Headquarters USA®

A Directory of Contact Information for Headquarters and Other Central Offices of Major Businesses & Organizations in the United States and in Canada

2009

31st EDITION

Volume 2: Classification by Subject

Mailing Addresses, Telephone Numbers, Toll-Free Phone Numbers, Fax Numbers, and World Wide Web Addresses for:

- Associations, Foundations, and Similar Organizations
- Businesses, Industries, and Professions of All Types
- Colleges, Universities, Vocational & Technical Schools, and Other Educational Institutions
- Electronic Resources, including Internet Companies, Organizations, and Web Sites
- Embassies, Consulates, and UN Missions & Agencies
- Government Agencies & Offices at All Levels—City, County, State, Federal
- Libraries, Museums & Galleries, Zoos & Botanical Gardens, Performing Arts Organizations & Facilities, and Other Cultural Institutions
- Media—Newspapers, Magazines, Newsletters; and Radio & Television Companies, Networks, Stations, and Syndicators
- Research Centers & Organizations, including Scientific, Public Policy, and Market Research
- Professional Sports Teams, Other Sports Organizations, and Sports Facilities

And also including an Area/Zip Code Guide Covering over 10,000 US Cities and Towns, as well as Area Code Tables in State & Numerical Order; and a detailed Index to Classified Headings under which listings are organized in the Directory's Classified Section

P.O. Box 31-1640, Detroit, Michigan 48231

Omnigraphics, Inc.

Lori Perez, *Assistant Editor*
Alicia Elkiss, *Editorial Associate*
Tiffany Delano and Sue Lynch, *Verification Assistants*

* * *

Peter E. Ruffner, *Publisher*
Matthew P. Barbour, *Senior Vice President*

* * *

Elizabeth Collins, *Research and Permissions Coordinator*
Kevin M. Hayes, *Operations Manager*
Allison Beckett, Mary Butler and Cherry Stockdale, *Research Associates*
Shirley Amore, Martha Johns, and Kirk Kauffman, *Administrative Staff*

ISSN 1531-2909

Printed in the United States of America

OMNIGRAPHICS, INC.
P.O. Box 31-1640 • Detroit, MI 48231
Phone Orders: 800-234-1340 • Fax Orders: 800-875-1340
Mail Orders: P.O. Box 625 • Holmes, PA 19043
www.omnigraphics.com

Table of Contents

Volume 1:
Alphabetical by Organization Name

Volume 2:
Classified by Subject

Classified Headings Table

Listed here are all of the headings under which listings are categorized in the Classified Section of this directory. The headings are numbered sequentially, and these numbers correspond to those printed in the "Class' column that accompanies listings in the Alphabetical Section. Just match the number in the "Class" column to the corresponding number printed in this table in order to identify the type of business or organization of any white pages listing. Use this table, too, to locate the page on which that subject category appears in the classified section.

For a more detailed list of classified headings, including "See" and "See also" references, please see the Index to Classified Headings at the back of this book.

A

B

Still can't find what you're looking for? *For a more detailed subject selection, see the Index to Classified Headings at the back of this directory.*

Still can't find what you're looking for? *For a more detailed subject selection, see the Index to Classified Headings at the back of this directory.*

Still can't find what you're looking for? *For a more detailed subject selection, see the Index to Classified Headings at the back of this directory.*

Still can't find what you're looking for? *For a more detailed subject selection, see the Index to Classified Headings at the back of this directory.*

Still can't find what you're looking for? *For a more detailed subject selection, see the Index to Classified Headings at the back of this directory.*

R

Still can't find what you're looking for? *For a more detailed subject selection, see the Index to Classified Headings at the back of this directory.*

Still can't find what you're looking for? *For a more detailed subject selection, see the Index to Classified Headings at the back of this directory.*

U

V

W

Z

Still can't find what you're looking for? *For a more detailed subject selection, see the Index to Classified Headings at the back of this directory.*

Classified Section

Listings in the Classified Section are organized alphabetically (or, where noted, by city or state names) under subject headings denoting a business or organization type. Alphabetizing is on a word-by-word rather than letter-by-letter basis.

For a detailed explanation of the scope and arrangement of listings, please refer to "How to Use This Directory" at the beginning of this book. Page elements and listing formats are illustrated on the sample pages with accompanying explanatory notes found just inside the back cover.

1 ABRASIVE PRODUCTS

Name / Address	City	State	ZIP	Phone	Fax
3M Abrasive Systems Div 3M Center Bldg 223-6N-01 **Fax Area Code:* 800 ■ *TF:* 866-599-4227 ■ *Web:* www.3m.com/us/mfg_industrial/abrasives	Saint Paul	MN	55144	651-737-6501	898-9841*
3M Manufacturing & Industry Solutions 3M Ctr *TF:* 888-364-3577 ■ *Web:* www.3m.com/US/mfg_industrial	Saint Paul	MN	55144	651-733-1110	733-9973
Acme Holding Co 24200 Marmon Ave *Web:* www.acmeabrasive.com	Warren	MI	48089	586-759-6555	759-3334
Avery Abrasives Inc 2225 Reservoir Ave **Fax:* Cust Svc	Trumbull	CT	06611	203-372-3513	372-3714*
Barker Bros Inc Bardo Products Div 1666 Summerfield St	Ridgewood	NY	11385	718-456-6400	366-2104
Bullard Abrasives Inc 6 Carol Dr *TF:* 800-227-4469 ■ *Web:* www.bullardabrasives.com	Lincoln	RI	02865	401-333-3000	333-3077
Camel Grinding Wheels 7525 N Oak Park Ave *TF:* 800-447-4248 ■ *Web:* www.cgwheels.com	Niles	IL	60714	847-647-5994	647-1861
CITCO Operations 357 Washington St *TF:* 800-242-7366 ■ *Web:* www.citcodiamond.com	Chardon	OH	44024	440-285-9181	285-3678
Comco Inc 2151 N Lincoln St *TF:* 800-796-6626 ■ *Web:* www.comcoinc.com	Burbank	CA	91504	818-841-5500	955-8365
Composition Materials Co Inc 125 Old Gate Ln *TF:* 800-262-7763 ■ *Web:* compomat.com	Milford	CT	06460	203-874-6500	874-6505
Diagrind Inc 10491 W 164th Pl *TF:* 800-790-4333 ■ *Web:* www.diagrind.com	Orland Park	IL	60467	708-460-4333	460-8842
Diamond Innovations 6325 Huntley Rd *TF Cust Svc:* 800-443-1455 ■ *Web:* www.abrasivesnet.com	Columbus	OH	43229	614-438-2000	438-2898
Eagle Grinding Wheel Corp 2519 W Fulton St *Web:* www.eaglegrindingwheel.com	Chicago	IL	60612	312-733-1770	733-5949
Ervin Industries Inc 3893 Research Pk Dr *TF:* 800-748-0055 ■ *Web:* www.ervinindustries.com	Ann Arbor	MI	48108	734-769-4600	663-0136
Formax Mfg Corp 168 Wealthy St SW *TF:* 800-242-2833 ■ *Web:* www.formaxmfg.com	Grand Rapids	MI	49503	616-456-5458	456-7507
Garfield Industries PO Box 839 *Web:* www.polishingbuffs.com	Caldwell	NJ	07007	973-575-8800	575-6840
Gemtex Abrasives 60 Belfield Rd *TF:* 800-387-5100 ■ *Web:* www.gemtexabrasives.com	Toronto	ON	M9W1G1	416-245-5605	245-3723
Glit/Microtron 809 Broad St *TF:* 800-431-2976 ■ *Web:* www.glit-microtron.com	Wrens	GA	30833	706-547-6555	547-6367
JacksonLea 1715 Conover Blvd E PO Box 699 *TF:* 800-438-6880 ■ *Web:* www.jacksonlea.com	Conover	NC	28613	828-464-1376	464-7094
Kennametal Inc 2879 Aero Park Dr **Fax:* Sales ■ *TF:* 800-662-2131 ■ *Web:* www.kennametal.com	Traverse City	MI	49686	231-946-2100	946-3025*
Klingspor Abrasives Inc 2555 Tate Blvd SE *TF:* 800-645-5555 ■ *Web:* www.klingspor.com	Hickory	NC	28602	828-322-3030	326-0296
Marvel Abrasive Products Inc 6230 S Oak Park Ave *TF:* 800-621-0673 ■ *Web:* www.marvelabrasives.com	Chicago	IL	60638	773-586-8700	586-0187
Mosher Co 15 Exchange St *Web:* www.mocomfg.com	Chicopee	MA	01014	413-598-8341	594-7647
Moyco Technologies Inc 200 Commerce Dr *TF:* 800-331-8837 ■ *Web:* www.moycotech.com	Montgomeryville	PA	18936	215-855-4300	362-3809
Norton Co 1 New Bond St *TF:* 800-543-4335 ■ *Web:* www.nortonabrasives.com	Worcester	MA	01606	508-795-5000	795-5741
Pacific Grinding Wheel Co 13120 State Ave *TF:* 800-688-9328 ■ *Web:* www.pacificgrindingwheel.com	Marysville	WA	98271	360-659-6201	653-3200
Radiac Abrasives Inc 1015 S College Ave **Fax:* Cust Svc ■ *TF:* 800-851-1095 ■ *Web:* www.radiac.com	Salem	IL	62881	618-548-4200	548-4207*
Raytech Industries 475 Smith St *TF Cust Svc:* 800-243-7163 ■ *Web:* www.raytech-ind.com	Middletown	CT	06457	860-632-2020	632-1699
Red Hill Grinding Wheel Corp PO Box 150	Pennsburg	PA	18073	215-679-7964	679-3715
Reed Minerals 5040 Louise Dr Suite 106 Rossmoyne Industrial Park **Fax Area Code:* 717 ■ *Web:* www.reedmin.com	Mechanicsburg	PA	17055	888-733-3646	763-6496*
Saint Gobian Abrasives 84 O'Leary Dr **Fax:* Cust Svc ■ *TF:* 800-323-6676	Bensenville	IL	60106	630-238-3300	238-3315*
Sancap Abrasives 16123 Armour St NE *TF:* 800-433-6663 ■ *Web:* www.sancapabrasives.com	Alliance	OH	44601	330-821-3510	821-3516
Sandusky-Chicago Abrasive Wheel Co 1100 W Barker Ave *TF:* 800-843-4980 ■ *Web:* www.sanduskychicago.com	Michigan City	IN	46360	219-879-6601	872-8139
Sax Stan Corp 101 S Waterman St *Web:* www.stansaxcorp.com	Detroit	MI	48209	313-841-7170	841-7171
Schaffner Mfg Co Inc 21 Herron Ave Schaffner Ctr *TF:* 800-292-9903 ■ *Web:* www.schaffnermfg.com	Pittsburgh	PA	15202	412-761-9902	761-8998
Spedecut Abrasives 10042 Rancho Rd *Web:* www.spedecut.com	Adelanto	CA	92301	760-246-6850	246-6889
Stan Sax Corp 101 S Waterman St *Web:* www.stansaxcorp.com	Detroit	MI	48209	313-841-7170	841-7171
Standard Abrasives Inc 4201 Guardian St **Fax:* Hum Res ■ *TF:* 800-423-5444 ■ *Web:* www.standardabrasives.com	Simi Valley	CA	93063	805-520-5800	577-7397*
TYROLIT Wickman Inc 10325 Capital Ave *TF:* 800-366-4431 ■ *Web:* www.wickmancorp.com	Oak Park	MI	48237	248-548-3822	548-3831
VSM Abrasives 1012 E Wabash St *TF:* 800-737-0176 ■ *Web:* www.vsmabrasives.com	O'Fallon	MO	63366	636-272-7432	272-7434
Washington Mills Electro Minerals Co 20 N Main St *Web:* www.washingtonmills.com	North Grafton	MA	01536	508-839-6511	839-7675

2 ACCOUNTING FIRMS

Name / Address	City	State	ZIP	Phone	Fax
Amper Politziner & Mattia 2015 Lincoln Hwy *Web:* www.amper.com	Edison	NJ	08818	732-287-1000	287-3200
Anchin Block & Anchin LLP 1375 Broadway 18th Fl *Web:* www.anchin.com	New York	NY	10018	212-840-3456	840-7066
Argy Wiltse & Robinson PC 8405 Greensboro Dr Suite 700 *Web:* www.awr.com	McLean	VA	22102	703-893-0600	893-2766
Armanino McKenna LLP 12667 Alcosta Blvd Suite 500 *Web:* amllp.com	San Ramon	CA	94583	925-790-2600	790-2601
Aronson & Co 700 King Farm Blvd 3rd Fl *Web:* www.aronsoncompany.com	Rockville	MD	20850	301-231-6200	231-7630
BDO Seidman LLP 1 Prudential Plaza 130 E Randolph St Suite 2800 *Web:* www.bdo.com	Chicago	IL	60601	312-240-1236	240-3311
Beers & Cutler PLLC 8219 Leesburg Pike Suite 800 *Web:* www.beersandcutler.com	Vienna	VA	22182	703-923-8300	923-8330
Berdon LLP 360 Madison Ave 8th Fl *Web:* www.berdonllp.com	New York	NY	10017	212-832-0400	371-1159
Berkowitz Dick Pollack & Brant LLP 200 S Biscayne Blvd 6th Fl *TF:* 800-999-1272 ■ *Web:* www.bdpb.com	Miami	FL	33131	305-379-7000	379-8200
BKD LLP 901 E Saint Louis St Suite 1800 *Web:* www.bkd.com	Springfield	MO	65806	417-831-7283	831-4763
Blackman Kallick 10 S Riverside Plaza Suite 900 *Web:* www.blackmankallick.com	Chicago	IL	60606	312-207-1040	207-1066
Blue & Co 12800 N Meridian St Suite 400 *TF:* 800-717-2583 ■ *Web:* www.blueandco.com	Carmel	IN	46032	317-848-8920	573-2458
Blum Shapiro 29 S Main St 4th Fl *TF:* 800-561-6889 ■ *Web:* www.bshapiro.com	West Hartford	CT	06107	860-561-4000	521-9241
bmc 2609 Keiser Blvd PO Box 311 *TF:* 800-267-9405 ■ *Web:* www.beardmiller.com	Reading	PA	19603	610-927-4910	927-9809
Bonadio Group The 171 Sully's Trail Suite 201 *Web:* www.bonadio.com	Pittsford	NY	14534	585-381-1000	381-3131
Burr Pilger & Mayer LLP 600 California St Suite 1300 *Web:* www.bpmllp.com	San Francisco	CA	94108	415-421-5757	288-6288
Carlin Charron & Rosen LLP 1400 Computer Dr *TF:* 800-888-2102 ■ *Web:* www.ccrgroup.com	Westborough	MA	01581	508-926-2200	616-4402
Carr Riggs & Ingram LLC 1117 Boll Weevil Cir PO Box 311070 *Web:* www.cricpa.com	Enterprise	AL	36331	334-347-0088	347-7650
CBIZ Inc 6050 Oak Tree Blvd S Suite 500 *NASDAQ: CBIZ* ■ *Web:* www.cbizinc.com	Cleveland	OH	44131	216-447-9000	447-9007
Cherry Bekaert & Holland LLP 1700 Bayberry Ct Suite 300 *TF:* 800-849-8281 ■ *Web:* www.cbh.com	Richmond	VA	23226	804-673-4224	673-4290
Citrin Cooperman & Co LLP 529 5th Ave 2nd Fl *Web:* www.citrincooperman.com	New York	NY	10017	212-697-1000	697-1004
Clark Schaefer Hackett & Co 160 N Breiel Blvd *Web:* www.cshco.com	Middletown	OH	45042	513-424-5000	422-7882
Clifton Gunderson LLP 301 SW Adams St Suite 900 *Web:* www.cliftoncpa.com	Peoria	IL	61602	309-671-4500	671-4508
Cohn JH LLP 4 Becker Farm Rd *TF:* 800-879-2571 ■ *Web:* www.jhcohn.com	Roseland	NJ	07068	973-228-3500	228-0330
Crowe Chizek & Co LLC 330 E Jefferson Blvd PO Box 7 *TF:* 800-276-9301 ■ *Web:* www.crowechizek.com	South Bend	IN	46624	574-232-3992	236-8692
Decosimo Joseph & Co PLLC 2 Union Sq Tallan Bldg Suite 1100 *TF:* 800-782-8382 ■ *Web:* www.decosimo.com	Chattanooga	TN	37402	423-756-7100	756-2939
Deloitte Touche Tohmatsu 1633 Broadway *Web:* www.deloitte.com	New York	NY	10019	212-489-1600	492-4154
Deloitte & Touche USA LLP 1633 Broadway *Web:* www.deloitte.com	New York	NY	10019	212-489-1600	489-1687
Dixon Hughes PLLC 500 Ridgefield Ct *TF:* 800-425-7182 ■ *Web:* www.dixon-hughes.com	Asheville	NC	28806	828-254-2254	254-6859
Doeren Mayhew 755 W Big Beaver Rd Suite 2300 *Web:* www.doeren.com	Troy	MI	48084	248-244-3000	244-3090
Ehrhardt Keefe Steiner & Hottman PC 7979 E Tufts Ave Suite 400 *TF:* 888-740-9400 ■ *Web:* www.eksh.com	Denver	CO	80237	303-740-9400	740-9009
Eide Bailly LLP 4310 17th Ave S *TF:* 888-777-9552 ■ *Web:* www.eidebailly.com	Fargo	ND	58103	701-239-8500	239-8600
Eisner LLP 750 3rd Ave *Web:* www.eisnerllp.com	New York	NY	10017	212-949-8700	891-4100
Elliott Davis LLC 200 E Broad St *TF:* 800-503-4721 ■ *Web:* www.elliottdavis.com	Greenville	SC	29601	864-242-3370	232-7161
Ernst & Young 5 Times Sq **Fax:* Mail Rm ■ *Web:* www.ey.com	New York	NY	10036	212-773-3000	773-6350*
Ernst & Young Ernst & Young Tower 222 Bay St PO Box 251 *TF:* 800-291-3380 ■ *Web:* www.ey.com	Toronto	ON	M5K1J7	416-864-1234	864-1174
Fiducial 1370 Ave of the Americas 31st Fl *TF:* 866-343-8242 ■ *Web:* www.fiducial.com	New York	NY	10019	212-207-4700	308-2613
Frank Rimerman & Co LLP 1801 Page Mill Rd *Web:* www.fr-co.com	Palo Alto	CA	94304	650-845-8100	494-1975
Friedman LLP 1700 Broadway 23rd Fl *Web:* www.friedmanllp.com	New York	NY	10019	212-842-7000	842-7001
Goldenberg Rosenthal LLP 101 West Ave PO Box 458 *Web:* www.grgrp.com	Jenkintown	PA	19046	215-881-8800	881-8801
Goodman & Co LLP 1 Commercial Pl Suite 800 *TF:* 888-899-5100 ■ *Web:* www.goodmanco.com	Norfolk	VA	23510	757-624-5100	624-5233
Grant Thornton LLP 175 W Jackson Blvd 20th Fl *Web:* www.grantthornton.com	Chicago	IL	60604	312-856-0001	602-8099
Habif Arogeti & Wynne LLP 5565 Glenridge Connector NE Suite 200 *TF:* 800-792-9651 ■ *Web:* www.hawcpa.com	Atlanta	GA	30342	404-892-9651	
Hein & Assoc LLP 717 17th St Suite 1600 *Web:* www.heincpa.com	Denver	CO	80202	303-298-9600	298-8118
Hill Barth & King LLC 7680 Market St *TF:* 800-733-8613 ■ *Web:* www.hbkcpa.com	Boardman	OH	44512	330-758-8613	758-0357

	City	State	Zip	Phone	Fax
Holthouse Carlin & Van Trigt LLP 1601 Cloverfield Blvd Suite 300-S	Santa Monica	CA	90404	310-566-1900	566-1901
Web: www.hcvt.com					
Holtz Rubenstein Reminick LLP 125 Baylis Rd	Melville	NY	11747	631-752-7400	752-1742
Web: www.hrcpa.com					
Honkamp Krueger & Co PC 2345 JFK Rd PO Box 699	Dubuque	IA	52004	563-556-0123	
TF: 888-556-0123 ■ *Web:* www.honkamp.com					
Horne LLP 200 E Capitol St Suite 1400	Jackson	MS	39201	601-948-0940	355-6521
Web: www.horne-llp.com					
JH Cohn LLP 4 Becker Farm Rd	Roseland	NJ	07068	973-228-3500	228-0330
TF: 800-879-2571 ■ *Web:* www.jhcohn.com					
Joseph Decosimo & Co PLLC 2 Union Sq Tallan Bldg Suite 1100	Chattanooga	TN	37402	423-756-7100	756-2939
TF: 800-782-8382 ■ *Web:* www.decosimo.com					
Katz Sapper & Miller 800 E 96th St Suite 500	Indianapolis	IN	46240	317-580-2000	580-2117
Web: www.ksmcpa.com					
Kaufman Rossin & Co PA 2699 S Bayshore Dr Suite 300	Miami	FL	33133	305-858-5600	856-3284
Web: www.krco-cpa.com					
Kemper CPA Group LLP 322 E Main	Greenfield	IN	46140	317-462-3401	
Web: www.kcpag.com					
Kennedy & Coe LLC 3030 Cortland Cir PO Box 1100	Salina	KS	67402	785-825-1561	825-5371
TF: 800-967-0098 ■ *Web:* www.kcoe.com					
KPMG LLP US 3 Chestnut Ridge Rd	Montvale	NJ	07645	201-307-7000	307-7575
Web: www.kpmg.com					
LarsonAllen LLP 220 S 6th St Suite 300	Minneapolis	MN	55402	612-376-4500	376-4850
TF: 888-335-6080 ■ *Web:* www.larsonallen.com					
Lattimore Black Morgan & Cain PC 5250 Virginia Way	Brentwood	TN	37027	615-377-4600	309-2500
Web: www.lbmc.com					
LeMaster & Daniels PLLC 601 W Riverside Ave Suite 700	Spokane	WA	99201	509-624-4315	624-8874
TF: 866-622-5553 ■ *Web:* www.lemasterdaniels.com					
Lurie Besikof Lapidus & Co LLP 2501 Wayzata Blvd	Minneapolis	MN	55405	612-377-4404	377-1325
Web: www.lblco.com					
Mahoney Cohen & Co 1065 Ave of the Americas	New York	NY	10018	212-790-5700	398-0267
Web: www.mahoneycohen.com					
Marcum & Kliegman LLP 10 Melville Park Rd	Melville	NY	11747	631-414-4000	414-4001
TF: 800-921-0777 ■ *Web:* www.mkllp.com					
Margolin Winer & Evens LLP 400 Garden City Plaza Suite 500	Garden City	NY	11530	516-747-2000	747-9184
Web: www.mwellp.com					
Marks Paneth & Shron LLP 622 3rd Ave 7th Fl	New York	NY	10017	212-503-8800	370-3759
Web: www.markspaneth.com					
Mohler Nixon & Williams 635 Campbell Technology Pkwy Suite 100	Campbell	CA	95008	408-369-2400	879-9485
Web: www.mohlernixon.com					
Morrison Brown Argiz & Farra LLP 1001 Brickell Bay Dr 9th Fl	Miami	FL	33131	305-373-5500	373-0056
TF: 800-239-3843 ■ *Web:* www.mbafcpa.com					
Moss Adams LLP 999 3rd Ave Suite 2800	Seattle	WA	98104	206-302-6500	622-9975
TF: 800-243-4936 ■ *Web:* www.mossadams.com					
Novogradac & Co LLP 246 1st St 5th Fl	San Francisco	CA	94105	415-356-8000	356-8001
Web: www.novoco.com					
O'Connor Davies Munns & Dobbins LLP 60 E 42nd St Lincoln Bldg 36th Fl	New York	NY	10165	212-286-2600	286-4080
Web: www.odmdllp.com					
Padgett Business Services 160 Hawthorne Park	Athens	GA	30606	706-548-1040	543-8537
TF: 800-723-4388 ■ *Web:* www.smallbizpros.com					
Parente Randolph LLC 2 Penn Center Suite 1800 1500 JFK Blvd	Philadelphia	PA	19102	215-972-0701	563-4925
Web: www.parentenet.com					
Plante & Moran PLLC 27400 Northwestern Hwy	Southfield	MI	48034	248-352-2500	352-0018
TF: 800-827-1280 ■ *Web:* www.plantemoran.com					
PRG-Schultz International Inc 600 Galleria Pkwy Suite 100	Atlanta	GA	30339	770-779-3900	779-3133
NASDAQ: PRGX ■ *TF:* 800-752-5894 ■ *Web:* www.prgx.com					
PricewaterhouseCoopers LLP 300 Madison Ave	New York	NY	10017	646-471-4000	286-6000*
**Fax Area Code:* 813 ■ *Web:* www.pwc.com					
Rachlin LLP 1 SE 3rd Ave 10th Fl	Miami	FL	33131	305-377-4228	377-8331
Web: www.rachlin.com					
Rehmann Group 5800 Gratiot St Suite 201	Saginaw	MI	48638	989-799-9580	799-0227
TF: 866-799-9580 ■ *Web:* www.rehmann.com					
Reznick Group PC 7700 Old Georgetown Rd Suite 400	Bethesda	MD	20814	301-652-9100	652-1848
Web: www.rfs.com					
RGL - Forensic Accountants & Consultants 5619 DTC Pkwy Suite 1010	Englewood	CO	80111	303-721-8898	721-8936
Web: www.rgl.com					
Rosen Seymour Shapss Martin & Co LLP 757 3rd Ave 6th Fl	New York	NY	10017	212-303-1800	755-5600
Web: www.rssmcpa.com					
Rothstein Kass 4 Becker Farm Rd	Roseland	NJ	07068	973-994-6666	994-0337
Web: www.rkco.com					
RSM/McGladrey & Pullen LLP 3600 American Blvd W 3rd Fl	Bloomington	MN	55431	952-835-9930	921-7702
TF: 866-835-9930 ■ *Web:* www.rsmmcgladrey.com					
RubinBrown LLP 1 N Brentwood Blvd Suite 1100	Saint Louis	MO	63105	314-290-3300	290-3400
TF: 800-678-3134 ■ *Web:* www.rubinbrown.com					
SC&H Group LLC 910 Ridgebrook Rd	Sparks	MD	21152	410-403-1500	403-1570
TF: 800-832-3008 ■ *Web:* www.scandh.com					
Schenck Business Solutions 200 E Washington St	Appleton	WI	54911	920-731-8111	731-8037
TF: 800-236-2246 ■ *Web:* www.schencksolutions.com					
Schneider Downs & Co Inc 1133 Penn Ave	Pittsburgh	PA	15222	412-261-3644	261-4876
Web: www.sdcpa.com					
Schonbraun McCann Group 750 Third Ave	New York	NY	10017	212-840-7383	731-1599*
**Fax Area Code:* 646 ■ *Web:* www.smgllp.com					
Seiler LLP 3 Lagoon Dr Suite 400	Redwood City	CA	94065	650-365-4646	368-4055
Web: www.seiler.com					
Sikich LLP 998 Corporate Blvd	Aurora	IL	60502	630-566-8400	566-8401
TF: 877-279-1900 ■ *Web:* www.sikich.com/sg					
Singer Lewak Greenbaum & Goldstein LLP 10960 Wilshire Blvd Suite 1100	Los Angeles	CA	90024	310-477-3924	478-6070
Web: www.slgg.com					
Smart & Assoc LLP 80 Lancaster Ave	Devon	PA	19333	610-254-0700	254-5292
Web: www.smartassociates.com					
Squar Milner Peterson Miranda & Williamson LLP 4100 Newport Place Dr 3rd Fl	Newport Beach	CA	92660	949-222-2999	222-2989
Web: www.squarmilner.com					
SS&G Financial Services Inc 32125 Solon Rd	Solon	OH	44139	440-248-8787	248-0841
Web: www.ssandg.com					
Stonefield Josephson Inc 2049 Century Park E Suite 400	Los Angeles	CA	90067	310-453-9400	453-1187
Web: www.sjaccounting.com					
Suby Von Haden & Assoc SC 1221 John Q Hammons Dr PO Box 44966	Madison	WI	53744	608-831-8181	831-4243
TF: 800-279-2616 ■ *Web:* www.sva.com					
Tofias PC 350 Massachusetts Ave	Cambridge	MA	02139	617-761-0600	761-0601
TF: 888-761-8835 ■ *Web:* www.tofias.com					
UHY Advisors Inc 30 S Wacker Dr Suite 2850	Chicago	IL	60606	312-578-9600	346-6500
Web: www.uhyllp-us.com					
Vavrinek Trine Day & Co LLP 8270 Aspen St	Rancho Cucamonga	CA	91730	909-466-4410	466-4431
Web: www.vtdcpa.com					
Virchow Krause & Co LLP 10 Terrace Ct	Madison	WI	53718	608-249-6622	249-8532
TF: 800-362-7301 ■ *Web:* www.virchowkrause.com					
Vitale Caturano & Co Ltd 80 City Sq	Boston	MA	02129	617-912-9000	912-9001
Web: www.vitale.com					
Warren Averett Kimbrough & Marino LLC 2500 Acton Rd	Birmingham	AL	35243	205-979-4100	979-6313
Web: www.wakm.com					
Watkins Meegan Drury & Co LLC 7700 Wisconsin Ave Suite 500	Bethesda	MD	20814	301-654-7555	656-9115
Web: www.wmdco.com					
Weaver & Tidwell LLP 1600 W 7th St Suite 300	Fort Worth	TX	76102	817-332-7905	429-5936
TF: 800-332-7952 ■ *Web:* www.weaverandtidwell.com					
Weiser LLP 135 W 50th St	New York	NY	10020	212-812-7000	375-6888
Web: www.mrweiser.com					
Wipfli LLP 11 Scott St Suite 400	Wausau	WI	54403	715-845-3111	842-7272
Web: www.wipfli.com					
WithumSmith+Brown 5 Vaughn Dr	Princeton	NJ	08540	609-520-1188	520-9882
Web: www.withum.com					

3 ADHESIVES & SEALANTS

	City	State	Zip	Phone	Fax
3M Automotive Aftermarket Div 3M Center Bldg 223-6N-01	Saint Paul	MN	55144	651-737-6515	699-7840*
**Fax Area Code:* 800 ■ *TF:* 800-364-3577 ■ *Web:* www.3m.com/us/auto_marine_aero/aad					
3M Canada Co PO Box 5757	London	ON	N6A4T1	519-451-2500	452-4714*
**Fax:* Library ■ *TF:* 800-265-1840 ■ *Web:* www.3m.com/ca/					
3M Manufacturing & Industry Solutions 3M Ctr	Saint Paul	MN	55144	651-733-1110	733-9973
TF: 888-364-3577 ■ *Web:* www.3m.com/US/mfg_industrial					
3M Transportation Div 3M Center	Saint Paul	MN	55144	651-733-1110	
TF: 888-364-3577					
Adhesives Research Inc 400 Seaks Run Rd PO Box 100	Glen Rock	PA	17327	717-235-7979	235-8320
TF: 800-445-6240 ■ *Web:* www.adhesivesresearch.com					
American Biltrite Inc Tape Products Div 105 Whittendale Dr	Moorestown	NJ	08057	856-778-0700	778-7485
Web: www.abitape.com					
Arclin 5865 McLaughlin Rd Suite 3	Mississauga	ON	L5R1B8	905-712-0900	712-0901
Web: www.dynea.com					
Arlon Adhesives & Films 2811 S Harbor Blvd	Santa Ana	CA	92704	714-540-2811	431-4305
TF: 800-854-0361 ■ *Web:* www.arlon.com					
Atlas Minerals & Chemicals Inc 1227 Valley Rd	Mertztown	PA	19539	610-682-7171	682-9200
TF Cust Svc: 800-523-8269 ■ *Web:* www.atlasmin.com					
Avery Dennison Corp 150 N Orange Grove Blvd	Pasadena	CA	91103	626-304-2000	304-2192
NYSE: AVY ■ *TF Cust Svc:* 800-252-8379 ■ *Web:* www.averydennison.com					
Axson North America Inc 1611 Hults Dr	Eaton Rapids	MI	48827	517-663-8191	663-0523
Web: www.axson-na.com					
BASF Building Systems 889 Valley Park Dr	Shakopee	MN	55379	952-496-6000	496-6067*
**Fax Area Code:* 800 ■ **Fax:* Cust Svc ■ *TF Cust Svc:* 800-433-9517 ■ *Web:* www.buildingsystems.basf.com					
Bondo Corp 3700 Atlanta Industrial Pkwy NW	Atlanta	GA	30331	404-696-2730	696-6814
TF: 800-622-8754 ■ *Web:* www.bondo-online.com					
Bostik Inc 11320 Watertown Plank Rd	Wauwatosa	WI	53226	414-774-2250	774-8075
TF: 800-558-4302 ■ *Web:* www.bostik-us.com					
Brady Coated Products 6555 W Good Hope Rd	Milwaukee	WI	53223	414-358-6600	292-2289*
**Fax Area Code:* 800 ■ *TF:* 800-635-7557 ■ *Web:* www.coatedproducts.com					
CFC International Inc 500 State St	Chicago Heights	IL	60411	708-891-3456	758-5989
NASDAQ: CFCI ■ *Web:* www.cfcintl.com					
Chase Corp 26 Summer St	Bridgewater	MA	02324	508-279-1789	697-6419
AMEX: CCF ■ *Web:* www.chasecorp.com					
Colloid Environmental Technologies Co (CETCO) 1500 W Shure Dr	Arlington Heights	IL	60004	847-392-5800	577-6150
TF: 800-527-9948 ■ *Web:* www.cetco.com					
Covalence Plastics 1401 W 94th St	Minneapolis	MN	55431	800-873-3941	
Web: www.covalenceplastics.com					
Custom Building Products 13001 Seal Beach Blvd	Seal Beach	CA	90740	562-598-8808	598-4008
TF: 800-272-8786 ■ *Web:* www.custombuildingproducts.com					
DAP Inc 2400 Boston St Suite 200	Baltimore	MD	21224	410-675-2100	558-1068*
**Fax:* Cust Svc ■ *TF Cust Svc:* 800-584-3840 ■ *Web:* www.dap.com					
Darex 62 Whittemore Ave	Cambridge	MA	02140	617-498-4571	499-2880
TF: 800-232-6100 ■ *Web:* www.gracedarex.com					
Devcon Inc 30 Endicott St	Danvers	MA	01923	978-777-1100	774-0516
TF: 800-626-7226 ■ *Web:* www.devcon.com					
Eclectic Products Inc 1075 Arrowsmith St 2nd Fl Suite B	Eugene	OR	97402	541-284-4667	746-1983
TF: 800-693-4667 ■ *Web:* www.eclecticproducts.com					
EFTEC North America LLC 2710 Bellingham Dr Suite 100	Troy	MI	48083	248-585-2200	585-3699
TF: 800-633-7789 ■ *Web:* www.eftec.com					
Elmer's Products Inc 180 E Broad St	Columbus	OH	43215	614-225-4000	225-3390
Web: www.elmers.com					
Euclid Chemical Co 19218 Redwood Rd	Cleveland	OH	44110	216-531-9222	531-9596
TF: 800-321-7628 ■ *Web:* www.euclidchemical.com					
Forbo Adhesives LLC 523 Davis Dr Suite 400	Durham	NC	27713	919-433-1300	433-1301
TF: 800-213-4805 ■ *Web:* www.forbo.com					
Foster Products Corp 1105 S Frontenac St	Aurora	IL	60504	800-231-9541	942-6856
Web: www.fosterproducts.com					
Fox Industries Inc 3100 Falls Cliff Rd	Baltimore	MD	21211	410-243-8856	243-2701
TF: 888-760-0369 ■ *Web:* www.fox-ind.com					
Franklin International 2020 Bruck St	Columbus	OH	43207	614-443-0241	445-1493
TF: 800-877-4583 ■ *Web:* www.franklini.com					
Geocel Corp PO Box 398	Elkhart	IN	46515	574-264-0645	264-3698
TF: 800-348-7615 ■ *Web:* www.geocelusa.com					
HB Fuller Co 1200 Willow Lake Blvd PO Box 64683	Saint Paul	MN	55164	651-236-5900	236-5898
NYSE: FUL ■ *TF:* 800-828-2981 ■ *Web:* www.hbfuller.com					
Henkel Corp 32100 Stephenson Hwy	Madison Heights	MI	48071	248-583-9300	583-2976
TF: 800-521-6895 ■ *Web:* www.henkel.com					
Henkel Corp 32150 Just Imagine Dr	Avon	OH	44011	440-937-7000	937-7077
TF: 800-321-1733 ■ *Web:* www.henkelca.com					
Hercules Chemical Co Inc 111 South St	Passaic	NJ	07055	973-778-5000	777-4115
TF: 800-221-9330 ■ *Web:* www.herchem.com					
Hexion Specialty Chemicals Inc 180 E Broad St	Columbus	OH	43215	614-225-4000	220-6693*
**Fax:* Hum Res ■ *Web:* www.hexionchem.com					
Houghton International Inc 945 Madison Ave PO Box 930	Valley Forge	PA	19482	610-666-4000	666-1376
TF: 888-459-9844 ■ *Web:* www.houghtonintl.com					
ICI Americas Inc 10 Finderne Ave	Bridgewater	NJ	08807	908-203-5000	685-5005
TF: 800-998-9986 ■ *Web:* www.ici.com/UnitedStatesofAmerica					
Illinois Tool Works Inc TACC Div 56 Air Station Industrial Pk	Rockland	MA	02370	781-878-7015	231-8222*
**Fax Area Code:* 800 ■ **Fax:* Cust Svc ■ *TF:* 800-503-6991 ■ *Web:* www.taccint.com					
IPS Corp 455 W Victoria St	Compton	CA	90220	310-898-3300	898-3390
TF: 800-421-2677 ■ *Web:* www.ipscorp.com					
ITW Insulcast Inc 565 Eagle Rock Ave	Roseland	NJ	07068	973-403-0603	403-0046
TF: 800-645-7546 ■ *Web:* www.insulcast.com					
Key Polymer Corp 17 Shepherd St	Lawrence	MA	01843	978-683-9411	686-7729
TF: 888-539-7659 ■ *Web:* www.keypolymer.com					
Kindt-Collins Co LLC 12651 Elmwood Ave	Cleveland	OH	44111	216-252-4122	252-5639*
**Fax:* Cust Svc ■ *TF:* 800-321-3170 ■ *Web:* www.kindt-collins.com					
L & L Products Inc PO Box 308	Romeo	MI	48065	586-336-1600	336-2060
LaPolla Industries Inc 15402 Vantage Pkwy E Suite 322	Houston	TX	77032	281-219-4100	219-4102
AMEX: LPA ■ *TF:* 800-382-4931 ■ *Web:* www.lapollaindustries.com					

Phone | Fax

Laticrete International Inc 91 Amity Rd .... Bethany CT 06524 203-393-0010 393-1684
TF: 800-243-4788 ■ Web: www.laticrete.com
Loctite Corp 1001 Trout Brook Crossing .... Rocky Hill CT 06067 860-571-5100 571-5465
TF: 800-842-0041 ■ Web: www.loctite.com
Loctite Corp North American Group
1001 Trout Brook Crossing .... Rocky Hill CT 06067 860-571-5100 571-5465
TF Cust Svc: 800-243-4874 ■ Web: www.loctite.com
Lord Corp 111 Lord Dr .... Cary NC 27511 919-468-5979
TF: 800-524-2885 ■ Web: www.lord.com
M-D Building Products Inc 4041 N Santa Fe Ave .... Oklahoma City OK 73118 405-528-4411 557-3541
TF Cust Svc: 800-654-8454 ■ Web: www.mdteam.com
MACCO Adhesives 15885 W Sprague Rd .... Strongsville OH 44136 440-297-7304 297-7319*
*Fax: Cust Svc ■ TF: 800-634-0015
MACtac 4560 Darrow Rd .... Stow OH 44224 330-688-1111 688-2540
TF: 800-762-2822 ■ Web: www.mactac.com
MAPEI Corp 1144 E Newport Center Dr .... Deerfield Beach FL 33442 954-246-8888 246-8830
TF: 800-426-2734 ■ Web: www.mapei.com
Mask-Off Co Inc 345 W Maple Ave .... Monrovia CA 91016 626-359-3261 359-7160
Web: www.mask-off.com
Morgan Adhesives Co DBA MACtac 4560 Darrow Rd .... Stow OH 44224 330-688-1111 688-2540
TF: 800-762-2822 ■ Web: www.mactac.com
National Casein Co 601 W 80th St .... Chicago IL 60620 773-846-7300 487-5709
Web: www.nationalcasein.com
National Starch & Chemical Co 10 Finderne Ave .... Bridgewater NJ 08807 908-685-5000 685-5005
TF: 800-797-4992 ■ Web: www.nationalstarch.com
Norton & Son Inc 148 E 5th St .... Bayonne NJ 07002 201-437-0770 437-2316
TF: 800-631-3440 ■ Web: www.muralo.com
Nylok Corp 15260 Hallmark Dr .... Macomb MI 48042 586-786-0100 786-0598
TF: 800-826-5161 ■ Web: www.nylok.com
Ohio Sealants Inc 7405 Production Dr .... Mentor OH 44060 440-255-8900 974-8774
TF: 800-321-3578 ■ Web: www.osisealants.com
Para-Chem Southern Inc PO Box 127 .... Simpsonville SC 29681 864-967-7691 963-1241
TF: 800-763-7272 ■ Web: www.parabond.com
Pecora Corp 165 Wambold Rd .... Harleysville PA 19438 215-723-6051 721-0286
TF: 800-523-6688 ■ Web: www.pecora.com
PrescoTech Industries 1001 W Oak St .... Louisville KY 40210 502-585-5866 587-1175
Red Devil Inc 1437 S Boulder Suite 750 Boulder Towers .... Tulsa OK 74361 918-585-8111 585-8120
TF: 800-423-3845 ■ Web: www.reddevil.com
Sika Corp 201 Polito Ave .... Lyndhurst NJ 07071 201-933-8800 933-9379*
*Fax: Acctg ■ TF: 800-933-7452 ■ Web: www.sikacorp.com
Solar Compounds Corp 1201 W Blancke St .... Linden NJ 07036 908-862-2813 862-8061
Web: www.solarcompounds.com
Super Glue Corp 9420 Santa Anita Ave .... Rancho Cucamonga CA 91730 909-987-0550 987-0490
TF: 800-538-3091 ■ Web: www.supergluecorp.com
Synkoloid Co 148 E 5th St .... Bayonne NJ 07002 201-437-0770 437-2316
TF: 800-631-3440
TACC Div Illinois Tool Works Inc 56 Air Station Industrial Pk ...... Rockland MA 02370 781-878-7015 231-8222*
*Fax Area Code: 800 ■ *Fax: Cust Svc ■ TF: 800-503-6991 ■ Web: www.taccint.com
TEC Specialty Products Inc
601 W Campas Dr Suite C-7 .... Arlington Heights IL 60004 800-832-9002 952-2368
TF: 800-832-9002 ■ Web: www.tecspecialty.com
Tremco Inc Roofing Div 3735 Green Rd .... Beachwood OH 44122 216-292-5000 760-3070*
*Fax Area Code: 800 ■ *Fax: Cust Svc ■ TF: 800-852-6013 ■
Web: www.tremcoroofing.com
Uniseal Inc PO Box 6288 .... Evansville IN 47719 812-425-1361 463-5232
TF: 800-443-6297 ■ Web: www.uniseal.com
Valspar Corp Packaging & Coatings Div 2001 Tracy St .... Pittsburgh PA 15233 412-766-9300 732-3131
TF: 800-873-5575
Worthen Industries Inc 3 E Spit Brook Rd .... Nashua NH 03060 603-888-5443 888-7945
TF: 800-967-8436 ■ Web: www.worthenind.com

4 ADVERTISING AGENCIES

SEE ALSO Public Relations Firms p. 2147

Phone | Fax

4WARD Intellect Inc 550 Alden Rd Suite 107 .... Markham ON L3R6A8 905-513-7360 513-7552
TF: 866-892-6297
A Web That Works 2733 Concession Rd 7 .... Bowmanville ON L1C3K6 905-263-2666 263-8989
TF: 800-579-9253 ■ Web: www.awebthatworks.com
Abelson-Taylor Inc 35 E Wacker Dr Suite 900 .... Chicago IL 60601 312-781-1700 894-5526
Web: www.abelson-taylor.com
Ackerman McQueen Inc
1601 Northwest Expy Suite 1100 .... Oklahoma City OK 73118 405-843-7777 848-8034
Web: www.am.com
Adair-Greene McCann Healthcare Communications
1575 Northside Dr NW 200 Atlanta Technology Ctr .... Atlanta GA 30318 404-351-8424 351-1495
Web: www.adair-greene.com
Adelle Lisa Design Inc 2828 Routh St Suite 650 .... Dallas TX 75201 214-969-0141 528-8344
Web: www.lisaadelledesign.com
AdMasters 16901 Dallas Pkwy Suite 204 .... Addison TX 75001 972-866-9300 866-9292
TF: 877-236-2783 ■ Web: www.admasters.com
Agent 16 79 5th Ave 16th Fl .... New York NY 10003 212-367-3800 367-3880
Web: www.agent16.com
AKQA Inc 118 King St 6th Fl .... San Francisco CA 94107 415-645-9400 645-9420
Web: www.akqa.com
Al Paul Lefton Co Inc 100 Independence Mall W .... Philadelphia PA 19106 215-923-9600 351-4298
Web: www.lefton.com
Allied Advertising 545 Boylston St 11th Fl .... Boston MA 02116 617-859-4800 247-8110
Web: www.alliedadvpub.com
AMPM Inc 1380 E Wackerly Rd .... Midland MI 48642 989-837-8800 832-0781
TF: 800-530-9100 ■ Web: www.ampminc.com
Anderson Communications 2245 Godby Rd .... Atlanta GA 30349 404-766-8000 767-5264
Web: www.andercom.com
Arnold Worldwide 101 Huntington Ave .... Boston MA 02199 617-587-8000 587-8070
TF: 800-782-4893 ■ Web: www.arnoldworldwide.com
Arnold Worldwide 110 5th Ave .... New York NY 10011 212-463-1000 463-1111
Web: www.arnoldworldwide.com
Aspen Marketing Services 1240 North Ave .... West Chicago IL 60185 630-293-3600
TF: 800-848-0212 ■ Web: www.aspenms.com
Avrett Free Ginsberg 885 2nd Ave 35th Fl .... New York NY 10017 212-832-3800 486-6518
Web: www.afg1.com
Bader Rutter & Assoc Inc 13845 Bishops Dr .... Brookfield WI 53005 262-784-7200 938-5595
Web: www.baderrutter.com
Barkley 1740 Main St .... Kansas City MO 64108 816-842-1500
Web: www.beap.com
BBDO Worldwide Inc 1285 Ave of the Americas .... New York NY 10019 212-459-5000 459-6645
Web: www.bbdo.com
Berenter Greenhouse & Webster Inc 300 Park Ave S 4th Fl .... New York NY 10010 212-727-5600 727-5601
Web: www.bgwad.com
Bernard Hodes Group 220 E 42 St .... New York NY 10017 212-999-9000 999-9484
TF: 888-438-9911 ■ Web: www.hodes.com

Phone | Fax

Bernstein-Rein 4600 Madison Ave Suite 1500 .... Kansas City MO 64112 816-756-0640 756-1753
TF: 800-571-6246 ■ Web: www.bernstein-rein.com
Brand Pharm 105 Madison Ave 18th Fl .... New York NY 10010 212-684-0909 213-4694
Web: www.brandpharmusa.com
Bravo Group 20 Cooper Sq 5th Fl .... New York NY 10003 212-780-5800 575-8339
Bromley Communications Inc 401 E Houston St .... San Antonio TX 78205 210-244-2000 244-2116
Web: www.bromleyville.com
Brouillard Communications Inc 466 Lexington Ave 7th Fl .... New York NY 10017 212-210-8563 210-8511
Web: www.brouillard.com
BuderEngel & Friends 128 King St 3rd Fl .... San Francisco CA 94107 415-658-2800 658-2815
Web: www.buderengel.com
Burnett Leo Co Inc 35 W Wacker Dr .... Chicago IL 60601 312-220-5959 220-3299
Web: www.leoburnett.com
Burrell 233 N Michigan Ave 29th Fl .... Chicago IL 60601 312-297-9600 297-9601
Web: www.burrell.com
Butler Shine Stern & Partners 10 Liberty Ship Way Suite 300 ..... Sausalito CA 94965 415-331-6049 331-3524
Web: www.bssp.com
Campbell-Ewald 30400 Van Dyke Ave .... Warren MI 48093 586-574-3400 558-5891*
*Fax: Hum Res ■ Web: www.cecom.com
Campbell Mithun 222 S 9th St .... Minneapolis MN 55402 612-347-1000 347-1515
Web: www.campbellmithun.com
Carmichael Lynch 800 Hennepin Ave .... Minneapolis MN 55403 612-334-6000 334-6126
Web: www.carmichaellynch.com
Carol H Williams Advertising 555 12th St Suite 1700 .... Oakland CA 94607 510-763-5200 763-9266
Web: www.carolhwilliams.com
Chicago Creative Partnership 314 W Superior St 5th Fl .... Chicago IL 60610 312-335-4330 335-8339
Web: www.chicagocp.com
Clarity Coverdale Fury
120 S 6th St 1 Financial Plaza Suite 1300 .... Minneapolis MN 55402 612-339-3902 359-4399
Web: www.ccf-ideas.com
Clear Ink 741 Alston Way .... Berkeley CA 94710 510-549-4200 549-4205
Web: www.clearink.com
Cliff Freeman & Partners 375 Hudson St 8th Fl .... New York NY 10014 212-463-3200 463-3225
Web: www.clifffreeman.com
Cline Davis & Mann Inc 220 E 42nd St .... New York NY 10017 212-907-4300 687-5411
Web: www.clinedavis.com
CMD 1631 NW Thurman St .... Portland OR 97209 503-223-6794 223-2430
Web: www.cmdpdx.com
CoActive Marketing Group Inc 75 9th Ave 3rd Fl .... New York NY 10011 516-465-4600 622-2888
NASDAQ: CMKG ■ TF: 800-680-9998 ■ Web: www.coactivemarketing.com
Cole & Weber United 221 Yale Ave N Suite 600 .... Seattle WA 98109 206-447-9595 233-0178
TF: 800-262-8515 ■ Web: www.coleweber.com
Colle & McVoy Inc 400 1st Ave N Suite 700 .... Minneapolis MN 55401 612-305-6000 305-6500
Web: www.collemcvoy.com
CommonHealth 400 Interpace Pkwy .... Parsippany NJ 07054 973-352-1000 352-2251
Web: www.commonhealth.com
Compas Inc 4300 Haddonfield Rd Suite 200 .... Pennsauken NJ 08109 856-667-8577 667-6112
Web: www.compasonline.com
Cooper DDB 806 Douglas Rd 11th Fl .... Coral Gables FL 33134 305-529-4300 529-4314
Corbett Accel Healthcare Group 211 E Chicago Ave 16th Fl .... Chicago IL 60611 312-664-5310 649-7232
Web: www.corbett.com
Cossette Communications 415 Madison Ave 3rd Fl .... New York NY 10017 212-753-4700 753-4996
Web: www.cossette.com
Cramer-Krasselt 733 N Van Buren St 4th Fl .... Milwaukee WI 53202 414-227-3500 276-8710
Web: www.c-k.com
Cranford Johnson Robinson Woods 303 W Capitol Ave .... Little Rock AR 72201 501-975-6251 975-4241
TF: 888-383-2579 ■ Web: www.cjrw.com
Creative Alliance Inc 437 W Jefferson St .... Louisville KY 40202 502-584-8787 589-9900
TF: 800-525-0294 ■ Web: www.cre8.com
Crispin Porter Bogusky 3390 Mary St Suite 300 .... Miami FL 33133 305-859-2070 854-3419
Web: www.cpbgroup.com
Dailey & Assoc 8687 Melrose Ave Suite G300 .... West Hollywood CA 90069 310-360-3100 360-0810*
*Fax: Acctg ■ Web: www.daileyads.com
Dale RJ Advertising & Public Relations
211 E Ontario St Suite 200 .... Chicago IL 60611 312-644-2316 644-2688
Web: www.rjdale.com
Davis Elen Advertising 865 S Figueroa St 12th Fl .... Los Angeles CA 90017 213-688-7000 688-7190
TF: 800-729-4322 ■ Web: www.daviselen.com
DDB Worldwide 437 Madison Ave .... New York NY 10022 212-415-2000 415-3414
TF: 800-332-3336 ■ Web: www.ddb.com
Della Femina/Rothschild/Jeary & Partners
902 Broadway 15th Fl .... New York NY 10010 212-506-0700 506-0755
Web: www.dfjp.com
Dentsu America Inc 666 5th Ave 9th Fl .... New York NY 10103 212-397-3333 397-3322
Web: www.dentsuamerica.com
Deutsch Inc 111 8th Ave 14th Fl .... New York NY 10011 212-981-7600 981-7525
TF: 800-287-3457 ■ Web: www.deutschinc.com
Dieste Harmel & Partners 1999 Bryan St Suite 2700 .... Dallas TX 75201 214-259-8000 259-8040
Web: www.dieste.com
Diversified Agency Services 437 Madison Ave .... New York NY 10022 212-415-3049 415-3530
Web: www.dasglobal.com
Doner Advertising 25900 Northwestern Hwy .... Southfield MI 48075 248-354-9700 827-0880*
*Fax: PR
Doremus & Co 200 Varick St 11th Fl .... New York NY 10014 212-366-3000 366-3660
Web: www.doremus.com
Dorland Global Corp 1 S Broad St 11th Fl .... Philadelphia PA 19107 215-625-0111 625-9037
Web: www.dorland.com
Draftfcb 633 N Saint Clair St .... Chicago IL 60611 312-944-3500 944-3566
TF: 800-288-8755 ■ Web: www.draftfcb.com
Dudnyk Co 100 Tournament Dr Suite 214 .... Horsham PA 19044 215-443-9406 443-7049
Web: www.dudnyk.com
Duffy & Shanley Inc 222 Richmond St 4th Fl .... Providence RI 02903 401-274-0001 274-3535
Web: www.duffyshanley.com
E Morris Communications Inc 820 N Orleans Suite 402 .... Chicago IL 60610 312-943-2900 943-5856
Web: www.emorris.com
Eric Mower & Assoc 500 Plum St .... Syracuse NY 13204 315-466-1000 466-2000
Web: www.mower.com
Euro RSCG Life 200 Madison Ave 9th Fl .... New York NY 10016 212-532-1000 251-2766
Web: www.eurorscglife.com
Euro RSCG Life Chelsea 75 9th Ave .... New York NY 10011 212-299-5000 299-5050
Web: www.eurorscg.com
Euro RSCG Worldwide 350 Hudson St 6th Fl .... New York NY 10014 212-886-2000 886-2016
TF: 800-263-7590 ■ Web: www.eurorscg.com
Exposed Brick 250 W Broadway 3rd Fl .... New York NY 10012 212-226-0060 226-0240
Web: www.exposedbrick.com
Fahlgren Inc 414 Walnut St Suite 1006 .... Cincinnati OH 45202 513-241-9200 241-5982
TF: 800-543-2663 ■ Web: www.fahlgren.com
Fallon 50 S 6th St Suite 2800 .... Minneapolis MN 55402 612-758-2345 758-2346
TF: 888-758-2345 ■ Web: www.fallon.com
FCB HealthCare 100 W 33rd St 7th Fl .... New York NY 10001 212-672-2300 672-2301
Web: www.fcbhealthcare.com
Fitzgerald & Co
1 Buckhead Plaza 3060 Peachtree Rd NW Suite 500 .... Atlanta GA 30305 404-504-6900 239-0548
Web: www.fitzco.com
Fogarty Klein Monroe 7155 Old Katy Rd Suite 100 .... Houston TX 77024 713-862-5100 869-6560
TF: 866-228-3252 ■ Web: www.fkmagency.com

Name / Address	City	State	Zip	Phone	Fax
Foth Ron Advertising 8100 N High St *TF:* 888-766-3684 ■ *Web:* www.ronfoth.com	Columbus	OH	43235	614-888-7771	888-5933
Freeman Cliff & Partners 375 Hudson St 8th Fl *Web:* www.clifffreeman.com	New York	NY	10014	212-463-3200	463-3225
Frogdesign Inc 3460 Hillview Ave *Web:* www.frogdesign.com	Palo Alto	CA	94305	650-391-1400	856-3763
FutureBrand 300 Park Ave S 7th Fl *Web:* www.futurebrand.com	New York	NY	10010	212-931-6300	931-6310
G2 Direct & Digital 777 3rd Ave *Web:* www.g2.com/directdigital	New York	NY	10017	212-537-3700	537-3737
G2 Promotional Marketing 1010 Washington Blvd 8th Fl *Web:* g2.com/promotionalmarketing	Stamford	CT	06901	203-352-0600	352-0798
GKV Advertising Inc 1030 Hull St 4th Fl *Web:* www.gkv.com	Baltimore	MD	21230	410-539-5400	234-2441
Global Hue 4000 Town Center 16th Fl *Web:* www.globalhue.com	Southfield	MI	48075	248-223-8900	304-5960
Goodby Silverstein & Partners 720 California St *Web:* www.goodbysilverstein.com	San Francisco	CA	94108	415-392-0669	788-4303
Gotham Inc 100 5th Ave *Web:* www.gothaminc.com	New York	NY	10011	212-414-7000	414-7095
Grafica Inc 525 E Main St *Web:* www.grafica.com	Chester	NJ	07930	908-879-2169	879-2569
Greer Margolis Mitchell Burns & Assoc 1010 Wisconsin Ave NW Suite 800 *TF:* 800-283-7606 ■ *Web:* www.gmmb.com	Washington	DC	20007	202-338-8700	338-2334
Grey Healthcare Group Inc 114 5th Ave *Web:* www.ghgroup.com	New York	NY	10011	212-886-3000	
Grey Worldwide 777 3rd Ave *Web:* greyglobalgroup.com	New York	NY	10017	212-546-2000	546-1495
Group360 Inc 10818 Midwest Industrial Blvd *TF:* 800-666-8243 ■ *Web:* www.group360.com	Saint Louis	MO	63132	314-423-9300	423-6104
GSD & M 828 W 6th St *Web:* www.gsdm.com	Austin	TX	78703	512-242-4736	242-4700
GSW Worldwide 500 Old Worthington Rd *Web:* www.gsw-w.com	Westerville	OH	43082	614-848-4848	848-3477
Hal Lewis Group 1700 Market St 6th Fl *TF:* 888-778-6115 ■ *Web:* www.hlg.com	Philadelphia	PA	19103	215-563-4461	563-1148
Hamilton Communications Group 20 N Wacker St Suite 1960 *Web:* www.hamiltongrp.com	Chicago	IL	60606	312-321-5000	321-5005
Hanft Raboy & Partners 205 Hudson St 7th Fl *Web:* www.hanftunlimited.com	New York	NY	10013	212-674-3100	228-7679
Harrison & Star 16 W 22nd St 8th Fl *Web:* www.hs-ideas.com	New York	NY	10010	212-727-1330	822-6690
HEILBrice Inc 4 Corporate Plaza Suite 100 *Web:* www.hbra.com	Newport Beach	CA	92660	949-644-7477	644-1828
Hill Holliday 200 Clarendon St John Hancock Tower 39th Fl *Web:* www.hillholliday.com	Boston	MA	02116	617-437-1600	859-4216
Hill Holliday 622 3rd Ave 14th Fl *Web:* www.hhcc.com	New York	NY	10017	212-905-7200	
Howard Merrell & Partners Inc 8521 Six Forks Rd Suite 400 *Web:* www.merrellgroup.com	Raleigh	NC	27615	919-848-2400	848-2420
HSR Business to Business 300 E-Business Way Suite 500 *TF:* 800-243-2648 ■ *Web:* www.hsrb2b.com	Cincinnati	OH	45241	513-671-3811	671-8163
Hyphen 711 3rd Ave 12th Fl *Web:* www.hyphenhealth.com	New York	NY	10017	212-856-8700	856-8602
Interpublic Group of Cos Inc 1114 Ave of the Americas *NYSE:* IPG ■ *Web:* www.interpublic.com	New York	NY	10036	212-704-1200	
J Walter Thompson 466 Lexington Ave *Web:* www.jwt.com	New York	NY	10017	212-210-7000	
JWT Specialized Communications 5200 W Century Blvd Suite 310 *TF:* 800-676-7080 ■ *Web:* www.jwtworks.com	Los Angeles	CA	90045	310-665-8700	216-2898
Kang & Lee Advertising 20 Cooper Sq *Web:* www.kanglee.com	New York	NY	10003	212-375-8111	375-8255
Kaplan Thaler Group Ltd 825 8th Ave *Web:* www.kaplanthaler.com	New York	NY	10019	212-474-5000	474-5400
Keller Crescent Co Inc 1100 E Louisiana St *Fax: Cust Svc ■ *TF:* 800-457-3837 ■ *Web:* www.kellercrescent.com	Evansville	IN	47711	812-464-2461	426-7601*
King Group Inc 1801 N Hampton Rd Suite 410	DeSoto	TX	75115	214-720-9046	720-1435
Kirshenbaum Bond & Partners 160 Varick St 4th Fl *Web:* www.kb.com	New York	NY	10013	212-633-0080	463-9097
Korey Kay & Partners 130 5th Ave 8th Fl *Web:* www.koreykay.com	New York	NY	10011	212-620-4300	620-7149
KPR 711 3rd Ave 12th Fl *Web:* www.kprny.com	New York	NY	10017	212-856-8400	856-8660
Kraus-Anderson Communications Group 523 S 8th St *Web:* www.kacommunications.com	Minneapolis	MN	55404	612-375-1080	342-2239
Laughlin/Constable Inc 207 E Michigan St *Web:* www.laughlin.com	Milwaukee	WI	53202	414-272-2400	272-3056
Lefton Al Paul Co Inc 100 Independence Mall W *Web:* www.lefton.com	Philadelphia	PA	19106	215-923-9600	351-4298
Leo Burnett Co Inc 35 W Wacker Dr *Web:* www.leoburnett.com	Chicago	IL	60601	312-220-5959	220-3299
Liggett-Stashower Inc 1228 Euclid Ave 2nd Fl *TF:* 800-877-4573 ■ *Web:* www.liggett.com	Cleveland	OH	44115	216-348-8500	861-1284
Lisa Adelle Design Inc 2828 Routh St Suite 650 *Web:* www.lisaadelledesign.com	Dallas	TX	75201	214-969-0141	528-8344
LLNS Inc 220 E 42nd St 3rd Fl *TF:* 800-599-0188 ■ *Web:* www.llns.com	New York	NY	10017	212-771-3000	771-3010
Lowe 150 E 42nd St *Fax: Hum Res ■ *Web:* www.loweworldwide.com	New York	NY	10017	212-605-8000	605-4703*
Maiden Lane 27 Maiden Ln *Web:* www.maidenlane.com	San Francisco	CA	94108	415-645-6800	645-6868
MARC USA 225 W Station Sq Dr Suite 500 *Web:* www.marc-usa.com	Pittsburgh	PA	15219	412-562-2000	562-2022
Marketing Drive Worldwide 800 Connecticut Ave 3rd Fl *Web:* www.marketingdrive.com	Norwalk	CT	06854	203-857-6100	
Marketing Support Inc 200 E Randolph Dr Suite 5000 *Web:* www.msinet.com	Chicago	IL	60601	312-565-0044	946-6100
Mars Advertising Co Inc 25200 Telegraph Rd *TF:* 800-521-9317 ■ *Web:* www.marsusa.com	Southfield	MI	48034	248-936-2200	936-2501
Marshad Technology Group 76 Laight St *Web:* www.marshad.com	New York	NY	10013	212-292-8910	292-8912
Martin Agency Inc 1 Shockoe Plaza *Web:* www.martinagency.com	Richmond	VA	23219	804-698-8000	698-8001
Martin-Williams Advertising 60 S 6th St Suite 2800 *TF:* 800-632-1388 ■ *Web:* www.martinwilliams.com	Minneapolis	MN	55402	612-340-0800	342-9700
Matlock Advertising & Public Relations 107 Luckie St *Web:* www.matlock-adpr.com	Atlanta	GA	30303	404-872-3200	876-4929
McCann-Erickson Worldwide Advertising 622 3rd Ave *Web:* www.mccann.com	New York	NY	10017	646-865-2000	487-9610
McKinney 318 Blackwell St *Web:* www.mckinney-silver.com	Durham	NC	27701	919-313-0802	313-0805
Medicus NY 1675 Broadway *Web:* www.medicusny.com	New York	NY	10019	212-468-3100	468-3208

Name / Address	City	State	Zip	Phone	Fax
Mendelsohn/Zien Advertising 11111 Santa Monica Blvd Suite 2150 *Web:* www.mzad.com	Los Angeles	CA	90025	310-444-1990	444-9888
Merkley & Partners 200 Varick St 12th Fl *Web:* www.merkleyandpartners.com	New York	NY	10014	212-366-3500	366-3637
MindShare 498 7th Ave *Web:* www.mindshareworld.com	New York	NY	10018	212-297-7000	297-8888
MMG Worldwide 4601 Madison Ave *Web:* www.mmgworldwide.com	Kansas City	MO	64112	816-472-5988	471-5395
Molecular Inc 343 Arsenal St *Web:* www.molecular.com	Watertown	MA	02472	617-218-6500	218-6700
Momentum Worldwide 161 6th Ave 8th Fl *Web:* www.momentum-ww.com	New York	NY	10013	212-367-4500	367-4501
Moroch Partners 3625 N Hall St Suite 1100 *TF:* 800-916-4327 ■ *Web:* www.moroch.com	Dallas	TX	75219	214-520-9700	520-5611
Morris E Communications Inc 820 N Orleans Suite 402 *Web:* www.emorris.com	Chicago	IL	60610	312-943-2900	943-5856
Mower Eric & Assoc 500 Plum St *Web:* www.mower.com	Syracuse	NY	13204	315-466-1000	466-2000
MRM Partners Worldwide 622 3rd Ave *Web:* www.mrmworldwide.com	New York	NY	10017	646-865-2000	487-9610
Mullen 36 Essex St *TF:* 800-363-6010 ■ *Web:* www.mullen.com	Wenham	MA	01984	978-468-1155	468-1133
Muse Communications Inc 5358 Melrose Ave West Bldg Ground Fl *Web:* www.museusa.com	Hollywood	CA	90038	323-960-4080	960-4081
NAS Recruitment Communications 1 Infinity Corporate Ctr Dr *TF:* 866-627-7327 ■ *Web:* www.nasrecruitment.com	Cleveland	OH	44125	216-478-0300	468-8280
Noble 2155 W Chesterfield Blvd *Web:* www.noble.net	Springfield	MO	65807	417-875-5000	875-5051
Northlich 720 E Pete Rose Way Suite 120 *Web:* www.northlich.com	Cincinnati	OH	45202	513-421-8840	287-1858
Ogilvy Healthworld 100 Ave of the Americas *Web:* www.ogilvyhealthworld.com	New York	NY	10013	212-625-4000	966-7755
Ogilvy Interactive 309 W 49th St Worldwide Plaza *Web:* www.ogilvy.com/o_interactive	New York	NY	10019	212-237-4000	237-5123
Ogilvy & Mather Worldwide 309 W 49th St Worldwide Plaza *Web:* www.ogilvy.com	New York	NY	10019	212-237-4000	237-5123
Ogilvy One Worldwide 309 W 49th St *Web:* www.ogilvy.com	New York	NY	10019	212-237-6000	237-5123
Pacific Communications 575 Anton Blvd Suite 900 *Web:* www.pacific-com.com	Costa Mesa	CA	92626	714-427-1900	427-1965
Pacifico Inc 3880 S Bascom Ave Suite 215 *Web:* www.pacifico.com	San Jose	CA	91525	408-559-8880	
Pedone & Partners 100 5th Ave 6th Fl *Web:* www.pedonepartners.com	New York	NY	10011	212-627-3300	627-3966
Periscope 921 Washington Ave S *TF:* 800-339-2103 ■ *Web:* www.periscope.com	Minneapolis	MN	55415	612-339-2100	399-0600
Prime Access Inc 345 7th Ave *Web:* www.primeaccess.net	New York	NY	10001	212-868-6800	868-9495
Publicis & Hal Riney 2001 Embarcadero *Web:* www.hrp.com	San Francisco	CA	94133	415-293-2001	293-2628
Publicis USA 4 Herald Sq 950 6th Ave *Web:* www.publicis.com	New York	NY	10001	212-279-5550	279-5560
Rare Method 1812 4th St SW Suite 500 *Web:* www.cogentmedia.com	Calgary	AB	T2S1W1	403-543-4500	532-3004
RealTime Solutions 12925 Prosperity Ave *Web:* www.realtime-solutions.net	Becker	MN	55308	763-262-3150	
Resource Interactive 343 N Front St *TF:* 800-550-5815 ■ *Web:* www.resource.com	Columbus	OH	43215	614-621-2888	621-2873
Richards Group 8750 N Central Expy Suite 1200 *Web:* www.richards.com	Dallas	TX	75231	214-891-5700	
Risdall Advertising Agency 550 Main St *TF:* 888-747-3255 ■ *Web:* www.risdall.com	New Brighton	MN	55112	651-631-1098	631-2561
Rives Carlberg 3900 Essex Ln Suite 350 *Web:* www.carlberg.com	Houston	TX	77027	713-965-0764	965-0135
RJ Dale Advertising & Public Relations 211 E Ontario St Suite 200 *Web:* www.rjdale.com	Chicago	IL	60611	312-644-2316	644-2688
RMGConnect 466 Lexington Ave *Web:* www.rmgconnect.com	New York	NY	10017	212-210-7000	210-5678
Rockett Burkhead & Winslow 8601 6 Forks Rd 7th Fl *Web:* www.dynamicbranding.com	Raleigh	NC	27615	919-848-2600	848-2614
Ron Foth Advertising 8100 N High St *TF:* 888-766-3684 ■ *Web:* www.ronfoth.com	Columbus	OH	43235	614-888-7771	888-5933
Rubin Postaer & Assoc 2525 Colorado Ave *Web:* www.rpa.com	Santa Monica	CA	90404	310-394-4000	917-2526
Saatchi & Saatchi 375 Hudson St *Web:* www.saatchiny.com	New York	NY	10014	212-463-2000	463-9856
Saint John & Partners Advertising & Public Relations 5220 Belfort Rd Suite 400 *TF:* 800-642-2828 ■ *Web:* www.sjp.com	Jacksonville	FL	32256	904-281-2500	281-0030
Sanders\Wingo Advertising Inc 221 N Kansas Suite 900 *Web:* www.sanderswingo.com	El Paso	TX	79901	915-533-9583	533-3601
Sawtooth Group 100 Woodbridge Ctr Dr Suite 102 *Web:* www.sawtoothgroup.com	Woodbridge	NJ	07095	732-636-6600	602-4212
Seiden Group 708 3rd Ave 13th Fl *Web:* www.seidenadvertising.com	New York	NY	10017	212-223-8700	223-1188
Shaker Recruitment Advertising & Communications 1100 Lake St 3rd Fl *TF:* 800-323-5170 ■ *Web:* www.shaker.com	Oak Park	IL	60301	708-383-5320	383-7670
Siegel & Gale 437 Madison Ave 12th Fl *Web:* www.siegelgale.com	New York	NY	10022	212-817-6650	817-6680
SPAR Group Inc 580 White Plains Rd 6th Fl *NASDAQ:* SGRP ■ *Web:* www.sparinc.com	Tarrytown	NY	10591	914-332-4100	332-0741
Stern Advertising Inc 29125 Chagrin Blvd 3rd Fl	Pepper Pike	OH	44122	216-464-4850	464-7859
Sudler & Hennessey 230 Park Ave S *Fax: Hum Res ■ *Web:* www.sudler.com	New York	NY	10003	212-614-4100	598-6930*
TBC (Trahan Burden & Charles Inc) 900 S Wolfe St *Web:* www.tbc.us	Baltimore	MD	21231	410-347-7500	986-1299
TBWA Chiat/Day Inc 488 Madison Ave 7th Fl *TF:* 877-666-2347 ■ *Web:* www.tbwachiat.com	New York	NY	10022	212-804-1000	804-1200
Team One 1960 E Grand Ave Suite 700 *Web:* www.teamoneadv.com	El Segundo	CA	90245	310-615-2000	322-7565
Ted Barkus Co 5017 Anderson St	Philadelphia	PA	19118	215-545-0616	
Ten United 1000 Legion Pl Suite 1250 *Web:* www.tenunited.com	Orlando	FL	32801	407-649-8101	649-8686
Ten United 375 N Front St Suite 400 *TF:* 866-415-1010 ■ *Web:* www.tenunited.com	Columbus	OH	43215	614-573-1010	573-1011
Ten United 420 Fort Duquesne Blvd Suite 1900 1Gateway Ctr *TF:* 800-937-3657 ■ *Web:* www.tenunited.com	Pittsburgh	PA	15222	412-471-5300	471-3308
Thompson J Walter 466 Lexington Ave *Web:* www.jwt.com	New York	NY	10017	212-210-7000	
Three Marketeers Advertising Inc 785 The Almeda *Web:* www.3marketeers.com	San Jose	CA	95126	408-293-3233	293-2433
Tinsley Advertising 2660 Brickell Ave *Web:* www.tinsley.com	Miami	FL	33129	305-856-6060	858-3877

				Phone	Fax
TM Advertising LP 6555 Sierra Dr *Web:* www.tm.com	Irving	TX	75039	972-556-1100	830-2619
Torre Lazur-McCann HealthCare Worldwide 20 Waterview Blvd Waterview Corp Ctr *Web:* www.torrelazur.com	Parsippany	NJ	07054	973-263-9100	263-4113
Trahan Burden & Charles Inc (TBC) 900 S Wolfe St *Web:* www.tbc.us	Baltimore	MD	21231	410-347-7500	986-1299
Tribal DDB Worldwide 437 Madison Ave 8th Fl *Web:* www.tribalddb.com	New York	NY	10022	212-515-8600	515-8660
Trone 4035 Piedmont Pkwy *TF:* 877-493-3043 ■ *Web:* www.trone.com	High Point	NC	27265	336-886-1622	886-4242
UniWorld Group Inc 100 Ave of the Americas 15th Fl *TF:* 800-900-2958 ■ *Web:* www.uniworldgroup.com	New York	NY	10013	212-219-1600	941-0650
VML 250 Richards Rd *TF:* 800-990-2468 ■ *Web:* www.vml.com	Kansas City	MO	64116	816-283-0700	283-0954
Vox Medica Inc 601 Walnut St Suite 250-E *TF:* 800-842-6482 ■ *Web:* www.voxmedica.com	Philadelphia	PA	19106	215-238-8500	592-4287
WeAreGigantic 411 Lafayette St 6th Fl *Web:* www.wearegigantic.com	New York	NY	10003	212-979-6600	475-3932
West Wayne 1170 Peachtree St NE Suite 1500 *Web:* www.westwayne.com	Atlanta	GA	30309	404-347-8700	347-8800
Wieden & Kennedy 224 NW 13th Ave *Web:* www.wk.com	Portland	OR	97209	503-937-7000	937-8000
Williams Carol H Advertising 555 12th St Suite 1700 *Web:* www.carolhwilliams.com	Oakland	CA	94607	510-763-5200	763-9266
WKP & Spier New York 460 Park Ave S *Web:* www.wkpadv.com	New York	NY	10016	212-686-2914	686-5652
WPP Group USA Inc 125 Park Ave 4th Fl	New York	NY	10017	212-632-2200	632-2222
Wyse Advertising 25 Prospect Ave W Suite 1700 **Fax:* Mktg ■ *Web:* www.wyseadv.com	Cleveland	OH	44115	216-696-2424	736-4440*
Y & R Inc 285 Madison Ave *Web:* www.yandr.com	New York	NY	10017	212-210-3000	490-9073
Zimmerman Advertising 2200 W Commercial Blvd Suite 300 *TF:* 800-248-8522 ■ *Web:* www.zadv.com	Fort Lauderdale	FL	33309	954-731-2900	731-2977

ADVERTISING DISPLAYS

SEE Displays - Exhibit & Trade Show p. 1589; Displays - Point-of-Purchase p. 1589; Signs p. 2317

5 ADVERTISING SERVICES - DIRECT MAIL

				Phone	Fax
Accurate Mailings Inc 215 O'Neill Ave *TF:* 800-732-3290 ■ *Web:* www.accuratemailings.com	Belmont	CA	94002	650-591-5601	594-8428
Acxiom Direct 822 Airpark Ctr Dr *TF:* 888-816-0925 ■ *Web:* www.acxiom.com	Nashville	TN	37217	615-850-3000	399-9867
Adtron Inc 1700 Morrissey Dr	Bloomington	IL	61704	309-662-1221	663-6691
Advanced Technology Marketing 400 N Continental Blvd Suite 200 *Web:* www.advancedtechmktg.com	El Segundo	CA	90245	310-642-1881	414-9436
ADVO Inc 1 Targeting Center *NYSE:* AD ■ **Fax:* Hum Res ■ *TF:* 800-238-6462 ■ *Web:* www.advo.com	Windsor	CT	06095	860-285-6100	298-5597*
American Mailers 100 American Way *Web:* www.americanmailers.com	Detroit	MI	48209	313-842-4000	842-2900
American Student List LLC 330 Old Country Rd *TF:* 888-462-5600 ■ *Web:* www.studentlist.com	Mineola	NY	11501	516-248-6100	248-6364
Americomm Direct Marketing 804 Greenbrier Cir *TF:* 800-527-6757 ■ *Web:* www.americomm.net	Chesapeake	VA	23320	757-622-2724	624-5713
Arista Information Systems Inc 1105 Fairchild Rd *Web:* www.aristainfo.com	Winston-Salem	NC	27105	336-776-1105	776-1104
Bennett Kuhn Varner Inc 2964 Peachtree Rd Suite 700 *Web:* www.bkv.com	Atlanta	GA	30305	404-233-0332	233-0302
Blair DL Inc 1051 Franklin Ave *Web:* www.dlblair.com	Garden City	NY	11530	516-746-3700	746-3889
Bloom Carl Assoc Inc 81 Main St Suite 126 *Web:* www.carlbloom.com	White Plains	NY	10601	914-761-2800	761-2744
Brierley & Partners 8401 N Central Expy Suite 1000 *Web:* www.brierley.com	Dallas	TX	75225	214-760-8700	743-5511
Carl Bloom Assoc Inc 81 Main St Suite 126 *Web:* www.carlbloom.com	White Plains	NY	10601	914-761-2800	761-2744
Catalina Marketing Corp 200 Carillon Pkwy *NYSE:* POS ■ *TF:* 888-322-3814 ■ *Web:* www.catmktg.com	Saint Petersburg	FL	33716	727-579-5000	556-2700
CBIZ The Leifer Group 11440 Tomahawk Creek Pkwy *Web:* www.cbiz.com/leifer/	Leawood	KS	66211	913-385-9200	234-1105
Centron Data Services Inc 1175 Devin Dr *TF Cust Svc:* 800-732-8787 ■ *Web:* www.centrondata.com	Norton Shores	MI	49441	231-798-1221	799-0092
Cenveo Inc 1 Canterberry Green *NYSE:* CVO ■ *Web:* www.cenveo.com	Stamford	CT	06901	203-595-3000	595-3070
ChoicePoint Precision Marketing 8600 N Industrial Rd *Web:* www.choicepointdirect.com	Peoria	IL	61615	309-689-1000	689-6969
City Directories 5711 S 86th Cir *TF:* 888-508-0866 ■ *Web:* www.infousacity.com	Omaha	NE	68127	402-593-4500	596-7677
Corcillo Direct Inc 65 East Ave *Web:* www.corcillodirect.com	Norwalk	CT	06851	203-854-9992	854-9625
Corporate Express Promotional Marketing 1400 N Price Rd *TF:* 800-325-1965 ■ *Web:* www.cepromotionalmarketing.com	Saint Louis	MO	63132	314-432-1800	432-1818
Creative Automation Co 220 Fencl Ln *TF:* 800-773-1588 ■ *Web:* www.cauto.com	Hillside	IL	60162	708-449-2800	449-2811
CTRAC Computer Services Inc 16855 Foltz Pkwy *Web:* www.ctrac.com	Strongsville	OH	44149	440-572-1000	572-3330
Denison Mailing Service 9601 Newton Ave S *Web:* www.denisonmailing.com	Minneapolis	MN	55431	952-888-1460	888-9641
Direct Media Inc 200 Pemberwick Rd *Web:* www.directmedia.com	Greenwich	CT	06830	203-532-1000	532-3866
DL Blair Inc 1051 Franklin Ave *Web:* www.dlblair.com	Garden City	NY	11530	516-746-3700	746-3889
DMW Worldwide LLC 1325 Morris Dr *TF:* 877-744-3699 ■ *Web:* www.dmw-w.com	Wayne	PA	19087	610-407-0407	407-0410
Draftfcb 101 E Erie St *Web:* www.draftfcb.com	Chicago	IL	60611	312-425-5000	425-5010
EBSCO Industries Inc Publisher Promotion & Fulfillment Div 5724 Hwy 280 E *TF:* 800-633-4931	Birmingham	AL	35242	205-991-6600	995-1588
FFwd 325 Arlington Ave Suite 700 *Web:* www.ffwdgroup.com	Charlotte	NC	28203	704-344-7900	344-7920
Focus Direct LLC 9707 Broadway *TF:* 800-299-9185 ■ *Web:* www.focusdirect.com	San Antonio	TX	78217	210-805-9185	
G2 Direct & Digital 777 3rd Ave *Web:* www.g2.com/directdigital	New York	NY	10017	212-537-3700	537-3737
GA Wright Inc Direct Marketing Div 10325 E 47th Ave *TF:* 800-824-5886 ■ *Web:* www.gawright.com	Denver	CO	80238	303-333-4453	393-5320
Gannett Direct Marketing Services Inc 3400 Robards Ct *TF:* 800-345-5654 ■ *Web:* www.gdms.com	Louisville	KY	40218	502-454-6660	459-7479
Haines & Co Inc 8050 Freedom Ave NW *TF:* 800-843-8452 ■ *Web:* www.haines.com	North Canton	OH	44720	330-494-9111	494-3862
Hallmark Data Systems 7300 N Linder Ave *Web:* www.halldata.com	Skokie	IL	60077	847-983-2000	763-9542
Harte-Hanks Inc PO Box 269 *NYSE:* HHS ■ *TF:* 800-456-9748 ■ *Web:* www.harte-hanks.com	San Antonio	TX	78291	210-829-9000	829-9403
Haynes & Partners Communications 5745 Lee Rd *Web:* www.hp-inc.com	Indianapolis	IN	46216	317-860-3000	860-3001
Hecks Direct Mail & Printing Service Inc 202 W Florence Ave *TF:* 800-997-4325 ■ *Web:* www.hecksprinting.com	Toledo	OH	43605	419-661-6000	661-6036
Heritage Publishing Co 2402 Wildwood Ave **Fax:* Hum Res ■ *TF:* 800-643-8822	Sherwood	AR	72120	501-835-5000	835-5834*
Hibbert Group 400 Pennington Ave *TF:* 888-442-2378 ■ *Web:* www.hibbertco.com	Trenton	NJ	08618	609-394-7500	392-9237
iDirect Marketing 9880 Research Dr Suite 100 *TF:* 877-339-3737 ■ *Web:* www.idirectmarketing.com	Irvine	CA	92618	949-753-7300	753-7523
Jacobs & Clevenger Inc 303 E Wacker Dr Suite 2350 *Web:* www.jacobsclevenger.com	Chicago	IL	60601	312-894-3000	894-3005
Johnson & Quin Inc 7460 N Lehigh Ave *TF:* 800-872-3769 ■ *Web:* www.johnsonandquin.com	Niles	IL	60714	847-588-4800	647-6949
JS & A Group Inc 3350 Palms Centre Dr *TF:* 800-323-6400	Las Vegas	NV	89103	702-798-9000	597-2002
King Organization 245 S 4th Ave *Web:* www.kinglitho.com	Mount Vernon	NY	10550	914-667-4200	667-5281
Klasek Letter Co 2850 S Jefferson Ave *TF:* 877-551-5596 ■ *Web:* www.klasek.com	Saint Louis	MO	63118	314-664-0023	664-9457
Lake Group Media Inc 411 Theodore Fremd Ave Suite 2-N *Web:* www.lakegroupmedia.com	Rye	NY	10580	914-925-2400	925-2499
Lewis Systems Inc 325 E Oliver St *TF:* 800-533-5394 ■ *Web:* www.lewisdirect.com	Baltimore	MD	21202	410-539-5100	685-5144
Lortz Direct Marketing Inc 13936 Gold Cir *TF:* 800-366-7686 ■ *Web:* www.lortzdirect.com	Omaha	NE	68144	402-334-9446	334-9622
Market Data Retrieval 1 Forest Pkwy *TF:* 800-333-8802 ■ *Web:* www.schooldata.com	Shelton	CT	06484	203-926-4800	926-0784
Marketing Drive Worldwide 800 Connecticut Ave 3rd Fl *Web:* www.marketingdrive.com	Norwalk	CT	06854	203-857-6100	
Marketing Resource Group Inc 225 S Washington Sq *Web:* www.mrgmi.com	Lansing	MI	48933	517-372-4400	372-5107
McCann-Erickson WorldGroup 622 3rd Ave *Web:* www.mccann.com	New York	NY	10017	646-865-2000	487-9610
Modern Printing & Mailing 3535 Enterprise St *Web:* home.pacbell.net/modprint/homepage.html	San Diego	CA	92110	619-222-0535	222-0657
Money Mailer LLC 12131 Western Ave *TF:* 800-234-2771 ■ *Web:* www.moneymailer.com	Garden Grove	CA	92841	714-889-3800	889-4618
Newgen Results Corp 10243 Genetic Center Dr *TF:* 800-763-9436 ■ *Web:* www.ngresults.com	San Diego	CA	92121	858-346-5000	346-6500
News America Marketing 1211 Ave of the Americas 5th Fl *TF:* 800-462-0852 ■ *Web:* www.newsamerica.com	New York	NY	10036	212-782-8000	575-5847
Odell Simms & Assoc 7704 Leesburg Pike *TF:* 800-662-7400 ■ *Web:* www.odellsimms.com	Falls Church	VA	22043	703-903-9797	903-8850
Ogilvy Action 350 W Mart Center Dr Suite 1150 *TF:* 888-414-1410 ■ *Web:* www.ogilvyaction.com	Chicago	IL	60654	312-527-3900	527-3327
Ogilvy One Worldwide 309 W 49th St *Web:* www.ogilvy.com	New York	NY	10019	212-237-6000	237-5123
Priority Publications 6700 France Ave S Suite 300 *TF:* 800-727-6397 ■ *Web:* www.prioritypub.com	Edina	MN	55435	952-920-9943	920-9930
Promotions Unlimited Corp PO Box 087601 *TF:* 800-992-9307 ■ *Web:* www.promot.com	Racine	WI	53408	262-681-7000	681-7001
Proven Direct W165 N5761 Ridgewood Dr *TF:* 866-890-6245 ■ *Web:* www.provendirect.com	Menomonee Falls	WI	53051	262-703-0760	703-0520
Publi-Sac Group 525 boul Lebeau *Web:* www.publisac.com	Saint-Laurent	QC	H4N1S2	514-337-6920	832-5083
Publishers Mailing Service 230 Aurora Ave N	Seattle	WA	98109	206-448-0411	441-4564
Rapp Collins Worldwide 437 Madison Ave 3rd & 4th Fl *Web:* www.rappcollins.com	New York	NY	10022	212-817-6800	817-6750
RDI Marketing Services 4350 Glendale Milford Rd Suite 250 *TF:* 800-388-7636 ■ *Web:* www.rdimarketing.com	Cincinnati	OH	45242	513-984-5927	984-6126
Reid Russ Co Inc 2 N Lake Ave Suite 600 *Web:* www.russreid.com	Pasadena	CA	91101	626-449-6100	449-6190
RR Donnelley Logistics 1000 Windham Pkwy *TF:* 888-744-7773 ■ *Web:* www.donnelleylogistics.com	Bolingbrook	IL	60490	630-226-6100	226-6555
RR Donnelley Response Marketing Services 3075 Highland Pkwy *TF:* 800-745-0780	Downers Grove	IL	60515	630-963-9494	
RSVP Publications 6730 W Linebaugh Ave Suite 201 *TF:* 800-360-7787 ■ *Web:* www.rsvppublications.com	Tampa	FL	33625	813-960-7787	549-3306
RTC Relationship Marketing 1055 Thomas Jefferson St NW Suite 500 *Web:* www.rtcdirect.com	Washington	DC	20007	202-625-2111	424-7900
Russ Reid Co Inc 2 N Lake Ave Suite 600 *Web:* www.russreid.com	Pasadena	CA	91101	626-449-6100	449-6190
Sherman & Assoc 333 Harmon Ave NW *Web:* www.shermanexperience.com	Warren	OH	44483	330-399-4500	399-6747
Simon Marketing Inc 5200 W Century Blvd Suite 420	Los Angeles	CA	90045	310-417-4660	417-4670
Sitel Operating Corp 3102 W End Ave Suite 1000 *TF:* 877-935-6442 ■ *Web:* www.sitel.com	Nashville	TN	37203	615-301-7100	301-7150
SourceLink Inc 500 Park Blvd Suite 415 **Fax Area Code:* 847 ■ *Web:* www.sourcelink.com	Itasca	IL	60143	866-947-6872	438-5016*
Step Saver Inc 213 Spring St *Web:* www.stepsaver.com	Southington	CT	06489	860-628-9645	621-1841
Summit Marketing 8515 Bluejacket St *TF:* 800-843-7347 ■ *Web:* www.summitmarketing.com	Lenexa	KS	66214	913-888-6222	888-2493
SuperCoups 350 Revolutionary Dr *TF:* 800-626-2620 ■ *Web:* www.supercoups.com	East Taunton	MA	02718	508-977-2000	977-0644
Tension Envelope Corp 819 E 19th St *TF:* 800-388-5122 ■ *Web:* www.tension.com	Kansas City	MO	64108	816-471-3800	283-1498
Transcontinental Distribution 525 boul Lebeau *Web:* www.publisac.com	Saint-Laurent	QC	H4N1S2	514-337-6920	832-5083
Tyme Direct Mail Services Inc 250 Hudson St 14th Fl *Web:* www.tymedirect.com	New York	NY	10013	212-691-4444	691-6747
United Advertising Publications Inc 2301 McDaniel Dr Suite 100 *Web:* www.unitedadvertising.com	Carrollton	TX	75006	972-280-0055	
United Letter Service Inc DBA United Graphics & **Mailing Group** 2200 Estes Ave *Web:* www.unitedletter.com	Elk Grove Village	IL	60007	312-427-3537	435-1192
United Marketing Solutions 7644 Dynatech Ct *TF:* 800-368-3501 ■ *Web:* www.unitedol.com	Springfield	VA	22153	703-644-0200	455-8519
Valpak Direct Marketing Systems Inc 8605 Largo Lakes Dr *TF:* 800-237-6266 ■ *Web:* www.valpak.com	Largo	FL	33773	727-393-1270	393-8060

Company	City	State	Zip	Phone	Fax
Vertis Communications 2901 Blackbridge Rd *TF:* 800-441-1850 ■ *Web:* www.usamailnow.com	York	PA	17406	717-852-1000	852-1030
Vertis Media & Marketing Services 21 Corporate Dr *Web:* www.vertisinc.com	Clifton Park	NY	12065	518-373-0419	373-5890
WA Wilde Co 201 Summer St **Fax:* Hum Res ■ *TF:* 800-933-9453 ■ *Web:* www.wilde.com	Holliston	MA	01746	508-429-5515	893-0375*
Western Graphics 7614 Lemon Ave *Web:* www.westerngraphics.org	Lemon Grove	CA	91945	619-466-4157	466-6428
Wilde WA Co 201 Summer St **Fax:* Hum Res ■ *TF:* 800-933-9453 ■ *Web:* www.wilde.com	Holliston	MA	01746	508-429-5515	893-0375*
World Marketing 7950 Joliet Rd Suite 200 *Web:* www.worldmarkinc.com	McCook	IL	60525	708-871-6000	871-6245
Wright GA Inc Direct Marketing Div 10325 E 47th Ave *TF:* 800-824-5886 ■ *Web:* www.gawright.com	Denver	CO	80238	303-333-4453	393-5320
Yeck Brothers Co 2222 Arbor Blvd *TF:* 800-417-2767 ■ *Web:* www.yeck.com	Dayton	OH	45439	937-294-4000	294-6985

6 ADVERTISING SERVICES - MEDIA BUYERS

Company	City	State	Zip	Phone	Fax
Allan Hackel Organization Inc 1330 Center St *Web:* www.hackelbarter.com	Newton Center	MA	02459	617-965-4400	527-6005
Arnold Romedy & Sullivan Advertising Inc 1001 Reads Lake Rd	Chattanooga	TN	37415	423-875-3743	875-5346
Berry Co 3170 Kettering Blvd *TF:* 800-366-2379 ■ *Web:* www.lmberry.com	Dayton	OH	45439	937-296-2121	
Carat USA 2450 Colorado Ave Suite 300 E *TF:* 800-847-6334 ■ *Web:* www.carat.com	Santa Monica	CA	90404	310-255-1000	255-1050
CBS Television Distribution Media Sales 1675 Broadway 17th Fl	New York	NY	10019	212-708-8212	708-8200
Corinthian Communications Inc 500 8th Ave 5th Fl *Web:* www.mediabuying.com	New York	NY	10018	212-279-5700	239-1772
Cybereps 505 Sansome St 2nd Fl *Web:* www.cybereps.com	San Francisco	CA	94111	415-268-9201	442-5049
EBSCO Industries Inc Publisher Promotion & Fulfillment Div 5724 Hwy 280 E *TF:* 800-633-4931	Birmingham	AL	35242	205-991-6600	995-1588
Hackel Allan Organization Inc 1330 Center St *Web:* www.hackelbarter.com	Newton Center	MA	02459	617-965-4400	527-6005
Horizon Media Inc 630 3rd Ave 3rd Fl *TF:* 800-282-0901 ■ *Web:* www.horizonmedia.net	New York	NY	10017	212-916-8600	916-8685
Interep National Radio Sales Inc 100 Park Ave 5th Fl *Web:* www.interep.com	New York	NY	10017	212-916-0700	
Katz Media Group Inc 125 W 55th St **Fax:* Hum Res ■ *Web:* www.katz-media.com	New York	NY	10019	212-424-6000	424-6110*
Lopito Ileana & Howie Inc PO Box 11856 *Web:* www.lih.com	San Juan	PR	00922	787-783-1160	783-8063
MAGNA Global USA 1 Dag Hammarskjold Plaza 7th Fl *Web:* www.magnaglobal.com	New York	NY	10017	917-542-7000	542-7001
Media Networks Inc 1 Station Pl 5th Fl *TF:* 800-225-3457 ■ *Web:* www.mni.com	Stamford	CT	06902	203-967-3100	967-6472
Millennium Sales & Marketing 125 W 55th St 6th Fl	New York	NY	10019	212-373-8200	
Petry Media 3 E 54th St *Web:* www.petrymedia.com	New York	NY	10022	212-688-0200	230-5843
PGR Media 34 Farnsworth St *Web:* www.pgrmedia.com	Boston	MA	02210	617-502-8400	451-0451
PHD USA 200 N Broadway 14th Fl	Saint Louis	MO	63102	314-444-2100	444-2199
Rainbow Advertising Sales Corp 530 5th Ave 6th Fl *Web:* www.rainbow-media.com/adsales/index.html	New York	NY	10036	212-382-6100	382-6128
RW Walker Co Inc 601 W 5th St Suite 205 *Web:* www.rwwcompany.com	Los Angeles	CA	90071	213-896-9210	896-9209
TaigMarks Inc 223 S Main St Suite 100 *Web:* www.taigmarks.com	Elkhart	IN	46516	574-294-8844	294-8855
Telerep Inc 885 2nd Ave *Web:* www.telerepinc.com	New York	NY	10017	212-759-8787	486-8746
Universal McCann Worldwide 622 3rd Ave *Web:* www.universalmccann.com	New York	NY	10017	646-865-5000	865-3728
Walker RW Co Inc 601 W 5th St Suite 205 *Web:* www.rwwcompany.com	Los Angeles	CA	90071	213-896-9210	896-9209
Winstar Interactive Media 100 Park Ave 5th Fl *TF Cust Svc:* 888-961-8800 ■ *Web:* www.winstarinteractive.com	New York	NY	10017	212-916-0700	896-8321
Working Mother Media Inc 60 E 42nd St 27th *TF:* 800-627-0690 ■ *Web:* www.workingmother.com	New York	NY	10165	212-351-6400	351-6487
Worldata 3000 N Military Trail *TF:* 800-331-8102 ■ *Web:* www.worldata.com	Boca Raton	FL	33431	561-393-8200	368-8345

7 ADVERTISING SERVICES - ONLINE

Company	City	State	Zip	Phone	Fax
24/7 Real Media Inc 132 W 31st St 9th Fl *NASDAQ: TFSM* ■ *TF:* 877-247-2477 ■ *Web:* www.247realmedia.com	New York	NY	10001	212-231-7100	760-1774
ACSYS Inc 6 Executive Dr Suite 106 *TF:* 866-497-3725 ■ *Web:* www.acsysweb.com	Farmington	CT	06032	860-679-9332	679-9344
Active Decisions Inc 1400 Fashion Island Blvd Suite 500 *TF:* 866-662-3847 ■ *Web:* www.activedecisions.com	San Mateo	CA	94404	650-342-0500	358-8600
Active Network 10182 Telesis Ct Suite 300 *TF Cust Svc:* 888-543-7223 ■ *Web:* www.theactivenetwork.com	San Diego	CA	92121	858-551-9916	964-3978
Acxiom Digital 177 Bovet Rd Suite 200 *TF:* 800-491-9320 ■ *Web:* www.acxiomdigital.com	San Mateo	CA	94402	650-356-3400	356-3410
Addis Group Inc 2515 9th St *Web:* www.addis.com	Berkeley	CA	94710	510-704-7500	704-7501
Advertising.com Inc 1020 Hull St Suite 100 *TF:* 877-835-6699 ■ *Web:* www.advertising.com	Baltimore	MD	21230	410-244-1370	244-1699
Agency.com Ltd 488 Madison Ave 22nd Fl *TF:* 800-736-4644 ■ *Web:* www.agency.com	New York	NY	10022	212-358-2600	358-2604
Aptimus Inc 2001 6th Ave Suite 3200 *NASDAQ: APTM* ■ *Web:* www.aptimus.com	Seattle	WA	98121	206-441-9100	441-9661
aQuantive Inc 821 2nd Ave Suite 1800 *NASDAQ: AQNT* ■ *Web:* www.aquantive.com	Seattle	WA	98104	206-816-8700	816-8808
Arc Worldwide 35 W Wacker Dr 15th Fl *Web:* www.arcww.com	Chicago	IL	60601	312-220-3200	220-1995
AspenMedia 13885-A Alton Pkwy *Web:* www.aspenmedia.com	Irvine	CA	92618	949-454-0124	
Beyond Interactive Inc 5405 Data Ct Suite 200 *Web:* www.gobeyond.com	Ann Arbor	MI	48108	734-205-0600	747-8621
BigBad Inc 321 Summer St *TF:* 877-296-4287 ■ *Web:* www.bigbad.com	Boston	MA	02210	617-338-7770	338-7787
Biggs/Gilmore Communications 261 E Kalamazoo Ave Suite 300 *Web:* www.biggs-gilmore.com	Kalamazoo	MI	49007	269-349-7711	349-3051
BigWorld Communications 650 N Dearborn St Suite 700 *Web:* www.bworld.com	Chicago	IL	60610	312-649-9408	649-9418
Blattner Brunner Inc 11 Stanwix St 5th Fl *TF:* 800-545-5372 ■ *Web:* www.blattnerbrunner.com	Pittsburgh	PA	15222	412-995-9500	995-9501
Blue Cat Design Inc 4753 Mast Woods Rd *Web:* www.bluecatdesign.com	Port Hope	ON	L1A3V5	905-753-1017	
Blue Diesel 500 Olde Worthington Rd *Web:* www.bluediesel.com	Westerville	OH	43082	614-540-4226	540-3155
Burst Media 8 New England Executive Pk *Web:* www.burstmedia.com	Burlington	MA	01803	781-272-5544	272-0897
Carve Media Inc 38 Miller Rd Suite 221 *Web:* www.carve.com	Mill Valley	CA	94941	415-389-9981	389-9961
Claria Corp 555 Broadway St *Web:* www.claria.com	Redwood City	CA	94063	650-980-1500	980-1599
Commission Junction Inc 530 E Montecito St *TF:* 800-761-1072 ■ *Web:* www.cj.com	Santa Barbara	CA	93103	805-730-8000	730-8001
CrossCurrent Solutions 1220 W 6th St Suite 407	Cleveland	OH	44113	216-902-8050	241-8190
D2 Creative 28 World's Fair Dr *Web:* www.nyd2.com	Somerset	NJ	08873	732-805-9297	805-0637
Digital Pulp Inc 220 E 23rd St Suite 900 *Web:* www.digitalpulp.com	New York	NY	10010	212-679-0676	679-6217
DigitalDay Creative Group 1653 Main St *Web:* www.digitaldaycreative.com	Peninsula	OH	44264	330-657-2565	657-2389
DoubleClick Inc 111 8th Ave 10th Fl *TF:* 866-683-0001 ■ *Web:* www.doubleclick.com/us	New York	NY	10011	212-271-2542	287-1203
E-centives Inc 6901 Rockledge Dr *TF:* 877-323-6848 ■ *Web:* www.e-centives.com	Bethesda	MD	20817	240-333-6100	
e21 corp 41900 Christy St *Web:* www.e21mm.com	Fremont	CA	94538	510-226-6780	226-0679
Enhance Interactive Inc 727 N 1550 East Suite 350 *TF:* 800-840-1012 ■ *Web:* www.enhance.com	Orem	UT	84097	801-705-7125	705-7138
Epsilon Interactive 315 Park Ave S 18th Fl *Web:* www.epsiloninteractive.com	New York	NY	10010	212-995-7500	995-7514
Euro RSCG 4D 350 Hudson St *Web:* www.eurorscg4d.com	New York	NY	10014	212-886-2000	886-2016
Focalex Inc 90 Bridge St *Web:* www.focalex.com	Newton	MA	02458	617-559-0155	559-0475
Freestyle Interactive Inc 475 Brannan St Suite 410 *Web:* www.freestyleinteractive.com	San Francisco	CA	94107	415-541-2710	975-0848
Fusionary Media 820 Monroe Ave NW Suite 212 *Web:* www.fusionary.com	Grand Rapids	MI	49503	616-454-2357	454-6827
Grey Interactive 111 5th Ave 6th Fl *Web:* www.greyinteractive.com	New York	NY	10003	212-420-5100	420-5151
GSI Commerce Inc 935 1st Ave *NASDAQ: GSIC* ■ *TF:* 877-708-4305 ■ *Web:* www.gsicommerce.com	King of Prussia	PA	19406	610-491-7000	265-2866
Hacker Group Inc 1110 112th Ave NE Suite 200 *Web:* www.hackergroup.com	Bellevue	WA	98004	425-454-8556	455-5694
HouseValues Inc 11332 NE 122nd Way *NASDAQ: SOLD* ■ *TF:* 877-450-0088 ■ *Web:* www.housevalues.com	Kirkland	WA	98034	425-852-5500	952-5694
IconNicholson LLC 22 4th St 9th Fl *TF:* 866-426-6871 ■ *Web:* www.iconmedialab.com	San Francisco	CA	94103	415-278-0471	278-0497
Interact Multimedia Corp 115 Highland Ave Suite 5 *Web:* www.interactmedical.com	Jersey City	NJ	07306	201-209-1569	
iProspect 311 Arsenal St *TF:* 800-522-1152 ■ *Web:* www.iprospect.com	Watertown	MA	02472	617-923-7000	923-7004
LinkShare Corp 215 Park Ave S 8th Fl *TF:* 800-875-5465 ■ *Web:* www.linkshare.com	New York	NY	10003	646-654-6000	602-0160
LiveWorld Inc 170 Knowles Dr Suite 211 *Web:* www.liveworld.com	Los Gatos	CA	95032	408-871-5200	871-5300
LSF Network Inc 395 Oyster Pt Blvd Suite 110 *TF:* 877-616-8226 ■ *Web:* www.lsfnetwork.com	South San Francisco	CA	94080	650-616-8226	624-5412
Macquarium Intelligent Communications 1800 Peachtree St NW Suite 250 *Web:* www.macquarium.com	Atlanta	GA	30309	404-554-4000	554-4001
Marchex Inc 413 Pine St Suite 500 *NASDAQ: MCHX* ■ *Web:* www.marchex.com	Seattle	WA	98101	206-331-3300	331-3695
mediSpecialty Inc 1050 George St Suite 14L *Web:* www.medispecialty.com	New Brunswick	NJ	08901	732-828-6382	828-6385
MetaDesign North America 615 Battery St 6th Fl *Web:* www.metadesign.com	San Francisco	CA	94111	415-627-0790	627-0795
Miva Inc 5220 Summerlin Commons Blvd Suite 500 *NASDAQ: MIVA* ■ *TF:* 888-882-3178 ■ *Web:* www.miva.com/us	Fort Myers	FL	33907	239-561-7229	561-7224
myGeek Inc 4130 E Van Buren St Suite 250 *TF:* 866-258-9245 ■ *Web:* www.mygeek.com	Phoenix	AZ	85008	602-265-5242	297-4219
MyPoints.com Inc 188 The Embarcadero 5th Fl *TF:* 888-262-4528 ■ *Web:* www.mypoints.com	San Francisco	CA	94105	415-615-1100	615-1122
NetGain Technology Inc 720 W Saint Germain St Suite 200 *Web:* www.netgaintechnology.com	Saint Cloud	MN	56301	320-251-4700	251-5030
non-linear creations Inc 987 Wellington St Suite 201 *TF:* 866-915-2997 ■ *Web:* www.nonlinear.ca	Ottawa	ON	K1Y2Y1	613-241-2067	241-3086
Organic Inc 555 Market St 4th Fl *Web:* www.organic.com	San Francisco	CA	94105	415-581-5300	581-5400
Pacifico Inc 3880 S Bascom Ave Suite 215 *Web:* www.pacifico.com	San Jose	CA	91525	408-559-8880	
Q Interactive Inc 360 N Michigan Ave Suite 1900 *TF:* 888-426-6654 ■ *Web:* www.coolsavings.com	Chicago	IL	60601	312-224-5000	224-5001
Renegade Marketing Group LLC 75 9th Ave 4th Fl *Web:* www.renegademarketing.com	New York	NY	10011	646-486-7700	486-7800
Return Path Inc 304 Park Ave S 7th Fl *Web:* www.returnpath.biz	New York	NY	10010	212-905-5500	905-5501
R/GA 350 W 39th St *Web:* www.rga.com	New York	NY	10018	212-946-4000	946-4010
RMGConnect 466 Lexington Ave *Web:* www.rmgconnect.com	New York	NY	10017	212-210-7000	210-5678
rpinteractive 2525 Colorado Ave 1st Fl *Web:* www.rpa.com	Santa Monica	CA	90404	310-394-4000	260-4660
SFI 10 Liberty Ship Way Suite 300 *Web:* www.sfinteractive.com	Sausalito	CA	94965	415-331-6049	331-3524
Siegel & Gale 437 Madison Ave 12th Fl *Web:* www.siegelgale.com	New York	NY	10022	212-817-6650	817-6680
Stein Rogan & Partners 432 Park Ave S 16th Fl *Web:* www.steinrogan.com	New York	NY	10016	212-213-1112	779-7305
Think Partnership Inc 100 N Waukegan Rd Suite 100 *AMEX: THK* ■ *Web:* www.thinkpartnership.com	Lake Bluff	IL	60044	847-615-2890	615-2980
Topica Inc 685 Market St Suite 300 *Web:* www.topica.com	San Francisco	CA	94105	415-344-0800	344-0900
ValueClick Inc 30699 Russell Ranch Rd Suite 250 *NASDAQ: VCLK* ■ *TF:* 877-825-8323 ■ *Web:* www.valueclick.com	Westlake Village	CA	91361	818-575-4500	575-4501
ValueClick Media 360 Olive St *Web:* www.valueclickmedia.com	Santa Barbara	CA	93101	805-568-5334	899-4720
Vendare Media 2101 Rosecrans Ave Suite 2000 **Fax Area Code:* 818 ■ *Web:* www.vendaremedia.com	El Segundo	CA	90245	310-647-6000	647-6001*
VentureDirect Worldwide Inc 60 Madison Ave *Web:* www.venturedirect.com	New York	NY	10010	212-684-4800	576-1129
Visibility Factor Inc 250 Storke Rd Suite 16 *Web:* www.visibilityfactor.com	Santa Barbara	CA	93117	805-961-8735	562-0023

Phone Fax

Yahoo! Search Marketing 74 N Pasadena Ave 3rd Fl .... Pasadena CA 91103 626-685-5600 685-5601
TF: 888-811-4686 ■ Web: searchmarketing.yahoo.com

yesmail inc 959 Skyway Rd Suite 150 .... San Carlos CA 94070 650-620-1200 620-1273
TF: 877-937-6245 ■ Web: www.yesmail.com

8 ADVERTISING SERVICES - OUTDOOR ADVERTISING

Phone Fax

Adams Outdoor Advertising Co 911 SW Adams St .... Peoria IL 61602 309-692-2482 692-8452
Web: www.adamsoutdoor.com

Attracta Sign Co 14680 James Rd .... Rogers MN 55374 763-428-6377 428-9097
TF: 866-339-0603

Bowlin Travel Centers Inc 150 Louisiana Blvd NE............ Albuquerque NM 87108 505-266-5985 266-7821
TF: 800-334-2236 ■ Web: www.bowlintc.com

CBS Outdoor 405 Lexington Ave 14th Fl .... New York NY 10174 212-297-6400 370-1817
TF: 800-926-8834 ■ Web: www.cbsoutdoor.com

Clear Channel Outdoor Holdings
2850 E Camelback Rd Suite 200 .... Phoenix AZ 85016 602-381-5700 381-5735
Web: www.clearchanneloutdoor.com

Colby Poster Printing Co Inc 1332 W 12th Pl .... Los Angeles CA 90015 213-747-5108 747-3209
Web: www.colbyposter.com

Diamond Outdoor Advertising 1200 E Golf Rd .... Des Plaines IL 60016 847-827-1771 827-6551
Web: www.diamondoutdoor.com

Fairway Outdoor Advertising 713 Broad St .... Augusta GA 30901 706-724-8987 724-6308
Web: www.fairwayoutdoor.com

Jim Pattison Media Group 1067 W Cordova St Suite 1800....... Vancouver BC V6C1C7 604-688-6764 694-6900
Web: www.jimpattison.com/medi/me__index.htm

Kubin-Nicholson Corp 8440 N 87th St .... Milwaukee WI 53224 414-586-4300 586-6808
TF: 800-858-9557 ■ Web: www.kubin.com

Lamar Advertising Co 5551 Corporate Blvd .... Baton Rouge LA 70808 225-926-1000 923-0658
NASDAQ: LAMR ■ TF: 800-235-2627 ■ Web: www.lamar.com

Lamar Outdoor Advertising 5953 Susquehanna Plaza Dr............. York PA 17406 717-252-1528 252-4832
TF: 800-632-9014 ■ Web: www.lamaroutdoor.com

May Advertising International Ltd 1200 Forum Way S.......... Fort Worth TX 76140 817-336-5671 877-0627
TF: 800-800-4629 ■ Web: www.mayadvertising.com

National Print Group Inc National Posters Div
1001 Latta St .... Chattanooga TN 37406 423-622-1106 624-4289
TF: 800-624-0408 ■ Web: www.nationalposters.com

NextMedia Group LLC
6312 S Fiddlers Green Cir Suite 360E .... Greenwood Village CO 80111 303-694-9118 694-4940
Web: www.nextmediagroup.net

Waitt Media Inc 1125 S 103rd St Suite 200 .... Omaha NE 68124 402-697-8000 697-8024
TF: 888-656-0634 ■ Web: www.waittmedia.com

Witt Sign Co Inc 306 McCowan Dr .... Lebanon TN 37087 615-444-3898 444-3980

9 ADVERTISING SPECIALTIES

SEE ALSO Signs p. 2317; Smart Cards p. 2318; Trophies, Plaques, Awards p. 2385

Phone Fax

Aakron Rule Corp 8 Indianola Ave .... Akron NY 14001 716-542-5483 542-1537
TF: 800-828-1570 ■ Web: www.aakronrule.com

Adco Litho Line Inc 2700 W Roosevelt Rd.................... Broadview IL 60155 708-345-8200 345-8297
TF: 800-875-2326 ■ Web: www.adcolitholine.com

Adimage Promotional Group 2300 Main St .... Hugo MN 55038 651-426-0820 896-9228*
*Fax Area Code: 800 ■ TF: 800-344-8809 ■ Web: www.promoxml.com

Adva-Lite Inc 7340 Bryan Dairy Rd............................ Largo FL 33777 727-546-5483 544-5316
Web: www.advalite.com

Adventures in Advertising 800 Winneconne Ave .... Neenah WI 54957 920-886-3700 886-3701
TF: 800-460-7836 ■ Web: www.advinadv.com

Advertising Specialty Co 1555 Industrial Way.................... Sparks NV 89431 775-826-2711 826-6647
Web: www.adspecreno.com

Airmate Co Inc 16280 County Rd D .... Bryan OH 43506 419-636-3184 636-4210
TF: 800-544-3614 ■ Web: www.airmatecompany.com

Alexander Mfg Co 12978 Tesson Ferry Rd....................... Saint Louis MO 63128 314-842-3344 467-6453*
*Fax Area Code: 800 ■ TF: 800-467-5343 ■ Web: www.alexandermc.com

Allen Co 712 E Main St....................................... Blanchester OH 45107 937-783-2491 783-4831
TF: 800-329-2491 ■ Web: www.allenmugs.com

American Identity 7500 W 110th St......................... Overland Park KS 66210 913-319-3100 319-4960
TF: 800-848-8028 ■ Web: www.americanidentity.com

Americanna Co 29 Aldrin Rd.................................... Plymouth MA 02360 508-747-5550 747-5578
TF Cust Svc: 888-747-5550 ■ Web: www.americanna.com

AmPro Inc 1511 S Garfield Pl .... Mason City IA 50401 641-422-9950 422-0244
TF: 800-325-3895 ■ Web: www.amprousa.com

Amsterdam Printing & Litho Corp 166 Wallins Corners Rd...... Amsterdam NY 12010 518-842-6000 843-5204
TF: 800-833-6231 ■ Web: www.amsterdamprinting.com

Arnold Pen Co PO Box 791.................................... Petersburg VA 23804 804-733-6612 658-4623*
*Fax Area Code: 800 ■ TF: 800-296-6612 ■ Web: www.arnoldpen.com

Arthur Blank & Co Inc 225 Rivermoor St......................... Boston MA 02132 617-325-9600 327-1235
TF: 800-776-7333 ■ Web: www.arthurblank.com

Atlantis Match Co 524 Center Rd.............................. Frankfort IL 60423 815-464-2187 469-7089
Web: www.matchbooks.com

Atlas Match LLC 1801 S Airport Cir........................... Euless TX 76040 817-267-1500 354-7478
TF: 800-628-2426 ■ Web: www.atlasmatch.com

Atlas Pen & Pencil Corp 3040 N 29th Ave .... Hollywood FL 33020 954-920-4444 920-8899
TF: 800-327-3232 ■ Web: www.atlaspen.com

Barlow Promotional Products Inc 5151 Moundview Dr........... Red Wing MN 55066 800-800-3372 770-2012
TF: 800-227-5691

Barrett LW Co Inc 55 S Zuni St .... Denver CO 80223 303-934-5755 934-5756
TF: 888-312-0888 ■ Web: www.lwbarrett.com

Barton Nelson Inc 13700 Wyandotte .... Kansas City MO 64145 816-942-3100 942-6995
TF: 800-821-6697 ■ Web: www.bebco.com

Bastian Co PO Box 250 .... Phelps NY 14532 315-548-2300 548-2310
TF: 800-609-0097 ■ Web: www.bastiancompany.com

Belaire Products Inc 763 S Broadway St.......................... Akron OH 44311 330-253-3116 376-7790
TF: 800-886-3224 ■ Web: www.belaireproducts.com

Bergamot Inc 820 E Wisconsin St .... Delavan WI 53115 262-728-5572 728-3750*
*Fax: Sales ■ TF Cust Svc: 800-922-6733 ■ Web: www.bergamot.net

Blank Arthur & Co Inc 225 Rivermoor St........................ Boston MA 02132 617-325-9600 327-1235
TF: 800-776-7333 ■ Web: www.arthurblank.com

Brown & Bigelow Inc 345 Plato Blvd E .... Saint Paul MN 55107 651-293-7000 293-7025*
*Fax: Hum Res ■ TF Cust Svc: 800-628-1755 ■ Web: www.brownandbigelow.com

Churchwell Co 814 S Edgewood Ave .... Jacksonville FL 32205 904-356-5721 354-2436
TF: 800-245-0075 ■ Web: www.churchwellcompany.com

Clear Channel Merchandising 1 Noyes Ave .... Rumford RI 02916 954-423-1909 424-0193
Web: www.clearchannel.com/Merchandising

Crown Products Inc 3107 Halls Mill Rd .... Mobile AL 36606 251-476-7777 471-2095
TF: 800-367-2769 ■ Web: www.crownprod.com

Phone Fax

Dard Products Inc 912 Custer Ave .... Evanston IL 60202 847-328-5000 328-7835
TF: 800-323-2925 ■ Web: www.tagmaster.net

Dunn Mfg Inc 1400 Goldmine Rd .... Monroe NC 28110 704-283-2147 289-6857
TF: 800-868-7111

EBSCO Creative Concepts 825 5th Ave S..................... Birmingham AL 35233 205-323-4618 226-8429
TF: 800-756-7023 ■ Web: www.ebscocreativeconcepts.com

Elliott Sales Corp 2502 S 12th St .... Tacoma WA 98405 253-383-3883 383-3130
TF: 800-576-3945 ■ Web: www.elliottsales.com

Ever-Lite Co Inc 1717 N Bayshore Dr Unit 1632 .... Miami FL 33132 305-577-0819 374-4252
TF: 800-891-4670 ■ Web: www.ever-lite.com

Exclusive Findings 29 Delaine St .... Providence RI 02909 401-331-8199 273-2940
TF: 800-342-9560

Flair Communications Agency Inc 214 W Erie St .... Chicago IL 60610 312-943-5959 943-0881
TF: 800-621-8317 ■ Web: www.flairagency.com

Francis & Lusky LLC 1437 Donelson Pike .... Nashville TN 37217 615-242-0501 256-0862
TF: 800-251-3711 ■ Web: www.promoville.com

Geiger 70 Mt Hope Ave .... Lewiston ME 04240 207-755-2000 755-2422
Web: www.geiger.com

Geiger Brothers Promotional Marketing 2010 Oakgrove Rd..... Hattiesburg MS 39402 601-264-1991 268-1175
TF: 800-264-9291

Gigunda Group 540 N Commercial St 3rd Fl................... Manchester NH 03101 603-314-5000 314-5001
Web: www.gigundagroup.com

Gold Bond Inc 5485 Hixson Pike................................ Hixson TN 37343 423-842-5844 729-4852*
*Fax Area Code: 800 ■ Web: www.goldbondinc.com

HALO Branded Solutions 1980 Industrial Dr.................... Sterling IL 61081 815-632-6800 632-6900
Web: www.halo.com

Hit Promotional Products Inc 7150 Bryan Dairy Rd .... Largo FL 33777 727-541-5561 541-5130
TF: 800-237-6305 ■ Web: www.hitpromo.net

House of Specialties 5451 Able Ct............................. Mobile AL 36693 251-438-2422 438-4809
TF: 800-348-2422 ■ Web: www.hos.cc

Imageworks Mfg Inc 49 South St.......................... Park Forest IL 60466 708-503-1122 503-1133
TF: 800-950-1122 ■ Web: www.imageworksmfg.com

Instant Imprints 9808 Waples St .... San Diego CA 92121 858-642-4848 453-6513
TF: 800-542-3437 ■ Web: www.instantimprints.com

Jordan Industries Inc Specialty Printing & Labeling Group
1751 Lake Cook Rd Suite 550 ArborLake Center .... Deerfield IL 60015 847-945-5591 945-5698
Web: www.jordanindustries.com

Lee Wayne Corp 1980 Industrial Dr .... Sterling IL 61081 815-625-0980 548-9193
Web: www.leewayne.com

Lewtan Industries Corp 30 High St........................... Hartford CT 06103 860-278-9800 278-9019
TF: 800-539-8268 ■ Web: www.lewtan8.com

LW Barrett Co Inc 55 S Zuni St .... Denver CO 80223 303-934-5755 934-5756
TF: 888-312-0888 ■ Web: www.lwbarrett.com

MARC Promotions 7172 Lakeview Pkwy W Dr................ Indianapolis IN 46268 317-290-3516 290-3525
TF: 866-627-2776 ■ Web: www.marcpromotions.com

Marco 2640 Commerce Dr .... Harrisburg PA 17110 717-545-1060 545-5672
TF: 800-232-1121 ■ Web: www.marcomeetings.com

Marietta Corp 37 Huntington St.............................. Cortland NY 13045 607-753-6746 756-0658*
*Fax Area Code: 800 ■ *Fax: Cust Svc ■ TF: 800-431-3023 ■
Web: www.mariettacorp.com

Maryland Match Corp 605 Alluvion St .... Baltimore MD 21230 410-752-8164 752-3441
TF: 800-423-0013 ■ Web: www.marylandmatch.com

Mid-America Merchandising Inc 204 W 3rd St.............. Kansas City MO 64105 816-471-5600 842-0952
TF: 800-333-6737 ■ Web: www.mmipromo.com

MMG Works/Status Promotions 4601 Madison Ave............ Kansas City MO 64112 816-472-5988 472-7107
TF: 800-945-4044 ■ Web: www.mmgworks.com

Morco Inc 125 High St .... Cochranton PA 16314 814-425-7476 425-7119
TF: 800-247-4093 ■ Web: www.morcoline.com

Myron Corp 205 Maywood Ave................................. Maywood NJ 07607 201-843-6464 843-8390
TF: 800-526-9766 ■ Web: www.myron.com

National Pen Corp 16885 Via Del Compo Ct Suite 100 .... San Diego CA 92127 858-675-3000 675-0890
TF: 800-854-1000 ■ Web: www.pens.com

Nationwide Advertising Specialty Inc 2025 S Cooper St .... Arlington TX 76010 817-275-2678 274-4301
Web: www.nationwideadvertising.net

Neely Mfg Inc 2178 Hwy 2.................................... Corydon IA 50060 641-872-1100 872-2039
TF: 800-247-1785 ■ Web: www.neelymfg.com

Newton Mfg Co 1123 1st Ave E .... Newton IA 50208 641-792-4121 792-6261
TF: 800-500-7227 ■ Web: www.newtonmfg.com

Norscot Group Inc 1000 W Donges Bay Rd PO Box 998........... Mequon WI 53092 262-241-3313 241-4904
TF: 800-653-3313 ■ Web: www.norscot.com

Norwood Promotional Products Inc
10 W Market St Suite 1400.................................. Indianapolis IN 46204 317-275-2500 275-2570
TF: 800-959-9138 ■ Web: www.norwood.com

Norwood Souvenir 202 F Ave NW........................... Cedar Rapids IA 52405 319-366-7831 831-6343*
*Fax Area Code: 800 ■ *Fax: Cust Svc ■ TF: 800-413-8371 ■ Web: www.norwood.com

Numo Mfg Co 1072 E Hwy 175................................ Kaufman TX 75142 972-962-5400 962-5436
TF: 800-253-0434 ■ Web: www.numomfg.com

Perrygraf Co 25 W 550 Geneva Rd .... Carol Stream IL 60188 630-784-0100 784-6690
TF: 800-423-5329 ■ Web: www.perrygraf.com

Pilgrim Plastic Products Co 1200 W Chestnut St .... Brockton MA 02301 508-436-6300 580-3542
TF: 877-343-7810 ■ Web: www.pilgrimplastics.com

Prime Resources Corp 1100 Boston Ave .... Bridgeport CT 06610 203-331-9100 330-0123
TF: 800-873-7746 ■ Web: www.primeline.com

Quick Point Inc 1717 Fenpark Dr .... Fenton MO 63026 636-343-9400 343-3587
Web: www.quickpoint.com

Quikey Mfg Co 1500 Industrial Pkwy .... Akron OH 44310 330-633-8106 633-6670
TF: 877-901-1200 ■ Web: www.quikey.com

Rainbow Magnetics Inc 3221 W MacArthur Blvd .... Santa Ana CA 92704 714-540-4777 545-5164
TF Sales: 800-248-6200 ■ Web: www.rainbowmagnetics.com

RM Crow Co 200 Factory Dr .... Waco TX 76710 254-772-5280 772-0941

Sanders Mfg Co 1422 Lebanon Rd............................ Nashville TN 37210 615-254-6611 242-3732
TF: 866-254-6611 ■ Web: www.samcoline.com

Shaw & Slavsky Inc 13821 Elmira Ave......................... Detroit MI 48227 313-834-3990 834-2680
TF: 800-521-7527

Signatures Network Inc 2 Bryant St Suite 300............. San Francisco CA 94105 415-247-7400 247-7407
Web: www.signaturesnetwork.com

Sport It Inc PO Box 50777 .... San Diego CA 92150 858-592-6532 592-6539
TF: 888-233-2659 ■ Web: www.sport-it.com

Universal Creative Concepts Corp 13700 State Rd .... North Royalton OH 44133 440-230-1366 230-1919
Web: www.uccadv.com

Vanguard East 1172 Azalea Garden Rd......................... Norfolk VA 23502 757-857-3600 857-0222
TF: 800-221-1264 ■ Web: www.vanguardmil.com

VATEX America 2395 Hermitage Rd .... Richmond VA 23220 804-353-9010 353-8939
Web: www.vatex.com

Vernon Co 1 Promotion Pl PO Box 600 .... Newton IA 50208 641-792-9000 792-6901
Web: www.vernoncompany.com

Virtronic/Four Seasons 4680 Parkway Dr Suite 200 .... Mason OH 45040 513-398-3695 398-7165
TF: 877-844-5032 ■ Web: www.v4s.com

Western Plastic Products Inc 1556 W Esther St............. Long Beach CA 90813 562-435-4881 495-2232
TF: 800-453-1881 ■ Web: www.westernplastic.com

AGRICULTURAL CHEMICALS

SEE Fertilizers & Pesticides p. 1635

AGRICULTURAL MACHINERY & EQUIPMENT

SEE Farm Machinery & Equipment - Mfr p. 1631; Farm Machinery & Equipment - Whol p. 1632

10 AGRICULTURAL PRODUCTS

SEE ALSO Fruit Growers p. 1678; Horse Breeders p. 1789; Horticultural Products Growers p. 1789; Seed Companies p. 2311

10-1 Cattle Ranches, Farms, Feedlots (Beef Cattle)

				Phone	Fax
A Duda & Sons Inc PO Box 620257	Oviedo	FL	32762	407-365-2111	365-2010
Web: www.duda.com					
Agri Beef Co 1555 Shoreline Dr 3rd Fl	Boise	ID	83702	208-338-2500	338-2605
TF: 800-657-6305 ■ *Web:* www.agribeef.com					
Agri Beef Co Boise Valley Feeders Div 2201 Ridgeway Rd	Parma	ID	83660	208-722-8090	722-8093
Web: www.agribeef.com/cattledivision/boisevalley.asp					
Agri Beef Co El Oro Cattle Feeders Div 18857 Rd 2.7 SE	Moses Lake	WA	98837	509-349-2321	349-2272
Web: www.agribeef.com/cattledivision/eloro.asp					
Ainsworth Feed Yards Co PO Box 267	Ainsworth	NE	69210	402-387-2455	387-0105
TF: 800-438-3148					
Ashland Feeders 2590 CRL	Ashland	KS	67831	620-635-2213	635-2291
Web: www.ashlandfeeders.com					
AzTx Cattle Co PO Box 390	Hereford	TX	79045	806-364-8871	364-3842
TF: 800-999-5065 ■ *Web:* www.aztx.com					
Bar G Feedyard PO Box 1797	Hereford	TX	79045	806-357-2241	357-2245
Web: www.bar-g.com					
Barton County Feeders Inc 1164 SE 40th Rd	Ellinwood	KS	67526	620-564-2200	564-2253
Beef Belt Feeders Inc 1350 E RD 70	Scott City	KS	67871	620-872-3059	872-7060
Web: www.beefbelt.com					
Beef Belt Feeders Inc Kansas Feed Yard Div PO Box 528	Scott City	KS	67871	620-872-2660	
Web: www.beefbelt.com/feedyard.htm					
Beef Land Feed Yard 12500 S Beef Land Rd	Garden City	KS	67846	620-275-2030	275-0272
Web: www.irsikanddoll.com					
Beef Northwest Feeders Inc 3455 Victorio Rd	Nyssa	OR	97913	541-372-2101	372-5661
Web: www.beefnw.com					
Beef Tech Cattle Feeders Inc 3476 Country Rd 9	Hereford	TX	79045	806-363-6080	363-6078
Bledsoe Cattle Co PO Box 406	Wray	CO	80758	970-332-4955	332-4837
Boise Valley Feeders Div Agri Beef Co 2201 Ridgeway Rd	Parma	ID	83660	208-722-8090	722-8093
Web: www.agribeef.com/cattledivision/boisevalley.asp					
Bracht Feedyards Inc 1931 'I' Rd	West Point	NE	68788	402-372-3662	372-3669
Brookover Feed Yards Inc PO Box 917	Garden City	KS	67846	620-276-6662	276-4447
Web: www.brookover.com					
Buffalo Feeders LLC PO Box 409	Buffalo	OK	73834	580-735-2511	735-6035
Web: www.buffalofeeders.com					
Cactus Feeders Inc PO Box 3050	Amarillo	TX	79116	806-373-2333	371-4775*
**Fax:* Hum Res ■ *Web:* www.cactusfeeders.com					
Canadian Feedyards Inc PO Box 866	Canadian	TX	79014	806-323-5333	323-8422
Caprock Industries Inc 151 N Main	Wichita	KS	67202	316-291-2500	291-1980
Carson County Feedyards Inc 1025 FM 2385	Panhandle	TX	79068	806-537-3531	537-5450
Cattlco PO Box 1271	Sterling	CO	80751	970-522-8260	522-8269
Cedar Bluff Cattle Feeders Inc RR 2 Box 71	Ellis	KS	67637	785-726-3100	
Christensen Cattle Co Inc 2967 Hwy 14	Fullerton	NE	68638	308-536-2405	536-2562
Cluck Dean Cattle Co Ltd 105 Dean Cluck Ave	Gruver	TX	79040	806-733-5021	733-2244
Coleman Natural Foods 1767 Denver West Blvd Suite 200	Golden	CO	80401	303-468-2500	
TF: 800-442-8666 ■ *Web:* www.colemannatural.com					
ContiBeef LLC 5408 Idylwild Trail	Boulder	CO	80301	303-516-1150	516-5939
Web: www.contigroup.com/cfd.html					
Coyote Lake Feedyard Inc 1287 FM 1731	Muleshoe	TX	79347	806-946-3321	946-3329
TF: 800-299-3321 ■ *Web:* www.coyotelakefeedyard.com					
CRI Feeders Inc Rt 2 Box 114	Guymon	OK	73942	580-545-3344	545-3642
Crist Feed Yard Inc 553 W Rd 40	Scott City	KS	67871	620-872-7271	872-5763
Darr Feedlot Inc 42826 Rd 759	Cozad	NE	69130	308-324-2363	324-2365
Web: www.darrfeedlot.com					
Dean Cluck Cattle Co Ltd 105 Dean Cluck Ave	Gruver	TX	79040	806-733-5021	733-2244
Dinklage Feed Yards Inc PO Box 274	Sidney	NE	69162	308-254-5941	254-6260
Web: www.dinklagefeedyards.com					
Double A Feeders Inc PO Box 220	Clayton	NM	88415	505-374-2591	374-8342
Web: www.doubleafeeders.com					
Duda A & Sons Inc PO Box 620257	Oviedo	FL	32762	407-365-2111	365-2010
Web: www.duda.com					
Dumas Cattle Feeders Inc 11301 US Hwy 287	Dumas	TX	79029	806-935-7993	935-7766
El Oro Cattle Feeders Div Agri Beef Co 18857 Rd 2.7 SE	Moses Lake	WA	98837	509-349-2321	349-2272
Web: www.agribeef.com/cattledivision/eloro.asp					
Fall River Feedyard LLC PO Box 892	Hot Springs	SD	57747	605-745-4109	745-3352
Ford County Feed Yard Inc 12466 US Hwy 400	Ford	KS	67842	620-369-2252	369-2250
TF: 800-783-2739					
Friona Feedyard PO Box 806	Friona	TX	79035	806-265-3574	265-3577
TF: 800-658-6086 ■ *Web:* www.frionaind.com/feedyard/friona.htm					
Friona Industries LP 500 S Taylor St Suite 601	Amarillo	TX	79101	806-374-1811	374-1324
TF: 800-658-6014 ■ *Web:* www.frionaind.com					
Garden City Feed Yard 1805 W Annie Scheer Rd	Garden City	KS	67846	620-275-4191	
TF: 800-272-4191					
Gottsch Feeding Corp 20507 Nicholas Rd Suite 100	Elkhorn	NE	68022	402-289-4421	289-4202
Gray County Feed Yard 23405 SR 23	Cimarron	KS	67835	620-855-3486	855-7739
Web: www.irsikanddoll.com					
Great Bend Feeding Inc 355 NW 30 Ave	Great Bend	KS	67530	620-792-2508	792-5047
Web: www.gbfeeding.com					
Hansford County Feeders LP 13800 County Rd 19	Spearman	TX	79081	806-733-5025	733-5281
Hays Feeders LLC PO Box 310	Hays	KS	67601	785-625-3415	625-0074
Web: www.prattfeeders.com					
Henry C Hitch Feedyards PO Box 1559	Guymon	OK	73942	580-338-2533	338-2718
TF: 800-951-2533 ■ *Web:* www.hitchok.com/HitchFeedyard.htm					
Heritage Feeders Co Inc PO Box 370	Wheeler	TX	79096	806-826-5591	826-3476
Hillside Farms PO Box 1830	Shavertown	PA	18708	570-696-3881	696-4850
Web: www.thelandsathillsidefarms.org					
Hitch Henry C Feedyards PO Box 1559	Guymon	OK	73942	580-338-2533	338-2718
TF: 800-951-2533 ■ *Web:* www.hitchok.com/HitchFeedyard.htm					
Hurd Co 83973 489th Ave	Bartlett	NE	68622	402-482-5931	482-5971
Ingalls Feed Yard 10505 US Hwy 50	Ingalls	KS	67853	620-335-5174	335-5232
TF: 800-477-6907 ■ *Web:* www.irsikanddoll.com					
Irsik & Doll PO Box 847	Cimarron	KS	67835	620-855-3111	855-3748
Web: www.irsikanddoll.com					
Irsik & Doll Feed Yard 8220 E Hwy 50	Garden City	KS	67846	620-275-7131	275-0800
Web: www.irsikanddoll.com					
JR Simplot Co 999 Main St	Boise	ID	83702	208-336-2110	389-7515
TF: 800-635-5008 ■ *Web:* www.simplot.com					
Kansas Feed Yard Div Beef Belt Feeders Inc PO Box 528	Scott City	KS	67871	620-872-2660	
Web: www.beefbelt.com/feedyard.htm					
Kearny County Feeders Inc PO Box 109	Lakin	KS	67860	620-355-6630	355-6995
Web: www.kearnycountyfeeders.com					
King Ranch Inc 2 Miles West of Hwy 141 PO Box 1090	Kingsville	TX	78364	361-592-6411	592-6885
TF: 800-375-6411 ■ *Web:* www.king-ranch.com					
Knight Feedlot Inc 1768 Ave J	Lyons	KS	67554	620-257-5106	257-3347
Lasley Walter & Sons Inc PO Box 168	Stratford	TX	79084	806-753-4411	753-4435
Web: www.walterlasleyandsons.com					
Littlefield Feedyard RR 1 Box 26	Amherst	TX	79312	806-385-5141	385-3485
TF: 800-687-5141 ■ *Web:* www.frionaind.com/feedyard/little_field.htm					
McElhaney Cattle Co 34673 E Country 9 St	Wellton	AZ	85356	928-785-3384	785-3843
McLean Feedyard Ltd PO Box 630	McLean	TX	79057	806-779-2405	779-2319
Web: www.ranches.org/McLean.htm					
Midwest Feeders Inc 05013 13th Rd	Ingalls	KS	67853	620-335-5790	
Web: www.midwest-feeders.com					
Morrison Enterprises PO Box 609	Hastings	NE	68902	402-463-3191	462-8542
North Platte Feeders Inc PO Box 1919	North Platte	NE	69103	308-963-4386	963-4301
Oshkosh Feed Yard PO Box 440	Oshkosh	NE	69154	308-772-3237	
Paco Feed Yard Inc PO Box 956	Friona	TX	79035	806-265-3281	265-3497
TF: 800-725-3433					
Perryton Feeders Inc 13210 Hwy 70 S	Perryton	TX	79070	806-435-5466	435-3197
Pinal Feeding Co Inc PO Box 609	Maricopa	AZ	85239	602-252-3467	252-0243
Pinneo Feed Lot Ltd Liability Co PO Box 384	Brush	CO	80723	970-842-0701	842-0720
PM Beef Group LLC 2850 Hwy 60 E	Windom	MN	56101	507-831-2761	831-6216
Web: www.pmholdings.com/b.html					
Pratt Feeders Inc PO Box 945	Pratt	KS	67124	620-672-6448	672-7797
Web: prattfeeders.com					
Premium Feeders Inc PO Box 230	Scandia	KS	66966	785-335-2222	335-2558
Web: www.premiumfeeders.com					
Pride Feeders I Ltd Rt 2 Box 67	Hooker	OK	73945	580-253-6381	253-6383
TF: 800-872-7251					
Quality Beef Producers PO Box 145	Wildorado	TX	79098	806-426-3325	426-3582
Web: www.qualitybeefproducers.com					
Rafter 3 Feedyard Inc PO Box 1127	Dimmitt	TX	79027	806-647-5103	
Randall County Feedyard 15000 FM 2219	Amarillo	TX	79119	806-499-3701	499-3439
TF: 800-658-6063 ■ *Web:* www.frionaind.com/feedyard/randall.htm					
Red Rock Feeding Co PO Box 1039	Red Rock	AZ	85245	520-682-3448	682-3830
Roberts Enterprises Inc PO Box 2192	Sacaton	AZ	85247	520-315-2125	315-2130
Royal Beef Feed Yard 11060 N Falcon Rd	Scott City	KS	67871	620-872-5371	872-3380
Web: www.irsikanddoll.com					
Runnells Peters Cattle Co Inc 22115 Miners Rd	Laredo	TX	78045	956-724-3637	724-5269
Schwertner Farms Inc PO Box 1	Schwertner	TX	76573	254-527-3342	527-4400
Web: www.cllnet.com					
Simplot JR Co 999 Main St	Boise	ID	83702	208-336-2110	389-7515
TF: 800-635-5008 ■ *Web:* www.simplot.com					
Snake River Cattle Feeders 2394 Feed Lot Rd	American Falls	ID	83211	208-226-5126	226-5128
Snake River Cattle Feeders Div Agri Beef Co 2394 Feed Lot Rd	American Falls	ID	83211	208-226-5126	226-5128
Sparrowk Livestock 18780 E Hwy 88	Clements	CA	95227	209-759-3530	759-3831
Web: www.sparrowk.com					
Sublette Feeders PO Box 917	Sublette	KS	67877	620-668-5501	
Sugarland Feed Yards Inc PO Box 186	Hereford	TX	79045	806-364-3381	363-6804
Supreme Cattle Feeders LLC RR 1 Box 64	Kismet	KS	67859	620-624-6296	624-4411
Swisher County Cattle Co PO Box 129	Tulia	TX	79088	806-627-4231	627-4254
TF: 800-658-6064 ■ *Web:* www.frionaind.com/feedyard/swisher.htm					
Taylor/Herring Co PO Box 2805	Amarillo	TX	79105	806-376-6347	376-6340
Tejas Feeders Ltd PO Box 1782	Pampa	TX	79066	806-665-2303	669-0210
Tejon Ranch Co PO Box 1000	Lebec	CA	93243	661-248-3000	248-3100
NYSE: TRC ■ *Web:* www.tejonranch.com					
Texas County Feed Yard LLC PO Box 1029	Guymon	OK	73942	580-338-7714	338-0782
Thomas County Feeders Inc 1762 US Hwy 83	Colby	KS	67701	785-462-3947	462-7606
TF: 800-257-2409					
Tri-State Feeders Inc PO Box 7	Turpin	OK	73950	580-778-3600	778-3750
Van de Graaf Ranches Inc 1691 Midvale Rd	Sunnyside	WA	98944	509-837-3151	837-7414
Walter Lasley & Sons Inc PO Box 168	Stratford	TX	79084	806-753-4411	753-4435
Web: www.walterlasleyandsons.com					
Weborg Cattle Inc 1737 V Rd	Pender	NE	68047	402-385-3441	385-2441
Western Feed Yard Inc 548 S Rd I	Johnson	KS	67855	620-492-6256	492-6239
Web: www.westernfeedyard.com					

10-2 Cotton Farms

				Phone	Fax
Burford Ranch 1443 W Sample Ave	Fresno	CA	93711	559-431-0902	431-1625
Cal-Organic Farms 12000 Main St	Lamont	CA	93241	661-845-2296	845-7414
Circle C Farms 1393 Yates Spring Rd	Brinson	GA	39825	229-246-7090	246-0605
Delta & Pine Land Co PO Box 157	Scott	MS	38772	662-742-3351	742-3795
NYSE: DLP ■ *TF:* 800-321-8989 ■ *Web:* www.deltaandpine.com					
E Ritter & Co Inc 106 Frisco St	Marked Tree	AR	72365	870-358-2200	358-4160
TF: 800-323-0355 ■ *Web:* www.ritteragri.com					
JG Boswell Co 101 W Walnut St	Pasadena	CA	91103	626-583-3000	583-3090
JR Norton Co 3200 E Camelback St Suite 389	Phoenix	AZ	85018	602-954-8812	954-8908
Langston Enterprises Inc 5267 E State Hwy 150	Blytheville	AR	72315	870-763-6670	763-1050
McCleskey Cotton Co LLC Hwy 118 PO Box 171	Bronwood	GA	39826	229-995-2616	995-5702
Salyer American 210 Oregon Ave	Corcoran	CA	93212	559-992-2131	992-5403
Web: www.salyeramerican.com					
Vignolo Farms 30988 Riverside St PO Box 1270	Shafter	CA	93263	661-325-8243	746-3643
Wesson Farms Inc 25 Victoria Rd	Victoria	AR	72370	870-563-2674	563-6927
Westlake Farms Inc 23311 Newton Ave	Stratford	CA	93266	559-947-3328	947-3590

10-3 Dairy Farms

				Phone	Fax
Big D Ranch 7590 S 10 Mile Rd	Meridian	ID	83642	208-888-1710	888-0075
Web: www.bigdranch.com					
Coach Farm Inc 105 Mill Hill Rd	Pine Plains	NY	12567	518-398-5325	398-5329
Web: www.coachfarm.com					
Fred Rau Dairy 10255 W Manning Ave	Fresno	CA	93706	559-237-3393	237-3879
Hollandia Dairy Inc 622 E Mission Rd	San Marcos	CA	92069	760-744-3222	744-2789
TF: 800-794-0978 ■ *Web:* www.hollandiadairy.com					
Inland Northwest Dairies 33 E Francis Ave PO Box 7310	Spokane	WA	99208	509-489-8600	482-3402
Kreider Farms 1461 Lancaster Rd	Manheim	PA	17545	717-665-4415	665-9614
TF: 888-665-4415 ■ *Web:* www.kreiderfarms.com					
Lawnel Farms Inc 2413 Craig Rd	Piffard	NY	14533	585-243-2448	
Luiz Everett & Sons Dairy Inc 18721 N Ray Rd	Lodi	CA	95242	209-369-9290	

Phone Fax

Marburger Farm Dairy Inc 1506 Mars Evans City Rd .... Evans City PA 16033 724-538-4752 538-3250
TF: 800-331-1295 ■ *Web:* www.marburgerdairy.com
Maytag Dairy Farms Inc 2282 E 8th N .... Newton IA 50208 641-792-1133 792-1567
TF: 800-247-2458
Meadow Gold Dairy 55 S Wakea Ave .... Kahului HI 96732 808-877-5541 877-0525
Web: www.lanimoo.com
Price's Producers Inc 201 E Main Dr Suite 1521 .... El Paso TX 79901 915-532-2296 532-1727
Shamrock Farms Co 40034 W Clayton Rd .... Stanfield AZ 85272 480-988-1452 988-1634
Web: www.shamrockfarms.net
Stencil Farms 4819 Glenview Rd .... Denmark WI 54208 920-863-6500 863-3621

10-4 General Farms

Phone Fax

ABF Farm Services Inc 7761 W Undine Rd .... Stockton CA 95206 209-462-0208 462-9429
Amana Society Inc PO Box 189 .... Amana IA 52203 319-622-7500 622-3090
Web: www.amanasociety.com
Belk Farms PO Box 24 .... Coachella CA 92236 760-399-5951 399-1223
Burford Ranch 1443 W Sample Ave .... Fresno CA 93711 559-431-0902 431-1625
DM Camp & Sons PO Box 80007 .... Bakersfield CA 93380 661-399-5511 393-5113
Web: www.dmcampandsons.com
Fisher Ranch Corp 10600 Ice Plant Rd .... Blythe CA 92225 760-922-4151 922-3080
Gilkey Enterprises PO Box 426 .... Corcoran CA 93212 559-992-2136 992-8266
Great American Farms Inc 1287 W Atlantic Blvd .... Pompano Beach FL 33069 954-785-9400 941-2977
Mercer Canyons Inc 46 Sonova Rd .... Prosser WA 99350 509-894-4773 894-4965
Millhaven Co Inc 1705 Millhaven Rd .... Sylvania GA 30467 912-829-4742 829-4745
TF: 800-421-8043
Morrison Enterprises PO Box 609 .... Hastings NE 68902 402-463-3191 462-8542
Nevada Nile Ranch Inc PO Box 1150 .... Lovelock NV 89419 775-273-2646 273-7208
Nickel Family LLC 15701 Hwy 178 .... Bakersfield CA 93386 661-872-5050 872-7141
Oji Brothers Farms Inc 8547 Sawtelle Ave .... Yuba City CA 95991 530-673-0845 673-8742
OPC Farms Inc PO Box 817 .... San Joaquin CA 93660 559-693-2700 693-2701
River Garden Farms Co 41758 County Rd 112 .... Knights Landing CA 95645 530-735-6274 735-6734
Stone Land Co 28521 Nevada Ave .... Stratford CA 93266 559-947-3185 945-9442
Sumner Peck Ranch Inc 14354 Rd 204 .... Madera CA 93638 559-822-2525
Tosh Farms 1586 Atlantic Ave .... Henry TN 38231 731-243-4861 243-4860
TF: 888-243-4885

10-5 Grain Farms

Phone Fax

AgriNorthwest 7404 W Hood Pl Suite B .... Kennewick WA 99336 509-734-1195 734-1092
TF: 800-333-8175
Agripro Seeds Inc 2369 330th St .... Slater LA 50244 877-247-4776
Web: www.agripro.com
Alger Farms 950 NW 8th St .... Homestead FL 33030 305-247-4334 247-4157
Busch Agricultural Resources Inc 2101 26th St S .... Moorhead MN 56560 218-233-8531 233-6082
Web: www.anheuser-busch.com/overview/bari.html
DuPont Agriculture & Nutrition
1007 Market St DuPont Bldg .... Wilmington DE 19898 302-774-1000 999-4399
TF: 800-441-7515
Erwin-Keith Inc 1529 Hwy 193 .... Wynne AR 72396 870-238-2079 238-8621
Fred Gutwein & Sons Inc 15691 W 600 S .... Francesville IN 47946 219-567-9141 567-2645
TF Cust Svc: 800-457-2700 ■ *Web:* www.gutwein.com
Golden Harvest Seeds Inc 100 JC Robinson Blvd .... Waterloo NE 68069 800-228-9906 779-3317*
**Fax Area Code:* 402 ■ *TF:* 800-747-2127 ■ *Web:* www.goldenharvestseeds.com
Gumz Richard Farms 8905 S Gumz Rd .... North Judson IN 46366 574-896-5441 896-5443
Gutwein Fred & Sons Inc 15691 W 600 S .... Francesville IN 47946 219-567-9141 567-2645
TF Cust Svc: 800-457-2700 ■ *Web:* www.gutwein.com
Heidrick Joe Enterprises Inc 36826 CR 24 .... Woodland CA 95695 530-662-3046 662-1715
Hoegemeyer Hybrids Inc 1755 Hoegemeyer Rd .... Hooper NE 68031 402-654-3399 654-3342
TF: 800-245-4631 ■ *Web:* www.corn1.com
Illinois Foundation Seeds Inc 1083 County Rd 900 N .... Tolono IL 61880 217-485-6260 485-3687
Web: www.ifsi.com
Joe Heidrick Enterprises Inc 36826 CR 24 .... Woodland CA 95695 530-662-3046 662-1715
Knight Management Inc 205 SW 1st St .... Belle Glade FL 33430 561-996-6262 992-8995
MFA Inc 201 Ray Young Dr .... Columbia MO 65201 573-874-5111 876-5430
Web: www.mfaincorporated.com
Minn-Dak Growers Ltd PO Box 13276 .... Grand Forks ND 58208 701-746-7453 780-9050
Web: www.minndak.com
Moews Seed Co Inc Rt 89 S .... Granville IL 61326 815-339-2201
TF: 800-663-9795 ■ *Web:* www.moews.com
Pfister Hybrid Corn Co 187 N Fayette St .... El Paso IL 61738 309-527-6010 527-5676
TF: 888-647-3478 ■ *Web:* www.pfisterhybrid.com
Pioneer Hi-Bred International Inc
400 Locust St Capital Sq Suite 800 .... Des Moines IA 50309 515-248-4800
TF: 800-247-6803 ■ *Web:* www.pioneer.com
Renk William F & Sons Inc 6809 Wilburn Rd .... Sun Prairie WI 53590 608-837-7351 825-6143
TF: 800-289-7365 ■ *Web:* www.renkseed.com
Richard Gumz Farms 8905 S Gumz Rd .... North Judson IN 46366 574-896-5441 896-5443
Wesson Farms Inc 25 Victoria Rd .... Victoria AR 72370 870-563-2674 563-6927
Westlake Farms Inc 23311 Newton Ave .... Stratford CA 93266 559-947-3328 947-3590
William F Renk & Sons Inc 6809 Wilburn Rd .... Sun Prairie WI 53590 608-837-7351 825-6143
TF: 800-289-7365 ■ *Web:* www.renkseed.com
Wyffels Hybrids Inc 13344 US Hwy 6 .... Geneseo IL 61254 309-944-8334 944-8338
TF: 800-369-7833 ■ *Web:* www.wyffels.com

10-6 Hog Farms

Phone Fax

Black River Farms PO Box 1 .... Harrells NC 28444 910-532-2814 532-2651
Cargill Inc 15407 McGinty Rd .... Wayzata MN 55391 952-742-7575 742-7209*
**Fax:* Cust Svc ■ *TF:* 800-227-4455 ■ *Web:* www.cargill.com
Christensen Farms 23971 County Rd 10 .... Sleepy Eye MN 56085 507-794-5310 794-2471
Web: www.christensenfarms.com
Clougherty Packing Co DBA Farmer John Meats
3049 E Vernon Ave .... Los Angeles CA 90058 323-583-4621 584-1699
TF Sales: 800-432-7637 ■ *Web:* www.farmerjohn.com
Coharie Farms 300 Westover Rd .... Clinton NC 28328 910-592-1122 592-0224
Farmer John Meats 3049 E Vernon Ave .... Los Angeles CA 90058 323-583-4621 584-1699
TF Sales: 800-432-7637 ■ *Web:* www.farmerjohn.com
Garland Farm Supply 250 Belgrade Ave PO Box 741 .... Garland NC 28441 910-529-9731 529-1844
Gold Kist Inc 244 Perimeter Ctr Pkwy NE .... Atlanta GA 30346 770-393-5000 393-5262
NASDAQ: GKIS ■ *Web:* goldkist.com
Hanor Co E 4614 Hwy 14-60 .... Spring Green WI 53588 608-588-9170 588-2308
Hastings Pork PO Box 67 .... Hastings NE 68902 402-463-0551 463-1349
Hitch Pork Production Inc HCR 4 Box 15 .... Guymon OK 73942 580-338-7613 338-7610
Hog Slat 206 Fayetteville St .... Newton Grove NC 28366 910-594-0219 594-1392
TF: 800-949-4647 ■ *Web:* www.hogslat.com
Iowa Select Farms LP PO Box 400 .... Iowa Falls IA 50126 641-648-4479 648-4251
Web: www.iowaselect.com
LL Murphrey Co 39 Vandiford-Thomas Rd .... Farmville NC 27828 252-753-5361 753-8759

Phone Fax

Murphy Brown LLC PO Box 759 .... Rose Hill NC 28458 910-289-2111 289-6400
TF: 800-311-9458 ■ *Web:* www.murphybrownllc.com
Murphy-Brown LLC 2822 W NC Hwy PO Box 856 .... Warsaw NC 28398 910-293-3434 293-7551
Web: www.murphybrownllc.com
NG Purvis Farms Inc 2504 Spies Rd .... Robbins NC 27325 910-948-2297 948-3213
PIC USA 100 Bluegrass Commons blvd Suite 2200 .... Hendersonville TN 37075 615-265-2700 265-2849
TF: 800-325-3398 ■ *Web:* www.pic.com/usa
Prestage Farms 4651 Taylors Bridge Hwy PO Box 438 .... Clinton NC 28329 910-592-5771 592-9552
Web: www.prestagefarms.com
Seaboard Farms Inc 9000 W 67th St Suite 200 .... Shawnee Mission KS 66202 913-261-2600 261-2626
Web: www.seaboardfoods.com
Smithfield Foods Inc 200 Commerce St .... Smithfield VA 23430 757-365-3000 365-3017*
NYSE: SFD ■ **Fax:* Cust Svc ■ *TF:* 800-276-6158 ■ *Web:* www.smithfieldfoods.com
Swine Graphics Enterprises LP 1620 Superior St .... Webster City IA 50595 515-832-5481 832-2237
Web: www.sgepork.com
Texas Farm Inc 4200 S Main St .... Perryton TX 79070 806-434-8936 435-3656
Tosh Farms 1586 Atlantic Ave .... Henry TN 38231 731-243-4861 243-4860
TF: 888-243-4885
TriOak Foods Inc 103 W Railroad St .... Oakville IA 52646 319-766-4411 766-4602
Web: www.trioak.com
Tyson Foods Inc 2210 W Oaklawn Dr .... Springdale AR 72762 479-290-4000 290-4217*
NYSE: TSN ■ **Fax:* Hum Res ■ *TF:* 800-643-3410 ■ *Web:* www.tyson.com
Wakefield Pork Inc 410 Main Ave E .... Gaylord MN 55334 507-237-5581 237-5584
Web: www.wakefieldpork.com

10-7 Mushroom Growers

Phone Fax

Modern Mushroom Farms Inc PO Box 340 .... Avondale PA 19311 610-268-3535 268-3099
Web: www.modernmush.com
Money's Mushrooms Ltd 24 Duncan St 5th Fl .... Toronto ON M5V2B8 416-977-1400 977-8722
TF: 800-661-8623
Monterey Mushrooms Inc 260 Westgate Dr .... Watsonville CA 95076 831-763-5300 763-0700
TF: 800-333-6874 ■ *Web:* www.montereymushrooms.com
Ostrom Mushroom Farms 8323 Steilacoom Rd SE .... Olympia WA 98513 360-491-1410 438-2594
TF: 800-640-7408 ■ *Web:* www.ostromfarms.com
Phillips Mushroom Farms Inc 1011 Kaolin Rd .... Kennett Square PA 19348 610-444-4492 925-0527
TF: 800-722-8818 ■ *Web:* www.phillipsmushroomfarms.com
Sylvan Inc 90 Glade Dr .... Kittanning PA 16201 724-543-3900 543-7583
TF: 866-352-7520 ■ *Web:* www.sylvaninc.com

10-8 Poultry & Eggs Production

Phone Fax

Allen's Hatchery Inc 126 N Shipley St .... Seaford DE 19973 302-629-9163 629-0514
TF: 800-777-8966 ■ *Web:* www.allenfamilyfoods.com
Amick Farms Inc PO Box 2309 .... Leesville SC 29070 803-532-1400 532-1492
TF: 800-926-4257 ■ *Web:* www.amickfarms.com
Aviagen Group 5015 Bradford Dr .... Huntsville AL 35805 256-890-3800 890-3919
TF: 800-826-9685 ■ *Web:* www.aviagen.com
Cagle's Farms Inc PO Box 38 .... Dalton GA 30722 706-278-2372 226-6169
Web: www.cagles.net
Cal-Maine Foods Inc PO Box 2960 .... Jackson MS 39207 601-948-6813 969-0905
NASDAQ: CALM ■ *Web:* www.calmainefoods.com
Cargill Turkey Products 1 Kratzer Rd .... Harrisonburg VA 22802 540-568-1400 568-1401
TF Cust Svc: 800-233-8457
Cobb-Vantress Inc PO Box 1030 .... Siloam Springs AR 72761 479-524-3166 524-3043
TF: 800-749-9719 ■ *Web:* www.cobb-vantress.com
Coleman Natural Foods 1767 Denver West Blvd Suite 200 .... Golden CO 80401 303-468-2500
TF: 800-442-8666 ■ *Web:* www.colemannatural.com
Cooper Farms 22348 County Rd 140 .... Oakwood OH 45873 419-594-3325 594-3372
TF: 888-594-8759 ■ *Web:* www.cooperfarms.com
Creighton Brothers LP PO Box 220 .... Atwood IN 46502 574-267-3101 267-6446
TF: 800-847-3447 ■ *Web:* www.cb-cl.com
Cuddy Farms Inc 1162 Bethel Rd .... Wadesboro NC 28170 704-694-6501 694-3665
Web: www.cuddyfarms.com
Culver Duck Farms Inc PO Box 910 .... Middlebury IN 46540 574-825-9537 825-2613
Web: www.culverduck.com
CWT Farms International Inc PO Box 1396 .... Gainesville GA 30503 770-532-3181 531-0555
Daylay Egg Farms Inc PO Box 5 .... West Mansfield OH 43358 937-355-6531 355-7911
Demler Egg Ranch 1455 N Warren Rd .... San Jacinto CA 92582 951-654-8166 487-9766
Diestel Turkey Ranch 22200 Lyons Bald Mountain Rd .... Sonora CA 95370 209-532-4950 532-6060
TF: 800-777-8966 ■ *Web:* www.diestelturkey.com
Dorothy Egg Farms LLC 271 Turkey Ln .... Winthrop ME 04364 207-377-9927
Durbin Marshall Farms Inc 2830 Commerce Blvd .... Irondale AL 35210 205-956-3505 380-3251
Web: www.marshalldurbin.com
Durbin Marshall Food Corp 2830 Commerce Blvd .... Irondale AL 35210 205-956-3505 380-3251
TF: 800-768-2456 ■ *Web:* www.marshalldurbin.com
Echo Lake Farm Produce Co
33102 S Honey Lake Rd PO Box 279 .... Burlington WI 53105 262-763-9551 763-4593
TF: 800-888-3447 ■ *Web:* www.echolakefoods.com
Esbenshade Farms 220 Eby Chiques Rd .... Mount Joy PA 17552 717-653-8061 653-6922
Feather Crest Farms Inc PO Box 129 .... Kurten TX 77862 979-589-2576 589-3052
Foster Farms Inc 1000 Davis St PO Box 457 .... Livingston CA 95334 209-394-7901 394-6342
Web: www.fosterfarms.com
Glenwood Foods LLC 20850 Jackson Ln .... Jetersville VA 23083 804-561-3447 561-3228
Harrison Poultry Inc Star St PO Box 550 .... Bethlehem GA 30620 770-867-7511 867-0999
Hickman's Egg Ranch Inc 6515 S Jackrabbit Trail .... Buckeye AZ 85236 623-872-1120 872-9220
TF: 800-224-2123 ■ *Web:* www.hickmanseggs.com
Hillandale Farms Inc PO Box 2109 .... Lake City FL 32056 386-397-1300 397-1130
Hubbard ISA PO Box 415 .... Walpole NH 03608 603-756-3311 756-9034
TF: 800-482-2442 ■ *Web:* www.hubbardbreeders.com
Hy-Line International 1755 W Lakes Pkwy .... West Des Moines IA 50266 515-225-6030 225-6425
Web: www.hy-line.com
ISA Breeders Inc Box 400 .... Cambridge ON C1R5V9 519-621-5191 621-9407
Jennie-O Turkey Store 2505 Willmar Ave SW .... Willmar MN 56201 320-235-2622 231-7100
TF: 800-328-1756 ■ *Web:* www.jennieoturkeystore.com
JFC Inc PO Box 1106 .... Saint Cloud MN 56302 320-251-3570 240-6250
TF: 800-328-8236
Kofkoff Egg Farm LLC 17 Schwartz Rd .... Bozrah CT 06334 860-886-2445 886-1138
Maple Leaf Farms Inc PO Box 308 .... Milford IN 46542 574-658-4121 658-2208
Web: www.mapleleaffarms.com
Mar-Jac Poultry Inc PO Box 1017 .... Gainesville GA 30503 770-536-0561 531-5049
TF: 800-226-0561 ■ *Web:* www.marjacpoultry.com
Marshall Durbin Farms Inc 2830 Commerce Blvd .... Irondale AL 35210 205-956-3505 380-3251
Web: www.marshalldurbin.com
Marshall Durbin Food Corp 2830 Commerce Blvd .... Irondale AL 35210 205-956-3505 380-3251
TF: 800-768-2456 ■ *Web:* www.marshalldurbin.com
McClain Enterprises Inc 801 S College St Suite 2 .... Mountain Home AR 72653 870-425-5700
Michael Foods Inc 301 Carlson Pkwy Suite 400 .... Minnetonka MN 55305 952-258-4000 258-4940
TF: 800-325-4270 ■ *Web:* www.michaelfoods.com
Midwest Hatchery & Poultry Farms Inc PO Box 247 .... Dassel MN 55325 320-275-3351
Midwest Poultry Services LP 9951 W SR 25 .... Mentone IN 46539 574-353-7651 353-7223
Murphy-Brown LLC 2822 W NC Hwy PO Box 856 .... Warsaw NC 28398 910-293-3434 293-7551
Web: www.murphybrownllc.com

Poultry & Eggs Production (Cont'd)

	City	State	ZIP	Phone	Fax
Nebraska Turkey Growers Co-op Assoc 12 Lawn Ave	Gibbon	NE	68840	308-468-5711	468-5715
Nicholas Turkey Breeding Farms 19449 Riverside Dr	Sonoma	CA	95476	707-938-1111	935-0144
Web: www.nicholas-turkey.com					
Norco Ranch Inc 1811 Mountain Ave	Norco	CA	92860	951-737-6735	737-9405
Web: www.norcoeggs.com					
Oakdell Egg Farms Inc 7401 N Glade Rd	Pasco	WA	99301	509-547-8665	547-9656
Papetti's Hygrade Egg Products Inc 1 Papetti Plaza	Elizabeth	NJ	07206	908-282-7900	354-8660
PECO Farms Inc PO Box 798	Gordo	AL	35466	205-364-7121	364-2158
PECO Foods Inc 3701 Kauloosa Ave	Tuscaloosa	AL	35403	205-345-3955	343-2401
Web: www.pecofoods.com					
Perdue Farms Inc PO Box 1537	Salisbury	MD	21802	410-543-3000	543-3212*
**Fax:* Sales ■ *TF:* 800-457-3738 ■ *Web:* www.perdue.com					
Peterson Farms Inc 250 S Main St	Decatur	AR	72722	479-752-5400	752-5650
Web: www.petersonfarms.com					
Pilgrim's Pride Corp 4845 US Hwy 271 PO Box 93	Pittsburg	TX	75686	903-434-1000	
NYSE: PPC ■ *Web:* www.pilgrimspride.com					
Plainville Farms Inc 7830 Plainville Rd	Plainville	NY	13137	315-635-3427	638-0659
Web: www.plainvillefarms.com					
Puglisi Egg Farms Inc 75 Easy St	Howell	NJ	07731	732-938-2373	938-2232
Ritewood Inc 3643 S 4000 East PO Box 120	Franklin	ID	83237	208-646-2213	646-2217
Rose Acre Farms Inc RR 5 PO Box 1250	Seymour	IN	47274	812-497-2557	497-3311
Web: www.roseacre.com					
Ross Breeders Inc 5015 Bradford Dr NW	Huntsville	AL	35805	256-890-3800	890-3919
TF: 800-826-9685 ■ *Web:* www.rossbreeders.com					
Sanderson Farms Inc PO Box 988	Laurel	MS	39441	601-649-4030	932-1461
NASDAQ: SAFM ■ *Web:* www.sandersonfarms.com					
Shinn Turkeys Inc Rt 63 Box 38	Dunning	NE	68833	308-533-2272	
Simpson's Eggs Inc 5015 E Hwy 218	Monroe	NC	28110	704-753-1478	753-4762
Sleepy Creek Farms Inc 938 Millers Chapel Rd PO Box 10009	Goldsboro	NC	27534	919-778-3130	778-8111
Tampa Farm Service Inc 14425 Haynes Rd	Dover	FL	33527	813-659-0605	659-0197
TF: 800-441-3447 ■ *Web:* www.4grain.com					
Tarheel Turkey Hatchery Inc Hwy 401 N Raeford PO Box 150	Raeford	NC	28376	910-875-8711	875-8712
Townsends Inc 919 N Market St Suite 420	Wilmington	DE	19801	302-777-6650	777-6660
Web: www.townsends.com					
Tyson Foods Inc 2210 W Oaklawn Dr	Springdale	AR	72762	479-290-4000	290-4217*
NYSE: TSN ■ **Fax:* Hum Res ■ *TF:* 800-643-3410 ■ *Web:* www.tyson.com					
Ward Egg Ranch Inc 2900 Harmony Grove Rd	Escondido	CA	92029	760-745-5689	745-5865
Wayne Farms LLC 4110 Continental Dr	Oakwood	GA	30566	678-450-3100	531-0858*
**Fax Area Code:* 770 ■ *TF:* 800-392-0844 ■ *Web:* www.waynefarmsllc.com					
Weiss Lake Egg Co Inc Hwy 411	Centre	AL	35960	256-927-5546	927-2596
Wilcox Farms Inc 40400 Harts Lake Valley Rd	Roy	WA	98580	360-458-7774	458-6950
TF: 800-568-6456 ■ *Web:* www.wilcoxfarms.com					
Willmar Poultry Co Inc PO Box 753	Willmar	MN	56201	320-235-8850	235-8869
TF: 800-328-8842 ■ *Web:* www.willmarpoultry.com/wpc.htm					
Willow Brook Foods Inc PO Box 50190	Springfield	MO	65805	417-862-3612	837-1675
TF: 800-423-2366 ■ *Web:* www.wbfoods.com					
Zacky Farms Inc 13200 Crossroads Pkwy N Suite 25	City of Industry	CA	91746	562-641-2900	641-2040
Web: www.zacky.com					
Zephyr Egg Co Inc 4622 Gall Blvd	Zephyrhills	FL	33542	813-782-1521	782-7070
TF: 800-488-6543					

10-9 Sugarcane & Sugarbeets Growers

	City	State	ZIP	Phone	Fax
A Duda & Sons Inc PO Box 620257	Oviedo	FL	32762	407-365-2111	365-2010
Web: www.duda.com					
Alico Inc PO Box 338	La Belle	FL	33975	863-675-2966	675-6928
NASDAQ: ALCO ■ *Web:* www.alicoinc.com					
Duda A & Sons Inc PO Box 620257	Oviedo	FL	32762	407-365-2111	365-2010
Web: www.duda.com					
Florida Crystals Corp 1 N Clematis St Suite 200	West Palm Beach	FL	33401	561-655-6303	659-3206
Web: www.floridacrystals.com					
Gay & Robinson Inc 1 Kaumakani Ave PO Box 156	Kaumakani	HI	96747	808-335-3133	335-6424
Heidrick Joe Enterprises Inc 36826 CR 24	Woodland	CA	95695	530-662-3046	662-1715
Joe Heidrick Enterprises Inc 36826 CR 24	Woodland	CA	95695	530-662-3046	662-1715
Knight Management Inc 205 SW 1st St	Belle Glade	FL	33430	561-996-6262	992-8995
Mueka Kea Agribusiness Co Inc PO Box 15	Papaikou	HI	96781	808-964-8405	964-8426
Sugar Cane Growers Co-op of Florida PO Box 666	Belle Glade	FL	33430	561-996-5556	996-4747
Web: www.scgc.org					
US Sugar Corp 111 Ponce de Leon Ave	Clewiston	FL	33440	863-983-8121	902-2889*
**Fax:* Hum Res ■ *Web:* www.ussugar.com					
Wedgworth Farms Inc 651 NW 9th St PO Box 2076	Belle Glade	FL	33430	561-996-2076	996-0613
TF: 800-477-2077					

10-10 Tree Nuts Growers

	City	State	ZIP	Phone	Fax
Agri-World Co-op 31545 Donald Ave	Madera	CA	93638	559-673-1306	673-1318
Baker Farming Co 45499 W Panoche Rd	Firebaugh	CA	93622	559-659-3942	659-7114
Big Valley Farm 450 CR 417	Goldthwaite	TX	76844	325-938-5560	938-5231
Blackwell Land Co 4900 California Ave Suite 370-B	Bakersfield	CA	93309	661-397-2622	397-2627
Blue Diamond Growers 1802 C St	Sacramento	CA	95814	916-442-0771	446-8620
TF: 888-285-1351 ■ *Web:* www.bluediamond.com					
Braden Farms Inc PO Box 1022	Hughson	CA	95326	209-883-4061	883-4862
Cummings Violich Inc 1750 Dayton Rd	Chico	CA	95928	530-894-5494	891-4946
Deseret Farms of California 6100 Wilson Landing Rd	Chico	CA	95973	530-343-5365	891-8037
Diamond Walnut Growers Inc PO Box 1727	Stockton	CA	95201	209-467-6000	467-6257
Web: www.diamondnuts.com					
Evans Farms Hwy 96 E & 50 Evans Rd PO Box 913	Fort Valley	GA	31030	478-825-2095	825-3670
Farmland Management Services 138 Regis St Suite A	Turlock	CA	95382	209-669-0742	669-0811
Green Valley Pecan Co 1625 E Sahuarita Rd	Sahuarita	AZ	85629	520-791-2852	791-2853
TF: 800-533-5269 ■ *Web:* www.greenvalleypecan.com					
Hammons Products Co 105 Hammons Dr PO Box 140	Stockton	MO	65785	417-276-5181	276-5187
TF: 888-429-6887 ■ *Web:* www.hammonsproducts.com					
Lassen Land Co 320 E South St PO Box 607	Orland	CA	95963	530-865-7676	865-8085
MacFarms of Hawaii LLC 89-406 Mamalahoa Hwy	Captain Cook	HI	96704	808-328-2435	328-8081
Web: www.macfarms.com					
Mauna Loa Macadamia Nut Corp HC01 Box 3	Hilo	HI	96720	808-982-6562	966-8410*
**Fax:* Cust Svc ■ *TF Cust Svc:* 800-832-9993 ■ *Web:* www.maunaloa.com					
ML Macadamia Orchards LP 26-238 Hawaii Belt Rd	Hilo	HI	96720	808-969-8057	969-8123
NYSE: NUT ■ *Web:* www.mlmacadamia.com					
Montpelier Orchards Management Co 1131 12th St	Modesto	CA	95354	209-577-2804	577-2320
Naraghi Farms PO Box 7	Escalon	CA	95320	209-577-5777	838-3299
Naumes Inc 2 Barnett Rd	Medford	OR	97501	541-772-6268	772-2135
Web: www.naumes.com					
Pandol & Sons 401 Rd 192	Delano	CA	93215	661-725-3755	725-4741
Web: www.pandol.com					
Paramount Farming Co 33141 E Lerdo Hwy	Bakersfield	CA	93308	661-399-4456	399-1735
Premiere Partners 2407 S Neil St PO Box 3009	Champaign	IL	61826	217-352-6000	352-9048
Spycher Brothers Farms 14827 W Harding Rd	Turlock	CA	95380	209-668-2471	668-4988
Web: www.spycherbros.com					
Stahmann Farms Inc 22500 S Hwy 28	La Mesa	NM	88044	505-526-2453	681-3955*
**Fax Area Code:* 888 ■ *Web:* www.stahmanns.com					
Sunnyland Farms Inc 2314 Wilson Rd	Albany	GA	31705	229-436-5654	888-8332
Web: www.sunnylandfarms.com					
Tejon Ranch Co PO Box 1000	Lebec	CA	93243	661-248-3000	248-3100
NYSE: TRC ■ *Web:* www.tejonranch.com					
Twelve Oaks Farm 31461 NE Bell Rd	Sherwood	OR	97140	503-538-8558	538-4393
Web: www.nutworld.com					

10-11 Vegetable Farms

	City	State	ZIP	Phone	Fax
A Duda & Sons Inc PO Box 620257	Oviedo	FL	32762	407-365-2111	365-2010
Web: www.duda.com					
Abe-El Produce 42143 Rd 120	Orosi	CA	93647	559-528-3030	528-6772
Accursio Sam S & Sons Farms PO Box 901767	Homestead	FL	33090	305-246-3455	245-2682
TF: 800-233-6826					
Agri-Empire Corp PO Box 490	San Jacinto	CA	92581	951-654-7311	654-7639
Web: www.agri-empire.com					
Amigo Farms 4245 E Hwy 80	Yuma	AZ	85365	928-726-3738	726-3744
Web: www.amigofarms.com					
Anderson Farms Inc 4600 2nd St	Davis	CA	95616	530-753-5695	753-5764
Anderson Produce 2302 N Closner Blvd	Edinburg	TX	78541	956-381-1421	381-1282
Anthony Farms Inc 290 Depot St	Scandinavia	WI	54977	715-467-2212	467-2626
TF: 800-826-0456 ■ *Web:* www.anthonyfarms.com					
Artesian Farms Inc PO Box 128	Ruskin	FL	33575	813-645-3211	645-7506
Barkley Co PO Box 2706	Yuma	AZ	85366	928-343-2918	343-2940
Web: www.barkleyag.com					
Barnes Farming Corp 7840 Old Barley Hwy	Spring Hope	NC	27882	252-459-3101	459-9020
Web: www.farmpak.com					
Bengard Tom Ranch Inc PO Box 80090	Salinas	CA	93912	831-422-9021	422-7782
TF: 800-546-3517					
Betteravia Farms PO Box 5079	Santa Maria	CA	93456	805-925-2417	922-7982
TF: 800-328-8816 ■ *Web:* www.bonipak.com					
Black Gold Farms 4575 32nd Ave S Suite 2A	Grand Forks	ND	58201	701-248-3788	
Web: www.blackgoldpotato.com					
Bo-Jac Seed Co 245 1500th Ave	Mount Pulaski	IL	62548	217-792-5001	792-5006
TF: 800-397-2069 ■ *Web:* www.bo-jac.com					
Bolthouse William Farms Inc 7200 E Brundage Ln	Bakersfield	CA	93307	661-366-7207	366-2834*
**Fax:* Sales ■ *Web:* www.bolthouse.com					
Borzynski Brothers Distributing Inc PO Box 133	Franksville	WI	53126	262-886-1623	886-2111
TF: 800-248-0420					
Boskovich Farms Inc PO Box 1352	Oxnard	CA	93032	805-487-2299	487-5189
Web: www.boskovichfarms.com					
Boutonnet Farms 10855 Ocean Mia Pkwy Suite B	Castroville	CA	95012	831-633-4977	633-4577
Buurma Farms Inc 3909 Kok Rd	Willard	OH	44890	419-935-6411	935-1918
TF: 888-428-8762 ■ *Web:* www.buurmafarms.com					
Byrd Foods Inc PO Box 318	Parksley	VA	23421	757-665-5194	665-6425
TF: 800-777-2973 ■ *Web:* www.byrdfoodsinc.com					
Capurro Frank & Son LLC PO Box 410	Moss Landing	CA	95039	831-728-3904	728-0241
Web: www.frankcapurroandson.com					
Cargil Produce Co PO Box 1146	Uvalde	TX	78802	830-278-5616	278-4935
Charles H West Farms Inc 2953 Tub Mill Pond Rd	Milford	DE	19963	302-335-3936	335-0438
Christopher Ranch 305 Bloomfield Ave	Gilroy	CA	95020	408-847-1100	847-5488
TF: 800-321-9333 ■ *Web:* www.christopherranch.com					
Circle C Farms 1393 Yates Spring Rd	Brinson	GA	39825	229-246-7090	246-0605
CROPP Cooperative 1 Organic Way	LaFarge	WI	54639	608-625-2602	625-2600
TF: 888-444-6455 ■ *Web:* www.organicvalley.coop					
D'Arrigo Brothers Co of California Inc PO Box 850	Salinas	CA	93902	831-424-3955	424-3136
Web: www.andyboy.com					
Dean Kincaid Inc N 2028 Hwy 106	Palmyra	WI	53156	262-495-3000	495-3002
Deardorff-Jackson Co Inc PO Box 1188	Oxnard	CA	93032	805-487-7801	483-1286
Web: www.deardorfffamilyfarms.com					
DiMare Florida Inc PO Box 900460	Homestead	FL	33090	305-245-4211	246-9740
Web: dimareinc.com/florida.htm					
Dole Fresh Vegetables Co PO Box 1759	Salinas	CA	93902	831-754-5244	757-0973
TF Sales: 800-333-5454 ■ *Web:* www.dole.com					
Doug Mellon Farms Inc 2197 S 4th Ave Suite 206	Yuma	AZ	85364	928-782-4482	782-0688
Dresick Farms Inc PO Box 1260	Huron	CA	93234	559-945-2513	945-9627
DuBois & Sons Farms Inc PO Box 740180	Boynton Beach	FL	33474	561-498-3000	498-5487
Duda A & Sons Inc PO Box 620257	Oviedo	FL	32762	407-365-2111	365-2010
Web: www.duda.com					
Earthbound Farm 1721 San Juan Hwy	San Juan Bautista	CA	95045	831-623-7880	623-4988
TF: 800-690-3200 ■ *Web:* www.ebfarm.com					
Elmore & Stahl Inc 4012 E Goodwin Rd	Mission	TX	78572	956-585-4540	585-5825
Everkrisp Vegetables Inc 9202 W Harrison St	Tolleson	AZ	85353	623-936-3321	936-1008
Farming Technology Corp 6950 Neuhaus St	Houston	TX	77061	713-923-5807	928-2437
TF: 800-395-2004					
Fordel Inc 1000 Airport Blvd	Mendota	CA	93640	559-655-3241	655-3045
Web: www.fordelinc.com					
FP Wood & Son Inc PO Box 159	Camden	NC	27921	252-335-4357	335-4075
Frank Capurro & Son LLC PO Box 410	Moss Landing	CA	95039	831-728-3904	728-0241
Web: www.frankcapurroandson.com					
Fresh Express Inc 950 E Blanco Rd	Salinas	CA	93901	831-422-5917	775-2331
TF Cust Svc: 800-242-5472 ■ *Web:* www.freshexpress.com					
Gargiulo Inc 15000 Old 41 N	Naples	FL	34110	239-597-3131	597-8963
Grant Family Farms 1020 W County Rd 72	Wellington	CO	80549	970-568-7654	568-7655
Web: www.grantfarms.com					
Greenheart Farms Inc PO Box 1510	Arroyo Grande	CA	93421	805-481-2234	481-7374
TF: 800-549-5531 ■ *Web:* www.greenheartfarms.com					
Griffin Ranches Inc 9490 W County 19th St	Somerton	AZ	85350	928-627-8809	627-8909
Grimmway Farms Inc PO Box 81498	Bakersfield	CA	93380	661-845-3724	845-9750
Web: www.grimmway.com					
Growers Marketing Service Inc PO Box 2595	Lakeland	FL	33806	863-644-2414	647-1086
TF: 800-476-2037					
Harris Farms Inc 23300 W Oakland Ave	Coalinga	CA	93210	559-884-2477	884-2267
TF: 800-691-1199 ■ *Web:* www.harrisfarms.com					
Hartung Brothers Inc 708 Hartland Trail Suite 2000	Madison	WI	53717	608-829-6000	829-6001
TF: 800-362-2522 ■ *Web:* www.hartungbrothers.com					
Hearne WP Produce Co Inc PO Box 1975	Salisbury	MD	21802	410-742-7363	749-6107
Heartland Farms Inc 907 3rd Ave	Hancock	WI	54943	715-249-5555	249-5265
Hundley Farms Inc PO Box H	Loxahatchee	FL	33470	561-996-6855	996-1158
Jack Brothers Co PO Box 116	Brawley	CA	92227	760-344-3781	344-2373
JET Farms Inc PO Box 1370	Loxahatchee	FL	33470	561-793-6216	793-4809
Long Farms Inc 2849 Lust Rd	Apopka	FL	32703	407-889-4141	889-5069
Major Farms Inc PO Box 719	Salinas	CA	93902	831-422-9616	422-9618
Martori Farms 7332 E Butherus Dr	Scottsdale	AZ	85260	480-998-1444	483-6723
TF: 800-627-8674 ■ *Web:* www.martorifarms.com					
McClure Farms/West Coast Tomato Inc 502 6th Ave W	Palmetto	FL	34221	941-722-4545	729-6778
Mecca Farms Inc PO Box 541779	Lake Worth	FL	33454	561-968-3605	968-3740
Mellon Doug Farms Inc 2197 S 4th Ave Suite 206	Yuma	AZ	85364	928-782-4482	782-0688
Merrill Farms PO Box 659	Salinas	CA	93902	831-424-7365	424-0447
Web: www.merrillfarms.com					

Phone Fax

Mount Dora Farms 1500 Port Blvd ... Miami FL 33132 305-530-4700 375-0971
Web: www.mountdorafarms.com
My-T Acres Inc 8127 Lewiston Rd ... Batavia NY 14020 585-343-1026 343-2051
Nash Produce Co 6160 S North Carolina 58 ... Nashville NC 27856 252-443-6011 443-6746
TF: 800-334-3032 ■ *Web:* www.nashproduce.com
Navajo Agricultural Products Industry PO Drawer 1318 ... Farmington NM 87499 505-566-2600 324-9458
Nunes Vegetables Inc PO Box 50956 ... Oxnard CA 93031 805-487-7472 487-8274
Ocean Mist Farms 10855 Ocean Mia Pkwy Suite A ... Castroville CA 95012 831-633-2144 633-0561
Web: www.oceanmist.com
Offutt RD Co PO Box 7160 ... Fargo ND 58106 701-237-6062 239-8787
TF: 877-444-7363
Pacific Tomato Growers PO Box 866 ... Palmetto FL 34220 941-722-3291 729-5849
Web: sunripe.sunripeproduce.com
Papen Farms Inc 847 Papen Ln ... Dover DE 19904 302-697-3291 697-2380
Paramount Farms Inc PO Box 188 ... Bancroft WI 54921 715-335-6357 335-6363
Web: www.paramountfarmsinc.com
Pasquinelli Produce Co PO Box 2949 ... Yuma AZ 85366 928-783-7813 343-4093
Pero Family Farms Inc 14095 SR-7 ... Delray Beach FL 33446 561-498-4533 496-4009
Petrocco Farms 14110 Brighton Rd ... Brighton CO 80601 303-659-6498 659-7645
TF: 888-876-2207 ■ *Web:* www.petroccofarms.com
Pine Bluff Farms Inc PO Box 38 ... Grand Marsh WI 53936 608-339-3616 339-3523
RC Farms PO Drawer R ... Gonzales CA 93926 831-455-9246 675-1915
RD Offutt Co PO Box 7160 ... Fargo ND 58106 701-237-6062 239-8787
TF: 877-444-7363
Rio Farms 1051 S Pacific Ave ... Oxnard CA 93030 805-240-1979 240-1953
Roth Farms Inc PO Box 1300 ... Belle Glade FL 33430 561-996-2991 996-8501
Web: www.rothfarms.com
Rousseau Farming Inc 9601 W Harrison Ave ... Tolleson AZ 85353 623-936-6249 936-5334
Royal Packing Co Inc PO Box 82157 ... Salinas CA 93912 831-424-0975 424-0762
Royvan Inc PO Box 619 ... Pahokee FL 33476 561-924-5551 924-5214
Russo Farms Inc 1962 S East Ave ... Vineland NJ 08360 856-692-5942 692-8534
Sackett Ranch Inc 2939 Neff Rd NE ... Stanton MI 48888 989-762-5049 762-5500
Sakata Farms Inc PO Box 508 ... Brighton CO 80601 303-659-1559 659-7865
Sam S Accursio & Sons Farms PO Box 901767 ... Homestead FL 33090 305-246-3455 245-2682
TF: 800-233-6826
San Miguel Produce Inc 4444 Naval Air Rd ... Oxnard CA 93033 805-488-0981 488-2103
TF: 888-347-3367 ■ *Web:* www.cutncleangreens.com
Sea Mist Farms 10855 Ocean Mia Pkwy Suite C ... Castroville CA 95012 831-633-2144 633-8163
Six L's Packing Co Inc 315 E New Market Rd ... Immokalee FL 34142 239-657-4221 657-6951
TF: 800-554-6606 ■ *Web:* www.sixls.com
SMT Farms PO Box 170 ... Yuma AZ 85366 928-341-9616 341-9644
Station Creek Co Inc 1529 Seaside Rd ... Saint Helena Island SC 29920 843-838-2883 838-7669
Sun World International Inc 16350 Driver Rd ... Bakersfield CA 93308 661-392-5000 392-4678
Web: www.sun-world.com
Suwannee Farms 19620 N County Rd 349 ... O'Brien FL 32071 386-776-1025 776-1089
Tanimura & Antle Inc PO Box 4070 ... Salinas CA 93912 831-455-2950 455-3639*
**Fax:* Hum Res ■ *TF:* 800-772-4542 ■ *Web:* www.taproduce.com
Taylor & Fulton Inc 932 5th Ave W ... Palmetto FL 34221 941-729-3883 723-2969
TF: 800-457-5577 ■ *Web:* www.taylorfulton.com
Teixeira Farms Inc 2600 Bonita Lateral Rd ... Santa Maria CA 93458 805-928-3801 928-9405
Web: www.teixeirafarms.com
Thomas Produce Co 9905 Clint Moore Rd ... Boca Raton FL 33496 561-482-1111 852-0018
Tom Bengard Ranch Inc PO Box 80090 ... Salinas CA 93912 831-422-9021 422-7782
TF: 800-546-3517
Torrey Farms Inc Maltby Rd Box 187 ... Elba NY 14058 585-757-9941 757-2528
Tri-Campbell Farms 15111 Hwy 17 ... Grafton ND 58237 701-352-3116 352-2008
TF: 877-999-7783 ■ *Web:* www.tricampbellfarms.com
Triple E Produce Corp PO Box 239 ... Tracy CA 95378 209-835-5123 835-7956
Turek Farms 8558 SR 90 ... King Ferry NY 13081 315-364-8735 364-5257
Twin Garden Farms 23017 Rt 173 ... Harvard IL 60033 815-943-7448 943-8024
Web: www.twingardenfarms.com
Village Farms LP 7 Christopher Way ... Eatontown NJ 07724 732-676-3000 676-3028
TF: 877-777-7718 ■ *Web:* www.villagefarms.com
Virginia Fork Produce Inc PO Box 148 ... Edenton NC 27932 252-482-2165 482-3515
TF: 800-334-7716
Wada Farms Potatoes Inc 2058 Jennie Lee Dr ... Idaho Falls ID 83404 208-542-2898 542-2893
TF: 800-657-5565 ■ *Web:* www.wadafarms.com
Walker Farms PO Box 129 ... Menan ID 83434 208-754-4696 754-4961
Waymon Farms Inc 9700 W Hwy 95 ... Somerton AZ 85350 928-627-8836 627-2988
Weber Farms 3559 Rd 'K' NW ... Quincy WA 98848 509-787-4578 787-4465
West Charles H Farms Inc 2953 Tub Mill Pond Rd ... Milford DE 19963 302-335-3936 335-0438
Wiers Farm Inc PO Box 385 ... Willard OH 44890 419-935-0131 933-2017
TF: 800-825-6525
William Bolthouse Farms Inc 7200 E Brundage Ln ... Bakersfield CA 93307 661-366-7207 366-2834*
**Fax:* Sales ■ *Web:* www.bolthouse.com
Wilson Farm Inc 10 Pleasant St ... Lexington MA 02421 781-862-3900 863-0469
Web: www.wilsonfarm.com
Wolfsen Inc 1269 W 'I' St ... Los Banos CA 93635 209-827-7700 827-7780
Web: www.wolfseninc.com
Wood FP & Son Inc PO Box 159 ... Camden NC 27921 252-335-4357 335-4075
Worzella & Sons Inc 2801 Hoover Ave ... Plover WI 54467 715-344-4098 344-4803
WP Hearne Produce Co Inc PO Box 1975 ... Salisbury MD 21802 410-742-7363 749-6107
Wysocki Produce Farm Inc 6320 3rd Ave ... Plainfield WI 54966 715-366-7175 366-7177
Zellwin Farms Co PO Box 188 ... Zellwood FL 32798 407-886-1891 889-2515

11 AGRICULTURAL SERVICES

11-1 Crop Preparation Services

Phone Fax

Allstate Packers Inc PO Box 350 ... Lodi CA 95241 209-369-3586 369-5465
American Raisin Packers Inc 2335 Chandler St PO Box 30 ... Selma CA 93662 559-896-4760 896-8942
Andrews Distribution Co 13650 Copus Rd ... Bakersfield CA 93313 661-858-2266 858-2965
Web: andrewsag.com
Baird-Neece Packing Corp 60 S 'E' St PO Box 791 ... Porterville CA 93258 559-784-3393 784-7773
Belair Packing House 1626 90th Ave ... Vero Beach FL 32966 772-567-1151 567-2719
TF: 800-567-1154
Bolthouse William Farms Inc 7200 E Brundage Ln ... Bakersfield CA 93307 661-366-7207 366-2834*
**Fax:* Sales ■ *Web:* www.bolthouse.com
Borg Produce Co 1601 E Olympic Blvd Bldg 100 Suite 101 ... Los Angeles CA 90021 213-688-9388 688-9381
TF: 800-808-2674 ■ *Web:* www.borgproduce.com
Calberi Inc 3605 W Pendleton Ave ... Santa Ana CA 92704 714-979-5221 641-7542
Web: www.calberi.com
California Family Foods LLC 6050 Struckmeyer Ave ... Arbuckle CA 95912 530-476-3326 476-3524
Cargill AgHorizons PO Box 9300 MS 19 ... Minneapolis MN 55440 952-742-7575 742-7313
TF: 800-227-4455 ■ *Web:* www.cargillaghorizons.com
Cecelia Packing Corp 24780 E South Ave ... Orange Cove CA 93646 559-626-5000 626-7561
Central Valley Processing Inc 3415 Chiles Ave ... Merced CA 95340 209-723-2950 723-4931
Charles G Watts Inc DBA Cream of the Crop 332 John St ... Salinas CA 93912 831-757-4955 757-2593
Chooljian Brothers Packing Co Inc 3192 S Indianola St ... Sanger CA 93657 559-875-5501 875-6618
Web: www.cal-raisin.com
Cream of the Crop 332 John St ... Salinas CA 93912 831-757-4955 757-2593

Phone Fax

Crop Production Services Inc PO Box 1467 ... Galesburg IL 61402 309-342-4100 342-4187
Web: www.cropproductionservices.com
Deardorff-Jackson Co Inc PO Box 1188 ... Oxnard CA 93032 805-487-7801 483-1286
Web: www.deardorfffamilyfarms.com
Delta Packing Co 6021 E Kettleman Ln ... Lodi CA 95240 209-334-1023 334-0811
Web: www.deltapacking.com
Diamond Fruit Growers Inc 3515 Chevron Dr ... Hood River OR 97031 541-354-5300 354-5394
Web: www.diamondfruit.com
DiMare Brothers/New England Farms Packing Co
84 New England Produce Ctr ... Chelsea MA 02150 617-889-3800 889-2067
Web: www.dimareinc.com
DiMare Florida Inc PO Box 900460 ... Homestead FL 33090 305-245-4211 246-9740
Web: dimareinc.com/florida.htm
DiMare Ruskin Inc 5715 US Hwy 41 N PO Box 967 ... Ruskin FL 33575 813-645-3241 645-4846
Dole Fresh Vegetables Co PO Box 1759 ... Salinas CA 93902 831-754-5244 757-0973
TF Sales: 800-333-5454 ■ *Web:* www.dole.com
Dundee Citrus Growers Assn 111 1st St N ... Dundee FL 33838 863-439-1574 439-1535
TF: 800-447-1574 ■ *Web:* www.dun-d.com
Emerald Packing Co Inc 2823 N Orange Blossom Trail ... Orlando FL 32804 407-423-0531 423-6426
Eppich Grain Inc 151 Canal Blvd ... Basin City WA 99343 509-269-4693 269-4200
Erwin-Keith Inc 1529 Hwy 193 ... Wynne AR 72396 870-238-2079 238-8621
Federal Dryer & Storage Co Hwy 165 ... England AR 72046 501-842-2301 842-2877
Fillmore-Piru Citrus Assoc 355 N Main St PO Box 350 ... Piru CA 93040 805-521-1781 521-0990
TF: 800-524-8787 ■ *Web:* www.fillmorepirucitrus.com
Food Technology Service Inc 502 Prairie Mine Rd ... Mulberry FL 33860 863-425-0039 425-5526
NASDAQ: VIFL ■ *Web:* www.foodtechservice.com
Fordel Inc 1000 Airport Blvd ... Mendota CA 93640 559-655-3241 655-3045
Web: www.fordelinc.com
Fresh Express Inc 950 E Blanco Rd ... Salinas CA 93901 831-422-5917 775-2331
TF Cust Svc: 800-242-5472 ■ *Web:* www.freshexpress.com
Germain's Technology Group North America 8333 Swanston Ln ... Gilroy CA 95020 408-847-1198 848-2124
Web: www.germains-usaseedcoat.com
Golden Peanut Co LLC 100 North Point Ctr E Suite 400 ... Alpharetta GA 30022 770-752-8160 752-8305
Web: www.goldenpeanut.com
Great Lakes Packers Inc 400 Great Lakes Pkwy PO Box 366 ... Bellevue OH 44811 419-483-2956 483-6922
TF: 800-624-8464
Grimmway Farms Inc PO Box 81498 ... Bakersfield CA 93380 661-845-3724 845-9750
Web: www.grimmway.com
GTC-GTC LLC 14574 Weld County Road 64 ... Greeley CO 80631 970-351-6000 351-6003
Haines City Citrus Growers Assn 8 Railroad Ave ... Haines City FL 33844 863-422-1174 422-3938
TF Sales: 800-422-4245 ■ *Web:* www.hilltopcitrus.com
Harllee Packing Inc 2308 US Hwy 301 N ... Palmetto FL 34221 941-722-7747 723-3027
Harris Woolf Almonds 26060 Colusa Rd ... Coalinga CA 93210 559-884-2147 884-2746
Hazelnut Growers of Oregon 401 N 26th Ave ... Cornelius OR 97113 503-648-4176 648-9515
TF: 800-273-4676 ■ *Web:* www.hazelnut.com
Hunt Brothers Co-op Inc 2404 Hunt Brothers Rd SE ... Lake Wales FL 33853 863-676-9471 676-8362
Index Fresh Inc 18184 Slover Ave ... Bloomington CA 92316 909-877-1577 877-0495
TF: 800-352-6931 ■ *Web:* www.indexfresh.com
Indian River Exchange Packers Inc 7355 9th St SW ... Vero Beach FL 32968 772-562-2252 569-7484
Web: www.irexp.com
Inland Fruit Co 300 N Frontage Rd ... Wapato WA 98951 509-877-2126 877-2045
Web: www.inlandfruit.com
JLG Harvesting Inc 1450 S Atlantic Ave ... Yuma AZ 85365 928-329-7548 329-7551
Kaprielian Brothers Packing Co 1750 S Buttonwillow Ave ... Reedley CA 93654 559-638-9277 638-6050
Keegan Inc 2570 Eldridge Ave ... Twin Falls ID 83303 208-733-5371 734-2754
Kingsburg Apple Packers Inc
10363 E Davis Ave PO Box 456 ... Kingsburg CA 93631 559-897-5132 897-4532
Kingston Cos 477 Shoup Ave Suite 207 ... Idaho Falls ID 83402 208-522-2365 522-7488
Klink Citrus Assn Inc 32921 Rd 159 PO Box 188 ... Ivanhoe CA 93235 559-798-1881 798-2226
LA Hearne Co Inc 512 Metz Rd ... King City CA 93930 831-385-5441 385-4377
Web: www.hearneco.com
Lake Region Packing Assn Inc 124 S Joanna Ave PO Box 1477 ... Tavares FL 32778 352-343-3111 343-1616
TF: 800-780-3400
Larson Fruit Co 109 N Wenas Rd PO Box 70 ... Selah WA 98942 509-697-7208 697-5281
Mann Packing Co Inc PO Box 690 ... Salinas CA 93902 831-422-7405 422-1131
TF: 800-285-1002 ■ *Web:* www.broccoli.com
Mariani Nut Co 709 Dutton St ... Winters CA 95694 530-795-4529 795-2681
Web: www.marianinut.com
Mariani Packing Co Inc 500 Crocker Dr ... Vacaville CA 95688 707-452-2800 452-8334
TF: 800-231-1287 ■ *Web:* www.marianifruit.com
Mesa Citrus Growers Assn 254 W Broadway Rd ... Mesa AZ 85210 480-964-8615 834-0764
Mooney Farms 1220 Fortress St ... Chico CA 95973 530-899-2661 899-7746
Web: www.mooneyfarms.com
Northern Fruit Co Inc 220 3rd St NE ... East Wenatchee WA 98802 509-884-6651 884-1990
TF: 800-234-6651 ■ *Web:* www.northernfruit.com
Packers of Indian River Ltd 5700 W Midway Rd ... Fort Pierce FL 34979 772-468-8835 466-0108
Phelan & Taylor Produce Co Inc
1860 Pacific Coast Hwy 1 PO Box 458 ... Oceano CA 93475 805-489-2413 489-0151
Pleasant Valley Potato Inc 275 E Elmore St PO Box 538 ... Aberdeen ID 83210 208-397-4194 397-4841
TF: 888-867-7783 ■ *Web:* www.pleasantvalleypotato.com
River Ranch Fresh Foods 1156 Abbott St ... Salinas CA 93901 831-758-1390 755-8281
TF: 800-538-5868 ■ *Web:* www.rrff.com
RPAC LLC PO Box 2138 ... Los Banos CA 93635 209-826-0272 826-3882
Web: www.rpacalmonds.com
Shoei Foods USA Inc 1900 Feather River Blvd ... Marysville CA 95901 530-742-7866 742-2873
Sun Pacific Packers Inc 1250 E Myer Rd ... Exeter CA 93221 559-592-5168 592-3852
Taplett Fruit Packing Inc 2301 5th St ... Wenatchee WA 98801 509-662-5570 662-3027
Taylor Fresh Foods Inc 911 Blanco Cir Suite B ... Salinas CA 93901 831-754-1715 754-0473
Tracy-Luckey Co Inc 110 N Hicks St PO Box 880 ... Harlem GA 30814 706-556-6216 556-6210
Web: www.tracy-luckey.com
Trout-Blue Chelan Inc 8 Houser Rd PO Box 669 ... Chelan WA 98816 509-682-2591 682-4620
Uni-Kool Partners 395 W Market St ... Salinas CA 93901 831-424-6613
Veg-Pro Inc 11800 Gordon Ave PO Box 635 ... Grant MI 49327 231-834-5657 834-8569
Verdelli Farms Inc 7505 Grayson Rd ... Harrisburg PA 17111 717-561-2900 561-2940*
**Fax:* Sales ■ *TF:* 800-422-8344 ■ *Web:* www.verdelli.com
Viterra Inc 201 Portage Ave PO Box 6600 ... Winnipeg MB R3C3A7 204-944-5411 944-5454
TF: 866-569-4411 ■ *Web:* www.viterra.ca
Wilco Peanut Co 3391 US Hwy 281 N PO Drawer B ... Pleasanton TX 78064 830-569-3808 569-2743
Web: www.wilcopeanut.com
William Bolthouse Farms Inc 7200 E Brundage Ln ... Bakersfield CA 93307 661-366-7207 366-2834*
**Fax:* Sales ■ *Web:* www.bolthouse.com

11-2 Livestock Improvement Services

Phone Fax

ABS Global Inc 1525 River Rd ... DeForest WI 53532 608-846-3721 846-6442
TF Cust Svc: 800-356-5331 ■ *Web:* www.absglobal.com
Accelerated Genetics E 10890 Penny Ln ... Baraboo WI 53913 608-356-8357 356-4387
TF: 800-451-9275 ■ *Web:* www.accelgen.com
Alta California PO Box 669 ... Hilmar CA 95324 209-632-5836 632-6499
Web: www.altacal.com
Alta Genetics Inc RR 2 ... Balzac AB T0M0E0 403-226-0666 226-4259
TF: 800-932-2855 ■ *Web:* www.altagenetics.com
AMS Genetics Inc 1048 State Rt 254 ... Milleville PA 17846 570-458-4571 458-5529
Web: www.amsgenetics.com

Livestock Improvement Services (Cont'd)

Phone | Fax

Certified Semen Services 401 Bernadette Dr PO Box 1033........ Columbia MO 65203 573-445-4406 446-2279
Web: www.naab-css.org

COBA/Select Sires Inc 1224 Alton Darby Creek Rd ....Columbus OH 43228 614-878-5333 870-2622
TF: 800-837-2621 ■ *Web:* www.cobaselect.com

Cobb-Vantress Inc PO Box 1030 .... Siloam Springs AR 72761 479-524-3166 524-3043
TF: 800-749-9719 ■ *Web:* www.cobb-vantress.com

Dairy One 730 Warren Rd ....Ithaca NY 14850 607-257-1272 257-6808
TF: 800-344-2697 ■ *Web:* www.dairyone.com

Equine Embryos Inc 2409 Alps Rd RR1 ....Ayr ON N0B1E0 519-624-7670 624-2097
Web: www.equineembryos.com

Flatness International Inc 104 Stony Mountain Rd.......... Tunkhannock PA 18657 570-836-3527 836-1549
Web: www.flatnessintl.com

Genex Co-op Inc/CRI 100 MBC Dr .... Shawano WI 54166 715-526-2141 526-4511
TF: 888-333-1783 ■ *Web:* genex.crinet.com

Hagyard-Davidson-McGee Assoc PSC 4250 Iron Works Rd ....Lexington KY 40511 859-255-8741 253-0196
Web: www.hagyard.com

National Assn of Animal Breeders (NAAB) PO Box 1033 .... Columbia MO 65205 573-445-4406 446-2279
Web: www.naab-css.org

National Dairy Herd Improvement Assn Inc
421 S 9 Mound Rd PO Box 930399 .... Verona WI 53593 608-848-6455 848-7675
Web: www.dhia.org

Newsham Genetics LC
5058 Grand Ridge Dr Suite 200 .... West Des Moines IA 50265 515-225-9420 225-9560
TF: 800-622-2627 ■ *Web:* www.newsham.com

Reproduction Enterprises Inc 908 N Prairie Rd................ Stillwater OK 74075 405-377-8037 377-4541
TF: 866-734-2855 ■ *Web:* agonline.com/rei

SEK Genetics 9525 70th Rd ....Galesburg KS 66740 620-763-2211 763-2231
TF: 800-443-6389 ■ *Web:* www.sekgenetics.com

Select Sires Inc 11740 US Hwy 42 N .... Plain City OH 43064 614-873-4683 873-5751
Web: www.selectsires.com

Simonsen Laboratories Inc 1180-C Day Rd ....Gilroy CA 95020 408-847-2002 847-4176
Web: www.simlab.com

Taurus Service Inc Grift Flat Rd PO Box 164................ Mehoopany PA 18629 570-833-5123 833-2690
TF: 800-836-5123 ■ *Web:* www.taurus-service.com

12 AIR CARGO CARRIERS

Phone | Fax

ABX Air Inc 145 Hunter Dr .... Wilmington OH 45177 937-382-5591 383-1233
NASDAQ: ABXA ■ *TF:* 800-736-3973 ■ *Web:* www.abxair.com

Aeronet Worldwide 42 Corporate Park PO Box 17239...............Irvine CA 92623 949-474-3000 474-1477
TF: 800-552-3869 ■ *Web:* www.aeronet.com

Air Canada Cargo LaGuardia International Airport Hangar 5B ....Flushing NY 11371 718-899-9128 651-5467
TF: 800-688-2274 ■ *Web:* www.aircanada.com/cargo/en/index.html

Air Jamaica Cargo Sales 1701 NW 66th Ave Bldg 709..............Miami FL 33126 305-526-2390 871-7214
Web: www.airjamaica.com/cargo

Air New Zealand Ltd 1960 E Grand Ave Suite 900............. El Segundo CA 90245 310-648-7000 648-7017
TF: 800-262-1234 ■ *Web:* www.airnz.com/default.htm

Air Traffic Management Inc 1924 Rankin Rd ....Houston TX 77073 281-821-2002 443-0938
TF Cust Svc: 800-231-0221 ■ *Web:* www.atmairfrt.com

Air Ukraine Cargo JFK International Airport Cargo Bldg 67 .... Jamaica NY 11430 718-376-1023 376-1073
Web: www.airukraine.com

Alaska Airlines Cargo Services 19300 International blvd .... Seattle WA 98188 206-433-3200 574-1950*
**Fax:* Hum Res ■ *TF:* 800-426-0333 ■ *Web:* www.alaskaair.com

Alex Nichols Agency 50 Carnation Ave Bldg 1................Floral Park NY 11001 516-488-8080 326-9696
TF: 800-765-8283 ■ *Web:* www.alexnicholsagency.com

Alitalia Executive Cargo Div
JFK International Airport N Boundry Rd Bldg 79................Jamaica NY 11430 718-244-8500 656-4257
TF: 800-221-4745 ■ *Web:* www.alitaliacargo.com

American Airlines Inc Cargo Div 4255 Amon Carter Blvd........Fort Worth TX 76155 817-967-2400 963-2143
TF: 800-227-4622 ■ *Web:* www.aacargo.com

Ameriflight Inc 4700 Empire Ave Hangar 1 ....Burbank CA 91505 818-980-5005 847-0305*
**Fax:* Cust Svc ■ *TF:* 800-800-4538 ■ *Web:* www.ameriflight.com

Amerijet International Inc 2800 S Andrews Ave........... Fort Lauderdale FL 33316 954-320-5300 765-3521
TF: 800-927-6059 ■ *Web:* www.amerijet.com

Arrow Air Inc 1701 NW 63rd Ave Bldg 712 ....Miami FL 33126 305-871-3116 526-0933
TF: 800-871-3370 ■ *Web:* www.arrowair.com

Atlas Air Worldwide Holdings Inc 2000 Westchester Ave......... Purchase NY 10577 914-701-8000 701-8001
Web: www.atlasair.com

Austrian Airlines Cargo
JFK International Airport Bldg 75 Area B.................... Jamaica NY 11430 718-995-2274 995-5007
TF: 800-637-2957 ■ *Web:* www.auacargo.com

British Airways World Cargo
JFK International Airport Cargo Bldg 66 .... Jamaica NY 11430 718-425-5000 425-5020
Web: www.baworldcargo.com

Capital Cargo International Airlines 7100 TPC Dr Suite 200 .... Orlando FL 32822 407-855-2004 855-6620
TF: 800-593-9119 ■ *Web:* www.capitalcargo.com

Cargo Services Inc 1601 NW 70th Ave ....Miami FL 33126 305-599-9333 599-6262
TF: 800-597-6010 ■ *Web:* www.cargo-services.com

Cargolux Airlines International 238 Lawrence Ave ..... South San Francisco CA 94080 650-225-0747 225-0988
TF: 800-722-2023 ■ *Web:* www.cargolux.com

Cathay Pacific Cargo 6040 Avion Dr Suite 338...............Los Angeles CA 90045 310-417-0052 348-9789
TF: 800-628-6960 ■ *Web:* www.cathaypacific.com/cgo

Cayman Airways Cargo Services 5915 NW 18th St Bldg 716-H ....Miami FL 33106 305-526-3190 871-7971
Web: www.caymanairways.com/cargo/index.html

Central Airlines Inc 411 Lou Holland Dr .... Kansas City MO 64116 816-472-7711 472-1682
Web: www.centralairsouthwest.com

China Airlines Cargo Sales & Service 11201 Aviation Blvd .....Los Angeles CA 90045 310-646-4293 215-5684*
**Fax:* Sales ■ *TF:* 800-421-1289 ■ *Web:* www.china-airlines.com/en

Continental Airlines Inc Cargo Div DBA Continental Cargo
1600 Smith St ....Houston TX 77002 713-324-5000
TF: 800-421-2456 ■ *Web:* www.cocargo.com/cocargo

Continental Cargo 1600 Smith St.............................Houston TX 77002 713-324-5000
TF: 800-421-2456 ■ *Web:* www.cocargo.com/cocargo

Delta Air Cargo 1600 Charles W Grant Pkwy ....Atlanta GA 30320 800-352-2746 714-7070*
**Fax Area Code:* 404 ■
Web: www.delta-air.com/business_programs_services/delta_cargo/index.jsp

East Coast Air Charter Inc 301 E Front St PO Box 7137 ....Statesville NC 28687 704-838-1991 838-1982
TF: 888-277-7434 ■ *Web:* www.eastcoastaircharter.com

Empire Airlines Inc 11559 N Atlas Rd ....Hayden ID 83835 208-292-3850 292-3851
Web: www.empireairlines.com

Evergreen International Airlines Inc 3850 Three-Mile Ln .... McMinnville OR 97128 503-472-0011 434-4210
TF: 800-383-5338 ■ *Web:* www.evergreenairlines.com

Evergreen International Aviation Inc 3850 Three Mile Ln....... McMinnville OR 97128 503-472-9361 472-1048
TF: 800-472-9361 ■ *Web:* www.evergreenaviation.com

Gemini Air Cargo 44965 Aviation Dr Suite 300 ....Dulles VA 20166 703-260-8100 260-8102
TF: 888-359-4221 ■ *Web:* www.gac-cargo.com

Gulf & Caribbean Air 6860 S Service Dr ....Waterford MI 48327 248-666-5910 666-9618

Iberia Air Cargo 5600 NW 36th Ave Bldg 56 Suite 201.............Miami FL 33122 305-526-6771 871-7712
TF: 800-221-6002

Phone | Fax

JAL Cargo America Region 944 N Field Rd .... San Francisco CA 94128 650-737-5100 737-0227
Web: www.jal.co.jp/en/jalcargo/ar

Kalitta Flying Service 818 Willow Run Airport ....Ypsilanti MI 48198 734-484-0088 484-7178
TF: 800-521-1590 ■ *Web:* www.kalittaair.com

Kitty Hawk Inc 1535 W 20th St ....DFW Airport TX 75261 972-456-2200 456-2259
AMEX: KHK ■ *TF:* 800-486-3780 ■ *Web:* www.khcargo.com

LanChile Cargo Group 6500 NW 22nd St.........................Miami FL 33122 305-871-4980 871-4381
TF: 800-735-5526 ■ *Web:* www.lancargo.cl

Lloyd Aereo Boliviano Airlines Cargo
5815 NW 18th St Bldg 716-J ....Miami FL 33126 305-526-5565 871-5760
TF Cust Svc: 800-489-4118

LOT Polish Airlines Cargo
JFK International Airport Cargo Bldg 21-B .... Jamaica NY 11430 718-656-2674 656-6063
Web: www.lot.com

Lufthansa Cargo USA
3400 Peachtree Rd Lenox Towers Suite 1225.................. Atlanta GA 30326 404-814-5311 814-5300
TF: 877-542-2746 ■ *Web:* www.lhcargo.com

Lynden Air Cargo LLC 6441 S Airpark Pl .... Anchorage AK 99502 907-243-6150 243-2143
TF: 888-243-7248 ■ *Web:* www.lac.lynden.com

Martinair Holland Cargo 500 Glades Rd Suite 500 .... Boca Raton FL 33431 561-391-1313 750-5221
TF: 800-366-3734

MartinAire Aviation LLC 4745 Frank Luke Dr................... Addison TX 75001 972-349-5700 349-5750
TF: 800-282-3828 ■ *Web:* www.martinaire.com

Northern Air Cargo Inc 3900 Old International Airport Rd........ Anchorage AK 99502 907-243-3331 249-5190
TF: 800-727-2141 ■ *Web:* www.northernaircargo.com

Northwest Airlines Cargo Div 5101 Northwest Dr .... Saint Paul MN 55111 800-692-2746
Web: www.nwa.com/services/shipping/cargo

Polar Air Cargo 2000 Westchester Ave......................... Purchase NY 10577 800-462-2012
Web: www.polaraircargo.com

Qantas Airways Cargo 6555 W Imperial Hwy.................Los Angeles CA 90045 310-665-2280 665-2201
TF: 800-227-0290

Rhoades Aviation Inc 4770 Ray Boll Blvd ....Columbus IN 47203 812-372-1819 378-2708
Web: www.rhoadesaviation.com

Ryan International Airlines Inc 4949 Harrison Ave............. Rockford IL 61108 815-316-5420 398-0192
TF: 800-727-0457 ■ *Web:* www.flyryan.com

SAS Cargo
International Cargo Center Newark International Airport
Brewster Rd Bldg 340 ....Newark NJ 07114 973-849-3300 849-3367
Web: www.sascargo.com

Service by Air Inc 222 Crossways Park Dr.................... Woodbury NY 11797 516-921-4101 921-4304
TF: 800-243-5545 ■ *Web:* www.servicebyair.com

Singapore Airlines Cargo 710 McDonnell Rd.............. San Francisco CA 94128 650-876-7350 875-0678
Web: www.siacargo.com

Southwest Airlines Air Cargo 8028 Aviation Pl ....Dallas TX 75235 214-792-5534 792-5534
TF: 800-533-1222 ■ *Web:* www.swacargo.com

STAF Airlines 1851 NW 68th Ave Bldg 706 Suite 225...............Miami FL 33126 305-871-0130 871-0118

Tampa Airlines Cargo 1850 NW 66th Ave Bldg 708 ....Miami FL 33122 305-526-6720 526-2720

Thai Airways International Cargo 6501 W Imperial Hwy........Los Angeles CA 90045 310-670-8591 670-1057
TF: 800-426-8678 ■ *Web:* www.thaicargo.com

United Airlines Cargo Services Div PO Box 66100 .... Chicago IL 60666 800-822-2746
Web: www.ualcargo.com

US Airways Inc 111 Rio Salado Pkwy........................... Tempe AZ 85284 480-693-0800 693-5506
TF: 800-428-4322 ■ *Web:* www.usairways.com

Virgin Atlantic Cargo 1983 Marcus Ave Suite 100 ....Lake Success NY 11042 516-775-2600 354-3760
TF: 800-828-6822 ■ *Web:* www.virgin-atlantic.com

13 AIR CHARTER SERVICES

SEE ALSO Aviation - Fixed-Base Operations p. 1364; Helicopter Transport Services p. 1776

Phone | Fax

40-Mile Air Ltd Mile 1313 Alaska Hwy PO Box 539...................Tok AK 99780 907-883-5191 883-5194
Web: outdoorsdirectory.com/akpages/40mileair

Active Aero Group 2068 E St ....Belleville MI 48111 734-547-7200 547-7222*
**Fax:* Hum Res ■ *TF Cust Svc:* 800-872-5387 ■ *Web:* www.activeaero.com

Actus Aviation LLC 2030 Airport Rd..............................Napa CA 94558 707-252-8152 254-3733
Web: www.actusaviationllc.com

Aero Air LLC 2050 NE 25th Ave .... Hillsboro OR 97124 503-640-3711 681-6514
TF: 800-448-2376 ■ *Web:* www.aeroair.com

Air America Jet Charter Inc 9000 Randolph St.................. Houston TX 77061 713-640-2900 532-2214
TF: 888-423-9110 ■ *Web:* www.airamericajetcharter.com

Air Charter Team 10015 NW Ambassador Dr Suite 202 .... Kansas City MO 64153 816-283-3280 283-3185
TF: 800-205-6610 ■ *Web:* www.airchartertearn.com

Air Orlando Aviation Inc 319 N Crystal Lake Dr.................. Orlando FL 32803 407-896-2799 896-7551
Web: www.flyairorlando.com

Air Palm Springs 145 S Gene Autry Trail Suite 14............Palm Springs CA 92262 760-322-1104 322-1204
Web: www.airps.com

Air Royale International Inc 9100 Wilshire Blvd Suite 420......Beverly Hills CA 90212 310-289-9800 289-9804
TF: 800-776-9253 ■ *Web:* www.airroyale.com

AirFlite Inc 3250 AirFlite Way.......................... Long Beach CA 90807 562-490-6200 490-6290
TF: 800-241-3548 ■ *Web:* www.airflight.com

Allegiant Air 3301 N Buffalo Dr Suite B-9 .... Las Vegas NV 89129 702-851-7300 851-7301
TF Resv: 800-432-3810 ■ *Web:* www.allegiantair.com

American Air Charter Network PO Box 32146......... Palm Beach Gardens FL 33420 516-768-3202 883-0071*
**Fax Area Code:* 323 ■ *TF:* 800-393-2884

American Jet Charter
5901 Philip J Rhoads Hanger 14 Wiley Post Airport .... Bethany OK 73008 405-495-5453 495-5472
TF: 800-495-5453 ■ *Web:* www.american-jet.com

Atkin Air 1420 Flightline Dr Suite B ....Lincoln CA 95648 916-645-6242 645-7132
TF: 800-924-2471 ■ *Web:* www.atkinair.com

Aviation Charter Services 6551 Pierson Dr................. Indianapolis IN 46241 317-244-7200 241-8091
TF: 800-522-2296 ■ *Web:* www.avcharter.com

Avstar Aviation 12 N Haven Ln......................... East Northport NY 11731 631-499-0048 499-0051
TF: 800-575-2359 ■ *Web:* www.avstaraviation.com

Berkshire Aviation Enterprises Inc
Great Barrington Airport PO Box 179 .... Great Barrington MA 01230 413-528-1010 528-1605
Web: www.berkshireaviation.net

Berry Aviation Inc 1807 Airport Dr..................... San Marcos TX 78666 512-353-2379 353-2593
TF: 800-229-2379 ■ *Web:* www.berryair.com

Bighorn Airways Inc 912 W Brundage Ln.......................Sheridan WY 82801 307-672-3421 674-4468
Web: www.bighornairways.com

Bluffton Flying Service Co 1080 Navajo Dr..................... Bluffton OH 45817 419-358-7045 358-6851
TF: 800-468-6359 ■ *Web:* www.blufftonflyingservice.com

Bridgeford Flying Services 2030 Airport Rd Napa County Airport.......Napa CA 94558 707-224-0887 257-7770
TF: 800-229-6272 ■ *Web:* www.bfsnapa.com

CAI (Chrysler Aviation Inc) 7120 Hayvenhurst Ave Suite 309 ...... Van Nuys CA 91406 818-989-7900
TF: 800-995-0825 ■ *Web:* www.chrysleraviation.com

Champion Air 8009 34th Ave S Suite 500 .... Bloomington MN 55425 952-814-8700 814-8990
TF: 800-922-2606 ■ *Web:* www.championair.com

Charter Flight Inc 5400 Airport Dr.......................... Charlotte NC 28208 704-359-9124 359-9128
TF: 800-521-3148 ■ *Web:* www.charterflightinc.com

	City	State	Zip	Phone	Fax
Charter Services Inc 8400 Airport Blvd Bldg 31 *TF:* 800-657-1555 ■ *Web:* www.csijets.com	Mobile	AL	36608	251-633-6090	633-6850
Chrysler Aviation Inc (CAI) 7120 Hayvenhurst Ave Suite 309 *TF:* 800-995-0825 ■ *Web:* www.chrysleraviation.com	Van Nuys	CA	91406	818-989-7900	
Clay Lacy Aviation 7435 Valjean Ave *TF:* 800-423-2904 ■ *Web:* www.claylacy.com	Van Nuys	CA	91406	818-989-2900	989-2953
Clintondale Aviation Inc 652 Rt 299 Suite 201 *Web:* www.clintondale.com	Highland	NY	12528	845-883-5277	883-5293
Colgan Air Services 2709 Fanta Reed Rd *TF:* 800-658-9498 ■ *Web:* www.colgan-air.com	La Crosse	WI	54603	608-783-8359	783-8050
Corporate Express Airline 305 Aviation Way NE	Calgary	AB	T2E2M4	403-216-4050	216-4055
Corporate Flight Inc 6150 Highland Rd *TF:* 800-767-2473 ■ *Web:* www.corporateflight.com	Waterford	MI	48327	248-666-8800	666-8804
Corporate Flight International 5220 Haven St Suite 104 *TF:* 800-869-8591 ■ *Web:* www.cfi-inc.com	Las Vegas	NV	89119	702-736-0077	736-6258
CSI Aviation Services Inc 3700 Rio Grand Blvd NW Suite 1 *TF:* 800-765-9464 ■ *Web:* www.airchartertravel.com	Albuquerque	NM	87107	505-761-9000	342-7377
East Coast Flight Services Inc 29111 Newman Rd Easton Municipal Airport *TF Sales:* 800-554-0550 ■ *Web:* www.eastcoastflight.com	Easton	MD	21601	410-820-6633	763-7404
Elite Aviation LLC 7501 Hayvenhurst Pl *TF:* 888-334-7777 ■ *Web:* www.eliteaviation.com	Van Nuys	CA	91406	818-988-5387	988-2111
Era Aviation Inc Louisiana Lake Charles Municipal Airport PO Box 6550 *TF:* 800-256-2372 ■ *Web:* www.flyera.com	Lake Charles	LA	70606	337-478-6131	474-3918
Exec Air Montana Inc 2430 Airport Rd *TF:* 800-513-2190 ■ *Web:* www.execairmontana.com	Helena	MT	59601	406-442-2190	442-2199
Executive Fliteways 1 Clark Dr *TF:* 800-533-3363 ■ *Web:* www.fly-efi.com	Ronkonkoma	NY	11779	631-588-5454	588-5527
Executive Jet 4556 Airport Rd *TF:* 800-451-2822 ■ *Web:* www.ejmjets.com	Cincinnati	OH	45226	513-979-6600	979-6662
Fairwind Air Charter 2555 SE Dixie Hwy *TF:* 800-989-9665 ■ *Web:* fairwindaircharter.com	Stuart	FL	34996	772-288-4130	288-4230
Flight Options 26180 Curtiss Wright Pkwy *TF:* 800-433-1285 ■ *Web:* www.flightoptions.com	Richmond Heights	OH	44143	216-261-3500	261-3595
Flightstar Corp 7 Airport Rd Willard Airport *TF:* 800-747-4777 ■ *Web:* www.flightstar.com	Savoy	IL	61874	217-351-7700	351-9843
Hop-A-Jet Inc 5525 NW 15th Ave Suite 150 *TF:* 800-556-6633 ■ *Web:* www.hopajet.com	Fort Lauderdale	FL	33309	954-771-5779	772-6981
International Charter Inc of Oregon 1860 Hawthorne Ave NE Suite 390 *Web:* www.icioregon.com	Salem	OR	97303	503-589-1437	371-7285
International Jet Aviation Services 12401 Aviator Way *TF:* 800-858-5891 ■ *Web:* www.internationaljet.com	Englewood	CO	80112	303-790-0414	790-4144
Jet Air Jet Charter 547 Perimeter Rd Hanger 2 PO Box 178207 *TF:* 888-812-6604	Nashville	TN	37217	615-361-1007	361-1090
Jet Aviation Business Jets Inc 112 Charles A Lindbergh Dr *TF:* 800-736-8538 ■ *Web:* www.jetaviation.com	Teterboro	NJ	07608	201-462-4100	462-4136
Jet Resource Inc 455 Wilmer Ave Lunken Airport Hangar 27 *TF:* 800-404-5387 ■ *Web:* www.jetresource.com	Cincinnati	OH	45226	513-762-6909	871-4181
JetCorp 18500 Edison Ave *TF:* 800-325-4811 ■ *Web:* www.jetcorp.com	Chesterfield	MO	63005	636-530-7000	530-7001
KaiserAir Inc 8735 Earhart Rd *TF:* 800-538-2625 ■ *Web:* www.kaiserair.com	Oakland	CA	94621	510-569-9622	569-9670
Key Air Inc 3 Juliano Dr Suite 201 Waterbury-Oxford Airport *TF:* 800-258-6975 ■ *Web:* www.keyair.com	Oxford	CT	06478	203-264-0605	264-0218
Lacy Clay Aviation 7435 Valjean Ave *TF:* 800-423-2904 ■ *Web:* www.claylacy.com	Van Nuys	CA	91406	818-989-2900	989-2953
Landmark Aviation 3821 N Liberty St **Fax:* Sales ■ *TF:* 800-393-4908 ■ *Web:* www.landmarkaviation.com	Winston-Salem	NC	27105	336-776-6060	776-6061*
LR Services 600 Hayden Cir *TF:* 888-675-9650 ■ *Web:* www.lrservices.com	Allentown	PA	18109	610-266-2500	266-3100
Lynx Air International 3402 SW 9th Ave *TF:* 888-596-9247 ■ *Web:* www.lynxair.com	Fort Lauderdale	FL	33315	954-772-9808	772-1141
Maguire Aviation Group 7155 Valjean Ave *TF:* 800-451-7270	Van Nuys	CA	91406	818-989-2300	902-9386
Maine Aviation Corp 1025 Westbrook St *TF:* 888-359-7600 ■ *Web:* www.maineaviation.com	Portland	ME	04102	207-780-1811	775-3359
Mar-El Aviation Inc DBA Jet Air Jet Charter 547 Perimeter Rd Hanger 2 PO Box 178207 *TF:* 888-812-6604	Nashville	TN	37217	615-361-1007	361-1090
Mayo Aviation Inc 7735 S Peoria St *TF:* 800-525-0194 ■ *Web:* www.mayoaviation.com	Englewood	CO	80112	303-790-9777	790-4909
Miami Air International Inc 5000 NW 36 St Suite 307 *Web:* www.miamiair.com	Miami	FL	33122	305-871-3300	871-4222
Million Air Interlink Inc 8501 Telephone Rd **Fax Area Code:* 866 ■ *TF:* 888-589-9059 ■ *Web:* www.millionair.com	Houston	TX	77061	713-640-4000	283-8274*
MissionAir 704 Southgate Rd *TF:* 877-231-2992	Saint Andrews	MB	R1A3P8	204-231-2992	338-3226
Mountainbird Inc DBA Salmon Air 29 Hamner Dr *TF:* 800-448-3413 ■ *Web:* www.salmonair.com	Salmon	ID	83467	208-756-6211	756-6219
Nashville Jet 1480 Murfreesboro Rd Hanger 14 *TF:* 800-824-4778 ■ *Web:* www.nashvillejetcharters.com	Nashville	TN	37209	615-350-8400	350-8408
NetJets Inc 581 Main St 5th Fl *Web:* www.netjets.com	Woodbridge	NJ	07095	732-326-3700	326-3777
New York Aviation PO Box 438 LaGuardia Airport *Web:* www.privatejetcharters.com	Flushing	NY	11371	718-279-4000	279-3814
Pacific Coast Jet Charter Inc PO Box 419074 *TF:* 800-655-3599 ■ *Web:* www.pacificjet.com	Rancho Cordova	CA	95741	916-631-6507	631-6687
Paragon Air Kahului Airport Commuter Airline Terminal PO Box 575 *Web:* www.paragon-air.com	Kahului	HI	96733	808-244-3356	573-8218
Pentastar Aviation 7310 Highland Rd **Fax:* Mktg ■ *TF:* 800-662-9612 ■ *Web:* www.pentastaraviation.com	Waterford	MI	48327	248-666-3630	666-9668*
Personal Jet Charter Inc 5401 E Perimeter Rd *TF:* 800-432-1538 ■ *Web:* www.personaljet.com	Fort Lauderdale	FL	33309	954-776-4515	491-5771
Planemasters Ltd 32 W 611 Tower Rd DuPage Airport *TF:* 800-994-6400 ■ *Web:* www.planemasters.com	West Chicago	IL	60185	630-513-2100	377-3283
Premier Air Charter 2544 Winchester Rd Hanger 4 *TF:* 866-468-8917 ■ *Web:* www.flypremierjets.com	Memphis	TN	38116	901-324-0046	345-7226
Premier Jets 2140 NE 25th Ave Hillsboro Airport *TF:* 800-635-8583 ■ *Web:* www.premierjets.com	Hillsboro	OR	97124	503-640-2927	681-3064
Presidential Aviation 1725 NW 51st Pl Fort Lauderdale Executive Airport Hangar 71 *TF:* 888-772-8622 ■ *Web:* www.presidential-aviation.com	Fort Lauderdale	FL	33309	954-772-8622	771-2622
Priester Aviation 1061 S Wolf Rd *TF:* 888-323-7887 ■ *Web:* www.priesterav.com	Wheeling	IL	60090	847-537-1133	459-0778
PrivatAir Inc 611 Access Rd *TF:* 800-380-4009 ■ *Web:* www.privatair.com	Stratford	CT	06615	203-337-4600	380-4017
Raytheon Aircraft Charter & Management 101 Webb Rd **Fax Area Code:* 800 ■ *TF:* 800-519-6283 ■ *Web:* www.raytheonaircraft.com	Wichita	KS	67207	316-676-3007	725-1116*
Ryan International Airlines Inc 4949 Harrison Ave *TF:* 800-727-0457 ■ *Web:* www.flyryan.com	Rockford	IL	61108	815-316-5420	398-0192
Salmon Air 29 Hamner Dr *TF:* 800-448-3413 ■ *Web:* www.salmonair.com	Salmon	ID	83467	208-756-6211	756-6219
San Juan Airlines Co 4000 Airport Rd Suite A *TF:* 800-874-4434 ■ *Web:* www.sanjuanairlines.com	Anacortes	WA	98221	360-293-4691	299-0981
Seneca Flight Operations 2262 Airport Dr *Web:* www.senecaflight.com	Penn Yan	NY	14527	315-536-4471	536-4558
Sentient Jet Inc 97 Libbey Pkwy 4th Fl Executive Jet Corporate Ctr *TF:* 866-473-6843 ■ *Web:* www.sentientjet.com	Weymouth	MA	02189	781-763-0200	871-8002
Skyservice Airlines Inc 31 Fasken Dr *TF:* 800-701-9448 ■ *Web:* www.skyserviceairlines.com	Etobicoke	ON	M9W1K6	416-679-5700	679-5920
Southwest Jet Aviation Ltd 14988 N 78th Way Suite 112 Scottsdale Municipal Airport *TF:* 800-991-7076 ■ *Web:* www.southwestjet.com	Scottsdale	AZ	85260	480-991-7076	991-8511
Spirit Aviation Inc 16233 Vanowen St Hangar 1 *TF:* 800-995-1865 ■ *Web:* www.flyspirit.com	Van Nuys	CA	91406	818-989-4642	785-9585
Sunbird Air Services Inc 1251 W Blee Rd *TF:* 800-537-2711 ■ *Web:* www.sunbirdcharter.com	Springfield	OH	45502	937-322-2711	322-6256
Sunset Aviation 351 Airport Rd *TF:* 800-359-7861 ■ *Web:* www.sunsetaviation.com	Novato	CA	94945	415-897-4522	898-9672
Superior Air Charter Inc 2070 Milligan Way *TF:* 800-793-1030 ■ *Web:* www.flysuperior.com	Medford	OR	97504	541-772-5660	772-8980
Tag Aviation USA Inc 111 Anza Blvd Suite 200 *TF:* 800-331-1930 ■ *Web:* www.tagaviation.com	Burlingame	CA	94010	650-342-1717	342-1767
Tas Group Inc DBA Air Charter Team 10015 NW Ambassador Dr Suite 202 *TF:* 800-205-6610 ■ *Web:* www.aircharterteam.com	Kansas City	MO	64153	816-283-3280	283-3185
Tavaero Jet Charter 7930 Airport Blvd *TF:* 800-343-3771 ■ *Web:* www.tavaero.com	Houston	TX	77061	713-643-6043	643-5398
TDM Inc DBA Colgan Air Services 2709 Fanta Reed Rd *TF:* 800-658-9498 ■ *Web:* www.colgan-air.com	La Crosse	WI	54603	608-783-8359	783-8050
Trans-Exec Air Service Inc 7240 Hayvenhurst Ave Suite 200 *Web:* www.transexec.com	Van Nuys	CA	91406	818-904-6900	904-6909
Tulip City Air Service Inc 1581 S Washington Ave *TF:* 800-748-0515 ■ *Web:* www.tulipcityair.com	Holland	MI	49423	616-392-7831	392-1841
Twin Cities Air Service 81 Airport Dr *TF:* 800-564-3882 ■ *Web:* www.flycharter.com	Auburn	ME	04210	207-782-3882	784-5326
United Executive Jet Inc DBA JetCorp 18500 Edison Ave *TF:* 800-325-4811 ■ *Web:* www.jetcorp.com	Chesterfield	MO	63005	636-530-7000	530-7001
Victory Aviation Inc 2710 County Rd 60 *Web:* www.victoryfbo.com	Auburn	IN	46706	260-927-4040	927-4048
West Coast Charters Inc 19711 Campus Dr Suite 200 *TF:* 800-352-6153 ■ *Web:* www.westcoastcharters.com	Santa Ana	CA	92707	949-852-8340	260-3999
World Airways Inc 101 World Dr HLH Bldg *TF:* 800-274-3601 ■ *Web:* www.worldairways.com	Peachtree City	GA	30269	770-632-8000	
Yellowstone Jetcenter 456 Gallatin Field Rd *TF:* 800-700-5381 ■ *Web:* www.ysjet.com	Belgrade	MT	59714	406-388-4152	388-6272

AIR CONDITIONING EQUIPMENT - AUTOMOTIVE

SEE Air Conditioning & Heating Equipment - Residential p. 1268

AIR CONDITIONING EQUIPMENT - WHOL

SEE Plumbing, Heating, Air Conditioning Equipment & Supplies - Whol p. 2126

14 AIR CONDITIONING & HEATING EQUIPMENT - COMMERCIAL/INDUSTRIAL

SEE ALSO Air Conditioning & Heating Equipment - Residential p. 1268; Refrigeration Equipment - Mfr p. 2209

	City	State	Zip	Phone	Fax
AAON Inc 2425 S Yukon Ave *NASDAQ: AAON* ■ *Web:* www.aaon.com	Tulsa	OK	74107	918-583-2266	583-6094
Absolut Aire Inc 5496 N Riverview Dr *TF:* 800-804-4000 ■ *Web:* www.absolutaire.com	Kalamazoo	MI	49004	269-382-1875	382-5291
AdobeAir Inc 1450 E Grant St *Web:* www.adobeair.com	Phoenix	AZ	85034	602-257-0060	257-1349
Advantage Engineering Inc 525 E Stop 18 Rd *Web:* www.advantageengineering.com	Greenwood	IN	46143	317-887-0729	881-1277
AEC Inc 2900 S 160th St *TF:* 800-783-7835 ■ *Web:* www.aecinternet.com	Schaumburg	IL	60173	847-273-7700	273-7804
Airtek Div Parker Hannifin Corp 4087 Walden Ave *TF:* 800-451-6023 ■ *Web:* www.airtek.com	Lancaster	NY	14086	716-685-4040	685-1010
Aitken Products Inc 566 N Eagle St PO Box 151 *TF:* 800-569-9341 ■ *Web:* www.aitkenproducts.com	Geneva	OH	44041	440-466-5711	466-5716
American Coolair Corp 3604 Mayflower St *Web:* www.coolair.com	Jacksonville	FL	32205	904-389-3646	387-3449
American Standard Cos Inc Heating & Cooling Products Div 6200 Troup Hwy	Tyler	TX	75711	903-581-3200	581-3482
Anderson-Snow Corp 9225 Ivanhoe St *TF:* 800-346-2645 ■ *Web:* www.anscorcoils.com	Schiller Park	IL	60176	847-678-3823	678-0413
Armstrong International Inc 2081 SE Ocean Blvd 4th Fl *Web:* www.armintl.com	Stuart	FL	34996	772-286-7175	286-1001
Baltimore Aircoil Co 7600 Dorsey Run Rd PO Box 7322 *Web:* www.baltaircoil.com	Baltimore	MD	21227	410-799-6200	799-6416
Birdwell Co 3708 Greenhouse Rd *TF:* 800-237-2095 ■ *Web:* www.birdwellco.com	Houston	TX	77084	281-492-1786	492-1036
Blissfield Mfg Co 626 Depot St *TF Cust Svc:* 800-626-1772 ■ *Web:* www.blissfield.com	Blissfield	MI	49228	517-486-2121	486-2128
Bristol Compressors Inc 15185 Industrial Park Rd *Web:* www.bristolcompressors.com	Bristol	VA	24202	276-466-4121	645-2423
Brooks Automation Inc Polycold Systems 3800 Lakeville Hwy *TF:* 888-476-5926 ■ *Web:* www.brooks.com	Petaluma	CA	94954	707-769-7000	769-1380
Bry-Air Inc 10793 SR 37 W *TF:* 877-427-9247 ■ *Web:* www.bry-air.com	Sunbury	OH	43074	740-965-2974	965-5470
Carnes Co 448 S Main St *Web:* www.carnes.com	Verona	WI	53593	608-845-6411	845-6470
Carrier Corp 1 Carrier Pl **Fax:* Hum Res ■ *TF:* 800-227-7437 ■ *Web:* www.carrier.com	Farmington	CT	06034	860-674-3000	674-3125*
ClimateMaster Inc 7300 SW 44th St **Fax:* Cust Svc ■ *TF:* 800-299-9747 ■ *Web:* www.climatemaster.com	Oklahoma City	OK	73179	405-745-6000	745-2006*
Colmac Coil Mfg Inc 370 N Lincoln St PO Box 571 *TF:* 800-845-6778 ■ *Web:* www.colmaccoil.com/coil	Colville	WA	99114	509-684-2595	684-8331

	City	State	Zip	Phone	Fax
Control Air Inc 7924 Reco Ave	Baton Rouge	LA	70814	225-612-7400	612-7407
Web: www.isomix.com					
Copeland Corp 1675 W Campbell Rd Box 669	Sidney	OH	45365	937-498-3011	498-3887*
**Fax:* Hum Res ■ *Web:* www.copeland-corp.com					
Danfoss Inc 7941 Corporate Dr	Baltimore	MD	21236	410-931-8250	931-8256
TF: 800-236-3677 ■ *Web:* www.danfoss.com					
Dectron Inc 4300 Poirier Blvd	Montreal	QC	H4R2C5	514-334-9609	334-9184
TF: 888-332-8766 ■ *Web:* www.dry-o-tron.com					
DiversiTech Inc 6650 Sugarloaf Pkwy Suite 100	Duluth	GA	30097	678-542-3600	542-3700
TF: 800-995-2222 ■ *Web:* www.diversitech.com					
Dometic Corp 2320 Industrial Pkwy PO Box 490	Elkhart	IN	46515	574-294-2511	293-9686
TF: 800-544-4881 ■ *Web:* www.dometic.com					
DRISTEEM Corp 14949 Technology Dr	Eden Prairie	MN	55344	952-949-2415	229-3200
TF: 800-328-4447 ■ *Web:* www.dristeem.com					
DRS Sustainment Systems Inc 7375 Industrial Rd	Florence	KY	41042	859-525-2102	525-6667
Web: www.kecoindustries.com					
Duro Dyne Corp 81 Spence St	Bay Shore	NY	11706	631-249-9000	249-8346
TF: 800-899-3876 ■ *Web:* www.durodyne.com					
EasyHeat Div EGS Electrical Group LLC 2 Connecticut S Dr	East Granby	CT	06026	860-653-1600	653-4938
TF: 800-523-7636 ■ *Web:* www.easyheat.com					
EGS Electrical Group LLC EasyHeat Div 2 Connecticut S Dr	East Granby	CT	06026	860-653-1600	653-4938
TF: 800-523-7636 ■ *Web:* www.easyheat.com					
Electro Impulse Laboratory Inc					
1805 State Hwy 33 PO Box 278	Neptune	NJ	07754	732-776-5800	776-6793
Web: www.electro-impulse.com					
Electrofilm Mfg Corp 25395 Rye Canyon Rd	Valencia	CA	91385	661-257-2242	257-7738
Web: www.ef-heaters.com/					
Ellis & Watts Inc 4400 Glen Willow Lake Ln	Batavia	OH	45103	513-752-9000	752-4983
Web: www.elliswatts.com					
Environmental Air Systems Inc 521 Banner Ave	Greensboro	NC	27401	336-273-1975	378-9859
Web: www.envairsys.com					
Factory Air Conditioning Corp 421 Culebra Rd	San Antonio	TX	78201	210-732-9984	732-9666
TF: 800-487-1037 ■ *Web:* www.facair.com					
Fieldhouse Refrigeration 9905 Express Dr	Highland	IN	46322	219-924-5000	922-8450
TF: 800-451-2377 ■ *Web:* fieldhouserefrigeration.com					
First Operations LP 8273 Moberly Ln	Dallas	TX	75227	214-388-5751	388-2255
Web: www.firstco.com					
Friedrich Air Conditioning Co					
4200 N Pan Am Expy PO Box 1540	San Antonio	TX	78295	210-225-2000	357-4480
TF: 800-541-6645 ■ *Web:* www.friedrich.com					
Fritze LLC 1 Chapin Rd	Pine Brook	NJ	07058	973-487-4800	808-0423
TF Cust Svc: 800-626-7799 ■ *Web:* www.fritzellc.com					
Goettl Air Conditioning Inc 1845 W 1st St	Tempe	AZ	85282	602-275-1515	231-8699*
**Fax:* Acctg ■ *TF:* 800-334-6494 ■ *Web:* www.goettl.com					
Governair Corp 4841 N Sewell Ave	Oklahoma City	OK	73118	405-525-6546	528-4724
Web: www.governair.com					
Hankison International 1000 Philadelphia St	Canonsburg	PA	15317	724-745-1555	745-6040
Web: www.hankisonintl.com					
Hastings HVAC Inc 3606 Yost Ave PO Box 669	Hastings	NE	68902	402-463-9821	463-6273
TF Cust Svc: 800-228-4243 ■ *Web:* www.hastingshvac.com					
Heat Controller Inc 1900 Wellworth Ave	Jackson	MI	49203	517-787-2100	787-9341
Web: www.heatcontroller.com					
Heatcraft Inc 3984 Hwy 51 S PO Box 948	Grenada	MS	38902	662-226-3421	229-2002
Web: www.heatcraft.com					
Henry Technologies 701 S Main St	Chatham	IL	62629	217-483-2406	483-2408
Web: www.henrytech.com					
Howden Buffalo Inc 2029 W Dekalb St	Camden	SC	29020	803-713-2200	713-2222
Web: www.howdenbuffalo.com					
ICE-CAP Inc 275 Grand Blvd	Westbury	NY	11590	718-729-7000	392-4193
Web: www.icecap.com					
International Environmental Corp 5000 I-40 W	Oklahoma City	OK	73128	405-947-7666	605-5001
TF: 800-226-5406 ■ *Web:* www.iec-okc.com					
IPAC Inc 2107 Liberty Dr	Niagara Falls	NY	14304	716-283-6464	283-1911
TF: 800-388-3211 ■ *Web:* www.ipacinc.com					
ITT Bell & Gossett 8200 N Austin Ave	Morton Grove	IL	60053	847-966-3700	966-9052*
**Fax:* Mktg ■ *Web:* www.bellgossett.com					
ITW Air Management 10125 Carver Rd	Cincinnati	OH	45242	513-891-7474	891-4092
TF: 800-745-5355 ■ *Web:* www.itw-air.com					
J & D Mfg Inc 6200 Hwy 12	Eau Claire	WI	54701	715-834-1439	834-3812
TF Cust Svc: 800-848-7998 ■ *Web:* www.jdmfg.com					
Kobelco Compressors (America) Inc 3000 Hammond Ave	Elkhart	IN	46516	574-295-3145	293-1641
Web: www.kocoa.com					
Kooltronic Inc 30 Pennington-Hopewell Rd	Pennington	NJ	08534	609-466-3400	466-1114
TF: 800-321-5665 ■ *Web:* www.kooltronic.com					
Krack Corp 401 S Rohlwing Rd	Addison	IL	60101	630-629-7500	629-0535
Web: www.krack.com					
Lakewood Engineering & Mfg Co 501 N Sacramento Blvd	Chicago	IL	60612	773-722-4300	722-1541
TF: 800-621-4277 ■ *Web:* www.lakewoodeng.com					
Lawler Mfg Corp 7 Kilmer Ct	Edison	NJ	08817	732-777-2040	777-4828
Web: www.lawler-mfg.com					
Layton Mfg Corp 864 E 52nd St	Brooklyn	NY	11203	718-498-6000	498-6003
TF: 800-545-8002 ■ *Web:* www.laytonmfg.com					
LE Rabjohn Inc 1833 N Daly St	Los Angeles	CA	90031	323-221-9163	223-5132
TF: 800-559-3737					
Lintern Corp 8685 Station St	Mentor	OH	44060	440-255-9333	255-6427
TF: 800-321-3638 ■ *Web:* www.lintern.com					
Lomanco Inc 2101 W Main St	Jacksonville	AR	72076	501-982-6511	982-1258
TF: 800-643-5596 ■ *Web:* www.lomanco.com					
Mammoth Inc 101 W 82nd St	Chaska	MN	55318	952-361-2711	361-2700
TF: 800-328-3321 ■ *Web:* www.mammoth-inc.com					
Maradyne Corp 4540 W 160th St	Cleveland	OH	44135	216-362-0755	362-0799
TF: 800-537-7444 ■ *Web:* www.maradyne.com					
Marc Climatic Controls Inc 1611 Elmview Dr	Houston	TX	77080	713-464-8587	468-8810
TF: 800-397-0131 ■ *Web:* www.marcclimatic.com					
Master-Bilt Products 908 Hwy 15 N	New Albany	MS	38652	662-534-9061	534-6049
TF: 800-647-1284 ■ *Web:* www.master-bilt.com					
Mestek Inc 260 N Elm St	Westfield	MA	01085	413-568-9571	562-7630
NYSE: MCC ■ *Web:* www.mestek.com					
Modine Manufacturing Co 1500 DeKoven Ave	Racine	WI	53403	262-636-1200	636-1424
Web: www.modine.com					
Munters Corp 210 6th St	Fort Myers	FL	33907	239-936-1555	936-2657*
**Fax:* Cust Svc ■ *TF:* 800-446-6868 ■ *Web:* www.munters.com					
Munters Corp DHI 79 Monroe St	Amesbury	MA	01913	978-388-0600	241-1215
TF Sales: 800-843-5360 ■ *Web:* www.munters.com					
Niagara Blower Co Inc 673 Ontario St	Buffalo	NY	14207	716-875-2000	875-1077
TF: 800-426-5169 ■ *Web:* www.niagarablower.com					
Nordyne Inc 8000 Phoenix Pkwy	O'Fallon	MO	63368	636-561-7300	561-7323*
**Fax:* Sales ■ *TF:* 800-422-4328 ■ *Web:* www.nordyne.com					
Packless Industries 8401 Imperial Dr PO Box 20668	Waco	TX	76702	254-666-7700	666-7893
TF Cust Svc: 800-347-4859 ■ *Web:* www.packless.com					
Packless Metal Hose Inc DBA Packless Industries					
8401 Imperial Dr PO Box 20668	Waco	TX	76702	254-666-7700	666-7893
TF Cust Svc: 800-347-4859 ■ *Web:* www.packless.com					
Peerless of America Inc 1201 Wabash Ave	Effingham	IL	62401	217-342-0400	342-0412
Web: www.peerlessofamerica.com					
Phelps Fan LLC 10701 I-30	Little Rock	AR	72209	501-568-5550	568-3363
TF: 800-742-6899 ■ *Web:* www.phelpsfan.com					
Phoenix Mfg Inc 3655 E Roeser Rd	Phoenix	AZ	85040	602-437-1034	437-4833
TF: 800-325-6952 ■ *Web:* www.evapcool.com					
Rabjohn LE Inc 1833 N Daly St	Los Angeles	CA	90031	323-221-9163	223-5132
TF: 800-559-3737					
RAE Corp Technical Systems Div 4492 Hunt St PO box 1206	Pryor	OK	74361	918-825-7222	825-0723
TF: 888-498-8922 ■ *Web:* www.rae-corp.com/tech_sys.htm					
Rama Corp 600 W Esplanade Ave	San Jacinto	CA	92583	951-654-7351	654-3748
TF: 800-472-5670 ■ *Web:* www.ramacorporation.com					
Refrigeration Research Inc 525 N 5th St	Brighton	MI	48116	810-227-1151	227-3700
Web: www.refresearch.com					
Rheem Mfg Co 1100 Abernathy Rd Suite 1400	Atlanta	GA	30328	770-351-3000	351-3003
Web: www.rheem.com					
Rheem Mfg Co Air Conditioning Div					
5600 Old Greenwood Rd PO Box 17010	Fort Smith	AR	72908	479-646-4311	648-4819*
**Fax:* Mktg ■ *Web:* www.rheemac.com					
Rink Systems Inc 1103 Hershey St	Albert Lea	MN	56007	507-373-9175	377-1060
TF: 800-944-7930 ■ *Web:* www.rinksystems.com					
Rovac Corp 1030 Stafford St PO Box 111	Rochdale	MA	01542	508-892-1121	892-7157
Russell Div HTP Group 221 S Berry St	Brea	CA	92821	714-529-1935	529-7203
Web: www.russellcoil.com					
Russell Div Ardco Inc 221 S Berry St	Brea	CA	92821	714-529-1935	529-7203
Web: www.russellcoil.com					
Ruud Mfg Co Air Conditioning Div 5600 Old Greenwood Rd	Fort Smith	AR	72908	479-648-4900	648-4155
Web: www.ruudac.com					
Sealed Unit Parts Co Inc 2230 Landmark Pl	Allenwood	NJ	08720	732-223-6644	223-1617
TF: 800-333-9125 ■ *Web:* www.supco.com					
Skuttle Mfg Co 101 Margaret St	Marietta	OH	45750	740-373-9169	373-9565
TF: 800-848-9786 ■ *Web:* www.skuttle.com					
Slant Fin Corp 100 Forest Dr	Greenvale	NY	11548	516-484-2600	484-2600
TF: 800-775-4552 ■ *Web:* www.slantfin.com					
Snyder Capital Corp 8409 Pickwick Ln Suite 379	Dallas	TX	75225	214-754-0500	754-0350
Standard Refrigeration Co 2050 N Ruby St	Melrose Park	IL	60160	708-345-5400	345-3513
Web: www.stanref.com					
Stone Air 72 Arizona Ave	Plattsburgh	NY	12903	518-561-0044	561-0055
Tecumotor 2700 W Wood St PO Box 1208	Paris	TN	38242	731-642-6394	644-8181
Temtrol Inc 15 E Oklahoma Ave PO Box 409	Okarche	OK	73762	405-263-7286	263-4924
Web: www.temtrol.com					
Thermo King Corp 314 W 90th St	Bloomington	MN	55420	952-887-2200	887-2615
Web: www.thermoking.com					
ThermoElectric Cooling America Corp 4048 W Schubert Ave	Chicago	IL	60639	773-342-4900	342-0191
TF: 888-832-2872 ■ *Web:* www.thermoelectric.com					
Trane Co 3600 Pammel Creek Rd	La Crosse	WI	54601	608-787-2000	
Web: www.trane.com					
Traulsen & Co Inc 4401 Blue Mound Rd	Fort Worth	TX	76106	817-625-9671	765-8728*
**Fax Area Code:* 800 ■ **Fax:* Cust Svc ■ *TF:* 800-825-8220 ■ *Web:* www.traulsen.com					
Tutco Inc 500 Gould Dr	Cookeville	TN	38506	931-432-4141	432-4140
TF: 877-262-4533 ■ *Web:* www.tutco.com					
United Electric Co LP 501 Galveston St	Wichita Falls	TX	76301	940-397-2100	397-2166
Web: www.magicaire.com					
Virginia KMP-Parker Hannifin Corp 1174 Security Dr	Dallas	TX	75247	214-330-7731	877-8567*
**Fax Area Code:* 800 ■ *TF:* 800-285-8567 ■ *Web:* www.virginiakmp.us					
Watsco Inc 2665 S Bayshore Dr Suite 901	Coconut Grove	FL	33133	305-714-4100	858-4492
NYSE: WSO ■ *TF:* 800-492-8726 ■ *Web:* www.watsco.com					
WEDJ Inc 491 E Princess St	York	PA	17403	717-845-8685	845-4953
TF: 877-905-1111 ■ *Web:* www.unitedcoolair.com					
WSA Engineered Systems 2018 S 1st St	Milwaukee	WI	53207	414-481-4120	481-4121
Web: www.wsaes.com					
York Airside Service 1237 Penn Ave	Hollsopple	PA	15935	814-479-4023	479-7113
York International Corp Engineered Systems Group					
5005 York Dr	Norman	OK	73069	405-364-4040	419-6214
TF: 877-874-7378 ■ *Web:* www.york.com					
York International Corp Unitary Products Group 5005 York Dr	Norman	OK	73069	405-364-4040	419-6214*
**Fax:* Hum Res ■ *TF:* 877-874-7378 ■ *Web:* www.york.com					

15 AIR CONDITIONING & HEATING EQUIPMENT - RESIDENTIAL

SEE ALSO Air Conditioning & Heating Equipment - Commercial/Industrial p. 1267

	City	State	Zip	Phone	Fax
Amana Appliances Inc 2800 220th Trail	Amana	IA	52204	319-622-5511	622-2180
TF Cust Svc: 800-843-0304 ■ *Web:* www.amana.com					
American Standard Cos Inc Heating & Cooling Products Div					
6200 Troup Hwy	Tyler	TX	75711	903-581-3200	581-3482
Armstrong Air Conditioning Inc 421 Monroe St	Bellevue	OH	44811	419-483-4840	483-3557
TF: 800-448-5872 ■ *Web:* www.aac-inc.com					
Bard Mfg Co Inc 1914 Randolph Dr	Bryan	OH	43506	419-636-1194	636-2640
Web: www.bardhvac.com					
Behr Climate Systems 5020 Augusta Dr	Fort Worth	TX	76106	817-624-7273	624-3328
TF: 800-247-6558 ■ *Web:* www.behrgroup.com					
Behr Dayton Thermal Products LLC 1600 Webster St	Dayton	OH	45404	937-369-2305	224-2447*
**Fax:* Hum Res					
Bergstrom Mfg Co 2390 Blackhawk Rd	Rockford	IL	61125	815-874-7821	874-2144
Web: www.bergstrominc.com					
Butler Vent-A-Matic Corp 100 Washington Rd	Mineral Wells	TX	76067	940-325-7887	325-9311
TF: 800-433-1626 ■ *Web:* www.bvc.com					
CalsonicKansei North America Inc 1 Calsonic Way	Shelbyville	TN	37160	931-684-4490	684-2724
Web: www.calsonic.com					
Carrier Corp Carrier Transicold Div					
6304 Thompson Rd Bldg TR-20	East Syracuse	NY	13057	315-432-6000	432-6207
TF: 800-255-7382 ■ *Web:* www.carrier.transicold.com					
Delphi Harrison Thermal Systems 200 Upper Mountain Rd	Lockport	NY	14094	716-439-2011	439-2885
Evans Tempcon Inc 701 Ann St NW	Grand Rapids	MI	49504	616-361-2681	361-9646
TF: 800-354-7088 ■ *Web:* www.evanstempcon.com					
Fedders Corp 505 Martinsville Rd Westgate Corporate Ctr	Liberty Corner	NJ	07938	908-604-8686	604-0715
NYSE: FJC ■ *Web:* www.fedders.com					
Friedrich Air Conditioning Co					
4200 N Pan Am Expy PO Box 1540	San Antonio	TX	78295	210-225-2000	357-4480
TF: 800-541-6645 ■ *Web:* www.friedrich.com					
GE Consumer Products Appliance Park Rm 129	Louisville	KY	40225	502-452-4311	452-0054*
**Fax:* Cust Svc ■ *TF:* 800-626-2000 ■ *Web:* www.geconsumerproducts.com					
Goodman Mfg Co LP 2550 N Loop W Suite 400	Houston	TX	77092	713-861-2500	861-7972
Web: www.goodmanmfg.com					
Hotstart Kim Mfg Co 5723 E Alki Ave	Spokane	WA	99212	509-534-6171	224-5550*
**Fax Area Code:* 800 ■ *Web:* www.kimhotstart.com					
Hunter Mfg Co 30525 Aurora Rd	Solon	OH	44139	440-248-6111	248-1691
Web: www.huntermfgco.com					
International Comfort Products Corp 650 Heil Quaker Ave	Lewisburg	TN	37091	931-359-3511	270-3312
TF: 800-458-6650 ■ *Web:* www.icpusa.com					
Johnson Controls Inc - YORK 631 S Richland Ave PO Box 1592	York	PA	17405	717-771-7890	771-7440
Web: www.johnsoncontrols.com					
Kim Hotstart Mfg Co 5723 E Alki Ave	Spokane	WA	99212	509-534-6171	224-5550*
**Fax Area Code:* 800 ■ *Web:* www.kimhotstart.com					

Company	City	State	Zip	Phone	Fax
Lennox Industries Inc 2100 Lake Park Blvd *Fax: Mail Rm ■ Web: www.davelennox.com	Richardson	TX	75080	972-497-5000	497-5299*
Lennox International Inc 2100 Lake Pk Blvd NYSE: LII ■ *Fax: Mail Rm ■ Web: www.davelennox.com	Richardson	TX	75380	972-497-5000	497-6668*
Modine Mfg Co 1500 De Koven Ave NYSE: MOD ■ Web: www.modine.com	Racine	WI	53403	262-636-1200	636-1424
National System of Garage Ventilation Inc 714 N Church St PO Box 1186 TF: 800-728-8368 ■ Web: www.nsgv.com	Decatur	IL	62521	217-423-7314	422-5387
Nortek Inc 50 Kennedy Plaza Web: www.nortek-inc.com	Providence	RI	02903	401-751-1600	751-4610
Proliance International Inc 100 Gando Dr AMEX: PLI ■ TF: 800-755-2160 ■ Web: www.pliii.com	New Haven	CT	06513	203-401-6450	865-3723
Rheem Mfg Co 1100 Abernathy Rd Suite 1400 Web: www.rheem.com	Atlanta	GA	30328	770-351-3000	351-3003
Rheem Mfg Co Air Conditioning Div 5600 Old Greenwood Rd PO Box 17010 *Fax: Mktg ■ Web: www.rheemac.com	Fort Smith	AR	72908	479-646-4311	648-4819*
Ruud Mfg Co Air Conditioning Div 5600 Old Greenwood Rd Web: www.ruudac.com	Fort Smith	AR	72908	479-648-4900	648-4155
Simpson Mfg Co Inc 5956 W Las Positas Blvd NYSE: SSD ■ TF: 800-925-5099 ■ Web: www.simpsonmfg.com	Pleasanton	CA	94588	925-560-9000	847-1603
TPI Corp PO Box 4973 TF: 800-251-0382 ■ Web: www.tpicorp.com	Johnson City	TN	37602	423-477-4131	477-0084
Trane Co Unitary Products Group 6200 Troup Hwy Web: www.trane.com	Tyler	TX	75707	903-581-3200	581-3482
Whirlpool Corp 2000 N M-63 NYSE: WHR ■ TF: 800-253-1301 ■ Web: www.whirlpoolcorp.com	Benton Harbor	MI	49022	269-923-5000	923-5443
York International Corp Unitary Products Group 5005 York Dr *Fax: Hum Res ■ TF: 877-874-7378 ■ Web: www.york.com	Norman	OK	73069	405-364-4040	419-6214*
Young Touchstone Inc 200 Smith Ln TF Sales: 800-238-8230 ■ Web: www.youngtouchstone.com	Jackson	TN	38301	731-424-5045	265-2302

16 AIR FARE CONSOLIDATORS

Company	City	State	Zip	Phone	Fax
Air by Pleasant 4025 Camino del Rio S Suite 210 TF: 800-877-8111 ■ Web: www.airbypleasant.com	San Diego	CA	92108	619-282-3455	282-4164
Air-Supply Inc 350 5th Ave Empire State Bldg Suite 6724 TF: 800-671-9961 ■ Web: www.air-supply.com	New York	NY	10118	212-695-1647	695-7756
Airline Consolidator.com 7401 E Brainerd Rd Suite 100 TF: 888-468-5385 ■ Web: www.airlineconsolidator.com	Chattanooga	TN	37421	423-485-1291	485-1420
BMD Travel Services Inc DBA Airline Consolidator.com 7401 E Brainerd Rd Suite 100 TF: 888-468-5385 ■ Web: www.airlineconsolidator.com	Chattanooga	TN	37421	423-485-1291	485-1420
Brazilian Travel Service 16 W 46th St 2nd Fl TF: 800-342-5746 ■ Web: www.btstravelonline.com	New York	NY	10036	212-730-1010	719-4142
C & H International 4751 Wilshire Blvd Suite 201 TF: 800-833-8888 ■ Web: www.cnhintl.com	Los Angeles	CA	90010	323-933-2288	939-2286
Centrav Inc 350 W Burnsville Pkwy Suite 250 TF: 800-874-2033 ■ Web: www.centrav.com	Burnsville	MN	55337	952-886-7650	886-7640
D-FW Tours Holiday House 7616 LBJ Fwy Suite 700 TF: 800-527-2589 ■ Web: www.dfwtours.com	Dallas	TX	75251	972-980-4540	386-3802
DER Travel Services 9501 W Devon Ave Suite 301 *Fax Area Code: 877 ■ TF: 800-782-2424 ■ Web: www.der.com	Rosemont	IL	60018	847-430-0000	268-3308*
Global Network Tours Inc DBA Air-Supply Inc 350 5th Ave Empire State Bldg Suite 6724 TF: 800-671-9961 ■ Web: www.air-supply.com	New York	NY	10118	212-695-1647	695-7756
GTT Global 4100 Spring Valley Rd Suite 202 TF: 800-485-6828 ■ Web: www.gttglobal.com	Dallas	TX	75244	972-490-3394	387-5847
International Travel Systems Inc 194 Boulevard 2nd Fl TF: 800-258-0135	Hasbrouck Heights	NJ	07604	201-727-0470	727-0473
Mill-Run Inc 424 Madison Ave 11th Fl TF: 800-645-5786 ■ Web: www5.millrun.com	New York	NY	10017	212-486-9840	223-8129
Picasso Travel 11099 S La Cienega Blvd Suite 210 TF: 800-742-2776 ■ Web: www.picassotravel.net	Los Angeles	CA	90045	310-645-4400	645-0412
Premier Gateway Inc 320 SW Stark St Suite 315 TF: 800-759-7515 ■ Web: www.premiergateway.com	Portland	OR	97204	503-294-6478	294-2199
Sky Bird Travel & Tours Inc 26500 Northwestern Hwy Suite 260 TF: 888-759-2473 ■ Web: www.skybird-travel.com	Southfield	MI	48076	248-372-4800	372-4810
Skylink Travel 265 Madison Ave 5th Fl TF: 800-247-6659 ■ Web: skylinkus.com	New York	NY	10016	212-573-8980	573-8878
Solar Tours 1629 K St NW Suite 604 TF: 800-388-7652 ■ Web: www.solartours.com	Washington	DC	20006	202-861-5864	452-0905
Trans Am Travel 4300 King St Suite 130 TF: 800-822-7600 ■ Web: www.transamtravel.com	Alexandria	VA	22302	703-998-7676	824-8190

17 AIR PURIFICATION EQUIPMENT - HOUSEHOLD

SEE ALSO Appliances - Small - Mfr p. 1280

Company	City	State	Zip	Phone	Fax
AAF International Corp 10300 Ormsby Park Pl Suite 600 *Fax Area Code: 888 ■ TF: 888-223-2003 ■ Web: www.aafintl.com	Louisville	KY	40223	502-637-0011	223-6500*
Air Quality Engineering Inc 7140 Northland Dr N TF: 800-328-0787 ■ Web: www.air-quality-eng.com	Brooklyn Park	MN	55428	763-531-9823	531-9900
Airguard Industries Inc 3807 Bishop Ln *Fax: Cust Svc ■ TF: 800-999-3458 ■ Web: www.airguard.com	Louisville	KY	40218	502-969-2304	995-3030*
ALFCO Div Home Care Industries Inc 1 Lisbon St TF Cust Svc: 800-240-7998 ■ Web: www.homecareind.com	Clifton	NJ	07013	973-365-1600	365-1770
Dayton Reliable Air Filter Inc 2294 N Moraine Dr TF Orders: 800-699-0747 ■ Web: www.reliablefilter.com	Dayton	OH	45439	937-293-4611	293-3975
Electrocorp 595 Portal St Suite A TF: 800-525-0711 ■ Web: www.electrocorp.net	Cotati	CA	94931	707-665-9616	665-9620
Gaylord Industries Inc 10900 SW Avery St TF: 800-547-9696 ■ Web: www.gaylordusa.com	Tualatin	OR	97062	503-691-2010	692-6048
General Filters Inc 43800 Grand River Ave Web: www.generalfilters.com	Novi	MI	48375	248-349-2481	349-2366
Glasfloss Industries Inc 400 S Hall St *Fax Area Code: 800 ■ Web: www.glasfloss.com	Dallas	TX	75226	214-741-7056	435-8377*
HEPA Corp 3071 E Coronado St Web: www.hepa.com	Anaheim	CA	92806	714-630-5700	630-2894
Home Care Industries Inc ALFCO Div 1 Lisbon St TF Cust Svc: 800-240-7998 ■ Web: www.homecareind.com	Clifton	NJ	07013	973-365-1600	365-1770
Indoor Purification Systems Inc 887 N McCormick Way Suite 3 TF: 888-812-1516 ■ Web: www.indoorpurifiers.com	Layton	UT	84041	801-444-0606	991-4838
Kaz Home Environment 250 Turnpike Rd Web: www.kaz.com	Southborough	MA	01772	508-490-7000	
Koch Filter Corp 625 W Hill St Web: www.kochfilter.com	Louisville	KY	40208	502-634-4796	637-2280
Lakewood Engineering & Mfg Co 501 N Sacramento Blvd TF: 800-621-4277 ■ Web: www.lakewoodeng.com	Chicago	IL	60612	773-722-4300	722-1541
Lau Industries Inc 4509 Springfield St Web: www.laufan.com	Dayton	OH	45431	937-476-6500	254-9519
Lipidex Corp 411 Plain St Web: www.aircycler.com	Marshfield	MA	02050	781-834-1600	834-1601
Permatron Group 1180 Pratt Blvd TF: 800-882-8012 ■ Web: www.permatron.com	Elk Grove Village	IL	60007	847-434-1421	451-1811
Praxair Trailigaz Ozone Co 8190 Beechmont Ave Suite 308 Web: www.praxair.com	Cincinnati	OH	45255	513-233-0444	233-9555
PuriTec 7251 W Lake Mead Blvd Suite 300 TF: 888-491-4100 ■ Web: www.puritec.com	Las Vegas	NV	89128	702-562-8802	446-4841
Purolator Products Air Filtration Co 880 Facet Rd *Fax Area Code: 800 ■ TF: 800-334-6659 ■ Web: www.purolatorair.com	Henderson	NC	27536	252-492-1141	356-2397*
Rena Ware International Inc PO Box 97050 TF: 877-736-2245 ■ Web: www.renaware.com	Redmond	WA	98073	425-881-6171	882-7500
Research Products Corp 1015 E Washington Ave TF: 800-334-6011	Madison	WI	53703	608-257-8801	257-4357
RPS Products Inc 281 Keyes Ave TF: 800-683-7030 ■ Web: www.rpsproducts.com	Hampshire	IL	60140	847-683-3400	683-3939
Spencer Turbine Co 600 Day Hill Rd TF: 800-232-4321 ■ Web: www.spencerturbine.com	Windsor	CT	06095	860-688-8361	688-0098
Sterilone 2125 Biscayne Blvd Suite 580 *Fax Area Code: 419 ■ TF: 877-271-1057 ■ Web: www.sterilone.com	Miami Beach	FL	33137	305-572-0660	831-2824*
Tjernlund Products Inc 1601 9th St TF: 800-255-4208 ■ Web: www.tjernlund.com	White Bear Lake	MN	55110	651-426-2993	426-9547
Trion Inc 101 McNeill Rd TF: 866-829-2440 ■ Web: www.trioninc.com	Sanford	NC	27330	919-775-2201	774-8771
United Air Specialists Inc 4440 Creek Rd TF: 800-252-4647 ■ Web: www.uasinc.com	Cincinnati	OH	45242	513-891-0400	891-4882
Vornado Air Circulation Systems Inc 415 E 13th St TF: 800-297-0883 ■ Web: www.vornado.com	Andover	KS	67002	316-733-0035	733-1544

18 AIR PURIFICATION EQUIPMENT - INDUSTRIAL

Company	City	State	Zip	Phone	Fax
AAF International Corp 10300 Ormsby Park Pl Suite 600 *Fax Area Code: 888 ■ TF: 888-223-2003 ■ Web: www.aafintl.com	Louisville	KY	40223	502-637-0011	223-6500*
Acme Engineering & Mfg Corp 1820 N York Web: www.acmefan.com	Muskogee	OK	74403	918-682-7791	682-0134
Advantec MFS Inc 6723 Sierra Ct Suite A TF: 800-334-7132 ■ Web: www.advantecmfs.com	Dublin	CA	94568	925-479-0625	479-0630
Aerovent Inc 5959 Trenton Ln Web: www.aerovent.com	Plymouth	MN	55442	763-551-7500	551-7501
Aget Mfg Co 1408 E Church St TF: 800-832-2438 ■ Web: www.agetmfg.com	Adrian	MI	49221	517-263-5781	263-7154
Air Quality Engineering Inc 7140 Northland Dr N TF: 800-328-0787 ■ Web: www.air-quality-eng.com	Brooklyn Park	MN	55428	763-531-9823	531-9900
Aircon Filter Mfg Co 441 Green St TF: 800-833-3019 ■ Web: www.filtersales.com	Philadelphia	PA	19123	215-922-5222	922-5316
Airflow Systems Inc 11221 Pagemill Rd TF: 800-818-6185 ■ Web: www.airflowsystems.com	Dallas	TX	75243	214-503-8008	503-9596
Airfoil Impellers Corp 2010 Fountain Ave Web: www.airfoil.com	Bryan	TX	77801	979-823-7556	775-5588
Airguard Industries Inc 3807 Bishop Ln *Fax: Cust Svc ■ TF: 800-999-3458 ■ Web: www.airguard.com	Louisville	KY	40218	502-969-2304	995-3030*
Airmaster Fan Co 1300 Falahee Rd *Fax Area Code: 800 ■ Web: www.airmasterfan.com	Jackson	MI	49203	517-764-2300	255-3084*
AirPol Inc 199 Pomeroy Rd Suite 103 Web: www.airpol.com	Parsippany	NJ	07054	973-599-4400	428-6048
Airtech Corp 4260 W Artesia Ave TF: 800-634-4453 ■ Web: www.airtechlaminarflow.com	Fullerton	CA	92833	714-562-9295	562-9273
Alanco Technologies Inc 15575 N 83rd Way Suite 3 NASDAQ: ALAN ■ Web: www.alanco.com	Scottsdale	AZ	85260	480-607-1010	607-1515
ALFCO Div Home Care Industries Inc 1 Lisbon St TF Cust Svc: 800-240-7998 ■ Web: www.homecareind.com	Clifton	NJ	07013	973-365-1600	365-1770
Amerex Industries Inc 119 VIP Dr Suite 204 TF: 800-359-2586 ■ Web: www.amerexind.com	Wexford	PA	15090	724-935-1300	935-1342
American Fan Co Inc 2933 Symmes Rd Web: www.amfan-woods.com	Fairfield	OH	45014	513-874-2400	870-6249
AMETEK Rotron Mil-Aero Products Div 55 Hasbrouck Ln Web: www.rotron.com	Woodstock	NY	12498	845-679-2401	679-7080
AMETEK Rotron Technical & Industrial Products 627 Lake St Web: www.rotronindustrial.com	Kent	OH	44240	330-673-3452	678-8227
Andersen 2000 Inc 306 Dividend Dr TF: 800-241-5424 ■ Web: www.crownandersen.com/Andersen.html	Peachtree City	GA	30269	770-486-2000	487-5066
Anguil Environmental Systems Inc 8855 N 55th St TF: 800-488-0230 ■ Web: www.anguil.com	Milwaukee	WI	53223	414-365-6400	365-6410
Arrow Pneumatics Inc 2111 W 21st St Web: www.arrowpneumatics.com	Broadview	IL	60155	708-343-9595	343-1907
Baghouse & Industrial Sheet Metal Services Inc 1731 Pomona Rd TF: 866-997-3784 ■ Web: www.1888baghouse.com	Corona	CA	92880	951-272-6610	272-1241
Barnebey & Sutcliffe Corp 835 N Cassady Ave TF: 800-886-2272 ■ Web: www.bscarbons.com	Columbus	OH	43219	614-258-9501	258-3464
Barron Industries Inc 105 19th St S TF: 800-226-3267 ■ Web: www.barronind.com	Irondale	AL	35210	205-956-3441	956-2265
Beckett Air Inc 37850 Beckett Pkwy TF: 800-831-7839 ■ Web: www.beckettair.com	North Ridgeville	OH	44039	440-327-9999	327-3569
Belco Technologies Corp 7 Entin Rd Web: www.belcotech.com	Parsippany	NJ	07054	973-884-4700	884-4775
Beltran Assoc Inc 1133 E 35th St Web: www.beltranassociates.com	Brooklyn	NY	11210	718-338-3311	253-9028
Blocksom & Co 450 St John Rd Suite 710 TF: 800-745-1408 ■ Web: www.blocksom.com	Michigan City	IN	46360	219-874-3231	874-9785
Bruning & Federle Mfg Co 2503 Northside Dr Web: www.bruning-federle.com	Statesville	NC	28625	704-873-7237	878-0647
Buffalo Air Handling Co 467 Zane Snead Dr Web: www.buffaloair.com	Amherst	VA	24521	434-946-7455	946-5486
Busch Co 10431 Perry Hwy Web: www.busch-co.com	Wexford	PA	15090	724-940-5024	940-4140
Camfil Farr Co 2121 E Paulhan St TF: 800-310-3277 ■ Web: www.camfilfarr.com	Rancho Dominguez	CA	90220	310-668-6300	609-2164
CECO Environmental Corp 3120 Forrer St NASDAQ: CECE ■ TF: 800-333-5475 ■ Web: www.cecoenviro.com	Cincinnati	OH	45209	513-458-2600	458-2647
Cincinnati Fan & Ventilator 7697 Snider Rd Web: www.cincinnatifan.com	Mason	OH	45040	513-573-0600	573-0640
Clarcor Inc 840 Crescent Center Dr Suite 600 NYSE: CLC ■ TF: 800-252-7267 ■ Web: www.clarcor.com	Franklin	TN	37067	615-771-3100	771-5616

	City	State	Zip	Phone	Fax
Cleanroom Systems 7000 Performance Dr	North Syracuse	NY	13212	315-452-7400	452-7420
TF: 800-825-3268 ■ *Web:* www.cleanroomsystems.com					
Clements National Co 6650 S Narragansett Ave	Chicago	IL	60638	708-594-5890	594-2481
TF: 800-966-0016 ■ *Web:* www.cadillacproducts.com					
CMI Schneible Co 714 N Saginaw St	Holly	MI	48442	248-634-8211	634-2240
TF: 800-627-6508 ■ *Web:* www.cmischneible.com					
Columbus Industries Inc 2938 SR-752	Ashville	OH	43103	740-983-2552	983-4622
TF: 800-766-2552 ■ *Web:* www.colind.com					
Comair Rotron Inc 2675 Customhouse Ct Suite F	San Diego	CA	92154	619-661-6688	661-6057
Web: www.comairrotron.com					
Cook Loren Co 2015 E Dale St	Springfield	MO	65803	417-869-6474	862-3820
Web: www.lorencook.com					
Corning Environmental Technologies 1 Riverfront Plaza	Corning	NY	14831	607-974-9000	974-8776
Web: www.corning.com/environmentaltechnologies					
Crown Andersen Inc 306 Dividend Dr	Peachtree City	GA	30269	770-486-2000	487-5066
TF: 800-241-5424 ■ *Web:* www.crownandersen.com					
CSM Worldwide Inc 269 Sheffield St Suite 1	Mountainside	NJ	07092	908-233-2882	233-1064
TF: 800-952-5227 ■ *Web:* www.csmworldwide.com					
CUNO Inc 400 Research Pkwy	Meriden	CT	06450	203-237-5541	238-8701
TF: 800-243-6894 ■ *Web:* www.cuno.com					
Daw Technologies Inc 1600 W 2200 South Suite 201	Salt Lake City	UT	84119	801-977-3100	973-6640
Web: www.dawtech.com					
Dectron Inc 4300 Poirier Blvd	Montreal	QC	H4R2C5	514-334-9609	334-9184
TF: 888-332-8766 ■ *Web:* www.dry-o-tron.com					
Disa Systems Inc 102 Transit Ave	Thomasville	NC	27360	336-889-5599	884-0017
TF: 800-532-0830 ■ *Web:* www.disagroup.com					
Donaldson Co 115 E Steels Corners Rd	Stow	OH	44224	330-928-4100	928-0122
Web: www.donaldson.com					
Duall Div Met-Pro Corp 1550 Industrial Dr	Owosso	MI	48867	989-725-8184	725-8188
Web: www.dualldiv.com					
Ducon Technologies Inc 19 Engineers Ln	Farmingdale	NY	11735	631-420-4900	420-4985
Web: www.ducon.com					
Dustex Corp 100 Chastain Center Blvd NW	Kennesaw	GA	30144	770-429-5575	429-5556
Web: www.dustex.com					
Dynamic Air Engineering Inc 620 E Dyer Rd	Santa Ana	CA	92705	714-540-1000	545-9145
Web: www.dynamic-air.com					
EBM Industries Inc 100 Hyde Rd	Farmington	CT	06034	860-674-1515	674-8536
Web: www.ebm.com					
Eco-Air Products Inc 9455 Cabot Dr	San Diego	CA	92126	858-271-8111	271-9617
TF: 800-284-8111 ■ *Web:* www.ecoair.info					
Electrocorp 595 Portal St Suite A	Cotati	CA	94931	707-665-9616	665-9620
TF: 800-525-0711 ■ *Web:* www.electrocorp.net					
Engineered Cooling Systems Inc 201 W Carmel Dr	Carmel	IN	46032	317-846-3438	846-3460
Web: www.ecsfans.com					
Environmental Air Systems Inc 521 Banner Ave	Greensboro	NC	27401	336-273-1975	378-9859
Web: www.envairsys.com					
Environmental Elements Corp 3700 Koppers St	Baltimore	MD	21227	410-368-7000	368-6721
TF: 800-333-4331 ■ *Web:* www.eec1.com					
Epcon Industrial Systems Inc 17777 Interstate 45 S	Conroe	TX	77385	936-273-1774	273-4600
TF: 800-447-7872 ■ *Web:* www.epconind.com					
Fedder RP Corp 740 Driving Park Ave	Rochester	NY	14613	585-288-1600	288-2481
TF: 800-288-1660 ■ *Web:* www.rpfedder.com					
Filtertech Inc 113 Fairgrounds Dr PO Box 527	Manlius	NY	13104	315-682-8815	682-8825
Web: www.filtertech.com					
Filtration Group Inc 912 E Washington St	Joliet	IL	60433	815-726-4600	518-1162*
**Fax Area Code:* 800 ■ *TF:* 800-739-4600 ■ *Web:* www.filtrationgroup.com					
Flanders Corp 531 Flanders Filters Rd	Washington	NC	27889	252-946-8081	946-3425
NASDAQ: FLDR ■ *Web:* www.flanderscorp.com					
Flex-Kleen Div Met-Pro Corp 955 Hawthorn Dr	Itasca	IL	60143	630-775-0707	875-3212
TF: 800-621-0734 ■ *Web:* www.flex-kleen.com					
Gardner Denver Blower Div 100 Gardner Park	Peachtree City	GA	30269	770-632-5000	632-5095
TF: 800-543-7736 ■ *Web:* www.gardnerdenver.com					
Gaylord Industries Inc 10900 SW Avery St	Tualatin	OR	97062	503-691-2010	692-6048
TF: 800-547-9696 ■ *Web:* www.gaylordusa.com					
General Filters Inc 43800 Grand River Ave	Novi	MI	48375	248-349-2481	349-2366
Web: www.generalfilters.com					
Glasfloss Industries Inc 400 S Hall St	Dallas	TX	75226	214-741-7056	435-8377*
**Fax Area Code:* 800 ■ *Web:* www.glasfloss.com					
Great Lakes Filters 301 Arch Ave	Hillsdale	MI	49242	517-437-8940	437-8942
TF: 800-521-8565 ■ *Web:* www.greatlakesfilters.com					
Greenheck Fan Corp 1100 Industrial Ave PO Box 410	Schofield	WI	54476	715-359-6171	355-2399
Web: www.greenheck.com					
Griffin Environmental Co Inc 7066 Interstate Island Rd	Syracuse	NY	13209	315-451-5300	451-2338
TF: 877-293-8789 ■ *Web:* www.griffinenviro.com					
Hardie-Tynes Co Inc 800 28th St N	Birmingham	AL	35203	205-252-5191	252-3254
Web: www.hardie-tynes.com					
Hartzell Fan Inc 910 S Downing St	Piqua	OH	45356	937-773-7411	773-8994
TF: 800-336-3267 ■ *Web:* www.hartzellfan.com					
HEPA Corp 3071 E Coronado St	Anaheim	CA	92806	714-630-5700	630-2894
Web: www.hepa.com					
Holming Co Inc 6900 N Teutonia Ave	Milwaukee	WI	53209	414-352-3250	352-1833
Home Care Industries Inc ALFCO Div 1 Lisbon St	Clifton	NJ	07013	973-365-1600	365-1770
TF Cust Svc: 800-240-7998 ■ *Web:* www.homecareind.com					
Honeyville Metal Inc 4200 S 900 West	Topeka	IN	46571	260-593-2266	593-2486
Web: www.honeyvillemetal.com					
Howden Buffalo Inc 2029 W Dekalb St	Camden	SC	29020	803-713-2200	713-2222
Web: www.howdenbuffalo.com					
King Engineering Corp 3201 S State St	Ann Arbor	MI	48106	734-662-5691	662-6652
TF Cust Svc: 800-959-0128 ■ *Web:* www.king-gage.com					
Koch Filter Corp 625 W Hill St	Louisville	KY	40208	502-634-4796	637-2280
Web: www.kochfilter.com					
La Calhene Inc 1325 Field Ave S	Rush City	MN	55069	320-358-4713	358-3549
TF: 800-322-7604 ■ *Web:* www.lacalhene.com					
Lakewood Engineering & Mfg Co 501 N Sacramento Blvd	Chicago	IL	60612	773-722-4300	722-1541
TF: 800-621-4277 ■ *Web:* www.lakewoodeng.com					
Lau Industries Inc 4509 Springfield St	Dayton	OH	45431	937-476-6500	254-9519
Web: www.laufan.com					
Loren Cook Co 2015 E Dale St	Springfield	MO	65803	417-869-6474	862-3820
Web: www.lorencook.com					
Lydall Inc 1 Colonial Rd	Manchester	CT	06042	860-646-1233	646-4917
NYSE: LDL ■ *TF:* 800-365-9325 ■ *Web:* www.lydall.com					
M-D Pneumatics Div Tuthill Corp 4840 W Kearney St	Springfield	MO	65803	417-865-8715	865-2950
TF: 800-825-6937 ■ *Web:* pneumatics.tuthill.com					
Mafi-Trench Corp 3037 Industrial Pkwy	Santa Maria	CA	93455	805-928-5757	925-3861
Web: www.mafi-trench.com					
Marsulex Environmental Technology 200 N 7th St	Lebanon	PA	17046	717-274-7000	274-7103
Web: www.met.marsulex.com					
McIntire Co 745 Clark Ave	Bristol	CT	06010	860-585-0050	314-4500
TF: 800-437-9247 ■ *Web:* www.mcintireco.com					
Met-Pro Corp Duall Div 1550 Industrial Dr	Owosso	MI	48867	989-725-8184	725-8188
Web: www.dualldiv.com					
Met-Pro Corp Flex-Kleen Div 955 Hawthorn Dr	Itasca	IL	60143	630-775-0707	875-3212
TF: 800-621-0734 ■ *Web:* www.flex-kleen.com					
Met-Pro Corp Systems Div 1555 Bustard Rd Box 325	Kulpsville	PA	19443	215-631-9500	631-1801
Web: www.met-prosystems.com					
Midwesco Filter Resources Inc 385 Battaile Dr	Winchester	VA	22601	540-667-8500	667-9074
TF: 800-336-7300 ■ *Web:* www.midwescofilter.com					

	City	State	Zip	Phone	Fax
Midwest International 105 Stover Rd Midwest Plaza	Charlevoix	MI	49720	231-547-4000	547-9453
Web: www.midwestmagic.com					
Morrison Products Inc 16900 S Waterloo Rd	Cleveland	OH	44110	216-486-4000	486-0631
NAO Inc 1284 E Sedgley Ave	Philadelphia	PA	19134	215-743-5300	743-3018
TF Cust Svc: 800-523-3495 ■ *Web:* www.nao.com					
National Filter Media Corp 691 N 400 West	Salt Lake City	UT	84103	801-363-6736	531-1293
TF: 800-777-4248 ■ *Web:* www.nfm-filter.com					
New York Blower Co 7660 Quincy St	Willowbrook	IL	60527	630-794-5700	794-5776
Web: www.nyb.com					
NMB Technologies Corp 9730 Independence Ave	Chatsworth	CA	91311	818-341-3355	341-8207
Web: www.nmbtech.com					
Parker Hannifin Corp Finite Filtratio & Separation Div					
500 Glaspie St	Oxford	MI	48371	248-628-6400	628-1850
TF: 800-521-4357 ■ *Web:* www.parker.com					
Paxton Products Corp 10125 Carver Rd	Cincinnati	OH	45242	513-891-7474	891-4092
TF: 800-441-7475 ■ *Web:* www.paxtonproducts.com					
Praxair Trailigaz Ozone Co 8190 Beechmont Ave Suite 308	Cincinnati	OH	45255	513-233-0444	233-9555
Web: www.praxair.com					
Precipitator Services Group Inc 1625 Broad St	Elizabethton	TN	37643	423-543-7331	543-8737
TF: 800-345-0484 ■ *Web:* www.psgtn.net					
Process Equipment Inc 2770 Welborn St	Pelham	AL	35124	205-663-5330	663-6037
TF: 800-765-9863 ■ *Web:* www.process-equip.com					
PSP Industries 300 Montague Expy Suite 200	Milpitas	CA	95035	408-942-1155	262-5388
Web: www.pspindustries.com					
Purafil Inc 2654 Weaver Way	Doraville	GA	30340	770-662-8545	263-6922
TF: 800-222-6367 ■ *Web:* www.purafil.com					
Purolator Products Air Filtration Co 880 Facet Rd	Henderson	NC	27536	252-492-1141	356-2397*
**Fax Area Code:* 800 ■ *TF:* 800-334-6659 ■ *Web:* www.purolatorair.com					
Revcor Inc 251 Edwards Ave	Carpentersville	IL	60110	847-428-4411	426-4630
TF: 800-323-8261 ■ *Web:* www.revcor.com					
Robinson Industries Inc 400 Robinson Dr	Zelienople	PA	16063	724-452-6121	452-0388
Web: www.robinsonfans.com					
Ross Air Systems Inc 370 Campus Dr	Somerset	NJ	08873	732-356-4555	356-6676
Web: www.rossairsystems.com					
RP Fedder Corp 740 Driving Park Ave	Rochester	NY	14613	585-288-1600	288-2481
TF: 800-288-1660 ■ *Web:* www.rpfedder.com					
RPS Products Inc 281 Keyes Ave	Hampshire	IL	60140	847-683-3400	683-3939
TF: 800-683-7030 ■ *Web:* www.rpsproducts.com					
Seneca Environmental Products Inc					
1685 S Seneca County Rd Airport Industrial Park	Tiffin	OH	44883	419-447-1282	448-4048
Web: www.senecaenvironmental.com					
Sly Inc 8300 Dow Cir	Strongsville	OH	44136	440-891-3200	891-3210
TF: 800-334-2957 ■ *Web:* www.slyinc.com					
Sonic Air Systems Inc 1050 Beacon St	Brea	CA	92821	714-255-0124	255-8366
TF: 800-827-6642 ■ *Web:* www.sonicairsystems.com					
Spencer Turbine Co 600 Day Hill Rd	Windsor	CT	06095	860-688-8361	688-0098
TF: 800-232-4321 ■ *Web:* www.spencerturbine.com					
SPX Air Treatment 4647 SW 40th Ave	Ocala	FL	34474	352-237-1220	873-5722
Web: www.spxairtreatment.com					
Sterling Blower Co 135 Vista Center Dr	Forest	VA	24551	434-316-5310	316-5910
Web: www.sterlingblower.com					
Strobic Air Corp 160 Cassell Rd PO Box 144	Harleysville	PA	19438	215-723-4700	723-6758
Web: www.strobicair.com					
Tek Air Systems Inc 41 Eagle Rd	Danbury	CT	06810	203-791-1400	798-6534
Web: www.tek-air.com					
Terra Universal Inc 800 S Ramon Ave	Fullerton	CA	92831	714-526-0100	992-2179
TF: 800-767-0100 ■ *Web:* www.terrauni.com					
Thermatrix Inc 5 Sentry Pkwy E Suite 204	Blue Bell	PA	19422	610-832-8713	834-0473
Web: www.thermatrix.com					
Tjernlund Products Inc 1601 9th St	White Bear Lake	MN	55110	651-426-2993	426-9547
TF: 800-255-4208 ■ *Web:* www.tjernlund.com					
Tri-Dim Filter Corp 93 Industrial Dr Bldg 2	Louisa	VA	23093	540-967-2600	967-9670
TF: 800-458-9835 ■ *Web:* www.tridim.com					
Tri-Mer Corp 1400 Monroe St	Owosso	MI	48867	989-723-7838	723-7844
TF: 800-688-7838 ■ *Web:* www.tri-mer.com					
Trion Inc 101 McNeill Rd	Sanford	NC	27330	919-775-2201	774-8771
TF: 866-829-2440 ■ *Web:* www.trioninc.com					
Turbosonic Technologies Inc 239 New Rd Bldg B-205	Parsippany	NJ	07054	973-244-9544	244-9545
Web: www.turbosonic.com					
Tuthill Corp M-D Pneumatics Div 4840 W Kearney St	Springfield	MO	65803	417-865-8715	865-2950
TF: 800-825-6937 ■ *Web:* pneumatics.tuthill.com					
Twin City Fan Cos Ltd 5959 Trenton Ln N	Minneapolis	MN	55442	763-551-7600	551-7601
Web: www.tcf.com					
United Air Specialists Inc 4440 Creek Rd	Cincinnati	OH	45242	513-891-0400	891-4882
TF: 800-252-4647 ■ *Web:* www.uasinc.com					
Venturedyne Ltd 600 College Ave	Pewaukee	WI	53072	262-691-9900	691-9901
Web: www.venturedyne.com					
Walton Enterprises Inc 125 W Central Ave	Bentonville	AR	72712	479-273-5743	464-1500
Wheelabrator Air Pollution Control Inc					
441 Smithfield St 5th Fl	Pittsburgh	PA	15222	412-562-7300	562-7254
Web: www.wapc.com					

19 AIR TRAFFIC CONTROL SERVICES

The Federal Aviation Administration (a US government agency) and NAV CANADA (a private, not-for-profit Canadian firm) provide air traffic services nationwide in the US and Canada, respectively. The types of services provided include aircraft routing, approach and departure instruction, and weather information.

	City	State	Zip	Phone	Fax
Apptis NJ Inc (TMA Inc) 314 Chris Gaupp Dr Suite 203	Galloway	NJ	08205	609-652-9211	652-5585
Web: www.apptis.com					
Federal Aviation Administration (FAA)					
800 Independence Ave SW	Washington	DC	20591	866-835-5322	
Web: www.faa.gov					
Air Traffic Organization					
800 Independence Ave SW Rm 1002	Washington	DC	20591	202-267-3666	267-5456
Web: www.faa.gov/about/office_org/headquarters_offices/ato					
Federal Aviation Administration Regional Offices					
Alaskan Region 222 W 7th Ave	Anchorage	AK	99513	907-271-5296	
Web: www.alaska.faa.gov					
Central Region Federal Bldg 901 Locust St	Kansas City	MO	64106	816-329-3050	329-3055
Web: www.faa.gov/cen					
Eastern Region 1 Aviation Plaza 159-30 Rockaway Blvd	Jamaica	NY	11434	718-553-3000	
Web: aea.faa.gov					
Great Lakes Region 2300 E Devon Ave	Des Plaines	IL	60018	847-294-7294	294-8490
Web: www.agl.faa.gov					
New England Region 12 New England Executive Pk	Burlington	MA	01803	781-238-7020	238-7005
Web: www.faa.gov/region/ane					
Northwest Mountain Region 1601 Lind Ave SW	Renton	WA	98057	425-227-2001	227-1006
Web: www.nw.faa.gov					

Phone Fax

Southern Region 1701 Columbia Ave .... College Park GA 30337 404-305-5000 305-5010
Web: www.faa.gov/aso

Western Pacific Region 15000 Aviation Blvd.......... Lawndale CA 90261 310-725-3550 725-6811
Web: www.awp.faa.gov

MILCOM Systems Corp 532 Viking Dr.......... Virginia Beach VA 23452 757-463-2800 463-3052
TF: 800-967-0966 ■ *Web:* www.milcomsystems.com

NAV CANADA 77 Metcalfe St.......... Ottawa ON K1P5L6 613-563-5588 563-3426
TF: 800-876-4693 ■ *Web:* www.navcanada.ca

TMA Inc (Apptis NJ Inc) 314 Chris Gaupp Dr Suite 203 .... Galloway NJ 08205 609-652-9211 652-5585
Web: www.apptis.com

20 AIRCRAFT

SEE ALSO Airships p. 1277

Phone Fax

Air Tractor Inc 1584 Airport Rd.......... Olney TX 76374 940-564-5616 564-5625
Web: airtractor.com

American Champion Aircraft Corp 32032 Washington Ave.......... Rochester WI 53167 262-534-6317 534-2395
Web: www.amerchampionaircraft.com

American Eurocopter Corp 2701 Forum Dr.......... Grand Prairie TX 75052 972-641-0000 641-3550
TF: 800-873-0001 ■ *Web:* www.eurocopterusa.com

Aviation General Inc
7200 NW 63 St Wiley Post Airport Hangar 8.......... Bethany OK 73008 405-440-2255 495-8383

Bell Helicopter Textron Inc PO Box 482.......... Fort Worth TX 76053 817-280-2011 280-2321
TF: 800-359-2355 ■ *Web:* www.bellhelicopter.textron.com

Boeing Business Jets PO Box 3707 MS 1E-77.......... Seattle WA 98124 206-662-4300 662-4330
Web: www.boeing.com/commercial/bbj

Boeing Co 100 N Riverside Plaza.......... Chicago IL 60606 312-544-2000 544-2082*
NYSE: BA ■ **Fax: PR* ■ *Web:* www.boeing.com

Boeing Co Commercial Airplane Group PO Box 3707.......... Seattle WA 98124 206-655-2121
Web: www.boeing.com/commercial

Boeing Commercial Airplane Group Douglas Products Div
3855 Lakewood Blvd.......... Long Beach CA 90846 562-593-5511

Bombardier Aerospace 400 Cote-Vertu Rd W.......... Dorval QC H4S1Y9 514-855-5000 855-7401
Web: www.aerospace.bombardier.com

Bombardier Aerospace Learjet 1 Learjet Way.......... Wichita KS 67209 316-946-2000 946-2163
TF: 800-289-5327 ■ *Web:* www.learjet.com

Bombardier Inc 800 boul Rene Levesque O Bureau 2900.......... Montreal QC H3B1Y8 514-861-9481 861-7053
TSX: BBD.a ■ *Web:* www.bombardier.com

Cessna Aircraft Co 1 Cessna Blvd.......... Wichita KS 67215 316-517-6000 517-7250
Web: cessna.com

Commander Aircraft Co 7200 NW 63rd St.......... Bethany OK 73008 405-495-8080 495-8383
Web: www.commanderair.com

Dassault Falcon Jet Corp PO Box 2000.......... South Hackensack NJ 07606 201-440-6700 541-4401*
**Fax: Hum Res* ■ *TF:* 800-526-7071 ■ *Web:* www.falconjet.com

Douglas Products Div Boeing Commercial Airplane Group
3855 Lakewood Blvd.......... Long Beach CA 90846 562-593-5511

Eclipse Aviation Corp 2503 Clark Carr Loop SE.......... Albuquerque NM 87106 505-245-7555 241-8800
Web: www.eclipseaviation.com

Embraer Aircraft Corp 276 SW 34th St.......... Fort Lauderdale FL 33315 954-359-3700 359-3701
TF: 800-362-7237 ■ *Web:* www.embraer.com

Enstrom Helicopter Corp USA 2209 22nd St PO Box 490.......... Menominee MI 49858 906-863-1200 863-6821
Web: www.enstromhelicopter.com

Erickson Air-Crane Co
3100 Willow Springs Rd PO Box 3247.......... Central Point OR 97502 541-664-5544 664-2312
TF: 800-424-2413 ■ *Web:* www.erickson-aircrane.com

Groen Brothers Aviation Inc
2640 W California Ave Suite A.......... Salt Lake City UT 84104 801-973-0177 973-4027
Web: www.groenbros.com

Gulfstream Aerospace Corp PO Box 2206.......... Savannah GA 31402 912-965-3000 965-3775
Web: www.gulfstream.com

Hawker Beechcraft Corp PO Box 85.......... Wichita KS 67201 316-676-7111 676-8867*
**Fax: PR* ■ *Web:* www.hawkerbeechcraft.com

Kaman Aerospace Corp Old Windsor Rd PO Box 2.......... Bloomfield CT 06002 860-242-4461 243-7514
Web: www.kamanaero.com

Kaman Aerospace International Corp PO Box 2.......... Bloomfield CT 06002 860-242-4461 243-7514
Web: www.kamanaero.com

Lockheed Martin Aeronautics Co PO Box 748.......... Fort Worth TX 76101 817-777-2000 777-2115
Web: www.lockheedmartin.com/aeronautics

Lockheed Martin Corp 6801 Rockledge Dr.......... Bethesda MD 20817 301-897-6000 897-6083
NYSE: LMT ■ *Web:* www.lockheedmartin.com

M7 Aerospace PO Box 790490.......... San Antonio TX 78279 210-824-9421 824-9476*
**Fax: Hum Res* ■ *Web:* www.m7aerospace.com

Mooney Aircraft Corp 165 Al Mooney Rd N.......... Kerrville TX 78028 830-896-6000 896-3133
TF: 800-456-3033 ■ *Web:* www.mooney.com

New Piper Aircraft Inc 2926 Piper Dr.......... Vero Beach FL 32960 772-567-4361 978-6584
Web: www.newpiper.com

Northrop Grumman Corp 1840 Century Park E.......... Los Angeles CA 90067 310-553-6262 201-3023
NYSE: NOC ■ *Web:* www.northropgrumman.com

Northrop Grumman Corp Military Aircraft Systems Div
1 Hornet Way.......... El Segundo CA 90245 310-332-1000 553-2076

Robinson Helicopter Co 2901 Airport Dr.......... Torrance CA 90505 310-539-0508 539-5198
Web: www.robinsonheli.com

Ryan Aerospace Corp PO Box 500261.......... Austin TX 78750 512-576-0427 219-6881
Web: www.ryanaerospace.com

Sabreliner Corp 3551 Doniphan Dr.......... Neosho MO 64850 417-451-1810 451-0192
TF: 800-325-4663 ■ *Web:* www.sabreliner.com

Scaled Composites Inc 1624 Flight Line Rd.......... Mojave CA 93501 661-824-4541 824-4174
Web: www.scaled.com

Schweizer Aircraft Corp 1250 Schweizer Rd.......... Horseheads NY 14845 607-739-3821 796-2488
Web: www.sacusa.com

Sikorsky Aircraft Corp 6900 Main St PO Box 9729.......... Stratford CT 06615 203-386-4000
Web: www.sikorsky.com

Snow Aviation International Inc
Rickenbacker International Airport 7201 Paul Tibbets St.......... Columbus OH 43217 614-492-7669 492-7679
Web: www.snowaviation.com

Textron Canada Ltd 40 Westminster St.......... Providence RI 02903 401-421-2800 421-2878
Web: www.textron.com

Thrush Aircraft Inc 300 Old Pretoria Rd.......... Albany GA 31706 229-883-1440 439-9790
Web: www.thrushaircraft.com

Tiger Aircraft LLC 226 Pilot Way.......... Martinsburg WV 25401 304-260-0038
TF: 877-808-4437 ■ *Web:* www.tigeraircraft.com

21 AIRCRAFT ENGINES & ENGINE PARTS

Phone Fax

A & B Aerospace Inc 612 Ayon Ave.......... Azusa CA 91702 626-334-2976 334-6539
TF: 888-999-9397

Phone Fax

AAR Corp 1100 N Wood Dale Rd 1 AAR Pl.......... Wood Dale IL 60191 630-227-2000 227-2019
NYSE: AIR ■ *TF:* 800-422-2213 ■ *Web:* www.aarcorp.com

ACR Industries Inc 15375 23-Mile Rd.......... Macomb MI 48042 586-781-2800 781-0152
Web: www.acrind.com

Airfoil Technologies International LLC
5910 Landerbrook Dr Landerbrook Corporate Center.......... Mayfield Heights OH 44124 440-446-8450 466-8451
Web: www.airfoiltech.com

Alpha Q Inc 87 Upton Rd.......... Colchester CT 06415 860-537-4681 537-4332

Barnes Aerospace 169 Kennedy Rd.......... Windsor CT 06095 860-298-7740 298-7738
Web: www.barnesaero.com

Beacon Industries Inc 85 Granby St.......... Bloomfield CT 06002 860-242-3453 242-2204

BH Aircraft Co Inc 2230 Smithtown Ave.......... Ronkonkoma NY 11779 631-981-4200 981-0221
Web: www.bhaircraft.com

Chromalloy Gas Turbine Corp 4430 Director Dr.......... San Antonio TX 78219 210-333-6010 359-5570

Delta Industries 39 Bradley Park Rd.......... East Granby CT 06026 860-653-5041 653-5792
Web: www.delta-industries-ct.com

Engine Components Inc 9503 Middlex Dr.......... San Antonio TX 78217 210-820-8100 820-8103
TF: 800-324-2359 ■ *Web:* www.eci2fly.com

GE Aircraft Engines 1 Neumann Way.......... Cincinnati OH 45215 513-243-2000 552-2177*
**Fax: Sales* ■ *Web:* www.geae.com

GE Aviation 1 Neumann Way.......... Cincinnati OH 45215 513-243-2000
Web: www.geaviation.com

Gentz Industries Inc 25250 Easy St.......... Warren MI 48089 586-772-2500 772-2913
Web: www.gentzindustries.com

Goodrich Corp Pump & Engine Control Systems Div
Charter Oak Blvd.......... West Hartford CT 06133 860-236-0651 236-1062

Goodrich Corp Turbo Machinery Products Div
323 S Bracken Ln.......... Chandler AZ 85224 480-899-8995 857-5780
Web: www.tmp.goodrich.com

Gros-Ite Industries 1790 New Britain Ave.......... Farmington CT 06032 860-677-2603 677-6316
TF: 800-242-1790 ■ *Web:* www.edactechnologies.com

Hamilton Sundstrand Aerospace PO Box 7002.......... Rockford IL 61125 815-226-6000 226-7278
Web: www.hamiltonsundstrandcorp.com

Hamilton Sundstrand Power Systems 4400 Ruffin Rd.......... San Diego CA 92123 858-627-6000 627-6918
Web: www.hs-powersystems.com

HEICO Corp 3000 Taft St.......... Hollywood FL 33021 954-987-6101 966-2169
NYSE: HEI ■ *Web:* www.heico.com

Heroux-Devtek Inc
1111 Saint-Charles St W Suite 658 East Tower.......... Longueuil QC J4K5G4 450-679-3330 679-3666
TSX: HRX ■ *Web:* www.herouxdevtek.com

Hitchcock Industries Inc 8701 Harriet Ave S.......... Bloomington MN 55420 952-881-1000 887-7858
Web: www.hitchcock-ind.com

Ketema Div Senior Aerospace 790 Greenfield Dr.......... El Cajon CA 92021 619-442-3451 440-1456
Web: www.sfketema.com

Kreisler Industrial Corp 180 Van Riper Ave.......... Elmwood Park NJ 07407 201-791-0700 791-8015
Web: www.kreisler-ind.com

Kreisler Mfg Corp 180 Van Riper Ave.......... Elmwood Park NJ 07407 201-791-0700 791-8015
NASDAQ: KRSL

Lear Romec Crane Corp 241 S Abbe Rd.......... Elyria OH 44035 440-323-3211 322-3378
Web: www.learromec.com

Lycoming Engines 652 Oliver St.......... Williamsport PA 17701 570-323-6181 327-7066*
**Fax: Mktg* ■ *TF:* 800-258-3279 ■ *Web:* www.lycoming.textron.com

Magellan Aerospace Corp 3160 Derry Rd E.......... Mississauga ON L4T1A9 905-677-1889 677-5658
Web: www.malaero.com

Meco Inc 2121 S Main St.......... Paris IL 61944 217-465-7575 465-5230

Middleton Aerospace Corp 206 S Main St.......... Middleton MA 01949 978-774-6000 777-5640

Moeller Mfg Co Inc Aircraft Div 30100 Beck Rd.......... Wixom MI 48393 248-960-3999 960-1593
Web: www.moelleraircraft.com

MTU Aero Engines North America 275 Richard St.......... Newington CT 06111 860-667-2134 667-0057
Web: www.mtu.de/en/standorte/north_america/

Nichols Airborne Div Parker Hannifin Corp
14 Robbins Pond Rd.......... Devens MA 01434 978-784-1200 784-1400
Web: www.parker.com/ag/NAD

Palmer Mfg Co Inc 243 Medford St.......... Malden MA 02148 781-321-0480 321-2226
Web: www.palmermfgco.com

Parker Gas Turbine Fuel Systems Div 124 Columbia St.......... Clyde NY 14433 315-923-2311 923-9306
Web: www.parker.com/gasturbine

Parker Hannifin Corp 6035 Parkland Blvd.......... Cleveland OH 44124 216-896-3000 896-4000
NYSE: PH ■ *TF Cust Svc:* 800-272-7537 ■ *Web:* www.parker.com

Parker Hannifin Corp Nichols Airborne Div
14 Robbins Pond Rd.......... Devens MA 01434 978-784-1200 784-1400
Web: www.parker.com/ag/NAD

Pratt & Whitney 400 Main St.......... East Hartford CT 06108 860-565-4321 565-6609*
**Fax: Sales* ■ *Web:* www.pratt-whitney.com

Pratt & Whitney Canada Inc 1000 Marie-Victorin Blvd.......... Longueuil QC J4G1A1 450-677-9411 647-2888
TF: 800-268-8000 ■ *Web:* www.pwc.ca

Pratt & Whitney Government Engines & Space Propulsion Div PO Box 109600.......... West Palm Beach FL 33410 561-796-2000 796-5876*
**Fax: Sales* ■ *TF:* 800-327-3246

Rolls-Royce North America 14850 Conference Ctr Dr Suite 100.......... Chantilly VA 20151 703-834-1700 709-6086
TF: 800-274-5387 ■ *Web:* www.rolls-royce.com

Senior Aerospace Ketema Div 790 Greenfield Dr.......... El Cajon CA 92021 619-442-3451 440-1456
Web: www.sfketema.com

Sifco Industries Inc 970 E 64th St.......... Cleveland OH 44103 216-881-8600 432-6281
AMEX: SIF ■ *Web:* www.sifco.com

Teledyne Continental Motors 2039 Broad St.......... Mobile AL 36615 251-438-3411 438-1623
Web: www.tcmlink.com

Teledyne Technologies Inc 12333 W Olympic Blvd.......... Los Angeles CA 90064 310-893-1600 893-1613
NYSE: TDY ■ *Web:* www.teledynetechnologies.com

Teleflex Aerospace Mfg Group 280 Adams St.......... Manchester CT 06040 860-643-2473 643-2477
Web: www.teleflexaerospace.com

Twigg Aerospace Components 659 E York St.......... Martinsville IN 46151 765-342-7126 342-1553
Web: www.twiggcorp.com

Unison Industries Inc 7575 Baymeadows Way.......... Jacksonville FL 32256 904-739-4000 739-4006
Web: www.unisonindustries.com

Valley-Todeco 12975 Bradley Ave.......... Sylmar CA 91342 818-367-2261 364-6036*
**Fax: Sales* ■ *Web:* www.valley-todeco.com

Wall Colmonoy Corp 30261 Stephenson Hwy.......... Madison Heights MI 48071 248-585-6400 585-7960
TF: 800-521-2412 ■ *Web:* www.wallcolmonoy.com

Williams International
2280 East West Maple Rd PO Box 200.......... Walled Lake MI 48390 248-624-5200 669-1577
Web: www.williams-int.com

Woodward 5001 N 2nd St.......... Loves Park IL 61111 815-877-7441 639-6033
NASDAQ: WGOV ■ *TF:* 888-273-8839 ■ *Web:* www.woodward.com

22 AIRCRAFT PARTS & AUXILIARY EQUIPMENT

SEE ALSO Precision Machined Products p. 2133

Phone Fax

AAR Cargo Systems 12633 Inkster Rd.......... Livonia MI 48150 734-522-2000 522-2240
TF: 800-247-1273 ■ *Web:* www.aarcorp.com/manufact/cargo.html

				Phone	Fax
AAR Composites 14201 Myerlake Cir *TF:* 888-227-3597 ■ *Web:* www.aarcorp.com/manufact/composites.html	Clearwater	FL	33760	727-539-8585	539-0316
AAR Corp 1100 N Wood Dale Rd 1 AAR Pl *NYSE: AIR* ■ *TF:* 800-422-2213 ■ *Web:* www.aarcorp.com	Wood Dale	IL	60191	630-227-2000	227-2019
Ace Clearwater Enterprises 19815 Magellan Dr *Web:* www.aceclearwater.com	Torrance	CA	90502	310-538-5380	323-2137
Acromil Corp 18421 Railroad St *Web:* www.acromil.com	City of Industry	CA	91748	626-964-2522	810-6100
Aero Parts Mfg & Repair Inc 431 Rio Rancho Blvd NE *TF:* 800-839-5505 ■ *Web:* www.aeroparts.net	Rio Rancho	NM	87124	505-891-6600	891-6650
Aeronca Inc 2320 Wedekind Dr *Web:* www.aeroncainc.com	Middletown	OH	45042	513-422-2751	422-0812
Aerospace Technologies Inc 7445 E Lancaster St	Fort Worth	TX	76112	817-451-0620	451-2563
Arkwin Industries Inc 686 Main St *Web:* www.arkwin.com	Westbury	NY	11590	516-333-2640	997-4053
Arrow Gear Co Inc 2301 Curtiss St *Web:* www.arrowgear.com	Downers Grove	IL	60515	630-969-7640	969-0253
Arrowhead Products Corp 4411 Katella Ave *Web:* www.arrowheadproducts.net	Los Alamitos	CA	90720	714-828-7770	220-6487
B/E Aerospace Inc 1400 Corporate Ctr Way *NASDAQ: BEAV* ■ *TF:* 888-223-2376 ■ *Web:* www.beaerospace.com	Wellington	FL	33414	561-791-5000	791-7900
Boeing Co Commercial Airplane Group PO Box 3707 *Web:* www.boeing.com/commercial	Seattle	WA	98124	206-655-2121	
BVR Technologies Co 3358-60 Publishers Dr *Web:* www.bvraero.com	Rockford	IL	61109	815-874-2471	874-8163
Castle Precision Industries 15148 Bledsoe St *Web:* www.castlepi.com	Sylmar	CA	91342	818-362-5665	367-8936
CEF Industries Inc 320 S Church St *TF:* 800-888-6419 ■ *Web:* www.cefind.com	Addison	IL	60101	630-628-2299	628-1386
Chem-Fab Corp 1923 Central Ave *Web:* www.chem-fab.com	Hot Springs	AR	71901	501-321-9325	321-2859
Cox & Co Inc 200 Varick St *Web:* www.coxandco.com	New York	NY	10014	212-366-0200	366-0222
CTL Aerospace Inc 5616 Spellmire Dr *Web:* www.ctlaerospace.com	Cincinnati	OH	45246	513-874-7900	874-2499
Curtiss-Wright Corp 4 Becker Farm Rd 3rd Fl *NYSE: CW* ■ *Web:* www.curtisswright.com	Roseland	NJ	07068	973-597-4700	597-4799
Curtiss-Wright Flight Systems 201 Old Boiling Springs Rd **Fax:* Cust Svc ■ *Web:* www.curtisswright.com	Shelby	NC	28152	704-481-1150	482-1903*
Ducommun Inc 23301 Wilmington Ave *NYSE: DCO* ■ *Web:* www.ducommun.com	Carson	CA	90745	310-513-7280	513-7279
Dukes Aerospace 9060 Winnetka Ave *Web:* www.dukesinc.com	Northridge	CA	91324	818-998-9811	700-8361
EDO M Tech 165 Veterans Way Suite 100 *Web:* www.nycedo.com	Warminster	PA	18974	267-960-2500	960-2501
Engineered Arresting Systems Corp 2550 Market St *Web:* www.esco-usa.com	Aston	PA	19014	610-494-8000	494-8989
Essex Cryogenic of Missouri Inc 8007 Chivvis Dr *Web:* www.essexind.com/cryo_frame.htm	Saint Louis	MO	63123	314-832-8077	832-8208
Fenn Technologies 300 Fenn Rd *Web:* www.fennmfg.com	Newington	CT	06111	860-594-4400	667-2103
FletchAir Inc Comfort Falls Aviation Estates 118 FM 1621 *TF:* 800-329-4647 ■ *Web:* www.fletchair.com	Comfort	TX	78013	713-649-8700	643-0070
Flight Safety Technologies Inc 28 Cottrell St *AMEX: FLT* ■ *Web:* www.flysafetech.com	Mystic	CT	06355	860-245-0191	536-6607
GE Aviation Systems Div 3290 Patterson Ave SE *Web:* www.geaviationsystems.com	Grand Rapids	MI	49512	616-241-7000	241-7533
GenMech Aerospace 60 Milbar Blvd	Farmingdale	NY	11735	631-249-7901	694-1849
Gill MC Corp 4056 Easy St *Web:* www.mcgillcorp.com	El Monte	CA	91731	626-443-6094	350-5880
GKN Aerospace Chem-tronics Inc 1150 W Bradley Ave *Web:* www.chem-tronics.com	El Cajon	CA	92020	619-448-2320	258-5270
Goodrich Aerospace Aerostructures Group 850 Lagoon Dr *Web:* www.aerostructures.goodrich.com	Chula Vista	CA	91910	619-691-4111	691-2905
Goodrich Corp Aircraft Interior Products Div 3414 S 5th St *TF:* 888-419-4344 ■ *Web:* www.aip.goodrich.com	Phoenix	AZ	85040	602-232-4000	232-4100
Goodrich Corp De-Icing & Specialty Systems Div 1555 Corporate Woods Pkwy *Web:* www.deicingsystems.goodrich.com	Uniontown	OH	44685	330-374-3040	374-2290
Goodrich Corp Landing Gear Div 8000 Marble Ave **Fax:* Hum Res ■ *Web:* www.lgd.goodrich.com	Cleveland	OH	44105	216-341-1700	429-4511*
Goodrich Corp Sensor Systems Div 14300 Judicial Rd *Web:* www.sensors.goodrich.com	Burnsville	MN	55306	952-892-4300	892-4800
Goodrich Corp Wheels & Brakes Div 101 Waco St *TF:* 800-448-2102 ■ *Web:* www.wheelsandbrakes.goodrich.com	Troy	OH	45373	937-339-3811	440-3257
Hamilton Sundstrand Aerospace PO Box 7002 *Web:* www.hamiltonsundstrandcorp.com	Rockford	IL	61125	815-226-6000	226-7278
Hartwell Corp 900 S Richfield Rd *Web:* www.hartwellcorp.com	Placentia	CA	92870	714-993-4200	579-4419
Hartzell Propeller Inc 1 Propeller Pl *Web:* www.hartzellprop.com	Piqua	OH	45356	937-778-4200	778-4271
Honeywell Aerospace 1944 E Sky Harbor Cir **Fax Area Code:* 602 ■ *Web:* www.honeywellaerospace.com	Phoenix	AZ	85034	800-601-3099	365-3343*
Honeywell Inc Aircraft Landing Systems 3520 Westmoor St *TF:* 800-707-4555	South Bend	IN	46628	574-231-2000	231-2020
HR Textron Inc 25200 W Rye Canyon Rd *TF:* 800-235-3330 ■ *Web:* www.systems.textron.com	Valencia	CA	91355	661-294-6000	259-9622
Hydro-Aire Inc 3000 Winona Ave *Web:* www.hydroaire.com	Burbank	CA	91504	818-526-2600	526-2284
K & F Industries Holdings Inc 50 Main St *NYSE: KFI*	White Plains	NY	10606	914-448-2700	448-2719
Kaman Aerospace Corp Old Windsor Rd PO Box 2 *Web:* www.kamanaero.com	Bloomfield	CT	06002	860-242-4461	243-7514
L-3 Communications Integrated Systems 10001 Jack Finney Blvd *Web:* www.l-3com.com/is	Greenville	TX	75402	903-455-3450	457-4413
Limco Airepair Inc 5304 S Lawton Ave *Web:* www.limcoairepair.com	Tulsa	OK	74107	918-445-4300	446-8704
LMI Aerospace Inc 3600 Mueller Rd *NASDAQ: LMIA* ■ *Web:* www.lmiaerospace.com	Saint Charles	MO	63301	636-946-6525	949-1576
Magellan Aerospace Corp 3160 Derry Rd E *Web:* www.malaero.com	Mississauga	ON	L4T1A9	905-677-1889	677-5658
MC Gill Corp 4056 Easy St *Web:* www.mcgillcorp.com	El Monte	CA	91731	626-443-6094	350-5880
Middle River Aircraft Systems 103 Chesapeake Pk Plaza *TF:* 800-880-9975 ■ *Web:* www.mras-usa.com	Baltimore	MD	21220	410-682-1500	
NORDAM Group 6911 N Whirlpool Dr PO Box 3365 **Fax:* Sales ■ *Web:* www.nordam.com	Tulsa	OK	74101	918-587-4105	878-4808*
Northrop Grumman Corp 1840 Century Park E *NYSE: NOC* ■ *Web:* www.northropgrumman.com	Los Angeles	CA	90067	310-553-6262	201-3023
Paramount Panels Inc 1531 E Cedar St *Web:* www.paramountpanels.com	Ontario	CA	91761	909-947-5168	947-8012
Parker Aerospace Group 14300 Alton Pkwy *Web:* www.parker.com/ag	Irvine	CA	92618	949-833-3000	851-3277
Pemco Air Support Services 100 Pemco Dr *Web:* www.pemcoaviationgroup.com	Dothan	AL	36303	334-983-7089	983-7042
Pratt & Whitney Auto Air Inc 5640 Enterprise Dr *Web:* www.autoair.com	Lansing	MI	48911	517-393-4040	393-2164
Sargent Fletcher Inc 9400 E Flair Dr *Web:* www.sargentfletcher.com	El Monte	CA	91731	626-443-7171	579-9183
Shaw Aero Devices 3580 Shaw Blvd *Web:* www.shawaero.com/devicehomepage.htm	Naples	FL	34117	239-304-1000	304-1088
Shimadzu Aircraft Equipment 3111 Lomita Blvd *Web:* www1.shimadzu.com/products/aircraft	Torrance	CA	90505	310-517-9910	517-9180
Sierracin/Sylmar Corp 12780 San Fernando Rd *Web:* www.sierracin.com	Sylmar	CA	91342	818-362-6711	362-7801
Stellex Bandy Machining Inc 3420 N San Fernando Blvd *Web:* www.bandy-machining.com	Burbank	CA	91510	818-846-9020	846-0621
Stellex Monitor Aerospace Inc 1000 New Horizons Blvd **Fax:* Hum Res ■ *Web:* www.monair.com	Amityville	NY	11701	631-957-2300	957-0179*
Symbolic Displays Inc 1917 E St Andrew Pl *Web:* www.symbolicdisplays.com	Santa Ana	CA	92705	714-258-2811	258-2810
Triumph Thermal Systems Inc 200 Railroad St *Web:* www.triumph-thermal.com	Forest	OH	45843	419-273-2511	273-3285
Universal Propulsion Co 25401 N Central Ave *Web:* www.upco.goodrich.com	Phoenix	AZ	85085	623-516-3340	516-3355
Vought Aircraft Industries Inc 9314 W Jefferson Blvd *Web:* www.voughtaircraft.com	Dallas	TX	75211	972-946-2011	

23 AIRCRAFT RENTAL

SEE ALSO Aviation - Fixed-Base Operations p. 1364

				Phone	Fax
AeroCentury Corp 1440 Chapin Ave Suite 310 *AMEX: ACY* ■ *Web:* www.aerocentury.com	Burlingame	CA	94010	650-340-1888	696-3929
AeroTurbine Inc 2323 NW 82nd Ave **Fax:* Cust Svc ■ *Web:* www.aeroturbine.com	Miami	FL	33122	305-590-2600	717-3568*
Aviation Capital Group Corp 610 Newport Center Dr 14th Fl *Web:* www.aviationcapital.com	Newport Beach	CA	92660	949-219-4600	759-5675
Aviation Leasing Group 8080 Ward Pkwy Suite 407 *Web:* www.algkc.com	Kansas City	MO	64114	816-931-7300	931-8200
GE Aviation Services 201 High Ridge Rd *Web:* www.gecas.com	Stamford	CT	06927	203-357-3776	316-7865
International Lease Finance Corp (ILFC) 10250 Constellation Blvd Suite 3400 *Web:* www.ilfc.com	Los Angeles	CA	90067	310-788-1999	788-1990
Jetscape Inc 10 S New River Dr E Suite 200 *TF:* 800-355-5387 ■ *Web:* www.jetscape.aero	Fort Lauderdale	FL	33301	954-763-4737	763-4757
Jones Aviation Service Inc 1234 Clyde Jones Rd *TF:* 800-945-6637 ■ *Web:* www.jonesav.com	Sarasota	FL	34243	941-355-8100	351-9700
Pinnacle Air 802 Airport Rd *TF:* 800-828-4462 ■ *Web:* www.pinnacleairservices.com	Springdale	AR	72764	479-751-4462	751-2646
US Airways Leasing & Sales Inc 2345 Crystal Dr	Arlington	VA	22227	703-872-7500	872-7515
Willis Lease Finance Corp 2320 Marinship Way Suite 300 *NASDAQ: WLFC* ■ **Fax:* Mktg ■ *Web:* www.wlfc.com	Sausalito	CA	94965	415-331-5281	331-0607*
Wright Air Service Inc PO Box 60142 *Web:* www.wrightair.net	Fairbanks	AK	99706	907-474-0502	474-0375

24 AIRCRAFT SERVICE & REPAIR

				Phone	Fax
AAR Aircraft Component Services 747 Zeckendorf Blvd *Web:* www.aarcorp.com	Garden City	NY	11530	516-222-9000	222-0987
AAR Aircraft Services 6611 S Meridian Ave *Web:* www.aarcorp.com/airframe/oklahoma.html	Oklahoma City	OK	73159	405-218-3000	218-3610
AAR Corp 1100 N Wood Dale Rd 1 AAR Pl *NYSE: AIR* ■ *TF:* 800-422-2213 ■ *Web:* www.aarcorp.com	Wood Dale	IL	60191	630-227-2000	227-2019
AAR Landing Gear Services 9371 NW 100th St *Web:* www.aarcorp.com	Miami	FL	33178	305-887-4027	887-9437
AAR Power Services 148 Industrial Park Dr *Web:* www.aarcorp.com	Frankfort	NY	13340	315-731-3700	731-3737
AeroThrust Corp 5300 NW 36th St PO Box 522236 *TF:* 800-228-0665 ■ *Web:* www.aerothrust.com	Miami	FL	33152	305-871-1790	526-7388
American Avionics 7023 Perimeter Rd S *TF Sales:* 800-518-5858 ■ *Web:* www.americanavionics.com	Seattle	WA	98108	206-763-8530	763-2036
Argo-Tech Corp Customer Support Operations Div 204 S Hindry Ave *Web:* www.argo-tech.com	Inglewood	CA	90301	310-670-4020	670-9633
b-Fast Corp PO Box 1616	Newtown	PA	18940	215-860-5600	968-6010
Basler Turbo Conversions LLC 255 W 35th St PO Box 2305 *Web:* www.baslerturbo.com	Oshkosh	WI	54903	920-236-7820	235-0381
Bridgestone Aircraft Tire USA Inc 802 S Ayersville Rd	Mayodan	NC	27027	336-548-8100	548-7441
Byerly Aviation 6100 EM Dirkson Pkwy *Web:* www.byerlyaviation.com	Peoria	IL	61607	309-697-6300	697-2779
Christiansen Aviation Inc PO Box 702412 *TF:* 800-331-5550 ■ *Web:* www.christiansenaviation.com	Tulsa	OK	74170	918-299-2687	299-0694
Composite Technology Inc 1001 Ave R *TF:* 888-284-1972 ■ *Web:* www.rotorblades.com	Grand Prairie	TX	75050	972-606-4400	606-4418
Curtiss-Wright Controls Inc 15800 John J Delaney Dr Suite 200 *TF:* 877-319-8468 ■ *Web:* www.cwcontrols.com	Charlotte	NC	28277	704-869-4600	869-4601
Cutter Aviation 2802 E Old Tower Rd *TF:* 800-234-5382 ■ *Web:* www.cutteraviation.com	Phoenix	AZ	85034	602-273-1237	275-4010
Duncan Aviation Inc 3701 Aviation Rd PO Box 81887 *TF:* 800-228-4277 ■ *Web:* www.duncanaviation.com	Lincoln	NE	68501	402-475-2611	475-5541
EADS Barfield Inc 4101 NW 29th St *TF:* 800-321-1039 ■ *Web:* www.barfield.eads.net	Miami	FL	33142	305-894-5400	894-5301
Elliott Aviation Inc PO Box 100 *TF:* 800-447-6711 ■ *Web:* www.elliottaviation.com	Moline	IL	61266	309-799-3183	799-2014
Emery Air Inc 1 Airport Cir PO Box 6067 *TF:* 800-435-8090 ■ *Web:* www.emeryair.net	Rockford	IL	61125	815-968-8287	968-2889
Empire Aero Center 394 Hangar Rd Bldg 101 Griffis Airport *Web:* www.empireacmro.com	Rome	NY	13441	315-838-1530	838-1515
Evergreen International Aviation Inc 3850 Three Mile Ln *TF:* 800-472-9361 ■ *Web:* www.evergreenaviation.com	McMinnville	OR	97128	503-472-9361	472-1048
Evergreen Maintenance Center Inc Pinal Air Park Rd *TF:* 800-624-6838 ■ *Web:* www.evergreenaviation.com/EAC	Marana	AZ	85653	520-682-4181	682-2056
GKN Aerospace Chem-tronics Inc 1150 W Bradley Ave *Web:* www.chem-tronics.com	El Cajon	CA	92020	619-448-2320	258-5270
Hamilton Aerospace Technologies Inc 6901 S Park Ave *Web:* www.hamaerotech.com	Tucson	AZ	85706	520-294-3481	741-1430
Hawker Pacific Aerospace 11240 Sherman Way *Web:* www.hawker.com	Sun Valley	CA	91352	818-765-6201	765-8073

Phone | Fax

Honeywell Inc Aircraft Landing Systems
3520 Westmoor St. ... South Bend IN 46628 574-231-2000 231-2020
TF: 800-707-4555
Jet Aviation 112 Charles A Lindbergh Dr ... Teterboro NJ 07608 201-288-8400 462-4005
TF: 800-538-0832 ■ *Web:* www.jetaviation.com
L-3 Communications Flight International Aviation LLC
1 Lear Dr ... Newport News VA 23602 757-886-5500 874-7481
TF: 800-358-4685 ■ *Web:* www.l-3com.com/fi
Mars Aircraft Radio Service 333 Industrial Ave. ... Teterboro NJ 07608 201-288-0222 288-4366
Martin Aviation 19300 Ike Jones Rd ... Santa Ana CA 92707 714-210-2945 557-0637
TF: 800-793-9191
Maytag Aircraft Corp 6145 Lehman Dr Suite 300 ... Colorado Springs CO 80918 719-593-1600 593-8518
McKinley Air Transport Inc PO Box 2406 ... North Canton OH 44720 330-499-3316 499-0444
TF: 800-225-6446
Mercury Air Group Inc 5456 McConnell Ave ... Los Angeles CA 90066 310-827-2737 827-5510
Web: www.mercuryairgroup.com
Million Air Interlink Inc 8501 Telephone Rd ... Houston TX 77061 713-640-4000 283-8274*
**Fax Area Code:* 866 ■ *TF:* 888-589-9059 ■ *Web:* www.millionair.com
NORDAM Group 6911 N Whirlpool Dr PO Box 3365 ... Tulsa OK 74101 918-587-4105 878-4808*
**Fax:* Sales ■ *Web:* www.nordam.com
Northern Air Inc 5500 44th St SE Bldg 403 ... Grand Rapids MI 49512 616-336-4700 336-4777
TF: 800-262-4953 ■ *Web:* www.northern-air.com
Pemco Aeroplex Inc 1943 50th St N ... Birmingham AL 35212 205-591-7870 592-6306
Web: www.pemcoaviationgroup.com
Pemco Aviation Group Inc 1943 50th St N ... Birmingham AL 35212 205-592-0011 592-0195
NASDAQ: PAGI ■ *Web:* www.pemcoaviationgroup.com
Pemco World Air Services 100 Pemco Dr ... Dothan AL 36303 334-983-4571 983-7046*
**Fax:* Hum Res ■ *Web:* www.pemcoaviationgroup.com
Precision Airmotive LLC 14800 40th Ave NE ... Marysville WA 98271 360-651-8282 651-8080*
**Fax:* Sales ■ *Web:* www.precisionairmotive.com
Priester Aviation 1061 S Wolf Rd ... Wheeling IL 60090 847-537-1133 459-0778
TF: 888-323-7887 ■ *Web:* www.priesterav.com
Rolls-Royce Engine Services Inc 7200 Earhart Rd ... Oakland CA 94621 510-613-1000 635-3221
TF: 800-622-2677 ■ *Web:* www.rolls-royce.com/northamerica/facilities
Sabreliner Corp 7733 Forsyth Blvd Suite 1500 ... Clayton MO 63105 314-863-6880 863-6887
TF: 800-325-4663 ■ *Web:* www.sabreliner.com
Segers 4705 NW 132nd St ... Miami FL 33054 305-688-1211 688-1992
Seneca Flight Operations 2262 Airport Dr ... Penn Yan NY 14527 315-536-4471 536-4558
Web: www.senecaflight.com
Servisair 111 Great Neck Rd Suite 600 ... Great Neck NY 11021 516-487-8610 487-4855
Web: www.servisair.com
Sierra Industries Inc 122 Howard Langford Dr ... Uvalde TX 78801 830-278-4381 278-7649
TF: 888-835-9377 ■ *Web:* www.sijet.com
Sifco Industries Inc 970 E 64th St ... Cleveland OH 44103 216-881-8600 432-6281
AMEX: SIF ■ *Web:* www.sifco.com
ST Mobile Aerospace Engineering Inc
2100 9th St Brookley Complex ... Mobile AL 36615 251-438-8888 438-8892
Standard Aero Ltd 33 Allen Dyne Rd ... Winnipeg MB R3H1A1 204-775-9711 885-2229
TF: 888-836-4433 ■ *Web:* www.standardaero.com
Summit Aviation Inc 4200 Summit Bridge Rd PO Box 258 ... Middletown DE 19709 302-834-5400 378-7035
TF: 800-441-9343 ■ *Web:* www.summit-aviation.com
TAG Aviation Inc 6855 34th Ave S ... Minneapolis MN 55450 612-726-1673 726-9532
TF: 800-726-1673 ■ *Web:* www.tagaviation.com
Telford Aviation Inc 154 Maine Ave ... Bangor ME 04401 207-262-6098 262-8708
TF: 800-639-4809 ■ *Web:* www.telfordaviation.com
TIMCO Aviation Services Inc 623 Radar Rd ... Greensboro NC 27410 336-668-4410 665-0134*
**Fax:* Hum Res
Triumph Accessory Services 411 N West Rd ... Wellington KS 67152 620-326-2235 326-3761
Web: www.triumphgroup.com
Triumph Group Inc 1550 Liberty Ridge Dr Suite 100 ... Wayne PA 19087 610-251-1000 251-1555
NYSE: TGI ■ *Web:* www.triumphgroup.com
Tulsair Beechcraft Inc 2845 N Sheridan Rd PO Box 582470 ... Tulsa OK 74158 918-835-7651 838-8913
TF: 800-331-4071 ■ *Web:* www.tulsair.com
Twin Air Inc 498 SW 34th St ... Fort Lauderdale FL 33315 954-359-8266 359-8271
Web: www.flytwinair.com
West Star Aviation Inc 796 Heritage Way ... Grand Junction CO 81506 970-243-7500 242-5178
TF: 800-255-4193 ■ *Web:* www.weststaraviation.com
Windsor Airmotive 7 Connecticut S Dr ... East Granby CT 06026 860-653-5531 653-0397
Web: www.windsorairmotive.com
Wood Group Turbo Power LLC 14820 NW 60th Ave ... Miami Lakes FL 33014 305-820-3225 820-0404
TF: 800-403-6737 ■ *Web:* www.woodgroupturbopower.com

25 AIRLINES - COMMERCIAL

SEE ALSO Air Cargo Carriers p. 1266; Air Charter Services p. 1266; Airlines - Frequent Flyer Programs p. 1274

Phone | Fax

Aer Lingus 538 Broadhollow Rd Suite 3 ... Melville NY 11747 631-577-5700 752-2044
TF: 800-474-7424 ■ *Web:* www.aerlingus.com
Aeroflot Russian International Airlines 1411 4th Ave Suite 420 ... Seattle WA 98101 206-464-1005 464-0452
Web: www.aeroflot.com
Aerolineas Argentinas 51 E 42nd St Suite 1600 ... New York NY 10017 212-542-8880 542-8881
TF: 800-333-0276 ■ *Web:* www.aeroargentinas.com
AeroMexico 3663 N Sam Houston Pkwy E Suite 500 ... Houston TX 77032 281-372-3420 372-3619
TF: 800-237-6639 ■ *Web:* www.aeromexico.com
Air Canada PO Box 14000 ... Dorval QC H4Y1H4 514-422-5000 237-3563*
**Fax Area Code:* 800 ■ *TF:* 888-247-2262 ■ *Web:* www.aircanada.ca
Air Canada Jazz 310 Goudey Dr ... Enfield NS B2T1E4 902-873-5000 873-2098
TF Cust Svc: 877-942-2274 ■ *Web:* www.flyjazz.ca
Air China 150 E 52 St ... New York NY 10022 212-371-9898 935-7951
TF: 800-982-8802 ■ *Web:* www.airchina.com.cn/en
Air France 125 W 55th St ... New York NY 10019 212-830-4000 830-4299*
**Fax:* Mktg ■ *TF Resv:* 800-237-2747 ■ *Web:* www.airfrance.us
Air India 570 Lexington Ave 15th Fl ... New York NY 10022 212-407-1300 407-1352
TF: 800-223-7776 ■ *Web:* www.airindia.com
Air Jamaica 95-25 Queens Blvd 7th FL ... Rego Park NY 11374 718-830-0622 275-8717
TF: 800-523-5585 ■ *Web:* www.airjamaica.com
Air Midwest Inc DBA US Airways Express 2203 Air Cargo Rd ... Wichita KS 67209 316-942-8137 945-0947
TF: 800-428-4322 ■ *Web:* www.usair.com
Air New Zealand Ltd 1960 E Grand Ave Suite 900 ... El Segundo CA 90245 310-648-7000 648-7017
TF: 800-262-1234 ■ *Web:* www.airnz.com/default.htm
Air Sunshine Inc PO Box 22237 ... Fort Lauderdale FL 33335 954-434-8900 359-8211
TF: 800-327-8900 ■ *Web:* www.airsunshine.com
Air Tahiti Nui 1990 E Grand Ave ... El Segundo CA 90245 310-662-1860 640-3683
TF Cust Svc: 877-824-4846 ■ *Web:* www.airtahitinui-usa.com
Air Wisconsin Airlines Corp W6390 Challenger Dr Suite 203 ... Appleton WI 54914 920-739-5123 749-4233
Web: www.airwis.com
AirTran Airways 9955 AirTran Blvd ... Orlando FL 32827 407-251-5600 251-5727
TF: 800-247-8726 ■ *Web:* www.airtran.com
Alaska Airlines Inc PO Box 68900 ... Seattle WA 98168 206-433-3200 392-5366*
**Fax:* Mktg ■ *TF Resv:* 800-252-7522 ■ *Web:* www.alaskaair.com

Phone | Fax

Alitalia Airlines 350 5th Ave 37th Fl ... New York NY 10118 212-903-3300 903-3541*
**Fax:* Mktg ■ *TF:* 800-223-5730 ■ *Web:* www.alitaliausa.com
All Nippon Airways Co Ltd 1251 Ave of the Americas 8th Fl ... New York NY 10020 800-235-9262 840-5858*
**Fax Area Code:* 212 ■ *Web:* www.ana.co.jp/eng/index.html
Allegiant Air 3301 N Buffalo Dr Suite B-9 ... Las Vegas NV 89129 702-851-7300 851-7301
TF Resv: 800-432-3810 ■ *Web:* www.allegiantair.com
American Airlines Inc PO Box 619616 ... DFW Airport TX 75261 817-963-1234 967-4162*
**Fax:* Cust Svc ■ *TF:* 800-433-7300 ■ *Web:* www.aa.com
American Eagle 835 Airport Dr ... San Luis Obispo CA 93401 805-541-1010 541-1756
Web: www.aa.com
Asiana Airlines Inc 3530 Wilshire Blvd Suite 1700 ... Los Angeles CA 90010 213-365-4500 365-9630
TF: 800-227-4262 ■ *Web:* us.flyasiana.com
Atlantic Southeast Airlines Inc
100 Hartsfield Ctr Pkwy Suite 800 ... Atlanta GA 30354 404-766-1400 209-0162
Web: www.flyasa.com
Austrian Airlines 1720 Whitestone Expy Suite 500 ... Whitestone NY 11357 718-670-8600 670-8619
TF: 800-843-0002 ■ *Web:* www.aua.com/us
Avianca Airlines 8350 NW 52nd Terr Suite 100 ... Miami FL 33166 800-284-2622 599-7282*
**Fax Area Code:* 305 ■ *Web:* www.avianca.com
Bearskin Airlines PO Box 1447 ... Sioux Lookout ON P8T1C1 807-737-3474 737-3093
TF: 800-465-2327 ■ *Web:* www.bearskinairlines.com
Bering Air PO Box 1650 ... Nome AK 99762 907-443-5422 443-5919
Web: www.beringair.com
Big Sky Airlines 1601 Aviation Pl ... Billings MT 59105 406-247-3910 247-3972*
**Fax:* Cust Svc ■ *TF:* 800-237-7788 ■ *Web:* www.bigskyair.com
British Airways 75-20 Astoria Blvd ... Jackson Heights NY 11370 347-418-4000 418-4395
TF: 800-247-9297 ■ *Web:* www.britishairways.com
BWIA International Airways 5805 Blue Lagoon Dr Suite 340 ... Miami FL 33126 305-261-0393 262-7458
TF: 800-327-0204 ■ *Web:* www.bwee.com
CanJet Airlines PO Box 980 ... Enfield NS B2T1R6 902-873-7800 973-6580
TF Resv: 800-809-7777 ■ *Web:* www.canjet.com
Cape Air 660 Barnstable Rd ... Hyannis MA 02601 508-771-6944 775-8815
TF: 800-352-0714 ■ *Web:* www.flycapeair.com
Cathay Pacific Airways 1960 E Grand Ave Suite 540 ... El Segundo CA 90245 310-615-1113 615-0042
TF: 800-233-2742 ■ *Web:* www.cathay-usa.com
Cathay Pacific Airways Canada 550 W 6th Ave Suite 500 ... Vancouver BC V5Z4S2 604-606-8888 606-2938
Web: www.cathaypacific.com
Cayman Airways Ltd 8400 NW 52nd St Suite 210 ... Miami FL 33166 305-266-6760 267-2925
TF: 800-422-9626 ■ *Web:* www.caymanairways.com
Chautauqua Airlines Inc 2500 S High School Rd Suite 160 ... Indianapolis IN 46241 317-484-6000 484-6040
Web: www.flychautauqua.com
China Airlines Ltd 200 Continental Blvd ... El Segundo CA 90245 310-322-3888 322-8888
TF: 800-227-5118 ■ *Web:* www.china-airlines.com
Comair Delta Connection 77 Comair Blvd ... Erlanger KY 41018 859-767-2550 767-2960
TF: 800-727-2550 ■ *Web:* www.comair.com
Continental Airlines Inc 1600 Smith St ... Houston TX 77002 713-324-5000 214-0506*
NYSE: CAL ■ **Fax Area Code:* 800 ■ *TF:* 800-525-0280 ■ *Web:* www.continental.com
Continental Express 1600 Smith St HQSCE ... Houston TX 77002 713-324-5000 324-4420
NYSE: XJT ■ *TF:* 877-324-2639 ■ *Web:* www.expressjet.com
Czech Airlines 1350 Ave of the Americas Suite 601 ... New York NY 10019 212-765-6545 765-6588
TF: 800-223-2365 ■ *Web:* www.csa.cz/en
Delta Air Lines Inc
PO Box 20706 Hartsfiled-Atlanta International Airport ... Atlanta GA 30320 404-715-2600 715-1400
TF: 800-221-1212 ■ *Web:* www.delta.com
Delta Connection 444 S River Rd ... Saint George UT 84790 435-634-3000 634-3506
TF: 800-221-1212 ■ *Web:* www.comair.com/about/deltaconnection/
EgyptAir 19 W 44th St Suite 170 ... New York NY 10036 212-581-5600 586-6599
TF: 800-334-6787 ■ *Web:* www.egyptair.com.eg
El Al Israel Airlines Ltd 15 E 26th St 6th Fl ... New York NY 10010 212-852-0600 768-9440
TF: 800-223-6700 ■ *Web:* www.elal.co.il
Era Aviation Inc 6160 Carl Brady Dr ... Anchorage AK 99502 907-243-6633 266-8350
TF: 800-866-8394 ■ *Web:* www.flyera.com
Ethiopian Airlines 336 E 45th St 3rd Fl ... New York NY 10017 212-867-0095 692-9589
TF: 800-445-2733 ■ *Web:* www.flyethiopian.com
EVA Airways 12440 E Imperial Hwy Suite 250 ... Norwalk CA 90650 562-565-6000 565-6120
TF: 800-695-1188 ■ *Web:* www.evaair.com
ExpressJet Airlines Inc 1600 Smith St HQSCE ... Houston TX 77002 713-324-5000 324-4420
NYSE: XJT ■ *TF:* 877-324-2639 ■ *Web:* www.expressjet.com
Finnair 228 E 45th St ... New York NY 10017 212-499-9000 499-9040
TF: 800-950-5000 ■ *Web:* www.finnair.fi
Frontier Airlines 7001 Tower Rd ... Denver CO 80249 720-374-4200 374-4622
TF: 800-265-5505 ■ *Web:* www.frontierairlines.com
Frontier Flying Service Inc 5245 Airport Industrial Rd ... Fairbanks AK 99709 907-450-7250 450-7274
TF Resv: 800-478-6779 ■ *Web:* www.frontierflying.com
Garuda Indonesian Airlines 3050 Post Oak Blvd Suite 1320 ... Houston TX 77056 713-877-1942 626-1905
TF: 800-342-7832 ■ *Web:* www.garuda-indonesia.com
Great Lakes Airlines 1022 Airport Pkwy ... Cheyenne WY 82001 307-432-7000 432-7071*
**Fax:* Hum Res ■ *TF:* 800-554-5111 ■ *Web:* www.greatlakesav.com
Great Lakes Aviation Ltd DBA Great Lakes Airlines
1022 Airport Pkwy ... Cheyenne WY 82001 307-432-7000 432-7071*
**Fax:* Hum Res ■ *TF:* 800-554-5111 ■ *Web:* www.greatlakesav.com
Grupo Taca PO Box 590628 ... Miami FL 33159 305-871-1587 871-2667
TF: 800-251-1351
Gulfstream International Airlines 3201 Griffin Rd 4th Fl ... Fort Lauderdale FL 33312 954-985-1500 985-5245
TF: 800-457-4853 ■ *Web:* www.gulfstreamair.com
Hawaiian Airlines Inc 3375 Koapaka St Suite G350 ... Honolulu HI 96819 808-835-3700 838-6777
AMEX: HA ■ *TF:* 800-367-5320 ■ *Web:* www.hawaiianair.com
Horizon Air Industries Inc
19521 International Blvd PO Box 68977 ... Seattle WA 98168 206-241-6757 431-4696
TF: 800-523-1223 ■ *Web:* www.alaskaair.com
Iberia Airlines of Spain 5835 Blue Lagoon Dr Suite 350 ... Miami FL 33126 305-267-7747 262-8763
TF: 800-772-4642 ■ *Web:* www.iberia.com
Icelandair 5950 Symphony Woods Rd Suite 410 ... Columbia MD 21044 410-715-1600 715-3547
TF: 800-223-5500 ■ *Web:* www.icelandair.net
Island Express Airlines 650 SW 34th St Suite 306 ... Fort Lauderdale FL 33315 954-359-0380 359-7944
Web: oii.net/islandexpress
Japan Airlines 461 5th Ave 6th Fl ... New York NY 10017 212-838-4400 310-1321
TF: 800-525-3663 ■ *Web:* www.japanair.com
Jat Airways 274 Madison Ave Suite 1500 ... New York NY 10016 212-689-1677 689-2583
Web: www.jat.com
JetBlue Airways 118-29 Queens Blvd ... Forest Hills NY 11375 718-286-7900 709-3621
TF: 800-538-2583 ■ *Web:* www.jetblue.com
Kenmore Air Harbor Inc 6321 NE 175th St ... Kenmore WA 98028 425-486-1257 485-4774
TF: 800-543-9595 ■ *Web:* www.kenmoreair.com
KLM Royal Dutch Airlines 2700 Lone Oak Pkwy ... Eagan MN 55121 612-726-2111 726-0776
TF: 800-225-2525 ■ *Web:* www.klm.com
Korean Air 6101 W Imperial Hwy ... Los Angeles CA 90045 310-417-5200 417-3051
TF: 800-438-5000 ■ *Web:* www.koreanair.com
Kuwait Airways 400 Kelby St 18th Fl ... Fort Lee NJ 07024 201-582-9222 947-8113
Web: www.kuwait-airways.com
L A B Flying Service Inc PO Box 272 ... Haines AK 99827 907-766-2222 766-2734
Web: labflying.com
LAB Airlines 225 SE 1st St ... Miami FL 33131 305-374-4600 503-8194*
**Fax:* Sales ■ *TF:* 800-337-0918 ■ *Web:* www.labairlines.com
LACSA 3600 Wilshire Blvd Suite 100P ... Los Angeles CA 90010 213-385-9424 385-5880
TF Sales: 800-225-2272 ■ *Web:* www.taca.com

	City	State	Zip	Phone	Fax
LanChile Airlines 6500 NW 22nd St 11th Fl. *TF:* 866-435-9526 ■ *Web:* www7.lan.com	Miami	FL	33122	305-670-1961	
LanPeru Airlines Miami International Airport Concourse A Level 2 *TF:* 800-735-5526 ■ *Web:* www7.lan.com	Miami	FL	33122	305-670-9999	670-5960
Lauda Air 1155 Connecticut Ave NW Suite 602 *TF:* 800-843-0002 ■ *Web:* www.aua.com/at/eng/Austrian/lauda	Washington	DC	20036	202-955-0023	293-0410
Lloyd Aereo Boliviano DBA LAB Airlines 225 SE 1st St **Fax:* Sales ■ *TF:* 800-337-0918 ■ *Web:* www.labairlines.com	Miami	FL	33131	305-374-4600	503-8194*
LOT Polish Airlines 500 5th Ave Suite 408 *TF:* 800-223-0593 ■ *Web:* www.lot.com	New York	NY	10110	212-869-1074	768-2981
LTU International Airways 20803 Biscayne Blvd Suite 401 *TF:* 866-266-5588 ■ *Web:* www.ltu.com	North Miami Beach	FL	33180	305-932-1595	932-1545
Lufthansa USA 1640 Hempstead Tpke **Fax:* Sales ■ *TF Resv:* 800-581-6400 ■ *Web:* www.lufthansa-usa.com	East Meadow	NY	11554	516-296-9200	296-9490*
Lynx Air International 3402 SW 9th Ave *TF:* 888-596-9247 ■ *Web:* www.lynxair.com	Fort Lauderdale	FL	33315	954-772-9808	772-1141
Malaysia Airlines 100 N Sepulveda Blvd Suite 400 *TF:* 800-552-9264 ■ *Web:* www.malaysiaairlines.com	El Segundo	CA	90245	310-535-9288	726-6260
Malev-Hungarian Airlines 90 John St Suite 312 *TF:* 800-223-6884 ■ *Web:* www.hungarianairlines.com	New York	NY	10038	212-566-9944	566-9950
Malev-Hungarian Airlines Canada 175 Bloor St E Suite 909 *Web:* www.malevhungarianairlines.com	Toronto	ON	M4W3R8	416-944-0093	944-0095
Martinair 5550 Glades Rd Suite 600 *TF:* 800-627-8462 ■ *Web:* www.martinairusa.com	Boca Raton	FL	33431	561-391-6165	750-3073
Mesa Airlines 410 N 44th St Suite 700 *TF:* 800-637-2247 ■ *Web:* www.mesa-air.com	Phoenix	AZ	85008	602-685-4000	685-4350
Mesaba Airlines Inc DBA Northwest Airlink 1000 Blue Gentian Rd Suite 200 *Web:* www.mesaba.com	Eagan	MN	55121	651-367-5000	367-5392
Mexicana Airlines 6151 W Century Blvd Suite 1124 *TF:* 800-531-7923 ■ *Web:* www.mexicana.com	Los Angeles	CA	90045	310-646-0401	216-5714
Midwest Airlines Inc 6744 S Howell Ave **Fax:* Mktg ■ *TF:* 800-452-2022 ■ *Web:* www.midwestairlines.com	Oak Creek	WI	53154	414-570-4000	570-0199*
New England Airlines Inc 56 Airport Rd *TF:* 800-243-2460 ■ *Web:* www.block-island.com/nea	Westerly	RI	02891	401-596-2460	596-7366
Northwest Airlines Inc 2700 Lone Oak Pkwy *TF:* 800-225-2525 ■ *Web:* www.nwa.com	Eagan	MN	55121	612-726-2111	726-0776
Northwest Airlink 1000 Blue Gentian Rd Suite 200 *Web:* www.mesaba.com	Eagan	MN	55121	651-367-5000	367-5392
Olympic Airways 7000 Austin St *TF:* 800-736-5717 ■ *Web:* www.olympicairlines.com	Forest Hills	NY	11375	718-269-2200	269-2212
Pacific Wings Kahului Airport Commuter Terminal 1 Kahului Airport Rd *TF:* 888-575-4547 ■ *Web:* www.pacificwings.com	Kahului	HI	96732	808-873-0877	873-7920
Pakistan International Airlines Corp 505 8th Ave 14th Fl *TF:* 800-221-2552 ■ *Web:* www.piac.com.pk	New York	NY	10018	212-760-8484	971-5434
Peninsula Airways Inc 6100 Boeing Ave *TF:* 800-448-4226 ■ *Web:* www.penair.com	Anchorage	AK	99502	907-243-2485	243-6848
Philippine Airlines Inc 116 McDonnell Rd *TF Resv:* 800-435-9725 ■ *Web:* www.philippineairlines.com	San Francisco	CA	94128	650-877-4818	871-2627
Piedmont Airlines Inc DBA US Airways Express 5443 Airport Terminal Rd *TF:* 800-354-3394 ■ *Web:* piedmont-airlines.com	Salisbury	MD	21804	410-742-2996	742-3968
Pinnacle Airlines Inc 1689 Nonconnah Blvd Suite 111 *NASDAQ: PNCL* ■ *TF:* 800-603-4594 ■ *Web:* www.nwairlink.com	Memphis	TN	38132	901-348-4100	348-4130
PSA Airlines Inc DBA US Airways Express 3400 Terminal Dr *TF:* 800-235-0986 ■ *Web:* www.psaairlines.net	Vandalia	OH	45377	937-454-1116	454-5828
Qantas Airways Ltd 6080 Center Dr Suite 400 *TF:* 800-227-4500 ■ *Web:* www.qantas.com	Los Angeles	CA	90045	310-726-1400	726-1485
Qatar Airways 399 Thornall St *TF:* 877-777-2827 ■ *Web:* www.qatarairways.com	Edison	NJ	08837	732-321-1701	321-0057
Royal Air Maroc 55 E 59th St Suite 17B *TF:* 800-344-6726 ■ *Web:* www.royalairmaroc.com	New York	NY	10022	212-750-5115	754-4215
Royal Jordanian Airlines 6 E 43rd St 27th Fl *TF:* 800-223-0470 ■ *Web:* www.rja.com.jo/	New York	NY	10017	212-949-0060	949-0488
Royal Nepal Airlines North America 16250 Ventura Blvd Suite 115 **Fax Area Code:* 818 ■ *Web:* www.royalnepal.com	Encino	CA	91436	800-266-3725	501-2098*
Saudi Arabian Airlines 12555 N Burrough Dr *TF:* 800-472-8342 ■ *Web:* www.saudiairlines.com	Houston	TX	77067	281-873-1000	873-1069
Scandinavian Airlines System 9 Polito Ave *TF:* 800-221-2350 ■ *Web:* www.scandinavian.net	Lyndhurst	NJ	07071	201-896-3600	896-3723
Singapore Airlines Ltd 5670 Wilshire Blvd 18th Fl *TF:* 800-742-3333 ■ *Web:* www.singaporeair.com	Los Angeles	CA	90036	323-934-8833	934-4482
Skyservice Airlines Inc 31 Fasken Dr *TF:* 800-701-9448 ■ *Web:* www.skyserviceairlines.com	Etobicoke	ON	M9W1K6	416-679-5700	679-5920
SkyWest Airlines 444 S River Rd *Web:* www.skywest.com	Saint George	UT	84790	435-634-3000	634-3506
Song Airways LLC PO Box 20504 *Web:* www.flysong.com	Atlanta	GA	30320	800-221-1212	
South African Airways 515 E Las Olas Blvd 16th Fl **Fax:* Sales ■ *TF:* 800-722-9675 ■ *Web:* www.flysaa.com/saa_home.jhtml	Fort Lauderdale	FL	33301	954-769-5000	769-5079*
Southwest Airlines Co 2702 Love Field Dr *NYSE: LUV* ■ *TF Resv:* 800-435-9792 ■ *Web:* www.southwest.com	Dallas	TX	75235	214-792-4000	792-5015
Spirit Airlines Inc 2800 Executive Way *TF:* 800-772-7117 ■ *Web:* www.spiritair.com	Miramar	FL	33025	954-447-7965	447-7979
SriLankan Airlines 111 Woods Ave S **Fax Area Code:* 732 ■ *TF:* 877-915-2652 ■ *Web:* www.srilankan.aero	Iselin	NJ	08830	877-915-2652	205-0299*
Sun Country Airlines Inc 1300 Mendota Heights Rd *TF:* 800-359-6786 ■ *Web:* www.suncountry.com	Mendota Heights	MN	55120	651-681-3900	681-3970
Surinam Airways Ltd 7270 NW 12th St Suite 255 *TF:* 800-327-6864 ■ *Web:* www.surinamairways.net	Miami	FL	33126	305-599-1196	591-3466
Swiss International Airlines Ltd 10 E 53rd St *Web:* www.swiss.com	New York	NY	10022	877-359-7947	
TACA International Airlines 7795 W Flagler St Suite 45 **Fax Area Code:* 504 ■ *TF:* 800-535-8780 ■ *Web:* www.taca.com	Miami	FL	33144	800-535-8780	888-3746*
TAP Air Portugal 399 Market St *TF Resv:* 800-221-7370 ■ *Web:* www.flytap.com	Newark	NJ	07105	973-344-4490	344-7344
Thai Airways International Ltd 222 N Sepulveda Blvd Suite 1950 **Fax:* Sales ■ *TF:* 800-426-5204 ■ *Web:* www.thaiair.com	El Segundo	CA	90245	310-640-0097	640-8202*
Turkish Airlines 437 Madison Ave **Fax Area Code:* 212 ■ *Web:* www.turkishairlines.com	New York	NY	10022	800-874-8875	339-9680*
Ukraine International Airlines 1643-A W Henderson St *TF:* 800-876-0114 ■ *Web:* www.ukraine-international.com/eng	Cleburne	TX	76033	817-641-3478	641-4477
United Airlines Inc PO Box 66100 *TF:* 800-241-6522 ■ *Web:* www.united.com	Chicago	IL	60666	847-700-4000	700-2214
United Express 1200 E Algonquin Rd *TF:* 800-241-6522	Elk Grove Township	IL	60007	847-700-4000	700-2534
US Airways Express 111 Rio Salado Pkwy *TF:* 800-428-4322 ■ *Web:* www.usairways.com	Tempe	AZ	85284	480-693-0800	693-5506
US Airways Express 2203 Air Cargo Rd *TF:* 800-428-4322 ■ *Web:* www.usair.com	Wichita	KS	67209	316-942-8137	945-0947
US Airways Express 5443 Airport Terminal Rd *TF:* 800-354-3394 ■ *Web:* piedmont-airlines.com	Salisbury	MD	21804	410-742-2996	742-3968
US Airways Express 3400 Terminal Dr *TF:* 800-235-0986 ■ *Web:* www.psaairlines.net	Vandalia	OH	45377	937-454-1116	454-5828
US Airways Inc 111 Rio Salado Pkwy *TF:* 800-428-4322 ■ *Web:* www.usairways.com	Tempe	AZ	85284	480-693-0800	693-5506
US Airways Shuttle Inc La Guardia Airport *TF:* 800-428-4322	Flushing	NY	11371	718-397-6200	397-6040
USA 3000 Airlines 335 Bishop Hollow Rd Suite 100 *TF:* 877-872-3000 ■ *Web:* www.usa3000.com	Newtown Square	PA	19073	610-325-1280	325-1285
Varig Brasil Airlines 14411 Commerce Way Suite 200 *TF:* 800-468-2744 ■ *Web:* www.varig.com	Miami Lakes	FL	33016	786-522-2400	522-2409
Virgin Atlantic Airways Ltd 747 Belden Ave **Fax:* Mktg ■ *TF:* 800-862-8621 ■ *Web:* www.virgin-atlantic.com	Norwalk	CT	06850	203-750-2000	750-6430*
WestJet Airlines Ltd 5055 11th St NE *TSX: WJA* ■ *TF:* 888-293-7853 ■ *Web:* www.westjet.com	Calgary	AB	T2E8N4	403-444-2600	444-2301

26 AIRLINES - FREQUENT FLYER PROGRAMS

	City	State	Zip	Phone	Fax
Aer Lingus Airlines Gold Circle Club 538 Broadhollow Rd **Fax Area Code:* 631 ■ *Web:* www.aerlingus.com	Melville	NY	11747	800-474-7424	752-2044*
AeroMexico Club Premier 3663 N Sam Houston Pkwy E Suite 500 **Fax Area Code:* 281 ■ *Web:* www.aeromexico.com	Houston	TX	77032	800-247-3737	372-3602*
Air Canada Aeroplan PO Box 7737 Station Terminal *TF:* 866-689-8080 ■ *Web:* www.aircanada.com/en/aeroplan/	Vancouver	BC	V6B5W9	800-361-5373	
Air China Companion Club 150 E 52nd St *TF:* 800-982-8802 ■ *Web:* ffp.airchina.com.cn/EN	New York	NY	10022	212-371-9898	935-7951
Air France Frequence Plus 235 King St E *TF:* 800-375-8723 ■ *Web:* www.airfrance.com	Kitchener	ON	N2G4N5	519-772-3570	744-9692
Air Jamaica 7th Heaven 8300 NW 33rd St Suite 440 *TF:* 800-523-5585 ■ *Web:* www.airjamaica.com	Miami	FL	33122	305-670-3222	669-6631
Air New Zealand Airpoints 1960 E Grand Ave Suite 300 *TF:* 800-223-9494 ■ *Web:* www.airnz.com/airpoints	El Segundo	CA	90245	800-262-1234	272-9494
AirTran Airways A-Plus Rewards 1224 Bob Harman Rd **Fax Area Code:* 912 ■ *Web:* www.airtran.com/programs/aplus	Savannah	GA	31408	888-327-5878	966-6376*
Alaska Airlines Mileage Plan PO Box 24948 Customer Service Ctr **Fax Area Code:* 206 ■ *Web:* www.alaskaair.com/mileageplan/MPtoc.asp	Seattle	WA	98124	800-654-5669	433-3477*
Alitalia Airlines MilleMiglia Club 350 5th Ave 36th Fl **Fax Area Code:* 212 ■ *TF:* 800-223-5730 ■ *Web:* www.alitaliausa.com/millemiglia/index.htm	New York	NY	10118	800-223-5730	903-3331*
All Nippon Airways Mileage Club (ANA) 2050 W 190th St Suite 100 *TF:* 800-262-4653 ■ *Web:* www.anaskyweb.com/us/e/amc/index.html	Torrance	CA	90504	310-782-3000	782-3185
American Airlines AAdvantage Program PO Box 619620 **Fax Area Code:* 817 ■ *Web:* www.aa.com	DFW Airport	TX	75261	800-882-8880	963-7882*
Asiana Airlines Asiana Club 3530 Wilshire Blvd Suite 1700 *TF Resv:* 800-227-4262 ■ *Web:* us.flyasiana.com	Los Angeles	CA	90010	213-365-4500	365-9630
British Airways Executive Club PO Box 1757 **Fax Area Code:* 763 ■ *Web:* www.britishairways.com	Minneapolis	MN	55440	800-955-2748	212-5494*
China Airlines Dynasty Flyer 6053 W Century Blvd Suite 800 **Fax Area Code:* 310 ■ *TF:* 800-227-5118 ■ *Web:* www.china-airlines.com	Los Angeles	CA	90045	800-227-5118	641-0864*
Club Tiare 1990 E Grand Ave Suite 320 *TF:* 877-824-4846 ■ *Web:* www.airtahitinui-usa.com	El Segundo	CA	90245	310-662-1860	640-3683
Continental Airlines OnePass 900 Grand Plaza Dr PO Box 4365 *TF:* 800-621-7467 ■ *Web:* www.continental.com/onepass	Houston	TX	77210	713-952-1630	
Czech Airlines OK Plus 1350 Ave of the Americas Suite 601 *TF:* 800-223-2365 ■ *Web:* www.csa.cz/en/okplus/okplus_home.htm	New York	NY	10019	212-765-6545	765-6588
Delta Air Lines SkyMiles SkyMiles Service Ctr Dept 654 PO Box 20532 **Fax Area Code:* 404 ■ *Web:* www.delta.com/skymiles	Atlanta	GA	30320	800-323-2323	773-1945*
EgyptAir Plus 19 W 44th St Suite 1701 *TF:* 800-334-6787 ■ *Web:* www.egyptair.com.eg/docs/frequent.htm	New York	NY	10036	212-581-5600	586-6599
El Al Israel Airlines Matmid Frequent Flyer Club 15 E 26th St *TF:* 800-223-6700 ■ *Web:* www.elal.co.il	New York	NY	10010	212-852-0604	852-0632
EVA Air Evergreen Club 12440 E Imperial Hwy Suite 250 *TF:* 800-695-1188 ■ *Web:* www.evaair.com	Norwalk	CA	90650	562-565-6000	565-6120
Finnair Plus 228 E 45th St **Fax Area Code:* 212 ■ *Web:* www.finnair.com	New York	NY	10017	800-950-3387	499-9036*
Frontier Airlines EarlyReturns PO Box 17304 *TF Cust Svc:* 800-265-5505 ■ *Web:* www.frontierairlines.com/travel/early_returns.asp	Denver	CO	80217	866-263-2759	
GlobalPass 6355 NW 36th St Suite 600 *TF:* 877-946-4537 ■ *Web:* www.globalpass.com	Miami	FL	33166	305-870-7500	870-7555
Hawaiian Airlines HawaiianMiles PO Box 30008 **Fax Area Code:* 808 ■ *Web:* www.hawaiianair.com/hawaiianmiles	Honolulu	HI	96820	877-426-4537	838-6735*
Iberia Airlines Plus Program 5835 Blue Lagoon Dr Suite 350 *TF:* 800-721-4122 ■ *Web:* www.iberia.com	Miami	FL	33126	800-271-4122	
Icelandair Customer Club 5950 Symphony Woods Rd Suite 410 **Fax Area Code:* 410 ■ *TF:* 800-223-5500 ■ *Web:* www.icelandair.com	Columbia	MD	21044	800-757-7242	715-3547*
Japan Airlines Mileage Bank 300 Continental Blvd Suite 401 **Fax Area Code:* 310 ■ *Web:* www.jal.co.jp/en/jalmile	El Segundo	CA	90245	800-525-6453	414-0149*
Jat Airways One Flight More 274 Madison Ave Suite 1500 *Web:* www.jat.com	New York	NY	10016	212-689-1677	689-2583
JetBlue TrueBlue 6322 S 3000 East Fl G-1 Suite G-10 *TF:* 800-538-2583 ■ *Web:* www.jetblue.com/trueblue	Salt Lake City	UT	84121	801-365-2528	365-2480
Korean Air Skypass 1813 Wilshire Blvd Suite 400 **Fax Area Code:* 213 ■ *Web:* www.koreanair.com	Los Angeles	CA	90057	800-525-4480	484-5790*
Kuwait Airways Oasis Club 400 Kelby St 18th Fl *Web:* www.oasisclub-ku.com	Fort Lee	NJ	07024	201-582-9222	947-8113
LanPass 6500 NW 2nd St *TF:* 866-435-9526 ■ *Web:* www.lan.com/lanpass/index.html	Miami	FL	33010	305-670-9999	
Mabuhay Miles 116 McDonnell Rd *Web:* www.mabuhaymiles.com	San Francisco	CA	94128	800-747-1959	
Malev Hungarian Airlines Duna Club 90 John St Suite 312 *TF:* 800-223-6884 ■ *Web:* www.hungarianairlines.com	New York	NY	10038	212-566-9944	566-9950
Mexicana Airlines Frecuenta 482 W San Ysidro Blvd Suite 754 **Fax Area Code:* 949 ■ *Web:* www.mexicana.com	San Ysidro	CA	92173	800-531-7901	608-6646*
Midwest Airlines Midwest Miles 6744 S Howell Ave Dept 16 *TF:* 800-452-2022 ■ *Web:* www.midwestairlines.com	Oak Creek	WI	53154	414-570-4000	570-0192
Miles & More PO Box 946 **Fax Area Code:* 661 ■ *Web:* www.milesandmore.com	Santa Clarita	CA	91380	800-581-6400	295-8719*
Northwest Airlines WorldPerks 601 Oak St **Fax Area Code:* 218 ■ *Web:* www.nwa.com/freqfly	Chisholm	MN	55719	800-447-3757	254-7567*
Qantas Airways Frequent Flyer Program 6080 Center Dr **Fax Area Code:* 310 ■ *TF:* 800-227-4220 ■ *Web:* www.qantas.com.au	Los Angeles	CA	90045	800-227-4220	726-1401*
Qatar Airways Privilege Club 399 Thornall St *TF:* 877-777-2827 ■ *Web:* www.qmiles.net	Edison	NJ	08837	732-321-1701	321-0057

Phone | Fax

Saudi Arabian Airlines Alfursan Program
12555 N Burrough Dr ... Houston TX 77067 281-873-1000 873-1069
TF: 800-472-8342 ■ *Web:* www.saudiairlines.com/alfursan/alfursanprogram.jsp

Scandinavian Airlines System EuroBonus (SAS) 9 Polito Ave ... Lyndhurst NJ 07071 800-437-5807 896-3729*
**Fax Area Code:* 201 ■ *Web:* www.scandinavian.net

Singapore Airlines KrisFlyer 5670 Wilshire Blvd Suite 1900 ... Los Angeles CA 90036 800-742-3333 934-4482*
**Fax Area Code:* 323 ■ *Web:* www.krisflyer.com

South African Airways Voyager
515 E Las Olas Blvd Sun Trust Bldg 16th Fl ... Fort Lauderdale FL 33301 954-769-5000 769-5079
TF: 800-359-7220 ■ *Web:* www.saa.co.za

Southwest Airlines Rapid Rewards PO Box 36657 ... Dallas TX 75235 214-792-4223 792-6560
Web: www.southwest.com/rapid_rewards

SriLankan Airlines Skywards 111 Wood Ave S ... Iselin NJ 08830 877-915-2652 205-0299*
**Fax Area Code:* 752 ■ *TF:* 877-915-2652 ■
Web: www.srilankan.aero/frequent/skywards.shtml

Thai Airways Royal Orchid Plus
222 N Sepulveda Blvd Suite 1950 ... El Segundo CA 90245 800-426-5204 322-8728*
**Fax Area Code:* 310 ■ *Web:* www.thaiair.com/Royal_Orchid_Plus/default.htm

Turkish Airlines Miles & Miles 437 Madison Ave ... New York NY 10022 800-874-8875 339-3680*
**Fax Area Code:* 212 ■ *Web:* www.flyturkish.com/codeshare.htm

Ukraine International Airlines Panorama Club
1643-A W Henderson ... Cleburne TX 76033 817-641-3478 641-4477
TF: 800-876-0114 ■ *Web:* www.ukraine-international.com/eng/club/club

United Airlines Mileage Plus PO Box 6120 ... Rapid City SD 57709 800-421-4655
Web: www.united.com

US Airways Dividend Miles Program PO Box 5 ... Winston-Salem NC 27102 800-428-4322 661-8216*
**Fax Area Code:* 336 ■ *TF:* 800-428-4322 ■ *Web:* www.usairways.com/dividendmiles

Varig Brasil Airlines Smiles Program
71 S Central Ave 2nd FL ... Valley Stream NY 11580 516-612-0339 612-0201
TF: 800-468-2744 ■ *Web:* www.tsbot.de/company_details_46_varig-brasil_eng.html

Virgin Atlantic Flying Club 747 Belden Ave ... Norwalk CT 06850 800-365-9500 750-6450*
**Fax Area Code:* 203 ■ *TF:* 800-365-9500 ■
Web: www.virgin-atlantic.com/en/us/frequentflyer/index.jsp

27 AIRPORTS

SEE ALSO Ports & Port Authorities p. 2130

Listings for airports in the US and Canada are organized by states and provinces, and then by city names within those groupings.

Phone | Fax

Birmingham International Airport (BHM) ... Birmingham AL 35212 205-595-0533 599-0538
Web: www.bhamintlairport.com

Huntsville International Airport (HSV) ... Huntsville AL 35824 256-772-9395 772-0305
Web: www.hsvairport.org/airport

Mobile Regional Airport (MOB) ... Mobile AL 36608 251-633-4510 639-7437
TF: 800-357-5373 ■ *Web:* www.mobairport.com

Montgomery Regional Airport (MGM) ... Montgomery AL 36108 334-281-5040 281-5041
Web: www.montgomeryairport.org

Ted Stevens Anchorage International Airport (ANC) ... Anchorage AK 99502 907-266-2526 266-2458
Web: www.anchorageairport.com

Fairbanks International Airport (FAI) ... Fairbanks AK 99709 907-474-2500 474-2513

Juneau International Airport (JNU) ... Juneau AK 99801 907-789-7821 789-1227
Web: www.juneau.org/airport/

Calgary International Airport (YYC) ... Calgary AB T2E6W5 403-735-1200 735-1281
TF: 877-254-7427 ■ *Web:* www.calgaryairport.com

Edmonton International Airport (YEG) ... Edmonton AB T5J2T2 780-890-8382 890-8269
TF: 800-268-7134 ■ *Web:* www.edmontonairports.com

Flagstaff Pulliam Airport (FLG) ... Flagstaff AZ 86001 928-774-7435 556-1288

Phoenix Sky Harbor International Airport (PHX) ... Phoenix AZ 85034 602-273-3300 683-4887
Web: phoenix.gov/AVIATION

Tucson International Airport (TUS) ... Tucson AZ 85706 520-573-8100 573-8008
Web: www.tucsonairport.org

Northwest Arkansas Regional Airport (XNA) Suite 100 ... Bentonville AR 72712 479-205-1000 205-1001
Web: www.nwara.com

Fort Smith Regional Airport (FSM) ... Fort Smith AR 72903 479-452-7000 452-7008
Web: www.fortsmithairport.com

Hot Springs Memorial Field (HOT) ... Hot Springs AR 71913 501-624-3306 321-6754
Web: www.hotspringsairport.net

Little Rock National Airport/Adams Field (LIT) ... Little Rock AR 72202 501-372-3439 372-0612
Web: lrn-airport.com

Vancouver International Airport (YVR) ... Vancouver BC V7B1Y7 604-207-7077
Web: www.yvr.ca

Meadows Field Airport (BFL) ... Bakersfield CA 93308 661-391-1800 391-1801
Web: www.meadowsfield.com

Bob Hope Airport (BUR) ... Burbank CA 91505 818-840-8840 848-1173
Web: www.bobhopeairport.com

Burbank-Glendale-Pasadena Airport ... Burbank CA 91505 818-840-8840 848-1173
Web: www.bobhopeairport.com

Fresno Yosemite International Airport (FYI) ... Fresno CA 93727 559-621-4500 251-4825
TF: 800-244-2359 ■ *Web:* www.flyfresno.org

Long Beach Airport (LGB) ... Long Beach CA 90808 562-570-2600 570-2601
Web: www.longbeach.gov/airport/

Los Angeles International Airport (LAX) ... Los Angeles CA 90045 310-646-5252 646-0523
Web: www.los-angeles-lax.com

Modesto City Airport (MOD) ... Modesto CA 95354 209-577-5318 576-1985
Web: www.modairport.com

Monterey Peninsula Airport (MRY) ... Monterey CA 93940 831-648-7000 373-2625
Web: www.montereyairport.com

Oakland International Airport (OAK) ... Oakland CA 94621 510-577-4000 430-9392
TF: 888-247-6255 ■ *Web:* www.flyoakland.com

Ontario International Airport (ONT) ... Ontario CA 91761 909-937-2700 937-2743
Web: www.lawa.org/ont

Oxnard Airport (OXR) ... Oxnard CA 93030 805-388-4274 382-9845
Web: www.ventura.org/airports/oxrmain.htm

Palm Springs International Airport (PSP) ... Palm Springs CA 92262 760-318-3800 318-3815
Web: www.palmspringsairport.com

Palo Alto Airport (PAO) ... Palo Alto CA 94303 650-856-7833 424-8071
Web: www.countyairports.org

Sacramento International Airport (SMF) ... Sacramento CA 95837 916-929-5411 648-0636
Web: www.sacairports.org

San Diego International Airport - Lindbergh Field (SAN) ... San Diego CA 92101 619-231-2100 400-2866
Web: www.san.org

San Francisco International Airport (SFO) ... San Francisco CA 94128 650-821-5041 821-5005
Web: www.sfoairport.com

Norman Y Mineta San Jose International Airport (SJC) ... San Jose CA 95110 408-501-7600 573-1675
Web: www.sjc.org

John Wayne Airport (SNA) ... Santa Ana CA 92707 949-252-5200 252-5290
Web: www.ocair.com

Colorado Springs Municipal Airport (COS) ... Colorado Springs CO 80916 719-550-1900 550-1901

Denver International Airport (DEN) ... Denver CO 80249 303-342-2000 342-2215
TF: 800-247-2336 ■ *Web:* www.flydenver.com

Fort Collins/Loveland Municipal Airport (FNL) ... Loveland CO 80538 970-962-2850 962-2855
Web: fcgov.com/airport

Tweed New Haven Regional Airport (HVN) ... New Haven CT 06512 203-466-8833 466-1199
Web: www.flytweed.com

Sikorsky Memorial Airport (BDR) ... Stratford CT 06615 203-576-8162 576-8166

Bradley International Airport (BDL) ... Windsor Locks CT 06096 860-292-2000 627-3594
TF: 888-624-1533 ■ *Web:* www.bradleyairport.com

Ronald Reagan Washington National Airport (DCA) ... Washington DC 20001 703-417-8000 417-8371*
**Fax:* PR ■ *Web:* www.mwaa.com/National/index.html

Washington Dulles International Airport (IAD) ... Washington DC 20041 703-572-2730 572-5718
Web: www.metwashairports.com/Dulles/

Saint Petersburg-Clearwater International Airport (PIE) ... Clearwater FL 33762 727-453-7800 453-7846
Web: www.fly2pie.com

Daytona Beach International Airport (DAB) ... Daytona Beach FL 32114 386-248-8069 248-8038
Web: www.flydaytonafirst.com

Fort Lauderdale Executive Airport (FXE) ... Fort Lauderdale FL 33309 954-828-4966 938-4974
Web: ci.ftlaud.fl.us/FXE

Fort Lauderdale/Hollywood International Airport (FLL) ... Fort Lauderdale FL 33315 954-359-1200 359-0027
Web: www.broward.org/airport

Southwest Florida International Airport (RSW) ... Fort Myers FL 33913 239-590-4800 590-4511
Web: www.flylcpa.com

Jacksonville International Airport (JAX) ... Jacksonville FL 32218 904-741-4902 741-2011
Web: www.jaa.aero

Key West International Airport (EYW) ... Key West FL 33040 305-296-5439 292-3578

Miami International Airport (MIA) ... Miami FL 33122 305-876-7515 876-8077
Web: www.miami-airport.com

Naples Municipal Airport (APF) ... Naples FL 34104 239-643-0733 643-4084
Web: www.flynaples.com

Orlando International Airport (MCO) ... Orlando FL 32827 407-825-2001 825-2202
Web: www.orlandoairports.net

Pensacola Regional Airport (PNS) ... Pensacola FL 32504 850-436-5000 436-5006
Web: www.flypensacola.com

Sarasota-Bradenton International Airport (SRQ) ... Sarasota FL 34243 941-359-5200 359-5054
Web: www.srq-airport.com

Tallahassee Regional Airport (TLH) ... Tallahassee FL 32310 850-891-7800 891-7837
Web: www.talgov.com/residents/transportation/airport.cfm

Tampa International Airport (TPA) ... Tampa FL 33607 813-870-8700 875-6670
TF: 800-767-8882 ■ *Web:* www.tampaairport.com

Palm Beach International Airport (PBI) ... West Palm Beach FL 33406 561-471-7412 471-7427
Web: www.pbia.org

Hartsfield-Jackson Atlanta International Airport (ATL) ... Atlanta GA 30320 404-530-6600 530-6803
Web: www.atlanta-airport.com

Augusta Regional Airport - Bush Field (AGS) ... Augusta GA 30906 706-798-2656 796-8933
Web: www.augustaregionalairport.com

Columbus Metropolitan Airport (CSG) ... Columbus GA 31909 706-324-2449 324-1016
Web: www.flycolumbusga.com

Middle Georgia Regional Airport (MCN) ... Macon GA 31297 478-788-3760 784-9338

Savannah/Hilton Head International Airport (SAV) ... Savannah GA 31408 912-964-0514 964-0877
TF: 877-359-2728 ■ *Web:* www.savannahairport.com

Honolulu International Airport (HNL) ... Honolulu HI 96819 808-836-6413 838-8734
Web: www.honoluluairport.com

Kona International Airport (KOA) ... Kailua-Kona HI 96740 808-327-9520 329-7414
Web: www.state.hi.us/dot/airports/hawaii/koa

Kahului Airport (OGG) ... Maui HI 96732 808-872-3830 872-3829

Boise Airport (BOI) ... Boise ID 83705 208-383-3110 343-9667
Web: www.cityofboise.org/transportation/airport

Pocatello Regional Airport (PIH) ... Pocatello ID 83204 208-234-6154 233-8418
Web: www.pocatello.us/Airport/Airport.htm

Chicago Midway Airport (MDW) ... Chicago IL 60638 773-838-0600 838-0587
Web: www.flychicago.com/midway/MidwayHomepage.shtm

O'Hare International Airport (ORD) ... Chicago IL 60666 773-686-2200 686-3424
Web: www.flychicago.com/Ohare/OhareHomepage.shtm

Greater Peoria Regional Airport (PIA) ... Peoria IL 61607 309-697-8272 697-8132
Web: www.flypia.com

Greater Rockford Airport (RFD) ... Rockford IL 61109 815-969-4000 969-4001
TF: 866-359-7331 ■ *Web:* www.flyrfd.com

Willard Airport (CMI) ... Savoy IL 61874 217-244-8689 244-8644
Web: www.flycmi.com

Abraham Lincoln Capital Airport (SPI) ... Springfield IL 62707 217-788-1063 788-8056
Web: www.flyspi.com

Evansville Regional Airport (EVV) ... Evansville IN 47725 812-421-4401 421-4412
Web: www.evvairport.com

Fort Wayne International Airport (FWA) ... Fort Wayne IN 46809 260-747-4146 747-1762
Web: www.fwairport.com

Indianapolis International Airport (IND) ... Indianapolis IN 46241 317-487-7243 487-5034
Web: indianapolisairport.com

South Bend Regional Airport (SBN) ... South Bend IN 46628 574-233-2185 239-2585
Web: www.sbnair.com

Eastern Iowa Airport (CID) ... Cedar Rapids IA 52404 319-362-3131 362-1670
Web: www.eiairport.org

Des Moines International Airport (DSM) ... Des Moines IA 50321 515-256-5050 256-5025
Web: www.dsmairport.com

Dubuque Regional Airport (DBQ) ... Dubuque IA 52003 563-589-4127 589-4108
Web: www.flydbq.com

Forbes Field (FOE) ... Topeka KS 66619 785-862-2362 862-1830
Web: www.mtaa-topeka.org

Midcontinent Airport (ICT) ... Wichita KS 67209 316-946-4700 946-4793
Web: www.flywichita.com

Blue Grass Airport (LEX) ... Lexington KY 40510 859-425-3114 233-1822
Web: www.bluegrassairport.com

Louisville International Airport (SDF) ... Louisville KY 40209 502-368-6524 367-0199
Web: www.flylouisville.com

Baton Rouge Metropolitan Airport (BTR) ... Baton Rouge LA 70807 225-355-0333 355-2334
Web: www.flybtr.com

Louis Armstrong New Orleans International Airport (MSY) ... Kenner LA 70062 504-464-0831 465-1264
Web: www.flymsy.com

Lafayette Regional Airport (LFT) ... Lafayette LA 70508 337-266-4400 266-4410
Web: www.lftairport.com

Shreveport Regional Airport (SHV) ... Shreveport LA 71109 318-673-5370 673-5377
Web: www.ci.shreveport.la.us/dept/airport/

Augusta State Airport (AUG) ... Augusta ME 04330 207-626-2306 626-2309

Bangor International Airport (BGR) ... Bangor ME 04401 207-947-0384 945-3607
TF: 866-359-2264 ■ *Web:* www.flybangor.com

Portland International Jetport (PWM) ... Portland ME 04102 207-774-7301 774-7740
Web: www.portlandjetport.org

Hancock County-Bar Harbor Airport (BHB) ... Trenton ME 04605 207-667-7329 667-0218
Web: www.bhbairport.com

Winnipeg James Armstrong Richardson International Airport (YWG) ... Winnipeg MB R3H1C2 204-987-9400 987-9401
Web: www.waa.ca

Baltimore/Washington International Thurgood Marshall Airport (BWI) ... Baltimore MD 21240 410-859-7111 859-4729
TF: 800-435-9294 ■ *Web:* www.bwiairport.com

Salisbury Ocean City-Wicomico County Regional Airport (SBY) ... Salisbury MD 21804 410-548-4827 548-4945
Web: www.flysby.com

Airport	City	State	ZIP	Phone	Fax
Logan International Airport (BOS)	Boston	MA	02128	617-561-1818	568-1022
TF: 800-235-6426 ■ *Web:* www.massport.com/logan					
Worcester Regional Airport (ORH)	Worcester	MA	01602	508-799-1741	799-1866
Web: www.flyworcester.com					
Alpena County Regional Airport (APN)	Alpena	MI	49707	989-354-2907	358-9988
Web: www.alpenaairport.com					
Coleman A Young International Airport (DET)	Detroit	MI	48213	313-628-2141	372-2448
Web: www.detroitmi.gov					
Detroit Metropolitan Airport (DTW)	Detroit	MI	48242	734-942-3685	942-3793
Web: www.metroairport.com					
Bishop International Airport (FNT)	Flint	MI	48507	810-235-6560	233-3065
Web: www.bishopairport.org					
Gerald R Ford International Airport (GRR)	Grand Rapids	MI	49512	616-336-4500	233-6025
Web: www.grr.org					
Capital City Airport (LAN)	Lansing	MI	48906	517-321-6121	321-6197
Web: www.flylansing.com					
Duluth International Airport (DLH)	Duluth	MN	55811	218-727-2968	727-2960
Web: www.duluthairport.com					
Rochester International Airport (RST)	Rochester	MN	55902	507-282-2328	282-2346
Web: www.rochesterintlairport.com					
Minneapolis-Saint Paul International Airport (MSP)	Saint Paul	MN	55111	612-726-5555	726-5527
Web: www.mspairport.com					
Gulfport/Biloxi International Airport (GPT)	Gulfport	MS	39503	228-863-5951	863-5953
TF: 866-447-8259 ■ *Web:* www.flygpt.com					
Jackson International Airport (JAN)	Jackson	MS	39208	601-939-5631	939-3713
Web: www.jmaa.com					
Hattiesburg-Laurel Regional Airport (PIB)	Moselle	MS	39459	601-649-2444	545-3155
Web: www.hlrairport.com					
Tupelo Regional Airport (TUP)	Tupelo	MS	38801	662-841-6570	841-6571
Web: www.flytupelo.com					
Columbia Regional Airport (COU)	Columbia	MO	65201	573-442-9770	874-0105
Kansas City International Airport (MCI)	Kansas City	MO	64153	816-243-5237	243-3170
Web: www.flykci.com					
Lambert Saint Louis International Airport (STL)	Saint Louis	MO	63145	314-426-8097	426-1221
Web: www.lambert-stlouis.com					
Springfield-Branson National Airport (SGF)	Springfield	MO	65803	417-869-0300	869-1031
Web: www.flyspringfield.com					
Billings Logan International Airport (BIL)	Billings	MT	59105	406-657-8495	657-8438
Web: www.flybillings.com					
Great Falls International Airport (GTF)	Great Falls	MT	59404	406-727-3404	727-6929
Web: www.gtfairport.com					
Helena Regional Airport (HLN)	Helena	MT	59602	406-442-2821	449-2340
Web: www.helenaairport.com					
Lincoln Airport (LNK)	Lincoln	NE	68524	402-458-2480	458-2490
Web: www.lincolnairport.com					
Eppley Airfield (OMA)	Omaha	NE	68110	402-661-8000	661-8025
Web: www.eppleyairfield.com					
McCarran International Airport (LAS)	Las Vegas	NV	89119	702-261-5743	597-9553
Web: mccarran.com					
Reno-Tahoe International Airport (RNO)	Reno	NV	89510	775-328-6400	328-6510
Web: www.renoairport.com					
Manchester Municipal Airport (MHT)	Manchester	NH	03103	603-624-6539	666-4101
Web: www.flymanchester.com					
Atlantic City International Airport (ACY)	Egg Harbor Township	NJ	08234	609-645-7895	641-4348
Web: www.acairport.com					
Newark Liberty International Airport (EWR)	Newark	NJ	07114	973-961-6007	961-6259
TF: 888-397-4636 ■ *Web:* www.newarkairport.com					
Albuquerque International Sunport (ABQ)	Albuquerque	NM	87106	505-842-4366	842-4278
Web: www.cabq.gov/airport/					
Las Cruces International Airport (LRU)	Las Cruces	NM	88007	505-541-2471	541-2472
Web: www.las-cruces.org/facilities/airport/					
Santa Fe Municipal Airport (SAF)	Santa Fe	NM	87504	505-955-2900	955-2905
Albany International Airport (ALB)	Albany	NY	12211	518-242-2200	242-2641
Web: www.albanyairport.com					
Buffalo Niagara International Airport (BUF)	Cheektowaga	NY	14225	716-630-6000	630-6070
Web: www.buffaloairport.com					
LaGuardia Airport (LGA)	Flushing	NY	11371	718-533-3400	533-3421
Web: www.panynj.gov/aviation/lgaframe.HTM					
John F Kennedy International Airport (JFK)	Jamaica	NY	11430	718-244-4444	244-3505
Web: www.panynj.gov/aviation/jfkframe.HTM					
Greater Rochester International Airport (ROC)	Rochester	NY	14624	585-464-6000	753-7008
Web: www.rocairport.com					
Long Island MacArthur Airport (ISP)	Ronkonkoma	NY	11779	631-467-3210	467-3348
Web: www.macarthurairport.com					
Syracuse Hancock International Airport (SYR)	Syracuse	NY	13212	315-454-3263	454-8757
Web: www.syrairport.org					
Westchester County Airport (HPN)	White Plains	NY	10604	914-995-4860	995-3980
Web: www.co.westchester.ny.us/airport					
Charlotte/Douglas International Airport (CLT)	Charlotte	NC	28208	704-359-4000	359-4030
Web: www.charmeck.org/Departments/Airport/Home.htm					
Asheville Regional Airport (AVL)	Fletcher	NC	28732	828-684-2226	684-3404
Web: www.flyavl.com					
Piedmont Triad International Airport (GSO)	Greensboro	NC	27409	336-665-5600	665-1425
Web: www.flyfrompti.com					
Raleigh-Durham International Airport (RDU)	Raleigh	NC	27623	919-840-2100	840-0175
Web: www.rdu.com					
Smith Reynolds Airport (INT)	Winston-Salem	NC	27105	336-767-6361	767-8556
Web: www.smithreynolds.org					
Bismarck Municipal Airport (BIS)	Bismarck	ND	58502	701-222-6502	221-6886
TF: 800-453-4244 ■ *Web:* www.bismarckairport.com					
Hector International Airport (FAR)	Fargo	ND	58102	701-241-1501	241-1538
Web: www.fargoairport.com					
Grand Forks International Airport (GFK)	Grand Forks	ND	58203	701-795-6981	795-6979
Web: www.gfkairport.com					
Halifax International Airport (YHZ)	Enfield	NS	B2T1K2	902-873-1234	873-4750
Web: www.hiaa.ca					
Cincinnati-Northern Kentucky International Airport (CVG)	Cincinnati	OH	45275	859-767-3151	767-3080
Web: www.cvgairport.com					
Cleveland Hopkins International Airport (CLE)	Cleveland	OH	44135	216-265-6000	265-6021
Web: www.clevelandairport.com					
Port Columbus International Airport (CMH)	Columbus	OH	43219	614-239-4000	239-2219
Web: www.port-columbus.com/home.asp					
Akron-Canton Airport (CAK)	North Canton	OH	44720	330-499-4059	499-5176
TF: 888-434-2359 ■ *Web:* www.akroncantonairport.com					
Toledo Express Airport (TOL)	Swanton	OH	43558	419-865-2351	867-8245
Web: www.toledoexpress.com					
Dayton International Airport (DAY)	Vandalia	OH	45377	937-454-8200	454-8284
TF: 877-359-3291 ■ *Web:* www.flydayton.com					
Youngstown-Warren Regional Airport (YNG)	Vienna	OH	44473	330-856-1537	539-4833
Web: www.yngwrnair.com					
Will Rogers World Airport (OKC)	Oklahoma City	OK	73159	405-680-3200	680-3319
Web: www.flyokc.com					
Tulsa International Airport (TUL)	Tulsa	OK	74115	918-838-5000	838-5199
Web: www.tulsaairports.com					
Ottawa Macdonald-Cartier International Airport (YOW)	Gloucester	ON	K1V9B4	613-248-2000	248-2003
Web: ottawa-airport.ca					
Lester B Pearson International Airport (YYZ)	Toronto	ON	L5P1C2	416-776-3000	776-7746
TF: 800-247-7678					
Eugene Airport (EUG)	Eugene	OR	97402	541-682-5430	682-6838
Portland International Airport (PDX)	Portland	OR	97218	503-460-4040	460-4124
Web: www.flypdx.com					
Lehigh Valley International Airport (ABE)	Allentown	PA	18109	610-266-6000	264-0115
TF: 888-359-5842 ■ *Web:* www.lvia.org					
Wilkes-Barre/Scranton International Airport (AVP)	Avoca	PA	18641	570-602-2000	602-2010
Web: www.flyavp.com					
Erie International Airport (ERI)	Erie	PA	16505	814-833-4258	833-0393
Web: www.erieairport.org					
Harrisburg International Airport (MDT)	Middletown	PA	17057	717-948-3900	948-4636
TF: 888-235-9442 ■ *Web:* www.flyhia.com					
Philadelphia International Airport (PHL)	Philadelphia	PA	19153	215-937-6937	937-6497
Web: www.phl.org					
Pittsburgh International Airport (PIT)	Pittsburgh	PA	15231	412-472-3525	472-3636
Web: www.pitairport.com					
Montreal-Pierre Elliott Trudeau International Airport (YUL)	Montreal	QC	H4Y1H1	514-394-7377	394-7356
Web: www.admtl.com					
Jean-Lesage International Airport (YQB)	Sainte-Foy	QC	G2G2T9	418-640-2600	640-2656
Theodore Francis Green State Airport (PVD)	Warwick	RI	02886	401-737-4000	732-3034
TF: 888-268-7222 ■ *Web:* www.pvdairport.com					
Charleston International Airport (CHS)	Charleston	SC	29418	843-767-1100	760-3020
Web: www.chs-airport.com					
Columbia Metropolitan Airport (CAE)	Columbia	SC	29170	803-822-5010	822-5140
Web: www.columbiaairport.com					
Greenville-Spartanburg Airport (GSP)	Greer	SC	29651	864-877-7426	848-6225
Web: www.gspairport.com					
Hilton Head Island Airport (HXD)	Hilton Head Island	SC	29926	843-689-5400	689-5411
Web: www.hiltonheadairport.com					
Myrtle Beach International Airport (MYR)	Myrtle Beach	SC	29577	843-448-1589	626-9096
Web: www.flymyrtlebeach.com					
Pierre Regional Airport (PIR)	Pierre	SD	57501	605-773-7447	773-7561
Web: www.pierreairport.com					
Rapid City Regional Airport (RAP)	Rapid City	SD	57703	605-394-4195	394-6190
Web: www.rcgov.org/Airport/pages/					
Sioux Falls Regional Airport (FSD)	Sioux Falls	SD	57104	605-336-0762	367-7374
Web: www.sfairport.com					
McGhee Tyson Airport (TYS)	Alcoa	TN	37701	865-342-3000	342-3050
Web: www.tys.org					
Tri-Cities Regional Airport (TRI)	Blountville	TN	37617	423-325-6000	325-6061
Web: www.triflight.com					
Chattanooga Metropolitan Airport (CHA)	Chattanooga	TN	37421	423-855-2200	855-2212
Web: www.chattairport.com					
Memphis International Airport (MEM)	Memphis	TN	38116	901-922-8000	922-8099
Web: www.memphisairport.org					
Nashville International Airport (BNA)	Nashville	TN	37214	615-275-1600	275-1499*
**Fax:* Hum Res ■ *Web:* www.flynashville.com					
Abilene Regional Airport (ABI)	Abilene	TX	79602	325-676-6367	676-6317
Web: www.abilenetx.com/airport/					
Rick Husband Amarillo International Airport (AMA)	Amarillo	TX	79111	806-335-1671	335-1672
Web: www.visitamarillotx.com/Airport-Airline					
Austin-Bergstrom International Airport (AUS)	Austin	TX	78719	512-530-2242	530-7686
Web: www.ci.austin.tx.us/austinairport					
Brownsville-South Padre Island International Airport (BRO)	Brownsville	TX	78521	956-542-4373	542-4374
Web: www.flybrownsville.com					
Corpus Christi International Airport (CRP)	Corpus Christi	TX	78406	361-289-0171	289-0251
Web: www.corpuschristiairport.com					
Dallas-Fort Worth International Airport (DFW)	Dallas	TX	75261	972-574-8888	574-5509
TF: 800-762-0238 ■ *Web:* www.dfwairport.com					
Dallas Love Field (DAL)	Dallas	TX	75235	214-670-6080	670-6051
Web: www.dallas-lovefield.com					
El Paso International Airport (ELP)	El Paso	TX	79925	915-772-4271	779-5452
Web: elpasoairport.com					
Bush Intercontinental Airport (IAH)	Houston	TX	77032	281-233-3000	233-1874
Web: www.fly2houston.com/iah					
William P Hobby Airport (HOU)	Houston	TX	77061	713-640-3000	641-7703
Web: www.fly2houston.com/hobbyHome					
Lubbock International Airport (LBB)	Lubbock	TX	79403	806-775-2035	775-3133
TF: 888-873-7485 ■ *Web:* www.flylia.com					
Midland International Airport (MAF)	Midland	TX	79711	432-560-2200	560-2237
Web: www.flymaf.com					
San Antonio International Airport (SAT)	San Antonio	TX	78216	210-207-3411	207-3500*
**Fax:* PR ■ *Web:* www.sanantonio.gov/airport					
Ogden-Hinckley Airport (OGD)	Ogden	UT	84405	801-629-8251	627-8104
Salt Lake City International Airport (SLC)	Salt Lake City	UT	84116	801-575-2400	575-2499
TF: 800-595-2442 ■ *Web:* www.slcairport.com					
Burlington International Airport (BTV)	South Burlington	VT	05403	802-863-2874	863-7947
Web: www.burlingtonintlairport.com					
Newport News/Williamsburg International Airport (PHF)	Newport News	VA	23602	757-877-0221	877-6369
Web: www.nnwairport.com					
Norfolk International Airport (ORF)	Norfolk	VA	23518	757-857-3351	857-3265
Web: www.norfolkairport.com					
Richmond International Airport (RIC)	Richmond	VA	23250	804-226-3052	652-2606*
**Fax:* Mail Rm ■ *Web:* www.flyrichmond.com					
Roanoke Regional Airport (ROA)	Roanoke	VA	24012	540-362-1999	563-4838
Web: www.roanokeairport.com					
Seattle-Tacoma International Airport (SEA)	Seattle	WA	98158	206-433-5388	433-4641
Web: www.portseattle.org/seatac					
Spokane International Airport (GEG)	Spokane	WA	99224	509-455-6455	624-6633
Web: www.spokaneairports.net					
Yeager Airport (CRW)	Charleston	WV	25311	304-344-8033	344-8034
Web: www.yeagerairport.com					
Morgantown Municipal Airport (MGW)	Morgantown	WV	26505	304-291-7461	291-7463
Web: www.morgantownairport.com					
Wheeling-Ohio County Airport (HLG)	Wheeling	WV	26003	304-234-3865	234-3867
Austin Straubel International Airport (GRB)	Green Bay	WI	54313	920-498-4800	498-8799
Web: www.co.brown.wi.us/airport/					
Dane County Regional Airport (MSN)	Madison	WI	53704	608-246-3380	246-3385
Web: www.msnairport.com					
General Mitchell International Airport (MKE)	Milwaukee	WI	53207	414-747-5300	747-4525
Web: www.mitchellairport.com					
Natrona County International Airport (CPR)	Casper	WY	82604	307-472-6688	472-1805
Web: www.iflycasper.com					
Cheyenne Regional Airport (CYS)	Cheyenne	WY	82001	307-634-7071	632-1206
Web: www.cheyenneairport.com					
Jackson Hole Airport (JAC)	Jackson	WY	83001	307-733-7682	733-9270
Web: www.jacksonholeairport.com					

28 AIRSHIPS

SEE ALSO Aircraft p. 1271

Company / Address	City	State	ZIP	Phone	Fax
21st Century Airships Inc PO Box 177 Main Stn *Web:* www.21stcenturyairships.com	Newmarket	ON	L3Y4X1	905-898-6274	898-7245
Advanced Hybrid Aircraft 15225 Marine Dr *Web:* www.ahausa.com	White Rock	BC	V4B1C7	604-541-8064	541-8064
American Blimp Corp 1900 NE 25th Ave Suite 5 *Web:* www.americanblimp.com	Hillsboro	OR	97124	503-693-1611	681-0906
Boland Balloon Post Mills Airport PO Box 51 *Web:* www.myairship.com/database/boland.html	Post Mills	VT	05058	802-333-9254	333-9254
Bosch Aerospace Inc 205 Lawler Dr *Web:* www.boschaero.com	Brownsboro	AL	35741	256-852-5033	852-5898
Cameron Balloons US PO Box 3672 **Fax Area Code:* 866 ■ *TF:* 866-423-6178 ■ *Web:* www.cameronballoons.com	Ann Arbor	MI	48106	734-426-5525	423-6179*
FireFly Balloons 810 Salisbury Rd *Web:* www.fireflyballoons.net	Statesville	NC	28677	704-878-9501	878-9505
Global Skyship Industries Inc 2 Soundview Dr *Web:* www.globalskyships.com	Greenwich	CT	06830	203-625-0074	625-0065
ILC Dover Inc 1 Moonwalker Rd *TF:* 800-631-9567 ■ *Web:* www.ilcdover.com	Frederica	DE	19946	302-335-3911	335-0762
Lindstrand Balloons USA 11440 Dandar St *Web:* www.lindstrand.com	Galena	IL	61036	815-777-6006	777-6004
Millennium Airship Inc Bremerton National Airport 8850 SW State Hwy 3 *Web:* www.millenniumairship.com	Port Orchard	WA	98367	360-674-2488	674-2494
TCOM LP 7115 Thomas Edison Dr *TF:* 800-767-8266 ■ *Web:* www.tcomlp.com	Columbia	MD	21046	410-312-2400	312-2455
Worldwide Aeros Corp 6005 Yolanda Ave *Web:* www.aerosml.com	Tarzana	CA	91356	818-993-5533	344-3933

29 ALL-TERRAIN VEHICLES

SEE ALSO Sporting Goods p. 2323

Company / Address	City	State	ZIP	Phone	Fax
American Honda Motor Co Inc 1919 Torrance Blvd **Fax:* Hum Res ■ *TF:* 800-999-1009 ■ *Web:* www.honda.com	Torrance	CA	90501	310-783-2000	783-2110*
American Suzuki Motor Corp 3251 E Imperial Hwy *Web:* www.suzuki.com	Brea	CA	92821	714-996-7040	524-2512
Arctic Cat Inc 601 Brooks Ave S *NASDAQ: ACAT* ■ *Web:* www.arctic-cat.com	Thief River Falls	MN	56701	218-681-8558	681-3162
Berrien Buggy Inc 10644 US Hwy 31 *Web:* www.berrienbuggy.com	Berrien Springs	MI	49103	269-471-1411	
Bombardier Recreational Products 565 de la Montagne *Web:* www.brp.com	Valcourt	QC	J0E2L0	450-532-2211	
Bush Hog LLC 2501 Griffin Ave PO Box 1039 *TF:* 800-363-6096 ■ *Web:* www.bushhog.com	Selma	AL	36702	334-872-6261	874-2701
Cycle Country Accessories Corp 2188 Hwy 86 PO Box 239 *AMEX: ATC* ■ *TF:* 800-841-2222 ■ *Web:* www.cyclecountry.com	Milford	IA	51351	712-338-2701	338-2601
Kawasaki Motors Corp USA PO Box 25252 *Web:* www.kawasaki.com	Santa Ana	CA	92799	949-770-0400	460-5600
Ontario Drive & Gear Ltd 220 Bergey Ct *Web:* www.argoatv.com	New Hamburg	ON	N3A2J5	519-662-2840	662-2421
Polaris Industries Inc 2100 Hwy 55 *NYSE: PII* ■ *Web:* www.polarisindustries.com	Medina	MN	55340	763-542-0500	542-0599
Recreatives Industries Inc 60 Depot St *TF:* 800-255-2511 ■ *Web:* www.maxatvs.com	Buffalo	NY	14206	716-855-2226	855-1094
Yamaha Motor Corp USA 6555 Katella Ave *TF Cust Svc:* 800-962-7926 ■ *Web:* www.yamaha-motor.com	Cypress	CA	90630	714-761-7300	761-7302

30 AMBULANCE SERVICES

Company / Address	City	State	ZIP	Phone	Fax
Acadian Ambulance & Air Med Services Inc PO Box 98000 **Fax:* Hum Res ■ *TF:* 800-259-3333 ■ *Web:* www.acadian.com	Lafayette	LA	70509	337-291-3333	291-3326*
Air Methods Corp 7301 S Peoria St *NASDAQ: AIRM* ■ *Web:* www.airmethods.com	Englewood	CO	80112	303-792-7400	790-0499
Air Response Inc 7211 S Peoria St Suite 200 **Fax Area Code:* 888 ■ *TF:* 800-631-6565 ■ *Web:* www.proflight.com	Englewood	CO	80112	303-858-9967	631-6565*
AirEvac Services Inc 2800 N 44th St Suite 800 *TF:* 800-421-6111 ■ *Web:* www.airevac.com	Phoenix	AZ	85008	602-244-9327	302-6721
American Medical Response (AMR) 6200 S Syracuse Way Suite 200 *TF:* 800-244-4890 ■ *Web:* www.amr.net	Greenwood Village	CO	80111	303-495-1200	495-1649
CJ Systems Aviation Group Inc 57 Allegheny County Airport *TF:* 800-245-0230 ■ *Web:* www.corpjet.com	West Mifflin	PA	15122	412-466-2500	466-1978
MedjetAssist 3500 Colonnade Pkwy Suite 500 *TF:* 800-527-7478 ■ *Web:* www.medjet.com	Birmingham	AL	35243	205-595-6626	595-6658
Metro Aviation Inc PO Box 7008 *Web:* www.metroaviation.com	Shreveport	LA	71137	318-222-5529	222-0503
National Air Ambulance 3495 SW 9th Ave *TF:* 800-525-0166 ■ *Web:* www.nationaljets.com/natjet/ambul	Fort Lauderdale	FL	33315	954-359-9400	359-0064
Omniflight Helicopters Inc 4650 Airport Pkwy *TF:* 800-727-4644 ■ *Web:* www.omniflight.com	Addison	TX	75001	972-776-0130	776-0131
Rural/Metro Corp 9221 E Via de Ventura *NASDAQ: RURL* ■ **Fax:* Hum Res ■ *TF:* 800-421-5718 ■ *Web:* www.ruralmetro.com	Scottsdale	AZ	85258	480-994-3886	606-3268*
Shock Trauma Air Rescue Society (STARS) 1441 Aviation Park NE *Web:* www.stars.ca	Calgary	AB	T2E8M7	403-295-1811	275-4891
Skyservice Airlines Inc 31 Fasken Dr *TF:* 800-701-9448 ■ *Web:* www.skyserviceairlines.com	Etobicoke	ON	M9W1K6	416-679-5700	679-5920

31 AMUSEMENT PARK COMPANIES

SEE ALSO Circus, Carnival, Festival Operators p. 1446

Company / Address	City	State	ZIP	Phone	Fax
Busch Entertainment Corp 231 S Bemiston St Suite 600 *Web:* www.4adventure.com	Saint Louis	MO	63105	314-577-2000	613-6089
Cedar Fair LP 1 Cedar Point Dr *NYSE: FUN* ■ *Web:* www.cedarfair.com	Sandusky	OH	44870	419-626-0830	627-2234
Herschend Family Entertainment Corp 399 Indian Point Rd **Fax:* Mktg ■ *TF:* 800-952-6626 ■ *Web:* sdcprops.silverdollarcity.com	Branson	MO	65616	417-338-2611	338-8080*
Hershey Entertainment & Resorts Co 300 Park Blvd *Web:* www.hersheypa.com	Hershey	PA	17033	717-534-3090	534-8991
Kennywood Entertainment Corp 4800 Kennywood Blvd *Web:* www.kennywoodentertainment.com	West Mifflin	PA	15122	412-461-0500	464-0719
Palace Entertainment Inc 4950 MacArthur Rd Suite 400 *Web:* www.palaceentertainment.com	Newport Beach	CA	92660	949-261-0404	261-1414
Paramount Parks Inc 8720 Red Oak Blvd Suite 315 *Web:* www.paramountparks.com	Charlotte	NC	28217	704-525-5250	525-2960
Ripley Entertainment Inc 7576 Kingspointe Pkwy *Web:* www.ripleys.com	Orlando	FL	32819	407-345-8010	345-0801
Santa Cruz Seaside Co 400 Beach St *Web:* www.beachboardwalk.com	Santa Cruz	CA	95060	831-423-5590	423-2438
Six Flags Inc 11501 NE Expy *NYSE: PKS* ■ *Web:* www.sixflags.com	Oklahoma City	OK	73131	405-475-2500	475-2555
Universal Parks & Resorts 100 Universal City Plaza *Web:* themeparks.universalstudios.com	Universal City	CA	91608	818-777-1000	
Walt Disney Parks & Resorts 500 S Buena Vista St *Web:* destinations.disney.go.com	Burbank	CA	91521	818-560-1000	560-1930

32 AMUSEMENT PARKS

Company / Address	City	State	ZIP	Phone	Fax
Adventure Island 1001 Malcolm McKinley Dr *TF:* 888-800-5447 ■ *Web:* www.adventureisland.com	Tampa	FL	33612	813-987-5600	987-5654
Adventure Landing 1944 Beach Blvd *Web:* www.adventurelanding.com	Jacksonville Beach	FL	32250	904-246-4386	249-1018
Adventure Landing 3311 Capital Blvd *Web:* www.adventurelanding.com	Raleigh	NC	27604	919-872-1688	872-3408
Adventuredome 2880 Las Vegas Blvd S *TF:* 800-634-3450 ■ *Web:* www.adventuredome.com	Las Vegas	NV	89119	702-794-3912	792-2846
Adventureland Park 305 34th Ave NW *TF:* 800-532-1286 ■ *Web:* www.adventureland-usa.com	Altoona	IA	50009	515-266-2121	266-9831
Alabama Adventure 4599 Alabama Adventure Pkwy *Web:* www.alabamaadventure.com	Bessemer	AL	35022	205-481-4750	481-4758
Astroland Amusement Park 1000 Surf Ave Coney Island *Web:* www.astroland.com	Brooklyn	NY	11224	718-265-2100	265-2155
Busch Gardens Tampa Bay 3605 Bougainvillea Ave *TF:* 888-800-5447 ■ *Web:* www.buschgardens.com	Tampa	FL	33612	813-987-5082	987-5111
Busch Gardens Williamsburg 1 Busch Gardens Blvd **Fax Area Code:* 757 ■ **Fax:* Mktg ■ *TF:* 800-343-7946 ■ *Web:* www.buschgardens.com	Williamsburg	VA	23187	800-343-7946	253-3399*
California's Great America 4701 Great America Pkwy **Fax:* Sales ■ *Web:* www.cagreatamerica.com	Santa Clara	CA	95054	408-988-1776	986-5855*
Casino Pier & Water Works 800 Ocean Terr *Web:* www.casinopiernj.com	Seaside Heights	NJ	08751	732-793-6488	793-0461
Castle Park 3500 Polk St *Web:* www.castlepark.com	Riverside	CA	92505	951-785-3000	785-3075
Cedar Point Amusement Park 1 Cedar Point Dr **Fax:* Mktg ■ *Web:* www.cedarpoint.com	Sandusky	OH	44870	419-626-0830	627-2200*
Children's Fairyland Theme Park 699 Bellevue Ave *Web:* www.fairyland.org	Oakland	CA	94610	510-452-2259	452-2261
Coney Island Park 6201 Kellogg Ave *Web:* www.coneyislandpark.com	Cincinnati	OH	45228	513-232-8230	231-1352
Cypress Gardens Adventure Park 6000 Cypress Gardens Blvd **Fax:* PR ■ *Web:* www.cypressgardens.com	Winter Haven	FL	33884	863-324-2111	595-2315*
Darien Lake Theme Park Resort 9993 Allegheny Rd PO Box 91 *Web:* www.godarienlake.com	Darien Center	NY	14040	585-599-4641	599-4053
Disneyland 1313 S Harbor Blvd *Web:* disneyland.disney.go.com	Anaheim	CA	92802	714-781-7290	
DisneyQuest 1486 E Lake Buena Vista Dr *Web:* www.disneyquest.com	Lake Buena Vista	FL	32830	407-828-4600	938-6202
Disney's Animal Kingdom 2901 Osceola Pkwy *Web:* disneyworld.disney.go.com	Lake Buena Vista	FL	32830	407-938-3000	938-4799
Disney's Blizzard Beach 1500 W Buena Vista Dr *Web:* www.disneyworld.com	Lake Buena Vista	FL	32830	407-824-4321	
Disney's California Adventure 1313 S Harbor Blvd *Web:* www.disneyland.com	Anaheim	CA	92803	714-781-7290	
Disney's Hollywood Studios 351 S Studio Dr *Web:* www.disneyworld.com	Lake Buena Vista	FL	32830	407-824-4321	
Disney's Typhoon Lagoon 1145 E Buena Vista Dr *Web:* www.disneyworld.com	Lake Buena Vista	FL	32830	407-560-7223	560-7405
Disney's Wide World of Sports 700 Victory Way *Web:* www.disneysports.com	Kissimmee	FL	34747	407-939-1500	
Dollywood 1020 Dollywood Ln **Fax:* Mktg ■ *TF:* 800-365-5996 ■ *Web:* www.dollywood.com	Pigeon Forge	TN	37863	865-428-9400	428-9494*
Dorney Park & Wildwater Kingdom 3830 Dorney Park Rd *TF:* 800-386-8463 ■ *Web:* www.dorneypark.com	Allentown	PA	18104	610-395-3724	391-7650
Dutch Wonderland Family Amusement Park 2249 Lincoln Hwy E *TF:* 866-386-2839 ■ *Web:* www.dutchwonderland.com	Lancaster	PA	17602	717-291-1888	291-1595
Elitch Gardens 2000 Elitch Cir *Web:* www.elitchgardens.com	Denver	CO	80204	303-595-4386	534-2221
EPCOT 200 E Epcot Center Dr *Web:* www.disneyworld.com	Lake Buena Vista	FL	32830	407-824-4321	
Family Kingdom Amusement Park & Oceanfront Water Park 300 S Ocean Blvd *Web:* www.family-kingdom.com	Myrtle Beach	SC	29577	843-626-3447	448-4548
Frontier City Theme Park 11501 Northeast Expy *Web:* www.frontiercity.com	Oklahoma City	OK	73131	405-478-2412	478-3104
Geauga Lake Wildwater Kingdom 1100 Squires Rd *Web:* www.geaugalake.com	Aurora	OH	44202	330-562-8303	
Grand Harbor Resort & Waterpark 350 Bell St *TF:* 866-690-4006 ■ *Web:* www.grandharborresort.com	Dubuque	IA	52001	563-690-4000	690-0558
Great Escape & Splashwater Kingdom 1172 Rt 9 *Web:* www.sixflags.com/parks/greatescape	Queensbury	NY	12084	518-792-3500	792-3404
Hersheypark 100 W Hersheypark Dr **Fax:* Mktg ■ *TF:* 800-437-7439 ■ *Web:* www.hersheypark.com	Hershey	PA	17033	717-534-3900	534-3165*
Holiday World & Splashin' Safari 452 E Christmas Blvd *TF:* 877-463-2645 ■ *Web:* www.holidayworld.com	Santa Claus	IN	47579	812-937-4401	937-4405
Holy Land Experience 4655 Vineland Rd *TF:* 800-447-7235 ■ *Web:* www.theholylandexperience.com	Orlando	FL	32811	407-872-2272	872-3393
Idlewild & Soak Zone Rt 30 E *Web:* www.idlewild.com	Ligonier	PA	15658	724-238-3666	238-6544
Indiana Beach 5224 E Indiana Beach Rd *TF:* 800-583-4306 ■ *Web:* www.indianabeach.com	Monticello	IN	47960	574-583-4141	583-4125
Islands of Adventure 6000 Universal Studios Plaza *TF:* 877-801-9720 ■ *Web:* themeparks.universalstudios.com	Orlando	FL	32819	407-363-8000	224-6942
Kennywood Park 4800 Kennywood Blvd *Web:* www.kennywood.com	West Mifflin	PA	15122	412-461-0500	464-0719

Phone | Fax

Knight's Action Park & Caribbean Water Adventure
1700 Recreation Dr .... Springfield IL 62711 217-546-8881 546-8995
Web: www.knightsactionpark.com
Knoebels Amusement Resort PO Box 317 .... Elysburg PA 17824 570-672-2572 672-3293
TF: 800-487-4386 ■ *Web:* www.knoebels.com
Knott's Berry Farm 8039 Beach Blvd .... Buena Park CA 90620 714-220-5220 220-5124
Web: www.knotts.com
Knott's Soak City San Diego 2052 Entertainment Cir .... Chula Vista CA 91911 619-661-7373 661-7393
Web: www.knotts.com/soakcity/sd/
Knott's Soak City USA 8039 Beach Blvd .... Buena Park CA 90620 714-220-5200 220-5028
Web: www.soakcityusa.com
Knott's Soak City USA 1500 S Gene Autry Trail .... Palm Springs CA 92264 760-327-0499 322-4191
Web: www.soakcityusa.com
La Ronde Theme Park Sainte-Helene Island 22 McDonald Rd .... Montreal QC H3C6A3 514-397-2000 397-7759
Web: www.laronde.com/en
Lagoon & Pioneer Village 375 N Lagoon Dr .... Farmington UT 84025 801-451-8000 451-8015
TF: 800-748-5246 ■ *Web:* www.lagoonpark.com
Lake Compounce Theme Park 271 Enterprise Dr .... Bristol CT 06010 860-583-3300 589-7974
Web: www.lakecompounce.com
Lake Winnepesaukah Amusement Park 1730 Lakeview Dr .... Rossville GA 30741 706-866-5681 858-0497
TF: 877-525-3946 ■ *Web:* www.lakewinnie.com
LEGOLAND California 1 Legoland Dr .... Carlsbad CA 92008 760-438-5346 918-5459
TF: 877-534-6526 ■ *Web:* www.legoland.com/california.htm
Magic Kingdom Park 1365 Monorail Way .... Lake Buena Vista FL 32830 407-824-4401
Web: www.disneyworld.com
Magic Springs Theme Park & Crystal Falls Water Park
1701 E Grand Ave .... Hot Springs AR 71901 501-624-0100 318-5367
Web: www.magicsprings.com
Marineland 7657 Portage Rd .... Niagara Falls ON L2E6X8 905-356-9565 374-6652
Web: www.marinelandcanada.com
Morey's Piers & Raging Waters Waterparks 3501 Boardwalk .... Wildwood NJ 08260 609-522-3900 522-0788
Web: www.moreyspiers.com
Myrtle Waves Water Park 3000 10th Ave N Ext .... Myrtle Beach SC 29577 843-913-9260
Web: www.myrtlewaves.com
NASCAR SpeedPark 1 Bass Pro Mills Dr .... Vaughan ON L4K5W4 905-669-7373 669-7371
Web: www.nascarspeedpark.com
Oaks Amusement Park 7805 SE Oaks Park Way .... Portland OR 97202 503-233-5777 236-9143
Web: www.oakspark.com
Paramount Canada's Wonderland 9580 Jane St .... Vaughan ON L6A1S6 905-832-7000 832-7519
Web: www.canadas-wonderland.com
Paramount's Carowinds 14523 Carowinds Blvd .... Charlotte NC 28273 704-588-2600 587-9034
TF: 800-888-4386 ■ *Web:* www.carowinds.com
Paramount's Kings Dominion 16000 Theme Pkwy .... Doswell VA 23047 804-876-5400 876-5864
TF: 800-553-7277 ■ *Web:* www.kingsdominion.com
Paramount's Kings Island
6300 Kings Island Dr PO Box 901 .... Kings Island OH 45034 513-754-5700 754-5710
TF: 800-288-0808 ■ *Web:* www.pki.com
Park at Mall of America 5000 Center Ct .... Bloomington MN 55425 952-883-8500 883-8683
Web: info.theparkatmoa.com/
Pharaoh's Theme & Water Park 1101 N California St .... Redlands CA 92374 909-335-7275 307-2622
Raging Waters 2333 S White Rd .... San Jose CA 95148 408-238-9900 270-2022
Web: www.rwsplash.com
Raging Waters Sacramento 1600 Exposition Blvd .... Sacramento CA 95815 916-924-3747 924-1314
Web: www.rwsac.com
Sandcastle Water Park 1000 Sandcastle Dr .... West Homestead PA 15120 412-462-6666 462-0827
Web: www.sandcastlewaterpark.com
Santa Cruz Beach Boardwalk 400 Beach St .... Santa Cruz CA 95060 831-423-5590 460-3335
Web: www.beachboardwalk.com
Schlitterbahn Beach Waterpark
33261 State Park Rd Hwy 100 .... South Padre Island TX 78597 956-772-7873 761-3960
Web: www.schlitterbahn.com
Schlitterbahn Waterpark Resort 381 E Austin St .... New Braunfels TX 78130 830-625-2351 625-3515
Web: www.schlitterbahn.com
SeaWorld Orlando 7007 Sea World Dr .... Orlando FL 32821 407-351-3600 363-2409*
**Fax:* Cust Svc ■ *TF:* 800-327-2424 ■ *Web:* www.seaworldorlando.com
SeaWorld San Antonio 10500 SeaWorld Dr .... San Antonio TX 78251 210-523-3000 523-3199*
**Fax:* Mktg ■ *TF:* 800-700-7786 ■ *Web:* www.seaworld.com
SeaWorld San Diego 500 SeaWorld Dr .... San Diego CA 92109 619-226-3901
TF: 800-257-4268 ■ *Web:* www.seaworld.com
Sesame Place 100 Sesame Rd .... Langhorne PA 19047 215-752-7070 741-5307
Web: www.sesameplace.com
Seven Peaks Water Park 1330 E 300 North .... Provo UT 84606 801-373-8777 373-8791
Web: www.sevenpeaks.com
Silver Springs 5656 E Silver Springs Blvd .... Silver Springs FL 34488 352-236-2121 236-2860
Web: www.silversprings.com
Six Flags America 13710 Central Ave .... Mitchellville MD 20721 301-249-1500 249-8853
Web: www.sixflags.com/parks/america/
Six Flags Discovery Kingdom 1001 Fairgrounds Dr .... Vallejo CA 94589 707-644-4000 644-0241
Web: www.sixflags.com/discoveryKingdom/
Six Flags Fiesta Texas 17000 IH-10 W .... San Antonio TX 78257 210-697-5000 697-5415
TF: 800-473-4378 ■ *Web:* www.sixflags.com/parks/fiestatexas
Six Flags Great Adventure Rt 537 .... Jackson NJ 08527 732-928-1821 928-2775
Web: www.sixflags.com/parks/greatadventure
Six Flags Great America 542 N Rt 21 .... Gurnee IL 60031 847-249-2133 249-2390
Web: www.sixflags.com/parks/greatamerica
Six Flags Hurricane Harbor Dallas 1800 E Lamar Blvd .... Arlington TX 76006 817-265-3356 607-6184
Web: www.sixflags.com/parks/hurricaneharbordallas
Six Flags Hurricane Harbor Los Angeles
26101 Magic Mountain Pkwy .... Valencia CA 91355 661-255-4100 255-4170
Web: www.sixflags.com/parks/hurricaneharborla
Six Flags Hurricane Harbor New Jersey Rt 537 .... Jackson NJ 08527 732-928-1821 928-2775
Web: www.sixflags.com/parks/hurricaneharbornj
Six Flags Kentucky Kingdom 937 Phillips Ln .... Louisville KY 40209 502-366-2231 366-8746
TF: 800-727-3267 ■ *Web:* www.sixflags.com/parks/kentuckykingdom
Six Flags Magic Mountain 26101 Magic Mountain Pkwy .... Valencia CA 91355 661-255-4100 255-4170
Web: www.sixflags.com/parks/magicmountain
Six Flags New England Route 159 1623 Main St .... Agawam MA 01001 413-786-9300 821-2402*
**Fax:* Mktg ■ *TF:* 800-370-7488 ■ *Web:* www.sixflags.com/parks/newengland
Six Flags Over Georgia 7561 Six Flags Pkwy .... Austell GA 30168 770-948-9290 948-4378
Web: www.sixflags.com/parks/overgeorgia
Six Flags Over Texas 2201 Road to Six Flags .... Arlington TX 76011 817-640-8900 607-6140
Web: www.sixflags.com/parks/overtexas
Six Flags Saint Louis 4900 Six Flags Rd .... Eureka MO 63025 636-938-5300 587-3617
Web: www.sixflags.com/parks/stlouis
Six Flags White Water Park 250 Cobb Pkwy N .... Marietta GA 30062 770-424-9283 424-7565
Web: www.sixflags.com/parks/whitewater
Six Flags Wild Safari Rt 537 .... Jackson NJ 08527 732-928-1821 928-2775
Web: www.sixflags.com/parks/wildsafari
Soak City 1 Cedar Point Dr .... Sandusky OH 44870 419-627-2350 627-2200*
**Fax:* Mktg ■ *Web:* www.experiencethepoint.com/soakcity
Splashtown Water Park 21300 IH-45 N .... Spring TX 77373 281-355-3300 353-7946
Web: www.splashtownpark.com
Splish Splash 2549 Splish Splash Dr .... Riverhead NY 11901 631-727-3600
Web: www.splishsplashlongisland.com
Universal Orlando 1000 Universal Studios Plaza .... Orlando FL 32819 407-363-8000 363-8006*
**Fax:* Hum Res ■ *TF:* 877-801-9720 ■ *Web:* themeparks.universalstudios.com

Phone | Fax

Universal Studios Hollywood 100 Universal City Plaza .... Universal City CA 91608 818-622-3801 866-1516*
**Fax:* Hum Res ■ *TF:* 800-864-8377 ■ *Web:* www.universalstudioshollywood.com
Universal's Islands of Adventure 6000 Universal Studios Plaza .... Orlando FL 32819 407-363-8000 224-6942
TF: 877-801-9720 ■ *Web:* themeparks.universalstudios.com
Valleyfair 1 Valleyfair Dr .... Shakopee MN 55379 952-445-7600 445-1539
TF: 800-386-7433 ■ *Web:* www.valleyfair.com
Village Vacances Valcartier
1860 Valcartier Blvd .... Saint-Gabriel-de-Valcarti QC G0A4S0 418-844-2200 844-1239
TF: 888-384-5524 ■ *Web:* www.valcartier.com
Wannado City 12801 W Sunrise Blvd Anchor D .... Sunrise FL 33323 954-838-7100 514-6055
TF: 888-926-6236 ■ *Web:* www.wannadocity.com
Water Country USA 176 Water Country Pkwy .... Williamsburg VA 23185 757-229-9300 220-2816
TF: 800-343-7946 ■ *Web:* www.watercountryusa.com
Waterworld California 1950 Waterworld Pkwy .... Concord CA 94520 925-609-1364 609-1360
Web: www.waterworldcalifornia.com
Weeki Wachee Springs 6131 Commercial Way .... Spring Hill FL 34606 352-596-2062 597-1388
Web: www.weekiwachee.com
Western Playland Amusement Park 1249 Futurity Dr .... Sunland Park NM 88063 575-589-3410 589-0877
Web: www.westernplayland.com
Wet 'n Wild Emerald Pointe 3910 S Holden Rd .... Greensboro NC 27406 336-852-9721 852-2391
TF: 800-555-5900 ■ *Web:* www.emeraldpointe.com
Wet 'n Wild Orlando 6200 International Dr .... Orlando FL 32819 407-351-1800 363-1147
TF: 800-992-9453 ■ *Web:* www.wetnwild.com
White Water 3505 W Hwy 76 .... Branson MO 65616 800-475-9370 336-7791*
**Fax Area Code:* 417 ■ *Web:* whitewater.silverdollarcity.com
White Water Bay 3908 W Reno Ave .... Oklahoma City OK 73107 405-943-0392
Web: www.whitewaterbay.com
Wild Waters 5656 E Silver Springs Blvd .... Silver Springs FL 34488 352-236-2121 236-1732
Web: www.wildwaterspark.com
Wild Waves/Enchanted Village 36201 Enchanted Pkwy S .... Federal Way WA 98003 253-661-8000 925-1332*
**Fax:* Hum Res ■ *Web:* www.wildwaves.com
Wonderland Amusement Park 2601 Dumas Dr .... Amarillo TX 79107 806-383-0832 383-8737
TF: 800-383-4712 ■ *Web:* www.wonderlandpark.com
Worlds of Fun & Oceans of Fun 4545 Worlds of Fun Ave .... Kansas City MO 64161 816-454-4545 454-4655
Web: www.worldsoffun.com

33 ANIMATION COMPANIES

SEE ALSO Motion Picture & Television Production p. 1979; Motion Picture Production - Special Interest p. 1978

Phone | Fax

Advanced Animations PO Box 34 Rt 107 .... Stockbridge VT 05772 802-746-8974 746-8971
Web: www.advancedanimations.com
Animatic Media 1907 W Burbank Blvd 2nd Fl .... Burbank CA 91506 818-842-0800 842-0864
Web: www.animaticmedia.com
Atomic Cartoons Inc 1125 Hove St Suite 250 .... Vancouver BC V6Z2K8 604-734-2866 734-2869
Web: www.atomiccartoons.com
Big Idea Inc 230 Franklin Rd Bldg 2A .... Franklin TN 37064 615-224-2200 224-2250
Web: www.bigidea.com
Bix Pix Entertainment Inc 1917 W Belmont .... Chicago IL 60657 773-248-5430 248-5480
Web: www.bixpix.com
Blue Sky Studios 44 S Broadway 17th Floor .... White Plains NY 10601 914-259-6500 259-6499
Web: www.blueskystudios.com
Blur Studio 589 Venice Blvd .... Venice CA 90291 310-581-8848 581-8850
Web: www.blur.com
Brilliant Digital Entertainment Inc
14011 Ventura Blvd Suite 501 .... Sherman Oaks CA 91423 818-386-2180 615-0995
Web: www.brilliantdigital.com
Camp Chaos Entertainment 613 Penn Ave .... Reading PA 19611 610-376-4050 376-5110
Web: www.campchaos.com
Cartoon Network 1050 Techwood Dr .... Atlanta GA 30318 404-885-2263
Web: www.cartoonnetwork.com
Central Park Media Corp 250 W 57th St Suite 317 .... New York NY 10107 646-957-8301 977-8709*
**Fax Area Code:* 212 ■ *TF:* 800-833-7456 ■ *Web:* www.centralparkmedia.com
CineGroupe 1151 rue Alexandre-DeSeve 5th Fl .... Montreal QC H2L2T7 514-849-5008 849-5001
Web: www.cinegroupe.com
Cookie Jar Group 266 King St W 2nd Fl .... Toronto ON M5V1H8 416-977-3238 977-4526
Web: www.thecookiejarcompany.com
Cuppa Coffee Animation 215 Spadina Ave Suite 400 .... Toronto ON M5T2C7 416-340-8869 340-9819
Web: www.cuppacoffee.com
Curious Pictures Div iNTELEFILM Inc 440 Lafayette St 6th Fl .... New York NY 10003 212-674-1400 674-0081
Web: www.curiouspictures.com
DIC Entertainment LP 4100 W Alameda Ave .... Burbank CA 91505 818-955-5400 955-5696
Web: www.dicentertainment.com
DNA Productions 2201 W Royal Lane Suite 275 .... Irving TX 75063 214-352-4694 496-9333
Web: www.dnahelix.com
Dreamworks Animation LLC 1000 Flower St .... Glendale CA 91201 818-695-5000 695-7574
NYSE: DWA ■ *Web:* www.dreamworks.com
DUCK 2205 Stoner Ave .... Los Angeles CA 90064 310-478-0771 478-0773
Web: www.duckstudios.com
Film Roman Inc 2950 N Hollywood Way 3rd Fl .... Burbank CA 91505 818-748-4000 748-4619
Web: www.filmroman.com
iNTELEFILM Inc Curious Pictures Div 440 Lafayette St 6th Fl .... New York NY 10003 212-674-1400 674-0081
Web: www.curiouspictures.com
Itoons 6348 N Milwaukee Ave Suite 345 .... Chicago IL 60646 773-598-5811
Web: www.snap2play.com/itoons
Jim Henson's Creature Shop 1416 N LaBrea Ave .... Hollywood CA 90028 323-802-1525 802-1891
Web: www.creatureshop.com
Klasky Csupo Inc 6353 Sunset Blvd .... Hollywood CA 90028 323-468-2600
Web: www.klaskycsupo.com
Krislin Co 23901 Calabasas Rd Suite 2090 .... Calabasas CA 91302 818-222-2660 222-2661
Web: www.krislincompany.com
Laika 1400 NW 22nd Ave .... Portland OR 97210 503-225-1130 226-3746
Web: www.laika.com
Loop Filmworks Inc 45 Main St 5th Floor Suite 504 .... Brooklyn NY 11201 718-522-5667 522-5668
Web: www.loopfilmworks.com
Lucasfilm Ltd Animation 1110 Gorgas St PO Box 29901 .... San Francisco CA 94129 415-662-1800
Web: www.lucasfilm.com/divisions/animation
Mainframe Entertainment Inc 2025 W Broadway Suite 200 .... Vancouver BC V6J1Z6 604-714-2600 714-2641
Web: www.mainframe.ca
Mercury Filmworks 740 Nicola St .... Vancouver BC V6G2Z1 604-684-9117 684-8339
Web: www.mercuryfilmworks.com
MTV Animation 1633 Broadway 31st Fl .... New York NY 10019 212-654-3000
Nelvana Ltd 135 Liberty Suite 101 .... Toronto ON M6K1A7 416-535-0935 530-2832
Web: www.nelvana.com
NestFamily 1461 S Beltline Rd Suite 500 .... Coppell TX 75019 972-402-7100 629-7181
TF: 800-447-5958 ■ *Web:* www.nestfamily.com
Nickelodeon 1515 Broadway 38th Fl .... New York NY 10036 212-258-8000 258-7705
Web: www.nick.com
Pixar Animation Studios 1200 Park Ave .... Emeryville CA 94608 510-752-3000 752-3151
NASDAQ: PIXR ■ *TF:* 800-888-9856 ■ *Web:* www.pixar.com

	City	State	Zip	Phone	Fax
Pixel Factory Inc PO Box 618413 *Web:* www.pixfactory.com	Orlando	FL	32861	407-835-1220	
Renegade Animation Inc 116 N Maryland Ave Lower Level *Web:* www.renegadeanimation.com	Glendale	CA	91206	818-551-2351	551-2350
Rhythm & Hues Inc 5404 Jandy Pl *Web:* www.rhythm.com	Los Angeles	CA	90066	310-448-7500	448-7600
Sony Pictures Animation 9050 W Washington Blvd *Web:* www.sonypictures.com/tv/kids/	Culver City	CA	90232	323-857-7801	
Topix 35 McCaul St Suite 200 *Web:* www.topix.com	Toronto	ON	M5T1V7	416-971-7711	971-9277
Universal Cartoon Studio 100 Universal City Plaza	Universal City	CA	91608	818-777-1000	
Walt Disney Feature Animation 500 S Buena Vista St MC 91521-4876	Burbank	CA	91521	818-560-1000	
Warner Bros Classic Animation 15301 Ventura Blvd Unit E	Sherman Oaks	CA	91403	818-977-8700	977-0125
Warner Bros Feature Animation 15301 Ventura Blvd Unit E	Sherman Oaks	CA	91403	818-977-8700	977-0125
Wild Brain Inc 660 Alabama St *Web:* www.wildbraininc.com	San Francisco	CA	94110	415-553-8000	553-8009

34 APPAREL FINDINGS

	City	State	Zip	Phone	Fax
Copen Assoc Inc 1 W 37th St 10th Fl *Web:* midso.com	New York	NY	10018	212-819-0008	819-0870
Cushman & Marden Inc 56 Pulaski St *Web:* www.cushmanandmarden.com	Peabody	MA	01960	978-532-1670	531-6773
Dallas Bias Fabrics Inc 1401 N Carroll Ave *Web:* dallasbias.com	Dallas	TX	75204	214-824-2036	821-5204
International Molders Inc 3578 Hayden Ave *Web:* www.internationalmoldersinc.com	Culver City	CA	90230	310-559-8300	559-0452
Metric Products Inc 4671 Leahy St *TF:* 800-763-8742 ■ *Web:* www.metric-products.com	Culver City	CA	90232	310-815-9000	838-0241
Modern Quilters Inc 62038 Minnesota Hwy 24 PO Box 570	Litchfield	MN	55355	320-693-7987	693-2288
QST Industries Inc 525 W Monroe Suite 1400 *Web:* www.qst.com	Chicago	IL	60661	312-930-9400	648-0312
Western Textile Cos 3400 Treecourt Industrial Blvd *TF:* 800-624-8731	Saint Louis	MO	63122	636-225-9400	225-9854

35 APPLIANCE & HOME ELECTRONICS STORES

SEE ALSO Computer Stores p. 1520; Department Stores p. 1586; Furniture Stores p. 1685; Home Improvement Centers p. 1788

	City	State	Zip	Phone	Fax
AAA Co Inc PO Box 35866 *TF:* 800-850-8776	Fayetteville	NC	28303	910-867-6111	487-1422
ABC Appliance Inc DBA ABC Warehouse 1 W Silverdome Industrial Pk **Fax:* Hum Res ■ *TF:* 800-981-3866 ■ *Web:* www.abcwarehouse.com	Pontiac	MI	48342	248-335-4222	335-2853*
ABC Warehouse 1 W Silverdome Industrial Pk **Fax:* Hum Res ■ *TF:* 800-981-3866 ■ *Web:* www.abcwarehouse.com	Pontiac	MI	48342	248-335-4222	335-2853*
Adray Appliance Photo & Sound Center 20219 Carlysle St *TF:* 800-652-3729 ■ *Web:* www.adray.com	Dearborn	MI	48124	313-274-9500	274-6875
American TV & Appliance of Madison Inc 2404 W Beltline Hwy *Web:* www.americantv.com	Madison	WI	53713	608-271-1000	275-7439
Arthur F Schultz Co 939 W 26th St *Web:* www.arthurfschultz.com	Erie	PA	16508	814-454-8171	454-3052
At Your Service 4400 Airport Fwy *TF:* 888-777-7115 ■ *Web:* www.ayselectronics.com	Fort Worth	TX	76117	817-831-3113	831-8118
Audio Direct 460 W Roger Rd Suite 105 **Fax Area Code:* 520 ■ *Web:* www.audio-direct.com	Tucson	AZ	85705	888-628-3467	292-6101*
Audio Graphic Systems Inc 2131 S Grove Ave Suite A *TF:* 800-854-8547 ■ *Web:* www.agspresents.com	Ontario	CA	91761	909-673-0070	673-0990
Audio King Corp 321 W 84th Ave Suite A *TF:* 800-260-2660 ■ *Web:* www.ultimateelectronics.com	Thornton	CO	80260	303-412-2500	412-2501
Auto Accents 6550 Pearl Rd *TF:* 800-567-3120 ■ *Web:* www.autoaccents.com	Cleveland	OH	44130	440-888-8886	888-4333
Batteries Plus LLC 925 Walnut Ridge Dr *TF:* 800-274-9155 ■ *Web:* www.batteriesplus.com	Hartland	WI	53029	262-369-0690	912-3100
Best Buy Co Inc 7601 Penn Ave S *NYSE: BBY* ■ **Fax Area Code:* 952 ■ **Fax:* Cust Svc ■ *TF:* 800-369-5050 ■ *Web:* www.bestbuy.com	Richfield	MN	55423	612-291-1000	238-3160*
BrandsMart USA Corp 3200 SW 42nd St *TF:* 800-432-8579 ■ *Web:* www.brandsmartusa.com	Hollywood	FL	33312	954-797-4000	797-4061
Circuit City Group 9950 Mayland Dr **Fax:* Acctg ■ *TF:* 800-251-2665 ■ *Web:* www.circuitcity.com	Richmond	VA	23233	804-527-4000	527-4171*
Conn's Inc 3295 College St *NASDAQ: CONN* ■ *TF Cust Svc:* 800-511-5750 ■ *Web:* www.conns.com	Beaumont	TX	77701	409-832-1696	832-4344
Cook's Inc PO Box 205 *TF:* 800-499-6001	Grand Haven	MI	49417	616-842-0180	842-1941
Cyberian Outpost Inc 25 N Main St *TF:* 877-688-7678 ■ *Web:* www.outpost.com	Kent	CT	06757	860-927-2050	927-8600
DeSears Appliances Inc 6430 14th St W *TF:* 800-337-3277	Bradenton	FL	34207	941-751-7525	756-4731
eCOST.com Inc 2555 W 190th St Suite 106 *TF:* 800-555-3613 ■ *Web:* www.ecost.com	Torrance	CA	90504	310-225-4044	225-4030
Eklund's Appliance & TV Co 1007 Central Ave W *Web:* www.eklundsappliance.com	Great Falls	MT	59404	406-761-3430	453-6942
Filco Inc 1433 Fulton Ave	Sacramento	CA	95825	916-483-4526	978-3455
Fry's Electronics 600 E Brokaw Rd **Fax:* PR ■ *Web:* www.frys.com	San Jose	CA	95112	408-487-4500	487-4700*
FS Appliance & TV Center 3805 Oakwood Mall Dr	Eau Claire	WI	54701	715-836-8270	836-8273
Future Shop Ltd 6200 McKay Ave Unit 144 *TF:* 800-663-2275 ■ *Web:* www.futureshop.ca	Burnaby	BC	V5H4L7	604-434-3844	434-2041
GNP Audio Video Inc 1254 E Colorado Blvd *Web:* www.gnpaudiovideo.com	Pasadena	CA	91106	626-577-7767	584-6994
Gregg Appliances Inc DBA HH Gregg 4151 E 96th St *TF:* 800-284-7344 ■ *Web:* www.hhgregg.com	Indianapolis	IN	46240	317-848-8710	848-8723
Harvey Electronics Inc 205 Chubb Ave *NASDAQ: HRVE* ■ *TF:* 800-254-7836 ■ *Web:* www.harveyonline.com	Lyndhurst	NJ	07071	201-842-0078	842-0660
Henshaw's Electronics Co 7622 Wornall Rd *TF:* 888-445-3434 ■ *Web:* www.henshaws.com	Kansas City	MO	64114	816-444-3434	363-4466
HH Gregg 4151 E 96th St *TF:* 800-284-7344 ■ *Web:* www.hhgregg.com	Indianapolis	IN	46240	317-848-8710	848-8723
Howard's Appliance & Big Screen Superstores 901 E Imperial Hwy *Web:* www.howards.com	La Habra	CA	90631	714-871-2700	871-2719
IbuyDigital.com Inc 252 Conover St *TF:* 866-243-4289 ■ *Web:* www.ibuydigital.com	Brooklyn	NY	11231	646-218-2200	
InPhonic Inc 1010 Wisconsin Ave NW Suite 600 *NASDAQ: INPC* ■ *Web:* www.inphonic.com	Washington	DC	20007	202-333-0001	333-5007
Interbond Corp of America 3200 SW 42nd St **Fax:* Hum Res ■ *TF:* 800-432-8579	Hollywood	FL	33312	954-797-4000	797-4061*
InterTAN Inc 3300 Hwy 7 Suite 904 Royal Center *Web:* www.intertan.com	Concord	ON	L4K4M3	905-760-9701	760-3620
Kitchen Resource LLC 3767 S 150 East *TF:* 800-692-6724 ■ *Web:* www.boschmixers.com	Salt Lake City	UT	84115	801-261-3222	261-3235
Let's Talk Inc 410 Townsend St Suite 100 *TF Orders:* 866-825-5460 ■ *Web:* www.letstalk.com	San Francisco	CA	94107	415-344-0227	344-0288
Midland Radio Corp 1120 Clay St **Fax Area Code:* 800 ■ *Web:* www.midlandradio.com	North Kansas City	MO	64116	816-241-8500	821-8528*
Moore Pete Appliance Inc 1615 W State St	Bristol	VA	24201	276-669-2106	466-4282
National Auto Sound Inc 11001 E Hwy 40 *Web:* www.nationalautosound.com	Independence	MO	64055	816-356-8700	356-7230
NationLink Wireless 342 Cool Springs Blvd Suite 200 *TF:* 800-496-2355 ■ *Web:* www.4nationlink.com	Franklin	TN	37067	615-567-2224	567-2230
Niederauer Inc DBA Western Appliance 1976 W San Carlos St *Web:* www.westernappliance.com	San Jose	CA	95128	408-297-2440	286-9436
PC Richard & Son Inc 150 Price Pkwy *TF:* 800-696-2000 ■ *Web:* www.pcrichard.com	Farmingdale	NY	11735	631-843-4300	843-4309
Pete Moore Appliance Inc 1615 W State St	Bristol	VA	24201	276-669-2106	466-4282
Pieratt's Inc 110 S Mt Tabor Rd *Web:* www.pieratts.net	Lexington	KY	40517	859-268-6000	268-9065
Queen City TV & Appliance Co Inc 2430 I-85 S *TF:* 800-365-6665 ■ *Web:* www.queencitytv.com	Charlotte	NC	28208	704-391-6000	391-6038
RadioShack 300 Radioshack Cir *TF:* 800-843-7422 ■ *Web:* www.radioshack.com	Fort Worth	TX	76102	817-415-3011	415-3240
RadioShack Corp 300 RadioShack Cir *NYSE: RSH* ■ *TF:* 800-843-7422 ■ *Web:* www.radioshackcorporation.com	Fort Worth	TX	76102	817-415-3011	415-3240
REX Stores Corp 2875 Needmore Rd *NYSE: RSC* ■ *TF:* 800-528-9739 ■ *Web:* www.rexstores.com	Dayton	OH	45414	937-276-3931	276-8643
Schultz Arthur F Co 939 W 26th St *Web:* www.arthurfschultz.com	Erie	PA	16508	814-454-8171	454-3052
Sharper Image Corp 650 Davis St *NASDAQ: SHRP* ■ **Fax:* Cust Svc ■ *TF:* 800-344-4444 ■ *Web:* www.sharperimage.com	San Francisco	CA	94111	415-445-6000	445-1508*
Simutek Inc 3136 E Fort Lowell Rd *Web:* www.simutek.com	Tucson	AZ	85716	520-321-9077	321-9078
Sound Advice Inc 2501 SW 32nd Terr *TF Cust Svc:* 800-749-1897 ■ *Web:* www.tweeter.com	Pembroke Park	FL	33023	954-922-4434	
Star Cellular 1371 S Bascom Ave *TF:* 800-969-0023	San Jose	CA	95128	408-288-8500	288-8556
Starsound Audio Inc 2679 Oddie Blvd *Web:* www.starsound.com	Reno	NV	89512	775-331-1010	331-1030
Tweeter Home Entertainment Group Inc 40 Pequot Way *NASDAQ: TWTR* ■ *TF:* 800-893-3837 ■ *Web:* www.tweeter.com	Canton	MA	02021	781-821-2900	821-9956
Ultimate Electronics Inc 321-A W 84th Ave *TF:* 800-260-2660 ■ *Web:* www.ultimateelectronics.com	Thornton	CO	80260	303-412-2500	412-2501
Western Appliance 1976 W San Carlos St *Web:* www.westernappliance.com	San Jose	CA	95128	408-297-2440	286-9436
Wireless Toyz Ltd 23399 Commerce Dr Suite B-1 *TF:* 866-237-2624 ■ *Web:* www.wirelesstoyz.com	Farmington Hills	MI	48335	248-426-8200	671-0346
Wireless Zone 34 Industrial Park Pl *TF:* 800-411-2355 ■ *Web:* www.wirelesszone.com	Middletown	CT	06457	860-632-9494	632-9343
Yale Electric Supply Co 296 Freeport St *TF:* 800-289-9253 ■ *Web:* www.yaleelectric.com	Dorchester	MA	02122	617-825-9253	825-6541

36 APPLIANCES - MAJOR - MFR

SEE ALSO Air Conditioning & Heating Equipment - Residential p. 1268

	City	State	Zip	Phone	Fax
AM Appliance Group PO Box 851805 *TF:* 800-898-1879 ■ *Web:* www.askousa.com	Richardson	TX	75085	972-644-8595	234-2709
Anaheim Mfg Co 4240 E La Palma Ave *TF Cust Svc:* 800-854-3229 ■ *Web:* www.anaheimmfg.com	Anaheim	CA	92807	714-524-7770	996-7073
AO Smith Corp 11270 W Park Pl Suite 170 *NYSE: AOS* ■ *TF:* 800-359-4065 ■ *Web:* www.aosmith.com	Milwaukee	WI	53224	414-359-4000	359-4180
AO Smith Water Products Co 500 Tennessee Waltz Pkwy *TF:* 800-365-8170 ■ *Web:* www.hotwater.com	Ashland City	TN	37015	615-792-4371	792-4371
Bradford White Corp 725 Talamore Dr *TF:* 800-523-2931 ■ *Web:* www.bradfordwhite.com	Ambler	PA	19002	215-641-9400	641-1612
Bradley Direct 7100 Jamesson Rd **Fax Area Code:* 706 ■ *Web:* www.grilllovers.com	Midland	GA	31820	800-252-8248	565-2121*
Brown Stove Works Inc 1422 Carolina Ave NE *TF:* 800-251-7485 ■ *Web:* www.fivestarrange.com	Cleveland	TN	37311	423-476-6544	476-6599
Cervitor Kitchens Inc 10775 Lower Azusa Rd *TF:* 800-523-2666 ■ *Web:* www.cervitor.com	El Monte	CA	91731	626-443-0184	443-0400
Char-Broil 1442 Belfast Ave **Fax:* Cust Svc ■ *TF Cust Svc:* 800-352-4111 ■ *Web:* www.charbroil.com	Columbus	GA	31904	706-324-0421	576-6355*
CookTek Inc 810 W Washington St *TF:* 888-266-5835 ■ *Web:* www.cooktek.com	Chicago	IL	60607	312-563-9600	432-6220
Crosley Corp 675 N Main St *TF:* 800-849-1112 ■ *Web:* www.crosley.com	Winston-Salem	NC	27101	336-722-1112	721-0685
Daewoo Electronics Corp of America 300 - 3E SR 17 S *TF:* 877-399-7823 ■ *Web:* www.dwe.co.kr	Lodi	NJ	07644	973-249-3410	249-3412
Dwyer Products Corp 1226 Michael Dr Suite S *TF:* 800-348-8508 ■ *Web:* www.dwyerkitchens.com	Wood Dale	IL	60191	630-741-7970	741-7974
Electric Heater Co 45 Seymour St *TF:* 800-647-3165 ■ *Web:* www.hubbellheaters.com	Stratford	CT	06615	203-378-2659	378-3593
Electrolux 20445 Emerald Pkwy Suite 250	Cleveland	OH	44135	216-898-1800	
Emerson Radio Corp 9 Entin Rd *AMEX: MSN* ■ *Web:* www.emersonradio.com	Parsippany	NJ	07054	973-884-5800	428-2067
Fisher & Paykel Appliances Inc 5900 Skylab Rd *TF:* 800-933-7718 ■ *Web:* usa.fisherpaykel.com	Huntington Beach	CA	92647	949-790-8900	790-8911
Frigidaire Home Products Co 250 Bobby Jones Expy *TF Sales:* 800-288-4924 ■ *Web:* www.frigidaire.com	Augusta	GA	30907	706-651-1751	651-7754
GE Consumer Products Appliance Park Rm 129 **Fax:* Cust Svc ■ *TF:* 800-626-2000 ■ *Web:* www.geconsumerproducts.com	Louisville	KY	40225	502-452-4311	452-0054*
In-Sink-Erator 4700 21st St *TF:* 800-558-5712 ■ *Web:* www.insinkerator.com	Racine	WI	53406	262-554-5432	554-3546
Jenn-Air Co 403 W 4th St N *TF:* 800-688-9900 ■ *Web:* www.jennair.com	Newton	IA	50208	641-792-7000	787-8395
KitchenAid Div Whirlpool Corp 2000 M-63 N *TF:* 800-253-1301 ■ *Web:* kitchenaid.com	Benton Harbor	MI	49022	269-923-5000	923-5443
LG Electronics USA Inc 1000 Sylvan Ave *TF Tech Supp:* 800-243-0000 ■ *Web:* us.lge.com/index.do	Englewood Cliffs	NJ	07632	201-816-2000	816-0636
Lochinvar Corp 300 Maddox Simpson Pkwy *Web:* www.lochinvar.com	Lebanon	TN	37090	615-889-8900	547-1000

Phone Fax

Maytag Appliances 403 W 4th St N. . . . . Newton IA 50208 641-792-7000 787-8395*
*Fax: Mail Rm ■ TF Cust Svc: 800-688-9900 ■ Web: www.maytag.com

Maytag-Cleveland Cooking Products 740 King Edward Ave . . . . . Cleveland TN 37320 423-472-3371 478-4680
TF: 800-688-1120

Maytag-Herrin Laundry Products 410 E Lyerla Dr . . . . . Herrin IL 62948 618-988-8431 942-2833

Maytag-Jackson Dishwashing Products
2500 Doctor FE Wright Dr. . . . . Jackson TN 38305 731-424-3500 424-5200

Maytag-Newton Laundry Products 403 West 4th St N . . . . . Newton IA 50208 641-792-7000 787-8317
TF: 800-866-9900

Miele Inc 9 Independence Way. . . . . Princeton NJ 08540 609-419-9898 419-4298
TF: 800-843-7231 ■ Web: www.miele.com

Multi-Pak Corp 180 Atlantic St. . . . . Hackensack NJ 07601 201-342-7474 342-6525
TF: 800-234-7441 ■ Web: www.compactors1.com

Northland Corp 701 Ranney Dr. . . . . Greenville MI 48838 616-754-5601 754-0970
TF: 800-223-3900 ■ Web: www.northlandnka.com

Peerless Premier Appliance Co 119 S 14th St . . . . . Belleville IL 62222 618-233-0475 235-1771
TF: 800-858-5844 ■ Web: www.premierrange.com

Rheem Mfg Co Water Heater Div 2600 Gunter Park Dr E. . . . . Montgomery AL 36109 334-260-1500 535-9538*
*Fax Area Code: 800 ■ *Fax: Orders ■ TF: 800-621-5622 ■ Web: rheem.com

Robert Bosch LLC 2800 S 25th Ave . . . . . Broadview IL 60155 708-865-5200 865-6430
Web: www.boschusa.com

Roper Corp 1507 Broomtown Rd . . . . . La Fayette GA 30728 706-638-5100 638-5767

Samsung Electronics America Inc 105 Challenger Rd. . . . . Ridgefield Park NJ 07660 201-229-4000 229-4029
TF: 800-726-7864 ■ Web: www.samsungusa.com

Sanyo Fisher Co 21605 Plummer St. . . . . Chatsworth CA 91311 818-998-7322 701-4194
Web: us.sanyo.com

Sharp Electronics Corp 1 Sharp Plaza . . . . . Mahwah NJ 07430 201-529-8200 529-8413
TF: 800-237-4277 ■ Web: www.sharpusa.com

Siemens Home Appliances 5551 McFadden Ave . . . . . Huntington Beach CA 92649 714-901-6600 901-5360
TF: 888-474-3636 ■ Web: www.siemens-home.com

Smith AO Corp 11270 W Park Pl Suite 170 . . . . . Milwaukee WI 53224 414-359-4000 359-4180
NYSE: AOS ■ TF: 800-359-4065 ■ Web: www.aosmith.com

Smith AO Water Products Co 500 Tennessee Waltz Pkwy. . . . . Ashland City TN 37015 615-792-4371 792-4371
TF: 800-365-8170 ■ Web: www.hotwater.com

Sub-Zero Freezer Co Inc 4717 Hammersley Rd. . . . . Madison WI 53711 608-271-2233 270-3362
TF Prod Info: 800-222-7820 ■ Web: www.subzero.com

Thermador 5551 McFadden Ave . . . . . Huntington Beach CA 92649 714-901-6600 901-5980
TF: 800-735-4328 ■ Web: www.thermador.com

Thetford Corp Recreational Vehicle Group PO Box 1285. . . . . Ann Arbor MI 48106 734-769-6000 769-2023

Vaughn Mfg Corp 26 Old Elm St. . . . . Salisbury MA 01952 978-462-6683 462-6497
TF: 800-282-8446 ■ Web: www.vaughncorp.com

WC Bradley Char-Broil 1442 Belfast Ave . . . . . Columbus GA 31904 706-324-0421 576-6355*
*Fax: Cust Svc ■ TF Cust Svc: 800-352-4111 ■ Web: www.charbroil.com

Weber-Stephen Products Co 200 E Daniels Rd . . . . . Palatine IL 60067 847-934-5700 934-3153
TF Cust Svc: 800-446-1071 ■ Web: www.weberbbq.com

Whirlpool Corp 2000 N M-63 . . . . . Benton Harbor MI 49022 269-923-5000 923-5443
NYSE: WHR ■ TF: 800-253-1301 ■ Web: www.whirlpoolcorp.com

Whirlpool Corp KitchenAid Div 2000 M-63 N . . . . . Benton Harbor MI 49022 269-923-5000 923-5443
TF: 800-253-1301 ■ Web: kitchenaid.com

Whirlpool Corp North American Region 2000 N M-63 . . . . . Benton Harbor MI 49022 269-923-5000 923-5443*
*Fax: Hum Res ■ TF: 800-253-1301 ■ Web: www.whirlpoolcorp.com

Wisco Industries Inc 736 Janesville St. . . . . Oregon WI 53575 608-835-3106 835-7399
TF: 800-999-4726 ■ Web: www.wiscoind.com

37 APPLIANCES - SMALL - MFR

SEE ALSO Air Purification Equipment - Household p. 1269; Vacuum Cleaners - Household p. 2396

Phone Fax

Abatement Technologies 605 Satellite Blvd Suite 300. . . . . Suwanee GA 30024 678-889-4200 358-2394*
*Fax Area Code: 800 ■ TF: 800-634-9091 ■ Web: www.abatement.com

Adams Mfg Co Inc 9790 Midwest Ave . . . . . Cleveland OH 44125 216-587-6801 587-6807
Web: www.adamsmanufacturing.com

Aisin World Corp of America 24330 Garnier St. . . . . Torrance CA 90505 310-326-8681 326-0678*
*Fax: Acctg ■ TF: 800-822-2726 ■ Web: www.aisinworld.com

Andis Co 1800 Renaissance Blvd . . . . . Sturtevant WI 53177 262-884-2600 884-1100
TF Cust Svc: 800-558-9441 ■ Web: www.andis.com

Applica Consumer Products Inc 3633 Flamingo Rd . . . . . Miramar FL 33027 954-883-1000 883-1070
TF Cust Svc: 800-231-9786 ■ Web: www.applicainc.com

Applica Inc 3633 Flamingo Rd . . . . . Miramar FL 33027 954-883-1000 883-1070
NYSE: APN ■ TF: 800-557-9463 ■ Web: www.applicainc.com

Bernina of America Inc 3702 Prairie Lake Ct. . . . . Aurora IL 60504 630-978-2500 978-8214
Web: www.berninausa.com

Bodum Inc 1860 Renaissance Blvd Suite 201. . . . . Sturtevant WI 53177 262-884-4650 884-4655
TF: 800-232-6386 ■ Web: www.bodum.com

Braun North America 1 Gillette Pk . . . . . Boston MA 02127 617-463-3000 796-4565*
*Fax Area Code: 800 ■ TF Cust Svc: 800-272-8611 ■ Web: www.braun.com/na

Broan-NuTone LLC 926 W State St. . . . . Hartford WI 53027 262-673-4340 673-8709
TF Cust Svc: 800-558-1711 ■ Web: www.broan.com

Brother International Corp 100 Somerset Corporate Blvd. . . . . Bridgewater NJ 08807 908-704-1700 704-8235
TF Cust Svc: 800-276-7746 ■ Web: www.brother-usa.com

Bunn-O-Matic Corp 1400 Stevenson Dr . . . . . Springfield IL 62703 217-529-6601 529-6622
TF: 800-637-8606 ■ Web: www.bunnomatic.com

Cadet Mfg Co Inc 2500 W 4th Plain Blvd. . . . . Vancouver WA 98660 360-693-2505 694-6939
TF: 800-442-2338 ■ Web: www.cadetco.com

Casablanca Fan Co 761 Corporate Center Dr. . . . . Pomona CA 91768 909-629-1477 629-3243
TF: 888-227-2178 ■ Web: www.casablancafanco.com

Chromalox Inc 103 Gamma Dr Ext. . . . . Pittsburgh PA 15238 412-967-3800 967-5148
TF Cust Svc: 800-368-2493 ■ Web: www.chromalox.com

Conair Corp 1 Cummings Pt Rd . . . . . Stamford CT 06902 203-351-9000 351-9180
TF: 800-726-6247 ■ Web: www.conair.com

Craftmade International Inc 650 S Royal Ln. . . . . Coppell TX 75019 972-393-3800 304-3750
NASDAQ: CRFT ■ TF: 800-527-2578 ■ Web: www.craftmade.com

Cuisinart Corp 1 Cummings Pt Rd . . . . . Stamford CT 06902 203-975-4600 975-4660
TF: 800-726-0190 ■ Web: www.cuisinart.com

Electrolux 20445 Emerald Pkwy Suite 250. . . . . Cleveland OH 44135 216-898-1800

Fan-Tastic Vent Corp 2083 S Almont Ave . . . . . Imlay City MI 48444 810-724-3818 724-3460
TF: 800-521-0298 ■ Web: www.fantasticvent.com

GE Consumer Products Appliance Park Rm 129. . . . . Louisville KY 40225 502-452-4311 452-0054*
*Fax: Cust Svc ■ TF: 800-626-2000 ■ Web: www.geconsumerproducts.com

Hamilton Beach/Proctor-Silex Inc 4421 Waterfront Dr . . . . . Glen Allen VA 23060 804-273-9777 527-7142
TF Cust Svc: 800-851-8900 ■ Web: www.hambeach.com

Hitachi Home Electronics Inc 900 Hitachi Way. . . . . Chula Vista CA 91914 619-591-5200 591-5201
TF: 800-981-2588

Holmes Group Inc 1 Holmes Way. . . . . Milford MA 01757 508-634-8050 634-1211
TF: 800-546-5637 ■ Web: www.holmesproducts.com

Hotronic USA Inc 25 Omega Dr . . . . . Williston VT 05495 802-862-7403 863-6519
Web: www.hotronic.com

Hunter Fan Co 2500 Frisco Ave . . . . . Memphis TN 38114 901-743-1360
TF: 800-448-6837 ■ Web: www.hunterfan.com

iRobot Corp 63 South Ave. . . . . Burlinton MA 01803 781-345-0200 345-0201
NASDAQ: IRBT ■ TF: 888-776-2687 ■ Web: www.irobot.com

Phone Fax

Kaz Home Environment 250 Turnpike Rd . . . . . Southborough MA 01772 508-490-7000
Web: www.kaz.com

Kaz Inc 1775 Broadway Suite 2405. . . . . New York NY 10019 212-586-1630 265-9248
TF Cust Svc: 800-241-1131 ■ Web: www.kaz.com

King Electrical Mfg Co 9131 10th Ave S. . . . . Seattle WA 98108 206-762-0400 763-7738
TF: 800-603-5464 ■ Web: www.king-electric.com

KitchenAid Div Whirlpool Corp 2000 M-63 N . . . . . Benton Harbor MI 49022 269-923-5000 923-5443
TF: 800-253-1301 ■ Web: kitchenaid.com

Krups North America 196 Boston Ave . . . . . Medford MA 02155 800-526-5377 396-1313*
*Fax Area Code: 781 ■ Web: www.krupsusa.com

Lasko Metal Products Inc 820 Lincoln Ave. . . . . West Chester PA 19380 610-692-7400 696-4648
TF: 800-394-3267 ■ Web: www.laskoproducts.com

LG Electronics USA Inc 1000 Sylvan Ave. . . . . Englewood Cliffs NJ 07632 201-816-2000 816-0636
TF Tech Supp: 800-243-0000 ■ Web: us.lge.com/index.do

Lifetime Brands Inc Farberware Div 1000 Stewart Ave. . . . . Garden City NY 11530 516-683-6000 683-6161
TF: 800-252-3390 ■ Web: www.farberware.com

Marley Engineered Products 470 Beauty Spot Rd E. . . . . Bennettsville SC 29512 843-479-4006 479-8912
TF: 800-452-4179 ■ Web: www.marleymeh.com

Marvin WB Mfg Co 211 Glenn Ave. . . . . Urbana OH 43078 937-653-7131 652-1375
TF: 800-733-1706 ■ Web: www.wbmarvin.com

Metal Ware Corp 1700 Monroe St. . . . . Two Rivers WI 54241 920-793-1368 793-1086
TF Cust Svc: 800-288-4545 ■ Web: www.nesco.com

Munsey Products Inc 9911 I-30. . . . . Little Rock AR 72209 501-568-7870 568-7876

National Presto Industries Inc 3925 N Hastings Way. . . . . Eau Claire WI 54703 715-839-2121 839-2122
NYSE: NPK ■ TF: 800-877-0441 ■ Web: www.presto-net.com

Panasonic Consumer Electronics Co 1 Panasonic Way. . . . . Secaucus NJ 07094 201-348-7000 392-6168
TF: 888-275-2595 ■ Web: www.panasonic.com/consumer_electronics/home

Philips Electronics North America Corp
1251 Ave of the Americas 20th Fl. . . . . New York NY 10020 212-536-0500 536-0559*
*Fax: Hum Res ■ TF: 800-223-1828 ■ Web: www.philips.com

Rival Co 1605 George Dieter St Suite 688 . . . . . El Paso TX 79936 800-557-4825 791-7929*
*Fax Area Code: 915 ■ Web: www.rivco.com

Rowenta Inc 196 Boston Ave . . . . . Medford MA 02155 781-396-0600 396-1313
TF: 800-769-3682 ■ Web: www.rowentausa.com

Salton Inc 1955 W Field Ct. . . . . Lake Forest IL 60045 847-803-4600 803-1186
NYSE: SFP ■ TF: 800-272-5629 ■ Web: www.saltoninc.com

Schawbel Corp 100 Crosby Dr Suite 102 . . . . . Bedford MA 01730 781-541-6900 541-6007
TF: 866-753-3837 ■ Web: www.thermacell.net

Sharp Electronics Corp 1 Sharp Plaza . . . . . Mahwah NJ 07430 201-529-8200 529-8413
TF: 800-237-4277 ■ Web: www.sharpusa.com

Singer Sewing Co 1224 Hill Quaker Blvd PO Box 7017 . . . . . La Vergne TN 37086 615-213-0880 213-0894
TF: 877-738-9869 ■ Web: www.singerco.com

Sunbeam Products Inc 2381 Executive Center Dr . . . . . Boca Raton FL 33431 561-912-4100 912-4567
Web: www.sunbeam.com

T-Fal Corp 1 Boland Dr Suite 101. . . . . West Orange NJ 07052 973-736-0300 736-9078
TF: 800-395-8325 ■ Web: www.t-falusa.com

Tatung Co of America Inc 2850 El Presidio St . . . . . Long Beach CA 90810 310-637-2105
TF: 800-827-2850 ■ Web: www.tatungusa.com

Vita-Mix Corp 8615 Usher Rd. . . . . Cleveland OH 44138 440-235-4840 235-3726
TF: 800-848-2649 ■ Web: www.vita-mix.com

Waring Products Inc 314 Ella T Grasso Ave. . . . . Torrington CT 06790 860-496-3100 496-9017
TF: 800-269-6640 ■ Web: www.waringproducts.com

WB Marvin Mfg Co 211 Glenn Ave. . . . . Urbana OH 43078 937-653-7131 652-1375
TF: 800-733-1706 ■ Web: www.wbmarvin.com

West Bend Housewares LLC 1100 Schmidt Rd . . . . . West Bend WI 53090 262-334-2311 334-6881
TF: 800-269-8805 ■ Web: www.westbend.com

Whirlpool Corp KitchenAid Div 2000 M-63 N . . . . . Benton Harbor MI 49022 269-923-5000 923-5443
TF: 800-253-1301 ■ Web: kitchenaid.com

World Dryer Corp 5700 McDermott Dr . . . . . Berkeley IL 60163 708-449-6950 449-6958
TF: 800-323-0701 ■ Web: www.worlddryer.com

38 APPLIANCES - WHOL

Phone Fax

Allison-Erwin Co 2920 N Tyron St PO Box 32308 . . . . . Charlotte NC 28232 704-334-8621 334-8381
TF Sales: 800-253-0370 ■ Web: www.allisonerwin.com

Almo Corp 2709 Commerce Way. . . . . Philadelphia PA 19154 215-698-4000 698-4080*
*Fax: Hum Res ■ TF: 800-345-2566 ■ Web: www.almo.com

Amco McLean Corp 561 S 4th Ave. . . . . Mount Vernon NY 10550 914-237-4000 237-4341
TF: 800-431-2010 ■ Web: amcomcleancorp.com

Autco Distributing Inc 10900 Midwest Industrial Blvd. . . . . Saint Louis MO 63132 314-426-6524 426-7378
TF: 800-443-0044 ■ Web: www.autco.com

Bermil Industries Corp DBA Wascomat of America
PO Box 960338 . . . . . Inwood NY 11096 516-371-4400 371-4204
TF: 800-645-2205

Blodgett Supply Co Inc 100 Ave D PO Box 759. . . . . Williston VT 05495 802-864-9831 864-3645
TF: 800-223-6911 ■ Web: www.blodgettsupply.com

Brady Marketing Co 80 Berry Dr Suite A. . . . . Pacheco CA 94553 925-676-1300 676-3082
TF: 800-326-6080 ■ Web: www.bradymarketing.com

Brooke Distributors Inc 16250 NW 52nd Ave . . . . . Miami FL 33014 305-624-9752 620-3988
TF: 800-275-8792 ■ Web: www.brooke.com

Carl Schaedel & Co Inc 4 Sperry Rd . . . . . Fairfield NJ 07004 973-244-1311 244-0822
TF: 800-783-6008 ■ Web: www.carlschaedel.com

Collins Appliance Parts Inc 1533 Metropolitan St. . . . . Pittsburgh PA 15233 412-321-3700 323-1232
TF: 800-366-9969 ■ Web: www.appliancepartscollins.com

Cunningham Distributing Inc 2015 Mills Ave. . . . . El Paso TX 79901 915-533-6993 545-1320

Electrical Distributing Inc 4600 NW St Helens Rd . . . . . Portland OR 97210 503-226-4044 226-4040
TF: 800-932-3774 ■ Web: www.edinw.com

Fogel MH & Co Inc 2839 Liberty Ave. . . . . Pittsburgh PA 15222 412-261-3921 261-3979
TF: 800-245-2954

Fretz Corp 2001 Woodhaven Rd. . . . . Philadelphia PA 19116 215-671-8300 671-8340
TF: 866-987-2121 ■ Web: www.fretz.com

Glindmeyer Distributing Co Inc 2910 Lausat St. . . . . Metairie LA 70001 504-832-2223 832-2228
TF: 800-466-1754 ■ Web: www.glindmeyer.com

Gold Star Distributors 520 N Central Expy . . . . . Richardson TX 75080 972-238-9541 699-9718
TF: 800-756-9337 ■ Web: www.homeappliances.com/goldstar

Goldberg Co Inc 2423-A Grenoble Rd. . . . . Richmond VA 23294 804-228-5700 228-5701
TF: 800-365-6533

Gotham Sales Co 302 Main St . . . . . Millburn NJ 07041 973-912-8412 912-0814
Web: www.gothamsales.com

GPX Inc 900 N 23 St. . . . . Saint Louis MO 63106 314-621-3314 621-0869
Web: www.gpx.com

H Schultz & Sons Inc 777 Lehigh Ave . . . . . Union NJ 07083 908-687-5400 687-1788
Web: www.housewaresandthings.com

Hamburg Brothers Inc 40 24th St. . . . . Pittsburgh PA 15222 412-227-6200 227-6258
TF: 800-568-4624 ■ Web: www.hamburgbrothers.com

Helen of Troy Ltd 1 Helen of Troy Plaza. . . . . El Paso TX 79912 915-225-8000 225-8011
NASDAQ: HELE ■ TF: 800-487-8432 ■ Web: www.hotus.com

Inter-Ocean Industries Inc Bldg 300-2 Unit C Rt 17 S . . . . . Lodi NJ 07644 973-458-8070 458-8085

King Kitchen Distributing Inc 6075 E Shelby Dr Suite 1. . . . . Memphis TN 38141 901-362-9651 362-9667

Klaus Radio Inc 8400 N Allen Rd. . . . . Peoria IL 61615 309-691-4840 693-1724
TF: 800-545-5287 ■ Web: www.klausco.com

Liberty Distributors Inc 520 S Commerce St PO Box 48168. . . . . Wichita KS 67201 316-264-7393 264-5210
TF: 800-633-9211

	City	State	Zip	Phone	Fax
MH Fogel & Co Inc 2839 Liberty Ave *TF:* 800-245-2954	Pittsburgh	PA	15222	412-261-3921	261-3979
Midwest Sales & Service Inc 917 S Chapin St *TF:* 800-772-7262	South Bend	IN	46601	574-287-3365	287-3429
Molay Supply Inc 801 1st Ave N	Birmingham	AL	35203	205-322-4321	322-4331
Nelson & Small Inc 212 Canco Rd *TF:* 800-341-0780 ■ *Web:* www.nelsonsmall.com	Portland	ME	04103	207-775-5666	775-4303
Oakton Distributors Inc 125 E Oakton St *TF:* 800-262-5866 ■ *Web:* www.oakton.com	Des Plaines	IL	60018	847-294-5858	294-6816
O'Rourke Sales Co 3885 Elmore Ave Suite 100 *TF:* 800-523-4730 ■ *Web:* www.orourkesales.com	Davenport	IA	52807	563-823-1501	823-1534
Peirce-Phelps Inc 2000 N 59th St *TF:* 800-222-2742 ■ *Web:* www.peirce.com	Philadelphia	PA	19131	215-879-7000	879-5141
Potter Distributing Inc 4037 Roger B Chaffee Blvd *TF:* 800-748-0568 ■ *Web:* www.potterdistributing.com	Grand Rapids	MI	49548	616-531-6860	531-9578
Precision Trading Corp 1430 NW 88th Ave *Web:* www.precisiontrading.com	Miami	FL	33172	305-592-4500	593-6169
Prudential Distributors Inc 3304 E Ferry PO Box 3088 *TF:* 800-767-5567	Spokane	WA	99220	509-535-2401	534-9145
Radio Distributing Co Inc 27015 Trolley Industrial Dr *TF:* 800-462-1544	Taylor	MI	48180	313-295-4500	295-0298
Roth Distributing Co 11300 W 47th St *TF:* 800-642-3227 ■ *Web:* www.rothdistributing.com	Minnetonka	MN	55343	952-933-4428	935-8795
Rott-Keller Supply Co Inc 6520 8th St PO Box 390 *TF:* 800-342-4709 ■ *Web:* www.rottkeller.com	Fargo	ND	58107	701-235-0563	232-7900
RTA International Inc 1008 Industrial Blvd	Chula Vista	CA	91911	619-424-6699	422-6929
Schaedel Carl & Co Inc 4 Sperry Rd *TF:* 800-783-6008 ■ *Web:* www.carlschaedel.com	Fairfield	NJ	07004	973-244-1311	244-0822
Schultz H & Sons Inc 777 Lehigh Ave *Web:* www.housewaresandthings.com	Union	NJ	07083	908-687-5400	687-1788
Servall Co 6761 E Ten Mile Rd *TF:* 800-989-7378 ■ *Web:* www.servallco.com	Center Line	MI	48015	586-754-1818	754-2260
Servco Pacific Inc 900 4th St Mall Suite 600 *Web:* www.servco.com	Honolulu	HI	96813	808-521-6511	523-3937
Speco Technologies 200 New Hwy *TF:* 800-645-5516 ■ *Web:* www.specotech.com	Amityville	NY	11701	631-957-8700	957-9142
Tacony Corp 1760 Gilsinn Ln *TF:* 800-482-2669 ■ *Web:* www.tacony.com	Fenton	MO	63026	636-349-3000	349-2333
Telerent Leasing Corp PO Box 26627 *Web:* www.telerent.com	Raleigh	NC	27611	919-772-8604	662-7070
Vermont Hardware Co Inc 180 Flynn Ave	Burlington	VT	05401	802-864-6835	864-7029
VSM Sewing Inc 31000 Viking Pkwy *TF:* 800-541-3357	Westlake	OH	44145	440-808-6550	847-0001
Warren Distributing Corp 2400 Atlantic Ave *TF:* 800-333-7227	Raleigh	NC	27604	919-828-9100	828-8896
Wascomat of America PO Box 960338 *TF:* 800-645-2205	Inwood	NY	11096	516-371-4400	371-4204
Web Service Co Inc 3690 Redondo Beach Ave *Fax Area Code: 310 ■ *TF:* 800-421-6897 ■ *Web:* www.weblaundry.com	Redondo Beach	CA	90278	323-772-5131	643-6958*
Westye Group 2615 E Beltline Rd PO Box 111400 *TF:* 800-441-9260 ■ *Web:* www.westye.com	Carrollton	TX	75011	972-416-6677	416-0661
Whirlpool Canada 1901 Minnesota Ct *Web:* www.whirlpoolcanada.com	Mississauga	ON	L5N3A7	905-821-6400	821-4151
Williams Distributing & Kitchen & Bath 658 Richmond St NW *TF:* 800-968-3718 ■ *Web:* www.williamskitchen.com	Grand Rapids	MI	49504	616-771-0505	771-0429
Woodson & Bozeman Inc 3870 New Getwell Rd *TF:* 800-876-4243 ■ *Web:* www.woodsonbozeman.com	Memphis	TN	38118	901-362-1500	362-1509

39 APPLICATION SERVICE PROVIDERS (ASPS)

Application Service Providers rent, deliver, license, manage, and/or host proprietary and/or third-party business software ("applications") and/or computer services to multiple users (customers). Included here are companies that host software applications as well as companies that provide the equipment necessary to do so.

	City	State	Zip	Phone	Fax
5 by 5 Networks 1455 McCarthy Blvd *Web:* www.5by5networks.com	Milpitas	CA	95053	408-433-5295	433-5298
AboutFace Corp 103 Longwood Ave *Web:* www.aboutface.com	Brookline	MA	02446	617-975-3800	344-6135
Access Data Corp 2 Chatham Ctr 11th Fl *TF:* 888-799-1744 ■ *Web:* www.accessdc.com	Pittsburgh	PA	15219	412-201-6000	201-6060
Alliance Commerce Inc 2141 N University Drt Suite 302 *TF:* 877-638-2777 ■ *Web:* www.alliancecommerce.net	Coral Springs	FL	33071	954-575-2300	
AllMeds Inc 151 Lafayette Dr Suite 401 *TF:* 888-343-6337 ■ *Web:* www.allmeds.com	Oak Ridge	TN	37830	865-482-1999	481-0921
Altiris Inc 588 W 400 South *NASDAQ: ATRS* ■ *TF:* 888-252-5551 ■ *Web:* www.altiris.com	Lindon	UT	84042	801-226-8500	226-8506
American Data Center Inc 25 W Palatine Rd	Palatine	IL	60067	847-358-7111	358-7635
Andale Inc 300 Ferguson Dr *Fax Area Code: 650 ■ *Web:* www.andale.com	Mountain View	CA	94043	888-326-3253	230-3090*
Application Consulting Group 121 Headquarters Plaza North Tower 2nd Fl *Web:* www2.acgi.com	Morristown	NJ	07960	973-898-0012	898-6647
AppStream Inc 2300 Geng Rd Suite 100 *Web:* www.appstream.com	Palo Alto	CA	94303	650-251-2500	251-2595
Aptas Inc 1517 Blake St 2nd Fl *Web:* www.aptas.com	Denver	CO	80202	303-572-1122	572-1123
Ariba Inc 807 11th Ave *NASDAQ: ARBA* ■ *TF:* 888-237-3131 ■ *Web:* www.ariba.com	Sunnyvale	CA	94089	650-390-1000	390-1100
Arsenal Digital Solutions Worldwide Inc 8000 Regency Pkwy Suite 110 *Web:* www.arsenaldigital.com	Cary	NC	27518	919-466-6700	466-6778
Atomz Corp 1111 Bayhill Dr Suite 285 *Web:* www.atomz.com	San Bruno	CA	94066	650-244-1400	244-1401
Avanade Inc 2211 Elliott Ave Suite 200 *Web:* www.avanade.com	Seattle	WA	98121	206-239-5600	239-5605
Avatech Solutions Inc 10715 Red Run Blvd Suite 101 *TF:* 800-520-8000 ■ *Web:* www.avat.com	Owings Mills	MD	21117	410-581-8080	581-8088
Avazpour Networking Services Inc 10895 Grandview Dr Suite 250 *Web:* www.avazpour.com	Overland Park	KS	66210	913-498-8777	498-8778
BizLand Inc 70 Blanchard Rd *TF:* 866-599-9964 ■ *Web:* www.bizland.com	Burlington	MA	01803	781-272-5585	272-2915
Blue Martini Software Inc 1615 S Congress Ave Suite 200 *Fax Area Code: 650 ■ *TF:* 800-258-3627 ■ *Web:* www.bluemartini.com	Del Ray Beach	FL	33445	561-265-2700	256-4001*
BluePoint Data Storage Inc 1200 N Federal Hwy Suite 200 *TF:* 866-786-7390 ■ *Web:* www.bluepointdata.com	Boca Raton	FL	33432	561-417-0324	417-0347
BlueSky Solutions LLC 106 Berrybush Dr *Web:* www.blueskyllc.us	Harrison City	PA	15636	724-858-1408	858-1408
Bluestreak Inc 155 S Main St Suite 100 *TF:* 866-258-3787 ■ *Web:* www.bluestreak.com	Providence	RI	02903	401-341-3300	849-3411
BrassRing Inc 343 Winter St *TF:* 888-265-6969 ■ *Web:* www.brassring.com	Waltham	MA	02451	781-530-5000	530-5500
BrightStar Information Technology Group Inc 6601 Owens Dr Suite 115 *Web:* www.brightstar.com	Pleasanton	CA	94588	925-251-0000	251-0001
BroadVision Inc 585 Broadway *NASDAQ: BVSN* ■ *Web:* www.broadvision.com	Redwood City	CA	94063	650-542-5100	542-5900
Canopy Systems Inc 5501 Dillard Ave *TF:* 800-757-1354 ■ *Web:* www.canopysystems.com	Cary	NC	27511	919-851-6177	233-1321
CareScience Inc 3600 Market St 7th Fl *TF:* 888-223-8247 ■ *Web:* www.carescience.com	Philadelphia	PA	19104	215-387-9401	387-9406
CaseCentral Inc 760 Market St Suite 200 *TF:* 800-714-2727 ■ *Web:* www.casecentral.com	San Francisco	CA	94102	415-989-2300	989-2373
Cayenta Canada Corp 4200 N Fraser Way Suite 201 *TF:* 866-229-3682 ■ *Web:* www.cayenta.com	Burnaby	BC	V5J5K7	604-570-4300	291-0742
CenterBeam Inc 30 Rio Robles Dr *Web:* www.centerbeam.com	San Jose	CA	95134	408-750-0500	750-0555
Centric Software Inc 50 Las Colinas Ln *TF:* 888-537-2639 ■ *Web:* www.centricsoftware.com	San Jose	CA	95119	408-574-7802	574-7809
Chemical Safety Corp 5901 Christie Ave Suite 502 *TF:* 888-594-1100 ■ *Web:* www.chemicalsafety.com	Emeryville	CA	94608	510-594-1000	594-1100
Citadon Inc 201 Mission St Suite 2700 *TF Sales:* 800-351-5231 ■ *Web:* www.citadon.com	San Francisco	CA	94105	415-882-1888	882-1899
CliniComp International 9655 Towne Ctr Dr *TF:* 800-350-8202 ■ *Web:* www.clinicomp.com	San Diego	CA	92121	858-546-8202	546-1801
Cogency Software Inc 500 Airport Blvd Suite 200 *Web:* www.cogencysoftware.com	Burlingame	CA	94010	650-685-2500	685-2515
College Central Network Inc 245 8th Ave Suite 892 *Web:* www.collegecentralnetwork.com	New York	NY	10011	800-442-3614	
Comergent Technologies Inc 1201 Radio Rd 2nd Fl *Web:* www.comergent.com	Redwood City	CA	94065	650-232-6000	232-6010
Computer Programs & Systems Inc (CPSI) 6600 Wall St *NASDAQ: CPSI* ■ *TF:* 800-711-2774 ■ *Web:* www.cpsinet.com	Mobile	AL	36695	251-639-8100	639-8214
Concur Technologies Inc 18400 NE Union Hill Rd *NASDAQ: CNQR* ■ *TF:* 800-358-0610 ■ *Web:* www.concur.com	Redmond	WA	98052	425-702-8808	702-8828
Connected Corp 100 Pennsylvania Ave *Fax: Sales ■ *TF:* 800-934-0956 ■ *Web:* www.connected.com	Framingham	MA	01701	508-808-7300	879-6653*
Connectria Corp 10845 Olive Blvd Suite 300 *TF:* 800-781-7820 ■ *Web:* www.connectria.com	Saint Louis	MO	63141	314-587-7000	587-7090
Corio Inc 959 Skyway Rd Suite 100 *TF Cust Svc:* 877-737-3700 ■ *Web:* www.corio.com	San Carlos	CA	94070	650-232-3000	232-3200
CPSI (Computer Programs & Systems Inc) 6600 Wall St *NASDAQ: CPSI* ■ *TF:* 800-711-2774 ■ *Web:* www.cpsinet.com	Mobile	AL	36695	251-639-8100	639-8214
Critical Path Inc 2 Harrison St 2nd Fl *Web:* www.cp.net	San Francisco	CA	94105	415-541-2500	541-2300
CustomerSat Inc 500 Ellis St *TF:* 800-372-7772 ■ *Web:* www.customersat.com	Mountain View	CA	94043	650-237-3300	934-0949
CyberData Inc 20 Max Ave *TF:* 877-942-8100 ■ *Web:* www.cyberdata.com	Hicksville	NY	11801	516-942-8000	942-0800
Cyveillance Inc 1555 Wilson Blvd Suite 406 *TF:* 888-243-0097 ■ *Web:* www.cyveillance.com	Arlington	VA	22209	703-351-1000	312-0536
Dakota Imaging Inc 7130 Minstrel Way *TF:* 800-833-3137 ■ *Web:* www.dakotaimaging.com	Columbia	MD	21045	410-381-3113	381-3114
DataServ LLC 12825 Flushing Meadows Dr Suite 100 *TF:* 877-700-3282 ■ *Web:* www.dataservsolution.com	Saint Louis	MO	63131	314-842-1155	842-6161
Digital River Inc 9625 W 76th St Suite 150 *NASDAQ: DRIV* ■ *Web:* www.digitalriver.com	Eden Prairie	MN	55344	952-253-8400	253-8760
DigitalWork.com Inc 130 S Jefferson St Suite 100 *TF:* 877-496-7571 ■ *Web:* www.digitalwork.com	Chicago	IL	60661	312-379-5950	379-5952
DocMan Technologies 31300 Bainbridge Rd *TF:* 888-636-2626 ■ *Web:* www.docmantech.com	Cleveland	OH	44139	440-542-9660	542-9668
E-Builder Inc 1800 NW 69 Ave Suite 201 *TF:* 800-580-9322 ■ *Web:* www.e-builder.net	Plantation	FL	33313	954-556-6701	792-5949
E-Markets Inc 1606 Golden Aspen Dr Suite 108 *TF:* 877-674-7419 ■ *Web:* www.e-markets.com	Ames	IA	50010	515-233-8720	956-9388
eApps 3850 Holcomb Bridge Rd Suite 250 *Web:* www.eapps.com	Norcross	GA	30092	770-448-2100	416-1570
eAttorney Inc 245 Peachtree Ctr Ave Suite 2415 *Fax Area Code: 404 ■ *Web:* www.eattorney.com	Atlanta	GA	30303	800-378-6101	215-5408*
eGain Communications Corp 345 E Middlefield Rd *TF:* 888-603-4246 ■ *Web:* www.egain.com	Mountain View	CA	94043	650-230-7500	230-7600
eJiva Inc 1000 Commerce Dr Suite 500 *TF:* 877-354-8226 ■ *Web:* www.ejiva.com	Pittsburgh	PA	15275	412-787-2100	494-9272
Electric Mail Co Inc 3999 Henning Dr Suite 300 *TF:* 800-419-7463 ■ *Web:* www.electricmail.com	Burnaby	BC	V5C6P9	604-482-1111	482-1110
Emdeon Corp 669 River Dr Center 2 *NASDAQ: HLTH* ■ *TF:* 877-469-3263 ■ *Web:* www.emdeon.com	Elmwood Park	NJ	07407	201-703-3400	703-3401
Employease Inc 3295 River Exchange Dr Suite 500 *TF:* 888-327-3638 ■ *Web:* www.employease.com	Norcross	GA	30092	770-325-7700	325-7702
ePlus Inc 13595 Dulles Technology Dr *NASDAQ: PLUS* ■ *TF:* 800-827-5711 ■ *Web:* www.eplus.com	Herndon	VA	20171	703-984-8400	984-8600
eProject Inc 1008 Western Ave Suite 500 *Web:* www.eproject.com	Seattle	WA	98104	206-341-9117	341-9123
eWork Exchange Inc 717 Market St Suite 500 *Web:* www.ework.com	San Francisco	CA	94103	415-546-4800	546-3889
Exenet Technologies Inc 220 W 42nd St 6th Fl *TF:* 877-393-6388 ■ *Web:* www.exenet.com	New York	NY	10036	212-763-5500	685-7636
FaceTime Communications Inc 1159 Triton Dr *TF:* 888-349-3223 ■ *Web:* www.facetime.net	Foster City	CA	94404	650-574-1600	574-2700
FinancialCAD Corp 13450 102nd Ave Suite 1750 *TF:* 800-304-0702 ■ *Web:* www.fincad.com	Surrey	BC	V3T5X3	604-957-1200	957-1201
Flying Aces Technology LLC 305 N Westgate Rd Suite 100 *Web:* www.flying-aces.com	Mount Prospect	IL	60056	847-299-7815	
Gelco Information Network Inc 10700 Prairie Lakes Dr *TF:* 800-444-6588 ■ *Web:* www.gelco.com	Eden Prairie	MN	55344	952-947-1500	947-1525
Glowpoint Inc 225 Long Ave *TF:* 866-456-9764 ■ *Web:* www.glowpoint.com	Hillside	NJ	07205	973-282-2000	282-2033
HealthMEDX 5100 N Towne Ctr Dr *TF:* 877-875-1200 ■ *Web:* www.healthmedx.com	Ozark	MO	65721	417-582-1816	582-0296
Hire.com Inc 200 Academy Dr *TF:* 800-953-4473 ■ *Web:* www.hire.com	Austin	TX	78704	512-583-4400	583-4401
I-Business Network LLC 2256 Northwest Pkwy Suite E *TF:* 877-336-4426 ■ *Web:* www.i-bn.net	Marietta	GA	30067	678-627-0646	627-0688
IE Discovery Inc 13640 Briarwick Dr Suite 250 *TF:* 800-656-8444 ■ *Web:* www.iediscovery.com	Austin	TX	78729	512-498-7400	498-7444
Imergent Inc 754 E Technology Ave *AMEX: IIG* ■ *Web:* www.imergentinc.com	Orem	UT	84097	801-227-0004	226-8848
Incentivecity 7370 Bramalea Rd Suite 3 *TF:* 877-387-2529 ■ *Web:* www.incentivecity.com	Mississauga	ON	L5S1N6	905-362-0951	362-0957
Incentra Solutions Inc 1140 Pearl St *TF Tech Supp:* 877-667-8720 ■ *Web:* www.incentrasolutions.com	Boulder	CO	80302	303-449-8279	

Phone Fax

Informative Inc 701 Gateway Blvd Suite 270 .... South San Francisco CA 94080 650-534-1010 534-1020
TF Sales: 800-829-1979 ■ *Web:* www.informative.com
InsynQ Inc 1127 Broadway Plaza Suite 202 .... Tacoma WA 98402 253-284-2000 722-5605
TF: 866-796-9925 ■ *Web:* www.insynq.com
Intacct Corp 125 S Market St Suite 600 .... San Jose CA 95113 408-878-0900 878-9010
TF: 877-968-0600 ■ *Web:* us.intacct.com
Integrity eLearning Inc
751 S Weir Canyon Rd Suite 157451 .... Anaheim Hills CA 92808 714-637-9480
Web: www.ielearning.com
Internap Network Services Corp 250 Williams St Suite E-100 .... Atlanta GA 30303 404-302-9700 475-0520
AMEX: IIP ■ *TF:* 877-843-7627 ■ *Web:* www.internap.com
Internet Operations Center Inc
200 Galleria Officentre Suite 109 .... Southfield MI 48034 248-204-8800 204-8801
TF: 800-485-4462 ■ *Web:* www.iocenter.net
IntraLinks Inc 1372 Broadway 11th Fl .... New York NY 10018 212-543-7700 543-7978
TF Tech Supp: 888-546-5383 ■ *Web:* www.intralinks.com
Intranets.com Inc 1 Van de Graaff Dr 6th Fl .... Burlington MA 01803 781-565-6000 565-6355
TF: 888-932-2600 ■ *Web:* www.intranets.com
Jamcracker Inc 4677 Old Ironsides Dr Suite 450 .... Santa Clara CA 95054 408-496-5500 456-9944
TF: 866-559-0035 ■ *Web:* www.jamcracker.com
Journyx Inc 9011 Mountain Ridge Suite 200 .... Austin TX 78759 512-834-8888 834-8858
TF: 800-755-9878 ■ *Web:* www.journyx.com
Kleinschmidt Inc 450 Lake Cook Rd .... Deerfield IL 60015 847-945-1000 945-4619
Web: www.kleinschmidt.com
LanVision Systems Inc 10200 Alliance Rd Suite 200 .... Cincinnati OH 45242 513-794-7100 794-7272
NASDAQ: LANV ■ *TF:* 800-878-5262 ■ *Web:* www.lanvision.com
Learningstation.com Inc 8008 Corporate Ctr Dr Suite 210 .... Charlotte NC 28226 704-926-5400 926-5401
TF: 888-679-7058 ■ *Web:* www.learningstation.com
Legal Systems Holding Co DBA Serengeti Law
2018 156th Ave NE Suite 100 .... Bellevue WA 98007 425-748-5115 748-5116
Web: www.serengetilaw.com
LivePerson Inc 462 7th Ave 2nd & 3rd Fl .... New York NY 10018 212-609-4200 609-4201
NASDAQ: LPSN ■ *Web:* www.liveperson.com
Management Dynamics Inc 1 Meadowlands Plaza .... East Rutherford NJ 07073 201-935-8588 935-5187
Web: www.managementdynamics.com
MarketSoft Corp 10 Maguire Rd Suite 330 .... Lexington MA 02421 781-674-0000 674-0090
Web: www.marketsoft.com
MedAvant Healthcare Solutions
1854 Shackleford Ct Suite 200 .... Norcross GA 30093 770-806-9918 806-4799
NASDAQ: PILL ■ *TF:* 800-882-0802 ■ *Web:* www.medavanthealth.com
Metier Ltd 3222 'N' St NW 5th Fl .... Washington DC 20007 202-965-9500 965-7600
TF: 877-965-9501 ■ *Web:* www.metier.com
MetraTech Corp 330 Bear Hill Rd .... Waltham MA 02451 781-839-8300 839-8301
Web: www.metratech.com
Mi8 Corp 601 W 26th St 11th Fl .... New York NY 10001 212-727-0911 727-0937
TF: 800-965-4648 ■ *Web:* www.mi8.com
Miva Inc 5220 Summerlin Commons Blvd Suite 500 .... Fort Myers FL 33907 239-561-7229 561-7224
NASDAQ: MIVA ■ *TF:* 888-882-3178 ■ *Web:* www.miva.com/us
Napster Inc 9044 Melrose Ave .... Los Angeles CA 90069 310-281-5000 281-5120
NASDAQ: NAPS ■ *TF:* 800-839-4210 ■ *Web:* www.napster.com
NaviSite Inc 400 Minuteman Rd .... Andover MA 01810 978-682-8300 688-8100
NASDAQ: NAVI ■ *TF:* 888-298-8222 ■ *Web:* www.navisite.com
NeoMedia Technologies Inc 2201 2nd St Suite 402 .... Fort Myers FL 33901 239-337-3434 337-3668
Web: www.neom.com
NetBase Corp 4443 Brookfield Corporate Dr Suite 200 .... Chantilly VA 20151 703-814-4040 814-4074
TF Cust Svc: 888-456-6528 ■ *Web:* www.netbasecorp.com
NetSuite Inc 2955 Campus Dr Suite 100 .... San Mateo CA 94403 650-627-1000 627-1001
TF: 800-762-5524 ■ *Web:* www.netsuite.com
Network Technology Group Inc 7127 Florida Blvd .... Baton Rouge LA 70806 225-214-3800 215-3800
Web: www.ntg.com
OneMind Connect Inc 2 Corporate Plaza Suite 100 .... Newport Beach CA 92660 949-640-0701 640-0711
TF: 877-658-5022 ■ *Web:* www.onemindconnect.com
onProject Inc 3 Wing Dr Suite 225 .... Cedar Knolls NJ 07927 973-971-9970 971-9971
TF: 877-936-6776 ■ *Web:* www.onproject.com
Open Solutions Inc 455 Winding Brook Dr .... Glastonbury CT 06033 860-652-3155 652-3156
NASDAQ: OPEN ■ *Web:* www.opensolutions.com
OpenAir Inc 211 Congress St 8th Fl .... Boston MA 02110 617-351-0230 351-0220
TF Sales: 888-367-1715 ■ *Web:* www.openair.com
Opsware Inc 599 N Mathilda Ave .... Sunnyvale CA 94085 408-744-7300 744-7379
NASDAQ: OPSW ■ *Web:* www.opsware.com
Optas Inc 500 Unicorn Park Dr .... Woburn MA 01801 781-937-9400 937-0490
Web: www.optas.com
Oracle Corp 500 Oracle Pkwy .... Redwood Shores CA 94065 650-506-7000 506-7200
NASDAQ: ORCL ■ *TF Sales:* 800-672-2531 ■ *Web:* www.oracle.com
Outstart Inc 745 Atlantic Ave 4th Fl .... Boston MA 02111 617-897-6800 897-6801
Web: www.outstart.com
Outtask Inc 209 Madison St Suite 400 .... Alexandria VA 22314 703-837-6100 837-6106
TF: 888-662-6248 ■ *Web:* www.outtask.com
Paramount Technologies Inc
2075 E West Maple Rd Suite B-203 .... Commerce Township MI 48390 248-960-0909 960-1919
TF: 800-725-4408 ■ *Web:* www.paramountusa.com
Passkey.com Inc 180 Old Colony Ave 3rd Fl .... Quincy MA 02170 617-237-8200 328-1212
TF Sales: 800-211-4234 ■ *Web:* www.passkey.com
PBM Corp 20600 Chagrin Blvd Suite 450 .... Cleveland OH 44122 216-283-7999 283-7931
TF: 800-341-5809 ■ *Web:* www.pbmcorp.com
PeopleSupport Inc 1100 Glendon Ave Suite 1250 .... Los Angeles CA 90024 310-824-6200 824-6299
NASDAQ: PSPT ■ *TF:* 877-914-5999 ■ *Web:* www.peoplesupport.com
Perfect Commerce Inc 2713 Magruder Blvd Suite A .... Hampton VA 23666 757-766-8211 865-3452
TF Sales: 877-871-3788 ■ *Web:* www.perfect.com
Perimeter Technology Inc 540 N Commercial St .... Manchester NH 03101 603-645-1616 645-1424
TF: 800-645-1650 ■ *Web:* www.ip-acd.com
PhDx Systems Inc 1001 University Blvd SE Suite 103 .... Albuquerque NM 87106 505-764-0174 764-0120
TF: 888-999-7439 ■ *Web:* www.phdx.com
PicoSearch LLC 10 Fawcett St .... Cambridge MA 02138 617-547-4020 576-7227
Web: www.picosearch.com
Pivotal Corp 858 Beatty St Suite 600 .... Vancouver BC V6B1C1 604-699-8000 699-8001
TF: 877-797-4595 ■ *Web:* www.pivotal.com
Plumtree Software Inc 500 Sansome St .... San Francisco CA 94111 415-263-8900 263-8991
TF: 800-810-7586 ■ *Web:* www.plumtree.com
Pointivity 4320 La Jolla Village Dr Suite 205 .... San Diego CA 92122 858-777-6900 777-6915
Web: www.pointivity.com
Premiere Global Services Inc 3399 Peachtree Rd NE Suite 700 .... Atlanta GA 30326 404-262-8400
NYSE: PGI ■ *Web:* www.premiereglobal.com
Prodata Systems Inc 3855 Monte Villa Pkwy Suite 105 .... Bothell WA 98021 425-487-8300 487-8355
TF: 866-487-8346 ■ *Web:* www.prodata.com
PureSafety 1321 Murfreesboro Rd Suite 200 .... Nashville TN 37217 615-367-4404 367-3887
TF: 888-202-3016 ■ *Web:* www.puresafety.com
PureWorks Inc DBA PureSafety
1321 Murfreesboro Rd Suite 200 .... Nashville TN 37217 615-367-4404 367-3887
TF: 888-202-3016 ■ *Web:* www.puresafety.com
Quality Care Solutions Inc (QCSI) 14647 S 50th St Suite 150 .... Phoenix AZ 85044 480-735-7000 735-7011
Web: www.qcsi.com
QuickArrow Inc 11675 Jollyville Rd Suite 200 .... Austin TX 78759 512-381-0600 381-0660
Web: www.quickarrow.com
Quovera 800 W El Camino Real Suite 100 .... Mountain View CA 94040 650-962-6300
Web: www.quovera.com

Phone Fax

Realm Business Solutions Inc 13727 Noel Rd Suite 800 .... Dallas TX 75240 469-791-1000 791-1810
TF: 866-697-3256 ■ *Web:* www.realm.com
Resource Development Corp 280 Daines St Suite 200 .... Birmingham MI 48009 248-646-2300 646-0789
TF: 800-360-7222 ■ *Web:* www.resourcedev.com
Responsys Inc 3 Lagwood Dr Suite 300 .... Redwood City CA 94065 650-801-7400 801-7401
TF: 800-624-5356 ■ *Web:* www.responsys.com
RightNow Technologies Inc 40 Enterprise Blvd .... Bozeman MT 59718 406-522-4200 522-4227
NASDAQ: RNOW ■ *TF:* 877-363-5678 ■ *Web:* www.rightnowtech.com
Salesforce.com Inc 1 Market St The Landmark Suite 300 .... San Francisco CA 94105 415-901-7000 901-7040
NYSE: CRM ■ *TF:* 800-667-6389 ■ *Web:* www.salesforce.com
Salesnet Inc 268 Summer St 4th Fl .... Boston MA 02210 617-979-6100 979-6188
TF: 877-350-0160 ■ *Web:* www.salesnet.com
SAVVIS Inc 1 SAVVIS Pkwy .... Town & Country MO 63017 314-628-7000
NASDAQ: SVVS ■ *TF:* 800-728-8471 ■ *Web:* www.savvis.net
Semtek Innovative Solutions 9340 Hazard Way Suite D .... San Diego CA 92123 858-300-3381 278-6004
Web: www.semtek.com
Serengeti Law 2018 156th Ave NE Suite 100 .... Bellevue WA 98007 425-748-5115 748-5116
Web: www.serengetilaw.com
SevenSpace/Nuclio Corp 20098 Ashbrook Pl .... Ashburn VA 20147 703-726-6777 726-6799
Shareholder.com 12 Clock Tower Pl Suite 300 .... Maynard MA 01754 978-461-3111 897-3739
TF: 800-990-6397 ■ *Web:* www.shareholder.com
Siemens E-Health 22010 SE 51st St 1st Fl .... Issaquah WA 98029 425-507-4260 507-4290
Siemens Health Services 51 Valley Stream Pkwy .... Malvern PA 19355 610-219-6300 219-3124
TF: 888-767-8326 ■ *Web:* www.smed.com
Siemens Medical Solutions Health Services Corp
51 Valley Stream Pkwy .... Malvern PA 19355 610-219-6300 219-3124
TF: 888-767-8326 ■ *Web:* www.smed.com
Siennax Inc 171 Saxony Rd Suite 204 .... Encinitas CA 92024 858-385-8900 385-8997
TF: 800-717-4565
SiteLite Corp 111 Theory 2nd Fl .... Irvine CA 92612 949-265-6200 265-6399
Web: www.sitelite.com
Smart Online Inc PO Box 12794 .... Research Triangle Park NC 27709 919-765-5000 765-5020
TF: 800-578-9000 ■ *Web:* www.smartonline.com
Spyre Infostructure Inc 25 Imperial St Suite 210 .... Toronto ON M5P1B9 416-487-7797 487-7706
TF: 888-467-7973 ■ *Web:* www.spyre.com
Storability Inc 118 Turnpike Rd .... Southborough MA 01772 508-229-1700 229-1701
Web: www.storability.com
StorageASP Inc 515 Consumers Rd Suite 405 .... Toronto ON M2J4Z2 416-750-4002 750-8802
Web: www.storageasp.com
Strategic Systems Consulting Inc DBA eApps
3850 Holcomb Bridge Rd Suite 250 .... Norcross GA 30092 770-448-2100 416-1570
Web: www.eapps.com
Syntrio 33 New Montgomery St Suite 1280 .... San Francisco CA 94105 415-951-7913 951-7915
TF: 888-858-2887 ■ *Web:* www.syntrio.com
Talisma Corp 411 108th Ave NE Suite 900 .... Bellevue WA 98004 425-688-3800 688-3899
TF: 877-934-3276 ■ *Web:* www.talisma.com
TALX Corp 11432 Lackland Dr .... Saint Louis MO 63146 314-214-7000 214-7588
NASDAQ: TALX ■ *TF:* 800-888-8277 ■ *Web:* www.talx.com
TeamOn Systems Inc 1180 NW Maple St Suite 330 .... Issaquah WA 98027 425-369-5700 837-8098
Web: www.teamon.com
Toolwire Inc 6120 Stoneridge Mall Rd Suite 110 .... Pleasanton CA 94588 925-227-8500 227-8501
TF: 866-935-8665 ■ *Web:* www.toolwire.com
TriZetto Group Inc 567 San Nicolas Dr Suite 360 .... Newport Beach CA 92660 949-719-2200 219-2197
NASDAQ: TZIX ■ *TF:* 800-569-1222 ■ *Web:* www.trizetto.com
UltraDNS Corp 1000 Marina Blvd Suite 600 .... Brisbane CA 94005 650-228-2300 745-2827
TF: 888-367-4812 ■ *Web:* www.ultradns.com
UnicornHRO 25B Hanover Rd .... Florham Park NJ 07932 973-360-0688 360-0699
TF: 800-343-6844 ■ *Web:* www.unicornhro.com
USA.NET Inc 1155 Kelly Johnson Blvd Suite 400 .... Colorado Springs CO 80920 719-265-2930 265-2922
TF: 800-653-0179 ■ *Web:* www.usa.net
USinternetworking Inc (USI Inc) 1 USi Plaza .... Annapolis MD 21401 410-897-4400 573-1906
TF: 800-839-4874 ■ *Web:* www.usi.net
Vcommerce Corp 10001 N 92nd St Suite 120 .... Scottsdale AZ 85258 480-922-9922 551-3791
TF Cust Svc: 800-821-6034 ■ *Web:* www.vcommerce.com
VeriCenter Inc 757 N Eldridge Pkwy Suite 200 .... Houston TX 77079 281-584-4500
TF Tech Supp: 866-823-6837 ■ *Web:* www.vericenter.com
Verso Technologies Inc 400 Galleria Pkwy Suite 200 .... Atlanta GA 30339 678-589-3500 589-3750
NASDAQ: VRSO ■ *Web:* www.verso.com
Vocus Inc 4296 Forbes Blvd .... Lanham MD 20706 301-459-2590 459-2827
NASDAQ: VOCS ■ *TF:* 800-345-5572 ■ *Web:* www.vocus.com
Webauthor.com LLC 2737 Misty Oakes Cir .... Royal Palm Beach FL 33411 561-282-3300
Web: www.webauthor.com
Webhire Inc 91 Hartwell Ave .... Lexington MA 02421 781-869-5000 869-5050
TF: 877-932-4473 ■ *Web:* www.webhire.com
WebMD Health Holdings Inc 111 8th Ave 7th Fl .... New York NY 10011 212-624-3700 624-3800
NASDAQ: WBMD ■ *Web:* www.webmd.com
Wizmo Inc 7646 Golden Triangle Dr .... Eden Prairie MN 55344 952-983-3300 983-3600
Web: www.wizmo.com
Workbrain Inc 3440 Preston Ridge Rd Suite 100 .... Alpharetta GA 30005 678-713-6014 713-6020
TF: 866-967-5272 ■ *Web:* www.workbrain.com
Workscape Inc 123 Selton St .... Marlborough MA 01752 508-861-5500 573-9500
TF: 888-605-9620 ■ *Web:* www.workscape.com
WTS Inc 1100 Olive Way Suite 1100 .... Seattle WA 98101 206-436-3300 436-3305
TF: 877-987-7253 ■ *Web:* www.wtservices.com
Zantaz Inc 5671 Gibraltar Dr .... Pleasanton CA 94588 925-598-3000 598-3145
TF: 800-636-0095 ■ *Web:* www.zantaz.com
ZLand Inc PO Box 3469 .... Costa Mesa CA 92628 888-682-0911

40 AQUARIUMS - PUBLIC

SEE ALSO Botanical Gardens & Arboreta p. 1391; Zoos & Wildlife Parks p. 2419

Phone Fax

Adventure Aquarium 1 Aquarium Dr .... Camden NJ 08103 856-365-3300 365-3311
TF: 800-616-5297 ■ *Web:* www.adventureaquarium.com
Albuquerque Aquarium 2601 Central Ave NW .... Albuquerque NM 87104 505-764-6200 848-7192
Web: www.cabq.gov/biopark/aquarium
Aquarium of the Bay
The Embarcadero at Beach St Pier 39 .... San Francisco CA 94133 415-623-5300 623-5324
TF: 888-732-3483 ■ *Web:* www.aquariumofthebay.com
Aquarium et Centre Marin de Shippagan 100 Aquarium St .... Shippagan NB E8S1H9 506-336-3013 336-3057
Web: www.gnb.ca/aquarium
Aquarium of the Pacific 100 Aquarium Way .... Long Beach CA 90802 562-590-3100 950-3109
Web: www.aquariumofpacific.org
Audubon Aquarium of the Americas 1 Canal St .... New Orleans LA 70130 504-581-4629 565-3010
TF: 800-774-7394 ■ *Web:* www.auduboninstitute.org/aoa
Birch Aquarium at Scripps 2300 Expedition Way .... La Jolla CA 92037 858-534-3474 534-7114
Web: aquarium.ucsd.edu
Cabrillo Marine Aquarium 3720 Stephen White Dr .... San Pedro CA 90731 310-548-7562 548-2649
Web: www.cabrilloaq.org

	City	State	Zip	Phone	Fax
Clearwater Marine Aquarium 249 Windward Passage	Clearwater	FL	33767	727-441-1790	447-4922
TF: 888-239-9414 ■ *Web:* www.cmaquarium.org					
Dallas Aquarium at Fair Park 1462 1st Ave & ML King Blvd Fair Park	Dallas	TX	75226	214-670-8443	670-8452
Web: www.dallas-zoo.org					
Dallas World Aquarium 1801 N Griffin St	Dallas	TX	75202	214-655-1444	720-2242
TF: 800-732-7957 ■ *Web:* www.dwazoo.com					
Dauphin Island Sea Lab Estuarium 101 Bienville Blvd	Dauphin Island	AL	36528	251-861-2141	861-4646
TF: 866-403-4400 ■ *Web:* www.disl.org					
Downtown Aquarium 410 Bagby St & Memorial Dr	Houston	TX	77002	713-223-3474	
Web: www.downtownaquarium.com					
Downtown Aquarium - Denver 700 Water St Qwest Park	Denver	CO	80211	303-561-4450	561-4650
Web: www.downtownaquariumdenver.com					
ECHO at the Leahy Center 1 College St	Burlington	VT	05401	802-864-1848	864-6832
Web: www.echovermont.org					
Florida Aquarium 701 Channelside Dr	Tampa	FL	33602	813-273-4000	273-4160
TF: 800-353-4741 ■ *Web:* www.flaquarium.org					
Fluvarium The Nagle's Place Box 5	Saint John's	NL	A1B2Z2	709-754-3474	754-5947
Web: fluvarium.ca					
Georgia Aquarium 225 Baker St	Atlanta	GA	30313	404-581-4000	
Web: www.georgiaaquarium.org					
Great Lakes Aquarium 353 Harbor Dr	Duluth	MN	55802	218-740-3474	740-2020
TF: 877-866-3474 ■ *Web:* www.glaquarium.org					
JL Scott Marine Education Center & Aquarium 703 E Beach Dr	Ocean Springs	MS	39564	228-818-8890	818-8894
Web: www.usm.edu/aquarium					
John G Shedd Aquarium 1200 S Lake Shore Dr	Chicago	IL	60605	312-939-2435	939-3793
Web: www.sheddaquarium.org					
Key West Aquarium 1 Whitehead St	Key West	FL	33040	305-296-2051	293-7094
TF: 800-868-7482 ■ *Web:* www.keywestaquarium.com					
Maria Mitchell Assn Aquarium 28 Washington St	Nantucket	MA	02554	508-228-5387	228-1031
Web: www.mmo.org/museums					
Marineland of Florida 9600 Ocean Shore Blvd	Saint Augustine	FL	32080	904-460-1275	471-1111
TF: 888-279-9194 ■ *Web:* www.marineland.net					
Marinelife Center of Juno Beach 14200 US Hwy 1 Loggerhead Park	Juno Beach	FL	33408	561-627-8280	627-8305
Web: www.marinelife.org					
Maritime Aquarium at Norwalk 10 N Water St	Norwalk	CT	06854	203-852-0700	838-5416
Web: www.maritimeaquarium.org					
Maui Ocean Center 192 Maalaea Rd	Wailuku	HI	96793	808-270-7000	270-7070
TF: 800-350-5634 ■ *Web:* www.mauioceancenter.com					
Miami Seaquarium 4400 Rickenbacker Cswy	Miami	FL	33149	305-361-5705	361-6077
Web: www.miamiseaquarium.com					
Monterey Bay Aquarium 886 Cannery Row	Monterey	CA	93940	831-648-4800	648-4810
TF: 800-555-3656 ■ *Web:* www.montereybayaquarium.org					
Moody Gardens 1 Hope Blvd	Galveston	TX	77554	409-744-4673	744-1631
TF: 800-582-4673 ■ *Web:* www.moodygardens.com					
Mystic Aquarium & Institute for Exploration 55 Coogan Blvd	Mystic	CT	06355	860-572-5955	572-5969
Web: www.mysticaquarium.org					
National Aquarium 14th & Constitution Ave NW Dept of Commerce Bld Rm B-077	Washington	DC	20230	202-482-2826	482-4946
Web: www.nationalaquarium.com					
National Aquarium in Baltimore 501 E Pratt St Pier 3	Baltimore	MD	21202	410-576-3800	576-8238
Web: www.aqua.org					
National Park Aquarium 209 Central Ave	Hot Springs	AR	71901	501-624-3474	
New England Aquarium Central Wharf	Boston	MA	02110	617-973-5200	720-5098
Web: www.neaq.org					
New York Aquarium W 8th St & Surf Ave Coney Island	Brooklyn	NY	11224	718-265-3474	265-2660
Web: www.nyaquarium.com					
Newport Aquarium One Aquarium Way	Newport	KY	41071	859-261-7444	261-5888
TF: 800-406-3474 ■ *Web:* www.newportaquarium.com					
North Carolina Aquarium at Fort Fisher 900 Loggerhead Rd	Kure Beach	NC	28449	910-458-8257	458-6812
TF: 866-301-3476 ■ *Web:* www.ncaquariums.com					
North Carolina Aquarium on Roanoke Island 374 Airport Rd PO Box 967	Manteo	NC	27954	252-473-3493	473-1980
TF: 866-332-3475 ■ *Web:* www.ncaquariums.com					
Ocean Life Center Aquarium 800 N New Hampshire Ave	Atlantic City	NJ	08401	609-348-2880	
Web: oceanlifecenter.com					
Oklahoma Aquarium 300 Aquarium Dr	Jenks	OK	74037	918-296-3474	296-3467
Web: www.okaquarium.org					
Oregon Coast Aquarium 2820 SE Ferry Slip Rd	Newport	OR	97365	541-867-3474	867-6846
Web: www.aquarium.org					
Pacific Undersea Gardens 490 Belleville St	Victoria	BC	V8V1W9	250-382-5717	382-5210
Web: www.pacificunderseagardens.com					
Parc Aquarium du Quebec 1675 des Hotels Ave	Quebec	QC	G1W4S3	418-659-5266	646-9238
Web: www.aquarium.qc.ca					
Pier Aquarium 800 2nd Ave NE 2nd Fl	Saint Petersburg	FL	33701	727-895-7437	894-1212
Web: www.stpete-pier.com/pieraquarium.php?LID=3					
Pittsburgh Zoo & PPG Aquarium 1 Wild Pl	Pittsburgh	PA	15206	412-665-3639	665-3661
TF: 800-474-4966 ■ *Web:* www.pittsburghzoo.com					
Point Defiance Zoo & Aquarium 5400 N Pearl St	Tacoma	WA	98407	253-591-5337	591-5448
Web: www.pdza.org					
Ripley's Aquarium 1110 Celebrity Cir Broadway at the Beach	Myrtle Beach	SC	29577	843-916-0888	916-0752
TF: 800-734-8888 ■ *Web:* www.ripleysaquarium.com					
Scott JL Marine Education Center & Aquarium 703 E Beach Dr	Ocean Springs	MS	39564	228-818-8890	818-8894
Web: www.usm.edu/aquarium					
Sea Life Park 41-202 Kalanianaole Hwy	Waimanalo	HI	96795	808-259-7933	259-7373
TF: 866-365-7446 ■ *Web:* www.sealifeparkhawaii.com					
Seattle Aquarium 1483 Alaskan Way Waterfront Park Pier 59	Seattle	WA	98101	206-386-4300	386-4328
Web: www.seattleaquarium.org					
SeaWorld Orlando 7007 Sea World Dr	Orlando	FL	32821	407-351-3600	363-2409*
*Fax: Cust Svc ■ *TF:* 800-327-2424 ■ *Web:* www.seaworldorlando.com					
SeaWorld San Antonio 10500 SeaWorld Dr	San Antonio	TX	78251	210-523-3000	523-3199*
*Fax: Mktg ■ *TF:* 800-700-7786 ■ *Web:* www.seaworld.com					
Shedd John G Aquarium 1200 S Lake Shore Dr	Chicago	IL	60605	312-939-2435	939-3793
Web: www.sheddaquarium.org					
South Carolina Aquarium 100 Aquarium Wharf	Charleston	SC	29401	843-720-1990	579-8503
TF: 800-722-6455 ■ *Web:* www.scaquarium.org					
Steinhart Aquarium California Academy of Sciences 875 Howard St	San Francisco	CA	94103	415-321-8000	321-8610
Web: www.calacademy.org/aquarium					
Tennessee Aquarium 1 Broad St	Chattanooga	TN	37401	423-265-0695	267-3561
TF: 800-262-0695 ■ *Web:* www.tennis.org					
Texas State Aquarium 2710 N Shoreline Blvd	Corpus Christi	TX	78402	361-881-1200	881-1257
TF: 800-477-4853 ■ *Web:* www.texasstateaquarium.org					
University of Georgia Aquarium 30 Ocean Science Cir	Savannah	GA	31411	912-598-2496	598-2302
Web: www.uga.edu/aquarium					
Vancouver Aquarium Marine Science Center 845 Avison Way	Vancouver	BC	V6G3E2	604-659-3474	659-3515
TF: 800-931-1186 ■ *Web:* www.vanaqua.org					
Virginia Aquarium & Marine Science Center 717 General Booth Blvd	Virginia Beach	VA	23451	757-437-4949	437-4976
Web: www.vmsm.com					
Waikiki Aquarium 2777 Kalakaua Ave	Honolulu	HI	96815	808-923-9741	923-1771
Web: www.waquarium.org					
ZooQuarium 674 Rte 28	West Yarmouth	MA	02673	508-775-8883	
Web: www.zooquariumcapecod.net					

41 ARBITRATION SERVICES - LEGAL

	City	State	Zip	Phone	Fax
American Arbitration Assn Inc (AAA) 1633 Broadway 10th Fl	New York	NY	10019	212-716-5800	716-5905
TF: 800-778-7879 ■ *Web:* www.adr.org					
Arbitration Forums Inc 3350 Buschwood Park Dr Suite 295	Tampa	FL	33618	813-931-4004	931-4618
TF Cust Svc: 800-967-8889 ■ *Web:* www.arbfile.org					
Council of Better Business Bureaus Inc Dispute Resolution Services & Mediation Training 4200 Wilson Blvd Suite 800	Arlington	VA	22203	703-276-0100	525-8277
TF: 800-537-4600 ■ *Web:* www.dr.bbb.org					
CPR Institute for Dispute Resolution 575 Lexington Ave 21st Fl	New York	NY	10022	212-949-6490	949-8859
Web: www.cpradr.org					
Federal Mediation & Conciliation Service 2100 K St NW	Washington	DC	20427	202-606-8100	606-4251
Web: www.fmcs.gov					
Inland Valley Arbitration & Mediation Service (IVAMS) 8287 White Oak Ave	Rancho Cucamonga	CA	91730	909-466-1665	466-1796
TF: 800-944-8267 ■ *Web:* www.ivams.com/					
JAMS/Endispute 500 N State College Blvd Suite 600	Orange	CA	92868	714-939-1300	939-1787
TF: 800-352-5267 ■ *Web:* www.jamsadr.com					
Judicate West 1851 E 1st St Suite 1450	Santa Ana	CA	92705	714-834-1340	834-1344
TF: 800-488-8805 ■ *Web:* www.adjudicateinc.com					
National Arbitration & Mediation 990 Stewart Ave	Garden City	NY	11530	516-794-8950	794-8518
TF: 800-358-2550 ■ *Web:* www.namadr.com					
Resolute Systems Inc 1550 N Prospect Ave	Milwaukee	WI	53202	414-276-4774	270-0932
TF: 800-776-6060 ■ *Web:* www.resolutesystems.com					

ARCHITECTS

SEE Engineering & Design p. 1619

ART - COMMERCIAL

SEE Graphic Design p. 1767

42 ART DEALERS & GALLERIES

	City	State	Zip	Phone	Fax
Abbozzo Gallery 179 Lakeshore Rd E	Oakville	ON	L6J1H5	905-844-4481	844-2036
TF: 866-844-4481 ■ *Web:* www.abbozzogallery.com					
ACA Galleries 529 W 20th St 5th Fl	New York	NY	10011	212-206-8080	206-8498
Web: www.acagalleries.com					
Acquavella Galleries Inc 18 E 79th St	New York	NY	10021	212-734-6300	794-9394
Web: www.acquavellagalleries.com					
Adams Davidson Galleries 2727 29th St NW Suite 504	Washington	DC	20008	202-965-3800	265-3395
Web: www.adgal.com					
Adams George Gallery 525 W 26th St	New York	NY	10001	212-564-8480	564-8485
Web: www.artnet.com/gadams.html					
Adler Rachel Fine Art 24 E 71st St	New York	NY	10021	212-308-0511	308-0516
Web: www.racheladlerfineart.com					
Albert White Gallery 80 Spadina Ave Suite 208	Toronto	ON	M5V2J4	416-703-1021	703-1675
Aldis Browne Fine Arts 1614 Crescent Pl	Venice	CA	90291	310-301-6976	301-0698
Alexander & Bonin LLC 132 10th Ave	New York	NY	10011	212-367-7474	367-7337
Web: www.alexanderandbonin.com					
Allan Stone Gallery 113 E 90th St	New York	NY	10128	212-987-4997	987-4946
Web: www.allanstonegallery.com					
Alpha Gallery 38 Newbury St	Boston	MA	02116	617-536-4465	536-5695
Web: www.alphagallery.com					
Ana Kustera/Jack Tilton Gallery 8 76th St	New York	NY	10021	212-737-2221	396-1725
Web: www.jacktiltongallery.com					
Angles Gallery 2230 Main St	Santa Monica	CA	90405	310-396-5019	396-3797
Web: www.anglesgallery.com					
Anna Kustera Gallery 520 W 21st St	New York	NY	10011	212-989-0082	989-0456
Web: www.annakustera.com					
Art Emporium 2928 Granville St	Vancouver	BC	V6H3J7	604-738-3510	733-5427
Web: www.theartemporium.ca					
Art Placement Inc 228 3rd Ave S	Saskatoon	SK	S7K1L9	306-664-3385	933-2521
Web: www.artplacement.com					
Atelier Gallery 2421 Granville St	Vancouver	BC	V6H3G5	604-732-3021	
Web: www.ateliergallery.ca					
Babcock Galleries 724 5th Ave 11th Fl	New York	NY	10019	212-767-1852	767-1857
Web: www.artnet.com/babcock.html					
Barbara Gladstone Gallery 515 W 24th St	New York	NY	10011	212-206-9300	206-9301
Web: www.gladstonegallery.com					
Barbara Krakow Gallery 10 Newbury St 5th Fl	Boston	MA	02116	617-262-4490	262-8971
Web: www.barbarakrakowgallery.com					
Barbara Mathes Gallery 22 E 80th St	New York	NY	10021	212-570-4190	570-4190
Web: www.bmathesgallery.com/					
Bau-Xi Gallery 3045 Granville St	Vancouver	BC	V6H3J9	604-733-7011	733-3211
Web: www.bau-xi.com					
Beckett Fine Art Ltd 120 Scollard St	Toronto	ON	M5R1G4	416-922-5582	922-9869
Web: www.beckettfineart.com					
Berggruen John Gallery 228 Grant Ave	San Francisco	CA	94108	415-781-4629	781-0126
Web: www.berggruen.com					
Berry-Hill Galleries Inc 11 E 70th St	New York	NY	10021	212-744-2300	744-2838
Web: www.berry-hill.com					
Boone Mary Gallery 745 5th Ave 4th Fl	New York	NY	10151	212-752-2929	752-3939
Web: www.maryboonegallery.com					
Brady WM & Co Inc 22 E 80th St 4th Fl	New York	NY	10021	212-249-7212	628-6587
Bransten Rena Gallery 77 Geary St	San Francisco	CA	94108	415-982-3292	982-1807
Web: www.renabranstengallery.com					
Brooke Alexander Editions 59 Wooster St	New York	NY	10012	212-925-4338	941-9565
Web: www.baeditions.com					
Browne Aldis Fine Arts 1614 Crescent Pl	Venice	CA	90291	310-301-6976	301-0698
Bulger Stephen Gallery 1026 Queen St W	Toronto	ON	M6J1H6	416-504-0575	504-8929
Web: www.bulgergallery.com					

Listing	City	State	Zip	Phone	Fax
Buschlen Mowatt Fine Arts Ltd 1445 W Georgia St	Vancouver	BC	V6G2T3	604-682-1234	682-6004
TF: 800-663-8071 ■ Web: www.buschlenmowatt.com					
Byron Gallery 25 E 83rd St	New York	NY	10028	212-249-0348	517-3004
C & M Arts 45 E 78th St	New York	NY	10021	212-861-0020	861-7858
Web: www.c-m-arts.com					
Castelli Leo Gallery 18 E 77th St	New York	NY	10021	212-249-4470	249-5220
Web: www.castelligallery.com					
Catriona Jeffries Gallery 274 E 1st Ave	Vancouver	BC	V5T1A6	604-736-1554	736-1054
Web: www.catrionajeffries.com					
CDS Gallery 76 E 79th St	New York	NY	10021	212-772-9555	772-9542
Charles Cowles Gallery Inc 537 W 24th St	New York	NY	10011	212-741-8999	741-6222
Web: www.cowlesgallery.com					
Cheim & Read 547 W 25th St	New York	NY	10001	212-242-7727	242-7737
Web: www.cheimread.com					
Christopher Cutts Gallery 21 Morrow Ave	Toronto	ON	M6R2H9	416-532-5566	532-7272
Web: www.cuttsgallery.com					
Christopher Virginia Galleries Ltd 816 11th Ave SW	Calgary	AB	T2R0E5	403-263-4346	263-4346
Web: www.virginiachristopherfineart.com					
Clark Garth Gallery 24 W 57th St Suite 305	New York	NY	10019	212-246-2205	489-5168
Web: www.garthclark.com					
Conner Rosenkranz LLC 19 E 74th St	New York	NY	10021	212-517-3710	734-7678
Web: www.crsculpture.com					
Cooper Paula Gallery 534 W 21st St	New York	NY	10011	212-255-1105	255-5156
Corkin Jane Gallery 55 Mill St Bldg 61	Toronto	ON	M5A3C4	416-979-1980	979-7018
Web: www.janecorkin.com					
Corkin Shopland Gallery 55 Mill St Bldg 61	Toronto	ON	M5A3C4	416-979-1980	979-7018
Web: www.janecorkin.com					
Cowles Charles Gallery Inc 537 W 24th St	New York	NY	10011	212-741-8999	741-6222
Web: www.cowlesgallery.com					
CRG Gallery 535 W 22nd St 3rd Fl	New York	NY	10011	212-229-2766	229-2788
Web: www.crggallery.com					
Cutts Christopher Gallery 21 Morrow Ave	Toronto	ON	M6R2H9	416-532-5566	532-7272
Web: www.cuttsgallery.com					
D'Amelio Terras 525 W 22nd St	New York	NY	10011	212-352-9460	352-9464
Web: www.damelioterras.com					
Danese 535 W 24th St 6th Fl	New York	NY	10011	212-223-2227	605-1016
Web: www.danese.com					
David Findlay Galleries Inc 984 Madison Ave	New York	NY	10021	212-249-2909	249-2912
Web: www.davidfindlaygalleries.com					
David Findlay Jr Fine Art 41 E 57th St Suite 1120	New York	NY	10022	212-486-7660	486-6377
Web: www.davidfindlayjr.com					
David Nolan Gallery 560 Broadway 6th Fl	New York	NY	10012	212-925-6190	334-9139
Web: www.davidnolangallery.com					
David Tunick Inc 19 E 66th St	New York	NY	10021	212-570-0090	744-8931
Web: www.tunickart.com					
David Zwirner Gallery 525 W 19th St	New York	NY	10011	212-727-2070	727-2072
Web: www.davidzwirner.com					
Davidson Maxwell Gallery 724 5th Ave 4th Fl	New York	NY	10019	212-759-7555	759-5824
Web: www.davidsongallery.com					
Davis & Langdale Co Inc 231 E 60th St	New York	NY	10022	212-838-0333	752-7764
Day Edward Gallery Inc 952 Queen St W	Toronto	ON	M6J1G8	416-921-6540	921-6624
Web: www.edwarddaygallery.com					
Dickinson Roundell Inc 19 E 66th St	New York	NY	10021	212-772-8083	772-8186
Web: www.simondickinson.com					
Didier Aaron Inc 32 E 67th St	New York	NY	10021	212-988-5248	737-3513
Web: www.didieraaron.com					
Donald Young Gallery 933 W Washington Blvd	Chicago	IL	60607	312-455-0100	455-0101
Web: www.donaldyoung.com					
Douglas Udell Gallery 10332 124th St	Edmonton	AB	T5N1R2	780-488-4445	488-8335
Web: www.douglasudellgallery.com					
Drabinsky Gallery 122 Scollard St	Toronto	ON	M5R1G2	416-324-5766	324-5770
Web: www.drabinskygallery.com					
Edward Day Gallery Inc 952 Queen St W	Toronto	ON	M6J1G8	416-921-6540	921-6624
Web: www.edwarddaygallery.com					
Edwynn Houk Gallery 745 5th Ave Suite 407	New York	NY	10151	212-750-7070	688-4848
Web: www.houkgallery.com					
Elkon Gallery Inc 18 E 81st St Suite 2-A	New York	NY	10028	212-535-3940	737-8479
Equinox Gallery 2321 Granville St	Vancouver	BC	V6H3G4	604-736-2405	736-0464
Web: www.equinoxgallery.com					
EV Thaw & Co Inc 726 Park Ave	New York	NY	10021	212-535-6333	535-1465
Feheley Fine Arts 14 Hazelton Ave	Toronto	ON	M5R2E2	416-323-1373	323-0121
Web: www.feheleyfinearts.com					
Feigen Contemporary 535 W 20th St	New York	NY	10011	212-929-0500	929-0065
Web: www.feigencontemporary.com					
Feigen Richard L & Co 34 E 69th St	New York	NY	10021	212-628-0700	249-4574
Web: www.rlfeigen.com					
Feldman Ronald Fine Arts Inc 31 Mercer St	New York	NY	10013	212-226-3232	941-1536
Web: www.feldmangallery.com					
Findlay David Galleries Inc 984 Madison Ave	New York	NY	10021	212-249-2909	249-2912
Web: www.davidfindlaygalleries.com					
Findlay David Jr Fine Art 41 E 57th St Suite 1120	New York	NY	10022	212-486-7660	486-6377
Web: www.davidfindlayjr.com					
Findlay Peter Gallery 41 E 57th St 8th Fl	New York	NY	10022	212-644-4433	644-1675
Web: www.findlay.com					
Fischbach Gallery 210 11th Ave Suite 801	New York	NY	10001	212-759-2345	366-1783
Web: www.fischbachgallery.com					
Forum Gallery 745 5th Ave 5th Fl	New York	NY	10151	212-355-4545	355-4547
Web: www.forumgallery.com					
Fraenkel Gallery 49 Geary St	San Francisco	CA	94108	415-981-2661	981-4014
Web: www.artnet.com/fraenkel.html					
Friedrich Petzel Gallery 535 W 22nd St	New York	NY	10011	212-680-9467	680-9473
Web: www.petzel.com					
Galerie Bernard Desroches Inc 2125 Crescent St	Montreal	QC	H3G2C1	514-842-8648	842-7951
Galerie Lelong 528 W 26th St	New York	NY	10001	212-315-0470	262-0624
Web: www.galerie-lelong.com					
Galerie Saint Etienne 24 W 57th St	New York	NY	10019	212-245-6734	765-8493
Web: www.gseart.com					
Galerie Saint Laurent + Hill 333 Cumberland St	Ottawa	ON	K1N7J3	613-789-7145	789-0976
Web: www.galeriestlaurentplushill.com					
Galerie Valentin 1490 Sherbrooke St W Suite 200	Montreal	QC	H3G1L3	514-939-0500	939-0413
Web: www.galerievalentin.com					
Galerie Walter Klinkhoff Inc 1200 Sherbrooke St W	Montreal	QC	H3A1H6	514-288-7306	288-5972
Web: www.klinkhoff.com					
Gallery 78 Inc 796 Queen St	Fredericton	NB	E3B1C6	506-454-5192	443-0199
TF: 888-883-8322 ■ Web: www.gallery78.com					
Gallery Moos Ltd 622 Richmond St W	Toronto	ON	M5V1Y9	416-504-5445	504-5446
Web: www.gallerymoos.com					
Gallery One 121 Scollard St	Toronto	ON	M5R1G4	416-929-3103	929-0278
Web: www.artgalleryone.com					
Gallery Paule Anglim 14 Geary St	San Francisco	CA	94108	415-433-2710	433-1501
Web: www.gallerypauleanglim.com					
Garth Clark Gallery 24 W 57th St Suite 305	New York	NY	10019	212-246-2205	489-5168
Web: www.garthclark.com					
George Adams Gallery 525 W 26th St	New York	NY	10001	212-564-8480	564-8485
Web: www.artnet.com/gadams.html					
Gibson Michael Gallery 157 Carling St	London	ON	N6A1H5	519-439-0451	439-2842
TF: 866-644-2766 ■ Web: www.gibsongallery.com					
Gladstone Barbara Gallery 515 W 24th St	New York	NY	10011	212-206-9300	206-9301
Web: www.gladstonegallery.com					
Godard Mira Gallery 22 Hazelton Ave	Toronto	ON	M5R2E2	416-964-8197	964-5912
Web: www.godardgallery.com					
Goodman James Gallery 41 E 57th St Suite 802	New York	NY	10022	212-593-3737	980-0195
Web: www.jamesgoodmangallery.com					
Goodman Marian Gallery 24 W 57th St	New York	NY	10019	212-977-7160	581-5187
Web: www.mariangoodman.com					
Graham James & Sons Inc 1014 Madison Ave	New York	NY	10021	212-535-5767	794-2454
Web: www.jamesgrahamandsons.com					
Gray Richard Gallery 875 N Michigan Ave Suite 2503	Chicago	IL	60611	312-642-8877	642-8488
Web: www.richardgraygallery.com					
Greenberg Van Doren Gallery 3540 Washington Ave	Saint Louis	MO	63103	314-361-7600	361-7743
Web: www.greenbergvandoren.com					
Greenberg Van Doren Gallery 730 5th Ave 7th Fl	New York	NY	10019	212-445-0444	445-0442
Web: www.agvdgallery.com					
Haime Nohra Gallery 41 E 57th St 6th Fl	New York	NY	10022	212-888-3550	888-7869
Hans P Kraus Jr Inc 962 Park Ave	New York	NY	10021	212-794-2064	744-2770
Heffel Gallery Ltd 2247 Granville St	Vancouver	BC	V6H3G1	604-732-6505	732-4245
TF: 800-528-9608 ■ Web: www.heffel.com/gallery					
Helman Joseph Gallery 20 W 57th St 2nd Fl	New York	NY	10019	212-245-2888	265-4592
Hirschl & Adler Galleries Inc 21 E 70th St	New York	NY	10021	212-535-8810	772-7237
Web: www.hirschlandadler.com					
Hobbs Susan Gallery Inc 137 Tecumseth St	Toronto	ON	M6J2H2	416-504-3699	504-8064
Web: www.susanhobbs.com					
Hoffman Nancy Gallery 429 W Broadway	New York	NY	10012	212-966-6676	334-5078
Web: www.nancyhoffmangallery.com					
Hoffman Rhona Gallery 118 N Peoria St	Chicago	IL	60607	312-455-1990	455-1727
Web: www.artnet.com/rhoffman.html					
Horan Vivian Fine Art 35 E 67th St 2nd Fl	New York	NY	10021	212-517-9410	772-6107
Houk Edwynn Gallery 745 5th Ave Suite 407	New York	NY	10151	212-750-7070	688-4848
Web: www.houkgallery.com					
Houston North Gallery 110 Montague St PO Box 1055	Lunenburg	NS	B0J2C0	902-634-8869	634-8332
TF: 866-634-8869 ■ Web: www.houston-north-gallery.ns.ca					
Hutton Leonard Galleries 41 E 57th St	New York	NY	10022	212-751-7373	832-2261
Web: www.leonardhuttongalleries.com					
Hyman Linda Fine Arts 44 E 67th St Apt 3A	New York	NY	10021	212-399-0112	399-1048
Web: www.lindahymanfinearts.com					
Inuit Gallery of Vancouver Ltd 206 Cambie St Gastown	Vancouver	BC	V6B2M9	604-688-7323	688-5404
TF: 888-615-8399 ■ Web: www.inuit.com					
Irving Galleries Inc 332 Worth Ave	Palm Beach	FL	33480	561-659-6221	659-0567
Jack Gallery 678 N Wells St	Chicago	IL	60610	312-943-8500	943-8587
TF: 877-252-2122 ■ Web: www.jackgallery.com					
Jack Kilgore & Co Inc 154 E 71st St 3rd Fl	New York	NY	10021	212-650-1149	650-1389
Jack Tilton Gallery 8 76th St	New York	NY	10021	212-737-2221	396-1725
Web: www.jacktiltongallery.com					
James Goodman Gallery 41 E 57th St Suite 802	New York	NY	10022	212-593-3737	980-0195
Web: www.jamesgoodmangallery.com					
James Graham & Sons Inc 1014 Madison Ave	New York	NY	10021	212-535-5767	794-2454
Web: www.jamesgrahamandsons.com					
Jan Krugier Gallery 980 Madison Ave	New York	NY	10021	212-755-7288	980-6079
Jason McCoy Inc 41 E 57th St 11th Fl	New York	NY	10022	212-319-1996	319-4799
Web: jasonmccoyinc.com					
Jean-Pierre Valentin Gallery 1490 Sherbrooke St W Suite 200	Montreal	QC	H3G1L3	514-939-0500	939-0413
Web: www.galerievalentin.com					
Jeffries Catriona Gallery 274 E 1st Ave	Vancouver	BC	V5T1A6	604-736-1554	736-1054
Web: www.catrionajeffries.com					
Jill Newhouse Gallery 12 E 86th St	New York	NY	10028	212-249-9216	734-4098
Web: www.jillnewhouse.com					
John Berggruen Gallery 228 Grant Ave	San Francisco	CA	94108	415-781-4629	781-0126
Web: www.berggruen.com					
Joseph Helman Gallery 20 W 57th St 2nd Fl	New York	NY	10019	212-245-2888	265-4592
June Kelly Gallery 591 Broadway	New York	NY	10012	212-226-1660	226-2433
Web: www.junekellygallery.com					
Kamen Leo Gallery 80 Spadina Ave Suite 406	Toronto	ON	M5V2J4	416-504-9515	504-3194
Web: www.leokamengallery.com					
Kelly June Gallery 591 Broadway	New York	NY	10012	212-226-1660	226-2433
Web: www.junekellygallery.com					
Kilgore Jack & Co Inc 154 E 71st St 3rd Fl	New York	NY	10021	212-650-1149	650-1389
Kind Phyllis Gallery 430 W 22nd St	New York	NY	10011	212-925-1200	941-7841
Web: www.phylliskindgallery.com					
Kinsman Robinson Galleries 108 Cumberland St	Toronto	ON	M5R1A6	416-964-2374	964-2374
TF: 800-895-4278 ■ Web: www.kinsmanrobinson.com					
Knoedler & Co 19 E 70th St	New York	NY	10021	212-794-0550	772-6932
Web: www.knoedlergallery.com					
Korper Olga Gallery 17 Morrow Ave	Toronto	ON	M6R2H9	416-538-8220	538-8772
Web: www.olgakorpergallery.com					
Krakow Barbara Gallery 10 Newbury St 5th Fl	Boston	MA	02116	617-262-4490	262-8971
Web: www.barbarakrakowgallery.com					
Kraus Hans P Jr Inc 962 Park Ave	New York	NY	10021	212-794-2064	744-2770
Kraushaar Galleries Inc 74 E 79th St	New York	NY	10021	212-288-2558	288-2557
Web: www.kraushaargalleries.com					
Krugier Jan Gallery 980 Madison Ave	New York	NY	10021	212-755-7288	980-6079
Kuhn Paul Gallery 724 11th Ave SW	Calgary	AB	T2R0E4	403-263-1162	262-9426
Web: www.paulkuhngallery.com					
LA Louver Inc 45 N Venice Blvd	Venice	CA	90291	310-822-4955	821-7529
Web: www.lalouver.com					
Langmann Uno Fine Arts Ltd 2117 Granville St	Vancouver	BC	V6H3E9	604-736-8825	736-8826
TF: 800-730-8825 ■ Web: www.langmann.com					
Laurence Miller Gallery 20 W 57th St 3rd Fl	New York	NY	10019	212-397-3930	397-3932
Web: www.laurencemillergallery.com					
Leavin Margo Gallery 812 N Robertson Blvd	Los Angeles	CA	90069	310-273-0603	273-9131
Lennon Weinberg Inc 514 W 25th St	New York	NY	10001	212-941-0012	929-3265
Web: www.lennonweinberg.com					
Leo Castelli Gallery 18 E 77th St	New York	NY	10021	212-249-4470	249-5220
Web: www.castelligallery.com					
Leo Kamen Gallery 80 Spadina Ave Suite 406	Toronto	ON	M5V2J4	416-504-9515	504-3194
Web: www.leokamengallery.com					
Leonard Hutton Galleries 41 E 57th St	New York	NY	10022	212-751-7373	832-2261
Web: www.leonardhuttongalleries.com					
Leslie Tonkonow Artworks & Projects 535 W 22nd St 6th Fl	New York	NY	10011	212-255-8450	414-8744
Web: www.tonkonow.com					
Lillian Heidenberg Fine Art 45 E 66th St	New York	NY	10021	212-628-6110	628-4958
Web: www.heidenbergfineart.com					
Linda Hyman Fine Arts 44 E 67th St Apt 3A	New York	NY	10021	212-399-0112	399-1048
Web: www.lindahymanfinearts.com					
Loch Gallery 16 Hazelton Ave	Toronto	ON	M5R2E2	416-964-9050	964-2778
TF: 877-227-9828 ■ Web: www.lochgallery.com					
Locks Gallery 600 Washington Sq S	Philadelphia	PA	19106	215-629-1000	629-3868
Web: www.locksgallery.com					
Long Meredith & Co 2323 San Felipe Blvd	Houston	TX	77019	713-523-6671	523-2355
Web: www.meredithlonggallery.com					
Luhring Augustine Gallery 531 W 24th St	New York	NY	10011	212-206-9100	206-9055
Web: www.luhringaugustine.com					
Manny Silverman Gallery 619 N Almont Dr	Los Angeles	CA	90069	310-659-8256	659-1001
Margo Leavin Gallery 812 N Robertson Blvd	Los Angeles	CA	90069	310-273-0603	273-9131

Name / Address	City	State	Zip	Phone	Fax
Marian Goodman Gallery 24 W 57th St	New York	NY	10019	212-977-7160	581-5187
Web: www.mariangoodman.com					
Marks Matthew Gallery 523 W 24th St	New York	NY	10011	212-243-0200	243-0047
Web: www.mmarks.com					
Mary-Anne Martin Fine Art 23 E 73rd St 4th Fl	New York	NY	10021	212-288-2213	861-7656
Web: www.mamfa.com					
Mary Boone Gallery 745 5th Ave 4th Fl	New York	NY	10151	212-752-2929	752-3939
Web: www.maryboonegallery.com					
Mary Ryan Gallery 24 W 57th St 2nd Fl	New York	NY	10019	212-397-0669	397-0766
Web: www.maryryangallery.com					
Masters Gallery Ltd 2115 4th St SW	Calgary	AB	T2S1W8	403-245-2064	244-1636
Web: www.mastersgalleryltd.com					
Mathes Barbara Gallery 22 E 80th St	New York	NY	10021	212-570-4190	570-4190
Web: www.bmathesgallery.com/					
Matthew Marks Gallery 523 W 24th St	New York	NY	10011	212-243-0200	243-0047
Web: www.mmarks.com					
Max Protetch Gallery 511 W 22nd St	New York	NY	10011	212-633-6999	691-4342
Web: www.maxprotetch.com					
Maxwell Davidson Gallery 724 5th Ave 4th Fl	New York	NY	10019	212-759-7555	759-5824
Web: www.davidsongallery.com					
Mazoh Stephen & Co Inc 19 Pink Ln	Rhinebeck	NY	12572	845-876-2723	876-5838
McCoy Jason Inc 41 E 57th St 11th Fl	New York	NY	10022	212-319-1996	319-4799
Web: jasonmccoyinc.com					
McKee Gallery 745 5th Ave 4th Fl	New York	NY	10151	212-688-5951	752-5638
Web: www.mckeegallery.com					
Meredith Long & Co 2323 San Felipe Blvd	Houston	TX	77019	713-523-6671	523-2355
Web: www.meredithlonggallery.com					
Metro Pictures Gallery 519 W 24th St	New York	NY	10011	212-206-7100	337-0070
Web: www.artnet.com/metropictures.html					
Michael Gibson Gallery 157 Carling St	London	ON	N6A1H5	519-439-0451	439-2842
TF: 866-644-2766 ■ *Web:* www.gibsongallery.com					
Michael Rosenfeld Gallery 24 W 57th St 7th Fl	New York	NY	10019	212-247-0082	247-0402
Web: www.michaelrosenfeldart.com					
Michael Werner Gallery 4 E 77th St 2nd Fl	New York	NY	10021	212-988-1623	988-1774
Web: www.michaelwerner.net					
Miller Laurence Gallery 20 W 57th St 3rd Fl	New York	NY	10019	212-397-3930	397-3932
Web: www.laurencemillergallery.com					
Miller Robert Gallery 524 W 26th St	New York	NY	10001	212-366-4774	366-4454
Web: www.robertmillergallery.com					
Mira Godard Gallery 22 Hazelton Ave	Toronto	ON	M5R2E2	416-964-8197	964-5912
Web: www.godardgallery.com					
Miriam Shiell Fine Art Ltd 16-A Hazelton Ave	Toronto	ON	M5R2E2	416-925-2461	925-2471
Web: www.miriamshiell.com					
Mitchell-Iness & Nash Gallery 1018 Madison Ave	New York	NY	10021	212-744-7400	744-7401
Web: www.miandn.com					
Modernism Inc 685 Market St Suite 290	San Francisco	CA	94105	415-541-0461	541-0425
Web: www.modernisminc.com					
Moeller Fine Art Ltd 36 E 64th St	New York	NY	10021	212-988-4500	644-2134
Web: www.moellerart.com					
Montgomery Gallery 406 Jackson St	San Francisco	CA	94111	415-788-8300	788-5469
Web: www.montgomerygallery.com					
Munson Gallery 225 Canyon Rd	Santa Fe	NM	87501	505-983-1657	988-9867
Web: www.munsongallery.com					
Nancy Hoffman Gallery 429 W Broadway	New York	NY	10012	212-966-6676	334-5078
Web: www.nancyhoffmangallery.com					
Naumann Otto Ltd 22 E 80th St 2nd Fl	New York	NY	10021	212-734-4443	535-0617
Web: www.dutchpaintings.com					
Newzones Gallery of Contemporary Art 730 11th Ave SW	Calgary	AB	T2R0E4	403-266-1972	266-1987
Web: www.newzones.com					
Nohra Haime Gallery 41 E 57th St 6th Fl	New York	NY	10022	212-888-3550	888-7869
Nouveau Gallery 2146 Albert St	Regina	SK	S4P2T9	306-569-9279	352-2453
Web: www.nouveaugallery.com					
Odon Wagner Gallery 196 Davenport Rd	Toronto	ON	M5R1J2	416-962-0438	962-1581
TF: 800-551-2465 ■ *Web:* www.odonwagnergallery.com					
O'Hara Gallery 41 E 57th St Suite 1302	New York	NY	10022	212-355-3330	355-3361
Olga Korper Gallery 17 Morrow Ave	Toronto	ON	M6R2H9	416-538-8220	538-8772
Web: www.olgakorpergallery.com					
Otto Naumann Ltd 22 E 80th St 2nd Fl	New York	NY	10021	212-734-4443	535-0617
Web: www.dutchpaintings.com					
Pace Prints 32 E 57th St 3rd Fl	New York	NY	10022	212-421-3237	832-5162
TF: 877-440-7223 ■ *Web:* www.paceprints.com					
Pace Wildenstein 32 E 57th St 4th Fl	New York	NY	10022	212-421-3292	421-0835
Web: www.pacewildenstein.com					
Paul Kuhn Gallery 724 11th Ave SW	Calgary	AB	T2R0E4	403-263-1162	262-9426
Web: www.paulkuhngallery.com					
Paula Cooper Gallery 534 W 21st St	New York	NY	10011	212-255-1105	255-5156
Peter Findlay Gallery 41 E 57th St 8th Fl	New York	NY	10022	212-644-4433	644-1675
Web: www.findlay.com					
Petzel Friedrich Gallery 535 W 22nd St	New York	NY	10011	212-680-9467	680-9473
Web: www.petzel.com					
Phyllis Kind Gallery 430 W 22nd St	New York	NY	10011	212-925-1200	941-7841
Web: www.phylliskindgallery.com					
Pilkington-Olsoff Fine Arts Inc 555 W 25th St	New York	NY	10001	212-647-1044	647-1043
Web: www.ppowgallery.com					
Prime Gallery 52 McCaul St	Toronto	ON	M5T1V9	416-593-5750	593-0942
Web: www.primegallery.ca					
Protetch Max Gallery 511 W 22nd St	New York	NY	10011	212-633-6999	691-4342
Web: www.maxprotetch.com					
Rachel Adler Fine Art 24 E 71st St	New York	NY	10021	212-308-0511	308-0516
Web: www.racheladlerfineart.com					
Rena Bransten Gallery 77 Geary St	San Francisco	CA	94108	415-982-3292	982-1807
Web: www.renabranstengallery.com					
Rhona Hoffman Gallery 118 N Peoria St	Chicago	IL	60607	312-455-1990	455-1727
Web: www.artnet.com/rhoffman.html					
Richard Gray Gallery 875 N Michigan Ave Suite 2503	Chicago	IL	60611	312-642-8877	642-8488
Web: www.richardgraygallery.com					
Richard L Feigen & Co 34 E 69th St	New York	NY	10021	212-628-0700	249-4574
Web: www.rlfeigen.com					
Riva Yares Gallery 123 Grant Ave	Santa Fe	NM	07501	505-984-0330	986-8661
Web: www.rivayaresgallery.com					
Robert Miller Gallery 524 W 26th St	New York	NY	10001	212-366-4774	366-4454
Web: www.robertmillergallery.com					
Roberts Gallery Ltd 641 Yonge St	Toronto	ON	M4Y1Z9	416-924-8731	
Web: www.robertsgallery.net					
Ronald Feldman Fine Arts Inc 31 Mercer St	New York	NY	10013	212-226-3232	941-1536
Web: www.feldmangallery.com					
Rosenfeld Michael Gallery 24 W 57th St 7th Fl	New York	NY	10019	212-247-0082	247-0402
Web: www.michaelrosenfeldart.com					
Russell Gallery of Fine Art 165 King St	Peterborough	ON	K9J2R8	705-743-0151	
Web: www.russellgallery.com					
Ryan Mary Gallery 24 W 57th St 2nd Fl	New York	NY	10019	212-397-0669	397-0766
Web: www.maryryangallery.com					
S2 Art Group Ltd 678 N Wells St	Chicago	IL	60610	312-943-8500	943-8587
TF: 877-252-2122 ■ *Web:* www.jackgallery.com					
Salander O'Reilly Galleries LLC 22 E 71st St	New York	NY	10021	212-879-6606	400-4490
Web: www.salander.com					
Schwarz Gallery 1806 Chestnut St	Philadelphia	PA	19103	215-563-4887	561-5621
Web: www.schwarzgallery.com					
Sheehan Susan Gallery 20 W 57th St 7th Fl	New York	NY	10019	212-489-3331	489-4009
Web: www.susansheehangallery.com					
Shiell Miriam Fine Art Ltd 16-A Hazelton Ave	Toronto	ON	M5R2E2	416-925-2461	925-2471
Web: www.miriamshiell.com					
Sikkema Jenkins & Co 530 W 22nd St	New York	NY	10011	212-929-2262	929-2340
Web: www.sikkemajenkinsco.com					
Silverman Manny Gallery 619 N Almont Dr	Los Angeles	CA	90069	310-659-8256	659-1001
Sperone Westwater 415 W 13th St 2nd Fl	New York	NY	10014	212-999-7337	999-7338
Web: www.speronewestwater.com					
Stair Sainty Matthiesen Inc 50 E 78th St	New York	NY	10021	212-288-1088	628-2449
Web: www.europeanpaintings.com					
Stephen Bulger Gallery 1026 Queen St W	Toronto	ON	M6J1H6	416-504-0575	504-8929
Web: www.bulgergallery.com					
Stephen Mazoh & Co Inc 19 Pink Ln	Rhinebeck	NY	12572	845-876-2723	876-5838
Stone Allan Gallery 113 E 90th St	New York	NY	10128	212-987-4997	987-4946
Web: www.allanstonegallery.com					
Susan Hobbs Gallery Inc 137 Tecumseth St	Toronto	ON	M6J2H2	416-504-3699	504-8064
Web: www.susanhobbs.com					
Susan Sheehan Gallery 20 W 57th St 7th Fl	New York	NY	10019	212-489-3331	489-4009
Web: www.susansheehangallery.com					
Tasende Gallery 820 Prospect St	La Jolla	CA	92037	858-454-3691	454-0589
Web: www.artnet.com/tasende.html					
Tatar Gallery 527 King St W Suite 300	Toronto	ON	M5V1K4	416-360-3822	360-3834
Web: www.tatargallery.com					
Thaw EV & Co Inc 726 Park Ave	New York	NY	10021	212-535-6333	535-1465
Thielsen Gallery 1038 Adelaide St N	London	ON	N5Y2M9	519-434-7681	434-8814
Web: www.thielsengallery.com					
Tibor de Nagy Gallery 724 5th Ave 12th Fl	New York	NY	10019	212-262-5050	262-1841
Web: tibordenagy.com					
TrepanierBaer Gallery 999 8th St SW Suite 105	Calgary	AB	T2R1J5	403-244-2066	244-2094
Web: www.trepanierbaer.com					
Tunick David Inc 19 E 66th St	New York	NY	10021	212-570-0090	744-8931
Web: www.tunickart.com					
Ubu Gallery 416 E 59th St	New York	NY	10022	212-753-4444	753-4470
Web: www.ubugallery.com					
Udell Douglas Gallery 10332 124th St	Edmonton	AB	T5N1R2	780-488-4445	488-8335
Web: www.douglasudellgallery.com					
Uno Langmann Fine Arts Ltd 2117 Granville St	Vancouver	BC	V6H3E9	604-736-8825	736-8826
TF: 800-730-8825 ■ *Web:* www.langmann.com					
Valley House Gallery Inc 6616 Spring Valley Rd	Dallas	TX	75254	972-239-2441	239-1462
Web: www.valleyhouse.com					
Virginia Christopher Galleries Ltd 816 11th Ave SW	Calgary	AB	T2R0E5	403-263-4346	263-4346
Web: www.virginiachristopherfineart.com					
Vivian Horan Fine Art 35 E 67th St 2nd Fl	New York	NY	10021	212-517-9410	772-6107
Waddington & Gorce Inc 7 Jackes Ave Suite 1707	Toronto	ON	M4T1E3	416-929-5591	
Web: www.waddingtongorce.com					
Wagner Odon Gallery 196 Davenport Rd	Toronto	ON	M5R1J2	416-962-0438	962-1581
TF: 800-551-2465 ■ *Web:* www.odonwagnergallery.com					
Wallace Galleries Ltd 500 5th Ave SW	Calgary	AB	T2P3L5	403-262-8050	264-7112
Web: www.wallacegalleries.com					
Wallack Galleries 203 Bank St	Ottawa	ON	K2P1W7	613-235-4339	235-0450
Werner Michael Gallery 4 E 77th St 2nd Fl	New York	NY	10021	212-988-1623	988-1774
Web: www.michaelwerner.net					
West End Gallery Ltd 12308 Jasper Ave	Edmonton	AB	T5N3K5	780-488-4892	488-4893
Web: www.westendgalleryltd.com					
White Albert Gallery 80 Spadina Ave Suite 208	Toronto	ON	M5V2J4	416-703-1021	703-1675
Winchester Galleries Ltd 2260 Oak Bay Ave	Victoria	BC	V8R1G7	250-595-2777	595-2310
Web: www.winchestergalleriesltd.com					
WM Brady & Co Inc 22 E 80th St 4th Fl	New York	NY	10021	212-249-7212	628-6587
Worthington Gallery Inc 645 N Michigan Suite 1040	Chicago	IL	60611	312-266-2424	266-2461
Wynick Tuck Gallery 401 Richmond St W Unit 128	Toronto	ON	M5V3A8	416-504-8716	504-8699
Web: www.wynicktuckgallery.ca					
Young Donald Gallery 933 W Washington Blvd	Chicago	IL	60607	312-455-0100	455-0101
Web: www.donaldyoung.com					
Zabriskie Gallery 41 E 57th St 4th Fl	New York	NY	10022	212-752-1223	752-1224
Web: www.zabriskiegallery.com					
Zolla Lieberman Gallery 325 W Huron St	Chicago	IL	60610	312-944-1990	944-8967
Web: www.zollaliebermangallery.com					
Zwickers Gallery 5415 Doyle St	Halifax	NS	B3J1H9	902-423-7662	422-3870
Web: www.zwickersgallery.ca					
Zwirner David Gallery 525 W 19th St	New York	NY	10011	212-727-2070	727-2072
Web: www.davidzwirner.com					

43 ART MATERIALS & SUPPLIES - MFR

SEE ALSO Pens, Pencils, Parts p. 2090

Name / Address	City	State	Zip	Phone	Fax
Adco Inc 13911 Distribution Way	Dallas	TX	75234	972-484-6177	484-1726
TF: 800-486-4583 ■ *Web:* www.gluestick.com					
Alvin & Co Inc 1335 Blue Hills Ave	Bloomfield	CT	06002	860-243-8991	777-2896*
**Fax Area Code:* 800 ■ *TF:* 800-444-2584 ■ *Web:* www.alvinco.com					
American Art Clay Co Inc (AMACO) 66 Guion Rd	Indianapolis	IN	46254	317-244-6871	248-9300
TF: 800-374-1600 ■ *Web:* www.amaco.com					
American Mat & Frame Co 760 E Lambert Suite F	La Habra	CA	90631	562-697-4700	694-3875
TF: 800-537-0984 ■ *Web:* www.americanmat.com					
American Metalcraft Inc 2074 George St	Melrose Park	IL	60160	708-345-1177	345-5758
TF: 800-333-9133 ■ *Web:* www.amnow.com					
Ampersand Art Supply 1500 E 4th St	Austin	TX	78702	512-322-0278	322-9928
TF: 800-822-1939 ■ *Web:* www.ampersandart.com					
ART Studio Clay Co 9320 Michigan Ave	Sturtevant	WI	53177	262-884-4278	884-4343
TF: 800-323-0212 ■ *Web:* www.artclay.com					
Artist Brand Canvas 2448 Loma Ave	South El Monte	CA	91733	626-579-2740	686-2658*
**Fax Area Code:* 323 ■ *TF Orders:* 888-579-2704 ■ *Web:* www.artistbrandcanvas.com					
Badger Air Brush Co 9128 W Belmont Ave	Franklin Park	IL	60131	847-678-3104	671-4352
TF: 800-222-7553 ■ *Web:* www.badgerairbrush.com					
Binney & Smith Inc 1100 Church Ln	Easton	PA	18044	610-253-6271	250-5768
TF: 800-272-9652 ■ *Web:* www.binney-smith.com					
Canson Inc 21 Industrial Dr	South Hadley	MA	01075	413-538-9250	533-6554
TF: 800-628-9283 ■ *Web:* www.canson-us.com					
Chartpak Inc 1 River Rd	Leeds	MA	01053	413-584-5446	584-6781
TF: 800-628-1910 ■ *Web:* www.chartpak.com					
Daler-Rowney USA Ltd 2 Corporate Dr	Cranbury	NJ	08512	609-655-5252	655-5852
Web: www.daler-rowney.com					
DecoArt Inc PO Box 297	Stanford	KY	40484	606-365-3193	365-9739
TF: 800-367-3047 ■ *Web:* www.decoart.com					
Duncan Enterprises 5673 E Shields Ave	Fresno	CA	93727	559-291-4444	291-9444
TF: 800-458-7010 ■ *Web:* www.duncancrafts.com					
Duro Art Industries Inc 1832 Juneway Terr	Chicago	IL	60626	773-743-3430	743-3882
TF: 800-621-5144					

	City	State	ZIP	Phone	Fax
Gare Inc 165 Rosemont St	Haverhill	MA	01832	978-373-9131	372-9432
TF: 888-511-4273 ■ *Web:* www.gare.com					
General Pencil Co Inc PO Box 5311	Redwood City	CA	94063	650-369-4889	369-7169
Web: www.generalpencil.com					
Georgie's Ceramic & Clay Co Inc 756 NE Lombard St	Portland	OR	97211	503-283-1353	283-1387
TF: 800-999-2529 ■ *Web:* www.georgies.com					
Golden Artists Colors Inc 188 Bell Rd	New Berlin	NY	13411	607-847-6154	847-6767
TF: 800-959-6543 ■ *Web:* www.goldenpaints.com					
Houston Art 10770 Moss Ridge Rd	Houston	TX	77043	713-462-1086	462-1783
TF Cust Svc: 800-272-3804 ■ *Web:* www.houstonart.com					
Jack Richeson & Co Inc 557 Marcella Dr	Kimberly	WI	54136	920-738-0744	738-9156
TF: 800-233-2404 ■ *Web:* www.richesonart.com					
Martin/F Weber Co 2727 Southampton Rd	Philadelphia	PA	19154	215-677-5600	677-3336
Web: www.weberart.com					
Masterpiece Artists Canvas Inc 1415 Bancroft Ave	San Francisco	CA	94124	415-822-8707	822-2124
Web: www.masterpiecearts.com					
National Artcraft Supply Co 7996 Darrow Rd	Twinsburg	OH	44087	330-963-6011	292-4916*
**Fax Area Code:* 800 ■ *TF Orders:* 800-526-7419 ■ *Web:* www.nationalartcraft.com					
Paasche Airbrush Co 4311 N Normandy	Chicago	IL	60634	773-867-9191	867-9198
TF Sales: 800-621-1907 ■ *Web:* www.paascheairbrush.com					
Plaid Enterprises Inc 3225 Westech Dr	Norcross	GA	30092	678-291-8100	291-8383
TF: 800-842-4197 ■ *Web:* www.plaidonline.com					
Richeson Jack & Co Inc 557 Marcella Dr	Kimberly	WI	54136	920-738-0744	738-9156
TF: 800-233-2404 ■ *Web:* www.richesonart.com					
Royal Brush Mfg Inc 6707 Broadway	Merrillville	IN	46410	219-660-4170	660-4181
TF: 800-247-2211 ■ *Web:* www.royalbrush.com					
Sanford Brands Div Newell Rubbermaid Inc					
2707 Butterfield Rd	Oak Brook	IL	60523	630-481-2200	481-2099*
**Fax:* Cust Svc ■ *TF:* 800-323-0749 ■ *Web:* www.sanford.com					
Sargent Art Inc 100 E Diamond Ave	Hazleton	PA	18201	570-454-3596	459-1752
TF: 800-424-3596 ■ *Web:* www.sargentart.com					
Sinopia Inc 3385 22nd St	San Francisco	CA	94110	415-824-3180	824-3280
Web: www.sinopia.com					
Smooth-On Inc 2000 Saint John St	Easton	PA	18042	610-252-5800	252-6200
TF: 800-766-6841 ■ *Web:* www.smooth-on.com					
Spraylat Corp One Shot LLC 5300 W 5th Ave	Gary	IN	46406	219-949-1684	949-1612
Web: www.1shot.com					
Staedtler Inc 21900 Plummer St	Chatsworth	CA	91311	818-882-6000	882-3767
TF: 800-800-3691 ■ *Web:* www.staedtler-usa.com					
Super Brush Co 165 Front St Suite 4	Chicopee	MA	01013	413-592-4195	594-2987
TF: 800-272-0591 ■ *Web:* www.superbrush.com					
Tara Materials Inc PO Box 646	Lawrenceville	GA	30046	770-963-5256	963-1044
TF: 800-241-8129 ■ *Web:* www.taramaterials.com					
Testor Corp 440 Blackhawk Park Ave	Rockford	IL	61104	815-962-6654	962-7401
TF: 800-962-3741 ■ *Web:* www.testors.com					
Tri-Chem Inc 681 Main St Bldg 24	Belleville	NJ	07109	973-751-9200	450-1260
Web: www.trichem.com					
Utrecht 6 Corporate Dr	Cranbury	NJ	08512	609-409-8001	409-8002
TF: 800-223-9132 ■ *Web:* www.utrecht.com					
Walbuck Crayon Co PO Box 367	Lawrence	MA	01842	978-974-0220	957-2421*
**Fax Area Code:* 800 ■ *TF:* 800-626-0099 ■ *Web:* www.walbuck.com					

44 ART MATERIALS & SUPPLIES - WHOL

	City	State	ZIP	Phone	Fax
American Hobby Craft Distributors Inc 2040 W North Ln	Phoenix	AZ	85021	602-861-1239	944-7124
Charrette LLC 31 Olympia Ave	Woburn	MA	01801	781-935-6000	626-7889*
**Fax Area Code:* 800 ■ *Web:* www.charrette.com					
Craft Wholesalers Inc 77 Cypress St SW	Reynoldsburg	OH	43068	740-964-6210	964-6212
TF: 800-666-5858 ■ *Web:* www.shopcwi.com					
Crafts Etc Ltd 7717 SW 44th St	Oklahoma City	OK	73179	405-745-1200	745-1225
TF: 800-888-0321 ■ *Web:* www.craftsetc.com					
Creative Hobbies Inc 900 Creek Rd	Bellmawr	NJ	08031	856-933-2540	992-7675*
**Fax Area Code:* 800 ■ *TF:* 800-843-5456 ■ *Web:* www.creative-hobbies.com					
D & L Stained Glass Supply Inc 4939 N Broadway	Boulder	CO	80304	303-449-8737	442-3429
TF: 800-525-0940 ■ *Web:* www.dlstainedglass.com					
Darice Inc 13000 Darice Pkwy	Strongsville	OH	44149	440-238-9150	238-1680
TF: 800-321-1494 ■ *Web:* www.darice.com					
Decorator & Craft Corp (DC & C) 428 S Zelta St	Wichita	KS	67207	316-685-6265	685-7606
TF: 800-835-3013 ■ *Web:* www.dcccrafts.com					
Howells-Craftland 6030 NE 112th Ave	Portland	OR	97220	503-255-2002	227-6956
TF: 800-547-0368 ■ *Web:* www.howells-craftland.com					
King Art & Craft Supply Co Inc 142 N Main St PO Box 671	Herkimer	NY	13350	315-866-5500	866-8062
TF: 800-777-1975 ■ *Web:* www.kingcraftco.com					
MacPherson's-Artcraft 1351 Ocean Ave	Emeryville	CA	94608	510-428-9011	768-6630
TF: 800-289-9800 ■ *Web:* www.macphersonart.com					
Pioneer Wholesale Co 500 W Bagley Rd	Berea	OH	44017	440-234-5400	234-5403
TF: 888-234-5400 ■ *Web:* www.pioneerwholesaleco.com					
Sax Arts & Crafts Inc 2725 S Moorland Rd Suite 101	New Berlin	WI	53151	262-784-6880	328-4729*
**Fax Area Code:* 800 ■ *TF Cust Svc:* 800-558-6696 ■ *Web:* www.saxarts.com					
Sbar's Inc 14 Sbar Blvd	Moorestown	NJ	08057	856-234-8220	234-9159
TF: 800-989-7227 ■ *Web:* www.sbarsonline.com					
Sepp Leaf Products Inc 381 Park Ave S Suite 1301	New York	NY	10016	212-683-2840	725-0308
TF: 800-971-7377 ■ *Web:* www.seppleaf.com					
Wholesale Art & Hobby Distributors Inc					
7207 114th Ave N Suite CF	Largo	FL	33773	727-548-1999	548-7676
TF: 800-227-2520 ■ *Web:* www.wholesaleartandhobby.com					
Zweigart-Joan Toggitt Ltd					
262 Old New Brunswick Rd Suite E	Piscataway	NJ	08854	732-562-8888	562-8866
Web: www.zweigart.com					

45 ART SUPPLY STORES

	City	State	ZIP	Phone	Fax
A & S Poliquin Inc DBA Artco 5401 6th Ave	Tacoma	WA	98406	253-759-9585	759-9713
Aaron Brothers Inc 1221 S Beltline Rd Suite 500	Coppell	TX	75019	972-409-1300	887-8441*
**Fax Area Code:* 323 ■ *TF:* 888-372-6464 ■ *Web:* www.aaronbrothers.com					
AC Moore Arts & Crafts Inc 130 AC Moore Dr	Berlin	NJ	08009	856-768-4930	753-4723
NASDAQ: ACMR ■ *Web:* www.acmoore.com					
Al Friedman Co Inc 44 W 18th St 4th Fl	New York	NY	10011	212-243-9000	929-7320
TF: 800-204-6352 ■ *Web:* www.aifriedman.com					
Alabama Art Supply Inc 1006 23rd St S	Birmingham	AL	35205	205-322-4741	254-3116
TF Cust Svc: 800-749-4741 ■ *Web:* www.alabamaart.com					
All Media Art Supply 417 E Main St	Kent	OH	44240	330-678-8078	678-0794
Arizona Art Supply 118 W Indian School Rd	Phoenix	AZ	85013	602-264-9514	264-1009
Web: www.arizonaartsupply.com					
Art Center 3101 E Yandell Dr	El Paso	TX	79903	915-566-2410	566-5628
Art Corner 264 Washington St	Salem	MA	01970	978-745-9524	
Art & Drafting Connection 2353 Schoenersville Rd	Bethlehem	PA	18017	610-882-0533	882-0566
Web: www.artanddrafting.com					
Art Essentials 32 E Victoria St	Santa Barbara	CA	93101	805-965-5456	965-3347
TF: 877-965-5456 ■ *Web:* www.sbartessentials.com					
Art Hardware 402 S Nevada Ave	Colorado Springs	CO	80903	719-635-2348	635-4857
TF: 800-355-4229 ■ *Web:* www.arthardware.com					
Art Supply Headquarters Inc 707 Monroe St	Jackson	MS	39202	601-948-4141	353-7973
Art Supply Warehouse 6672 Westminster Blvd	Westminster	CA	92683	714-891-3626	895-6701
TF: 800-854-6467 ■ *Web:* www.artsupplywarehouse.com					
Art & Woodcrafters Supply 671 Hwy 165	Branson	MO	65616	417-335-8382	335-8367
TF Orders: 800-786-4818 ■ *Web:* www.artwoodcrafter.com					
Artco 5401 6th Ave	Tacoma	WA	98406	253-759-9585	759-9713
Artistic Alternative 16-C Mountain Ave	Bloomfield	CT	06002	860-286-9640	286-9641
TF: 800-927-8258					
Artmart 2325 S Hanley Rd	Saint Louis	MO	63144	314-781-9999	781-3121
Web: www.artmartstl.com					
Asel Art Supply 2701 Cedar Springs Rd	Dallas	TX	75201	214-871-2425	871-0007
TF: 888-273-5278 ■ *Web:* www.aselart.com					
Ben Franklin Stores Promotions Unlimited Corp 087601	Racine	WI	53408	262-681-7000	
Web: www.benfranklinstores.com					
Blaine's Art Supply 2803 Spenard Rd	Anchorage	AK	99503	907-561-5344	562-5988
Web: www.blainesart.com					
Blick Dick Co PO Box 1267	Galesburg	IL	61402	309-343-6181	343-5785
TF Orders: 800-447-8192 ■ *Web:* www.dickblick.com					
Brudno Art Supply 29 E Balbo Ave	Chicago	IL	60605	312-787-0030	341-1345
Web: www.brudnoartsupply.com					
Champion's Craft & Decorating 9750 Regency Sq Blvd	Jacksonville	FL	32225	904-725-3020	725-5489
Charrette LLC 31 Olympia Ave	Woburn	MA	01801	781-935-6000	626-7889*
**Fax Area Code:* 800 ■ *Web:* www.charrette.com					
Commercial Art Supply 935 Erie Blvd E	Syracuse	NY	13210	315-474-1000	474-5311
TF: 800-669-2787					
Continental Art Supplies 7041 Reseda Blvd	Reseda	CA	91335	818-345-1044	345-5004
TF: 800-499-5146 ■ *Web:* www.continentalart.com					
Crafts Frames & Things 108 Owen Dr	Fayetteville	NC	28304	910-485-4833	485-4833
Web: www.craftsframesandthings.com					
Deck The Walls Inc 101 S Hanley Rd Suite 1280	Saint Louis	MO	63105	314-719-8200	
TF: 866-719-8200 ■ *Web:* www.deckthewalls.com					
Dick Blick Co PO Box 1267	Galesburg	IL	61402	309-343-6181	343-5785
TF Orders: 800-447-8192 ■ *Web:* www.dickblick.com					
Douglas & Sturgess Inc 730 Bryant St	San Francisco	CA	94107	415-896-6283	896-6379
TF: 888-278-7883 ■ *Web:* www.artstuf.com					
Evergreen Art Works 3280 Middle Rd	Bettendorf	IA	52722	563-359-8324	359-8901
TF: 800-468-7280 ■ *Web:* www.bettoffice.com/evart.html					
Fastframe USA Inc 1200 Lawrence Dr Suite 300	Newbury Park	CA	91320	805-498-4463	498-8983
TF: 888-863-7263 ■ *Web:* www.fastframe.com					
Flax Art & Design 240 Valley Dr	Brisbane	CA	94005	800-343-3529	352-9123
Web: www.flaxart.com					
Framing & Art Centre 1800 Appleby Line Rd	Burlington	ON	L7L6A1	800-563-7263	565-5755
Web: www.framingartcentre.com					
Friedman Al Co Inc 44 W 18th St 4th Fl	New York	NY	10011	212-243-9000	929-7320
TF: 800-204-6352 ■ *Web:* www.aifriedman.com					
G & H Art Co 4300 Hamilton Rd	Columbus	GA	31904	706-576-5551	576-4848
Georgie's Ceramic & Clay Co Inc 756 NE Lombard St	Portland	OR	97211	503-283-1353	283-1387
TF: 800-999-2529 ■ *Web:* www.georgies.com					
Great Frame Up The 101 S Hanley Rd Suite 1280	Saint Louis	MO	63105	314-719-8200	
TF: 866-719-8200 ■ *Web:* www.greatframeup.com					
Herweck's Art & Drafting Supplies 300 Broadway St	San Antonio	TX	78205	210-227-1349	227-8533
TF: 800-725-1349 ■ *Web:* www.herwecks.com					
Hobby Lobby Creative Centers 7707 SW 44th St	Oklahoma City	OK	73179	405-745-1100	745-1547
Web: www.hobbylobby.com					
Hobbytown USA 6301 S 58th St	Lincoln	NE	68516	402-434-5385	
TF: 800-869-0424 ■ *Web:* www.hobbytown.com					
HR Meininger Co 499 Broadway	Denver	CO	80203	303-698-3838	871-8676
TF: 800-950-2787 ■ *Web:* www.meininger.com					
Hungates Inc 102 Hungate Dr	Greenville	NC	27858	252-756-9565	756-2397
Web: www.hungates.com					
Jerry's Artarama 5325 Departure Dr	Raleigh	NC	27616	919-878-6782	790-6676
TF: 800-827-8478 ■ *Web:* www.jerrysartarama.com					
Jo-Ann Fabrics & Crafts 5555 Darrow Rd	Hudson	OH	44236	330-656-2600	463-6660
TF: 888-739-4120 ■ *Web:* www.jo-ann.com					
Lance's Art Supplies 345 Calhoun St	Cincinnati	OH	45219	513-861-0667	861-0500
Lee's Art Shop Inc 220 W 57th St	New York	NY	10019	212-247-0110	247-0507
Web: www.leesartshop.com					
Meininger HR Co 499 Broadway	Denver	CO	80203	303-698-3838	871-8676
TF: 800-950-2787 ■ *Web:* www.meininger.com					
Miami Clay Co 270 NE 183rd St	Miami	FL	33179	305-651-4695	652-8498
TF: 800-651-4695 ■ *Web:* www.miamiclay.net					
Michaels Stores Inc 8000 Bent Branch Dr	Irving	TX	75063	972-409-1300	409-7570*
NYSE: MIK ■ **Fax:* Hum Res ■ *TF Cust Svc:* 800-642-4235 ■ *Web:* www.michaels.com					
Millers Artist Supplies 33332 W 12 Mile Rd	Farmington Hills	MI	48334	248-489-8070	489-8643
Web: www.millersart.com					
Moore AC Arts & Crafts Inc 130 AC Moore Dr	Berlin	NJ	08009	856-768-4930	753-4723
NASDAQ: ACMR ■ *Web:* www.acmoore.com					
National Art Shop 509 S National Ave	Springfield	MO	65802	417-866-3743	866-3748
New York Central Art Supply 62 3rd Ave	New York	NY	10003	212-473-7705	475-2542
TF: 800-950-6111 ■ *Web:* www.nycentralart.com					
Pat Catan's Craft Centers 13000 Darice Pkwy	Strongsville	OH	44149	440-238-9150	238-8320
TF: 800-321-1494 ■ *Web:* www.patcatans.com					
Paul's Arts & Crafts 4039 E Little Creek Rd	Chesapeake	VA	23518	757-588-2800	
Pearl Paint Co Inc 308 Canal St	New York	NY	10013	212-431-7932	274-8290
TF: 800-221-6845 ■ *Web:* www.pearlpaint.com					
Plaza Art 633 Middleton St	Nashville	TN	37203	615-254-3368	254-1814
Web: www.plazaart.com					
Plaza Art Supply 519 York Rd	Baltimore	MD	21204	410-823-6406	823-5635
Plaza Artists Materials 173 Madison Ave	New York	NY	10016	212-689-2870	689-3386
TF: 800-327-3200 ■ *Web:* www.pla-za.com					
Rag Shops Inc 111 Wagaraw Rd	Hawthorne	NJ	07506	973-423-1303	427-6568*
**Fax:* Orders ■ *Web:* www.ragshop.com					
Rex Artist Supplies 3160 Coral Way	Miami	FL	33145	305-445-1413	445-1412
TF: 800-739-2782 ■ *Web:* www.rexart.com					
Richards Art & Crafts 4502 Las Positas Rd	Livermore	CA	94550	925-447-0471	447-0999
Web: www.richardscrafts.com					
RISD Store Art Supplies 30 N Main St	Providence	RI	02903	401-454-6465	454-6453
Riverside Art Shop 1600 Grand Army Hwy	Somerset	MA	02726	508-672-6735	672-6797
TF: 800-354-9899 ■ *Web:* www.riversideart.com					
Searle Art 639-B Lighthouse Ave	New Monterey	CA	93940	831-373-0126	646-9184
Spokane Art Supply Inc N 1303 Monroe St	Spokane	WA	99201	509-327-6622	327-6629
TF: 800-556-5568 ■ *Web:* www.myartsupply.com					
Starvin' Artist Supplies 651 Graceland Ave	Des Plaines	IL	60016	847-294-1300	795-8760
TF: 800-427-8478 ■ *Web:* www.starvinartistsupply.com					
Sterling Art Supply 18871 Teller Ave	Irvine	CA	92612	949-553-0101	553-0387
TF: 800-953-2953 ■ *Web:* www.sterlingart.com					
Suder's Art Store 1309 Vine St	Cincinnati	OH	45202	513-241-0800	
Tandy Leather Co 3847 E Loop 820 S	Fort Worth	TX	76119	817-451-1480	451-5254
TF: 888-890-1611 ■ *Web:* www.tandyleather.com					
Texas Art Supply 2001 Montrose Blvd	Houston	TX	77006	713-526-5221	524-7474
TF: 800-888-9278 ■ *Web:* www.texasart.com					
Thomson's Art Store 184 Mamaroneck Ave	White Plains	NY	10601	914-949-4885	949-4978
TF: 800-287-4885					

Phone Fax

Tidwell Art Supply Center 343 King St. ..... Charleston SC 29401 843-722-0647 722-7328
Top Notch Art Center 411 S Craig St ..... Pittsburgh PA 15213 412-683-4444 683-2831
Trinity Ceramic Supply Inc 9016 Diplomacy Row ..... Dallas TX 75247 214-631-0540 637-6463
Web: www.trinityceramic.com
Village Art Supply 715 Hahman Dr. ..... Santa Rosa CA 95405 707-575-4501 568-2112
Web: www.villageartsupply.com
Wet Paint Inc 1684 Grand Ave ..... Saint Paul MN 55105 651-698-6431 698-8041
Web: www.wetpaintart.com
Woodcraft Supply LLC 1177 Rosemar Rd PO Box 1686 ..... Parkersburg WV 26105 304-422-5412 428-8271
TF Cust Svc: 800-535-4482 ■ *Web:* www.woodcraft.com
World Supply Inc 3425 W Cahuenga Blvd ..... Hollywood CA 90068 323-851-1350 851-1922
TF: 800-399-6753 ■ *Web:* www.worldsupply.org

46 ASPHALT PAVING & ROOFING MATERIALS

Phone Fax

AE Stone Inc 1435 Doughty Rd ..... Egg Harbor Township NJ 08234 609-641-2781 641-0374
Web: www.aestone.com
American Asphalt Paving Co 500 Chase Rd ..... Shavertown PA 18708 570-696-1181 696-3486
TF: 800-326-9362 ■ *Web:* www.amerasphalt.com
Antioch Building Materials Co PO Box 870 ..... Antioch CA 94509 925-432-0171 432-9441
APAC Inc 900 Ashwood Pkwy Suite 700 ..... Atlanta GA 30338 770-392-5300 392-5393
TF: 800-241-7074 ■ *Web:* www.apac.com
Atlas Roofing Corp 2322 Valley Rd ..... Meridian MS 39307 601-483-7111 483-7344
TF Cust Svc: 800-478-0258 ■ *Web:* www.atlasroofing.com
Barrett Paving Materials Inc PO Box 13591 ..... Dayton OH 45413 937-279-3200 279-3205
Web: www.barrettpaving.com
Baxter's Asphalt & Concrete Inc PO Box 938 ..... Marianna FL 32447 850-482-4621 485-5080
Bellco Materials Inc 453 N Ash St PO Box 466 ..... Nowata OK 74048 918-273-1416 273-1460
Brannan Sand & Gravel Co 2500 E Brannan Way ..... Denver CO 80229 303-534-1231 534-1231
Web: www.brannan1.com
Brewer Co 1354 US Hwy 50 ..... Milford OH 45150 513-576-6300 576-1414
TF: 800-394-0017 ■ *Web:* www.brewercote.com
Brox Industries Inc 1471 Methuen St ..... Dracut MA 01826 978-454-9105 805-9720
Web: www.broxindustries.com
Burkholder Paving 621 Martindale Rd ..... Ephrata PA 17522 717-354-1340 428-7469*
**Fax Area Code:* 888 ■ *TF:* 866-839-3426 ■ *Web:* www.burkholderpaving.com
Capitol Aggregates Ltd 11551 Nacogdoches Rd ..... San Antonio TX 78217 210-655-3010 599-0560
TF: 800-292-5315 ■ *Web:* www.capaggltd.com
CertainTeed Corp 750 E Swedesford Rd ..... Valley Forge PA 19482 610-341-7000 341-7797
TF Prod Info: 800-782-8777 ■ *Web:* www.certainteed.com
Community Asphalt Corp 14005 NW 186th St ..... Hialeah FL 33018 305-829-0700 829-8772
TF: 800-741-0806 ■ *Web:* www.cacorp.net
Consolidated Fiberglass Products Co 3801 Standard St ..... Bakersfield CA 93308 661-323-6026 324-2635
Web: www.conglas.com
Crafco Inc 420 N Roosevelt Ave ..... Chandler AZ 85226 602-276-0406 961-0513*
**Fax Area Code:* 480 ■ *TF:* 800-528-8242 ■ *Web:* www.crafco.com
Cushing Stone Co Inc 725 State Hwy 5 S ..... Amsterdam NY 12010 518-887-2521 887-2520
Dalrymple Gravel & Contracting Co Inc 2105 S Broadway ..... Pine City NY 14871 607-737-6200 737-1056
Web: www.dalrymplecompanies.com
Dalton Enterprises Inc 131 Willow St ..... Cheshire CT 06410 203-272-3221 271-3396
TF: 800-851-5606 ■ *Web:* www.latexite.com
Dewitt Products Co 5860 Plumer Ave ..... Detroit MI 48209 313-554-0575 554-2171
TF Cust Svc: 800-962-8599 ■ *Web:* www.dewittproducts.com
Elk Premium Building Products Inc 14911 Quorum Dr Suite 600 ..... Dallas TX 75254 972-851-0500 851-0550
Web: www.elkcorp.com
Elk Premium Roofing 14911 Quorum Dr Suite 600 ..... Dallas TX 75254 972-851-0500 851-0550
Web: www.elkcorp.com
Emulsicoat Inc 705 E University Ave ..... Urbana IL 61802 217-344-7775 344-4174
Fields Co LLC 2240 Taylor Way ..... Tacoma WA 98421 253-627-4098 383-2181
TF: 800-627-4098 ■ *Web:* www.fieldscorp.com
GAF Materials Corp 1361 Alps Rd ..... Wayne NJ 07470 973-628-3000 628-3577*
**Fax:* Hum Res ■ *TF:* 800-365-7353 ■ *Web:* www.gaf.com
Gardner Asphalt Corp 4161 E 7th Ave ..... Tampa FL 33605 813-248-2101
TF: 800-237-1155 ■ *Web:* www.gardnerasphalt.com
Garland Co Inc 3800 E 91st St ..... Cleveland OH 44105 216-641-7500 641-0633
TF: 800-321-9336 ■ *Web:* www.garlandco.com
General Asphalt Co Inc 4850 NW 72nd Ave ..... Miami FL 33166 305-592-3480 477-4675
Glenn O Hawbaker Inc PO Box 135 ..... State College PA 16804 814-237-1444
TF: 800-221-1355 ■ *Web:* www.goh-inc.com
Granite Construction Inc PO Box 50085 ..... Watsonville CA 95077 831-724-1011 722-9657
NYSE: GVA ■ *Web:* www.graniteconstruction.com
Hempt Brothers Inc 205 Creek Rd ..... Camp Hill PA 17011 717-737-3411 761-5019
Henry Co 909 N Sepulveda Blvd Suite 650 ..... El Segundo CA 90245 310-955-9200 640-7663
TF: 800-598-7663 ■ *Web:* www.henry.com
HRI Inc 1750 W College Ave ..... State College PA 16801 814-238-5071 238-0131
Web: www.hrico.com
Jax Asphalt Inc PO Box 1725 ..... Mount Vernon IL 62864 618-244-0500 244-0833
JPS Elastomerics Corp 9 Sullivan Rd ..... Holyoke MA 01040 413-533-8100 552-1199
TF: 800-621-7663 ■ *Web:* www.jpselastomerics.com
Karnak Corp 330 Central Ave ..... Clark NJ 07066 732-388-0300 388-9422
TF: 800-526-4236 ■ *Web:* www.karnakcorp.com
Kool Seal Inc 1499 Enterprise Pkwy ..... Twinsburg OH 44087 330-425-4717 296-5665*
**Fax Area Code:* 888 ■ *TF:* 888-321-5665 ■ *Web:* www.koolseal.com
Koppers Inc 436 7th Ave ..... Pittsburgh PA 15219 412-227-2001 227-2333
NYSE: KOP ■ *TF:* 800-321-9876 ■ *Web:* www.koppers.com
Lunday-Thagard Co PO Box 1519 ..... South Gate CA 90280 562-928-7000 806-4032
Malarkey Roofing Products 3131 N Columbia Blvd ..... Portland OR 97217 503-283-1191 289-7644
TF: 800-545-1191 ■ *Web:* www.malarkey-rfg.com
Marathon Petroleum LLC 539 S Main St ..... Findlay OH 45840 419-422-2121 425-7040
Web: www.mapllc.com
Martin Asphalt Co 2 Riverway Suite 400 ..... South Houston TX 77056 713-350-6800 350-6801
TF: 800-662-0987 ■ *Web:* www.gsac.net
McClinton Anchor Co PO Box 1367 ..... Fayetteville AR 72702 479-587-3300 521-2826
TF: 877-241-9703
Midland Asphalt Materials Inc 640 Young St ..... Tonawanda NY 14150 716-692-0730 692-0613
TF: 800-573-0400 ■ *Web:* www.midlandasphalt.com
Neyra Industries 10700 Evendale Dr ..... Cincinnati OH 45241 513-733-1000 733-3989
TF: 800-543-7077 ■ *Web:* www.neyra.com
Owatonna Construction Co 900 30th Pl PO Box 246 ..... Owatonna MN 55060 507-451-8950 451-0575
Web: www.owatonnaconstruction.com
Pace Products Inc 4510 W 89th St Suite 1100-S ..... Overland Park KS 66207 913-469-5588 469-4067
TF: 888-389-8203 ■ *Web:* www.paceproducts.com
Package Pavement Co Inc PO Box 408 ..... Stormville NY 12582 845-221-2224 221-0433
TF: 800-724-8193 ■ *Web:* www.packagepavement.com
Palmer Asphalt Co 196 W 5th St PO Box 58 ..... Bayonne NJ 07002 201-339-0855 339-8320
TF: 800-352-9898 ■ *Web:* www.palmerasphalt.com
Peckham Industries Inc 20 Haarlem Ave ..... White Plains NY 10603 914-949-2000 949-2075
Web: www.peckham.com
Pike Industries Inc 3 Eastgate Park Rd ..... Belmont NH 03220 603-527-5100 527-5101
TF: 800-283-7453 ■ *Web:* www.pikeindustries.com
Quaker Sales Corp PO Box 880 ..... Johnstown PA 15907 814-539-1376 535-1685
Rason Asphalt Inc PO Box 530 ..... Old Bethpage NY 11804 631-293-6210 293-6849

Phone Fax

Rochester Asphalt Materials Inc 1150 Penfield Rd ..... Rochester NY 14625 585-381-7010 381-0208
Russell Standard Corp PO Box 479 ..... Bridgeville PA 15017 412-221-7300 221-3811
TF: 800-323-3053 ■ *Web:* www.russellstandard.com
Saint Gobain Technical Fabrics 1795 Baseline Rd ..... Grand Island NY 14072 716-775-3900 775-3901
TF: 800-762-6694 ■ *Web:* www.sgtf.com
Sarnafil Inc 100 Dan Rd ..... Canton MA 02021 781-828-5400 828-5365
TF: 800-451-2504 ■ *Web:* www.sarnafilus.com
Seaboard Asphalt Products Co 3601 Fairfield Rd ..... Baltimore MD 21226 410-355-0330 355-5864
TF: 800-536-0332 ■ *Web:* www.seaboardasphalt.com
Shelly Materials PO Box 938 ..... Lima OH 45802 419-229-2736 229-8390
South State Inc PO Box 68 ..... Bridgeton NJ 08302 856-451-5300 455-3461
Staker & Parson Cos 2350 S 1900 W ..... Ogden UT 84401 801-731-1111 731-8800
TF: 800-748-4100 ■ *Web:* www.stakerparson.com
Stavola Contracting PO Box 482 ..... Red Bank NJ 07701 732-542-2328 389-6083
Web: www.stavola.com
Stone Industries Inc 400 Central Ave PO Box 8310 ..... Haledon NJ 07538 973-595-6250 595-6920
Web: www.braenstone.com
Suit-Kote Corp 1911 Lorings Crossing Rd ..... Cortland NY 13045 607-753-1100 756-8611
TF: 800-622-5636 ■ *Web:* www.suit-kote.com
Tilcon Connecticut Inc PO Box 1357 ..... New Britain CT 06050 860-224-6005 225-1865
Web: www.tilconct.com
US Intec Inc PO Box 2845 ..... Port Arthur TX 77643 409-724-7024 271-6588*
**Area Code:* 877 ■ **Fax:* Cust Svc ■ *TF Tech Supp:* 800-624-6832 ■
Web: www.usintec.com
Vance Bros Inc PO Box 300107 ..... Kansas City MO 64130 816-923-4325 923-6472
TF: 800-821-8549 ■ *Web:* www.vancebrothers.com
Vulcan Materials Co
1200 Urban Center Dr PO Box 385014 ..... Birmingham AL 35238 205-298-3000 298-2942
NYSE: VMC ■ *Web:* www.vulcanmaterials.com
Vulcan Materials Co Western Div 3200 San Fernando Rd ..... Los Angeles CA 90065 323-258-2777 258-1583
TF: 800-225-6280 ■ *Web:* www.vulcanmaterials.com
Weldon Materials 141 Central Ave ..... Westfield NJ 07090 908-233-4444 233-9440
Web: www.weldonmat.com

47 ASSOCIATION MANAGEMENT COMPANIES

Phone Fax

Able Management Solutions Inc 5310 E Main St Suite 104 ..... Columbus OH 43213 614-868-1144 868-1177
Web: www.ablemgt.com
Administrative Systems Inc
5204 Fairmount Ave Suite 208 ..... Downers Grove IL 60515 630-655-0112 493-0798
Web: www.asihq.com
Advanced Management Concepts 136 S Keowee St ..... Dayton OH 45402 937-222-1024 222-5794
Web: www.advmgtconcepts.com
Alampi & Assoc Management Corp 66 Morris Ave Suite 2A ..... Springfield NJ 07081 973-379-1100 379-6507
Web: www.alampimgt.com
Allen Marketing & Management 810 E 10th St PO Box 1897 ..... Lawrence KS 66044 785-843-1235 843-1274
TF: 800-627-0932 ■ *Web:* www.allenmm.com
Alliance Management Group 1701 L St Suite 570 ..... Washington DC 20036 202-293-7642 293-0495
Web: www.alliancemg.com
Amber Association Partners LLC 801 N Fairfax St Suite 211 ..... Alexandria VA 22314 703-299-0000 299-9233
American PressWorks Inc 2020 N 14th St ..... Arlington VA 22201 703-812-8989 812-9455
Web: www.americanpressworks.com
AMP (Applied Measurement Professionals Inc)
18000 W 105th St ..... Olathe KS 66061 913-895-4600 895-4650
Web: www.goamp.com
AMR Management Services 201 E Main St Suite 1405 ..... Lexington KY 40507 859-514-9150 514-9207
Web: www.amrinc.net
Anthony J Jannetti Inc 200 E Holly Ave ..... Sewell NJ 08080 856-256-2300 589-7463
Web: www.ajj.com
Applied Measurement Professionals Inc (AMP)
18000 W 105th St ..... Olathe KS 66061 913-895-4600 895-4650
Web: www.goamp.com
APT Inc 2900 E Broadway Suite 5 ..... Bismarck ND 58501 701-224-1815 224-9824
Web: www.aptnd.com
ARDEL Group PO Box 24267 ..... Minneapolis MN 55424 763-765-2300 765-2329
Web: www.ardel.com
Association Assoc Inc 1 AAA Dr Suite 102 ..... Trenton NJ 08691 609-890-9207 581-8244
Web: www.hq4u.com
Association Enterprise Inc 1801 N Mill St Suite R ..... Naperville IL 60563 630-369-3772 369-3773
Web: www.aeinc.org
Association Headquarters Inc
15000 Commerce Pkwy Suite C ..... Mount Laurel NJ 08054 856-439-0500 439-0525
Web: www.associationheadquarters.com
Association Insight 4536 114th St ..... Urbandale IA 50322 515-727-0648 251-8657
Web: www.associationinsight.com
Association Management Bureau Inc
8405 Greensboro Dr Suite 800 ..... McLean VA 22102 703-506-3260 506-3266
Web: www.coultercos.com
Association Management Center 4700 W Lake Ave ..... Glenview IL 60025 847-375-4700 586-7616*
**Fax Area Code:* 866 ■ *Web:* www.amctec.com
Association Management Centre 1603 10th Ave SW Suite 200 ..... Calgary AB T3C0J7 403-244-7831 228-2018
Web: www.assocworldwide.com
Association Management & Communications
349 Granada Rd ..... West Palm Beach FL 33401 561-802-4310 659-1824
Web: www.association-management.net
Association Management Consultants Inc
409 Granville St Suite 218 ..... Vancouver BC V6C1T2 604-669-5344 669-5343
TF: 866-668-5344 ■ *Web:* www.amcdirectory.com
Association Management Group Inc 8201 Greensboro Dr 3rd Fl ..... McLean VA 22102 703-610-9000 610-9005
Web: www.amg-inc.com
Association Management Ltd 100 E Grand Ave Suite 330 ..... Des Moines IA 50309 515-243-1558 243-2049
Web: www.aml.org
Association Management Resources
2810 Industrial Plaza Dr ..... Tallahassee FL 32301 850-656-8848 656-3038
Web: www.mgmtresources.org
Association Management Solutions Inc
1951 W Camelback Rd Suite 445 ..... Phoenix AZ 85015 602-995-1442 995-1449
Web: nonprofitmanager.org
Association Management Solutions LLC
48377 Freemont Blvd Suite 117 ..... Fremont CA 94538 510-492-4000 492-4001
Web: www.amsl.com
Association Management Specialists
275 E Hillcrest Dr Suite 215 ..... Thousand Oaks CA 91360 805-557-1111 557-1133
Web: www.assoc-mgmt.net
Association Management Systems Inc 214 N Hale St ..... Wheaton IL 60187 630-510-4500 510-4501
Web: www.association-mgmt.com
Association Managers Inc 12427 Hedges Run Dr Suite 104 ..... Lake Ridge VA 22192 703-426-8100 426-8400
TF: 800-403-3374 ■ *Web:* www.assnmgrs.com
Association Resource Center 785 Orchard Dr Suite 225 ..... Folsom CA 95630 916-932-2200 932-2209
Web: www.assocresourcecenter.com
Association Resources Inc 342 N Main St ..... West Hartford CT 06117 860-586-7500 586-7550
Web: www.associationresources.com

Company / Address	City	State	ZIP	Phone	Fax
Association Services Management Co 2640 W 26th Ave Suite 17-C	Denver	CO	80211	720-259-3432	370-4055*
*Fax Area Code: 775 ■ Web: www.assn-services.com					
Association & Society Management International Inc 201 Park Washington Ct	Falls Church	VA	22046	703-533-0251	241-5603
Web: www.asmii.com					
Association Solutions Ltd 4513 Lincoln Ave Suite 213	Lisle	IL	60532	630-241-3100	241-0142
Web: www.associationsolutions.com					
Association Xpertise Inc 105-150 Crowfoot Crescent NW Suite 867	Calgary	AB	T3G3T2	403-374-1822	374-1823
Web: www.axi.ca					
AssociationsFirst Ltd 39 River St	Toronto	ON	M5A3P1	416-646-1600	646-9460
Web: www.associationsfirst.com					
Bannister & Assoc Inc 34 N High St	New Albany	OH	43054	614-895-1355	895-3466
Web: www.bannister.com					
BB & C Association Management Services 6835 Century Ave 2nd Fl	Mississauga	ON	L5N2L2	905-826-6665	826-4873
Web: www.bbandc.com					
BLF Management Ltd 1152 Goodale Blvd	Columbus	OH	43216	614-221-9580	221-2335
TF: 866-298-3576 ■ Web: www.blfmanagement.com					
Bostrom Corp 230 E Ohio St Suite 400	Chicago	IL	60611	312-644-0828	644-8557
Web: www.bostrom.com					
Boylan & Assoc LLC 308 E Lancaster Ave	Wynnewood	PA	19096	610-642-0607	
BTF Enterprises Inc 3540 Soquel Ave Suite A	Santa Cruz	CA	95062	831-464-4880	464-4881
Web: www.btfenterprises.com					
Calabrese & Heuser Organizational Resource Group 4305 N 6th St Suite A-2	Harrisburg	PA	17110	717-238-9989	238-9985
Web: www.calabreseheuser.org					
Center for Association Growth 1926 Waukegan Rd Suite 1	Glenview	IL	60025	847-657-6700	657-6819
TF: 800-492-6462 ■ Web: www.tcag.com					
Center for Association Resources Inc 1901 N Roselle Rd	Schaumburg	IL	60195	847-885-5680	885-5681
TF: 888-705-1434 ■ Web: www.association-resources.com					
Certified Association Management Co 900 Fox Valley Dr Suite 100	Longwood	FL	32779	407-774-0207	774-6751
Web: www.associationoffice.net					
Challenge Management Inc 12300 Ford Rd Suite 135	Dallas	TX	75234	972-755-2560	755-2561
Web: www.challenge-management.com					
Clarion Management Resources Inc 515 King St Suite 420	Alexandria	VA	22314	703-684-5570	684-6048
Web: www.clarionmanagement.com					
Clemons & Assoc Inc 5024 Campbell Blvd Suite R	Baltimore	MD	21236	410-931-8100	931-8111
Web: www.clemonsmgmt.com					
CM Services Inc 800 Roosevelt Rd Bldg C Suite 312	Glen Ellyn	IL	60137	630-858-7337	790-3095
TF: 800-613-6672 ■ Web: www.cmservices.com					
Crow-Segal Management Co 341 N Maitland Ave Suite 130	Maitland	FL	32751	407-647-8839	629-2502
Web: www.crowsegal.com					
Custom Management Group LLC 2365 Hunters Way	Charlottesville	VA	22911	434-971-4788	977-0899
Web: www.custommanagement.com					
Degnon Assoc Inc 6728 Old McLean Village Dr	McLean	VA	22101	703-550-9225	550-8729
Web: www.degnon.org					
DeSantis Management Group 1950 Old Tustin Ave	Santa Ana	CA	92705	714-550-9155	550-9234
Web: www.desantisgroup.com					
Diversified Management Services 525 SW 5th St Suite A	Des Moines	IA	50309	515-282-8192	282-9117
Web: www.assoc-mgmt.com					
Drake & Co 16020 Swingley Ridge Rd Suite 300	Chesterfield	MO	63017	636-449-5050	449-5051
Web: www.drakeco.com					
Drohan Management Group 12100 Sunset Hills Rd Suite 130	Reston	VA	20190	703-437-4377	435-4390
Web: www.drohanmgmt.com					
Droz Group LLC 511 San Nicholas Ct	Laguna Beach	CA	92651	949-715-6932	715-6931
Web: www.thedrozgroup.com					
eGroupManager 16476 Chesterfield Airport Rd	Chesterfield	MO	63017	636-530-7700	530-7777
TF: 800-992-8044 ■ Web: www.egroupmanager.com					
Ewald Consulting Group Inc 1000 Westgate Dr Suite 252	Saint Paul	MN	55114	651-290-6260	290-2266
Web: www.ewald.com					
Executive Administration Inc 85 W Algonquin Rd Suite 550	Arlington Heights	IL	60005	847-427-9600	427-9656
Executive Director Inc 555 E Wells St	Milwaukee	WI	53202	414-276-6445	276-3349
Web: www.execinc.com					
Executive Management Assoc 210 N Glenoaks Blvd Suite C	Burbank	CA	91502	818-843-5660	843-7423
Web: www.emaoffice.com					
Fanning Group Inc 1280 Main St 2nd Fl	Hanson	MA	02341	781-293-4100	294-0808
Web: www.fanningnet.com					
Fernley & Fernley Inc 100 N 20th St 4th Fl	Philadelphia	PA	19103	215-564-3484	564-2175
Web: www.fernley.com					
Franklin Management Co Inc 19 W Boscawen St	Winchester	VA	22601	540-678-9944	678-9940
TF: 866-703-2004 ■ Web: www.franklinmanagement.com					
FSA Group LLC 304 W Liberty St Suite 201	Louisville	KY	40202	502-583-3783	589-3602
TF: 800-620-6422 ■ Web: www.fsagroup.net					
Gilstrap Motta & Cole LLC 815 N 1st Ave Suite 1	Phoenix	AZ	85003	602-712-9822	712-1252
Web: www.gilstrapmottacole.com					
Giuffrida Assoc Inc 204 'E' St NE	Washington	DC	20002	202-547-6340	547-6348
Web: www.giuffrida.org					
Guild Assoc Inc 389 Main St Suite 202	Malden	MA	02148	781-397-8870	397-8887
Harrington Co 4248 Park Glen Rd	Minneapolis	MN	55416	952-928-4666	929-1318
Web: www.harringtoncompany.com					
Harrington Management Inc 305 2nd Ave Suite 200	Waltham	MA	02451	781-895-9080	895-9088
Hauck & Assoc Inc 1255 23rd St NW Suite 200	Washington	DC	20037	202-452-8100	833-3636
Web: www.hauck.com					
IMI Association Executives Inc 2501 Aerial Center Pkwy Suite 103	Morrisville	NC	27560	919-459-2070	459-2075
Web: www.imiae.com					
Interactive Management Inc 11166 Huron St Suite 27	Denver	CO	80234	303-433-4446	458-0002
TF: 800-243-1233 ■ Web: www.imigroup.org					
J Edgar Eubanks & Assoc 1 Windsor Cove Suite 305	Columbia	SC	29223	803-252-5646	765-0860
TF: 800-445-8629 ■ Web: www.jee.com					
JMP Productions Inc 6277 Franconia Rd	Alexandria	VA	22310	703-971-1116	971-7772
Kellen Co 1156 15th St NW Suite 900	Washington	DC	20005	202-785-3232	331-2714
Web: www.kellencompany.com					
King Stringfellow Group 2105 Laurel Bush Rd Suite 200	Bel Air	MD	21015	443-640-1030	640-1031
Web: www.ksgroup.org					
Lagniappe Assoc Inc 1016 Rosser St	Conyers	GA	30012	770-388-7979	761-1720
Web: www.lagniappeassociates.com					
LoBue & Majdalany Management Group 572B Ruger St PO Box 29920	San Francisco	CA	94129	415-561-6110	561-6120
Web: www.lm-mgmt.com					
Madeleine Crouch & Co Inc 14070 Proton Rd Suite 100	Dallas	TX	75244	972-233-9107	490-4219
Web: www.madcrouch.com					
Management Solutions Plus Inc 15245 Shady Grove Rd Suite 130	Rockville	MD	20850	301-258-9210	990-9771
Web: www.mgmtsol.com					
McBride & Assoc Inc 1633 Normandy Ct Suite A-200	Lincoln	NE	68512	402-476-3852	476-6547
Web: www.mcbridemanagement.com					
Melby Cameron & Hull Co 23607 Hwy 99 Suite 2C	Edmonds	WA	98026	425-774-7479	771-9588
Web: www.melbycameronhull.com					
Milde Rollins & Assoc LLC 505 Beach St Suite 130	San Francisco	CA	94133	415-674-4500	674-4539
Multiservice Management Co 994 Old Eagle School Rd Suite 1019	Wayne	PA	19087	610-971-4850	971-4859
Web: www.multiservicemgmt.com					
National Administration Co DBA eGroupManager 16476 Chesterfield Airport Rd	Chesterfield	MO	63017	636-530-7700	530-7777
TF: 800-992-8044 ■ Web: www.egroupmanager.com					
NeuStar Secretariat Services 46000 Center Oak Plaza	Sterling	VA	20166	571-434-5400	
Web: www.foretec.com					
NonProfit Team Inc 10 W Market St Suite 1720	Indianapolis	IN	46204	317-464-5156	464-5146
Web: www.npteam.org					
OEI Association Management Co 1711 W County Rd B Suite 300N	Roseville	MN	55113	651-635-0206	635-0307
Offinger Management Co 1100-H Brandywine Blvd	Zanesville	OH	43701	740-452-4541	452-2552
Web: www.offinger.com					
Organization Management Group 638 Independence Pkwy Suite 100	Chesapeake	VA	23320	757-473-8701	473-9897
Web: www.managegroup.com					
PAI Management Corp 5272 River Rd Suite 630	Bethesda	MD	20816	301-656-4224	656-0989
Web: www.paimgmt.com					
Pathfinder Group 6009 Quinpool Rd Suite 700	Halifax	NS	B3K5J7	902-425-2445	425-2441
Web: www.pathfinder-group.com					
Peripheral Services Inc PO Box 539	Webster	NY	14580	585-545-6920	545-6927
Web: www.peripheralservices.com					
Prime Management Services 3416 Primm Ln	Birmingham	AL	35216	205-823-6106	823-2760
Web: www.primemanagement.net					
Professional Management Assoc LLC 203 Towne Centre Dr	Hillsborough	NJ	08844	908-359-1184	359-7619
Web: www.profmgmt.com					
Queen Communications LLC 1215 Anthony Ave	Columbia	SC	29201	803-779-0340	254-3773
Web: www.queencommunicationsllc.com					
Raybourn Group International Inc 7150 Winton Dr Suite 300	Indianapolis	IN	46268	317-328-4421	280-8527
TF: 800-362-2546 ■ Web: www.raybourn.com					
Rees Group Inc 2810 Crossroads Dr Suite 3800	Madison	WI	53718	608-443-2468	443-2478
Web: www.reesgroupinc.com					
REM Association Services 2001 Jefferson Davis Hwy Suite 1004	Arlington	VA	22202	703-416-0010	416-0014
Web: www.remservices.biz					
Resource Center for Associations 10200 W 44th Ave Suite 304	Wheat Ridge	CO	80033	303-422-2615	422-8894
TF: 877-382-7823 ■ Web: www.resourcenter.com					
Resource Management Plus Inc 100 N 20th St 4th Fl	Philadelphia	PA	19103	215-545-1985	545-8107
TF: 800-408-8951 ■ Web: www.rmpinc.com					
Roberts Group LLC 1620 'I' St NW Suite 925	Washington	DC	20006	202-293-5800	463-8998
Web: www.therobertsgroup.net					
Robstan Group Inc 14 W 3rd St Suite 200	Kansas City	MO	64105	816-472-8870	472-7765
Web: www.robstan.com					
Ruggles Service Corp 2209 Dickens Rd	Richmond	VA	23230	804-282-0062	282-0090
Web: www.societyhq.com					
S & S Management Services Inc 1 Regency Dr	Bloomfield	CT	06002	860-243-3977	286-0787
Web: www.ssmgt.com					
Sanford Organization Inc 1000 N Rand Rd Suite 214	Wauconda	IL	60084	847-526-2010	526-3993
Web: www.tso.net					
Sherwood Group Inc 60 Revere Dr Suite 500	Northbrook	IL	60062	847-480-9080	480-9282
Web: www.sherwood-group.com					
SmithBucklin Corp 401 N Michigan Ave Suite 2200	Chicago	IL	60611	312-644-6610	245-1080
TF: 800-539-9740 ■ Web: www.smithbucklin.com					
Solutions for Associations Inc 140 N Bloomingdale Rd	Bloomingdale	IL	60108	630-351-8669	351-8490
Web: www.solutions-for-assoc.com					
STAT Association Marketing & Management Inc 11240 Waples Mill Rd Suite 200	Fairfax	VA	22030	703-934-0160	359-7562
Web: www.statmarketing.com					
Synergy Resource Group Inc 491 3rd St SW	Delano	MN	55328	612-619-4110	566-5780*
*Fax Area Code: 763 ■ TF: 888-990-9959 ■ Web: www.synergy-resource.com					
Talley Management Group Inc 19 Mantua Rd	Mount Royal	NJ	08061	856-423-7222	423-3420
TF: 888-423-4233 ■ Web: www.talley.com					
Technical Enterprises Inc 7044 S 13th St	Oak Creek	WI	53154	414-768-8000	768-8001
Web: www.techenterprises.net					
TH Management Inc 212 S Tryon St Suite 1150	Charlotte	NC	28281	704-365-3622	365-3678
Web: www.associationoffices.com					
Thomas Assoc Inc 1300 Sumner Ave	Cleveland	OH	44115	216-241-7333	241-0105
Web: www.taol.com					
Total Management Solutions Inc 55 Harristown Rd	Glen Rock	NJ	07452	201-447-0707	447-3831
Web: www.totmgtsol.com					
Trade Association Management Inc 25 N Broadway	Tarrytown	NY	10591	914-332-0040	332-1541
Web: www.taminc.com					
Virtual Inc 401 Edgewater Pl Suite 600	Wakefield	MA	01880	781-246-0500	224-1239
Web: www.virtualmgmt.com					
Wanner Assoc Inc 908 N 2nd St	Harrisburg	PA	17102	717-236-2050	236-2046
Web: www.wannerassoc.com					
Ward Management Group Inc 10293 N Meridian St Suite 175	Indianapolis	IN	46290	317-816-1619	816-1633
Web: www.wardmanage.com					
Wherry Assoc 30200 Detroit Rd	Cleveland	OH	44145	440-899-0010	892-1404
Web: www.wherryassoc.com					
Williams Management Resources Inc 1755 Park St Suite 260	Naperville	IL	60563	630-416-1166	416-9798
Web: www.wmrhq.com					
Willow Group 1485 Laperriere Ave	Ottawa	ON	K1Z7S8	613-722-8796	729-6206
Web: www.thewillowgroup.com					
XMi Association Management 618 Church St Suite 220	Nashville	TN	37219	615-254-3687	254-7047
Web: www.xmi-amc.com					

48 ASSOCIATIONS & ORGANIZATIONS - GENERAL

SEE ALSO Performing Arts Organizations p. 2098; Political Action Committees p. 2128; Political Parties (Major) p. 2129

48-1 Accreditation & Certification Organizations

Organization / Address	City	State	ZIP	Phone	Fax
AACSB International - Assn to Advance Collegiate Schools of Business (AACSB) 777 S Harbour Island Blvd Suite 750	Tampa	FL	33602	813-769-6500	769-6559
Web: www.aacsb.edu					
ABET Inc 111 Market Pl Suite 1050	Baltimore	MD	21202	410-347-7700	625-2238
Web: www.abet.org					
ABIM (American Board of Internal Medicine) 510 Walnut St Suite 1700	Philadelphia	PA	19106	215-446-3500	446-3590
TF: 800-441-2246 ■ Web: www.abim.org					
ABMS (American Board of Medical Specialties) 1007 Church St Suite 404	Evanston	IL	60201	847-491-9091	328-3596
Web: www.abms.org					
Accreditation Assn for Ambulatory Health Care (AAAHC) 3201 Old Glenview Rd Suite 300	Wilmette	IL	60091	847-853-6060	853-9028
Web: www.aaahc.org					

Organization	City	State	Zip	Phone	Fax
Accreditation Commission for Acupuncture & Oriental Medicine (ACAOM) 7501 Greenway Center Dr Suite 820	Greenbelt	MD	20770	301-313-0855	313-0912
Web: www.acaom.org					
Accreditation Council for Accountancy & Taxation (ACAT) 1010 N Fairfax St	Alexandria	VA	22314	703-549-2228	549-2984
TF: 888-289-7763 ■ *Web:* www.acatcredentials.org					
Accreditation Council for Continuing Medical Education (ACCME) 515 N State St Suite 2150	Chicago	IL	60610	312-755-7401	755-7496
TF: 800-475-2761 ■ *Web:* www.accme.org					
Accreditation Council for Graduate Medical Education (ACGME) 515 N State St Suite 2000	Chicago	IL	60610	312-755-5000	755-7498
Web: www.acgme.org					
Accreditation Council for Occupational Therapy Education (ACOTE) 4720 Montgomery Ln	Bethesda	MD	20824	301-652-6611	652-7711
Web: www.aota.org					
Accreditation Council on Optometric Education (ACOE) 243 N Lindbergh Blvd	Saint Louis	MO	63141	314-991-4100	991-4101
Web: www.aoa.org					
Accreditation Council for Pharmacy Education 20 N Clark St Suite 2500	Chicago	IL	60602	312-664-3575	664-4652
Web: www.acpe-accredit.org					
Accreditation Review Commission on Education for the Physician Assistant Inc (ARC-PA) 12000 Findley Rd Suite 240	Duluth	GA	30097	770-476-1224	476-1738
Web: www.arc-pa.org					
Accrediting Bureau of Health Education Schools (ABHES) 7777 Leesburg Pike Suite 314 N	Falls Church	VA	22043	703-917-9503	917-4109
Web: www.abhes.org					
Accrediting Commission of Career Schools & Colleges of Technology (ACCSCT) 2101 Wilson Blvd Suite 302	Arlington	VA	22201	703-247-4212	247-4533
Web: www.accsct.org					
Accrediting Council for Continuing Education & Training (ACCET) 1722 'N' St NW	Washington	DC	20036	202-955-1113	955-1118
Web: www.accet.org					
Accrediting Council on Education in Journalism & Mass Communications (ACEJMC) Univ of Kansas School of Journalism Stauffer-Flint Hall 1435 Jayhawk Blvd	Lawrence	KS	66045	785-864-3986	864-5225
Web: www2.ku.edu/acejmc					
Accrediting Council for Independent Colleges & Schools (ACICS) 750 1st St NE Suite 980	Washington	DC	20002	202-336-6780	842-2593
Web: www.acics.org					
American Academy for Liberal Education (AALE) 1050 17th St NW Suite 400	Washington	DC	20036	202-452-8611	452-8620
Web: www.aale.org					
American Assn for Accreditation of Ambulatory Surgery Facilities Inc (AAAASF) 5101 Washington St Suite 2F PO Box 9500	Gurnee	IL	60031	888-545-5222	775-1985*
**Fax Area Code:* 847 ■ *Web:* www.aaaasf.org					
American Assn for Laboratory Accreditation (A2LA) 5301 Buckeystown Pike Suite 350	Frederick	MD	21704	301-644-3248	662-2974
Web: www.a2la.org					
American Board of Funeral Service Education (ABFSE) 3432 Ashland Ave Suite U	Saint Joseph	MO	64506	816-233-3747	233-3703
Web: www.abfse.org					
American Board of Internal Medicine (ABIM) 510 Walnut St Suite 1700	Philadelphia	PA	19106	215-446-3500	446-3590
TF: 800-441-2246 ■ *Web:* www.abim.org					
American Board of Medical Specialties (ABMS) 1007 Church St Suite 404	Evanston	IL	60201	847-491-9091	328-3596
Web: www.abms.org					
American College of Nurse-Midwives Div of Accreditation 8403 Colesville Rd Suite 1550	Silver Spring	MD	20910	240-485-1800	485-1818
Web: www.midwife.org					
American Council for Construction Education (ACCE) 1717 N Loop 1604 East Suite 320	San Antonio	TX	78232	210-495-6161	495-6168
Web: acce-hq.org					
American Culinary Federation Inc (ACF) 180 Center Place Way	Saint Augustine	FL	32095	904-824-4468	825-4758
TF: 800-624-9458 ■ *Web:* www.acfchefs.org					
American Library Assn Committee on Accreditation 50 E Huron St	Chicago	IL	60611	800-545-2433	280-2433*
**Fax Area Code:* 312 ■ *Web:* www.ala.org/ala/accreditation					
American National Standards Institute (ANSI) 25 W 43rd St 4th Fl	New York	NY	10036	212-642-4900	398-0023
Web: www.ansi.org					
American Osteopathic Assn (AOA) 142 E Ontario St	Chicago	IL	60611	312-202-8000	202-8200
TF: 800-621-1773 ■ *Web:* www.osteopathic.org					
American Psychological Assn Committee on Accreditation 750 1st St NE	Washington	DC	20002	202-336-5979	336-5978
Web: www.apa.org/ed					
American Veterinary Medical Assn Council on Education 1931 N Meacham Rd Suite 100	Schaumburg	IL	60173	847-925-8070	925-1329
TF: 800-248-2862 ■ *Web:* www.avma.org					
Association of Advanced Rabbinical & Talmudic Schools (AARTS) 11 Broadway	New York	NY	10004	212-363-1991	533-5335
Association for Assessment & Accreditation of Laboratory Animal Care International 11300 Rockville Pike Suite 1211	Rockville	MD	20852	301-231-5353	231-8282
TF: 800-926-0066 ■ *Web:* www.aaalac.org					
Association for Biblical Higher Education (AABC) 5575 S Semoran Blvd Suite 26	Orlando	FL	32822	407-207-0808	207-0840
Web: www.abhe.org					
Association for Clinical Pastoral Education (ACPE) 1549 Clairmont Rd Suite 103	Decatur	GA	30033	404-320-1472	320-0849
Web: www.acpe.edu					
Association of Collegiate Business Schools & Programs (ACBSP) 7007 College Blvd Suite 420	Overland Park	KS	66211	913-339-9356	339-6226
Web: www.acbsp.org					
Association of Specialized & Professional Accreditors (ASPA) 1020 W Byron St Suite 8G	Chicago	IL	60613	773-525-2160	525-2162
Web: www.aspa-usa.org					
Association of Theological Schools in the US & Canada (ATS) 10 Summit Park Dr	Pittsburgh	PA	15275	412-788-6505	788-6510
Web: www.ats.edu					
Canadian Architectural Certification Board 1 Nicholas St Suite 1508	Ottawa	ON	K1N7B7	613-241-8399	241-7991
Web: cacb.ca					
Canadian Assn of Occupational Therapists (CAOT) 1125 Colonel By Dr Suite 3400	Ottawa	ON	K1S5R1	613-523-2268	523-2552
Web: www.caot.ca					
Canadian Assn of Speech-Language Pathologists & Audiologists (CASLPA) 401-200 Elgin St	Ottawa	ON	K2P1L5	613-567-9968	567-2859
Web: www.caslpa.ca					
Canadian Council for Accreditation of Pharmacy Programs (CCAPP) 123 Thorvaldson Bldg 110 Science Pl	Saskatoon	SK	S7N5C9	306-966-6388	966-6377
Web: www.ccapp-accredit.ca					
Canadian Council of Professional Engineers 180 Elgin St Suite 1100	Ottawa	ON	K2P2K3	613-232-2474	230-5759
Web: www.ccpe.ca					
Canadian Forestry Accreditation Board 18 Pommel Crescent	Kanata	ON	K2M1A2	613-599-7259	599-8107
Web: www.cfab.ca					
Canadian Information Processing Society (CIPS) 280 Skymark Ave Suite 402	Mississauga	ON	L4W5A6	905-602-1370	602-7884
Web: www.cips.ca					
Certified Financial Planner Board of Standards Inc 1670 Broadway Suite 600	Denver	CO	80202	303-830-7500	860-7388
TF: 888-237-6275 ■ *Web:* www.cfp.net					
Commission on Accreditation of Allied Health Education Programs (CAAHEP) 1361 Park St	Clearwater	FL	33756	727-210-2350	210-2354
Web: www.caahep.org					
Commission on Accreditation for Dietetics Education 120 S Riverside Plaza Suite 2000	Chicago	IL	60606	312-899-0040	899-4758
Web: www.eatright.org					
Commission on Accreditation of Healthcare Management Education 2000 14th St N Suite 780	Arlington	VA	22201	703-894-0960	894-0941
Web: www.cahmeweb.org					
Commission on Accreditation for Law Enforcement Agencies (CALEA) 10302 Eaton Pl Suite 100	Fairfax	VA	22030	703-352-4225	591-2206
TF: 800-368-3757 ■ *Web:* www.calea.org					
Commission on Accreditation in Physical Therapy Education (CAPTE) 1111 N Fairfax St	Alexandria	VA	22314	703-706-3245	838-8910
Web: www.apta.org					
Commission on Accreditation of Rehabilitation Facilities (CARF) 4891 E Grant Rd	Tucson	AZ	85712	520-325-1044	318-1129
TF: 888-281-6531 ■ *Web:* www.carf.org					
Commission on Collegiate Nursing Education 1 Dupont Cir NW Suite 530	Washington	DC	20036	202-887-6791	887-8476
Web: www.aacn.nche.edu					
Commission on Dental Accreditation 211 E Chicago Ave 18th Fl	Chicago	IL	60611	312-440-2500	440-2800
TF: 800-621-8099 ■ *Web:* www.ada.org/prof/ed					
Commission on Dental Accreditation of Canada 1815 Alta Vista Dr	Ottawa	ON	K1G3Y6	613-523-7114	523-7736
Web: www.cda-adc.ca					
Commission on English Language Program Accreditation 1725 Duke St Suite 500	Alexandria	VA	22314	703-519-2070	683-8099
Web: www.cea-accredit.org					
Commission on Massage Therapy Accreditation 1007 Church St Suite 302	Evanston	IL	60201	847-869-5039	869-6739
Web: www.comta.org					
Commission on Office Laboratory Accreditation (COLA) 9881 Broken Land Pkwy Suite 200	Columbia	MD	21046	410-381-6581	381-8611*
**Fax:* Hum Res ■ *TF:* 800-981-9883 ■ *Web:* www.cola.org					
Commission on Opticianry Accreditation 8665 Sudley Rd Suite 341	Manassas	VA	20110	703-940-9134	
Web: www.coaccreditation.com					
Committee on Accreditation of Educational Programs for the Emergency Medical Services Professions 1248 Hardwood Rd	Bedford	TX	76021	817-283-9403	354-8519
Web: www.coaemsp.org					
Community Health Accreditation Program Inc (CHAP) 1700 Diagonal Rd Suite 725	Alexandria	VA	22314	800-656-9656	480-8832*
**Fax Area Code:* 212 ■ *TF:* 800-656-9656 ■ *Web:* www.chapinc.org					
Continuing Care Accreditation Commission (CARF-CCAC) 1730 Rhode Island Ave NW Suite 209	Washington	DC	20036	202-587-5001	587-5009
TF: 866-888-1122 ■ *Web:* www.carf.org					
Council on Academic Accreditation in Audiology & Speech-Language Pathology 10801 Rockville Pike	Rockville	MD	20852	301-897-5700	571-0457
TF: 800-498-2071					
Council on Accreditation (COA) 120 Wall St 11th Fl	New York	NY	10005	212-797-3000	797-1428
TF: 866-262-8088 ■ *Web:* www.coanet.org					
Council on Accreditation of Nurse Anesthesia Educational Programs 222 S Prospect Ave	Park Ridge	IL	60068	847-692-7050	692-6968
Web: www.aana.com					
Council on Aviation Accreditation (CAA) 3410 Skyway Dr	Auburn	AL	36830	334-844-2431	844-2432
Web: www.caaaccreditation.org					
Council on Chiropractic Education Commission on Accreditation 8049 N 85th Way	Scottsdale	AZ	85258	480-443-8877	483-7333
Web: www.cce-usa.org					
Council on Education for Public Health 800 'I' St NW Suite 202	Washington	DC	20001	202-789-1050	789-1895
Web: www.ceph.org					
Council for Higher Education Accreditation (CHEA) 1 Dupont Cir NW Suite 510	Washington	DC	20036	202-955-6126	955-6129
Web: www.chea.org					
Council on Naturopathic Medical Education PO Box 178	Great Barrington	MA	01230	413-528-8877	528-8880
Web: www.cnme.org					
Council on Occupational Education 41 Perimeter Ctr East NE Suite 640	Atlanta	GA	30346	770-396-3898	396-3790
TF: 800-917-2081 ■ *Web:* www.council.org					
Council on Podiatric Medical Education (CPME) 9312 Old Georgetown Rd	Bethesda	MD	20814	301-581-9200	530-2752
Council on Quality & Leadership in Support for People with Disabilities 100 West Rd Suite 406	Towson	MD	21204	410-583-0060	583-0063
Web: www.thecouncil.org					
Council on Rehabilitation Education Commission on Standards and Accreditation 1835 Rohlwing Rd Suite E	Rolling Meadows	IL	60008	847-394-1785	394-2108
Web: www.core-rehab.org					
Council of the Section of Legal Education & Admissions to the Bar 321 N Clark St 21st Fl	Chicago	IL	60610	312-988-6738	988-5681
Web: www.abanet.org/legaled					
Distance Education & Training Council (DETC) 1601 18th St NW Suite 2	Washington	DC	20009	202-234-5100	332-1386
Web: www.detc.org					
Emergency Management Accreditation Program (EMAP) 2760 Research Park Dr	Lexington	KY	40511	859-244-8222	244-8239
Web: www.emaponline.org					
Foundation for Interior Design Education Research (FIDER) 146 Monroe Ctr NW Suite 1318	Grand Rapids	MI	49503	616-458-0400	458-0460
Web: www.fider.org					
Intersocietal Commission for the Accreditation of Vascular Laboratories (ICAVL) 8830 Stanford Blvd Suite 306	Columbia	MD	21045	410-872-0100	872-0030
Web: www.icavl.org					
Joint Commission on Accreditation of Healthcare Organizations (JCAHO) 1 Renaissance Blvd	Oakbrook Terrace	IL	60181	630-792-5000	792-5005
Web: www.jointcommission.org					
Joint Review Committee on Education in Radiologic Technology (JRCERT) 20 N Wacker Dr Suite 2850	Chicago	IL	60606	312-704-5300	704-5304
Web: www.jrcert.org					
Joint Review Committee on Educational Programs in Nuclear Medicine Technology 716 Black Point Rd PO Box 1149	Polson	MT	59860	406-883-0003	883-0022
Web: www.jrcnmt.org					

Accreditation & Certification Organizations (Cont'd)

Organization	City	State	ZIP	Phone	Fax
Landscape Architectural Accreditation Board (LAAB) 636 'I' St NW *Web:* www.asla.org/nonmembers/education.cfm	Washington	DC	20001	202-898-2444	898-1185
Liaison Committee on Medical Education (LCME) American Medical Assn 515 N State St *TF:* 800-621-8335 ■ *Web:* www.lcme.org	Chicago	IL	60610	312-464-4657	464-5830
Middle States Assn of Colleges & Schools 3624 Market St **Fax Area Code:* 215 ■ *TF:* 800-355-1258 ■ *Web:* www.msche.org	Philadelphia	PA	19104	267-284-5000	662-5501*
Midwifery Education Accreditation Council (MEAC) 515 E Birch Ave *Web:* www.meacschools.org	Flagstaff	AZ	86001	928-214-0997	773-9694
Montessori Accreditation Council for Teacher Education 506 7th St *Web:* www.macte.org	Racine	WI	53403	262-898-1846	898-1849
National Accreditation Council for Agencies Serving People with Blindness or Visual Impairment (NACASB) 21475 Lorain Rd Suite 300 *Web:* www.nacasb.org	Fairview Park	OH	44126	440-409-0340	409-0173
National Accrediting Agency for Clinical Laboratory Sciences (NAACLS) 8410 W Bryn Mawr Ave Suite 670 *Web:* www.naacls.org	Chicago	IL	60631	773-714-8880	714-8886
National Accrediting Commission of Cosmetology Arts & Sciences (NACCAS) 4401 Ford Ave Suite 1300 *Web:* www.naccas.org	Alexandria	VA	22302	703-600-7600	379-2200
National Architectural Accrediting Board (NAAB) 1735 New York Ave NW *Web:* www.naab.org	Washington	DC	20006	202-783-2007	783-2822
National Assn for the Education of Young Children (NAEYC) 1313 L St NW Suite 500 *TF:* 800-424-2460 ■ *Web:* www.naeyc.org	Washington	DC	20005	202-232-8777	328-1846
National Assn of Industrial Technology (NAIT) 3300 Washtenaw Ave Suite 220 *Web:* www.nait.org	Ann Arbor	MI	48104	734-677-0720	677-0046
National Assn of Nurse Practitioners in Women's Health Council on Accreditation 505 C St NE *Web:* www.npwh.org	Washington	DC	20002	202-543-9693	543-9858
National Assn of Schools of Art & Design (NASAD) 11250 Roger Bacon Dr Suite 21 *Web:* nasad.arts-accredit.org	Reston	VA	20190	703-437-0700	437-6312
National Assn of Schools of Dance (NASD) 11250 Roger Bacon Dr Suite 21 *Web:* nasd.arts-accredit.org	Reston	VA	20190	703-437-0700	437-6312
National Assn of Schools of Music (NASM) 11250 Roger Bacon Dr Suite 21 *Web:* nasm.arts-accredit.org	Reston	VA	20190	703-437-0700	437-6312
National Assn of Schools of Public Affairs & Administration Commission on Peer Review & Accreditation 1029 Vermont Ave NW Suit 1100 *Web:* www.naspaa.org	Washington	DC	20005	202-628-8965	626-4978
National Board of Trial Advocacy (NBTA) 200 Stonewall Blvd Suite 1 *TF:* 866-384-6565 ■ *Web:* www.nbtanet.org	Wrentham	MA	02093	508-384-6565	384-8022
National Certification Commission for Acupuncture & Oriental Medicine (NCCAOM) 11 Canal Center Plaza Suite 300 *Web:* www.nccaom.org	Alexandria	VA	22314	703-548-9004	548-9079
National Commission on Certification of Physician Assistants (NCCPA) 12000 Findley Rd Suite 200 *Web:* www.nccpa.net	Duluth	GA	30097	678-417-8100	417-8135
National Council for Accreditation of Teacher Education (NCATE) 2010 Massachusetts Ave NW Suite 500 *Web:* www.ncate.org	Washington	DC	20036	202-466-7496	296-6620
National Federation of Nonpublic School State Accrediting Assns 6300 Father Tribou St *Web:* www.nfnssaa.org	Little Rock	AR	72205	501-664-0340	664-9075
National League for Nursing Accrediting Commission Inc (NLNAC) 61 Broadway 33rd Fl *TF:* 800-669-1656 ■ *Web:* www.nlnac.org	New York	NY	10006	212-363-5555	812-0390
National Recreation & Park Assn/American Assn for Leisure & Recreation Council on Accreditation 22377 Belmont Ridge Rd *Web:* www.nrpa.org	Ashburn	VA	20148	703-858-0784	858-0794
NBTA (National Board of Trial Advocacy) 200 Stonewall Blvd Suite 1 *TF:* 866-384-6565 ■ *Web:* www.nbtanet.org	Wrentham	MA	02093	508-384-6565	384-8022
NCCPA (National Commission on Certification of Physician Assistants) 12000 Findley Rd Suite 200 *Web:* www.nccpa.net	Duluth	GA	30097	678-417-8100	417-8135
New England Assn of Schools & Colleges (NEASC) 209 Burlington Rd *Web:* www.neasc.org	Bedford	MA	01730	781-271-0022	271-0950
North Central Assn Commission on Accreditation & School Improvement (NCA CASI) Arizona State Univ PO Box 871008 *TF:* 800-525-9517 ■ *Web:* www.ncacasi.org	Tempe	AZ	85287	480-773-6900	
North Central Assn Higher Learning Commission 30 N La Salle St Suite 2400 *TF:* 800-621-7440 ■ *Web:* www.ncacihe.org	Chicago	IL	60602	312-263-0456	263-7462
Northwest Assn of Accredited Schools (NAAS) 1510 Robert St Suite 103 *Web:* www.northwestaccreditation.org	Boise	ID	83705	208-493-5077	334-3228
Northwest Commission on Colleges & Universities (NWCCU) 8060 165th Ave NE Suite 100 *Web:* www.nwccu.org	Redmond	WA	98052	425-558-4224	376-0596
Office of Social Work Accreditation and Education Excellence 1725 Duke St Suite 500 *Web:* www.cswe.org	Alexandria	VA	22314	703-683-8080	739-9048
Society of Accredited Marine Surveyors Inc (SAMS) 4605 Cardina Blvd *TF:* 800-344-9077 ■ *Web:* www.marinesurvey.org	Jacksonville	FL	32210	904-384-1494	388-3958
Society of American Foresters (SAF) 5400 Grosvenor Ln *Web:* www.safnet.org	Bethesda	MD	20814	301-897-8720	897-3690
Southern Assn of Colleges & Schools 1866 Southern Ln *TF:* 800-248-7701 ■ *Web:* www.sacs.org	Decatur	GA	30033	404-679-4500	679-4556
Teacher Education Accreditation Council (TEAC) 1 Dupont Cir Suite 320 *Web:* www.teac.org	Washington	DC	20036	202-466-7236	466-7238
Transnational Assn of Christian Colleges & Schools (TRACS) PO Box 328 *Web:* www.tracs.org	Forest	VA	24551	434-525-9539	525-9538
URAC 1220 L St NW Suite 400 *Web:* www.urac.org	Washington	DC	20005	202-216-9010	216-9006
Western Assn of Schools & Colleges (WASC) 985 Atlantic Ave Suite 100 *Web:* www.wascweb.org	Alameda	CA	94501	510-748-9001	748-9797

48-2 Agricultural Organizations

Organization	City	State	ZIP	Phone	Fax
Agricultural Retailers Assn (ARA) 1156 15th St NW Suite 302 *Web:* www.aradc.org	Washington	DC	20005	202-457-0825	457-0864
Agriculture Council of America (ACA) 11020 King St Suite 205 *TF:* 888-982-4329 ■ *Web:* www.agday.org	Overland Park	KS	66210	913-491-1895	491-6502
American Agricultural Economics Assn (AAEA) 415 S Duff Ave Suite C *Web:* www.aaea.org	Ames	IA	50010	515-233-3202	233-3101
American Angus Assn (AAA) 3201 Frederick Ave *TF:* 800-821-5478 ■ *Web:* www.angus.org	Saint Joseph	MO	64506	816-383-5100	233-9703
American Assn of Bovine Practitioners (AABP) PO Box 1755 *TF:* 800-269-2227 ■ *Web:* www.aabp.org	Rome	GA	30162	706-232-2220	232-2232
American Assn of Crop Insurers (AACI) 1 Massachusetts Ave NW Suite 800 *Web:* www.cropinsurers.org	Washington	DC	20001	202-789-4100	408-7763
American Dairy Assn 10255 W Higgins Rd Suite 900 *Web:* www.ilovecheese.com	Rosemont	IL	60018	847-803-2000	803-2077
American Dairy Goat Assn (ADGA) 209 W Main St PO Box 865 *Web:* www.adga.org	Spindale	NC	28160	828-286-3801	287-0476
American Dairy Science Assn (ADSA) 1111 N Dunlap Ave *Web:* www.adsa.org	Savoy	IL	61874	217-356-5146	398-4119
American Egg Board (AEB) 1460 Renaissance Dr Suite 301 *Web:* www.aeb.org	Park Ridge	IL	60068	847-296-7043	296-7007
American Farm Bureau Federation 600 Maryland Ave SW Suite 1000-W *Web:* www.fb.org	Washington	DC	20024	202-406-3600	406-3606
American Farmland Trust (AFT) 1200 18th St NW Suite 800 *TF:* 800-431-1499 ■ *Web:* www.farmland.org	Washington	DC	20036	202-331-7300	659-8339
American Feed Industry Assn (AFIA) 1501 Wilson Blvd Suite 1100 *Web:* www.afia.org	Arlington	VA	22209	703-524-0810	524-1921
American Fisheries Society (AFS) 5410 Grosvenor Ln Suite 110 *Web:* www.fisheries.org	Bethesda	MD	20814	301-897-8616	897-8096
American Forage & Grassland Council (AFGC) PO Box 94 **Fax Area Code:* 512 ■ *Web:* www.afgc.org	Georgetown	TX	78627	800-944-2342	931-1166*
American Forest Foundation (AFF) 1111 19th St NW Suite 780 *TF:* 888-889-4466 ■ *Web:* www.affoundation.org	Washington	DC	20036	202-463-2462	463-2461
American Forest & Paper Assn (AF&PA) 1111 19th St NW Suite 800 *TF:* 800-878-8878 ■ *Web:* www.afandpa.org	Washington	DC	20036	202-463-2700	463-2785
American Gelbvieh Assn 10900 Dover St *Web:* www.gelbvieh.org	Westminster	CO	80021	303-465-2333	465-2339
American Hereford Assn 1501 Wyandotte St *Web:* www.hereford.org	Kansas City	MO	64108	816-842-3757	842-6931
American-International Charolais Assn (AICA) PO Box 20247 *Web:* www.charolaisusa.com	Kansas City	MO	64195	816-464-5977	464-5759
American Jersey Cattle Assn 6486 E Main St *Web:* www.usjersey.com	Reynoldsburg	OH	43068	614-861-3636	861-8040
American Land Rights Assn (ALRA) 30218 NE 82nd Ave PO Box 400 *Web:* www.landrights.org	Battle Ground	WA	98604	360-687-3087	687-2973
American National CattleWomen Inc (ANCW) PO Box 3881 *Web:* www.ancw.org	Englewood	CO	80155	303-694-0313	694-2390
American Nursery & Landscape Assn (ANLA) 1000 Vermont Ave NW Suite 300 *Web:* www.anla.org	Washington	DC	20005	202-789-2900	789-1893
American Poultry International Ltd PO Box 16805 *Web:* www.apipoultry.com	Jackson	MS	39236	601-956-1715	956-1755
American Red Poll Assn PO Box 147 *Web:* www.redpollusa.org	Bethany	MO	64424	660-425-7318	425-8374
American Royal Assn 1701 American Royal Ct *TF:* 800-821-5857 ■ *Web:* www.americanroyal.com	Kansas City	MO	64102	816-221-9800	221-8189
American Seed Trade Assn (ASTA) 225 Reinekers Ln Suite 650 *TF:* 888-890-7333 ■ *Web:* www.amseed.com	Alexandria	VA	22314	703-837-8140	837-9365
American Sheep Industry Assn (ASI) 9785 Maroon Cir Suite 360 *Web:* www.sheepusa.org	Englewood	CO	80112	303-771-3500	771-8200
American Simmental Assn (ASA) 1 Simmental Way *Web:* www.simmental.org	Bozeman	MT	59718	406-587-4531	587-9301
American Society of Agricultural & Biological Engineers (ASABE) 2950 Niles Rd *TF Orders:* 800-695-2723 ■ *Web:* www.asabe.org	Saint Joseph	MI	49085	269-429-0300	429-3852
American Society of Agricultural Consultants (ASAC) 950 S Cherry St Suite 508 *Web:* www.agconsultants.org	Denver	CO	80246	303-759-5091	758-0190
American Society of Agronomy (ASA) 677 S Segoe Rd *Web:* www.agronomy.org	Madison	WI	53711	608-273-8080	273-2021
American Society of Animal Science (ASAS) 1111 N Dunlap Ave *Web:* www.asas.org	Savoy	IL	61874	217-356-9050	398-4119
American Society of Farm Managers & Rural Appraisers (ASFMRA) 950 S Cherry St Suite 508 *Web:* www.asfmra.org	Denver	CO	80246	303-758-3513	758-0190
American Society for Horticultural Science (ASHS) 113 South West St Suite 200 *Web:* www.ashs.org	Alexandria	VA	22314	703-836-4606	836-2024
American Society of Landscape Architects (ASLA) 636 'I' St NW *TF:* 888-999-2752 ■ *Web:* www.asla.org	Washington	DC	20001	202-898-2444	898-1185
American Soybean Assn (ASA) 12125 Woodcrest Executive Dr Suite 100 *TF:* 800-688-7692 ■ *Web:* www.amsoy.org	Saint Louis	MO	63141	314-576-1770	576-2786
American Sugar Cane League PO Box 938 *Web:* www.amscl.org	Thibodaux	LA	70302	985-448-3707	448-3722
ASABE (American Society of Agricultural & Biological Engineers) 2950 Niles Rd *TF Orders:* 800-695-2723 ■ *Web:* www.asabe.org	Saint Joseph	MI	49085	269-429-0300	429-3852
ASFMRA (American Society of Farm Managers & Rural Appraisers) 950 S Cherry St Suite 508 *Web:* www.asfmra.org	Denver	CO	80246	303-758-3513	758-0190
Association of Consulting Foresters of America (ACF) 312 Montgomery St Suite 208 *TF:* 888-540-8733 ■ *Web:* www.acf-foresters.org	Alexandria	VA	22314	703-548-0990	548-6395
Association of Farmworker Opportunity Programs (AFOP) 1726 M St NW Suite 800 *Web:* www.afop.org	Washington	DC	20036	202-828-6006	828-6005
Association of Water Technologies (AWT) 8201 Greensboro Dr Suite 300 *TF:* 800-858-6683 ■ *Web:* www.awt.org	McLean	VA	22102	703-610-9012	610-9005

Phone Fax

Beefmaster Breeders United (BBU)
6800 Park Ten Blvd Suite 290-W San Antonio TX 78213 210-732-3132 732-7711
Web: www.beefmasters.org
Beet Sugar Development Foundation 800 Grant St Suite 300 Denver CO 80203 303-832-4460 832-4468
Web: www.bsdf-assbt.org
Brown Swiss Cattle Breeders Assn of the USA 800 Pleasant St Beloit WI 53511 608-365-4474 365-5577
Web: www.brownswiss.com
Burley Tobacco Growers Cooperative Assn 620 S Broadway Lexington KY 40508 859-252-3561 231-9804
Web: www.burleytobacco.com
California Redwood Assn (CRA) 405 Enfrente Dr Suite 200 Novato CA 94949 415-382-0662 382-8531
TF: 888-225-7339 ■ *Web:* www.calredwood.org
Corn Refiners Assn Inc (CRA)
1701 Pennsylvania Ave NW Suite 950 Washington DC 20006 202-331-1634 331-2054
Web: www.corn.org
Cotton Council International 1521 New Hampshire Ave NW Washington DC 20036 202-745-7805 483-4040
Web: www.cottonusa.org
Cotton Inc 6399 Weston Pkwy Cary NC 27513 919-678-2220 678-2230
TF: 800-334-5868 ■ *Web:* www.cottoninc.com
Crop Science Society of America (CSSA) 677 S Segoe Rd Madison WI 53711 608-273-8080 273-2021
Web: www.crops.org
CropLife America 1156 15th St NW Suite 400 Washington DC 20005 202-296-1585 463-0474
TF: 888-295-1588 ■ *Web:* www.croplifeamerica.org
Dairy Management Inc (DMI) 10255 W Higgins Rd Suite 900 Rosemont IL 60018 847-803-2000 803-2077
Web: www.dairyinfo.com
Farm Aid 11 Ward St Suite 200 Somerville MA 02143 617-354-2922 354-6992
TF: 800-327-6243 ■ *Web:* www.farmaid.org
Farm Equipment Manufacturers Assn (FEMA)
1000 Executive Pkwy Suite 100 Saint Louis MO 63141 314-878-2304 878-1742
Web: www.farmequip.org
Farmers Educational & Cooperative Union of America
500 DTC Pkwy Suite 300 Greenwood Village CO 80111 303-337-5500 771-1770
TF: 800-347-1961 ■ *Web:* www.nfu.org
Fertilizer Institute (TFI) 820 1st St NE Suite 430 Washington DC 20002 202-962-0490 962-0577
Web: www.tfi.org
Forest Products Society 2801 Marshall Ct Madison WI 53705 608-231-1361 231-2152
TF: 800-354-7164 ■ *Web:* www.forestprod.org
Georgia Peanut Commission 110 E 4th St PO Box 967 Tifton GA 31793 229-386-3470 386-3501
Web: www.gapeanuts.com
Golf Course Superintendents Assn of America (GCSAA)
1421 Research Park Dr Lawrence KS 66049 785-841-2240 832-4455
TF: 800-472-7878 ■ *Web:* www.gcsaa.org
Hawaii Agriculture Research Center (HARC)
99-193 Aiea Heights Dr Suite 300 Aiea HI 96701 808-487-5561 486-5020
Web: www.hawaiiag.org/harc
Herb Growing & Marketing Network (HGMN) PO Box 245 Silver Spring PA 17575 717-393-3295 393-9261
Web: www.herbworld.com
Holstein Assn USA Inc 1 Holstein Pl Brattleboro VT 05302 802-254-4551 254-8251
TF Orders: 800-952-5200 ■ *Web:* www.holsteinusa.com
Hoo-Hoo International PO Box 118 Gurdon AR 71743 870-353-4997 353-4151
TF: 800-979-9950
Humane Farming Assn (HFA) PO Box 3577 San Rafael CA 94912 415-771-2253 485-0106
Web: www.hfa.org
International Banana Assn
1901 Pennsylvania Ave NW Suite 1100 Washington DC 20006 202-303-3400 303-3433
Web: www.eatmorebananas.com
International Brangus Breeders Assn (IBBA)
5750 Epsilon PO Box 696020 San Antonio TX 78269 210-696-4343 696-8718
Web: www.int-brangus.org
International Fertilizer Development Center (IFDC)
PO Box 2040 Muscle Shoals AL 35662 256-381-6600 381-7408
Web: www.ifdc.org
International Plant Nutrition Institute (IPNI)
3500 Parkway Ln Suite 550 Norcross GA 30092 770-447-0335 448-0439
Web: www.ipni.net
International Society of Arboriculture (ISA)
1400 W Anthony Dr PO Box 3129 Champaign IL 61826 217-355-9411 355-9516
TF: 888-472-8733 ■ *Web:* www.isa-arbor.com
IPNI (International Plant Nutrition Institute)
3500 Parkway Ln Suite 550 Norcross GA 30092 770-447-0335 448-0439
Web: www.ipni.net
Irrigation Assn (IA) 6540 Arlington Blvd Falls Church VA 22042 703-536-7080 536-7019
Web: www.irrigation.org
Landscape Nursery Council 1611 Creekview Dr Florence KY 41042 859-525-1809 525-9114
Livestock Marketing Assn (LMA)
10510 NW Ambassador Dr Kansas City MO 64153 816-891-0502 891-7926
TF: 800-821-2048 ■ *Web:* www.lmaweb.com
Milk Industry Foundation (MIF) 1250 H St NW Suite 900 Washington DC 20005 202-737-4332 331-7820
Mohair Council of America 233 W Twohig Rd PO Box 5337 San Angelo TX 76902 325-655-3161 655-4761
TF: 800-583-3161 ■ *Web:* www.mohairusa.com
National Agri-Marketing Assn (NAMA)
11020 King St Suite 205 Overland Park KS 66210 913-491-6500 491-6502
TF: 800-530-5646 ■ *Web:* www.nama.org
National Agricultural Aviation Assn (NAAA) 1005 'E' St SE Washington DC 20003 202-546-5722 546-5726
Web: www.agaviation.org
National Alliance of Independent Crop Consultants (NAICC)
349 E Nolley Dr Collierville TN 38017 901-861-0511 861-0512
Web: www.naicc.org
National Assn of Wheat Growers (NAWG)
415 2nd St NE Suite 300 Washington DC 20002 202-547-7800 546-2638
Web: www.wheatworld.org
National Cattlemen's Beef Assn (NCBA)
9110 E Nichols Ave Suite 300 Centennial CO 80112 303-694-0305 694-2851
Web: www.beef.org
National Chicken Council 1015 15th St NW Suite 930 Washington DC 20005 202-296-2622 293-4005
Web: www.eatchicken.com
National Christmas Tree Assn (NCTA)
16020 Swingley Ridge Rd Suite 300 Chesterfield MO 63017 636-449-5070 449-5051
Web: www.realchristmastrees.org
National Corn Growers Assn (NCGA) 632 Cepi Dr Chesterfield MO 63005 636-733-9004 733-9005
Web: www.ncga.com
National Cotton Council of America 1918 North Pkwy Memphis TN 38112 901-274-9030 725-0510
TF: 800-377-9030 ■ *Web:* www.cotton.org
National Cottonseed Products Assn (NCPA)
104 Timber Creek Dr Suite 200 Cordova TN 38108 901-682-0800 682-2856
Web: www.cottonseed.com
National Council of Agricultural Employers (NCAE)
1112 16th St NW Suite 920 Washington DC 20036 202-728-0300 728-0303
Web: www.ncaeonline.org
National Council of Farmer Cooperatives (NCFC)
50 F St NW Suite 900 Washington DC 20001 202-626-8700 626-8722
Web: www.ncfc.org
National Crop Insurance Services (NCIS)
8900 Indian Creek Pkwy Suite 600 Overland Park KS 66210 913-685-2767 685-3080
TF: 800-951-6247 ■ *Web:* www.ag-risk.org
National Dairy Council (NDC) 10255 W Higgins Rd Suite 900 Rosemont IL 60018 847-803-2000 803-2077
Web: www.nationaldairycouncil.org

Phone Fax

National Endangered Species Act Reform Coalition (NESARC)
1050 Thomas Jefferson St 7th Fl Washington DC 20007 202-333-7481 338-2416
Web: www.nesarc.org
National Family Farm Coalition (NFFC)
110 Maryland Ave NE Suite 307 Washington DC 20002 202-543-5675 543-0978
Web: www.nffc.net
National Farmers Organization (NFO)
528 Billy Sunday Rd Suite 100 PO Box 2508 Ames IA 50010 515-292-2000 292-7106
TF: 800-247-2110 ■ *Web:* www.nfo.org
National Farmers Union 500 DTC Pkwy Suite 300 Greenwood Village CO 80111 303-337-5500 771-1770
TF: 800-347-1961 ■ *Web:* www.nfu.org
National FFA Organization 6060 FFA Dr Indianapolis IN 46268 317-802-6060 802-6061
TF: 800-772-0939 ■ *Web:* www.ffa.org
National Fisheries Institute Inc (NFI)
7918 Jones Branch Dr Suite 700 McLean VA 22102 703-752-8880 752-7583
Web: www.aboutseafood.com
National Grain & Feed Assn (NGFA)
1250 'I' St NW Suite 1003 Washington DC 20005 202-289-0873 289-5388
TF: 800-680-9223 ■ *Web:* www.ngfa.org
National Grange 1616 H St NW Washington DC 20006 202-628-3507 347-1091
TF: 888-447-2643 ■ *Web:* www.grange.org
National Oilseed Processors Assn (NOPA)
1300 L St NW Suite 1020 Washington DC 20005 202-842-0463 842-9126
Web: www.nopa.org
National Onion Assn (NOA) 822 7th St Suite 510 Greeley CO 80631 970-353-5895 353-5897
Web: www.onions-usa.org
National Renderers Assn (NRA) 801 N Fairfax St Suite 207 Alexandria VA 22314 703-683-0155 683-2626
Web: www.renderers.org
National Turkey Federation (NTF)
1225 New York Ave NW Suite 400 Washington DC 20005 202-898-0100 898-0203
Web: www.eatturkey.com
National Woodland Owners Assn (NWOA)
374 Maple Ave E Suite 310 Vienna VA 22180 703-255-2700 281-9200
TF: 800-476-8733 ■ *Web:* www.woodlandowners.org
NCIS (National Crop Insurance Services)
8900 Indian Creek Pkwy Suite 600 Overland Park KS 66210 913-685-2767 685-3080
TF: 800-951-6247 ■ *Web:* www.ag-risk.org
North American Blueberry Council (NABC)
2390 E Bidwell St Suite 300 Folsom CA 95630 916-983-0111 983-9370
Web: www.blueberry.org
North American Limousin Foundation (NALF)
7383 S Alton Way Suite 100 Englewood CO 80112 303-220-1693 220-1884
Web: www.nalf.org
Organic Trade Assn (OTA) 60 Wells St PO Box 547 Greenfield MA 01302 413-774-7511 774-6432
Web: www.ota.com
Professional Landcare Network (PLANET)
950 Herndon Pkwy Suite 450 Herndon VA 20170 703-736-9666 736-9668
TF: 800-395-2522 ■ *Web:* www.landcarenetwork.org
Red Angus Assn of America 4201 N I-35 Denton TX 76207 940-387-3502 383-4036
Web: redangus.org
Rural Coalition 1012 14th St NW Suite 1100 Washington DC 20005 202-628-7160 393-1816
Web: www.ruralco.org
Santa Gertrudis Breeders International PO Box 1257 Kingsville TX 78364 361-592-9357 592-8572
Web: santagertrudis.com
Society of American Foresters (SAF) 5400 Grosvenor Ln Bethesda MD 20814 301-897-8720 897-3690
Web: www.safnet.org
Soil Science Society of America (SSSA) 677 S Segoe Rd Madison WI 53711 608-273-8080 273-2021
Web: www.soils.org
Southern Forest Products Assn (SFPA) 2900 Indiana Ave Kenner LA 70065 504-443-4464 443-6612
Web: www.sfpa.org
Sugar Assn 1300 L St NW Suite 1001 Washington DC 20005 202-785-1122 785-5019
Web: www.sugar.org
Supima 4141 E Broadway Rd Phoenix AZ 85040 602-437-1364 437-0143
Web: www.supima.com
Texas Longhorn Breeders Assn of America (TLBAA)
2315 N Main St Suite 402 Fort Worth TX 76106 817-625-6241 625-1388
Web: www.tlbaa.org
Tobacco Associates Inc 1306 Annapolis Dr Suite 102 Raleigh NC 27605 919-821-7670 821-7674
Web: www.tobaccoassociatesinc.org
Tobacco Merchants Assn (TMA) PO Box 8019 Princeton NJ 08543 609-275-4900 275-8379
Web: www.tma.org
United Fresh Fruit & Vegetable Assn
1901 Pennsylvania Ave NW Suite 1100 Washington DC 20006 202-303-3400 303-3433
Web: www.uffva.org
United Producers Inc 5909 Cleveland Ave Columbus OH 43231 614-890-6666 890-4776
TF: 800-456-3276 ■ *Web:* www.uproducers.com
United Soybean Board (USB)
16640 Chesterfield Grove Rd Suite 130 Chesterfield MO 63005 636-530-1777 530-1560
TF: 800-989-8721 ■ *Web:* www.unitedsoybean.org
US Apple Assn 8233 Old Courthouse Rd Suite 200 Vienna VA 22182 703-442-8850 790-0845
TF: 800-781-4443 ■ *Web:* www.usapple.org
US Grains Council 1400 K St NW Suite 1200 Washington DC 20005 202-789-0789 898-0522
Web: www.grains.org
US Potato Board (USPB) 7555 E Hampden Ave Suite 412 Denver CO 80231 303-369-7783 369-7718
Web: www.uspotatoes.com
US Poultry & Egg Assn 1530 Cooledge Rd Tucker GA 30084 770-493-9401 493-9257
Web: www.poultryegg.org
US Wheat Associates (USW) 3103 10th St N Suite 300 Arlington VA 22201 202-463-0999 524-4399*
**Fax Area Code:* 703 ■ *Web:* www.uswheat.org
USA Rice Federation 4301 N Fairfax Dr Suite 425 Arlington VA 22203 703-236-2300 236-2301
Web: www.usarice.com
Western Wood Products Assn (WWPA)
522 SW 5th Ave Yeon Bldg Suite 500 Portland OR 97204 503-224-3930 224-3934
Web: www.wwpa.org
Wheat Quality Council 106 W Capitol Suite 2 Pierre SD 57501 605-224-5187 224-0517
Web: www.wheatqualitycouncil.org
Wild Blueberry Assn of North America (WBANA) PO Box 100 Old Town ME 04468 207-570-3535 581-3499
Web: www.wildblueberries.com

48-3 Animals & Animal Welfare Organizations

Phone Fax

African Wildlife Foundation (AWF)
1400 16th St NW Suite 120 Washington DC 20036 202-939-3333 939-3332
TF: 888-494-5354 ■ *Web:* www.awf.org
AHI (Animal Health Institute) 1325 G St NW Suite 700 Washington DC 20005 202-637-2440 393-1667
Web: www.ahi.org
Alaska Wildlife Alliance PO Box 202022 Anchorage AK 99520 907-277-0897 277-7423
Web: www.akwildlife.org
American Animal Hospital Assn (AAHA) 12575 W Bayaud Ave Lakewood CO 80228 303-986-2800 986-1700
TF: 800-252-2242 ■ *Web:* www.aahanet.org
American Assn of Equine Practitioners (AAEP)
4075 Iron Works Pkwy Lexington KY 40511 859-233-0147 233-1968
TF: 800-443-0177 ■ *Web:* www.aaep.org
American Boarding Kennels Assn (ABKA)
1702 E Pikes Peak Ave Colorado Springs CO 80909 719-667-1600 667-0116
TF: 877-570-7788 ■ *Web:* www.abka.com

Animals & Animal Welfare Organizations (Cont'd)

Organization	City	State	Zip	Phone	Fax
American Buckskin Registry Assn Inc (ABRA) 1141 Hartnell Ave PO Box 3850 *Web:* www.americanbuckskin.org	Redding	CA	96049	530-223-1420	
American Cetacean Society (ACS) PO Box 1391 *Web:* www.acsonline.org	San Pedro	CA	90733	310-548-6279	548-6950
American Donkey & Mule Society (ADMS) PO Box 1210 *Web:* www.lovelongears.com	Lewisville	TX	75067	972-219-0781	420-9980
American Horse Council (AHC) 1616 H St NW 7th Fl *Web:* www.horsecouncil.org	Washington	DC	20006	202-296-4031	296-1970
American Humane Assn (AHA) 63 Inverness Dr E *TF:* 800-227-4645 ■ *Web:* www.americanhumane.org	Englewood	CO	80112	303-792-9900	792-5333
American Miniature Horse Assn (AMHA) 5601 S I-35 W *Web:* www.amha.org	Alvarado	TX	76009	817-783-5600	783-6403
American Morgan Horse Assn (AMHA) 122 Bostwick Rd *Web:* www.morganhorse.com	Shelburne	VT	05482	802-985-4944	985-8897
American Ornithologists' Union (AOU) 1313 Dolley Madison Blvd Suite 402 *Web:* www.aou.org	McLean	VA	22101	703-790-1745	790-2672
American Paint Horse Assn (APHA) PO Box 961023 *Web:* www.apha.com	Fort Worth	TX	76161	817-834-2742	834-3152
American Quarter Horse Assn (AQHA) PO Box 200 *TF:* 800-414-7433 ■ *Web:* www.aqha.com	Amarillo	TX	79168	806-376-4811	349-6404
American Rabbit Breeders Assn (ARBA) PO Box 426 *Web:* www.arba.net	Bloomington	IL	61702	309-664-7500	664-0941
American Saddlebred Horse Assn (ASHA) 4093 Iron Works Pkwy *Web:* www.saddlebred.com	Lexington	KY	40511	859-259-2742	259-1628
American Shetland Pony Club (ASPC) 81-B E Queenwood Rd *Web:* www.shetlandminiature.com	Morton	IL	61550	309-263-4044	263-5113
American Shorthorn Assn 8288 Hascall St *Web:* www.shorthorn.org	Omaha	NE	68124	402-393-7200	393-7203
American Society for the Prevention of Cruelty to Animals (ASPCA) 424 E 92nd St **Fax:* Hum Res ■ *Web:* www.aspca.org	New York	NY	10128	212-876-7700	876-0014*
American Warmblood Registry (AWR) PO Box 211735 *Web:* www.americanwarmblood.com	Royal Palm Beach	FL	33421	561-333-5848	
American Zoo & Aquarium Assn (AZA) 8403 Colesville Rd Suite 710 *Web:* www.aza.org	Silver Spring	MD	20910	301-562-0777	562-0888
Animal Alliance of Canada 221 Broadview Ave Suite 101 *Web:* www.animalalliance.ca	Toronto	ON	M4M2G3	416-462-9541	462-9647
Animal Health Institute (AHI) 1325 G St NW Suite 700 *Web:* www.ahi.org	Washington	DC	20005	202-637-2440	393-1667
Animal Protection Institute (API) 1122 'S' St *TF:* 800-348-7387 ■ *Web:* www.api4animals.org	Sacramento	CA	95814	916-447-3085	447-3070
Appaloosa Horse Club (ApHC) 2720 W Pullman Rd *Web:* www.appaloosa.com	Moscow	ID	83843	208-882-5578	882-8150
Arabian Horse Assn (AHA) 10805 E Bethany Dr *Web:* www.arabianhorses.org	Aurora	CO	80014	303-696-4500	696-4599
Arabian Horse Registry of America 10805 E Bethany Dr *Web:* www.arabianhorses.org	Aurora	CO	80014	303-450-4748	450-2841
ASPCA (American Society for the Prevention of Cruelty to Animals) 424 E 92nd St **Fax:* Hum Res ■ *Web:* www.aspca.org	New York	NY	10128	212-876-7700	876-0014*
ASPCA Animal Poison Control Center 1717 S Philo Rd Suite 36 *TF:* 888-426-4435 ■ *Web:* www.aspca.org	Urbana	IL	61802	217-337-5030	337-0599
Atlantic Salmon Federation (ASF) PO Box 5200 *TF:* 800-565-5666 ■ *Web:* www.asf.ca	Saint Andrews	NB	E5B3S8	506-529-1033	529-4438
Bat Conservation International (BCI) PO Box 162603 *TF:* 800-538-2287 ■ *Web:* www.batcon.org	Austin	TX	78716	512-327-9721	327-9724
Belgian Draft Horse Corp of America PO Box 335 *Web:* www.belgiancorp.com	Wabash	IN	46992	260-563-3205	
Bird Studies Canada PO Box 160 *TF:* 888-448-2473 ■ *Web:* www.bsc-eoc.org	Port Rowan	ON	N0E1M0	519-586-3531	586-3532
Canadian Federation of Humane Societies (CFHS) 30 Concourse Gate Suite 102 *TF:* 888-678-2347 ■ *Web:* cfhs.ca	Ottawa	ON	K2E7V7	613-224-8072	723-0252
Canadian Kennel Club (CKC) 200 Ronson Dr Suite 400 *TF:* 800-250-8040 ■ *Web:* www.ckc.ca	Etobicoke	ON	M9W5Z9	416-675-5511	675-6506
Canadian Peregrine Foundation 1450 O'Connor Dr Bldg B Suite 214 *TF:* 888-709-3944 ■ *Web:* www.peregrine-foundation.ca	Toronto	ON	M4B2T8	416-481-1233	481-7158
Certified Horsemanship Assn (CHA) 5318 Old Bullard Rd *TF:* 800-399-0138 ■ *Web:* www.cha-ahse.org	Tyler	TX	75703	903-509-2473	509-2474
Defenders of Wildlife 1130 17th St NW *TF:* 800-989-8981 ■ *Web:* www.defenders.org	Washington	DC	20036	202-682-9400	682-1331
Delta Waterfowl Foundation P.O. Box 3128 *TF:* 888-987-3695 ■ *Web:* www.deltawaterfowl.org	Bismarck	ND	58501	701-222-8857	223-4645
Dian Fossey Gorilla Fund International 800 Cherokee Ave SE *TF:* 800-851-0203 ■ *Web:* www.gorillafund.org	Atlanta	GA	30315	404-624-5881	624-5999
Ducks Unlimited Inc 1 Waterfowl Way *TF:* 800-453-8257 ■ *Web:* www.ducks.org	Memphis	TN	38120	901-758-3825	758-3850
Friends of Animals Inc (FoA) 777 Post Rd Suite 205 *TF:* 800-321-7387 ■ *Web:* www.friendsofanimals.org	Darien	CT	06820	203-656-1522	656-0267
Fund for Animals Inc 200 W 57th St *TF:* 888-405-3863 ■ *Web:* www.fundforanimals.org	New York	NY	10019	212-246-2096	246-2633
Great Bear Foundation 802 E Front St PO Box 9383 *Web:* www.greatbear.org	Missoula	MT	59807	406-829-9378	829-9379
Greyhound Friends Inc 167 Saddle Hill Rd *Web:* www.greyhound.org	Hopkinton	MA	01748	508-435-5969	435-0547
Hawk Mountain Sanctuary Assn 1700 Hawk Mountain Rd *Web:* www.hawkmountain.org	Kempton	PA	19529	610-756-6961	756-4468
Humane Farming Assn (HFA) PO Box 3577 *Web:* www.hfa.org	San Rafael	CA	94912	415-771-2253	485-0106
Humane Society of the US (HSUS) 2100 L St NW *Web:* www.hsus.org	Washington	DC	20037	202-452-1100	778-6132
In Defense of Animals (IDA) 131 Camino Alto Suite E *Web:* www.idausa.org	Mill Valley	CA	94941	415-388-9641	388-0388
International Fund for Animal Welfare (IFAW) 411 Main St PO Box 193 *TF:* 800-932-4329 ■ *Web:* www.ifaw.org	Yarmouth Port	MA	02675	508-744-2000	744-2009
International Primate Protection League (IPPL) PO Box 766 *Web:* www.ippl.org	Summerville	SC	29484	843-871-2280	871-7988
International Society for Animal Rights (ISAR) 965 Griffin Pond Rd *TF:* 800-543-4727 ■ *Web:* www.isaronline.org	Clarks Summit	PA	18411	570-586-2200	586-9580
International Society for the Protection of Mustangs & Burros (ISPMB) PO Box 55 *Web:* www.ispmb.org	Lantry	SD	57636	605-964-6866	365-6991
International Veterinary Acupuncture Society (IVAS) PO Box 271395 *Web:* www.ivas.org	Fort Collins	CO	80527	970-266-0666	266-0777
International Wildlife Coalition (IWC) 70 E Falmouth Hwy *Web:* www.iwc.org	East Falmouth	MA	02536	508-457-1898	457-1898
Jane Goodall Institute for Wildlife Research Education & Conservation (JGI) 4245 N Fairfax Dr Suite 600 *TF:* 800-592-5263 ■ *Web:* www.janegoodall.org	Arlington	VA	22203	703-682-9220	682-9312
Missouri Fox Trotting Horse Breed Assn Inc PO Box 1027 *Web:* www.mfthba.com	Ava	MO	65608	417-683-2468	683-6144
Mountain Lion Foundation PO Box 1896 *TF:* 800-319-7621 ■ *Web:* www.mountainlion.org	Sacramento	CA	95812	916-442-2666	442-2871
National Animal Control Assn 132 S Cherry St *Web:* www.nacanet.org	Olathe	KS	66061	913-768-1319	768-1378
National Anti-Vivisection Society (NAVS) 53 W Jackson Blvd Suite 1552 *TF:* 800-888-6287 ■ *Web:* www.navs.org	Chicago	IL	60604	312-427-6065	427-6524
National Assn of Animal Breeders (NAAB) PO Box 1033 *Web:* www.naab-css.org	Columbia	MO	65205	573-445-4406	446-2279
National Cutting Horse Assn (NCHA) 260 Bailey Ave *Web:* www.nchacutting.com	Fort Worth	TX	76107	817-244-6188	244-2015
National Disaster Search Dog Foundation 206 N Signal St Suite R *Web:* www.searchdogfoundation.org	Ojai	CA	93023	805-646-1015	640-1848
National Dog Registry (NDR) PO Box 116 *TF:* 800-637-3647 ■ *Web:* www.nationaldogregistry.com	Woodstock	NY	12498	800-637-3647	
National Reining Horse Assn (NRHA) 3000 NW 10th St *Web:* www.nrha.com	Oklahoma City	OK	73107	405-946-7400	946-8410
National Wild Turkey Federation (NWTF) 770 Augusta Rd PO Box 530 *TF Cust Svc:* 800-843-6983 ■ *Web:* www.nwtf.com	Edgefield	SC	29824	803-637-3106	637-0034
National Wildlife Federation (NWF) 11100 Wildlife Center Dr *TF:* 800-822-9919 ■ *Web:* www.nwf.org	Reston	VA	20190	703-438-6000	438-3570
Paso Fino Horse Assn 101 N Collins St *Web:* www.pfha.org	Plant City	FL	33566	813-719-7777	719-7872
People for the Ethical Treatment of Animals (PETA) 501 Front St *TF Orders:* 800-483-4366 ■ *Web:* www.peta-online.org	Norfolk	VA	23510	757-622-7382	628-0782
Performing Animal Welfare Society (PAWS) PO Box 849 *Web:* www.pawsweb.org	Galt	CA	95632	209-745-2606	745-1809
Pet Sitters International (PSI) 201 E King St *Web:* www.petsit.com	King	NC	27021	336-983-9222	983-5266
Pinto Horse Assn of America (PtHA) 7330 NW 23rd St *Web:* www.pinto.org	Bethany	OK	73008	405-491-0111	787-0773
Racking Horse Breeders Assn of America (RHBAA) 67 Horse Ctr Rd *Web:* www.rackinghorse.com	Decatur	AL	35603	256-353-7225	353-7266
Ruffed Grouse Society (RGS) 451 McCormick Rd *TF:* 888-564-6747 ■ *Web:* www.ruffedgrousesociety.org	Coraopolis	PA	15108	412-262-4044	262-9207
Save the Manatee Club (SMC) 500 N Maitland Ave *TF:* 800-432-5646 ■ *Web:* www.savethemanatee.org	Maitland	FL	32751	407-539-0990	539-0871
Tennessee Walking Horse Breeders' & Exhibitors' Assn (TWHBEA) PO Box 286 *TF:* 800-359-1574 ■ *Web:* www.twhbea.com	Lewisburg	TN	37091	931-359-1574	359-2539
Thoroughbred Owners & Breeders Assn (TOBA) PO Box 4367 *TF:* 888-606-8622 ■ *Web:* www.toba.org	Lexington	KY	40544	859-276-2291	276-2462
Trout Unlimited (TU) 1300 N 17th St Suite 500 *TF:* 800-834-2419 ■ *Web:* www.tu.org	Arlington	VA	22209	703-522-0200	284-9400
Wildlife Conservation Society (WCS) 2300 Southern Blvd *TF:* 800-234-5128 ■ *Web:* www.wcs.org	Bronx	NY	10460	718-220-5100	220-2685
Wildlife Forever 2700 Freeway Blvd Suite 1000 *Web:* www.wildlifeforever.org	Brooklyn Center	MN	55430	763-253-0222	560-9961
Wildlife Management Institute (WMI) 1146 19th St NW Suite 700 *Web:* www.wildlifemanagementinstitute.org	Washington	DC	20036	202-371-1808	408-5059
Wildlife Society 5410 Grosvenor Ln Suite 200 *Web:* www.wildlife.org	Bethesda	MD	20814	301-897-9770	530-2471
World Society for the Protection of Animals (WSPA) 34 Deloss St *TF:* 800-883-9772 ■ *Web:* www.wspa.org.uk	Framingham	MA	01702	508-879-8350	620-0786
World Wildlife Fund (WWF) 1250 24th St NW Suite 500 *TF:* 800-225-5993 ■ *Web:* www.worldwildlife.org	Washington	DC	20037	202-293-4800	293-9211
World Wildlife Fund Canada 245 Eglinton Ave E Suite 410 *TF:* 800-267-2632 ■ *Web:* www.wwf.ca	Toronto	ON	M4P3J1	416-489-8800	489-3611
Zoocheck Canada 2646 St. Clair Ave E *Web:* www.zoocheck.com	Toronto	ON	M4B3M1	416-285-1744	285-4670

48-4 Arts & Artists Organizations

Organization	City	State	Zip	Phone	Fax
Academy of Motion Picture Arts & Sciences 8949 Wilshire Blvd *Web:* www.oscars.org	Beverly Hills	CA	90211	310-247-3000	859-9619
Actors' Equity Assn 165 W 46th St *Web:* www.actorsequity.org	New York	NY	10036	212-869-8530	719-9815
ADAA (Art Dealers Assn of America) 205 Lexington Ave Suite 901 **Fax Area Code:* 646 ■ *Web:* www.artdealers.org	New York	NY	10016	212-488-5550	688-6809*
Alliance of Motion Picture & Television Producers (AMPTP) 15503 Ventura Blvd *Web:* www.amptp.org	Encino	CA	91436	818-995-3600	
American Academy of Arts & Letters 633 W 155th St	New York	NY	10032	212-368-5900	491-4615
American Academy of Arts & Sciences 136 Irving St *Web:* www.amacad.org	Cambridge	MA	02138	617-576-5000	576-5050
American Accordionists Assn (AAA) 152 Homefair Dr *Web:* www.ameraccord.com	Fairfield	CT	06825	203-335-2045	335-2048
American Antiquarian Society (AAS) 185 Salisbury St *Web:* www.americanantiquarian.org	Worcester	MA	01609	508-755-5221	753-3311
American Arts Alliance 1211 Connecticut Ave NW Suite 200 *Web:* www.americanartsalliance.org	Washington	DC	20036	202-207-3850	833-1543
American Assn of Community Theatre (AACT) 8402 BriarWood Cir *TF:* 866-687-2228 ■ *Web:* www.aact.org	Lago Vista	TX	78645	512-267-0711	267-0712
American Assn of Museums (AAM) 1575 'I' St NW Suite 400 *TF:* 866-266-2150 ■ *Web:* www.aam-us.org	Washington	DC	20005	202-289-1818	289-6578
American Assn for State & Local History (AASLH) 1717 Church St *Web:* www.aaslh.org	Nashville	TN	37203	615-320-3203	327-9013
American Ceramic Society (ACerS) 735 Ceramic Pl Suite 100 *Web:* www.ceramics.org	Westerville	OH	43081	614-890-4700	899-6109
American Choral Directors Assn (ACDA) 545 Couch Dr PO Box 2720 *Web:* www.acdaonline.org	Oklahoma City	OK	73101	405-232-8161	232-8162
American College of Musicians PO Box 1807 *Web:* pianoguild.com	Austin	TX	78767	512-478-5775	478-5843

Phone Fax

American Composers Alliance (ACA) 648 Broadway Rm 803 ...... New York NY 10012 212-925-0458 925-6798
Web: www.composers.com
American Craft Council 72 Spring St 6th Fl. ...... New York NY 10012 212-274-0630 274-0650
TF: 800-836-3470 ■ *Web:* www.craftcouncil.org
American Design Drafting Assn (ADDA) 105 E Main St. ...... Newbern TN 38059 731-627-0802 627-9321
Web: www.adda.org
American Federation of Arts (AFA) 305 E 47th St 10th Fl ...... New York NY 10017 212-988-7700 861-2487
Web: www.afaweb.org
American Federation of Musicians of the US & Canada (AFM)
1501 Broadway Suite 600 ...... New York NY 10036 212-869-1330 764-6134
TF: 800-762-3444 ■ *Web:* www.afm.org
American Film Institute (AFI) 2021 N Western Ave. ...... Los Angeles CA 90027 323-856-7600 467-4578
Web: www.afi.com
American Guild of Musical Artists (AGMA)
1430 Broadway 14th Fl ...... New York NY 10018 212-265-3687 262-9088
TF: 800-543-2462 ■ *Web:* www.musicalartists.org
American Guild of Organists (AGO)
475 Riverside Dr Suite 1260 ...... New York NY 10115 212-870-2310 870-2163
TF: 800-246-5115 ■ *Web:* www.agohq.org
American Guild of Variety Artists (AGVA)
363 7th Ave 17th Fl ...... New York NY 10001 212-675-1003 633-0097
American Institute of Architects (AIA)
1735 New York Ave NW ...... Washington DC 20006 202-626-7300 626-7547
TF Orders: 800-242-3837 ■ *Web:* www.aia.org
American Institute for Conservation of Historic & Artistic Works (AIC) 1156 15th St NW Suite 320 ...... Washington DC 20005 202-452-9545 452-9328
Web: aic.stanford.edu
American Institute of Graphic Arts (AIGA) 164 5th Ave ...... New York NY 10010 212-807-1990 807-1799
TF: 800-548-1634 ■ *Web:* www.aiga.org
American Music Center (AMC) 30 W 26th St Suite 1001 ...... New York NY 10010 212-366-5260 366-5265
Web: www.amc.net
American Music Conference (AMC) 5790 Armada Dr ...... Carlsbad CA 92008 760-431-9124 438-7237
Web: www.amc-music.com
American Musicological Society (AMS) 6010 College Station. .... Brunswick ME 04011 207-798-4243 798-4254
TF: 888-679-7648 ■ *Web:* www.ams-net.org
American Society of Artists PO Box 1326 ...... Palatine IL 60078 312-751-2500
Web: www.americansocietyofartists.org
American Society of Cinematographers (ASC)
1782 N Orange Dr ...... Hollywood CA 90028 323-969-4333 882-6391
TF: 800-448-0145 ■ *Web:* www.theasc.com
American Society of Composers Authors & Publishers (ASCAP)
1 Lincoln Plaza ...... New York NY 10023 212-621-6000 724-9064
TF: 800-952-7227 ■ *Web:* www.ascap.com
American Society of Interior Designers (ASID)
608 Massachusetts Ave NE ...... Washington DC 20002 202-546-3480 546-3240
Web: www.asid.org
Americans for the Arts 1000 Vermont Ave NW 6th Fl. ...... Washington DC 20005 202-371-2830 371-0424
Web: ww3.artsusa.org
Archives of American Art 750 9th St NW Suite 2200 ...... Washington DC 20001 202-633-7940 633-7994
Web: artarchives.si.edu
ARSC (Association for Recorded Sound Collections)
PO Box 543 ...... Annapolis MD 21404 410-757-0488 349-0175
Web: www.arsc-audio.org
Art Dealers Assn of America (ADAA)
205 Lexington Ave Suite 901 ...... New York NY 10016 212-488-5550 688-6809*
**Fax Area Code: 646* ■ *Web:* www.artdealers.org
Art Dealers Assn of Canada (ADAC) 111 Peter St Suite 501 ...... Toronto ON M5V2H1 416-934-1583 934-1584
Web: www.ad-ac.ca
Art Directors Guild (ADG) 11969 Ventura Blvd Suite 200. ...... Studio City CA 91604 818-762-9995 762-9997
Web: www.artdirectors.org
Arts & Business Council of Americans for the Arts
1 E 53rd St 2nd Fl ...... New York NY 10022 212-279-5910 980-4857
Web: www.artsandbusiness.org
Associated Actors & Artistes of America 165 W 46th St. ...... New York NY 10036 212-869-0358 869-1746
Association of Children's Museums (ACM)
1300 L St NW Suite 975 ...... Washington DC 20005 202-898-1080 898-1086
Web: www.childrensmuseums.org
Association of Film Commissioners International (AFCI)
314 N Main St Suite 307 ...... Helena MT 59601 406-495-8040 495-8039
Web: www.afci.org
Association for Information Media & Equipment (AIME)
PO Box 9844 ...... Cedar Rapids IA 52409 319-654-0608 654-0609
Web: www.aime.org
Association of Performing Arts Presenters
1211 Connecticut Ave NW Suite 200. ...... Washington DC 20036 202-833-2787 833-1543
Web: www.artspresenters.org
Association for Recorded Sound Collections (ARSC)
PO Box 543 ...... Annapolis MD 21404 410-757-0488 349-0175
Web: www.arsc-audio.org
Association of Talent Agents 9255 Sunset Blvd Suite 930 ...... Los Angeles CA 90069 310-274-0628 274-5063
Web: www.agentassociation.com
Authors Guild 31 E 32nd St 7th Fl ...... New York NY 10016 212-563-5904 564-5363
Web: www.authorsguild.org
Ballet Theatre Foundation
American Ballet Theatre 890 Broadway 3rd Fl. ...... New York NY 10003 212-477-3030 254-5938
Web: www.abt.org
Bix Beiderbecke Memorial Society PO Box 3688 ...... Davenport IA 52808 563-324-7170 326-1732
TF: 888-249-5487 ■ *Web:* www.bixsociety.org
Broadcast Music Inc (BMI) 320 W 57th St ...... New York NY 10019 212-586-2000 489-2368
Web: www.bmi.com
Broadway League 226 W 47th St. ...... New York NY 10036 212-764-1122 719-4389
Web: www.broadwayleague.com
Business Committee for the Arts Inc (BCA)
29-27 Queens Plaza N 4th Fl. ...... Long Island City NY 11101 718-482-9900 482-9911
Web: www.bcainc.org
Chamber Music America (CMA) 305 7th Ave 5th Fl. ...... New York NY 10001 212-242-2022 242-7955
Web: www.chamber-music.org
Choristers Guild 2834 W Kingsley Rd. ...... Garland TX 75041 972-271-1521 840-3113
Web: www.choristersguild.org
Chorus America 1156 15th St NW Suite 310. ...... Washington DC 20005 202-331-7577 331-7599
Web: www.chorusamerica.org
Clowns of America International (COAI) PO Box C ...... Richeyville PA 15358 888-522-5696
Web: www.coai.org
College Art Assn (CAA) 275 7th Ave. ...... New York NY 10001 212-691-1051 627-2381
Web: www.collegeart.org
Conductors Guild 5300 Glenside Dr Suite 2207 ...... Richmond VA 23228 804-553-1378 553-1876
Web: www.conductorsguild.org
Country Music Assn (CMA) 1 Music Cir S ...... Nashville TN 37203 615-244-2840 726-0314
TF: 800-998-4636 ■ *Web:* www.cmaworld.com
Dance/USA 1111 16 St NW Suite 300. ...... Washington DC 20036 202-833-1717 833-2686
Web: www.danceusa.org
Design Management Institute (DMI) 29 Temple Pl 2nd Fl. ...... Boston MA 02111 617-338-6380 338-6570
Web: www.dmi.org
Dramatists Guild of America Inc 1501 Broadway Suite 701 ...... New York NY 10036 212-398-9366 944-0420
Web: www.dramaguild.com
Drum Corps International (DCI) 470 S Irmen Dr ...... Addison IL 60101 630-628-7888 628-7971
TF Orders: 800-495-7469 ■ *Web:* www.dci.org

Phone Fax

Earshot Jazz 3429 Fremont Pl Suite 309 ...... Seattle WA 98103 206-547-6763 547-6286
Web: www.earshot.org
Educational Theatre Assn 2343 Auburn Ave ...... Cincinnati OH 45219 513-421-3900 421-7077
Web: www.etassoc.org
Entertainment Services & Technology Assn (ESTA)
875 Sixth Ave Suite 1005 ...... New York NY 10001 212-244-1505 244-1502
Web: www.esta.org
Folk Alliance 510 S Main St 1st Fl. ...... Memphis TN 38103 901-522-1170 522-1172
Web: www.folk.org
Frank Lloyd Wright Foundation Taliesin West PO Box 4430 ...... Scottsdale AZ 85261 480-860-2700 860-8472
Web: www.franklloydwright.org
Glass Art Society (GAS) 3131 Western Ave Suite 414 ...... Seattle WA 98121 206-382-1305 382-2630
Web: www.glassart.org
Gold Coast Jazz Society 1350 E Sunrise Blvd ...... Fort Lauderdale FL 33304 954-524-0805 525-7880
Web: www.goldcoastjazz.org
Gospel Music Assn (GMA) 1205 Division St. ...... Nashville TN 37203 615-242-0303 254-9755
Web: www.gospelmusic.org
Graphic Artists Guild Inc 90 John St Suite 403 ...... New York NY 10038 212-791-3400 791-0333
Web: www.gag.org
Guild of American Luthiers 8222 South Park Ave ...... Tacoma WA 98408 253-472-7853
Web: www.luth.org
Hollywood Foreign Press Assn 646 N Robertson Blvd. ...... West Hollywood CA 90069 310-657-1731 657-5576
Web: www.hfpa.org
Independent Feature Project (IFP) 104 W 29th St 12th Fl ...... New York NY 10001 212-465-8200 465-8525
Web: www.ifp.org
Independent Film & Television Alliance (IFTA)
10850 Wilshire Blvd 9th Fl. ...... Los Angeles CA 90024 310-446-1000 446-1600
Web: www.ifta-online.org
Indian Arts & Crafts Assn (IACA)
4010 Carlisle Blvd NE Suite C ...... Albuquerque NM 87107 505-265-9149 265-8251
Web: www.iaca.com
International Alliance for Women in Music (IAWM)
Rollins College Box 2731 1000 Holt Ave. ...... Winter Park FL 32789 407-646-2233
Web: www.iawm.org
International Assn of Jazz Education (IAJE) PO Box 724 ...... Manhattan KS 66505 785-776-8744 776-6190
Web: www.iaje.org
International Brotherhood of Magicians (IBM)
11155-C South Towne Sq ...... Saint Louis MO 63123 314-845-9200 845-9220
Web: www.magician.org
International Center of Medieval Art (ICMA)
799 Fort Washington Ave The Cloisters Fort Tryon Park ...... New York NY 10040 212-928-1146 928-9946
Web: www.medievalart.org
International Federation for Choral Music (IFCM)
Univ of Illinois at Chicago Dept of Performing Arts 1040 W Harrison St MC 255 ...... Chicago IL 60607 312-996-8744 996-0954
Web: ifcm.net
International Interior Design Assn (IIDA)
222 Merchandise Mart Plaza Suite 13-500 ...... Chicago IL 60654 312-467-1950 467-0779
TF: 888-799-4432 ■ *Web:* www.iida.org
International Piano Guild 808 Rio Grande St. ...... Austin TX 78701 512-478-5775 478-5843
Web: www.pianoguild.com
International Society of Bassists (ISB)
13140 Coit Rd Suite 320 LB 120. ...... Dallas TX 75240 972-233-9107 490-4219
Web: www.isbworldoffice.com
International Society for the Performing Arts Foundation (ISPA)
17 Purdy Ave PO Box 909 ...... Rye NY 10580 914-921-1550 921-1593
Web: www.ispa.org
International Ticketing Assn (INTIX)
330 W 38th St Suite 605. ...... New York NY 10018 212-629-4036 629-8532
Web: www.intix.org
Kansas City Jazz Ambassadors PO Box 36181 ...... Kansas City MO 64111 913-967-6767
Web: www.jazzkc.org
League of American Orchestras 33 W 60th St 5th Fl ...... New York NY 10023 212-262-5161 262-5198
Web: www.americanorchestras.org
League of Resident Theatres (LORT)
1501 Broadway Suite 2401 ...... New York NY 10036 212-944-1501 768-0785
Web: www.lort.org
Metropolitan Opera Guild 70 Lincoln Ctr Plaza 6th Fl ...... New York NY 10023 212-769-7000 769-7002
Web: www.metopera.org/guild
Motion Picture Assn (MPA) 15503 Ventura Blvd ...... Encino CA 91436 818-995-6600 382-1799
TF: 800-662-6797 ■ *Web:* www.mpaa.org
Motion Picture Assn of America (MPAA) 15503 Ventura Blvd ...... Encino CA 91436 818-995-6600
TF: 800-662-6797 ■ *Web:* www.mpaa.org
Motion Picture & Television Fund 23388 Mulholland Dr ...... Woodland Hills CA 91364 818-876-1888
Web: www.mptvfund.org
Mystery Writers of America Inc (MWA) 17 E 47th St 6th Fl ...... New York NY 10017 212-888-8171 888-8107
Web: www.mysterywriters.org
National Academy of Recording Arts & Sciences
3402 Pico Blvd. ...... Santa Monica CA 90405 310-392-3777 392-2306
TF: 800-423-2017 ■ *Web:* www.grammy.com
National Academy of Television Arts & Sciences
111 W 57th St Suite 600. ...... New York NY 10019 212-586-8424 246-8129
Web: www.emmyonline.org
National Assn of Pastoral Musicians (NPM)
962 Wayne Ave Suite 210 ...... Silver Spring MD 20910 240-247-3000 247-3001
Web: www.npm.org
National Assn of Science Writers (NASW) PO Box 890. ...... Hedgesville WV 25427 304-754-5077 754-5076
Web: www.nasw.org
National Assn of Theatre Owners (NATO)
750 1st St NE Suite 1130 ...... Washington DC 20002 202-962-0054 962-0370
TF: 800-282-6286 ■ *Web:* www.natoonline.org
National Council for the Traditional Arts (NCTA)
1320 Fenwick Ln Suite 200 ...... Silver Spring MD 20910 301-565-0654 565-0472
Web: www.ncta.net
National Federation of Music Clubs (NFMC)
1336 N Delaware St. ...... Indianapolis IN 46202 317-638-4003 638-0503
Web: www.nfmc-music.org
National Guild of Piano Teachers PO Box 1807 ...... Austin TX 78767 512-478-5775 478-5843
Web: pianoguild.com
National Humanities Alliance (NHA)
21 Dupont Cir NW Suite 604. ...... Washington DC 20036 202-296-4994 872-0884
Web: www.nhalliance.org
National League of American Pen Women Inc
1300 17th St NW. ...... Washington DC 20036 202-785-1997 452-8868
Web: www.americanpenwomen.org
National Music Center & Museum Foundation
801 K St NW Suite 600 ...... Washington DC 20005 202-383-1860 223-4720
Web: www.nationalmusiccenter.org
National Music Publishers' Assn (NMPA)
101 Constitution Ave NW Suite 705 East ...... Washington DC 20001 202-742-4375 742-4377
Web: www.nmpa.org
National Speakers Assn (NSA) 1500 S Priest Dr ...... Tempe AZ 85281 480-968-2552 968-0911
Web: www.nsaspeaker.org
National Writers Union (NWU) 113 University Pl 6th Fl ...... New York NY 10003 212-254-0279 254-0673
Web: www.nwu.org
Percussive Arts Society (PAS) 701 NW Ferris Ave ...... Lawton OK 73507 580-353-1455 353-1456
Web: www.pas.org

Arts & Artists Organizations (Cont'd)

Phone Fax

Professional Photographers of America Inc (PPA)
229 Peachtree St NE Suite 2200 Atlanta GA 30303 404-522-8600 614-6400
TF: 800-786-6277 ■ *Web:* www.ppa.com

Professional Picture Framers Assn (PPFA) 3000 Picture Pl Jackson MI 49201 517-788-8100 788-8371
Web: www.ppfa.com

Recording Industry Assn of America Inc (RIAA)
1025 F St NW 10th Fl Washington DC 20004 202-775-0101 775-7253
Web: www.riaa.com

Research & Engineering Council of the Graphic Arts Industry
PO Box 1086 White Stone VA 22578 804-436-9922 436-9511
Web: www.recouncil.org

Sacramento Traditional Jazz Society (STJS)
2787 Del Monte St West Sacramento CA 95691 916-372-5277 372-3479
Web: www.sacjazz.com

Screen Actors Guild (SAG) 5757 Wilshire Blvd Los Angeles CA 90036 323-954-1600 549-6775
Web: www.sag.org

SESAC Inc 55 Music Sq E Nashville TN 37203 615-320-0055 963-3527
TF: 800-826-9996 ■ *Web:* www.sesac.com

SITE Santa Fe 1606 Paseo de Peralta Santa Fe NM 87501 505-989-1199 989-1188
Web: www.sitesantafe.org

Society of American Archivists (SAA) 527 S Wells St 5th Fl Chicago IL 60607 312-922-0140 347-1452
Web: www.archivists.org

Society of Animal Artists Inc 47 5th Ave New York NY 10003 212-741-2880 741-2262
Web: www.societyofanimalartists.com

Society for Ethnomusicology (SEM)
Indiana University 1165 E 3rd St Morrison Hall 005 Bloomington IN 47405 812-855-6672 855-6673
Web: www.ethnomusicology.org

Society of Glass & Ceramic Decorators (SGCD) 47 N 4th St Zanesville OH 43701 740-588-9882 588-0245
Web: www.sgcd.org

Society for the History of Authorship Reading & Publishing (SHARP) PO Box 30 Wilmington NC 28402 910-254-0308
Web: www.sharpweb.org

Society of Motion Picture & Television Engineers (SMPTE)
3 Barker Ave White Plains NY 10601 914-761-1100 761-3115
Web: www.smpte.org

Songwriters Guild of America 209 10th Ave S Suite 321 Nashville TN 37203 615-742-9945 742-9948
Web: www.songwritersguild.com

Stuntwomen's Assn of Motion Pictures
12457 Ventura Blvd Suite 208 Studio City CA 91604 818-762-0907 762-9534
Web: www.stuntwomen.com

Sundance Institute PO Box 3630 Salt Lake City UT 84110 801-328-3456 575-5175
Web: www2.sundance.org

Tucson Jazz Society (TJS) PO Box 1069 Tucson AZ 85702 520-903-1265 903-1266
Web: www.tucsonjazz.org

Visual Artists & Galleries Assn 350 5th Ave Suite 2820 New York NY 10118 212-736-6666 736-6767

Wedding & Portrait Photographers International (WPPI)
1312 Lincoln Blvd Santa Monica CA 90401 310-451-0090 395-9058
Web: www.wppionline.com

Women in Film (WIF) 8857 W Olympic Blvd Suite 201 Beverly Hills CA 90211 310-657-5144 657-5154
Web: www.wif.org

World Monuments Fund (WMF) 95 Madison Ave 9th Fl New York NY 10016 646-424-9594 424-9593
TF: 800-547-9171 ■ *Web:* www.wmf.org

Writers Guild of America East (WGAE)
555 W 57th St Suite 1230 New York NY 10019 212-767-7800 582-1909
Web: www.wgaeast.org

Writers Guild of America West (WGAw) 7000 W 3rd St Los Angeles CA 90048 323-951-4000 782-4800
TF: 800-548-4532 ■ *Web:* www.wga.org

Young Audiences Inc 115 E 92nd St New York NY 10128 212-831-8110 289-1202
Web: www.youngaudiences.org

48-5 Charitable & Humanitarian Organizations

Phone Fax

ACDI/VOCA 50 F St NE Suite 1075 Washington DC 20001 202-638-4661 626-8726
TF: 800-929-8622 ■ *Web:* www.acdivoca.org

Action Against Hunger 247 W 37th St 10th Fl New York NY 10018 212-967-7800 967-5480
TF: 877-777-1420 ■ *Web:* www.aah-usa.org

Adventist Community Services 12501 Old Columbia Pike Silver Spring MD 20904 301-680-6438 680-6125
TF: 877-227-2702 ■ *Web:* northamerica.adventist.org/acs.htm

Adventist Development & Relief Agency International (ADRA) 12501 Old Columbia Pike Silver Spring MD 20904 301-680-6380 680-6370
TF: 800-424-2372 ■ *Web:* www.adra.org

African Medical & Research Foundation (AMREF)
4 W 43rd St 2nd Fl New York NY 10036 212-768-2440 768-4230
Web: www.amref.org

Africare Inc 440 R St NW Washington DC 20001 202-462-3614 387-1034
Web: www.africare.org

Aga Khan Foundation USA (AKF) 1825 K St NW Suite 901 Washington DC 20006 202-293-2537 785-1752
Web: www.akdn.org/agency/akf.html

Aid to Artisans Inc (ATA) 331 Wethersfield Ave Hartford CT 06114 860-947-3344 947-3350
Web: aidtoartisans.org

Air Serv International 6583 Merchant Pl Suite 100 Warrenton VA 20187 540-428-2323 428-2326
Web: www.airserv.org

Alan Guttmacher Institute (AGI) 125 Maiden Ln 7th Fl New York NY 10038 212-248-1111 248-1951
TF: 800-355-0244 ■ *Web:* www.guttmacher.org

American Anti-Slavery Group Inc 198 Tremont St Suite 421 Boston MA 02116 617-426-8161 507-8257
TF: 800-884-0719 ■ *Web:* www.iabolish.com

American Assn of Fund-Raising Counsel (AAFRC)
4700 W Lake Ave Glenview IL 60025 847-375-4709 263-7316*
**Fax Area Code:* 866 ■ *TF:* 800-462-2372 ■ *Web:* www.aafrc.org

American Council for Voluntary International Action
1400 16th St Nw Suite 210 Washington DC 20036 202-667-8227 667-8236
Web: www.interaction.org

American Friends Service Committee (AFSC)
1501 Cherry St Philadelphia PA 19102 215-241-7000 241-7275
Web: www.afsc.org

American Institute of Philanthropy (AIP) PO Box 578460 Chicago IL 60657 773-529-2300 529-0024
Web: www.charitywatch.org

American Jewish Joint Distribution Committee (JDC)
711 3rd Ave 10th Fl New York NY 10017 212-687-6200 370-5467
Web: www.jdc.org

American Jewish World Service (AJWS) 45 W 36th St 11th Fl New York NY 10018 212-736-2597 792-2930
TF: 800-889-7146 ■ *Web:* www.ajws.org

American Lebanese Syrian Associated Charities (ALSAC)
501 St Jude Pl Memphis TN 38105 901-578-2000 578-2805
TF: 800-822-6344 ■ *Web:* www.stjude.org

American Leprosy Missions (ALM) 1 ALM Way Greenville SC 29601 864-271-7040 271-7062
TF: 800-543-3135 ■ *Web:* www.leprosy.org

American Near East Refugee Aid (ANERA)
1522 K St NW Suite 600 Washington DC 20005 202-842-2766 842-4064
Web: www.anera.org

American ORT 75 Maiden Ln 10th Fl New York NY 10038 212-505-7700 674-2057
TF: 800-364-9678 ■ *Web:* www.aort.org

Phone Fax

American Red Cross 2025 'E' St NW Washington DC 20006 202-303-4498 303-0044
Web: www.redcross.org

American Refugee Committee (ARC)
430 Oak Grove St Suite 204 Minneapolis MN 55403 612-872-7060 607-6499
TF: 800-875-7060 ■ *Web:* www.arcrelief.org

AmeriCares Foundation 88 Hamilton Ave Stamford CT 06902 203-658-9500 327-5200
TF: 800-486-4357 ■ *Web:* www.americares.org

America's Development Foundation (ADF)
101 N Union St Suite 200 Alexandria VA 22314 703-836-2717 836-3379
Web: www.adfusa.org

America's Second Harvest 35 E Wacker Dr Suite 2000 Chicago IL 60601 312-263-2303 263-5626
TF: 800-771-2303 ■ *Web:* www.secondharvest.org

Amigos de las Americas 5618 Star Ln Houston TX 77057 713-782-5290 782-9267
TF: 800-231-7796 ■ *Web:* www.amigoslink.org

Amnesty International USA (AIUSA) 5 Penn Plaza 14th Fl New York NY 10001 212-807-8400 627-1451
TF: 800-266-3789 ■ *Web:* www.amnestyusa.org

ANGELCARE PO Box 600370 San Diego CA 92160 619-795-6234 795-6238
TF: 888-264-5227 ■ *Web:* www.angelcare.org

Applied Research Ethics National Assn (ARENA)
126 Brookline Ave Suite 202 Boston MA 02215 617-423-4112 423-1185
Web: www.primr.org/membership/overview.html

Arms Control Assn 1313 L St NW Suite 130 Washington DC 20005 202-463-8270 463-8273
Web: www.armscontrol.org

Association of Fundraising Professionals (AFP)
1101 King St Suite 700 Alexandria VA 22314 703-684-0410 684-0540
TF: 800-666-3863 ■ *Web:* www.afpnet.org

Association of Gospel Rescue Missions (AGRM)
1045 Swift Ave Kansas City MO 64116 816-471-8020 471-3718
TF: 800-624-5156 ■ *Web:* www.agrm.org

Bread for the World 50 F St NW Suite 500 Washington DC 20001 202-639-9400 639-9401
TF Cust Svc: 800-822-7323 ■ *Web:* www.bread.org

Brother's Brother Foundation 1200 Galveston Ave Pittsburgh PA 15233 412-321-3160 321-3325
TF: 888-323-1916 ■ *Web:* www.brothersbrother.org

Canadian Council for International Cooperation (CCIC)
1 Nicholas St Suite 300 Ottawa ON K1N7B7 613-241-7007 241-5302
Web: www.ccic.ca

Canadian National Institute for the Blind (CNIB)
1929 Bayview Ave Toronto ON M4G3E8 416-486-2500 480-7019
Web: www.cnib.ca

CARE USA 151 Ellis St NE Atlanta GA 30303 404-681-2552 589-2630*
**Fax:* Hum Res ■ *TF:* 800-422-7385 ■ *Web:* www.care.org

Catholic Charities USA 1731 King St Alexandria VA 22314 703-549-1390 549-1656
Web: www.catholiccharitiesusa.org

Catholic Medical Mission Board (CMMB) 10 W 17th St New York NY 10011 212-242-7757 807-9161
TF: 800-678-5659 ■ *Web:* www.cmmb.org

Catholic Relief Services (CRS) 209 W Fayette St Baltimore MD 21201 410-625-2220 685-1635
TF: 800-235-2772 ■ *Web:* www.crs.org

Center for Community Change (CCC) 1536 U St NW Washington DC 20009 202-339-9300 387-4891
TF: 877-777-1536 ■ *Web:* www.communitychange.org

Center for Human Services
University Research Co 7200 Wisconsin Ave Suite 600 Bethesda MD 20814 301-654-8338 941-8427
TF: 800-444-2969 ■ *Web:* www.chs-urc.org

Centre for Development & Population Activities (CEDPA)
1133 21st St NW Suite 800 Washington DC 20036 202-667-1142 332-4496
Web: www.cedpa.org

Child Health Foundation
10630 Little Patuxent Pkwy Century Plaza Suite 126 Columbia MD 21044 301-596-4514 992-5641*
**Fax Area Code:* 410 ■ *Web:* www.childhealthfoundation.org

Children Inc PO Box 5381 Richmond VA 23220 804-359-4562 353-7541
TF: 800-538-5381 ■ *Web:* www.children-inc.org

Children International 2000 E Red Bridge Rd Kansas City MO 64131 816-942-2000 942-3714
TF: 800-888-3089 ■ *Web:* children.org

Children's Miracle Network 4220 Steeles Ave W Suite C18 Woodbridge ON L4L3S8 905-265-9750 265-9749
Web: www.childrensmiraclenetwork.ca

Children's Miracle Network 4525 S 2300 East Salt Lake City UT 84117 801-278-8900 277-8787
Web: www.childrensmiraclenetwork.org

Christian Appalachian Project 322 Crab Orchard St Lancaster KY 40444 859-792-3051 792-6560
TF: 866-270-4227 ■ *Web:* www.chrisapp.org

Christian Blind Mission International (CBMI) 450 E Park Ave Greenville SC 29601 864-239-0065 239-0069
TF: 800-937-2264 ■ *Web:* www.cbmiusa.org

Christian Disaster Response International PO Box 564 Lake Alfred FL 33850 863-967-4357 968-1414
TF: 800-430-1235 ■ *Web:* www.cdresponse.org

Christian Reformed World Relief Committee (CRWRC)
2850 Kalamazoo Ave SE Grand Rapids MI 49560 616-224-0740 224-0806
TF: 800-552-7972 ■ *Web:* www.crwrc.org

Christian Relief Services 2550 Huntington Ave Suite 200 Alexandria VA 22303 703-317-9086 317-9690
TF: 800-337-3543 ■ *Web:* www.christianrelief.org

Church World Service 28606 Phillips St PO Box 968 Elkhart IN 46515 574-264-3102 262-0966
TF: 800-297-1516 ■ *Web:* www.churchworldservice.org

Church World Service Emergency Response Program
475 Riverside Dr Suite 700 New York NY 10115 212-870-3151 870-2236
TF: 800-297-1516 ■ *Web:* www.cwserp.org

Citizens Network for Foreign Affairs (CNFA)
1828 L St NW Suite 710 Washington DC 20036 202-296-3920 296-3948
TF: 888-872-2632

Coalition on Human Needs (CHN)
1120 Connecticut Ave NW Suite 910 Washington DC 20036 202-223-2532 223-2538
Web: www.chn.org

Community Action Partnership
1140 Connecticut Ave NW Suite 1210 Washington DC 20036 202-265-7546 265-5048
Web: www.communityactionpartnership.com

Community Health Charities 200 N Glebe Rd Suite 801 Arlington VA 22203 703-528-1007 528-1365
TF: 800-654-0845 ■ *Web:* www.healthcharities.org

Compassion International PO Box 65000 Colorado Springs CO 80965 719-487-7000 481-5738
TF: 800-336-7539 ■ *Web:* www.compassion.com

Concern America PO Box 1790 Santa Ana CA 92702 714-953-8575 953-1242
TF: 800-266-2376 ■ *Web:* www.concernamerica.org

Concern Worldwide US Inc 104 E 40th St Suite 903 New York NY 10016 212-557-8000 557-8004
Web: www.concernusa.org

Congressional Hunger Center
400 N Capitol St NW Suite G-100 Washington DC 20001 202-547-7022 547-7575
Web: www.hungercenter.org

Council on Foundations 2121 Crystal Dr Suite 700 Arlington VA 22202 703-879-0600 879-0800
TF: 800-673-9036 ■ *Web:* www.cof.org

CRISTA Ministries 19303 Fremont Ave N Seattle WA 98133 206-546-7200 546-7214
TF: 800-442-4003 ■ *Web:* www.crista.org

Direct Relief International 27 S La Patera Ln Santa Barbara CA 93117 805-964-4767 681-4838
TF: 800-676-1638 ■ *Web:* www.directrelief.org

Doctors Without Borders USA Inc 333 7th Ave 2nd Fl New York NY 10001 212-679-6800 679-7016
TF: 888-392-0392 ■ *Web:* www.doctorswithoutborders.org

Doctors of the World 80 Maiden Ln New York NY 10038 212-226-9890 226-7026
Web: www.doctorsoftheworld.org

Dress for Success Worldwide 32 E 31st St 7th Fl New York NY 10016 212-532-1922 684-9563
Web: www.dressforsuccess.org

Elton John AIDS Foundation PO Box 17139 Beverly Hills CA 90209 310-535-1775
Web: www.ejaf.org

Organization	City	State	Zip	Phone	Fax
Enersol Inc 55 Middlesex St Suite 221 *Web:* www.enersol.org	Chelmsford	MA	01863	978-251-1828	251-5291
Enterprise Foundation 10227 Wincopin Cir Suite 500 *TF:* 800-624-4298 ■ *Web:* www.enterprisefoundation.org	Columbia	MD	21044	410-964-1230	964-1918
EnterpriseWorks/VITA 1825 Connecticut Ave NW Suite 630 *Web:* www.enterpriseworks.org	Washington	DC	20009	202-293-4600	293-4598
Episcopal Migration Ministries (EMM) 815 2nd Ave *TF:* 800-334-7626 ■ *Web:* www.episcopalchurch.org/emm	New York	NY	10017	212-716-6258	972-0860
Episcopal Relief & Development 815 2nd Ave **Fax Area Code:* 212 ■ *Web:* www.er-d.org	New York	NY	10017	800-334-7626	983-6377*
Ethiopian Community Development Council Inc (ECDC) 901 S Highland St *Web:* www.ecdcinternational.org	Arlington	VA	22204	703-685-0510	685-0529
Evangelical Council for Financial Accountability (ECFA) 440 W Jubal Early Dr Suite 130 *TF:* 800-323-9473 ■ *Web:* www.ecfa.org	Winchester	VA	22601	540-535-0103	535-0533
Fair Labor Assn (FLA) 1707 L St NW Suite 200S *Web:* www.fairlabor.org	Washington	DC	20036	202-898-1000	898-9050
Family Health International (FHI) PO Box 13950 *Web:* www.fhi.org	Research Triangle Park	NC	27709	919-544-7040	544-7261
Farm Aid 11 Ward St Suite 200 *TF:* 800-327-6243 ■ *Web:* www.farmaid.org	Somerville	MA	02143	617-354-2922	354-6992
Feed the Children PO Box 36 *TF:* 800-627-4556 ■ *Web:* www.feedthechildren.org	Oklahoma City	OK	73101	405-942-0228	945-4177
FHI (Family Health International) PO Box 13950 *Web:* www.fhi.org	Research Triangle Park	NC	27709	919-544-7040	544-7261
First Book 1319 F St NW Suite 1000 *Web:* www.firstbook.org	Washington	DC	20004	202-393-1222	628-1258
First Voice International (FVI) 8515 Georgia Ave 9th Fl *Web:* www.firstvoiceint.org	Silver Spring	MD	20910	301-960-1273	960-1157
Food for All 201 Park Washington Ct *TF:* 800-896-5101 ■ *Web:* www.foodforall.org	Falls Church	VA	22046	703-237-3677	237-4163
Food First 398 60th St *Web:* www.foodfirst.org	Oakland	CA	94618	510-654-4400	654-4551
Food for the Hungry Inc 1224 E Washington St *TF:* 800-248-6437 ■ *Web:* www.fh.org	Phoenix	AZ	85034	480-998-3100	889-5401
Food for the Poor Inc (FFP) 550 SW 12th Ave Bldg 4 *Web:* www.foodforthepoor.org	Deerfield Beach	FL	33442	954-427-2222	570-7654
Foundation for International Community Assistance (FINCA) 1101 14th St NW 11th Fl *Web:* www.villagebanking.org	Washington	DC	20005	202-682-1510	682-1535
Freedom from Hunger 1644 DaVinci Ct *TF:* 800-708-2555 ■ *Web:* www.freefromhunger.org	Davis	CA	95616	530-758-6200	758-6241
Friends of the World Food Programme 1819 L St NW Suite 900 *Web:* www.friendsofwfp.org	Washington	DC	20036	202-530-1694	530-1698
Fund for Peace 1701 K St NW Suite 1100 *Web:* www.fundforpeace.org	Washington	DC	20006	202-223-7940	223-7947
Gifts In Kind International 333 N Fairfax St Suite 100 **Fax Area Code:* 877 ■ *Web:* www.giftsinkind.org	Alexandria	VA	22314	703-836-2121	798-3192*
Global Children's Organization PO Box 67583 **Fax Area Code:* 323 ■ *Web:* www.globalchild.org	Los Angeles	CA	90067	310-581-2234	934-0305*
Global Health Council 1111 19th St NW Suite 1120 *Web:* www.globalhealth.org	Washington	DC	20036	202-833-5900	833-0075
Goodwill Industries International Inc 15810 Indianola Dr *TF:* 800-741-0197 ■ *Web:* www.goodwill.org	Rockville	MD	20855	301-530-6500	530-1516
Grantmakers in Health (GIH) 1100 Connecticut Ave NW Suite 1200 *Web:* www.gih.org	Washington	DC	20036	202-452-8331	452-8340
Guttmacher Alan Institute 125 Maiden Ln 7th Fl *TF:* 800-355-0244 ■ *Web:* www.guttmacher.org	New York	NY	10038	212-248-1111	248-1951
Habitat for Humanity International Inc 121 Habitat St *TF:* 800-422-4828 ■ *Web:* www.habitat.org	Americus	GA	31709	229-924-6935	924-6541
Healing the Children (HTC) PO Box 9065 *TF:* 800-992-0324 ■ *Web:* www.healingthechildren.org	Spokane	WA	99209	509-327-4281	327-4284
Heart to Heart International 401 S Clairborne Rd Suite 302 *TF:* 800-764-5220 ■ *Web:* www.hearttoheart.org	Olathe	KS	66062	913-764-5200	764-0809
Hebrew Immigrant Aid Society (HIAS) 333 7th Ave 16th Fl *TF:* 800-442-7714 ■ *Web:* www.hias.org	New York	NY	10001	212-967-4100	967-4483
Heifer Project International (HPI) PO Box 1692 *TF:* 800-422-0474 ■ *Web:* www.heifer.org	Merrifield	VA	22116	501-907-2900	907-2902
Helen Keller International 352 Park Ave S Suite 1200 *TF:* 877-535-5374 ■ *Web:* www.hki.org	New York	NY	10010	212-532-0544	532-5860
HELP USA 5 Hanover Sq *Web:* www.helpusa.org	New York	NY	10004	212-400-7000	400-7005
Hole in the Wall Gang Camps Inc 265 Church St Suite 503 *Web:* www.holeinthewallcamps.org	New Haven	CT	06510	203-562-1203	562-1207
HOPE worldwide 353 W Lancaster Ave Suite 200 *Web:* www.hopeww.org	Wayne	PA	19087	610-254-8800	254-8989
Housing Assistance Council (HAC) 1025 Vermont Ave NW Suite 606 *TF:* 800-989-4422 ■ *Web:* www.ruralhome.org	Washington	DC	20005	202-842-8600	347-3441
Hunger Project The 5 Union Sq W *TF:* 800-228-6691 ■ *Web:* www.thp.org	New York	NY	10003	212-251-9100	532-9785
I Have a Dream Foundation (IHAD) 330 7th Ave 20th Fl *Web:* www.ihad.org	New York	NY	10001	212-293-5480	293-5478
Independent Charities of America 21 Tamal Vista Blvd Suite 209 **Fax Area Code:* 415 ■ *Web:* www.independentcharities.org	Corte Madera	CA	94925	800-477-0733	924-1379*
Independent Order of Foresters (IOF) 789 Don Mills Rd *TF:* 800-828-1540 ■ *Web:* www.foresters.com	Toronto	ON	M3C1T9	416-429-3000	429-3896
Independent Sector 1200 18th St NW Suite 200 *TF Orders:* 888-860-8118 ■ *Web:* www.independentsector.org	Washington	DC	20036	202-467-6100	467-6101
INMED Partnerships for Children 45449 Severn Way Suite 161 *TF:* 800-521-1175 ■ *Web:* www.inmed.org	Sterling	VA	20166	703-444-4477	444-4471
Institute for Food & Development Policy 398 60th St *Web:* www.foodfirst.org	Oakland	CA	94618	510-654-4400	654-4551
InterAction 1400 16th St Nw Suite 210 *Web:* www.interaction.org	Washington	DC	20036	202-667-8227	667-8236
Interchurch Medical Assistance Inc (IMA) 500 Main St PO Box 429 *Web:* www.interchurch.org	New Windsor	MD	21776	410-635-8720	635-8726
International Aid Inc 17011 W Hickory St *TF:* 800-968-7490 ■ *Web:* www.internationalaid.org	Spring Lake	MI	49456	616-846-7490	846-3842
International Catholic Migration Commission (ICMC) c/o MRS/US Conference of Catholic Bishops 3211 4th St NE *Web:* www.icmc.net	Washington	DC	20017	202-541-3389	541-3222
International Eye Foundation (IEF) 10801 Connecticut Ave *Web:* www.iefusa.org	Kensington	MD	20895	240-290-0263	290-0269
International Institute of Rural Reconstruction (IIRR) 40 Exchange Pl Suite 1111 *Web:* www.iirr.org	New York	NY	10005	212-880-9147	880-9148
International Medical Corps (IMC) 1919 Santa Monica Blvd Suite 300 *TF:* 800-481-4462 ■ *Web:* www.imcworldwide.org	Santa Monica	CA	90404	310-826-7800	442-6622
International Orthodox Christian Charities (IOCC) 110 West Rd Suite 360 *TF:* 877-803-4622 ■ *Web:* www.iocc.org	Baltimore	MD	21204	410-243-9820	243-9824
International Planned Parenthood Federation - Western Hemisphere Region (IPPF/WHR) 120 Wall St 9th Fl *Web:* www.ippfwhr.org	New York	NY	10005	212-248-6400	248-4221
International Rescue Committee (IRC) 122 E 42nd St 12th Fl *Web:* www.theirc.org	New York	NY	10168	212-551-3000	551-3179
Jesuit Refugee Service - North America (JRS) 1016 16th St NW Suite 500 *Web:* www.jesref.org	Washington	DC	20036	202-462-0400	328-9212
Katalysis Bootstrap Fund 3601 Pacific Ave **Fax Area Code:* 866 ■ *Web:* www.katalysis.org	Stockton	CA	95211	209-644-6245	403-6571*
Landmine Survivors Network (LSN) 2100 M St NW Suite 302 *Web:* www.landminesurvivors.org	Washington	DC	20037	202-464-0007	464-0011
Lutheran Disaster Response 8765 W Higgins Rd **Fax Area Code:* 773 ■ *TF:* 800-638-3522 ■ *Web:* www.ldr.org	Chicago	IL	60631	800-638-3522	380-2270*
Lutheran Immigration & Refugee Service (LIRS) 700 Light St *Web:* www.lirs.org	Baltimore	MD	21230	410-230-2700	230-2890
Lutheran World Relief (LWR) 700 Light St *TF:* 800-597-5972 ■ *Web:* www.lwr.org	Baltimore	MD	21230	410-230-2700	230-2882
Make-A-Wish Foundation of America 3550 N Central Ave Suite 300 *TF:* 800-722-9474 ■ *Web:* www.wish.org	Phoenix	AZ	85012	602-279-9474	279-0855
MAP International PO Box 215000 *TF:* 800-225-8550 ■ *Web:* www.map.org	Brunswick	GA	31521	912-265-6010	265-6170
Marine Toys for Tots Foundation 715 Broadway St *Web:* www.toysfortots.org	Quantico	VA	22134	703-640-9433	640-0917
Meals on Wheels Assn of America (MOWAA) 203 S Union St *Web:* www.mowaa.org	Alexandria	VA	22314	703-548-5558	548-8024
Medecins Sans Frontieres 333 7th Ave 2nd Fl *TF:* 888-392-0392 ■ *Web:* www.doctorswithoutborders.org	New York	NY	10001	212-679-6800	679-7016
Medical Care Development International (MCDI) 8401 Colesville Rd Suite 425 *Web:* mcdi.mcd.org	Silver Spring	MD	20910	301-562-1920	562-1921
Mennonite Central Committee (MCC) 21 S 12th St PO Box 500 *TF:* 888-563-4676 ■ *Web:* www.mcc.org	Akron	PA	17501	717-859-1151	859-2171
Mennonite Disaster Service (MDS) 1018 Main St *Web:* mds.mennonite.net	Akron	PA	17501	717-859-2210	859-4910
MENTOR/National Mentoring Partnership 1600 Duke St Suite 300 *Web:* www.mentoring.org	Alexandria	VA	22314	703-224-2200	226-2581
Mercy Corps 3015 SW 1st Ave *TF:* 800-292-3355 ■ *Web:* www.mercycorps.org	Portland	OR	97201	503-796-6800	796-6844
Mercy-USA for Aid & Development Inc (M-USA) 44450 Pinetree Dr Suite 201 *TF:* 800-556-3729 ■ *Web:* www.mercyusa.org	Plymouth	MI	48170	734-454-0011	454-0303
Migration & Refugee Services US Conference of Catholic Bishops 3211 4th St NE *Web:* www.nccbuscc.org/mrs	Washington	DC	20017	202-541-3000	722-8755
National Alliance to End Homelessness 1518 K St NW Suite 410 *Web:* www.endhomelessness.org	Washington	DC	20005	202-638-1526	638-4664
National AMBUCS Inc (AMBUCS) 4285 Regency Ct *Web:* www.ambucs.org	High Point	NC	27265	336-852-0052	852-6830
National Assn for the Exchange of Industrial Resources (NAEIR) 560 McClure St *TF:* 800-562-0955 ■ *Web:* www.naeir.org	Galesburg	IL	61401	309-343-0704	343-7316
National Benevolent Assn (NBA) 149 Weldon Pkwy Suite 115 *Web:* www.nbacares.org	Maryland Heights	MO	63043	314-993-9000	993-9018
National Children's Advocacy Center (NCAC) 210 Pratt Ave *Web:* www.nationalcac.org	Huntsville	AL	35801	256-533-5437	534-6883
National Coalition for the Homeless (NCH) 2201 P St NW *Web:* www.nationalhomeless.org	Washington	DC	20037	202-462-4822	462-4823
National Committee on Planned Giving (NCPG) 233 McCrea St Suite 400 *Web:* www.ncpg.org	Indianapolis	IN	46225	317-269-6274	269-6276
National Committee for Responsive Philanthropy (NCRP) 2001 'S' St NW Suite 620 *Web:* www.ncrp.org	Washington	DC	20009	202-387-9177	332-5084
National Hunger Clearinghouse 505 8th Ave Suite 2100 *TF:* 866-348-6479 ■ *Web:* www.worldhungeryear.org/nhc	New York	NY	10018	212-629-3392	465-9274
National Peace Corps Assn (NPCA) 1900 L St NW Suite 404 *TF:* 800-424-8580 ■ *Web:* www.rpcv.org	Washington	DC	20036	202-293-7728	293-7554
National Peace Foundation (NPF) 666 11th St NW Suite 202 *TF:* 800-237-3223 ■ *Web:* www.nationalpeace.org	Washington	DC	20001	202-783-7030	783-7040
National Student Campaign Against Hunger & Homelessness (NSCAHH) 233 N Pleasant St Suite 32 *TF:* 800-664-8647 ■ *Web:* www.nscahh.org	Amherst	MA	01002	413-253-6417	256-6435
Near East Foundation (NEF) 90 Broad St 15th Fl *Web:* www.neareast.org	New York	NY	10004	212-425-2205	425-2350
NewTithing Group 1 Market Stewart Tower Suite 2105 *Web:* www.newtithing.org	San Francisco	CA	94105	415-274-2765	274-2756
Northwest Medical Teams International (NWMTI) PO Box 10 *TF:* 800-959-4325 ■ *Web:* www.medicalteams.org	Portland	OR	97207	503-624-1000	624-1001
Nuclear Age Peace Foundation (NAPF) 1187 Coast Village Rd Suite 1 PMB 121 *Web:* www.wagingpeace.org	Santa Barbara	CA	93108	805-965-3443	568-0466
OIC International 240 W Tulpehocken St *TF:* 800-653-6424 ■ *Web:* www.oicinternational.org	Philadelphia	PA	19144	215-842-0860	849-7033
Operation USA 8320 Melrose Ave Suite 200 *TF:* 800-678-7255 ■ *Web:* www.opusa.org	Los Angeles	CA	90069	323-658-8876	653-7846
ORBIS International Inc 520 8th Ave 11th Fl *TF:* 800-672-4787 ■ *Web:* www.orbis.org	New York	NY	10018	646-674-5500	674-5599
Outreach International PO Box 210 *TF:* 888-833-1235 ■ *Web:* www.outreach-international.org	Independence	MO	64051	816-833-0883	833-0103
Oxfam America 26 West St *TF:* 800-776-9326 ■ *Web:* www.oxfamamerica.org	Boston	MA	02111	617-482-1211	728-2594
Pan American Development Foundation (PADF) 1889 F St NW 2nd Fl *Web:* www.padf.org	Washington	DC	20006	202-458-3969	458-6316
Partners of the Americas 1424 K St NW Suite 700 *TF:* 800-322-7844 ■ *Web:* www.partners.net	Washington	DC	20005	202-628-3300	628-3306
Pathfinder International 9 Galen St Suite 217 *Web:* www.pathfind.org	Watertown	MA	02472	617-924-7200	924-3833
Peace Action 1100 Wayne Ave Suite 1020 *Web:* www.peace-action.org	Silver Spring	MD	20910	301-565-4050	565-0850
People-to-People Health Foundation 255 Carter Hall Ln *TF:* 800-544-4673 ■ *Web:* www.projhope.org	Millwood	VA	22646	540-837-2100	837-1813
Physicians for Human Rights (PHR) 2 Arrow St Suite 301 *Web:* www.phrusa.org	Cambridge	MA	02138	617-301-4200	301-4250

Charitable & Humanitarian Organizations (Cont'd)

Organization	City	State	ZIP	Phone	Fax
Physicians for Social Responsibility (PSR) 1875 Connecticut Ave NW Suite 1012 *Web:* www.psr.org	Washington	DC	20009	202-667-4260	667-4201
Points of Light Foundation & Volunteer Center National Network 1400 'I' St NW Suite 800 *TF:* 800-750-7653 ■ *Web:* www.pointsoflight.org	Washington	DC	20005	202-729-8000	729-8100
Population Action International (PAI) 1300 19th St NW 2nd Fl *Web:* www.populationaction.org	Washington	DC	20036	202-557-3400	728-4177
Population Communication 1250 E Walnut St Suite 220	Pasadena	CA	91106	626-793-4750	793-4791
Population Connection 2120 L St NW Suite 5001 *TF:* 800-767-1956 ■ *Web:* www.populationconnection.org	Washington	DC	20037	202-332-2200	332-2302
Population Resource Center (PRC) 1731 Connecticut Ave NW 4th Fl *Web:* www.prcdc.org	Washington	DC	20009	202-467-5030	467-5034
Presbyterian Disaster Assistance (PDA) 100 Witherspoon St *TF:* 888-728-7228 ■ *Web:* www.pcusa.org/pda	Louisville	KY	40202	502-569-5839	569-8039
Private Agencies Collaborating Together (PACT) 1200 18th St NW Suite 350 *Web:* www.pactworld.org	Washington	DC	20036	202-466-5666	466-5669
Project Concern International 5151 Murphy Canyon Rd Suite 320 *Web:* www.projectconcern.org	San Diego	CA	92123	858-279-9690	694-0294
Project HOPE 255 Carter Hall Ln *TF:* 800-544-4673 ■ *Web:* www.projhope.org	Millwood	VA	22646	540-837-2100	837-1813
ProLiteracy Worldwide 1320 Jamesville Ave *TF:* 800-448-8878 ■ *Web:* www.proliteracy.org	Syracuse	NY	13210	315-422-9121	422-6369
Rainbow/PUSH Coalition Inc 930 E 50th St *Web:* www.rainbowpush.org	Chicago	IL	60615	773-373-3366	373-3571
Random Acts of Kindness Foundation 1727 Tremont Pl *TF:* 800-660-2811 ■ *Web:* www.actsofkindness.org	Denver	CO	80202	303-297-1964	297-2919
REACT International Inc 5210 Auth Rd Suite 403 *Web:* www.reactintl.org	Suitland	MD	20746	301-316-2900	316-2903
Rebuilding Together 1536 16th St NW *TF:* 800-473-4229 ■ *Web:* www.rebuildingtogether.org	Washington	DC	20036	202-483-9083	483-9081
Refugees International (RI) 2001 S St NW Suite 700-K *TF:* 800-733-8433 ■ *Web:* www.refugeesinternational.org	Washington	DC	20009	202-828-0110	828-0819
Research!America 1101 King St Suite 520 *TF:* 800-366-2873 ■ *Web:* www.researchamerica.org	Alexandria	VA	22314	703-739-2577	739-2372
Resource Foundation PO Box 3006 *Web:* www.resourcefnd.org	Larchmont	NY	10538	914-834-5810	
RESULTS 440 1st St NW Suite 1040 *Web:* www.results.org	Washington	DC	20001	202-783-7100	783-2818
Ronald McDonald House Charities (RMHC) 1 Kroc Dr Dept 014 *Web:* www.rmhc.org	Oak Brook	IL	60523	630-623-7048	623-7488
Rotary Foundation 1560 Sherman Ave *Web:* www.rotary.org/foundation	Evanston	IL	60201	847-866-3000	328-4101
Salvation Army PO Box 269 *TF:* 800-725-2769 ■ *Web:* www.salvationarmyusa.org	Alexandria	VA	22313	703-684-5500	684-3478
Save the Children Federation Inc 54 Wilton Rd *TF:* 800-728-3843 ■ *Web:* www.savethechildren.org	Westport	CT	06880	203-221-4000	
Senior Gleaners Inc 1951 Bell Ave *TF:* 800-585-1530 ■ *Web:* www.seniorgleaners.org	Sacramento	CA	95838	916-925-3240	568-1528
Sertoma International 1912 E Meyer Blvd *TF:* 800-593-5646 ■ *Web:* www.sertoma.org	Kansas City	MO	64132	816-333-8300	333-4320
Service & Development Agency Inc (SADA) 1134 11th St NW Suite 101 *Web:* www.amecnet.org/sada/sada.htm	Washington	DC	20001	202-371-8722	371-0981
SHARE Foundation 598 Bosworth St Suite 1 *Web:* www.share-elsalvador.org	San Francisco	CA	94131	415-239-2595	239-0785
Share Our Strength 1730 M St NW Suite 700 *TF:* 800-969-4767 ■ *Web:* www.strength.org	Washington	DC	20036	202-393-2925	347-5868
Smile Train Inc 245 5th Ave Suite 2201 *TF:* 877-543-7645 ■ *Web:* www.smiletrain.org	New York	NY	10016	212-689-9199	689-9299
Society of Saint Andrew 3383 Sweet Hollow Rd *TF:* 800-333-4597 ■ *Web:* www.endhunger.org	Big Island	VA	24526	434-299-5956	299-5949
Soroptimist International of the Americas 1709 Spruce St *Web:* www.soroptimist.org	Philadelphia	PA	19103	215-893-9000	893-5200
Southeast Asia Resource Action Center (SEARAC) 1628 16th St NW 3rd Fl *TF:* 800-600-9188 ■ *Web:* www.searac.org	Washington	DC	20009	202-667-4690	667-6449
Southern Baptist Disaster Relief 4200 North Point Pkwy *TF:* 800-749-7479 ■ *Web:* www.namb.net/site/c.9qKILUOzEpH/b.224451/k.A400/Disaster_Relief.htm	Alpharetta	GA	30022	770-410-6442	410-6014
Special Wish Foundation Inc 5340 E Main St Suite 208 *TF:* 800-486-9474 ■ *Web:* www.spwish.org	Columbus	OH	43213	614-575-9474	575-1866
Synergos Institute Inc 51 Madison Ave 21st Fl *Web:* www.synergos.org	New York	NY	10010	212-447-8111	447-8119
TechnoServe 49 Day St *TF:* 800-999-6757 ■ *Web:* www.technoserve.org	Norwalk	CT	06854	203-852-0377	838-6717
Tolstoy Foundation Inc 104 Lake Rd *Web:* www.tolstoyfoundation.org	Valley Cottage	NY	10989	845-268-6722	268-6937
Trickle Up Program Inc 104 W 27th St 12th Fl *TF:* 866-246-9980 ■ *Web:* www.trickleup.org	New York	NY	10001	212-255-9980	255-9974
UNICEF (United Nations Children's Fund) 3 UN Plaza *TF Orders:* 800-553-1200 ■ *Web:* www.unicef.org	New York	NY	10017	212-326-7000	888-7465
Unitarian Universalist Service Committee (UUSC) 130 Prospect St *TF:* 800-388-3920 ■ *Web:* www.uusc.org	Cambridge	MA	02139	617-868-6600	868-7102
United Methodist Committee on Relief (UMCOR) 475 Riverside Dr Rm 330 *TF:* 800-554-8583 ■ *Web:* gbgm-umc.org/umcor	New York	NY	10115	212-870-3814	870-3624
United Nations Children's Fund (UNICEF) 3 UN Plaza *TF Orders:* 800-553-1200 ■ *Web:* www.unicef.org	New York	NY	10017	212-326-7000	888-7465
United Nations Foundation (UNF) 1800 Massachusetts Ave NW Suite 400 *Web:* www.unfoundation.org	Washington	DC	20036	202-887-9040	887-9021
United Way of America 701 N Fairfax St *TF:* 800-892-2757 ■ *Web:* national.unitedway.org	Alexandria	VA	22314	703-836-7100	683-7840
United Way International 701 N Fairfax St *Web:* www.uwint.org	Alexandria	VA	22314	703-519-0092	519-0097
US Committee for Refugees & Immigrants (USCRI) 1717 Massachusetts Ave NW Suite 200 *Web:* www.refugees.org	Washington	DC	20036	202-347-3507	797-2363
US Fund for UNICEF 125 Maiden Ln *Web:* www.unicefusa.org	New York	NY	10016	212-922-2649	779-1679
USA for UNHCR 1775 K St NW Suite 290 *TF:* 800-770-1100 ■ *Web:* www.usaforunhcr.org	Washington	DC	20006	202-296-1115	296-1081
Veterans for Peace Inc (VFP) 216 S Meramec Ave *Web:* www.veteransforpeace.org	Saint Louis	MO	63105	314-725-6005	725-7103
Voices of September 11th 161 Cherry St *TF:* 866-505-3911 ■ *Web:* www.voicesofsept11.org	New Canaan	CT	06840	203-966-3911	966-5701
Volunteers of America 1660 Duke St *TF:* 800-899-0089 ■ *Web:* www.voa.org	Alexandria	VA	22314	703-341-5000	341-7000
War Resisters League 339 Lafayette St *Web:* www.warresisters.org	New York	NY	10012	212-228-0450	228-6193
Women's Action for New Directions (WAND) 691 Massachusetts Ave *Web:* www.wand.org	Arlington	MA	02476	781-643-6740	643-6744
World Concern 19303 Fremont Ave N *TF:* 800-755-5022 ■ *Web:* www.worldconcern.org	Seattle	WA	98133	206-546-7201	546-7269
World Education Inc 44 Farnsworth St *Web:* www.worlded.org	Boston	MA	02210	617-482-9485	482-0617
World Hunger Year Inc (WHY) 505 8th Ave Suite 2100 *TF:* 800-548-6479 ■ *Web:* www.worldhungeryear.org	New York	NY	10018	212-629-8850	465-9274
World Learning 1015 18th St NW Suite 1000 *TF:* 800-826-0196 ■ *Web:* www.worldlearning.org/delphi	Washington	DC	20036	202-898-0950	842-0885
World Neighbors Inc 4127 NW 122nd St *TF:* 800-242-6387 ■ *Web:* www.wn.org	Oklahoma City	OK	73120	405-752-9700	752-9393
World Opportunities International/Help the Children 1875 Century Park E Suite 700 *TF:* 800-464-7187	Los Angeles	CA	90067	323-466-7187	871-1546
World Peace Prayer Society 26 Benton Rd *Web:* www.worldpeace.org	Wassaic	NY	12592	845-877-6093	877-6862
World Relief 7 E Baltimore St *Web:* www.wr.org	Baltimore	MD	21202	443-451-1900	451-1995
World Vision Inc PO Box 9716 **Fax:* Cust Svc ■ *TF:* 800-777-5777 ■ *Web:* www.worldvision.org	Federal Way	WA	98063	253-815-1000	815-5951*

48-6 Children & Family Advocacy Organizations

Organization	City	State	ZIP	Phone	Fax
AARP 601 'E' St NW *TF:* 888-687-2277 ■ *Web:* www.aarp.org	Washington	DC	20049	202-434-2277	434-7597
AARP Grandparent Information Center 601 E St NW *TF:* 888-687-2277 ■ *Web:* www.aarp.org/grandparents	Washington	DC	20049	202-434-2296	434-6474
ABA Center on Children & the Law 740 15th St NW 9th Fl *TF:* 800-285-2221 ■ *Web:* www.abanet.org/child	Washington	DC	20005	202-662-1720	662-1755
ABA Commission on Law & Aging (COLA) 740 15th St NW 8th Fl *Web:* www.abanet.org/aging	Washington	DC	20005	202-662-8690	662-8698
Adopt America Network 1025 N Reynolds Rd *TF:* 800-246-1731 ■ *Web:* www.adoptamericanetwork.org	Toledo	OH	43615	419-534-3350	534-2995
Adoption ARC Inc 4701 Pine St Suite J-7 *TF:* 800-884-4004 ■ *Web:* www.adoptionarc.com	Philadelphia	PA	19143	215-748-1441	842-9881
Adoption Crossroads 444 E 76th St *Web:* www.adoptioncrossroads.org	New York	NY	10021	212-988-0110	988-0291
Adoptive Families of America 39 W 37th St 15th Fl *Web:* www.adoptivefamilies.com	New York	NY	10018	646-366-0830	366-0842
Alliance for Aging Research 2021 K St NW Suite 305 *TF:* 800-639-2421 ■ *Web:* www.agingresearch.org	Washington	DC	20006	202-293-2856	785-8574
Alliance for Children & Families Inc 11700 W Lake Park Dr *Web:* www.alliance1.org	Milwaukee	WI	53224	414-359-1040	359-1074
Alliance for Retired Americans 815 16th St NW 4th Fl *TF:* 888-373-6497 ■ *Web:* www.retiredamericans.org	Washington	DC	20006	202-637-5399	637-5398
American Academy of Pediatrics (AAP) 141 Northwest Point Blvd *TF:* 800-433-9016 ■ *Web:* www.aap.org	Elk Grove Village	IL	60007	847-434-4000	434-8000
American Adoption Congress (AAC) PO Box 42730 *Web:* www.americanadoptioncongress.org	Washington	DC	20015	202-483-3399	
American Assn of Homes & Services for the Aging (AAHSA) 2519 Connecticut Ave NW *TF:* 800-508-9442 ■ *Web:* www2.aahsa.org	Washington	DC	20008	202-783-2242	783-2255
American Assn for Marriage & Family Therapy (AAMFT) 112 S Alfred St *Web:* www.aamft.org	Alexandria	VA	22314	703-838-9808	838-9805
American Assn of Retired Persons 601 'E' St NW *TF:* 888-687-2277 ■ *Web:* www.aarp.org	Washington	DC	20049	202-434-2277	434-7597
American Coalition for Fathers & Children (ACFC) 1420 Spring Hill Rd **Fax Area Code:* 703 ■ *Web:* www.acfc.org	McLean	VA	22102	800-978-3237	442-5313*
American Culinary Federation Chef & Child Foundation 180 Center Place Way *TF:* 800-624-9458 ■ *Web:* www.acfchefs.org/Content/ACFPrograms/ChefandChild	Saint Augustine	FL	32095	904-824-4468	825-4758
American Humane Assn (AHA) 63 Inverness Dr E *TF:* 800-227-4645 ■ *Web:* www.americanhumane.org	Englewood	CO	80112	303-792-9900	792-5333
American Professional Society on the Abuse of Children (APSAC) PO Box 30669 **Fax Area Code:* 803 ■ *TF:* 877-402-7722 ■ *Web:* apsac.fmhi.usf.edu	Charleston	SC	29417	843-764-2905	753-9823*
American Senior Fitness Assn (SFA) PO Box 2575 *TF:* 800-243-1478 ■ *Web:* www.seniorfitness.net	New Smyrna Beach	FL	32170	386-423-6634	427-0613
American Seniors Housing Assn (ASHA) 5100 Wisconsin Ave NW Suite 307 *Web:* www.seniorshousing.org	Washington	DC	20016	202-237-0900	237-1616
American SIDS Institute 509 Augusta Dr *TF:* 800-232-7437 ■ *Web:* www.sids.org	Marietta	GA	30067	770-426-8746	426-1369
American Society on Aging (ASA) 833 Market St Suite 511 *TF:* 800-537-9728 ■ *Web:* www.asaging.org	San Francisco	CA	94103	415-974-9600	974-0300
America's Promise - The Alliance for Youth 909 N Washington St Suite 400 *TF:* 800-365-0153 ■ *Web:* www.americaspromise.org	Alexandria	VA	22314	703-684-4500	535-3900
Association for Children for Enforcement of Support (ACES) PO Box 7842 **Fax Area Code:* 540 ■ *Web:* www.childsupport-aces.org	Fredericksburg	VA	22404	800-738-2237	582-3386*
Association for Couples in Marriage Enrichment (ACME) PO Box 21374 *TF:* 800-634-8325 ■ *Web:* www.bettermarriages.org	Winston-Salem	NC	27120	336-724-1526	721-4746
Association of Jewish Aging Services (AJAS) 316 Pennsylvania Ave SE Suite 402 *Web:* www.ajas.org	Washington	DC	20003	202-543-7500	543-4090
Athletes & Entertainers for Kids (AEFK) 14340 Bolsa Chica Rd Unit C *Web:* www.aefk.org	Westminster	CA	92683	714-894-5450	
Believe In Tomorrow National Children's Foundation 6601 Frederick Rd *TF:* 800-933-5470 ■ *Web:* www.believeintomorrow.org	Baltimore	MD	21228	410-744-1032	744-1984
Big Brothers Big Sisters of America (BBBSA) 230 N 13th St *Web:* www.bbbs.org	Philadelphia	PA	19107	215-567-7000	567-0394
Cal Farley's Boys Ranch 600 W 11th St PO Box 1890 *TF:* 800-687-3722 ■ *Web:* www.calfarleysboysranch.org	Amarillo	TX	79174	806-372-2341	372-6638
Campaign for a Commercial-Free Childhood (CCFC) Judge Baker Children's Center 3 Parker Hill Ave *Web:* www.commercialexploitation.org	Boston	MA	02120	617-278-4172	232-7343
CARP: Canada's Assn for the Fifty-Plus 1304-27 Queen St E *TF:* 800-363-9736 ■ *Web:* www.50plus.com	Toronto	ON	M5C2M6	416-363-8748	363-8747

Organization	City	State	Zip	Phone	Fax
Child Alert Foundation (CAF) Rt 87 S Box 357 *Web:* www.childalert.org	Dushore	PA	18614	570-928-8422	928-8110
Child Find of America Inc 7 Cummings Ln *TF:* 800-426-5678 ■ *Web:* www.childfindofamerica.org	Highland	NY	12528	845-691-4666	691-7766
Child Find Canada 212-2211 McPhillips St *TF:* 800-387-7962 ■ *Web:* www.childfind.ca	Winnipeg	MB	R2V0M5	204-339-5584	339-5587
Child Lures Prevention 5166 Shelburne Rd *Web:* www.childlures.org	Shelburne	VT	05482	802-985-8458	985-8418
Child Quest International 307 Orchard City Dr Suite 108 *TF:* 888-818-4673 ■ *Web:* www.childquest.org	Campbell	CA	95008	408-287-4673	287-4676
Child Trends 4301 Connecticut Ave NW Suite 100 *Web:* www.childtrends.org	Washington	DC	20008	202-572-6000	362-8420
Child Welfare League of America (CWLA) 2345 Crystal Dr Suite 250 *Web:* www.cwla.org	Arlington	VA	22202	703-412-2430	412-2401
Childhelp USA 15757 N 78th St Suite B *TF:* 800-422-4453 ■ *Web:* www.childhelpusa.org	Scottsdale	AZ	85260	480-922-8212	922-7061
Children of Aging Parents PO Box 167 **Fax Area Code:* 215 ■ *TF:* 800-227-7294 ■ *Web:* www.caps4caregivers.org	Richboro	PA	18954	800-227-7294	945-8720*
Children Awaiting Parents Inc (CAP) 595 Blossom Rd Suite 306 *TF:* 888-835-8802 ■ *Web:* www.capbook.org	Rochester	NY	14610	585-232-5110	232-2634
Children of Deaf Adults International Inc (CODA) PO Box 30715 *Web:* www.coda-international.org	Santa Barbara	CA	93130	805-682-0997	
Children Inc PO Box 5381 *TF:* 800-538-5381 ■ *Web:* www.children-inc.org	Richmond	VA	23220	804-359-4562	353-7541
Children of the Night 14530 Sylvan St *TF:* 800-551-1300 ■ *Web:* www.childrenofthenight.org	Van Nuys	CA	91411	818-908-4474	908-1468
Children's Defense Fund (CDF) 25 'E' St NW *TF:* 800-233-1200 ■ *Web:* www.childrensdefense.org	Washington	DC	20001	202-628-8787	662-3510
Children's Rights Council (CRC) 6200 Editors Park Dr Suite 103 *TF:* 800-787-5437 ■ *Web:* www.gocrc.com	Hyattsville	MD	20782	301-559-3120	559-3124
Christian Children's Fund Inc (CCF) 2821 Emerywood Pkwy *TF:* 800-776-6767 ■ *Web:* www.christianchildrensfund.org	Richmond	VA	23294	804-756-2700	756-2718
Christian Foundation for Children & Aging (CFCA) 1 Elmwood Ave *TF:* 800-875-6564 ■ *Web:* www.cfcausa.org	Kansas City	KS	66103	913-384-6500	384-2211
CityKids Foundation 57 Leonard St *Web:* www.citykids.com	New York	NY	10013	212-925-3320	925-0128
CODA (Children of Deaf Adults International Inc) PO Box 30715 *Web:* www.coda-international.org	Santa Barbara	CA	93130	805-682-0997	
Committee for Mother & Child Rights Inc 6536 Colgate Ave	Los Angeles	CA	90048	323-634-0543	
Common Sense About Kids & Guns 1225 'I' St NW Suite 1100 *TF:* 877-955-5437 ■ *Web:* www.kidsandguns.org	Washington	DC	20005	202-546-0200	371-9615
Communities in Schools Inc (CIS) 277 S Washington St Suite 210 *TF:* 800-247-4543 ■ *Web:* www.cisnet.org	Alexandria	VA	22314	703-519-8999	519-7537
Consortium for Citizens with Disabilities (CCD) 1660 L St NW Suite 701 *Web:* c-c-d.org	Washington	DC	20036	202-783-2229	783-8250
Corps Network The 666 11th St NW Suite 1000 *TF:* 800-666-2722 ■ *Web:* www.corpsnetwork.org	Washington	DC	20001	202-737-6272	737-6277
Council for Equal Rights in Adoption 444 E 76th St *Web:* www.adoptioncrossroads.org	New York	NY	10021	212-988-0110	988-0291
Covenant House 5 Penn Plaza 3rd Fl **Fax:* Hum Res ■ *TF:* 800-999-9999 ■ *Web:* www.covenanthouse.org	New York	NY	10001	212-727-4000	727-6516*
Creative Grandparenting Inc 100 W 10th St Suite 1007 *Web:* www.creativegrandparenting.org	Wilmington	DE	19801	302-656-2122	656-2123
Dads & Daughters (DADs) 2 W 1st St Suite 101 *Web:* www.dadsanddaughters.org	Duluth	MN	55802	218-722-3942	728-0314
Donaldson Evan B Adoption Institute 120 E 38th St **Fax Area Code:* 775 ■ *Web:* www.adoptioninstitute.org	New York	NY	10016	212-925-4089	796-6592*
Dream Factory Inc 1218 S 3rd St *TF:* 800-456-7556 ■ *Web:* www.dreamfactoryinc.com	Louisville	KY	40203	502-637-8700	637-8744
Eden Alternative 742 Turnpike Rd **Fax Area Code:* 607 ■ *Web:* www.edenalt.com	Sherburne	NY	13460	907-747-4888	674-6723*
Evan B Donaldson Adoption Institute 120 E 38th St **Fax Area Code:* 775 ■ *Web:* www.adoptioninstitute.org	New York	NY	10016	212-925-4089	796-6592*
Experience Works Inc 2200 Clarendon Blvd Suite 1000 *TF:* 866-397-9757 ■ *Web:* www.experienceworks.org	Arlington	VA	22201	703-522-7272	522-0141
FaithTrust Institute 2400 N 45th St Suite 101 *TF:* 877-860-2255 ■ *Web:* www.faithtrustinstitute.org	Seattle	WA	98103	206-634-1903	634-0115
Family & Home Network PO Box 545 *Web:* www.familyandhome.org	Merrifield	VA	22116	703-352-1072	352-1076
Family Research Council (FRC) 801 G St NW *TF:* 800-225-4008 ■ *Web:* www.frc.org	Washington	DC	20001	202-393-2100	393-2134
Family Support America 205 W Randolph St Suite 2222	Chicago	IL	60606	312-338-0900	338-1522
Family Violence Prevention Fund (FVPF) 383 Rhode Island St Suite 304 *Web:* endabuse.org	San Francisco	CA	94103	415-252-8900	252-8991
Federation of Families for Children's Mental Health 9605 Medical Center Dr Suite 280 *Web:* www.ffcmh.org	Rockville	MD	28050	240-403-1901	403-1909
Find the Children 2656 29th St Suite 203 *TF:* 888-477-6721 ■ *Web:* www.findthechildren.com	Santa Monica	CA	90405	310-314-3213	314-3169
First Candle/SIDS Alliance 1314 Bedford Ave Suite 210 *TF:* 800-221-7437 ■ *Web:* www.firstcandle.org	Baltimore	MD	21208	410-653-8226	653-8709
Focus on the Family 8605 Explorer Dr *TF Sales:* 800-232-6459 ■ *Web:* www.family.org	Colorado Springs	CO	80920	719-531-3400	548-4670
Food Research & Action Center (FRAC) 1875 Connecticut Ave NW Suite 540 *Web:* www.frac.org	Washington	DC	20009	202-986-2200	986-2525
Generations United (GU) 1333 H St NW Suite 500-W *Web:* www.gu.org	Washington	DC	20005	202-289-3979	289-3952
Girls & Boys Town 14100 Crawford St *TF:* 800-448-3000 ■ *Web:* www.girlsandboystown.org	Boys Town	NE	68010	402-498-1300	498-1348
Girls Inc 120 Wall St 3rd Fl *TF:* 800-374-4475 ■ *Web:* www.girlsinc.org	New York	NY	10005	212-509-2000	509-8708
Grandparents Rights Organization (GRO) 100 W Long Lake Rd Suite 250 *Web:* www.grandparentsrights.org	Bloomfield Hills	MI	48304	248-646-7177	646-9722
Gray Panthers 1612 K St NW Suite 300 *TF:* 800-280-5362 ■ *Web:* www.graypanthers.org	Washington	DC	20006	202-737-6637	737-1160
Healing Alliance PO Box 429 *Web:* www.healingall.org	Pewee Valley	KY	40056	502-241-5544	
Healthy Teen Network 509 2nd St NE *Web:* www.healthyteennetwork.org	Washington	DC	20002	202-547-8814	547-8815
Hear My Voice 1100 N Main St Suite 201 *Web:* www.hearmyvoice.org	Ann Arbor	MI	48104	734-747-9654	747-9559
HMHB (National Healthy Mothers Healthy Babies Coalition) 121 N Washington St Suite 300 *Web:* www.hmhb.org	Alexandria	VA	22314	703-836-6110	836-3470
Human Life International (HLI) 4 Family Life Ln *TF Orders:* 800-549-5433 ■ *Web:* www.hli.org	Front Royal	VA	22630	540-635-7884	622-6247
International MOMS Club 1464 Madera Rd Suite N-191 *Web:* www.momsclub.org	Simi Valley	CA	93065	805-526-2725	
International Soundex Reunion Registry PO Box 2312 *Web:* www.isrr.net	Carson City	NV	89702	775-882-7755	
Jewish Assn for Services for the Aged (JASA) 132 W 31st St 15th Fl *Web:* www.jasa.org	New York	NY	10001	212-273-5272	695-9070
Jewish Board of Family & Children Services (JBFCS) 120 W 57th St *TF:* 888-523-2769 ■ *Web:* www.jbfcs.org	New York	NY	10019	212-582-9100	956-5676
Jimmy Ryce Center for Victims of Predatory Abduction (JRC) 908 Coquina Ln *TF:* 800-546-7923 ■ *Web:* www.jimmyryce.org	Vero Beach	FL	32963	772-492-0200	492-0210
Joint Custody Assn (JCA) 10606 Wilkins Ave	Los Angeles	CA	90024	310-475-5352	475-6541
Kempe Children's Center 1825 Marion St *Web:* www.kempecenter.org	Denver	CO	80218	303-864-5300	864-5302
KlaasKids Foundation PO Box 925 *Web:* www.klaaskids.org	Sausalito	CA	94966	415-331-6867	331-5633
Margaret Sanger Center International (MSCI) 26 Bleecker St *Web:* www.margaretsangercenterinternational.org	New York	NY	10012	212-274-7239	274-7299
Men Against Destruction Defending Against Drugs & Social Disorder Inc (MAD DADS) 555 Stockton St *Web:* www.maddads.com	Jacksonville	FL	32204	904-388-8171	
Mentoring USA 5 Hanover Sq *Web:* www.helpusa.org	New York	NY	10004	212-400-8294	400-8278
MENTOR/National Mentoring Partnership 1600 Duke St Suite 300 *Web:* www.mentoring.org	Alexandria	VA	22314	703-224-2200	226-2581
MOPS International 2370 S Trenton Way *TF:* 800-929-1287 ■ *Web:* www.mops.org	Denver	CO	80231	303-733-5353	733-5770
Mothers Against Drunk Driving (MADD) 511 E John Carpenter Fwy Suite 700 **Fax Area Code:* 972 ■ *TF:* 800-438-6233 ■ *Web:* www.madd.org	Irving	TX	75062	214-744-6233	869-2207*
Mothers & More PO Box 31 *Web:* www.mothersandmore.org	Elmhurst	IL	60126	630-941-3553	941-3551
Mothers of Supertwins (MOST) PO Box 306 *Web:* www.mostonline.org	East Islip	NY	11730	631-859-1110	
NAMES Project Foundation/AIDS Memorial Quilt 101 Krog St *Web:* www.aidsquilt.org	Atlanta	GA	30307	404-688-5500	688-5552
National Adoption Center 1500 Walnut St Suite 701 *Web:* www.adopt.org	Philadelphia	PA	19102	215-735-9988	735-9410
National Adult Day Services Assn (NADSA) 8201 Greensboro Dr Suite 300 *TF:* 800-424-9046 ■ *Web:* www.nadsa.org	McLean	VA	22102	703-610-9000	610-9005
National Alliance for Caregiving 4720 Montgomery Ln 5th Fl *Web:* www.caregiving.org	Bethesda	MD	20814	301-718-8444	652-7711
National Assn of Child Care Professionals (NACCP) 7610 Hwy 71 W Suite E *TF:* 800-537-1118 ■ *Web:* www.naccp.org	Austin	TX	78735	512-301-5557	301-5080
National Assn of Child Care Resource & Referral Agencies (NACCRRA) 3101 Wilson Blvd Suite 350 *TF:* 800-424-2246 ■ *Web:* www.naccrra.org	Arlington	VA	22201	703-341-4100	341-4101
National Assn for Family Child Care (NAFCC) 5202 Pinemont Dr *TF:* 800-359-3817 ■ *Web:* www.nafcc.org	Salt Lake City	UT	84123	801-269-9338	268-9507
National Assn for Hispanic Elderly 1452 W Temple St Suite 100	Los Angeles	CA	90026	213-202-5900	202-5905
National Assn for Home Care & Hospice (NAHC) 228 7th St SE *Web:* www.nahc.org	Washington	DC	20003	202-547-7424	547-3540
National Caregiving Foundation 801 N Pitt St Suite 116 *TF:* 800-930-1357 ■ *Web:* www.caregivingfoundation.org	Alexandria	VA	22314	703-299-9300	299-9304
National Caucus & Center on Black Aged Inc (NCBA) 1220 L St NW Suite 800 *Web:* www.ncba-aged.org	Washington	DC	20005	202-637-8400	347-0895
National Center for Children in Poverty (NCCP) 215 W 125th St 3rd Fl *Web:* www.nccp.org	New York	NY	10027	646-284-9600	284-9623
National Center on Elder Abuse (NCEA) 297 Graham Hall *Web:* www.elderabusecenter.org	Newark	DE	19716	302-831-3525	831-4225
National Center for Family Literacy (NCFL) 325 W Main St Suite 300 *TF:* 877-326-5481 ■ *Web:* www.famlit.org	Louisville	KY	40202	502-584-1133	584-0172
National Center for Missing & Exploited Children (NCMEC) 699 Prince St *TF:* 800-843-5678 ■ *Web:* www.missingkids.com	Alexandria	VA	22314	703-274-3900	274-2200
National Child Abuse Hotline 15757 N 78th St Suite B *TF:* 800-422-4453 ■ *Web:* www.childhelpusa.org	Scottsdale	AZ	85260	480-922-8212	922-7061
National Child Care Assn (NCCA) 2025 M St NW Suite 800 *TF:* 800-543-7161 ■ *Web:* www.nccanet.org	Washington	DC	20036	202-367-1133	367-2133
National Child Safety Council (NCSC) 4065 Page Ave *TF:* 800-327-5107	Jackson	MI	49204	517-764-6070	764-3068
National Child Support Enforcement Assn (NCSEA) 1109 Spring St Suite 700 **Fax Area Code:* 301 ■ *Web:* www.ncsea.org	Silver Spring	MD	20910	240-595-6600	587-1683*
National Coalition Against Domestic Violence (NCADV) 1201 E Colfax Ave Suite 385 *TF:* 800-799-7233 ■ *Web:* www.ncadv.org	Denver	CO	80218	303-839-1852	831-9251
National Coalition for the Protection of Children & Families (NCPCF) 800 Compton Rd Suite 9224 *Web:* www.eos.net/ncpcf	Cincinnati	OH	45231	513-521-6227	521-6337
National Council for Adoption (NCFA) 225 N Washington St *TF:* 866-212-3678 ■ *Web:* www.adoptioncouncil.org	Alexandria	VA	22314	703-299-6633	299-6004
National Council on the Aging (NCOA) 1901 L St NW 4th Fl *TF:* 800-424-9046 ■ *Web:* www.ncoa.org	Washington	DC	20036	202-479-1200	479-0735
National Council on Family Relations (NCFR) 3989 Central Ave NE Suite 550 *TF:* 888-781-9331 ■ *Web:* www.ncfr.com	Minneapolis	MN	55421	763-781-9331	781-9348
National Court Appointed Special Advocate Assn (CASA) 100 W Harrison St North Tower Suite 500 *TF:* 800-628-3233 ■ *Web:* www.nationalcasa.org	Seattle	WA	98119	206-270-0072	270-0078
National Dissemination Center for Children with Disabilities 1825 Connecticut Ave *TF:* 800-695-0285 ■ *Web:* www.nichcy.org	Washington	DC	20009	202-884-8200	884-8441
National Domestic Violence Hotline (NDVH) PO Box 161810 *TF:* 800-799-7233 ■ *Web:* www.ndvh.org	Austin	TX	78716	512-794-1133	453-8541
National Family Caregivers Assn (NFCA) 10400 Connecticut Ave Suite 500 *TF:* 800-896-3650 ■ *Web:* www.nfcacares.org	Kensington	MD	20895	301-942-6430	942-2302
National Foster Parent Assn (NFPA) 7512 Stanich Ln Suite 6 *TF:* 800-557-5238 ■ *Web:* www.nfpainc.org	Gig Harbor	WA	98335	253-853-4000	853-4001
National Healthy Mothers Healthy Babies Coalition (HMHB) 121 N Washington St Suite 300 *Web:* www.hmhb.org	Alexandria	VA	22314	703-836-6110	836-3470

Children & Family Advocacy Organizations (Cont'd)

Phone | Fax

National Hispanic Council on Aging (NHCOA)
734 15th St NW Suite 1050 Washington DC 20005 202-347-9733 347-9735
Web: www.nhcoa.org

National Independent Living Assn (NILA)
4203 Southpoint Blvd Jacksonville FL 32216 904-296-1038 296-1953
Web: www.nilausa.org

National Indian Council on Aging (NICOA)
10501 Montgomery Blvd NE Suite 210 Albuquerque NM 87111 505-292-2001 292-1922
Web: www.nicoa.org

National Inhalant Prevention Coalition (NIPC)
322-A Thompson St Chattanooga TN 37405 423-265-4662 265-4889
TF: 800-269-4237 ■ *Web:* www.inhalants.org

National Interfaith Coalition on Aging (NICA)
1901 L St NW 4th Fl Washington DC 20036 202-479-1200 479-0735
TF: 800-424-9046 ■ *Web:* www.ncoa.org

National Network for Youth 1319 F St NW Suite 401 Washington DC 20004 202-783-7949 783-7955
Web: www.nn4youth.org

National Organization of Mothers of Twins Clubs Inc (NOMOTC)
PO Box 700860 Plymouth MI 48170 248-231-4480
TF: 877-540-2200 ■ *Web:* www.nomotc.org

National Organization of Single Mothers PO Box 68 Midland NC 28107 704-888-5437
Web: singlemothers.org

National Resource Center on Domestic Violence (NRCDV)
6400 Flank Dr Suite 1300 Harrisburg PA 17112 717-545-6400 545-9456
TF: 800-537-2238 ■ *Web:* www.nrcdv.org

National Resource Center on Native American Aging (NRCNAA) 501 N Columbia Rd Rm 4535 Grand Forks ND 58202 701-777-3437 777-6779
TF: 800-896-7628 ■ *Web:* www.med.und.nodak.edu/depts/rural//nrcnaa

National Resource Center on Nutrition Physical Activity & Aging
Florida International Univ 11200 SW 8th St Bldg OE200 Miami FL 33199 305-348-1517 348-1518
Web: nutritionandaging.fiu.edu

National Resource Center for Special Needs Adoptions
16250 Northland Dr Suite 120 Southfield MI 48075 248-443-7080 443-7099
TF: 877-767-5437 ■ *Web:* www.spaulding.org

National Runaway Switchboard (NRS) 3080 N Lincoln Ave Chicago IL 60657 773-880-9860 929-5150
TF: 800-621-4000 ■ *Web:* www.nrscrisisline.org

National SAFE KIDS Campaign
1301 Pennsylvania Ave NW Suite 1000 Washington DC 20004 202-662-0600 393-2072
Web: www.safekids.org

National Senior Citizens Law Center (NSCLC)
1444 'I' St Suite 1100 Washington DC 20005 202-289-6976 289-7224
Web: www.nsclc.org

National Urban Technology Center 80 Maiden Ln Suite 606 New York NY 10038 212-528-7350 528-7355
TF: 800-998-3212 ■ *Web:* www.urbantech.org

National WIC Assn (NWA) 2001 'S' St NW Suite 580 Washington DC 20009 202-232-5492 387-5281
Web: www.nwica.org

National Youth Advocacy Coalition (NYAC)
1638 R St NW Suite 300 Washington DC 20009 202-319-7596 319-7365
TF: 800-541-6922 ■ *Web:* www.nyacyouth.org

North America Missing Children Assn Inc 136 Rt 420 Hwy South Esk NB E1V4N8 800-260-0753
Web: www.namca.com

North American Council on Adoptable Children (NACAC)
970 Raymond Ave Suite 106 Saint Paul MN 55114 651-644-3036 644-9848
Web: www.nacac.org

Older Women's League (OWL) 3300 N Fairfax Dr Suite 218 Arlington VA 22201 703-812-7990 628-0458*
**Fax Area Code:* 202 ■ *TF:* 800-825-3695 ■ *Web:* www.owl-national.org

Orphan Foundation of America (OFA)
12020-D N Shore Dr Tall Oaks Village Ctr Reston VA 20190 571-203-0270 203-0273
TF: 800-950-4673 ■ *Web:* www.orphan.org

Parents Helping Parents (PHP) 3041 Olcott St Santa Clara CA 95054 408-727-5775 727-0182
Web: www.php.com

Parents of Murdered Children (POMC)
100 E 8th St Suite B-41 Cincinnati OH 45202 513-721-5683 345-4489
TF: 888-818-7662 ■ *Web:* www.pomc.com

Parents Without Partners (PWP)
1650 S Dixie Hwy Suite 510 Boca Raton FL 33432 561-391-8833 395-8557
TF: 800-637-7974 ■ *Web:* www.parentswithoutpartners.org

Pension Rights Center 1350 Connecticut Ave NW Suite 206 Washington DC 20036 202-296-3776 833-2472
Web: www.pensionrights.org

Plan USA 155 Plan Way Warwick RI 02886 401-738-5600 738-5608
TF: 800-556-7918 ■ *Web:* www.planusa.org

Planned Parenthood Federation of America 434 W 33rd St New York NY 10001 212-541-7800 245-1845
TF: 800-829-7732 ■ *Web:* www.plannedparenthood.org

Prevent Child Abuse America 200 S Michigan Ave 17th Fl Chicago IL 60604 312-663-3520 939-8962
TF: 800-244-5373 ■ *Web:* www.preventchildabuse.org

Program on Women & Aging
Brandeis University Institute on Assets & Social Policy MS 035 Waltham MA 02454 781-736-3826
Web: iasp.brandeis.edu/womenandaging

Promise Keepers 4045 Pecos St PO Box 11798 Denver CO 80211 303-964-7600 433-1036
TF: 800-888-7595 ■ *Web:* www.promisekeepers.org

Rainbows 2100 Golf Rd Suite 370 Rolling Meadows IL 60008 847-952-1770 952-1774
TF: 800-266-3206 ■ *Web:* www.rainbows.org

RAINN (Rape Abuse & Incest National Network)
2000 L St NW Suite 406 Washington DC 20036 202-544-1034 544-3556
TF: 800-656-4673 ■ *Web:* www.rainn.org

Rape Abuse & Incest National Network (RAINN)
2000 L St NW Suite 406 Washington DC 20036 202-544-1034 544-3556
TF: 800-656-4673 ■ *Web:* www.rainn.org

Rolling Readers USA 4007 Camino Del Rio S Suite 203 San Diego CA 92108 619-516-4095 516-4096
Web: www.rollingreaders.org

Sanger Margaret Center International 26 Bleecker St New York NY 10012 212-274-7239 274-7299
Web: www.margaretsangercenterinternational.org

Seniors Coalition 4401 Fair Lakes Ct Suite 210 Fairfax VA 22033 703-631-4211 631-4283
TF: 800-325-9891 ■ *Web:* www.senior.org

SER - Jobs for Progress National Inc
5215 N O'Connor Blvd Suite 2550 Irving TX 75039 972-506-7815 506-7832
TF: 800-427-2306 ■ *Web:* www.ser-national.org

SOS Children's Villages-USA
1317 F St NW1200 6th St NW Suite 550 Washington DC 20005 202-347-7920 347-7334*
**Fax:* Hum Res ■ *TF:* 800-886-5767 ■ *Web:* www.sos-childrensvillages.org

Spaulding for Children 16250 Northland Dr Suite 120 Southfield MI 48075 248-443-7080 443-7099
TF: 877-767-5437 ■ *Web:* www.spaulding.org

Stand For Children 516 SE Morrison St Suite 206 Portland OR 97214 503-235-2305 963-9517
TF: 800-663-4032 ■ *Web:* www.stand.org

Stars of David International Inc
3175 Commercial Ave Suite 100 Northbrook IL 60062 800-782-7349 274-1527*
**Fax Area Code:* 773 ■ *TF:* 800-782-7349 ■ *Web:* www.starsofdavid.org

Stepfamily Assn of America (SAA) 650 J St Suite 205 Lincoln NE 68508 402-477-7837 477-8317
TF: 800-735-0329 ■ *Web:* www.saafamilies.org

Stepfamily Foundation 333 West End Ave Suite 11C New York NY 10023 212-877-3244 362-7030
TF: 800-759-7837 ■ *Web:* www.stepfamily.org

Phone | Fax

Students Against Destructive Decisions (SADD)
255 Main St Marlborough MA 01752 508-481-3568 481-5759
TF: 877-723-3462 ■ *Web:* www.sadd.org

Triplet Connection PO Box 429 Spring City UT 84662 435-851-1105 462-7466
Web: www.tripletconnection.org

Vanished Children's Alliance (VCA)
991 W Hedding St Suite 101 San Jose CA 95126 408-296-1113 296-1117
TF: 800-826-4743 ■ *Web:* www.vca.org

Voices for America's Children
1000 Vermont Ave NW Suite 700 Washington DC 20005 202-289-0777 289-0776
Web: www.voicesforamericaschildren.org

Well Spouse Foundation 63 W Main St Suite H Freehold NJ 07728 732-577-8899 577-8644
TF: 800-838-0879 ■ *Web:* www.wellspouse.org

YMCA of the USA 101 N Wacker Dr 14th Fl Chicago IL 60606 312-977-0031 977-9063
TF: 800-872-9622 ■ *Web:* www.ymca.net

Youth Crime Watch of America 9200 S Dadeland Blvd Suite 417 Miami FL 33156 305-670-2409 670-3805
Web: www.ycwa.org

YWCA USA 1015 18th St NW Suite 1100 Washington DC 20036 202-467-0801 467-0802
TF: 800-992-2871 ■ *Web:* www.ywca.org

48-7 Civic & Political Organizations

Phone | Fax

ACU (American Conservative Union) 1007 Cameron St Alexandria VA 22314 703-836-8602 836-8606
TF: 800-228-7345 ■ *Web:* www.conservative.org

Advocates for Self-Government 213 S Erwin St Cartersville GA 30120 770-386-8372 386-8373
Web: www.self-gov.org

AIDS Action 1730 M St NW Suite 611 Washington DC 20036 202-530-8030 530-8031
Web: www.aidsaction.org

AIPAC (American Israel Public Affairs Committee)
251 H St Washington DC 20001 202-639-5200 347-4918
Web: www.aipac.org

Alliance for Justice (AFJ) 11 Dupont Cir NW 2nd Fl Washington DC 20036 202-822-6070 822-6068
Web: www.afj.org

Alliance of Nonprofit Mailers (ANM)
1211 Connecticut Ave NW Ste 620 Washington DC 20036 202-462-5132 462-0423
Web: www.nonprofitmailers.org

American Assn of Political Consultants (AAPC)
600 Pennsylvania Ave SE Suite 330 Washington DC 20003 202-544-9815 544-9816
Web: www.theaapc.org

American Cause The 501 Church St Suite 217-A Vienna VA 22180 703-255-2632 255-2219
Web: www.theamericancause.org

American Conservative Union (ACU) 1007 Cameron St Alexandria VA 22314 703-836-8602 836-8606
TF: 800-228-7345 ■ *Web:* www.conservative.org

American Council for an Energy-Efficient Economy (ACEEE)
1001 Connecticut Ave NW Suite 801 Washington DC 20036 202-429-8873 429-2248
Web: www.aceee.org

American Israel Public Affairs Committee (AIPAC)
251 H St Washington DC 20001 202-639-5200 347-4918
Web: www.aipac.org

American Jewish Congress 825 3rd Ave Suite 1800 New York NY 10022 212-879-4500 758-1633
Web: www.ajcongress.org

American Legislative Exchange Council (ALEC)
1101 Vermont Ave NW 11th Fl Washington DC 20005 202-466-3800 466-3801
Web: www.alec.org

Americans for Democratic Action (ADA)
1625 K St NW Suite 210 Washington DC 20006 202-785-5980 785-5969
TF: 800-787-2734 ■ *Web:* www.adaction.org

Americans for Fair Taxation PO Box 27487 Houston TX 77227 713-963-9023 963-8403
TF: 800-324-7829 ■ *Web:* www.fairtax.org

Americans for Peace Now (APN) 1101 14th St NW 6th Fl Washington DC 20005 202-728-1893 728-1895
Web: www.peacenow.org

Americans United for Separation of Church & State
518 C St NE Washington DC 20002 202-466-3234 466-2587
TF: 800-875-3707 ■ *Web:* www.au.org

ANM (Alliance of Nonprofit Mailers)
1211 Connecticut Ave NW Ste 620 Washington DC 20036 202-462-5132 462-0423
Web: www.nonprofitmailers.org

Association of Community Organizations for Reform Now (ACORN) 739 8th St SE Washington DC 20003 202-547-2500 546-2483
TF: 877-552-2676 ■ *Web:* www.acorn.org

Brady Campaign to Prevent Gun Violence
1225 'I' St NW Suite 1100 Washington DC 20005 202-898-0792 371-9615
Web: www.bradycampaign.org

Brady Center to Prevent Gun Violence
1225 'I' St NW Suite 1100 Washington DC 20005 202-289-7319 408-1851
Web: www.bradycenter.org

Campaign Legal Center
Media Policy Program Campaign Legal Ctr 1640 Rhode Island Ave NW Suite 650 Washington DC 20036 202-736-2200 736-2222
Web: www.campaignlegalcenter.org

CapitolWatch PO Box 650911 Potomac Falls VA 20165 202-544-2600 430-6378*
**Fax Area Code:* 703 ■ *TF:* 888-468-9282 ■ *Web:* www.capitolwatch.org

Center for Democracy & Technology (CDT)
1634 'I' St NW 11th Fl Washington DC 20006 202-637-9800 637-0968
Web: www.cdt.org

Center for Government Reform (CGR)
2915 Hunter Mill Rd Suite 23 Oakton VA 22124 703-319-0009 319-8842
Web: www.govreform.org

Center for Third World Organizing (CTWO) 1218 E 21st St Oakland CA 94606 510-533-7583 533-0923
Web: www.ctwo.org

Christian Coalition of America PO Box 37030 Washington DC 20013 202-479-6900 479-4260
TF: 888-440-2262 ■ *Web:* www.cc.org

Citizens Against Government Waste (CAGW)
1301 Connecticut Ave NW Suite 400 Washington DC 20036 202-467-5300 467-4253
TF: 800-232-6479 ■ *Web:* www.cagw.org

Citizens Committee for the Right to Keep & Bear Arms (CCRKBA)
12500 NE 10th Pl Bellevue WA 98005 425-454-4911 451-3959
TF: 800-426-4302 ■ *Web:* www.ccrkba.org

Citizens for Tax Justice (CTJ) 1616 P St NW Suite 200-B Washington DC 20036 202-299-1066 299-1065
TF: 888-626-2622 ■ *Web:* www.ctj.org

Clinton Presidential Foundation 55 W 125th St New York NY 10027 212-348-8882 348-9245
Web: www.clintonpresidentialcenter.org

Close Up Foundation Inc 44 Canal Ctr Plaza Alexandria VA 22314 703-706-3300 706-0000
TF: 800-256-7387 ■ *Web:* www.closeup.org

Coalition to Stop Gun Violence
1023 15th St NW Suite 301 Washington DC 20005 202-408-0061 408-0062
Web: www.csgv.org

Committee of Concerned Scientists 145 W 79th St Suite 4D New York NY 10024 212-362-4441 441-1759*
**Fax Area Code:* 917 ■ *Web:* www.libertynet.org/ccs

Common Cause 1133 19th St NW 9th Fl Washington DC 20036 202-833-1200 659-3716
TF: 800-926-1064 ■ *Web:* www.commoncause.org

Community Associations Institute
225 Reinekers Ln Suite 300 Alexandria VA 22314 703-548-8600 684-1581
Web: www.caionline.org

				Phone	Fax
Concord Coalition 1011 Arlington Blvd Suite 300	Arlington	VA	22209	703-894-6222	894-6231
TF: 888-333-4248 ■ *Web:* www.concordcoalition.org					
Congress Watch 215 Pennsylvania Ave SE 3rd Fl	Washington	DC	20003	202-546-4996	547-7392
TF: 800-289-3787 ■ *Web:* www.citizen.org/congress					
Constitutional Rights Foundation 601 S Kingsley Dr	Los Angeles	CA	90005	213-487-5590	386-0459
TF: 800-488-4273 ■ *Web:* www.crf-usa.org					
Consumers for World Trade 1707 L St NW Suite 570	Washington	DC	20036	202-293-2944	293-0495
Web: www.cwt.org					
Council on American-Islamic Relations (CAIR) 453 New Jersey Ave SE	Washington	DC	20003	202-488-8787	488-0833
Council of the Americas 680 Park Ave	New York	NY	10065	212-628-3200	249-5868
TF: 800-733-2342					
Council of Canadians 170 Laurier Ave W Suite 700	Ottawa	ON	K1P5V5	613-233-2773	233-6776
TF: 800-387-7177 ■ *Web:* www.canadians.org					
Democracy 21 1875 'I' St NW Suite 500	Washington	DC	20006	202-429-2008	429-9574
Web: democracy21.org					
Democratic Congressional Campaign Committee (DCCC) 430 S Capitol St SE	Washington	DC	20003	202-863-1500	485-3536
Web: www.dccc.org					
Democratic Governors Assn (DGA) 1401 K St NW Suite 200	Washington	DC	20005	202-772-5600	772-5602
Web: www.democraticgovernors.org					
Democratic Senatorial Campaign Committee (DSCC) 120 Maryland Ave NE	Washington	DC	20002	202-224-2447	969-0354
Web: www.dscc.org					
Do Something 24-32 Union Sq E 4th Fl S	New York	NY	10003	212-254-2390	254-2391
Web: www.dosomething.org					
DSCC (Democratic Senatorial Campaign Committee) 120 Maryland Ave NE	Washington	DC	20002	202-224-2447	969-0354
Web: www.dscc.org					
EMILY's List 1120 Connecticut Ave NW Suite 1100	Washington	DC	20036	202-326-1400	326-1415
TF: 800-683-6459 ■ *Web:* www.emilyslist.org					
Evangelicals for Social Action (ESA) 10 E Lancaster Ave	Wynnewood	PA	19096	610-645-9390	649-8090
TF: 800-650-6600 ■ *Web:* www.esa-online.org					
Families USA 1201 New York Ave NW Suite 1100	Washington	DC	20005	202-628-3030	347-2417
TF: 800-593-5041 ■ *Web:* www.familiesusa.org					
Federation for American Immigration Reform (FAIR) 25 Massachusetts Ave NW Suite 330	Washington	DC	20009	202-328-7004	387-3447
TF: 877-627-3247 ■ *Web:* www.fairus.org					
FM Policy Focus 555 13th St NW	Washington	DC	20004	202-637-8281	637-5910
Web: www.fmpolicyfocus.org					
Foreign Policy Assn (FPA) 470 Park Ave S 2nd Fl	New York	NY	10016	212-481-8100	481-9275
TF: 800-628-5754 ■ *Web:* www.fpa.org					
Foundation for Moral Law Inc PO Box 231264	Montgomery	AL	36123	334-262-1245	262-1708
TF: 866-317-0800 ■ *Web:* www.morallaw.org					
Freedom Forum 1101 Wilson Blvd	Arlington	VA	22209	703-528-0800	284-3770
Web: www.freedomforum.org					
FreedomWorks 601 Pennsylvania Ave NW Suite 700-N	Washington	DC	20004	202-783-3870	942-7649
TF: 888-564-6273 ■ *Web:* www.freedomworks.org					
Girls Nation American Legion Auxiliary 777 N Meridian St 3rd Fl	Indianapolis	IN	46204	317-955-3845	955-3884
Web: www.legion-aux.org					
Global Exchange 2017 Mission St Suite 303	San Francisco	CA	94110	415-255-7296	255-7498
TF: 800-497-1994 ■ *Web:* www.globalexchange.org					
HALT - An Organization of Americans for Legal Reform 1612 K St NW Suite 510	Washington	DC	20006	202-887-8255	887-9699
TF: 888-367-4258 ■ *Web:* www.halt.org					
Interfaith Alliance 1212 New York Ave 7th Fl	Washington	DC	20005	202-238-3300	238-3301
TF: 800-510-0969 ■ *Web:* www.interfaithalliance.org					
International Society of Political Psychology (ISPP) Syracuse Univ Moynihan Institute of Global Affairs 346 Eggers Hall	Syracuse	NY	13244	315-443-4470	443-9085
Web: ispp.org					
Interreligious Foundation for Community Organization (IFCO) 418 W 145th St	New York	NY	10031	212-926-5757	926-5842
Web: www.ifconews.org					
Judicial Watch Inc 501 School St SW	Washington	DC	20024	202-646-5172	646-5199
TF: 888-593-8442 ■ *Web:* www.judicialwatch.org					
Junior Chamber International (JCI) 15645 Olive Blvd	Chesterfield	MO	63017	636-449-3100	449-3107
TF: 800-905-5499 ■ *Web:* www.jci.cc					
Keep America Beautiful Inc 1010 Washington Blvd	Stamford	CT	06901	203-323-8987	325-9199
Web: www.kab.org					
Landmark Volunteers PO Box 455	Sheffield	MA	02157	413-229-0255	229-2050
Web: www.volunteers.com					
League of Conservation Voters 1920 L St NW Suite 800	Washington	DC	20030	202-785-8683	835-0491
Web: www.lcv.org					
League of Women Voters (LWV) 1730 M St NW Suite 1000	Washington	DC	20036	202-429-1965	429-0854
TF: 800-249-8683 ■ *Web:* www.lwv.org					
National Assn of Neighborhoods (NAN) 1300 Pennsylvania Ave NW Suite 700	Washington	DC	20004	202-332-7766	332-2314
Web: www.nanworld.org					
National Assn of Town Watch (NATW) 1 E Wynnewood Rd Suite 102	Wynnewood	PA	19096	610-649-7055	649-5456
TF: 800-648-3688 ■ *Web:* www.nationaltownwatch.org					
National Center for Neighborhood Enterprise (NCNE) 1625 K St Suite 1200	Washington	DC	20006	202-518-6500	588-0314
TF: 866-518-1263 ■ *Web:* www.cneonline.org					
National Civic League (NCL) 1445 Market St Suite 300	Denver	CO	80202	303-571-4343	571-4404
Web: www.ncl.org					
National Coalition on Black Civic Participation Inc (NCBCP) 1900 L St NW Suite 700	Washington	DC	20036	202-659-4929	659-5025
Web: www.bigvote.org					
National Committee to Preserve Social Security & Medicare (NCPSSM) 10 G St NE Suite 600	Washington	DC	20002	202-216-0420	216-0451
TF: 800-966-1935 ■ *Web:* www.ncpssm.org					
National Community Action Foundation (NCAF) 810 1st St NE Suite 530	Washington	DC	20002	202-842-2092	842-2095
Web: www.ncaf.org					
National Conference of Black Mayors (NCBM) 1151 Cleveland Ave Suite D	East Point	GA	30344	404-765-6444	765-6430
Web: www.blackmayors.org					
National Council on Public History (NCPH) 425 University Blvd 327 Cavanaugh Hall	Indianapolis	IN	46202	317-274-2716	278-5230
Web: www.ncph.org					
National Council of Women of the US Inc (NCW) 777 UN Plaza	New York	NY	10017	212-697-1278	972-0164
Web: www.ncw-us.org					
National Endowment for Democracy (NED) 1025 F St NW Suite 800	Washington	DC	20004	202-378-9700	
Web: www.ned.org					
National Federation of Democratic Women (NFDW) PO Box 72	Bastrop	LA	71221	318-281-2356	281-2736
Web: www.nfdw.com					
National Federation of Republican Women (NFRW) 124 N Alfred St	Alexandria	VA	22314	703-548-9688	548-9836
Web: www.nfrw.org					
National Taxpayers Union (NTU) 108 N Alfred St	Alexandria	VA	22314	703-683-5700	683-5722
TF: 800-829-4258 ■ *Web:* www.ntu.org					
National Women's Political Caucus (NWPC) PO Box 50476	Washington	DC	20091	202-785-1100	370-6306
Web: www.nwpc.org					
Native American Community Board (NACB) PO Box 572	Lake Andes	SD	57356	605-487-7072	487-7964
Web: www.nativeshop.org					
OMB Watch 1742 Connecticut Ave NW	Washington	DC	20009	202-234-8494	234-8584
Web: www.ombwatch.org					
Organization of American States (OAS) 1889 F St NW	Washington	DC	20006	202-458-3000	458-3967
Web: www.oas.org					
People for the American Way (PFAW) 2000 M St NW Suite 400	Washington	DC	20036	202-467-4999	293-2672
TF: 800-326-7329 ■ *Web:* www.pfaw.org					
Population-Environment Balance Inc 2000 P St NW Suite 600	Washington	DC	20036	202-955-5700	955-6161
TF: 800-866-6269 ■ *Web:* www.balance.org					
Population Reference Bureau (PRB) 1875 Connecticut Ave NW Suite 520	Washington	DC	20009	202-483-1100	328-3937
TF: 800-877-9881 ■ *Web:* www.prb.org					
Preservation Action 401 F Street NW Suite 324	Washington	DC	20001	202-637-7873	637-6874
Web: www.preservationaction.org					
Project Vote 2101 S Main St	Little Rock	AR	72206	800-546-8683	376-3952*
**Fax Area Code:* 501 ■ *TF:* 800-546-8683 ■ *Web:* www.projectvote.org					
Project Vote Smart 1 Common Ground	Philipsburg	MT	59858	406-859-8683	859-8680
TF: 888-868-3762 ■ *Web:* votesmart.org					
Public Affairs Council (PAC) 2033 K St NW Suite 700	Washington	DC	20006	202-872-1790	835-8343
Web: www.pac.org					
Public Citizen 1600 20th St NW	Washington	DC	20009	202-588-1000	588-7796
Web: www.citizen.org					
Public Forum Institute 2300 M St NW Suite 900	Washington	DC	20037	202-467-2774	293-5717
Web: www.publicforuminstitute.org					
Public Service Research Foundation 320-D Maple Ave E	Vienna	VA	22180	703-242-3575	242-3579
Web: www.psrf.org					
Republican Governors Assn (RGA) 1747 Pennsylvania Ave NW Suite 250	Washington	DC	20006	202-662-4140	662-4925
Web: www.rga.org					
Ripon Society 1300 L St NW Suite 900	Washington	DC	20005	202-216-1008	216-0036
Web: www.riponsoc.org					
Rock the Vote (RTV) 10635 Santa Monica Blvd Suite 150	Los Angeles	CA	90025	310-234-0665	234-0666
Web: www.rockthevote.com					
Seniors Against Federal Extravagance (SAFE) 413 Delaware Ave	Wilmington	DE	19803	302-478-0676	
Web: www.s-a-f-e.org					
Sister Cities International (SCI) 1301 Pennsylvania Ave NW Suite 850	Washington	DC	20004	202-347-8630	393-6524
Web: www.sister-cities.org					
US Junior Chamber of Commerce PO Box 7	Tulsa	OK	74102	918-584-2481	584-4422
TF: 800-529-2337 ■ *Web:* www.usjaycees.org					
US Term Limits (USTL) 9900 Main St Suite 303	Fairfax	VA	22031	703-383-0907	383-5288
TF: 800-733-6440 ■ *Web:* www.ustl.org					
Violence Policy Center (VPC) 1730 Rhode Island Ave NW Suite 1014	Washington	DC	20036	202-822-8200	
Web: www.vpc.org					
William J Clinton Presidential Foundation 55 W 125th St	New York	NY	10027	212-348-8882	348-9245
Web: www.clintonpresidentialcenter.org					
WISH List 333 N Fairfax St Suite 302	Alexandria	VA	22314	703-778-5550	778-5554
TF: 800-756-9474 ■ *Web:* www.thewishlist.org					
Women's Campaign Fund (WCF) 734 15th St NW Suite 500	Washington	DC	20005	202-393-8164	393-0649
TF: 800-446-8170 ■ *Web:* www.wcfonline.org					
Young America's Foundation 110 Elden St	Herndon	VA	20170	703-318-9608	318-9122
TF: 800-292-9231 ■ *Web:* www.yaf.org					
Young Democrats of America PO Box 77496	Washington	DC	20013	202-639-8585	318-3221
Web: www.yda.org					
Young Republican National Federation Inc (YRNF) 525 G St SE Suite 17	Washington	DC	20003	202-608-1417	
Web: www.yrnf.com					

48-8 Civil & Human Rights Organizations

				Phone	Fax
AAI (Arab American Institute) 1600 K St NW Ste 601	Washington	DC	20006	202-429-9210	429-9214
Web: www.aaiusa.org					
ACLU (American Civil Liberties Union) 125 Broad St 18th Fl	New York	NY	10004	212-549-2500	549-2580
Web: www.aclu.org					
ACT UP 332 Bleecker St Suite G5	New York	NY	10014	212-966-4873	
Web: www.actupny.org					
AIDS Coalition to Unleash Power 332 Bleecker St Suite G5	New York	NY	10014	212-966-4873	
Web: www.actupny.org					
Alliance for Consumer Rights 132 Nassau St Rm 200	New York	NY	10038	212-349-9204	608-2310
Alliance of Guardian Angels 717 5th Ave Suite 401	New York	NY	10022	212-860-5575	223-8180
Web: www.guardianangels.org					
American-Arab Anti Discrimination Committee (ADC) 1732 Wisconsin Ave	Washington	DC	20007	202-244-2990	244-3196
Web: www.adc.org					
American Civil Liberties Union (ACLU) 125 Broad St 18th Fl	New York	NY	10004	212-549-2500	549-2580
Web: www.aclu.org					
American Jewish Committee (AJC) 165 E 56th St	New York	NY	10022	212-751-4000	750-0326
Web: www.ajc.org					
American Society of Access Professionals (ASAP) 1444 'I' St NW Suite 700	Washington	DC	20005	202-712-9054	216-9646
Web: www.accesspro.org					
Americans for Effective Law Enforcement (AELE) 841 W Touhy Ave	Park Ridge	IL	60068	847-685-0700	685-9700
TF: 800-763-2802 ■ *Web:* www.aele.org					
Americans for Tax Reform (ATR) 1920 L St NW Suite 200	Washington	DC	20036	202-785-0266	785-0261
Web: www.atr.org					
Amnesty International USA (AIUSA) 5 Penn Plaza 14th Fl	New York	NY	10001	212-807-8400	627-1451
TF: 800-266-3789 ■ *Web:* www.amnestyusa.org					
Anti-Defamation League (ADL) 605 3rd Ave	New York	NY	10158	212-885-7700	867-0779
Web: www.adl.org					
Arab American Institute (AAI) 1600 K St NW Ste 601	Washington	DC	20006	202-429-9210	429-9214
Web: www.aaiusa.org					
Asian American Legal Defense & Education Fund (AALDEF) 99 Hudson St 12th Fl	New York	NY	10013	212-966-5932	966-4303
TF: 800-966-5946 ■ *Web:* www.aaldef.org					
Association for Women's Rights in Development (AWID) 215 Spadina Ave Suite 150	Toronto	ON	M5T2C7	416-594-3773	594-0330
Web: www.awid.org					
Becket Fund for Religious Liberty 1350 Connecticut Ave NW Suite 605	Washington	DC	20036	202-955-0095	955-0090
TF: 800-232-5385 ■ *Web:* www.becketfund.org					
Center for Democratic Renewal PO Box 50469	Atlanta	GA	30302	404-221-0025	221-0045
Web: www.thecdr.org					
Center for Economic & Social Rights (CESR) 162 Montague St 2nd Fl	Brooklyn	NY	11201	718-237-9145	237-9147
Web: www.cesr.org					
Center for Individual Rights (CIR) 1233 20th St NW Suite 300	Washington	DC	20036	202-833-8400	833-8410
TF: 877-426-2665 ■ *Web:* www.cir-usa.org					

Civil & Human Rights Organizations (Cont'd)

Phone | Fax

Center for Reproductive Rights 120 Wall St 14th Fl............New York NY 10005 917-637-3600 637-3666
TF: 800-786-9711 ■ *Web:* www.crlp.org

Children's Rights Council (CRC)
6200 Editors Park Dr Suite 103.......................... Hyattsville MD 20782 301-559-3120 559-3124
TF: 800-787-5437 ■ *Web:* www.gocrc.com

Congress of Racial Equality (CORE) 817 Broadway 3rd Fl........New York NY 10003 212-598-4000 529-3568
Web: www.core-online.org

Corporate Accountability International 46 Plympton St...........Boston MA 02118 617-695-2525 695-2626
TF: 800-688-8797 ■ *Web:* www.stopcorporateabuse.org/cms/index.cfm?group_id=1000

Crime Stoppers International PO Box 614...................Arlington TX 76004 817-451-9229 446-1576
TF: 800-245-0009 ■ *Web:* www.c-s-i.org

Cultural Survival Inc 215 Prospect St.....................Cambridge MA 02139 617-441-5400 441-5417
Web: www.cs.org

Digital Freedom Network (DFN) 520 Broad St 3rd FL.............Newark NJ 07102 973-438-7345 969-9900*
*Fax Area Code: 202 ■ *Web:* www.dfn.org

Disability Rights Center Inc 18 Low Ave.......................Concord NH 03301 603-228-0432 225-2077
TF: 800-834-1721 ■ *Web:* www.drcnh.org

Drug Policy Alliance 70 W 36th St 16th Fl..................New York NY 10018 212-613-8020 613-8021
Web: www.drugpolicy.org

Ethics Resource Center 2345 Crystal Dr Suite 201.............Arlington VA 22202 703-647-2185 647-2180
Web: www.ethics.org

Facing History & Ourselves National Foundation Inc
16 Hurd Rd..Brookline MA 02445 617-232-1595 232-0281
TF: 800-856-9039 ■ *Web:* www.facing.org

Families Against Mandatory Minimums (FAMM)
1612 K St NW Suite 700...............................Washington DC 20006 202-822-6700 822-6704
Web: www.famm.org

Gay & Lesbian Alliance Against Defamation (GLAAD)
104 W 29th St 4th Fl.....................................New York NY 10001 212-629-3322 629-3225
Web: www.glaad.org

Grandparents Rights Organization (GRO)
100 W Long Lake Rd Suite 250......................Bloomfield Hills MI 48304 248-646-7177 646-9722
Web: www.grandparentsrights.org

Human Rights Campaign 1640 Rhode Island Ave NW..........Washington DC 20036 202-628-4160 347-5323
TF: 800-777-4723 ■ *Web:* www.hrc.org

Human Rights Watch 350 5th Ave 34th Fl.....................New York NY 10118 212-290-4700 736-1300
Web: www.hrw.org

Institute for Health Freedom 1875 'I' St NW Suite 500........Washington DC 20006 202-429-6610 861-1973
TF: 888-616-1976 ■ *Web:* www.forhealthfreedom.org

Integrative Strategies Forum (ISF)
11426 Rockville Pike Suite 306........................... Rockville MD 20852 301-770-6375 770-6377
Web: www.isforum.org

International Gay & Lesbian Human Rights Commission (IGLHRC) 80 Maiden Ln Suite 1505..................New York NY 10038 212-268-8040 430-6060
Web: www.iglhrc.org

International Organization for Migration
1752 'N' St NW Suite 700.............................Washington DC 20036 202-862-1826 862-1879
Web: www.iom.int

International Task Force on Euthanasia & Assisted Suicide
PO Box 760...Steubenville OH 43952 740-282-3810 282-0769
TF: 800-958-5678 ■ *Web:* www.internationaltaskforce.org

Joint Custody Assn (JCA) 10606 Wilkins Ave................Los Angeles CA 90024 310-475-5352 475-6541

King Center The 449 Auburn Ave NE...........................Atlanta GA 30312 404-524-1956 526-8969
Web: www.thekingcenter.org

Lambda Legal Defense & Education Fund
120 Wall St Suite 1500.................................New York NY 10005 212-809-8585 809-0055
Web: www.lambdalegal.org

Leadership Conference on Civil Rights (LCCR)
1629 K St NW Suite 1000.............................Washington DC 20006 202-466-3311 466-3435
Web: www.civilrights.org/lccr/index.html

Legal Counsel for the Elderly 601 'E' St NW Bldg A 4th Fl.....Washington DC 20049 202-434-2170 434-6464
Web: www.aarp.org/aarp/lce/

Media Watch PO Box 618.................................Santa Cruz CA 95061 831-423-6355
TF: 800-631-6355 ■ *Web:* www.mediawatch.com

Medicare Rights Center (MRC) 520 8th Ave N Wing 3rd Fl.......New York NY 10018 212-869-3850 869-3532
TF hotline: 800-333-4114 ■ *Web:* www.medicarerights.org

Migrant Legal Action Program (MLAP)
1001 Connecticut Ave NW Suite 915.....................Washington DC 20036 202-775-7780 775-7784
Web: www.mlap.org

NAACP (National Assn for the Advancement of Colored People)
4805 Mount Hope Dr.....................................Baltimore MD 21215 410-358-8900 486-9255
TF: 877-622-2798 ■ *Web:* www.naacp.org

NARAL Pro-Choice America (NARAL)
1156 15th St NW Suite 700.............................Washington DC 20005 202-973-3000 973-3096
Web: www.naral.org

National Abortion Federation (NAF)
1660 L St NW Suite 450................................Washington DC 20036 202-667-5881 667-5890
TF: 800-772-9100 ■ *Web:* www.prochoice.org

National Assn to Advance Fat Acceptance (NAAFA)
PO Box 22510.. Oakland CA 94609 916-558-6880 558-6881
Web: www.naafa.org

National Assn for the Advancement of Colored People (NAACP)
4805 Mount Hope Dr.....................................Baltimore MD 21215 410-358-8900 486-9255
TF: 877-622-2798 ■ *Web:* www.naacp.org

National Center for Juvenile Justice (NCJJ)
3700 S Water St Suite 200............................. Pittsburgh PA 15203 412-227-6950 227-6955
TF: 800-577-6903 ■ *Web:* www.ncjj.org

National Center for Victims of Crime (NCVC)
2000 M St NW Suite 480................................Washington DC 20036 202-467-8700 467-8701
TF: 800-394-2255 ■ *Web:* www.ncvc.org

National Coalition to Abolish the Death Penalty (NCADP)
1705 DeSales St NW 5th Fl............................Washington DC 20033 202-331-4090 331-4099
TF: 888-286-2237 ■ *Web:* www.ncadp.org

National Coalition Against Censorship (NCAC)
275 7th Ave 9th Fl.......................................New York NY 10001 212-807-6222 807-6245
Web: www.ncac.org

National Coalition Against Domestic Violence (NCADV)
1201 E Colfax Ave Suite 385..............................Denver CO 80218 303-839-1852 831-9251
TF: 800-799-7233 ■ *Web:* www.ncadv.org

National Conference on Citizenship (NCOC)
1828 L St NW 11th Fl..................................Washington DC 20036 202-467-8833 467-8900
Web: www.ncoc.net

National Consumer Law Center (NCLC) 77 Summer St 10th Fl.......Boston MA 02110 617-542-8010 542-8028
Web: www.consumerlaw.org

National Council on Crime & Delinquency (NCCD)
1970 Broadway Suite 500.................................Oakland CA 94612 510-208-0500 208-0511
Web: www.nccd-crc.org

National Court Appointed Special Advocate Assn (CASA)
100 W Harrison St North Tower Suite 500..................Seattle WA 98119 206-270-0072 270-0078
TF: 800-628-3233 ■ *Web:* www.nationalcasa.org

National Crime Prevention Council (NCPC)
2345 Crystal Dr Suite 500...............................Arlington VA 22202 202-466-6272 296-1356
Web: www.ncpc.org

Phone | Fax

National Freedom of Information Coalition
Univ of Missouri 133 Neff Annex..........................Columbia MO 65211 573-882-4856 884-6204
Web: foi.missouri.edu

National Gay & Lesbian Task Force (NGLTF)
1325 Massachusetts Ave NW Suite 600..................Washington DC 20005 202-393-5177 393-2241
Web: www.thetaskforce.org

National Immigration Forum 50 F St NW Suite 300...........Washington DC 20001 202-347-0040 347-0058
Web: www.immigrationforum.org

National Organization for the Reform of Marijuana Laws (NORML) 1600 K St NW Suite 501...................Washington DC 20006 202-483-5500 483-0057
TF: 888-676-6765 ■ *Web:* www.norml.org

National Organization for Victim Assistance (NOVA)
510 King St Suite 424..................................... Alexandria VA 22314 703-535-6682 535-5500
TF: 800-879-6682 ■ *Web:* www.trynova.org

National Right to Life Committee Inc (NRLC)
512 10th St NW...Washington DC 20004 202-626-8800 737-9189
Web: www.nrlc.org

National Urban League Inc 120 Wall St 8th Fl..................New York NY 10005 212-558-5300 344-5332
Web: www.nul.org

NCAC (National Coalition Against Censorship)
275 7th Ave 9th Fl.......................................New York NY 10001 212-807-6222 807-6245
Web: www.ncac.org

No Peace Without Justice (NPWJ) 866 UN Plaza Suite 408.......New York NY 10017 212-980-2558 980-1072
Web: www.npwj.org

NORML (National Organization for the Reform of Marijuana Laws) 1600 K St NW Suite 501.........................Washington DC 20006 202-483-5500 483-0057
TF: 888-676-6765 ■ *Web:* www.norml.org

Nuclear Information & Resource Service (NIRS)
6930 Carroll Ave Suite 340...........................Takoma Park MD 20919 301-270-6477 270-4291
Web: www.nirs.org

Osborne Assn 36-31 38th St.......................... Long Island City NY 11101 718-707-2600 707-3103
Web: www.osborneny.org

Parents Families & Friends of Lesbians & Gays (PFLAG)
1726 M St NW Suite 400...............................Washington DC 20036 202-467-8180 467-8194
Web: www.pflag.org

PEN American Center 588 Broadway.........................New York NY 10012 212-334-1660 334-2181
Web: www.pen.org

Prison Fellowship Ministries (PF) PO Box 1550................Merrifield VA 22116 703-478-0100 478-2709
TF: 877-498-0100 ■ *Web:* www.pfm.org

Pro-Life Action League 6160 N Cicero Ave Suite 600............ Chicago IL 60646 773-777-2900 777-3061
Web: www.prolifeaction.org

Project Equality Inc 7132 Main St.........................Kansas City MO 64114 816-361-9222 361-8997
Web: www.projectequality.org

Rutherford Institute PO Box 7482.................... Charlottesville VA 22906 434-978-3888 978-1789
TF: 800-225-1791 ■ *Web:* www.rutherford.org

Second Amendment Foundation 12500 NE 10th Pl...............Bellevue WA 98005 425-454-7012 451-3959
TF: 800-426-4302 ■ *Web:* www.saf.org

Sentencing Project 514 10th St NW Suite 1000..............Washington DC 20004 202-628-0871 628-1091
Web: www.sentencingproject.org

Simon Wiesenthal Center 9786 W Pico Blvd..................Los Angeles CA 90035 310-553-9036 772-7655
TF: 800-900-9036 ■ *Web:* www.wiesenthal.com

Southern Poverty Law Center (SPLC) 400 Washington Ave..... Montgomery AL 36104 334-956-8200 956-8483
Web: www.splcenter.org

Thomas Jefferson Center for the Protection of Free Expression 400 Worrell Dr........................... Charlottesville VA 22911 434-295-4784 296-3621
Web: www.tjcenter.org

Urban Land Institute (ULI)
1025 Thomas Jefferson St NW Suite 500W..............Washington DC 20007 202-624-7000 624-7140
TF Orders: 800-321-5011 ■ *Web:* www.uli.org

US Privacy Council PO Box 302............................Cabin John MD 20818 301-229-7002 229-8011

WeTip Inc PO Box 1296...........................Rancho Cucamonga CA 91729 909-987-5005 987-2477
TF: 800-782-7463 ■ *Web:* www.wetip.com

Wiesenthal Simon Center 9786 W Pico Blvd..................Los Angeles CA 90035 310-553-9036 772-7655
TF: 800-900-9036 ■ *Web:* www.wiesenthal.com

48-9 Computer & Internet Organizations

Phone | Fax

1394 Trade Assn 1111 S Main St.............................Grapevine TX 76051 817-416-2200 410-5757
Web: www.1394ta.org

ACM (Association for Computing Machinery)
2 Penn Plaza Suite 701...................................New York NY 10121 212-626-0500 944-1318
TF: 800-342-6626 ■ *Web:* www.acm.org

Advanced Network & Services Inc
200 South Rd Suite 44-193............................Poughkeepsie NY 12601 845-795-2090 795-2180
Web: www.advanced.org

AFCOM 742 E Chapman Ave.....................................Orange CA 92866 714-997-7966 997-9743
Web: www.afcom.com

Alliance for Public Technology (APT)
919 18th St NW 10th Fl...............................Washington DC 20006 202-263-2970 263-2960
Web: apt.org

American Assn for Artificial Intelligence (AAAI)
445 Burgess Dr Suite 100............................. Menlo Park CA 94025 650-328-3123 321-4457
Web: www.aaai.org

American Registry for Internet Numbers (ARIN)
3635 Concorde Pkwy Suite 200...........................Chantilly VA 20151 703-227-9840 227-0676
Web: www.arin.net

American Society for Information Science & Technology (ASIS&T) 1320 Fenwick Ln Suite 510............... Silver Spring MD 20910 301-495-0900 495-0810
Web: www.asis.org

Apache Software Foundation (ASF) 1901 Munsey Dr........... Forest Hill MD 21050 410-420-0140 803-2258
Web: www.apache.org

Association for Computing Machinery (ACM)
2 Penn Plaza Suite 701...................................New York NY 10121 212-626-0500 944-1318
TF: 800-342-6626 ■ *Web:* www.acm.org

Association of Service & Computer Dealers International (ASCDI) 131 NW 1st Ave Suite 206..................... Delray Beach FL 33444 561-266-9016 266-9017
Web: www.ascdi.com

Association of Shareware Professionals (ASP)
PO Box 1522.. Martinsville IN 46151 765-349-4740 349-4744
Web: www.asp-shareware.org

Association of Support Professionals 122 Barnard Ave......... Watertown MA 02472 617-924-3944 924-7288
Web: www.asponline.com

Association for Women in Computing (AWC)
41 Sutter St Suite 1006............................ San Francisco CA 94104 415-905-4663
Web: www.awc-hq.org

Black Data Processing Associates (BDPA)
6301 Ivy Ln Suite 700....................................Greenbelt MD 20770 301-220-2180 220-2185
TF: 800-727-2372 ■ *Web:* www.bdpa.org

Business Software Alliance (BSA)
1150 18th St NW Suite 700............................Washington DC 20036 202-872-5500 872-5501
TF: 888-667-4722 ■ *Web:* www.bsa.org

CALICO (Computer Assisted Language Instruction Consortium)
601 University Dr 214 Centennial Hall.................... San Marcos TX 78666 512-245-2360 245-8298
Web: www.calico.org

Phone Fax

CANARIE 110 O'Connor St 4th Fl. Ottawa ON K1P5M9 613-943-5454 943-5443
Web: www.canarie.ca

Coalition for Networked Information
21 Dupont Cir NW Euram Bldg Suite 800 Washington DC 20036 202-296-5098 872-0884
Web: www.cni.org

CommerceNet 510 Logue Ave Mountain View CA 94043 650-962-2600 962-2601
TF: 888-255-1900 ■ *Web:* www.commerce.net

CompTIA (Computing Technology Industry Assn)
1815 S Meyers Rd Suite 300 Oakbrook Terrace IL 60181 630-678-8300 678-8384
Web: www.comptia.org

Computer Assisted Language Instruction Consortium (CALICO)
601 University Dr 214 Centennial Hall San Marcos TX 78666 512-245-2360 245-8298
Web: www.calico.org

Computer Law Assn (CLA) 3028 Javier Rd Suite 402 Fairfax VA 22031 703-560-7747 207-7028
Web: www.cla.org

Computer Measurement Group (CMG)
151 Fries Mill Rd Suite 104 Turnersville NJ 08012 856-401-1700 401-1708
TF: 800-436-7264 ■ *Web:* www.cmg.org

Computer Professionals for Social Responsibility (CPSR)
PO Box 717 Palo Alto CA 94302 650-322-3778 322-4748
Web: www.cpsr.org

Computer Security Institute (CSI) 600 Harrison St 6th Fl San Francisco CA 94107 415-947-6000 905-2218
Web: www.gocsi.com

Computing Research Assn 1100 17th St NW Suite 507 Washington DC 20036 202-234-2111 667-1066
Web: www.cra.org

Computing Technology Industry Assn (CompTIA)
1815 S Meyers Rd Suite 300 Oakbrook Terrace IL 60181 630-678-8300 678-8384
Web: www.comptia.org

Consortium for School Networking (CoSN)
1025 Vermont Ave NW Suite 1010 Washington DC 20005 202-861-2676 393-2011
TF: 866-267-8747 ■ *Web:* www.cosn.org

Corporation for National Research Initiatives (CNRI)
1895 Preston White Dr Suite 100 Reston VA 20191 703-620-8990 620-0913
Web: www.cnri.reston.va.us

Data Interchange Standards Assn (DISA)
7600 Leesburg Pike Suite 430 Falls Church VA 22043 703-970-4480 970-4488
Web: www.disa.org

Document Management Industries Assn (DMIA)
433 E Monroe Ave Alexandria VA 22301 703-836-6232 836-2241
TF: 800-336-4641 ■ *Web:* www.dmia.org

DSL Forum 39355 California St Suite 307 Fremont CA 94538 510-608-5905 608-5917
Web: www.dslforum.org

EDUCAUSE 1150 18th St NW Suite 1010 Washington DC 20036 202-872-4200 872-4318
Web: www.educause.edu

Electronic Frontier Foundation Inc (EFF) 454 Shotwell St San Francisco CA 94110 415-436-9333 436-9993
Web: www.eff.org

Electronic Privacy Information Center (EPIC)
1718 Connecticut Ave NW Suite 200 Washington DC 20009 202-483-1140 483-1248
Web: epic.org

Encompass 401 N Michigan Ave 22nd Fl Chicago IL 60611 312-321-5151 673-4609
TF: 877-354-9887 ■ *Web:* www.encompassus.org

Entertainment Software Assn (ESA)
575 7th St NW Suite 300 Washington DC 20004 202-223-2400 223-2401
Web: www.theesa.com

ESA (Entertainment Software Assn)
575 7th St NW Suite 300 Washington DC 20004 202-223-2400 223-2401
Web: www.theesa.com

ICANN (Internet Corp for Assigned Names & Numbers)
4676 Admiralty Way Suite 330 Marina del Rey CA 90292 310-823-9358 823-8649
Web: www.icann.org

IEEE Computer Society IEEE Operations Ctr 445 Hoes Ln Piscataway NJ 08854 732-981-0060 981-1721
Web: www.computer.org

Independent Computer Consultants Assn (ICCA)
11131 S Towne Sq Suite F Saint Louis MO 63123 314-892-1675 487-1345
TF: 800-774-4222 ■ *Web:* www.icca.org

Information Systems Audit & Control Assn (ISACA)
3701 Algonquin Rd Suite 1010 Rolling Meadows IL 60008 847-253-1545 253-1443
Web: www.isaca.org

Information Technology Assn of America (ITAA)
1401 Wilson Blvd Suite 1100 Arlington VA 22209 703-522-5055 525-2279
Web: www.itaa.org

Information Technology Industry Council (ITI)
1250 'I' St NW Suite 200 Washington DC 20005 202-737-8888 638-4922
Web: www.itic.org

Institute for Certification of Computing Professionals (ICCP)
2350 E Devon Ave Suite 115 Des Plaines IL 60018 847-299-4227 299-4280
TF: 800-843-8227 ■ *Web:* www.iccp.org

Institute for Women & Technology (IWT)
1501 Page Mill Rd MS 1105 Palo Alto CA 94304 650-236-4756 852-8172
Web: www.iwt.org

Interex PO Box 3439 Sunnyvale CA 94088 408-747-0227 747-0947
TF: 800-468-3739

International Academy of Digital Arts & Sciences
3515 24th St San Francisco CA 94110 415-824-2268 826-9111
Web: www.iadas.net

International Assn for Computer Systems Security
6 Swarthmore Ln Dix Hills NY 11746 631-499-1616 462-9178
Web: www.iacss.com

International Disk Drive Equipment & Materials Assn (IDEMA)
470 Lakeside Dr Suite A Sunnyvale CA 94085 408-991-9430 991-9434
Web: www.idema.org

International Tandem Users' Group (ITUG) 401 N Michigan Chicago IL 60611 312-321-6851 321-5158
TF: 800-845-4884 ■ *Web:* www.itug.org

International Webmasters Assn (IWA) 119 E Union St Suite F Pasadena CA 91103 626-449-3709 449-8308
Web: www.iwanet.org

Internet Assigned Numbers Authority (IANA)
4676 Admiralty Way Suite 330 Marina del Rey CA 90292 310-823-9358 823-8649
Web: www.iana.org

Internet Corp for Assigned Names & Numbers (ICANN)
4676 Admiralty Way Suite 330 Marina del Rey CA 90292 310-823-9358 823-8649
Web: www.icann.org

Internet Engineering Task Force (IETF)
1895 Preston White Dr Suite 100 Reston VA 20191 703-620-8990 620-0913
Web: www.ietf.cnri.reston.va.us

Internet Scambusters 197 New Market Ctr Suite 115 Boone NC 28607 828-262-5885
Web: www.scambusters.com

Internet Society (ISOC) 1775 Wiehle Ave Suite 102 Reston VA 20190 703-326-9880 326-9881
Web: www.isoc.org

Internet2 3025 Boardwalk Suite 200 Ann Arbor MI 48108 734-913-4250 913-4255
Web: www.internet2.edu

IWA (International Webmasters Assn) 119 E Union St Suite F Pasadena CA 91103 626-449-3709 449-8308
Web: www.iwanet.org

Mozilla Foundation 1350 Villa St Suite C Mountain View CA 94041 650-903-0800 903-0875
TF Tech Supp: 888-586-4539 ■ *Web:* www.mozilla.org

National Assn of Computer Consultant Businesses (NACCB)
1800 Diagonal Rd Suite 520 Alexandria VA 22314 703-838-2050 838-3610
Web: www.naccb.org

National Urban Technology Center 80 Maiden Ln Suite 606 New York NY 10038 212-528-7350 528-7355
TF: 800-998-3212 ■ *Web:* www.urbantech.org

Network & Systems Professionals Assn Inc (NaSPA)
7044 S 13th St Oak Creek WI 53154 414-768-8000 768-8001
Web: www.naspa.com

Object Management Group (OMG) 250 1st Ave Suite 100 Needham MA 02494 781-444-0404 444-0320
Web: www.omg.org

Online Privacy Alliance (OPA)
c/o Hogan & Hartson LLP 555 13th St NW Washington DC 20004 202-637-5600 637-5710
Web: www.privacyalliance.org

Open Applications Group Inc (OAGi) PO Box 4897 Marietta GA 30061 678-715-7588 234-6036*
**Fax Area Code: 770* ■ *Web:* www.openapplications.org

Open Group 44 Montgomery St Suite 960 San Francisco CA 94104 415-374-8280 374-8293
Web: www.opengroup.org

Personal Computer Memory Card International Assn (PCMCIA)
2635 N 1st St Suite 218 San Jose CA 95134 408-433-2273 433-9558
Web: www.pcmcia.org

Portable Computer & Communications Assn (PCCA)
PO Box 680 Hood River OR 97031 541-490-5140
Web: www.pcca.org

Society for Information Display (SID) 610 S 2nd St San Jose CA 95112 408-977-1013 977-1531
Web: www.sid.org

Society for Information Management (SIM)
401 N Michigan Ave Suite 2400 Chicago IL 60611 312-527-6734 644-6363
Web: www.simnet.org

Society for Modeling & Simulation International (SCS)
4838 Ronson Ct Suite L PO Box 17900 San Diego CA 92111 858-277-3888 277-3930
Web: www.scs.org

Software & Information Industry Assn (SIIA)
1090 Vermont Ave NW 6th Fl Washington DC 20005 202-289-7442 289-7097
Web: www.siia.net

Software Productivity Consortium
2214 Rock Hill Rd Suite 1 SPC Bldg Herndon VA 20170 703-742-8877 742-7200
Web: www.software.org

Software in the Public Interest Inc PO Box 502761 Indianapolis IN 46250 317-578-8882 578-8920
Web: www.spi-inc.org

TechNet 2600 E Bayshore Rd 1st Fl Palo Alto CA 94303 650-213-1160 213-9059
Web: www.technet.org

TeleManagement Forum
240 Headquarters Plaza N East Tower 10th Fl Morristown NJ 07960 973-944-5100 944-5110
Web: www.tmforum.org

Transaction Processing Performance Council (TPC)
PO Box 29920 San Francisco CA 94129 415-561-6272 561-6120
Web: www.tpc.org

TRUSTe 685 Market St Suite 560 San Francisco CA 94105 415-618-3400 618-3420
Web: www.truste.org

UCAID (University Consortium for Advanced Internet Development) 3025 Boardwalk Suite 200 Ann Arbor MI 48108 734-913-4250 913-4255
Web: www.internet2.edu

UniForum Assn PO Box 3177 Annapolis MD 21043 410-715-9500 465-0207*
**Fax Area Code: 240* ■ *TF:* 800-333-8649 ■ *Web:* www.uniforum.org

University Consortium for Advanced Internet Development (UCAID) 3025 Boardwalk Suite 200 Ann Arbor MI 48108 734-913-4250 913-4255
Web: www.internet2.edu

Urban & Regional Information Systems Assn (URISA)
1460 Renaissance Dr Suite 305 Park Ridge IL 60068 847-824-6300 824-6363
Web: www.urisa.org

US Internet Industry Assn (USIIA)
5810 Kingstowne Center Dr Suite 120 PMB 212 Alexandria VA 22315 703-924-0006 924-4203
Web: www.usiia.org

USENIX Assn 2560 9th St Suite 215 Berkeley CA 94710 510-528-8649 548-5738
Web: www.usenix.org

Video Electronics Standards Assn 860 Hillview Ct Suite 150 Milpitas CA 95035 408-957-9270 957-9277
Web: www.vesa.org

Webby Awards 3515 24th St San Francisco CA 94110 415-824-2268 707-2015
Web: www.webbyawards.com

World Wide Web Consortium (W3C)
MIT Laboratory for Computer Science 77 Massachusetts Ave Bldg 32 Cambridge MA 02139 617-253-2613 258-5999
Web: www.w3.org

Xplor International 24238 Hawthorne Blvd Torrance CA 90505 310-373-3633 375-4240
TF: 800-669-7567 ■ *Web:* www.xplor.org

48-10 Consumer Interest Organizations

Phone Fax

Accuracy in Media Inc (AIM)
4455 Connecticut Ave NW Suite 330 Washington DC 20008 202-364-4401 364-4098
TF: 800-787-4567 ■ *Web:* www.aim.org

Advocates for Highway & Auto Safety
750 1st St NE Suite 901 Washington DC 20002 202-408-1711 408-1699
TF: 800-659-2247 ■ *Web:* www.saferoads.org

Alliance Against Fraud in Telemarketing & Electronic Commerce (AAFT) 1701 K St NW Suite 1200 Washington DC 20006 202-835-3323 835-0747
Web: www.fraud.org/aaft/aaftinfo.htm

Alliance for Consumer Rights 132 Nassau St Rm 200 New York NY 10038 212-349-9204 608-2310

American Council on Consumer Interests (ACCI)
415 S Duff Ave Suite C Ames IA 50010 515-956-4666 233-3101
Web: consumerinterests.org

American Council on Science & Health (ACSH)
1995 Broadway 2nd Fl New York NY 10023 212-362-7044 362-4919
Web: www.acsh.org

American Homeowners Assn (AHA) 1 Stamford Plaza 9th Fl Stamford CT 06901 203-323-7715 323-4558
TF Cust Svc: 800-470-2242 ■ *Web:* www.ahahome.com

Auriton Solutions 1700 W Hwy 36 Suite 301 Roseville MN 55113 651-631-8000 697-7955
TF: 877-332-8700 ■ *Web:* auriton.org

BBB OnLine 4200 Wilson Blvd Suite 800 Arlington VA 22203 703-247-9370 525-8277
Web: www.bbbonline.org

Call for Action 5272 River Rd Suite 300 Bethesda MD 20816 301-657-8260 657-2914
TF: 800-647-1756 ■ *Web:* www.callforaction.org

Carpet & Rug Institute (CRI) 310 S Holiday Ave Dalton GA 30720 706-278-3176 278-8835
TF: 800-882-8846 ■ *Web:* www.carpet-rug.com

Center for Auto Safety (CAS)
1825 Connecticut Ave NW Suite 330 Washington DC 20009 202-328-7700 387-0140
Web: www.autosafety.org

Center for Science in the Public Interest (CSPI)
1875 Connecticut Ave NW Suite 300 Washington DC 20009 202-332-9110 265-4954
Web: www.cspinet.org

Consumer Federation of America 1620 I St NW Suite 200 Washington DC 20006 202-387-6121 265-7989
Web: www.consumerfed.org

Consumers' Research Council of America
2020 Pennsylvania Ave NW Suite 300A Washington DC 20006 202-835-9698 835-9739
Web: www.consumersresearchcncl.org

Council of Better Business Bureaus (CBBB)
4200 Wilson Blvd Suite 800 Arlington VA 22203 703-276-0100 525-8277
Web: www.bbb.org

Consumer Interest Organizations (Cont'd)

Phone | Fax

Council of Better Business Bureaus Inc Wise Giving Alliance
4200 Wilson Blvd Suite 800 Arlington VA 22203 703-276-0100 525-8277
Web: www.give.org
Drug Information Assn (DIA) 800 Enterprise Rd Suite 200 Horsham PA 19044 215-442-6100 442-6199
Web: www.diahome.org
Essential Information PO Box 19405 Washington DC 20036 202-387-8030 234-5176
Web: www.essential.org
Family Support America 205 W Randolph St Suite 2222 Chicago IL 60606 312-338-0900 338-1522
Funeral Consumers Alliance 33 Patchen Rd South Burlington VT 05403 802-865-8300 865-2626
TF: 800-765-0107 ■ *Web:* www.funerals.org
Funeral Service Consumer Assistance Program
13625 Bishops Dr Brookfield WI 53005 800-662-7666
Green Seal 1001 Connecticut Ave NW Suite 827 Washington DC 20036 202-872-6400 872-4324
Web: www.greenseal.org
Insurance Information Institute (III) 110 William St 24th Fl New York NY 10038 212-346-5500 732-1916
TF: 800-331-9146 ■ *Web:* www.iii.org
International Fabricare Institute (IFI) 14700 Sweitzer Ln Laurel MD 20707 301-622-1900 295-4200*
*Fax Area Code: 240 ■ *TF:* 800-638-2627 ■ *Web:* www.ifi.org
Internet Alliance (IA) 1615 L St NW Suite 1100 Washington DC 20036 202-861-2476
Web: www.internetalliance.org
Internet Fraud Watch
c/o National Fraud Information Ctr 1701 K St NW
Suite 1200 Washington DC 20006 202-835-3323 835-0747
TF: 800-876-7060 ■ *Web:* www.fraud.org/internet/intinfo.htm
Investor Responsibility Research Center (IRRC)
1350 Connecticut Ave NW Suite 1101 Washington DC 20036 202-833-0700 833-3555
Web: www.irrc.org
Myvesta.org Inc PO Box 8587 Gaithersburg MD 20898 301-762-5270
Web: www.myvesta.org
National Assn of Child Care Resource & Referral Agencies (NACCRRA) 3101 Wilson Blvd Suite 350 Arlington VA 22201 703-341-4100 341-4101
TF: 800-424-2246 ■ *Web:* www.naccrra.org
National Center for Employee Ownership (NCEO)
1736 Franklin St 8th Fl Oakland CA 94612 510-208-1300 272-9510
Web: www.nceo.org
National Committee for Quality Assurance (NCQA)
1100 13th St NW Suite 1000 Washington DC 20005 202-955-3500 955-3599
TF: 800-275-7585 ■ *Web:* www.ncqa.org
National Consumer Law Center (NCLC) 77 Summer St 10th Fl Boston MA 02110 617-542-8010 542-8028
Web: www.consumerlaw.org
National Consumers League (NCL)
1701 K St NW Suite 1200 Washington DC 20006 202-835-3323 835-0747
TF: 800-876-7060 ■ *Web:* www.natlconsumersleague.org
National Endowment for Financial Education (NEFE)
5299 DTC Blvd Suite 1300 Greenwood Village CO 80111 303-741-6333 220-0838
Web: www.nefe.org
National Fireworks Assn (NFA) 8224 NW Bradford Ct Kansas City MO 64151 816-505-3589 741-1348
Web: www.nationalfireworks.org
National Foundation for Credit Counseling (NFCC)
801 Roeder Rd Suite 900 Silver Spring MD 20910 301-589-5600 495-5623
TF: 800-388-2227 ■ *Web:* www.nfcc.org
National Fraud Information Center (NFIC)
1701 K St NW Suite 1200 Washington DC 20006 202-835-3323 835-0747
TF: 800-876-7060 ■ *Web:* www.fraud.org
NeighborWorks America 1325 G St NW Suite 800 Washington DC 20005 202-220-2300 376-2600
Web: www.nw.org
Philanthropic Research Inc 4801 Courthouse St Suite 220 Williamsburg VA 23188 757-229-4631 229-8912
TF: 800-784-9378 ■ *Web:* www.guidestar.org
Privacy Rights Clearinghouse 3100 5th Ave Suite B San Diego CA 92103 619-298-3396 298-5681
Web: www.privacyrights.org
Private Citizen Inc PO Box 233 Naperville IL 60566 630-393-1555
TF: 800-288-5865 ■ *Web:* privatecitizen.com
Public Citizen 1600 20th St NW Washington DC 20009 202-588-1000 588-7796
Web: www.citizen.org
Public Citizen Health Research Group 1600 20th St NW Washington DC 20009 202-588-1000 588-7796
Web: www.citizen.org/hrg
SOCAP International 675 N Washington St Suite 200 Alexandria VA 22314 703-519-3700 549-4886
Web: www.socap.org
US Metric Assn Inc (USMA) 10245 Andasol Ave Northridge CA 91325 818-363-5606
Web: lamar.colostate.edu/hillger

48-11 Educational Associations & Organizations

Phone | Fax

A Better Chance 240 W 35th St 9th Fl New York NY 10001 646-346-1310 346-1311
TF: 800-543-7181 ■ *Web:* www.abetterchance.org
AACSB International - Assn to Advance Collegiate Schools of Business (AACSB) 777 S Harbour Island Blvd Suite 750 Tampa FL 33602 813-769-6500 769-6559
Web: www.aacsb.edu
Academy for Educational Development (AED)
1825 Connecticut Ave NW Suite 800 Washington DC 20009 202-884-8000 884-8400
Web: www.aed.org
Academy of Political Science 475 Riverside Dr Suite 1274 New York NY 10115 212-870-2500 870-2202
Advanced Network & Services Inc
200 South Rd Suite 44-193 Poughkeepsie NY 12601 845-795-2090 795-2180
Web: www.advanced.org
AED (Academy for Educational Development)
1825 Connecticut Ave NW Suite 800 Washington DC 20009 202-884-8000 884-8400
Web: www.aed.org
AFS International Inc 71 W 23rd St 17th Fl New York NY 10010 212-807-8686 807-1001
Web: www.afs.org
Alliance for Excellent Education
1201 Connecticut Ave Suite 901 Washington DC 20036 202-828-0828 828-0821
Web: www.all4ed.org
Alliance for International Educational & Cultural Exchange
1776 Massachusetts Ave NW Suite 620 Washington DC 20036 202-293-6141 293-6144
Web: www.alliance-exchange.org
American Academy of Political & Social Science
3814 Walnut St Philadelphia PA 19104 215-746-6500 573-3003
Web: www.aapss.org
American Indian College Fund 8333 Greenwood Blvd Denver CO 80221 303-426-8900 426-1200
TF: 800-776-3863 ■ *Web:* www.collegefund.org
American Institute for Foreign Study (AIFS) 9 W Broad St Stamford CT 06902 203-399-5000 399-5590
TF: 800-727-2437 ■ *Web:* www.aifs.org
American Montessori Society (AMS) 281 Park Ave S 6th Fl New York NY 10010 212-358-1250 358-1256
Web: www.amshq.org
American Philosophical Society (APS) 104 S 5th St Philadelphia PA 19106 215-440-3400 440-3436
Web: www.amphilsoc.org
Americas Society 680 Park Ave New York NY 10021 212-249-8950 249-1880
Web: www.americas-society.org
Archaeological Institute of America (AIA) 656 Beacon St 4th Fl Boston MA 02215 617-353-9361 353-6550
Web: www.archaeological.org

Phone | Fax

Associated Collegiate Press (ACP)
2221 University Ave SE Suite 121 Minneapolis MN 55414 612-625-8335 626-0720
Web: studentpress.journ.umn.edu
Association for Asian Studies (AAS) 1021 E Huron St Ann Arbor MI 48104 734-665-2490 665-3801
Web: www.aasianst.org
Association of Boarding Schools (TABS)
9 SW Pack Sq Suite 201 Asheville NC 28801 828-258-5354 258-6428
Web: www.schools.com
Association for Humanistic Psychology (AHP)
1516 Oak St Suite 320A Alameda CA 94501 510-769-6495 769-6433
Web: ahpweb.org
Association of Jesuit Colleges & Universities (AJCU)
1 Dupont Cir NW Suite 405 Washington DC 20036 202-862-9893 862-8523
Web: www.ajcunet.edu
Association of Writers & Writing Programs (AWP)
George Mason Univ 4400 University Dr Tallwood House
MS 1E3 Fairfax VA 22030 703-993-4301 993-4302
Web: awpwriter.org
Astronomical Society of the Pacific 390 Ashton Ave San Francisco CA 94112 415-337-1100 337-5205
Web: www.astrosociety.org
Bands of America Inc (BOA) 39 W Jackson Pl Suite 150 Indianapolis IN 46225 317-636-2263 524-6200
TF: 800-848-2263 ■ *Web:* www.bands.org
Braille Institute of America Inc 741 N Vermont Ave Los Angeles CA 90029 323-663-1111 663-0867
TF: 800-272-4553 ■ *Web:* www.brailleinstitute.org
Breakthrough Collaborative 40 1st St 5th Fl San Francisco CA 94105 415-442-0600 442-0609
Web: www.breakthroughcollaborative.org
Center for Education Reform 910 17th St NW Suite 1120 Washington DC 20006 202-822-9000 822-5077
TF: 800-521-2118 ■ *Web:* www.edreform.com
Challenger Center for Space Science Education
1250 N Pitt St Alexandria VA 22314 703-683-9740 683-7546
TF: 800-987-8277 ■ *Web:* www.challenger.org
College Board 45 Columbus Ave New York NY 10023 212-713-8000 713-8184*
*Fax: PR ■ *TF:* 800-927-4302 ■ *Web:* www.collegeboard.com
College Parents of America (CPA) 2000 N 14th St Suite 800 Arlington VA 22201 888-761-6702 875-2199*
*Fax Area Code: 703 ■ *TF:* 888-256-4627 ■ *Web:* www.collegeparents.org
Columbia Scholastic Press Assn (CSPA)
Columbia University MC 5711 New York NY 10027 212-854-9400 854-9401
Web: www.columbia.edu/cu/cspa
Committee for Education Funding (CEF)
122 C St NW Suite 280 Washington DC 20001 202-383-0083 383-0097
Web: www.cef.org
Communities in Schools Inc (CIS)
277 S Washington St Suite 210 Alexandria VA 22314 703-519-8999 519-7537
TF: 800-247-4543 ■ *Web:* www.cisnet.org
Council for Opportunity in Education
1025 Vermont Ave NW Suite 900 Washington DC 20005 202-347-7430 347-0786
Web: www.trioprograms.org
DAAD (German Academic Exchange Service)
871 United Nations Plaza 14th Fl New York NY 10017 212-758-3223 755-5780
Web: www.daad.org
Education Development Center Inc (EDC) 55 Chapel St Suite 1 Newton MA 02458 617-969-7100 969-3401
Web: www.edc.org
Education Trust 1250 H St NW Suite 700 Washington DC 20005 202-293-1217 293-2605
Web: www2.edtrust.org/edtrust
Facing History & Ourselves National Foundation Inc
16 Hurd Rd Brookline MA 02445 617-232-1595 232-0281
TF: 800-856-9039 ■ *Web:* www.facing.org
Family Career & Community Leaders of America (FCCLA)
1910 Association Dr Reston VA 20191 703-476-4900 860-2713
TF: 800-234-4425 ■ *Web:* www.fcclainc.org
FBLA (Future Business Leaders of America - Phi Beta Lambda Inc) 1912 Association Dr Reston VA 20191 703-860-3334 758-0749
TF: 800-325-2946 ■ *Web:* www.fbla-pbl.org
FIRST 200 Bedford St Manchester NH 03101 603-666-3906 666-3907
TF: 800-871-8326 ■ *Web:* www.usfirst.org
Foundation Center 79 5th Ave 2nd Fl New York NY 10003 212-620-4230 807-3691
TF: 800-424-9836 ■ *Web:* foundationcenter.org
Future Business Leaders of America - Phi Beta Lambda Inc (FBLA-PBL) 1912 Association Dr Reston VA 20191 703-860-3334 758-0749
TF: 800-325-2946 ■ *Web:* www.fbla-pbl.org
German Academic Exchange Service (DAAD)
871 United Nations Plaza 14th Fl New York NY 10017 212-758-3223 755-5780
Web: www.daad.org
Graduate Management Admission Council (GMAC)
1600 Tyson Blvd Suite 1400 McLean VA 22102 703-749-0131 749-0169
Web: www.gmac.com
Great Books Foundation 35 E Wacker Dr Suite 2300 Chicago IL 60601 312-332-5870 407-0334
TF: 800-222-5870 ■ *Web:* www.greatbooks.org
Health Occupations Students of America (HOSA)
6021 Morriss Rd Suite 111 Flower Mound TX 75028 972-874-0062 874-0063
TF: 800-321-4672 ■ *Web:* www.hosa.org
IDRA (Intercultural Development Research Assn)
5815 Callaghan Rd Suite 101 San Antonio TX 78228 210-444-1710 444-1714
Web: www.idra.org
Institute of Consumer Financial Education PO Box 34070 San Diego CA 92163 619-232-8811 239-1401
Web: www.financial-education-icfe.org
Institute for Education & the Arts
1156 15th St NW Suite 600 Washington DC 20005 202-223-9721 223-4720
Web: www.edartsinstitute.org
Institute of General Semantics (IGS) 2260 College Ave Fort Worth TX 76110 817-922-9950 922-9903
Web: www.generalsemantics.org
Institute of International Education (IIE) 809 UN Plaza New York NY 10017 212-883-8200 984-5452
Web: www.iie.org
Intercollegiate Studies Institute (ISI) 3901 Centerville Rd Wilmington DE 19807 302-652-4600 652-1760
TF: 800-526-7022 ■ *Web:* www.isi.org
Intercultural Development Research Assn (IDRA)
5815 Callaghan Rd Suite 101 San Antonio TX 78228 210-444-1710 444-1714
Web: www.idra.org
International Studies Assn (ISA)
Univ of Arizona 324 Social Sciences Tucson AZ 85721 520-621-7715 621-5780
Web: www.isanet.org
JA Worldwide 1 Education Way Colorado Springs CO 80906 719-540-8000 540-6229
Web: www.ja.org
JACAN (Junior Achievement of Canada) 1 Eva Rd Suite 218 Toronto ON M9C4Z5 416-622-4602 622-6861
TF: 800-265-0699 ■ *Web:* www.jacan.org
Jewish Education Service of North America (JESNA)
111 8th Ave Suite 11-E New York NY 10011 212-284-6950 284-6951
Web: www.jesna.org
Junior Achievement of Canada (JACAN) 1 Eva Rd Suite 218 Toronto ON M9C4Z5 416-622-4602 622-6861
TF: 800-265-0699 ■ *Web:* www.jacan.org
Junior State of America (JSA)
400 S El Camino Real Suite 300 San Mateo CA 94402 650-347-1600 347-7200
TF: 800-334-5353 ■ *Web:* www.jsa.org
League for Innovation in the Community College
4505 E Chandler Blvd Suite 250 Phoenix AZ 85048 480-705-8200 705-8201
Web: www.league.org

Phone | Fax

Linguistic Society of America (LSA)
1325 18th St NW Suite 211 .... Washington DC 20036 202-835-1714 835-1717
Web: www.lsadc.org

Medieval Academy of America 104 Mount Auburn St 5th Fl ..... Cambridge MA 02138 617-491-1622 492-3303
Web: www.medievalacademy.org

Montessori Foundation
2400 Miguel Bay Dr PO Box 130 .... Terra Ceia Island FL 34250 941-729-9565 729-9594
Web: www.montessori.org

National Alliance of Blind Students Inc
1155 15th St NW Suite 1004 .... Washington DC 20005 202-467-5081 467-5085
TF: 800-424-8666 ■ *Web:* www.blindstudents.org

National Assn for Year-Round Education (NAYRE)
PO Box 711386 .... San Diego CA 92171 619-276-5296 571-5754*
**Fax Area Code:* 858 ■ *Web:* www.nayre.org

National Center for Education Information (NCEI)
4401-A Connecticut Ave NW Suite 212 .... Washington DC 20008 202-822-8280 822-8284
Web: www.ncei.com

National Center for Family Literacy (NCFL)
325 W Main St Suite 300 .... Louisville KY 40202 502-584-1133 584-0172
TF: 877-326-5481 ■ *Web:* www.famlit.org

National Congress of Parents & Teachers (PTA)
541 N Fairbanks Ct Suite 1300 .... Chicago IL 60611 312-670-6782 670-6783
TF: 800-307-4782 ■ *Web:* www.pta.org

National Forensic League (NFL) 125 Watson St PO Box 38 .... Ripon WI 54971 920-748-6206 748-9478
Web: www.nflonline.org

National Head Start Assn (NHSA) 1651 Prince St .... Alexandria VA 22314 703-739-0875 739-0878
TF: 800-355-6472 ■ *Web:* www.nhsa.org

National Honor Society (NHS) 1904 Association Dr .... Reston VA 20191 703-860-0200 476-5432
TF: 800-253-7746 ■ *Web:* www.nhs.us

National Research Council (NRC) 500 5th St NW .... Washington DC 20001 202-334-2000
Web: www.nationalacademies.org/nrc

National Scholastic Press Assn (NSPA)
2221 University Ave SE Suite 121 .... Minneapolis MN 55414 612-625-8335 626-0720
Web: www.studentpress.org/nspa

National Society for Experiential Education (NSEE)
515 King St Suite 420 .... Alexandria VA 22314 703-706-9552 684-6048
Web: www.nsee.org

North-American Interfraternity Conference (NIC)
3901 W 86th St Suite 390 .... Indianapolis IN 46268 317-872-1112 872-1134
Web: www.nicindy.org

NRC (National Research Council) 500 5th St NW .... Washington DC 20001 202-334-2000
Web: www.nationalacademies.org/nrc

Public Education Network (PEN)
601 13th St NW Suite 710-S .... Washington DC 20005 202-628-7460 628-1893
Web: www.publiceducation.org

Reading Is Fundamental Inc (RIF)
1825 Connecticut Ave NW Suite 400 .... Washington DC 20009 877-743-7323 287-3196*
**Fax Area Code:* 202 ■ *TF:* 877-743-7323 ■ *Web:* www.rif.org

Rolling Readers USA 4007 Camino Del Rio S Suite 203 .... San Diego CA 92108 619-516-4095 516-4096
Web: www.rollingreaders.org

Scholarship America 1 Scholarship Way .... Saint Peter MN 56082 507-931-1682 931-9168
TF: 800-537-4180 ■ *Web:* www.scholarshipamerica.org

SkillsUSA PO Box 3000 .... Leesburg VA 20177 703-777-8810 777-8999
TF Orders: 800-321-8422 ■ *Web:* www.skillsusa.org

TABS (Association of Boarding Schools)
9 SW Pack Sq Suite 201 .... Asheville NC 28801 828-258-5354 258-6428
Web: www.schools.com

United Negro College Fund Inc (UNCF)
8260 Willow Oaks Corporate Dr Suite 400 .... Fairfax VA 22031 703-205-3400 205-3507
TF: 800-331-2244 ■ *Web:* www.uncf.org

US Student Assn (USSA)
1211 Connecticut Ave NW Suite 406 .... Washington DC 20036 202-640-6570 233-4005
Web: www.usstudents.org

White House Historical Assn 740 Jackson Pl NW .... Washington DC 20506 202-737-8292 789-0440
Web: www.whitehousehistory.org

Wilson Woodrow National Fellowship Foundation
PO Box 5281 .... Princeton NJ 08543 609-452-7007 452-0066
Web: www.woodrow.org

Woodrow Wilson National Fellowship Foundation
PO Box 5281 .... Princeton NJ 08543 609-452-7007 452-0066
Web: www.woodrow.org

World Assn of International Studies (WAIS)
Hoover Institution 766 Santa Ynez St .... Stanford CA 94305 650-322-2026 723-1687
Web: wais.stanford.edu

World Learning International Development Programs
1015 15th St NW Suite 750 .... Washington DC 20005 202-408-5420 408-5397
Web: www.worldlearning.org

Young Astronaut Council 5200 27th St NW .... Washington DC 20015 301-617-0923 776-0858
Web: www.youngastronauts.org/yac

Youth for Understanding International Exchange
6400 Goldsboro Rd Suite 100 .... Bethesda MD 20817 240-235-2100 235-2104
TF: 800-424-3691 ■ *Web:* www.yfu.org

48-12 Energy & Natural Resources Organizations

Phone | Fax

Air & Waste Management Assn (A&WMA)
420 Fort Duquesne Blvd 1 Gateway Ctr 3rd Fl .... Pittsburgh PA 15222 412-232-3444 232-3450
TF: 800-270-3444 ■ *Web:* www.awma.org

Alliance to Save Energy (ASE) 1850 M St NW Suite 600 .... Washington DC 20036 202-857-0666 331-9588
Web: www.ase.org

American Academy of Environmental Engineers
130 Holiday Ct Suite 100 .... Annapolis MD 21401 410-266-3311 266-7653
Web: www.aaee.net

American Assn of Petroleum Geologists (AAPG)
1444 S Boulder Ave .... Tulsa OK 74119 918-584-2555 560-2694*
**Fax:* Cust Svc ■ *TF:* 800-364-2274 ■ *Web:* www.aapg.org

American Assn of Professional Landmen (AAPL)
4100 Fossil Creek Blvd .... Fort Worth TX 76137 817-847-7700 847-7704
TF: 888-566-2275 ■ *Web:* www.landman.org

American Coal Ash Assn (ACAA) 15200 E Girard Ave Suite 3050 ..... Aurora CO 80014 720-870-7897 870-7889
Web: www.acaa-usa.org

American Coke & Coal Chemicals Institute (ACCCI)
1140 Connecticut Ave NW Suite 705 .... Washington DC 20036 202-452-7198 463-6573
Web: www.accci.org

American Gas Assn (AGA) 400 N Capitol St NW 4th Fl .... Washington DC 20001 202-824-7000 824-7115
Web: www.aga.org

American Hydrogen Assn (AHA) 1739 W 7th Ave .... Mesa AZ 85202 480-827-7915
Web: www.clean-air.org

American Institute of Mining Metallurgical & Petroleum Engineers (AIME) 8307 Shaffer Pkwy PO Box 270728 .... Littleton CO 80127 303-948-4255 948-4260
Web: www.aimehq.org

American Oil Chemists Society (AOCS) 2710 S Boulder .... Urbana IL 61802 217-359-2344 351-8091
TF: 800-336-2627 ■ *Web:* www.aocs.org

American Petroleum Institute (API) 1220 L St NW 9th Fl ...... Washington DC 20005 202-682-8000 682-8029
Web: api-ec.api.org

American Public Gas Assn (APGA)
201 Massachusetts Ave NE Suite C-4 .... Washington DC 20002 202-464-2742 464-0246
TF: 800-927-4204 ■ *Web:* www.apga.org

American Public Power Assn (APPA)
1875 Connecticut Ave Suite 1200 .... Washington DC 20009 202-467-2900 467-2910
Web: www.appanet.org

American Solar Energy Society (ASES)
2400 Central Ave Suite A .... Boulder CO 80301 303-443-3130 443-3212
Web: www.ases.org

American Water Works Assn (AWWA) 6666 W Quincy Ave .... Denver CO 80235 303-794-7711 347-0804
TF: 800-926-7337 ■ *Web:* www.awwa.org

American Wind Energy Assn (AWEA)
1101 14th St NW 12th Fl .... Washington DC 20005 202-383-2500 383-2505
Web: www.awea.org

ASE (Alliance to Save Energy) 1850 M St NW Suite 600 .... Washington DC 20036 202-857-0666 331-9588
Web: www.ase.org

Association of Energy Engineers (AEE)
4025 Pleasantdale Rd Suite 420 .... Atlanta GA 30340 770-447-5083 446-3969
Web: www.aeecenter.org

Association of Energy Service Companies (AESC)
10200 Richmond Ave Suite 275 .... Houston TX 77042 713-781-0758 781-7542
TF: 800-692-0771 ■ *Web:* www.aesc.net

Automatic Meter Reading Assn (AMRA)
60 Revere Dr Suite 500 .... Northbrook IL 60062 847-480-9628 480-9282
Web: www.amra-intl.org

Bituminous Coal Operators Assn 1776 I St NW .... Washington DC 20006 202-783-3195 783-4862

Center for Energy & Economic Development (CEED)
333 John Carlyle St Suite 530 .... Alexandria VA 22314 703-684-6292 684-6297
Web: www.ceednet.org

Coalition for Fair Lumber Imports (CFLI) 975 F St NW .... Washington DC 20004 202-862-3686 862-1093
Web: www.fairlumbercoalition.org

Cooling Technology Institute (CTI)
2611 FM 1960 RD W Suite A-101 .... Houston TX 77068 281-583-4087 537-1721
Web: www.cti.org

Edison Electric Institute (EEI) 701 Pennsylvania Ave NW .... Washington DC 20004 202-508-5000 508-5051
TF: 800-334-4688 ■ *Web:* www.eei.org

Electric Power Supply Assn (EPSA)
1401 New York Ave NW 11th Fl .... Washington DC 20005 202-628-8200 628-8260
Web: www.epsa.org

Electricity Consumers Resource Council (ELCON)
1333 H St NW West Tower 8th Fl .... Washington DC 20005 202-682-1390 289-6370
Web: www.elcon.org

Environmental Industry Assns
4301 Connecticut Ave NW Suite 300 .... Washington DC 20008 202-244-4700 966-4818
Web: www.envasns.org

Environmental Technology Council (ETC)
734 15th St NW Suite 720 .... Washington DC 20005 202-783-0870 737-2038
Web: www.etc.org

EPSA (Electric Power Supply Assn)
1401 New York Ave NW 11th Fl .... Washington DC 20005 202-628-8200 628-8260
Web: www.epsa.org

Gas Processors Assn (GPA) 6526 E 60th St .... Tulsa OK 74145 918-493-3872 493-3875
Web: www.gasprocessors.com

Gas Processors Suppliers Assn (GPSA) 6526 E 60th St .... Tulsa OK 74145 918-493-3872 493-3875
Web: gpsa.gasprocessors.com

Independent Petroleum Assn of America (IPAA)
1201 15th St NW Suite 300 .... Washington DC 20005 202-857-4722 857-4799
TF: 800-433-2851 ■ *Web:* www.ipaa.org

Institute of Clean Air Companies (ICAC)
1730 M St NW Suite 206 .... Washington DC 20036 202-457-0911 331-1388
Web: icac.com

Institute of Hazardous Materials Management (IHMM)
11900 Parklawn Dr Suite 450 .... Rockville MD 20852 301-984-8969 984-1516
Web: www.ihmm.org

Institute of Nuclear Power Operations
700 Galleria Pkwy SE Suite 100 .... Atlanta GA 30339 770-644-8000 644-8549
Web: www.eh.doe.gov/inpo

Institute of Scrap Recycling Industries Inc (ISRI)
1615 L St NW Suite 600 .... Washington DC 20036 202-662-8500 626-0900
Web: www.isri.org

Integrated Waste Services Assn (IWSA)
1331 H St NW Suite 801 .... Washington DC 20005 202-467-6240 467-6225
Web: www.wte.org

International Institute for Energy Conservation (IIEC)
10005 Leamoore Ln Suite 100 .... Vienna VA 22181 703-281-7263 938-5153
Web: www.iiec.org

Interstate Oil & Gas Compact Commission (IOGCC)
900 NE 23rd St PO Box 53127 .... Oklahoma City OK 73152 405-525-3556 525-3592
TF: 800-822-4015 ■ *Web:* www.iogcc.oklaosf.state.ok.us

Methanol Institute (MI) 4100 N Fairfax Dr Suite 740 .... Arlington VA 22203 703-248-3636 248-3997
TF: 888-275-0768 ■ *Web:* www.methanol.org

National Assn of Regulatory Utility Commissioners (NARUC)
1101 Vermont Ave NW Suite 200 .... Washington DC 20005 202-898-2200 898-2213
Web: www.naruc.org

National Assn of State Utility Consumer Advocates (NASUCA) 8380 Colesville Rd Suite 101 .... Silver Spring MD 20910 301-589-6313 589-6380
Web: www.nasuca.org

National Assn of Water Companies (NAWC)
2001 L St NW Suite 850 .... Washington DC 20036 202-833-8383 331-7442
Web: www.nawc.com

National Energy Services Assn (NESA)
6430 FM 1960 W Suite 213 .... Houston TX 77069 713-856-6525 856-6199
Web: www.nesanet.org

National Ground Water Assn (NGWA) 601 Dempsey Rd .... Westerville OH 43081 614-898-7791 898-7786
TF: 800-551-7379 ■ *Web:* www.ngwa.org

National Mining Assn (NMA)
101 Constitution Ave NW Suite 500-E .... Washington DC 20001 202-463-2600 463-2666
Web: www.nma.org

National Ocean Industries Assn (NOIA)
1120 G St NW Suite 900 .... Washington DC 20005 202-347-6900 347-8650
Web: www.noia.org

National Petrochemical & Refiners Assn (NPRA)
1899 L St NW Suite 1000 .... Washington DC 20036 202-457-0480 457-0486
Web: www.npradc.org

National Propane Gas Assn (NPGA)
1150 17th St NW Suite 310 .... Washington DC 20036 202-466-7200 466-7205
Web: www.npga.org

National Rural Electric Cooperative Assn (NRECA)
4301 Wilson Blvd .... Arlington VA 22203 703-907-5500 907-5528
TF: 866-673-2299 ■ *Web:* www.nreca.org

National Rural Water Assn (NRWA) 2915 S 13th St .... Duncan OK 73533 580-252-0629 255-4476
Web: www.nrwa.org

National Water Resources Assn (NWRA)
3800 N Fairfax Dr Suite 4 .... Arlington VA 22203 703-524-1544 524-1548
Web: www.nwra.org

Natural Gas Supply Assn (NGSA) 805 15th St NW Suite 510 ..... Washington DC 20005 202-326-9300 326-9330
Web: www.ngsa.org

Energy & Natural Resources Organizations (Cont'd)

Organization	City	State	Zip	Phone	Fax
NGWA (National Ground Water Assn) 601 Dempsey Rd. *TF:* 800-551-7379 ■ *Web:* www.ngwa.org	Westerville	OH	43081	614-898-7791	898-7786
North American Electric Reliability Council (NERC) 116-390 Village Blvd *TF:* 800-726-8060 ■ *Web:* www.nerc.com	Princeton	NJ	08540	609-452-8060	452-9550
Nuclear Energy Institute (NEI) 1776 'I' St NW Suite 400 *Web:* www.nei.org	Washington	DC	20006	202-739-8000	785-4019
Petroleum Technology Transfer Council (PTTC) 16010 Barkers Point Ln Suite 220 *TF:* 888-843-7882 ■ *Web:* www.pttc.org	Houston	TX	77079	281-921-1720	921-1723
Renewable Fuels Assn (RFA) 1 Massachusetts Ave NW Suite 820 *Web:* www.ethanolrfa.org	Washington	DC	20001	202-289-3835	289-7519
Society of Exploration Geophysicists (SEG) 8801 S Yale Ave *Web:* www.seg.org	Tulsa	OK	74137	918-493-3516	497-5557
Society of Petroleum Engineers (SPE) 222 Palisades Creek Dr *TF:* 800-456-6863 ■ *Web:* www.spe.org	Richardson	TX	75080	972-952-9393	952-9435
Society of Petrophysicists & Well Log Analysts (SPWLA) 8866 Gulf Fwy Suite 320 *Web:* www.spwla.org	Houston	TX	77017	713-947-8727	947-7181
Solar Energy Industries Assn (SEIA) 805 15th St NW Suite 510 *Web:* www.seia.org	Washington	DC	20005	202-682-0556	628-7779
Solid Waste Assn of North America (SWANA) 1100 Wayne Ave Suite 700 *TF:* 800-467-9262 ■ *Web:* www.swana.org	Silver Spring	MD	20910	301-585-2898	589-7068
SWANA (Solid Waste Assn of North America) 1100 Wayne Ave Suite 700 *TF:* 800-467-9262 ■ *Web:* www.swana.org	Silver Spring	MD	20910	301-585-2898	589-7068
US Energy Assn (USEA) 1300 Pennsylvania Ave NW Suite 550 *Web:* www.usea.org	Washington	DC	20004	202-312-1230	682-1826
Water Quality Assn 4151 Naperville Rd *Web:* www.wqa.org	Lisle	IL	60532	630-505-0160	505-9637
Western Forestry & Conservation Assn 4033 SW Canyon Rd *TF:* 888-722-9416 ■ *Web:* www.westernforestry.org	Portland	OR	97221	503-226-4562	226-2515

48-13 Environmental Organizations

Organization	City	State	Zip	Phone	Fax
Adirondack Council 103 Hand Ave Suite 3 *TF:* 877-873-2240 ■ *Web:* www.adirondackcouncil.org	Elizabethtown	NY	12932	518-873-2240	873-6675
Alaska Wilderness League 122 C St NW Suite 240 *Web:* www.alaskawild.org	Washington	DC	20001	202-544-5205	544-5197
Alliance for Responsible Atmospheric Policy 2111 Wilson Blvd Ste 850 *Web:* www.arap.org	Arlington	VA	22201	703-243-0344	243-2874
Alouette River Management Society (ARMS) PO Box 21117	Maple Ridge	BC	V2X1P7	604-467-6401	467-6478
America the Beautiful Fund 1730 K St NW Suite 1002 *TF:* 800-522-3557 ■ *Web:* www.america-the-beautiful.org	Washington	DC	20006	202-638-1649	638-2175
American Cave Conservation Assn 119 E Main St PO Box 409 *Web:* www.cavern.org/acca/accahome.html	Horse Cave	KY	42749	270-786-1466	786-1467
American Conservation Assn 30 Rockefeller Plaza 56th Fl	New York	NY	10112	212-649-5819	649-5729
American Farmland Trust (AFT) 1200 18th St NW Suite 800 *TF:* 800-431-1499 ■ *Web:* www.farmland.org	Washington	DC	20036	202-331-7300	659-8339
American Forests 734 15th St NW Suite 800 PO Box 2000 *TF:* 800-368-5748 ■ *Web:* www.americanforests.org	Washington	DC	20013	202-737-1944	737-2457
American Lands Alliance 726 7th St SE *Web:* www.americanlands.org	Washington	DC	20002	202-547-9400	547-9213
American Littoral Society (ALS) Sandy Hook Bldg 18 *Web:* www.littoralsociety.org	Highlands	NJ	07732	732-291-0055	291-3551
American Public Information on the Environment 316 Oak St PO Box 676 *TF:* 800-320-2743 ■ *Web:* www.americanpie.org	Northfield	MN	55057	507-645-5613	645-5724
American Rivers 1101 14th St NW Suite 1400 *TF:* 877-347-7550 ■ *Web:* www.americanrivers.org	Washington	DC	20005	202-347-7550	347-9240
American Shore & Beach Preservation Assn (ASBPA) 5460 Beaujolais Ln *Web:* www.asbpa.org	Fort Myers	FL	33919	239-489-2616	489-9917
American Wildlands 321 East Main St Suite 418 *Web:* www.wildlands.org	Bozeman	MT	59715	406-586-8175	586-8242
Appalachian Mountain Club (AMC) 5 Joy St *TF Orders:* 800-262-4455 ■ *Web:* www.outdoors.org	Boston	MA	02108	617-523-0655	523-0722
APVA Preservation Virginia (APVA) 204 W Franklin St *Web:* www.apva.org	Richmond	VA	23220	804-648-1889	775-0802
Archaeological Conservancy 5301 Central Ave NE Suite 902 *Web:* www.americanarchaeology.com/aaabout.html	Albuquerque	NM	87108	505-266-1540	266-0311
Audubon Naturalist Society 8940 Jones Mill Rd *Web:* www.audubonnaturalist.org	Chevy Chase	MD	20815	301-652-9188	951-7179
Beyond Pesticides 701 'E' St SE Suite 200 *Web:* www.beyondpesticides.org	Washington	DC	20003	202-543-5450	543-4791
Big Bend Natural History Assn PO Box 196 *Web:* www.bigbendbookstore.org	Big Bend National Park	TX	79834	432-477-2236	477-2234
Canadian Parks & Wilderness Society (CPAWS) 250 City Center Ave Suite 506 *Web:* www.cpaws.org	Ottawa	ON	K1R6K7	613-569-7226	569-7098
Canadian Water Resources Assn (CWRA) 280 Albert St Suite 900 *Web:* www.cwra.org	Ottawa	ON	K1P5G8	613-237-9363	594-5190
Canadian Wildlife Federation (CWF) 350 Michael Cowpland Dr *TF:* 800-563-9453 ■ *Web:* www.cwf-fcf.org	Kanata	ON	K2M2W1	613-599-9594	599-4428
Center for Plant Conservation (CPC) 4344 Shaw Blvd *Web:* www.centerforplantconservation.org	Saint Louis	MO	63110	314-577-9450	577-9465
Charles A & Anne Morrow Lindbergh Foundation 2150 3rd Ave N Suite 310 *Web:* www.lindberghfoundation.org	Anoka	MN	55303	763-576-1596	576-1664
Circumpolar Conservation Union (CCU) 1730 Rhode Island Ave NW Suite 707 *Web:* www.circumpolar.org	Washington	DC	20036	202-775-5671	775-2179
Citizens Network for Sustainable Development (CitNet) 11426 Rockville Pike Suite 306 *Web:* www.citnet.org	Rockville	MD	20852	301-770-6375	770-6377
Civil War Preservation Trust (CWPT) 1331 H St NW Suite 1001 *TF:* 888-606-1400 ■ *Web:* www.civilwar.org	Washington	DC	20005	202-367-1861	367-1865
Clean Water Action 4455 Connecticut Ave NW Suite A-300 *TF:* 800-709-2837 ■ *Web:* www.cleanwateraction.org	Washington	DC	20008	202-895-0420	895-0438
Clean Water Fund (CWF) 4455 Connecticut Ave NW Suite A300-16 *TF:* 800-709-2837 ■ *Web:* www.cleanwaterfund.org	Washington	DC	20008	202-895-0432	895-0438
Co-op America 1612 K St NW Suite 600 *TF:* 800-584-7336 ■ *Web:* www.coopamerica.org	Washington	DC	20006	202-872-5307	331-8166
Coalition for Responsible Waste Incineration (CRWI) 1615 L St NW Suite 1350 *Web:* www.crwi.org	Washington	DC	20036	202-452-1241	887-8044
Coastal Conservation Association (CCA) 6919 Portwest Dr Suite 100 *TF:* 800-201-3474 ■ *Web:* www.joincca.org	Houston	TX	77024	713-626-4234	626-5852
Conservation Fund 1655 N Fort Myer Dr Suite 1300 *Web:* www.conservationfund.org	Arlington	VA	222092157	703-525-6300	525-4610
Conservation International (CI) 2011 Crystal Drive Suite 500 *TF:* 800-406-2306 ■ *Web:* www.conservation.org	Arlington	VA	22202	703-341-2400	
Conservation Treaty Support Fund (CTSF) 3705 Cardiff Rd *TF:* 800-654-3150 ■ *Web:* www.conservationtreaty.org	Chevy Chase	MD	20815	301-654-3150	652-6390
Consortium for Oceanographic Research & Education (CORE) 1201 New York Ave NW Suite 420 *Web:* www.coreocean.org	Washington	DC	20005	202-332-0063	332-8887
Corporation for Jefferson's Poplar Forest DBA Thomas Jefferson's Poplar Forest PO Box 419 *Web:* www.poplarforest.org	Forest	VA	245510419	434-525-1806	525-7252
Cousteau Society 710 Settlers Landing Rd *TF:* 800-441-4395 ■ *Web:* www.cousteausociety.org	Hampton	VA	23669	757-722-9300	722-8185
Earth Day Network (EDN) 1616 P St NW Suite 340 *Web:* www.earthday.net	Washington	DC	20036	202-518-0044	518-8794
Earth Island Institute 300 Broadway Suite 28 *Web:* www.earthisland.org	San Francisco	CA	941333312	415-788-3666	788-7324
Earth Share 7735 Old Georgetown Rd Suite 900 *TF:* 800-875-3863 ■ *Web:* www.earthshare.org	Bethesda	MD	20814	240-333-0300	333-0301
Earthjustice 426 17th St 6th Fl *TF:* 800-584-6460 ■ *Web:* www.earthjustice.org	Oakland	CA	94612	510-550-6700	550-6740
EarthRights International 1612 K St NW Suite 401 *Web:* www.earthrights.org	Washington	DC	20006	202-466-5188	466-5189
Earthwatch Institute 3 Clock Tower Pl Suite 100 PO Box 75 *TF:* 800-776-0188 ■ *Web:* www.earthwatch.org	Maynard	MA	01754	978-461-0081	461-2332
Educational Communications Inc PO Box 351419 *Web:* www.ecoprojects.org	Los Angeles	CA	90035	310-559-9160	559-9160
Environmental Careers Organization (ECO) 30 Windsor St 6th Fl *Web:* www.eco.org	Boston	MA	02108	617-426-4375	423-0998
Environmental Defense 257 Park Ave S *TF:* 800-505-0703 ■ *Web:* www.environmentaldefense.org	New York	NY	10010	212-505-2100	505-2375
Environmental Information Assn (EIA) 6935 Wisconsin Ave Suite 306 *TF:* 888-343-4342 ■ *Web:* www.eia-usa.org	Chevy Chase	MD	208156113	301-961-4999	961-3094
Environmental Law Institute (ELI) 2000 L St NW Suite 620 *TF:* 800-433-5120 ■ *Web:* www.eli.org	Washington	DC	20036	202-939-3800	939-3868
Environmental Protection Information Center (EPIC) 351 Sprowl Creek Rd PO Box 397 *Web:* www.wildcalifornia.org	Garberville	CA	95542	707-923-2931	923-4210
Forest Guild PO Box 519 *Web:* forestguild.org	Santa Fe	NM	87504	505-983-8992	986-0798
Forest History Society 701 William Vickers Ave *Web:* www.foresthistory.org	Durham	NC	277013162	919-682-9319	682-2349
Forest Landowners Assn (FLA) 3776 La Vista Rd Suite 250 *TF:* 800-325-2954 ■ *Web:* www.forestlandowners.com	Tucker	GA	30084	404-325-2954	325-2955
Freshwater Society 2500 Shadywood Rd *TF:* 888-471-9773 ■ *Web:* www.freshwater.org	Excelsior	MN	55331	952-471-9773	471-7685
Friends of the Earth 1717 Massachusetts Ave NW Suite 600 *TF:* 877-843-8687 ■ *Web:* www.foe.org	Washington	DC	20036	202-783-7400	783-0444
Friends of the Earth Canada 260 Saint Patrick St Suite 300 *TF:* 888-385-4444 ■ *Web:* www.foecanada.org	Ottawa	ON	K1N5K5	613-241-0085	241-7998
Friends of the Everglades 7800 Red Rd Suite 215K *Web:* www.everglades.org	South Miami	FL	33143	305-669-0858	669-4108
Friends of the River 915 20th St *TF:* 888-464-2477 ■ *Web:* www.friendsoftheriver.org	Sacramento	CA	95814	916-442-3155	442-3396
Grand Canyon Trust 2601 N Fort Valley Rd *TF:* 888-428-5550 ■ *Web:* www.grandcanyontrust.org	Flagstaff	AZ	86001	928-774-7488	774-7570
Great Lakes United (GLU) Buffalo State College Cassety Hall 1300 Elmwood Ave *TF:* 800-846-0142 ■ *Web:* www.glu.org	Buffalo	NY	14222	716-886-0142	886-0303
Greater Yellowstone Coalition (GYC) 13 S Willson Ave, Suite 2 PO Box 1874 *TF:* 800-775-1834 ■ *Web:* www.greateryellowstone.org	Bozeman	MT	59715	406-586-1593	556-2839
Greenpeace Canada 250 Dundas St W Suite 605 *TF:* 800-320-7183 ■ *Web:* www.greenpeace.ca	Toronto	ON	M5T2Z5	416-597-8408	597-8422
Greenpeace USA 702 H St NW Suite 300 *TF:* 800-326-0959 ■ *Web:* www.greenpeace.org	Washington	DC	20001	202-462-1177	462-4507
Ground Water Protection Council (GWPC) 13308 N MacArthur Blvd *Web:* www.gwpc.org	Oklahoma City	OK	73142	405-516-4972	516-4973
Hells Canyon Preservation Council 105 Fir St Suite 327 PO Box 2768 *Web:* www.hellscanyon.org	La Grande	OR	97850	541-963-3950	963-0584
Heritage Canada Foundation 5 Blackburn Ave *Web:* www.heritagecanada.org	Ottawa	ON	K1N8A2	613-237-1066	237-5987
Historic New England 141 Cambridge St *Web:* www.historicnewengland.org	Boston	MA	02114	617-227-3956	227-9204
International Assn of Wildland Fire (IAWF) PO Box 261 *Web:* www.iawfonline.org	Hot Springs	SD	577470261	605-890-2348	
International Society of Tropical Foresters (ISTF) 5400 Grosvenor Ln *TF:* 866-897-8720 ■ *Web:* www.istf-bethesda.org	Bethesda	MD	20814	301-897-8720	897-3690
Island Nature Trust PO Box 265 *Web:* www.islandnaturetrust.ca	Charlottetown	PE	C1A7K4	902-566-9150	628-6331
Izaak Walton League of America (IWLA) 707 Conservation Ln *TF:* 800-453-5463 ■ *Web:* www.iwla.org	Gaithersburg	MD	20878	301-548-0150	548-0146
Land Trust Alliance (LTA) 1331 H St NW Suite 400 *Web:* www.lta.org	Washington	DC	200054734	202-638-4725	638-4730
League to Save Lake Tahoe 955 Emerald Bay Rd *Web:* www.keeptahoeblue.org	South Lake Tahoe	CA	96150	530-541-5388	541-5454
Montana Wilderness Assn (MWA) 324 Fuller St PO Box 635 *Web:* www.wildmontana.org	Helena	MT	59624	406-443-7350	443-0750
Mount Rushmore National Memorial Society 825 Saint Joseph St Suite 300 PO Box 1524 *Web:* www.mountrushmoresociety.com	Rapid City	SD	57709	605-341-8883	341-8883
National Alliance of Preservation Commissions 325 S Lumpkin St Founders Garden House *Web:* www.uga.edu/sed/pso/programs/napc/napc.htm	Athens	GA	30602	706-542-4731	583-0320
National Arbor Day Foundation 100 Arbor Ave *TF:* 888-448-7337 ■ *Web:* www.arborday.org	Nebraska City	NE	68410	402-474-5655	474-0820
National Assn for Olmsted Parks 1111 16th St NW Suite 310 *TF:* 866-666-6905 ■ *Web:* www.olmsted.org	Washington	DC	20036	202-223-9113	223-9112

Organization	City	State	Zip	Phone	Fax
National Assn for PET Container Resources (NAPCOR) 17474 Sonoma Hwy PO Box 1327 *Web:* www.napcor.com	Sonoma	CA	95476	707-996-4207	935-1998
National Audubon Society (NAS) 700 Broadway *Web:* www.audubon.org	New York	NY	10003	212-979-3000	979-3188
National Council for Air & Stream Improvement Inc (NCASI) 4815 Emperor Blvd Suite 110 *Web:* www.ncasi.org	Research Triangle Park	NC	27703	919-941-6400	941-6401
National Fish & Wildlife Foundation 1120 Connecticut Ave NW Suite 900 *Web:* www.nfwf.org	Washington	DC	20036	202-857-0166	857-0162
National Forest Foundation 27 Fort Missoula Rd Bldg 27 Suite 3 *TF:* 866-733-4633 ■ *Web:* www.natlforests.org	Missoula	MT	59804	406-542-2805	542-2810
National Marine Sanctuary Foundation 8601 Georgia Ave Suite 501 *Web:* www.nmsfocean.org	Silver Spring	MD	20910	301-608-3040	608-3044
National Park Foundation (NPF) 11 Dupont Cir NW Suite 600 *Web:* www.nationalparks.org	Washington	DC	20036	202-238-4200	234-3103
National Park Trust (NPT) 51 Monroe St Suite 110 *Web:* www.parktrust.org	Rockville	MD	20850	301-279-7275	279-7211
National Parks Conservation Assn (NPCA) 1300 19th St NW Suite 300 *TF:* 800-628-7275 ■ *Web:* www.npca.org	Washington	DC	20036	202-223-6722	659-0650
National Trust for Historic Preservation 1785 Massachusetts Ave NW *TF:* 800-944-6847 ■ *Web:* www.nationaltrust.org	Washington	DC	20036	202-588-6000	588-6038
National Wildlife Refuge Assn (NWRA) 1901 Pennsylvania Ave Suite 407 *TF:* 877-396-6972 ■ *Web:* www.refugenet.org	Washington	DC	20006	202-333-9075	333-9077
Natural Areas Assn (NAA) PO Box 1504 *Web:* www.naturalarea.org	Bend	OR	97709	541-317-0199	317-0140
Natural Resources Council of America (NRCA) 1616 P St Suite 340 *Web:* www.naturalresourcescouncil.org	Washington	DC	20036	202-232-6531	
Natural Resources Defense Council (NRDC) 40 W 20th St *Web:* www.nrdc.org	New York	NY	10011	212-727-2700	727-1773
Nature Canada 85 Albert St Suite 900 *Web:* www.naturecanada.ca	Ottawa	ON	K1P6A4	613-562-3447	562-3371
Nature Conservancy 4245 N Fairfax Dr Suite 100 *TF Cust Svc:* 800-628-6860 ■ *Web:* www.nature.org	Arlington	VA	22203	703-841-5300	841-1283
Nature Conservancy of Canada 110 Eglinton Ave W Suite 400 *TF:* 800-465-0029 ■ *Web:* www.natureconservancy.ca	Toronto	ON	M4R1A3	416-932-3202	932-3208
Negative Population Growth (NPG) 2861 Duke St Suite 36 *Web:* www.npg.org	Alexandria	VA	22314	703-370-9510	370-9514
New England Wild Flower Society 180 Hemenway Rd *Web:* www.newfs.org	Framingham	MA	01701	508-877-7630	
Ocean Conservancy 2029 K St NW *TF:* 800-519-1541 ■ *Web:* www.oceanconservancy.org	Washington	DC	20006	202-429-5609	
Ocean Futures Society 325 Chapala St *Web:* www.oceanfutures.org	Santa Barbara	CA	93101	805-899-8899	899-8898
Open Space Institute (OSI) 1350 Broadway Suite 201 *Web:* www.osiny.org	New York	NY	10018	212-290-8200	244-3441
Pacific Rivers Council (PRC) 540 Oak St Suite E *Web:* www.pacrivers.org	Eugene	OR	97441	541-345-0119	345-0710
Pew Charitable Trust 1200 18th St NW 5th Fl *Web:* www.pewtrusts.org	Washington	DC	20036	202-887-8800	887-8877
Pollution Probe 625 Church St Suite 402 *Web:* www.pollutionprobe.org	Toronto	ON	M4Y2G1	416-926-1907	926-1601
Project for Public Spaces 700 Broadway 4th Fl *Web:* www.pps.org	New York	NY	10003	212-620-5660	620-3821
Public Lands Foundation (PLF) PO Box 7226 *Web:* www.publicland.org	Arlington	VA	22207	703-790-1988	821-3490
Rails-to-Trails Conservancy (RTC) 1100 17th St NW 10th Fl *Web:* www.railtrails.org	Washington	DC	20036	202-331-9696	
Rainforest Action Network (RAN) 221 Pine St Fifth Floor *TF:* 800-989-7246 ■ *Web:* www.ran.org	San Francisco	CA	94104	415-398-4404	398-2732
Renewable Natural Resources Foundation (RNRF) 5430 Grosvenor Ln *Web:* www.rnrf.org	Bethesda	MD	20814	301-493-9101	493-6148
River Management Society 200 Pattee Canyon Dr PO Box 9048 *Web:* www.river-management.org	Missoula	MT	59807	406-549-0514	542-6208
Royal Oak Foundation 26 Broadway Suite 950 *TF:* 800-913-6565 ■ *Web:* www.royal-oak.org	New York	NY	10004	212-480-2889	785-7234
Save America's Forests 4 Library Ct SE *Web:* www.saveamericasforests.org	Washington	DC	20003	202-544-9219	544-7462
Save-the-Redwoods League 114 Sansome St Rm 1200 *TF:* 888-836-0005 ■ *Web:* www.savetheredwoods.org	San Francisco	CA	94104	415-362-2352	362-7017
Scenic America 1634 'I' St NW Suite 510 *Web:* www.scenic.org	Washington	DC	20006	202-638-0550	638-3171
Sea Grant Assn (SGA) 5784 York Complex University of Maine *Web:* www.sga.seagrant.org	Orono	ME	04469	207-581-1435	581-1426
Sierra Club 85 2nd St 2nd Fl *Web:* www.sierraclub.org	San Francisco	CA	94105	415-977-5500	977-5799
Sierra Club of Canada 1 Nicholas St Suite 412 *TF:* 888-810-4204 ■ *Web:* www.sierraclub.ca	Ottawa	ON	K1N7B7	613-241-4611	241-2292
Sierra Club Foundation 85 2nd St Suite 750 *TF:* 800-216-2110 ■ *Web:* www.sierraclub.org/foundation	San Francisco	CA	94105	415-995-1780	995-1791
Sierra Legal Defense Fund 131 Water St Suite 214 *TF:* 800-926-7744 ■ *Web:* www.sierralegal.org	Vancouver	BC	V6B4M3	604-685-5618	685-7813
Society of Architectural Historians (SAH) 1365 N Astor St *Web:* www.sah.org	Chicago	IL	60610	312-573-1365	573-1141
Society for Ecological Restoration International (SERI) 285 W 18th St Suite 1 *Web:* www.ser.org	Tucson	AZ	85701	520-622-5485	622-5491
Society Promoting Environmental Conservation (SPEC) 2150 Maple St *Web:* www.spec.bc.ca	Vancouver	BC	V6J3T3	604-736-7732	736-7115
Soil & Water Conservation Society (SWCS) 945 SW Ankeny Rd *Web:* www.swcs.org	Ankeny	IA	50021	515-289-2331	289-1227
Southern Utah Wilderness Alliance (SUWA) 425 East 100 South *Web:* www.suwa.org	Salt Lake City	UT	84111	801-486-3161	
Student Conservation Assn (SCA) 689 River Rd PO Box 550 *TF:* 888-722-9675 ■ *Web:* www.thesca.org	Charlestown	NH	03603	603-543-1700	543-1828
Tall Timbers 13093 Henry Beadel Dr *Web:* www.talltimbers.org	Tallahassee	FL	32312	850-893-4153	893-6470
Thomas Jefferson's Poplar Forest PO Box 419 *Web:* www.poplarforest.org	Forest	VA	245510419	434-525-1806	525-7252
Thornton W Burgess Society 6 Discovery Hill Rd *Web:* www.thorntonburgess.org	East Sandwich	MA	02537	508-888-6870	888-1919
Tongass Conservation Society (TCS) PO Box 23377 *Web:* www.tongassconservation.org	Ketchikan	AK	99901	907-225-3275	
Tree Care Industry Assn (TCIA) 3 Perimeter Rd Unit 1 *TF:* 800-733-2622 ■ *Web:* www.treecareindustry.org	Manchester	NH	03103	603-314-5380	314-5386
Trust for Public Land (TPL) 116 New Montgomery St 4th Fl *TF:* 800-714-5263 ■ *Web:* www.tpl.org	San Francisco	CA	94105	415-495-4014	495-4103
Union of Concerned Scientists (UCS) 2 Brattle Sq 6th Fl *TF:* 800-664-8276 ■ *Web:* www.ucsusa.org	Cambridge	MA	02238	617-547-5552	864-9405
Upper Mississippi River Conservation Committee (UMRCC) 555 Lester Ave *Web:* www.mississippi-river.com/umrcc	Onalaska	WI	54650	608-783-8432	
US Committee of the International Council on Monuments & Sites (US/ICOMOS) National Building Museum 401 F St NW Rm 331 *Web:* www.icomos.org/usicomos	Washington	DC	20001	202-842-1866	842-1866
Walden Woods Project 44 Baker Farm Rd *TF:* 800-554-3569 ■ *Web:* www.walden.org	Lincoln	MA	01773	781-259-4700	259-4710
Water Environment Federation (WEF) 601 Wythe St *TF:* 800-666-0206 ■ *Web:* www.wef.org	Alexandria	VA	22314	703-684-2400	684-2492
Western Canada Wilderness Committee (WCWC) 227 Abbott St *TF:* 800-661-9453 ■ *Web:* www.wildernesscommittee.org	Vancouver	BC	V6B2K7	604-683-8220	683-8229
Wilderness Society 1615 M St NW *TF:* 800-843-8443 ■ *Web:* www.wilderness.org	Washington	DC	20036	202-833-2300	429-3958
Wildlands Project 52 Bridge St PO Box 455 *Web:* www.wildlandsproject.org	Richmond	VT	05477	802-434-4077	434-5980
Wildlife Habitat Council (WHC) 8737 Colesville Rd Suite 800 *Web:* www.wildlifehc.org	Silver Spring	MD	20910	301-588-8994	588-4629
World Forestry Center 4033 SW Canyon Rd *Web:* www.worldforestry.org	Portland	OR	97221	503-228-1367	228-4608
World Resources Institute (WRI) 10 G St NE Suite 800 *Web:* www.wri.org	Washington	DC	20002	202-729-7600	729-7610
Yosemite Assn (YA) 5020 El Portal Rd PO Box 230 *Web:* www.yosemite.org	El Portal	CA	95318	209-379-2646	379-2486

48-14 Ethnic & Nationality Organizations

Organization	City	State	Zip	Phone	Fax
AAI (Arab American Institute) 1600 K St NW Ste 601 *Web:* www.aaiusa.org	Washington	DC	20006	202-429-9210	429-9214
Africa-America Institute (AAI) 420 Lexington Ave Suite 1706 *Web:* www.aaionline.org	New York	NY	10170	212-949-5666	682-6174
American Folklore Society (AFS) Ohio State Univ Mershon Ctr 1501 Neil Ave *Web:* www.afsnet.org	Columbus	OH	43201	614-292-3375	292-2407
American Hellenic Educational Progressive Assn (AHEPA) 1909 Q St NW Suite 500 *Web:* www.ahepa.org	Washington	DC	20009	202-232-6300	232-2140
American Historical Society of Germans from Russia 631 D St *Web:* www.ahsgr.org	Lincoln	NE	68502	402-474-3363	474-7229
American Latvian Assn in the US 400 Hurley Ave *Web:* www.alausa.org	Rockville	MD	20850	301-340-1914	340-8732
Arab American Institute (AAI) 1600 K St NW Ste 601 *Web:* www.aaiusa.org	Washington	DC	20006	202-429-9210	429-9214
Armenian Assembly of America 1140 19th St NW Suite 600 *Web:* www.aaainc.org	Washington	DC	20036	202-393-3434	638-4904
Armenian General Benevolent Union (AGBU) 55 E 59th St 7th Fl *Web:* www.agbu.org	New York	NY	10022	212-319-6383	319-6507
ASPIRA Assn Inc 1444 'I' St NW Suite 800 *Web:* www.aspira.org	Washington	DC	20005	202-835-3600	835-3613
Assembly of Turkish American Assns (ATAA) 1526 18th St NW *Web:* www.ataa.org	Washington	DC	20036	202-483-9090	483-9092
Association on American Indian Affairs (AAIA) 2009 S Dakota Hwy 10 Suite B *Web:* www.indian-affairs.org	Sisseton	SD	57262	605-698-3998	698-3316
Association of American Indian Physicians (AAIP) 1225 Sovereign Row Suite 103 *TF:* 800-943-4299 ■ *Web:* www.aaip.com	Oklahoma City	OK	73108	405-946-7072	946-7651
Association of Jewish Aging Services (AJAS) 316 Pennsylvania Ave SE Suite 402 *Web:* www.ajas.org	Washington	DC	20003	202-543-7500	543-4090
Center for Cuban Studies 124 W 23rd St *Web:* www.cubaupdate.org	New York	NY	10011	212-242-0559	242-1937
China Institute in America 125 E 65th St *Web:* www.chinainstitute.org	New York	NY	10065	212-744-8181	628-4159
Colombian-American Assn 30 Vesey St Suite 506 *Web:* www.colombianamerican.org	New York	NY	10007	212-233-7776	233-7779
Congress of Russian-Americans 2460 Sutter St *Web:* www.russian-americans.org	San Francisco	CA	94115	415-928-5841	928-5831
Croatian Fraternal Union of America (CFU) 100 Delaney Dr *Web:* www.croatianfraternalunion.org	Pittsburgh	PA	15235	412-351-3909	823-1594
Cuban American National Council 1223 SW 4th St *Web:* www.cnc.org	Miami	FL	33135	305-642-3484	642-9122
Cuban American National Foundation 1312 SW 27th Ave Suite 301 *Web:* www.canfnet.org	Miami	FL	33145	305-642-2220	592-7889
Ecuadorian-American Assn 30 Vesey St Suite 506	New York	NY	10007	212-233-7776	233-7779
First Nations Development Institute 2300 Fallhill Ave Suite 412 *Web:* www.firstnations.org	Fredericksburg	VA	22401	540-371-5615	371-3505
Foundation for Jewish Culture 330 7th Ave 21st Fl *Web:* www2.jewishculture.org	New York	NY	10001	212-629-0500	629-0508
French Institute Alliance Francaise (FIAF) 22 E 60th St *Web:* www.fiaf.org	New York	NY	10022	212-355-6100	935-4119
German-American National Congress (DANK) 4740 N Western Ave 2nd Fl *Web:* www.dank.org	Chicago	IL	60625	773-275-1100	275-4010
Hispanic Society of America 613 W 155th St *Web:* www.hispanicsociety.org	New York	NY	10032	212-926-2234	690-0743
Ibero-American Action League Inc 911 E Main St *Web:* www.iaal.org	Rochester	NY	14605	585-256-8900	256-0120
Japan Society 333 E 47th St *Web:* www.japansociety.org	New York	NY	10017	212-832-1155	755-6752
Japanese American Citizens League (JACL) 1765 Sutter St *Web:* www.jacl.org	San Francisco	CA	94115	415-921-5225	931-4671
Korean American Coalition (KAC) 3727 W 6th St Suite 515 *Web:* www.kacla.org	Los Angeles	CA	90020	213-380-6175	380-7990
Kurdish Heritage Foundation of America 345 Park Pl	Brooklyn	NY	11238	718-783-7930	398-4365
Latin American Studies Assn (LASA) Univ of Pittsburgh 946 William Pitt Union *Web:* lasa.international.pitt.edu	Pittsburgh	PA	15260	412-648-7929	624-7145

Ethnic & Nationality Organizations (Cont'd)

Organization	City	State	Zip	Phone	Fax
Lithuanian-American Community Inc PO Box 2376 *Fax Area Code: 815 ■ Web: lietuviu-bendruomene.org	Naperville	IL	60567	410-663-0158	327-8881*
Mexican American Legal Defense & Educational Fund (MALDEF) 634 S Spring St Web: maldef.org	Los Angeles	CA	90014	213-629-2512	629-0266
Mexican-American Opportunity Foundation 401 N Garfield Ave Web: www.maof.org	Montebello	CA	90640	323-890-9600	890-9637
National Congress of American Indians (NCAI) 1301 Connecticut Ave NW Suite 200 Web: www.ncai.org	Washington	DC	20036	202-466-7767	466-7797
National Council of La Raza (NCLR) 1126 16th St NW 6th Fl Web: www.nclr.org	Washington	DC	20036	202-785-1670	776-1792
National Hispanic Institute (NHI) PO Box 220 Web: www.nhi-net.org	Maxwell	TX	78656	512-357-6137	357-2206
National Indian Council on Aging (NICOA) 10501 Montgomery Blvd NE Suite 210 Web: www.nicoa.org	Albuquerque	NM	87111	505-292-2001	292-1922
National Puerto Rican Coalition Inc (NPRC) 1901 L St NW Suite 802 Web: www.bateylink.org/overview.htm	Washington	DC	20036	202-223-3915	429-2223
National Slovak Society of the USA (NSS) 351 Valley Brook Rd TF: 800-488-1890 ■ Web: www.nsslife.com	McMurray	PA	15317	724-731-0094	731-0145
Order Sons of Italy in America (OSIA) 219 'E' St NE Web: www.osia.org	Washington	DC	20002	202-547-2900	546-8168
Organization of Chinese Americans (OCA) 1322 18th St NW Web: www.ocanatl.org	Washington	DC	20036	202-223-5500	296-0540
Polish American Congress 5711 N Milwaukee Ave Web: www.polamcon.org	Chicago	IL	60646	773-763-9944	763-7114
Scottish Heritage USA PO Box 457 Web: www.sandhillsonline.com/shusa	Pinehurst	NC	28370	910-295-4448	295-3147
Sons of Norway 1455 W Lake St 2nd Fl TF: 800-945-8851 ■ Web: www.sofn.com	Minneapolis	MN	55408	612-827-3611	827-0658
Swedish Council of America 2600 Park Ave Web: www.swedishcouncil.org	Minneapolis	MN	55407	612-871-0593	871-0687
Tolstoy Foundation Inc 104 Lake Rd Web: www.tolstoyfoundation.org	Valley Cottage	NY	10989	845-268-6722	268-6937
Ukrainian National Assn PO Box 280 TF: 800-253-9862 ■ Web: www.unamember.com	Parsippany	NJ	07054	973-292-9800	292-0900
US Hispanic Chamber of Commerce 2175 K St NW Suite 100 TF: 800-874-2286 ■ Web: www.ushcc.com	Washington	DC	20037	202-842-1212	842-3221
US Pan Asian American Chamber of Commerce (USPAACC) 1329 18th St NW Web: www.uspaacc.com	Washington	DC	20036	202-296-5221	296-5225
Venezuelan-American Assn of the US 30 Vesey St Suite 506 Web: www.venezuelanamerican.org	New York	NY	10007	212-233-7776	233-7779

48-15 Fraternal & Social Organizations

Organization	City	State	Zip	Phone	Fax
American Mensa Ltd 1229 Corporate Dr W TF: 800-666-3672 ■ Web: www.us.mensa.org	Arlington	TX	76006	817-607-0060	649-5232
Association of Junior Leagues International Inc (AJLI) 80 Maiden Ln Suite 305 TF: 800-955-3248 ■ Web: www.ajli.org	New York	NY	10038	212-683-1515	481-7196
Athletes in Action 651 Taylor Dr Web: www.aia.com	Xenia	OH	45385	937-352-1000	352-1101
Benevolent & Protective Order of Elks of the USA 2750 N Lakeview Ave Web: www.elks.org	Chicago	IL	60614	773-755-4700	755-4790
Boy Scouts of America (BSA) PO Box 152079 Web: www.scouting.org	Irving	TX	75015	972-580-2000	580-2502
Boys & Girls Clubs of America 1230 W Peachtree St NW TF: 800-854-2582 ■ Web: www.bgca.org	Atlanta	GA	30309	404-487-5700	487-5757
Camp Fire USA 1100 Walnut St Suite 1900 TF: 800-669-6884 ■ Web: www.campfire.org	Kansas City	MO	64106	816-285-2010	285-9444
Civitan International PO Box 130744 TF: 800-248-4826 ■ Web: www.civitan.org	Birmingham	AL	35213	205-591-8910	592-6307
Cosmopolitan International 7341 W 80th St TF: 800-648-4331 ■ Web: www.cosmopolitan.org	Overland Park	KS	66204	913-648-4330	648-4630
DeMolay International 10200 NW Ambassabor Dr TF Orders: 800-336-6529 ■ Web: www.demolay.org	Kansas City	MO	64153	816-891-8333	891-9062
English-Speaking Union of the US 144 E 39th St Web: www.english-speakingunion.org	New York	NY	10016	212-818-1200	867-4177
FOP (Fraternal Order of Police) 1410 Donelson Pike Suite A-17 TF: 800-451-2711 ■ Web: www.grandlodgefop.org	Nashville	TN	37217	615-399-0900	399-0400
Fraternal Order of Police (FOP) 1410 Donelson Pike Suite A-17 TF: 800-451-2711 ■ Web: www.grandlodgefop.org	Nashville	TN	37217	615-399-0900	399-0400
Friars Club 57 E 55th St Web: www.friarsclub.com	New York	NY	10022	212-751-7272	355-0217
General Grand Chapter Order of the Eastern Star 1618 New Hampshire Ave NW TF: 800-648-1182 ■ Web: www.easternstar.org/ggc/frame.html	Washington	DC	20009	202-667-4737	462-5162
Girl Scouts of the USA 420 5th Ave TF: 800-223-0624 ■ Web: www.girlscouts.org	New York	NY	10018	212-852-8000	852-6517
Grand Aerie Fraternal Order of Eagles 1623 Gateway Cir S Web: www.foe.com	Grove City	OH	43123	614-883-2200	883-2201
Imperial Council AAONMS 2900 N Rocky Point Dr *Fax: Acctg ■ Web: www.shrinershq.org	Tampa	FL	33607	813-281-0300	281-2519*
Independent Order of Odd Fellows 422 Trade St TF: 800-235-8358 ■ Web: www.ioof.org	Winston-Salem	NC	27101	336-725-5955	722-7317
International Assn of Lions Clubs 300 W 22nd St Web: www.lionsclubs.org	Oak Brook	IL	60523	630-571-5466	571-8890
Key Club International 3636 Woodview Trace TF: 800-549-2647 ■ Web: www.keyclub.org	Indianapolis	IN	46268	317-875-8755	879-0204
Knights of Columbus 1 Columbus Plaza TF: 800-524-3611 ■ Web: www.kofc.org	New Haven	CT	06510	203-752-4000	752-4100
Loyal Order of Moose Rt 31 Web: www.mooseintl.org	Mooseheart	IL	60539	630-859-2000	859-6618
Masonic Service Assn of North America (MSANA) 8120 Fenton St Web: www.msana.com	Silver Spring	MD	20910	301-588-4010	608-3457
Moose International Inc Rt 31 Web: www.mooseintl.org	Mooseheart	IL	60539	630-859-2000	859-6618
National 4-H Council 7100 Connecticut Ave Web: www.fourhcouncil.edu	Chevy Chase	MD	20815	301-961-2800	961-2848
National Exchange Club 3050 W Central Ave TF: 800-924-2643 ■ Web: www.nationalexchangeclub.com	Toledo	OH	43606	419-535-3232	535-1989
National Grange 1616 H St NW TF: 888-447-2643 ■ Web: www.grange.org	Washington	DC	20006	202-628-3507	347-1091
Optimist International 4494 Lindell Blvd TF: 800-500-8130 ■ Web: www.optimist.org	Saint Louis	MO	63108	314-371-6000	371-6006
Procrastinators' Club of America PO Box 712 Web: www.geocities.com/procrastinators_club_of_america	Bryn Athyn	PA	19009	215-947-9020	947-7210
Quota International 1420 21st St NW Web: www.quota.org	Washington	DC	20036	202-331-9694	331-4395
Rotary International 1560 Sherman Ave Web: www.rotary.org	Evanston	IL	60201	847-866-3000	328-8554
Ruritan National PO Box 487 TF Orders: 877-787-8727 ■ Web: www.ruritan.org	Dublin	VA	24084	540-674-5431	674-2304
Shrine of North America 2900 N Rocky Point Dr *Fax: Acctg ■ Web: www.shrinershq.org	Tampa	FL	33607	813-281-0300	281-2519*
TelecomPioneers PO Box 13888 Web: www.telecompioneers.org	Denver	CO	80201	303-571-1200	572-0520
Toastmasters International 23182 Arroyo Vista Web: www.toastmasters.org	Rancho Santa Margarita	CA	92688	949-858-8255	858-1207
Up With People 1600 Broadway Suite 1460 TF: 877-264-8856 ■ Web: www.upwithpeople.org	Denver	CO	80202	303-460-7100	225-4649

48-16 Greek Letter Societies

Organization	City	State	Zip	Phone	Fax
Alpha Beta Gamma International Business Honor Society 75 Grasslands Rd Web: www.abg.org	Valhalla	NY	10595	914-606-6877	606-6481
Alpha Chi National College Honor Scholarship Society Harding University Box 12249 TF: 800-477-4225 ■ Web: www.harding.edu/alphachi	Searcy	AR	72149	501-279-4443	279-4589
Alpha Chi Omega 5939 Castle Creek Pkwy N Dr Web: www.alphachiomega.org	Indianapolis	IN	46250	317-579-5050	579-5051
Alpha Chi Rho Fraternity Inc 109 Oxford Way Web: alphachirho.org	Neptune	NJ	07753	732-869-1895	988-5357
Alpha Chi Sigma 2141 N Franklin Rd Web: www.alphachisigma.org	Indianapolis	IN	46219	317-357-5944	351-9702
Alpha Delta Phi International Fraternity 6126 Lincoln Ave Web: www.alphadeltaphi.org	Morton Grove	IL	60053	847-965-1832	965-1871
Alpha Delta Pi 1386 Ponce de Leon Ave NE Web: www.alphadeltapi.org	Atlanta	GA	30306	404-378-3164	373-0084
Alpha Epsilon Delta (AED) James Madison University 601 University Blvd MSC 9015 Web: www.jmu.edu/orgs/nationalaed	Harrisonburg	VA	22807	540-568-2594	568-2595
Alpha Epsilon Phi Sorority (AEPhi) 11 Lake Ave Ext Suite 1-A Web: www.aephi.org	Danbury	CT	06811	203-748-0029	748-0039
Alpha Epsilon Pi Fraternity Inc 8815 Wesleyan Rd TF: 800-223-2374 ■ Web: www.aepi.org	Indianapolis	IN	46268	317-876-1913	876-1057
Alpha Gamma Delta 8701 Founders Rd Web: www.alphagammadelta.org	Indianapolis	IN	46268	317-872-2655	875-5824
Alpha Gamma Rho 10101 N Ambassador Dr Web: www.agrs.org	Kansas City	MO	64153	816-891-9200	891-9401
Alpha Kappa Alpha Sorority Inc 5656 S Stony Island Ave Web: www.aka1908.com	Chicago	IL	60637	773-684-1282	288-8251
Alpha Kappa Psi (AKPsi) 7801 E 88th St Web: www.akpsi.com	Indianapolis	IN	46256	317-872-1553	872-1567
Alpha Omega International Dental Fraternity 191 Clarksville Rd *Fax Area Code: 619 ■ TF: 800-677-8468 ■ Web: www.ao.org	Princeton	NJ	08550	877-677-8468	799-7032*
Alpha Omicron Pi Fraternity 5390 Virginia Way Web: www.alphaomicronpi.org	Brentwood	TN	37027	615-370-0920	371-9736
Alpha Phi Alpha Fraternity Inc 2313 Saint Paul St Web: www.alphaphialpha.net	Baltimore	MD	21218	410-554-0040	554-0054
Alpha Phi Delta Fraternity Inc 3901 W 86th St Suite 390 Web: www.apd.org	Indianapolis	IN	46268	317-876-4688	872-1134
Alpha Phi International Fraternity 1930 Sherman Ave Web: www.alphaphi.org	Evanston	IL	60201	847-475-0663	475-6820
Alpha Phi Omega (APO) 14901 E 42nd St Web: www.apo.org	Independence	MO	64055	816-373-8667	373-5975
Alpha Sigma Alpha (ASA) 9550 Zionsville Rd Suite 160 Web: www.alphasigmaalpha.org	Indianapolis	IN	46268	317-871-2920	871-2924
Alpha Sigma Kappa 1009 University Ave SE Web: www.alpha-sigma-kappa.org	Minneapolis	MN	55414	612-378-4759	
Alpha Sigma Phi National Fraternity 710 Adams St TF: 800-800-1845 ■ Web: www.alphasigmaphi.org	Carmel	IN	46032	317-843-1911	843-2966
Alpha Sigma Tau Sorority 1929 Canyon Rd Web: www.alphasigmatau.org	Birmingham	AL	35216	205-978-2179	978-2182
Alpha Tau Omega Fraternity (ATO) 1 N Pennsylvania St 12th Fl Web: www.ato.org	Indianapolis	IN	46204	317-684-1865	684-1862
Alpha Xi Delta Women's Fraternity 8702 Founders Rd Web: www.alphaxidelta.org	Indianapolis	IN	46268	317-872-3500	872-2947
Beta Alpha Psi Palladian I 220 Leigh Farm Rd Web: www.bap.org	Durham	NC	27707	919-402-4044	402-4040
Beta Beta Beta National Biological Honor Society Univ of North Alabama Box 5079 Web: www.tri-beta.org	Florence	AL	35632	256-765-6220	765-6221
Beta Gamma Sigma Inc 125 Weldon Pkwy Web: www.betagammasigma.org	Maryland Heights	MO	63043	314-432-5650	432-7083
Beta Phi Mu Florida State Univ School of Information Studies Web: www.beta-phi-mu.org	Tallahassee	FL	32306	850-644-3907	644-9763
Beta Theta Pi 5134 Bonham Rd TF: 800-800-2382 ■ Web: www.betathetapi.org	Oxford	OH	45056	513-523-7591	523-2381
Chi Alpha Campus Ministries USA 1445 Booneville Ave Web: www.chialpha.com	Springfield	MO	65802	417-862-2781	865-9947
Chi Omega Fraternity 3395 Players Club Pkwy Web: www.chiomega.com	Memphis	TN	38125	901-748-8600	748-8686
Chi Phi Fraternity 850 Indian Trail Rd NW Web: www.chiphi.org	Lilburn	GA	30047	404-231-1824	237-5090
Chi Psi Fraternity 147 Maple Row Blvd Suite 200 Web: www.chipsi.org	Hendersonville	TN	37075	615-826-9966	826-9986
Delta Chi Fraternity Inc 314 Church St PO Box 1817 Web: www.deltachi.com	Iowa City	IA	52244	319-337-4811	337-5529
Delta Delta Delta Fraternity 2331 Brookhollow Plaza Dr PO Box 5987 Web: www.tridelta.org	Arlington	TX	76005	817-633-8001	652-0212
Delta Gamma 3250 Riverside Dr PO Box 21397 Web: www.deltagamma.org	Columbus	OH	43221	614-481-8169	481-0133
Delta Kappa Epsilon Fraternity (DKE) PO Box 8360 Web: www.dke.org	Ann Arbor	MI	48107	734-302-4210	
Delta Nu Alpha Transportation Fraternity (DNA) 1451 Elm Hill Pike Suite 255 Web: www.deltanualpha.org	Nashville	TN	37210	615-360-6863	360-1891

Organization	City	State	Zip	Phone	Fax
Delta Phi Epsilon International Sorority 16A Worthington Dr *Web:* www.dphie.org	Maryland Heights	MO	63043	314-275-2626	275-2655
Delta Phi Fraternity Inc PO Box 81521 *Web:* deltaphi.org	Athens	GA	30608	706-552-1444	
Delta Pi Epsilon (DPE) PO Box 4340 *Web:* www.dpe.org	Little Rock	AR	72214	501-219-1866	219-1876
Delta Sigma Phi Fraternity 1331 N Delaware St *Web:* www.deltasig.org	Indianapolis	IN	46202	317-634-1899	634-1410
Delta Sigma Pi 330 S Campus Ave Box 230 *Web:* www.dspnet.org	Oxford	OH	45056	513-523-1907	523-7292
Delta Sigma Theta Sorority Inc 1707 New Hampshire Ave NW *Web:* www.deltasigmatheta.org	Washington	DC	20009	202-986-2400	986-2513
Delta Tau Delta Fraternity 10000 Allisonville Rd *Web:* www.delts.org	Fishers	IN	46038	317-284-0203	284-0214
Delta Theta Phi 38640 Butternut Ridge Rd *TF:* 800-783-2600 ■ *Web:* www.deltathetaphi.org	Elyria	OH	44035	440-458-4381	458-4380
Delta Upsilon International Fraternity 8705 Founders Rd PO Box 68942 *Web:* www.deltau.org	Indianapolis	IN	46268	317-875-8900	876-1629
Delta Zeta Sorority 202 E Church St *Web:* www.deltazeta.org	Oxford	OH	45056	513-523-7597	523-1921
Epsilon Sigma Phi PO Box 357340 *Web:* espnational.org	Gainesville	FL	32635	352-378-6665	375-0722
Eta Sigma Gamma 2000 University Ave *TF:* 800-715-2559 ■ *Web:* www.bsu.edu/web/esg	Muncie	IN	47306	765-285-2258	285-3210
Fraternity of Alpha Kappa Lambda 4735 Statesmen Dr Suite F **Fax Area Code:* 866 ■ *Web:* www.akl.org	Indianapolis	IN	46250	317-585-4911	556-8719*
Gamma Beta Phi Society 78A Mitchell Rd *TF:* 800-628-9920 ■ *Web:* www.gammabetaphi.org	Oak Ridge	TN	37830	865-483-6212	483-9801
Gamma Phi Beta International Sorority 12737 E Euclid Dr *Web:* www.gammaphibeta.org	Centennial	CO	80111	303-799-1874	799-1876
International Fraternity of Phi Gamma Delta 1201 Red Mile Rd PO Box 4599 *Web:* www.phigam.org	Lexington	KY	40544	859-255-1848	253-0779
Kappa Alpha Order PO Box 1865 *Web:* www.kappaalphaorder.org	Lexington	VA	24450	540-463-1865	463-2140
Kappa Alpha Psi Fraternity Inc 2322 N Broad St *Web:* www.kappaalphapsi.com	Philadelphia	PA	19132	215-228-7184	228-7181
Kappa Alpha Theta Fraternity 8740 Founders Rd *TF:* 800-526-1870 ■ *Web:* www.kappaalphatheta.org	Indianapolis	IN	46268	317-876-1870	876-1925
Kappa Delta Epsilon (KDE) 3108 Castle Maine Dr *Web:* www.kappadeltaepsilon.org	Charlotte	NC	28269	704-503-1370	
Kappa Delta Pi 3707 Woodview Trace *TF:* 800-284-3167 ■ *Web:* www.kdp.org	Indianapolis	IN	46268	317-871-4900	704-2323
Kappa Delta Sorority 3205 Players Ln *TF:* 800-536-1897 ■ *Web:* www.kappadelta.org	Memphis	TN	38125	901-748-1897	748-0949
Kappa Kappa Gamma 530 E Town St PO Box 38 *TF:* 866-554-1870 ■ *Web:* www.kappakappagamma.org	Columbus	OH	43216	614-228-6515	228-7809
Kappa Kappa Iota 1875 E 15th St *TF:* 800-678-0389 ■ *Web:* www.kappakappaiota.org	Tulsa	OK	74104	918-744-0389	744-0578
Kappa Kappa Psi National Honorary Band Fraternity PO Box 849 *TF:* 800-543-6505 ■ *Web:* www.kkpsi.org	Stillwater	OK	74076	405-372-2333	372-2363
Kappa Psi Pharmaceutical Fraternity 100 Campus Dr *Web:* www.kappa-psi.org	Weatherford	OK	73096	580-774-7170	774-7125
Kappa Sigma Fraternity PO Box 5066 *Web:* www.kappasigma.org	Charlottesville	VA	22905	434-295-3193	296-9557
Lambda Chi Alpha International Fraternity 8741 Founders Rd *TF:* 800-209-6837 ■ *Web:* www.lambdachi.org	Indianapolis	IN	46268	317-872-8000	875-3828
Mu Phi Epsilon International Music Fraternity 4705 N Sonora Ave Suite 114 *TF:* 888-259-1471 ■ *Web:* home.muphiepsilon.org	Fresno	CA	93722	559-277-1898	277-2825
National Alpha Lambda Delta PO Box 4403 *Web:* www.mercer.edu/ald	Macon	GA	31208	478-744-9595	744-9924
National Fraternity of Kappa Delta Rho 331 S Main St *TF:* 800-536-5371 ■ *Web:* www.kdr.com	Greensburg	PA	15601	724-838-7100	838-7101
Omega Psi Phi Fraternity Inc 3951 Snapfinger Pkwy *Web:* www.oppf.org	Decatur	GA	30035	404-284-5533	284-0333
Omicron Delta Epsilon PO Box 1486 *TF:* 800-584-5514 ■ *Web:* www.omicrondeltaepsilon.org	Hattiesburg	MS	39403	601-264-3115	264-3669
Phi Alpha Delta Law Fraternity International 345 N Charles St *Web:* www.pad.org	Baltimore	MD	21201	410-347-3118	347-3119
Phi Alpha Theta Univ of South Florida 4202 E Fowler Ave SOC 107 *TF:* 800-394-8195 ■ *Web:* www.phialphatheta.org	Tampa	FL	33620	813-974-8212	974-8215
Phi Beta Kappa Society 1606 New Hampshire Ave NW *Web:* staging.pbk.org	Washington	DC	20009	202-265-3808	986-1601
Phi Beta Sigma Fraternity Inc 145 Kennedy St NW *Web:* www.pbs1914.org	Washington	DC	20011	202-726-5434	882-1681
Phi Chi Theta 1508 E Beltline Rd Suite 104 *Web:* www.phichitheta.org	Carrollton	TX	75006	972-245-7202	
Phi Delta Kappa International (PDK) 408 N Union St PO Box 789 *TF:* 800-766-1156 ■ *Web:* www.pdkintl.org	Bloomington	IN	47402	812-339-1156	339-0018
Phi Delta Phi International Legal Fraternity 1426 21st St NW *TF:* 800-368-5606 ■ *Web:* www.phideltaphi.org	Washington	DC	20036	202-223-6801	223-6808
Phi Delta Theta 2 S Campus Ave *Web:* www.phideltatheta.org	Oxford	OH	45056	513-523-6345	523-9200
Phi Eta Sigma National Honor Society 1906 College Heights Blvd #11062 *Web:* www.phietasigma.org	Bowling Green	KY	42101	270-745-6540	745-3893
Phi Kappa Psi 510 Lockerbie St *TF:* 800-486-1852 ■ *Web:* www.phikappapsi.com	Indianapolis	IN	46202	317-632-1852	637-1898
Phi Kappa Sigma International Fraternity Inc 2 Timber Dr *Web:* www.pks.org	Chester Springs	PA	19425	610-469-3282	469-3286
Phi Kappa Tau 5221 Morning Sun Rd *TF:* 800-758-1906 ■ *Web:* www.phikappatau.org	Oxford	OH	45056	513-523-4193	523-9325
Phi Kappa Theta National Fraternity 9640 N Augusta Dr Suite 420 *Web:* www.phikaps.org	Carmel	IN	46032	317-872-9934	879-1889
Phi Mu Alpha Sinfonia Fraternity of America Inc 10600 Old State Rd *Web:* www.sinfonia.org	Evansville	IN	47711	812-867-2433	867-0633
Phi Mu Fraternity 400 Westpark Dr *TF:* 888-744-6836 ■ *Web:* www.phimu.org	Peachtree City	GA	30269	770-632-2090	632-2136
Phi Sigma Kappa 2925 E 96th St *Web:* www.phisigmakappa.org	Indianapolis	IN	46240	317-573-5420	573-5430
Phi Sigma Pi National Honor Fraternity Inc 2119 Ambassador Cir *Web:* www.phisigmapi.org	Lancaster	PA	17603	717-299-4710	390-3054
Phi Sigma Sigma Fraternity Inc 8178 Lark Brown Rd Suite 202 *Web:* www.phisigmasigma.org	Elkridge	MD	21075	410-799-1224	799-9186
Phi Theta Kappa International Honor Society 1625 Eastover Dr PO Box 13729 *Web:* www.ptk.org	Jackson	MS	39236	601-984-3504	984-3550
Pi Beta Phi Fraternity for Women 1154 Town & Country Commons Dr *Web:* www.pibetaphi.org	Town and Country	MO	63017	636-256-0680	256-8095
Pi Kappa Alpha Fraternity 8347 W Range Cove *Web:* www.pka.com	Memphis	TN	38125	901-748-1868	748-3100
Pi Kappa Phi Fraternity 2102 Cambridge Beltway Dr Suite A PO Box 240526 *Web:* www.pikapp.org	Charlotte	NC	28224	704-504-0888	504-0880
Pi Lambda Phi Fraternity Inc 36 Mill Plain Rd Suite 309 *TF:* 800-394-7573 ■ *Web:* www.pilambdaphi.org	Danbury	CT	06811	203-740-1044	740-1644
Pi Lambda Theta PO Box 6626 **Fax Area Code:* 812 ■ *Web:* www.pilambda.org	Bloomington	IN	47407	800-487-3411	339-3462*
Pi Sigma Alpha 1527 New Hampshire Ave NW *Web:* www.apsanet.org/~psa	Washington	DC	20036	202-483-2512	483-2657
Pi Sigma Epsilon (PSE) 3747 S Howell Ave *TF:* 800-761-9350 ■ *Web:* www.pse.org	Milwaukee	WI	53207	414-328-1952	328-1953
Psi Chi National Honor Society in Psychology PO Box 709 *Web:* www.psichi.org	Chattanooga	TN	37401	423-756-2044	265-1529
Psi Upsilon Fraternity 3003 E 96th St *TF:* 800-394-1833 ■ *Web:* www.psiu.org	Indianapolis	IN	46240	317-571-1833	844-5170
Sigma Alpha Epsilon Fraternity (SAE) 1856 Sheridan Rd *TF:* 800-233-1856 ■ *Web:* www.saefraternity.org	Evanston	IL	60201	847-475-1856	475-2250
Sigma Alpha Iota (SAI) 1 Tunnel Rd *Web:* www.sai-national.org	Asheville	NC	28805	828-251-0606	251-0644
Sigma Alpha Mu Fraternity 9245 N Meridian St Suite 105 *TF:* 888-369-9361 ■ *Web:* www.sam.org	Indianapolis	IN	46260	317-846-0600	846-9462
Sigma Chi Fraternity 1714 Hinman Ave PO Box 469 *Web:* www.sigmachi.org	Evanston	IL	60204	847-869-3655	869-4906
Sigma Delta Tau 714 Adams St *Web:* www.sigmadeltatau.com	Carmel	IN	46032	317-846-7747	575-5562
Sigma Gamma Rho Sorority Inc 1000 S Hill Dr Suite 200 *TF:* 888-747-1922 ■ *Web:* www.sgrho1922.org	Cary	NC	27513	919-678-9720	678-9721
Sigma Kappa Sorority 8733 Founders Rd *Web:* www.sigmakappa.org	Indianapolis	IN	46268	317-872-3275	872-0716
Sigma Nu Fraternity Inc 9 Lewis St PO Box 1869 *Web:* www.sigmanu.org	Lexington	VA	24450	540-463-1869	463-1669
Sigma Phi Epsilon Fraternity 310 South Blvd *TF:* 800-313-1901 ■ *Web:* www.sigep.org	Richmond	VA	23220	804-353-1901	359-8160
Sigma Pi Fraternity PO Box 1897 **Fax Area Code:* 615 ■ *Web:* www.sigmapi.org	Brentwood	TN	37024	888-744-6274	373-8949*
Sigma Tau Gamma Fraternity Inc PO Box 54 *Web:* www.sigmataugamma.org	Warrensburg	MO	64093	660-747-2222	747-9599
Sigma Theta Tau International 550 W North St *TF:* 888-634-7575 ■ *Web:* www.nursingsociety.org	Indianapolis	IN	46202	317-634-8171	634-8188
Sigma Xi Scientific Research Society 3106 E NC Hwy 54 PO Box 13975 *TF:* 800-243-6534 ■ *Web:* www.sigmaxi.org	Research Triangle Park	NC	27709	919-549-4691	549-0090
Tau Alpha Chi 82 Thompson St *Web:* www.taualphachi.org	Alpharetta	GA	30004	770-475-4253	475-4408
Tau Beta Pi Assn PO Box 2697 *Web:* www.tbp.org	Knoxville	TN	37901	865-546-4578	546-4579
Tau Beta Sigma National Honorary Band Sorority PO Box 849 *TF:* 800-543-6505 ■ *Web:* www.kkytbs.org/tbs	Stillwater	OK	74076	405-372-2333	372-2363
Tau Kappa Epsilon (TKE) 8645 Founders Rd *Web:* www.tke.org	Indianapolis	IN	46268	317-872-6533	875-8353
Theta Delta Chi Inc 214 Lewis Wharf *TF:* 800-999-1847 ■ *Web:* www.tdx.org	Boston	MA	02110	617-742-8886	742-8868
Theta Phi Alpha Fraternity Inc 27025 Knickerbocker Rd *TF:* 877-843-8274 ■ *Web:* www.thetaphialpha.org	Bay Village	OH	44140	440-899-9282	899-9293
Theta Tau Professional Engineering Fraternity 815 Brazos St Suite 710 *TF:* 800-264-1904 ■ *Web:* www.thetatau.org	Austin	TX	78701	512-472-1904	472-4820
Theta Xi Fraternity PO Box 411134 *TF:* 800-783-6294 ■ *Web:* www.thetaxi.org	Saint Louis	MO	63141	314-993-6294	993-8760
Zeta Beta Tau Fraternity Inc (ZBT) 3905 Vincennes Rd Suite 300 *Web:* www.zbt.org	Indianapolis	IN	46268	317-334-1898	334-1899
Zeta Phi Beta Sorority Inc 1734 New Hampshire Ave NW *TF:* 000-300-5772 ■ *Web:* www.zphib1920.org	Washington	DC	20009	202-387-3103	232-4593
Zeta Psi Fraternity of North America 15 S Henry St *TF:* 800-477-1847 ■ *Web:* www.zetapsi.org	Pearl River	NY	10965	845-735-1847	735-1989
Zeta Tau Alpha Fraternity (ZTA) 3450 Founders Rd *Web:* www.zetataualpha.org	Indianapolis	IN	46268	317-872-0540	876-3948

48-17 Health & Health-Related Organizations

Organization	City	State	Zip	Phone	Fax
Acoustic Neuroma Assn (ANA) 600 Peachtree Pkwy Suite 108 *Web:* anausa.org	Cumming	GA	30041	770-205-8211	205-0239
AIDS Treatment Data Network 611 Broadway Suite 613 *Web:* www.atdn.org	New York	NY	10012	212-260-8868	260-8869
Alexander Graham Bell Assn for the Deaf & Hard of Hearing (AG Bell) 3417 Volta Pl NW *Web:* www.agbell.org	Washington	DC	20007	202-337-5220	337-8314
Alliance for Aging Research 2021 K St NW Suite 305 *TF:* 800-639-2421 ■ *Web:* www.agingresearch.org	Washington	DC	20006	202-293-2856	785-8574
Alliance for Lupus Research (ALA) 28 W 44th St Suite 501 *Web:* www.lupusresearch.org	New York	NY	10036	212-218-2840	218-2848
ALS Assn 27001 Agoura Rd Suite 150 *TF:* 800-782-4747 ■ *Web:* www.alsa.org	Calabasas Hills	CA	91301	818-880-9007	880-9006
Alzheimer's Assn 225 N Michigan Ave Suite 1700 *TF:* 800-272-3900 ■ *Web:* www.alz.org	Chicago	IL	60601	312-335-8700	335-1110
American Academy for Cerebral Palsy & Developmental Medicine (AACPDM) 555 E Wells St Suite 1100 *Web:* aacpdm.org	Milwaukee	WI	53202	414-276-4445	276-3349
American Academy of Medical Acupuncture (AAMA) 4929 Wilshire Blvd Suite 428 *Web:* www.medicalacupuncture.org	Los Angeles	CA	90010	323-937-5514	937-0959
American Academy of Sleep Medicine (AASM) 1 Westbrook Corporate Center Suite 920 *Web:* www.aasmnet.org	Westchester	IL	60154	708-492-0930	492-0943
American Amputee Foundation (AAF) PO Box 250218 Hillcrest Stn *Web:* www.americanamputee.org	Little Rock	AR	72225	501-666-2523	666-8367
American Assn of Drugless Practitioners (AADP) 2200 Market St Suite 329 *TF:* 888-764-2237 ■ *Web:* www.aadp.net	Galveston	TX	77550	409-621-2600	
American Assn on Intellectual & Developmental Disabilities (AAIDD) 444 N Capitol St NW Suite 846 *TF:* 800-424-3688 ■ *Web:* www.aaidd.org	Washington	DC	20001	202-387-1968	387-2193

Health & Health-Related Organizations (Cont'd)

Organization	City	State	ZIP	Phone	Fax
American Assn of Naturopathic Physicians (AANP) 4435 Wisconsin Ave NW Suite 403 *TF:* 866-538-2267 ■ *Web:* www.naturopathic.org	Washington	DC	20016	202-237-8150	237-8152
American Assn of Oriental Medicine (AAOM) PO Box 162340 *TF:* 866-455-7999 ■ *Web:* www.aaom.org	Sacramento	CA	95816	916-443-4770	443-4766
American Assn of Suicidology (AAS) 5221 Wisconsin Ave NW 2nd Fl *Web:* www.suicidology.org	Washington	DC	20015	202-237-2280	237-2282
American Autoimmune Related Disease Assn (AARDA) 22100 Gratiot Ave *TF:* 800-598-4668 ■ *Web:* www.aarda.org	Eastpointe	MI	48021	586-776-3900	776-3903
American Bone Marrow Donor Registry 2733 North St *TF:* 800-745-2452 ■ *Web:* www.charityadvantage.com/abmdr	Mandeville	LA	70448	985-626-1749	626-7414
American Botanical Council PO Box 144345 *TF:* 800-373-7105 ■ *Web:* www.herbalgram.org	Austin	TX	78714	512-926-4900	926-2345
American Brain Tumor Assn (ABTA) 2720 River Rd *TF:* 800-886-2282 ■ *Web:* hope.abta.org	Des Plaines	IL	60018	847-827-9910	827-9918
American Cancer Society (ACS) 1599 Clifton Rd NE *TF:* 800-227-2345 ■ *Web:* www.cancer.org	Atlanta	GA	30329	404-320-3333	325-9341
American Chronic Pain Assn (ACPA) PO Box 850 *TF:* 800-533-3231 ■ *Web:* www.theacpa.org	Rocklin	CA	95677	916-632-0922	632-3208
American Council on Alcoholism (ACA) 1000 E Indian School Rd *Fax Area Code: 602 ■ *Web:* www.aca-usa.org	Phoenix	AZ	85014	800-527-5344	264-7403*
American Council of the Blind (ACB) 1155 15th St NW Suite 1004 *TF:* 800-424-8666 ■ *Web:* www.acb.org	Washington	DC	20005	202-467-5081	467-5085
American Council for Drug Education (ACDE) c/o Phoenix House 164 W 74th St *TF:* 800-378-4435 ■ *Web:* www.acde.org	New York	NY	10023	212-595-5810	721-7384
American Council on Exercise (ACE) 4851 Paramount Dr *TF:* 800-825-3636 ■ *Web:* www.acefitness.org	San Diego	CA	92123	858-279-8227	279-8064
American Council for Headache Education (ACHE) 19 Mantua Rd *TF:* 800-255-2243 ■ *Web:* www.achenet.org	Mount Royal	NJ	08061	856-423-0258	423-0082
American Diabetes Assn (ADA) 1701 N Beauregard St *TF:* 800-232-3472 ■ *Web:* www.diabetes.org	Alexandria	VA	22311	703-549-1500	836-2464
American Dietetic Assn (ADA) 120 S Riverside Plaza Suite 2000 *TF:* 800-877-1600 ■ *Web:* www.eatright.org	Chicago	IL	60606	312-899-0040	899-4899
American Epilepsy Society (AES) 342 N Main St *Web:* www.aesnet.org	West Hartford	CT	06117	860-586-7505	586-7550
American Foundation for AIDS Research (amfAR) 120 Wall St 13th Fl *Web:* www.amfar.org	New York	NY	10005	212-806-1600	806-1601
American Foundation for the Blind (AFB) 11 Penn Plaza Suite 300 *TF:* 800-232-5463 ■ *Web:* www.afb.org	New York	NY	10001	212-502-7600	502-7777
American Foundation for Suicide Prevention (AFSP) 120 Wall St 22nd Fl *TF:* 888-333-2377 ■ *Web:* www.afsp.org	New York	NY	10005	212-363-3500	363-6237
American Hair Loss Council (AHLC) 125 7th St Suite 625 *Web:* www.ahlc.org	Pittsburgh	PA	15222	412-765-3666	765-3669
American Hearing Research Foundation 8 S Michigan Ave Suite 814 *Web:* www.american-hearing.org	Chicago	IL	60603	312-726-9670	726-9695
American Heart Assn (AHA) 7272 Greenville Ave *TF:* 800-242-8721 ■ *Web:* www.americanheart.org	Dallas	TX	75231	214-373-6300	706-1191
American Herbalists Guild (AHG) 141 Nob Hill Rd *Web:* www.americanherbalistsguild.com	Cheshire	CT	06410	203-272-6731	272-8550
American Holistic Health Assn (AHHA) PO Box 17400 *Web:* ahha.org	Anaheim	CA	92817	714-779-6152	
American Holistic Medical Assn (AHMA) 12101 Menaul Blvd NE Suite C *Web:* www.holisticmedicine.org	Albuquerque	NM	87112	505-292-7788	293-7582
American Holistic Nurses' Assn (AHNA) 323 N San Francisco St Suite 201 *TF:* 800-278-2462 ■ *Web:* ahna.org	Flagstaff	AZ	86001	928-526-2196	526-2752
American Institute of Stress (AIS) 124 Park Ave *Web:* www.stress.org	Yonkers	NY	10703	914-963-1200	965-6267
American Juvenile Arthritis Organization (AJAO) 1330 W Peachtree St Suite 100 *TF:* 800-283-7800 ■ *Web:* www.arthritis.org/communities	Atlanta	GA	30309	404-965-7538	872-9559
American Kidney Fund (AKF) 6110 Executive Blvd Suite 1010 *TF:* 800-638-8299 ■ *Web:* www.akfinc.org	Rockville	MD	20852	301-881-3052	881-0898
American Leprosy Missions (ALM) 1 ALM Way *TF:* 800-543-3135 ■ *Web:* www.leprosy.org	Greenville	SC	29601	864-271-7040	271-7062
American Liver Foundation (ALF) 75 Maiden Ln Suite 603 *TF:* 800-465-4837 ■ *Web:* www.liverfoundation.org	New York	NY	10038	212-668-1000	483-8179
American Lung Assn (ALA) 61 Broadway 6th Fl *TF:* 800-586-4872 ■ *Web:* www.lungusa.org	New York	NY	10006	212-315-8700	315-8872
American Massage Therapy Assn (AMTA) 500 Davis St Suite 900 *TF:* 877-905-2700 ■ *Web:* www.amtamassage.org	Evanston	IL	60201	847-864-0123	864-1178
American Menopause Foundation Inc 350 5th Ave Suite 2822 *Web:* www.americanmenopause.org	New York	NY	10118	212-714-2398	
American Music Therapy Assn (AMTA) 8455 Colesville Rd Suite 1000 *Web:* www.musictherapy.org	Silver Spring	MD	20910	301-589-3300	589-5175
American Naturopathic Medical Assn (ANMA) PO Box 96273 *Web:* www.anma.com	Las Vegas	NV	89193	702-897-7053	897-7140
American Organization for Bodywork Therapies of Asia (AOBTA) 1010 Haddonfield-Berlin Rd Suite 408 *Web:* www.aobta.org	Voorhees	NJ	08043	856-782-1616	782-1653
American Orthotic & Prosthetic Assn (AOPA) 330 John Carlyle St Suite 200 *Web:* www.aopanet.org	Alexandria	VA	22314	571-431-0876	431-0899
American Pain Society (APS) 4700 W Lake Ave *Fax Area Code: 877 ■ *Web:* www.ampainsoc.org	Glenview	IL	60025	847-375-4715	734-8758*
American Parkinson Disease Assn (APDA) 35 Parkinson Ave *TF:* 800-223-2732 ■ *Web:* www.apdaparkinson.org	Staten Island	NY	10305	718-981-8001	981-4399
American Polarity Therapy Assn (APTA) PO Box 19858 *Web:* www.polaritytherapy.org	Boulder	CO	80308	303-545-2080	545-2161
American Prostate Society 7188 Ridge Rd PO Box 870 *TF:* 800-308-1106 ■ *Web:* www.ameripros.org	Hanover	MD	21076	410-859-3735	850-0818
American Self-Help Group Clearinghouse Saint Claires Health Services 100 E Hanover Ave Suite 202 *Web:* www.mentalhelp.net/selfhelp	Cedar Knolls	NJ	07927	973-326-8853	326-9467
American SIDS Institute 509 Augusta Dr *TF:* 800-232-7437 ■ *Web:* www.sids.org	Marietta	GA	30067	770-426-8746	426-1369
American Sleep Apnea Assn (ASAA) 1424 K St NW Suite 302 *Web:* www.sleepapnea.org	Washington	DC	20005	202-293-3650	293-3656
American Social Health Assn (ASHA) PO Box 13827 *TF:* 800-277-8922 ■ *Web:* www.ashastd.org	Research Triangle Park	NC	27709	919-361-8400	361-8425
American Society of Alternative Therapists (ASAT) PO Box 703 *Web:* www.asat.org	Rockport	MA	01966	978-281-4400	282-1144
American Therapeutic Recreation Assn (ATRA) 1414 Prince St Suite 204 *Web:* www.atra-tr.org	Alexandria	VA	22314	703-683-9420	683-9431
American Tinnitus Assn (ATA) PO Box 5 *TF:* 800-634-8978 ■ *Web:* www.ata.org	Portland	OR	97207	503-248-9985	248-0024
American Urological Assn Foundation (AUA Foundation) 1000 Corporate Blvd *TF:* 800-828-7866 ■ *Web:* www.auafoundation.org	Linthicum	MD	21090	410-689-3990	689-3998
American Yoga Assn (AYA) PO Box 19986 *Web:* www.americanyogaassociation.org	Sarasota	FL	34276	941-927-4977	921-9844
Americans for Better Care of the Dying (ABCD) 1700 Diagonal Rd Suite 635 *Web:* www.abcd-caring.org	Alexandria	VA	22314	703-647-8505	837-1233
Americans for Nonsmokers' Rights (ANR) 2530 San Pablo Ave Suite J *Web:* www.no-smoke.org	Berkeley	CA	94702	510-841-3032	841-3071
Anxiety Disorders Assn of America (ADAA) 8730 Georgia Ave Suite 600 *Web:* www.adaa.org	Silver Spring	MD	20910	240-485-1001	485-1035
Arc of the US 1010 Wayne Ave Suite 650 *TF:* 800-433-5255 ■ *Web:* www.thearc.org	Silver Spring	MD	20910	301-565-3842	565-3843
Arthritis Foundation 1330 W Peachtree St Suite 100 *TF:* 800-283-7800 ■ *Web:* www.arthritis.org	Atlanta	GA	30309	404-872-7100	872-0457
Associated Bodywork & Massage Professionals (ABMP) 1271 Sugarbush Dr *TF:* 800-458-2267 ■ *Web:* www.abmp.com	Evergreen	CO	80439	303-674-8478	674-0859
Association for the Advancement of the Blind & Retarded (AABR) 1508 College Pt Blvd *Web:* www.aabr.org	College Point	NY	11356	718-321-3800	321-8688
Association for Applied & Therapeutic Humor (AATH) 5 Independence Way Suite 300 *Web:* www.aath.org	Princeton	NJ	08540	609-514-5141	514-5131
Association for Children with Down Syndrome Inc (ACDS) 4 Fern Pl *Web:* www.acds.org	Plainview	NY	11803	516-933-4700	933-9524
Association for Macular Diseases Inc 210 E 64th St 8th Fl *Web:* www.macula.org	New York	NY	10021	212-605-3719	605-3795
Association of Natural Medicine Pharmacists (ANMP) 7 Mt Lassen Dr Suite C-116 *Web:* www.anmp.org	San Rafael	CA	94915	415-479-1512	472-2559
Association for Research & Enlightenment (ARE) 215 67th St *TF:* 800-333-4499 ■ *Web:* www.edgarcayce.org	Virginia Beach	VA	23451	757-428-3588	422-6921
Asthma & Allergy Foundation of America (AAFA) 1233 20th St NW Suite 402 *TF:* 800-727-8462 ■ *Web:* www.aafa.org	Washington	DC	20036	202-466-7643	466-8940
Attention Deficit Disorder Assn (ADDA) PO Box 543 *Fax Area Code: 610 ■ *Web:* www.add.org	Pottstown	PA	19464	484-945-2101	970-7520*
Autism Research Institute (ARI) 4182 Adams Ave *Web:* www.autism.com	San Diego	CA	92116	619-281-7165	563-6840
Autism Society of America (ASA) 7910 Woodmont Ave Suite 300 *TF:* 800-328-8476 ■ *Web:* www.autism-society.org	Bethesda	MD	20814	301-657-0881	
BACCHUS Network PO Box 100430 *Web:* bacchusgamma.org	Denver	CO	80250	303-871-0901	871-0907
BEGINNINGS for Parents of Children Who Are Deaf or Hard of Hearing Inc 3714 A Benson Dr *Web:* www.ncbegin.org	Raleigh	NC	27609	919-850-2746	850-2804
Bell Alexander Graham Assn for the Deaf & Hard of Hearing 3417 Volta Pl NW *Web:* www.agbell.org	Washington	DC	20007	202-337-5220	337-8314
Better Hearing Institute (BHI) 515 King St Suite 420 *TF:* 888-432-7435 ■ *Web:* www.betterhearing.org	Alexandria	VA	22314	703-684-3391	684-6048
Better Sleep Council 501 Wythe St *Web:* www.bettersleep.org	Alexandria	VA	22314	703-683-8371	683-4503
Better Vision Institute (BVI) Vision Council of America 1700 Diagonal Rd Suite 500 *TF:* 800-424-8422 ■ *Web:* www.visionsite.org	Alexandria	VA	22314	703-548-4560	548-4580
Birth Defect Research for Children 930 Woodcock Rd Suite 225 *Web:* www.birthdefects.org	Orlando	FL	32803	407-895-0802	895-0824
Bloch RA Cancer Foundation 4400 Main St *TF:* 800-433-0464 ■ *Web:* www.blochcancer.org	Kansas City	MO	64111	816-932-8453	931-7486
Brain Injury Assn of America 8201 Greensboro Dr Suite 611 *TF:* 800-444-6443 ■ *Web:* www.biausa.org	McLean	VA	22102	703-761-0750	761-0755
Brooks Kristin Hope Center 615 7th St NE *TF:* 800-784-2433 ■ *Web:* www.hopeline.com	Washington	DC	20002	202-536-3200	536-3206
Campaign for Tobacco-Free Kids 1400 'I' St NW Suite 1200 *TF:* 800-284-5437 ■ *Web:* www.tobaccofreekids.org	Washington	DC	20005	202-296-5469	296-5427
Cancer Care Inc 275 7th Ave 22nd Fl *TF:* 800-813-4673 ■ *Web:* www.cancercare.org	New York	NY	10001	212-712-8400	712-8495
Cancer Research & Prevention Foundation 1600 Duke St Suite 500 *TF:* 800-227-2732 ■ *Web:* www.preventcancer.org	Alexandria	VA	22314	703-836-4412	836-4413
Candlelighters Childhood Cancer Foundation PO Box 498 *TF:* 800-366-2223 ■ *Web:* www.candlelighters.org	Kensington	MD	20895	301-962-3520	962-3521
Canine Companions for Independence (CCI) 2965 Dutton Ave *TF:* 800-572-2275 ■ *Web:* www.caninecompanions.org	Santa Rosa	CA	95407	707-577-1700	577-1711
Carbon Monoxide Referral & Resources 618 Wyndhurst Ave Suite 2 *Web:* www.mcsrr.org	Baltimore	MD	21210	410-889-6666	889-4944
Carcinoid Cancer Foundation Inc 333 Mamaroneck Ave Suite 492 *TF:* 888-722-3132 ■ *Web:* www.carcinoid.org	White Plains	NY	10605	212-722-3132	
Center on Human Policy 805 S Crouse Ave *TF:* 800-894-0826 ■ *Web:* thechp.syr.edu	Syracuse	NY	13244	315-443-3851	443-4338
Center for Jewish Genetic Diseases Mt Sinai School of Medicine Box 1497 One Gustave L Levy Pl *Web:* www.nfjgd.org	New York	NY	10029	212-659-6774	
Center for Practical Bioethics 1100 Walnut St Suite 2900 *TF:* 800-344-3829 ■ *Web:* www.practicalbioethics.org	Kansas City	MO	64106	816-221-1100	221-2002
CFIDS Assn of America Inc 6827 Fairview Rd Suite A *Web:* www.cfids.org	Charlotte	NC	28210	704-364-0466	365-9755

	City	State	Zip	Phone	Fax
Child & Adolescent Bipolar Foundation (CABF) 1000 Skokie Blvd Suite 425 *Web:* www.bpkids.org	Wilmette	IL	60091	847-256-8525	920-9498
Children & Adults with Attention-Deficit/Hyperactivity Disorder (CHADD) 8181 Professional Pl Suite 150 *TF:* 800-233-4050 ■ *Web:* www.chadd.org	Landover	MD	20785	301-306-7070	306-7090
Children's Eye Foundation PO Box 193832 *Web:* www.childrenseyefoundation.org	San Francisco	CA	94119	415-561-8568	561-8531
Children's Leukemia Research Assn 585 Stewart Ave Suite 18 *Web:* www.childrensleukemia.org	Garden City	NY	11530	516-222-1944	222-0457
Children's Organ Transplant Assn (COTA) 2501 Cota Dr *TF:* 800-366-2682 ■ *Web:* www.cota.org	Bloomington	IN	47403	812-336-8872	336-8885
Children's Tumor Foundation 95 Pine St 16th Fl *TF:* 800-323-7938 ■ *Web:* www.ctf.org	New York	NY	10005	212-344-6633	747-0004
Children's Wish Foundation International 8615 Roswell Rd *TF:* 800-323-9474 ■ *Web:* www.childrenswish.org	Atlanta	GA	30350	770-393-9474	393-0683
Christopher Reeve Foundation 636 Morris Tpke *TF:* 800-225-0292 ■ *Web:* www.christopherreeve.org	Short Hills	NJ	07078	973-379-2690	912-9433
Cleft Palate Foundation (CPF) 1504 E Franklin St Suite 102 *TF:* 800-242-5338 ■ *Web:* www.cleftline.org	Chapel Hill	NC	27514	919-933-9044	933-9604
Compassion & Choices PO Box 101810 *TF:* 800-247-7421 ■ *Web:* www.compassionandchoices.org	Denver	CO	80250	303-639-1202	639-1224
Conjoined Twins International PO Box 10895	Prescott	AZ	86304	928-445-2777	
Cornelia de Lange Syndrome Foundation Inc (CdLS) 302 W Main St Suite 100 *TF:* 800-753-2357 ■ *Web:* www.cdlsusa.org	Avon	CT	06001	860-676-8166	676-8337
Council for Affordable Health Insurance (CAHI) 127 S Peyton St Suite 210 *Web:* www.cahi.org	Alexandria	VA	22314	703-836-6200	836-6550
Council on Size & Weight Discrimination PO Box 305 *Web:* www.cswd.org	Mount Marion	NY	12456	845-679-1209	679-1206
Creutzfeldt-Jakob Disease Foundation Inc PO Box 5312 *TF:* 800-659-1991 ■ *Web:* www.cjdfoundation.org	Akron	OH	44334	330-665-5590	668-2474
Crohn's & Colitis Foundation of America (CCFA) 386 Park Ave S 17th Fl *TF:* 800-932-2423 ■ *Web:* www.ccfa.org	New York	NY	10016	212-685-3440	779-4098
Cystic Fibrosis Foundation 6931 Arlington Rd Suite 200 *TF:* 800-344-4823 ■ *Web:* www.cff.org	Bethesda	MD	20814	301-951-4422	951-6378
DBSA (Depression & Bipolar Support Alliance) 730 N Franklin St Suite 501 *TF:* 800-826-3632 ■ *Web:* www.dbsalliance.org	Chicago	IL	60610	312-642-0049	642-7243
Deafness Research Foundation (DRF) 641 Lexington Ave 15th Fl *Web:* www.drf.org	New York	NY	10022	212-328-9480	
Delta Society 875 124th Ave NE Suite 101 *Web:* www.deltasociety.org	Bellevue	WA	98005	425-226-7357	235-1076
Depression & Bipolar Support Alliance (DBSA) 730 N Franklin St Suite 501 *TF:* 800-826-3632 ■ *Web:* www.dbsalliance.org	Chicago	IL	60610	312-642-0049	642-7243
Diabetes Exercise & Sports Assn (DESA) 8001 Montcastle Dr *Fax Area Code: 615 ■ *Web:* www.diabetes-exercise.org	Nashville	TN	37221	800-898-4322	673-2077*
Disability Rights Center Inc 18 Low Ave *TF:* 800-834-1721 ■ *Web:* www.drcnh.org	Concord	NH	03301	603-228-0432	225-2077
Disabled & Alone/Life Services for the Handicapped 61 Broadway Suite 510 *TF:* 800-995-0066 ■ *Web:* www.disabledandalone.org	New York	NY	10006	212-532-6740	532-3588
Drug Information Assn (DIA) 800 Enterprise Rd Suite 200 *Web:* www.diahome.org	Horsham	PA	19044	215-442-6100	442-6199
Dystonia Medical Research Foundation 1 E Wacker Dr Suite 2430 *TF:* 800-863-4863 ■ *Web:* www.dystonia-foundation.org	Chicago	IL	60601	312-755-0198	803-0138
Easter Seals 230 W Monroe St Suite 1800 *TF:* 800-221-6827 ■ *Web:* www.easterseals.com	Chicago	IL	60606	312-726-6200	726-1494
ECRI 5200 Butler Pike *Web:* www.ecri.org	Plymouth Meeting	PA	19462	610-825-6000	834-1275
Eden Alternative 742 Turnpike Rd *Fax Area Code: 607 ■ *Web:* www.edenalt.com	Sherburne	NY	13460	907-747-4888	674-6723*
Elizabeth Glaser Pediatric AIDS Foundation 2950 31st St Suite 125 *TF:* 888-499-4673 ■ *Web:* www.pedaids.org	Santa Monica	CA	90405	310-314-1459	314-1469
Endometriosis Assn 8585 N 76th Pl *TF:* 800-992-3636 ■ *Web:* www.endometriosisassn.org	Milwaukee	WI	53223	414-355-2200	355-6065
EngenderHealth 440 9th Ave 13th Fl *TF:* 800-564-2872 ■ *Web:* www.engenderhealth.org	New York	NY	10001	212-561-8000	561-8067
Epilepsy Foundation 4351 Garden City Dr *TF:* 800-332-1000 ■ *Web:* www.epilepsyfoundation.org	Landover	MD	20785	301-459-3700	577-2684
Euthanasia Research & Guidance Organization (ERGO) 24829 Norris Ln *Web:* www.finalexit.org	Junction City	OR	97448	541-998-1873	
FaithTrust Institute 2400 N 45th St Suite 101 *TF:* 877-860-2255 ■ *Web:* www.faithtrustinstitute.org	Seattle	WA	98103	206-634-1903	634-0115
Families of Spinal Muscular Atrophy PO Box 196 *TF:* 800-886-1762 ■ *Web:* www.fsma.org	Libertyville	IL	60048	847-367-7620	367-7623
Family of the Americas Foundation PO Box 1170 *TF:* 800-443-3395 ■ *Web:* www.familyplanning.net	Dunkirk	MD	20754	301-627-3346	627-0847
Family Caregiver Alliance (FCA) 180 Montgomery St Suite 1100 *TF:* 800-445-8106 ■ *Web:* www.caregiver.org	San Francisco	CA	94104	415-434-3388	
Feingold Assn of the US 540 E Main St Suite N *TF:* 800-321-3287 ■ *Web:* www.feingold.org	Riverhead	NY	11901	631-369-9340	369-2988
First Candle/SIDS Alliance 1314 Bedford Ave Suite 210 *TF:* 800-221-7437 ■ *Web:* www.firstcandle.org	Baltimore	MD	21208	410-653-8226	653-8709
Food Allergy & Anaphylaxis Network (FAAN) 11781 Lee Jackson Hwy Suite 160 *TF:* 800-929-4040 ■ *Web:* www.foodallergy.org	Fairfax	VA	22033	703-691-3179	691-2713
Foundation Fighting Blindness 11435 Cron Hill Dr *TF:* 800-683-5555 ■ *Web:* www.blindness.org	Owings Mills	MD	21117	410-568-0150	363-2393
Freedom From Fear (FFF) 308 Seaview Ave *Web:* www.freedomfromfear.org	Staten Island	NY	10305	718-351-1717	667-8893
Gay Men's Health Crisis (GMHC) 119 W 24th St *TF:* 800-243-7692 ■ *Web:* www.gmhc.org	New York	NY	10011	212-367-1000	367-1220
Genetic Alliance Inc 4301 Connecticut Ave NW Suite 404 *TF:* 800-336-4363 ■ *Web:* www.geneticalliance.org	Washington	DC	20008	202-966-5557	966-8553
Gift of Life Bone Marrow Foundation 7700 Congress Ave Suite 2201 *Web:* www.giftoflife.org	Boca Raton	FL	33487	561-988-0100	988-0140
Gilda Radner Familial Ovarian Cancer Registry Roswell Park Cancer Institute Elm & Carlton Sts *TF:* 800-682-7426 ■ *Web:* www.ovariancancer.com	Buffalo	NY	14263	716-845-4503	845-8266
Glaucoma Foundation (TGF) 80 Maiden Ln Suite 700 *Web:* www.glaucomafoundation.org	New York	NY	10038	212-285-0080	651-1888
Glaucoma Research Foundation 251 Post St Suite 600 *TF:* 800-826-6693 ■ *Web:* www.glaucoma.org	San Francisco	CA	94108	415-986-3162	986-3763
Gluten Intolerance Group (GIG) 31214 124th Ave SE *Web:* www.gluten.net	Auburn	WA	98092	206-833-6655	833-6675
Guide Dog Foundation for the Blind Inc 371 E Jericho Tkpe *TF:* 800-548-4337 ■ *Web:* www.guidedog.org	Smithtown	NY	11787	631-265-2121	930-9009
Guide Dogs of America 13445 Glenoaks Blvd *TF:* 800-459-4843 ■ *Web:* www.guidedogsofamerica.org	Sylmar	CA	91342	818-362-5834	362-6870
Guide Dogs for the Blind 350 Los Ranchitos Rd *TF:* 800-295-4050 ■ *Web:* www.guidedogs.com	San Rafael	CA	94903	415-499-4000	499-4035
Guillain-Barre Syndrome Foundation International PO Box 262 *Web:* www.guillain-barre.com	Wynnewood	PA	19096	610-667-0131	667-7036
Head Injury Hotline 212 Pioneer Bldg *Web:* www.headinjury.com	Seattle	WA	98104	206-621-8558	329-4355
Health Physics Society 1313 Dolley Madison Blvd Suite 402 *Web:* www.hps.org	McLean	VA	22101	703-790-1745	790-2672
Healthcare Leadership Council (HLC) 1001 Pennsylvania Ave NW Suite 550 S *Web:* hlc.org	Washington	DC	20004	202-452-8700	296-9561
HEATH Resource Center George Washington Univ 2134 G St NW *TF:* 800-544-3284 ■ *Web:* www.heath.gwu.edu	Washington	DC	20052	202-973-0904	994-3365
Hepatitis Foundation International (HFI) 504 Blick Dr *TF:* 800-891-0707 ■ *Web:* www.hepfi.org	Silver Spring	MD	20904	301-622-4200	622-4702
Herb Research Foundation (HRF) 4140 15th St *Web:* www.herbs.org	Boulder	CO	80304	303-449-2265	449-7849
Hereditary Disease Foundation (HDF) 1303 Pico Blvd *Web:* www.hdfoundation.org	Santa Monica	CA	90405	310-450-9913	450-9532
HMHB (National Healthy Mothers Healthy Babies Coalition) 121 N Washington St Suite 300 *Web:* www.hmhb.org	Alexandria	VA	22314	703-836-6110	836-3470
Hospice Assn of America (HAA) 228 7th St SE *Web:* www.nahc.org/HAA	Washington	DC	20003	202-546-4757	547-3540
Hospice Education Institute 3 Unity Sq PO Box 98 *TF:* 800-331-1620 ■ *Web:* www.hospiceworld.org	Machiasport	ME	04655	207-255-8800	255-8008
Human Factors & Ergonomics Society (HFES) PO Box 1369 *Web:* www.hfes.org	Santa Monica	CA	90406	310-394-1811	394-2410
Human Growth Foundation 997 Glen Cove Ave Suite 5 *TF:* 800-451-6434 ■ *Web:* www.hgfound.org	Glen Head	NY	11545	516-671-4041	671-4055
Huntington's Disease Society of America (HDSA) 505 8th Ave Suite 902 *TF:* 800-345-4372 ■ *Web:* www.hdsa.org	New York	NY	10018	212-242-1968	239-3430
Hysterectomy Educational Resources & Services Foundation (HERS) 422 Bryn Mawr Ave *TF:* 888-750-4377 ■ *Web:* www.hersfoundation.com	Bala Cynwyd	PA	19004	610-667-7757	667-8096
Immune Deficiency Foundation (IDF) 40 W Chesapeake Ave Suite 308 *TF:* 800-296-4433 ■ *Web:* www.primaryimmune.org	Towson	MD	21204	410-321-6647	321-9165
Institute for International Medical Education 106 Corporate Park Dr Suite 100 *Web:* www.iime.org	White Plains	NY	10604	914-253-6633	253-6644
International Assn for the Study of Pain (IASP) 111 Queen Anne Ave N Suite 501 *Web:* www.iasp-pain.org	Seattle	WA	98109	206-283-0311	283-9403
International Center for the Disabled (ICD) 340 E 24th St *Web:* www.icdnyc.org	New York	NY	10010	212-585-6000	585-6262
International Cesarean Awareness Network Inc (ICAN) 1304 Kingsdale Ave *TF:* 800-686-4226 ■ *Web:* www.ican-online.org	Redondo Beach	CA	90278	310-542-6400	542-5368
International Childbirth Education Assn (ICEA) PO Box 20048 *Web:* www.icea.org	Minneapolis	MN	55420	952-854-8660	854-8772
International Dyslexia Assn (IDA) 8600 LaSalle Rd Chester Bldg Suite 382 *TF:* 800-222-3123 ■ *Web:* www.interdys.org	Baltimore	MD	21286	410-296-0232	321-5069
International Hearing Society (IHS) 16880 Middlebelt Rd Suite 4 *TF:* 800-521-5247 ■ *Web:* ihsinfo.org	Livonia	MI	48154	734-522-7200	522-0200
Iron Overload Diseases Assn (IOD) 433 Westwind Dr *Web:* www.ironoverload.org	North Palm Beach	FL	33408	561-840-8512	842-9881
Juvenile Diabetes Research Foundation International (JDRF) 120 Wall St *TF:* 800-533-2873 ■ *Web:* www.jdrf.org	New York	NY	10005	212-785-9500	785-9595
Kristin Brooks Hope Center (KBHC) 615 7th St NE *TF:* 800-784-2433 ■ *Web:* www.hopeline.com	Washington	DC	20002	202-536-3200	536-3206
La Leche League International Inc (LLL) 1400 N Meacham Rd *TF:* 800-525-3243 ■ *Web:* www.lalecheleague.org	Schaumburg	IL	60173	847-519-7730	519-0035
Lamaze International 2025 M St NW Suite 800 *TF:* 800-368-4404 ■ *Web:* www.lamaze.org	Washington	DC	20036	202-367-1128	367-2128
Learning Disabilities Assn of America (LDA) 4156 Library Rd *TF:* 888-300-6710 ■ *Web:* www.ldanatl.org	Pittsburgh	PA	15234	412-341-1515	344-0224
Leukemia & Lymphoma Society 475 Park Ave S 8th Fl *TF:* 800-955-4572 ■ *Web:* www.leukemia-lymphoma.org	New York	NY	10016	212-448-9206	448-9214
Lifespire 350 5th Ave Suite 301 *Web:* www.lifespire.org	New York	NY	10118	212-741-0100	463-9814
Light for Life Foundation International PO Box 644 *Web:* www.yellowribbon.org	Westminster	CO	80036	303-429-3530	426-4496
Lighthouse International 111 E 59th St *Fax: Hum Res ■ *TF:* 800-829-0500 ■ *Web:* www.lighthouse.org	New York	NY	10022	212-821-9200	821-9707*
Little People of America (LPA) 5289 NE Elam Young Pkwy Suite F-700 *TF:* 888-572-2001 ■ *Web:* www.lpaonline.org	Hillsboro	OR	97124	503-846-1562	846-1590
Living Bank PO Box 6725 *TF:* 800-528-2971 ■ *Web:* www.livingbank.org	Houston	TX	77625	713-961-9431	961-0979
Lupus Foundation of America Inc (LFA) 2000 L St NW Suite 710 *TF:* 800-558-0121 ■ *Web:* www.lupus.org	Washington	DC	20036	202-349-1155	349-1156
Lyme Disease Foundation Inc (LDF) Box 332 *TF:* 800-886-5963 ■ *Web:* www.lyme.org	Tolland	CT	06084	860-525-2000	870-0080
Lymphoma Research Foundation 8800 Venice Blvd Suite 207 *TF:* 800-500-9976 ■ *Web:* www.lymphoma.org	Los Angeles	CA	90034	310-204-7040	204-7043
Macula Foundation Inc 210 E 64th St 8th Fl *Web:* www.macula.org	New York	NY	10021	212-605-3777	605-3795
Make Today Count St John's Mid-America Cancer Center 1235 E Cherokee St *TF:* 800-432-2273	Springfield	MO	65804	417-820-3324	888-7426
Male Survivor 5505 Connecticut Ave NW PMB 103 *TF:* 800-738-4181 ■ *Web:* www.malesurvivor.org	Washington	DC	20015	800-738-4181	
March of Dimes Birth Defects Foundation 1275 Mamaroneck Ave *Web:* www.marchofdimes.com	White Plains	NY	10605	914-428-7100	428-8203
Marrow Foundation 3001 Broadway St NE Suite 100 *Fax Area Code: 202 ■ *Web:* www.themarrowfoundation.org	Minneapolis	MN	55413	612-627-5800	638-0641*
MCS Referral & Resources Inc 618 Wyndhurst Ave Suite 2 *Web:* www.mcsrr.org	Baltimore	MD	21210	410-889-6666	889-4944
MedicAlert Foundation International 2323 Colorado Ave *TF Cust Svc:* 800-432-5378 ■ *Web:* www.medicalert.org	Turlock	CA	95382	209-668-3333	669-2495

Health & Health-Related Organizations (Cont'd)

Phone | Fax

Medicare Rights Center (MRC) 520 8th Ave N Wing 3rd Fl .... New York NY 10018 212-869-3850 869-3532
TF hotline: 800-333-4114 ■ *Web:* www.medicarerights.org

Mended Hearts 7272 Greenville Ave .... Dallas TX 75231 214-706-1442 360-6145
TF: 888-432-7899 ■ *Web:* www.mendedhearts.org

Migraine Awareness Group: A National Understanding for Migraineurs (MAGNUM) 113 S Saint Asaph St Suite 100 .... Alexandria VA 22314 703-739-9384 739-2432
Web: www.migraines.org

Mothers Supporting Daughters with Breast Cancer (MSDBC)
21710 Bayshore Rd .... Chestertown MD 21620 410-778-1982 778-1411
Web: www.mothersdaughters.org

Multiple Sclerosis Foundation (MSF)
6350 N Andrews Ave .... Fort Lauderdale FL 33309 954-776-6805 938-8708
TF: 800-225-6495 ■ *Web:* www.msfacts.org

Muscular Dystrophy Assn (MDA) 3300 E Sunrise Dr .... Tucson AZ 85718 520-529-2000 529-5300
TF: 800-572-1717 ■ *Web:* www.mda.org

Myasthenia Gravis Foundation of America (MGFA)
1821 University Ave W Suite S256 .... Saint Paul MN 55104 651-917-6256 917-1835
TF: 800-541-5454 ■ *Web:* www.myasthenia.org

NAPWA (National Assn of People with AIDS)
8401 Colesville Rd Suite 750 .... Silver Spring MD 20910 240-247-0880 247-0574
Web: www.napwa.org

Narcolepsy Network Inc PO Box 294 .... Pleasantville NY 10570 401-667-2523 633-6567
Web: www.narcolepsynetwork.org

NARIC (National Rehabilitation Information Center)
4200 Forbes Blvd Suite 202 .... Lanham MD 20706 301-459-5900 459-4263
TF: 800-346-2742 ■ *Web:* www.naric.com

National Adrenal Diseases Foundation (NADF)
505 Northern Blvd .... Great Neck NY 11021 516-487-4992
Web: www.medhelp.org/nadf

National Allergy Bureau (NAB) 555 E Wells St 11th Fl .... Milwaukee WI 53202 414-272-6071 272-6070
Web: www.aaaai.org/nab

National Alliance for Hispanic Health 1501 16th St NW .... Washington DC 20036 202-387-5000 797-4353
Web: www.hispanichealth.org

National Alliance on Mental Illness (NAMI)
2107 Wilson Blvd Suite 300 .... Arlington VA 22201 703-524-7600 524-9094
TF: 800-950-6264 ■ *Web:* www.nami.org

National Alopecia Areata Foundation (NAAF)
14 Mitchell Blvd .... San Rafael CA 94903 415-472-3780 472-5343
Web: www.naaf.org

National Amputation Foundation 40 Church St .... Malverne NY 11565 516-887-3600 887-3667
Web: www.nationalamputation.org

National Assn of Anorexia Nervosa & Associated Disorders (ANAD) PO Box 7 .... Highland Park IL 60035 847-831-3438 433-4632
Web: www.anad.org

National Assn for Biomedical Research (NABR)
818 Connecticut Ave NW Suite 200 .... Washington DC 20006 202-857-0540 659-1902
Web: www.nabr.org

National Assn of Certified Natural Health Professionals
714 E Winona Ave .... Warsaw IN 46580 800-321-1005 268-5393*
**Fax Area Code:* 574 ■ *Web:* www.cnhp.org

National Assn for Continence (NAFC) PO Box 1019 .... Charleston SC 29402 843-377-0900 377-0905
TF: 800-252-3337 ■ *Web:* www.nafc.org

National Assn of the Deaf (NAD)
814 Thayer Ave Suite 250 .... Silver Spring MD 20910 301-587-1788 587-1791
Web: www.nad.org

National Assn on Drug Abuse Problems Inc (NADAP)
355 Lexington Ave 2nd Fl .... New York NY 10017 212-986-1170 697-2939
Web: www.nadap.org

National Assn for Holistic Aromatherapy (NAHA)
3327 W Indian Trail Rd .... Spokane WA 99208 509-325-3419 325-3479
TF: 888-275-6242 ■ *Web:* www.naha.org

National Assn for Parents of Children with Visual Impairments (NAPVI) PO Box 317 .... Watertown MA 02471 617-972-7441 972-7444
TF: 800-562-6265 ■ *Web:* www.spedex.com/napvi

National Assn of People with AIDS (NAPWA)
8401 Colesville Rd Suite 750 .... Silver Spring MD 20910 240-247-0880 247-0574
Web: www.napwa.org

National Assn of Protection & Advocacy Systems
900 2nd St NE Suite 211 .... Washington DC 20002 202-408-9514 408-9520
Web: www.napas.org

National Assn for Visually Handicapped (NAVH)
22 W 21st St 6th Fl .... New York NY 10010 212-889-3141 727-2931
Web: www.navh.org

National Breast Cancer Coalition (NBCC)
1101 17th St NW Suite 1300 .... Washington DC 20036 202-296-7477 265-6854
TF: 800-622-2838 ■ *Web:* www.stopbreastcancer.org

National Cancer Registrars Assn (NCRA)
1340 Braddock Pl Suite 203 .... Alexandria VA 22314 703-299-6640 299-6620
Web: www.ncra-usa.org

National Center for Assault Prevention (NCAP) 900 Hollydell Ct .... Sewell NJ 08080 856-582-8282 582-3588
TF: 800-258-3189 ■ *Web:* www.ncap.org

National Center for Disability Services (NCDS)
201 IU Willets Rd .... Albertson NY 11507 516-747-5400 393-2668*
**Fax:* Hum Res ■ *Web:* www.ncds.org

National Center for Homeopathy (NCH)
801 N Fairfax St Suite 306 .... Alexandria VA 22314 703-548-7790 548-7792
TF: 877-624-0613 ■ *Web:* www.homeopathic.org

National Center for Stuttering (NCS) 200 E 33rd St .... New York NY 10016 212-532-1460 683-1372
TF: 800-221-2483 ■ *Web:* www.stuttering.com

National Children's Cancer Society (NCCS)
1015 Locust St Suite 600 .... Saint Louis MO 63101 314-241-1600 241-6949
TF: 800-532-6459 ■ *Web:* www.nationalchildrenscancersociety.com

National Chronic Pain Outreach Assn (NCPOA) PO Box 274 .... Millboro VA 24460 540-862-9437 862-9485
Web: www.chronicpain.org

National Citizens' Coalition for Nursing Home Reform (NCCNHR) 1828 L St NW Suite 801 .... Washington DC 20036 202-332-2275 332-2949
Web: www.nccnhr.org

National Coalition for Adult Immunization (NCAI)
4733 Bethesda Ave Suite 750 .... Bethesda MD 20814 301-656-0003 907-0878

National Coalition for Cancer Survivorship (NCCS)
1010 Wayne Ave Suite 770 .... Silver Spring MD 20910 301-650-9127 565-9670
Web: www.canceradvocacy.org

National Coalition on Health Care
1200 G St NW Suite 750 .... Washington DC 20005 202-638-7151 638-7166
Web: www.nchc.org

National Committee for Quality Assurance (NCQA)
1100 13th St NW Suite 1000 .... Washington DC 20005 202-955-3500 955-3599
TF: 800-275-7585 ■ *Web:* www.ncqa.org

National Council on Alcoholism & Drug Dependence (NCADD)
244 E 58th St 4th Fl .... New York NY 10022 212-269-7797 269-7510
TF: 800-622-2255 ■ *Web:* www.ncadd.org

National Deaf Education Center (NDEC) 800 Florida Ave NE .... Washington DC 20002 202-651-5051 651-5708
Web: clerccenter.gallaudet.edu

Phone | Fax

National Dissemination Center for Children with Disabilities
1825 Connecticut Ave .... Washington DC 20009 202-884-8200 884-8441
TF: 800-695-0285 ■ *Web:* www.nichcy.org

National Down Syndrome Congress (NDSC)
1370 Center Dr Suite 102 .... Atlanta GA 30338 770-604-9500 604-9898
TF: 800-232-6372 ■ *Web:* www.ndsccenter.org

National Down Syndrome Society (NDSS)
666 Broadway 8th Fl .... New York NY 10012 212-460-9330 979-2873
TF: 800-221-4602 ■ *Web:* www.ndss.org

National Eating Disorders Assn 603 Stewart St Suite 803 .... Seattle WA 98101 206-382-3587 829-8501
TF: 800-931-2237 ■ *Web:* www.nationaleatingdisorders.org

National Federation of the Blind (NFB) 1800 Johnson St .... Baltimore MD 21230 410-659-9314 685-5653
Web: www.nfb.org

National Fibromyalgia Partnership Inc (NFP)
140 Zinn Way PO Box 160 .... Linden VA 22642 866-725-4404 666-2727
Web: www.fmpartnership.org

National Fire Protection Assn (NFPA) 1 Batterymarch Pk .... Quincy MA 02169 617-770-3000 770-0700
TF: 800-344-3555 ■ *Web:* www.nfpa.org

National Foundation of Dentistry for the Handicapped (NFDH)
1800 15th St Unit 100 .... Denver CO 80202 303-534-5360 534-5290
TF: 888-471-6334 ■ *Web:* www.nfdh.org

National Gaucher Foundation (NGF) 61 General Early Dr .... Harpers Ferry WV 25425 800-428-2437 725-6429*
**Fax Area Code:* 304 ■ *Web:* www.gaucherdisease.org

National Headache Foundation (NHF)
820 N Orleans St Suite 217 .... Chicago IL 60610 888-643-5552 640-9049*
**Fax Area Code:* 312 ■ *Web:* www.headaches.org

National Health Assn (NHA) PO Box 30630 .... Tampa FL 33630 813-855-6607 855-8052
Web: www.healthscience.org

National Health Council (NHC) 1730 M St NW Suite 500 .... Washington DC 20036 202-785-3910 785-5923
TF: 800-684-6814 ■ *Web:* www.nhcouncil.org

National Healthy Mothers Healthy Babies Coalition (HMHB)
121 N Washington St Suite 300 .... Alexandria VA 22314 703-836-6110 836-3470
Web: www.hmhb.org

National Hearing Conservation Assn (NHCA)
7995 E Prentice Ave Suite 100 .... Greenwood Village CO 80111 303-224-9022 770-1614
Web: www.hearingconservation.org

National Hemophilia Foundation (NHF)
116 W 32nd St 11th Fl .... New York NY 10001 212-328-3700 328-3777
TF: 800-424-2634 ■ *Web:* www.hemophilia.org

National Herpes Resource Center (HRC)
PO Box 13827 .... Research Triangle Park NC 27709 919-361-8488 361-8425
TF: 800-227-8922 ■ *Web:* www.ashastd.org/hrc

National HPV & Cervical Cancer Prevention Resource Center PO Box 13827 .... Research Triangle Park NC 27709 919-361-8400 361-8425
TF: 800-277-8922 ■ *Web:* www.ashastd.org/hpvccrc

National Industries for the Blind (NIB) 1310 Braddock Pl .... Alexandria VA 22314 703-310-0500
TF Cust Svc: 800-433-2304 ■ *Web:* www.nib.org

National Inhalant Prevention Coalition (NIPC)
322-A Thompson St .... Chattanooga TN 37405 423-265-4662 265-4889
TF: 800-269-4237 ■ *Web:* www.inhalants.org

National Institute for Rehabilitation Engineering (NIRE)
PO Box T .... Hewitt NJ 07421 973-853-6585 832-2894*
**Fax Area Code:* 928 ■ *TF:* 800-736-2216 ■ *Web:* www.angelfire.com/nj/nire2

National Kidney Foundation (NKF) 30 E 33rd St 8th Fl .... New York NY 10016 212-889-2210 779-0068
TF: 800-622-9010 ■ *Web:* www.kidney.org

National Marfan Foundation (NMF) 22 Manhasset Ave .... Port Washington NY 11050 516-883-8712 883-8040
TF: 800-862-7326 ■ *Web:* www.marfan.org

National Marrow Donor Program (NMDP)
3001 Broadway St NE Suite 500 .... Minneapolis MN 55413 612-627-5800 627-5877
TF: 800-526-7809 ■ *Web:* www.marrow.org

National Mental Health Assn (NMHA)
2001 N Beauregard St 12th Fl .... Alexandria VA 22311 703-684-7722 684-5968
TF Help Line: 800-969-6642 ■ *Web:* www.nmha.org

National Minority AIDS Council (NMAC) 1931 13th St NW .... Washington DC 20009 202-483-6622 483-1135
Web: www.nmac.org

National Multiple Sclerosis Society 733 3rd Ave 3rd Fl .... New York NY 10017 212-986-3240 986-7981
TF: 800-344-4867 ■ *Web:* www.nmss.org

National Native American AIDS Prevention Center (NNAAPC)
436 14th St Suite 1020 .... Oakland CA 94612 510-444-2051 444-1593
Web: www.nnaapc.org

National Niemann-Pick Disease Foundation (NNPDF)
415 Madison Ave .... Fort Atkinson WI 53538 920-563-0930 563-0931
TF: 877-287-3672 ■ *Web:* www.nnpdf.org

National Odd Shoe Exchange PO Box 1120 .... Chandler AZ 85244 480-892-3484 892-3568

National Oral Health Information Clearinghouse (NOHIC)
1 NOHIC Way .... Bethesda MD 20892 301-402-7364 480-4098
Web: www.healthfinder.gov/orgs/HR2457.htm

National Organization for Albinism & Hypopigmentation (NOAH) PO Box 959 .... East Hampstead NH 03826 603-887-2310 887-6049
TF: 800-648-2310 ■ *Web:* www.albinism.org

National Organization of Circumcision Information Resource Centers (NOCIRC) PO Box 2512 .... San Anselmo CA 94979 415-488-9883 488-9660
Web: www.nocirc.org

National Organization on Disability (NOD)
910 16th St NW Suite 600 .... Washington DC 20006 202-293-5960 293-7999
Web: www.nod.org

National Organization for Rare Disorders (NORD)
55 Kenosia Ave PO Box 1968 .... Danbury CT 06813 203-744-0100 798-2291
TF: 800-999-6673 ■ *Web:* www.rarediseases.org

National Organization of Restoring Men (NORM)
3205 Northwood Dr Suite 209 .... Concord CA 94520 925-827-4077 827-4119
Web: www.norm.org

National Osteoporosis Foundation (NOF) 1232 22nd St NW .... Washington DC 20037 202-223-2226 223-2237
TF: 800-221-4222 ■ *Web:* www.nof.org

National Ovarian Cancer Coalition (NOCC)
500 NE Spanish River Blvd Suite 8 .... Boca Raton FL 33431 561-393-0005 393-7275
TF: 888-682-7426 ■ *Web:* www.ovarian.org

National Parkinson Foundation (NPF) 1501 NW 9th Ave .... Miami FL 33136 305-547-6666 243-5595
TF: 800-327-4545 ■ *Web:* www.parkinson.org

National Pesticide Information Center (NPIC)
333 Weniger Hall .... Corvallis OR 97331 800-858-7378 737-0761*
**Fax Area Code:* 541 ■ *Web:* npic.orst.edu

National Psoriasis Foundation (NPF)
6600 SW 92nd Ave Suite 300 .... Portland OR 97223 503-244-7404 245-0626
TF: 800-723-9166 ■ *Web:* www.psoriasis.org

National Rehabilitation Assn (NRA) 633 S Washington St .... Alexandria VA 22314 703-836-0850 836-0848
Web: www.nationalrehab.org

National Rehabilitation Information Center (NARIC)
4200 Forbes Blvd Suite 202 .... Lanham MD 20706 301-459-5900 459-4263
TF: 800-346-2742 ■ *Web:* www.naric.com

National Reye's Syndrome Foundation (NRSF) 426 N Lewis St .... Bryan OH 43506 419-636-2679 636-9897
TF: 800-233-7393 ■ *Web:* www.reyessyndrome.org

National Rosacea Society 800 S Northwest Hwy Suite 200 .... Barrington IL 60010 847-382-8971 382-5567
TF: 888-662-5874 ■ *Web:* www.rosacea.org

National SAFE KIDS Campaign
1301 Pennsylvania Ave NW Suite 1000 .... Washington DC 20004 202-662-0600 393-2072
Web: www.safekids.org

Phone | Fax

National Safety Council (NSC) 1121 Spring Lake Dr ... Itasca IL 60143 630-285-1121 285-1315
TF: 800-621-7619 ■ *Web:* www.nsc.org

National Self-Help Clearinghouse 365 5th Ave Suite 3300 ... New York NY 10016 212-817-1822 817-1561
Web: www.selfhelpweb.org

National Sleep Foundation (NSF) 1522 K St NW Suite 500 ... Washington DC 20005 202-347-3471 347-3472
Web: www.sleepfoundation.org

National Society of Genetic Counselors (NSGC)
401 N Michigan Ave ... Chicago IL 60611 312-321-6834 673-6972
Web: www.nsgc.org

National Spinal Cord Injury Assn (NSCIA)
6701 Democracy Blvd Suite 300-9 ... Bethesda MD 20817 800-962-9629 963-1265*
**Fax Area Code:* 301 ■ *Web:* www.spinalcord.org

National Stroke Assn (NSA) 9707 E Easter Ln ... Englewood CO 80112 303-649-9299 649-1328
TF: 800-787-6537 ■ *Web:* www.stroke.org

National Stuttering Assn (NSA) 119 W 40th St 14th Fl ... New York NY 10018 212-944-4050 944-8244
TF: 800-937-8888 ■ *Web:* www.nsastutter.org

National Tay-Sachs & Allied Diseases Assn (NTSAD)
2001 Beacon St Suite 204 ... Brighton MA 02135 617-277-4463 277-0134
TF: 800-906-8723 ■ *Web:* www.ntsad.org

National Vaccine Information Center (NVIC) 421-E Church St ... Vienna VA 22180 703-938-3783 938-5768
TF: 800-909-7468 ■ *Web:* www.909shot.com

National Wellness Institute (NWI)
1300 College Ct PO Box 827 ... Stevens Point WI 54481 715-342-2969 342-2979
TF: 800-243-8694 ■ *Web:* www.nationalwellness.org

NISH 8401 Old Courthouse Rd ... Vienna VA 22182 703-560-6800 849-8916
Web: www.nish.org

North American Menopause Society (NAMS)
5900 Landerbrook Dr Suite 195 ... Mayfield Heights OH 44124 440-442-7550 442-2660
Web: www.menopause.org

Obesity Society 8630 Fenton St ... Silver Spring MD 20910 301-563-6526 563-6595
TF: 800-986-2373 ■ *Web:* www.obesity.org

Obsessive Compulsive Foundation (OCF) PO Box 961029 ... Boston MA 02196 617-973-5801 973-5803
Web: www.ocfoundation.org

Oley Foundation Albany Medical Ctr 214 Hun Memorial MC A-28 ... Albany NY 12208 518-262-5079 262-5528
TF: 800-776-6539 ■ *Web:* www.oley.org

Oral Health America 410 N Michigan Ave Suite 352 ... Chicago IL 60611 312-836-9900 836-9986
Web: www.oralhealthamerica.org

Paget Foundation for Paget's Disease of Bone & Related Disorders 120 Wall St Suite 1602 ... New York NY 10005 212-509-5335 509-8492
TF: 800-237-2438 ■ *Web:* www.paget.org

Parkinson's Disease Foundation (PDF) 1359 Broadway ... New York NY 10018 212-923-4700 923-4778
TF: 800-457-6676 ■ *Web:* www.pdf.org

Partnership for a Drug-Free America
405 Lexington Ave Suite 1601 ... New York NY 10174 212-922-1560 922-1570
TF: 888-575-3115 ■ *Web:* www.drugfree.org

Pedorthic Footwear Assn (PFA)
7150 Columbia Gateway Dr Suite G ... Columbia MD 21046 410-381-7278 381-1167
TF: 800-673-8447 ■ *Web:* www.pedorthics.org

Phoenix Society for Burn Survivors
1835 RW Berends Dr SW ... Grand Rapids MI 49519 616-458-2773 458-2831
TF: 800-888-2876 ■ *Web:* www.phoenix-society.org

Physicians Committee for Responsible Medicine (PCRM)
5100 Wisconsin Ave NW Suite 400 ... Washington DC 20016 202-686-2210 686-2216
TF: 866-416-7276 ■ *Web:* www.pcrm.org

Postpartum Support International 927 N Kellogg Dr ... Santa Barbara CA 93111 805-967-7636 967-0608
Web: www.postpartum.net

Prader-Willi Syndrome Assn (USA)
5700 Midnight Pass Rd Suite 6 ... Sarasota FL 34242 941-312-0400 312-0142
TF: 800-926-4797 ■ *Web:* www.pwsausa.org

Prevent Blindness America 211 W Wacker Dr Suite 1700 ... Chicago IL 60606 312-363-6001 636-6052
TF: 800-331-2020 ■ *Web:* www.preventblindness.org

Program for Appropriate Technology in Health (PATH)
1455 NW Leary Way ... Seattle WA 98107 206-285-3500 285-6619
Web: www.path.org

Project Inform 205 13th St Suite 2001 ... San Francisco CA 94103 415-558-8669 558-0684
Web: www.projinf.org

Public Citizen Health Research Group 1600 20th St NW ... Washington DC 20009 202-588-1000 588-7796
Web: www.citizen.org/hrg

Public Health Institute 555 12th St 10th Fl ... Oakland CA 94607 510-285-5500 285-5501
Web: www.phi.org

RA Bloch Cancer Foundation 4400 Main St ... Kansas City MO 64111 816-932-8453 931-7486
TF: 800-433-0464 ■ *Web:* www.blochcancer.org

Radner Gilda Familial Ovarian Cancer Registry
Roswell Park Cancer Institute Elm & Carlton Sts ... Buffalo NY 14263 716-845-4503 845-8266
TF: 800-682-7426 ■ *Web:* www.ovariancancer.com

Recording for the Blind & Dyslexic (RFB&D) 20 Roszel Rd ... Princeton NJ 08540 609-452-0606 987-8116
TF: 800-221-4792 ■ *Web:* www.rfbd.org

Reeve Christopher Paralysis Foundation 636 Morris Tpke ... Short Hills NJ 07078 973-379-2690 912-9433
TF: 800-225-0292 ■ *Web:* www.christopherreeve.org

Registry of Interpreters for the Deaf Inc (RID)
333 Commerce St ... Alexandria VA 22314 703-838-0030 838-0454
Web: www.rid.org

Rehabilitation Engineering & Assistive Technology Society of North America (RESNA) 1700 N Moore St Suite 1540 ... Arlington VA 22209 703-524-6686 524-6630
Web: www.resna.org

Research to Prevent Blindness Inc (RPB)
645 Madison Ave 21st Fl ... New York NY 10022 212-752-4333 688-6231
TF: 800-621-0026 ■ *Web:* www.rpbusa.org

RESOLVE: National Infertility Assn
7910 Woodmont Ave Suite 1350 ... Bethesda MD 20814 301-652-8505 652-9375
Web: www.resolve.org

Restless Legs Syndrome Foundation Inc 819 2nd St SW ... Rochester MN 55902 507-287-6465 287-6312
TF: 877-463-6757 ■ *Web:* www.rls.org

Retinitis Pigmentosa International Society for Degenerative Eye Disease & Related Disorders Inc
PO Box 900 ... Woodland Hills CA 91365 818-992-0500 992-3265
Web: www.rpinternational.org

Rolf Institute of Structural Integration
5055 Chaparral Ct Suite 103 ... Boulder CO 80301 303-449-5903 449-5978
TF: 800-530-8875 ■ *Web:* www.rolf.org

Safe Tables Our Priority (STOP) PO Box 4352 ... Burlington VT 05406 802-863-0555 264-9055
TF: 800-350-7867 ■ *Web:* www.safetables.org

SAVE - Suicide Awareness Voices of Education
9001 E Bloomington Fwy Suite 150 ... Bloomington MN 55420 952-946-7998 829-0841
TF: 888-511-7283 ■ *Web:* www.save.org

Scleroderma Foundation 300 Rosewood Dr Suite 105 ... Danvers MA 01923 978-463-5843 463-5809
TF: 800-722-4673 ■ *Web:* www.scleroderma.org

Scoliosis Assn Inc 2500 N Military Trail ... Boca Raton FL 33431 561-994-4435 994-2455
TF: 800-800-0669 ■ *Web:* www.scoliosis-assoc.org

Self Help for Hard of Hearing People (SHHH)
7910 Woodmont Ave Suite 1200 ... Bethesda MD 20814 301-657-2248 913-9413
Web: www.hearingloss.org

Seventh-day Adventist Dietetic Assn (SDADA)
6100 Leoni Rd ... Grizzly Flats CA 95636 530-626-3610 626-8524
Web: www.sdada.org

Sexuality Information & Education Council of the US (SIECUS)
90 John St Suite 704 ... New York NY 10038 212-819-9770 819-9776
Web: www.siecus.org

Sickle Cell Disease Assn of America (SCDAA)
231 E Baltimore St Suite 800 ... Baltimore MD 21202 410-528-1555 528-1495
TF: 800-421-8453 ■ *Web:* www.sicklecelldisease.org

Simon Foundation for Incontinence PO Box 815 ... Wilmette IL 60091 847-864-3913 864-9758
TF: 800-237-4666 ■ *Web:* www.simonfoundation.org

Skin Cancer Foundation 149 Madison Ave Suite 901 ... New York NY 10016 212-725-5176 725-5751
TF: 800-754-6490 ■ *Web:* www.skincancer.org

Society for Women's Health Research
1025 Connecticut Ave Suite 701 ... Washington DC 20036 202-223-8224 833-3472
Web: www.womenshealthresearch.org

Spina Bifida Assn of America (SBAA)
4590 MacArthur Blvd NW Suite 250 ... Washington DC 20007 202-944-3285 944-3295
TF: 800-621-3141 ■ *Web:* www.sbaa.org

Starlight Starbright Children's Foundation
1850 Sawtelle Blvd Suite 450 ... Los Angeles CA 90025 310-479-1212 479-1235
TF: 800-274-7827 ■ *Web:* www.starlight.org

Stuttering Foundation of America
3100 Walnut Grove Rd Suite 603 ... Memphis TN 38111 901-452-7343 452-3931
TF: 800-992-9392 ■ *Web:* www.stuttersfa.org

Support Dogs Inc 11645 Lilburn Pk Rd ... Saint Louis MO 63146 314-997-2325 997-7202
Web: www.supportdogs.org

Susan G Komen Breast Cancer Foundation
5005 LBJ Fwy Suite 250 ... Dallas TX 75244 972-855-1600 855-4372
Web: www.komen.org

TASH 29 W Susquehanna Ave Suite 210 ... Baltimore MD 21204 410-828-8274 828-6706
Web: www.tash.org

Thyroid Foundation of America Inc (TFA)
1 Longfellow Pl Suite 1518 ... Boston MA 02114 617-534-1500 534-1515
TF: 800-832-8321 ■ *Web:* www.tsh.org

TOPS Club Inc 4575 S 5th St ... Milwaukee WI 53207 414-482-4620 482-1655
TF: 800-932-8677 ■ *Web:* www.tops.org

Touch for Health Kinesiology Assn PO Box 392 ... New Carlisle OH 45344 937-845-3404 845-3909
TF: 800-466-8342 ■ *Web:* www.tfhka.org

Tourette Syndrome Assn Inc 42-40 Bell Blvd Suite 205 ... Bayside NY 11361 718-224-2999 279-9596
TF: 888-486-8738 ■ *Web:* www.tsa-usa.org

Trichotillomania Learning Center Inc (TLC)
303 Potrero St Suite 51 ... Santa Cruz CA 95060 831-457-1004 426-4383
Web: www.trich.org

Turner Syndrome Society of the US 14450 TC Jester Suite 260 ... Houston TX 77014 832-249-9988 249-9987
TF: 800-345-9944 ■ *Web:* www.turner-syndrome-us.org

UCP (United Cerebral Palsy) 1660 L St NW Suite 700 ... Washington DC 20036 202-776-0406 776-0414
TF: 800-872-5827 ■ *Web:* www.ucp.org

Undersea & Hyperbaric Medical Society (UHMS)
10020 Southern Maryland Blvd Suite 204 PO Box 1020 ... Dunkirk MD 20754 410-257-6606 257-6617
Web: www.uhms.org

United Cerebral Palsy (UCP) 1660 L St NW Suite 700 ... Washington DC 20036 202-776-0406 776-0414
TF: 800-872-5827 ■ *Web:* www.ucp.org

United Network for Organ Sharing (UNOS) 700 N 4th St ... Richmond VA 23219 804-330-8500 782-4817
TF: 888-894-6361 ■ *Web:* www.unos.org

Vegan Action PO Box 4288 ... Richmond VA 23220 804-502-8736
Web: www.vegan.org

Vegetarian Resource Group (VRG) PO Box 1463 ... Baltimore MD 21203 410-366-8343 366-8804
Web: www.vrg.org

Vocational Evaluation & Career Assessment Professionals (VECAP) PO Box 26273 ... Colorado Springs CO 80936 719-638-4787 638-6153
Web: www.vecap.org

Voice of the Retarded (VOR)
5005 Newport Dr Suite 108 ... Rolling Meadows IL 60008 847-253-6020 253-6054
Web: www.vor.net

Washington Business Group on Health (WBGH)
50 F St NW Suite 600 ... Washington DC 20001 202-628-9320 628-9244
Web: wbgh.org

Well Spouse Foundation 63 W Main St Suite H ... Freehold NJ 07728 732-577-8899 577-8644
TF: 800-838-0879 ■ *Web:* www.wellspouse.org

White Lung Assn (WLA) PO Box 1483 ... Baltimore MD 21203 410-243-5864
Web: www.whitelung.org

Women Alive 1566 S Burnside Ave ... Los Angeles CA 90019 323-965-1564 965-9886
TF: 800-554-4876 ■ *Web:* www.women-alive.org

Xeroderma Pigmentosum Society Inc (XPS)
437 Snydertown Rd ... Craryville NY 12521 518-851-2612
TF: 877-977-2873 ■ *Web:* www.xpc.org

Y-ME National Breast Cancer Organization
212 W Van Buren St ... Chicago IL 60607 312-986-8338 294-8597
TF: 800-221-2141 ■ *Web:* www.y-me.org

Yellow Ribbon Suicide Prevention Program PO Box 644 ... Westminster CO 80036 303-429-3530 426-4496
Web: www.yellowribbon.org

48-18 Hobby Organizations

Phone | Fax

Academy of Model Aeronautics (AMA) 5161 E Memorial Dr ... Muncie IN 47302 765-287-1256 289-4248
TF: 800-435-9262 ■ *Web:* www.modelaircraft.org

American Bonanza Society (ABS)
1922 Midfield Rd PO Box 12888 ... Wichita KS 67277 316-945-1700 945-1710
Web: www.bonanza.org

American Contract Bridge League (ACBL) 2990 Airways Blvd ... Memphis TN 38116 901-332-5586 398-7754
TF Sales: 800-264-2743 ■ *Web:* www.acbl.org

American Craft Council 72 Spring St 6th Fl ... New York NY 10012 212-274-0630 274-0650
TF: 800-836-3470 ■ *Web:* www.craftcouncil.org

American Federation of Astrologers (AFA) 6535 S Rural Rd ... Tempe AZ 85283 480-838-1751 838-8293
TF: 888-301-7630 ■ *Web:* www.astrologers.com

American Horticultural Society (AHS) 7931 E Boulevard Dr ... Alexandria VA 22308 703-768-5700 768-8700
TF: 800-777-7931 ■ *Web:* www.ahs.org

American Kennel Club (AKC) 260 Madison Ave 4th Fl ... New York NY 10016 212-696-8200 696-8299
Web: www.akc.org

American Numismatic Assn (ANA) 818 N Cascade Ave ... Colorado Springs CO 80903 719-632-2646 634-4085
TF: 800-367-9723 ■ *Web:* www.money.org

American Philatelic Society (APS) 100 Match Factory Pl ... Bellefonte PA 16823 814-933-3803 933-6128
Web: www.stamps.org

American Radio Relay League (ARRL) 225 Main St ... Newington CT 06111 860-594-0200 594-0259
Web: www.arrl.org

American Rose Society (ARS) 8877 Jefferson Paige Rd ... Shreveport LA 71119 318-938-5402 938-5405
TF: 800-637-6534 ■ *Web:* www.ars.org

American Stamp Dealers Assn Inc (ASDA)
3 School St Suite 205 ... Glen Cove NY 11542 516-759-7000 759-7014
Web: www.asdaonline.com

Antique Automobile Club of America (AACA)
501 W Governor Rd PO Box 417 ... Hershey PA 17033 717-534-1910 534-9101
Web: www.aaca.org

Art & Creative Materials Institute Inc (ACMI)
1280 Main St PO Box 479 ... Hanson MA 02341 781-293-4100 294-0808
Web: www.acminet.org

Hobby Organizations (Cont'd)

Organization	City	State	ZIP	Phone	Fax
Barbershop Harmony Society 7930 Sheridan Rd *TF:* 800-876-7464 ■ *Web:* www.barbershop.org	Kenosha	WI	53143	262-653-8440	654-5552
BMW Motorcycle Owners of America PO Box 3982 *Web:* www.bmwmoa.org	Ellisville	MO	63022	636-394-7277	391-1811
Craft & Hobby Assn (CHA) 319 E 54th St *TF:* 800-822-0494 ■ *Web:* www.craftandhobby.org	Elmwood Park	NJ	07407	201-794-1133	797-0657
Embroiderers Guild of America (EGA) 335 W Broadway Suite 100 *Web:* www.egausa.org	Louisville	KY	40202	502-589-6956	584-7900
Experimental Aircraft Assn (EAA) 3000 Poberezny Rd *TF:* 800-236-4800 ■ *Web:* www.eaa.org	Oshkosh	WI	54902	920-426-4800	426-4828
Glass Art Society (GAS) 3131 Western Ave Suite 414 *Web:* www.glassart.org	Seattle	WA	98121	206-382-1305	382-2630
Handweavers Guild of America (HGA) 1255 Buford Hwy Suite 211 *Web:* www.weavespindye.org	Suwanee	GA	30024	678-730-0010	730-0836
Knitting Guild of America (TKGA) 1100-H Brandywine Blvd PO Box 3388 *TF:* 800-969-6069 ■ *Web:* www.tkga.com	Zanesville	OH	43702	740-452-4541	452-2552
National Craft Assn (NCA) 2012 Ridge Rd E Suite 120 *TF:* 800-715-9594 ■ *Web:* www.craftassoc.com	Rochester	NY	14622	585-266-5472	785-3231
National Garden Clubs Inc (NGC) 4401 Magnolia Ave *TF:* 800-550-6007 ■ *Web:* www.gardenclub.org	Saint Louis	MO	63110	314-776-7574	776-5108
National Gardening Assn (NGA) 1100 Dorset St *TF:* 800-538-7476 ■ *Web:* www.garden.org	South Burlington	VT	05403	802-863-5251	864-6889
National Genealogical Society (NGS) 3108 Columbia Pike Suite 300 *TF:* 800-473-0060 ■ *Web:* www.ngsgenealogy.org	Arlington	VA	22204	703-525-0050	525-0052
National Model Railroad Assn (NMRA) 4121 Cromwell Rd *Web:* www.nmra.org	Chattanooga	TN	37421	423-892-2846	899-4869
National NeedleArts Assn (TNNA) 1100-H Brandywine Blvd *TF:* 800-889-8662 ■ *Web:* www.tnna.org	Zanesville	OH	43701	740-455-6773	452-2552
National Scrabble Assn 403 Front St PO Box 700 *Web:* www.scrabble-assoc.com	Greenport	NY	11944	631-477-0033	477-0294
National Wood Carvers Assn (NWCA) 7424 Miami Ave *Web:* www.chipchats.org	Cincinnati	OH	45243	513-561-9051	
Philatelic Foundation 70 W 40th St 15th Fl *Web:* www.philatelicfoundation.org	New York	NY	10018	212-221-6555	221-6208
Society of Decorative Painters 393 N McLean Blvd *Web:* www.decorativepainters.org	Wichita	KS	67203	316-269-9300	269-9191
Sports Car Club of America (SCCA) PO Box 19400 *TF:* 800-770-2055 ■ *Web:* www.scca.com	Topeka	KS	66619	785-357-7222	232-7228
Sweet Adelines International 9110 S Toledo Ave *TF:* 800-992-7464 ■ *Web:* www.sweetadelineintl.org	Tulsa	OK	74137	918-622-1444	665-0894
US Chess Federation PO Box 3967 *TF Sales:* 800-388-5464 ■ *Web:* www.uschess.org	Crossville	TN	38557	931-787-1234	787-1200
World Pen Pals PO Box 337 *Web:* www.world-pen-pals.com	Saugerties	NY	12477	845-246-7828	246-7828

48-19 Military, Veterans, Patriotic Organizations

Organization	City	State	ZIP	Phone	Fax
Air Force Assn (AFA) 1501 Lee Hwy *TF:* 800-727-3337 ■ *Web:* www.afa.org	Arlington	VA	22209	703-247-5800	247-5853
Air Force Sergeants Assn (AFSA) 5211 Auth Rd *TF:* 800-638-0594 ■ *Web:* www.afsahq.org	Suitland	MD	20746	301-899-3500	899-8136
Alpha-66 2250 SW 8th St *Web:* www.alpha66.org	Miami	FL	33135	305-541-5433	541-2252
American Legion 700 N Pennsylvania St *TF Cust Svc:* 800-433-3318 ■ *Web:* www.legion.org	Indianapolis	IN	46204	317-630-1200	630-1223
American Legion Auxiliary 777 N Meridian St 3rd Fl *Web:* www.legion-aux.org	Indianapolis	IN	46204	317-955-3845	955-3884
American Logistics Assn (ALA) 1133 15th St NW Suite 640 *Web:* www.ala-national.org	Washington	DC	20005	202-466-2520	296-4419
American Society of Military Comptrollers (ASMC) 415 N Alfred *TF:* 800-462-5637 ■ *Web:* www.asmconline.org	Alexandria	VA	22314	703-549-0360	549-3181
AMVETS 4647 Forbes Blvd *TF:* 877-726-8387 ■ *Web:* www.amvets.org	Lanham	MD	20706	301-459-9600	459-7924
Armed Forces Communications & Electronics Assn (AFCEA) 4400 Fair Lakes Ct *TF:* 800-336-4583 ■ *Web:* www.afcea.org	Fairfax	VA	22033	703-631-6100	631-4693
Armed Services Mutual Benefit Assn (ASMBA) PO Box 160384 *TF:* 800-251-8434 ■ *Web:* www.asmba.com	Nashville	TN	37216	615-851-0800	851-9484
Army Aviation Assn of America (AAAA) 755 Main St Suite 4D *Web:* www.quad-a.org	Monroe	CT	06468	203-268-2450	268-5870
Army Distaff Foundation 6200 Oregon Ave NW *TF:* 800-541-4255 ■ *Web:* www.armydistaff.org	Washington	DC	20015	202-541-0105	541-0128
Association of Civilian Technicians (ACT) 12620 Lake Ridge Dr *Web:* www.actnat.com	Woodbridge	VA	22192	703-494-4845	494-0961
Association of Naval Aviation (ANA) 2550 Huntington Ave Suite 201 *Web:* www.anahq.org	Alexandria	VA	22303	703-960-2490	960-4490
Association of Old Crows (AOC) 1000 N Payne St Suite 300 *TF:* 888-653-2769 ■ *Web:* www.crows.org	Alexandria	VA	22314	703-549-1600	549-2589
Association of the US Army (AUSA) 2425 Wilson Blvd *TF:* 800-336-4570 ■ *Web:* www.ausa.org	Arlington	VA	22201	703-841-4300	525-9039
Delta Phi Epsilon Professional Foreign Service Fraternity Inc PO Box 25401 *Web:* www.deltaphiepsilon.net/National_Fraternity.html	Washington	DC	20027	202-337-7116	
Disabled American Veterans (DAV) 3725 Alexandria Pike *TF:* 877-426-2838 ■ *Web:* www.dav.org	Cold Spring	KY	41076	859-441-7300	441-1416
Enlisted Assn of the National Guard of the US (EANGUS) 3133 Mt Vernon Ave *TF:* 800-234-3264 ■ *Web:* www.eangus.org	Alexandria	VA	22305	703-519-3846	519-3849
Fleet Reserve Assn (FRA) 125 N West St *TF:* 800-372-1924 ■ *Web:* www.fra.org	Alexandria	VA	22314	703-683-1400	549-6610
Marine Corps Assn (MCA) PO Box 1775 *TF:* 800-336-0291 ■ *Web:* www.mca-marines.org	Quantico	VA	22134	703-640-6161	640-0823
Marine Corps League (MCL) PO Box 3070 *TF:* 800-625-1775 ■ *Web:* www.mcleague.org	Merrifield	VA	22116	703-207-9588	207-0047
Marine Corps Reserve Assn (MCRA) 337 Potomac Ave *TF:* 800-927-6270 ■ *Web:* www.usmcra.org	Quantico	VA	22134	703-630-3772	630-1904
Military Benefit Assn (MBA) PO Box 221110 *TF:* 800-336-0100 ■ *Web:* www.militarybenefit.org	Chantilly	VA	20153	703-968-6200	968-6423
Military Officers Assn of America (MOAA) 201 N Washington St *TF:* 800-234-6622 ■ *Web:* www.moaa.org	Alexandria	VA	22314	703-549-2311	838-8173
MOAA (Military Officers Assn of America) 201 N Washington St *TF:* 800-234-6622 ■ *Web:* www.moaa.org	Alexandria	VA	22314	703-549-2311	838-8173
National Assn for Uniformed Services (NAUS) 5535 Hempstead Way *TF:* 800-842-3451 ■ *Web:* www.naus.org	Springfield	VA	22151	703-750-1342	354-4380
National Committee for Employer Support of the Guard & Reserve (ESGR) 1555 Wilson Blvd Suite 200 *TF:* 800-336-4590 ■ *Web:* www.esgr.org	Arlington	VA	22209	703-696-1386	696-1411
National Defense Industrial Assn (NDIA) 2111 Wilson Blvd Suite 400 *Web:* www.ndia.org	Arlington	VA	22201	703-522-1820	522-1885
National Fallen Firefighters Foundation PO Drawer 498 *Web:* www.firehero.org	Emmitsburg	MD	21727	301-447-1365	447-1645
National Guard Assn of the US (NGAUS) 1 Massachusetts Ave NW Suite 200 *TF:* 888-226-4287 ■ *Web:* www.ngaus.org	Washington	DC	20001	202-789-0031	682-9358
National League of Families of American Prisoners & Missing in Southeast Asia 1005 N Glebe Rd Suite 170 *Web:* www.pow-miafamilies.org	Arlington	VA	22201	703-465-7432	465-7433
National Medical War Memorial Project PO Box 14492 *Web:* www.medicalwarmemorial.org	Kansas City	MO	64152	816-452-0606	454-0897
National Society Daughters of the American Revolution (DAR) 1776 D St NW *Web:* www.dar.org	Washington	DC	20006	202-628-1776	879-3252
National Society of the Sons of the American Revolution (SAR) 1000 S 4th St *Web:* www.sar.org	Louisville	KY	40203	502-589-1776	589-1671
Naval Enlisted Reserve Assn (NERA) 6703 Farragut Ave *TF:* 800-776-9020 ■ *Web:* www.nera.org	Falls Church	VA	22042	703-534-1329	534-3617
Naval Reserve Assn (NRA) 1619 King St **Fax Area Code:* 866 ■ *TF:* 866-672-4968 ■ *Web:* www.navy-reserve.org	Alexandria	VA	22314	703-548-5800	683-3647*
Navy League of the US 2300 Wilson Blvd *TF:* 800-356-5760 ■ *Web:* www.navyleague.org	Arlington	VA	22201	703-528-1775	528-2333
Navy-Marine Corps Relief Society (NMCRS) 4015 Wilson Blvd 10th Fl *TF:* 800-654-8364 ■ *Web:* www.nmcrs.org	Arlington	VA	22203	703-696-4904	696-0144
Non-Commissioned Officers Assn (NCOA) 10635 IH-35 N *TF Cust Svc:* 800-662-2620 ■ *Web:* www.ncoausa.org	San Antonio	TX	78233	210-653-6161	637-3337
Paralyzed Veterans of America (PVA) 801 18th St NW **Fax:* PR ■ *TF:* 800-424-8200 ■ *Web:* www.pva.org	Washington	DC	20006	202-872-1300	416-7641*
Reserve Officers Assn of the US (ROA) 1 Constitution Ave NE *TF:* 800-809-9448 ■ *Web:* www.roa.org	Washington	DC	20002	202-479-2200	547-1641
Retired Enlisted Assn (TREA) 13130 E Colfax Ave *Web:* www.trea.org	Aurora	CO	80011	303-340-3939	340-4516
Society of American Military Engineers (SAME) 607 Prince St *TF:* 800-336-3097 ■ *Web:* www.same.org	Alexandria	VA	22314	703-549-3800	684-0231
Society of Military Widows (SMW) 5535 Hempstead Way *TF:* 800-842-3451 ■ *Web:* www.militarywidows.org	Springfield	VA	22151	703-750-1342	354-4380
Tailhook Assn 9696 Businesspark Ave *TF:* 800-322-4665 ■ *Web:* www.tailhook.org	San Diego	CA	92131	858-689-9223	578-8839
TREA (Retired Enlisted Assn) 13130 E Colfax Ave *Web:* www.trea.org	Aurora	CO	80011	303-340-3939	340-4516
United Service Organizations (USO) 2111 Wilson Blvd Suite 1200 *Web:* www.uso.org	Arlington	VA	22201	703-908-6400	908-6401
US Coast Guard Chief Petty Officers Assn 5520-G Hempstead Way *Web:* www.uscgcpoa.org	Springfield	VA	22151	703-941-0395	941-0397
US Naval Institute 291 Wood Rd *TF:* 800-233-8764 ■ *Web:* www.usni.org	Annapolis	MD	21402	410-268-6110	269-7940
Veterans of Foreign Wars of the US (VFW) 406 W 34th St *Web:* www.vfw.com	Kansas City	MO	64111	816-756-3390	968-1149
Veterans for Peace Inc (VFP) 216 S Meramec Ave *Web:* www.veteransforpeace.org	Saint Louis	MO	63105	314-725-6005	725-7103
VFW (Veterans of Foreign Wars of the US) 406 W 34th St *Web:* www.vfw.com	Kansas City	MO	64111	816-756-3390	968-1149
Vietnam Veterans of America (VVA) 8605 Cameron St Suite 400 *TF:* 800-882-1316 ■ *Web:* www.vva.org	Silver Spring	MD	20910	301-585-4000	585-0519
Women in Military Service for America Memorial Foundation Inc Dept 560 *TF:* 800-222-2294 ■ *Web:* www.womensmemorial.org	Washington	DC	20042	703-533-1155	931-4208

48-20 Religious Organizations

Organization	City	State	ZIP	Phone	Fax
92nd St Young Men's & Young Women's Hebrew Assn 1395 Lexington Ave *Web:* www.92y.org	New York	NY	10128	212-415-5500	
American Academy of Religion (AAR) 825 Houston Mill Rd NE Suite 300 *Web:* www.aarweb.org	Atlanta	GA	30329	404-727-3049	727-7959
American Baptist Assn (ABA) 4605 N State Line Ave *TF:* 800-264-2482 ■ *Web:* www.abaptist.org	Texarkana	TX	75503	903-792-2783	792-8128
American Baptist Churches USA PO Box 851 *TF:* 800-222-3872 ■ *Web:* www.abc-usa.org	Valley Forge	PA	19482	610-768-2000	768-2275
American Bible Society 1865 Broadway *TF:* 800-242-5375 ■ *Web:* www.americanbible.org	New York	NY	10023	212-408-1200	408-1512
American Council of Christian Churches (ACCC) PO Box 5455 *Web:* www.amcouncilcc.org	Bethlehem	PA	18015	610-865-3009	865-3033
American Theological Library Assn (ATLA) 250 S Wacker Dr Suite 1600 *TF:* 888-665-2852 ■ *Web:* www.atla.com	Chicago	IL	60606	312-454-5100	454-5505
American Tract Society (ATS) 1624 N 1st St *TF:* 800-548-7228 ■ *Web:* www.atstracts.org	Garland	TX	75040	972-276-9408	272-9642
Antiochian Orthodox Christian Archdiocese of North America 358 Mountain Rd *Web:* www.antiochian.org	Englewood	NJ	07631	201-871-1355	871-7954
Armenian Church of America 630 2nd Ave *Web:* www.armenianchurch.org	New York	NY	10016	212-686-0710	779-3558
Assemblies of God (A/G) 1445 N Boonville Ave *TF:* 800-641-4310 ■ *Web:* ag.org	Springfield	MO	65802	417-862-2781	862-8558
Association of Gospel Rescue Missions (AGRM) 1045 Swift Ave *TF:* 800-624-5156 ■ *Web:* www.agrm.org	Kansas City	MO	64116	816-471-8020	471-3718
Association of Professional Chaplains (APC) 1701 E Woodfield Rd Suite 760 *Web:* www.professionalchaplains.org	Schaumburg	IL	60173	847-240-1014	240-1015
Avant Ministries 10000 N Oak Trafficway *TF:* 800-468-1892 ■ *Web:* www.avantministries.org	Kansas City	MO	64155	816-734-8500	734-4601
Baptist Bible Fellowship International (BBFI) PO Box 191 *Web:* www.bbfi.org	Springfield	MO	65801	417-862-5001	865-0794
Baptist General Conference (BGC) 2002 S Arlington Heights Rd *TF:* 800-323-4215 ■ *Web:* www.bgcworld.org	Arlington Heights	IL	60005	847-228-0200	228-5376

Organization	City	State	Zip	Phone	Fax
Baptist Mid-Missions PO Box 308011 *Web:* www.bmm.org	Cleveland	OH	44130	440-826-3930	826-4457
Baptist Missionary Assn of America (BMA) PO Box 30910 *Web:* www.bmaam.com	Little Rock	AR	72260	501-455-4977	455-3636
Baptist World Alliance 405 N Washington St *Web:* www.bwanet.org	Falls Church	VA	22046	703-790-8980	790-5719
Bible League PO Box 28000 *TF:* 866-825-4636 ■ *Web:* www.bibleleague.org	Chicago	IL	60628	708-367-8500	367-8600
Billy Graham Evangelistic Assn 1 Billy Graham Pkwy PO Box 1270 *TF:* 877-247-2426 ■ *Web:* www.billygraham.org	Charlotte	NC	28201	704-401-2432	401-2140
B'nai B'rith International 2020 K St NW 7th Fl *TF:* 888-388-4224 ■ *Web:* bnaibrith.org	Washington	DC	20006	202-857-6600	857-6609
B'nai B'rith Youth Organization (BBYO) 2020 K St NW *Web:* www.bbyo.org	Washington	DC	20006	202-857-6633	857-6568
Buddhist Churches of America 1710 Octavia St *Web:* www.buddhistchurchesofamerica.org	San Francisco	CA	94109	415-776-5600	771-6293
Campus Crusade for Christ International 100 Lake Hart Dr *TF:* 877-924-7478 ■ *Web:* www.ccci.org	Orlando	FL	32832	407-826-2000	
Canon Law Society of America (CLSA) 108 N Payne St Suite C *Web:* www.clsa.org	Alexandria	VA	22314	703-739-2560	739-2562
Catholic Biblical Assn of America 620 Michigan Ave NE 433 Caldwell Hall *Web:* studentorg.cua.edu/cbib	Washington	DC	20064	202-319-5519	319-4799
Catholic Church Extension Society of the USA 150 S Wacker Dr 20th Fl *TF:* 800-842-7804 ■ *Web:* www.catholic-extension.org	Chicago	IL	60606	312-236-7240	236-5276
Central Conference of American Rabbis (CCAR) 355 Lexington Ave 18th Fl *TF:* 800-935-2227 ■ *Web:* ccarnet.org	New York	NY	10017	212-972-3636	692-0819
Christian Aid Ministries PO Box 360	Berlin	OH	44610	330-892-2428	893-2305
Christian Church (Disciples of Christ) PO Box 1986 *Web:* www.disciples.org	Indianapolis	IN	46206	317-635-3100	635-3700
Christian Endeavor International 424 E Main St *TF:* 800-260-3234 ■ *Web:* www.teamce.com	Edmore	MI	48829	989-427-3737	427-5530
Christian & Missionary Alliance PO Box 35000 *Web:* www.cmalliance.org	Colorado Springs	CO	80935	719-599-5999	
Christian Reformed Church in North America (CRC) 2850 Kalamazoo Ave SE *TF:* 800-272-5125 ■ *Web:* www.crcna.org	Grand Rapids	MI	49560	616-241-1691	224-0834
Christophers The 5 Hanover Sq 11th Fl *TF:* 888-298-4050 ■ *Web:* www.christophers.org	New York	NY	10004	212-759-4050	838-5073
Church of the Brethren 1451 Dundee Ave *TF:* 800-323-8039 ■ *Web:* www.brethren.org	Elgin	IL	60120	847-742-5100	742-6103
Church of God in Christ Inc 938 Mason St *Web:* www.cogic.org	Memphis	TN	38126	901-947-9300	947-9359
Church of God Ministries 1201 E 5th St *TF:* 800-848-2464 ■ *Web:* www.chog.org	Anderson	IN	46012	765-642-0256	642-5652
Church of God World Missions PO Box 8016 *TF:* 800-345-7492 ■ *Web:* www.cogwm.org	Cleveland	TN	37320	423-478-7190	478-7155
Church of Jesus Christ of Latter-Day Saints 50 E North Temple St *Web:* www.lds.org	Salt Lake City	UT	84150	801-240-1000	240-2033
Church of the Nazarene 6401 The Paseo *Web:* www.nazarene.org	Kansas City	MO	64131	816-333-7000	
Church Women United (CWU) 475 Riverside Dr Rm 1626 *TF:* 800-298-5551 ■ *Web:* www.churchwomen.org	New York	NY	10115	212-870-2347	870-2338
Community of Christ 1001 W Walnut St **Fax:* Hum Res ■ *TF:* 800-825-2806 ■ *Web:* www.cofchrist.org	Independence	MO	64050	816-833-1000	521-3085*
Connecting Businessmen to Christ (CBMC) 5746 Marlin Rd Suite 602 Osborne Center *TF:* 800-575-2262 ■ *Web:* www.cbmc.com	Chattanooga	TN	37411	423-698-4444	629-4434
Courage 210 W 31st St *Web:* couragerc.net	New York	NY	10001	212-268-1010	268-7150
Episcopal Church USA 815 2nd Ave *TF:* 800-334-7626 ■ *Web:* www.episcopalchurch.org	New York	NY	10017	212-716-6000	867-0395
Evangelical Church Alliance (ECA) PO Box 9 *Web:* www.ecainternational.org	Bradley	IL	60915	815-937-0720	937-0001
Evangelical Fellowship of Canada (EFC) Markham Industrial Park Box 3745 *Web:* www.evangelicalfellowship.ca	Markham	ON	L3R0Y4	905-479-5885	
Evangelical Lutheran Church in America (ELCA) 8765 W Higgins Rd *TF:* 800-638-3522 ■ *Web:* www.elca.org	Chicago	IL	60631	773-380-2700	380-1465
Evangelical Training Assn (ETA) 1620 Penny Ln **Fax Area Code:* 847 ■ *TF:* 800-369-8291 ■ *Web:* www.etaworld.org	Schaumburg	IL	60173	630-540-7840	882-3506*
Fellowship of Christian Athletes (FCA) 8701 Leeds Rd *TF:* 800-289-0909 ■ *Web:* www.fca.org	Kansas City	MO	64129	816-921-0909	921-8755
First Church of Christ Scientist 175 Huntington Ave *Web:* www.tfccs.com	Boston	MA	02115	617-450-2000	450-2281
General Assn of Regular Baptist Churches (GARBC) 1300 N Meacham Rd *Web:* www.garbc.org	Schaumburg	IL	60173	847-843-1600	843-3757
Graham Billy Evangelistic Assn 1 Billy Graham Pkwy PO Box 1270 *TF:* 877-247-2426 ■ *Web:* www.billygraham.org	Charlotte	NC	28201	704-401-2432	401-2140
Greek Orthodox Archdiocese of America 8 E 79th St *Web:* www.goarch.org	New York	NY	10021	212-570-3500	570-3569
Hadassah Women's Zionist Organization of America Inc 50 W 58th St *TF:* 888-303-3640 ■ *Web:* www.hadassah.org	New York	NY	10019	212-355-7900	303-8282
IFCA International PO Box 810 *TF:* 800-347-1840 ■ *Web:* www.ifca.org	Grandville	MI	49468	616-531-1840	531-1814
International Bible Society (IBS) 1820 Jet Stream Dr *TF Cust Svc:* 800-524-1588 ■ *Web:* www.ibs.org	Colorado Springs	CO	80921	719-488-9200	488-0870
International Church of the Foursquare Gospel (ICFG) 1910 W Sunset Blvd Suite 200 *TF:* 888-635-4234 ■ *Web:* www.foursquare.org	Los Angeles	CA	90026	213-989-4234	989-4590
International Lutheran Laymen's League 660 Mason Ridge Ctr Dr *TF:* 800-944-3450 ■ *Web:* www.lhm.org	Saint Louis	MO	63141	314-317-4100	317-4291
International Pentecostal Holiness Church (IPHC) PO Box 12609 *Web:* www.iphc.org	Oklahoma City	OK	73157	405-787-7110	789-3957
InterVarsity Christian Fellowship/USA 6400 Schroeder Rd *Web:* www.intervarsity.org	Madison	WI	53711	608-274-9001	274-7882
Jehovah's Witnesses 25 Columbia Heights *Web:* www.watchtower.org	Brooklyn	NY	11201	718-560-5000	560-8030
Jewish Community Centers Assn of North America 520 8th Ave *Web:* www.jcca.org	New York	NY	10018	212-532-4949	481-4174
Jewish Federation of Metropolitan Chicago 1 S Franklin St *Web:* www.juf.org	Chicago	IL	60606	312-346-6700	
Jewish National Fund (JNF) 42 E 69th St *TF:* 800-542-8733 ■ *Web:* www.jnf.org	New York	NY	10021	212-879-9300	
Jewish Reconstructionist Federation (JRF) 101 Greenwood Ave Suite 430 *Web:* www.jrf.org	Jenkintown	PA	19046	215-885-5601	885-5603
Jews for Jesus 60 Haight St *Web:* www.jewsforjesus.org	San Francisco	CA	94102	415-864-2600	552-8325
Jimmy Swaggart Ministries (JSM) 8919 World Ministry Blvd *TF Orders:* 800-288-8350 ■ *Web:* www.jsm.org	Baton Rouge	LA	70810	225-768-8300	769-2244
King Benevolent Fund Inc 1119 Commonwealth Ave *TF:* 800-321-9234 ■ *Web:* www.kingbf.org	Bristol	VA	24201	276-466-3014	466-0108
Lutheran Church Missouri Synod (LCMS) 1333 S Kirkwood Rd *TF:* 888-843-5267 ■ *Web:* www.lcms.org	Saint Louis	MO	63122	314-965-9000	996-1016
Mission Aviation Fellowship (MAF) 1849 N Wabash Ave *TF:* 800-359-7623 ■ *Web:* www.maf.org	Redlands	CA	92374	909-794-1151	794-3016
Nation of Islam 7351 S Stony Island *Web:* www.noi.org	Chicago	IL	60649	773-324-6000	324-6309
National Assn of Congregational Christian Churches (NACCC) 8473 S Howell Ave *TF:* 800-262-1620 ■ *Web:* www.naccc.org	Oak Creek	WI	53154	414-764-1620	764-0319
National Assn of Evangelicals (NAE) 701 G St SW *Web:* www.nae.net	Washington	DC	20024	202-789-1011	842-0392
National Assn of Free Will Baptists (NAFWB) 5233 Mt View Rd *TF:* 877-767-7659 ■ *Web:* www.nafwb.org	Antioch	TN	37013	615-731-6812	731-0771
National Baptist Convention of America Inc 1320 Pierre Ave *Web:* www.nbcamerica.net	Shreveport	LA	71103	318-221-3701	222-7512
National Baptist Convention USA Inc 1700 Baptist World Center Dr *TF:* 866-531-3054 ■ *Web:* www.nationalbaptist.com	Nashville	TN	37207	615-228-6292	
National Conference on Ministry to the Armed Forces 7708 Griffin Pond Ct *Web:* www.ncmaf.org	Springfield	VA	22153	703-455-7908	455-7948
National Council of the Churches of Christ in the USA (NCCCUSA) 475 Riverside Dr Suite 880 *Web:* www.ncccusa.org	New York	NY	10115	212-870-2227	870-2030
National Spiritual Assembly of the Baha'is of the US 1233 Central St *Web:* www.bahai.us	Evanston	IL	60201	847-869-9039	869-0247
Navigators PO Box 6000 *Web:* www.navigators.org	Colorado Springs	CO	80934	719-598-1212	260-0479
New Tribes Mission (NTM) 1000 E 1st St *TF:* 800-321-5375 ■ *Web:* www.ntm.org	Sanford	FL	32771	407-323-3430	330-0376
North American Christian Convention (NACC) 110 Boggs Ln Suite 330 *Web:* www.naccteconnectingplace.org	Cincinnati	OH	45246	513-772-9970	772-9980
Orthodox Union (OU) 11 Broadway *Web:* www.ou.org	New York	NY	10004	212-563-4000	564-9058
Peale Center for Christian Living 66 E Main St	Pawling	NY	12564	845-855-5000	855-1036
Pentecostal World Fellowship (PWF) PO Box 12609 *Web:* pentecostalworldfellowship.org	Oklahoma City	OK	73157	405-787-7110	789-3957
Presbyterian Church in America (PCA) 1700 N Brown Rd Suite 105 *Web:* www.pcanet.org	Lawrenceville	GA	30043	678-825-1000	825-1001
Presbyterian Church (USA) 100 Witherspoon St *TF:* 888-728-7228 ■ *Web:* www.pcusa.org	Louisville	KY	40202	502-569-5000	569-5018
Progressive National Baptist Convention Inc (PNBC) 601 50th St NE *TF:* 800-876-7622 ■ *Web:* pnbc.org	Washington	DC	20019	202-396-0558	398-4998
Promise Keepers 4045 Pecos St PO Box 11798 *TF:* 800-888-7595 ■ *Web:* www.promisekeepers.org	Denver	CO	80211	303-964-7600	433-1036
Rabbinical Assembly 3080 Broadway *Web:* www.rabbinicalassembly.org	New York	NY	10027	212-280-6000	
Reconstructionist Rabbinical Assn (RRA) 1299 Church Rd *Web:* www.therra.org	Wyncote	PA	19095	215-576-5210	576-8051
Reformed Church in America 475 Riverside Dr 18th Fl *TF:* 800-722-9977 ■ *Web:* www.rca.org	New York	NY	10115	212-870-3071	870-2499
Religious Science International (RSI) 901 E 2nd Ave Suite 301 *TF:* 800-662-1348 ■ *Web:* www.rsintl.org	Spokane	WA	99202	509-624-7000	624-9322
Salvation Army PO Box 269 *TF:* 800-725-2769 ■ *Web:* www.salvationarmyusa.org	Alexandria	VA	22313	703-684-5500	684-3478
Seat of the Soul Foundation 1257 Siskiyou Blvd Suite 57 *TF:* 888-440-7685 ■ *Web:* www.seatofthesoul.org	Ashland	OR	97520	541-482-8000	482-0176
Seventh-day Adventist World Church 12501 Old Columbia Pike *Web:* www.adventist.org	Silver Spring	MD	20904	301-680-6000	680-6090
Society of Biblical Literature (SBL) The Luce Center 825 Houston Mill Rd *Web:* www.sbl-site.org	Atlanta	GA	30329	404-727-3100	727-3101
Southern Baptist Convention (SBC) 901 Commerce St *Web:* www.sbc.net	Nashville	TN	37203	615-244-2355	742-8919
Standing Conference of Canonical Orthodox Bishops in the Americas 8 E 79th St *Web:* www.scoba.us	New York	NY	10075	212-570-3500	774-0202
Swaggart Jimmy Ministries 8919 World Ministry Blvd *TF Orders:* 800-288-8350 ■ *Web:* www.jsm.org	Baton Rouge	LA	70810	225-768-8300	769-2244
Traditional Values Coalition (TVC) 139 C St SE *Web:* www.traditionalvalues.org	Washington	DC	20003	202-547-8570	546-6403
Union of Orthodox Rabbis of the US & Canada 235 E Broadway	New York	NY	10002	212-964-6337	
Union for Reformed Judaism 633 3rd Ave *Web:* urj.org	New York	NY	10017	212-650-4000	650-4159
Unitarian Universalist Assn (UUA) 25 Beacon St *Web:* www.uua.org	Boston	MA	02108	617-742-2100	367-3237
United Church of Christ (UCC) 700 Prospect Ave *TF:* 866-822-8224 ■ *Web:* www.ucc.org	Cleveland	OH	44115	216-736-2100	736-2103
United Jewish Communities (UJC) 111 8th Ave Suite 11E *Web:* www.ujc.org	New York	NY	10011	212-284-6500	284-6835
United Pentecostal Church International (UPCI) 8855 Dunn Rd *Web:* www.upci.org	Hazelwood	MO	63042	314-837-7300	837-4503
United Synagogue of Conservative Judaism 155 5th Ave *Web:* www.uscj.org	New York	NY	10010	212-533-7800	353-9439
Urban Alternative PO Box 4000 *TF:* 800-800-3222 ■ *Web:* www.tonyevans.org	Dallas	TX	75208	214-943-3868	943-2632
US Conference of Catholic Bishops (USCCB) 3211 4th St NE *Web:* www.usccb.org	Washington	DC	20017	202-541-3000	541-3322
US National Committee to the International Dairy Federation PO Box 930398 *Web:* www.usnac.org	Verona	WI	53593	608-848-6455	848-7675
Watchtower Bible & Tract Society 25 Columbia Heights *Web:* www.watchtower.org	Brooklyn	NY	11201	718-560-5000	560-8030
Wheat Ridge Ministries 1 Pierce Pl Suite 250E *TF:* 800-762-6748 ■ *Web:* www.wheatridge.org	Itasca	IL	60143	630-766-9066	766-9622

Religious Organizations (Cont'd)

Organization	City	State	ZIP	Phone	Fax
Wider Church Ministries 700 Prospect Ave 7th Fl *TF:* 866-822-8224 ■ *Web:* www.ucc.org/wcm	Cleveland	OH	44115	216-736-3200	736-3203
Wisconsin Evangelical Lutheran Synod (WELS) 2929 N Mayfair Rd *Web:* www.wels.net	Milwaukee	WI	53222	414-256-3888	256-3899
Woman's Missionary Union (WMU) 100 Missionary Ridge *TF:* 800-968-7301 ■ *Web:* www.wmu.com	Birmingham	AL	35242	205-991-8100	991-4990
World Gospel Mission PO Box 948 *Web:* www.wgm.org	Marion	IN	46952	765-664-7331	671-7230
World Methodist Council PO Box 518 *Web:* www.worldmethodistcouncil.org	Lake Junaluska	NC	28745	828-456-9432	456-9433
WorldVenture 1501 W Mineral Ave *Web:* www.worldventure.com	Littleton	CO	80120	720-283-2000	283-2111
Wycliffe Bible Translators PO Box 628200 *TF:* 800-992-5433 ■ *Web:* www.wycliffe.org	Orlando	FL	32862	407-852-3611	852-3601
Youth for Christ/USA PO Box 4478 *TF:* 800-735-3252 ■ *Web:* community.gospelcom.net/Brix/yfcusa/public	Englewood	CO	80155	303-843-9000	843-9002

48-21 Self-Help Organizations

Organization	City	State	ZIP	Phone	Fax
ABIL Inc (Agoraphobics Building Independent Lives Inc) 2501 Fox Harbor Ct *Web:* www.anxietysupport.org	Richmond	VA	23235	804-353-3964	353-3687
Adult Children of Alcoholics World Service Organization Inc (ACA) PO Box 3216 *Web:* www.adultchildren.org	Torrance	CA	90510	310-534-1815	
Agoraphobics Building Independent Lives Inc (ABIL Inc) 2501 Fox Harbor Ct *Web:* www.anxietysupport.org	Richmond	VA	23235	804-353-3964	353-3687
Al-Anon Family Group Headquarters Inc 1600 Corporate Landing Pkwy *TF:* 888-425-2666 ■ *Web:* www.al-anon.org	Virginia Beach	VA	23454	757-563-1600	563-1655
Alateen 1600 Corporate Landing Pkwy *TF:* 888-425-2666 ■ *Web:* www.alateen.org	Virginia Beach	VA	23454	757-563-1600	563-1655
Alcoholics Anonymous (AA) 475 Riverside Dr 11th Fl *Web:* www.aa.org	New York	NY	10115	212-870-3400	870-3003
Alcoholics Victorious (AV) 1045 Swift Ave *Web:* av.iugm.org	Kansas City	MO	64116	816-471-8020	471-3718
ARTS Anonymous (ARTS) PO Box 230175 *Web:* www.artsanonymous.org	New York	NY	10023	212-873-7075	
Bereaved Parents of the USA PO Box 95 *Web:* www.bereavedparentsusa.org	Park Forest	IL	60466	708-748-7866	
Burns United Support Group PO Box 36416	Grosse Pointe	MI	48236	313-881-5577	417-8702
Calix Society 2555 Hazelwood Ave *TF:* 800-398-0524 ■ *Web:* www.calixsociety.org	Saint Paul	MN	55109	651-773-3117	777-3069
Candlelighters Childhood Cancer Foundation PO Box 498 *TF:* 800-366-2223 ■ *Web:* www.candlelighters.org	Kensington	MD	20895	301-962-3520	962-3521
Chemically Dependent Anonymous (CDA) PO Box 423 *TF:* 800-232-4673 ■ *Web:* www.cdaweb.org	Severna Park	MD	21146	800-232-4673	
Children of Lesbians & Gays Everywhere (COLAGE) 3543 18th St Suite 1 *Web:* www.colage.org	San Francisco	CA	94110	415-861-5437	255-8345
Cleptomaniacs & Shoplifters Anonymous Inc (CASA) PO Box 250008 *Web:* www.shopliftersanonymous.com	Franklin	MI	48205	248-358-8508	
Clutterers Anonymous World Service Organization (CLA) PO Box 91413 *Web:* www.clutterersanonymous.net	Los Angeles	CA	90009	310-281-6064	
Co-Anon Family Groups PO Box 12722 *TF:* 800-898-9985 ■ *Web:* www.co-anon.org	Tucson	AZ	85732	520-513-5028	
Co-Dependents Anonymous Inc (CODA) PO Box 33577 *Web:* www.codependents.org	Phoenix	AZ	85067	602-277-7991	
Cocaine Anonymous World Services Inc (CA) 3740 Overland Ave Suite C *TF:* 800-347-8998 ■ *Web:* www.ca.org	Los Angeles	CA	90034	310-559-5833	559-2554
Compassionate Friends PO Box 3696 *TF:* 877-969-0010 ■ *Web:* www.compassionatefriends.com	Oak Brook	IL	60522	630-990-0010	990-0246
Compulsive Eaters Anonymous - HOW (CEA-HOW) 5500 E Atherton St Suite 227B *Web:* www.ceahow.org	Long Beach	CA	90815	562-342-9344	342-9346
Concerned United Birthparents Inc (CUB) PO Box 503475 **Fax Area Code:* 858 ■ *Web:* www.cubirthparents.org	San Diego	CA	92150	800-822-2777	435-4863*
Concerns of Police Survivors Inc (COPS) 3096 S State Hwy 5 PO Box 3199 *Web:* www.nationalcops.org	Camdenton	MO	65020	573-346-4911	346-1414
Crystal Meth Anonymous General Service Organization 8205 Santa Monica Blvd PMB 1-114 *Web:* www.crystalmeth.org	West Hollywood	CA	90046	213-488-4455	
Debtors Anonymous (DA) PO Box 920888 *Web:* www.debtorsanonymous.org	Needham	MA	02492	781-453-2743	453-2745
Depressed Anonymous PO Box 17414 *Web:* www.depressedanon.com	Louisville	KY	40217	502-569-1989	
DignityUSA Inc 721 8th St Se **Fax Area Code:* 781 ■ *TF:* 800-877-8797 ■ *Web:* www.dignityusa.org	Washington	DC	20003	202-861-0017	397-0584*
Domestic Violence Anonymous PO Box 29011	San Francisco	CA	94129	415-681-4850	
Double Trouble in Recovery Inc PO Box 245055 *Web:* www.doubletroubleinrecovery.org	Brooklyn	NY	11224	718-373-2684	
Emotions Anonymous International (EA) 2233 University Ave W Suite 402 PO Box 4245 *Web:* www.emotionsanonymous.org	Saint Paul	MN	55104	651-647-9712	647-1593
Families Anonymous (FA) PO Box 3475 *TF:* 800-736-9805 ■ *Web:* www.familiesanonymous.org	Culver City	CA	90231	310-815-8010	815-9682
Food Addicts Anonymous (FAA) 4623 Forest Hill Blvd Suite 109-4 *Web:* www.foodaddictsanonymous.org	West Palm Beach	FL	33415	561-967-3871	967-9815
Food Addicts In Recovery Anonymous (FA) 6 Pleasant St Suite 402 *Web:* www.foodaddicts.org	Malden	MA	02148	781-321-9118	321-9223
Gam-Anon International Service Office Inc PO Box 157 *Web:* gam-anon.org	Whitestone	NY	11357	718-352-1671	746-2571
Gamblers Anonymous (GA) PO Box 17173 *TF:* 888-424-3577 ■ *Web:* www.gamblersanonymous.org	Los Angeles	CA	90017	213-386-8789	386-0030
GROW Inc 2403 W Springfield Ave Box 3667 *Web:* www.growinamerica.org	Champaign	IL	61826	217-352-6989	352-8530
HEARTBEAT/Survivors After Suicide Inc 2015 Devon St *Web:* www.heartbeatsurvivorsaftersuicide.org	Colorado Springs	CO	80909	719-596-2575	
Homosexuals Anonymous Fellowship Services PO Box 7881 *Web:* members.aol.com/hawebpage	Reading	PA	19603	610-779-2500	921-0470
Incest Survivors Anonymous (ISA) PO Box 17245 *Web:* www.lafn.org/medical/isa	Long Beach	CA	90807	562-428-5599	
Intercongregational Alcoholism Program (ICAP) 7777 Lake St Suite 115	River Forest	IL	60305	708-488-9770	488-9774
International Lawyers in Alcoholics Anonymous (ILAA) PO Box 552212 *Web:* www.ilaa.org	Las Vegas	NV	89155	702-455-4827	455-5597
International Pharmacists Anonymous 11 Dewey Ln *Web:* mywebpages.comcast.net/ipa/ipapage.htm	Glen Gardner	NJ	08826	908-537-4295	537-2449
Jewish Alcoholics Chemically Dependent Persons & Significant Others (JACS) 120 W 57th St 6th Fl *Web:* www.jacsweb.org	New York	NY	10019	212-397-4197	399-3525
LifeRing Secular Recovery 1440 Broadway Suite 312 *Web:* www.unhooked.com	Oakland	CA	94612	510-763-0779	763-1513
Lightning Strike & Electric Shock Survivors International Inc (LSESSI) PO Box 1156 *Web:* www.lightning-strike.org	Jacksonville	NC	28541	910-346-4708	
Manic Depressives Anonymous PO Box 73	Audubon	NJ	08106	856-869-5508	
Marijuana Anonymous World Services (MA) PO Box 2912 *Web:* www.marijuana-anonymous.org	Van Nuys	CA	91404	800-766-6779	
MISS Foundation PO Box 5333 *Web:* www.missfoundation.org	Peoria	AZ	85385	623-979-1000	979-1001
Moderation Management Network Inc (MM) 22 W 27th St 5th Fl *Web:* www.moderation.org	New York	NY	10001	212-871-0974	213-6582
Nar-Anon World Service Office 22527 Crenshaw Blvd Suite 200B *Web:* www.naranon.com	Torrance	CA	90505	310-534-8188	
Narcotics Anonymous World Services (NA) 19737 Nordhoff Pl *Web:* www.na.org	Chatsworth	CA	91311	818-773-9999	700-0700
Native American Indian General Service Office of Alcoholics Anonymous (NAIGSO-AA) PO Box 1253 *Web:* www.naigso-aa.org	Lakeside	CA	92040	951-927-2626	
Nicotine Anonymous World Services 419 Main St PMB 370 *Web:* www.nicotine-anonymous.org	Huntington Beach	CA	92648	415-750-0328	
Obsessive-Compulsive Anonymous (OCA) PO Box 215 *Web:* hometown.aol.com/_ht_a/west24th	New Hyde Park	NY	11040	516-739-0662	
Overcomers in Christ PO Box 34460 *Web:* www.overcomersinchrist.org	Omaha	NE	68134	402-573-0966	573-0960
Overcomers Outreach PO Box 2208 *TF:* 800-310-3001 ■ *Web:* www.overcomersoutreach.org	Oakhurst	CA	93644	559-692-2630	
Overeaters Anonymous Inc (OA) PO Box 44020 *Web:* www.oa.org	Rio Rancho	NM	87174	505-891-2664	891-4320
Parents Anonymous Inc 675 W Foothill Blvd Suite 220 *Web:* www.parentsanonymous.org	Claremont	CA	91711	909-621-6184	625-6304
Pathways to Peace Inc PO Box 259 *TF:* 800-775-4212 ■ *Web:* www.pathwaystopeaceinc.com	Cassadaga	NY	14718	716-595-3884	595-3886
Rational Recovery PO Box 800 *TF:* 800-303-2873 ■ *Web:* www.rational.org	Lotus	CA	95651	530-621-2667	622-4296
Recoveries Anonymous PO Box 1212 *Web:* www.r-a.org	East Northport	NY	11731	516-261-1212	
Recovering Couples Anonymous (RCA) PO Box 11029 *Web:* www.recovering-couples.org	Oakland	CA	94611	510-663-2312	
Recovering Racists Network 517 Loon Dr *Web:* www.rrnet.org	Petaluma	CA	94954	415-577-8331	
Recovery Inc 802 N Dearborn St *Web:* www.recovery-inc.com	Chicago	IL	60610	312-337-5661	337-5756
reFocus Inc PO Box 2180 *Web:* www.refocus.org	Flagler Beach	FL	32136	386-439-7541	439-7537
Rest Ministries Inc PO Box 502928 **Fax Area Code:* 800 ■ *TF:* 888-751-7378 ■ *Web:* www.restministries.org	San Diego	CA	92150	858-486-4685	933-1078*
S-Anon International Family Groups Inc PO Box 111242 *Web:* www.sanon.org	Nashville	TN	37222	615-833-3152	
Secular Organizations for Sobriety (SOS) 4773 Hollywood Blvd *Web:* www.cfiwest.org/sos	Hollywood	CA	90027	323-666-4295	
Sex Addicts Anonymous (SAA) PO Box 70949 *TF:* 800-477-8191 ■ *Web:* www.saa-recovery.org	Houston	TX	77270	713-869-4902	869-4176
Sex & Love Addicts Anonymous (SLAA) PO Box 338 *Web:* www.slaafws.org	Norwood	MA	02062	781-255-8825	255-9190
Sexaholics Anonymous (SA) PO Box 3565 *Web:* www.sa.org	Brentwood	TN	37024	615-370-6062	370-0882
SHARE Pregnancy & Infant Loss Support Inc St Joseph's Health Ctr 300 1st Capitol Dr *TF:* 800-821-6819 ■ *Web:* www.nationalshareoffice.com	Saint Charles	MO	63301	636-947-6164	947-7486
Single Mothers by Choice Inc (SMC) PO Box 1642 Gracie Square Stn *Web:* mattes.home.pipeline.com	New York	NY	10028	212-988-0993	
Sisters Network Inc 8787 Woodway Dr Suite 4206 *Web:* sistersnetworkinc.org	Houston	TX	77063	713-781-0255	780-8998
SMART Recovery 7537 Mentor Ave Suite 306 *TF:* 866-951-5357 ■ *Web:* www.smartrecovery.org	Mentor	OH	44060	440-951-5357	951-5358
Social Workers Helping Social Workers PO Box 486 *Web:* www.socialworkershelping.org	Nora Springs	IA	50458	641-422-7797	422-7516
Spenders Anonymous PO Box 2405 Loop Station *Web:* www.spenders.org	Minneapolis	MN	55402	651-649-4573	
Straight Spouse Network (SSN) 8215 Terrace Dr *Web:* www.straightspouse.org	El Cerrito	CA	94530	510-525-0200	525-4831
Survivors of Incest Anonymous (SIA) PO Box 190 *Web:* www.siawso.org	Benson	MD	21018	410-893-3322	
Survivors Network of Those Abused by Priests (SNAP) PO Box 6416 *TF:* 877-762-7432 ■ *Web:* www.snapnetwork.org	Chicago	IL	60680	312-409-2720	
Take Root PO Box 930 *TF:* 888-766-8674 ■ *Web:* www.takeroot.org	Kalama	WA	98625	360-673-3720	673-3732
TOPS Club Inc 4575 S 5th St *TF:* 800-932-8677 ■ *Web:* www.tops.org	Milwaukee	WI	53207	414-482-4620	482-1655
Twinless Twins Support Group International (TTSG) PO Box 980481 *Web:* www.twinlesstwins.org	Ypsilanti	MI	48198	888-205-8962	
White Bison Inc 6145 Lehman Dr Suite 200 *Web:* www.whitebison.org	Colorado Springs	CO	80918	719-548-1000	548-9407
Wings Foundation 8725 W 14th Ave Suite 150 *TF:* 800-373-8671 ■ *Web:* www.wingsfound.org	Lakewood	CO	80215	303-238-8660	
Wings of Light Inc 16845 N 29th Ave Suite 1 *Web:* www.wingsoflight.org	Phoenix	AZ	85053	623-516-1115	
Women for Sobriety Inc (WFS) PO Box 618 *Web:* www.womenforsobriety.org	Quakertown	PA	18951	215-536-8026	
Workaholics Anonymous World Service Organization PO Box 289 *Web:* www.workaholics-anonymous.org	Menlo Park	CA	94026	510-273-9253	

48-22 Sports Organizations

Organization	City	State	ZIP	Phone	Fax
Adventure Cycling Assn 150 E Pine St PO Box 8308 *TF:* 800-755-2453 ■ *Web:* www.adventurecycling.org	Missoula	MT	59807	406-721-1776	721-8754

Phone Fax

Aerobics & Fitness Assn of America (AFAA)
15250 Ventura Blvd Suite 200 Sherman Oaks CA 91403 818-905-0040 990-5468
TF: 877-968-7263 ■ *Web:* www.afaa.com
Amateur Athletic Union of the US (AAU)
PO Box 22409 Lake Buena Vista FL 32830 407-934-7200 934-7242
Web: www.aausports.org
Amateur Softball Assn of America Inc (ASA)
2801 NE 50th St Oklahoma City OK 73111 405-424-5266 424-3855
TF: 800-654-8337 ■ *Web:* www.softball.org
Amateur Trapshooting Assn (ATA) 601 W National Rd Vandalia OH 45377 937-898-4638 898-5472
Web: www.shootata.com
American Alliance for Health Physical Education Recreation & Dance (AAHPERD) 1900 Association Dr Reston VA 20191 703-476-3400 476-9527
TF: 800-213-7193 ■ *Web:* www.aahperd.org
American Amateur Baseball Congress (AABC)
100 W Broadway Farmington NM 87401 505-327-3120 327-3132
Web: www.aabc.us
American Baseball Coaches Assn (ABCA)
108 S University Ave Suite 3 Mount Pleasant MI 48858 989-775-3300 775-3600
Web: www.abca.org
American Bicycle Assn (ABA) 1645 W Sunrise Blvd Gilbert AZ 85233 480-961-1903 961-1842
TF: 800-886-1269 ■ *Web:* www.ababmx.com
American Canoe Assn (ACA)
7432 Alban Station Blvd Suite B-232 Springfield VA 22150 703-451-0141 451-2245
TF: 800-929-5162 ■ *Web:* www.americancanoe.org
American Council on Exercise (ACE) 4851 Paramount Dr San Diego CA 92123 858-279-8227 279-8064
TF: 800-825-3636 ■ *Web:* www.acefitness.org
American Football Coaches Assn (AFCA) 100 Legends Ln Waco TX 76706 254-754-9900 754-7373
Web: www.afca.com
American Grandprix Assn (AGA) 1301 6th Ave W Suite 406 Bradenton FL 34205 941-744-5465 744-0874
TF: 800-237-8924 ■ *Web:* www.stadiumjumping.com/aga
American Legion Baseball PO Box 1055 Indianapolis IN 46206 317-630-1213 630-1369
American Motorcyclist Assn (AMA) 13515 Yarmouth Dr Pickerington OH 43147 614-856-1900 856-1920
TF: 800-262-5646 ■ *Web:* www.ama-cycle.org
American Poolplayers Assn (APA)
1000 Lake St Louis Blvd Suite 325 Lake Saint Louis MO 63367 636-625-8611 625-2975
TF: 800-372-2536 ■ *Web:* www.poolplayers.com
American Running Assn 4405 East-West Hwy Suite 405 Bethesda MD 20814 301-913-9517 913-9520
TF: 800-776-2732 ■ *Web:* www.americanrunning.org
American Senior Fitness Assn (SFA) PO Box 2575 New Smyrna Beach FL 32170 386-423-6634 427-0613
TF: 800-243-1478 ■ *Web:* www.seniorfitness.net
American Society of Golf Course Architects (ASGCA)
125 N Executive Dr Suite 106 Brookfield WI 53005 262-786-5960 786-5919
Web: www.asgca.org
American Sportfishing Assn (ASA)
225 Reinekers Ln Suite 420 Alexandria VA 22314 703-519-9691 519-1872
Web: www.asafishing.org
American Sports Institute (ASI) PO Box 1837 Mill Valley CA 94942 415-383-5750 383-5785
Web: www.amersports.org
American Volkssport Assn (AVA)
1001 Pat Booker Rd Suite 101 Universal City TX 78148 210-659-2112 659-1212
TF: 800-830-9255 ■ *Web:* www.ava.org
American Watercraft Assn PO Box 1993 Ashburn VA 20147 800-913-2921 421-9889*
**Fax Area Code:* 703 ■ *Web:* www.awahq.org
American Youth Soccer Organization (AYSO)
12501 S Isis Ave Hawthorne CA 90250 310-643-6455 643-5310
TF Cust Svc: 800-872-2976 ■ *Web:* soccer.org
Aquatic Exercise Assn (AEA) PO Box 1609 Nokomis FL 34274 941-486-8600 486-8820
TF: 888-232-9283 ■ *Web:* aeawave.com
Association of Professional Ball Players of America
1820 W Orangewood Ave Suite 206 Orange CA 92868 714-935-9993 935-0431
Web: www.apbpa.org
Association of Surfing Professionals (ASP)
PO Box 309 Huntington Beach CA 92648 714-848-8851 848-8861
Web: www.aspworldtour.com
ATP Tour Inc 201 ATP Tour Blvd Ponte Vedra Beach FL 32082 904-285-8000 285-5966
TF: 800-527-4811 ■ *Web:* www.atptennis.com
Babe Ruth League Inc 1770 Brunswick Pike Trenton NJ 08638 609-695-1434 695-2505
TF: 800-880-3142 ■ *Web:* www.baberuthleague.org
Billiard Congress of America 4345 Beverly St Suite D Colorado Springs CO 80918 719-264-8300 264-0900
Web: www.bca-pool.com
Boat Owners Assn of the US 880 S Pickett St Alexandria VA 22304 703-823-9550 461-2847
TF: 800-395-2628 ■ *Web:* www.boatus.com
Continental Basketball Assn (CBA) 195 Washington Ave Albany NY 12210 518-694-0100 694-0101
Web: www.cbahoopsonline.com
Cross Country Ski Areas Assn 259 Bolton Rd Winchester NH 03470 603-239-4341 239-6387
TF: 877-779-2754 ■ *Web:* www.xcski.org
Disabled Sports USA (DS/USA) 451 Hungerford Dr Suite 100 Rockville MD 20850 301-217-0960 217-0968
Web: www.dsusa.org
Fellowship of Christian Athletes (FCA) 8701 Leeds Rd Kansas City MO 64129 816-921-0909 921-8755
TF: 800-289-0909 ■ *Web:* www.fca.org
Harness Horsemen International 64 Rt 33 Manalapan NJ 07726 732-683-1580 683-1578
Hockey North America (HNA) PO Box 78 Sterling VA 20167 703-430-8100 421-9205
TF: 800-446-2539 ■ *Web:* www.hna.com
Ice Skating Institute (ISI) 17120 Dallas Pkwy Suite 140 Dallas TX 75248 972-735-8800 735-8815
Web: www.skateisi.com
IDEA Inc 10455 Pacific Ctr Ct San Diego CA 92121 858-535-8979 535-8234
TF: 800-999-4332 ■ *Web:* www.ideafit.com
IMSA (International Motor Sports Assn) 1394 Broadway Ave Braselton GA 30517 706-658-2120 658-2130
Web: www.imsaracing.net
Indy Racing League 4565 W 16th St Indianapolis IN 46222 317-492-6526 492-6525
Web: www.indycar.com/indycar/
International Assn of Approved Basketball Officials (IAABO)
12321 Middlebrook Rd Suite 290 Germantown MD 20875 301-540-5180 540-5182
Web: www.iaabo.org
International Collegiate Licensing Assn (ICLA)
24651 Detroit Rd Westlake OH 44145 440-892-4000 892-4007
TF: 800-996-2232 ■ *Web:* nacda.collegesports.com/icla/nacda-icla.html
International Health Racquet & Sportsclub Assn (IHRSA)
263 Summer St 8th Fl Boston MA 02210 617-951-0055 951-0056
TF: 800-228-4772 ■ *Web:* www.ihrsa.org
International Hot Rod Assn (IHRA) 9 1/2 E Main St Norwalk OH 44857 419-663-6666 663-4472
Web: www.ihra.com
International Motor Sports Assn (IMSA) 1394 Broadway Ave Braselton GA 30517 706-658-2120 658-2130
Web: www.imsaracing.net
International Professional Rodeo Assn (IPRA)
PO Box 83377 Oklahoma City OK 73148 405-235-6540 235-6577
Web: www.iprarodeo.com
International Shooting Coaches Assn 17446 SW Granada Dr Beaverton OR 97007 503-642-5873 649-5182
International Sports Sciences Assn (ISSA) 1015 Mark Ave Carpinteria CA 93013 805-884-8111 884-8119
TF: 800-892-4772 ■ *Web:* www.issaonline.com
Jockey Club 40 E 52nd St 15th Fl New York NY 10022 212-371-5970 371-6123
Web: www.jockeyclub.com
Jockeys' Guild Inc PO Box 150 Monrovia CA 91017 626-305-5605 305-5615
TF: 866-465-6257

Ladies Professional Golf Assn (LPGA)
100 International Golf Dr Daytona Beach FL 32124 386-274-6200 274-1099
Web: www.lpga.com
League of American Bicyclists 1612 K St NW Suite 800 Washington DC 20006 202-822-1333 822-1334
Web: www.bikeleague.org
Little League Baseball Inc
539 US Rt 15 Hwy PO Box 3485 Williamsport PA 17701 570-326-1921 326-1074
Web: www.littleleague.org
Maccabi USA/Sports for Israel 1926 Arch St Suite 4R Philadelphia PA 19103 215-561-6900 561-5470
Web: www.maccabiusa.com
Major Indoor Soccer League (MISL) 1175 Post Rd E Suite 2 Westport CT 06880 203-222-4900 221-7300
TF: 866-647-5638 ■ *Web:* www.misl.net
Major League Baseball Players Assn (MLBPA)
12 E 49th St 24th Fl New York NY 10017 212-826-0808 752-4378
Web: mlbplayers.mlb.com/NASApp/mlb/pa/index.jsp
NASCAR (National Assn for Stock Car Auto Racing)
1801 W International Speedway Blvd Daytona Beach FL 32114 386-253-0611 947-6712*
**Fax:* Mktg ■ *Web:* www.nascar.com
National Aeronautic Assn (NAA) 1737 King St Suite 220 Alexandria VA 22314 703-527-0226 527-0229
TF: 800-644-9777 ■ *Web:* www.naa-usa.org
National Alliance for Youth Sports 2050 Vista Pkwy West Palm Beach FL 33411 561-684-1141 684-2546
TF: 800-729-2057 ■ *Web:* www.nays.org
National Assn of Basketball Coaches (NABC)
1111 Main St Suite 1000 Kansas City MO 64105 816-878-6222 878-6223
Web: nabc.ocsn.com
National Assn of Collegiate Directors of Athletics (NACDA)
24651 Detroit Rd Westlake OH 44145 440-892-4000 892-4007
TF: 800-996-2232 ■ *Web:* nacda.collegesports.com
National Assn for Girls & Women in Sport (NAGWS)
1900 Association Dr Reston VA 20191 703-476-3400 476-4566
TF: 800-213-7193 ■ *Web:* www.aahperd.org
National Assn of Intercollegiate Athletics (NAIA)
23500 W 105th St Olathe KS 66061 913-791-0044 791-9555
Web: www.naia.org
National Assn of Police Athletic Leagues (PAL)
658 Indiantown Rd Suite 201 Jupiter FL 33458 561-745-5535 745-3147
TF: 800-725-7743 ■ *Web:* www.nationalpal.org
National Assn of Professional Baseball Leagues
201 Bayshore Dr SE Saint Petersburg FL 33701 727-822-6937 821-5819
Web: www.minorleaguebaseball.com
National Assn of Sports Officials (NASO) 2017 Lathrop Ave Racine WI 53405 262-632-5448 632-5460
TF: 800-733-6100 ■ *Web:* www.naso.org
National Assn for Stock Car Auto Racing (NASCAR)
1801 W International Speedway Blvd Daytona Beach FL 32114 386-253-0611 947-6712*
**Fax:* Mktg ■ *Web:* www.nascar.com
National Assn of Underwater Instructors (NAUI) 1232 Tech Blvd Tampa FL 33619 813-628-6284 628-8253
TF: 800-553-6284 ■ *Web:* www.naui.org
National Athletic Trainers Assn (NATA)
2952 Stemmons Fwy Suite 200 Dallas TX 75247 214-637-6282 637-2206
TF: 800-879-6282 ■ *Web:* www.nata.org
National Basketball Players Assn (NBPA)
310 Lennox Ave 3rd Fl New York NY 10027 212-655-0880 655-0881
Web: www.nbpa.com
National Baton Twirling Assn PO Box 266 Janesville WI 53547 608-754-2238 754-1986
National Center for Bicycling & Walking (NCBW)
8120 Woodmont Ave Suite 650 Bethesda MD 20814 301-656-4220 656-4225
Web: www.bikewalk.org
National Collegiate Athletic Assn (NCAA)
700 W Washington St PO Box 6222 Indianapolis IN 46206 317-917-6222 917-6888
Web: www.ncaa.org
National Congress of State Games
1631 Mesa Ave Suite E Colorado Springs CO 80906 719-634-7333 634-5198
Web: www.stategames.org
National Dart Assn (NDA) 5613 W 74th St Indianapolis IN 46278 317-387-1299 387-0999
TF: 800-808-9884 ■ *Web:* www.ndadarts.com
National Disability Sports Alliance (NDSA)
25 W Independence Way Kingston RI 02881 401-792-7130 792-7132
Web: www.ndsaonline.org
National Federation of State High School Assns (NFHS)
PO Box 690 Indianapolis IN 46206 317-972-6900 822-5700
TF Cust Svc: 800-776-3462 ■ *Web:* www.nfhs.org
National Football League Players Assn (NFLPA)
2021 L St NW Suite 600 Washington DC 20036 202-463-2200 857-0380
TF: 800-372-2000 ■ *Web:* www.nflpa.org
National Golf Foundation (NGF) 1150 S US Hwy 1 Suite 401 Jupiter FL 33477 561-744-6006 744-6107
TF: 800-733-6006 ■ *Web:* www.ngf.org
National Greyhound Assn (NGA) PO Box 543 Abilene KS 67410 785-263-4660 263-4689
Web: www.ngagreyhounds.com
National Health Club Assn 640 Plaza Dr Suite 300 Highlands Ranch CO 80129 303-753-6422 986-6813
TF: 800-765-6422
National Hockey League Players Assn (NHLPA) 20 Bay St Toronto ON M5J2N8 800-363-4625
Web: www.nhlpa.com
National Intramural-Recreational Sports Assn (NIRSA)
4185 SW Research Way Corvallis OR 97333 541-766-8211 766-8284
Web: www.nirsa.org
National Junior College Athletic Assn (NJCAA)
1755 Telstar Dr Suite 103 Colorado Springs CO 80920 719-590-9788 590-7324
Web: www.njcaa.org
National Little Britches Rodeo Assn (NLBRA)
5050 Edison Ave Suite 105 Colorado Springs CO 80915 719-389-0333 578-1367
TF: 800-763-3694 ■ *Web:* www.nlbra.org
National Rifle Assn of America (NRA) 11250 Waples Mill Rd Fairfax VA 22030 703-267-1000 267-3957
TF Membership: 800-672-3888 ■ *Web:* www.nra.org
National Senior Golf Assn (NSGA)
3672 Nottingham Way Hamilton Square NJ 08690 609-631-8145 584-8950
TF: 800-282-6772 ■ *Web:* www.nsgatour.com
National Shooting Sports Foundation (NSSF) 11 Mile Hill Rd Newtown CT 06470 203-426-1320 426-1087
Web: www.nssf.org
National Soccer Coaches Assn of America (NSCAA)
6700 Squibb Rd Suite 215 Mission KS 66202 913-362-1747 362-3439
TF: 800-458-0678 ■ *Web:* www.nscaa.com
National Strength & Conditioning Assn (NSCA)
1885 Bob Johnson Dr Colorado Springs CO 80906 719-632-6722 632-6367
TF: 800-815-6826 ■ *Web:* www.nsca-lift.org
National Thoroughbred Racing Assn (NTRA)
2525 Harrodsburg Rd Lexington KY 40504 859-223-5444 223-3945
TF: 800-722-3287 ■ *Web:* www.ntra.com
National Tractor Pullers Assn (NTPA) 6155-B Huntley Rd Columbus OH 43229 614-436-1761 436-0964
Web: www.ntpapull.com
National Youth Sports Coaches Assn (NYSCA)
2050 Vista Pkwy West Palm Beach FL 33411 561-684-1141 684-2546
TF: 800-729-2057 ■ *Web:* www.nays.org
National Youth Sports Safety Foundation (NYSSF)
1 Beacon St Suite 3333 Boston MA 02108 617-367-6677 722-9999
Web: www.nyssf.org

Sports Organizations (Cont'd)

Organization	City	State	ZIP	Phone	Fax
NBPA (National Basketball Players Assn) 310 Lennox Ave 3rd Fl *Web:* www.nbpa.com	New York	NY	10027	212-655-0880	655-0881
New York Arm Wrestling Assn (NYAWA) PO Box 670952 *TF:* 877-692-2767 ■ *Web:* www.nycarms.com	Flushing	NY	11367	718-544-4592	261-8111
North American Youth Sport Institute (NAYSI) 4985 Oak Garden Dr *TF:* 800-767-4916 ■ *Web:* www.naysi.com	Kernersville	NC	27284	336-784-4926	784-5546
PBA (Professional Bowlers Assn) 719 2nd Ave Suite 701 *Web:* www.pba.com	Seattle	WA	98104	206-332-9688	654-6030
PGA of America 100 Ave of the Champions *TF:* 800-477-6465 ■ *Web:* www.pga.com	Palm Beach Gardens	FL	33418	561-624-8400	624-8439
PGA Tour Inc 112 PGA Tour Blvd *Web:* www.pgatour.com	Ponte Vedra Beach	FL	32082	904-285-3700	
PONY Baseball/Softball Inc 300 Clare Dr PO Box 225 *Web:* www.pony.org	Washington	PA	15301	724-225-1060	225-9852
Pop Warner Little Scholars Inc 586 Middletown Blvd Suite C-100 *Web:* www.popwarner.com	Langhorne	PA	19047	215-752-2691	752-2879
Professional Assn of Diving Instructors International (PADI) 30151 Tomas St *TF Sales:* 800-729-7234 ■ *Web:* www.padi.com	Rancho Santa Margarita	CA	92688	949-858-7234	858-0106
Professional Bowlers Assn (PBA) 719 2nd Ave Suite 701 *Web:* www.pba.com	Seattle	WA	98104	206-332-9688	654-6030
Professional Rodeo Cowboys Assn (PRCA) 101 Pro Rodeo Dr *Web:* www.prorodeo.com	Colorado Springs	CO	80919	719-593-8840	548-4876
Professional Tennis Registry PO Box 4739 *TF:* 800-421-6289 ■ *Web:* www.ptrtennis.org	Hilton Head Island	SC	29938	843-785-7244	686-2033
Roller Skating Assn International (RSAI) 6905 Corporate Dr *Web:* www.rollerskating.org	Indianapolis	IN	46278	317-347-2626	347-2636
Senior Softball USA 2701 K St Suite 101A *Web:* www.seniorsoftball.com	Sacramento	CA	95816	916-326-5303	326-5304
Special Olympics Inc 1133 19th St NW 11th Fl *TF:* 800-700-8585 ■ *Web:* www.specialolympics.org	Washington	DC	20036	202-628-3630	824-0200
Sports Turf Managers Assn 805 New Hampshire St Suite E *TF:* 800-323-3875 ■ *Web:* www.sportsturfmanager.com	Lawrence	KS	66044	785-843-2549	843-2977
Thoroughbred Racing Assns (TRA) 420 Fair Hill Dr Suite 1 *Web:* www.tra-online.com	Elkton	MD	21921	410-392-9200	398-1366
United States Bowling Congress (USBC) 5301 S 76th St **Fax Area Code:* 414 ■ *TF:* 800-514-2695 ■ *Web:* www.bowl.com	Greendale	WI	53129	800-514-2695	421-8560*
US Assn of Blind Athletes 33 N Institute St *Web:* www.usaba.org	Colorado Springs	CO	80903	719-630-0422	630-0616
US Auto Club (USAC) 4910 W 16th St *Web:* www.usacracing.com	Speedway	IN	46224	317-247-5151	247-0123
US Biathlon Assn 29 Ethan Allen Ave *TF:* 800-242-8456 ■ *Web:* www.usbiathlon.org	Colchester	VT	05446	802-654-7833	654-7830
US Bobsled & Skeleton Federation (USBSF) 196 Old Military Rd PO Box 828 *TF:* 800-262-7533 ■ *Web:* www.usbsf.com	Lake Placid	NY	12946	518-523-1842	523-9491
US Curling Assn PO Box 866 *TF:* 888-287-5377 ■ *Web:* www.usacurl.org	Stevens Point	WI	54481	715-344-1199	344-2279
US Diving Inc 201 S Capitol Ave Suite 430 *Web:* www.usadiving.org	Indianapolis	IN	46225	317-237-5252	237-5257
US Equestrian Federation Inc 4047 Iron Works Pkwy *Web:* www.usef.org	Lexington	KY	40511	859-225-6900	231-6662
US Equestrian Team (USET) PO Box 355 *Web:* www.uset.org	Gladstone	NJ	07934	908-234-1251	234-9417
US Fencing Assn (USFA) 1 Olympic Plaza *Web:* www.usfencing.org	Colorado Springs	CO	80909	719-866-4511	632-5737
US Field Hockey Assn 1 Olympic Plaza *Web:* www.usfieldhockey.com	Colorado Springs	CO	80909	719-866-4567	632-0979
US Figure Skating Assn (USFSA) 20 1st St *Web:* www.usfsa.org	Colorado Springs	CO	80906	719-635-5200	635-9548
US Golf Assn (USGA) 77 Liberty Corner Rd *TF Orders:* 800-336-4446 ■ *Web:* www.usga.org	Far Hills	NJ	07930	908-234-2300	234-9687
US Luge Assn 57 Church St *Web:* www.usaluge.org	Lake Placid	NY	12946	518-523-2071	523-4106
US Olympic Committee (USOC) 1 Olympic Plaza *Web:* www.olympic-usa.org	Colorado Springs	CO	80909	719-632-5551	866-4677
US Parachute Assn (USPA) 1440 Duke St *TF:* 800-371-8772 ■ *Web:* www.uspa.org	Alexandria	VA	22314	703-836-3495	836-2843
US Power Squadrons (USPS) PO Box 30423 **Fax Area Code:* 888 ■ *TF:* 888-367-8777 ■ *Web:* www.usps.org	Raleigh	NC	27622	919-821-0281	304-0813*
US Professional Tennis Assn (USPTA) 3535 Briarpark Dr Suite 1 *TF:* 800-877-8248 ■ *Web:* www.uspta.org	Houston	TX	77042	713-978-7782	978-7780
US Racquet Stringers Assn (USRSA) 330 Main St *TF:* 888-900-3545 ■ *Web:* www.racquettech.com	Vista	CA	92084	760-536-1177	536-1171
US Racquetball Assn (USRA) 1685 W Uintah St *TF:* 800-234-5396 ■ *Web:* www.usra.org	Colorado Springs	CO	80904	719-635-5396	635-0685
US Rowing Assn 201 S Capitol Ave Suite 400 *TF:* 800-314-4769 ■ *Web:* www.usrowing.org	Indianapolis	IN	46225	317-237-5656	237-5646
US Sailing Assn 15 Maritime Dr PO Box 1260 *TF:* 800-877-2451 ■ *Web:* www.ussailing.org	Portsmouth	RI	02871	401-683-0800	683-0840
US Ski & Snowboard Assn PO Box 100 *Web:* www.usskiteam.com	Park City	UT	84060	435-649-9090	649-3613
US Soccer Federation 1801 S Prairie Ave *TF:* 800-759-9636 ■ *Web:* www.ussoccer.com	Chicago	IL	60616	312-808-1300	808-1301
US Speedskating PO Box 450639 *TF:* 800-634-4766 ■ *Web:* www.usspeedskating.org	Westlake	OH	44145	440-899-0128	899-0109
US Squash Racquets Assn (USSRA) 23 Cynwyd Rd PO Box 1215 *Web:* www.us-squash.org/squash	Bala Cynwyd	PA	19004	610-667-4006	667-6539
US Synchronized Swimming 201 S Capitol Ave Suite 901 *Web:* www.usasynchro.org	Indianapolis	IN	46225	317-237-5700	237-5705
US Taekwondo Union 1 Olympic Plaza Suite 104C *Web:* www.ustu.org	Colorado Springs	CO	80909	719-866-4632	866-4642
US Tennis Assn (USTA) 70 W Red Oak Ln *TF:* 800-990-8782 ■ *Web:* www.usta.com	White Plains	NY	10604	914-696-7000	696-7167
US Trotting Assn (USTA) 750 Michigan Ave *TF:* 800-887-8782 ■ *Web:* www.ustrotting.com	Columbus	OH	43215	614-224-2291	224-4575
USA Archery (NAA) 1 Olympic Plaza *Web:* www.usarchery.org	Colorado Springs	CO	80909	719-866-4576	632-4733
USA Baseball PO Box 1133 *Web:* www.usabaseball.com	Durham	NC	27702	919-474-8721	474-8822
USA Basketball 5465 Mark Dabling Blvd *Web:* www.usabasketball.com	Colorado Springs	CO	80918	719-590-4800	590-4811
USA Boxing Inc 1 Olympic Plaza *Web:* www.usaboxing.org	Colorado Springs	CO	80909	719-866-4506	632-3426
USA Canoe/Kayak 301 S Tryon St Suite 1750 *Web:* www.usacanoekayak.org	Charlotte	NC	28282	704-348-4330	348-4418
USA Cycling Inc 1 Olympic Plaza *Web:* www.usacycling.org	Colorado Springs	CO	80909	719-866-4581	866-4628
USA Deaf Sports Federation 102 N Krohn Pl *Web:* www.usadsf.org	Sioux Falls	SD	57103	605-367-5760	367-5958
USA Gymnastics 201 S Capitol Ave Suite 300 *TF:* 800-345-4719 ■ *Web:* www.usa-gymnastics.org	Indianapolis	IN	46225	317-237-5050	237-5069
USA Hockey 1775 Bob Johnson Dr *Web:* www.usahockey.com	Colorado Springs	CO	80906	719-576-8724	538-1160
USA Judo Inc 1 Olympic Plaza Suite 505 *Web:* www.usjudo.org	Colorado Springs	CO	80909	719-866-4730	866-4733
USA Karate Federation 1300 Kenmore Blvd *Web:* www.usakarate.org	Akron	OH	44314	330-753-3114	753-6888
USA Roller Sports 4730 South St *Web:* www.usarollersports.org	Lincoln	NE	68506	402-483-7551	483-1465
USA Swimming 1 Olympic Plaza *Web:* www.usaswimming.org	Colorado Springs	CO	80909	719-866-4578	866-4669
USA Table Tennis 1 Olympic Plaza *Web:* www.usatt.org	Colorado Springs	CO	80909	719-866-4583	632-6071
USA Team Handball 1 Olympic Plaza *Web:* www.usateamhandball.org	Colorado Springs	CO	80909	719-866-4036	866-4055
USA Track & Field (USATF) 1 RCA Dome Suite 140 *Web:* www.usatf.org	Indianapolis	IN	46225	317-261-0500	261-0481
USA Triathlon 1365 Garden of the Gods Rd Suite 250 *Web:* www.usatriathlon.org	Colorado Springs	CO	80907	719-597-9090	597-2121
USA Water Polo 1631 Mesa Ave Suite A-1 *Web:* www.usawaterpolo.com	Colorado Springs	CO	80906	719-634-0699	634-0866
USA Water Ski 1251 Holy Cow Rd *TF:* 800-533-2972 ■ *Web:* www.usawaterski.org	Polk City	FL	33868	863-324-4341	325-8259
USA Weightlifting 1 Olympic Plaza *Web:* www.usaweightlifting.org	Colorado Springs	CO	80909	719-866-4508	866-4741
USA Wrestling 6155 Lehman Dr *TF:* 800-999-8531 ■ *Web:* www.usawrestling.org	Colorado Springs	CO	80918	719-598-8181	598-9440
USATF (USA Track & Field) 1 RCA Dome Suite 140 *Web:* www.usatf.org	Indianapolis	IN	46225	317-261-0500	261-0481
USPS (US Power Squadrons) PO Box 30423 **Fax Area Code:* 888 ■ *TF:* 888-367-8777 ■ *Web:* www.usps.org	Raleigh	NC	27622	919-821-0281	304-0813*
Western Golf Assn (WGA) 1 Briar Rd *Web:* www.westerngolfassociation.com	Golf	IL	60029	847-724-4600	724-7133
Wheelchair Sports USA 1668 320th Way *Web:* www.wsusa.org	Earlham	IA	50072	515-833-2450	
Women's Sports Foundation Eisenhower Pk *TF:* 800-227-3988 ■ *Web:* www.womenssportsfoundation.org	East Meadow	NY	11554	516-542-4700	542-4716
WTA Tour Inc 1 Progress Plaza Suite 1500 *TF:* 800-764-8579 ■ *Web:* www.wtatour.com	Saint Petersburg	FL	33701	727-895-5000	894-1982
YMCA of the USA 101 N Wacker Dr 14th Fl *TF:* 800-872-9622 ■ *Web:* www.ymca.net	Chicago	IL	60606	312-977-0031	977-9063

48-23 Travel & Recreation Organizations

Organization	City	State	ZIP	Phone	Fax
AAA (American Automobile Assn) 1000 AAA Dr *Web:* www.aaa.com	Heathrow	FL	32746	407-444-4240	444-4247
Access Fund PO Box 17010 *TF:* 888-863-6237 ■ *Web:* www.accessfund.org	Boulder	CO	80308	303-545-6772	545-6774
Adirondack Mountain Club 814 Goggins Rd *TF Orders:* 800-395-8080 ■ *Web:* www.adk.org	Lake George	NY	12845	518-668-4447	668-3746
Alberta Hotel & Lodging Assn 5241 Calgary Trail S Suite 401-Centre 104 *Web:* www.albertahotels.ab.ca	Edmonton	AB	T6H5G8	780-436-6112	436-5404
America Outdoors 5816 Kingston Pike *TF:* 800-524-4814 ■ *Web:* www.americoutdoors.org	Knoxville	TN	37919	865-558-3595	558-3598
American Amusement Machine Assn (AAMA) 450 E Higgins Rd Suite 201 *TF:* 866-372-5190 ■ *Web:* www.coin-op.org	Elk Grove Village	IL	60007	847-290-9088	290-9121
American Assn for Physical Activity & Recreation (AAPAR) 1900 Association Dr *TF:* 800-213-7193 ■ *Web:* www.aahperd.org/aapar/	Reston	VA	20191	703-476-3400	476-9527
American Automobile Assn (AAA) 1000 AAA Dr *Web:* www.aaa.com	Heathrow	FL	32746	407-444-4240	444-4247
American Camp Assn (ACA) 5000 SR-67 N *TF:* 800-428-2267 ■ *Web:* www.acacamps.org	Martinsville	IN	46151	765-342-8456	349-6357
American Gaming Assn (AGA) 1299 Pennsylvania Ave NW Suite 1175 *Web:* www.americangaming.org	Washington	DC	20004	202-552-2675	552-2676
American Hiking Society (AHS) 1422 Fenwick Ln *Web:* www.americanhiking.org	Silver Spring	MD	20910	301-565-6704	565-6714
American Hotel & Lodging Assn (AH&LA) 1201 New York Ave NW Suite 600 *Web:* www.ahla.com	Washington	DC	20005	202-289-3100	289-3185
American Park & Recreation Society (APRS) c/o National Recreation & Park Assn 22377 Belmont Ridge Rd *TF:* 800-626-6772 ■ *Web:* www.nrpa.org/aprs	Ashburn	VA	20148	703-858-4731	858-0794
American Recreation Coalition (ARC) 1225 New York Ave NW Ste 450 *Web:* www.funoutdoors.com	Washington	DC	20005	202-682-9530	682-9529
American Society of Travel Agents (ASTA) 1101 King St Suite 200 *TF:* 800-440-2782 ■ *Web:* www.asta.org	Alexandria	VA	22314	703-739-2782	684-8319
American Trails PO Box 491797 *Web:* www.americantrails.org	Redding	CA	96049	530-547-2060	547-2035
American Whitewater (AW) PO Box 1540 *TF:* 866-262-8429 ■ *Web:* www.americanwhitewater.org	Cullowhee	NC	28723	828-586-1930	586-2840
Amusement & Music Operators Assn (AMOA) 33 W Higgins Rd Suite 830 *TF:* 800-937-2662 ■ *Web:* amoa.com	South Barrington	IL	60010	847-428-7699	428-7719
Appalachian Mountain Club (AMC) 5 Joy St *TF Orders:* 800-262-4455 ■ *Web:* www.outdoors.org	Boston	MA	02108	617-523-0655	523-0722
Appalachian Trail Conservancy (ATC) 799 Washington St PO Box 807 *Web:* www.appalachiantrail.org	Harpers Ferry	WV	25425	304-535-6331	535-2667
ARC (American Recreation Coalition) 1225 New York Ave NW Ste 450 *Web:* www.funoutdoors.com	Washington	DC	20005	202-682-9530	682-9529
Association of Corporate Travel Executives (ACTE) 515 King St Suite 440 *TF:* 800-228-3669 ■ *Web:* www.acte.org	Alexandria	VA	22314	703-683-5322	683-2720
Association of Destination Management Executives (ADME) PO Box 2307 *Web:* www.adme.org	Dayton	OH	45401	937-586-3727	586-3699
Back Country Horsemen of America (BCHA) PO Box 1367 *TF:* 888-893-5161 ■ *Web:* www.backcountryhorse.com	Graham	WA	98338	360-832-2461	832-2471
Boat Owners Assn of the US 880 S Pickett St *TF:* 800-937-9307 ■ *Web:* www.boatus.com	Alexandria	VA	22304	703-823-9550	461-2847
BoatUS 880 S Pickett St *TF:* 800-937-9307 ■ *Web:* www.boatus.com	Alexandria	VA	22304	703-823-9550	461-2847

Phone *Fax*

Bowling Proprietors Assn of America Inc (BPAA)
PO Box 5802 .... Arlington TX 76005 817-649-5105 633-2940
TF: 800-343-1329 ■ *Web:* www.bpaa.com

Canadian Automobile Assn (CAA) 1145 Hunt Club Rd Suite 200 ..... Ottawa ON K1V0Y3 613-247-0117 247-0118
Web: www.caa.ca

Canadian Parks & Recreation Assn (CPRA)
2197 Riverside Dr Suite 404 .... Ottawa ON K1H7X3 613-523-5315 523-1182
Web: www.cpra.ca

Colorado Dude & Guest Ranch Assn PO Box D .... Shawnee CO 80475 866-942-3472
Web: www.coloradoranch.com

Continental Divide Trail Society 3704 N Charles St Suite 601 ..... Baltimore MD 21218 410-235-9610 243-1960
Web: www.cdtsociety.org

Cruise Lines International Assn (CLIA)
910 SE 17th St Suite 400 .... Fort Lauderdale FL 33316 754-224-2200 224-2250
Web: www.cruising.org

Destination Marketing Assn International
2025 M St NW Suite 500 .... Washington DC 20036 202-296-7888 296-7889
TF: 888-275-3140 ■ *Web:* www.destinationmarketing.org

Dude Ranchers' Assn PO Box 2307 .... Cody WY 82414 307-587-2339 587-2776
TF: 866-399-2339 ■ *Web:* www.duderanch.org

Elderhostel Inc 11 Ave de Lafayette .... Boston MA 02111 617-426-7788 426-2166*
**Fax Area Code:* 877 ■ *TF:* 877-426-8056 ■ *Web:* www.elderhostel.org

Environmental Traveling Companions (ETC)
Fort Mason Ctr Building C .... San Francisco CA 94123 415-474-7662 474-3919
Web: www.etctrips.org

Escapees RV Club 100 Rainbow Dr .... Livingston TX 77399 936-327-8873 327-4388
TF: 800-231-9896 ■ *Web:* www.escapees.com

Family Campers & RVers (FCRV) 4804 Transit Rd Bldg 2 .... Depew NY 14043 716-668-6242
TF: 800-245-9755 ■ *Web:* www.fcrv.org

Family Motor Coach Assn (FMCA) 8291 Clough Pike .... Cincinnati OH 45244 513-474-3622 474-2332
TF: 800-543-3622 ■ *Web:* www.fmca.com

Good Sam Recreational Vehicle Club PO Box 6888 .... Englewood CO 80155 800-234-3450 728-7306*
**Fax Area Code:* 303 ■ *TF:* 800-234-3450 ■ *Web:* www.goodsamclub.com

Hostelling International USA - American Youth Hostels (HI-AYH) 8401 Colesville Rd Suite 600 .... Silver Spring MD 20910 301-495-1240 495-6697
Web: www.hiusa.org

Ice Age Park & Trail Foundation
306 East Wilson St Lower Level .... Madison WI 53703 608-663-8278 663-1283
TF: 800-227-0046 ■ *Web:* www.iceagetrail.org

International Airline Passengers Assn (IAPA)
5204 Tennyson Pkwy .... Plano TX 75024 972-404-9980 233-5348
TF: 800-821-4272 ■ *Web:* www.iapa.com

International Assn of Amusement Parks & Attractions (IAAPA)
1448 Duke St .... Alexandria VA 22314 703-836-4800 836-4801
Web: www.iaapa.org

International Assn of Fairs & Expositions (IAFE)
3043 E Cairo .... Springfield MO 65802 417-862-5771 862-0156
TF: 800-516-0313 ■ *Web:* www.fairsandexpos.com

International Assn for Medical Assistance to Travellers (IAMAT)
40 Regal Rd .... Guelph ON N1K1B5 519-836-0102 836-3412
Web: www.iamat.org

International Ecotourism Society (TIES)
1333 H St NW Suite 300 E Tower .... Washington DC 20005 202-347-9203 789-7279
Web: www.ecotourism.org

International Festivals & Events Assn (IFEA)
2603 W Eastover Terr .... Boise ID 83706 208-433-0950 433-9812
Web: www.ifea.com

International Gay & Lesbian Travel Assn (IGLTA)
915 Middle River Dr Suite 306 .... Fort Lauderdale FL 33304 954-630-1637 630-1652
TF: 800-448-8550 ■ *Web:* www.iglta.org

International Mountain Bicycling Assn (IMBA)
207 Canyon Blvd Suite 301 PO Box 7578 .... Boulder CO 80306 303-545-9011 545-9026
TF: 888-442-4622 ■ *Web:* www.imba.com

International Society of Travel Medicine (ISTM)
2386 Clover St Suite A-102 .... Snellville GA 30078 770-736-7060 736-0313
Web: www.istm.org

Leave No Trace Center for Outdoor Ethics Inc PO Box 997 .... Boulder CO 80306 303-442-8222 442-8217
TF: 800-332-4100 ■ *Web:* www.lnt.org

Lewis & Clark Trail Heritage Foundation
4201 Giant springs Rd .... Great Falls MT 59405 406-454-1234 771-9237
TF: 888-701-3434 ■ *Web:* www.lewisandclark.org

Lincoln Highway Assn 136 N Elm St .... Franklin Grove IL 61031 815-456-3030
Web: www.lincolnhighwayassoc.org

Loners on Wheels (LoW) 1795 O'Kelley Rd SE .... Deming NM 88030 575-546-4058 546-6542
Web: www.lonersonwheels.com

Mountaineers 300 3rd Ave W .... Seattle WA 98119 206-284-6310 284-4977
Web: www.mountaineers.org

National Assn of Commissioned Travel Agents (NACTA)
1101 King St Suite 200 .... Alexandria VA 22314 703-739-6826 739-6861
Web: www.nacta.org

National Assn of RV Parks & Campgrounds 113 Park Ave .... Falls Church VA 22046 703-241-8801 241-1004
Web: www.arvc.org

National Business Travel Assn (NBTA) 110 N Royal St 4th Fl .... Alexandria VA 22314 703-684-0836 684-0263
Web: www.nbta.org

National Caves Assn PO Box 280 .... Park City KY 42160 270-749-2228 749-2428
Web: www.cavern.com

National Club Assn (NCA) 1201 15th St NW Suite 450 .... Washington DC 20005 202-822-9822 822-9808
TF: 800-625-6221 ■ *Web:* www.natlclub.org

National Forest Recreation Assn (NFRA) PO Box 488 .... Woodlake CA 93286 559-564-2365 564-2048
Web: www.nfra.org

National Golf Course Owners Assn (NGCOA)
291 Seven Farms Dr 2nd Fl .... Charleston SC 29492 843-881-9956 881-9958
TF: 800-933-4262 ■ *Web:* www.ngcoa.org

National Indian Gaming Assn (NIGA) 224 2nd St SE .... Washington DC 20003 202-546-7711 546-1755
TF: 800-286-6442 ■ *Web:* www.indiangaming.org

National Recreation & Park Assn (NRPA)
22377 Belmont Ridge Rd .... Ashburn VA 20148 703-858-0784 858-0794
TF: 800-626-6772 ■ *Web:* www.nrpa.org

National Ski Areas Assn (NSAA)
133 S Van Gordon St Suite 300 .... Lakewood CO 80228 303-987-1111 986-2345
Web: www.nsaa.org

National Ski Patrol System Inc (NSP)
133 S Van Gordon St Suite 100 .... Lakewood CO 80228 303-988-1111 988-3005
Web: www.nsp.org

National Society for Park Resources (NSPR)
c/o National Recreation & Park Assn 22377 Belmont Ridge Rd .... Ashburn VA 20148 703-858-0784 858-0794
TF: 800-626-6772

National Tour Assn (NTA) 546 E Main St .... Lexington KY 40508 859-226-4444 226-4404
TF: 800-682-8886 ■ *Web:* www.ntaonline.com

North Country Trail Association 229 E. Main St .... Lowell MI 49331 616-897-5987 897-6605
TF: 866-445-3628 ■ *Web:* www.northcountrytrail.org

NTA (National Tour Assn) 546 E Main St .... Lexington KY 40508 859-226-4444 226-4404
TF: 800-682-8886 ■ *Web:* www.ntaonline.com

Oregon-California Trails Assn PO Box 1019 .... Independence MO 64051 816-252-2276 836-0989
TF: 888-811-6282 ■ *Web:* www.octa-trails.org

Phone *Fax*

Pacific Crest Trail Assn (PCTA)
5325 Elkhorn Blvd PMB 256 .... Sacramento CA 95842 916-349-2109 349-1268
TF: 888-728-7245 ■ *Web:* www.pcta.org

Pennsylvania AAA Federation 600 N 3rd St .... Harrisburg PA 17105 717-238-7192 238-6574
Web: www.aaapa.org

Relais & Chateaux Assn 10 E 53rd St .... New York NY 10022 212-319-4880 319-4666
TF: 800-735-2478 ■ *Web:* www.relaischateaux.com

RVing Women PO Box 1940 .... Apache Junction AZ 85217 480-671-6226 671-6230
TF: 888-557-8464 ■ *Web:* www.rvingwomen.org

Santa Fe Trail Assn c/o Santa Fe Trail Ctr 1349 K-156 Hwy .... Larned KS 67550 620-285-2054
Web: www.santafetrail.org

Shenandoah National Park Assn 3655 US Hwy 211 E .... Luray VA 22835 540-999-3582 999-3583
Web: www.snpbooks.org

Society of Incentive & Travel Executives (SITE)
401 N Michigan Ave Suite 2400 .... Chicago IL 60611 312-321-5148 527-6783
Web: www.site-intl.org

Society of Park & Recreation Educators (SPRE)
c/o National Recreation & Park Assn 22377 Belmont Ridge Rd .... Ashburn VA 20148 703-858-0784 858-0794
TF: 800-626-6772 ■ *Web:* www.nrpa.org

Special Military Active Retired Travel Club (SMART)
600 University Office Blvd Suite 1A .... Pensacola FL 32504 850-478-1986
TF: 800-354-7681 ■ *Web:* www.smartrving.net

Statue of Liberty-Ellis Island Foundation
17 Battery Pl Suite 210 .... New York NY 10004 212-561-4588 779-1990
Web: www.statueofliberty.org

Travel Industry Assn of America (TIA)
1100 New York Ave NW Suite 450 .... Washington DC 20005 202-408-8422 408-1255
Web: www.tia.org

Travel Institute 148 Linden St Suite 305 .... Wellesley MA 02482 781-237-0280 237-3860
TF: 800-542-4282 ■ *Web:* www.thetravelinstitute.com

US Tour Operators Assn (USTOA)
275 Madison Ave Suite 2014 .... New York NY 10016 212-599-6599 599-6744
Web: www.ustoa.com

Washington Trails Assn (WTA) 2019 3rd Ave Suite 100 .... Seattle WA 98121 206-625-1367 625-9249
Web: www.wta.org

Western National Parks Assn (WNPA)
12880 N Vistoso Village Dr .... Tucson AZ 85755 520-622-1999 623-9519
Web: www.wnpa.org

Wilderness Inquiry (WI) 808 14th Ave SE .... Minneapolis MN 55414 612-676-9400 676-9401
TF: 800-728-0719 ■ *Web:* www.wildernessinquiry.org

48-24 Women's Organizations

Phone *Fax*

9to5 National Assn of Working Women
207 E Buffalo St Suite 211 .... Milwaukee WI 53202 414-274-0925 272-2870
TF: 800-522-0925 ■ *Web:* www.9to5.org

Association for Women's Rights in Development (AWID)
215 Spadina Ave Suite 150 .... Toronto ON M5T2C7 416-594-3773 594-0330
Web: www.awid.org

Business & Professional Women/USA (BPW/USA)
1900 M St NW Suite 310 .... Washington DC 20036 202-293-1100 861-0298
Web: www.bpwusa.org

Center for Women Policy Studies
1776 Masachusetts Ave NW Suite 410 .... Washington DC 20036 202-872-1770 296-8962
Web: www.centerwomenpolicy.org

Coalition of Labor Union Women (CLUW)
815 16th St NW 2nd Fl .... Washington DC 20006 202-508-6969 508-6968
Web: www.cluw.org

Equal Rights Advocates (ERA) 1663 Mission St Suite 250 .... San Francisco CA 94103 415-621-0672 621-6744
TF: 800-839-4372 ■ *Web:* www.equalrights.org

Feminist Majority Foundation (FMF)
1600 Wilson Blvd Suite 801 .... Arlington VA 22209 703-522-2214 522-2219
Web: www.feminist.org

General Federation of Women's Clubs (GFWC)
1734 'N' St NW .... Washington DC 20036 202-347-3168 835-0246
Web: www.gfwc.org

Girls Inc 120 Wall St 3rd Fl .... New York NY 10005 212-509-2000 509-8708
TF: 800-374-4475 ■ *Web:* www.girlsinc.org

Inter-American Commission of Women
1889 F St NW Rm 350 .... Washington DC 20006 202-458-6084 458-6094
Web: www.oas.org/CIM/

International Alliance for Women (TIAW)
8405 Greensboro Dr Suite 800 .... McLean VA 22102 703-506-3284 305-1548*
**Fax Area Code:* 905 ■ *TF:* 866-533-8429 ■ *Web:* www.tiaw.org

International Center for Research on Women (ICRW)
1120 20th St NW Suite 500-N .... Washington DC 20036 202-797-0007 797-0020
Web: www.icrw.org

Ms Foundation for Women 120 Wall St 33rd Fl .... New York NY 10005 212-742-2300 742-1653
Web: www.ms.foundation.org

National Assn for Female Executives (NAFE)
60 E 42nd St 27th Fl .... New York NY 10165 212-351-6400 351-6487
TF: 800-927-6233 ■ *Web:* www.nafe.com

National Congress of Neighborhood Women
249 Manhattan Ave .... Brooklyn NY 11211 718-388-8915 388-0285

National Council of Jewish Women (NCJW)
475 Riverside Dr Suite 520 .... New York NY 10115 212-645-4048 645-7466
TF: 800-829-6259 ■ *Web:* www.ncjw.org

National Council of Negro Women Inc (NCNW)
633 Pennsylvania Ave NW .... Washington DC 20004 202-737-0120 737-0476
Web: www.ncnw.org

National Council of Women of the US Inc (NCW)
777 UN Plaza .... New York NY 10017 212-697-1278 972-0164
Web: www.ncw-us.org

National Organization for Women (NOW)
1100 H St NW 3rd Fl .... Washington DC 20005 202-628-8669 785-8576
Web: www.now.org

National Partnership for Women & Families
1875 Connecticut Ave NW Suite 650 .... Washington DC 20009 202-986-2600 986-2539
Web: www.nationalpartnership.org

National Woman's Party 144 Constitution Ave NE .... Washington DC 20002 202-546-1210 546-3997
Web: www.sewallbelmont.org

National Women's Law Center (NWLC)
11 Dupont Cir NW Suite 800 .... Washington DC 20036 202-588-5180 588-5185
Web: www.nwlc.org

New Ways to Work Inc 103 Morris St Suite A .... Sebastopol CA 95472 707-824-4000 824-4410
Web: www.nww.org

Ninety-Nines Inc 4300 Amelia Earhart Rd .... Oklahoma City OK 73159 405-685-7969 685-7985
Web: www.ninety-nines.org

NOW (National Organization for Women)
1100 H St NW 3rd Fl .... Washington DC 20005 202-628-8669 785-8576
Web: www.now.org

Program on Women & Aging
Brandeis University Institute on Assets & Social Policy MS 035 .... Waltham MA 02454 781-736-3826
Web: iasp.brandeis.edu/womenandaging

Women's Organizations (Cont'd)

				Phone	Fax
Wider Opportunities for Women (WOW)					
1001 Connecticut Ave NW Suite 930	Washington	DC	20036	202-464-1596	464-1660
Web: www.w-o-w.org					
Women Employed 111 N Wabash Ave Suite 1300	Chicago	IL	60602	312-782-3902	782-5249
Web: www.womenemployed.org					
Women Work! National Network for Women's Employment					
1625 K St NW Suite 300	Washington	DC	20006	202-467-6346	467-5366
TF: 800-235-2732 ■ *Web:* www.womenwork.org					
Women's Economic Agenda Project (WEAP)					
449 15th St 2nd Fl	Oakland	CA	94612	510-986-8620	986-8628
Web: www.weap.org					
Women's Research & Education Institute (WREI)					
3300 N Fairfax Dr Suite 218	Arlington	VA	22201	703-812-7990	812-0687
Web: www.wrei.org					
Women's Sports Foundation Eisenhower Pk	East Meadow	NY	11554	516-542-4700	542-4716
TF: 800-227-3988 ■ *Web:* www.womenssportsfoundation.org					
YWCA USA 1015 18th St NW Suite 1100	Washington	DC	20036	202-467-0801	467-0802
TF: 800-992-2871 ■ *Web:* www.ywca.org					
Zonta International 557 W Randolph St	Chicago	IL	60661	312-930-5848	930-0951
Web: www.zonta.org					

49 ASSOCIATIONS & ORGANIZATIONS - PROFESSIONAL & TRADE

SEE ALSO Bar Associations - State p. 1372; Dental Associations - State p. 1585; Labor Unions p. 1881; Library Associations - State & Province p. 1912; Medical Associations - State p. 1952; Nurses Associations - State p. 2033; Pharmacy Associations - State p. 2112; Realtor Associations - State p. 2206; Veterinary Medical Associations - State p. 1952

49-1 Accountants Associations

				Phone	Fax
AACE International - Assn for the Advancement of Cost					
Engineering (AACE) 209 Prairie Ave Suite 100	Morgantown	WV	26501	304-296-8444	291-5728
TF: 800-858-2678 ■ *Web:* www.aacei.org					
Accountants Global Network 2851 S Parker Rd Suite 850	Aurora	CO	80014	303-743-7880	743-7660
TF: 800-782-2272 ■ *Web:* www.agn-na.org					
AGN International-North America 2851 S Parker Rd Suite 850	Aurora	CO	80014	303-743-7880	743-7660
TF: 800-782-2272 ■ *Web:* www.agn-na.org					
American Accounting Assn 5717 Bessie Dr	Sarasota	FL	34233	941-921-7747	923-4093
Web: aaahq.org					
American Institute of Certified Public Accountants (AICPA)					
1211 Ave of the Americas	New York	NY	10036	212-596-6200	596-6213
TF: 888-777-7077 ■ *Web:* www.aicpa.org					
American Institute of Professional Bookkeepers (AIPB)					
6001 Montrose Rd Suite 500	Rockville	MD	20852	301-770-7300	541-0066*
**Fax Area Code:* 800 ■ *TF:* 800-622-0121 ■ *Web:* www.aipb.org					
American Society of Women Accountants (ASWA)					
1760 Old Meadows Rd Suite 500	McLean	VA	22102	703-506-3265	506-3266
Web: www.aswa.org					
American Woman's Society of Certified Public Accountants					
(AWSCPA) 136 S Keowee St	Dayton	OH	45402	937-222-1872	222-5794
TF: 800-297-2721 ■ *Web:* www.awscpa.org					
Association for Accounting Administration (AAA)					
136 S Keowee St	Dayton	OH	45402	937-222-0030	222-5794
Web: www.cpaadmin.org					
Association of Certified Fraud Examiners (ACFE) 716 West Ave	Austin	TX	78701	512-478-9070	478-9297
TF: 800-245-3321 ■ *Web:* www.acfe.com					
Association of Chartered Accountants in the US (ACAUS)					
341 Lafayette St Suite 4246	New York	NY	10012	212-334-2078	431-5786
Web: www.acaus.org					
Association of Government Accountants (AGA)					
2208 Mt Vernon Ave	Alexandria	VA	22301	703-684-6931	548-9367
TF: 800-242-7211 ■ *Web:* www.agacgfm.org					
Association of Healthcare Internal Auditors (AHIA)					
10200 W 44th Ave Suite 304	Wheat Ridge	CO	80063	303-327-7546	422-8894
TF: 888-275-2442 ■ *Web:* www.ahia.org					
BKR International 19 Fulton St Suite 306	New York	NY	10038	212-964-2115	964-2133
TF: 800-257-4685 ■ *Web:* www.bkr.com					
Construction Financial Management Assn (CFMA)					
29 Emmons Dr Suite F-50	Princeton	NJ	08540	609-452-8000	452-0474
Web: www.cfma.org					
CPA Associates International Inc 301 Rt 17 N 7th Fl	Rutherford	NJ	07070	201-804-8686	804-9222
Web: www.cpaai.com					
CPA Auto Dealer Consultants Assn (CADCA)					
624 Grassmere Park Suite 15	Nashville	TN	37211	615-373-9880	377-7092
TF: 888-475-4476 ■ *Web:* www.autodealercpas.com					
CPA Manufacturing Services Assn					
624 Grassmere Park Suite 15	Nashville	TN	37211	615-373-9880	377-7092
TF: 888-475-4476 ■ *Web:* www.manufacturingcpas.com					
CPAmerica International 11801 Research Dr	Alachua	FL	32615	386-418-4001	418-4002
TF: 800-992-2324 ■ *Web:* www.cpamerica.org					
FASB (Financial Accounting Standards Board)					
401 Merritt 7 PO Box 5116	Norwalk	CT	06856	203-847-0700	849-9714
TF: 800-748-0659 ■ *Web:* www.fasb.org					
Financial Accounting Foundation (FAF)					
401 Merritt 7 PO Box 5116	Norwalk	CT	06856	203-847-0700	849-9714
TF: 800-748-0659 ■ *Web:* www.fasb.org/facts					
Financial Accounting Standards Board (FASB)					
401 Merritt 7 PO Box 5116	Norwalk	CT	06856	203-847-0700	849-9714
TF: 800-748-0659 ■ *Web:* www.fasb.org					
Foundation for Accounting Education 3 Park Ave 18th Fl	New York	NY	10016	212-719-8300	719-3365
TF: 800-537-3635					
Hospitality Financial & Technology Professionals (HFTP)					
11709 Boulder Ln Suite 110	Austin	TX	78726	512-249-5333	646-4387
TF: 800-856-4242 ■ *Web:* www.hftp.org					
IGAF Worldwide 3235 Satellite Blvd Bldg 400 Suite 300	Duluth	GA	30096	678-417-7730	417-6977
TF: 800-272-4423 ■ *Web:* www.igaf.org					
Institute of Internal Auditors (IIA) 247 Maitland Ave	Altamonte Springs	FL	32701	407-937-1100	937-1101
Web: www.theiia.org					
Institute of Management Accountants Inc (IMA)					
10 Paragon Dr	Montvale	NJ	07645	201-573-9000	474-1600
TF: 800-638-4427 ■ *Web:* www.imanet.org					
International Federation of Accountants (IFAC)					
545 5th Ave 14th Fl	New York	NY	10017	212-286-9344	286-9570
Web: www.ifac.org					

				Phone	Fax
National Accounting & Finance Council (NAFC)					
American Trucking Assns 950 N Glebe Rd	Arlington	VA	22307	703-838-1915	836-0751
Web: truckline.com					
National Assn of Black Accountants (NABA)					
7249-A Hanover Pkwy	Greenbelt	MD	20770	301-474-6222	474-3114
Web: www.nabainc.org					
National Assn of State Boards of Accountancy (NASBA)					
150 4th Ave N Suite 700	Nashville	TN	37219	615-880-4200	880-4290
TF: 800-272-3926 ■ *Web:* www.nasba.org					
National Assn of Tax Professionals (NATP) 720 Association Dr	Appleton	WI	54914	920-749-1040	747-0001*
**Fax Area Code:* 800 ■ *TF:* 800-558-3402 ■ *Web:* www.natptax.com					
National CPA Health Care Advisors Assn (HCAA)					
624 Grassmere Park Suite 15	Nashville	TN	37211	615-373-9880	377-7092
TF: 888-475-4476 ■ *Web:* www.hcaa.com					
National Society of Accountants (NSA) 1010 N Fairfax St	Alexandria	VA	22314	703-549-6400	549-2984
TF: 800-966-6679 ■ *Web:* www.nsacct.org					
Not-for-Profit Services Assn (NSA)					
624 Grassmere Park Suite 15	Nashville	TN	37211	615-373-9880	377-7092
TF: 888-475-4476 ■ *Web:* www.nonprofitcpas.com					
Polaris International 9200 S Dadeland Blvd Suite 510	Miami	FL	33156	305-670-0580	670-3818
Web: www.accountants.org					
Tax Executives Institute (TEI) 1200 G St NW Suite 300	Washington	DC	20005	202-638-5601	638-5607
Web: www.tei.org					

49-2 Banking & Finance Professionals Associations

				Phone	Fax
ABA (American Bankers Assn) 1120 Connecticut Ave NW	Washington	DC	20036	202-663-5000	828-5045*
**Fax:* Hum Res ■ *TF Cust Svc:* 800-226-5377 ■ *Web:* www.aba.com					
ABA Marketing Network 1120 Connecticut Ave NW	Washington	DC	20036	202-663-5000	828-5053
TF: 800-226-5377 ■ *Web:* www.aba.com/MarketingNetwork					
ACA International - Assn of Credit & Collection					
Professionals PO Box 390106	Minneapolis	MN	55439	952-926-6547	926-1624
Web: www.acainternational.org					
AFSA (American Financial Services Assn)					
919 18th St NW Suite 300	Washington	DC	20006	202-296-5544	223-0321
Web: www.afsaonline.org					
American Assn of Daily Money Managers (AADMM)					
174 Crestview Dr	Bellefonte	PA	16823	877-326-5991	355-2452*
**Fax Area Code:* 814 ■ *Web:* www.aadmm.com					
American Assn of Individual Investors (AAII)					
625 N Michigan Ave Suite 1900	Chicago	IL	60611	312-280-0170	280-9883
TF: 800-428-2244 ■ *Web:* www.aaii.com					
American Bankers Assn (ABA) 1120 Connecticut Ave NW	Washington	DC	20036	202-663-5000	828-5045*
**Fax:* Hum Res ■ *TF Cust Svc:* 800-226-5377 ■ *Web:* www.aba.com					
American Benefits Council					
1212 New York Ave NW Suite 1250	Washington	DC	20005	202-289-6700	289-4582
Web: www.americanbenefitscouncil.org					
American Council for Capital Formation (ACCF)					
1750 K St NW Suite 400	Washington	DC	20006	202-293-5811	785-8165
Web: www.accf.org					
American Economic Assn (AEA) 2014 Broadway Suite 305	Nashville	TN	37203	615-322-2595	343-7590
Web: www.aeaweb.org					
American Finance Assn (AFA) Blackwell Publishing 350 Main St	Malden	MA	02148	781-388-8599	388-8232
TF: 800-835-6770 ■ *Web:* www.afajof.org					
American Financial Services Assn (AFSA)					
919 18th St NW Suite 300	Washington	DC	20006	202-296-5544	223-0321
Web: www.afsaonline.org					
American Institute of Certified Planners (AICP)					
1776 Massachusetts Ave NW Suite 400	Washington	DC	20036	202-872-0611	872-0643
Web: www.planning.org/aicp					
America's Community Bankers (ACB)					
1120 Connecticut Ave NW	Washington	DC	20036	202-857-3100	296-8716
TF: 800-226-5377 ■ *Web:* www.acbankers.org					
Association for Financial Professionals (AFP)					
4520 East West Hwy Suite 750	Bethesda	MD	20814	301-907-2862	907-2864
Web: www.afponline.org					
Bank Administration Institute (BAI) 1 N Franklin St Suite 1000	Chicago	IL	60606	312-553-4600	683-2321*
**Fax:* Cust Svc ■ *TF Cust Svc:* 800-224-9889 ■ *Web:* www.bai.org					
Bankers' Assn for Finance & Trade (BAFT)					
1120 Connecticut Ave NW	Washington	DC	20036	202-663-7575	663-5538
Web: www.baft.org					
Better Investing PO Box 220	Royal Oak	MI	48068	248-583-6242	583-4880
TF: 877-275-6242 ■ *Web:* www.betterinvesting.org					
Certified Financial Planner Board of Standards Inc					
1670 Broadway Suite 600	Denver	CO	80202	303-830-7500	860-7388
TF: 888-237-6275 ■ *Web:* www.cfp.net					
CFA Institute 560 Ray C Hunt Dr PO Box 3668	Charlottesville	VA	22903	434-951-5499	951-5262
TF: 800-247-8132 ■ *Web:* www.cfainstitute.org					
Commercial Finance Assn (CFA) 225 W 34th St Suite 1815	New York	NY	10122	212-594-3490	564-6053
Web: www.cfa.com					
Community Banking Advisory Network (CBAN)					
624 Grassmere Park Dr Suite 15	Nashville	TN	37211	615-377-3392	377-7092
TF: 888-475-4476 ■ *Web:* www.bankingcpas.com					
Consumer Bankers Assn (CBA) 1000 Wilson Blvd Suite 2500	Arlington	VA	22209	703-276-1750	528-1290
Web: www.cbanet.org					
Consumer Data Industry Assn (CDIA)					
1090 Vermont Ave NW Suite 200	Washington	DC	20005	202-371-0910	371-0134
Web: www.cdiaonline.org					
Council of Institutional Investors					
888 17th St NW Suite 500	Washington	DC	20006	202-822-0800	822-0801
Web: www.cii.org					
Credit Professionals International 525B N Laclede Stn Rd	Saint Louis	MO	63119	314-961-0031	961-0040
Web: www.creditprofessionals.org					
Credit Research Foundation (CRF) 8840 Columbia 100 Pkwy	Columbia	MD	21045	410-740-5499	740-4620
TF: 866-557-3242 ■ *Web:* www.crfonline.org					
Credit Union Executives Society (CUES)					
5510 Research Park Dr	Madison	WI	53711	608-271-2664	271-2303
TF: 800-252-2664 ■ *Web:* www.cues.org					
Credit Union National Assn (CUNA) 5710 Mineral Point Rd	Madison	WI	53705	608-231-4000	231-4858*
**Fax:* PR ■ *TF:* 800-356-9655 ■ *Web:* www.cuna.org					
EFTA (Electronic Funds Transfer Assn)					
11350 Random Hills Rd Suite 800	Fairfax	VA	22030	703-934-6052	934-6058
Web: www.efta.org					
Electronic Funds Transfer Assn (EFTA)					
11350 Random Hills Rd Suite 800	Fairfax	VA	22030	703-934-6052	934-6058
Web: www.efta.org					
Emerging Markets Traders Assn (EMTA)					
360 Madison Ave 18th Fl	New York	NY	10017	212-313-1100	313-1016
Web: www.emta.org					
Farm Credit Council 50 F St NW Suite 900	Washington	DC	20001	202-626-8710	626-8718
Web: www.fccouncil.com					
Financial Executives International (FEI)					
200 Campus Dr PO Box 674	Florham Park	NJ	07932	973-765-1000	765-1018
Web: www.financialexecutives.org					

Organization / Address	City	State	Zip	Phone	Fax
Financial Industry Regulatory Authority (FINRA) 9509 Key West Ave *Web:* www.finra.org	Rockville	MD	20850	301-590-6500	
Financial Management Assn International (FMA) USF College of Business Admin 4202 E Fowler Ave Suite 3331 *Web:* www.fma.org	Tampa	FL	33620	813-974-2084	974-3318
Financial Managers Society (FMS) 100 W Monroe St Suite 810 *TF Cust Svc:* 800-275-4367 ■ *Web:* www.fmsinc.org	Chicago	IL	60603	312-578-1300	578-1308
Financial Planning Assn (FPA) 4100 E Mississippi Ave Suite 400 *TF:* 800-945-4237 ■ *Web:* www.fpanet.org	Denver	CO	80246	303-759-4900	759-0749
Financial Service Centers of America Inc (FiSCA) 21 Main St 1st Fl *Web:* www.fisca.org	Hackensack	NJ	07602	201-487-0412	487-3954
Financial Services Roundtable 1001 Pennsylvania Ave NW Suite 500-S *Web:* www.fsround.org	Washington	DC	20004	202-289-4322	628-2507
Financial Women International (FWI) 1027 W Roselawn Ave *TF:* 866-236-2007 ■ *Web:* www.fwi.org	Roseville	MN	55113	651-487-7632	489-1322
FINRA 1735 K St NW *TF:* 800-289-9999 ■ *Web:* www.finra.org	Washington	DC	20006	202-728-8000	
Futures Industry Assn (FIA) 2001 Pennsylvania Ave NW Suite 600 *Web:* www.fiafii.org	Washington	DC	20006	202-466-5460	296-3184
Independent Community Bankers of America (ICBA) 1615 L St NW Suite 900 *TF:* 800-422-8439 ■ *Web:* www.icba.org	Washington	DC	20036	202-659-8111	861-5503
Industry Council for Tangible Assets (ICTA) PO Box 1365 *Web:* www.ictaonline.org	Severna Park	MD	21146	410-626-7005	626-7007
Institute of International Bankers 299 Park Ave 17th Fl *Web:* www.iib.org	New York	NY	10171	212-421-1611	421-1119
Institute of International Finance (IIF) 1333 H St NW Suite 800-E *Web:* www.iif.com	Washington	DC	20005	202-857-3600	775-1430
International Financial Services Assn (IFSA) 9 Sylvan Way 1st Fl *Web:* www.ifsa.org	Parsippany	NJ	07054	973-656-1900	656-1915
International Swaps & Derivatives Assn (ISDA) 360 Madison Ave 16th Fl *Web:* www.isda.org	New York	NY	10017	212-901-6000	901-6001
Investment Company Institute (ICI) 1401 H St NW 12th Fl *Web:* www.ici.org	Washington	DC	20005	202-326-5800	326-5985
Investment Management Consultants Assn (IMCA) 5619 DTC Pkwy Suite 500 *Web:* www.imca.org	Greenwood Village	CO	80111	303-770-3377	770-1812
Investment Program Assn (IPA) 1140 Connecticut Ave NW Suite 1040 *Web:* www.theipaonline.org	Washington	DC	20036	202-775-9750	331-8446
Investor Protection Trust 919 18th St NW Suite 300 *Web:* www.investorprotection.org	Washington	DC	20006	202-775-2111	
Life Insurance Settlement Assn (LISA) 1011 E Colonial Dr Suite 500 *Web:* www.lisassociation.org	Orlando	FL	32803	407-894-3797	897-1325
Managed Funds Assn (MFA) 2025 M St NW Suite 800 *Web:* www.mfainfo.org	Washington	DC	20036	202-367-1140	367-2140
Mortgage Bankers Assn (MBA) 1919 Pennsylvania Ave NW *Fax: Cust Svc ■ *TF:* 800-793-6222 ■ *Web:* www.mortgagebankers.org	Washington	DC	20006	202-557-2700	721-0247*
Municipal Securities Rulemaking Board (MSRB) 1900 Duke St Suite 600 *Web:* www.msrb.org	Alexandria	VA	22314	703-797-6600	797-6700
Mutual Fund Education Alliance (MFEA) 100 NW Englewood Rd Suite 130 *Web:* www.mfea.com	Kansas City	MO	64118	816-454-9422	454-9322
NACHA - Electronic Payments Assn (NACHA) 13665 Dulles Technology Dr Suite 300 *TF:* 800-487-9180 ■ *Web:* www.nacha.org	Herndon	VA	20171	703-561-1100	787-0996
National Assn of Credit Management (NACM) 8840 Columbia 100 Pkwy *TF:* 800-955-8815 ■ *Web:* www.nacm.org	Columbia	MD	21045	410-740-5560	740-5574
National Assn of Development Organizations (NADO) 400 N Capitol St NW Suite 390 *Web:* www.nado.org	Washington	DC	20001	202-624-7806	624-8813
National Assn of Federal Credit Unions (NAFCU) 3138 10th St N *TF:* 800-336-4644 ■ *Web:* www.nafcu.org	Arlington	VA	22201	703-522-4770	524-1082
National Assn of Financial & Estate Planning (NAFEP) 545 E 4500 South Suite E-220 *Web:* www.nafep.com	Salt Lake City	UT	84107	801-266-9900	266-1019
National Assn of Government Guaranteed Lenders (NAGGL) 215 E 9th Ave *Web:* www.naggl.org	Stillwater	OK	74074	405-377-4022	377-3931
National Assn of Mortgage Brokers (NAMB) 7900 Westpark Dr Suite T-309 *Web:* www.namb.org	McLean	VA	22102	703-342-5900	342-5905
National Assn of Personal Financial Advisors (NAPFA) 3250 N Arlington Heights Rd Suite 109 *TF:* 800-366-2732 ■ *Web:* www.napfa.org	Arlington Heights	IL	60004	847-483-5400	483-5415
National Assn of Professional Surplus Lines Offices (NAPSLO) 200 NE 54th St Suite 2000 *Web:* www.napslo.org	Kansas City	MO	64118	816-741-3910	741-5409
National Assn of Small Business Investment Companies (NASBIC) 666 11th St NW Suite 750 *Web:* www.nasbic.org	Washington	DC	20001	202-628-5055	628-5080
National Assn of Stock Plan Professionals (NASPP) PO Box 21639 *Web:* www.naspp.com	Concord	CA	94521	925-685-9271	685-5402
National Automated Clearing House Assn 13665 Dulles Technology Dr Suite 300 *TF:* 800-487-9180 ■ *Web:* www.nacha.org	Herndon	VA	20171	703-561-1100	787-0996
National Federation of Community Development Credit Unions (NFCDCU) 116 John St 33rd Fl *TF:* 800-437-8711 ■ *Web:* www.natfed.org	New York	NY	10038	212-809-1850	809-3274
National Futures Assn (NFA) 300 S Riverside Plaza Suite 1800 *TF:* 800-366-6321 ■ *Web:* www.nfa.futures.org	Chicago	IL	60606	312-781-1300	781-1467
National Investment Company Service Assn (NICSA) 2 Mt Royal Ave Suite 320 *Web:* www.nicsa.org	Marlborough	MA	01752	508-485-1500	485-1560
National Investor Relations Institute (NIRI) 8020 Towers Crescent Dr Suite 250 *Web:* www.niri.org	Vienna	VA	22182	703-506-3570	506-3571
National Venture Capital Assn (NVCA) 1655 N Fort Myer Dr Suite 850 *Web:* www.nvca.org	Arlington	VA	22209	703-524-2549	524-3940
North American Securities Administrators Assn (NASAA) 750 1st St NE Suite 1140 *TF:* 888-846-2722 ■ *Web:* www.nasaa.org	Washington	DC	20002	202-737-0900	783-3571
Pension Real Estate Assn (PREA) 100 Pearl St 13th Fl *Web:* www.prea.org	Hartford	CT	06103	860-692-6341	692-6351
RMA - Risk Management Assn 1801 Market St Suite 300 *TF Cust Svc:* 800-677-7621 ■ *Web:* www.rmahq.org	Philadelphia	PA	19103	215-446-4000	446-4101
Savings Coalition of America 1050 17th St NW Suite 1000 *Web:* www.savingscoalition.org	Washington	DC	20036	202-223-2632	223-2634
Securities Industry & Financial Markets Assn (SIFMAA) 120 Broadway 35th Fl *Web:* www.sifma.org	New York	NY	10271	212-313-1200	313-1301
Security Traders Assn (STA) 420 Lexington Ave Suite 2334 *Web:* www.securitytraders.org	New York	NY	10170	212-867-7002	867-7030
Smart Card Alliance Inc 191 Clarkville Rd *TF:* 800-556-6828 ■ *Web:* www.smartcardalliance.org	Princeton Junction	NJ	08550	609-799-5654	799-7032
Western Economic Assn International (WEAI) 18837 Brookhurst St Suite 304 *Web:* www.weainternational.org	Fountain Valley	CA	92708	714-965-8800	965-8829
World Council of Credit Unions Inc (WOCCU) 5710 Mineral Point Rd *Web:* www.woccu.org	Madison	WI	53705	608-395-2000	395-2001

49-3 Construction Industry Associations

Organization / Address	City	State	Zip	Phone	Fax
AGC (Associated General Contractors of America) 2300 Wilson Blvd Suite 400 *TF:* 800-242-1766 ■ *Web:* www.agc.org	Arlington	VA	22201	703-548-3118	548-3119
Air Conditioning Contractors of America (ACCA) 2800 Shirlington Rd Suite 300 *Web:* www.acca.org	Arlington	VA	22206	703-575-4477	575-8107
Air Movement & Control Assn International Inc (AMCA) 30 W University Dr *Web:* www.amca.org	Arlington Heights	IL	60004	847-394-0150	253-0088
AMD (Association of Millwork Distributors) 10047 Robert Trent Jones Pkwy *TF:* 800-786-7274 ■ *Web:* www.nsdja.com	New Port Richey	FL	34655	727-372-3665	372-2879
American Architectural Manufacturers Assn (AAMA) 1827 Walden Office Sq Suite 550 *Web:* www.aamanet.org	Schaumburg	IL	60173	847-303-5664	303-5774
American Concrete Institute International (ACI) 38800 Country Club Dr PO Box 9094 *Web:* www.concrete.org	Farmington Hills	MI	48331	248-848-3700	848-3701
American Concrete Pavement Assn (ACPA) 5420 Old Orchard Rd Suite A-100 *Web:* www.pavement.com	Skokie	IL	60077	847-966-2272	966-9970
American Concrete Pipe Assn 1303 W Walnut Ln Suite 305 *Web:* www.concrete-pipe.org	Irving	TX	75038	972-506-7216	506-7682
American Congress on Surveying & Mapping (ACSM) 6 Montgomery Village Ave Suite 403 *Web:* www.acsm.net	Gaithersburg	MD	20879	240-632-9716	632-1321
American Fence Assn (AFA) 800 Roosevelt Rd Bldg C-312 *TF:* 800-822-4342 ■ *Web:* www.americanfenceassociation.com	Glen Ellyn	IL	60137	630-942-6598	790-3095
American Fire Sprinkler Assn (AFSA) 12750 Merit Dr Suite 350 *Web:* www.firesprinkler.org	Dallas	TX	75251	214-349-5965	343-8898
American Institute of Constructors (AIC) PO Box 26334 *Web:* aicnet.org	Alexandria	VA	22314	703-683-4999	683-5480
American Institute of Steel Construction (AISC) 1 E Wacker Dr Suite 3100 *Web:* www.aisc.org	Chicago	IL	60601	312-670-2400	670-5403
American Institute of Timber Construction (AITC) 7012 S Revere Pkwy Suite 140 *Web:* www.aitc-glulam.org	Centennial	CO	80112	303-792-9559	792-0669
American Lumber Standard Committee Inc (ALSC) 19715 Waters Rd *Web:* www.alsc.org	Germantown	MD	20874	301-972-1700	540-8004
American Road & Transportation Builders Assn (ARTBA) 1219 28th St NW *Web:* www.artba-hq.org	Washington	DC	20007	202-289-4434	289-4435
American Society of Heating Refrigerating & Air-Conditioning Engineers Inc (ASHRAE) 1791 Tullie Cir NE *TF Cust Svc:* 800-527-4723 ■ *Web:* www.ashrae.org	Atlanta	GA	30329	404-636-8400	321-5478
American Society of Home Inspectors (ASHI) 932 Lee St Suite 101 *TF:* 800-743-2744 ■ *Web:* www.ashi.org	Des Plaines	IL	60016	847-759-2820	759-1620
American Society of Plumbing Engineers (ASPE) 8614 W Catalpa Ave Suite 1007 *Web:* www.aspe.org	Chicago	IL	60656	773-693-2773	695-9007
American Society of Professional Estimators (ASPE) 2525 Perimeter Place Dr Suite 103 *Web:* www.aspenational.com	Nashville	TN	37214	615-316-9200	316-9800
American Subcontractors Assn (ASA) 1004 Duke St *Web:* www.asaonline.com	Alexandria	VA	22314	703-684-3450	836-3482
American Welding Society (AWS) 550 NW Le Jeune Rd *TF:* 800-443-9353 ■ *Web:* www.aws.org	Miami	FL	33126	305-443-9353	443-7559
APA - Engineered Wood Assn 7011 S 19th St W *Web:* www.apawood.org	Tacoma	WA	98466	253-565-6600	565-7265
Architectural Precast Assn (APA) 6710 Winkler Rd Suite 8 *Web:* www.archprecast.org	Fort Myers	FL	33919	239-454-6989	454-6787
Architectural Woodwork Institute (AWI) 1952 Isaac Newton Sq W *Web:* www.awinet.org	Reston	VA	20190	703-733-0600	733-0584
Asphalt Institute 2696 Research Park Dr *Web:* www.asphaltinstitute.org	Lexington	KY	40511	859-288-4960	288-4999
Asphalt Recycling & Reclaiming Assn (ARRA) 3 Church Cir PMB 250 *Web:* www.arra.org	Annapolis	MD	21401	410-267-0023	267-7546
Asphalt Roofing Manufacturers Assn (ARMA) 1156 15th St NW Suite 900 *TF:* 800-785-3255 ■ *Web:* www.asphaltroofing.org	Washington	DC	20005	202-207-0917	223-9741
Associated Builders & Contractors Inc (ABC) 4250 N Fairfax Dr 9th Fl *Web:* www.abc.org	Arlington	VA	22203	703-812-2000	812-8203
Associated General Contractors of America (AGC) 2300 Wilson Blvd Suite 400 *TF:* 800-242-1766 ■ *Web:* www.agc.org	Arlington	VA	22201	703-548-3118	548-3119
Associated Locksmiths of America (ALOA) 3500 Easy St *TF:* 800-532-2562 ■ *Web:* aloa.org	Dallas	TX	75254	214-819-9733	819-9736
Association of Millwork Distributors (AMD) 10047 Robert Trent Jones Pkwy *TF:* 800-786-7274 ■ *Web:* www.nsdja.com	New Port Richey	FL	34655	727-372-3665	372-2879
Association for Retail Environment (ARE) 4651 Sheridan St Suite 470 *Web:* www.retailenvironments.org	Hollywood	FL	33021	954-893-7300	893-7500

Construction Industry Associations (Cont'd)

Phone Fax

Association of the Wall & Ceiling Industries International (AWCI) 513 W Broad St Suite 210........................Falls Church VA 22046 703-534-8300 534-8307
Web: www.awci.org

Brick Industry Assn (BIA) 1850 Centennial Park Dr Suite 301........ Reston VA 20191 703-620-0010 620-3928
Web: www.gobrick.com

Building & Construction Trades Dept AFL-CIO
815 16th St NW Suite 600.............................. Washington DC 20006 202-347-1461 628-0724
Web: www.buildingtrades.org

Building Material Dealers Assn (BMDA)
12540 SW Main St Suite 200 ....Tigard OR 97223 503-624-0561 620-1016
TF: 800-666-2632 ■ *Web:* www.bmda.com

Cedar Shake & Shingle Bureau 7101 Horne St Suite 2........... Mission BC V2V7A2 604-820-7700 820-0266
Web: www.cedarbureau.org

Ceilings & Interior Systems Construction Assn (CISCA)
405 Illinois Ave Unit 2-B .... Saint Charles IL 60174 630-584-1919 584-2003
Web: cisca.org

Cement Assn of Canada 1500-60 Queen St.......................... Ottawa ON K1P5Y7 613-236-9471 563-4498
Web: www.cement.ca

Cement Kiln Recycling Coalition (CKRC) PO Box 7553........... Arlington VA 22207 703-534-0892 466-5009*
**Fax Area Code:* 202 ■ *Web:* www.ckrc.org

Central Station Alarm Assn (CSAA) 440 Maple Ave E Suite 201...... Vienna VA 22180 703-242-4670 242-4675
Web: www.csaaul.org

Composite Panel Assn 19465 Deerfield Ave Suite 306 .... Leesburg VA 20176 703-724-1128 274-1588
TF: 866-426-6767 ■ *Web:* www.pbmdf.com

Concrete Reinforcing Steel Institute (CRSI)
933 N Plum Grove Rd .... Schaumburg IL 60173 847-517-1200 517-1206
Web: www.crsi.org

Construction Financial Management Assn (CFMA)
29 Emmons Dr Suite F-50.............................. Princeton NJ 08540 609-452-8000 452-0474
Web: www.cfma.org

Construction Specifications Institute (CSI)
99 Canal Ctr Plaza Suite 300............................ Alexandria VA 22314 703-684-0300 684-0465
TF: 800-689-2900 ■ *Web:* www.csinet.org

Distribution Contractors Assn (DCA)
101 W Renner Rd Suite 460..............................Richardson TX 75082 972-680-0261 680-0461
Web: www.dca-online.org

Door & Hardware Institute (DHI)
14150 Newbrook Dr Suite 200 ....Chantilly VA 20151 703-222-2010 222-2410
Web: www.dhi.org

Forest Resources Assn Inc 600 Jefferson Plaza Suite 350 .... Rockville MD 20852 301-838-9385 838-9481
Web: www.forestresources.org

Hardwood Plywood & Veneer Assn (HPVA)
1825 Michael Faraday Dr...................................... Reston VA 20195 703-435-2900 435-2537
Web: www.hpva.org

Interlocking Concrete Pavement Institute (ICPI)
1444 'I' St NW Suite 700.............................. Washington DC 20005 202-712-9036 408-0285
TF: 800-241-3652 ■ *Web:* icpi.org

International Assn of Drilling Contractors (IADC)
10370 Richmond Ave Suite 760 ....Houston TX 77042 713-292-1945 292-1946
Web: www.iadc.org

International Assn of Electrical Inspectors (IAEI)
901 Waterfall Way Suite 602..............................Richardson TX 75080 972-235-1455 235-6858
TF: 800-786-4234 ■ *Web:* www.iaei.org

International Code Council (ICC)
500 New Jersey Ave NW 6th Fl........................... Washington DC 20001 888-422-7233 783-2348*
**Fax Area Code:* 292 ■ *Web:* www.iccsafe.org

International Council of Employers of Bricklayers & Allied Craftworkers PO Box 21462....................... Washington DC 20009 202-457-9040 457-9051
Web: www.icebac.org

International Council of Shopping Centers (ICSC)
1221 Ave of the Americas 41st Fl ....New York NY 10020 646-728-3800 589-5555*
**Fax Area Code:* 212 ■ *Web:* www.icsc.org

International District Energy Assn (IDEA)
24 Lyman St suite 230 .... Westborough MA 01581 508-366-9339 366-0019
Web: www.districtenergy.org

International Institute of Ammonia Refrigeration (IIAR)
1110 N Glebe Rd Suite 250................................Arlington VA 22201 703-312-4200 312-0065
Web: www.iiar.org

International Masonry Institute (IMI)
James Brice House 42 East St.............................Annapolis MD 21401 410-280-1305 261-2855*
**Fax Area Code:* 301 ■ *TF:* 800-803-0295 ■ *Web:* www.imiweb.org

International Road Federation (IRF)
500 Mongomery St Suite 525............................ Alexandria VA 22314 703-535-1001 535-1007
Web: www.irfnet.org

International Union of Elevator Constructors (IUEC)
7154 Columbia Gateway Dr .... Columbia MD 21046 410-953-6150 953-6169
Web: www.iuec.org

International Wood Products Assn (IWPA) 4214 King St W ...... Alexandria VA 22302 703-820-6696 820-8550
Web: www.iwpawood.org

Log Home Builder's Assn of North America 22203 State Rt 203 .... Monroe WA 98272 360-794-4469
Web: www.loghomebuilders.org

Manufactured Housing Institute (MHI)
2101 Wilson Blvd Suite 610 .... Arlington VA 22201 703-558-0400 558-0401
TF: 800-505-5500 ■ *Web:* www.manufacturedhousing.org

Marble Institute of America (MIA)
28901 Clemens Rd Suite 100 .... Westlake OH 44145 440-250-9222 250-9223
Web: www.marble-institute.com

Mason Contractors Assn of America (MCAA)
33 S Roselle Rd .... Schaumburg IL 60193 847-301-0001 301-1110
TF: 800-536-2225 ■ *Web:* www.masoncontractors.org

Mechanical Contractors Assn of America (MCAA)
1385 Piccard Dr.. Rockville MD 20850 301-869-5800 990-9690
TF: 800-556-3653 ■ *Web:* www.mcaa.org

Metal Building Manufacturers Assn (MBMA)
1300 Sumner Ave .... Cleveland OH 44115 216-241-7333 241-0105
Web: www.mbma.com

MHI (Manufactured Housing Institute)
2101 Wilson Blvd Suite 610 .... Arlington VA 22201 703-558-0400 558-0401
TF: 800-505-5500 ■ *Web:* www.manufacturedhousing.org

Monument Builders of North America (MBNA) 136 S Keowee St..... Dayton OH 45402 800-233-4472 222-5794*
**Fax Area Code:* 937 ■ *TF:* 800-233-4472 ■ *Web:* www.monumentbuilders.org

National Assn of Home Builders (NAHB) 1201 15th St NW....... Washington DC 20005 202-266-8200 266-8586
TF: 800-368-5242 ■ *Web:* www.nahb.org

National Assn of Home Inspectors Inc (NAHI)
4248 Park Glen Rd.................................... Minneapolis MN 55416 952-928-4641 929-1318
TF: 800-448-3942 ■ *Web:* www.nahi.org

National Assn of Minority Contractors
666 11th St NW Suite 520.............................. Washington DC 20001 202-347-8259 628-1876
TF: 866-688-6262 ■ *Web:* www.namconline.org

National Assn of the Remodeling Industry (NARI)
780 Lee St Suite 200.................................. Des Plaines IL 60016 847-298-9200 298-9225
TF: 800-611-6274 ■ *Web:* www.nari.org

National Assn of Tower Erectors (NATE) 8 2nd St SE.......... Watertown SD 57201 605-882-5865 886-5184
TF: 888-882-5865 ■ *Web:* www.natehome.com

National Assn of Women in Construction (NAWIC)
327 S Adams St.......................................Fort Worth TX 76104 817-877-5551 877-0324
TF: 800-552-3506 ■ *Web:* www.nawic.org

National Burglar & Fire Alarm Assn (NBFAA)
2300 Valley View Ln Suite 230 .... Irving TX 75062 214-260-5970 260-5979
TF: 888-447-1689 ■ *Web:* www.alarm.org

National Concrete Masonry Assn 13750 Sunrise Valley Dr.........Herndon VA 20171 703-713-1900 713-1910
Web: www.ncma.org

National Conference of States on Building Codes & Standards (NCSBCS) 505 Huntmar Park Dr Suite 210 ....Herndon VA 20170 703-481-2038 481-3596
TF: 800-362-2633 ■ *Web:* www.ncsbcs.org

National Corrugated Steel Pipe Assn (NCSPA)
14070 Proton Rd Suite 100.................................... Dallas TX 75244 972-850-1907 490-4219
Web: www.ncspa.org

National Council of Examiners for Engineering & Surveying (NCEES) 280 Seneca Creek Rd...............................Clemson SC 29631 864-654-6824 654-6033
TF: 800-250-3196 ■ *Web:* www.ncees.org

National Electrical Contractors Assn (NECA)
3 Bethesda Metro Ctr Suite 1100 .... Bethesda MD 20814 301-657-3110 215-4500
Web: www.necanet.org

National Elevator Industry Inc 1677 County Rd 64 PO Box 838.......Salem NY 12865 518-854-3100 854-3257
Web: www.neii.org

National Fire Sprinkler Assn (NFSA) 40 Jon Barrett Rd........... Patterson NY 12563 845-878-4200 878-4215
Web: www.nfsa.org

National Frame Builders Assn (NFBA)
4840 Bob Billings Pkwy Suite 1000....................... Lawrence KS 66049 785-843-2444 843-7555
TF: 800-557-6957 ■ *Web:* www.nfba.org

National Hardwood Lumber Assn (NHLA)
6830 Raleigh-LaGrange Rd .... Memphis TN 38134 901-377-1818 382-6419
TF: 800-933-0318 ■ *Web:* www.natlhardwood.org

National Housing Conference (NHC)
1801 K St NW Suite M-100.............................. Washington DC 20006 202-466-2121 466-2122
Web: www.nhc.org

National Institute of Building Sciences (NIBS)
1090 Vermont Ave NW Suite 700 .... Washington DC 20005 202-289-7800 289-1092
Web: www.nibs.org

National Insulation Assn (NIA)
99 Canal Center Plaza Suite 222 .... Alexandria VA 22314 703-683-6422 549-4838
TF: 877-968-7642 ■ *Web:* www.insulation.org

National Kitchen & Bath Assn (NKBA)
687 Willow Grove St ....Hackettstown NJ 07840 908-852-0033 852-1695
TF: 800-843-6522 ■ *Web:* www.nkba.org

National Parking Assn (NPA) 1112 16th St NW Suite 840 ...... Washington DC 20036 202-296-4336 396-3102
TF: 800-647-7275 ■ *Web:* www.npapark.org

National Precast Concrete Assn (NPCA)
10333 N Meridian St Suite 272.......................... Indianapolis IN 46290 317-571-9500 571-0041
TF: 800-366-7731 ■ *Web:* www.precast.org

National Ready Mixed Concrete Assn (NRMCA)
900 Spring St....................................... Silver Spring MD 20910 301-587-1400 585-4219
TF: 888-846-7622 ■ *Web:* www.nrmca.org

National Roofing Contractors Assn (NRCA)
10255 W Higgins Rd Suite 600.......................... Rosemont IL 60018 847-299-9070 299-1183
TF Cust Svc: 800-323-9545 ■ *Web:* www.nrca.net

National Stone Sand & Gravel Assn (NSSGA) 1605 King St...... Alexandria VA 22314 703-525-8788 525-7782
TF: 800-342-1415 ■ *Web:* www.nssga.org

National Utility Contractors Assn (NUCA)
4301 N Fairfax Dr Suite 360 .... Arlington VA 22203 703-358-9300 358-9307
TF: 800-662-6822 ■ *Web:* www.nuca.com

National Wood Flooring Assn (NWFA)
111 Chesterfield Industrial Blvd........................ Chesterfield MO 63005 636-519-9663 519-9664
TF: 800-422-4556 ■ *Web:* www.woodfloors.org

North American Building Material Distribution Assn (NBMDA)
401 N Michigan Ave Suite 2400 .... Chicago IL 60611 312-644-6610 321-6869
TF: 888-747-7862 ■ *Web:* www.nbmda.org

North American Insulation Manufacturers Assn (NAIMA)
44 Canal Center Plaza Suite 310 .... Alexandria VA 22314 703-684-0084 684-0427
Web: www.naima.org

North American Wholesale Lumber Assn (NAWLA)
3601 Algonquin Rd Suite 400........................Rolling Meadows IL 60008 847-870-7470 870-0201
TF: 800-527-8258 ■ *Web:* www.lumber.org

Operative Plasterers' & Cement Masons' International Assn of the US & Canada (OPCMIA) 11720 Beltsville Dr Suite 700 ....Beltsville MD 20705 301-623-1000 623-1032
Web: www.opcmia.org

Painting & Decorating Contractors of America (PDCA)
1801 Park 270th Dr Suite 220...........................Saint Louis MO 63146 314-514-7322 514-9417
TF: 800-332-7322 ■ *Web:* www.pdca.com

Partnership for Air-Conditioning Heating Refrigeration Accreditation 4100 N Fairfax Dr Suite 200 .... Arlington VA 22203 703-524-8800 528-3816
Web: www.ari.org

Plumbing-Heating-Cooling Contractors National Assn (PHCC)
180 S Washington St.................................Falls Church VA 22040 703-237-8100 237-7442
TF: 800-533-7694 ■ *Web:* www.phccweb.org

Plumbing Manufacturers Institute (PMI)
1921 Rohlwing Rd Unit G ....Rolling Meadows IL 60008 847-481-5500 481-5501
Web: www.pmihome.org

Portland Cement Assn (PCA) 5420 Old Orchard Rd................ Skokie IL 60077 847-966-6200 966-9781
Web: www.cement.org

Precast/Prestressed Concrete Institute (PCI)
209 W Jackson Blvd Suite 500 .... Chicago IL 60606 312-786-0300 786-0353
Web: www.pci.org

Precision Metalforming Assn (PMA) 6363 Oak Tree Blvd......Independence OH 44131 216-901-8800 901-9190
Web: www.metalforming.com

Refrigeration Service Engineers Society (RSES)
1666 Rand Rd .... Des Plaines IL 60016 847-297-6464 297-5038
TF: 800-297-5660 ■ *Web:* www.rses.org

Sheet Metal & Air Conditioning Contractors' National Assn (SMACNA) 4201 Lafayette Center Dr ....Chantilly VA 20151 703-803-2980 803-3732
Web: www.smacna.org

Sheet Metal Workers International Assn (SMWIA)
1750 New York Ave NW 6th Fl .... Washington DC 20006 202-783-5880 662-0894
TF: 800-457-7694 ■ *Web:* www.smwia.org

Single Ply Roofing Institute (SPRI)
411 Waverly Oaks Rd Suite 331-B ....Waltham MA 02452 781-647-7026 647-7222
Web: www.spri.org

Steel Framing Alliance 1201 15th St NW Suite 320........... Washington DC 20005 202-785-2022 785-3856
Web: www.steelframingalliance.com

Tile Council of America Inc (TCA)
100 Clemson Research Blvd .... Anderson SC 29625 864-646-8453 646-2821
Web: www.tileusa.com

Tilt-up Concrete Assn (TCA) 113 1st St W PO Box 204 ...... Mount Vernon IA 52314 319-895-6911 213-5555*
**Fax Area Code:* 320 ■ *Web:* www.tilt-up.org

US Society on Dams 1616 17th St Suite 483........................ Denver CO 80202 303-628-5430 628-5431
Web: www.ussdams.org

Window & Door Manufacturers Assn (WDMA)
401 N Michigan Ave 24th Fl .... Chicago IL 60611 847-299-5200 299-1286
TF: 800-223-2301 ■ *Web:* www.wdma.com

Phone Fax

Wood Moulding & Millwork Producers Assn (WMMPA)
507 First St ... Woodland CA 95695 530-661-9591 661-9586
TF: 800-550-7889 ■ *Web:* wmmpa.com

Wood Products Manufacturers Assn (WPMA) PO Box 761 ... Westminster MA 01473 978-874-5445 874-9946
Web: www.wpma.org

Wood Truss Council of America (WTCA) 6300 Enterprise Ln ... Madison WI 53719 608-274-4849 274-3329
Web: www.sbcindustry.com

49-4 Consumer Sales & Service Professionals Associations

Phone Fax

Advanced Medical Technology Assn
701 Pennsylvania Ave NW Suite 800 ... Washington DC 20004 202-783-8700 783-8750
Web: www.advamed.org

AeA: Advancing the Business of Technology
400 Great America Pkwy Suite 400 ... Santa Clara CA 95054 408-987-4200 987-4298
TF: 800-284-4232 ■ *Web:* www.aeanet.org

AHFA (American Home Furnishings Alliance)
317 W High Ave 10th Fl ... High Point NC 27260 336-884-5000 884-5303
Web: www.ahfa.us

AHRI - Air-Conditioning Heating & Refrigeration Institute (AHRI)
4100 N Fairfax Dr Suite 200 ... Arlington VA 22203 703-524-8800 528-3816
Web: www.ahrinet.org

American Apparel & Footwear Assn (AAFA)
1601 N Kent St Suite 1200 ... Arlington VA 22209 703-524-1864 522-6741
TF: 800-520-2262 ■ *Web:* www.apparelandfootwear.org

American Bio-Recovery Assn (ABRA) PO Box 828 ... Ipswich MA 01938 888-979-2272 356-4606*
**Fax Area Code:* 987 ■ *TF:* 888-979-2217 ■ *Web:* americanbiorecovery.com

American Boat & Yacht Council Inc (ABYC)
613 3rd St Suite 10 ... Annapolis MD 21403 410-990-4460 990-4466
Web: www.abycinc.org

American Gem Society (AGS) 8881 W Sahara Ave ... Las Vegas NV 89117 702-255-6500 255-7420
TF: 866-805-6500 ■ *Web:* www.americangemsociety.org

American Gem Trade Assn (AGTA) 3030 LBJ Fwy Suite 840 ... Dallas TX 75234 214-742-4367 742-7334
TF: 800-972-1162 ■ *Web:* www.agta.org

American Hardware Manufacturers Assn (AHMA)
801 N Plaza Dr ... Schaumburg IL 60173 847-605-1025 605-1030
Web: www.ahma.org

American Health & Beauty Aids Institute (AHBAI)
PO Box 19510 ... Chicago IL 60619 708-633-6328 633-6329
Web: www.proudlady.org

American Home Furnishings Alliance (AHFA)
317 W High Ave 10th Fl ... High Point NC 27260 336-884-5000 884-5303
Web: www.ahfa.us

American Institute of Floral Designers (AIFD) 720 Light St ... Baltimore MD 21230 410-752-3318 752-8295
Web: www.aifd.org

American Lighting Assn (ALA) 2050 Stemmons Fwy Suite 10046 ... Dallas TX 75207 214-698-9898
TF: 800-605-4448 ■ *Web:* www.americanlightingassoc.com

American Pet Products Manufacturers Assn (APPMA)
255 Glenville Rd ... Greenwich CT 06831 203-532-0000 532-0551
TF: 800-452-1225 ■ *Web:* www.appma.org

American Rental Assn (ARA) 1900 19th St ... Moline IL 61265 309-764-2475 764-1533
TF: 800-334-2177 ■ *Web:* www.ararental.org

American Sportfishing Assn (ASA)
225 Reinekers Ln Suite 420 ... Alexandria VA 22314 703-519-9691 519-1872
Web: www.asafishing.org

American Watchmakers-Clockmakers Institute (AWI)
701 Enterprise Dr ... Harrison OH 45030 513-367-9800 367-1414
TF: 866-367-2924 ■ *Web:* www.awci.com

Aspirin Foundation of America 807 National Press Bldg ... Washington DC 20045 800-432-3247 737-8406*
**Fax Area Code:* 202 ■ *Web:* www.aspirin.org

Association of Home Appliance Manufacturers (AHAM)
1111 19th St NW Suite 402 ... Washington DC 20036 202-872-5955 872-9354
Web: www.aham.org

Association of International Automobile Manufacturers (AIAM)
2111 Wilson Blvd Suite 1150 ... Arlington VA 22201 703-525-7788 525-8817
Web: www.aiam.org

Association for Linen Management
2161 Lexington Rd Suite 2 ... Richmond KY 40475 859-624-0177 624-3580
TF: 800-669-0863 ■ *Web:* www.almnet.org

Association of Pool & Spa Professionals (APSP)
2111 Eisenhower Ave Suite 500 ... Alexandria VA 22314 703-838-0083 549-0493
TF: 800-323-3996 ■ *Web:* www.theapsp.org

Association of Specialists in Cleaning & Restoration (ASCR)
9810 Patuxent Woods Dr Suite K ... Columbia MD 21046 443-878-1000 878-1010
TF: 800-272-7012 ■ *Web:* www.ascr.org

Automotive Recyclers Assn (ARA) 3975 Fair Ridge Dr Suite 20N ... Fairfax VA 22033 703-385-1001 385-1494
TF: 888-385-1005 ■ *Web:* www.a-r-a.org

Awards & Recognition Assn (ARA) 4700 W Lake Ave ... Glenview IL 60025 847-375-4800 375-6480
TF: 800-344-2148 ■ *Web:* www.ara.org

Carpet & Rug Institute (CRI) 310 S Holiday Ave ... Dalton GA 30720 706-278-3176 278-8835
TF: 800-882-8846 ■ *Web:* www.carpet-rug.com

Cigar Assn of America Inc 1707 H St NW Suite 800 ... Washington DC 20006 202-223-8204 833-0379

Clothing Manufacturers Assn of the USA
730 Broadway 10th Fl ... New York NY 10003 212-529-0823

Coin Laundry Assn (CLA) 1315 Butterfield Rd Suite 212 ... Downers Grove IL 60515 630-963-5547 963-5864
TF: 800-570-5629 ■ *Web:* www.coinlaundry.org

Consumer Healthcare Products Assn (CHPA)
900 19th St NW Suite 700 ... Washington DC 20006 202-429-9260 223-6835
Web: www.chpa-info.org

Contact Lens Manufacturers Assn PO Box 29398 ... Lincoln NE 68529 402-465-4122 465-4187
TF: 800-344-9060 ■ *Web:* www.clma.net

Cosmetic Toiletry & Fragrance Assn (CTFA)
1101 17th St NW Suite 300 ... Washington DC 20036 202-331-1770 331-1969
Web: www.ctfa.org

Cremation Assn of North America (CANA)
401 N Michigan Ave Suite 2400 ... Chicago IL 60611 312-644-6610 321-4098
Web: www.cremationassociation.org

CTFA (Cosmetic Toiletry & Fragrance Assn)
1101 17th St NW Suite 300 ... Washington DC 20036 202-331-1770 331-1969
Web: www.ctfa.org

Dental Trade Alliance (DTA) 2300 Clarendon Blvd Suite 1003 ... arlington VA 22201 703-379-7755 931-9429
Web: www.dentaltradealliance.org

Diamond Council of America (DCA)
3212 West End Ave Suite 202 ... Nashville TN 37203 615-385-5301 385-4955
TF: 877-283-5669 ■ *Web:* www.diamondcouncil.org

Diving Equipment & Marketing Assn (DEMA)
3750 Convoy St Suite 310 ... San Diego CA 92111 858-616-6408 616-6495
TF: 800-862-3483 ■ *Web:* www.dema.org

Envelope Manufacturers Assn (EMA)
500 Montgomery St Suite 550 ... Alexandria VA 22314 703-739-2200 739-2209
Web: www.envelope.org

Extra Touch Florist Assn (ETF)
137 N Larchmont Blvd Suite 529 ... Los Angeles CA 90019 323-735-7272
TF: 888-419-1515 ■ *Web:* www.etfassociation.org

Phone Fax

Fashion Group International Inc (FGI) 8 W 40th St 7th Fl ... New York NY 10018 212-302-5511 302-5533
Web: www.fgi.org

Footwear Distributors & Retailers of America (FDRA)
1319 F St NW Suite 700 ... Washington DC 20004 202-737-5660 638-2615
Web: www.fdra.org

Fragrance Foundation 145 E 32nd St ... New York NY 10016 212-725-2755 779-9058
Web: www.fragrance.org

Gemological Institute of America (GIA) 5345 Armada Dr ... Carlsbad CA 92008 760-603-4000 603-4003
TF: 800-421-7250 ■ *Web:* www.gia.edu

Hearth Patio & Barbecue Assn (HPBA)
1901 N Moore St Suite 600 ... Arlington VA 22209 703-522-0086 522-0548
Web: www.hpba.org

Home Furnishings Independents Assn (HFIA)
2050 Stemmons World Trade Center Suite 170 PO
Box 420807 ... Dallas TX 75342 214-741-7632 742-9103
TF: 800-942-4663 ■ *Web:* www.hfia.com

Hosiery Assn 7421 Carmel Executive Park Suite 200-B ... Charlotte NC 28226 704-365-0913 362-2056
Web: www.hosieryassociation.com

Independent Jewelers Organization (IJO) 25 Seir Hill Rd ... Norwalk CT 06850 203-846-4215 846-8571
TF: 800-624-9252 ■ *Web:* www.independentjewelers.com

Independent Office Products & Furniture Dealers Assn (IOPFDA) 301 N Fairfax St Suite 200 ... Alexandria VA 22314 703-549-9040 683-7552
TF: 800-542-6672 ■ *Web:* www.iopfda.org

Institute of Inspection Cleaning & Restoration Certification (IICRC) 2715 E Mill Plain Blvd ... Vancouver WA 98661 360-693-5675 693-4858
Web: www.iicrc.org

International Assn of Lighting Designers (IALD)
200 World Trade Ctr Merchandise Mart Suite 9-104 ... Chicago IL 60654 312-527-3677 527-3680
Web: www.iald.org

International Card Manufacturers Assn (ICMA)
191 Clarksville Rd ... Princeton Junction NJ 08550 609-799-4900 799-7032
Web: www.icma.com

International Cemetery Cremation & Funeral Assn (ICCFA)
107 Carpenter Dr Suite 100 ... Sterling VA 20164 703-391-8400 391-8416
TF: 800-645-7700 ■ *Web:* www.iccfa.com

International Engraved Graphics Assn 305 Plus Park Blvd ... Nashville TN 37217 615-366-1094 366-4192
TF x209: 800-821-3138 ■ *Web:* www.iega.org

International Executive Housekeepers Assn (IEHA)
1001 Eastwind Dr Suite 301 ... Westerville OH 43081 614-895-7166 895-1248
TF: 800-200-6342 ■ *Web:* www.ieha.org

International Fabricare Institute (IFI) 14700 Sweitzer Ln ... Laurel MD 20707 301-622-1900 295-4200*
**Fax Area Code:* 240 ■ *TF:* 800-638-2627 ■ *Web:* www.ifi.org

International Furniture Rental Assn (IFRA)
5229 College Hill Rd ... Woodstock VT 05091 802-457-1658
Web: www.ifra.org

International Housewares Assn (IHA)
6400 Shafer Ct Suite 650 ... Rosemont IL 60018 847-292-4200 292-4211
Web: www.housewares.org

International Order of the Golden Rule (OGR)
13523 Lakefront Dr ... Earth City MO 63045 314-209-7142 209-1289
TF: 800-637-8030 ■ *Web:* www.ogr.org

International Precious Metals Institute (IPMI)
5101 N 12th Ave Suite C216 ... Pensacola FL 32504 850-476-1156 476-1548
Web: www.ipmi.org

International Sign Assn (ISA) 1001 N Fairfax St Suite 301 ... Alexandria VA 22314 703-836-4012 836-8353
TF: 888-472-7446 ■ *Web:* www.signs.org

International Sleep Products Assn (ISPA) 501 Wythe St ... Alexandria VA 22314 703-683-8371 683-4503
Web: www.sleepproducts.org

Japan Automobile Manufacturers Assn (JAMA)
1050 17th St NW Suite 410 ... Washington DC 20036 202-296-8537 872-1212
Web: www.jama.org

Jewelers of America (JA) 52 Vanderbilt Ave 19th Fl ... New York NY 10017 646-658-0246 658-0256
TF: 800-223-0673 ■ *Web:* www.jewelers.org

Jewelers Board of Trade (JBT) 95 Jefferson Blvd ... Warwick RI 02888 401-467-0055 467-1199
Web: www.jewelersboard.com

Jewish Funeral Directors of America (JFDA)
150 Lynnway Suite 506 ... Lynn MA 01902 781-477-9300 477-9393
Web: www.jfda.org

Juvenile Products Manufacturers Assn (JPMA)
15000 Commerce Pkwy Suite C ... Mount Laurel NJ 08054 856-638-0420 439-0525
Web: www.jpma.org

Leather Industries of America (LIA)
3050 K St NW Suite 400 ... Washington DC 20007 202-342-8497 342-8583
Web: www.leatherusa.com

Manufacturing Jewelers & Suppliers of America (MJSA)
45 Royal Little Dr ... Providence RI 02904 401-274-3840 274-0265
TF: 800-444-6572 ■ *Web:* www.mjsa.org

National Assn of Diaper Services (NADS)
994 Old Eagle School Rd Suite 1019 ... Wayne PA 19087 610-971-4850 971-4859
Web: www.diapernet.com

National Assn of Professional Band Instrument Repair Technicians (NAPBIRT) PO Box 51 ... Normal IL 61761 309-452-4257 452-4825
Web: www.napbirt.org

National Assn of Professional Organizers (NAPO)
15000 Commerce Pkwy Suite C ... Mount Laurel NJ 08054 856-380-6828 439-0525
Web: www.napo.net

National Beauty Culturists' League Inc (NBCL)
25 Logan Cir NW ... Washington DC 20005 202-332-2695 332-0940
Web: www.nbcl.org

National Bicycle Dealers Assn (NBDA)
777 W 19th St Suite O ... Costa Mesa CA 92627 949-722-6909 722-1747
Web: nbda.com

National Cleaners Assn 252 W 29th St 2nd Fl ... New York NY 10001 212-967-3002 967-2240
TF: 800-888-1622 ■ *Web:* www.nca-i.com

National Cosmetology Assn 401 N Michigan Ave 22nd Fl ... Chicago IL 60611 312-527-6765 464-6118
Web: www.ncacares.org

National Funeral Directors Assn (NFDA) 13625 Bishop's Dr ... Brookfield WI 53005 262-789-1880 789-6977
TF: 800-228-6332 ■ *Web:* www.nfda.org

National Funeral Directors & Morticians Assn (NFDMA)
3951 Snapfinger Pkwy Suite 570 ... Decatur GA 30035 404-286-6680 286-6573
TF: 800-434-0958 ■ *Web:* www.nfdma.com

National Home Furnishings Assn (NHFA)
3910 Tinsley Dr Suite 101 ... High Point NC 27265 336-886-6100 801-6102
TF: 800-888-9590 ■ *Web:* www.nhfa.org

National Pest Management Assn Inc (NPMA) 10460 North St ... Fairfax VA 22030 703-573-8330 352-3031
Web: www.pestworld.org

National Shoe Retailers Assn (NSRA)
7150 Columbia Gateway Dr Suite G ... Columbia MD 21046 410-381-8282 381-1167
TF: 800-673-8446 ■ *Web:* nsra.org

National Sporting Goods Assn (NSGA)
1601 Feehanville Dr Suite 300 ... Mount Prospect IL 60056 847-296-6742 391-9827
TF: 800-815-5422 ■ *Web:* www.nsga.org

National Volunteer Fire Council (NVFC)
7582 Walker Dr Suite 450 ... Greenbelt MD 20770 202-887-5700 887-5291
TF: 888-275-6832 ■ *Web:* www.nvfc.org

Outdoor Industry Assn (OIA) 4909 Pearl East Cir Suite 200 ... Boulder CO 80301 303-444-3353 444-3284
Web: www.outdoorindustry.org

Consumer Sales & Service Professionals Associations (Cont'd)

Phone | Fax

Outdoor Power Equipment Institute Inc (OPEI)
341 S Patrick St. Alexandria VA 22314 703-549-7600 549-7604
Web: opei.mow.org

Paint & Decorating Retailers Assn (PDRA) 403 Axminster Dr. Fenton MO 63026 636-326-2636 326-1823
TF: 800-737-0107 ■ *Web:* www.pdra.org

Pedorthic Footwear Assn (PFA)
7150 Columbia Gateway Dr Suite G. Columbia MD 21046 410-381-7278 381-1167
TF: 800-673-8447 ■ *Web:* www.pedorthics.org

Pet Food Institute (PFI) 2025 M St NW Suite 800. Washington DC 20036 202-367-1120 367-2120
Web: www.petfoodinstitute.org

Pet Industry Joint Advisory Council (PIJAC)
1220 19th St NW Suite 400. Washington DC 20036 202-452-1525 293-4377
TF: 800-553-7387 ■ *Web:* www.pijac.org

Piano Technicians Guild 4444 Forest Ave. Kansas City KS 66106 913-432-9975 432-9986
Web: www.ptg.org

Professional Assn of Innkeepers International (PAII)
207 White Horse Pike. Haddon Heights NJ 08035 856-310-1102 310-1105
TF: 800-468-7244 ■ *Web:* www.paii.org

Recreation Vehicle Industry Assn (RVIA) 1896 Preston White Dr. Reston VA 20191 703-620-6003 620-5071
TF: 800-336-0154 ■ *Web:* www.rvia.org

Salon Assn (TSA) 15825 N 71st St Suite 100. Scottsdale AZ 85254 480-281-0424 905-0708
TF: 800-211-4872 ■ *Web:* www.probeauty.org/salonspa

Security Industry Assn (SIA) 635 Slaters Ln Suite 110. Alexandria VA 22314 703-683-2075 683-2469
TF: 866-817-8888 ■ *Web:* www.siaonline.org

Selected Independent Funeral Homes
500 Lake Cook Rd Suite 205. Deerfield IL 60015 847-236-9401 236-9968
TF: 800-323-4219 ■ *Web:* www.selectedfuneralhomes.org

SGMA International 1150 17th St NW Suite 850. Washington DC 20036 202-775-1762 296-7462
Web: www.sgma.com

Shoe Service Institute of America (SSIA) 18 School St. North Brookfield MA 01535 508-867-7731 867-4600
Web: www.ssia.info

Silver Institute 1200 G St NW Suite 800. Washington DC 20005 202-835-0185 835-0155
Web: www.silverinstitute.org

SnowSports Industries America (SIA) 8377-B Greensboro Dr. McLean VA 22102 703-556-9020 821-8276
Web: www.snowsports.org

Soap & Detergent Assn (SDA) 1500 K St NW Suite 300. Washington DC 20005 202-347-2900 347-4110
Web: www.cleaning101.com

Society of American Florists (SAF) 1601 Duke St. Alexandria VA 22314 703-836-8700 836-8705
TF: 800-336-4743 ■ *Web:* www.safnow.org

Specialty Sleep Assn (SSA) 46639 Jones Ranch Rd. Friant CA 93626 559-868-4187 868-4185
Web: www.sleepinformation.org

Textile Rental Services Assn (TRSA)
1800 Diagonal Rd Suite 200. Alexandria VA 22314 703-519-0029 519-0026
TF: 800-868-8772 ■ *Web:* www.trsa.org

Tire Industry Assn (TIA) 1532 Pointer Ridge Pl Suite E. Bowie MD 20716 301-430-7280 430-7283
TF: 800-876-8372 ■ *Web:* www.tireindustry.org

Toy Industry Assn 1115 Broadway Suite 400. New York NY 10010 212-675-1141 633-1429
Web: www.toy-tia.org

Uniform & Textile Service Assn (UTSA)
1501 Lee Hwy Suite 304. Arlington VA 22209 703-247-2600 841-4750
TF: 800-486-6745 ■ *Web:* www.utsa.com

Vision Council of America (VCA)
1700 Diagonal Rd Suite 500. Alexandria VA 22314 703-548-4560 548-4580
TF: 800-424-8422 ■ *Web:* www.visionsite.org

Wallcoverings Assn 401 N Michigan Ave Suite 2200. Chicago IL 60611 312-644-6610 527-6705
Web: www.wallcoverings.org

Western-English Trade Assn (WETA) 451 E 58th Ave Suite 4323. Denver CO 80216 303-295-2001 295-6108
Web: www.wetaonline.com

WETA (Western-English Trade Assn) 451 E 58th Ave Suite 4323. Denver CO 80216 303-295-2001 295-6108
Web: www.wetaonline.com

World Floor Covering Assn (WFCA) 2211 Howell Ave. Anaheim CA 92806 714-978-6440 978-6066
TF: 800-624-6880 ■ *Web:* www.wfca.org

World Gold Council 444 Madison Ave Suite 301. New York NY 10022 212-317-3800 688-0410
Web: www.gold.org

World Shoe Assn (WSA) 15821 Ventura Blvd Suite 415. Encino CA 91436 818-379-9400 379-9410
Web: www.wsashow.com

49-5 Education Professionals Associations

Phone | Fax

ACUTA - Assn for Communications Technology Professionals in Higher Education 152 W Zandale Dr Suite 200. Lexington KY 40503 859-278-3338 278-3268
Web: www.acuta.org

American Anthropological Assn (AAA)
2200 Wilson Blvd Suite 600. Arlington VA 22201 703-528-1902 528-3546
Web: www.aaanet.org

American Assn for Adult & Continuing Education (AAACE)
10111 ML King Jr Hwy Suite 200-C. Bowie MD 20720 301-459-6261 459-6241
Web: www.aaace.org

American Assn of Colleges of Nursing (AACN)
1 Dupont Cir NW Suite 530. Washington DC 20036 202-463-6930 785-8320
Web: www.aacn.nche.edu

American Assn of Colleges of Pharmacy (AACP)
1727 King St 2nd Fl. Alexandria VA 22314 703-739-2330 836-8982
Web: www.aacp.org

American Assn of Colleges for Teacher Education (AACTE)
1307 New York Ave NW Suite 300. Washington DC 20005 202-293-2450 457-8095
Web: www.aacte.org

American Assn of Collegiate Registrars & Admissions Officers (AACRAO) 1 Dupont Cir NW Suite 520. Washington DC 20036 202-293-9161 872-8857
Web: www.aacrao.org

American Assn of Community Colleges (AACC)
1 Dupont Cir NW Suite 410. Washington DC 20036 202-728-0200 833-2467
Web: www.aacc.nche.edu

American Assn of Family & Consumer Sciences (AAFCS)
400 N Columbus St Suite 202. Alexandria VA 22314 703-706-4600 706-4663
TF: 800-424-8080 ■ *Web:* www.aafcs.org

American Assn of Physics Teachers (AAPT)
1 Physics Ellipse. College Park MD 20740 301-209-3300 209-0845
Web: www.aapt.org

American Assn of School Administrators (AASA)
801 N Quincy St Suite 700. Arlington VA 22203 703-528-0700 841-1543
TF: 800-771-1162 ■ *Web:* www.aasa.org

American Assn of State Colleges & Universities (AASCU)
1307 New York Ave NW 5th Fl. Washington DC 20005 202-293-7070 296-5819
TF: 800-542-2062 ■ *Web:* www.aascu.org

American Assn of Teachers of Arabic (AATA)
College of William & Mary Dept of Modern Languages & Literatures PO Box 8795. Williamsburg VA 23187 757-221-3145 221-3637
Web: www.wm.edu/aata

American Assn of Teachers of French (AATF)
Southern Illinois Univ MC 4510. Carbondale IL 62901 618-453-5731 453-5733
Web: www.frenchteachers.org

Phone | Fax

American Assn of Teachers of German (AATG)
112 Haddontowne Ct Suite 104. Cherry Hill NJ 08034 856-795-5553 795-9398
Web: www.aatg.org

American Assn of Teachers of Spanish & Portuguese (AATSP)
423 Exton Commons. Exton PA 19341 610-363-7005 363-7116
Web: www.aatsp.org

American Assn of University Professors (AAUP)
1012 14th St NW Suite 500. Washington DC 20005 202-737-5900 737-5526
TF: 800-424-2973 ■ *Web:* www.aaup.org

American Assn of University Women (AAUW)
1111 16th St NW. Washington DC 20036 202-785-7700 872-1425
TF: 800-326-2289 ■ *Web:* www.aauw.org

American College Personnel Assn (ACPA)
1 Dupont Cir NW Suite 300. Washington DC 20036 202-835-2272 296-3286
Web: www.acpa.nche.edu

American Council on Education (ACE)
1 Dupont Cir NW Suite 800. Washington DC 20036 202-939-9300 833-4760
Web: www.acenet.edu

American Council on the Teaching of Foreign Languages (ACTFL) 1001 N Fairfax St Suite 200. Alexandria VA 22314 703-894-2900 894-2905
Web: www.actfl.org

American Councils for International Education
1776 Massachusetts Ave NW Suite 700. Washington DC 20036 202-833-7522 833-7523
Web: www.americancouncils.org

American Dental Education Assn (ADEA)
1400 K St NW Suite 1100. Washington DC 20005 202-289-7201 289-7204
TF: 800-353-2237 ■ *Web:* www.adea.org

American Educational Research Assn (AERA)
1430 K St NW. Washington DC 20005 202-238-3200 238-3250
Web: www.aera.net

American Federation of School Administrators (AFSA)
1101 17th St NW Suite 408. Washington DC 20036 202-986-4209 986-4211
TF: 800-354-2372 ■ *Web:* www.admin.org

American Historical Assn (AHA) 400 A St SE. Washington DC 20003 202-544-2422 544-8307
Web: www.historians.org

American Library Assn (ALA) 50 E Huron St. Chicago IL 60611 312-944-6780 944-2641
TF: 800-545-2433 ■ *Web:* www.ala.org

American Medical Student Assn (AMSA) 1902 Association Dr. Reston VA 20191 703-620-6600 620-5873
TF: 800-767-2266 ■ *Web:* www.amsa.org

American Philological Assn (APA)
Univ of Pennsylvania 292 Logan Hall 249 S 36th St. Philadelphia PA 19104 215-898-4975 573-7874
Web: www.apaclassics.org

American Political Science Assn (APSA)
1527 New Hampshire Ave NW. Washington DC 20036 202-483-2512 483-2657
Web: www.apsanet.org

American School Counselor Assn (ASCA)
1101 King St Suite 625. Alexandria VA 22314 703-683-2722 683-1619
TF: 800-306-4722 ■ *Web:* www.schoolcounselor.org

American School Health Assn (ASHA)
7263 State Rt 43 PO Box 708. Kent OH 44240 330-678-1601 678-4526
TF: 800-445-2742 ■ *Web:* www.ashaweb.org

American Society for Engineering Education (ASEE)
1818 'N' St NW Suite 600. Washington DC 20036 202-331-3500 265-8504
Web: www.asee.org

American Society for Training & Development (ASTD)
1640 King St 3rd Fl Box 1443. Alexandria VA 22313 703-683-8100 683-1523
TF: 800-628-2783 ■ *Web:* www.astd.org

American Sociological Assn (ASA)
1307 New York Ave NW Suite 700. Washington DC 20005 202-383-9005 638-0882
Web: www.asanet.org

American String Teachers Assn (ASTA) 4153 Chain Bridge Rd. Fairfax VA 22030 703-279-2113 279-2114
Web: www.astaweb.com

American Studies Assn (ASA) 1120 19th St NW Suite 301. Washington DC 20036 202-467-4783 467-4786
Web: www.georgetown.edu/crossroads/asainfo.html

American Translators Assn (ATA)
225 Reinekers Ln Suite 590. Alexandria VA 22314 703-683-6100 683-6122
Web: www.atanet.org

APPA: Assn of Higher Education Facilities Officers
1643 Prince St. Alexandria VA 22314 703-684-1446 549-2772
Web: www.appa.org

Association of Advanced Rabbinical & Talmudic Schools (AARTS) 11 Broadway. New York NY 10004 212-363-1991 533-5335

Association for Advanced Training in the Behavioral Sciences (AATBS) 5126 Ralston St. Ventura CA 93003 805-676-3030 676-3033
TF: 800-472-1931 ■ *Web:* www.aatbs.com

Association for the Advancement of Computing in Education (AACE) PO Box 1545. Chesapeake VA 23327 757-366-5606 997-8760*
**Fax Area Code:* 703 ■ *Web:* www.aace.org

Association of American Colleges & Universities (AAC&U)
1818 R St NW. Washington DC 20009 202-387-3760 265-9532
Web: www.aacu.org

Association of American Law Schools (AALS)
1201 Connecticut Ave NW Suite 800. Washington DC 20036 202-296-8851 296-8869
Web: www.aals.org

Association of American Medical Colleges (AAMC)
2450 'N' St NW. Washington DC 20037 202-828-0400 828-1125
Web: www.aamc.org

Association of American Universities (AAU)
1200 New York Ave NW Suite 550. Washington DC 20005 202-408-7500 408-8184
Web: www.aau.edu

Association of Ancient Historians
Mercyhurst College Dept of History 501 E 38th St. Erie PA 16546 814-824-2345
Web: www.trentu.ca/ahc/aah

Association for Career & Technical Education (ACTE)
1410 King St. Alexandria VA 22314 703-683-3111 683-7424
TF: 800-826-9972 ■ *Web:* www.acteonline.org

Association for Childhood Education International (ACEI)
17904 Georgia Ave Suite 215. Olney MD 20832 301-570-2111 570-2212
TF: 800-423-3563 ■ *Web:* www.acei.org

Association of Christian Schools International (ACSI)
731 Chapel Hills Dr. Colorado Springs CO 80920 719-528-6906 531-0631
TF Cust Svc: 800-367-0798 ■ *Web:* www.acsi.org

Association of College Unions International (ACUI)
120 W 7th St 1 City Center Suite 200. Bloomington IN 47404 812-245-2284 245-6710
Web: www.acui.org

Association of College & University Housing Officers International (ACUHO-I) 941 Chatham Ln Suite 318. Columbus OH 43221 614-292-0099 292-3205
Web: www.acuho.ohio-state.edu

Association of Collegiate Schools of Architecture (ACSA)
1735 New York Ave NW 3rd Fl. Washington DC 20006 202-785-2324 628-0448
Web: www.acsa-arch.org

Association of Community College Trustees (ACCT)
1233 20th St NW Suite 605. Washington DC 20036 202-775-4667 223-1297
Web: www.acct.org

Association for Continuing Higher Education (ACHE)
PO Box 118067. Charleston SC 29423 800-807-2243 574-6470*
**Fax Area Code:* 843 ■ *TF:* 800-807-2243 ■ *Web:* www.acheinc.org

Phone Fax

Association for Educational Communications & Technology (AECT) 1800 N Stonelake Dr Suite 2 .... Bloomington IN 47404 812-335-7675 335-7678
TF: 877-677-2328 ■ Web: www.aect.org

Association of Fraternity Advisors (AFA)
9640 N Augusta Dr Suite 433 .... Carmel IN 46032 317-876-1632 876-3981
Web: www.fraternityadvisors.org

Association for Gerontology in Higher Education (AGHE)
1220 L St NW Suite 901 .... Washington DC 20005 202-289-9806 289-9824
Web: www.aghe.org

Association of Governing Boards of Universities & Colleges (AGB) 1133 20th St NW Suite 300 .... Washington DC 20036 202-296-8400 223-7053
TF: 800-356-6317 ■ Web: www.agb.org

Association for Practical & Professional Ethics
618 E 3rd St.. Bloomington IN 47405 812-855-6450 856-4969
Web: www.indiana.edu/appe

Association of Program Directors in Internal Medicine (APDIM) 2501 M St NW Suite 550 .... Washington DC 20037 202-887-9450 861-9731
TF: 800-622-4558 ■ Web: www.im.org/APDIM

Association of Research Libraries (ARL)
21 Dupont Cir NW Suite 800.............................. Washington DC 20036 202-296-2296 872-0884
Web: www.arl.org

Association of School Business Officials International (ASBO)
11401 N Shore Dr .... Reston VA 20190 703-478-0405 478-0205
TF: 866-682-2729 ■ Web: asbointl.org

Association of Schools of Public Health (ASPH)
1101 15th St NW Suite 910.............................. Washington DC 20005 202-296-1099 296-1252
Web: www.asph.org

Association for Science Teacher Education (ASTE)
Ball State University Dept of Biology.......................... Muncie IN 47306 765-288-9044 285-8804
Web: aste.chem.pitt.edu

Association for Supervision & Curriculum Development (ASCD)
1703 N Beauregard St.................................. Alexandria VA 22311 703-578-9600 575-5400
TF: 800-933-2723 ■ Web: www.ascd.org

Association of Test Publishers
601 Pennsylvania Ave NW Suite 900...................... Washington DC 20004 866-240-7909
Web: www.testpublishers.org

Association of Theological Schools in the US & Canada (ATS)
10 Summit Park Dr .... Pittsburgh PA 15275 412-788-6505 788-6510
Web: www.ats.edu

Association of Universities for Research in Astronomy (AURA)
1200 New York Ave NW Suite 350 .... Washington DC 20005 202-483-2101 483-2106
Web: www.aura-astronomy.org

Association of University Centers on Disabilities (AUCD)
1010 Wayne Ave Suite 920 .... Silver Spring MD 20910 301-588-8252 588-2842
Web: www.aucd.org

Broadcast Education Assn (BEA) 1771 'N' St NW .... Washington DC 20036 202-243-2339 775-2981
TF: 888-380-7222 ■ Web: www.beaweb.org

Business-Higher Education Forum
2025 M St NW Suite 800 .... Washington DC 20036 202-367-1189 367-2269
Web: www.bhef.com

Business Professionals of America 5454 Cleveland Ave..........Columbus OH 43231 614-895-7277 895-1165
TF: 800-334-2007 ■ Web: www.bpa.org

Career College Assn (CCA)
1101 Connecticut Ave NW Suite 900...................... Washington DC 20036 202-336-6700 336-6828
Web: www.career.org

Christian Schools International (CSI)
3350 E Paris Ave SE .... Grand Rapids MI 49512 616-957-1070 957-5022
TF: 800-635-8288 ■ Web: www.csionline.org

CIES (Council for International Exchange of Scholars)
3007 Tilden St NW Suite 5L .... Washington DC 20008 202-686-4000 362-3442
Web: www.cies.org

College Music Society (CMS) 312 E Pine St .... Missoula MT 59802 406-721-9616 721-9419
TF: 800-729-0235 ■ Web: www.music.org

College & University Professional Assn for Human Resources (CUPA-HR) 1811 Commons Point Dr....................... Knoxville TN 37932 865-637-7673 637-7674
TF: 877-287-2474 ■ Web: www.cupahr.org

Conference on College Composition & Communication (CCCC)
1111 W Kenyon Rd .... Urbana IL 61801 217-328-3870 278-3763
TF: 800-369-6283 ■ Web: www.ncte.org/groups/cccc

Council of Administrators of Special Education (CASE)
Fort Valley State Univ 1005 State University Dr .... Fort Valley GA 31030 478-825-7667 825-7811
TF: 800-585-1753 ■ Web: www.casecec.org

Council for Advancement & Support of Education (CASE)
1307 New York Ave NW Suite 1000 .... Washington DC 20005 202-328-5900 387-4973
TF Orders: 800-554-8536 ■ Web: www.case.org

Council of Chief State School Officers (CCSSO)
1 Massachusetts Ave NW Suite 700 .... Washington DC 20001 202-408-5505 408-8072
Web: www.ccsso.org

Council for Christian Colleges & Universities (CCCU)
321 8th St NE .... Washington DC 20002 202-546-8713 546-8913
Web: www.cccu.org

Council for Exceptional Children (CEC)
1110 N Glebe Rd Suite 300.............................. Arlington VA 22201 703-620-3660 264-9494
TF: 888-232-7733 ■ Web: www.cec.sped.org

Council of Graduate Schools (CGS)
1 Dupont Cir NW Suite 230.............................. Washington DC 20036 202-223-3791 331-7157
Web: www.cgsnet.org

Council of the Great City Schools
1301 Pennsylvania Ave NW Suite 702...................... Washington DC 20004 202-393-2427 393-2400
Web: www.cgcs.org

Council of Independent Colleges (CIC)
1 Dupont Cir NW Suite 320.............................. Washington DC 20036 202-466-7230 466-7238
Web: www.cic.edu

Council on International Educational Exchange (CIEE)
300 Fore St 2nd Fl.. Portland ME 04101 207-553-4000 553-5272
TF Cust Svc: 888-268-6245 ■ Web: www.ciee.org

Council for International Exchange of Scholars (CIES)
3007 Tilden St NW Suite 5L .... Washington DC 20008 202-686-4000 362-3442
Web: www.cies.org

Council for Professional Recognition 2460 16th St NW........ Washington DC 20009 202-265-9090 265-9161
TF: 800-424-4310 ■ Web: www.cdacouncil.org

Council on Social Work Education (CSWE)
1725 Duke St Suite 500................................ Alexandria VA 22314 703-683-8080 683-8099
Web: www.cswe.org

DECA (Distributive Education Clubs of America)
1908 Association Dr.. Reston VA 20191 703-860-5000 860-4013
Web: www.deca.org

Distance Education & Training Council (DETC)
1601 18th St NW Suite 2 .... Washington DC 20009 202-234-5100 332-1386
Web: www.detc.org

Distributive Education Clubs of America (DECA)
1908 Association Dr.. Reston VA 20191 703-860-5000 860-4013
Web: www.deca.org

Econometric Society
Northwestern Univ Dept of Economics 2003 Sheridan Rd .... Evanston IL 60208 847-491-3615 491-5427
Web: www.econometricsociety.org

Phone Fax

Economic History Assn (EHA)
Santa Clara University Dept of Economics 500 El Camino Real...................................... Santa Clara CA 95053 408-554-4348 554-2331
Web: eh.net/EHA

Education Commission of the States (ECS)
700 Broadway Suite 810 .... Denver CO 80203 303-299-3600 296-8332
Web: www.ecs.org

Foundation for Independent Higher Education
1920 'N' St NW Suite 210............................. Washington DC 20036 202-367-0333 367-0334
Web: www.fihe.org

Hispanic Assn of Colleges & Universities (HACU)
8415 Datapoint Dr Suite 400.......................... San Antonio TX 78229 210-692-3805 692-0823
TF: 800-780-4228 ■ Web: www.hacu.net

Independent Educational Consultants Assn (IECA)
3251 Old Lee Hwy Suite 510.................................. Fairfax VA 22030 703-591-4850 591-4860
TF: 800-808-4322 ■ Web: www.educationalconsulting.org

International Council on Hotel Restaurant & Institutional Education (CHRIE) 2810 N Parham Rd Suite 230............. Richmond VA 23294 804-346-4800 346-5009
Web: www.chrie.org

International Reading Assn (IRA)
800 Barksdale Rd PO Box 8139 .... Newark DE 19714 302-731-1600 737-0878
TF: 800-336-7323 ■ Web: www.reading.org

International Society for Technology in Education (ISTE)
480 Charnelton St .... Eugene OR 97401 541-302-3777 302-3778
TF: 800-336-5191 ■ Web: www.iste.org

International Technology Education Assn (ITEA)
1914 Association Dr Suite 201 .... Reston VA 20191 703-860-2100 860-0353
Web: www.iteawww.org

Languages Canada 5886 169 A St.................................. Surrey BC V3S6Z8 604-574-1532 277-0522*
*Fax Area Code: 888 ■ Web: www.languagescanada.ca

Law School Admission Council Inc (LSAC) PO Box 40 .... Newtown PA 18940 215-968-1101 968-1169
Web: www.lsac.org

MENC: National Assn for Music Education
1806 Robert Fulton Dr....................................... Reston VA 20191 703-860-4000 860-1531
TF: 800-336-3768 ■ Web: www.menc.org

Middle States Assn of Colleges & Schools 3624 Market St..... Philadelphia PA 19104 267-284-5000 662-5501*
*Fax Area Code: 215 ■ TF: 800-355-1258 ■ Web: www.msche.org

Modern Language Assn (MLA) 26 Broadway 3rd Fl .... New York NY 10004 646-576-5000 458-0030
Web: www.mla.org

Music Teachers National Assn (MTNA)
441 Vine St Suite 3100 .... Cincinnati OH 45202 513-421-1420 421-2503
TF: 888-512-5278 ■ Web: www.mtna.org

NAFSA: Assn of International Educators
1307 New York Ave NW 8th Fl .... Washington DC 20005 202-737-3699 737-3657
Web: www.nafsa.org

National Academy of Education 500 5th St NW Suite 333...... Washington DC 20001 202-334-2341 334-2350
Web: www.nae.nyu.edu

National Art Education Assn (NAEA) 1916 Association Dr........... Reston VA 20191 703-860-8000 860-2960
TF: 800-299-8321 ■ Web: www.naea-reston.org

National Assn for Bilingual Education (NABE)
1313 L St Nw Suite 210 .... Washington DC 20005 202-898-1829 789-2866
Web: www.nabe.org

National Assn of Biology Teachers (NABT)
12030 Sunrise Valley Dr Suite 110 .... Reston VA 20191 703-264-9696 264-7778
TF: 800-406-0775 ■ Web: www.nabt.org

National Assn for Campus Activities (NACA) 13 Harbison Way .... Columbia SC 29212 803-732-6222 749-1047
TF: 800-845-2338 ■ Web: www.naca.org

National Assn of Catholic School Teachers (NACST)
1700 Sansom St Suite 903 .... Philadelphia PA 19103 215-665-0993 568-8270
TF: 800-996-2278 ■ Web: www.nacst.com

National Assn for College Admission Counseling (NACAC)
1631 Prince St... Alexandria VA 22314 703-836-2222 836-8015
TF: 800-822-6285 ■ Web: www.nacac.com

National Assn of College Auxiliary Services (NACAS)
7 Boars Head Ln .... Charlottesville VA 22903 434-245-8425 245-8453
Web: www.nacas.org

National Assn of College & University Business Officers (NACUBO) 1110 Vermont Ave NW Suite 800............... Washington DC 20005 202-861-2500 861-2583
TF: 800-462-4916 ■ Web: www.nacubo.org

National Assn of Colleges & Employers (NACE)
62 Highland Ave.. Bethlehem PA 18017 610-868-1421 868-0208
TF: 800-544-5272 ■ Web: www.naceweb.org

National Assn for the Education of Young Children (NAEYC)
1313 L St NW Suite 500 .... Washington DC 20005 202-232-8777 328-1846
TF: 800-424-2460 ■ Web: www.naeyc.org

National Assn of Elementary School Principals (NAESP)
1615 Duke St... Alexandria VA 22314 703-684-3345 548-6021
TF: 800-386-2377 ■ Web: www.naesp.org

National Assn of Independent Colleges & Universities (NAICU) 1025 Connecticut Ave NW Suite 700.............. Washington DC 20036 202-785-8866 835-0003
Web: www.naicu.edu

National Assn of Independent Schools (NAIS)
1620 L St NW Suite 1100 .... Washington DC 20036 202-973-9700 973-9790
Web: www.nais.org

National Assn of Schools of Art & Design (NASAD)
11250 Roger Bacon Dr Suite 21 .... Reston VA 20190 703-437-0700 437-6312
Web: nasad.arts-accredit.org

National Assn of Schools of Dance (NASD)
11250 Roger Bacon Dr Suite 21 .... Reston VA 20190 703-437-0700 437-6312
Web: nasd.arts-accredit.org

National Assn of Schools of Music (NASM)
11250 Roger Bacon Dr Suite 21 .... Reston VA 20190 703-437-0700 437-6312
Web: nasm.arts-accredit.org

National Assn of Secondary School Principals (NASSP)
1904 Association Dr.. Reston VA 20191 703-860-0200 476-5432
TF: 800-253-7746 ■ Web: www.principals.org

National Assn of State Boards of Education (NASBE)
277 S Washington St Suite 100 .... Alexandria VA 22314 703-684-4000 836-2313
TF: 800-368-5023 ■ Web: www.nasbe.org

National Assn of State Directors of Special Education (NASDSE) 1800 Diagonal Rd Suite 320 .... Alexandria VA 22314 703-519-3800 519-3808
Web: www.nasdse.org

National Assn of State Universities & Land Grant Colleges
1307 New York Ave NW Suite 400 .... Washington DC 20005 202-478-6040 478-6046
Web: www.nasulgc.org

National Assn of Student Activity Advisors 1904 Association Dr.... Reston VA 20191 703-860-0200 476-5432

National Assn of Student Financial Aid Administrators (NASFAA) 1101 Connecticut Ave Suite 1100 .... Washington DC 20036 202-785-0453 785-1487
Web: www.nasfaa.org

National Assn of Student Personnel Administrators (NASPA)
1875 Connecticut Ave NW Suite 418........................ Washington DC 20009 202-265-7500 797-1157
Web: www.naspa.org

National Business Education Assn (NBEA) 1914 Association Dr...... Reston VA 20191 703-860-8300 620-4483
Web: www.nbea.org

National Catholic Educational Assn (NCEA)
1077 30th St NW Suite 100................................ Washington DC 20007 202-337-6232 333-6706
Web: www.ncea.org

Education Professionals Associations (Cont'd)

Phone | Fax

National Coalition of Girls' Schools (NCGS) 57 Main St ... Concord MA 01742 978-287-4485 287-6014
Web: www.ncgs.org

National Communication Assn (NCA) 1765 'N' St NW ... Washington DC 20036 202-464-4622 464-4600
Web: www.natcom.org

National Community Education Assn (NCEA)
3929 Old Lee Hwy Suite 91-A ... Fairfax VA 22030 703-359-8973 359-0972
Web: www.ncea.com

National Council on Economic Education (NCEE)
1140 6th Ave 2nd Fl ... New York NY 10036 212-730-7007 730-1793
TF: 800-338-1192 ■ *Web:* www.ncee.net

National Council for the Social Studies (NCSS)
8555 16th St Suite 500 ... Silver Spring MD 20910 301-588-1800 588-2049
TF: 800-296-7840 ■ *Web:* www.ncss.org

National Council of Supervisors of Mathematics (NCSM)
6000 E Evans Ave Suite 3-205 ... Denver CO 80222 303-758-9611 758-9616
Web: www.ncsmonline.org

National Council of Teachers of English (NCTE)
1111 W Kenyon Rd ... Urbana IL 61801 217-328-3870 328-0977
TF: 800-369-6283 ■ *Web:* www.ncte.org

National Council of Teachers of Mathematics (NCTM)
1906 Association Dr ... Reston VA 20191 703-620-9840 476-2970
TF Orders: 800-235-7566 ■ *Web:* www.nctm.org

National Education Assn (NEA) 1201 16th St NW ... Washington DC 20036 202-833-4000 822-7974
Web: www.nea.org

National Environmental Safety & Health Training Assn (NESHTA)
2720 E Thomas Rd ... Phoenix AZ 85016 602-956-6099 956-6399
Web: neshta.org

National Guild of Community Schools of the Arts
520 8th Ave Suite 302 ... New York NY 10018 212-268-3337 268-3995
Web: www.nationalguild.org

National Middle School Assn (NMSA)
4151 Executive Pkwy Suite 300 ... Westerville OH 43081 614-895-4730 895-4750
TF: 800-528-6672 ■ *Web:* www.nmsa.org

National School Boards Assn (NSBA) 1680 Duke St ... Alexandria VA 22314 703-838-6722 683-7590
Web: www.nsba.org

National School Public Relations Assn (NSPRA)
15948 Derwood Rd ... Rockville MD 20855 301-519-0496 519-0494
Web: www.nspra.org

National Science Teachers Assn (NSTA) 1840 Wilson Blvd ... Arlington VA 22201 703-243-7100 243-7177
TF Sales: 800-722-6782 ■ *Web:* www.nsta.org

National Staff Development Council (NSDC) 504 S Locust St ... Oxford OH 45056 513-523-6029 523-0638
TF: 800-727-7288 ■ *Web:* www.nsdc.org

North Central Assn Higher Learning Commission
30 N La Salle St Suite 2400 ... Chicago IL 60602 312-263-0456 263-7462
TF: 800-621-7440 ■ *Web:* www.ncacihe.org

Oak Ridge Associated Universities (ORAU)
130 Badger Ave PO Box 117 ... Oak Ridge TN 37831 865-576-3000 576-3643
Web: www.orau.org

Organization of American Historians (OAH)
112 N Bryan Ave PO Box 5457 ... Bloomington IN 47408 812-855-7311 855-0696
Web: www.oah.org

Organization for Tropical Studies (OTS) 410 Swift Ave ... Durham NC 27705 919-684-5774 684-5661
Web: www.ots.duke.edu

Registry of Interpreters for the Deaf Inc (RID)
333 Commerce St ... Alexandria VA 22314 703-838-0030 838-0454
Web: www.rid.org

Research Libraries Group Inc (RLG)
2029 Stierlin Ct Suite 100 ... Mountain View CA 94043 650-991-2333 964-0943
TF: 800-537-7546 ■ *Web:* www.rlg.org

Society for Academic Emergency Medicine (SAEM)
901 N Washington Ave ... Lansing MI 48906 517-485-5484 485-0801
Web: www.saem.org

Society for American Archaeology (SAA)
900 2nd St NE Suite 12 ... Washington DC 20002 202-789-8200 789-0284
Web: www.saa.org

Society for College & University Planning (SCUP)
339 E Liberty St Suite 300 ... Ann Arbor MI 48104 734-998-7832 998-6532
Web: www.scup.org

Society for History Education PO Box 1578 ... Borrego Springs CA 92004 760-767-5938
Web: www.thehistoryteacher.org

Society of Park & Recreation Educators (SPRE)
c/o National Recreation & Park Assn 22377 Belmont
Ridge Rd ... Ashburn VA 20148 703-858-0784 858-0794
TF: 800-626-6772 ■ *Web:* www.nrpa.org

Society for Research in Child Development (SRCD)
3131 S State St Suite 302 ... Ann Arbor MI 48108 734-998-6578 998-6569
Web: www.srcd.org

Southern Assn of Colleges & Schools 1866 Southern Ln ... Decatur GA 30033 404-679-4500 679-4556
TF: 800-248-7701 ■ *Web:* www.sacs.org

Surratt Society PO Box 427 ... Clinton MD 20735 301-868-1121 868-8177
Web: www.surratt.org/su_scty.html

Teach For America 315 W 36th St 7th Fl ... New York NY 10018 212-279-2080 279-2081
Web: www.teachforamerica.org

Teachers of English to Speakers of Other Languages (TESOL)
700 S Washington St Suite 200 ... Alexandria VA 22314 703-836-0774 836-7864
TF: 888-547-3369 ■ *Web:* www.tesol.org

Torah Umesorah-National Society for Hebrew Day Schools
1090 Coney Island Ave ... Brooklyn NY 11230 212-227-1000 406-6934

Trees for Tomorrow (TFT) 519 Sheridan St E PO Box 609 ... Eagle River WI 54521 715-479-6456 479-2318
TF: 800-838-9472 ■ *Web:* www.treesfortomorrow.com

University Continuing Education Assn (UCEA)
1 Dupont Cir NW Suite 615 ... Washington DC 20036 202-659-3130 785-0374
Web: www.ucea.edu

Western Assn of Schools & Colleges (WASC)
985 Atlantic Ave Suite 100 ... Alameda CA 94501 510-748-9001 748-9797
Web: www.wascweb.org

Women's College Coalition (WCC) 1678 Asylum Ave W ... Hartford CT 06117 860-231-5247
Web: www.womenscolleges.org

49-6 Food & Beverage Industries Professional Associations

Phone | Fax

American Assn of Cereal Chemists Inc (AACC)
3340 Pilot Knob Rd ... Saint Paul MN 55121 651-454-7250 454-0766
Web: www.aaccnet.org

American Bakers Assn (ABA) 1300 'I' St NW Suite 700-W ... Washington DC 20005 202-789-0300 898-1164
Web: www.americanbakers.org

American Beverage Assn 1101 16th St NW ... Washington DC 20036 202-463-6732 463-8178
Web: www.ameribev.org

American Beverage Licensees (ABL) 5101 River Rd Suite 108 ... Bethesda MD 20816 301-656-1494 656-7539
TF: 800-311-8999 ■ *Web:* www.ablusa.org

Phone | Fax

American Culinary Federation Inc (ACF)
180 Center Place Way ... Saint Augustine FL 32095 904-824-4468 825-4758
TF: 800-624-9458 ■ *Web:* www.acfchefs.org

American Dairy Products Institute (ADPI)
116 N York St Suite 200 ... Elmhurst IL 60126 630-530-8700 530-8707
Web: www.adpi.org

American Frozen Food Institute (AFFI)
2000 Corporate Ridge Suite 1000 ... McLean VA 22102 703-821-0770 821-1350
Web: www.affi.com

American Institute of Baking
1213 Bakers Way PO Box 3999 ... Manhattan KS 66505 785-537-4750 537-1493
TF: 800-633-5137 ■ *Web:* www.aibonline.org

American Malting Barley Assn (AMBA)
740 N Plankinton Ave Suite 830 ... Milwaukee WI 53203 414-272-4640
Web: www.ambainc.org

American Meat Institute (AMI)
1150 Connecticut Ave NW Suite 1200 ... Washington DC 20036 202-587-4200 587-4300
Web: www.meatami.com

American Peanut Shellers Assn 2336 Lake Park Dr ... Albany GA 31707 229-888-2508 888-5150
Web: www.peanut-shellers.org

American Seafood Distributors Assn
7918 Jones Branch Dr Suite 700 ... McLean VA 22102 703-752-8880 752-7583
TF: 877-206-2732 ■ *Web:* www.freetradeinseafood.org

American Society for Nutrition (ASNS)
9650 Rockville Pike Suite L3503A ... Bethesda MD 20814 301-634-7029 634-7099
TF: 800-433-2732 ■ *Web:* www.nutrition.org

American Spice Trade Assn (ASTA)
2025 M St NW Suite 800 ... Washington DC 20036 202-367-1127 367-2127
Web: www.astaspice.org

American Wine Society (AWS) 113 S Perry St ... Lawrenceville GA 30045 678-377-7070 377-7005
Web: www.americanwinesociety.org

Association of Food Industries Inc (AFI)
3301 Rt 66 Bldg C Suite 205 ... Neptune NJ 07753 732-922-3008 922-3590
Web: afi.mytradeassociation.org

At-sea Processors Assn (APA) 4039 21st Ave W Suite 400 ... Seattle WA 98199 206-285-5139 285-1841
Web: www.atsea.org

Beer Institute 122 C St NW Suite 350 ... Washington DC 20001 202-737-2337 737-7004
TF: 800-379-2739 ■ *Web:* www.beerinstitute.org

Biscuit & Cracker Manufacturers Assn (B&CMA)
6325 Woodside Ct Suite 125 ... Columbia MD 21046 443-545-1645 290-8585*
*Fax Area Code: 410 ■ *Web:* www.thebcma.org

Chocolate Manufacturers Assn (CMA)
8320 Old Courthouse Rd Suite 300 ... Vienna VA 22182 703-790-5011 790-5752
TF: 800-433-1200 ■ *Web:* www.chocolateusa.org

CIES - Food Business Forum 8455 Colesville Rd Suite 705 ... Silver Spring MD 20910 301-563-3383 563-3386
Web: www.ciesnet.com

Confrerie de la Chaine des Rotisseurs 285 Madison Ave ... Madison NJ 07940 973-360-9200 360-9330
Web: www.chaineus.org

Council for Responsible Nutrition (CRN)
1828 L St NW Suite 900 ... Washington DC 20036 202-776-7929 204-7980
Web: www.crnusa.org

Distilled Spirits Council of the US Inc (DISCUS)
1250 'I' St NW Suite 400 ... Washington DC 20005 202-628-3544 682-8888
TF: 888-862-7597 ■ *Web:* www.discus.org

Flavor & Extract Manufacturers Assn of the US (FEMA)
1620 'I' St NW Suite 925 ... Washington DC 20006 202-293-5800 463-8998
Web: www.femaflavor.org

Food Institute 1 Broadway 2nd Fl ... Elmwood Park NJ 07407 201-791-5570 791-5222
Web: www.foodinstitute.com

Food Marketing Institute (FMI) 2345 Crystal Dr Suite 800 ... Arlington VA 22202 202-220-0600 429-4519
Web: www.fmi.org

Foodservice Group 630 Village Trace Bldg 15 Suite A ... Marietta GA 30067 770-989-0049 956-7498
Web: www.fsgroup.com

GMA/FPA (Grocery Manufacterers Assn/Food Products Assn)
1350 'I' St NW Suite 300 ... Washington DC 20005 202-337-9400 337-4508
Web: www.gmabrands.com

Grocery Manufacterers Assn/Food Products Assn (GMA/FPA)
1350 'I' St NW Suite 300 ... Washington DC 20005 202-337-9400 337-4508
Web: www.gmabrands.com

Institute of Food Technologists (IFT)
525 W Van Buren St Suite 1000 ... Chicago IL 60607 312-782-8424 782-8348
TF: 800-438-3663 ■ *Web:* www.ift.org

International Assn of Culinary Professionals (IACP)
455 S 4th St Suite 650 ... Louisville KY 40202 502-583-3783 589-3602
TF: 800-928-4227 ■ *Web:* www.iacp.com

International Assn for Food Protection (IAFP)
6200 Aurora Ave Suite 200W ... Des Moines IA 50322 515-276-3344 276-8655
TF: 800-369-6337 ■ *Web:* www.foodprotection.org

International Bottled Water Assn (IBWA)
1700 Diagonal Rd Suite 650 ... Alexandria VA 22314 703-683-5213 683-4074
TF: 800-928-3711 ■ *Web:* www.bottledwater.org

International Dairy-Deli-Bakery Assn (IDDBA) 636 Science Dr ... Madison WI 53711 608-238-7908 238-6330
Web: www.iddba.org

International Dairy Foods Assn (IDFA)
1250 H St NW Suite 900 ... Washington DC 20005 202-737-4332 331-7820
Web: www.idfa.org

International Food Information Council (IFIC)
1100 Connecticut Ave NW Suite 430 ... Washington DC 20036 202-296-6540 296-6547
Web: www.ific.org

International Food Service Executives Assn (IFSEA)
8155 Briar Cliff Dr ... Castle Pines North CO 80108 720-733-8001 733-8999
TF: 800-893-5499 ■ *Web:* www.ifsea.com

International Foodservice Distributors Assn (IFDA)
1410 Spring Hill Rd Suite 210 ... McLean VA 22102 703-532-9400 538-4673
Web: www.ifdaonline.org

International Foodservice Manufacturers Assn (IFMA)
180 N Stetson Ave 2 Prudential Plaza Suite 4400 ... Chicago IL 60601 312-540-4400 540-4401
Web: www.ifmaworld.com

International Ice Cream Assn 1250 H St NW Suite 900 ... Washington DC 20005 202-737-4332 331-7820

Master Brewers Assn of the Americas (MBAA)
3340 Pilot Knob Rd ... Saint Paul MN 55121 651-454-7250 454-0766
Web: www.mbaa.com

National Assn of Catering Executives (NACE)
9881 Broken Land Pkwy Suite 101 ... Columbia MD 21046 410-290-5410 290-5460
Web: www.nace.net

National Assn of Pizzeria Operators 908 S 8th St Suite 200 ... Louisville KY 40203 502-736-9500 736-9501
TF: 800-489-8324 ■ *Web:* www.napo.com

National Assn for the Specialty Food Trade Inc (NASFT)
120 Wall St 27th Fl ... New York NY 10005 212-482-6440 482-6459
TF: 800-627-3869 ■ *Web:* www.specialtyfoodmarket.com

National Beer Wholesalers Assn (NBWA)
1101 King St Suite 600 ... Alexandria VA 22314 703-683-4300 683-8965
TF: 800-300-6417 ■ *Web:* www.nbwa.org

National Cheese Institute 1250 H St NW Suite 900 ... Washington DC 20005 202-737-4332 331-7820

National Coffee Assn of USA Inc (NCA)
15 Maiden Ln Suite 1405 ... New York NY 10038 212-766-4007 766-5815
Web: www.ncausa.org

Organization	City	State	ZIP	Phone	Fax
National Confectioners Assn (NCA) 8320 Old Courthouse Rd Suite 300 *TF:* 800-433-1200 ■ *Web:* www.candyusa.org	Vienna	VA	22182	703-790-5750	790-5752
National Frozen & Refrigerated Foods Assn (NFRA) 4755 Linglestown Rd Suite 300 *Web:* www.nfraweb.org	Harrisburg	PA	17112	717-657-8601	657-9862
National Grocers Assn (NGA) 1005 N Glebe Rd Suite 250 *Web:* www.nationalgrocers.org	Arlington	VA	22201	703-516-0700	516-0115
National Meat Assn (NMA) 1970 Broadway Suite 825 *Web:* www.nmaonline.org	Oakland	CA	94612	510-763-1533	763-6186
National Milk Producers Federation (NMPF) 2101 Wilson Blvd Suite 400 *Web:* www.nmpf.org	Arlington	VA	22201	703-243-6111	841-9328
National Pork Producers Council (NPPC) 122 C St NW Suite 875 *Web:* www.nppc.org	Washington	DC	20001	202-347-3600	347-5265
National Products Assn 2112 E 4th St Suite 200 *TF:* 800-966-6632 ■ *Web:* www.naturalproductsassoc.org	Santa Ana	CA	92705	714-460-7732	460-7444
National Restaurant Assn (NRA) 1200 17th St NW *TF:* 800-424-5156 ■ *Web:* www.restaurant.org	Washington	DC	20036	202-331-5900	331-2429
North American Meat Processors Assn (NAMP) 1910 Association Dr *Web:* www.namp.com	Reston	VA	20191	703-758-1900	758-8001
North American Millers Assn (NAMA) 600 Maryland Ave SW Suite 825-W *Web:* www.namamillers.org	Washington	DC	20024	202-484-2200	488-7416
Popcorn Board 401 N Michigan Ave *TF:* 877-767-2568 ■ *Web:* www.popcorn.org	Chicago	IL	60611	312-644-6610	527-6658
Produce Marketing Assn (PMA) 1500 Casho Mill Rd *Web:* www.pma.com	Newark	DE	19711	302-738-7100	731-2409
RBA - Retailer's Bakery Assn 8201 Greensboro Dr Suite 300 *TF:* 800-638-0924 ■ *Web:* www.rbanet.com	McLean	VA	22102	703-610-9035	610-9005
Retail Confectioners International (RCI) 1807 Glenview Rd Suite 204 *TF:* 800-545-5381 ■ *Web:* www.retailconfectioners.org	Glenview	IL	60025	847-724-6120	724-2719
Salt Institute 700 N Fairfax St Suite 600 *Web:* www.saltinstitute.org	Alexandria	VA	22314	703-549-4648	548-2194
School Nutrition Assn (SNA) 700 S Washington St Suite 300 *TF:* 800-877-8822 ■ *Web:* www.schoolnutrition.org	Alexandria	VA	22314	703-739-3900	739-3915
Snack Food Assn 1600 Wilson Blvd Suite 650 *TF:* 800-628-1334 ■ *Web:* www.sfa.org	Arlington	VA	22209	703-836-4500	836-8262
Specialty Coffee Assn of America (SCAA) 330 Golden Shore Ave Suite 50 *Web:* www.scaa.org	Long Beach	CA	90802	562-624-4100	624-4101
Tea Assn of the USA Inc 362 5th Ave Suite 801 *Web:* www.teausa.com	New York	NY	10001	212-986-9415	697-8658
Tea Council of the USA Inc 362 5th Ave Suite 801 *Web:* www.teausa.com	New York	NY	10001	212-986-6998	697-8658
US Dairy Export Council 2101 Wilson Blvd Suite 400 *Web:* www.usdec.org	Arlington	VA	22201	703-528-3049	528-3705
US Meat Export Federation Inc (USMEF) 1050 17th St Suite 2200 *Web:* www.usmef.org	Denver	CO	80265	303-623-6328	623-0297
USA Poultry & Egg Export Council (USAPEEC) 2300 W Park Place Blvd Suite 100 *Web:* www.usapeec.org	Stone Mountain	GA	30087	770-413-0006	413-0007
Wheat Foods Council 10841 S Crossroads Dr Suite 105 *Web:* www.wheatfoods.org	Parker	CO	80134	303-840-8787	840-6877
Wine Institute 425 Market St Suite 1000 *Web:* www.wineinstitute.org	San Francisco	CA	94105	415-512-0151	442-0742
Wine & Spirits Shippers Assn Inc (WSSA) 11800 Sunrise Valley Dr Suite 332 *TF:* 800-368-3167 ■ *Web:* www.wssa.com	Reston	VA	22091	703-860-2300	860-2422
Wine & Spirits Wholesalers of America Inc (WSWA) 805 15th St NW Suite 430 *Web:* www.wswa.org	Washington	DC	20005	202-371-9792	789-2405
WineAmerica 1212 New York Ave NW Suite 425 *TF:* 800-879-4637 ■ *Web:* www.wineamerica.org	Washington	DC	20005	202-783-2756	347-6341
World Cocoa Foundation (WCF) 8320 Old Courthouse Rd Suite 300 *Web:* www.worldcocoafoundation.org	Vienna	VA	22182	703-790-5012	790-0168

49-7 Government & Public Administration Professional Associations

Organization	City	State	ZIP	Phone	Fax
American Assn of Motor Vehicle Administrators (AAMVA) 4301 Wilson Blvd Suite 400 *TF:* 800-515-8881 ■ *Web:* www.aamva.org	Arlington	VA	22203	703-522-4200	522-1553
American Assn of State Highway & Transportation Officials (AASHTO) 444 N Capitol St NW Suite 249 *Web:* www.transportation.org	Washington	DC	20001	202-624-5800	624-5806
American Conference of Governmental Industrial Hygienists (ACGIH) 1330 Kemper Meadows Dr *Web:* www.acgih.org	Cincinnati	OH	45240	513-742-2020	742-3355
American Correctional Assn (ACA) 206 N Washington St Suite 200 *TF:* 800-222-5646 ■ *Web:* www.aca.org	Alexandria	VA	22314	703-224-0000	224-0010
American Federation of Police & Concerned Citizens 6350 Horizon Dr *Web:* www.aphf.org/afp_cc.html	Titusville	FL	32780	321-264-0911	264-0033
American Foreign Service Assn (AFSA) 2101 'E' St NW *TF:* 800-704-2372 ■ *Web:* www.afsa.org	Washington	DC	20037	202-338-4045	338-6820
American Foreign Service Protective Assn 1716 'N' St NW *Web:* www.afspa.org	Washington	DC	20036	202-833-4910	833-4918
American Jail Assn (AJA) 1135 Professional Ct *Web:* www.aja.org	Hagerstown	MD	21740	301-790-3930	790-2941
American Public Human Services Assn (APHSA) 810 1st St NE Suite 500 *Web:* www.aphsa.org	Washington	DC	20002	202-682-0100	289-6555
American Public Works Assn (APWA) 2345 Grand Blvd Suite 500 *Web:* www.apwa.net	Kansas City	MO	64108	816-472-6100	472-1610
American Society for Public Administration (ASPA) 1301 Pennsylvania Ave NW Suite 840 *Web:* www.aspanet.org	Washington	DC	20004	202-393-7878	638-4952
APCO International 351 N Williamson Blvd *TF:* 888-272-6911 ■ *Web:* www.apcointl.org	Daytona Beach	FL	32114	386-322-2500	322-2501
Association of Conservation Engineers (ACE) Missouri Department of Conservation PO Box 180 *Web:* conservationengineers.org	Jefferson City	MO	65102	573-522-4115	522-2324
Association of Local Air Pollution Control Officials (ALAPCO) 444 N Capitol St NW Suite 307 *Web:* www.cleanairworld.org	Washington	DC	20001	202-624-7864	624-7863
Association of Maternal & Child Health Programs (AMCHP) 1220 19th St NW Suite 801 *Web:* www.amchp.org	Washington	DC	20036	202-775-0436	466-5471
Association of Public Health Laboratories (APHL) 8515 Georgia Ave Suite 700 *Web:* www.aphl.org	Silver Spring	MD	20910	240-485-2745	485-2700
Association of Public-Safety Communications Officials International Inc 351 N Williamson Blvd *TF:* 888-272-6911 ■ *Web:* www.apcointl.org	Daytona Beach	FL	32114	386-322-2500	322-2501
Association of Racing Commissioners International (ARCI) 2343 Alexandria Dr Suite 200 *Web:* www.arci.com	Lexington	KY	40504	859-224-7070	224-7071
Association of Social Work Boards (ASWB) 400 Southridge Pkwy Suite B *TF:* 800-225-6880 ■ *Web:* www.aswb.org	Culpeper	VA	22701	540-829-6880	829-0142
Association of State & Interstate Water Pollution Control Administrators (ASIWPCA) 1221 Connecticut Ave NW 2nd Fl *Web:* www.asiwpca.org	Washington	DC	20036	202-756-0600	898-0929
Association of State & Provincial Psychology Boards (ASPPB) PO Box 241245 *TF:* 800-448-4069 ■ *Web:* www.asppb.org	Montgomery	AL	36124	334-832-4580	269-6379
Association of State & Territorial Health Officials (ASTHO) 2231 Crystal Dr Suite 450 **Fax Area Code:* 571 ■ *Web:* www.astho.org	Arlington	VA	22203	202-371-9090	527-3189*
Association of State & Territorial Solid Waste Management Officials (ASTSWMO) 444 N Capitol St NW Suite 315 *Web:* www.astswmo.org	Washington	DC	20001	202-624-5828	624-7875
Association of State Wetland Managers 2 Basin Rd *Web:* www.aswm.org	Windham	ME	04062	207-892-3399	892-3089
Commission on Accreditation for Law Enforcement Agencies (CALEA) 10302 Eaton Pl Suite 100 *TF:* 800-368-3757 ■ *Web:* www.calea.org	Fairfax	VA	22030	703-352-4225	591-2206
Conference of Radiation Control Program Directors (CRCPD) 205 Capitol Ave *Web:* www.crcpd.org	Frankfort	KY	40601	502-227-4543	227-7862
Conference of State Bank Supervisors (CSBS) 1155 Connecticut Ave NW 5th Fl *TF:* 800-886-2727 ■ *Web:* www.csbs.org	Washington	DC	20036	202-296-2840	296-1928
Council on Licensure Enforcement & Regulation (CLEAR) 403 Marquis Ave Suite 100 *Web:* www.clearhq.org	Lexington	KY	40502	859-269-1289	231-1943
Council of State Governments (CSG) 2760 Research Park Dr *TF Sales:* 800-800-1910 ■ *Web:* www.csg.org	Lexington	KY	40578	859-244-8000	244-8001
Council of State & Territorial Epidemiologists (CSTE) 2872 Woodcock Blvd Suite 303 *Web:* www.cste.org	Atlanta	GA	30341	770-458-3811	458-8516
CSBS (Conference of State Bank Supervisors) 1155 Connecticut Ave NW 5th Fl *TF:* 800-886-2727 ■ *Web:* www.csbs.org	Washington	DC	20036	202-296-2840	296-1928
Federal Bureau of Investigation Agents Assn (FBIAA) PO Box 12650 *Web:* www.fbiaa.org	Arlington	VA	22219	703-247-2173	247-2175
Federal Law Enforcement Officers Assn (FLEOA) PO Box 326 *Web:* www.fleoa.org	Lewisberry	PA	17339	717-938-2300	932-2262
Federal Managers Assn (FMA) 1641 Prince St *Web:* www.fedmanagers.org	Alexandria	VA	22314	703-683-8700	683-8707
Federally Employed Women Inc (FEW) 1666 K St NW Suite 440 **Fax Area Code:* 703 ■ *Web:* www.few.org	Washington	DC	20006	202-898-0994	299-9233*
Federation of State Medical Boards of the US Inc (FSMB) 400 Fuller Wiser Rd Suite 300 *TF:* 800-876-5396 ■ *Web:* www.fsmb.org	Euless	TX	76039	817-868-4000	868-4099
Federation of Tax Administrators (FTA) 444 N Capitol St NW Suite 348 *Web:* www.taxadmin.org	Washington	DC	20001	202-624-5890	624-7888
Forest Service Employees for Environmental Ethics (FSEEE) PO Box 11615 *Web:* www.fseee.org	Eugene	OR	97440	541-484-2692	484-3004
Government Finance Officers Assn (GFOA) 203 N LaSalle St Suite 2700 *Web:* www.gfoa.org	Chicago	IL	60601	312-977-9700	977-4806
International Assn of Arson Investigators (IAAI) 2151 Priest Bridge Dr Suite 25 *Web:* www.firearson.com	Crofton	MD	21114	410-451-3473	451-9049
International Assn of Assessing Officers (IAAO) 314 W 10th St *TF:* 800-616-4226 ■ *Web:* www.iaao.org	Kansas City	MO	64105	816-701-8100	701-8149
International Assn of Auto Theft Investigators (IAATI) PO Box 223 *Web:* www.iaati.org	Clinton	NY	13323	315-853-1913	793-0048
International Assn of Chiefs of Police (IACP) 515 N Washington St *TF:* 800-843-4227 ■ *Web:* www.theiacp.org	Alexandria	VA	22314	703-836-6767	836-4543
International Assn of Fire Chiefs (IAFC) 4025 Fair Ridge Dr Suite 300 *TF:* 866-385-9110 ■ *Web:* www.iafc.org	Fairfax	VA	22033	703-273-0911	273-9363
International Assn of Fish & Wildlife Agencies (IAFWA) 444 N Capitol St NW Suite 725 *Web:* www.fishwildlife.org	Washington	DC	20001	202-624-7890	624-7891
International Assn of Plumbing & Mechanical Officials (IAPMO) 5001 E Philadelphia St *Web:* www.iapmo.org	Ontario	CA	91761	909-472-4100	472-4150
International Bridge Tunnel & Turnpike Assn (IBTTA) 1146 19th St NW Suite 800 *Web:* www.ibtta.org	Washington	DC	20036	202-659-4620	659-0500
International City/County Management Assn (ICMA) 777 N Capitol St NE Suite 500 *Web:* www.icma.org	Washington	DC	20002	202-289-4262	962-3500
International Conference of Funeral Service Examining Boards Inc 1885 Shelby Ln *Web:* www.theconferenceonline.org	Fayetteville	AR	72704	479-442-7076	442-7090
International Institute of Municipal Clerks (IIMC) 8331 Utica Ave Suite 200 *TF:* 800-251-1639 ■ *Web:* www.iimc.com	Rancho Cucamonga	CA	91730	909-944-4162	944-8545
International Municipal Signal Assn (IMSA) 165 E Union St PO Box 539 *TF:* 800-723-4672 ■ *Web:* www.imsasafety.org	Newark	NY	14513	315-331-2182	331-8205
International Narcotic Enforcement Officers Assn (INEOA) 112 State St Suite 1200 *Web:* www.ineoa.org	Albany	NY	12207	518-463-6232	432-3378
International Society of Fire Service Instructors (ISFSI) 2425 Hwy 49 E **Fax Area Code:* 615 ■ *Web:* www.isfsi.org	Pleasant View	TN	37146	800-435-0005	746-1170*
Kansas Assn of Counties (KAC) 300 SW 8th St 3rd Fl *Web:* www.kansascounties.org	Topeka	KS	66603	785-272-2585	272-3585
Maryland Assn of Counties (MACo) 169 Conduit St *Web:* www.mdcounties.org	Annapolis	MD	21401	410-269-0043	268-1775

Government & Public Administration Professional Associations (Cont'd)

Phone | Fax

Midwest Association of Fish & Wildlife Agencies
Wisconsin Department of Natural Resources 107 Sutliff Ave. .... Rhinelander WI 54501 715-365-8924 365-8932
Web: mafwa.iafwa.org

NACCHO (National Assn of County & City Health Officials)
1100 17th St 2nd Fl. .... Washington DC 20036 202-783-5550 783-1583
Web: www.naccho.org

NAGE (National Assn of Government Employees)
159 Burgin Pkwy .... Quincy MA 02169 617-376-0220 376-0285
Web: www.nage.org

National Academy of Public Administration
900 7th St NW Suite 600 .... Washington DC 20001 202-347-3190 393-0993
TF: 800-883-3190 ■ *Web:* www.napawash.org

National Alcohol Beverage Control Assn (NABCA)
4401 Ford Ave Suite 700 .... Alexandria VA 22302 703-578-4200 820-3551
Web: www.nabca.org

National American Indian Housing Council (NAIHC)
50 F St NW Suite 3300 .... Washington DC 20001 202-789-1754 789-1758
TF: 800-284-9165 ■ *Web:* www.naihc.net

National Assembly of State Arts Agencies (NASAA)
1029 Vermont Ave NW 2nd Fl. .... Washington DC 20005 202-347-6352 737-0526
Web: www.nasaa-arts.org

National Assn of Area Agencies on Aging (N4A)
1730 Rhode Island Ave NW Suite 1200 .... Washington DC 20036 202-872-0888 872-0057
Web: www.n4a.org

National Assn of Attorneys General (NAAG)
2030 M St NW 8th Fl. .... Washington DC 20036 202-326-6000 331-1427
TF: 888-245-6224 ■ *Web:* www.naag.org

National Assn of Boards of Examiners of Long Term Care Administrators (NAB) 1444 'I' St NW Suite 700 .... Washington DC 20005 202-712-9040 216-9646
Web: www.nabweb.org

National Assn of Boards of Pharmacy (NABP)
1600 Feehanville Dr .... Mount Prospect IL 60056 847-391-4406 391-4502
Web: www.nabp.net

National Assn of Chiefs of Police (NACOP) 6350 Horizon Dr .... Titusville FL 32780 321-264-0911 264-0033
Web: www.aphf.org/nacop.html

National Assn of Clean Water Agencies (NACWA)
1816 Jefferson Pl NW .... Washington DC 20036 202-833-2672 833-4657
Web: www.nacwa.org

National Assn of Conservation Districts (NACD)
509 Capitol Ct NE. .... Washington DC 20002 202-547-6223 547-6450
TF: 888-695-2433 ■ *Web:* www.nacdnet.org

National Assn of Counties (NACo)
25 Massachusetts Ave NW Suite 500 .... Washington DC 20001 202-393-6226 393-2630
Web: www.naco.org

National Assn of County & City Health Officials (NACCHO)
1100 17th St 2nd Fl. .... Washington DC 20036 202-783-5550 783-1583
Web: www.naccho.org

National Assn of Government Archives & Records Administrators (NAGARA) 90 State St Suite 1009 .... Albany NY 12207 518-463-8644 463-8656
Web: www.nagara.org

National Assn of Government Employees (NAGE)
159 Burgin Pkwy .... Quincy MA 02169 617-376-0220 376-0285
Web: www.nage.org

National Assn of Housing & Redevelopment Officials (NAHRO)
630 'I' St NW .... Washington DC 20001 202-289-3500 289-8181
TF: 877-866-2476 ■ *Web:* www.nahro.org

National Assn of Insurance Commissioners (NAIC)
2301 McGee St Suite 800 .... Kansas City MO 64108 816-842-3600 783-8175
Web: www.naic.org

National Assn of Latino Elected & Appointed Officials (NALEO) 1122 W Washington Blvd 3rd Fl .... Los Angeles CA 90015 213-747-7606 747-7664
Web: www.naleo.org

National Assn of Local Housing Finance Agencies (NALHFA)
2025 M St NW Suite 800 .... Washington DC 20036 202-367-1197 367-2197
Web: www.nalhfa.org

National Assn of Postal Supervisors (NAPS)
1727 King St Suite 400 .... Alexandria VA 22314 703-836-9660 836-9665
Web: www.naps.org

National Assn of Postmasters of the US (NAPUS)
8 Herbert St .... Alexandria VA 22305 703-683-9027 683-6820
Web: www.napus.org

National Assn of Regional Councils (NARC)
1666 Connecticut Ave NW Suite 300 .... Washington DC 20009 202-986-1032 986-1038
Web: www.narc.org

National Assn of Regulatory Utility Commissioners (NARUC)
1101 Vermont Ave NW Suite 200 .... Washington DC 20005 202-898-2200 898-2213
Web: www.naruc.org

National Assn of Rehabilitation Providers & Agencies (NARA)
12100 Sunset Hills Rd Suite 130 .... Reston VA 20190 703-437-4377 435-4390
Web: www.naranet.org

National Assn for Search & Rescue (NASAR)
4500 Southgate Pl Suite 100 .... Chantilly VA 20151 703-222-6277 222-6283
TF: 877-893-0702 ■ *Web:* www.nasar.org

National Assn of Social Workers (NASW)
750 1st St NE Suite 700 .... Washington DC 20002 202-408-8600 336-8311
TF: 800-638-8799 ■ *Web:* www.naswdc.org

National Assn of State Alcohol & Drug Abuse Directors (NASADAD) 808 17th St NW Suite 410 .... Washington DC 20006 202-293-0090 293-1250
Web: www.nasadad.org

National Assn of State Auditors Comptrollers & Treasurers (NASACT) 449 Lewis Hargett Cir Suite 290 .... Lexington KY 40503 859-276-1147 278-0507
Web: www.nasact.org

National Assn of State Aviation Officials (NASAO)
Reagan National Airport Hangar 7 Suite 218 .... Washington DC 20001 703-417-1880 417-1885
Web: www.nasao.org

National Assn of State Budget Officers (NASBO)
444 N Capitol St NW Suite 642 .... Washington DC 20001 202-624-5382 624-7745
Web: www.nasbo.org

National Assn of State Chief Information Officers
201 E Main St Suite 1405 .... Lexington KY 40507 859-514-9156 514-9166
Web: www.nascio.org

National Assn of State Departments of Agriculture (NASDA)
1156 15th St NW Suite 1020 .... Washington DC 20005 202-296-9680 296-9686
Web: www.nasda.org

National Assn of State Fire Marshals (NASFM)
1319 F St NW Suite 301 .... Washington DC 20004 202-737-1226 393-1296
TF: 877-996-2736 ■ *Web:* www.firemarshals.org

National Assn of State Foresters (NASF)
444 N Capitol St NW Suite 540 .... Washington DC 20001 202-624-5415 624-5407
Web: www.stateforesters.org

National Assn of State Mental Health Program Directors (NASMHPD) 66 Canal Center Plaza Suite 302 .... Alexandria VA 22314 703-739-9333 548-9517
Web: www.nasmhpd.org

National Assn of State Procurement Officials (NASPO)
201 E Main St Suite 1405 .... Lexington KY 40507 859-514-9159
Web: www.naspo.org

National Assn of State Units on Aging
1201 15th St NW Suite 350 .... Washington DC 20005 202-898-2578 898-2583
Web: www.nasua.org

National Assn of State Workforce Agencies
444 N Capitol St NW Suite 142 .... Washington DC 20001 202-434-8020 434-8033
Web: www.naswa.org

National Assn of Towns & Townships (NATaT)
1130 Connecticut Ave NW Suite 300 .... Washington DC 20036 202-454-3954 331-1598
TF: 866-830-0008 ■ *Web:* www.natat.org

National Assn of Unclaimed Property Administrators (NAUPA)
2760 Research Park Dr .... Lexington KY 40511 859-244-8150 244-8053
Web: www.unclaimed.org

National Board of Boiler & Pressure Vessel Inspectors
1055 Crupper Ave .... Columbus OH 43229 614-888-8320 847-1147*
**Fax:* Cust Svc ■ *Web:* www.nationalboard.org

National Center for State Courts (NCSC) 300 Newport Ave. .... Williamsburg VA 23185 757-253-2000 564-2022
TF: 800-616-6164 ■ *Web:* www.ncsconline.org

National Conference of State Historic Preservation Officers
444 N Capitol St NW Suite 342 .... Washington DC 20001-1512 202-624-5465 624-5419
Web: www.ncshpo.org

National Conference of State Legislatures 7700 E 1st Pl .... Denver CO 80230 303-364-7700 364-7800
Web: www.ncsl.org

National Conference of States on Building Codes & Standards (NCSBCS) 505 Huntmar Park Dr Suite 210 .... Herndon VA 20170 703-481-2038 481-3596
TF: 800-362-2633 ■ *Web:* www.ncsbcs.org

National Council of Architectural Registration Boards (NCARB) 1801 K St NW Suite 700-K .... Washington DC 20006 202-783-6500 783-0290
Web: www.ncarb.org

National Council of State Housing Agencies (NCSHA)
444 N Capitol St NW Suite 438 .... Washington DC 20001 202-624-7710 624-5899
Web: www.ncsha.org

National Council of State Tourism Directors (NCSTD)
1100 New York Ave NW Suite 450 .... Washington DC 20005 202-408-8422 408-1255
Web: www.tia.org/councils/ncstd.asp

National District Attorneys Assn (NDAA)
99 Canal Center Plaza Suite 510 .... Alexandria VA 22314 703-549-9222 836-3195
Web: www.ndaa.org

National Emergency Management Assn (NEMA)
PO Box 11910 .... Lexington KY 40578 859-244-8000 244-8002
Web: www.nemaweb.org

National Environmental Health Assn (NEHA)
720 S Colorado Blvd 100 N Tower .... Denver CO 80246 303-756-9090 691-9490
Web: www.neha.org

National Fire Protection Assn (NFPA) 1 Batterymarch Pk .... Quincy MA 02169 617-770-3000 770-0700
TF: 800-344-3555 ■ *Web:* www.nfpa.org

National Forum for Black Public Administrators (NFBPA)
777 N Capitol St NE Suite 807 .... Washington DC 20002 202-408-9300 408-8558
Web: www.nfbpa.org

National Governors Assn (NGA)
444 N Capitol St NW Suite 267 .... Washington DC 20001 202-624-5300 624-5313
Web: www.nga.org

National Institute of Governmental Purchasing (NIGP)
151 Spring St. .... Herndon VA 20170 703-736-8900 736-9644
TF: 800-367-6447 ■ *Web:* www.nigp.org

National League of Cities (NLC)
1301 Pennsylvania Ave NW Suite 550 .... Washington DC 20004 202-626-3000 626-3043
Web: www.nlc.org

National Organization of Black Law Enforcement Executives (NOBLE) 4609 Pinecrest Office Park Dr Suite F .... Alexandria VA 22312 703-658-1529 658-9479
Web: www.noblenatl.org

National Recreation and Park Association (NACPRO)
22377 Belmont Ridge Rd. .... Ashburn VA 20148 703-858-0784 858-0794
Web: www.nrpa.org

National Sheriffs' Assn (NSA) 1450 Duke St .... Alexandria VA 22314 703-836-7827 683-6541
TF: 800-424-7827 ■ *Web:* www.sheriffs.org

National Ski Patrol System Inc (NSP)
133 S Van Gordon St Suite 100 .... Lakewood CO 80228 303-988-1111 988-3005
Web: www.nsp.org

National Volunteer Fire Council (NVFC)
7582 Walker Dr Suite 450 .... Greenbelt MD 20770 202-887-5700 887-5291
TF: 888-275-6832 ■ *Web:* www.nvfc.org

North American Assn of State & Provincial Lotteries (NASPL)
6 N Broadway .... Geneva OH 44041 440-466-5630 466-5649
Web: www.naspl.org

Opportunity Finance Network 620 Chestnut St Suite 572 .... Philadelphia PA 19106 215-923-4754 923-4755
Web: www.opportunityfinance.net

Police Executive Research Forum (PERF)
1120 Connecticut Ave NW Suite 930 .... Washington DC 20036 202-466-7820 466-7826
TF: 888-202-4563 ■ *Web:* www.policeforum.org

Public Employees Roundtable (PER) PO Box 75248 .... Washington DC 20013 202-927-4926 927-4920
Web: www.theroundtable.org

Public Risk Management Assn (PRIMA)
500 Montgomery St Suite 750 .... Alexandria VA 22314 703-528-7701 739-0200
Web: www.primacentral.org

Public Technology Inc
1301 Pennsylvania Ave NW Suite 830 .... Washington DC 20004 202-626-2400 626-2498
Web: www.pti.org

State & Territorial Air Pollution Program Administrators (STAPPA) 444 N Capitol St NW Suite 307 .... Washington DC 20001 202-624-7864 624-7863
Web: www.cleanairworld.org

United Federation of Police Officers 540 N State Rd .... Briarcliff Manor NY 10510 914-941-4103 941-4472
TF: 800-227-4291 ■ *Web:* www.policefederation.com

US Conference of Mayors 1620 'I' St NW Suite 400 .... Washington DC 20006 202-293-7330 293-2352
Web: www.usmayors.org

US Ombudsman Assn (USOA) 5619 NW 86th St Suite 600 .... Johnston IA 50131 515-225-2323 225-6363
Web: www.usombudsman.org

West Virginia Assn of Counties 2211 Washington St .... Charleston WV 25311 304-346-0591 346-0592
Web: www.wvcounties.org

49-8 Health & Medical Professionals Associations

Phone | Fax

AABB: Advancing Transfusion and Cellular Therapies Worldwide
8101 Glenbrook Rd .... Bethesda MD 20814 301-907-6977 907-6895
Web: www.aabb.org

Academic Orthopaedic Society (AOS)
6300 N River Rd Suite 505 .... Rosemont IL 60018 847-318-7330 318-7339

Academy of General Dentistry (AGD)
211 E Chicago Ave Suite 900 .... Chicago IL 60611 312-440-4300 440-0559
TF: 888-243-3368 ■ *Web:* www.agd.org

Academy for International Health Studies (AIHS)
37 Aspen Dr. .... South Glastonbury CT 06073 860-430-1388 430-1420
Web: www.aihs.com

Organization / Address	City	State	Zip	Phone	Fax
Academy of Managed Care Pharmacy (AMCP)					
100 N Pitt St Suite 400	Alexandria	VA	22314	703-683-8416	683-8417
TF: 800-827-2627 ■ *Web:* www.amcp.org					
Academy of Osseointegration					
85 W Algonquin Rd Suite 550	Arlington Heights	IL	60005	847-439-1919	439-1569
TF: 800-656-7736 ■ *Web:* www.osseo.org					
Academy of Pharmacy Practice & Management					
American Pharmacists Assn 1100 15th St NW Suite 400	Washington	DC	20005	202-628-4410	783-2351
TF: 800-237-2742 ■ *Web:* www.pharmacist.com					
Academy of Students of Pharmacy					
American Pharmacists Assn 1100 15th St NW Suite 400	Washington	DC	20005	202-628-4410	783-2351
TF: 800-237-2742 ■ *Web:* www.pharmacist.com					
AcademyHealth 1150 17th St NW Suite 600	Washington	DC	20036	202-292-6700	292-6800
Web: www.academyhealth.org					
Aerospace Medical Assn (AsMA) 320 S Henry St	Alexandria	VA	22314	703-739-2240	739-9652
Web: www.asma.org					
AHA (American Hospital Assn) 1 N Franklin St	Chicago	IL	60606	312-422-3000	422-4796
TF: 800-424-4301 ■ *Web:* www.aha.org					
AMA (American Medical Assn) 515 N State St	Chicago	IL	60610	312-464-5000	464-4184
TF: 800-621-8335 ■ *Web:* www.ama-assn.org					
American Academy of Allergy Asthma & Immunology (AAAAI)					
611 E Wells St 4th Fl	Milwaukee	WI	53202	414-272-6071	272-6070
TF: 800-822-2762 ■ *Web:* www.aaaai.org					
American Academy of Ambulatory Care Nursing (AAACN)					
200 E Holly Ave Box 56	Pitman	NJ	08071	856-256-2350	589-7463
TF: 800-262-6877 ■ *Web:* www.aaacn.org					
American Academy of Audiology (AAA)					
11730 Plaza America Dr Suite 300	Reston	VA	20190	703-790-8466	790-8631
TF: 800-222-2336 ■ *Web:* www.audiology.org					
American Academy of Cosmetic Dentistry (AACD)					
5401 World Dairy Dr	Madison	WI	53718	608-222-8583	222-9540
TF: 800-543-9220 ■ *Web:* www.aacd.com					
American Academy of Cosmetic Surgery (AACS)					
737 N Michigan Ave Suite 2100	Chicago	IL	60611	312-981-6760	981-6787
Web: www.cosmeticsurgery.org					
American Academy of Dental Group Practice (AADGP)					
2525 E Arizona Biltmore Cir Suite 127	Phoenix	AZ	85016	602-381-1185	381-1093
Web: www.aadgp.org					
American Academy of Dermatology (AAD)					
930 E Woodfield Rd PO Box 4014	Schaumburg	IL	60168	847-330-0230	330-0050
Web: www.aad.org					
American Academy of Disability Evaluating Physicians (AADEP)					
150 N Wacker Dr Suite 1420	Chicago	IL	60606	312-658-1171	658-1175
TF: 800-456-6095 ■ *Web:* www.aadep.org					
American Academy of Facial Plastic & Reconstructive Surgery					
(AAFPRS) 310 S Henry St	Alexandria	VA	22314	703-299-9291	299-8898
TF: 800-332-3223 ■ *Web:* www.aafprs.org					
American Academy of Family Physicians (AAFP)					
11400 Tomahawk Creek Pkwy	Leawood	KS	66211	913-906-6000	906-6075
TF: 800-274-2237 ■ *Web:* www.aafp.org					
American Academy of Home Care Physicians (AAHCP)					
PO Box 1037	Edgewood	MD	21040	410-676-7966	
Web: www.aahcp.org					
American Academy of Hospice & Palliative Medicine (AAHPM)					
4700 W Lake Ave	Glenview	IL	60025	847-375-4712	734-8671*
**Fax Area Code:* 877 ■ *Web:* www.aahpm.org					
American Academy of Neurology (AAN) 1080 Montreal Ave	Saint Paul	MN	55116	651-695-1940	695-2791
TF: 800-879-1960 ■ *Web:* www.aan.com					
American Academy of Nurse Practitioners (AANP)					
PO Box 12846	Austin	TX	78711	512-442-4262	442-6469
Web: www.aanp.org					
American Academy of Ophthalmology 655 Beach St	San Francisco	CA	94109	415-561-8500	561-8575
TF: 866-561-8558 ■ *Web:* www.aao.org					
American Academy of Optometry (AAO)					
6110 Executive Blvd Suite 506	Rockville	MD	20852	301-984-1441	984-4737
Web: www.aaopt.org					
American Academy of Orthopaedic Surgeons (AAOS)					
6300 N River Rd	Rosemont	IL	60018	847-823-7186	823-8125
Web: www.aaos.org					
American Academy of Orthotists & Prosthetists (AAOP)					
526 King St Suite 201	Alexandria	VA	22314	703-836-0788	836-0737
Web: www.oandp.org					
American Academy of Otolaryngology-Head & Neck Surgery					
(AAO-HNS) 1 Prince St	Alexandria	VA	22314	703-836-4444	683-5100
Web: www.entnet.org					
American Academy of Pain Management (AAPM)					
13947 Mono Way Suite A	Sonora	CA	95370	209-533-9744	533-9750
Web: www.aapainmanage.org					
American Academy of Pediatric Dentistry (AAPD)					
211 E Chicago Ave Suite 700	Chicago	IL	60611	312-337-2169	337-6329
Web: www.aapd.org					
American Academy of Pediatrics (AAP)					
141 Northwest Point Blvd	Elk Grove Village	IL	60007	847-434-4000	434-8000
TF: 800-433-9016 ■ *Web:* www.aap.org					
American Academy of Periodontology (AAP)					
737 N Michigan Ave Suite 800	Chicago	IL	60611	312-787-5518	787-3670
TF: 800-282-4867 ■ *Web:* www.perio.org					
American Academy of Physical Medicine & Rehabilitation					
(AAPM&R) 1 IBM Plaza Suite 2500	Chicago	IL	60611	312-464-9700	464-0227
TF: 877-227-6799 ■ *Web:* www.aapmr.org					
American Academy of Physician Assistants (AAPA)					
950 N Washington St	Alexandria	VA	22314	703-836-2272	684-1924
Web: www.aapa.org					
American Assn of Bioanalysts (AAB)					
906 Olive St Suite 1200	Saint Louis	MO	63101	314-241-1445	241-1449
Web: www.aab.org					
American Assn for Cancer Research (AACR)					
615 Chestnut St 17th Fl	Philadelphia	PA	19106	215-440-9300	440-7228
TF: 866-423-3965 ■ *Web:* www.aacr.org					
American Assn of Clinical Endocrinologists (AACE)					
1000 Riverside Ave Suite 205	Jacksonville	FL	32204	904-353-7878	353-8185
Web: www.aace.com					
American Assn of Colleges of Osteopathic Medicine					
(AACOM) 5550 Friendship Blvd Suite 310	Chevy Chase	MD	20815	301-968-4100	968-4101
Web: www.aacom.org					
American Assn of Colleges of Podiatric Medicine (AACPM)					
15850 Crabbs Branch Way Suite 320	Rockville	MD	20855	800-922-9266	948-1928*
**Fax Area Code:* 301 ■ *TF:* 800-922-9266 ■ *Web:* www.aacpm.org					
American Assn of Critical-Care Nurses (AACN)					
101 Columbia	Aliso Viejo	CA	92656	949-362-2000	362-2020
TF: 800-809-2273 ■ *Web:* www.aacn.org					
American Assn of Diabetes Educators (AADE)					
100 W Monroe St Suite 400	Chicago	IL	60603	312-424-2426	424-2427
TF: 800-338-3633 ■ *Web:* www.aadenet.org					
American Assn of Endodontists (AAE)					
211 E Chicago Ave Suite 1100	Chicago	IL	60611	312-266-7255	266-9867
TF: 800-872-3636 ■ *Web:* www.aae.org					
American Assn of Gynecological Laparoscopists (AAGL)					
6757 Katella Ave	Cypress	CA	90630	714-503-6200	503-6201
TF: 800-554-2245 ■ *Web:* www.aagl.com					
American Assn of Healthcare Consultants (AAHC)					
5938 N Drake Ave	Chicago	IL	60659	888-350-2242	463-3552*
**Fax Area Code:* 773 ■ *Web:* www.aahc.net					
American Assn for Homecare 625 Slaters Ln Suite 200	Alexandria	VA	22314	703-836-6263	836-6730
Web: www.aahomecare.org					
American Assn of Immunologists (AAI) 9650 Rockville Pike	Bethesda	MD	20814	301-634-7178	634-7887
Web: www.aai.org					
American Assn of Integrated Healthcare Delivery Systems Inc					
(AAIHDS) 4435 Waterfront Dr Suite 101	Glen Allen	VA	23060	804-747-5823	747-5316
Web: www.aaihds.org					
American Assn of Medical Assistants (AAMA)					
20 N Wacker Dr Suite 1575	Chicago	IL	60606	312-899-1500	899-1259
TF: 800-228-2262 ■ *Web:* www.aama-ntl.org					
American Assn of Medical Review Officers					
(AAMRO) PO Box 12873	Research Triangle Park	NC	27709	919-489-5407	490-1010
TF: 800-489-1839 ■ *Web:* www.aamro.com					
American Assn of Medical Society Executives (AAMSE)					
555 E Wells St Suite 1100	Milwaukee	WI	53202	414-221-9275	276-3349
Web: www.aamse.org					
American Assn of Neurological Surgeons (AANS)					
5550 Meadowbrook Dr	Rolling Meadows	IL	60008	847-378-0500	378-0600
TF: 888-566-2267 ■ *Web:* www.aans.org					
American Assn of Neuromuscular & Electrodiagnostic					
Medicine (AANEM) 421 1st Ave SW Suite 300E	Rochester	MN	55902	507-288-0100	288-1225
Web: www.aanem.org					
American Assn of Neuroscience Nurses (AANN)					
4700 W Lake Ave	Glenview	IL	60025	847-375-4733	734-8677*
**Fax Area Code:* 877 ■ *TF:* 888-557-2266 ■ *Web:* www.aann.org					
American Assn of Nurse Anesthetists (AANA)					
222 S Prospect Ave	Park Ridge	IL	60068	847-692-7050	692-6968
Web: www.aana.com					
American Assn of Nutritional Consultants (AANC)					
401 Kings Hwy	Winona Lake	IN	46590	574-269-6165	268-2120
TF: 888-828-2262 ■ *Web:* www.aanc.net					
American Assn of Occupational Health Nurses (AAOHN)					
2920 Brandywine Rd Suite 100	Atlanta	GA	30341	770-455-7757	455-7271
TF: 888-646-4631 ■ *Web:* www.aaohn.org					
American Assn of Oral & Maxillofacial Surgeons (AAOMS)					
9700 W Bryn Mawr Ave	Rosemont	IL	60018	847-678-6200	678-6286
TF: 800-822-6637 ■ *Web:* www.aaoms.org					
American Assn of Oriental Medicine (AAOM)					
PO Box 162340	Sacramento	CA	95816	916-443-4770	443-4766
TF: 866-455-7999 ■ *Web:* www.aaom.org					
American Assn of Orthodontists (AAO)					
401 N Lindbergh Blvd	Saint Louis	MO	63141	314-993-1700	997-1745
TF: 800-424-2841 ■ *Web:* www.braces.org					
American Assn of Physician Specialists Inc (AAPS)					
2296 Henderson Mill Rd Suite 206	Atlanta	GA	30345	770-939-8555	939-8559
TF: 800-447-9397 ■ *Web:* www.aapsga.org					
American Assn of Poison Control Centers (AAPCC)					
3201 New Mexico Ave Suite 330	Washington	DC	20016	202-362-7217	362-3240
TF: 800-222-1222 ■ *Web:* www.aapcc.org					
American Assn of Preferred Provider Organizations (AAPPO)					
222 S 1st St Suite 303	Louisville	KY	40202	502-403-1122	403-1129
Web: www.aappo.org					
American Assn for Respiratory Care (AARC)					
9425 N MacArthur Blvd Suite 100	Irving	TX	75063	972-243-2272	484-2720
Web: www.aarc.org					
American Assn for the Study of Liver Diseases (AASLD)					
1729 King St Suite 200	Alexandria	VA	22314	703-299-9766	299-9622
Web: www.aasld.org					
American Assn for Thoracic Surgery (AATS)					
900 Cummings Center Suite 221-U	Beverly	MA	01915	978-927-8330	524-8890
Web: www.aats.org					
American Assn of Tissue Banks (AATB)					
1320 Old Chain Bridge Rd Suite 450	McLean	VA	22101	703-827-9582	356-2198
Web: www.aatb.org					
American Auditory Society 352 Sundial Ridge Cir	Dammeron Valley	UT	84783	435-574-0062	574-0063
Web: www.amauditorysoc.org					
American Autoimmune Related Disease Assn (AARDA)					
22100 Gratiot Ave	Eastpointe	MI	48021	586-776-3900	776-3903
TF: 800-598-4668 ■ *Web:* www.aarda.org					
American Board of Physician Nutrition Specialists (ABPNS)					
Univ of Alabama Birmingham Dept of Nutrition Sciences					
439 Susan Mott Webb Nutrition Sciences Bldg	Birmingham	AL	35194	205-966-2513	934-7050
Web: main.uab.edu/ipnec/show.asp?durki=37725					
American Burn Assn (ABA) 625 N Michigan Ave Suite 2550	Chicago	IL	60611	312-642-9260	642-9130
Web: www.ameriburn.org					
American Cancer Society (ACS) 1599 Clifton Rd NE	Atlanta	GA	30329	404-320-3333	325-9341
TF: 800-227-2345 ■ *Web:* www.cancer.org					
American Chiropractic Assn (ACA)					
1701 Clarendon Blvd 2nd Fl	Arlington	VA	22209	703-276-8800	243-2593
TF: 800-986-4636 ■ *Web:* www.amerchiro.org					
American Cleft Palate-Craniofacial Assn					
1504 E Franklin St Suite 102	Chapel Hill	NC	27514	919-933-9044	933-9604
TF: 800-242-5338 ■ *Web:* www.acpa-cpf.org					
American College for Advancement in Medicine (ACAM)					
23121 Verdugo Dr Suite 204	Laguna Hills	CA	92653	949-583-7666	455-9679
TF: 800-532-3688 ■ *Web:* www.acam.org					
American College of Allergy Asthma & Immunology					
(ACAAI) 85 W Algonquin Rd Suite 550	Arlington Heights	IL	60005	847-427-1200	427-1294
TF: 800-842-7777 ■ *Web:* www.acaai.org					
American College of Cardiology (ACC)					
9111 Old Georgetown Rd	Bethesda	MD	20814	301-897-5400	897-9745
TF Cust Svc: 800-253-4636 ■ *Web:* www.acc.org					
American College of Chest Physicians (ACCP)					
3300 Dundee Rd	Northbrook	IL	60062	847-498-1400	498-5460
TF: 800-343-2227 ■ *Web:* www.chestnet.org					
American College of Clinical Pharmacy (ACCP)					
3101 Broadway Suite 650	Kansas City	MO	64111	816-531-2177	531-4990
Web: www.accp.com					
American College of Dentists (ACD)					
839 Quince Orchard Blvd Suite J	Gaithersburg	MD	20878	301-977-3223	977-3330
TF: 888-223-1920 ■ *Web:* www.facd.org					
American College of Emergency Physicians (ACEP)					
PO Box 619911	Dallas	TX	75261	972-550-0911	580-2816
TF: 800-798-1822 ■ *Web:* www.acep.org					
American College of Eye Surgeons/American Board of					
Eye Surgery (ACES) 334 East Lake Rd Suite 135	Palm Lake Harbor	FL	34685	727-480-8542	786-6622
Web: www.aces-abes.org					
American College of Foot & Ankle Surgeons (ACFAS)					
8725 W Higgins Rd Suite 555	Chicago	IL	60631	773-693-9300	693-9304
TF: 800-421-2237 ■ *Web:* www.acfas.org					

Health & Medical Professionals Associations (Cont'd)

Organization	City	State	ZIP	Phone	Fax
American College of Forensic Examiners (ACFE) 2750 E Sunshine St *TF:* 800-423-9737 ■ *Web:* www.acfei.com	Springfield	MO	65804	417-881-3818	881-4702
American College of Gastroenterology (ACG) 6400 Goldsboro Rd Suite 450 *Web:* www.acg.gi.org	Bethesda	MD	20817	301-263-9000	263-9025
American College Health Assn (ACHA) PO Box 28937 *Web:* www.acha.org	Baltimore	MD	21240	410-859-1500	859-1510
American College of Health Care Administrators (ACHCA) 300 N Lee St Suite 301 *TF:* 888-882-2422 ■ *Web:* www.achca.org	Alexandria	VA	22314	703-739-7900	739-7901
American College of Healthcare Executives (ACHE) 1 N Franklin St Suite 1700 *Web:* www.ache.org	Chicago	IL	60606	312-424-2800	424-0023
American College of Managed Care Medicine (ACMCM) 4435 Waterfront Dr Suite 101 *Web:* www.acmcm.org	Glen Allen	VA	23060	804-527-1906	747-5316
American College of Nurse-Midwives (ACNM) 8403 Colesville Rd Suite 1550 *Web:* www.midwife.org	Silver Spring	MD	20910	240-485-1800	485-1818
American College of Nutrition 300 S Duncan Ave Suite 225 *Web:* www.am-coll-nutr.org	Clearwater	FL	33755	727-446-6086	446-6202
American College of Obstetricians & Gynecologists (ACOG) 409 12th St SW PO Box 96920 *Web:* www.acog.com	Washington	DC	20090	202-638-5577	863-4284
American College of Occupational & Environmental Medicine (ACOEM) 25 Northwest Point Blvd Suite 700 *Web:* www.acoem.org	Elk Grove Village	IL	60007	847-818-1800	818-9266
American College of Osteopathic Family Physicians (ACOFP) 330 E Algonquin Rd Suite 1 *TF:* 800-323-0794 ■ *Web:* www.acofp.org	Arlington Heights	IL	60005	847-228-6090	228-9755
American College of Physician Executives (ACPE) 4890 W Kennedy Blvd Suite 200 *TF:* 800-562-8088 ■ *Web:* www.acpe.org	Tampa	FL	33609	813-287-2000	287-8993
American College of Physicians (ACP) 190 N Independence Mall W *TF:* 800-523-1546 ■ *Web:* www.acponline.org	Philadelphia	PA	19106	215-351-2400	351-2594
American College of Preventive Medicine (ACPM) 1307 New York Ave NW Suite 200 *Web:* www.acpm.org	Washington	DC	20005	202-466-2044	466-2662
American College of Radiology (ACR) 1891 Preston White Dr *TF:* 800-227-5463 ■ *Web:* www.acr.org	Reston	VA	20191	703-648-8900	295-6772
American College of Rheumatology (ACR) 1800 Century Pl Suite 250 *Web:* www.rheumatology.org	Atlanta	GA	30345	404-633-3777	633-1870
American College of Sports Medicine (ACSM) 401 W Michigan St *Web:* www.acsm.org	Indianapolis	IN	46202	317-637-9200	634-7817
American College of Surgeons (ACS) 633 N Saint Clair St *TF:* 800-621-4111 ■ *Web:* www.facs.org	Chicago	IL	60611	312-202-5000	202-5001
American College of Toxicology 9650 Rockville Pike *Web:* www.actox.org	Bethesda	MD	20814	301-634-7840	634-7852
American Congress of Community Supports & Employment Services (ACCSES) 1501 M St NW 7th Fl *Web:* www.accses.org	Washington	DC	20005	202-466-3355	466-7571
American Dental Assistants Assn (ADAA) 35 E Wacker Dr Suite 1730 *TF:* 877-874-3785 ■ *Web:* www.dentalassistant.org	Chicago	IL	60601	312-541-1550	541-1496
American Dental Assn (ADA) 211 E Chicago Ave **Fax:* Hum Res ■ *Web:* www.ada.org	Chicago	IL	60611	312-440-2500	440-2395*
American Dental Hygienists' Assn (ADHA) 444 N Michigan Ave Suite 3400 *TF:* 800-243-2342 ■ *Web:* www.adha.org	Chicago	IL	60611	312-440-8900	467-1806
American Diabetes Assn (ADA) 1701 N Beauregard St *TF:* 800-232-3472 ■ *Web:* www.diabetes.org	Alexandria	VA	22311	703-549-1500	836-2464
American Dietetic Assn (ADA) 120 S Riverside Plaza Suite 2000 *TF:* 800-877-1600 ■ *Web:* www.eatright.org	Chicago	IL	60606	312-899-0040	899-4899
American Embryo Transfer Assn (AETA) 1111 N Dunlap Ave *Web:* www.aeta.org	Savoy	IL	61847	217-398-2217	398-4119
American Endodontic Society Box 5523 *Web:* www.aesoc.com	Fullerton	CA	92838	714-778-2338	738-1098
American Epilepsy Society (AES) 342 N Main St *Web:* www.aesnet.org	West Hartford	CT	06117	860-586-7505	586-7550
American Federation for Aging Research (AFAR) 55 W 39th St 16th Fl *TF:* 888-582-2327 ■ *Web:* www.afar.org	New York	NY	10018	212-703-9977	997-0330
American Federation for Medical Research (AFMR) 900 Cummings Ctr Suite 221-U *Web:* www.afmr.org	Beverly	MA	01915	978-927-8330	524-8890
American Gastroenterological Assn (AGA) 4930 Del Ray Ave *Web:* www.gastro.org	Bethesda	MD	20814	301-654-2055	654-5920
American Geriatrics Society (AGS) 350 5th Ave Empire State Bldg Suite 801 *Web:* www.americangeriatrics.org	New York	NY	10018	212-308-1414	832-8646
American Headache Society (AHS) 19 Mantua Rd *Web:* www.americanheadachesociety.org	Mount Royal	NJ	08061	856-423-0043	423-0082
American Health Care Assn (AHCA) 1201 L St NW *TF:* 800-321-0343 ■ *Web:* www.ahca.org	Washington	DC	20005	202-842-4444	842-3860
American Health Information Management Assn (AHIMA) 233 N Michigan Ave Suite 2150 *TF:* 800-335-5535 ■ *Web:* www.ahima.org	Chicago	IL	60601	312-233-1100	233-1090
American Health Quality Assn (AHQA) 1155 21st St NW *Web:* www.ahqa.org	Washington	DC	20036	202-331-5790	331-9334
American Healthcare Radiology Administrators (AHRA) 490-B Boston Post Rd Suite 101 *TF:* 800-334-2472 ■ *Web:* www.ahraonline.org	Sudbury	MA	01776	978-443-7591	443-8046
American Heart Assn (AHA) 7272 Greenville Ave *TF:* 800-242-8721 ■ *Web:* www.americanheart.org	Dallas	TX	75231	214-373-6300	706-1191
American Herbal Products Assn (AHPA) 8484 Georgia Ave Suite 370 *Web:* www.ahpa.org	Silver Spring	MD	20910	301-588-1171	588-1174
American Hospital Assn (AHA) 1 N Franklin St *TF:* 800-424-4301 ■ *Web:* www.aha.org	Chicago	IL	60606	312-422-3000	422-4796
American Institute of Ultrasound in Medicine (AIUM) 14750 Sweitzer Ln Suite 100 *TF:* 800-638-5352 ■ *Web:* www.aium.org	Laurel	MD	20707	301-498-4100	498-4450
American Lung Assn (ALA) 61 Broadway 6th Fl *TF:* 800-586-4872 ■ *Web:* www.lungusa.org	New York	NY	10006	212-315-8700	315-8872
American Medical Assn (AMA) 515 N State St *TF:* 800-621-8335 ■ *Web:* www.ama-assn.org	Chicago	IL	60610	312-464-5000	464-4184
American Medical Directors Assn (AMDA) 10480 Little Patuxent Pkwy Suite 760 *TF:* 800-876-2632 ■ *Web:* www.amda.com	Columbia	MD	21044	410-740-9743	740-4572
American Medical Group Assn (AMGA) 1422 Duke St *Web:* www.amga.org	Alexandria	VA	22314	703-838-0033	548-1890
American Medical Informatics Assn (AMIA) 4915 Saint Elmo Ave Suite 401 *Web:* www.amia.org	Bethesda	MD	20814	301-657-1291	657-1296
American Medical Rehabilitation Providers Assn (AMRPA) 1710 'N' St NW *TF:* 888-346-4624 ■ *Web:* www.amrpa.org	Washington	DC	20036	202-223-1920	223-1925
American Medical Technologists (AMT) 710 Higgins Rd *TF:* 800-275-1268 ■ *Web:* www.amt1.com	Park Ridge	IL	60068	847-823-5169	823-0458
American Medical Women's Assn (AMWA) 801 N Fairfax St Suite 400 *Web:* www.amwa-doc.org	Alexandria	VA	22314	703-838-0500	549-3864
American Nephrology Nurses Assn (ANNA) 200 E Holly Ave *TF:* 888-600-2662 ■ *Web:* www.annanurse.org	Pitman	NJ	08080	856-256-2320	589-7463
American Neurological Assn (ANA) 5841 Cedar Lake Rd Suite 204 *Web:* www.aneuroa.org	Minneapolis	MN	55416	952-545-6284	545-6073
American Nurses Assn (ANA) 8515 Georgia Ave Suite 400 *TF:* 800-274-4262 ■ *Web:* www.ana.org	Silver Spring	MD	20910	301-628-5000	628-5001
American Occupational Therapy Assn Inc (AOTA) 4720 Montgomery Ln PO Box 31220 *Web:* www.aota.org	Bethesda	MD	20824	301-652-2682	652-7711
American Optometric Assn (AOA) 243 N Lindbergh Blvd *Web:* www.aoa.org	Saint Louis	MO	63141	314-991-4100	991-4101
American Organization of Nurse Executives (AONE) 1 N Franklin St 32nd Fl *Web:* www.aone.org	Chicago	IL	60606	312-422-2800	422-4503
American Orthopaedic Assn (AOA) 6300 N River Rd Suite 505 *Web:* www.aoassn.org	Rosemont	IL	60018	847-318-7330	318-7339
American Orthopaedic Society for Sports Medicine (AOSSM) 6300 N River Rd Suite 500 *TF:* 877-321-3500 ■ *Web:* www.sportsmed.org	Rosemont	IL	60018	847-292-4900	292-4905
American Osteopathic Assn (AOA) 142 E Ontario St *TF:* 800-621-1773 ■ *Web:* www.osteopathic.org	Chicago	IL	60611	312-202-8000	202-8200
American Pain Society (APS) 4700 W Lake Ave **Fax Area Code:* 877 ■ *Web:* www.ampainsoc.org	Glenview	IL	60025	847-375-4715	734-8758*
American Pharmacists Assn (APhA) 1100 15th St NW Suite 400 *TF:* 800-237-2742 ■ *Web:* www.pharmacist.com	Washington	DC	20005	202-628-4410	783-2351
American Physical Therapy Assn (APTA) 1111 N Fairfax St *TF:* 800-999-2782 ■ *Web:* www.apta.org	Alexandria	VA	22314	703-706-3245	838-8910
American Physiological Society (APS) 9650 Rockville Pike *Web:* www.the-aps.org	Bethesda	MD	20814	301-634-7164	634-7241
American Podiatric Medical Assn (APMA) 9312 Old Georgetown Rd *TF:* 800-275-2762 ■ *Web:* www.apma.org	Bethesda	MD	20814	301-581-9200	530-2752
American Professional Practice Assn (APPA) 350 Fairway Dr Suite 200 *TF:* 800-221-2168 ■ *Web:* www.appa-assn.com	Deerfield Beach	FL	33441	954-571-1877	571-8582
American Prosthodontic Society (APS) 426 Hudson St *TF:* 877-499-3500 ■ *Web:* www.prostho.org	Hackensack	NJ	07601	201-440-7699	440-7963
American Psychiatric Nurses Assn (APNA) 1555 Wilson Blvd Suite 602 *Web:* www.apna.org	Arlington	VA	22209	703-243-2443	243-3390
American Public Health Assn (APHA) 800 'I' St NW *Web:* www.apha.org	Washington	DC	20001	202-777-2742	777-2533
American Registry of Diagnostic Medical Sonographers (ARDMS) 51 Monroe St Plaza East 1 *TF:* 800-541-9754 ■ *Web:* www.ardms.org	Rockville	MD	20850	301-738-8401	738-0312
American Roentgen Ray Society (ARRS) 44211 Slatestone Ct *TF:* 800-438-2777 ■ *Web:* www.arrs.org	Leesburg	VA	20176	703-729-3353	729-4839
American Society of Abdominal Surgeons (ASAS) 1 E Emerson St *Web:* www.abdominalsurg.org	Melrose	MA	02176	781-665-6102	665-4127
American Society of Addiction Medicine (ASAM) 4601 N Park Ave Upper Arcade Suite 101 *Web:* www.asam.org	Chevy Chase	MD	20815	301-656-3920	656-3815
American Society for Aesthetic Plastic Surgery (ASAPS) 11081 Winners Cir *TF:* 800-364-2147 ■ *Web:* www.surgery.org	Los Alamitos	CA	90720	562-799-2356	799-1098
American Society of Andrology (ASA) 1111 N Plaza Dr Suite 550 *Web:* www.andrologysociety.com	Schaumburg	IL	60173	847-619-4909	517-7229
American Society of Anesthesiologists (ASA) 520 N Northwest Hwy *Web:* www.asahq.org	Park Ridge	IL	60068	847-825-5586	825-1692
American Society of Bariatric Physicians (ASBP) 2821 S Parker Rd Suite 625 *Web:* www.asbp.org	Aurora	CO	80014	303-770-2526	779-4834
American Society for Bone & Mineral Research (ASBMR) 2025 M St NW Suite 800 *Web:* www.asbmr.org	Washington	DC	20036	202-367-1161	367-2161
American Society of Cataract & Refractive Surgery (ASCRS) 4000 Legato Rd Suite 700 *TF:* 800-451-1339 ■ *Web:* www.ascrs.org	Fairfax	VA	22033	703-591-2220	591-0614
American Society of Clinical Hypnosis (ASCH) 140 N Bloomingdale Rd *Web:* www.asch.net	Bloomingdale	IL	60108	630-980-4740	351-8490
American Society for Clinical Investigation (ASCI) PO Box 7226 *TF:* 866-660-2724 ■ *Web:* www.asci-jci.org	Ann Arbor	MI	48107	734-222-6050	222-6058
American Society for Clinical Laboratory Science (ASCLS) 6701 Democracy Blvd Suite 300 *Web:* www.ascls.org	Bethesda	MD	20817	301-657-2768	657-2909
American Society of Clinical Oncology (ASCO) 1900 Duke St Suite 200 *TF:* 888-282-2552 ■ *Web:* www.asco.org	Alexandria	VA	22314	703-299-0150	299-1044
American Society for Clinical Pathology (ASCP) 2100 W Harrison St *TF Cust Svc:* 800-621-4142 ■ *Web:* www.ascp.org	Chicago	IL	60612	312-738-1336	738-1619
American Society for Colposcopy & Cervical Pathology (ASCCP) 152 W Washington St *TF:* 800-787-7227 ■ *Web:* www.asccp.org	Hagerstown	MD	21740	301-733-3640	733-5775
American Society of Consultant Pharmacists (ASCP) 1321 Duke St *TF:* 800-355-2727 ■ *Web:* www.ascp.com	Alexandria	VA	22314	703-739-1300	739-1321
American Society of Contemporary Medicine Surgery & Ophthalmology 7250 N Cicero Ave Lower Level 6 *TF:* 800-621-4002	Lincolnwood	IL	60712	847-677-9093	677-9094
American Society for Dermatologic Surgery (ASDS) 5550 Meadowbrook Dr Suite 120 *Web:* www.asds-net.org	Rolling Meadows	IL	60008	847-956-0900	956-0999

Phone Fax

American Society of Dermatopathology (ASDP)
60 Revere Dr Suite 500 .... Northbrook IL 60062 847-400-5820 480-9282
Web: www.asdp.org

American Society of Echocardiography (ASE)
1500 Sunday Dr Suite 102 .... Raleigh NC 27607 919-861-5574 787-4916
Web: asecho.org

American Society for Gastrointestinal Endoscopy (ASGE)
1520 Kensington Rd Suite 202 .... Oak Brook IL 60523 630-573-0600 573-0691
TF: 866-353-2743 ■ *Web:* www.asge.org

American Society of Health-System Pharmacists (ASHP)
7272 Wisconsin Ave .... Bethesda MD 20814 301-657-3000 664-8877
TF: 866-279-0681 ■ *Web:* www.ashp.org

American Society for Healthcare Engineering (ASHE)
1 N Franklin St 28th Fl .... Chicago IL 60606 312-422-3800 422-4571
Web: www.ashe.org

American Society of Hematology (ASH)
1900 M St NW Suite 200 .... Washington DC 20036 202-776-0544 776-0545
Web: www.hematology.org

American Society for Histocompatibility & Immunogenetics (ASHI) 15000 Commerce Pkwy Suite C .... Mount Laurel NJ 08054 856-638-0428 439-0525
Web: www.ashi-hla.org

American Society of Hypertension (ASH)
148 Madison Ave 5th Fl .... New York NY 10016 212-696-9099 696-0711
Web: www.ash-us.org

American Society for Laser Medicine & Surgery (ASLMS)
2100 Stewart Ave Suite 240 .... Wausau WI 54401 715-845-9283 848-2493
Web: www.aslms.org

American Society for Microbiology (ASM) 1752 'N' St NW .... Washington DC 20036 202-737-3600
Web: www.asm.org

American Society of Nephrology (ASN)
1725 'I' St NW Suite 510 .... Washington DC 20006 202-659-0599 659-0709
Web: www.asn-online.com

American Society of Neuroradiology (ASNR)
2210 Midwest Rd Suite 207 .... Oak Brook IL 60523 630-574-0220 574-0661
Web: www.asnr.org

American Society of Nuclear Cardiology (ASNC)
9111 Old Georgetown Rd .... Bethesda MD 20814 301-493-2360 493-2376
Web: www.asnc.org

American Society for Parenteral & Enteral Nutrition (ASPEN)
8630 Fenton St Suite 412 .... Silver Spring MD 20910 301-587-6315 587-2365
TF: 800-727-4567 ■ *Web:* www.nutritioncare.org

American Society of PeriAnesthesia Nurses (ASPAN)
10 Melrose Ave Suite 110 .... Cherry Hill NJ 08003 856-616-9600 616-9601
TF: 877-737-9696 ■ *Web:* www.aspan.org

American Society for Pharmacology & Experimental Therapeutics (ASPET) 9650 Rockville Pike .... Bethesda MD 20814 301-634-7060 634-7061
Web: www.aspet.org

American Society of Plastic Surgeons (ASPS)
444 E Algonquin Rd .... Arlington Heights IL 60005 847-228-9900 228-9131
TF: 888-475-2784 ■ *Web:* www.plasticsurgery.org

American Society of Radiologic Technologists (ASRT)
15000 Central Ave SE .... Albuquerque NM 87123 505-298-4500 298-5063
TF: 800-444-2778 ■ *Web:* www.asrt.org

American Society of Regional Anesthesia & Pain Medicine (ASRA) 520 N Northwest Hwy .... Park Ridge IL 60068 847-825-7246
Web: www.asra.com

American Society for Reproductive Medicine (ASRM)
1209 Montgomery Hwy .... Birmingham AL 35216 205-978-5000 978-5005
Web: www.asrm.org

American Society for Surgery of the Hand (ASSH)
6300 N River Rd Suite 600 .... Rosemont IL 60018 847-384-8300 384-1435
TF: 888-576-2774 ■ *Web:* www.assh.org

American Society for Therapeutic Radiology & Oncology (ASTRO)
12500 Fair Lakes Cir Suite 375 .... Fairfax VA 22033 703-502-1550 502-7852
TF: 800-962-7876 ■ *Web:* www.astro.org

American Society of Transplantation (AST)
15000 Commerce Pkwy Suite C .... Mount Laurel NJ 08054 856-439-9986 439-9982
Web: www.a-s-t.org

American Society of Tropical Medicine & Hygiene (ASTMH)
60 Revere Dr Suite 500 .... Northbrook IL 60062 847-480-9592 480-9282
Web: www.astmh.org

American Speech-Language-Hearing Assn (ASHA)
10801 Rockville Pike .... Rockville MD 20852 301-897-5700 571-0457
TF: 800-498-2071 ■ *Web:* www.asha.org

American Thoracic Society (ATS) 61 Broadway 4th Fl .... New York NY 10006 212-315-8600 315-6498
Web: www.thoracic.org

American Trauma Society
8903 Presidential Pkwy Suite 512 .... Upper Marlboro MD 20772 301-420-4189 420-0617
TF: 800-556-7890 ■ *Web:* www.amtrauma.org

American Urological Assn (AUA) 1000 Corporate Blvd .... Linthicum MD 21090 410-689-3700 689-3800
TF: 866-746-4282 ■ *Web:* www.auanet.org

American Veterinary Medical Assn (AVMA)
1931 N Meacham Rd Suite 100 .... Schaumburg IL 60173 847-925-8070 925-1329
TF: 800-925-8070 ■ *Web:* www.avma.org

America's Blood Centers (ABC) 725 15th St NW Suite 700 .... Washington DC 20005 202-393-5725 393-1282
TF: 888-872-5663 ■ *Web:* www.americasblood.org

AORN Inc 2170 S Parker Rd Suite 300 .... Denver CO 80231 303-755-6300 750-3212*
**Fax:* Cust Svc ■ *TF:* 800-755-2676 ■ *Web:* www.aorn.org

Arthroscopy Assn of North America (AANA)
6300 N River Rd Suite 104 .... Rosemont IL 60018 847-292-2262 292-2268
Web: www.aana.org

Assisted Living Federation of America (ALFA)
11200 Waples Mill Rd Suite 150 .... Fairfax VA 22030 703-691-8100 691-8106
Web: www.alfa.org

Association of Academic Health Centers (AHC)
1400 16th St NW Suite 720 .... Washington DC 20036 202-265-9600 265-7514
TF: 800-925-4755 ■ *Web:* www.aahcdc.org

Association for the Advancement of Medical Instrumentation (AAMI) 1110 N Glebe Rd Suite 220 .... Arlington VA 22201 703-525-4890 276-0793
TF: 800-332-2264 ■ *Web:* www.aami.org

Association of Air Medical Services (AAMS)
526 King St Suite 415 .... Alexandria VA 22314 703-836-8732 836-8920
Web: www.aams.org

Association of American Indian Physicians (AAIP)
1225 Sovereign Row Suite 103 .... Oklahoma City OK 73108 405-946-7072 946-7651
TF: 800-943-4299 ■ *Web:* www.aaip.com

Association for Applied Psychophysiology & Biofeedback (AAPB) 10200 W 44th Ave Suite 304 .... Wheat Ridge CO 80033 303-422-8436 422-8894
TF: 800-477-8892 ■ *Web:* www.aapb.org

Association of Black Cardiologists (ABC)
6849 Peachtree Dunwoody Rd NE Bldg 2 .... Atlanta GA 30328 678-302-4222 302-4223
TF: 800-753-9222 ■ *Web:* www.abcardio.org

Association of Clinical Research Professionals (ACRP)
500 Montgomery St Suite 800 .... Alexandria VA 22314 703-254-8100 254-8101
Web: www.acrpnet.org

Phone Fax

Association of Community Cancer Centers (ACCC)
11600 Nebel St Suite 201 .... Rockville MD 20852 301-984-9496 770-1949
Web: www.accc-cancer.org

Association for Death Education & Counseling (ADEC)
60 Revere Dr Suite 1500 .... Northbrook IL 60062 847-509-0403 480-9282
Web: www.adec.org

Association of Emergency Physicians (AEP) 911 Whitewater Dr .... Mars PA 16046 724-772-1818
TF: 866-772-1818 ■ *Web:* www.aep.org

Association for Healthcare Documentation Integrity (AHDI)
4230 Kiernan Ave Suite 130 .... Modesto CA 95356 209-527-9620 527-9633
TF: 800-982-2182 ■ *Web:* www.aamt.org

Association for Healthcare Philanthropy (AHP)
313 Park Ave Suite 400 .... Falls Church VA 22046 703-532-6243 532-7170
Web: www.ahp.org

Association of Military Surgeons of the US (AMSUS)
9320 Old Georgetown Rd .... Bethesda MD 20814 301-897-8800 530-5446
TF: 800-761-9320 ■ *Web:* www.amsus.org

Association of Nurses in AIDS Care (ANAC) 3538 Ridgewood Rd .... Akron OH 44333 330-670-0101 670-0109
TF: 800-260-6780 ■ *Web:* www.anacnet.org

Association of Osteopathic Directors & Medical Educators (AODME) 142 E Ontario St .... Chicago IL 60611 312-202-8211 202-8224
Web: www.aodme.org

Association for Professionals in Infection Control & Epidemiology Inc (APIC) 1275 K St NW Suite 1000 .... Washington DC 20005 202-789-1890 789-1899
Web: www.apic.org

Association of Program Directors in Internal Medicine (APDIM) 2501 M St NW Suite 550 .... Washington DC 20037 202-887-9450 861-9731
TF: 800-622-4558 ■ *Web:* www.im.org/APDIM

Association of Rehabilitation Nurses (ARN) 4700 W Lake Ave .... Glenview IL 60025 847-375-4710 734-9384*
**Fax Area Code:* 877 ■ *TF:* 800-229-7530 ■ *Web:* www.rehabnurse.org

Association of Reproductive Health Professionals (ARHP)
2401 Pennsylvania Ave NW Suite 350 .... Washington DC 20037 202-466-3825 466-3826
Web: www.arhp.org

Association for Research in Vision & Ophthalmology (ARVO)
12300 Twinbrook Pkwy Suite 250 .... Rockville MD 20852 240-221-2900 221-0370
Web: www.arvo.org

Association of Schools of Allied Health Professions (ASAHP)
4400 Jenifer St NW Suite 333 .... Washington DC 20015 202-237-6481 237-6485
TF: 800-497-8080 ■ *Web:* www.asahp.org

Association of Schools & Colleges of Optometry (ASCO)
6110 Executive Blvd Suite 420 .... Rockville MD 20852 301-231-5944 770-1828
Web: www.opted.org

Association of Staff Physician Recruiters (ASPR)
1711 W County Rd B Suite 300N .... Roseville MN 55113 651-635-0359 635-0307
TF: 800-830-2777 ■ *Web:* www.aspr.org

Association of Surgical Technologists (AST)
6 W Dry Creek Cir Suite 200 .... Littleton CO 80120 303-694-9130 694-9169
Web: www.ast.org

Association of University Programs in Health Administration (AUPHA) 2000 N 14th St Suite 780 .... Arlington VA 22201 703-894-0940 894-0941
Web: www.aupha.org

Association of Women's Health Obstetric & Neonatal Nurses (AWHONN) 2000 L St NW Suite 740 .... Washington DC 20036 202-261-2400 728-0575
TF: 800-673-8499 ■ *Web:* www.awhonn.org

Asthma & Allergy Foundation of America (AAFA)
1233 20th St NW Suite 402 .... Washington DC 20036 202-466-7643 466-8940
TF: 800-727-8462 ■ *Web:* www.aafa.org

Canada's Research-Based Pharmaceutical Companies (Rx&D)
55 Metcalfe St Suite 1220 .... Ottawa ON K1P6L5 613-236-0455 236-6756
Web: www.canadapharma.org

Canadian Academy of Sport Medicine (CASM)
5330 Canotek Rd Unit 4 .... Ottawa ON K1T9C1 613-748-5851 748-5792
TF: 877-585-2394 ■ *Web:* www.casm-acms.org

Canadian Assn of Emergency Physicians (CAEP)
1785 Alta Vista Dr Suite 104 .... Ottawa ON K1G3Y6 613-523-3343 523-0190
TF: 800-463-1158 ■ *Web:* www.caep.ca

Canadian Medical Assn (CMA) 1867 Alta Vista Dr .... Ottawa ON K1G5W8 613-731-9331 731-7314
TF: 800-663-7336 ■ *Web:* www.cma.ca

Canadian Veterinary Medical Assn (CVMA) 339 Booth St .... Ottawa ON K1R7K1 613-236-1162 236-9681
Web: canadianveterinarians.net

Case Management Society of America (CMSA)
8201 Cantrell Rd Suite 230 .... Little Rock AR 72227 501-225-2229 221-9068
Web: www.cmsa.org

Catholic Health Assn of the US (CHA) 4455 Woodson Rd .... Saint Louis MO 63134 314-427-2500 427-0029
Web: www.chausa.org

Certification Board for Nutrition Specialists
300 S Duncan Ave Suite 225 .... Clearwater FL 33755 727-446-6086 446-6202
Web: www.cert-nutrition.org

Children's Hospice International (CHI)
901 N Pitt St Suite 230 .... Alexandria VA 22314 703-684-0330 684-0226
TF: 800-242-4453 ■ *Web:* www.chionline.org

Christian Medical & Dental Assns (CMDA) PO Box 7500 .... Bristol TN 37621 423-844-1000 844-1005
TF: 888-231-2637 ■ *Web:* www.cmdahome.org

Clinical Immunology Society (CIS)
555 E Wells St Suite 1100 .... Milwaukee WI 53202 414-224-8095 272-6070
Web: www.clinimmsoc.org

Clinical & Laboratory Standards Institute (CLSI)
940 W Valley Rd Suite 1400 .... Wayne PA 19087 610-688-0100 688-0700
TF: 877-447-1888 ■ *Web:* www.clsi.org

CMA (Canadian Medical Assn) 1867 Alta Vista Dr .... Ottawa ON K1G5W8 613-731-9331 731-7314
TF: 800-663-7336 ■ *Web:* www.cma.ca

College of American Pathologists (CAP) 325 Waukegan Rd .... Northfield IL 60093 847-832-7000 832-8000
TF: 800-323-4040 ■ *Web:* www.cap.org

Commission on Office Laboratory Accreditation (COLA)
9881 Broken Land Pkwy Suite 200 .... Columbia MD 21046 410-381-6581 381-8611*
**Fax:* Hum Res ■ *TF:* 800-981-9883 ■ *Web:* www.cola.org

Dietary Managers Assn (DMA) 406 Surrey Woods Dr .... Saint Charles IL 60174 630-587-6336 587-6308
TF: 800-323-1908 ■ *Web:* www.dmaonline.org

Emergency Nurses Assn (ENA) 915 Lee St .... Des Plaines IL 60016 847-460-4000 460-4001
TF: 800-900-9659 ■ *Web:* www.ena.org

Endocrine Society 8401 Connecticut Ave Suite 900 .... Chevy Chase MD 20815 301-941-0200 941-0259
Web: www.endo-society.org

Eye Bank Assn of America (EBAA)
1015 18th St NW Suite 1010 .... Washington DC 20036 202-775-4999 429-6036
Web: www.restoresight.org

Federal Nurses Assn (FedNA) 8515 Georgia Ave Suite 400 .... Silver Spring MD 20910 301-628-5333 628-5001
Web: www.nursingworld.org/Fedna

Federation of American Hospitals
801 Pennsylvania Ave NW Suite 245 .... Washington DC 20004 202-624-1500 737-6462
TF: 877-219-6800 ■ *Web:* www.fahs.com

Federation of State Medical Boards of the US Inc (FSMB)
400 Fuller Wiser Rd Suite 300 .... Euless TX 76039 817-868-4000 868-4099
TF: 800-876-5396 ■ *Web:* www.fsmb.org

Gerontological Society of America
1220 L St NW Suite 901 .... Washington DC 20005 202-842-1275 842-1150
Web: www.geron.org

Health & Medical Professionals Associations (Cont'd)

Phone *Fax*

Gynecologic Oncology Group (GOG)
1600 JFK Blvd Suite 1020 .... Philadelphia PA 19103 215-854-0770 854-0716
TF: 800-225-3053 ■ *Web:* www.gog.org

Health Industry Business Communications Council (HIBCC)
2525 E Arizona Biltmore Cir Suite 127 .... Phoenix AZ 85016 602-381-1091 381-1093
Web: www.hibcc.org

Healthcare Financial Management Assn (HFMA)
2 Westbrook Corporate Ctr Suite 700 .... Westchester IL 60154 708-531-9600 531-0032
TF: 800-252-4362 ■ *Web:* www.hfma.org

Healthcare Information & Management Systems Society (HIMSS)
230 E Ohio St Suite 500 .... Chicago IL 60611 312-664-4467 664-6143
Web: www.himss.org

Heart Rhythm Society 1400 K St NW Suite 500 .... Washington DC 20005 202-464-3400 464-3401
Web: www.hrsonline.org

Hospice Foundation of America (HFA)
1621 Connecticut Ave NW Suite 300 .... Washington DC 20009 202-638-5419 638-5312
TF: 800-854-3402 ■ *Web:* www.hospicefoundation.org

Hospice & Palliative Nurses Assn (HPNA)
Penn Ctr W 1 Suite 229 .... Pittsburgh PA 15276 412-787-9301 787-9305
Web: www.hpna.org

Infectious Diseases Society of America (IDSA)
66 Canal Center Plaza Suite 600 .... Alexandria VA 22314 703-299-0200 299-0204
Web: www.idsociety.org

Infusion Nurses Society (INS) 220 Norwood Pk S .... Norwood MA 02062 781-440-9408 440-9409
TF: 800-694-0298 ■ *Web:* www.ins1.org

Institute for the Advancement of Human Behavior (IAHB)
4370 Alpine Rd Suite 209 .... Portola Valley CA 94028 650-851-8411 851-0406
TF: 800-258-8411 ■ *Web:* www.ibh.com

Institute for Healthcare Improvement (IHI)
20 University Rd 7th Fl .... Cambridge MA 02138 617-301-4800 301-4848
TF: 866-787-0831 ■ *Web:* www.ihi.org

Institute of Medicine 500 5th St NW .... Washington DC 20001 202-334-2352 334-1412
Web: www.iom.edu

Interamerican College of Physicians & Surgeons (ICPS)
233 Broadway Suite 806 .... New York NY 10279 212-777-3642 267-5394
Web: www.icps.org

International Academy of Compounding Pharmacists (IACP)
PO Box 1365 .... Sugar Land TX 77487 281-933-8400 495-0602
TF: 800-927-4227 ■ *Web:* www.iacprx.org

International Academy of Pathology (IAP)
Armed Forces Institute of Pathology Walter Reed
Compound 6825 16th St NW .... Washington DC 20306 202-782-2503 782-7166
Web: www.iaphomepage.org

International Anesthesia Research Society (IARS)
2 Summit Park Dr Suite 140 .... Cleveland OH 44131 216-642-1124 642-1127
Web: www.iars.org

International Assn for Dental Research (IADR) 1619 Duke St .... Alexandria VA 22314 703-548-0066 548-1883
Web: www.iadr.com

International Assn of Ocular Surgeons
7250 N Cicero Ave LL-6 .... Lincolnwood IL 60712 847-677-9093 677-9094
TF: 800-621-4002

International Assn of Physicians in AIDS Care (IAPAC)
33 N LaSalle St Suite 1700 .... Chicago IL 60602 312-795-4930 795-4938
Web: www.iapac.org

International Atherosclerosis Society (IAS)
6535 Fannin St Suite 754-A .... Houston TX 77030 713-797-0401 796-8853
Web: www.athero.org

International Chiropractors Assn (ICA)
1110 N Glebe Rd Suite 650 .... Arlington VA 22201 703-528-5000 528-5023
TF: 800-423-4690 ■ *Web:* www.chiropractic.org

International College of Dentists (ICD)
51 Monroe St Suite 1400 .... Rockville MD 20850 301-251-8861 738-9143
Web: www.icd.org

International College of Surgeons (ICS) 1516 N Lake Shore Dr .... Chicago IL 60610 312-642-3555 787-1624
Web: www.icsglobal.org

International Congress of Oral Implantologists (ICOI)
248 Lorraine Ave 3rd Fl .... Upper Montclair NJ 07043 973-783-6300 783-1175
TF: 800-442-0525 ■ *Web:* www.icoi.org

International Nurses Society on Addictions (IntNSA)
PO Box 10752 .... Raleigh NC 27605 919-821-1292 833-5743
Web: www.intnsa.org

International Society for Heart & Lung Transplantation (ISHLT)
14673 Midway Rd Suite 200 .... Addison TX 75001 972-490-9495 490-9499
Web: www.ishlt.org

International Society for Magnetic Resonance in Medicine (ISMRM) 2118 Millvia St Suite 201 .... Berkeley CA 94704 510-841-1899 841-2340
Web: www.ismrm.org

International Society for Peritoneal Dialysis (ISPD) 66 Martin St .... Milton ON L9T2R2 905-875-2456 875-2864
TF: 888-834-1001 ■ *Web:* www.ispd.org

International Society for Pharmacoeconomics & Outcomes Research (ISPOR) 3100 Princeton Pike Bldg 3 Suite E .... Lawrenceville NJ 08648 609-219-0773 219-0774
Web: www.ispor.org

International Society for Pharmacoepidemiology (ISPE)
5272 River Rd Suite 630 .... Bethesda MD 20816 301-718-6500 656-0989
Web: www.pharmacoepi.org

International Society of Refractive Surgery (ISRS)
655 Beach St .... San Francisco CA 94109 415-561-8581 561-8575
Web: www.isrs.org

International Society of Travel Medicine (ISTM)
2386 Clover St Suite A-102 .... Snellville GA 30078 770-736-7060 736-0313
Web: www.istm.org

International Transplant Nurses Society (ITNS)
1739 E Carson St Box 351 .... Pittsburgh PA 15203 412-343-4867 343-3959
Web: www.itns.org

Islamic Medical Assn of North America (IMANA)
101 W 22nd St Suite 106 .... Lombard IL 60148 630-932-0000 932-0005
Web: www.imana.org

Lamaze International 2025 M St NW Suite 800 .... Washington DC 20036 202-367-1128 367-2128
TF: 800-368-4404 ■ *Web:* www.lamaze.org

Medical Group Management Assn (MGMA)
104 Inverness Terr E .... Englewood CO 80112 303-799-1111 643-4439
TF: 877-275-6462 ■ *Web:* www.mgma.com

Medical Records Institute (MRI) 425 Boylston St 4th Fl .... Boston MA 02116 617-964-3923 964-3926
Web: www.medrecinst.com

National Abortion Federation (NAF)
1660 L St NW Suite 450 .... Washington DC 20036 202-667-5881 667-5890
TF: 800-772-9100 ■ *Web:* www.prochoice.org

National Assn of Addiction Treatment Providers (NAATP)
313 West Liberty St Suite 129 .... Lancaster PA 17603 717-392-8480 392-8481
Web: www.naatp.org

National Assn of Certified Healthcare Business Consultants (NSCHBC) 12100 Sunset Hills Rd Suite 130 .... Reston VA 20190 703-234-4099 435-4390
Web: www.healthcon.org

Phone *Fax*

National Assn of Children's Hospitals & Related Institutions (NACHRI) 401 Wythe St .... Alexandria VA 22314 703-684-1355 684-1589
Web: www.childrenshospitals.net

National Assn of Community Health Centers (NACHC)
7200 Wisconsin Ave Suite 210 .... Bethesda MD 20814 301-347-0400 347-0459
Web: www.nachc.com

National Assn of Dental Laboratories (NADL)
325 John Knox Rd Suite L-103 .... Tallahassee FL 32303 850-205-5626 222-0053
TF: 800-950-1150 ■ *Web:* www.nadl.org

National Assn of Directors of Nursing Administration in Long Term Care (NADONA/LTC) 10101 Alliance Rd Suite 140 .... Cincinnati OH 45242 513-791-3679 791-3699
TF: 800-222-0539 ■ *Web:* www.nadona.org

National Assn of Health Data Organizations (NAHDO)
375 Chipeta Way Suite A .... Salt Lake City UT 84108 801-587-9104 587-9125
Web: www.nahdo.org

National Assn for Healthcare Quality (NAHQ)
4700 W Lake Ave .... Glenview IL 60025 847-375-4720 218-7939*
**Fax Area Code:* 877 ■ *TF:* 800-966-9392 ■ *Web:* www.nahq.org

National Assn for Home Care & Hospice (NAHC)
228 7th St SE .... Washington DC 20003 202-547-7424 547-3540
Web: www.nahc.org

National Assn of Managed Care Physicians (NAMCP)
4435 Waterfront Dr Suite 101 PO Box 4765 .... Glen Allen VA 23060 804-527-1905 747-5316
TF: 800-722-0376 ■ *Web:* www.namcp.com

National Assn Medical Staff Services (NAMSS)
2025 M St NW Suite 800 .... Washington DC 20036 202-367-1196 367-2196
Web: www.namss.org

National Assn of Neonatal Nurses (NANN) 4700 W Lake Ave .... Glenview IL 60025 847-375-3660 477-6266*
**Fax Area Code:* 888 ■ *TF:* 800-451-3795 ■ *Web:* www.nann.org

National Assn of Nurse Practitioners in Women's Health
505 C St NE .... Washington DC 20002 202-543-9693 543-9858
Web: www.npwh.org

National Assn of Orthopaedic Nurses (NAON)
401 N Michigan Ave Suite 2200 .... Chicago IL 60611 800-289-6266 527-6658*
**Fax Area Code:* 312 ■ *Web:* www.orthonurse.org

National Assn of Physician Recruiters (NAPR)
PO Box 150127 .... Altamonte Springs FL 32715 407-774-7880 774-6440
TF: 800-726-5613 ■ *Web:* www.napr.org

National Assn of Professional Geriatric Care Managers (GCM)
1604 N Country Club Rd .... Tucson AZ 85716 520-881-8008 325-7925
Web: www.caremanager.org

National Assn of Public Hospitals & Health Systems (NAPH)
1301 Pennsylvania Ave NW Suite 950 .... Washington DC 20004 202-585-0100 585-0101
Web: www.naph.org

National Assn of School Nurses (NASN) PO Box 1300 .... Scarborough ME 04070 207-883-2117 883-2683
TF: 877-627-6476 ■ *Web:* www.nasn.org

National Assn of Subacute & Post Acute Care (NASPAC)
1960 Gallows Rd Suite 120 .... Vienna VA 22182 703-790-8989 790-8485
Web: www.naspac.net

National Assn for the Support of Long Term Care (NASL)
1321 Duke St Suite 304 .... Alexandria VA 22314 703-549-8500 549-8342
Web: www.nasl.org

National Assn of Vascular Access Networks (NAVAN)
11441 S State St Suite A113 .... Draper UT 84020 801-576-1824 553-9137
TF: 888-576-2826 ■ *Web:* www.avainfo.org

National Board of Medical Examiners (NBME)
3750 Market St .... Philadelphia PA 19104 215-590-9500
Web: www.nbme.org

National Coalition for Adult Immunization (NCAI)
4733 Bethesda Ave Suite 750 .... Bethesda MD 20814 301-656-0003 907-0878

National Community Pharmacists Assn (NCPA)
100 Daingerfield Rd .... Alexandria VA 22314 703-683-8200 683-3619
TF: 800-544-7447 ■ *Web:* www.ncpanet.org

National Council on Problem Gambling Inc
216 G St NE Suite 200 .... Washington DC 20002 202-547-9204 547-9206
TF: 800-522-4700 ■ *Web:* www.ncpgambling.org

National Council of State Boards of Nursing (NCSBN)
111 E Wacker Dr Suite 2900 .... Chicago IL 60601 312-525-3600 279-1032
Web: www.ncsbn.org

National EMS Pilots Assn (NEMSPA) 526 King St Suite 415 .... Alexandria VA 22314 703-836-8930 836-8920
Web: www.nemspa.org

National Foundation for Infectious Diseases (NFID)
4733 Bethesda Ave Suite 750 .... Bethesda MD 20814 301-656-0003 907-0878
Web: www.nfid.org

National Home Infusion Assn (NHIA) 100 Daingerfield Rd .... Alexandria VA 22314 703-549-3740 683-1484
TF: 800-544-7447 ■ *Web:* www.nhianet.org

National Hospice & Palliative Care Organization (NHPCO)
1700 Diagonal Rd Suite 625 .... Alexandria VA 22314 703-837-1500 837-1233
TF Help Line: 800-658-8898 ■ *Web:* www.nhpco.org

National Kidney Foundation (NKF) 30 E 33rd St 8th Fl .... New York NY 10016 212-889-2210 779-0068
TF: 800-622-9010 ■ *Web:* www.kidney.org

National League for Nursing (NLN) 61 Broadway 33rd Fl .... New York NY 10006 212-363-5555 812-0391
TF: 800-669-1656 ■ *Web:* www.nln.org

National Medical Assn (NMA) 1012 10th St NW .... Washington DC 20001 202-347-1895 842-3293
TF: 800-662-0554 ■ *Web:* www.nmanet.org

National Nursing Staff Development Organization (NNSDO)
7794 Grow Dr .... Pensacola FL 32514 850-474-0995 484-8762
TF: 800-489-1995 ■ *Web:* www.nnsdo.org

National Nutrition Alliance 300 S Duncan Ave Suite 225 .... Clearwater FL 33755 727-446-6086 446-6202
Web: www.am-coll-nutr.org/nna/nna.htm

National Organization for Rare Disorders (NORD)
55 Kenosia Ave PO Box 1968 .... Danbury CT 06813 203-744-0100 798-2291
TF: 800-999-6673 ■ *Web:* www.rarediseases.org

National Pharmaceutical Council (NPC) 1894 Preston White Dr .... Reston VA 20191 703-620-6390 476-0904
Web: www.npcnow.org

National Pharmacy Technicians Assn (NPTA)
3707 FM 1960 W Suite 460 .... Houston TX 77068 281-866-7900 895-7320
TF: 888-247-8700 ■ *Web:* www.pharmacytechnician.org

National Renal Administrators Assn (NRAA) 1904 Naomi Pl .... Prescott AZ 86303 928-717-2772 441-3857
Web: www.nraa.org

National Rural Health Assn (NRHA)
1 W Armour Blvd Suite 203 .... Kansas City MO 64111 816-756-3140 756-3144
Web: www.nrharural.org

National Student Nurses Assn (NSNA) 45 Main St Suite 606 .... Brooklyn NY 11201 718-210-0705 210-0710
Web: www.nsna.org

North American Menopause Society (NAMS)
5900 Landerbrook Dr Suite 195 .... Mayfield Heights OH 44124 440-442-7550 442-2660
Web: www.menopause.org

North American Spine Society (NASS) 22 Calendar Ct 2nd Fl .... La Grange IL 60525 708-588-8080 588-1080
TF: 877-774-6337 ■ *Web:* www.spine.org

Oncology Nursing Society (ONS) 125 Enterprise Dr .... Pittsburgh PA 15275 412-859-6100 369-5497*
**Fax Area Code:* 877 ■ *TF:* 866-257-4667 ■ *Web:* www.ons.org

Optical Laboratories Assn (OLA) 11096 Lee Hwy Suite A-101 .... Fairfax VA 22030 703-359-2830 359-2834
TF: 800-477-5652 ■ *Web:* www.ola-labs.org

Optical Society of America (OSA)
2010 Massachusetts Ave NW .... Washington DC 20036 202-223-8130 223-1096
TF: 800-762-6960 ■ *Web:* www.osa.org

	City	State	Zip	Phone	Fax
Opticians Assn of America (OAA) 441 Carlisle Dr *Web:* www.oaa.org	Herndon	VA	20170	703-437-8780	437-0727
PDA PO Box 79465 *Web:* www.pda.org	Baltimore	MD	21279	301-986-0293	986-1093
Pharmaceutical Care Management Assn (PCMA) 601 Pennsylvania Ave NW Suite 740 *Web:* www.pcmanet.org	Washington	DC	20004	202-207-3610	207-3623
Pharmaceutical Research & Manufacturers of America (PhRMA) 950 F St NW Suite 3000 *Web:* www.phrma.org	Washington	DC	20004	202-835-3400	835-3414
Physiatric Assn of Spine Sports & Occupational Rehabilitation (PASSOR) 1 IBM Plaza Suite 2500 *Web:* www.aapmr.org/passor.htm	Chicago	IL	60611	312-464-9700	464-0227
Physicians Committee for Responsible Medicine (PCRM) 5100 Wisconsin Ave NW Suite 400 *TF:* 866-416-7276 ■ *Web:* www.pcrm.org	Washington	DC	20016	202-686-2210	686-2216
Physicians for Social Responsibility (PSR) 1875 Connecticut Ave NW Suite 1012 *Web:* www.psr.org	Washington	DC	20009	202-667-4260	667-4201
Plasma Protein Therapeutics Assn (PPTA) 147 Old Solomon's Island Rd Suite 100 *Web:* www.pptaglobal.org	Annapolis	MD	21401	410-263-8296	263-2298
Radiological Society of North America (RSNA) 820 Jorie Blvd *TF:* 800-381-6660 ■ *Web:* www.rsna.org	Oak Brook	IL	60523	630-571-2670	571-7837
Radiology Business Management Assn (RBMA) 8001 Irvine Center Dr Suite 1060 *TF:* 888-224-7262 ■ *Web:* rbma.org	Irvine	CA	92618	949-340-5000	340-5001
Regulatory Affairs Professionals Society (RAPS) 5635 Fishers Ln Suite 550 *Web:* www.raps.org	Rockville	MD	20852	301-770-2920	770-2924
Renal Physicians Assn (RPA) 1700 Rockville Pike Suite 220 *Web:* www.renalmd.org	Rockville	MD	20852	301-468-3515	468-3511
Society for Academic Emergency Medicine (SAEM) 901 N Washington Ave *Web:* www.saem.org	Lansing	MI	48906	517-485-5484	485-0801
Society of American Gastrointestinal Endoscopic Surgeons (SAGES) 11300 W Olympic Blvd Suite 600 *Web:* www.sages.org	Los Angeles	CA	90064	310-437-0544	437-0585
Society of Cardiovascular Anesthesiologists (SCA) 2209 Dickens Rd *Web:* www.scahq.org	Richmond	VA	23230	804-282-0084	282-0090
Society of Critical Care Medicine (SCCM) 701 Lee St Suite 200 *Web:* www.sccm.org	Des Plaines	IL	60016	847-827-6869	827-6886
Society of Diagnostic Medical Sonography (SDMS) 2745 N Dallas Pkwy Suite 350 *TF:* 800-229-9506 ■ *Web:* www.sdms.org	Plano	TX	75093	214-473-8057	473-8563
Society of Gastroenterology Nurses & Associates Inc (SGNA) 401 N Michigan Ave *TF:* 800-245-7462 ■ *Web:* www.sgna.org	Chicago	IL	60611	312-321-5165	527-6658
Society for Healthcare Epidemiology of America (SHEA) 66 Canal Center Plaza Suite 600 *Web:* www.shea-online.org	Alexandria	VA	22314	703-684-1006	684-1009
Society for Healthcare Strategy & Market Development American Hospital Assn 1 N Franklin St 28th Fl *TF:* 800-242-2626 ■ *Web:* www.shsmd.org	Chicago	IL	60606	312-422-3888	422-4579
Society of Interventional Radiology (SIR) 3975 Fair Rdige Dr Suite 400 North *TF:* 800-488-7284 ■ *Web:* www.sirweb.org	Fairfax	VA	22033	703-691-1805	691-1855
Society for Investigative Dermatology Inc (SID) 820 W Superior Ave 7th Fl *Web:* www.sidnet.org	Cleveland	OH	44113	216-579-9300	579-9333
Society of Laparoendoscopic Surgeons (SLS) 7330 SW 62nd Pl Suite 410 *TF:* 800-446-2659 ■ *Web:* www.sls.org	South Miami	FL	33143	305-665-9959	667-4123
Society for Medical Decision Making 100 N 20th St 4th Fl *Web:* www.smdm.org	Philadelphia	PA	19103	215-545-7697	564-2175
Society for Neuroscience (SFN) 1121 14th St NW Suite 1010 *Web:* web.sfn.org	Washington	DC	20005	202-962-4000	962-4941
Society of Nuclear Medicine (SNM) 1850 Samuel Morse Dr *TF:* 800-487-5620 ■ *Web:* www.snm.org	Reston	VA	20190	703-708-9000	708-9015
Society for Surgery of the Alimentary Tract (SSAT) 900 Cummings Ctr Suite 221-U *Web:* www.ssat.com	Beverly	MA	01915	978-927-8330	524-8890
Society of Teachers of Family Medicine (STFM) 11400 Tomahawk Creek Pkwy Suite 540 *Web:* www.stfm.org	Leawood	KS	66211	913-906-6000	906-6096
Society of Thoracic Surgeons (STS) 633 N Saint Clair St Suite 2320 *Web:* www.sts.org	Chicago	IL	60611	312-202-5800	202-5801
Society of Toxicology (SOT) 1821 Michael Faraday Dr Suite 300 *Web:* www.toxicology.org	Reston	VA	20190	703-438-3115	438-3113
Society of Urologic Cryosurgeons 1950 Old Tustin Ave	Santa Ana	CA	92705	714-550-9155	550-9234
Society for Vascular Surgery (SVS) 633 N St Clair 24th Fl *TF:* 800-258-7188 ■ *Web:* svs.vascularweb.org	Chicago	IL	60611	312-202-5600	202-5610
Southern Medical Assn (SMA) 35 W Lakeshore Dr *TF:* 800-423-4992 ■ *Web:* www.sma.org	Birmingham	AL	35209	205-945-1840	942-0642
Special Care Dentistry Assn 401 N Michigan Ave 22nd Fl *Web:* www.scdonline.org	Chicago	IL	60611	312-527-6764	673-6663
Sports Cardiovascular & Wellness Nutritionists (SCAN) PO Box 8088 *TF:* 800-249-2875 ■ *Web:* www.scandpg.org	Chicago	IL	60690	847-441-7200	556-0352
Therapeutic Communities of America (TCA) 1601 Connecticut Ave NW Suite 803 *Web:* www.therapeuticcommunitiesofamerica.org	Washington	DC	20009	202-296-3503	518-5475
United American Nurses AFL-CIO (UAN) 8515 Georgia Ave Suite 400 *Web:* www.uannurse.org	Silver Spring	MD	20910	301-628-5118	628-5347
US Pharmacopeia (USP) 12601 Twinbrook Pkwy **Fax:* Hum Res ■ *TF:* 800-877-6209 ■ *Web:* www.usp.org	Rockville	MD	20852	301-881-0666	816-8525*
Visiting Nurse Assns of America (VNAA) 99 Summer St Suite 1700 *TF:* 800-426-2547 ■ *Web:* www.vnaa.org	Boston	MA	02110	617-737-3200	737-1144
World Allergy Organization (WAO) 555 E Wells St *Web:* www.worldallergy.org	Milwaukee	WI	53202	414-276-1791	276-3349
World Foundation for Medical Studies in Female Health (WFFH) 405 Main St Suite 8 *Web:* www.wffh.org	Port Washington	NY	11050	516-944-8655	944-8663
Wound Ostomy & Continence Nurses Society (WOCN) 15000 Commerce Pkwy Suite C **Fax Area Code:* 866 ■ *Web:* www.wocn.org	Mount Laurel	NJ	08054	888-224-9626	615-8560*

49-9 Insurance Industry Associations

	City	State	Zip	Phone	Fax
ACORD 2 Blue Hill Plaza 3rd Fl *TF:* 800-444-3341 ■ *Web:* www.acord.org	Pearl River	NY	10965	845-620-1700	620-3600
American Academy of Actuaries 1100 17th St NW 7th Fl *Web:* www.actuary.org	Washington	DC	20036	202-223-8196	872-1948
American Assn of Crop Insurers (AACI) 1 Massachusetts Ave NW Suite 800 *Web:* www.cropinsurers.org	Washington	DC	20001	202-789-4100	408-7763
American Assn of Insurance Services (AAIS) 1745 S Naperville Rd *TF:* 800-564-2247 ■ *Web:* www.aaisonline.com	Wheaton	IL	60189	630-681-8347	681-8356
American Assn of Managing General Agents (AAMGA) 150 S Warner Rd Suite 156 *Web:* www.aamga.org	King of Prussia	PA	19406	610-225-1999	225-1996
American Council of Life Insurers (ACLI) 101 Constitution Ave NW Suite 700 W *Web:* www.acli.com	Washington	DC	20001	202-624-2000	624-2319
American Institute for CPCU & Insurance Institute of America (AICPCU/IIA) 720 Providence Rd Suite 100 *TF:* 800-644-2101 ■ *Web:* www.aicpcu.org	Malvern	PA	19355	610-644-2100	640-9576
American Institute of Marine Underwriters (AIMU) 14 Wall St 8th Fl *Web:* www.aimu.org	New York	NY	10005	212-233-0550	227-5102
American Insurance Assn (AIA) 1130 Connecticut Ave NW Suite 1000 *Web:* www.aiadc.org	Washington	DC	20036	202-828-7100	293-1219
American Nuclear Insurers (ANI) 95 Glastonbury Blvd *TF:* 866-301-1301 ■ *Web:* www.amnucins.com	Glastonbury	CT	06033	860-682-1301	659-0002
American Society for Healthcare Risk Management (ASHRM) 1 N Franklin St *Web:* www.ashrm.org	Chicago	IL	60606	312-422-3980	422-4580
America's Health Insurance Plans (AHIP) 601 Pennsylvania Ave NW Suite 500 *TF Cust Svc:* 877-291-2247 ■ *Web:* www.ahip.org	Washington	DC	20004	202-778-3200	331-7487
Associated Risk Managers International (ARMI) 2 Pierce Pl *Web:* www.armnet.com	Itasca	IL	60143	630-285-4186	285-3590
Association for Advanced Life Underwriting (AALU) 2901 Telestar Ct Suite 400 *TF:* 888-275-0092 ■ *Web:* www.aalu.org	Falls Church	VA	22042	703-641-9400	641-9885
Association of Health Insurance Advisors (AHIA) 2901 Telestar Ct *Web:* www.ahia.net	Falls Church	VA	22042	703-770-8200	770-8201
Blue Cross & Blue Shield Assn 225 N Michigan Ave *TF:* 888-663-2583 ■ *Web:* www.bluecares.com	Chicago	IL	60601	312-297-6000	297-6609
Casualty Actuarial Society (CAS) 4350 N Fiarfax Dr Suite 250 *Web:* www.casact.org	Arlington	VA	22203	703-276-3100	276-3108
Coalition Against Insurance Fraud 1012 14th St NW Suite 200 *Web:* www.insurancefraud.org	Washington	DC	20005	202-393-7330	318-9189
Consumer Credit Industry Assn (CCIA) 542 S Dearborn St Suite 400 *Web:* www.cciaonline.com	Chicago	IL	60605	312-939-2242	939-8287
Council for Affordable Health Insurance (CAHI) 127 S Peyton St Suite 210 *Web:* www.cahi.org	Alexandria	VA	22314	703-836-6200	836-6550
Council of Insurance Agents & Brokers 701 Pennsylvania Ave NW Suite 750 *TF:* 888-919-4400 ■ *Web:* www.ciab.com	Washington	DC	20004	202-783-4400	783-4410
CPCU Society 720 Providence Rd **Fax Area Code:* 610 ■ *TF:* 800-932-2728 ■ *Web:* www.cpcusociety.org	Malvern	PA	19355	800-932-2728	251-2780*
Delta Dental Plans Assn 1515 W 22nd St Suite 450 *Web:* www.deltadental.com	Oak Brook	IL	60523	630-574-6001	
GAMA International 2901 Telestar Ct Suite 140 *TF Cust Svc:* 800-345-2687 ■ *Web:* www.gamaweb.com	Falls Church	VA	22042	703-770-8184	770-8182
Independent Insurance Agents & Brokers of America Inc (IIABA) 127 S Peyton St *TF:* 800-221-7917 ■ *Web:* www.iiaba.org	Alexandria	VA	22314	703-683-4422	683-7556
Institute for Business & Home Safety (IBHS) 4775 E Fowler Ave *TF:* 866-657-4247 ■ *Web:* www.disastersafety.org	Tampa	FL	33617	813-286-3400	286-9960
Insurance Information Institute (III) 110 William St 24th Fl *TF:* 800-331-9146 ■ *Web:* www.iii.org	New York	NY	10038	212-346-5500	732-1916
Insurance Institute for Highway Safety 1005 N Glebe Rd Suite 800 *Web:* www.iihs.org	Arlington	VA	22201	703-247-1500	247-1678
Insurance Marketing Communications Assn (IMCA) 4916 Pt Fosdick Dr NW Suite 180 *Web:* imcanet.com	Gig Harbor	WA	98335	206-219-9811	210-2481
Insurance Research Council (IRC) 718 Providence Rd PO Box 3025 *TF:* 800-644-2101 ■ *Web:* www.ircweb.org	Malvern	PA	19355	610-644-2212	644-5388
Life Insurance Settlement Assn (LISA) 1011 E Colonial Dr Suite 500 *Web:* www.lisassociation.org	Orlando	FL	32803	407-894-3797	897-1325
LIMRA International Inc 300 Day Hill Rd *Web:* www.limra.com	Windsor	CT	06095	860-688-3358	298-9555
LOMA 2300 Windy Ridge Pkwy Suite 600 *TF:* 800-275-5662 ■ *Web:* www.loma.org	Atlanta	GA	30339	770-951-1770	984-0441
Million Dollar Round Table (MDRT) 325 W Touhy Ave *TF:* 800-879-6378 ■ *Web:* www.mdrt.org	Park Ridge	IL	60068	847-692-6378	518-8921
Mortgage Insurance Companies of America (MICA) 1425 K St NW Suite 210 *Web:* www.privatemi.com	Washington	DC	20005	202-682-2683	842-9252
National Assn of Dental Plans (NADP) 8111 LBJ Fwy Suite 935 *Web:* www.nadp.org	Dallas	TX	75251	972-458-6998	458-2258
National Assn of Health Underwriters (NAHU) 2000 N 14th St Suite 450 *Web:* www.nahu.org	Arlington	VA	22201	703-276-0220	841-7797
National Assn of Insurance Commissioners (NAIC) 2301 McGee St Suite 800 *Web:* www.naic.org	Kansas City	MO	64108	816-842-3600	783-8175
National Assn of Insurance & Financial Advisors (NAIFA) 2901 Telestar Ct *TF Sales:* 877-866-2432 ■ *Web:* www.naifa.org	Falls Church	VA	22042	703-770-8100	770-8224
National Assn of Insurance Women (International) 9393 E 95th Ct S *TF:* 800-766-6249 ■ *Web:* www.naiw.org	Tulsa	OK	74133	918-294-3700	294-3711
National Assn of Mutual Insurance Companies (NAMIC) 3601 Vincennes Rd PO Box 68700 *TF:* 800-336-2642 ■ *Web:* www.namic.org	Indianapolis	IN	46268	317-875-5250	879-8408
National Assn of Professional Insurance Agents (PIA) 400 N Washington St *TF:* 800-742-6900 ■ *Web:* www.pianet.com	Alexandria	VA	22314	703-836-9340	836-1279
National Assn of Surety Bond Producers (NASBP) 1828 L St NW Suite 720 *Web:* www.nasbp.org	Washington	DC	20036	202-686-3700	686-3656

Insurance Industry Associations (Cont'd)

Organization	City	State	Zip	Phone	Fax
National Assn for Variable Annuities (NAVA) 11710 Plaza America Dr Suite 100 *Web:* www.navanet.org	Reston	VA	20190	703-707-8830	707-8831
National Council for Prescription Drug Programs (NCPDP) 9240 E Raintree Dr *Web:* www.ncpdp.org	Scottsdale	AZ	85260	480-477-1000	767-1042
National Crop Insurance Services (NCIS) 8900 Indian Creek Pkwy Suite 600 *TF:* 800-951-6247 ■ *Web:* www.ag-risk.org	Overland Park	KS	66210	913-685-2767	685-3080
National Insurance Crime Bureau (NICB) 1111 E Touhy Ave Suite 400 *Fax: Hum Res ■ *TF:* 800-447-6282 ■ *Web:* www.nicb.org	Des Plaines	IL	60018	847-544-7000	544-7102*
National Organization of Life & Health Insurance Guaranty Assns (NOLHGA) 13873 Park Center Rd Suite 329 *Web:* www.nolhga.com	Herndon	VA	20171	703-481-5206	481-5209
NCIS (National Crop Insurance Services) 8900 Indian Creek Pkwy Suite 600 *TF:* 800-951-6247 ■ *Web:* www.ag-risk.org	Overland Park	KS	66210	913-685-2767	685-3080
Physician Insurers Assn of America 2275 Research Blvd Suite 250 *Web:* www.piaa.us	Rockville	MD	20850	301-947-9000	947-9090
Professional Insurance Marketing Assn (PIMA) 230 E Ohio St Suite 400 *Web:* www.pima-assn.org	Chicago	IL	60611	817-569-7462	569-7461
Professional Liability Underwriting Society 5353 Wayzata Blvd Suite 600 *TF:* 800-845-0778 ■ *Web:* www.plusweb.org	Minneapolis	MN	55416	952-746-2580	746-2599
Property Casualty Insurers Assn of America 2600 S River Rd *Web:* www.pciaa.net	Des Plaines	IL	60018	847-297-7800	297-5064
Property Loss Research Bureau (PLRB) 3025 Highland Pkwy Suite 800 *TF:* 888-711-7572 ■ *Web:* www.plrb.org	Downers Grove	IL	60515	630-724-2200	724-2260
Reinsurance Assn of America (RAA) 1301 Pennsylvania Ave NW Suite 900 *TF:* 800-638-3651 ■ *Web:* www.reinsurance.org	Washington	DC	20004	202-638-3690	638-0936
Risk & Insurance Management Society Inc (RIMS) 1065 Ave of the Americas 13th Fl *TF:* 800-711-0317 ■ *Web:* www.rims.org	New York	NY	10018	212-286-9292	986-9716
Self-Insurance Institute of America Inc (SIIA) PO Box 1237 *TF:* 800-851-7789 ■ *Web:* www.siia.org	Simpsonville	SC	29681	864-962-2208	962-2483
Society of Actuaries (SOA) 475 N Martingale Rd Suite 600 *Web:* www.soa.org	Schaumburg	IL	60173	847-706-3500	706-3599
Society of Certified Insurance Counselors PO Box 27027 *TF:* 800-633-2165	Austin	TX	78755	512-345-7932	349-6194
Society of Financial Service Professionals (SFSP) 17 Campus Blvd Suite 201 *TF:* 800-392-6900 ■ *Web:* www.financialpro.org	Newtown Square	PA	19073	610-526-2500	527-4010
Surety & Fidelity Assn of America (SFAA) 1101 Connecticut Ave NW Suite 800 *Web:* www.surety.org	Washington	DC	20036	202-463-0600	463-0606
Workmen's Circle/Arbeter Ring 45 E 33rd St 4th Fl *TF:* 800-922-2558 ■ *Web:* www.circle.org	New York	NY	10016	212-889-6800	532-7518

49-10 Legal Professionals Associations

Organization	City	State	Zip	Phone	Fax
ABA (American Bar Assn) 321 N Clark St *TF:* 800-285-2221 ■ *Web:* www.abanet.org	Chicago	IL	60610	312-988-5522	988-6281
ABA Commission on Domestic Violence 740 15th St NW 9th Fl *TF:* 800-799-7233 ■ *Web:* www.abanet.org/domviol	Washington	DC	20005	202-662-1000	
ABA Commission on Law & Aging (COLA) 740 15th St NW 8th Fl *Web:* www.abanet.org/aging	Washington	DC	20005	202-662-8690	662-8698
American Academy of Psychiatry & the Law (AAPL) 1 Regency Dr PO Box 30 *TF:* 800-331-1389 ■ *Web:* www.aapl.org	Bloomfield	CT	06002	860-242-5450	286-0787
American Arbitration Assn Inc (AAA) 1633 Broadway 10th Fl *TF:* 800-778-7879 ■ *Web:* www.adr.org	New York	NY	10019	212-716-5800	716-5905
American Assn for Justice (AAJ) 1050 31st St NW *TF:* 800-424-2725 ■ *Web:* www.justice.org	Washington	DC	20007	202-965-3500	625-7313
American Bankruptcy Institute (ABI) 44 Canal Center Plaza Suite 400 *Web:* www.abiworld.org	Alexandria	VA	22314	703-739-0800	739-1060
American Bar Assn (ABA) 321 N Clark St *TF:* 800-285-2221 ■ *Web:* www.abanet.org	Chicago	IL	60610	312-988-5522	988-6281
American College of Trust & Estate Counsel (ACTEC) 3415 S Sepulveda Blvd Suite 330 *Web:* www.actec.org	Los Angeles	CA	90034	310-398-1888	572-7280
American Health Lawyers Assn (AHLA) 1025 Connecticut Ave NW Suite 600 *Web:* www.healthlawyers.org	Washington	DC	20036	202-833-1100	833-1105
American Immigration Lawyers Assn (AILA) 918 F St NW *Web:* www.aila.org	Washington	DC	20004	202-216-2400	783-7853
American Intellectual Property Law Assn (AIPLA) 241 18th St S Suite 700 *Web:* www.aipla.org	Arlington	VA	22202	703-415-0780	415-0786
American Judicature Society (AJS) Drake Univ Opperman Ctr 2700 University Ave *TF:* 800-626-4089 ■ *Web:* www.ajs.org	Des Moines	IA	50311	515-271-2281	279-3090
American Land Title Assn (ALTA) 1828 L St NW Suite 705 *TF:* 800-787-2582 ■ *Web:* www.alta.org	Washington	DC	20036	202-296-3671	223-5843
American Law Institute (ALI) 4025 Chestnut St *TF:* 800-253-6397 ■ *Web:* www.ali.org	Philadelphia	PA	19104	215-243-1600	243-1636
American Society of International Law (ASIL) 2223 Massachusetts Ave NW *Web:* www.asil.org	Washington	DC	20008	202-939-6000	797-7133
American Tort Reform Assn (ATRA) 1101 Connecticut Ave NW Suite 400 *Web:* www.atra.org	Washington	DC	20036	202-682-1163	682-1022
Association of American Law Schools (AALS) 1201 Connecticut Ave NW Suite 800 *Web:* www.aals.org	Washington	DC	20036	202-296-8851	296-8869
Association for Conflict Resolution (ACR) 5151 Wisconsin Ave NW Suite 5001 *Web:* www.acrnet.org	Washington	DC	20016	202-464-9700	464-9720
Association of Corporate Counsel (ACC) 1025 Connecticut Ave NW Suite 200 *Web:* www.acc.com	Washington	DC	20036	202-293-4103	293-4701
Association of Legal Administrators (ALA) 75 Tri-State International Suite 222 *Web:* www.alanet.org	Lincolnshire	IL	60069	847-267-1252	267-1329
Battered Women's Justice Project 1801 Nicollet Ave S Suite 102 *TF:* 800-903-0111 ■ *Web:* www.bwjp.org	Minneapolis	MN	55403	612-824-8768	824-8965
Christian Legal Society (CLS) 8001 Braddock Rd Suite 300 *Web:* www.clsnet.org	Springfield	VA	22151	703-642-1070	642-1075
Commercial Law League of America (CLLA) 70 E Lake St Suite 630 *TF:* 800-978-2552 ■ *Web:* www.clla.org	Chicago	IL	60601	312-781-2000	781-2010
Defense Research Institute (DRI) 150 N Michigan Ave Suite 300 *TF:* 800-667-8108 ■ *Web:* www.dri.org	Chicago	IL	60601	312-795-1101	795-0749
Environmental Law Institute (ELI) 2000 L St NW Suite 620 *TF:* 800-433-5120 ■ *Web:* www.eli.org	Washington	DC	20036	202-939-3800	939-3868
False Claims Act Legal Center 1220 19th St NW Suite 501 *TF:* 800-873-2573 ■ *Web:* www.taf.org	Washington	DC	20036	202-296-4826	296-4838
Federalist Society for Law & Public Policy Studies 1015 18th St NW Suite 425 *Web:* www.fed-soc.org	Washington	DC	20036	202-822-8138	296-8061
Food & Drug Law Institute (FDLI) 1155 15th St NW Suite 800 *TF:* 800-956-6293 ■ *Web:* www.fdli.org	Washington	DC	20005	202-371-1420	371-0649
Hispanic National Bar Assn (HNBA) 1111 Pennsylvania Ave NW 3rd Fl *Web:* www.hnba.com	Washington	DC	20004	202-223-4777	223-2324
Institute of Judicial Administration NYU School of Law 40 Washington Sq S Vanderbilt Hall	New York	NY	10012	212-998-6196	995-4036
Institute for Professionals in Taxation (IPT) 600 N Park Town Center 1200 Abernathy Rd NE Suite L-2 *Web:* www.ipt.org	Atlanta	GA	30328	404-240-2300	240-2315
International Assn of Defense Counsel (IADC) 1 N Franklin St Suite 1205 *Web:* www.iadclaw.org	Chicago	IL	60606	312-368-1494	368-1854
International Intellectual Property Alliance (IIPA) 2101 L St NW Suite 1000 *Web:* www.iipa.com	Washington	DC	20037	202-833-4198	261-0151
International Law Institute (ILI) 1055 Thomas Jefferson St NW Suite M-100 *Web:* www.ili.org	Washington	DC	20007	202-247-6006	247-6010
International Municipal Lawyers Assn (IMLA) 7910 Woodmont Ave Suite 1440 *Web:* www.imla.org	Bethesda	MD	20814	202-466-5424	785-0152
Justice Research & Statistics Assn (JRSA) 777 N Capitol St NE Suite 801 *Web:* www.jrsainfo.org	Washington	DC	20002	202-842-9330	842-9329
Lawyers for Civil Justice (LCJ) 1140 Connecticut Ave NW Suite 503 *Web:* www.lfcj.com	Washington	DC	20036	202-429-0045	429-6892
Lawyers' Committee for Civil Rights Under Law 1401 New York Ave NW Suite 400 *Web:* www.lawyerscommittee.org	Washington	DC	20005	202-662-8600	783-0857
Media Law Resource Center (MLRC) 520 8th Ave 20th Fl *Web:* www.medialaw.org	New York	NY	10011	212-337-0200	337-9893
NALS - Assn for Legal Professionals 8159 E 41st St *Web:* www.nals.org	Tulsa	OK	74145	918-582-5188	582-5907
National Academy of Elder Law Attorneys (NAELA) 1604 N Country Club Rd *Web:* www.naela.com	Tucson	AZ	85716	520-881-4005	325-7925
National Assn of Bond Lawyers (NABL) 230 W Monroe St Suite 320 *Web:* www.nabl.org	Chicago	IL	60606	312-648-9590	648-9588
National Assn of College & University Attorneys (NACUA) 1 Dupont Cir NW Suite 620 *Web:* www.nacua.org	Washington	DC	20036	202-833-8390	296-8379
National Assn for Community Mediation (NAFCM) PO Box 3263 NW *Web:* www.nafcm.org	Washington	DC	20010	202-545-8866	545-8873
National Assn for Court Management (NACM) National Center for State Courts 300 Newport Ave *TF:* 800-616-6165 ■ *Web:* www.nacmnet.org	Williamsburg	VA	23185	757-259-1841	259-1520
National Assn of Criminal Defense Lawyers (NACDL) 1150 18th St NW Suite 950 *Web:* www.nacdl.org	Washington	DC	20036	202-872-8600	872-8690
National Assn of Enrolled Agents (NAEA) 1120 Connecticut Ave NW Suite 460 *Web:* www.naea.org	Washington	DC	20036	202-822-6232	822-6270
National Assn of Estate Planners & Councils (NAEPC) 1120 Chester Ave Suite 470 *Fax Area Code: 216 ■ *TF:* 866-226-2224 ■ *Web:* www.naepc.org	Cleveland	OH	44114	866-226-2224	696-2582*
National Assn for Law Placement (NALP) 1025 Connecticut Ave NW Suite 1110 *Web:* www.nalp.org	Washington	DC	20036	202-835-1001	835-1112
National Assn of Legal Assistants (NALA) 1516 S Boston Ave Suite 200 *Web:* www.nala.org	Tulsa	OK	74119	918-587-6828	582-6772
National Assn of Professional Process Servers (NAPPS) PO Box 4547 *TF:* 800-477-8211 ■ *Web:* www.napps.org	Portland	OR	97208	503-222-4180	222-3950
National Bar Assn (NBA) 1225 11th St NW *Web:* www.nationalbar.org	Washington	DC	20001	202-842-3900	289-6170
National Center for Juvenile Justice (NCJJ) 3700 S Water St Suite 200 *TF:* 800-577-6903 ■ *Web:* www.ncjj.org	Pittsburgh	PA	15203	412-227-6950	227-6955
National Council of Juvenile & Family Court Judges (NCJFCJ) Univ of Nevada PO Box 8970 *Web:* www.ncjfcj.org	Reno	NV	89507	775-784-6012	784-6628
National Court Reporters Assn (NCRA) 8224 Old Courthouse Rd *TF:* 800-272-6272 ■ *Web:* www.ncraonline.org	Vienna	VA	22182	703-556-6272	556-6291
National Employment Lawyers Assn (NELA) 44 Montgomery St Suite 2080 *Web:* www.nela.org	San Francisco	CA	94104	415-296-7629	677-9445
National Federation of Paralegal Assns (NFPA) 23607 Hwy 99 Suite 2-C *Web:* www.paralegals.org	Edmonds	WA	98020	425-967-0045	771-9588
National Legal Aid & Defender Assn (NLADA) 1140 Connecticut Ave NW Suite 900 *Web:* www.nlada.org	Washington	DC	20036	202-452-0620	872-1031
National Network of Estate Planning Attorneys Inc (NNEPA) 3500 DePauw Blvd Suite 2090 *Fax Area Code: 402 ■ *TF:* 800-638-8681 ■ *Web:* www.nnepa.com	Indianapolis	IN	46268	800-638-8681	964-3800*
National Partnership for Women & Families 1875 Connecticut Ave NW Suite 650 *Web:* www.nationalpartnership.org	Washington	DC	20009	202-986-2600	986-2539

Phone Fax

National Senior Citizens Law Center (NSCLC)
1444 'I' St Suite 1100 .... Washington DC 20005 202-289-6976 289-7224
Web: www.nsclc.org

Native American Rights Fund (NARF) 1506 Broadway St .... Boulder CO 80302 303-447-8760 443-7776
Web: www.narf.org

Pension Rights Center 1350 Connecticut Ave NW Suite 206..... Washington DC 20036 202-296-3776 833-2472
Web: www.pensionrights.org

Practising Law Institute (PLI) 810 7th Ave 26th Fl ....New York NY 10019 212-824-5700 477-0300*
*Fax Area Code: 800 ■ *Fax: Cust Svc ■ *TF:* 800-260-4754 ■ *Web:* www.pli.edu

Taxpayers Against Fraud Education Fund (TAF)
1220 19th St NW Suite 501............ Washington DC 20036 202-296-4826 296-4838
TF: 800-873-2573 ■ *Web:* www.taf.org

Vera Institute of Justice 233 Broadway 12th Fl ....New York NY 10279 212-334-1300 941-9407
Web: www.vera.org

World Jurist Assn (WJA) 7910 Woodmont Ave Suite 1440 .... Bethesda MD 20814 202-466-5428 452-8540
Web: www.worldjurist.org

49-11 Library & Information Science Associations

Phone Fax

American Assn of Law Libraries (AALL)
53 W Jackson Blvd Suite 940 .... Chicago IL 60604 312-939-4764 431-1097
Web: www.aallnet.org

American Assn of School Librarians (AASL) 50 E Huron St .... Chicago IL 60611 312-280-4386 664-7459
TF: 800-545-2433 ■ *Web:* www.ala.org/aasl

American Library Assn (ALA) 50 E Huron St .... Chicago IL 60611 312-944-6780 944-2641
TF: 800-545-2433 ■ *Web:* www.ala.org

American Theological Library Assn (ATLA)
250 S Wacker Dr Suite 1600.............. Chicago IL 60606 312-454-5100 454-5505
TF: 888-665-2852 ■ *Web:* www.atla.com

Association of College & Research Libraries (ACRL)
50 E Huron St .... Chicago IL 60611 312-280-2519 280-2520
TF: 800-545-2433 ■ *Web:* www.ala.org/acrl.html

Association of Jewish Libraries 330 7th Ave 21st Fl ....New York NY 10001 212-725-5359
Web: www.jewishlibraries.org

Association for Library Collections & Technical Services (ALCTS)
50 E Huron St .... Chicago IL 60611 312-280-5038 280-5033
TF: 800-545-2433 ■ *Web:* www.ala.org/alcts

Association for Library & Information Science Education (ALISE)
65 E Wacker Pl Suite 1900 .... Chicago IL 60601 312-795-0996 419-8950
Web: www.alise.org

Association for Library Service to Children (ALSC)
50 E Huron St .... Chicago IL 60611 312-280-2163 944-7671
TF: 800-545-2433 ■ *Web:* www.ala.org/alsc

Association for Library Trustees & Advocates (ALTA)
50 E Huron St .... Chicago IL 60611 312-280-2161 280-3256
Web: www.ala.org/alta

Association of Specialized & Cooperative Library Agencies (ASCLA) 50 E Huron St .... Chicago IL 60611 312-280-4395 944-8085
TF: 800-545-2433 ■ *Web:* www.ala.org/ascla

Canadian Assn of Children's Librarians (CACL) 328 Frank St........ Ottawa ON K2P0X8 613-232-9625 563-9895
Web: www.cla.ca/divisions/capl/cacl.htm

Canadian Assn of College & University Libraries (CACUL)
328 Frank St............ Ottawa ON K2P0X8 613-232-9625 563-9895
Web: www.cla.ca/divisions/cacul/index.htm

Canadian Assn of Law Libraries (CALL) PO Box 1570............Kingston ON K7L5C8 613-531-9338 531-0626
Web: www.callacbd.ca

Canadian Assn of Public Libraries (CAPL) 328 Frank St........... Ottawa ON K2P0X8 613-232-9625 563-9895
Web: www.cla.ca/divisions/capl/index.htm

Canadian Assn of Special Libraries & Information Services (CASLIS) 328 Frank St .... Ottawa ON K2P0X8 613-232-9625 563-9895
Web: www.cla.ca/caslis/index.htm

Canadian Health Libraries Assn (CHLA) 39 River St .... Toronto ON M5A3P1 416-646-1600 646-9460
Web: www.chla-absc.ca

Canadian Library Assn (CLA) 328 Frank St.................... Ottawa ON K2P0X8 613-232-9625 563-9895
Web: www.cla.ca

Canadian Library Trustees Assn (CLTA) 328 Frank St.............. Ottawa ON K2P0X8 613-232-9625 563-9895
Web: www.cla.ca/divisions/clta/clta.htm

Canadian School Library Assn (CSLA) 328 Frank St .... Ottawa ON K2P0X8 613-232-9625 563-9895
Web: www.cla.ca/divisions/csla

Friends of Libraries USA (FOLUSA)
1420 Walnut St Suite 450 .... Philadelphia PA 19102 215-790-1674 545-3821
TF: 800-936-5872 ■ *Web:* www.folusa.com

Library Administration & Management Assn (LAMA)
50 E Huron St .... Chicago IL 60611 312-280-5036 280-5033
TF: 800-545-2433 ■ *Web:* www.ala.org/lama

Library & Information Technology Assn (LITA) 50 E Huron St...... Chicago IL 60611 312-280-4270 280-3257
TF: 800-545-2433 ■ *Web:* www.lita.org

Medical Library Assn (MLA) 65 E Wacker Pl Suite 1900........... Chicago IL 60601 312-419-9094 419-8950
Web: www.mlanet.org

Music Library Assn (MLA) 8551 Research Way Suite 180.........Middleton WI 53562 608-836-5825 831-8200
Web: www.musiclibraryassoc.org

New England Library Assn (NELA) PO Box 709 .... Marblehead MA 01945 781-631-1578 631-1579
Web: www.nelib.org

Online Computer Library Center Inc (OCLC) 6565 Kilgour Pl......... Dublin OH 43017 614-764-6000 764-6096
TF: 800-848-5878 ■ *Web:* www.oclc.org

Public Library Assn (PLA) 50 E Huron St.................... Chicago IL 60611 312-280-5752 280-5029
TF: 800-545-2433 ■ *Web:* www.pla.org

Reference & User Services Assn (RUSA) 50 E Huron St........... Chicago IL 60611 312-280-4398 944-8085
TF: 800-545-2433 ■ *Web:* www.ala.org/rusa

Special Libraries Assn (SLA) 331 S Patrick St............ Alexandria VA 22314 703-647-4900 647-4901
Web: www.sla.org

Urban Libraries Council (ULC) 125 S Wacker Dr Suite 1050........ Chicago IL 60606 847-866-9999 866-9989
Web: www.urbanlibraries.org

Young Adult Library Services Assn (YALSA) 50 E Huron St .... Chicago IL 60611 312-280-4390 664-7459
TF: 800-545-2433 ■ *Web:* www.ala.org/yalsa

49-12 Management & Business Professional Associations

Phone Fax

Academy of Management 235 Elm Rd Rm 109........... Briarcliff Manor NY 10510 914-923-2607 923-2615
Web: www.aomonline.org

American Business Conference (ABC)
1828 L St NW Suite 908............ Washington DC 20036 202-822-9300 467-4070
Web: www.americanbusinessconference.org

American Business Women's Assn (ABWA)
9100 Ward Pkwy .... Kansas City MO 64114 816-361-6621 361-4991
TF: 800-228-0007 ■ *Web:* www.abwa.org

American Businesspersons Assn (ABA)
350 Fairway Dr Suite 200 .... Deerfield Beach FL 33441 954-571-1877 571-8582
TF: 800-221-2168 ■ *Web:* www.aba-assn.com

American Cash Flow Assn (ACFA) 255 S Orange Ave Suite 600..... Orlando FL 32801 407-206-6523 206-6507
TF: 800-253-1294 ■ *Web:* acfa-cashflow.org

American Chamber of Commerce Executives (ACCE)
4875 Eisenhower Ave Suite 250 .... Alexandria VA 22304 703-998-0072 212-9512
TF: 800-394-2223 ■ *Web:* www.acce.org

American Management Assn (AMA) 1601 Broadway............New York NY 10019 212-586-8100 903-8168
TF: 800-262-9699 ■ *Web:* www.amanet.org

American Payroll Assn (APA) 660 N Main Ave Suite 100 ....San Antonio TX 78205 210-226-4600 226-4027
Web: www.americanpayroll.org

American Seminar Leaders Assn (ASLA)
2405 E Washington Blvd .... Pasadena CA 91104 626-791-1211 798-0701
TF: 800-735-0511 ■ *Web:* www.asla.com

American Society of Association Executives (ASAE)
1575 'I' St NW............ Washington DC 20005 202-626-2723 371-8825
TF: 888-950-2723 ■ *Web:* www.asaecenter.org

American Society of Notaries (ASN) PO Box 5707 .... Tallahassee FL 32314 850-671-5164 671-5165
TF: 800-522-3392 ■ *Web:* www.notaries.org

American Society of Pension Professionals & Actuaries (ASPPA)
4245 N Fairfax Dr Suite 750 .... Arlington VA 22203 703-516-9300 516-9308
Web: www.asppa.org

American Staffing Assn (ASA)
277 S Washington St Suite 200 .... Alexandria VA 22314 703-253-2020 253-2053
Web: www.americanstaffing.net

Appraisers Assn of America (AAA)
386 Park Ave S Suite 2000............New York NY 10016 212-889-5404 889-5503
Web: www.appraisersassoc.org

APQC 123 N Post Oak Ln Suite 300............Houston TX 77024 713-681-4020 681-8578
TF: 800-776-9676 ■ *Web:* www.apqc.org

ARMA International 13725 W 109th St Suite 101.................Lenexa KS 66215 913-341-3808 341-3742
TF: 800-422-2762 ■ *Web:* www.arma.org

ASIS International 1625 Prince St .... Alexandria VA 22314 703-519-6200 519-6299
Web: www.asisonline.org

Association for Business Communication (ABC)
PO Box 6143 ....Nacogdoches TX 75962 936-468-6280 468-6281
Web: www.businesscommunication.org

Association for Corporate Growth (ACG)
616 N North Ct Suite 200 .... Palatine IL 60067 847-934-5425 934-6089
TF: 800-699-1331 ■ *Web:* www.acg.org

Association of Executive Search Consultants (AESC)
12 E 41st St 17th Fl............New York NY 10017 212-398-9556 398-9560
TF: 877-843-2372 ■ *Web:* www.aesc.org

Association of Fundraising Professionals (AFP)
1101 King St Suite 700 .... Alexandria VA 22314 703-684-0410 684-0540
TF: 800-666-3863 ■ *Web:* www.afpnet.org

Association of Management (AoM)
920 S Battlefield Blvd Suite 100 .... Chesapeake VA 23322 757-482-2273 482-0325
Web: www.aom-iaom.org

Association of Management Consulting Firms (AMCF)
380 Lexington Ave Suite 1700............New York NY 10168 212-551-7887 551-7934
Web: www.amcf.org

Association for Manufacturing Excellence (AME)
3115 N Wilke Rd Suite G............Arlington Heights IL 60004 224-232-5980 232-5981
Web: www.ame.org

Association for Manufacturing Technology (AMT)
7901 Westpark Dr .... McLean VA 22102 703-893-2900 893-1151
TF: 800-524-0475 ■ *Web:* www.amtonline.org

Association of Proposal Management Professionals (APMP)
PO Box 668 ....Dana Point CA 92629 949-493-9398
Web: www.apmp.org

Association for Services Management International (AFSMI)
11031 Via Frontera Suite A .... San Diego CA 92127 858-207-8667 946-0005
TF: 800-333-9786 ■ *Web:* www.afsmi.org

Business Council for International Understanding (BCIU)
1212 Ave of the Americas 10th Fl............New York NY 10036 212-490-0460 697-8526
Web: www.bciu.org

Business Executives for National Security (BENS)
1717 Pennsylvania Ave NW Suite 350............ Washington DC 20006 202-296-2125 296-2490
TF: 800-296-2125 ■ *Web:* www.bens.org

Business Forms Management Assn (BFMA)
319 SW Washington St Suite 710............Portland OR 97204 503-227-3393 274-7667
Web: www.bfma.org

Business Roundtable 1717 Rhode Island Ave NW Suite 800..... Washington DC 20036 202-872-1260 466-3509
Web: www.brtable.org

Chief Executives Organization 7920 Norfolk Ave Suite 400 .... Bethesda MD 20814 301-656-9220 656-9221
TF: 800-634-2655 ■ *Web:* www.ceo.org

Christian Leadership Alliance
635 Camino De Los Mares Suite 205............San Clemente CA 92673 949-487-0900 487-0927
TF: 800-727-4262 ■ *Web:* www.christianleadershipalliance.com

Club Managers Assn of America (CMAA) 1733 King St .... Alexandria VA 22314 703-739-9500 739-0124
Web: www.cmaa.org

Coalition of Publicly Traded Partnerships
1801 K St NW Suite 500............ Washington DC 20006 202-973-3150 973-3101
Web: www.ptpcoalition.org

Coalition of Service Industries (CSI)
1090 Vermont Ave NW Suite 420 .... Washington DC 20005 202-289-7460 775-1726
Web: www.uscsi.org

Conference Board Inc 845 3rd Ave ....New York NY 10022 212-759-0900 980-7014
Web: www.conference-board.org

Council for Community & Economic Research (C2ER)
3330 N Washington Blvd 2nd Fl .... Arlington VA 22201 703-522-4980 522-4985
Web: www.c2er.org/

Council on State Taxation (COST) 122 C St NW Suite 330..... Washington DC 20001 202-484-5222 484-5229
Web: www.statetax.org

DRI International 1331 H St NW .... Washington DC 20005 202-962-3979
Web: www.drii.org

Electronic Industries Alliance (EIA) 2500 Wilson Blvd .... Arlington VA 22201 703-907-7500 907-7501
Web: www.eia.org

Employee Assistance Professionals Assn Inc (EAPA)
4350 N Fairfax Dr Suite 410 .... Arlington VA 22203 703-387-1000 522-4585
Web: www.eapassn.org

Employee Involvement Assn (EIA)
11 W Monument Ave Suite 510............ Dayton OH 45402 937-586-3724 586-3699
Web: www.eianet.org

Employee Relocation Council (ERC)
4401 Wilson Blvd Suite 510 .... Arlington VA 22203 703-842-3400 527-1553
TF: 888-372-2255 ■ *Web:* www.erc.org

Employee Services Management Assn (ESM Assn)
568 Spring Rd Suite D............ Elmhurst IL 60126 630-559-0020 559-0025
Web: www.esmassn.org

Employers Council on Flexible Compensation (ECFC)
927 15th St NW Suite 100............ Washington DC 20005 202-659-4300 371-1467
Web: www.ecfc.org

ESOP Assn 1726 M St NW Suite 501 .... Washington DC 20036 202-293-2971 293-7568
TF: 866-366-3832 ■ *Web:* www.esopassociation.org

Executive Women International
515 South 700 East Suite 2-A............Salt Lake City UT 84102 801-355-2800 355-2852
TF: 877-439-4669 ■ *Web:* www.executivewomen.org

Family Firm Institute (FFI) 200 Lincoln St Suite 201.............. Boston MA 02111 617-482-3045 482-3049
Web: www.ffi.org

Management & Business Professional Associations (Cont'd)

Organization	City	State	Zip	Phone	Fax
Foundation on Economic Trends 4520 East West Hwy Suite 600 *Web:* www.foet.org	Bethesda	MD	20814	301-656-6272	654-0208
GS1 US 1009 Lenox Dr Suite 202 *Web:* www.gs1us.org	Lawrenceville	NJ	08648	609-620-0200	620-1200
Human Resource Planning Society (HRPS) 317 Madison Ave Suite 1509 *Web:* www.hrps.org	New York	NY	10017	212-490-6387	682-6851
Institute for a Drug-Free Workplace 8614 Westwood Center Dr Suite 950 *Web:* www.drugfreeworkplace.org	Vienna	VA	22182	703-288-4300	
Institute for Alternative Futures (IAF) 100 N Pitt St Suite 235 *Web:* www.altfutures.com	Alexandria	VA	22314	703-684-5880	684-0640
Institute of Business Appraisers (IBA) 6950 Cypress Rd Suite 209 *TF:* 800-299-4130 ■ *Web:* www.go-iba.org	Plantation	FL	33317	954-584-1144	584-1184
Institute of Certified Professional Managers (ICPM) James Madison University MSC 5504 *TF:* 800-568-4120 ■ *Web:* www.icpm.biz	Harrisonburg	VA	22807	540-568-3247	801-8650
Institute of Management Consultants USA Inc (IMC USA) 2025 M St NW Suite 800 *TF:* 800-221-2557 ■ *Web:* www.imcusa.org	Washington	DC	20036	202-367-1134	367-2134
Institute for Supply Management (ISM) 2055 Centennial Cir *TF Cust Svc:* 800-888-6276 ■ *Web:* www.ism.ws	Tempe	AZ	85284	480-752-6276	752-7890
International Assn of Administrative Professionals (IAAP) 10502 NW Ambassador Dr *Web:* www.iaap-hq.org	Kansas City	MO	64153	816-891-6600	891-9118
International Assn of Assembly Managers (IAAM) 635 Fritz Dr Suite 100 *TF:* 800-935-4226 ■ *Web:* iaam.org	Coppell	TX	75019	972-906-7441	906-7418
International Assn of Association Management Companies (IAAMC) 100 N 20th St 4th Fl *Web:* www.iaamc.org	Philadelphia	PA	19103	215-564-3484	963-9784
International Assn of Business Communicators (IABC) 1 Hallidie Plaza Suite 600 *TF:* 800-766-4222 ■ *Web:* www.iabc.com	San Francisco	CA	94102	415-544-4700	544-4747
International Assn of Conference Centers (IACC) 243 N Lindbergh Blvd *Web:* www.iacconline.org	Saint Louis	MO	63141	314-993-8575	993-8919
International Assn for Human Resource Information Management (IHRIM) PO Box 1086 *TF:* 800-946-6363 ■ *Web:* www.ihrim.org	Burlington	MA	01803	781-273-3697	998-8011
International Assn for Impact Assessment (IAIA) 1330 23rd St S Suite C *Web:* www.iaia.org	Fargo	ND	58103	701-297-7908	297-7917
International Assn of Workforce Professionals (IAPES) 1801 Louisville Rd *TF:* 888-898-9960 ■ *Web:* www.iawponline.org	Frankfort	KY	40601	502-223-4459	223-4127
International Council of Shopping Centers (ICSC) 1221 Ave of the Americas 41st Fl **Fax Area Code:* 212 ■ *Web:* www.icsc.org	New York	NY	10020	646-728-3800	589-5555*
International Customer Service Assn (ICSA) 24 Wernik Pl *TF:* 800-360-4272 ■ *Web:* www.icsa.com	Metuchen	NJ	08840	732-767-0330	
International Economic Development Council (IEDC) 734 15th St NW Suite 900 *Web:* www.iedconline.org	Washington	DC	20005	202-223-7800	223-4745
International Facility Management Assn (IFMA) 1 E Greenway Plaza Suite 1100 *Web:* www.ifma.org	Houston	TX	77046	713-623-4362	623-6124
International Foundation of Employee Benefit Plans (IFEBP) 18700 W Bluemond Rd PO Box 69 **Fax:* Mktg ■ *TF:* 888-334-3327 ■ *Web:* www.ifebp.org	Brookfield	WI	53008	262-786-6700	786-8670*
International Graphoanalysis Society (IGAS) 842 5th Ave **Fax Area Code:* 206 ■ *Web:* www.igas.com	New Kensington	PA	15068	724-472-9701	339-6573*
International Network of M&A Partners (IMAP) 525 SW 5th St Suite A *Web:* www.imap.com	Des Moines	IA	50309	515-282-8192	282-9117
International Public Management Assn for Human Resources (IPMA-HR) 1617 Duke St *TF:* 800-220-4762 ■ *Web:* www.ipma-hr.org	Alexandria	VA	22314	703-549-7100	684-0948
International Society of Certified Employee Benefit Specialists (ISCEBS) 18700 W Bluemond Rd PO Box 209 *TF:* 888-334-3327 ■ *Web:* www.iscebs.org	Brookfield	WI	53008	262-786-8771	786-8650
International Society for Performance Improvement (ISPI) 1400 Spring St Suite 260 *Web:* www.ispi.org	Silver Spring	MD	20910	301-587-8570	587-8573
International Trademark Assn (INTA) 655 3rd Ave 10th Fl *Web:* www.inta.org	New York	NY	10017	212-768-9887	768-7796
Labor & Employment Relations Assn (LERA) 121 Labor & Industrial Relations Bldg 504 E Armory Ave *Web:* www.lera.uiuc.edu	Champaign	IL	61820	217-333-0072	265-5130
Latin Business Assn (LBA) 120 S San Pedro St Suite 530 *Web:* www.lbausa.com	Los Angeles	CA	90012	213-628-8510	628-8519
Manufacturers Alliance/MAPI Inc 1600 Wilson Blvd Suite 1100 *Web:* www.mapi.net	Arlington	VA	22209	703-841-9000	841-9514
Meeting Professionals International (MPI) 3030 LBJ Fwy Suite 1700 *Web:* www.mpiweb.org	Dallas	TX	75234	972-702-3000	702-3070
National Assn for Business Economics (NABE) 1233 20th St NW Suite 505 *Web:* www.nabe.com	Washington	DC	20036	202-463-6223	463-6239
National Assn of Certified Valuation Analysts (NACVA) 1111 E Brickyard Rd Suite 200 *TF:* 800-677-2009 ■ *Web:* www.nacva.com	Salt Lake City	UT	84106	801-486-0600	486-7500
National Assn of Corporate Directors (NACD) 1133 21st St NW Suite 700 *Web:* www.nacdonline.org	Washington	DC	20036	202-775-0509	775-4857
National Assn of Ecumenical & Interreligious Staff PO Box 7093 *Web:* www.naeis.org	Tacoma	WA	98406	253-759-0141	759-9689
National Assn for Female Executives (NAFE) 60 E 42nd St 27th Fl *TF:* 800-927-6233 ■ *Web:* www.nafe.com	New York	NY	10165	212-351-6400	351-6487
National Assn of Home Based Businesses (NAHBB) 3 Woodthorne Ct Suite 12 *Web:* www.usahomebusiness.com	Owings Mills	MD	21117	410-363-3698	
National Assn of Manufacturers (NAM) 1331 Pennsylvania Ave NW Suite 600 *TF:* 800-814-8468 ■ *Web:* www.nam.org	Washington	DC	20004	202-637-3000	637-3182
National Assn of Parliamentarians (NAP) 213 S Main St *TF:* 888-627-2929 ■ *Web:* www.parliamentarians.org	Independence	MO	64050	816-833-3892	833-3893
National Assn of Personnel Services (NAPS) 131 Prominence Ln Suite 130 **Fax Area Code:* 866 ■ *Web:* www.recruitinglife.com	Dawsonville	GA	30534	706-531-0060	739-4750*
National Assn of Professional Employer Organizations (NAPEO) 901 N Pitt St Suite 150 *Web:* www.napeo.org	Alexandria	VA	22314	703-836-0466	836-0976
National Assn for the Self-Employed (NASE) PO Box 612067 DFW Airport **Fax:* Cust Svc ■ *Web:* www.nase.org	Dallas	TX	75261	800-232-6273	551-4446*
National Assn of Service Managers (NASM) PO Box 250796 *Web:* www.nasm.com	Milwaukee	WI	53225	414-466-6060	466-0840
National Assn of Women Business Owners (NAWBO) 8405 Greensboro Dr Suite 800 *TF:* 800-556-2926 ■ *Web:* www.nawbo.org	McLean	VA	22102	703-506-3268	506-3266
National Assn of Workforce Development Professionals (NAWDP) 810 1st St NE Suite 525 *Web:* www.nawdp.org	Washington	DC	20002	202-589-1790	589-1799
National Black MBA Assn (NBMBAA) 180 N Michigan Ave Suite 1400 *Web:* www.nbmbaa.org	Chicago	IL	60601	312-236-2622	236-0390
National Business Assn (NBA) 5151 Beltline Rd Suite 1150 *Web:* www.nationalbusiness.org	Dallas	TX	75254	972-458-0900	960-9149
National Business Coalition on Health (NBCH) 1015 18th St NW Suite 730 *TF:* 877-775-6224 ■ *Web:* www.nbch.org	Washington	DC	20036	202-775-9300	775-1569
National Business Incubation Assn (NBIA) 20 E Circle Dr Box 37198 *Web:* www.nbia.org	Athens	OH	45701	740-593-4331	593-1996
National Coalition of Black Meeting Planners (NCBMP) 8630 Fenton St Suite 126 **Fax Area Code:* 301 ■ *Web:* www.ncbmp.com	Silver Spring	MD	20910	202-628-3952	588-0011*
National Contract Management Assn (NCMA) 21740 Beaumeade Cir Suite 125 **Fax Area Code:* 703 ■ *TF:* 800-344-8096 ■ *Web:* www.ncmahq.org	Ashburn	VA	20147	571-382-0082	448-0939*
National Cooperative Business Assn (NCBA) 1401 New York Ave NW Suite 1100 *Web:* www.ncba.coop	Washington	DC	20005	202-638-6222	638-1374
National Council for Advanced Manufacturing (NACFAM) 2025 M St NW Suite 800 *Web:* www.nacfam.org	Washington	DC	20036	202-429-2220	429-2422
National Federation of Independent Business (NFIB) 1201 F St NW Suite 200 *TF:* 800-552-6342 ■ *Web:* www.nfib.com	Washington	DC	20004	202-554-9000	554-0496
National Institute for Work & Learning (NIWL) 1825 Connecticut Ave NW 7th Fl *Web:* www.niwl.org	Washington	DC	20009	202-884-8186	884-8422
National Management Assn (NMA) 2210 Arbor Blvd *Web:* www.nma1.org	Dayton	OH	45439	937-294-0421	294-2374
National Minority Business Council Inc (NMBC) 120 Broadway 19th Fl *Web:* www.nmbc.org	New York	NY	10271	212-693-5050	693-5048
National Notary Assn (NNA) 9350 DeSoto Ave *TF:* 800-876-6827 ■ *Web:* www.nationalnotary.org	Chatsworth	CA	91313	818-739-4000	700-1830
National Right to Work Committee (NRTWC) 8001 Braddock Rd Suite 500 *TF:* 800-325-7892 ■ *Web:* www.right-to-work.org	Springfield	VA	22160	703-321-8510	321-7342
National Small Business Assn (NSBA) 1156 15th St NW Suite 1100 *TF:* 800-345-6728 ■ *Web:* www.nsba.biz	Washington	DC	20005	202-293-8830	872-8543
National Society of Compliance Professionals Inc (NSCP) 22 Kent Rd *Web:* www.nscp.org	Cornwall Bridge	CT	06754	860-672-0843	672-3005
New York Celebrity Assistants 459 Columbus Ave Suite 216 *Web:* www.nycelebrityassistants.org	New York	NY	10024	212-803-5444	
Organization for International Investment (OFII) 1225 19th St NW Suite 501 *Web:* www.ofii.org	Washington	DC	20033	202-659-1903	659-2293
PRISM International 1418 Aversboro Rd Suite 201 *TF:* 800-336-9793 ■ *Web:* www.prismintl.org	Garner	NC	27529	919-771-0657	771-0457
Product Development & Management Assn (PDMA) 15000 Commerce Pkwy Suite C *TF:* 800-232-5241 ■ *Web:* www.pdma.org	Mount Laurel	NJ	08054	856-439-0500	439-0525
Professional Convention Management Assn (PCMA) 2301 S Lake Shore Dr Suite 1001 *TF:* 877-827-7262 ■ *Web:* www.pcma.org	Chicago	IL	60616	312-423-7262	423-7222
Professional Records & Information Services Management International 1418 Aversboro Rd Suite 201 *TF:* 800-336-9793 ■ *Web:* www.prismintl.org	Garner	NC	27529	919-771-0657	771-0457
Professional Services Council (PSC) 4401 Wilson Blvd Suite 1110 *Web:* www.pscouncil.org	Arlington	VA	22203	703-875-8059	875-8922
Profit Sharing/401(k) Council of America (PSCA) 20 N Wacker Dr Suite 3700 *Web:* www.psca.org	Chicago	IL	60606	312-419-1863	419-1864
Project Management Institute (PMI) 14 Campus Blvd *TF:* 866-276-4764 ■ *Web:* www.pmi.org	Newtown Square	PA	19073	610-356-4600	356-4647
Religious Conference Management Assn Inc (RCMA) 7702 Woodland Dr Suite 120 *Web:* www.rcmaweb.org	Indianapolis	IN	46278	317-632-1888	632-7909
Relocation Directors Council Inc (RDC) 8 S Michigan Ave Suite 1000 *Web:* relocationdirectorscouncil.org	Chicago	IL	60603	312-726-7410	580-0165
SCORE Assn 1175 Herndon Pkwy Suite 900 **Fax Area Code:* 703 ■ *TF:* 800-634-0245 ■ *Web:* www.score.org	Herndon	VA	20170	800-634-0245	487-3066*
Service Industry Assn (SIA) 2164 Historic Decatur Rd Villa 19 *Web:* www.servicenetwork.org	San Diego	CA	92106	619-221-9200	221-8201
Small Business & Entrepreneurship Council 2944 Hunter Mill Rd Suite 204 *Web:* www.sbsc.org	Oakton	VA	22124	703-242-5840	242-5841
Small Business Legislative Council (SBLC) 1100 H St NW Suite 540 *Web:* www.sblc.org	Washington	DC	20005	202-639-8500	296-5333
Society for Advancement of Management (SAM) Texas A&M Univ Corpus Christi College of Business 6300 Ocean Dr FC111 *TF:* 888-827-6077 ■ *Web:* www.cob.tamucc.edu/sam	Corpus Christi	TX	78412	361-825-6045	825-2725
Society of Competitive Intelligence Professionals (SCIP) 1700 Diagonal Rd Suite 600 *Web:* www.scip.org	Alexandria	VA	22314	703-739-0696	739-2524
Society of Corporate Secretaries & Governance Professionals Inc 521 5th Ave 32nd Fl *Web:* www.governanceprofessionals.org	New York	NY	10175	212-681-2000	681-2005
Society for Human Resource Management (SHRM) 1800 Duke St *TF:* 800-283-7476 ■ *Web:* www.shrm.org	Alexandria	VA	22314	703-548-3440	836-0367

Phone Fax

Society of Professional Benefit Administrators (SPBA)
2 Wisconsin Cir Suite 670 ... Chevy Chase MD 20815 301-718-7722 718-9440
Web: users.erols.com/spba

SOLE - International Society of Logistics
8100 Professional Pl Suite 111 ... Hyattsville MD 20785 301-459-8446 459-1522
Web: www.sole.org

US-ASEAN Business Council 1101 17th St NW Suite 411 ... Washington DC 20036 202-289-1911 289-0519
Web: www.us-asean.org

US Business & Industry Council (USBIC)
910 16th St NW Suite 300 ... Washington DC 20006 202-728-1980 728-1981
Web: www.usbusiness.org

US-China Business Council 1818 N St NW Suite 200 ... Washington DC 20036 202-429-0340 775-2476
Web: www.uschina.org

US Council for International Business (USCIB)
1212 Ave of the Americas 18th Fl ... New York NY 10036 212-354-4480 575-0327
Web: www.uscib.org

US-Japan Business Council 2000 L St NW Suite 515 ... Washington DC 20036 202-728-0068 728-0073
Web: www.usjbc.org

US-Russia Business Council
1701 Pennsylvania Ave NW Suite 520 ... Washington DC 20006 202-739-9180 659-5920
Web: www.usrbc.org

US-Saudi Arabian Business Council 8081 Wolftrap Rd Suite 300 ... Vienna VA 22182 703-962-9300 204-0332
Web: www.us-sabc.org

Vistage International 11452 El Camino Real Suite 400 ... San Diego CA 92130 858-532-6800 532-6802
TF: 800-274-2367 ■ *Web:* www.vistage.com

World Trade Centers Assn (WTCA)
420 Lexington Ave Suite 518 ... New York NY 10170 212-432-2626 488-0064
Web: world.wtca.org

WorldatWork 14040 N Northsight Blvd ... Scottsdale AZ 85260 480-951-9191 483-8352
TF: 877-951-9191 ■ *Web:* www.worldatwork.org

Worldwide Employee Benefits Network Inc (WEB)
1700 Pennsylvania Ave Suite 400 ... Washington DC 20006 202-349-2049 318-8778
Web: www.webnetwork.org

Young Presidents' Organization (YPO)
600 E Las Colinas Blvd Suite 1000 ... Irving TX 75039 972-587-1500 587-1600
TF: 800-773-7976 ■ *Web:* www.ypo.org

YPO-WPO 600 E Las Colinas Blvd Suite 1000 ... Irving TX 75039 972-587-1500 587-1600
Web: www.wpo.org

49-13 Manufacturing Industry Professional & Trade Associations

Phone Fax

Adhesive & Sealant Council Inc (ASC)
7979 Old Georgetown Rd Suite 500 ... Bethesda MD 20814 301-986-9700 986-9795
Web: www.ascouncil.org

Alliance for the Polyurethanes Industry (API)
1300 Wilson Blvd ... Arlington VA 22209 703-741-5656 741-5655
Web: www.polyurethane.org

Aluminum Assn 1528 Wilson Blvd Suite 600 ... Arlington VA 22209 703-358-2960 358-2961
Web: www.aluminum.org

Aluminum Extruders Council (AEC)
1000 N Rand Rd Suite 214 ... Wauconda IL 60084 847-526-2010 526-3993
Web: aec.org

American Assn of Textile Chemists & Colorists (AATCC) 1 Davis Dr PO Box 12215 ... Research Triangle Park NC 27709 919-549-8141 549-8933
Web: www.aatcc.org

American Boiler Manufacturers Assn (ABMA)
4001 N 9th St Suite 226 ... Arlington VA 22203 703-522-7350 522-2665
Web: www.abma.com

American Chemistry Council (ACC) 1300 Wilson Blvd ... Arlington VA 22209 703-741-5000 741-6000
Web: www.americanchemistry.com

American Composites Manufacturers Assn (ACMA)
1010 N Glebe Rd Suite 450 ... Arlington VA 22201 703-525-0511 525-0743
Web: www.acmanet.org

American Electroplaters & Surface Finishers Society Inc (AESF)
3660 Maguire Blvd Suite 250 ... Orlando FL 32803 407-281-6441 281-6446
Web: www.aesf.org

American Fiber Manufacturers Assn Inc (AFMA)
1530 Wilson Blvd Suite 690 ... Arlington VA 22209 703-875-0432 875-0907
Web: www.afma.org

American Foundry Society (AFS) 1695 N Penny Ln ... Schaumburg IL 60173 847-824-0181 824-7848
TF: 800-537-4237 ■ *Web:* www.afsinc.org

American Galvanizers Assn (AGA) 6881 S Holly Cir Suite 108 ... Centennial CO 80112 720-554-0900 554-0909
TF: 800-468-7732 ■ *Web:* www.galvanizeit.org

American Gear Manufacturers Assn (AGMA)
500 Montgomery St Suite 350 ... Alexandria VA 22314 703-684-0211 684-0242
Web: www.agma.org

American Industrial Hygiene Assn (AIHA)
2700 Prosperity Ave Suite 250 ... Fairfax VA 22031 703-849-8888 207-3561
Web: www.aiha.org

American Iron & Steel Institute (AISI)
1140 Connecticut Ave NW Suite 705 ... Washington DC 20036 202-452-7100 463-6573
Web: www.steel.org

American Plastics Council (APC) 1300 Wilson Blvd ... Arlington VA 22209 703-741-5000
Web: www.americanplasticscouncil.org

American Society for Quality (ASQ) 600 N Plankinton Ave ... Milwaukee WI 53201 414-272-8575 272-1734
TF: 800-248-1946 ■ *Web:* www.asq.org

American Textile Machinery Assn (ATMA)
201 Park Washington Ct ... Falls Church VA 22046 703-538-1789 241-5603
Web: www.atmanet.org

American Wire Producers Assn (AWPA)
801 N Fairfax St Suite 211 ... Alexandria VA 22314 703-299-4434 299-9233
Web: www.awpa.org

APICS - Assn for Operations Management 5301 Shawnee Rd ... Alexandria VA 22312 703-354-8851 354-8106
TF: 800-444-2742 ■ *Web:* www.apics.org

Asia America MultiTechnology Assn (AAMA)
3300 Zanker Rd MD SJ2F8 ... San Jose CA 95134 408-955-4505 955-4516
Web: www.aamasv.com

ASM International 9639 Kinsman Rd ... Materials Park OH 44073 440-338-5151 338-4634
TF: 800-336-5152 ■ *Web:* www.asminternational.org

Association of Equipment Manufacturers (AEM)
111 E Wisconsin Ave Suite 1000 ... Milwaukee WI 53202 414-272-0943 272-1170
Web: www.aem.org

Association for Facilities Engineering (AFE)
8160 Corporate Park Dr Suite 125 ... Cincinnati OH 45242 513-489-2473 247-7422
Web: afe.org

Association of Industrial Metallizers Coaters & Laminators (AIMCAL) 201 Springs St ... Fort Mill SC 29715 803-802-7820 802-7821
Web: aimcal.org

Association for Iron & Steel Technology (AIST)
186 Thorn Hill Rd ... Warrendale PA 15086 724-776-1535 776-0430
Web: www.aist.org

Association of Rotational Molders International (ARM)
2000 Spring Rd Suite 511 ... Oak Brook IL 60523 630-571-0611 571-0616
Web: www.rotomolding.org

Phone Fax

Association of Vacuum Equipment Manufacturers International (AVEM) 71 Pinon Hill Pl NE ... Albuquerque NM 87122 505-856-6924 856-6716
Web: www.avem.org

Basic Acrylic Monomer Manufacturers Inc (BAMM)
941 Rhonda Pl SE ... Leesburg VA 20175 703-669-5688 669-5689
Web: www.bamm.net

Building Service Contractors Assn International (BSCAI)
10201 Lee Hwy Suite 225 ... Fairfax VA 22030 703-359-7090 352-0493
TF: 800-368-3414 ■ *Web:* www.bscai.org

Business & Institutional Furniture Manufacturers Assn (BIFMA) 2680 Horizon Dr SE Suite A-1 ... Grand Rapids MI 49546 616-285-3963 285-3765
Web: www.bifma.com

Can Manufacturers Institute (CMI)
1730 Rhode Island Ave NW Suite 1000 ... Washington DC 20036 202-232-4677 232-5756
Web: www.cancentral.com

Chlorine Institute Inc 1300 Wilson Blvd ... Arlington VA 22209 703-741-5760 741-6068
Web: www.chlorineinstitute.org

Color Pigments Manufacturers Assn PO Box 20839 ... Alexandria VA 22320 703-684-4044 684-1795
Web: www.pigments.org

Composite Can & Tube Institute (CCTI)
50 S Pickett St Suite 110 ... Alexandria VA 22310 703-823-7234 823-7237
Web: www.cctiwdc.org

Compressed Gas Assn (CGA) 4221 Walney Rd 5th Fl ... Chantilly VA 20151 703-788-2700 961-1831
Web: www.cganet.com

Consortium for Advanced Manufacturing - International (CAM-I)
119 NE Wilshire Blvd ... Burleson TX 76028 817-426-5744 426-5799
Web: www.cam-i.com

Consumer Specialty Products Assn (CSPA)
900 17th St NW Suite 300 ... Washington DC 20006 202-872-8110 872-8114
Web: www.cspa.org

Copper Development Assn Inc 260 Madison Ave 16th Fl ... New York NY 10016 212-251-7200 251-7234
TF: 800-232-3282 ■ *Web:* www.copper.org

Cordage Institute 994 Old Eagle School Rd Suite 1019 ... Wayne PA 19087 610-971-4854 971-4859
Web: www.ropecord.com

Council of Industrial Boiler Owners (CIBO)
6035 Burke Center Pkwy Suite 360 ... Burke VA 22015 703-250-9042 239-9042
Web: www.cibo.org

Crane Manufacturers Assn of America (CMAA)
8720 Red Oak Blvd Suite 201 ... Charlotte NC 28217 704-676-1190 676-1199
TF: 800-345-1815 ■ *Web:* www.mhia.org/psc

Ductile Iron Pipe Research Assn (DIPRA)
245 Riverchase Pkwy E Suite 'O' ... Birmingham AL 35244 205-402-8700 402-8730
Web: www.dipra.org

Edison Welding Institute (EWI) 1250 Arthur E Adams Dr ... Columbus OH 43221 614-688-5000 688-5001
Web: www.ewi.org

Engine Manufacturers Assn (EMA) 2 N LaSalle St Suite 2200 ... Chicago IL 60602 312-827-8700 827-8737
Web: www.enginemanufacturers.org

Equipment & Tool Institute (ETI)
10 Laboratory Dr ... Research Triangle Park NC 27709 919-406-8844 406-1306
Web: www.etools.org

Expandable Polystyrene Resin Suppliers Council (ERSC)
1300 Wilson Blvd 8th Fl ... Arlington VA 22209 703-741-5649 741-5651

Fabricators & Manufacturers Assn International (FMA)
833 Featherstone Rd ... Rockford IL 61107 815-399-8700 484-7700
TF: 800-432-2832 ■ *Web:* www.fmanet.org

Federation of Societies for Coatings Technology (FSCT)
492 Norristown Rd ... Blue Bell PA 19422 610-940-0777 940-0292
Web: www.coatingstech.org

Fibre Box Assn (FBA) 2850 Golf Rd Suite 412 ... Rolling Meadows IL 60008 847-364-9600 364-9639
Web: www.fibrebox.org

Flexible Packaging Assn (FPA) 971 Corporate Blvd Suite 403 ... Linthicum MD 21090 410-694-0800 694-0900
Web: www.flexpack.org

Fluid Controls Institute (FCI) 1300 Sumner Ave ... Cleveland OH 44115 216-241-7333 241-0105
Web: www.fluidcontrolsinstitute.org

Fluid Power Distributors Assn (FPDA) PO Box 1420 ... Cherry Hill NJ 08034 856-424-8998 424-9248
Web: www.fpda.org

Food Processing Machinery Assn (FPMA)
200 Daingerfield Rd ... Alexandria VA 22314 703-684-1080 548-6563
TF: 800-833-4337 ■ *Web:* www.foodprocessingmachinery.com

Foodservice & Packaging Institute (FPI)
150 S Washington St Suite 204 ... Falls Church VA 22046 703-538-2800 538-2187
Web: www.fpi.org

Forging Industry Assn (FIA) 25 W Prospect Ave Suite 300 ... Cleveland OH 44115 216-781-6260 781-0102
Web: www.forging.org

Glass Assn of North America (GANA)
2945 SW Wanamaker Dr Suite A ... Topeka KS 66614 785-271-0208 271-0166
Web: www.glasswebsite.com

Glass Packaging Institute (GPI) 515 King St Suite 420 ... Alexandria VA 22314 703-684-6359 684-6048
Web: www.gpi.org

Gypsum Assn 810 1st St NE Suite 510 ... Washington DC 20002 202-289-5440 289-3707
Web: www.gypsum.org

Homeland Security Industries Assn
666 11th St NW Suite 315 ... Washington DC 20001 202-331-3096 331-8191
Web: www.hsianet.org

Hydronics Institute 35 Russo Pl PO Box 218 ... Berkeley Heights NJ 07922 908-464-8200 464-7818

Illuminating Engineering Society of North America (IESNA)
120 Wall St 17th Fl ... New York NY 10005 212-248-5000 248-5017
Web: www.iesna.org

INDA: Assn of the Nonwoven Fabrics Industry
1200 Crescent Green Suite 100 ... Cary NC 27511 919-233-1210 233-1282
Web: www.inda.org

Independent Battery Manufacturers Assn (IBMA)
401 N Michigan Ave 24th Fl ... Chicago IL 60611 312-245-1074 527-6640
TF: 800-237-6126 ■ *Web:* www.batterycouncil.org

Independent Lubricant Manufacturers Assn (ILMA)
651 S Washington St ... Alexandria VA 22314 703-684-5574 836-8503
Web: www.ilma.org

Industrial Designers Society of America (IDSA)
45195 Business Ct Suite 250 ... Dulles VA 20166 703-707-6000 787-8501
Web: www.idsa.org

Industrial Diamond Assn of America (IDA) PO Box 29460 ... Columbus OH 43229 614-797-2265 797-2264
Web: www.superabrasives.org

Industrial Fabrics Assn International (IFAI)
1801 County Rd 'B' W ... Roseville MN 55113 651-222-2508 631-9334
TF: 800-225-4324 ■ *Web:* www.ifai.com

Institute of Caster & Wheel Manufacturers (ICWM)
8720 Red Oak Blvd Suite 201 ... Charlotte NC 28217 704-676-1190 676-1199
TF: 800-345-1815 ■ *Web:* www.mhia.org/psc

Institute of Industrial Engineers (IIE)
3577 Parkway Ln Suite 200 ... Norcross GA 30092 770-449-0460 441-3295
TF Cust Svc: 800-494-0460 ■ *Web:* www.iienet2.org

Institute of Makers of Explosives (IME)
1120 19th St NW Suite 310 ... Washington DC 20036 202-429-9280 293-2420
Web: www.ime.org

Institute of Packaging Professionals (IoPP)
1601 N Bond St Suite 101 ... Naperville IL 60563 630-544-5050 544-5055
TF: 800-432-4085 ■ *Web:* www.iopp.org

Manufacturing Industry Professional & Trade Associations (Cont'd)

	City	State	Zip	Phone	Fax
Institute of Paper Science & Technology (IPST) 500 10th St NW *TF:* 800-558-6611 ■ *Web:* www.ipst.gatech.edu	Atlanta	GA	30332	404-894-5700	894-4778
International AntiCounterfeiting Coalition (IACC) 1730 M St NW Suite 1020 *Web:* www.iacc.org	Washington	DC	20006	202-223-6667	223-6668
International Copper Assn 260 Madison Ave 16th Fl *Web:* www.copperinfo.com	New York	NY	10016	212-251-7240	251-7245
International Ground Source Heat Pump Assn (IGSHPA) Oklahoma State University 374 Cordell S *TF:* 800-626-4747 ■ *Web:* www.igshpa.okstate.edu	Stillwater	OK	74078	405-744-5175	744-5283
International Institute of Synthetic Rubber Producers Inc (IISRP) 2077 S Gessner Rd Suite 133 *Web:* www.iisrp.com	Houston	TX	77063	713-783-7511	783-7253
International Magnesium Assn (IMA) 1000 N Rand Rd Suite 214 *Web:* www.intlmag.org	Wauconda	IL	60084	847-526-2010	526-3993
Investment Casting Institute (ICI) 136 Summit Ave *Web:* www.investmentcasting.org	Montvale	NJ	07645	201-573-9770	573-9771
Material Handling Equipment Distributors Assn (MHEDA) 201 US Hwy 45 *Web:* www.mheda.org	Vernon Hills	IL	60061	847-680-3500	362-6989
Material Handling Industry of America (MHIA) 8720 Red Oak Blvd Suite 201 *TF:* 800-345-1815 ■ *Web:* www.mhia.org	Charlotte	NC	28217	704-676-1190	676-1199
Metal Powder Industries Federation (MPIF) 105 College Rd E *Web:* www.mpif.org	Princeton	NJ	08540	609-452-7700	987-8523
Metals Service Center Institute (MSCI) 4201 Euclid Ave *Web:* www.msci.org	Rolling Meadows	IL	60008	847-485-3000	485-3001
Minerals Metals & Materials Society (TMS) 184 Thorn Hill Rd *Web:* www.tms.org	Warrendale	PA	15086	724-776-9000	776-3770
NACE International: Corrosion Society 1440 S Creek Dr *Web:* www.nace.org	Houston	TX	77084	281-228-6200	228-6300
National Assn of Metal Finishers (NAMF) 3660 Maguire Blvd Suite 250 *Web:* www.namf.org	Orlando	FL	32803	407-281-6445	281-7345
National Assn of Steel Pipe Distributors (NASPD) 1501 E Mockingbird Ln Suite 307 *Fax Area Code: 832 ■ *Web:* www.naspd.com	Victoria	TX	77904	361-574-7878	201-9479*
National Coil Coating Assn (NCCA) 1300 Sumner Ave *Web:* www.coilcoating.org	Cleveland	OH	44115	216-241-7333	241-0105
National Council of Textile Organizations (NCTO) 910 17th St NW Suite 1020 *Web:* www.ncto.org	Washington	DC	20006	202-822-8028	822-8029
National Electrical Manufacturers Assn (NEMA) 1300 N 17th St Suite 1847 *Web:* www.nema.org	Rosslyn	VA	22209	703-841-3200	841-5900
National Fluid Power Assn (NFPA) 3333 N Mayfair Rd Suite 211 *Web:* www.nfpa.com	Milwaukee	WI	53222	414-778-3344	778-3361
National Glass Assn (NGA) 8200 Greensboro Dr Suite 302 *TF:* 866-342-5642 ■ *Web:* www.glass.org	McLean	VA	22102	703-442-4890	442-0630
National Marine Electronics Assn (NMEA) 7 Riggs Ave *Web:* www.nmea.org	Severna Park	MD	21146	410-975-9425	975-9450
National Paint & Coatings Assn (NPCA) 1500 Rhode Island Ave NW *Web:* www.paint.org	Washington	DC	20005	202-462-6272	462-8549
National Paperbox Assn (NPA) 113 S West St 3rd Fl *Web:* www.paperbox.org	Alexandria	VA	22314	703-684-2212	683-6920
National Textile Assn (NTA) 6 Beacon St Suite 1125 *Web:* www.nationaltextile.org	Boston	MA	02108	617-542-8220	542-2199
National Tooling & Machining Assn (NTMA) 9300 Livingston Rd *TF:* 800-248-6862 ■ *Web:* www.ntma.org	Fort Washington	MD	20744	301-248-6200	248-7104
National Wooden Pallet & Container Assn (NWPCA) 329 S Patrick St *Web:* www.nwpca.com	Alexandria	VA	22314	703-519-6104	519-4720
NDMAC 1111 Prince of Wales Dr Suite 406 *Web:* www.ndmac.ca	Ottawa	ON	K2C3T2	613-723-0777	723-0779
Nonprescription Drug Manufacturers Assn of Canada 1111 Prince of Wales Dr Suite 406 *Web:* www.ndmac.ca	Ottawa	ON	K2C3T2	613-723-0777	723-0779
North American Assn of Food Equipment Manufacturers (NAFEM) 161 N Clark St Suite 2020 *Web:* www.nafem.org	Chicago	IL	60601	312-821-0201	821-0202
North American Die Casting Assn (NADCA) 241 Holbrook Dr *Web:* www.diecasting.org	Wheeling	IL	60090	847-279-0001	279-0002
Packaging Machinery Manufacturers Institute (PMMI) 4350 N Fairfax Dr Suite 600 *TF:* 800-275-7664 ■ *Web:* www.pmmi.org	Arlington	VA	22203	703-243-8555	243-8556
Paper Industry Management Assn (PIMA) 4700 W Lake Ave *Fax Area Code: 877 ■ *Web:* pima-online.org	Glenview	IL	60025	847-375-6860	527-5973*
Paperboard Packaging Council (PPC) 201 N Union St Suite 220 *Web:* www.ppcnet.org	Alexandria	VA	22314	703-836-3300	836-3290
Petroleum Equipment Institute (PEI) PO Box 2380 *Web:* www.peinet.org	Tulsa	OK	74101	918-494-9696	491-9895
Plastics Institute of America (PIA) 333 Aiken St *Web:* www.plasticsinstitute.org	Lowell	MA	01854	978-934-3130	458-4141
Polystyrene Packaging Council (PSPC) 1300 Wilson Blvd *Web:* www.polystyrene.org	Arlington	VA	22209	703-741-5000	741-6000
Polyurethane Foam Assn (PFA) 9724 Kingston Pike Suite 503 *Web:* www.pfa.org	Knoxville	TN	37922	865-690-4648	690-4649
Polyurethane Manufacturers Assn (PMA) 1123 N Water St *Web:* www.pmahome.org	Milwaukee	WI	53202	414-431-3094	
Portable Rechargeable Battery Assn (PRBA) 1000 Parkwood Cir Suite 430 *Web:* www.prba.org	Atlanta	GA	30339	770-612-8826	612-8841
Precision Machined Products Assn (PMPA) 6700 W Snowville Rd *Web:* www.pmpa.org	Brecksville	OH	44141	440-526-0300	526-5803
Process Equipment Manufacturers Assn (PEMA) 201 Park Washington Ct *Web:* www.pemanet.org	Falls Church	VA	22046	703-538-1796	241-5603
Recycled Paperboard Technical Assn 920 Davis Rd Suite 306	Elgin	IL	60123	847-622-2544	622-2546
Reusable Industrial Packaging Assn (RIPA) 8401 Corporate Dr Suite 450 *TF:* 800-533-3786 ■ *Web:* www.reusablepackaging.org	Landover	MD	20785	301-577-3786	577-6476
Rigid Plastics Packaging Institute (RPPI) 179 S Kenilworth Ave *Web:* www.rigidplasticpackaging.org	Elmhurst	IL	60126	630-833-5894	833-5896
Rubber Manufacturers Assn (RMA) 1400 K St NW Suite 900 *TF:* 800-220-7622 ■ *Web:* www.rma.org	Washington	DC	20005	202-682-4800	682-4854
Sewn Products Equipment Suppliers Assn (SPESA) 5107 Falls of the Neuse Suite B15 *TF:* 888-447-7372 ■ *Web:* www.spesa.org	Raleigh	NC	27609	919-872-8909	872-1915
Society of Manufacturing Engineers (SME) 1 SME Dr *TF:* 800-733-4763 ■ *Web:* www.sme.org	Dearborn	MI	48121	313-271-1500	425-3400
Society for Mining Metallurgy & Exploration Inc (SME) 8307 Shaffer Pkwy *TF:* 800-763-3132 ■ *Web:* www.smenet.org	Littleton	CO	80127	303-973-9550	973-3845
Society of Plastics Engineers (SPE) 14 Fairfield Dr *Web:* www.4spe.org	Brookfield	CT	06804	203-775-0471	775-8490
Society of the Plastics Industry Inc (SPI) 1667 K St NW Suite 1000 *Web:* www.plasticsindustry.org	Washington	DC	20006	202-974-5200	296-7005
Society of Tribologists & Lubrication Engineers (STLE) 840 Busse Hwy *Web:* www.stle.org	Park Ridge	IL	60068	847-825-5536	825-1456
Society of Vacuum Coaters (SVC) 71 Pinon Hill Pl NE *Web:* www.svc.org	Albuquerque	NM	87122	505-856-7188	856-6716
Spring Manufacturers Institute (SMI) 2001 Midwest Rd Suite 106 *Web:* www.smihq.org	Oak Brook	IL	60523	630-495-8588	495-8595
SSPC: Society for Protective Coatings 40 24th St 6th Fl *Web:* www.sspc.org	Pittsburgh	PA	15222	412-281-2331	281-9995
Steel Founders' Society of America (SFSA) 780 McArdle Dr Suite G *Web:* www.sfsa.org	Crystal Lake	IL	60014	815-455-8240	455-8241
Steel Manufacturers Assn (SMA) 1150 Connecticut Ave NW Suite 715 *Web:* www.steelnet.org	Washington	DC	20036	202-296-1515	296-2506
Steel Plate Fabricators Assn (SPFA) 570 Oakwood Rd *Web:* www.spfa.org	Lake Zurich	IL	60047	847-438-8265	438-8766
Steel Tank Institute (STI) 570 Oakwood Rd *TF:* 800-275-1300 ■ *Web:* www.steeltank.com	Lake Zurich	IL	60047	847-438-8265	438-8766
Sulphur Institute (TSI) 1140 Connecticut Ave NW Suite 612 *Web:* www.sulphurinstitute.org	Washington	DC	20036	202-331-9660	293-2940
Technical Assn of the Pulp & Paper Industry (TAPPI) 15 Technology Pkwy S *TF Sales:* 800-332-8686 ■ *Web:* www.tappi.org	Norcross	GA	30092	770-446-1400	446-6947
TRI/Princeton PO Box 625 *Web:* www.triprinceton.org	Princeton	NJ	08542	609-924-3150	683-7836
Valve Manufacturers Assn of America (VMA) 1050 17th St NW Suite 280 *Web:* www.vma.org	Washington	DC	20036	202-331-8105	296-0378
Vinyl Institute 1300 Wilson Blvd *Web:* www.vinylinfo.org	Arlington	VA	22209	703-741-5670	741-5672
Vinyl Siding Institute (VSI) 1201 15th St NW Suite 220 *TF:* 888-367-8741 ■ *Web:* www.vinylsiding.org	Washington	DC	20005	202-587-5100	
Wire Assn International (WAI) 1570 Boston Post Rd PO Box 578 *Web:* www.wirenet.org	Guilford	CT	06437	203-453-2777	453-8384
Wiring Harness Manufacturers Assn (WHMA) 7500 Flying Cloud Dr Suite 900 *Web:* www.whma.org	Eden Prairie	MN	55344	952-253-6225	835-4774
Wood Machinery Manufacturers of America (WMMA) 100 N 20th St 4th Fl *Web:* www.wmma.org	Philadelphia	PA	19103	215-564-3484	963-9785

49-14 Media Professionals Associations

	City	State	Zip	Phone	Fax
Academy of Television Arts & Sciences 5220 Lankershim Blvd *Web:* www.emmys.tv	North Hollywood	CA	91601	818-754-2800	761-2827
Accuracy in Media Inc (AIM) 4455 Connecticut Ave NW Suite 330 *TF:* 800-787-4567 ■ *Web:* www.aim.org	Washington	DC	20008	202-364-4401	364-4098
American Federation of Television & Radio Artists (AFTRA) 260 Madison Ave 7th Fl *Web:* www.aftra.com	New York	NY	10016	212-532-0800	532-2242
American Medical Writers Assn (AMWA) 40 W Gude Dr Suite 101 *Web:* www.amwa.org	Rockville	MD	20850	301-294-5303	294-9006
American Radio Relay League (ARRL) 225 Main St *Web:* www.arrl.org	Newington	CT	06111	860-594-0200	594-0259
American Society of Journalists & Authors (ASJA) 1501 Broadway Suite 302 *Web:* www.asja.org	New York	NY	10036	212-997-0947	937-2315
American Society of Media Photographers (ASMP) 150 N 2nd St *Web:* www.asmp.org	Philadelphia	PA	19106	215-451-2767	451-0880
American Society of Newspaper Editors (ASNE) 11690-B Sunrise Valley Dr *Web:* www.asne.org	Reston	VA	20191	703-453-1122	453-1133
American Women in Radio & Television (AWRT) 8405 Greensboro Dr Suite 800 *Web:* www.awrt.org	McLean	VA	22102	703-506-3290	506-3266
Association of Alternative Newsweeklies (AAN) 1250 'I' St NW Suite 804 *Web:* aan.org	Washington	DC	20005	202-289-8484	289-2004
Association of Independents in Radio (AIR) 42 Charles St 2nd Fl *Web:* www.airmedia.org	Dorchester	MA	02125	617-825-4400	
Association for Maximum Service Television (MSTV) 4100 Wisconsin Ave NW 1st Fl *Web:* www.mstv.org	Washington	DC	20016	202-966-1956	966-9617
Association of Public Television Stations (APTS) 2100 Crystal Dr Suite 700 *Web:* www.apts.org	Arlington	VA	22202	202-654-4200	654-4236
Association for Women in Communications (AWC) 3337 Duke St *Web:* www.womcom.org	Alexandria	VA	22314	703-370-7436	370-7437
Broadcast Cable Financial Management Assn (BCFM) 550 W Frontage Rd Suite 3600 *Web:* www.bcfm.com	Northfield	IL	60093	847-716-7000	716-7004
Broadcast Design Assn (BDA) 9000 W Sunset Blvd Suite 900 *Web:* www.promax.tv	Los Angeles	CA	90069	310-788-7600	788-7616
Cable & Telecommunications Assn for Marketing (CTAM) 201 N Union St Suite 440 *Web:* www.ctam.com	Alexandria	VA	22314	703-549-4200	684-1167
Cable Television Laboratories Inc 858 Coal Creek Cir *Web:* www.cablelabs.com	Louisville	CO	80027	303-661-9100	661-9199

Phone Fax

Catholic Press Assn (CPA) 205 W Monroe St Suite 470 .... Chicago IL 60606 312-380-6789 361-0256
Web: www.catholicpress.org
Center for Media Literacy 23852 Pacific Coast Hwy Suite 472....... Malibu CA 90265 310-456-1225 456-0020
Web: www.medialit.org
Content Delivery & Storage Assn 182 Nassau St Suite 204 .... Princeton NJ 08542 609-279-1700 279-1999
Web: www.contentdeliveryandstorage.org
Country Radio Broadcasters Inc (CRB) 819 18th Ave S .... Nashville TN 37203 615-327-4487 329-4492
Web: www.crb.org
Essential Information PO Box 19405 .... Washington DC 20036 202-387-8030 234-5176
Web: www.essential.org
Foundation for American Communications (FACS)
85 S Grand Ave .... Pasadena CA 91105 626-584-0010 584-0627
Web: www.facsnet.org
Inter American Press Assn (IAPA) 1801 SW 3rd Ave 8th Fl .... Miami FL 33129 305-634-2465 635-2272
Web: sipiapa.org
Intercollegiate Broadcasting System Inc (IBS)
367 Windsor Hwy .... New Windsor NY 12553 845-565-0003 565-7446
Web: www.ibsradio.org
International Communication Assn (ICA) 1500 21st St NW ..... Washington DC 20036 202-955-1444 955-1448
Web: www.icahdq.org
International Newspaper Marketing Assn (INMA)
10300 N Central Expy Suite 467 .... Dallas TX 75231 214-373-9111 373-9112
Web: www.inma.org
International Radio & Television Society Foundation Inc (IRTS)
420 Lexington Ave Suite 1601.................... New York NY 10170 212-867-6650 867-6653
Web: www.irts.org
Media Coalition Inc 275 7th Ave Suite 1504 .... New York NY 10001 212-587-4025 587-2436
Web: www.mediacoalition.org
Media Communications Assn International (MCA-I)
2810 Crossroads Dr Suite 3800 .... Madison WI 53718 608-443-2464 443-2478
Web: www.mca-i.org
National Assn of Broadcasters (NAB) 1771 'N' St NW .... Washington DC 20036 202-429-5300
Web: www.nab.org
National Assn of Hispanic Journalists (NAHJ)
529 14th St NW National Press Bldg Suite 1000 .... Washington DC 20045 202-662-7145 662-7144
Web: www.nahj.org
National Assn of Television Program Executives (NATPE)
5757 Wilshire Blvd PH-10 .... Los Angeles CA 90036 310-453-4440 453-5258
Web: www.natpe.org
National Cable & Telecommunications Assn (NCTA)
25 Massachusetts Ave NW Suite 100 .... Washington DC 20001 202-222-2300
Web: www.ncta.com
National Cable Television Cooperative Inc (NCTC)
11200 Corporate Ave.................... Lenexa KS 66219 913-599-5900 599-5903
TF: 800-888-6282 ■ *Web:* www.cabletvco-op.org
National Federation of Community Broadcasters (NFCB)
1970 Broadway Suite 1000 .... Oakland CA 94612 510-451-8200 451-8208
TF: 888-280-6322 ■ *Web:* www.nfcb.org
National Newspaper Assn (NNA) 127 Neff Annex PO Box 7540..... Columbia MO 65205 573-882-5800 884-5490
TF: 800-829-4662 ■ *Web:* www.nna.org
National Newspaper Publishers Assn (NNPA)
3200 13th St NW.................... Washington DC 20010 202-588-8764 588-8960
Web: www.nnpa.org
National Press Club (NPC)
National Press Bldg 529 14th St NW 13th Fl .... Washington DC 20045 202-662-7500 662-7569
Web: www.press.org
National Press Photographers Assn (NPPA)
3200 Croasdaile Dr Suite 306 .... Durham NC 27705 919-383-7246 383-7261
Web: www.nppa.org
National Public Radio (NPR) 635 Massachusetts Ave NW....... Washington DC 20001 202-513-2000 513-3329
Web: www.npr.org
National Religious Broadcasters (NRB) 9510 Technology Dr ...... Manassas VA 20110 703-330-7000 330-7100
Web: www.nrb.org
Newsletter & Electronic Publishers Assn (NEPA)
8229 Boone Blvd suite 260 .... Vienna VA 22182 703-992-9339 992-7512
TF: 800-356-9302 ■ *Web:* www.newsletters.org
Newspaper Assn of America (NAA)
4401 Wilson Blvd Suite 900 .... Arlington VA 22203 571-366-1000 366-1195
Web: www.naa.org
Overseas Press Club of America (OPC) 40 W 45th St............ New York NY 10036 212-626-9220 626-9210
Web: www.opcofamerica.org
Parents Television Council (PTC)
707 Wilshire Blvd Suite 2075 .... Los Angeles CA 90017 213-629-9255 629-9254
Web: www.parentstv.org
Radio-Television News Directors Assn (RTNDA)
1600 K St NW Suite 700.................... Washington DC 20006 202-659-6510 223-4007
TF: 800-807-8632 ■ *Web:* www.rtnda.org
Satellite Broadcasting & Communications Assn (SBCA)
1730 M St NW Suite 600 .... Washington DC 20036 202-349-3620 349-3621
TF: 800-541-5981 ■ *Web:* www.sbca.com
Society of Broadcast Engineers (SBE)
9102 N Meridian St Suite 150.................... Indianapolis IN 46260 317-846-9000 846-9120
Web: www.sbe.org
Society of Environmental Journalists (SEJ)
321 Old York Rd Suite 200.................... Jenkintown PA 19046 215-884-8174 884-8175
Web: www.sej.org
Society for News Design (SND)
1130 Ten Rod Rd Suite D-202 .... North Kingstown RI 02852 401-294-5233 294-5238
Web: www.snd.org
Society of Professional Journalists (SPJ) 3909 Meridian St..... Indianapolis IN 46208 317-927-8000 920-4789
Web: www.spj.org
Society for Technical Communication (STC)
901 N Stuart St Suite 904.................... Arlington VA 22203 703-522-4114 522-2075
Web: www.stc.org
White House News Photographers' Assn (WHNPA)
PO Box 7119 Ben Franklin Stn .... Washington DC 20044 202-785-5230
Web: www.whnpa.org
Women in Cable & Telecommunications (WICT)
14555 Avion Pkwy Suite 250.................... Chantilly VA 20151 703-234-9810 817-1595
Web: www.wict.org

49-15 Mental Health Professionals Associations

Phone Fax

Administrators in Academic Psychiatry (AAP)
Univ of Michigan Dept of Psychiatry UH9C 9151 .... Ann Arbor MI 48109 734-936-4860 936-6880
Web: www.adminpsych.org
American Academy of Addiction Psychiatry (AAAP)
345 Blackstone Blvd 1st Fl.................... Providence RI 02906 401-524-3076 272-0922
Web: www.aaap.org
American Academy of Child & Adolescent Psychiatry (AACAP) 3615 Wisconsin Ave NW.................... Washington DC 20016 202-966-7300 966-2891
TF: 800-333-7636 ■ *Web:* www.aacap.org
American Academy of Psychiatry & the Law (AAPL)
1 Regency Dr PO Box 30.................... Bloomfield CT 06002 860-242-5450 286-0787
TF: 800-331-1389 ■ *Web:* www.aapl.org
American Assn for Geriatric Psychiatry (AAGP)
7910 Woodmont Ave Suite 1050.................... Bethesda MD 20814 301-654-7850 654-4137
Web: www.aagpgpa.org
American College of Psychiatrists
122 Michigan Ave Suite 1360 .... Chicago IL 60603 312-662-1020 662-1025
Web: www.acpsych.org
American Council of Hypnotist Examiners 700 S Central Ave ...... Glendale CA 91204 818-242-1159 247-9379
TF: 800-894-9766 ■ *Web:* www.hypnotistexaminers.org
American Counseling Assn (ACA) 5999 Stevenson Ave.......... Alexandria VA 22304 703-823-9800 823-0252
TF: 800-347-6647 ■ *Web:* www.counseling.org
American Group Psychotherapy Assn (AGPA)
25 E 21st St 6th Fl.................... New York NY 10010 212-477-2677 979-6627
TF: 877-668-2472 ■ *Web:* www.agpa.org
American Mental Health Counselors Assn (AMHCA)
801 N Fairfax St Suite 304.................... Alexandria VA 22314 703-548-6002 548-4775
TF: 800-326-2642 ■ *Web:* www.amhca.org
American Orthopsychiatric Assn
Dept of Psychology Box 871104 Arizona State University .... Tempe AZ 85287 480-727-7518
Web: www.amerortho.org
American Psychiatric Assn (APA)
1000 Wilson Blvd Suite 1825 .... Arlington VA 22209 703-907-7300 907-1085
TF: 888-357-7924 ■ *Web:* www.psych.org
American Psychiatric Nurses Assn (APNA)
1555 Wilson Blvd Suite 602 .... Arlington VA 22209 703-243-2443 243-3390
Web: www.apna.org
American Psychoanalytic Assn (APsaA) 309 E 49th St........... New York NY 10017 212-752-0450 593-0571
Web: www.apsa.org
American Psychological Assn (APA) 750 1st St NE .... Washington DC 20002 202-336-5500 336-5962
TF: 800-374-2721 ■ *Web:* www.apa.org
American Psychological Society (APS)
1010 Vermont Ave NW Suite 1100 .... Washington DC 20005 202-783-2077 783-2083
Web: www.psychologicalscience.org
American Society for Adolescent Psychiatry (ASAP)
PO Box 570218 .... Dallas TX 75357 972-613-0985 613-5532
Web: www.adolpsych.org
Association for Advancement of Behavior Therapy (AABT)
305 7th Ave 16th Fl.................... New York NY 10001 212-647-1890 647-1865
TF: 800-685-2228 ■ *Web:* www.aabt.org
Association for Play Therapy (APT) 3198 Willow Ave Suite 110....... Clovis CA 93612 559-294-2128 294-2129
Web: www.a4pt.org
Association for Psychological Type (APT) 9650 Rockville Pike .... Bethesda MD 20814 301-634-7450 634-7455
TF: 800-847-9943 ■ *Web:* www.aptcentral.org
Depression & Related Affective Disorders Assn (DRADA)
8201 Greensboro Dr Suite 300 .... McLean VA 22102 703-610-9026
Web: www.drada.org
Federation of Families for Children's Mental Health
9605 Medical Center Dr Suite 280.................... Rockville MD 28050 240-403-1901 403-1909
Web: www.ffcmh.org
International Assn of Marriage & Family Counselors (IAMFC)
c/o American Counseling Assn 5999 Stevenson Ave .... Alexandria VA 22304 703-823-9800 823-0252
TF: 800-545-2223 ■ *Web:* www.iamfc.com
International Neuropsychological Society (INS)
700 Ackerman Rd Suite 625 .... Columbus OH 43202 614-263-4200 263-4366
Web: www.the-ins.org
International Society for Traumatic Stress Studies (ISTSS)
111 Deer Lake Rd Suite 100.................... Deerfield IL 60015 847-480-9028 480-9282
Web: www.istss.org
International Transactional Analysis Assn (ITAA)
2186 Rheem Dr Suite B-1 .... Pleasanton CA 94588 925-600-8110 600-8112
Web: www.itaa-net.org
NAADAC - Assn for Addiction Professionals
1001 N Fairfax St Suite 201.................... Alexandria VA 22314 703-741-7686 377-1136*
**Fax Area Code:* 800 ■ *TF:* 800-548-0497 ■ *Web:* naadac.org
National Assn of Psychiatric Health Systems (NAPHS)
701 13th St NW Suite 950.................... Washington DC 20005 202-393-6700 783-6041
Web: www.naphs.org
National Assn of School Psychologists (NASP)
4340 East West Hwy Suite 402.................... Bethesda MD 20814 301-657-0270 657-0275
TF: 866-331-6277 ■ *Web:* www.nasponline.org
National Council for Community Behavioral Healthcare
12300 Twinbrook Pkwy Suite 320.................... Rockville MD 20852 301-984-6200 881-7159
Web: www.nccbh.org
National Council for Therapeutic Recreation Certification Inc (NCTRC) 7 Elmwood Dr .... New City NY 10066 845-639-1439 639-1471
Web: www.nctrc.org
National Psychological Assn for Psychoanalysis (NPAP)
150 W 13th St.................... New York NY 10011 212-924-7440 989-7543
Web: www.npap.org
National Resource Center on Homelessness & Mental Illness (NRC) 189 Wells Ave Suite 200.................... Newton Centre MA 02459 617-467-6014 467-6015
TF: 800-444-7415 ■ *Web:* www.nrchmi.samhsa.gov
SAVE - Suicide Awareness Voices of Education
9001 E Bloomington Fwy Suite 150 .... Bloomington MN 55420 952-946-7998 829-0841
TF: 888-511-7283 ■ *Web:* www.save.org
Society of Behavioral Medicine (SBM)
555 E Wells St Suite 1100.................... Milwaukee WI 53202 414-918-3156 276-3349
Web: www.sbm.org
Society for Social Work Leadership in Health Care
100 N 20th St 4th Fl .... Philadelphia PA 19103 215-599-6134 564-2175
TF: 866-237-9542 ■ *Web:* www.sswlhc.org

49-16 Publishing & Printing Professional Associations

Phone Fax

American Book Producers Assn (ABPA)
611 Broadway Suite 611 .... New York NY 10012 212-645-2368 802-2893
TF: 800-209-4575 ■ *Web:* www.abpaonline.org
American Business Media (ABM) 675 3rd Ave 7th Fl .... New York NY 10017 212-661-6360 370-0736
Web: www.americanbusinessmedia.com
American Society of Business Publication Editors (ASBPE)
214 N Hale St.................... Wheaton IL 60187 630-510-4588 510-4501
Web: www.asbpe.org
American Society of Indexers (ASI)
10200 W 44th Ave Suite 304.................... Wheat Ridge CO 80033 303-463-2887 422-8894
Web: www.asindexing.org
Associated Church Press (ACP) PO Box 621001 .... Oviedo FL 32762 407-341-6615 386-3236
Web: www.theacp.org
Association of American Publishers Inc (AAP) 71 5th Ave........ New York NY 10003 212-255-0200 255-7007
Web: www.publishers.org
Association of American University Presses (AAUP)
71 W 23rd St Suite 901.................... New York NY 10010 212-989-1010 989-0275
Web: www.aaupnet.org
Association of Directory Publishers (ADP) 116 Cass St .... Traverse City MI 49684 800-267-9002 486-2182*
**Fax Area Code:* 231 ■ *Web:* www.adp.org
Binding Industries Assn International (BIA) 200 Deer Run Rd..... Sewickley PA 15143 412-741-6860 741-2311
TF: 800-910-4283 ■ *Web:* www.bindingindustries.org

Publishing & Printing Professional Associations (Cont'd)

Organization	City	State	Zip	Phone	Fax
Book Industry Study Group Inc (BISG) 370 Lexington Ave Suite 900 *Web:* www.bisg.org	New York	NY	10017	646-336-7141	336-6214
Book Manufacturers Institute Inc (BMI) 2 Armand Beach Dr Suite 1-B *Web:* www.bmibook.org	Palm Coast	FL	32137	386-986-4552	986-4553
Canadian Community Newspapers Assn 8 Market St Suite 300 *TF:* 877-305-2262 ■ *Web:* www.ccna.ca	Toronto	ON	M5E1M6	416-482-1090	482-1908
Canadian Newspaper Assn 890 Yonge St Suite 200 *Web:* www.cna-acj.ca	Toronto	ON	M4W3P4	416-923-3567	923-7206
Children's Book Council (CBC) 12 W 37th St 2nd Fl *TF Orders:* 800-999-2160 ■ *Web:* www.cbcbooks.org	New York	NY	10018	212-966-1990	966-2073
Copyright Clearance Center Inc (CCC) 222 Rosewood Dr *Web:* www.copyright.com	Danvers	MA	01923	978-750-8400	646-8600
Copyright Society of the USA 352 7th Ave Suite 739 *Web:* www.csusa.org	New York	NY	10001	212-354-6401	354-2847
Editorial Freelancers Assn (EFA) 71 W 23rd St 4th Fl *TF:* 866-929-5400 ■ *Web:* www.the-efa.org	New York	NY	10010	212-929-5400	929-5439
Evangelical Christian Publishers Assn (ECPA) 9633 S 48th St Suite 140 *Web:* www.ecpa.org	Phoenix	AZ	85044	480-966-3998	966-1944
Flexographic Technical Assn (FTA) 900 Marconi Ave *Web:* www.flexography.org	Ronkonkoma	NY	11779	631-737-6020	737-6813
Gravure Assn of America (GAA) 1200-A Scottsville Rd *Web:* www.gaa.org	Rochester	NY	14624	585-436-2150	436-7689
Greeting Card Assn (GCA) 1156 15th St NW Suite 900 *Web:* www.greetingcard.org	Washington	DC	20005	202-393-1778	223-9741
IDEAlliance (International Digital Enterprise Alliance) 1421 Prince St Suite 230 *Web:* www.idealliance.org	Alexandria	VA	22314	703-837-1070	837-1072
International Assn of Printing House Craftsmen (IAPHC) 7042 Brooklyn Blvd *TF:* 800-466-4274 ■ *Web:* www.iaphc.org	Minneapolis	MN	55429	763-560-1620	560-1350
International Digital Enterprise Alliance (IDEAlliance) 1421 Prince St Suite 230 *Web:* www.idealliance.org	Alexandria	VA	22314	703-837-1070	837-1072
International Publishing Management Assn (IPMA) 710 Regency Dr Suite 6 *Web:* www.ipma.org	Kearney	MO	64060	816-902-4762	902-4766
International Reprographic Assn (IRgA) 401 N Michigan Ave Suite 2200 *TF:* 800-833-4742 ■ *Web:* www.irga.com	Chicago	IL	60611	312-245-1026	673-6724
IPA - Assn of Graphic Solution Providers 7200 France Ave S Suite 223 *TF:* 800-255-8141 ■ *Web:* www.ipa.org	Edina	MN	55435	952-896-1908	
Magazine Publishers of America (MPA) 810 7th Ave 24th Fl *TF:* 888-567-3228 ■ *Web:* www.magazine.org	New York	NY	10019	212-872-3700	888-4217
National Assn of Printing Ink Manufacturers (NAPIM) 581 Main St 5th Fl *Web:* www.napim.org	Woodbridge	NJ	07095	732-855-1525	855-1838
National Assn for Printing Leadership (NAPL) 75 W Century Rd *TF Cust Svc:* 800-642-6275 ■ *Web:* www.napl.org	Paramus	NJ	07652	201-634-9600	634-0324
National Assn of Quick Printers (NAQP) 2250 E Devon Ave Suite 302 *TF:* 800-234-0040 ■ *Web:* www.naqp.com	Des Plaines	IL	60018	847-298-8680	298-8705
National Information Standards Organization (NISO) 1 N Charles St Suite 1905 **Fax Area Code:* 410 ■ *Web:* www.niso.org	Baltimore	MD	21201	301-654-2512	685-5278*
National Press Foundation (NPF) 1211 Connecticut Ave NW Suite 310 *Web:* www.nationalpress.org	Washington	DC	20036	202-663-7280	530-2855
NPES: Assn for Suppliers of Printing Publishing & Converting Technologies 1899 Preston White Dr *TF:* 866-381-9839 ■ *Web:* www.npes.org	Reston	VA	20191	703-264-7200	620-0994
Online Publishers Assn (OPA) 249 W 17th St 14th Fl *Web:* www.online-publishers.org	New York	NY	10011	212-204-1488	204-1514
Printing Industries of America/Graphic Arts Technical Foundation (PIA/GATF) 200 Deer Run Rd *TF:* 800-910-4283 ■ *Web:* www.gain.net	Sewickley	PA	15143	412-741-6860	741-2311
Publishers Marketing Assn (PMA) 627 Aviation Way *Web:* www.pma-online.org	Manhattan Beach	CA	90266	310-372-2732	374-3342
Society for Imaging Science & Technology 7003 Kilworth Ln *Web:* www.imaging.org	Springfield	VA	22151	703-642-9090	642-9094
Society of Publication Designers Inc (SPD) 17E 47th St 6th Fl *Web:* www.spd.org	New York	NY	10017	212-223-3332	223-5880
Society for Scholarly Publishing (SSP) 10200 W 44th Ave Suite 304 *Web:* www.sspnet.org	Wheat Ridge	CO	80033	303-422-3914	422-8894
Specialty Graphic Imaging Assn (SGIA) 10015 Main St *TF:* 888-385-3588 ■ *Web:* www.sgia.org	Fairfax	VA	22031	703-385-1335	273-0456
Web Offset Assn (WOA) 200 Deer Run Rd *TF:* 800-910-4283 ■ *Web:* www.gain.net/PIA_GATF/WOA/main.html	Sewickley	PA	15143	412-741-6860	741-2311
Yellow Pages Assn (YPA) 820 Kirts Blvd Suite 100 *TF:* 800-841-0639	Troy	MI	48084	248-244-6200	244-0700

49-17 Real Estate Professionals Associations

Organization	City	State	Zip	Phone	Fax
AIR Commercial Real Estate Assn 800 W 6th St Suite 800 *Web:* www.airea.com	Los Angeles	CA	90017	213-687-8777	687-8616
American Homeowners Foundation (AHF) 6776 Little Falls Rd *TF:* 800-489-7776 ■ *Web:* www.americanhomeowners.org	Arlington	VA	22213	703-536-7776	536-7079
American Planning Assn (APA) 1776 Massachusetts Ave NW Suite 400 *Web:* www.planning.org	Washington	DC	20036	202-872-0611	872-0643
American Resort Development Assn (ARDA) 1201 15th St NW Suite 400 *Web:* www.arda.org	Washington	DC	20005	202-371-6700	289-8544
American Society of Appraisers (ASA) 555 Herndon Pkwy Suite 125 *TF:* 800-272-8258 ■ *Web:* www.appraisers.org	Herndon	VA	20170	703-478-2228	742-8471
Appraisal Institute 550 W Van Buren St Suite 1000 *Web:* www.appraisalinstitute.org	Chicago	IL	60607	312-335-4100	335-4400
Building Owners & Managers Assn International (BOMA) 1101 15th St NW Suite 800 *TF:* 800-426-6292 ■ *Web:* www.boma.org	Washington	DC	20005	202-408-2662	326-6377
Building Owners & Managers Institute 1 Park Pl Suite 475 *TF:* 800-235-2664 ■ *Web:* www.bomi-edu.org	Annapolis	MD	21401	410-974-1410	974-1935
CCIM Institute 430 N Michigan Ave Suite 800 *TF:* 800-621-7027 ■ *Web:* www.ccim.com	Chicago	IL	60611	312-321-4460	321-4530
CoreNet Global Inc 260 Peachtree St NW Suite 1500 *TF:* 800-726-8111 ■ *Web:* www.corenetglobal.org	Atlanta	GA	30303	404-589-3200	589-3201
Council of Real Estate Brokerage Managers (CRB) 430 N Michigan Ave Suite 300 **Fax Area Code:* 312 ■ *TF:* 800-621-8738 ■ *Web:* www.crb.com	Chicago	IL	60611	800-621-8738	329-8882*
Council of Residential Specialists 430 N Michigan Ave Suite 300 *TF:* 800-462-8841 ■ *Web:* www.crs.com	Chicago	IL	60611	312-321-4400	329-8882
Counselors of Real Estate (CRE) 430 N Michigan Ave 2nd Fl *Web:* www.cre.org	Chicago	IL	60611	312-329-8427	329-8881
Institute of Business Appraisers (IBA) 6950 Cypress Rd Suite 209 *TF:* 800-299-4130 ■ *Web:* www.go-iba.org	Plantation	FL	33317	954-584-1144	584-1184
Institute of Real Estate Management (IREM) 430 N Michigan Ave **Fax Area Code:* 800 ■ *TF:* 800-837-0706 ■ *Web:* www.irem.org	Chicago	IL	60611	312-329-6000	338-4736*
International Downtown Assn (IDA) 1250 H St NW 10th Fl *Web:* ida-downtown.org	Washington	DC	20005	202-393-6801	393-6869
International Right of Way Assn (IRWA) 19750 S Vermont Ave Suite 220 *Web:* www.irwaonline.org	Torrance	CA	90502	310-538-0233	538-1471
National Apartment Assn (NAA) 4300 Wilson Blvd Suite 400 *Web:* www.naahq.org	Arlington	VA	22203	703-518-6141	248-9440
National Assn of Exclusive Buyer Agents (NAEBA) 1481 N Eliseo C Felix Jr Way Suite 223 *TF:* 888-623-2299 ■ *Web:* www.naeba.org	Avondale	AZ	85323	623-932-0098	932-0212
National Assn of Housing Cooperatives (NAHC) 1444 'I' St NW Suite 700 *Web:* www.coophousing.org	Washington	DC	20005	202-737-0797	216-9646
National Assn of Independent Fee Appraisers (NAIFA) 401 N Michigan Ave Suite 2200 *Web:* www.naifa.com	Chicago	IL	60611	312-321-6830	673-6652
National Assn of Industrial & Office Properties (NAIOP) 2201 Cooperative Way 3rd Fl *TF:* 800-666-6780 ■ *Web:* www.naiop.org	Herndon	VA	20171	703-904-7100	904-7942
National Assn of Master Appraisers 303 W Cypress St *TF:* 800-229-6262 ■ *Web:* www.masterappraisers.org	San Antonio	TX	78212	210-271-0781	271-0791
National Assn of Real Estate Companies (NAREC) 216 W Jackson Blvd Suite 625 *Web:* www.narec.org	Chicago	IL	60606	312-263-1755	750-1203
National Assn of Real Estate Investment Trusts (NAREIT) 1875 'I' St NW Suite 600 *TF:* 800-362-7348 ■ *Web:* www.nareit.com	Washington	DC	20006	202-739-9400	739-9401
National Assn of REALTORS 430 N Michigan Ave **Fax:* Mktg ■ *TF:* 800-874-6500 ■ *Web:* www.realtor.org	Chicago	IL	60611	312-329-8200	329-8390*
National Assn of Residential Property Managers (NARPM) 638 Independence Pkwy Suite 100 *TF:* 800-782-3452 ■ *Web:* www.narpm.org	Chesapeake	VA	23320	757-473-9700	473-9897
National Assn of Royalty Owners (NARO) 15 W 6th St Suite 2626 *TF:* 800 558 0557 ■ *Web:* www.naro-us.org	Tulsa	OK	74119	918-794-1660	794-1662
National Assn of Screening Agencies (NASA) 3337 Duke St *Web:* www.n-a-s-a.com	Alexandria	VA	22314	703-370-7436	
National Council of Exchangors (NCE) PO Box 668 **Fax Area Code:* 866 ■ *TF:* 800-324-1031 ■ *Web:* www.infoville.com/nce	Morro Bay	CA	93443	805-772-4662	332-3004*
National Housing & Rehabilitation Assn (NH&RA) 1400 16th St NW Suite 420 *Web:* housingonline.com	Washington	DC	20036	202-939-1750	265-4435
National Multi Housing Council (NMHC) 1850 M St NW Suite 540 *Web:* www.nmhc.org	Washington	DC	20036	202-974-2300	775-0112
Real Estate Buyer's Agent Council (REBAC) 430 N Michigan Ave *TF:* 800-648-6224 ■ *Web:* www.rebac.net	Chicago	IL	60611	312-329-8656	329-8632
Real Estate Educators Assn (REEA) 19 Mantua Rd *Web:* www.reea.org	Mount Royal	NJ	08061	856-423-3215	423-3420
Real Estate Roundtable 801 Pennsylvania Ave NW Suite 720 *Web:* www.rer.org	Washington	DC	20004	202-639-8400	639-8442
Realtors Land Institute 430 N Michigan Ave *TF:* 800-441-5263 ■ *Web:* www.rliland.com	Chicago	IL	60611	312-329-8446	329-8633
SIOR (Society of Industrial & Office REALTORS) 1201 New York Ave NW Suite 350 *Web:* www.sior.com	Washington	DC	20005	202-449-8200	216-9325
Society of Industrial & Office REALTORS (SIOR) 1201 New York Ave NW Suite 350 *Web:* www.sior.com	Washington	DC	20005	202-449-8200	216-9325
Vacation Rental Managers Assn (VRMA) PO Box 1202 *TF:* 800-871-8762 ■ *Web:* www.vrma.com	Santa Cruz	CA	95061	831-426-8762	458-3637
Women's Council of REALTORS (WCR) 430 N Michigan Ave *TF:* 800-245-8512 ■ *Web:* www.wcr.org	Chicago	IL	60611	312-329-8483	329-3290

49-18 Sales & Marketing Professional Associations

Organization	City	State	Zip	Phone	Fax
ABA (American Booksellers Assn) 200 White Plains Rd *TF:* 800-637-0037 ■ *Web:* www.bookweb.org	Tarrytown	NY	10591	914-591-2665	591-2720
ABC (Audit Bureau of Circulations) 900 N Meacham Rd *Web:* www.accessabc.com	Schaumburg	IL	60173	847-605-0909	605-0483
Ad Council 261 Madison Ave 11th Fl *Web:* www.adcouncil.org	New York	NY	10016	212-922-1500	922-1676
Advertising Council Inc 261 Madison Ave 11th Fl *Web:* www.adcouncil.org	New York	NY	10016	212-922-1500	922-1676
Advertising Research Foundation (ARF) 432 Park Ave S 6th Fl	New York	NY	10016	212-751-5656	319-5265
Agricultural Retailers Assn (ARA) 1156 15th St NW Suite 302 *Web:* www.aradc.org	Washington	DC	20005	202-457-0825	457-0864
American Advertising Federation (AAF) 1101 Vermont Ave NW Suite 500 *TF:* 800-999-2231 ■ *Web:* www.aaf.org	Washington	DC	20005	202-898-0089	898-0159
American Assn of Advertising Agencies (AAAA) 405 Lexington Ave 18th Fl *Web:* www.aaaa.org	New York	NY	10174	212-682-2500	682-8391
American Assn of Exporters & Importers (AAEI) 1050 17th St NW Suite 810 *Web:* www.aaei.org	Washington	DC	20036	202-857-8009	857-7843
American Assn of Franchisees & Dealers (AAFD) 3500 5th Ave Suite 103 *TF:* 800-733-9858 ■ *Web:* www.aafd.org	San Diego	CA	92103	619-209-3775	209-3777
American Booksellers Assn (ABA) 200 White Plains Rd *TF:* 800-637-0037 ■ *Web:* www.bookweb.org	Tarrytown	NY	10591	914-591-2665	591-2720
American Hardwood Export Council (AHEC) 1111 19th St NW Suite 800 *Web:* www.ahec.org	Washington	DC	20036	202-463-2720	463-2787
American International Automobile Dealers Assn (AIADA) 211 N Union St Suite 300 *TF:* 800-462-4232 ■ *Web:* www.aiada.org	Alexandria	VA	22314	703-519-7800	519-7810

Organization / Address	City	State	Zip	Phone	Fax
American Machine Tool Distributors' Assn (AMTDA) 1445 Research Blvd Suite 450 — *TF:* 800-878-2683 ■ *Web:* www.amtda.org	Rockville	MD	20850	301-738-1200	738-9499
American Marketing Assn (AMA) 311 S Wacker Dr Suite 5800 — *TF:* 800-262-1150 ■ *Web:* www.marketingpower.com	Chicago	IL	60606	312-542-9000	542-9001
American Supply Assn (ASA) 222 Merchandise Mart Plaza Suite 1400 — *Web:* www.asa.net	Chicago	IL	60654	312-464-0090	464-0091
American Wholesale Marketers Assn (AWMA) 2750 Prosperity Ave Suite 530 — *TF:* 800-482-2962 ■ *Web:* www.awmanet.org	Fairfax	VA	22031	703-208-3358	573-5738
Associated Equipment Distributors (AED) 615 W 22nd St — *TF:* 800-388-0650 ■ *Web:* www.aednet.org	Oak Brook	IL	60523	630-574-0650	574-0132
Association of National Advertisers Inc (ANA) 708 3rd Ave — *Web:* www.ana.net	New York	NY	10017	212-697-5950	687-7310
Association for Postal Commerce 1901 N Fort Myer Dr Suite 401 — *Web:* www.postcom.org	Arlington	VA	22209	703-524-0096	524-1871
Association of Progressive Rental Organizations (APRO) 1504 Robin Hood Trail — *TF:* 800-204-2776 ■ *Web:* www.rtohq.org	Austin	TX	78703	512-794-0095	794-0097
Association of Retail Marketing Services 10 Drs James Parker Blvd Suite 103 — *TF:* 866-231-6310 ■ *Web:* www.narms.com	Red Bank	NJ	07701	732-842-5070	219-1938
Audit Bureau of Circulations (ABC) 900 N Meacham Rd — *Web:* www.accessabc.com	Schaumburg	IL	60173	847-605-0909	605-0483
Automotive Distribution Network DBA Parts Plus 5050 Poplar Ave Suite 2020 — *TF:* 800-727-8112	Memphis	TN	38157	901-682-9090	682-9098
Beauty & Barber Supply Institute (BBSI) 15825 N 71st St Suite 100 — *TF:* 800-468-2274 ■ *Web:* www.bbsi.org/index2.html	Scottsdale	AZ	85254	480-281-0424	905-0708
BPA Worldwide 2 Corporate Dr Suite 900 — *Web:* www.bpaww.com	Shelton	CT	06484	203-447-2800	447-2900
Brick Industry Assn (BIA) 1850 Centennial Park Dr Suite 301 — *Web:* www.gobrick.com	Reston	VA	20191	703-620-0010	620-3928
Business Marketing Assn (BMA) 400 N Michigan Ave 15th Fl — *TF:* 800-664-4262 ■ *Web:* www.marketing.org	Chicago	IL	60611	312-822-0005	822-0054
Business Technology Assn (BTA) 12411 Wornall Rd — *TF:* 800-316-9721 ■ *Web:* www.bta.org	Kansas City	MO	64145	816-941-3100	941-2829
Cabletelevision Advertising Bureau (CAB) 830 3rd Ave 2nd Fl — *Web:* www.cabletvadbureau.com	New York	NY	10022	212-508-1200	832-3268
Canadian Assn of Chemical Distributors (CACD) 627 Lyons Ln Suite 301 — *Web:* www.cacd.ca	Oakville	ON	L6J5Z7	905-844-9140	844-5706
CBA International 9240 Explorer Dr — *TF:* 800-252-1950 ■ *Web:* www.cbaonline.org	Colorado Springs	CO	80920	719-265-9895	272-3510
Center for Exhibition Industry Research (CEIR) 401 N Michigan Ave Suite 2200 — *Web:* www.ceir.org	Chicago	IL	60611	312-527-6735	673-6722
Chain Drug Marketing Assn (CDMA) 43157 W Nine-Mile Rd PO Box 995 — *TF:* 800-935-2362 ■ *Web:* www.chaindrug.com	Novi	MI	48376	248-449-9300	449-4634
Christian Booksellers Assn 9240 Explorer Dr — *TF:* 800-252-1950 ■ *Web:* www.cbaonline.org	Colorado Springs	CO	80920	719-265-9895	272-3510
Clio Awards Inc 770 Broadway 6th Fl — *TF:* 800-946-2546 ■ *Web:* www.clioawards.com	New York	NY	10003	212-683-4300	683-4796
Coalition for Employment through Exports (CEE) 1100 Connecticut Ave NW Suite 810 — *Web:* usaexport.org	Washington	DC	20036	202-296-6107	296-9709
Coalition for Government Procurement 1990 M St NW Suite 450 — *Web:* www.coalgovpro.org	Washington	DC	20036	202-331-0975	822-9788
Color Marketing Group (CMG) 5845 Richmond Hwy Suite 410 — *Web:* www.colormarketing.org	Alexandria	VA	22303	703-329-8500	329-0155
Council of Supply Chain Management Professionals 2805 Butterfield Rd Suite 200 — *Web:* www.cscmp.org	Oak Brook	IL	60523	630-574-0985	574-0989
Direct Marketing Assn Inc (DMA) 1120 Ave of the Americas — *Web:* www.the-dma.org	New York	NY	10036	212-768-7277	302-6714
Direct Selling Assn (DSA) 1667 K St NW Suite 1100 — *Web:* www.dsa.org	Washington	DC	20006	202-452-8866	452-9010
Electronic Retailing Assn (ERA) 2000 N 14th St Suite 300 — *Web:* www.retailing.org	Arlington	VA	22201	703-841-1751	841-1860
Electronics Representatives Assn (ERA) 444 N Michigan Ave Suite 1960 — *TF:* 800-776-7377 ■ *Web:* www.era.org	Chicago	IL	60611	312-527-3050	527-3783
Equipment Leasing Assn of America (ELA) 4301 N Fairfax Dr Suite 550 — *Web:* www.elaonline.com	Arlington	VA	22203	703-527-8655	527-2649
Exhibit Designers & Producers Assn (EDPA) 5775 Peachtree Dunwoody Rd Bldg G Suite 500 — *Web:* www.edpa.com	Atlanta	GA	30342	404-303-7310	252-0774
Food Marketing Institute (FMI) 2345 Crystal Dr Suite 800 — *Web:* www.fmi.org	Arlington	VA	22202	202-220-0600	429-4519
Gases & Welding Distributors Assn (GAWDA) 100 N 20th St 4th Fl — *Web:* www.gawda.org	Philadelphia	PA	19103	215-564-3484	963-9785
General Merchandise Distributors Council (GMDC) 1275 Lake Plaza Dr — *Web:* www.gmdc.com	Colorado Springs	CO	80906	719-576-4260	576-2661
Global Offset & Countertrade Assn (GOCA) 818 Connecticut Ave NW 12th Fl — *Web:* www.globaloffset.org	Washington	DC	20006	202-887-9011	872-8324
Health Industry Distributors Assn (HIDA) 310 Montgomery St — *TF:* 800-549-4432 ■ *Web:* www.hida.org	Alexandria	VA	22314	703-549-4432	549-6495
Healthcare Convention & Exhibitors Assn (HCEA) 5775 Peachtree-Dunwoody Rd Bldg G Suite 500 — *Web:* www.hcea.org	Atlanta	GA	30342	404-252-3663	252-0774
Healthcare Distribution Management Assn (HDMA) 901 N Glebe Rd Suite 1000 — *Web:* www.healthcaredistribution.org	Arlington	VA	22203	703-787-0000	935-3200
Healthcare Marketing & Communications Council (HMC) 1525 Valley Ctr Pkwy Suite 150 — *Web:* www.hmc-council.org	Bethlehem	PA	18017	610-868-8299	868-8387
Heating Airconditioning & Refrigeration Distributors International (HARDI) 1389 Dublin Rd — *TF:* 888-253-2128 ■ *Web:* www.hardinet.org	Columbus	OH	43215	614-488-1835	488-0482
Hospitality Sales & Marketing Assn International (HSMAI) 8201 Greensboro Dr Suite 300 — *Web:* www.hsmai.org	McLean	VA	22102	703-610-9024	610-9005
International Advertising Assn (IAA) 275 Madison Ave Suite 2102 — *Web:* www.iaaglobal.org	New York	NY	10016	212-557-1133	983-0455
International Assn for Exhibition Management (IAEM) 8111 LBJ Pkwy Suite 750 — *Web:* www.iaem.org	Dallas	TX	75251	972-458-8002	458-8119
International Assn of Plastics Distributors (IAPD) 4707 College Blvd Suite 105 — *Web:* www.iapd.org	Leawood	KS	66211	913-345-1005	345-1006
International Federation of Pharmaceutical Wholesalers (IFPW) 10569 Crestwood Dr — *Web:* www.ifpw.com	Manassas	VA	20109	703-331-3714	331-3715
International Foodservice Distributors Assn (IFDA) 1410 Spring Hill Rd Suite 210 — *Web:* www.ifdaonline.org	McLean	VA	22102	703-532-9400	538-4673
International Franchise Assn (IFA) 1501 K St NW Suite 350 — *TF:* 800-543-1038 ■ *Web:* www.franchise.org	Washington	DC	20005	202-628-8000	628-0812
International Furniture Suppliers Assn (IFSA) 164 S Main St Suite 310 — *Web:* www.ifsa-info.com	High Point	NC	27261	336-884-1566	884-1350
International Home Furnishings Representatives Assn (IHFRA) 209 S Main St — *TF:* 800-931-3920 ■ *Web:* www.ihfra.org	High Point	NC	27260	336-889-3920	883-8245
International Sanitary Supply Assn (ISSA) 7373 N Lincoln Ave — *TF:* 800-225-4772 ■ *Web:* www.issa.com	Lincolnwood	IL	60712	847-982-0800	982-1012
Licensing Executives Society (LES) 1800 Diagonal Rd Suite 280 — *Web:* www.usa-canada.les.org	Alexandria	VA	22314	703-836-3106	836-3107
Machinery Dealers National Assn (MDNA) 315 S Patrick St — *TF:* 800-872-7807 ■ *Web:* www.mdna.org	Alexandria	VA	22314	703-836-9300	836-9303
Mailing & Fulfillment Service Assn (MFSA) 1421 Prince St Suite 410 — *TF:* 800-333-6272 ■ *Web:* www.mfsanet.org	Alexandria	VA	22314	703-836-9200	548-8204
Manufacturers' Agents National Assn (MANA) 1 Spectrum Pointe Dr Suite 150 — *TF:* 877-626-2776 ■ *Web:* www.manaonline.org	Lake Forest	CA	92630	949-859-4040	855-2973
Marketing Research Assn (MRA) 110 National Dr 2nd Fl — *Web:* www.mra-net.org	Glastonbury	CT	06033	860-682-1000	682-1010
Medical Marketing Assn (MMA) 575 Market St Suite 2125 — *TF:* 800-551-2173 ■ *Web:* www.mmanet.org	San Francisco	CA	94105	415-764-4807	927-5734
Metals Service Center Institute (MSCI) 4201 Euclid Ave — *Web:* www.msci.org	Rolling Meadows	IL	60008	847-485-3000	485-3001
Multi-Level Marketing International Assn (MLMIA) 119 Stanford Ct — *Web:* www.mlmia.com	Irvine	CA	92612	949-854-0484	854-7687
NAMM - International Music Products Assn 5790 Armada Dr — *TF:* 800-767-6266 ■ *Web:* www.namm.org	Carlsbad	CA	92008	760-438-8001	438-7327
National Agri-Marketing Assn (NAMA) 11020 King St Suite 205 — *TF:* 800-530-5646 ■ *Web:* www.nama.org	Overland Park	KS	66210	913-491-6500	491-6502
National Art Materials Trade Assn 15806 Brookway Dr Suite 300 — *Web:* www.namta.org	Huntersville	NC	28078	704-892-6244	892-6247
National Assn of Chain Drug Stores (NACDS) 413 N Lee St — *TF:* 800-678-6223 ■ *Web:* www.nacds.org	Alexandria	VA	22314	703-549-3001	836-4869
National Assn of Chemical Distributors (NACD) 1560 Wilson Blvd Suite 1250 — *Web:* www.nacd.com	Arlington	VA	22209	703-527-6223	527-7747
National Assn of College Stores (NACS) 500 E Lorain St — *TF:* 800-622-7498 ■ *Web:* www.nacs.org	Oberlin	OH	44074	440-775-7777	775-4769
National Assn of Convenience Stores (NACS) 1600 Duke St — *TF Cust Svc:* 800-966-6227 ■ *Web:* www.nacsonline.com	Alexandria	VA	22314	703-684-3600	836-4564
National Assn of Educational Buyers (NAEB) 5523 Research Pk Dr Suite 340 — *Web:* www.naepnet.org	Baltimore	MD	21228	443-543-5540	543-5550
National Assn of Electrical Distributors Inc (NAED) 1100 Corporate Square Dr Suite 100 — *TF:* 888-791-2512 ■ *Web:* www.naed.org	Saint Louis	MO	63132	314-991-9000	991-3060
National Assn of Federally Licensed Firearms Dealers 2400 E Las Olas Blvd Suite 397 — *Web:* www.amfire.com	Fort Lauderdale	FL	33311	954-467-9994	463-2501
National Assn of Fire Equipment Distributors (NAFED) 104 S Michigan Ave Suite 300 — *Web:* www.nafed.org	Chicago	IL	60603	312-263-8100	263-8111
National Assn of General Merchandise Representatives (NAGMR) 766 W Algonquin Rd — *Web:* www.nagmr.org	Arlington Heights	IL	60005	847-434-0951	434-0960
National Assn of Recording Merchandisers (NARM) 9 Eves Dr Suite 120 — *Web:* www.narm.com	Marlton	NJ	08053	856-596-2221	596-3268
National Assn for Retail Marketing Services (NARMS) PO Box 906 — *TF:* 888-526-2767 ■ *Web:* www.narms.com	Plover	WI	54467	715-342-0948	342-1943
National Assn of Steel Pipe Distributors (NASPD) 1501 E Mockingbird Ln Suite 307 — **Fax Area Code:* 832 ■ *Web:* www.naspd.com	Victoria	TX	77904	361-574-7878	201-9479*
National Assn of Wholesaler-Distributors (NAWD) 1325 G St NW Suite 1000 — *Web:* www.naw.org	Washington	DC	20005	202-872-0885	785-0586
National Auctioneers Assn (NAA) 8880 Ballentine St — *TF:* 888-541-8084 ■ *Web:* www.auctioneers.org	Overland Park	KS	66214	913-541-8084	894-5281
National Auto Auction Assn (NAAA) 5320-D Spectrum Dr — *Web:* www.naaa.com	Frederick	MD	21703	301-696-0400	631-1359
National Automatic Merchandising Assn (NAMA) 20 N Wacker Dr Suite 3500 — *Web:* www.vending.org	Chicago	IL	60606	312-346-0370	704-4140
National Automobile Dealers Assn (NADA) 8400 Westpark Dr — *TF:* 800-252-6232 ■ *Web:* www.nada.org	McLean	VA	22102	703-821-7000	821-7075
National Cotton Council of America 1918 North Pkwy — *TF:* 800-377-9030 ■ *Web:* www.cotton.org	Memphis	TN	38112	901-274-9030	725-0510
National Electrical Manufacturers Representatives Assn (NEMRA) 660 White Plains Rd — *Web:* www.nemra.org	Tarrytown	NY	10591	914-524-8650	524-8655
National Electronic Distributors Assn (NEDA) 1111 Alderman Dr Suite 400 — *TF:* 800-347-6332 ■ *Web:* www.nedassoc.org	Alpharetta	GA	30005	678-393-9990	393-9998
National Electronics Service Dealers Assn (NESDA) 3608 Pershing Ave — *TF:* 800-946-0201 ■ *Web:* www.nesda.com	Fort Worth	TX	76107	817-921-9061	921-3741
National Foreign Trade Council (NFTC) 1625 K St NW Suite 200 — *Web:* www.nftc.org	Washington	DC	20006	202-887-0278	452-8160
National Independent Automobile Dealers Assn (NIADA) 2521 Brown Blvd — *TF:* 800-682-3837 ■ *Web:* www.niada.com	Arlington	TX	76006	817-640-3838	649-5866

Sales & Marketing Professional Associations (Cont'd)

Association	City	State	Zip	Phone	Fax
National Independent Flag Dealers Assn (NIFDA) 214 N Hale St. *TF:* 877-544-3524 ■ *Web:* www.flaginfo.com	Wheaton	IL	60187	630-510-4500	510-4501
National Luggage Dealers Assn (NLDA) 1817 Elmdale Ave *TF:* 866-998-6869 ■ *Web:* www.nlda.com	Glenview	IL	60026	847-998-6869	998-6884
National Lumber & Building Material Dealers Assn (NLBMDA) 2025 M St NW *TF:* 800-634-8645 ■ *Web:* www.dealer.org	Washington	DC	20036	202-367-1159	367-2169
National Mail Order Assn (NMOA) 2807 Polk St NE *Web:* www.nmoa.org	Minneapolis	MN	55418	612-788-1673	788-1147
National Marine Representatives Assn (NMRA) 1333 Delany Rd Suite 500 *Web:* www.nmraonline.org	Gurnee	IL	60031	847-662-3167	336-7146
National Minority Supplier Development Council (NMSDC) 1040 Ave of the Americas 2nd Fl *TF:* 888-396-1110 ■ *Web:* www.nmsdcus.org	New York	NY	10018	212-944-2430	719-9611
National Retail Federation (NRF) 325 7th St NW Suite 1100 *TF:* 800-673-4692 ■ *Web:* www.nrf.com	Washington	DC	20004	202-783-7971	737-2849
National Retail Hardware Assn (NRHA) 5822 W 74th St *TF Cust Svc:* 800-772-4424 ■ *Web:* www.nrha.org	Indianapolis	IN	46278	317-290-0338	328-4354
National School Supply & Equipment Assn (NSSEA) 8380 Colesville Rd Suite 250 *TF:* 800-395-5550 ■ *Web:* www.nssea.org	Silver Spring	MD	20910	301-495-0240	495-3330
National Shoe Retailers Assn (NSRA) 7150 Columbia Gateway Dr Suite G *TF:* 800-673-8446 ■ *Web:* nsra.org	Columbia	MD	21046	410-381-8282	381-1167
Network of Ingredient Marketing Specialists Inc (NIMS) 304 W Liberty St Suite 201 *Web:* www.nimsgroup.com	Louisville	KY	40202	502-583-3783	589-3602
North American Building Material Distribution Assn (NBMDA) 401 N Michigan Ave Suite 2400 *TF:* 888-747-7862 ■ *Web:* www.nbmda.org	Chicago	IL	60611	312-644-6610	321-6869
North American Equipment Dealers Assn (NAEDA) 1195 Smizer Mill Rd *Web:* www.naeda.com	Fenton	MO	63026	636-349-5000	349-5443
North American Graphic Arts Suppliers Assn (NAGASA) PO Box 934483 *Web:* www.nagasa.org	Margate	FL	33093	954-971-1383	971-4362
North American Retail Dealers Assn (NARDA) 10 E 22nd St Suite 310 *TF:* 800-621-0298 ■ *Web:* www.narda.com	Lombard	IL	60148	630-953-8950	953-8957
North American Wholesale Lumber Assn (NAWLA) 3601 Algonquin Rd Suite 400 *TF:* 800-527-8258 ■ *Web:* www.lumber.org	Rolling Meadows	IL	60008	847-870-7470	870-0201
NPTA Alliance 500 Bi-County Blvd Suite 200E *TF:* 800-355-6782 ■ *Web:* www.gonpta.com	Farmingdale	NY	11735	631-777-2223	777-2224
Office Products Wholesalers Assn (OPWA) 5024 Campbell Blvd Suite R *Web:* www.opwa.org	Baltimore	MD	21236	410-931-8100	931-8111
Outdoor Advertising Assn of America (OAAA) 1850 M St NW Suite 1040 *Web:* www.oaaa.org	Washington	DC	20036	202-833-5566	833-1522
Paint & Decorating Retailers Assn (PDRA) 403 Axminister Dr *TF:* 800-737-0107 ■ *Web:* www.pdra.org	Fenton	MO	63026	636-326-2636	326-1823
Parts Plus 5050 Poplar Ave Suite 2020 *TF:* 800-727-8112	Memphis	TN	38157	901-682-9090	682-9098
Pet Industry Distributors Assn (PIDA) 2105 Laurel Bush Rd Suite 200 *Web:* www.pida.org	Bel Air	MD	21015	443-640-1060	640-1086
Petroleum Marketers Assn of America (PMAA) 1901 N Fort Myer Dr Suite 500 *TF:* 800-300-7622 ■ *Web:* www.pmaa.org	Arlington	VA	22209	703-351-8000	351-9160
Photo Marketing Assn International (PMA) 3000 Picture Pl *TF:* 800-762-9287 ■ *Web:* www.pmai.org	Jackson	MI	49201	517-788-8100	788-8371
Point-of-Purchase Advertising International (POPAI) 1600 Duke St Suite 400 *TF:* 888-407-6724 ■ *Web:* www.popai.com	Alexandria	VA	22314	703-373-8800	373-8801
PostCom 1901 N Fort Myer Dr Suite 401 *Web:* www.postcom.org	Arlington	VA	22209	703-524-0096	524-1871
Power Transmission Distributors Assn (PTDA) 250 S Wacker Dr Suite 300 *Web:* www.ptda.org	Chicago	IL	60606	312-876-9461	876-9490
Private Label Manufacturers Assn (PLMA) 630 3rd Ave 4th Fl *Web:* www.plma.com	New York	NY	10017	212-972-3131	983-1382
PROMAX 9000 W Sunset Blvd Suite 900 *Web:* www.promax.org	Los Angeles	CA	90069	310-788-7600	788-7616
Promotion Marketing Assn Inc (PMA) 257 Park Ave S Suite 1102 *Web:* www.pmalink.org	New York	NY	10010	212-420-1100	533-7622
Promotional Products Assn International (PPAI) 3125 Skyway Cir N *TF:* 888-492-6891 ■ *Web:* www.ppa.org	Irving	TX	75038	972-252-0404	258-3004
Public Relations Society of America (PRSA) 33 Maiden Ln 11th Fl *TF:* 800-937-7772 ■ *Web:* www.prsa.org	New York	NY	10038	212-460-1400	995-0757
Qualitative Research Consultants Assn Inc (QRCA) PO Box 967 *TF:* 888-674-7722 ■ *Web:* www.qrca.org	Camden	TN	38320	731-584-8080	584-7882
Radio Advertising Bureau (RAB) 125 W 55th St 21st Fl *TF:* 800-252-7234 ■ *Web:* www.rab.com	New York	NY	10019	212-681-7200	681-7223
Recreation Vehicle Dealers Assn (RVDA) 3930 University Dr 3rd Fl *TF:* 800-336-0355 ■ *Web:* www.rvda.org	Fairfax	VA	22030	703-591-7130	591-0734
Retail Advertising & Marketing Assn (RAMA) 325 7th St NW Suite 1100 *TF:* 800-673-4692 ■ *Web:* www.rama-nrf.org	Washington	DC	20004	202-661-3052	737-2849
Retail Industry Leaders Assn (RILA) 1700 N Moore St Suite 2250 *Web:* www.retail-leaders.org	Arlington	VA	22209	703-841-2300	841-1184
Retail Solutions Providers Assn (RSPA) 415 Taggart Creek Rd *Web:* www.rspassn.org	Charlotte	NC	28208	704-357-3124	357-3127
Society of Independent Gasoline Marketers of America (SIGMA) 11495 Sunset Hills Rd Suite 215 *Web:* www.sigma.org	Reston	VA	20190	703-709-7000	709-7007
Society for Marketing Professional Services (SMPS) 99 Canal Center Plaza Suite 330 *TF:* 800-292-7677 ■ *Web:* www.smps.org	Alexandria	VA	22314	703-549-6117	549-2498
Souvenirs Gifts & Novelties Trade Assn 10 E Athens Ave Suite 208 *TF:* 800-284-5451	Ardmore	PA	19003	610-645-6940	645-6943
Specialty Tools & Fasteners Distributors Assn (STAFDA) 500 Elm Grove Rd Suite 210 *TF:* 800-352-2981 ■ *Web:* www.stafda.org	Elm Grove	WI	53122	262-784-4774	784-5059
Television Bureau of Advertising (TVB) 3 E 54th St 10th Fl *Web:* www.tvb.org	New York	NY	10022	212-486-1111	935-5631
Trade Show Exhibitors Assn (TSEA) 2301 S Lake Shore Dr Suite 1005 *Web:* www.tsea.org	Chicago	IL	60616	312-842-8732	842-8744
Traffic Audit Bureau for Media Measurement (TAB) 271 Madison Ave Suite 1504 *Web:* www.tabonline.com	New York	NY	10016	212-972-8075	
United Assn of Equipment Leasing (UAEL) 78120 Calle Estado Suite 201 *Web:* www.uael.org	La Quinta	CA	92253	760-564-2227	564-2206
Video Software Dealers Assn (VSDA) 16530 Ventura Blvd Suite 400 *TF:* 800-955-8732 ■ *Web:* www.idealink.org/Resource.phx/public/aboutvsda.htx	Encino	CA	91436	818-385-1500	385-0567
Wholesale Florist & Florist Supplier Assn (WF&FSA) 147 Old Solomons Island Rd Suite 302 *TF:* 888-289-3372 ■ *Web:* www.wffsa.org	Annapolis	MD	21401	410-573-0400	573-5001
World Wide Pet Industry Assn Inc (WWPIA) 406 S 1st Ave *TF:* 800-999-7295 ■ *Web:* www.wwpia.org	Arcadia	CA	91006	626-447-2222	447-8350

49-19 Technology, Science, Engineering Professionals Associations

Association	City	State	Zip	Phone	Fax
ABET Inc 111 Market Pl Suite 1050 *Web:* www.abet.org	Baltimore	MD	21202	410-347-7700	625-2238
Acoustical Society of America (ASA) 2 Huntington Quadrangle Suite 1NO1 *Web:* asa.aip.org	Melville	NY	11747	516-576-2360	576-2377
AIIM - Enterprise Content Management Assn 1100 Wayne Ave Suite 1100 *TF:* 800-477-2446 ■ *Web:* www.aiim.org	Silver Spring	MD	20910	301-587-8202	587-2711
AIM Global - Assn for Automatic Identification & Mobility (AIM) 125 Warrendale-Bayne Rd Suite 100 *TF:* 800-338-0206 ■ *Web:* www.aimglobal.org	Warrendale	PA	15086	724-934-4470	934-4495
American Assn for the Advancement of Science (AAAS) 1200 New York Ave NW *TF:* 800-731-4939 ■ *Web:* www.aaas.org	Washington	DC	20005	202-326-6400	682-0816
American Assn for Clinical Chemistry Inc (AACC) 1850 K St NW Suite 625 *TF Cust Svc:* 800-892-1400 ■ *Web:* www.aacc.org	Washington	DC	20006	202-857-0717	887-5093
American Assn of Engineering Societies (AAES) 1620 'I' St NW Suite 210 *TF Orders:* 888-400-2237 ■ *Web:* www.aaes.org	Washington	DC	20006	202-296-2237	296-1151
American Assn for Laboratory Accreditation (A2LA) 5301 Buckeystown Pike Suite 350 *Web:* www.a2la.org	Frederick	MD	21704	301-644-3248	662-2974
American Assn for Laboratory Animal Science (AALAS) 9190 Crestwyn Hills Dr *Web:* www.aalas.org	Memphis	TN	38125	901-754-8620	753-0046
American Assn of Pharmaceutical Scientists (AAPS) 2107 Wilson Blvd Suite 700 *TF:* 877-998-2277 ■ *Web:* www.aaps.org	Arlington	VA	22201	703-243-2800	243-9650
American Assn of Physicists in Medicine (AAPM) 1 Physics Ellipse *Web:* www.aapm.org	College Park	MD	20740	301-209-3350	209-0862
American Assn of Variable Star Observers (AAVSO) 49 Bay State Rd *Web:* www.aavso.org	Cambridge	MA	02138	617-354-0484	354-0665
American Astronomical Society (AAS) 2000 Florida Ave NW Suite 400 *Web:* www.aas.org	Washington	DC	20009	202-328-2010	234-2560
American Chemical Society (ACS) 1155 16th St NW *TF:* 800-227-5558 ■ *Web:* www.acs.org	Washington	DC	20036	202-872-4600	872-4615
American Council of Engineering Companies (ACEC) 1015 15th St NW 8th Fl *Web:* www.acec.org	Washington	DC	20005	202-347-7474	898-0068
American Council of Independent Laboratories (ACIL) 1629 K St NW Suite 400 *Web:* www.acil.org	Washington	DC	20006	202-887-5872	887-0021
American Council on Science & Health (ACSH) 1995 Broadway 2nd Fl *Web:* www.acsh.org	New York	NY	10023	212-362-7044	362-4919
American Geological Institute (AGI) 4220 King St *Web:* www.agiweb.org	Alexandria	VA	22302	703-379-2480	379-7563
American Geophysical Union (AGU) 2000 Florida Ave NW *TF:* 800-966-2481 ■ *Web:* www.agu.org	Washington	DC	20009	202-462-6900	328-0566
American Indian Science & Engineering Society (AISES) 2305 Renard SE Suite 200 *Web:* www.aises.org	Albuquerque	NM	87106	505-765-1052	765-5608
American Institute of Aeronautics & Astronautics (AIAA) 1801 Alexander Bell Dr Suite 500 *TF:* 800-639-2422 ■ *Web:* www.aiaa.org	Reston	VA	20191	703-264-7500	264-7657
American Institute of Biological Sciences (AIBS) 1444 'I' St NW Suite 200 *TF:* 800-992-2427 ■ *Web:* www.aibs.org	Washington	DC	20005	202-628-1500	628-1509
American Institute of Chemical Engineers (AIChE) 3 Park Ave 19th Fl **Fax:* Cust Svc ■ *TF Cust Svc:* 800-242-4363 ■ *Web:* www.aiche.org	New York	NY	10016	212-591-8100	591-8888*
American Institute of Chemists (AIC) 315 Chestnut St *Web:* www.theaic.org	Philadelphia	PA	19106	215-873-8224	925-1954
American Institute of Engineers (AIE) 4630 Appian Way Suite 206 *Web:* www.members-aie.org	El Sobrante	CA	94803	510-758-6240	
American Institute of Physics 1 Physics Ellipse *Web:* www.aip.org	College Park	MD	20740	301-209-3100	209-0843
American Institute of Professional Geologists (AIPG) 1400 W 122nd Ave Suite 250 *Web:* www.aipg.org	Westminster	CO	80234	303-412-6205	253-9220
American Mathematical Society (AMS) 201 Charles St PO Box 6248 *TF Cust Svc:* 800-321-4267 ■ *Web:* www.ams.org	Providence	RI	02940	401-455-4000	331-3842
American Meteorological Society (AMS) 45 Beacon St *Web:* www.ametsoc.org	Boston	MA	02108	617-227-2425	742-8718
American Nuclear Society (ANS) 555 N Kensington Ave *TF:* 800-323-3044 ■ *Web:* www.ans.org	La Grange Park	IL	60526	708-352-6611	352-0499
American Physical Society (APS) 1 Physics Ellipse *Web:* www.aps.org	College Park	MD	20740	301-209-3200	209-0865
American Phytopathological Society (APS) 3340 Pilot Knob Rd *Web:* www.apsnet.org	Saint Paul	MN	55121	651-454-7250	454-0766
American Rock Mechanics Assn (ARMA) 600 Woodland Terr *Web:* www.armarocks.org	Alexandria	VA	22302	703-683-1808	683-1815

Organization / Address	City	State	ZIP	Phone	Fax
American Society for Biochemistry & Molecular Biology (ASBMB) 9650 Rockville Pike — *Web:* www.asbmb.org	Bethesda	MD	20814	301-634-7145	634-7126
American Society for Cell Biology (ASCB) 8120 Woodmont Ave Suite 750 — *Web:* www.ascb.org	Bethesda	MD	20814	301-347-9300	347-9310
American Society for Engineering Education (ASEE) 1818 'N' St NW Suite 600 — *Web:* www.asee.org	Washington	DC	20036	202-331-3500	265-8504
American Society of Human Genetics (ASHG) 9650 Rockville Pike — *TF:* 866-486-4363 ■ *Web:* www.ashg.org	Bethesda	MD	20814	301-634-7300	634-7079
American Society of Ichthyologists & Herpetologists Florida International Univ Biology Dept 11200 SW 8th St — *Web:* www.asih.org	Miami	FL	33199	305-348-1235	348-1986
American Society of Limnology & Oceanography (ASLO) 5400 Bosque Blvd Suite 680 — *TF:* 800-929-2756 ■ *Web:* aslo.org	Waco	TX	76710	254-399-9635	776-3767
American Society of Mechanical Engineers (ASME) 3 Park Ave — *TF Cust Svc:* 800-843-2763 ■ *Web:* www.asme.org	New York	NY	10016	212-591-7722	591-7739
American Society for Nondestructive Testing Inc (ASNT) 1711 Arlingate Ln — *TF Orders:* 800-222-2768 ■ *Web:* www.asnt.org	Columbus	OH	43228	614-274-6003	274-6899
American Society for Photobiology (ASP) 810 E 10th St — *TF:* 800-627-0629 ■ *Web:* www.photobiology.org	Lawrence	KS	66044	785-843-1234	843-1274
American Society for Photogrammetry & Remote Sensing (ASPRS) 5410 Grosvenor Ln Suite 210 — *Web:* www.asprs.org	Bethesda	MD	20814	301-493-0290	493-0208
American Society of Plant Biologists (ASPB) 15501 Monona Dr — *Web:* www.aspb.org	Rockville	MD	20855	301-251-0560	279-2996
American Society of Safety Engineers (ASSE) 1800 E Oakton St — *Web:* www.asse.org	Des Plaines	IL	60018	847-699-2929	768-3434
American Statistical Assn (ASA) 732 N Washington St — *TF:* 888-231-3473 ■ *Web:* www.amstat.org	Alexandria	VA	22314	703-684-1221	684-2037
AOAC International 481 N Frederick Ave Suite 500 — *TF:* 800-379-2622 ■ *Web:* www.aoac.org	Gaithersburg	MD	20877	301-924-7077	924-7089
ASFE 8811 Colesville Rd Suite G106 — *Web:* www.asfe.org	Silver Spring	MD	20910	301-565-2733	589-2017
ASME International Gas Turbine Institute (IGTI) 6525 The Corners Pkwy — *Web:* igti.asme.org	Norcross	GA	30092	404-847-0072	847-0151
Association of American Geographers (AAG) 1710 16th St NW — *Web:* www.aag.org	Washington	DC	20009	202-234-1450	234-2744
Association of Consulting Chemists & Chemical Engineers (ACC&CE) PO Box 297 — *Web:* www.chemconsult.org	Sparta	NJ	07871	973-729-6671	729-7088
Association of Science-Technology Centers Inc (ASTC) 1025 Vermont Ave NW Suite 500 — *Web:* www.astc.org	Washington	DC	20005	202-783-7200	783-7207
Association of University Technology Managers (AUTM) 111 Deer Lake Rd SDuite 100 — *Web:* www.autm.net	Deerfield	IL	60062	847-559-0846	480-9282
Association for Women in Science Inc (AWIS) 1200 New York Ave NW Suite 650 — *TF:* 800-886-2947 ■ *Web:* www.awis.org	Washington	DC	20005	202-326-8940	326-8960
ASTM International 100 Barr Harbor Dr PO Box C700 — *Web:* www.astm.org	West Conshohocken	PA	19428	610-832-9500	832-9555
Audio Engineering Society 60 E 42nd St Rm 2520 — *TF:* 800-541-7299 ■ *Web:* www.aes.org	New York	NY	10165	212-661-8528	682-0477
AVS Science & Technology Society 120 Wall St 32nd Fl — *Web:* www.avs.org	New York	NY	10005	212-248-0200	248-0245
Biophysical Society (BPS) 9650 Rockville Pike — *Web:* www.biophysics.org	Bethesda	MD	20814	301-634-7114	634-7133
Biotechnology Industry Organization (BIO) 1201 Maryland Ave SW Suite 900 — *TF:* 800-255-3304 ■ *Web:* www.bio.org	Washington	DC	20024	202-962-9200	488-6301
Center for Chemical Process Safety 3 Park Ave — *Web:* www.aiche.org/CCPS/index.aspx	New York	NY	10016	212-591-7319	591-7699
Center for Science in the Public Interest (CSPI) 1875 Connecticut Ave NW Suite 300 — *Web:* www.cspinet.org	Washington	DC	20009	202-332-9110	265-4954
Clinical Laboratory Management Assn (CLMI) 989 Old Eagle School Rd Suite 815 — *Web:* www.clma.org	Wayne	PA	19087	610-995-9580	
Clinical Ligand Assay Society (CLAS) 3139 S Wayne Rd — *Web:* www.clas.org	Wayne	MI	48184	734-722-6290	722-7006
Commission on Professionals in Science & Technology (CPST) 1200 New York Ave NW Suite 113 — *Web:* www.cpst.org	Washington	DC	20005	202-326-7080	842-1603
Committee of Concerned Scientists 145 W 79th St Suite 4D — **Fax Area Code:* 917 ■ *Web:* www.libertynet.org/ccs	New York	NY	10024	212-362-4441	441-1759*
Controlled Release Society (CRS) 3340 Pilot Knob Rd — *Web:* www.controlledreleasesociety.org	Saint Paul	MN	55121	651-454-7250	454-0766
Coordinating Research Council Inc (CRC) 3650 Mansell Rd Suite 140 — *Web:* www.crcao.com	Alpharetta	GA	30022	678-795-0506	795-0509
Council for Chemical Research Inc (CCR) 1730 Rhode Island Ave NW Suite 302 — *Web:* www.ccrhq.org	Washington	DC	20036	202-429-3971	429-3976
Council for Responsible Genetics (CRG) 5 Upland Rd Suite 3 — *Web:* www.gene-watch.org	Cambridge	MA	02140	617-868-0870	491-5344
Cryogenic Society of America (CSA) 218 Lake St — *Web:* www.cryogenicsociety.org	Oak Park	IL	60302	708-383-6220	383-9337
Custom Electronic Design & Installation Assn (CEDIA) 7150 Winton Dr Suite 300 — *TF:* 800-669-5329 ■ *Web:* www.cedia.net	Indianapolis	IN	46268	317-328-4336	735-4012
Drug Chemical & Associated Technologies Assn (DCAT) 1 Washington Blvd Suite 7 — *Web:* www.dcat.org	Robbinsville	NJ	08691	609-448-1000	448-1944
Earthquake Engineering Research Institute (EERI) 499 14th St Suite 320 — *Web:* www.eeri.org	Oakland	CA	94612	510-451-0905	451-5411
Ecological Society of America (ESA) 1707 H St NW Suite 400 — *Web:* www.esa.org	Washington	DC	20006	202-833-8773	833-8775
Electrical Apparatus Service Assn (EASA) 1331 Baur Blvd — *Web:* www.easa.com	Saint Louis	MO	63132	314-993-2220	993-1269
Electrochemical Society 65 S Main St Bldg D — *Web:* www.electrochem.org	Pennington	NJ	08534	609-737-1902	737-2743
Electronics Technicians Assn International (ETA) 5 Depot St — *TF:* 800-288-3824 ■ *Web:* www.eta-i.org	Greencastle	IN	46135	765-653-8262	653-4287
Electrophoresis Society 1202 Ann St — *TF:* 800-462-3417 ■ *Web:* www.aesociety.org	Madison	WI	53713	608-258-1565	258-1569
Engineering Contractors' Assn (ECA) 8310 Florence Ave — *TF:* 800-293-2240 ■ *Web:* www.ecaonline.net/ECA_Homex.html	Downey	CA	90240	562-861-0929	923-6179
Entomological Society of America 10001 Derekwood Ln Suite 100 — *Web:* www.entsoc.org	Lanham	MD	20706	301-731-4535	731-4538
Federation of American Scientists (FAS) 1725 DeSales St NW 6th Fl — *Web:* www.fas.org	Washington	DC	20036	202-546-3300	315-5847
Federation of American Societies for Experimental Biology (FASEB) 9650 Rockville Pike — *TF:* 800-433-2732 ■ *Web:* www.faseb.org	Bethesda	MD	20814	301-634-7000	634-7001
Foundation for Advanced Education in the Sciences (FAES) 1 Cloister Ct Suite 230 — *Web:* www.faes.org	Bethesda	MD	20814	301-496-7976	402-0174
Fragrance Materials Assn of the US 1620 'I' St NW Suite 925 — *Web:* www.fmafragrance.org	Washington	DC	20006	202-293-5800	463-8998
Generic Pharmaceutical Assn (GPhA) 2300 Clarendon Blvd Suite 400 — *Web:* www.gphaonline.org	Arlington	VA	22201	703-647-2480	647-2481
Genetics Society of America (GSA) 9650 Rockville Pike — *TF:* 866-486-4363 ■ *Web:* www.genetics-gsa.org	Bethesda	MD	20814	301-634-7300	634-7079
Geological Society of America (GSA) 3300 Penrose Pl PO Box 9140 — *TF:* 800-472-1988 ■ *Web:* www.geosociety.org	Boulder	CO	80301	303-447-2020	357-1070
Geospatial Information & Technology Assn (GITA) 14456 E Evans Ave — *Web:* www.gita.org	Aurora	CO	80014	303-337-0513	337-1001
Government Electronics & Information Technology Assn (GEIA) 1401 Wilson Blvd Suite 1100 — *Web:* www.geia.org	Arlington	VA	22209	703-907-7566	522-6694
IEEE Aerospace & Electronics Systems Society IEEE Operations Ctr 445 Hoes Ln — *TF:* 800-678-4333 ■ *Web:* www.ewh.ieee.org/soc/aes	Piscataway	NJ	08854	732-981-0060	981-1721
IEEE Antennas & Propagation Society (APS) IEEE Operations Ctr 445 Hoes Ln — *TF:* 800-678-4333 ■ *Web:* www.ieeeaps.org	Piscataway	NJ	08854	732-981-0060	981-1721
IEEE Broadcast Technology Society (BTS) IEEE Operations Ctr 445 Hoes Ln — *TF:* 800-678-4333 ■ *Web:* www.ieee.org/organizations/society/bt	Piscataway	NJ	08854	732-981-0060	981-1721
IEEE Circuits & Systems Society (CAS) IEEE Operations Ctr 445 Hoes Ln — *TF:* 800-678-4333 ■ *Web:* www.ieee-cas.org	Piscataway	NJ	08854	732-981-0060	981-1721
IEEE Communications Society (COMSOC) IEEE Operations Ctr 445 Hoes Ln — *TF:* 800-678-4333 ■ *Web:* www.comsoc.org	Piscataway	NJ	08854	732-981-0060	981-1721
IEEE Components Packaging & Manufacturing Technology Society 445 Hoes Ln PO Box 1331 — *TF:* 800-678-4333 ■ *Web:* www.cpmt.org	Piscataway	NJ	08855	732-562-5529	981-1769
IEEE Computational Intelligence Society (CIS) 9330 Scranton Rd Suite 150 — *Web:* ieee-cis.org	San Diego	CA	92121	858-455-6449	455-1560
IEEE Computer Society IEEE Operations Ctr 445 Hoes Ln — *Web:* www.computer.org	Piscataway	NJ	08854	732-981-0060	981-1721
IEEE Consumer Electronics Society (CES) IEEE Operations Ctr 445 Hoes Ln — *TF:* 800-678-4333 ■ *Web:* www.ewh.ieee.org/soc/ces	Piscataway	NJ	08854	732-981-0060	981-1721
IEEE Control Systems Society (CSS) IEEE Operations Ctr 445 Hoes Ln — *TF:* 800-678-4333 ■ *Web:* ieeecss.org	Piscataway	NJ	08854	732-981-0060	981-1721
IEEE Dielectrics & Electrical Insulation Society IEEE Operations Ctr 445 Hoes Ln — *TF:* 800-678-4333 ■ *Web:* tdei.sju.edu/deis	Piscataway	NJ	08854	732-981-0060	981-1721
IEEE Education Society (ES) IEEE Operations Ctr 445 Hoes Ln — *TF:* 800-678-4333 ■ *Web:* www.ewh.ieee.org/soc/es	Piscataway	NJ	08854	732-981-0060	981-1721
IEEE Electromagnetic Compatibility Society (EMC) IEEE Operations Ctr 445 Hoes Ln — *TF:* 800-678-4333 ■ *Web:* www.ewh.ieee.org/soc/emcs	Piscataway	NJ	08854	732-981-0060	981-1721
IEEE Electron Devices Society (EDS) IEEE Operations Ctr 445 Hoes Ln — *TF:* 800-678-4333 ■ *Web:* www.ieee.org/organizations/society/eds	Piscataway	NJ	08854	732-981-0060	981-1721
IEEE Engineering Management Society (EMS) IEEE Operations Ctr 445 Hoes Ln — *TF:* 800-678-4333 ■ *Web:* www.ewh.ieee.org/soc/ems	Piscataway	NJ	08854	732-981-0060	981-1721
IEEE Engineering in Medicine & Biology Society (EMB) IEEE Operations Ctr 445 Hoes Ln — *TF:* 800-678-4333 ■ *Web:* embs.gsbme.unsw.edu.au	Piscataway	NJ	08854	732-981-0060	981-1721
IEEE Geoscience & Remote Sensing Society (GRSS) IEEE Operations Ctr 445 Hoes Ln — *TF:* 800-678-4333 ■ *Web:* www.ewh.ieee.org/soc/grss	Piscataway	NJ	08854	732-981-0060	981-1721
IEEE Industrial Electronics Society (IES) IEEE Operations Ctr 445 Hoes Ln — *TF:* 800-678-4333 ■ *Web:* www.ewh.ieee.org/soc/ies	Piscataway	NJ	08854	732-981-0060	981-1721
IEEE Industry Applications Society IEEE Operations Ctr 445 Hoes Ln — *TF:* 800-678-4333 ■ *Web:* www.ewh.ieee.org/soc/ias	Piscataway	NJ	08854	732-981-0060	981-1721
IEEE Information Theory Society (IT) IEEE Operations Ctr 445 Hoes Ln — *TF:* 800-678-4333 ■ *Web:* golay.uvic.ca	Piscataway	NJ	08854	732-981-0060	981-1721
IEEE Instrumentation & Measurement Society (IM) IEEE Operations Ctr 445 Hoes Ln — *TF:* 800-678-4333 ■ *Web:* www.ewh.ieee.org/soc/im	Piscataway	NJ	08854	732-981-0060	981-1721
IEEE Lasers & Electro-Optics Society (LEOS) IEEE Operations Ctr 445 Hoes Ln — *TF:* 800-678-4333 ■ *Web:* www.i-LEOS.org	Piscataway	NJ	08854	732-981-0060	981-1721
IEEE Magnetics Society IEEE Operations Ctr 445 Hoes Ln — *TF:* 800-678-4333 ■ *Web:* www.ieeemagnetics.org	Piscataway	NJ	08854	732-981-0060	981-1721
IEEE Microwave Theory & Techniques Society (MTT-S) IEEE Operations Ctr 445 Hoes Ln — *TF:* 800-678-4333 ■ *Web:* www.mtt.org	Piscataway	NJ	08854	732-981-0060	981-1721
IEEE Nuclear & Plasma Sciences Society (NPSS) IEEE Operations Ctr 445 Hoes Ln — *TF:* 800-678-4333 ■ *Web:* ewh.ieee.org/soc/nps	Piscataway	NJ	08854	732-981-0060	981-1721
IEEE Oceanic Engineering Society (OES) IEEE Operations Ctr 445 Hoes Ln — *TF:* 800-678-4333 ■ *Web:* www.oceanicengineering.org	Piscataway	NJ	08854	732-981-0060	981-1721
IEEE Power Electronics Society (PELS) IEEE Operations Ctr 445 Hoes Ln — *TF:* 800-678-4333 ■ *Web:* www.pels.org	Piscataway	NJ	08854	732-981-0060	981-1721

Technology, Science, Engineering Professionals Associations (Cont'd)

Phone Fax

IEEE Power Engineering Society (PES)
IEEE Operations Ctr 445 Hoes Ln Piscataway NJ 08854 732-562-3883 562-3881
TF: 800-678-4333 ■ *Web:* www.ieee.org/portal/index.jsp?pageID=pes_home

IEEE Product Safety Engineering Society
IEEE Operations Ctr 445 Hoes Ln Piscataway NJ 08854 732-981-0060 981-1721
TF: 800-678-4333 ■ *Web:* ewh.ieee.org/soc/pses

IEEE Professional Communication Society (PCS)
IEEE Operations Ctr 445 Hoes Ln Piscataway NJ 08854 732-981-0060 981-1721
TF: 800-678-4333 ■ *Web:* www.ieeepcs.org

IEEE Reliability Society (RS)
IEEE Operations Ctr 445 Hoes Ln Piscataway NJ 08854 732-981-0060 981-1721
TF: 800-678-4333 ■ *Web:* www.ewh.ieee.org/soc/rs

IEEE Robotics & Automation Society (RAS)
IEEE Operations Ctr 445 Hoes Ln Piscataway NJ 08854 732-981-0060 981-1721
TF: 800-678-4333 ■ *Web:* www.ncsu.edu/IEEE-RAS

IEEE Signal Processing Society
IEEE Operations Ctr 445 Hoes Ln Piscataway NJ 08854 732-981-0060 981-1721
TF: 800-678-4333 ■ *Web:* www.ieee.org/organizations/society/sp

IEEE Society on Social Implications of Technology (SSIT)
IEEE Operations Ctr 445 Hoes Ln Piscataway NJ 08854 732-981-0060 981-1721
TF: 800-678-4333 ■ *Web:* www.ieeessit.org

IEEE Solid State Circuits Society (SSCS)
IEEE Operations Ctr 445 Hoes Ln Piscataway NJ 08854 732-981-0060 981-1721
TF: 800-678-4333 ■ *Web:* sscs.org

IEEE Systems Man & Cybernetics Society (SMC)
IEEE Operations Ctr 445 Hoes Ln Piscataway NJ 08854 732-981-0060 981-1721
TF: 800-678-4333 ■ *Web:* www.ieeesmc.org

IEEE Ultrasonics Ferroelectrics & Frequency Control Society
IEEE Operations Ctr 445 Hoes Ln Piscataway NJ 08854 732-981-0060 981-1721
TF: 800-678-4333 ■ *Web:* www.ieee-uffc.org

IEEE Vehicular Technology Society (VTS)
IEEE Operations Ctr 445 Hoes Ln Piscataway NJ 08854 732-981-0060 981-1721
TF: 800-678-4333 ■ *Web:* www.vtsociety.org

IMAPS (International Microelectronics & Packaging Society)
611 2nd St NE Washington DC 20002 202-548-4001 548-6115
Web: www.imaps.org

Industrial Research Institute Inc (IRI)
2200 Clarendon Blvd Suite 1102 Arlington VA 22201 703-647-2580 647-2581
Web: www.iriinc.org

Institute of Electrical & Electronics Engineers (IEEE)
3 Park Ave 17th Fl New York NY 10016 212-419-7900 752-4929
TF: 800-678-4333 ■ *Web:* www.ieee.org

Institute of Environmental Sciences & Technology (IEST) 2340 S Arlington Heights Rd Suite 100 Arlington Heights IL 60005 847-981-0100 981-4130
Web: www.iest.org

Institute for Operations Research & the Management Sciences (INFORMS) 7240 Parkway Dr Suite 310 Hanover MD 21076 443-757-3500 757-3515
TF: 800-446-3676 ■ *Web:* www.informs.org

International Biometric Society (IBS)
1444 'I' St NW Suite 700 Washington DC 20005 202-712-9049 216-9646
Web: www.tibs.org

International Center for Technology Assessment (ICTA)
660 Pennsylvania Ave SE Suite 302 Washington DC 20003 202-547-9359 547-9429
TF: 800-600-6664 ■ *Web:* www.icta.org

International Engineering Consortium (IEC)
300 W Adams St Suite 1210 Chicago IL 60606 312-559-4100 559-4111
Web: www.iec.org

International Lead Zinc Research Organization (ILZRO)
2525 Meridian Pkwy Suite 100 Durham NC 27713 919-361-4647 361-1957
Web: www.ilzro.org

International Microelectronics & Packaging Society (IMAPS)
611 2nd St NE Washington DC 20002 202-548-4001 548-6115
Web: www.imaps.org

International Society of Certified Electronics Technicians (ISCET) 3608 Pershing Ave Fort Worth TX 76107 817-921-9101 921-3741
TF: 800-946-0201 ■ *Web:* www.iscet.org

International Society for Pharmaceutical Engineering (ISPE)
3109 W Dr ML King Jr Blvd Suite 250 Tampa FL 33607 813-960-2105 264-2816
Web: www.ispe.org

International Titanium Assn (ITA)
2655 W Midway Blvd Suite 300 Broomfield CO 80020 303-404-2221 404-9111
Web: www.titanium.org

IPC - Assn Connecting Electronics Industries
3000 Lakeside Dr Suite 309 Bannockburn IL 60015 847-509-9700 615-7105
Web: www.ipc.org

ISA - Instrumentation Systems & Automation Society 67 Alexander Dr Research Triangle Park NC 27709 919-549-8411 549-8288
Web: www.isa.org

Laser Institute of America (LIA) 13501 Ingenuity Dr Suite 128 Orlando FL 32826 407-380-1553 380-5588
TF: 800-345-2737 ■ *Web:* www.laserinstitute.org

Materials Properties Council (MPC) PO Box 201547 Shaker Heights OH 44120 216-658-3847 658-3854
Web: www.forengineers.org/mpc/index.html

Materials Research Society (MRS) 506 Keystone Dr Warrendale PA 15086 724-779-3003 779-8313
Web: www.mrs.org

Mathematical Assn of America (MAA) 1529 18th St NW Washington DC 20036 202-387-5200 265-2384
TF: 800-331-1622 ■ *Web:* www.maa.org

Microscopy Society of America (MSA) 230 E Ohio St Suite 400 Chicago IL 60611 312-644-1527 644-8557
TF: 800-538-3672 ■ *Web:* www.msa.microscopy.org

MTM Assn for Standards & Research
1111 E Touhy Ave Suite 280 Des Plaines IL 60018 847-299-1111 299-3509
Web: www.mtm.org

National Academies 500 5th St NW Washington DC 20001 202-334-2138 334-2229
TF: 800-624-6242 ■ *Web:* www.nas.edu

National Academy of Engineering 500 5th Ave Washington DC 20001 202-334-3200 334-2290
Web: www.nae.edu

National Assn of Radio & Telecommunications Engineers (NARTE) 840 Queen St New Bern NC 28560 252-672-0200 672-0111
TF: 800-896-2783 ■ *Web:* www.narte.org

National Council on Radiation Protection & Measurements (NCRP) 7910 Woodmont Ave Suite 400 Bethesda MD 20814 301-657-2652 907-8768
TF: 800-229-2652 ■ *Web:* www.ncrponline.org

National Environmental Balancing Bureau (NEBB)
8575 Grovemont Cir Gaithersburg MD 20877 301-977-3698 977-9589
TF: 866-497-4447 ■ *Web:* www.nebb.org

National Geographic Society 1145 17th St NW Washington DC 20036 202-857-7000 775-6141
TF Orders: 800-647-5463 ■ *Web:* www.nationalgeographic.com

National Hydrogen Assn (NHA)
1211 Connecticut Ave NW Suite 600 Washington DC 20036 202-223-5547 223-5537
Web: www.hydrogenus.org

National Institute for Women in Trades Technology & Science (IWITTS) 1150 Ballena Blvd Suite 102 Alameda CA 94501 510-749-0200 749-0500
Web: www.iwitts.com

National Society of Black Physicists (NSBP)
1110 N Glebe Rd Suite 1010 Arlington VA 22201 703-536-4207 536-4203
Web: www.nsbp.org

National Society of Professional Engineers (NSPE)
1420 King St Alexandria VA 22314 703-684-2800 836-4875
TF: 888-285-6773 ■ *Web:* www.nspe.org

National Space Society (NSS) 1620 'I' St NW Suite 615 Washington DC 20006 202-429-1600 463-8497
Web: www.nss.org

New York Academy of Medicine (NYAM) 1216 5th Ave New York NY 10029 212-822-7200 423-0275
Web: www.nyam.org

New York Academy of Sciences 250 Greenwich St 40th Fl New York NY 10007 212-298-8600 298-3610
TF: 800-843-6927 ■ *Web:* www.nyas.org

Plasma Protein Therapeutics Assn (PPTA)
147 Old Solomon's Island Rd Suite 100 Annapolis MD 21401 410-263-8296 263-2298
Web: www.pptaglobal.org

Robotic Industries Assn (RIA) 900 Victors Way Suite 140 Ann Arbor MI 48108 734-994-6088 994-3338
Web: www.roboticsonline.com

Scientific Equipment & Furniture Assn (SEFA)
1205 Franklin Ave Suite 320 Garden City NY 11530 516-294-5424 294-2758
Web: www.sefalabs.com

Semiconductor Environmental Safety & Health Assn (SESHA)
1313 Dolley Madison Blvd Suite 402 McLean VA 22101 703-790-1745 790-2672
Web: seshaonline.org

Semiconductor Equipment & Materials International (SEMI)
3081 Zanker Rd San Jose CA 95134 408-943-6900 428-9600
TF: 800-974-7364 ■ *Web:* www.semi.org

Semiconductor Industry Assn (SIA) 181 Metro Dr Suite 450 San Jose CA 95110 408-436-6600 436-6646
Web: www.sia-online.org

Silicones Environmental Health & Safety Council of North America 11921 Freedom Dr Suite 550 Reston VA 20190 703-904-4322 925-5955
Web: www.sehsc.com

Society for the Advancement of Material & Process Engineering (SAMPE) 1161 Park View Dr Suite 200 Covina CA 91724 626-331-0616 332-8929
TF: 800-562-7360 ■ *Web:* www.sampe.org

Society for Biomaterials 15000 Commerce Pkwy Suite C Mount Laurel NJ 08054 856-439-0826 439-0525
Web: www.biomaterials.org

Society of Cable Telecommunications Engineers (SCTE)
140 Philips Rd Exton PA 19341 610-363-6888 363-5898
TF: 800-542-5040 ■ *Web:* www.scte.org

Society of Cosmetic Chemists (SCC) 120 Wall St Suite 2400 New York NY 10005 212-668-1500 668-1504
Web: www.scconline.org

Society of Environmental Toxicology & Chemistry (SETAC)
1010 N 12th Ave Pensacola FL 32501 850-469-1500 469-9778
Web: www.setac.org

Society for Experimental Mechanics Inc (SEM) 7 School St Bethel CT 06801 203-790-6373 790-4472
Web: www.sem.org

Society of Hispanic Professional Engineers (SHPE)
5400 E Olympic Blvd Suite 210 Los Angeles CA 90022 323-725-3970 725-0316
Web: www.shpe.org

Society for Industrial & Applied Mathematics (SIAM)
3600 Market St 6th Fl Philadelphia PA 19104 215-382-9800 386-7999
TF: 800-447-7426 ■ *Web:* www.siam.org

Society for Integrative & Comparative Biology (SICB)
1313 Dolley Madison Blvd Suite 402 McLean VA 22101 703-790-1745 790-2672
Web: www.sicb.org

Society for Risk Analysis (SRA)
1313 Dolley Madison Blvd Suite 402 McLean VA 22101 703-790-1745 790-2672
Web: www.sra.org

Society for Sedimentary Geology (SEPM)
6128 E 38th St Suite 308 Tulsa OK 74135 918-610-3361 621-1685
TF: 800-865-9765 ■ *Web:* www.sepm.org

Society of Women Engineers (SWE) 230 E Ohio St Suite 400 Chicago IL 60611 312-596-5223 596-5252
Web: www.societyofwomenengineers.org

SPIE - International Society for Optical Engineering
1000 20th St Bellingham WA 98225 360-676-3290 647-1445
Web: www.spie.org

Synthetic Organic Chemical Manufacturers Assn (SOCMA)
1850 M St NW Suite 700 Washington DC 20036 202-721-4100 296-8120
TF: 888-377-0778 ■ *Web:* www.socma.com

Universities Research Assn Inc (URA)
1111 19th St NW Suite 400 Washington DC 20036 202-293-1382 293-5012
Web: www.ura-hq.org

Universities Space Research Assn (USRA)
10211 Wincopin Cir Suite 500 Columbia MD 21044 410-730-2656 730-3496
Web: www.usra.edu

Vibration Institute 6262 S Kingery Hwy Suite 212 Willowbrook IL 60527 630-654-2254 654-2271
Web: www.vibinst.org/vabout.htm

Women in Technology International (WITI)
13351-D Riverside Dr Suite 441 Sherman Oaks CA 91423 818-788-9484 788-9410
TF: 800-334-9484 ■ *Web:* www.witi.com

World Future Society 7910 Woodmont Ave Suite 450 Bethesda MD 20814 301-656-8274 951-0394
TF: 800-989-8274 ■ *Web:* www.wfs.org

49-20 Telecommunications Professionals Associations

Phone Fax

ACUTA - Assn for Communications Technology Professionals in Higher Education 152 W Zandale Dr Suite 200 Lexington KY 40503 859-278-3338 278-3268
Web: www.acuta.org

Alliance for Telecommunications Industry Solutions (ATIS)
1200 G St NW Suite 500 Washington DC 20005 202-628-6380 393-5453
TF: 888-429-7517 ■ *Web:* www.atis.org

American Public Communications Council Inc (APCC)
625 Slaters Ln Suite 104 Alexandria VA 22314 703-739-1322 739-1324
TF: 800-868-2722 ■ *Web:* www.apcc.net

Communications Supply Service Assn (CSSA)
5700 Murray St Little Rock AR 72209 501-562-7666 562-7616
TF: 800-252-2772 ■ *Web:* www.cssa.net

COMPTEL 900 17th St NW Suite 400 Washington DC 20006 202-296-6650 296-7585
Web: www.comptel.org

Computer & Communications Industry Assn (CCIA)
900 17th St NW Suite 1100 Washington DC 20006 202-783-0070 783-0534
Web: www.ccianet.org

CTIA - Wireless Assn 1400 16th St NW Suite 600 Washington DC 20036 202-785-0081 785-0721
Web: www.ctia.org

Enterprise Wireless Alliance (EWA)
8484 Westpark Dr Suite 630 McLean VA 22102 703-528-5115 524-1074
TF: 800-482-8282 ■ *Web:* www.enterprisewireless.org

Forest Industries Telecommunications (FIT) 1565 Oak St Eugene OR 97401 541-485-8441 485-7556
Web: www.landmobile.com

International Communications Industries Assn (ICIA)
11242 Waples Mill Rd Suite 200 Fairfax VA 22030 703-273-7200 278-8082
TF: 800-659-7469 ■ *Web:* www.infocomm.org

National Systems Contractors Assn (NSCA)
625 1st St SE Suite 420 Cedar Rapids IA 52401 319-366-6722 366-4164
TF: 800-446-6722 ■ *Web:* www.nsca.org

	City	State	Zip	Phone	Fax
National Telecommunications Cooperative Assn (NTCA) 4121 Wilson Blvd 10th Fl. *Web:* www.ntca.org	Arlington	VA	22203	703-351-2000	351-2001
Organization for the Promotion & Advancement of Small Telecommunications Companies (OPASTCO) 21 Dupont Cir NW Suite 700 *Web:* www.opastco.org	Washington	DC	20036	202-659-5990	659-4619
PCIA - Wireless Infrastructure Assn 901 N Washington St Suite 600 *TF:* 800-759-0300 ■ *Web:* www.pcia.com	Alexandria	VA	22314	703-739-0300	836-1608
Society of Telecommunications Consultants (STC) PO Box 70 *TF:* 800-782-7670 ■ *Web:* www.stcconsultants.org	Old Station	CA	96071	530-335-7313	335-7360
Telecommunications Industry Assn (TIA) 2500 Wilson Blvd Suite 300 *Web:* www.tiaonline.org	Arlington	VA	22201	703-907-7700	907-7727
US Telecom Assn (USTA) 607-14th St NW Suite 400 *Web:* www.usta.org	Washington	DC	20005	202-326-7300	326-7333
Utilities Telecom Council (UTC) 1901 Pennsylvania Ave NW 5th Fl. *Web:* www.utc.org	Washington	DC	20006	202-872-0030	872-1331
Wireless Communications Assn International (WCA) 1333 H St NW Suite 700W *Web:* www.wcai.com	Washington	DC	20005	202-452-7823	452-0041

49-21 Transportation Industry Associations

	City	State	Zip	Phone	Fax
Aerospace Industries Assn of America (AIA) 1000 Wilson Blvd Suite 1700 *Web:* www.aia-aerospace.org	Arlington	VA	22209	703-358-1000	358-1011
Air Traffic Control Assn (ATCA) 1101 King St Suite 300 *Web:* www.atca.org	Alexandria	VA	22314	703-299-2430	299-2437
Air Transport Assn of America (ATA) 1301 Pennsylvania Ave NW Suite 1100 *TF:* 800-319-2463 ■ *Web:* www.air-transport.org	Washington	DC	20004	202-626-4000	626-4068
Aircraft Electronics Assn (AEA) 4217 S Hocker Dr *Web:* www.aea.net	Independence	MO	64055	816-373-6565	478-3100
Aircraft Owners & Pilots Assn (AOPA) 421 Aviation Way *TF:* 800-872-2672 ■ *Web:* www.aopa.org	Frederick	MD	21701	301-695-2000	695-2375
Airlines Reporting Corp (ARC) 4100 N Fairfax Dr Suite 600 *Web:* www.arccorp.com	Arlington	VA	22203	703-816-8000	816-8104
Airports Council International of North America (ACI-NA) 1775 K St NW Suite 500 *Web:* www.aci-na.org	Washington	DC	20006	202-293-8500	331-1362
American Ambulance Assn (AAA) 8201 Greensboro Dr Suite 300 *TF:* 800-523-4447 ■ *Web:* www.the-aaa.org	McLean	VA	22102	703-610-9018	610-9005
American Assn of Airport Executives (AAAE) 601 Madison St Suite 400 *TF:* 800-367-2223 ■ *Web:* www.aaae.org	Alexandria	VA	22314	703-824-0500	820-1395
American Assn of Port Authorities (AAPA) 1010 Duke St *Web:* www.aapa-ports.org	Alexandria	VA	22314	703-684-5700	684-6321
American Assn of State Highway & Transportation Officials (AASHTO) 444 N Capitol St NW Suite 249 *Web:* www.transportation.org	Washington	DC	20001	202-624-5800	624-5806
American Boat & Yacht Council Inc (ABYC) 613 3rd St Suite 10 *Web:* www.abycinc.org	Annapolis	MD	21403	410-990-4460	990-4466
American Bureau of Shipping (ABS) 16855 Northchase Dr *Web:* www.eagle.org	Houston	TX	77060	281-877-6000	877-6001
American Cotton Shippers Assn (ACSA) 88 Union Ave Suite 1204 *Web:* www.acsa-cotton.org	Memphis	TN	38103	901-525-2272	527-8803
American Helicopter Society International (AHS) 217 N Washington St *Web:* www.vtol.org	Alexandria	VA	22314	703-684-6777	739-9279
American Highway Users Alliance 1101 14th St NW Suite 750 *Web:* www.highways.org	Washington	DC	20005	202-857-1200	857-1220
American International Automobile Dealers Assn (AIADA) 211 N Union St Suite 300 *TF:* 800-462-4232 ■ *Web:* www.aiada.org	Alexandria	VA	22314	703-519-7800	519-7810
American Maritime Congress 400 N Capitol St NW Suite G-50 *Web:* www.us-flag.org	Washington	DC	20001	202-347-8020	347-1550
American Moving & Storage Assn (AMSA) 1611 Duke St *Web:* www.promover.org	Alexandria	VA	22314	703-683-7410	683-7527
American Pilots' Assn 499 S Capitol St SW Suite 409 *TF:* 800-527-4568 ■ *Web:* www.americanpilots.org	Washington	DC	20003	202-484-0700	484-9320
American Public Transportation Assn (APTA) 1666 K St NW Suite 1100 *Web:* www.apta.com	Washington	DC	20006	202-496-4800	496-4321
American Railway Engineering & Maintenance-of-Way Assn (AREMA) 8201 Corporate Dr Suite 1125 *Web:* www.arema.org	Landover	MD	20785	301-459-3200	459-8077
American Shipbuilding Assn (ASA) 600 Pennsylvania Ave SE Suite 305 *Web:* www.americanshipbuilding.com	Washington	DC	20003	202-544-8170	544-8252
American Short Line & Regional Railroad Assn (ASLRRA) 50 F St NW Suite 7020 *Web:* www.aslrra.org	Washington	DC	20001	202-628-4500	628-6430
American Society of Naval Engineers (ASNE) 1452 Duke St *Web:* www.navalengineers.org	Alexandria	VA	22314	703-836-6727	836-7491
American Society of Transportation & Logistics (ASTL) 1700 N Moore St Suite 1900 *Web:* www.astl.org	Arlington	VA	22209	703-524-5011	524-5017
American Traffic Safety Services Assn (ATSSA) 15 Riverside Pkwy Suite 100 *TF:* 800-272-8772 ■ *Web:* www.atssa.com	Fredericksburg	VA	22406	540-368-1701	368-1717
American Trucking Assns (ATA) 2200 Mill Rd *TF:* 800-282-5463 ■ *Web:* www.trucking.org	Alexandria	VA	22314	703-838-1700	684-5751
American Waterways Operators (AWO) 801 N Quincy St Suite 200 *Web:* www.americanwaterways.com	Arlington	VA	22203	703-841-9300	841-0389
Association of American Railroads (AAR) 50 F St NW *Web:* www.aar.org	Washington	DC	20001	202-639-2100	639-2466
Association of Diesel Specialists (ADS) 10 Laboratory Dr PO Box 13966 *Web:* www.diesel.org	Research Triangle Park	NC	27709	919-549-4800	549-4824
Association of International Automobile Manufacturers (AIAM) 2111 Wilson Blvd Suite 1150 *Web:* www.aiam.org	Arlington	VA	22201	703-525-7788	525-8817
Association of Retail Travel Agents (ARTA) 73 White Bridge Rd Box 238 **Fax Area Code:* 615 ■ *Web:* www.artaonline.com	Nashville	TN	37205	800-969-6069	985-0600*
Automatic Transmission Rebuilders Assn (ATRA) 2400 Latigo Ave *Web:* www.atra.com	Oxnard	CA	93030	805-604-2000	604-2003
Automotive Aftermarket Industry Assn (AAIA) 7101 Wisconsin Ave *Web:* www.aftermarket.org	Bethesda	MD	20814	301-654-6664	654-3299
Automotive Engine Rebuilders Assn (AERA) 330 Lexington Dr *TF:* 888-326-2372 ■ *Web:* www.aera.org	Buffalo Grove	IL	60089	847-541-6550	541-5808
Automotive Fleet & Leasing Assn 1000 Westgate Dr Suite 252 *Web:* www.aflaonline.org	Saint Paul	MN	55114	651-203-7247	290-2266
Automotive Industry Action Group (AIAG) 26200 Lahser Rd Suite 200 *Web:* www.aiag.org	Southfield	MI	48034	248-358-3570	358-3253
Automotive Oil Change Assn (AOCA) 12810 Hillcrest Rd Suite 221 *TF:* 800-331-0329 ■ *Web:* www.aoca.org	Dallas	TX	75230	972-458-9468	458-9539
Automotive Parts Remanufacturers Assn (APRA) 4215 Lafayette Center Dr Suite 3 *Web:* www.apra.org	Chantilly	VA	20151	703-968-2772	968-2878
Automotive Recyclers Assn (ARA) 3975 Fair Ridge Dr Suite 20N *TF:* 888-385-1005 ■ *Web:* www.a-r-a.org	Fairfax	VA	22033	703-385-1001	385-1494
Automotive Service Assn (ASA) 1901 Airport Fwy *TF Cust Svc:* 800-272-7467 ■ *Web:* www.asashop.org	Bedford	TX	76021	817-283-6205	685-0225
Brotherhood of Railroad Signalmen 917 Shenandoah Shores Rd *Web:* www.brs.org	Front Royal	VA	22630	540-622-6522	622-6532
Car Care Council 7101 Wisconsin Ave **Fax Area Code:* 301 ■ *Web:* www.carcare.org	Bethesda	MD	20814	240-333-1088	614-3299*
Cargo Airline Assn 1220 19th St NW Suite 400	Washington	DC	20036	202-293-1030	293-4377
Center for Auto Safety (CAS) 1825 Connecticut Ave NW Suite 330 *Web:* www.autosafety.org	Washington	DC	20009	202-328-7700	387-0140
Coalition Against Bigger Trucks (CABT) 901 N Pitt St Suite 310 *TF:* 888-222-8123 ■ *Web:* www.cabt.org	Alexandria	VA	22314	703-535-3131	535-3322
Coalition for Auto Repair Equality (CARE) 119 Oronoco St Suite 300 *TF:* 800-229-5380 ■ *Web:* www.careauto.org	Alexandria	VA	22314	703-519-7555	519-7747
Community Transportation Assn of America (CTAA) 1341 G St NW Suite 1000 *TF:* 800-891-0590 ■ *Web:* www.ctaa.org	Washington	DC	20005	202-628-1480	737-9197
Containerization & Intermodal Institute 960 Holmdel Rd Bldg 2	Holmdel	NJ	07733	732-817-9131	817-9133
Dangerous Goods Advisory Council (DGAC) 1100 H St NW Suite 740 *TF:* 800-634-1598 ■ *Web:* www.dgac.org	Washington	DC	20005	202-289-4550	289-4074
Distribution & LTL Carriers Assn 4218 Roanoke Rd Suite 200 *Web:* www.dltlca.com	Kansas City	MO	64111	816-753-0411	931-4339
Electric Drive Transportation Assn 1101 Vermont Ave NW Suite 401 *Web:* www.electricdrive.org	Washington	DC	20005	202-408-0774	408-7610
Flight Safety Foundation 601 Madison St Suite 300 *Web:* www.flightsafety.org	Alexandria	VA	22314	703-739-6700	739-6708
General Aviation Manufacturers Assn (GAMA) 1400 K St NW Suite 801 *Web:* www.gama.aero	Washington	DC	20005	202-393-1500	842-4063
Helicopter Assn International (HAI) 1635 Prince St *TF:* 800-435-4976 ■ *Web:* www.rotor.com	Alexandria	VA	22314	703-683-4646	683-4745
I-CAR Inter-Industry Conference on Auto Collision Repair (I-CAR) 5125 Trillium Blvd *TF:* 800-422-7872 ■ *Web:* www.i-car.com	Hoffman Estates	IL	60192	847-590-1191	590-1215
Independent Liquid Terminals Assn (ILTA) 1444 'I' St NW Suite 400 *Web:* www.ilta.org	Washington	DC	20005	202-842-9200	326-8660
Institute of International Container Lessors (IICL) 555 Pleasantville Rd Suite 140S *Web:* www.iicl.org	Briarcliff Manor	NY	10510	914-747-9100	747-4600
Institute of Navigation (ION) 3975 University Dr Suite 390 *Web:* www.ion.org	Fairfax	VA	22030	703-383-9688	383-9689
Institute of Transportation Engineers (ITE) 1099 14th St NW Suite 300W *Web:* www.ite.org	Washington	DC	20005	202-289-0222	289-7722
Insurance Institute for Highway Safety 1005 N Glebe Rd Suite 800 *Web:* www.iihs.org	Arlington	VA	22201	703-247-1500	247-1678
Intelligent Transportation Society of America (ITS) 1100 17th St NW Suite 1200 *Web:* www.itsa.org	Washington	DC	20036	202-484-4847	484-3483
Intermodal Assn of North America (IANA) 11785 Beltsville Dr Suite 1100 *Web:* www.intermodal.org	Calverton	MD	20705	301-982-3400	982-4815
International Air Cargo Assn (TIACA) 5600 NW 36th St Suite 620 *Web:* www.tiaca.org	Miami	FL	33159	786-265-7011	265-7012
International Air Transport Assn (IATA) 800 Pl Victoria PO Box 113 *Web:* www.iata.org	Montreal	QC	H4Z1M1	514-874-0202	874-9632
International Airlines Travel Agent Network (IATAN) 800 Place Victoria Suite 800 PO Box 113 *TF:* 877-734-2826 ■ *Web:* www.iatan.org	Montreal	QC	H4Z1M1	514-868-8800	868-8858
International Assn of Refrigerated Warehouses (IARW) 1500 King St Suite 201 *Web:* www.iarw.org	Alexandria	VA	22314	703-373-4300	373-4301
International Carwash Assn 401 N Michigan Ave *Web:* www.carwashes.com	Chicago	IL	60611	312-321-5199	245-1085
International Motor Coach Group Inc (IMG) 8645 College Blvd Suite 220 *TF:* 888-447-3466 ■ *Web:* www.imgcoach.com	Overland Park	KS	66210	913-906-0111	906-0115
International Parking Institute (IPI) 701 Kenmore Ave Suite 200 *Web:* www.parking.org	Fredericksburg	VA	22401	540-371-7535	371-8022
International Safe Transit Assn (ISTA) 1400 Abbott Rd Suite 160 *Web:* www.ista.org	East Lansing	MI	48823	517-333-3437	333-3813
International Warehouse Logistics Assn (IWLA) 2800 S River Rd Suite 260 *TF:* 800-525-0165 ■ *Web:* www.iwla.com	Des Plaines	IL	60018	847-813-4699	813-0115
Interstate Natural Gas Assn of America (INGAA) 10 G St NE Suite 700 *Web:* www.ingaa.org	Washington	DC	20002	202-216-5900	216-0870
IWLA (International Warehouse Logistics Assn) 2800 S River Rd Suite 260 *TF:* 800-525-0165 ■ *Web:* www.iwla.com	Des Plaines	IL	60018	847-813-4699	813-0115

Transportation Industry Associations (Cont'd)

Phone *Fax*

Japan Automobile Manufacturers Assn (JAMA)
1050 17th St NW Suite 410 Washington DC 20036 202-296-8537 872-1212
Web: www.jama.org
Jewelers Shipping Assn (JSA) 125 Carlsbad St Cranston RI 02920 401-943-6490 943-1490
TF: 800-688-4572 ■ *Web:* www.jewelersshipping.com
Mid-West Truckers Assn Inc 2727 N Dirksen Pkwy Springfield IL 62702 217-525-0310 525-0342
Web: www.mid-westtruckers.com
Mobile Air Conditioning Society Worldwide (MACS)
225 S Broad St Lansdale PA 19446 215-631-7020 631-7017
Web: www.macsw.org
Motor & Equipment Manufacturers Assn (MEMA)
10 Laboratory Dr PO Box 13966 Research Triangle Park NC 27709 919-549-4800 549-4824
Web: www.mema.org
Motorcycle Industry Council (MIC) 2 Jenner St Suite 150 Irvine CA 92618 949-727-4211 727-3313
Web: www.mic.org
Motorcycle Safety Foundation (MSF) 2 Jenner St Suite 150 Irvine CA 92618 949-727-3227 727-4217
Web: www.msf-usa.org
National Air Carrier Assn (NACA)
1000 Wilson Blvd Suite 1700 Arlington VA 22209 703-358-8060 358-8070
Web: www.naca.cc
National Air Traffic Controllers Assn (NATCA)
1325 Massachusetts Ave NW Washington DC 20005 202-628-5451 628-5767
TF: 800-266-0895 ■ *Web:* www.natca.org
National Air Transportation Assn (NATA) 4226 King St. Alexandria VA 22302 703-845-9000 845-8176
TF: 800-808-6282 ■ *Web:* www.nata.aero
National Assn of Cruise Oriented Agencies (NACOA)
7600 Red Rd Suite 126 Miami FL 33143 305-663-5626 663-5625
Web: www.nacoaonline.com
National Assn of Fleet Administrators (NAFA)
100 Wood Ave S Suite 310 Iselin NJ 08830 732-494-8100 494-6789
Web: www.nafa.org
National Assn of Marine Surveyors Inc (NAMS)
PO Box 9306 Chesapeake VA 23321 757-638-9638 638-9639
TF: 800-822-6267 ■ *Web:* www.nams-cms.org
National Auto Auction Assn (NAAA) 5320-D Spectrum Dr. Frederick MD 21703 301-696-0400 631-1359
Web: www.naaa.com
National Automobile Dealers Assn (NADA) 8400 Westpark Dr McLean VA 22102 703-821-7000 821-7075
TF: 800-252-6232 ■ *Web:* www.nada.org
National Automotive Radiator Service Assn (NARSA)
15000 Commerce Pkwy Suite C Mount Laurel NJ 08054 856-439-1575 439-9596
TF: 800-551-3232 ■ *Web:* www.narsa.org
National Business Aviation Assn (NBAA)
1200 18th St NW Suite 400 Washington DC 20036 202-783-9000 331-8364
Web: www.nbaa.org
National Cargo Bureau Inc (NCB) 17 Battery Pl Suite 1232 New York NY 10004 212-785-8300 785-8333
Web: www.natcargo.org
National Customs Brokers & Forwarders Assn of America Inc (NCBFAA) 1200 18th St NW Suite 901 Washington DC 20036 202-466-0222 466-0226
Web: www.ncbfaa.org
National EMS Pilots Assn (NEMSPA) 526 King St Suite 415 Alexandria VA 22314 703-836-8930 836-8920
Web: www.nemspa.org
National Industrial Transportation League (NITL)
1700 N Moore St Suite 1900 Arlington VA 22209 703-524-5011 524-5017
Web: www.nitl.org
National Marine Manufacturers Assn (NMMA)
200 E Randolph Dr Suite 5100 Chicago IL 60601 312-946-6200 946-0388
TF: 800-985-2401 ■ *Web:* www.nmma.org
National Motor Freight Traffic Assn (NMFTA) 2200 Mill Rd. Alexandria VA 22314 703-838-1810 683-1094
Web: www.nmfta.org
National Motorists Assn (NMA) 402 W 2nd St. Waunakee WI 53597 608-849-6000 849-8697
TF: 800-882-2785 ■ *Web:* www.motorists.org
National Private Truck Council (NPTC)
2200 Mill Rd Suite 350 Alexandria VA 22314 703-683-1300 683-1217
Web: www.nptc.org
National Tank Truck Carriers Inc 2200 Mill Rd Suite 620 Alexandria VA 22314 703-838-1960 684-5753
Web: www.tanktruck.org
National Truck Equipment Assn (NTEA)
37400 Hills Tech Dr. Farmington Hills MI 48331 248-489-7090 489-8590
TF: 800-441-6832 ■ *Web:* www.ntea.com
National Waterways Conference Inc (NWC)
4650 Washington Blvd Suite 608 Arlington VA 22201 703-243-4090 243-4155
Web: www.waterways.org
NATSO Inc 1737 King St Suite 200 Alexandria VA 22314 703-549-2100 684-4525
TF: 888-275-2876 ■ *Web:* www.natso.com
Owner-Operator Independent Drivers Assn (OOIDA)
1 NW OOIDA Dr. Grain Valley MO 64029 816-229-5791 229-0518
TF: 800-444-5791 ■ *Web:* www.ooida.com
Passenger Vessel Assn (PVA) 801 N Quincy St Suite 200 Arlington VA 22203 703-807-0100 807-0103
TF: 800-807-8360 ■ *Web:* www.passengervessel.com
Professional Aviation Maintenance Assn (PAMA)
717 Princess St Alexandria VA 22314 703-683-3171 683-0018
TF: 866-865-7262 ■ *Web:* www.pama.org
Propeller Club of the US 3927 Old Lee Hwy Suite 101-A Fairfax VA 22030 703-691-2777 691-4173
Web: www.propellerclubhq.com
Railway Supply Institute Inc (RSI) 50 F St NW Suite 7030 Washington DC 20001 202-347-4664 347-0047
Web: www.rsiweb.org
Recreation Vehicle Dealers Assn (RVDA)
3930 University Dr 3rd Fl. Fairfax VA 22030 703-591-7130 591-0734
TF: 800-336-0355 ■ *Web:* www.rvda.org
Recreation Vehicle Industry Assn (RVIA) 1896 Preston White Dr. Reston VA 20191 703-620-6003 620-5071
TF: 800-336-0154 ■ *Web:* www.rvia.org
Regional Airline Assn (RAA) 2025 M St NW Suite 800 Washington DC 20036 202-367-1100 367-2170
Web: www.raa.org
Self Storage Assn (SSA) 1900 N Beauregard St Suite 110 Alexandria VA 22311 703-575-8000 575-8901
TF: 888-735-3784 ■ *Web:* www.selfstorage.org
Shipbuilders Council of America (SCA)
1455 F St NW Suite 225 Washington DC 20005 202-347-5462 347-5464
Web: www.shipbuilders.org
Shipowners Claims Bureau (SCB) 1 Battery Park Plaza 31st Fl New York NY 10004 212-847-4500 847-4599
Web: www.american-club.com
Society of Automotive Engineers Inc (SAE)
400 Commonwealth Dr Warrendale PA 15096 724-776-4841 776-0790
TF: 877-606-7323 ■ *Web:* www.sae.org
Society of Government Travel Professionals
6935 Wisconsin Ave Suite 200 Bethesda MD 20815 301-654-8595 654-6663
Web: www.government-travel.org
Society of Naval Architects & Marine Engineers (SNAME)
601 Pavonia Ave 4th Fl Jersey City NJ 07306 201-798-4800 798-4975
Web: www.sname.org
Specialized Carriers & Rigging Assn (SC&RA)
2750 Prosperity Ave Suite 620 Fairfax VA 22031 703-698-0291 698-0297
Web: www.scranet.org
Specialty Equipment Market Assn 1575 S Valley Vista Dr Diamond Bar CA 91765 909-396-0289 860-0184
Web: www.sema.org

Phone *Fax*

Specialty Vehicle Institute of America (SVIA)
2 Jenner St Suite 150 Irvine CA 92618 949-727-3727 727-4216
TF: 800-887-2887 ■ *Web:* www.atvsafety.org
Technology & Maintenance Council (TMC)
American Trucking Assns 2200 Mill Rd Alexandria VA 22314 703-838-1761 684-4328
Web: www.truckline.com/aboutata/councils/tmc
Towing & Recovery Assn of America (TRAA)
2121 Eisenhower Ave Suite 200 Alexandria VA 22314 703-684-7734 684-6720
TF: 800-728-0136 ■ *Web:* www.towserver.net
Transportation Consumer Protection Council Inc (TCPC)
120 Main St Huntington NY 11743 631-427-0100 549-8962
Web: transportlaw.com/tcpc
Transportation Institute 5201 Auth Way Camp Springs MD 20746 301-423-3335 423-0634
Web: www.trans-inst.org
Transportation Intermediaries Assn (TIA)
1625 Prince St Suite 200 Alexandria VA 22314 703-299-5700 836-0123
Web: www.tianet.org
Transportation Research Board (TRB) 500 5th St NW Washington DC 20001 202-334-2934 334-2519
Web: www.trb.org
Truck Renting & Leasing Assn (TRALA)
675 N Washington St Suite 410 Alexandria VA 22314 703-299-9120 299-9115
Web: www.trala.org
Truckload Carriers Assn (TCA) 2200 Mill Rd 3rd Fl. Alexandria VA 22314 703-838-1950 836-6610
Web: www.truckload.org
United Motorcoach Assn (UMA) 113 S West St 4th Fl Alexandria VA 22314 703-838-2929 838-2950
TF: 800-424-8262 ■ *Web:* www.uma.org
Warehousing Education & Research Council (WERC)
1100 Jorie Blvd Suite 170 Oak Brook IL 60523 630-990-0001 990-0256
Web: www.werc.org

50 ATTRACTIONS

SEE ALSO Amusement Parks p. 1277; Aquariums - Public p. 1282; Art Dealers & Galleries p. 1283; Botanical Gardens & Arboreta p. 1391; Cemeteries - National p. 1412; Libraries - Presidential Libraries p. 1893; Libraries - Special Collections Libraries p. 1906; Museums p. 1985; Museums & Halls of Fame - Sports p. 2007; Museums - Children's p. 2006; Parks - National - Canada p. 2049; Parks - National - US p. 2050; Parks - State p. 2055; Performing Arts Facilities p. 2090; Planetariums p. 2117; Zoos & Wildlife Parks p. 2419

50-1 Churches, Cathedrals, Synagogues, Temples

Phone *Fax*

Antioch Baptist Church 1057 Texas Ave Shreveport LA 71101 318-222-7090 222-5738
Arch Street Meeting House 320 Arch St Philadelphia PA 19106 215-627-2667 627-3624
Web: www.archstreetfriends.org
Baltimore Basilica 409 Cathedral St. Baltimore MD 21201 410-727-3565 539-0407
Web: www.baltimorebasilica.org
Basilica of the Assumption 409 Cathedral St Baltimore MD 21201 410-727-3565 539-0407
Web: www.baltimorebasilica.org
Basilica of the National Shrine of Immaculate Conception
400 Michigan Ave NE Washington DC 20017 202-526-8300 526-8313
Web: www.nationalshrineinteractive.com
Basilica of Saint Mary of the Immaculate Conception
232 Chapel St. Norfolk VA 23504 757-622-4487 625-7969
Web: www.basilicaofstmary.org
Big Zion African Methodist Episcopal Zion Church
112 S Bayou St Mobile AL 36602 251-433-8431
Black Madonna Shrine St Joseph's Hill Rd PO Box 181 Eureka MO 63025 636-938-5361 587-2789
Web: www.franciscancaring.org/blackmadonnaforward.html
Carmel Mission 3080 Rio Rd Carmel CA 93923 831-624-1271 624-8050
Web: www.carmelmission.org
Cathedral Basilica of Notre-Dame 56 Guigues Ave. Ottawa ON K1N5H5 613-241-7496 241-1627
Cathedral Basilica of the Sacred Heart 89 Ridge St Newark NJ 07104 973-484-4600 483-8253
Web: www.cathedralbasilica.org
Cathedral Basilica of Saint Joseph 80 S Market St San Jose CA 95113 408-283-8100 283-8110
Web: www.stjosephcathedral.org
Cathedral Basilica of Saint Louis (New Cathedral)
4431 Lindell Blvd Saint Louis MO 63108 314-373-8200 373-8290
Web: www.cathedralstl.org
Cathedral of the Blessed Sacrament 1017 11th St. Sacramento CA 95814 916-444-3070 443-2749
Web: www.blessedsaccathedral.org
Cathedral of Christ the King 299 Colony Blvd. Lexington KY 40502 859-268-2861 268-8061
Web: cathedral.cdlex.org
Cathedral Church of All Saints Martello St & University Ave Halifax NS B3H1X3 902-423-6002 423-1437
Web: www.cathedralchurchofallsaints.com
Cathedral Church of Saint John the Divine
1047 Amsterdam Ave. New York NY 10025 212-316-7540 932-7348
Web: www.stjohndivine.org
Cathedral Church of Saint Mark 231 E 100 South Salt Lake City UT 84111 801-322-3400 322-3410
Web: www.stmarkscathedral-ut.org
Cathedral of the Immaculate Conception 2 S Claiborne St Mobile AL 36602 251-434-1565 434-1588
Web: www.mobilecathedral.org
Cathedral of the Immaculate Conception 125 Eagle St Albany NY 12202 518-463-4447 436-5177
Web: www.cathedralic.com
Cathedral of the Madeleine 331 E South Temple St. Salt Lake City UT 84111 801-328-8941 364-6504
Web: www.saltlakecathedral.org
Cathedral of Our Lady of the Angels 555 W Temple St Los Angeles CA 90012 213-680-5200 620-1982
Web: www.olacathedral.org
Cathedral of Saint John 271 N Main St. Providence RI 02903 401-331-4622 831-8425
Cathedral of Saint Mary of the Immaculate Conception
607 NE Madison Ave Peoria IL 61603 309-682-5823 682-6030
Web: www.cdop.org
Cathedral of Saint Paul 239 Selby Ave Saint Paul MN 55102 651-228-1766 228-9942
Web: www.cathedralsaintpaul.org
Cathedral of Saints Peter & Paul 30 Fenner St. Providence RI 02903 401-331-2434 273-0687
Center Church 675 Main St. Hartford CT 06103 860-249-5631 246-3915
Web: www.centerchurchhartford.org
Christ Church 118 N Washington St. Alexandria VA 22314 703-549-1450 549-5883
Web: www.historicchristchurch.org
Christ Church Cathedral 690 Burrard St Vancouver BC V6C2L1 604-682-3848 682-8377
Web: www.cathedral.vancouver.bc.ca
Christ Church Cathedral 45 Church St. Hartford CT 06103 860-527-7231 527-5313
Web: www.cccathedral.org
Christ Church Cathedral 125 Monument Cir Indianapolis IN 46204 317-636-4577 635-1040
Web: www.cccindy.org
Christ Church Cathedral 1210 Locust St Saint Louis MO 63103 314-231-3454 231-3142
Web: www.yourcathedral.org
Christ Church Cathedral 1414 Union Ave. Montreal QC H3A2B8 514-843-6577 843-6344
Web: www.montreal.anglican.org/cathedral/

Name / Address	City	State	Zip	Phone	Fax
Christ Church in Philadelphia 20 N American St *Web:* www.christchurchphila.org	Philadelphia	PA	19106	215-922-1695	922-3578
Christ Episcopal Church S State & Water Sts *Web:* www.christchurchdover.org	Dover	DE	19901	302-734-5731	734-7702
Christ Episcopal Church 10 N Church St *Web:* www.ccgsc.org	Greenville	SC	29601	864-271-8773	242-0879
Church of the Transfiguration 1 E 29th St *Web:* www.littlechurch.org	New York	NY	10016	212-684-6770	684-1662
Circular Congregational Church 150 Meeting St *Web:* www.circularchurch.org	Charleston	SC	29401	843-577-6400	958-0594
Congregation Beth Elohim 90 Hasell St *Web:* www.kkbe.org	Charleston	SC	29401	843-723-1090	723-0537
Congregation Mikveh Israel 44 N 4th St *Web:* www.mikvehisrael.org	Philadelphia	PA	19106	215-922-5446	922-1550
Crystal Cathedral 12141 Lewis St **Fax:* Hum Res ■ *TF:* 877-456-7900 ■ *Web:* www.crystalcathedral.org	Garden Grove	CA	92840	714-971-4000	971-4906*
Dagom Gaden Tensung-Ling Monastery 102 Clubhouse Dr *Web:* www.ganden.org	Bloomington	IN	47404	812-339-0857	323-8803
Dexter Avenue King Memorial Baptist Church 454 Dexter Ave *Web:* www.dexterkingmemorial.org	Montgomery	AL	36104	334-263-3970	263-5223
Duke Memorial United Methodist Church 504 W Chapel Hill St *Web:* www.dukememorial.org	Durham	NC	27701	919-683-3467	682-3349
Ebenezer Baptist Church 407 Auburn Ave NE *Web:* www.historicebenezer.org	Atlanta	GA	30312	404-688-7263	521-1129
Emanuel African Methodist Episcopal Church 110 Calhoun St *Web:* www.cr.nps.gov/nr/travel/charleston/ema.htm	Charleston	SC	29401	843-722-2561	722-1869
First Congregational Church 62 Centre St	Nantucket	MA	02554	508-228-0950	228-0095
First Unitarian Church of Philadelphia 2125 Chestnut St *Web:* www.firstuu-philly.org	Philadelphia	PA	19103	215-563-3980	563-4209
Franciscan Monastery 1400 Quincy St NE *Web:* www.myfranciscan.com	Washington	DC	20017	202-526-6800	529-9889
Historic Trinity Lutheran Church 812 Soulard St *Web:* www.historictrinitystlouis.org	Saint Louis	MO	63104	314-231-4092	231-5430
Holy Trinity Catholic Church 315 Marshall St *Web:* www.holytrinity-shreveport.com	Shreveport	LA	71101	318-221-5990	221-3545
Jewish Heritage Center of the Southwest 564 S Stone Ave *Web:* www.jewishheritagecenter.net	Tucson	AZ	85701	520-670-9073	670-9078
King's Chapel 58 Tremont St *Web:* www.kings-chapel.org	Boston	MA	02108	617-227-2155	227-4101
Landmark on the Park Sanctuary 160 Central Park W *Web:* www.landmarkonthepark.org	New York	NY	10023	212-595-1658	595-0134
Ling Shen Ching Tze Temple 17012 NE 40th Ct	Redmond	WA	98052	425-882-0916	
Mesa Arizona Temple 101 S LeSueur St *Web:* www.ldschurchtemples.com	Mesa	AZ	85204	480-833-1211	827-2828
Mission Dolores 3321 16th St *Web:* www.missiondolores.org	San Francisco	CA	94114	415-621-8204	621-2294
Mission of Nombre de Dios & Shrine of Our Lady of La Leche 27 Ocean Ave *TF:* 800-342-6529 ■ *Web:* www.missionandshrine.org	Saint Augustine	FL	32084	904-824-2809	829-0819
Mission San Fernando Rey De Espana 15151 San Fernando Mission Blvd	Mission Hills	CA	93145	818-361-0186	
Mission San Jose 701 E Pyron Ave *Web:* www.nps.gov/saan/visit/MissionSanJose.htm	San Antonio	TX	78214	210-922-0543	932-2271
Mission San Luis Rey de Francia 4050 Mission Ave *Web:* sanluisrey.org	Oceanside	CA	92057	760-757-3651	757-4613
Mormon Tabernacle 50 E North Temple St *TF:* 800-537-9703 ■ *Web:* www.ldschurchtemples.com	Salt Lake City	UT	84150	801-240-3221	240-4886
Mother Bethel AME Church 419 S 6th St *Web:* www.motherbethel.org	Philadelphia	PA	19147	215-925-0616	925-1402
National Shrine of Our Lady of Lebanon 2759 N Lipkey Rd *Web:* www.ourladyoflebanonshrine.org	North Jackson	OH	44451	330-538-3351	538-0455
National Shrine of Our Lady of the Snows 442 S De Mazenod Dr *TF:* 800-682-2879 ■ *Web:* www.snows.org	Belleville	IL	62223	618-397-6700	398-6549
National Shrine of Saint John Neumann 1019 N 5th St *TF:* 888-315-1860 ■ *Web:* www.stjohnneumann.org	Philadelphia	PA	19123	215-627-3080	627-3296
New England Peace Pagoda 100 Cave Hill Rd *Web:* www.peacepagoda.org	Leverett	MA	01054	413-367-2202	367-9369
Oakland Mormon Temple 4770 Lincoln Ave *Web:* www.ldschurchtemples.com	Oakland	CA	94602	510-531-1475	531-7625
Old Dutch Church of Sleepy Hollow 430 N Broadway *Web:* www.sleepyhollowchamber.com	Sleepy Hollow	NY	10591	914-631-1123	
Old First Reformed Church 151 N 4th St *Web:* www.oldfirstucc.org	Philadelphia	PA	19106	215-922-4566	922-6366
Old Mission San Jose 43300 Mission Blvd	Fremont	CA	94539	510-657-1797	651-8332
Old North Church 193 Salem St *Web:* www.oldnorth.com	Boston	MA	02113	617-523-6676	725-0559
Old North Church 62 Centre St	Nantucket	MA	02554	508-228-0950	228-0095
Old Pine Street Presbyterian Church 412 Pine St *Web:* www.oldpine.org	Philadelphia	PA	19106	215-925-8051	922-7120
Old Saint Ferdinand's Shrine 1 Rue St Francois	Florissant	MO	63031	314-839-3829	
Old Saint Joseph's Church 321 Willings Alley *Web:* www.oldstjoseph.org	Philadelphia	PA	19106	215-923-1733	574-8529
Old Saint Mary's Church 123 E 13th St *Web:* www.oldstmarys.org	Cincinnati	OH	45202	513-721-2988	721-0436
Old Saint Patrick's Church 700 W Adams St *Web:* www.oldstpats.org	Chicago	IL	60661	312-648-1021	648-9025
Old Whaling Church 89 Main St *Web:* www.mvpreservation.org	Edgartown	MA	02539	508-627-4440	627-8088
Our Lady Queen of the Most Holy Rosary Cathedral 2535 Collingwood Blvd *Web:* www.rosarycathedral.org	Toledo	OH	43610	419-244-9575	242-1901
Queen of Angels Monastery 840 S Main St *Web:* www.benedictine-srs.org	Mount Angel	OR	97362	503-845-6141	845-6585
Saint George's Anglican Church 1101 Stanley St *Web:* www.st-georges.org	Montreal	QC	H3B2S6	514-866-7113	866-6096
Saint George's Church 2222 Brunswick St *Web:* www.roundchurch.ca	Halifax	NS	B3K2Z3	902-423-1059	423-0897
Saint James Meeting House 375 Boardman-Poland Rd *Web:* www.boardmanpark.com	Boardman	OH	44512	330-726-8107	726-4562
Saint Joan of Arc Chapel Marquette University Ministry 1442 W Wisconsin Ave *Web:* www.marquette.edu/chapel	Milwaukee	WI	53233	414-288-7039	288-3696
Saint Joseph Cathedral 521 N Duluth Ave	Sioux Falls	SD	57104	605-336-7390	
Saint Louis Cathedral 615 Pere Antoine Alley *Web:* www.stlouiscathedral.org	New Orleans	LA	70116	504-525-9585	525-9583
Saint Mary's Cathedral 203 E 10th St *Web:* www.saintmaryscathedral.org	Austin	TX	78701	512-476-6182	476-8799
Saint Mary's Catholic Church 155 Market St	Memphis	TN	38105	901-522-9420	522-8314
Saint Matthew's Church 1479 Barrington St *Web:* www.stmatts.ns.ca	Halifax	NS	B3J1Z2	902-423-9209	423-2833
Saint Patrick's Cathedral 14 E 51st St *Web:* www.saintpatrickscathedral.org	New York	NY	10022	212-753-2261	755-4128
Saint Paul's Episcopal Church 1430 J St *Web:* www.stpaulssacramento.org	Sacramento	CA	95814	916-446-2620	
Saint Photios Greek Orthodox National Shrine 41 Saint George St PO Box 1960 *Web:* www.stphotios.com	Saint Augustine	FL	32085	904-829-8205	829-8707
Salt Lake Temple 50 E North Temple St *TF:* 800-537-9703 ■ *Web:* www.ldschurchtemples.com	Salt Lake City	UT	84150	801-240-3221	240-4886
San Gabriel Mission 428 S Mission Dr *Web:* www.sangabrielmission.org	San Gabriel	CA	91776	626-457-3035	282-5308
San Miguel Mission 401 Old Santa Fe Trail	Santa Fe	NM	87501	505-983-3974	
San Xavier Del Bac Mission 1950 W San Xavier Rd *Web:* www.sanxaviermission.org	Tucson	AZ	85746	520-294-2624	294-3438
Santuario de Guadalupe 100 S Guadalupe St	Santa Fe	NM	87501	505-988-2027	
Scottish Rite Cathedral 160 S Scott Ave	Tucson	AZ	85701	520-622-8364	
Sixteenth Street Baptist Church 1530 6th Ave N	Birmingham	AL	35203	205-251-9402	251-9811
Socorro Mission 328 S Nevarez St	El Paso	TX	79927	915-859-7718	859-9452
Temple Square 50 W North Temple St *TF:* 800-453-3860 ■ *Web:* www.visittemplesquare.com	Salt Lake City	UT	84150	801-240-1245	240-1471
Touro Synagogue National Historic Site 85 Touro St *Web:* www.tourosynagogue.org	Newport	RI	02840	401-847-4794	841-6790
Trinity Cathedral 2230 Euclid Ave *Web:* www.trinitycleveland.org	Cleveland	OH	44115	216-771-3630	771-3657
Union Chapel Narragansett Ave *Web:* www.mvpreservation.org	Oak Bluffs	MA	02539	508-627-4440	627-8088
Union Church of Pocantico Hills 555 Bedford Rd *Web:* www.hudsonvalley.org	Sleepy Hollow	NY	10591	914-631-8200	631-0089
Wayfarers Chapel 5755 Palos Verdes Dr S *Web:* www.wayfarerschapel.org	Rancho Palos Verdes	CA	90275	310-377-1650	541-1435
White Church Christian Church 2200 N 85th St	Kansas City	KS	66109	913-299-4056	299-1066
Ysleta Mission 131 S Zaragosa Rd *Web:* ysletamission.org	El Paso	TX	79907	915-859-9848	860-9340

50-2 Cultural & Arts Centers

Arizona

Name / Address	City	State	Zip	Phone	Fax
Deer Valley Rock Art Center 3711 W Deer Valley Rd *Web:* www.asu.edu/clas/shesc/dvrac/	Glendale	AZ	85308	623-582-8007	582-8831
Mesa Arts Center 1 E Main St PO Box 1466 *Web:* www.mesaartscenter.com	Mesa	AZ	85211	480-644-6501	644-6503

Arkansas

Name / Address	City	State	Zip	Phone	Fax
Arkansas Arts Center 501 E 9th St *TF:* 800-264-2787 ■ *Web:* www.arkarts.com	Little Rock	AR	72202	501-372-4000	375-8053
Center for Art & Education 104 N 13th St *Web:* www.art-ed.org	Van Buren	AR	72956	479-474-7767	474-4411

California

Name / Address	City	State	Zip	Phone	Fax
Aerie Art Garden 71-255 Aerie Rd *Web:* www.aerieartgarden.com	Palm Desert	CA	92260	760-568-6366	
African American Art & Culture Complex 762 Fulton St Suite 300 *Web:* www.aaacc.org	San Francisco	CA	94102	415-922-2049	922-5130
Huntington Beach Arts Center 538 Main St	Huntington Beach	CA	92648	714-374-1650	374-5304
Jurupa Mountains Cultural Center 7621 Granite Hill Dr *Web:* www.jmcc.us	Riverside	CA	92509	951-685-5818	685-1240
La Raza Galeria Posada 1022-1024 22nd St *Web:* www.larazagaleriaposada.org	Sacramento	CA	95816	916-446-5133	446-1324
Mission Cultural Center for Latino Arts 2868 Mission St *Web:* www.missionculturalcenter.org	San Francisco	CA	94110	415-821-1155	648-0933
Oakland Asian Cultural Center 388 9th St Suite 290 *Web:* www.oacc.cc	Oakland	CA	94607	510-637-0455	637-0459
Roy & Edna Disney/CALARTS Theater (REDCAT) 631 W 2nd St *Web:* www.redcat.org	Los Angeles	CA	90012	213-237-2800	680-1320
Skirball Cultural Center 2701 N Sepulveda Blvd *Web:* www.skirball.org	Los Angeles	CA	90049	310-440-4500	440-4595

Colorado

Name / Address	City	State	Zip	Phone	Fax
Anasazi Heritage Center 27501 Hwy 184 *Web:* www.co.blm.gov/ahc	Dolores	CO	81323	970-882-5600	882-7035
Anderson Ranch Arts Center 5263 Owl Creek Rd *Web:* www.andersonranch.org	Snowmass Village	CO	81615	970-923-3181	923-3871
Dairy Center for the Arts 2590 Walnut St *Web:* www.thedairy.org	Boulder	CO	80302	303-440-7826	440-7104
Durango Arts Center 802 E 2nd Ave *Web:* durangoarts.org	Durango	CO	81301	970-259-2606	259-6571
Southern Ute Cultural Center & Museum 14826 Hwy 172 *Web:* www.southernutemuseum.org	Ignacio	CO	81137	970-563-9583	563-4641

Connecticut

Name / Address	City	State	Zip	Phone	Fax
Charter Oak Cultural Center 21 Charter Oak Ave *Web:* www.charteroakcenter.org	Hartford	CT	06106	860-249-1207	524-8014
Rowayton Arts Center 145 Rowayton Ave *Web:* www.rowaytonartscenter.org	Rowayton	CT	06853	203-866-2744	866-1123
Silvermine Guild Arts Center 1037 Silvermine Rd *Web:* www.silvermineart.org	New Canaan	CT	06840	203-966-9700	966-2763
Westport Arts Center 51 Riverside Ave *Web:* westportartscenter.org	Westport	CT	06880	203-222-7070	222-7999

Delaware

Name / Address	City	State	Zip	Phone	Fax
Delaware Center for the Contemporary Arts 200 S Madison St *Web:* www.thedcca.org	Wilmington	DE	19801	302-656-6466	656-6944

Cultural & Arts Centers (Cont'd)

Florida

				Phone	Fax
African-American Research Library & Cultural Center 2650 NW Sistrunk Blvd *Web:* www.broward.org/library/aarlcc.htm	Fort Lauderdale	FL	33311	954-625-2800	625-2803
Armory Art Center 1700 Parker Ave *Web:* www.armoryart.org	West Palm Beach	FL	33401	561-832-1776	832-0191
Art Center South Florida 924 Lincoln Rd Suite 205 *Web:* www.artcentersf.org	Miami Beach	FL	33139	305-674-8278	674-8772
ArtSouth 240 N Krome Ave *Web:* www.artsouthhomestead.org	Homestead	FL	33033	305-247-9406	247-7308
Lighthouse Center for the Arts 373 Tequesta Dr Gallery Sq N *Web:* www.lighthousearts.org	Tequesta	FL	33469	561-746-3101	746-3241
Maitland Art Center 231 W Packwood Ave *Web:* www.maitlandartcenter.org	Maitland	FL	32751	407-539-2181	539-1198

Georgia

				Phone	Fax
Atlanta Contemporary Art Center 535 Means St NW *Web:* www.thecontemporary.org	Atlanta	GA	30318	404-688-1970	577-5856
Callanwolde Fine Arts Center 980 Briarcliff Rd NE *Web:* www.callanwolde.org	Atlanta	GA	30306	404-872-5338	872-5175
Center for Puppetry Arts 1404 Spring St NW *Web:* www.puppet.org	Atlanta	GA	30309	404-873-3089	873-9907
City Market Art Center 219 W Bryan St Suite 207 *Web:* www.savannahcitymarket.com/art.html	Savannah	GA	31401	912-232-4903	232-2142

Idaho

				Phone	Fax
Pocatello Art Center 444 N Main St. *Web:* www.pocatelloartctr.org	Pocatello	ID	83204	208-232-0970	

Illinois

				Phone	Fax
Chicago Cultural Center 78 E Washington *Web:* www.ci.chi.il.us/Tourism/CultureCenterTour/	Chicago	IL	60602	312-744-6630	744-2089
Illinois Mennonite Heritage Center 675 SR-116 *Web:* imhgs.org	Metamora	IL	61548	309-367-2551	
Irish American Heritage Center 4626 N Knox Ave *Web:* www.irishamhc.com	Chicago	IL	60630	773-282-7035	282-0380
North Lakeside Cultural Center 6219 N Sheridan Rd *Web:* www.northlakesidecc.org	Chicago	IL	60660	773-743-4477	743-1484
South Shore Cultural Center 7059 S Shore Dr *Web:* www.chicagoparkdistrict.com	Chicago	IL	60649	773-256-0149	256-1163

Indiana

				Phone	Fax
Indianapolis Art Center 820 E 67th St *Web:* www.indianapolisartcenter.org	Indianapolis	IN	46220	317-255-2464	254-0486
John Waldron Arts Center 122 S Walnut St *Web:* www.artlives.org	Bloomington	IN	47404	812-334-3100	323-2787
Tibetan Cultural Center 3655 Snoddy Rd *Web:* www.tibetancc.com	Bloomington	IN	47401	812-331-0014	334-7046

Kentucky

				Phone	Fax
Capital Gallery of Contemporary Art 314 Lewis St	Frankfort	KY	40601	502-223-2649	
Kentucky Center for African American Heritage 315 Guthrie Green *Web:* www.kcaah.com	Louisville	KY	40202	502-583-4100	583-4112
Kentucky Museum of Art & Craft 715 W Main St *Web:* www.kentuckyarts.org	Louisville	KY	40202	502-589-0102	589-0154

Louisiana

				Phone	Fax
Acadiana Center for the Arts 101 W Vermilion St *Web:* www.acadianaartscouncil.org	Lafayette	LA	70501	337-233-7060	233-7062
Barnwell Garden & Art Center 601 Clyde Fant Pkwy *Web:* www.barnwellcenter.com	Shreveport	LA	71101	318-673-7703	673-7707
Cannes Brulee Native American Center 303 Williams Blvd Rivertown *Web:* www.rivertownkenner.com	Kenner	LA	70062	504-468-7231	471-2159

Maine

				Phone	Fax
Maine Folklife Center 5773 S Stevens Hall University of Maine *Web:* www.umaine.edu/folklife/	Orono	ME	04469	207-581-1891	581-1823

Manitoba

				Phone	Fax
Jewish Heritage Center of Western Canada C116-123 Doncaster St *Web:* www.jhcwc.mb.ca	Winnipeg	MB	R3N2B2	204-477-7460	477-7465
Saint Norbert Arts & Cultural Centre 100 rue des Ruines du Monastere *Web:* www.snac.mb.ca	Winnipeg	MB	R3V1L6	204-269-0564	261-1927

Maryland

				Phone	Fax
Elizabeth Myers Mitchell Art Gallery 60 College Ave	Annapolis	MD	21401	410-626-2556	
Eubie Blake National Jazz Institute & Cultural Center 847 N Howard St *Web:* www.eubieblake.org	Baltimore	MD	21201	410-225-3130	225-3139
Maryland Art Place 8 Market Pl Suite 100 *Web:* www.mdartplace.org	Baltimore	MD	21202	410-962-8565	244-8017
Maryland Federation of Art Circle Gallery 18 State Cir *Web:* www.mdfedart.org	Annapolis	MD	21401	410-268-4566	268-4570

Massachusetts

				Phone	Fax
Worcester Center for Crafts 25 Sagamore Rd *Web:* www.worcestercraftcenter.org	Worcester	MA	01605	508-753-8183	797-5626

Michigan

				Phone	Fax
Ann Arbor Art Center 117 W Liberty St *Web:* www.annarborartcenter.org	Ann Arbor	MI	48104	734-994-8004	994-3610
Detroit Gallery of Contemporary Crafts Fisher Bldg 3011 W Grand Blvd Suite 104	Detroit	MI	48202	313-873-7888	
Flint Cultural Center 1178 Robert T Longway Blvd *TF:* 888-823-6837 ■ *Web:* www.flintculturalcenter.com	Flint	MI	48503	810-237-7333	237-7335
Lansing Art Gallery 113 S Washington Sq *Web:* www.lansingartgallery.org	Lansing	MI	48933	517-374-6400	374-6385
Nokomis Learning Center 5153 Marsh Rd *Web:* www.nokomis.org	Okemos	MI	48864	517-349-5777	349-8560
Oakland University Art Gallery Oakland University Wilson Hall Rm 208 *Web:* www.oakland.edu/ouag/	Rochester	MI	48309	248-370-3005	370-4208

Minnesota

				Phone	Fax
Rochester Art Center 40 Civic Center Dr SE *Web:* www.rochesterartcenter.org	Rochester	MN	55904	507-282-8629	282-7737

Mississippi

				Phone	Fax
Mississippi Arts Center 201 E Pascagoula St	Jackson	MS	39201	601-960-1500	960-1352
Municipal Art Gallery 839 N State St	Jackson	MS	39202	601-960-1582	960-2066

Missouri

				Phone	Fax
Center of Contemporary Arts 524 Trinity Ave *Web:* www.cocastl.org	Saint Louis	MO	63130	314-725-6555	725-6222
Portfolio Gallery & Educational Center 3514 Delmar Blvd *Web:* www.portfolio-stl.com	Saint Louis	MO	63103	314-533-3323	531-3401

Nebraska

				Phone	Fax
Bemis Center for Contemporary Arts 724 S 12th St *Web:* www.bemiscenter.org/	Omaha	NE	68102	402-341-7130	341-9791
Gerald R Ford Conservation Center 1326 S 32nd St *Web:* www.nebraskahistory.org/sites/ford	Omaha	NE	68105	402-595-1180	595-1178

New Jersey

				Phone	Fax
Atlantic City Art Center Boardwalk & New Jersey Ave *Web:* www.acartcenter.org	Atlantic City	NJ	08401	609-347-5837	347-5844
Great Falls Historic District Cultural Center 65 McBride Ave Ext	Paterson	NJ	07501	973-279-9587	279-0587

New Mexico

				Phone	Fax
Branigan Cultural Center 500 N Water St *Web:* www.salemart.org	Las Cruces	NM	88001	505-541-2155	541-2152
National Hispanic Cultural Center 1701 4th St SW *Web:* www.nhccnm.org	Albuquerque	NM	87102	505-246-2261	246-2613
South Broadway Cultural Center 1025 Broadway SE *Web:* www.cabq.gov/sbcc	Albuquerque	NM	87102	505-848-1320	848-1329

New York

				Phone	Fax
African American Cultural Center of Buffalo Inc 350 Masten Ave *Web:* www.africancultural.org	Buffalo	NY	14209	716-884-2013	885-2590
Burchfield-Penney Art Center 1300 Elmwood Ave Buffalo State College Rockwell Hall *Web:* www.burchfield-penney.org	Buffalo	NY	14222	716-878-6011	878-6003
Hallwalls Contemporary Arts Center 341 Delaware Ave *Web:* www.hallwalls.org	Buffalo	NY	14202	716-854-1694	854-1696
Rochester Contemporary 137 East Ave *Web:* www.rochestercontemporary.org	Rochester	NY	14604	585-461-2222	461-2223

North Carolina

				Phone	Fax
African American Cultural Complex 119 Sunnybrook Rd *Web:* www.aaccmuseum.org	Raleigh	NC	27610	919-231-0625	212-3598
Afro-American Cultural Center 401 N Meyers St *Web:* www.aacc-charlotte.org	Charlotte	NC	28202	704-374-1565	374-9273
Center for Visual Arts - Greensboro 200 N Davie St Box 13 *Web:* www.greensboroart.org	Greensboro	NC	27401	336-333-7475	333-7477
Delta Arts Center 2611 New Walkertown Rd *Web:* www.deltafinearts.org	Winston-Salem	NC	27101	336-722-2625	722-9449
Green Hill Center for North Carolina Art 200 N Davie St *Web:* www.greenhillcenter.org	Greensboro	NC	27401	336-333-7460	333-2612
Greensboro Cultural Center at Festival Park 200 N Davie St *Web:* www.greensboro-nc.gov/Departments/Executive/events/hosting/culturalcenter/	Greensboro	NC	27401	336-373-2712	373-4187

	City	State	ZIP	Phone	Fax
Pack Place 2 S Pack Sq	Asheville	NC	28801	828-257-4500	251-5652
Web: www.packplace.org					
Page-Walker Arts & History Center 119 Ambassador Loop	Cary	NC	27513	919-460-4963	
Web: townofcary.org					
Sawtooth Center for Visual Arts 226 N Marshall St Suite D	Winston-Salem	NC	27101	336-723-7395	773-0132
Web: www.sawtooth.org					
Sertoma Arts Center 1400 W Millbrook Rd	Raleigh	NC	27612	919-420-2329	420-2330
Southeastern Center for Contemporary Art 750 Marguerite Dr	Winston-Salem	NC	27106	336-725-1904	722-6059
Web: www.secca.org					
Spirit Square Center for Arts & Education 345 N College St	Charlotte	NC	28202	704-348-5750	348-5828

Ohio

	City	State	ZIP	Phone	Fax
Contemporary Arts Center 44 E 6th St	Cincinnati	OH	45202	513-345-8400	721-7418
Web: www.contemporaryartscenter.org					
Dayton Cultural Center 40 S Edwin C Moses Blvd	Dayton	OH	45402	937-333-2489	333-7072
Dayton Visual Arts Center 118 N Jefferson St	Dayton	OH	45402	937-224-3822	224-3822
Web: www.daytonvisualarts.org					
King Arts Complex 867 Mt Vernon Ave	Columbus	OH	43203	614-645-5464	645-0672
Web: www.thekingartscomplex.com					
Riverbend Arts Center 1301 E Siebenthaler Ave	Dayton	OH	45414	937-333-7000	333-3158

Oklahoma

	City	State	ZIP	Phone	Fax
City Arts Center 3000 Pershing Blvd	Oklahoma City	OK	73107	405-951-0000	951-0003
Web: www.cityartscenter.org					
Greenwood Cultural Center 322 N Greenwood Ave	Tulsa	OK	74120	918-596-1020	596-1029
Web: www.greenwoodculturalcenter.com					
Red Earth Museum 2100 NE 52nd St	Oklahoma City	OK	73111	405-427-5228	427-8079
Web: www.redearth.org					

Oregon

	City	State	ZIP	Phone	Fax
Bush Barn Art Center 600 Mission St SE	Salem	OR	97302	503-581-2228	371-3342
Maude Kerns Art Center 1910 E 15th Ave	Eugene	OR	97403	541-345-1571	345-6248
Web: www.mkartcenter.org					
Portland Institute for Contemporary Art 224 NW 13th Ave Suite 305	Portland	OR	97209	503-242-1419	243-1167
Web: www.pica.org					

Pennsylvania

	City	State	ZIP	Phone	Fax
Painted Bride Art Center 230 Vine St	Philadelphia	PA	19106	215-925-9914	925-7402
Web: www.paintedbride.org					
Pittsburgh Center for the Arts 6300 5th Ave	Pittsburgh	PA	15232	412-361-0873	361-8338
Web: www.pittsburgharts.org					
Silver Eye Center for Photography 1015 E Carson St	Pittsburgh	PA	15203	412-431-1810	431-5777
Web: www.silvereye.org					

Quebec

	City	State	ZIP	Phone	Fax
L'Eglise du Gesu 1202 rue de Bleury	Montreal	QC	H3B3J3	514-861-4378	866-4853
Web: www.gesu.net					

South Dakota

	City	State	ZIP	Phone	Fax
Dahl Arts Center 713 7th St	Rapid City	SD	57701	605-394-4101	394-6121
Web: www.thedahl.org					
Horse Barn Arts Center 309 E Falls Park Dr	Sioux Falls	SD	57104	605-977-2002	
Web: www.siouxempireartscouncil.com					
Multi-Cultural Center of Sioux Falls 515 N Main Ave	Sioux Falls	SD	57104	605-367-7400	367-7404
Web: www.multi-culturalcenter.org					

Tennessee

	City	State	ZIP	Phone	Fax
Beck Cultural Exchange Center Inc 1927 Dandridge Ave	Knoxville	TN	37915	865-524-8461	524-8462
Web: www.discoveret.org/beckcec/					

Texas

	City	State	ZIP	Phone	Fax
Art Center of Corpus Christi 100 N Shoreline Dr	Corpus Christi	TX	78401	361-884-6406	884-8836
Web: www.artcentercc.org					
ArtCentre of Plano 1039 E 15th St	Plano	TX	75074	972-423-7809	424-0745
Web: www.artcentreofplano.org					
Bath House Cultural Center 521 E Lawther Dr	Dallas	TX	75218	214-670-8749	670-8751
Web: www.bathhousecultural.com					
Blue Star Contemporary Arts Center 116 Blue Star Rd	San Antonio	TX	78204	210-227-6960	229-9412
Web: www.bluestarart.org					
Carver Community Cultural Center 226 N Hackberry St	San Antonio	TX	78202	210-207-7211	207-4412
Web: www.thecarver.org					
Center for Contemporary Arts 220 Cypress St	Abilene	TX	79601	325-677-8389	677-1171
Web: www.center-arts.com					
Dallas Center for Contemporary Art 2801 Swiss Ave	Dallas	TX	75204	214-821-2522	821-9103
Web: www.thecontemporary.net					
Dougherty Arts Center 1110 Barton Springs Rd	Austin	TX	78704	512-397-1468	397-1475
Web: www.cityofaustin.org/dougherty					
Guadalupe Cultural Arts Center 1300 Guadalupe St	San Antonio	TX	78207	210-271-3151	271-3480
Web: www.guadalupeculturalarts.org					
Ice House Cultural Center 1004 W Page St	Dallas	TX	75208	214-670-7524	670-0550
Web: www.dallasculture.org/iceHouseCulturalCenter.cfm					
La Villita Historic Arts Village 418 Villita St	San Antonio	TX	78205	210-207-8610	207-4390
Web: lavillita.com					
Latino Cultural Center 2600 Live Oak	Dallas	TX	75204	214-671-0045	670-0633
Web: www.dallasculture.org/latinocc					
Louise Hopkins Underwood Center for the Arts (LHUCA) 511 Ave K	Lubbock	TX	79401	806-762-8606	762-8622
Web: www.theunderwoodcenter.org					
McKinney Avenue Contemporary (The MAC) 3120 McKinney Ave	Dallas	TX	75204	214-953-1212	953-1873
Web: www.the-mac.org					
Nasher Sculpture Center 2001 Flora St	Dallas	TX	75201	214-242-5100	242-5155
Web: www.nashersculpturecenter.org					

Utah

	City	State	ZIP	Phone	Fax
Eccles Community Art Center 2580 Jefferson Ave	Ogden	UT	84401	801-392-6935	392-5295
Web: www.ogden4arts.org					

Virginia

	City	State	ZIP	Phone	Fax
Arlington Arts Center 3550 Wilson Blvd	Arlington	VA	22201	703-248-6800	248-6849
Web: www.arlingtonartscenter.org					
Contemporary Art Center of Virginia 2200 Parks Ave	Virginia Beach	VA	23451	757-425-0000	425-8186
Web: www.cacv.org					
Ellipse Arts Center 4350 N Fairfax Dr Suite 125	Arlington	VA	22203	703-228-7710	516-4468
Web: www.arlingtonarts.org/arts_comm/exhibitions.htm					
Peninsula Fine Arts Center 101 Museum Dr	Newport News	VA	23606	757-596-8175	596-0807
Web: www.pfac-va.org					

Washington

	City	State	ZIP	Phone	Fax
Art Concepts on Broadway 924 Broadway Plaza	Tacoma	WA	98402	253-272-2202	272-0899
TF: 800-758-7459 ■ *Web:* www.artconceptsonbroadway.com					
Corbin Art Center 507 W 7th Ave	Spokane	WA	99204	509-625-6677	
Web: www.spokaneparks.org					
Daybreak Star Arts Center PO Box 99100	Seattle	WA	98199	206-285-4425	282-3640
Web: www.unitedindians.org					

West Virginia

	City	State	ZIP	Phone	Fax
Artisan Center 1400 Main St Heritage Sq	Wheeling	WV	26003	304-232-1810	232-1812
Web: www.artisancenter.com					
Artworks Around Town Gallery & Art Center 2200 Market St	Wheeling	WV	26003	304-233-7540	
Web: www.artworksaroundtown.org					
Monongalia Arts Center 107 High St	Morgantown	WV	26507	304-292-3325	292-3326
Web: www.monartscenter.com					
Oglebay Institute's Stifel Fine Arts Center 1330 National Rd	Wheeling	WV	26003	304-242-7700	242-7747
TF: 888-696-4283 ■ *Web:* www.oionline.com					

Wisconsin

	City	State	ZIP	Phone	Fax
Irish Cultural & Heritage Center of Wisconsin 2133 W Wisconsin Ave	Milwaukee	WI	53233	414-345-8800	345-8805
Web: www.ichc.net					

50-3 Historic Homes & Buildings

Alabama

	City	State	ZIP	Phone	Fax
Battle-Friedman House & Gardens 1010 Greensboro Ave	Tuscaloosa	AL	35401	205-758-6138	
Web: www.historictuscaloosa.org					
Conde-Charlotte Museum House 104 Theatre St	Mobile	AL	36602	251-432-4722	
Fort Gaines Historic Site 51 Bienville Blvd	Dauphin Island	AL	36528	251-861-6992	861-6993
Web: www.dauphinisland.org/fort.htm					
Old Alabama Town 301 Columbus St	Montgomery	AL	36104	334-240-4500	240-4519
TF: 888-240-1850 ■ *Web:* www.oldalabamatown.com					
Tannehill Ironworks Historical State Park 12632 Confederate Pkwy	McCalla	AL	35111	205-477-5711	477-9400
Web: www.tannehill.org					

Alaska

	City	State	ZIP	Phone	Fax
Gold Dredge Number Eight 1755 Old Steese Hwy N	Fairbanks	AK	99712	907-457-6058	457-8888
Web: www.golddredgeno8.com					

Arizona

	City	State	ZIP	Phone	Fax
Cosanti Historic Site 6433 Doubletree Ranch Rd	Paradise Valley	AZ	85253	480-948-6145	998-4312
TF: 800-752-3187 ■ *Web:* www.arcosanti.org/expCosanti					
Goldfield Ghost Town & Mine 4650 N Mammouth Rd Hwy 88	Apache Junction	AZ	85219	480-983-0333	834-7947
Web: www.goldfieldghosttown.com					
OK Corral 326 E Allen St	Tombstone	AZ	85638	520-457-3456	457-3456
TF: 800-518-1566 ■ *Web:* www.ok-corral.com					
Phoenix Heritage Square 115 N 6th St	Phoenix	AZ	85004	602-262-5071	534-1786
Web: www.ci.phoenix.az.us/PARKS/heritage.html					
Taliesin West 12621 N Frank Lloyd Wright Blvd	Scottsdale	AZ	85259	480-860-2700	391-4009
Web: www.franklloydwright.org					
Wrigley Mansion 2501 E Telawa Trail	Phoenix	AZ	85016	602-955-4079	956-8439
TF: 888-879-7201 ■ *Web:* www.wrigleymansionclub.com					

Arkansas

	City	State	ZIP	Phone	Fax
Arkansas Governor's Mansion 1800 Center St	Little Rock	AR	72206	501-324-9805	324-9808
Web: www.arkansasgovernorsmansion.com					
Belle Grove Historic District bounded by N 5th N 'H' N 8th & N 'C' Sts	Fort Smith	AR	72901	479-783-8888	784-2421
TF: 800-637-1477 ■ *Web:* www.fortsmith.org/attractions/bellegrove.asp					
Clayton House 514 N 6th St	Fort Smith	AR	72901	479-783-7643	
Miss Laura's Visitor Center 2 N 'B' St	Fort Smith	AR	72901	479-783-8888	784-2421
TF: 800-637-1477 ■ *Web:* www.fortsmith.org/attractions/misslaurasvc.asp					
Quapaw Quarter Curran Hall 615 E Capitol Ave	Little Rock	AR	72202	501-371-0075	374-8142
Web: www.quapaw.com					

Historic Homes & Buildings (Cont'd)

California

				Phone	Fax

Camron-Stanford House 1418 Lakeside Dr ... Oakland CA 94612 510-874-7802 874-7803
Web: www.cshouse.org
Casa del Herrero 1387 E Valley Rd ... Santa Barbara CA 93108 805-565-5653 969-2371
Web: www.casadelherrero.com
Cohen-Bray House 1440 29th Ave ... Oakland CA 94601 510-536-1703
Web: www.cohen-brayhouse.info
Coit Tower 1 Telegraph Hill Blvd ... San Francisco CA 94133 415-362-0808 421-7795
Web: www.coittower.org
Dunsmuir Historic Estate 2960 Peralta Oaks Ct ... Oakland CA 94615 510-615-5555 562-8294
Web: www.dunsmuir.org
Ennis-Brown House 2655 Glendower Ave ... Los Angeles CA 90027 323-660-0607 660-3646
Web: www.ennishouse.org
Fallon House 175 W Saint John St ... San Jose CA 95110 408-993-8300 993-8088
Web: www.historysanjose.org/visiting_hsj/peralta_fallon
George White & Anna Gunn Marston House 3525 7th Ave ... San Diego CA 92103 619-298-3142
Kimberly Crest House & Gardens
1325 Prospect Dr PO Box 206 ... Redlands CA 92373 909-792-2111 798-1716
Web: www.kimberlycrest.org
McCallum Adobe
221 S Palm Canyon Dr Village Green Heritage Center ... Palm Springs CA 92262 760-323-8297 320-2561
Web: www.palmspringshistoricalsociety.org
McHenry Mansion 906 15th St ... Modesto CA 95354 209-577-5344 491-4407
Web: www.mchenrymuseum.org
Old Sacramento Historic District 1111 2nd St Suite 300 ... Sacramento CA 95814 916-264-7031 264-7286
Web: www.oldsacramento.com
Old Sacramento Schoolhouse 1200 Front St ... Sacramento CA 95814 916-483-8818 972-7041
Web: www.scoe.net/oldsacschoolhouse
Olivas Adobe Historical Park 4200 Olivas Park Dr ... Ventura CA 93001 805-644-4346
Web: www.olivasadobe.org
Peralta Adobe 175 W Saint John St ... San Jose CA 95110 408-993-8300 993-8088
Web: www.historysanjose.org/visiting_hsj/peralta_fallon
Tor House & Hawk Tower 26304 Ocean View Ave ... Carmel CA 93923 831-624-1813 624-3696
Web: www.torhouse.org
Village Green Heritage Center 221 S Palm Canyon Dr ... Palm Springs CA 92262 760-323-8297 320-2561
Web: www.palmspringshistoricalsociety.org
Winchester Mystery House 525 S Winchester Blvd ... San Jose CA 95128 408-247-2000 247-2090
Web: www.winchestermysteryhouse.com

Colorado

				Phone	Fax

Centennial House 1671 Galena St ... Aurora CO 80010 303-739-6660
Pearce-McAllister Cottage 1880 Gaylord St ... Denver CO 80206 303-322-1053 322-3704

Connecticut

				Phone	Fax

Bates-Scofield Homestead 45 Old King's Hwy N ... Darien CT 06820 203-655-9233 656-3892
Bush-Holley House 39 Strickland Rd ... Cos Cob CT 06807 203-869-6899 861-9720
Web: www.hstg.org
Captain David Judson House 967 Academy Hill ... Stratford CT 06615 203-378-0630 378-2562
Web: www.stratfordhistoricalsociety.com
Harriet Beecher Stowe House & Library 77 Forest St ... Hartford CT 06105 860-525-9317 522-9259
Web: www.harrietbeecherstowecenter.org
Hoyt-Barnum House 713 Bedford St ... Stamford CT 06905 203-329-1183 322-1607
Isham-Terry House 211 High St ... Hartford CT 06103 860-247-8996 249-4907
Web: www.hartnet.org/als/
Mill Hill Historic Park & Museum 2 E Wall St ... Norwalk CT 06851 203-846-0525
Web: www.norwalkhistoricalsociety.org
Ogden House & Gardens 1520 Bronson Rd ... Fairfield CT 06824 203-259-1598 255-2716
Web: www.fairfieldhistoricalsociety.org/ogdonhouse.html
Old State House 800 Main St ... Hartford CT 06103 860-522-6766 522-2812
Web: www.ctosh.org
Pardee-Morris House 325 Lighthouse Rd ... New Haven CT 06512 203-562-4183 562-2002
Sheffield Island Lighthouse 132 Water St ... South Norwalk CT 06854 203-838-9444 855-1017
Web: www.seaport.org/sheffield_island.htm
Wheeler House 25 Avery Pl ... Westport CT 06880 203-222-1424 221-0981
Web: westporthistory.org

Delaware

				Phone	Fax

Amstel House 2 E 4th St ... New Castle DE 19720 302-322-2794 322-8923
Web: www.newcastlehistory.org/houses/amstel.html
Dutch House 32 E 3rd St ... New Castle DE 19720 302-322-9168 322-8923
Web: www.newcastlehistory.org/houses/dutch.html
George Read II House & Garden 42 The Strand ... New Castle DE 19720 302-322-8411 322-8557
Web: www.hsd.org/read.htm
Gibraltar Estate & Gardens 1405 Greenhill Ave ... Wilmington DE 19806 302-651-9617 651-9603
Web: www.preservationde.org/gibraltar
Greenbank Mill 500 Greenbank Rd ... Wilmington DE 19808 302-999-9001
Web: www.greenbankmill.org
John Dickinson Plantation 340 Kitts Hummock Rd ... Dover DE 19901 302-739-3277 739-3173
Web: www.destatemuseums.org/jdp

District of Columbia

				Phone	Fax

Dumbarton House 2715 Q St NW ... Washington DC 20007 202-337-2288 337-0348
Web: www.dumbartonhouse.org
Old Stone House 3051 M St NW ... Washington DC 20007 202-426-6851 426-0215
Web: www.nps.gov/rocr/oldstonehouse/
Tudor Place Historic House & Garden 1644 31st St NW ... Washington DC 20007 202-965-0400 965-0164
Web: www.tudorplace.org
US Capitol Capitol Hill ... Washington DC 20510 202-225-6827
Web: www.aoc.gov

Florida

				Phone	Fax

Ann Norton Sculpture Gardens 253 Barcelona Rd ... West Palm Beach FL 33401 561-832-5328 835-9305
Web: www.ansg.org
Brokaw-McDougall House 329 N Meridian St ... Tallahassee FL 32301 850-891-3900 891-3902
Web: www.taltrust.org/brokaw.htm
Ernest Hemingway Home & Museum 907 Whitehead St ... Key West FL 33040 305-294-1136 294-2755
Web: www.hemingwayhome.com
Gonzalez-Alvarez House - The Oldest House
14 Saint Francis St ... Saint Augustine FL 32084 904-824-2872 824-2569
Web: www.staugustinehistoricalsociety.org
Historic Pensacola Village Church & Tarragona Sts ... Pensacola FL 32502 850-595-5985 595-5989
Web: www.historicpensacola.org
King-Cromartie House 229 SW 2nd Ave ... Fort Lauderdale FL 33301 954-463-4431 523-6228
Merrick House 907 Coral Way ... Coral Gables FL 33134 305-460-5361
Mission San Luis de Apalachee 2020 W Mission Rd ... Tallahassee FL 32304 850-487-3711 488-8015
Web: dhr.dos.state.fl.us/archaeology/sanluis
Old Saint Augustine Village 246 Saint George St ... Saint Augustine FL 32084 904-823-9722 823-9938
Web: www.old-staug-village.com
Oldest House - The Gonzalez-Alvarez House
14 Saint Francis St ... Saint Augustine FL 32084 904-824-2872 824-2569
Web: www.staugustinehistoricalsociety.org
Oldest Wooden School House 14 Saint George St ... Saint Augustine FL 32084 904-824-0192 808-0549
TF: 888-653-7245
Pablo Historical Park 380 Pablo Ave ... Jacksonville Beach FL 32250 904-241-5657 241-6243
Ponce de Leon Inlet Lighthouse 4931 S Peninsula Dr ... Ponce Inlet FL 32127 386-761-1821 761-3121
Web: www.ponceinlet.org
Ponce de Leon's Fountain of Youth 11 Magnolia Ave ... Saint Augustine FL 32084 904-829-3168 826-1913
TF: 800-356-8222 ■ *Web:* www.fountainofyouthflorida.com
Sugar Mill Ruins 600 Mission Rd ... New Smyrna Beach FL 32168 386-736-5953 943-7012

Georgia

				Phone	Fax

Andrew Low House 329 Abercorn St ... Savannah GA 31401 912-233-6854 233-1828
Web: www.andrewlowhouse.com
Boyhood Home of President Woodrow Wilson 419 7th St ... Augusta GA 30901 706-722-9828 724-3083
Web: www.wilsonboyhoodhome.org
Ezekiel Harris House 1822 Broad St ... Augusta GA 30901 706-722-8454 737-2820
Web: www.augustamuseum.org/eh.htm
Gordon-Lee Mansion 217 Cove Rd ... Chickamauga GA 30707 706-375-4728 357-9499
Web: www.gordon-leemansion.com
Green-Meldrim House 14 W Macon St ... Savannah GA 31401 912-232-1251 232-5559
Hammonds House 503 Peeples St SW ... Atlanta GA 30310 404-752-8730 752-8733
Web: www.hammondshouse.org
Hay House 934 Georgia Ave ... Macon GA 31201 478-742-8155 745-4277
Web: www.georgiatrust.org
Herndon Home 587 University Pl NW ... Atlanta GA 30314 404-581-9813
Historic Roswell District 617 Atlanta St ... Roswell GA 30075 770-640-3253 640-3252
TF: 800-776-7935 ■ *Web:* www.cvb.roswell.ga.us/attractions.html
Juliette Gordon Low Girl Scout National Center
10 E Oglethorpe Ave ... Savannah GA 31401 912-233-4501 233-4659
Web: www.popeleighey1940.org
Ma Rainey House 805 5th Ave ... Columbus GA 31901 706-322-0756
Margaret Mitchell House & Museum 990 Peachtree St NE ... Atlanta GA 30309 404-249-7012 249-7118
Web: www.gwtw.org
Old Fort Jackson 1 Fort Jackson Rd ... Savannah GA 31404 912-232-3945 236-5126
Web: www.chsgeorgia.org/jackson
Owens-Thomas House 124 Abercorn St ... Savannah GA 31401 912-233-9743
Web: www.telfair.org/buildings/ot_house.asp
Pebble Hill Plantation Hwy 319 ... Thomasville GA 31792 229-226-2344 226-0780
Web: www.pebblehill.com
Sidney Lanier Cottage 935 High St ... Macon GA 31201 478-743-3851
Web: www.cityofmacon.net/Living/slcottage.htm
Smith Plantation Home 935 Alpharetta St ... Roswell GA 30075 770-641-3978 641-3974
Web: www.archibaldsmithplantation.org
Stately Oaks Plantation 100 Carriage Ln ... Jonesboro GA 30236 770-473-0197 473-9855
Swan House Atlanta History Center 130 W Paces Ferry Rd ... Atlanta GA 30305 404-814-4000 814-2041
Web: www.atlantahistorycenter.com
Woodruff House 988 Bond St ... Macon GA 31201 478-301-2715 301-4124
TF: 800-837-2911

Hawaii

				Phone	Fax

Queen Emma Summer Palace 2913 Pali Hwy ... Honolulu HI 96817 808-595-6291 595-4395
Web: www.daughtersofhawaii.org

Idaho

				Phone	Fax

Old Idaho Penitentiary State Historic Site
2445 Old Penitentiary Rd ... Boise ID 83712 208-334-2844 334-3225
Web: www.idahohistory.net/oldpen.html

Illinois

				Phone	Fax

Dana-Thomas House 301 E Lawrence Ave ... Springfield IL 62703 217-782-6776 788-9450
Web: www.dana-thomas.org
Jane Addams Hull-House Museum 800 S Halsted St ... Chicago IL 60607 312-413-5353 413-2092
Web: www.uic.edu/jaddams/hull/hull_house.html
John C Flanagan House 942 NE Glen Oak Ave ... Peoria IL 61603 309-674-0322 674-1882
Lewis & Clark State Historic Site 1 Lewis & Clark Trail ... Hartford IL 62048 618-251-5811
Web: www.campriverdubois.com
Lincoln-Herndon Law Offices State Historic Site
6th & Adams ... Springfield IL 62701 217-785-7289
Web: www.illinoishistory.gov/hs/lincoln_herndon.htm
Sears Tower 233 S Wacker Dr ... Chicago IL 60606 312-875-9449 906-8193
TF: 877-759-3325 ■ *Web:* www.theskydeck.com
Stephen Mack Home & Whitman Trading Post
2221 Freeport Rd ... Rockton IL 61072 815-624-4200
Web: www.macktownlivinghistory.com

Indiana

				Phone	Fax

Allen County Courthouse 715 S Calhoun St ... Fort Wayne IN 46802 260-449-7211 449-7919*
**Fax:* County Clerk
Morris-Butler House 1204 N Park Ave ... Indianapolis IN 46202 317-636-5409 636-2630
TF: 800-450-4534
President Benjamin Harrison Home 1230 N Delaware St ... Indianapolis IN 46202 317-631-1898 632-5488
Web: www.presidentbenjaminharrison.org
Swinney Homestead 1424 W Jefferson Blvd ... Fort Wayne IN 46802 260-424-7212
Web: www.settlersinc.org

Iowa

Name / Address	City	State	ZIP	Phone	Fax
Brucemore 2160 Linden Dr SE	Cedar Rapids	IA	52403	319-362-7375	362-9481
Web: www.brucemore.org					
Eisenhower Mamie Doud Birthplace 709 Carroll St.	Boone	IA	50036	515-432-1896	
Web: www.booneiowa.com					
Mamie Doud Eisenhower Birthplace 709 Carroll St.	Boone	IA	50036	515-432-1896	
Web: www.booneiowa.com					
Mathias Ham House Historic Site 2241 Lincoln Ave	Dubuque	IA	52001	563-557-9545	583-1241
TF: 800-226-3369 ■ *Web:* www.mississippirivermuseum.com/hamhouse.htm					
Seminole Valley Farm 1400 Seminole Valley Rd NE	Cedar Rapids	IA	52411	319-378-9240	
Sherman Hill National Historic District 756 16th St	Des Moines	IA	50314	515-284-5717	
Web: www.shermanhill.org					
Wallace House 756 16th St	Des Moines	IA	50314	515-243-7063	243-8927
Web: www.wallace.org					

Kansas

Name / Address	City	State	ZIP	Phone	Fax
Cedar Crest Governor's Mansion 1 SW Cedar Crest Rd	Topeka	KS	66606	785-296-3636	272-9024
Web: www.ksgovernor.org					

Kentucky

Name / Address	City	State	ZIP	Phone	Fax
Ashland-The Henry Clay Estate 120 Sycamore Rd	Lexington	KY	40502	859-266-8581	268-7266
Web: www.henryclay.org					
Berry Hill Mansion 700 Louisville Rd	Frankfort	KY	40601	502-564-3000	564-6505
Web: www.historicproperties.ky.gov					
Brennan House Historic Home 631 S 5th St	Louisville	KY	40202	502-540-5145	540-5165
Web: thebrennanhouse.org					
Daniel Boone's Grave 215 E Main St	Frankfort	KY	40601	502-227-2403	
Hopemont The Hunt-Morgan House 201 N Mill St.	Lexington	KY	40508	859-233-3290	259-9210
Web: www.cr.nps.gov/nr/travel/lexington/hun.htm					
Locust Grove Historic Home 561 Blankenbaker Ln	Louisville	KY	40207	502-897-9845	897-0103
Web: www.locustgrove.org					
Loudoun House 209 Castlewood Dr.	Lexington	KY	40505	859-254-7024	254-7214
TF: 800-914-7990 ■ *Web:* www.lexingtonartleague.org/loudounhousegallery.htm					
Mary Todd Lincoln House 578 W Main St	Lexington	KY	40507	859-233-9999	252-2269
Web: www.mtlhouse.org					
Old Louisville Historic Preservation District 1340 S 4th St	Louisville	KY	40208	502-635-5244	635-5245
Web: www.oldlouisville.com					
Orlando Brown House 202 Wilkinson St.	Frankfort	KY	40601	502-227-2560	227-3348
TF: 888-516-5101 ■ *Web:* www.libertyhall.org					
Riverside Farnsley-Moremen Landing 7410 Moorman Rd.	Louisville	KY	40272	502-935-6809	935-6821
Web: www.riverside-landing.org					

Louisiana

Name / Address	City	State	ZIP	Phone	Fax
Beauregard-Keyes House 1113 Chartres St	New Orleans	LA	70116	504-523-7257	523-7257
Destrehan Plantation 13034 River Rd	Destrehan	LA	70047	985-764-9315	725-1929
TF: 877-453-2095 ■ *Web:* www.destrehanplantation.org					
Elms Mansion 3029 St Charles Ave	New Orleans	LA	70115	504-895-5493	899-3231
Web: www.elmsmansion.com					
Greenwood Plantation 6838 Highland Rd.	Saint Francisville	LA	70775	225-655-4475	655-3292
TF: 800-259-4475 ■ *Web:* www.greenwoodplantation.com					
Hermann-Grima House 820 Saint Louis St	New Orleans	LA	70112	504-525-5661	568-9735
Web: www.hgghh.org					
Houmas House Plantation & Gardens 40136 Hwy 942	Darrow	LA	70725	225-473-7841	473-7891
TF: 866-850-5654 ■ *Web:* www.houmashouse.com					
Rosedown Plantation State Historic Site 12501 Hwy 10	Saint Francisville	LA	70775	225-635-3332	784-1382
TF: 888-376-1867 ■ *Web:* www.crt.state.la.us/parks/irosedown.aspx					

Maine

Name / Address	City	State	ZIP	Phone	Fax
Blaine House 192 State St	Augusta	ME	04330	207-287-2121	287-6420
Fort Knox Historical Site 711 Fort Knox Rd.	Prospect	ME	04981	207-469-7719	469-7719
Isaac Farrar Mansion 17 2nd St.	Bangor	ME	04401	207-941-2808	941-2812
Neal Dow Memorial 714 Congress St.	Portland	ME	04102	207-773-7773	
Portland Head Light 12 Captain Strout Cir PO Box 6260	Cape Elizabeth	ME	04107	207-799-2661	799-2800
Web: www.portlandheadlight.com					
Victoria Mansion 109 Danforth St	Portland	ME	04101	207-772-4841	772-6290
Web: www.victoriamansion.org					
Wadsworth-Longfellow House 487 Congress St.	Portland	ME	04101	207-879-0427	775-4301
Web: www.mainehistory.org/house_overview.shtml					

Maryland

Name / Address	City	State	ZIP	Phone	Fax
Barracks The 43 Pinkney St	Annapolis	MD	21401	410-267-7619	267-6189
TF: 800-603-4020 ■ *Web:* www.annapolis.org					
Charles Carroll House 107 Duke of Gloucester St	Annapolis	MD	21401	410-269-1737	
Web: www.charlescarrollhouse.com					
Chase-Lloyd House 22 Maryland Ave	Annapolis	MD	21401	410-263-2723	
Evergreen House 4545 N Charles St.	Baltimore	MD	21210	410-516-0341	516-0864
Web: www.jhu.edu/~evrgreen/evergreen.html					
Waterfront Warehouse 4 Pinkney St.	Annapolis	MD	21401	410-267-7619	267-6189
TF: 800-603-4020 ■ *Web:* www.annapolis.org/tour-properties.html					
William Paca House & Garden 186 Prince George St	Annapolis	MD	21401	410-263-5553	626-1030
TF: 800-603-4020 ■ *Web:* www.annapolis.org/paca-house.html					

Massachusetts

Name / Address	City	State	ZIP	Phone	Fax
Barnstable Court House 3195 Main St.	Barnstable	MA	02630	508-375-6685	362-7754
Captain Bangs Hallett House 11 Strawberry Ln.	Yarmouth Port	MA	02675	508-362-3021	
Web: www.hsoy.org					
Freedom Trail 99 Chauncy St Suite 401	Boston	MA	02111	617-357-8300	357-8303
Web: www.thefreedomtrail.org					
Grange Hall State Rd.	West Tisbury	MA	02575	508-627-4440	627-8088
Web: www.mvpreservation.org					
Hadwen House 96 Main St	Nantucket	MA	02554	508-228-1894	228-5618
Web: www.nha.org					
House of the Seven Gables 54 Turner St.	Salem	MA	01970	978-744-0991	741-4350
Web: www.7gables.org					
Hoxie House 18 Water St	Sandwich	MA	02563	508-888-1173	
Mitchell House 1 Vestal St	Nantucket	MA	02554	508-228-2896	228-1031
Web: www.mmo.org/museums/michhouse.php					
Olde Colonial Courthouse Rendezvous Ln & Rte 6A	Barnstable	MA	02630	508-362-8927	
Salisbury Mansion 40 Highland St	Worcester	MA	01609	508-753-8278	753-9070
Web: www.worcesterhistory.org/mansion.html					
Wistariahurst Museum 238 Cabot St	Holyoke	MA	01040	413-322-5660	534-2344
Web: www.wistariahurst.org					

Michigan

Name / Address	City	State	ZIP	Phone	Fax
Applewood - The CS Mott Estate 1400 E Kearsley St	Flint	MI	48503	810-233-3031	232-6937
Edsel & Eleanor Ford House 1100 Lake Shore Rd.	Grosse Pointe Shores	MI	48236	313-884-4222	884-5977
Web: www.fordhouse.org					
Ford Edsel & Eleanor House 1100 Lake Shore Rd.	Grosse Pointe Shores	MI	48236	313-884-4222	884-5977
Web: www.fordhouse.org					
Heritage Hill Historic District 126 College Ave SE	Grand Rapids	MI	49503	616-459-8950	459-2409
Web: www.heritagehillweb.org					
Meyer May House 450 Madison Ave SE	Grand Rapids	MI	49503	616-246-4821	
Turner-Dodge House & Heritage Center 100 E North St	Lansing	MI	48906	517-483-4220	483-6081
Web: www.parks.cityoflansingmi.com/tdodge					
Whaley Historical House 624 E Kearsley St	Flint	MI	48502	810-235-6841	235-6186
Web: www.gfn.org/whaley/					

Minnesota

Name / Address	City	State	ZIP	Phone	Fax
Alexander Ramsey House 265 S Exchange St	Saint Paul	MN	55102	651-296-8760	296-0100
Web: www.mnhs.org/places/sites/arh					
Ard Godfrey House Central Ave & University Ave SE	Minneapolis	MN	55414	612-870-8001	813-5336
Web: www.ardgodfreyhouse.com					
Comstock Historic House 506 8th St S	Moorhead	MN	56560	218-291-4211	
Web: www.mnhs.org/places/sites/ch/index.html					
Glensheen Mansion 3300 London Rd.	Duluth	MN	55804	218-726-8910	726-8911
TF: 888-454-4536 ■ *Web:* www.d.umn.edu/glen					
Godfrey Ard House Central Ave & University Ave SE	Minneapolis	MN	55414	612-870-8001	813-5336
Web: www.ardgodfreyhouse.com					
Historic Fort Snelling Hwy 55 E of Airport.	Saint Paul	MN	55111	612-726-1171	725-2429
Web: www.mnhs.org/places/sites/hfs/index.html					
James J Hill House 240 Summit Ave	Saint Paul	MN	55102	651-297-2555	297-5655
TF: 888-727-8386 ■ *Web:* www.mnhs.org/places/sites/jjhh					
Mayowood Mansion 3720 Mayowood Rd SW	Rochester	MN	55902	507-282-9447	289-5481
Web: olmstedhistory.com/mayowood.htm					
Plummer House 1091 SW Plummer Ln.	Rochester	MN	55902	507-328-2525	328-2535
Web: www.ci.rochester.mn.us/park/Plummer/plummer.htm					
Purcell-Cutts House 2328 Lake Pl	Minneapolis	MN	55405	612-870-3131	
Web: www.artsmia.org/unified-vision/purcell-cutts-house					

Mississippi

Name / Address	City	State	ZIP	Phone	Fax
Isaac Carter Cabin 1701 Old Richton Rd	Petal	MS	39465	601-583-3306	

Missouri

Name / Address	City	State	ZIP	Phone	Fax
1859 Jail Marshal's Home & Museum 217 N Main St	Independence	MO	64050	816-252-1892	252-1510
Web: www.jchs.org/jail/museum.html					
Fort Osage National Historic Landmark 105 Osage St	Sibley	MO	64088	816-650-5737	795-7938
Web: www.historicfortosage.com					
Frank Lloyd Wright House in Ebbsworth Park 120 N Ballas Rd	Kirkwood	MO	63122	314-822-8359	
Web: www.ebsworthpark.org					
General Daniel Bissell House 10225 Bellefontaine Rd.	Saint Louis	MO	63137	314-544-5714	638-5009
Web: www.co.st-louis.mo.us/parks/cg-bissellhouse.html					
Harris-Kearney House 4000 Baltimore St	Kansas City	MO	64111	816-561-1821	
Web: www.westporthistorical.org/house.html					
Historic Christopher Hawken House 1155 S Rock Hill Rd.	Saint Louis	MO	63119	314-968-1857	968-1857
Web: www.historicwebster.org/hawken_house.shtml					
Historic Hanley House 7600 Westmoreland St.	Clayton	MO	63105	314-290-8501	290-8517
Historic Samuel Cupples House 3673 W Pine Mall	Saint Louis	MO	63108	314-977-3575	977-3581
Web: www.slu.edu/the_arts/cupples					
Oakland House 7801 Genesta St.	Saint Louis	MO	63123	314-352-5654	
Web: www.afftonoaklandhouse.com					
Saint Louis Union Station 1820 Market St	Saint Louis	MO	63103	314-421-6655	421-3314
Web: www.stlouisunionstation.com					
Vaile Mansion 1500 N Liberty St	Independence	MO	64050	816-325-7430	
Web: vailemansion.org					

Montana

Name / Address	City	State	ZIP	Phone	Fax
Moss Mansion 914 Division St	Billings	MT	59101	406-256-5100	252-0091
Web: www.mossmansion.com					

Nebraska

Name / Address	City	State	ZIP	Phone	Fax
General Crook House Museum 5730 N 30th St Bldg 11B	Omaha	NE	68111	402-455-9990	453-9448
Web: omahahistory.org/museum.htm					
Joslyn Castle 3902 Davenport St	Omaha	NE	68106	402-595-2199	
Web: www.joslyncastle.com					
Thomas P Kennard House 1627 H St	Lincoln	NE	68508	402-471-4764	
Web: www.nebraskahistory.org/sites/kennard/index.htm					

Nevada

Name / Address	City	State	ZIP	Phone	Fax
Bowers Mansion 4005 US 395 S	Carson City	NV	89701	775-828-6642	849-9568

New Hampshire

Name / Address	City	State	ZIP	Phone	Fax
Kimball-Jenkins Estate 266 N Main St.	Concord	NH	03301	603-225-3932	225-9288
Web: www.kimballjenkins.com					

Historic Homes & Buildings (Cont'd)

New Jersey

	City	State	ZIP	Phone	Fax
Absecon Lighthouse 31 S Rhode Island Ave *Web:* www.abseconlighthouse.org	Atlantic City	NJ	08401	609-449-1360	449-1919
Ballantine House 49 Washington St *Web:* www.newarkmuseum.org	Newark	NJ	07102	973-596-6550	642-0459
Batsto Historic Village 4110 Nesco Rd Wharton State Forest *Web:* www.batstovillage.org	Hammonton	NJ	08037	609-561-0024	567-8116
Dey Mansion 199 Totowa Rd	Wayne	NJ	07470	973-696-1776	696-1365
Durand Hedden House 523 Ridgewood Rd	Maplewood	NJ	07040	973-763-7712	
Israel Crane House c/o Montclair Historical Society 110 Orange Rd *Web:* www.montclairhistorical.org	Montclair	NJ	07042	973-783-1717	783-9419
Pennsylvania Station 1 Raymond Plaza W	Newark	NJ	07107	973-491-8757	
Van Riper-Hopper House 533 Berdan Ave	Wayne	NJ	07470	973-694-7192	694-9100
William Trent House 15 Market St *Web:* www.williamtrenthouse.org	Trenton	NJ	08611	609-989-3027	278-7890

New Mexico

	City	State	ZIP	Phone	Fax
Coronado State Monument 485 Kuaua Rd *Web:* www.nmmonuments.org	Bernalillo	NM	87004	505-867-5351	867-1733
Picuris Pueblo Hwy 75	Penasco	NM	87553	505-587-2519	587-1071
Santa Fe Southern Railway 410 S Guadalupe St *TF:* 888-989-8600 ■ *Web:* www.sfsr.com	Santa Fe	NM	87501	505-989-8600	983-7620
Taos Pueblo 120 Veterans Hwy *Web:* www.taospueblo.com	Taos	NM	87571	505-758-1028	758-4604

New York

	City	State	ZIP	Phone	Fax
Browns Race Historic District 60 Browns Race	Rochester	NY	14614	585-325-2030	325-2414
Campbell-Whittlesey House 123 S Fitzhugh St	Rochester	NY	14608	585-546-7028	586-4788
Edgar Allan Poe Cottage E Kingsbridge Rd Grand Concourse	Bronx	NY	10458	718-881-8900	881-4827
Frank Lloyd Wright's Darwin D Martin House 125 Jewett Pkwy *TF:* 877-377-3858 ■ *Web:* www.darwinmartinhouse.org	Buffalo	NY	14214	716-856-3858	856-4009
George Eastman House & Gardens 900 East Ave *Web:* www.eastmanhouse.org	Rochester	NY	14607	585-271-3361	271-3970
Glenview Mansion 511 Warburton Ave Hudson River Museum *Web:* www.hrm.org/mansion.html	Yonkers	NY	10701	914-963-4550	
Gracie Mansion 88th St & East End Ave *Web:* www.nyc.gov/html/om/html/gracie.html	New York	NY	10128	212-570-4751	570-4493
Jacob Purdy House 60 Park Ave	White Plains	NY	10603	914-328-1776	
Kingsland Homestead 143-35 37th Ave *Web:* www.queenshistoricalsociety.org/kingsland.html	Flushing	NY	11354	718-939-0647	539-9885
Kykuit - The Rockefeller Estate Rt 9 *Web:* www.hudsonvalley.org	Sleepy Hollow	NY	10591	914-631-9491	
Lighthouse at Sleepy Hollow Palmer Ave Kingsland Point Park	Sleepy Hollow	NY	10549	914-366-5109	
Lyndhurst 635 S Broadway *Web:* www.lyndhurst.org	Tarrytown	NY	10591	914-631-4481	
Philipsburg Manor Rt 9 *Web:* www.hudsonvalley.org	Sleepy Hollow	NY	10591	914-631-3992	
Philipse Manor Hall 29 Warburton Ave	Yonkers	NY	10701	914-965-4027	965-6485
Poe Edgar Allan Cottage E Kingsbridge Rd Grand Concourse	Bronx	NY	10458	718-881-8900	881-4827
Pruyn House 207 Old Niskayuna Rd *Web:* www.colonie.com/pruyn	Newtonville	NY	12128	518-783-1435	783-1437
Sleepy Hollow Cemetery 540 N Broadway *Web:* www.sleepyhollowcemetery.org	Sleepy Hollow	NY	10591	914-631-0081	631-0085
Washington Irving's Sunnyside W Sunnyside Ln *Web:* www.hudsonvalley.org	Tarrytown	NY	10591	914-591-8763	591-4436
Washington's Heaquarters/Miller House 140 Virginia Rd	White Plains	NY	10603	914-949-1236	
Wilcox Octagon House 5420 W Genesee St	Camillus	NY	13031	315-488-7800	
Woodside Mansion 485 East Ave *Web:* rochesterhistory.org	Rochester	NY	14607	585-271-2705	271-9089

North Carolina

	City	State	ZIP	Phone	Fax
Biltmore Estate 1 Approach Rd *TF Resv:* 800-411-3812 ■ *Web:* www.biltmore.com	Asheville	NC	28803	828-225-1333	225-1629
Blandwood Mansion 447 W Washington St *Web:* www.blandwood.org	Greensboro	NC	27401	336-272-5003	272-8049
Castle McCulloch 3925 Kivett Dr *Web:* www.castlemcculloch.com	Jamestown	NC	27282	336-887-5413	887-5429
Haywood Hall House & Gardens 211 New Bern Pl *Web:* www.haywoodhall.org	Raleigh	NC	27601	919-832-8357	
Historic Latta Plantation 5225 Sample Rd *Web:* www.lattaplantation.org	Huntersville	NC	28078	704-875-2312	875-1724
James K Polk Memorial State Historic Site 12031 Lancaster Hwy *Web:* www.ah.dcr.state.nc.us/sections/hs/polk/polk.htm	Pineville	NC	28134	704-889-7145	889-3057
Mendenhall Plantation 603 W Main St *Web:* www.mendenhallplantation.org	Jamestown	NC	27282	336-454-3819	
Mordecai Historic Park 1 Mimosa St *Web:* www.raleighnc.gov/mordecai	Raleigh	NC	27604	919-857-4364	
Reed Gold Mine State Historic Site 9621 Reed Mine Rd *Web:* www.ah.dcr.state.nc.us/sections/hs/reed/reed.htm	Midland	NC	28107	704-721-4653	721-4657
Tannenbaum Historic Park 2200 New Garden Rd *Web:* www.greensboro-nc.gov/Departments/Parks/facilities/tannenbaum/default.htm	Greensboro	NC	27410	336-545-5315	545-5314
Thomas Wolfe Memorial 52 N Market St *Web:* www.wolfememorial.com	Asheville	NC	28801	828-253-8304	252-8171
Vance Birthplace State Historic Site 911 Reems Creek Rd *Web:* www.ah.dcr.state.nc.us/sections/hs/vance/vance.htm	Weaverville	NC	28787	828-645-6706	645-0936

Ohio

	City	State	ZIP	Phone	Fax
Fort Meigs State Memorial 29100 W River Rd *TF:* 800-283-8916 ■ *Web:* www.fortmeigs.org	Perrysburg	OH	43551	419-874-4121	874-9446
German Village 588 S 3rd St *Web:* www.germanvillage.org	Columbus	OH	43215	614-221-8888	222-4747
John Brown Home 514 Diagonal Rd	Akron	OH	44320	330-535-1120	535-0250
Loghurst Farm 3967 Boardman-Canfield Rd *Web:* www.wrhs.org/loghurst	Canfield	OH	44406	330-533-4330	
Paul Laurence Dunbar House 219 N Paul Laurence Dunbar St *TF:* 800-860-0148	Dayton	OH	45402	937-224-7061	224-4256
Perkins Stone Mansion 550 Copley Rd	Akron	OH	44320	330-535-1120	535-0250
SunWatch Indian Village/Archaeological Park 2301 W River Rd *Web:* www.sunwatch.org	Dayton	OH	45418	937-268-8199	268-1760

Oklahoma

	City	State	ZIP	Phone	Fax
Oklahoma Heritage Center 1400 N Classen Dr *TF:* 888-501-2059 ■ *Web:* www.oklahomaheritage.com	Oklahoma City	OK	73106	405-235-4458	235-2714

Ontario

	City	State	ZIP	Phone	Fax
Zion Schoolhouse 1091 Finch Ave E	Toronto	ON	M2J2X3	416-395-7435	395-1208

Oregon

	City	State	ZIP	Phone	Fax
Brunk House 5705 Salem-Dallas Hwy NW *Web:* www.open.org/~pchs/Brunk.html	Salem	OR	97304	503-371-8586	
Deepwood Estate 1116 Mission St SE *Web:* www.oregonlink.com/deepwood	Salem	OR	97302	503-363-1825	363-3586
Mission Mill Museum 1313 Mill St SE *Web:* www.missionmill.org	Salem	OR	97301	503-585-7012	588-9902
Shelton-McMurphey-Johnson House 303 Willamette St *Web:* www.smjhouse.org	Eugene	OR	97401	541-484-0808	984-1413

Pennsylvania

	City	State	ZIP	Phone	Fax
Besty Ross House 239 Arch Street *Web:* www.betsyrosshouse.org	Philadelphia	PA	19106	215-686-1252	686-1256
Bishop White House 309 Walnut St	Philadelphia	PA	19106	215-597-0068	
Carpenters' Hall 320 Chestnut St *Web:* www.ushistory.org/carpentershall	Philadelphia	PA	19106	215-925-0167	925-3880
Cashier's House 417 State St *Web:* www.eriecountyhistory.org	Erie	PA	16501	814-454-1813	454-6890
Declaration House 7th & Market Sts	Philadelphia	PA	19106	215-597-0068	597-2744
Eastern State Penitentiary Historic Site 22nd St & Fairmount Ave *Web:* www.easternstate.org	Philadelphia	PA	19130	215-236-5111	236-5289
Fallingwater 1491 Mill Run Rd *Web:* www.wpconline.org/fallingwaterhome.htm	Mill Run	PA	15464	724-329-8501	329-0553
Fort Hunter Mansion & Park 5300 N Front St *Web:* www.forthunter.org	Harrisburg	PA	17110	717-599-5751	599-5838
Franklin Court 322 Market St *Web:* www.nps.gov/inde/Franklin_Court	Philadelphia	PA	19106	215-597-2761	
Glen Foerd on the Delaware 5001 Grant Ave *Web:* www.glenfoerd.org	Philadelphia	PA	19114	215-632-5330	632-2312
Hans Herr House & Museum 1849 Hans Herr Dr *Web:* www.hansherr.org	Willow Street	PA	17584	717-464-4438	
Hartwood Mansion 200 Hartwood Acres	Pittsburgh	PA	15238	412-767-9200	767-0171
Historic Rock Ford Plantation 881 Rockford Rd *Web:* www.rockfordplantation.org	Lancaster	PA	17602	717-392-7223	392-7283
Independence Hall & Congress Hall Chestnut St-between 5th & 6th Sts *Web:* www.nps.gov/inde	Philadelphia	PA	19106	215-597-0068	597-8976
Jennie Wade House 548 Baltimore St *Web:* www.gettysburgbattlefieldtours.com	Gettysburg	PA	17325	717-334-6296	334-9100
John Chadds House 1719 Creek Rd	Chadds Ford	PA	19317	610-388-7376	388-7480
John Harris Mansion 219 S Front St *Web:* www.dauphincountyhistoricalsociety.org	Harrisburg	PA	17104	717-233-3462	233-6059
Liberty Bell Shrine 622 Hamilton St *Web:* www.libertybellmuseum.org	Allentown	PA	18101	610-435-4232	435-5061
Physick House 321 S 4th St *Web:* www.philalandmarks.org	Philadelphia	PA	19106	215-925-7866	925-7909
Powel House 244 S 3rd St *Web:* www.philalandmarks.org/powel.aspx	Philadelphia	PA	19106	215-627-0364	627-1733
Scranton Iron Furnace 159 Cedar Ave	Scranton	PA	18505	570-963-4804	963-4194
Todd House 4th & Walnut Sts	Philadelphia	PA	19106	215-965-2305	597-1548
Wheatland - Home of President James Buchanan 1120 Marietta Ave *Web:* www.wheatland.org	Lancaster	PA	17603	717-392-8721	295-8825

Quebec

	City	State	ZIP	Phone	Fax
Artillery Park Heritage Site 2 D'Auteuil St PO Box 10 Station B *Web:* www.pc.gc.ca/lhn-nhs/qc/artiller	Quebec	QC	G1K7A1	418-648-4205	648-4285
Fortifications of Quebec National Historic Site 100 Saint-Louis St PO Box 10 Station B *Web:* www.museocapitale.qc.ca	Quebec	QC	G1K7A1	418-648-7016	948-9068
Parliament Building (Hotel du Parlement) Grande-Allee & Honore-Mercier Ave *TF:* 866-337-8837 ■ *Web:* www.assnat.qc.ca	Quebec	QC	G1A1A4	418-643-7239	641-2638

Rhode Island

	City	State	ZIP	Phone	Fax
Astors' Beechwood Mansion 580 Bellevue Ave *Web:* www.astorsbeechwood.com	Newport	RI	02840	401-846-3772	849-6998
Belcourt Castle 657 Bellevue Ave *Web:* www.belcourtcastle.com	Newport	RI	02840	401-846-0669	846-5345
Chateau-Sur-Mer 474 Bellevue Ave *Web:* www.newportmansions.org	Newport	RI	02840	401-847-1000	847-1361
Edward King House 35 King St *TF:* 866-878-6954 ■ *Web:* www.edwardkinghouse.com	Newport	RI	02840	401-846-7426	846-5308
Hunter House 54 Washington St *Web:* www.newportmansions.org	Newport	RI	02840	401-847-1000	847-1361
John Brown House Museum 52 Power St *Web:* www.rihs.org	Providence	RI	02906	401-273-7507	751-2307
Marble House 596 Bellevue Ave *Web:* www.newportmansions.org	Newport	RI	02840	401-847-1000	847-1361
Nightingale-Brown House 357 Benefit St *Web:* www.brown.edu/Research/JNBC	Providence	RI	02903	401-863-1177	
Rose Island Lighthouse *Web:* www.roseislandlighthouse.org	Rose Island	RI	02840	401-847-4242	
Samuel Whitehorne House 416 Thames St *Web:* www.newportrestoration.com	Newport	RI	02840	401-849-7300	849-0125

				Phone	Fax
Whitehorne Samuel House 416 Thames St	Newport	RI	02840	401-849-7300	849-0125
Web: www.newportrestoration.com					

South Carolina

				Phone	Fax
Aiken-Rhett House 48 Elizabeth St	Charleston	SC	29401	843-723-1159	
Web: www.historiccharleston.org					
Beattie House 8 Bennett St	Greenville	SC	29601	864-233-9977	
Boone Hall Plantation 1235 Long Point Rd	Mount Pleasant	SC	29464	843-884-4371	884-0475
Web: www.boonehallplantation.com					
Fort Hill - The John C Calhoun House Clemson University Fort Hill St	Clemson	SC	29634	864-656-2475	656-1026
Gassaway Mansion 106 Dupont Dr	Greenville	SC	29607	864-271-0188	242-9935
Web: www.gassawaymansion.com					
Hampton-Preston Mansion & Garden 1616 Blanding St	Columbia	SC	29201	803-252-1770	929-7695
Heyward-Washington House 87 Church St	Charleston	SC	29401	843-722-0354	
Kilgore-Lewis House 560 N Academy St PO Box 681	Greenville	SC	29602	864-232-3020	
Web: www.kilgore-lewis.org					
Mann-Simons Cottage 1403 Richland St	Columbia	SC	29201	803-252-7742	929-7695
Mills Robert House 1616 Blanding St	Columbia	SC	29201	803-252-7742	929-7695
Nathaniel Russell House 51 Meeting St	Charleston	SC	29401	843-724-8481	805-6732
Web: www.historiccharleston.org/experience/nrh/					
Old Exchange & Provost Dungeon 122 E Bay St	Charleston	SC	29401	843-727-2165	727-2163
TF: 888-763-0448 ■ *Web:* www.oldexchange.com					
Robert Mills House 1616 Blanding St	Columbia	SC	29201	803-252-7742	929-7695
Seibels House 1601 Richland St	Columbia	SC	29201	803-252-7742	929-7695
Web: www.historiccolumbia.org/rentals/seibels.html					
South Carolina State House 1100 Gervais St	Columbia	SC	29201	803-734-2430	734-2439
Woodrow Wilson Family Home 1705 Hampton St	Columbia	SC	29201	803-252-7742	929-7695
Web: www.historiccolumbia.org/history/wilson.html					

South Dakota

				Phone	Fax
Corn Palace 604 N Main St	Mitchell	SD	57301	605-996-5031	996-8273
TF: 800-257-2676 ■ *Web:* www.cornpalace.org					

Tennessee

				Phone	Fax
Armstrong-Lockett House 2728 Kingston Pike	Knoxville	TN	37919	865-637-3163	637-1709
Belmont Mansion 1900 Belmont Blvd	Nashville	TN	37212	615-460-5459	460-5688
Web: www.belmontmansion.com					
Blount Mansion 200 W Hill Ave	Knoxville	TN	37901	865-525-2375	546-5315
TF: 888-654-0016 ■ *Web:* www.blountmansion.org					
Carnton Plantation 1345 Carnton Ln	Franklin	TN	37064	615-794-0903	794-6563
Web: www.carnton.org					
Carter House 1140 Columbia Ave	Franklin	TN	37064	615-791-1861	794-1327
Confederate Memorial Hall 3148 Kingston Pike	Knoxville	TN	37919	865-522-2371	
Web: www.knoxvillecmh.org					
Davies Manor House 9336 Davies Plantation Rd	Memphis	TN	38133	901-386-0715	388-4677
Web: www.daviesmanorplantation.org					
Hunt-Phelan Home 533 Beale St	Memphis	TN	38103	901-525-8225	527-9120
Web: www.huntphelan.com					
Lauderdale Courts-Former Home of Elvis Presley 185 Winchester Apt 328	Memphis	TN	38105	901-523-8662	523-8299
Web: www.lauderdalecourts.com					
Ramsey House 2614 Thorngrove Pike	Knoxville	TN	37914	865-546-0745	546-1851
Web: www.ramseyhouse.org					
Tipton-Haynes State Historic Site 2620 S Roan St	Johnson City	TN	37601	423-926-3631	
Web: www.tipton-haynes.org					
Travellers Rest Plantation & Museum 636 Farrell Pkwy	Nashville	TN	37220	615-832-8197	832-8169
TF: 866-832-8197 ■ *Web:* www.travellersrestplantation.org					
Woodruff-Fontaine House 680 Adams Ave	Memphis	TN	38105	901-526-1469	755-6075

Texas

				Phone	Fax
French-Galvan House 1581 N Chaparral St	Corpus Christi	TX	78401	361-826-3410	826-4301
Web: www.co.nueces.tx.us/histcomm/frenchgalvanhouse.asp					
Fulton Mansion 317 S Fulton Beach Rd	Rockport	TX	78382	361-729-0386	729-6581
Web: www.tpwd.state.tx.us/park/fulton					
Guenther House 205 E Guenther St	San Antonio	TX	78204	210-227-1061	351-6372
TF: 800-235-8186 ■ *Web:* www.guentherhouse.com					
Jalufka-Govatos House 1513 N Chaparral St	Corpus Christi	TX	78401	361-826-3410	826-4301
King William Historic District 1032 S Alamo St	San Antonio	TX	78210	210-227-8786	227-8030
Magoffin Homestead 1120 Magoffin Ave	El Paso	TX	79901	915-533-5147	544-4398
McCampbell House 1501 N Chaparral St	Corpus Christi	TX	78401	361-826-3410	826-4301
Neill-Cochran House 2310 San Gabriel St	Austin	TX	78705	512-478-2335	478-1865
Web: www.neill-cochranmuseum.org					
Old German Free School Building 507 E 10th St	Austin	TX	78701	512-482-0927	482-0636
TF: 866-482-4847 ■ *Web:* www.gths.net/school.html					
Sidbury House 1609 N Chaparral St	Corpus Christi	TX	78401	361-826-3410	826-4301
Thistle Hill 1509 Pennsylvania Ave	Fort Worth	TX	76104	817-336-1212	335-5338
Web: thistlehill.org					

Utah

				Phone	Fax
This is the Place Heritage Park 2601 E Sunnyside Ave	Salt Lake City	UT	84108	801-582-1847	583-1869
Web: www.thisistheplace.org					

Vermont

				Phone	Fax
Chimney Point State Historic Site 7305 Vermont Rt 125	Addison	VT	05491	802-759-2412	759-2547
Web: www.historicvermont.org					
Ethan Allen Homestead Ethan Allen Homestead	Burlington	VT	05408	802-865-4556	865-0661
Web: www.ethanallenhomestead.org					
President Chester A Arthur State Historic Site 4588 Chester Arthur Rd	Fairfield	VT	05455	802-828-3051	828-3206
Web: www.historicvermont.org/html/arthur.html					
Shelburne Farms 1611 Harbor Rd	Shelburne	VT	05482	802-985-8442	985-8123
Web: www.shelburnefarms.org					

Virginia

				Phone	Fax
Adam Thoroughgood House 1636 Parish Rd	Virginia Beach	VA	23455	757-460-7588	460-7644
Web: eteamz.active.com/AdamThoroughgood					
Athenaeum The 201 Prince St	Alexandria	VA	22314	703-548-0035	
Web: www.nvfaa.org					
Capitol Square 9th & Grace Sts	Richmond	VA	23219	804-698-1788	698-1906
Web: www.historicrichmond.com/capitolsquare.html					
Francis Land House 3131 Virginia Beach Blvd	Virginia Beach	VA	23452	757-431-4000	431-3733
Web: www.vbgov.com/dept/arts/francis_land					
Frank Lloyd Wright's Pope-Leighey House 9000 Richmond Hwy Woodlawn Plantation	Alexandria	VA	22309	703-780-4000	780-8509
Web: www.popeleighey1940.org					
George Washington's Mount Vernon Estate & Gardens George Washington Memorial Pkwy PO Box 110	Mount Vernon	VA	22121	703-780-2000	
Web: www.mountvernon.org					
Historic Fort Norfolk Front St	Norfolk	VA	23510	757-441-1852	
Web: www.norfolkhistorical.org/fort					
James Madison's Montpelier 11407 Constitution Hwy	Montpelier Station	VA	22957	540-672-2728	672-0411
Web: www.montpelier.org					
John Marshall House 818 E Marshall St	Richmond	VA	23219	804-648-7998	648-5880
Web: www.apva.org/marshall					
Lynnhaven House 4405 Wishart Rd	Virginia Beach	VA	23455	757-460-7109	460-7537
Web: www.apva.org/lynnhaven/					
Monticello 931 Thomas Jefferson Pkwy PO Box 316	Charlottesville	VA	22902	434-984-9822	977-7757
Web: www.monticello.org					
Old Cape Henry Lighthouse 583 Atlantic Ave	Fort Story	VA	23459	757-422-9421	
Pope-Leighey House 9000 Richmond Hwy	Alexandria	VA	22309	703-780-4000	780-8509
Web: www.popeleighey1940.org					
Shirley Plantation 501 Shirley Plantation Rd	Charles City	VA	23030	804-829-5121	829-6322
TF: 800-232-1613 ■ *Web:* www.shirleyplantation.com					
Sully Plantation 3650 Historic Sully Way	Chantilly	VA	20151	703-437-1794	787-3314
Web: www.fairfaxcounty.gov/parks/sully/					
Virginia House 4301 Sulgrave Rd	Richmond	VA	23221	804-353-4251	354-8247
Web: www.vahistorical.org					
Willoughby-Baylor House 601 E Freemason St	Norfolk	VA	23501	757-441-1526	
Woodlawn Plantation 9000 Richmond Hwy	Alexandria	VA	22309	703-780-4000	780-8509
Web: www.woodlawn1805.org					

Washington

				Phone	Fax
Covington House 4201 Main St	Vancouver	WA	98663	360-695-6750	

West Virginia

				Phone	Fax
Eckhart House 810 Main St Old Town	Wheeling	WV	26003	304-232-5439	
TF: 888-700-0118 ■ *Web:* www.eckharthouse.com					
Pearl S Buck Birthplace Rt 219 PO Box 126	Hillsboro	WV	24946	304-653-4430	
Web: www.pearlsbuckbirthplace.com					

Wisconsin

				Phone	Fax
Kilbourntown House 4400 N Estabrook Dr Estabrook Park	Milwaukee	WI	53211	414-273-8288	
Pabst Mansion 2000 W Wisconsin Ave	Milwaukee	WI	53233	414-931-0808	931-1005
Web: www.pabstmansion.com					
Taliesin 5607 County Hwy C	Spring Green	WI	53588	608-588-7090	588-7514
Web: www.taliesinpreservation.org					

50-4 Monuments, Memorials, Landmarks

				Phone	Fax
African-American Civil War Memorial & Museum 1200 U St NW	Washington	DC	20001	202-667-2667	667-6771
Web: www.afroamcivilwar.org					
Alcatraz Island c/o Alcatraz Cruises LLC Pier 33 Hornblower Alcatraz Landing	San Francisco	CA	94133	415-981-7625	
Web: www.nps.gov/alcatraz					
Amistad Memorial 165 Church St	New Haven	CT	06510	203-387-0370	397-2539
Arkansas Post National Memorial 1741 Old Post Rd	Gillett	AR	72055	870-548-2207	548-2431
Web: www.nps.gov/arpo/					
Arlington House-Robert E Lee Memorial George Washington Memorial Pkwy Turkey Run Park	McLean	VA	22101	703-235-1530	
Web: www.nps.gov/arho/					
Armed Forces Memorial 232 E Main St Town Point Park	Norfolk	VA	23510	757-664-6620	
Buffalo & Erie County Naval & Military Park 1 Naval Park Cove	Buffalo	NY	14202	716-847-1773	847-6405
Web: www.buffalonavalpark.org					
Bunker Hill Monument Monument Sq	Charlestown	MA	02129	617-242-5641	242-6006
Web: www.nps.gov/bost/Bunker_Hill.htm					
Chamizal National Memorial 800 S San Marcial St	El Paso	TX	79905	915-532-7273	532-7240
Web: www.nps.gov/cham/					
Coronado National Memorial 4101 E Montezuma Canyon Rd	Hereford	AZ	85615	520-366-5515	366-5705
Web: www.nps.gov/coro/					
Crazy Horse Memorial Ave of the Chiefs	Crazy Horse	SD	57730	605-673-4681	673-2185
Web: www.crazyhorsememorial.org					
De Soto National Memorial 3000 75th St NW	Bradenton	FL	34209	941-792-0458	792-5094
Web: www.nps.gov/deso/					
Desert Holocaust Memorial Fred Waring & San Pablo Sts Palm Desert Civic Park	Palm Desert	CA	92260	760-324-4737	324-3154
Web: www.palmsprings.com/points/holocaust/					
Empire State Building 350 5th Ave Suite 3210	New York	NY	10118	212-736-3100	967-6167
Web: www.esbnyc.com					
Federal Hall National Memorial 26 Wall St	New York	NY	10005	212-825-6888	825-6874
Web: www.nps.gov/feha/					
Flight 93 National Memorial National Park Service 109 W Main St - Suite 104	Somerset	PA	15501	814-443-4557	443-2180
Web: www.flight93memorialproject.org					
Fort Caroline National Memorial 12713 Fort Caroline Rd	Jacksonville	FL	32225	904-641-7155	641-3798
Web: www.nps.gov/foca/					
Franklin Delano Roosevelt Memorial 1850 W Basin Dr SW Potomac Park	Washington	DC	20042	202-376-6700	376-6702
Web: www.nps.gov/fdrm					
Gateway Arch 11 N 4th St	Saint Louis	MO	63102	314-655-1700	655-1641
Web: www.nps.gov/jeff					
General Grant National Memorial Riverside Dr & W 122nd St	New York	NY	10027	212-666-1640	932-9631
Web: www.nps.gov/gegr/					
George Washington Masonic National Memorial 101 Callahan Dr	Alexandria	VA	22301	703-683-2007	519-9270
Web: www.gwmemorial.org					
Golden Gate Bridge PO Box 9000	Presidio Station	CA	94129	415-921-5858	
Web: www.goldengate.org					

Monuments, Memorials, Landmarks (Cont'd)

				Phone	Fax
Grauman's Chinese Theatre 6925 Hollywood Blvd	Hollywood	CA	90028	323-461-3331	463-0879
Web: www.manntheatres.com/chinese					
Hamilton Grange National Memorial 122 St @ Riverside Dr.	New York	NY	10027	212-666-1640	
Web: www.nps.gov/hagr/					
Henry J Kaiser Shipyard Memorial & Interpretive Center					
Columbia Way Marine Park	Vancouver	WA	98661	360-619-1127	696-8009
Holocaust Memorial 1933-1945 Meridian Ave	Miami Beach	FL	33139	305-538-1663	538-2423
Web: www.holocaustmmb.org					
Hoover Dam Hwy 93	Boulder City	NV	89006	702-494-2517	494-2587
TF: 866-730-9097 ■ *Web:* www.usbr.gov/lc/hooverdam/					
Idaho Anne Frank Human Rights Memorial					
S end of 8th St at the Boise River	Boise	ID	83702	208-345-0304	433-1221
Web: www.idaho-humanrights.org/Memorial/memorial.html					
Illinois Korean War Memorial 1441 Monument Ave	Springfield	IL	62702	217-782-2717	
Web: www.state.il.us/agency/dva/memorial.htm					
Illinois Vietnam Veterans Memorial Oak Ridge Cemetery	Springfield	IL	62702	217-782-2717	524-3738
Web: www.state.il.us/agency/dva/memorial.htm					
Jefferson Barracks National Cemetery 2900 Sheridan Rd	Saint Louis	MO	63125	314-260-8691	260-8723
TF: 800-535-1117					
Jefferson Memorial E Basin Dr SW	Washington	DC	20242	202-426-6841	252-0051
Web: www.nps.gov/thje					
Jefferson National Expansion Memorial 11 N 4th St	Saint Louis	MO	63102	314-655-1700	655-1641
Web: www.nps.gov/jeff/					
John Brown Statue 27th St & Sewell Ave.	Kansas City	KS	66104	913-321-5800	
John F Kennedy Memorial Ocean St.	Hyannis	MA	02601	508-362-9484	
Johnstown Flood National Memorial 733 Lake Rd	South Fork	PA	15956	814-495-4643	495-7463
Web: www.nps.gov/jofl/					
Korean-Vietnam War Memorial 91st & Leavenworth Rd	Kansas City	KS	66109	913-596-7077	
Korean War Veterans Memorial					
c/o National Capital Parks - Central 900 Ohio Dr SW	Washington	DC	20004	202-426-6841	
Web: www.nps.gov/kowa/					
Lewis & Clark Monument Frontier Park	Saint Charles	MO	63303	800-366-2427	949-3217*
**Fax Area Code:* 636					
Liberty Bell Center 6th & Market Sts	Philadelphia	PA	19106	215-965-2305	861-4950
Web: www.nps.gov/inde					
Lincoln Boyhood National Memorial					
2916 E. South St PO Box 1816	Lincoln City	IN	47552	812-937-4541	937-9929
Web: www.nps.gov/libo/					
Lincoln Memorial					
c/o National Capitol Parks - Central 900 Ohio Dr SW	Washington	DC	20024	202-426-6841	724-0764
Web: www.nps.gov/linc/					
Lincoln Memorial Shrine 125 W Vine St	Redlands	CA	92373	909-798-7632	798-7566
Web: www.lincolnshrine.org					
Lincoln Tomb Oak Ridge Cemetery 1500 Monument Ave.	Springfield	IL	62702	217-782-2717	524-3738
Web: www.illinoishistory.gov/hs/lincoln_tomb.htm					
Lyndon Baines Johnson Memorial Grove on the Potomac					
Turkey Run Park George Washington Memorial Pkwy	McLean	VA	22101	703-289-2500	289-2598
Web: www.nps.gov/lyba/					
Martin Luther King Jr Memorial at Battle Garden					
800 S Stadium Blvd	Columbia	MO	65203	573-874-7460	874-7640
Mason-Dixon Historical Park 61 Buckeye Rd	Core	WV	26529	304-879-4101	
Web: www.vicoa.com/mason-dixon					
Minnesota Vietnam Veterans' Memorial					
State Capitol Grounds	Saint Paul	MN	55082	651-777-0686	
Web: www.mvvm.org					
Missouri Veterans Memorial Capitol Bldg Rm B-2	Jefferson City	MO	65101	573-751-3779	751-6836
Mormon Battalion Visitors Center 2510 Juan St.	San Diego	CA	92110	619-298-3317	298-5866
Mormon Trail Center at Historic Winter Quarter 3215 State St	Omaha	NE	68112	402-453-9372	453-1538
National War Memorial & Tomb of the Unknown Soldier					
Elgin & Wellington Sts Confederation Sq	Ottawa	ON	K1P5A1	613-992-7468	
Web: www.vac-acc.gc.ca/remembers					
New Haven Crypt 250 Temple St	New Haven	CT	06511	203-787-0121	787-2187
Web: www.newhavencenterchurch.org/crypt.html					
New Mexico Veterans Memorial 1100 Louisiana Blvd SE	Albuquerque	NM	87108	505-256-2042	294-6617
Perry's Victory & International Peace Memorial					
93 Delaware Ave PO Box 549	Put-in-Bay	OH	43456	419-285-2184	285-2516
Web: www.nps.gov/pevi/					
Philadelphia Vietnam Veterans Memorial					
Columbus Blvd & Spruce St	Philadelphia	PA	19104	215-535-0643	
Pilgrim Monument & Provincetown Museum					
1 High Pole Hill Rd	Provincetown	MA	02657	508-487-1310	487-4702
Web: pilgrim-monument.org					
Roger Williams National Memorial 282 N Main St	Providence	RI	02903	401-521-7266	521-7239
Web: www.nps.gov/rowi/					
Rosedale Memorial Arch Springfield & Memorial Dr	Kansas City	KS	66103	913-596-7077	677-3437
Soldiers & Sailors Memorial Arch 88 Trinity St Bushnell Park	Hartford	CT	06106	860-232-6710	
Web: www.bushnellpark.org/poi/smarch.html					
Space Needle 400 Broad St	Seattle	WA	98109	206-905-2200	905-2107
TF Resv: 800-937-9582 ■ *Web:* spaceneedle.com					
Statue of Liberty National Monument & Ellis Island					
Liberty Island	New York	NY	10004	212-363-3200	
Web: www.nps.gov/stli/					
Texas State Cemetery 909 Navasota St	Austin	TX	78702	512-463-0605	463-8811
Web: www.cemetery.state.tx.us					
Thaddeus Kosciuszko National Memorial					
c/o Independence National Historical Park 143 S 3rd St	Philadelphia	PA	19106	215-597-9618	861-4950
Web: www.nps.gov/thko/					
Theodore Roosevelt Island Park					
c/o Turkey Run Park George Washington Memorial Pkwy	McLean	VA	22101	703-289-2500	289-2598
Web: www.nps.gov/this/					
Trenton Battle Monument					
Rt 206 & Rt 31 N Warren & N Broad St.	Trenton	NJ	08638	609-737-0623	
US Marine Corps War Memorial Iwo Jima					
Meade St & Marshall Dr	Arlington	VA	22211	703-289-2500	289-2598
Web: www.nps.gov/gwmp/usmc.htm					
US Navy Memorial & Naval Heritage Center					
701 Pennsylvania Ave NW Suite 123	Washington	DC	20004	202-737-2300	737-2308
TF: 800-821-8892 ■ *Web:* www.lonesailor.org					
USS Alabama Battleship Memorial Park 2703 Battleship Pkwy	Mobile	AL	36602	251-433-2703	433-2777
TF: 800-426-4929 ■ *Web:* www.ussalabama.com					
USS Arizona Memorial 1 Arizona Memorial Pl	Honolulu	HI	96818	808-422-0561	483-8608
Web: www.nps.gov/usar/					
USS Indianapolis Memorial Walnut & Senate Ave	Indianapolis	IN	46204	317-232-7615	233-4258
Web: www.ussindianapolis.org/memorial.htm					
USS Kidd Veterans Memorial & Museum 305 S River Rd	Baton Rouge	LA	70802	225-342-1942	342-2039
Web: www.usskidd.com					
USS Missouri Memorial 63 Cowpens St	Honolulu	HI	96818	808-423-2263	455-1598
TF: 888-877-6477 ■ *Web:* www.ussmissouri.com					
USS Potomac 540 Water St Jack London Sq	Oakland	CA	94607	510-627-1215	839-4729
Web: www.usspotomac.org					
USS South Dakota Battleship Memorial					
12th St & Kiwanis Ave Sherman Park	Sioux Falls	SD	57104	605-367-7060	367-4326
Vietnam Veterans' Memorial					
Arkansas State Capitol Woodlane & Capitol Ave	Little Rock	AR	72201	501-682-5080	
Vietnam Veterans Memorial					
c/o National Capitol Park - Central 900 Ohio Drive SW	Washington	DC	20024	202-426-6841	426-1844
Web: www.thewall-usa.com					
Vietnam Veterans Memorial 43rd & Broadway	Kansas City	MO	64111	816-561-8387	
Vietnam Women's Memorial 5 Constitution Ave SW	Washington	DC	20004	202-426-6841	724-0764
Web: www.nps.gov/vive/memorial/women.htm					
Washington Monument					
c/o National Capitol Park - Central 900 Ohio Dr SW	Washington	DC	20024	202-426-6841	
Web: www.nps.gov/wamo/					
Women in Military Service for America Memorial					
Memorial Dr Arlington National Cemetery	Arlington	VA	22211	703-533-1155	892-7202
TF: 800-222-2294 ■ *Web:* www.womensmemorial.org					
Women's Memorial Memorial Dr Arlington National Cemetery	Arlington	VA	22211	703-533-1155	892-7202
TF: 800-222-2294 ■ *Web:* www.womensmemorial.org					
Wright Brothers National Memorial 1401 National Park Dr	Manteo	NC	27954	252-473-2111	473-2595
Web: www.nps.gov/wrbr/					

50-5 Nature Centers, Parks, Other Natural Areas

				Phone	Fax
Anita Purves Nature Center 1505 N Broadway	Urbana	IL	61801	217-384-4062	384-1052
Web: www.urbanaparks.org					
Anne Kolb Nature Center 751 Sheridan St	Hollywood	FL	33019	954-926-2410	926-2491
Web: www.broward.org/parks					
Ansonia Nature & Recreation Center 10 Deerfield Rd	Ansonia	CT	06401	203-736-1053	734-1672
Web: ansonianaturecenter.org					
Aurora Reservoir 5800 S Powhaton Rd	Aurora	CO	80016	303-690-1286	690-1654
Balboa Park 1549 El Prado Suite 1	San Diego	CA	92101	619-239-0512	525-2254
Web: www.balboapark.org					
Bear Creek Nature Center 245 Bear Creek Rd	Colorado Springs	CO	80906	719-520-6387	636-8968
Web: adm.elpasoco.com/Parks					
Beaver Lake Nature Center 8477 E Mud Lake Rd	Baldwinsville	NY	13027	315-638-2519	638-7488
Web: onondagacountyparks.com					
Biscayne Nature Center 6767 Crandon Blvd	Key Biscayne	FL	33149	305-361-6767	365-8434
Web: www.biscaynenaturecenter.org					
Black Hills Caverns 2600 Cavern Rd	Rapid City	SD	57702	605-343-0542	
TF: 800-837-9358 ■ *Web:* www.blackhillscaverns.com					
Blandford Nature Center 1715 Hillburn Ave NW	Grand Rapids	MI	49504	616-735-6240	735-6255
Web: www.mixedgreens.org					
Bluebonnet Swamp Nature Center					
10503 N Oak Hills Pkwy	Baton Rouge	LA	70810	225-757-8905	757-9390
Boulder Reservoir 5100 N 51st St	Boulder	CO	80301	303-441-3461	441-1807
Web: www.bouldercolorado.gov					
Box Springs Mountain Park					
9699 Box Springs Mountain Rd	Moreno Valley	CA	92557	951-955-4310	955-4305
Web: www.riversidecountyparks.org					
Boyd Hill Nature Park 1101 Country Club Way S	Saint Petersburg	FL	33705	727-893-7326	893-7720
Boyden Caverns 74101 E Kings Canyon Rd	Kings Canyon Natl Park	CA	93633	209-736-2708	736-0330
Web: www.caverntours.com					
Butterfly House 15193 Olive Blvd	Chesterfield	MO	63017	636-530-0076	530-1516
Web: www.butterflyhouse.org					
Butterfly House 11455 Obee Rd	Whitehouse	OH	43571	419-877-2733	
Web: www.butterfly-house.com					
Butterfly World 3600 W Sample Rd Tradewinds Park S	Coconut Creek	FL	33073	964-977-4400	977-4501
Web: www.butterflyworld.com					
Camelback Mountain & Echo Canyon Recreation Area					
5950 N Echo Canyon Pkwy	Phoenix	AZ	85018	602-261-8318	495-5561
Capen Hill Nature Sanctuary 56 Capen Rd PO Box 218	Charlton City	MA	01508	508-248-5516	248-5516
Web: www.capenhill.org					
Carson Hot Springs 1500 Hot Springs Rd	Carson City	NV	89706	775-885-8844	887-0617
TF: 888-917-3711 ■ *Web:* www.carsonhotspringsresort.com					
Cascade Caverns Park 226 Cascade Caverns Rd	Boerne	TX	78006	830-755-8080	755-2400
Web: www.cascadecaverns.com					
Cave of the Mounds					
2975 Cave of the Mounds Rd PO Box 148	Blue Mounds	WI	53517	608-437-3038	437-4181
Web: www.caveofthemounds.com					
Cave of the Winds W Hwy 24 PO Box 826	Manitou Springs	CO	80829	719-685-5444	685-1712
Web: www.caveofthewinds.com					
Centennial Olympic Park 265 Park Ave W NW	Atlanta	GA	30313	404-222-7275	223-4499
Web: www.centennialpark.com					
Central Park 830 5th Ave	New York	NY	10065	212-360-8111	830-7860
Web: www.centralparknyc.org					
Chattahoochee Nature Center 9135 Willeo Rd	Roswell	GA	30075	770-992-2055	552-0926
Web: www.chattnaturecenter.com					
Cherry Springs Nature Area					
Caribou-Targhee National Forest 4350 Cliffs Dr	Pocatello	ID	83204	208-236-7500	236-7555
Connecticut Audubon Society Nature Center 2325 Burr St	Fairfield	CT	06824	203-259-6305	254-7365
Web: www.ctaudubon.org					
Cypress Gardens 3030 Cypress Gardens Rd	Moncks Corner	SC	29461	843-553-0515	569-0644
Web: www.cypressgardens.info					
Darien Nature Center Inc 120 Brookside Rd PO Box 1603	Darien	CT	06820	203-655-7459	655-3185
Web: dnc.darien.org/					
DeGraaf Nature Center 600 Graafschap Rd	Holland	MI	49423	616-355-1057	355-1069
Devil's Den Preserve 33 Pent Rd	Weston	CT	06883	203-226-4991	226-4807
Dodge Nature Center 365 W Marie Ave	West Saint Paul	MN	55118	651-455-4531	455-2575
Web: www.dodgenaturecenter.org					
Domaine Maizerets 2000 Montmorency Blvd	Quebec	QC	G1J5E7	418-641-6117	660-6295
Eagle River Nature Center 32750 Eagle River Rd	Eagle River	AK	99577	907-694-2108	694-2119
Web: www.ernc.org					
Earthplace 10 Woodside Ln PO Box 165	Westport	CT	06881	203-227-7253	227-8909
Web: www.earthplace.org					
El Dorado East Regional Park & Nature Center					
7550 E Spring St	Long Beach	CA	90815	562-570-1745	570-8530
Everglades Holiday Park 21940 Griffin Rd	Southwest Ranches	FL	33332	954-434-8111	434-4252
TF: 800-226-2244 ■ *Web:* www.evergladesholidaypark.com					
Falls Park on the Reedy S Main St & Camperdown Way	Greenville	SC	29601	864-467-4350	467-4185
Web: www.fallspark.com					
Fern Forest Nature Center 201 Lyons Rd S	Coconut Creek	FL	33063	954-970-0150	970-0111
Web: www.broward.org/parks/					
Forest Park Nature Center 5809 Forest Park Dr	Peoria Heights	IL	61616	309-686-3360	686-8820
Fort DeSoto Park 3500 Pinellas Bayway S	Tierra Verde	FL	33715	727-582-2267	866-2485
Web: fortdesoto.com					
Fuller State Park 1500 Mitchell Rd	Memphis	TN	38109	901-543-7581	785-8485
Web: www.tennessee.gov/environment/parks/TOFuller/					
Golden Gate Park 501 Stanyan St	San Francisco	CA	94117	415-831-2700	831-2096
Web: www.nps.gov/goga/					
Great Plains Nature Center 6232 E 29th St North	Wichita	KS	67220	316-683-5499	688-9555
Web: www.gpnc.org					
Green Mountain Audubon Center 255 Sherman Hollow Rd	Huntington	VT	05462	802-434-3068	434-4686
Web: www.vt.audubon.org					
Gulf Branch Nature Center 3608 N Military Rd	Arlington	VA	22207	703-228-3403	228-4401
Gumbo Limbo Nature Center 1801 N Ocean Blvd	Boca Raton	FL	33432	561-338-1473	338-1483
Web: www.gumbolimbo.org					
Hanauma Bay Nature Preserve 100 Hanauma Bay Rd	Honolulu	HI	96825	808-396-4229	395-0468
Web: www.co.honolulu.hi.us/parks/facility/hanaumabay					
Harlem Hills Nature Preserve Nimtz Rd & Flora Dr	Loves Park	IL	61111	815-964-6666	964-6661

Name / Address	City	State	ZIP	Phone	Fax
Hemlock Bluffs Nature Preserve 2616 Kildaire Farm Rd	Cary	NC	27518	919-387-5980	
Heritage Square 65 E Central Blvd	Orlando	FL	32801	407-836-8500	836-8550
Houston Arboretum & Nature Center 4501 Woodway Dr	Houston	TX	77024	713-681-8433	681-1191
TF: 866-510-7219 ■ *Web:* www.houstonarboretum.org					
Ijams Nature Center 2915 Island Home Ave	Knoxville	TN	37920	865-577-4717	577-1683
Web: www.ijams.org					
Indian Creek Nature Center 6665 Otis Rd SE	Cedar Rapids	IA	52403	319-362-0664	362-2876
Web: www.indiancreeknaturecenter.org					
Jefferson Barracks County Park 345 North Rd	Saint Louis	MO	63125	314-544-5714	638-5009
Web: www.stlouisco.com/parks/j-b.html					
Katharine Ordway Preserve 165 Goodhill Rd	Weston	CT	06883	203-226-4991	226-4807
Web: www.nature.org					
Lava Hot Springs 430 E Main St PO Box 669	Lava Hot Springs	ID	83246	208-776-5221	776-5273
TF: 800-423-8597 ■ *Web:* www.lavahotsprings.com					
Lewis & Clark National Historic Trail c/o National Park Service 601 Riverfront Dr	Omaha	NE	68102	402-661-1804	661-1805
TF: 888-237-3252 ■ *Web:* www.nps.gov/lecl					
Lewis & Clark National Historic Trail Interpretive Center 4201 Giant Springs Rd	Great Falls	MT	59405	406-727-8733	453-6157
Web: www.fs.fed.us/r1/lewisclark/lcic					
Lincoln Memorial Garden & Nature Center 2301 E Lake Shore Dr	Springfield	IL	62712	217-529-1111	529-0134
Web: www.lmgnc.org					
Linville Caverns US 221 N	Marion	NC	28752	828-756-4171	756-4171
TF: 800-419-0540 ■ *Web:* www.linvillecaverns.com					
Long Branch Nature Center 625 S Carlin Springs Rd	Arlington	VA	22204	703-228-6535	845-2654
Long Wharf Nature Preserve Long Wharf Dr	New Haven	CT	06511	203-946-5713	
Lost River Caverns 726 Durham St PO Box M	Hellertown	PA	18055	610-838-8767	838-2961
Web: www.lostcave.com					
Martin Park Nature Center 5000 W Memorial Rd	Oklahoma City	OK	73142	405-755-0676	749-3072
Web: www.okc.gov/parks/martin_park					
McKelligon Canyon 3 McKelligon Canyon Rd	El Paso	TX	79930	915-534-0609	
Minnehaha Falls 4825 Minnehaha Ave S	Minneapolis	MN	55417	612-230-6400	230-6513
Mississippi Petrified Forest 124 Forest Park Rd	Flora	MS	39071	601-879-8189	879-3282
Web: www.mspetrifiedforest.com					
Morikami Museum & Japanese Gardens 4000 Morikami Park Rd	Delray Beach	FL	33446	561-495-0233	499-2557
Web: www.morikami.org					
Morrison-Knudsen Nature Center 600 S Walnut St	Boise	ID	83706	208-334-2225	287-2905
Mount Airy Forest & Arboretum 5083 Colerain Ave	Cincinnati	OH	45223	513-352-4080	352-4096
Web: www.cinci-parks.org/parks					
Mount Saint Helens National Volcanic Monument 42218 NE Yale Bridge Rd	Amboy	WA	98601	360-449-7800	449-7801
Web: www.fs.fed.us/gpnf/mshnvm					
Natural Bridge Caverns 26495 Natural Bridge Caverns Rd	Natural Bridge Caverns	TX	78266	210-651-6101	651-6144
Web: www.naturalbridgecaverns.com					
New Canaan Nature Center 144 Oenoke Ridge	New Canaan	CT	06840	203-966-9577	966-6536
Web: www.newcanaannature.org					
Niagara Falls Prospect Park	Niagara Falls	NY	14303	716-278-1796	278-1744
Web: www.nysparks.state.ny.us					
Nisqually Reach Nature Center 4949 D'Milluhr Rd NE	Olympia	WA	98412	360-459-0387	
Web: www.nisquallyestuary.org					
Oahe Dam & Reservoir 6 miles N on Hwy 1804	Pierre	SD	57501	605-224-5862	224-5945
Ogden Nature Center 966 W 12th St	Ogden	UT	84404	801-621-7595	621-1867
Web: www.ogdennaturecenter.org					
Olentangy Indian Caverns 1779 Home Rd	Delaware	OH	43015	740-548-7917	548-4572
Web: www.olentangyindiancaverns.com					
Oxbow Meadows Environmental Learning Center 3535 S Lumpkin St	Columbus	GA	31907	706-687-4090	687-3020
Web: oxbow.colstate.edu					
Parkersville Landing Historical Park 24 S 'A' St	Washougal	WA	98671	360-834-4792	835-2197
Pike National Forest 601 S Weber St	Colorado Springs	CO	80903	719-636-1602	477-4233
Web: www.fs.fed.us/r2/psicc					
Pine Jog Environmental Education Center 6301 Summit Blvd	West Palm Beach	FL	33415	561-686-6600	687-4968
Web: www.pinejog.org					
Plains Conservation Center 21901 E Hampden Ave	Aurora	CO	80013	303-693-3621	693-3379
Web: www.plainsconservationcenter.org					
Powder Valley Conservation Nature Center 11715 Cragwold Rd	Saint Louis	MO	63122	314-301-1500	301-1501
Web: mdc.mo.gov/areas/cnc/powder/					
Prairie Wetlands Learning Center 602 State Hwy 210 E	Fergus Falls	MN	56537	218-736-0938	736-0941
Web: midwest.fws.gov/pwlc					
Provo Canyon N Hwy 189	Provo	UT	84606	801-851-2100	851-2109
Pruyn Sanctuary Butterfly & Hummingbird Garden 275 Millwood Rd	Chappaqua	NY	10514	914-666-6503	666-7430
Web: www.sawmillriveraudubon.org/Pruyn.html					
Quarry Hill Nature Center 701 NE Silver Creek Rd	Rochester	MN	55906	507-281-6114	287-1345
Web: www.qhnc.org					
Raccoon Mountain Caverns 319 W Hills Dr	Chattanooga	TN	37419	423-821-9403	825-1289
TF: 800-823-2267 ■ *Web:* www.raccoonmountain.com					
Randall Davey Audubon Center 1800 Upper Canyon Rd	Santa Fe	NM	87501	505-983-4609	983-2355
Web: www.audubon.org/chapter/nm/nm/rdac/					
Red Rock Canyon National Conservation Area HCR 33 Box 5500	Las Vegas	NV	89124	702-515-5350	363-6779
Web: www.nv.blm.gov/redrockcanyon					
Riveredge Nature Center 4458 W Hawthorne Dr PO Box 26	Newburg	WI	53060	262-375-2715	375-2714
TF: 800-287-8098 ■ *Web:* www.riveredgenaturecenter.org					
Rock City Gardens 1400 Patten Rd	Lookout Mountain	GA	30750	706-820-2531	820-2533
TF: 800-854-0675 ■ *Web:* www.seerockcity.com					
Ruby Falls 1720 S Scenic Hwy	Chattanooga	TN	37409	423-821-2544	825-1958
TF: 800-755-7105 ■ *Web:* www.rubyfalls.com					
Runge Conservation Nature Center PO Box 180	Jefferson City	MO	65101	573-526-5544	526-4496
Web: mdc.mo.gov/areas/cnc/runge					
Rushmore Cave 13622 Hwy 40	Keystone	SD	57751	605-255-4384	
Web: www.beautifulrushmorecave.com					
Sabino Canyon 5700 N Sabino Canyon Rd	Tucson	AZ	85750	520-749-8700	749-7723
Web: www.fs.fed.us/r3/coronado					
Saint Marks Historic Railroad State Trail W of 363 S of 319 (Capital Circle)	Tallahassee	FL	32301	850-245-2052	245-2083
TF: 877-822-5208					
Schilling Wildlife Management Area 17614 Schilling Refuge Rd	Plattsmouth	NE	68048	402-296-0041	
Web: www.ngpc.state.ne.us/wildlife/places/schilling.asp					
Schlitz Audubon Nature Center 1111 E Brown Deer Rd	Bayside	WI	53217	414-352-2880	352-6091
Web: www.schlitzauduboncenter.com					
Sea Lion Caves 91560 Hwy 101	Florence	OR	97439	541-547-3111	547-3545
Web: www.sealioncaves.com					
Secret Woods Nature Center 2701 W State Rd 84	Dania Beach	FL	33312	954-791-1030	791-1092
Web: www.broward.org/parks/					
Seven Falls 2850 S Cheyenne Canyon Rd	Colorado Springs	CO	80906	719-632-0765	632-0781
Web: www.sevenfalls.com					
Severson Dells Nature Center 8786 Montague Rd	Rockford	IL	61102	815-335-2915	335-2471
Web: www.seversondells.org					
Sitting Bull Crystal Caverns 13745 S Hwy 16	Rapid City	SD	57701	605-342-2777	
Web: www.sittingbullcrystalcaverns.com					
Snake River Birds of Prey National Conservation Area Swan Falls Rd	Kuna	ID	83634	208-384-3300	384-3326
Web: www.birdsofprey.blm.gov					
Springfield Conservation Nature Center 4600 S Chrisman Ave	Springfield	MO	65804	417-888-4237	888-4241
Web: mdc.mo.gov/areas/cnc/springfd/					
Stepping Stone Falls 5161 Branch Rd	Flint	MI	48506	810-736-7100	736-7275
TF: 800-648-4242 ■ *Web:* www.geneseecountyparks.org/stepping_stone.htm					
Stone Mountain Park Hwy 78 E	Stone Mountain	GA	30086	770-498-5690	498-5735
TF: 800-317-2006 ■ *Web:* www.stonemountainpark.org					
Tacoma Nature Center 1919 S Tyler St	Tacoma	WA	98405	253-591-6439	593-4152
Thunderhead Falls 10940 W Hwy 44	Rapid City	SD	57702	605-343-0081	
Web: www.blackhillsbadlands.com/thfalls					
Tree Hill Nature Center 7152 Lone Star Rd	Jacksonville	FL	32211	904-724-4646	724-9132
Web: www.treehill.org					
Vickers Nature Preserve Rt 224	Ellsworth Township	OH	44416	330-702-3000	702-3010
Web: www.millcreekmetroparks.com/vickers.htm					
Vista House 40700 E Historic Columbia River Hwy	Corbett	OR	97019	503-695-2230	695-2250
Web: www.vistahouse.com					
Weedon Island Preserve Cultural & Natural History Center 1800 Weedon Dr NE	Saint Petersburg	FL	33702	727-453-6500	
Web: www.weedonislandcenter.org					
Wehr Nature Center 9701 W College Ave	Franklin	WI	53132	414-425-8550	425-6992
Web: www.countyparks.com/horticulture/wehr/					
Western North Carolina Nature Center 75 Gashes Creek Rd	Asheville	NC	28805	828-298-5600	298-2644
Web: wildwnc.org					
Westwood Hills Nature Center 8300 W Franklin Ave	Saint Louis Park	MN	55426	952-924-2544	797-9691
Woldumar Nature Center 5739 Old Lansing Rd	Lansing	MI	48917	517-322-0030	322-9394
Web: www.woldumar.org					
Woodcock Nature Center 56 Deer Run Rd	Wilton	CT	06897	203-762-7280	834-0062
Web: www.woodcocknaturecenter.org					
World Bird Sanctuary 125 Bald Eagle Ridge Rd	Valley Park	MO	63088	636-861-3225	861-3240
Web: www.worldbirdsanctuary.org					

50-6 Shopping/Dining/Entertainment Districts

Name / Address	City	State	ZIP	Phone	Fax
Aloha Tower Marketplace 1 Aloha Tower Dr	Honolulu	HI	96813	808-528-5700	524-8334
Web: www.alohatower.com					
Bannister's Wharf 1 Bannister's Wharf	Newport	RI	02840	401-846-4500	849-8750
Web: www.bannisterswharf.net					
Barefoot Landing 4898 Hwy 17 S	North Myrtle Beach	SC	29582	843-272-8349	272-1052
TF: 800-272-2320 ■ *Web:* www.bflanding.com					
Bayside Marketplace 401 Biscayne Blvd	Miami	FL	33132	305-577-3344	577-0306
Web: www.baysidemarketplace.com					
Bazaar del Mundo 4133 Taylor St	San Diego	CA	92110	619-296-3161	296-3113
Web: www.bazaardelmundo.com					
Beale Street Historic District Downtown Memphis	Memphis	TN	38103	901-526-0110	526-0125
Web: www.bealestreet.com					
Belmar 355 S Teller St	Lakewood	CO	80226	303-742-1500	742-1502
Web: www.belmarcolorado.com					
BOB The (Big Old Building) 20 Monroe Ave NW	Grand Rapids	MI	49503	616-356-2000	493-2011
Web: www.thebob.com					
Bricktown N of Reno Ave & W of Stiles Rd	Oklahoma City	OK	73104	405-236-8666	602-3800
Web: www.bricktownokc.com					
Brightleaf Square Gregson & Main Sts	Durham	NC	27701	919-682-9229	
Broadway at the Beach 1325 Celebrity Cir	Myrtle Beach	SC	29577	843-444-3200	444-3222
TF: 800-444-3200 ■ *Web:* www.broadwayatthebeach.com					
Cannery at Del Monte Square 2801 Leavenworth St	San Francisco	CA	94133	415-771-3112	771-2424
Web: www.delmontesquare.com					
Cannery Row 765 Wave St	Monterey	CA	93940	831-649-6690	373-4812
Web: www.canneryrow.com					
Captain's Cove Seaport 1 Bostwick Ave	Bridgeport	CT	06605	203-335-1433	335-6793
Web: www.captainscoveseaport.com					
Center in the Square 1 Market Sq SE	Roanoke	VA	24011	540-342-5700	224-1238
Web: www.centerinthesquare.org					
Centro Ybor 1600 E 8th Ave	Tampa	FL	33605	813-242-4660	242-4664
Web: www.centroybor.com					
Channelside 615 Channelside Dr	Tampa	FL	33602	813-223-4250	221-2161
Web: www.channelsidetampa.com					
Citigroup Center 53rd St & Lexington Ave	New York	NY	10022	212-751-1007	751-1012
City Market 219 W Bryan St	Savannah	GA	31401	912-232-4903	232-2142
Web: www.savannahcitymarket.com					
CityPlace 700 S Rosemary Ave	West Palm Beach	FL	33401	561-366-1000	366-1001
Web: www.cityplace.com					
CocoWalk 3015 Grand Ave	Coconut Grove	FL	33133	305-444-0777	441-8936
Web: www.galleryatcocowalk.com					
Cooper-Young Historic District Cooper & Young Sts	Memphis	TN	38104	901-276-7222	
Web: www.cooperyoung.com					
Country Club Plaza 4745 Central St	Kansas City	MO	64112	816-753-0100	753-4625
Web: www.countryclubplaza.com					
Crocker Park 25 Main St	Westlake	OH	44145	440-871-6880	835-9024
Web: www.crockerpark.com					
Deep Ellum 2630 Commerce St	Dallas	TX	75226	214-748-4332	
Web: www.deepellumtx.com					
Desert Passage at Aladdin 3663 Las Vegas Blvd S	Las Vegas	NV	89109	702-866-0710	866-0717
TF: 888-800-8284 ■ *Web:* www.desertpassage.com					
Desert Ridge Marketplace 21001 N Tatum Blvd	Phoenix	AZ	85050	480-513-7586	563-1829
Web: www.shopdesertridge.com					
District The 11 S 10th St	Columbia	MO	65201	573-442-6816	499-0421
Web: www.discovertheddistrict.com					
Dole Cannery Square 650 Iwilei Rd Suite 540	Honolulu	HI	96817	808-548-4811	548-6668
Web: www.dole-cannery.com					
Downtown Disney S Disneyland Dr	Anaheim	CA	92802	714-781-4565	
Web: disneyland.disney.go.com					
Downtown Disney 1449 E Buena Vista Dr	Lake Buena Vista	FL	32830	407-828-1076	
Web: disney.go.com					
Downtown at the Gardens 3501 PGA Blvd	Palm Beach Gardens	FL	33410	561-282-5000	282-5001
Web: www.downtownatthegardens.com					
East Town 770 N Jefferson St	Milwaukee	WI	53202	414-271-1416	271-6401
Web: www.easttown.com					
Faneuil Hall Marketplace 4 S Market Bldg 5th Fl	Boston	MA	02109	617-523-1300	523-1779
Web: www.faneuilhallmarketplace.com					
Fifth Street Public Market 296 E 5th Ave	Eugene	OR	97401	541-484-0383	686-1220
Findlay Market Race & Elder Sts	Cincinnati	OH	45210	513-665-4839	665-4840
Web: www.findlaymarket.org					
Flatiron Crossing 1 W Flatiron Cir	Broomfield	CO	80021	720-887-9900	887-0707
Web: www.flatironcrossing.com					
Flats The 1283 Riverbed St	Cleveland	OH	44113	216-566-1046	566-0222
Web: www.clevelandflats.org					
Fort Worth Stockyards National Historic District N Main & Exchange Sts	Fort Worth	TX	76106	817-624-4741	624-4793
Web: www.fortworthstockyards.org					
Fourth Avenue 4th Ave-between University Blvd & 9th St	Tucson	AZ	85705	520-624-5004	624-5933
TF: 800-933-2477 ■ *Web:* www.fourthavenue.org					

Shopping/Dining/Entertainment Districts (Cont'd)

Name / Address	City	State	ZIP	Phone	Fax
Gaslamp Quarter 5th Ave & Market St *Web:* www.gaslamp.org	San Diego	CA	92101	619-233-5227	233-4693
Gateway The 90 S 400 West *Web:* www.boyercompany.com/gateway	Salt Lake City	UT	84101	801-456-0000	456-0005
Ghirardelli Square 900 N Point St Suite 100 *Web:* www.ghirardellisq.com	San Francisco	CA	94109	415-775-5500	775-0912
Great Lakes Crossing 4000 Baldwin Rd *Web:* www.shopgreatlakescrossing.com	Auburn Hills	MI	48326	248-454-5000	745-8719
Harborplace & The Gallery 200 E Pratt St *TF:* 800-427-2671 ■ *Web:* www.harborplace.com	Baltimore	MD	21202	410-332-4191	547-7317
Hillcrest Historic District Kavanaugh & Beechwood Sts	Little Rock	AR	72205	501-371-0075	
Hollywood & Highland 6801 Hollywood Blvd *Web:* www.hollywoodandhighland.com	Hollywood	CA	90028	323-817-0220	460-6003
Hyde Park Village 742 S Village Cir *Web:* www.hydeparkvillage.net	Tampa	FL	33606	813-251-3500	251-4158
International Plaza & Bay Street 2223 N West Shore Blvd *Web:* www.shopinternationalplaza.com	Tampa	FL	33607	813-342-3790	342-3788
Jacksonville Landing 2 Independent Dr *Web:* www.jacksonvillelanding.com	Jacksonville	FL	32202	904-353-1188	353-1558
John's Pass Village & Boardwalk 150 John's Pass Boardwalk Pl *TF:* 800-755-0677 ■ *Web:* www.johnspass.com	Madeira Beach	FL	33708	727-398-6577	398-2416
Jordan Commons 9400 S State St *Web:* www.jordancommons.com	Sandy	UT	84070	801-304-4577	304-4515
Laclede's Landing 710 N 2nd St *Web:* www.lacledeslanding.org	Saint Louis	MO	63102	314-241-5875	241-2313
Larimer Square 1430 Larimer St Suite 200 *Web:* www.larimersquare.com	Denver	CO	80202	303-534-2367	623-1041
Las Olas Riverfront 300 SW 1st Ave *Web:* www.riverfrontfl.com	Fort Lauderdale	FL	33301	954-522-6556	522-1899
Main Gate Square University Blvd-between Park & Euclid *Web:* www.maingatesquare.com	Tucson	AZ	85719	520-622-8613	622-0124
Market Street at Celebration 610 Sycamore St Suite 310 *Web:* www.celebrationfl.com/market_street/home.html	Orlando	FL	34747	407-566-2200	566-4705
Mellwood Arts & Entertainment Center 1860 Mellwood Ave *Web:* www.mellwoodartcenter.com	Louisville	KY	40206	502-895-3650	895-3680
Metreon 101 4th St *Web:* westfield.com/metreon/	San Francisco	CA	94103	415-369-6000	369-6025
New Roc City 33 LeCount Pl *Web:* www.newroccity.com	New Rochelle	NY	10801	914-637-7575	637-1048
Newport on the Levee 1 Levee Way Suite 1113 *TF:* 866-538-3359 ■ *Web:* www.newportonthelevee.com	Newport	KY	41071	859-291-0550	291-7020
Ocean Walk Shoppes at the Village 250 N Atlantic Ave *Web:* www.oceanwalkshoppes.com	Daytona Beach	FL	32118	877-845-9255	
Old Sacramento Historic District 1111 2nd St Suite 300 *Web:* www.oldsacramento.com	Sacramento	CA	95814	916-264-7031	264-7286
Old Town San Felipe & Old Town Rd *Web:* www.oldtownalbuquerque.com	Albuquerque	NM	87104	505-243-3215	
Peabody Place 150 Peabody Pl *Web:* www.belz.com/peabody	Memphis	TN	38103	901-261-7529	259-5570
Penn's Landing 121 N Columbus Blvd *Web:* www.pennslandingcorp.com	Philadelphia	PA	19106	215-923-8181	923-2801
Pier 39 Beach & Embarcadero Sts *Web:* www.pier39.com	San Francisco	CA	94133	415-981-7437	
Pier The 800 2nd Ave NE *Web:* www.stpete-pier.com	Saint Petersburg	FL	33701	727-821-6164	821-6451
Pike Place Market 1st Ave & Pike St *Web:* www.pikeplacemarket.org	Seattle	WA	98101	206-682-7453	625-0646
Pike at Rainbow Harbor 95 S Pine Ave *Web:* www.shopthepike.com	Long Beach	CA	90802	562-432-8325	432-8374
Pioneer Square 202 Yesler Way *Web:* www.pioneersquare.org	Seattle	WA	98104	206-667-0687	667-9739
Pointe Orlando 9101 International Dr Suite 1040 *Web:* www.pointeorlandofl.com	Orlando	FL	32819	407-248-2838	248-0078
Ports O'Call Village Berth 77	San Pedro	CA	90731	310-732-7696	
Power Plant Live! 34 Market St *TF:* 800-733-5444 ■ *Web:* www.powerplantlive.com	Baltimore	MD	21202	410-752-5444	659-9491
Quincy Market between Chatham & Clinton Sts	Boston	MA	02109	617-523-1300	
Red River District Downtown Shreveport Riverfront	Shreveport	LA	71101	318-220-0711	424-2382
Renaissance Center Detroit River *Web:* marriott.com/property/propertypage/DTWDT	Detroit	MI	48243	313-568-5600	568-5606
River Walk *Web:* thesanantonioriverwalk.com	San Antonio	TX	78204	210-227-4262	212-7602
Rivertown 405 Williams Blvd *Web:* www.rivertownkenner.com	Kenner	LA	70062	504-468-7231	471-2159
Saint Armands Circle 300 Madison Dr Suite 201 *Web:* www.starmandscircleassoc.com	Sarasota	FL	34236	941-388-1554	388-2855
Sakura Square 1255 19th St	Denver	CO	80202	303-295-0305	295-0304
Santana Row 355 Santana Row *Web:* www.santanarow.com	San Jose	CA	95128	408-551-4600	551-4616
Seaport Village 849 W Harbor Dr Suite D *Web:* www.spvillage.com	San Diego	CA	92101	619-235-4014	696-0025
Shops at Columbus Circle 10 Columbus Cir Suite 310 *Web:* www.shopsatcolumbuscircle.com	New York	NY	10019	212-823-6300	823-6050
Shoreline Village 429-P Shoreline Village Dr *Web:* www.shorelinevillage.com	Long Beach	CA	90802	562-435-2668	435-6445
South Street Seaport Market Place 19 Fulton St *Web:* www.southstreetseaport.com	New York	NY	10038	212-732-8257	964-8056
SouthSide Works Sidney St-between 26th & Hot Metal Sts *TF:* 877-977-8800 ■ *Web:* www.thesouthsideworks.com	Pittsburgh	PA	15235	412-481-1750	481-1786
Station Square 100 W Station Sq Dr *TF:* 800-859-8959 ■ *Web:* www.stationsquare.com	Pittsburgh	PA	15219	412-261-2811	261-2825
Stockyards Station 130 E Exchange Ave *Web:* www.stockyardsstation.com	Fort Worth	TX	76106	817-625-9715	625-9744
Streets at Southpoint & Main Street 6910 Fayetteville Rd *Web:* www.thestreetsatsouthpoint.com	Durham	NC	27713	919-572-8800	572-8818
Sundance Square 201 Main St *Web:* www.sundancesquare.com	Fort Worth	TX	76102	817-255-5700	390-8709
Underground Atlanta 50 Upper Alabama St Suite 007 *Web:* www.underground-atlanta.com	Atlanta	GA	30303	404-523-2311	523-0507
Union Station 50 Massachusetts Ave NE *Web:* www.unionstationdc.com	Washington	DC	20002	202-289-1908	
Universal Studios CityWalk 1000 Universal Studios Plaza *Web:* themeparks.universalstudios.com	Orlando	FL	32819	407-363-8000	
Universal Studios CityWalk Hollywood Universal Center Dr *Web:* www.citywalkhollywood.com	Los Angeles	CA	91608	818-622-4455	
Walt Disney World Boardwalk 2101 N Epcot Resorts Blvd *Web:* disneyworld.disney.go.com/wdw/	Lake Buena Vista	FL	32830	407-939-5100	939-5150
Water Tower Place 835 N Michigan Ave *Web:* www.shopwatertower.com	Chicago	IL	60611	312-440-3165	440-1259
Waterside Festival Marketplace 333 Waterside Dr *Web:* www.watersidemarketplace.com	Norfolk	VA	23510	757-627-3300	627-3981
West End MarketPlace 603 Munger Ave *Web:* www.dallaswestend.org	Dallas	TX	75202	214-748-4801	748-4803
West Port Plaza I-270 & Page Blvd *Web:* www.westportstl.com	Saint Louis	MO	63146	314-576-7100	542-4095
Westport Historic District 40th St to 43rd St-between Main St & SW Trafficway *Web:* www.westporthistorical.org	Kansas City	MO	64111	816-561-1821	

50-7 Wineries

The wineries listed in this category feature wine-tasting as an attraction.

Name / Address	City	State	ZIP	Phone	Fax
A Nonini Winery 2640 N Dickenson Ave *Web:* www.noniniwinery.com	Fresno	CA	93722	559-275-1936	241-7119
Adams County Winery 251 Peach Tree Rd *Web:* www.adamscountywinery.com	Orrtanna	PA	17353	717-334-4631	334-4026
Arbor Crest Winery 4705 N Fruithill Rd *Web:* www.arborcrest.com	Spokane	WA	99217	509-927-9463	927-0574
Bogle Vineyards & Winery 37783 County Rd 144 *Web:* www.boglewinery.com	Clarksburg	CA	95612	916-744-1139	744-1187
Butler Winery 1022 N College Ave *Web:* www.butlerwinery.com	Bloomington	IN	47404	812-339-7233	
Cap*Rock Winery 408 E Woodrow Rd *Web:* www.caprockwinery.com	Lubbock	TX	79423	806-863-2704	863-2712
Casa Rondena Winery 733 Chavez Rd NW *TF:* 800-706-1699 ■ *Web:* www.casarondena.com	Albuquerque	NM	87107	505-344-5911	343-1823
Caterina Winery 905 N Washington St *Web:* www.caterinawinery.com	Spokane	WA	99201	509-328-5069	328-9694
Chaddsford Winery 632 Baltimore Pike *Web:* www.chaddsford.com	Chadds Ford	PA	19317	610-388-6221	388-0360
Chateau Elan Winery 100 Tour de France *TF:* 800-233-9463 ■ *Web:* www.chateauelan.com	Braselton	GA	30517	678-425-0900	425-6000
Chateau Julien Wine Estate 8940 Carmel Valley Rd *TF:* 800-966-2601 ■ *Web:* www.chateaujulien.com	Carmel	CA	93923	831-624-2600	624-6138
Chateau Morrisette Winery 287 Winery Rd SW *Web:* www.chateaumorrisette.com	Floyd	VA	24091	540-593-2865	593-2868
Chateau Saint Jean 8555 Sonoma Hwy PO Box 293 *Web:* www.chateaustjean.com	Kenwood	CA	95452	707-833-4134	833-4200
Chateau Ste Michelle Winery 14111 NE 145th St *TF:* 800-267-6793 ■ *Web:* www.ste-michelle.com	Woodinville	WA	98072	425-415-3300	415-3657
Cherry Hill Winery 7867 Crowley Rd *Web:* www.cherryhillwinery.com	Rickreall	OR	97371	503-623-7867	623-7878
Columbia Winery 14030 NE 145th St PO Box 1248 *TF:* 800-488-2347 ■ *Web:* www.columbiawinery.com	Woodinville	WA	98072	425-488-2776	488-3460
Countryside Vineyards Winery 658 Henry Harr Rd	Blountville	TN	37617	423-323-1660	323-1660
Denali Winery 1301 E Dowling Rd Suite 107 *Web:* www.denaliwinery.com	Anchorage	AK	99518	907-563-9434	563-9501
Easley Winery 205 N College Ave *Web:* www.easleywine.com	Indianapolis	IN	46202	317-636-4516	974-0128
Eola Hills Wine Cellars 501 S Pacific Hwy 99 West *TF:* 800-291-6730 ■ *Web:* www.eolahillswinery.com	Rickreall	OR	97371	503-623-2405	623-0350
Forks of Cheat Winery 2811 Stewart Town Rd *TF:* 877-989-4637 ■ *Web:* www.wvwines.com	Morgantown	WV	26508	304-598-2019	598-2019
Georgia Winery 6469 Battlefield Pkwy *Web:* www.georgiawines.com	Ringgold	GA	30736	706-937-2177	937-9860
Gruet Winery 8400 Pan American Fwy NE *TF:* 888-857-9463 ■ *Web:* www.gruetwinery.com	Albuquerque	NM	87113	505-821-0055	857-0066
Honeywood Winery 1350 Hines St SE *TF:* 800-726-4101 ■ *Web:* www.honeywoodwinery.com	Salem	OR	97302	503-362-4111	362-4112
Huber's Orchard & Winery 19816 Huber Rd *TF:* 800-345-9463	Starlight	IN	47106	812-923-9463	923-3013
J Lohr Winery 1000 Lenzen Ave *Web:* www.jlohr.com	San Jose	CA	95126	408-288-5057	993-2276
James Arthur Vineyards & Winery 2001 W Raymond Rd *Web:* www.jamesarthurvineyards.com	Raymond	NE	68428	402-783-5255	783-5256
King Estate Winery 80854 Territorial Rd *TF:* 800-884-4441 ■ *Web:* www.kingestate.com	Eugene	OR	97405	541-942-9874	942-9867
La Vina Winery 4201 S Hwy 28 *Web:* www.lavinawinery.com	La Union	NM	88021	505-882-7632	882-7632
Latah Creek Winery 13030 E Indiana Ave *TF:* 800-528-2427 ■ *Web:* www.latahcreek.com	Spokane	WA	99216	509-926-0164	926-0710
LaVelle Vineyards 89697 Sheffler Rd *TF:* 800-645-8463 ■ *Web:* www.lavelle-vineyards.com	Elmira	OR	97437	541-935-9406	935-7202
Llano Estacado Winery FM 1585 3.2 miles E of US 87 S *TF:* 800-634-3854 ■ *Web:* www.llanowine.com	Lubbock	TX	79404	806-745-2258	748-1674
Lone Canary Winery 109 S Scott St Suite B2 *TF:* 866-822-6279 ■ *Web:* www.lonecanary.com	Spokane	WA	99202	509-534-9062	534-9066
Mazza Vineyards 11815 E Lake Rd Rt 5 *TF:* 800-796-9463 ■ *Web:* www.mazzawines.com	North East	PA	16428	814-725-8695	725-3948
Michael-David Vineyards 4580 W Hwy 12 *TF:* 888-707-9463 ■ *Web:* www.lodivineyards.com	Lodi	CA	95242	209-368-7384	368-5801
Mount Hope Estate & Winery 2775 Lebanon Rd	Manheim	PA	17545	717-665-7021	664-3466
Mountain Dome Winery 16315 E Temple Rd *Web:* www.mountaindome.com	Spokane	WA	99217	509-928-2788	922-8078
Nassau Valley Vineyards 32165 Winery Way *Web:* www.nassauvalley.com	Lewes	DE	19958	302-645-9463	645-6666
Oak Ridge Winery 6100 E Hwy 12 *Web:* www.oakridgewinery.com	Lodi	CA	95240	209-369-4758	369-0202
Oliver Winery 8024 N SR-37 *TF:* 800-258-2783 ■ *Web:* www.oliverwinery.com	Bloomington	IN	47404	812-876-5800	876-9309
Orfila Vineyards & Winery 13455 San Pasqual Rd *TF:* 800-868-9463 ■ *Web:* www.orfila.com	Escondido	CA	92025	760-738-6500	745-3773
Penn Shore Vineyards & Winery 10225 E Lake Rd Rt 5 *Web:* www.pennshore.com	North East	PA	16428	814-725-8688	725-8689
Redhawk Winery 2995 Michigan City Ave NW *Web:* www.redhawkwine.com	Salem	OR	97304	503-362-1596	589-9189
Saint Innocent Winery 5657 Zena Rd NW *Web:* www.stinnocentwine.com	Salem	OR	97304	503-378-1526	378-1041
Sakonnet Vineyards 162 W Main Rd *TF:* 800-919-4637 ■ *Web:* www.sakonnetwine.com	Little Compton	RI	02837	401-635-8486	635-2101
San Sebastian Winery 157 King St *TF:* 888-352-9463 ■ *Web:* www.sansebastianwinery.com	Saint Augustine	FL	32084	904-826-1594	826-1595
Silvan Ridge/Hinman Vineyards 27012 Briggs Hill Rd *TF:* 866-574-5826 ■ *Web:* www.silvanridge.com	Eugene	OR	97405	541-345-1945	345-6174
Stone Hill Winery 601 State Hwy 165 *TF:* 888-926-9463 ■ *Web:* www.stonehillwinery.com	Branson	MO	65616	417-334-1897	334-1942
Talon Winery & Vineyards 7086 Tates Creek Rd *Web:* www.talonwine.com	Lexington	KY	40515	859-971-3214	971-8787
Westbend Vineyards 5394 Williams Rd *TF:* 866-901-5032 ■ *Web:* www.westbendvineyards.com	Lewisville	NC	27023	336-945-5032	945-5294
Williamsburg Winery Ltd 5800 Wessex Hundred *Web:* www.williamsburgwinery.com	Williamsburg	VA	23185	757-229-0999	229-0911
Winery at Wolf Creek 2637 S Cleveland-Massillon Rd *TF:* 800-436-0426 ■ *Web:* www.wineryatwolfcreek.com	Norton	OH	44203	330-666-9285	665-1445

Phone Fax

Woodbridge Winery 5950 E Woodbridge Rd .... Acampo CA 95220 209-365-2839 365-8036
Web: www.woodbridgewines.com

51 AUCTIONS

Phone Fax

Abidon Inc 5301 E State St Suite 215 .... Rockford IL 61108 815-226-8700 226-8769
Ableauctions.com Inc 1963 Lougheed Hwy.......................Coquitlam BC V3K3T8 604-521-2253 520-6706
AMEX: AAC ■ *TF:* 888-599-2253 ■ *Web:* www.ableauctions.com
ADESA Inc 13085 Hamilton Crossing Blvd .... Carmel IN 46032 317-815-1100 249-4600
NYSE: KAR ■ *TF:* 800-923-3725 ■ *Web:* www.adesa.com
Auction Block 1502 S I-35 Suite 200.........................Lancaster TX 75146 972-230-0400 230-7733
TF: 866-890-0400 ■ *Web:* www.auctionblocktx.com
Auction Systems Auctioneers & Appraisers Inc
2324 E University Dr .... Phoenix AZ 85034 602-252-4842 275-8548
TF: 800-801-8880 ■ *Web:* www.auctionandappraise.com
Bates Rene Auctioneers Inc 4660 County Rd 1006 ....McKinney TX 75071 972-548-9636 542-5495
Web: www.renebates.com
Biddington's Inc 425 E 50th St.............................New York NY 10022 212-838-3572
Web: www.biddingtons.com
BidWay.com Inc 401 N Brand Blvd Suite 540 ....Glendale CA 91203 877-424-3229 287-4107*
**Fax Area Code:* 661 ■ *TF:* 877-424-3229 ■ *Web:* www.bidway.com
Bonhams & Butterfields 220 San Bruno Ave............... San Francisco CA 94103 415-861-7500 861-8951
TF: 800-223-2854 ■ *Web:* www.bonhams.com/americas
Boos Frank H Gallery 2830 W Maple Rd .... Troy MI 48084 248-643-1900
Web: www.boosgallery.com
Christie's Inc 20 Rockefeller Plaza ....New York NY 10020 212-636-2000 636-2399
Web: www.christies.com
Collectors Universe Inc PO Box 6280 .... Newport Beach CA 92658 949-567-1234 833-7955
NASDAQ: CLCT ■ *TF:* 800-325-1121 ■ *Web:* www.collectors.com
Copart Inc 4665 Business Center Dr.......................... Fairfield CA 94534 707-639-5000 639-5188
NASDAQ: CPRT ■ *Web:* www.copart.com
Dalton Auction Co Inc 1815 S Dixie Rd PO Box 1462.............. Dalton GA 30722 706-278-7441 275-9744
Davis Harry & Co 1725 Blvd of Allies .... Pittsburgh PA 15219 412-765-1170 765-0910
TF: 800-775-2289 ■ *Web:* www.harrydavis.com
DoveBid Inc 1241 E Hillsdale Blvd ....Foster City CA 94404 650-571-7400 356-6700
TF: 800-665-1042 ■ *Web:* www.dovebid.com
Doyle New York 175 E 87th St..............................New York NY 10128 212-427-2730 369-0892
TF: 800-808-0902 ■ *Web:* www.doylenewyork.com
Dumouchelle Art Galleries Co 409 E Jefferson Ave................ Detroit MI 48226 313-963-6255 963-8199
Web: www.dumouchelles.com
Earl's Auction Co 5199 Lafayette Rd........................ Indianapolis IN 46254 317-291-5843 291-5844
Web: www.earlsauction.com
eBay Inc 2145 Hamilton Ave................................. San Jose CA 95125 408-558-7400 376-7401
NASDAQ: EBAY ■ *TF:* 800-322-9266 ■ *Web:* www.ebay.com
Escala Group Inc 775 Passaic Ave .... West Caldwell NJ 07006 973-882-0004 882-3499
NASDAQ: ESCL ■ *TF:* 800-221-0243 ■ *Web:* www.escalagroup.com
Fasig-Tipton Co Inc 2400 Newtown Pike PO Box 13610..........Lexington KY 40583 859-255-1555 254-0794
Web: www.fasigtipton.com
Frank H Boos Gallery 2830 W Maple Rd .... Troy MI 48084 248-643-1900
Web: www.boosgallery.com
Freeman/Fine Arts of Philadelphia 1808 Chestnut St..........Philadelphia PA 19103 215-563-9275 563-8236
Web: www.freemansauction.com
Gallery of History Inc 3601 W Sahara Ave Suite 207 .... Las Vegas NV 89102 702-364-1000 364-1285
NASDAQ: HIST ■ *TF:* 800-425-5379 ■ *Web:* www.galleryofhistory.com
Gordon Brothers 101 Huntington Ave............................ Boston MA 02199 617-426-3233 422-6287
TF: 800-487-4882 ■ *Web:* www.gordonbrothers.com
Harry Davis & Co 1725 Blvd of Allies .... Pittsburgh PA 15219 412-765-1170 765-0910
TF: 800-775-2289 ■ *Web:* www.harrydavis.com
Henderson Auctions Co 13340 Florida Blvd PO Box 336......... Livingston LA 70754 225-686-2252 686-0647
TF: 800-850-2252 ■ *Web:* www.hendersonauctions.com
Heritage Place Inc 2829 S MacArthur ....Oklahoma City OK 73128 405-682-4551 686-1267
Web: www.heritageplace.com
icollector.com 1963 Lougheed Hwy..........................Coquitlam BC V3K3T8 604-521-3369 521-4911
TF: 866-313-0123 ■ *Web:* www.icollector.com
Insurance Auto Auctions Inc
2 Westbrook Corporate Center Suite 500 ....Westchester IL 60154 708-492-7000 492-7979
TF: 800-872-1501 ■ *Web:* www.iaai.com
Kennedy-Wilson Inc 9601 Wilshire Blvd Suite 220 ....Beverly Hills CA 90210 310-887-6400 887-6414
TF: 800-522-6664 ■ *Web:* www.kennedywilson.com
Kruse International 5540 County Rd 11A......................... Auburn IN 46706 260-925-5600 925-5467
TF: 800-968-4444 ■ *Web:* www.kruseinternational.com
Liquidity Services Inc 1920 L St NW 6th Fl................. Washington DC 20036 202-467-6868 467-5475
NASDAQ: LQDT ■ *Web:* www.liquidityservicesinc.com
Manheim Auctions Inc 6205 Peachtree Dunwoody Rd .... Atlanta GA 30328 678-645-0000 645-3171*
**Fax:* Mktg ■ *TF:* 800-777-2053 ■ *Web:* www.manheimauctions.com
NexTag.com Inc 1300 S El Camino Real Suite 600 ....San Mateo CA 94402 650-645-4700 341-3779
Web: www.nextag.com
Priceline.com Inc 800 Connecticut Ave .... Norwalk CT 06854 203-299-8000 299-8955*
NASDAQ: PCLN ■ **Fax:* Mktg ■ *TF:* 800-774-2354 ■ *Web:* www.priceline.com
Rene Bates Auctioneers Inc 4660 County Rd 1006 ....McKinney TX 75071 972-548-9636 542-5495
Web: www.renebates.com
Ritchie Brothers Auctioneers Inc 6500 River Rd .... Richmond BC V6X4G5 604-273-7564
NYSE: RBA ■ *TF:* 800-663-1739 ■ *Web:* www.rbauction.com
Rouse Asset Services 361 S Robertson Blvd.................Beverly Hills CA 90211 310-360-9200 855-7854
TF: 800-421-0816 ■ *Web:* www.rouseservices.com
Skinner Inc 357 Main St.................................... Bolton MA 01740 978-779-6241 779-5144
Web: www.skinnerinc.com
Sotheby's Inc 1334 York Ave ....New York NY 10021 212-606-7000 606-7028
Web: www.sothebys.com
Spear Auctioneers Inc PO Box 1052 ....Russellville AR 72811 479-968-2028 967-0573
Web: www.spearauctioneers.com
Swann Galleries Inc 104 E 25th St...........................New York NY 10010 212-254-4710 979-1017
Web: www.swanngalleries.com
Theriault's 2148 Renard Ct PO Box 151......................Annapolis MD 21404 410-224-3655 224-2515
TF: 800-966-3655 ■ *Web:* www.theriaults.com
uBid Inc 8725 W Higgins Rd 9th Fl .... Chicago IL 60631 773-272-5000 272-4000
TF: 866-946-8243 ■ *Web:* www.ubid.com
Yahoo! Auctions 701 1st Ave .... Sunnyvale CA 94089 408-349-3300 349-3301
TF: 866-562-7219 ■ *Web:* auctions.yahoo.com

52 AUDIO & VIDEO EQUIPMENT

Phone Fax

Alesis Corp 300 Corporate Pointe Suite 300..................Culver City CA 90230 310-693-7005 693-7040
Web: www.alesis.com
Alpine Electronics of America 19145 Gramercy Pl...............Torrance CA 90501 310-326-8000 212-0884*
**Fax:* Hum Res ■ *TF:* 800-257-4631 ■ *Web:* www.alpine-usa.com
Altec Lansing Technologies Inc 535 Rt 6 & 209 .... Milford PA 18337 570-296-6444 296-1222
TF: 800-258-3288 ■ *Web:* www.altecmm.com
Amplifier Technologies Inc 1749 Chapin Rd ....Montebello CA 90640 323-278-0001 278-0083
Web: www.bgw.com
AmpliVox Sound Systems LLC 3995 Commercial Ave...........Northbrook IL 60062 847-498-9000 498-6691
TF: 800-267-5486 ■ *Web:* www.ampli.com
Andrea Electronics Corp 65 Orville Dr Suite 1...................Bohemia NY 11716 631-719-1800 719-1998
AMEX: AND ■ *TF:* 800-442-7787 ■ *Web:* www.andreaelectronics.com
Applied Research & Technology 215 Tremont St ....Rochester NY 14608 585-436-2720 436-3942
Web: www.artroch.com
Atlas Sound 1601 Jack McKay Blvd .... Ennis TX 75119 972-875-8413 765-3435*
**Fax Area Code:* 800 ■ *TF:* 800-876-3333 ■ *Web:* www.atlassound.com
Audio Command Systems 694 Main St.......................Westbury NY 11590 516-997-5800 997-2195
TF: 800-382-2939 ■ *Web:* www.audiocommand.com
Audio Research Corp 3900 Annapolis Ln N ....Plymouth MN 55447 763-577-9700 577-0323
Web: www.audioresearch.com
Audio-Video Corp 213 Broadway.............................. Albany NY 12204 518-449-7213 449-1205
Web: www.audiovideocorp.com
Audiosears Corp 2 South St .... Stamford NY 12167 607-652-7305 652-3653
TF: 800-533-7863 ■ *Web:* www.audiosears.com
Audiovox Corp 150 Marcus Blvd.........................Hauppauge NY 11788 631-231-7750 434-3995
NASDAQ: VOXX ■ *TF:* 800-645-4994 ■ *Web:* www.audiovox.com
Automated Voice Systems Inc (AVSI) 17059 El Cajon Ave ......Yorba Linda CA 92886 714-524-4488 996-1127
TF: 888-505-2026 ■ *Web:* www.mastervoice.com
AVSI (Automated Voice Systems Inc) 17059 El Cajon Ave ......Yorba Linda CA 92886 714-524-4488 996-1127
TF: 888-505-2026 ■ *Web:* www.mastervoice.com
Biamp Systems Inc 10074 SW Arctic Dr ....Beaverton OR 97005 503-641-7287 626-0281
TF: 800-826-1457 ■ *Web:* www.biamp.com
Blaupunkt Div Robert Bosch Corp 2800 S 25th Ave .... Broadview IL 60155 708-865-5200 865-5296*
**Fax:* Sales ■ *TF Sales:* 800-323-1943 ■ *Web:* www.blaupunktusa.com
Bogen Communications International Inc 50 Spring St .... Ramsey NJ 07446 201-934-8500 934-6532
TF: 800-999-2809 ■ *Web:* www.bogen.com
Bose Corp The Mountain...............................Framingham MA 01701 508-879-7330 766-7543
TF Sales: 800-444-2673 ■ *Web:* www.bose.com
Boston Acoustics Inc 300 Jubilee Dr..........................Peabody MA 01960 978-538-5000 538-5199
TF: 800-288-6148 ■ *Web:* www.bostonacoustics.com
Cambridge Soundworks Inc 100 Brickstone Sq 5th Fl............. Andover MA 01810 978-623-4400 475-7219
TF: 800-945-4434 ■ *Web:* www.cambridgesoundworks.com
Casio Inc 570 Mt Pleasant Ave................................ Dover NJ 07801 973-361-5400 537-8910*
**Fax:* Hum Res ■ *TF Cust Svc:* 800-634-1895 ■ *Web:* www.casio.com
Cerwin-Vega Inc 3000 SW 42nd St .... Hollywood FL 33312 954-316-1501 316-1590
Web: www.cerwinvega.com
Citizen Systems America Corp 363 Van Ness Way Suite 404.......Torrance CA 90501 310-781-1460 781-9152*
**Fax:* Sales ■ *TF:* 800-421-6516 ■ *Web:* www.cbma.com
Clarion Corp of America 6200 Gateway Dr .... Cypress CA 90630 310-327-9100 327-1999
TF: 800-347-8667 ■ *Web:* www.clarion.com
Community Light & Sound Inc 333 E 5th St ....Chester PA 19013 610-876-3400 874-0190
TF: 800-523-4934 ■ *Web:* www.community.chester.pa.us
Creative Labs Inc 1901 McCarthy Blvd............................ Milpitas CA 95035 408-428-6600 428-6611
TF Cust Svc: 800-998-1000 ■ *Web:* us.creative.com
Crest Electronics Inc 3706 Alliance Dr.................... Greensboro NC 27407 336-855-6422 855-6676
TF: 800-873-2121 ■ *Web:* www.crestelectronics.com
Daewoo Electronics Corp of America 300 - 3E SR 17 S .... Lodi NJ 07644 973-249-3410 249-3412
TF: 877-399-7823 ■ *Web:* www.dwe.co.kr
dbx Professional Products 8760 S Sandy Pkwy ....Sandy UT 84070 801-566-8800 566-7005
TF: 800-931-1117 ■ *Web:* www.dbxpro.com
Denon Electronics Ltd 100 Corporate Dr .... Mahwah NJ 07430 201-762-6500 762-6670
TF: 877-386-3666 ■ *Web:* www.denon.com
Digidesign Inc 2001 Junipero Serra Blvd .... Daly City CA 94014 650-731-6300 731-6399
TF: 800-333-2137 ■ *Web:* www.digidesign.com
Digit Professional Inc 3926 Varsity Dr......................... Ann Arbor MI 48108 734-677-0840 677-3027
TF: 877-767-8862 ■ *Web:* www.digitprofessional.com
Digital Innovations 3436 N Kennicott Suite 200 ....Arlington Heights IL 60004 847-463-9000 463-9001
TF: 888-762-7858 ■ *Web:* www.digitalinnovations.com
Digital Video Systems Inc 357 Castro St Suite 5...........Mountain View CA 94041 650-938-8815 938-8829
Web: www.dvsystems.com
Directed Electronics Inc 1 Viper Way ....Vista CA 92081 760-598-6200 598-6400
NASDAQ: DEIX ■ *TF:* 800-876-0800 ■ *Web:* www.directed.com
Dolby Laboratories Inc 100 Potrero Ave.................. San Francisco CA 94103 415-558-0200 645-4000
NYSE: DLB ■ *Web:* www.dolby.com
DTS Inc (DTS) 5171 Clareton Dr ....Agoura Hills CA 91301 818-706-3525 706-1868
NASDAQ: DTSI ■ *TF:* 800-959-4109 ■ *Web:* www.dtsonline.com
Dynamic Instruments Inc 3860 Calle Fortunada................... San Diego CA 92123 858-278-4900 278-6700
TF: 800-793-3358 ■ *Web:* www.dynamicinst.com
Echo Corp 6450 Via Real Suite 1 .... Carpinteria CA 93013 805-684-4593 684-6628
Web: www.echoaudio.com
Educational Technology Inc 300 Bedford Ave...................Bellmore NY 11710 516-221-8440 221-9404
TF Cust Svc: 800-942-2136 ■ *Web:* www.educationaltechnology.com
Eiger Technology Inc 144 Front St W Suite 700 .... Toronto ON M5J2L7 416-216-8659 216-1164
TSX: AXA ■ *Web:* www.eigertechnology.com
Emergent Technologies Inc 2508 Ashley Worth Blvd Suite 200.......Austin TX 78738 512-263-3232 263-3236
Web: www.emergenttechnologies.com
Emerson Radio Corp 9 Entin Rd..........................Parsippany NJ 07054 973-884-5800 428-2067
AMEX: MSN ■ *Web:* www.emersonradio.com
Eminence Speaker LLC 838 Mulberry Pike PO Box 360 .... Eminence KY 40019 502-845-5622 845-5653
Web: www.eminence-speaker.com
Euphonix Inc 220 Portage Ave .... Palo Alto CA 94306 650-855-0400 855-0410
TF: 800-579-7836 ■ *Web:* www.euphonix.com
Extron Electronics USA 1230 S Lewis St ....Anaheim CA 92805 714-491-1500 491-1517
TF Tech Supp: 800-633-9876 ■ *Web:* www.extron.com
Foster Electric America 1000 E State Pkwy Suite G .... Schaumburg IL 60173 847-310-8200 310-8212
Fujitsu Ten Corp of America 19600 S Vermont Ave ....Torrance CA 90502 310-327-2151 767-4375
TF: 800-233-2216 ■ *Web:* www.eclipse-web.com
Funai Corp 201 Rt 17 N Suite 903 .... Rutherford NJ 07070 201-288-2063 288-8019
Web: www.funai-corp.com
Furman Sound LLC 1690 Corporate Cir......................... Petaluma CA 94954 707-763-1010 763-1310
TF: 877-486-4738 ■ *Web:* www.furmansound.com
Gemini Sound Products Corp 120 Clover Pl........................ Edison NJ 08837 732-738-9003 738-9006
Web: www.geminidj.com
GlobalMedia Group LLC 8281 E Gelding Dr .... Scottsdale AZ 85260 480-922-0044 922-1090
Web: www.globalmedia.com
Harman International Industries Inc
1101 Pennsylvania Ave NW Suite 1010................... Washington DC 20004 202-393-1101 393-3064
NYSE: HAR ■ *TF Cust Svc:* 800-336-4525 ■ *Web:* www.harman.com
Harman Kardon Inc 250 Crossways Park Dr.................... Woodbury NY 11797 516-496-3400 682-3510
Web: www.harmankardon.com
Harman Music Group 8760 S Sandy Pkwy ....Sandy UT 84070 801-566-8800 566-7005
TF: 800-931-1117 ■ *Web:* www.dbxpro.com
Harman/Becker Automotive Systems
39001 W 12 Mile Rd .... Farmington Hills MI 48331 248-994-2100 994-2900
Web: www.harman.com
Hitachi Home Electronics Inc 900 Hitachi Way ....Chula Vista CA 91914 619-591-5200 591-5201
TF: 800-981-2588
Infinity Systems Inc 250 Crossways Park Dr................... Woodbury NY 11797 516-496-3400 682-3510
Web: www.infinitysystems.com
JBL Consumer 250 Crossways Park Dr........................ Woodbury NY 11797 516-496-3400 682-3521
Web: www.jbl.com
JBL Professional 8400 Balboa Blvd .... Northridge CA 91329 818-894-8850 830-1220
TF: 800-852-5776 ■ *Web:* www.jblpro.com

	City	State	Zip	Phone	Fax
JVC Co of America 1700 Valley Rd *Fax Area Code: 956 ■ *Fax: Cust Svc ■ TF: 800-252-5722 ■ Web: www.jvc.com	Wayne	NJ	07470	800-526-5308	682-4360*
JVC Professional Products Co 1700 Valley Rd *Fax Area Code: 956 ■ Web: pro.jvc.com/prof	Wayne	NJ	07470	800-252-5722	682-4360*
Kenwood USA Corp 2201 E Flamingo St PO Box 22745 *Fax: Hum Res ■ TF: 800-536-9663 ■ Web: www.kenwoodusa.com	Long Beach	CA	90801	310-639-9000	608-5445*
KLH Audio Systems 11131 Dora St TF: 800-854-4441 ■ Web: www.klhaudio.com	Sun Valley	CA	91352	818-767-2843	767-8246
Klipsch LLC 137 County Rd 278 TF: 800-554-7724 ■ Web: www.klipsch.com	Hope	AR	71801	870-777-6751	777-6753
Koss Corp 4129 N Port Washington Ave NASDAQ: KOSS ■ TF: 800-872-5677 ■ Web: www.koss.com	Milwaukee	WI	53212	414-964-5000	964-8615
Krell Industries Inc 45 Connair Rd Web: www.krellonline.com	Orange	CT	06477	203-799-9954	799-9796
KSC Industries Inc 881 Kuhn Dr Suite 200 Web: www.kscind.com	Chula Vista	CA	91914	619-671-0110	671-0330
Law Enforcement Associates Corp 100 Hunter Pl AMEX: AID ■ TF: 800-354-9669 ■ Web: www.leacorp.com	Youngsville	NC	27596	919-554-4700	556-6240
Lenoxx Electronics Corp 35 Brunswick Ave *Fax Area Code: 732 ■ Web: www.lenoxx.com	Edison	NJ	08817	800-315-5885	777-0889*
Lexicon Inc 3 Oak Park Web: www.lexicon.com	Bedford	MA	01730	781-280-0300	280-0490
Line 6 26580 Agoura Rd Web: www.line6.com	Calabasas	CA	91302	818-575-3600	575-3601
LKG Industries Inc 3660 Publisher's Dr TF: 800-645-2262 ■ Web: www.crankinpower.com	Rockford	IL	61109	815-874-2301	874-2896
Logitech Inc 6505 Kaiser Dr TF Sales: 800-231-7717 ■ Web: www.logitech.com	Fremont	CA	94555	510-795-8500	792-8901
LOUD Technologies Inc 16220 Wood Red Rd NE NASDAQ: LTEC ■ TF: 800-258-6883 ■ Web: www.loudtechinc.com	Woodinville	WA	98072	425-487-4333	487-4337
Loudspeaker Components Corp 7596 US Hwy 61 S	Lancaster	WI	53813	608-723-2127	723-7775
Lowell Mfg Co 100 Integram Dr TF: 800-325-9660 ■ Web: www.lowellmfg.com	Pacific	MO	63069	636-257-3400	257-6606
M & S Systems Inc 1950 Camino Vida Roble Suite 150 TF: 800-421-1587 ■ Web: www.mssystems.com	Carlsbad	CA	92008	760-438-7000	931-1340
M2 America Corp 470 Riverside St Web: www.m2america.com	Portland	ME	04103	207-797-2600	797-2604
Magna-Tech Electronic Co Inc 5600 NW 32nd Ave Web: www.magna-tech.com	Miami	FL	33142	305-573-7339	573-8101
Marantz America Inc 100 Corporate Dr Web: www.marantz.com	Mahwah	NJ	07430	201-762-6500	762-6670
Matsushita Communication Industrial Corp of USA 776 Hwy 74 S Web: www.panasonic.com	Peachtree City	GA	30269	770-487-3356	487-3357
Matsushita Electric Corp of America 1 Panasonic Way TF: 888-275-2595	Secaucus	NJ	07094	201-348-7000	392-6007
McIntosh Laboratory Inc 2 Chambers St TF: 800-538-6576 ■ Web: www.mcintoshlabs.com	Binghamton	NY	13903	607-723-3512	724-0549
Metra Electronics Corp 460 Walker St TF Sales: 800-221-0932 ■ Web: www.metraonline.com	Holly Hill	FL	32117	386-257-1186	255-3965
Meyer Sound Laboratories Inc 2832 San Pablo Ave Web: www.meyersound.com	Berkeley	CA	94702	510-486-1166	486-8356
Mitsubishi Digital Electronics America Inc 9351 Jeronimo Rd *Fax: Sales ■ TF: 800-332-2119 ■ Web: www.mitsubishi-tv.com	Irvine	CA	92618	949-465-6000	465-6155*
Mitsubishi Electric & Electronics USA Inc Elevator & Escalator Div 5665 Plaza Dr Web: www.mitsubishi-elevator.com	Cypress	CA	90630	714-220-4822	220-4812
Monster Cable Products Inc 455 Valley Dr TF: 877-800-8989 ■ Web: www.monstercable.com	Brisbane	CA	94005	415-840-2000	
MTX Corp 4545 E Baseline Rd TF: 800-225-5689 ■ Web: www.mtxaudio.com	Phoenix	AZ	85042	602-438-4545	438-8692
Mustek Inc 15271 Barranca Pkwy TF: 800-308-7226 ■ Web: www.mustek.com	Irvine	CA	92618	949-790-3800	788-3670
Nady Systems Inc 6701 Shellmound St Web: www.nadywireless.com	Emeryville	CA	94608	510-652-2411	652-5075
NCT Group Inc 375 Bridgeport Ave 2nd Fl TF: 800-278-3526 ■ Web: www.nctgroupinc.com	Shelton	CT	06484	203-944-9533	944-9733
Nu-Way Speaker Products Inc 945 Anita Ave Web: www.nuway-speaker.com	Antioch	IL	60002	847-395-5141	395-8862
Omnitronics LLC 6573 Cochran Rd PO Box I TF: 888-872-3104 ■ Web: www.omnitronics-llc.com	Solon	OH	44139	440-349-4900	593-6724
OSRAM Sylvania Inc 100 Endicott St Web: www.sylvania.com	Danvers	MA	01923	978-777-1900	750-2152
Otari USA Sales Inc 21110 Nordhoff St Suite G/H Web: www.otari.com	Chatsworth	CA	91311	818-734-1785	594-7208
Panasonic Avionics Corp 26200 Enterprise Way TF: 800-755-2684 ■ Web: www.mascorp.com	Lake Forest	CA	92630	949-672-2000	462-7100
Panasonic Communications & Systems Co 1 Panasonic Way *Fax: Hum Res ■ TF Cust Svc: 800-211-7262 ■ Web: www.panasonic.com	Secaucus	NJ	07094	201-348-7000	392-6007*
Panasonic Consumer Electronics Co 1 Panasonic Way TF: 888-275-2595 ■ Web: www.panasonic.com/consumer_electronics/home	Secaucus	NJ	07094	201-348-7000	392-6168
Peavey Electronics Corp 5022 Hartley Peavey Dr TF: 877-732-8391 ■ Web: www.peavey.com	Meridian	MS	39305	601-483-5365	486-1278
Philips Consumer Electronics 64 Perimeter Center E *Fax Area Code: 404 ■ TF Cust Svc: 800-531-0039 ■ Web: www.consumer.philips.com	Atlanta	GA	30346	770-821-2400	601-3863*
Philips Electronics North America Corp 1251 Ave of the Americas 20th Fl *Fax: Hum Res ■ TF: 800-223-1828 ■ Web: www.philips.com	New York	NY	10020	212-536-0500	536-0559*
Pictorvision 7701 Haskel Ave Suite B TF: 800-876-5583 ■ Web: www.pictorvision.com	Van Nuys	CA	91406	818-785-9282	785-9787
Pioneer Electronics (USA) Inc 2265 E 220th St TF Cust Svc: 800-421-1404 ■ Web: www.pioneerelectronics.com	Long Beach	CA	90810	310-952-2000	952-2402
Polk Audio Inc 5601 Metro Dr TF: 800-377-7655 ■ Web: www.polkaudio.com	Baltimore	MD	21215	410-358-3600	764-5266
Primo Microphones Inc 1805 Couch Dr TF: 800-767-7466 ■ Web: www.primomic.com	McKinney	TX	75069	972-548-9807	548-1351
QSC Audio Products Inc 1675 MacArthur Blvd *Fax: Mktg ■ TF: 800-854-4079 ■ Web: www.qscaudio.com	Costa Mesa	CA	92626	714-754-6175	754-6174*
Quam-Nichols Co Inc 234 E Marquette Rd TF: 800-633-3669 ■ Web: www.quamspeakers.com	Chicago	IL	60637	773-488-5800	488-6944
Rane Corp 10802 47th Ave W Web: www.rane.com	Mukilteo	WA	98275	425-355-6000	347-7757
Record Play Tek Inc 110 E Vistula St Web: www.recordplaytek.com	Bristol	IN	46507	574-848-5233	848-5333
ReQuest Inc 100 Saratoga Village Blvd Suite 44 TF Cust Svc: 800-236-2812 ■ Web: www.request.com/us/	Ballston Spa	NY	12020	518-899-1254	899-1205
Roanwell Corp 2564 Park Ave Web: www.roanwellcorp.com	Bronx	NY	10451	718-401-0288	401-0663
Robert Bosch Corp Blaupunkt Div 2800 S 25th Ave *Fax: Sales ■ TF Sales: 800-323-1943 ■ Web: www.blaupunktusa.com	Broadview	IL	60155	708-865-5200	865-5296*
Robert Bosch LLC 2800 S 25th Ave Web: www.boschusa.com	Broadview	IL	60155	708-865-5200	865-6430
Rockford Corp 600 S Rockford Dr NASDAQ: ROFO ■ TF: 800-669-9899 ■ Web: www.rockfordcorp.com	Tempe	AZ	85281	480-967-3565	966-3983
Rodin 9200 N Decatur St *Fax: Sales ■ TF: 800-950-1449 ■ Web: www.rodinaudio.com/	Portland	OR	97203	503-286-9300	978-3380*
Samsung Electronics America Inc 105 Challenger Rd TF: 800-726-7864 ■ Web: www.samsungusa.com	Ridgefield Park	NJ	07660	201-229-4000	229-4029
Sanyo Fisher Co 21605 Plummer St Web: us.sanyo.com	Chatsworth	CA	91311	818-998-7322	701-4194
Sanyo Mfg Corp 3333 Sanyo Rd *Fax: Hum Res ■ TF: 800-877-5036	Forrest City	AR	72335	870-633-5030	633-3179*
Sanyo North America Corp 2055 Sanyo Ave Web: www.sanyo.com	San Diego	CA	92154	619-661-1134	661-6795
SDI Technologies Inc 1299 Main St *Fax: Hum Res ■ TF Cust Svc: 800-888-4491 ■ Web: www.sdidirect.com	Rahway	NJ	07065	732-574-9000	574-1716*
Sharp Electronics Corp 1 Sharp Plaza TF: 800-237-4277 ■ Web: www.sharpusa.com	Mahwah	NJ	07430	201-529-8200	529-8413
Sherwood America 13101 Moore St TF: 800-777-8755 ■ Web: www.sherwoodamerica.com	Cerritos	CA	90703	562-741-0960	741-0967
Shure Inc 5800 W Touhy Ave TF: 800-257-4873 ■ Web: www.shure.com	Niles	IL	60714	847-866-2200	600-1212
Sima Products Corp 140 Pennsylvania Ave Bldg 5 TF: 800-345-7462 ■ Web: www.simacorp.com	Oakmont	PA	15139	412-828-3700	828-3775
SLS International Inc 1650 W Jackson St AMEX: SLS ■ Web: www.slsloudspeakers.com	Ozark	MO	65721	417-883-4549	883-2723
Sony of Canada Ltd 115 Gordon Baker Rd Web: www.sony.ca	Toronto	ON	M2H3R6	416-499-1414	499-1774
Sony Corp of America 550 Madison Ave TF: 800-282-2848 ■ Web: www.sony.com	New York	NY	10022	212-833-6800	
Sony Electronics Inc 1 Sony Dr *Fax: Hum Res ■ TF Cust Svc: 800-222-7669 ■ Web: www.sony.com	Park Ridge	NJ	07656	201-930-1000	358-4058*
Southern Audio Services 14763 Florida Blvd TF: 800-843-8823 ■ Web: www.bazooka.com	Baton Rouge	LA	70819	225-272-7135	272-9844
Stancil Corp 2644 S Croddy Way TF: 800-782-6245 ■ Web: www.stancilcorp.com	Santa Ana	CA	92704	714-546-2002	546-2092
Sunfire Corp 1920 Bickford Ave Web: www.sunfire.com	Snohomish	WA	98290	425-335-4748	335-4746
Tatung Co of America Inc 2850 El Presidio St TF: 800-827-2850 ■ Web: www.tatungusa.com	Long Beach	CA	90810	310-637-2105	
TDK USA Corp 901 Franklin Ave PO Box 9302 *Fax: Sales ■ TF: 800-835-8273 ■ Web: www.tdk.com	Garden City	NY	11530	516-535-2600	294-7751*
TEAC America Inc 7733 Telegraph Rd Web: www.teac.com	Montebello	CA	90640	323-726-0303	727-7656
Telex Communications Inc 12000 Portland Ave S TF Sales: 800-828-6107 ■ Web: www.telex.com	Burnsville	MN	55337	952-884-4051	884-0043
Toshiba America Inc 1251 Ave of the Americas Suite 4100 TF: 800-457-7777 ■ Web: www.toshiba.com	New York	NY	10020	212-596-0600	593-3875
Universal Electronics Inc 1864 Enterprise Pkwy W NASDAQ: UEIC ■ *Fax: Cust Svc ■ Web: www.ueic.com	Twinsburg	OH	44087	330-487-1110	963-7881*
Vrex Inc 3 Westchester Plaza Web: www.vrex.com	Elmsford	NY	10523	914-345-8877	345-9558
Xantech Corp 13100 Telfair Ave 2nd Fl TF Sales: 800-843-5465 ■ Web: www.xantech.com	Sylmar	CA	91342	818-362-0353	362-9506
Yamaha Electronics Corp 6660 Orangethorpe Ave *Fax Area Code: 800 ■ TF Cust Svc: 800-292-2982 ■ Web: www.yamaha.com/yec	Buena Park	CA	90620	714-522-9888	634-0355*
Zenith Electronics Corp 2000 Millbrook Dr Web: www.zenith.com	Lincolnshire	IL	60069	847-391-7000	941-8763

53 AUTO CLUBS

	City	State	Zip	Phone	Fax
AAA (American Automobile Assn) 1000 AAA Dr Web: www.aaa.com	Heathrow	FL	32746	407-444-4240	444-4247
AAA Akron 111 W Center St Web: www.aaa.com	Akron	OH	44308	330-762-0631	762-5965
AAA Alabama 2400 Acton Rd TF: 800-521-8124 ■ Web: www.aaa.com	Birmingham	AL	35243	205-978-7000	978-7026
AAA Alliance Auto Club 2322 S Union Ave Web: www.aaa.com	Alliance	OH	44601	330-823-9820	
AAA Allied Group Inc 15 W Central Pkwy TF: 800-543-2345 ■ Web: www.aaacincinnati.com	Cincinnati	OH	45202	513-762-3100	762-3282
AAA Arizona 3144 N 7th Ave *Fax: PR ■ TF: 800-352-5382 ■ Web: www.aaa.com	Phoenix	AZ	85013	602-274-1116	277-1194*
AAA Ashland County 502 Claremont Ave TF: 800-222-4357 ■ Web: www.aaa.com	Ashland	OH	44805	419-289-8133	281-1326
AAA Auto Club South 1515 N Westshore Blvd Web: www.aaasouth.com	Tampa	FL	33607	813-289-5000	289-5015
AAA Blue Grass/Kentucky 155 N MLK Blvd TF: 800-568-5222 ■ Web: www.aaa.com	Lexington	KY	40507	859-233-1111	281-1410
AAA Carolinas 6600 AAA Dr TF: 800-477-4222 ■ Web: www.aaacarolinas.com	Charlotte	NC	28212	704-569-3600	532-5822
AAA Central Penn 2023 Market St TF: 877-848-9990 ■ Web: www.aaa.com	Harrisburg	PA	17103	717-236-4021	236-0468
AAA Chicago Motor Club 975 Meridian Lake Dr TF: 866-968-7222 ■ Web: www.autoclubgroup.com/chicago	Aurora	IL	60504	630-328-7000	499-8200
AAA Colorado 4100 E Arkansas Ave TF: 877-244-9790 ■ Web: www.aaacolo.com	Denver	CO	80222	303-753-8800	758-8515
AAA Columbiana County 216 Broadway St TF: 800-222-4357 ■ Web: www.aaa.com	East Liverpool	OH	43920	330-385-2020	385-9718
AAA Connecticut Motor Club 2276 Whitney Ave Web: www.aaact.com	Hamden	CT	06518	203-765-4222	288-0079
AAA East Central 5900 Baum Blvd Web: www.aaa.com	Pittsburgh	PA	15206	412-363-5100	362-8943
AAA East Penn 1020 Hamilton St TF: 800-552-6679 ■ Web: www.aaa.com	Allentown	PA	18101	610-434-5141	778-3390
AAA East Tennessee 100 W 5th Ave TF: 800-234-1222 ■ Web: www.aaaet.com	Knoxville	TN	37917	865-637-1910	524-7866
AAA Hawaii 1130 N Nimitz Hwy Suite A-170 TF: 800-736-2886 ■ Web: www.aaa-hawaii.com	Honolulu	HI	96817	808-593-2221	591-9359
AAA Hoosier Motor Club 3750 Guion Rd *Fax: Cust Svc ■ TF: 800-624-9820 ■ Web: www.aaa.com	Indianapolis	IN	46222	317-923-3311	923-1351*
AAA Hudson Valley 618 Delaware Ave Web: www.aaa.com	Albany	NY	12209	518-426-1000	426-1595
AAA Kentucky 435 E Broadway TF: 800-727-2552 ■ Web: www.aaa.com	Louisville	KY	40202	502-582-3311	584-1455
AAA Massillon Auto Club 1972 Wales Rd NE TF: 800-222-4357 ■ Web: www.aaa.com	Massillon	OH	44646	330-833-1084	833-5542
AAA Merrimack Valley 49 Orchard Hill Rd Web: www.aaa.com	North Andover	MA	01845	978-681-9200	688-4891
AAA Miami Valley 825 S Ludlow St TF: 800-624-2321 ■ Web: www.aaa.com	Dayton	OH	45402	937-224-2801	224-2892
AAA Michigan 1 Auto Club Dr TF: 800-222-6424 ■ Web: www.autoclubgroup.com/michigan	Dearborn	MI	48126	313-336-1234	336-1809
AAA Mid-Atlantic 1 River Pl *Fax Area Code: 215 ■ TF: 800-222-4357 ■ Web: www.aaamidatlantic.com	Wilmington	DE	19801	302-299-4000	864-5170*
AAA Minneapolis 5400 Auto Club Way Web: www.aaa.com	Minneapolis	MN	55416	952-927-2600	927-2559
AAA Minnesota/Iowa 600 W Travelers Trail TF: 800-222-1333 ■ Web: www.autoclubgroup.com/mnia	Burnsville	MN	55337	952-707-4500	707-4220

	City	State	ZIP	Phone	Fax
AAA Missouri 12901 N Forty Dr *TF:* 800-222-4357 ■ *Web:* www.ouraaa.com	Saint Louis	MO	63141	314-523-7350	523-7427
AAA MountainWest 2100 11th Ave *TF:* 800-332-6119 ■ *Web:* www.aaa.com	Helena	MT	59062	406-447-8100	442-5671
AAA Nebraska 910 N 96th St **Fax:* Cust Svc ■ *TF:* 800-222-6327 ■ *Web:* www.autoclubgroup.com/nebraska	Omaha	NE	68114	402-390-1000	390-6023*
AAA New Mexico Inc 10501 Montgomery Blvd NE *TF:* 800-846-0377 ■ *Web:* www.aaa-newmexico.com	Albuquerque	NM	87111	505-291-6611	291-6706
AAA Niagara-Orleans Auto Club 7135 Rochester Rd *Web:* www.aaa.com	Lockport	NY	14094	716-434-2865	434-3452
AAA North Dakota 4950 13th Ave S Suite 15 *TF:* 800-342-4254 ■ *Web:* www.aaa.com	Fargo	ND	58103	701-282-6222	282-8952
AAA North Jersey 418 Hamburg Tpke *TF:* 800-222-4357 ■ *Web:* www.aaa.com	Wayne	NJ	07470	973-956-2200	956-2232
AAA North Penn 1035 N Washington Ave *Web:* www.aaa.com	Scranton	PA	18509	570-348-2511	348-2563
AAA Northampton County 3914 Hecktown Rd *Web:* www.aaa.com	Easton	PA	18045	610-258-2371	258-5256
AAA of Northern California Nevada & Utah 150 Van Ness Ave **Fax:* Hum Res ■ *TF Cust Svc:* 800-922-8228 ■ *Web:* www.csaa.com	San Francisco	CA	94102	415-565-2012	431-7572*
AAA Northern New England 68 Marginal Way *TF:* 800-222-4357 ■ *Web:* www.aaanne.com	Portland	ME	04104	207-780-6800	780-6986
AAA Northway 112 Railroad St *Web:* www.aaa.com	Schenectady	NY	12305	518-374-4575	374-3140
AAA Northwest Ohio 7150 W Central Ave *TF:* 800-428-0060 ■ *Web:* www.aaanwohio.com	Toledo	OH	43617	419-843-1200	843-1249
AAA Ohio Auto Club 90 E Wilson Bridge Rd *TF:* 800-282-0585 ■ *Web:* www.aaaohio.com	Worthington	OH	43085	614-431-7800	431-7918
AAA Oklahoma 2121 E 15th St *TF:* 800-222-2582 ■ *Web:* www.aaaoklahoma.com	Tulsa	OK	74104	918-748-1000	748-1111
AAA Oregon/Idaho 600 SW Market St *TF Cust Svc:* 800-452-1643 ■ *Web:* www.aaaorid.com	Portland	OR	97201	503-222-6734	219-6222
AAA Reading-Berks 920 Van Reed Rd *Web:* www.aaa.com	Wyomissing	PA	19610	610-374-4531	374-1325
AAA Schuylkill County 340 S Centre St *Web:* www.aaa.com	Pottsville	PA	17901	570-622-4991	622-8179
AAA Shelby County 920 Wapakoneta Ave *Web:* www.aaa.com	Sidney	OH	45365	937-492-3167	492-7297
AAA South Dakota 1300 Industrial Ave *TF:* 800-222-4545 ■ *Web:* www.aaasouthdakota.com	Sioux Falls	SD	57104	605-336-3690	332-4055
AAA South Jersey 700 Laurel Oak Rd *Web:* www.aaa.com	Voorhees	NJ	08043	856-783-4222	627-9100
AAA Southern New England 110 Royal Little Dr *TF:* 800-222-7448 ■ *Web:* www.aaa.com	Providence	RI	02904	401-868-2000	868-2085
AAA Southern New York 21 Washington St *Web:* www.aaa.com	Binghamton	NY	13901	607-722-7255	724-6935
AAA Southern Pennsylvania 2840 Eastern Blvd *TF:* 800-222-1469 ■ *Web:* www.aaa.com	York	PA	17402	717-600-8700	755-2142
AAA Susquehanna Valley 1001 Market St *Web:* www.aaa.com	Sunbury	PA	17801	570-286-4507	286-1130
AAA Texas 6555 N State Hgwy 161 *Web:* www.aaa-texas.com	Irving	TX	75039	469-221-6006	221-6033
AAA Tidewater Virginia 5366 Virginia Beach Blvd *Web:* www.aaa.com	Virginia Beach	VA	23462	757-233-3800	233-3896
AAA Tri County Motor Club 195 Oneida St Suite A *Web:* www.aaa.com	Oneonta	NY	13820	607-432-4512	432-9123
AAA Tuscarawas County 1112 4th St NW *Web:* www.aaa.com	New Philadelphia	OH	44663	330-343-4481	364-1116
AAA Utica & Central New York 409 Court St *Web:* www.aaa.com	Utica	NY	13502	315-797-5000	797-5005
AAA Washington-Inland 1745 114th Ave SE *TF:* 800-562-2582 ■ *Web:* www.aaawa.com	Bellevue	WA	98004	425-462-2222	646-2169
AAA Western & Central New York 100 International Dr *TF:* 800-836-2582	Buffalo	NY	14221	716-633-9860	633-4439
AAA Wisconsin 8401 Excelsior Dr *TF:* 800-236-1300 ■ *Web:* www.autoclubgroup.com/wisconsin	Madison	WI	53717	608-836-6555	828-2443
AARP Motoring Plan 200 N Martingale Rd *Web:* www.aarpmotoring.com	Schaumburg	IL	60173	800-555-1121	
ACA (Auto Club of America Corp) 9411 N Georgia St *TF:* 800-411-2007 ■ *Web:* www.autoclubofamerica.com	Oklahoma City	OK	73120	405-751-4430	751-4462
Allstate Motor Club 51 W Higgins Rd *TF:* 800-255-2582 ■ *Web:* allstatemotorclub.com	South Barrington	IL	60010	847-551-2300	
American Automobile Assn (AAA) 1000 AAA Dr *Web:* www.aaa.com	Heathrow	FL	32746	407-444-4240	444-4247
Auto Club of America Corp (ACA) 9411 N Georgia St *TF:* 800-411-2007 ■ *Web:* www.autoclubofamerica.com	Oklahoma City	OK	73120	405-751-4430	751-4462
Auto Club Ltd 106 E 6th St Suite 900 **Fax Area Code:* 512 ■ *TF:* 866-247-3728 ■ *Web:* www.theautoclub.com	Austin	TX	78701	866-247-3728	697-0661*
Auto Club of New York Inc 1415 Kellum Pl *Web:* www.aaany.com	Garden City	NY	11530	516-746-7730	873-2320
Auto Club of Pioneer Valley 150 Capital Dr	West Springfield	MA	01089	413-785-1381	205-2306
Automobile Club of Southern California 2601 S Figueroa St *TF:* 800-400-4222 ■ *Web:* www.aaa-calif.com	Los Angeles	CA	90007	213-741-3686	741-4151
AutoVantage 100 Connecticut Ave *Web:* www.autovantage.com	Norwalk	CT	06850	800-876-7787	
BCAA (British Columbia Automobile Assn) 4567 Canada Way *TF:* 800-222-4357 ■ *Web:* www.bcaa.com	Burnaby	BC	V5G4T1	604-268-5000	268-5569
BP MotorClub 200 N Martingale Rd **Fax Area Code:* 847 ■ *Web:* www.bpmotorclub.com	Schaumburg	IL	60196	800-334-3300	605-4864*
Brickell Financial Services Motor Club Inc DBA Road America Motor Club 7300 Corporate Ctr Dr Suite 601 *TF:* 800-262-7262 ■ *Web:* www.road-america.com	Miami	FL	33126	305-392-4300	302-4301
British Columbia Automobile Assn (BCAA) 4567 Canada Way *TF:* 800-222-4357 ■ *Web:* www.bcaa.com	Burnaby	BC	V5G4T1	604-268-5000	268-5569
CAA Alberta Motor Assn 10310 39A Ave NW *TF:* 800-642-3810 ■ *Web:* www.ama.ab.ca	Edmonton	AB	T6J6R7	780-430-5555	430-5676
CAA Central Ontario 60 Commerce Valley Dr E *TF:* 800-268-3750 ■ *Web:* www.central.on.caa.ca	Thornhill	ON	L3T7P9	905-771-3000	771-3101
CAA Manitoba 870 Empress St *TF:* 800-222-4357 ■ *Web:* www.caamanitoba.com	Winnipeg	MB	R3C2Z3	204-262-6166	774-9961
CAA Maritimes 378 Westmorland Rd *TF:* 800-561-8807 ■ *Web:* www.caa.maritimes.ca	Saint John	NB	E2J2G4	506-634-1400	653-9500
CAA Mid-Western Ontario 148 Manitou Dr *TF:* 800-265-8975 ■ *Web:* www.caamwo.com	Kitchener	ON	N2G4W8	519-894-2582	893-5512
CAA Niagara 3271 Schmon Pkwy *TF:* 800-263-7272 ■ *Web:* www.caa.niagara.net	Thorold	ON	L2V4Y6	905-984-8585	688-0289
CAA North & East Ontario 2525 Carling Ave *TF:* 800-267-8713 ■ *Web:* www.caaneo.on.ca	Ottawa	ON	K2B7Z2	613-820-1890	820-4646
CAA Quebec 444 Bouvier St *TF:* 800-686-9243 ■ *Web:* www.caaquebec.com	Quebec	QC	G2J1E3	418-624-2424	623-7331
CAA Saskatchewan 200 Albert St N *TF:* 800-564-6222 ■ *Web:* www.caasask.sk.ca	Regina	SK	S4R5E2	306-791-4321	949-4461
CAA South Central Ontario 163 Centennial Pkwy N *Web:* www.caasco.on.ca	Hamilton	ON	L8E1H8	905-525-1210	525-1654
California State Automobile Assn 150 Van Ness Ave **Fax:* Hum Res ■ *TF Cust Svc:* 800-922-8228 ■ *Web:* www.csaa.com	San Francisco	CA	94102	415-565-2012	431-7572*
Canadian Automobile Assn (CAA) 1145 Hunt Club Rd Suite 200 *Web:* www.caa.ca	Ottawa	ON	K1V0Y3	613-247-0117	247-0118
Chevron Travel Club Inc PO Box 5010 **Fax Area Code:* 925 ■ *Web:* www.chevroncreditcard.com	Concord	CA	94524	800-222-0585	827-6367*
Cross Country Automotive Services 1 Cabot Rd **Fax Area Code:* 781 ■ *Web:* www.crosscountry-auto.com	Medford	MA	02155	800-833-5500	395-6706*
Exxon Travel Club PO Box 660460 *Web:* www.exxon.com	Dallas	TX	75266	800-833-9966	
Findlay Automobile Club 1550 Tiffin Ave *Web:* www.aaa.com	Findlay	OH	45840	419-422-4961	422-5620
Ford Auto Club Inc PO Box 660460	Dallas	TX	75226	800-348-5220	
GE Motor Club Inc 200 N Martingale Rd *TF:* 800-616-9286 ■ *Web:* www.gemotorclub.com	Schaumburg	IL	60173	800-616-9286	
GM Motor Club PO Box 1049 *Web:* www.gmmotorclub.com	Winston-Salem	NC	27102	800-705-0055	
Gulf Motor Club Inc 929 N Plum Grove Rd **Fax Area Code:* 847	Schaumburg	IL	60173	800-633-3224	240-2114*
Motor Club of America Enterprises Inc 3200 Wilshire Blvd	Oklahoma City	OK	73156	800-288-2889	
NAC (National Automobile Club) 1151 E Hillsdale Blvd *Web:* www.nationalautoclub.com	Foster City	CA	94404	650-294-7000	294-7040
National Automobile Club (NAC) 1151 E Hillsdale Blvd *Web:* www.nationalautoclub.com	Foster City	CA	94404	650-294-7000	294-7040
National Motor Club of America Inc 6500 Beltline Rd Suite 200 *TF:* 800-523-4582 ■ *Web:* www.nmca.com	Irving	TX	75063	972-999-4400	999-4405
New Jersey Auto Club 1 Hanover Rd *Web:* www.aaamidatlantic.com	Florham Park	NJ	07932	973-377-7200	377-7204
Ohio Motorists Assn 5700 Brecksville Rd *TF:* 800-711-5370	Independence	OH	44131	216-606-6100	606-6182
Pennsylvania AAA Federation 600 N 3rd St *Web:* www.aaapa.org	Harrisburg	PA	17105	717-238-7192	238-6574
Pinnacle Motor Club 130 E John Carpenter Fwy *Web:* www.pinnaclemotorclub.com	Irving	TX	75062	800-446-1289	
Road America Motor Club 7300 Corporate Ctr Dr Suite 601 *TF:* 800-262-7262 ■ *Web:* www.road-america.com	Miami	FL	33126	305-392-4300	302-4301
Roadgard Motor Club 11222 Quail Roost Dr	Miami	FL	33157	800-432-8603	
Travelers Motor Club 720 NW 50th St *TF:* 800-654-9208 ■ *Web:* www.travelersmotorclub.com	Oklahoma City	OK	73154	405-848-1711	
Trilegiant Corp DBA AutoVantage 100 Connecticut Ave *Web:* www.autovantage.com	Norwalk	CT	06850	800-876-7787	
US Auto Club Motoring Div Inc PO Box 660460	Dallas	TX	75226	800-348-2761	

54 AUTO SUPPLY STORES

	City	State	ZIP	Phone	Fax
Advance Auto Parts Inc 5673 Airport Rd *NYSE: AAP* ■ **Fax:* Hum Res ■ *Web:* www.advance-auto.com	Roanoke	VA	24012	540-362-4911	561-6930*
Advance Stores Co Inc 5673 Airport Rd *NYSE: AAP* ■ **Fax:* Hum Res ■ *Web:* www.advance-auto.com	Roanoke	VA	24012	540-362-4911	561-6930*
Am-Pac Tire Pros Inc 917 6th Ave N *TF:* 800-875-4655 ■ *Web:* www.tirepros.com	Birmingham	AL	35203	205-322-4651	521-9051
Anderson Auto Parts Co 102 Brown Rd	Anderson	SC	29621	864-225-1475	231-9553
Auto Barn 13 Harbor Park Dr *Web:* www.autobarn.com	Port Washington	NY	11050	516-484-9500	484-4341
AutoZone Inc 123 S Front St *NYSE: AZO* ■ *TF:* 800-288-6966 ■ *Web:* www.autozone.com	Memphis	TN	38103	901-495-6500	495-8300
Bennett Auto Supply Inc 3141 SW 10th St **Fax:* Hum Res ■ *TF:* 800-766-5913 ■ *Web:* www.bennettauto.com	Pompano Beach	FL	33069	954-335-8700	335-8834*
Benny's Inc 340 Waterman Ave *Web:* www.hellobennys.com	Smithfield	RI	02917	401-231-1000	231-1080
Blue Star Automobile Stores Inc 2001 S State St	Chicago	IL	60616	312-225-7174	225-7474
Bond Auto Parts 272 Morrison Rd PO Box 687 *TF:* 800-639-1982 ■ *Web:* www.bondauto.com	Barre	VT	05641	802-479-0571	476-1308
Canadian Tire Corp Ltd PO Box 770 Stn K *TSX: CTR* ■ *TF:* 800-387-8803 ■ *Web:* www2.canadiantire.ca	Toronto	ON	M4P2V8	416-480-3000	544-7715
CARQUEST Corp 2635 E Millbrook Rd **Fax:* Mktg ■ *TF:* 800-876-1291 ■ *Web:* www.carquest.com	Raleigh	NC	27604	919-573-3000	573-3558*
Crow-Burlingame Co Inc 190 E Roosevelt St *TF:* 877-282-6591	Little Rock	AR	72203	501-372-5275	376-2769
CSK Auto Corp 645 E Missouri Ave Suite 400 *NYSE: CAO* ■ **Fax:* Hum Res ■ *Web:* www.cskauto.com	Phoenix	AZ	85012	602-631-7000	631-7321*
Discount Tire Co 20225 N Scottsdale Rd **Fax:* Cust Svc ■ *TF:* 800-347-4348 ■ *Web:* www.discounttire.com	Scottsdale	AZ	85255	480-606-6000	443-3162*
Hedahls Inc 100 E Broadway *TF:* 800-433-2457 ■ *Web:* www.hedahls.com	Bismarck	ND	58502	701-223-8393	221-4251
Knecht's Auto Parts 3400 Main St *Web:* www.knechts.com	Springfield	OR	97478	541-746-4532	746-0884
KOI Warehouse Inc 2701 Spring Grove Ave *TF:* 800-354-0408 ■ *Web:* www.koiautoparts.com	Cincinnati	OH	45225	513-357-2400	412-3554
Merle's Automotive Supply Inc 33 W University Blvd *TF:* 800-447-7202 ■ *Web:* www.merlesauto.com	Tucson	AZ	85705	520-622-3526	622-2760
Murray's Discount Auto Stores 8080 Hagerty Rd *TF:* 800-946-8772 ■ *Web:* www.murraysdiscount.com	Belleville	MI	48111	734-957-8080	957-8156
NAPA Auto Parts Stores 2999 Circle 75 Pkwy NW *Web:* www.napaonline.com	Atlanta	GA	30339	770-956-2200	956-2212
O'Reilly Automotive Inc 233 S Patterson Ave *NASDAQ: ORLY* ■ **Fax:* Cust Svc ■ *Web:* www.oreillyauto.com	Springfield	MO	65802	417-862-3333	874-7179*
Original Parts Group Inc 5252 Bolsa Ave *TF:* 800-243-8355 ■ *Web:* www.originalpartsgroup.com	Huntington Beach	CA	92649	714-230-6000	230-6050
Peerless Tyre Co 5000 Kingston St *TF:* 800-999-7810 ■ *Web:* www.peerlesstyreco.com	Denver	CO	80239	303-371-4300	371-4749
Pep Boys - Manny Moe & Jack 3111 W Allegheny Ave *NYSE: PBY* ■ **Fax:* Hum Res ■ *TF:* 800-737-2697 ■ *Web:* www.pepboys.com	Philadelphia	PA	19132	215-227-9000	227-7513*
Rent-A-Tire Rent-A-Wheel 15350 Sherman Way Suite 260 *Web:* www.rentawheel.com	Van Nuys	CA	91406	818-786-7906	786-7458
Rex Auto Parts 1233 Gordon Park Rd *Web:* www.rexautoparts.com	Augusta	GA	30901	706-722-7526	724-0181
Schuck's Auto Supply Inc 2402 R St NW Suite 100 *Web:* www.cskauto.com	Auburn	WA	98001	253-833-1115	833-9533
Strauss Discount Auto 9-A Brick Plant Rd *TF:* 800-947-2637 ■ *Web:* www.straussauto.com	South River	NJ	08882	732-390-9000	390-9056
Tire Warehouse Central Inc 492 Main St *Web:* www.tirewarehouse.net	Keene	NH	03431	603-352-4478	357-5108
Town Fair Tire Co Inc 460 Coe Ave *TF:* 800-972-2245 ■ *Web:* www.townfair.com	East Haven	CT	06512	203-467-8600	467-1630
United Auto Supply Inc 625 3rd St S	La Crosse	WI	54601	608-784-9198	784-4760
VIP Discount Auto Center 12 Lexington St *Web:* www.vipauto.com	Lewiston	ME	04240	207-784-5423	784-9178

55 AUTOMATIC MERCHANDISING EQUIPMENT & SYSTEMS

SEE ALSO Food Service p. 1664

				Phone	Fax
AIR-serv Group LLC 1370 Mendota Heights Rd	Mendota Heights	MN	55120	651-454-0518	454-9542
TF: 800-227-5336 ■ Web: www.air-serv.com					
American Coin Merchandising Inc DBA SugarLoaf Creations 397 S Taylor Ave	Louisville	CO	80027	303-444-2559	247-1728
American Vending Sales Inc 750 Morse Ave	Elk Grove Village	IL	60007	847-439-9400	439-9405
TF: 800-441-0009 ■ Web: www.americanvending.com					
Automatic Products International Ltd 75 Plato Blvd W	Saint Paul	MN	55107	651-224-4391	224-5559*
*Fax: Sales ■ TF: 800-523-8363 ■ Web: www.automaticproducts.com					
Betson Enterprises Inc 303 Paterson Plank Rd	Carlstadt	NJ	07072	201-438-1300	438-4837
TF: 800-524-2343 ■ Web: www.betson.com					
Birmingham Vending Co 540 2nd Ave N	Birmingham	AL	35204	205-324-7526	322-6639
TF: 800-288-7635 ■ Web: www.bhmvending.com					
Coin Acceptors Inc 300 Hunter Ave	Saint Louis	MO	63124	314-725-0100	725-6636
TF: 800-325-2646 ■ Web: www.coinco.com					
Coinstar Inc 1800 114th Ave SE	Bellevue	WA	98004	425-943-8000	943-8030*
NASDAQ: CSTR ■ *Fax: Mktg ■ TF: 800-928-2274 ■ Web: www.coinstar.com					
Crane Merchandising Systems 12955 Enterprise Way	Bridgeton	MO	63044	314-298-3500	298-3505*
*Fax: Sales ■ TF: 800-325-8811 ■ Web: www.cranems.com					
Dixie-Narco Inc PO Drawer 719	Williston	SC	29853	803-266-5000	266-5040
TF: 800-688-9090 ■ Web: www.dixienarco.com					
Fawn Vendors Inc 8040 University Blvd	Des Moines	IA	50325	515-274-3641	274-5180*
*Fax: Sales ■ TF: 800-247-1787 ■ Web: www.fawnvendors.com					
Federal Machine Corp 8040 University Blvd	Des Moines	IA	50325	515-274-1555	274-5180*
*Fax: Sales ■ TF: 800-247-2446 ■ Web: www.federalmachine.com					
Glacier Water Services Inc 1385 Park Ctr Dr	Vista	CA	92081	760-560-1111	560-3333
TF: 800-452-2437 ■ Web: www.glacierwater.com					
Harcourt Outlines Inc 7765 S 175 West PO Box 128	Milroy	IN	46156	765-629-2625	278-5165*
*Fax Area Code: 800 ■ TF: 800-428-6584 ■ Web: www.harcourtoutlines.com					
LM Becker & Co Inc PO Box 1459	Appleton	WI	54912	920-739-5269	739-2418
TF: 888-869-6569 ■ Web: www.toynjoy.com					
Mars Electronics International (MEI) 1301 Wilson Dr	West Chester	PA	19380	610-430-2500	430-2694
TF Cust Svc: 800-345-8215 ■ Web: www.meiglobal.com					
Melo-Tone Vending Inc 130 Broadway	Somerville	MA	02145	617-666-4900	666-4906
TF: 800-322-7741 ■ Web: melotone.com					
Money Controls Inc 34099 Melinz Pkwy	Eastlake	OH	44095	440-946-3000	946-9829
TF: 800-321-0765 ■ Web: www.moneycontrols.com					
Northwestern Corp 922 E Armstrong St	Morris	IL	60450	815-942-1300	942-4477
TF: 800-942-1316 ■ Web: www.nwcorp.com					
Rowe International Inc 1500 Union Ave SE	Grand Rapids	MI	49507	616-243-3633	247-6531*
*Fax: Sales ■ TF: 800-636-2787 ■ Web: www.roweami.com					
SugarLoaf Creations 397 S Taylor Ave	Louisville	CO	80027	303-444-2559	247-1728
Universal Distributing of Nevada Inc 745 Grier Dr	Las Vegas	NV	89119	702-361-3166	361-3403
Web: www.udnslots.com					

56 AUTOMATIC TELLER MACHINES (ATMS)

				Phone	Fax
Cardtronics Inc 3110 Hayes Rd Suite 300	Houston	TX	77082	281-596-9988	596-9984
TF: 800-786-9666 ■ Web: www.cardtronics.com					
Cash Systems Inc 3201 W County Rd 42 Suite 106	Burnsville	MN	55306	952-895-8399	895-7308
NASDAQ: CKNN ■ TF Sales: 877-600-8399 ■ Web: www.cashsystemsinc.com					
Diebold Inc 5995 Mayfair Rd	North Canton	OH	44720	330-490-4000	
NYSE: DBD ■ TF: 800-999-3600 ■ Web: www.diebold.com					
Electronic Cash Systems Inc 30052 Aventura	Rancho Santa Margarita	CA	92688	888-327-2860	888-8024*
*Fax Area Code: 949 ■ TF: 888-327-2864 ■ Web: www.ecsatm.com					
Frisco Bay Industries Ltd 160 Graveline St	Saint-Laurent	QC	H4T1R7	514-738-7300	735-7039
TF: 800-463-7472 ■ Web: www.friscobay.com					
Fujitsu Transaction Solutions Inc 2801 Network Blvd	Frisco	TX	75034	972-963-2300	963-2651
TF: 800-538-8716 ■ Web: www.ftxs.fujitsu.com					
Global Cash Access Holdings Inc 3525 E Post Rd Suite 120	Las Vegas	NV	89120	702-855-3000	672-4371*
NYSE: GCA ■ *Fax Area Code: 866 ■ TF: 800-833-7110 ■ Web: www.globalcashaccess.com					
NCR Corp 1700 S Patterson Blvd	Dayton	OH	45479	937-445-5000	445-5617*
NYSE: NCR ■ *Fax: Cust Svc ■ TF Cust Svc: 800-531-2222 ■ Web: www.ncr.com					
Tidel Engineering Inc 2310 McDaniel Dr	Carrollton	TX	75006	972-484-3358	484-1014
TF: 800-678-7577 ■ Web: www.tidel.com					
Tidel Technologies Inc 2900 Wilcrest Dr Suite 205	Houston	TX	77042	713-783-8200	783-6003
TF: 800-753-3440					
Tranax Technologies Inc 44320 Nobel Dr	Fremont	CA	94538	510-770-2227	770-2240
TF: 888-340-2484 ■ Web: www.tranax.com					

57 AUTOMOBILE DEALERS & GROUPS

SEE ALSO Automobile Sales & Related Services - Online p. 1359

				Phone	Fax
32 Ford Mercury Inc 610 W Main St	Batavia	OH	45103	513-732-2124	732-1029
Web: www.32fordmercury.com					
#1 Cochran of Monroeville 4520 William Penn Hwy	Monroeville	PA	15146	412-373-3333	
TF: 877-262-4726 ■ Web: www.1cochran.com					
Allan Vigil Ford 6790 Mt Zion Blvd	Marrow	GA	30260	678-364-3673	364-3333
TF: 800-222-3597 ■ Web: www.vigilford.com					
Allen Samuels Auto Group 301 Owen Ln	Waco	TX	76710	254-761-6800	761-6899
TF: 800-762-8850 ■ Web: www.allensamuels.com					
America's Car-Mart Inc 1501 SE Walton Blvd Suite 213	Bentonville	AR	72712	479-464-9944	273-7556
NASDAQ: CRMT ■ TF: 800-264-2535 ■ Web: www.car-mart.com					
Ancira Enterprises Inc 6111 Bandera Rd	San Antonio	TX	78238	210-681-4900	681-9413
TF: 800-299-5286 ■ Web: www.ancira.com					
Anderson Automotive Group 9101 Glenwood Ave	Raleigh	NC	27617	919-787-0099	
TF: 800-706-2713 ■ Web: www.andersonautomotive.com					
Asbury Automotive Group Inc 622 3rd Ave 37th Fl	New York	NY	10017	212-885-2500	885-2652
NYSE: ABG ■ Web: www.asburyauto.com					
AutoFair Automotive Group 33 Auto Center Rd	Manchester	NH	03103	603-634-1000	622-2929
Web: www.autofairusa.com					
Autofocus Inc 5994 W Las Positas Blvd Suite 221	Pleasanton	CA	94588	925-924-1105	
AutoNation Inc 110 SE 6th St	Fort Lauderdale	FL	33301	954-769-6000	769-6537*
NYSE: AN ■ *Fax: PR ■ TF: 800-899-4911 ■ Web: corp.autonation.com					
Balise Motor Sales Co 1102 Riverdale St	West Springfield	MA	01089	413-733-8604	739-6441
Web: www.baliseauto.com					
Barrett Holdings Inc 15423 I-10 W	San Antonio	TX	78249	210-341-2800	341-4144
TF: 800-234-3466					
Beck Automotive Group 5141 E Independence Blvd	Charlotte	NC	28212	704-535-6400	532-1926
TF: 800-532-0595 ■ Web: www.beckautogroup.com					
Bella Automotive Group 5895 NW 167th St	Hialeah	FL	33015	305-364-9800	364-9823
TF: 800-779-8696					
Bergstrom Automotive 1 Neenah Ctr	Neenah	WI	54956	920-725-4444	729-5145
Web: www.bergstromauto.com					
Bill Heard Enterprises 200 Brookstone Ctr Pkwy Suite 205	Columbus	GA	31904	706-323-1111	321-9488
TF: 800-833-0479 ■ Web: www.billheard.com					
Bob Baker Auto Group 591 Camino de la Reina Suite 1100	San Diego	CA	92108	619-297-1001	299-1049
Web: www.bobbaker.com					
Bob Rohrman Auto Group 701 Sagamore Pkwy S	Lafayette	IN	47905	765-448-1000	449-2266
TF: 800-488-3534 ■ Web: www.rohrman.com					
Bommarito Automotive Group 15736 Manchester Rd	Ellisville	MO	63011	636-391-7200	227-9340
Boucher Group Inc 4141 S 108th St	Greenfield	WI	53228	414-427-4141	427-4140
Web: www.boucherautos.com					
Boyland Auto Group Inc 710 W Marine Dr	Astoria	OR	97103	503-325-6411	
TF: 888-760-9303					
Braman Management Assn 2060 Biscayne Blvd 2nd Fl	Miami	FL	33137	305-576-1889	576-9898
Brandon Dodge Inc 9207 Adamo Dr E	Tampa	FL	33619	813-620-4300	622-7258
Web: www.brandon.fivestardealers.com					
Buchanan Automotive Group 707 S Washington Blvd	Sarasota	FL	34236	941-366-5230	955-5934
TF: 800-282-5633 ■ Web: www.buchananautomotivegroup.com					
Burt Automotive Network 10301 E Arapahoe Rd	Centennial	CO	80112	303-789-6700	789-6395
TF: 800-535-2878 ■ Web: www.burt.com					
Cable-Dahmer Chevrolet Inc 1834 S Noland Rd	Independence	MO	64055	816-254-3860	521-7638
Web: www.cabledahmer.com					
Capital Ford Inc 4900 Capital Blvd	Raleigh	NC	27616	919-790-4600	790-4668
TF: 800-849-3166 ■ Web: www.capitalford.com					
CarMax Inc 12800 Tuckahoe Creek Pkwy	Richmond	VA	23238	804-747-0422	217-6819
NYSE: KMX ■ Web: www.carmax.com					
Chapman Auto Group 20 Cumberland St	Lebanon	PA	17042	610-272-9400	
Web: www.chapmanautogroup.com					
Chapman Automotive Group LLC 1150 N 54th St Chandler	Scottsdale	AZ	85225	480-970-0740	994-4096
Web: www.chapmanchoice.com					
Chastang Enterprises Inc 6200 N Loop E	Houston	TX	77026	713-671-0101	671-9703
Checkered Flag Motor Car Corp 6541 E Virginia Beach Blvd	Norfolk	VA	23502	757-687-3452	
Web: www.checkeredflag.com					
Collins Auto Group 4220 Bardstown Rd	Louisville	KY	40218	502-459-9550	459-1966
TF: 800-258-2455 ■ Web: www.collinsautogroup.com					
Conant Auto Retail Group 18500 Studebaker Rd	Cerritos	CA	90703	562-402-3844	402-0442
Courtesy Chevrolet 1233 E Camelback Rd	Phoenix	AZ	85014	602-279-3232	604-3063
TF: 800-555-9322 ■ Web: www.houseofcourtesy.com					
Cutter Management Co 1100 Alakea St PH 2	Honolulu	HI	96813	808-529-2000	529-2010
Web: www.cuttercars.com					
DarCars Ltd 12210 Cherry Hill Rd	Silver Spring	MD	20904	301-622-0300	622-4915
Web: www.darcars.com					
Dave Smith Auto Group 210 N Division St	Kellogg	ID	83837	208-784-1208	783-1226
Web: www.usautosales.com					
Day Automotive Group 1600 Golden Mile Hwy	Monroeville	PA	15146	724-327-0900	327-0765*
*Fax: Acctg ■ Web: www.dayauto.com					
Desert Sun Motors Inc 2600 N White Sands Blvd	Alamagordo	NM	88310	505-437-7530	434-2097
TF: 800-682-5266 ■ Web: www.desertsunmotors.com					
Dothan Chrysler-Dodge Inc 4074 Ross Clark Cir NW	Dothan	AL	36303	334-794-0606	794-2600
TF: 800-792-3007 ■ Web: www.dothanchrysler.com					
DriveTime Corp 4020 E Indian School Rd	Phoenix	AZ	85018	602-852-6600	852-6696
TF: 800-863-7483 ■ Web: www.drivetime.com					
Earnhardt Auto Centers 1301 N Arizona Ave	Gilbert	AZ	85233	480-926-4000	558-4050*
*Fax: Sales ■ TF: 800-497-8740 ■ Web: www.earnhardt.com					
Ed Morse Automotive Group Inc 6363 NW 6th Way Suite 400	Fort Lauderdale	FL	33309	954-351-0055	771-5980*
*Fax: Mktg ■ TF: 800-336-6773 ■ Web: www.edmorse.com					
Elder Automotive Group 777 John R	Troy	MI	48083	248-585-4000	585-4039
TF: 800-585-4005 ■ Web: www.elderautomotivegroup.com					
Family Automotive Group Inc 33395 Camino Capistrano	San Juan Capistrano	CA	92675	949-493-4100	240-2445
Faulkner Organization 4437 Street Rd	Trevose	PA	19053	215-364-3980	364-0706
Web: www.tobesure.com					
Ferman Automotive Group 1306 W Kennedy Blvd	Tampa	FL	33606	813-251-2765	254-4798
Web: www.fermanauto.com					
Findlay Automotive Group 310 N Gibson Rd	Henderson	NV	89014	702-558-8888	558-8812
Web: www.findlayauto.com					
Fletcher Jones Automotive Group 7300 W Sahara Ave	Las Vegas	NV	89117	702-739-9800	739-0486
Web: www.fletcherjones.com					
Folsom Lake Ford Inc 12755 Folsom Blvd	Folsom	CA	95630	916-353-2000	353-2080
TF: 800-655-0555 ■ Web: www.folsomlakeford.com					
Freehold Chevrolet 3712 Rt 9 S PO Box 6697	Freehold	NJ	07728	732-462-1324	462-8993
TF: 800-648-8656 ■ Web: www.freeholdchevy.com					
Galloway Family of Dealerships PO Box 70	Fort Myers	FL	33902	239-936-2193	274-2210
TF: 800-220-2598 ■ Web: www.gallowayfamily.com					
Galpin Motors Inc 15505 Roscoe Blvd	North Hills	CA	91343	818-787-3800	778-2211*
*Fax: Acctg ■ TF: 800-464-2574 ■ Web: www.gogalpin.com					
Germain Motor Co 4130 Morse Crossing	Columbus	OH	43219	614-478-2002	478-5370
TF: 866-771-2178 ■ Web: www.germaincars.com					
Gettel Automotive Group 3480 Bee Ridge Rd	Sarasota	FL	34239	941-921-2655	927-1532
TF: 888-468-8696 ■ Web: www.gettelsupercenter.com					
Gillman Cos 10595 W Sam Houston Pkwy S	Houston	TX	77099	713-776-7000	776-6361*
*Fax: Acctg ■ TF: 800-933-7809 ■ Web: www.gillmanauto.com					
Gonzales Automotive Group 5800 Firestone Blvd	South Gate	CA	90280	562-776-2330	776-2331
TF: 888-318-5337 ■ Web: www.casadegonzales.com					
Greenway Automotive Group 9001 E Colonial Dr	Orlando	FL	32817	407-275-3200	515-6464
Web: www.greenwayfordoforlando.com					
Group 1 Automotive Inc 950 Echo Ln Suite 100	Houston	TX	77024	713-647-5700	647-5868*
NYSE: GPI ■ *Fax: Hum Res ■ Web: www.group1auto.com					
Gulf States Toyota Inc 7701 Wilshire Pl Dr PO Box 40306	Houston	TX	77040	713-580-3300	580-3332
Gunn Automotive Group 227 Broadway	San Antonio	TX	78205	210-472-2501	472-2514
Web: www.gunnauto.com					
Gus Machado Ford 1200 W 49th St	Hialeah	FL	33012	305-822-3211	827-2116
Web: www.gusmachadoford.com					
Hall Automotive 441 Viking Dr	Virginia Beach	VA	23452	757-431-9944	431-9950
TF: 800-242-4255 ■ Web: www.hallauto.com					
Hendrick Automotive Group 6000 Monroe Rd Suite 100	Charlotte	NC	28212	704-568-5550	566-3295
Web: www.hendrickauto.com					
Herb Chambers Cos 259 McGrath Hwy	Somerville	MA	02145	617-666-8333	666-8448
Web: www.herbchambers.com					
Hertrich Family of Automobile Dealerships Rt 13 S	Seaford	DE	19973	302-629-5100	629-8428
Web: www.hertrich.com					
Hitchcock Automotive Resources 17340 E Gale Ave	City of Industry	CA	91748	626-839-8401	913-0105
Web: www.phford.com					
Holler Automotive Group PO Box 1720	Winter Park	FL	32790	407-539-6500	629-9213
Holman Enterprises 7411 Maple Ave	Pennsauken	NJ	08109	856-663-5200	663-1409*
*Fax: Hum Res ■ Web: www.holmanauto.com					
Huffines Auto Group 4500 W Plano Pkwy	Plano	TX	75093	972-867-6000	867-6001
TF: 866-522-5138 ■ Web: www.huffines.net					
Jeff Wyler Dealer Group Inc 829 Eastgate S Dr	Cincinnati	OH	45245	513-752-7450	752-1923
Web: www.wyler.com					
Jim Ellis Auto Dealerships 5901 Peachtree Industrial Blvd	Atlanta	GA	30341	770-458-6811	234-8187
Web: www.jimellis.com					

	City	State	ZIP	Phone	Fax
Jim Koons Automotive Group 2000 Chain Bridge Rd *Web:* www.koons.com	Vienna	VA	22182	703-448-7000	442-5777
Jim Pattison Automotive Group 1067 W Cordova St Suite 1800 *Web:* www.jimpattison.com	Vancouver	BC	V6C1C7	604-688-6764	687-2601
JM Family Enterprises 100 Jim Moran Blvd *Web:* www.jmfamily.com	Deerfield Beach	FL	33442	954-429-2000	429-2300
Kahlig Enterprises 9207 San Pedro St *TF:* 800-880-6756	San Antonio	TX	78216	210-341-8841	340-2507
Kelley Automotive Group 633 Ave of Autos *TF:* 800-434-4750 ■ *Web:* www.kelleyautogroup.com	Fort Wayne	IN	46804	260-434-4700	434-4601
Ken Garff Automotive Group 195 E University Pkwy *TF:* 888-323-5869 ■ *Web:* www.kengarff.com	Orem	UT	84058	801-374-1751	377-7109
Kenny Ross Automotive Group 11250 Rt 30 *Web:* www.kennyross.com	North Huntingdon	PA	15642	724-863-9000	863-9488
Kenwood Dealer Group Inc 9500 Kings Automall Rd	Cincinnati	OH	45249	513-683-5484	683-3671
Kerry Automotive Group 155 W Kemper Rd *TF:* 800-641-7400	Cincinnati	OH	45246	513-671-6400	671-6608
Keyes Automotive Group 5855 Van Nuys Blvd *TF:* 800-974-7709 ■ *Web:* www.keyesdirect.com	Van Nuys	CA	91401	818-782-0122	907-4170
Kuni Automotive Group 3725 SW Cedar Hills Blvd *Web:* www.kuniauto.com	Beaverton	OR	97005	503-643-1543	546-9149
Larry H Miller Automotive Group 9350 South 150 E Suite 1000 *Web:* www.lhmauto.com	Sandy	UT	84070	801-563-4100	563-4198
Lia Auto Group 1258 Central Ave *Web:* www.liacars.com	Albany	NY	12205	518-489-2111	489-2112
Lithia Motors Inc 360 E Jackson St *NYSE: LAD* ■ *Web:* www.lithia.com	Medford	OR	97501	541-776-6401	776-6897
Lloyd A Wise Cos 10550 International Blvd *Web:* www.lloydawise.com	Oakland	CA	94603	510-638-4000	
Lou Bachrodt Automotive Group 1801 W Atlantic Blvd *Web:* www.bachrodt.com	Pompano Beach	FL	33069	954-971-3000	977-3500
Lou Fusz Automotive Network Inc 925 N Lindbergh Blvd *TF:* 800-371-7819 ■ *Web:* www.fusz.com	Saint Louis	MO	63141	314-994-1500	993-8641
Lou Sobh Automotive 2473 Pleasant Hill Rd *Web:* www.lousobh.com	Duluth	GA	30096	770-232-0099	232-2695
Love Chrysler Plymouth Inc 4331 S Staples St *TF:* 866-460-5683 ■ *Web:* www.lovechrysler.com	Corpus Christi	TX	78411	361-991-5683	991-2351
Lupient Automotive Group 750 Pennsylvania Ave S *TF:* 800-328-0608 ■ *Web:* www.lupient.com	Minneapolis	MN	55426	763-544-6666	513-5517
Mac Haik Auto Group 10333 Katy Freeway *Web:* www.machaik.com	Houston	TX	77024	713-932-4225	
Machado Gus Ford 1200 W 49th St *Web:* www.gusmachadoford.com	Hialeah	FL	33012	305-822-3211	827-2116
Magnussen Dealership Group 545 Middlefield Rd Suite 240	Menlo Park	CA	94025	650-327-4100	
March/Hodge Automotive 77 Liebert Rd *Web:* www.marchhodgeauto.com	Hartford	CT	06120	860-249-1301	249-5466
Martin Automotive Group Inc 1065 Ashley St Suite 100 *Web:* www.martingp.com	Bowling Green	KY	42103	270-783-8080	783-8006
Marty Franich Auto Center 550 Auto Center Dr	Watsonville	CA	95076	831-722-4181	724-1853
Metro Ford Inc 9000 NW 7th Ave *Web:* www.metroford.com	Miami	FL	33150	305-751-9711	757-4819
Mike Shaw Chevrolet Buick Saab 1080 S Colorado Blvd *TF:* 800-223-1615 ■ *Web:* www.mikeshawauto.com	Denver	CO	80246	303-757-6161	757-7845
New Country Motor Car Group 358 Broadway *Web:* www.newcountry.com	Saratoga Springs	NY	12866	518-584-7700	
Noarus Auto Group 6701 Center Dr W Suite 925 *Web:* www.noarus.com	Los Angeles	CA	90045	310-258-0920	337-4860
Ourisman Automotive Group 4400 Branch Ave **Fax: Acctg* ■ *Web:* www.ourisman.com	Marlow Heights	MD	20748	301-423-4000	423-1845*
Paramount Auto Group 17805 North Fwy **Fax Area Code: 832* ■ *Web:* www.paramountautogroup.com	Houston	TX	77090	281-569-2200	484-9567*
Paul Young Auto Group 3701 E Saunders St PO Box 2965 *Web:* www.paulyoungautomall.com	Laredo	TX	78044	956-727-1192	796-0684
Penske Automotive Group 3534 N Peck Rd **Fax: Sales* ■ *TF:* 800-355-6646 ■ *Web:* www.penskeautomotive.com	El Monte	CA	91731	626-580-6000	580-6137*
Performance Cos 153 Treeline Pk Suite 300	San Antonio	TX	78209	210-829-1800	829-5001
Phil Long Dealerships 1212 Motor City Dr **Fax: Sales* ■ *TF:* 800-685-5664 ■ *Web:* phillong.com	Colorado Springs	CO	80906	719-575-7100	575-2807*
Phil Smith Automotive Group 4250 N Federal Hwy *Web:* www.philsmithauto.com	Lighthouse Point	FL	33064	954-867-1234	
Piazza Auto Group 401 S Schuylkill Ave *Web:* www.piazzaautogroup.com	Norristown	PA	19403	610-630-7911	
Piercey Automotive Group 13600 Beach Blvd *Web:* www.pierceyautogroup.com	Westminster	CA	92683	714-896-9777	896-9779
Plaza Automall 2740 Nostrand Ave *TF:* 800-999-5901 ■ *Web:* www.plazaautomall.com	Brooklyn	NY	11210	718-253-8400	677-9087
Pohanka Automotive Group 4608 St Barnabas Rd *Web:* www.pohanka.com	Marlow Heights	MD	20748	301-899-0941	702-8926
Popular Ford Sales Inc 2505 Coney Island Ave *TF:* 888-622-9122 ■ *Web:* www.popularfordny.com	Brooklyn	NY	11223	718-376-5600	376-9691
Potamkin Automotive Group 6600 Cow Pen Rd Suite 200 *Web:* www.planetautomotive.com	Miami Lakes	FL	33014	305-774-7690	774-4673
Prestige Automotive Group 444 James L Hart Pkwy *Web:* www.prestigeautomotive.com	Ypsilanti	MI	48197	734-438-0322	
Prestige Management Services 400 Sette Dr	Paramus	NJ	07652	201-265-7800	
Priority Auto Group 1495 S Military Hwy *Web:* www.priorityauto.com	Chesapeake	VA	23320	757-424-1102	
Ray Catena Motor Car Corp 910 Rt 1 N *Web:* www.raycatena.com	Edison	NJ	08817	732-549-6600	549-9387
Ray Childress Auto Group LP 900 Business Hwy 290 N **Fax Area Code: 979*	Hempstead	TX	77445	713-350-0976	826-7971*
Red McCombs Automotive Group 755 E Mulberry Ave Suite 600 *TF:* 800-460-4883 ■ *Web:* www.redmccombs.com	San Antonio	TX	78212	210-821-6523	821-5860
Ricart Automotive Group 4255 S Hamilton Rd PO Box 27130 *TF:* 800-332-5872 ■ *Web:* www.ricart1.com	Columbus	OH	43227	614-836-5321	836-6635
Rick Case Automotive Group 875 N SR 7 *Web:* www.rickcase.com	Fort Lauderdale	FL	33317	954-587-1111	587-6381
Ron Carter Automotive Group 3205 FM 528 *Web:* www.roncarter.com	Alvin	TX	77511	281-331-3111	331-4569
Ron Tonkin Dealerships 122 NE 122nd Ave *TF:* 800-460-5328 ■ *Web:* www.tonkin.com	Portland	OR	97230	503-255-4100	252-4899
Rosatti Auto Group DBA Plaza Automall 2740 Nostrand Ave *TF:* 800-999-5901 ■ *Web:* www.plazaautomall.com	Brooklyn	NY	11210	718-253-8400	677-9087
Rosenthal Automotive Organization 1100 S Glebe Rd *Web:* www.rosenthalauto.com	Arlington	VA	22204	703-553-4300	553-8435
Roundtree Automotive Group LLC 8660 Fern Ave Suite 200	Shreveport	LA	71105	318-798-6500	798-5424
Russ Darrow Group W133 N8569 Executive Pkwy *TF:* 800-732-7769 ■ *Web:* www.russdarrow.com	Menomonee Falls	WI	53051	262-250-9600	253-7530
Ryan Automotive LLC 200 Carter Dr *Web:* www.ryanautogroup.com	Edison	NJ	08817	732-650-1550	
Sam Swope Auto Group LLC 10 Swope Auto Ctr *TF:* 800-228-9086 ■ *Web:* www.samswope.com	Louisville	KY	40299	502-499-5000	499-3894
Sansone Auto Network 90-100 Route 1 N *Web:* www.sansoneauto.com	Avenel	NJ	07001	732-815-2270	
Scott-McRae Group 701 Riverside Pk Pl Suite 200 *Web:* www.smag.com	Jacksonville	FL	32204	904-354-4000	354-4730
Serra Automotive Group 9709 Parkway E Suite D *Web:* www.serraautomotive.com	Birmingham	AL	35215	205-836-6775	
Serra Automotive Inc 3118 E Hill Rd	Grand Blanc	MI	48439	810-694-1720	694-6405
Servco Pacific Inc 900 4th St Mall Suite 600 *Web:* www.servco.com	Honolulu	HI	96813	808-521-6511	523-3937
Shammas Automotive Group 1801 S Figueroa St	Los Angeles	CA	90015	213-748-8951	
Sheehy Auto Stores 12701 Fair Lakes Cir Suite 250 *Web:* www.sheehy.com	Fairfax	VA	22033	703-802-3480	802-3481
Shelly Automotive Group 2030 Main St Suite 1650 *Web:* www.shellygroup.com	Irvine	CA	92614	949-387-8242	
Silver Star Automotive Group 3905 Auto Mall Dr *TF:* 800-995-5175 ■ *Web:* www.silverstarauto.com	Thousand Oaks	CA	91362	805-371-5400	371-5451
Sonic Automotive Inc 6415 Idlewild Rd Suite 109 *NYSE: SAH* ■ *Web:* www.sonicautomotive.com	Charlotte	NC	28212	704-566-2400	536-4665
Staluppi Auto Group 2010 Ave B	Riviera Beach	FL	33404	561-844-7148	844-6473
Suburban Collection 1810 Maplelawn Dr *Web:* www.suburbancollection.com	Troy	MI	48084	248-643-0070	643-8058
Sullivan Automotive Group 2440 Santa Monica Blvd *Web:* www.sullivanautomotivegroup.com	Santa Monica	CA	90404	310-829-1888	
Sunland Park Pontiac-Buick-GMC 955 Crockett Way	El Paso	TX	79922	915-584-8419	581-9203
Tamiami Automotive Group 8250 SW 8th St *TF:* 800-845-2886 ■ *Web:* tamiami.fivestardealers.com	Miami	FL	33144	305-266-5500	266-5604
Toresco Enterprises Inc 170 Rt 22 E *Web:* www.autoland-usa.com	Springfield	NJ	07081	973-467-2900	467-1824
Tuttle-Click Automotive Group 41 Auto Center Dr *TF:* 800-926-8253 ■ *Web:* www.tuttleclick.com	Irvine	CA	92618	949-598-4800	830-0980
United Auto Group Inc 2555 Telegraph Rd *NYSE: UAG* ■ *Web:* www.unitedauto.com	Bloomfield Hills	MI	48302	248-648-2500	648-2035
Van Enterprises 8500 Shawnee Mission Pkwy Suite 200 *TF:* 800-747-4400 ■ *Web:* www.vanenterprises.com	Shawnee Mission	KS	66202	913-432-6400	789-1039
Victory Automotive Group 5496 W Andrew Johnson Hwy *Web:* www.victoryautomotivegroup.com	Morristown	TN	37814	423-586-9657	
Vista Auto 21501 Ventura Blvd *Web:* www.vistaauto.com	Woodland Hills	CA	91364	818-884-7600	883-2975
VT Inc DBA Van Enterprises 8500 Shawnee Mission Pkwy Suite 200 *TF:* 800-747-4400 ■ *Web:* www.vanenterprises.com	Shawnee Mission	KS	66202	913-432-6400	789-1039
Warnock Automotive Group 175 Rt 10 *Web:* www.warnockauto.com	East Hanover	NJ	07936	973-884-2100	884-9590
West-Herr Automotive Group Inc S-5025 Camp Rd *TF:* 800-933-5701 ■ *Web:* www.westherr.com	Hamburg	NY	14075	716-649-5640	649-7883
Wilde Automotive Group 1603 E Moreland Blvd *TF:* 800-236-5567 ■ *Web:* www.wildeauto.com	Waukesha	WI	53186	262-542-0771	542-0882
Wilson Automotive Group 1400 N Tustin St *Web:* www.toyotaoforange.com	Orange	CA	92867	714-639-6750	997-9200
Wolfe Automotive Group 1011 W 103rd St *Web:* www.jaywolfe.com	Kansas City	MO	64114	816-943-6060	942-5399
World Auto Group 3057 Route 10 E *Web:* www.denvillenissan.com	Denville	NJ	07834	973-442-0500	
World Class Automotive Group PO Box 62609	Houston	TX	77205	281-443-3443	

AUTOMOBILE LEASING

SEE Credit & Financing - Commercial p. 1580; Credit & Financing - Consumer p. 1581; Fleet Leasing & Management p. 1640

58 AUTOMOBILE SALES & RELATED SERVICES - ONLINE

SEE ALSO Automobile Dealers & Groups p. 1358

	City	State	ZIP	Phone	Fax
Autobytel Inc 18872 MacArthur Blvd *NASDAQ: ABTL* ■ *TF:* 888-422-8999 ■ *Web:* www.autobytel.com	Irvine	CA	92612	949-225-4500	225-4541
Autofusion Corp 9605 Scranton Rd Suite 450 *TF:* 800-410-7354 ■ *Web:* www.autofusion.com	San Diego	CA	92121	858-270-9444	270-6116
Automobile Consumer Services Inc 6249 Stewart Rd *TF:* 800-223-4882 ■ *Web:* www.acscorp.com	Cincinnati	OH	45227	513-527-7700	527-7705
Automotive Information Center 18872 MacArthur Blvd *TF:* 888-422-8999 ■ *Web:* www.autosite.com	Irvine	CA	92612	949-862-1335	757-8920
AUTOPEDIA 5455 Production Dr *Web:* autopedia.com	Huntington Beach	CA	92649	714-892-0969	
AutoTrader.com LLC 5775 Peachtree Dunwoody Rd Suite A-200 *TF:* 800-353-9350 ■ *Web:* www.autotrader.com	Atlanta	GA	30342	404-269-8000	845-8680
AutoVIN Inc 50 Mansell Ct Suite 200 *TF:* 877-428-8684 ■ *Web:* www.autovin.com	Roswell	GA	30076	678-585-8000	585-8201
Autoweb.com Inc 18872 MacArthur Blvd *TF:* 888-422-8999 ■ *Web:* www.autoweb.com	Irvine	CA	92612	949-225-4500	225-4541
Carfax Inc 10304 Eaton Pl Suite 500 *TF:* 800-274-2277 ■ *Web:* www.carfax.com	Fairfax	VA	22030	703-934-2664	218-2853
CarPrices.com c/o AutoFusion Corp 9605 Scranton Rd Suite 450 *TF:* 800-410-7354 ■ *Web:* www.carprices.com	San Diego	CA	92121	858-270-9444	270-6116
Cars.com c/o Classified Ventures LLC 175 W Jackson Blvd Suite 800 *Web:* www.cars.com	Chicago	IL	60604	312-601-5000	
CarsDirect.com Inc 909 N Sepulveda Blvd 11th Fl *TF Cust Svc:* 800-431-2500 ■ *Web:* www.carsdirect.com	El Segundo	CA	90245	310-280-4000	
CarSmart 18872 MacArthur Blvd *TF:* 888-422-8999 ■ *Web:* www.carsmart.com	Irvine	CA	92612	949-862-1335	757-8920
DealerNet c/o Cobalt Group Inc 2200 1st Ave S Suite 400 *TF:* 800-909-8244 ■ *Web:* www.dealernet.com	Seattle	WA	98134	206-269-6363	269-6350
Edmunds.com Inc 1620 26th St Suite 400 South Tower *Web:* www.edmunds.com	Santa Monica	CA	90404	310-309-6300	309-6400
IntelliChoice Inc 1901 S Bascom Ave Suite 600 *Web:* www.intellichoice.com	Campbell	CA	95008	408-377-4300	377-4303
Kelley Blue Book Co Inc 195 Technology Dr *TF:* 800-258-3266 ■ *Web:* www.kbb.com	Irvine	CA	92623	949-770-7704	837-1904
MotorPlace.com 2200 1st Ave S *Web:* www2.motorplace.com	Seattle	WA	98134	206-269-6363	

59 AUTOMOBILES - MFR

SEE ALSO All-Terrain Vehicles p. 1277; Motor Vehicles - Commercial & Special Purpose p. 1982; Motorcycles & Motorcycle Parts & Accessories p. 1983; Snowmobiles p. 2318

				Phone	Fax
4 Guys Inc 230 Industrial Park Rd PO Box 90 — *Web:* www.4guysfire.com	Meyersdale	PA	15552	814-634-8373	634-0076
Acura Div American Honda Motor Co Inc 1919 Torrance Blvd — **Fax:* Hum Res ■ *TF:* 800-999-1009 ■ *Web:* www.acura.com	Torrance	CA	90501	310-783-2000	783-2010*
AM General LLC 105 N Niles Ave PO Box 7025 — *Web:* www.amgeneral.com	South Bend	IN	46617	574-237-6222	284-2814
American Honda Motor Co Inc 1919 Torrance Blvd — **Fax:* Hum Res ■ *TF:* 800-999-1009 ■ *Web:* www.honda.com	Torrance	CA	90501	310-783-2000	783-2110*
American Honda Motor Co Inc Acura Div 1919 Torrance Blvd — **Fax:* Hum Res ■ *TF:* 800-999-1009 ■ *Web:* www.acura.com	Torrance	CA	90501	310-783-2000	783-2010*
American Suzuki Motor Corp 3251 E Imperial Hwy — *Web:* www.suzuki.com	Brea	CA	92821	714-996-7040	524-2512
Aston Martin Lagonda of North America Inc 553 MacArthur Blvd — *TF:* 800-637-6837 ■ *Web:* www.astonmartin.com	Mahwah	NJ	07430	201-818-8351	818-8328
Audi of America 3800 Hamlin Rd — **Fax:* Hum Res ■ *TF:* 800-367-2834 ■ *Web:* www.audiusa.com	Auburn Hills	MI	48326	248-340-5000	754-6521*
Bentley Motors Ltd 3800 Hamlin Rd — *TF:* 800-777-6923 ■ *Web:* www.bentleymotors.com	Auburn Hills	MI	48326	248-754-6464	659-1508
BMW of North America LLC 300 Chestnut Ridge Rd — *TF:* 800-526-0818 ■ *Web:* www.bmwusa.com	Woodcliff Lake	NJ	07677	201-307-4000	307-4095
Buick Motor Div General Motors Corp 300 Renaissance Center — **Fax Area Code:* 248 ■ *TF Cust Svc:* 800-521-7300 ■ *Web:* www.buick.com	Detroit	MI	48265	313-556-5000	696-4984*
Cadillac Motor Car Div General Motors Corp 300 Renaissance Center — **Fax Area Code:* 248 ■ *TF Cust Svc:* 800-458-8006 ■ *Web:* www.cadillac.com	Detroit	MI	48265	313-556-5000	696-4984*
Chevrolet Motor Div General Motors Corp 300 Renaissance Center — **Fax Area Code:* 248 ■ *TF Cust Svc:* 800-222-1020 ■ *Web:* www.chevrolet.com	Detroit	MI	48265	313-556-5000	696-4984*
DaimlerChrysler Canada Inc 2199 Chrysler Center — **Fax:* Sales ■ *TF:* 800-265-6904 ■ *Web:* www.daimlerchrysler.ca	Windsor	ON	N9A4H6	519-973-2000	973-2799*
DaimlerChrysler Corp 1000 Chrysler Dr — *NYSE:* DCX ■ **Fax:* Cust Svc ■ *TF:* 800-992-1997 ■ *Web:* www.daimlerchrysler.com	Auburn Hills	MI	48326	248-576-5741	512-8084*
DaimlerChrysler Corp Dodge Div 1000 Chrysler Dr — **Fax:* Cust Svc ■ *TF Cust Svc:* 800-992-1997 ■ *Web:* www.dodge.com	Auburn Hills	MI	48321	248-576-5741	512-8840*
DaimlerChrysler Corp Jeep Div PO Box 21-8004 — *TF Cust Svc:* 800-992-1997 ■ *Web:* www.jeep.com	Auburn Hills	MI	48321	248-576-5741	
DaimlerChrysler Corp Plymouth Div PO Box 21-8004 — *TF Cust Svc:* 800-992-1997	Auburn Hills	MI	48321	248-576-5741	
Dodge Div DaimlerChrysler Corp 1000 Chrysler Dr — **Fax:* Cust Svc ■ *TF Cust Svc:* 800-992-1997 ■ *Web:* www.dodge.com	Auburn Hills	MI	48321	248-576-5741	512-8840*
Ferrari North America Inc 250 Sylvan Ave — *Web:* www.ferrarina.com	Englewood Cliffs	NJ	07632	201-816-2600	816-2626
Fiat USA Inc 7 Times Sq Tower Suite 4306 — *Web:* www.fiat.com	New York	NY	10036	212-355-2600	755-6152
Ford Motor Co 1 American Rd PO Box 6248 — *NYSE:* F ■ *TF:* 800-392-3673 ■ *Web:* www.ford.com	Dearborn	MI	48126	313-322-3000	845-6073
Ford Motor Co of Canada Ltd PO Box 2000 — **Fax:* Mail Rm ■ *Web:* www.ford.ca	Oakville	ON	L6J5E4	905-845-2511	844-8085*
General Motors of Canada Ltd 1908 Colonel Sam Dr — **Fax:* PR ■ *TF:* 800-263-3777 ■ *Web:* www.gmcanada.com	Oshawa	ON	L1H8P7	905-644-5000	644-5731*
General Motors Corp (GMC) 300 Renaissance Center — *NYSE:* GM ■ **Fax Area Code:* 248 ■ *Web:* www.gm.com	Detroit	MI	48265	313-556-5000	696-7300*
General Motors Corp Buick Motor Div 300 Renaissance Center — **Fax Area Code:* 248 ■ *TF Cust Svc:* 800-521-7300 ■ *Web:* www.buick.com	Detroit	MI	48265	313-556-5000	696-4984*
General Motors Corp Cadillac Motor Car Div 300 Renaissance Center — **Fax Area Code:* 248 ■ *TF Cust Svc:* 800-458-8006 ■ *Web:* www.cadillac.com	Detroit	MI	48265	313-556-5000	696-4984*
General Motors Corp Chevrolet Motor Div 300 Renaissance Center — **Fax Area Code:* 248 ■ *TF Cust Svc:* 800-222-1020 ■ *Web:* www.chevrolet.com	Detroit	MI	48265	313-556-5000	696-4984*
General Motors Corp Pontiac Div 300 Renaissance Center — **Fax:* Mktg ■ *TF Cust Svc:* 800-762-2737 ■ *Web:* www.pontiac.com	Detroit	MI	48265	313-556-5000	667-4001*
General Motors Corp Pontiac-GMC Div 300 Renaissance Center — **Fax Area Code:* 248 ■ *TF Cust Svc:* 800-462-4782 ■ *Web:* www.gmc.com	Detroit	MI	48265	313-556-5000	696-4984*
General Motors Corp Saturn Corp Div 100 Saturn Pkwy MD 371-999-S24 — *TF Cust Svc:* 800-553-6000 ■ *Web:* www.saturn.com	Spring Hill	TN	37174	931-486-5000	489-4245
Honda Canada Inc 715 Milner Ave — *Web:* www.honda.ca	Toronto	ON	M1B2K8	416-284-8110	286-1322
Hyundai Motor America 10550 Talbert Ave — **Fax:* Mktg ■ *TF Cust Svc:* 800-633-5151 ■ *Web:* www.hyundaiusa.com	Fountain Valley	CA	92708	714-965-3000	965-3843*
Infiniti Div Nissan Motor Corp USA 333 Commerce St — *TF:* 800-647-7263 ■ *Web:* www.infiniti.com	Nashville	TN	37201	615-725-1000	723-3343
Isuzu Motors America Inc 13340 183rd St — **Fax:* Hum Res ■ *TF Cust Svc:* 800-255-6727 ■ *Web:* www.isuzu.com	Cerritos	CA	90702	562-229-5000	229-5463*
Jaguar Cars North America 555 MacArthur Blvd — *TF Cust Svc:* 800-452-4827 ■ *Web:* www.jaguar.com/us	Mahwah	NJ	07430	201-818-8500	818-9770
Jeep Div DaimlerChrysler Corp PO Box 21-8004 — *TF Cust Svc:* 800-992-1997 ■ *Web:* www.jeep.com	Auburn Hills	MI	48321	248-576-5741	
Kia Motors America Inc 9801 Muirlands Blvd — *TF:* 800-225-5542 ■ *Web:* www.kia.com	Irvine	CA	92619	949-470-7000	470-2802
Land Rover North America Inc 555 MacArthur Blvd — *TF:* 800-637-6837 ■ *Web:* www.landrover.com	Mahwah	NJ	07430	201-818-8500	818-9770
Lexus Div Toyota Motor Sales USA Inc 19001 S Western Ave — *TF Cust Svc:* 800-331-4331 ■ *Web:* www.lexus.com	Torrance	CA	90501	310-468-4000	468-7800
Lincoln-Mercury Co 16800 Executive Plaza Dr PO Box 6248 — *Web:* www.lincolnmercury.com	Dearborn	MI	48121	800-521-4140	
Lotus Cars USA Inc 2236 Northmont Pkwy — *TF:* 800-245-6887 ■ *Web:* www.lotuscars.com	Duluth	GA	30096	770-476-6540	476-6541
Mazda North American Operations 7755 Irvine Center Dr — *TF Cust Svc:* 800-222-5500 ■ *Web:* www.mazdausa.com	Irvine	CA	92618	949-727-1990	727-6101
Mercedes-Benz USA 1 Mercedes Dr — *TF Cust Svc:* 800-222-0100 ■ *Web:* www.mbusa.com	Montvale	NJ	07645	201-573-0600	573-2337
Mitsubishi Canada Ltd 200 Granville St Suite 2800 — *Web:* www.mitsubishi.ca	Vancouver	BC	V6C1G6	604-654-8000	654-8222
Mitsubishi Motors America Inc 6400 Katella Ave — *Web:* www.mitsubishi-motors.co.jp	Cypress	CA	90630	714-372-6000	
New United Motor Mfg Inc (NUMMI) 45500 Fremont Blvd — *Web:* www.nummi.com	Fremont	CA	94538	510-498-5500	
Nissan Canada Inc 5290 Orbitor Dr — *TF:* 800-387-0122 ■ *Web:* www.nissancanada.com	Mississauga	ON	L4W4Z5	905-629-2888	629-2888
Nissan Motor Corp USA Infiniti Div 333 Commerce St — *TF:* 800-647-7263 ■ *Web:* www.infiniti.com	Nashville	TN	37201	615-725-1000	723-3343
Nissan North America Inc 333 Commerce St — *TF:* 800-647-7263 ■ *Web:* www.nissanusa.com	Nashville	TN	37201	615-725-1000	723-3343
NUMMI (New United Motor Mfg Inc) 45500 Fremont Blvd — *Web:* www.nummi.com	Fremont	CA	94538	510-498-5500	
Peugeot Motors of America Inc 150 Clove Rd Overlook at Great Notch — *TF:* 800-223-0587 ■ *Web:* www.peugeot.com	Little Falls	NJ	07424	973-812-4444	812-2280
Plymouth Div DaimlerChrysler Corp PO Box 21-8004 — *TF Cust Svc:* 800-992-1997	Auburn Hills	MI	48321	248-576-5741	
Pontiac Div General Motors Corp 300 Renaissance Center — **Fax:* Mktg ■ *TF Cust Svc:* 800-762-2737 ■ *Web:* www.pontiac.com	Detroit	MI	48265	313-556-5000	667-4001*
Pontiac-GMC Div General Motors Corp 300 Renaissance Center — **Fax Area Code:* 248 ■ *TF Cust Svc:* 800-462-4782 ■ *Web:* www.gmc.com	Detroit	MI	48265	313-556-5000	696-4984*
Porsche Cars North America Inc 980 Hammond Dr Suite 1000 — *TF:* 800-545-8039 ■ *Web:* www.porsche.com/usa	Atlanta	GA	30328	770-290-3500	290-3708
Saab Cars USA Inc 100 Renaissance Ctr — *TF:* 800-722-2872 ■ *Web:* www.saabusa.com	Detroit	MI	48265	313-556-5000	665-0550
Saturn Corp Div General Motors Corp 100 Saturn Pkwy MD 371-999-S24 — *TF Cust Svc:* 800-553-6000 ■ *Web:* www.saturn.com	Spring Hill	TN	37174	931-486-5000	489-4245
Subaru of America Inc 2235 Rt 70 W PO Box 6000 — **Fax:* Mktg ■ *TF Cust Svc:* 800-782-2783 ■ *Web:* www.subaru.com	Cherry Hill	NJ	08034	856-488-8500	488-3274*
Toyota Canada Inc 1 Toyota Pl — *TF Cust Svc:* 888-869-6828 ■ *Web:* www.toyota.ca	Scarborough	ON	M1H1H9	416-438-6320	431-1867
Toyota Motor Sales USA Inc 19001 S Western Ave — *TF Cust Svc:* 800-331-4331 ■ *Web:* www.toyota.com	Torrance	CA	90501	310-468-4000	468-7814
Toyota Motor Sales USA Inc Lexus Div 19001 S Western Ave — *TF Cust Svc:* 800-331-4331 ■ *Web:* www.lexus.com	Torrance	CA	90501	310-468-4000	468-7800
Volkswagen of America Inc 3800 Hamlin Rd — *TF:* 800-822-8987 ■ *Web:* www.vw.com	Auburn Hills	MI	48326	248-754-5000	
Volkswagen Canada Inc 777 Bayly St W — *TF:* 800-822-8987 ■ *Web:* www.vw.ca	Ajax	ON	L1S7G7	905-428-6700	428-5898
Volvo Cars of North America 1 Volvo Dr — *TF Cust Svc:* 800-458-1552 ■ *Web:* www.volvocars.com	Rockleigh	NJ	07647	201-768-7300	768-1385

60 AUTOMOTIVE PARTS & SUPPLIES - MFR

SEE ALSO Carburetors, Pistons, Piston Rings, Valves p. 1407; Electrical Equipment for Internal Combustion Engines p. 1606; Engines & Turbines p. 1624; Gaskets, Packing, Sealing Devices p. 1689; Hose & Belting - Rubber or Plastics p. 1790; Motors (Electric) & Generators p. 1983

				Phone	Fax
AAM (American Axle & Mfg Inc) 1 Dauch Dr — *NYSE:* AXL ■ *TF:* 800-299-2953 ■ *Web:* www.aam.com	Detroit	MI	48211	313-758-3600	
Aamp of America Inc 13160 56th Ct Suite 508 — *TF:* 800-477-2267 ■ *Web:* www.aampofamerica.com	Clearwater	FL	33760	727-572-9255	573-9326
Acadia Polymers Inc Park at Valley Pointe 5251 Concourse Dr Suite 3 — *TF:* 800-444-6165 ■ *Web:* www.acadiapolymers.com	Roanoke	VA	24019	540-265-2700	265-2764
Accuride Corp 7140 Office Cir — *NYSE:* ACW ■ *TF Cust Svc:* 800-626-7096 ■ *Web:* www.accuridecorp.com	Evansville	IN	47715	812-962-5000	962-5400
Affinia Group Inc 1101 Technology Dr — *Web:* www.affiniagroup.com	Ann Arbor	MI	48108	734-827-5400	827-5407
Aftermarket Technology Corp 1400 Opus Pl Suite 600 — *NASDAQ:* ATAC ■ *Web:* www.atcaff.com	Downers Grove	IL	60515	630-271-8100	271-9999
Airtex Products 407 W Main St — *TF:* 800-880-3056 ■ *Web:* www.airtexproducts.com	Fairfield	IL	62837	618-842-2111	842-4069
Aisin World Corp of America 24330 Garnier St — **Fax:* Acctg ■ *TF:* 800-822-2726 ■ *Web:* www.aisinworld.com	Torrance	CA	90505	310-326-8681	326-0678*
Alcoa Automotive 36555 Corporate Dr Suite 185	Farmington Hills	MI	48331	248-489-4900	
Allison Transmission Div General Motors Corp 4700 W 10th St — *Web:* www.allisontransmission.com	Indianapolis	IN	46206	317-242-5000	242-0262
Alma Products Co 2000 Michigan Ave — **Fax Area Code:* 800 ■ *TF:* 877-427-2624 ■ *Web:* www.almaproducts.com	Alma	MI	48801	989-463-1151	457-2719*
Aluminum Casting & Engineering Co Inc 2039 S Lenox St — *Web:* www.alumcast.com	Milwaukee	WI	53207	414-744-3902	744-6411
AMBAC International Inc 910 Spears Creek Ct — *TF:* 800-628-6894 ■ *Web:* www.ambac.net	Elgin	SC	29045	803-735-1400	735-2163
American Axle & Mfg Inc (AAM) 1 Dauch Dr — *NYSE:* AXL ■ *TF:* 800-299-2953 ■ *Web:* www.aam.com	Detroit	MI	48211	313-758-3600	
American Racing Equipment Inc 19067 S Reyes Ave — *TF:* 800-421-5800 ■ *Web:* www.americanracing.com	Rancho Dominguez	CA	90221	310-635-7806	764-9417
Amerigon Inc 5462 Irwindale Ave — *NASDAQ:* ARGN ■ *Web:* www.amerigon.com	Irwindale	CA	91706	626-815-7400	815-7441
AMSTED Industries Inc 180 N Stetson St Suite 1800 — **Fax:* Hum Res ■ *Web:* www.amsted.com	Chicago	IL	60601	312-645-1700	819-8504*
ARC Automotive Inc 1601 Midpark Rd Suite 100 — *Web:* www.arcautomotive.com	Knoxville	TN	37921	865-583-7711	583-7611
ArvinMeritor Inc 2135 W Maple Rd — *NYSE:* ARM ■ *Web:* www.arvinmeritor.com	Troy	MI	48084	248-435-1000	435-1393
ASC Inc 18500 Walnut St — *Web:* www.ascglobal.com	Southgate	MI	48195	734-285-4911	246-0029
ASF-Keystone Inc 1700 Walnut St — *Web:* www.asf-usa.com	Granite City	IL	62040	618-452-2111	452-7115
Autocam Corp 4070 E Paris Ave — *TF:* 800-747-6978 ■ *Web:* www.autocam.com	Kentwood	MI	49512	616-698-0707	698-6876
Avis Industrial Corp 1909 S Main St — *Web:* www.avisindustrial.com	Upland	IN	46989	765-998-8100	998-8111
Baldwin Filters 4400 E Hwy 30 — **Fax Area Code:* 800 ■ *TF:* 800-822-5394 ■ *Web:* www.baldwinfilter.com	Kearney	NE	68848	308-234-1951	828-4453*
Bean John Co 309 Exchange Ave — *TF:* 800-362-8326 ■ *Web:* www.johnbean.com	Conway	AR	72032	501-450-1500	450-1585
Black River Mfg Inc 2625 20th St — *Web:* www.blackrivermfg.com	Port Huron	MI	48060	810-982-9812	982-2074
Blackhawk Automotive Plastics Inc 800 Pennsylvania Ave — *Web:* www.blackhawkplastics.com	Salem	OH	44460	330-337-9961	332-6579
Blount Industrial & Power Equipment Group 535 Mack Todd Rd — *TF:* 800-254-8173 ■ *Web:* www.blount.com/Induspg.html	Zebulon	NC	27597	919-269-7421	269-0257
Blue Water Automotive Systems Inc 1515 Busha Hwy — *Web:* www.bwasi.com	Marysville	MI	48040	810-364-4550	364-4556
BorgWarner Automatic Transmission Systems 3800 Automation Ave — *Web:* www.borgwarner.com	Auburn Hills	MI	48326	248-754-9600	
BorgWarner Inc 3850 Hamlin Rd — *NYSE:* BWA ■ *Web:* www.bwauto.com	Auburn Hills	MI	48326	248-754-9200	
BorgWarner Morse TEC 800 Warren Rd — *Web:* www.bwauto.com	Ithaca	NY	14850	607-257-6700	257-3359
BorgWarner TorqTransfer Systems 3800 Automation Ave — *Web:* www.borgwarner.com	Auburn Hills	MI	48326	248-754-9600	754-9356
Cadence Innovation 977 E 14 Mile Rd — *Web:* www.cadenceinnovation.com	Troy	MI	48083	248-457-4400	

Company	City	State	Zip	Phone	Fax
Capsonic Automotive Inc 460 S 2nd St	Elgin	IL	60123	847-888-7300	888-7543
TF: 888-981-1500 ■ *Web:* www.capsonic.com					
Cardone Industries Inc 5501 Whitaker Ave	Philadelphia	PA	19124	215-912-3000	912-3498
TF Cust Svc: 800-777-4780 ■ *Web:* www.cardone.com					
Carlisle Cos Inc 13925 Ballantyne Corporate Pl Suite 400	Charlotte	NC	28277	704-501-1100	501-1190
NYSE: CSL ■ *Web:* www.carlisle.com					
Carlisle Industrial Brake 1031 E Hillside Dr	Bloomington	IN	47401	812-336-3811	334-8775
TF: 800-873-6361 ■ *Web:* www.carlislebrake.com					
Casco Products Corp 1 Waterview Dr	Shelton	CT	06484	203-922-3200	922-3201
Web: www.cascoglobal.com					
Champion Laboratories Inc 200 S 4th St	Albion	IL	62806	618-445-6011	445-4040
Web: www.champlabs.com					
Clarcor Inc 840 Crescent Center Dr Suite 600	Franklin	TN	37067	615-771-3100	771-5616
NYSE: CLC ■ *TF:* 800-252-7267 ■ *Web:* www.clarcor.com					
Collins & Aikman 26533 Evergreen Rd	Southfield	MI	48076	248-728-4500	
Web: www.collinsaikman.com					
Commercial Vehicle Group Inc 6530 W Campus Oval	New Albany	OH	43054	614-289-5360	289-5361
NASDAQ: CVGI ■ *Web:* www.cvgrp.com					
Consolidated Metco Inc 13940 N Rivergate Blvd	Portland	OR	97203	503-286-5741	240-5488*
**Fax:* Sales ■ *TF Sales:* 800-547-9473 ■ *Web:* www.conmet.com					
CONTECH US LLC 8001 Angling Rd Suite 2-C	Portage	MI	49024	269-327-9990	327-9993
TF: 800-314-4779 ■ *Web:* www.contech-global.com					
Cooper-Standard Automotive Fluid Systems Div 2110 Executive Hills Ct	Auburn Hills	MI	48326	248-836-9400	836-9116
Web: www.cooperstandard.com					
Cooper-Standard Automotive Inc 39550 Orchard Hill Place Dr	Novi	MI	48375	248-596-5900	596-6540*
**Fax:* Hum Res ■ *Web:* www.cooperstandard.com					
Cummins Filtration 2931 Elm Hill Pike	Nashville	TN	37214	615-367-0040	399-3650
TF: 800-777-7064 ■ *Web:* www.cumminsfiltration.com					
Cummins Inc 1000 5th St PO Box 3005	Columbus	IN	47201	812-377-5000	377-3334
NYSE: CMI ■ *TF:* 800-343-7357 ■ *Web:* www.cummins.com					
CWC Textron 1085 W Sherman Blvd	Muskegon	MI	49441	231-733-1331	739-2649
TF: 800-892-9871					
Dacco Inc 741 Dacco Dr PO Box 2789	Cookeville	TN	38502	931-528-7581	528-9777
TF: 800-443-2226 ■ *Web:* www.daccoatparts.com					
Dana Corp 4500 Dorr St PO Box 1000	Toledo	OH	43697	419-535-4500	535-4643
NYSE: DCN ■ *Web:* www.dana.com					
Danaher Corp 2099 Pennsylvania Ave NW 12th Fl	Washington	DC	20006	202-828-0850	828-0860
NYSE: DHR ■ *Web:* www.danaher.com					
Dayton Parts LLC 3500 Industrial Rd PO Box 5795	Harrisburg	PA	17110	717-255-8500	255-8568
TF Cust Svc: 800-225-2159 ■ *Web:* www.daytonparts.com					
Decoma International Inc 50 Casmir Ct	Concord	ON	L4K4J5	905-669-2888	669-4992
TF: 800-461-3967 ■ *Web:* www.decoma.com					
Delphi Aftermarket Operations 1441 W Long Lake Rd	Troy	MI	48098	248-267-8800	
Delphi Corp 5725 Delphi Dr	Troy	MI	48098	248-813-2000	813-6866
Web: www.delphi.com					
Delphi Energy & Chassis Systems 5725 Delphi Dr	Troy	MI	48098	248-813-2000	813-6866
Web: www.delphi.com					
Delphi Saginaw Steering Systems 3900 E Holland Rd	Saginaw	MI	48601	989-757-5000	757-5115
Web: www.delphi.com					
Denso International America Inc 24777 Denso Dr	Southfield	MI	48033	248-350-7500	213-2337
TF: 866-874-3104 ■ *Web:* www.densocorp-na.com					
Detroit Steel Products Co Inc 511 N Rangeline Rd	Morristown	IN	46161	765-763-6089	763-6551
Web: www.detroitsteel.com					
Dexter Axle 2900 Industrial Pkwy E	Elkhart	IN	46515	574-295-7888	295-8666
Web: www.dexteraxle.com					
Dura Automotive Systems Inc 2791 Research Dr	Rochester Hills	MI	48309	248-299-7500	299-7501
NASDAQ: DRRA ■ *TF:* 800-362-3872 ■ *Web:* www.duraauto.com					
Dura Convertible Systems 1365 E Beecher St	Adrian	MI	49221	517-263-7864	266-3214
Durakon Industries Inc 2101 N Lapeer Rd	Lapeer	MI	48446	810-664-0850	667-7735*
**Fax:* Cust Svc ■ *TF Cust Svc:* 800-955-3993 ■ *Web:* www.durakon.com					
Eagle-Picher Industries Inc 2424 John Daly Rd	Inkster	MI	48141	313-278-5956	278-5982
Web: www.epcorp.com					
Eagle-Picher Industries Inc Hillsdale Div 2424 John Daly Rd	Inkster	MI	48141	313-278-5956	278-5982
Web: www.epcorp.com					
East Penn Mfg Co Inc PO Box 147	Lyon Station	PA	19536	610-682-6361	682-4781
Web: www.eastpenn-deka.com					
Eaton Corp 1111 Superior Ave Eaton Center	Cleveland	OH	44114	216-523-5000	523-4787
NYSE: ETN ■ *Web:* www.eaton.com					
Edelbrock Corp 2700 California St	Torrance	CA	90503	310-781-2222	320-1187
TF: 800-739-3737 ■ *Web:* www.edelbrock.com					
EnPro Industries Inc 5605 Carnegie Blvd Suite 500	Charlotte	NC	28209	704-731-1500	731-1511
NYSE: NPO ■ *TF:* 866-663-6776 ■ *Web:* www.enproindustries.com					
Faurecia Exhaust Systems Inc 543 Matzinger Rd	Toledo	OH	43612	419-727-5000	727-5025
Web: www.faurecia.com					
Federal-Mogul Corp 26555 Northwestern Hwy	Southfield	MI	48034	248-354-7700	354-8950
TF Cust Svc: 800-560-1400 ■ *Web:* www.federalmogul.com					
Filtran Div SPX Corp 875 Seegers Rd	Des Plaines	IL	60016	847-635-6670	635-7724
Web: www.spxfiltran.com					
Findlay Industries Inc 4000 Fostoria Rd	Findlay	OH	45840	419-422-1302	422-0385
Web: www.findlayindustries.com					
Firestone Industrial Products Co 310 E 96th St	Indianapolis	IN	46240	317-818-8600	818-8645
TF: 800-888-0650 ■ *Web:* www.firestoneindustrial.com					
Fleetline Products 784 Bill Jones Industrial Dr	Springfield	TN	37172	615-384-4338	382-1430
TF: 800-332-6653 ■ *Web:* www.fontainefl.com					
Flex-N-Gate Corp 1306 E University Ave	Urbana	IL	61802	217-278-2600	278-2616
Web: www.flex-n-gate.com					
Fontaine International Inc 5000 Grantswood Rd Suite 200	Irondale	AL	35210	205-421-4300	421-4400
TF: 800-874-9780 ■ *Web:* www.fifthwheel.com					
Fontaine Truck Equipment Co 2490 Pinson Valley Pkwy	Birmingham	AL	35217	205-841-8582	849-9615
TF: 800-824-3033 ■ *Web:* www.fontaine.com					
French JL Corp 3101 S Taylor Dr	Sheboygan	WI	53081	920-458-7724	458-0140
TF: 800-236-1117 ■ *Web:* www.jlfrench.com					
Freudenberg-NOK General Partnership 47690 E Anchor Ct	Plymouth	MI	48170	734-451-0020	451-0125
TF: 800-533-5656 ■ *Web:* www.freudenberg-nok.com					
GDX Automotive Inc 36600 Corporate Dr	Farmington Hills	MI	48331	248-553-5300	553-5105
Web: www.gdxautomotive.com					
General Motors Corp Allison Transmission Div 4700 W 10th St	Indianapolis	IN	46206	317-242-5000	242-0262
Web: www.allisontransmission.com					
GenTek Inc 90 E Hasley Rd	Parsippany	NJ	07054	973-515-1977	515-1997
NASDAQ: GETI ■ *TF:* 800-631-8050 ■ *Web:* www.gentek-global.com					
GKN Driveline North America Inc 3300 University Dr	Auburn Hills	MI	48326	248-377-1200	377-1370
Web: www.gknplc.com					
Glasstite Inc 600 Hwy 4 N	Dunnell	MN	56127	507-695-2378	695-2980
TF Cust Svc: 800-533-0450 ■ *Web:* www.glasstite.com					
Grote Industries Inc 2600 Lanier Dr	Madison	IN	47250	812-273-2121	265-8440
TF: 800-628-0809 ■ *Web:* www.grote.com					
Gunite Corp 302 Peoples Ave	Rockford	IL	61104	815-490-6364	964-0775
TF: 800-677-3786 ■ *Web:* www.gunite.com					
Hastings Mfg Co 325 N Hanover St	Hastings	MI	49058	269-945-2491	945-4667
TF: 800-776-1088 ■ *Web:* www.hastingsmfg.com					
HAWK Corp 200 Public Sq Suite 1500	Cleveland	OH	44114	216-861-3553	861-4546
AMEX: HWK ■ *Web:* www.hawkcorp.com					
Hayden Automotive 1241 Old Temescal Rd Suite 101	Corona	CA	92881	951-736-2665	736-2608*
**Fax:* Cust Svc ■ *TF:* 800-621-3233 ■ *Web:* www.haydenauto.com					

Company	City	State	Zip	Phone	Fax
Hayes Lemmerz International Inc 15300 Centennial Dr	Northville	MI	48168	734-737-5000	737-2099
NASDAQ: HAYZ ■ *TF:* 800-521-0515 ■ *Web:* www.hayes-lemmerz.com					
Hendrickson International 800 S Frontage Rd	Woodridge	IL	60517	630-910-2800	910-2899
Web: www.hendrickson-intl.com					
Hennessy Industries Inc 1601 JP Hennesey Dr	La Vergne	TN	37086	615-641-5122	641-5104
TF: 800-688-6359 ■ *Web:* www.ammcoats.com					
Hilite International 1671 S Broadway	Carrollton	TX	75006	972-242-2116	242-2902
Web: www.hilite-ind.com					
Hitachi Automotive Products (USA) Inc 955 Warwick Rd	Harrodsburg	KY	40330	859-734-9451	734-5309
Web: www.hap.com					
Holley Performance Products Inc 1801 Russellville Rd	Bowling Green	KY	42101	270-782-2900	781-9940*
**Fax:* Cust Svc ■ *TF Sales:* 800-638-0032 ■ *Web:* www.holley.com					
Honeywell Friction Materials 900 W Maple Rd	Troy	MI	48084	248-362-7000	362-7198
Honeywell Hobbs Corp 1034 E Ash St	Springfield	IL	62703	217-753-7600	753-7771
Web: content.honeywell.com/sensing/hss/hobbscorp					
Honeywell Transportation Systems 23326 Hawthorne Blvd Suite 200	Torrance	CA	90505	310-791-9101	791-7806
Honeywell Turbo Technologies 23326 Hawthorne Blvd Bldg 10 Suite 200	Torrance	CA	90505	310-791-9101	
Web: www.egarrett.com					
Hopkins Mfg Corp 428 Peyton St	Emporia	KS	66801	620-342-7320	340-8590
TF: 800-524-1458 ■ *Web:* www.hopkinsmfg.com					
Hutchens Industries Inc 215 N Patterson Ave	Springfield	MO	65802	417-862-5012	862-2317*
**Fax:* Cust Svc ■ *TF:* 800-654-8824 ■ *Web:* www.hutch-susp.com					
Indian Head Industries Inc 8530 Cliff Cameron Dr	Charlotte	NC	28269	704-547-7411	547-9367
TF: 800-527-1534 ■ *Web:* www.indianheadindustries.com					
Indian Head Industries Inc MGM Brakes Div 8530 Cliff Cameron Dr	Charlotte	NC	28269	704-547-7411	547-9367
TF: 800-527-1534 ■ *Web:* www.mgmbrakes.com					
Intier Automotive Inc 39600 Lewis Dr	Novi	MI	48377	248-567-4000	
Web: www.intier.com					
ITW ChronoTherm 935 N Oaklawn Ave	Elmhurst	IL	60126	630-993-9990	993-9399
Web: www.itwchronotherm.com					
ITW Fibre Glass-Evercoat 6600 Cornell Rd	Cincinnati	OH	45242	513-489-7600	489-9229
TF: 800-729-7600 ■ *Web:* www.evercoat.com					
Jacobs Vehicle Systems Inc 22 E Dudley Town Rd	Bloomfield	CT	06002	860-243-1441	243-7632
Web: www.jakebrake.com					
Jason Inc 411 E Wisconsin Ave Suite 2120	Milwaukee	WI	53202	414-277-9300	277-9445
Web: www.jasoninc.com					
JASPER Engines & Transmissions 815 Wernsing Rd PO Box 650	Jasper	IN	47547	812-482-1041	634-1820
TF: 800-827-7455 ■ *Web:* www.jasperengines.com					
JL French Corp 3101 S Taylor Dr	Sheboygan	WI	53081	920-458-7724	458-0140
TF: 800-236-1117 ■ *Web:* www.jlfrench.com					
John Bean Co 309 Exchange Ave	Conway	AR	72032	501-450-1500	450-1585
TF: 800-362-8326 ■ *Web:* www.johnbean.com					
Johnson Controls Inc 5757 N Green Bay Ave	Milwaukee	WI	53209	414-524-1200	524-3232
NYSE: JCI ■ *TF:* 800-972-8040 ■ *Web:* www.johnsoncontrols.com					
Johnson Controls Inc Automotive Systems Group 49200 Halyard Dr	Plymouth	MI	48170	734-254-5000	254-5843*
**Fax:* Hum Res ■ *Web:* www.johnsoncontrols.com/asg-intro					
JSJ Corp 700 Robbins Rd	Grand Haven	MI	49417	616-842-6350	847-3112
Web: www.jsjcorp.com					
KONI North America 1961-A International Way	Hebron	KY	41048	859-586-4100	334-3340
Web: www.koni-na.com					
LDI Inc 4311 Patterson Ave SE	Grand Rapids	MI	49512	616-957-2570	957-5011
Web: www.ldiinc.com					
Lear Corp 21557 Telegraph Rd	Southfield	MI	48034	248-447-1500	447-1722
NYSE: LEA ■ *Web:* www.lear.com					
Linamar Corp 287 Speedvale Ave W	Guelph	ON	N1H1C5	519-836-7550	824-8479
Web: www.linamar.com					
LuK USA LLC 3401 Old Airport Rd	Wooster	OH	44691	330-264-4383	264-4333
Web: www.lukusa.com					
Lund International Holdings Inc 300 Horizon Dr	Suwanee	GA	30024	678-804-3767	438-3788*
**Fax Area Code:* 800 ■ **Fax:* Cust Svc ■ *TF:* 800-377-5863 ■ *Web:* www.lundinternational.com					
MacLean-Fogg Co 1000 Allanson Rd	Mundelein	IL	60060	847-566-0010	949-0285
TF: 800-323-4536 ■ *Web:* www.maclean-fogg.com					
Magna International of America 600 Wilshire Dr	Troy	MI	48084	248-729-2400	729-2410
Web: www.magna.com					
Magna International Inc 337 Magna Dr	Aurora	ON	L4G7K1	905-726-2462	726-7164
NYSE: MGA ■ *Web:* www.magnaint.com					
Magna Powertrain Inc 1775 Research Dr	Troy	MI	48083	248-680-4900	680-4924
Web: www.magnapowertrain.com					
Magneti Marelli Powertrain USA Inc 2101 Nash St	Sanford	NC	27331	919-776-4111	775-6339*
**Fax:* Mktg ■ *Web:* www.marelliusa.com					
MAHLE Clevite Inc 1350 Eisenhower Pl	Ann Arbor	MI	48108	734-975-4777	975-7820
TF: 800-338-8786 ■ *Web:* www.clevite.com					
MAHLE Engine Components USA Inc 2001 Sanford St	Muskegon	MI	49443	231-722-1300	724-1940
TF: 800-717-5398 ■ *Web:* www.us.mahle.com					
MAHLE Engine Components USA Inc 17226 CR-57	Caldwell	OH	43724	740-732-2311	732-2520
Web: www.us.mahle.com					
Mark IV Industries Inc 501 John James Audubon Pkwy	Amherst	NY	14226	716-689-4972	689-6098
Web: www.mark-iv.com					
Marmon-Herrington Co 13001 Magisterial Dr	Louisville	KY	40223	502-253-0277	253-0317
TF: 800-227-0727 ■ *Web:* www.marmon-herrington.com					
Masterack-Crown Inc 7315 E Lincon Way	Apple Creek	OH	44606	330-262-6010	262-4095
TF Cust Svc: 800-321-4934 ■ *Web:* www.crown-na.com					
Melling Tool Co 2620 Saradan St PO Box 1188	Jackson	MI	49204	517-787-8172	787-5304
TF: 800-777-8172 ■ *Web:* www.melling.com					
Meridian Automotive Systems Inc 999 Republic Dr	Allen Park	MI	48101	313-336-4182	336-4184
Metaldyne Corp 47603 Halyard Dr	Plymouth	MI	48170	734-207-6200	207-6500
Web: www.metaldyne.com					
MGM Brakes Div Indian Head Industries Inc 8530 Cliff Cameron Dr	Charlotte	NC	28269	704-547-7411	547-9367
TF: 800-527-1534 ■ *Web:* www.mgmbrakes.com					
Mid-South Mfg Co 301 Industrial Park	Marked Tree	AR	72365	870-358-3473	358-3398
Mitsuba Bardstown Inc 901 Withrow Ct	Bardstown	KY	40004	502-348-3100	348-3204
TF: 800-307-8787 ■ *Web:* www.mitsuba.co.jp					
Moroso Performance Products Inc 80 Carter Dr	Guilford	CT	06437	203-453-6571	453-6906*
**Fax:* Cust Svc ■ *Web:* www.moroso.com					
Neapco Inc 740 Queen St PO Box 399	Pottstown	PA	19464	610-323-6000	327-2551
TF: 800-821-2374 ■ *Web:* www.neapco.com					
Newcor Inc 4850 Coolidge Hwy Suite 100	Royal Oak	MI	48073	248-435-4269	435-5385
Web: www.newcor.com					
Noble International Ltd 28213 Van Dyke Ave	Warren	MI	48093	586-751-5600	751-5601
NASDAQ: NOBL ■ *Web:* www.nobleintl.com					
Omni Gear 7502 Mesa Rd	Houston	TX	77028	713-635-6331	635-6360
Web: www.omnigear.com					
Penda Corp 2344 W Wisconsin St	Portage	WI	53901	608-742-5301	742-9402*
**Fax:* Hum Res ■ *TF:* 800-356-7704 ■ *Web:* www.pendacorp.com					
Perfection Clutch Co 100 Perfection Way	Timmonsville	SC	29161	843-326-5544	326-5581
TF: 800-258-8312 ■ *Web:* www.perfectionclutch.com					
Peterson Mfg Co 4200 E 135th St	Grandview	MO	64030	816-765-2000	761-6693
TF: 800-821-3490 ■ *Web:* www.pmlights.com					
Powers & Sons LLC 1613 Magda Dr	Montpelier	OH	43543	419-485-3151	485-5490
Web: www.powersandsonsllc.com					

Company	City	State	Zip	Phone	Fax
Pretty Products Inc 437 Cambridge Rd *TF:* 800-837-9160 ■ *Web:* www.rubberqueen.com	Coshocton	OH	43812	740-622-3522	623-4737
R & B Inc 3400 E Walnut St *NASDAQ: RBIN* ■ *TF:* 800-868-5777 ■ *Web:* www.rbinc.com	Colmar	PA	18915	215-997-1800	997-1741
Raybestos Products Co 1204 Darlington Ave *TF:* 800-428-0825 ■ *Web:* www.raybestosproducts.com	Crawfordsville	IN	47933	765-362-3500	362-9574
Remy International Inc 2902 Enterprise Dr **Fax Area Code:* 888 ■ **Fax:* Cust Svc ■ *TF:* 800-372-5131 ■ *Web:* www.remyinc.com	Anderson	IN	46013	765-778-6499	372-3077*
Rieter Automotive North America Inc 38555 Hills Tech Dr *TF:* 888-743-8370 ■ *Web:* www.rieter.com	Farmington Hills	MI	48331	248-848-0100	848-0130
Robert Bosch LLC 2800 S 25th Ave *Web:* www.boschusa.com	Broadview	IL	60155	708-865-5200	865-6430
Rush Metals Inc Hwy 15 E PO Box 398	Billings	OK	74630	580-725-3295	725-3217
SAF-Holland USA 1950 Industrial Blvd *TF:* 888-396-6501 ■ *Web:* www.safholland.us	Muskegon	MI	49443	231-773-3271	767-8843
Sauer-Danfoss Inc 2800 E 13th St *NYSE: SHS* ■ *Web:* www.sauer-danfoss.com	Ames	IA	50010	515-239-6000	239-6318
Siemens VDO Automotive Corp 2400 Executive Hills Blvd *TF Cust Svc:* 800-879-8079 ■ *Web:* www.siemensvdo.com	Auburn Hills	MI	48326	248-253-1000	253-4040
SmarTire Systems Inc 13151 Vanier Pl Suite 150 *TF:* 888-982-3001 ■ *Web:* www.smartire.com	Richmond	BC	V5V2J1	604-276-9884	276-2350
Sports Resorts International Inc 951 Aiken Rd *TF:* 800-433-3604 ■ *Web:* www.sportsresortsinternational.com	Owosso	MI	48867	989-725-8354	729-6234
SPX Corp Filtran Div 875 Seegers Rd *Web:* www.spxfiltran.com	Des Plaines	IL	60016	847-635-6670	635-7724
Stanadyne Corp 92 Deerfield Rd *TF:* 800-929-0919 ■ *Web:* www.stanadyne.com	Windsor	CT	06095	860-525-0821	683-4500
Standard Motor Products Inc 37-18 Northern Blvd *NYSE: SMP* ■ *Web:* www.smpcorp.com	Long Island City	NY	11101	718-392-0200	729-4549
Stemco LP 300 Industrial Blvd PO Box 1989 **Fax:* Sales ■ *TF:* 800-527-8492 ■ *Web:* www.stemco.com	Longview	TX	75606	903-758-9981	232-3508*
Stoneridge Inc 9400 E Market St *NYSE: SRI* ■ *Web:* www.stoneridge.com	Warren	OH	44484	330-856-2443	856-3618
Strattec Security Corp 3333 W Good Hope Rd *NASDAQ: STRT* ■ *TF:* 888-710-5770 ■ *Web:* www.strattec.com	Milwaukee	WI	53209	414-247-3333	247-3329
Summit Polymers Inc 6717 S Sprinkle Rd *Web:* www.summitpolymers.com	Portage	MI	49002	269-324-9323	324-9322
Superior Industries International Inc 7800 Woodley Ave *NYSE: SUP* ■ *TF:* 800-545-9882 ■ *Web:* www.superiorindustries.com	Van Nuys	CA	94106	818-781-4973	780-3500
TAG Holdings LLC 2075 W Big Beaver Rd Suite 500 *Web:* www.taghold.com	Troy	MI	48084	248-822-8010	822-8012
Taylor Devices Inc 90 Taylor Dr PO Box 748 *NASDAQ: TAYD* ■ *Web:* www.shockandvibration.com	North Tonawanda	NY	14120	716-694-0800	695-6015
TBDN Tennessee Co 1410 Hwy 70 Bypass *Web:* www.tbdn.com	Jackson	TN	38301	731-427-4774	421-4879
Teleflex Automotive Group Inc 700 Stephenson Hwy *Web:* www.tfxauto.com	Troy	MI	48083	248-616-3800	616-3810
Teleflex Power Systems 3831 No 6 Rd *Web:* www.teleflexpower.com	Richmond	BC	V6V1P6	604-270-6899	270-7172
Teleflex Canada 3831 No 6 Rd *Web:* www.teleflexpower.com	Richmond	BC	V6V1P6	604-270-6899	270-7172
TeleflexGFI Control Systems LP 100 Hollinger Crescent *TF:* 800-667-4275 ■ *Web:* www.teleflexgfi.com	Kitchener	ON	N2K2Z3	519-576-4270	576-7045
Tenneco Inc 500 N Field Dr *NYSE: TEN* ■ *TF:* 800-777-9564 ■ *Web:* www.tenneco.com	Lake Forest	IL	60045	847-482-5000	843-4169
TFX Marine Inc 101 Western Maryland Pkwy *Web:* www.tfxmarine.com	Hagerstown	MD	21740	301-790-2708	790-2652
ThyssenKrupp Budd Co 3155 W Big Beaver Rd PO Box 2601 *Web:* www.buddcompany.com	Troy	MI	48007	248-643-3500	643-3593
TI Automotive 12345 E Nine-Mile Rd **Fax:* Hum Res ■ *TF:* 800-521-2500 ■ *Web:* www.tiauto.com	Warren	MI	48090	586-758-4511	755-8375*
Titan International Inc 2701 Spruce St *NYSE: TWI* ■ **Fax:* Cust Svc ■ *TF:* 800-872-2327 ■ *Web:* www.titan-intl.com	Quincy	IL	62301	217-228-6011	228-9331*
Titan Wheel Corp 2701 Spruce St **Fax:* Cust Svc ■ *TF:* 800-518-4826 ■ *Web:* www.titan-intl.com	Quincy	IL	62301	217-228-6011	228-9331*
Trelleborg Automotive Americas 400 Aylworth Ave *TF:* 800-456-0557 ■ *Web:* www.trelleborg.com/automotive	South Haven	MI	49090	269-637-2116	637-8315
Triangle Suspension Systems Inc Maloney Rd *TF:* 800-458-6077 ■ *Web:* www.trianglegroup.com	Du Bois	PA	15801	814-375-7211	371-4495
Trico Products Corp 3255 W Hamlin Rd *TF:* 888-565-9632 ■ *Web:* www.tricoproducts.com	Rochester Hills	MI	48309	248-371-1700	371-8300
Trim Systems LLC 5700 Perimeter Dr Suite A *Web:* www.trimsystems.com	Dublin	OH	43017	614-880-2100	985-1841
TRW Automotive 12025 Tech Center Dr *Web:* www.trwauto.com	Livonia	MI	48150	734-855-2600	855-5702
TRW Automotive Holdings Corp 12025 Tech Center Dr *NYSE: TRW* ■ *Web:* www.trwauto.com	Livonia	MI	48150	734-855-2600	855-5702
TS Trim Industries Inc 59 Gender Rd *Web:* www.tstrim.com	Canal Winchester	OH	43110	614-837-4114	837-4127
Tuthill Transport Technologies 1205 Industrial Park Dr *TF Cust Svc:* 800-753-0050 ■ *Web:* transport.tuthill.com	Mount Vernon	MO	65712	417-466-2178	466-3964
United Components Inc 14601 Hwy 41 N *Web:* www.ucinc.com	Evansville	IN	47725	812-867-4156	867-4157
Unitek Sealing Solutions 315 Brighton St *TF:* 800-348-8842	LaPorte	IN	46350	219-326-1315	324-4010
Universal Mfg Co 405 Diagonal St PO Box 190 *TF:* 800-545-9350 ■ *Web:* www.universalmanf.com	Algona	IA	50511	515-295-3557	295-5537
US Chemical & Plastics 600 Nova Dr SE PO Box 709 *TF:* 800-321-0672 ■ *Web:* www.uschem.com	Massillon	OH	44648	330-830-6000	830-6005
US Mfg Corp 28201 Van Dyke Ave *Web:* www.usmfg.com	Warren	MI	48093	586-467-1600	467-1630
Valeo Inc 3000 University Dr **Fax:* Hum Res ■ *Web:* www.valeo.com	Auburn Hills	MI	48326	248-340-3000	340-3190*
Visteon Corp 1 Village Center Dr *NYSE: VC* ■ **Fax Area Code:* 313 ■ *TF:* 800-847-8366 ■ *Web:* www.visteon.com	Van Buren Township	MI	48111	734-710-2020	755-7983*
Voith Turbo Inc 25 Winship Rd *Web:* www.usa.voithturbo.com	York	PA	17406	717-767-3200	767-3210
Webasto Roof Systems Inc 1757 Northfield Dr *Web:* www.webastoroofsystems.com	Rochester Hills	MI	48309	248-997-5100	997-5101
Webb Wheel Products Inc 2310 Industrial Dr SW **Fax:* Sales ■ *TF:* 800-633-3256 ■ *Web:* www.webbwheel.com	Cullman	AL	35055	256-739-6660	739-6246*
Wells Mfg LP 26 S Brooke St PO Box 70 *TF:* 800-558-9770 ■ *Web:* www.wellsmfgcorp.com	Fond du Lac	WI	54936	920-922-5900	922-3585
Wescast Industries Inc 100 Water St *Web:* www.wecast.com	Wingham	ON	N0G2W0	519-357-4447	357-4127
Westport Innovations Inc 1750 W 75th Ave Suite 101 *TSX: WPT* ■ *Web:* www.westport.com	Vancouver	BC	V6P6G2	604-718-2000	718-2001
Williams Controls Inc 14100 SW 72nd Ave *TF Cust Svc:* 800-547-1889 ■ *Web:* wmco.com	Portland	OR	97224	503-684-8600	684-3879
Wix Filtration Products 1 Wix Way PO Box 1967 **Fax:* Cust Svc ■ *Web:* www.wixfilters.com	Gastonia	NC	28053	704-864-6711	864-1843*
Worthington Precison Metals Inc 8229 Tyler Blvd *Web:* www.w-pm.com	Mentor	OH	44060	440-255-6700	255-4263

61 AUTOMOTIVE PARTS & SUPPLIES - WHOL

Company	City	State	Zip	Phone	Fax
Aapco Automotive Warehouse 2997 E La Palma Ave	Anaheim	CA	92806	714-630-5600	666-2913
Ace Tool Co 7337 Bryan Dairy Rd *TF:* 800-777-5910 ■ *Web:* www.acetoolco.com	Largo	FL	33777	727-544-4331	544-6211
Arrow Speed Warehouse 686 S Adams St *TF:* 800-255-4606 ■ *Web:* www.arrow-speed.com	Kansas City	KS	66105	913-321-1200	321-7729
Automotive Parts Headquarters 2815 Clearwater Rd *TF:* 800-247-0339	Saint Cloud	MN	56301	320-252-5411	252-4256
Automotive Supply Assoc Inc 129 Manchester St	Concord	NH	03301	603-225-4000	225-2484
AW Imported Auto Parts Inc 52 Hwy 35 *TF:* 800-631-5589	Eatontown	NJ	07724	732-542-5600	542-6050
Balkamp Inc 2601 S Holt Rd *Web:* www.balkamp.com	Indianapolis	IN	46241	317-244-7241	381-2200
Barron Motor Inc 1850 McCloud Pl NE *TF:* 800-332-7953 ■ *Web:* www.barronmotorsupply.com	Cedar Rapids	IA	52402	319-393-6220	393-4864
Bell Industries Inc 1960 E Grand Ave Suite 560 *AMEX: BI* ■ *TF:* 800-782-2355 ■ *Web:* www.bellind.com	El Segundo	CA	90245	310-563-2355	648-7280
Bell Industries Inc Recreational Products Group 580 Yankee Doodle Rd Suite 1200 *TF:* 800-388-2355 ■ *Web:* www.bellrpg.com	Eagan	MN	55121	651-450-9020	450-0844
Bendix Commercial Vehicle Systems LLC 901 Cleveland St *TF:* 800-247-2725 ■ *Web:* www.bendix.com	Elyria	OH	44035	440-329-9000	329-9557
Birmingham Electric Battery Co 2221 2nd Ave S *TF:* 800-446-0919 ■ *Web:* www.bebco.net	Birmingham	AL	35233	205-458-0581	458-1522
Brake & Wheel Parts Industries Inc 2415 W 21st St *TF:* 800-621-8836 ■ *Web:* www.bwpindustries.com	Chicago	IL	60608	773-847-7000	847-5149
CAP Warehouse 3108 Losee Rd *TF:* 800-879-7901	North Las Vegas	NV	89030	702-642-7801	642-9174
Carolina Rim & Wheel Co 1308 Upper Asbury Ave *TF:* 800-532-6219 ■ *Web:* www.carolinarim.com	Charlotte	NC	28206	704-334-7276	334-7270
Carolinas Auto Supply House Inc 2135 Tipton Dr **Fax Area Code:* 800 ■ *TF:* 800-438-4070 ■ *Web:* www.autosupplyhouse.com	Charlotte	NC	28206	704-334-4646	377-7016*
CARQUEST Corp 2635 E Millbrook Rd **Fax:* Mktg ■ *TF:* 800-876-1291 ■ *Web:* www.carquest.com	Raleigh	NC	27604	919-573-3000	573-3558*
Charleston Auto Parts Inc DBA CAP Warehouse 3108 Losee Rd *TF:* 800-879-7901	North Las Vegas	NV	89030	702-642-7801	642-9174
Tri-State University 1 University Blvd **Fax:* Admissions ■ *TF:* 800-347-4878 ■ *Web:* www.tristate.edu	Angola	IN	46703	260-665-4100	665-4578*
University of Evansville 1800 Lincoln Ave **Fax:* Admissions ■ *TF:* 800-423-8633 ■ *Web:* www.evansville.edu	Evansville	IN	47722	812-488-2000	488-4076*
University of Indianapolis 1400 E Hanna Ave **Fax:* Admissions ■ *TF:* 800-232-8634 ■ *Web:* www.uindy.edu	Indianapolis	IN	46227	317-788-3368	788-3300*
University of Notre Dame 220 Main Bldg **Fax:* Admissions ■ *Web:* www.nd.edu	Notre Dame	IN	46556	574-631-7505	631-8665*
University of Saint Francis 2701 Spring St **Fax:* Admissions ■ *TF:* 800-729-4732 ■ *Web:* www.sfc.edu	Fort Wayne	IN	46808	260-434-3100	434-7526*
University of Southern Indiana 8600 University Blvd *TF:* 800-467-1965 ■ *Web:* www.usi.edu	Evansville	IN	47712	812-464-1765	465-7154
Valparaiso University 1700 Chapel Dr **Fax:* Admissions ■ *TF:* 888-468-2576 ■ *Web:* www.valpo.edu	Valparaiso	IN	46383	219-464-5011	464-6898*
Wabash College 410 W Wabash Ave PO Box 352 **Fax:* Admissions ■ *TF:* 800-345-5385 ■ *Web:* www.wabash.edu	Crawfordsville	IN	47933	765-361-6225	361-6437*
Coast Distribution System 350 Woodview Ave *AMEX: CRV* ■ **Fax Area Code:* 800 ■ *TF:* 800-495-5858	Morgan Hill	CA	95037	408-782-6686	778-1150*
Custom Chrome Inc 16100 Jacqueline Ct *TF:* 800-729-3332 ■ *Web:* www.customchrome.com	Morgan Hill	CA	95037	408-778-0500	359-5700
Distributors Warehouse Inc 1900 N 10th St *TF:* 800-892-9966	Paducah	KY	42001	270-442-8201	442-4914
Dorian Drake International Inc 2 Gannett Dr *Web:* www.doriandrake.com	White Plains	NY	10604	914-697-9800	697-9683
Dreyco Inc 263 Veterans Blvd *Web:* www.dreycoinc.com	Carlstadt	NJ	07072	201-896-9000	896-1378
Drive Train Industries Inc 3301 Brighton Blvd *TF:* 800-525-6177 ■ *Web:* www.drivetrainindustries.com	Denver	CO	80216	303-292-5176	297-0473
Edwards Frank Co 3626 Parkway Blvd *TF:* 800-366-8851	West Valley City	UT	84120	801-736-8000	736-8051
Fisher Auto Parts Inc 512 Greenville Ave PO Box 2246 *Web:* www.fisherautoparts.com	Staunton	VA	24401	540-885-8901	885-1808
Flowers Auto Parts Co 935 Hwy 70 SE *TF Cust Svc:* 800-395-6272	Hickory	NC	28601	828-322-5414	322-9070
Frank Edwards Co 3626 Parkway Blvd *TF:* 800-366-8851	West Valley City	UT	84120	801-736-8000	736-8051
General Truck Parts & Equipment Co 3835 W 42nd St *TF:* 800-621-3914 ■ *Web:* www.generaltruckparts.com	Chicago	IL	60632	773-247-6900	247-2632
Genuine Parts Co 2999 Circle 75 Pkwy *NYSE: GPC* ■ *Web:* www.genpt.com	Atlanta	GA	30339	770-953-1700	956-2211
Global Motorsport Group 16100 Jacqueline Ct **Fax:* Mktg ■ *TF:* 800-359-5700	Morgan Hill	CA	95037	408-778-0500	778-7370*
Globe Motorists Supply Co Inc 560 S 3rd Ave *TF:* 888-884-7278 ■ *Web:* www.tviparts.com	Mount Vernon	NY	10550	914-668-6430	668-0376
Gooch Brake & Equipment Co 506 Grand Blvd *TF:* 800-444-3216 ■ *Web:* www.goochbrake.com	Kansas City	MO	64106	816-421-3085	421-7970
Hahn Automotive Warehouse Inc 415 W Main St *TF:* 800-456-0365 ■ *Web:* www.hahnauto.com	Rochester	NY	14608	585-235-1595	235-1865
Hedahls Inc 100 E Broadway *TF:* 800-433-2457 ■ *Web:* www.hedahls.com	Bismarck	ND	58502	701-223-8393	221-4251
Henderson Wheel & Warehouse Supply 1825 S 300 West *TF:* 800-748-5111 ■ *Web:* www.hendersonwheel.com	Salt Lake City	UT	84115	801-486-2073	486-0353
InterAmerican Motor Corp 8901 Canoga Ave **Fax:* Sales ■ *TF:* 800-874-8925 ■ *Web:* www.imcparts.com	Canoga Park	CA	91304	818-678-1200	678-1330*
International Brake Industries Inc 1840 McCullough St **Fax:* Cust Svc ■ *TF:* 800-537-2838 ■ *Web:* www.ibilima.com	Lima	OH	45801	419-227-4421	993-8177*
Interstate Batteries 12770 Merit Dr Suite 400 *TF:* 800-541-8419 ■ *Web:* www.interstatebatteries.com	Dallas	TX	75251	972-991-1444	455-6533
Intraco Corp 530 Stephenson Hwy *TF:* 800-595-6900 ■ *Web:* www.intracousa.com	Troy	MI	48083	248-585-6900	585-6920
J Korber & Co 2400 Menaul Blvd NE	Albuquerque	NM	87107	505-884-4652	884-4681
Johnson Industries 5944 Peachtree Corners E *TF Orders:* 800-922-8111 ■ *Web:* www.teamji.com	Norcross	GA	33071	770-441-1128	248-2896
Keystone Automotive Industries Inc 700 E Bonita Ave *NASDAQ: KEYS* ■ *TF:* 800-772-5557 ■ *Web:* www.keystone-auto.com	Pomona	CA	91767	909-624-8041	624-9136
LKQ Corp 120 N LaSalle St Suite 3300 *NASDAQ: LKQX* ■ *TF:* 877-557-2677 ■ *Web:* www.lkqcorp.com	Chicago	IL	60602	312-621-1950	621-1969
Midwest Truck & Auto Parts 1001 W Exchange **Fax Area Code:* 800 ■ *TF:* 800-934-2727 ■ *Web:* www.midwesttruck.com	Chicago	IL	60609	312-225-1550	526-4885*
Mighty Distributing System of America Inc 650 Engineering Dr *TF:* 800-829-3900 ■ *Web:* www.mightyautoparts.com	Norcross	GA	30092	770-448-3900	446-8627
Mutual Wheel Co Inc 2345 4th Ave *Web:* www.mutualwheel.com	Moline	IL	61265	309-757-1200	757-1241
NAPA (National Automotive Parts Assn) 2999 Cir 75 Pkwy NW *Web:* www.napaonline.com	Atlanta	GA	30339	770-956-2200	956-2212

Name / Address	City	State	Zip	Phone	Fax
National Automotive Parts Assn (NAPA) 2999 Cir 75 Pkwy NW	Atlanta	GA	30339	770-956-2200	956-2212
Web: www.napaonline.com					
PACCAR Parts 750 Houser Way N	Renton	WA	98055	425-254-4400	254-6200
TF: 800-477-0251 ■ Web: www.paccar.com/parts					
PAM Div US Oil Co Inc 200 S Petro Ave	Sioux Falls	SD	57107	605-336-1788	339-9909
TF: 800-456-2660 ■ Web: www.pam-companies.com					
Parts Central Inc 3243 Whitfield St	Macon	GA	31204	478-745-0878	746-1177
TF: 800-226-9396 ■ Web: www.partscentral.net					
Pioneer Inc 5184 Pioneer Rd	Meridian	MS	39301	601-483-5211	821-2303*
*Fax Area Code: 800 ■ TF: 800-647-6272 ■ Web: www.pioneerautoinc.com					
Plaza Fleet Parts Inc 1520 S Broadway	Saint Louis	MO	63104	314-231-5047	231-5109
TF: 800-325-7618					
Quaker City Motor Parts Co 680 N Broad St	Middletown	DE	19709	302-378-9834	378-0726
TF: 800-538-6272 ■ Web: www.qcmponline.com					
Replacement Parts Inc 1901 E Roosevelt Rd	Little Rock	AR	72206	501-375-1215	372-5555*
*Fax: Cust Svc ■ TF: 877-282-6591 ■ Web: www.btbautoparts.com					
Ridge Co Inc 1535 S Main St	South Bend	IN	46613	574-234-3143	234-4227
TF: 800-348-2409 ■ Web: www.ridgeautoparts.com					
Rim & Wheel Service Inc 1014 Gest St	Cincinnati	OH	45203	513-721-6940	721-4160
TF: 800-783-6940 ■ Web: www.rimwheel.com					
Six Robblees' Inc 11010 Tukwila International Blvd	Tukwila	WA	98168	206-767-7970	763-7416
TF: 800-275-7499 ■ Web: www.sixrobblees.com					
Six States Distributors Inc 247 W 1700 South	Salt Lake City	UT	84115	801-488-4666	488-4676
TF: 800-453-5703 ■ Web: www.sixstates.com					
SKD Automotive Group 1450 W Long Lake Rd Suite 210	Troy	MI	48098	248-267-9670	267-9686
Web: www.skdautomotive.com					
Tucker Rocky Distributing Inc 4900 Alliance Gateway Fwy	Fort Worth	TX	76177	817-258-9000	304-1020*
*Fax Area Code: 800 ■ *Fax: Cust Svc ■ TF: 800-283-8787 ■ Web: www.tuckerrocky.com					
Twinco Romax 4635 Willow Dr	Medina	MN	55340	763-478-2360	478-3411
TF: 800-682-3800 ■ Web: www.twincoromax.com					
UAP Inc 7025 rue Ontario E	Montreal	QC	H1N2B3	514-256-5031	256-8469
Web: www.uapinc.com					
Wetherill Assoc Inc 1101 Enterprise Dr	Royersford	PA	19468	610-495-2200	495-4000
TF: 800-948-6121 ■ Web: www.wai-wetherill.com					
White Brothers 24845 Corbit Pl	Yorba Linda	CA	92887	714-692-3404	692-5220*
*Fax: Sales ■ TF: 800-854-1899 ■ Web: www.whitebros.com					

62 AUTOMOTIVE SERVICES

SEE ALSO Gas Stations p. 1687

62-1 Appearance Care - Automotive

Name / Address	City	State	Zip	Phone	Fax
American Auto Wash Inc DBA Gentle Touch Car Wash 512 E King Rd	Malvern	PA	19355	610-296-4126	296-2854
Autobell Car Wash Inc 1521 E 3rd St	Charlotte	NC	28204	704-527-9274	333-0526
TF: 800-582-8096 ■ Web: www.autobell.com					
Blue Beacon International Inc 500 Graves Blvd	Salina	KS	67401	785-825-2221	825-0801
Web: www.bluebeacon.com					
Carnett's Car Washes 631-B Indian Trail Rd	Lilburn	GA	30047	770-381-6900	717-5860
Web: www.carnetts.com					
Classic Car Wash Corp 871 E Hamilton Ave Suite C	Campbell	CA	95008	408-371-2414	371-4337
Web: www.classiccarwash.com					
Clean Machine Car Care Center Inc 1181-3 Worcester Rd	Framingham	MA	01701	508-872-5830	
Color-Glo International 7111 Ohms Ln	Minneapolis	MN	55439	952-835-1338	835-1395
TF: 800-328-6347 ■ Web: www.colorglo.com					
Creative Colors International Inc 19015 S Jodi Rd Suite E	Mokena	IL	60448	708-478-1437	478-1636
TF: 800-933-2656 ■ Web: www.creativecolorsintl.com					
Danny's Family Carousel Car Wash 7373 E Shea Blvd	Scottsdale	AZ	85254	480-348-2223	348-9110
Don's Car Washes Inc 1802 Main Ave Suite A	Fargo	ND	58103	701-237-0133	237-9552
Dr Vinyl & Assoc Ltd 201 NW Victoria Dr	Lee's Summit	MO	64086	816-525-6060	525-6333
TF: 800-531-6600 ■ Web: www.drvinyl.com					
Flagstop Corp 11031 Ironbridge Rd	Chester	VA	23831	804-768-0090	768-0094
Web: flagstopcarwash.com					
Fleetwash Inc 273 Passaic Ave	Fairfield	NJ	07004	973-882-8314	882-0585
TF: 800-847-3735 ■ Web: www.fleetwash.com					
Gentle Touch Car Wash 512 E King Rd	Malvern	PA	19355	610-296-4126	296-2854
Hoffman Car Wash 1757 Central Ave	Albany	NY	12205	518-809-3218	809-3574
Web: www.hoffmancarwash.com					
Jax Car Wash Inc 28845 Telegraph Rd	Southfield	MI	48034	248-353-4700	353-8591
TF: 866-529-5273 ■ Web: www.jaxcarwash.net					
Kaady Car Washes 7400 SW Barbur Blvd	Portland	OR	97219	503-246-7735	245-0851
Web: www.kaady.com					
MARS International Inc 2001 E Division St Suite 101	Arlington	TX	76011	817-226-6277	230-2859*
*Fax Area Code: 800 ■ Web: www.marsinternational.com					
Mike's Carwash Inc 10251 Hague Rd	Indianapolis	IN	46256	317-572-9250	572-9251
TF: 888-285-9274 ■ Web: www.mikescarwash.com					
Mister Car Wash 3561 E Sunrise Dr Suite 125	Tucson	AZ	85718	520-615-4000	615-4001
TF: 866-254-3229 ■ Web: www.mistercarwash.com					
Oasis Carwash LLC 3425 E Flamingo Rd	Las Vegas	NV	89121	702-433-3680	433-3682
Web: www.oasiscarwash.com					
Precision Auto Care Inc 748 Miller Dr SE	Leesburg	VA	20175	703-777-9095	771-7108
TF: 800-438-8863 ■ Web: www.precisionac.com					
ScrubaDub Auto Wash Centers Inc 172 Worcester Rd	Natick	MA	01760	508-650-1155	655-9261
Web: www.scrubadub.com					
Sikder Inc 24795 Alicia Pkwy	Laguna Hills	CA	92653	949-859-5851	859-5727
Simoniz Car Wash 435 Eastern Ave	Malden	MA	02148	781-321-1900	339-2760*
*Fax Area Code: 800 ■ Web: www.washdepot.com					
Super Wash Inc 707 W Lincolnway	Morrison	IL	61270	815-772-2111	772-7160
Web: www.superwash.com					
Triangle Car Wash Inc 973 E Main St	Palmyra	PA	17078	717-838-7125	838-7131
TF: 800-331-9274 ■ Web: www.trianglecarwashes.com					
Vizzawash Inc DBA Wash Tub 16035 University Oak	San Antonio	TX	78249	210-493-8822	493-7835
TF: 866-493-8822 ■ Web: www.washtub.net					
Wash Depot Holdings Inc 14 Summer St	Malden	MA	02148	781-324-2000	321-5483
TF: 800-339-3949 ■ Web: www.washdepot.com					
Wash Tub 16035 University Oak	San Antonio	TX	78249	210-493-8822	493-7835
TF: 866-493-8822 ■ Web: www.washtub.net					
Wonder Wash/Wonder Lube Management Inc 1601 Caledonia St Suite 1	La Crosse	WI	54603	608-783-5525	783-5709
TF: 800-261-9274 ■ Web: www.wonderwash-wonderlube.com					
Ziebart International Corp 1290 E Maple Rd	Troy	MI	48083	248-588-4100	588-2513*
*Fax: Orders ■ TF: 800-877-1312 ■ Web: www.ziebart.com					

62-2 Glass Replacement - Automotive

Name / Address	City	State	Zip	Phone	Fax
ABRA Auto Body & Glass 6601 Shingle Creek Pkwy Suite 200	Brooklyn Center	MN	55430	763-561-7220	585-6455*
*Fax: Hum Res ■ TF: 888-872-2272 ■ Web: www.abraauto.com					
All Star Glass Co Inc 1845 Morena Blvd	San Diego	CA	92110	619-275-3343	275-1546
TF: 800-225-4185 ■ Web: www.allstarglass.net					
Auto Glass National 1537 W Alameda	Denver	CO	80223	303-722-9600	722-9900
TF: 800-388-0104 ■ Web: www.autoglassnational.com					
Auto Glass Specialists IncSafelight Auto Glass 2400 Farmers Dr 2nd Fl	Columbus	OH	43235	614-210-9000	
TF: 800-558-1000					
Cindy Rowe Auto Glass 4750 Lindle Rd	Harrisburg	PA	17111	717-939-7551	939-8617
TF: 800-882-4639 ■ Web: www.cindyrowe.com					
City Auto Glass Inc 116 S Concord Exchange	South Saint Paul	MN	55075	651-552-1000	552-1080
TF: 888-552-4272 ■ Web: www.cityautoglass.com					
Diamond/Triumph Auto Glass Inc 220 Division St	Kingston	PA	18704	570-287-9915	283-3813
TF: 800-234-4527 ■ Web: www.diamondtriumphglass.com					
Ding Doctor Windshield Repair PO Box 855	La Vernia	TX	78121	210-225-3464	
Web: www.dingdoctor.biz					
Glass Doctor 1020 N University Parks Dr	Waco	TX	76707	254-745-2480	745-5073
TF: 800-280-9959 ■ Web: www.glassdoctor.com					
Glass Doctor 1020 N University Parks Dr	Waco	TX	76707	254-745-2480	745-5073
TF: 800-280-9959 ■ Web: www.glassdoctor.com					
Glass Specialty System Inc PO Box 737	Bloomington	IL	61702	309-664-1087	662-1246
TF: 800-500-0500 ■ Web: www.glassspecialty.com					
Guardian Glass Co 23919 Freeway Park Dr	Farmington Hills	MI	48335	248-471-0180	471-7247
TF: 800-621-8682 ■ Web: www.guardianautoglass.com					
Harmon Autoglass 4000 Olson Memorial Hwy Suite 600	Minneapolis	MN	55422	763-521-5100	521-2394
TF: 800-352-0777 ■ Web: www.harmonautoglass.com					
Martin Glass Co 25 Center Plaza	Belleville	IL	62220	618-277-1946	277-6742
TF: 800-325-1946 ■ Web: www.martinglass.net					
NOVUS Auto Glass Eagle Creek Commerce Ctr 12800 Hwy 13 S Suite 500	Minneapolis	MN	55378	952-944-8000	944-2542
TF: 800-328-1137 ■ Web: www.novusglass.com					
Rowe Cindy Auto Glass 4750 Lindle Rd	Harrisburg	PA	17111	717-939-7551	939-8617
TF: 800-882-4639 ■ Web: www.cindyrowe.com					
Royal Glass Co 9241 Hampton Overlook	Capital Heights	MD	20743	301-808-2855	333-6570
TF: 800-509-4495 ■ Web: www.royalglass.com					
Safelite Glass Corp 2400 Farmers Dr 5th Fl	Columbus	OH	43235	614-210-9465	210-9451
TF: 800-835-2257 ■ Web: www.safelite.com					
Speedy Auto & Glass Inc 9655 SE 36th St Suite 103	Mercer Island	WA	98040	206-232-9500	232-6404
TF: 800-533-6545 ■ Web: www.windshields.com					
SuperGlass Windshield Repair Inc 6101 Chancellor Dr Suite 200	Orlando	FL	32809	407-240-1920	240-3266
TF: 866-557-7497 ■ Web: www.sgwr.com					
Synergistic International Inc DBA Glass Doctor 1020 N University Parks Dr	Waco	TX	76707	254-745-2480	745-5073
TF: 800-280-9959 ■ Web: www.glassdoctor.com					

62-3 Mufflers & Exhaust Systems Repair - Automotive

Name / Address	City	State	Zip	Phone	Fax
Car-X Assoc Corp 1375 E Woodfield Rd Suite 500	Schaumburg	IL	60173	847-273-8920	619-3310
TF: 800-359-2359 ■ Web: www.carx.com					
Cole Muffler Inc 103 Kuhn Rd	Syracuse	NY	13208	315-455-7468	454-0373
Meineke Car Care Centers 128 S Tryon St Suite 900	Charlotte	NC	28202	704-377-8855	377-1490
TF: 800-275-5200 ■ Web: www.meineke.com					
Midas Inc 1300 Arlington Heights Rd	Itasca	IL	60143	630-438-3000	438-3703
NYSE: MDS ■ Web: www.midasinc.com					
Midas International Corp 1300 Arlington Heights Rd	Itasca	IL	60143	630-438-3000	438-3700
TF: 800-621-0144 ■ Web: www.midas.com					
Monro Muffler Brake Inc 200 Holleder Pkwy	Rochester	NY	14615	585-647-6400	647-0945
NASDAQ: MNRO ■ TF: 800-876-6676 ■ Web: www.monro.com					
Walt's Radiator & Muffler LLC 2588 Pacific Hwy E	Tacoma	WA	98424	253-922-5111	926-0112

62-4 Paint & Body Work - Automotive

Name / Address	City	State	Zip	Phone	Fax
1-Day Paint & Body Centers Inc 21801 S Western Ave	Torrance	CA	90501	310-328-0390	212-5493
TF: 800-448-1908 ■ Web: www.1daypaint.com					
ABRA Auto Body & Glass 6601 Shingle Creek Pkwy Suite 200	Brooklyn Center	MN	55430	763-561-7220	585-6455*
*Fax: Hum Res ■ TF: 888-872-2272 ■ Web: www.abraauto.com					
Caliber Collision Centers 17771 Cowan Ave Suite 100	Irvine	CA	92614	949-224-0300	224-0313
TF: 888-225-3237 ■ Web: www.calibercollision.com					
CARSTAR Quality Collision Service 8400 W 110th St Suite 200	Overland Park	KS	66210	913-451-1294	451-4436
TF: 800-227-7827 ■ Web: www.carstar.com					
Collex Collision Experts 44700 Enterprise Dr	Clinton Township	MI	48038	586-954-3850	493-5375
TF: 888-426-5539 ■ Web: www.collexcollision.com					
Colors on Parade 642 Century Cir	Conway	SC	29526	843-347-8818	347-0349
TF: 800-929-3363 ■ Web: www.colorsonparade.com					
Dent Clinic Canada Inc 711 48th Ave SE Suite 6	Calgary	AB	T2G4X2	403-255-3111	258-3555
TF: 888-722-3368 ■ Web: www.dentclinic.com					
Dent Doctor Inc 11301 W Markham St	Little Rock	AR	72211	501-224-0500	224-0507
TF: 800-946-3368 ■ Web: www.dentdoctor.com					
Dent Wizard International 4710 Earth City Expway	Bridgeton	MO	63044	314-592-1800	592-1951
TF: 800-336-8949 ■ Web: www.dentwizard.com					
Earl Scheib Inc 15206 Ventura Blvd Suite 200	Sherman Oaks	CA	91403	818-981-9992	981-8863*
*Fax: Sales ■ TF: 800-639-3275 ■ Web: www.earlscheib.com					
Gerber Auto Collision & Glass Centers Inc 8250 Skokie Blvd	Skokie	IL	60077	847-679-0510	679-0549
TF: 800-479-1230 ■ Web: www.gerbercollision.com					
Holmes Body Shop Inc 1095 E Colorado Blvd	Pasadena	CA	91106	626-795-6447	795-2123
Web: www.holmesbodyshop.com					
MAACO LLC 381 Brooks Rd	King of Prussia	PA	19406	610-265-6606	337-6113
TF: 800-523-1180 ■ Web: www.maaco.com					
Master Collision Group LLC 2980 Empire Ln	Plymouth	MN	55447	763-509-0900	509-9022
Mike Rose's Auto Body Inc 2260 Via de Marcardos	Concord	CA	94520	925-689-1739	689-0991
Web: www.mautobody.com					
Miracle Auto Painting Inc 2343 Lincoln Ave	Hayward	CA	94545	510-887-2211	887-3092
Web: www.miracleautopainting.com					
Peach Auto Painting & Collision Inc 506 Manchester Expwy Suite A-4	Columbus	GA	31904	706-324-0103	324-0105
Seidner's Collision Centers 2525 E Workman Ave	West Covina	CA	91791	626-915-7878	967-0243
Web: www.seidnerscc.com					
Service King Collision Repair Centers 808 S Central Expy	Richardson	TX	75080	972-960-7595	980-4266
Web: www.serviceking.com					
True2Form Collision Repair Centers 4853 Galaxy Pkwy Suite E	Cleveland	OH	44128	216-591-0730	591-0731
TF: 888-223-8783 ■ Web: www.true2form.com					

62-5 Repair Service (General) - Automotive

Name / Address	City	State	Zip	Phone	Fax
All Tune & Lube Brakes & More Inc 8334 Veteran's Hwy	Millersville	MD	21108	410-987-1011	987-9080
TF: 800-935-8863 ■ Web: www.alltuneandlube.com					

Repair Service (General) - Automotive (Cont'd)

				Phone	Fax
All Tune and Lube International Inc ATL International Inc					
8334 Veterans Hwy	Millersville	MD	21108	410-987-1011	987-9080
TF: 800-935-8863 ■ *Web:* www.alltuneandlube.com					
Allied Tire & Service Inc 4857 Edgewater Dr	Orlando	FL	32804	407-290-3389	
Web: www.alliedtires.com					
Basin Tire & Auto Inc 2700 E Main St	Farmington	NM	87402	505-326-2231	325-9105
TF: 800-589-2414					
Bauer Radiator Inc 3805 Walden Ave	Lancaster	NY	14086	716-681-9777	684-7423
TF: 800-462-1837 ■ *Web:* www.bauer-radiator.com					
Belle Tire Inc 3500 Enterprise Dr	Allen Park	MI	48101	313-271-9400	271-6793
TF: 800-352-7946 ■ *Web:* www.belletire.com					
Bergey's Inc 462 Harleysville Pike	Franconia	PA	18924	215-723-6071	721-3479
TF: 800-237-4397 ■ *Web:* www.bergeys.com					
Big 10 Tire Co Inc 3938 Government Blvd Suite 102	Mobile	AL	36693	251-666-9938	666-9431
Web: www.big10tires.com					
Big O Tires Inc 12650 E Briarwood Ave Suite 2D	Englewood	CO	80112	303-728-5500	728-5700
TF: 800-321-2446 ■ *Web:* www.bigotires.com					
Bob Sumerel Tires & Service Inc 3646 E Broad St	Columbus	OH	43213	614-237-6325	237-6328
TF: 800-858-0421 ■ *Web:* www.bobsumereltire.com					
Bridgestone Americas Holding Inc 535 Marriott Dr	Nashville	TN	37214	615-937-5000	937-3621
TF Cust Svc: 800-543-7522 ■ *Web:* www.bridgestone-firestone.com					
Bruce Scher's Goodyear 2120 E Warm Springs Rd	Las Vegas	NV	89119	702-263-2300	614-0039
Web: www.vegasgoodyear.com					
Cassidy Tire & Service 344 N Canal St	Chicago	IL	60606	312-226-4395	715-1702
Web: www.cassidytire.com/					
Clark Tire & Auto Supply Co Inc 220 S Center St	Hickory	NC	28602	828-322-2303	327-2783
TF: 800-968-3092 ■ *Web:* www.clarktire.com					
Craven Tire & Auto Inc 2728 Dorr Ave	Fairfax	VA	22031	703-698-8505	876-2871
TF: 800-284-6211 ■ *Web:* www.craventire.com					
Cross-Midwest Tire Inc 3570 Gardener Ave	Kansas City	MO	64120	816-231-6511	231-6393
Web: www.crossmidwest.com					
Divine Corp 203 W 3rd Ave	Spokane	WA	99201	509-455-8622	455-4327
Econo Lube N' Tune Inc PO Box 2470	Newport Beach	CA	92658	949-851-2259	851-0435
TF: 800-478-3795 ■ *Web:* www.econolube.com					
Express Oil Change 1880 S Park Dr	Hoover	AL	35244	205-945-1771	940-6025
TF: 888-945-1771 ■ *Web:* www.expressoil.com					
Fyda Freightliner Youngstown Inc 5260 76th Dr	Youngstown	OH	44515	330-797-0224	797-0230
TF: 800-837-3932 ■ *Web:* www.fydafreightliner.com					
Grease Monkey International Inc					
7100 E Belleview Ave Suite 305	Greenwood Village	CO	80111	303-308-1660	308-5908
TF: 800-822-7706 ■ *Web:* www.greasemonkey.net					
Heartland Automotive Services Inc 11308 Davenport St	Omaha	NE	68154	402-333-0990	333-2338
TF: 800-417-7308					
Jack Williams Tire Co Inc PO Box 3655	Scranton	PA	18505	570-457-5000	457-2852
TF: 800-833-5051 ■ *Web:* www.jackwilliams.com					
Jensen Tire & Auto 10609 'I' St	Omaha	NE	68127	402-339-2917	339-8815
Web: jensentire.com					
Jiffy Lube International Inc 700 Milam St	Houston	TX	77002	713-546-4000	
TF: 800-327-9532 ■ *Web:* www.jiffylube.com					
Jubitz Corp 33 NE Middlefield Rd	Portland	OR	97211	503-283-1111	240-5834
TF: 800-399-5480 ■ *Web:* www.jubitz.com					
Kolstad Co Inc 8501 Naples St NE	Blaine	MN	55449	763-792-1033	792-3799
Lamb Ventures LP 10313 Lake Creek Pkwy	Austin	TX	78750	512-257-2350	257-1895
TF: 800-325-5262 ■ *Web:* www.lambstire.com					
Les Schwab Tire Centers Inc					
646 NW Madras Hwy PO Box 667	Prineville	OR	97754	541-447-4136	416-5157*
**Fax:* Cust Svc ■ *Web:* www.lesschwab.com					
Lucor Inc 790 Pershing Rd	Raleigh	NC	27608	919-828-9511	828-2433
TF: 800-216-2553 ■ *Web:* www.jiffylube-lucor.com					
Meineke Car Care Centers 128 S Tryon St Suite 900	Charlotte	NC	28202	704-377-8855	377-1490
TF: 800-275-5200 ■ *Web:* www.meineke.com					
Merchant's Tire & Auto Centers 823 Donald Ross Rd	Juno Beach	FL	33408	561-842-4290	368-1658*
**Fax Area Code:* 703 ■ *TF:* 800-368-3130 ■ *Web:* www.merchantstire.com					
Merlin 200,000 Mile Shops 1 N River Lane Suite 206	Geneva	IL	60134	630-208-9900	208-8601
TF: 800-637-5467 ■ *Web:* www.merlins.com					
Merlin Corp 1 N River Lane Suite 206	Geneva	IL	60134	630-208-9900	208-8601
TF: 800-637-5467 ■ *Web:* www.merlins.com					
Midas Inc 1300 Arlington Heights Rd	Itasca	IL	60143	630-438-3000	438-3703
NYSE: MDS ■ *Web:* www.midasinc.com					
Morgan Tire & Auto Inc 2021 Sunnydale Blvd	Clearwater	FL	33765	727-442-8388	443-2401
TF: 800-269-4424 ■ *Web:* www.tiresplus.com					
Mountain View Tire & Service Inc 8140 Masi Dr	Rancho Cucamonga	CA	91730	909-484-9777	484-3973
Web: www.mountainviewtire.com					
Mr Tire Auto Service Centers Inc 200 Holleder Pkwy	Rochester	NY	14615	800-876-6676	647-1416*
**Fax Area Code:* 585 ■ *Web:* www.mrtire.com					
National Tire & Battery (NTB) 823 Donald Ross Rd	Juno Beach	FL	33408	561-842-4290	
Web: www.ntb.com					
Oil Butler International Corp 1599 Rt 22	Union	NJ	07083	908-687-3283	687-7617
Web: www.oilbutlerinternational.com					
Parrish Tire Co Inc 5130 Indiana Ave	Winston-Salem	NC	27106	336-767-0202	744-2716
TF: 800-849-8473 ■ *Web:* www.parrishtire.com					
Perry Brothers Tire Service Inc 610 Wicker St	Sanford	NC	27330	919-775-7225	774-4853
Web: www.perrybros.com					
Precision Auto Care Inc 748 Miller Dr SE	Leesburg	VA	20175	703-777-9095	771-7108
TF: 800-438-8863 ■ *Web:* www.precisionac.com					
Purcell's Western States Tires & Automotive Service Inc					
1700 N 23rd Ave	Phoenix	AZ	85009	602-252-5757	252-2316
TF: 888-787-2355 ■ *Web:* www.purcelltire.com					
Schwab Les Tire Centers Inc					
646 NW Madras Hwy PO Box 667	Prineville	OR	97754	541-447-4136	416-5157*
**Fax:* Cust Svc ■ *Web:* www.lesschwab.com					
Somerset Tire Services Inc 400 W Main St	Bound Brook	NJ	08805	732-356-8500	356-8821
TF: 800-445-1434 ■ *Web:* www.ststire.com					
Sullivan Tire Co Inc 41 Accord Park Dr	Norwell	MA	02061	781-982-1550	871-6250
TF: 800-892-1955 ■ *Web:* www.sullivantire.com					
Sumerel Bob Tires & Service Inc 3646 E Broad St	Columbus	OH	43213	614-237-6325	237-6328
TF: 800-858-0421 ■ *Web:* www.bobsumereltire.com					
Sun Devil Auto Inc 1830 E Elliott Rd Suite 104	Tempe	AZ	85284	480-491-4210	491-4204
Web: www.sundevilauto.com					
Ted Wiens Tire & Auto Centers Inc 1701 Las Vegas Blvd S	Las Vegas	NV	89104	702-732-2382	735-4061
Web: www.tedwiens.com					
Tire Distribution Systems Inc 4000 W 44th Ave	Wheat Ridge	CO	80033	303-422-2300	463-8448
TF: 800-541-8473					
Tire Kingdom Inc 823 Donald Ross Rd	Juno Beach	FL	33408	561-842-4290	
Web: www.tirekingdom.com					
Tire-Rama Inc 1401 Industrial Ave PO Box 23509	Billings	MT	59104	406-245-4006	245-0257
TF: 800-828-1642 ■ *Web:* www.tirerama.com					
Tires Plus 2021 Sunnydale Blvd	Clearwater	FL	33765	727-441-3727	443-2401
TF: 800-269-4424 ■ *Web:* www.tiresplus.com					
Tires Plus Total Car Care 2021 Sunnydale Blvd	Clearwater	FL	33765	727-441-3727	443-2401
TF: 800-269-4424 ■ *Web:* www.tiresplus.com					
Transtek Inc 4303 Lewis Rd PO Box 4174	Harrisburg	PA	17111	717-564-6151	564-1118
TF: 800-871-1935					
Tuffy Assoc Corp 1414 Baronial Plaza Dr	Toledo	OH	43615	419-865-6900	865-7343
TF: 800-228-8339 ■ *Web:* www.tuffy.com					
VIP Parts Tires & Service 12 Lexington St	Lewiston	ME	04240	207-784-5423	784-9178
Web: www.vipauto.com/					
Warren Tire Service Center Inc 4 Highland Ave Suite 3	Queensbury	NY	12804	518-792-0316	792-8982
Wiens Ted Tire & Auto Centers Inc 1701 Las Vegas Blvd S	Las Vegas	NV	89104	702-732-2382	735-4061
Web: www.tedwiens.com					
Williams Jack Tire Co Inc PO Box 3655	Scranton	PA	18505	570-457-5000	457-2852
TF: 800-833-5051 ■ *Web:* www.jackwilliams.com					
Wingfoot Commercial Tire Systems LLC 1000 S 21st St	Fort Smith	AR	72901	479-788-6400	788-6486
TF: 800-643-7330 ■ *Web:* www.treadco.com					
Ziegler Tire & Supply Co Inc 4150 Millennium Blvd SE	Massillon	OH	44646	330-834-3332	834-3342

62-6 Transmission Repair - Automotive

				Phone	Fax
AAMCO Transmissions Inc 1 Presidential Blvd	Bala Cynwyd	PA	19004	610-668-2900	664-1226
TF Cust Svc: 800-523-0401 ■ *Web:* www.aamcotransmissions.com					
All Tune Transmissions 8334 Veteran's Hwy	Millersville	MD	21108	410-987-1011	987-9080
TF: 800-935-8863 ■ *Web:* www.alltuneandlube.com					
Certified Transmission Rebuilders Inc 1801 S 54th St	Omaha	NE	68106	402-558-2117	558-2202
TF: 800-554-7520 ■ *Web:* www.certifiedtransmissions.com					
Cottman Transmission Systems LLC					
201 Gibraltar Rd Suite 150	Horsham	PA	19044	215-643-5885	643-2519
TF: 800-394-6116 ■ *Web:* www.cottman.com					
Lee Myles Assoc Corp 650 From Rd 4th Fl South Lobby	Paramus	NJ	07652	201-262-0555	262-5177
TF: 800-533-6953 ■ *Web:* www.leemyles.com					
Mr Transmission 9675 Yonge St 2nd Fl	Richmond Hill	ON	L4C1V7	905-884-1511	884-4727
TF: 800-373-8432 ■ *Web:* www.mistertransmission.com					

62-7 Van Conversions

				Phone	Fax
Clock Conversions 6700 Clay Ave	Grand Rapids	MI	49548	616-698-9400	698-9495
TF: 800-732-5625 ■ *Web:* www.clockconversions.com/					
Eclipse Conversions 135 E County Rd 6	Elkhart	IN	46514	574-262-1223	262-9578
Web: www.eclipseconversions.com/index.html					
Marathon Coach Inc 91333 Coburg Industrial Way	Coburg	OR	97408	541-343-9991	343-2401
Web: www.marathoncoach.com					
Mobility Van Conversions 3012 Calumet Dr	Orlando	FL	32810	407-625-5438	
Web: www.mobilityvan.com/					
Monaco Coach Corp 91320 Coburg Industrial Way	Coburg	OR	97408	541-686-8011	681-8037*
NYSE: MNC ■ **Fax:* Hum Res ■ *TF:* 800-634-0855 ■ *Web:* www.monaco-online.com					
Rollx Vans 6591 Hwy 13 W	Savage	MN	55378	952-890-7851	890-1903
TF: 800-956-6668 ■ *Web:* www.rollxvans.com					
Sherrod Vans Inc 3151 Industrial Blvd	Wayross	GA	31503	912-490-1210	490-1212
TF: 800-824-6333 ■ *Web:* www.sherrodvans.com					
Sidewinder Conversions 45681Yale Rd W	Chilliwack	BC	V2P2N1	604-792-2082	792-8920
TF: 888-266-2299 ■ *Web:* www.sidewinder-conversions.com/					
Unique Conversions Inc PO Box 672	Mansfield	TX	76063	817-477-5251	477-2711
Van Conversions Inc 925 S Trooper Rd	Norristown	PA	19403	610-666-9100	666-9102
Web: www.vanconinc.com/					
Vantage Mobility International (VMI) 5202 S 28th Pl	Phoenix	AZ	85040	602-243-2700	304-3290
TF: 800-348-8267 ■ *Web:* www.vantagemobility.com/					
Waldoch Crafts Inc 13821 Lake Dr NE	Forest Lake	MN	55025	651-464-3215	464-1117
Web: www.waldoch.com					

63 AVIATION - FIXED-BASE OPERATIONS

SEE ALSO Air Cargo Carriers p. 1266; Air Charter Services p. 1266; Aircraft Rental p. 1272; Aircraft Service & Repair p. 1272

				Phone	Fax
A & M Aviation Inc 130 S Clow International Pkwy Suite B	Bolingbrook	IL	60490	630-759-1555	759-2281
Web: www.aandmaviation.com					
Abilene Aero 2850 Airport Blvd	Abilene	TX	79602	325-677-2601	671-8018
Web: www.abileneaero.com					
ACM Aviation Inc 1475 Airport Blvd	San Jose	CA	95110	408-286-3832	286-1629
TF: 800-359-7538 ■ *Web:* www.acmaviation.com					
Aero Industries Inc					
5690 Clarkson Rd Richmond International Airport	Richmond	VA	23250	804-222-7211	236-1670
TF: 800-845-1308 ■ *Web:* www.aeroind.com					
Aerodynamics Inc 6544 Highland Rd	Waterford	MI	48327	248-666-3500	666-9041
TF: 800-235-9234 ■ *Web:* www.flyadi.com					
AG Spanos Jet Center 4800 S Airport Way	Stockton	CA	95206	209-982-1550	983-4710
Air America Fuel & Service Inc					
Grant County International Airport 7810 Andrews St NE					
Suite 134	Moses Lake	WA	98837	509-762-2626	762-2299
Web: www.airamericafuelservice.com					
Aircraft Specialists Inc 6005 Propeller Ln	Sellersburg	IN	47172	812-246-4696	246-4365
Web: www.asicharter.com					
Aire Shannon Inc 3380 Shannon Airport Cir	Fredericksburg	VA	22408	540-373-4431	373-0035
American Aviation 2495 Broad St	Brooksville	FL	34604	352-796-5173	799-4681
Web: www.americanaviation.com					
Anniston Aviation Anniston Metropolitan Airport PO Box 2185	Anniston	AL	36202	256-831-4410	831-4411
Arcadia Aviation 170 Aviation Way	Martinsburg	WV	25401	304-262-4710	262-4715
TF: 800-550-2507 ■ *Web:* www.arcadiaaviation.com					
Arlins Aircraft Service Inc 36 Gallatin Field	Belgrade	MT	59714	406-388-1351	388-7417
Web: www.arlins.com					
Atlantic Aviation					
10510 Superfortress Ave Sacramento Mather Airport	Mather	CA	95655	916-368-1455	368-5770
TF: 800-565-2647 ■ *Web:* www.atlanticaviation.com					
Atlantic Aviation					
George Bush Intercontinental Airport 17725 JFK Blvd	Houston	TX	77032	281-443-3434	821-9149
Web: www.atlanticaviation.com					
Atlantic Aviation Corp					
New Orleans International Airport PO Box 1897	New Orleans	LA	70141	504-466-1700	465-9699
Web: www.atlanticaviation.com					
Atlantic Aviation Services					
19711 Campus Dr Suite 100 John Wayne Airport	Santa Ana	CA	92707	949-851-5061	851-1450
TF: 800-500-5061 ■ *Web:* www.atlanticaviation.com/sna.html					
Aurora Aviation Aurora State Airport PO Box 127	Aurora	OR	97002	503-678-1217	678-1219
Web: www.auroraaviation.com					
Avion Flight Centre Inc 2506 N Pliska Dr	Midland	TX	79711	432-563-2033	563-4765
TF: 800-759-3359 ■ *Web:* www.avionflight.com					
Banyan Air Service 5360 NW 20th Terr	Fort Lauderdale	FL	33309	954-491-3170	771-0281
TF: 800-200-2031 ■ *Web:* www.banyanair.com					
Basler Flight Service Wittman Regional Airport PO Box 2464	Oshkosh	WI	54903	920-236-7827	236-7833
Web: www.baslerflightservice.com					

Phone Fax

Bet-Ko Air Inc 3681 S Burch Way Yuma AZ 85365 928-726-1116 726-0421
Web: www.betkoair.com
BMG Aviation Inc 984 S Kirby Rd Bloomington IN 47403 812-825-7979 825-7978
TF: 888-457-3787 ■ Web: www.bmgaviation.com
Boca Aviation 3700 Airport Rd Boca Raton FL 33431 561-368-1110 392-7113
TF: 800-335-2622 ■ Web: www.bocaaviation.com
Brookville Air Park 9386 W National Rd Brookville OH 45309 937-833-2590
Cav-Air LLC 2011 S Perimeter Rd Suite L Fort Lauderdale FL 33309 954-491-4454 772-1626
TF: 800-537-4454 ■ Web: www.cavair.com
Central Flying Service Inc 1501 Bond St Little Rock AR 72202 501-375-3245 375-7274
TF: 800-888-5387 ■ Web: www.flycfs.com
Channel Islands Aviation 305 Durley Ave Camarillo Airport Camarillo CA 93010 805-987-1301 987-8301
Web: www.flycia.com
Co-Mar Aviation 1065 Ashley St Suite 100 Bowling Green KY 42103 270-783-8080 781-4792
Web: www.comaraviation.com
Colonial Air 1605 Airport Rd New Bedford MA 02746 508-997-0620 990-2582
Web: www.colonial-air.com
Columbia Air Services
175 Tower Ave Groton-New London Airport Groton CT 06340 860-449-1400 405-7269
TF: 800-787-5001 ■ Web: www.columbiaairservices.com
Columbia Air Services LLC 112 Caruso Dr Trenton ME 04605 207-667-5534 667-4222
TF: 888-756-8648 ■ Web: www.columbiaairservices.com
Concord Aviation Services 71 Airport Rd Concord NH 03301 603-228-2267 228-2268
Cook Aviation Inc 970 S Kirby Rd Bloomington IN 47403 812-825-2392 825-3701
TF: 800-880-3499 ■ Web: www.cookaviation.com
Corporate Air LLC 15 Allegheny County Airport West Mifflin PA 15122 412-469-6800 469-0877
TF: 888-429-5377 ■ Web: www.travelredefined.com
Corporate Wings 355 Richmond Rd Cleveland OH 44143 216-261-1111 261-4260
TF: 800-261-1115 ■ Web: www.corporatewings.com
Craig Air Center 855-14 St John's Bluff Rd N Jacksonville FL 32225 904-641-0300 642-2012
TF: 888-277-6326 ■ Web: apro-fbo.com
Crow Executive Air Inc
28331 Lemoyne Rd Toledo Metcalf Airport Millbury OH 43447 419-838-6921 838-6911
TF: 800-972-2769 ■ Web: www.crowair.com
Dassault Falcon
191 N DuPont Hwy New Castle County Airport New Castle DE 19720 302-322-7000 322-7331
TF: 800-441-9390 ■ Web: www.atlanticaviation.com
DB Aviation Inc 3550 N McAree Rd Waukegan IL 60087 847-263-5600 263-6486
TF: 800-638-4990 ■ Web: www.dbaviation.com
De Gol Jet Center Inc 580 S Loyalsock Ave Montoursville PA 17754 570-368-2651 368-8651
TF: 800-872-3599
Deer Horn Aviation Ltd Co DBA Avion Flight Centre Inc
2506 N Pliska Dr Midland TX 79711 432-563-2033 563-4765
TF: 800-759-3359 ■ Web: www.avionflight.com
Del Monte Aviation Inc DBA Monterey Bay Aviation
514 Airport Way Monterey CA 93940 831-373-3201 373-2352
Web: www.montereybayaviation.com
Dodgen Aircraft 740 Grand St Allegan MI 49010 269-673-4157 673-4157
Web: www.dodgenaircraft.com
Dolphin Aviation Inc
8191 N Tamiami Tr Sarasota Bradenton International Airport Sarasota FL 34243 941-355-7715 351-7197*
*Fax: Cust Svc ■ Web: www.dolphinaviation.com
Dulles Aviation Inc
10501 Observation Rd Manassas Regional Airport Manassas VA 20110 703-361-2171 361-4478
TF: 888-835-9324 ■ Web: www.dullesaviation.com/default.htm
Dunkirk Aviation Sales & Service Inc 3389 Middle Rd Dunkirk NY 14048 716-366-6938 366-6986
Web: www.dkk.com
Dyersburg Avionics of Caruthersville 2204 Airport Dr Caruthersville MO 63830 573-333-4296 333-0674
Web: www.dyersburgavionics.com
Eagle Aviation
2861 Aviation Way Columbia Metropolitan Airport West Columbia SC 29170 803-822-5577 822-5592
TF: 800-848-6359 ■ Web: www.eagle-aviation.com
Edwards Jet Center 1691 Aviation Pl Billings MT 59105 406-252-0508 245-9491
TF: 800-755-9624 ■ Web: www.edwardsjetcenter.com
Encore FBO Frederick 330 Aviation Way Frederick MD 21701 301-662-8156 662-3101
TF: 800-545-9393 ■ Web: www.encorefbo.com
Encore FBO Sioux Falls 3501 Aviation Ave Sioux Falls SD 57104 605-336-7791 336-8009
TF: 800-888-1646 ■ Web: www.encorefbo.com
Epps Aviation Inc 1 Aviation Way DeKalb Peachtree Airport Atlanta GA 30341 770-458-9851 458-0320
TF: 800-462-0104 ■ Web: www.eppsaviation.com
Executive Air
2131 Airport Dr Austin Straubel International Airport Green Bay WI 54313 920-498-4880 498-4890
Web: www.executiveair.com
Felts Field Aviation Inc 5829 E Rutter Ave Spokane WA 99212 509-535-9011 535-9014
TF: 800-676-5538 ■ Web: www.feltsfield.com
Flightcraft Inc 90454 Boeing Dr Eugene OR 97402 541-688-9291 688-5749
TF: 800-776-6312 ■ Web: www.flightcraft.com
Flightline of Dothan Inc PO Box 9044 Dothan AL 36304 334-983-5555 983-6666
TF: 866-466-5903 ■ Web: www.flightlineofdothan.com
Flightline Group Inc
3256 SW Capital Cir Tallahassee Regional Airport Tallahassee FL 32310 850-574-4444 576-4210
Web: www.flightlinegroup.com
Fournet Paul Air Service Inc
118 John Glen Dr Lafayette Regional Airport Lafayette LA 70508 337-237-0520 232-1188
Web: www.fournet.com
Galvin Flying Services 7149 Perimeter Rd Seattle WA 98108 206-763-0350 767-9333
TF: 800-341-4102 ■ Web: www.galvinflying.com
Gibbs Flying Service 8906 Aero Dr San Diego CA 92123 858-277-0162 277-0854
Web: gibbsflyingservice.com
Grand Aire Express Inc 11777 W Airport Service Rd Swanton OH 43558 419-865-1780 865-2965
TF: 800-704-7263 ■ Web: www.grandaire.com
Grand Strand Aviation DBA Ramp 66
2800 Terminal St North Myrtle Beach SC 29582 843-272-5337 272-5822
TF: 800-433-8918 ■ Web: www.ramp66.com
Hagerstown Aviation Services Inc 18627 Jarkey Dr Hagerstown MD 21742 301-733-5200 733-6981
TF: 800-889-6094 ■ Web: www.hagerstownaviation.com
Holman Aviation Co 1940 Airport Ct Great Falls MT 59404 406-453-7613 453-7204
TF: 800-843-7613 ■ Web: www.holmanaviation.com
Hunt Pan Am Aviation Inc
505 S Minnesota Ave Brownsville/South Padre
International Airport Brownsville TX 78521 956-542-9111 542-9133
TF: 800-888-7524 ■ Web: www.huntpanam.com
Inter-State Aviation 4800 Airport Complex N Airport Rd Pullman WA 99163 509-332-6596 334-1751
Interstate Aviation 62 Johnson Ave Plainville CT 06062 860-747-5519 589-1853
TF: 800-573-5519 ■ Web: www.interstateaviation.com
Jet Aviation 1515 Perimeter Rd West Palm Beach FL 33406 561-233-7233 233-7222
TF: 800-758-5387 ■ Web: www.jetaviation.com
Jet Harbor Inc 1475 Airport Rd Gallatin TN 37066 615-452-6699 230-0414
Web: www.jetharbor.com
JetDirect Aviation 1 Earhart Dr Suite 1 Coatesville PA 19320 610-384-9000 384-7083
TF: 866-538-3473 ■ Web: www.jetdirect.net
Kansas City Aviation Center Inc
15325 Pflumm Rd Johnson County Executive Airport Olathe KS 66062 913-782-0530 782-9462
TF Sales: 800-720-5222 ■ Web: www.kcac.com
Keystone Aviation Services Inc 288 Christian St Oxford CT 06478 203-264-6525 264-0295
TF: 866-436-2177

Phone Fax

Landmark Aviation 4360 Agar Dr Richmond BC V7B1A3 604-279-9922 279-9942
TF: 888-298-7326 ■ Web: www.fbovancouver.com
Landmark Aviation 6201 W Imperial Hwy Los Angeles CA 90045 310-568-3700 568-3790
TF: 800-942-7738 ■ Web: www.landmarkaviation.com
Landmark Aviation 3821 N Liberty St Winston-Salem NC 27105 336-776-6060 776-6061*
*Fax: Sales ■ TF: 800-393-4908 ■ Web: www.landmarkaviation.com
Lane Aviation Corp 4389 International Gateway Columbus OH 43219 614-237-3747 237-2048*
*Fax: Cust Svc ■ TF: 800-848-6263 ■ Web: www.wingsonline.com/lanehp.cfm
Leading Edge Aviation Service Inc 6582 Eureka Springs Rd Tampa FL 33610 813-626-1515 623-6483
Web: www.leadingedgeaviation.com
Loyd's Aviation Services Inc PO Box 80958 Bakersfield CA 93380 661-393-1334 393-0824
TF: 800-284-1334 ■ Web: www.loydsaviation.com
M7 Aerospace LP 10823 NE Entrance Rd San Antonio TX 78216 210-824-9421 824-9476*
*Fax: Hum Res ■ TF: 800-327-2313 ■ Web: www.m7aerospace.com
Maine Instrument Flight Augusta State Airport PO Box 2 Augusta ME 04332 207-622-1211 622-7858
TF: 888-643-3597 ■ Web: www.mif.aero
Malloy Air East Inc Francis S Gabreski Airport Westhampton Beach NY 11978 631-288-5410 288-1470
TF: 888-673-9888 ■ Web: malloyaireast.com
McCall Aviation 300 Deinhard Ln McCall ID 83638 208-634-7137 634-3917
TF: 800-992-6559 ■ Web: www.mccallair.com
Mercury Air Centers Inc 2161 E Avion St Ontario CA 91761 909-390-2370 390-4508
Web: www.mercuryairgroup.com
Miami Executive Aviation Inc 15001 NW 42 Ave Miami FL 33054 305-687-8410 769-5815
TF: 800-861-1343 ■ Web: www.miamiexecutive.com
Mid-Ohio Aviation 6020 N Honeytown Rd Smithville OH 44677 330-669-2671 669-2402
TF: 800-669-4243 ■ Web: www.midohioaviation.com
Midwest Corporate Aviation 3512 N Webb Rd Wichita KS 67226 316-636-9700 636-9747
TF: 800-435-9622 ■ Web: www.midwestaviation.com
Millenium Aviation 2365 Bernville Rd Reading Regional Airport Reading PA 19605 610-374-0100 374-7580
TF: 800-366-9419 ■ Web: www.majets.com
Million Air 4300 Westgrove Dr Addison TX 75001 972-248-1600 733-5803
TF: 800-248-1602 ■ Web: www.millionair.com
Minuteman Aviation Inc 5225 Hwy 10 W Airport Box 16 Missoula MT 59808 406-728-9363 728-6981
Web: www.minutemanaviation.com
Miracle Strip Aviation - Avitat Destin 1001 Airport Rd Destin FL 32541 850-837-6135 654-0618
Web: www.avitat.com
Mobile Air Center Bates Field West Ramp PO Box 88027 Mobile AL 36608 251-633-5000 633-2225
TF: 800-566-9411 ■ Web: www.mobileaircenter.com
Monroe Air Center 5410 Operations Rd Monroe LA 71203 318-387-0222 325-1538
TF: 800-223-3895 ■ Web: www.monroeair.com
Monroeville Aviation PO Box 189 Monroeville AL 36460 251-575-4235 575-1907
Monterey Bay Aviation 514 Airport Way Monterey CA 93940 831-373-3201 373-2352
Web: www.montereybayaviation.com
Montgomery Aviation Corp 4525 Selma Hwy Montgomery AL 36108 334-288-7334 288-7337
TF: 800-392-8044 ■ Web: www.montgomeryaviation.com
National Jets Air Center 3495 SW 9th Ave Fort Lauderdale FL 33315 954-359-9400 359-0039
TF: 800-525-0166 ■ Web: www.nationaljets.com/natjet/jet/index.html
Newton Aviation Lewistown Municipal Airport 410 Skyline Dr Lewistown MT 59457 406-538-8150 538-8166
Web: www.lewistownairport.com
North Coast Air 4645 W 12th St Erie International Airport Erie PA 16505 814-836-9220 836-9901
Web: www.ncair.com
Northeast Airmotive Inc 1011 Westbrook St Portland ME 04102 207-774-6318 874-4714
TF: 800-397-6786 ■ Web: www.northeastairmotive.com
Northside Aviation Inc McCollum Airport PO Box 490 Kennesaw GA 30156 770-422-4300 422-4382
TF: 800-754-4300 ■ Web: atlantanorthsideaviation.com
Ocean Aire RJ Miller Airpark PO Box 1245 Toms River NJ 08754 732-797-1077 797-1076
Web: www.oceanaire.net
Panorama Flight Service Inc 67 Tower Rd White Plains NY 10604 914-328-9800 328-9684
TF: 888-359-7266 ■ Web: www.flypfs.com
Paul Fournet Air Service Inc
118 John Glen Dr Lafayette Regional Airport Lafayette LA 70508 337-237-0520 232-1188
Web: www.fournet.com
Pelican Aviation 1314 Hangar Dr New Iberia LA 70560 337-367-1401 367-1404
Pensacola Aviation Center Inc 4145 Jerry L Maygarden Rd Pensacola FL 32504 850-434-0636 434-3984
TF: 800-874-6580 ■ Web: www.pensacolaaviation.com
Personal Jet Charter Inc 5401 E Perimeter Rd Fort Lauderdale FL 33309 954-776-4515 491-5771
TF: 800-432-1538 ■ Web: www.personaljet.com
Phoenix Aviation Inc 701 Wilson Pt Rd Box 37 Middle River MD 21220 410-574-3897 574-3810
Web: www.phoenixaviation.com
Pike Aviation Inc 301 Airport Rd Troy AL 36079 334-566-3470
Premier Jet Center 3301A NE Cornell Rd Hillsboro OR 97124 503-693-1096 640-0167
Web: www.premierjetcenter.com
Prior Aviation Service Inc 50 N Airport Dr Buffalo NY 14225 716-633-1000 633-1543
TF: 800-621-2923 ■ Web: www.prioraviation.com
Private Sky Aviation Services Inc 1 Private Skyway Fort Myers FL 33913 239-225-6100 225-0798
Web: www.privatesky.net
PS Air Inc 3435 Beech Way Cedar Rapids IA 52404 319-846-3600 846-3605
Web: www.psair.com
Ramp 66 2800 Terminal St North Myrtle Beach SC 29582 843-272-5337 272-5822
TF: 800-433-8918 ■ Web: www.ramp66.com
Regional Jet Center 12344 Tower Dr Bentonville AR 72712 479-205-1100 205-1101
TF: 866-962-3835 ■ Web: www.regionaljetcenter.com
Richmor Aviation Inc 1142 Rt 9 H Columbia County Airport Hudson NY 12534 518-828-9461 828-1303
TF: 800-331-6101 ■ Web: www.richmor.com
Robinson Aviation 50 Thompson Ave East Haven CT 06512 203-467-9555 467-6346
Web: www.robinsonaviation.com
Ronson Aviation Inc Trenton Mercer Airport Trenton NJ 08628 609-771-9500 771-0885*
*Fax: Cust Svc ■ TF: 800-257-0416 ■ Web: www.ronsonaviation.com
Saint Paul Flight Center 270 Airport Rd Saint Paul MN 55107 651-227-8108 227-6195
TF: 800-368-0107 ■ Web: www.stpaulflight.com
Sanford Aircraft Services Inc 701 Rod Sullivan Rd Sanford NC 27330 919-708-5549 774-9627
TF: 888-871-1947 ■ Web: www.sanfordaircraft.com
Santa Fe Air Center Inc 121 Aviation Dr Bldg 3005 Santa Fe NM 87507 505-471-2525 438-0671
TF: 800-263-7695 ■ Web: www.santafejet.biz
Servicecenter Inc 7301 NW 50th St Wiley Post Airport Oklahoma City OK 73132 405-789-5000 789-5995
TF: 800-299-8546 ■ Web: www.thescinc.com
SheltAir Aviation Services Fort Lauderdale
1100 Lee Wagener Blvd Fort Lauderdale FL 33315 954-359-3200 359-3211
TF: 800-394-5388 ■ Web: www.sheltairaviation.com/aviation/fll.html
Showalter Flying Service
Orlando Executive Airport 400 Herndon Ave Orlando FL 32803 407-894-7331 894-5094
TF: 800-894-7331 ■ Web: www.showalter.com
Signature Flight Support 201 S Orange Ave Suite 1100-S Orlando FL 32801 407-648-7200 206-8428*
*Fax: Hum Res ■ TF: 800-428-5597 ■ Web: www.bba-aviation.com/flightsupport
Silverhawk Aviation Inc 1751 W Kearney Ave Lincoln NE 68524 402-475-8600 475-1422
TF: 800-479-5851 ■ Web: www.silverhawkaviation.com
Sky Bright 65 Aviation Dr Gilford NH 03249 603-528-6818 528-1814
TF: 800-639-6012 ■ Web: www.skybright.com
Skyservice Airlines Inc 31 Fasken Dr Etobicoke ON M9W1K6 416-679-5700 679-5920
TF: 800-701-9448 ■ Web: www.skyserviceairlines.com
SkyTech Inc 550 Airport Rd Rock Hill SC 29732 803-366-5108 366-1519
TF: 888-386-3596 ■ Web: www.skytechinc.com
Smyrna Air Center 300 Doug Warpoole Rd Smyrna TN 37167 615-459-3337 625-7020
Web: www.smyrnaaircenter.com
Snohomish Flying Service Inc 9900 Airport Way Snohomish WA 98296 360-568-1541 568-6034
Web: www.snohomishflying.com

				Phone	Fax
Southwest Airport Services Inc 11811 N Brantly St Ellington Field Bldg 500 *TF:* 800-426-5237 ■ *Web:* www.swjetops.com	Houston	TX	77034	281-484-6551	484-8184
Space Coast Jet Center 7003 Challenger Ave *TF:* 800-559-5473 ■ *Web:* www.spacecoastjetcenter.com	Titusville	FL	32780	321-267-6043	267-0129
Spanaflight 16715 Meridian E Bldg H *Web:* www.spanaflight.com	Puyallup	WA	98375	253-848-2020	840-5843
Spanos AG Jet Center 4800 S Airport Way	Stockton	CA	95206	209-982-1550	983-4710
Statesville Flying Service PO Box 5056	Statesville	NC	28687	704-873-1111	873-1113
Stetson Aviation 1 Airport Rd *TF:* 877-520-8118 ■ *Web:* www.stetsonaviation.com	Kenedy	TX	78119	830-583-9897	583-9749
Stevens Aviation Inc 600 Delaware St Donaldson Industrial Pk *TF:* 800-359-7838 ■ *Web:* www.stevensaviation.com	Greenville	SC	29605	864-879-6000	879-6195
Stuart Jet Center LLC 2501 SE Aviation Way *TF:* 877-735-9538 ■ *Web:* www.stuartjet.com	Stuart	FL	34996	772-288-6700	288-3782
Sun Valley Aviation Friedman Memorial Airport PO Box 1085 *Web:* www.7bar.com/service/sunvalley	Hailey	ID	83333	208-788-9511	788-1399
Sundance Aviation Inc 12210 N Sara Rd Sundance Airpark *Web:* www.sundanceairpark.com	Yukon	OK	73099	405-373-3886	373-3893
Swift Aviation 2710 E Old Tower Rd *Web:* www.swiftaviation.com	Phoenix	AZ	85034	602-273-3770	273-3773
Tejas Avco Inc 503 McKeever Rd Suite 1505 *TF:* 800-511-6062	Arcola	TX	77583	281-431-2581	431-2845
Telford Aviation Inc 154 Maine Ave *TF:* 800-639-4809 ■ *Web:* www.telfordaviation.com	Bangor	ME	04401	207-262-6098	262-8708
Top Gun Aviation Inc Hammond Municipal Airport PO Box 2032	Hammond	LA	70404	985-542-0719	542-2077
Tri State Airmotive LLC 20 Tri State Rd Carroll County Airport	Berryville	AR	72616	870-423-4911	
Truman Arnold Cos 701 S Robison Rd *TF:* 800-235-5343 ■ *Web:* www.tacair.com	Texarkana	TX	75504	903-794-3835	832-7226
Vee Neal Aviation Inc 148 Aviation Ln Suite 109 *TF:* 800-278-2710 ■ *Web:* www.veeneal.com	Latrobe	PA	15650	724-539-4533	539-5501
Western Aircraft Inc 4300 S Kennedy St *TF:* 800-333-3442 ■ *Web:* www.westair.com	Boise	ID	83705	208-338-1800	338-1830
Western Cardinal Inc 205 Durley Ave *TF:* 800-882-3018 ■ *Web:* www.wciline.com	Camarillo	CA	93010	805-482-2586	484-2713
Wilson Air Center 2930 Winchester Rd Memphis International Airport *TF:* 800-464-2992 ■ *Web:* www.wilsonair.com	Memphis	TN	38118	901-345-2992	345-1088
Wings Air Charter 3620 1st St S Alexander Field *Web:* www.wingsaircharter.com	Wisconsin Rapids	WI	54494	715-424-3737	424-3737
Wisconsin Aviation Inc 1741 River Dr *TF:* 800-657-0761 ■ *Web:* www.wisconsinaviation.com	Watertown	WI	53094	920-261-4567	206-6386
Woodland Aviation Inc 17992 County Rd 94B Watts-Woodland Airport *TF:* 800-442-1333 ■ *Web:* www.woodlandaviation.com	Woodland	CA	95695	530-662-9631	662-3035

64 BABY PRODUCTS

SEE ALSO Clothing & Accessories - Mfr - Children's & Infants' Clothing p. 1450; Furniture - Mfr - Household Furniture p. 1682; Paper Products - Sanitary p. 2048; Toys, Games, Hobbies p. 2375

				Phone	Fax
Baby Jogger Co 8575 Magellan Parkway Suite 1000 **Fax Area Code:* 804 ■ *TF:* 800-241-1848 ■ *Web:* www.babyjogger.com	Richmond	VA	23227	800-241-1848	262-6277*
Baby Trend Inc 1567 S Campus Ave **Fax Area Code:* 909 ■ *TF Cust Svc:* 800-328-7363 ■ *Web:* www.babytrend.com	Ontario	CA	91761	800-328-7363	773-0108*
Baby's Dream Furniture Inc 411 Industrial Blvd PO Box 579 *TF:* 800-835-2742 ■ *Web:* www.babysdream.com	Buena Vista	GA	31803	229-649-4404	649-2007
BabySwede LLC 5700 Lombardo Center Dr Rock Run North Suite 202 *TF:* 866-424-0200 ■ *Web:* www.babyswede.com	Cleveland	OH	44131	216-447-9140	
BabyUniverse Inc 5601 NW 9th Ave Suite 104 *NASDAQ: POSH* ■ *TF:* 877-615-2229 ■ *Web:* investor.babyuniverse.com	Fort Lauderdale	FL	33309	954-771-5160	523-9881
Ball Bounce and Sport Inc/Hedstrom Plastics 1401 Jacobson Ave **Fax:* Sales ■ *TF:* 800-765-9665 ■ *Web:* www.hedstrom.com	Ashland	OH	44805	419-289-9310	281-3371*
Basic Comfort Inc 5151 Franklin St *TF:* 800-456-8687 ■ *Web:* www.basiccomfort.com	Denver	CO	80216	303-778-7535	778-0143
BebeSounds 15 W 36th St *TF:* 800-430-0222 ■ *Web:* www.bebesounds.com	New York	NY	10018	212-736-6760	736-6762
Britax Child Safety Inc 13501 S Ridge Dr **Fax Area Code:* 800 ■ **Fax:* Cust Svc ■ *TF:* 888-427-4829 ■ *Web:* www.britaxusa.com	Charlotte	NC	28273	704-409-1700	246-1962*
C.D.M. Over the Shoulder Baby Holder P.O. Box 5191 *TF:* 800-637-9426 ■ *Web:* www.babyholder.com	San Clemente	CA	92673	949-361-1089	361-1336
Cardinal Gates 15 St John's Circle *TF:* 800-318-3380 ■ *Web:* www.cardinalgates.com	Newnan	GA	30265	770-252-4200	252-4122
Central Specialties Ltd 220-D Exchange Dr *TF:* 800-873-4370 ■ *Web:* www.csltd.com	Crystal Lake	IL	60014	815-459-6000	459-6562
Chicco USA 1817 Colonial Village Ln **Fax Area Code:* 717 ■ *TF:* 877-424-4226 ■ *Web:* www.chiccousa.com	Lancaster	PA	17601	877-424-4226	735-0888*
Combi USA Inc 1962 Highway 160 West Suite 100 *TF:* 800-992-6624 ■ *Web:* www.combi-intl.com	Fort Mill	SC	297088028	803-548-6633	548-3663
Crown Crafts Infant Products Inc 711 W Walnut St **Fax:* Cust Svc ■ *TF:* 800-421-0526 ■ *Web:* www.ccipinc.com	Compton	CA	90220	310-763-8100	537-2272*
Delta Enterprise Corp 114 West 26th St *TF:* 800-377-3777 ■ *Web:* www.deltaenterprise.com	New York	NY	10001	212-736-7000	627-0352
Dolly Inc 320 N 4th St *TF:* 888-463-6559 ■ *Web:* www.dolly.com	Tipp City	OH	45371	937-667-5711	667-5328
Dorel Industries Inc 1255 Greene Ave Suite 300 *NASDAQ: DIIB* ■ *Web:* www.dorel.com	Montreal	QC	H3Z2A4	514-934-3034	934-9379
Dorel Juvenile Group USA 2525 State St *TF:* 800-544-1108 ■ *Web:* www.djgusa.com	Columbus	IN	47201	812-372-0141	372-0911
Evenflo Co Inc 1801 Commerce Dr **Fax:* Hum Res ■ *TF:* 800-233-5921 ■ *Web:* www.evenflo.com	Piqua	OH	45356	937-415-3300	415-3112*
Fisher-Price Inc 636 Girard Ave *TF:* 800-432-5437 ■ *Web:* www.fisher-price.com	East Aurora	NY	14052	716-687-3000	687-3476
Gerber Products Co 445 State St *TF:* 800-443-7237 ■ *Web:* www.gerber.com	Fremont	MI	49413	231-928-2000	928-2723
GRACO Children's Products Inc 150 Oaklands Blvd *TF:* 800-345-4109 ■ *Web:* www.gracobaby.com	Exton	PA	19341	610-884-8000	884-8700
Infantino LLC 4920 Carroll Canyon Rd Suite 200 *TF:* 800-365-8182 ■ *Web:* www.infantino.com	San Diego	CA	92121	858-457-9797	457-0181
Inglesina USA Inc 414 Eagle Rock Ave Suite 308 *TF:* 877-486-5112 ■ *Web:* www.inglesina.com	West Orange	NJ	070524229	973-243-0234	243-7234
International Playthings Inc 75D Lackawanna Ave *TF:* 800-631-1272 ■ *Web:* www.intplay.com	Parsippany	NJ	07054	973-316-2500	316-5883
Kelty 6235 Lookout Rd **Fax Area Code:* 800 ■ *TF:* 800-423-2320 ■ *Web:* www.kelty.com	Boulder	CO	80301	303-262-3320	504-2745*
KidCo Inc 1013 Technology Way *TF:* 800-553-5529 ■ *Web:* www.kidcoinc.com	Libertyville	IL	60048	847-549-8600	549-8660
Kids II 555 North Point Center East Suite 600 *TF:* 877-325-7056 ■ *Web:* www.kidsii.com	Alpharetta	GA	300228237	770-751-0442	751-0543
Kolcraft Enterprises Inc 10832 NC Hwy 211 E *TF Cust Svc:* 800-453-7673 ■ *Web:* www.kolcraft.com	Aberdeen	NC	28315	910-944-9345	
Lan Enterprises LLC Zooper North America 10140-10200 SW Allen Blvd **Fax Area Code:* 503 ■ *TF:* 888-742-9899 ■ *Web:* www.zooperstrollers.com	Beaverton	OR	97005	888-742-9899	248-9471*
Learning Curve International Inc 1111 W 22nd St Suite 320 *TF:* 800-704-8697 ■ *Web:* www.learningcurve.com	Oak Brook	IL	60523	630-573-7200	573-7575
Little Tikes Co 2180 Barlow Rd *TF Cust Svc:* 800-321-0183 ■ *Web:* www.littletikes.com	Hudson	OH	44236	330-650-3000	650-3877
Maclaren USA Inc 4 Testa Place *TF:* 877-442-4622 ■ *Web:* www.maclarenbaby.com	South Norwalk	CT	06854	203-354-4400	354-4415
Manhattan Toy 430 1st Ave N Suite 500 *TF:* 800-541-1345 ■ *Web:* www.manhattantoy.com	Minneapolis	MN	55401	612-337-9600	341-4457
Maya Group Inc Exclusive Distributor of Tiny Love 12622 Monarch St *TF:* 888-846-9568 ■ *Web:* www.tinylove.com	Garden Grove	CA	92841	714-898-0807	898-7945
Newell Rubbermaid Inc Home & Family Group 10B Glenlake Pkwy Suite 300 *TF:* 800-434-4314 ■ *Web:* www.newellrubbermaid.com	Atlanta	GA	30328	770-407-3800	407-3970
North States Industries Inc 1507 92nd Ln NE *TF:* 800-848-8421 ■ *Web:* www.northstatesind.com	Blaine	MN	55449	763-486-1754	486-1763
Peg-Perego USA Inc 3625 Independence Dr *TF Cust Svc:* 800-671-1701 ■ *Web:* www.perego.com	Fort Wayne	IN	46808	260-482-8191	484-2940
Playtex Products Inc 300 Nyala Farms Rd *NYSE: PYX* ■ **Fax:* Hum Res ■ *TF:* 800-999-9700 ■ *Web:* www.playtexproductsinc.com	Westport	CT	06880	203-341-4000	341-4027*
Prince Lionheart Inc 2421 S Westgate Rd *TF:* 800-544-1132 ■ *Web:* www.princelionheart.com	Santa Maria	CA	93455	805-922-2250	922-9442
RC2 Brands DBA First Years 100 Technology Center Dr **Fax Area Code:* 508 ■ *TF:* 800-225-0382 ■ *Web:* www.thefirstyears.com	Stoughton	MA	02072	800-225-0382	583-9067*
REI *TF:* 800-426-4840 ■ *Web:* www.rei.com	Sumner	WA	983520001	253-891-2500	891-2523
Safety 1st Inc 45 Dan Rd *TF:* 800-962-7233 ■ *Web:* www.safety1st.com	Canton	MA	02021	781-364-3100	364-3833
Sassy Inc 2305 Breton Industrial Park Dr SE *TF:* 800-323-6336 ■ *Web:* www.sassybaby.com	Kentwood	MI	49508	616-243-0767	243-1042
Step2 Co 10010 Aurora-Hudson Rd *TF Cust Svc:* 800-347-8372 ■ *Web:* www.step2.com	Streetsboro	OH	44241	330-656-0440	655-9685
Storkcraft Baby 11511 Number Five Rd *TF:* 877-274-0277 ■ *Web:* www.storkcraft.com	Richmond	BC	V7A4E8	604-274-5121	274-9727
Summer Infant Inc 582 Great Rd *TF:* 800-268-6237 ■ *Web:* www.summerinfant.com	North Smithsfield	RI	02896	401-334-9966	671-6051
Tough Traveler Ltd 1012 State St *TF Cust Svc:* 800-468-6844 ■ *Web:* www.toughtraveler.com	Schenectady	NY	12307	518-377-8526	377-5434
Triboro Quilt Mfg Inc 172 S Broadway *TF:* 800-227-2077 ■ *Web:* www.cuddletime.com	White Plains	NY	10605	914-428-7551	428-0610
Triple Play Products LLC 904 Main St Suite 330 *TF:* 800-829-1625 ■ *Web:* www.tripleplayproducts.com	Hopkins	MN	55343	952-938-0531	935-4835
Unisar Inc DBA BebeSounds 15 W 36th St *TF:* 800-430-0222 ■ *Web:* www.bebesounds.com	New York	NY	10018	212-736-6760	736-6762

65 BAGS - PAPER

				Phone	Fax
AJM Packaging Corp E4111 Andover Rd Suite 100 *Web:* www.ajmpack.com	Bloomfield Hills	MI	48302	248-901-0040	901-0061
Ampac Corp 30 Coldenham Rd *TF:* 800-472-2247 ■ *Web:* www.ampaconline.com	Walden	NY	12586	845-778-5511	778-2369
Bancroft Bag Inc 425 Bancroft Blvd **Fax:* Cust Svc ■ *TF:* 800-551-4950 ■ *Web:* www.bancroftbag.com	West Monroe	LA	71292	318-387-2550	324-2316*
Bemis Co Inc 1 Neenah Center 4th Fl PO Box 669 *NYSE: BMS* ■ *Web:* www.bemis.com	Neenah	WI	54957	920-727-4100	
Bemis Co Inc Paper Packaging Div 2445 Deer Park Blvd *TF:* 800-541-4303 ■ *Web:* www.bemispaper.com	Omaha	NE	68105	402-938-2500	938-2609
Bonita Pioneer Packaging Products Inc 7333 SW Bonita Rd **Fax Area Code:* 800 ■ *TF:* 800-677-7725 ■ *Web:* www.bonitapioneer.com	Portland	OR	97224	503-684-6542	323-6027*
Brown Paper Goods Co Inc 3530 Birchwood Dr *TF:* 800-323-9099 ■ *Web:* www.brownpapergoods.com	Waukegan	IL	60085	847-688-1450	688-1458
Colonial Bag Co 1 Ocean Pond Ave PO Box 929 *TF:* 800-392-4875 ■ *Web:* www.colonial-bag.com	Lake Park	GA	31636	229-559-8484	559-0085
Duro Bag Mfg Co 7600 Empire Dr *TF:* 800-879-3876 ■ *Web:* www.durobag.com	Florence	KY	41042	859-371-2150	
El Dorado Paper Bag Mfg Co Inc 204 Prescolite Dr	El Dorado	AR	71730	870-862-4977	862-8520
Hood Packaging Corp 25 Woodgreen Pl *TF:* 800-321-8115 ■ *Web:* www.hoodpackaging.com	Madison	MS	39110	601-853-7260	853-7299
K Yamada Distributors (KYD Inc) 2949 Koapaka St *Web:* www.kydinc.com	Honolulu	HI	96819	808-836-3221	833-8995
KYD Inc (K Yamada Distributors) 2949 Koapaka St *Web:* www.kydinc.com	Honolulu	HI	96819	808-836-3221	833-8995
Longview Fibre Paper & Packaging Co 300 Fibre Way PO Box 639 *Web:* www.longviewfibre.com	Longview	WA	98632	360-425-1550	575-5934
Master Design Corp 163 13th St	Brooklyn	NY	11215	718-499-9717	788-3498
Mid-America Packaging LLC 3501 Jefferson Pkwy *TF:* 800-469-5120	Pine Bluff	AR	71602	870-541-5120	541-5148
Pacific Bag Inc 15300 Woodinville Redmond Rd NE Suite A *TF:* 800-562-2247 ■ *Web:* www.pacificbag.com	Woodinville	WA	98072	425-455-1128	990-8582
Portco Corp 3601 SE Columbia Way Suite 260 *TF:* 800-676-8666 ■ *Web:* www.portco.com	Vancouver	WA	98661	360-696-1641	695-4849
Roses Southwest Papers Inc 1701 2nd St SW *Web:* www.rosessouthwest.com	Albuquerque	NM	87102	505-842-0134	242-0342
Ross & Wallace Paper Products Inc 204 Old Covington Hwy *TF:* 800-854-2300 ■ *Web:* www.rossandwallace.com	Hammond	LA	70403	985-345-1321	345-1370
Stewart Sutherland Inc 5411 E 'V' Ave *TF:* 800-253-1034 ■ *Web:* www.ssbags.com	Vicksburg	MI	49097	269-649-0530	649-3961
Uniflex Holdings 383 W John St *TF:* 800-223-0564 ■ *Web:* www.uniflexbags.com	Hicksville	NY	11802	516-932-2000	932-3129
Werthan Packaging Inc 1515 5th Ave N *Web:* www.werthan.com	Nashville	TN	37208	615-259-9331	726-1093
Weyerhaeuser Co 33663 Weyerhaeuser Way S *NYSE: WY* ■ *TF:* 800-525-5440 ■ *Web:* www.weyerhaeuser.com	Federal Way	WA	98003	253-924-2345	924-2685
White Bag Co Inc 8027 Hwy 161 N *TF:* 800-527-1733 ■ *Web:* www.whitebag.com	North Little Rock	AR	72117	501-835-1444	835-2226
Wright Packaging Inc 4818 Kimmel Dr	Davenport	IA	52802	563-324-5727	324-5960
Zenith Specialty Bag Co Inc 17625 E Railroad St *TF:* 800-962-2247 ■ *Web:* www.zsb.com	City of Industry	CA	91748	626-912-2481	810-5136

66 BAGS - PLASTICS

Company	City	State	Zip	Phone	Fax
Aabaco Plastics Inc 9520 Midwest Ave **Fax:* Sales ■ *Web:* www.aabacoplastics.com	Garfield Heights	OH	44125	216-663-9494	663-9475*
Admiral Packaging inc 10 Admiral St *TF:* 800-556-6454 ■ *Web:* www.admiralpkg.com	Providence	RI	02908	401-274-7000	331-1910
American Transparent Plastics Corp 180 National Rd *TF Orders:* 800-942-8725	Edison	NJ	08817	732-287-3000	287-1421
Ampac Packaging LLC 12025 Tricon Rd **Fax:* Cust Svc ■ *TF:* 800-543-7030 ■ *Web:* www.ampaconline.com	Cincinnati	OH	45246	513-671-1777	671-2920*
Armand Mfg Inc 2399 Silver Wolf Dr *TF:* 800-343-7982 ■ *Web:* www.armandmfg.com	Henderson	NV	89015	702-565-7500	565-3838
Associated Bag Co 400 W Boden St **Fax Area Code:* 800 ■ *TF:* 800-926-6100 ■ *Web:* www.associatedbag.com	Milwaukee	WI	53207	414-769-1000	926-4610*
Bema Film Systems Inc 744 N Oaklawn Ave *TF:* 800-833-6657	Elmhurst	IL	60126	630-279-7800	279-0284
Bemis Co Inc 1 Neenah Center 4th Fl PO Box 669 *NYSE:* BMS ■ *Web:* www.bemis.com	Neenah	WI	54957	920-727-4100	
Bemis Co Inc Milprint Div 3550 Moser St PO Box 2968 *Web:* www.milprint.com	Oshkosh	WI	54903	920-527-2300	527-2310
Clear View Bag Co 7137 Prospect Church Rd *TF:* 800-670-6483 ■ *Web:* www.clearviewbag.com	Thomasville	NC	27361	336-885-8131	885-1044
Clorox Co 1221 Broadway *NYSE:* CLX ■ *TF Cust Svc:* 800-292-2808 ■ *Web:* www.thecloroxcompany.com	Oakland	CA	94612	510-271-7000	832-1463
Covalence Plastics 1401 W 94th St *Web:* www.covalenceplastics.com	Minneapolis	MN	55431	800-873-3941	
CPI Plastics Group Ltd 151 Courtney Park Dr W **Fax Area Code:* 800 ■ *TF:* 800-251-9566 ■ *Web:* www.cpiplastics.com	Mississauga	ON	L5W1Y5	905-795-5505	251-9577*
Duro Bag Mfg Co 7600 Empire Dr *TF:* 800-879-3876 ■ *Web:* www.durobag.com	Florence	KY	41042	859-371-2150	
Excelsior Packing Group 159 Alexander St	Yonkers	NY	10701	914-968-1300	968-6567
FlexSol Packaging Corp 560 Ferry St *TF:* 800-496-1998 ■ *Web:* www.flexsolpackaging.com	Newark	NJ	07105	973-465-0266	465-7901
Fortune Plastics Inc Williams Ln PO Box 637 *TF:* 800-243-0306 ■ *Web:* www.fortuneplastics.com	Old Saybrook	CT	06475	860-388-3426	388-9930
GB Plastics & Papers Inc 9927 Honeywell St	Houston	TX	77074	713-772-0739	772-4088
Glad Products Co 1221 Broadway *Web:* www.glad.com	Oakland	CA	94612	510-271-7000	832-1463
Heritage Bags 1648 Diplomat Dr *TF:* 800-527-2247 ■ *Web:* www.heritage-bag.com	Carrollton	TX	75006	972-241-5525	241-5543
Home Care Industries Inc 1 Lisbon St *TF:* 888-772-2100 ■ *Web:* www.homecareind.com	Clifton	NJ	07013	973-365-1600	365-1770
Hood Packaging Corp 25 Woodgreen Pl *TF:* 800-321-8115 ■ *Web:* www.hoodpackaging.com	Madison	MS	39110	601-853-7260	853-7299
International Poly Bag Inc 990 Park Ctr Dr Suite F *TF:* 800-976-5922 ■ *Web:* www.intlpolybag.com	Vista	CA	92081	760-598-2468	598-2469
K Yamada Distributors (KYD Inc) 2949 Koapaka St *Web:* www.kydinc.com	Honolulu	HI	96819	808-836-3221	833-8995
KYD Inc (K Yamada Distributors) 2949 Koapaka St *Web:* www.kydinc.com	Honolulu	HI	96819	808-836-3221	833-8995
Mercury Plastics Inc 14825 Salt Lake Ave *TF:* 800-831-2517 ■ *Web:* www.mercurybags.com	City of Industry	CA	91746	626-961-0165	333-4513
Mercury Plastics Inc 123 Willamette Ln *TF:* 800-347-0338 ■ *Web:* www.mercurybags.com	Bowling Green	KY	42101	270-782-8026	782-7478
Milprint Div Bemis Co Inc 3550 Moser St PO Box 2968 *Web:* www.milprint.com	Oshkosh	WI	54903	920-527-2300	527-2310
Omega Plastics Corp 901 Commerce Cir	Shelbyville	KY	40065	502-633-0168	633-6797
Pacific Bag Inc 15300 Woodinville Redmond Rd NE Suite A *TF:* 800-562-2247 ■ *Web:* www.pacificbag.com	Woodinville	WA	98072	425-455-1128	990-8582
Pactiv Corp 1900 W Field Ct *NYSE:* PTV ■ *TF:* 888-828-2850 ■ *Web:* www.pactiv.com	Lake Forest	IL	60045	847-482-2000	482-4738
Pitt Plastics Inc 1400 Atkinson Ave *TF:* 800-835-0366 ■ *Web:* www.pittplastics.com	Pittsburg	KS	66762	620-231-4030	231-7612
Plastic Packaging Inc 1246 Main Ave SE **Fax:* Sales ■ *Web:* www.ppi-hky.com	Hickory	NC	28602	828-328-2466	322-1830*
Poly-America Inc 2000 W Marshall Dr *TF:* 800-527-3322 ■ *Web:* www.poly-america.com	Grand Prairie	TX	75051	972-337-7100	337-7410
Poly-Pak Industries Inc 125 Spagnoli Rd *TF:* 800-969-1995 ■ *Web:* www.poly-pak.com	Melville	NY	11747	631-293-6767	454-6366
Portco Corp 3601 SE Columbia Way Suite 260 *TF:* 800-676-8666 ■ *Web:* www.portco.com	Vancouver	WA	98661	360-696-1641	695-4849
Presto Products Co 670 N Perkins St *TF:* 800-558-3525 ■ *Web:* www.prestoproducts.com	Appleton	WI	54912	920-739-9471	738-1458
Putnam Plastics Inc 255 S Alex Rd *TF:* 800-457-3099 ■ *Web:* www.putnamfarm.com	West Carrollton	OH	45449	937-866-6261	866-9365
Ronpak Inc 4301 New Brunswick Ave *Web:* www.ronpak.com	South Plainfield	NJ	07080	732-968-8000	752-6097
Shields Bag & Printing Co 1009 Rock Ave *TF:* 800-541-8630 ■ *Web:* www.shieldsbag.com	Yakima	WA	98902	509-248-7500	248-6304
Southeastern Plastics Corp 15 Home News Row *TF:* 800-966-2247	New Brunswick	NJ	08901	732-846-8500	846-9795
Star Packaging Corp 453 85th Cir *TF:* 800-252-5414 ■ *Web:* www.starpackagingcorp.com	College Park	GA	30349	404-763-2800	763-1914
Uniflex Holdings 383 W John St *TF:* 800-223-0564 ■ *Web:* www.uniflexbags.com	Hicksville	NY	11802	516-932-2000	932-3129
Webster Industries Inc 58 Pulaski St *TF:* 800-225-0796 ■ *Web:* www.websterindustries.com	Peabody	MA	01960	978-532-2000	531-3354
Western Summit Mfg Corp 13290 Daum Dr	City of Industry	CA	91746	626-333-3333	961-2247
White Bag Co Inc 8027 Hwy 161 N *TF:* 800-527-1733 ■ *Web:* www.whitebag.com	North Little Rock	AR	72117	501-835-1444	835-2226

67 BAGS - TEXTILE

SEE ALSO Handbags, Totes, Backpacks p. 1769; Luggage, Bags, Cases p. 1923

Company	City	State	Zip	Phone	Fax
A Rifkin Co 1400 Sans Souci Pkwy *TF Cust Svc:* 800-458-7300 ■ *Web:* www.arifkin.com	Wilkes-Barre	PA	18706	570-825-9551	825-5282
Aceco Industrial Packaging 166 Frelinghuysen Ave *TF:* 800-832-2247	Newark	NJ	07114	973-242-2200	242-1044
American Bag & Burlap Co DBA Corman Bag Co 32 Arlington St *Web:* www.cormanbag.com	Chelsea	MA	02150	617-884-7600	437-7917
Bag Bazaar 1 E 33rd St	New York	NY	10016	212-689-3508	696-2098
Bearse Mfg Co 3815 W Cortland St *Web:* www.bearseusa.com	Chicago	IL	60647	773-235-8710	235-8716
Bulk Lift International Inc 1013 Tamarac Dr *TF:* 800-879-2247 ■ *Web:* www.bulklift.com	Carpentersville	IL	60110	847-428-6059	428-7180
Central Bag Co 1323 W 13th St	Kansas City	MO	64102	816-471-0388	842-5501
Corman Bag Co 32 Arlington St *Web:* www.cormanbag.com	Chelsea	MA	02150	617-884-7600	437-7917
Fox Packaging Co 2200 Fox Dr *TF:* 800-336-6369 ■ *Web:* www.foxbag.com	McAllen	TX	78504	956-682-6176	682-5768
Fulton-Denver Co 3500 Wynkoop St *TF:* 800-776-6715	Denver	CO	80216	303-294-9292	292-9470
GEM Group 9 International Way *TF:* 800-800-3200 ■ *Web:* www.gemlinebags.com	Lawrence	MA	01843	978-691-2000	691-2085
Halsted Corp 78 Halladay St *TF:* 800-843-5184	Jersey City	NJ	07304	201-433-3323	333-0670
Harry Miller Co Inc 850 Albany St *TF:* 800-225-5598 ■ *Web:* www.harrymiller.com	Boston	MA	02119	617-427-2300	442-1152
HBD Inc 3901 Riverdale Rd *TF:* 800-403-2247 ■ *Web:* www.hbdinc.com	Greensboro	NC	27406	336-275-4800	275-7242
Indian Valley Industries Inc 60-100 Corliss Ave *TF:* 800-659-5111 ■ *Web:* www.iviindustries.com	Johnson City	NY	13790	607-729-5111	729-5158
J & M Industries Inc 300 Ponchatoula Pkwy *TF:* 800-989-1002 ■ *Web:* www.jm-ind.com	Ponchatoula	LA	70454	985-386-6000	386-9066
Langston Cos Inc 1760 S 3rd St *TF Cust Svc:* 800-444-7046	Memphis	TN	38101	901-774-4440	942-5402
LBU Inc 217 Brook Ave *TF:* 800-678-4528 ■ *Web:* www.lbuinc.com	Passaic	NJ	07055	973-773-4800	773-6005
Max Katz Inc 235 S LaSalle St *TF:* 800-225-3729	Indianapolis	IN	46201	317-635-9561	635-3458
Menardi 1 Maxwell Dr *TF:* 800-321-3218 ■ *Web:* www.menardifilters.com	Trenton	SC	29847	803-663-6551	663-4029
Mid-America Packaging LLC 3501 Jefferson Pkwy *TF:* 800-469-5120	Pine Bluff	AR	71602	870-541-5120	541-5148
Miller Harry Canvas Co Inc 850 Albany St *TF:* 800-225-5598 ■ *Web:* www.harrymiller.com	Boston	MA	02119	617-427-2300	442-1152
Morgan Brothers Bag Co Inc 3412 W Moore St PO Box 25577 *TF:* 800-368-2247	Richmond	VA	23260	804-355-9107	355-9100
NYP Corp 805 E Grand St *TF:* 800-524-1052 ■ *Web:* www.nyp-corp.com	Elizabeth	NJ	07201	908-351-6550	351-0108
Sacramento Bag Mfg Co 530 Q St *TF:* 800-287-2247 ■ *Web:* www.sacbag.com	Sacramento	CA	95814	916-441-6121	448-3141
Super Sack Mfg Corp 11510 Data Dr *TF:* 800-331-9200 ■ *Web:* www.bagcorp.com	Dallas	TX	75218	214-340-7060	340-4598

68 BAKERIES

Company	City	State	Zip	Phone	Fax
Andre Boudin Bakeries Inc 221 Main St Suite 1230 *Web:* www.boudinbakery.com	San Francisco	CA	94105	415-882-1849	913-1818
Atlanta Bread Co International Inc 1955 Lake Park Dr Suite 400 *TF:* 800-398-3728 ■ *Web:* www.atlantabread.com	Smyrna	GA	30080	770-432-0933	444-1991
Au Bon Pain 19 Fid Kennedy Ave *TF:* 800-825-5227 ■ *Web:* www.aubonpain.com	Boston	MA	02210	617-423-2100	423-7879
Auntie Anne's Inc 160-A Rt 41 *Web:* www.auntieannes.com	Gap	PA	17527	717-442-4766	442-4139
Awrey Bakeries Inc 12301 Farmington Rd *TF:* 800-950-2253 ■ *Web:* www.awrey.com	Livonia	MI	48150	734-522-1100	522-1453
Big Apple Bagels 500 Lake Cook Rd Suite 475 *TF:* 800-251-6101 ■ *Web:* www.babcorp.com	Deerfield	IL	60015	847-948-7520	405-8140
Bruegger's Enterprises 159 Bank St *Web:* www.brueggers.com	Burlington	VT	05401	802-660-4020	652-9293
Busken Bakery Inc 2675 Madison Rd *Web:* www.busken.com	Cincinnati	OH	45208	513-871-5330	871-2662
C-Street Bakery 2930 W Maple St *TF:* 800-336-1320 ■ *Web:* www.hotstufffoods.com/OurBrands	Sioux Falls	SD	57107	605-336-6961	336-0141
Cheryl & Co 646 McCorkle Blvd *TF:* 800-443-8124 ■ *Web:* www.cherylandco.com	Westerville	OH	43082	614-891-8822	891-8699
Cinnabon Inc 200 Glenridge Point Pkwy Suite 200 *Web:* www.cinnabon.com	Atlanta	GA	30342	404-255-3250	255-4978
Collin Street Bakery Inc 401 W 7th Ave *TF Sales:* 800-504-1896 ■ *Web:* www.collinstreetbakery.com	Corsicana	TX	75110	903-872-8111	872-6879
Cookies in Bloom Inc 7208 La Casa Rd *TF:* 800-222-3104 ■ *Web:* www.cookiesinbloom.com	Dallas	TX	75248	972-490-8644	490-8646
Cookies By Design Inc 1865 Summit Ave Suite 605 *TF:* 800-945-2665 ■ *Web:* www.cookiesbydesign.com	Plano	TX	75074	972-398-9536	398-9542
Corner Bakery Cafe 6820 LBJ Fwy *Web:* www.cornerbakery.com	Dallas	TX	75240	972-980-9917	770-9593
Crest Foods Inc DBA Nestle Toll House Cafe by Chip 101 W Renner Rd Suite 240 *Web:* www.nestlecafe.com	Richardson	TX	75802	214-495-9533	853-5347
Damascus Bakery Inc 56 Gold St *TF:* 800-367-7482 ■ *Web:* www.damascusbakery.com	Brooklyn	NY	11201	718-855-1457	403-0948
Daylight Donut Flour Co LLC 11707 E 11th St *TF:* 800-331-2245 ■ *Web:* www.daylightdonuts.com	Tulsa	OK	74128	918-438-0800	438-0804
Dunkin' Donuts 130 Royall St *TF Cust Svc:* 800-859-5339 ■ *Web:* www.dunkindonuts.com	Canton	MA	02021	781-737-3000	737-4000
Eatzi's Market & Bakery LLC 2508 Highlander Way Suite 220 *Web:* www.eatzis.com	Carrollton	TX	75006	972-248-5200	248-5249
Einstein/Noah Bagel Corp 1687 Cole Blvd *TF Cust Svc:* 800-660-3200 ■ *Web:* www.einsteinbros.com	Golden	CO	80401	303-568-8000	568-8039
Gold Medal Bakery Inc 21 Penn St *TF:* 800-642-7568 ■ *Web:* www.goldmedalbakery.com	Fall River	MA	02724	508-674-5766	674-6090
Gonnella Baking Co 2002 W Erie St *TF:* 800-262-3442 ■ *Web:* www.gonnella.com	Chicago	IL	60612	312-733-2020	733-7056
Great American Cookie Co Inc 4685 Frederick Dr SW *TF:* 800-332-4856 ■ *Web:* www.greatamericancookies.com	Atlanta	GA	30336	404-696-1700	699-0887
Great Harvest Bread Co 28 S Montana St *TF:* 800-442-0424 ■ *Web:* www.greatharvest.com	Dillon	MT	59725	406-683-6842	683-5537
Haas Baking Co 9769 Reavis Park Dr *TF:* 800-325-3171 ■ *Web:* www.haasbaking.com	Saint Louis	MO	63123	314-631-6100	631-3464
Honey Dew Assoc Inc 2 Taunton St *TF:* 800-946-6393 ■ *Web:* www.honeydewdonuts.com	Plainville	MA	02762	508-699-3900	699-3949
J & J Restaurant Group LLC 505 W Roseville Rd *TF:* 800-233-0128	Lancaster	PA	17601	717-299-0968	299-1476
Just Desserts Inc 550 85th Ave *Web:* www.justdesserts.com	Oakland	CA	94621	510-567-2910	567-2911
Koffee Kup Bakery Inc 436 Riverside Ave	Burlington	VT	05401	802-863-2696	860-0116
Krispy Kreme Doughnuts Corp 370 Knollwood St Suite 500 *NYSE:* KKD ■ *TF:* 800-334-1243 ■ *Web:* www.krispykreme.com	Winston-Salem	NC	27103	336-725-2981	733-3796
La Madeleine Inc 6688 N Central Expy Suite 700 **Fax:* Cust Svc ■ *TF:* 800-400-5840 ■ *Web:* www.lamadeleine.com	Dallas	TX	75206	214-696-6962	696-0485*
Manhattan Bagel Co Inc 100 Horizon Ctr Blvd *TF:* 800-308-2457 ■ *Web:* www.manhattanbagel.com	Hamilton	NJ	08691	609-631-7000	631-7068
Maple Donuts Inc 3455 E Market St *TF:* 800-627-5348 ■ *Web:* www.mapledonuts.com	York	PA	17402	717-757-7826	755-8725

	City	State	Zip	Phone	Fax
Middle East Bakery Inc 30 International Way	Lawrence	MA	01841	978-688-2221	683-7954
Mrs Fields Original Cookies Inc					
2855 E Cottonwood Pkwy Suite 400	Salt Lake City	UT	84121	801-736-5600	736-5970
TF: 800-348-6311 ■ *Web:* www.mrsfields.com					
Nestle Toll House Cafe by Chip					
101 W Renner Rd Suite 240	Richardson	TX	75802	214-495-9533	853-5347
Web: www.nestlecafe.com					
New Mount Pleasant Bakery Inc 941 Crane St	Schenectady	NY	12303	518-374-7577	374-5548
Olde Tyme Pastries 2225 Geer Rd	Turlock	CA	95382	209-668-0928	668-2741
Web: www.otpastries.com					
Panera Bread Co 6710 Clayton Rd	Richmond Heights	MO	63117	314-633-7100	633-7280
NASDAQ: PNRA ■ *TF:* 800-301-5566 ■ *Web:* www.panerabread.com					
Quality Naturally Foods 18830 E San Jose Ave	City of Industry	CA	91748	626-854-6363	965-0978
TF: 877-541-5554 ■ *Web:* www.qnfoods.com					
Rotella's Italian Bakery Inc 6949 S 108th St	La Vista	NE	68128	402-592-6600	592-2989
TF: 800-759-0360 ■ *Web:* www.rotellas-bakery.com					
Saint Louis Bread Co 6710 Clayton Rd	Richmond Heights	MO	63117	314-633-7100	633-7280
TF: 800-301-5566 ■ *Web:* www.stlouisbread.com					
Southern Maid Donut Flour Co 3615 Cavalier Dr	Garland	TX	75042	972-272-6425	276-3549
TF: 800-936-6887 ■ *Web:* www.southernmaiddonuts.com					
Tip Top Cafe & Bakery Corp 3173 Akahi St	Lihue	HI	96766	808-245-2333	246-8988
Treats International Franchise Corp					
1550-A Laperriere Ave Suite 201	Ottawa	ON	K1Z7T2	613-563-4073	563-1982
TF: 800-461-4003 ■ *Web:* www.treats.com					
Vie de France Yamazaki Inc 2070 Chain Bridge Rd Suite 500	Vienna	VA	22182	703-442-9205	821-2695
TF: 800-446-4404 ■ *Web:* www.vdfy.com					
Wetzel's Pretzels LLC 35 Hugus Alley Suite 300	Pasadena	CA	91103	626-432-6900	432-6904
Web: www.wetzels.com					
Zaro's Bread Basket Inc 138 Bruckner Blvd	Bronx	NY	10454	718-993-5600	292-9353

69 BANKING-RELATED SERVICES

	City	State	Zip	Phone	Fax
Automatic Funds Transfer Services 151 S Landers St Suite C	Seattle	WA	98134	206-254-0975	254-0968
TF: 800-275-2033 ■ *Web:* www.afts.com					
Bankserv 222 Kearny St Suite 400	San Francisco	CA	94108	415-217-4581	277-9904
TF: 888-877-7703 ■ *Web:* www.bankserv.com					
Comdata Corp 5301 Maryland Way	Brentwood	TN	37027	615-370-7000	370-7828
TF: 800-741-3939 ■ *Web:* www.comdata.com					
Credit Union 24 Inc 2252 Killearn Center Blvd Suite 300	Tallahassee	FL	32309	850-701-2824	701-2424
TF: 877-570-2824 ■ *Web:* www.cu24.com					
First Data Integrated Payment Systems Financial					
Services Div 6200 S Quebec St	Greenwood Village	CO	80111	303-488-8000	488-8705
TF: 800-735-3362 ■ *Web:* www.firstdata.com					
Fiserv Inc 255 Fiserv Dr PO Box 979	Brookfield	WI	53008	262-879-5000	879-5000
NASDAQ: FISV ■ *TF Mktg:* 800-872-7882 ■ *Web:* www.fiserv.com					
Game Financial Corp 1550 Utica Ave S Suite 100	Saint Louis Park	MN	55416	952-591-3000	322-5086*
**Fax Area Code:* 801 ■ *TF:* 800-363-3372 ■ *Web:* www.gamecash.com					
Lydian Trust Co 3801 PGA Blvd	Palm Beach Gardens	FL	33410	561-776-8860	776-6378
TF: 877-998-2265 ■ *Web:* www.lydian.com					
MoneyGram International Inc					
1550 Utica Ave S Suite 100	Saint Louis Park	MN	55416	952-591-3000	591-3121
NYSE: MGI ■ *TF:* 800-328-5678 ■ *Web:* www.moneygram.com					
NetBank Payment Systems Inc 200 Briarwood W Dr	Jackson	MS	39206	601-956-1222	957-9006
TF: 800-523-2104 ■ *Web:* www.netbankpaymentsystems.com					
NYCE Corp 400 Plaza Dr	Secaucus	NJ	07094	201-865-9000	330-3374
TF: 800-522-6923 ■ *Web:* www.nyce.net					
OANDA Corp 140 Broadway 46th Fl	New York	NY	10005	416-593-9436	593-0185
Web: www.oanda.com					
Pershing LLC 95 Christopher Columbus Dr	Jersey City	NJ	07302	201-413-2000	413-3103*
**Fax:* Hum Res ■ *TF:* 800-443-4342 ■ *Web:* www.pershing.com					
PULSE EFT Assn 1301 McKinney St	Houston	TX	77010	713-223-1400	223-1204
TF: 800-420-2122 ■ *Web:* www.pulse-eft.com					
Star Systems Inc 495 N Keller Rd Suite 500	Maitland	FL	32751	321-263-3000	263-4114*
**Fax:* Hum Res ■ *TF:* 888-233-7337 ■ *Web:* www.star-system.com					
Travelex Worldwide Money 29 Broadway	New York	NY	10006	212-363-6206	701-0497
TF: 800-815-1795 ■ *Web:* www.travelex.com					
Universal Money Centers Inc 6800 Squibb Rd	Shawnee Mission	KS	66201	913-831-2055	831-0248
TF: 800-234-6860 ■ *Web:* www.universalmoney.com					
Western Union Co 12500 E Belford Ave	Englewood	CO	80112	720-332-1000	332-4753
NYSE: WU ■ *TF Cust Svc:* 800-325-6000 ■ *Web:* www.westernunion.com					

70 BANKS - COMMERCIAL & SAVINGS

SEE ALSO Credit & Financing - Commercial p. 1580; Credit & Financing - Consumer p. 1581; Credit Unions p. 1582; Holding Companies - Bank Holding Companies p. 1776

	City	State	Zip	Phone	Fax
1st Community Bank 2911 N Westwood Blvd	Poplar Bluff	MO	63901	573-778-0101	778-9138
TF: 888-831-3620 ■ *Web:* www.1stcombank.com					
1st Source Bank 100 N Michigan St	South Bend	IN	46601	574-235-2000	235-2948*
**Fax:* Mktg ■ *Web:* www.1stsource.com					
Acacia Federal Savings Bank					
7600 Leesburg Pike East Bldg Suite 200	Falls Church	VA	22043	703-506-8100	506-8160
TF: 800-950-0270 ■ *Web:* www.afsbonline2.com					
Advanta Bank PO Box 15555	Wilmington	DE	19850	302-529-6673	529-6540
TF: 800-544-8205 ■ *Web:* www.advanta.com					
Alliance Bank 541 Lawrence Rd	Broomall	PA	19008	610-353-2900	359-6908
NASDAQ: ALLB ■ *TF:* 800-550-4387 ■ *Web:* www.alliancebk.com					
Allied Irish Banks 405 Park Ave	New York	NY	10022	212-339-8000	339-8008
Web: www.aib.ie					
Amalgamated Bank of New York 10 E 14th St	New York	NY	10003	212-823-8708	924-5631
TF: 800-662-0860 ■ *Web:* www.amalgamatedbank.com					
Amarillo National Bank 410 S Taylor St Plaza One	Amarillo	TX	79101	806-378-8000	373-7505*
**Fax:* Cust Svc ■ *TF:* 800-262-3733 ■ *Web:* www.anb.com					
Amboy National Bank 3590 US Hwy 9 S	Old Bridge	NJ	08857	732-591-8700	591-0726
TF: 800-942-6269 ■ *Web:* www.amboybank.com					
AMCORE Bank NA 501 7th St	Rockford	IL	61104	815-968-1259	961-7748*
**Fax:* Mktg ■ *TF:* 888-426-2673 ■ *Web:* www.amcore.com					
Amegy Bank of Texas 4400 Post Oak Pkwy	Houston	TX	77027	713-235-8800	232-5948
TF: 800-287-0301 ■ *Web:* www.amegybank.com					
American Bank 4029 W Tilghman St	Allentown	PA	18104	610-366-1800	366-1900
TF Cust Svc: 888-366-6622 ■ *Web:* www.pcbanker.com					
American Express Centurion Bank 4315 S 2700 West	Salt Lake City	UT	84184	801-945-3000	
TF: 800-542-0779 ■ *Web:* home.americanexpress.com					
American Savings Bank FSB 915 Fort St PO Box 2300	Honolulu	HI	96804	808-531-6262	536-3141
TF: 800-272-2566 ■ *Web:* www.asbhawaii.com					
Ameriserv Financial 216 Franklin St	Johnstown	PA	15901	814-533-5300	533-5283
TF: 800-837-2265 ■ *Web:* www.ameriservfinancial.com					
AmTrust Bank 1801 E 9th St	Cleveland	OH	44114	216-622-4100	622-4417*
**Fax:* Hum Res ■ *TF:* 888-268-2878 ■ *Web:* www.amtrust.com					
AnchorBank PO Box 7933	Madison	WI	53703	608-252-8700	252-8783
TF: 800-252-6246 ■ *Web:* www.anchorbank.com					
Apple Bank for Savings 122 E 42nd St 9th Fl	New York	NY	10168	212-224-6400	224-6592*
**Fax:* Hum Res ■ *TF:* 800-722-6888 ■ *Web:* www.theapplebank.com					
Applied Bank 50 Applied Card Way	Glen Mills	PA	19342	302-326-4200	467-4985*
**Fax:* Cust Svc ■ *TF:* 800-334-3180 ■ *Web:* www.appliedcardbank.com					
Arvest Bank 201 NE A St	Bentonville	AR	72712	479-271-1291	271-1315
TF: 800-333-9369 ■ *Web:* www.arvest.com					
Ascenia Bank PO Box 436029	Louisville	KY	40253	502-499-4800	499-4811
TF: 877-369-2265 ■ *Web:* www.ascenciabank.com					
Associated Bank 2870 Holmgren Way	Green Bay	WI	54304	262-879-0133	
TF: 800-682-4989 ■ *Web:* www.associatedbank.com					
Associated Bank Green Bay NA 200 N Adams St	Green Bay	WI	54301	920-433-3200	433-3060
TF: 800-236-3479 ■ *Web:* www.associatedbank.com					
Associated Bank Illinois NA 612 N Main St	Rockford	IL	61103	815-987-3500	987-3536
TF: 800-236-8866 ■ *Web:* www.associatedbank.com					
Associated Bank Milwaukee 401 E Kilbourn Ave	Milwaukee	WI	53202	414-271-1786	283-2204
TF: 800-236-8866 ■ *Web:* www.associatedbank.com					
Associated Bank North 303 S 1st Ave	Wausau	WI	54402	715-845-4301	842-8840
TF: 800-236-8866 ■ *Web:* www.associatedbank.com					
Astoria Federal Savings & Loan Assn					
1 Astoria Federal Plaza	Lake Success	NY	11042	516-327-3000	327-7860
TF: 800-278-6742 ■ *Web:* www.astoriafederal.com					
Atlantic Bank of New York 960 Ave of the Americas	New York	NY	10001	212-967-7425	563-2729
TF: 800-535-2269 ■ *Web:* www.abny.com					
Australia & New Zealand Banking Group Ltd					
1177 Ave of the Americas 6th Fl	New York	NY	10036	212-801-9800	801-9859
Web: www.anz.com					
Banca di Roma 34 E 51st St	New York	NY	10022	212-407-1600	407-1677
Banca Intesa 1 William St	New York	NY	10004	212-607-3500	809-9785
Web: www.bancaintesa.us					
BancFirst Corp 101 N Broadway Ave Suite 500	Oklahoma City	OK	73102	405-270-1086	270-1089
NASDAQ: BANF ■ *Web:* www.bancfirst.com					
Banco Bilbao Vizcaya Argentaria SA					
1345 Ave of the Americas 45th Fl	New York	NY	10105	212-728-1500	333-2906
NYSE: BBV ■ *Web:* www.bbva.es					
Banco Popular de Puerto Rico PO Box 36-2708	San Juan	PR	00936	787-765-9800	758-0710*
**Fax:* Cust Svc ■ *TF:* 888-724-3650 ■ *Web:* www.bancopopular.com					
Banco de Santander 45 E 53rd St	New York	NY	10022	212-350-3500	350-3535
Web: www.santander.com					
Banco Santander Puerto Rico PO Box 362589	San Juan	PR	00936	787-759-7070	765-7426
TF: 800-726-8263 ■ *Web:* www.santandernet.com					
Bancorp Bank 405 Silverside Rd Suite 105	Wilmington	DE	19809	302-385-5000	385-5194
NASDAQ: TBBK ■ *TF Cust Svc:* 800-545-0289 ■ *Web:* secure.thebancorp.com					
BancorpSouth 201 S Spring St	Tupelo	MS	38804	662-680-2000	678-7263
TF: 888-797-7711 ■ *Web:* www.bancorpsouthonline.com					
Bangor Savings Bank PO Box 930	Bangor	ME	04402	207-942-5211	941-2752*
**Fax:* Cust Svc ■ *TF:* 877-226-4671 ■ *Web:* www.bangor.com					
Bank of America NA 699 S Mill Ave Suite 101	Tempe	AZ	85281	480-804-9481	642-5736
TF: 800-432-1000 ■ *Web:* www.bankofamerica.com					
Bank of America NA 101 S Tryon St	Charlotte	NC	28255	704-386-5478	386-9928
TF: 800-432-1000 ■ *Web:* www.bankofamerica.com					
Bank of the Carolinas 135 Boxwood Village Dr	Mocksville	NC	27028	336-751-5755	751-1116
NASDAQ: BCAR ■ *TF:* 877-751-5755 ■ *Web:* www.bankofthecarolinas.com					
Bank of East Asia Ltd 202 Canal St	New York	NY	10013	212-233-8833	219-3378
Bank Financial 6415 W 95th St	Chicago Ridge	IL	60415	708-747-2000	675-6421
TF: 888-409-5100 ■ *Web:* www.bankfinancial.com					
Bank of Hawaii 111 S King St	Honolulu	HI	96813	808-538-4171	693-1285
TF: 888-643-3888 ■ *Web:* www.boh.com					
Bank Leumi USA 579 5th Ave	New York	NY	10017	917-542-2343	542-2254
TF: 800-892-5430 ■ *Web:* www.leumiusa.com					
Bank of Marin 50 Madera Blvd	Corte Madera	CA	94925	415-927-2265	927-8920
NASDAQ: BMRC ■ *TF:* 800-654-5111 ■ *Web:* www.bankofmarin.com					
Bank of McKenney 20718 1st St	McKenney	VA	23872	804-478-4434	478-4704
NASDAQ: BOMK ■ *Web:* www.bankofmckenney.com					
Bank Midwest NA 1111 Main St Suite 350	Kansas City	MO	64105	816-471-9800	842-6291
Web: www.bankmw.com					
Bank of Montreal 3 Times Sq	New York	NY	10036	212-758-6300	702-1193
TF: 800-363-9992 ■ *Web:* www.bmo.com					
Bank of Montreal 119 Saint Jacques St	Montreal	QC	H2Y1L6	514-877-7373	877-8118
NYSE: BMO ■ *TF:* 800-363-9992 ■ *Web:* www.bmo.com					
Bank of New York 1 Wall St	New York	NY	10286	212-495-1784	635-1200
TF: 866-269-1784 ■ *Web:* www.bankofny.com					
Bank of Newport PO Box 450	Newport	RI	02840	401-846-3400	845-0696
TF: 800-234-8586 ■ *Web:* www.banknewport.com					
Bank of North Dakota 1200 Memorial Hwy	Bismarck	ND	58504	701-328-5600	328-5632
TF: 800-472-2166 ■ *Web:* www.banknd.com					
Bank of Nova Scotia 1 Liberty Plaza 26th Fl	New York	NY	10006	212-225-5000	225-5090
TF: 800-472-6842 ■ *Web:* www.scotiabank.com					
Bank of Nova Scotia 44 King St W	Toronto	ON	M5H1H1	416-866-6161	866-3750
NYSE: BNS ■ *TF:* 800-472-6842 ■ *Web:* www.scotiabank.ca					
Bank of Oak Ridge 2211 Oak Ridge Rd	Oak Ridge	NC	27310	336-644-9944	644-6644
NASDAQ: BKOR ■ *Web:* www.bankofoakridge.com					
Bank of Oklahoma NA PO Box 2300	Tulsa	OK	74192	918-588-6000	588-6962*
**Fax:* Cust Svc ■ *TF Cust Svc:* 800-234-6181 ■ *Web:* www.bankofoklahoma.com					
Bank of Scotland 565 5th Ave	New York	NY	10017	212-450-0800	557-9460
Web: www.bankofscotland.co.uk					
Bank of the Sierra PO Box 1930	Porterville	CA	93258	559-782-4900	782-4994
TF: 888-454-2265 ■ *Web:* www.bankofthesierra.com					
Bank of Tokyo-Mitsubishi Ltd 1251 Ave of the Americas	New York	NY	10020	212-782-4000	782-6419*
**Fax:* Hum Res ■ *Web:* www.btmna.com					
Bank of Virginia 11730 Hull Street Rd	Midlothian	VA	23112	804-744-7576	744-2306
NASDAQ: BOVA ■ *Web:* www.bankofva.com					
Bank of the West 1450 Treat Blvd	Walnut Creek	CA	94597	925-942-8300	
TF: 800-575-6677 ■ *Web:* www.bankofthewest.com					
BankAtlantic 2100 W Cypress Creek Rd	Fort Lauderdale	FL	33309	954-760-5000	940-5840
TF: 800-741-1700 ■ *Web:* www.bankatlantic.com					
BankUnited FSB 255 Alhambra Cir	Coral Gables	FL	33134	305-569-2000	569-2018
TF: 800-440-9646 ■ *Web:* www.bankunited.com					
Banner Bank PO Box 907	Walla Walla	WA	99362	509-526-8731	524-5980*
**Fax:* Hum Res ■ *TF:* 800-272-9933 ■ *Web:* www.bannerbank.com					
BB & T Bank 3233 Thomasville Rd	Tallahassee	FL	32308	850-385-3300	386-5241
TF: 888-385-3301 ■ *Web:* www.bbt.com					
Beal Bank SSB 6000 Legacy Dr	Plano	TX	75024	469-467-5000	312-8922*
**Fax Area Code:* 972 ■ *TF:* 800-404-4494 ■ *Web:* www.bealbank.com					
Beneficial Bank 3 Sunset Rd	Burlington	NJ	08016	609-387-2728	239-2977
TF: 888-742-5272 ■ *Web:* www.thebeneficial.com					
Beneficial Mutual Savings Bank 530 Walnut St	Philadelphia	PA	19106	215-864-6000	864-6198
TF: 800-784-8490 ■ *Web:* www.thebeneficial.com					
Berkshire Bank PO Box 1308	Pittsfield	MA	01202	413-443-5601	447-1799
TF: 800-773-5601 ■ *Web:* www.berkshirebank.com					
Branch Banking & Trust Co 200 W 2nd St	Winston-Salem	NC	27101	336-733-2500	733-2190*
**Fax:* Hum Res ■ *TF:* 800-226-5228 ■ *Web:* www.bbandt.com					

Phone Fax

Branch Banking & Trust Co of South Carolina PO Box 408.......Greenville SC 29602 864-242-8000 282-3309
TF: 800-226-5228 ■ *Web:* www.bbandt.com
Branch Banking & Trust Co of Virginia 500 E Main St.............Norfolk VA 23510 757-823-7800 626-0405
TF: 800-226-5228 ■ *Web:* www.bbandt.com
Brookline Bank 160 Washington St.........................Brookline MA 02445 617-730-3500 730-3569
TF: 888-730-3554 ■ *Web:* www.brooklinebank.com
Brown Brothers Harriman & Co 140 Broadway.................New York NY 10005 212-483-1818 493-7287*
**Fax:* Hum Res ■ *Web:* www.bbh.com
Busey Bank 201 W Main St..................................Urbana IL 61801 217-365-4500 365-4061
TF: 800-672-8739 ■ *Web:* www.busey.com
California Bank & Trust 11622 El Camino Real Suite 200........San Diego CA 92130 858-793-7400 793-7438
TF: 800-400-6080 ■ *Web:* www.calbanktrust.com
California National Bank 221 S Figueroa St.................Los Angeles CA 90012 213-440-1400 965-6216*
**Fax Area Code:* 323 ■ *TF:* 866-373-7838 ■ *Web:* www.calnationalbank.com
Calyon 1301 Ave of the Americas..........................New York NY 10019 212-261-7000 459-3182
Web: www.lcl.fr
Cambridge Savings Bank 1374 Massachusetts Ave.............Cambridge MA 02138 617-864-8700 441-4316*
**Fax:* Cust Svc ■ *TF:* 800-864-2265 ■ *Web:* www.cambridgesavings.com
Canadian Imperial Bank of Commerce
199 Bay St Commerce Court W...............................Toronto ON M5L1G9 416-980-2777
NYSE: BCM ■ *TF:* 800-465-2422 ■ *Web:* www.cibc.com
Canadian Western Bank 10303 Jasper Ave Suite 2300..........Edmonton AB T5J3X6 780-423-8888 423-8897
TSX: CWB ■ *TF:* 800-663-1124 ■ *Web:* www.cwbank.com
Cape Bank 201 Shore Rd PO Box 279.........................Linwood NJ 08221 609-601-8553 601-8554
TF: 888-720-2265 ■ *Web:* www.boardwalkbank.com
Cape Cod Five Cents Savings Bank 19 West Rd.................Orleans MA 02653 508-240-0555 240-1895*
**Fax:* Mktg ■ *TF:* 800-678-1855 ■ *Web:* www.capecodfive.com
Capital City Bank 2111 N Monroe St......................Tallahassee FL 32303 850-402-7700 402-7798
TF: 888-402-7000 ■ *Web:* www.ccbg.com
Capital Crossing Bank 101 Summer St........................Boston MA 02110 617-880-1000 880-1010
NASDAQ: CAPX ■ *TF:* 888-880-3880 ■ *Web:* www.capitalcrossing.com
Capital One FSB 15000 Capital One Dr......................Richmond VA 23238 804-967-1000
Capitol Federal Savings Bank 700 S Kansas Ave...............Topeka KS 66603 785-235-1341 231-6329
TF: 800-432-2926 ■ *Web:* www.capfed.com
Cardinal State Bank 3710 University Dr Suite 100............Durham NC 27707 919-403-2833 403-2783
NASDAQ: CSNC ■ *TF:* 866-803-9554 ■ *Web:* www.cardinalstatebank.com
Carolina First Bank 102 S Main St........................Greenville SC 29601 864-255-7900 239-6401
TF: 800-476-6400 ■ *Web:* www.carolinafirst.com
Carolina Trust Bank 901 E Main St........................Lincolnton NC 28092 704-735-1104 735-1258
NASDAQ: CART ■ *Web:* www.carolinatrust.com
Carver FSB 75 W 125th St..................................New York NY 10027 212-876-4747 426-6162
Web: www.carverbank.com
Cathay Bank 777 N Broadway...............................Los Angeles CA 90012 213-625-4791 625-1368
TF: 800-922-8429 ■ *Web:* www.cathaybank.com
Central Pacific Bank PO Box 3590...........................Honolulu HI 96811 808-544-0500
NYSE: CPF ■ *TF Cust Svc:* 800-342-8422 ■ *Web:* www.centralpacificbank.com
Century National Bank 14 S 5th St........................Zanesville OH 43701 740-454-2521 455-7201
TF: 800-321-7061 ■ *Web:* www.centurynationalbank.com
Charter One Bank 1215 Superior Ave........................Cleveland OH 44114 216-566-5300 566-1453
TF: 800-553-8981 ■ *Web:* www.charteronebank.com
CharterBank 1233 OG Skinner Dr...........................West Point GA 31833 706-645-1391 645-1370
TF: 800-763-4444 ■ *Web:* www.charterbank.net
Chase Bank 1 Chase Manhattan Plaza........................New York NY 10081 212-270-6000 270-1043*
**Fax:* PR ■ *TF:* 800-935-9935 ■ *Web:* www.chase.com
Cheviot Financial Corp 3723 Glenmore Ave...................Cheviot OH 45211 513-661-0457 389-3312
NASDAQ: CHEV ■ *Web:* www.cheviotsavings.com
Chevy Chase Bank FSB 7501 Wisconsin Ave...................Bethesda MD 20814 240-497-4102 497-4110
TF: 800-987-2265 ■ *Web:* www.chevychasebank.com
Chiba Bank Ltd 1133 Ave of the Americas 15th Fl...............New York NY 10036 212-354-7777 354-8575
Chinatrust Bank USA 22939 Hawthorne Blvd..................Torrance CA 90505 310-791-2828 791-2880
TF: 888-839-9000 ■ *Web:* www.chinatrustusa.com
Chittenden Bank 2 Burlington Sq PO Box 820.................Burlington VT 05402 802-658-4000 660-1285*
**Fax:* Mktg ■ *TF:* 800-752-0006 ■ *Web:* www.chittenden.com
Citibank (Delaware) 1 Penns Way..........................New Castle DE 19720 302-323-3600 827-3122*
**Fax Area Code:* 646 ■ *TF:* 800-341-4727 ■ *Web:* www.citi.com
Citibank FSB 245 Market St..............................San Francisco CA 94105 866-248-4937
Web: www.citi.com
Citibank NA 399 Park Ave.................................New York NY 10022 800-627-3999
Web: www.citibank.com
Citibank (Nevada) NA 8701 W Sahara Ave...................Las Vegas NV 89117 866-248-4937
Web: www.citi.com
Citibank (South Dakota) NA 701 E 60th St N................Sioux Falls SD 57117 605-331-2626 357-2073
TF: 800-950-5114 ■ *Web:* www.citi.com
Citibank Texas 2800 S Texas Ave Suite 200...................Bryan TX 77802 979-361-6200 361-6205
TF: 800-299-0062 ■ *Web:* www.citibank.com
Citibank (West) FSB 590 Market St.......................San Francisco CA 94104 866-248-4937
Web: www.citibank.com/domain/calfed_converts.htm
Citizens Bank 919 N Market St............................Wilmington DE 19801 302-421-2228 421-2294*
**Fax:* Hum Res ■ *TF:* 888-910-4100 ■ *Web:* www.citizensbank.com
Citizens Bank 328 S Saginaw St 1 Citizens Banking Ctr..............Flint MI 48502 810-766-7500 768-4724*
**Fax:* Cust Svc ■ *TF:* 800-825-7200 ■ *Web:* www.cbclientsfirst.com
Citizens Bank 2425 E Grand River Ave........................Lansing MI 48912 800-825-7200 483-6654*
**Fax Area Code:* 517 ■ *TF:* 888-722-7377 ■ *Web:* www.citizensbanking.com
Citizens Bank of Massachusetts 28 State St....................Boston MA 02109 617-725-5500
TF: 800-922-9999 ■ *Web:* www.citizensbank.com
Citizens Bank New Hampshire 875 Elm St..................Manchester NH 03101 603-634-6000 634-7191
TF: 800-862-5000 ■ *Web:* www.citizensbank.com
Citizens Bank of Rhode Island 1 Citizens Plaza...............Providence RI 02903 401-456-7000 455-5715
TF Cust Svc: 800-922-9999 ■ *Web:* www.citizensbank.com
Citizens Business Bank 701 N Haven Ave......................Ontario CA 91764 909-980-4030 481-2130
TF: 888-222-5432 ■ *Web:* www.citizensbusinessbank.com
Citizens Financial Services 707 Ridge Rd.....................Munster IN 46321 219-836-5500 836-0265
TF: 888-226-5237 ■ *Web:* www.bankcfs.com
Citizens First Savings Bank 525 Water St...................Port Huron MI 48060 810-987-8300 987-7537
TF: 800-462-2786 ■ *Web:* www.cfsbank.com
Citizens Trust Bank PO Box 4485...........................Atlanta GA 30302 404-406-4000 575-8269
TF: 800-547-1344 ■ *Web:* www.ctbatl.com
City Bank PO Box 97007....................................Lynnwood WA 98046 425-745-5933 742-9797
NASDAQ: CTBK ■ *TF:* 800-569-0006 ■ *Web:* www.citybank.com
City National Bank 400 N Roxbury Dr......................Beverly Hills CA 90210 310-888-6000 888-6045*
**Fax:* Mktg ■ *TF Cust Svc:* 800-773-7100 ■ *Web:* www.cnb.com
City National Bank of Florida
450 E Las Olas Blvd Suite 160.........................Fort Lauderdale FL 33301 954-467-6667 524-8247
TF: 800-762-2489 ■ *Web:* www.mycitynational.com
City National Bank of West Virginia 3601 McCorckle Ave.......Charleston WV 25304 304-926-3300 925-8073
TF: 877-203-8700 ■ *Web:* www.cityholding.com
Coast Capital Savings 645 Tyee Rd Suite 400..................Victoria BC V9A6X5 250-483-8100 482-8180
TF: 888-517-7000 ■ *Web:* www.coastcapitalsavings.com
Cole Taylor Bank 1965 N Milwaukee Ave.......................Chicago IL 60647 773-927-7000 278-2183
TF: 800-727-2265 ■ *Web:* www.coletaylor.com
College Savings Bank 5 Vaughn Dr..........................Princeton NJ 08540 609-987-3700 987-3760
TF: 800-888-2723 ■ *Web:* www.collegesavings.com
Colonial Bank 100 Colonial Bank Blvd.....................Montgomery AL 36117 334-240-5000 277-1063*
**Fax:* Hum Res ■ *TF:* 877-502-2265 ■ *Web:* www.colonialbank.com
Columbia Bank 7168 Columbia Gateway Dr....................Columbia MD 21046 410-730-5000 730-6178
TF: 800-314-7714 ■ *Web:* www.columbank.com

Phone Fax

Columbia Savings Bank 19-01 Rt 208........................Fair Lawn NJ 07410 201-796-3600 794-5812
TF Cust Svc: 800-747-4428 ■ *Web:* www.columbiabankonline.com
Columbia State Bank PO Box 2156...........................Tacoma WA 98401 253-305-1900 396-6960
TF: 800-305-1905 ■ *Web:* www.columbiabank.com
Columbus Bank & Trust Co 1148 Broadway....................Columbus GA 31901 706-649-2012 649-2481*
**Fax:* Cust Svc ■ *TF:* 800-334-9007 ■ *Web:* www.columbusbankandtrust.com
Comerica Bank 500 Woodward Ave...........................Detroit MI 48226 248-371-5000
TF: 800-643-4418 ■ *Web:* www.comerica.com
Comerica Bank-California 333 W Santa Clara St................San Jose CA 95113 408-556-5000 556-5870*
**Fax:* Hum Res ■ *TF:* 800-521-1190 ■ *Web:* www.comerica.com
Comerica Bank-Texas 753 W Illinois Ave........................Dallas TX 75224 214-630-3030 946-9111
TF: 800-925-2160 ■ *Web:* www.comerica.com
Commerce Bank NA 922 Walnut St.........................Kansas City MO 64106 816-234-2000 234-2019*
**Fax:* Hum Res ■ *TF Cust Svc:* 800-453-2265 ■ *Web:* www.commercebank.com
Commerce Bank NA 1701 Rt 70 E..........................Cherry Hill NJ 08034 856-751-9000 751-0226
TF: 888-751-9000 ■ *Web:* www.commerceonline.com
Commerzbank AG 2 World Financial Ctr......................New York NY 10281 212-266-7200 266-7235
Web: www.commerzbank.com
Commonwealth Bank of Australia 599 Lexington Ave 17th Fl......New York NY 10022 212-848-9200 336-7722
Web: www.commbank.com.au/ie.htm
Community Bank NA PO Box 509...............................Canton NY 13617 315-386-4553 386-8176*
**Fax:* Hum Res ■ *TF:* 800-835-2993 ■ *Web:* www.communitybankna.com
Community Trust Bank NA 346 N Mayo Trail....................Pikeville KY 41501 606-432-1414 433-4749*
**Fax:* Cust Svc ■ *TF:* 800-422-1090 ■ *Web:* www.ctbi.com
Compass Bank 15 S 20th St.............................Birmingham AL 35233 205-933-3000 558-6306
TF Cust Svc: 800-266-7277 ■ *Web:* www.compassweb.com
Corus Bank NA 3959 N Lincoln Ave..........................Chicago IL 60613 773-549-7100 832-3499*
**Fax:* Hum Res ■ *TF:* 800-555-5710 ■ *Web:* www.corusbank.com
Country Bank for Savings 75 Main St.........................Ware MA 01082 413-967-6221 967-7132
TF: 800-322-8233 ■ *Web:* www.countrybank.com
DBS Bank Ltd 445 S Figueroa St Suite 3550.................Los Angeles CA 90071 213-627-0222 627-0228
Web: www.dbs.com
Desert Community Bank 12530 Hesperia Rd...................Victorville CA 92395 760-243-2140 243-5048*
NASDAQ: DCBK ■ **Fax:* Cust Svc ■ *TF:* 888-895-5650 ■ *Web:* www.dcbk.org
Deutsche Bank Canada 199 Bay Street Suite 4700 PO Box 263.....Toronto ON M5L1E9 416-682-8000 682-8383
Web: www.db.com
Dexia Bank 445 Park Ave 8th Fl............................New York NY 10022 212-705-0700 705-0701
Web: www.dexia.com
Dime Savings Bank of Williamsburgh 275 S 5th St.............Brooklyn NY 11211 718-782-6200 782-5814
TF: 800-321-3463 ■ *Web:* www.dimewill.com
Discover Bank 12 Read's Way............................New Castle DE 19720 302-323-7110 323-7393
TF: 800-347-7000 ■ *Web:* discoverbank.com
Dollar Bank FSB 3 Gateway Ctr...........................Pittsburgh PA 15222 412-261-4900 261-4900
TF: 800-828-5527 ■ *Web:* www.dollarbank.com
Doral Bank 1451 FD Roosevelt Ave.........................San Juan PR 00920 787-474-6200 474-6889
Web: www.doralbank.com
Downey Savings & Loan Assn FA 3501 Jamboree Rd.......Newport Beach CA 92660 949-854-3100 725-0921
Web: www.downeysavings.com
Dresdner Bank AG 1301 Ave of the Americas..................New York NY 10019 212-429-2000
Web: www.dresdner-bank.com
E*Trade Bank 671 N Glebe Rd..............................Arlington VA 22203 703-247-3700 236-7210
TF: 800-387-2331 ■ *Web:* bankus.etrade.com/e/t/bank/home
East West Bank 942 N Broadway..........................Los Angeles CA 90012 213-617-8688 626-5663
Web: www.eastwestbank.com
East-West Bank 135 N Los Robles Ave........................Pasadena CA 91101 626-768-6000 683-7134
TF: 800-888-3932 ■ *Web:* www.eastwestbank.com
Eastern Bank 195 Market St.................................Lynn MA 01901 781-599-2100 598-7697
TF: 800-327-8376 ■ *Web:* www.easternbank.com
ebank.com Inc 2410 Paces Ferry Rd SE Suite 190................Atlanta GA 30339 770-863-9225 863-9228
TF: 888-278-9898 ■ *Web:* www.ebank.com
El Dorado Savings Bank 4040 El Dorado Rd...................Placerville CA 95667 530-622-1492 621-1659
TF: 800-874-9779 ■ *Web:* www.eldoradosavingsbank.com
Elmira Savings Bank FSB 333 E Water St......................Elmira NY 14901 607-734-3374 732-4007
NASDAQ: ESBK ■ *TF:* 888-372-9299 ■ *Web:* www.elmirasavingsbank.com
Emigrant Savings Bank 5 E 42nd St..........................New York NY 10017 212-850-4000 986-6587*
**Fax:* Acctg ■ *TF:* 800-836-1998 ■ *Web:* www.emigrant.com
Encore Bank 9 Greenway Plaza Suite 1000....................Houston TX 77046 713-787-3100 787-3192
TF: 800-308-6709 ■ *Web:* www.encorebank.com
ESB Bank 600 Lawrence Ave..............................Ellwood City PA 16117 724-758-5584 758-0576
TF: 800-533-4193 ■ *Web:* www.esbbank.com
Farmers & Merchants Bank of Long Beach 302 Pine Ave......Long Beach CA 90802 562-437-0011 437-8672
Web: www.fmb.com
Fidelity Bank 100 E English St..............................Wichita KS 67201 316-265-2261 268-7492
TF: 800-658-1637 ■ *Web:* www.fidelitybank.com
Fifth Third Bank 38 Fountain Sq Plaza......................Cincinnati OH 45263 513-579-5300 579-6701*
**Fax:* Mktg ■ *TF:* 800-972-3030 ■ *Web:* www.53.com
Fifth Third Bank Central Ohio 21 E State St................Columbus OH 43215 614-341-2595 744-7516
TF: 800-972-3030 ■ *Web:* www.53.com
Fifth Third Bank Inc 100 Brighton Park Blvd..................Frankfort KY 40601 502-695-0882 695-9124
TF: 800-972-3030 ■ *Web:* www.53.com
Fifth Third Bank Northwestern Ohio 550 N Summit St..............Toledo OH 43604 419-259-7890 259-7624*
**Fax:* Mktg ■ *TF Cust Svc:* 800-972-3030 ■ *Web:* www.53.com
Fifth Third Bank Western Ohio 110 N Main St...................Dayton OH 45402 937-227-6500 449-2678*
**Fax:* Hum Res ■ *TF:* 800-972-3030 ■ *Web:* www.53.com
Fireside Bank 5050 Hopyard Rd Suite 200...................Pleasanton CA 94588 925-460-9020 730-3505
TF: 800-825-1862 ■ *Web:* www.firesidebank.com
First American Bank 261 S Western Ave..................Carpentersville IL 60110 847-426-6300 426-1066
Web: www.firstambank.com
First Bank 11901 Olive Blvd..............................Creve Coeur MO 63141 314-995-8700 567-7341
TF: 800-760-2265 ■ *Web:* firstbanks.com
First Calgary Savings 510 16th Ave NE Suite 200...............Calgary AB T2E1K4 403-230-2783 276-6338
TF: 866-923-4778 ■ *Web:* www.1stcalgary.com
First Citizens Bank & Trust Co 3128 Smoketree Ct................Raleigh NC 27604 919-716-7000 716-7379*
**Fax:* Cust Svc ■ *TF Cust Svc:* 888-323-4732 ■ *Web:* www.firstcitizens.com
First Citizens Bank & Trust Co Inc 1230 Main St PO Box 29......Columbia SC 29201 803-771-8700 733-2763
TF: 888-612-4444 ■ *Web:* www.firstcitizensonline.com
First Federal Bank of Arkansas FA 1401 Hwy 62 65 N...........Harrison AR 72601 870-741-7641 365-8369
TF: 800-345-2539 ■ *Web:* www.ffbh.com
First Federal Bank of California FSB 401 Wilshire Blvd.......Santa Monica CA 90401 310-319-6000 319-5973
TF: 800-637-5540 ■ *Web:* www.firstfedca.com
First Federal Bank of the Midwest 601 Clinton St PO Box 248.....Defiance OH 43512 419-782-5015 782-5145
TF: 800-472-6292 ■ *Web:* www.first-fed.com
First Federal Savings & Loan Assn of Charleston
2440 Mall Dr.......................................North Charleston SC 29406 843-529-5800 529-5775
TF: 800-768-3248 ■ *Web:* www.firstfederal.com
First Federal Savings & Loan Assn of Lakewood
14806 Detroit Ave...Lakewood OH 44107 216-221-7300 226-0622
TF: 800-966-7300 ■ *Web:* www.ffl.net
First Financial Bank 1 First Financial Plaza.................Terre Haute IN 47807 812-238-6000 232-5336
TF: 800-511-0045 ■ *Web:* www.first-online.com
First Financial Bank 300 High St............................Hamilton OH 45011 513-867-4700 867-3111*
**Fax:* Cust Svc ■ *TF Cust Svc:* 800-543-2265 ■ *Web:* bankatfirst.com
First Hawaiian Bank 999 Bishop St..........................Honolulu HI 96813 808-525-7000 525-8708*
**Fax:* Mktg ■ *TF:* 888-844-4444 ■ *Web:* www.fhb.com
First Internet Bank of Indiana
7820 Innovation Blvd Suite 210..........................Indianapolis IN 46278 317-532-7900 644-8678*
**Fax Area Code:* 888 ■ **Fax:* Cust Svc ■ *TF:* 888-873-3424 ■ *Web:* www.firstib.com

				Phone	Fax
First Interstate Bank 401 N 31st St *Fax: Hum Res ■ TF: 888-752-3336 ■ Web: www.firstinterstatebank.com	Billings	MT	59101	406-255-5000	255-5213*
First Midwest Bank NA 1 Pierce Pl Suite 1500 TF: 800-322-3623 ■ Web: www.firstmidwest.com	Itasca	IL	60143	630-875-7200	875-7474
First National Bank Alaska 101 W 36 Ave TF: 800-856-4362 ■ Web: www.fnbalaska.com	Anchorage	AK	99503	907-276-6300	777-3528
First National Bank of Nevada 2510 S Maryland Pkwy TF: 866-213-2112 ■ Web: www.fnbnonline.com	Las Vegas	NV	89109	702-792-2200	792-4316
First National Bank of Omaha 1620 Dodge St TF: 800-228-4411 ■ Web: www.fnbomaha.com	Omaha	NE	68197	402-341-0500	636-6033
First Niagara Bank 6950 S Transit Rd TF: 800-421-0004 ■ Web: www.fnfg.com	Lockport	NY	14094	716-625-7500	434-0160
First Place Bank 185 E Market St *Fax: Cust Svc ■ TF: 800-995-2646 ■ Web: www.firstplace.net	Warren	OH	44481	330-373-1221	373-9990*
First Republic Bank 111 Pine St 3rd Fl NYSE: FRC ■ TF: 888-408-0288 ■ Web: www.firstrepublic.com	San Francisco	CA	94111	415-392-1400	392-1413
First Tennessee Bank 165 Madison Ave *Fax: Mktg ■ TF: 800-382-5465 ■ Web: www.firsttennessee.com	Memphis	TN	38103	901-523-4444	523-4145*
FirstBank Puerto Rico 1519 Ponce de Leon Ave Stop 23 Web: www.firstbankpr.com	Santurce	PR	00908	787-729-8200	729-8205
Firstrust Savings Bank 1931 Cottman Ave TF: 800-220-2265 ■ Web: www.firstrust.com	Philadelphia	PA	19111	215-722-4000	728-8332
Fiserv ISS 717 17th St Suite 1700 TF: 800-525-2124 ■ Web: www.fiserviss.com	Denver	CO	80202	303-293-2223	297-3658
Flagstar Bank FSB 5151 Corporate Dr *Fax: Hum Res ■ TF: 800-945-7700 ■ Web: www.flagstar.com	Troy	MI	48098	248-312-2000	312-6842*
Flushing Savings Bank FSB 1979 Marcus Ave Suite E-140 *Fax Area Code: 516 ■ Web: www.flushingsavings.com	Lake Success	NY	11042	718-961-5400	358-4361*
Franklin Bank NA 24725 W 12-Mile Rd Web: www.franklinbank.com	Southfield	MI	48034	248-358-5170	354-6353
Franklin Federal Savings & Loan Assn of Richmond PO Box 5310 Web: www.franklinfederal.com	Glen Allen	VA	23058	804-967-7000	967-7050
Fremont Investment & Loan 2727 E Imperial Hwy TF: 800-373-6668 ■ Web: www.1800fremont.com	Brea	CA	92821	714-961-5000	961-7515
Frontier Bank 332 SW Everett Mall Way Web: www.frontierbank.com	Everett	WA	98204	425-514-0731	514-0718
Frost Bank 100 W Houston St *Fax: Mktg ■ TF: 800-562-6732 ■ Web: www.frostbank.com	San Antonio	TX	78205	210-220-4011	220-4673*
Fulton Bank 1 Penn Sq *Fax: Hum Res ■ TF: 800-322-2595 ■ Web: www.fultonbank.com	Lancaster	PA	17602	717-581-3000	291-2608*
Giantbank.com 6300 NE 1st Ave Suite 300 TF: 877-446-4200 ■ Web: www.giantbank.com/	Fort Lauderdale	FL	33303	954-958-0001	958-0190
Great Southern Bank FSB 1451 E Battlefield Rd TF: 800-749-7113 ■ Web: www.greatsouthernbank.com	Springfield	MO	65804	417-887-4400	888-4533
Guaranty Bank 8333 Douglas Ave TF: 800-999-1726 ■ Web: www.bank.guarantygroup.com	Dallas	TX	75225	214-360-3360	369-1004
Guaranty Bank SSB 4000 W Brown Deer Rd TF: 800-840-0770 ■ Web: www.guarantybanking.com	Brown Deer	WI	53209	414-362-4000	365-6779
Gunma Bank Ltd 780 3rd Ave 6th Fl	New York	NY	10017	212-949-8690	867-1081
Hancock Bank 2510 14th St *Fax: Mktg ■ TF: 800-448-8812 ■ Web: www.hancockbank.com	Gulfport	MS	39501	228-868-4000	563-7975*
Harleysville National Bank & Trust Co 483 Main St PO Box 195 TF: 800-423-3955 ■ Web: www.harleysvillebank.com	Harleysville	PA	19438	215-256-8851	
Harris Trust & Savings Bank 111 W Monroe St TF: 888-340-2265 ■ Web: www4.harrisbank.com	Chicago	IL	60603	312-461-2121	
Hickory Point Bank & Trust FSB PO Box 2548 TF Cust Svc: 888-424-1976 ■ Web: www.hickoryptbank.com	Decatur	IL	62525	217-875-3131	872-6250
Hingham Institution for Savings 55 Main St NASDAQ: HIFS ■ TF: 877-447-2265 ■ Web: www.hinghamsavings.com	Hingham	MA	02043	781-749-2200	740-4889
Hokuriku Bank Ltd 780 3rd Ave 28th Fl	New York	NY	10017	212-355-3883	355-3204
Home Federal Bank 225 S Main Ave PO Box 5000 TF: 800-244-2149 ■ Web: www.homefederal.com	Sioux Falls	SD	57117	605-333-7500	333-7591
Home Federal Bank of Tennessee FSB 515 Market St Web: www.homefederalbanktn.com	Knoxville	TN	37902	865-546-0330	541-6962
Home Federal Savings Bank 715 N Broadway TF: 888-422-4117 ■ Web: www.justcallhome.com	Spring Valley	MN	55975	507-346-7345	346-9711
Home Savings & Loan Co of Youngstown 275 Federal Plaza W TF: 888-822-4751 ■ Web: www.homesavings.com	Youngstown	OH	44501	330-742-0500	742-0615
HomeFederal 222 W 2nd St TF: 877-626-7000 ■ Web: www.homf.com	Seymour	IN	47274	812-522-1592	522-9561
HomeStreet Bank 601 Union St 2 Union Sq Suite 2000 TF: 800-654-1075 ■ Web: www.homestreetbank.com	Seattle	WA	98101	206-623-3050	389-7701
Horizon Bank 1500 Cornwall Ave TF: 800-955-9194 ■ Web: www.horizonbank.com	Bellingham	WA	98225	360-733-3050	733-7019
HSBC Bank Canada 885 W Georgia St Suite 200 TF: 888-310-4722 ■ Web: www.hsbc.ca	Vancouver	BC	V6C3G1	604-685-1000	641-2506
HSBC Bank USA 1 HSBC Center *Fax: Mtkg ■ TF: 800-975-4722 ■ Web: www.us.hsbc.com	Buffalo	NY	14203	716-841-2424	841-4746*
Hudson City Savings Bank W 80 Century Rd TF: 866-448-9498 ■ Web: www.hudsoncitysavingsbank.com	Paramus	NJ	07652	201-967-1900	967-9136
Hudson Valley Bank 21 Scarsdale Rd Web: www.hvbank.com	Yonkers	NY	10707	914-961-6100	779-7350
Huntington National Bank 41 S High St TF: 800-480-2265 ■ Web: www.huntington.com	Columbus	OH	43287	614-480-8300	480-5746
HypoVereinsbank 150 E 42nd St 29th Fl TF: 800-493-2203 ■ Web: www.hypovereinsbank.de	New York	NY	10017	212-672-6000	672-5500
IBERIABANK 1101 E Admiral Doyle Dr TF: 888-447-0770 ■ Web: www.iberiabank.com	New Iberia	LA	70560	337-365-2361	367-9929
Imperial Capital Bank 888 Prospect St Suite 110 *Fax: Hum Res ■ TF: 888-551-4852 ■ Web: www.imperialcapitalbank.com	La Jolla	CA	92037	858-551-0511	551-0631*
Independence Federal Savings Bank 1229 Connecticut Ave NW NASDAQ: IFSB ■ TF: 888-922-6537 ■ Web: www.ifsb.com	Washington	DC	20036	202-628-5500	626-7106
Industrial Bank NA 4812 Georgia Ave NW Web: www.industrial-bank.com	Washington	DC	20011	202-722-2000	722-2040
InsurBanc 10 Executive Dr TF: 866-467-2262 ■ Web: www.insurbanc.com	Farmington	CT	06032	860-677-9701	677-9793
Integra Bank NA 21 SE 3rd St TF Cust Svc: 800-467-1928 ■ Web: www.integrabank.com	Evansville	IN	47708	812-464-9800	461-9133
International Bank of Commerce 1200 San Bernardo Ave *Fax Area Code: 210 ■ Web: www.ibc.com	Laredo	TX	78040	956-722-7611	804-7410*
INTRUST Bank NA 105 N Main St *Fax: Hum Res ■ TF: 800-895-2265 ■ Web: www.intrustbank.com	Wichita	KS	67202	316-383-1111	383-5805*
Investors Savings Bank 101 JFK Pkwy TF: 800-252-8119 ■ Web: www.isbnj.com	Short Hills	NJ	07078	973-376-5100	376-5357
Irwin Union Bank & Trust Co 500 Washington St *Fax: Hum Res ■ TF: 888-879-5900 ■ Web: www.irwinunion.com	Columbus	IN	47201	812-372-0111	376-1705*
Israel Discount Bank of New York (IDB Bank) 511 5th Ave Web: www.idbny.com	New York	NY	10017	212-551-8500	
jNational City Bank 100 S 2nd St TF: 800-226-4376 ■ Web: www.nationalcity.com	Fort Pierce	FL	34950	772-461-2414	460-7056
Johnson Bank 4001 N Main St TF: 800-236-8586 ■ Web: www.johnsonbank.com	Racine	WI	53402	262-639-6010	681-4627

				Phone	Fax
JP Morgan Chase 270 Park Ave Web: www.jpmorgan.com	New York	NY	10017	212-483-2323	648-5230
JP Morgan Chase 500 Neville St Web: www.jpmorganchase.com	Beckley	WV	25801	304-256-2157	256-2263
KBC Bank 177 Avenue of the Americas 8th Fl *Fax: Hum Res ■ Web: www.kbc.be	New York	NY	10036	212-541-0600	956-5580*
Kearny Federal Savings Bank 614 Kearny Ave TF: 800-273-3406 ■ Web: www.kearnyfederalsavings.com	Kearny	NJ	07032	201-991-4100	991-6713
Key Bank 65 Dutch Hill Rd TF Cust Svc: 800-616-3491 ■ Web: www.key.com	Orangeburg	NY	10962	845-365-4816	365-2130
Key Bank USA NA 127 Public Sq *Fax Area Code: 800 ■ TF: 800-625-3256 ■ Web: www.keybank.com	Cleveland	OH	44144	216-813-5850	762-7409*
KeyBank NA 127 Public Sq TF: 800-523-7247 ■ Web: www.keybank.com	Cleveland	OH	44114	216-689-3000	689-4037
Laredo National Bank 700 San Bernardo Ave TF: 888-723-1151 ■ Web: www.lnb.com	Laredo	TX	78040	956-723-1151	723-1151
LaSalle Bank NA 135 S LaSalle St TF: 800-643-9600 ■ Web: www.lasallebanks.com	Chicago	IL	60603	312-443-2000	904-2579
Laurentian Bank of Canada 1981 ave McGill College TSX: LB ■ TF: 877-522-3863 ■ Web: www.laurentianbank.ca	Montreal	QC	H3A3K3	514-284-4500	284-3988
Lehman Brothers Bank FSB 1000 West St Suite 200 TF: 800-372-8464 ■ Web: www.lehmanbrothersbank.com	Wilmington	DE	19801	302-654-6179	654-4318
Liberty Bank 315 Main St *Fax: Cust Svc ■ TF: 800-622-6732 ■ Web: www.liberty-bank.com	Middletown	CT	06457	860-344-7200	704-2132*
Liberty Savings Bank FSB 647 Fife Ave TF: 800-436-6300 ■ Web: libertysavingsbank.portalvault.com	Wilmington	OH	45177	937-382-6993	383-2208
Lloyds Bank Plc 1251 6th Ave 39th Fl Web: www.lloydstsb.com	New York	NY	10020	212-930-5000	930-5098
Luther Burbank Savings Bank 804 4th St Web: www.lutherbsavings.com	Santa Rosa	CA	95404	707-578-9216	573-0316
M & I Bank 135 N Pennsylvania St First Indiana Plaza TF: 888-464-5463 ■ Web: www.mibank.com	Indianapolis	IN	46204	317-269-1200	269-1683
M & I Bank Northeast 310 W Walnut St TF: 888-464-5463 ■ Web: www.mibank.com	Green Bay	WI	54303	920-436-1800	436-1941
M & I Marshall & Ilsley Bank 770 N Water St TF: 800-342-2265 ■ Web: www.mibank.com	Milwaukee	WI	53202	414-765-7700	765-7436
M & T Bank Corp 67 Jackson St TF: 800-433-2265 ■ Web: www.mandtbank.com	Fishkill	NY	12524	845-896-7644	896-4708
Manufacturers & Traders Trust Co 1 M & T Plaza TF: 800-724-2440 ■ Web: www.mandtbank.com	Buffalo	NY	14203	716-842-4470	842-5834
Maspeth Federal Savings & Loan Assn 56-18 69th St TF: 888-558-1300 ■ Web: www.maspethfederal.com	Maspeth	NY	11378	718-335-1300	335-4629
MASSBANK 123 Haven St TF: 800-447-1052 ■ Web: www.massbank.com	Reading	MA	01867	781-662-0100	942-8194
Mayflower Co-operative Bank 30 S Main St PO Box 311 NASDAQ: MFLR ■ TF: 800-552-4344 ■ Web: www.mayflowerbank.com	Middleboro	MA	02346	508-947-4343	923-0864
MB Financial Bank 1200 N Ashland Ave *Fax Area Code: 773 ■ TF: 888-422-6562 ■ Web: www.mbfinancial.com	Chicago	IL	60622	888-422-6562	278-4066*
Mechanics Bank 3170 Hilltop Mall Rd TF: 800-797-6324 ■ Web: www.mechbank.com	Richmond	CA	94806	510-262-7251	262-7941
Mellon 1st Business Bank 601 W 5th St Web: www.mellon.com/mfbb	Los Angeles	CA	90071	213-489-1000	
Mercantil Commercebank NA 220 Alhambra Cir TF: 888-629-0810 ■ Web: www.mercantilcb.com	Coral Gables	FL	33134	305-460-8701	629-1400
Merrill Lynch Bank & Trust Co 800 Scudders Mill Rd	Plainsboro	NJ	08536	609-282-2265	282-0942
Middlesex Savings Bank 36 Summer St TF: 877-463-6287 ■ Web: www.middlesexbank.com	Natick	MA	01760	508-653-0300	653-4789
MidFirst Bank PO Box 76149 *Fax: Cust Svc ■ TF: 888-643-3477 ■ Web: www.midfirst.com	Oklahoma City	OK	73147	405-943-8002	840-0862*
Mitsubishi Trust & Banking Corp 520 Madison Ave 25th Fl Web: www.tr.mufg.jp/english	New York	NY	10022	212-838-7700	755-2349
Mizuho Corporate Bank Ltd 1251 Ave of the Americas	New York	NY	10020	212-282-3000	282-4250
Mizuho Financial Group 1251 Ave of the Americas Web: www.mizuho-fg.co.jp/english	New York	NY	10020	212-282-3000	282-4250
Monarch Community Bancorp Inc 375 N Willowbrook Rd NASDAQ: MCBF ■ TF: 800-882-2911 ■ Web: www.monarchcb.com	Coldwater	MI	49036	517-278-4566	279-0221
Monroe Bank & Trust 102 E Front St *Fax: Hum Res ■ TF: 800-321-0032 ■ Web: www.mbandt.com	Monroe	MI	48161	734-241-3431	242-3811*
Mouvement des caisses Desjardins 100 des Commandeurs TF: 866-835-8444 ■ Web: www.desjardins.com	Levis	QC	G6V7N5	418-835-8444	833-5873
National Australia Bank Americas 245 Park Ave 28th Fl Web: www.national.com.au	New York	NY	10167	212-916-9500	983-1969
National Bank of Arizona 335 N Wilmot Rd TF: 800-365-7455 ■ Web: www.nbarizona.com	Tucson	AZ	85711	520-571-1500	513-0134
National Bank of Canada 600 rue de la Gauchetière O TSX: NA ■ TF: 800-361-8688 ■ Web: www.nbc.ca	Montreal	QC	H3B4L2	514-394-5000	394-8258
National Bank of South Carolina 1 Broad St TF: 800-708-5687 ■ Web: www.nationalbanksc.com	Sumter	SC	29150	803-778-8259	778-8304
National City Bank 2650 Warrenville Rd Suite 500 TF: 800-925-9259 ■ Web: www.nationalcity.com	Downers Grove	IL	60515	630-325-7300	325-0372
National City Bank 1 E 4th St *Fax: Cust Svc ■ TF: 888-622-4932 ■ Web: www.nationalcity.com	Cincinnati	OH	45202	513-455-2800	345-7333*
National City Bank 1900 E 9th St *Fax: Mktg ■ TF: 800-738-3888 ■ Web: www.nationalcity.com	Cleveland	OH	44114	216-222-2000	420-9512*
National City Bank Indiana 101 W Washington St *Fax: Hum Res ■ TF: 800-777-2424 ■ Web: www.nationalcity.com	Indianapolis	IN	46255	317-267-7900	267-6156*
National City Bank of Kentucky 101 S 5th St TF: 800-727-8686 ■ Web: www.nationalcity.com	Louisville	KY	40202	502-581-4200	
National City Bank of Michigan/Illinois 2595 Waukegan Rd TF Cust Svc: 800-925-9259 ■ Web: www.nationalcity.com	Bannockburn	IL	60015	847-317-2350	317-2356
National City Bank Northeast 1900 E 9th St TF: 800-738-3888 ■ Web: www.nationalcity.com	Cleveland	OH	44114	216-222-2223	
National City Bank of Pennsylvania 20 Sandwix St Web: www.nationalcity.com	Pittsburgh	PA	15222	412-644-7922	
National InterBank PO Box 1245 *Fax Area Code: 877 ■ TF: 877-468-7265 ■ Web: www.nationalinterbank.com	Indianapolis	IN	46206	317-229-4011	435-8083*
National Penn Bank PO Box 547 *Fax: Mktg ■ TF: 800-822-3321 ■ Web: www.natpennbank.com	Boyertown	PA	19512	610-367-6001	369-6501*
NBT Bank NA 52 S Broad St *Fax Area Code: 607 ■ Web: www.nbtbank.com	Norwich	NY	13815	800-628-2265	336-8670*
NetBank Inc 1015 Windward Ridge Pkwy NASDAQ: NTBK ■ TF Cust Svc: 888-256-6932 ■ Web: www.netbank.com	Alpharetta	GA	30005	770-343-6006	343-6464
Nevada State Bank PO Box 990 TF: 800-727-4743 ■ Web: www.nsbank.com	Las Vegas	NV	89125	702-383-0009	
New South Federal Savings Bank 2000 Crestwood Blvd TF: 800-366-1010 ■ Web: www.newsouthfederal.com	Irondale	AL	35210	205-951-4000	951-1027
New York Community Bank 615 Merrick Ave *Fax: Mktg ■ Web: www.mynycb.com	Westbury	NY	11590	516-942-6000	942-9351*
NewAlliance Bank 195 Church St *Fax: Mktg ■ TF: 800-892-2096 ■ Web: www.newalliancebank.com	New Haven	CT	06510	203-787-1111	784-5059*
Nexity Bank 3500 Blue Lake Dr Suite 330 TF: 877-738-6391 ■ Web: www.nexitybank.com	Birmingham	AL	35243	205-298-6391	298-6395
North American Savings Bank FSB 12498 S 71 Hwy *Fax: Cust Svc ■ TF: 800-677-6272 ■ Web: www.nasb.com	Grandview	MO	64030	816-765-2200	316-4503*
North Fork Bank 275 Broad Hollow Rd *Fax: Cust Svc ■ TF: 877-694-9111 ■ Web: www.northforkbank.com	Melville	NY	11747	631-844-1000	844-1375*

	City	State	ZIP	Phone	Fax
North Shore Bank FSB 15700 W Bluemound Rd **Fax:* Cust Svc ■ *TF:* 800-236-4672 ■ *Web:* www.northshorebank.com	Brookfield	WI	53005	262-785-1600	797-3850*
Northern Trust Bank of Florida NA 700 Brickell Ave **Fax:* Mktg ■ *TF:* 800-468-2352 ■ *Web:* www.ntrs.com	Miami	FL	33131	305-372-1000	789-6233*
Northern Trust Co 50 S LaSalle St **Fax:* Mktg ■ *TF:* 888-289-6542 ■ *Web:* www.ntrs.com	Chicago	IL	60603	312-630-6000	630-1779*
Northrim BanCorp Inc 3111 C St *NASDAQ: NRIM* ■ **Fax:* Mktg ■ *TF:* 800-478-3311 ■ *Web:* www.northrim.com	Anchorage	AK	99503	907-562-0062	261-3594*
Northwest Savings Bank 108 Liberty St **Fax:* Mktg ■ *TF:* 800-822-2009 ■ *Web:* www.northwestsavingsbank.com	Warren	PA	16365	814-726-2140	728-7708*
NOVA Savings Bank 1535 Locust St *TF:* 877-482-2650 ■ *Web:* www.novasavingsbank.com	Philadelphia	PA	19102	215-893-1000	569-1595
Ocean Bank 780 NW 42nd Ave *TF:* 877-688-2265 ■ *Web:* www.oceanbank.com	Miami	FL	33126	305-442-2660	446-3192
OceanFirst Bank 975 Hooper Ave *TF:* 888-623-2633 ■ *Web:* www.oceanfirstonline.com	Toms River	NJ	08753	732-240-4500	341-2579
Ocwen Federal Bank FSB 1661 Worthington Rd Suite 100 **Fax Area Code:* 407 ■ **Fax:* Hum Res ■ *TF:* 800-280-3863 ■ *Web:* www.ocwen.com	West Palm Beach	FL	33409	561-682-8000	737-6211*
Ohio Legacy Corp 305 W Liberty St PO Box 959 *NASDAQ: OLCB* ■ *TF:* 877-965-1113 ■ *Web:* www.ohiolegacybank.com	Wooster	OH	44691	330-263-1955	263-0063
Old National Bank 1 Main St **Fax:* Cust Svc ■ *TF:* 800-731-2265 ■ *Web:* www.oldnational.com	Evansville	IN	47708	812-464-1200	464-1551*
OneUnited Bank 133 Federal St 8th Fl *TF:* 877-663-8648 ■ *Web:* www.oneunited.com	Boston	MA	02110	617-457-4400	457-4430
Oriental Bank & Trust PO Box 195115 **Fax:* Cust Svc ■ *TF:* 800-981-5554 ■ *Web:* www.orientalonline.com	San Juan	PR	00919	787-771-6800	771-6808*
Oversea-Chinese Banking Corp Ltd 1700 Broadway 18th Fl *Web:* www.ocbc.com	New York	NY	10019	212-586-6222	586-0636
Pacific Capital Bank 30343 Canwood St Suite 100 *TF:* 800-272-7200 ■ *Web:* www.pacificcapitalbank.com	Agoura Hills	CA	91301	818-865-3300	865-3232
Park National Bank 50 N 3rd St **Fax:* Cust Svc ■ *TF:* 800-762-2616 ■ *Web:* www.parknationalbank.com	Newark	OH	43055	740-349-8451	349-3931*
Parkvale Bank 4220 William Penn Hwy **Fax:* Hum Res ■ *Web:* www.parkvale.com	Monroeville	PA	15146	412-373-7200	856-3943*
Parkvale Savings Bank DBA Parkvale Bank 4220 William Penn Hwy **Fax:* Hum Res ■ *Web:* www.parkvale.com	Monroeville	PA	15146	412-373-7200	856-3943*
Penn Federal Savings Bank 36 Ferry St *TF:* 800-722-0351 ■ *Web:* www.pennfsb.com	Newark	NJ	07105	973-589-8616	589-1202
Peoples First Community Bank 2305 Hwy 77 *TF:* 800-624-9699 ■ *Web:* www.peoplesfirst.com	Panama City	FL	32405	850-769-5261	769-3603
People's United Bank 850 Main St Bridgeport Ctr *NASDAQ: PBCT* ■ *TF:* 800-772-1090 ■ *Web:* www.peoples.com	Bridgeport	CT	06604	203-338-7171	338-2310
PFF Bank & Trust 9337 Milliken Ave **Fax Area Code:* 909 ■ *Web:* www.pffbank.com	Rancho Cucamonga	CA	91730	888-733-5465	941-5527*
Piedmont Federal Savings & Loan Assn 16 W 3rd St *Web:* www.piedmontfederal.com	Winston-Salem	NC	27101	336-770-1000	770-1108
PNC Bank 2 Hopkins Plaza *TF:* 888-762-2265 ■ *Web:* www.pnc.com	Baltimore	MD	21201	410-237-5569	237-5364
PNC Bank 110 Thomas Johnson Dr **Fax:* Cust Svc ■ *TF:* 888-762-2265 ■ *Web:* www.pnc.com/	Frederick	MD	21702	301-698-4603	695-3081*
PNC Bank 702 Russell Ave Suite 200 *TF Cust Svc:* 888-762-2265 ■ *Web:* www.pnc.com	Gaithersburg	MD	20877	301-963-7600	963-7683
PNC Bank 600 Grant St **Fax Area Code:* 202 ■ *TF:* 800-368-5800 ■ *Web:* www.pncbank.com	Pittsburgh	PA	15219	888-762-2265	835-5270*
PNC Bank Advisors NA 99 High St 27th Fl *TF:* 800-762-3374 ■ *Web:* www.pncadvisors.com	Boston	MA	02110	617-338-6030	338-6384
PNC Bank Delaware 300 Delaware Ave *TF:* 888-762-2265 ■ *Web:* www.pnc.com	Wilmington	DE	19801	302-429-1361	429-2872
PNC Bank NA 249 5th Ave 1 PNC Plaza *TF:* 888-762-2265 ■ *Web:* www.pncbank.com	Pittsburgh	PA	15222	412-762-2021	762-5798
Preferred Bank Los Angeles 601 S Figueroa St 20th Fl *NASDAQ: PFBC* ■ *TF:* 877-773-3663 ■ *Web:* www.preferredbank.com	Los Angeles	CA	90017	213-891-1188	622-0369
Presidential Online Bank 4520 East-West Hwy *TF:* 800-383-6266 ■ *Web:* www.presidential.com	Bethesda	MD	20814	301-652-0700	951-3582
Provident Bank 830 Bergen Ave **Fax Area Code:* 973 ■ *TF Cust Svc:* 800-448-7768 ■ *Web:* www.providentnj.com	Jersey City	NJ	07306	201-333-1000	748-7001*
Provident Bank 38 New Main St *Web:* www.providentbanking.com	Haverstraw	NY	10927	845-942-3880	942-3885
Provident Bank of Maryland 114 E Lexington St *TF:* 800-962-9644 ■ *Web:* www.provbank.com	Baltimore	MD	21202	410-281-7000	576-2747
Provident Savings Bank FSB 3756 Central Ave *TF:* 800-245-2217 ■ *Web:* www.myprovident.com	Riverside	CA	92506	951-686-6060	782-6157
Queens County Savings Bank 136-65 Roosevelt Ave **Fax:* Cust Svc ■ *Web:* www.mynycb.com	Flushing	NY	11354	718-460-4800	460-4844*
Rabo Bank 1026 Grand Ave PO Box 6002 *TF:* 800-473-7788 ■ *Web:* www.rabobankamerica.com	Arroyo Grande	CA	93421	805-473-7710	473-7751
RBC Financial Group 200 Bay St *NYSE: RY* ■ *TF:* 800-769-2599 ■ *Web:* www.rbc.com	Toronto	ON	M5J2J5	416-974-5151	974-6400
RBC Royal Bank 1 Liberty Plaza *TF:* 800-769-2540 ■ *Web:* www.royalbank.com	New York	NY	10006	212-428-6200	428-2304
RBC Royal Bank 1 pl Ville-Marie *Web:* www.royalbank.com	Montreal	QC	H3C3B5	800-769-2599	
Regions Bank 417 20th St N **Fax:* Hum Res ■ *TF:* 800-734-4667 ■ *Web:* www.regionsbank.com	Birmingham	AL	35202	205-326-7100	326-7756*
Regions Bank 1900 5th Ave N *TF:* 800-284-4100 ■ *Web:* www.regions.com	Birmingham	AL	35203	205-326-5300	320-7185
Renasant Bank 209 Troy St *TF:* 800-680-1601 ■ *Web:* www.renasantbank.com	Tupelo	MS	38804	662-680-1001	680-1234
Republic Bank & Trust Co 601 W Market St *TF:* 888-584-3600 ■ *Web:* www.republicbank.com	Louisville	KY	40202	502-584-3600	584-3753
Richmond County Savings Bank 1214 Castleton Ave *Web:* www.mynycb.com	Staten Island	NY	10310	718-448-2800	569-4238
Ridgewood Savings Bank 71-02 Forest Ave *TF:* 800-250-4832 ■ *Web:* www.ridgewoodbank.com	Ridgewood	NY	11385	718-240-4800	240-4877
Riverview Community Bank 315 SW 5th Ave Suite 201 *TF:* 800-822-2076 ■ *Web:* www.riverviewbank.com	Portland	OR	97204	503-221-5801	221-6242
Rockland Trust Co 288 Union St **Fax:* Hum Res ■ *TF:* 800-826-6100 ■ *Web:* www.rocklandtrust.com	Rockland	MA	02370	781-878-6100	982-6424*
Royal Bank America 732 Montgomery Ave *TF:* 800-417-5198 ■ *Web:* www.royalbankamerica.com	Narberth	PA	19072	610-668-4700	668-1185
Royal Bank of Canada 200 Bay St *NYSE: RY* ■ *TF:* 800-769-2599 ■ *Web:* www.rbc.com	Toronto	ON	M5J2J5	416-974-5151	974-6400
Royal Bank of Scotland 101 Park Ave 10th Fl *TF:* 800-741-9607 ■ *Web:* www.royalbankscot.co.uk	New York	NY	10178	212-401-3200	
S & T Bank 800 Philadelphia St *TF Cust Svc:* 800-325-2265 ■ *Web:* www.stbank.com	Indiana	PA	15701	724-349-1800	465-1417
Safra National Bank of New York 546 5th Ave *Web:* www.safra.com	New York	NY	10036	212-704-5500	704-5527
Salem Five & Savings Bank 210 Essex St *TF:* 800-322-2265 ■ *Web:* www.salemfive.com	Salem	MA	01970	978-745-5555	744-7941
San Diego National Bank 1420 Kettner Blvd *TF:* 888-724-7362 ■ *Web:* www.sdnb.com	San Diego	CA	92101	619-231-4989	233-7017
Sandy Spring National Bank of Maryland 17801 Georgia Ave *TF:* 800-399-5919 ■ *Web:* www.sandyspringbank.com	Olney	MD	20832	301-774-6400	260-0044
Santa Barbara Bank & Trust 20 E Carrillo St *TF Cust Svc:* 888-400-7228 ■ *Web:* www.sbbt.com	Santa Barbara	CA	93101	805-564-6300	564-6439
Scotiabank 1 Liberty Plaza 26th Fl *TF:* 800-472-6842 ■ *Web:* www.scotiabank.com	New York	NY	10006	212-225-5000	225-5090
Scotiabank 44 King St W *NYSE: BNS* ■ *TF:* 800-472-6842 ■ *Web:* www.scotiabank.ca	Toronto	ON	M5H1H1	416-866-6161	866-3750
Scotiabank de Puerto Rico 273 Ponce de Leon Ave *Web:* www.scotiabankpr.com	Hato Rey	PR	00936	787-758-8989	766-7879
Seaway Bank & Trust Co 645 E 87th St *Web:* www.seawaybank.us/	Chicago	IL	60619	773-487-4800	487-0452
Shizuoka Bank Ltd 600 Lexington Ave 4th Fl *Web:* www.shizuokabank.co.jp	New York	NY	10022	212-319-6260	319-6270
Signature Bank 565 5th Ave 12th Fl *NASDAQ: SBNY* ■ *TF:* 866-744-5463 ■ *Web:* www.signatureny.com	New York	NY	10017	646-822-1500	822-1447
Silicon Valley Bank 3003 Tasman Dr **Fax:* Mktg ■ *Web:* www.svb.com	Santa Clara	CA	95054	408-654-7400	654-6209*
Skandinaviska Enskilda Banken Corp 245 Park Ave 42nd Fl	New York	NY	10167	212-907-4700	370-1642
Societe Generale USA 1221 Ave of the Americas *TF:* 800-942-7575 ■ *Web:* www.sgcib.com	New York	NY	10020	212-278-6000	278-6789
Southwest Bank of Saint Louis 2301 S Kingshighway Blvd *TF:* 888-811-3196 ■ *Web:* www.mysouthwestbank.com	Saint Louis	MO	63110	314-776-5200	776-2146
Sovereign Bank FSB PO Box 12646 *TF Cust Svc:* 877-768-2265 ■ *Web:* www.sovereignbank.com	Reading	PA	19612	610-320-8400	208-6195
Spencer Savings Bank SLA 34 Outwater Ln *TF:* 800-363-8115 ■ *Web:* www.spencersavings.com	Garfield	NJ	07026	973-772-6700	772-2411
Standard Chartered Bank 1 Madison Ave *TF:* 800-269-3101 ■ *Web:* www.standardchartered.com	New York	NY	10010	212-667-0700	667-0770
State Farm Financial Services FSB PO Box 2316 *Web:* www.statefarm.com/bank/bank.htm	Bloomington	IL	61702	877-734-2265	
State Street Bank 200 Clarendon St *Web:* www.statestreet.com	Boston	MA	02116	617-330-6700	330-6033
State Street Corp 1 Lincoln St **Fax:* Mktg ■ *Web:* www.statestreet.com	Boston	MA	02111	617-786-3000	664-6316*
Sterling Bank 15000 Northwest Fwy *TF:* 888-777-8735 ■ *Web:* www.banksterling.com	Houston	TX	77040	713-466-8300	466-0765
Sterling Bank & Trust FSB 1 Town Sq 17th Fl *Web:* www.sterlingbank.com	Southfield	MI	48076	248-355-2400	355-3915
Sterling Savings Bank 111 N Wall St **Fax:* Hum Res ■ *TF:* 800-650-7141 ■ *Web:* www.sterlingsavingsbank.com	Spokane	WA	99201	509-624-4114	358-6161*
Stonebridge Bank PO Box 2425 *TF:* 800-807-1666 ■ *Web:* www.stonebridgebank.com	West Chester	PA	19380	610-280-4700	719-8225
Sumitomo Mitsui Banking Corp 277 Park Ave 6th Fl *Web:* www.smbcgroup.com	New York	NY	10172	212-224-4000	593-9522
Sumitomo Trust & Banking Co (USA) 111 River St *Web:* www.sumitomotrustusa.com	Hoboken	NJ	07030	201-595-8886	420-8596
Sun National Bank 226 Landis Ave *TF:* 800-691-7701 ■ *Web:* www.sunnb.com	Vineland	NJ	08360	856-691-7700	786-9066
SunTrust Bank 25 Park Pl NE **Fax:* Mktg ■ *TF:* 800-688-7878 ■ *Web:* www.suntrust.com	Atlanta	GA	30303	404-588-7230	724-3330*
Suntrust Bank PO Box 4418 **Fax Area Code:* 901 ■ *Web:* www.suntrust.com	Atlanta	GA	30302	800-786-8787	523-3310*
Susquehanna Bank 307 International Cir Suite 600 *TF:* 800-787-0020 ■ *Web:* www.susquehanna.net	Hunt Valley	MD	21030	410-316-0000	
Susquehanna Bank 26 N Cedar St *TF:* 800-311-3182 ■ *Web:* www.susquehanna.net	Lititz	PA	17543	717-626-4735	626-7318
Svenska Handelsbanken 875 3rd Ave 4th Fl *Web:* www.handelsbanken.se	New York	NY	10022	212-326-5100	326-5196
Swedbank 1 Penn Plaza 15th Fl *Web:* www.swedbank.com	New York	NY	10119	212-486-8400	486-3220
TCF National Bank 801 Marquette Ave **Fax:* Mktg ■ *TF:* 800-533-1723 ■ *Web:* www.tcfbank.com	Minneapolis	MN	55402	612-661-6500	661-8271*
TD Banknorth Massachusetts 295 Park Ave *TF Cust Svc:* 800-747-7000 ■ *Web:* www.tdbanknorth.com	Worcester	MA	01609	508-752-2584	751-8090
TD Canada Trust 161 Bay St 35th Fl *TF:* 866-222-3456 ■ *Web:* www.tdcanadatrust.com	Toronto	ON	M5J2T2	416-361-5400	361-5355
TD Waterhouse Bank NA 1 Harborside Financial Plaza 4A 8th Fl **Fax Area Code:* 201 ■ *Web:* www.tdwaterhouse.com/banking/welcome	Jersey City	NJ	07310	888-327-9962	369-8903*
Texas Capital Bank 6060 N Central Expy Suite 800 **Fax Area Code:* 877 ■ *TF:* 877-839-2265 ■ *Web:* www.texascapitalbank.com	Dallas	TX	75206	972-560-4501	839-2738*
Texas State Bank 3900 N 10th St *TF Cust Svc:* 877-546-9911 ■ *Web:* www.texasstatebank.com	McAllen	TX	78501	956-632-7693	631-7326
The Bank of New York Mellon Corp 500 Grant St 1 Mellon Ctr **Fax:* Cust Svc ■ *TF:* 800-635-5662 ■ *Web:* www.bnymellon.com	Pittsburgh	PA	15258	412-234-5000	236-4491*
Third Federal Savings Bank 3 Penns Trail *TF:* 800-786-5310 ■ *Web:* www.thirdfedbank.com	Newtown	PA	18940	215-579-4600	579-4748
Third Federal Savings & Loan Assn of Cleveland 7007 Broadway Ave *TF:* 888-844-7333 ■ *Web:* www.thirdfederal.com	Cleveland	OH	44105	216-441-6000	429-5096
TierOne Bank PO Box 83009 *TF:* 800-288-0722 ■ *Web:* www.tieronebank.com	Lincoln	NE	68501	402-475-0521	473-6242
Tompkins Trust Co 110 N Tioga St Ithaca Commons *AMEX: TMP* ■ *TF:* 888-273-3210 ■ *Web:* www.tompkinstrust.com	Ithaca	NY	14850	607-273-3210	277-6874
Toronto-Dominion Bank 55 King St W *NYSE: TD* ■ *Web:* www.td.com	Toronto	ON	M5K1A2	416-982-8222	944-6931
Trustco Bank NA 5 Sarnowski Dr *TF:* 800-670-3110 ■ *Web:* www.trustcobank.com	Glenville	NY	12302	518-377-3311	381-3630
Trustmark National Bank 248 E Capitol St **Fax:* Hum Res ■ *TF:* 800-844-2000 ■ *Web:* www.trustmark.com	Jackson	MS	39201	601-208-5111	208-6684*
UBS AG 299 Park Ave *TF:* 888-827-7275 ■ *Web:* www.ubs.com	New York	NY	10171	212-821-3000	821-3285
UMB Bank NA 1010 Grand Blvd *TF:* 800-821-2171 ■ *Web:* www.umb.com	Kansas City	MO	64106	816-860-7000	860-3589
Umpqua Bank 1 SW Columbia Suite 1200 *TF:* 866-486-7782 ■ *Web:* www.umpquabank.com	Portland	OR	97258	503-727-4100	546-2498
Union Bank of California NA 400 California St 1st Fl *TF:* 800-238-4486 ■ *Web:* www.uboc.com	San Francisco	CA	94104	415-765-3434	765-3507
Union Savings Bank 226 Main St *TF:* 800-860-6670 ■ *Web:* www.unionsavings.com	Danbury	CT	06810	203-830-4200	731-3168
Union Savings Bank 8534 E Kemper Rd *TF:* 800-582-9702 ■ *Web:* www.unionsavingsbank.com	Cincinnati	OH	45249	513-247-0300	247-9730
United Bank 11185 Main St *TF:* 800-724-3259 ■ *Web:* www.unitedbankdcmetro.com	Fairfax	VA	22030	703-219-4850	352-8730
United Commercial Bank 711 Van Ness Ave *TF:* 800-821-3899 ■ *Web:* www.ibankunited.com	San Francisco	CA	94102	415-929-6070	885-5248
United Overseas Bank Ltd 592 5th Ave 10th Fl *TF:* 800-222-2121 ■ *Web:* www.uob.com.sg	New York	NY	10036	212-382-0088	382-1881
United Security Bancshares 2126 Inyo St Dept 98 *NASDAQ: UBFO* ■ *TF:* 888-683-6030 ■ *Web:* www.unitedsecuritybank.com	Fresno	CA	93721	559-248-4943	320-1220
United Western Bank 700 17th St Suite 100 *TF:* 800-594-2079 ■ *Web:* www.uwbank.com	Denver	CO	80202	720-956-6500	956-6599
US Bank NA 800 Nicollet Mall *TF:* 800-872-2657 ■ *Web:* www.usbank.com	Minneapolis	MN	55402	651-466-3000	
US Bank NA 505 2nd Ave N *Web:* www.usbank.com	Fargo	ND	58102	701-280-3655	280-3532

Phone | Fax

USAA FSB 10750 McDermott Fwy — San Antonio TX 78288 — 210-498-2211 — 531-5717*
*Fax Area Code: 800 ■ TF: 800-531-8722 ■ Web: www.usaa.com

Valley National Bank 615 Main Ave — Passaic NJ 07055 — 973-777-6768 — 777-2785
TF: 800-522-4100 ■ Web: www.valleynationalbank.com

Vantus Bank 329 Pierce St — Sioux City IA 51101 — 712-277-0200 — 277-0224
TF: 800-352-4620 ■ Web: www.vantusbank.com

Vectra Bank Colorado NA 2000 S Colorado Blvd — Denver CO 80222 — 720-947-7500 — 947-7760
TF Cust Svc: 888-648-7850 ■ Web: www.vectrabank.com

Vineyard National Bancorp 9590 Foothill Blvd — Rancho Cucamonga CA 91730 — 909-987-0177 — 989-4554
NASDAQ: VNBC ■ TF: 888-665-2266 ■ Web: www.vineyardbank.com

VirtualBank
3801 PGA Blvd Suite 700 PO Box 109638 — Palm Beach Gardens FL 33410 — 561-776-8860 — 776-6378
TF: 877-998-2265 ■ Web: www.virtualbank.com

Wachovia Bank 301 S College St — Charlotte NC 28202 — 704-335-3878
TF: 800-922-4684 ■ Web: www.wachovia.com

Wachovia Bank NA
301 S College St Suite 4000 1 Wachovia Center — Charlotte NC 28288 — 704-374-6161
TF: 800-922-4684 ■ Web: www.wachovia.com

Wachovia Dealer Services 15750 Alton Pkwy — Irvine CA 92618 — 949-727-1000 — 727-2342
TF: 800-922-4684 ■ Web: www.wachoviadealer.com

Wainwright Bank & Trust Co 63 Franklin St — Boston MA 02110 — 617-478-4000 — 478-4010*
NASDAQ: WAIN ■ *Fax: Hum Res ■ TF: 800-444-2265 ■ Web: www.wainwrightbank.com

Washington Federal Savings & Loan Assn 425 Pike St — Seattle WA 98101 — 206-624-7930 — 624-2334*
*Fax: Hum Res ■ TF: 800-324-9375 ■ Web: www.washingtonfederal.com

Washington Mutual Bank 1301 2nd Ave — Seattle WA 98101 — 206-461-2000 — 461-5739
TF: 800-788-7000 ■ Web: www.wamu.com

Washington Mutual Bank FA 400 E Main St — Stockton CA 95202 — 209-460-2888 — 460-2531
TF Cust Svc: 800-788-7000 ■ Web: www.wamu.com

Washington Mutual Inc 1301 2nd Ave — Seattle WA 98101 — 206-461-2000
NYSE: WM ■ TF: 800-788-7000 ■ Web: www.wamu.com

Washington Savings Bank FSB 4201 Mitchellville Rd Suite 100 — Bowie MD 20716 — 301-352-3130 — 352-3110
AMEX: WSB ■ TF: 800-843-7250 ■ Web: www.twsb.com

Washington Trust Bank PO Box 2127 — Spokane WA 99210 — 509-353-3875 — 353-3836
TF: 800-788-4578 ■ Web: www.watrust.com

Wauwatosa Savings Bank 11200 W Plank Ct — Wauwatosa WI 53226 — 414-918-0500 — 918-0905
TF: 888-686-7272 ■ Web: www.wsbonline.com

Webster Bank 145 Bank St Webster Plaza — Waterbury CT 06702 — 203-578-2200 — 753-6511*
*Fax: Mktg ■ TF: 800-325-2424 ■ Web: www.websterbank.com

Wells Fargo Alaska PO Box 196127 — Anchorage AK 99519 — 907-276-1132 — 265-2068
TF: 800-411-4932 ■ Web: www.wellsfargo.com

Wells Fargo Bank 5622 3rd St — Katy TX 77493 — 281-391-2101 — 391-1338
TF: 800-869-3557 ■ Web: www.wellsfargo.com

Wells Fargo Bank Indiana NA 111 E Wayne St — Fort Wayne IN 46802 — 260-461-6401 — 461-6709
TF: 800-869-3557 ■ Web: www.wellsfargo.com

Wells Fargo Bank Iowa NA 666 Walnut St PO Box 837 — Des Moines IA 50309 — 515-245-3071 — 245-8118*
*Fax: Cust Svc ■ TF: 800-869-3557 ■ Web: www.wellsfargo.com

Wells Fargo Bank Minnesota South NA 21 1st St SW — Rochester MN 55902 — 507-285-2800 — 285-2974*
*Fax: Hum Res ■ TF: 800-869-3557 ■ Web: www.wellsfargo.com

Wells Fargo Bank Montana NA 175 N 27th St — Billings MT 59101 — 406-657-1903 — 657-3624
TF: 888-809-3557 ■ Web: www.wellsfargo.com

Wells Fargo Bank NA 420 Montgomery St — San Francisco CA 94104 — 415-396-3053 — 397-2987
TF: 800-869-3557 ■ Web: www.wellsfargo.com

Wells Fargo Bank Nebraska NA 1919 Douglas St — Omaha NE 68102 — 402-536-2022 — 536-2317
TF: 800-869-3557 ■ Web: www.wellsfargo.com

Wells Fargo Bank North Dakota NA 406 Main Ave — Fargo ND 58126 — 701-293-4200 — 280-8821
TF: 800-869-3557 ■ Web: www.wellsfargo.com

Wells Fargo Bank South Dakota NA 101 N Phillips Ave — Sioux Falls SD 57104 — 605-575-6900 — 575-6060
TF: 800-869-3557 ■ Web: www.wellsfargo.com

Wells Fargo Bank Texas NA 40 NE Loop 410 — San Antonio TX 78216 — 210-856-5000 — 856-5038
TF: 800-869-3557 ■ Web: www.wellsfargo.com

Wells Fargo Bank West NA 1740 Broadway — Denver CO 80274 — 303-861-8811 — 863-4605
TF: 800-444-4823 ■ Web: www.wellsfargo.com

Wells Fargo Bank Wisconsin NA 735 W Wisconsin Ave — Milwaukee WI 53233 — 414-224-4429 — 224-4110
TF: 800-869-3557 ■ Web: www.wellsfargo.com

Wells Fargo Bank Wyoming NA 234 E 1st St — Casper WY 82601 — 307-235-7630 — 235-7626
Web: www.wellsfargo.com

WesBanco Bank Inc 1 Bank Plaza — Wheeling WV 26003 — 304-234-9000 — 234-9298
TF: 800-328-3369 ■ Web: www.wesbanco.com/bank/index.htm

West Coast Bank 506 SW Coast Hwy — Newport OR 97365 — 541-265-6666 — 265-8656
TF Cust Svc: 800-895-3345 ■ Web: www.westcoastbancorp.com

West Suburban Bank 711 S Westmore Ave — Lombard IL 60148 — 630-629-4200 — 629-0278
Web: www.westsuburbanbank.com

Westamerica Bank 4560 Mangels Blvd — Fairfield CA 94534 — 707-863-6113 — 863-6065
TF: 800-848-1088 ■ Web: www.westamerica.com

Western Security Bank 2812 1st Ave N — Billings MT 59101 — 406-238-8100 — 371-8225
TF: 800-366-5120 ■ Web: www.westernsecuritybank.com

Westernbank Puerto Rico PO Box 1180 — Mayaguez PR 00681 — 787-834-8000 — 831-5958
Web: www.wbpr.com

Westpac Banking Corp Americas Div 575 5th Ave 39th Fl — New York NY 10017 — 212-551-1800 — 551-1999
TF: 800-937-8722 ■ Web: www.westpac.com.au

Whitney National Bank 228 St Charles Ave — New Orleans LA 70130 — 504-586-7272 — 586-7383
TF: 800-347-7272 ■ Web: www.whitneybank.com

Wilmington Savings Fund Society FSB 838 N Market St — Wilmington DE 19801 — 302-792-6000 — 792-6198
TF: 800-292-9594 ■ Web: www.wsfsbank.com

Wilmington Trust Co 1100 N Market St — Wilmington DE 19890 — 302-651-1000 — 651-8937*
*Fax: Hum Res ■ TF: 800-441-7120 ■ Web: www.wilmingtontrust.com

Wilshire State Bank 3200 Wilshire Blvd — Los Angeles CA 90010 — 213-387-3200 — 427-6562*
*Fax: Cust Svc ■ Web: www.wilshirebank.com

World Savings Bank FSB 11601 Wilshire Blvd — Los Angeles CA 90025 — 310-477-8004 — 477-7324
TF: 866-467-3776 ■ Web: www.worldsavings.com

WSFS Bank 838 N Market St — Wilmington DE 19801 — 302-792-6000 — 792-6198
TF: 800-292-9594 ■ Web: www.wsfsbank.com

Yadkin Valley Bank & Trust Co 209 N Bridge St PO Box 888 — Elkin NC 28621 — 336-526-6312 — 835-8858
NASDAQ: YAVY ■ Web: www.yadkinvalleybank.com

Yakima Federal Savings & Loan Assn 118 E Yakima Ave — Yakima WA 98901 — 509-248-2634 — 575-8405
TF: 800-331-3225 ■ Web: www.yakimafed.com

Yardville National Bank 2465 Kuser Rd — Hamilton NJ 08690 — 609-585-5100
TF: 800-548-9545 ■ Web: www.yanb.com

Zions First National Bank 1 S Main St — Salt Lake City UT 84111 — 801-524-4711 — 524-4914
TF: 800-974-8800 ■ Web: www.zionsbank.com

71 BANKS - FEDERAL RESERVE

Phone | Fax

Federal Reserve System 20th & C St — Washington DC 20551 — 202-452-3000 — 452-3819
Web: www.federalreserve.gov

Federal Reserve Bank of Atlanta 1000 Peachtree St NE — Atlanta GA 30309 — 404-498-8500 — 498-8550*
*Fax: PR ■ TF: 877-521-8500 ■ Web: www.frbatlanta.org
Birmingham Branch 524 Liberty Pkwy — Birmingham AL 35242 — 205-968-6700 — 968-6175
TF: 877-658-6700
Jacksonville Branch PO Box 929 — Jacksonville FL 32204 — 904-632-1000
Miami Branch 9100 NW 36th St — Miami FL 33178 — 305-591-2065 — 471-6240
Nashville Branch 301 8th Ave N — Nashville TN 37203 — 615-251-7100 — 251-7189
New Orleans Branch 525 St Charles Ave — New Orleans LA 70130 — 504-593-3200 — 593-3213
TF: 800-562-9023

Federal Reserve Bank of Boston 600 Atlantic Ave — Boston MA 02210 — 617-973-3000 — 973-3487
Web: www.bos.frb.org

Federal Reserve Bank of Chicago 230 S LaSalle St — Chicago IL 60604 — 312-322-5322 — 322-5091
Web: www.chicagofed.org
Des Moines Branch 2200 Rittenhouse St Suite 150 — Des Moines IA 50321 — 515-256-6100 — 256-6116
Detroit Branch 160 W Fort St — Detroit MI 48226 — 313-961-6880

Federal Reserve Bank of Cleveland
1455 E 6th St PO Box 6387 — Cleveland OH 44101 — 216-579-2000 — 579-3172
TF: 888-333-2538 ■ Web: www.clevelandfed.org
Cincinnati Branch 150 E 4th St — Cincinnati OH 43202 — 513-721-4787 — 455-4583
TF: 800-432-1343
Pittsburgh Branch 717 Grant St PO Box 867 — Pittsburgh PA 15219 — 412-261-7800
TF: 888-333-7488

Federal Reserve Bank of Dallas 2200 N Pearl St PO Box 655906 — Dallas TX 75265 — 214-922-6000 — 922-5268
TF: 800-333-4460 ■ Web: www.dallasfed.org
El Paso Branch 301 E Main St — El Paso TX 79901 — 915-521-5200 — 521-8284
Web: www.dallasfed.org
Houston Branch 1801 Allen Pkwy — Houston TX 77019 — 713-659-4433 — 483-3638
TF: 800-392-4162 ■ Web: www.houstonfed.org
San Antonio Branch 126 E Nueva St — San Antonio TX 78204 — 210-978-1200 — 978-1407
Web: www.dallasfed.org

Federal Reserve Bank of Kansas City 925 Grand Blvd — Kansas City MO 64198 — 816-881-2000 — 881-2846
TF: 800-333-1010 ■ Web: www.kc.frb.org
Denver Branch 1020 16th St — Denver CO 80202 — 303-572-2300 — 572-2491
TF: 800-333-1020
Oklahoma City Branch 226 Dean A McGee Ave — Oklahoma City OK 73102 — 405-270-8400 — 270-8676
TF: 800-333-1030
Omaha Branch 2201 Farnam St — Omaha NE 68102 — 402-221-5500 — 221-5715
TF: 800-333-1040

Federal Reserve Bank of Minneapolis 90 Hennepin Ave — Minneapolis MN 55401 — 612-204-5000 — 204-5339
TF: 800-553-9656 ■ Web: www.minneapolisfed.org
Helena Branch 100 Neill Ave — Helena MT 59601 — 406-447-3800 — 447-3808

Federal Reserve Bank of New York 33 Liberty St — New York NY 10045 — 212-720-5000 — 720-5780
Web: www.newyorkfed.org
Buffalo Branch 40 Fountain Plaza Suite 650 — Buffalo NY 14202 — 716-849-5000 — 849-5021
TF: 800-234-2931

Federal Reserve Bank of Philadelphia
10 Independence Mall — Philadelphia PA 19106 — 215-574-6000 — 574-6034
Web: www.phil.frb.org

Federal Reserve Bank of Richmond 701 E Byrd St — Richmond VA 23219 — 804-697-8000
Web: www.richmondfed.org
Baltimore Branch 502 S Sharp St — Baltimore MD 21201 — 410-576-3300 — 576-3353
Charlotte Branch 530 E Trade St — Charlotte NC 28202 — 704-358-2100 — 358-2486

Federal Reserve Bank of Saint Louis 1421 Dr ML King Dr — Saint Louis MO 63106 — 314-444-8444 — 444-8430
TF: 800-333-0810 ■ Web: www.stlouisfed.org
Little Rock Branch
111 Center St Suite 1000 Stephens Bldg — Little Rock AR 72201 — 501-324-8300 — 324-8201
TF: 800-332-0813 ■ Web: www.stlouisfed.org
Louisville Branch 101 S 5th St Suite 1920 — Louisville KY 40202 — 502-568-9200 — 568-9247
Web: www.stlouisfed.org
Memphis Branch 200 N Main St PO Box 407 — Memphis TN 38101 — 901-523-7171 — 579-2406

Federal Reserve Bank of San Francisco
101 Market St PO Box 7702 — San Francisco CA 94105 — 415-974-2000 — 974-3340
TF: 800-227-4133 ■ Web: www.frbsf.org
Los Angeles Branch 950 S Grand Ave — Los Angeles CA 90015 — 213-683-2300 — 683-2488
Portland Branch 1500 SW 1st Ave Suite 100 — Portland OR 97201 — 503-276-3000 — 276-3002
Salt Lake City Branch 120 S State St — Salt Lake City UT 84111 — 801-322-7900 — 322-7845
Seattle Branch 1015 2nd Ave PO Box 3567 — Seattle WA 98104 — 206-343-3600 — 343-3822
TF: 800-227-4133

72 BAR ASSOCIATIONS - STATE

SEE ALSO Associations & Organizations - Professional & Trade - Legal Professionals Associations p. 1332

Phone | Fax

Alabama 415 Dexter Ave — Montgomery AL 36104 — 334-269-1515 — 261-6310
Web: www.alabar.org

Alaska 550 W 7th Ave Suite 1900 — Anchorage AK 99501 — 907-272-7469 — 272-2932
Web: www.alaskabar.org

Arizona 4201 N 24th St Suite 200 — Phoenix AZ 85016 — 602-252-4804 — 271-4930
TF: 866-482-9227 ■ Web: www.azbar.org

Arkansas 400 W Markham St — Little Rock AR 72201 — 501-375-4606 — 375-4901
Web: www.arkbar.com

California 180 Howard St — San Francisco CA 94105 — 415-538-2000 — 538-2304
Web: www.calbar.org

Colorado 1900 Grant St Suite 900 — Denver CO 80203 — 303-860-1115 — 894-0821
Web: www.cobar.org

Connecticut 30 Bank St — New Britain CT 06051 — 860-223-4400 — 223-4488
Web: www.ctbar.org

Delaware 301 N Market St — Wilmington DE 19801 — 302-658-5279 — 658-5212
Web: www.dsba.org

District of Columbia 1250 H St NW 6th Fl — Washington DC 20005 — 202-737-4700 — 626-3471
TF: 877-333-2227 ■ Web: www.dcbar.org

Florida 651 E Jefferson St — Tallahassee FL 32399 — 850-561-5600 — 561-1141
TF: 800-342-8060 ■ Web: www.flabar.org

Georgia 104 Marietta St NW Suite 100 — Atlanta GA 30303 — 404-527-8700 — 527-8717
TF: 800-334-6865 ■ Web: www.gabar.org

Hawaii 1132 Bishop St Suite 906 — Honolulu HI 96813 — 808-537-1868 — 521-7936
Web: hsba.org

Idaho 525 W Jefferson — Boise ID 83702 — 208-334-4500 — 334-4515
TF: 800-221-3295 ■ Web: www2.state.id.us/isb

Illinois 424 S 2nd St Illinois Bar Ctr — Springfield IL 62701 — 217-525-1760 — 525-0712
Web: www.illinoisbar.org

Indiana 1 Indiana Sq Suite 530 — Indianapolis IN 46204 — 317-639-5465 — 266-2588
TF: 800-266-2581 ■ Web: www.inbar.org

Iowa 521 E Locust St 3rd Fl — Des Moines IA 50309 — 515-243-3179 — 243-2511
Web: www.iowabar.org

Kansas 1200 SW Harrison St — Topeka KS 66612 — 785-234-5696 — 234-3813
Web: www.ksbar.org

Kentucky 514 W Main St — Frankfort KY 40601 — 502-564-3795 — 564-3225
Web: www.kybar.org

Louisiana 601 St Charles Ave — New Orleans LA 70130 — 504-566-1600 — 566-0930
TF: 800-421-5722 ■ Web: www.lsba.org

Maine 124 State St — Augusta ME 04330 — 207-622-7523 — 623-0083
TF: 800-475-7523 ■ Web: www.mainebar.org

Maryland 520 W Fayette St — Baltimore MD 21201 — 410-685-7878 — 685-1016
TF: 800-492-1964 ■ Web: www.msba.org

Massachusetts 20 West St — Boston MA 02111 — 617-338-0500 — 338-0650
TF: 866-627-7577 ■ Web: www.massbar.org

	City	State	Zip	Phone	Fax
Michigan 306 Townsend St *TF:* 800-968-1442 ■ *Web:* www.michbar.org	Lansing	MI	48933	517-372-9030	482-6248
Minnesota 600 Nicollet Mall Suite 380 *TF:* 800-882-6722 ■ *Web:* www.mnbar.org	Minneapolis	MN	55402	612-333-1183	333-4927
Mississippi 643 N State St *Web:* www.msbar.org	Jackson	MS	39202	601-948-4471	355-8635
Missouri 326 Monroe St *Web:* www.mobar.org	Jefferson City	MO	65101	573-635-4128	635-2811
Montana PO Box 577 *Web:* www.montanabar.org	Helena	MT	59624	406-442-7660	442-7763
Nebraska 635 S 14th St *TF:* 800-927-0117 ■ *Web:* www.nebar.com	Lincoln	NE	68501	402-475-7091	475-7098
Nevada 600 E Charleston Blvd *TF:* 800-254-2797 ■ *Web:* www.nvbar.org	Las Vegas	NV	89104	702-382-2200	385-2878
New Hampshire 112 Pleasant St *Web:* www.nhbar.org	Concord	NH	03301	603-224-6942	224-2910
New Jersey 1 Constitution Sq New Jersey Law Ctr *Web:* www.njsba.com	New Brunswick	NJ	08901	732-249-5000	249-2815
New Mexico 5121 Masthead St NE *TF:* 800-876-6227 ■ *Web:* www.nmbar.org	Albuquerque	NM	87109	505-797-6000	828-3765
New York 1 Elk St *TF:* 800-342-3661 ■ *Web:* www.nysba.org	Albany	NY	12207	518-463-3200	463-4276
North Carolina 208 Fayetteville St Mall *TF:* 800-662-7407 ■ *Web:* www.ncbar.com	Raleigh	NC	27601	919-828-4620	821-9168
North Dakota PO Box 2136 *Web:* www.sband.org	Bismarck	ND	58502	701-255-1404	224-1621
Ohio 1700 Lake Shore Dr *TF:* 800-282-6556 ■ *Web:* www.ohiobar.org	Columbus	OH	43204	614-487-2050	487-1008
Oklahoma PO Box 53036 *TF:* 800-522-8065 ■ *Web:* www.okbar.org	Oklahoma City	OK	73152	405-416-7000	416-7001
Oregon 5200 SW Meadows Rd *Web:* www.osbar.org	Lake Oswego	OR	97035	503-620-0222	684-1366
Pennsylvania 100 South St *TF:* 800-932-0311 ■ *Web:* www.pabar.org	Harrisburg	PA	17101	717-238-6715	238-1204
Puerto Rico Apartado 9021900	San Juan	PR	00902	787-721-3358	725-0330
Rhode Island 115 Cedar St *Web:* www.ribar.com	Providence	RI	02903	401-421-5740	421-2703
South Carolina 950 Taylor St *Web:* www.scbar.org	Columbia	SC	29202	803-799-6653	799-4118
South Dakota 222 E Capitol Ave *Web:* www.sdbar.org	Pierre	SD	57501	605-224-7554	224-0282
Tennessee 221 4th Ave N Suite 400 *TF:* 800-899-6993 ■ *Web:* www.tba.org	Nashville	TN	37219	615-383-7421	297-8058
Texas 1414 Colorado St *TF:* 800-204-2222 ■ *Web:* www.texasbar.com	Austin	TX	78701	512-463-1463	463-1475
Utah 645 S 200 East Suite 310 *Web:* www.utahbar.org	Salt Lake City	UT	84111	801-531-9077	531-0660
Vermont 35-37 Court St *Web:* www.vtbar.org	Montpelier	VT	05602	802-223-2020	223-1573
Virginia 707 E Main St Suite 1500 *Web:* www.vsb.org	Richmond	VA	23219	804-775-0500	775-0501
Washington 1325 4th Ave Suite 400 *TF:* 800-945-9722 ■ *Web:* www.wsba.org	Seattle	WA	98101	206-727-8200	727-8320
West Virginia 2006 Kanawha Blvd E *Web:* www.wvbar.org	Charleston	WV	25311	304-558-2456	558-2467
Wisconsin 5302 Eastpark Blvd *TF:* 800-728-7788 ■ *Web:* www.wisbar.org	Madison	WI	53718	608-257-3838	257-5502
Wyoming 500 Randall Ave *Web:* www.wyomingbar.org	Cheyenne	WY	82001	307-632-9061	632-3737

73 BASKETS, CAGES, RACKS, ETC - WIRE

SEE ALSO Pet Products p. 2106

	City	State	Zip	Phone	Fax
Adrian Fabricators Inc Cargotainer Div PO Box 518 *TF:* 800-221-3794 ■ *Web:* www.cargotainer.com	Adrian	MI	49221	517-266-5700	266-5751
Apco Products Inc PO Box 236 *Web:* www.apco-products.com	Essex	CT	06426	860-767-2108	767-7259
Archer Wire International Corp 7300 S Narragansett Ave *Web:* www.archerwire.com	Bedford Park	IL	60638	708-563-1700	563-1740
Bright Coop Inc 803 W Seale St *TF:* 800-562-0730 ■ *Web:* www.brightcoop.com	Nacogdoches	TX	75964	936-564-8378	564-3281
Cargotainer Div Adrian Fabricators PO Box 518 *TF:* 800-221-3794 ■ *Web:* www.cargotainer.com	Adrian	MI	49221	517-266-5700	266-5751
Equipment Fabricating Corp 729 45th Ave *Web:* www.equipmentfabricating.com	Oakland	CA	94601	510-261-0343	261-0715
Glamos Wire Products Co Inc 5561 N 152nd St *TF:* 800-428-6353 ■ *Web:* www.glamoswire.com	Hugo	MN	55038	651-429-5386	429-7733
InterMetro Industries Corp 651 N Washington St **Fax:* Hum Res ■ *TF Cust Svc:* 800-992-1776 ■ *Web:* www.metro.com	Wilkes-Barre	PA	18705	570-825-2741	824-7520*
Kaspar Wire Works Inc PO Box 667 *TF:* 800-337-0610 ■ *Web:* www.kwire.com/wirewrk.htm	Shiner	TX	77984	361-594-3327	594-3311
Kewanna Metal Specialties Inc (KMS) PO Box 367 *Web:* www.kmswire.com	Kewanna	IN	46939	574-653-2554	653-2556
Lab Products Inc 742 Sussex Ave *TF:* 800-526-0469 ■ *Web:* www.labproductsinc.com	Seaford	DE	19973	302-628-4300	628-4309
Marlboro Wire Ltd PO Box 5058 *Web:* www.marlborowire.com	Quincy	IL	62305	217-224-7989	224-7990
Midwest Wire Products Inc 800 Woodward Heights *TF:* 800-989-9881 ■ *Web:* www.midwestwire.com	Ferndale	MI	48220	248-399-5100	542-7104
Nashville Wire Products Mfg Co 199 Polk Ave *TF:* 888-743-2595 ■ *Web:* www.nashvillewire.com	Nashville	TN	37210	615-743-2500	242-4225
Nestaway 9501 Granger Rd *Web:* www.nestawaywire.com	Cleveland	OH	44125	216-587-1500	587-2774
Progress Wire Products Inc 3535 W 140th St *Web:* www.progresswire.com	Cleveland	OH	44111	216-251-2181	251-2699
Stevens Wire Products Inc 351 NW 'F' St PO Box 1146 *Web:* www.stevenswire.com	Richmond	IN	47375	765-966-5534	962-3586
Technibilt Corp PO Box 310 *TF Cust Svc:* 800-351-2278 ■ *Web:* www.technibilt.com	Newton	NC	28658	828-464-7388	464-7603
Tote Cart Co Inc 1802 Preston St *TF:* 800-435-5709 ■ *Web:* www.totecart.com	Rockford	IL	61102	815-963-3414	963-3892
Unarco Industries Inc 400 SE 15th St *Web:* www.unarco.com	Wagoner	OK	74467	918-485-9531	485-3853
United Steel & Wire Co 4909 Wayne Rd *TF:* 800-227-7887 ■ *Web:* www.unitedsteelandwire.com	Battle Creek	MI	49015	269-962-5571	962-5577
Wirefab Inc 75 Blackstone River Rd *TF Sales:* 877-877-4445 ■ *Web:* www.wirefab.com	Worcester	MA	01607	508-754-5359	797-3620

74 BATTERIES

	City	State	Zip	Phone	Fax
Atlantic Battery Co Inc 80 Elm St *TF:* 800-924-2450	Watertown	MA	02472	617-924-2868	924-5200
Bren-Tronics Inc 10 Brayton Ct *Web:* www.bren-tronics.com	Commack	NY	11725	631-499-5155	499-5504
C & D Technologies Inc 1400 Union Meeting Rd PO Box 3053 *NYSE: CHP* ■ *TF:* 800-543-8630 ■ *Web:* www.cdtechno.com	Blue Bell	PA	19422	215-619-2700	619-7840
Continental Battery Corp 4919 Woodall St *TF:* 800-442-0081 ■ *Web:* www.continentalbattery.com	Dallas	TX	75247	214-631-5701	634-7846
Crown Battery Mfg Co 1445 Majestic Dr *TF:* 800-487-2879 ■ *Web:* www.crownbattery.com	Fremont	OH	43420	419-334-7181	334-7416
Douglas Battery Mfg Co 500 Battery Dr **Fax:* Hum Res ■ *TF:* 800-368-4527 ■ *Web:* www.douglasbattery.com	Winston-Salem	NC	27107	336-650-7000	650-7057*
Duracell 14 Research Dr Berkshire Corporate Park *TF:* 800-243-9540 ■ *Web:* www.duracell.com	Bethel	CT	06801	203-796-4000	796-4483
Eagle-Picher Industries Inc 2424 John Daly Rd *Web:* www.epcorp.com	Inkster	MI	48141	313-278-5956	278-5982
Eagle-Picher Technologies LLC 1261 West C St **Fax:* Sales ■ *Web:* www.eaglepicher.com/EaglePicherInternet/Technologies	Joplin	MO	64801	417-623-8000	623-0850*
East Penn Mfg Co Inc PO Box 147 *Web:* www.eastpenn-deka.com	Lyon Station	PA	19536	610-682-6361	682-4781
Ener1 Inc 500 W Cypress Creek Rd Suite 100 *Web:* www.ener1.com	Fort Lauderdale	FL	33309	954-556-4020	556-4031
Energizer Holdings Inc 533 Maryville University Dr *NYSE: ENR* ■ *TF:* 800-383-7323 ■ *Web:* www.energizer.com	Saint Louis	MO	63141	314-985-2000	985-2200
EnerSys 2366 Bernville Rd *NYSE: ENS* ■ *TF:* 800-538-3627 ■ *Web:* www.enersysinc.com	Reading	PA	19605	610-208-1991	372-8457
EnerSys Inc 617 N Ridgeview Dr *Web:* www.enersysreservepower.com	Warrensburg	MO	64093	660-429-2165	429-2253
Exide Technologies 13000 Deerfield Pkwy *NASDAQ: XIDE* ■ *TF:* 866-289-0645 ■ *Web:* www.exideworld.com	Atlanta	GA	30004	678-566-9000	566-9680
Johnson Controls Inc 5757 N Green Bay Ave *NYSE: JCI* ■ *TF:* 800-972-8040 ■ *Web:* www.johnsoncontrols.com	Milwaukee	WI	53209	414-524-1200	524-3232
Keystone Battery Corp 35 Holton St *Web:* www.keystonebattery.com	Winchester	MA	01890	781-729-8333	721-0127
MarathonNorco Aerospace Inc 8301 Imperial Dr *Web:* www.mnaerospace.com	Waco	TX	76712	254-776-0650	776-6558
Medis Technologies Ltd 805 3rd Ave 15th Fl *NASDAQ: MDTL* ■ *Web:* www.medisel.com	New York	NY	10022	212-935-8484	935-9216
Medtronic Energy & Component Center (MECC) 6700 Shingle Creek Pkwy *TF:* 800-328-2518	Brooklyn Center	MN	55430	763-514-1000	514-1170
Millennium Cell Inc 1 Industrial Way W Bldg E *NASDAQ: MCEL* ■ *TF:* 866-532-2783 ■ *Web:* www.millenniumcell.com	Eatontown	NJ	07724	732-542-4000	542-4010
Power Battery Co Inc 25 McLean Blvd **Fax:* Sales ■ *TF:* 800-783-7697 ■ *Web:* www.powbat.com	Paterson	NJ	07514	973-523-8630	523-3023*
Powersafe Standby Batteries 444 Foxon Rd *TF:* 800-538-3677	East Haven	CT	06512	203-777-0037	773-1010
Reaco Battery Service Corp 17217 Rt 37 *TF:* 800-957-3226	Johnston City	IL	62951	618-983-5441	983-8888
Seiko Instruments USA Inc Electronic Components Div 2990 Lomita Blvd *Web:* www.siielectroniccomponents.com	Torrance	CA	90505	310-517-7771	517-7709
Spectrum Brands Inc 601 Rayovac Dr *NYSE: SPC* ■ *TF:* 800-237-7000 ■ *Web:* www.rayovac.com	Madison	WI	53711	608-275-3340	275-4577
Staab Battery Mfg Co 931 S 11th St *Web:* www.staabbattery.com	Springfield	IL	62703	217-528-0421	
Tadiran Batteries 2 Seaview Blvd Suite 102 *TF:* 800-537-1368 ■ *Web:* www.tadiranbat.com	Port Washington	NY	11050	516-621-4980	621-4517
TNR Technical Inc 301 Central Park Dr *TF:* 800-346-0601 ■ *Web:* www.batterystore.com	Sanford	FL	32771	407-321-3011	321-3208
Trojan Battery Co 12380 Clark St *TF Cust Svc:* 800-423-6569 ■ *Web:* www.trojanbattery.com	Santa Fe Springs	CA	90670	562-946-8381	946-9061
Ultralife Batteries Inc 2000 Technology Pkwy *NASDAQ: ULBI* ■ *TF:* 800-332-5000 ■ *Web:* www.ulbi.com	Newark	NY	14513	315-332-7100	331-7800
US Battery Mfg Corp 1675 Sampson Ave *TF:* 800-695-0945 ■ *Web:* www.usbattery.com	Corona	CA	92879	951-371-8090	371-4671
Valence Technology Inc 12201 Technology Blvd Suite 150 *NASDAQ: VLNC* ■ *TF:* 888-825-3623 ■ *Web:* www.valence-tech.com	Austin	TX	78727	512-527-2900	527-2910
Voltmaster Co Inc 2185 Hwy 2 PO Box 288	Corydon	IA	50060	641-872-2011	872-2661
Yardney Technical Products Inc 82 Mechanic St *Web:* www.yardney.com/yardney	Pawcatuck	CT	06379	860-599-1100	599-3903

75 BEARINGS - BALL & ROLLER

	City	State	Zip	Phone	Fax
Accurate Bushing Co Inc 443 North Ave *TF Sales:* 800-932-0076 ■ *Web:* www.smithbearing.com	Garwood	NJ	07027	908-789-1121	789-9429
Aetna Bearing Co 4600 W Schubert Ave **Fax:* Sales ■ *Web:* www.aetnabearing.com	Chicago	IL	60639	773-227-2410	227-2640*
Alinabal Inc 28 Woodmont Rd *TF:* 800-254-6763 ■ *Web:* www.alinabal.com	Milford	CT	06460	203-877-3241	874-5063
American Roller Bearing Co 150 Gamma Dr *Web:* www.amroll.com	Pittsburgh	PA	15238	412-781-1190	963-0616
AST Bearings 115 Main Rd *TF:* 800-526-1250 ■ *Web:* www.astbearings.com	Montville	NJ	07045	973-335-2230	335-6987
Axsys Technologies Inc 175 Capital Blvd Suite 103 *NASDAQ: AXYS* ■ *Web:* www.axsys.com	Rocky Hill	CT	06067	860-257-0200	594-5750
Barnes Engineering Co 2715 Delta Pl *TF:* 800-995-6050 ■ *Web:* www.slimtrack.com	Colorado Springs	CO	80910	719-390-6500	390-6700
Bearing Inspection Inc 4422 Corporate Ctr Dr *TF:* 800-416-8881 ■ *Web:* www.bearinginspect.com	Los Alamitos	CA	90720	714-484-2400	484-2428
Bearing Service Co of Pennsylvania 630 Alpha Dr CIDC Industrial Park *TF:* 800-783-2327 ■ *Web:* www.bearing-service.com	Pittsburgh	PA	15238	412-963-7710	963-8005
Berliss Bearing Co 644 Rt 10 *Web:* www.berliss.com	Livingston	NJ	07039	973-992-4242	992-6669
Brenco Inc 2580 Frontage Rd PO Box 389 *TF:* 800-238-4712 ■ *Web:* www.brencoqbs.com	Petersburg	VA	23804	804-732-0202	861-6989
C & S Engineering Corp 956 Old Colony Rd	Meriden	CT	06451	203-235-5727	237-7498
Carolina Forge PO Box 370 *Web:* home.carolinaforgeco.com/nucorbearing/	Wilson	NC	27894	252-237-8181	237-2777
Emerson Power Transmission McGill Mfg Div 909 N Lafayette St	Valparaiso	IN	46383	219-465-2200	465-2290
FAG Bearings Corp 200 Park Ave *TF:* 800-243-7512	Danbury	CT	06810	203-790-5474	830-8168
Freeway Corp 9301 Allen Dr **Fax:* Sales ■ *Web:* www.freewaycorp.com	Cleveland	OH	44125	216-524-9700	524-7396*
Gear Products Inc 1111 N 161st East Ave *Web:* www.gearproducts.com	Tulsa	OK	74116	918-234-3044	234-3455

Company	City	State	Zip	Phone	Fax
General Bearing Corp 44 High St	West Nyack	NY	10994	845-358-6000	358-6277
TF Sales: 800-431-1766 ■ *Web:* www.generalbearing.com					
Hartford Technologies 1022 Elm St	Rocky Hill	CT	06067	860-571-3601	571-3609
TF: 888-840-9565 ■ *Web:* www.hartfordtechnologies.com					
INA USA Corp 308 Springhill Farm Rd	Fort Mill	SC	29715	803-548-8500	548-8599
Web: www.ina.com/us					
Industrial Tectonics Bearings Corp					
18301 S Santa Fe Ave	Rancho Dominguez	CA	90221	310-537-3750	537-2909
TF: 800-654-2597 ■ *Web:* www.rbcbearings.com					
Ingersoll-Rand Co 155 Chestnut Ridge Rd	Montvale	NJ	07645	201-573-0123	573-3172
NYSE: IR ■ *Web:* www.irco.com					
Kaydon Corp 315 E Eisenhower Pkwy Suite 300	Ann Arbor	MI	48108	734-747-7025	747-6565
NYSE: KDN ■ *Web:* www.kaydon.com					
Kilian Mfg Corp PO Box 6974	Syracuse	NY	13217	315-432-0700	432-1312
Koyo Corp of USA 29570 Clemens Rd	Westlake	OH	44145	440-835-1000	835-9347
TF: 800-321-3102 ■ *Web:* www.koyousa.com					
LSB Industries Inc 16 S Pennsylvania Ave	Oklahoma City	OK	73107	405-235-4546	235-5067
AMEX: LXU ■ *Web:* www.lsb-okc.com					
Lutco Bearings Inc 130 Higgins St	Worcester	MA	01606	508-853-2114	853-1105
Lutco Inc 677 Cambridge St	Worcester	MA	01610	508-756-6296	799-6848
TF: 888-588-0099 ■ *Web:* www.lutco.com					
Messinger Bearings Corp 10385 Drummond Rd	Philadelphia	PA	19154	215-739-6880	426-7515
TF: 800-203-2729 ■ *Web:* www.messingerbearings.com					
MRC Bearings Inc 402 Chandler St	Jamestown	NY	14701	716-661-2600	661-2740
TF Cust Svc: 800-672-7000 ■ *Web:* www.mrcbearings.com					
Nachi America Inc 715 Pushville Rd	Greenwood	IN	46143	888-340-2747	734-1206
TF: 888-340-2747 ■ *Web:* www.nachi.com					
National Bearing Co PO Box 4726	Lancaster	PA	17604	717-569-0485	569-1605
Web: www.nationalbearing.com					
New Hampshire Ball Bearings Inc 175 Jaffrey Rd	Peterborough	NH	03458	603-924-3311	924-4419*
**Fax:* Cust Svc ■ *Web:* www.nhbb.com					
Nice Ball Bearings Inc 400 Sullivan Way	West Trenton	NJ	08628	800-390-3300	882-5533*
**Fax Area Code:* 608 ■ *TF:* 800-321-6423					
NSK Corp 4200 Goss Rd	Ann Arbor	MI	48105	734-761-9500	913-7500
TF: 800-521-0605 ■ *Web:* www.nsk-corp.com					
NTN Bearing Corp of America 1600 E Bishop Ct	Mount Prospect	IL	60056	847-298-7500	699-9744
TF: 800-468-6528 ■ *Web:* www.ntnamerica.com					
Oiles America Corp 44099 Plymouth Oaks Blvd Suite 109	Plymouth	MI	48170	734-414-7400	414-7484
TF: 888-645-3726 ■ *Web:* www.oiles.com					
Peer Bearing Co 2200 Norman Dr S	Waukegan	IL	60085	847-578-1000	578-1200
TF: 800-433-7337 ■ *Web:* www.peerbearing.com					
Professional Instruments Co 7800 Powell Rd	Hopkins	MN	55343	952-933-1222	933-3315
Web: www.airbearings.com					
RBC Bearings Inc 1 Tribology Ctr	Oxford	CT	06478	203-267-7001	267-5000
NASDAQ: ROLL ■ *TF:* 800-352-0079 ■ *Web:* www.rbcbearings.com					
Roller Bearing Co of America 400 Sullivan Way	West Trenton	NJ	08628	609-882-5050	882-5533
Web: www.rbcbearings.com					
Rotek Inc 1400 S Chillicothe Rd PO Box 312	Aurora	OH	44202	330-562-4000	562-4620*
**Fax:* Sales ■ *TF:* 800-221-8043 ■ *Web:* www.rotek-inc.com					
Schatz Bearing Corp 10 Fairview Ave	Poughkeepsie	NY	12601	845-452-6000	452-1660
TF: 800-554-1406					
Sealmaster Bearings Co PO Box 1588	Aurora	IL	60507	630-898-9620	898-6064*
**Fax:* Cust Svc					
SKF USA Inc 1111 Adams Ave	Norristown	PA	19403	610-630-2800	630-2801
Web: www.skfusa.com					
SKF USA Inc Roller Bearing Div 20 Industrial Dr	Hanover	PA	17331	717-637-8981	637-3395
Timken Co 1835 Dueber Ave SW	Canton	OH	44706	330-438-3000	471-3810
NYSE: TKR ■ *TF:* 800-223-1954 ■ *Web:* www.timken.com					
Timken Rail Bearing Service 2122 Holston Bend Dr	Mascot	TN	37806	865-932-5800	932-5774
Web: www.timken.com/products/bearings/					
Timken Super Precision PO Box 547	Keene	NH	03431	603-352-0310	355-4554
Web: www.timken.com/industries/superprecision					
Tuthill Corp 8500 S Madison St	Burr Ridge	IL	60527	630-382-4900	382-4999
TF: 800-888-4455 ■ *Web:* www.tuthill.com					
Universal Bearings Inc 431 N Birkey St	Bremen	IN	46506	574-546-2261	546-5085
Web: www.univbrg.com					
Virginia Industries Inc 1022 Elm St	Rocky Hill	CT	06067	860-571-3600	571-3604
Winsted Precision Ball Corp 159 Colebrook River Rd	Winsted	CT	06098	860-379-2788	379-9650
TF: 800-462-3075 ■ *Web:* www.winball.com					

76 BEAUTY SALON EQUIPMENT & SUPPLIES

Company	City	State	Zip	Phone	Fax
Aerial Co Inc 2300 Aerial Dr	Marinette	WI	54143	715-735-9323	735-9112
TF: 800-950-9565 ■ *Web:* www.aerialcompany.com					
B & S Distributing 1911 Rice St	Roseville	MN	55113	651-488-7261	488-9656
TF: 800-328-9653					
Beaute Craft Supply Co 600 W Maple Rd	Troy	MI	48084	248-362-0400	362-7996*
**Fax:* Cust Svc ■ *TF Cust Svc:* 800-331-8277 ■ *Web:* www.beaute-craft.com					
Belvedere USA Corp 1 Belvedere Blvd	Belvidere	IL	61008	815-544-3131	544-6747
TF: 800-435-5491 ■ *Web:* www.belvedere.com					
Betty Dain Creations Inc 3300 NW 110th St	Miami	FL	33167	305-769-3451	769-1180
TF: 800-327-5256 ■ *Web:* www.bettydain.com					
Burmax Co 28 Barretts Ave	Holtsville	NY	11742	631-447-8700	289-7590
TF: 800-645-5118 ■ *Web:* www.burmax.com					
Collins Mfg Co 2000 Bowser Rd	Cookeville	TN	38506	931-528-5151	528-5472
TF: 800-292-6450 ■ *Web:* www.collinsmfgco.com					
Dain Betty Creations Inc 3300 NW 110th St	Miami	FL	33167	305-769-3451	769-1180
TF: 800-327-5256 ■ *Web:* www.bettydain.com					
Dr Kern USA Inc 221 S Franklin Rd	Indianapolis	IN	46219	317-472-0867	472-0873
TF: 800-908-9885 ■ *Web:* www.drkern.com					
European Touch Ltd II 8301 W Parkland Ct	Milwaukee	WI	53223	414-357-7016	357-6360
TF: 800-626-6912 ■ *Web:* www.etspa.com					
Kaemark Inc 1338 County Rd 208	Giddings	TX	78942	979-542-3651	542-0039
Web: www.kaemark.com					
Living Earth Crafts 3210 Executive Ridge Dr	Vista	CA	92081	760-597-2155	599-7374
TF: 800-358-8292 ■ *Web:* www.livingearthcrafts.com					
Marvy William Co Inc 1540 St Clair Ave	Saint Paul	MN	55105	651-698-0726	698-4048
TF: 800-874-2651 ■ *Web:* www.wmmarvyco.com					
National Salon Resources Inc 3109 Louisiana Ave N	Minneapolis	MN	55427	763-546-9500	546-5212
TF: 800-622-0003 ■ *Web:* www.nationalsalon.com					
Pibbs Industries 133-15 32nd Ave	Flushing	NY	11354	718-445-8046	461-3910
TF: 800-551-5020 ■ *Web:* www.pibbs.com					
Sally Beauty Co Inc 3001 Colorado Blvd	Denton	TX	76210	940-297-2000	297-2110
TF: 800-777-5706 ■ *Web:* www.sallybeauty.com					
Takara Belmont USA Inc 101 Belmont Dr	Somerset	NJ	08873	732-469-5000	469-9430
Web: www.takara-belmont.com					
TouchAmerica PO Box 1304	Hillsborough	NC	27278	919-732-6968	732-1173
TF: 800-678-6824 ■ *Web:* www.touchamerica.com					
Valley Barber & Beauty Supply 413 W Harrison St	Harlingen	TX	78550	956-423-0727	423-0757
TF: 800-292-7548					
William Marvy Co Inc 1540 St Clair Ave	Saint Paul	MN	55105	651-698-0726	698-4048
TF: 800-874-2651 ■ *Web:* www.wmmarvyco.com					

77 BEAUTY SALONS

Company	City	State	Zip	Phone	Fax
Anthony Mark Inc 559 Jones Franklin Rd Suite 150	Raleigh	NC	27606	919-851-0962	851-2308
Web: www.mitchellshair.com					
Beauty Management Inc DBA Perfect Look Salons					
270 Beavercreek Rd Suite 100	Oregon City	OR	97405	503-723-3200	723-3232
TF: 888-268-7577 ■ *Web:* www.perfectlooksalons.com					
Bumble & Bumble LLC 146 E 56th St	New York	NY	10022	212-521-6500	759-0867
TF: 800-728-6253 ■ *Web:* www.bumbleandbumble.com					
Cost Cutters Family Hair Salon Div Regis Corp					
7201 Metro Blvd	Minneapolis	MN	55439	952-947-7777	947-7801
TF: 888-888-7778 ■ *Web:* www.costcutters.com					
Elizabeth Arden Red Door Spas 3822 E University Dr Suite 5	Phoenix	AZ	85034	602-864-8191	437-4220
TF: 800-592-7336 ■ *Web:* www.reddoorspas.com					
Fantastic Sams Inc 50 Dunham Rd 3rd Fl	Beverly	MA	01915	978-232-5600	232-5601
Web: www.fantasticsams.com					
Fiesta Salons Inc 6363 Fiesta Dr	Columbus	OH	43235	614-766-6363	766-5657
TF: 800-825-6363 ■ *Web:* www.fiestasalons.com					
First Choice Haircutters 6465 Millcreek Dr Suite 210	Mississauga	ON	L5N5R6	905-821-8555	567-7000
TF: 800-361-2887 ■ *Web:* www.firstchoice.com					
Frederic Fekkai & Co 714 5th Ave 4th Fl	New York	NY	10019	212-753-9500	583-3370
Web: www.fredericfekkai.com					
Georgette Klinger Inc 501 Madison Ave	New York	NY	10022	212-838-3200	838-1181
TF: 800-554-6437 ■ *Web:* www.georgetteklinger.com					
Gino Morena Enterprises 111 Starlite St	South San Francisco	CA	94080	650-871-0363	871-1379
Web: www.ginomorena.com					
Great Clips Inc 7700 France Ave S Suite 425	Minneapolis	MN	55435	952-893-9088	844-3444
TF: 800-999-5959 ■ *Web:* www.greatclips.com					
Holiday Hair 7201 Metro Blvd	Minneapolis	MN	55439	952-947-7777	947-7301
Web: www.holidayhair.com					
John Frieda Professional Hair Care Inc 333 Ludlow St	Stamford	CT	06902	203-762-1233	762-2262
TF Cust Svc: 800-521-3189 ■ *Web:* www.johnfrieda.com					
Klinger Georgette Inc 501 Madison Ave	New York	NY	10022	212-838-3200	838-1181
TF: 800-554-6437 ■ *Web:* www.georgetteklinger.com					
Las Olas Beauty 1501 E Las Olas Blvd	Fort Lauderdale	FL	33301	954-779-2616	832-0165
Web: www.lasolasbeauty.com					
Lemon Tree Inc 1 Division Ave	Levittown	NY	11756	516-735-2828	735-1851
TF: 800-345-9156 ■ *Web:* www.lemontree.com					
Lord's & Lady's Hair Salons 450 Belgrade Ave	Boston	MA	02132	617-323-4700	323-4059
Web: www.lordsandladys.com					
Mark Anthony Inc 559 Jones Franklin Rd Suite 150	Raleigh	NC	27606	919-851-0962	851-2308
Web: www.mitchellshair.com					
MasterCuts Div Regis Corp 7201 Metro Blvd	Minneapolis	MN	55439	952-947-7777	947-7801
TF: 888-888-7778 ■ *Web:* www.mastercuts.com					
Michael of the Carlyle 750 Citadel Dr E Suite 1008	Colorado Springs	CO	80909	719-591-6188	
Morena Gino Enterprises 111 Starlite St	South San Francisco	CA	94080	650-871-0363	871-1379
Web: www.ginomorena.com					
Premier Salons International 8341 10th Ave N	Golden Valley	MN	55427	800-542-4247	
Web: www.premierspacollection.com					
Premier Salons International 3762 14th Ave Suite 200	Markham	ON	L3R0G7	905-470-7850	470-8174
TF: 800-749-0805 ■ *Web:* www.premierspacollection.com					
Ratner Cos 1577 Spring Hill Rd Suite 500	Vienna	VA	22182	703-698-7090	269-5416
TF: 800-874-6288 ■ *Web:* www.ratnerco.com					
Regis Corp 7201 Metro Blvd	Minneapolis	MN	55439	952-947-7777	
NYSE: RGS ■ *TF:* 888-888-7778 ■ *Web:* www.regiscorp.com					
Regis Corp Cost Cutters Family Hair Salon Div					
7201 Metro Blvd	Minneapolis	MN	55439	952-947-7777	947-7801
TF: 888-888-7778 ■ *Web:* www.costcutters.com					
Regis Corp MasterCuts Div 7201 Metro Blvd	Minneapolis	MN	55439	952-947-7777	947-7801
TF: 888-888-7778 ■ *Web:* www.mastercuts.com					
Regis Corp Pro-Cuts Div 7201 Metro Blvd	Minneapolis	MN	55439	952-947-7777	
TF: 888-888-7778 ■ *Web:* www.pro-cuts.com					
Regis Corp Regis Hairstylists Div 7201 Metro Blvd	Minneapolis	MN	55439	952-947-7777	
TF: 888-888-7778 ■ *Web:* www.regishairstylists.com					
Regis Corp SmartStyle Div 7201 Metro Blvd	Minneapolis	MN	55439	952-947-7777	
TF: 888-888-7778 ■ *Web:* www.smartstyle.com					
Regis Corp Supercuts Div 7201 Metro Blvd	Minneapolis	MN	55439	952-947-7777	947-7801
TF: 888-888-7778 ■ *Web:* www.supercuts.com					
Regis Corp Trade Secret Div 7201 Metro Blvd	Minneapolis	MN	55439	952-947-7777	
TF: 888-888-7778 ■ *Web:* www.tradesecret.com					
Regis Hairstylists Div Regis Corp 7201 Metro Blvd	Minneapolis	MN	55439	952-947-7777	
TF: 888-888-7778 ■ *Web:* www.regishairstylists.com					
Rios Golden Cut Inc 121 N Park Blvd	San Antonio	TX	78204	210-227-4996	
SmartStyle Div Regis Corp 7201 Metro Blvd	Minneapolis	MN	55439	952-947-7777	
TF: 888-888-7778 ■ *Web:* www.smartstyle.com					
Sport Clips Inc 110 Briarwood Dr	Georgetown	TX	78628	512-869-1201	869-0366
TF: 800-872-4247 ■ *Web:* www.sportclips.com					
Steiner Leisure Ltd 770 S Dixie Hwy Suite 200	Coral Gables	FL	33146	305-358-9002	372-9310
NASDAQ: STNR ■ *Web:* www.steinerleisure.com					
Stewart School of Cosmetology 604 N West Ave	Sioux Falls	SD	57104	605-336-2775	357-0288
TF: 800-537-2625 ■ *Web:* www.stewartschool.com					
Supercuts Div Regis Corp 7201 Metro Blvd	Minneapolis	MN	55439	952-947-7777	947-7801
TF: 888-888-7778 ■ *Web:* www.supercuts.com					
Toni & Guy USA Inc 2311 Midway Rd	Carrollton	TX	75006	972-931-1567	248-0798
TF: 800-256-9391 ■ *Web:* www.tigihaircare.com					
Trade Secret Div Regis Corp 7201 Metro Blvd	Minneapolis	MN	55439	952-947-7777	
TF: 888-888-7778 ■ *Web:* www.tradesecret.com					
Vidal Sassoon Salons 14 Newbury St 4th Fl	Boston	MA	02116	617-536-5496	536-6197
Web: www.vidalsassoon.com					
Visible Changes Inc 1303 Campbell Rd	Houston	TX	77055	713-984-8800	984-2632
Web: www.visiblechanges.com					

78 BETTER BUSINESS BUREAUS - CANADA

Company	City	Prov	Postal Code	Phone	Fax
Canadian Council of Better Business Bureaus					
2 St Clair Ave E Suite 800	Toronto	ON	M4T2T5	416-644-4936	644-4945
Web: www.ccbbb.ca					
Alberta (Central & Northern) 9707 110th St 888 Capital Pl	Edmonton	AB	T5K2L9	780-482-2341	482-1150
Web: www.edmontonbbb.org					
Alberta (Southern) 7330 Fisher St SE Suite 350	Calgary	AB	T2H2H8	403-531-8784	640-2514
Web: www.betterbusinessbureau.ca					
British Columbia (Mainland) 788 Beatty St Suite 404	Vancouver	BC	V6B2M1	604-682-2711	681-1544
Web: www.bbbvan.org					
Montreal 1370 Notre-Dame St	Montreal	QC	H3C1K8	514-286-9281	323-1511
Web: www.bbb-bec.com					
Nova Scotia 1888 Brunswick St Suite 805	Halifax	NS	B3J3J8	902-422-6581	429-6457
Web: www.bbbmp.ca					
Ontario (Eastern) & the Outaouais 700 Industrial Ave Suite 505	Ottawa	ON	K1G0Y9	613-237-4856	237-4878
Web: www.ottawa.bbb.org					

	City	State	Zip	Phone	Fax
Ontario (Mid-Western) 354 Charles St E	Kitchener	ON	N2G4L5	519-579-3080	570-0072
TF: 800-459-8875 ■ *Web:* www.bbbmwo.ca					
Ontario (South Central) 100 King St E	Hamilton	ON	L8N1A8	905-526-1112	526-1225
Web: www.thebbb.ca					
Ontario (Western) 200 Queens Ave Suite 308 PO Box 2153	London	ON	N6A4E3	519-673-3222	673-5966
Web: www.bbblondon.on.ca					
Saskatchewan 2080 Broad St Suite 201	Regina	SK	S4P1Y3	306-352-7601	565-6236
Web: www.bbbsask.com					
Vancouver Island 1175 Cook St Suite 220	Victoria	BC	V8V4A1	250-386-6348	386-2367
TF: 877-826-4222 ■ *Web:* www.bbbvanisland.org					
Windsor & Southwestern Ontario 880 Ouellette Ave Suite 302	Windsor	ON	N9A1C7	519-258-7222	258-1198
Web: www.windsorbbb.com					
Winnipeg & Manitoba 1030B Empress St	Winnipeg	MB	R3G3H4	204-989-9010	989-9016
TF: 800-385-3074 ■ *Web:* www.bbbmanitoba.ca					

79 BETTER BUSINESS BUREAUS - US

SEE ALSO Associations & Organizations - General - Consumer Interest Organizations p. 1301

	City	State	Zip	Phone	Fax
BBB OnLine 4200 Wilson Blvd Suite 800	Arlington	VA	22203	703-247-9370	525-8277
Web: www.bbbonline.org					
Abilene Area 3300 S 14th St Suite 307	Abilene	TX	79605	325-691-1533	691-0309
Web: www.abilene.bbb.org					
Acadiana 4007 W Congress St Suite B	Lafayette	LA	70506	337-981-3497	981-7559
Web: www.acadiana.bbb.org					
Akron Area 222 W Market St	Akron	OH	44303	330-253-4590	253-6249
TF: 800-825-8887 ■ *Web:* www.akronbbb.org					
Alabama (Central) & the Wiregrass Area 1210 S 20th St	Birmingham	AL	35205	205-558-2238	558-2239
Web: www.birmingham-al.bbb.org					
Alabama (Central) & the Wiregrass Area Dothan Branch 118 Woodburn Dr	Dothan	AL	36305	334-794-0492	794-0659
TF: 800-824-5274 ■ *Web:* www.birmingham-al.bbb.org					
Alabama (Central) & the Wiregrass Area Montgomery Branch 500 Eastern Blvd Suite 128	Montgomery	AL	36117	334-273-5530	273-5546
TF: 800-824-5274 ■ *Web:* www.birmingham-al.bbb.org					
Alabama (Northern) 107 Lincoln St	Huntsville	AL	35804	256-533-1640	533-1177
Web: www.northalabama.bbb.org					
Alabama (Southern) 3361 Cottage Hill Rd Suite E	Mobile	AL	36606	251-433-5494	438-3191
TF: 800-544-4714 ■ *Web:* www.bbbsouthal.org					
Alaska 3601 C St Suite 1378	Anchorage	AK	99503	907-562-0704	644-5222
Web: www.alaska.bbb.org					
Arizona (Central Northeast Northwest & Southwest) 4428 N 12th St	Phoenix	AZ	85014	602-264-1721	
Web: www.arizonabbb.org					
Ark-La-Tex 401 Edwards St Suite 135	Shreveport	LA	71101	318-222-7575	222-7576
TF: 800-372-4222 ■ *Web:* www.shreveport.bbb.org					
Arkansas 12521 Kanis Rd	Little Rock	AR	72211	501-664-7274	664-0024
Web: www.arkansas.bbb.org					
Asheville/Western North Carolina 112 Executive Park	Asheville	NC	28801	828-253-2392	252-5039
Web: www.asheville.bbb.org					
Atlanta (Metropolitan) 503 Oak Pl Suite 590	Atlanta	GA	30349	404-766-0875	768-1085
Web: www.atlanta.bbb.org					
Bakersfield Area 1601 H St Suite 101	Bakersfield	CA	93301	661-322-2074	322-8318
Web: www.bakersfield.bbb.org					
Better Business Bureau of Metropolitan New York 257 Park Ave S	New York	NY	10010	212-533-6200	477-4912
Web: www.newyork.bbb.org					
Better Business Bureau of the Mid-Hudson 150 White Plains Rd Suite 107	Tarrytown	NY	11735	212-533-6200	477-4912
Web: www.newyork.bbb.org					
Better Business Bureau of Rockford 810 E State St 3rd Fl	Rockford	IL	61104	815-963-2222	963-0329
Web: www.rockford.bbb.org					
Brazos Valley & Deep East Texas 418 Tarrow	College Station	TX	77840	979-260-2222	846-0276
Web: www.bryan.bbb.org					
California (Northeast) 3075 Beacon Blvd	West Sacramento	CA	95691	916-443-6843	443-0376
Web: www.necal.bbb.org					
Canton Region/West Virginia 1434 Cleveland Ave NW	Canton	OH	44711	330-454-9401	456-8957
TF: 800-362-0494 ■ *Web:* canton.bbb.org/					
Carolinas (Southern Piedmont) 13860 Ballantyne Corporate Pl Suite 225	Charlotte	NC	28277	704-927-8611	927-8615
Web: www.charlotte.bbb.org					
Chicago & Northern Illinois 330 N Wabash Ave Suite 2006	Chicago	IL	60611	312-832-0500	832-9985
Web: www.chicago.bbb.org					
Cincinnati 7 W 7th St Suite 1600	Cincinnati	OH	45202	513-421-3015	621-0907
Web: www.cinbbb.org					
Connecticut 94 S Turnpike Rd	Wallingford	CT	06492	203-269-2700	294-3694
Web: www.ctbbb.org					
Council of Better Business Bureaus (CBBB) 4200 Wilson Blvd Suite 800	Arlington	VA	22203	703-276-0100	525-8277
Web: www.bbb.org					
Dallas (Metropolitan) & Northeast Texas 1601 Elm St Suite 3838	Dallas	TX	75201	214-220-2000	740-0321
Web: www.dallas.bbb.org					
Dayton/Miami Valley 15 W 4th St Suite 300	Dayton	OH	45402	937-222-5825	222-3338
Web: www.dayton.bbb.org					
Delaware 60 Reads Way	New Castle	DE	19720	302-230-0108	230-0116
Web: www.wilmington.bbb.org					
Denver-Boulder Metro Area 1020 Cherokee St	Denver	CO	80204	303-758-2100	758-8321
Web: www.denver.bbb.org					
Detroit & Eastern Michigan 30555 Southfield Rd Suite 200	Southfield	MI	48076	248-644-9100	644-5026
Web: www.easternmichiganbbb.org					
Eastern Washington North Idaho & Montana Inc 152 S Jefferson St Suite 200	Spokane	WA	99201	509-455-4200	838-1079
Web: www.bbb.org/					
El Paso 221 N Kansas St Suite 1101	El Paso	TX	79901	915-577-0191	577-0209
Web: www.bbbelpaso.com					
Florida (Central) 1600 S Grant St	Longwood	FL	32750	407-621-3300	786-2625
Web: www.orlando.bbb.org					
Florida (Northeast) 4417 Beach Blvd Suite 202	Jacksonville	FL	32207	904-721-2288	721-7373
TF: 800-940-1315 ■ *Web:* www.bbbnefla.org					
Florida (Northwest) 912 E Gadsden St	Pensacola	FL	32501	850-429-0002	429-0006
Web: www.nwfl.bbb.org					
Florida (Southeast) 4411 Beacon Cir Suite 4	West Palm Beach	FL	33407	561-842-1918	845-7234
TF: 800-834-6286 ■ *Web:* www.seflorida.bbb.org					
Florida (West) PO Box 7950	Clearwater	FL	33758	727-535-5522	539-6301
TF: 800-525-1447 ■ *Web:* www.westflorida.bbb.org					
Fort Worth Area 101 Summit Ave Suite 707	Fort Worth	TX	76102	817-332-7585	882-0566
Web: www.fortworth.bbb.org					
Four Corners & Grand Junction Colorado 308 N Locke Ave	Farmington	NM	87401	505-326-6501	327-7731
Web: www.farmington.bbb.org					
Georgia (Central) 277 ML King Jr Blvd Suite 102	Macon	GA	31201	478-742-7999	742-8191
Web: www.centralgeorgia.bbb.org					
Georgia (Southeast) & South Carolina (Southeast) 6606 Abercorn St Suite 108C	Savannah	GA	31405	912-354-7522	354-5068
TF: 800-353-1192 ■ *Web:* www.savannah.bbb.org					
Georgia (Southwest) PO Box 808	Albany	GA	31702	229-883-0744	438-8222
Web: www.columbus-ga.bbb.org					
Georgia (West) & Alabama (East) PO Box 2587	Columbus	GA	31902	706-324-0712	324-2181
TF: 800-768-4888 ■ *Web:* www.columbus-ga.bbb.org					
Hampton Roads (Greater) 586 Virginian Dr	Norfolk	VA	23505	757-531-1300	531-1388
Web: www.hamptonroadsbbb.org					
Hawaii 1132 Bishop St Suite 1507	Honolulu	HI	96813	808-536-6956	523-2335
Web: www.hawaii.bbb.org					
Houston 1333 W Loop S Suite 1200	Houston	TX	77027	713-868-9500	867-4947
Web: www.bbbhou.org					
Idaho (Southwest) & Oregon (Eastern) 4355 Emerald St Suite 290	Boise	ID	83706	208-342-4649	342-5116
Web: www.boise.bbb.org					
Illinois (Central) 112 Harrison St	Peoria	IL	61602	309-688-3741	681-7290
Web: www.peoria.bbb.org					
Indiana (Central) 22 E Washington St Suite 200	Indianapolis	IN	46204	317-488-2222	713-0533
Web: www.indianapolis.bbb.org					
Indiana (Northeastern) 4011 Parnell Ave	Fort Wayne	IN	46805	260-423-4433	423-3301
Web: www.neindiana.bbb.org					
Indiana (Northwest) 7863 Broadway Suite 124	Merrillville	IN	46410	260-423-4433	884-2123*
**Fax Area Code:* 219 ■ *Web:* www.nwin.bbb.org					
Iowa (Central & Eastern) 505 5th Ave Suite 950	Des Moines	IA	50309	515-243-8137	243-2227
TF: 800-222-1600 ■ *Web:* www.iowa.bbb.org					
Kansas City (Greater) 8080 Ward Pkwy Suite 401	Kansas City	MO	64114	816-421-7800	472-5442
Web: www.kansascity.bbb.org					
Kansas (Except the Northeast) 328 Laura St	Wichita	KS	67211	316-263-3146	263-3063
TF: 800-856-2417 ■ *Web:* www.wichita.bbb.org					
Kansas (Northeast) 501 SE Jefferson St Suite 24	Topeka	KS	66607	785-232-0454	232-9677
Web: www.topeka.bbb.org					
Kentucky (Central & Eastern) 1460 Newtown Pike	Lexington	KY	40511	859-259-1008	259-1639
TF: 800-866-6668 ■ *Web:* www.ky.bbb.org					
Lancaster 1337 N Front St	Harrisburg	PA	17102	717-364-3250	364-3251
Web: www.easternpa.bbb.org					
Lehigh Div 528 N New St	Bethlehem	PA	18018	610-866-8780	868-8668
Web: www.mybbb.org					
Louisiana (Central) 5220-C Rue Verdun	Alexandria	LA	71303	318-473-4494	473-8906
TF: 800-372-4222 ■ *Web:* www.alexandria-la.bbb.org					
Louisiana (Northeast) 212 Walnut St Suite 210	Monroe	LA	71201	318-387-4600	361-0461
TF: 800-960-7756 ■ *Web:* www.bbbnela.org					
Louisiana (South Central) 748 Main St	Baton Rouge	LA	70802	225-346-5222	346-1029
Web: www.batonrouge.bbb.org					
Louisiana (Southwest) 2309 E Prien Lake Rd	Lake Charles	LA	70601	337-478-6253	474-8981
TF: 800-542-7085 ■ *Web:* www.lakecharles.bbb.org					
Louisville Southern Indiana & Western Kentucky 844 S 4th St	Louisville	KY	40203	502-583-6546	589-9940
Web: www.ky-in.bbb.org					
Maine 235 W Central St	Natick	MA	01760	508-652-4800	652-4820
Web: www.boston.bbb.org					
Maryland (Greater) 1414 Key Hwy Suite 100	Baltimore	MD	21230	410-347-3990	347-3936
Web: www.baltimore.bbb.org					
Massachusetts (Eastern) Maine & Vermont 235 W Central St Suite 1	Natick	MA	01760	508-652-4800	652-4820
Web: www.boston.bbb.org					
Massachusetts (Western) 333 Park St Suite A	West Springfield	MA	01089	413-734-3114	734-2006
Michiana 4011 Parnell Ave	Fort Wayne	IN	46801	260-423-4433	423-3301
Web: www.michiana.bbb.org					
Michigan (Western) 40 Pearl St NW Suite 354	Grand Rapids	MI	49503	616-774-8236	774-2014
TF: 800-684-3222 ■ *Web:* www.grandrapids.bbb.org					
Minnesota & North Dakota 2706 Gannon Rd	Saint Paul	MN	55116	651-699-1111	699-7665
Web: www.mnd.bbb.org					
Mississippi PO Box 3302	Ridgeland	MS	39158	601-856-9357	856-9331
Web: ms.bbb.org					
Missouri (Eastern) & Illinois (Southern) 15 Sunnen Dr Suite 107	Saint Louis	MO	63143	314-645-3300	645-2666
TF: 866-996-3887 ■ *Web:* www.stlouis.bbb.org					
Missouri (Southwest) 1516 E Saint Louis St	Springfield	MO	65802	417-862-4222	869-5544
Web: southwestmissouri.bbb.org					
Mountain States 8020 S County Rd 5 Suite 100	Fort Collins	CO	80528	970-484-1348	221-1239
TF: 800-564-0371 ■ *Web:* www.mountainstates.bbb.org					
Nebraska (Northern) & Iowa (Southwest) 11811 P St	Omaha	NE	68137	402-391-7612	391-7535
Web: www.bbbnebraska.org					
Nebraska (Southern) 3633 'O' St Suite 1	Lincoln	NE	68510	402-436-2345	476-8221
Web: www.lincoln.bbb.org					
Nevada (Northern) 991 Bible Way	Reno	NV	89502	775-322-0657	322-8163
Web: reno.bbb.org					
Nevada (Southern) 2301 Palomino Ln	Las Vegas	NV	89107	702-320-4500	320-4560
Web: www.vegas.bbb.org					
New England (Central) & Connecticut (Northeast) 339 Main St	Worcester	MA	01608	508-755-3340	754-4158
Web: central-westernma.bbb.org					
New Hampshire 25 Hall St Suite 102	Concord	NH	03301	603-228-3789	
Web: www.concord.bbb.org/					
New Jersey (Central & Southern) 1700 Whitehorse-Hamilton Sq Rd Suite D-5	Trenton	NJ	08690	609-588-0808	588-0546
Web: www.trenton.bbb.org					
New Mexico 2625 Pennsylvania St NE Suite 2050	Albuquerque	NM	87110	505-346-0110	346-0696
Web: www.bbbsw.org					
New Orleans (Greater) 710 Baronne St Suite C	New Orleans	LA	70113	504-581-6222	524-9110
Web: www.neworleans.bbb.org					
New York (Western) & the Capital District 741 Delaware Ave Suite 100	Buffalo	NY	14209	716-881-5222	883-5349
TF: 800-828-5000 ■ *Web:* www.upstateny.bbb.org					
North Carolina (Central) 3608 W Friendly Ave	Greensboro	NC	27410	336-852-4240	852-7540
Web: www.greensboro.bbb.org					
North Carolina (Eastern) 5540 Munford Rd Suite 130	Raleigh	NC	27612	919-277-4222	277-4221
Web: easternnc.bbb.org/					
North Carolina (Northwest) 500 W 5th St Suite 202	Winston-Salem	NC	27101	336-725-8348	777-3727
Web: www.nwnc.bbb.org					
North & South Carolina (Coastal) 314 Laurel St Suite 203	Conway	SC	29526	843-488-2227	488-0998
Web: myrtlebeach.bbb.org					
Ohio (Central) 1169 Dublin Rd	Columbus	OH	43215	614-486-6336	486-6631
TF: 800-759-2400 ■ *Web:* www.columbus-oh.bbb.org					
Ohio (Northeast) 2217 E 9th St Suite 200	Cleveland	OH	44115	216-241-7678	861-6365
Web: www.cleveland.bbb.org					
Ohio (Northwest) & Michigan (Southeast) 3103 Executive Pkwy Suite 200	Toledo	OH	43606	419-531-3116	578-6001
TF: 800-743-4222					
Ohio (West Central) 219 N McDonel St	Lima	OH	45801	419-223-7010	229-2029
Web: www.wcohio.bbb.org					
Oklahoma (Central) 17 S Dewey Ave	Oklahoma City	OK	73102	405-239-6081	235-5891
Web: www.oklahomacity.bbb.org					
Oklahoma (Eastern) 1722 S Carson Ave Suite 3200	Tulsa	OK	74119	918-492-1266	492-1276
TF: 800-928-4222 ■ *Web:* www.tulsa.bbb.org					

Phone | Fax

Oregon & Western Washington PO Box 1000 .... Dupont WA 98327 206-431-2222 431-2211
Web: www.alaskaoregonwesternwashington.bbb.org/
Pennsylvania (Eastern) 1608 Walnut St Suite 402 .... Philadelphia PA 19103 215-985-9313 893-9312
Web: www.mybbb.org
Pennsylvania (Northeastern & Central) 4099 Birney Ave .... Moosic PA 18507 570-342-9129 342-1282
TF: 888-229-3222 ■ *Web:* www.nepa.bbb.org
Pennsylvania (Western) 300 6th Ave Suite 100-UL .... Pittsburgh PA 15222 412-456-2700 456-2739
Web: www.westernpennsylvania.bbb.org
Permian Basin Area of West Texas PO Box 60206 .... Midland TX 79711 432-563-1880 561-9435
Web: www.permianbasinbbb.org
Pike's Peak Region 25 N Wahsatch Ave .... Colorado Springs CO 80903 719-636-1155 636-5078
TF: 866-206-1800 ■ *Web:* www.bbbsc.org
Rhode Island 120 Lavan St .... Warwick RI 02888 401-785-1212 785-3061
Web: www.rhodeisland.bbb.org
San Angelo Area 3134 Executive Dr .... San Angelo TX 76904 325-949-2989 949-3514
Web: www.sanangelo.bbb.org
San Diego & Imperial Counties
5050 Murphy Canyon Rd Suite 110 .... San Diego CA 92123 858-637-6199 496-2141
Web: www.sandiego.bbb.org
San Joaquin Valley 4201 W Shaw Ave Suite 107 .... Fresno CA 93722 559-222-8111 228-6518
Web: www.cencal.bbb.org
San Luis Obispo Santa Barbara & Ventura Counties
PO Box 129 .... Santa Barbara CA 93102 805-963-8657 962-8557
Web: www.santabarbara.bbb.org
San Mateo County 1000 Broadway Suite 625 .... Oakland CA 94607 510-844-2000 844-2100
TF: 866-411-2221 ■ *Web:* www.bbbgoldengate.org
Santa Clara Valley 700 Empey Way Suite 110 .... San Jose CA 95128 408-278-7400 278-7444
Web: www.sanjose.bbb.org/
South Carolina (Central) & the Charleston Area PO Box 8326 .... Columbia SC 29202 803-254-2525 779-3117
Web: www.columbia.bbb.org
South Carolina (Upstate) 408 N Church St Suite C .... Greenville SC 29601 864-242-5052 271-9802
Web: www.greenville.bbb.org
South Central Area 1800 NE Loop 410 Suite 400 .... San Antonio TX 78217 210-828-9441 828-3101
Web: www.sanantonio.bbb.org
Tennessee (Greater East) PO Box 31377 .... Knoxville TN 37930 865-692-1600 692-1590
Web: www.knoxville.bbb.org
Tennessee (Middle) 201 4th Ave N Suite 100 PO Box 198436 .... Nashville TN 37219 615-242-4222 250-4245
Web: www.gobbb.org
Tennessee (Southeast) & Georgia (Northwest)
1010 Market St Suite 200 .... Chattanooga TN 37402 423-266-6144 267-1924
Web: www.chattanooga.bbb.org
Tennessee (West) Mississippi (North) & Arkansas (Eastern)
3693 Tyndale Dr .... Memphis TN 38125 901-759-1300 757-2997
Web: www.midsouth.bbb.org
Texas (Central) 1005 LaPosada Dr Suite 302 .... Austin TX 78752 512-445-2911 445-2096
Web: www.centraltx.bbb.org
Texas (Central East) 3600 Old Bullard Rd Bldg 1 .... Tyler TX 75701 903-581-5704 534-8644
Web: www.tyler.bbb.org
Texas (Central East) Longview Branch
2401 Judson Rd Suite 102 .... Longview TX 75605 903-758-3222 758-3226
Web: www.longview.bbb.org
Texas (Coastal Bend) 101 N Shoreline Blvd Suite 216 .... Corpus Christi TX 78401 361-852-4949 885-0628
TF: 800-379-4222 ■ *Web:* bbb.caller.com
Texas (Heart of) 2210 Washington Ave .... Waco TX 76701 254-755-7772 755-7774
Web: www.waco.bbb.org
Texas (North Central) 4245 Kemp Blvd Suite 900 .... Wichita Falls TX 76308 940-691-1172 691-1175
Web: www.wichitafalls.bbb.org
Texas Panhandle 720 S Tyler St Suite B-112 .... Amarillo TX 79105 806-379-6222 379-8206
Web: www.amarillo.bbb.org
Texas (South) 2110 W 6th St .... Weslaco TX 78596 956-968-3678 968-7638
Web: www.weslaco.bbb.org
Texas (South Plains) 3333 66th St .... Lubbock TX 79413 806-763-0459 744-9748
Texas (Southeast) 550 Fannin St Suite 100 .... Beaumont TX 77701 409-835-5348 838-6858
Web: www.bbbsetexas.org
Torrance PO Box 970 .... Colton CA 92324 909-825-7280 825-6246
Web: www.labbb.org
Tri-Parish Area 801 Barrow St Suite 400 .... Houma LA 70360 985-868-3456 876-7664
Web: www.houma.bbb.org
Tri-State 5401 Vogel Rd Suite 410 .... Evansville IN 47715 812-473-0202 473-3080
Web: www.evansville.bbb.org
Tucson Area 434 S Williams Blvd Suite 102 .... Tucson AZ 85711 520-888-5353 888-6262
Web: www.tucson.bbb.org
Utah 5673 S Redwood Rd Suite 22 .... Salt Lake City UT 84123 801-892-6009 892-6002
Web: www.utah.bbb.org
Virginia (Central) 701 E Franklin St Suite 712 .... Richmond VA 23219 804-648-0016 648-3115
Web: www.richmond.bbb.org
Virginia (Western) 31 W Campbell Ave Suite G .... Roanoke VA 24011 540-342-3455 345-2289
Web: www.vabbb.org
Washington DC (Metro) & Eastern Pennsylvania
1411 K St NW Suite 1000 .... Washington DC 20005 202-393-8000 393-1198
Web: www.mybbb.org
Wisconsin 10101 W Greenfield Ave Suite 125 .... Milwaukee WI 53214 414-847-6000 302-0355
TF: 800-273-1002 ■ *Web:* www.wisconsin.bbb.org
Youngstown Area PO Box 1495 .... Youngstown OH 44501 330-744-3111 744-7336
Web: www.youngstown.bbb.org

80 BEVERAGES - MFR

SEE ALSO Breweries p. 1397; Water - Bottled p. 2413

80-1 Liquor - Mfr

Phone | Fax

Bacardi Corp PO Box 363549 .... San Juan PR 00936 787-788-1500 788-0340
Web: www.bacardi.com
Bacardi USA Inc 2100 Biscayne Blvd .... Miami FL 33137 305-573-8511 573-7507
TF: 800-222-2734 ■ *Web:* www.bacardi.com
Black Prince Distillery Inc PO Box 1999 .... Clifton NJ 07015 973-365-2050 365-0746
Web: www.blackprincedistillery.com
Bowman A Smith Distillery Inc 1 Bowman Dr .... Fredericksburg VA 22408 540-373-4555 371-2236
Web: www.bowmanco.com
Brown-Forman Beverages Worldwide 850 Dixie Hwy .... Louisville KY 40210 502-585-1100 774-7189*
**Fax:* Hum Res ■ *Web:* www.brown-forman.com
Consolidated Distilled Products 2600 W 35th St .... Chicago IL 60632 773-254-9000 890-8889*
**Fax:* Hum Res ■ *TF:* 800-944-9450
Diageo North America 801 Main Ave .... Norwalk CT 06851 203-229-2100 967-7682*
**Fax:* Hum Res ■ *TF:* 800-847-4109 ■ *Web:* www.diageo.com
Dickel George A Co PO Box 490 .... Tullahoma TN 37388 931-857-3124 857-9313
Web: www.dickel.com
Early Times Distillery Co PO Box 1105 .... Louisville KY 40201 502-774-2960 774-2103
Web: www.earlytimes.com
Florida Distillers Co 530 Dakota Ave PO Box 1447 .... Lake Alfred FL 33850 863-956-1116 956-3979
Web: www.todhunter.com
Heavenhill Distilleries Inc PO Box 729 .... Bardstown KY 40004 502-348-3921 349-1512
Web: www.heaven-hill.com
Jack Daniel Distillery PO Box 199 .... Lynchburg TN 37352 931-759-4221 759-6321
Web: www.jackdaniels.com
Jacquin Charles et Cie 2633 Trenton Ave .... Philadelphia PA 19125 215-425-9300 425-9438
TF: 800-523-3811
Jim Beam Brands Worldwide Inc 510 Lake Cook Rd .... Deerfield IL 60015 847-948-8888 948-7883
TF: 866-522-6246 ■ *Web:* www.jimbeam.com
Laird & Co Inc 1 Laird Rd .... Scobeyville NJ 07724 732-542-0312 542-2244
TF: 877-438-5247 ■ *Web:* www.lairdandco.com
Maker's Mark Distillery Inc 3350 Burke Spring Rd .... Loretto KY 40037 270-865-2881 865-2196
Web: www.makersmark.com
McCormick Distilling Co Inc 1 McCormick Ln .... Weston MO 64098 816-640-2276 640-3085
Web: www.mccormickdistilling.com
Montebello Brands Inc 1919 Willow Spring Rd .... Baltimore MD 21222 410-282-8800 282-8809
Paramount Distillers Inc 3116 Berea Rd .... Cleveland OH 44111 216-671-6300 671-2299
TF: 800-821-2989 ■ *Web:* www.paramountdistillers.com
Pernod Ricard USA 100 Manhattanville Rd .... Purchase NY 10577 914-848-4800 848-4777
TF: 800-488-7539 ■ *Web:* www.pernod-ricard-usa.com
Sazerac Co Inc 803 Jefferson Hwy .... Jefferson LA 70121 504-831-9450 831-2383
Web: www.sazerac.com
Skyy Spirits Inc 1 Beach St Suite 300 .... San Francisco CA 94133 415-315-8000 315-8001
TF: 800-367-7599 ■ *Web:* www.skyy.com
Takara Sake USA Inc 708 Addison St .... Berkeley CA 94710 510-540-8250 486-8758
Web: www.takarasake.com
Walker MS Inc 20 3rd Ave .... Somerville MA 02143 617-776-6700 776-5808
TF: 800-776-5808 ■ *Web:* www.mswalker.com
White Rock Distilleries Inc PO Box 1829 .... Lewiston ME 04241 207-783-1433 783-8409
TF: 800-628-5441 ■ *Web:* www.whiterockdistilleries.com
Wild Turkey Distillery PO Box 180 .... Lawrenceburg KY 40342 502-839-4544 839-3902
Web: www.wildturkeybourbon.com

80-2 Soft Drinks - Mfr

Phone | Fax

Adirondack Beverages Inc 701 Corporations Pk .... Scotia NY 12302 518-370-3621 370-3762
Web: www.adirondackbeverages.com
American Beverage Corp 1 Daily Way .... Verona PA 15147 412-828-9020 828-8876
Web: www.ambev.com
American Water Star Inc 2580 Anthem Village Dr Suite B-1 .... Henderson NV 89052 702-588-5965
AMEX: AMW ■ *Web:* www.americanwaterstar.com
AriZona Beverage Co 5 Dakota Dr Suite 205 .... Lake Success NY 11024 516-812-0300 326-4988
TF: 800-832-3775 ■ *Web:* www.arizonabev.com
Beverage Corp International 3505 NW 107th St .... Miami FL 33167 305-714-7000
TF: 800-226-5061 ■ *Web:* www.bcibeverages.com
Big Red/Seven Up Bottling of South Texas
4518 Seguin Rd .... San Antonio TX 78219 210-661-4271 666-0911
TF: 800-580-7333 ■ *Web:* www.dpsubg.com
Coca-Cola Co 1 Coca-Cola Plaza .... Atlanta GA 30313 404-676-2121 676-6792
NYSE: KO ■ *TF:* 800-438-2653 ■ *Web:* www.coca-cola.com
Cott Corp 207 Queen's Quay W Suite 340 .... Toronto ON M5J1A7 416-203-3898 203-8171
NYSE: COT ■ *TF:* 800-994-2688 ■ *Web:* www.cott.com
Davis Beverage Group 1530-A Bobali Dr .... Harrisburg PA 17104 717-914-1295 914-1296
TF: 800-360-7056
Double Cola Co USA 537 Market St Suite 100 .... Chattanooga TN 37402 423-267-5691 267-0793
TF: 877-325-2659 ■ *Web:* www.double-cola.com
Dr Pepper/Seven-Up Inc 5301 Legacy Dr .... Plano TX 75024 972-673-7000 673-7698*
**Fax:* Hum Res ■ *TF:* 800-527-7096 ■ *Web:* www.dpsu.com
Everfresh/Lacroix Beverages Inc 6600 E 9-Mile Rd .... Warren MI 48091 586-755-9500 755-4587
TF: 800-323-3416
Faygo Beverages Inc 3579 Gratiot Ave .... Detroit MI 48207 313-925-1600 571-7611
TF: 800-347-6591 ■ *Web:* www.faygo.com
Ferolito Vultaggio & Sons 5 Dakota Dr Suite 205 .... Lake Success NY 11024 516-812-0300 326-4988
TF: 800-832-3775 ■ *Web:* www.arizonabev.com
Global Beverage Co 130 Linden Oaks Dr .... Rochester NY 14625 585-381-3560 381-4025
Web: www.joltcola.com
Hansen Natural Corp 1010 Railroad St .... Corona CA 92882 951-739-6200 739-6210
NASDAQ: HANS ■ *TF:* 800-426-7367 ■ *Web:* www.hansens.com
Monarch Beverage Co 3424 Peachtree Rd Suite 1450 .... Atlanta GA 30326 404-262-4040 262-4001
TF: 800-241-3732
National Beverage Corp 1 N University Dr .... Fort Lauderdale FL 33324 954-581-0922 473-4710
AMEX: FIZ ■ *TF:* 888-462-2349 ■ *Web:* www.nbcfiz.com
Pepsi Bottling Group Inc 1 Pepsi Way .... Somers NY 10589 914-767-6000 767-7761
NYSE: PBG ■ *TF PR:* 800-433-2652 ■ *Web:* www.pbg.com
Pepsi QTG Canada 77 City Center Dr .... Mississauga ON L5B1M5 905-804-5200
PepsiAmericas Inc 60 S 6th St Suite 4000 .... Minneapolis MN 55402 612-661-3830 661-3825
NYSE: PAS ■ *Web:* www.pepsiamericas.com
PepsiCo Beverages North America 700 Anderson Hill Rd .... Purchase NY 10577 914-253-2000 253-2070
Web: www.pepsi.com
Polar Beverages Inc 1001 Southbridge St .... Worcester MA 01610 508-753-4300 793-0813
TF Cust Svc: 800-225-7410 ■ *Web:* www.polarbev.com
Shasta Beverages Inc 26901 Industrial Blvd .... Hayward CA 94545 510-783-3200 785-3228*
**Fax:* Sales ■ *TF:* 800-326-8640 ■ *Web:* www.shastapop.com
Snapple Beverage Corp 900 King St .... Rye Brook NY 10573 800-964-7842 612-4100*
**Fax Area Code:* 914 ■ *Web:* www.snapple.com
South Beach Beverage Co 40 Richards Ave .... Norwalk CT 06854 203-899-7111 899-7177
TF Cust Svc: 800-588-0548 ■ *Web:* www.sobebev.com
White Rock Products Corp 141-07 20th Ave .... Whitestone NY 11357 718-746-3400 767-0413
TF: 800-969-7625 ■ *Web:* www.whiterockbeverages.com
Yoo-Hoo Chocolate Beverage Corp 600 Commercial Ave .... Carlstadt NJ 07072 201-933-0070 933-5360
TF: 800-966-4669 ■ *Web:* www.drinkyoo-hoo.com

80-3 Wines - Mfr

Phone | Fax

Archery Summit Winery 18955 NE Archery Summit Rd .... Dayton OR 97114 503-864-4300 864-4285
Web: www.archerysummit.com
Banfi Vintners USA 1111 Cedar Swamp Rd .... Old Brookville NY 11545 516-626-9200 626-9218
TF: 800-645-6511 ■ *Web:* www.banfivintners.com
Beaulieu Vineyard 1960 St Helena Hwy .... Rutherford CA 94573 707-967-5200 963-5920
TF: 800-264-6918 ■ *Web:* www.bvwines.com
Benziger Family Winery 1883 London Ranch Rd .... Glen Ellen CA 95442 707-935-3000 935-3016
TF: 888-490-2739 ■ *Web:* www.benziger.com
Beringer Blass Wine Estates 610 Airpark Rd PO Box 4500 .... Napa CA 94558 707-259-4500 259-4542
Web: www.beringer.com
Bronco Wine Co 6342 Bystrum Rd .... Ceres CA 95307 209-538-3131 538-2178
TF: 800-692-5780
Brotherhood America's Oldest Winery Ltd
100 Brotherhood Plaza Dr PO Box 190 .... Washingtonville NY 10992 845-496-9101
Web: www.brotherhoodwinery.net
Brown-Forman Beverages Worldwide 850 Dixie Hwy .... Louisville KY 40210 502-585-1100 774-7189*
**Fax:* Hum Res ■ *Web:* www.brown-forman.com

Company	City	State	ZIP	Phone	Fax
Bully Hill Vineyards 8843 Greyton H Taylor Memorial Dr *Web:* www.bullyhill.com	Hammondsport	NY	14840	607-868-3610	868-3205
Canandaigua Wine Co Inc 235 N Bloomfield Rd *TF:* 888-659-7900 ■ *Web:* www.cwine.com	Naples	NY	14512	585-396-7600	396-7833
Clos du Bois Wines 19410 Geyserville Ave PO Box 940 *TF Sales:* 800-222-3189 ■ *Web:* closdubois.com	Geyserville	CA	95441	707-857-1651	857-1667
Columbia Crest Winery PO Box 231 *TF:* 888-309-9463 ■ *Web:* www.columbia-crest.com	Paterson	WA	99345	509-875-2061	875-2869
Delicato Vineyards 12001 S Hwy 99 *TF:* 888-599-4637 ■ *Web:* www.delicato.com	Manteca	CA	95336	209-824-3600	824-3400
Diageo Chateau & Estate Wines Co 240 Gateway Rd W *Web:* www.diageowines.com	Napa	CA	94558	707-299-2600	299-2777
Distillerie Stock USA Ltd 58-58 Laurel Hill Blvd *TF:* 800-323-1884 ■ *Web:* www.stockusaltd.com	Woodside	NY	11377	718-651-9800	651-7806
Domaine Chandon Inc 1 California Dr *TF:* 800-736-2892 ■ *Web:* www.chandon.com	Yountville	CA	94599	707-944-8844	944-1123
E & J Gallo Winery 600 Yosemite Blvd *TF:* 800-322-2389 ■ *Web:* www.gallo.com	Modesto	CA	95354	209-341-3111	341-3307
F Korbel & Bros Inc 13250 River Rd *TF:* 800-656-7235 ■ *Web:* www.korbel.com	Guerneville	CA	95446	707-824-7000	869-2981
Fetzer Vineyards 13601 Old River Rd *TF:* 800-846-8637 ■ *Web:* www.fetzer.com	Hopland	CA	95449	707-744-1250	744-7605
Franciscan Estates 1178 Galleron Rd *TF:* 800-529-9463 ■ *Web:* www.franciscan.com	Saint Helena	CA	94574	707-963-7111	963-7867
Franzia Winery 1887 N Mooney Blvd	Tulare	CA	93274	559-688-1766	688-8034
Freixenet USA Inc 2355 Hwy 121 PO Box 1427 *Web:* www.freixenetusa.com	Sonoma	CA	95476	707-996-7256	996-0720
Gallo E & J Winery 600 Yosemite Blvd *TF:* 800-322-2389 ■ *Web:* www.gallo.com	Modesto	CA	95354	209-341-3111	341-3307
Giumarra Vineyards Corp 11220 Edison Hwy	Edison	CA	93220	661-395-7000	366-7134
Heineman Beverages Inc 407 Short St *TF:* 800-734-9115	Port Clinton	OH	43452	419-734-9100	732-2211
Hogue Cellars 2800 Lee Rd *TF:* 800-565-9779 ■ *Web:* www.hoguecellars.com	Prosser	WA	99350	509-786-4557	786-4580
J Filippi Vintage Co 12467 Base Line Rd *Web:* www.josephfilippiwinery.com	Rancho Cucamonga	CA	91739	909-899-5755	899-9196
Kendall-Jackson Wine Estates Ltd 425 Aviation Blvd *TF:* 800-544-4413 ■ *Web:* www.kj.com	Santa Rosa	CA	95403	707-544-4000	569-0105
Kenwood Vineyards 9592 Sonoma Hwy PO Box 447 *Web:* www.kenwoodvineyards.com	Kenwood	CA	95452	707-833-5891	833-1146
Korbel Champagne Cellars 13250 River Rd *TF:* 800-656-7235 ■ *Web:* www.korbel.com	Guerneville	CA	95446	707-824-7000	869-2981
Louis M Martini Winery 254 S St Helena Hwy PO Box 112 *TF:* 800-321-9463 ■ *Web:* www.louismartini.com	Saint Helena	CA	94574	707-963-2736	963-8750
Malibu Hills Vineyards 29000 Newton Canyon Rd **Fax Area Code:* 949 ■ *TF:* 800-814-0733 ■ *Web:* www.rosenthalestatewines.com	Malibu	CA	90265	310-463-9532	916-1858*
Meier's Wine Cellars Inc 6955 Plainfield Rd *TF:* 800-346-2941 ■ *Web:* www.meierswinecellars.com	Silverton	OH	45236	513-891-2900	891-6370
Mendocino Wine Co 501 Parducci Rd *TF:* 888-362-9463 ■ *Web:* www.mendocinowinecompany.com/Parducci.html	Ukiah	CA	95482	707-463-5350	462-7260
Ozeki Sake (USA) Inc 249 Hillcrest Rd *Web:* www.ozekisake.com	Hollister	CA	95023	831-637-9217	637-0953
Pine Ridge Winery LLC 5901 Silverado Trail *TF:* 800-575-9779 ■ *Web:* www.pineridgewinery.com	Napa	CA	94558	707-253-7500	
Ravenswood Winery Inc 26200 Arnold Dr *Web:* www.ravenswood-wine.com	Sonoma	CA	95476	707-938-1960	933-2380
Raymond Vineyard & Cellar Inc 849 Zinfandel Ln **Fax Area Code:* 800 ■ *TF:* 800-525-2659 ■ *Web:* www.raymondwine.com	Saint Helena	CA	94574	707-963-3141	525-5339*
Renault Winery 72 N Bremen Ave *Web:* www.renaultwinery.com	Egg Harbor City	NJ	08215	609-965-2111	965-1847
Robert Mondavi Co 7801 St Helena Hwy PO Box 106 *TF:* 888-766-6328 ■ *Web:* www.mondavi.com	Oakville	CA	94562	888-766-6328	
Rodney Strong Vineyards 1145 Old Redwood Hwy *TF:* 800-474-9463 ■ *Web:* www.rodneystrong.com	Healdsburg	CA	95448	707-433-6511	433-0939
Round Hill Vineyards & Cellars 1680 Silverado Trail *TF:* 800-778-0424 ■ *Web:* www.roundhillwines.com	Saint Helena	CA	94574	707-963-5251	963-0834
Royal Wine Corp 63 Le Fante Ln *TF:* 800-382-8299 ■ *Web:* www.kedem.com	Bayonne	NJ	07002	718-384-2400	384-5329
Sebastiani Vineyards Inc 389 4th St E *TF:* 800-888-5532 ■ *Web:* www.sebastiani.com	Sonoma	CA	95476	707-938-5532	933-3370
Simi Winery 16275 Healdsburg Ave *TF:* 800-746-4880 ■ *Web:* www.simiwinery.com	Healdsburg	CA	95448	707-433-6981	433-6253
Ste Michelle Wine Estates 14111 NE 145th St *TF:* 800-267-6793 ■ *Web:* www.ste-michelle.com	Woodinville	WA	98072	425-488-1133	415-3657
Strong Rodney Vineyards 1145 Old Redwood Hwy *TF:* 800-474-9463 ■ *Web:* www.rodneystrong.com	Healdsburg	CA	95448	707-433-6511	433-0939
Trefethen Vineyards Winery Inc 1160 Oak Knoll Ave *TF:* 800-556-4847 ■ *Web:* www.trefethen.com	Napa	CA	94558	707-255-7700	255-0793
Trinchero Family Estates 100 Saint Helena Hwy S PO Box 248 **Fax:* Mktg ■ *Web:* www.tfewines.com	Saint Helena	CA	94574	707-963-3104	963-2381*
Vie-Del Co 11903 S Chestnut	Fresno	CA	93725	559-834-2525	834-1348
Vincor International Inc 441 Courtneypark Dr E *TSX:* VN ■ **Fax:* Sales ■ *TF:* 800-265-9463 ■ *Web:* www.vincorinternational.com	Mississauga	ON	L5T2V3	905-564-6900	564-6909*
Warner Vineyards Inc 706 S Kalamazoo St *TF:* 800-756-5357 ■ *Web:* www.warnerwines.com	Paw Paw	MI	49079	269-657-3165	657-4154
Weibel Vineyards 1 Winemaster Way *TF:* 800-932-9463 ■ *Web:* www.weibel.com	Lodi	CA	95240	209-365-9463	365-9469
Widmer's Wine Cellars Inc 235 N Bloomfield Rd *TF:* 800-836-5253 ■ *Web:* www.widmerwine.com	Naples	NY	14512	585-374-6311	374-2028
Willamette Valley Vineyards Inc 8800 Enchanted Way SE *NASDAQ:* WVVI ■ *TF Sales:* 800-344-9463 ■ *Web:* www.willamettevalleyvineyards.com	Turner	OR	97392	503-588-9463	588-8894
Windsor Vineyards 9600 Bell Rd PO Box 368 *TF:* 800-289-9463 ■ *Web:* www.windsorwines.com	Windsor	CA	95492	707-836-5000	836-5924
Wine Group Inc 240 Stockton St Suite 800	San Francisco	CA	94108	415-986-8700	986-4305

81 BEVERAGES - WHOL

81-1 Beer & Ale - Whol

Company	City	State	ZIP	Phone	Fax
Ace Beverage Corp 401 S Anderson St	Los Angeles	CA	90033	323-264-6000	264-9789
All State Beverage Co 1580 Parallel St *TF:* 800-489-1021	Montgomery	AL	36104	334-265-0507	263-2367
Allentown Beverage Co Inc 1249 N Quebec St	Allentown	PA	18109	610-432-4581	821-8311
Anheuser-Busch International Inc 1 Busch Pl *Web:* www.budweiser.com	Saint Louis	MO	63118	314-577-2000	577-2900
Arkansas Distributing Co LLC 800 E Barton Ave *TF:* 877-735-3506	West Memphis	AR	72301	870-735-3506	735-0052
Associated Distributors LLC 401 Woodlake Dr *TF:* 800-268-4200	Chesapeake	VA	23320	757-424-6300	424-4616
Atlas Distributing Corp 44 Southbridge St *TF:* 800-649-6221 ■ *Web:* www.atlasdistributing.com	Auburn	MA	01501	508-791-6221	791-0812
Banko Beverage Co 2124 Hanover Ave *TF:* 800-322-9295 ■ *Web:* www.bankobeverage.com	Allentown	PA	18109	610-434-0147	434-2348
Barringer RH Distributing Inc 1620 Fairfax Rd *TF:* 800-273-0555	Greensboro	NC	27407	336-854-0555	854-4199
Beauchamp Distributing Co 1911 S Santa Fe Ave *TF:* 800-734-5102	Compton	CA	90221	310-639-5320	537-8641
Bellavance Beverage Co Inc 120 Northwest Blvd	Nashua	NH	03063	603-882-9722	882-0414
Beloit Beverage Co Inc 4059 W Bradley Rd	Milwaukee	WI	53209	414-362-5000	362-5016
Bergseth Brothers Co 501 23rd St N	Fargo	ND	58102	701-232-8818	232-8684
Beverage Solutions Inc 13813 W Laurel Dr *TF:* 800-842-4050	Lake Forest	IL	60045	847-247-0121	247-0129
Big Sky Distributors Inc 14220 Wyandotte St **Fax Area Code:* 913 ■ *TF:* 800-926-4233 ■ *Web:* www.bigskydist.net	Kansas City	MO	64145	816-941-3300	897-3095*
Bissman Co Inc 193 N Main St	Mansfield	OH	44901	419-524-2337	524-2337
Blach Distributing Co 131 Main St *TF:* 888-812-5224 ■ *Web:* www.abwholesaler.com/blach	Elko	NV	89801	775-738-7111	738-6731
Blue Ridge Beverage Co Inc 4446 Barley Dr PO Box 700 *TF Cust Svc:* 800-868-0354 ■ *Web:* www.blueridgebeverage.com	Salem	VA	24153	540-380-2000	380-2546
Bob Hall LLC 5600 SE Crane Hwy *TF:* 800-451-6508	Upper Marlboro	MD	20772	301-627-1900	627-0613
Bonanza Beverage Co 6333 Ensworth St *TF Cust Svc:* 800-677-4166	Las Vegas	NV	89119	702-361-4166	361-6408
Brewery Products Co Inc 1017 N Sherman St *TF Cust Svc:* 800-233-9433 ■ *Web:* www.breweryproducts.com	York	PA	17402	717-757-3515	840-4328
Buck Distributing Co Inc 15827 Commerce Ct *TF Cust Svc:* 800-750-2825 ■ *Web:* www.buckdistributing.com	Upper Marlboro	MD	20774	301-952-0400	627-5380
Burke Beverages Inc 4900 S Vernon	McCook	IL	60525	708-688-2000	688-2050
Busch International Sales Co 1 Busch Pl	Saint Louis	MO	63118	314-577-2000	577-2900
Calumet Breweries Inc 6535 Osborn Ave *TF Cust Svc:* 800-882-2739	Hammond	IN	46320	219-845-2242	845-2338
Capital Beverage Co 2424 Del Monte St *TF Cust Svc:* 800-954-2667	West Sacramento	CA	95691	916-371-8164	371-0636
Carenbauer Distributing Corp 1900 Jacob St *Web:* www.abwholesaler.com/carenbauerwholesale	Wheeling	WV	26003	304-232-3000	232-3630
Carter Distributing Co 1307 Broad St	Chattanooga	TN	37402	423-266-0056	265-1501
Central Distributors Inc 15 Foss Rd *TF Cust Svc:* 800-427-5757 ■ *Web:* www.centraldistributors.com	Lewiston	ME	04240	207-784-4026	784-7869
Central European Distribution Corp 2 Bala Plaza Suite 300 *NASDAQ:* CEDC ■ *Web:* www.ced-c.com	Bala Cynwyd	PA	19004	610-660-7817	667-3308
Cherokee Distributing Co Inc 200 Miller Main Cir *TF:* 800-362-9459	Knoxville	TN	37919	865-588-7641	558-8941
Chicago Beverage Systems Inc 441 N Kilbourn Ave	Chicago	IL	60624	773-826-4100	826-8023
City Beverage LLC 1105 E Lafayette St *TF:* 800-272-2635	Bloomington	IL	61701	309-662-1373	663-6790
City Beverages of Orlando 10928 Florida Crown Dr *TF:* 800-717-7267 ■ *Web:* www.citybeverages.com	Orlando	FL	32824	407-851-7100	251-4089
Clare Rose Inc 72 Clare Rose Blvd *TF:* 800-427-2833 ■ *Web:* www.clarerose.com	Patchogue	NY	11772	631-475-1840	475-1837
Classic City Beverages LLC 530 Calhoun Dr *TF:* 800-300-0218	Athens	GA	30601	706-353-1650	353-1655
Coastal Beverage Co Inc 301 Harley Rd PO Box 10159 *TF:* 800-229-3884	Wilmington	NC	28404	910-799-3011	392-3674
Columbia Distributing Co 6840 N Cutter Cir *TF:* 800-275-4494 ■ *Web:* www.columbia-dist.com	Portland	OR	97217	503-289-9600	240-8666
Commercial Distributing Co Inc 46 S Broad St *TF Cust Svc:* 800-332-8999	Westfield	MA	01085	413-562-9691	562-4618
Consolidated Beverages Inc 12 Saint Mark St *TF:* 800-922-8128	Auburn	MA	01501	508-832-5311	832-9831
Coors Distributing Co 5400 N Pecos St *TF:* 800-642-6116 ■ *Web:* www.coors.com	Denver	CO	80221	303-433-6541	964-5577
Couch Distributing Co Inc 104 Lee Rd *Web:* www.couchdistributing.com	Watsonville	CA	95076	831-724-0649	724-4293
Crescent Crown Distributing 5900 Almonaster Ave	New Orleans	LA	70136	504-240-5900	240-5500
Crest Beverage Co 7598 Trade St *Web:* crest.bevonline.com	San Diego	CA	92121	858-566-1800	547-7350
Cunningham Wholesale Co Inc 901 Berryhill Rd	Charlotte	NC	28208	704-392-8371	392-2626
D Canale Beverages Inc 45 Crump Blvd *Web:* www.abwholesaler.com/dcanalebeverages	Memphis	TN	38106	901-948-4543	948-6907
Dearing Beverage Co Inc 331 Victory Rd *TF Cust Svc:* 800-552-9550	Winchester	VA	22602	540-662-0561	662-0595
DeBauge Brothers Inc 2915 W 15th Ave	Emporia	KS	66801	620-342-4663	342-3312
Delaware Importers Inc 615 Lambson Ln *TF:* 800-292-7890	New Castle	DE	19720	302-656-4407	656-0291
Desert Eagle Distributors 6949 Market St	El Paso	TX	79915	915-772-4246	775-0985
DET Distributing Co 301 Great Circle Rd *Web:* www.detdist.com	Nashville	TN	37228	615-244-4113	555-0122
Dutchess Beer Distributors Inc 5 Laurel St *TF Cust Svc:* 800-427-6308	Poughkeepsie	NY	12603	845-452-0940	452-0958
Dwan & Co Inc 142 Industrial Ln PO Box 96	Torrington	CT	06790	860-489-3149	489-4805
Eagle Brands Inc 3201 NW 72nd Ave	Miami	FL	33122	305-599-2337	597-0221
Eagle Distributing Co Inc 1100 S Bud Blvd *TF:* 877-377-2283	Fremont	NE	68025	402-721-9723	721-0620
Eagle Distributing Co Inc 310 Radford Pl *TF:* 800-467-3301	Knoxville	TN	37917	865-637-3311	525-9530
Eastown Distributors Co 14400 Oakland Ave *TF:* 800-417-0080 ■ *Web:* www.eastown.com	Highland Park	MI	48203	313-867-6900	867-6020
Fox Henry A Sales Co 4494 36th St SE *TF:* 800-762-8730	Kentwood	MI	49512	616-949-1210	949-7209
Frank B Fuhrer Wholesale Co 3100 E Carson St *TF:* 800-837-2212 ■ *Web:* www.fuhrerwholesale.com	Pittsburgh	PA	15203	412-488-8844	488-0195
Fuhrer Frank B Wholesale Co 3100 E Carson St *TF:* 800-837-2212 ■ *Web:* www.fuhrerwholesale.com	Pittsburgh	PA	15203	412-488-8844	488-0195
Gambrinus Co 14800 San Pedro Ave 3rd Fl *TF:* 800-596-6486 ■ *Web:* www.gambrinusco.com	San Antonio	TX	78232	210-490-9128	490-9984
Gate City Beverage Distributors 2505 Steele St *TF:* 800-500-4283 ■ *Web:* www.gcbev.com	San Bernardino	CA	92408	909-799-1600	799-1615
General Beverage & Beer Sales Co 6169 McKee Rd PO Box 44326 *TF:* 800-362-3636	Madison	WI	53744	608-271-1234	271-8625
General Distributing Co 5350 W Amelia Earhart Dr	Salt Lake City	UT	84116	801-531-7895	363-4924
General Wholesale Beer Co 1271 Tacoma Dr NW *TF:* 800-801-0772	Atlanta	GA	30318	404-351-3626	350-6550
Georgia Crown Distributing 100 Georgia Crown Dr *TF:* 800-332-4830 ■ *Web:* www.georgiacrown.com	McDonough	GA	30253	770-302-3000	305-9438
Giglio Distributing Co Inc 155 MLK Pkwy *TF:* 800-725-2337	Beaumont	TX	77701	409-838-1654	838-4018
Girardi Distributors LLC 5 Railroad Pl *TF:* 800-322-1229	Athol	MA	01331	978-249-3581	249-7894
Gold Coast Beverage Distributors Inc 3325 NW 70th Ave *Web:* www.goldcoastbeverage.com	Miami	FL	33122	305-591-9800	593-2392
Golden Brand Beverage Distributors 2225 Jerrold Ave *Web:* www.goldenbrands.com	San Francisco	CA	94124	415-643-9900	643-9397
Golden Eagle of Arkansas Inc 1900 E 15th St	Little Rock	AR	72202	501-372-2800	376-2404
Golden Eagle Distributors Inc 705 E Ajo Way *TF:* 800-274-4283 ■ *Web:* www.gedaz.com	Tucson	AZ	85713	520-884-5999	884-1804

Beer & Ale - Whol (Cont'd)

	City	State	Zip	Phone	Fax
Goldring Gulf Distributing Co 675 S Pace Blvd *Web:* www.goldringgulf.com	Pensacola	FL	32501	850-429-7000	429-7013
Grantham Distributing Co Inc 2685 Hansrob Rd	Orlando	FL	32804	407-299-6446	295-7104
Great Bay Distributors Inc 2310 Starkey Rd *TF:* 800-231-4283 ■ *Web:* www.greatbaybud.com	Largo	FL	33771	727-584-8626	585-9425
Gretz Beer Co 710 E Main St **Fax Area Code:* 866 ■ *TF:* 866-473-8926 ■ *Web:* www.gretzbeer.com	Norristown	PA	19401	610-275-0285	808-0075*
Grey Eagle Distributors Inc 2340 Millpark Dr *Web:* www.greyeagle.com	Maryland Heights	MO	63043	314-429-9100	429-9137
Grosslein Beverages Inc 13554 Tungsten St NW *TF Cust Svc:* 800-421-5804	Anoka	MN	55303	763-421-5804	427-5555
Guiffre Distributing Co 6839 Industrial Rd	Springfield	VA	22151	703-642-1700	642-2855
Gusto Brands Inc 707 Douglas St *TF:* 800-241-3232	LaGrange	GA	30240	706-882-2573	882-2412
H Dennert Distributing Corp 351 Wilmer Ave *TF Cust Svc:* 800-837-5659 ■ *Web:* www.hdennert.com	Cincinnati	OH	45226	513-871-7272	871-4432
Halo Distributing Co 200 Lombrano St	San Antonio	TX	78207	210-735-1111	737-2139
Hartford Distributors Inc 131 Chapel Rd *TF:* 800-832-7211	Manchester	CT	06042	860-643-2337	646-3780
Hayes Beer Distributing Co 12160 S Central Ave	Alsip	IL	60803	708-389-8200	389-8287
Heidelberg Distributing Co 1518 Dalton St *TF Cust Svc:* 800-486-1518 ■ *Web:* www.heidelbergdist.com	Cincinnati	OH	45214	513-421-5000	421-5194
Heineken USA 360 Hamilton Ave Suite 1103 *TF:* 800-811-4951 ■ *Web:* www.heineken.com	White Plains	NY	10601	914-681-4100	681-1900
Hensley & Co 4201 N 45th Ave **Fax Area Code:* 623 ■ *Web:* www.hensley.com	Phoenix	AZ	85031	602-264-1635	247-7094*
High Grade Beverage Inc 891 Georges Rd *TF:* 800-221-1194 ■ *Web:* www.highgradebeverage.com	Monmouth Junction	NJ	08852	732-821-7600	821-5953
High Life Sales Co 1325 N Topping Ave	Kansas City	MO	64120	816-483-3700	241-1789
Hill Distributing Co 2555 Harrison Rd *Web:* www.hilldistributing.com	Columbus	OH	43204	614-276-6533	276-8888
House of La Rose Inc 6745 Southpoint Pkwy *TF:* 800-642-4379	Becksville	OH	44141	440-746-7500	746-7501
House of Schwan Inc 3636 Comotara St *TF:* 800-373-7773	Wichita	KS	67226	316-636-9100	636-6210
Hub City Distributing Co 6 Princess Rd *TF:* 800-551-0668	Lawrenceville	NJ	08648	609-844-9600	844-9669
Hubert Distributors Inc 1200 Auburn Rd *Web:* www.abwholesaler.com/hubertdistributors	Pontiac	MI	48342	248-858-2340	858-7777
InBev USA 101 Merritt 7 PO Box 5075 *TF Cust Svc:* 800-769-5337 ■ *Web:* www.inbev.com	Norwalk	CT	06856	203-750-6600	750-6699
Iron City Distributing Co 2670 Commercial Ave *TF Cust Svc:* 800-759-2671 ■ *Web:* www.ironcitydist.com	Mingo Junction	OH	43938	740-598-4171	598-4677
JJ Taylor Cos Inc 655 N AIA *Web:* www.jjtaylor.com	Jupiter	FL	33477	561-354-2900	354-2999
JJ Taylor Distributing of Florida Inc 501 W 1st St **Fax:* Mktg ■ *Web:* www.jjtaylor.com	Tampa	FL	33619	813-247-4000	248-1231*
Joe G Maloof & Co Inc 701 Comanche Rd NE *TF:* 800-760-2293	Albuquerque	NM	87107	505-243-2293	768-1552
Koerner Distributors Inc 1305 W Wabash St *TF:* 800-475-5162 ■ *Web:* www.koernerdistributor.com	Effingham	IL	62401	217-347-7113	347-8736
Kramer Beverage Co Inc 161 S 2nd Rd *TF Cust Svc:* 800-321-4522 ■ *Web:* www.kramerbev.com	Hammonton	NJ	08037	609-704-7000	704-7100
Kunda Beverage 349 S Henderson Rd *TF:* 800-262-2323 ■ *Web:* www.kundabev.com	King of Prussia	PA	19406	610-265-3113	265-3190
L & M Distributors Inc 2300 Hoover Dr	Modesto	CA	95354	209-521-2350	521-5073
Labatt Breweries of Canada 207 Queen's Quay W Suite 299 *TF:* 800-268-2337 ■ *Web:* www.labatt.ca	Toronto	ON	M5J1A7	416-361-5050	361-5200
Lake Beverage Corp 900 John St *TF:* 800-476-4049 ■ *Web:* www.lakebeverage.com	West Henrietta	NY	14586	585-427-0090	427-0693
Leon Farmer & Co 100 Rail Ridge Rd PO Box 1352 *TF:* 800-282-7009 ■ *Web:* www.leonfarmer.com	Athens	GA	30603	706-353-1166	369-8922
Lion Brewery Inc 700 N Pennsylvania Ave *TF:* 800-233-8327 ■ *Web:* www.lionbrewery.com	Wilkes-Barre	PA	18705	570-823-8801	823-6686
Louis Glunz Beer Inc 7100 N Capitol Dr *Web:* www.glunzbeer.com	Lincolnwood	IL	60712	847-676-9500	675-5678
Luce & Son Inc 2399 Valley Rd *TF:* 888-296-7570	Reno	NV	89512	775-785-7810	785-7834
M & M Distributors Inc 3901 S Creyts Rd	Lansing	MI	48917	517-322-9010	322-0359
Maloof Joe G & Co Inc 701 Comanche Rd NE *TF:* 800-760-2293	Albuquerque	NM	87107	505-243-2293	768-1552
Maple City Ice Co Inc 371 Cleveland Rd *TF Cust Svc:* 800-736-6091	Norwalk	OH	44857	419-668-2531	668-5291
Mark VII Distributors Inc 475 Prior Ave N	Saint Paul	MN	55104	651-646-6063	646-6036
Markstein Beverage Co 505 S Pacific St *Web:* www.abwholesaler.com/markstein	San Marcos	CA	92079	760-744-9100	744-0082
Mautino Distributing Co 500 N Richards St *TF Cust Svc:* 800-851-2756	Spring Valley	IL	61362	815-664-4311	664-2224
MBC United Wholesale 966 E I65 Service Rd N	Mobile	AL	36607	251-471-3486	479-5423
McLaughlin & Moran Inc 40 Slater Rd	Cranston	RI	02920	401-463-5454	463-3770
Merrimack Valley Distributing Co 50 Prince St *TF:* 800-698-0250	Danvers	MA	01923	978-777-2213	774-7487
Mesa Distributing Co Inc 8870 Liquid Ct *TF:* 800-275-1071 ■ *Web:* www.mesadistributing.com	San Diego	CA	92121	858-452-2300	452-6242
Metropolitan Distributing Co Inc 911 N Summit St	Toledo	OH	43604	419-241-6111	241-2334
Metz Beverage Co Inc 302 N Custer St *TF:* 800-821-4010	Sheridan	WY	82801	307-672-5848	672-6405
Mission Beverage Co 550 S Mission Rd	Los Angeles	CA	90033	323-266-6238	266-6559
Moon Distributors Inc 2800 Vance St	Little Rock	AR	72206	501-375-8291	375-7035
Mt Hood Beverage Co 3601 NW Yeon Ave *TF:* 800-788-9992 ■ *Web:* www.mhbco.com	Portland	OR	97210	503-274-9990	727-3210
Muller Inc 2800 Grant Ave *TF:* 800-729-5483	Philadelphia	PA	19114	215-676-7575	698-0414
Nackard Beverage Inc 5660 E Pensdock Ave *TF:* 800-622-5273	Flagstaff	AZ	86004	928-526-2229	522-2171
Nebraska Wine & Spirits Inc 4444 S 94th St	Omaha	NE	68127	402-339-9444	593-0209
Nevada Beverage Co Inc 3940 W Tropicana Ave **Fax:* Sales	Las Vegas	NV	89103	702-739-9474	739-7345*
New Hampshire Distributors Inc 65 Regional Dr *TF:* 800-852-3781	Concord	NH	03301	603-224-9991	224-0415
NKS Distributors Inc 399 New Churchmans Rd *TF:* 800-292-9509 ■ *Web:* www.abwholesaler.com/nksdistributors	New Castle	DE	19720	302-322-1811	324-4024
Odom Corp 10500 NE 8th St Suite 2000 *TF:* 800-767-6366 ■ *Web:* www.odomcorp.com	Bellevue	WA	98004	425-456-3535	456-3536
Pacific Beverage Co 5305 Ekwill St *TF Cust Svc:* 800-325-2278	Santa Barbara	CA	93111	805-964-0611	683-4304
Paradise Beverages Inc 94-1450 Moaniani St **Fax:* Sales ■ *TF:* 800-252-3723	Waipahu	HI	96797	808-678-4000	677-8280*
Pepin Distributing Co 4121 N 50th St *Web:* www.pepindistributing.com	Tampa	FL	33610	813-626-6176	626-5800
Pike Distributors Inc 401 E John St PO Box 465	Newberry	MI	49868	906-293-8611	
Pine State Trading Co 8 Ellis Ave *TF:* 800-873-3825 ■ *Web:* www.pinestatetrading.com	Augusta	ME	04330	207-622-3741	626-0150
Powers Distributing Co Inc 3700 Giddings Rd *TF:* 800-498-4008 ■ *Web:* www.powers-dist.com/	Orion	MI	48359	248-393-3700	393-1503
Premier Beverage Co of Florida 9801 Premier Pkwy *TF:* 800-432-2002 ■ *Web:* www.premier-bev.com	Miramar	FL	33025	954-436-9200	266-2351
Premium Beverage Co Inc 928 N Railroad Ave	Opelika	AL	36801	334-745-4521	745-2179
Premium Distributors of Maryland LLC 530 Monocacy Blvd *TF:* 800-352-9165 ■ *Web:* www.reyesholdings.com/maryland_dist.html	Frederick	MD	21701	301-662-0372	663-9488
Premium Distributors of Virginia 15001 Northridge Dr	Chantilly	VA	20151	703-227-1200	227-1202
Premium Distributors of Washington DC LLC 3500 Fort Lincoln Dr NE *TF:* 888-524-5483	Washington	DC	20018	202-526-3900	526-7417
Quality Beverage Inc 525 Miles Standish Blvd PO Box 671 *TF:* 800-525-8989	Taunton	MA	02780	508-822-6200	822-7051
RH Barringer Distributing Co Inc 1620 Fairfax Rd *TF:* 800-273-0555	Greensboro	NC	27407	336-854-0555	854-4199
Richland Beverage Assoc 2415 Midway Rd Suite 115 *TF:* 877-357-0248 ■ *Web:* www.richland-trading.com	Carrollton	TX	75006	214-357-0248	357-9581
Ritchie & Page Distributing Co Inc 292 3rd St *TF:* 800-257-9360	Trenton	NJ	08611	609-392-1146	392-8541
Sapporo USA Inc 11 E 44 St Suite 508 *Web:* www.sapporousa.com	New York	NY	10017	212-922-9165	922-9576
Saratoga Eagle Sales & Service Inc 319 Corinth Rd *TF:* 800-342-9565 ■ *Web:* www.abwholesaler.com/SARATOGAEAGLE	Glens Falls	NY	12804	518-792-3112	792-3247
Savannah Distributing Co Inc 5 Interchange Ct PO Box 1388 *TF:* 800-551-0777 ■ *Web:* www.gawine.com	Savannah	GA	31402	912-233-1167	233-1157
Seneca Beverage Corp 388 Upper Oakwood Ave *TF:* 800-724-0350	Elmira	NY	14903	607-734-6111	734-2415
Silver Eagle Distributors LP 7777 Washington Ave *Web:* www.abwslr.com/SILVEREAGLE5	Houston	TX	77007	713-869-4361	867-8112
Silver State Liquor & Wine Inc 100 Distribution Dr *TF:* 800-543-3867 ■ *Web:* www.renotahoedrinks.com	Sparks	NV	89441	775-331-3400	331-3474
Skokie Valley Beverage Co 199 Shepard Ave	Wheeling	IL	60090	847-541-1500	541-2059
Southern Wine & Spirits of Colorado 5270 Fox St PO Box 5603 *TF:* 800-332-9956 ■ *Web:* www.southernwine.com	Denver	CO	80217	303-292-1711	297-9967
Southwest Services 4370 S Valley View Blvd	Las Vegas	NV	89103	702-367-7777	367-1143
Standard Beverage Corp 2416 E 37th St N *TF:* 800-999-7707 ■ *Web:* www.stdbev.com	Wichita	KS	67219	316-838-7707	838-1396
Standard Sales Co Inc 4800 E 42nd St Suite 400	Odessa	TX	79762	432-367-7662	367-9526
Star Distributors Inc 10 Eder Rd *TF:* 800-922-3501	West Haven	CT	06516	203-932-3636	932-5977
Stoudt Co 1618 Judson Rd PO Box 4147	Longview	TX	75606	903-753-7239	758-6479
Superior Distributing Co 22116 Washington Township Rd 218	Fostoria	OH	44830	419-435-1938	435-5231
Supreme Beverage Co 2100-A Jackson Ave *TF:* 800-281-1482	Huntsville	AL	35805	256-534-1482	534-0291
Three Lakes Distributing Co 111 Overton St	Hot Springs	AR	71901	501-623-8201	624-4499
Town & Country Distributors Inc 1050 W Ardmore Ave	Itasca	IL	60143	630-250-0590	250-8946
Tri-County Beverage Co 14301 Prospect Ave *Web:* www.tricountybeverage.com	Dearborn	MI	48126	313-584-7100	584-8364
United Distributors Inc 206 7th St PO Box 1077 *TF:* 800-749-7694	Macon	GA	31202	478-746-7694	746-1852
United Distributors Inc 5500 United Dr *TF:* 800-282-7950	Smyrna	GA	30082	678-305-2000	305-2050
Virginia Distributing Co 2401 Patterson Ave SW *Web:* www.virginiadistributing.com	Roanoke	VA	24016	540-342-3105	345-1738
Watson Kunda & Sons Inc DBA Kunda Beverage 349 S Henderson Rd *TF:* 800-262-2323 ■ *Web:* www.kundabev.com	King of Prussia	PA	19406	610-265-3113	265-3190
Wayne Distributing Co 45 Sharpe Dr	Cranston	RI	02920	401-463-7020	463-3466
Western Beverages Inc 4545 E 51st Ave *TF:* 877-701-2337 ■ *Web:* www.westernbev.net	Denver	CO	80216	303-388-5751	336-3336
Western Wyoming Beverages Inc 100 Reliance Rd *TF:* 800-551-8244	Rock Springs	WY	82901	307-362-6332	362-6335
Williams Distributing Corp 880 Burnett Rd *TF:* 800-332-9634	Chicopee	MA	01020	413-594-4900	594-4911
Wright Wisner Distributing Corp 3165 Brighton-Henrietta Town Line Rd	Rochester	NY	14623	585-427-2880	272-1216

81-2 Soft Drinks - Whol

	City	State	Zip	Phone	Fax
Admiral Beverage Corp PO Box 726 *Web:* www.admiralbeverage.com	Worland	WY	82401	307-347-4201	347-3571
All-American Bottling Corp 1400 N Shartel Suite 1200 *TF:* 800-471-2652	Oklahoma City	OK	73103	405-232-1158	232-1523
All State Beverage Co 1580 Parallel St *TF:* 800-489-1021	Montgomery	AL	36104	334-265-0507	263-2367
Atlas Distributing Corp 44 Southbridge St *TF:* 800-649-6221 ■ *Web:* www.atlasdistributing.com	Auburn	MA	01501	508-791-6221	791-0812
Beverages Direct Inc 20 Danada Sq W *Web:* www.beveragesdirect.com	Wheaton	IL	60187	630-510-8925	
Bissman Co Inc 193 N Main St	Mansfield	OH	44901	419-524-2337	524-2337
Buffalo Rock Co PO Box 10048 *TF Sales:* 800-822-9799 ■ *Web:* www.buffalorock.com	Birmingham	AL	35202	205-942-3435	942-2601
Carolina Canners Inc PO Box 1628	Cheraw	SC	29520	843-537-5281	537-6743
Coca-Cola Bottling Co of Chattanooga PO Box 11128 *TF:* 800-747-2653	Chattanooga	TN	37401	423-624-4681	622-6134
Coca-Cola Bottling Co Consolidated 4100 Coca-Cola Plaza *NASDAQ: COKE* ■ *TF:* 800-777-2653 ■ *Web:* www.cokeconsolidated.com	Charlotte	NC	28211	704-551-4400	557-4646
Coca-Cola Bottling Co of New York 3 Skyline Dr **Fax:* Cust Svc	Hawthorne	NY	10532	914-345-3900	789-1814*
Coca-Cola Bottling Co United Inc 4600 East Lake Blvd	Birmingham	AL	35201	205-849-4722	849-4728
Coca-Cola Enterprises Inc 2500 Windy Ridge Pkwy *NYSE: CCE* ■ *Web:* www.cokecce.com	Atlanta	GA	30339	770-989-3000	989-3597
Coca-Cola Enterprises Inc Central US/Eastern Canada Group PO Box 132008 **Fax:* Hum Res	Dallas	TX	75313	214-357-1781	902-2736*
Coca-Cola Enterprises Inc Eastern US Group PO Box 723040	Atlanta	GA	31139	770-989-3000	989-3363
Coca-Cola Enterprises Inc Western US/Western Canada Group 1334 S Central Ave *TF:* 800-647-2653	Los Angeles	CA	90021	213-746-5555	745-6141
Cunningham Wholesale Co Inc 901 Berryhill Rd	Charlotte	NC	28208	704-392-8371	392-2626
Dr Pepper Bottling Co of Texas 2304 Century Ctr Blvd *TF:* 800-696-5891 ■ *Web:* www.drpep.com	Irving	TX	75062	972-579-1024	721-8147
Dr Pepper/Seven-Up Bottling Group Inc 5950 Sherry Ln Suite 500	Dallas	TX	75225	214-530-5000	530-5035
F & V Distributing 700 Columbia St	Brooklyn	NY	11231	718-386-4200	532-4234
Farrell Louis E Co Inc 20 Karen Dr *TF:* 800-473-7741	South Burlington	VT	05403	802-864-6000	658-7773
Flavia Beverage Systems 1301 Wilson Dr *TF:* 800-882-6629 ■ *Web:* www.flavia.net	West Chester	PA	19380	610-430-2500	430-2652
General Beverage & Beer Sales Co 6169 McKee Rd PO Box 44326 *TF:* 800-362-3636	Madison	WI	53744	608-271-1234	271-8625
Grant-Lydick Beverage Co 3411 Hidalgo St	Austin	TX	78702	512-385-4477	385-8751
Gulf States Canners Inc 1006 Industrial Park	Clinton	MS	39056	601-924-0511	924-7746

				Phone	Fax
Gusto Brands Inc 707 Douglas St	LaGrange	GA	30240	706-882-2573	882-2412
TF: 800-241-3232					
High Grade Beverage Inc 891 Georges Rd	Monmouth Junction	NJ	08852	732-821-7600	821-5953
TF: 800-221-1194 ■ Web: www.highgradebeverage.com					
Honickman Affiliates 8275 Rt 130	Pennsauken	NJ	08110	856-665-6200	661-4560
Leading Brands Inc 1500 W Georgia St Suite 1800	Vancouver	BC	V6G2Z6	604-685-5200	685-5249
NASDAQ: LBIX ■ TF: 866-685-5200 ■ Web: www.lbix.com					
Louis E Farrell Co Inc 20 Karen Dr	South Burlington	VT	05403	802-864-6000	658-7773
TF: 800-473-7741					
Made-Rite Co PO Box 3283	Longview	TX	75606	903-753-8604	236-9743
Malolo Beverages & Supplies Ltd 120 Sand Island Access Rd	Honolulu	HI	96819	808-845-4830	845-4835
Markstein Beverage Co 505 S Pacific St	San Marcos	CA	92079	760-744-9100	744-0082
Web: www.abwholesaler.com/markstein					
Meadowbrook Distributing Corp 550 New Horizons Blvd	Amityville	NY	11701	631-226-9000	226-4233
Metz Beverage Co Inc 302 N Custer St	Sheridan	WY	82801	307-672-5848	672-6405
TF: 800-821-4010					
Nehi Royal Crown Bottling & Distributing Co Inc					
PO Box 1687	Bowling Green	KY	42102	270-842-8106	842-2877
TF: 800-626-5255					
Noel Canning Corp 1001 S 1st St	Yakima	WA	98901	509-248-4545	248-2843
Nor-Cal Beverage Co Inc 2286 Stone Blvd	West Sacramento	CA	95691	916-372-0600	374-2602
Web: www.ncbev.com					
Pepsi Bottling Ventures LLC 4700 Homewood Ct Suite 200	Raleigh	NC	27609	919-782-9271	783-6925
PepsiAmericas Inc 60 S 6th St Suite 4000	Minneapolis	MN	55402	612-661-3830	661-3825
NYSE: PAS ■ Web: www.pepsiamericas.com					
PepsiCo International 700 Anderson Hill Rd	Purchase	NY	10577	914-253-2000	253-2070
Philadelphia Coca-Cola Bottling Co 725 E Erie Ave	Philadelphia	PA	19134	215-427-4500	427-4496*
*Fax: Hum Res ■ TF Cust Svc: 888-551-6800 ■ Web: www.phillycoke.com					
Seltzer & Rydholm Inc 191 Merrow Rd	Auburn	ME	04210	207-784-5791	784-8685
Seven Up Bottling Group of Kansas 2900 S Hydraulic St	Wichita	KS	67216	316-529-3777	529-1608
TF: 800-540-0001					
Southeast-Atlantic Corp 6001 Bowdendale Ave	Jacksonville	FL	32216	904-739-1000	737-9125
TF: 800-329-2067					
Southwest Canners Inc PO Box 809	Portales	NM	88130	505-356-6623	356-2365
TF: 800-658-2085					
Southwest Services 4370 S Valley View Blvd	Las Vegas	NV	89103	702-367-7777	367-1143
Swire Coca-Cola USA 12634 S 265 West	Draper	UT	84020	801-816-5300	816-5423
TF: 800-530-2653					
Western Wyoming Beverages Inc 100 Reliance Rd	Rock Springs	WY	82901	307-362-6332	362-6335
TF: 800-551-8244					
Wis-Pak Inc 860 West St	Watertown	WI	53094	920-262-6300	262-9273
Wright Wisner Distributing Corp					
3165 Brighton-Henrietta Town Line Rd	Rochester	NY	14623	585-427-2880	272-1216

81-3 Wine & Liquor - Whol

				Phone	Fax
Alabama Crown Distributing 421 Industrial Ln	Birmingham	AL	35211	205-941-1155	942-3767
TF: 800-548-1869					
Allied Beverage Group LLC 600 Washington Ave	Carlstadt	NJ	07072	201-842-6200	842-6331*
*Fax: Cust Svc ■ TF: 800-272-1323 ■ Web: www.alliedbeverage.com					
Bacardi Bottling Corp 12200 N Main St PO Box 26368	Jacksonville	FL	32226	904-757-1290	751-1397
Badger Liquor Co Inc 850 S Morris St	Fond du Lac	WI	54936	920-922-0550	923-8169
TF: 800-242-9708 ■ Web: www.badgerliquor.com					
Badger West Wine & Spirits LLC					
5400 Old Town Hall Rd PO Box 869	Eau Claire	WI	54701	715-836-8600	836-8609
TF: 800-472-6674 ■ Web: www.badgerwest.com					
Barton Inc 1 S Dearborn St Suite 1700	Chicago	IL	60603	312-346-9200	855-1220
TF: 800-949-7837 ■ Web: www.bartoninc.com					
Ben Arnold Sunbelt Beverage Co 101 Beverage Blvd	Ridgeway	SC	29130	803-337-3500	337-5741*
*Fax: Cust Svc ■ TF: 888-262-9787 ■ Web: www.benarnold-sunbelt.com					
Beverage Distributors Co 14200 E Montcrieff Pl Suite D	Aurora	CO	80011	303-371-3421	375-9484
TF: 888-576-6464 ■ Web: www.beveragedistr.com					
Blue Ridge Beverage Co Inc 4446 Barley Dr PO Box 700	Salem	VA	24153	540-380-2000	380-2546
TF Cust Svc: 800-868-0354 ■ Web: www.blueridgebeverage.com					
Brotherhood America's Oldest Winery Ltd					
100 Brotherhood Plaza Dr PO Box 190	Washingtonville	NY	10992	845-496-9101	
Web: www.brotherhoodwinery.net					
Capitol-Husting Co Inc 12001 W Carmen Ave	Milwaukee	WI	53225	414-353-1000	353-0768
TF: 800-242-2231 ■ Web: www.capitol-husting.com					
Castle Brands Inc 570 Lexington Ave 29th Fl	New York	NY	10022	646-356-0200	356-0222
AMEX: ROX ■ TF: 800-882-8140 ■ Web: www.castlebrandsinc.com					
Central Distributors Inc 15 Foss Rd	Lewiston	ME	04240	207-784-4026	784-7869
TF Cust Svc: 800-427-5757 ■ Web: www.centraldistributors.com					
Charmer Industries Inc 19-50 48th St	Astoria	NY	11105	718-726-2500	726-3101
TF: 800-834-3546 ■ Web: www.charmer.com					
Columbia Distributing Co 6840 N Cutter Cir	Portland	OR	97217	503-289-9600	240-8666
TF: 800-275-4494 ■ Web: www.columbia-dist.com					
Consolidated Distilled Products 2600 W 35th St	Chicago	IL	60632	773-254-9000	890-8889*
*Fax: Hum Res ■ TF: 800-944-9450					
Constellation Brands Inc 370 Woodcliff Dr Suite 300	Fairport	NY	14450	585-218-3600	218-2155
NYSE: STZ ■ TF: 888-724-2169 ■ Web: www.cbrands.com					
Cruzan International Inc 222 Lakeview Ave Suite 110	West Palm Beach	FL	33402	561-655-8977	655-9718
AMEX: RUM ■ Web: www.todhunter.com					
David Sherman Corp 5050 Kemper Ave	Saint Louis	MO	63139	314-772-2626	772-6021
Web: www.davidsherman.com					
Delaware Importers Inc 615 Lambson Ln	New Castle	DE	19720	302-656-4487	656-0291
TF: 800-292-7890					
Diageo Chateau & Estate Wines Co 240 Gateway Rd W	Napa	CA	94558	707-299-2600	299-2777
Web: www.diageowines.com					
Eber Brothers Wine & Liquor Corp 155 Paragon Dr	Rochester	NY	14624	585-349-7700	349-7720
TF: 800-776-3237 ■ Web: www.eberbros.com					
Edison Liquor Corp 21125 Enterprise Ave	Brookfield	WI	53045	262-821-0600	821-0363
Fedway Assoc Inc 56 Hackensack Ave	South Kearny	NJ	07032	973-624-6444	589-3556
TF: 800-433-3929 ■ Web: www.fedway.com					
Fox Henry A Sales Co 4494 36th St SE	Kentwood	MI	49512	616-949-1210	949-7209
TF: 800-762-8730					
Frederick Wildman & Sons Ltd 307 E 53rd St	New York	NY	10022	212-355-0700	355-4719
TF: 800-733-9463 ■ Web: www.frederickwildman.com					
General Beverage & Beer Sales Co					
6169 McKee Rd PO Box 44326	Madison	WI	53744	608-271-1234	271-8625
TF: 800-362-3636					
General Wholesale Beer Co 1271 Tacoma Dr NW	Atlanta	GA	30318	404-351-3626	350-6550
TF: 800-801-0772					
General Wine & Liquor Co 373 Victor Ave	Highland Park	MI	48203	313-867-0521	867-4039
Web: www.gwlc.com					
Georgia Crown Distributing 100 Georgia Crown Dr	McDonough	GA	30253	770-302-3000	305-9438
TF: 800-332-4830 ■ Web: www.georgiacrown.com					
Glazer's Wholesale Drug Co Inc 14911 Quorum Dr Suite 400	Dallas	TX	75254	972-392-8200	702-8508
TF: 800-275-2854 ■ Web: www.glazers.com					
Goldring Gulf Distributing Co 675 S Pace Blvd	Pensacola	FL	32501	850-429-7000	429-7013
Web: www.goldringgulf.com					
Grant William & Sons Inc 130 Fieldcrest Ave Raritan Center	Edison	NJ	08837	732-225-9000	225-0950
Web: www.grantusa.com					
Grantham Distributing Co Inc 2685 Hansrob Rd	Orlando	FL	32804	407-299-6446	295-7104
Hammer Co Inc 9450 Rosemont Dr	Streetsboro	OH	44241	330-422-9463	422-4727
TF: 800-258-9463					
Heidelberg Distributing Co 1518 Dalton St	Cincinnati	OH	45214	513-421-5000	421-5194
TF Cust Svc: 800-486-1518 ■ Web: www.heidelbergdist.com					
Horizon Wine & Spirits Nashville 337 28th Ave N	Nashville	TN	37209	615-320-7292	321-4173
Web: www.horizonwineandspirits.com					
Johnson Brothers Wholesale Liquor Co 1999 Shepard Rd	Saint Paul	MN	55116	651-649-5800	649-5894
TF: 800-723-2424 ■ Web: www.johnsonbrothers.com					
Judge & Dolph 1501 Michael Dr	Wood Dale	IL	60191	847-228-9000	928-1985
TF: 800-548-8041 ■ Web: www.judgedolph.com					
Kings Liquor Inc 2810 W Berry St	Fort Worth	TX	76109	817-923-3737	927-0021
Web: www.kingsliquor.com					
Koerner Distributors Inc 1305 W Wabash St	Effingham	IL	62401	217-347-7113	347-8736
TF: 800-475-5162 ■ Web: www.koernerdistributor.com					
L & M Distributors Inc 2300 Hoover Dr	Modesto	CA	95354	209-521-2350	521-5073
Majestic Distilling Co Inc 2200 Monumental Rd	Baltimore	MD	21227	410-242-0200	247-7831
Web: www.majesticdistilling.com					
Major Brands Inc 1502 Business 70 W	Columbia	MO	65202	573-443-3169	874-1035
TF: 800-264-9988 ■ Web: www.majorbrands.com					
Major Brands Inc 550 E 13th Ave	North Kansas City	MO	64116	816-221-1070	421-1062
TF: 800-467-1070 ■ Web: www.majorbrands.com					
MBC United Wholesale 2500 W I65 Service Rd N	Mobile	AL	36607	251-471-3486	479-5423
Mendez & Co PO Box 363348	San Juan	PR	00936	787-793-8888	783-9498
Merrimack Valley Distributing Co 50 Prince St	Danvers	MA	01923	978-777-2213	774-7487
TF: 800-698-0250					
Millenium Import LLC 25 Main St SE	Minneapolis	MN	55414	612-331-6230	623-1644
Moet Hennessy USA 85 10th Ave	New York	NY	10011	212-251-8200	251-8388
Web: www.mhusa.com					
Moon Distributors Inc 2800 Vance St	Little Rock	AR	72206	501-375-8291	375-7035
Mt Hood Beverage Co 3601 NW Yeon Ave	Portland	OR	97210	503-274-9990	727-3210
TF: 800-788-9992 ■ Web: www.mhbco.com					
Nackard Beverage Inc 5660 E Pensdock Ave	Flagstaff	AZ	86004	928-526-2229	522-2171
TF: 800-622-5273					
National Distributing Co Inc 1 National Dr SW	Atlanta	GA	30336	404-696-9440	505-1013
TF: 800-282-3548 ■ Web: www.ndcweb.com					
National Wine & Spirits Inc PO Box 1602	Indianapolis	IN	46206	317-636-6092	685-8810
TF: 800-562-7359 ■ Web: www.nwscorp.com					
Nebraska Wine & Spirits Inc 4444 S 94th St	Omaha	NE	68127	402-339-9444	593-0209
NKS Distributors Inc 399 New Churchmans Rd	New Castle	DE	19720	302-322-1811	324-4024
TF: 800-292-9509 ■ Web: www.abwholesaler.com/nksdistributors					
Odom Corp 10500 NE 8th St Suite 2000	Bellevue	WA	98004	425-456-3535	456-3536
TF: 800-767-6366 ■ Web: www.odomcorp.com					
Olinger Distributing Co 5337 W 78th St	Indianapolis	IN	46268	317-876-1188	876-3638
TF: 800-366-1090 ■ Web: www.olingerindiana.com					
Paradise Beverages Inc 94-1450 Moaniani St	Waipahu	HI	96797	808-678-4000	677-8280*
*Fax: Sales ■ TF: 800-252-3723					
Paterno Wines International 900 Armour Dr	Lake Bluff	IL	60044	847-604-8900	604-5829
TF: 800-950-7676 ■ Web: www.paternoimports.com					
Peerless Importers Inc 16 Bridgewater St	Brooklyn	NY	11222	718-383-5500	441-5596*
*Fax Area Code: 800 ■ TF: 800-338-3880 ■ Web: www.peerimp.com					
Pernod Ricard USA 100 Manhattanville Rd	Purchase	NY	10577	914-848-4800	848-4777
TF: 800-488-7539 ■ Web: www.pernod-ricard-usa.com					
Phillips Distributing Corp 3010 Nob Hill Rd	Madison	WI	53713	608-222-9177	222-0558
TF: 800-236-7269 ■ Web: www.phillipsdistributing.com					
Premier Beverage Co of Florida 9801 Premier Pkwy	Miramar	FL	33025	954-436-9200	266-2351
TF: 800-432-2002 ■ Web: www.premier-bev.com					
Premium Beverage Co Inc 928 N Railroad Ave	Opelika	AL	36801	334-745-4521	745-2179
Quality Beverage Inc 525 Miles Standish Blvd PO Box 671	Taunton	MA	02780	508-822-6200	822-7051
TF: 800-525-8989					
R & R Marketing LLC 10 Patton Dr	West Caldwell	NJ	07006	973-228-5100	403-8679
TF: 800-772-2096					
Remy Cointreau USA Inc 1290 Ave of the Americas	New York	NY	10104	212-399-4200	399-6909
TF: 800-858-9898 ■ Web: www.remycointreau.com					
Republic Beverage Co 4320 S 94th St	Omaha	NE	68127	402-339-9100	597-7289
TF: 800-572-3664					
Republic National Distributing Co (RNDC)					
6511 Tri County Pkwy	Schertz	TX	78154	210-224-7531	227-7810
TF: 800-749-7532 ■ Web: www.rndc-usa.com					
Sainte-Michelle Wine Estates 14111 NE 145th St	Woodinville	WA	98072	425-488-1133	415-3657
Web: www.stimson-lane.com					
Savannah Distributing Co Inc 5 Interchange Ct PO Box 1388	Savannah	GA	31402	912-233-1167	233-1157
TF: 800-551-0777 ■ Web: www.gawine.com					
Silver State Liquor & Wine Inc 100 Distribution Dr	Sparks	NV	89441	775-331-3400	331-3474
TF: 800-543-3867 ■ Web: www.renotahoedrinks.com					
Southern Wine & Spirits of America Inc 1600 NW 163rd St	Miami	FL	33169	305-625-4171	621-0388*
*Fax: Cust Svc ■ TF: 800-432-6431 ■ Web: www.southernwine.com					
Southern Wine & Spirits of Colorado 5270 Fox St PO Box 5603	Denver	CO	80217	303-292-1711	297-9967
TF: 800-332-9956 ■ Web: www.southernwine.com					
Southern Wine & Spirits of Illinois					
300 E Crossroads Pkwy Bolingbrook Corp Ctr	Bolingbrook	IL	60440	630-685-3000	685-3700
TF: 800-776-0180 ■ Web: www.southernwine.com					
Southern Wine & Spirits of New York 345 Underhill Blvd	Syosset	NY	11791	516-921-9005	
Web: www.southernwine.com					
Southwest Services 4370 S Valley View Blvd	Las Vegas	NV	89103	702-367-7777	367-1143
Standard Beverage Corp 2416 E 37th St N	Wichita	KS	67219	316-838-7707	838-1396
TF: 800-999-7707 ■ Web: www.stdbev.com					
Sterling Distributing Co 4433 S 96th St	Omaha	NE	68127	402-339-2300	339-3772
Sunbelt Beverage Corp 60 E 42nd St Suite 1915	New York	NY	10165	212-699-7000	699-7099
Web: www.charmer-sunbelt.com					
Terlato Wine Group 900 Armour Dr	Lake Bluff	IL	60044	847-604-8900	604-5829
TF: 800-950-7676 ■ Web: www.twg.com					
Union Beverage Co 2600 W 35th St	Chicago	IL	60632	773-254-9000	890-8889
TF: 800-685-6868					
United Distributors Inc 206 7th St PO Box 1077	Macon	GA	31202	478-746-7694	746-1852
TF: 800-749-7694					
United Liquors Ltd 175 Campanelli Dr	Braintree	MA	02185	781-348-8000	356-4172
TF: 800-323-9666 ■ Web: www.unitedliquors.com					
Virginia Distributing Co 2401 Patterson Ave SW	Roanoke	VA	24016	540-342-3105	345-1738
Web: www.virginiadistributing.com					
Wayne Distributing Co 45 Sharpe Dr	Cranston	RI	02920	401-463-7020	463-3466
Wet Planet Beverages 130 Linden Oaks Dr Suite C	Rochester	NY	14625	585-381-3560	381-4025
Web: www.wetplanet.com					
Wildman Frederick & Sons Ltd 307 E 53rd St	New York	NY	10022	212-355-0700	355-4719
TF: 800-733-9463 ■ Web: www.frederickwildman.com					
William Grant & Sons Inc 130 Fieldcrest Ave Raritan Center	Edison	NJ	08837	732-225-9000	225-0950
Web: www.grantusa.com					
Wisconsin Distributors Inc 900 Progress Way	Sun Prairie	WI	53590	608-834-2337	834-2300
TF: 800-373-2921 ■ Web: www.wdbud.com					
Young's Market Co LLC 2164 N Batavia St	Orange	CA	92865	714-283-4933	283-6175*
*Fax: Hum Res ■ TF: 800-317-6150 ■ Web: www.youngsmarket.com					

82 BICYCLES & BICYCLE PARTS & ACCESSORIES

SEE ALSO Sporting Goods p. 2323; Toys, Games, Hobbies p. 2375

Company	City	State	Zip	Phone	Fax
Aero-Fast Bicycle Co PO Box 3812 *TF:* 800-656-2376 ■ *Web:* www.aerofast.com	Jacksonville	FL	32206	904-354-3339	354-3488
Answer Products Inc 28209 Ave Stanford *TF Cust Svc:* 800-423-0273 ■ *Web:* www.answerproducts.com	Valencia	CA	91355	661-257-4411	294-4180
Burley Design Co-op Inc 4020 Steward Rd *TF:* 800-423-8445 ■ *Web:* www.burley.com	Eugene	OR	97402	541-687-1644	687-0436
Cane Creek Cycling Components 355 Cane Creek Rd *TF:* 800-234-2725 ■ *Web:* www.canecreek.com	Fletcher	NC	28732	828-684-3551	684-1057
Diamondback Div Raleigh America Inc 6004 S 190th St Suite 101 *Fax Area Code: 800 ■ *TF:* 800-222-5527 ■ *Web:* www.diamondback.com	Kent	WA	98032	253-395-1100	851-0807*
EV Global Motors Co 4826 4th St *TF:* 800-871-4545 ■ *Web:* www.evglobal.com	Irwindale	CA	91706	626-813-9505	813-9506
Fuji Bikes 10940 Dutton Rd *Web:* www.fujibikes.com/	Philadelphia	PA	19154	215-824-3854	824-1051
Giant Bicycle Inc 3587 Old Conejo Rd *Fax Area Code: 800 ■ *TF:* 800-874-4268 ■ *Web:* www.giant-bicycle.com	Newbury Park	CA	91320	805-267-4600	637-9704*
Haro Bicycles 1230 Avenida Chelsea *Web:* www.harobikes.com/	Vista	CA	92081	760-599-0544	599-1237
Huffy Bicycle Co 225 Byers Rd *Fax Area Code: 937 ■ *TF:* 800-872-2453 ■ *Web:* www.huffybikes.com	Springboro	OH	45342	800-872-2453	865-5470*
K2 Bike 19215 Vashon Hwy SW *TF:* 800-426-1617 ■ *Web:* www.k2bike.com	Vashon	WA	98070	206-463-3631	463-8272
Marwi USA Co 11614 McBean Dr *Web:* www.marwiusa.com	El Monte	CA	91732	626-401-1335	401-1339
Pacific Cycle LLC 4902 Hammersley Rd *Web:* www.pacific-cycle.com	Madison	WI	53711	608-268-2468	268-8955
Raleigh America Inc Diamondback Div 6004 S 190th St Suite 101 *Fax Area Code: 800 ■ *TF:* 800-222-5527 ■ *Web:* www.diamondback.com	Kent	WA	98032	253-395-1100	851-0807*
Raleigh USA 6004 S 190th St Suite 101 *Fax Area Code: 800 ■ *TF:* 800-222-5527 ■ *Web:* www.raleighusa.com	Kent	WA	98032	253-395-1100	851-0807*
Serotta Competition Bicycles 41 Geyser Rd *Web:* www.serotta.com/	Saratoga Springs	NY	12866	518-584-1221	584-8900
Shimano American Corp 1 Holland Dr *Web:* www.shimano.com	Irvine	CA	92618	949-951-5003	768-0920
Smith Mfg Co DBA Aero-Fast Bicycle Co PO Box 3812 *TF:* 800-656-2376 ■ *Web:* www.aerofast.com	Jacksonville	FL	32206	904-354-3339	354-3488
Specialized Bicycle Components 15130 Concord Cir *TF:* 877-808-8154 ■ *Web:* www.specialized.com	Morgan Hill	CA	95037	408-779-6229	779-1631
SRAM Corp 1333 N Kingsbury St 4th Fl *Web:* www.sram.com	Chicago	IL	60622	312-664-8800	664-8826
Terry Precision Bicycles for Women Inc 1657 E Park Dr *TF Orders:* 800-289-8379 ■ *Web:* www.terrybicycles.com/	Macedon	NY	14502	315-986-2103	986-2104
Trek Bicycle Corp 801 W Madison St *Web:* www.trekbikes.com	Waterloo	WI	53594	920-478-2191	478-2774
Wald Mfg Co Inc 800 E 5th St *Fax: Sales ■ *Web:* www.waldllc.com	Maysville	KY	41056	606-564-4077	564-5248*
Worksman Trading Corp 94-15 100th St *Web:* www.worksman.com	Ozone Park	NY	11416	718-322-2000	529-4803

83 BIO-RECOVERY SERVICES

Companies listed here provide services for managing and eliminating biohazard dangers that may be present after a death or injury. These services include cleaning, disinfecting, and deodorizing biohazard scenes resulting from accidents, homicides, suicides, natural deaths, and similar events.

Company	City	State	Zip	Phone	Fax
AA Trauma Cleaning Service Inc 5500 NW 15th St M4 *Web:* www.aatraumacleaning.com	Margate	FL	33063	954-973-9502	973-8975
Advanced Ozone Engineering Inc 6038 Oakwood Ave *TF:* 800-588-3871 ■ *Web:* www.advancedozone.com	Cincinnati	OH	45224	513-681-3871	681-3991
Bio Cleaning Specialists Inc PO Box 18622 *TF:* 888-283-8895 ■ *Web:* www.biocsi.com	Minneapolis	MN	55418	651-765-2429	998-1166
Bio Pro LLC 955 W Sherri Dr *Fax Area Code: 480	Gilbert	AZ	85233	602-234-6856	926-4985*
Bio-Recovery Corp 51-49 47th St *TF:* 877-246-2532 ■ *Web:* www.biorecovery.com	Woodside	NY	11377	718-729-2600	472-1588
Bio-Recovery Services of America LLC 552 Danberry St *TF:* 800-699-6522 ■ *Web:* www.biorecovery.net	Toledo	OH	43609	419-381-8255	381-8361
Bio-Scene Recovery Inc 13191 Meadow St NE Suite A *TF:* 877-380-5500 ■ *Web:* www.bioscene.com	Alliance	OH	44601	330-823-5500	823-4405
Biocare Inc PO Box 817 *TF:* 800-875-9396	Easley	SC	29641	864-855-3400	855-1185
BioClean Inc PO Box 3062 *TF:* 888-412-6300 ■ *Web:* www.biocleanwa.com	Arlington	WA	98223	360-435-8170	435-8180
Clean Scene Services LLC 9300 Hwy 23	Belle Chasse	LA	70037	504-433-5777	
Commercial Detail Cleaning 11836 Judd Ct Suite 320 *Web:* www.cdcllc.com	Dallas	TX	75243	214-575-5060	
Crime & Death Scene Cleaning PO Box 828 *TF:* 877-366-8348 ■ *Web:* www.cadsc.com	Ipswich	MA	01938	978-356-7007	356-4606
Critical Cleaning Services Inc 1760 Palm Ave Suite D *Web:* www.ccserv.net/splash_02.asp	San Diego	CA	92154	619-424-3220	424-8424
Distress Scene Cleanup LLC 6001 Wichita Dr	Knoxville	TN	37921	865-694-4114	694-4186
Emergi-Clean PO Box 2136 *Web:* www.we-cleanall.com/company_overview.htm	Linden	NJ	07036	908-587-0980	
Grangeville Environmental Services 585 McAllister St *TF:* 866-437-5151 ■ *Web:* www.grangevilleenvironmental.com	Hanover	PA	17331	717-637-6152	630-2713
JNL Cleaning & Restoration 4320 Chinchilla Ct *Web:* www.jnl.us	Middleburg	FL	32068	904-282-9617	
JP Maguire Associates 266 Brookside Rd *Web:* www.jpmaguire.com	Waterbury	CT	06708	203-755-2297	573-8547
Loss Recovery Systems Inc 10 Dwight Pk Dr *TF:* 800-724-3473 ■ *Web:* www.lrs911.com	Syracuse	NY	13209	315-451-9111	451-9222
Metro Restoration Inc PO Box 115 *TF:* 877-570-1315 ■ *Web:* www.metrocleaningservice.com	Thornton	IL	60476	708-339-6300	339-7551
Midwest Crisis Cleaning Inc 590 Meyerwood Rd *TF:* 877-937-4862 ■ *Web:* www.midwestcrisiscleaning.com	Festus	MO	63028	636-937-4862	
Peerless Cleaners Inc 519 N Monroe St *TF:* 800-879-7056 ■ *Web:* www.peerlessrestoration.com	Decatur	IL	62522	217-423-7703	
Red Alert Bio-Response Service Inc PO Box 941629 *TF:* 800-570-1833 ■ *Web:* www.wecleanall.com	Houston	TX	77094	281-993-0016	232-2551
Richey Restoration Inc PO Box 833 *Web:* www.richeyrestoration.com	Mount Juliet	TN	37121	615-758-8760	754-7160
Rocky Mountain Remediation Contractors LLC 5870 S Walden Ct *Fax Area Code: 720 ■ *Web:* www.rockymountainmold.com	Centennial	CO	80015	303-667-0400	870-2696*
Timbertown Cleaning & Restoration 106 Hoyt Ave *TF:* 800-832-7060 ■ *Web:* www.timbertownservices.com	Saginaw	MI	48607	989-753-5139	754-0418
Trade-Winds Environmental Restoration Inc 100 Sweeneydale Ave *TF:* 800-282-8701 ■ *Web:* www.twer.com/index.cfm?fuseaction=home	Bay Shore	NY	11706	631-435-8900	435-4337
Trauma Scene Restoration Inc PO Box 2136 *Web:* www.traumascene.net	Linden	NJ	07036	215-742-4221	742-1481

84 BIOMETRIC IDENTIFICATION EQUIPMENT & SOFTWARE

Company	City	State	Zip	Phone	Fax
AcSys Biometrics Corp 399 Pearl St *TF:* 877-842-7687 ■ *Web:* www.acsysbiometrics.com	Burlington	ON	L7R2M8	905-634-4111	634-1101
Aspect Business Solutions 7550 IH-10 W 14th Fl *TF:* 800-609-8113 ■ *Web:* 4aspect.com	San Antonio	TX	78229	210-256-8300	682-2137
AuthenTec Inc 709 S Harbor City Blvd Suite 400 *Web:* www.authentec.com	Melbourne	FL	32901	321-308-1300	308-1430
BIO-key International Inc 300 Nickerson Rd *Web:* www.bio-key.com	Marlborough	MA	01752	508-460-4000	
Bio Medic Data Systems Inc 1 Silas Rd *TF:* 800-526-2637 ■ *Web:* www.bmds.com	Seaford	DE	19973	302-628-4100	628-4110
BioLink Technologies International Inc 599 Lexington Ave 38th Fl *TF:* 866-994-3843 ■ *Web:* www.biolinkusa.com	New York	NY	10022	212-572-6344	572-6499
Biometric Access Corp 2555 IH-35 Suite 200 *TF:* 800-873-4133 ■ *Web:* www.biometricaccess.com	Round Rock	TX	78664	512-246-3760	246-3768
Bioscrypt Inc 505 Cochrane Dr *TSX: BYT* ■ *TF:* 800-845-0096 ■ *Web:* www.bioscrypt.com	Markham	ON	L3R8E3	905-940-7750	940-7642
BNX Systems Corp 1953 Gallows Rd Suite 500 *TF:* 800-397-7561 ■ *Web:* www.bnx.com	Vienna	VA	22182	703-734-9200	734-6565
Cogent Inc 209 Fair Oaks Ave *NASDAQ: COGT* ■ *Web:* www.cogentsystems.com	South Pasadena	CA	91030	626-799-8090	799-8996
Communication Intelligence Corp 275 Shoreline Dr Suite 500 *TF Sales:* 800-888-8242 ■ *Web:* www.cic.com	Redwood Shores	CA	94065	650-802-7888	802-7777
Count Me In LLC 601 W Golf Rd Suite 108 *TF:* 800-958-8779 ■ *Web:* www.countmeinllc.com	Mount Prospect	IL	60056	847-981-8779	981-8870
Cross Match Technologies 3950 RCA Blvd Suite 5001 *Web:* www.crossmatch.net	Palm Beach Gardens	FL	33410	561-622-1650	622-9938
Datastrip Inc 211 Welsh Pool Rd Suite 100 *TF:* 800-548-2517 ■ *Web:* www.datastrip.com	Exton	PA	19341	610-594-6130	594-6065
Digital Persona Inc 720 Bay Rd Suite 100 *TF:* 877-378-2738 ■ *Web:* www.digitalpersona.com	Redwood City	CA	94063	650-474-4000	298-8313
Graphco Holdings Corp 321 Norristown Rd Suite 205 *Web:* www.graphcotech.com	Ambler	PA	19002	215-591-6550	591-6565
Honeywell Aerospace 1944 E Sky Harbor Cir *Fax Area Code: 602 ■ *Web:* www.honeywellaerospace.com	Phoenix	AZ	85034	800-601-3099	365-3343*
Identix Inc 5600 Rowland Rd *NASDAQ: IDNX* ■ *Web:* www.identix.com	Minnetonka	MN	55343	952-932-0888	932-7181
International Biometric Group LLC 1 Battery Park Plaza *TF:* 888-424-8424 ■ *Web:* www.biometricgroup.com	New York	NY	10004	212-809-9491	809-6197
I/O Software Inc 6711 Lee Hwy Suite 214 *Web:* www.iosoftware.com	Arlington	VA	22205	703-738-9267	852-7914
Iridian Technologies Inc 1245 N Church St Suite 3 *TF:* 866-474-3426 ■ *Web:* www.iridiantech.com	Moorestown	NJ	08057	856-222-9090	222-9020
Lightning Powder Co Inc 13386 International Pkwy *Web:* www.redwop.com	Jacksonville	FL	32218	904-741-5400	741-5403
NEC Corp of America 10850 Gold Center Dr Suite 200 *TF:* 800-632-4636 ■ *Web:* www.necam.com	Rancho Cordova	CA	95670	916-463-7000	636-5656
Recognition Systems Inc 1520 Dell Ave *Web:* www.recogsys.com	Campbell	CA	95008	408-341-4100	341-4101
SAFLINK Corp 777 108th Ave NE Suite 2100 *NASDAQ: SFLK* ■ *TF:* 800-762-9595 ■ *Web:* www.saflink.com	Bellevue	WA	98004	425-278-1100	278-1300
Sagem Morpho Inc 1145 Broadway Suite 200 *TF:* 800-346-2674 ■ *Web:* www.morpho.com	Tacoma	WA	98402	253-383-3617	272-2934
SecuGen Corp 2356 Walsh Ave *TF:* 866-942-8800 ■ *Web:* www.secugen.com	Santa Clara	CA	95051	408-727-7787	727-7105
Security First Corp 22362 Gilberto Suite 130 *Web:* www.securityfirstcorp.com	Rancho Santa Margarita	CA	92688	949-858-7525	858-7092
Sensory Inc 1991 Russell Ave *Web:* www.sensoryinc.com	Santa Clara	CA	95054	408-327-9000	727-4748
SIRCHIE Finger Print Laboratories Inc 100 Hunter Pl *TF:* 800-356-7311 ■ *Web:* www.sirchie.com	Youngsville	NC	27596	919-554-2244	554-2266
Ultra-Scan Corp 4240 Ridge Lea Rd Suite 10 *Web:* www.ultra-scan.com	Amherst	NY	14226	716-832-6269	832-2810
Veridicom Inc 999 3rd Ave *TF:* 800-363-1418 ■ *Web:* www.veridicom.com	Seattle	WA	98104	206-224-6206	224-6207
Viisage Technology Inc 296 Concord Rd 3rd Fl *NASDAQ: VISG* ■ *Web:* www.viisage.com	Billerica	MA	01821	978-932-2200	932-2225
Visiphor Corp 4710 Kingsway Suite 1100 *Web:* www.imagistechnologies.com	Bernaby	BC	V5H4M2	604-684-2449	684-9314

85 BIOTECHNOLOGY COMPANIES

SEE ALSO Diagnostic Products p. 1587; Medicinal Chemicals & Botanical Products p. 1957; Pharmaceutical Companies p. 2109; Pharmaceutical Companies - Generic Drugs p. 2111

Company	City	State	Zip	Phone	Fax
Aastrom Biosciences Inc 24 Frank Lloyd Wright Dr *NASDAQ: ASTM* ■ *Web:* www.aastrom.com	Ann Arbor	MI	48105	734-930-5777	665-0485
ACADIA Pharmaceuticals Inc 3911 Sorrento Valley Blvd *NASDAQ: ACAD* ■ *Web:* www.acadia-pharm.com	San Diego	CA	92121	858-558-2871	558-2872
Access Pharmaceuticals Inc 2600 Stemmons Fwy Suite 176 *AMEX: AKC* ■ *Web:* www.accesspharma.com	Dallas	TX	75207	214-905-5100	905-5101
Acorda Therapeutics Inc 15 Skyline Dr *NASDAQ: ACOR* ■ *Web:* www.acorda.com	Hawthorne	NY	10532	914-347-4300	347-4560
Acusphere Inc 500 Arsenal St *NASDAQ: ACUS* ■ *TF:* 800-388-9429 ■ *Web:* www.acusphere.com	Watertown	MA	02472	617-648-8800	926-4750
Adherex Technologies Inc 4620 Creekstone Dr Suite 200 *AMEX: ADH* ■ *Web:* www.adherex.com	Durham	NC	27703	919-484-8484	484-8001
Adolor Corp 700 Pennsylvania Dr *NASDAQ: ADLR* ■ *TF:* 800-563-4450 ■ *Web:* www.adolor.com	Exton	PA	19341	484-595-1500	595-1520

Company	City	State	Zip	Phone	Fax
ADVENTRX Pharmaceuticals Inc 6725 Mesa Ridge Rd Suite 100 *AMEX: ANX* ■ *Web:* www.adventrx.com	San Diego	CA	92121	858-552-0866	552-0876
Aeolus Pharmaceuticals Inc 23811 Inverness Pl. *TF:* 888-290-0528 ■ *Web:* www.aeoluspharma.com	Laguna Niguel	CA	92677	949-481-9825	481-9829
AEterna Zentaris Inc 1405 Parc Technologique Blvd *NASDAQ: AEZS* ■ *Web:* www.aeternazentaris.com	Quebec	QC	G1P4P5	418-652-8525	652-0881
Affymax Inc 4001 Miranda Ave *Web:* www.affymax.com	Palo Alto	CA	94304	650-812-8700	424-0832
Alexion Pharmaceuticals Inc 352 Knotter Dr. *NASDAQ: ALXN* ■ *Web:* www.alxn.com	Cheshire	CT	06410	203-272-2596	271-8190
Alexza Pharmaceuticals Inc 2091 Stierlin Ct. *NASDAQ: ALXA* ■ *Web:* www.alexza.com	Mountain View	CA	94043	650-944-7000	944-7999
Alfacell Corp 300 Atrium Dr *NASDAQ: ACEL* ■ *Web:* www.alfacell.com	Somerset	NJ	08873	732-652-4525	652-4575
Alkermes Inc 88 Sidney St *NASDAQ: ALKS* ■ *Web:* www.alkermes.com	Cambridge	MA	02139	617-494-0171	494-9263
Alliance Pharmaceutical Corp 6175 Lusk Blvd *Web:* www.allp.com	San Diego	CA	92121	858-410-5200	410-5201
Allos Therapeutics Inc 11080 Circle Point Rd Suite 200 *NASDAQ: ALTH* ■ *TF:* 888-255-6702 ■ *Web:* www.allos.com	Westminster	CO	80020	303-426-6262	412-9160
Alnylam Pharmaceuticals Inc 300 3rd St 3rd Fl *NASDAQ: ALNY* ■ *Web:* www.alnylam.com	Cambridge	MA	02142	617-551-8200	551-8101
Alseres Pharmaceuticals Inc 85 Main St. *Web:* www.alseres.com	Hopkinton	MA	01748	508-497-2360	497-9964
Amarillo Biosciences Inc 4134 Business Pk Dr. *Web:* www.amarbio.com	Amarillo	TX	79110	806-376-1741	376-9301
Ambrilia Biopharma Inc 1000 chemin du Golf *TSX: AMB* ■ *TF:* 877-776-2966 ■ *Web:* www.ambrilia.com	Verdun	QC	H3E1H4	514-751-2003	751-2502
American Bio Medica Corp 122 Smith Rd *NASDAQ: ABMC* ■ *TF:* 800-227-1243 ■ *Web:* www.americanbiomedica.com	Kinderhook	NY	12106	518-758-8158	758-8171
Amgen Canada Inc 6775 Financial Dr Suite 100 **Fax Area Code:* 866 ■ *TF:* 800-665-4273 ■ *Web:* www.amgen.com	Mississauga	ON	L5N0A4	905-285-3000	912-6436*
Amgen Inc 1 Amgen Ctr Dr *NASDAQ: AMGN* ■ *TF:* 800-926-4369 ■ *Web:* www.amgen.com	Thousand Oaks	CA	91320	805-447-1000	447-1010
Anesiva Inc 650 Gateway Blvd *NASDAQ: ANSV* ■ *Web:* www.anesiva.com	South San Francisco	CA	94080	650-624-9600	624-7540
Antibodies Inc PO Box 1560 *TF:* 800-824-8540 ■ *Web:* www.antibodiesinc.com	Davis	CA	95617	530-758-4400	758-6307
Antigenics Inc 162 5th Ave Suite 900 *NASDAQ: AGEN* ■ *Web:* www.antigenics.com	New York	NY	10010	212-994-8200	994-8299
Applera Corp 301 Merritt 7 *TF:* 800-761-5381 ■ *Web:* www.applera.com	Norwalk	CT	06856	203-840-2000	841-2014
Applied Molecular Evolution Inc (AME) 3520 Dunhill St. *Web:* www.amevolution.com	San Diego	CA	92121	858-597-4990	597-4950
Arboretum The 1102 S Goodwin Ave Rm N-409 University of Illinois at Urbana-Champaign *Web:* www.arboretum.uiuc.edu	Urbana	IL	61801	217-333-7579	244-3469
Ardea Biosciences Inc 4939 Directors Pl. *Web:* www.ardeabiosciences.com	San Diego	CA	92121	858-652-6500	625-0760
Arena Pharmaceuticals Inc 6166 Nancy Ridge Dr. *NASDAQ: ARNA* ■ *Web:* www.arenapharm.com	San Diego	CA	92121	858-453-7200	453-7210
ARIAD Pharmaceuticals Inc 26 Landsdowne St. *NASDAQ: ARIA* ■ *Web:* www.ariad.com	Cambridge	MA	02139	617-494-0400	494-8144
ArQule Inc 19 Presidential Way *NASDAQ: ARQL* ■ *TF:* 800-644-5000 ■ *Web:* www.arqule.com	Woburn	MA	01801	781-994-0300	376-6019
Array BioPharma Inc 3200 Walnut St. *NASDAQ: ARRY* ■ *TF:* 877-633-2436 ■ *Web:* www.arraybiopharma.com	Boulder	CO	80301	303-381-6600	449-5376
Aspreva Pharmaceuticals Corp 4464 Markham St Suite 1203 *NASDAQ: ASPV* ■ *Web:* www.aspreva.com	Victoria	BC	V8Z7X8	250-744-2488	744-2498
Assay Designs Inc 5777 Hines Dr. *TF Orders:* 877-423-4548 ■ *Web:* www.assaydesigns.com	Ann Arbor	MI	48108	734-668-6113	669-0134
AtheroGenics Inc 8995 Westside Pkwy *NASDAQ: AGIX* ■ *Web:* www.atherogenics.com	Alpharetta	GA	30004	678-336-2500	336-2501
AtriCure Inc 6033 Schumacher Park Dr *NASDAQ: ATRC* ■ *TF:* 866-349-2342 ■ *Web:* www.atricure.com	West Chester	OH	45069	513-755-4100	755-4108
Autoimmune Technologies LLC 1010 Common St Suite 1705 *Web:* www.autoimmune.com	New Orleans	LA	70112	504-529-9944	529-8982
Avalon Pharmaceuticals Inc 20358 Seneca Meadows Pkwy *NASDAQ: AVRX* ■ *Web:* www.avalonrx.com	Germantown	MD	20876	301-556-9900	556-9910
AVANIR Pharmaceuticals 101 Enterprise Suite 300 *AMEX: AVN* ■ *Web:* www.avanir.com	Aliso Viejo	CA	92656	[illegible]	[illegible]
AVANT Immunotherapeutics Inc 119 4th Ave *NASDAQ: AVAN* ■ *Web:* www.avantimmune.com	Needham	MA	02494	781-433-0771	433-0262
AVAX Technologies Inc 2000 Hamilton St Suite 204	Philadelphia	PA	19130	215-241-9760	241-9684
Avecia Biotechnology Inc 125 Fortune Blvd *Web:* www.avecia.com	Milford	MA	01757	508-532-2500	532-2503
AVI BioPharma Inc 1 SW Columbia St Suite 1105 *NASDAQ: AVII* ■ *Web:* www.avibio.com	Portland	OR	97258	503-227-0554	227-0751
Avigen Inc 1301 Harbor Bay Pkwy *NASDAQ: AVGN* ■ *Web:* www.avigen.com	Alameda	CA	94502	510-748-7150	748-7155
Bayer CropScience 2 TW Alexander Dr *Web:* www.bayercropscienceus.com	Research Triangle Park	NC	27709	919-549-2000	
BD Biosciences PharMingen 10975 Torreyana Rd. *TF:* 800-848-6227 ■ *Web:* www.bdbiosciences.com/pharmingen	San Diego	CA	92121	858-812-8800	812-8888
BioCryst Pharmaceuticals Inc 2190 Pkwy Lake Dr *NASDAQ: BCRX* ■ *Web:* www.biocryst.com	Birmingham	AL	35244	205-444-4600	444-4640
BioDelivery Sciences International Inc 801 Corporate Center Dr Suite 210 *NASDAQ: BDSI* ■ *Web:* www.bdsinternational.com	Raleigh	NC	27607	919-582-9050	582-9051
Biogen Idec Inc 14 Cambridge Ctr *NASDAQ: BIIB* ■ *TF:* 800-262-4363 ■ *Web:* www.biogenidec.com	Cambridge	MA	02142	617-679-2000	679-2617
BioMarin Pharmaceutical Inc 105 Digital Dr *NASDAQ: BMRN* ■ *TF:* 800-803-9514 ■ *Web:* www.biomarinpharm.com	Novato	CA	94949	415-884-6700	
Bioniche Life Sciences Inc PO Box 1570 *TSX: BNC* ■ *TF:* 800-265-5464 ■ *Web:* www.bioniche.com	Belleville	ON	N8N5J2	613-966-8058	966-4177
BioNumerik Pharmaceuticals Inc 8122 Datapoint Dr Suite 1250 *Web:* www.bionumerik.com	San Antonio	TX	78229	210-614-1701	615-8030
Biopure Corp 11 Hurley St *NASDAQ: BPUR* ■ *Web:* www.biopure.com	Cambridge	MA	02141	617-234-6500	234-6505
Bioqual Corp 9600 Medical Ctr Dr Suite 200 *Web:* www.bioqual.com	Rockville	MD	20850	301-251-2801	251-1260
BioReliance Corp 14920 Broschart Rd *TF:* 800-553-5372 ■ *Web:* www.bioreliance.com	Rockville	MD	20850	301-738-1000	738-1036
BioSphere Medical Inc 1050 Hingham St *NASDAQ: BSMD* ■ *TF:* 800-394-0295 ■ *Web:* www.biospheremed.com	Rockland	MA	02370	781-681-7900	792-2745
BioTime Inc 6121 Hollis St *Web:* www.biotimeinc.com	Emeryville	CA	94608	510-350-2940	350-2948
BioVeris Corp 16020 Industrial Dr *NASDAQ: BIOV* ■ *TF:* 800-339-4436 ■ *Web:* www.bioveris.com	Gaithersburg	MD	20877	301-869-9800	230-0158
Calgene LLC 1920 5th St.	Davis	CA	95616	530-753-6313	792-2453
Callisto Pharmaceuticals Inc 420 Lexington Ave Suite 1609 *AMEX: KAL* ■ *Web:* www.callistopharma.com	New York	NY	10170	212-297-0010	297-0020
Cangene Corp 180 Attwell Dr Suite 360 *TSX: CNJ* ■ *Web:* www.cangene.com	Toronto	ON	M9W6A9	416-675-8300	675-8301
Cardiome Pharma Corp 6190 Agronomy Rd 6th Fl *NASDAQ: CRME* ■ *TF:* 800-330-9928 ■ *Web:* www.cardiome.com	Vancouver	BC	V6T1Z3	604-677-6905	677-6915
CardioTech International Inc 229 Andover St *AMEX: CTE* ■ *Web:* www.cardiotech-inc.com	Wilmington	MA	01887	978-657-0075	657-0074
CEL-SCI Corp 8229 Boone Blvd Suite 802 *AMEX: CVM* ■ *Web:* www.cel-sci.com	Vienna	VA	22182	703-506-9460	506-9471
Celera Genomics Group 45 W Gude Dr *NYSE: CRA* ■ *TF:* 877-235-3721 ■ *Web:* www.celera.com	Rockville	MD	20850	240-453-3000	453-4000
Celgene Corp 86 Morris Ave *NASDAQ: CELG* ■ *TF:* 800-742-3107 ■ *Web:* www.celgene.com	Summit	NJ	07901	908-673-9000	673-9001
Celgene Corp Signal Research Div 4550 Town Ctr Ct. *Web:* www.signalpharm.com	San Diego	CA	92121	858-558-7500	552-8775
Cell Genesys Inc 500 Forbes Blvd *NASDAQ: CEGE* ■ *TF:* 800-648-6747 ■ *Web:* www.cellgenesys.com	South San Francisco	CA	94080	650-266-3000	266-3010
Cell Therapeutics Inc 501 Elliott Ave W Suite 400 *NASDAQ: CTIC* ■ *TF:* 800-215-2355 ■ *Web:* www.cticseattle.com	Seattle	WA	98119	206-282-7100	284-6206
Centocor Inc 200 Great Valley Pkwy. *TF:* 800-972-9063 ■ *Web:* www.centocor.com	Malvern	PA	19355	610-651-6000	651-6100
Cephalon Inc 41 Moores Rd *NASDAQ: CEPH* ■ *TF:* 800-782-3656 ■ *Web:* www.cephalon.com	Frazer	PA	19355	610-344-0200	344-0065
Cerus Corp 2411 Stanwell Dr *NASDAQ: CERS* ■ *TF:* 888-268-6115 ■ *Web:* www.cerus.com	Concord	CA	94520	925-288-6000	288-6001
Chesapeake Biological Laboratories Inc (CBL) 1111 S Paca St *TF:* 800-441-4225 ■ *Web:* www.cblinc.com	Baltimore	MD	21230	410-843-5000	843-4414
Cima Labs Inc 10000 Valley View Rd *Web:* www.cimalabs.com	Eden Prairie	MN	55344	952-947-8700	947-8770
CMC ICOS Biologics 22021 20th Ave SE *Web:* www.icos.com	Bothell	WA	98021	425-485-1900	485-1961
Cogenics 100 Perimeter Park Dr Suite C *TF:* 877-226-4364 ■ *Web:* www.cogenics.com	Morrisville	NC	27560	919-379-5462	468-8766
CollaGenx Pharmaceuticals Inc 41 University Dr Suite 200 *NASDAQ: CGPI* ■ *TF:* 800-613-7847 ■ *Web:* www.collagenex.com	Newtown	PA	18940	215-579-7388	579-8577
Colorado Serum Co 4950 York St PO Box 16428 *TF Orders:* 800-525-2065 ■ *Web:* www.colorado-serum.com	Denver	CO	80216	303-295-7527	295-1923
CombiMatrix Corp 6500 Harbour Heights Pkwy Suite 303 *NASDAQ: CBMX* ■ *TF:* 800-985-2269 ■ *Web:* www.combimatrix.com	Mukilteo	WA	98275	425-493-2000	493-2010
ConjuChem Inc 225 President Kennedy Ave Suite 3950 *TSX: CJC* ■ *Web:* www.conjuchem.com	Montreal	QC	H2X3Y8	514-844-5558	844-1119
Cook Biotech Inc 1425 Innovation Pl *TF:* 888-299-4224 ■ *Web:* www.cookbiotech.com	West Lafayette	IN	47906	765-497-3355	497-2361
Corcept Therapeutics Inc 149 Commonwealth Dr *NASDAQ: CORT* ■ *Web:* www.corcept.com	Menlo Park	CA	94025	650-327-3270	327-3218
Covance Inc 210 Carnegie Center *NYSE: CVD* ■ *TF:* 888-268-2623 ■ *Web:* www.covance.com	Princeton	NJ	08540	609-452-8550	452-9375
CryoCor Inc 9717 Pacific Heights Blvd *NASDAQ: CRYO* ■ *TF:* 866-909-2796 ■ *Web:* www.cryocor.com	San Diego	CA	92121	858-909-2200	909-2300
Cryolife Inc 1655 Roberts Blvd NW *NYSE: CRY* ■ *TF:* 800-438-8285 ■ *Web:* www.cryolife.com	Kennesaw	GA	30144	770-419-3355	
Cubist Pharmaceuticals Inc 65 Hayden Ave *NASDAQ: CBST* ■ *TF:* 877-528-2478 ■ *Web:* www.cubist.com	Lexington	MA	02421	781-860-8660	861-0566
Curacyte Inc 109 Connor Dr Bldg 1 Suite 2102 *Web:* www.curacyte.com	Chapel Hill	NC	27514	919-405-4002	405-4010
CuraGen Corp 322 E Main St *NASDAQ: CRGN* ■ *Web:* www.curagen.com	Branford	CT	06405	203-481-1104	483-2552
Curis Inc 45 Moulton St *NASDAQ: CRIS* ■ *Web:* www.curis.com	Cambridge	MA	02138	617-503-6500	503-6501
CV Therapeutics Inc 3172 Porter Dr *NASDAQ: CVTX* ■ *TF:* 877-475-2790 ■ *Web:* www.cvt.com	Palo Alto	CA	94304	650-384-8500	858-0390
Cypress Bioscience Inc 4350 Executive Dr Suite 325 *NASDAQ: CYPB* ■ *TF:* 800-452-7646 ■ *Web:* www.cypressbio.com	San Diego	CA	92121	858-452-2323	452-1222
Cytogen Corp 650 College Rd E Suite 3100 *NASDAQ: CYTO* ■ **Fax:* Mktg ■ *TF:* 800-833-3533 ■ *Web:* www.cytogen.com	Princeton	NJ	08540	609-750-8200	452-2476*
Cytokinetics Inc 280 E Grand Ave *NASDAQ: CYTK* ■ *TF:* 877-394-2986 ■ *Web:* www.cytokinetics.com	South San Francisco	CA	94080	650-624-3000	624-3010
Cytomedix Inc 416 Hungerford Dr Suite 330 *AMEX: GTF* ■ *TF:* 866-298-6633 ■ *Web:* www.cytomedix.com	Rockville	MD	20850	240-499-2680	499-2690
Cytori Therapeutics Inc 3020 Callan Rd. *NASDAQ: CYTX* ■ *Web:* www.cytoritx.com	San Diego	CA	92121	858-458-0900	458-0994
CytRx Corp 11726 San Vicente Blvd Suite 650 *NASDAQ: CYTR* ■ *Web:* www.cytrx.com	Los Angeles	CA	90049	310-826-5648	826-6139
Danisco US Inc Genencor Division 925 Page Mill Rd *Web:* www.genencor.com	Palo Alto	CA	94304	650-846-7500	845-0500
Delcath Systems Inc 600 5th Ave 23rd Fl Rockefeller Center *NASDAQ: DCTH* ■ *Web:* www.delcath.com	New York	NY	10020	212-489-2100	489-2102
Dendreon Corp 3005 1st Ave *NASDAQ: DNDN* ■ *TF:* 877-256-4545 ■ *Web:* www.dendreon.com	Seattle	WA	98121	206-256-4545	256-0571
DepoMed Inc 1360 O'Brien Dr *NASDAQ: DEPO* ■ *Web:* www.depomedinc.com	Menlo Park	CA	94025	650-462-5900	462-9993
DexCom Inc 6340 Sequence Dr *NASDAQ: DXCM* ■ *TF:* 877-339-2664 ■ *Web:* www.dexcom.com	San Diego	CA	92121	858-200-0200	200-0201
diaDexus Inc 343 Oyster Point Blvd *Web:* www.diadexus.com	South San Francisco	CA	94080	650-246-6400	246-6499
Discovery Laboratories Inc 2600 Kelly Rd Suite 100 *NASDAQ: DSCO* ■ *TF:* 877-266-2411 ■ *Web:* www.discoverylabs.com	Warrington	PA	18976	215-488-9300	488-9301
Diversa Corp 4955 Directors Pl *TF:* 800-523-2990 ■ *Web:* www.verenium.com	San Diego	CA	92121	858-526-5000	526-5551
DOR BioPharma Inc 850 Bear Tavern Rd Suite 201 *AMEX: DOR* ■ *Web:* www.dorbiopharma.com	Ewing	NJ	08628	609-538-8200	538-8205
DOV Pharmaceutical Inc 150 Pierce St *NASDAQ: DOVP* ■ *Web:* www.dovpharm.com	Somerset	NJ	08873	732-907-3600	
Dow AgroSciences LLC 9330 Zionsville Rd **Fax Area Code:* 800 ■ *TF:* 800-258-1470 ■ *Web:* www.dowagro.com	Indianapolis	IN	46268	317-337-3000	905-7326*
Draxis Health Inc 16751 Transcanada Hwy *NASDAQ: DRAX* ■ *Web:* www.draxis.com	Kirkland	QC	H9H4J4	514-630-7210	694-8201
DURECT Corp 2 Results Way *NASDAQ: DRRX* ■ *Web:* www.durect.com	Cupertino	CA	95014	408-777-1417	777-3577
DUSA Pharmaceuticals Inc 25 Upton Dr *NASDAQ: DUSA* ■ *Web:* www.dusapharma.com	Wilmington	MA	01887	978-657-7500	657-9193
Dyadic International Inc 140 Intracoastal Pointe Dr Suite 404 *AMEX: DIL* ■ *Web:* www.dyadic-group.com	Jupiter	FL	33477	561-743-8333	743-8343
Dyax Corp 300 Technology Sq *NASDAQ: DYAX* ■ *Web:* www.dyax.com	Cambridge	MA	02139	617-225-2500	225-2501
Elan Pharmaceutical Research Corp 1300 Gould Dr. *NYSE: ELN* ■ *Web:* www.elan.com	Gainesville	GA	30504	770-534-8239	534-8247
Elite Pharmaceuticals Inc 165 Ludlow Ave *AMEX: ELI* ■ *Web:* www.elitepharma.com	Northvale	NJ	07647	201-750-2646	750-2755
Embrex Inc Pfizer Poultry Health Div 1040 Swabia Ct *NASDAQ: EMBX* ■ *TF:* 800-849-3629 ■ *Web:* www.embrex.com	Durham	NC	27703	919-941-5185	941-5186
EMD Serono Inc 1 Technology Pl *TF:* 800-283-8088 ■ *Web:* www.emdserono.com	Rockland	MA	02370	781-982-9000	681-2914
Emergent Biosolutions Inc 2273 Research Blvd Suite 400 *Web:* www.emergentbiosolutions.com	Rockville	MD	20850	301-795-1800	795-1899
Emisphere Technologies Inc 765 Old Saw Mill River Rd. *NASDAQ: EMIS* ■ *Web:* www.emisphere.com	Tarrytown	NY	10591	914-347-2220	593-8290

Company	City	State	ZIP	Phone	Fax
Encore Medical Corp 9800 Metric Blvd *NASDAQ: ENMC* ■ *Web:* www.encoremed.com	Austin	TX	78758	512-832-9500	834-6300
Encysive Pharmaceuticals Inc 4848 Loop Central Dr Suite 700 *NASDAQ: ENCY* ■ *Web:* www.encysive.com	Houston	TX	77081	713-796-8822	796-8232
EntreMed Inc 9640 Medical Ctr Dr *NASDAQ: ENMD* ■ *TF:* 888-368-7363 ■ *Web:* www.entremed.com	Rockville	MD	20850	240-864-2600	864-2601
Enzo Biochem Inc 60 Executive Blvd *NYSE: ENZ* ■ *TF:* 800-522-5052 ■ *Web:* www.enzo.com	Farmingdale	NY	11735	631-755-5500	
Enzon Pharmaceuticals Inc 685 Rt 202-206 *NASDAQ: ENZN* ■ *Web:* www.enzon.com	Bridgewater	NJ	08807	732-541-8600	575-9457
Eurand 845 Center Dr *Web:* www.eurand.com	Vandalia	OH	45377	937-898-9669	898-9529
Exelixis Inc 210 E Grand Ave *NASDAQ: EXEL* ■ *Web:* www.exelixis.com	South San Francisco	CA	94080	650-837-7000	837-8300
Favrille Inc 10421 Pacific Center Ct *NASDAQ: FVRL* ■ *Web:* www.favrille.com	San Diego	CA	92121	858-526-8000	597-7040
Forbes Medi-Tech Inc 750 W Pender St Suite 200 *NASDAQ: FMTI* ■ *Web:* www.forbesmedi.com	Vancouver	BC	V6C2T8	604-689-5899	689-7641
Genaera Corp 5110 Campus Dr *NASDAQ: GENR* ■ *TF:* 800-522-8973 ■ *Web:* www.genaera.com	Plymouth Meeting	PA	19462	610-941-4020	941-5399
Genelabs Technologies Inc 505 Penobscot Dr *NASDAQ: GNLB* ■ *Web:* www.genelabs.com	Redwood City	CA	94063	650-369-9500	368-0709
Genentech Inc 1 DNA Way *NYSE: DNA* ■ *TF:* 800-551-2231 ■ *Web:* www.gene.com	South San Francisco	CA	94080	650-225-1000	225-6000
Generex Biotechnology Corp 33 Harbour Sq Suite 202 *NASDAQ: GNBT* ■ *TF:* 800-391-6755 ■ *Web:* www.generex.com	Toronto	ON	M5J2G2	416-364-2551	364-9363
Genitope Corp 6900 Dumbarton Cir *NASDAQ: GTOP* ■ *TF:* 866-436-4867 ■ *Web:* www.genitope.com	Fremont	CA	94555	510-284-3000	284-3100
Genomic Health Inc 301 Penobscot Dr *NASDAQ: GHDX* ■ *TF:* 866-662-6897 ■ *Web:* www.genomichealth.com	Redwood City	CA	94063	650-556-9300	556-1073
Genomic Solutions Inc 4355 Varsity Dr Suite E *TF:* 877-436-6642 ■ *Web:* www.genomicsolutions.com	Ann Arbor	MI	48108	734-975-4800	975-4808
Genta Inc 2 Connell Dr *NASDAQ: GNTA* ■ *TF:* 888-322-2264 ■ *Web:* www.genta.com	Berkeley Heights	NJ	07922	908-286-9800	464-1701
GenVec Inc 65 W Watkins Mill Rd *NASDAQ: GNVC* ■ *TF:* 877-943-6832 ■ *Web:* www.genvec.com	Gaithersburg	MD	20878	240-632-0740	632-0735
Genzyme Corp 500 Kendall St *NASDAQ: GENZ* ■ *TF:* 800-326-7002 ■ *Web:* www.genzyme.com	Cambridge	MA	02142	617-252-7500	252-7600
Genzyme Oncology 55 Cambridge Pkwy *Web:* www.genzyme.com/molecularoncology.asp	Cambridge	MA	02142	617-252-7811	761-8783
Geron Corp 230 Constitution Dr *NASDAQ: GERN* ■ *Web:* www.geron.com	Menlo Park	CA	94025	650-473-7700	473-7750
Gilead Sciences Inc 333 Lakeside Dr *NASDAQ: GILD* ■ *TF:* 800-445-3235 ■ *Web:* www.gilead.com	Foster City	CA	94404	650-574-3000	578-9264
Grifols USA Inc 2410 Lillyvale Ave *TF:* 800-421-0008 ■ *Web:* www.grifolsusa.com	Los Angeles	CA	90032	323-225-2221	441-7968
GTC Biotherapeutics Inc 175 Crossing Blvd Suite 410 *NASDAQ: GTCB* ■ *Web:* www.gtc-bio.com	Framingham	MA	01702	508-620-9700	370-3797
GTx Inc 3 N Dunlap St *NASDAQ: GTXI* ■ *Web:* www.gtxinc.com	Memphis	TN	38163	901-523-9700	523-9772
Helix Biopharma Corp 305 Industrial Pkwy S Unit 3 *Web:* www.helixbiopharma.com	Aurora	ON	L4G6X7	905-841-2300	841-2244
Hemispherx Biopharma Inc 1617 JFK Blvd Suite 660 *AMEX: HEB* ■ *Web:* www.hemispherx.net	Philadelphia	PA	19103	215-988-0080	988-1739
Hemosol Inc 2585 Meadowpine Blvd *NASDAQ: HMSL* ■ *Web:* www.hemosol.com	Mississauga	ON	O5N8H9	905-286-6200	286-6300
Hollis-Eden Pharmaceuticals Inc 4435 Eastgate Mall Suite 400 *NASDAQ: HEPH* ■ *Web:* holliseden.com	San Diego	CA	92121	858-587-9333	558-6470
i3 Innovus 10 Cabot Rd Suite 304 *Web:* www.innovus.com	Medford	MA	02155	781-338-9700	338-9522
Idenix Pharmaceuticals Inc 60 Hampshire St *NASDAQ: IDIX* ■ *TF:* 877-443-6491 ■ *Web:* www.idenix.com	Cambridge	MA	02139	617-995-9800	995-9801
Idera Pharmaceuticals Inc 167 Sidney St *AMEX: IDP* ■ *TF:* 800-223-3771 ■ *Web:* www.iderapharma.com	Cambridge	MA	02139	617-679-5500	679-5592
IDM Pharma Inc 9 Parker Suite 100 *NASDAQ: IDMI* ■ *Web:* www.idm-biotech.com	Irvine	CA	92618	949-470-4751	470-6470
Illumina Inc 9885 Towne Centre Dr *NASDAQ: ILMN* ■ *TF:* 800-809-4566 ■ *Web:* www.illumina.com	San Diego	CA	92121	858-202-4500	202-4545
ImClone Systems Inc 180 Varick St 6th Fl *NASDAQ: IMCL* ■ *Web:* www.imclone.com	New York	NY	10014	212-645-1405	645-2054
IMCOR Pharmaceutical Co 4660 La Jolla Village Dr Suite 500	San Diego	CA	92122	858-546-2955	546-2933
ImmunoGen Inc 128 Sidney St *NASDAQ: IMGN* ■ *Web:* www.immunogen.com	Cambridge	MA	02139	617-995-2500	995-2510
Immunomedics Inc 300 American Rd *NASDAQ: IMMU* ■ *TF:* 800-327-7211 ■ *Web:* www.immunomedics.com	Morris Plains	NJ	07950	973-605-8200	605-8282
Incyte Corp Rt 141 & Henry Clay Rd Bldg E-336 *NASDAQ: INCY* ■ *Web:* www.incyte.com	Wilmington	DE	19880	302-498-6700	425-2750
Indevus Pharmaceuticals Inc 33 Hayden Ave *NASDAQ: IDEV* ■ *TF:* 800-370-4742 ■ *Web:* www.indevus.com	Lexington	MA	02421	781-861-8444	861-3830
Inflazyme Pharamceuticals Ltd 5600 Parkwood Way Suite 425 *TF:* 800-315-3660 ■ *Web:* www.inflazyme.com	Richmond	BC	V6V2M2	604-279-8511	279-8711
Inhibitex Inc 9005 Westside Pkwy *NASDAQ: INHX* ■ *TF:* 866-784-3510 ■ *Web:* www.inhibitex.com	Alpharetta	GA	30004	678-746-1100	746-1299
Innovus Research Inc 1016-A Sutton Dr *Web:* www.innovus.com	Burlington	ON	L7L6B8	905-331-9911	331-9912
Inovio Biomedical Corp 11494 Sorrento Valley Rd *AMEX: INO* ■ *TF:* 877-446-6846 ■ *Web:* www.inovio.com	San Diego	CA	92121	858-597-6006	597-0451
INSMED Inc 8720 Stony Point Pkwy Suite 200 *NASDAQ: INSM* ■ *Web:* www.insmed.com	Richmond	VA	23235	804-565-3000	565-3500
Inspire Pharmaceuticals Inc 4222 Emperor Blvd Suite 200 *NASDAQ: ISPH* ■ *TF:* 877-800-4536 ■ *Web:* www.inspirepharm.com	Durham	NC	27703	919-941-9777	941-9797
Integra LifeSciences Holdings Corp 311 Enterprise Dr *NASDAQ: IART* ■ *TF:* 800-654-2873 ■ *Web:* www.integra-ls.com	Plainsboro	NJ	08536	609-275-0500	799-3297
Introgen Therapeutics Inc 301 Congress Ave Suite 1850 *NASDAQ: INGN* ■ *TF:* 800-320-5010 ■ *Web:* www.introgen.com	Austin	TX	78701	512-708-9310	708-9311
Invitrogen Corp 5791 Van Allen Way *NASDAQ: IVGN* ■ *TF Sales:* 800-955-6288 ■ *Web:* www.invitrogen.com	Carlsbad	CA	92008	760-603-7200	603-7229
Iomai Corp 20 Firstfield Rd Suite 250 *NASDAQ: IOMI* ■ *Web:* www.iomai.com	Gaithersburg	MD	20878	301-556-4500	556-4501
Isis Pharmaceuticals Inc 1896 Rutherford Rd *NASDAQ: ISIS* ■ *Web:* www.isispharm.com	Carlsbad	CA	92008	760-931-9200	603-2700
Isolagen Inc 405 Eagleview Blvd *AMEX: ILE* ■ *Web:* www.isolagen.com	Exton	PA	19341	484-713-6000	713-6001
ISTA Pharmaceuticals Inc 15295 Alton Pkwy Suite 100 *NASDAQ: ISTA* ■ *TF:* 866-264-8568 ■ *Web:* www.istavision.com	Irvine	CA	92618	949-788-6000	788-6010
Ivers-Lee Inc 31 Hansen Rd S *TF:* 800-387-1188 ■ *Web:* ivers-lee.com	Brampton	ON	L6W3H7	905-451-5535	451-1255
Kosan Biosciences Inc 3832 Bay Center Pl *NASDAQ: KOSN* ■ *Web:* www.kosan.com	Hayward	CA	94545	510-732-8400	732-8401
KV Pharmaceutical Co 2503 S Hanley Rd *NYSE: KV* ■ *Web:* www.kvpharmaceutical.com	Saint Louis	MO	63144	314-645-6600	644-2419
La Jolla Pharmaceutical Co 6455 Nancy Ridge Dr *NASDAQ: LJPC* ■ *Web:* www.ljpc.com	San Diego	CA	92121	858-452-6600	554-0234
Labopharm Inc 480 Armand Frappier Blvd *TF:* 888-686-1017 ■ *Web:* www.labopharm.com	Laval	QC	H7V4B4	450-686-1017	686-9201
Leo Pharma Inc 123 Commerce Valley Dr E Suite 400 *TF:* 800-668-7234 ■ *Web:* www.leo-pharma.com	Thornhill	ON	L3T7W8	905-886-9822	886-6622
Lescarden Inc 420 Lexington Ave Suite 212 *TF:* 888-581-2076 ■ *Web:* www.lescarden.com	New York	NY	10170	212-687-1050	687-1051
Lexicon Pharmaceuticals Inc 8800 Technology Forest Pl *NASDAQ: LEXG* ■ *TF:* 800-578-1972 ■ *Web:* www.lexicon-genetics.com	The Woodlands	TX	77381	281-863-3000	863-8088
LifeCore Biomedical Inc 3515 Lyman Blvd *NASDAQ: LCBM* ■ *TF Cust Svc:* 800-752-2663 ■ *Web:* www.lifecore.com	Chaska	MN	55318	952-368-4300	368-3411
Ligand Pharmaceuticals Inc 10275 Science Ctr Dr *NASDAQ: LGND* ■ *TF:* 800-964-5793 ■ *Web:* www.ligand.com	San Diego	CA	92121	858-550-7500	550-7506
LiphaTech Inc 3600 W Elm St **Fax Area Code: 414* ■ *Web:* www.liphatech.com	Milwaukee	WI	53209	888-331-7900	247-8166*
Lipid Sciences Inc 7068 Koll Center Pkwy Suite 401 *NASDAQ: LIPD* ■ *TF:* 866-254-7437 ■ *Web:* www.lipidsciences.com	Pleasanton	CA	94566	925-249-4000	249-4040
Lonza Biologics Inc 97 South St *Web:* www.lonza.com	Hopkinton	MA	01748	508-497-0700	435-8498
Lorus Therapeutics Inc 2 Meridian Rd *AMEX: LRP* ■ *Web:* www.lorusthera.com	Toronto	ON	M9W4Z7	416-798-1200	798-2200
Lundbeck Canada Inc 413 St-Jacques St W Suite FB-230 *Web:* www.lundbeck.com	Montreal	QC	H2Y1N9	514-844-8515	844-5495
MacroChem Corp 40 Washington St Suite 220 *Web:* www.macrochem.com	Wellesley Hills	MA	02481	781-489-7310	489-7311
MannKind Corp 28903 N Ave Paine *NASDAQ: MNKD* ■ *TF:* 866-428-7348 ■ *Web:* www.mannkindcorp.com	Valencia	CA	91355	661-775-5300	775-2081
Martek Biosciences Corp 6480 Dobbin Rd *NASDAQ: MATK* ■ *Web:* www.martekbio.com	Columbia	MD	21045	410-740-0081	740-2985
Maxygen Inc 515 Galveston Dr *NASDAQ: MAXY* ■ *TF:* 888-629-9436 ■ *Web:* www.maxygen.com	Redwood City	CA	94063	650-298-5300	364-2715
MDS Inc 2700 Matheson Blvd E Suite 300 W Tower *NYSE: MDZ* ■ *TF:* 877-675-6777 ■ *Web:* www.mdsintl.com	Mississauga	ON	L4W4V9	416-675-6777	675-0688
Medarex Inc 707 State Rd *NASDAQ: MEDX* ■ *Web:* www.medarex.com	Princeton	NJ	08540	609-430-2880	430-2850
Medicines Co 8 Campus Dr *NASDAQ: MDCO* ■ *TF:* 800-388-1183 ■ *Web:* www.themedicinescompany.com	Parsippany	NJ	07054	973-656-1616	656-9898
MediGene Inc 10660 Scripts Ranch Blvd Suite 200 *TF:* 888-586-1050 ■ *Web:* www.medigene.com	San Diego	CA	92131	858-586-2240	586-2241
MedImmune Inc 1 MedImmune Way *NASDAQ: MEDI* ■ *TF:* 877-633-4411 ■ *Web:* www.medimmune.com	Gaithersburg	MD	20878	301-398-0000	398-9000
Memory Pharmaceuticals Corp 100 Phillips Pkwy *NASDAQ: MEMY* ■ *Web:* www.memorypharma.com	Montvale	NJ	07645	201-802-7100	802-7190
Mera Pharmaceuticals Inc 73-4460 Queen Kaahumanu Hwy Suite 110 *TF:* 800-480-6515 ■ *Web:* www.merapharma.com	Kailua-Kona	HI	96740	808-326-9301	326-9401
Metabasis Therapeutics Inc 11119 N Torrey Pines Rd *NASDAQ: MBRX* ■ *Web:* www.mbasis.com	La Jolla	CA	92037	858-587-2770	622-5556
Microbix Biosystems Inc 341 Bering Ave *TF:* 800-794-6694 ■ *Web:* www.microbix.com	Toronto	ON	M8Z3A8	416-234-1624	234-1626
MicroIslet Inc 6370 Nancy Ridge Dr Suite 112 *AMEX: MII* ■ *Web:* www.microislet.com	San Diego	CA	92121	858-657-0287	657-0288
Micromet Inc 6707 Democracy Blvd Suite 505 *NASDAQ: MITI* ■ *Web:* www.micromet-inc.com	Bethesda	MD	20817	240-752-1420	752-1425
Millennium Pharmaceuticals Inc 40 Lansdowne St *NASDAQ: MLNM* ■ *Web:* www.mlnm.com	Cambridge	MA	02139	617-679-7000	374-7788
Millipore Corp 290 Concord Rd *NYSE: MIL* ■ **Fax Area Code: 800* ■ *TF:* 800-645-5476 ■ *Web:* www.millipore.com	Billerica	MA	01821	978-715-4321	645-5439*
Momenta Pharmaceuticals Inc 675 W Kendall St *NASDAQ: MNTA* ■ *Web:* www.momentapharma.com	Cambridge	MA	02142	617-491-9700	621-0431
MultiCell Technologies Inc 701 George Washington Hwy *Web:* www.multicelltech.com	Lincoln	RI	02865	401-333-0610	333-0659
Myriad Genetics Inc 320 Wakara Way *NASDAQ: MYGN* ■ *TF:* 800-469-7423 ■ *Web:* www.myriad.com	Salt Lake City	UT	84108	801-582-3400	584-3615
Nabi Biopharmaceuticals 12276 Wilkins Ave *NASDAQ: NABI* ■ *TF:* 800-685-5579 ■ *Web:* www.nabi.com	Rockville	MD	20852	301-770-3099	770-3097
Nanogen Inc 10398 Pacific Ctr Ct *NASDAQ: NGEN* ■ *TF:* 877-626-6436 ■ *Web:* www.nanogen.com	San Diego	CA	92121	858-410-4600	410-4848
Nastech Pharmaceutical Co Inc 3830 Monte Villa Pkwy *NASDAQ: NSTK* ■ *TF:* 888-627-2579 ■ *Web:* www.nastech.com	Bothell	WA	98021	425-908-3600	908-3650
Nektar Therapeutics 150 Industrial Rd *NASDAQ: NKTR* ■ *TF:* 800-457-1806 ■ *Web:* www.nektar.com	San Carlos	CA	94070	650-631-3100	631-3150
NeoPharm Inc 1850 Lakeside Dr *NASDAQ: NEOL* ■ *Web:* www.neophrm.com	Waukegan	IL	60085	847-887-0800	887-9281
Neose Technologies Inc 102 Rock Rd *NASDAQ: NTEC* ■ *Web:* www.neose.com	Horsham	PA	19044	215-315-9000	315-9100
Neurobiological Technologies Inc 2000 Powell St Suite 800 *NASDAQ: NTII* ■ *Web:* www.ntii.com	Emeryville	CA	94608	510-595-6000	595-6006
Neurochem Inc 275 Armand Frappier Blvd *NASDAQ: NRMX* ■ *TF:* 877-680-4500 ■ *Web:* www.neurochem.com	Laval	QC	H7V4A7	450-680-4500	680-4501
Neurocrine Biosciences Inc 12790 El Camino Real *NASDAQ: NBIX* ■ *TF:* 800-876-3522 ■ *Web:* www.neurocrine.com	San Diego	CA	92130	858-617-7600	617-7602
Neurogen Corp 35 NE Industrial Rd *NASDAQ: NRGN* ■ *Web:* www.neurogen.com	Branford	CT	06405	203-488-8201	481-8683
NexMed Inc 89 Twin Rivers Dr *NASDAQ: NEXM* ■ *Web:* www.nexmed.com	East Windsor	NJ	08520	609-371-8123	426-9116
NitroMed Inc 45 Hayden Ave *NASDAQ: NTMD* ■ *TF:* 888-992-4338 ■ *Web:* www.nitromed.com	Lexington	MA	02421	781-266-4000	274-8080
Northfield Laboratories Inc 1560 Sherman Ave Suite 1000 *NASDAQ: NFLD* ■ *Web:* www.northfieldlabs.com	Evanston	IL	60201	847-864-3500	864-3577
Novartis Vaccines & Diagnostics 4560 Horton St *TF:* 800-524-4766 ■ *Web:* www.novartis-vaccines.com	Emeryville	CA	94608	510-655-8730	655-9910
Novavax Inc 9920 Belward Campus Dr *NASDAQ: NVAX* ■ *TF:* 888-669-9111 ■ *Web:* www.novavax.com	Rockville	MA	20850	240-268-2000	268-2100
Novogen Inc 59 Grove St Suite 2i *NASDAQ: NVGN* ■ *Web:* www.novogen.com	New Cannon	CT	06860	203-966-2556	966-2558
NPS Pharmaceuticals Inc 550 Hills Dr 3rd Fl *NASDAQ: NPSP* ■ *Web:* www.npsp.com	Bedminster	NJ	07921	908-450-5300	450-5351
Nucro-Technics 2000 Ellesmere Rd Unit 16 *Web:* www.nucro-technics.com	Scarborough	ON	M1H2W4	416-438-6727	438-3463
NUCRYST Pharmaceuticals Corp 50 Audubon Rd Suite B *NASDAQ: NCST* ■ *TF:* 877-630-1234 ■ *Web:* www.nucryst.com	Wakefield	MA	01880	781-224-1444	246-6002
Nuvelo Inc 201 Industrial Rd Suite 310 *NASDAQ: NUVO* ■ *Web:* www.nuvelo.com	San Carolos	CA	94070	650-517-8000	
Nuvo Research Inc 7560 Airport Rd Suite 10 *TSX: NRI* ■ *TF:* 888-398-3463 ■ *Web:* www.nuvoresearch.com	Mississauga	ON	L4T4H4	905-673-6980	673-1842
Nycomed Canada Inc 435 N Service Rd W 1st Fl *TF:* 888-367-3331 ■ *Web:* www.nycomed.ca	Oakville	ON	L6M4X8	905-469-9333	469-4883
Nymox Pharmaceutical Corp 9900 Cavendish Blvd Suite 306 *NASDAQ: NYMX* ■ *TF:* 800-936-9669 ■ *Web:* www.nymox.com	Saint-Laurent	QC	H4M2V2	514-332-3222	332-2227
Oakwood Laboratories LLC 7670 1st Pl Suite A *TF:* 888-625-9352 ■ *Web:* www.oakwoodlabs.com	Oakwood Village	OH	44146	440-359-0000	359-0001
Oncolytics Biotech Inc 1167 Kensington Crescent NW Suite 210 *NASDAQ: ONCY* ■ *Web:* www.oncolyticsbiotech.com	Calgary	AB	T2N1X7	403-670-7377	283-0858

Phone Fax

Oncothyreon Inc 110 110th Ave NE Suite 625 ... Bellevue WA 98004 425-450-0370 450-0371
Web: www.oncothyreon.com
Onyx Pharmaceuticals Inc 2100 Powell St ... Emeryville CA 94608 510-597-6500 597-6600
NASDAQ: ONXX ■ *Web:* www.onyx-pharm.com
Oragenics Inc 13700 Progress Blvd ... Alachua FL 32615 386-418-4018 418-1660
AMEX: ONI ■ *Web:* www.oragenics.com
OraPharma Inc 732 Louis Dr ... Warminster PA 18974 215-956-2200 443-9531
TF: 866-273-7846 ■ *Web:* www.orapharma.com
Organogenesis Inc 150 Dan Rd ... Canton MA 02021 781-575-0775 575-0440
Web: www.organogenesis.com
Organon Canada Ltd 300 Consilium Pl Suite 1000 ... Scarborough ON M1H3G2 416-290-6131 290-6133
Web: www.organon.ca
Ortho BioTech Products LP 430 Rt 22 E PO Box 6914 ... Bridgewater NJ 08807 908-541-4000
TF Cust Svc: 800-325-7504 ■ *Web:* www.orthobiotech.com/us.html
Oscient Pharmaceuticals Corp 1000 Winter St ... Waltham MA 02451 781-398-2300 893-9535
NASDAQ: OSCI ■ *Web:* www.oscient.com
OSI Pharmaceuticals Inc 41 Pinelawn Rd ... Melville NY 11747 631-962-2000 752-3880
NASDAQ: OSIP ■ *TF:* 800-572-1932 ■ *Web:* www.osip.com
Osteotech Inc 51 James Way ... Eatontown NJ 07724 732-542-2800
NASDAQ: OSTE ■ *Web:* www.osteotech.com
OXiGENE Inc 230 3rd Ave ... Waltham MA 02451 781-547-5900 547-6800
NASDAQ: OXGN ■ *Web:* www.oxigene.com
Oxis International Inc 323 Vintage Park Dr Suite B ... Foster City CA 94404 650-212-2568 212-2569
TF: 800-547-3686 ■ *Web:* www.oxis.com
Pacira Inc 10450 Science Ctr Dr ... San Diego CA 92121 858-625-2424 625-2439
Web: www.pacira.com
Palatin Technologies Inc 4-C Cedar Brook Dr ... Cranbury NJ 08512 609-495-2200 495-2201
AMEX: PTN ■ *Web:* www.palatin.com
Panacos Pharmaceuticals Inc 134 Coolidge Ave ... Watertown MA 02472 617-926-1551 923-2245
NASDAQ: PANC ■ *Web:* www.panacos.com
PDL BioPharma Inc 1400 Seaport Blvd ... Redwood City CA 94063 650-454-1000 454-2000
NASDAQ: PDLI ■ *Web:* www.pdl.com
Penwest Pharmaceuticals Co 39 Old Ridgebury Rd Suite 11 ... Danbury CT 06810 203-796-3700 794-1393
NASDAQ: PPCO ■ *TF:* 877-736-9378 ■ *Web:* www.penw.com
Peregrine Pharmaceuticals Inc 14272 Franklin Ave Suite 100 ... Tustin CA 92780 714-508-6000 838-9433
NASDAQ: PPHM ■ *TF:* 800-694-5334 ■ *Web:* peregrineinc.com
Pharmachem Corp 719 Stefko Blvd ... Bethlehem PA 18018 610-867-4654 867-2971
Web: www.pharmachemcorp.com
Pharmacopeia Drug Discovery Inc Box 5350 ... Princeton NJ 08543 609-452-3600
NASDAQ: PCOP ■ *Web:* www.pharmacopeia.com
Pharmacyclics Inc 995 E Arques Ave ... Sunnyvale CA 94085 408-774-0330 774-0340
NASDAQ: PCYC ■ *TF:* 800-458-0330 ■ *Web:* www.pharmacyclics.com
Poniard Pharmaceuticals Inc
7000 Shoreline Ct Suite 270 ... South San Francisco CA 94080 650-583-3774 583-3789
NASDAQ: PARD ■ *Web:* www.poniard.com
Pozen Inc 1414 Raleigh Rd Suite 400 ... Chapel Hill NC 27517 919-913-1030 913-1039
NASDAQ: POZN ■ *Web:* www.pozen.com
PRA International 4141 Parklake Ave Suite 530 ... Raleigh NC 27612 919-786-8200 786-8201
NASDAQ: PRAI ■ *Web:* www.prainternational.com
PreMD Inc 4211 Yonge St Suite 615 ... Toronto ON M2P2A9 416-222-3449 222-4533
AMEX: PME ■ *Web:* www.premdinc.com
Pressure BioSciences Inc 14 Norfolk Ave ... South Easton MA 02375 508-230-1828 230-1829
NASDAQ: PBIO ■ *Web:* www.pressurebiosciences.com
Pro-Pharmaceuticals Inc 7 Wells Ave Suite 34 ... Newton MA 02459 617-559-0033 928-3450
AMEX: PRW ■ *TF:* 800-488-6445 ■ *Web:* www.pro-pharmaceuticals.com
Progenics Pharmaceuticals Inc 777 Old Saw Mill River Rd ... Tarrytown NY 10591 914-789-2800 789-2817
NASDAQ: PGNX ■ *Web:* www.progenics.com
Protein Polymer Technologies Inc 10655 Sorrento Valley Rd ... San Diego CA 92121 858-558-6064 558-6477
Web: www.ppti.com
Protein Sciences Corp 1000 Research Pkwy ... Meriden CT 06450 203-686-0800 686-0268
Web: www.proteinsciences.com
Proteome Systems Inc 6 Gill St ... Woburn MA 01801 781-932-9477 932-9294
TF: 866-779-7836 ■ *Web:* www.proteomesystems.com
pSivida Inc 400 Pleasant St ... Watertown MA 02472 617-926-5000 926-5050
NASDAQ: PSDV ■ *Web:* www.psivida.com
Psychemedics Corp 125 Nagog Park Suite 200 ... Acton MA 01720 978-206-8220 264-9236
AMEX: PMD ■ *TF:* 800-628-8073 ■ *Web:* www.psychemedics.com
QLT Inc 887 Great Northern Way ... Vancouver BC V5T4T5 604-707-7000 707-7001
TSX: QLT ■ *TF:* 800-663-5486 ■ *Web:* www.qltinc.com
Questcor Pharmaceuticals Inc 3260 Whipple Rd ... Union City CA 94587 510-400-0700 400-0799
AMEX: QSC ■ *TF:* 800-411-3065 ■ *Web:* www.questcor.com
Raven Laboratories 8607 Park Dr ... Omaha NE 68127 402-593-0781 593-0921
TF: 800-728-5702 ■ *Web:* www.ravenlabs.com
Regeneron Pharmaceuticals Inc 777 Old Saw Mill River Rd ... Tarrytown NY 10591 914-347-7000 347-2847
NASDAQ: REGN ■ *TF:* 800-637-8322 ■ *Web:* www.regeneron.com
Renovis Inc 2 Corporate Dr ... South San Francisco CA 94080 650-266-1400 266-1460
NASDAQ: RNVS ■ *Web:* www.renovis.com
Repligen Corp 41 Seyon St ... Waltham MA 02453 781-250-0111 250-0115
NASDAQ: RGEN ■ *TF Sales:* 800-622-2259 ■ *Web:* www.repligen.com
Repros Therapeutics Inc 2408 Timberloch Pl Suite B-7 ... The Woodlands TX 77380 281-719-3400 719-3446
NASDAQ: RPRX ■ *Web:* www.reprosrx.com
Research Triangle Park Laboratories 8109 Ebenezer Chruch Rd ... Raleigh NC 27612 919-510-0228 510-0141
Web: www.rtp-labs.com
Revivicor Inc 1700 Kraft Dr Suite 2400 ... Blacksburg VA 24060 540-961-5559 961-7958
Web: www.revivicor.com
Rigel Pharmaceuticals Inc 1180 Veterans Blvd ... South San Francisco CA 94080 650-624-1100 624-1101
NASDAQ: RIGL ■ *Web:* www.rigel.com
Roche Palo Alto LLC 3431 Hillview Ave ... Palo Alto CA 94304 650-855-5050 855-5526
Web: paloalto.roche.com
RTI Biologics Inc 11621 Research Cir ... Alachua FL 32615 386-418-8888 418-0342
NASDAQ: RTIX ■ *TF:* 877-343-6832 ■ *Web:* www.rtix.com
SAFC 3050 Spruce St ... Saint Louis MO 63103 314-534-4900 652-0000
TF: 800-244-1173 ■ *Web:* www.safcglobal.com
Samaritan Pharmaceuticals Inc
101 Convention Center Dr Suite 310 ... Las Vegas NV 89109 702-735-7001 737-7016
AMEX: LIV ■ *Web:* www.samaritanpharma.com
Sangamo BioSciences Inc 501 Canal Blvd Suite A100 ... Richmond CA 94804 510-970-6000 236-8951
NASDAQ: SGMO ■ *Web:* www.sangamo.com
Sanofi-Aventis Canada 2150 St Elzear Blvd W ... Laval QC H7L4A8 514-331-9220 334-8016
TF: 800-363-6364 ■ *Web:* www.sanofi-aventis.ca
Sanofi Pasteur Inc Discovery Dr ... Swiftwater PA 18370 570-839-7187 839-0561*
**Fax: Hum Res* ■ *TF Orders:* 800-822-2463 ■ *Web:* www.sanofi-pasteur.us
Santarus Inc 3721 Valley Centre Dr Suite 400 ... San Diego CA 92130 858-314-5700 314-5701
NASDAQ: SNTS ■ *TF:* 888-778-0887 ■ *Web:* www.santarus.com
Scios Inc 6500 Paseo Padre Pkwy ... Fremont CA 94555 650-564-4800 248-2389*
**Fax Area Code:* 510 ■ *TF:* 800-972-4670 ■ *Web:* www.sciosinc.com
SCOLR Pharma Inc 3625 132nd Ave SE Suite 400 ... Bellevue WA 98006 425-373-0171 373-0181
AMEX: DDD ■ *Web:* www.scolr.com
Seattle Genetics Inc 21823 30th Dr SE ... Bothell WA 98021 425-527-4000 527-4001
NASDAQ: SGEN ■ *Web:* www.seattlegenetics.com
Sequenom Inc 3595 John Hopkins Ct ... San Diego CA 92121 858-202-9000 202-9001
NASDAQ: SQNM ■ *TF:* 877-443-6663 ■ *Web:* www.sequenom.com
SGX Pharmaceuticals Inc 10505 Roselle St ... San Diego CA 92121 858-558-4850 558-4859
NASDAQ: SGXP ■ *Web:* www.sgxpharma.com
Signal Research Div Celgene Corp 4550 Town Ctr Ct ... San Diego CA 92121 858-558-7500 552-8775
Web: www.signalpharm.com

Phone Fax

Signalife Inc 531 S Main St Suite 301 ... Greenville SC 29601 864-233-2300 233-2100
AMEX: SGN ■ *Web:* www.signalife.com
Sirna Therapeutics Inc 2950 Wilderness Pl ... Boulder CO 80301 303-449-6500 449-8829
NASDAQ: RNAI ■ *Web:* www.sirna.com
Spectrum Pharmaceuticals Inc 157 Technology Dr ... Irvine CA 92618 949-788-6700 788-6706
NASDAQ: SPPI ■ *TF:* 888-622-6368 ■ *Web:* www.spectrumpharm.com
SuperGen Inc 4140 Dublin Blvd Suite 200 ... Dublin CA 94568 925-560-0100 560-0101
NASDAQ: SUPG ■ *TF:* 800-353-1075 ■ *Web:* www.supergen.com
Supernus Pharmaceuticals Inc 1550 E Gude Dr ... Rockville MD 20850 301-838-2500 838-2501
Web: www.supernuspharmaceuticals.com
Synthetech Inc 1290 Industrial Way ... Albany OR 97322 541-967-6575 967-9424
NASDAQ: NZYM ■ *Web:* www.synthetech.com
Targeted Genetics Corp 1100 Olive Way Suite 100 ... Seattle WA 98101 206-623-7612 223-0288
NASDAQ: TGEN ■ *TF:* 800-828-6022 ■ *Web:* www.targen.com
Tekmira Pharmaceuticals Corp 8900 Glenlyon Pkwy Suite 200 ... Burnaby BC V5J5J8 604-419-3200 419-3201
Web: www.tekmirapharm.com
Telik Inc 3165 Porter Dr ... Palo Alto CA 94304 650-845-7700 845-7800
NASDAQ: TELK ■ *TF:* 800-254-2598 ■ *Web:* www.telik.com
Thallion Pharmaceuticals Inc 7150 Alexander-Fleming ... Montreal QC H4S2C8 514-940-3600 228-3622
Web: www.thallion.com
Theratechnologies Inc 2310 Blvd of Fred Nobel ... Montreal QC H4S2A4 514-336-7800 336-7242
Web: www.theratech.com
Theravance Inc 901 Gateway Blvd ... South San Francisco CA 94080 650-808-6000 827-8690
NASDAQ: THRX ■ *Web:* www.theravance.com
Therics Inc 283 E Waterloo ... Akron OH 44319 330-773-7677 773-7697
Web: www.therics.com
Third Wave Technologies Inc 502 S Rosa Rd ... Madison WI 53719 608-273-8933 273-8618
NASDAQ: TWTI ■ *TF:* 888-898-2357 ■ *Web:* www.twt.com
Threshold Pharmaceuticals Inc 1300 Seaport Blvd 5th Fl ... Redwood City CA 94063 650-474-8200 474-2529
NASDAQ: THLD ■ *Web:* www.thresholdpharm.com
Titan Pharmaceuticals Inc
400 Oyster Point Blvd Suite 505 ... South San Francisco CA 94080 650-244-4990 244-4956
AMEX: TTP ■ *TF:* 800-500-6608 ■ *Web:* www.titanpharm.com
TolerRx Inc 300 Technology Sq 3rd Fl ... Cambridge MA 02139 617-354-8100 354-8300
Web: www.tolerrx.com
Trimeris Inc 3500 Paramount Pkwy ... Morrisville NC 27560 919-419-6050 419-1816
NASDAQ: TRMS ■ *Web:* www.trimeris.com
Unigene Laboratories Inc 110 Little Falls Rd ... Fairfield NJ 07004 973-882-0860 227-6088
Web: www.unigene.com
United Biomedical Inc 25 Davids Dr ... Hauppauge NY 11788 631-273-2828 273-1717
Web: www.unitedbiomedical.com
Urigen Pharmaceuticals Inc 875 Mahler Rd Suite 235 ... Burlingame CA 94010 650-259-0239 259-0901
Web: www.urigen.com
Vasogen Inc 2505 Meadowvale Blvd ... Mississauga ON L5N5S2 905-569-2265 569-9231
NASDAQ: VSGN ■ *TF:* 866-282-3770 ■ *Web:* www.vasogen.com
VaxGen Inc 349 Oyster Point Blvd ... South San Francisco CA 94080 650-624-1000
TF: 877-282-9436 ■ *Web:* www.vaxgen.com
Vermillion Inc 6611 Dumbarton Cir ... Fremont CA 94555 510-505-2100 505-2101
TF: 888-864-3770 ■ *Web:* www.vermillion.com
Vertex Pharmaceuticals Inc 130 Waverly St ... Cambridge MA 02139 617-444-6100 444-6180
NASDAQ: VRTX ■ *TF:* 800-294-2465 ■ *Web:* www.vrtx.com
ViaCell Inc 245 1st St 15th Fl ... Cambridge MA 02142 617-577-7744 565-2243*
NASDAQ: VIAC ■ **Fax Area Code:* 866 ■ **Fax:* Mktg ■ *TF:* 866-874-2235 ■
Web: www.viacellinc.com
Vical Inc 10390 Pacific Ctr Ct ... San Diego CA 92121 858-646-1100 646-1150
NASDAQ: VICL ■ *Web:* www.vical.com
Vion Pharmaceuticals Inc 4 Science Park ... New Haven CT 06511 203-498-4210 498-4211
NASDAQ: VION ■ *Web:* www.vionpharm.com
Virexx Medical Corp 8223 Roper Rd NW ... Edmonton AB T6E6S4 780-433-4411 436-0068
Web: www.virexx.com
ViroPharma Inc 397 Eagleview Blvd ... Exton PA 19341 610-458-7300 458-7380
NASDAQ: VPHM ■ *TF:* 888-651-0201 ■ *Web:* www.viropharma.com
Viventia Biotech Inc 5060 Spectrum Way Suite 405 ... Mississauga ON L4W5N5 905-361-8686 361-2673
Web: www.viventia.com
Wyeth Pharmaceuticals 500 Arcola Rd ... Collegeville PA 19426 484-865-5000
Web: www.wyeth.com
Xenogen Corp 2601 Challenger Dr ... Alameda CA 94501 510-291-6100 291-6232
NASDAQ: XGEN ■ *TF:* 877-936-6436 ■ *Web:* www.xenogen.com
XenoPort Inc 3410 Central Expy ... Santa Clara CA 95051 408-616-7200 616-7210
NASDAQ: XNPT ■ *Web:* www.xenoport.com
XOMA (US) LLC 2910 7th St ... Berkeley CA 94710 510-204-7200 644-2011
NASDAQ: XOMA ■ *TF:* 800-544-9662 ■ *Web:* www.xoma.com
YM Biosciences Inc 5045 Orbitor Dr Bldg 11 Suite 400 ... Mississauga ON L4W4Y4 905-629-9761 629-4959
AMEX: YMI ■ *Web:* www.ymbiosciences.com
ZymoGenetics Inc 1201 Eastlake Ave E ... Seattle WA 98102 206-442-6600 442-6608
NASDAQ: ZGEN ■ *TF:* 800-775-6686 ■ *Web:* www.zymogenetics.com

86 BLANKBOOKS & BINDERS

SEE ALSO Checks - Personal & Business p. 1440

Phone Fax

Abco Inc 1621 Wall St ... Dallas TX 75215 214-565-1191 428-8996
TF: 800-969-2226 ■ *Web:* www.abcoinc.com
ACCO Brands Corp 300 Tower Pkwy ... Lincolnshire IL 60069 847-541-9500 478-0073
NYSE: ABD ■ *TF:* 800-222-6462 ■ *Web:* www.acco.com
ACCO Canada Inc 5 Precido Ct ... Brampton ON L6S6B7 905-595-3100 595-3130
TF: 800-268-3447 ■ *Web:* www.acco.ca
Acme Sample Books Inc 2410 Schirra Pl ... High Point NC 27263 336-883-4187 883-4565
Web: www.acmesample.com
AD Industries Inc 12160 Sherman Way ... North Hollywood CA 91605 818-765-4200 765-4370
TF: 800-233-4201 ■ *Web:* www.adind.com
Advanced Looseleaf Technologies Inc 1424 Somerset Ave ... Dighton MA 02715 508-669-6354 669-6143
TF: 800-339-6354 ■ *Web:* www.binder.com
Allison Payment Systems LLC 2200 Production Dr ... Indianapolis IN 46241 317-808-2400 808-2477
TF: 800-755-2440 ■ *Web:* www.apsllc.com
American Thermoplastic Co 106 Gamma Dr ... Pittsburgh PA 15238 412-967-0900 967-9990
TF: 800-245-6600 ■ *Web:* www.binders.com
Antioch Co PO Box 1839 ... Saint Cloud MN 56301 320-251-3822 529-5863
TF: 800-328-2344 ■ *Web:* www.antiochcompany.com
Antioch Publishing Co 888 Dayton St ... Yellow Springs OH 45387 937-767-7379 767-6289
TF: 800-543-2397 ■ *Web:* www.antioch.com
Art Leather Mfg Co Inc 45-10 94th St ... Elmhurst NY 11373 718-699-6300 882-5286*
**Fax Area Code:* 800 ■ *TF:* 888-252-5286 ■ *Web:* www.artleather.com
Avery Dennison Corp 150 N Orange Grove Blvd ... Pasadena CA 91103 626-304-2000 304-2192
NYSE: AVY ■ *TF Cust Svc:* 800-252-8379 ■ *Web:* www.averydennison.com
Blackbourn Media Packaging Div Fey Industries
200 4th Ave N ... Edgerton MN 56128 800-842-7550 442-4313*
**Fax Area Code:* 507 ■ *Web:* www.blackbourn.com
Blair Packaging Inc 116 E Missouri St ... Scott City MO 63780 573-264-2146 264-3730
TF: 800-624-3150 ■ *Web:* www.blairpkg.com
Bobley Harmann Publishing Co 311 Crossways Park Dr ... Woodbury NY 11797 516-364-1800 364-1899
TF Cust Svc: 800-323-1692

Phone | Fax

Cardinal Brands Inc 643 Massachusetts St Suite 200 Lawrence KS 66044 785-344-1400 344-1200
TF: 800-364-8713 ■ *Web:* www.cardinalbrands.com
Chilcote Co 2140-60 Superior Ave Cleveland OH 44114 216-781-6000 771-2572
TF Sales: 800-827-5679
Colad Group 801 Exchange St Buffalo NY 14210 716-961-1776 961-1753
TF: 800-950-1755 ■ *Web:* www.colad.com
Columbia Loose Leaf Corp 50-02 5th St Long Island City NY 11101 718-937-8585 937-8589
Web: www.columbialooseleaf.com
Colwell Industries Inc 123 N 3rd St Minneapolis MN 55401 612-340-0365 340-0231
Web: www.colwellindustries.com
Consolidated Looseleaf Inc 649 Alden St Fall River MA 02722 508-676-8580 677-0130
TF: 800-289-3523
Continental Binder & Specialty Corp 407 W Compton Blvd Gardena CA 90248 310-324-8227 715-6740
TF: 800-872-2897 ■ *Web:* www.continentalbinder.com
Continental Loose Leaf Inc 1122 16th Ave SE Minneapolis MN 55414 612-378-4800 378-7680
Web: www.continentallooseleaf.com
CR Gibson Inc 404 BNA Dr Bldg 100 Suite 600 Nashville TN 37217 615-724-2900 871-0501
TF: 800-243-6004 ■ *Web:* www.crgibson.com
Custom Cover Service Inc 1600 W 92nd St Bloomington MN 55431 952-884-5511 888-9014
Web: www.lithotechusa.com
Customcraft Binder Corp 21 Addison Ln Greenvale NY 11548 516-484-4020 621-5008
TF: 800-428-0934 ■ *Web:* www.customcraftbinder.com
D Davis Kenny Co Inc 4810 Greatland San Antonio TX 78218 210-662-9882 662-9887
Web: www.topflightalbums.com
Daret Inc 33 Daret Dr Ringwood NJ 07456 973-962-6001 962-6091
Data Management Inc 537 New Britain Ave Farmington CT 06034 860-677-8586 428-1951*
**Fax Area Code:* 800 ■ *TF Orders:* 800-243-1969 ■ *Web:* www.datamanage.com
Day Runner Inc 101 O'Neil Rd Sydney NY 13838 607-563-9411 563-8811
TF: 800-323-0500 ■ *Web:* www.dayrunner.com
Day-Timers Inc 1 Willow Ln East Texas PA 18046 610-398-1151 530-6500*
**Fax:* Hum Res ■ *TF:* 800-457-5702 ■ *Web:* www.daytimer.com
Dayton Legal Blank Inc 875 Congress Pk Dr Dayton OH 45459 937-435-4405 435-8352
TF: 800-262-8480 ■ *Web:* www.dlbinc.com
Dilley Mfg Co 215 E 3rd St Des Moines IA 50309 515-288-7289 288-4210
TF: 800-247-5087 ■ *Web:* www.dilleymfg.com
EBSCO Industries Inc Vulcan Information Packaging Div
PO Box 29 Vincent AL 35178 205-672-2241 672-1276
TF: 800-633-4526 ■ *Web:* www.vulcan-online.com
Eckhart & Co Inc 4011 W 54th St Indianapolis IN 46254 317-347-2665 347-2666
TF: 800-443-3791 ■ *Web:* www.eckhartandco.com
Esko Inc 700 Liberty Ln Dayton OH 45449 937-865-0498 865-0070
TF: 800-783-7526 ■ *Web:* www.esko.com
Esselte Corp 48 S Service Rd Suite 400 Melville NY 11747 631-675-5700 675-3456
TF Cust Svc: 800-645-6051 ■ *Web:* www.esselte.com
Esselte Pendaflex Corp 1625 E Duane Blvd Kankakee IL 60901 815-933-3351 933-7922
TF: 800-888-2115
Executive Greetings Inc 120 Greenwoods Industrial Pk New Hartford CT 06057 860-379-9911 379-7124
TF Cust Svc: 800-562-5468 ■ *Web:* www.executive-greetings.com
Federal Business Products Inc 95 Main Ave Clifton NJ 07014 973-667-9800 667-7756
TF: 800-927-5123 ■ *Web:* www.feddirect.com
Fey Industries Blackbourn Media Packaging Div
200 4th Ave N Edgerton MN 56128 800-842-7550 442-4313*
**Fax Area Code:* 507 ■ *Web:* www.blackbourn.com
Fey Industries Inc 200 4th Ave N Edgerton MN 56128 507-442-4311 442-3686
TF: 800-533-5340
Forbes Products Corp 45 High Tech Dr Rush NY 14543 585-334-4800 334-6180
TF: 800-836-7237 ■ *Web:* www.forbesproducts.com
Formflex Inc PO Box 218 Bloomingdale IN 47832 765-498-8900 498-5200
TF: 800-255-7659 ■ *Web:* www.formflexproducts.com
General Binding Corp 1 GBC Plaza Northbrook IL 60062 847-272-3700 914-8178*
**Fax Area Code:* 800 ■ *TF Orders:* 800-723-4000 ■ *Web:* www.gbcconnect.com
General Loose Leaf Bindery Co 3811 Hawthorn Ct Waukegan IL 60087 847-244-9700 244-9741
TF: 800-621-0493 ■ *Web:* www.looseleaf.com
General Products 4045 N Rockwell St Chicago IL 60618 773-463-2424 463-3028
TF: 800-888-1934 ■ *Web:* www.gpalbums.com
HC Miller Co 3030 Lowell Dr Green Bay WI 54311 800-829-6555 465-3035*
**Fax Area Code:* 920 ■ *Web:* www.hcmiller.com
Holum & Sons Co Inc 740 N Burr Oak Dr Westmont IL 60559 630-654-8222 654-2929
TF: 800-447-4479 ■ *Web:* www.holumandsons.com
Kenny D Davis Co Inc 4810 Greatland San Antonio TX 78218 210-662-9882 662-9887
Web: www.topflightalbums.com
Kunz Business Products Co 813 Green Ave Altoona PA 16603 814-643-4320 643-8521
TF: 800-458-3442 ■ *Web:* www.jbkunz.com
Kurtz Brothers Co Inc PO Box 392 Clearfield PA 16830 814-765-6561 765-8690
TF: 800-252-3811 ■ *Web:* www.kurtzbros.com
Leed Selling Tools Corp 9700 Hwy 57 Evansville IN 47725 812-867-4340 867-4353
M & F Case International Inc 717 School St Pawtucket RI 02860 401-722-4830 725-8652
TF Cust Svc: 800-343-8820
MeadWestvaco Consumer & Office Products
4751 Hempstead Station Dr Kettering OH 45429 937-495-6323 495-3168
TF: 800-648-6323 ■ *Web:* www.meadwestvaco.com/cop.nsf
Michael Lewis Simon Products Co Inc 201 Mittel Dr Wood Dale IL 60191 630-350-1060 350-1089
TF: 800-323-8808 ■ *Web:* www.mlco.com
Miller HC Co 3030 Lowell Dr Green Bay WI 54311 800-829-6555 465-3035*
**Fax Area Code:* 920 ■ *Web:* www.hcmiller.com
NAPCO Inc 120 Trojan Ave Sparta NC 28675 336-372-5228 372-8890
TF: 800-854-8621 ■ *Web:* www.napcousa.com
Northeast Data Services 1316 College Ave Elmira NY 14901 607-733-5541 735-4540
TF Cust Svc: 800-845-3720 ■ *Web:* www.artisticlabels.com
Pioneer Photo Albums Inc 9801 Deering Ave Chatsworth CA 91311 818-882-2161 882-6239
TF: 800-366-3686 ■ *Web:* www.pioneerphotoalbums.com
Roaring Spring Blank Book Co 740 Spang St PO Box 35 Roaring Spring PA 16673 814-224-5141 224-5429
TF Cust Svc: 800-441-1653 ■ *Web:* www.rspaperproducts.com
Rogers Loose Leaf Co Inc 1555 W Fulton St Chicago IL 60607 312-226-1947 226-3005
Samsill Corp 5740 Hartman Rd Fort Worth TX 76119 817-536-1906 535-6900
TF: 800-255-1100 ■ *Web:* www.samsill.com
Southwest Plastic Binding Co Inc 109 Millwell Ct Maryland Heights MO 63043 314-739-4400 942-2010*
**Fax Area Code:* 800 ■ *TF:* 800-325-3628 ■ *Web:* www.swplastic.com
Spiral Binding Co Inc 1 Maltese Dr Totowa NJ 07511 973-256-0666 256-5981*
**Fax:* Cust Svc ■ *TF:* 800-631-3572 ■ *Web:* www.spiralbinding.com
Superior Press Inc 11930 Hamden Pl Santa Fe Springs CA 90670 562-948-1866 948-4966
TF: 888-590-7998 ■ *Web:* www.superior-press.com
Trendex Inc 240 E Maryland Ave Suite 100 Saint Paul MN 55117 651-489-4655 489-4423
TF: 800-328-9200 ■ *Web:* www.trendexinc.com
Twentieth Century Plastics Inc 205 S Puente St Brea CA 92821 714-441-4500 786-7939*
**Fax Area Code:* 800 ■ *TF:* 800-767-0777
Unified Packaging Inc 711 Topeka Way Castle Rock CO 80109 303-733-1000 733-6789
Web: www.unifiedpackaginginc.com
Union Group 649 Alden St Fall River MA 02722 508-676-8580 677-0130
TF: 800-289-3523 ■ *Web:* www.theuniongroup.com
US Ring Binder 6800 Arsenal St Saint Louis MO 63139 314-645-7880 645-7239
Web: www.usringbinder.com
ViaTech Publishing Solutions 1440 5th Ave Bay Shore NY 11706 631-968-8500 968-8522
TF: 800-645-8558 ■ *Web:* www.viatechpub.com
Vulcan Information Packaging Div EBSCO Industries Inc
PO Box 29 Vincent AL 35178 205-672-2241 672-1276
TF: 800-633-4526 ■ *Web:* www.vulcan-online.com

West Coast Samples Inc 14450 Central Ave Chino CA 91710 909-464-1616 465-9982
Web: www.wcsample.com
Western Looseleaf Div Cal/West United Inc
12160 Sherman Way North Hollywood CA 91605 818-765-4200 765-4370
TF: 800-233-4201 ■ *Web:* www.westernlooseleaf.com
Winthrop-Atkins Co Inc 35 E Main St Middleboro MA 02346 508-947-4600 431-1890*
**Fax Area Code:* 888 ■ *TF:* 888-463-7888 ■ *Web:* www.winthropatkins.com

87 BLINDS & SHADES

Phone | Fax

Aeroshade Inc 433 Oakland Ave Waukesha WI 53186 262-547-2101 547-0546
TF: 800-331-7179 ■ *Web:* www.aeroshade.com
Beauti-Vue Products Inc 8555 194th Ave Bristol Industrial Park Bristol WI 53104 262-857-2306 329-9431*
**Fax Area Code:* 800 ■ *TF:* 800-558-9431 ■ *Web:* www.beautivue.com
Budget Blinds Inc 1927 N Glassell St Orange CA 92865 714-637-2100 637-1400
TF: 800-800-9250 ■ *Web:* www.budgetblinds.com
C-Mor Co 7 Jewell St Garfield NJ 07026 973-478-3900 478-0249
TF: 800-631-3830
Comfortex Window Fashions Inc 21 Elm St Maplewood NY 12189 518-273-3333 336-4580*
**Fax Area Code:* 800 ■ *TF Cust Svc:* 800-843-4151 ■ *Web:* www.comfortex.com
Delaine James Inc 10200 McKalla Pl Suite 400 Austin TX 78758 512-835-5333 999-5555*
**Fax Area Code:* 800 ■ *TF:* 800-999-5444 ■ *Web:* www.delainejames.com
Dixon Blind & Awning Service 1800 Sunset Ave Rocky Mount NC 27804 252-442-2145 442-2146
Draper Shade & Screen Co 411 S Pearl St Spiceland IN 47385 765-987-7999 987-7142
TF: 800-238-7999 ■ *Web:* www.draperinc.com
Fashion Tech Inc 2010 SE 8th Ave Portland OR 97214 503-238-0666 231-6366
TF: 800-444-8822 ■ *Web:* www.fashiontech.com
Friedland Ralph & Brothers Inc 17 Industrial Dr Cliffwood Beach NJ 07735 732-290-9800 290-2933
TF: 800-631-2162
Gotcha Covered 1611 N Stemmons Fwy Suite 318 Carrollton TX 75006 972-466-2544 446-6774
Web: www.gotchacoveredblinds.com
Hunter Douglas 2 Parkway & Rt 17 S Upper Saddle River NJ 07458 201-327-8200 327-7938
TF: 800-436-7366 ■ *Web:* www.hunterdouglas.com
Kenney Mfg Co 1000 Jefferson Blvd Warwick RI 02886 401-739-2200 821-4240
TF Cust Svc: 800-753-6639 ■ *Web:* www.kenney.com
Lafayette Venetian Blind Inc 3000 Klondike Rd West Lafayette IN 47906 765-464-2500 464-2680
TF: 800-342-5523 ■ *Web:* www.lafvb.com
Levolor Kirsch Window Fashions 4110 Premier Dr High Point NC 27265 336-812-8181 881-5991
TF: 800-232-2028 ■ *Web:* www.levolor.com
Mark Window Products Inc 2900 S Fairview St Santa Ana CA 92704 714-641-1411 754-6117
TF: 800-427-4127 ■ *Web:* www.markwindow.com
Mill Supply Div 264 Morse St Hamden CT 06517 203-777-7668 777-4515
TF: 800-243-6648 ■ *Web:* www.millsupplydiv.com
Nationwide Floorcover & Window Coverings
111 E Kilbourn Ave Suite 2400 Milwaukee WI 53202 414-765-9900 765-1300
TF: 800-366-8088 ■ *Web:* www.floorsandwindows.com
Ralph Friedland & Brothers Inc 17 Industrial Dr Cliffwood Beach NJ 07735 732-290-9800 290-2933
TF: 800-631-2162
Southland Window Fashions 408 Arlington St Houston TX 77007 713-863-7761 299-7761*
**Fax Area Code:* 800 ■ *TF:* 800-299-9030 ■ *Web:* www.southlandwf.com
Springs Global US Inc 205 N White St Fort Mill SC 29715 803-547-1500 547-1579*
**Fax:* Mktg ■ *TF:* 888-926-7888 ■ *Web:* www.springs.com
Sun Control Products Inc 1908 2nd St SW Rochester MN 55902 507-282-2620 282-2377
TF: 800-533-0010
Superior Shade & Blind Co Inc 1541 N Powerline Rd Pompano Beach FL 33069 954-975-8122 975-2938
TF: 800-325-9018 ■ *Web:* www.superiorshade.com
Warm Co 5529 186th Pl SW Lynnwood WA 98037 425-248-2424 248-2422
TF: 800-234-9276 ■ *Web:* www.warmcompany.com
Warren Steven Window Fashions 600 NE Hoover St Minneapolis MN 55413 612-331-5939 331-9116
TF: 800-937-0008 ■ *Web:* www.warrensteven.com

88 BLISTER PACKAGING

Phone | Fax

Andex Industries Inc 1911 4th Ave N Escanaba MI 49829 906-786-6070 786-3133
TF: 800-338-9882 ■ *Web:* www.andex.net
Bryan Mfg Co Inc 71 Leonard St Norton MA 02766 508-285-4587 285-2750
Card Pak Inc 29601 Solon Rd Solon OH 44139 440-542-3100 542-3399
TF: 800-824-3342 ■ *Web:* www.cardpak.com
Display Pack 1340 Monroe Ave NW Grand Rapids MI 49505 616-451-3061 451-8907
Web: www.displaypack.com
Dot Group 6223 Constitution Dr Fort Wayne IN 46804 260-432-3822 432-0083
Dot Packaging Group Inc 1500 Paramount Pkwy Batavia IL 60510 630-879-0121 879-7000
TF: 800-323-6160 ■ *Web:* www.dotpack.com
Jay Packaging Group 100 Warwick Industrial Dr Warwick RI 02886 401-739-7200 738-5104*
**Fax:* Cust Svc ■ *Web:* www.jaypack.com
Placon Corp 6096 McKee Rd Madison WI 53719 608-271-5634 271-3162
TF: 800-541-1535 ■ *Web:* www.placon.com
Plastic Concept Inc 15602 Container Ln Huntington Beach CA 92649 714-895-4722 895-2129
Sealed Air Corp 200 Riverfront Blvd Elmwood Park NJ 07407 201-791-7600
NYSE: SEE ■ *Web:* www.sealedaircorp.com
Sharp Corp 23 Carland Rd Conshohocken PA 19428 610-279-3550 279-4712
TF: 800-892-6197 ■ *Web:* www.sharpcorporation.com

89 BLOOD CENTERS

SEE ALSO Laboratories - Drug-Testing p. 1883; Laboratories - Genetic Testing p. 1883; Laboratories - Medical p. 1883

The centers listed here are members of America's Blood Centers (ABC), the national network of non-profit, independent community blood centers. ABC members are licensed and regulated by the US Food & Drug Administration.

Phone | Fax

Belle Bonfils Memorial Blood Center 717 Yosemite St Denver CO 80230 303-341-4000 340-2751
TF: 800-365-0006 ■ *Web:* www.bonfils.org
Blood Assurance Inc 705 E 4th St Chattanooga TN 37403 423-756-0966 752-8460
TF: 800-962-0628 ■ *Web:* www.bloodassurance.org
Blood Bank of Alaska 4000 Laurel St Anchorage AK 99508 907-222-5600 563-1371
Web: www.bloodbankofalaska.org
Blood Bank of Delmarva 100 Hygeia Dr Newark DE 19713 302-737-8406 737-8233
TF: 888-825-6638 ■ *Web:* www.bloodbankofdelaware.org

	City	State	Zip	Phone	Fax
Blood Bank of Hawaii 2043 Dillingham Blvd	Honolulu	HI	96819	808-845-9966	848-4737
TF: 800-372-9966 ■ *Web:* www.bbh.org					
Blood Bank of the Redwoods 2324 Bethards Dr	Santa Rosa	CA	95405	707-545-1222	575-8178
TF: 800-425-6634 ■ *Web:* bbr.org					
Blood Center The 312 S Johnson St	New Orleans	LA	70112	504-524-1322	592-1580
Web: www.thebloodcenter.org					
Blood Center of Iowa 431 E Locust St	Des Moines	IA	50309	515-288-0276	288-0833
TF: 800-287-4903 ■ *Web:* www.bloodonor.org					
Blood Center of New Jersey 45 S Grove St	East Orange	NJ	07018	973-676-4700	676-4933
TF: 800-652-5663 ■ *Web:* www.bloodnj.org					
Blood Center of Northcentral Wisconsin 211 Forest St	Wausau	WI	54403	715-842-0761	845-6429
Blood Centers of the Pacific 270 Masonic Ave	San Francisco	CA	94118	415-567-6400	749-6620
TF: 888-393-4483 ■ *Web:* www.bloodcenters.org					
Blood Systems 6210 E Oak St PO Box1867	Scottsdale	AZ	85257	480-946-4201	675-5767
Web: www.unitedbloodservices.org					
Blood & Tissue Center of Central Texas 4300 N Lamar Blvd	Austin	TX	78756	512-206-1266	458-3859
Web: www.bloodandtissue.org					
BloodCenter of Wisconsin 638 N 18th St	Milwaukee	WI	53233	414-933-5000	937-6332
TF: 800-257-3840 ■ *Web:* www.bloodctrwise.org					
BloodSource 1625 Stockton Blvd	Sacramento	CA	95816	916-456-1500	739-8219*
**Fax Area Code: 401* ■ *TF:* 800-995-4420 ■ *Web:* www.smfbc.org					
Carter BloodCare 2205 Hwy 121	Bedford	TX	76021	817-412-5000	412-5992
TF: 800-366-2834 ■ *Web:* www.carterbloodcare.org					
Cascade Regional Blood Services 220 S 'I' St	Tacoma	WA	98401	253-383-2553	572-6340
TF: 877-242-5663 ■ *Web:* www.cascadebloodcenters.org					
Central California Blood Center 3445 N 1st St	Fresno	CA	93726	559-224-2900	225-1602
TF: 800-404-2500 ■ *Web:* www.cencalblood.org					
Central Illinois Community Blood Center 1134 S 7th St	Springfield	IL	62703	217-753-1530	753-8116
TF: 866-448-3256					
Central Jersey Blood Center 494 Sycamore Ave	Shrewsbury	NJ	07702	732-842-5750	842-1617
Web: www.cjbc.org					
Central Kentucky Blood Center 330 Waller Ave	Lexington	KY	40504	859-276-2534	233-4166
TF: 800-775-2522 ■ *Web:* www.ckbc.org					
Central Pennsylvania Blood Bank 8167 Adams Dr	Hummelstown	PA	17036	717-566-6161	566-7850
TF: 800-771-0059 ■ *Web:* www.cpbb.org					
Coastal Bend Blood Center 209 N Padre Island Dr	Corpus Christi	TX	78415	361-855-4943	855-2641
TF: 800-299-4943 ■ *Web:* www.communitybloodbank.com					
Coffee Memorial Blood Center 7500 Wallace Drive	Amarillo	TX	79106	806-358-4563	358-2982
TF: 800-658-6178 ■ *Web:* www.thegiftoflife.org					
Community Blood Bank of the Lancaster County Medical Society					
100 N 84th St	Lincoln	NE	68505	402-486-9400	486-9429
TF: 877-486-9414 ■ *Web:* www.don8bld.org					
Community Blood Bank of Northwest Pennsylvania 2646 Peach St	Erie	PA	16508	814-456-4206	452-3966
Web: www.fourhearts.org					
Community Blood Center 4040 Main St	Kansas City	MO	64111	816-753-4040	968-4047
TF: 888-647-4040 ■ *Web:* www.savealifenow.org					
Community Blood Center 349 S Main St	Dayton	OH	45402	937-461-3450	461-9217
TF: 800-388-4483 ■ *Web:* www.cbccts.org					
Blue Springs Center 1124 W 40th Hwy	Blue Springs	MO	64015	816-224-0728	224-0944
Web: www.bloodislife.org					
Gladstone Center 7265 N Oak Trafficway	Gladstone	MO	64118	816-468-9813	
Web: www.savealifenow.org					
Jefferson City Center 751 W Stadium Blvd Suite D	Jefferson City	MO	65109	573-556-5550	632-7049
Web: www.savealifenow.org					
Lawrence Center 1410 Kasold Rd	Lawrence	KS	66049	785-843-5383	
Web: www.savealifenow.org					
Olathe Center 1463 E 151st St	Olathe	KS	66061	913-829-3724	
Web: www.savealifenow.org					
Saint Joseph Center 3122 Frederick Ave	Saint Joseph	MO	64506	816-232-6791	232-3324
TF: 800-725-6791 ■ *Web:* www.bloodislife.org					
Topeka Center 800 Southwest Ln	Topeka	KS	66606	785-233-0195	233-5953
Web: www.savealifenow.org					
Community Blood Center Inc 4406 W Spencer St	Appleton	WI	54914	920-738-3131	738-3139
Web: www.communityblood.org					
Community Blood Center of the Ozarks 2230 S Glenstone	Springfield	MO	65804	417-227-5000	227-5400
TF: 800-280-5337 ■ *Web:* www.cbco.org					
Community Blood Centers of South Florida 1700 N SR 7	Lauderhill	FL	33313	954-735-9600	733-6331
TF: 800-357-4483 ■ *Web:* www.cbcsf.org					
Community Blood Services 970 Linwood Ave W	Paramus	NJ	07652	201-444-3900	670-6174
Web: www.communitybloodservices.org					
Community Blood Services of Illinois 1408 W University Ave	Urbana	IL	61801	217-367-2202	367-6403
TF: 800-217-4483 ■ *Web:* www.bloodservices.org					
Delta Blood Bank 65 N Commerce St	Stockton	CA	95201	209-943-3831	462-0221
TF: 800-244-6794 ■ *Web:* www.deltabloodbank.org					
Florida Blood Services 10100 Dr ML King Jr St N	Saint Petersburg	FL	33716	727-568-5433	568-1177
TF: 800-682-5663 ■ *Web:* www.fbsblood.org					
Florida Georgia Blood Alliance 536 W 10th St	Jacksonville	FL	32206	904-353-8263	355-6853
TF: 800-447-1479 ■ *Web:* www.fgba.org					
Florida's Blood Centers 345 W Michigan St Suite 106	Orlando	FL	32806	407-835-5501	835-5505
TF: 888-936-6283 ■ *Web:* www.floridasbloodcenters.org					
Gulf Coast Regional Blood Center 1400 La Concha Ln	Houston	TX	77054	713-790-1200	790-1007
TF: 888-482-5663 ■ *Web:* www.giveblood.org					
Heartland Blood Centers 1200 N Highland Ave	Aurora	IL	60506	630-892-7055	892-4590
TF: 800-786-4483 ■ *Web:* www.heartlandbc.org					
Hemacare Corp 4954 Van Nuys Blvd	Sherman Oaks	CA	91403	818-986-3883	986-1417
TF: 888-481-1538 ■ *Web:* www.hemacare.com					
Houchin Blood Services 2600 G St	Bakersfield	CA	93301	661-327-8541	327-0509
Web: www.hcbb.com					
Hoxworth Blood Center University of Cincinnati Medical Center					
3130 Highland Ave ML0055	Cincinnati	OH	45267	513-558-1200	558-1300
TF: 800-265-1515 ■ *Web:* www.hoxworth.org					
Imperial Valley Blood Services 1415 Ross Ave	El Centro	CA	92243	760-353-3554	339-7390
Inland Northwest Blood Center 1341 Northwood Ctr Ct	Coeur d'Alene	ID	83814	208-667-5461	292-6103
TF: 800-423-0151 ■ *Web:* www.inbc2.org					
Inland Northwest Blood Center 210 W Cataldo Ave	Spokane	WA	99201	509-624-0151	232-4523
TF: 800-423-0151 ■ *Web:* www.inbc2.org					
Institute for Transfusion Medicine 3636 Blvd of the Allies	Pittsburgh	PA	15213	412-209-7300	209-7330
TF: 800-431-0608 ■ *Web:* www.itxm.org					
Lane Memorial Blood Bank 2211 Willamette St	Eugene	OR	97405	541-484-9111	484-6976
Web: www.lanecountyblood.org					
Lifeblood Mid-South Regional Blood Center					
1040 Madison Ave	Memphis	TN	38104	901-522-8585	523-8671
TF: 888-543-3256 ■ *Web:* www.lifeblood.org					
Blytheville Center 320 N 6th St	Blytheville	AR	72315	870-763-8585	763-4117
Web: www.lifeblood.org					
DeSoto Center 577 Goodman Rd Suite 5	Southaven	MS	38671	662-349-0662	349-2427
Web: www.lifeblood.org					
LIFELINE Blood Services 828 North Pkwy	Jackson	TN	38305	731-427-4431	422-4712
TF: 800-924-6572 ■ *Web:* www.lifelinebloodserv.org					
LifeShare Blood Centers 1523 Doctors Dr	Bossier City	LA	71111	318-742-4636	741-6980
TF: 877-256-4115 ■ *Web:* www.lifeshare.org					
LifeShare Blood Centers 1404 S Vienna St	Ruston	LA	71279	318-254-1167	255-6367
Web: www.lifeshare.org					
LifeShare Blood Centers 107 N Service Rd	Ruston	LA	71270	318-322-4445	651-4435
TF: 800-256-5433 ■ *Web:* www.lifeshare.org					
LifeShare Blood Centers 8910 Linwood Ave	Shreveport	LA	71106	318-222-7770	222-8886
TF: 800-256-4483 ■ *Web:* www.lifeshare.org					
LifeShare Community Blood Services 105 Cleveland St	Elyria	OH	44035	440-322-5700	322-6240
TF: 866-644-5433 ■ *Web:* www.lifeshare.cc					
LifeSource Blood Services 1205 N Milwaukee Ave	Glenview	IL	60025	847-298-9660	298-4473
TF: 800-486-0680 ■ *Web:* www.lifesource.org					
LifeSouth Community Blood Centers 1221 NW 13th St	Gainesville	FL	32601	352-334-1000	334-1066
Web: www.crbs.org					
LifeSouth Community Blood Centers Atlanta					
4891 Ashford Dunwoody Rd	Atlanta	GA	30338	404-329-1994	329-1707
TF: 888-795-1707 ■ *Web:* www.lifesouth.org					
Manatee Community Blood Center 216 Manatee Ave E	Bradenton	FL	34208	941-746-7195	748-1711
Web: www.manateeblood.org					
Memorial Blood Centers of Minnesota 737 Pelham Blvd	Saint Paul	MN	55114	651-332-7000	332-7001
Web: www.memorialbloodcenters.org					
Michigan Community Blood Centers 1036 Fuller Ave NE	Grand Rapids	MI	49503	616-774-2300	233-8567
TF: 866-642-5663 ■ *Web:* miblood.org					
Michigan Community Blood Centers 4005 Orchard Dr	Midland	MI	48670	989-839-3490	839-1315
TF: 866-642-5663 ■ *Web:* www.miblood.org					
Michigan Community Blood Centers Northwest					
2575 Aero Pk Dr	Traverse City	MI	49686	231-935-3030	935-1690
TF: 800-642-5663 ■ *Web:* www.miblood.org					
Miller-Keystone Blood Center 1465 Valley Ctr Pkwy	Bethlehem	PA	18017	610-691-5850	691-5423
TF: 800-223-6667 ■ *Web:* www.hcsc.org/blood					
Mississippi Blood Services 1995 Lakeland Dr	Jackson	MS	39216	601-981-3232	984-3783
TF: 888-902-5663 ■ *Web:* www.msblood.com					
Mississippi Valley Regional Blood Center					
5500 Lakeview Pkwy	Davenport	IA	52807	563-359-5401	359-8603
TF: 800-747-5401 ■ *Web:* www.bloodcenter.org					
New York Blood Center 310 E 67th St	New York	NY	10021	212-570-3000	570-3195
Web: www.nybloodcenter.org					
Northern California Community Blood Bank 2524 Harrison Ave	Eureka	CA	95501	707-443-8004	443-8007
Northwest Florida Blood Center 2201 N 9th Ave	Pensacola	FL	32503	850-434-2535	432-8941
Web: www.nfbcblood.org					
Oklahoma Blood Institute 1001 N Lincoln Blvd	Oklahoma City	OK	73104	405-297-5700	297-5513
TF: 800-827-5693 ■ *Web:* www.obi2.org					
Puget Sound Blood Center 921 Terry Ave	Seattle	WA	98104	206-292-6500	292-8030
TF: 800-366-2831 ■ *Web:* www.psbc.org					
Rhode Island Blood Center 405 Promenade St	Providence	RI	02908	401-453-8360	453-8557
TF: 800-283-8385 ■ *Web:* www.ribc.org					
Rock River Valley Blood Center 419 N 6th St	Rockford	IL	61107	815-965-8751	965-8756
TF: 866-889-9073 ■ *Web:* www.rrvbc.org					
San Diego Blood Bank 440 Upas St	San Diego	CA	92103	619-296-6393	296-0126
TF: 800-479-3902 ■ *Web:* www.sandiegobloodbank.org					
SeraCare Life Sciences Inc 375 West St	West Bridgewater	MA	02379	508-580-1900	580-2202
NASDAQ: SRLS ■ *TF:* 800-676-1881 ■ *Web:* www.seracare.com					
Shepeard Community Blood Center 1533 Wrightsboro Rd	Augusta	GA	30904	706-737-4551	733-5214
Web: www.shepeardblood.org					
Siouxland Community Blood Bank 1019 Jones St	Sioux City	IA	51105	712-252-4208	252-1013
TF: 800-798-4208 ■ *Web:* www.siouxlandbloodbank.org					
South Texas Blood & Tissue Center 6211 IH-10 W	San Antonio	TX	78201	210-731-5555	731-5501
TF: 800-292-5534 ■ *Web:* www.bloodntissue.org					
Southeast Iowa Blood Center 1007 Pennsylvania Ave	Ottumwa	IA	52501	641-682-8149	682-9791
TF: 800-452-1097					
Southeastern Community Blood Center 1731 Riggins Rd	Tallahassee	FL	32308	850-877-7181	877-7435
TF: 800-722-2218 ■ *Web:* www.scbcinfo.org					
Stewart Regional Blood Center 815 S Baxter Ave	Tyler	TX	75701	903-535-5400	535-5450
TF: 800-252-5584 ■ *Web:* www.unitedbloodservices.org					
Suncoast Communities Blood Bank 1760 Mound St	Sarasota	FL	34236	941-954-1600	951-2629
Web: www.scbb.org					
Texoma Regional Blood Center 3911 N Texoma Pkwy	Sherman	TX	75090	903-893-4314	893-8628
Tri-Counties Blood Bank 945 S Main St	Salinas	CA	93901	831-751-1993	751-1985
Web: www.unitedbloodservices.org					
Tri-Counties Blood Bank 4119 Broad St Suite 100	San Luis Obispo	CA	93401	805-543-4290	543-4926
Web: www.unitedbloodservices.org					
United Blood Services 6210 E Oak St PO Box1867	Scottsdale	AZ	85257	480-946-4201	675-5767
United Blood Services of Arizona					
Chandler 1989 W Elliot Rd Suite 33	Chandler	AZ	85224	480-732-9007	732-9009
Web: www.unitedbloodservices.org					
Glendale 18583 N 59th Ave Suite 113	Glendale	AZ	85308	602-843-1303	843-1476
Web: www.unitedbloodservices.org					
Mesa 1337 S Gilbert Rd Suite 101-103	Mesa	AZ	85204	480-892-6577	892-8343
TF: 800-288-2199 ■ *Web:* www.unitedbloodservices.org					
Phoenix 5757 N Black Canyon Hwy	Phoenix	AZ	85015	602-242-4007	242-7020
Web: www.unitedbloodservices.org					
United Blood Services of Arkansas					
Fort Smith 5300 S 'U' St	Fort Smith	AR	72903	479-452-5880	452-0572
TF: 800-934-9415 ■ *Web:* www.unitedbloodservices.org					
Hot Springs 1635 Higdon Ferry Rd Suite 3	Hot Springs	AR	71913	501-624-0667	624-2714
TF: 800-286-2116 ■ *Web:* www.unitedbloodservices.org					
United Blood Services of California					
216 Moorpark Ave Suite 109	Moorpark	CA	93021	805-531-9902	531-9917
Web: www.unitedbloodservices.org					
United Blood Services of Colorado 146 Sawyer Dr	Durango	CO	81301	970-385-4601	385-4837
TF: 800-863-4524 ■ *Web:* www.unitedbloodservices.org					
United Blood Services of Louisiana					
Baton Rouge 8234 1 Calais Ave	Baton Rouge	LA	70806	225-769-7233	769-8633
Web: www.unitedbloodservices.org					
Lafayette 1503 Bertrand Dr	Lafayette	LA	70506	337-235-5433	232-5352
Web: www.unitedbloodservices.org					
Morgan City 1234 David Dr Suite 102	Morgan City	LA	70380	985-384-5671	384-5672
Web: www.unitedbloodservices.org					
United Blood Services of Mississippi					
Hattiesburg 805 S 28th Ave	Hattiesburg	MS	39402	601-264-0743	264-6717
Web: www.unitedbloodservices.org					
Jackson 3 Riverbend Pl	Flowood	MS	39208	601-939-3336	939-0855
TF: 800-880-3326 ■ *Web:* www.unitedbloodservices.org					
Laurel 1215 Jefferson St	Laurel	MS	39440	601-426-2224	649-8495
Web: www.unitedbloodservices.org					
Meridian 1115 25th Ave	Meridian	MS	39301	601-482-2482	483-4204
TF: 877-582-2482 ■ *Web:* www.unitedbloodservices.org					
Tupelo 4326 S Eason Blvd	Tupelo	MS	38803	662-842-8870	680-9161
TF: 800-844-8870 ■ *Web:* www.unitedbloodservices.org					
United Blood Services of Montana					
Billings 1444 Grand Ave	Billings	MT	59102	406-248-9168	248-1025
TF: 800-365-4450 ■ *Web:* www.unitedbloodservices.org					
Butte 2201 Harrison Ave	Butte	MT	59701	406-723-3264	782-4475
Web: www.unitedbloodservices.org					
United Blood Services of Nevada					
Carson City 256 E Winnie Ln	Carson City	NV	89701	775-887-9111	887-9134
Web: www.unitedbloodservices.org					
Green Valley 601 Whitney Ranch Dr Bldg D Suite 20	Henderson	NV	89014	702-434-1838	434-1007
Web: www.unitedbloodservices.org					
Las Vegas 4950 W Craig Rd Suite 1	Las Vegas	NV	89130	702-645-3600	645-3716
Web: www.unitedbloodservices.org					
Las Vegas 3935 E Charleston Blvd	Las Vegas	NV	89104	702-438-9850	438-0642
Web: www.unitedbloodservices.org					

Phone Fax

Las Vegas 6930 W Charleston Blvd. Las Vegas NV 89117 702-228-4483 228-2374
Web: www.unitedbloodservices.org
Reno 1125 Terminal Way. Reno NV 89502 775-329-6451 324-6480
TF: 800-627-4928 ■ Web: www.unitedbloodservices.org

United Blood Services of New Mexico
Albuquerque 1515 University Blvd NE Albuquerque NM 87102 505-843-6227 247-8835
TF: 800-333-8037 ■ Web: www.unitedbloodservices.org
Farmington 475 E 20th St Suite A Farmington NM 87401 505-325-1505 327-1889
Web: www.unitedbloodservices.org
Las Cruces 1200 Commerce Dr Las Cruces NM 88011 505-527-1322 527-5210
TF: 800-236-8053 ■ Web: www.unitedbloodservices.org
Rio Rancho 3301 Southern Blvd SE Suite 300 Rio Rancho NM 87124 505-892-3329 892-7793
Web: www.unitedbloodservices.org
Roswell 3 Grand Plaza Ave Roswell NM 88201 505-625-9743 625-1377
Web: www.unitedbloodservices.org
Sante Fe 2801 Rodeo Rd Suite B-10 Santa Fe NM 87505 505-438-0678 438-0783
Web: www.unitedbloodservices.org

United Blood Services of North Dakota
Bismarck 517 S 7th St. Bismarck ND 58502 701-258-4512 223-0557
TF: 800-456-6159 ■ Web: www.unitedbloodservices.org
Fargo 1320 1st Ave N Fargo ND 58102 701-293-9453 293-9564
TF: 800-293-8203 ■ Web: www.unitedbloodservices.org
Minot 1919 N Broadway Minot ND 58703 701-852-2161 839-1503
Web: www.unitedbloodservices.org

United Blood Services of South Dakota
Mitchell 200 W 7th St Mitchell SD 57301 605-996-3688
Web: www.unitedbloodservices.org
Rapid City 2209 W Omaha St Rapid City SD 57702 605-342-8585 342-6662
Web: www.unitedbloodservices.org

United Blood Services of Texas
Brownsville 2370 Central Blvd Brownsville TX 78520 956-504-3809 504-3827
Web: www.unitedbloodservices.org
El Paso 424 S Mesa Hills El Paso TX 79912 915-544-5422 544-5509
TF: 800-582-3146 ■ Web: www.unitedbloodservices.org
Lubbock 2523 48th St Lubbock TX 79413 806-797-6804 797-1824
Web: www.unitedbloodservices.org
McAllen 1312 Pecan Blvd McAllen TX 78501 956-682-1314 682-7578
TF: 888-827-4376 ■ Web: www.unitedbloodservices.org
San Angelo 2020 W Beauregard St San Angelo TX 76901 325-223-7500 223-7522
TF: 800-756-0024 ■ Web: www.unitedbloodservices.org

United Blood Services of Wyoming
Casper 167 S Conwell Casper WY 82601 307-237-2328 237-1321
Web: www.unitedbloodservices.org
Cheyenne 112 E 8th Ave Cheyenne WY 82001 307-638-3326 635-6919
Web: www.unitedbloodservices.org

Virginia Blood Services 2401 Hydraulic Rd Charlottesville VA 22903 434-977-8956 979-4860
TF: 800-989-4438 ■ Web: www.vablood.org
Virginia Blood Services 2201 Westwood Ave Richmond VA 23230 804-359-5100 358-2786
Web: www.vablood.org
West Tennessee Regional Blood Center Inc 828 North Pkwy Jackson TN 38305 731-427-4431 422-4712
TF: 800-924-6572 ■ Web: www.lifelinebloodserv.org
Western Kentucky Regional Blood Center
3015 Old Hartford Rd Owensboro KY 42303 270-684-9296 684-4901
TF: 888-684-9296 ■ Web: www.wkrbc.org

90 BOATS - RECREATIONAL

Phone Fax

Action Craft Inc 2603 Andalusia Blvd Cape Coral FL 33909 239-574-7008 574-1152
Web: www.actioncraft.com
Advanced Outdoors Inc 1250 NE 6th St Hamlin TX 79520 325-576-2144 576-2339
Web: www.advancedoutdoorsinc.com
Albemarle Sportfishing Boats Inc 140 Midway Dr Edenton NC 27932 252-482-7600 482-8289
Web: www.albemarleboats.com
Albin Marine Inc 143 River Rd PO Box 228 Cos Cob CT 06807 203-661-4341 661-6040
Web: www.albinmarine.com
Albury Brothers Boats 1401 Broadway Riviera Beach FL 33404 561-863-7006 863-7746
Web: www.alburybrothers.com
Alumacraft Boat Co 315 W Saint Julien St Saint Peter MN 56082 507-931-1050 931-9056
Web: www.alumacraft.com
Alumaweld Boats Inc 2000 Rouge River Dr Eagle Point OR 97524 541-826-7171 826-6701
TF: 800-401-2628 ■ Web: www.alumaweldboats.com
American Marine Sports LLC 20150 Independence Blvd Groveland FL 34736 352-429-8989 429-8988
Web: www.americanmarinesports.com
Angler Boat Corp 7400 NW 37th Ave Miami FL 33147 305-691-9975 691-9377
Web: www.anglerboats.com
Aquasport Marine Corp 1651 Whitfield Ave Sarasota FL 34243 941-755-5800 751-7822
TF: 800-755-1099 ■ Web: www.aquasport.com
Arima Marine International Inc 47 37th St NE Auburn WA 98002 253-939-7980 939-1364
TF: 800-811-6440 ■ Web: www.arimaboats.com
B & B Boats Inc 3568 Old Winter Garden Rd Orlando FL 32805 407-299-2190 208-9800
Web: www.flycraft-boats.com
B & D Boatworks Inc PO Box 550 Wanchese NC 27981 252-473-6446 473-1595
Web: www.banddboatworks.com
Baha Cruiser Boats Inc 668 N Fletcher Ave PO Box 1387 Mayo FL 32066 386-294-2447 294-1311
Web: www.bahacruisers.com
Baja Marine Corp 1520 Isaac Beal Rd PO Box 151 Bucyrus OH 44820 419-562-5377 562-0846
Web: www.bajamarine.com
Bay Craft Inc 1785 Langley Ave DeLand FL 32724 386-943-8877 943-8617
Web: www.baycraftinc.com
Beneteau USA Inc 1313 W Hwy 76 Marion SC 29571 843-629-5300 629-5309
Web: www.beneteauusa.com
Bertram Yacht Inc 3663 NW 21st St Miami FL 33142 305-633-8011 633-2868
Web: www.bertram.com
Blue Wave Boats HC 60 Box 25 Checotah OK 74426 918-473-6768 473-2274
TF: 800-432-6768 ■ Web: www.bluewaveboats.com
Bluewater Inc 811 E Maple Ave Mora MN 55051 320-679-3811 679-3820
TF: 800-733-7127 ■ Web: www.bluewateryacht.com
Bone Boats 2901 N Interstate 10 Service Rd E Metairie LA 70002 504-828-5089 828-8986
Web: www.boneboats.com
Boston Whaler Inc 100 Whaler Way Edgewater FL 32141 386-426-1400
Web: www.whaler.com
Briggs Boat Works Inc 370 Harbor Rd Wanchese NC 27981 252-473-2393 473-2392
Web: www.briggsboatworks.com
Brunswick Boat Group 800 S Gay St 17th Fl Knoxville TN 37929 865-582-2200 582-2301
Web: www.brunswick.com/boats.html
Brunswick Corp 1 N Field Ct Lake Forest IL 60045 847-735-4700 735-4765
NYSE: BC ■ Web: www.brunswick.com
Brunswick Corp Sea Ray Group 2600 Sea Ray Blvd Knoxville TN 37914 865-522-4181 971-6434
Web: www.searay.com
C & C Mfg 6725 Bayline Dr Panama City FL 32404 850-769-0311 769-0731
Web: www.cobiaboats.com
Cabo Yachts Inc 9780 Rancho Rd Adelanto CA 92301 760-246-8917 246-8970
Web: www.caboyachts.com
Cape Cod Shipbuilding Co PO Box 152 Wareham MA 02571 508-295-3550 295-3551
Web: www.capecodshipbuilding.com
Caravelle Marine Inc PO Box 1899 Americus GA 31709 229-924-1185 924-1030
Web: www.caravelleboats.com
Caribiana Sea Skiffs 8920 County Rd 65 Foley AL 36535 251-981-4442 981-3039
TF: 888-203-4883 ■ Web: www.caribiana.com
Carolina Classic Boats Inc 109 Anchors Way Dr PO Box 968 Edenton NC 27932 252-482-3699
Web: www.carolinaclassicboats.com
Carolina Skiff Inc 3231 Fulford Rd Waycross GA 31503 912-287-0547 287-0533
TF: 800-422-7543 ■ Web: www.carolina-skiff.com/
Carver Boat Corp 790 Markham Dr PO Box 1010 Pulaski WI 54162 920-822-9000 822-8800
Web: www.carveryachts.com
Catalina Yachts Inc 21200 Victory Blvd Woodland Hills CA 91367 818-884-7700 884-3810
Web: www.catalinayachts.com
Catamarans New Zealand Ltd 5021 Newport Ave San Diego CA 92107 619-523-8891 223-9215
Web: www.powercatswest.com
Cavileer Boatworks 2143 River Rd Lower Bank NJ 08215 609-965-8650 965-7480
Web: www.cavileer.com
Champion Boats Inc 880 Butler Dr Murfreesboro TN 37127 615-494-2090 494-2061
Web: www.championboats.com
Chaparral Boats PO Drawer 928 Nashville GA 31639 229-686-7481 686-3660
Web: www.chaparralboats.com
Chris-Craft Boats 8161 15th St E Sarasota FL 34243 941-351-4900 358-3782
Web: www.chriscraftboats.com
Cigarette Racing Team Inc 4355 NW 128th St Opa Locka FL 33054 305-931-4564 935-0276
TF: 800-347-4327 ■ Web: www.cigaretteracing.com
Cobalt Boats 1715 N 8th St Neodesha KS 66757 620-325-2653 325-3342
TF: 800-835-0256 ■ Web: www.cobaltboats.com
Concept Boats Corp 2410 NW 147th St Opa Locka FL 33054 305-635-8712 635-9543
TF: 888-635-8712 ■ Web: www.conceptboats.com
Correct Craft Inc 6100 S Orange Ave Orlando FL 32809 407-855-4141 851-7844
TF: 800-346-2092 ■ Web: skinautique.com
Crestliner Inc 609 13th Ave NE Little Falls MN 56345 320-632-6686 632-2127
Web: www.crestliner.com
Crownline Boats Inc 11884 Country Club Rd West Frankfort IL 62896 618-937-6426 932-3426
Web: www.crownlineboats.com
Cruisers Div KCS International Inc 804 Pecor St Oconto WI 54153 920-834-2211 834-2105*
*Fax: Hum Res ■ TF: 800-743-3478 ■ Web: www.cruiseryachts.com
Defiant Marine 2234 Industrial Blvd Sarasota FL 34234 941-351-8581 359-1516
Web: www.defiantmarine.com
Donzi Marine PO Box 987 Tallevast FL 34270 941-727-0622 758-5417
TF Cust Svc: 800-446-6725 ■ Web: www.donzimarine.com
Edey & Duff Ltd 128 Aucoot Rd Mattapoisett MA 02739 508-758-2743 758-6330
Web: www.edeyandduff.com
EdgeWater Power Boats 211 Dale St Edgewater FL 32132 386-426-5457 427-9783
Web: www.edgewaterpowerboats.com
Egg Harbor Yachts Inc
801 Philadelphia Ave Po Box 702 Egg Harbor City NJ 08215 609-965-2300 965-3517
Web: www.eggharboryachts.com
Egret Boat Co 2051 NW 11th St Miami FL 33125 305-643-0334
Ercoa Industries Inc 40800 Hwy 65 NE Braham MN 55006 320-396-3386 396-4107
Web: www.ercoa.com
Everglades Boats 544 Air Park Rd Edgewater FL 32132 386-409-2202 409-7939
Web: www.evergladesboats.com
Famous Craft Inc 7921 15th St E Sarasota FL 34243 941-358-3121 351-5479
TF: 888-244-3244 ■ Web: www.famouscraft.com
Fiberglass Engineering Inc DBA Cobalt Boats 1715 N 8th St Neodesha KS 66757 620-325-2653 325-3342
TF: 800-835-0256 ■ Web: www.cobaltboats.com
Flats Cat Boats 1565 Patton Rd Rosenberg TX 77471 281-342-3940
Web: www.flatscat.com
Fountain Powerboat Industries Inc PO Drawer 457 Washington NC 27889 252-975-2000 975-6793
AMEX: FPB ■ Web: www.fountainpowerboats.com
Four Winns Inc 925 Frisbie St Cadillac MI 49601 231-775-1351 779-2348
Web: www.fourwinns.com
Garlington Landeweer Marine Inc 3370 SE Slater St Stuart FL 34997 772-283-7124 220-1049
Web: www.garlingtonyachts.com
Genmar Industries Inc 80 S 8th St 2900 IDS Ctr Minneapolis MN 55402 612-339-7600 337-1930
TF: 800-328-5557 ■ Web: www.genmar.com
Gibson Boats Inc 308 Church St Goodlettsville TN 37072 615-859-1351 851-0739
Web: www.gibsonboats.com
Glacier Bay Catamarans 14298 169th Dr SE Monroe WA 98272 360-794-0444 794-6674
Web: www.glacierbaycats.com
Glastron Boats PO Box 460 Little Falls MN 56345 320-632-8395 632-1438
Web: www.glastron.com
Godfrey Marine 4500 Middlebury St Elkhart IN 46516 574-522-8381 522-5120
Web: www.godfreymarine.com
Grady-White Boats Inc PO Box 1527 Greenville NC 27835 252-752-2111 752-4217
Web: www.gradywhite.com
Grand Banks Yachts Ltd 2100 Westlake Ave N Suite 107 Seattle WA 98109 206-352-0116
Web: www.grandbanks.com
HarrisKayot Inc 2801 W State Blvd Fort Wayne IN 46808 260-432-4555 436-6907
Web: www.harriskayot.com
Hatteras Yachts Inc 110 N Glenburnie Rd New Bern NC 28560 252-633-3101 634-4813
Web: www.hatterasyachts.com
Hinckley Co 130 Shore Rd Southwest Harbor ME 04679 207-244-5531 244-9833
TF: 888-456-2553 ■ Web: www.hinckleyyachts.com
Hobie Cat Co 4925 Oceanside Blvd Oceanside CA 92056 760-758-9100 758-1841
TF: 800-462-4349 ■ Web: www.hobiecat.com
Hunter Marine Corp PO Box 1030 Alachua FL 32616 386-462-3077 462-4077
TF: 800-771-5556 ■ Web: www.huntermarine.com
Hydroswift II 3383 W 12600 South Riverton UT 84065 801-254-1535 262-4255
Iguana Marine 9110 NW 13th St Plantation FL 33322 954-622-1115
Intrepid Powerboats 11700 S Belcher Rd Largo FL 33773 727-548-1260 544-1796
Web: www.intrepidboats.com
Island Runner Boats 1177 W Blue Heron Blvd Riviera Beach FL 33404 561-863-9989 863-9987
Web: www.islandrunner.com
Jefferson Yachts Inc 700 E Market St PO Box 790 Jeffersonville IN 47131 812-282-8111 288-7783
Web: www.jeffersonyachts.com
Johnson Outdoors Inc 555 Main St Racine WI 53403 262-631-6600 631-6601
NASDAQ: JOUT ■ TF: 800-299-2592 ■ Web: www.johnsonoutdoors.com
Johnson Outdoors Watercraft Sport & Leisure Group
5960 Tahoe Dr Suite 500 Grand Rapids MI 49546 616-942-8998 575-0241
TF: 800-552-6287 ■ Web: www.jowatercraft.com
KCS International Inc Cruisers Div 804 Pecor St Oconto WI 54153 920-834-2211 834-2105*
*Fax: Hum Res ■ TF: 800-743-3478 ■ Web: www.cruiseryachts.com
KenCraft Manufacturing Inc 4155 Dixie Inn Rd Wilson NC 27893 252-291-0271 291-0815
Web: www.kencraftboats.com
Key West Boats Inc 593 Ridgeville Rd PO Box 399 Ridgeville SC 29472 843-873-0112 821-6334
Web: www.keywestboatsinc.com
Klamath Boat Co Inc Mare Island Station PO Box 2093 Vallejo CA 94592 707-643-0447 643-0483
TF: 800-326-5526 ■ Web: www.klamathboats.com
L & H Boats Inc 3350 SE Slater St Stuart FL 34997 772-288-2291 288-9878
Web: www.lhboats.com
Larson Boats 700 Paul Larson Memorial Dr Little Falls MN 56345 320-632-5481 632-1439
TF: 800-255-3622 ■ Web: www.larsonboats.com
Livingston Boats PO Box 819 Elma WA 98541 360-482-5580 482-5411
TF: 866-482-5580 ■ Web: www.livingstonboats.com

Company	City	State	ZIP	Phone	Fax
Lowe Boats 2900 Industrial Dr *TF:* 800-641-4372 ■ *Web:* www.loweboats.com	Lebanon	MO	65536	417-532-9101	532-8992
Luhrs Corp 255 Diesel Rd *TF:* 800-829-5847 ■ *Web:* www.luhrs.com	Saint Augustine	FL	32084	904-829-0500	827-2156
Lund Boat Co 318 W Gilman St PO Box 248 *Web:* www.lundboats.com	New York Mills	MN	56567	218-385-2235	385-2227
Magnum Marine Corp 2900 NE 188th St *Web:* www.magnummarine.com	Aventura	FL	33180	305-931-4292	931-0088
Mainship Corp 255 Diesel Rd *TF:* 800-829-5847 ■ *Web:* www.mainship.com	Saint Augustine	FL	32084	904-829-0500	829-0683
Marine Manufacturing Inc 1815 Peterson Ave *Web:* www.capecraftfishingboats.com	Douglas	GA	31535	912-384-8943	384-8974
Marine Products Corp 2170 Piedmont Rd NE *NYSE:* MPX ■ *Web:* www.marineproductscorp.com	Atlanta	GA	30324	404-321-2140	321-5483
Marine Safety Corp PO Box 465	Farmingdale	NJ	07727	732-938-5661	938-4839
MarineMax Inc 18167 US 19 N Suite 300 *NYSE:* HZO ■ *Web:* www.marinemax.com	Clearwater	FL	33764	727-531-1700	531-0123
Maritime Skiff Inc PO Box 218 *Web:* www.maritimeskiff.com	Duxbury	MA	02331	781-934-0010	934-0257
MasterCraft Boat Co 100 Cherokee Cove Dr *TF:* 800-443-8774 ■ *Web:* www.mastercraftboats.com	Vonore	TN	37885	423-884-2221	884-2295
Maurell Products Inc PO Box 190 *Web:* www.crestpontoonboats.com	Owosso	MI	48867	989-725-5188	725-6849
Maverick Boat Co Inc 3207 Industrial 29th St *TF:* 888-742-5569 ■ *Web:* www.maverickboats.com	Fort Pierce	FL	34946	772-465-0631	489-2168
May-Craft Fiberglass Products Inc PO Box 450 *Web:* www.maycraftboats.com	Smithfield	NC	27577	919-934-3000	934-9014
McKee Craft Boats 404 Sandy St PO Box 623 *Web:* www.mckeecraft.com	Fairmont	NC	28430	910-628-0926	628-9598
Melges Boatworks Inc PO Box 1 *Web:* www.melges.com	Zenda	WI	53195	262-275-1110	275-8012
Merritt's Boat & Engine Works Inc 2931 NE 16th St *Web:* www.merrittboat.com/	Pompano Beach	FL	33062	954-941-0118	942-1531
Mitzi Skiff Boat Co 709 Talleyrand Ave *Web:* www.mitziskiffs.com	Jacksonville	FL	32202	904-270-0589	338-0134
Monterey Boats 1579 SW 18th St *Web:* www.montereyboats.com	Williston	FL	32696	352-528-2628	529-2628
Monza Marine Inc 3230 NW 42nd St *Web:* www.monzaboats.com	Miami	FL	33142	305-634-0518	634-0738
Ocean Yachts Inc PO Box 312 *Web:* www.oceanyachtsinc.com	Egg Harbor City	NJ	08215	609-965-4616	965-4914
Pacific Seacraft Corp 1301 E Orangethorpe Ave *Web:* www.pacificseacraft.com	Fullerton	CA	92831	714-879-1610	879-5454
Palmer Marine of Washington Inc 5611 Imperial Way SW *Web:* www.shamrockboats.com	Port Orchard	WA	98367	360-674-7090	674-7119
Parker Marine Enterprises Inc PO Box 2129 *Web:* www.parkerboats.net	Beaufort	NC	28516	252-728-5621	728-2770
Playbuoy Pontoon Mfg Inc 903 Michigan Ave PO Box 698 *TF:* 800-334-2913 ■ *Web:* www.playbuoy.com	Alma	MI	48801	989-463-2112	463-8226
Porta-Bote International 1074 Independence Ave *Web:* www.porta-bote.com	Mountain View	CA	94043	650-961-5334	961-3800
PowerPlay Marine Inc 2740 NW 29th Terr *Web:* www.powerplaymarine.com	Fort Lauderdale	FL	33311	954-733-2500	733-2700
Pro-Line Boats Inc PO Box 1348 *TF:* 800-344-1281 ■ *Web:* www.prolineboats.com	Crystal River	FL	34423	352-795-4111	795-4374
Pursuit Boats 3901 St Lucie Blvd *TF:* 800-947-8778 ■ *Web:* www.pursuitboats.com	Fort Pierce	FL	34946	772-465-6006	465-6177
Ranger Boats PO Box 179 *Web:* www.rangerboats.com	Flippin	AR	72634	870-453-2222	453-2306
Regal Marine Industries Inc 2300 Jetport Dr **Fax:* Sales ■ *TF:* 800-877-3425 ■ *Web:* www.regalboats.com	Orlando	FL	32809	407-851-4360	857-1256*
Renaissance Marine Inc 2400 NW 150th St *Web:* www.renaissancecats.com	Opa Locka	FL	33054	305-769-3010	769-3055
Rinalli Boats Ltd 1600 N King St *TF:* 866-746-2554 ■ *Web:* www.rinalliboats.com	Seguin	TX	78155	830-372-3300	
Rybovich Spencer Group 4200 N Flagler Dr *Web:* www.rybovich.com	West Palm Beach	FL	33407	561-844-1800	844-8393
Sabre Corp PO Box 134 *Web:* www.sabreyachts.com	South Casco	ME	04077	207-655-3831	655-5050
Scout Boats Inc 2531 Hwy 78 W *Web:* www.scoutboats.com	Summerville	SC	29483	843-821-0068	821-4786
Sea Cat Boats Inc 1005 Marina Rd *Web:* seacatboats.com	Titusville	FL	32796	321-268-2628	269-8483
Sea Craft 1181 Old Caroleen Rd *Web:* www.seacraft-boats.com	Forest City	NC	28043	828-288-6500	245-3961
Sea Fox Boat Co Inc 2550 Hwy 52 *Web:* www.seafoxboats.com	Moncks Corner	SC	29461	843-761-6090	761-6139
Sea Ray Group Brunswick Corp 2600 Sea Ray Blvd *Web:* www.searay.com	Knoxville	TN	37914	865-522-4181	971-6434
Sea Sport Inc 4654 Guide Meridian PO Box 30678 *Web:* www.seasportboats.com	Bellingham	WA	98228	360-733-3380	733-3653
SeaArk Boats PO Box 803 *Web:* www.seaarkboats.com	Monticello	AR	71657	870-367-5317	460-3200
Seaswirl Boats PO Box 167 **Fax:* Cust Svc ■ *Web:* www.seaswirl.com	Culver	OR	97734	541-546-5011	546-7249*
Seminole Marine 2501 Milestone Industrial Park *Web:* www.sailfishboats.com	Cairo	GA	39828	229-377-2125	377-1855
Silverton Marine Corp 301 Riverside Dr **Fax:* Mktg ■ *Web:* www.silverton.com	Millville	NJ	08332	856-825-4117	825-2064*
Skeeter Products Inc 1 Skeeter Rd *Web:* www.skeeterboats.com	Kilgore	TX	75662	903-984-0541	984-7856
Smoker Craft Inc PO Box 65 *Web:* www.smokercraft.com	New Paris	IN	46553	574-831-2103	831-7003
Sonic USA 3600 N 29th Ave *Web:* www.sonicusaboats.com	Hollywood	FL	33020	954-922-5535	922-0578
Stamas Yacht Inc 300 Pampas Ave *TF Sales:* 800-782-6271 ■ *Web:* www.stamas.com	Tarpon Springs	FL	34689	727-937-4118	934-1339
Starcraft Marine LLC 201 Starcraft Dr PO Box 517 *TF:* 800-535-5722 ■ *Web:* www.starcraftmarine.com	Topeka	IN	46571	260-593-2500	593-2816
Stratos Boat Co 880 Butler Rd *Web:* stratosboats.com	Murfreesboro	TN	37127	615-895-5190	494-2060
Sundance Boats Inc 6131 Sundance Rd *Web:* www.sundanceboats.com	Blackshear	GA	31516	912-449-0033	449-0038
Tartan Yachts 1920 Fairport Nursery Rd *Web:* www.tartanyachts.com	Fairport Harbor	OH	44077	440-354-3111	354-6162
Thunderbird Products Inc 2200 W Monroe St *Web:* www.formulaboats.com	Decatur	IN	46733	260-724-9111	724-1166
Tiara Yachts Inc 725 E 40th St *Web:* www.tiarayachts.com	Holland	MI	49423	616-392-7163	394-7466
Tracker Marine Group LLC 2500 E Kearney St **Fax:* Mktg ■ *Web:* www.tracker-marine.com	Springfield	MO	65803	417-873-5900	873-5068*
Triton Boats 15 Bluegrass Dr *TF:* 888-887-4866 ■ *Web:* www.tritonboats.com	Ashland City	TN	37015	615-792-6767	792-9053
Triumph Boats 100 Golden Dr *TF:* 800-564-4225 ■ *Web:* www.triumphboats.com	Durham	NC	27705	919-382-3149	382-0585
Valiant Yachts Inc 500 Harbour View Rd *Web:* www.valiantsailboats.com	Gordonville	TX	76245	903-523-4899	523-4077
Venture Marine Inc 1525 53rd St *TF:* 800-960-3434 ■ *Web:* www.venturemarine.com	West Palm Beach	FL	33407	561-845-8557	842-4239
Viking Yacht Co Inc 5738 US Hwy 9 *Web:* www.vikingyachts.com	New Gretna	NJ	08224	609-296-6000	296-3956
Vivian Industries Inc 680 S Pardue St *TF:* 800-256-7579 ■ *Web:* www.vipboats.com	Vivian	LA	71082	318-375-3241	375-4619
WCC Group Inc 1090 W Saint James St *TF:* 866-485-8899 ■ *Web:* www.worldclasscat.com	Tarboro	NC	27886	252-641-8000	641-9866
Weeres Industries Corp 1045 33rd St S *TF:* 800-397-6686 ■ *Web:* www.weeres.com	Saint Cloud	MN	56301	320-251-3551	654-9188
Wellcraft Marine Corp 1651 Whitfield Ave **Fax:* Sales ■ *TF:* 800-755-1099 ■ *Web:* www.wellcraft.com	Sarasota	FL	34243	941-753-7811	751-7808*
Willard Marine Inc 1250 N Grove St *Web:* willardmarine.com	Anaheim	CA	92806	714-666-2150	632-8136
Wood Mfg Co Inc DBA Ranger Boats PO Box 179 *Web:* www.rangerboats.com	Flippin	AR	72634	870-453-2222	453-2306
Wooldridge Boats Inc 1303 S 96th St *Web:* www.wooldridgeboats.com	Seattle	WA	98108	206-722-8998	
Yellowfin Yachts Inc 6611 19th St E *Web:* www.yellowfinyachts.com	Sarasota	FL	34243	941-753-7828	753-2540
Zodiac of North America 540 Thompson Creek Rd *Web:* www.zodiac.com	Stevensville	MD	21666	410-643-4141	643-4491

91 BOILER SHOPS

Company	City	State	ZIP	Phone	Fax
Ace Tank & Fueling Equipment 6703 E Marginal Way South *TF:* 800-426-2880 ■ *Web:* www.acetank.com	Seattle	WA	98108	206-281-5000	281-5030
Adamson Global Technology Corp 13101 N Enon Church Rd *TF:* 800-525-7703 ■ *Web:* www.adamsontank.com	Chester	VA	23836	804-748-6453	796-2037
Aerofin Corp 4621 Murray Pl PO Box 10819 **Fax:* Sales ■ *TF:* 800-237-6346 ■ *Web:* www.aerofin.com	Lynchburg	VA	24506	434-845-7081	528-6242*
Aesys Technologies LLC 693 N Hills Rd *Web:* www.aesystech.com	York	PA	17402	717-755-1081	755-0020
Air-X-Changers PO Box 1804 *Web:* www.airx.com	Tulsa	OK	74101	918-619-8000	384-5000
AlfaLaval Inc 5400 International Trade Dr *Web:* www.alfalaval.com	Richmond	VA	23231	804-222-5300	236-3276
ALSTOM Power Inc 2000 Day Hill Rd *Web:* www.power.alstom.com	Windsor	CT	06095	860-688-1911	285-3110
American Welding & Tank Co 4718 Old Gettysburg Rd Suite 300 *TF:* 800-586-2657 ■ *Web:* www.awtank.com	Mechanicsburg	PA	17001	717-763-5080	763-5081
Amtrol Inc 1400 Division Rd *Web:* www.amtrol.com	West Warwick	RI	02893	401-884-6300	885-2567
API Heat Transfer Inc 2777 Walden Ave *TF:* 877-274-4328 ■ *Web:* www.apiheattransfer.com	Buffalo	NY	14225	716-684-9700	684-2129
Armstrong Engineering Assoc Inc PO Box 566 *Web:* www.rmarmstrong.com	West Chester	PA	19381	610-436-6080	436-0374
Arrow Tank & Engineering Co 650 N Emerson St *TF:* 888-892-7769 ■ *Web:* www.arrowtank.com	Cambridge	MN	55008	763-689-3360	689-1263
AustinMohawk & Co Inc 2175 Beechgrove Pl *TF:* 800-765-3110 ■ *Web:* www.austinmohawk.com	Utica	NY	13501	315-793-3000	793-9370
Autoclave Engineers Div Snap-Tite 8325 Hessinger Dr *TF:* 800-458-0409 ■ *Web:* www.snap-tite.com/divisions/ae/index.html	Erie	PA	16509	814-838-5700	833-0145
Babcock Power Inc 155 Ferncroft Rd Suite 210 *Web:* www.babcockpower.com	Danvers	MA	01923	978-646-3300	646-3301
Babcock & Wilcox Co 20 S Van Buren Ave *TF:* 800-222-2625 ■ *Web:* www.babcock.com	Barberton	OH	44203	330-753-4511	860-1886
Baltimore Aircoil Co 7600 Dorsey Run Rd PO Box 7322 *Web:* www.baltaircoil.com	Baltimore	MD	21227	410-799-6200	799-6416
Beaird Co Ltd 601 Benton Kelly St *Web:* www.beairdco.com	Shreveport	LA	71106	318-671-5400	671-5583
Bristol Metals LP 390 Bristol Metals Rd *Web:* www.brismet.com	Bristol	TN	37620	423-968-2151	989-4742
Bryan Steam LLC 783 N Chili Ave *Web:* www.bryanboilers.com	Peru	IN	46970	765-473-6651	473-3074
Burgett C & Assoc Inc 104 Baker Ave PO Box 579 *Web:* www.shreve.net/~cobbfab/	Scottsville	TX	75688	903-938-6638	938-4881
C Burgett & Assoc Inc 104 Baker Ave PO Box 579 *Web:* www.shreve.net/~cobbfab/	Scottsville	TX	75688	903-938-6638	938-4881
Caldwell Tanks Inc 4000 Tower Rd *Web:* www.caldwelltanks.com	Louisville	KY	40219	502-964-3361	966-8732
CB Mills Div Chicago Boiler Co 1300 Northwestern Ave *TF:* 800-969-7343 ■ *Web:* www.cbmills.com	Gurnee	IL	60031	847-662-4000	662-4003
Chart Industries Inc 1 Infinity Corporate Centre Dr Suite 300 *Web:* www.chart-ind.com	Garfield Heights	OH	44125	440-753-1490	753-1491
Chicago Boiler Co 1300 Northwestern Ave *TF:* 800-969-7343	Gurnee	IL	60031	847-662-4000	662-4003
Chicago Boiler Co CB Mills Div 1300 Northwestern Ave *TF:* 800-969-7343 ■ *Web:* www.cbmills.com	Gurnee	IL	60031	847-662-4000	662-4003
Clawson Tank Co 4545 Clawson Tank Dr *TF:* 800-325-8700 ■ *Web:* www.clawsontank.com	Clarkston	MI	48346	248-625-8700	625-3066
Cleaver Brooks 11950 W Lake Park Dr	Milwaukee	WI	53224	414-359-0600	577-3171
Cleaver Brooks Thomasville 221 Law St *Web:* www.cleaver-brooks.com	Thomasville	GA	31792	229-226-3024	226-3027
Coen Co Inc 1510 Tanforan Ave *Web:* www.coen.com	Woodland	CA	95776	530-668-2100	668-2171
Columbia Boiler Co of Pottstown 390 Old Reading Pike PO Box 1070 *Web:* www.columbiaboiler.com	Pottstown	PA	19464	610-323-2700	323-7292
Columbian Tectank 2101 S 21st St PO Box 996 *TF:* 800-421-2788 ■ *Web:* www.tanks.com	Parsons	KS	67357	620-421-0200	421-9122
Connell LP 1 International Pl 31st Fl *TF:* 800-276-4746 ■ *Web:* www.connell-lp.com	Boston	MA	02110	617-737-2700	737-1617
CP Industries Inc 12767 Industrial Dr PO Box 690 *Web:* www.cpind.com	Granger	IN	46530	574-273-3000	273-4000
CP Industries Inc (CPI) 2214 Walnut St **Fax:* Sales ■ *Web:* www.cp-industries.com	McKeesport	PA	15132	412-664-6604	664-6653*
DCI Inc 600 N 54th Ave *Web:* www.dciinc.com	Saint Cloud	MN	56303	320-252-8200	252-0866
Delta Industries 39 Bradley Park Rd *Web:* www.delta-industries-ct.com	East Granby	CT	06026	860-653-5041	653-5792
Eaton Metal Products Co 4800 York St *TF:* 800-208-2657 ■ *Web:* www.eatonsalesservice.com	Denver	CO	80216	303-296-4800	296-5736
Ecodyne MRM 8203 Market St *Web:* www.ecodynemrm.com	Houston	TX	77029	713-675-3511	675-7922
Enerfab Inc 4955 Spring Grove Ave *TF:* 800-966-7323 ■ *Web:* www.enerfab.com	Cincinnati	OH	45232	513-641-0500	641-1821
Energy Exchanger Co 1844 N Garnett Rd *Web:* www.energyexchanger.com	Tulsa	OK	74116	918-437-3000	437-7144
Engineered Storage Products Co 345 Harvestore Dr *Web:* www.engstorage.com	DeKalb	IL	60115	815-756-1551	756-7821

				Phone	Fax
Erdle Perforating Co 100 Pixley Industrial Pkwy	Rochester	NY	14624	585-247-4700	247-4716
TF: 800-627-4700 ■ *Web:* www.erdle.com					
Fabsco Shell & Tube LLC 2410 Industrial Rd PO Box 988	Sapulpa	OK	74066	918-224-7550	224-3564
Fafco Inc 435 Otterson Dr	Chico	CA	95928	530-332-2100	332-2109
TF: 800-994-7652 ■ *Web:* www.fafco.com					
Fisher Tank Co 3131 W 4th St	Chester	PA	19013	610-494-7200	485-0157
Web: www.fishertank.com					
Gardner Cryogenics 2136 City Line Rd	Bethlehem	PA	18017	610-264-4523	266-3752
Web: www.gardnercryo.com					
GE Nuclear Energy 1989 Little Orchard St	San Jose	CA	95125	408-925-1000	925-5721
TF: 800-626-2004 ■ *Web:* www.gepower.com/dhtml/nuclear/en_us					
GEA Rainey Corp 5202 W Channel Rd	Catoosa	OK	74015	918-266-3060	266-2464
Web: www.gearainey.com					
Geiger & Peters Inc 761 S Sherman Dr PO Box 33807	Indianapolis	IN	46203	317-359-9521	359-9525
Web: www.gpsteel.com					
General Welding Works Inc					
2060 N Loop W Suite 200 PO Box 925749	Houston	TX	77292	713-869-6401	869-5405
Web: www.generalwelding.com					
Goodhart Sons Inc 2515 Horseshoe Rd	Lancaster	PA	17605	717-656-2404	656-3301
Web: www.goodhartsons.com					
Hague International 6 Ivy Ct PO Box 449	Kennebunk	ME	04043	207-985-3540	985-9007
Web: www.hague.com					
HB Smith Co Inc 47 Westfield Industrial Pk Rd	Westfield	MA	01085	413-568-3148	568-0525
Highland Tank & Mfg Co 1 Highland Rd	Stoystown	PA	15563	814-893-5701	893-6126
Web: www.highlandtank.com					
Holman Boiler Works Inc 1956 Singleton Blvd	Dallas	TX	75212	214-637-0020	631-2742
TF Sales: 800-331-1956 ■ *Web:* www.hbw-inc.com					
Hughes-Anderson Heat Exchangers Inc 1001 N Fulton Ave	Tulsa	OK	74115	918-836-1681	836-5967
Web: www.hughesanderson.com					
Imperial Fabricating Co Inc 160 Kirby Rd	Portland	TN	37148	615-325-9224	325-4819
Web: www.o-mmfg.com					
Indeck Energy Services Inc					
600 N Buffalo Grove Rd Suite 300	Buffalo Grove	IL	60089	847-520-3212	520-9883
Web: www.indeck-energy.com					
ITT Standard 175 Standard Pkwy	Cheektowaga	NY	14227	716-897-2800	897-1777
TF: 800-447-7700 ■ *Web:* www.ittstandard.com					
James Machine Works Inc 1521 Adams St	Monroe	LA	71201	318-322-6104	388-4245
TF: 800-259-6104 ■ *Web:* www.jmwinc.net					
Joseph Oat Corp 2500 Broadway	Camden	NJ	08104	856-541-2900	541-0864
Web: www.josephoat.com					
Koch Chemical Technology Group LLC 4111 E 37th St N	Wichita	KS	67220	316-828-5500	828-4704
Web: www.kochchemtech.com					
Koch Heat Transfer Co LP 12602 FM 529	Houston	TX	77041	713-466-3535	466-3701
Web: www.kochheattransfer.com					
Krueger Engineering & Mfg Co					
12001 Hirsch Rd PO Box 11308	Houston	TX	77293	281-442-2537	442-6668
Web: www.kemco.net					
Loveless Mfg Co 1314 N Wheeling Ave	Tulsa	OK	74110	918-583-9129	583-6208
Mark Steel Corp 1230 W 200 South	Salt Lake City	UT	84104	801-521-0670	303-2040
Web: www.marksteel.net					
MiTek Industries Inc 14515 N Outer 40 Rd Suite 300	Chesterfield	MO	63017	314-434-1200	434-9110
TF: 800-325-8075 ■ *Web:* www.mii.com/unitedstates					
Mitternight Boiler Works Inc 5301 Hwy 43 N PO Box 489	Satsuma	AL	36572	251-675-2550	675-2671
Web: www.mitternight.com					
Modern Welding Co Inc 2880 New Hartford Rd	Owensboro	KY	42303	270-685-4404	684-6972
TF: 800-922-1932 ■ *Web:* www.modweldco.com					
Nebraska Boiler Co Inc 6940 Cornhusker Hwy	Lincoln	NE	68507	402-434-2000	434-2064
Web: www.neboiler.com					
Oat Joseph Corp 2500 Broadway	Camden	NJ	08104	856-541-2900	541-0864
Web: www.josephoat.com					
Ohmstede Ltd 895 N Main St	Beaumont	TX	77701	409-833-6375	839-4948
TF: 800-568-2328 ■ *Web:* www.ohmstede.com					
Patterson-Kelley 100 Burson St	East Stroudsburg	PA	18301	570-421-7500	421-8735
Web: www.patkelco.com					
Pentair Water Treatment 200 Industrial Pkwy	Chardon	OH	44024	440-286-4116	942-7659*
**Fax Area Code:* 800 ■ *TF:* 800-922-8265 ■ *Web:* www.pentair.com/water.html					
Plant Maintenance Service Corp 3000 Fite Rd	Memphis	TN	38127	901-353-9880	353-0882
TF: 800-459-9131 ■ *Web:* www.pmscmphs.com					
Precision Custom Components 500 Lincoln St	York	PA	17404	717-848-1126	843-5733*
**Fax:* Mktg ■ *Web:* www.pcc-york.com					
Pressed Steel Tank Co Inc 1445 S 66th St	West Allis	WI	53214	414-476-0500	476-7191
Web: www.pressedsteel.com					
PVI Industries LLC 3209 Galvez Ave PO Box 7124	Fort Worth	TX	76111	817-335-9531	332-6742
TF: 800-784-8326 ■ *Web:* www.pvi.com					
Q3 JMC Inc 605 Miami St	Urbana	OH	43078	937-652-2181	653-8352
TF: 800-767-1422					
Reco Constructors Inc 710 Hospital St	Richmond	VA	23219	804-644-2611	643-3561
Web: www.recoconstructors.com					
Redman Equipment & Mfg Co 19800 Normandie Ave	Torrance	CA	90502	310-329-1134	324-5656
Web: www.redmaneq.com					
Ross Technology Corp 104 N Maple Ave	Leola	PA	17540	717-656-2095	656-3281
TF: 800-345-8170 ■ *Web:* www.rosstechnology.com					
Roy E Hanson Jr Mfg 1600 E Washington Blvd	Los Angeles	CA	90021	213-747-7514	747-7724
TF: 800-421-9395 ■ *Web:* www.hansontank.com					
Sivalls Inc 2200 E 2nd St	Odessa	TX	79761	432-337-3571	337-2624
Web: www.sivalls.com					
Smith HB Co Inc 47 Westfield Industrial Pk Rd	Westfield	MA	01085	413-568-3148	568-0525
Smithco Engineering Inc 6312 S 39th West Ave	Tulsa	OK	74132	918-446-4406	445-2857
Web: www.smithco-eng.com					
Snap-Tite Autoclave Engineers Div 8325 Hessinger Dr	Erie	PA	16509	814-838-5700	833-0145
TF: 800-458-0409 ■ *Web:* www.snap-tite.com/divisions/ae/index.html					
SPX Cooling Technologies 7401 W 129th St	Overland Park	KS	66213	913-664-7400	664-7753
TF: 800-462-7539 ■ *Web:* www.marleyct.com					
Structural Composites Industries 325 Enterprise Pl	Pomona	CA	91768	909-594-7777	594-3939
Web: www.scicomposites.com					
Structural Steel Services					
6215 Saint Louis St South Industrial Park	Meridian	MS	39307	601-482-8181	482-1520
Super Steel Products Corp 7900 W Tower Ave	Milwaukee	WI	53223	414-355-4800	355-0372
Web: www.supersteel.com					
Superior Boiler Works Inc 3524 E 4th St PO Box 1527	Hutchinson	KS	67504	620-662-6693	662-7586
TF: 800-444-6693 ■ *Web:* www.superiorboiler.com					
Superior Die Set Corp 900 W Drexel Ave	Oak Creek	WI	53154	414-764-4900	657-0855*
**Fax Area Code:* 800 ■ *TF:* 800-558-6040 ■ *Web:* www.supdie.com					
Superior Fabricators Inc 155 Gordy Ln PO Box 0539	Baldwin	LA	70514	337-923-7271	923-7517
TF: 800-960-7271 ■ *Web:* www.superiorfabricators.com					
Sussman Automatic Corp 43-20 34th St	Long Island City	NY	11101	718-937-4500	786-4051
TF: 800-727-8326					
Tampa Tank Inc 5205 Adamo Dr	Tampa	FL	33619	813-623-2675	622-7514
Web: www.tampatank.com					
Taylor Forge Engineered Systems Inc 208 N Iron St	Paola	KS	66071	913-294-5331	294-5337
Web: www.tfes.com					
Taylor-Wharton 4718 Old Gettysburg Rd Suite 300	Mechanicsburg	PA	17055	717-763-5060	731-7988
Web: www.taylorwharton.com					
Thermal Engineering International Inc					
10375 Slusher Dr	Santa Fe Springs	CA	90670	323-726-0641	726-9592
Web: www.thermalengint.com					
Thermal Transfer Corp 50 N Linden St	Duquesne	PA	15110	412-460-4004	466-2899
Web: www.hamon-thermaltransfer.com					
Thermasys Heat Transfer 2760 Gunter Park Dr W	Montgomery	AL	36109	334-277-1810	244-9248
TF: 800-233-3201 ■ *Web:* www.thermasys.com					
Thermodynetics Inc 651 Day Hill Rd	Windsor	CT	06095	860-683-2005	285-0139
Web: www.thermodynetics.com					
Titanium Fabrication Corp 110 Lehigh Dr	Fairfield	NJ	07004	973-227-5300	227-6541
Web: www.titaniumfabrication.com					
Tranter Inc 1900 Old Burk Hwy	Wichita Falls	TX	76307	940-723-7125	723-5131
TF: 800-414-6908 ■ *Web:* us.tranter.com					
Trinity Industries Inc LPG Containers Div					
2525 N Stemmons Fwy	Dallas	TX	75207	214-589-8213	589-8303
TF: 888-558-8265 ■ *Web:* www.trinitylpg.com					
Ultraflote Corp 8558 Katy Fwy Suite 100	Houston	TX	77024	713-461-2100	461-2213
TF: 877-461-2100 ■ *Web:* www.ultraflote.com					
Weben-Jarco Inc 4007 Platinum Way	Dallas	TX	75237	214-637-0530	330-6864
TF: 800-527-6449 ■ *Web:* www.weben-jarco.com					
Weil-McLain Co 500 Blaine St	Michigan City	IN	46360	219-879-6561	879-4025
Web: www.weil-mclain.com					
Winbco Tank Co 1200 E Main St PO Box 618	Ottumwa	IA	52501	641-683-1855	683-8265
Web: www.winbco.com					
Worthington Cylinder Corp 200 Old E Wilson Bridge Rd	Columbus	OH	43085	614-438-3013	438-3083
TF: 800-323-6224 ■ *Web:* www.worthingtoncylinders.com					

92 BOOK BINDING & RELATED WORK

SEE ALSO Printing Companies - Book Printers p. 1503

				Phone	Fax
Area Trade Bindery Co 157 W Providencia Ave	Burbank	CA	91502	818-846-5581	849-3733*
**Fax Area Code:* 313 ■ *TF:* 800-225-1343 ■ *Web:* www.atbbindery.com					
Bindagraphics Inc 2701 Wilmarco Ave	Baltimore	MD	21223	410-362-7200	362-7233
TF: 800-326-0300 ■ *Web:* www.bindagraphics.com					
Bookbinders Co 2808 S Vail Ave	Los Angeles	CA	90040	323-838-8900	838-8905
Booklet Binding Inc 2200 W 16th St	Broadview	IL	60155	708-345-0110	345-0289
Web: www.bookletbinding.com					
Booksource Inc 1230 Macklind Ave	Saint Louis	MO	63110	314-647-0600	647-1923*
**Fax Area Code:* 800 ■ *TF:* 800-444-0435 ■ *Web:* www.booksource.com					
Bound to Stay Bound Books Inc 1880 W Morton Ave	Jacksonville	IL	62650	217-245-5191	747-2872*
**Fax Area Code:* 800 ■ *TF:* 800-637-6586 ■ *Web:* www.btsb.com					
Brewer-Cantelmo Co Inc 350 7th Ave 4th Fl	New York	NY	10001	212-244-4600	244-1640
Web: www.brewer-cantelmo.com					
California Sample Service Inc 13020 Pierce St	Pacoima	CA	91331	818-899-3503	899-2011
Chilcote Co 2140-60 Superior Ave	Cleveland	OH	44114	216-781-6000	771-2572
TF Sales: 800-827-5679					
Continental Bindery Corp 700 Fargo Ave	Elk Grove Village	IL	60007	847-439-6811	439-6847
Dekker Bookbinding 2941 Clydon Ave SW	Grand Rapids	MI	49519	616-538-5160	538-0720
TF: 800-299-2463 ■ *Web:* www.dekkerbook.com					
Finishing Plus Inc 4546 W 47th St	Chicago	IL	60632	773-523-5510	523-9155
Form House Inc 7200 S Leamington Ave	Bedford Park	IL	60638	708-594-7300	594-7390
Web: www.theformhouse.com					
Hart Bindery Services Co 3290 E 26th St	Los Angeles	CA	90023	323-268-9250	268-0793
Web: www.hartbindery.com					
Heckman Bindery Inc 1010 N Sycamore St	North Manchester	IN	46962	260-982-2107	982-1130
TF: 800-334-3628 ■ *Web:* www.boundtoplease.com					
Kater-Crafts Bookbinders Inc 4860 Gregg Rd	Pico Rivera	CA	90660	562-692-0665	692-7920
Web: www.katercrafts.com					
Kolbus America Inc 812 Huron Rd E Suite 750	Cleveland	OH	44115	216-931-5100	931-5101
Web: www.kolbus.com					
Lake Book Mfg Inc 2085 N Cornell Ave	Melrose Park	IL	60160	708-345-7000	345-1544
Web: www.lakebook.com					
Library Binding Service 1801 Thompson Ave	Des Moines	IA	50316	515-262-3191	262-3839*
**Fax Area Code:* 888 ■ *TF:* 800-247-5323 ■ *Web:* www.lbsbind.com					
Macke Brothers Inc 10355 Spartan Dr	Cincinnati	OH	45215	513-771-7500	771-3830
Web: www.mackebrothers.com					
Marshall & Bruce Printing Co 689 Davidson St	Nashville	TN	37213	615-256-3661	256-6803
Web: www.marbruco.com					
McCain Bindery Systems Inc 3802 W 128th St	Alsip	IL	60803	708-824-9600	824-0771
TF Cust Svc: 800-225-9363 ■ *Web:* www.mccainbindery.com					
National Library Bindery Co 100 Hembree Park Dr	Roswell	GA	30076	770-442-5490	442-0183
TF: 800-422-7908					
Oxford Bookbinding Co 3101 Red Lion Rd	Philadelphia	PA	19114	215-632-0400	632-1811
Web: www.oxfordbookbinding.com					
Perma-Bound 617 E Vandalia Rd	Jacksonville	IL	62650	217-243-5451	551-1169*
**Fax Area Code:* 800 ■ *TF:* 800-637-6581 ■ *Web:* www.perma-bound.com					
Precision Technology Inc 39 Sheep Davis Rd	Pembroke	NH	03275	603-224-9989	226-0172
TF: 800-362-7717 ■ *Web:* www.precisiontechnology.com					
Reindl Bindery Co Inc 111 E Reindl Way	Glendale	WI	53212	414-906-1111	906-1110
TF: 800-878-1121 ■ *Web:* www.reindlbindery.com					
Rickard Circular Folding Co 325 N Ashland Ave	Chicago	IL	60607	312-243-6300	243-6323
Web: www.rickardbindery.com					
Riverside Group 655 Driving Park Ave	Rochester	NY	14613	585-458-2090	458-2123
TF: 800-777-2463 ■ *Web:* www.riversidegroup.com					
Rotherwood Corp 301 Carlson Pkwy Suite 103	Minnetonka	MN	55305	952-835-2115	893-9036
Sagebrush Education Resources 2101 N Topeka Blvd	Topeka	KS	66608	785-233-4252	257-2665*
**Fax Area Code:* 877 ■ *TF:* 800-255-3502 ■ *Web:* www.sagebrushcorp.com					
Talas Inc 20 W 20th St 5th Fl	New York	NY	10011	212-219-0770	219-0735
Web: www.talas-nyc.com					
United Bindery Service Inc 1845 W Carroll Ave	Chicago	IL	60612	312-243-0240	243-3080
Wert Bookbinding Inc 9975 Allentown Blvd	Grantville	PA	17028	717-469-0626	469-0629
TF Cust Svc: 800-344-9378 ■ *Web:* www.wertbookbinding.com					
Zonne Bookbinders Inc 5410 W Roosevelt Rd Suite 211	Chicago	IL	60644	773-261-5470	261-5475

93 BOOK, MUSIC, VIDEO CLUBS

				Phone	Fax
African American Literature Book Club (AALBC)					
55 W 116th St Suite 195	Harlem	NY	10026	866-603-8394	
Web: www.aalbc.com					
Architects & Designers Book Service 1225 S Market St	Mechanicsburg	PA	17055	717-918-2665	
Behavioral Science Book Service 1225 S Market St	Mechanicsburg	PA	17055	717-918-2665	
Web: www.healthbookclubs.com					
Black Expressions 1225 S Market St	Mechanicsburg	PA	17055	717-918-2665	
Web: www.blackexpressions.com					
BMG Music Service PO Box 1958	Indianapolis	IN	46291	317-692-9200	542-6090
Web: www.bmgmusic.com					
Book-of-the-Month Club Inc 1225 S Market St	Mechanicsburg	PA	17055	717-918-2665	
Web: www.bomc.com					

				Phone	Fax
Booksfree.com 8453P Tyco Rd. *Web:* www.booksfree.com	Vienna	VA	22182	703-748-2390	748-2394
BOOKSPAN 1225 S Market St *Web:* www.bookspan.com	Mechanicsburg	PA	17055	717-918-2665	
Children's Book-of-the-Month Club 1225 S Market St *Web:* www.cbomc.com	Mechanicsburg	PA	17055	717-918-2665	
Columbia House Co 1400 N Fruitridge Ave **Fax:* Hum Res ■ *Web:* www.columbiahouse.com	Terre Haute	IN	47811	812-466-8111	466-6409*
Conservative Book Club PO Box 97197 *TF:* 877-222-1964 ■ *Web:* www.conservativebookclub.com	Washington	DC	20090	202-216-0600	216-0615
Country Homes & Gardens Book Club 15 E 26th St Time Life Bldg 3rd Fl *Web:* www.countryhomesandgardens.com	New York	NY	10010	212-651-7400	
Crossings Book Club 1225 S Market St *Web:* www.crossings.com	Mechanicsburg	PA	17055	717-918-2665	
Disney Movie Club PO Box 738 *TF:* 800-362-4587 ■ *Web:* disney.videos.go.com	Neenah	WI	54957	920-521-4015	521-4020
Doubleday Book Club Doubleday Direct Inc 1225 S Market St *Web:* www.doubledaybookclub.com	Mechanicsburg	PA	17055	800-688-4442	
Doubleday Direct Inc 1225 S Market St	Mechanicsburg	PA	17055	719-918-2665	
Doubleday Large Print Home Library Doubleday Direct Inc 1225 S Market St *Web:* www.doubledaylargeprint.com	Mechanicsburg	PA	17055	717-918-2665	
DVD Avenue PO Box 820 *TF:* 800-990-4159 ■ *Web:* www.dvdavenue.com	Clinton	MD	20735	301-856-4159	856-4153
Early Childhood Teachers' Club PO Box 6375 *Web:* www.educationbookclubs.com	Camp Hill	PA	17012	717-918-2665	
eMusic.com Inc 100 Park Ave 17th Fl *Web:* www.emusic.com	New York	NY	10017	212-201-9240	201-9204
GameFly Inc PO Box 60018 **Fax Area Code:* 310 ■ *Web:* www.gamefly.com	City of Industry	CA	91716	888-986-6400	664-6788*
Gameznflix Inc 1535 Blackjack Rd **Fax Area Code:* 270 ■ *Web:* www.gameznflix.com	Franklin	KY	42134	888-542-6817	778-0025*
Good Cook 1225 S Market St *TF:* 800-233-1066 ■ *Web:* www.thegoodcook.com	Mechanicsburg	PA	17055	717-918-2665	
History Book Club 15 E 26th St *Web:* www.historybookclub.com	New York	NY	10010	212-651-7400	
HomeStyle Books 1225 S Market St *Web:* www.homestylebooks.com	Mechanicsburg	PA	17055	717-918-2665	
Intelliflix Inc 1401 Forum Way Suite 503 *Web:* www.intelliflix.com	West Palm Beach	FL	33401	561-697-8325	697-8320
Library of Science Book Club 1225 S Market St	Mechanicsburg	PA	17055	717-918-2665	
Library of Speech-Language Pathology PO Box 6375 *Web:* www.educationbookclubs.com	Camp Hill	PA	17012	717-918-2665	
Literary Guild Doubleday Direct Inc 1225 S Market St *Web:* www.literaryguild.com	Mechanicsburg	PA	17055	717-918-2665	
Military Book Club Doubleday Direct Inc 1225 S Market St *Web:* www.militarybookclub.com	Mechanicsburg	PA	17055	717-918-2665	
Musical Heritage Society 1710 Hwy 35 *TF Cust Svc:* 800-333-4647 ■ *Web:* www.musicalheritage.com	Oakhurst	NJ	07755	732-531-7000	517-1488
Mystery Guild Doubleday Direct Inc 1225 S Market St *Web:* www.mysteryguild.com	Mechanicsburg	PA	17055	717-918-2665	
NetFlix Inc 100 Winchester Cir *NASDAQ: NFLX* ■ **Fax Area Code:* 408 ■ *TF:* 888-638-3549 ■ *Web:* www.netflix.com	Los Gatos	CA	95032	888-638-3549	317-3737*
One Spirit Book Club 15 E 26th St *Web:* www.onespirit.com	New York	NY	10010	212-651-7400	
Primary Teachers' Book Club PO Box 6375 *Web:* www.educationbookclubs.com	Camp Hill	PA	17012	717-918-2665	
Quality Paperback Book Club 1225 S Market St *Web:* www.qpb.com	Mechanicsburg	PA	10119	717-918-2665	
Reader's Subscription 1225 S Market St	Mechanicsburg	PA	17055	717-918-2665	
Rhapsody Book Club Bookspan 1225 S Market St *Web:* www.rhapsodybookclub.com	Mechanicsburg	PA	17055	717-918-2665	
Scholastic Arrow Book Club 555 Broadway **Fax Area Code:* 800 ■ *TF Orders:* 800-724-6527 ■ *Web:* teacher.scholastic.com/clubs	New York	NY	10012	212-343-6100	223-4011*
Scholastic Firefly Book Club 555 Broadway **Fax Area Code:* 800 ■ *TF Orders:* 800-724-6527 ■ *Web:* teacher.scholastic.com/clubs	New York	NY	10012	212-343-6100	223-4011*
Scholastic Lucky Book Club 555 Broadway **Fax Area Code:* 800 ■ *TF Orders:* 800-724-6527 ■ *Web:* teacher.scholastic.com/clubs	New York	NY	10012	212-343-6100	223-4011*
Scholastic Seesaw Book Club 555 Broadway **Fax Area Code:* 800 ■ *TF:* 800-724-2424 ■ *Web:* teacher.scholastic.com/clubs	New York	NY	10012	212-343-6100	223-4011*
Scholastic TAB Book Club 555 Broadway **Fax Area Code:* 800 ■ *TF Orders:* 800-724-6527 ■ *Web:* teacher.scholastic.com/clubs	New York	NY	10012	212-343-6100	223-4022*
Science Fiction Book Club Doubleday Direct Inc 1225 S Market St *Web:* www.sfbc.com	Mechanicsburg	PA	17055	717-918-2665	
Writer's Digest Book Club 4700 E Galbraith Rd *TF Cust Svc:* 800-888-6880 ■ *Web:* www.writersdigest.com/wdbc	Cincinnati	OH	45236	513-531-2690	531-4082

94 BOOK PRODUCERS

Book producers, or book packagers, work with authors, editors, printers, publishers, and others to provide all publication services except sales and order fulfillment. These publication services include editing of manuscripts, formatting of computer disks, producing books as a finished product, and helping the book publisher to develop marketing plans. Book producers listed here are members of the American Book Producers Association.

				Phone	Fax
Agincourt Press 25 Main St	Chatham	NY	12037	518-392-2898	
AGS BookWorks PO Box 460313 *Web:* www.agsbookworks.com	San Francisco	CA	94146	415-285-8799	285-8790
Amaranth PO Box 573	Port Townsend	WA	98368	360-385-5014	
Archetype Press Inc 11 Waters Edge - Coral Hwy	Fenwick Island	DE	19944	302-537-1900	537-1175
Ardent Media Inc 522 E 82nd St	New York	NY	10028	212-861-1501	861-0998
Ariel Books 1916 Post Rd 2nd Fl	Fairfield	CT	06824	203-259-1600	259-7053
becker&mayer! Ltd 11010 Northup Way *Web:* www.beckermayer.com	Bellevue	WA	98004	425-827-7120	828-9659
Beth Allen Assoc Inc 347 W 22nd St Suite 9	New York	NY	10011	212-206-1138	989-5157
Book Builders LLC 425 Madison Ave Suite 1901	New York	NY	10017	212-371-1110	893-8680
Book Creation LLC 216 E 49th St 3rd Fl	New York	NY	10017	212-935-1954	935-1958
Byron Preiss Visual Publications Inc 24 W 25th St 11th Fl	New York	NY	10010	212-645-9870	645-9874
Charles Davey Design LLC 2 Deertrack Ln	Irvington	NY	10533	914-231-5120	
CMD Publishing 1250 Broadway 36th Fl *Web:* www.cmdny.com	New York	NY	10001	212-771-7300	849-1180
Current Medical Directions Inc 1250 Broadway 36th Fl *Web:* www.cmdny.com	New York	NY	10001	212-771-7300	849-1180
Design Press Savannah College of Art & Design 516 Abercorn St PO Box 3146 *Web:* www.designpressbooks.com	Savannah	GA	31402	912-525-5212	525-5211
Dimensional Illustrators Inc 362 2nd St Pike Suite 112	Southampton	PA	18966	215-953-1415	953-1697
Dovetail Books 24 Harstrom Pl *Web:* www.dovetailbooks.com	Rowayton	CT	06853	203-852-1640	852-1694
DreamBooks PO Box 10626 *Web:* www.belmaj.com	Burbank	CA	91510	818-841-9291	841-9691
Emprise Publishing Inc 4700 Marshall Dr W	Vestal	NY	13850	607-772-0559	
Evanston Publishing Inc 4824 Brownsboro Center *TF:* 800-594-5190 ■ *Web:* www.evanstonpublishing.com	Louisville	KY	40207	502-899-1919	896-0246
Fair Street Productions 127 W 26th St	New York	NY	10001	212-633-2266	633-2069
Focus Strategic Communications Inc 535 Tipperton Crescent *TF:* 866-263-6287 ■ *Web:* www.focussc.com	Oakville	ON	L6L5E1	905-825-8757	825-5724
Garden Bench Books 109 Bell St	Seattle	WA	98121	206-443-8856	443-8862
GGP Publishing Inc 138 Chatsworth Ave Suite 3-5	Larchmont	NY	10538	914-834-8896	834-7566
gonzalez defino 7 E 14th St Suite 20-S *Web:* www.gonzalezdefino.com	New York	NY	10003	212-414-1058	414-0876
Grace Associates 945 4th Ave Suite 200A	Huntington	WV	25701	304-697-3236	697-3399
Hall Nancy Inc 23 E 22nd St 4th Fl	New York	NY	10010	212-674-3408	353-1521
innovative USA Inc 18 Ann St *Web:* www.innovativeusa.com	Norwalk	CT	06854	203-838-6400	855-5582
Jump Start Press 144 W 27th St Suite 7R	New York	NY	10001	212-352-9870	352-2834
Learning Source Ltd 644 10th St *Web:* www.learningsourceltd.com	Brooklyn	NY	11215	718-768-0231	369-3467
Lief Philip Group Inc 130 Wall St *Web:* www.philipliefgroup.com	Princeton	NJ	08540	609-430-1000	430-0300
Lone Wolf Enterprises Ltd 13 Gurnett Rd *Web:* www.lonewolfent.net	Brunswick	ME	04011	207-373-1415	798-5070
Mountain Lion Inc 94 Voorhees Ct PO Box 799 *Web:* www.mtlioninc.com	Pennington	NJ	08534	609-730-1665	730-1286
MTM Publishing Inc 121 W 27th St Suite 802 *Web:* www.mtmpublishing.com	New York	NY	10016	212-645-2900	684-2526
Nancy Hall Inc 23 E 22nd St 4th Fl	New York	NY	10010	212-674-3408	353-1521
Palace Press International Packaging 17 Paul Dr *Web:* www.palacepress.com	San Rafael	CA	94903	415-526-1370	526-1394
Parachute Publishing LLC 156 5th Ave Suite 302 *Web:* www.parachutepublishing.com	New York	NY	10010	212-691-1421	645-8769
Pen & Pencil Books 13 Maple St Ext PO Box 709	Kent	CT	06757	860-927-0096	927-3704
Philip Lief Group Inc 130 Wall St *Web:* www.philipliefgroup.com	Princeton	NJ	08540	609-430-1000	430-0300
Pneuma Books LLC PO Box 1110 *Web:* www.pneumabooks.com	North East	MD	21901	410-287-3120	287-2359
Preiss Byron Visual Publications Inc 24 W 25th St 11th Fl	New York	NY	10010	212-645-9870	645-9874
Pro Media Ltd DBA Progressive Publishing 4126 John Young Pkwy *Web:* www.promedialtd.com	Orlando	FL	32804	407-852-7000	294-1490
Progressive Publishing 4126 John Young Pkwy *Web:* www.promedialtd.com	Orlando	FL	32804	407-852-7000	294-1490
Quirk Packaging 119 W 23rd St Suite 1001 *Web:* www.quirkpackaging.com	New York	NY	10011	212-352-0484	352-0461
rosa + wesley inc 128 S County Farm Rd Suite E *Web:* www.rosawesley.com	Wheaton	IL	60187	630-588-9801	588-9804
Roundtable Press Inc 80 5th Ave *Web:* www.roundtablepressinc.com	New York	NY	10011	212-691-0500	691-1298
Schlager Group Inc 1640 W Oakland Park Blvd Suite 401 *Web:* www.schlagergroup.com	Oakland Park	FL	33311	954-730-8214	730-8212
Scientific American Inc 415 Madison Ave *TF Cust Svc:* 800-333-1199 ■ *Web:* www.sciam.com	New York	NY	10017	212-451-8550	755-1976
Shoreline Publishing Group 125 Santa Rosa Pl *Web:* www.shorelinepublishing.com	Santa Barbara	CA	93109	805-564-1004	564-1156
Sideshow Media 611 Broadway Suite 611 *Web:* www.sideshowbooks.com	New York	NY	10012	212-674-5335	674-6116
Smallwood & Stewart Inc 5 E 20th St *Web:* www.smallwoodandstewart.com	New York	NY	10003	212-505-3268	505-3624
Spooky Cheetah Press 33 Glendale Dr *Web:* www.spookycheetah.com	Stamford	CT	06906	203-357-1160	357-8096
Stonesong Press LLC 27 W 24th St Suite 510 *Web:* www.stonesong.com	New York	NY	10010	212-929-4600	486-9123
Toy Department 52 Main St	Kingston	NY	12401	845-331-1782	331-1666
Victory Productions Inc 55 Linden St *Web:* www.victoryprd.com	Worcester	MA	01609	508-755-0051	755-0025
Welcome Enterprises Inc 6 W 18th St 3rd Fl *Web:* www.welcomebooks.com	New York	NY	10011	212-989-3200	989-3205

95 BOOK STORES

				Phone	Fax
Alibris Inc 1250 45th St Suite 100 *Web:* www.alibris.com	Emeryville	CA	94608	510-594-4500	652-2403
Amazon.com Inc 1200 12th Ave S Suite 1200 *NASDAQ: AMZN* ■ **Fax:* Hum Res ■ *TF Cust Svc:* 800-201-7575 ■ *Web:* www.amazon.com	Seattle	WA	98144	206-266-1000	266-7601*
Antigone Books 411 N 4th Ave *Web:* www.antigonebooks.com	Tucson	AZ	85705	520-792-3715	882-8802
Archambault Group Inc 500 rue Sainte-Catherine E *TF:* 877-849-8589 ■ *Web:* www.archambault.ca	Montreal	QC	H2L2C6	514-849-6206	849-0764
Atlantic Book Warehouse 979 Bethlehem Pike *TF:* 800-237-7323 ■ *Web:* www.atlanticbooks.us	Montgomeryville	PA	18936	215-661-0450	661-0472
B Dalton Bookseller Inc 122 5th Ave **Fax:* Cust Svc	New York	NY	10011	212-633-3300	807-6105*
Barnes & Noble College Bookstores Inc 120 Mountain View Blvd *Web:* www.bkstore.com	Basking Ridge	NJ	07920	908-991-2665	
Barnes & Noble Inc 122 5th Ave *NYSE: BKS* ■ **Fax:* Cust Svc ■ *Web:* www.barnesandnoble.com	New York	NY	10011	212-633-3300	807-6105*
barnesandnoble.com Inc 76 9th Ave 9th Fl *TF:* 800-843-2665 ■ *Web:* www.book.com	New York	NY	10011	212-414-6000	414-6018
Bear Pond Books 77 Main St *Web:* www.bearpondbooks.com	Montpelier	VT	05602	802-229-0774	229-1069
Berean Christian Stores 9415 Meridian Way *Web:* www.berean.com	West Chester	OH	45069	513-729-1500	728-6974
Book Loft 631 S 3rd St *Web:* www.bookloft.com	Columbus	OH	43206	614-464-1774	464-3443
Book Passage 51 Tamal Vista Blvd *TF:* 800-999-7909 ■ *Web:* www.bookpassage.com	Corte Madera	CA	94925	415-927-0960	927-3069
Book Revue 313 New York Ave *Web:* www.bookrevue.com	Huntington	NY	11743	631-271-1442	271-5890
Book Soup 8818 Sunset Blvd *TF:* 800-764-2665 ■ *Web:* www.booksoup.com	West Hollywood	CA	90069	310-659-3110	659-3410
BookBuyers 317 Castro St *Web:* www.bookbuyers.com	Mountain View	CA	94041	650-968-7323	

Company	City	State	Zip	Phone	Fax
BookCloseouts Inc 340 Welland Ave	Saint Catharines	ON	L2R7L9	905-680-6834	680-7218
TF: 888-402-7323 ■ *Web:* www.bookcloseouts.com					
BookPeople 603 N Lamar	Austin	TX	78703	512-472-5050	482-8495
TF: 800-853-9757 ■ *Web:* www.bookpeople.com					
Books-A-Million Inc 402 Industrial Ln	Birmingham	AL	35211	205-942-3737	945-1772
NASDAQ: BAMM ■ *Web:* www.booksamillion.com					
Books & Books 265 Aragon Ave	Coral Gables	FL	33134	305-442-4408	444-9751
TF: 888-626-6576 ■ *Web:* www.booksandbooks.com					
Books on the Square 471 Angell St	Providence	RI	02906	401-331-9097	331-2845
TF: 888-669-9660 ■ *Web:* www.booksq.com					
BookSense.com 200 White Plains Rd	Tarrytown	NY	10591	914-591-2665	591-2720
TF: 800-637-0037 ■ *Web:* www.booksense.com					
Borders Group Inc 100 Phoenix Dr	Ann Arbor	MI	48108	734-477-1100	477-1313
NYSE: BGP ■ *TF Cust Svc:* 800-566-6616 ■ *Web:* www.bordersgroupinc.com					
Borders Inc 100 Phoenix Dr	Ann Arbor	MI	48108	734-477-1100	477-1313
TF Cust Svc: 800-566-6616 ■ *Web:* www.bordersstores.com					
Boulder Book Store 1107 Pearl St	Boulder	CO	80302	303-447-2074	447-3946
TF: 800-244-4651 ■ *Web:* www.boulderbookstore.com					
Brazos Bookstore 2421 Bissonnet	Houston	TX	77005	713-523-0701	523-1829
Web: www.brazosbookstore.com					
Brookline Booksmith 279 Harvard St	Brookline	MA	02446	617-566-6660	734-9125
Web: www.brooklinebooksmith.com/					
Changing Hands Bookstore 6428 S McClintock Dr	Tempe	AZ	85283	480-730-0205	730-1196
Web: www.changinghands.com					
Chaucer's Books 3321 State St	Santa Barbara	CA	93105	805-682-6787	682-1129
Web: www.chaucers.booksense.com					
City Lights Booksellers 261 Columbus Ave	San Francisco	CA	94133	415-362-8193	362-4921
Web: www.citylights.com					
Cody's Books Inc 1730 4th St	Berkeley	CA	94710	510-559-9500	
TF: 800-995-1180 ■ *Web:* www.codysbooks.com					
Cover to Cover 221 Petro Ave	Sioux Falls	SD	57107	605-336-3000	336-7279
Curious George Goes to WordsWorth 1 JFK St	Cambridge	MA	02138	617-498-0062	498-0061
TF: 800-899-2202 ■ *Web:* www.curiousg.com					
Dakota News Inc DBA Cover to Cover 221 Petro Ave	Sioux Falls	SD	57107	605-336-3000	336-7279
Deseret Book Co PO Box 30178	Salt Lake City	UT	84130	801-534-1515	453-3876*
**Fax Area Code: 800* ■ *TF Sales:* 800-453-4532 ■ *Web:* deseretbook.com					
Dickens Books Ltd DBA Harry W Schwartz Bookshops					
219 N Milwaukee St	Milwaukee	WI	53202	414-270-3434	274-8685
Web: www.schwartzbooks.com					
EBSCO Book Services PO Box 1943	Birmingham	AL	35201	205-991-6600	991-1479
TF Cust Svc: 800-815-9627 ■ *Web:* www.ebsco.com/home/books					
eFollett.com 1818 Swift Dr	Oak Brook	IL	60522	800-381-5151	279-2569*
**Fax Area Code: 630* ■ *Web:* www.efollett.com					
Elliott Bay Book Company 101 S Main St	Seattle	WA	98104	206-624-6600	903-1601
TF: 800-962-5311 ■ *Web:* www.elliottbaybook.com					
Family Christian Stores Inc 5300 Patterson Ave	Grand Rapids	MI	49530	616-554-8700	554-8608
Web: www.familychristian.com					
Follett Corp 2233 West St	River Grove	IL	60171	708-583-2000	452-0169
TF: 800-621-4345 ■ *Web:* www.follett.com					
Follett Higher Education Group 1818 Swift Dr	Oak Brook	IL	60523	630-279-2330	279-2569
TF: 800-323-4506 ■ *Web:* www.fheg.follett.com					
Full Circle Bookstore 1900 Northwest Expy	Oklahoma City	OK	73118	405-842-2900	842-2894
TF: 800-683-7323 ■ *Web:* www.fullcirclebooks.com					
Goerings Book Store 1717 NW 1st Ave	Gainesville	FL	32603	352-372-3975	271-9274
Web: www.goerings.com					
Grason PO Box 669007	Charlotte	NC	28266	800-487-0433	401-3031*
**Fax Area Code: 704* ■ *Web:* www.grason.org					
Half Price Books Records & Magazines Inc					
5803E Northwest Hwy	Dallas	TX	75231	214-360-0833	379-8010
Web: www.halfpricebooks.com					
Half.com Inc PO Box 1469	Draper	UT	84020	800-545-9857	349-5782*
**Fax Area Code: 877* ■ *TF:* 800-545-9857 ■ *Web:* www.half.ebay.com					
Hall of Cards & Books Inc 2232 S 11th St	Niles	MI	49120	269-684-5115	684-8428
Harry W Schwartz Bookshops 219 N Milwaukee St	Milwaukee	WI	53202	414-270-3434	274-8685
Web: www.schwartzbooks.com					
Harvard Coop Society 1400 Massachusetts Ave	Cambridge	MA	02238	617-499-2000	499-2016
TF: 800-242-1882 ■ *Web:* www.thecoop.com					
Hastings Entertainment Inc 3601 Plains Blvd	Amarillo	TX	79102	806-351-2300	351-2211
NASDAQ: HAST ■ *TF Cust Svc:* 877-427-8464 ■ *Web:* www.gohastings.com					
Indigo Books & Music Inc 468 King St W Suite 500	Toronto	ON	M5V1L8	416-364-4499	364-0355
TSX: IDG ■ *Web:* www.chapters.indigo.ca					
Joseph-Beth Booksellers 1727 Eastern Ave	Cincinnati	OH	45202	513-412-5700	412-5712
Web: www.josephbeth.com					
Kinokuniya Bookstores 1581 Webster St	San Francisco	CA	94115	415-567-7626	567-4109
Kinokuniya Bookstores 10 W 49th St	New York	NY	10020	212-765-1461	541-9335
Web: www.kinokuniya.com					
Lee Booksellers 1265 S Cotner Blvd	Lincoln	NE	68510	402-488-4416	489-2770
TF: 888-665-0999 ■ *Web:* www.leebooksellers.com					
Left Bank Books 399 N Euclid Ave	Saint Louis	MO	63108	314-367-6731	367-3256
Web: www.left-bank.com					
LibertyTree 100 Swan Way	Oakland	CA	94621	510-568-6047	568-6040
TF: 800-927-8733 ■ *Web:* www.liberty-tree.org					
LibrairieSmith 468 King St W Suite 500	Toronto	ON	M5V1L8	416-364-4499	364-0355
Matthews Book Co Inc 11559 Rock Island Ct	Maryland Heights	MO	63043	314-432-1400	432-7044
TF: 800-633-2665 ■ *Web:* www.matthewsbooks.com					
Matthews Medical & Scientific Book Inc					
11559 Rock Island Ct	Maryland Heights	MO	63043	314-432-1400	432-7044
TF: 800-633-2665 ■ *Web:* www.matthewsbooks.com					
Micawber Books 110-114 Nassau St	Princeton	NJ	08542	609-577-0319	
Web: www.micawber.com					
Moe's Books 2476 Telegraph Ave	Berkeley	CA	94704	510-849-2087	849-9938
Web: www.moesbooks.com					
Newbury Comics Inc 5 Guest St	Brighton	MA	02135	617-254-1666	254-2540
Web: www.newbury.com					
Northshire Bookstore 4869 Main St	Manchester Center	VT	05255	802-362-2200	362-1233
TF: 800-437-3700 ■ *Web:* www.northshire.com					
Olsson's Books & Records 106 S Union St	Alexandria	VA	22314	703-684-0030	
TF: 800-989-8084 ■ *Web:* www.olssons.com					
Page One Bookstore 11018 Montgomery Blvd NE	Albuquerque	NM	87111	505-294-2026	323-9849
TF: 800-521-4122 ■ *Web:* page1book.com					
Parable Christian Stores 3563 Empleo St	San Luis Obispo	CA	93401	805-543-2644	543-2136
TF: 888-644-0500 ■ *Web:* www.parable.com					
Poisoned Pen Bookstore 4014 N Goldwater Blvd	Scottsdale	AZ	85251	480-947-2974	945-1023
TF: 888-560-9919 ■ *Web:* www.poisonedpen.com					
Politics & Prose Bookstore 5015 Connecticut Ave NW	Washington	DC	20008	202-364-1919	966-7532
TF: 800-722-0790 ■ *Web:* www.politics-prose.com					
Powell's Books Inc 7 NW 9th Ave	Portland	OR	97209	503-228-0540	228-1142
TF: 800-878-7323 ■ *Web:* www.powells.com					
Powell's City of Books 1005 W Burnside St	Portland	OR	97209	503-228-4651	228-4631
TF: 800-878-7323 ■ *Web:* www.powells.com					
Prairie Lights Bookstore 15 S Dubuque St	Iowa City	IA	52240	319-337-2681	887-3084
TF: 800-295-2665 ■ *Web:* www.prairielights.com					
Regulator Bookshop 720 9th St	Durham	NC	27705	919-286-2700	286-6063
Web: www.regbook.com					
Seminary Co-op Bookstore 5757 S University Ave	Chicago	IL	60637	773-752-4381	752-8507
Web: semcoop.booksense.com					
Shaman Drum Bookshop 311-315 S State St	Ann Arbor	MI	48104	734-662-7407	662-0017
TF: 800-490-7023 ■ *Web:* www.shamandrum.com					
Skylight Books 1818 N Vermont Ave	Los Angeles	CA	90027	323-660-1175	660-0232
Web: www.skylightbooks.com					
Social Studies School Service					
10200 Jefferson Blvd Box 802	Culver City	CA	90232	310-839-2436	944-5432*
**Fax Area Code: 800* ■ *TF:* 800-421-4246 ■ *Web:* www.socialstudies.com					
Square Books 160 Courthouse Sq	Oxford	MS	38655	662-236-2262	234-9630
TF: 800-648-4001 ■ *Web:* www.squarebooks.com					
Stacey's 581 Market St	San Francisco	CA	94105	415-421-4687	777-5017
TF: 800-926-6511 ■ *Web:* www.staceys.com					
Steve's Books & Magazines 2612 S Harvard	Tulsa	OK	74114	918-743-3544	743-5912
TF: 888-743-0989 ■ *Web:* www.stevesbooksmags.com					
Tatnuck Bookseller & Sons 18 Lyman St	Westborough	MA	01581	508-366-4959	366-7929
TF: 800-642-6657 ■ *Web:* www.tatnuck.com					
Tattered Cover Book Store Inc 1628 16th St	Denver	CO	80202	303-436-1070	629-1704
TF: 800-833-9327 ■ *Web:* www.tatteredcover.com					
That Bookstore in Blytheville 316 W Main St	Blytheville	AR	72315	870-763-3333	763-1125
Web: www.tbib.com					
University Press Books 2430 Bancroft Way	Berkeley	CA	94704	510-548-0585	849-9214
TF: 800-676-8722 ■ *Web:* www.universitypressbooks.com					
US Government Printing Office (GPO) Online Bookstore					
732 N Capitol St NW	Washington	DC	20401	202-512-1800	512-2104
Web: bookstore.gpo.gov					
Valley Books 220 N Pleasant St	Amherst	MA	01002	413-256-1508	
Web: www.valleybooks.com					
Varsity Group Inc 1850 M St NW Suite 1150	Washington	DC	20036	202-667-3400	332-5498
NASDAQ: VSTY ■ *TF:* 877-827-2665 ■ *Web:* www.varsitybooks.com					
Viewpoint Books 548 Washington St	Columbus	IN	47201	812-376-0778	376-1089
Web: www.viewpointbooks.com					
Walden Book Co Inc 100 Phoenix Dr	Ann Arbor	MI	48108	734-477-1100	973-4541*
**Fax:* Hum Res ■ *TF:* 800-566-6616					
World's Biggest Book Store 468 King St W Suite 500	Toronto	ON	M5V1L8	416-364-4499	364-0355

96 BOOKS, PERIODICALS, NEWSPAPERS - WHOL

Company	City	State	Zip	Phone	Fax
Advanced Marketing Services Inc 5880 Oberlin Dr Suite 400	San Diego	CA	92121	858-457-2500	452-2237
NYSE: MKT ■ *TF:* 800-695-3580 ■ *Web:* www.advmkt.com					
Anderson News Co 6016 Brookvale Ln Suite 151	Knoxville	TN	37919	865-584-9765	450-3159
Web: www.andersonnews.com					
AT & T Directory Sales Center					
2200 Riverchase Center Suite 600	Birmingham	AL	35244	800-241-4558	
Austin News Agency Inc 4414 E Saint Elmo Rd	Austin	TX	78744	512-447-6026	447-2769
TF: 800-542-0060					
Baker & Taylor Inc 2550 W Tyvola Rd Suite 300	Charlotte	NC	28217	704-998-3100	998-3316
TF: 800-775-1800 ■ *Web:* www.btol.com					
Blackwell North America Inc 6024 SW Jean Rd Bldg G	Lake Oswego	OR	97035	503-684-1140	639-2481
TF: 800-547-6426 ■ *Web:* www.blackwell.com					
BMI Educational Services PO Box 800	Dayton	NJ	08810	732-329-6991	986-9393*
**Fax Area Code: 800* ■ *TF:* 800-222-8100 ■ *Web:* www.bmiedserv.com					
Book Wholesalers Inc DBA BWI 1847 Mercer Rd Suite D	Lexington	KY	40511	859-231-9789	888-6319*
**Fax Area Code: 800* ■ *TF:* 800-888-4478 ■ *Web:* www.bwibooks.com					
Bookazine Co Inc 75 Hook Rd	Bayonne	NJ	07002	201-339-7777	339-7778
TF: 800-221-8112 ■ *Web:* www.bookazine.com					
Booksource Inc 1230 Macklind Ave	Saint Louis	MO	63110	314-647-0600	647-1923*
**Fax Area Code: 800* ■ *TF:* 800-444-0435 ■ *Web:* www.booksource.com					
Brodart Co Book Services Div 500 Arch St	Williamsport	PA	17701	570-326-2461	326-6769
TF: 800-233-8467 ■ *Web:* www.books.brodart.com					
BWI 1847 Mercer Rd Suite D	Lexington	KY	40511	859-231-9789	888-6319*
**Fax Area Code: 800* ■ *TF:* 800-888-4478 ■ *Web:* www.bwibooks.com					
Capitol Fiber Inc 6610 Electronics Dr	Springfield	VA	22151	703-658-0200	658-0212
Chas Levy Circulating Co 815 Ogden Ave	Lislee	IL	60532	800-549-5389	353-2699*
**Fax Area Code: 630* ■ **Fax:* Cust Svc ■ *Web:* www.chaslevy.com					
Directory Distributing Assoc (DDA) 160 Corporate Woods Ct	Bridgeton	MO	63044	314-592-8600	592-8790
TF: 800-325-1964 ■ *Web:* www.ddai.com					
EBSCO Magazine Express					
2517 State Hwy 35 Bldg C Suite 201	Manasquan	NJ	08736	732-223-7177	223-7178
Web: www.magazineexpress.com					
EBSCO Reception Room Subscription Services					
PO Box 830460	Birmingham	AL	35283	800-527-5901	995-1621*
**Fax Area Code: 205* ■ *Web:* www.ebsco.com/errss					
EBSCO Subscription Services PO Box 1943	Birmingham	AL	35201	205-991-1220	995-1518
Web: www.ebsco.com/home/about/ess.asp					
Educational Development Corp 10302 E 55th Pl	Tulsa	OK	74146	918-622-4522	665-7919
NASDAQ: EDUC ■ *TF:* 800-611-1655 ■ *Web:* www.edcpub.com					
Fall River News Co 25 Westwood Ave	New London	CT	06320	860-442-4394	439-0773
Follett Corp 2233 West St	River Grove	IL	60171	708-583-2000	452-0169
TF: 800-621-4345 ■ *Web:* www.follett.com					
Follett Educational Services 1433 International Pkwy	Woodridge	IL	60517	630-972-5600	638-4424*
**Fax Area Code: 800* ■ *TF:* 800-621-4272 ■ *Web:* www.fes.follett.com					
Follett Library Resources 1340 Ridgeview Dr	McHenry	IL	60050	815-759-1700	759-9831
TF: 888-511-5114 ■ *Web:* www.flr.follett.com					
Harlequin Enterprises Ltd Distribution Center 3010 Walden Ave	Depew	NY	14043	716-684-1800	684-5066
TF: 800-873-8635 ■ *Web:* www.eharlequin.com					
Hudson News Co 1305 Paterson Plank Rd	North Bergen	NJ	07047	201-867-3600	867-0067
TF: 800-225-0910					
Independent Publishers Group 814 N Franklin St	Chicago	IL	60610	312-337-0747	337-5985
TF Orders: 800-888-4741 ■ *Web:* www.ipgbook.com					
Ingram Book Group 1 Ingram Blvd	La Vergne	TN	37086	615-793-5000	213-7140
TF: 800-937-8000 ■ *Web:* www.ingrambookgroup.com					
JA Majors Co 1401 Lakeway Dr	Lewisville	TX	75057	972-353-1100	353-1300
TF: 800-633-1851 ■ *Web:* www.majors.com					
Jim Pattison News Group 3320 S Service Rd 2nd Fl	Burlington	ON	L7N3M6	905-681-1113	323-2420*
**Fax Area Code: 888*					
Kable News Co Inc 505 Park Ave 7th Fl	New York	NY	10022	212-705-4600	705-4666
Web: www.kable.com					
Levy Home Entertainment LLC 4201 Raymond Dr	Hillside	IL	60162	708-547-4400	547-4503
Web: www.levybooks.com					
MBS Textbook Exchange Inc 2711 W Ash St	Columbia	MO	65203	573-445-2243	446-5256
TF Cust Svc: 800-325-0530 ■ *Web:* www.mbsbooks.com					
Midwest Library Service Inc 11443 St Charles Rock Rd	Bridgeton	MO	63044	314-739-3100	739-1326
TF: 800-325-8833 ■ *Web:* www.midwestls.com					
MindBranch Inc 131 Ashland St Suite 200	North Adams	MA	01247	413-662-3700	664-9791
TF: 800-774-4410 ■ *Web:* www.mindbranch.com					
National Telephone Directory Co 3 Executive Dr	Somerset	NJ	08873	732-302-3000	302-9436
Nebraska Book Co 4700 S 19th St	Lincoln	NE	68512	402-421-7300	869-0399*
**Fax Area Code: 800* ■ *TF:* 800-869-0366 ■ *Web:* www.nebook.com					
NetLibrary Inc 4888 Pearl East Cir Suite 103	Boulder	CO	80301	303-415-2548	381-8600
TF: 800-413-4557 ■ *Web:* www.netlibrary.com					
News Group 2032 Gateway Blvd	Charlotte	NC	28208	704-391-1742	391-1745
Product Development Corp 20 Ragsdale Dr Suite 100	Monterey	CA	93940	831-333-1100	333-1122
Publishers Group Inc 1400 65th St Suite 250	Emeryville	CA	94608	510-595-3664	595-4228
TF: 800-788-3123 ■ *Web:* www.avalonpub.com					

Phone Fax

Publishers Group West 1400 65th St Suite250 ... Emeryville CA 94608 510-595-3664 595-4228
TF: 800-788-3123 ■ *Web:* www.pgw.com
Publishers' Warehouse PO Box 101927 ... Irondale AL 35210 205-956-2078 956-7265
TF: 800-956-2078
Quality Books Inc 1003 West Pines Rd ... Oregon IL 61061 815-732-4450 732-4499
TF Cust Svc: 800-323-4241 ■ *Web:* www.quality-books.com
Rittenhouse Book Distributors Inc 511 Feheley Dr ... King of Prussia PA 19406 610-277-1414 223-7488*
**Fax Area Code:* 800 ■ **Fax:* Orders ■ *TF Cust Svc:* 800-345-6425 ■
Web: www.rittenhouse.com
Saint Marie's Gopher News Co 9000 10th Ave N ... Minneapolis MN 55427 763-546-5300 525-3100
TF: 800-279-2665
Scholastic Book Fairs Inc 1080 Greenwood Blvd ... Lake Mary FL 32746 407-829-7300 829-7898*
**Fax:* Mktg ■ *TF:* 800-874-4809 ■ *Web:* www.scholastic.com/bookfairs
Source Interlink Cos Inc 27500 Riverview Ctr Blvd ... Bonita Springs FL 34134 239-949-4450 949-7633
NASDAQ: SORC ■ *TF:* 866-276-5584 ■ *Web:* www.sourceinterlink.com
Southwestern/Great American 2451 Atrium Way ... Nashville TN 37214 615-391-2500 391-2503*
**Fax:* Cust Svc ■ *TF Cust Svc:* 800-251-1542 ■ *Web:* www.southwestern.com
Spring Arbor Distributors 1 Ingram Blvd ... La Vergne TN 37086 800-395-4340 213-7140*
**Fax Area Code:* 615 ■ **Fax:* Sales ■ *Web:* www.springarbor.com
Swets Information Services 160 9th Ave ... Runnemede NJ 08078 856-312-2690 312-2000
TF: 800-645-6595 ■ *Web:* informationservices.swets.com
Texas Book Co 8501 Technology Cir ... Greenville TX 75403 903-455-6937 454-2442
TF: 800-527-1016
Tulare County News Agency Inc 637 S Lovers Ln ... Visalia CA 93292 559-734-9206 734-5732
Web: www.tularecountynews.net
Turtleback Books 5701 Manufacturers Dr ... Madison WI 53704 800-448-8939 828-0401*
**Fax:* Orders ■ *Web:* www.turtlebackbooks.com
Verizon Publishing 621 Mid-Atlantic Pkwy ... Martinsburg WV 25401 304-267-1100 267-1104
Vulcan Service PO Box 522 ... Birmingham AL 35201 205-991-1374 980-3891
TF: 800-841-9600 ■ *Web:* www.vulcanservice.com
YBP Library Services 999 Maple St ... Contoocook NH 03229 603-746-3102 746-5628
TF: 800-258-3774 ■ *Web:* www.ybp.com

97 BOTANICAL GARDENS & ARBORETA

SEE ALSO Zoos & Wildlife Parks p. 2419

Phone Fax

Adkins Arboretum 12610 Eveland Rd PO Box 100 ... Ridgely MD 21660 410-634-2847 634-2878
Web: www.adkinsarboretum.org
Afton Villa Gardens 9247 N Hwy 61 ... Saint Francisville LA 70775 225-635-6773
Airlie Gardens 300 Airlie Rd ... Wilmington NC 28401 910-798-7700
Web: www.airliegardens.org
Alaska Botanical Garden 461 Campbell Rd ... Anchorage AK 99520 907-770-3692 770-0555
Web: www.alaskabg.org
Aldridge Gardens 3530 Lorna Rd ... Hoover AL 35216 205-682-8019 682-8085
Web: www.aldridgegardens.com
Alexandra Botanic Gardens Wellesley College 106 Central St ... Wellesley MA 02481 781-283-3094 283-3642
Web: www.wellesley.edu/FOH/greenhouse.html
Alfred B Maclay State Gardens 3540 Thomasville Rd ... Tallahassee FL 32309 850-487-4556 487-8808
Web: www.ssnow.com/maclay
Allan Gardens Conservatory 19 Horticultural Ave ... Toronto ON M5A2P2 416-392-7288 392-0318
Web: collections.ic.gc.ca/gardens
Alta Vista Gardens PO Box 1988 ... Vista CA 92085 760-945-3954
Web: www.altavistagardens.org
Amarillo Botanical Gardens 1400 Streit Dr ... Amarillo TX 79106 806-352-6513 352-6227
Web: www.amarillobotanicalgardens.org
Amy BH Greenwell Ethnobotanical Garden
82-6188 Mamalahoa Hwy PO Box 1053 ... Captain Cook HI 96704 808-323-3318 323-2394
Web: www.bishopmuseum.org/greenwell
Anderson Japanese Gardens 318 Spring Creek Rd ... Rockford IL 61107 815-229-9390 229-9391
Web: www.andersongardens.org
Anna Scripps Whitcomb Conservatory Belle Isle Park ... Detroit MI 48207 313-852-4064 852-4074
Annmarie Garden 13480 Dowell Rd PO Box 99 ... Dowell MD 20629 410-326-4640 326-4887
Web: www.annmariegarden.org
Applewood - The CS Mott Estate 1400 E Kearsley St ... Flint MI 48503 810-233-3031 232-6937
Arboretum The Arboretum Rd University of Guelph ... Guelph ON N1G2W1 519-824-4120 763-9598
Web: www.uoguelph.ca/arboretum/
Arboretum at Arizona State University
826 E Apache Blvd PO Box 875112 ... Tempe AZ 85287 480-965-8467 965-9470
Web: www.asu.edu/fm/arboretum.htm
Arboretum of the Barnes Foundation 300 N Latch's Ln ... Merion PA 19066 610-667-0290 664-4026
Web: www.barnesfoundation.org/
Arboretum at California State University Fresno
2351 E Barstow Ave ... Fresno CA 93740 559-278-6930 278-7698
Arboretum at Flagstaff 4001 S Woody Mountain Rd ... Flagstaff AZ 86001 928-774-1442 774-1441
Web: www.thearb.org
Arboretum at Penn State 101 Ferguson Bldg ... University Park PA 16802 814-865-9118 865-3725
Web: www.arboretum.psu.edu
Arboretum at Penn State Erie 5091 Station Rd Glenhill Farmhouse ... Erie PA 16563 814-898-6160 898-6461
Web: www.pserie.psu.edu/aboutPS/arboretum.htm
Arboretum at the University of California Santa Cruz
1156 High St ... Santa Cruz CA 95064 831-427-2998 427-1524
Web: www2.ucsc.edu/arboretum
Arizona-Sonora Desert Museum 2021 N Kinney Rd ... Tucson AZ 85743 520-883-1380 883-2500
Web: www.desertmuseum.org
Arnold Arboretum of Harvard University 125 Arborway ... Jamaica Plain MA 02130 617-524-1718 524-1418
Web: www.arboretum.harvard.edu
Assiniboine Park Conservatory 15 Conservatory Dr ... Winnipeg MB R3P2N5 204-986-5537 986-6761
Atlanta Botanical Garden 1345 Piedmont Ave NE ... Atlanta GA 30309 404-876-5859 876-7472
Web: www.atlantabotanicalgarden.org
Awbury Arboretum & Historic Estate
1 Awbury Rd Francis Cope House ... Philadelphia PA 19138 215-849-2855 849-0213
Web: www.awbury.org
Bancroft Ruth Garden 1500 Bancroft Rd PO Box 30845 ... Walnut Creek CA 94598 925-210-9663
Web: www.ruthbancroftgarden.org
Bartlett Arboretum & Gardens 151 Brookdale Rd ... Stamford CT 06903 203-322-6971 595-9168
Web: bartlett.arboretum.uconn.edu
Bayard Cutting Arboretum State Park PO Box 466 ... Oakdale NY 11769 631-581-1002
Web: nysparks.state.ny.us/parks/info.asp?parkId=43
Beal WJ Botanical Garden
Michigan State University 412 Olds Hall ... East Lansing MI 48824 517-355-9582 432-1090
Web: www.cpp.msu.edu/beal
Beardsley Zoo 1875 Noble Ave ... Bridgeport CT 06610 203-394-6565 394-6566
Web: www.beardsleyzoo.org
Bellagio Conservatory & Botanical Gardens
3600 S Las Vegas Blvd ... Las Vegas NV 89109 702-693-7111 693-8508
Web: www.bellagiolasvegas.com/pages/attrac_highgardens.asp
Bellevue Botanical Garden 12001 Main St ... Bellevue WA 98005 425-452-2750 452-2748
Web: www.bellevuebotanical.org
Bellingrath Gardens & Home 12401 Bellingrath Garden Rd ... Theodore AL 36582 251-973-2217 973-0540
TF: 800-247-8420 ■ *Web:* www.bellingrath.org

Phone Fax

Belmont - The Gari Melchers Estate & Memorial Gallery
224 Washington St ... Fredericksburg VA 22405 540-654-1015 654-1785
Web: www.umw.edu/belm/
Berkshire Botanical Garden Rt 102 & 183 PO Box 826 ... Stockbridge MA 01262 413-298-3926 298-4897
Web: www.berkshirebotanical.org
Bernheim Arboretum & Research Forest
State Hwy 245 PO Box 130 ... Clermont KY 40110 502-955-8512 955-4039
Web: www.bernheim.org
Berry Botanic Garden 11505 SW Summerville Ave ... Portland OR 97219 503-636-4112 636-7496
Web: www.berrybot.org
Better Homes & Gardens Test Garden 15th St & Grand Ave ... Des Moines IA 50309 515-284-3994
Betty Ford Alpine Gardens 183 Gore Creek Dr ... Vail CO 81657 970-476-0103 476-1685
Web: www.bettyfordalpinegardens.org
Bicentennial Gardens 1105 Hobbs Rd ... Greensboro NC 27410 336-297-4162 299-7940
Bickelhaupt Arboretum 340 S 14th St ... Clinton IA 52732 563-242-4771 243-0392
Web: www.bickarb.org
Birmingham Botanical Gardens 2612 Lane Park Rd ... Birmingham AL 35223 205-414-3900 414-3906
Web: www.bbgardens.org
Blithewold Mansion Gardens & Arboretum 101 Ferry Rd ... Bristol RI 02809 401-253-2707 253-0412
Web: www.blithewold.org
Bloedel Floral Conservatory
33rd Ave & Cambie St Queen Elizabeth Park ... Vancouver BC V5X1C5 604-257-8584 257-2412
Web: www.city.vancouver.bc.ca/parks/parks/bloedel/index.htm
Bloedel Reserve 7571 NE Dolphin Dr ... Bainbridge Island WA 98110 206-842-7631 842-8970
Web: www.bloedelreserve.org
Boerner Botanical Gardens 9400 Boerner Dr ... Hales Corners WI 53130 414-525-5601 525-5610
Web: www.boernerbotanicalgardens.org
Botanic Garden of Smith College Smith College ... Northampton MA 01063 413-585-2740 585-2744
Web: www.smith.edu/garden
Botanica The Wichita Gardens 701 Amidon St ... Wichita KS 67203 316-264-0448 264-0587
Web: www.botanica.org
Botanical Garden of the Ozarks
44 N School Ave PO Box 3079 ... Fayetteville AR 72702 479-750-2620 443-6665
Web: www.bgso.org
Botanical Gardens at Asheville 151 WT Weaver Blvd ... Asheville NC 28804 828-252-5190
Web: www.ashevillebotanicalgardens.org
Botanical Research Institute of Texas 509 Pecan St ... Fort Worth TX 76102 817-332-4441 332-4112
Web: www.brit.org
Bowman's Hill Wildflower Preserve
1635 River Rd PO Box 685 ... New Hope PA 18938 215-862-2924 862-1846
Web: www.bhwp.org
Boxerwood Gardens 963 Ross Rd ... Lexington VA 24450 540-463-2697 463-1953
Web: www.boxerwood.org
Boyce Thompson Southwestern Arboretum 37615 Hwy 60 ... Superior AZ 85273 520-689-2632 689-5858
Web: ag.arizona.edu/bta/
Brenton Arboretum 2629 Palo Cir ... Dallas Center IA 50063 515-992-4211 992-3303
Web: www.thebrentonarboretum.org
Bright Carleen Arboretum 9001 Bosque Blvd ... Woodway TX 76712 254-399-9204 399-9216
Brookgreen Gardens 1931 Brookgreen Dr ... Murrells Inlet SC 29576 843-235-6000 235-6039
TF: 800-849-1931 ■ *Web:* www.brookgreen.org
Brooklyn Botanic Garden 1000 Washington Ave ... Brooklyn NY 11225 718-623-7200 857-2430
Web: www.bbg.org
Brookside Gardens 1800 Glenallan Ave ... Wheaton MD 20902 301-962-1400
Web: www.mc-mncppc.org/parks/brookside
Buffalo & Erie County Botanical Gardens 2655 S Park Ave ... Buffalo NY 14218 716-827-1584
Web: www.buffalogardens.com
Butchart Gardens 800 Benvenuto Ave ... Brentwood Bay BC V8M1J8 250-652-4422 652-7751
TF: 866-652-4422 ■ *Web:* www.butchartgardens.bc.ca
Cabrillo College Environmental Horticultural Center & Botanic Gardens 6500 Soquel Dr ... Aptos CA 95003 831-477-5671
Web: www.cabrillo.edu/academics/horticulture/hortcenterhome.html
Calgary Zoo Botanical Garden & Prehistoric Park
1300 Zoo Rd NE ... Calgary AB T2E7V6 403-232-9300 237-7582
TF: 800-661-1678 ■ *Web:* www.calgaryzoo.ab.ca
Callaway Gardens PO Box 2000 ... Pine Mountain GA 31822 706-663-2281 663-6812
TF: 800-225-5292 ■ *Web:* www.callawaygardens.com
Camden Children's Garden 3 Riverside Dr ... Camden NJ 08103 856-365-8733 365-9750
Web: www.camdenchildrensgarden.org
Cape Fear Botanical Garden 536 N Eastern Blvd ... Fayetteville NC 28301 910-486-0221 486-4209
Web: www.capefearbg.org
Carleen Bright Arboretum 9001 Bosque Blvd ... Woodway TX 76712 254-399-9204 399-9216
Carrier Edith J Arboretum 181 Patterson St MSC 7015 ... Harrisonburg VA 22807 540-568-3194 568-7111
Web: www.jmu.edu/arboretum
Casa del Herrero 1387 E Valley Rd ... Santa Barbara CA 93108 805-565-5653 969-2371
Web: www.casadelherrero.com
Cathedral Church of Saint Peter & Saint Paul
3101 Wisconsin Ave NW ... Washington DC 20016 202-537-6200
TF: 800-622-6304 ■ *Web:* www.cathedral.org/cathedral
Cave Hill Cemetery & Arboretum 701 Baxter Ave ... Louisville KY 40204 502-451-5630 451-5655
Web: www.cavehillcemetery.com
CDRI (Chihuahuan Desert Research Institute)
43869 State Hwy 118 PO Box 905 ... Fort Davis TX 79734 432-364-2499 364-2686
Web: www.cdri.org
Cedar Crest College 100 College Dr ... Allentown PA 18104 610-437-4471 606-4647*
**Fax:* Admissions ■ *TF Admissions:* 800-360-1222 ■ *Web:* www.cedarcrest.edu
Cedar Valley Arboretum & Botanic Gardens 3641 Kimball Ave ... Waterloo IA 50702 319-226-4966 226-4966
Centennial Conservatory 1601 Dease St ... Thunder Bay ON P7E6S4 807-622-7036 622-7602
Chanticleer Garden 786 Church Rd ... Wayne PA 19087 610-687-4163 293-0149
Web: www.chanticleergarden.org
Charlotte Botanical Gardens & Sculpture Garden
Biology Dept University of North Carolina Charlotte 9201 University City Blvd ... Charlotte NC 28223 704-687-2364 687-3128
Web: gardens.uncc.edu
Chatham County Botanical Garden 1388 Eisenhower Dr ... Savannah GA 31406 912-356-3591
Cheekwood Museum of Art & Botanical Garden
1200 Forrest Park Dr ... Nashville TN 37205 615-356-8000 353-0919
Web: www.cheekwood.org
Chesapeake Arboretum 624 Oak Grove Rd ... Chesapeake VA 23328 757-382-7060
Web: www.chesapeakearboretum.com
Cheyenne Botanic Gardens 710 S Lions Park Dr ... Cheyenne WY 82001 307-637-6458 637-6453
Web: botanic.org
Chicago Botanic Garden 1000 Lake Cook Rd ... Glencoe IL 60022 847-835-5440 835-4484
Web: www.chicago-botanic.org
Chihuahuan Desert Research Institute (CDRI)
43869 State Hwy 118 PO Box 905 ... Fort Davis TX 79734 432-364-2499 364-2686
Web: www.cdri.org
Chimney Rock Park Hwy 64/74A PO Box 39 ... Chimney Rock NC 28720 828-625-9611 625-9610
TF: 800-277-9611 ■ *Web:* www.chimneyrockpark.com
Cincinnati Zoo & Botanical Garden 3400 Vine St ... Cincinnati OH 45220 513-281-4701 559-7790
TF: 800-944-4776 ■ *Web:* www.cincyzoo.org
Clark County Museum 1830 S Boulder Hwy ... Henderson NV 89015 702-455-7955 455-7948
Cleveland Botanical Garden 11030 East Blvd ... Cleveland OH 44106 216-721-1600 721-2056
TF: 888-853-7091 ■ *Web:* www.cbgarden.org
Cleveland Metroparks Zoo 3900 Wildlife Way ... Cleveland OH 44109 216-661-6500 661-3312
Web: www.clemetzoo.com
Clovis Botanical Garden 945 N Clovis Ave ... Clovis CA 93611 559-299-0392
Web: www.clovisbotanicalgarden.org

				Phone	Fax
Coastal Maine Botanical Gardens 1 Alice West Dr PO Box 234 *Web:* www.mainegardens.org	Boothbay	ME	04537	207-633-4333	633-2366
Colasanti's Tropical Gardens PO Box 40 *Web:* www.colasanti.com	Ruthven	ON	N0P2G0	519-326-3287	322-2302
Columbus Topiary Garden 480 E Town St *Web:* www.topiarygarden.org	Columbus	OH	43215	614-645-0197	
Como Zoo & Conservatory 1225 Estabrook Dr *Web:* www.ci.stpaul.mn.us/depts/parks/comopark/	Saint Paul	MN	55103	651-487-8200	487-8254
Connecticut College Arboretum 270 Mohegan Ave Box 5201 *Web:* camel2.conncoll.edu/ccrec/greennet/arbo	New London	CT	06320	860-439-5020	
Conservatory of Flowers San Francisco Recreation & Park Dept 501 Stanyan St Golden Gate Park *Web:* www.conservatoryofflowers.org	San Francisco	CA	94117	415-666-7077	666-7257
Conservatory Garden 5th Ave & 105th St Central Park *Web:* www.centralparknyc.org	New York	NY	10029	212-860-1382	860-1388
Cooley Gardens 225 W Main St *Web:* www.cooleygardens.org	Lansing	MI	48933	517-483-4277	
Cornell Plantations 1 Plantations Rd *Web:* www.plantations.cornell.edu	Ithaca	NY	14850	607-255-3020	255-2404
Cox Arboretum & Gardens MetroPark 6733 Springboro Pike *Web:* www.coxarboretum.org	Dayton	OH	45449	937-434-9005	434-4361
Crosby Arboretum 370 Ridge Rd *Web:* www.msstate.edu/dept/crec/camain.html	Picayune	MS	39466	601-799-2311	799-2372
Crow Canyon Gardens 105 Park Pl	San Ramon	CA	94583	925-314-0362	314-9825
Cullen Gardens & Miniature Village 300 Taunton Rd W *Web:* www.cullengardens.com	Whitby	ON	L1T2A9	905-668-6606	668-0510
CW Post Community Arboretum Long Island University 720 Northern Blvd *Web:* www.cwpost.liunet.edu/cwis/cwp/arboretum	Brookville	NY	11548	516-299-2340	
Cylburn Arboretum 4915 Greenspring Ave *Web:* www.cylburnassociation.org	Baltimore	MD	21209	410-396-0180	367-8039
Dallas Arboretum & Botanical Garden 8525 Garland Rd *Web:* www.dallasarboretum.org	East Dallas	TX	75218	214-515-6500	515-6522
Daniel Stowe Botanical Garden 6500 S New Hope Rd *Web:* www.stowegarden.org	Belmont	NC	28012	704-825-4490	829-1240
Dawes Arboretum 7770 Jacksontown Rd SE *TF:* 800-443-2937 ■ *Web:* www.dawesarb.org	Newark	OH	43056	740-323-2355	323-4058
Delaware Center for Horticulture 1810 N DuPont St *Web:* www.dehort.org	Wilmington	DE	19806	302-658-6262	658-6267
Denver Botanic Gardens 1005 York St *Web:* www.botanicgardens.org	Denver	CO	80206	720-865-3500	865-3713
Des Moines Botanical Center 909 Robert D Ray Dr *Web:* www.botanicalcenter.com	Des Moines	IA	50316	515-323-6291	323-6275
Descanso Gardens 1418 Descanso Dr *Web:* www.descanso.com	La Canada	CA	91011	818-949-4200	790-3291
Desert Botanical Garden 1201 N Galvin Pkwy *Web:* www.dbg.org	Phoenix	AZ	85008	480-941-1225	481-8124
Devonian Botanic Garden University of Alberta *Web:* www.devonian.ualberta.ca	Edmonton	AB	T6G2E1	780-987-3054	987-4141
Devonian Gardens 317 7th Ave SW *Web:* www.calgary.ca/parks/devonian	Calgary	AB	T2P2Y9	403-221-3782	
Dixon Gallery & Gardens 4339 Park Ave *Web:* www.dixon.org/	Memphis	TN	38117	901-761-5250	682-0943
Donald M Kendall Sculpture Gardens at PepsiCo Headquarters 700 Anderson Hill Rd	Purchase	NY	10577	914-253-2082	
Dothan Area Botanical Gardens 5130 Headland Ave *Web:* www.dabg.com	Dothan	AL	36303	334-793-3224	793-5275
Dow Gardens 1018 W Main St *TF:* 800-362-4874 ■ *Web:* www.dowgardens.org	Midland	MI	48640	989-631-2677	631-0675
Dr Sun Yat-Sen Classical Chinese Garden 578 Carrall St *Web:* www.vancouverchinesegarden.com	Vancouver	BC	V6B5K2	604-662-3207	682-4008
Dubuque Arboretum & Botanical Gardens 3800 Arboretum Dr *Web:* www.dubuquearboretum.com	Dubuque	IA	52001	563-556-2100	556-2443
Duke Farms 80 US Rt 206 S *Web:* fdncenter.org/grantmaker/dorisduke	Hillsborough	NJ	08844	908-722-3700	
Dumbarton Oaks 1703 32nd St NW *Web:* www.doaks.org	Washington	DC	20007	202-339-6401	339-6419
Dyck Arboretum of the Plains 177 W Hickory St *Web:* www.dyckarboretum.org	Hesston	KS	67062	620-327-8127	327-3151
Earl Burns Miller Japanese Garden 1250 Bellflower Blvd *Web:* www.csulb.edu/~jgarden	Long Beach	CA	90840	562-985-8885	985-4893
East Tennessee State University Arboretum Dept of Biological Studies Box 70703 *Web:* www.etsu.edu/arboretum	Johnson City	TN	37614	423-439-8635	
East Texas Arboretum 1601 Patterson Rd *Web:* www.eastexasarboretum.org	Athens	TX	75751	903-675-5630	675-1618
Edith J Carrier Arboretum & Botanical Gardens 181 Patterson St MSC 7015 *Web:* www.jmu.edu/arboretum	Harrisonburg	VA	22807	540-568-3194	568-7111
Elizabeth Gamble Garden 1431 Waverley St *Web:* www.gamblegarden.org	Palo Alto	CA	94301	650-329-1356	329-1688
Elizabeth Park Rose Gardens 150 Walbridge St *Web:* www.elizabethpark.org/rose_garden.htm	West Hartford	CT	06102	860-722-6541	
Elizabethan Gardens 1411 National Pk Dr *Web:* www.elizabethangardens.org	Manteo	NC	27954	252-473-3234	473-3244
Enid A Haupt Glass Garden 400 E 34th St NYU Medical Center Rusk Institute of Rehabilitative Medicine	New York	NY	10016	212-263-6058	263-2091
Erie Zoo 423 W 38th St *Web:* www.eriezoo.org	Erie	PA	16508	814-864-4091	864-1140
FA Seiberling Nature Realm 1828 Smith Rd	Akron	OH	44313	330-865-8065	865-8070
Fairchild Tropical Botanic Garden 10901 Old Cutler Rd *Web:* www.ftg.org	Coral Gables	FL	33156	305-667-1651	661-8953
Fell Arboretum at Illinois State University Campus Box 9000 *Web:* www.ilstu.edu/depts/arboretum	Normal	IL	61790	309-438-3632	438-2089
Fellows Riverside Gardens 123 McKinley Ave	Youngstown	OH	44509	330-740-7116	740-7128
Fernwood Botanical Gardens & Nature Preserve 13988 Range Line Rd *Web:* www.fernwoodbotanical.org	Niles	MI	49120	269-695-6491	695-6688
Fetzer Vineyards 13601 Old River Rd *TF:* 800-846-8637 ■ *Web:* www.fetzer.com	Hopland	CA	95449	707-744-1250	744-7605
Filoli Formal Garden 86 Canada Rd *Web:* www.filoli.org	Woodside	CA	94062	650-364-8300	367-0724
Flamingo Gardens 3750 S Flamingo Rd *Web:* www.flamingogardens.org	Davie	FL	33330	954-473-2955	473-1738
Florida Botanical Gardens 12175 125th St N *Web:* www.flbg.org	Largo	FL	33774	727-582-2100	582-2149
Foellinger-Freimann Botanical Conservatory 1100 S Calhoun St *Web:* www.botanicalconservatory.org	Fort Wayne	IN	46802	260-427-6440	427-6450
For-Mar Nature Preserve & Arboretum 2142 N Genesee Rd *Web:* www.geneseecountyparks.org/formar.htm	Burton	MI	48509	810-789-8567	743-0541
Forestiere Underground Gardens 5021 W Shaw Ave *Web:* www.undergroundgardens.com	Fresno	CA	93722	559-271-0734	
Fort Worth Botanic Garden 3220 Botanic Garden Blvd *Web:* www.fwbg.com	Fort Worth	TX	76107	817-871-7686	871-7638
Foster Botanical Garden 50 N Vineyard Blvd *Web:* www.honolulu.gov/parks/hbg/fbg.htm	Honolulu	HI	96817	808-522-7066	522-7050
Founders Memorial Garden University of Georgia School of Environmental Design Caldwell Hall *Web:* www.uga.edu/gardenclub/Founder.html	Athens	GA	30602	706-542-8972	
Franklin Park Conservatory & Botanical Garden 1777 E Broad St *TF:* 800-241-7275 ■ *Web:* www.fpconservatory.org	Columbus	OH	43203	614-645-8733	645-5921
Frederik Meijer Gardens & Sculpture Park 1000 East Beltline Ave NE *TF:* 888-974-1580 ■ *Web:* www.meijergardens.org	Grand Rapids	MI	49525	616-957-1580	957-5792
Frelinghuysen Arboretum 53 E Hanover Ave PO Box 1295 *Web:* parks.morris.nj.us/parks/frelarbmain.htm	Morristown	NJ	07962	973-326-7600	644-9627
Fruit & Spice Park 24801 SW 187th Ave *Web:* www.floridaplants.com/fruit&spice/	Homestead	FL	33031	305-247-5727	245-3369
Fullerton Arboretum 1900 Associated Rd *Web:* www.arboretum.fullerton.edu	Fullerton	CA	92831	714-278-3579	278-7066
Gamble Elizabeth Garden 1431 Waverley St *Web:* www.gamblegarden.org	Palo Alto	CA	94301	650-329-1356	329-1688
Ganna Walska Lotusland 695 Ashley Rd *Web:* www.lotusland.org	Santa Barbara	CA	93108	805-969-3767	969-4423
Gardens of the American Rose Center 8877 Jefferson-Paige Rd *TF:* 800-637-6534 ■ *Web:* www.ars.org/ARC/gardens.htm	Shreveport	LA	71119	318-938-5402	938-5405
Gardens on Spring Creek 2145 S Centre Ave *Web:* fcgov.com/horticulture	Fort Collins	CO	80526	970-416-2486	416-2280
Garfield Park Conservatory 300 N Central Park Ave *Fax Area Code: 773 ■ *Web:* www.garfield-conservatory.org	Chicago	IL	60624	312-746-5100	638-1777*
Garvan Woodland Gardens 550 Arkridge Rd PO Box 22240 *TF:* 800-366-4664 ■ *Web:* www.garvangardens.org	Hot Springs	AR	71903	501-262-9300	262-9301
George Eastman House & Gardens 900 East Ave *Web:* www.eastmanhouse.org	Rochester	NY	14607	585-271-3361	271-3970
George L Luthy Memorial Botanical Gardens 2218 N Prospect Rd	Peoria	IL	61603	309-686-3362	685-6240
Georgeson Botanical Garden 117 W Tanana Dr University of Alaska Fairbanks Campus *Web:* www.uaf.edu/salrm/gbg	Fairbanks	AK	99775	907-474-7034	474-1841
Georgia Golf Hall of Fame Botanical Gardens 1 11th St *TF:* 888-874-4443 ■ *Web:* www.gghf.org	Augusta	GA	30901	706-724-4443	724-4428
Georgia Southern Botanical Garden 1505 Bland Ave PO Box 8039 *Web:* welcome.georgiasouthern.edu/garden	Statesboro	GA	30460	912-871-1149	871-1777
Getty J Paul Museum 1200 Getty Center Dr *Fax: Hum Res ■ *Web:* www.getty.edu/museum	Los Angeles	CA	90049	310-440-7300	440-7720*
Gibraltar Estate & Gardens 1405 Greenhill Ave *Web:* www.preservationde.org/gibraltar	Wilmington	DE	19806	302-651-9617	651-9603
Gifford Arboretum 1301 Memorial Dr Rm 190 University of Miami *Web:* www.bio.miami.edu/arboretum/	Coral Gables	FL	33124	305-284-5364	284-3039
Gilroy Gardens Family Theme Park 3050 Hecker Pass Hwy *Web:* www.gilroygardens.org	Gilroy	CA	95020	408-840-7100	
Ginter Lewis Botanical Garden 1800 Lakeside Ave *Web:* www.lewisginter.org	Richmond	VA	23228	804-262-9887	262-6329
Glacier Gardens Rainforest Adventure 7600 Glacier Hwy *Web:* www.glaciergardens.com	Juneau	AK	99801	907-790-3377	790-3907
Goodstay Gardens 2600 Pennsylvania Ave University of Delaware Goodstay Center	Wilmington	DE	19806	302-573-4450	652-0116
Goodwood Museum & Gardens 1600 Miccosukee Rd *Web:* www.goodwoodmuseum.org	Tallahassee	FL	32308	850-877-4202	877-3090
Graver Arboretum of Muhlenberg College 1581 Bushkill Center Rd *Web:* www.muhlenberg.edu/cultural/graver	Bath	PA	18014	610-759-3132	
Greater Philadelphia Gardens 100 E Northwestern Ave c/o Morris Arboretum *Web:* www.greaterphiladelphiagardens.org	Philadelphia	PA	19118	215-247-5777	
Green Bay Botanical Garden 2600 Larsen Rd PO Box 12644 *TF:* 877-355-4224 ■ *Web:* www.gbbg.org	Green Bay	WI	54307	920-490-9457	490-9461
Green Spring Gardens Park 4603 Green Spring Rd *Web:* www.greenspring.org	Alexandria	VA	22312	703-642-5173	642-8095
Greensboro Arboretum 401 Asland Dr	Greensboro	NC	27403	336-373-2199	292-2824
Grotto The 8840 NE Skidmore St *Web:* www.thegrotto.org	Portland	OR	97220	503-254-7371	254-7948
Guadalupe River Park & Gardens 438 Coleman Ave *Web:* www.grpg.org	San Jose	CA	95110	408-298-7657	288-9048
Halifax Public Gardens 5711 Sackville *Web:* www.halifaxpublicgardens.ca	Halifax	NS	B3H2C9	902-490-6509	435-8327
Harry P Leu Gardens 1920 N Forest Ave *Web:* www.leugardens.org	Orlando	FL	32803	407-246-2620	246-2849
Haverford College Arboretum 370 Lancaster Ave *Web:* www.haverford.edu/Arboretum/home.htm	Haverford	PA	19041	610-896-1101	896-1095
Hawaii Tropical Botanical Garden 27-717 Old Mamalahoa Hwy PO Box 80 *Web:* www.hawaiigarden.com	Papaikou	HI	96781	808-964-5233	964-1338
Heathcote Botanical Gardens 210 Savannah Rd *Web:* www.heathcotebotanicalgardens.org	Fort Pierce	FL	34982	772-464-4672	489-2748
Helen Avalynne Tawes Garden 580 Taylor Ave *TF:* 800-830-3974 ■ *Web:* www.dnr.state.md.us/publiclands/tawesgarden.html	Annapolis	MD	21401	410-260-8189	260-8191
Hendricks Park & Gardens 1800 Skyline Blvd *Web:* www.ci.eugene.or.us/parks/hendricks	Eugene	OR	97403	541-682-5324	
Henry Schmieder Arboretum 700 E Butler Ave Delaware Valley College *Web:* www.devalcol.edu/Arboretum	Doylestown	PA	18901	215-489-2283	
Hershey Gardens 170 Hotel Rd *Web:* www.hersheygardens.org	Hershey	PA	17033	717-534-3492	533-8289
Hidden Lake Gardens 6214 W Monroe Rd M-50 *Web:* hiddenlakegardens.msu.edu/	Tipton	MI	49287	517-431-2060	431-9148
Highline Garden 13735 24th Ave S *Web:* www.highlinegarden.org	SeaTac	WA	98168	206-391-4003	
Highstead Arboretum 127 Lonetown Rd PO Box 1097 *Web:* pages.prodigy.net/highsteadarboretum	Redding	CT	06875	203-938-8809	938-0343
Hill Polly Arboretum 809 State Rd PO Box 561 *Web:* www.pollyhillarboretum.org	West Tisbury	MA	02575	508-693-9426	693-5772
Hilltop Arboretum 11855 Highland Rd *Web:* www.lsu.edu/hilltop	Baton Rouge	LA	70810	225-767-6916	768-7740
Hilltop Garden & Nature Center 2301 E 10th St Indiana University Campus *Web:* www.indiana.edu/~hilltop	Bloomington	IN	47405	812-855-2799	855-3998
Hillwood Museum & Gardens 4155 Linnean Ave NW *TF:* 877-445-5966 ■ *Web:* www.hillwoodmuseum.org	Washington	DC	20008	202-686-8500	966-7846
Historic Bartram's Garden 54th St & Lindbergh Blvd *Web:* www.bartramsgarden.org	Philadelphia	PA	19143	215-729-5281	729-1047
Historic Bok Sanctuary 1151 Tower Blvd *Web:* www.boktower.org	Lake Wales	FL	33853	863-676-1408	676-6770

	City	State	ZIP	Phone	Fax
Hofstra University Arboretum 129 Hofstra University	Hempstead	NY	11549	516-463-5924	463-5302
Web: www.hofstra.edu/COM/Arbor					
Holden Arboretum 9500 Sperry Rd	Kirtland	OH	44094	440-946-4400	602-3857
Web: www.holdenarb.org					
Holmdel Arboretum 4000 Kozloski Rd PO Box 5033	Freehold	NJ	07728	732-431-7910	866-3558
Honolulu Botanical Gardens 50 N Vineyard Blvd	Honolulu	HI	96817	808-522-7060	522-7050
Web: www.honolulu.gov/parks/hbg/					
Hoyt Arboretum 4000 SW Fairview Blvd	Portland	OR	97221	503-865-8733	823-4213
Web: www.hoytarboretum.org					
Hudson Gardens & Event Center 6115 S Santa Fe Dr	Littleton	CO	80120	303-797-8565	797-8647
Web: www.hudsongardens.org					
Humber Arboretum 205 Humber College Blvd	Toronto	ON	M9W5L7	416-675-6622	675-6187
Web: www.humberarboretum.on.ca					
Humboldt Botanical Gardens PO Box 6117	Eureka	CA	95502	707-442-5139	442-6634
Web: www.hbgf.org					
Huntington Library-Art Collections & Botanical Gardens					
1151 Oxford Rd	San Marino	CA	91108	626-405-2100	405-0225
Web: www.huntington.org					
Huntington Museum of Art Inc 2033 McCoy Rd	Huntington	WV	25701	304-529-2701	529-7447
Web: www.hmoa.org					
Huntsville Botanical Garden 4747 Bob Wallace Ave	Huntsville	AL	35805	256-830-4447	830-5314
TF: 877-930-4447 ■ *Web:* www.hsvbg.org					
Hywet Stan Hall & Gardens 714 N Portage Path	Akron	OH	44403	330-836-5533	836-2680
TF: 888-836-5533 ■ *Web:* www.stanhywet.org					
Idaho Botanical Garden 2355 N Penitentiary Rd	Boise	ID	83712	208-343-8649	343-3601
TF: 877-527-8233 ■ *Web:* www.idahobotanicalgarden.org					
Inniswood Metro Gardens 940 S Hempstead Rd	Westerville	OH	43081	614-895-6216	895-6352
Web: www.inniswood.org					
International Peace Garden Hwy 10 S PO Box 419	Boissevain	MB	R0K0E0	204-534-2510	263-3169*
**Fax Area Code:* 701 ■ *TF:* 888-432-6733 ■ *Web:* www.peacegarden.com					
International Peace Garden Rt 1 Box 116	Dunseith	ND	58329	701-263-4390	263-3169
TF: 888-432-6733 ■ *Web:* www.peacegarden.com					
Iowa Arboretum 1875 Peach Ave	Madrid	IA	50156	515-795-3360	795-2619
J Paul Getty Museum 1200 Getty Center Dr	Los Angeles	CA	90049	310-440-7300	440-7720*
**Fax:* Hum Res ■ *Web:* www.getty.edu/museum					
James Madison's Montpelier					
11407 Constitution Hwy	Montpelier Station	VA	22957	540-672-2728	672-0411
Web: www.montpelier.org					
Japanese Garden 611 SW Kingston Ave	Portland	OR	97201	503-223-4070	223-8303
Web: www.japanesegarden.com					
JC Raulston Arboretum					
North Carolina State University PO Box 7522	Raleigh	NC	27695	919-513-7457	515-5361
Web: www.ncsu.edu/jcraulstonarboretum/					
Jenkins Arboretum 631 Berwyn Baptist Rd	Devon	PA	19333	610-647-8870	647-6664
Web: www.jenkinsarboretum.org					
JJ Neilson Arboretum					
Ridgetown College University of Guelph 120 Main St E	Ridgetown	ON	N0P2C0	519-674-1500	674-1515
Web: www.ridgetownc.on.ca/jjneilson					
Journey Museum 222 New York St	Rapid City	SD	57701	605-394-6923	394-6940
Web: www.journeymuseum.org					
Jungle Gardens Hwy 329	Avery Island	LA	70513	337-373-6158	369-6524
Jungle Island 1111 Parrot Jungle Trail	Miami	FL	33132	305-400-7000	400-7290
Web: www.jungleisland.com					
Juniper Level Botanic Gardens 9241 Sauls Rd	Raleigh	NC	27603	919-772-4794	662-0370
Web: www.plantdelights.com					
Kalmia Gardens of Coker College 1624 W Carolina Ave	Hartsville	SC	29550	843-383-8145	383-8149
Web: www.coker.edu/kalmia					
KC Irving Environmental Science Centre & Harriet Irving Botanical Gardens Acadia University 32 University Ave PO Box 48	Wolfville	NS	B4P2R6	902-585-5242	585-1034
Web: www.acadiau.ca/KCIrving_Centre/main.html					
Kenilworth Aquatic Gardens 1550 Anacostia Ave NE	Washington	DC	20019	202-426-6905	426-5991
Web: www.nps.gov/nace/keaq/					
Key West Forest & Botanical Garden 5210 College Rd	Key West	FL	33040	305-296-1504	296-2242
Web: www.keywestbotanicalgarden.org					
Kingwood Center 900 Park Ave W	Mansfield	OH	44906	419-522-0211	
Web: www.kingwoodcenter.org					
Klehm Arboretum & Botanical Garden 2701 Clifton Ave	Rockford	IL	61102	815-965-8146	965-5914
TF: 888-419-0782 ■ *Web:* www.klehm.org					
Kruckeberg Botanic Garden 20312 15th Ave NW	Shoreline	WA	98177	206-542-4777	
Web: www.kruckeberg.org					
Ladew Topiary Gardens 3535 Jarettsville Pike	Monkton	MD	21111	410-557-9466	557-7763
Web: www.ladewgardens.com					
Lady Bird Johnson Wildflower Center 4801 LaCrosse Ave	Austin	TX	78739	512-292-4200	292-4627
TF: 877-945-3357 ■ *Web:* www.wildflower.org					
Lake Erie Arboretum at Frontier Park 1650 Norcross Rd	Erie	PA	16510	814-825-1700	825-0775
Web: www.leaferie.org					
Lake Wilderness Arboretum 22520 SE 248th St Box 72	Maple Valley	WA	98038	425-413-2572	
Web: www.lakewildernessarboretum.org					
Lakewold Gardens 12317 Gravelly Lake Dr SW	Lakewood	WA	98499	253-584-4106	584-3021
TF: 888-858-4106 ■ *Web:* www.lakewold.org					
Landis Arboretum 174 Lape Rd PO Box 186	Esperance	NY	12066	518-875-6935	875-6394
Web: www.landisarboretum.org					
Lauritzen Gardens Omaha's Botanical Center 100 Bancroft St	Omaha	NE	68108	402-346-4002	346-8948
Web: www.omahabotanicalgardens.org					
Leach Botanical Garden 6704 SE 122 Ave	Portland	OR	97236	503-823-9503	823-9504
Web: www.portlandparks.org/Gardens/LeachBotanicalGar.htm					
Leila Arboretum 928 W Michigan Ave	Battle Creek	MI	49017	269-969-0270	969-0616
Web: www.leilaarboretumsociety.org					
Lewis Ginter Botanical Garden 1800 Lakeside Ave	Richmond	VA	23228	804-262-9887	262-6329
Web: www.lewisginter.org					
Liberty Forge Arboretum PO Box 1229	Camp Hill	PA	17001	717-795-9880	763-1336
Web: www.libertyforge.net/garden.htm					
Lincoln Botanical Garden & Arboretum					
University of Nebraska 1340 N 17th St	Lincoln	NE	68588	402-472-2679	472-9615
Web: bga.unl.edu					
Living Desert Zoo & Gardens 47900 Portola Ave	Palm Desert	CA	92260	760-346-5694	568-9685
Web: www.livingdesert.org					
Lockerly Arboretum 1534 Irwinton Rd	Milledgeville	GA	31061	478-452-2112	
Web: www.lockerlyarboretum.org					
Locust Grove - Samuel Morse Historic Site					
2683 South Rd	Poughkeepsie	NY	12601	845-454-4500	485-7122
Web: www.morsehistoricsite.org					
Long House Reserve 133 Hands Creek Rd	East Hampton	NY	11937	631-329-3568	329-4299
Web: www.longhouse.org					
Longue Vue House & Gardens 7 Bamboo Rd	New Orleans	LA	70124	504-488-5488	486-7015
Web: www.longuevue.com					
Longwood Gardens 1001 Longwood Rd PO Box 501	Kennett Square	PA	19348	610-388-1000	388-2183
TF: 800-737-5500 ■ *Web:* www.longwoodgardens.com					
Los Angeles County Arboretum & Botanic Garden					
301 N Baldwin Ave	Arcadia	CA	91007	626-821-3222	445-1217
Web: www.arboretum.org					
Los Angeles Zoo & Botanical Gardens 5333 Zoo Dr	Los Angeles	CA	90027	323-644-4200	662-9786
Web: www.lazoo.org					
Lubbock Memorial Arboretum 4111 University Ave	Lubbock	TX	79413	806-797-4520	
Web: lubbockarboretum.org					
Luther Burbank Home & Gardens					
Santa Rosa & Sonoma Aves	Santa Rosa	CA	95404	707-524-5445	543-3139
Web: www.lutherburbank.org					
Mabery Gelvin Botanical Gardens					
506 N Lombard St PO Box 1040	Mahomet	IL	61853	217-586-4630	586-6852
Web: www.ccfpd.org/gardens.htm					
Maclay Alfred B State Gardens 3540 Thomasville Rd	Tallahassee	FL	32309	850-487-4556	487-8808
Web: www.ssnow.com/maclay					
Magnolia Plantation & Gardens 3550 Ashley River Rd	Charleston	SC	29414	843-571-1266	571-5346
TF: 800-367-3517 ■ *Web:* www.magnoliaplantation.com					
Marie Selby Botanical Gardens 811 S Palm Ave	Sarasota	FL	34236	941-366-5731	366-9807
Web: www.selby.org					
Marjorie McNeely Conservatory at Como Park					
1225 Esta Brook Dr	Saint Paul	MN	55103	651-487-8201	
Markham Regional Arboretum 1202 La Vista Ave	Concord	CA	94521	925-681-2968	
Web: home.earthlink.net/~markhamarboretum/					
Marywood University Arboretum 2300 Adams Ave	Scranton	PA	18509	570-348-6218	
Web: www.marywood.edu					
Matthaei Botanical Gardens 1800 N Dixboro Rd	Ann Arbor	MI	48105	734-998-7061	998-6205
Web: www.lsa.umich.edu/mbg					
McCrory Gardens South Dakota State University	Brookings	SD	57007	605-688-5136	
McKee Botanical Garden 350 US Hwy 1	Vero Beach	FL	32962	772-794-0601	794-0602
Web: www.mckeegarden.org					
Meadowlark Botanical Gardens 9750 Meadowlark Gardens Ct	Vienna	VA	22182	703-255-3631	255-2392
Web: www.nvrpa.org/meadowlark.html					
Meijer Frederik Gardens & Sculpture Park					
1000 East Beltline Ave NE	Grand Rapids	MI	49525	616-957-1580	957-5792
TF: 888-974-1580 ■ *Web:* www.meijergardens.org					
Memorial Park Arboretum & Garden 1313 E Witzke Blvd	Appleton	WI	54911	920-993-1900	993-9492
Web: www.the-arb.org					
Memorial University of Newfoundland Botanical Garden					
Memorial University 306 Mt Scio Rd	Saint John's	NL	A1C5S7	709-737-8590	737-8596
Web: www.mun.ca/botgarden					
Memphis Botanic Garden 750 Cherry Rd	Memphis	TN	38117	901-576-4100	576-4100
Web: www.memphisbotanicgarden.com					
Mendocino Coast Botanical Gardens 18220 N Hwy 1	Fort Bragg	CA	95437	707-964-4352	964-3114
Web: www.gardenbythesea.org					
Mepkin Abbey Botanical Garden					
1098 Mepkin Abbey Rd	Moncks Corner	SC	29461	843-761-8509	761-6719
Mercer Arboretum & Botanic Gardens					
22306 Aldine Westfield Rd	Humble	TX	77338	281-443-8731	209-9767
Web: www.hcp4.net/mercer/					
Miami Beach Botanical Garden					
2000 Convention Center Dr	Miami Beach	FL	33139	305-673-7256	
Web: www.miamibeachbotanicalgarden.org					
Minnesota Landscape Arboretum 3675 Arboretum Dr	Chaska	MN	55318	952-443-1400	443-2521
Web: www.arboretum.umn.edu					
Missouri Botanical Garden 4344 Shaw Blvd	Saint Louis	MO	63110	314-577-5100	
TF: 800-642-8842 ■ *Web:* www.mobot.org					
Missouri State Arboretum					
Northwest Missouri State University 800 University Dr	Maryville	MO	64468	660-562-1329	562-1100
Web: www.nwmissouri.edu/arboretum					
Mitchell Park Horticultural Conservatory 524 S Layton Blvd	Milwaukee	WI	53215	414-649-9830	649-8616
Mobile Botanical Gardens 5151 Museum Dr	Mobile	AL	36689	251-342-0555	342-3149
Web: www.mobilebotanicalgardens.org					
Montgomery Botanical Center 11901 Old Cutler Rd	Miami	FL	33156	305-667-3800	661-5984
Web: www.montgomerybotanical.org					
Monticello 931 Thomas Jefferson Pkwy PO Box 316	Charlottesville	VA	22902	434-984-9822	977-7757
Web: www.monticello.org					
Montreal Botanical Garden 4101 Sherbrooke St E	Montreal	QC	H1X2B2	514-872-1452	872-1455
Web: www.ville.montreal.qc.ca/jardin/jardin.htm					
Morris Arboretum of the University of Pennsylvania					
100 E Northwestern Ave	Philadelphia	PA	19118	215-247-5777	
Web: www.business-services.upenn.edu/arboretum/					
Morton Arboretum 4100 Illinois Rt 53	Lisle	IL	60532	630-968-0074	719-2433
Web: www.mortonarb.org					
Morven Museum & Gardens 55 Stockton St	Princeton	NJ	08540	609-924-8144	924-8331
Web: www.historicmorven.org/					
Mount Holyoke College Botanic Garden 50 College St	South Hadley	MA	01075	413-538-2116	538-3243
Web: www.mtholyoke.edu/offices/botan					
Mount Pisgah Arboretum 34901 Frank Parrish Rd	Eugene	OR	97405	541-747-1504	741-4904
Web: members.efn.org/~mtpisgah					
Mount Vernon Gardens 10th & Y Sts	Omaha	NE	68107	402-444-5900	444-4921
Mountain Top Arboretum PO Box 379 Rt 23C	Tannersville	NY	12485	518-589-3903	
Web: www.mtarbor.org					
Mounts Botanical Garden 531 N Military Trail	West Palm Beach	FL	33415	561-233-1749	233-1782
Web: www.mounts.org					
Muttart Conservatory 9626 96A St	Edmonton	AB	T6C4L8	780-496-8755	496-8747
Mynelle Gardens 4736 Clinton Blvd	Jackson	MS	39209	601-960-1894	922-5759
Web: www.city.jackson.ms.us/Visitors/mynelle.htm					
Myriad Botanical Gardens/Crystal Bridge Tropical Conservatory 301 W Reno	Oklahoma City	OK	73102	405-297-3995	297-3620
Web: www.myriadgardens.com					
Naples Botanical Garden 4820 Bayshore Dr	Naples	FL	34112	239-643-7275	649-7306
Web: www.naplesgarden.org					
National Garden 245 1st St SW	Washington	DC	20024	202-226-4083	225-7910
Web: www.nationalgarden.org					
National Tropical Botanical Garden 3530 Papalina Rd	Kalaheo	HI	96741	808-332-7324	332-9765
Web: www.ntbg.org					
Native Plant Center at Westchester Community College					
75 Grasslands Rd	Valhalla	NY	10595	914-606-6600	
Web: www.nativeplantcenter.org					
Nebraska Statewide Arboretum					
University of Nebraska 206 Biochemistry Hall	Lincoln	NE	68583	402-472-2971	472-8095
Web: arboretum.unl.edu					
Neilson JJ Arboretum					
Ridgetown College University of Guelph 120 Main St E	Ridgetown	ON	N0P2C0	519-674-1500	674-1515
Web: www.ridgetownc.on.ca/jjneilson					
New Brunswick Botanical Gardens 33 Principale St	Saint-Jacques	NB	E7B1A3	506-737-5383	737-5389
Web: www.umce.ca/jardin/					
New England Tropical Conservatory PO Box 4715	Bennington	VT	05201	802-447-7419	
Web: www.netrop.org					
New England Wild Flower Society Garden in the Woods					
180 Hemenway Rd	Framingham	MA	01701	508-877-7630	
Web: www.newfs.org					
Niagara Parks Botanical Gardens					
2565 Niagara Pkwy N PO box 150	Niagara Falls	ON	L2E6T2	905-356-8554	356-5488
TF: 877-642-7275 ■ *Web:* niagaraparks.com/horticulture					
Nichols Arboretum					
1610 Washington Heights University of Michigan	Ann Arbor	MI	48104	734-998-9540	998-9536
Web: sitemaker.umich.edu/mbgna					
Nikka Yuko Japanese Garden PO Box 751	Lethbridge	AB	T1J3Z6	403-328-3511	328-0511
Web: www.japanesegarden.ab.ca					
Norfolk Botanical Garden 6700 Azalea Garden Rd	Norfolk	VA	23518	757-441-5830	853-8294
Web: www.nbgs.org					

Phone *Fax*

Normandale Community College Japanese Garden
9700 France Ave S ... Bloomington MN 55431 952-487-8106
Web: www.normandale.mnscu.edu/japanesegarden

North Carolina Arboretum 100 Frederick Law Olmsted Way ... Asheville NC 28806 828-665-2492 665-2371
Web: www.ncarboretum.org

North Carolina Botanical Garden
CB 3375 Totten Center University of North Carolina ... Chapel Hill NC 27599 919-962-0522 962-3531
Web: www.ncbg.unc.edu

Oak Hill & Martha Berry Museum PO Box 490189 ... Mount Berry GA 30149 706-291-1883 802-0902
Web: www.berry.edu/oakhill/index.asp

Oklahoma Botanical Garden & Arboretum
Oklahoma State University Dept of Horticulture 360 Ag Hall ... Stillwater OK 74078 405-744-5415 744-9709
Web: home.okstate.edu/Okstate/dasnr/hort/hortlahome.nsf/toc/obga/

Olbrich Botanical Gardens 3330 Atwood Ave ... Madison WI 53704 608-246-4551 246-4719
Web: www.olbrich.org

Old City Cemetery Museums & Arboretum 401 Taylor St ... Lynchburg VA 24501 434-847-1465 856-2004
Web: www.gravegarden.org

Oldfields - Lilly House & Gardens 4000 Michigan Rd ... Indianapolis IN 46208 317-923-1331 931-1978
Web: www.ima-art.org

Oregon Garden 879 W Main St PO Box 155 ... Silverton OR 97381 503-874-8100 874-8200
TF: 877-674-2733 ■ *Web:* www.oregongarden.org

Overfelt Gardens 2145 McKee Rd ... San Jose CA 95116 408-251-3323 251-2865
Web: www.sanjoseca.gov/prns/regionalparks/og/index.htm

Park & Tilford Gardens 333 Brooksbank Ave Suite 440 ... North Vancouver BC V7J3S8 604-984-8200 984-6099

Philbrook Museum of Art & Gardens 2727 S Rockford Rd ... Tulsa OK 74114 918-749-7941 743-4230
TF: 800-324-7941 ■ *Web:* www.philbrook.org

Phipps Conservatory & Botanical Gardens 1 Schenley Park ... Pittsburgh PA 15213 412-622-6915 665-2368
Web: www.phipps.conservatory.org

Pierre Native Plant Arboretum Izaak Walton Rd ... Pierre SD 57501 605-773-3594 773-4003
TF: 800-228-5254

Pikake Gardens 27537 Villa Sierra Rd ... Valley Center CA 92082 760-749-4819 749-5386
Web: members.cox.net/pikakegardens

Pine Tree State Arboretum 153 Hospital St ... Augusta ME 04330 207-621-0031 621-8245
Web: dir.gardenweb.com/directory/ptsa

Pinecrest Gardens 11000 Red Rd ... Pinecrest FL 33156 305-669-6942 669-6944
Web: www.pinecrest-fl.gov/gardens.htm

Polly Hill Arboretum 809 State Rd PO Box 561 ... West Tisbury MA 02575 508-693-9426 693-5772
Web: www.pollyhillarboretum.org

Polynesian Cultural Center 55-370 Kamehameha Hwy ... Laie HI 96762 808-293-3000 293-3027
TF: 800-367-7060 ■ *Web:* www.polynesia.com

Powell Gardens 1609 NW US Hwy 50 ... Kingsville MO 64061 816-697-2600 697-2619
Web: www.powellgardens.org

Quad City Botanical Center 2525 4th Ave ... Rock Island IL 61201 309-794-0991 794-1572
Web: www.qcgardens.com

Quail Botanical Gardens 230 Quail Gardens Dr ... Encinitas CA 92024 760-436-3036 632-0917
Web: www.qbgardens.com

Quarryhill Botanical Garden
12841 Sonoma Hwy PO Box 232 ... Glen Ellen CA 95442 707-996-3802 996-3198
Web: www.quarryhillbg.org

Queen Elizabeth II Sunken Gardens 2450 McDougall Rd ... Windsor ON N8X3N6 519-253-2300 255-7990

Queens Botanical Garden 43-50 Main St ... Flushing NY 11355 718-886-3800 463-0263
Web: www.queensbotanical.org

Rancho Santa Ana Botanic Garden 1500 N College Ave ... Claremont CA 91711 909-625-8767 626-7670
Web: www.rsabg.org

Raulston JC Arboretum
North Carolina State University PO Box 7522 ... Raleigh NC 27695 919-513-7457 515-5361
Web: www.ncsu.edu/jcraulstonarboretum/

Red Butte Garden & Arboretum
300 Wakara Way University of Utah ... Salt Lake City UT 84108 801-581-4747 585-6491
Web: www.redbuttegarden.org

Reeves-Reed Arboretum 165 Hobart Ave ... Summit NJ 07901 908-273-8787 273-6869
Web: www.reeves-reedarboretum.org

Reflection Riding Arboretum & Botanical Garden
400 Garden Rd ... Chattanooga TN 37419 423-821-9582
Web: www.reflectionriding.org

Reiman Gardens Iowa State University 1407 Elwood Dr ... Ames IA 50011 515-294-2710 294-4817
Web: www.reimangardens.iastate.edu

Reynolda Gardens of Wake Forest University
100 Reynolda Village ... Winston-Salem NC 27106 336-758-5593 758-4132
Web: www.wfu.edu/gardens

Rhododendron Species Botanical Garden
2525 S 336th St PO Box 3798 ... Federal Way WA 98063 253-838-4646 838-4686
Web: www.rhodygarden.org

Rio Grande Botanic Garden 2601 Central Ave NW ... Albuquerque NM 87104 505-764-6200 848-7192
Web: www.cabq.gov/biopark/garden

Riverbanks Zoo & Botanical Garden 500 Wildlife Pkwy ... Columbia SC 29210 803-779-8717 253-6381
Web: www.riverbanks.org

Robert Allerton Park & Conference Center
515 Old Timber Rd ... Monticello IL 61856 217-762-2721 762-3632
Web: www.allerton.uiuc.edu

Rockingham County Botanical Garden 113 North Rd ... Brentwood NH 03833 603-679-5616

Rockwood Mansion Park 610 Shipley Rd ... Wilmington DE 19809 302-761-4340 761-4345
Web: www.co.new-castle.de.us

Rodef Shalom Biblical Botanical Garden 4905 5th Ave ... Pittsburgh PA 15213 412-621-6566

Rotary Gardens 1455 Palmer Dr ... Janesville WI 53545 608-752-3885 752-3853
Web: www.rotarygardens.org

Royal Botanical Gardens 680 Plains Rd W ... Burlington ON L7T4H4 905-527-1158 577-0375
Web: www.rbg.ca

Royal Roads University Botanical Garden 2005 Sooke Rd ... Victoria BC V9B5Y2 250-391-2511

Rutgers Gardens
112 Ryders Ln Cook College/Rutgers University ... New Brunswick NJ 08901 732-932-8453 932-7060
Web: aesop.rutgers.edu/~rugardens

Ruth Bancroft Garden 1500 Bancroft Rd PO Box 30845 ... Walnut Creek CA 94598 925-210-9663
Web: www.ruthbancroftgarden.org

Salisbury University Arboretum 1101 Camden Ave ... Salisbury MD 21801 410-543-6323

San Antonio Botanical Garden & Lucile Halsell Conservatory
555 Funston Pl ... San Antonio TX 78209 210-207-3250 207-3274
Web: www.sabot.org

San Francisco Botanical Garden 9th Ave & Lincoln Way ... San Francisco CA 94122 415-661-1316 661-3539
Web: www.sfbotanicalgarden.org

San Jose Heritage Rose Garden Taylor & Spring Sts ... San Jose CA 95110 408-298-7657 288-9048

San Luis Obispo Botanical Garden PO Box 4957 ... San Luis Obispo CA 93403 805-546-3501
Web: www.slobg.org

Sandhills Horticultural Gardens 3395 Airport Rd ... Pinehurst NC 28374 910-695-3883 695-3894
Web: www.sandhills.cc.nc.us/lsg/hort.html

Santa Barbara Botanic Garden 1212 Mission Canyon Rd ... Santa Barbara CA 93105 805-682-4726 563-0352
Web: www.santabarbarabotanicgarden.org

Sarah P Duke Gardens 426 Anderson St ... Durham NC 27708 919-684-3698 668-3610
Web: www.hr.duke.edu/dukegardens

Sawtooth Botanical Garden PO Box 928 ... Sun Valley ID 83353 208-726-9358 726-5435
Web: www.sbgarden.org

Schedel Arboretum & Gardens
19255 W Portage River South Rd ... Elmore OH 43416 419-862-3182
Web: www.schedel-gardens.org

Schoepfle Garden 12882 Diagonal Rd ... La Grange OH 44050 440-965-7237
Web: www.loraincountymetroparks.com

Phone *Fax*

Schreiner's Iris Gardens 3625 Quinaby Rd NE ... Salem OR 97303 503-393-3232 393-5590
TF: 800-525-2367 ■ *Web:* www.oregonlink.com/iris/index.html

Scott Arboretum of Swarthmore College 500 College Ave ... Swarthmore PA 19081 610-328-8025
Web: www.scottarboretum.org

Secrest Arboretum 1680 Madison Ave ... Wooster OH 44691 330-263-3761
Web: secrest.osu.edu

Selby Marie Botanical Gardens 811 S Palm Ave ... Sarasota FL 34236 941-366-5731 366-9807
Web: www.selby.org

Seymour WW Botanical Conservatory 316 S 'G' St ... Tacoma WA 98405 253-591-5330 627-2192

Shambhala Mountain Center 4921 County Rd 68C ... Red Feather Lakes CO 80545 970-881-2184 881-2909
TF: 888-788-7221 ■ *Web:* www.shambhalamountain.org

Shangri La Botanical Gardens & Nature Center PO Box 1044 ... Orange TX 77630 409-670-9113 670-9341
Web: www.shangrilagardens.org

Sherman Library & Gardens 2647 E Coast Hwy ... Corona del Mar CA 92625 949-673-2261 675-5458
Web: www.slgardens.org

Sherwood Fox Arboretum
University of Western Ontario 110 Staging Bldg ... London ON N6A5B7 519-661-2111
Web: www.uwo.ca/arboretum

Shinzen Japanese Friendship Gardens 7775 N Friant Rd ... Fresno CA 93755 559-621-2900 498-1588
Web: www.shinzenjapanesegarden.org

Sister Mary Grace Burns Arboretum 900 Lakewood Ave ... Lakewood NJ 08701 732-364-2200
Web: www.georgian.edu/arboretum/index.html

Skylands PO Box 302 ... Ringwood NJ 07456 973-962-7527
Web: www.njskylands.com/pkskygar.htm

Slayton Arboretum of Hilsdale College 33 E College St ... Hillsdale MI 49242 517-607-2241
Web: www.hillsdale.edu/arboretum

Sonnenberg Gardens 151 Charlotte St ... Canandaigua NY 14424 585-394-4922 394-2192
Web: www.sonnenberg.org

South Carolina Botanical Garden
102 Garden Trail Clemson University ... Clemson SC 29634 864-656-3405 656-6230
Web: virtual.clemson.edu/groups/scbg

South Coast Botanic Garden
26300 Crenshaw Blvd ... Palos Verdes Peninsula CA 90274 310-544-6815 544-6820
Web: www.palosverdes.com/botanicgardens

South Texas Botanical Gardens & Nature Center
8545 S Staples St ... Corpus Christi TX 78413 361-852-2100 852-7875
Web: stxbot.org

Stan Hywet Hall & Gardens 714 N Portage Path ... Akron OH 44403 330-836-5533 836-2680
TF: 888-836-5533 ■ *Web:* www.stanhywet.org

State Arboretum of Virginia 400 Blandy Farm Ln ... Boyce VA 22620 540-837-1758 837-1523
Web: www.virginia.edu/blandy

State Botanical Garden of Georgia 2450 S Milledge Ave ... Athens GA 30605 706-542-1244 542-3091
Web: www.uga.edu/botgarden

Staten Island Botanical Garden 1000 Richmond Terr ... Staten Island NY 10301 718-273-8200 442-3645
Web: www.sibg.org

Stonecrop Gardens 81 Stonecrop Ln ... Cold Spring NY 10516 845-265-2000 265-2405
Web: www.stonecrop.org

Stranahan Arboretum 4131 Tantara Dr University of Toledo ... Toledo OH 43623 419-841-1007
Web: www.arboretum.utoledo.edu

Sunken Gardens 1825 4th St N ... Saint Petersburg FL 33704 727-551-3100 551-3104
Web: www.stpete.org/fun/parks/sunken.htm

Texas Discovery Gardens 3601 ML King Blvd Fair Park ... Dallas TX 75210 214-428-7476 428-5338
Web: www.texasdiscoverygardens.org

Thompson Boyce Southwestern Arboretum 37615 Hwy 60 ... Superior AZ 85273 520-689-2632 689-5858
Web: ag.arizona.edu/bta/

Tofino Botanical Gardens 1084 Pacific Rim Hwy PO Box 886 ... Tofino BC V0R2Z0 250-725-1220 725-2435
Web: www.tofinobotanicalgardens.com

Tohono Chul Park 7366 N Paseo del Norte ... Tucson AZ 85704 520-742-6455 797-1213
Web: www.tohonochulpark.org

Toledo Botanical Garden 5403 Elmer Dr ... Toledo OH 43615 419-936-2986 936-2987
Web: www.toledogarden.org

Tower Hill Botanic Garden 11 French Dr PO Box 598 ... Boylston MA 01505 508-869-6111 869-0314
Web: www.towerhillbg.org

Tryon Palace Historic Sites & Gardens 610 Pollock St ... New Bern NC 28562 252-514-4900 514-4876
TF: 800-767-1560 ■ *Web:* www.tryonpalace.org

Tucson Botanical Gardens 2150 N Alvernon Way ... Tucson AZ 85712 520-326-9255 324-0166
Web: www.tucsonbotanical.org

Tulsa Garden Center 2435 S Peoria Ave ... Tulsa OK 74114 918-746-5125 746-5128
Web: www.tulsagardencenter.com

Tyler Arboretum 515 Painter Rd ... Media PA 19063 610-566-5431 891-1490
Web: www.tylerarboretum.org

UC Davis Arboretum University of California La Ru Rd ... Davis CA 95616 530-752-4880 752-5796
Web: arboretum.ucdavis.edu

Unbelievable Acres Botanic Gardens
470 63rd Trail N PO Box 2695 ... Palm Beach FL 33480 561-242-1686

University of Alabama Arboretum
4801 Arboretum Way PO Box 870344 ... Tuscaloosa AL 35487 205-553-3278 553-3728
Web: bama.ua.edu/~arbor/

University of Arizona Campus Arboretum PO Box 210036 ... Tucson AZ 85721 520-621-7074 621-7186
Web: arboretum.arizona.edu/index.html

University of British Columbia Botanical Garden & Centre for Plant Research 6804 SW Marine Dr ... Vancouver BC V6T1Z4 604-822-9666 822-2016
Web: www.ubcbotanicalgarden.org

University of California Berkeley Botanical Garden
200 Centennial Dr ... Berkeley CA 94720 510-643-2755 642-5045
Web: botanicalgarden.berkeley.edu

University of California Riverside Botanic Gardens
900 University Ave ... Riverside CA 92521 951-827-4650 784-6962
Web: www.gardens.ucr.edu

University of Chicago Botanic Garden 5555 S Ellis Ave ... Chicago IL 60637 773-702-1700
Web: www.uchicago.edu

University of Delaware Botanic Garden
University of Delaware Plant & Soil Science Dept 152 Townsend Hall ... Newark DE 19716 302-831-2531 831-0605
Web: ag.udel.edu/udbg

University of Idaho Arboretum & Botanical Garden
875 Perimeter Dr PO Box 442281 ... Moscow ID 83844 208-885-6633 885-5748
Web: www.uidaho.edu/arboretum

University of Kentucky Lexington-Fayette Urban County Government Arboretum Dorotha Oatts Visitors Center 500 Alumni Dr ... Lexington KY 40503 859-257-9339 257-6955
Web: www.uky.edu/Arboretum/

University of Missouri Botanic Garden General Services Bldg ... Columbia MO 65211 573-882-4240

University of Rochester Arboretum 612 Wilson Blvd ... Rochester NY 14627 585-273-5627 461-3055
Web: www.facilities.rochester.edu/arboretum

University of South Florida Botanical Gardens
4202 E Fowler Ave ... Tampa FL 33620 813-974-2329 974-2184
Web: www.cas.usf.edu/garden

University of Southern Maine Arboretum 37 College Ave ... Gorham ME 04038 207-780-5443
Web: www.usm.maine.edu/arboretum

University of Tennessee Arboretum 901 S Illinois Ave ... Oak Ridge TN 37830 865-483-3571
Web: forestry.tennessee.edu/arboretum

University of Tennessee Gardens 2431 Joe Johnson Dr ... Knoxville TN 37996 865-974-7324
Web: utgardens.tennessee.edu

University of Wisconsin Arboretum 1207 Seminole Hwy ... Madison WI 53711 608-263-7888 262-5209
Web: wiscinfo.doit.wisc.edu/arboretum

Phone Fax

US Botanic Garden 245 1st St SW Washington DC 20024 202-225-8333 225-1561
Web: www.aoc.gov
US National Arboretum 3501 New York Ave NE Washington DC 20002 202-245-2726 245-4575
Web: www.usna.usda.gov
Utah Botanical Center 4870 Old Main Hill Utah State University Logan UT 84322 435-797-1984
Web: www.usu.edu/ubc
Van Vleck House & Gardens 21 Van Vleck St Montclair NJ 07042 973-744-0837
Web: www.vanvleck.org
Vander Veer Botanical Park 214 W Central Park Davenport IA 52803 563-326-7818 326-7955
Web: www.cityofdavenportiowa.com/leisure/parks/botanical.htm
Vanderbilt University 2305 W End Ave Nashville TN 37203 615-322-7311 343-7765*
**Fax:* Admissions ■ *TF Admissions:* 800-288-0432 ■ *Web:* www.vanderbilt.edu
Vermont Botanical Garden 1100 Dorset St South Burlington VT 05403 802-864-5206
Vines Botanical Gardens 3500 Oak Grove Rd Loganville GA 30052 770-466-7532 466-7854
Web: www.vinesbotanicalgardens.com
Virginia Tech Horticulture Garden
Virginia Tech 301 Saunders Hall Blacksburg VA 24061 540-231-5970
Web: www.hort.vt.edu/VTHG
Waddell Barnes Botanical Gardens
100 College Station Dr Macon State College Macon GA 31206 478-471-2780
Walska Ganna Lotusland 695 Ashley Rd Santa Barbara CA 93108 805-969-3767 969-4423
Web: www.lotusland.org
Washington Park Arboretum 2300 Arboretum Dr E Seattle WA 98112 206-543-8800 325-8893
Web: depts.washington.edu/wpa
Washington Park Botanical Garden 1740 W Fayette Springfield IL 62704 217-753-6228 544-9506
Web: www.springfieldparks.org/garden
Wave Hill W 249th St & Independence Ave Bronx NY 10471 718-549-3200 884-8952
Web: www.wavehill.org
Wegerzyn Gardens MetroPark 1375 E Siebenthaler Ave Dayton OH 45414 937-275-7275 277-6546
Web: www.metroparks.org
Welkinweir 1368 Prizer Rd Pottstown PA 19465 610-469-7543 469-2218
Web: greenvalleys.org/welkinweir.asp
West Virginia Botanic Garden 714 Venture Dr Morgantown WV 26508 304-376-2717
Web: www.wvbg.org
Whitcomb Anna Scripps Conservatory Belle Isle Park Detroit MI 48207 313-852-4064 852-4074
White River Gardens 1200 W Washington St Indianapolis IN 46222 317-630-2001 630-5153
Web: www.whiterivergardens.com
Wing Haven Gardens & Bird Sanctuary 248 Ridgewood Ave Charlotte NC 28209 704-331-0664 331-9368
Web: www.winghavengardens.com
Winterthur Museum & Country Estate 5105 Kennett Pike Winterthur DE 19735 302-888-4600 888-4880
TF: 800-448-3883 ■ *Web:* www.winterthur.org
WJ Beal Botanical Garden
Michigan State University 412 Olds Hall East Lansing MI 48824 517-355-9582 432-1090
Web: www.cpp.msu.edu/beal
Woodland Arboretum 118 Woodland Ave Dayton OH 45409 937-228-3221 222-7259
Web: www.woodlandarboretum.org
Wrigley Memorial & Botanical Garden 125 Claressa Ave Avalon CA 90704 310-510-2595 510-2325
Web: www.catalina.com/memorial.html
WW Seymour Botanical Conservatory 316 S 'G' St Tacoma WA 98405 253-591-5330 627-2192
Wynton M Blount Cultural Park 6000 Vaughn Rd Montgomery AL 36116 334-244-5700 273-9666
Web: www.blountculturalpark.org
Yale University Marsh Botanical Gardens
Yale University Corner of Prospect & Hillside St New Haven CT 06520 203-432-6320
Yat-Sen Dr Sun Classical Chinese Garden 578 Carrall St Vancouver BC V6B5K2 604-662-3207 682-4008
Web: www.vancouverchinesegarden.com
Yew Dell Gardens 6220 Old LaGrange Rd PO Box 1334 Crestwood KY 40014 502-241-4788 241-8338
Web: www.yewdellgardens.org
Zilker Botanical Garden 2220 Barton Springs Rd Austin TX 78746 512-477-8672 481-8253
Web: www.zilkergarden.org
ZooMontana & Botanical Gardens 2100 S Shiloh Rd Billings MT 59106 406-652-8100 652-9281
Web: www.zoomontana.org

BOTTLES - GLASS

SEE Glass Jars & Bottles p. 1691

98 BOTTLES - PLASTICS

Phone Fax

Abbott Industries Inc 1-11 Morris St Paterson NJ 07501 973-345-1116 345-9154
Alcoa Kama Inc 600 Dietrich Ave Hazleton PA 18201 570-455-2020 455-0178
Web: www.alcoa.com/kama/
Alpha Packaging 1555 Page Industrial Blvd Saint Louis MO 63132 314-427-4300 427-5445
TF: 800-421-4772 ■ *Web:* www.alphap.com
Amcor PET Packaging 10521 S Hwy M-52 Manchester MI 48158 734-428-9741 428-4622
TF: 800-666-7741 ■ *Web:* www.amcor.com/petpackaging
American Quality Products 13920 Mica St Santa Fe Springs CA 90670 562-946-1616 903-0606
TF: 800-245-3737 ■ *Web:* www.waterbottles.com
Apollo Packaging Inc 30 Moffitt St Stratford CT 06615 203-381-7980 378-1723
Ball Plastic Container Corp 9300 W 108th Cir Westminster CO 80021 303-469-5511
Web: www.ball.com
Broadway Cos Inc 6161 Bentnor Ave PO Box 13418 Dayton OH 45413 937-890-1888 890-9846
CKS Packaging Inc 5750 E Front St Kansas City MO 64120 816-241-6161 231-5448
TF: 800-668-8501 ■ *Web:* www.ckspackaging.com
Colt's Plastics Co 969 N Main St PO Box 429 Dayville CT 06241 860-774-2277 779-0782
TF: 800-222-2658 ■ *Web:* www.coltsplastics.com
Constar International Inc 1 Crown Way Philadelphia PA 19154 215-552-3700 552-3715
NASDAQ: CNST ■ *Web:* www.constar.net
Contour Packaging Corp 637 W Rockland St Philadelphia PA 19120 215-457-1600 457-5040
Web: www.contourpackaging.com
Custom Bottle Inc 10 Great Hill Rd Naugatuck CT 06770 203-723-6681 723-6687
TF: 800-453-7626 ■ *Web:* www.bottles.com
Drug Plastics & Glass Co Inc 1 Bottle Dr Boyertown PA 19512 610-367-5000 367-9800
Web: www.drugplastics.com
Fink RN Mfg Co Inc 1530 Noble Rd PO Box 245 Williamston MI 48895 517-655-4351 655-5119
Web: www.rnfink.com
Graham Packaging Co 2401 Pleasant Valley Rd York PA 17402 717-849-8500 854-4269
Web: www.grahampackaging.com
Henlopen Mfg Co Inc 20 Melville Park Rd Melville NY 11747 631-249-2500 531-5777
Metamora Products Corp Industrial Park Elkland PA 16920 814-258-7122 258-7661
Midland Mfg Co Inc 101 E County Line Rd PO Box 899 Monroe IA 50170 641-259-2625 259-3216
Web: www.midlandmfgco.com
NEW Plastics Corp 112 4th St Luxemburg WI 54217 920-845-2326 845-2439
TF: 800-666-5207 ■ *Web:* www.renewplastics.com/new.html
Novapak Corp 370 Stevers Crossing Rd Philmont NY 12565 518-672-7721 672-7728
TF: 800-672-7721 ■ *Web:* www.novapakcorp.com
Nutrifaster Inc 209 S Bennett St Seattle WA 98108 206-767-5054 762-2209
TF: 800-800-2641 ■ *Web:* www.nutrifaster.com
Paradigm Packaging 202 Washington Ave Carlstadt NJ 07072 201-507-0900 460-2059
Web: www.paradigmpackaging.com
Penn Bottle & Supply Co 710 E 3rd St Essington PA 19029 610-521-6000 521-7200
TF: 888-277-7366 ■ *Web:* www.pennbottle.com
Plastic Industries Inc 12400 Industry St Garden Grove CA 92841 714-897-2111 894-0124
Web: www.geocities.com/plasticindustriesinc
Plastipak Packaging Inc 41605 Ann Arbor Rd PO Box 2500C Plymouth MI 48170 734-455-3600 354-7391
Web: www.plastipak.com
Pluto Corp PO Box 391 French Lick IN 47432 812-936-9988 936-2828
Web: www.plutocorp.com
Portola Packaging Inc 97 E Brokaw Rd Suite 250 San Jose CA 95112 408-454-4961 454-4969
TF: 800-767-8652 ■ *Web:* www.portpack.com
Progressive Plastics Inc 14801 Emery Ave Cleveland OH 44135 216-252-5595 252-6327
TF: 800-252-0053 ■ *Web:* www.progressive-plastics.com
PVC Container Corp 2 Industrial Way Eatontown NJ 07724 732-542-0060 542-7706
TF: 800-975-2784 ■ *Web:* www.pvcc.com
Quality Containers of New England
247 Portland St Suite 300 Yarmouth ME 04096 207-846-5420 846-3755
TF: 800-639-1550 ■ *Web:* www.qualitycontainersne.com
RN Fink Mfg Co Inc 1530 Noble Rd PO Box 245 Williamston MI 48895 517-655-4351 655-5119
Web: www.rnfink.com
Silgan Plastics Corp 14515 N Outer Forty Suite 210 Chesterfield MO 63017 314-542-9223 523-4363
TF: 800-274-5426 ■ *Web:* www.silganplastics.com
Suscon Inc 600 Railway St Williamsport PA 17701 570-326-2003 326-6030
Weatherchem Corp 2222 Highland Rd Twinsburg OH 44087 330-425-4206 425-1385
Web: www.weatherchem.com
Weber International Packing 318 Cornelia St Plattsburgh NY 12901 518-561-8282 561-4509
Web: www.weberintl.com
Western Container Corp 1600 1st Ave Big Spring TX 79720 432-263-8361 263-8075

99 BOWLING CENTERS

Phone Fax

AMF Bowling Worldwide Inc 8100 AMF Dr Mechanicsville VA 23111 804-730-4000 730-0923
TF: 800-342-5263 ■ *Web:* www.amf.com
Bowl America Inc 6446 Edsall Rd Alexandria VA 22312 703-941-6300 256-2430
AMEX: BWLa ■ *Web:* www.bowl-america.com
Brunswick Bowling & Billiards 1 N Field Ct Lake Forest IL 60045 847-735-4700 735-4501
Web: www.brunswick.com
Don Carter Premier Bowling Centers 1389 NW 136 Ave Sunrise FL 33323 954-846-8400 846-0131
Web: www.doncarterbowling.com
Mardi-Bob Management Inc PO Box 69 Poughkeepsie NY 12602 845-471-2920 471-7202

100 BOXES - CORRUGATED & SOLID FIBER

Phone Fax

Advance Packaging Corp
4459 40th St SE PO Box 888311 Grand Rapids MI 49588 616-949-6610 954-7373
Web: www.advancepkg.com
Advanced Design & Packaging Inc 5090 McDougall Dr SW Atlanta GA 30336 404-699-1952 699-1825
TF: 800-331-7835
Akers Packaging Service Inc 2820 Lefferson Rd Middletown OH 45044 513-422-6312 422-2829
Web: www.akers-pkg.com
Aldelano Packaging Corp 2010 S Lynx Ave Ontario CA 91761 909-861-3970 861-6039
TF: 800-972-2599 ■ *Web:* www.aldelano.com
Amcor Sunclipse 6600 Valley View St Buena Park CA 90620 714-562-6000 562-6059
Anchor Bay Packaging Corp 30905 23 Mile Rd New Baltimore MI 48047 586-949-4040 949-9997
Web: www.anchorbaypackaging.com
Artistic Carton Co 1975 Big Timber Rd Elgin IL 60123 847-741-0247 741-8529
TF: 877-784-7842 ■ *Web:* www.artisticcarton.com
Arvco Container Corp 845 Gibson St Kalamazoo MI 49001 269-381-0900 381-2919
TF: 800-968-9128 ■ *Web:* www.arvco.com
Atlas Container Corp 8140 Telegraph Rd Severn MD 21144 410-551-6300 551-2703
TF: 800-394-4894 ■ *Web:* www.atlascontainer.com
Bates Container 6433 Davis Blvd North Richland Hills TX 76180 817-498-3200 581-8802
TF: 800-792-8736 ■ *Web:* www.batescontainer.com
Bay Cities Container Corp 8315 Hanan Way Pico Rivera CA 90660 562-948-3751 948-1503
Beacon Container Corp 700 W 1st St Birdsboro PA 19508 610-582-2222 582-3992
TF: 800-422-8383 ■ *Web:* www.beaconcontainer.com
Bell Container Corp 615 Ferry St Newark NJ 07105 973-344-4400 344-0817
Web: www.bellcontainer.com
Buckeye Container Inc 3350 Long Rd Wooster OH 44691 330-264-6336 264-0127
TF: 800-686-8692 ■ *Web:* www.buckeyecontainer.com
Buckeye Corrugated Inc 275 Springside Dr Akron OH 44333 330-576-0590 576-0600
Web: www.buckeyecorrugated.com
Cameo Container Corp 1415 W 44th St Chicago IL 60609 773-254-1030 254-9092
TF: 800-621-1030
Carolina Container Co 909 Prospect St High Point NC 27260 336-883-7146 883-7576
TF: 800-627-0825 ■ *Web:* www.carolinacontainer.com
Chesapeake Corp 1021 E Carey St Richmond VA 23219 804-697-1000 697-1199
NYSE: CSK ■ *Web:* www.cskcorp.com
Colorado Container Corp 4221 Monaco St Denver CO 80216 303-331-0400 331-9455
Web: www.coloradocontainer.com
Commander Packaging Corp 25777 S Cleveland Ave Monee IL 60449 708-367-4000 367-4010
Cornell Paper & Box Co 162 Van Dyke St Brooklyn NY 11231 718-875-3202 875-3281
Corrugated Supplies Corp 5043 W 67th St Bedford Park IL 60638 708-458-5525 458-0013
TF: 888-826-2738 ■ *Web:* www.csclive.com
Delta Corrugated Paper Products Corp
W Ruby & Railroad Ave Palisades Park NJ 07650 201-941-1910 941-9399
TF: 800-932-6937 ■ *Web:* www.deltacorrugated.com
El Morro Corrugated Box Corp PO Box 907 Vega Alta PR 00692 787-883-3760 883-6532
Elgin Corrugated Box Co Inc 824 Raymond St Elgin IL 60120 847-741-2200 741-3052
Franks Industries Inc 924 S Meridian St PO Box 127 Sunman IN 47041 812-623-1140 623-1158
TF: 800-446-4844 ■ *Web:* www.franksindustries.com
Georgia-Pacific Corp 133 Peachtree St NE Atlanta GA 30303 404-652-4000 230-5774
Web: www.gp.com
Gibraltar Packaging Group Inc DBA Great Plains Packaging Co
2000 Summit Ave Hastings NE 68901 402-463-1366 463-2467
TF: 800-456-1366 ■ *Web:* www.gppkg.com
Great Lakes Packaging Corp W 190 N 11393 Carnegie Dr Germantown WI 53022 262-255-2100 255-7290
TF: 800-261-4572 ■ *Web:* www.glpc.com
Great Northern Corp 395 Stroebe Rd Appleton WI 54914 920-739-3671 739-7096
TF: 800-236-3671 ■ *Web:* www.greatnortherncorp.com
Green Bay Packaging Inc 1700 N Webster Ct Green Bay WI 54302 920-433-5111
TF: 800-558-4008 ■ *Web:* www.gbp.com
HP Neun Co Inc 75 N Main St Fairport NY 14450 585-388-1360 388-0184
TF: 800-724-2641
Integrated Packaging Corp 122 Quentin Ave New Brunswick NJ 08901 732-247-5200 247-9559
Web: www.ipcboxes.com
Interstate Container Brunswick LLC 501 Finnegans Ln North Brunswick NJ 08902 732-821-8100 821-4040
Web: www.iripaper.com

	City	State	Zip	Phone	Fax
Interstate Resources Inc 1800 N Kent St Suite 1200	Arlington	VA	22209	703-243-3355	243-4681
Web: www.iripaper.com					
Key Container Corp 21 Campbell St	Pawtucket	RI	02861	401-723-2000	725-5980
TF: 800-343-8811 ■ *Web:* www.keycontainercorp.com					
Lawrence Paper Co 2801 Lakeview Rd	Lawrence	KS	66049	785-843-8111	749-3904
TF: 800-535-4553 ■ *Web:* www.lpco.net					
Liberty Carton Co 870 Louisiana Ave S	Minneapolis	MN	55426	763-540-9600	540-9628
TF: 800-328-1784 ■ *Web:* www.libertycarton.com					
Lone Star Corrugated Container Corp 700 N Wildwood Dr	Irving	TX	75061	972-579-1551	554-6081
TF: 800-552-6937 ■ *Web:* www.lonestarcontainer.com					
Longview Fibre Paper & Packaging Co					
300 Fibre Way PO Box 639	Longview	WA	98632	360-425-1550	575-5934
Web: www.longviewfibre.com					
Love Box Co Inc 700 E 37th St N	Wichita	KS	67219	316-832-3275	832-3269
TF: 800-937-5229 ■ *Web:* www.lovebox.com					
Massillon Container Co 49 Ohio St	Navarre	OH	44662	330-879-5653	879-2772
McLean Packaging Corp 3450 Salmon St	Philadelphia	PA	19134	215-423-7800	423-7809
Web: www.mcleanpackaging.com					
Menasha Corp 1645 Bergstrom Rd	Neenah	WI	54956	920-751-1000	751-1236
TF: 800-558-5073 ■ *Web:* www.menasha.com					
Menasha Packaging Co 1645 Bergstrom Rd	Neenah	WI	54956	920-751-1000	751-2349
TF: 800-558-5073 ■ *Web:* www.menashapackaging.com					
Multi-Wall Corp Div Real Reel Corp 50 Taylor Dr	East Providence	RI	02916	401-434-1070	438-5203
TF Cust Svc: 800-992-4166 ■ *Web:* www.multiwall.com					
National Packaging Cos Display Group 105 Ave L	Newark	NJ	07105	973-589-2155	589-2414
TF: 800-589-5808					
Neun HP Co Inc 75 N Main St	Fairport	NY	14450	585-388-1360	388-0184
TF: 800-724-2641					
Norampac Inc 1061 Parent St	Saint Bruno	QC	J3V6R7	450-461-8600	461-8636
TF: 866-735-2635 ■ *Web:* www.norampac.com					
North American Container Corp 1811 W Oak Pkwy Suite D	Marietta	GA	30062	770-431-4858	431-6957
TF: 800-929-3468 ■ *Web:* www.nacontainer.com					
Packaging Corp of America 1900 W Field Ct	Lake Forest	IL	60045	847-482-2000	615-6379
NYSE: PKG ■ *TF:* 888-828-2850 ■ *Web:* www.packagingcorp.com					
Pactiv Corp 1900 W Field Ct	Lake Forest	IL	60045	847-482-2000	482-4738
NYSE: PTV ■ *TF:* 888-828-2850 ■ *Web:* www.pactiv.com					
Rand-Whitney Container Corp 1 Agrand St	Worcester	MA	01607	508-791-2301	792-1578
TF: 800-370-9111 ■ *Web:* www.randwhitney.com					
Real Reel Corp Multi-Wall Corp Div 50 Taylor Dr	East Providence	RI	02916	401-434-1070	438-5203
TF Cust Svc: 800-992-4166 ■ *Web:* www.multiwall.com					
Royal Group 1301 S 47th Ave	Cicero	IL	60804	708-656-2020	656-2108
Web: www.royalbox.com					
Schiffenhaus Packaging Corp 2013 McCarter Hwy	Newark	NJ	07104	973-484-5000	481-3630
Web: www.schifpack.com					
Smurfit-Stone Container Corp 6 City Pl	Saint Louis	MO	63141	314-656-5300	
NASDAQ: SSCC ■ *TF:* 877-772-2999 ■ *Web:* www.smurfit-stone.com					
Smurfit-Stone Container Corp Corrugated Container Div					
6 City Pl	Saint Louis	MO	63141	314-656-5300	
TF: 877-772-2999 ■ *Web:* www.smurfit-stone.com					
Southern Container Corp 115 Engineers Rd	Hauppauge	NY	11788	631-231-0400	231-0174
Web: www.southern-container.com					
Southern Container Ltd 10410 Papalote St Suite 130	Houston	TX	77041	713-466-5661	466-4223
Web: www.southerncontainer.com					
Stephen Gould Paper Co Inc 35 S Jefferson Rd	Whippany	NJ	07981	973-428-1500	428-1610
TF: 800-253-1961 ■ *Web:* www.stephengould.com					
Stronghaven Inc 5090 McDougall Dr SW	Atlanta	GA	30336	404-699-9680	699-1825
TF: 800-233-2487 ■ *Web:* www.stronghaven.com					
Tecumseh Packaging Solutions Inc 707 S Evans St	Tecumseh	MI	49286	517-423-2126	423-7240
TF: 800-866-8660					
Temple-Inland Inc 1300 S Mopac Expy	Austin	TX	78746	512-434-5800	434-8723
NYSE: TIN ■ *TF:* 800-826-8807 ■ *Web:* www.temple-inland.com					
Tharco Inc 2222 Grant Ave	San Lorenzo	CA	94580	510-276-8600	322-4862*
**Fax Area Code:* 800 ■ *TF:* 800-772-2332 ■ *Web:* www.tharco.com					
TimBar Packaging & Display 148 N Penn St PO Box 449	Hanover	PA	17331	717-632-4727	632-1243
TF: 800-572-6061 ■ *Web:* www.timbar.com					
Tri-Wall 2626 County Rd 71	Butler	IN	46721	260-868-2151	868-2953
TF: 888-874-9255 ■ *Web:* www.triwall.com					
Unicorr 455 Sackett Point Rd	North Haven	CT	06473	203-248-2161	248-0241
TF: 800-229-4269 ■ *Web:* www.unicorr.com					
US Corrugated Inc 3391 Town Point Dr Suite 195	Kennesaw	GA	30144	770-218-7600	218-7610
Web: www.uscorr.com					
Welch Packaging Group 1020 Herman St	Elkhart	IN	46516	574-295-2460	295-1527
TF: 800-246-2475 ■ *Web:* www.welchpkg.com					
York Container Co 138 Mt Scion Rd	York	PA	17402	717-757-7611	755-8090
TF: 800-772-9675 ■ *Web:* www.yorkcontainer.com					

101 BOXES - PAPERBOARD

Products made by these companies include setup, folding, and nonfolding boxes.

	City	State	Zip	Phone	Fax
A Klein & Co 1 Heart Dr PO Box 610	Claremont	NC	28610	828-459-9261	459-9608
Advance Paper Box Co 6100 S Gramercy Pl	Los Angeles	CA	90047	323-750-2550	752-8133
Web: www.advancepaperbox.com					
AGI Inc 1950 N Ruby St	Melrose Park	IL	60160	708-344-9100	344-9113
TF: 800-677-9110 ■ *Web:* www.agiinc.com					
Aldelano Packaging Corp 2010 S Lynx Ave	Ontario	CA	91761	909-861-3970	861-6039
TF: 800-972-2599 ■ *Web:* www.aldelano.com					
Altivity Packaging LLC 450 E North Ave	Carol Stream	IL	60188	888-801-2579	
Web: www.altivity.com/					
Americraft Carton Group Inc 4323 Clary Blvd	Kansas City	MO	64130	816-924-5700	924-7032
Apex Paper Box Co 5601 Walworth Ave	Cleveland	OH	44102	216-631-4000	416-2140*
**Fax:* Sales ■ *TF Cust Svc:* 800-438-2269					
Arkay Packaging Corp 22 Arkay Dr	Hauppauge	NY	11788	631-273-2000	273-2478
TF: 888-327-5296 ■ *Web:* www.arkay.com					
Astronics Corp 130 Commerce Way	East Aurora	NY	14052	716-805-1599	655-0309
NASDAQ: ATRO ■ *Web:* www.astronics.com					
Boelter Industries Inc 202 Galewski Dr Airport Industrial Park	Winona	MN	55987	507-452-2315	452-2649
Web: www.boelterindustries.com					
Boutwell Owens & Co Inc 251 Authority Dr	Fitchburg	MA	01420	978-343-3067	343-9132
Web: www.boutwellowens.com					
Burd & Fletcher Co Inc 5151 E Geospace Dr	Independence	MO	64056	816-257-0291	257-9928
TF: 800-821-2776 ■ *Web:* www.burdfletcher.com					
Cadmus Communications Corp Whitehall Group Div					
2750 Whitehall Park Dr	Charlotte	NC	28273	704-583-6600	583-6781*
**Fax:* Sales ■ *TF:* 800-733-4318 ■ *Web:* www.cadmuswhitehall.com					
Calpine Containers Inc 3478 Buskirk Ave Suite 336	Pleasant Hill	CA	94523	925-287-8800	279-1272
Caraustar Carton Co 555 N Tripp Ave	Chicago	IL	60624	773-722-0555	722-3510
Web: www.caraustar.com					
Caraustar Industries Inc					
5000 Austell-Powder Sprngs Rd Suite 300	Austell	GA	30106	770-948-3100	
NASDAQ: CSAR ■ *Web:* www.caraustar.com					
Carton Service - Packaging Insights First Quality Dr	Shelby	OH	44875	419-342-5010	342-4804
TF: 800-533-7744 ■ *Web:* www.cartonservice.com					
Cascades Boxboard Group Inc					
772 Sherbrooke St W Suite 300	Montreal	QC	H3A1G1	514-284-9800	289-1773
TF: 800-465-9917 ■ *Web:* www.cascades.com					
Colbert Packaging Corp 28355 N Bradley Rd	Lake Forest	IL	60045	847-367-5990	367-4403
Web: www.colbertpkg.com					
Complemar Partners 500 Lee Rd Suite 200	Rochester	NY	14606	585-647-5800	647-5800
TF: 866-742-5274 ■ *Web:* www.complemar.com					
Cornell Paper & Box Co 162 Van Dyke St	Brooklyn	NY	11231	718-875-3202	875-3281
Cortegra 6 Commerce Rd	Fairfield	NJ	07004	973-808-8000	808-8010
Web: www.cortegra.com					
Curtis Packaging Corp 44 Berkshire Rd	Sandy Hook	CT	06482	203-426-5861	426-2684
Web: www.curtispackaging.com					
Dee Paper Co Inc 100 Broomall St	Chester	PA	19013	610-876-9285	876-7040
TF: 800-359-0041 ■ *Web:* www.deepaper.com					
Diamond Packaging Co Inc 111 Commerce Dr PO Box 23620	Rochester	NY	14692	585-334-8030	334-9141
TF: 800-333-4079 ■ *Web:* www.diamondpkg.com					
Economy Folding Box Corp 2601 S La Salle St	Chicago	IL	60616	312-225-2000	225-3082
Web: www.economyfoldingboxcorp.com					
F & S Carton Co PO Box 8606	Grand Rapids	MI	49518	616-538-9400	538-2650
Web: www.fscarton.com					
FC Meyer Packaging LLC 1000 Thomas Ave	Jeannette	PA	15644	724-523-5565	527-3575
FM Howell & Co 79 Pennsylvania Ave	Elmira	NY	14904	607-734-6291	734-8667
Web: www.howellpkg.com					
Franks Industries Inc 924 S Meridian St PO Box 127	Sunman	IN	47041	812-623-1140	623-1158
TF: 800-446-4844 ■ *Web:* www.franksindustries.com					
Fuller Box Co 150 Chestnut St	North Attleboro	MA	02760	508-695-2525	695-2187
Web: www.fullerbox.com					
Gibraltar Packaging Group Inc DBA Great Plains Packaging Co					
2000 Summit Ave	Hastings	NE	68901	402-463-1366	463-2467
TF: 800-456-1366 ■ *Web:* www.gppkg.com					
Gift Box Corp of America 7 W 34th St	New York	NY	10001	212-684-5113	684-5117
TF: 800-443-8269 ■ *Web:* www.800giftbox.com					
Graphic Packaging International 814 Livingston Ct	Marietta	GA	30067	770-644-3000	215-0766*
NYSE: GPK ■ **Fax Area Code:* 303 ■ *TF:* 800-677-2886 ■ *Web:* www.graphicpkg.com					
Great Plains Packaging Co 2000 Summit Ave	Hastings	NE	68901	402-463-1366	463-2467
TF: 800-456-1366 ■ *Web:* www.gppkg.com					
Harvard Folding Box Co Inc 71 Linden St	Lynn	MA	01905	781-598-1600	598-2950
TF: 800-876-1246					
House of Packaging Inc 13170 Temple Ave	City of Industry	CA	91746	626-369-3371	333-6115
Web: www.hopbox.com					
Howell FM & Co 79 Pennsylvania Ave	Elmira	NY	14904	607-734-6291	734-8667
Web: www.howellpkg.com					
HP Neun Co Inc 75 N Main St	Fairport	NY	14450	585-388-1360	388-0184
TF: 800-724-2641					
Hub Folding Box Co Inc 774 Norfolk St	Mansfield	MA	02048	508-339-0005	339-0102
TF: 800-334-1113					
Interstate Resources Inc 1800 N Kent St Suite 1200	Arlington	VA	22209	703-243-3355	243-4681
Web: www.iripaper.com					
Jordan Industries Inc Specialty Printing & Labeling Group					
1751 Lake Cook Rd Suite 550 ArborLake Center	Deerfield	IL	60015	847-945-5591	945-5698
Web: www.jordanindustries.com					
Klein A & Co 1 Heart Dr PO Box 610	Claremont	NC	28610	828-459-9261	459-9608
Knight Paper Box Co Inc 4651 W 72nd St	Chicago	IL	60629	773-585-2035	585-3824
Kramer Carton Co Inc 1800 61st St	Sacramento	CA	95817	916-452-5363	451-3561
Web: www.kramercarton.com					
Los Angeles Paper Box 6027 S Eastern Ave	City of Commerce	CA	90040	323-685-8900	724-2181
Web: www.lapb.com					
Love Box Co Inc 700 E 37th St N	Wichita	KS	67219	316-832-3275	832-3269
TF: 800-937-5229 ■ *Web:* www.lovebox.com					
Mafcote Industries Inc 108 Main St	Norwalk	CT	06851	203-847-8500	849-9177
TF Cust Svc: 800-221-3056 ■ *Web:* www.mafcote.com					
Malnove Inc 13434 F St	Omaha	NE	68137	402-330-1100	330-2941
TF: 800-228-9877 ■ *Web:* www.malnove.com					
Massillon Container Co 49 Ohio St	Navarre	OH	44662	330-879-5653	879-2772
McLean Packaging Corp 3450 Salmon St	Philadelphia	PA	19134	215-423-7800	423-7809
Web: www.mcleanpackaging.com					
MeadWestvaco Corp 5 High Ridge Pk	Stamford	CT	06905	203-461-7400	
NYSE: MWV ■ *TF:* 800-958-4785 ■ *Web:* www.meadwestvaco.com					
MeadWestvaco Packaging Systems 1040 W Marietta St NW	Atlanta	GA	30318	404-875-2711	897-6383
Web: www.meadwestvaco.com/packagingsystems.nsf					
Menasha Corp 1645 Bergstrom Rd	Neenah	WI	54956	920-751-1000	751-1236
TF: 800-558-5073 ■ *Web:* www.menasha.com					
MOD-PAC Corp 1801 Elmwood Ave	Buffalo	NY	14207	716-873-0640	873-6008
NASDAQ: MPAC ■ *TF Cust Svc:* 800-666-3722 ■ *Web:* www.modpac.com					
Neun HP Co Inc 75 N Main St	Fairport	NY	14450	585-388-1360	388-0184
TF: 800-724-2641					
Pactiv Corp 1900 W Field Ct	Lake Forest	IL	60045	847-482-2000	482-4738
NYSE: PTV ■ *TF:* 888-828-2850 ■ *Web:* www.pactiv.com					
Panoramic Inc 1500 N Parker Dr	Janesville	WI	53545	608-754-8850	754-5703
TF: 800-333-1394 ■ *Web:* www.panoramicinc.com					
Paragon Packaging Inc 49-B Sherwood Terr	Lake Bluff	IL	60044	847-615-0065	615-0099
TF: 888-615-0065 ■ *Web:* www.paragonpackaging.com					
Pharmagraphics 1072 Boulder Rd	Greensboro	NC	27409	336-292-4555	292-1727
Web: www.pharmagraphics.com					
Rex Packaging 136 Eastport Rd	Jacksonville	FL	32218	904-757-5210	757-5353
TF: 800-821-0798 ■ *Web:* www.rexcorp.com					
Rice Packaging Inc 356 Somers Rd	Ellington	CT	06029	860-872-8341	871-6834*
**Fax:* Sales ■ *TF:* 800-367-6725 ■ *Web:* www.ricepackaging.com					
Rock-Tenn Co 504 Thrasher St PO Box 4098	Norcross	GA	30091	770-448-2193	263-4483
NYSE: RKT ■ *TF:* 800-762-5836 ■ *Web:* www.rocktenn.com					
Rose City Printing & Packaging Inc 3100 NW Industrial St	Portland	OR	97210	503-241-6486	241-3604
TF: 800-704-8693 ■ *Web:* www.rcpp.com					
Royal Paper Box Co of California Inc PO Box 458	Montebello	CA	90640	323-728-7041	722-2646
Web: www.royalpaperbox.com					
RTS Packaging LLC 504 Thrasher St	Norcross	GA	30071	770-448-2244	449-0261
TF: 800-558-6984 ■ *Web:* www.rtspackaging.com					
Saint Joseph Packaging Inc 4515 Easton Rd	Saint Joseph	MO	64503	816-233-3181	233-2475
TF: 800-383-3000 ■ *Web:* www.stjpkg.com					
Seaboard Folding Box Corp 35 Daniels St	Fitchburg	MA	01420	978-342-8921	342-1105
TF: 800-225-6313					
Sheboygan Paper Box Co 716 Clara Ave PO Box 326	Sheboygan	WI	53082	920-458-8373	458-2901
TF: 800-458-8373 ■ *Web:* www.spbox.com					
Simkins Industries Inc 260 East St	New Haven	CT	06511	203-787-7171	787-7402
Web: www.simkinsindustries.com					
Smurfit-Stone Container Corp 6 City Pl	Saint Louis	MO	63141	314-656-5300	
NASDAQ: SSCC ■ *TF:* 877-772-2999 ■ *Web:* www.smurfit-stone.com					
Sonoco 1 N 2nd St	Hartsville	SC	29550	843-383-7000	383-7008*
NYSE: SON ■ **Fax:* PR ■ *TF:* 800-377-2692 ■ *Web:* www.sonoco.com					
Southern Standard Cartons Inc					
2415 Plantside Dr PO Box 99037	Louisville	KY	40269	502-491-2760	491-2767
Standard Group 75-20 Astoria Blvd	Jackson Heights	NY	11370	718-335-5500	507-6430
Stephen Gould Paper Co Inc 35 S Jefferson Rd	Whippany	NJ	07981	973-428-1500	428-1610
TF: 800-253-1961 ■ *Web:* www.stephengould.com					
Sterling Paper Co 2155 E Castor Ave	Philadelphia	PA	19134	215-744-5350	533-9577
TF: 800-745-5350					

Company	City	State	ZIP	Phone	Fax
Tetra Pak Inc 101 Corporate Woods Pkwy *TF:* 800-358-3872 ■ *Web:* www.tetrapak.com	Vernon Hills	IL	60061	847-955-6000	955-6500
Triumph Packaging Group 515 W Crossroads Pkwy *Web:* www.triumphpackaging.com	Bolingbrook	IL	60440	630-771-0900	771-0522
Tropical Paper Box Co 7000 NW 25th St	Miami	FL	33122	305-592-5520	599-8966
Unicorr 455 Sackett Point Rd *TF:* 800-229-4269 ■ *Web:* www.unicorr.com	North Haven	CT	06473	203-248-2161	248-0241
Utah Paper Box Co Inc 340 W 200 South *Web:* www.upbslc.com	Salt Lake City	UT	84101	801-363-0093	363-9212
Whitehall Group Div Cadmus Communications Corp 2750 Whitehall Park Dr **Fax:* Sales ■ *TF:* 800-733-4318 ■ *Web:* www.cadmuswhitehall.com	Charlotte	NC	28273	704-583-6600	583-6781*
Winchester Carton Corp PO Box 597 *TF:* 800-633-5967 ■ *Web:* www.winchestercarton.com	Eutaw	AL	35462	205-372-3337	372-9226

102 BREWERIES

SEE ALSO Malting Products p. 1944

Company	City	State	ZIP	Phone	Fax
Abita Brewing Co 21084 Hwy 36 *TF:* 800-737-2311 ■ *Web:* www.abita.com	Covington	LA	70433	985-893-3143	898-3546
Alaskan Brewing Co 5429 Shaune Dr *Web:* www.alaskanbeer.com	Juneau	AK	99801	907-780-5866	780-4514
Anchor Brewing Co 1705 Mariposa St *Web:* www.anchorbrewing.com	San Francisco	CA	94107	415-863-8350	552-7094
Anheuser-Busch Inc 1 Busch Pl *TF Cust Svc:* 800-342-5283 ■ *Web:* www.anheuser-busch.com	Saint Louis	MO	63118	314-577-2000	
Asahi Beer USA Inc 20000 Mariner Ave Suite 300 *Web:* www.asahibeerusa.com	Torrance	CA	90503	310-921-4000	921-4001
Boston Beer Co 75 Arlington St *NYSE:* SAM ■ *TF:* 800-372-1131 ■ *Web:* www.samueladams.com	Boston	MA	02116	617-368-5000	368-5500
Boulder Beer Co 2880 Wilderness Pl *Web:* www.boulderbeer.com	Boulder	CO	80301	303-444-8448	444-4796
Boulevard Brewing Co 2501 Southwest Blvd *Web:* www.blvdbeer.com	Kansas City	MO	64108	816-474-7095	474-1722
Breckinridge Brewery Denver 2220 Blake St *Web:* www.breckbrew.com	Denver	CO	80205	303-297-3644	297-2341
BridgePort Brewing Co 1318 NW Northrup St *TF:* 888-834-7546 ■ *Web:* www.bridgeportbrew.com	Portland	OR	97209	503-241-7179	241-0625
Brooklyn Brewery 79 N 11th St *Web:* www.brooklynbrewery.com	Brooklyn	NY	11211	718-486-7422	486-7440
Capital Brewery 7734 Terrace Ave *Web:* www.capital-brewery.com	Middleton	WI	53562	608-836-7100	831-9155
Coors Brewing Co 1225 17th St Suite 1875 *TF:* 800-642-6116 ■ *Web:* www.coors.com	Denver	CO	80202	303-279-6565	277-6246
Deschutes Brewery Inc 1044 NW Bond St *Web:* www.deschutesbrewery.com	Bend	OR	97701	541-382-9242	383-4505
DG Yuengling & Son Inc 5th & Mahantongo St *Web:* www.yuengling.com	Pottsville	PA	17901	570-622-4141	622-4011
DL Geary Brewing Co Inc 38 Evergreen Dr *Web:* www.gearybrewing.com	Portland	ME	04103	207-878-2337	878-2388
Flying Dog Brewery LLC 2401 Blake St *Web:* www.flyingdogales.com	Denver	CO	80205	303-292-5027	296-0164
Full Sail Brewing Co 506 Columbia St *TF:* 888-244-2337 ■ *Web:* www.fullsailbrewing.com	Hood River	OR	97031	541-386-2281	386-7316
Great Lakes Brewing Co 2516 Market Ave *Web:* www.greatlakesbrewing.com	Cleveland	OH	44113	216-771-4404	771-2799
Harpoon Brewery 306 Northern Ave *TF:* 888-427-7666 ■ *Web:* www.harpoonbrewery.com	Boston	MA	02210	617-574-9551	482-9361
Heineken USA 360 Hamilton Ave Suite 1103 *TF:* 800-811-4951 ■ *Web:* www.heineken.com	White Plains	NY	10601	914-681-4100	681-1900
High Falls Brewing Co 445 Saint Paul St *Web:* www.highfalls.com	Rochester	NY	14605	585-546-1030	546-5011
Humboldt Brews 856 10th St	Arcata	CA	95521	707-826-2739	826-2045
InBev USA 101 Merritt 7 PO Box 5075 *TF Cust Svc:* 800-769-5337 ■ *Web:* www.inbev.com	Norwalk	CT	06856	203-750-6600	750-6699
Jacob Leinenkugel Brewing Co Hwy 124 N PO Box 368 *TF:* 888-534-6437 ■ *Web:* www.leinie.com	Chippewa Falls	WI	54729	715-723-5557	
John I Haas Inc P O Box 1441 *Web:* www.johnihaas.com	Yakima	WA	08007	500 460 4000	400 4000
Jones Brewing Co 260 2nd St *Web:* www.stoneysbeer.com	Smithton	PA	15479	724-872-6626	872-6538
Kirin Brewery of America LLC 970 W 190 St Suite 890 *Web:* www.kirin.com	Torrance	CA	90502	310-354-2400	354-5955
Labatt Breweries of Canada 207 Queen's Quay W Suite 299 *TF:* 800-268-2337 ■ *Web:* www.labatt.ca	Toronto	ON	M5J1A7	416-361-5050	361-5200
Latrobe Brewing Co 119 Jefferson St *Web:* www.rollingrock.com	Latrobe	PA	15650	724-537-5545	537-4035
Lion Brewery Inc 700 N Pennsylvania Ave *TF:* 800-233-8327 ■ *Web:* www.lionbrewery.com	Wilkes-Barre	PA	18705	570-823-8801	823-6686
Long Trail Brewing Co 5520 US Rt 4 *Web:* www.longtrail.com	Bridgewater Corners	VT	05035	802-672-5011	672-5012
Malt Products Corp 88 Market St *TF:* 800-526-0180 ■ *Web:* www.maltproducts.com	Saddle Brook	NJ	07663	201-845-4420	845-0028
Matt Brewing Co 811 Edward St *Web:* www.saranac.com	Utica	NY	13502	315-624-2400	624-2401
McMenamins Pubs & Breweries Inc 430 N Killingsworth *Web:* www.mcmenamins.com	Portland	OR	97217	503-223-0109	294-0837
Mendocino Brewing Co 1601 Airport Rd *Web:* www.mendobrew.com	Ukiah	CA	95482	707-463-2627	463-2465
Miller Brewing Co 3939 W Highland Blvd *Web:* www.millerbrewing.com	Milwaukee	WI	53208	414-931-2000	931-3735
Minhas Craft Brewery 1208 14th Ave *Web:* minhasbrewery.com	Monroe	WI	53566	608-325-3191	325-3198
Molson Coors Brewing Co 1225 17th St Suite 1875 *NYSE:* TAP ■ *TF:* 800-642-6116 ■ *Web:* www.molsoncoors.com	Denver	CO	80202	303-279-6565	277-6246
New Belgium Brewing Co 500 Linden St *TF:* 888-622-4044 ■ *Web:* www.newbelgium.com	Fort Collins	CO	80524	970-221-0524	221-0535
Odell Brewing Co 800 E Lincoln Ave *TF:* 888-887-2797 ■ *Web:* www.odells.com	Fort Collins	CO	80524	970-498-9070	498-0706
Pabst Brewing Co 121 Interpark Blvd Suite 300 *TF:* 800-935-2337 ■ *Web:* www.pabst.com	San Antonio	TX	78216	210-226-0231	226-0231
Pittsburgh Brewing Co 3340 Liberty Ave *Web:* www.pittsburghbrewingco.com	Pittsburgh	PA	15201	412-682-7400	692-1189
Prairie Malt Ltd PO Box 1150 *Web:* www.prairiemaltltd.com	Biggar	SK	S0K0M0	306-948-3500	948-3969
Pyramid Breweries Inc 91 S Royal Brougham Way *NASDAQ:* PMID ■ *TF:* 800-603-3336 ■ *Web:* www.pyramidbrew.com	Seattle	WA	98134	206-682-8322	682-8420
Redhook Ale Brewery Inc 14300 NE 145th St *NASDAQ:* HOOK ■ *Web:* www.redhook.com	Woodinville	WA	98072	425-483-3232	485-0761
Rogue Ales Co 2320 OSU Dr *TF:* 800-850-1115 ■ *Web:* www.rogueales.com	Newport	OR	97365	541-867-3660	867-3260
Saint Stan's Brewery 821 L St *Web:* www.st-stans.com	Modesto	CA	95354	209-524-2337	524-4827
Sierra Nevada Brewing Co 1075 E 20th St *Web:* www.sierranevada.com	Chico	CA	95928	530-893-3520	893-1275
Summit Brewing Co 910 Montreal Cir *Web:* www.summitbrewing.com	Saint Paul	MN	55102	651-265-7800	265-7801
Widmer Bros Brewing Co 929 N Russell St *TF:* 800-943-6371 ■ *Web:* www.widmer.com	Portland	OR	97227	503-281-2437	281-1496

BROKERS

SEE Commodity Contracts Brokers & Dealers p. 1499; Electronic Communications Networks (ECNs) p. 1609; Insurance Agents, Brokers, Services p. 1857; Mortgage Lenders & Loan Brokers p. 1397; Real Estate Agents & Brokers p. 1397; Securities Brokers & Dealers p. 2307

103 BRUSHES & BROOMS

SEE ALSO Art Materials & Supplies - Mfr p. 1285

Company	City	State	ZIP	Phone	Fax
A & B Brush Mfg Corp 1150 Three Ranch Rd	Duarte	CA	91010	626-303-8856	303-1207
ABCO Products Inc 6800 NW 36th Ave *TF:* 888-694-2226 ■ *Web:* www.abcoproducts.com	Miami	FL	33147	305-694-2226	694-0451
Advanced Products Co 1015 Spring Garden St	Philadelphia	PA	19123	215-232-5926	232-3019
AJ Siris Corp Inc 10 Essex St PO Box AV *TF:* 800-526-5300 ■ *Web:* www.ajsiris.com	Paterson	NJ	07509	973-684-7700	684-3251
American Brush Co Inc 112 Industrial Blvd *TF:* 800-225-0392	Claremont	NH	03743	603-542-9951	542-2086
Anderson Products Inc 1040 Southbridge St **Fax Area Code:* 800 ■ *TF:* 800-755-6101 ■ *Web:* www.andersonproducts.com	Worcester	MA	01610	508-755-6100	729-4694*
Arnold SM Inc 7901 Michigan Ave *TF Cust Svc:* 800-325-7865 ■ *Web:* www.smarnold.com	Saint Louis	MO	63111	314-544-4103	544-3159
Bestt Liebco Corp 13201 N Lombard St *TF:* 800-523-9095 ■ *Web:* www.paintbrushes.com	Portland	OR	97202	503-286-8217	286-5336
Brush Research Mfg Co Inc 4642 E Floral Dr *Web:* www.brushresearch.com	Los Angeles	CA	90022	323-261-2193	268-6587
Brushes Corp 5400 Smith Rd *TF:* 800-967-9697 ■ *Web:* www.brushescorp.com	Brook Park	OH	44142	216-267-8084	267-9077
Brushtech Inc PO Box 1130 *TF Cust Svc:* 800-346-0818	Plattsburgh	NY	12901	518-563-8420	563-0581
Butler Home Products Inc 311 Hopping Brook Rd PO Box 8000 *TF:* 800-343-3368 ■ *Web:* www.thebutler.com	Holliston	MA	01746	508-429-8100	429-1289
Carlisle Sanitary Maintenance Products 402 S Black River St *TF:* 800-356-8366 ■ *Web:* www.carlislesmp.com	Sparta	WI	54656	608-269-2151	269-3293
Cleveland Wood Products 3871 W 150th St *TF:* 800-969-9695	Cleveland	OH	44111	216-252-1190	252-6205
Cosgrove Enterprises 16000 NW 49th Ave *TF:* 800-888-3396	Miami	FL	33014	305-623-6700	623-6935
Crystal Lake Mfg Inc 2225 Hwy 14 W PO Box 159 *TF:* 800-633-8720 ■ *Web:* www.crystallakemfg.com	Autaugaville	AL	36003	334-365-3342	365-3332
Danline Inc 1 Silver Ct *TF:* 800-552-7874 ■ *Web:* danlinebrushes.com	Springfield	NJ	07081	973-376-1000	376-9888
Detroit Quality Brush Mfg 32165 Schoolcraft Rd *TF:* 800-722-3037	Livonia	MI	48150	734-525-5660	525-0437
Felton Brush Inc 7 Burton Dr *TF:* 800-258-9702 ■ *Web:* www.feltonbrush.com	Londonderry	NH	03053	603-425-0200	425-0242
Fuller Brush Co 1 Fuller Way *TF Cust Svc:* 800-438-5537 ■ *Web:* www.fuller.com	Great Bend	KS	67530	620-792-1711	792-1906
Gordon Brush Mfg Co Inc 6247 Randolph St *TF:* 800-950-7950 ■ *Web:* www.gordonbrush.com	Commerce	CA	90040	323-724-7777	724-1111
Greenwood Mop & Broom Inc 312 Palmer St PO Drawer 1426 *TF:* 000-035-0049 ■ *Web:* www.greenwoodmopandbroom.com	Greenwood	SC	29648	864-227-8411	227-3200
Hamburg Industries Inc 218 Pine St *Web:* www.hamburgindustries.com	Hamburg	PA	19526	610-562-3031	562-0209
Harper Brush Works Inc 400 N 2nd *TF:* 800-223-7894 ■ *Web:* www.harper-brush.com	Fairfield	IA	52556	641-472-5186	472-3187
Industrial Brush Co Inc PO Box 869 *TF:* 800-241-9860 ■ *Web:* www.indbrush.com	Fairfield	NJ	07007	973-575-0455	575-6169
Industrial Brush Corp PO Box 2608 *TF:* 800-228-6146 ■ *Web:* www.industrialbrush.com	Pomona	CA	91769	909-591-9341	627-8916
Industries for the Blind 3220 W Vliet St *TF:* 800-642-8778 ■ *Web:* www.ibmilw.com	Milwaukee	WI	53208	414-933-4319	933-4316
Industries of the Blind Inc 920 W Lee St *Web:* www.industriesoftheblind.com	Greensboro	NC	27403	336-274-1591	274-9207
Keystone Plastics Inc 3451 S Clinton Ave *TF:* 800-635-5238 ■ *Web:* www.keystonesweeperbrushes.com	South Plainfield	NJ	07080	908-561-1300	561-3404
Laitner Brush Co 1561 Laitner Dr *TF Cust Svc:* 800-423-6805 ■ *Web:* www.laitner.com	Traverse City	MI	49686	231-929-3300	929-7219
Libman Co 220 N Sheldon St *TF:* 800-646-6262 ■ *Web:* www.mamalibman.com	Arcola	IL	61910	217-268-4200	268-3439
Linzer Products Corp 248 Wyandanch Ave *TF:* 800-221-0787 ■ *Web:* www.linzerproducts.com	Wyandanch	NY	11798	631-253-3333	253-9750
Magnolia Brush Mfg Inc 1001 N Cedar PO Box 932 *TF:* 800-248-2261 ■ *Web:* www.magnoliabrush.com	Clarksville	TX	75426	903-427-2261	427-5230
Mill-Rose Co 7995 Tyler Blvd *TF:* 800-321-3533 ■ *Web:* www.millrose.com	Mentor	OH	44060	440-255-9171	255-5039
Milwaukee Dustless Brush Co 10930 W Lapham St *TF:* 800-632-3220 ■ *Web:* www.milwaukeedustless.com	Milwaukee	WI	53214	414-476-1147	476-1760
Newell Rubbermaid Inc Shur-Line Div 4051 S Iowa Ave *TF:* 800-558-3958 ■ *Web:* www.shurline.com	Saint Francis	WI	53235	414-481-4500	481-7642
O-Cedar/Vileda Inc 505 N Railroad Ave *TF:* 800-543-8105 ■ *Web:* www.ocedar.com	North Lake	IL	60164	708-452-4100	452-9967
Ohio Brush Co 2680 Lisbon Rd *TF:* 888-411-3265 ■ *Web:* www.ohiobrush.com	Cleveland	OH	44104	216-791-3265	791-6615
Osborn International 5401 Hamilton Ave *TF Cust Svc:* 800-720-3358 ■ *Web:* www.osborn.com	Cleveland	OH	44114	216-361-1900	361-1913
Padco Inc 2220 Elm St SE *TF:* 800-328-5513 ■ *Web:* www.padco.com	Minneapolis	MN	55414	612-378-7270	378-9388
Pasco Industries Inc 17501 S Denver Ave	Gardena	CA	90248	310-323-8660	329-3537
PFERD Milwaukee Brush Co Inc 30 Jytek Dr *TF:* 800-336-3444 ■ *Web:* www.advance-milwaukee.com	Leominster	MA	01453	978-840-6420	840-6421
Prager Brush Co Inc 730 Echo St NW *TF:* 800-241-5696 ■ *Web:* www.pragerbrush.com	Atlanta	GA	30318	404-875-9292	872-1161
Rubberset Co 26466 Silver Ln *Web:* www.rubberset.com	Crisfield	MD	21817	410-968-1050	968-0861

Company	City	State	Zip	Phone	Fax
Rutland Products 86 Center St PO Box 340 *TF:* 800-544-1307 ■ *Web:* www.rutland.com	Rutland	VT	05702	802-775-5519	775-5262
Sanderson-MacLeod Inc 1199 S Main St *TF:* 866-522-3481 ■ *Web:* www.sandersonmacleod.com	Palmer	MA	01069	413-283-3481	289-1919
Shur-Line Div Newell Rubbermaid Inc 4051 S Iowa Ave *TF:* 800-558-3958 ■ *Web:* www.shurline.com	Saint Francis	WI	53235	414-481-4500	481-7642
Signature Works Inc 1 Signature Dr *TF:* 800-647-2468	Hazlehurst	MS	39083	601-894-1771	894-2993
Siris AJ Corp Inc 10 Essex St PO Box AV *TF:* 800-526-5300 ■ *Web:* www.ajsiris.com	Paterson	NJ	07509	973-684-7700	684-3251
SM Arnold Inc 7901 Michigan Ave *TF Cust Svc:* 800-325-7865 ■ *Web:* www.smarnold.com	Saint Louis	MO	63111	314-544-4103	544-3159
Stough Broom & Mop Co 163 N Wesson St	Tallassee	AL	36078	334-283-2170	283-2408
Super Brush Co 165 Front St Suite 4 *TF:* 800-272-0591 ■ *Web:* www.superbrush.com	Chicopee	MA	01013	413-592-4195	594-2987
Superior Brush Co 3453 W 140th St	Cleveland	OH	44111	216-252-5144	252-8838
Sweepster Inc 2800 N Zeeb Rd *TF:* 800-456-7100 ■ *Web:* www.sweepster.com	Dexter	MI	48130	734-996-9116	996-9014
Universal Brush Mfg Co 16200 Dixie Hwy *TF:* 800-323-3474 ■ *Web:* www.universalbrush.com	Markham	IL	60428	708-331-1700	331-4923
Weiler Corp 1 Wildwood Dr *TF:* 800-835-9999 ■ *Web:* www.weilercorp.com	Cresco	PA	18326	570-595-7495	595-2002
Wilen Products Inc 3760 S Side Industrial Pkwy *Web:* www.wilen.com	Atlanta	GA	30354	404-366-2111	361-8832
Wooster Brush Co 604 Madison Ave *TF:* 800-392-7246 ■ *Web:* www.woosterbrush.com	Wooster	OH	44691	330-264-4440	263-0495
Zephyr Mfg Co Inc 200 Mitchell Rd *TF:* 800-821-7197 ■ *Web:* www.zephyrmfg.com	Sedalia	MO	65301	660-827-0352	827-0713

104 BUILDING MAINTENANCE SERVICES

SEE ALSO Cleaning Services p. 1447

Company	City	State	Zip	Phone	Fax
ABM Industries Inc 160 Pacific Ave Suite 222 *NYSE: ABM* ■ *Web:* www.abm.com	San Francisco	CA	94111	415-733-4000	733-7333
Acme Building Maintenance 941 Catherine St *Web:* www.acmeco.com	Alviso	CA	95002	408-263-5911	946-6484
Aid Maintenance Co 300 Roosevelt Ave PO Box 476 *Web:* www.aidmaintenance.com	Pawtucket	RI	02860	401-722-6627	723-6860
American Building Maintenance Co 160 Pacific Ave Suite 222	San Francisco	CA	94111	415-733-4000	733-7333
Centennial One Inc 851 Brightseat Rd *Web:* www.centennialone.com	Landover	MD	20785	301-808-6700	808-6921
Colin Service Systems Inc 170 Hamilton Ave *TF:* 800-873-2654	White Plains	NY	10601	914-289-2000	
D & A Building Services Inc 983 Explorer Cove	Altamonte Springs	FL	32710	407-831-5388	831-1377
Denali Ventures Inc 5613 DTC Pkwy Suite 200 **Fax Area Code: 303* ■ *Web:* www.denaliventures.com	Greenwood Village	CO	80111	877-290-5590	716-5145*
FBG Service Corp 407 S 27th Ave *TF:* 800-777-8326 ■ *Web:* www.fbgservices.com	Omaha	NE	68131	402-346-4422	595-5044
Janitronics Building Services 29 Sawyer Rd *Web:* www.janitronics.com	Waltham	MA	02453	781-647-5570	893-5878
Laro Service Systems Inc 271 Skip Ln *Web:* www.laro.com	Bay Shore	NY	11706	631-667-0900	667-0881
OneSource 1600 Parkwood Cir Suite 400 *TF:* 800-424-4477 ■ *Web:* www.one-source.com	Atlanta	GA	30339	770-436-9900	226-8512
Temco Service Industries Inc 1 Park Ave	New York	NY	10016	212-889-6353	213-9854

105 BUILDINGS - PREFABRICATED - METAL

Company	City	State	Zip	Phone	Fax
American Buildings Co 1150 State Docks Rd **Fax: Sales* ■ *TF:* 888-307-4338 ■ *Web:* www.americanbuildings.com	Eufaula	AL	36027	334-687-2032	688-2185*
American Modular Technologies 6306 Old 421 Rd *Web:* americanmodular.org	Liberty	NC	27298	336-622-6200	622-6473
American Steel Building Co Inc 12218 Robin Blvd *TF:* 800-877-8335 ■ *Web:* www.americansteelbuildingco.com	Houston	TX	77045	713-433-5661	433-0847
Behlen Mfg Co 4025 E 23rd St *TF:* 800-553-5520 ■ *Web:* www.behlenmfg.com	Columbus	NE	68601	402-564-3111	563-7405
Butler Mfg Co 1540 Genessee St **Fax: Hum Res* ■ *Web:* www.butlermfg.com	Kansas City	MO	64102	816-968-3000	968-6506*
Ceco Building Systems 2400 Hwy 45 N *Web:* www.cecobuildings.com	Columbus	MS	39705	662-328-6722	243-2781
Clearspan Components Inc 6110 Old Hwy 80 W *Web:* www.clearspaninc.com	Meridian	MS	39307	601-483-3941	693-7493
Conley's Mfg & Sales Inc 4344 E Mission Blvd *TF:* 800-377-8441 ■ *Web:* www.conleys.com	Montclair	CA	91763	909-627-0981	628-3774
Dean Steel Buildings Inc 2929 Industrial Ave *Web:* www.deanintl.com	Fort Myers	FL	33901	239-334-1051	334-0932
DeRaffele Mfg Co Inc 2525 Palmer Ave	New Rochelle	NY	10801	914-636-6850	636-6596
Dura-Bilt Products Inc PO Box 188 *TF:* 800-233-4251 ■ *Web:* www.durabilt.com	Wellsburg	NY	14894	570-596-2000	596-3296
Erect-A-Tube Inc 701 W Park St *TF:* 800-624-9219 ■ *Web:* www.erect-a-tube.com	Harvard	IL	60033	815-943-4091	943-4095
Four Seasons Solar Products LLC 5005 Veterans Memorial Hwy *TF:* 800-368-7732 ■ *Web:* www.fourseasonssunrooms.com	Holbrook	NY	11741	631-563-4000	563-4010
Garco Building Systems 2714 S Garfield Rd *TF:* 800-941-2291 ■ *Web:* www.garcobuildings.com	Airway Heights	WA	99001	509-244-5611	244-2850
Gichner Shelter Systems 490 E Locust St	Dallastown	PA	17313	717-244-7611	246-5475
Gichner Systems Group Inc 490 E Locust St *Web:* www.gichner.us	Dallastown	PA	17313	717-244-7611	246-5475
Gulf States Manufacturers 101 Airport Rd PO Box 1128 *TF:* 800-844-4853 ■ *Web:* www.acedells.com/gulf.htm	Starkville	MS	39760	662-323-8021	324-2984
Imperial Industries Inc 505 Industrial Park Ave *TF:* 800-558-2945 ■ *Web:* www.imperialind.com	Rothschild	WI	54474	715-359-0200	355-5349
International Building Systems Inc 7150 Almeda Genoa Rd *Web:* www.internationalbuildings.com	Houston	TX	77075	713-991-7900	991-3939
Jewell Building Systems Inc 1932 Jordache Ct *Web:* www.jewellsteel.com	Dallas	NC	28052	704-922-8652	922-3237
Kay Home Products 26210 Emery Rd Suite 101 *TF:* 800-600-7009 ■ *Web:* www.kayhomeproducts.com	Cleveland	OH	44128	216-896-6900	896-6903
Kirby Building Systems Inc 124 Kirby Dr *TF:* 800-820-6449 ■ *Web:* www.kirby-abs.com	Portland	TN	37148	615-325-4165	325-4700
Lark Builders Inc 409 Dixon St *TF:* 800-841-7844 ■ *Web:* www.larkbuilders.com	Vidalia	GA	30474	912-538-1888	538-0057
Ludwig Buildings Inc 521 Timesaver Ave	Harahan	LA	70123	504-733-6260	733-7458
Madison Industries Inc of Georgia 1035 Iris Dr *Web:* www.madisonind.com	Conyers	GA	30094	770-483-4401	785-6622
Mesco Metal Buildings 400 N Kimball Ave PO Box 93629 *TF:* 800-556-3726 ■ *Web:* www.mescobldg.com	Southlake	TX	76092	817-488-8511	329-2335
Metal Building Components Inc 10943 Sam Houston Pkwy W *TF:* 877-713-6224 ■ *Web:* www.mbci.com	Houston	TX	77064	281-897-7788	477-9672
Metal Sales Mfg Corp 7800 State Rd 60 *TF:* 800-406-7387 ■ *Web:* www.mtlsales.com	Sellersburg	IN	47172	812-246-1935	246-1862
Metecno-ASI 725 Summerhill Dr *TF:* 888-882-5862 ■ *Web:* www.alumashield.com	DeLand	FL	32724	386-626-6789	734-3289
Mid-West Steel Building Co 7301 Fairview St *TF:* 800-777-9378 ■ *Web:* www.mid-weststeel.com	Houston	TX	77041	713-466-7788	466-3194
Miracle Steel Corp 600 Oakwood Rd PO Box 1266 *TF:* 888-508-4545 ■ *Web:* www.miracletruss.com	Watertown	SD	57201	605-886-7885	886-3036
Mobile Mini Inc 7420 S Kyrene Rd Suite 101 *NASDAQ: MINI* ■ *TF:* 800-288-5669 ■ *Web:* www.mobilemini.com	Tempe	AZ	85283	480-894-6311	894-1505
Morton Buildings Inc 252 W Adams St *TF:* 800-426-6686 ■ *Web:* www.mortonbuildings.com	Morton	IL	61550	309-263-7474	266-5123
National Greenhouse Co 6 Industrial Dr *TF:* 800-826-9314	Pana	IL	62557	217-562-9333	562-2841
NCI Building Systems Inc 7301 Fairview St *NYSE: NCS* ■ *TF:* 800-777-9378 ■ *Web:* www.ncilp.com	Houston	TX	77041	713-466-7788	466-3194
Nucor Building Systems 305 Industrial Pkwy *Web:* www.nucorbuildingsystems.com	Waterloo	IN	46793	260-837-7891	837-7384
Pacific Building Systems 2100 N Pacific Hwy *TF:* 800-727-7844 ■ *Web:* www.pbsbuildings.com	Woodburn	OR	97071	503-981-9581	981-9584
Package Industries Inc 15 Harback Rd *TF:* 800-225-7242 ■ *Web:* www.packagesteel.com	Sutton	MA	01590	508-865-5871	865-9130
Parkline Inc PO Box 65 *TF:* 800-786-4855 ■ *Web:* www.parkline.com	Winfield	WV	25213	304-586-2113	586-3842
Porta-Fab Corp 18080 Chesterfield Airport Rd *TF:* 800-325-3781 ■ *Web:* www.portafab.com	Chesterfield	MO	63005	636-537-5555	537-2955
PorterCorp 4240 N 136th Ave *TF:* 800-354-7721 ■ *Web:* www.portercorp.com	Holland	MI	49424	616-399-1963	399-9123
Red Dot Corp 1209 W Corsicana St *TF Cust Svc:* 800-657-2234 ■ *Web:* www.reddotbuildings.com	Athens	TX	75751	903-675-9181	675-9180
Rigid Building Systems Ltd 18933 Aldine Westfield Rd *TF:* 888-467-4443 ■ *Web:* www.rigidbuilding.com	Houston	TX	77073	281-443-9065	443-9064
Ruffin Building Systems Inc 6914 Hwy 2 **Fax: Cust Svc* ■ *TF Sales:* 800-421-4232 ■ *Web:* www.ruffinbuildingsystems.com	Oak Grove	LA	71263	318-428-2305	428-2231*
Smith XS Inc PO Box X *TF:* 800-631-2226 ■ *Web:* www.xssmith.com	Red Bank	NJ	07701	732-222-4600	222-7288
Southern Structures LLC 918 Young St *TF:* 800-264-5981 ■ *Web:* www.southernstructures.com	Broussard	LA	70518	337-856-5981	856-5980
Star Building Systems 8600 S I-35 *TF:* 800-879-7827 ■ *Web:* www.starbuildings.com	Oklahoma City	OK	73149	405-636-2010	636-2419
Stuppy Greenhouse Mfg Inc 120 E 12th Ave *TF:* 800-877-5025 ■ *Web:* www.stuppy.com	North Kansas City	MO	64116	816-842-3071	472-1512
Super Secur Mfg Co 15125 Proctor Ave *TF:* 800-591-9880 ■ *Web:* www.supersecur.com	City of Industry	CA	91746	626-333-2543	855-4860
Tampa Tank Inc 5205 Adamo Dr *Web:* www.tampatank.com	Tampa	FL	33619	813-623-2675	622-7514
Temo Sunrooms Inc 20400 Hall Rd *TF:* 800-344-8366 ■ *Web:* www.temosunrooms.com	Clinton Township	MI	48038	586-286-0410	286-5409
Trachte Building Systems Inc 314 Wilburn Rd *TF:* 800-356-5824 ■ *Web:* www.trachte.com	Sun Prairie	WI	53590	608-837-7899	837-0251
Truss-T Structures Inc DBA Pacific Building Systems 2100 N Pacific Hwy *TF:* 800-727-7844 ■ *Web:* www.pbsbuildings.com	Woodburn	OR	97071	503-981-9581	981-9584
Tyler Building Systems LP 3535 Shiloh Rd *TF:* 800-442-8979 ■ *Web:* www.tylerbuilding.com	Tyler	TX	75707	903-561-3000	561-7686
VP Buildings Inc 3200 Players Club Cir *Web:* www.vp.com	Memphis	TN	38125	901-748-8000	748-9323
WedgCor Building Systems Inc 6800 E Hampden Ave *Web:* www.wedgcor.com	Denver	CO	80224	303-759-3200	759-3025
Whirlwind Building Systems Inc 8234 Hansen Rd **Fax Area Code: 832* ■ *TF:* 800-324-9992 ■ *Web:* www.wwbldgsys.com	Houston	TX	77075	713-946-7140	553-4600*
Winandy Greenhouse Co 2211 Peacock Rd	Richmond	IN	47374	765-935-2111	935-2110
XS Smith Inc PO Box X *TF:* 800-631-2226 ■ *Web:* www.xssmith.com	Red Bank	NJ	07701	732-222-4600	222-7288

106 BUILDINGS - PREFABRICATED - WOOD

Company	City	State	Zip	Phone	Fax
Adrian Home Builders Inc 404 Hwy 80 E PO Box 266 *TF:* 800-642-7380 ■ *Web:* www.adrianhomesmfg.com	Adrian	GA	31002	478-668-3231	668-4943
All American Homes LLC 309 S 13th St *Web:* www.allamericanhomes.com	Decatur	IN	46733	260-724-8044	724-8987
American Standard Building Systems Inc 700 Commerce St PO Box 4908 *TF:* 800-888-4908 ■ *Web:* www.asbsystems.com	Martinsville	VA	24115	276-638-3991	638-3983
AmerLink Log Homes Ltd 7991 Beasley Rd *TF:* 800-872-4254 ■ *Web:* www.amerlink.com	Whitakers	NC	27891	252-977-2545	972-3188
Barden & Robeson Corp 103 Kelly Ave *TF:* 800-724-0141 ■ *Web:* www.bardenhomes.com	Middleport	NY	14105	716-735-3732	735-3752
Cardinal Homes Inc 525 Barnesville Hwy PO Box 10 *Web:* www.cardinalhomes.com	Wylliesburg	VA	23976	434-735-8111	735-8824
Craftech Building Systems Inc DBA Heckaman Homes Corp 2676 E Market St PO Box 229 *Web:* www.heckamanhomes.com	Nappanee	IN	46550	574-773-4167	773-2546
Deck House Inc 930 Main St *TF:* 800-727-3325 ■ *Web:* www.deckhouse.com	Acton	MA	01720	978-263-7000	263-4159
Deluxe Building Systems Inc 499 W 3rd St *TF:* 800-843-7372 ■ *Web:* www.deluxehomes.com	Berwick	PA	18603	570-752-5914	752-1525
Design Homes Inc 600 N Marquette Rd *TF:* 800-627-9443 ■ *Web:* www.designhomes.com	Prairie du Chien	WI	53821	608-326-6041	326-4233
Dickinson Homes Inc 404 S Stephenson Ave Hwy US-2 *TF:* 800-343-8179 ■ *Web:* www.dickinsonhomes.com	Iron Mountain	MI	49801	906-774-5800	774-5207
Doupnik Gary Mfg Inc 3237 Rippey Rd PO Box 527 *Web:* www.gdmfg.com	Loomis	CA	95650	916-652-9291	652-9021
Dynamic Homes LLC 525 Roosevelt Ave **Fax: Orders* ■ *TF:* 800-492-4833 ■ *Web:* www.dynamichomes.com	Detroit Lakes	MN	56501	218-847-2611	847-2617*
Farwest Homes 887 NW State Ave PO Box 480 *TF:* 800-752-0500 ■ *Web:* www.farwesthomes.com	Chehalis	WA	98532	360-748-3351	748-6443
Fleetwood Homes of California Inc 7007 Jurupa Ave *TF:* 800-999-9265 ■ *Web:* www.fleetwoodhomes.com	Riverside	CA	92504	951-688-5353	351-0378
Foremost Industries Inc 2375 Buchanan Trail W *TF:* 877-284-5334 ■ *Web:* www.foremosthomes.com	Greencastle	PA	17225	717-597-7166	597-5579
Gary Doupnik Mfg Inc 3237 Rippey Rd PO Box 527 *Web:* www.gdmfg.com	Loomis	CA	95650	916-652-9291	652-9021
Haven Homes Inc 554 Eagle Valley Rd PO Box 178 *TF:* 800-424-2836 ■ *Web:* www.havenhomes.com	Beech Creek	PA	16822	570-962-2111	962-3181
Heckaman Homes Corp 2676 E Market St PO Box 229 *Web:* www.heckamanhomes.com	Nappanee	IN	46550	574-773-4167	773-2546

Name / Address	City	State	Zip	Phone	Fax
Heritage Log Homes Inc 1 Heritage Pl *TF:* 800-456-4663 ■ *Web:* www.heritagelog.com	Kodak	TN	37764	865-453-0140	429-4434
Homes by Keystone Inc 13338 Midvale Rd PO Box 69 *TF:* 800-890-7926 ■ *Web:* www.homesbykeystone.com	Waynesboro	PA	17268	717-762-1104	762-1106
International Homes of Cedar Inc PO Box 886 *TF:* 800-767-7674 ■ *Web:* www.ihoc.com	Woodinville	WA	98072	360-668-8511	668-5562
KanBuild Inc DBA All American KanBuild 126 Nichols Rd PO Box 259 *TF:* 800-343-2783 ■ *Web:* www.kanbuild.com	Osage City	KS	66523	785-528-4163	528-4795
KIT HomeBuilders West LLC 1124 Garber St *TF:* 800-859-0347 ■ *Web:* www.kitwest.com	Caldwell	ID	83605	208-454-5000	455-2995
Lester Building Systems LLC 1111 2nd Ave S *TF:* 800-826-4439 ■ *Web:* www.lesterbuildings.com	Lester Prairie	MN	55354	320-395-2531	395-2969
Lindal Cedar Homes Inc 4300 S 104th Pl *TF Prod Info:* 800-426-0536 ■ *Web:* www.lindal.com	Seattle	WA	98178	206-725-0900	725-1615
Manufactured Structures Corp 3089 E Fort Wayne Rd PO Box 350 *TF:* 800-662-5344 ■ *Web:* www.mscoffice.com	Rochester	IN	46975	574-223-4794	223-9051
Mascot Homes Inc 800 Blue Ridge St *TF:* 800-472-8958 ■ *Web:* www.mascothomesinc.com	Gramling	SC	29348	864-472-2041	472-8958
Miller Building Systems Inc 58120 CR 3 S *TF:* 800-423-2559 ■ *Web:* www.mbsionline.com	Elkhart	IN	46517	574-295-1214	295-2232
Mod-U-Kraf Homes LLC 260 Weaver St PO Box 573 *TF:* 888-663-5723 ■ *Web:* www.mod-u-kraf.com	Rocky Mount	VA	24151	540-483-0291	483-2228
Modtech Holdings Inc 2830 Barrett Ave *NASDAQ: MODT* ■ *Web:* www.modtech.com	Perris	CA	92571	951-943-4014	940-0427
Morgan Building Systems Inc 2800 McCree Rd *TF:* 800-935-0321 ■ *Web:* www.morganusa.com	Garland	TX	75041	972-864-7300	864-7307
Muncy Homes Inc 1567 Rt 442 *TF:* 800-788-1555 ■ *Web:* www.muncyhomesinc.com	Muncy	PA	17756	570-546-2261	546-5903
Nationwide Custom Homes 1100 Rives Rd *TF:* 800-216-7001 ■ *Web:* www.nationwide-homes.com	Martinsville	VA	24115	276-632-7101	632-1181
New England Homes 270 Ocean Rd *TF:* 800-800-8831 ■ *Web:* www.newenglandhomes.net	Greenland	NH	03840	603-436-8830	431-8540
North American Housing Corp 5724 Industry Ln *Web:* www.northamericanhousing.com	Frederick	MD	21704	301-694-9100	694-7570
Northeastern Log Homes Inc 2312 Scott Hwy *TF:* 800-992-6526 ■ *Web:* www.northeasternlog.com	Groton	VT	05046	802-584-3336	584-3200
Northern Log Homes Inc 300 Bomarc Rd *TF:* 800-553-7311 ■ *Web:* www.northernloghomes.net	Bangor	ME	04401	207-942-6869	942-1576
Original Lincoln Logs Ltd 5 Riverside Dr *TF:* 800-833-2461 ■ *Web:* www.lincolnlogs.com	Chestertown	NY	12817	518-494-5500	494-3008
Pacific Modern Homes Inc PO Box 670 *TF Sales:* 800-395-1011 ■ *Web:* www.pmhi.com	Elk Grove	CA	95759	916-685-9514	685-1306
Pan Abode Cedar Homes Inc 4350 Lake Washington Blvd N *TF:* 800-782-2633 ■ *Web:* www.panabodeworldwide.com	Renton	WA	98056	425-255-8260	255-8630
Phoenix Building Solutions Inc 630 Hay Ave *TF:* 800-833-4096 ■ *Web:* www.phoenixbuildingsolutions.com	Brookville	OH	45309	937-833-4091	833-5268
Pittsville Homes Inc 5094 2nd Ave PO Box C *TF:* 877-248-8371 ■ *Web:* www.pittsvillehomes.com	Pittsville	WI	54466	715-884-2511	884-2136
Porta-Kamp International LP 555 Gelhorn Dr *Web:* www.portakamp.com	Houston	TX	77029	713-674-3163	674-4844
RJ Taylor Corp 9410 S Meridian	Clarklake	MI	49234	517-529-4007	529-4705
Rocky Mountain Log Homes 1883 Hwy 93 S *Web:* www.rmlh.com	Hamilton	MT	59840	406-363-5680	363-2109
Simplex Industries Inc 1 Simplex Dr *TF:* 800-233-4233 ■ *Web:* www.simplexind.com	Scranton	PA	18504	570-346-5113	346-3731
Sterling Building Systems PO Box 1967	Wausau	WI	54402	715-359-7108	359-2867
Stratford Homes LP 402 S Weber Ave *TF:* 800-448-1524 ■ *Web:* www.stratfordhomes.com	Stratford	WI	54484	715-687-3133	687-3453
Sun Building Systems 9 Stauffer Industrial Park *TF:* 888-740-8218 ■ *Web:* www.sunmodular.com	Taylor	PA	18517	570-562-0110	562-0737
Taylor RJ Corp 9410 S Meridian	Clarklake	MI	49234	517-529-4007	529-4705
Timberland Homes Inc 1201 37th St NW *TF:* 800-488-5036 ■ *Web:* www.timberland-homes.com	Auburn	WA	98001	253-735-3435	939-8803
Town & Country Cedar Homes 4772 US Hwy 131 S *TF:* 800-968-3178 ■ *Web:* www.cedarhomes.com	Petoskey	MI	49770	231-347-4360	347-7255
Unibilt Industries Inc 4641 Poplar Creek Rd *TF:* 800-777-9942 ■ *Web:* www.unibilt.com	Vandalia	OH	45377	937-890-7570	890-0574
Ward Cedar Log Homes 39 Bangor St PO Box 72 *TF Cust Svc:* 800-341-1566 ■ *Web:* www.wardcedarloghomes.com	Houlton	ME	04730	207-532-6531	532-7806
Wausau Homes Inc PO Box 8005 *Web:* www.wausauhomes.com	Wausau	WI	54402	715-359-7272	359-2867
Whitley Mfg Inc 201 W 1st St PO Box 496 *Web:* www.whitleyman.com	South Whitley	IN	46787	260-723-5131	723-6949
Wick Building Systems Inc 405 Walter Rd **Fax:* Sales ■ *TF:* 800-356-9682 ■ *Web:* www.wickbuildings.com	Mazomanie	WI	53560	608-795-4281	795-2294*
Wisconsin Homes Inc 425 W McMillan St *Web:* www.wisconsinhomesinc.com	Marshfield	WI	54449	715-384-2161	387-3627

107 BUS SERVICES - CHARTER

Name / Address	City	State	Zip	Phone	Fax
A Yankee Line 370 W 1st St *TF:* 800-942-8890 ■ *Web:* www.yankeeline.us	Boston	MA	02127	617-268-8890	268-6960
Action Transit Enterprises Inc 330 Poplar St *Web:* www.actiontransit.com	Pittsburgh	PA	15223	412-781-7906	781-8230
Agape Tours Inc 1210 US Hwy 281 **Fax:* Sales ■ *TF:* 800-460-2641 ■ *Web:* www.agapetoursinc.com	Wichita Falls	TX	76310	940-767-4935	692-8477*
All Aboard America 10615 W County Rd 127 *TF:* 800-848-4728 ■ *Web:* www.allaboardamerica.com	Odessa	TX	79765	432-561-8529	563-4287
All West Coachlines Inc 7701 Wilbur Way *TF:* 800-843-2121	Sacramento	CA	95828	916-423-4000	689-5926
Alpha Omega Tours & Charters 419 N Jefferson St PO Box 97 *TF:* 800-351-1060 ■ *Web:* www.alphaomegatoursandcharters.com	Medical Lake	WA	99022	509-299-5595	299-5545
American Coach Lines Inc 2328 10th Ave N Suite 501 *Web:* www.americancoachlines.com	Lake Worth	FL	33460	561-721-1170	721-2390
Anderson Coach & Travel 1 Anderson Plaza *TF:* 800-345-3435 ■ *Web:* www.goanderson.com	Greenville	PA	16125	724-588-8310	588-0257
Arrow Line Inc 19 George St *TF:* 800-243-9560 ■ *Web:* www.arrowline.com	East Hartford	CT	06108	860-289-1531	289-1535
Arrow Stage Lines 720 E Norfolk Ave *TF:* 800-672-8302 ■ *Web:* www.arrowstagelines.com	Norfolk	NE	68701	402-371-3850	371-3267
Atlantic Coach 600 S Military Hwy *TF:* 800-258-9061 ■ *Web:* www.goatlanticcoach.com	Virginia Beach	VA	23464	757-420-3135	424-9331
Atlantic Express Transportation Group Inc 7 North St *TF:* 800-336-3886 ■ *Web:* www.atlanticexpress.com	Staten Island	NY	10302	718-442-7000	442-7672
Audubon Trails Coach Lines Inc 1807 Moll Ln *TF:* 800-255-5234 ■ *Web:* www.audubontrailscoachlines.com	Evansville	IN	47725	812-867-2098	867-2833
B & C Bus Lines 427 Continental Dr *TF:* 877-812-2287	Maryville	TN	37804	865-983-4653	983-5354
Badger Bus 5501 Femrite Dr *TF:* 800-442-8259 ■ *Web:* www.badgerbus.com	Madison	WI	53718	608-255-1511	258-3484
Bieber Carl R Tourways Inc 320 Fair St *TF:* 800-243-2374 ■ *Web:* www.biebertourways.com	Kutztown	PA	19530	610-683-7333	683-5384
Blue Lakes Charters & Tours 12154 N Saginaw Rd *TF:* 800-282-4287 ■ *Web:* www.bluelakes.com	Clio	MI	48420	810-686-4287	686-9772
Boise-Winnemucca Stage Lines Inc 1105 La Pointe St *TF:* 800-448-5692	Boise	ID	83706	208-336-3300	336-3303
Brown Coach Inc 50 Venner Rd *Web:* www.browntours.com	Amsterdam	NY	12010	518-843-4700	843-3600
Butler Motor Transit Co Inc PO Box 1602 *Web:* www.coachusa.com/butler/	Butler	PA	16003	724-282-1000	282-3080
C & H Bus Lines Inc 448 Pine St	Macon	GA	31201	478-746-6441	743-5597
Carl R Bieber Tourways Inc 320 Fair St *TF:* 800-243-2374 ■ *Web:* www.biebertourways.com	Kutztown	PA	19530	610-683-7333	683-5384
Central West of Texas Inc 3426 S Gilbert Rd *TF:* 800-533-1939 ■ *Web:* www.bus-charter.com/centralwest.html	Grand Prairie	TX	75050	972-399-1059	986-7262
Chenango Valley Bus Lines Inc 105 Chenango St *TF:* 800-647-6471	Binghamton	NY	13901	607-723-9408	723-8883
Chippewa Trails 510 E South Ave *TF:* 800-657-4469 ■ *Web:* www.chippewatrailstours.com	Chippewa Falls	WI	54729	715-726-2440	726-2455
Citizen Auto Stage Co 67 E Baffert Dr	Nogales	AZ	85621	520-281-0400	281-4818
Classic Transportation Group 1600 Locust Ave *TF:* 800-666-4949 ■ *Web:* www.classictrans.com	Bohemia	NY	11716	631-567-5100	567-3722
Coach Tours Ltd 475 Federal Rd *TF:* 800-822-6224 ■ *Web:* www.coachtour.com	Brookfield	CT	06804	203-740-1118	775-6851
Coach USA Inc 160 S Rt 17 N **Fax:* Sales ■ *TF:* 800-877-1888 ■ *Web:* www.coachusa.com	Paramus	NJ	07652	201-225-7500	225-7502*
Colorado Charter Lines & Tours 4960 Locust St *TF:* 800-821-7491 ■ *Web:* www.bus-charter.com/colorado.html	Commerce City	CO	80022	303-287-0239	287-2819
Croswell Bus Lines Inc 975 W Main St *TF:* 800-782-8747 ■ *Web:* www.croswell-bus.com	Williamsburg	OH	45176	513-724-2206	724-3261
Cyr Bus Lines 153 Gilman Falls Ave *TF:* 800-244-2335 ■ *Web:* www.cyrbustours.com	Old Town	ME	04468	207-827-2335	827-6763
DATTCO Inc 583 South St *TF:* 800-229-4879 ■ *Web:* www.dattco.com	New Britain	CT	06051	860-229-4878	826-1115
Delta Bus Lines Inc 3107 Hwy 82E	Greenville	MS	38701	662-335-2633	335-2174
Elite Coach 1685 W Main St *TF:* 800-722-6206 ■ *Web:* www.elitecoach.com	Ephrata	PA	17522	717-733-7710	733-7133
Excellent Adventures Inc 6215 Commodity Ct *TF:* 800-552-3893 ■ *Web:* www.excellentadventuresinc.com	Fort Wayne	IN	46818	260-489-3556	489-2582
Eyre Bus Service Inc 13600 Triadelphia Rd *TF:* 800-321-3973 ■ *Web:* www.eyre.com	Glenelg	MD	21737	410-442-1330	442-0010
Flack Tours PO Box 725 *TF:* 800-842-9747	Waddington	NY	13694	315-393-7160	388-4207
Free Enterprise System Inc 1254 S West St *TF:* 800-255-1337 ■ *Web:* www.freeenterprisesystem.com	Indianapolis	IN	46225	317-634-7433	632-6557
Good Time Tours 455 Corday St *TF:* 800-446-0886 ■ *Web:* www.goodtimetours.com	Pensacola	FL	32503	850-476-0046	476-7637
Gray Line of Portland 11655 SW Pacific Hwy *TF:* 888-684-3322 ■ *Web:* www.raztrans.com	Portland	OR	97223	503-684-3322	968-3223
Gray Line Worldwide 1835 Gaylord St *Web:* www.grayline.com	Denver	CO	80206	303-394-6920	394-6950
Great American Coach Co 4220 Howard Ave *TF:* 866-596-2698	New Orleans	LA	70125	504-212-5925	212-5920
Great Southern Coaches Inc 900 Burke Ave *TF:* 800-251-5569	Jonesboro	AR	72401	870-935-5569	935-5572
Greene Coach Charters & Tours Inc 126 Bohannon Ave *TF:* 800-338-5469 ■ *Web:* www.greenecoach.com	Greeneville	TN	37745	423-638-8271	638-5541
Greyhound Canada Transportation Corp 180 Dundas St W Suite 300 *Web:* www.greyhound.ca	Toronto	ON	M5G1Z8	416-594-0343	594-0345
Greyhound Lines Inc PO Box 660606 *Web:* www.greyhound.com	Dallas	TX	75266	972-789-7000	387-1874
Hampton Jitney Inc 395 County Rd 39A Suite 6 *Web:* www.hamptonjitney.com	Southampton	NY	11968	631-283-4600	
Harran Transportation Co Inc 30 Mahan St *TF:* 800-666-4287 ■ *Web:* www.harran.com	West Babylon	NY	11704	631-491-9100	491-9057
Hawkeye Stages Inc 703 Dudley St *TF:* 800-323-3368 ■ *Web:* www.hawkeyestages.com	Decorah	IA	52101	563-382-3639	382-3945
Hertz Northern Bus 333-A 105th St E *Web:* hertznorthernbus.com	Saskatoon	SK	S7N1Z4	306-374-5161	374-2442
Indian Trails Inc 109 E Comstock St *TF:* 800-292-3831 ■ *Web:* www.indiantrails.com	Owosso	MI	48867	989-725-5105	725-9584
Industrial Bus Lines DBA All Aboard America 10615 W County Rd 127 *TF:* 800-848-4728 ■ *Web:* www.allaboardamerica.com	Odessa	TX	79765	432-561-8529	563-4287
Jack Rabbit Lines Inc 301 N Dakota Ave *TF:* 800-678-6543 ■ *Web:* www.jackrabbitlines.com	Sioux Falls	SD	57104	605-336-3339	336-1444
James River Bus Lines 915 N Allen Ave *TF:* 877-342-7300 ■ *Web:* www.jrbl.com	Richmond	VA	23220	804-342-7300	342-7373
Kerrville Bus Co 1 N Main St *TF:* 800-474-3352 ■ *Web:* www.iridekbc.com	Del Rio	TX	78840	830-775-7515	
King Ward Coach Lines 70 Justin Dr *TF:* 800-639-4805 ■ *Web:* www.kingwardcoachlines.com	Chicopee	MA	01022	413-539-5858	535-5172
Krapf Bus Cos 495 Thomas Jones Way Suite 300 *Web:* www.krapfbus.com	Exton	PA	19341	610-594-2664	594-5011
Lamers Bus Lines Inc 2407 S Point Rd *TF:* 800-236-1240 ■ *Web:* www.golamers.com	Green Bay	WI	54313	920-496-3600	496-3611
Leprechaun Lines PO Box 2628 *TF:* 800-624-4217 ■ *Web:* www.leprechaunlines.com	Newburgh	NY	12550	845-565-7900	565-1220
Marin Charter & Tours 8 Lovell Ave *Web:* www.marinairporter.com	San Rafael	CA	94901	415-256-8830	256-8839
Martz First Class Coach Co Inc DBA Martz Tampa Bay 4783 37th St N *TF:* 800-282-8020 ■ *Web:* www.martzfirstclass.com	Saint Petersburg	FL	33714	727-526-9086	522-5548
Martz Group 239 Old River Rd *TF:* 800-334-9608 ■ *Web:* www.martzgroup.com	Wilkes-Barre	PA	18702	570-821-3838	821-3835
Martz Tampa Bay 4783 37th St N *TF:* 800-282-8020 ■ *Web:* www.martzfirstclass.com	Saint Petersburg	FL	33714	727-526-9086	522-5548
Mid-America Charter Lines 2513 E Higgins Rd *TF:* 800-323-0312 ■ *Web:* www.bus-charter.com/midamerica.html	Elk Grove Village	IL	60007	847-437-3779	437-4978
Mid-American Coaches Inc PO Box 1609 *TF:* 866-316-9508 ■ *Web:* www.mid-americancoaches.com	Washington	MO	63090	636-239-4700	239-9542
MV Transportation Inc 360 Campus Ln Suite 201 *Web:* www.mvtransit.com	Fairfield	CA	94534	707-863-8980	863-8944
New World Tours Inc 7920 Gainsford Ct *TF:* 800-322-7733 ■ *Web:* www.newworldtours.com	Bristow	VA	20136	703-392-8687	643-9527
Northern Tours 2740 Bauer St *TF:* 800-735-8687 ■ *Web:* www.gonortherntours.com	Eau Claire	WI	54701	715-834-1463	834-8222
Northfield Lines Inc 32611 Northfield Blvd *TF:* 888-670-8068 ■ *Web:* www.northfieldlines.com	Northfield	MN	55057	507-645-5267	645-5635
Northwest Iowa Transportation Inc 2755 200th St PO Box 911 *TF:* 877-776-1700 ■ *Web:* www.nwitour.com	Fort Dodge	IA	50501	515-576-6494	955-1983
Northwestern Stage Lines Inc 1105 La Pointe St *Web:* user.nwadv.com/northw	Boise	ID	83706	208-336-3300	336-3303
Onondaga Coach Corp PO Box 277 *TF:* 800-451-1570 ■ *Web:* www.onondagacoach.com	Auburn	NY	13021	315-255-2216	255-0925

Company	City	State	Zip	Phone	Fax
Orange Belt Stages 2134 E Mineral King Ave *TF:* 800-266-7433 ■ *Web:* www.orangebelt.com	Visalia	CA	93292	559-733-4408	733-0538
Pacific Western Transportation Ltd 6999 Ordan Dr *TF:* 800-387-6787 ■ *Web:* www.pacificwesterntoronto.com	Mississauga	ON	L5T1K6	905-564-3232	564-5959
Peoria Charter Coach Co 2600 NE Adams St *TF:* 800-448-0572 ■ *Web:* www.peoriacharter.com	Peoria	IL	61603	309-688-9523	688-9520
Peter Pan Bus Lines Inc 1776 Main St *TF:* 800-237-8747 ■ *Web:* www.peterpanbus.com	Springfield	MA	01103	413-781-2900	731-9721
Premier Coach Co Inc 67 Champlain Dr *TF:* 800-532-1811 ■ *Web:* www.premiercoach.net	Colchester	VT	05446	802-655-4456	655-4213
Raz Transportation 11655 SW Pacific Hwy *TF:* 888-684-3322 ■ *Web:* www.raztrans.com	Portland	OR	97223	503-684-3322	968-3223
Red Carpet Charters PO Box 94626 *TF:* 888-878-5100 ■ *Web:* www.redcarpetcharters.com	Oklahoma City	OK	73143	405-672-5100	672-9613
Rimrock Stages Inc PO Box 988 *TF:* 800-255-7655 ■ *Web:* www.rimrocktrailways.com	Billings	MT	59103	406-245-5392	245-7696
Riteway Bus Service Inc Motorcoach Div W201 N13900 Fond du Lac Ave **Fax Area Code: 262* ■ *TF:* 800-776-7026 ■ *Web:* www.ritewaybus.com	Richfield	WI	53076	414-677-3282	677-1570*
Rockland Coaches Inc 180 Old Hook Rd *Web:* www.coachusa.com/rockland	Westwood	NJ	07675	201-263-1254	664-8036
Rohrer Bus Service 190 Pic Rite Ln *TF:* 800-487-8687 ■ *Web:* www.rohrerbusservice.com	Lewisburg	PA	17837	570-524-5800	524-5855
Rolling V Transportation Services PO Box 110 *Web:* www.rollingv.com	South Fallsburg	NY	12779	845-434-0511	434-0259
Royal American Charter Lines Inc 17727 Volbrecht Rd *TF:* 800-323-5281 ■ *Web:* www.royalride.com	Lansing	IL	60438	708-474-7474	331-8454
S & O Coach Lines Inc 6630 Fly Rd *Web:* www.coachusa.com/cny/	East Syracuse	NY	13057	315-431-4462	431-4502
Salter Bus Lines Inc 212 Hudson Ave *TF:* 800-223-8056 ■ *Web:* www.salter.us	Jonesboro	LA	71251	318-259-2522	259-2522
SBS Transit Inc 3747 Colorado Ave *TF:* 800-548-5304 ■ *Web:* www.sbstransit.com	Sheffield Village	OH	44054	440-949-8121	949-2979
Shafer's Bus Lines Div Southern Bus Stages Inc 750 Harry L Dr *TF:* 800-287-8986 ■ *Web:* www.shaferbus.com	Johnson City	NY	13790	607-797-2006	797-1183
Sierra Nevada Stage Lines 2050 Glendale Ave *TF:* 800-822-6009	Sparks	NV	89431	775-331-2877	331-8695
Silver Fox Tours & Motorcoaches 3 Silver Fox Dr *TF:* 800-342-5998 ■ *Web:* www.silverfoxcoach.com	Millbury	MA	01527	508-865-6000	865-4660
Southeastern Stages Inc 260 University Ave SW *Web:* www.southeasternstages.com	Atlanta	GA	30315	404-874-2741	591-2745
Southern Bus Stages Inc Shafer's Bus Lines Div 750 Harry L Dr *TF:* 800-287-8986 ■ *Web:* www.shaferbus.com	Johnson City	NY	13790	607-797-2006	797-1183
Southern Coach Co 1300 E Pettigrew St *TF:* 800-222-4793 ■ *Web:* www.southerncoach.com	Durham	NC	27701	919-688-1230	688-5305
Star of America 8111 N SR 37 *TF:* 800-933-0097 ■ *Web:* www.charterstaramerica.com	Bloomington	IN	47404	812-876-7851	876-9397
Starr Tours 2531 E State St *TF:* 800-782-7703 ■ *Web:* www.starrtours.com	Trenton	NJ	08619	609-587-0626	587-3052
Storer Coachways 3519 McDonald Ave *TF:* 800-621-3383 ■ *Web:* www.storercoachways.com	Modesto	CA	95358	209-521-8250	578-4888
Sun Valley Stages Inc PO Box 936 *TF:* 800-574-8661 ■ *Web:* www.sunvalleystages.cc	Twin Falls	ID	83303	208-733-3921	733-3993
Swarthout Coaches Inc 115 Graham Rd *TF:* 800-772-7267 ■ *Web:* www.goswarthout.com	Ithaca	NY	14850	607-257-2277	257-0218
Terrian Transportation Inc DBA King Ward Coach Lines 70 Justin Dr *TF:* 800-639-4805 ■ *Web:* www.kingwardcoachlines.com	Chicopee	MA	01022	413-539-5858	535-5172
Texas New Mexico & Oklahoma Coaches Inc PO Box 1800 *Web:* www.tnmo.com	Lubbock	TX	79408	806-763-5389	687-4535
Trailways Transportation System Inc 3554 Chain Bridge Rd Suite 301 *TF:* 877-467-3346 ■ *Web:* www.trailways.com	Fairfax	VA	22030	703-691-3052	691-9047
Triple J Tours Inc 4455 S Cameron St *Web:* www.lasvegasbus.com	Las Vegas	NV	89103	702-261-0131	736-5103
Van Galder Bus Co 715 S Pearl St *TF:* 800-747-7407 ■ *Web:* www.vangalderbus.com	Janesville	WI	53548	608-752-5407	752-7120
Vermont Transit Co Inc 345 Pine St *TF:* 800-552-8737 ■ *Web:* www.vermonttransit.com	Burlington	VT	05401	802-862-9671	862-7812
VIP Tour & Charter Bus Co 129-137 Fox St *TF:* 800-337-4457 ■ *Web:* www.vipchartercoaches.com	Portland	ME	04101	207-772-4457	772-7020
Wilson Bus Lines Inc PO Box 415 *TF:* 800-253-5235 ■ *Web:* www.wilsonbus.com	East Templeton	MA	01438	978-632-3894	632-9005
Winn Transportation 1831 Westwood Ave *TF:* 800-296-9466 ■ *Web:* www.winnbus.com	Richmond	VA	23227	804-358-9466	353-2606
Wisconsin Coach Lines Inc 1520 Arcadian Ave *TF:* 877-324-7767 ■ *Web:* www.wisconsincoach.com	Waukesha	WI	53186	262-542-8861	542-2036
Young Transportation & Tours 843 Riverside Dr *TF:* 800-622-5444 ■ *Web:* www.youngtransportation.com	Asheville	NC	28804	828-258-0084	252-3342

108 BUS SERVICES - INTERCITY & RURAL

SEE ALSO Bus Services - School p. 1400; Mass Transportation (Local & Suburban) p. 1947

Company	City	State	Zip	Phone	Fax
88 Transit Lines Inc 100 Arentzen Blvd	Charleroi	PA	15022	724-489-4418	489-0990
Adirondack Trailways 499 Hurley Ave *TF:* 800-858-8555 ■ *Web:* www.trailwaysny.com	Hurley	NY	12443	845-339-4230	225-6815
Ames Transit Agency 1700 W 6th St *Web:* www.cyride.com	Ames	IA	50014	515-292-1100	239-5578
Bonanza Bus Lines Inc 1 Bonanza Way *TF:* 888-331-7500 ■ *Web:* www.bonanzabus.com	Providence	RI	02904	401-331-7500	
Brazos Transit District 504 E 27th St *Web:* www.btd.org	Bryan	TX	77803	979-779-7443	822-7758
Capitol Trailways Inc PO Box 3353 *TF:* 800-333-8444 ■ *Web:* www.capitoltrailways.com	Harrisburg	PA	17105	717-233-7673	233-7716
Carolina Coach Trailways Inc 1201 S Blount St *Web:* www.trailways.com/member-company.asp?cid=25	Raleigh	NC	27601	919-833-3601	833-0627
City Bus 1500 W 3rd St *TF:* 800-248-9287 ■ *Web:* www.citybus.org	Williamsport	PA	17701	570-326-2500	326-9885
Coach USA Inc 160 S Rt 17 N **Fax: Sales* ■ *TF:* 800-877-1888 ■ *Web:* www.coachusa.com	Paramus	NJ	07652	201-225-7500	225-7502*
Colorado Valley Transit Inc 108 Cardinal Ln PO Box 940 *TF:* 800-548-1068 ■ *Web:* www.gotransit.org	Columbus	TX	78934	979-732-6281	732-6283
Command Bus Co Inc 12755 Flatlands Ave *Web:* www.commandbus.com	Brooklyn	NY	11208	718-277-8100	277-8210
Community & Rural Transportation Inc (CART) 850 Denver St	Idaho Falls	ID	83402	208-522-2278	529-5918
Concho Coaches Inc 31 W Concho Ave	San Angelo	TX	76903	325-655-4159	653-9046
CyRide 1700 W 6th St *Web:* www.cyride.com	Ames	IA	50014	515-292-1100	239-5578
FirstGroup America 705 Central Ave Suite 300 *Web:* www.firstgroupamerica.com	Cincinnati	OH	45202	513-241-2200	381-0149
Geauga County Transit 12555 Merritt Rd *TF:* 888-287-7190 ■ *Web:* www.geaugatransit.org	Chardon	OH	44024	440-279-2150	285-9476
Green Bus Lines Inc 165-25 147th Ave *Web:* www.greenbus.com	Jamaica	NY	11434	718-995-4700	995-4712
Greyhound Canada Transportation Corp 180 Dundas St W Suite 300 *Web:* www.greyhound.ca	Toronto	ON	M5G1Z8	416-594-0343	594-0345
Greyhound Lines Inc PO Box 660606 *Web:* www.greyhound.com	Dallas	TX	75266	972-789-7000	387-1874
Jamaica Buses Inc 114-15 Guy R Brewer Blvd *Web:* www.jamaicabus.com	Jamaica	NY	11434	718-526-0800	739-3361
Jefferson Lines 2100 E 26th St *TF Cust Svc:* 800-767-5333 ■ *Web:* www.jeffersonlines.com	Minneapolis	MN	55404	612-359-3400	359-3437
Jefferson Partners LP 2100 E 26th St *TF Cust Svc:* 800-767-5333 ■ *Web:* www.jeffersonlines.com	Minneapolis	MN	55404	612-359-3400	359-3437
Laidlaw Transit Services Inc 5360 College Blvd Suite 200 *TF:* 800-821-3451 ■ *Web:* www.laidlawtransit.com	Overland Park	KS	66211	913-345-1986	345-9974
Lamers Bus Lines Inc 2407 S Point Rd *TF:* 800-236-1240 ■ *Web:* www.golamers.com	Green Bay	WI	54313	920-496-3600	496-3611
Lassen County Public Transit System 701-980 Johnstonville Rd *Web:* www.lrbs.com	Susanville	CA	96130	530-252-7433	257-6333
Martha's Vineyard Regional Transit Authority RR 1 Box 10 11 A St MV Business Pk *Web:* www.vineyardtransit.com	Edgartown	MA	02539	508-693-9440	693-9953
Martz Group 239 Old River Rd *TF:* 800-334-9608 ■ *Web:* www.martzgroup.com	Wilkes-Barre	PA	18702	570-821-3838	821-3835
Martz Trailways 239 Old River Rd *Web:* www.martztrailways.com	Wilkes-Barre	PA	18702	570-821-3838	821-3835
Mat-Su Community Transit PO Box 871590 *Web:* matsutransit.com	Wasilla	AK	99687	907-376-5000	373-5999
Merced Transportation Co 300 Grogan Ave	Merced	CA	95340	209-384-2575	384-3805
Ozark Regional Transit 2423 E Robinson Ave *TF:* 800-865-5901 ■ *Web:* www.ozark.org	Springdale	AR	72764	479-756-5901	756-2901
Pacific Transit System 216 N 2nd St *Web:* www.pacifictransit.org	Raymond	WA	98577	360-875-9418	942-3193
Parker County Transportation Service Inc PO Box 1055 **Fax Area Code: 940*	Mineral Wells	TX	76068	866-521-1391	328-1392*
Pelivan Transit 333 S Oak St PO Drawer B *TF:* 800-482-4594	Big Cabin	OK	74332	918-783-5793	783-5786
Peter Pan Bus Lines Inc 1776 Main St *TF:* 800-237-8747 ■ *Web:* www.peterpanbus.com	Springfield	MA	01103	413-781-2900	731-9721
Pima County Dept of Transportation Transportation Systems Div 201 N Stone Ave 5th Fl *Web:* www.dot.co.pima.az.us/transsys	Tucson	AZ	85701	520-740-6403	740-6341
Powder River Transportation 1700 E Hwy 14-16 PO Box 218 *TF:* 800-442-3682 ■ *Web:* www.coachusa.com	Gillette	WY	82717	307-682-0960	682-4422
Red Ball Stage Line Inc PO Box 1799	Klamath Falls	OR	97601	541-884-6460	884-6460
Rides Mass Transit District (RMTD) PO Box 190 *TF:* 877-667-6122 ■ *Web:* www.ridesmtd.com	Rosiclare	IL	62982	618-285-3342	285-3340
Rimrock Stages Inc PO Box 988 *TF:* 800-255-7655 ■ *Web:* www.rimrocktrailways.com	Billings	MT	59103	406-245-5392	245-7696
Rural Community Transportation Inc 492 Bay St *Web:* www.riderct.org	Saint Johnsbury	VT	05819	802-748-8170	748-5275
Rural Transit Enterprises Coordinated Inc (RTEC) 100 Main St PO Box 746 *TF:* 800-321-7832 ■ *Web:* www.4rtec.com	Mount Vernon	KY	40456	606-256-9835	256-2181
Southeastern Stages Inc 260 University Ave SW *Web:* www.southeasternstages.com	Atlanta	GA	30315	404-874-2741	591-2745
Southeastern Trailways Inc 1810 W 16th St	Indianapolis	IN	46202	317-635-8671	687-2569
Suburban Transit Corp 750 Somerset St *TF:* 800-222-0492 ■ *Web:* www.suburbantransit.com	New Brunswick	NJ	08901	732-249-1100	545-7015
Thunderbird Rural Public Transportation System 5002 Knickerbocker St PO Box 60050 *TF:* 877-947-8286 ■ *Web:* www.cvcog.org/transportation.htm	San Angelo	TX	76906	325-944-9666	947-8286
Trans-Bridge Lines Inc 2012 Industrial Dr *TF:* 800-962-9135 ■ *Web:* www.transbridgebus.com	Bethlehem	PA	18017	610-868-6001	868-9057
Transit System Inc PO Box 332 *TF:* 800-952-8729	Glen Rose	TX	76043	254-897-2964	897-7922
Tri-State Coach/United Limo 2101 W 37th Ave *TF:* 800-248-8747 ■ *Web:* www.coachusa.com/tristateunitedlimo	Gary	IN	46408	219-884-0054	887-1541
Triangle Transportation Co Inc 1611 Central Ave NW **Fax Area Code: 701*	East Grand Forks	MN	56721	218-773-2631	772-1296*
Triboro Coach Corp 85-01 24th Ave *Web:* www.triborocoach.com	Jackson Heights	NY	11369	718-335-1000	397-1995
Union Street Bus Co Inc 65 Potomska St	New Bedford	MA	02740	508-999-5211	997-2341
Valley Transit Co Inc 219 N 'A' St *TF:* 800-580-4710 ■ *Web:* www.valleytransitcompany.com	Harlingen	TX	78550	956-423-4710	423-4888
Viking Trailways 201 Glendale Rd *TF:* 800-400-2779 ■ *Web:* www.trailways.com/member-company.asp?cid=68	Joplin	MO	64804	417-781-2779	781-2778
Wallowa Valley Stage Line LLC 918 Lostline Rd PO Box 156	Lostine	OR	97857	541-569-2284	569-2476
White Mountain Passenger Lines Inc 1041 E Hall St PO Box 460 *TF:* 866-255-4819 ■ *Web:* www.wmlines.com	Show Low	AZ	85902	928-537-4539	532-6683
Williamsport Bureau of Transportation 1500 W 3rd St *TF:* 800-248-9287 ■ *Web:* www.citybus.org	Williamsport	PA	17701	570-326-2500	326-9885
Wisconsin Coach Lines Inc 1520 Arcadian Ave *TF:* 877-324-7767 ■ *Web:* www.wisconsincoach.com	Waukesha	WI	53186	262-542-8861	542-2036

109 BUS SERVICES - SCHOOL

Company	City	State	Zip	Phone	Fax
A & E Transport Services Inc 101 W Utica St Suite 2 *TF:* 800-724-0614	Oswego	NY	13126	315-343-2804	343-0067
Action Transit Enterprises Inc 330 Poplar St *Web:* www.actiontransit.com	Pittsburgh	PA	15223	412-781-7906	781-8230
Atlantic Express Transportation Group Inc 7 North St *TF:* 800-336-3886 ■ *Web:* www.atlanticexpress.com	Staten Island	NY	10302	718-442-7000	442-7672
Beck Bus Transportation Corp 2201 Brownsville Rd PO Box 768	Mount Vernon	IL	62864	618-242-5685	242-4523
Birnie Bus Service Inc 248 Otis St *TF:* 800-734-3950 ■ *Web:* birniebus.tripod.com	Rome	NY	13441	315-336-3950	339-5957
Brown Bus Co 2111 E Sherman Ave *Web:* www.brownbuscompany.com	Nampa	ID	83686	208-466-4181	466-2861
Carroll George M Inc 7 SR 17K	Newburgh	NY	12550	845-565-8300	565-3196
Cook-Illinois Corp 4845 167th St Suite 300	Oak Forest	IL	60452	708-560-9840	560-0661
Cyr John T & Sons Inc 153 Gilman Falls Ave *TF:* 800-244-2335 ■ *Web:* www.cyrbustours.com	Old Town	ME	04468	207-827-2335	827-6763

				Phone	Fax
DATTCO Inc School Bus Div 583 South St	New Britain	CT	06051	860-229-4878	826-1115
TF: 800-229-4879 ■ *Web:* www.dattco.com					
Davidsmeyer Bus Service 2513 E Higgins Rd	Elk Grove Village	IL	60007	847-437-3767	437-4978
TF: 800-323-0312					
Dean Transportation Inc 4812 Aurelius Rd	Lansing	MI	48910	517-319-8300	319-8385
TF: 800-282-3326					
Durham School Services Inc 4130 Opus Pl Suite 200	Downers Grove	IL	60515	630-435-8000	435-8106
TF: 800-950-0485 ■ *Web:* www.durhamschoolservices.com					
First Student 16103 66th St NW	Edmonton	AB	T5E5S7	780-473-7670	472-7524
First Student Inc 177 Rt 94 S	Lafayette	NJ	07848	973-579-1197	579-2346
First Student Inc 705 Central Ave Suite 300	Cincinnati	OH	45202	513-241-2200	381-0149
Web: www.firststudentinc.com					
George M Carroll Inc 7 SR 17K	Newburgh	NY	12550	845-565-8300	565-3196
H & L Bloom Inc School Bus Div 28 Grovenor St	Taunton	MA	02780	508-822-1442	822-5702
TF: 800-323-3009 ■ *Web:* www.bloombus.com					
Hastings Bus Co 425 31st St E	Hastings	MN	55033	651-437-1888	438-3319
TF: 888-290-2429 ■ *Web:* www.minnesotacoaches.com					
Hertz Northern Bus 333-A 105th St E	Saskatoon	SK	S7N1Z4	306-374-5161	374-2442
Web: hertznorthernbus.com					
Holmes WT Transportation Co 22 Myrtle St	Norfolk	MA	02056	508-528-4550	528-4728
Independent Coach Corp 25 Wanser Ave	Inwood	NY	11096	516-239-1100	239-8641
John T Cyr & Sons Inc 153 Gilman Falls Ave	Old Town	ME	04468	207-827-2335	827-6763
TF: 800-244-2335 ■ *Web:* www.cyrbustours.com					
Johnson School Bus Services Inc 2151 W Washington St PO Box 285	West Bend	WI	53095	262-334-3146	334-8019
Web: www.johnsonschoolbus.com					
Kobussen Buses Ltd W914 County Rd CE	Kaukauna	WI	54130	920-766-0606	766-0797
TF: 800-447-0116 ■ *Web:* www.kobussen.com					
Krapf Bus Cos School Bus Div 120 Springton Rd	Glenmoore	PA	19343	610-269-3897	942-2545
Web: www.krapfbus.com					
Krise Bus Service Inc 119 Bus Ln	Punxsutawney	PA	15767	814-938-5250	938-5323
Web: www.krisebus.com					
Laidlaw International Inc School Bus Div 3221 N Service Rd	Burlington	ON	L7R3Y8	905-336-1800	336-3976
TF: 800-563-6072 ■ *Web:* www.laidlawschoolbus.com					
Lakeside Buses of Wisconsin 7300 W Green Tree Rd	Milwaukee	WI	53224	414-442-4210	536-2049
Lenon Bus Service Inc PO Box 8	Lake Geneva	WI	53147	262-248-3289	248-6447
Michael's Transportation Service Inc 140 Yolano Dr	Vallejo	CA	94589	707-643-2099	643-1906
TF: 800-295-2448 ■ *Web:* www.bustransportation.com					
Mid-Columbia Bus Co 73458 Bus Barn Ln	Pendleton	OR	97801	541-276-5621	276-5205
TF: 888-291-7513 ■ *Web:* www.midcobus.com					
Monroe School Transportation 970 Emerson St	Rochester	NY	14606	585-458-3230	458-9159
New York Bus Service I-95 at Exit 13	Bronx	NY	10475	718-994-5500	994-6927
Web: www.nybus.com					
Palmer Bus Service Inc 521 County Rd 15 E	Saint Clair	MN	56080	507-386-0210	386-0211
Pioneer Transportation Corp 2890 Arthur Kill Rd	Staten Island	NY	10309	718-984-8077	984-6588
Ridge Road Express Inc 5355 Junction Rd	Lockport	NY	14094	716-625-9211	433-0965
TF: 800-847-4887 ■ *Web:* www.grsbuses.com					
Riteway Bus Service Inc Motorcoach Div W201 N13900 Fond du Lac Ave	Richfield	WI	53076	414-677-3282	677-1570*
**Fax Area Code:* 262 ■ *TF:* 800-776-7026 ■ *Web:* www.ritewaybus.com					
Rocky Mountain Transportation Inc 1410 E Edgewood Dr	Whitefish	MT	59937	406-863-1200	863-1213
Web: www.rockymountaintrans.com					
Rolling V Transportation Services PO Box 110	South Fallsburg	NY	12779	845-434-0511	434-0259
Web: www.rollingv.com					
Romano's School Bus Service 1065 Belvoir Rd	Plymouth Meeting	PA	19462	610-272-7671	272-3871
TF: 800-877-2871 ■ *Web:* www.romanos-bus.com					
Royal Coach Lines Inc 924 Broadway PO Box 191	Thornwood	NY	10594	914-747-9494	747-9497
Safe-Way Bus Co 6030 Carmen Ave	Inver Grove Heights	MN	55076	651-451-1375	451-3525
Safety Bus Service 7200 Park Ave	Pennsauken	NJ	08109	856-665-2662	665-0658
Web: www.safetytours.com					
SBS Transit Inc 3747 Colorado Ave	Sheffield Village	OH	44054	440-949-8121	949-2979
TF: 800-548-5304 ■ *Web:* www.sbstransit.com					
Septran Inc 2000 W 96th St	Bloomington	MN	55431	952-881-9555	948-0126
Sheppard Bus Service 35 Rockville Rd	Bridgeton	NJ	08302	856-451-4004	453-1620
Stock Transportation 1670 Comstock Rd	Gloucester	ON	K1B5L2	613-749-3777	749-3075
Web: www.stocktransportation.com					
Stock Transportation Ltd 360 Shirley Ave	Kitchener	ON	N2B2E1	519-742-6224	579-2530
Web: www.stocktransportation.com					
Stock Transportation Ltd 25 Millard Ave W	Newmarket	ON	L3Y7R6	905-952-0878	952-0892
Web: www.stock-transport.com					
Student Transportation of America Inc 3349 Hwy 138 Bldg B Suite D	Wall	NJ	07719	732-280-4200	280-4214
TF: 888-942-2250 ■ *Web:* www.ridesta.com					
Suffolk Transportation Service Inc 10 Moffitt Blvd	Bay Shore	NY	11706	631-665-3245	665-3186
Web: www.suffolkbus.com					
TNT Bus Service 655 Walck Rd	North Tonawanda	NY	14120	716-695-7898	695-7506
WE Transport Inc 75 Commercial St	Plainview	NY	11803	516-349-8200	349-8275
Web: www.wetransport.com					
Williams Bus Lines Inc PO Box 1272	Springfield	VA	22151	703-560-5355	560-7851
Web: www.williamsbus.com					
WT Holmes Transportation Co 22 Myrtle St	Norfolk	MA	02056	508-528-4550	528-4728

110 BUSINESS FORMS

SEE ALSO Printing Companies - Commercial Printers p. 1503

				Phone	Fax
Ace Forms of Kansas Inc 2900 N Rotary Terr	Pittsburg	KS	66762	620-232-9290	232-1111
TF: 800-223-9287 ■ *Web:* www.aceforms.com					
Adams Business Forms Inc 200 Jackson St	Topeka	KS	66603	785-233-4101	233-4291
TF: 800-444-0038					
Allied Business Documents 333 Bucklin St	Providence	RI	02907	401-461-1700	785-8214
TF: 800-556-6310					
Allison Payment Systems LLC 2200 Production Dr	Indianapolis	IN	46241	317-808-2400	808-2477
TF: 800-755-2440 ■ *Web:* www.apsllc.com					
Amsterdam Printing & Litho Corp 166 Wallins Corners Rd	Amsterdam	NY	12010	518-842-6000	843-5204
TF: 800-833-6231 ■ *Web:* www.amsterdamprinting.com					
Apex Color 200 N Lee St	Jacksonville	FL	32204	904-358-2928	358-8811
TF: 800-367-6790 ■ *Web:* www.apexcolor.net					
Apperson Print Management Services 6855 E Gage Ave	Los Angeles	CA	90040	562-927-4718	927-2169
TF: 800-877-2341 ■ *Web:* www.appersonprint.com					
B & D Litho Inc 3820 N 38th Ave	Phoenix	AZ	85019	602-269-2526	269-2520
TF Cust Svc: 800-735-0375 ■ *Web:* www.bndlitho.com					
Bankers Systems Inc 6815 Saukview Dr	Saint Cloud	MN	56303	320-251-3060	251-8110
TF: 800-397-2341 ■ *Web:* www.bankerssystems.com					
BBF Printing Solutions 10950 S Belcher Rd	Largo	FL	33777	727-541-4641	541-1780
Web: www.bbfprinting.com					
Beldar Business Forms Inc 5 Fur Ct	Oakland	NJ	07436	201-405-2217	405-0038
Bernadette Business Forms Inc 8950 Pershall Rd	Saint Louis	MO	63042	314-522-1700	524-6161*
**Fax:* Mktg ■ *TF:* 800-862-7288 ■ *Web:* www.bbf.com					
Bestforms Inc 1135 Avenida Acaso	Camarillo	CA	93012	805-388-0503	987-5280
TF: 800-350-0618 ■ *Web:* www.bestforms.com					
Business Forms Inc 3498 Grand Ave	Pittsburgh	PA	15225	412-331-3300	331-5566
TF: 800-451-8086					
Calibrated Forms Co Inc 537 N East Ave	Columbus	KS	66725	800-237-7576	752-4396
Web: www.calforms.com					
CCH Insurance Services 130 Turner St Bldg 3 4th Fl	Waltham	MA	02453	781-907-6677	925-6159*
**Fax Area Code:* 260 ■ *TF:* 800-481-1522 ■ *Web:* www.insurance.cch.com					
Central States Business Forms Inc 2500 Industrial Pkwy	Dewey	OK	74029	918-534-1280	534-3470
TF: 800-331-0920 ■ *Web:* www.centralstates.net					
Champion Industries Inc 2450-90 1st Ave	Huntington	WV	25703	304-528-2791	528-2746*
NASDAQ: CHMP ■ **Fax:* Cust Svc ■ *TF:* 800-624-3431 ■ *Web:* www.champion-industries.com					
Computer Stock Forms Inc 324 S Washington St	Greenfield	OH	45123	937-981-7751	981-2159
TF: 800-543-5565 ■ *Web:* www.computerstockformsinc.com					
Corporate Express Document & Print Management 4205 S 96th St	Omaha	NE	68127	402-339-0900	898-6360
TF: 800-228-9277 ■ *Web:* www.corporate-express.com					
Curtis 1000 Inc 1725 Breckinridge Pkwy Suite 500	Duluth	GA	30096	678-380-9095	594-0518*
**Fax Area Code:* 800 ■ **Fax:* Mktg ■ *TF:* 800-683-8162 ■ *Web:* www.curtis1000.com					
Custom Business Forms Inc 210 Edge Pl	Minneapolis	MN	55418	612-789-0002	789-6321
TF: 800-234-1221 ■ *Web:* www.cbfnet.com					
Data Business Forms Ltd 9195 Torbram Rd	Brampton	ON	L6S6H2	905-791-6944	638-8373*
**Fax Area Code:* 800 ■ *Web:* www.dbf.com					
Data Papers Inc 468 Industrial Park Rd	Muncy	PA	17756	570-546-2201	546-2366*
**Fax Area Code:* 888 ■ *TF:* 800-233-3032 ■ *Web:* www.datapapers.com					
Data Source Inc 1400 Universal Ave	Kansas City	MO	64120	816-483-3282	483-3284
TF: 800-829-3369 ■ *Web:* www.data-source.com					
Datatel Resources Corp 1729 Pennsylvania Ave	Monaca	PA	15061	724-775-5300	775-0688
TF: 800-245-2688 ■ *Web:* www.datatelcorp.com					
DFS Group 12 South St	Townsend	MA	01469	800-225-9528	876-6337
Web: www.dfsbusiness.com					
Donnelley RR & Sons Co 111 S Wacker Dr	Chicago	IL	60601	312-326-8000	326-8543*
NYSE: RRD ■ **Fax:* Mail Rm ■ *Web:* www.rrdonnelley.com					
DSFI 450 S Lombard Rd	Addison	IL	60101	630-627-7777	828-9511*
**Fax Area Code:* 800 ■ **Fax:* Cust Svc ■ *TF Cust Svc:* 800-828-1411 ■ *Web:* www.dsfiforms.com					
Dupli-Systems Inc 8260 Dow Cir	Strongsville	OH	44136	440-234-9415	234-2350
TF: 800-321-1610 ■ *Web:* www.dupli-systems.com					
Eagle Graphics Inc 150 N Moyer St	Annville	PA	17003	717-867-5576	867-5579
Web: www.eaglegraphic.com					
Eastern Business Forms Inc 530 Old Sulphur Springs Rd	Greenville	SC	29607	864-288-2451	297-6492
Ennis Inc 2441 Residential Pkwy	Midlothian	TX	76065	972-872-3100	872-3195
NYSE: EBF ■ *Web:* www.ennis.com					
Executive Greetings Inc 120 Greenwoods Industrial Pk	New Hartford	CT	06057	860-379-9911	379-7124
TF Cust Svc: 800-562-5468 ■ *Web:* www.executive-greetings.com					
Falcon Business Forms Inc PO Box 326	Corsicana	TX	75151	903-874-6583	872-7960
TF: 800-442-6262					
Federal Business Products Inc 95 Main Ave	Clifton	NJ	07014	973-667-9800	667-7756
TF: 800-927-5123 ■ *Web:* www.feddirect.com					
Flesh Co 2118 59th St	Saint Louis	MO	63110	314-781-4400	781-5546*
**Fax:* Sales ■ *TF:* 800-869-3330 ■ *Web:* www.fleshco.com					
Forms Manufacturers Inc 312 E Forest Ave	Girard	KS	66743	620-724-8225	724-8188
TF: 800-835-0614					
Freedom Graphic Services Inc 1101 S Janesville St	Milton	WI	53563	608-868-7007	868-7006
TF: 800-334-3540 ■ *Web:* www.freedomgraphicsystems.com					
General Credit Forms Inc 3595 Rider Trail S	Earth City	MO	63045	314-216-8600	216-8570
TF: 800-325-1158 ■ *Web:* www.gcfinc.com					
Genoa Business Forms Inc 445 Park Ave	Sycamore	IL	60178	815-895-2800	895-8206
TF: 800-383-2801 ■ *Web:* www.genoabusforms.com					
Gulf Business Forms Inc 2460 S IH-35 PO Box 1073	San Marcos	TX	78667	512-353-8313	353-8866
TF: 800-433-4853 ■ *Web:* www.gulfforms.com					
Harland John H Co 2939 Miller Rd	Decatur	GA	30035	770-981-9460	593-5347
NYSE: JH ■ *TF:* 800-723-3690 ■ *Web:* www.harland.net					
Highland Computer Forms Inc 1025 W Main St	Hillsboro	OH	45133	937-393-4215	842-6485*
**Fax Area Code:* 800 ■ **Fax:* Sales ■ *TF:* 800-669-5213 ■ *Web:* www.hcf.com					
Holden Graphic Services 607 Washington Ave N	Minneapolis	MN	55401	612-339-0241	349-0433
TF: 800-423-1099 ■ *Web:* www.holdengraphics.com					
Hospital Forms & Systems Corp 8900 Ambassador Row	Dallas	TX	75247	214-634-8900	905-3819
TF: 800-527-5081 ■ *Web:* www.hforms.com					
Howard Press Inc 450 W 1st Ave	Roselle	NJ	07203	908-245-4400	245-1139
TF: 800-223-0648 ■ *Web:* www.howardpress.com					
Hygrade Business Group Inc 232 Entin Rd	Clifton	NJ	07014	973-249-6700	249-6109
TF: 800-836-7714 ■ *Web:* www.hygradebusiness.com					
Imperial Graphics Inc 3100 Walkent Dr NW	Grand Rapids	MI	49544	616-784-0100	784-8256
TF: 800-777-2591 ■ *Web:* www.impgraphics.com					
Integrated Print & Graphics 645 Stevenson Rd	South Elgin	IL	60177	847-695-6777	741-4090
Web: www.ipandginc.com					
Interform Solutions 1901 Mayview Rd	Bridgeville	PA	15017	412-221-3300	221-6585*
**Fax:* Mktg ■ *TF:* 800-945-7746 ■ *Web:* www.interformsolutions.com					
International Business Systems Inc 431 Yerkes Rd	King of Prussia	PA	19406	610-265-7997	265-7997
TF: 800-220-1255 ■ *Web:* www.ibs4cmyk.com					
John H Harland Co 2939 Miller Rd	Decatur	GA	30035	770-981-9460	593-5347
NYSE: JH ■ *TF:* 800-723-3690 ■ *Web:* www.harland.net					
Kaye-Smith PO Box 956	Renton	WA	98057	425-228-8600	271-0203
TF: 800-822-9987 ■ *Web:* www.kayesmith.com					
Maggio Data Forms Printing Ltd 1735 Expy Dr N	Hauppauge	NY	11788	631-348-0343	348-7529
TF: 800-783-6313 ■ *Web:* www.maggio.com					
Miami Systems Corp 10001 Alliance Rd	Cincinnati	OH	45242	513-793-0110	793-1140
TF: 800-543-4540 ■ *Web:* www.miamisystems.com					
Moore North America 1200 Lakeside Dr	Bannockburn	IL	60015	847-607-6000	607-7060*
**Fax:* Sales ■ *TF:* 800-745-0780 ■ *Web:* www.moore.com					
National Business Forms Inc 100 Pennsylvania Ave	Greeneville	TN	37743	423-638-7691	638-7782
TF Cust Svc: 800-722-8544					
NCP Solutions 5200 E Lake Blvd	Birmingham	AL	35217	205-849-5200	849-2907
Web: www.ncpsolutions.com					
NCR Corp Systemedia Div 1700 S Patterson Blvd	Dayton	OH	45479	937-445-5000	253-1846*
**Fax Area Code:* 800 ■ **Fax:* Cust Svc					
New England Business Service Inc (NEBS) 500 Main St	Groton	MA	01471	978-448-6111	333-4376*
**Fax Area Code:* 800 ■ **Fax:* Cust Svc ■ *TF Sales:* 800-225-6380 ■ *Web:* www.nebs.com					
New Jersey Business Forms Mfg Co 55 W Sheffield Ave	Englewood	NJ	07631	201-569-4500	569-1137
TF: 800-466-6523 ■ *Web:* www.njbf.com					
Northstar Computer Forms Inc 7130 Northland Cir N	Brooklyn Park	MN	55428	763-531-7340	535-5671
TF: 800-765-6787 ■ *Web:* www.nscf.com					
Paris Business Products 800 Highland Dr	Mount Holly	NJ	08060	609-265-9200	261-4853
TF Cust Svc: 800-523-6454 ■ *Web:* www.pariscorp.com					
Paris Corp 800 Highland Dr	Mount Holly	NJ	08060	609-387-7300	387-2114
Web: www.pariscorp.com					
Patterson Office Supplies 3310 N Duncan Rd PO Box 9009	Champaign	IL	60826	217-351-5400	843-3676*
**Fax Area Code:* 800 ■ *TF Cust Svc:* 800-637-1140 ■ *Web:* www.pattersonofficesupplies.com					
Performance Office Papers 21673 Cedar Ave	Lakeville	MN	55044	952-469-1400	488-5058*
**Fax Area Code:* 800 ■ *TF:* 800-458-7189 ■ *Web:* www.perfpapers.com					
PrintEdd Products of North America 2641 Forum Dr	Grand Prairie	TX	75052	972-988-3133	641-2564
TF: 800-367-6728 ■ *Web:* www.printedd.com					
Printegra Inc 403 Westpark Ct Suite A	Peachtree City	GA	30269	770-631-6070	631-6188
TF: 800-422-6070 ■ *Web:* www.printegra.com					
Printgraphics Inc 1170 Industrial Park Dr	Vandalia	OH	45377	937-898-3008	898-3071
TF: 800-543-7510 ■ *Web:* www.printgraphics.com					

				Phone	Fax
Pummill Business Forms Inc 903 Chicago Dr *TF:* 888-786-6455 ■ *Web:* www.pummill.com	Grand Rapids	MI	49509	616-475-9000	475-0491
Quality Forms 4317 W US Rt 36 **Fax Area Code:* 888 ■ *Web:* www.qualforms.com	Piqua	OH	45356	937-773-4595	550-3937*
Rapidforms Inc 301 Grove Rd **Fax Area Code:* 800 ■ *TF Cust Svc:* 800-257-8354 ■ *Web:* www.rapidforms.com	Thorofare	NJ	08086	856-384-1144	348-8113*
Rotary Forms Press Inc 835 S High St *TF:* 800-654-2876 ■ *Web:* www.rotaryformspress.com	Hillsboro	OH	45133	937-393-3426	393-8473
Royal Business Forms Inc 3301 Ave 'E' East *TF:* 800-255-9303	Arlington	TX	76011	817-640-5248	633-2164
RR Donnelley & Sons Co 111 S Wacker Dr *NYSE: RRD* ■ **Fax:* Mail Rm ■ *Web:* www.rrdonnelley.com	Chicago	IL	60601	312-326-8000	326-8543*
Safeguard Business Systems Inc 8585 N Stemmons Fwy Suite 600 N *TF:* 800-338-0636 ■ *Web:* www.safeguard.org	Dallas	TX	75247	214-905-3935	630-6821
SFI Inc 225 W Olney Rd **Fax Area Code:* 757 ■ *TF:* 800-899-8713 ■ *Web:* www.sfinet.com	Norfolk	VA	23510	866-789-8999	622-8899*
Socrates Media LLC DBA Made E-Z Products LLC 227 W Monroe St Suite 500 *TF:* 800-822-4566 ■ *Web:* www.socrates.com	Chicago	IL	60606	312-762-5600	762-5601
Source4 4141 S Peoria St *Web:* www.source4.com	Chicago	IL	60609	773-247-4141	247-1313
Specialized Printed Forms Inc 352 Center St *TF:* 800-688-2381 ■ *Web:* www.spforms.com	Caledonia	NY	14423	585-538-2381	538-4922
Standard Register Co PO Box 1167 *NYSE: SR* ■ **Fax:* Sales ■ *TF:* 800-755-6405 ■ *Web:* www.stdreg.com	Dayton	OH	45401	937-221-1000	221-4427*
Sterling Business Forms 5300 Crater Lake Ave *TF Cust Svc:* 800-759-3676 ■ *Web:* www.sbfnet.com	Central Point	OR	97502	541-779-3173	772-2409
Stry-Lenkoff Co Inc 1100 W Broadway St *TF:* 800-626-8247 ■ *Web:* www.strylenkoff.com	Louisville	KY	40232	502-587-6804	587-6822
Tinker Business Forms 192 Chandalar Place Dr	Pelham	AL	35124	205-663-9979	663-9923
United Business Forms Inc 8482 W Allens Bridge Rd *TF:* 800-547-5351	Greeneville	TN	37743	423-639-5551	639-7217
Unz & Co 201 Circle Dr N Suite 104 *TF:* 800-631-3098 ■ *Web:* www.unzco.com	Piscataway	NJ	08854	732-868-0706	868-0607
Victor Printing Inc 1 Victor Way *TF:* 800-443-2845 ■ *Web:* www.victorptg.com	Sharon	PA	16146	724-342-2106	342-6147
Ward-Kraft Inc 2401 Cooper St *TF:* 800-821-4021 ■ *Web:* www.wardkraft.com	Fort Scott	KS	66701	620-223-5500	223-6953
Web Graphics PO Box 308 *TF:* 800-833-8863 ■ *Web:* www.printatweb.com	Glens Falls	NY	12801	518-792-6501	792-9353
Wilmer Service Line 515 W Sycamore St **Fax Area Code:* 800 ■ *Web:* www.4wilmer.com	Coldwater	OH	45828	888-494-5637	553-4849*
Wise Business Forms Inc 555 McFarland 400 Dr *TF:* 888-815-9473 ■ *Web:* www.wbf.com	Alpharetta	GA	30004	770-442-1060	442-9849
Witt Printing Co Inc 301 Oak St *TF:* 800-641-4342 ■ *Web:* www.wittprinting.com	El Dorado Springs	MO	64744	417-876-4721	876-4794
WorkflowOne 220 E Monument Ave *TF:* 866-789-8999 ■ *Web:* www.workflowone.com	Dayton	OH	45402	877-735-4966	
Wright Business Forms Inc 2525 Braga Dr *TF:* 800-487-2204	Broadview	IL	60155	708-865-7600	865-7626
Wright Business Graphics 18440 NE San Rafael St *TF:* 800-547-8397 ■ *Web:* www.wrightbg.com	Portland	OR	97230	503-661-2525	661-0515

111 BUSINESS MACHINES - MFR

SEE ALSO Business Machines - Whol p. 1402; Calculators - Electronic p. 1404; Computer Equipment p. 1500; Photocopying Equipment & Supplies p. 2113

				Phone	Fax
Agissar Corp 526 Benton St *TF:* 800-627-8256 ■ *Web:* www.agissar.com	Stratford	CT	06615	203-375-8662	375-5345
Allegheny Paper Shredders Corp PO Box 80 *TF:* 800-245-2497 ■ *Web:* www.alleghenyshredders.com	Delmont	PA	15626	724-468-4300	468-5919
Amano Cincinnati Inc 140 Harrison Ave *TF:* 800-526-2559 ■ *Web:* www.amano.com	Roseland	NJ	07068	973-403-1900	364-1086
Atlantic Zeiser Inc 15 Patton Dr *Web:* www.atlanticzeiserusa.com	West Caldwell	NJ	07006	973-228-0800	228-9064
Better Packages Inc 255 Canal St **Fax:* Cust Svc ■ *TF:* 800-237-9151 ■ *Web:* betterpackages.com	Shelton	CT	06484	203-926-3700	926-3705*
Bidwell Industrial Group Inc 2055 S Main St *TF:* 800-235-0999 ■ *Web:* www.bidwellinc.com	Middletown	CT	06457	860-346-9283	347-8775
Bind-It Corp 150 Commerce Dr *TF:* 800-645-5110 ■ *Web:* www.bindit.com	Hauppauge	NY	11788	631-234-2500	234-3279
BOWE Bell + Howell 3791 S Alston Ave *TF:* 800-220-3030 ■ *Web:* www.bellhowell.com	Durham	NC	27713	919-767-7595	
Brother International Corp 100 Somerset Corporate Blvd *TF Cust Svc:* 800-276-7746 ■ *Web:* www.brother-usa.com	Bridgewater	NJ	08807	908-704-1700	704-8235
Burn James International 211 Cottage St **Fax Area Code:* 800 ■ *TF:* 800-431-4610 ■ *Web:* www.wire-o.com	Poughkeepsie	NY	12601	845-454-8200	562-8630*
Canon USA Inc 1 Canon Plaza *NYSE: CAJ* ■ **Fax:* Hum Res ■ *TF:* 800-828-4040 ■ *Web:* www.usa.canon.com	Lake Success	NY	11042	516-488-6700	328-4669*
CP Bourg Inc 50 Samuel Barnet Blvd *Web:* www.cpbourg.com	New Bedford	MA	02745	508-998-2171	998-2391
Cummins-Allison Corp 891 Feehanville Dr *TF:* 800-786-5528 ■ *Web:* www.cumminsallison.com	Mount Prospect	IL	60056	847-299-9550	299-4939
De La Rue Cash Systems Inc 705 S 12th St *Web:* www.delarue.com	Watertown	WI	53094	920-261-1780	261-1783
Diagraph Corp 1 Missouri Research Park Dr **Fax Area Code:* 636 ■ *Web:* www.diagraph.com	Saint Charles	MO	63304	800-526-2531	300-2005*
Dictaphone Corp 3191 Broadbridge Ave **Fax:* Mktg ■ *TF:* 800-942-6374 ■ *Web:* www.dictaphone.com	Stratford	CT	06614	203-381-7000	386-8597*
Dynetics Engineering Corp 515 Bond St *TF:* 800-888-8110 ■ *Web:* www.dyneticsengineering.com	Lincolnshire	IL	60069	847-541-7300	541-7488
Ecco Business Systems Inc 60 W 38th St 4th Fl *TF:* 800-682-3226 ■ *Web:* www.eccobusiness.com	New York	NY	10018	212-921-4545	921-2198
ECRM Inc 554 Clark Rd *Web:* www.ecrm.com	Tewksbury	MA	01876	978-851-0207	851-7016
Fellowes Inc 1789 Norwood Ave **Fax:* Cust Svc ■ *TF:* 800-945-4545 ■ *Web:* www.fellowes.com	Itasca	IL	60143	630-893-1600	893-1718*
Frisco Bay Industries Ltd 160 Graveline St *TF:* 800-463-7472 ■ *Web:* www.friscobay.com	Saint-Laurent	QC	H4T1R7	514-738-7300	735-7039
General Binding Corp 1 GBC Plaza **Fax Area Code:* 800 ■ *TF Orders:* 800-723-4000 ■ *Web:* www.gbcconnect.com	Northbrook	IL	60062	847-272-3700	914-8178*
Global Payment Technologies Inc 425 B Oser Ave *NASDAQ: GPTX* ■ *TF:* 800-472-2506 ■ *Web:* www.gptx.com	Hauppauge	NY	11788	631-231-1177	434-1771
Gradco USA Inc 871 Coronado Center Dr Suite 200 *Web:* www.gradco.com	Henderson	NV	89052	702-940-2266	952-0400
Imagistics International Inc 100 Oakview Dr *TF:* 800-945-9708 ■ *Web:* www.imagistics.com	Trumbull	CT	06611	203-365-7000	365-2329
Industrial Paper Shredders Inc 707 S Ellsworth Ave PO Box 180 *TF:* 888-637-4733 ■ *Web:* www.industrialshredders.com	Salem	OH	44460	330-332-0024	332-4535
International Business Machines Corp (IBM) 1 New Orchard Rd *NYSE: IBM* ■ *TF:* 800-426-4968 ■ *Web:* www.ibm.com/us	Armonk	NY	10504	914-766-1900	
James Burn International 211 Cottage St **Fax Area Code:* 800 ■ *TF:* 800-431-4610 ■ *Web:* www.wire-o.com	Poughkeepsie	NY	12601	845-454-8200	562-8630*
Lathem Time Corp 200 Selig Dr SW **Fax Area Code:* 800 ■ *TF:* 800-241-4990 ■ *Web:* www.lathem.com	Atlanta	GA	30336	404-691-0400	252-2208*
Lexmark International Inc 740 W New Circle Rd *NYSE: LXK* ■ *TF Cust Svc:* 800-539-6275 ■ *Web:* www.lexmark.com	Lexington	KY	40550	859-232-2000	
Lynde-Ordway Co Inc 3308 W Warner Ave *TF:* 800-762-7057 ■ *Web:* www.lynde-ordway.com	Santa Ana	CA	92704	714-957-1311	433-2166
Martin Yale Industries Inc 251 Wedcor Ave *TF:* 800-225-5644 ■ *Web:* www.martinyale.com	Wabash	IN	46992	260-563-0641	563-4575
Michael Business Machines Corp 3134 Industry Dr *TF Cust Svc:* 800-223-2508 ■ *Web:* www.mbmcorp.com	North Charleston	SC	29418	843-552-2700	552-2974
Neopost Inc 30955 Huntwood Ave *TF Cust Svc:* 800-827-4543 ■ *Web:* www.neopost.com	Hayward	CA	94544	510-489-6800	475-5701
Neopost Inc Canada 150 Steelcase Rd W *TF:* 800-636-7678 ■ *Web:* www.neopost.ca	Markham	ON	L3R3J9	905-475-3722	475-7699
Paymaster Technologies Inc 900 Pratt Blvd *TF:* 800-462-4477 ■ *Web:* www.paymastertech.com	Elk Grove Village	IL	60007	847-758-1234	758-0123
Pitney Bowes Inc 1 Elmcroft Rd *NYSE: PBI* ■ *TF:* 800-672-6937 ■ *Web:* www.pb.com	Stamford	CT	06926	203-356-5000	460-3851
Pubco Corp 3830 Kelley Ave *TF:* 800-837-4323	Cleveland	OH	44114	216-881-5300	881-8380
Royal Consumer Information Products Inc 379 Campus Dr 2nd Fl *TF Sales:* 888-261-4555 ■ *Web:* www.royal.com	Somerset	NJ	08875	732-627-9977	667-1556
Security Check 261 Jackson Ave W PO Box 1211 *TF:* 877-892-4325 ■ *Web:* www.security-check.com	Oxford	MS	38655	662-234-0440	234-2469
Security Engineered Machinery Co Inc 5 Walkup Dr PO Box 1045 *TF Sales:* 800-225-9293 ■ *Web:* www.semshred.com	Westborough	MA	01581	508-366-1488	836-4154
Sharp Electronics Corp 1 Sharp Plaza *TF:* 800-237-4277 ■ *Web:* www.sharpusa.com	Mahwah	NJ	07430	201-529-8200	529-8413
Staplex Co 777 5th Ave *TF Cust Svc:* 800-221-0822 ■ *Web:* www.staplex.com	Brooklyn	NY	11232	718-768-3333	965-0750
Swintec Corp 320 W Commercial Ave *TF:* 800-225-0867 ■ *Web:* www.swintec.com	Moonachie	NJ	07074	201-935-0115	933-9745
Toshiba TEC America 4401-A Bankers Cir *Web:* www.toshibatecusa.com	Atlanta	GA	30360	770-449-3040	449-1152
Varitronic Systems Inc 6835 Winnetka Cir *TF:* 800-328-0585 ■ *Web:* www.varitronicsystems.com	Brooklyn Park	MN	55428	763-536-6400	536-0769

112 BUSINESS MACHINES - WHOL

SEE ALSO Business Machines - Mfr p. 1402; Computer Equipment & Software - Whol p. 1504; Photocopying Equipment & Supplies p. 2113

				Phone	Fax
3M Canada Co PO Box 5757 **Fax:* Library ■ *TF:* 800-265-1840 ■ *Web:* www.3m.com/ca/	London	ON	N6A4T1	519-451-2500	452-4714*
Canon Business Solutions-Central 425 N Martingale Rd Suite 1400 **Fax:* Hum Res ■ *TF:* 800-706-3303 ■ *Web:* www.solutions.canon.com/central	Schaumburg	IL	60173	847-706-3400	706-3419*
Canon Business Solutions-Northeast Inc 125 Park Ave 9th Fl **Fax:* Mktg ■ *TF:* 800-627-2679 ■ *Web:* www.solutions.canon.com/northeast	New York	NY	10017	212-850-1000	661-2779*
Canon Business Solutions-Southeast Inc 300 Commerce Sq Blvd **Fax:* Mktg ■ *TF:* 800-220-4000 ■ *Web:* www.solutions.canon.com/southeast	Burlington	NJ	08016	609-387-8700	239-6489*
Canon Business Solutions-West 110 W Walnut St *Web:* www.solutions.canon.com/west	Gardena	CA	90248	310-217-3000	715-7050
Cash Register Sales Inc 4851 White Bear Pkwy *TF:* 800-333-4949 ■ *Web:* www.crs-usa.com	Saint Paul	MN	55110	651-294-2700	294-2900
Daisy IT Supplies Sales & Service 10742 Edison Ct *TF:* 800-266-5585 ■ *Web:* www.itsdaisy.com	Rancho Cucamonga	CA	91730	909-989-5585	989-7251
Danka Office Imaging Co Inc 7940 Marshall Dr *TF:* 800-336-4323 ■ *Web:* www.danka.com	Lenexa	KS	66214	913-495-5000	495-5087
Datamax Office Systems Inc 6717 Waldemar Ave *TF:* 800-325-9299 ■ *Web:* www.datamaxstlouis.com	Saint Louis	MO	63139	314-647-2500	633-1402
Dieterich-Post Co 616 Monterey Pass Rd **Fax Area Code:* 800 ■ *TF:* 800-955-3729 ■ *Web:* www.dieterich-post.com	Monterey Park	CA	91754	626-289-5021	688-3729*
Dresco Reproduction Inc 12603 Allard St *TF:* 800-423-5834 ■ *Web:* www.dresco.com	Santa Fe Springs	CA	90670	562-863-6677	868-9757
El Dorado Trading Group Inc 760 San Antonio Rd *TF:* 800-227-8292 ■ *Web:* www.edtg.com	Palo Alto	CA	94303	650-494-6600	494-1995
FDC Corp 360 Bonnie Ln *TF:* 800-848-5622 ■ *Web:* www.fdccorp.com	Elk Grove Village	IL	60007	847-437-3990	437-3995
FP Mailing Solutions 140 N Mitchell Ct *TF:* 800-341-6052 ■ *Web:* www.fpusa.com	Addison	IL	60101	630-827-5500	241-9091
Global Imaging Systems Inc 3820 Northdale Blvd Suite 200A *NASDAQ: GISX* ■ *TF:* 888-628-7834 ■ *Web:* www.global-imaging.com	Tampa	FL	33624	813-960-5508	264-7877
IKON Office Solutions Inc 70 Valley Stream Pkwy *NYSE: IKN* ■ *TF:* 800-983-2898 ■ *Web:* www.ikon.com	Malvern	PA	19355	610-296-8600	408-7026
Konica Minolta Business Solutions USA Inc 100 Williams Dr *Web:* www.kmbs.konicaminolta.us	Ramsey	NJ	07446	201-825-4000	
Lewan & Assoc Inc 1400 S Colorado Blvd *TF:* 800-553-9265 ■ *Web:* www.lewan.com	Denver	CO	80222	303-759-5440	759-0285
Merchants Solutions Co 4422 Roosevelt Rd *TF:* 800-486-3214 ■ *Web:* www.merchants-solutions.com	Hillside	IL	60162	708-449-6650	449-1432
New Age Electronics Inc 21950 Arnold Center Rd *TF:* 800-234-0300 ■ *Web:* www.newageinc.com	Carson	CA	90810	310-549-0000	549-5722
Numeridex Inc 632 Wheeling Rd *TF:* 800-323-7737 ■ *Web:* www.numeridex.com	Wheeling	IL	60090	847-541-8840	541-8392
Pitney Bowes Inc 1 Elmcroft Rd *NYSE: PBI* ■ *TF:* 800-672-6937 ■ *Web:* www.pb.com	Stamford	CT	06926	203-356-5000	460-3851
Ricoh Americas Corp 2300 Parklake Dr NE *Web:* www.ricoh-usa.com	Atlanta	GA	30345	770-496-9500	938-1020
Secap USA Inc 10 Clipper Rd *TF:* 800-523-0320 ■ *Web:* www.secapusa.com	West Conshohocken	PA	19428	610-825-6205	825-1397
Standard Duplicating Machines Corp 10 Connector Rd *TF:* 800-526-4774 ■ *Web:* www.sdmc.com	Andover	MA	01810	978-470-1920	475-1900
Stewart Engineering Supply Inc 3221 E Pioneer Pkwy *TF:* 800-533-1265 ■ *Web:* www.stewartengineering.com	Arlington	TX	76010	817-640-1767	633-7231

Phone Fax

Torex Retail Americas 5800 Ambler Dr Suite 215 ... Mississauga ON L4W4J4 905-507-4333 507-2325
TF: 800-387-3262 ■ Web: www.torexretail.com

BUSINESS ORGANIZATIONS

SEE Associations & Organizations - Professional & Trade - Management & Business Professional Associations p. 1333; Chambers of Commerce - Canadian p. 1413; Chambers of Commerce - International p. 1415; Chambers of Commerce - US - Local p. 1416; Chambers of Commerce - US - State p. 1440

113 BUSINESS SERVICE CENTERS

Phone Fax

Advanced Business Fulfillment Inc (ABF Inc)
3183 Rider Trail S ... Earth City MO 63045 314-770-2986 770-2654
TF: 800-804-7430 ■ Web: www.abfhealth.com
AIM Mail Centers 15550-D Rockfield Blvd ... Irvine CA 92618 949-837-4151 837-4537
TF: 800-669-4246 ■ Web: www.aimmailcenters.com
Allegra Network LLC 21680 Haggerty Rd ... Northville MI 48167 248-596-8600 596-8601
TF: 800-726-9050 ■ Web: www.allegranetwork.com
AlphaGraphics Inc 268 S State St Suite 300 ... Salt Lake City UT 84111 801-595-7270 595-7271
TF: 800-955-6246 ■ Web: www.alphagraphics.com
Color Reflections 3773 Richmond Ave ... Houston TX 77046 713-626-4045 623-6810
Web: www.colorreflections.com
Craters & Freighters 331 Corporate Cir Suite J ... Golden CO 80401 800-736-3335 399-9964*
*Fax Area Code: 303 ■ Web: www.cratersandfreighters.com
Duncan-Parnell Inc 900 S McDowell St ... Charlotte NC 28204 704-372-7766 333-3845
TF: 800-849-7708 ■ Web: www.duncan-parnell.com
FedEx Kinko's Office & Print Services Inc
13155 Noel Rd Suite 1600 ... Dallas TX 75240 214-550-7000 550-7001
TF Cust Svc: 800-254-6567 ■ Web: www.fedexkinkos.com
Group O Inc 4905 77th Ave ... Milan IL 61264 309-736-8300 736-8301
TF: 800-752-0730 ■ Web: www.groupo.com
Handle With Care Packaging Stores
5675 DTC Blvd Suite 280 ... Greenwood Village CO 80111 303-741-6626 741-6653
TF: 800-525-6309 ■ Web: www.gopackagingstore.com
Kinko's (now FedEx Kinko's Office & Print Services Inc)
13155 Noel Rd Suite 1600 ... Dallas TX 75240 214-550-7000 550-7001
TF Cust Svc: 800-254-6567 ■ Web: www.fedexkinkos.com
Mail Boxes Etc 6060 Cornerstone Ct W ... San Diego CA 92121 858-455-8800 546-7493
TF: 800-789-4623 ■ Web: www.mbe.com
Navis Logistics Network 5675 DTC Blvd Suite 280 ... Greenwood Village CO 80111 303-741-6626 741-6653
TF: 800-525-6309 ■ Web: www.gonavis.com
Navis Pack & Ship Centers
5675 DTC Blvd Suite 280 ... Greenwood Village CO 80111 303-741-6626 741-6653
TF: 800-525-6309 ■ Web: www.gonavis.com
Office Depot Inc 2200 Old Germantown Rd ... Delray Beach FL 33445 561-438-4800 438-4406*
NYSE: ODP ■ *Fax: Hum Res ■ TF: 800-937-3600 ■ Web: www.officedepot.com
Pak Mail Centers of America Inc
7173 S Havana St Suite 600 ... Englewood CO 80112 303-957-1000 790-9445
TF: 800-778-6665 ■ Web: pakmail.com
Parcel Plus Inc 12715 Telge Rd ... Cypress TX 77429 281-256-4100 373-4450
TF: 800-662-5553 ■ Web: www.parcelplus.com
Postal Connections of America
1081 Camino del Rio S Suite 109 ... San Diego CA 92108 619-294-7550 294-4550
TF: 800-767-8257 ■ Web: www.postalconnections.com
PostalAnnex+ Inc 7580 Metropolitan Dr Suite 200 ... San Diego CA 92108 619-563-4800 563-9850
TF: 800-456-1525 ■ Web: www.postalannex.com
PostNet International Franchise Corp 1819 Wazee St ... Denver CO 80202 303-771-7100 771-7133
TF: 800-841-7171 ■ Web: www.postnet.com
Sir Speedy Inc 26722 Plaza Dr ... Mission Viejo CA 92691 949-348-5000 348-5010
TF: 800-854-8297 ■ Web: www.sirspeedy.com
Staples Inc 500 Staples Dr ... Framingham MA 01702 508-253-5000 253-8989
NASDAQ: SPLS ■ TF: 800-378-2753 ■ Web: www.staples.com
TRM Corp 5208 NE 122nd Ave ... Portland OR 97230 503-257-8766 998-3712*
NASDAQ: TRMM ■ *Fax Area Code: 800 ■ TF: 800-877-8762 ■ Web: www.trm.com
UPS Store The 6060 Cornerstone Ct W ... San Diego CA 92121 858-455-8800 546-7492
Web: theupsstore.com

114 BUYER'S GUIDES - ONLINE

SEE ALSO Investment Guides - Online p. 1876

Phone Fax

Active Buyers Guide 1400 Fashion Island Blvd Suite 500 ... San Mateo CA 94404 650-342-0500 358-8600
Web: www.activebuyersguide.com
Bankrate.com 11760 US Hwy 1 Suite 500 ... North Palm Beach FL 33408 561-630-2400 625-4540
TF: 800-243-7720 ■ Web: www.bankrate.com
CardWeb.com Inc 10 N Jefferson St ... Frederick MD 21701 301-631-9100
TF: 800-260-7448 ■ Web: www.cardweb.com
ConsumerREVIEW Inc 2121 S El Camino Real Suite 400 ... San Mateo CA 94403 650-212-8600 341-6023
Web: www.consumerreview.com
Dr Toy 268 Bush St ... San Francisco CA 94104 800-551-8697 540-0171*
*Fax Area Code: 510 ■ Web: drtoy.com/main
Epinions Inc 8000 Marina Blvd 5th Fl ... Brisbane CA 94005 650-616-6500
Web: www.epinions.com
ePublicEye.com 1010 N Central Ave ... Glendale CA 91202 818-547-0222
Web: www.epubliceye.com
InsWeb Inc 11290 Pyrites Way Suite 200 ... Gold River CA 95670 916-853-3300 853-3325
NASDAQ: INSW ■ TF: 888-446-7932 ■ Web: www.insweb.com
mySimon Inc 235 2nd St ... San Francisco CA 94105 415-344-2000
Web: www.mysimon.com
PriceSCAN.com Inc 564 Nutt Rd Suite 103 ... Phoenixville PA 19460 610-651-0760
Web: www.pricescan.com
Shopping.com Inc 8000 Marina Blvd 5th Fl ... Brisbane CA 94005 650-616-6500 616-6510
Web: www.shopping.com

115 CABINETS - WOOD

SEE ALSO Construction - Special Trade Contractors - Carpentry & Flooring Contractors p. 1539; Furniture - Mfr - Household Furniture p. 1682

Phone Fax

American Woodmark Corp 3102 Shawnee Dr ... Winchester VA 22601 540-665-9100 665-9176
NASDAQ: AMWD ■ TF: 800-388-2483 ■ Web: www.americanwoodmark.com
Ampco Products Inc 11400 NW 36th Ave ... Miami FL 33167 305-821-5700 557-0764
Web: www.ampco.com
Armstrong Wood Products Inc 2500 Columbia Ave ... Lancaster PA 17603 717-396-0611 396-6344
Bertch Cabinet Mfg Inc PO Box 2280 ... Waterloo IA 50704 319-296-2987 296-2315
Web: www.bertch.com
Bloch Industries 140 Commerce Dr ... Rochester NY 14623 585-334-9600 521-9505*
*Fax Area Code: 800 ■ TF: 800-992-5624 ■ Web: www.blochindustries.com
Brandom Cabinets Co 404 Hawkins St ... Hillsboro TX 76645 254-580-1200 959-2801*
*Fax Area Code: 800 ■ TF Cust Svc: 800-366-8001 ■ Web: brandom.com
Cabinet Supply Inc 1700 NW 5th St ... Richmond IN 47374 765-966-6893 966-3283
Web: www.cabinetsupplyinc.com
Cal Door 400 Cochrane Cir ... Morgan Hill CA 95037 408-782-5700 782-9000
TF: 888-225-3667 ■ Web: www.caldoor.com
California Kitchen Cabinet Door Corp 400 Cochrane Cir ... Morgan Hill CA 95037 408-782-5700 782-9000
TF: 888-225-3667 ■ Web: www.caldoor.com
Cana Inc 29194 Phillips St ... Elkhart IN 46514 574-262-4664 262-0945
Canac A Kohler Co 360 John St ... Thornhill ON L3T3M9 905-881-2153 881-9725
TF: 800-226-2248 ■ Web: www.canackitchens.com
Canyon Creek Cabinet Co 16726 Tye St SE ... Monroe WA 98272 425-481-6860 674-0801*
*Fax Area Code: 206 ■ TF: 800-228-1830 ■ Web: www.canyoncreek.com
Cardell Cabinetry PO Box 200850 ... San Antonio TX 78220 210-225-0290 212-5823
Web: www.cardellcabinetry.com
Chandlers Plywood Products Inc PO Box 9009 ... Huntington WV 25704 304-429-1311 429-5886
TF: 800-624-3502 ■ Web: www.chandlerkitchens.com
Columbia Showcase & Cabinet Co 11034 Sherman Way ... Sun Valley CA 91352 818-765-9710 255-0750
Web: www.columbiashowcase.com
Commercial Wood Products Co 10019 Yucca Rd ... Adelanto CA 92301 760-246-4530 246-8226
Web: www.commercialwood.com
Conestoga Wood Specialties Inc 245 Reading Rd ... East Earl PA 17519 717-445-6701 638-7198*
*Fax Area Code: 800 ■ Web: www.conestogawood.com
Continental Cabinet Inc 2841 Pierce St ... Dallas TX 75233 214-467-4444 467-1132
TF: 800-786-6421 ■ Web: www.ccabinc.com
Coppes Napanee Co 455 E Lincoln St ... Nappanee IN 46550 574-773-4141 775-2889
Crystal Cabinet Works Inc 1100 Crystal Dr ... Princeton MN 55371 763-389-4187 389-5846
TF: 800-347-5045 ■ Web: www.ccworks.com
Custom Bilt Cabinet & Supply Inc PO Box 8969 ... Shreveport LA 71148 318-865-1412 865-1354
Dalia Kitchen Design Inc 1 Design Center Pl Suite 643 ... Boston MA 02210 617-482-2566 482-2744
Web: www.alno.com
Decore-ative Specialties Inc 2772 S Peck Rd ... Monrovia CA 91016 626-254-9191 254-1515
TF: 800-729-7277 ■ Web: www.decore.com
Dewils Industries Inc 6307 NE 127th Ave ... Vancouver WA 98682 360-892-0300 253-2096
Web: www.dewils.com
Dura Supreme Inc 300 Dura Dr ... Howard Lake MN 55349 320-543-3872 543-3310
Web: www.durasupreme.com
Dutch Made Custom Cabinetry 10415 Roth Rd ... Grabill IN 46741 260-657-3311 657-5778
Web: www.dutchmade.com
Evans Cabinet Corp 1321 N Franklin St ... Dublin GA 31021 478-272-2530 272-2731
Web: www.evanscabinet.com
Fashion Cabinet Mfg Inc 5440 W Axel Pk Rd ... West Jordan UT 84088 801-280-0646 280-8934
Web: www.fashioncabinet.com
Fixture Exchange Corp 3000 W Pafford St ... Fort Worth TX 76110 817-429-2496 927-8451
Fortune Brands Home & Hardware Inc 520 Lake Cook Rd ... Deerfield IL 60015 847-484-4400
Web: www.fortunebrands.com
Grabill Cabinet Co Inc PO Box 40 ... Grabill IN 46741 260-627-2131 627-3539
Web: www.grabillcabinets.com
Grandview Products Co 1601 Superior Dr ... Parsons KS 67357 620-421-6950 421-4211
TF: 800-247-9105 ■ Web: www.grandviewcabinets.com
Haas Cabinet Co Inc 625 W Utica St ... Sellersburg IN 47172 812-246-4431 246-5420
TF: 800-457-6458 ■ Web: www.haascabinet.com
HomeCrest Cabinetry 1002 Eisenhower Dr N ... Goshen IN 46526 574-535-9300 533-3667
TF: 800-960-3660 ■ Web: www.homecrestcab.com
Huntwood Industries 23800 E Apple Way ... Liberty Lake WA 99019 509-924-5858 928-6647
TF: 800-873-7350 ■ Web: www.huntwood.com
Kabinart Corp 3650 Trousdale Dr ... Nashville TN 37204 615-833-1961 834-8268
Kent Moore Cabinets Ltd 1460 Fountain Ave ... Bryan TX 77801 979-775-2906 775-0519
TF: 800-366-9233 ■ Web: www.kentmoorecabinets.com
Kinzee Industries Inc 1 Paul Kohner Pl ... Elmwood Park NJ 07407 201-797-4700 797-1360
Kitchen Craft of Canada Ltd 1180 Springfield Rd ... Winnipeg MB R2C2Z2 204-224-3211 222-7608
TF: 800-463-9707 ■ Web: www.kitchencraft.com
Kitchen Kompact Inc 911 E 11th St ... Jeffersonville IN 47130 812-282-6681 282-7880
Web: www.kitchenkompact.com
Kraftmaid Cabinetry Inc PO Box 1055 ... Middlefield OH 44062 440-632-5333 632-5648
Web: www.kraftmaid.com
Legacy Cabinets LLC PO Box 730 ... Eastaboga AL 36260 256-831-4888 831-4896
TF: 800-813-1112
Marsh Furniture Co 1001 S Centennial St ... High Point NC 27260 336-884-7363 884-0883
TF: 800-756-2774 ■ Web: www.marshfurniture.com
Martin Cabinet Inc 336 S Washington St ... Plainville CT 06062 860-747-5769 747-9595
Masco Corp 21001 Van Born Rd ... Taylor MI 48180 313-274-7400 792-6135
NYSE: MAS ■ Web: www.masco.com
MasterBrand Cabinets Inc 1 MasterBrand Cabinets Dr ... Jasper IN 47546 812-482-2527 482-5977
Web: www.mbcabinets.com
MasterBrand Industries Inc PO Box 420 ... Jasper IN 47547 812-482-2527 482-5977
Web: www.masterbrand.com
Mastercraft Industries Inc 120 W Allen St ... Rice Lake WI 54868 715-234-8111 234-6370
Web: www.mastercraftindustries.com
McConnell Cabinets Inc 13110 Louden Ln ... City of Industry CA 91746 626-937-2200 937-2207
TF: 800-794-7895 ■ Web: www.mcconnellinc.com
Medallion Cabinetry 180 Industrial Blvd ... Waconia MN 55387 952-442-5171 442-4998
TF: 800-543-4074 ■ Web: www.medallioncabinetry.com
Merillat Industries LLC PO Box 1946 ... Adrian MI 49221 517-263-0771 265-3325
TF: 866-850-8557 ■ Web: www.merillat.com
Mid-America Cabinet Inc PO Box 219 ... Gentry AR 72734 479-736-2671 736-8086
Web: www.midamericacabinets.com
Millbrook Kitchens 3565 Rt 20 PO Box 570 ... Nassau NY 12123 518-766-3033 766-3919
Web: www.millbrookkitchens.com
Millbrook Millwork Inc DBA Millbrook Kitchens
3565 Rt 20 PO Box 570 ... Nassau NY 12123 518-766-3033 766-3919
Web: www.millbrookkitchens.com
Mouser Custom Cabinetry 2112 N Hwy 31 W ... Elizabethtown KY 42701 270-737-7477 737-7446
TF: 800-345-7537 ■ Web: www.mousercc.com
Norcraft Cos LLC 3020 Denmark Ave Suite 100 ... Eagan MN 55121 651-234-3300
TF: 800-297-0661 ■ Web: www.norcraftcompanies.com
Omega Cabinetry Ltd 1205 Peters Dr ... Waterloo IA 50703 319-235-5700 235-5853*
*Fax: Cust Svc ■ Web: www.omegacab.com
Patella Industries 161 Stirling Ave ... LaSalle QC H8R3P3 514-364-1964 364-1906
Web: www.patella.com

Company	City	State	Zip	Phone	Fax
Patrick Industries Inc 107 W Franklin St	Elkhart	IN	46515	574-294-7511	522-5213
NASDAQ: PATK ■ *TF:* 800-331-2151 ■ *Web:* www.patrickind.com					
Plain & Fancy Custom Cabinetry Inc PO Box 519	Schaefferstown	PA	17088	717-949-6571	949-2114
TF: 800-447-9006 ■ *Web:* www.plainfancycabinetry.com					
Plato Woodwork Inc PO Box 98	Plato	MN	55370	320-238-2193	238-2131
TF: 800-328-5924 ■ *Web:* www.platowoodwork.com					
Prestige Inc 101 S 8th St	Neodesha	KS	66757	620-325-8500	325-8506
TF: 800-328-4006 ■ *Web:* www.prestigecabinets.com					
Quality Cabinets 515 Big Stone Gap Rd	Duncanville	TX	75137	972-298-6103	709-7753
TF: 800-284-3888 ■ *Web:* www.qualitycabinets.com					
Quality Custom Cabinetry Inc 125 Peters Rd	New Holland	PA	17557	717-656-2721	661-6901
TF: 800-909-6006 ■ *Web:* www.qcc.com					
Quality Wood Products Inc 7400 E 12th St	Kansas City	MO	64126	816-231-4601	231-4858
TF: 800-806-8531 ■ *Web:* www.qwpi.com					
Regal Kitchens Inc 8600 NW South River Dr	Miami	FL	33166	305-885-0111	885-7419
TF: 800-432-0731 ■ *Web:* www.regalkitchensinc.com					
Republic Industries Inc 1400 Warren Dr	Marshall	TX	75672	903-935-3680	935-3697
Web: www.republicind.com					
Rich Maid Kabinetry LLC 633 W Lincoln Ave	Myerstown	PA	17067	717-866-2112	866-5962
TF: 800-295-2912 ■ *Web:* richmaidkabinetry.com					
Rosebud Mfg Co Inc 111 W Center St	Madison	SD	57042	605-256-4561	256-3842
TF: 800-256-4561 ■ *Web:* www.rosebudmfg.com					
Royal Cabinets 1299 E Phillips Blvd	Pomona	CA	91766	909-629-8565	629-7762
Web: www.royalcabinets.com					
RSI Home Products Inc 400 E Orangethorpe Ave	Anaheim	CA	92801	714-449-2200	449-2222*
**Fax:* Cust Svc ■ *TF:* 888-774-8062 ■ *Web:* www.rsihomeproducts.com					
Rutt HandCrafted Cabinetry 215 Diller Ave	New Holland	PA	17557	717-351-1700	351-1714
Web: www.rutt1.com					
Rynone Mfg Corp PO Box 128	Sayre	PA	18840	570-888-5272	888-1175
Web: www.rynone.com					
Shamrock Cabinet & Fixture Corp 10201 E 65th St	Raytown	MO	64133	816-737-2300	356-7835
Web: www.shamrockcabinet.com					
Starmark Inc 600 E 48th St N	Sioux Falls	SD	57104	605-335-8600	336-5574
Web: www.starmarkcabinetry.com					
Thomasville Furniture Industries Inc					
401 E Main St PO Box 339	Thomasville	NC	27361	336-472-4000	472-4085
Web: www.thomasville.com					
Tri-Star Cabinet & Top Co Inc 1000 S Cedar	New Lenox	IL	60451	815-485-2564	485-5747
Web: www.tristarcabinets.com					
Ultracraft Co 6163 Old 421 Rd	Liberty	NC	27298	336-622-4281	622-3474
TF: 800-262-4046 ■ *Web:* www.ultracraft.com					
US Home Systems Inc					
405 State Hwy 121 Bypass Bldg A Suite 250	Louisville	TX	75067	214-488-6300	315-3739*
NASDAQ: USHS ■ **Fax Area Code:* 972 ■ *Web:* www.ushomesystems.com					
Valley Cabinet Inc 845 Prosper Rd	De Pere	WI	54115	920-336-3174	336-5956
TF: 800-236-8981 ■ *Web:* www.valleycabinetinc.com					
Wellborn Cabinet Inc 38669 Hwy 77	Ashland	AL	36251	256-354-7151	354-7022
TF: 800-762-4475 ■ *Web:* www.wellborn.com					
Wood-Mode Inc 1 2nd St	Kreamer	PA	17833	570-374-2711	374-2700
Web: www.wood-mode.com					
Woodcase Fine Cabinetry Inc 3255 W Osborn Rd	Phoenix	AZ	85017	602-269-9731	269-1242
Web: www.woodcaseinc.net					
Woodcraft Industries Inc 525 Lincoln Ave SE	Saint Cloud	MN	56304	320-252-1503	252-1504
Web: www.woodcraftind.com					
WW Wood Products Inc PO Box 50	Dudley	MO	63936	573-624-7090	624-8576
Yorktowne Inc 100 Redco Ave	Red Lion	PA	17356	717-244-4011	
TF: 800-777-0065 ■ *Web:* www.yorktowneinc.com					

116 CABLE & OTHER PAY TELEVISION SERVICES

Company	City	State	Zip	Phone	Fax
Advance/Newhouse Communications PO Box 4739	Syracuse	NY	13221	315-463-7675	463-4127
Armstrong Cable Services 660 S Benbrook Rd	Butler	PA	16001	724-482-4480	482-4884
Web: www.armstrongonewire.com					
Armstrong Group of Cos 1 Armstrong Pl	Butler	PA	16001	724-283-0925	283-9655
Web: www.armstrongonewire.com					
Astral Media Inc 2100 Rue Sainte-Catherine O Bureau 1000	Montreal	QC	H3H2T3	514-939-5000	939-1515
TSX: ACM.A ■ *Web:* www.astral.com					
BellSouth Entertainment 660 Hembree Pkwy Suite 120	Roswell	GA	30076	770-360-4990	360-4877
TF: 877-463-4448 ■ *Web:* www.bims.bellsouth.net					
Bresnan Communications 1 Manhattanville Rd	Purchase	NY	10577	914-641-3300	641-3301
TF: 888-909-4357 ■ *Web:* www.bresnan.com					
Buckeye CableSystem 5566 Southwick Blvd	Toledo	OH	43614	419-724-9802	724-7074
Web: www.buckeyecablesystem.com					
Buford Media Group 6125 Paluxy Dr	Tyler	TX	75703	903-561-4411	561-4031
Cable Line Inc 311 N 7th St PO Box 95	Perkasie	PA	18944	215-258-1380	258-1388
Web: www.cable-line.com					
Cable One Inc 1314 N 3rd St 3rd Fl	Phoenix	AZ	85004	602-364-6000	364-6010
Web: www.cableone.net					
CableAmerica Corp 4120 E Valley Auto Dr	Mesa	AZ	85206	480-558-7260	892-7775
TF: 800-327-4375 ■ *Web:* www.cableamerica.com					
Cablevision Systems Corp 1111 Stewart Ave	Bethpage	NY	11714	516-803-2300	803-3134*
NYSE: CVC ■ **Fax:* Hum Res ■ *Web:* www.cablevision.com					
Capitol Connection					
George Mason University Television 4400 University Dr					
MS 1D2	Fairfax	VA	22030	703-993-3100	273-2417
Web: www.capitolconnection.gmu.edu					
Charter Communications Inc 12405 Powerscourt Dr	Saint Louis	MO	63131	314-965-0555	543-2468*
NASDAQ: CHTR ■ **Fax:* Cust Svc ■ *Web:* www.chartercom.com					
Cogeco Cable Inc 5 Pl Ville-Marie Suite 915	Montreal	QC	H3B2G2	514-874-2600	874-2625
TF: 866-874-2600 ■ *Web:* www.cogeco.ca					
Comcast Cable Communications Inc 200 Cresson Blvd	Oaks	PA	19456	610-650-3000	650-1151
TF Cust Svc: 800-266-2278 ■ *Web:* www.comcast.com					
Comcast Corp Cable Div 1500 Market St	Philadelphia	PA	19102	215-665-1700	981-7790
Web: www.comcast.com					
Cox Communications Inc 1400 Lake Hearn Dr	Atlanta	GA	30319	404-843-5000	843-5777
Web: www.cox.com					
DIRECTV Inc 2230 E Imperial Hwy	El Segundo	CA	90245	310-535-5000	535-5315*
**Fax:* Hum Res ■ *TF Cust Svc:* 800-531-5000 ■ *Web:* www.directv.com					
DISH Network 9601 S Meridian Blvd	Englewood	CO	80112	303-723-1000	723-2727*
**Fax:* Cust Svc ■ *TF:* 800-333-3474 ■ *Web:* www.dishnetwork.com					
EchoStar Communications Corp 9601 S Meridian Blvd	Englewood	CO	80112	303-723-1000	723-1399*
NASDAQ: DISH ■ **Fax:* Hum Res ■ *TF:* 800-333-3474 ■ *Web:* www.dishnetwork.com					
Fanch Communications Inc 1873 S Bellaire St Suite 1550	Denver	CO	80222	303-756-5600	692-9807
Galaxy Cablevision PO Box 1007	Sikeston	MO	63801	573-472-8200	471-0119
TF Cust Svc: 800-365-6988 ■ *Web:* www.galaxycable.com					
Insight Communications Co Inc 810 7th Ave 41st Fl	New York	NY	10019	917-286-2300	286-2301
Web: www.insight-com.com					
Insight Interactive 5601 N MacArthur Blvd Suite 201	Irving	TX	75038	469-524-0116	518-1676*
**Fax Area Code:* 972 ■ **Fax:* Hum Res ■ *TF:* 877-494-6077 ■					
Web: www.insight-interactive.com					
James Cable LLC 901 Tower Dr Suite 310	Troy	MI	48098	248-641-1770	641-1631
TF: 877-834-9487					
Knology Inc 1241 OG Skinner Dr	West Point	GA	31833	706-645-8553	645-1446
NASDAQ: KNOL ■ *Web:* www.knology.com					
Level 3 Communications Inc 1 Technology Ctr	Tulsa	OK	74103	918-547-5760	547-1114
TF: 800-364-0807 ■ *Web:* www.level3.com					
LodgeNet Entertainment Corp 3900 W Innovation St	Sioux Falls	SD	57107	605-988-1330	988-1532
NASDAQ: LNET ■ *TF:* 888-563-4363 ■ *Web:* www.lodgenet.com					
Mediacom Communications Corp 100 Crystal Run Rd	Middletown	NY	10941	845-695-2600	695-2679
NASDAQ: MCCC ■ *TF:* 888-692-9090 ■ *Web:* www.mediacomcc.com					
Midcontinent Communications 5111 S Louise Ave	Sioux Falls	SD	57106	605-229-1775	330-4089*
**Fax:* Cust Svc ■ *TF:* 800-888-1300 ■ *Web:* www.midcocomm.com					
Millennium Digital Media Holdings LLC					
16305 Swingley Ridge Rd	Chesterfield	MO	63017	636-534-7400	534-7300
Web: www.mdm.net					
Northland Communications Corp 101 Stewart St Suite 700	Seattle	WA	98101	206-674-3900	623-9015
TF: 800-448-0273 ■ *Web:* www.northlandcabletv.com					
Oceanic Time Warner Cable 200 Akamainui St	Mililani	HI	96789	808-625-2100	625-5888
Web: www.oceanic.com					
Omega Communications Inc 41 E Washington Suite 110	Indianapolis	IN	46204	317-264-4010	264-4020
TF: 800-622-6728 ■ *Web:* www.omegac.com					
On Command Corp 4610 S Ulster St 6th Fl	Denver	CO	80237	720-873-3200	873-3299
TF: 800-797-7654 ■ *Web:* www.oncommand.com					
Pencor Services Inc 613 3rd St	Palmerton	PA	18071	610-826-2552	826-7626
TF: 800-634-6572					
Persona Inc 17 Duffy Pl PO Box 12155 Station A	Saint John's	NL	A1B4L1	709-754-3775	754-3883
TF: 866-737-7662 ■ *Web:* www.personainc.ca					
Phoenix Cable Inc 17 S Franklin Tpke Suite 100B	Ramsey	NJ	07446	201-825-9090	825-8794
Quebecor Media Inc 612 rue Saint-Jacques	Montreal	QC	H3C4M8	514-877-9777	594-8844
Web: www.quebecor.com					
RCN Corp 196 Van Buren St Suite 300	Herndon	VA	20170	703-434-8200	434-8462
NASDAQ: RCNI ■ *TF Cust Svc:* 800-746-4726 ■ *Web:* www.rcn.com					
Resort Television Cable Co Inc DBA Wehco Video Inc					
115 E Capitol Ave	Little Rock	AR	72201	501-378-3529	376-8594
Rifkin & Assoc Inc 360 S Monroe St Suite 600	Denver	CO	80209	303-333-1215	322-3553
Web: www.rifkinco.com					
Rogers Communications Inc 333 Bloor St E 10th Fl	Toronto	ON	M4W1G9	416-935-7777	935-3599
NYSE: RCI ■ *TF:* 888-620-7777 ■ *Web:* www.rogers.com					
Service Electric Cable TV & Communications 2260 Ave A	Bethlehem	PA	18017	610-865-9100	865-7888
TF: 800-232-9100 ■ *Web:* www.sectv.com					
Shaw Communications Inc 630 3rd Ave SW Suite 900	Calgary	AB	T2P4L4	403-750-4500	750-4501*
NYSE: SJR ■ **Fax:* Mktg ■ *TF:* 888-750-7429 ■ *Web:* www.shaw.ca					
Suddenlink PO Box 139400	Tyler	TX	75713	800-999-8876	561-5485*
**Fax Area Code:* 903 ■ *TF:* 877-423-2743 ■ *Web:* www.suddenlink.com					
Superstar PO Box 35728	Tulsa	OK	74153	800-395-9557	824-3289*
**Fax Area Code:* 888 ■ *Web:* www.superstar.com					
Sutton Capital Assoc Inc 1 Rockefeller Plaza Suite 3300	New York	NY	10020	212-218-4350	218-4355
Tele-Media Corp PO Box 39	Bellefonte	PA	16823	814-355-4729	353-2072
Web: www.tele-media.com					
Time Warner Cable 290 Harbor Dr	Stamford	CT	06902	203-328-0600	328-0690
TF: 800-950-2266 ■ *Web:* www.timewarnercable.com					
Time Warner Cable of New York City 120 E 23rd St	New York	NY	10010	212-598-7200	
Time Warner Communications Inc 1266 Dublin Rd	Columbus	OH	43215	614-481-5050	481-5044
TF: 800-492-9324 ■ *Web:* www.timewarnercable.com/Columbus					
TiVo Inc 2160 Gold St	Alviso	CA	95002	408-519-9100	519-5330
NASDAQ: TIVO ■ *TF:* 877-367-8486 ■ *Web:* www.tivo.com					
US Cable Corp 28 W Grand Ave	Montvale	NJ	07645	201-930-9000	930-9232
Web: www.uscablegroup.com					
Videotron Ltee 405 Ogilvy Ave	Montreal	QC	H2X3W4	514-281-1232	773-1877*
**Fax Area Code:* 800 ■ **Fax:* Cust Svc ■ *Web:* www.videotron.com					
Wireless Cable International Inc 5 Mountain Blvd Suite 6	Warren	NJ	07059	908-769-1731	769-4078

117 CABLE REELS

Company	City	State	Zip	Phone	Fax
American Reeling Devices Inc 15 Airpark Vista Blvd	Dayton	NV	89403	775-246-1000	246-1002
TF Sales: 800-354-7335 ■ *Web:* www.americanreeling.com					
Carris Reels Inc PO Box 696	Rutland	VT	05702	802-773-9111	770-3581
Web: www.carris.com					
Conductix 10102 F St	Omaha	NE	68127	402-339-9300	339-9627
TF: 800-521-4888 ■ *Web:* www.conductix.us					
Coxreels 6720 S Clementine Ct	Tempe	AZ	85283	480-820-6396	820-5132
TF Cust Svc: 800-269-7335 ■ *Web:* www.coxreels.com					
Cumberland Wood Products Inc PO Box 68	Helenwood	TN	37755	423-569-6363	569-9131
TF: 800-635-7335					
Gleason Reel Corp PO Box 26	Mayville	WI	53050	920-387-4120	387-4189
TF: 800-571-0166 ■ *Web:* www.hubbell-gleason.com					
Hannay Reels Inc 553 SR 143	Westerlo	NY	12193	518-797-3791	733-5464*
**Fax Area Code:* 800 ■ *TF:* 877-467-3357 ■ *Web:* www.hannay.com					
Reelcraft Industries Inc 1 Reelcraft Ctr PO Box 248	Columbia City	IN	46725	260-248-8188	248-2605
TF: 800-444-3134 ■ *Web:* www.reelcraft.com					
Tayloreel Corp PO Box 476	Oakwood	GA	30566	770-503-1612	503-9614
TF: 877-503-1612 ■ *Web:* www.tayloreel.com					

118 CALCULATORS - ELECTRONIC

Company	City	State	Zip	Phone	Fax
Calculated Industries Inc 4840 Hytech Dr	Carson City	NV	89706	775-885-4900	885-4949
TF: 800-854-8075 ■ *Web:* www.calculated.com					
Casio Inc 570 Mt Pleasant Ave	Dover	NJ	07801	973-361-5400	537-8910*
**Fax:* Hum Res ■ *TF Cust Svc:* 800-634-1895 ■ *Web:* www.casio.com					
Royal Consumer Information Products Inc					
379 Campus Dr 2nd Fl	Somerset	NJ	08875	732-627-9977	667-1556
TF Sales: 888-261-4555 ■ *Web:* www.royal.com					
Sharp Electronics Corp 1 Sharp Plaza	Mahwah	NJ	07430	201-529-8200	529-8413
TF: 800-237-4277 ■ *Web:* www.sharpusa.com					
Texas Instruments Inc 12500 TI Blvd	Dallas	TX	75243	972-995-2011	917-7792*
NYSE: TXN ■ **Fax:* Hum Res ■ *TF Cust Svc:* 800-336-5236 ■ *Web:* www.ti.com					
Victor Technology Inc 780 W Belden Ave	Addison	IL	60101	630-268-8400	268-8450
TF: 800-628-2420 ■ *Web:* www.victortech.com					

119 CAMERAS & RELATED SUPPLIES - RETAIL

Company	City	State	Zip	Phone	Fax
Abe's of Maine Cameras & Electronics					
1957 Coney Island Ave	Brooklyn	NY	11223	718-645-0900	998-5216
TF: 800-227-0400 ■ *Web:* www.abesofmaine.com					

Phone Fax

Adorama Camera Inc 42 W 18th St .... New York NY 10011 212-741-0052 463-7223
TF: 800-223-2500 ■ *Web:* www.adorama.com

B & H Photo-Video-Pro Audio Corp 420 9th Ave .... New York NY 10001 212-444-6600 239-7770
TF: 800-947-9954 ■ *Web:* www.bhphotovideo.com

Beach Camera 203 Rt 22 E .... Green Brook NJ 08812 732-968-6400 968-7709
Web: www.beachcamera.com

Black Photo Corp 371 Gough Rd .... Markham ON L3R4B6 905-475-2777 475-8814
TF: 800-668-3826 ■ *Web:* www.blackphoto.com

Brooks Cameras Inc 125 Kearny St .... San Francisco CA 94108 415-362-4708 362-1436
Web: www.brookscameras.com

Calumet Photographic Inc 890 Supreme Dr .... Bensenville IL 60106 630-860-7447 860-7481
TF Cust Svc: 800-453-2550 ■ *Web:* www.calumetphoto.com

Camasco Group 550-B Guy St .... Granby QC J2G7J8 800-361-4472
TF: 877-361-4472 ■ *Web:* www.cameraexpert.com

Cambridge Camera 34 Franklin Ave .... Brooklyn NY 11205 718-858-5002 858-5437
TF: 800-221-2253 ■ *Web:* www.cambridgeworld.com

Camera Corner Inc PO Box 1899 .... Burlington NC 27216 336-228-0251 222-8011
TF: 800-868-2462 ■ *Web:* www.camcor.com

Camera Expert 550-B Guy St .... Granby QC J2G7J8 800-361-4472
TF: 877-361-4472 ■ *Web:* www.cameraexpert.com

CameraWorld.com 2010 Main St Suite 400 .... Irvine CA 92614 949-442-0202 442-0210
TF: 800-226-3721 ■ *Web:* www.cameraworld.com

Canoga Camera Corp 22065 Sherman Way .... Canoga Park CA 91303 818-346-5506 346-9376
TF: 800-201-4201 ■ *Web:* www.canogacamera.com

Central Camera Co 230 S Wabash Ave .... Chicago IL 60606 312-427-5580 427-1898
TF: 800-421-1899 ■ *Web:* www.central-camera.com

Cress Photo PO Box 4262 .... Wayne NJ 07474 973-694-1280 694-6965
TF: 888-480-3456 ■ *Web:* www.flashbulbs.com

Dodd Co DBA Dodd Camera & Video 2077 E 30th St .... Cleveland OH 44115 216-361-6817 361-6819
TF: 800-507-1676 ■ *Web:* www.doddcamera.com

Dury's 701 Ewing Ave .... Nashville TN 37203 615-255-3456 255-3506
TF: 800-824-2379 ■ *Web:* www.durys.com

F-11 Photographic Supplies 16 E Main St .... Bozeman MT 59715 406-587-1300 587-3277
TF Sales: 800-548-0203 ■ *Web:* www.f11photo.com

Focus Camera Inc 905 McDonald Ave .... Brooklyn NY 11219 718-431-7900 437-8895
TF: 800-221-0828 ■ *Web:* focuscamera.com

Foto Source Canada Inc 1075 Meyerside Dr Unit 10 .... Mississauga ON L5T1M3 905-795-1771 795-0433
Web: www.fotosource.com

Get Smart Products 578 Nepperham Ave .... Yonkers NY 10701 914-709-0600 827-0673*
**Fax Area Code:* 866 ■ *TF:* 800-827-0673 ■ *Web:* www.pfile.com

Helix Ltd 310 S Racine Ave .... Chicago IL 60607 312-421-6000 421-1586
TF: 800-334-3549 ■ *Web:* www.helixphoto.com

Island Camera & Gift Shop Inc 670 Queen St .... Honolulu HI 96813 808-592-4800 592-4858

KEH Camera Brokers Inc 2310 Marietta Blvd NW .... Atlanta GA 30318 404-892-5522 892-1251
Web: www.keh.com

Kenmore Camera Inc 18031 67th Ave NE .... Kenmore WA 98028 425-485-7447 489-2843
TF: 888-485-7447 ■ *Web:* www.kcamera.com

Lawrence Photo & Video Inc 2550 S Campbell St .... Springfield MO 65807 417-883-8300 883-8305
Web: www.lawrencephotovideo.com

Light Impressions Inc PO Box 787 .... Brea CA 92822 714-441-4539 786-7939*
**Fax Area Code:* 800 ■ *TF:* 800-828-6216 ■ *Web:* www.lightimpressionsdirect.com

Porter's Camera Store PO Box 628 .... Cedar Falls IA 50613 319-268-0104 277-5254
TF: 800-553-2001 ■ *Web:* www.porterscamerastore.com

Projector Solution 181 Avenida La Pata Suite 100 .... San Clemente CA 92673 949-940-2400 492-8240
TF: 800-701-9869 ■ *Web:* www.projectorsolution.com

Ritz Camera Centers Inc 6711 Ritz Way .... Beltsville MD 20705 301-419-0000 419-2995
TF Orders: 877-690-0099 ■ *Web:* www.ritzcamera.com

Samy's Camera Inc 431 S Fairfax Ave .... Los Angeles CA 90036 323-938-2420 692-0750
TF: 800-321-4726 ■ *Web:* www.samys.com

Unique Photo Inc 11 Vreeland Rd .... Florham Park NJ 07932 973-377-5555 377-8800
TF: 800-631-0300 ■ *Web:* www.uniquephoto.com

Wright Images 3333 W Henrietta Rd Southtown Plaza .... Rochester NY 14623 585-424-3160 424-3165

120 CAMPERS, TRAVEL TRAILERS, MOTOR HOMES

Phone Fax

Airstream Inc 419 W Pike St .... Jackson Center OH 45334 937-596-6111 596-6092
Web: www.airstream-rv.com

Alaskan Campers Inc 420 NE Alaskan Way .... Chehalis WA 98532 360-748-6494 748-1475
Web: www.alaskancamper.net

Alfa Leisure Inc 13501 5th St .... Chino CA 91710 909-628-5574
TF: 800-373-3372 ■ *Web:* www.alfaleisure.com

Beaver Coaches Inc 91320 Coburg Industrial Way .... Coburg OR 97408 541-686-8011 995-1157
TF Sales: 800-423-2837 ■ *Web:* www.beavermotorcoaches.com

Coach House Inc 3480 Technology Dr .... Nokomis FL 34275 941-485-0984 488-4095
TF: 800-235-0984 ■ *Web:* www.coachhouserv.com

Coachmen Industries Inc 2831 Dexter Dr .... Elkhart IN 46514 574-262-0123 262-8823
NYSE: COA ■ *Web:* www.coachmen.com

Coachmen Recreational Vehicle Co LLC 423 N Main St .... Middlebury IN 46540 574-825-8500 825-7868
TF: 800-353-7383 ■ *Web:* www.coachmenrv.com

Cool Amphibious Manufacturers International LLC
31 Hawkes Rd .... Bluffton SC 29910 843-757-4133 757-6774
TF: 888-926-6553 ■ *Web:* www.camillc.com

Cruise America 11 W Hampton Ave .... Mesa AZ 85210 480-464-7300 464-7321
TF: 800-327-7799 ■ *Web:* www.cruiseamerica.com

Custom Fiberglass Mfg Corp 1711 Harbor Ave .... Long Beach CA 90813 562-432-5454 435-2992
TF: 800-768-4867 ■ *Web:* www.snugtop.com

Dexter Chassis Group 501 S Miller Dr .... White Pigeon MI 49099 269-483-7681 483-9089
TF: 800-669-7681 ■ *Web:* www.dexterchassisgroup.com

Dutchmen Mfg Inc 305 Steury Ave .... Goshen IN 46528 574-534-1224 533-3807
Web: www.dutchmen-rv.com

Fleetwood Enterprises Inc 3125 Myers St .... Riverside CA 92503 951-351-3500 351-3690
NYSE: FLE ■ *Web:* www.fleetwood.com

Fleetwood Folding Trailers Inc 258 Beacon St .... Somerset PA 15501 814-445-9661 443-7320
Web: www.fleetwoodrv.com

Forest River Inc 58277 SR 19 S .... Elkhart IN 46517 574-296-7700 295-8749
Web: www.forestriverinc.com

Foretravel Motorcoach Inc 1221 NW Stallings Dr .... Nacogdoches TX 75964 936-564-8367 564-0391
TF: 800-955-6226 ■ *Web:* www.foretravel.com

Four Wheel Campers 1460 Churchill Downs Ave .... Woodland CA 95776 530-666-1442 666-1486
TF: 800-242-1442 ■ *Web:* www.fourwheelcampers.com

Georgie Boy Mfg Inc 21888 BeckDr .... Elkhart IN 45616 574-295-7344 295-8687
TF: 877-876-9024 ■ *Web:* www.georgieboy.com/

Gulf Stream Coach Inc 503 S Oakland Ave PO Box 1005 .... Nappanee IN 46550 574-773-7761 773-5761
TF: 800-289-8787 ■ *Web:* www.gulfstreamcoach.com

Holiday Rambler Div Monaco Coach Corp 606 Nelson's Pkwy .... Wakarusa IN 46573 574-862-7211 862-7579*
**Fax:* Sales ■ *TF:* 800-650-7337 ■ *Web:* www.holidayrambler.com

Jayco Inc 903 S Main St .... Middlebury IN 46540 574-825-5861 825-7354
TF Cust Svc: 800-283-8267 ■ *Web:* www.jayco.com

Keystone RV Co 2642 Hackberry Dr .... Goshen IN 46526 574-535-2100 535-2199
TF: 866-425-4369 ■ *Web:* www.keystonerv.com

Lance Camper Mfg Corp 43120 Venture St .... Lancaster CA 93535 661-949-3322 949-1262
TF: 800-423-7996 ■ *Web:* www.lancecampers.com

Phone Fax

Monaco Coach Corp 91320 Coburg Industrial Way .... Coburg OR 97408 541-686-8011 681-8037*
NYSE: MNC ■ **Fax:* Hum Res ■ *TF:* 800-634-0855 ■ *Web:* www.monaco-online.com

Monaco Coach Corp Holiday Rambler Div 606 Nelson's Pkwy .... Wakarusa IN 46573 574-862-7211 862-7579*
**Fax:* Sales ■ *TF:* 800-650-7337 ■ *Web:* www.holidayrambler.com

National RV Holdings Inc 3411 N Perris Blvd .... Perris CA 92571 951-943-6007 943-8498
NYSE: NVH ■ *TF:* 800-322-6007 ■ *Web:* www.nrvh.com

New Horizons RV Corp 2618 Mid America Dr .... Junction City KS 66441 785-238-7575 238-4992
TF: 800-235-3140 ■ *Web:* www.horizonsrv.com

Newell Coach Corp PO Box 511 .... Miami OK 74354 918-542-3344 542-2028
TF: 888-363-9355 ■ *Web:* www.newellcoach.com

Newmar Corp 355 Delaware St .... Nappanee IN 46550 574-773-7791 773-2007
TF: 800-731-8300 ■ *Web:* www.newmarcorp.com

Nu-Wa Industries Inc 3701 Johnson Rd .... Chanute KS 66720 620-431-2088 431-2513
TF: 800-835-0676 ■ *Web:* www.nuwa.com

Palomino RV 1047 E M86 .... Colon MI 49040 269-432-3271 432-2516
Web: www.palominorv.com

Peterson Industries Inc 616 E Hwy 36 .... Smith Center KS 66967 785-282-6825 282-3810
TF: 800-368-3759 ■ *Web:* www.petersonind.com

Renegade/Kibbi LLC 52216 State Rd 15 .... Bristol IN 46507 574-848-1126 848-1127
TF: 888-522-1126 ■ *Web:* www.kibbi.com

Rexhall Industries Inc 46147 7th St W .... Lancaster CA 93534 661-726-0565 726-5811*
**Fax:* Sales ■ *TF:* 800-444-9720 ■ *Web:* www.rexhall.com

Skyline Corp 2520 By-Pass Rd .... Elkhart IN 46514 574-294-6521 295-8601
NYSE: SKY ■ *TF:* 800-348-7469 ■ *Web:* www.skylinecorp.com

Starcraft RV Inc 536 Michigan St PO Box 458 .... Topeka IN 46571 260-593-2550 593-2876
TF: 800-945-4787 ■ *Web:* www.starcraftrv.com

Sunline Coach Co Inc 245 S Muddy Creek Rd .... Denver PA 17517 717-336-2858 336-0527
TF: 800-827-6406 ■ *Web:* www.sunlinerv.com

Teton Homes 3283 N Nine-Mile Rd .... Casper WY 82604 307-235-1525 733-3792*
**Fax Area Code:* 800 ■ *Web:* www.tetonhomes.com

Thor Industries Inc 419 W Pike St .... Jackson Center OH 45334 937-596-6849 596-7929
NYSE: THO ■ *Web:* www.thorindustries.com

Tiffin Motor Homes Inc 105 2nd St NW .... Red Bay AL 35882 256-356-8661 356-8219
Web: www.tiffinmotorhomes.com

Viking Recreational Vehicles LLC
580 W Burr Oak St PO Box 549 .... Centreville MI 49032 269-467-6321 467-6021
Web: www.vikingrv.com

Western Recreational Vehicles Inc 3401 W Washington Ave .... Yakima WA 98903 509-457-4133 457-8184
TF: 800-888-4133 ■ *Web:* www.wrv.com

Winnebago Industries Inc 605 W Crystal Lake Rd .... Forest City IA 50436 641-585-3535 585-6960
NYSE: WGO ■ *TF:* 800-643-4892 ■ *Web:* www.winnebagoind.com

Zieman Mfg Co 12425 E Whittier Blvd .... Whittier CA 90608 562-696-1186 696-4789
Web: www.zieman.com

121 CAMPGROUND OPERATORS

Phone Fax

Holiday Trails Resorts Inc 53730 Bridal Falls Rd .... Rosedale BC V0X1X0 604-794-7876 794-3756
TF: 800-663-2265 ■ *Web:* www.holidaytrailsresorts.com

Kampgrounds of America Inc (KOA) PO Box 30558 .... Billings MT 59114 406-248-7444 248-7414
Web: www.koakampgrounds.com

Leisure Systems Inc DBA Yogi Bear's Jellystone Park Camp Resorts 50 W Techne Center Dr Suite G .... Milford OH 45150 513-831-2100 576-8670
TF Sales: 800-626-3720 ■ *Web:* www.leisuresystemsinc.com

Outdoor Resorts of America Inc
79-687 Country Club Rd Suite 201 .... Bermuda Dunes CA 92201 760-345-2046
TF: 800-541-2582 ■ *Web:* www.outdoor-resorts.com

Thousand Trails Inc 3801 Parkwood Blvd Suite 100 .... Frisco TX 75034 214-618-7200 618-7324
TF: 800-328-6226 ■ *Web:* www.thousandtrails.com

Western Horizon Resorts 103 W Tomichi Ave Suite 201A .... Gunnison CO 81230 970-642-4515 641-0929
Web: www.whresorts.com

Yogi Bear's Jellystone Park Camp Resorts
50 W Techne Center Dr Suite G .... Milford OH 45150 513-831-2100 576-8670
TF Sales: 800-626-3720 ■ *Web:* www.leisuresystemsinc.com

122 CANDLES

SEE ALSO Gift Shops p. 1690

Phone Fax

Blyth Inc 1 E Weaver St .... Greenwich CT 06831 203-661-1926 661-1969
NYSE: BTH ■ *Web:* www.blyth.com

Candle-Lite Div Lancaster Colony Corp PO Box 42364 .... Cincinnati OH 45242 513-563-1113 563-9639
TF: 800-718-7018 ■ *Web:* www.candle-lite.com

Candleman Corp 15025 Glazier Ave Suite 400 .... Apple Valley MN 55124 800-328-3453 997-6224*
**Fax Area Code:* 952 ■ *TF:* 800-328-3453 ■ *Web:* www.candleman.com

Continental Candle Co Inc 1420 W Walnut St .... Compton CA 90220 310-537-9300 537-6055
TF: 800-421-1035

Dadant & Sons Inc 51 S 2nd St .... Hamilton IL 62341 217-847-3324 847-3660
TF: 800-922-1293 ■ *Web:* www.dadant.com

General Wax & Candle Co
6858 Beck Ave PO Box 9398 .... North Hollywood CA 91609 818-765-5808 764-3878
TF: 800-543-0642 ■ *Web:* candles.genwax.com

Home Fragrance Holdings 8323 Fairbanks White Oak Rd .... Houston TX 77040 713-466-4600 849-6562
TF Cust Svc: 800-256-5689 ■ *Web:* www.hfh.cc

Knorr Beeswax Products Inc 1965 Kellogg Ave .... Carlsbad CA 92008 760-431-2007 431-8977
TF: 800-807-2337 ■ *Web:* www.knorrbeeswax.com

Lancaster Colony Corp Candle-Lite Div PO Box 42364 .... Cincinnati OH 45242 513-563-1113 563-9639
TF: 800-718-7018 ■ *Web:* www.candle-lite.com

Lumi-Lite Candle Co Inc 102 Sundale Rd PO Box 97 .... Norwich OH 43767 740-872-3248 872-3312
TF: 800-288-2340

Mack-Miller Candle Co Inc 202 SHeridan Rd .... Liverpool NY 13090 315-453-9665
TF: 800-522-6353 ■ *Web:* mysite.verizon.net/vzeecmkb

Mason Candlelight Co 8729 Aviation Blvd .... Inglewood CA 90301 800-556-2766 348-0135*
**Fax Area Code:* 310 ■ *Web:* www.masoncandle.com

Muench-Kreuzer Candle Co 617 E Hiawatha Blvd .... Syracuse NY 13208 315-471-4515 471-4581
TF: 800-448-7884

Prayer Candle Co 29 Ash St .... Brooklyn NY 11222 718-389-7707 389-8769

Reed Candle Co 1531 W Poplar St PO Box 7261 .... San Antonio TX 78207 210-734-4243 734-2342

Root Candles Co 623 W Liberty St .... Medina OH 44256 330-725-6677 725-5624
TF: 800-289-7668 ■ *Web:* www.rootcandles.com

Swans Candles 8933 Gravelly Lake Dr SW .... Lakewood WA 98499 253-584-4666 584-2874
TF: 888-848-7926 ■ *Web:* www.swanscandles.com

White Barn Candle Co 7 Limited Pkwy E .... Reynoldsburg OH 43068 614-856-6000 856-6313
TF: 800-395-1001 ■ *Web:* www.limitedbrands.com

Will & Baumer Inc 100 Buckley St .... Liverpool NY 13288 315-451-1000 451-0120
TF: 800-733-7337 ■ *Web:* www.will-baumer.com

Yankee Candle Co Inc 16 Yankee Candle Way .... South Deerfield MA 01373 413-665-8306 665-4815
NYSE: YCC ■ *TF:* 800-839-6038 ■ *Web:* www.yankeecandle.com

123 CANDY STORES

Phone | Fax

Candy Bouquet International Inc 423 E 3rd St .... Little Rock AR 72201 501-375-9990 375-9998
TF: 877-226-3901 ■ *Web:* www.candybouquet.com

Candy Express 3320 Greencastle Rd........................ Burtonsville MD 20866 301-384-5889 384-1788
Web: www.candyexpress.com

Gardners Candies Inc 2600 Adams Ave........................... Tyrone PA 16686 814-684-3925 684-3928
TF: 800-242-2639 ■ *Web:* www.gardnerscandies.com

Gertrude Hawk Chocolates Inc 9 Keystone Park .... Dunmore PA 18512 570-342-7556 342-0261
TF: 800-822-2032 ■ *Web:* www.gertrudehawkchocolates.com

Gorant Candies Inc 8301 Market St ....Youngstown OH 44512 330-726-8821 726-0325
TF: 800-572-4139

Hebert Candy Mansion 575 Hartford Tpke .... Shrewsbury MA 01545 508-845-8051 842-3065
TF: 800-642-7702 ■ *Web:* www.hebertcandies.com

JaCiva's Chocolate & Pastries 4733 SE Hawthorne Blvd .... Portland OR 97215 503-234-8115 234-6076
Web: www.jacivas.com

Karmelkorn Shoppes Inc 7505 Metro Blvd.................. Minneapolis MN 55439 952-830-0200 830-0270
Web: www.karmelkorn.com

Kilwin's Quality Confections 355 N Division Rd .... Petoskey MI 49770 231-347-3800 347-6951
TF: 800-454-5946 ■ *Web:* www.kilwins.com

Lammes Candies Since 1885 Inc 200 B Parker Dr Suite 500 ....Austin TX 78728 512-310-1885 310-2280
TF: 800-252-1885 ■ *Web:* www.lammes.com

Nirvana Chocolates 66 Central St Suite 7 .... Wellesley MA 02181 781-283-5787 237-1787
Web: www.nirvanachocolates.com

Provide Commerce Inc 5005 Wateridge Vista Dr............... San Diego CA 92121 858-638-4900 638-4724
TF Cust Svc: 800-776-3569 ■ *Web:* www.prvd.com

Quality Candy Shoppes Inc PO Box 070581................... Milwaukee WI 53207 414-483-4500 483-4137
TF: 800-972-2658 ■ *Web:* www.qcbs.com

Rocky Mountain Chocolate Factory Inc 265 Turner Dr............Durango CO 81303 970-259-0554 259-5895
NASDAQ: RMCF ■ *TF Cust Svc:* 888-525-2462 ■ *Web:* www.rmcf.com

See's Candies Inc 210 El Camino Real.............. South San Francisco CA 94080 650-761-2490 875-6825
TF Cust Svc: 800-951-7337 ■ *Web:* www.sees.com

Sweets From Heaven USA LP PO Box 882829.......... Steamboat Springs CO 80486 970-870-2770 870-8618
TF: 877-247-2770 ■ *Web:* www.sweetsfromheaven.com

Tropik Sun Fruit & Nut Stores
14052 Petronella Dr Suite 102........................... Libertyville IL 60048 847-968-4415 968-5535
Web: www.tropiksun.com/

Van Duyn Chocolate Inc 2360 NW Quimby St................... Portland OR 97210 503-227-1927 227-1510
Web: www.vanduyns.com

124 CANS - METAL

SEE ALSO Containers - Metal (Barrels, Drums, Kegs) p. 1555

Phone | Fax

Alcoa Rigid Packaging Div
900 S Gay St Riverview Tower Suite 1100.................. Knoxville TN 37902 865-594-4700 594-4755

Allstate Can Corp 1 Wood Hollow Rd ....Parsippany NJ 07054 973-560-9030 560-9217
Web: www.allstatecan.com

Ball Metal Beverage Container Corp 9675 W 108th Cir........Westminster CO 80021 303-469-5511 460-5256
Web: www.ball.com

Ball Metal Food Container Corp 9675 W 108th Cir............Westminster CO 80021 303-469-5511 460-5443
Web: www.ball.com

Bertels Can Co 485 Stewart Rd .... Wilkes-Barre PA 18706 570-829-0524 829-6544*
**Fax Area Code:* 800 ■ *TF Cust Svc:* 800-829-0578 ■ *Web:* www.bertelscan.com

BWAY Corp 8607 Roberts Dr Suite 250 .... Atlanta GA 30350 770-645-4800 645-4810
TF: 800-527-2267 ■ *Web:* www.bwaycorp.com

BWAY Corp 8607 Roberts Dr Suite 250 .... Atlanta GA 30350 770-645-4800 645-4810
TF: 800-385-8792 ■ *Web:* www.bwaycorp.com

Can Corp of America Inc PO Box 170.......................... Blandon PA 19510 610-926-3044 926-5041
TF: 800-441-0876

CCL Industries Inc 105 Gordon Baker Rd Suite 800 .... Willowdale ON M2H3P8 416-756-8500 756-8555
TSX: CCLa ■ *Web:* www.cclind.com

Central Can Co 3200 S Kilbourn Ave .... Chicago IL 60623 773-254-8700 254-9127

Champion Container Corp 180 Essex Ave PO Box 90 .... Avenel NJ 07001 732-636-6700 855-8663
Web: www.championcontainer.com

Container Supply Co Inc PO Box 5367.....................Garden Grove CA 92846 714-892-8321 892-3824

Crown Cork & Seal Co 1 Crown Way.......................Philadelphia PA 19154 215-698-5100 698-5201
NYSE: CCK ■ *TF:* 800-523-3644 ■ *Web:* www.crowncork.com

Crown Holdings Inc DBA Crown Cork & Seal Co
1 Crown Way.......................................Philadelphia PA 19154 215-698-5100 698-5201
NYSE: CCK ■ *TF:* 800-523-3644 ■ *Web:* www.crowncork.com

Eagle Mfg Co Inc 2400 Charles St..........................Wellsburg WV 26070 304-737-3171 737-1752
Web: www.eagle-mfg.com

Independent Can Co 1300 Brass Mill Rd ....Belcamp MD 21017 410-272-0090 273-7500
Web: www.independentcan.com

Intrapac Corp 20 Ashton Ave ....Swedesboro NJ 08085 856-467-0485 467-1683

ITW Sexton Can Co 3101 Sexton Rd .... Decatur AL 35603 256-355-5850 351-8730
TF: 888-739-8662 ■ *Web:* www.sextoncan.com

JL Clark Mfg Co 923 23rd Ave .... Rockford IL 61104 815-962-8861 962-6356
TF: 877-878-1940 ■ *Web:* www.jlclark.com

JL Clark Mfg Co Lancaster Div 303 N Plum St.................. Lancaster PA 17602 717-392-4125 392-5587
Web: www.jlclark.com

Metal Container Corp 3636 S Geyer Rd.....................Saint Louis MO 63127 314-957-9500 957-9319

Penny Plate Inc 603 Kresson Rd .... Cherry Hill NJ 08034 856-429-7583 429-7166

Protectoseal Co 225 W Foster Ave..........................Bensenville IL 60106 630-595-0800 595-8059
TF: 800-323-2268 ■ *Web:* www.protectoseal.com

Rexam Beverage Can Americas 8770 W Bryn Mawr Ave .... Chicago IL 60631 773-399-3000

Rexam Inc 4201 Congress St Suite 340....................... Charlotte NC 28209 704-551-1500 551-1571
TF: 800-289-2800 ■ *Web:* www.rexam.com

Ring Container Technology 1 Industrial Pk Dr.................. Oakland TN 38060 901-465-3607 465-1179*
**Fax:* Hum Res ■ *TF:* 800-280-6333

Silgan Containers Corp 21800 Oxnard St Suite 600 .... Woodland Hills CA 91367 818-348-3700 593-2255
Web: www.silgancontainers.com

Silgan Holdings Inc 4 Landmark Sq Suite 400................. Stamford CT 06901 203-975-7110 975-7902
NASDAQ: SLGN ■ *Web:* www.silganholdings.com

Simmons Metal Container 103 E Benge Rd .... Fort Gibson OK 74434 918-478-2117 478-4526

Spartanburg Steel Products Inc PO Box 6428................Spartanburg SC 29304 864-585-5216 583-5641
TF: 800-334-6318

125 CANS, TUBES, DRUMS - PAPER (FIBER)

Phone | Fax

Acme Spirally Wound Paper Products Inc
4810 W 139th St PO Box 35320.......................... Cleveland OH 44135 216-267-2950 267-0239
TF: 800-274-2797 ■ *Web:* www.acmespiral.com

American Paper Products Co Inc 2113 E Rush St .... Philadelphia PA 19134 215-739-5718 739-3019
Web: www.americanpaperproducts.com

American Tube & Paper Co Inc PO Box 68..........................Totowa NJ 07511 973-256-3600 785-3341

Armbrust Paper Tubes Inc 6255 S Harlem Ave .... Chicago IL 60638 773-586-3232 586-8997
Web: www.tubesrus.com

Callenor Co Inc N 60 W 15725 Kohler Ln ....Menomonee Falls WI 53051 262-252-3343 252-3873
Web: www.callenor.com

Caraustar Industries Inc
5000 Austell-Powder Sprngs Rd Suite 300..................... Austell GA 30106 770-948-3100
NASDAQ: CSAR ■ *Web:* www.caraustar.com

Chicago Mailing Tube Co 400 N Leavitt St .... Chicago IL 60612 312-243-6050 243-6545
Web: www.mailing-tube.com

Custom Paper Tubes Inc PO Box 35140 .... Cleveland OH 44135 216-362-2964 362-2980
TF: 800-766-2527 ■ *Web:* www.custompapertubes.com

Englehard Hexcore 101 Wood Ave S .... Iselin NJ 08830 732-205-5000 321-1161

FiberCorp Inc 670 17th St NW .... Massillon OH 44647 330-837-5151 837-9109

Greif Inc 425 Winter Rd .... Delaware OH 43015 740-549-6000 549-6100
NYSE: GEF ■ *TF:* 800-354-7343 ■ *Web:* www.greif.com

Industrial Paper Tube Inc 1335 E Bay Ave .... Bronx NY 10474 718-893-5000 378-0055
TF: 800-345-0960 ■ *Web:* www.mailingtubes-ipt.com

Jackson Co Inc 767 Airport Rd............................. Fall River MA 02720 508-679-5256 673-6588

Laminations 3010 E Venture Dr ....Appleton WI 54911 920-831-0596 831-0612
TF: 800-925-2626 ■ *Web:* www.laminations-net.com

LCH Packaging Corp 2360 Pilot Knob Rd............... Mandota Heights MN 55120 651-994-4593 994-2592
Web: www.lchpackaging.com

Marshall Paper Tube Co PO Box 304......................... Randolph MA 02368 781-963-5555 961-7291

Master Package Corp 200 Madson St .... Owen WI 54460 715-229-2156 229-2689
Web: www.masterpackage.com

Michael's Cooperage Co Inc 363 W Pershing Rd .... Chicago IL 60609 773-268-6281 268-9609
TF: 800-262-6281 ■ *Web:* www.michaelscooperage.com

Midwest Paper Tube & Can Corp PO Box 510006 ....New Berlin WI 53151 262-782-7300 782-7330
TF Cust Svc: 800-577-1400

Multi-Wall Corp Div Real Reel Corp 50 Taylor Dr..........East Providence RI 02916 401-434-1070 438-5203
TF Cust Svc: 800-992-4166 ■ *Web:* www.multiwall.com

New England Paper Tube Co Inc PO Box 186................. Pawtucket RI 02862 401-725-2610 726-4920

NYSCO Products Inc 2350 Lafayette Ave .... Bronx NY 10473 718-792-9000 792-7732
TF: 800-227-8685 ■ *Web:* www.nysco.com

Ohio Paper Tube Co 3422 Navarre Rd SW...................... Canton OH 44706 330-478-5171 478-9511
Web: www.ohiopapertube.com

Ox Paper Tube & Core Inc 331 Maple Ave..................... Hanover PA 17331 717-630-0230 630-0820
TF: 800-414-2476 ■ *Web:* www.mailingtube.com

Pacific Paper Tube Inc 1025 98th Ave .... Oakland CA 94603 510-562-8823 562-9002
TF: 888-377-8823 ■ *Web:* www.pacificpapertube.com

Precision Paper Tube Co Inc 1033 S Noel Ave................ Wheeling IL 60090 847-537-4250 537-5777
Web: www.pptube.com

Precision Paper Tube Co Resinite Corp Div 1033 S Noel Ave ..... Wheeling IL 60090 847-537-4250 537-5777
Web: www.pptube.com

Real Reel Corp Multi-Wall Corp Div 50 Taylor Dr..........East Providence RI 02916 401-434-1070 438-5203
TF Cust Svc: 800-992-4166 ■ *Web:* www.multiwall.com

Resinite Corp Div Precision Paper Tube Co 1033 S Noel Ave ..... Wheeling IL 60090 847-537-4250 537-5777
Web: www.pptube.com

Self-Seal Container Corp 401 E 4th St...................... Bridgeport PA 19405 610-275-2300 275-4430
TF: 800-334-1428 ■ *Web:* www.selfsealtubes.com

Sonoco 1 N 2nd St .... Hartsville SC 29550 843-383-7000 383-7008*
NYSE: SON ■ **Fax:* PR ■ *TF:* 800-377-2692 ■ *Web:* www.sonoco.com

Stonington Corp 111 Mosher St.............................. Holyoke MA 01040 413-493-1500 339-6803*
**Fax Area Code:* 843 ■ *TF Cust Svc:* 800-370-2673

TEKPAK Inc 1410 S Washington St .... Marion AL 36756 334-683-6121 683-9920
TF: 800-876-8841 ■ *Web:* www.tekpakinc.com

Trend-Pak of Canada 71 Railside Rd .... Toronto ON M3A1B2 416-510-3129 510-8371
Web: www.trendpak.com

Yankee Containers 110-A Republic Dr.....................North Haven CT 06473 203-288-3851 288-9936
Web: www.yankeecontainers.com

Yazoo Mills Inc PO Box 369............................. New Oxford PA 17350 717-624-8993 624-4420
TF Cust Svc: 800-242-5216 ■ *Web:* www.yazoomills.com

Yorktowne Paperboard Corp 1001 Loucksmill Rd .... York PA 17402 717-843-8061 843-3426

126 CAR RENTAL AGENCIES

SEE ALSO Fleet Leasing & Management p. 1640; Truck Rental & Leasing p. 2385

Phone | Fax

Ace Rent-A-Car 5806 W Washington St.................... Indianapolis IN 46241 317-243-6336 248-5691
TF: 800-242-7368 ■ *Web:* www.acerentacar.com

Advantage Rent-A-Car 1343 Hallmark Dr....................San Antonio TX 78216 210-344-4712 341-9716
TF Cust Svc: 800-777-5500 ■ *Web:* www.arac.com

Affordable Car Rental System Inc 105 Hwy 36.............. Eatontown NJ 07724 732-380-0888 380-0404
TF: 800-631-2290 ■ *Web:* www.sensiblecarrental.com

Alamo Rent A Car Inc 6929 N Lakewood Ave Suite 100 .... Tulsa OK 74117 918-401-6000
TF: 800-327-9633 ■ *Web:* www.alamo.com

Auto Europe 39 Commercial St............................. Portland ME 04101 207-842-2000 842-2222
TF: 800-223-5555 ■ *Web:* www.autoeurope.com

Avis Budget Group Inc 6 Sylvan Way..................... Parsippany NJ 07054 973-496-3500
NYSE: CAR ■ *Web:* www.avisbudgetgroup.com

Avis Rent A Car System Inc 6 Sylvan Way.................Parsippany NJ 07054 973-496-3500 496-3785*
**Fax:* Sales ■ *TF:* 800-331-1212 ■ *Web:* www.avis.com

Budget Rent A Car System Inc 6 Sylvan Way ....Parsippany NJ 07054 973-496-3500 496-3895
TF: 800-527-0700 ■ *Web:* www.budget.com

Car Rental Express 2817 138th St.............................. Surrey BC V4P1T6 604-714-5911 731-5772
TF: 888-557-8188 ■ *Web:* www.carrentalexpress.com

Discount Car & Truck Rentals Ltd 720 Arrow Rd ....North York ON M9M2M1 416-744-0123 744-0624
TF: 866-742-5968 ■ *Web:* www.discountcar.com

Dollar Rent A Car Inc 5330 E 31st St .... Tulsa OK 74135 918-669-3000 669-3007*
**Fax:* Sales ■ *TF:* 800-800-4000 ■ *Web:* www.dollarcar.com

Dollar Thrifty Automotive Group Inc 5330 E 31st St.............. Tulsa OK 74135 918-660-7700 669-3387
NYSE: DTG ■ *Web:* www.dtag.com

Enterprise Rent-A-Car 600 Corporate Park Dr ....Saint Louis MO 63105 314-512-5000 512-5940
TF: 800-325-8007 ■ *Web:* www.enterprise.com

Europe by Car Inc 62 William St 7th Fl ....New York NY 10005 212-581-3040 246-1458
TF: 800-223-1516 ■ *Web:* www.europebycar.com

Hertz Global Holdings Inc 225 Brae Blvd ....Park Ridge NJ 07656 201-307-2000 307-2644
NYSE: HTZ ■ *TF:* 800-654-3131 ■ *Web:* www.hertz.com

Kemwel Inc 39 Commercial St .... Portland ME 04112 207-842-2285 842-2147
TF: 800-678-0678 ■ *Web:* www.kemwel.com

National Car Rental 6929 N Lakewood Ave Suite 100............... Tulsa OK 74117 918-401-6000
TF: 800-227-7368 ■ *Web:* www.nationalcar.com

Payless Car Rental System Inc 2350-N 34th St N......... Saint Petersburg FL 33713 727-321-6352 322-6540
TF: 800-729-5255 ■ *Web:* www.paylesscarrental.com

Rent-A-Wreck of America LLC 105 Main St.......................Laurel MD 20707 240-581-1350
TF: 800-944-7501 ■ *Web:* www.rentawreck.com

Sensible Car Rental 105 Hwy 36 .... Eatontown NJ 07724 732-380-0888 380-0404
TF: 800-631-2290 ■ *Web:* www.sensiblecarrental.com

	City	State	Zip	Phone	Fax
Thrifty Car Rental 5310 E 31st St **Fax:* Hum Res ■ *TF:* 800-367-2277 ■ *Web:* www.thrifty.com	Tulsa	OK	74135	918-665-3930	669-2228*
Triangle Rent A Car Co 4226A South Blvd *TF:* 800-643-7368 ■ *Web:* www.trianglerentacar.com	Charlotte	NC	28209	704-527-1900	527-7325
U-Save Auto Rental of America Inc 4780 I-55 N Suite 300 *TF:* 800-438-2300 ■ *Web:* www.usave.com	Jackson	MS	39211	601-713-4333	713-4317
Vanguard Car Rental USA 6929 N Lakewood Ave Suite 100 *TF:* 800-837-0032 ■ *Web:* www.vanguardcar.com	Tulsa	OK	74117	918-401-6000	

127 CARBON & GRAPHITE PRODUCTS

	City	State	Zip	Phone	Fax
Advance Carbon Products Inc 2036 National Ave *TF:* 800-283-1249 ■ *Web:* www.advancecarbon.com	Hayward	CA	94545	510-293-5930	293-5939
Calcarb Inc 110 Indel Ave *TF:* 800-732-5432 ■ *Web:* www.calcarb.com	Rancocas	NJ	08073	609-261-4325	261-6111
Carbone of America Corp 400 Myrtle Ave *TF Cust Svc:* 800-526-0877 ■ *Web:* www.carbonebrush.com	Boonton	NJ	07005	973-334-0700	334-6394
Carbone of America Graphite Materials Div 215 Stackpole St	Saint Marys	PA	15857	814-781-1234	781-8570
Energy Conversion Systems 1 Morganite Dr *Web:* www.ecs-global.net	Dunn	NC	28334	910-892-8081	892-9600
Fiber Materials Inc 5 Morin St *Web:* www.fibermaterialsinc.com	Biddeford	ME	04005	207-282-5911	282-7529
GrafTech International Ltd 1521 Concord Pike Suite 301 *NYSE: GTI* ■ *Web:* www.graftech.com	Wilmington	DE	19803	302-778-8242	778-8237
Graphite Systems Inc 1613 Danciger Dr	Fort Worth	TX	76112	817-457-1851	457-2664
Helwig Carbon Products Inc 8900 W Tower Ave *TF:* 800-365-3113 ■ *Web:* www.helwigcarbon.com	Milwaukee	WI	53224	414-354-2411	354-2421
Micro Mech Inc 33 Turnpike Rd *Web:* www.micro-mech.com	Ipswich	MA	01938	978-356-2966	356-4019
Morgan AM & T 441 Hall Ave *Web:* www.morganamt.com	Saint Marys	PA	15857	814-781-1573	781-9249
National Electrical Carbon Products Inc 251 Forrester Dr *TF:* 800-543-6322 ■ *Web:* www.nationalelectrical.com	Greenville	SC	29607	864-458-7700	281-0180
Oxbow Carbon & Minerals Inc 1601 Forum Pl Suite 1400 *Web:* www.oxbow.com	West Palm Beach	FL	33401	561-697-4300	640-8727
Process Engineering Corp PO Box 279 *Web:* www.proengcorp.com	Crystal Lake	IL	60039	815-459-1734	459-3676
Pyrotek Inc 9503 E Montgomery Ave *TF:* 800-797-6835 ■ *Web:* www.pyrotek-inc.com	Spokane	WA	99206	509-926-6212	927-2408
Saint Marys Carbon Co 259 Eberl St *Web:* www.stmaryscarbon.com	Saint Marys	PA	15857	814-781-7333	834-9201
Saturn Industries Inc 157 Union Tpke *TF:* 800-775-1651 ■ *Web:* www.saturnedm.com	Hudson	NY	12534	518-828-9956	828-9868
SGL Carbon Corp 307 Jamestown Rd **Fax:* Sales ■ *TF:* 800-828-6601 ■ *Web:* www.sglcarbon.com	Morganton	NC	28655	828-437-3221	432-5885*
Superior Graphite Co 10 S Riverside Plaza Suite 1470 *TF Orders:* 800-325-0337 ■ *Web:* www.graphitesgc.com	Chicago	IL	60606	312-559-2999	559-9064
US Graphite Inc 1620 E Holland Ave *Web:* www.usgraphite.net	Saginaw	MI	48601	989-755-0441	755-0445
Zoltek Cos Inc 3101 McKelvey Rd *NASDAQ: ZOLT* ■ *TF:* 800-325-4409 ■ *Web:* www.zoltek.com	Bridgeton	MO	63044	314-291-5110	291-8536

128 CARBURETORS, PISTONS, PISTON RINGS, VALVES

SEE ALSO Aircraft Engines & Engine Parts p. 1271; Automotive Parts & Supplies - Mfr p. 1360

	City	State	Zip	Phone	Fax
C Lee Cook Co 916 S 8th St *TF:* 877-266-5226 ■ *Web:* www.cleecook.com	Louisville	KY	40203	502-587-6783	515-6992
France Compressor Products 4410 Greenbriar Dr *TF:* 800-675-6646 ■ *Web:* www.francecomp.com	Stafford	TX	77477	281-207-4600	207-4611
Grant Piston Rings 1360 N Jefferson St *TF:* 800-854-3540 ■ *Web:* www.grantpistonrings.com	Anaheim	CA	92807	714-996-0050	524-6607
Grover Corp 2759 S 28th St *TF:* 800-776-3602 ■ *Web:* www.grovercorp.com	Milwaukee	WI	53234	414-384-9472	384-0201
Hastings Mfg Co 325 N Hanover St *TF:* 800-776-1088 ■ *Web:* www.hastingsmfg.com	Hastings	MI	49058	269-945-2491	945-4667
Holley Performance Products Inc 1801 Russellville Rd **Fax:* Cust Svc ■ *TF Sales:* 800-638-0032 ■ *Web:* www.holley.com	Bowling Green	KY	42101	270-782-2900	781-9940*
Hydreco 2915 Whitehall Park Dr *Web:* www.hydreco.com	Charlotte	NC	28273	704-295-7575	295-7574
IMPCO Technologies Inc 3030 S Susan St *NASDAQ: IMCO* ■ **Fax:* Sales ■ *Web:* www.impcotechnologies.com	Santa Ana	CA	92704	714-656-1200	656-1400*
Intercoastal Mfg Co 5825 SW Arctic Dr *TF:* 800-547-6644	Beaverton	OR	97005	503-574-2200	574-2210
Jones LE Co 1200 34th Ave *TF:* 800-535-6637 ■ *Web:* www.lejones.com	Menominee	MI	49858	906-863-4411	863-4867
LE Jones Co 1200 34th Ave *TF:* 800-535-6637 ■ *Web:* www.lejones.com	Menominee	MI	49858	906-863-4411	863-4867
MAHLE Engine Components USA Inc 2001 Sanford St *TF:* 800-717-5398 ■ *Web:* www.us.mahle.com	Muskegon	MI	49443	231-722-1300	724-1940
MAHLE Inc 1 Mahle Dr *Web:* www.us.mahle.com	Morristown	TN	37814	423-581-6603	587-2635
Martin Wells Industries PO Box 01406 *TF:* 800-421-6000	Los Angeles	CA	90001	323-581-6266	589-2334
Pacific Piston Ring Co Inc 3620 Eastham Dr	Culver City	CA	90232	310-836-3322	836-3327
Safety Seal Piston Ring Co 4000 Airport Rd **Fax:* Sales ■ *TF Sales:* 800-962-3631 ■ *Web:* www.sswesco.com	Marshall	TX	75672	903-938-9241	938-9317*
United Engine & Machine Co Inc 4909 Goni Rd *TF:* 800-648-7970 ■ *Web:* www.kb-silvolite.com	Carson City	NV	89706	775-882-7790	882-7773
Wiseco Piston Inc 7201 Industrial Park Blvd *TF:* 800-321-1364 ■ *Web:* www.wiseco.com	Mentor	OH	44060	440-951-6600	951-6606
Woodward Rockford 5001 N 2nd St *Web:* www.woodward.com	Loves Park	IL	61111	815-877-7443	639-6033
Zenith Fuel Systems Inc 14570 Industrial Park Rd *Web:* www.zenithfuelsystems.com	Bristol	VA	24202	276-669-5555	669-0082

129 CARD SHOPS

SEE ALSO Gift Shops p. 1690

	City	State	Zip	Phone	Fax
American Greetings Corp Carlton Cards Div 1 American Rd *TF Sales:* 800-321-3040 ■ *Web:* www.carltoncards.com	Cleveland	OH	44144	216-252-7300	252-6778
AmericanGreetings.com Inc 1 American Rd *TF:* 888-749-5884 ■ *Web:* www.americangreetings.com	Cleveland	OH	44144	216-252-7300	252-6778
CardSmart Retail Corp 430 Pine St **Fax Area Code:* 401 ■ *Web:* www.cardsmart.com	Central Falls	RI	02863	877-227-3762	726-2384*
CardStore.com 1195 Park Ave Suite 211 *TF:* 877-822-2737 ■ *Web:* www.cardstore.com	Emeryville	CA	94608	510-595-6775	595-6657
Carlton Cards Div American Greetings Corp 1 American Rd *TF Sales:* 800-321-3040 ■ *Web:* www.carltoncards.com	Cleveland	OH	44144	216-252-7300	252-6778
Elm Tree Cards & Gifts Inc 4300 Prince William Pkwy	Woodbridge	VA	22192	703-680-2548	730-2439
Evenson Card Shops Inc PO Box 419218	Kansas City	MO	64141	816-274-3512	274-4800
Factory Card & Party Outlet Corp 2727 Diehl Rd *NASDAQ: FCPO* ■ *Web:* www.factorycard.com	Naperville	IL	60563	630-579-2000	579-2400
Hallmark Cards Inc 2501 McGee St **Fax:* Mail Rm ■ *TF:* 800-425-5627 ■ *Web:* www.hallmark.com	Kansas City	MO	64108	816-274-5111	545-2305*
Papyrus Franchise Corp 500 Chadbourne Rd *TF:* 800-333-6724 ■ *Web:* www.papyrusonline.com	Fairfield	CA	94533	707-428-8006	428-0641
Putnam Card & Gift 67 Millbrook St	Worcester	MA	01606	508-791-1200	791-5100
Recycled Paper Greetings Inc 3636 N Broadway *TF Cust Svc:* 800-777-9494 ■ *Web:* www.recycledpapergreetings.com	Chicago	IL	60613	773-348-6410	929-7123
Scribbles & Giggles 1 American Rd *TF Cust Svc:* 800-777-4891	Cleveland	OH	44144	216-252-8800	252-0653

130 CARDS - GREETING - MFR

	City	State	Zip	Phone	Fax
Alfred Mainzer Inc 27-08 40th Ave *TF:* 800-222-2737 ■ *Web:* www.mainzerdressedcats.com	Long Island City	NY	11101	718-392-4200	392-2681
Alice Briggs Illustration 11 Possum Hollow Ln *Web:* www.alicebriggs-illustration.com	Natick	MA	01760	508-651-1607	647-0090
Allen & John Inc 2505 N Shirk Rd	Visalia	CA	93278	800-803-7527	421-5291
Amber Lotus Publishing PO Box 11329 *TF:* 800-326-2375 ■ *Web:* www.amberlotus.com	Portland	OR	97211	503-284-6400	284-6417
American Artists Group Inc PO Box 49313 *Web:* www.americanartistsgroup.com	Athens	GA	30604	706-227-0708	
American Greetings Corp 1 American Rd *NYSE: AM* ■ *TF Sales:* 800-321-3040 ■ *Web:* corporate.americangreetings.com	Cleveland	OH	44144	216-252-7300	252-6778
Ancient Images Greeting Cards 44 N 100 West *TF:* 800-891-6635 ■ *Web:* www.ancientimagescards.com	Moab	UT	84532	435-259-4087	259-6635
Anne Taintor Inc PO Box 9 *Web:* www.annetaintor.com	Youngsville	NM	87064	505-638-5919	
AtticSalt Greetings Inc 1548 Erie St *Web:* www.atticsaltgreetings.com	North Kansas City	MO	64116	816-587-1600	587-1121
Avanti Press Inc 155 W Congress St Suite 200 **Fax Area Code:* 800 ■ *TF:* 800-228-2684 ■ *Web:* www.avantipress.com	Detroit	MI	48226	313-961-0022	875-9690*
B Designs Inc 23 Noel St Suite 2 *TF:* 800-978-3575 ■ *Web:* www.bdesignsinc.com	Amesbury	MA	01913	978-388-1052	388-3759
Backyard Oaks 401 E 8th St Suite 310 *TF:* 800-456-8208 ■ *Web:* www.backyardoaks.com	Sioux Falls	SD	57103	605-338-1968	336-1154
Bayview Press 30 Knox St PO Box 153 *TF:* 800-903-2346 ■ *Web:* www.bayviewpress.com	Thomaston	ME	04861	207-354-9919	354-9919
Birchcraft Studios Inc 10 Railroad St **Fax Area Code:* 800 ■ *TF:* 800-333-0405 ■ *Web:* www.birchcraft.com	Abington	MA	02351	781-878-5152	678-5151*
Birchcraft Studios Inc PO Box 328 **Fax Area Code:* 800 ■ *TF:* 800-333-0405 ■ *Web:* www.birchcraft.com	Rockland	MA	02370	781-878-5151	678-5151*
Bizou PhotoGreetings 29311 Castle Hill Dr *Web:* www.bizouphoto.com	Agoura Hills	CA	91301	818-640-7575	889-5881
Blue Mountain Arts Inc PO Box 4549 **Fax:* Cust Svc ■ *TF Sales:* 800-545-8573 ■ *Web:* www.bluemountain.com	Boulder	CO	80306	303-449-0536	417-6496*
Blue Turtle Studio 4884 Broiles Rd *Web:* www.blueturtlestudio.com	Christiana	TN	37037	615-896-9830	890-0191
Bonair Daydreams PO Box 3741 *TF:* 888-226-6247 ■ *Web:* www.bonairdaydreams.com	Farmington	NM	87499	505-326-7177	326-1683
Candy Care Inc W 58th St *TF:* 888-423-8823 ■ *Web:* www.candycare.com	New York	NY	10019	212-421-1234	421-1191
Caravan International & EthnoGraphics PO Box 768 *TF:* 800-442-0036	Colleyville	TX	76034	817-577-2988	577-4503
CardInTheBox 350 S Rohlwing Rd Suite 200 *TF:* 877-212-1121 ■ *Web:* www.cardinthebox.com	Addison	IL	60101	630-953-8882	678-6451
CardMakers PO Box 236 *Web:* www.cardmakers.com	Lyme	NH	03768	603-795-4422	795-4222
Carole Joy Creations Inc 1087 Federal Rd Unit 8 *TF Sales:* 800-223-6945 ■ *Web:* www.carolejoy.com	Brookfield	CT	06801	203-740-4400	740-4405
Caspari Inc 116 E 27th St 11th Fl *TF Sales:* 800-227-7274	New York	NY	10016	212-685-9798	685-9401
Charnette Messe Embracing Life 100 Phoenix Dr *Web:* www.charnettemesse.com	Groton	CT	06340	860-449-0798	
Checkerboard Ltd 216 W Boylston St	West Boylston	MA	01583	508-835-2475	835-4843
ClaudiaM Publications PO Box 925 *Web:* www.claudiampublications.com	Huntington	NY	11743	631-424-7074	
Closerie Publishing 1952 S La Cienega Blvd *TF:* 800-295-9909 ■ *Web:* www.closerie.com	Los Angeles	CA	90034	310-559-9704	559-7702
Cockeyed Creations 1442-A Walnut St Suite 412 *Web:* www.cockeyedcreations.com	Berkeley	CA	94709	510-559-1897	525-9509
Colors By Design 7723 Densmore Ave *TF:* 800-832-8436 ■ *Web:* www.cbdcards.com	Van Nuys	CA	91406	818-376-1226	376-1669
Copperplate Publishing Inc 1901 Lexington Ave N *TF:* 888-772-6001 ■ *Web:* www.tokensofaffection.com	Roseville	MN	55113	651-487-8575	487-8576
Cow Pie Greeting Cards PO Box 655	Springville	UT	84663	801-491-4300	226-6214
Creative Contrasts 303 W Lancaster Ave PMB #316 *Web:* www.creativecontrasts.com	Wayne	PA	19087	610-220-0081	975-0864
Curiosities Greeting Cards 21 Ashwood Ct *TF:* 877-424-4401 ■ *Web:* www.curiosities.com	Lancaster	NY	14086	716-681-2801	685-2141
DaySpring Cards Inc PO Box 1010 *TF:* 800-944-8000 ■ *Web:* www.dayspring.com	Siloam Springs	AR	72761	479-524-9301	524-8813
Design Design Inc 19 La Grave SE *TF:* 800-334-3348 ■ *Web:* www.designdesign.us	Grand Rapids	MI	49503	616-774-2448	774-4020
Designer Greetings Inc 250 Arlington Ave PO Box 140729 *TF:* 800-654-6960 ■ *Web:* www.designergreetings.com	Staten Island	NY	10314	718-981-7700	981-0151
Different Drumbeats 400 Murrasy Hollow Rd *TF:* 800-957-6548	Shushan	NY	12873	518-854-7446	
Eclectik 2506 N Clark St Suite 290 *Web:* www.eclectik.com	Chicago	IL	60614	773-480-0911	
Egreetings Network Inc 1 American Rd *TF:* 800-321-3040 ■ *Web:* www.egreetings.com	Cleveland	OH	44144	216-252-7300	252-6778
Erica Marston Handmade Greetings 3109 W 50th St Suite 285	Minneapolis	MN	55410	612-805-9104	724-2835
Eunco 168 Mason Way Suite B-3 *Web:* www.eunco.com	Industry	CA	91746	626-435-0177	435-0178
Executive Greetings Inc 120 Greenwoods Industrial Pk *TF Cust Svc:* 800-562-5468 ■ *Web:* www.executive-greetings.com	New Hartford	CT	06057	860-379-9911	379-7124
Family Cards USA 892 Riverside St *TF:* 877-765-3422	Portland	ME	04103	207-797-9738	879-1155
Fantus Paper Products DBA PS Greetings Inc 5730 N Tripp Ave *TF Sales:* 800-621-8823 ■ *Web:* www.psg-fpp.com	Chicago	IL	60646	773-267-6069	267-6055

Phone Fax

Fat Pat Productions LLC 4313 Columbine Dr. Austin TX 78727 800-856-0234
Web: www.fatpatcards.com

Fotofolio Inc 561 Broadway New York NY 10012 212-226-0923 226-0072
TF Sales: 800-955-3686 ■ *Web:* www.fotofolio.com

Freedom Greeting Card Co Inc 774 American Dr. Bensalem PA 19020 215-604-0300 604-0436
TF Sales: 800-359-3301 ■ *Web:* www.freedomgreetings.com

FSG Crest LLC 354 W Armory Dr South Holland IL 60473 708-210-0800 210-0808
TF: 877-747-1225 ■ *Web:* www.fsgcrest.com

Gallant Greetings Corp 4300 United Pkwy Schiller Park IL 60176 847-671-6500 671-5900
TF: 800-621-4279 ■ *Web:* www.gallantgreetings.com

Gina B Designs Inc 12700 Industrial Pk Blvd Suite 40 Plymouth MN 55441 763-559-7595 559-3899
TF: 800-228-4856 ■ *Web:* www.ginabdesigns.com

Goodge Street Press PO Box 9172 Peoria IL 61612 309-674-5477 674-1799
Web: www.goodge.com

Graphique De France 9 State St Woburn MA 01801 781-935-3405 935-5145
TF Sales: 800-444-1464 ■ *Web:* www.graphiquedefrance.com

Great Arrow Graphics 2495 Main St Suite 457 Buffalo NY 14214 716-836-0408 836-0702
TF: 800-835-0490 ■ *Web:* www.greatarrow.com

Hallmark Cards Inc 2501 McGee St Kansas City MO 64108 816-274-5111 545-2305*
**Fax:* Mail Rm ■ *TF:* 800-425-5627 ■ *Web:* www.hallmark.com

Hallmark International 2501 McGee St Kansas City MO 64108 816-274-5111 545-2305
TF: 800-425-5627 ■ *Web:* www.hallmark.com

Hazy Jean Inc 41 Crewe Ave Toronto ON M4C2J2 416-429-4977 429-5882
Web: www.hazyjean.com

Head Cards 1 Morton Sq Bronx NY 10014 917-952-3491
Web: www.headcards.com

Heart-Felt Greetings II Inc 1367 Fairview Blvd Fairview TN 37062 615-799-8562 799-7945
TF: 800-818-9099 ■ *Web:* www.heartfeltgreetings.com

Heart's Desire Press 55 Kyleswood Pl PO Box 883 Inverness CA 94937 415-663-5443 663-9282
Web: www.heartsdesirepress.com

Highland Creations Inc PO Box 3512 Westport MA 02790 617-262-3225
Web: www.highlandcreations.com

Hunkydory Paper Products PO Box 90081 San Antonio TX 78209 210-828-3370 828-3369
TF: 866-617-1259 ■ *Web:* www.hunkydorycards.com

Idesign Greetings Inc 12020 W Ripley Ave Milwaukee WI 53226 414-475-7176 475-7566
TF: 800-432-3301

Illustrated Dog The 1203 Brownstone Ln Santa Maria CA 93454 805-614-4530
Web: www.illustrateddog.com

InterArt Distribution DBA Sunrise Greetings
1145 Sunrise Greetings Ct Bloomington IN 47404 812-336-9900 336-8712
TF Sales: 800-457-4045 ■ *Web:* www.interartdistribution.com

IntroKnocks Corp 210 W 101st St New York NY 10025 212-967-6185 967-6083

ITB Solutions DBA CardInTheBox 350 S Rohlwing Rd Suite 200 Addison IL 60101 630-953-8882 678-6451
TF: 877-212-1121 ■ *Web:* www.cardinthebox.com

JewishCard 304 Darwin St Santa Cruz CA 95062 831-469-8883 469-8803
Web: www.jewishcard.com

Karen & Co Greeting Cards Inc PO Box 972 East Stroudsburg PA 18301 570-424-8528 424-8529
Web: www.sistathingcards.com

KDi Studios LLC 206 New Rd Avon CT 06001 860-913-4123 693-1952
Web: www.kdistudios.com

Kenzig Kards Inc 2300 Julia Goldbach Ave Ronkonkoma NY 11779 631-737-1584

Kisses To You Greetings 300 DeWittshire Rd S DeWitt NY 13214 315-210-6302 256-9210
Web: www.kissestoyougreetings.com

Krause Design Inc PO Box 240-319 Dorchester MA 02124 617-436-2661 436-2661
TF: 877-572-8730

Lacy Hummingbird Vine Farm 500 Arrowhead Pass Wimberley TX 78676 512-847-1353

Laughing Elephant 3645 Interlake Ave N Seattle WA 98103 206-447-9229 447-9189
TF: 800-354-0400 ■ *Web:* www.laughingelephant.com

Laura & Co Inc PO Box 1238 Yelm WA 98597 360-894-1418 894-1419
TF: 866-439-1715 ■ *Web:* www.lauraandcompany.com

Laurel Ink 911 N 145th St Seattle WA 98133 206-767-4000 763-4299
TF: 800-850-0081 ■ *Web:* www.laurelink.com

Leanin' Tree Inc 6055 Longbow Dr Boulder CO 80301 303-530-1442 530-7283
TF: 800-777-8716 ■ *Web:* www.leanintree.com

Legacy Greetings LLC PO Box 2196 Horsham PA 19044 215-677-7111 677-7119
Web: www.legacygreetings.com

LPG Greetings Inc 4000 Porett Dr Gurnee IL 60031 847-244-4414

Maid In The Shade PO Box 341 Church St Station New York NY 10008 201-659-1269 962-1420*
**Fax Area Code:* 212

Marian Heath Greeting Cards Inc 9 Kendrick Rd Wareham MA 02571 508-291-0766 291-2976
TF Sales: 800-338-3740 ■ *Web:* www.marianheath.com

Masterpiece Studios 2080 Lookout Dr Box 8240 North Mankato MN 56002 507-388-8788 344-4601
TF: 800-447-0219 ■ *Web:* www.masterpiecestudios.com

Max & Lucy 1737 E Washington St Suite B Phoenix AZ 85034 602-275-5050 275-5700
TF: 877-975-5050 ■ *Web:* www.maxandlucy.com

Meri Meri 525 Harbor Blvd Belmont CA 94002 650-508-2300 508-2301
TF: 800-733-4770 ■ *Web:* www.merimeri.com

Miya & Me 29 Floribel Ave San Anselmo CA 94960 415-460-1668 460-1658
Web: www.miyaandme.com

Morning Center Cards 37 Stratford Dr Brick NJ 08724 732-295-3923 295-3922
Web: www.morningcentercards.com

Mountain Girl Designs 1618 SE Ellis St Portland OR 97202 503-235-5492

Museum Facsimiles 117 4th St Pittsfield MA 01201 413-499-0020 442-3011
TF: 800-499-0020 ■ *Web:* www.museumfacsimiles.com

Naos Graphics Inc 103 Edgevale Rd Baltimore MD 21210 410-435-0031 435-1849
Web: www.naosgraphics.com

Natural Habitats 4269 Stern Ave Sherman Oaks CA 91423 818-783-4776 369-3776*
**Fax Area Code:* 310

NCPL Inc DBA Northern Cards 5694 Ambler Dr Mississauga ON L4W2K9 905-625-4944 625-5995
TF: 877-627-7444 ■ *Web:* www.northerncards.com

New England Art Publisher Inc DBA Birchcraft Studios Inc
PO Box 328 Rockland MA 02370 781-878-5151 678-5151*
**Fax Area Code:* 800 ■ *TF:* 800-333-0405 ■ *Web:* www.birchcraft.com

No Name Girl 691 Bridgeway Sausalito CA 94965 415-332-7633 332-1263
Web: www.nonamegirl.com

NobleWorks Inc 123 Grand St Hoboken NJ 07030 201-420-0095 420-0679
TF Sales: 800-346-6253 ■ *Web:* www.nobleworksinc.com

Northern Cards 5694 Ambler Dr Mississauga ON L4W2K9 905-625-4944 625-5995
TF: 877-627-7444 ■ *Web:* www.northerncards.com

Northern Cards 5694 Ambler Dr Mississauga ON L4W2K9 905-625-4944 625-5995
TF: 877-627-7444 ■ *Web:* www.northerncards.com

Northern Exposure Greeting Cards
2301 Circadian Way Suite 300 Santa Rosa CA 95407 707-546-2153 546-0875
TF: 800-237-3524 ■ *Web:* www.northernexposurecards.com

Nouvelles Images Inc 22 Eagle Rd Danbury CT 06810 203-730-1004 730-0516
TF: 800-345-1383

NRN Designs 5142 Argosy Ave Huntington Beach CA 92649 714-898-6363 898-0015
TF: 800-421-6958 ■ *Web:* nrninvitations.com

Nu-Art Publishers Inc 6247 W 74th St Bedford Park IL 60638 708-496-4900 496-8058
TF: 800-323-0398 ■ *Web:* www.nu-art.net

Oatmeal Studios Inc 440 State Garage Rd PO box 138 Rochester VT 05767 802-767-3171 767-9890
TF Cust Svc: 800-628-6325 ■ *Web:* www.oatmealstudios.com

Ooh La Lu! 1377 N Trail Creek Way Eagle ID 83616 208-939-8940 939-8708
TF: 866-664-5258 ■ *Web:* www.oohlalu.com

Palm Press Inc 1442A Walnut St PMB 120 Berkeley CA 94709 510-486-0502 486-1158
TF: 800-322-7256 ■ *Web:* www.palmpressinc.com

Paper Magic Group Inc 401 Adams Ave Suite 501 Scranton PA 18510 570-961-3863 961-2628*
**Fax:* Cust Svc ■ *TF Cust Svc:* 800-258-1044 ■ *Web:* www.papermagic.com

Paper Prince 2001 Kennedy St NE Minneapolis MN 55413 612-378-4691 617-4155
TF: 800-717-1574

Paperdoll Co 4944 Encino Ave Encino CA 91316 818-906-8411 907-0225
TF: 866-223-1145

PaperTroupe Ltd 1710 Wildwood Ln Hanover Park IL 60133 630-289-4348 338-3808*
**Fax Area Code:* 708

Paradachs Pictures Inc 17 W 64th St Suite 9C New York NY 10023 877-896-7877 657-2808*
**Fax Area Code:* 845 ■ *Web:* www.paradachs.com

Paramount Cards Inc 400 Pine St Pawtucket RI 02860 401-726-0800 727-0370*
**Fax:* Hum Res ■ *TF:* 800-554-5017 ■ *Web:* www.paramountcards.com

Parker Publications Inc PO Box 483 North Salem NY 10560 914-763-6933
TF: 866-968-7872

Patriot Greetings LLC 13736 Santa Rosa Ct Manassas VA 20112 703-725-6642 852-7229
Web: www.patriotgreetings.com

Peaceable Kingdom Press 950 Gilman St Berkeley CA 94710 510-558-2051 558-2052
TF: 800-444-7778 ■ *Web:* www.pkpress.com

Penny Laine Papers 2211 Century Ctr Blvd Suite 110 Irving TX 75062 972-812-3000 812-3004
TF: 800-456-6484

Perma-Greetings Inc 2470 Schuetz Rd Maryland Heights MO 63043 314-567-4606 567-0674

Persimmon Press PO Box 297 Belmont CA 94002 800-910-5080 910-5095
Web: www.persimmoncards.com

Pixel Ditties LLC 3980 S Bellaire St Cherry Hills Village CO 80113 303-757-8097 759-3895
Web: www.pdphotographystudio.com/pixelditties.htm

Portal Publications Ltd 201 Alameda Del Prado PO Box 6172 Novato CA 94948 415-884-6200 382-3377
TF: 800-227-1720 ■ *Web:* www.portalpub.com

Postcards from the Moon 1525 Summit Ave Seattle WA 98122 206-861-1971 861-1973
TF: 800-872-1410 ■ *Web:* www.postcardsfromthemoon.com

PostMark Press Inc 16 Spruce St Watertown MA 02472 617-924-3520 924-1371
TF: 888-924-3520 ■ *Web:* www.postmarkpress.com

Posty Cards Inc 1600 Olive St Kansas City MO 64127 816-231-2323 483-8135*
**Fax:* Sales ■ *TF Sales:* 800-554-5018 ■ *Web:* www.postycards.com

Potluck Press 1229 21st Ave E Seattle WA 98112 206-323-8310 328-4633
TF: 877-818-5500 ■ *Web:* www.potluckpress.com

Princeton Mint Inc PO Drawer M Jackson NJ 08527 732-928-2777 928-2660
Web: www.princetonmint.com

PS Greetings Inc 5730 N Tripp Ave Chicago IL 60646 773-267-6069 267-6055
TF Sales: 800-621-8823 ■ *Web:* www.psg-fpp.com

Queen of Cards 10008 S 67th E Pl Tulsa OK 74133 918-299-1850 299-1827
TF: 888-899-2508 ■ *Web:* www.queenofcards.com

Recycled Paper Greetings Inc 3636 N Broadway Chicago IL 60613 773-348-6410 929-7123
TF Cust Svc: 800-777-9494 ■ *Web:* www.recycledpapergreetings.com

Red Farm Studio Co Inc 1135 Roosevelt Ave Pawtucket RI 02862 401-728-9300 728-0350
TF: 800-556-7090 ■ *Web:* www.redfarmstudio.com

Renaissance Greeting Cards Inc 10 Renaissance Way Sanford ME 04073 207-324-4153 324-9564
TF: 800-688-9998 ■ *Web:* www.rencards.com

Saltbox Illustrations 75 Green St Box 299 Clinton MA 01510 978-368-8711 368-7867
TF: 800-322-3866 ■ *Web:* www.saltboxillustrations.com

Scarlet's Feathers PO Box 638 Montclair NJ 07042 973-509-9427
Web: www.scarletsfeathers.com

Schurman Fine Papers 500 Chadbourne Rd Box 6030 Fairfield CA 94533 707-428-0200 428-0641
TF Sales: 800-333-6724 ■ *Web:* www.papyrusonline.com

Sillies Greeting Card Co 14762 Oak Run Ln Burnsville MN 55306 952-892-5666 435-8036
TF: 800-355-9148

Silver Ink 222 Primrose Ave Mount Vernon NY 10552 914-667-5423

Smorganbord Ltd/Pumps Greetings 165 N Canal Suite 519 Chicago IL 60606 312-382-1557 382-1614
Web: www.pumpsgreetings.com

Sole Source Inc 1 Idea Way Caldwell ID 83607 800-285-1657 455-0642
TF: 800-285-1657 ■ *Web:* www.sole-source.com

Sourire PO Box 1659 Old Chelsea Station New York NY 10011 718-573-4624 455-8898
Web: www.capitalmindz.com/sourire/index.html

Spirit Inspired PO Box 7904 Atlanta GA 30357 404-792-3664 792-8168
TF: 877-474-8460 ■ *Web:* www.spiritinspired.com

StellArt 2012 Waltzer Rd Santa Rosa CA 95403 707-569-1378 569-1379
TF: 866-621-1987 ■ *Web:* www.stellart.com

Studio 1970 Inc 1813 Clarence St Suite 8 Dallas TX 75215 214-207-3465 565-1766
Web: www.studio1970.com

Sunrise Greetings 1145 Sunrise Greetings Ct Bloomington IN 47404 812-336-9900 336-8712
TF Sales: 800-457-4045 ■ *Web:* www.interartdistribution.com

Sunshine Art Studios Inc 270 Main St Agawam MA 01001 413-821-8700 525-5598
TF: 800-873-7681 ■ *Web:* www.sunshinecards.com

Sunshine Girl Creations Inc 11115 Excelsior Blvd Hopkins MN 55343 952-931-2464 931-2575
TF: 866-899-3632 ■ *Web:* www.sunshinegirlcreations.com

Suzy's Zoo Corp 2355 Northside Dr Suite 202 San Diego CA 92108 619-282-9401 285-5730
TF Cust Svc: 800-780-9066 ■ *Web:* www.suzyszoo.com

Tagline Greetings 1100 Irvine Blvd Suite 123 Tustin CA 92780 323-857-5337 857-5338

Touchstone Designs 111 Providence St Mendon MA 01756 508-243-3824 473-6489
Web: www.touchstonedesigns.com

Up With Paper 6049 Hi-Tek Ct Mason OH 45040 513-759-7473 293-8471*
**Fax Area Code:* 800 ■ *TF:* 800-852-7677 ■ *Web:* www.upwithpaper.com

US Allegiance Inc 63075 NE 18th St Bend OR 97701 541-330-6282 330-6268
TF: 800-327-1402 ■ *Web:* www.ipledge.com

USA Greetings Inc 268 Bush St Suite 3438 San Francisco CA 94104 415-269-6931 707-2103
Web: www.usagreetings.com

Victorian Trading Co 15600 W 99th St Lenexa KS 66219 913-438-3995 724-7697*
**Fax Area Code:* 800 ■ *TF Cust Svc:* 800-700-2035 ■ *Web:* www.victoriantradingco.com

Viktorina Cards 89 Stonehurst Ave Suite 311 Ottawa ON K1Y4R6 613-627-4149
Web: www.amazzzingcards.com

Vivyland 350 Detroit St Suite 206 Denver CO 80206 303-893-8038 329-0877
TF: 888-621-5266 ■ *Web:* www.vivyland.com

William Arthur Inc 7 Alewive Park Rd PO Box 460 West Kennebunk ME 04094 207-985-6581 985-0407
TF: 800-985-6581 ■ *Web:* www.williamarthur.com

Willow Creek Press Inc 9931 Hwy 70 W PO Box 147 Minocqua WI 54548 715-358-7010 358-2807
TF: 800-850-9453 ■ *Web:* www.willowcreekpress.com

World Paper Inc 76 Ethel Ave Hawthorne NJ 07506 973-238-1750 238-1740
TF: 800-385-5911

Yahoo! Greetings 701 1st Ave Sunnyvale CA 94089 408-349-3300 349-3301
Web: www.yahoo.americangreetings.com

Your True Greetings 2215 Farmersville Rd Bethlehem PA 18020 610-694-8028 694-8708
TF: 800-241-2704

ZPR International Inc 24000 Mercantile Rd Unit 8 Beachwood OH 44122 216-464-2667 464-2668

131 CARPETS & RUGS

SEE ALSO Flooring - Resilient p. 1640; Tile - Ceramic (Wall & Floor) p. 2367

The companies listed here include carpet finishers and makers of mats and padding.

Phone Fax

Aladdin Mills Inc 2001 Antioch Rd Dalton GA 30720 706-277-1100 252-3364*
**Fax Area Code:* 800 ■ *TF:* 800-241-4072

Company / Address	City	State	Zip	Phone	Fax
Apache Mills Inc 18 Passaic Ave Unit 1 TF: 800-456-7791	Fairfield	NJ	07004	973-227-9080	808-8330
Artisans Inc 716 River St *TF:* 800-311-8756 ■ *Web:* www.artisanscarpet.com	Calhoun	GA	30701	706-629-9265	629-4247
Atlas Carpet Mills Inc 2200 Saybrook Ave *TF:* 800-272-8527 ■ *Web:* www.atlascarpetmills.com	City of Commerce	CA	90040	323-724-9000	724-4526
Barrett Carpet Mills Inc 2216 Abutment Rd *TF:* 800-241-4064 ■ *Web:* www.barrettcarpet.com	Dalton	GA	30720	706-277-2114	277-3250
Beaulieu of America Inc 1502 Coronet Dr *Web:* www.beaulieu-usa.com	Dalton	GA	30720	706-695-4624	
Bentley Prince Street 14641 E Don Julian Rd **Fax Area Code:* 800 ■ *TF:* 800-423-4709 ■ *Web:* www.bentleymills.com	City of Industry	CA	91746	626-333-4585	741-7420*
Bigelow Commercial Div Mohawk Industries Inc 160 S Industrial Blvd **Fax Area Code:* 800 ■ *TF Cust Svc:* 800-233-4490 ■ *Web:* www.bigelowcommercial.com	Calhoun	GA	30703	706-629-7721	432-4036*
Blue Ridge Carpet Mills 1546 Progress Rd *TF:* 800-241-5945 ■ *Web:* www.blueridgecarpet.com	Ellijay	GA	30540	706-276-2001	276-2005
Camelot Carpet Mills Inc 17111 Red Hill Ave *TF:* 800-854-3258 ■ *Web:* www.camelotcarpetmills.com	Irvine	CA	92614	949-477-2299	553-8238
Capel Inc 831 N Main St *TF:* 800-334-3711 ■ *Web:* www.capelrugs.com	Troy	NC	27371	910-572-7000	572-7040
Carousel Carpet Mills Inc 1 Carousel Ln *TF:* 866-227-6873	Ukiah	CA	95482	707-485-0333	485-5911
Collins & Aikman 26533 Evergreen Rd *Web:* www.collinsaikman.com	Southfield	MI	48076	248-728-4500	
Collins & Aikman Corp Floorcoverings Div 1735 Cleveland Hwy PO Box 1447 **Fax:* Mktg ■ *TF:* 800-241-4902 ■ *Web:* www.powerbond.com	Dalton	GA	30722	706-259-9711	259-2099*
Couristan Inc 2 Executive Dr **Fax:* Orders ■ *TF:* 800-223-6186 ■ *Web:* www2.couristan.com	Fort Lee	NJ	07024	201-585-8500	585-8552*
Delaware Valley Corp 500 Broadway *Web:* www.dvc500.com	Lawrence	MA	01842	978-688-6995	688-5825
Dixie Group Inc 104 Nowlin Ln Suite 101 PO Box 25107 *NASDAQ: DXYN* ■ *TF:* 866-606-7475 ■ *Web:* www.thedixiegroup.com	Chattanooga	TN	37422	423-510-7000	510-7015
Dorsett Industries Inc 1304 May St *TF:* 800-241-4035 ■ *Web:* www.dorsettcarpet.com	Dalton	GA	30721	706-278-1961	217-1775
Durkan Patterned Carpet Inc 405 Virgil Dr *TF:* 800-241-4580 ■ *Web:* www.durkan.com	Dalton	GA	30722	706-278-7037	428-8270
F Schumacher & Co 79 Madison Ave *TF:* 800-523-1200 ■ *Web:* www.fschumacher.com	New York	NY	10016	212-213-7900	213-7848
General Fibers & Fabrics Inc 1404 Orchard Hill Rd	LaGrange	GA	30240	706-882-8801	882-8803
Glenoit LLC 1 Linde Dr *TF:* 800-223-1999	Goldsboro	NC	27530	919-735-7111	713-7209
Gulistan Carpet Inc 3140 Hwy 5 *TF:* 800-869-2727 ■ *Web:* www.gulistan.com	Aberdeen	NC	28315	910-944-2371	944-6359
Interface Inc 2859 Paces Ferry Rd Suite 2000 *NASDAQ: IFSIA* ■ *Web:* www.interfaceinc.com	Atlanta	GA	30339	770-437-6800	803-6950
J & J Industries Inc 818 J & J Dr *TF:* 800-241-4585 ■ *Web:* www.jjindustries.com	Dalton	GA	30721	706-278-4454	275-4433
Karastan Div Mohawk Industries Inc 335 Summit Rd **Fax Area Code:* 800 ■ **Fax:* Cust Svc ■ *TF Cust Svc:* 800-845-8877 ■ *Web:* www.karastan.com	Eden	NC	27288	336-627-7200	533-3263*
Langhorne Carpet Co 201 W Lincoln Hwy *Web:* www.langhornecarpets.com	Penndel	PA	19047	215-757-5155	757-2212
Lees Carpets Div Mohawk Industries Inc 706 Green Valley Rd Suite 300 **Fax Area Code:* 866 ■ *TF:* 800-523-5647 ■ *Web:* www.leescarpets.com	Greensboro	NC	27408	336-378-9162	250-3590*
Len-Dal Carpets Inc 3090 Hwy 411 N PO Box 39 *TF:* 800-241-4030	Chatsworth	GA	30705	706-695-4533	695-0072
Log Cabin Co 1001 Poly Pac Dr *TF:* 800-697-4824	Dalton	GA	30720	706-259-4824	259-8075
Mannington Commercial 345 Marine Dr PO Box 12281 *TF:* 800-241-2262 ■ *Web:* www.mannington.com	Calhoun	GA	30703	706-629-7301	629-2365
Maples Industries Inc 2210 Moody Ridge Rd *TF:* 800-537-3304	Scottsboro	AL	35768	256-259-1327	259-2072
Marglen Industries Inc 1748 Ward Mountain Rd NE	Rome	GA	30161	706-295-5621	295-0706
Masland Carpets Inc 716 Bill Myles Dr *TF:* 800-633-0468 ■ *Web:* www.maslandcarpets.com	Saraland	AL	36571	251-675-9080	675-5808
Milliken & Co 920 Milliken Rd **Fax:* Hum Res ■ *Web:* www.milliken.com	Spartanburg	SC	29303	864-503-2020	503-2100*
Milliken & Co KEX Div 201 Lukken Industrial Dr W MS 801 **Fax Area Code:* 706 ■ *Web:* www.milliken-kex.com	LaGrange	GA	30240	800-342-5539	880-5358*
Mohawk Carpet Corp 160 S Industrial Blvd *TF:* 800-241-4494 ■ *Web:* www.mohawkcarpet.com	Calhoun	GA	30701	706-629-7721	
Mohawk Commercial Business 443 Nathaniel Dr **Fax:* Cust Svc ■ *TF:* 800-554-6637 ■ *Web:* www.mohawkcommercial.com	East Dublin	GA	31027	478-272-7711	275-9539*
Mohawk Home 3032 Sugar Valley Rd NW *TF:* 800-843-4473 ■ *Web:* www.mohawkhome.com	Sugar Valley	GA	30746	706-629-7916	625-3544
Mohawk Industries Inc 160 S Industrial Blvd *NYSE: MHK* ■ **Fax:* Hum Res ■ *TF:* 800-241-4494 ■ *Web:* www.mohawkind.com	Calhoun	GA	30703	706-629-7721	625-4576*
Mohawk Industries Inc Bigelow Commercial Div 160 S Industrial Blvd **Fax Area Code:* 800 ■ *TF Cust Svc:* 800-233-4490 ■ *Web:* www.bigelowcommercial.com	Calhoun	GA	30703	706-629-7721	432-4036*
Mohawk Industries Inc Karastan Div 335 Summit Rd **Fax Area Code:* 800 ■ **Fax:* Cust Svc ■ *TF Cust Svc:* 800-845-8877 ■ *Web:* www.karastan.com	Eden	NC	27288	336-627-7200	533-3263*
Mohawk Industries Inc Lees Carpets Div 706 Green Valley Rd Suite 300 **Fax Area Code:* 866 ■ *TF:* 800-523-5647 ■ *Web:* www.leescarpets.com	Greensboro	NC	27408	336-378-9162	250-3590*
Natco Products Corp 155 Brookside Ave	West Warwick	RI	02893	401-828-0300	823-7670
Oriental Weavers Group Sphinx Div 3252 Lower Dug Gap Rd SW *TF:* 800-832-8020 ■ *Web:* www.owsphinx.com	Dalton	GA	30720	706-277-9666	277-9665
Patcraft Commercial Div Queen Carpet Co 616 Duvall Rd *TF:* 800-241-4014 ■ *Web:* www.patcraft.com	Chatsworth	GA	30705	706-279-4000	279-4031
Philadelphia Carpet Co 616 E Walnut Ave *TF:* 800-742-9872	Dalton	GA	30721	706-278-3812	275-3040
Queen Carpet Co Patcraft Commercial Div 616 Duvall Rd *TF:* 800-241-4014 ■ *Web:* www.patcraft.com	Chatsworth	GA	30705	706-279-4000	279-4031
Rieter Automotive North America - Carpet 480 W 5th St	Bloomsburg	PA	17815	570-784-4100	784-4106
Rogers Finishing LLC 1001 Riverland Rd PO Box 665	Dalton	GA	30722	706-278-8338	
Royalty Carpet Mills Inc 17111 Red Hill Ave *TF:* 800-854-8331 ■ *Web:* www.royaltycarpetmills.com	Irvine	CA	92614	949-474-4000	553-8238
S & S Mills Inc 3007 Parquet Dr PO Box 1568 *TF:* 800-392-6890 ■ *Web:* www.ssmills.com	Dalton	GA	30722	706-277-3677	277-3922
Shaw Industries Inc 616 E Walnut Ave **Fax:* Mail Rm ■ *TF:* 800-720-7429 ■ *Web:* www.shawfloors.com	Dalton	GA	30721	706-278-3812	275-3040*
Stainmaster 175 Town Park Dr **Fax Area Code:* 770 ■ *TF:* 800-438-7668 ■ *Web:* www.stainmaster.com	Kennesaw	GA	30144	877-446-8478	792-4215*
Tuftex Carpet 15305 Valley View Ave *TF:* 877-224-7429 ■ *Web:* www.shawfloors.com/AboutShaw/LabelsandLinks/Tuftex.asp	Santa Fe Springs	CA	90670	562-921-0951	921-9444
Unique Carpets Ltd 7360 Jurupa Ave *TF:* 800-547-8266 ■ *Web:* www.uniquecarpetsltd.com	Riverside	CA	92504	951-352-8125	352-8140
World Carpets Inc 160 S Industrial Blvd *TF:* 800-241-4494	Calhoun	GA	30701	706-278-8000	

132 CASINO COMPANIES

SEE ALSO Games & Gaming p. 1686

Company / Address	City	State	Zip	Phone	Fax
Alliance Gaming Corp 6601 S Bermuda Rd *NYSE: AGI* ■ **Fax:* Hum Res ■ *TF:* 877-462-2559 ■ *Web:* www.ally.com	Las Vegas	NV	89119	702-896-7700	896-7838*
Ameristar Casinos Inc 3773 Howard Hughes Pkwy Suite 490-S *NASDAQ: ASCA* ■ *TF:* 866-921-9229 ■ *Web:* www.ameristarcasinos.com	Las Vegas	NV	89169	702-567-7000	369-8860
Archon Corp 4336 Losee Rd Suite 5 *Web:* www.archoncorporation.com	North Las Vegas	NV	89030	702-732-9120	732-9465
Argosy Gaming Co 219 Piasa St *NYSE: AGY* ■ *TF:* 800-336-7568 ■ *Web:* www.pngaming.com	Alton	IL	62002	618-474-7500	474-7636
Aztar Corp 2390 E Camelback Rd *NYSE: AZR* ■ *Web:* www.aztar.com	Phoenix	AZ	85016	602-381-4100	381-4108
Barden Cos Inc 163 Madison Ave Suite 2000	Detroit	MI	48226	313-496-2900	496-8400
Black Hawk Gaming & Development Co Inc 240 Main St PO Box 50 *TF:* 877-711-1177	Black Hawk	CO	80422	303-582-1771	582-0236
Boomtown Inc PO Box 399 **Fax:* Hum Res ■ *TF:* 800-648-3790 ■ *Web:* www.boomtowncasinos.com	Verdi	NV	89439	775-345-6000	345-8695*
Boyd Gaming Corp 2950 Industrial Rd *NYSE: BYD* ■ **Fax:* Hum Res ■ *TF:* 800-695-2455 ■ *Web:* www.boydgaming.com	Las Vegas	NV	89109	702-792-7200	792-7354*
Century Casinos Inc 200-220 E Bennett Ave *NASDAQ: CNTY* ■ *TF:* 888-966-2257 ■ *Web:* www.cnty.com	Cripple Creek	CO	80813	719-689-0333	689-3282
Coast Casinos Inc 4500 W Tropicana Ave *TF:* 888-365-7111 ■ *Web:* www.coastcasinos.com	Las Vegas	NV	89103	702-365-7111	365-7102
Delaware North Cos Gaming & Entertainment 40 Fountain Plaza *TF:* 800-828-7240 ■ *Web:* www.delawarenorth.com	Buffalo	NY	14202	716-858-5000	858-5926
Empire Resorts Inc Monticello Raceway Rt 17B *NASDAQ: NYNY* ■ *Web:* www.empireresorts.com	Monticello	NY	12701	845-794-4100	791-1402
Exber Inc 600 E Freemont St *TF:* 800-634-6703	Las Vegas	NV	89101	702-385-5200	474-3632
Fond du Lac Band of Lake Superior Chippewa 1720 Big Lake Rd *TF:* 800-365-1613	Cloquet	MN	55720	218-879-4593	879-4146
Full House Resorts Inc 4670 S Fort Apache Rd Suite 190 *AMEX: FLL* ■ *Web:* www.fullhouseresorts.com	Las Vegas	NV	89147	702-221-7800	221-8101
Granite Gaming Group 115 N 1st St	Las Vegas	NV	89101	702-385-4250	385-4935
Great Canadian Gaming Corp 13775 Commerce Pkwy Suite 200 *TSX: GCD* ■ *Web:* www.greatcanadiancasinos.com	Richmond	BC	V6V2V4	604-303-1000	279-8505
Harrah's Entertainment Inc 1 Harrah's Ct *NYSE: HET* ■ *TF:* 800-442-6443 ■ *Web:* www.harrahs.com	Las Vegas	NV	89119	702-407-6000	407-6022
Ho-Chunk Nation PO Box 667 *TF:* 800-294-9343 ■ *Web:* ho-chunknation.com	Black River Falls	WI	54615	715-284-9343	284-9465
Hyatt Gaming Corp 71 S Wacker Dr	Chicago	IL	60606	312-750-1234	780-5278
Imperial Palace Inc 3535 Las Vegas Blvd S *TF:* 800-634-6441 ■ *Web:* www.imperialpalace.com	Las Vegas	NV	89109	702-731-3311	735-8328
Isle of Capri Casinos Inc 1641 Popps Ferry Rd Suite B-1 *NASDAQ: ISLE* ■ *TF:* 800-843-4753 ■ *Web:* www.theislecorp.com	Biloxi	MS	39532	228-396-7000	396-2640
Kerzner International Ltd 1000 S Pine Island Rd Suite 800 *NYSE: KZL* ■ *TF:* 800-321-3000 ■ *Web:* www.kerzner.com	Plantation	FL	33324	954-809-2000	809-2331
Lakes Entertainment Inc 130 Cheshire Ln Suite 101 *TF:* 800-946-9464 ■ *Web:* www.lakesentertainment.com	Minnetonka	MN	55305	952-449-9092	449-9353
Majestic Investor Holdings LLC 1 Buffington Harbor Dr *TF:* 888-225-8259 ■ *Web:* www.majesticstar.com	Gary	IN	46406	219-977-7777	977-7811
Mashantucket Pequot Gaming Enterprise Inc PO Box 3777 *TF:* 800-752-9244	Mashantucket	CT	06338	860-312-3000	312-4965
MGM Mirage Inc 3600 Las Vegas Blvd S *NYSE: MGM* ■ *Web:* www.mgmmirage.com	Las Vegas	NV	89109	702-693-7120	693-8626
Mille Lacs Band of Ojibwe 43408 Oodena Dr *TF:* 800-709-6445 ■ *Web:* www.millelacsojibwe.org	Onamia	MN	56359	320-532-4181	532-7505
MTR Gaming Group Inc PO Box 358 *NASDAQ: MNTG* ■ *TF:* 800-804-0468 ■ *Web:* www.mtrgaming.com	Chester	WV	26034	304-387-8300	387-8001
Nevada Gold & Casinos Inc 3040 Post Oak Blvd Suite 675 *AMEX: UWN* ■ *Web:* www.nevadagold.com	Houston	TX	77056	713-621-2245	621-6919
Palace Casino 158 Howard Ave **Fax:* Mktg ■ *TF:* 800-725-2239 ■ *Web:* www.palacecasinoresort.com	Biloxi	MS	39530	228-432-8888	386-2314*
Penn National Gaming Inc 825 Berkshire Blvd Suite 200 *NASDAQ: PENN* ■ *Web:* www.pnrc.com	Wyomissing	PA	19610	610-373-2400	373-4966
Peppermill Casinos Inc 90 W Grove St Suite 200 *TF:* 000-040-0992	Reno	NV	89509	775-689-8900	824-2718
Pinnacle Entertainment Inc 3800 Howard Hughes Pkwy Suite 1800 *NYSE: PNK* ■ *Web:* www.pnkinc.com	Las Vegas	NV	89109	702-784-7777	784-7778
President Casinos Inc 1000 N Lenor K Sullivan Blvd *TF:* 800-772-3647 ■ *Web:* www.presidentcasino.com	Saint Louis	MO	63102	314-622-3000	622-1833
Primm Valley Resorts 31900 S Las Vegas Blvd *TF:* 800-386-7867 ■ *Web:* www.primmvalleyresorts.com	Primm	NV	89019	702-386-7867	679-5633
Red Lake Gaming Enterprises Inc PO Box 543 *TF:* 800-568-6649	Red Lake	MN	56671	218-679-2111	679-2191
Saint Croix Chippewa Tribe of Wisconsin 24663 Angeline Ave *TF:* 800-236-2195	Webster	WI	54893	715-349-2195	349-5768
Station Casinos Inc 2411 W Sahara Ave *NYSE: STN* ■ *TF:* 800-544-2411 ■ *Web:* www.stationcasinos.com	Las Vegas	NV	89102	702-367-2411	367-2478
Trump Hotels & Casino Resorts Inc 1000 Boardwalk *Web:* www.trump.com	Atlantic City	NJ	08401	609-449-6515	449-6586

133 CASINOS

SEE ALSO Games & Gaming p. 1686

Listings for casinos are alphabetized by states.

Company / Address	City	State	Zip	Phone	Fax
Baccarat Casino 10128 104th Ave	Edmonton	AB	T5J4Y8	780-413-3178	413-3177
Deerfoot Inn & Casino 11500 35th St SE *TF:* 877-236-5225 ■ *Web:* www.deerfootinn.com	Calgary	AB	T2Z3W4	403-236-7529	252-4767
Palace Casino 2710 8882-170th St West Edmonton Mall *Web:* www.palacecasino.com	Edmonton	AB	T5T4J2	780-444-2112	444-1155
Stampede Casino 1801 Big Four Trail SE Big Four Bldg Stampede Park *Web:* www.stampedecasino.com	Calgary	AB	T2G2W1	403-261-0422	262-9409
Casino Arizona at Salt River 524 N 92nd St *TF:* 877-724-4687 ■ *Web:* www.casinoaz.com	Scottsdale	AZ	85256	480-850-7777	850-7741
Fort McDowell Casino 10424 N Fort McDowell Rd **Fax:* Mktg ■ *TF:* 800-843-3678 ■ *Web:* www.fortmcdowellcasino.com	Scottsdale	AZ	85264	480-837-1424	837-4756*
Harrah's Ak-Chin Casino Resort 15406 Maricopa Rd *TF:* 888-302-3293 ■ *Web:* www.harrahs.com	Maricopa	AZ	85239	480-802-5000	802-5048

Phone Fax

River Rock Casino Resort 8811 River Rd. Richmond BC V6X3P8 604-247-8900 247-2641
TF: 866-748-3718 ■ *Web:* www.greatcanadiancasinos.com/riverrock
Agua Caliente Casino 32-250 Bob Hope Dr. Rancho Mirage CA 92270 760-321-2000 202-2697
Web: www.hotwatercasino.com
Augustine Casino 84-001 Ave 54 Coachella CA 92236 760-391-9500 398-4447
TF: 888-752-9294 ■ *Web:* www.augustinecasino.com
Barona Valley Ranch Resort & Casino
1932 Wildcat Canyon Rd Lakeside CA 92040 619-443-2300 443-1794
TF: 888-722-7662 ■ *Web:* www.barona.com
Bicycle Casino 7301 Eastern Ave Bell Gardens CA 90201 562-806-4646 806-3576
TF: 800-292-0015 ■ *Web:* www.thebike.com
Chumash Casino 3400 E Hwy 246 Santa Ynez CA 93460 805-686-0855 686-3881
TF: 800-728-9997 ■ *Web:* www.chumashcasino.com
Commerce Casino 6131 Telegraph Rd Commerce CA 90040 323-721-2100 838-3472
Web: www.commercecasino.com
Eagle Mountain Casino 681 S Tule Reservation Rd. Porterville CA 93257 559-788-6220 788-6223
TF: 800-903-3353 ■ *Web:* www.eaglemtncasino.com
Fantasy Springs Resort Casino 84-245 Indio Springs Pkwy Indio CA 92203 760-342-5000 347-7880
TF: 800-827-2946 ■ *Web:* www.fantasyspringsresort.com
Harrah's Rincon Casino & Resort
777 Harrah's Rincon Way Valley Center CA 92082 760-751-3100 751-3200
TF: 877-777-2457 ■ *Web:* www.harrahs.com/our_casinos/rin
Hawaiian Gardens Casino 11871 Carson St. Hawaiian Gardens CA 90716 562-860-5887 860-6762
Web: www.hgcasino.com
Morongo Casino Resort & Spa
49500 Seminole Dr PO Box 366 Cabazon CA 92230 951-849-3080 849-3181
TF: 800-252-4499 ■ *Web:* www.morongocasinoresort.com
Pala Casino Resort & Spa 11154 Hwy 76 PO Box 40 Pala CA 92059 760-510-5100 510-5190
TF: 877-946-7252 ■ *Web:* www.palacasino.com
Pechanga Resort & Casino 45000 Pechanga Pkwy Temecula CA 92592 951-693-1819 695-7410
TF: 877-711-2946 ■ *Web:* www.pechanga.com
San Manuel Indian Bingo & Casino 777 San Manuel Blvd Highland CA 92346 909-864-5050 864-9528
TF: 800-359-2464 ■ *Web:* www.sanmanuel.com
Spa Hotel & Casino 100 N Indian Canyon Dr. Palm Springs CA 92262 760-325-1461 325-3344
TF: 800-854-1279 ■ *Web:* www.sparesortcasino.com
Spa Resort Casino 401 E Amado Rd Palm Springs CA 92262 760-883-1000 883-1250
TF: 800-854-1279 ■ *Web:* www.sparesortcasino.com
Spotlight 29 Casino 46-200 Harrison Pl. Coachella CA 92236 760-775-5566 775-7677
TF: 866-878-6729 ■ *Web:* www.spotlight29.com
Sycuan Casino & Resort 5469 Casino Way El Cajon CA 92019 619-445-6002 445-1961
TF: 800-279-2826 ■ *Web:* www.sycuancasino.com
Sycuan Resort & Casino 3007 Dehesa Rd El Cajon CA 92019 619-442-3425 442-9574
TF: 800-457-5568 ■ *Web:* www.sycuan.com/sycuan_resort
Viejas Casino 5000 Willows Rd Alpine CA 91901 619-445-5400 659-1954
TF: 800-847-6537 ■ *Web:* viejas.com
Black Hawk Station Casino 141 Gregory St. Black Hawk CO 80422 303-582-5582
Bronco Billy's Casino 233 E Bennett Ave PO Box 590 Cripple Creek CO 80813 719-689-2142 689-2869
TF: 877-989-2142 ■ *Web:* www.broncobillyscasino.com
Bullpen Casino 101 Gregory St. Black Hawk CO 80422 303-271-2733 271-2501
TF: 800-426-2855
Bullwhackers Casino 101 Gregory St. Black Hawk CO 80422 303-271-2506 271-2801
TF: 800-426-2855 ■ *Web:* www.bullwhackers.com
Canyon Casino 131 Main St Black Hawk CO 80422 303-777-1111 582-0311
Web: www.canyoncasino.com
Colorado Central Station Casino 340 Main St PO Box 22. Black Hawk CO 80422 303-582-3000 582-2171
Web: www.coloradocentralstation.com
Doc Holliday Casino 131 Main St. Central City CO 80427 303-582-1400 582-3800
Dostal Alley Casino 1 Dostal Alley Central City CO 80427 303-582-1610
Web: www.centralcitycolorado.com
Double Eagle Hotel & Casino 442 E Bennett Ave Cripple Creek CO 80813 719-689-5000 689-5096
TF: 800-711-7234 ■ *Web:* www.doubleeaglehotelandcasino.com
Easy Street Casino 120 Main St PO Box 399. Central City CO 80427 303-582-5914 582-0447
Eureka Casino 211 Gregory St Black Hawk CO 80422 303-582-1040 582-5988
Famous Bonanza Casino 107 Main St Central City CO 80427 303-582-5914 582-0447
Web: www.famousbonanza.com
Fitzgeralds Casino 101 Main St Black Hawk CO 80422 303-582-3203 582-6170
TF: 800-538-5825 ■ *Web:* www.fitzgeraldsbh.com
Fortune Valley Hotel & Casino 321 Gregory St. Central City CO 80427 303-582-0800 582-5860
TF: 800-924-6646 ■ *Web:* www.fortunevalleycasino.com
Gilpin Hotel Casino 111 Main St Black Hawk CO 80422 303-582-1133 582-1154
Golden Gates Casino 300 Main St Black Hawk CO 80422 303-582-1650 582-5700
Web: www.goldencasinogroup.com
Golden Gulch Casino 321 Main St Black Hawk CO 80422 303-582-1800 582-1801
Web: www.goldencasinogroup.com
Grande Plateau Casino 131 Main St. Black Hawk CO 80422 303-777-1111 582-1173
Isle of Capri Casino 401 Main St. Black Hawk CO 80422 303-998-7777 580-0614
TF: 800-843-4753 ■ *Web:* www.isleofcapricasinos.com
Lodge Casino 240 Main St Black Hawk CO 80422 303-582-1771 582-2300
Web: www.thelodgecasino.com
Mardi Gras Casino 300 Main St Black Hawk CO 80422 303-582-5600 582-5700
Web: www.goldencasinogroup.com
Midnight Rose Hotel & Casino 256 E Bennett Ave Cripple Creek CO 80813 719-689-2446 689-3413
TF: 888-461-7529 ■ *Web:* www.triplecrowncasinos.com/Default.asp
Mountain High Casino 111 Richman St Black Hawk CO 80422 303-567-1234 946-4030*
**Fax Area Code:* 720
Red Dolly Casino 530 Gregory St. Black Hawk CO 80422 303-582-1100 582-1435
Riviera Casino 444 Main St PO Box 9 Black Hawk CO 80422 303-582-1000 406-3812*
**Fax Area Code:* 720 ■ *Web:* www.rivierablackhawk.com
Silver Hawk Casino 101 Gregory St PO Box 49 Black Hawk CO 80422 303-271-2500 716-5501
Sky Ute Casino 14826 Hwy 172 N Ignacio CO 81137 970-563-3000 563-9546
TF: 888-842-4180 ■ *Web:* www.skyutecasino.com
Ute Mountain Casino 3 Weeminuche Dr. Towaoc CO 81334 970-565-8800 565-6553
TF: 800-258-8007 ■ *Web:* www.utemountaincasino.com
Wild Card Saloon & Casino 120 Main St PO Box 513 Black Hawk CO 80422 303-582-3412 582-3508
Web: www.wildcardcasino.com
Wild Horse Casino 353 Myers Ave PO Box 1890 Cripple Creek CO 80813 719-687-7777 689-0305
Web: www.thewildhorsecasino.com
Foxwoods Resort Casino 39 Norwich Westerly Rd Ledyard CT 06339 860-312-3000 396-3639
TF: 800-752-9244 ■ *Web:* www.foxwoods.com
Mohegan Sun Resort & Casino 1 Mohegan Sun Blvd Uncasville CT 06382 860-862-8000 862-7824
TF: 888-226-7711 ■ *Web:* www.mohegansun.com
Palm Beach Casino Line 1 E 11th St Suite 500. Riviera Beach FL 33404 561-845-2101 845-2188
TF: 800-841-7447 ■ *Web:* www.pbcasino.com
SeaEscape Entertainment Inc 3045 N Federal Hwy. Fort Lauderdale FL 33306 954-453-2200 453-6555*
**Fax:* Sales ■ *TF:* 877-732-3722 ■ *Web:* www.seaescape.com
Seminole Casino Hollywood 4150 N State Rd 7 Hollywood FL 33021 954-961-3220 961-3401
TF: 866-222-7466 ■ *Web:* www.seminoletribe.com/enterprises/hollywood/casino.shtml
Seminole Casino Immokalee 506 S 1st St. Immokalee FL 34143 800-218-0007 658-1515*
**Fax Area Code:* 239 ■ *Web:* www.theseminolecasino.com
Seminole Coconut Creek Casino 5550 NW 40th St. Coconut Creek FL 33073 954-977-6700 970-7721
TF: 877-937-6700
Seminole Hard Rock Hotel & Casino Hollywood
1 Seminole Way Hollywood FL 33314 954-327-7625 327-7655
TF: 800-937-0010 ■ *Web:* www.seminolehardrock.com
Seminole Hard Rock Hotel & Casino Tampa 5223 N Orient Rd Tampa FL 33610 813-621-1302 623-6862
TF: 800-282-7016 ■ *Web:* www.hardrockhotelcasinotampa.com

Phone Fax

SunCruz Casino 647 E Dania Beach Blvd Dania Beach FL 33004 954-929-3880 929-3830
TF: 800-474-3423 ■ *Web:* www.suncruzcasino.com
SunCruz Casino - Port Canaveral 610 Glen Cheek Dr Cape Canaveral FL 32920 321-783-2770 783-8368
TF: 800-474-3423 ■ *Web:* www.suncruzcasino.com
Argosy's Alton Belle Casino 219 Piasa St Alton IL 62002 800-711-4263
Web: www.argosycasinos.com
Casino Queen 200 S Front St East Saint Louis IL 62201 618-874-5000 874-5008
TF: 800-777-0777 ■ *Web:* www.casinoqueen.com
Empress Casino 2300 Empress Dr Joliet IL 60436 815-744-9400 744-9456
TF: 888-436-7737 ■ *Web:* www.argosycasinos.com
Grand Victoria Casino Elgin 250 S Grove Ave. Elgin IL 60120 847-888-1000 531-7747
Web: www.grandvictoria-elgin.com
Harrah's Joliet 151 N Joliet St Joliet IL 60432 815-740-7800 740-2223
TF: 800-427-7247 ■ *Web:* www.harrahs.com/our_casinos/jol
Harrah's Metropolis Casino 100 E Front St Metropolis IL 62960 618-524-2628 524-6150
TF: 800-929-5905 ■ *Web:* www.harrahs.com/our_casinos/met
Par-A-Dice Riverboat Casino 21 Blackjack Blvd. East Peoria IL 61611 309-698-7711 699-0711
TF: 800-727-2342 ■ *Web:* www.par-a-dice.com
Argosy Casino Cincinnati 777 Argosy Pkwy Lawrenceburg IN 47025 812-539-8000 539-8441
TF Resv: 888-274-6797 ■ *Web:* www.argosycasinos.com
Belterra Casino Resort 777 Belterra Dr Florence IN 47020 812-427-7777 427-7812*
**Fax:* Hum Res ■ *TF Resv:* 888-235-8377 ■ *Web:* www.belterracasino.com
Blue Chip Casino Inc 2 Easy St Michigan City IN 46360 219-879-7711 877-2112
TF: 888-879-7711 ■ *Web:* www.bluechip-casino.com
Casino Aztar 421 NW Riverside Dr Evansville IN 47708 812-433-4000 433-4384
TF: 800-342-5386 ■ *Web:* www.casinoaztar.com
Grand Victoria Casino & Resort by Hyatt
600 Grand Victoria Dr Rising Sun IN 47040 812-438-1234 438-5151
TF: 800-472-6311 ■ *Web:* www.hyatt.com
Horseshoe Casino 777 Casino Center Dr Hammond IN 46320 219-473-7000 473-6115
TF: 866-711-7463 ■ *Web:* www.horseshoe.com
Majestic Star Casino 1 Buffington Harbor Dr Gary IN 46406 219-977-7777 977-7211
TF: 888-218-7867 ■ *Web:* www.majesticstar.com
Resorts East Chicago 777 Resorts Blvd. East Chicago IN 46312 219-378-3000 378-3498*
**Fax:* Hum Res ■ *TF:* 877-496-1777 ■ *Web:* www.resortseastchicago.com
Ameristar Casino Hotel Council Bluffs 2200 River Rd Council Bluffs IA 51501 712-328-8888 329-6984*
**Fax:* Mktg ■ *TF:* 877-462-7827 ■ *Web:* www.ameristarcasinos.com
Harrah's Council Bluffs 1 Harrah's Blvd. Council Bluffs IA 51501 712-329-6000 329-6491
TF: 888-598-8451 ■ *Web:* www.harrahs.com/our_casinos/cou
Horseshoe Council Bluffs 2701 23rd Ave. Council Bluffs IA 51501 712-323-2500
Web: www.harrahs.com
Meskwaki Bingo Hotel Casino 1504 305th St Tama IA 52339 641-484-2108 484-1618
TF: 800-728-4263 ■ *Web:* www.meskwaki.com
Rhythm City Casino 101 W River Dr. Davenport IA 52801 563-322-2628 322-2583
TF: 800-262-8711 ■ *Web:* www.rhythmcitycasino.com
Harrah's Prairie Band Casino & Hotel 12305 150th Rd Mayetta KS 66509 785-966-7777 966-7799
TF: 800-427-7247 ■ *Web:* www.harrahs.com/our_casinos/top
Belle of Baton Rouge Casino 103 France St Baton Rouge LA 70802 225-378-6000 344-8056
TF: 800-676-4847 ■ *Web:* www.belleofbatonrouge.com
Boomtown Casino New Orleans 4132 Peters Rd Harvey LA 70058 504-366-7711 364-8796
TF: 800-366-7711 ■ *Web:* www.boomtownneworleans.com
Boomtown Hotel Casino 300 Riverside Dr Bossier City LA 71111 318-746-0711 226-9434
TF: 877-862-4428 ■ *Web:* www.boomtownbossier.com
Coushatta Casino Resort 777 Coushatta Dr PO Box 1510. Kinder LA 70648 337-738-7300 738-7386
TF: 800-584-7263 ■ *Web:* www.gccoushatta.com
Eldorado Resort Casino Shreveport 451 Clyde Fant Pkwy. Shreveport LA 71101 318-220-0711 220-0160
TF: 877-602-0711 ■ *Web:* www.eldoradoshreveport.com
Harrah's New Orleans 8 Canal St New Orleans LA 70130 504-533-6000 533-6174
TF: 800-847-5299 ■ *Web:* www.harrahs.com/our_casinos/nor
Hollywood Casino Baton Rouge 1717 River Rd N Baton Rouge LA 70802 225-709-7777 709-7770
TF: 800-447-6843 ■ *Web:* www.casinorouge.com
Horseshoe Casino & Hotel 711 Horseshoe Blvd Bossier City LA 71111 318-742-0711 741-7728*
**Fax:* Mktg ■ *Web:* www.harrahs.com
Isle of Capri Casino & Hotel 711 Isle of Capri Blvd Bossier City LA 71111 318-678-7777 424-1470
TF: 800-843-4753 ■ *Web:* www.isleofcapricasino.com/Bossier_City
Isle of Capri Lake Charles 100 W Lake Ave West Lake LA 70669 337-430-0711 430-0083
TF: 800-843-4753 ■ *Web:* www.isleofcapricasino.com/Lake_Charles
Paragon Casino Resort 711 Paragon Pl Marksville LA 71351 318-253-1946 253-2028
TF: 800-946-1946 ■ *Web:* www.paragoncasinoresort.com
Sam's Town Hotel & Casino Shreveport
315 Clyde Fant Pkwy Shreveport LA 71101 318-424-7777 424-5658
TF: 877-429-0711 ■ *Web:* www.samstownshreveport.com
Treasure Chest Casino 5050 Williams Blvd Kenner LA 70065 504-443-8000 469-4115
TF: 800-298-0711 ■ *Web:* www.treasurechest.com
Kewadin Casinos 3015 Mackinac Tr Saint Ignace MI 49781 906-643-7071 643-8472
TF: 800-539-2346 ■ *Web:* www.kewadin.com
Leelanau Sands Casino 2521 NW Bayshore Dr Suttons Bay MI 49682 231-534-8000 271-4136
TF: 800-922-2946 ■ *Web:* www.casino2win.com
MGM Grand Detroit 1300 John C Lodge. Detroit MI 48226 313-393-7777 394-4210*
**Fax:* Hum Res ■ *TF:* 877-888-2121 ■ *Web:* www.mgmgranddetroit.com/
MotorCity Casino 2901 Grand River Ave Detroit MI 48201 313-237-7711 961-0966
TF: 877-777-0711 ■ *Web:* www.motorcitycasino.com
Soaring Eagle Casino & Resort
6800 E Soaring Eagle Blvd. Mount Pleasant MI 48858 989-775-5777 775-5483
TF: 877-232-4532 ■ *Web:* www.soaringeaglecasino.com
Black Bear Casino Resort 1785 Hwy 210 PO Box 777 Carlton MN 55718 218-878-2327 878-2414
TF: 888-771-0777 ■ *Web:* www.blackbearcasinohotel.com
Grand Casino Hinckley 777 Lady Luck Dr Hinckley MN 55037 320-384-7777 384-4775
TF: 800-472-6321 ■ *Web:* www.grandcasinomn.com
Grand Casino Mille Lacs 777 Grand Ave PO Box 343 Onamia MN 56359 320-532-7777 532-8103
TF: 800-626-5825 ■ *Web:* www.grandcasinomn.com
Jackpot Junction Casino Hotel
39375 County Hwy 24 PO Box 420 Morton MN 56270 507-644-3000 644-2529
TF: 800-946-2274 ■ *Web:* www.jackpotjunction.com
Mystic Lake Casino Hotel 2400 Mystic Lake Blvd Prior Lake MN 55372 952-445-9000 403-5210
TF: 800-262-7799 ■ *Web:* www.mysticlake.com
Treasure Island Resort & Casino 5734 Sturgeon Lake Rd Welch MN 55089 651-388-6300 385-2906
TF: 800-222-7077 ■ *Web:* www.treasureislandcasino.com
Ameristar Casino Hotel Vicksburg 4116 Washington St Vicksburg MS 39180 601-638-1000 630-3742*
**Fax:* Mktg ■ *TF:* 800-700-7770 ■ *Web:* www.ameristarcasinos.com
Bally's Casino Tunica 1450 Bally's Blvd Casino Center Robinsonville MS 38664 662-357-1500 357-1756
TF: 800-382-2559 ■ *Web:* www.ballystunica.com
Bayou Caddy's Jubilee Casino 242 S Walnut St Greenville MS 38701 662-335-1111 335-2700
Boomtown Casino Biloxi 676 Bayview Ave. Biloxi MS 39530 228-435-7000 435-7964
TF: 800-627-0777 ■ *Web:* www.boomtownbiloxi.com
Fitzgeralds Casino & Hotel Tunica 711 Lucky Ln Robinsonville MS 38664 662-363-5825 363-3579
TF: 888-766-5825 ■ *Web:* www.fitzgeraldstunica.com
Gold Strike Casino Resort 1010 Casino Center Dr. Tunica Resorts MS 38664 662-357-1111 357-1306
TF Resv: 888-245-7829 ■ *Web:* www.goldstrikemississippi.com
Grand Casino Biloxi 280 Beach Blvd. Biloxi MS 39530 228-436-2946 436-2896
TF: 800-946-2946 ■ *Web:* www.harrahs.com
Grand Casino Tunica 13615 Old Hwy 61 N Robinsonville MS 38664 662-363-2788 357-3464
TF: 800-946-4946 ■ *Web:* www.harrahs.com
Hard Rock Hotel & Casino Biloxi 777 Beach Blvd. Biloxi MS 39530 228-276-7625 276-7007
TF: 877-877-6256 ■ *Web:* www.hardrockbiloxi.com
Hollywood Casino Bay Saint Louis 711 Hollywood Blvd Bay Saint Louis MS 39520 228-467-9257 467-3080*
**Fax:* Hum Res ■ *TF:* 866-758-2591 ■ *Web:* www.hollywoodcasinobsl.com

Name / Address	City	State	Zip	Phone	Fax
Hollywood Casino & Hotel					
1150 Casino Strip Blvd PO Box 218	Robinsonville	MS	38664	662-357-7700	357-7800
TF: 800-871-0711 ■ *Web:* www.hollywoodtunica.com					
Horizon Casino Hotel 1310 Mulberry St	Vicksburg	MS	39180	601-636-3423	630-2194
TF: 800-843-2343 ■ *Web:* www.horizonvicksburg.com					
Horseshoe Casino & Hotel 1021 Casino Center Dr	Robinsonville	MS	38664	662-357-5500	357-5561
TF: 800-303-7463 ■ *Web:* www.horseshoecasinos.com					
IP Casino Resort & Spa 850 Bayview Ave	Biloxi	MS	39530	228-436-3000	432-3260
TF: 800-436-3000 ■ *Web:* www.ipbiloxi.com					
Island View Casino Resort 3300 W Beach Blvd	Gulfport	MS	39501	228-314-2100	314-2221
TF: 877-774-8439 ■ *Web:* www.islandviewcasino.com					
Isle of Capri Casino 777 Isle of Capri Pkwy	Lula	MS	38644	662-363-4600	337-2845
TF: 800-789-5825 ■ *Web:* www.isleofcapricasino.com/lula					
Isle of Capri Casino Resort 151 Beach Blvd	Biloxi	MS	39530	228-435-5400	436-7834
TF: 800-843-4753 ■ *Web:* www.isleofcapricasino.com/Biloxi					
Lighthouse Point Casino 199 N Lakefront Rd	Greenville	MS	38701	662-334-7711	378-2024
TF: 800-878-1777 ■ *Web:* www.lighthouse-casino.com/					
Pearl River Resort 13541 Hwy 16 W	Philadelphia	MS	39350	601-650-1234	650-1351*
**Fax:* Mktg ■ *TF:* 800-557-0711 ■ *Web:* www.pearlriverresort.com					
Resorts Tunica 1100 Casino Strip Blvd PO Box 750	Robinsonville	MS	38664	662-363-7777	357-2300
TF Resv: 866-797-7111 ■ *Web:* www.resortstunica.com					
Sam's Town Hotel & Gambling Hall					
1477 Casino Strip Blvd	Robinsonville	MS	38664	662-363-0700	363-0895*
**Fax:* Hum Res ■ *TF:* 800-456-0711 ■ *Web:* www.samstowntunica.com					
Sheraton Casino & Hotel 1107 Casino Center Dr	Robinsonville	MS	38664	662-363-4900	363-8043
TF: 800-391-3777 ■ *Web:* www.starwood.com/sheraton					
Silver Slipper Casino 5000 S Beach Blvd	Lakeshore	MS	39558	228-469-2777	469-2805
TF: 866-775-4773 ■ *Web:* www.silverslipper-ms.com					
Treasure Bay Casino & Hotel 1980 Beach Blvd	Biloxi	MS	39531	228-385-6000	385-6082
TF: 800-747-2839 ■ *Web:* treasurebay.com					
Ameristar Casino Saint Charles					
1260 S Main St PO Box 720	Saint Charles	MO	63301	636-940-4300	940-4391
TF: 800-325-7777 ■ *Web:* www.ameristarcasinos.com					
Argosy Casino Kansas City 777 NW Argosy Pkwy	Riverside	MO	64150	816-746-3100	741-5423
TF: 800-900-3423 ■ *Web:* www.argosycasinos.com					
Casino Magic 2025 E Chestnut Expy	Springfield	MO	65802	417-886-2442	889-1888
TF: 866-657-1863					
Harrah's Saint Louis Casino & Hotel					
777 Casino Center Dr	Maryland Heights	MO	63043	314-770-8100	770-8399
TF: 800-427-7247 ■ *Web:* www.harrahs.com/our_casinos/stl					
Isle of Capri Casino 1800 E Front St	Kansas City	MO	64120	816-855-7777	855-4247
TF: 800-843-4753 ■ *Web:* www.isleofcapricasino.com/Kansas_City					
President Casino on the Admiral 802 N 1st St	Saint Louis	MO	63102	314-622-1111	622-3029
TF: 800-772-3647 ■ *Web:* www.presidentcasino.com/stlouis/					
Aquarius Casino Resort 1900 S Casino Dr	Laughlin	NV	89029	702-298-5111	
TF: 888-662-5825 ■ *Web:* www.aquariuscasinoresort.com					
Arizona Charlie's Boulder Casino & Hotel 4575 Boulder Hwy	Las Vegas	NV	89121	702-951-9000	951-1046
TF: 800-362-4040 ■ *Web:* www.arizonacharliesboulder.com					
Arizona Charlie's Decatur Casino & Hotel					
740 S Decatur Blvd	Las Vegas	NV	89107	702-258-5111	258-5192
TF: 800-342-2695 ■ *Web:* www.arizonacharliesdecatur.com					
Atlantis Casino Resort 3800 S Virginia St	Reno	NV	89502	775-825-4700	332-2211
TF: 800-723-6500 ■ *Web:* www.atlantiscasino.com					
Bally's Las Vegas 3645 Las Vegas Blvd S	Las Vegas	NV	89109	702-739-4111	967-4405
TF Resv: 800-225-5977 ■ *Web:* www.harrahs.com					
Binion's Horseshoe Hotel & Casino 128 E Fremont St	Las Vegas	NV	89101	702-382-1600	384-1574
TF: 800-237-6537 ■ *Web:* www.binions.com					
Boomtown Casino & Hotel Reno 2100 Garson Rd	Verdi	NV	89439	775-345-6000	345-8696
TF: 800-648-3790 ■ *Web:* www.boomtownreno.com					
Boulder Station Hotel & Casino 4111 Boulder Hwy	Las Vegas	NV	89121	702-432-7777	432-7744
TF: 800-683-7777 ■ *Web:* www.boulderstation.com					
Buffalo Bill's Resort & Casino 31700 S Las Vegas Blvd	Primm	NV	89019	702-382-1111	679-7766
TF: 800-386-7867 ■ *Web:* www.primmvalleyresorts.com/pages/bb_home.asp					
Cactus Jack's Casino 420 N Carson St	Carson City	NV	89702	775-882-8770	882-9147
Cactus Pete's Resort Casino 1385 Hwy 93 PO Box 508	Jackpot	NV	89825	775-755-2321	755-2740
TF: 800-821-1103 ■ *Web:* www.ameristarcasinos.com					
Caesars Palace Las Vegas 3570 Las Vegas Blvd S	Las Vegas	NV	89109	702-731-7110	866-1700
TF: 800-634-6661 ■ *Web:* www.harrahs.com					
California Hotel & Casino 12 Ogden Ave	Las Vegas	NV	89101	702-385-1222	388-2660
TF: 800-634-6255 ■ *Web:* www.thecal.com					
Cannery Casino & Hotel 2121 E Craig Rd	North Las Vegas	NV	89030	702-507-5700	507-5750
TF: 866-999-4899 ■ *Web:* www.cannerycasinos.com					
Carson Horseshoe Club Casino 402 N Carson St	Carson City	NV	89702	775-883-2211	883-2262
Carson Nugget Casino 507 N Carson St	Carson City	NV	89706	775-882-1626	883-1106
TF: 800-426-5239 ■ *Web:* www.ccnugget.com					
Casino Fandango 3800 S Carson St	Carson City	NV	89701	775-885-7000	885-7008
Web: www.casinofandango.com					
Casino Royale Hotel 3411 Las Vegas Blvd S	Las Vegas	NV	89109	702-737-3500	650-4743
Web: www.casinoroyalehotel.com					
Circus Circus Hotel & Casino Reno 500 N Sierra St	Reno	NV	89503	775-329-0711	328-9652
TF: 800-648-5010 ■ *Web:* www.circusreno.com					
Circus Circus Hotel Casino & Theme Park Las Vegas					
2880 Las Vegas Blvd S	Las Vegas	NV	89109	702-734-0410	794-3816
TF Resv: 800-634-3450 ■ *Web:* www.circuscircus.com					
Colorado Belle Hotel & Casino 2100 S Casino Dr	Laughlin	NV	89029	702-298-4000	298-3697*
**Fax:* Hum Res ■ *TF Resv:* 800-477-4837 ■ *Web:* www.coloradobelle.com					
Don Laughlin's Riverside Resort & Casino 1650 Casino Dr	Laughlin	NV	89029	702-298-2535	298-2695
TF: 800-227-3849 ■ *Web:* www.riversideresort.com					
Edgewater Hotel & Casino 2020 S Casino Dr	Laughlin	NV	89028	702-298-2453	298-5606
TF: 800-677-4837 ■ *Web:* www.edgewater-casino.com					
El Cortez Hotel & Casino 600 E Fremont St	Las Vegas	NV	89101	702-385-5200	474-3633
TF: 800-634-6703 ■ *Web:* www.elcortezhotelcasino.com					
Eldorado Hotel Casino 345 N Virginia St	Reno	NV	89501	775-786-5700	322-7124
TF Resv: 800-648-5966 ■ *Web:* www.eldoradoreno.com					
Excalibur Hotel & Casino 3850 Las Vegas Blvd S	Las Vegas	NV	89109	702-597-7777	597-7009
TF Resv: 800-937-7777 ■ *Web:* www.excalibur.com					
Fiesta Henderson Casino Hotel 777 W Lake Mead Pkwy	Henderson	NV	89015	702-558-7000	567-7373
TF: 888-899-7770 ■ *Web:* henderson.fiestacasino.com					
Fiesta Rancho Casino Hotel 2400 N Rancho Dr	Las Vegas	NV	89130	702-631-7000	638-3645
TF: 800-731-7333 ■ *Web:* www.fiestacasino.com					
Fitzgeralds Casino & Hotel Reno 255 N Virginia St PO Box 40130	Reno	NV	89504	775-785-3300	785-3318
TF: 800-535-5825 ■ *Web:* www.fitzgeraldsreno.com					
Flamingo Las Vegas 3555 Las Vegas Blvd S	Las Vegas	NV	89109	702-733-3111	733-3528
TF Resv: 800-732-2111 ■ *Web:* www.harrahs.com					
Fremont Hotel & Casino 200 E Fremont St	Las Vegas	NV	89101	702-385-3232	385-6270
TF: 800-634-6182 ■ *Web:* www.fremontcasino.com					
Gold Coast Hotel & Casino 4000 W Flamingo Rd	Las Vegas	NV	89103	702-367-7111	367-8575
TF: 888-402-6278 ■ *Web:* www.goldcoastcasino.com					
Gold Ranch Casino & RV Resort Hwy 80 W Exit 2 PO Box 160	Verdi	NV	89439	775-345-6789	345-2356
Web: www.goldranchrvcasino.com					
Gold Spike Hotel & Casino 400 E Ogden Ave	Las Vegas	NV	89101	702-384-8444	382-5242
TF: 877-467-7453 ■ *Web:* www.goldspikehotelcasino.com					
Gold Strike Hotel & Gambling Hall 1 Main St PO Box 19278	Jean	NV	89019	702-477-5000	671-1665
TF: 800-634-1359 ■ *Web:* www.goldstrike-jean.com					
Golden Nugget Hotel 129 E Fremont St	Las Vegas	NV	89101	702-385-7111	385-7111
TF: 800-634-3454 ■ *Web:* www.goldennugget.com					
Golden Nugget Laughlin 2300 S Casino Dr	Laughlin	NV	89029	702-298-7111	298-7122
TF: 800-237-1739 ■ *Web:* www.goldennugget.com/laughlin/					
Grand Sierra Resort & Casino 2500 E 2nd St	Reno	NV	89595	775-789-2000	789-1678
TF: 800-501-2651 ■ *Web:* www.grandsierraresort.com					
Green Valley Ranch Resort Casino & Spa					
2300 Paseo Verde Pkwy	Henderson	NV	89052	702-617-7777	617-7778
TF: 866-617-0777 ■ *Web:* www.greenvalleyranchresort.com					
Harrah's Lake Tahoe PO Box 8	Stateline	NV	89449	775-588-6611	586-6607
TF: 800-427-7247 ■ *Web:* www.harrahs.com/our_casinos/tah/					
Harrah's Las Vegas 3475 Las Vegas Blvd S	Las Vegas	NV	89109	702-369-5000	369-6014
TF: 800-427-7247 ■ *Web:* www.harrahs.com/our_casinos/					
Harrah's Laughlin 2900 S Casino Dr	Laughlin	NV	89029	702-298-4600	298-6802
TF: 800-427-7247 ■ *Web:* www.harrahs.com/our_casinos/					
Harrah's Reno 219 N Center St	Reno	NV	89501	775-786-3232	788-2815
TF: 800-427-7247 ■ *Web:* www.harrahs.com/our_casinos/ren					
Harveys Resort Hotel & Casino Hwy 50 PO Box 128	Stateline	NV	89449	775-588-2411	588-6643
TF: 800-427-8397 ■ *Web:* www.harrahs.com/our_casinos/hlt/					
Hyatt Regency Lake Tahoe Resort & Casino					
111 Country Club Dr	Incline Village	NV	89451	775-832-1234	831-2171
TF: 800-233-1234 ■ *Web:* www.hyatt.com					
Imperial Palace Hotel & Casino 3535 Las Vegas Blvd S	Las Vegas	NV	89109	702-731-3311	735-8328
TF: 800-634-6441 ■ *Web:* www.imperialpalace.com					
John Ascuaga's Nugget Hotel Casino 1100 Nugget Ave	Sparks	NV	89431	775-356-3300	356-3434
TF: 800-648-1177 ■ *Web:* www.janugget.com					
Lake Tahoe Horizon Casino 50 Hwy 50	Stateline	NV	89449	775-588-6211	588-3110
Web: www.horizoncasino.com/					
Las Vegas Club 18 E Fremont St	Las Vegas	NV	89101	702-385-1664	380-5793
TF: 800-634-6532 ■ *Web:* www.vegasclubcasino.net					
Las Vegas Hilton 3000 Paradise Rd	Las Vegas	NV	89109	702-732-5111	732-5778
TF: 800-732-7117 ■ *Web:* www.lvhilton.com					
Luxor Hotel & Casino 3900 Las Vegas Blvd S	Las Vegas	NV	89119	702-262-4000	262-4404
TF Resv: 800-288-1000 ■ *Web:* www.luxor.com					
Mandalay Bay Resort & Casino 3950 Las Vegas Blvd S	Las Vegas	NV	89119	702-632-7777	632-7234
TF: 877-632-7800 ■ *Web:* www.mandalaybay.com					
MGM Grand Hotel & Casino 3799 Las Vegas Blvd S	Las Vegas	NV	89109	702-891-1111	891-3036
TF: 800-929-1111 ■ *Web:* www.mgmgrand.com					
MontBleu Resort Casino & Spa 55 Hwy 50 PO Box 5800	Stateline	NV	89449	775-588-3515	586-4695
TF: 800-648-3353 ■ *Web:* www.montbleuresort.com					
Monte Carlo Resort & Casino 3770 Las Vegas Blvd S	Las Vegas	NV	89109	702-730-7777	730-7200
TF: 800-311-8999 ■ *Web:* www.montecarlo.com					
Nevada Landing Hotel & Casino 2 Goodsprings Rd	Jean	NV	89019	702-387-5000	671-1407
TF: 800-628-6682 ■ *Web:* www.nevadalanding.com					
New Frontier The 3120 Las Vegas Blvd S	Las Vegas	NV	89109	702-794-8200	794-8327
TF: 800-634-6966 ■ *Web:* www.frontierlv.com					
New York New York Hotel & Casino 3790 Las Vegas Blvd S	Las Vegas	NV	89109	702-740-6969	740-6700
TF: 800-693-6763 ■ *Web:* www.nynyhotelcasino.com					
Orleans Las Vegas Hotel & Casino 4500 W Tropicana Ave	Las Vegas	NV	89103	702-365-7111	365-7500
TF: 888-365-7111 ■ *Web:* www.orleanscasino.com					
Palace Station Hotel & Casino 2411 W Sahara Ave	Las Vegas	NV	89102	702-367-2411	367-2478
TF: 800-634-3101 ■ *Web:* www.palacestation.com					
Palms Casino Resort 4321 W Flamingo Rd	Las Vegas	NV	89103	702-942-7777	942-7001
TF: 866-942-7777 ■ *Web:* www.palms.com					
Paris Las Vegas 3655 Las Vegas Blvd S	Las Vegas	NV	89109	702-946-7000	946-4259
TF: 888-266-5687 ■ *Web:* www.harrahs.com					
Peppermill Hotel & Casino 2707 S Virginia St	Reno	NV	89502	775-826-2121	826-5205
TF: 800-282-2444 ■ *Web:* www.peppermillreno.com					
Planet Hollywood Resort & Casino 3667 Las Vegas Blvd S	Las Vegas	NV	89109	702-785-5555	785-9600
TF: 866-919-7472 ■ *Web:* www.planethollywoodresort.com					
Railroad Pass Hotel & Casino 2800 S Boulder Hwy	Henderson	NV	89002	702-294-5000	294-0092
TF: 800-654-0877 ■ *Web:* www.railroadpass.com					
Red Rock Resort Spa & Casino 11011 W Charleston Blvd	Las Vegas	NV	89126	702-797-7777	797-7890
Web: www.redrocklasvegas.com					
Rio All-Suite Hotel & Casino 3700 W Flamingo Rd	Las Vegas	NV	89103	702-777-7777	777-6565
TF: 888-746-7482 ■ *Web:* www.harrahs.com/our-casinos/					
River Palms Resort & Casino 2700 S Casino Dr	Laughlin	NV	89029	702-298-2242	298-2117
TF: 800-835-7904 ■ *Web:* www.river-palms.com					
Riviera Hotel & Casino 2901 Las Vegas Blvd S	Las Vegas	NV	89109	702-734-5110	794-9663
TF Resv: 800-634-6753 ■ *Web:* www.rivierahotel.com					
Sahara Hotel & Casino 2535 Las Vegas Blvd S	Las Vegas	NV	89109	702-737-2111	737-1017
TF: 888-696-2121 ■ *Web:* www.saharavegas.com					
Sam's Town Hotel & Gambling Hall 5111 Boulder Hwy	Las Vegas	NV	89122	702-456-7777	454-8107
TF: 800-634-6371 ■ *Web:* www.samstownlv.com					
Sands Regency Casino Hotel 345 N Arlington Ave	Reno	NV	89501	775-348-2200	348-2226
TF Resv: 800-648-3553 ■ *Web:* www.sandsregency.com					
Santa Fe Station 4949 N Rancho Dr	Las Vegas	NV	89130	702-658-4900	658-4919
TF: 866-767-7771 ■ *Web:* santafe.stationcasinos.com					
Silver Legacy Resort & Casino 407 N Virginia St	Reno	NV	89501	775-329-4777	325-7474
TF: 800-687-8733 ■ *Web:* www.silverlegacy.com					
Silverton Hotel & Casino 3333 Blue Diamond Rd	Las Vegas	NV	89139	702-263-7777	263-7002
TF: 800-588-7711 ■ *Web:* www.silvertoncasino.com					
Slots-A-Fun Casino 2890 Las Vegas Blvd S	Las Vegas	NV	89109	702-734-0410	794-3816
South Coast Hotel & Casino 9777 Las Vegas Blvd S	Las Vegas	NV	89123	702-796-7111	797-8041
TF: 866-796-7111 ■ *Web:* www.coastcasinos.com					
Stratosphere Tower Hotel & Casino 2000 S Las Vegas Blvd	Las Vegas	NV	89104	702-380-7777	383-4755*
**Fax:* Sales ■ *TF:* 800-998-6937 ■ *Web:* www.stratospherehotel.com					
Suncoast Hotel & Casino 9090 Alta Dr	Las Vegas	NV	89145	702-636-7111	636-7288
TF: 877-677-7111 ■ *Web:* www.suncoastcasino.com					
Sunset Station Hotel & Casino 1301 W Sunset Rd	Henderson	NV	89014	702-547-7777	547-7744
TF: 888-786-7389 ■ *Web:* www.sunsetstation.com					
Texas Station Gambling Hall & Hotel					
2101 Texas Star Ln	North Las Vegas	NV	89032	702-631-1000	631-8120
TF Resv: 800-654-8888 ■ *Web:* www.texasstation.com					
Treasure Island Hotel & Casino 3300 Las Vegas Blvd S	Las Vegas	NV	89109	702-894-7111	894-7414
TF: 800-944-7444 ■ *Web:* www.treasureisland.com					
Tropicana Express 2121 S Casino Dr	Laughlin	NV	89029	702-298-4200	298-6403
TF: 800-243-6846 ■ *Web:* www.tropicanax.com					
Tropicana Resort & Casino 3801 Las Vegas Blvd S	Las Vegas	NV	89109	702-739-2222	739-3648
TF Resv: 888-826-8767 ■ *Web:* tropicanalv.com					
Tuscany Suites & Casino 255 E Flamingo Rd	Las Vegas	NV	89109	702-893-8933	947-5994
TF Resv: 877-887-2261 ■ *Web:* www.sunsetstation.com					
Western Village Inn & Casino 815 Nichols Blvd	Sparks	NV	89434	775-331-1069	331-4834*
**Fax:* PR ■ *TF:* 800-648-1170					
Westin Casuarina Las Vegas Hotel Casino & Spa					
160 E Flamingo Rd	Las Vegas	NV	89109	702-836-5900	836-9776
Whiskey Pete's Hotel & Casino 100 W Primm Blvd	Primm	NV	89019	702-382-4388	679-5195
TF: 800-386-7867 ■ *Web:* www.primmvalleyresorts.com					
Wynn Las Vegas 3131 Las Vegas Blvd S	Las Vegas	NV	89109	702-770-7000	770-1571
TF: 888-320-7123 ■ *Web:* www.wynnlasvegas.com					
Atlantic City Hilton Casino Resort Pacific & Boston	Atlantic City	NJ	08401	609-347-7111	340-7128
TF: 877-432-7139 ■ *Web:* www.hiltonac.com					
Bally's Atlantic City 1900 Boardwalk	Atlantic City	NJ	08401	609-340-2000	340-1725
TF: 800-772-7777 ■ *Web:* www.harrahs.com					
Borgata Hotel Casino & Spa 1 Borgata Way	Atlantic City	NJ	08401	609-317-1000	317-1035
TF: 866-692-6742 ■ *Web:* www.theborgata.com					
Caesars Atlantic City Hotel Casino 2100 Pacific Ave	Atlantic City	NJ	08401	609-348-4411	343-2405
TF: 800-443-0104 ■ *Web:* www.harrahs.com					

Phone | Fax

Harrah's Atlantic City 777 Harrah's Blvd ... Atlantic City NJ 08401 609-441-5000 340-8621
TF: 800-427-7247 ■ *Web:* www.harrahs.com/our_casinos/atl
Resorts Atlantic City 1133 Boardwalk ... Atlantic City NJ 08401 609-344-6000 340-6847
TF: 800-336-6378 ■ *Web:* www.resortsac.com
Showboat Atlantic City 801 Boardwalk ... Atlantic City NJ 08401 609-343-4000 343-3409
TF: 800-427-7247 ■ *Web:* www.harrahs.com/our_casinos/sac
Tropicana Casino & Resort 2831 Boardwalk ... Atlantic City NJ 08401 609-340-4000 340-4457
TF: 800-843-8767 ■ *Web:* www.tropicana.net
Trump Marina Hotel & Casino Huron Ave & Brigantine Blvd. ... Atlantic City NJ 08401 609-441-2000 345-7604
TF Resv: 800-777-8477 ■ *Web:* www.trumpmarina.com
Trump Plaza Hotel & Casino 2225 Boardwalk ... Atlantic City NJ 08401 609-441-6000 441-7881
TF: 800-677-7378 ■ *Web:* www.trumpplaza.com
Trump Taj Mahal Casino Resort 1000 Boardwalk & Virginia Ave ... Atlantic City NJ 08401 609-449-1000 449-6818
TF Resv: 800-825-8786 ■ *Web:* www.trumptaj.com
Camel Rock Casino 17486A Hwy 84/285 ... Santa Fe NM 87506 505-984-8414 989-9234
Web: www.camelrockcasino.com
Cities of Gold Casino 10-B Cities of Gold Rd. ... Santa Fe NM 87506 505-455-3313 455-7188
TF: 800-455-3313 ■ *Web:* www.citiesofgold.com
Route 66 Casino 14500 Central Ave ... Albuquerque NM 87121 505-352-7866 352-7880
Web: www.rt66casino.com
Sandia Casino 30 Rainbow Rd NE ... Albuquerque NM 87113 505-796-7500 796-7605
TF: 800-526-9366 ■ *Web:* www.sandiacasino.com
Seneca Niagara Casino 310 4th St. ... Niagara Falls NY 14303 716-299-1100 299-1099
Web: www.senecaniagaracasino.com
Turning Stone Casino Resort 5218 Patrick Rd. ... Verona NY 13478 315-361-7711 361-7901
TF: 800-771-7711 ■ *Web:* www.turning-stone.com
Harrah's Cherokee Casino & Hotel 777 Casino Dr ... Cherokee NC 28719 828-497-7777 497-5076
TF: 800-427-7247 ■ *Web:* www.harrahs.com/our_casinos/che
Prairie Knights Casino & Resort 7932 Hwy 24 ... Fort Yates ND 58538 701-854-7777 854-7786
TF: 800-425-8277 ■ *Web:* www.prairieknights.com
Casino Nova Scotia 1983 Upper Water St ... Halifax NS B3J3Y5 902-425-7777 428-7846
TF: 888-642-6376 ■ *Web:* www.casinonovascotia.com
Cherokee Casino & Resort 777 W Cherokee St. ... Catoosa OK 74015 918-384-7800 266-3038
TF: 800-760-6700 ■ *Web:* www.cherokeecasino.com
Osage Nation Million Dollar Elm Casino 301 Blackjack Dr ... Sand Springs OK 74063 918-699-7777 699-7700
TF: 877-246-8777 ■ *Web:* www.milliondollarelm.com
Casino Niagara 5705 Falls Ave ... Niagara Falls ON L2G7M9 905-374-3598 353-6727
TF: 888-946-3255 ■ *Web:* discoverniagara.com/casino
Casino Windsor 377 Riverside Dr E ... Windsor ON N9A7H7 519-258-7878 258-0434
TF: 800-991-7777 ■ *Web:* www.casinowindsor.com
Niagara Fallsview Casino Resort 6380 Fallsview Blvd. ... Niagara Falls ON L2G7X5 905-358-3255 371-7952
TF: 888-325-5788 ■ *Web:* www.fallsviewcasinoresort.com
Presque Isle Downs Casino & Racetrack 8199 Perry Hwy ... Erie PA 16509 814-860-8999
TF: 866-374-3886 ■ *Web:* www.presqueisledowns.com/
Speaking Rock Casino & Entertainment Centre 122 S Old Pueblo Rd ... El Paso TX 79907 915-860-7777 860-7745
TF: 800-772-2646 ■ *Web:* www.speakingrockcasino.com
Emerald Queen Casino 2024 E 29th St. ... Tacoma WA 98404 253-594-7777 272-6725
TF: 888-831-7655 ■ *Web:* www.emeraldqueen.com
Great American Casino 10117 S Tacoma Way ... Lakewood WA 98499 253-396-0500 882-1001
Web: www.greatamericancasino.com
Lucky Eagle Casino 12888 188th Ave SW ... Rochester WA 98579 360-273-2000 273-2366
TF: 800-720-1788 ■ *Web:* www.luckyeagle.com
Muckleshoot Indian Casino 2402 Auburn Way S ... Auburn WA 98002 253-804-4444 939-7702
TF: 800-804-4944 ■ *Web:* www.muckleshootcasino.com
Northern Quest Casino 100 N Hayford Rd ... Airway Heights WA 99001 509-242-7000 343-2163
Web: www.northernquest.net
Red Wind Casino 12819 Yelm Hwy ... Olympia WA 98513 360-412-5000 455-0364
Web: redwindcasino.com
Skagit Valley Casino Resort 5984 N Darrk Ln. ... Bow WA 98232 360-724-7777 724-0116
TF: 877-275-2448 ■ *Web:* www.theskagit.com
Tulalip Casino 10200 Quil Ceda Blvd ... Tulalip WA 98271 360-651-1111 651-3119
TF: 888-272-1111 ■ *Web:* www.tulalipcasino.com
Ho-Chunk Casino S 3214 Hwy 12 ... Baraboo WI 53913 608-356-6210 355-1500
TF: 800-746-2486 ■ *Web:* www.ho-chunk.com
Lake of the Torches Resort Casino 510 Old Abe Rd. ... Lac du Flambeau WI 54538 715-588-7070 588-9508
TF: 800-258-6724 ■ *Web:* www.180025torch.com
Oneida Bingo & Casino 2020 Airport Dr. ... Oneida WI 54313 920-497-8118 496-3745
TF: 800-238-4263 ■ *Web:* www.oneidanation.org
Saint Croix Casino & Hotel 777 US Hwys 8 & 63 ... Turtle Lake WI 54889 715-986-4777 986-2877
TF: 800-846-8946 ■ *Web:* www.stcroixcasino.com

134 CASKETS & VAULTS

SEE ALSO Mortuary, Crematory, Cemetery Products & Services p. 1977

Phone | Fax

American Wilbert Vault Corp 1015 Troost Ave ... Forest Park IL 60130 708-366-3210 366-3281
Astral Industries Inc 7375 US 27 S PO Box 638 ... Lynn IN 47355 765-874-2525 874-1999
TF Sales: 800-874-1070
Balanced Line Casket Co 15 S Boundary St ... Cambridge City IN 47327 765-478-3501 478-3231
TF: 800-382-6934
Batesville Casket Co 1 Batesville Blvd ... Batesville IN 47006 812-934-7500 934-8300
Web: www.batesville.com
Brown-Wilbert Inc 2280 Hamline Ave N ... Saint Paul MN 55113 651-631-1234 631-1428
Web: www.wilbertvault.com
Casket Royale 137 Lafayette Rd ... Hampton Falls NH 03844 603-929-1515 926-8690
TF: 800-791-4169 ■ *Web:* www.casketroyale.com
Casket Shells Inc 432 1st St ... Eynon PA 18403 570-876-2642 876-5613
Web: www.casketshells.com
Clark Grave Vault Co 375 E 5th Ave ... Columbus OH 43201 614-294-3761 299-2324
TF: 800-848-3570 ■ *Web:* www.clarkvault.com
DeltAurora LLC 10944 Marsh Rd PO Box 29 ... Aurora IN 47001 812-926-1111 457-1191*
**Fax Area Code:* 800 ■ **Fax:* Cust Svc ■ *TF Cust Svc:* 800-457-5111 ■
Web: www.deltaurora.com
JM Hutton & Co Inc PO Box 129 ... Richmond IN 47375 765-962-3591 966-0149
Web: www.jmhutton.com
Loretto Casket Co 110 W Commerce St. ... Loretto TN 38469 931-853-6921 853-6924
TF: 800-225-9105
Matthews International Corp 2 Northshore Ctr Suite 200 ... Pittsburgh PA 15212 412-442-8200 442-8291
NASDAQ: MATW ■ *TF:* 800-223-4964 ■ *Web:* www.matthewsinternational.com
Norwalk-Wilbert Vault Co 136 James St ... Bridgeport CT 06604 203-366-5678 337-5433
TF: 800-826-9406 ■ *Web:* www.norwalkwilbertvault.com
Paul Casket Co 505 S Green St ... Cambridge City IN 47327 765-478-3991 962-0911
TF: 800-521-8202
Pettigrew & Sons Casket Co 6151 Power Inn Rd ... Sacramento CA 95824 916-383-0777 383-2445
Web: www.pettigrewcaskets.com
Providence Casket Co 1 Industrial Cir ... Lincoln RI 02865 401-726-1700 726-1702
TF: 800-848-2999
Sound Casket Inc 20350 71st Ave NE Suite F ... Arlington WA 98223 425-259-6012 403-7939*
**Fax Area Code:* 360 ■ *TF:* 800-735-7274 ■ *Web:* www.soundcasket.com
Wilbert Funeral Services Inc 2913 Gardner Rd. ... Broadview IL 60155 708-865-1600 865-1646
TF: 800-323-7188 ■ *Web:* www.wilbertonline.com
Wilbert Inc PO Box 147 ... Forest Park IL 60130 708-865-1600 865-1646
TF: 800-323-7188
York Group Inc 2 Northshore Ctr Suite 100 ... Pittsburgh PA 15212 412-995-1600 201-4338*
**Fax Area Code:* 800 ■ *TF:* 800-223-4964 ■ *Web:* www.yorkgrp.com
Zane Casket Co 1201 Hall Ave ... Zanesville OH 43702 740-452-4680 452-8993

135 CEMENT

Phone | Fax

Alamo Cement Co PO Box 34807 ... San Antonio TX 78265 210-208-1880 208-1881
Alamo Concrete Products Ltd PO Box 34210 ... San Antonio TX 78265 210-208-1880 208-1501
Ash Grove Cement Co PO Box 25900 ... Overland Park KS 66225 913-451-8900 451-8324
TF: 800-545-1886 ■ *Web:* www.ashgrove.com
Ash Grove Texas LP PO Box 520 ... Midlothian TX 76065 972-723-7200 723-7209
TF: 800-545-1882 ■ *Web:* www.ashgrove.com
Buzzi Unicem USA Inc 100 Brodhead Rd Suite 230 ... Bethlehem PA 18017 610-866-4400 866-9430
Web: www.buzziunicem.com
California Portland Cement Co 2025 E Financial Way Suite 200 ... Glendora CA 91741 626-852-6200 691-2269
TF: 800-272-1891 ■ *Web:* www.calportland.com
Capitol Aggregates Ltd 11551 Nacogdoches Rd ... San Antonio TX 78217 210-655-3010 599-0560
TF: 800-292-5315 ■ *Web:* www.capaggltd.com
Carter-Waters Corp 2440 W Pennway St ... Kansas City MO 64108 816-471-2570 421-2946
TF: 800-444-2570 ■ *Web:* www.carter-waters.com
Cemex Puerto Rico Inc
RT 165 KM 2.7 Industrial Amelia Park ... Bucahna Guaynabo PR 00968 787-783-3000 781-8850
Web: www.cemex.com
Cemex USA 840 Gessner Suite 1400 ... Houston TX 77024 713-650-6200 722-5105
NYSE: CX ■ *TF:* 800-999-8529 ■ *Web:* www.cemex.com
Centex Corp 2728 N Harwood St ... Dallas TX 75201 214-981-5000 981-6859*
NYSE: CTX ■ **Fax:* Investor Rel ■ *TF:* 888-847-5130 ■ *Web:* www.centex.com
CGM Inc 1445 Ford Rd ... Bensalem PA 19020 215-638-4400 638-7949
TF: 800-523-6570 ■ *Web:* www.cgmbuildingproducts.com
Coastal Cement Corp 36 Drydock Ave ... Boston MA 02210 617-350-0183 350-0186
TF: 800-828-8352
Continental Cement Co LLC 14755 N Outer 40 Suite 514 ... Chesterfield MO 63017 636-532-7440 532-7445
TF: 800-625-1144 ■ *Web:* www.continentalcement.com
Devcon International Corp 1350 E Newport Ctr Dr Suite 201 ... Deerfield Beach FL 33442 954-429-1500 429-1506
NASDAQ: DEVC ■ *Web:* www.devc.com
Dragon Products Co 38 Preble St ... Portland ME 04101 207-774-6355 761-5694
TF: 800-828-8352 ■ *Web:* www.dragonproducts.com
Eagle Materials Inc 3811 Turtle Creek Blvd Suite 1100 ... Dallas TX 75219 214-432-2000 432-2100
NYSE: EXP ■ *TF:* 800-759-7625 ■ *Web:* www.eaglematerials.com
Eastern Cement Corp 13250 Eastern Ave ... Palmetto FL 34221 941-729-7311 729-8124
TF: 800-282-7798
ESSROC Materials Inc 3251 Bath Pike ... Nazareth PA 18064 610-837-6725 837-9614
TF: 800-523-9238 ■ *Web:* www.essroc.com
Federal White Cement Ltd PO Box 1609 ... Woodstock ON N4S0A8 519-485-5410 485-5892
TF Sales: 800-265-1806 ■ *Web:* www.federalwhitecement.com
GCC Dacotah 501 N Saint Onge St ... Rapid City SD 57702 605-721-7100 721-7012
TF: 800-843-8324 ■ *Web:* www.gcc.com
Giant Cement Holding Inc 320-D Midland Pkwy ... Summerville SC 29485 843-851-9898 851-9881
TF: 800-845-1174
Glens Falls Lehigh Cement Co 313 Warren St. ... Glens Falls NY 12801 518-792-1137 792-0731
TF: 800-833-4157 ■ *Web:* www.gfcement.com
Hawaiian Cement 99-1300 Halawa Valley St ... Aiea HI 96701 808-532-3400 532-3490
Web: www.hawaiiancement.com
Holcim (US) Inc 6211 Ann Arbor Rd ... Dundee MI 48131 800-831-9507 821-7057*
**Fax Area Code:* 734 ■ *TF:* 800-831-9507 ■ *Web:* www2.holcim.com/USA
Illinois Cement Co PO Box 442 ... La Salle IL 61301 815-224-2112 224-4358
Keystone Cement Co PO Box A ... Bath PA 18014 610-837-1881 837-2267
TF: 800-523-5442
Knife River Corp 1150 W Century Ave ... Bismarck ND 58503 701-530-1400 530-1451
TF: 800-982-5339 ■ *Web:* www.kniferiver.com
Lafarge North America Inc 12950 Worldgate Dr Suite 600 ... Herndon VA 20170 703-480-3600 796-2214
NYSE: LAF ■ *Web:* www.lafargenorthamerica.com
Lehigh Cement Co North America 7660 Imperial Way ... Allentown PA 18195 610-366-4600 366-4799*
**Fax:* Hum Res ■ *TF:* 800-523-5488 ■ *Web:* www.lehighcement.com
Lehigh Inland Cement Ltd 12640 Inland Way ... Edmonton AB T5V1K2 780-420-2500 420-2550
TF: 800-252-9304 ■ *Web:* www.lehighinland.com
Lehigh Northwest Cement Ltd 3600 Lysander Ln Suite 320 ... Richmond BC V7B1C3 604-279-6600 261-7241
Web: www.lehighnw.com
Lehigh Southwest Cement Co 2300 Clayton Rd Suite 300 ... Concord CA 94520 925-609-6920 609-6930
TF: 888-554-5010 ■ *Web:* www.calaverascement.com
Monarch Cement Co 449 1200 St PO Box 1000 ... Humboldt KS 66748 620-473-2222 473-2447
TF: 800-362-0570 ■ *Web:* www.monarchcement.com
National Cement Co Inc PO Box 530010 ... Birmingham AL 35253 205-423-2600 870-5777
Phoenix Cement Co 8800 E Chaparral Rd Suite 155 ... Scottsdale AZ 85250 480-850-5757 850-5758
Web: www.srmaterials.com
Prairie Group Inc 7601 W 79th St ... Bridgeview IL 60455 708-458-0400 458-6007
TF Sales: 800-649-3690 ■ *Web:* www.prairiegroup.com
Rinker Materials Corp 1501 Belvedere Rd ... West Palm Beach FL 33406 561-833-5555 820-8666
TF: 800-226-5521 ■ *Web:* www.rinker.com
Rio Grande Portland Cement Co
4253 Montgomery Blvd NE Suite 210 ... Albuquerque NM 87109 505-881-5303 881-5304
TF: 800-234-2266
Saint Lawrence Cement Group Inc 1945 Graham Blvd ... Mont-Royal QC H3R1H1 514-340-1881 342-8154
TSX: STa ■ *Web:* www.stlawrencecement.com
Signal Mountain Cement Co 1201 Suck Creek Rd. ... Chattanooga TN 37405 423-886-0800 866-4651
Texas Industries Inc 1341 W Mockingbird Ln Suite 700W ... Dallas TX 75247 972-647-6700 647-3878
NYSE: TXI ■ *Web:* www.txi.com
Texas-Lehigh Cement Co PO Box 610 ... Buda TX 78610 512-295-6111 295-3102
TF: 800-388-5408 ■ *Web:* www.texaslehigh.com
Titan America Inc 1151 Azalea Garden Rd ... Norfolk VA 23502 757-858-6500 855-7707
TF: 800-468-7622 ■ *Web:* www.titanamerica.com
TXI Riverside Cement Co PO Box 51479 ... Ontario CA 91761 909-635-1800 635-1898*
**Fax:* Sales ■ *TF:* 800-442-4910

136 CEMETERIES - NATIONAL

SEE ALSO Attractions - Historic Homes & Buildings p. 1347; Parks - National - US p. 2050

Phone | Fax

Alexandria National Cemetery 209 E Shamrock St ... Pineville LA 71360 318-449-1793 449-9327
Web: www.cem.va.gov/nchp/alexandriala.htm
Alexandria National Cemetery 1450 Wilkes St ... Alexandria VA 22314 703-221-2183 221-2185
Alton National Cemetery 600 Pearl St ... Alton IL 62003 314-260-8691 260-8723
TF: 800-535-1117 ■ *Web:* www.cem.va.gov/nchp/alton.htm

Phone Fax

Annapolis National Cemetery 800 West St ... Annapolis MD 21401 410-644-9696 644-1563
Web: www.cem.va.gov/nchp/annapolis.htm
Arlington National Cemetery Arlington Cemetery ... Arlington VA 22211 703-607-8000 614-6339
Web: www.arlingtoncemetery.org
Balls Bluff National Cemetery Rt 7 ... Leesburg VA 22075 540-825-0027 825-6684
Web: www.cem.va.gov/nchp/ballsbluff.htm
Baltimore National Cemetery 5501 Frederick Ave ... Baltimore MD 21228 410-644-9696 644-1563
Web: www.cem.va.gov/nchp/baltimore.htm
Barrancas National Cemetery Naval Air Station 80 Hovey Rd ... Pensacola FL 32508 850-453-4108 453-4635
Web: www.cem.va.gov/nchp/barrancas.htm
Bath National Cemetery VA Medical Center ... Bath NY 14810 607-664-4853 664-4761
Web: www.cem.va.gov/nchp/bath.htm
Baton Rouge National Cemetery 220 N 19th St ... Baton Rouge LA 70806 225-389-9520
Battleground National Cemetery 6625 Georgia Ave NW ... Washington DC 20240 202-895-6070
Web: www.nps.gov/batt/index.htm
Bay Pines National Cemetery 10000 Bay Pines Blvd N ... Saint Petersburg FL 33708 727-398-9426 398-9520
Web: www.cem.va.gov/nchp/baypines.htm
Beaufort National Cemetery 1601 Boundary St ... Beaufort SC 29902 843-524-3925 524-8538
Web: www.cem.va.gov/nchp/beaufort.htm
Beverly National Cemetery 916 Bridgeboro Rd ... Beverly NJ 08010 609-880-0827 871-4691
Web: www.cem.va.gov/nchp/beverly.htm
Biloxi National Cemetery 400 Veterans Ave ... Biloxi MS 39531 228-388-6668 523-5784
Web: www.cem.va.gov/nchp/biloxi.htm
Black Hills National Cemetery 20901 Pleasant Valley Dr ... Sturgis SD 57785 605-347-3830 720-7298
Web: www.cem.va.gov/nchp/blackhills.htm
Calverton National Cemetery 210 Princeton Blvd ... Calverton NY 11933 631-727-5410 727-5815
Web: www.cem.va.gov/nchp/calverton.htm
Camp Butler National Cemetery 5063 Camp Butler Rd ... Springfield IL 62707 217-492-4070 492-4072
Web: www.cem.va.gov/pdf/cbutler.pdf
Camp Nelson National Cemetery 6980 Danville Rd ... Nicholasville KY 40356 859-885-5727 887-4860
Web: www.cem.va.gov/nchp/campnelson.htm
Cave Hill National Cemetery 701 Baxter Ave ... Louisville KY 40204 502-893-3852 893-6612
Web: www.cem.va.gov/nchp/cavehill.htm
Chattanooga National Cemetery 1200 Bailey Ave ... Chattanooga TN 37404 423-855-6590 855-6597
Web: www.cem.va.gov/pdf/chatnga.pdf
City Point National Cemetery 10th Ave & Davis St ... Hopewell VA 23860 804-795-2031 795-1064
Web: www.cem.va.gov/nchp/citypoint.htm
Cold Harbor National Cemetery 6038 Cold Harbor Rd ... Mechanicsville VA 23111 804-795-2031 795-1064
Web: www.cem.va.gov/nchp/coldharbor.htm
Corinth National Cemetery 1551 Horton St ... Corinth MS 38834 901-386-8311 382-0750
Web: www.cem.va.gov/nchp/corinth.htm
Crown Hill National Cemetery 700 W 38th St ... Indianapolis IN 46208 765-674-0284 674-4521
Web: www.cem.va.gov/nchp/crownhill.htm
Culpeper National Cemetery 305 US Ave ... Culpeper VA 22701 540-825-0027 825-6684
Web: www.cem.va.gov/nchp/culpeper.htm
Cypress Hills National Cemetery 625 Jamaica Ave ... Brooklyn NY 11208 631-454-4949 694-5422
Web: www.cem.va.gov/nchp/cypresshills.htm
Danville National Cemetery 1900 E Main St ... Danville IL 61832 217-554-4550 554-4803
Web: www.cem.va.gov/nchp/danvilleil.htm
Danville National Cemetery 721 Lee St ... Danville VA 24541 704-636-2661 636-1115
Web: www.cem.va.gov/nchp/danvilleva.htm
Dayton National Cemetery 4100 W 3rd St ... Dayton OH 45428 937-262-2115 262-2187
Web: www.cem.va.gov/nchp/dayton.htm
Eagle Point National Cemetery 2763 Riley Rd ... Eagle Point OR 97524 541-826-2511 826-2888
Web: www.cem.va.gov/nchp/eaglepoint.htm
Fayetteville National Cemetery 700 Government Ave ... Fayetteville AR 72701 479-444-5051 444-5094
Web: www.cem.va.gov/nchp/fayetteville.htm
Finn's Point National Cemetery Fort Mott Rd RD 3 Box 542 ... Salem NJ 08079 609-880-0827 871-4691
Web: www.cem.va.gov/nchp/finnspoint.htm
Florence National Cemetery 803 E National Cemetery Rd ... Florence SC 29506 843-669-8783 662-8318
Web: www.cem.va.gov/nchp/florence.htm
Florida National Cemetery 6502 SW 102nd Ave ... Bushnell FL 33513 352-793-7740 793-9560
Web: www.cem.va.gov/nchp/florida.htm
Fort Bayard National Cemetery PO Box 189 ... Fort Bayard NM 88036 915-564-0201 564-3746
Web: www.cem.va.gov/nchp/ftbayard.htm
Fort Bliss National Cemetery PO Box 6342 ... El Paso TX 79906 915-564-0201 564-3746
Web: www.cem.va.gov/nchp/ftbliss.htm
Fort Custer National Cemetery 15501 Dickman Rd ... Augusta MI 49012 269-731-4164 731-2428
Web: www.cem.va.gov/nchp/ftcuster.htm
Fort Gibson National Cemetery 1423 Cemetery Rd ... Fort Gibson OK 74434 918-478-2334 478-2661
Web: www.cem.va.gov/nchp/ftgibson.htm
Fort Harrison National Cemetery 8620 Varina Rd ... Richmond VA 23231 804-795-2031 795-1064
Web: www.cem.va.gov/nchp/ftharrision.htm
Fort Leavenworth National Cemetery 395 Biddle Blvd ... Fort Leavenworth KS 66027 913-758-4105 758-4136
Web: www.cem.va.gov/nchp/ftleavenworth.htm
Fort Logan National Cemetery 3698 S Sheridan Blvd ... Denver CO 80235 303-761-0117 781-9378
Web: www.cem.va.gov/nchp/ftlogan.htm
Fort Lyon National Cemetery 15700 County Rd HH ... Las Animas CO 81054 303-761-0117 781-9378
Web: www.cem.va.gov/nchp/ftlyon.htm
Fort Mitchell National Cemetery 553 Hwy 165 ... Fort Mitchell AL 36856 334-855-4731 855-4740
Web: www.cem.va.gov/nchp/ftmitchell.htm
Fort Richardson National Cemetery PO Box 5-498 ... Fort Richardson AK 99505 907-384-7075 384-7111
Web: www.cem.va.gov/nchp/ftrichardson.htm
Fort Rosecrans National Cemetery PO Box 6237 ... San Diego CA 92166 619-553-2084 553-6593
Web: www.cem.va.gov/nchp/ftrosecrans.htm
Fort Sam Houston National Cemetery
1520 Harry Wurzbach Rd ... San Antonio TX 78209 210-820-3891 820-3445
Web: www.cem.va.gov/nchp/ftsamhouston.htm
Fort Scott National Cemetery PO Box 917 ... Fort Scott KS 66701 620-223-2840 223-2505
Web: www.cem.va.gov/nchp/ftscott.htm
Fort Smith National Cemetery 522 Garland Ave ... Fort Smith AR 72901 479-783-5345 785-4189
Web: www.cem.va.gov/nchp/ftsmith.htm
Fort Snelling National Cemetery 7601 34th Ave S ... Minneapolis MN 55450 612-726-1127 726-9119
Web: www.cem.va.gov/nchp/ftsnelling.htm
Glendale National Cemetery 8301 Willis Church Rd ... Richmond VA 23231 804-795-2031 795-1064
Web: www.cem.va.gov/nchp/glendale.htm
Golden Gate National Cemetery 1300 Sneath Ln ... San Bruno CA 94066 650-589-7737 873-6578
Web: www.cem.va.gov/nchp/goldengate.htm
Grafton National Cemetery 431 Walnut St ... Grafton WV 26354 304-265-2044 265-4336
Web: www.cem.va.gov/nchp/grafton.htm
Hampton National Cemetery Cemetery Rd at Marshall Ave ... Hampton VA 23669 757-723-7104 728-3144
Web: www.cem.va.gov/nchp/hampton.htm
Houston National Cemetery 10410 Veterans Memorial Dr ... Houston TX 77038 281-447-8686 447-0580
Web: www.cem.va.gov/nchp/houston.htm
Indiantown Gap National Cemetery RR 2 Box 484 ... Annville PA 17003 717-865-5254 865-5256
Web: www.cem.va.gov/nchp/indiantowngap.htm
Jefferson Barracks National Cemetery 2900 Sheridan Rd ... Saint Louis MO 63125 314-260-8691 260-8723
Web: www.cem.va.gov/nchp/jeffersonbarracks.htm
Jefferson City National Cemetery 1024 E McCarty St ... Jefferson City MO 65101 314-260-8691 260-8723
Web: www.cem.va.gov/nchp/jeffersoncity.htm
Keokuk National Cemetery 1701 J St ... Keokuk IA 52632 309-782-2094 782-2097
Web: www.cem.va.gov/nchp/keokuk.htm
Kerrville National Cemetery 3600 Memorial Blvd ... Kerrville TX 78028 210-820-3891 820-3445
Web: www.cem.va.gov/nchp/kerrville.htm
Knoxville National Cemetery 939 Tyson St NW ... Knoxville TN 37917 423-855-6590 855-6597
Web: www.cem.va.gov/nchp/knoxville.htm
Leavenworth National Cemetery PO Box 1694 ... Leavenworth KS 66048 913-758-4105 758-4136
Web: www.cem.va.gov/nchp/leavenworth.htm
Lebanon National Cemetery 20 Hwy 208 ... Lebanon KY 40033 502-893-3852 893-6012
Web: www.cem.va.gov/nchp/lebanon.htm
Little Rock National Cemetery 2623 Confederate Blvd ... Little Rock AR 72206 501-324-6401 324-7182
Web: www.cem.va.gov/nchp/littlerock.htm
Long Island National Cemetery 2040 Wellwood Ave ... Farmingdale NY 11735 631-454-4949 694-5422
Web: www.cem.va.gov/nchp/longisland.htm
Los Angeles National Cemetery 950 S Sepulveda Blvd ... Los Angeles CA 90049 310-268-4494 268-3257
Web: www.cem.va.gov/nchp/losangeles.htm
Loudon Park National Cemetery 3445 Frederick Rd ... Baltimore MD 21228 410-644-9696 644-1563
Web: www.cem.va.gov/nchp/loudonpark.htm
Marietta National Cemetery 500 Washington Ave ... Marietta GA 30060 770-428-3258 426-6092
Web: www.cem.va.gov/nchp/marietta.htm
Marion National Cemetery 1700 E 38th St ... Marion IN 46953 765-674-0284 674-4521
Web: www.cem.va.gov/nchp/marion.htm
Massachusetts National Cemetery Connary Ave ... Bourne MA 02532 508-563-7113 564-9946
Web: www.cem.va.gov/nchp/massachuetts.htm
Memphis National Cemetery 3568 Townes Ave ... Memphis TN 38122 901-386-8311 382-0750
Web: www.cem.va.gov/nchp/memphis.htm
Mill Springs National Cemetery 9044 W Hwy 80 ... Nancy KY 42544 859-885-5727 887-4860
Web: www.cem.va.gov/nchp/millsprings.htm
Mobile National Cemetery 1202 Virginia St ... Mobile AL 36604 850-453-4108 453-4635
Web: www.cem.va.gov/nchp/mobile.htm
Mound City National Cemetery Hwy 37 & 51 PO Box 128 ... Mound City IL 62963 314-260-8691 260-8723
Web: www.cem.va.gov/nchp/moundcity.htm
Mountain Home National Cemetery PO Box 8 ... Mountain Home TN 37684 423-979-3535 979-3521
Web: www.cem.va.gov/nchp/mountainhome.htm
Nashville National Cemetery 1420 Gallatin Rd S ... Madison TN 37115 615-860-0086 860-8691
Web: www.cem.va.gov/nchp/nashville.htm
Natchez National Cemetery 41 Cemetery Rd ... Natchez MS 39120 601-445-4981 445-8815
Web: www.cem.va.gov/nchp/natchez.htm
National Memorial Cemetery of Arizona 23029 N Cave Creek Rd ... Phoenix AZ 85024 480-513-3600 513-1412
Web: www.cem.va.gov/nchp/nmca.htm
National Memorial Cemetery of the Pacific 2177 Puowaina Dr ... Honolulu HI 96813 808-532-3720 532-3756
New Albany National Cemetery 1943 Ekin Ave ... New Albany IN 47150 502-893-3852 893-6612
Web: www.cem.va.gov/nchp/newalbany.htm
New Bern National Cemetery 1711 National Ave ... New Bern NC 28560 252-637-2912 637-7145
Web: www.cem.va.gov/nchp/newbern.htm
Philadelphia National Cemetery Haines St & Limekiln Pike ... Philadelphia PA 19138 609-880-0827 871-4691
Web: www.cem.va.gov/nchp/philadelphia.htm
Poplar Grove National Cemetery 1539 Hickory Hill Rd ... Petersburg VA 23803 804-732-3531 732-3615
Web: www.nps.gov/pogr/index.htm
Port Hudson National Cemetery 20978 Port Hickey Rd ... Zachary LA 70791 225-654-3767 654-3728
Web: www.cem.va.gov/nchp/porthudson.htm
Prescott National Cemetery 500 Hwy 89 N ... Prescott AZ 86313 480-513-3600 513-1412
Web: www.cem.va.gov/nchp/prescott.htm
Quantico National Cemetery 18424 Joplin Rd ... Triangle VA 22172 703-221-2183 221-2185
Web: www.cem.va.gov/nchp/quantico.htm
Quincy National Cemetery 36th & Main Sts ... Quincy IL 62301 309-782-2094 782-2097
Web: www.cem.va.gov/nchp/quincy.htm
Raleigh National Cemetery 501 Rock Quarry Rd ... Raleigh NC 27610 252-637-2912 637-7145
Web: www.cem.va.gov/nchp/raleigh.htm
Richmond National Cemetery 1701 Williamsburg Rd ... Richmond VA 23231 804-795-2031 795-1064
Web: www.cem.va.gov/nchp/richmond.htm
Riverside National Cemetery 22495 Van Buren Blvd ... Riverside CA 92518 951-653-8417 683-5233
Web: www.cem.va.gov/nchp/riverside.htm
Rock Island National Cemetery PO Box 737 ... Moline IL 61265 309-782-2094 782-2097
Web: www.cem.va.gov/nchp/rockisland.htm
Roseburg National Cemetery 913 Garden Valley Blvd ... Roseburg OR 97470 541-826-2511 826-2888
Web: www.cem.va.gov/nchp/roseburg.htm
Saint Augustine National Cemetery 104 Marine St ... Saint Augustine FL 32084 352-793-7740 793-9560
Web: www.cem.va.gov/CEM/cems/nchp/staugustine.asp
Salisbury National Cemetery 501 Statesville Blvd ... Salisbury NC 28144 704-636-2661 636-1115
Web: www.cem.va.gov/nchp/salisbury.htm
San Antonio National Cemetery
c/o Port San Houston National Cemetery 1520 Harry
Wurzback Rd ... San Antonio TX 78209 210-820-3891 820-3445
San Francisco National Cemetery
Presidio of San Francisco 1 Lincoln Blvd ... San Francisco CA 94129 650-589-7737 873-6578
Web: www.cem.va.gov/nchp/sanfrancisco.htm
San Joaquin Valley National Cemetery 32053 W McCabe Rd ... Santa Nella CA 95322 209-854-1040 854-3944
Web: www.cem.va.gov/nchp/sanjoaquinvalley.htm
Santa Fe National Cemetery 501 N Guadalupe St ... Santa Fe NM 87501 505-988-6400 988-6497
Web: www.cem.va.gov/nchp/santafe.htm
Seven Pines National Cemetery 400 E Williamsburg Rd ... Sandston VA 23150 804-795-2031 795-1064
Web: www.cem.va.gov/nchp/sevenpines.htm
Sitka National Cemetery 803 Sawmill Creek Rd ... Sitka AK 99835 907-384-7075 384-7111
Web: www.cem.va.gov/nchp/sitka.htm
Springfield National Cemetery 1702 E Seminole St ... Springfield MO 65804 417-881-9499 881-7862
Web: www.cem.va.gov/pdf/springfield.pdf
Staunton National Cemetery 901 Richmond Ave ... Staunton VA 24401 540-825-0027 825-6684
Web: www.cem.va.gov/nchp/staunton.htm
Tahoma National Cemetery 18600 SE 240th St ... Kent WA 98042 425-413-9614 413-9618
Web: www.cem.va.gov/nchp/tahoma.htm
Togus National Cemetery VA Regional Office Center ... Togus ME 04330 508-563-7113 564-9946
Web: www.cem.va.gov/nchp/togus.htm
West Virginia National Cemetery Rt 2 Box 127 ... Grafton WV 26354 304-265-2044 265-4336
Web: www.cem.va.gov/nchp/westvirginia.htm
Willamette National Cemetery 11800 SE Mt Scott Blvd ... Portland OR 97266 503-273-5250 273-5330
Web: www.cem.va.gov/nchp/willamette.htm
Wilmington National Cemetery 2011 Market St ... Wilmington NC 28403 910-815-4877 637-7145*
**Fax Area Code: 252* ■ *Web:* www.cem.va.gov/nchp/wilmington.htm
Winchester National Cemetery 401 National Ave ... Winchester VA 22601 540-825-0027 825-6684
Web: www.cem.va.gov/nchp/winchester.htm
Wood National Cemetery 5000 W National Ave Bldg 1301 ... Milwaukee WI 53295 414-382-5300 382-5321
Web: www.cem.va.gov/nchp/wood.htm
Woodlawn National Cemetery 1825 Davis St ... Elmira NY 14901 607-732-5411 732-1769
Web: www.cem.va.gov/nchp/woodlawn.htm
Yorktown National Cemetery PO Box 210 ... Yorktown VA 23690 757-898-2410 898-3400
Web: www.nps.gov/york/index.htm
Zachary Taylor National Cemetery 4701 Brownboro Rd ... Louisville KY 40207 502-893-3852 893-6612
Web: www.cem.va.gov/nchp/zacharytaylor.htm

137 CHAMBERS OF COMMERCE - CANADIAN

Listings are organized by provinces and then are alphabetized within each province grouping according to the name of the city in which each chamber is located.

Phone Fax

Brooks & District Chamber of Commerce Box 400 ... Brooks AB T1R1B4 403-362-7641 362-6893
Web: www.brookschamber.ab.ca

	City	Prov	Postal Code	Phone	Fax
Calgary Chamber of Commerce 100 6th Ave SW *Web:* www.calgarychamber.com	Calgary	AB	T2P0P5	403-750-0400	266-3413
Alberta Chambers of Commerce 10025 - 102A Ave Suite 1808 Edmonton Ctr *Web:* www.abchamber.ca	Edmonton	AB	T5J2Z2	780-425-4180	429-1061
Edmonton Chamber of Commerce 9990 Jasper Ave Suite 600 *Web:* www.edmontonchamber.com	Edmonton	AB	T5J1P7	780-426-4620	424-7946
Fort McMurray Chamber of Commerce 9612 Franklin Ave Suite 304 *Web:* www.fortmcmurraychamber.ca	Fort McMurray	AB	T9H2J9	780-743-3100	790-9757
Grande Prairie & District Chamber of Commerce 11330 106th St Suite 217 *Web:* www.grandeprairiechamber.com	Grande Prairie	AB	T8V7X9	780-532-5340	532-2926
Lethbridge Chamber of Commerce 529 6th St S Suite 200 *Web:* lethbridgechamber.com	Lethbridge	AB	T1J2E1	403-327-1586	327-1001
Medicine Hat & District Chamber of Commerce 413 6th Ave SE *Web:* www.medicinehatchamber.com	Medicine Hat	AB	T1A2S7	403-527-5214	527-5182
Peace River Chamber of Commerce PO Box 6599 *Web:* www.peaceriverchamber.com	Peace River	AB	T8S1S4	780-624-4166	624-4663
Red Deer Chamber of Commerce 3017 Gaetz Ave *Web:* www.reddeerchamber.com	Red Deer	AB	T4N5Y6	403-347-4491	343-6188
Saint Albert Chamber of Commerce 71 St Albert Rd *Web:* www.stalbertchamber.com	Saint Albert	AB	T8N6L5	780-458-2833	458-6515
Abbotsford Chamber of Commerce 32900 S Fraser Way Unit 207 *Web:* www.abbotsfordchamber.com	Abbotsford	BC	V2S5A1	604-859-9651	850-6880
Burnaby Board of Trade 4555 Kings Way Suite 201 *Web:* www.burnabyboardoftrade.com	Burnaby	BC	V5H4T8	604-412-0100	412-0102
Campbell River & District Chamber of Commerce 900 Alder St PO Box 400 *Web:* www.campbellriverchamber.ca	Campbell River	BC	V9W5B6	250-287-4636	286-6490
Chilliwack Chamber of Commerce 46093 Yale Rd Suite 201 *Web:* www.chilliwackchamber.com	Chilliwack	BC	V2P2L8	604-793-4323	793-4303
Tri-Cities Chamber of Commerce 1209 Pinetree Way *Web:* www.tricitieschamber.com	Coquitlam	BC	V3B7Y3	604-464-2716	464-6796
Comox Valley Chamber of Commerce 2040 Cliffe Ave *TF:* 888-357-4471 ■ *Web:* www.comoxvalleychamber.com	Courtenay	BC	V9N2L3	250-334-3234	334-4908
Delta Chamber of Commerce 6201 60th Ave *Web:* www.deltachamber.com	Delta	BC	V4K4E2	604-946-4232	946-5285
Duncan Cowichan Chamber of Commerce 381 Trans Canada Hwy *Web:* duncancc.bc.ca	Duncan	BC	V9L3R5	250-748-1111	746-8222
Fort Saint John & District Chamber of Commerce 9325 100th St Suite 202 *Web:* www.fortstjohnchamber.com	Fort Saint John	BC	V1J4N4	250-785-6037	785-6050
Kamloops Chamber of Commerce 1290 W Trans-Canada Hwy *Web:* www.kamloopschamber.bc.ca/	Kamloops	BC	V2C6R3	250-372-7722	828-9500
Kelowna Chamber of Commerce 544 Harvey Ave *Web:* www.kelownachamber.org	Kelowna	BC	V1Y6C9	250-861-3627	861-3624
Langley Chamber of Commerce 5761 Glover Rd Unit 1 *Web:* www.langleychamber.com	Langley	BC	V3A8M8	604-530-6656	530-7066
Maple Ridge Chamber of Commerce 22238 Lougheed Hwy *Web:* www.mrpmchamber.ca	Maple Ridge	BC	V2X2T2	604-463-3366	463-3201
Mission Regional Chamber of Commerce 34033 Lougheed Hwy *Web:* www.missionchamber.bc.ca	Mission	BC	V2V5X8	604-826-6914	826-5916
Greater Nanaimo Chamber of Commerce 2133 Bowen Rd *Web:* www.nanaimochamber.bc.ca	Nanaimo	BC	V9S1H8	250-756-1191	756-1584
New Westminster Chamber of Commerce 601 Queens Ave *Web:* www.newwestchamber.com	New Westminster	BC	V3M1L1	604-521-7781	521-0057
North Vancouver Chamber of Commerce 124 W 1st St Suite 102 *TF:* 877-880-4699 ■ *Web:* www.nvchamber.bc.ca	North Vancouver	BC	V7M3N3	604-987-4488	987-8272
Parksville Chamber of Commerce PO Box 99 *Web:* www.chamber.parksville.bc.ca	Parksville	BC	V9P2G3	250-248-3613	248-5210
Penticton & Wine Country Chamber of Commerce 553 Railway St *TF:* 800-663-5052 ■ *Web:* www.penticton.org	Penticton	BC	V2A8S3	250-492-4103	492-6119
Alberni Valley Chamber of Commerce 2533 Port Alberni Hwy *Web:* www.avcoc.com	Port Alberni	BC	V9Y8P2	250-724-6535	724-6560
Prince George Chamber of Commerce 890 Vancouver St *Web:* www.pgchamber.bc.ca	Prince George	BC	V2L2P5	250-562-2454	562-6510
Richmond Chamber of Commerce 5811 Cooney Rd Suite 101 *Web:* www.richmondchamber.ca	Richmond	BC	V6X3M1	604-278-2822	278-2972
Saanich Peninsula Chamber of Commerce PO Box 2014 *Web:* www.spcoc.org	Sidney	BC	V8L3S3	250-656-3616	656-7111
Surrey Board of Trade 14439 104th Ave Suite 101 *Web:* www.surreychamber.org	Surrey	BC	V3R1M1	604-581-7130	588-7549
British Columbia Chamber of Commerce 750 W Pender St Suite 1201 *Web:* www.bcchamber.org	Vancouver	BC	V6C2T8	604-683-0700	683-0416
Vancouver Board Of Trade 999 Canada Pl Suite 400 *Web:* www.vancouver.boardoftrade.com	Vancouver	BC	V6C3E1	604-681-2111	681-0437
Greater Vernon Chamber of Commerce 701 Hwy 97 S *Web:* www.vernonchamber.ca	Vernon	BC	V1B3W4	250-545-0771	545-3114
Greater Victoria Chamber of Commerce 852 Fort St Suite 100 *Web:* www.victoriachamber.ca	Victoria	BC	V8W1H8	250-383-7191	385-3552
West Shore Chamber of Commerce 2830 Aldwynd Rd *TF:* 877-912-1780 ■ *Web:* westshore.bc.ca	Victoria	BC	V9B3S7	250-478-1130	478-1584
West Vancouver Chamber of Commerce 1846 Marine Dr *TF:* 888-471-9996 ■ *Web:* www.westvanchamber.com	West Vancouver	BC	V7V1J6	604-926-6614	925-7220
Westbank & District Chamber of Commerce 2375 Pamela Rd Unit 4 *TF:* 866-768-3378 ■ *Web:* www.westbankchamber.com	Westbank	BC	V4T2H9	250-768-3378	768-3465
Brandon Chamber of Commerce 1043 Rosser Ave *Web:* www.brandonchamber.ca	Brandon	MB	R7A0L5	204-571-5340	571-5347
Portage & District Chamber of Commerce 11 2nd St NE *Web:* www.portagechamber.com	Portage la Prairie	MB	R1N1R8	204-857-7778	857-4095
Saint-Boniface Chamber of Commerce 383 boul Provencher Box 204 *Web:* www.ccfsb.mb.ca	Saint-Boniface	MB	R2H3B4	204-235-1406	233-1017
Selkirk & District Chamber of Commerce 200 Eaton Ave *Web:* www.selkirkchamber.com	Selkirk	MB	R1A0W6	204-482-7176	482-5448
Manitoba Chambers of Commerce 227 Portage Ave *Web:* www.mbchamber.mb.ca	Winnipeg	MB	R3B2A6	204-948-0100	948-0110
Winnipeg Chamber of Commerce 259 Portage Ave Suite 100 *Web:* www.winnipeg-chamber.com	Winnipeg	MB	R3B2A9	204-944-8484	944-8492
Enterprise Fredericton 570 Queen St Suite 102 *TF:* 800-200-1180 ■ *Web:* www.gfedc.nb.ca	Fredericton	NB	E3B6Z6	506-444-4686	444-4649
Fredericton Chamber of Commerce 270 Rookwood Rd PO Box 275 *Web:* www.frederictonchamber.ca/	Fredericton	NB	E3B4Y9	506-458-8006	451-1119
Miramichi Chamber of Commerce PO Box 342 *Web:* www.greatermiramichi.com	Miramichi	NB	E1N3A7	506-622-5522	622-5959
Atlantic Provinces Chamber of Commerce 236 Saint George St Suite 21 *Web:* www.apcc.ca	Moncton	NB	E1C1W1	506-857-3980	859-6131
Greater Moncton Chamber of Commerce 910 Main St Suite 100 *Web:* www.gmcc.nb.ca	Moncton	NB	E1C1G6	506-857-2883	857-9209
Saint John Board of Trade 40 King St PO Box 6037 *Web:* www.sjboardoftrade.com	Saint John	NB	E2L4R5	506-634-8111	632-2008
Greater Corner Brook Board of Trade 11 Confederation Dr PO Box 475 *Web:* www.gcbbt.com	Corner Brook	NL	A2H6E6	709-634-5831	639-9710
Gander & Area Chamber of Commerce 109 Trans Canada Hwy *Web:* www.ganderchamber.nf.ca	Gander	NL	A1V1P6	709-256-7110	256-4080
Exploits Regional Chamber of Commerce PO Box 272	Grand Falls-Windsor	NL	A2A2J7	709-489-7512	489-7532
Saint John's Board of Trade PO Box 5127	Saint John's	NL	A1C5V5	709-726-2961	726-2003
Northwest Territories Chamber of Commerce 4910 50th Ave YK Center PO Box 13 *Web:* www.nwtchamber.com	Yellowknife	NT	X1A3S5	867-920-9505	873-4174
Bridgewater & Area Chamber of Commerce 220 North St *Web:* www.bridgewaterchamber.com	Bridgewater	NS	B4V2V6	902-543-4263	543-1156
Metropolitan Halifax Chamber of Commerce 656 Windmill Rd Suite 200 *Web:* www.halifaxchamber.com	Dartmouth	NS	B3B1B8	902-468-7111	468-7333
Pictou County Chamber of Commerce 980 E River Rd *Web:* www.pictouchamber.com	New Glasgow	NS	B2H3S8	902-755-3463	755-2848
Sydney & Area Chamber of Commerce PO Box 131 *Web:* www.sydneyareachamber.ca	Sydney	NS	B1P6G9	902-564-6453	539-7487
Truro & District Chamber of Commerce 605 Prince St PO Box 54 *Web:* www.trurochamber.com	Truro	NS	B2N1G2	902-895-6328	897-6641
Yarmouth Chamber of Commerce PO Box 532 *Web:* www.yarmouthchamber.ca	Yarmouth	NS	B5A4B4	902-742-3074	749-1383
Aurora Chamber of Commerce 6-14845 Yonge St Suite 321 *Web:* www.aurorachamber.on.ca	Aurora	ON	L4G6H8	905-727-7262	841-6217
Greater Barrie Chamber of Commerce 97 Toronto St *Web:* www.barriechamber.com	Barrie	ON	L4N1V1	705-721-5000	726-0973
Belleville & District Chamber of Commerce 5 Moira St E *TF:* 888-852-9992 ■ *Web:* www.bellevillechamber.ca	Belleville	ON	K8N5B3	613-962-4597	962-3911
Caledon Chamber of Commerce PO Box 626 *Web:* www.caledonchamber.com	Bolton	ON	L7E5T5	905-857-7393	857-7405
Brampton Board of Trade 33 Queen St W 2nd Fl *Web:* www.bramptonbot.com	Brampton	ON	L6Y1L9	905-451-1122	450-0295
Chamber of Commerce Brantford Brant 77 Charlotte St *Web:* www.brcc.ca	Brantford	ON	N3T2W8	519-753-2617	753-0921
Burlington Chamber of Commerce 414 Locust St Suite 201 *Web:* www.burlingtonchamber.com	Burlington	ON	L7S1T7	905-639-0174	333-3956
Cambridge Chamber of Commerce 750 Hespeler Rd *TF:* 800-749-7560 ■ *Web:* www.cambridgechamber.com	Cambridge	ON	N3H5L8	519-622-2221	622-0662
Chatham-Kent Chamber of Commerce 54 4th St *Web:* www.chatham-kentchamber.ca	Chatham	ON	N7M2G2	519-352-7540	352-8741
Vaughan Chamber of Commerce 160 Applewood Crescent Unit 32 *TF:* 888-828-4426 ■ *Web:* www.vaughanchamber.ca	Concord	ON	L4K4H2	905-761-1366	761-1918
Cornwall & Area Chamber of Commerce 113 2nd St E *Web:* www.chamber.cornwall.on.ca	Cornwall	ON	K6J1Y5	613-933-4004	933-8466
Dryden District Chamber of Commerce 284 Government St *Web:* www.cityofdryden.on.ca	Dryden	ON	P8N2P3	807-223-2622	223-2626
Halton Hills Chamber of Commerce 328 Guelph St *Web:* www.haltonhillschamber.on.ca	Georgetown	ON	L7G4B5	905-877-5116	877-5117
Guelph Chamber of Commerce 485 Silver Creek Pkwy N Unit 15 *Web:* www.guelphchamber.com	Guelph	ON	N1H7K5	519-822-8081	822-8451
Hamilton Chamber of Commerce 555 Bay St N *Web:* www.hamiltonchamber.on.ca	Hamilton	ON	L8L1H1	905-522-1151	522-1154
Greater Kingston Chamber of Commerce 67 Brock St *Web:* www.kingstonchamber.on.ca	Kingston	ON	K7L1R8	613-548-4453	548-4743
Chamber of Commerce of Kitchener & Waterloo 80 Queen St N PO Box 2367 *TF:* 888-672-4282 ■ *Web:* www.greaterkwchamber.com	Kitchener	ON	N2H6L4	519-576-5000	742-4760
Leamington District Chamber of Commerce PO Box 321 *TF:* 800-250-3336 ■ *Web:* www.leamingtonchamber.com	Leamington	ON	N8H3W3	519-326-2721	326-3204
London Chamber of Commerce 244 Pall Mall St Suite 101 *Web:* www.londonchamber.com	London	ON	N6A5P6	519-432-7551	432-8063
Markham Board of Trade 80 F Centurian Dr Suite 206 *Web:* www.markhamboard.com	Markham	ON	L3R8C1	905-474-0730	474-0685
Southern Georgia Bay Chamber of Commerce 208 King St *Web:* www.southerngeorgianbay.on.ca	Midland	ON	L4R3L9	705-526-7884	526-1744
Milton Chamber of Commerce 251 Main St E Suite 104 *Web:* www.chamber.milton.on.ca	Milton	ON	L9T1P1	905-878-0581	878-4972
Mississauga Board of Trade 77 City Centre Dr Suite 701 *Web:* www.mbot.com	Mississauga	ON	L5B1M5	905-273-6151	273-4937
Newmarket Chamber of Commerce 470 Davis Dr *Web:* www.newmarketchamber.com	Newmarket	ON	L3Y2P3	905-898-5900	853-7271
Niagara Falls Canada Chamber of Commerce 4056 Dorchester Rd *Web:* www.niagarafallschamber.com	Niagara Falls	ON	L2E6M9	905-374-3666	374-2972
North Bay & District Chamber of Commerce 1375 Seymour St PO Box 747 *TF:* 888-249-8998 ■ *Web:* www.northbaychamber.com	North Bay	ON	P1B8J8	705-472-8480	472-8027
Oakville Chamber of Commerce 2521 Wyecroft Rd *Web:* www.oakvillechamber.com	Oakville	ON	L6L6P8	905-845-6613	845-6475
Greater Dufferin Area Chamber of Commerce PO Box 101 *Web:* www.gdacc.ca	Orangeville	ON	L9W2Z5	519-941-0490	941-0492
Greater Oshawa Chamber of Commerce 44 Richmond St W Suite 100 *Web:* www.oshawachamber.com	Oshawa	ON	L1G1C7	905-728-1683	432-1259
Canadian Chamber of Commerce 350 Albert St Suite 420 *Web:* www.chamber.ca	Ottawa	ON	K1R7X7	613-238-4000	238-7643
Ottawa (Greater) Chamber of Commerce 1701 Woodward Dr Suite LL-20 *Web:* www.ottawachamber.ca	Ottawa	ON	K2C0R4	613-236-3631	236-7498
Upper Ottawa Valley Chamber of Commerce 2 International Dr. *Web:* www.upperottawavalleychamber.com	Pembroke	ON	K8A6W5	613-732-1492	732-5793
Perth & District Chamber of Commerce 34 Herriott St *Web:* www.perthchamber.com	Perth	ON	K7H1T2	613-267-3200	267-6797
Greater Peterborough Chamber of Commerce 175 George St N *TF:* 877-640-4037 ■ *Web:* www.peterboroughchamber.ca	Peterborough	ON	K9J3G6	705-748-9771	743-2331
Port Colborne-Wainfleet Chamber of Commerce 76 Main St W *Web:* www.pcwchamber.com	Port Colborne	ON	L3K3V2	905-834-9765	834-1542
Richmond Hill Chamber of Commerce 376 Church St S *Web:* www.rhcoc.com	Richmond Hill	ON	L4C9V8	905-884-1961	884-1962
Saint Catharines Chamber of Commerce 1 Saint Paul St PO Box 940 *Web:* www.scchamberofcommerce.com	Saint Catharines	ON	L2R6Z4	905-684-2361	684-2100
Saint Thomas & District Chamber of Commerce 555 Talbot St *Web:* www.stthomaschamber.on.ca	Saint Thomas	ON	N5P1C5	519-631-1981	631-0466
Sault Sainte Marie Chamber of Commerce 334 Bay St *Web:* www.ssmcoc.com	Sault Sainte Marie	ON	P6A1X1	705-949-7152	759-8166
Scarborough Chamber of Commerce 940 Progress Ave *Web:* www.scarboroughchamber.com	Scarborough	ON	M1G3T5	416-439-4140	439-4147
Timmins Chamber of Commerce PO Box 985 *Web:* www.timminschamber.on.ca	Schumacher	ON	P4N7H6	705-360-1900	360-1193

Phone | Fax

Simcoe & District Chamber of Commerce 95 Queensway W — Simcoe ON N3Y2M8 519-426-5867 428-7718
Web: www.simcoechamber.on.ca
Stratford & District Chamber of Commerce 55 Lorne Ave E — Stratford ON N5A6S4 519-273-5250 273-2229
Web: www.stratfordchamber.com
Greater Sudbury Chamber of Commerce 40 Elm St Suite 1 — Sudbury ON P3C1S8 705-673-7133 673-2944
Web: www.sudburychamber.ca
Thunder Bay Chamber of Commerce
200 Syndicated Ave S Suite 102 — Thunder Bay ON P7E1C9 807-624-2626 622-7752
Web: www.tb-chamber.on.ca
Canadian Chamber of Commerce Toronto Office
55 University Ave Suite 901 — Toronto ON M5J2H7 416-868-6415 868-0189
Web: www.chamber.ca
Ontario Chamber of Commerce 180 Dundas St W Suite 505 — Toronto ON M5G1Z8 416-482-5222 482-5879
Web: occ.on.ca
Toronto Board of Trade 1 First Canadian Pl PO Box 60 — Toronto ON M5X1C1 416-366-6811 366-6460
Web: www.bot.com
Flamborough Chamber of Commerce PO Box 1030 — Waterdown ON L0R2H0 905-689-7650 689-1313
Web: www.flamboroughchamber.ca
Welland/Pelham Chamber of Commerce 32 E Main St — Welland ON L3B3W3 905-732-7515 732-7175
Web: www.chamber.iaw.com
Whitby Chamber of Commerce 128 Brock St S — Whitby ON L1N4J8 905-668-4506 668-1894
Web: www.whitbychamber.org
Windsor & District Chamber of Commerce 2575 Ouellette Pl — Windsor ON N8X1L9 519-966-3696 966-0603
Web: www.windsorchamber.org
Woodstock District Chamber of Commerce
425 Dundas St Suite 3 — Woodstock ON N4S1B8 519-539-9411 456-1611
Web: www.woodstockchamber.on.ca
Greater Charlottetown Area Chamber of Commerce
PO Box 67 — Charlottetown PE C1A7K2 902-628-2000 368-3570
Web: www.charlottetownchamber.com
Chicoutimi Chamber of Commerce 194 rue Price O — Chicoutimi QC G7J1H1 418-543-5941 543-5576
Web: www.ccchic.qc.ca
La Chambre de Commerce de Drummond
234 rue Saint Marcel CP 188 — Drummondville QC J2B6V7 819-477-7822 477-2823
Web: www.ccid.qc.ca
Chambre de Commerce et d'Industrie de l'Outaouais
45 de Ville Bois Bureau 100 — Gatineau QC J8T8G7 819-243-2246 243-3346
Chambre de Commerce Haute-Yamaska Region
650 rue Principale — Granby QC J2G8L4 450-372-6100 372-3161
Web: www.chambredecommerce.org
Laval Chamber of Commerce 1555 boul Chomedey Bureau 200 — Laval QC H7V3Z1 450-682-5255 682-5735
Web: www.ccilaval.qc.ca
Mont-Laurier Chamber of Commerce 445 rue Du Pont — Mont-Laurier QC G9L2R8 819-623-3642 623-6102
Web: www.mont-laurier.net
Board of Trade of Metropolitan Montreal
380 Saint-Antoine St W Suite 6000 — Montreal QC H2Y3X7 514-871-4000 871-1255
Web: www.btmm.qc.ca
Canadian Chamber of Commerce Montreal Office
1155 University St Suite 709 — Montreal QC H3B3A7 514-866-4334 866-7296
Web: www.chamber.ca
Chambre de Commerce du Quebec
249 rue Saint Jacques Bureau 302 — Montreal QC H2Y1M6 514-522-1885 522-9468
TF: 888-595-8110 ■ *Web:* www.ccquebec.ca
Chambre de Commerce et d'Industrie du Quebec Metropolitain
17 Saint-Louis St — Quebec QC G1R3Y8 418-692-3853 694-2286
Web: www.ccquebec.ca
Haut-Richelieu Chamber of Commerce
315 rue MacDonald Bureau 232 — Saint-Jean-sur-Richelieu QC J3B8J3 450-346-2544 346-3812
Web: www.cchautrichelieu.qc.ca
Sept-Iles Chamber of Commerce 700 boul Laure Bureau 237 — Sept-Iles QC G4R1Y1 418-968-3488 968-3432
Chambre de Commerce de la Region Sherbrookoise
75 rue Welligton N Suite 402 — Sherbrooke QC J1H5A9 819-822-6151 822-6156
Web: www.ccsherbrooke.ca
Trois-Rivieres & District Chamber of Commerce
168 rue Bonaventure CP 1045 — Trois-Rivieres QC G9A5K4 819-375-9628 375-9083
Web: www.ccdtr.com
Moose Jaw & District Chamber of Commerce
88 Saskatchewan St E — Moose Jaw SK S6H0V4 306-692-6414 694-6463
Web: www.mjchamber.com
Battlefords Chamber of Commerce PO Box 1000 — North Battleford SK S9A3E6 306-445-6226 445-6633
Web: www.battlefordschamber.com
Prince Albert & District Chamber of Commerce
1084 Central Ave Suite 347 — Prince Albert SK S6V7P3 306-764-6222 922-4727
Web: www.thechamberofcom.com
Regina Chamber of Commerce 2145 Albert St — Regina SK S4P2V1 306-757-4658 757-4668
Web: www.reginachamber.com
Greater Saskatoon Chamber of Commerce 345 3rd Ave S — Saskatoon SK S7K1M6 306-244-2151 244-8366
Web: www.eboardoftrade.com
Whitehorse Chamber of Commerce 302 Steele St Suite 101 — Whitehorse YT Y1A2C5 867-667-7545 667-4507
Web: www.whitehorsechamber.com
Yukon Chamber of Commerce 307 Jarvis St Suite 101 — Whitehorse YT Y1A2H3 867-667-2000 667-2001
Web: www.yukonchamber.com

138 CHAMBERS OF COMMERCE - INTERNATIONAL

SEE ALSO Chambers of Commerce - Canadian p. 1413

Included here are organizations that work to promote business and trade relationships between the United States and other countries.

Phone | Fax

African Chamber of Commerce Dallas/Fort Worth
1402 Coringh St Suite 249 — Dallas TX 75215 214-421-6155 421-6158
Web: www.africanchamberdfw.org
America-Israel Chamber of Commerce - Chicago
247 S State St 15th Fl — Chicago IL 60604 312-235-0586 641-0724
Web: www.americaisrael.org
America-Israel Chamber of Commerce & Industry
3 New York Plaza 10th Fl — New York NY 10004 212-232-8440 365-3366*
**Fax Area Code:* 646 ■ *Web:* www.aicci.net
American Egyptian Cooperation Foundation
870 Market St Suite 855 — San Francisco CA 94102 415-837-0989 837-0989
Web: www.americanegyptiancoop.org
American Egyptian Cooperation Foundation
28 E Jackson Blvd Suite 809 — Chicago IL 60604 312-427-9368
Web: www.americanegyptiancoop.org
American Egyptian Cooperation Foundation
330 E 39th St Suite 32L — New York NY 10016 212-867-2323 697-0465
Web: www.americanegyptiancoop.org
American Egyptian Cooperation Foundation
1535 West Loop S Suite 200 — Houston TX 77027 713-624-7113
Web: www.americanegyptiancoop.org

Phone | Fax

American-Indonesian Chamber of Commerce
317 Madison Ave Suite 1619 — New York NY 10017 212-687-4505 687-5844
Web: www.aiccusa.org
American-Israel Chamber of Commerce & Industry of Minnesota 13100 Wayzata Blvd Suite 130 — Minnetonka MN 55305 952-593-8666 593-8668
Web: www.aiccmn.org
American-Israel Chamber of Commerce Southeast Region
1150 Lake Hearn Dr Suite 130 — Atlanta GA 30342 404-843-9426 843-1416
Web: www.aiccse.org
American-Russian Chamber of Commerce & Industry
1101 Pennsylvania Ave NW 6th Fl — Washington DC 20004 202-756-4943 362-4634
Web: www.arcci.org
Argentine-American Chamber of Commerce Inc
630 5th Ave 25th Fl — New York NY 10111 212-698-2238 698-2239
Web: www.argentinechamber.org
Association of American Chambers of Commerce in Latin America (AACCLA) 1615 H St NW 3rd Fl — Washington DC 20062 202-463-5485 463-3126
Web: www.aaccla.org
Australian-American Chamber of Commerce of Hawaii
1000 Bishop St — Honolulu HI 96813 808-526-2242 534-0475
Web: lava.net/aacc
Australian American Chamber of Commerce of Houston
PO Box 130261 — Houston TX 77219 713-527-9688 527-9688
Web: www.aacc-houston.org
Australian-American Chamber of Commerce of San Francisco PO Box 210508 — San Francisco CA 94121 415-485-6718 485-6832
Web: www.sfaussies.com
Australian New Zealand American Chambers of Commerce (ANZACC) c/o Embassy of Australia 1601 Massachusetts Ave NW — Washington DC 20036 202-797-3028 797-3457
Web: www.anzaccnational.com
Belgian-American Chamber of Commerce in the US (BACC)
101 Hudson St 21st Fl — Jersey City NJ 07302 201-631-8065 631-8067
Web: www.belcham.org
Brazilian-American Chamber of Commerce of Florida PO Box 310038 — Miami FL 33231 305-579-9030 579-9756
Web: www.brazilchamber.org
Brazilian-American Chamber of Commerce of Georgia
PO Box 93411 — Atlanta GA 30377 404-880-1551 880-1555
Web: www.bacc-ga.com
Brazilian-American Chamber of Commerce Inc
509 Madison Ave Suite 304 — New York NY 10022 212-751-4691 751-7692
Web: www.brazilcham.com
British-American Business Council (BABC)
52 Vanderbilt Ave 20th Fl — New York NY 10017 212-661-4060 661-4074
Web: www.babc.org
British-American Business Council of Los Angeles
11766 Wilshire Blvd Suite 1230 — Los Angeles CA 90025 310-312-1962 312-1914
Web: www.babcla.org
British-American Chamber of Commerce Great Lakes Region
1120 Chester Ave Suite 470 — Cleveland OH 44114 216-621-0222 696-2582
Web: www.baccgl.org
British-American Chamber of Commerce of Miami
200 S Biscayne Blvd Suite 4143 — Miami FL 33131 305-377-0992 448-7605
British-American Chamber of Commerce of San Francisco
235 Montgomery St Suite 907 — San Francisco CA 94104 415-296-8645 296-9649
Web: www.baccsf.org
Camara de Comercio Latina de Estados Unidos 1417 W Flagler St — Miami FL 33135 305-642-3870 642-0653
Web: www.camacol.org
Central American Chamber of Commerce 1395 Brickell Ave 13th Fl — Miami FL 33131 305-569-9113 735-2445
Chile-US Chamber of Commerce 800 Brickell Ave Suite 900 — Miami FL 33131 786-419-2092 374-4270*
**Fax Area Code:* 305 ■ *Web:* www.chileus.org
Chinese Chamber of Commerce of Hawaii 42 N King St — Honolulu HI 96817 808-533-3181 533-6967
Web: www.ccchi.org
Chinese Chamber of Commerce of Los Angeles
977 N Broadway Suite E — Los Angeles CA 90012 213-617-0396 617-2128
Web: www.lachinesechamber.org
Chinese Chamber of Commerce of San Francisco
730 Sacramento St — San Francisco CA 94108 415-982-3000 982-4720
Colombian American Chamber of Commerce
250 Catalonia Ave Suite 407 — Coral Gables FL 33134 305-446-2542 446-2038
Web: www.colombiachamber.com
Danish-American Chamber of Commerce 885 2nd Ave 18th Fl — New York NY 10017 212-705-4945 754-1904
Web: www.daccny.com
Ecuadorian-American Chamber of Commerce of Greater Miami
1390 Brickell Ave Suite 220 — Miami FL 33131 305-539-0010 539-8001
Web: www.ecuachamber.com
European-American Business Council 1325 G St Suite 500 — Washington DC 20005 202-449-4405 449-7704
Web: www.eabc.org
Finnish American Chamber of Commerce Inc
866 United Nations Plaza — New York NY 10017 212-821-0225 750-4418
Web: www.finlandtrade.com
Finnish-American Chamber of Commerce on the Pacific Coast
PO Box 3058 — Tustin CA 92781 714-573-0604 242-9153
Web: www.faccpacific.com
French-American Chamber of Commerce of Atlanta
321 Pharr Rd Suite G — Atlanta GA 30305 404-846-2500 846-2555
Web: www.facc-atlanta.com
French-American Chamber of Commerce of Chicago
35 E Wacker Dr Suite 670 — Chicago IL 60601 312-578-0444 578-0445
Web: www.facc-chicago.com
French-American Chamber of Commerce of Dallas
2665 Villa Creek Dr Suite 214 — Dallas TX 75234 972-241-0111 241-0901
Web: www.faccdallas.com
French-American Chamber of Commerce of Florida
14 NE 1st Ave Suite 1005 — Miami FL 33132 305-374-5000 358-8203
Web: www.faccmiami.com
French-American Chamber of Commerce of Houston
5373 W Alabama St Suite 209 — Houston TX 77056 713-960-0575 960-0495
Web: www.facchouston.com
French-American Chamber of Commerce of Los Angeles
8222 Melrose Ave Suite 203 — Los Angeles CA 90046 323-651-4741 651-2547
Web: www.frenchchamberla.org
French-American Chamber of Commerce of Louisiana
2 Canal St Suite 2426 — New Orleans LA 70130 504-561-0070 592-9999
Web: www.ccife.org/usa/louisiane
French-American Chamber of Commerce of New York
122 E 42nd St Suite 2015 — New York NY 10168 212-867-0123 867-9050
Web: www.ccife.org/usa/new_york
French-American Chamber of Commerce of the Pacific Northwest
2200 Alaskan Way Suite 490 — Seattle WA 98121 206-443-4703 448-4218
Web: www.ccife.org/usa/seattle
French-American Chamber of Commerce of Philadelphia
2000 Market St Suite 2850 — Philadelphia PA 19103 215-419-5559 419-5533
Web: www.faccphila.org
French-American Chamber of Commerce of San Francisco
703 Market St Suite 450 — San Francisco CA 94103 415-442-4717 442-4621
Web: www.faccsf.com

	City	ST	ZIP	Phone	Fax
German-American Chamber of Commerce Inc 75 Broad St 21st Fl *Web:* www.gaccny.com	New York	NY	10004	212-974-8830	974-8867
German-American Chamber of Commerce Inc - Philadelphia 1600 JFK Blvd Suite 200 4 Penn Center *Web:* www.gaccphiladelphia.com	Philadelphia	PA	19103	215-665-1585	665-0375
German-American Chamber of Commerce of the Midwest Inc 401 N Michigan Ave Suite 3330 *Web:* www.gaccom.org	Chicago	IL	60611	312-644-2662	644-0738
German-American Chamber of Commerce of the Southern US Inc 530 Means St NW Suite 120 *Web:* www.gaccsouth.com	Atlanta	GA	30318	404-586-6800	586-6820
Hellenic-American Chamber of Commerce 960 Ave of the Americas 9th Fl *Web:* www.hellenicamerican.cc	New York	NY	10001	212-629-6380	564-9281
Honolulu-Japanese Chamber of Commerce 2454 S Beretania St Suite 201 *Web:* www.honolulujapanesechamber.org	Honolulu	HI	96826	808-949-5531	949-3020
Hungarian-American Chamber of Commerce of New England Inc 111 Huntington Ave 26th Fl *Web:* www.hungarianamericanchamber.com	Boston	MA	02199	508-347-2742	347-3831
Hungarian-American Chamber of Commerce in the US Inc 205 De Anza Blvd PMB 157	San Mateo	CA	94402	650-573-7351	
Icelandic-American Chamber of Commerce 800 3rd Ave 36th Fl *Web:* www.iceland.org/us/nyc/consulate-general/chamber-of-commerce	New York	NY	10022	212-593-2700	593-6269
Ireland Chamber of Commerce in the US 556 Central Ave *Web:* www.iccusa.org	New Providence	NJ	07974	908-286-1300	286-1200
Ireland-US Council for Commerce & Industry 1156 Ave of the Americas	New York	NY	10036	212-921-1414	730-2232
Italian American Chamber of Commerce of Chicago 30 S Michigan Ave Suite 504 *Web:* www.italianchamber.us	Chicago	IL	60603	312-553-9137	553-9142
Italy-America Chamber of Commerce Inc 730 5th Ave Suite 600 *Web:* www.italchamber.org	New York	NY	10019	212-459-0044	459-0090
Italy-America Chamber of Commerce Southeast Inc 270 NE 4th St Suite 2 *Web:* www.iacc-miami.com	Miami	FL	33132	305-577-9868	577-3956
Italy-America Chamber of Commerce of Texas Inc 1800 W Loop S Suite 1120 *Web:* www.iacctexas.com	Houston	TX	77027	713-626-9303	626-9309
Italy-America Chamber of Commerce West Inc 10350 Santa Monica Blvd Suite 210 *Web:* www.italchambers.net/losangeles	Los Angeles	CA	90025	310-557-3017	557-1217
Japanese Chamber of Commerce & Industry of Chicago 541 N Fairbanks Ct Suite 2050 *Web:* www.jccc-chi.org/en	Chicago	IL	60611	312-245-8344	245-8355
Japanese Chamber of Commerce & Industry of Hawaii 400 Hualani St Suite 20B	Hilo	HI	96720	808-934-0177	934-0178
Japanese Chamber of Commerce & Industry of New York Inc 145 W 57th St 6th Fl *Web:* www.jcciny.org	New York	NY	10019	212-246-8001	246-8002
Japanese Chamber of Commerce of Northern California 1875 S Grant St Suite 760 *Web:* www.jccnc.org	San Mateo	CA	94402	650-522-8500	522-8300
Korean Chamber of Commerce 3440 Wilshire Blvd Suite 520	Los Angeles	CA	90010	213-480-1115	480-7521
Korean Chamber of Commerce & Industry in the USA Inc 460 Park Ave Suite 410 *Web:* www.kocham.org	New York	NY	10022	212-644-0140	644-9106
Latin Chamber of Commerce of the US (CAMACOL) 1417 W Flagler St *Web:* www.camacol.org	Miami	FL	33135	305-642-3870	642-0653
Luxembourg-American Chamber of Commerce 17 Beekman Pl *Web:* www.luxembourgbusiness.org	New York	NY	10022	212-888-6701	935-5896
National US-Arab Chamber of Commerce 8921 S Sepulveda Blvd Suite 206 *Web:* www.nusacc.org	Los Angeles	CA	90045	310-646-1499	646-2462
National US-Arab Chamber of Commerce 1023 15th St NW Suite 400 *Web:* www.nusacc.org	Washington	DC	20005	202-289-5920	289-5938
National US-Arab Chamber of Commerce 420 Lexington Ave Suite 2034 *Web:* www.nusacc.org	New York	NY	10170	212-986-8024	986-0216
National US-Arab Chamber of Commerce 1330 Post Oak Blvd Suite 1600 *Web:* www.nusacc.org	Houston	TX	77056	713-963-4620	963-4609
Netherlands Chamber of Commerce in the US Inc 267 5th Ave Suite 301 *Web:* www.netherlands.org	New York	NY	10016	212-265-6460	265-6402
Nicaraguan-American Chamber of Commerce 16161 SW 144th Terrace *Web:* www.naccflorida.com	Miami	FL	33196	305-599-2737	969-4509
North American-Chilean Chamber of Commerce 30 Vesey St Suite 506	New York	NY	10007	212-233-7776	233-7779
Norwegian-American Chamber of Commerce Inc 835 3rd Ave 38th Fl *Web:* www.nacc.no	New York	NY	10022	212-421-1655	838-0374
Norwegian-American Chamber of Commerce Northern California Chapter 20 California St 6th Fl *Web:* www.nacc.no/sanfrancisco	San Francisco	CA	94111	415-986-0770	986-7875
Norwegian-American Chamber of Commerce Southern California Chapter PO Box 3251 *Web:* www.naccla.org	Thousand Oaks	CA	91359	818-735-0019	735-0032
Norwegian-American Chamber of Commerce Southwest Chapter 2777 Allen Pkwy Suite 1185 *Web:* nacchouston.org	Houston	TX	77019	713-526-6222	521-9473
Norwegian-American Chamber of Commerce Upper Midwest Chapter 821 Marquette Ave Suite 800	Minneapolis	MN	55402	612-332-3338	332-1386
Peruvian American Chamber of Commerce 9737 NW 41st St PMB 348 *Web:* www.peruvianchamber.org	Doral	FL	33178	786-221-5890	221-5834
Philippine American Chamber of Commerce Inc 317 Madison Ave Suite 520 *Web:* www.philamchamber.org	New York	NY	10017	212-972-9326	687-5844
Portugal-US Chamber of Commerce 590 5th Ave 4th Fl *Web:* portugal-us.com	New York	NY	10036	212-354-4627	575-4737
Puerto Rican Chamber of Commerce of South Florida 3550 Biscayne Blvd Suite 306 *Web:* www.puertoricanchamber.com	Miami	FL	33137	305-571-8006	571-8007
Representative of German Industry & Trade 1627 'I' St NW Suite 550 *Web:* www.rgit-usa.com	Washington	DC	20006	202-659-4777	659-4779
Russian-American Chamber of Commerce 1552 Pennsylvania St *Web:* www.russianamericanchamber.org	Denver	CO	80203	303-831-0829	831-0830
Spain-US Chamber of Commerce 350 5th Ave Suite 2600 *Web:* www.spainuscc.org	New York	NY	10118	212-967-2170	564-1415
Swedish-American Chamber of Commerce Atlanta Inc 4775 Peachtree Industrial Blvd Bldg 300 Suite 300 *Web:* sacc-atlanta.org	Norcross	GA	30092	770-670-2480	670-2500
Swedish-American Chamber of Commerce in Colorado 4525 S Decatour St *Web:* sacc-usa.org/colorado	Englewood	CO	80110	720-338-2381	889-2606
Swedish-American Chamber of Commerce of Greater Los Angeles Inc 10940 Wilshire Blvd Suite 700 *Web:* www.sacc-gla.org	Los Angeles	CA	90024	310-478-8613	444-0424
Swedish-American Chamber of Commerce Inc Chicago Chapter 150 N Michigan Ave Suite 2800" *Web:* www.sacc-usa.org/chicago	Chicago	IL	60601	312-863-8592	624-7701
Swedish-American Chamber of Commerce Inc Minnesota Chapter American Swedish Institute 2600 Park Ave *Web:* www.sacc-minnesota.org	Minneapolis	MN	55407	612-991-3001	333-3914
Swedish-American Chamber of Commerce Inc New England Chapter 49 Walnut St Bldg 4 *Web:* www.sacc-ne.org	Wellesley	MA	02481	781-239-3555	239-3555
Swedish-American Chamber of Commerce Inc New York Chapter 570 Lexington Ave 20th Fl *Web:* www.saccny.org	New York	NY	10022	212-838-5530	755-7953
Swedish-American Chamber of Commerce Inc San Francisco Chapter 564 Market St Suite 305 *Web:* www.sacc-usa.org/sf	San Francisco	CA	94104	415-781-4188	781-4189
Swedish-American Chamber of Commerce Inc Washington DC Chapter 1501 M St NW 9th Fl *Web:* sacc-usa.org	Washington	DC	20005	202-467-2638	467-2688
Swedish-American Chamber of Commerce San Diego/Tijuana Chapter 1020 Symphony Towers 750 B St *Web:* www.sacc-sandiego.org	San Diego	CA	92101	619-338-4020	233-9890
Swedish-American Chambers of Commerce USA Inc 1403 King St *Web:* www.sacc-usa.org	Alexandria	VA	22314	703-836-6560	836-6561
Swiss-American Chamber of Commerce 500 5th Ave Rm 1800 *Web:* www.amcham.ch	New York	NY	10110	212-246-7789	246-1366
US-Angola Chamber of Commerce 1100 Connecticut Ave NW Suite 1000 *Web:* www.us-angola.org	Washington	DC	20036	202-223-0540	223-0551
US-Austrian Chamber of Commerce 165 W 46th St *Web:* www.usatchamber.com	New York	NY	10036	212-819-0117	819-0345
US Federation of Philippine American Chambers of Commerce Inc 2887 College Ave Suite 1 Box 106 *Web:* www.fpacc.com	Berkeley	CA	94705	510-548-7952	845-9901
US-Mexico Chamber of Commerce 1300 Pennsylvania Ave NW Suite 0003 *Web:* www.usmcoc.org	Washington	DC	20004	202-312-1520	312-1530
US-Mexico Chamber of Commerce California Pacific Chapter 2450 Colorado Ave Suite 400E *Web:* www.usmcocca.org	Santa Monica	CA	90404	310-586-7901	586-7800
US-Mexico Chamber of Commerce Inter-American Chapter 7001 SW 97th Ave *Web:* www.usmcoc.org	Miami	FL	33173	305-275-1536	275-1480
USA-China Chamber of Commerce 55 W Monroe St Suite 630 *Web:* www.usccc.org	Chicago	IL	60603	312-368-9030	368-9922
Venezuelan-American Chamber of Commerce of the US 2332 Galiano St 2nd Fl *Web:* venezuelanchamber.org	Coral Gables	FL	33134	305-728-7042	728-7043
Vietnamese-American Chamber of Commerce of Hawaii PO Box 2011 *Web:* www.vacch.org	Honolulu	HI	96805	808-545-1889	734-2315

139 CHAMBERS OF COMMERCE - US - LOCAL

SEE ALSO Associations & Organizations - General - Civic & Political Organizations p. 1298

Chambers listed here represent areas with a population of 25,000 or more. Listings are organized by states and then are alphabetized within each state grouping according to the name of the city in which each chamber is located.

Alabama

	City	ST	ZIP	Phone	Fax
Alexander City-Lake Martin Area Chamber of Commerce PO Box 926 *Web:* www.alexandercity.org	Alexander City	AL	35011	256-234-3461	234-0094
Calhoun County Chamber of Commerce 1330 Quintard Ave *TF:* 800-489-1087 ■ *Web:* www.calhounchamber.com	Anniston	AL	36201	256-237-3536	337-0126
Athens-Limestone County Chamber of Commerce PO Box 150 *Web:* www.tourathens.com	Athens	AL	35612	256-232-2600	232-2609
Auburn Chamber of Commerce PO Box 1370 *Web:* www.auburnchamber.com	Auburn	AL	36831	334-887-7011	821-5500
North Baldwin Chamber of Commerce 301 McMeans Ave *Web:* www.northbaldwinchamber.com	Bay Minette	AL	36507	251-937-5665	937-5670
Bessemer Area Chamber of Commerce 321 N 18th St *TF:* 888-423-7736 ■ *Web:* www.bessemerchamber.com	Bessemer	AL	35020	205-425-3253	425-4979
Birmingham Regional Chamber of Commerce 505 N 20th St Suite 200 *Web:* www.birminghamchamber.com	Birmingham	AL	35203	205-324-2100	324-2560
Chilton County Chamber of Commerce 500 5th Ave N *TF:* 800-553-0493 ■ *Web:* www.chiltoncountychamber.com	Clanton	AL	35045	205-755-2400	755-8444
Cullman Area Chamber of Commerce 301 2nd Ave SW *TF:* 800-313-5114 ■ *Web:* www.cullmanchamber.org	Cullman	AL	35056	256-734-0454	737-7443
Eastern Shore Chamber of Commerce 29750 Larry Dee Cawyer Dr. *Web:* www.eschamber.com	Daphne	AL	36521	251-621-8222	621-8001
Decatur-Morgan County Chamber of Commerce 515 6th Ave NE *TF:* 800-353-0005 ■ *Web:* www.dcc.org	Decatur	AL	35601	256-353-5312	353-2384
Dothan Area Chamber of Commerce 102 Jamestown Blvd *TF:* 800-221-1027 ■ *Web:* www.dothan.com	Dothan	AL	36301	334-792-5138	794-4796
Eufaula/Barbour County Chamber of Commerce 333 E Broad St *TF:* 800-524-7529 ■ *Web:* www.eufaula-barbourchamber.com	Eufaula	AL	36027	334-687-6664	687-5240
Shoals Chamber of Commerce 20 Hightower Pl *TF:* 877-764-4661 ■ *Web:* www.shoalschamber.com	Florence	AL	35630	256-764-4661	766-9017

Phone | Fax

South Baldwin Chamber of Commerce 104 N McKenzie St. Foley AL 36535 251-943-3291 943-6810
Web: www.southbaldwinchamber.com
Chamber - Gadsden & Etowah County PO Box 185 Gadsden AL 35902 256-543-3472 543-9887
TF: 800-238-6924 ■ *Web:* www.gadsdenchamber.com
Greenville Area Chamber of Commerce 1 Depot Sq Greenville AL 36037 334-382-3251 382-3181
TF: 800-959-0717
Hoover Chamber of Commerce PO Box 36005 Hoover AL 35236 205-988-5672 988-8383
Web: www.hooverchamber.org
Chamber of Commerce of Huntsville/Madison County
PO Box 408 Huntsville AL 35804 256-535-2000 535-2015
Web: www.huntsvillealabamausa.com
Walker County Chamber of Commerce 204 19th St E Suite 101 Jasper AL 35501 205-384-4571 384-4901
TF: 888-384-4571 ■ *Web:* www.walkerchamber.us
Greater Valley Area Chamber of Commerce PO Box 205 Lanett AL 36863 334-642-1411 642-1410
Web: www.greatervalleyarea.com
Mobile Area Chamber of Commerce 451 Government St Mobile AL 36602 251-433-6951 432-1143
TF: 800-422-6951 ■ *Web:* www.mobilechamber.com
Monroeville Area Chamber of Commerce
63 N Mt Pleasant Ave Monroeville AL 36460 251-743-2879 743-2189
Web: www.monroecountyal.com
Montgomery Area Chamber of Commerce
41 Commerce St Box 79 Montgomery AL 36101 334-834-5200 265-4745
Web: www.montgomerychamber.com
Lawrence County Chamber of Commerce 12001 AL Hwy 157 Moulton AL 35650 256-974-1658 974-2400
Web: www.lawrencealabama.com
Blount County-Oneonta Chamber of Commerce
227 2nd Ave E PO Box 1487 Oneonta AL 35121 205-274-2153 274-2099
Web: www.blountoneontachamber.org
Ozark Area Chamber of Commerce 294 Painter Ave Ozark AL 36360 334-774-9321 774-8736
TF: 800-582-8497 ■ *Web:* www.ozarkareacoc.com
Greater Shelby County Chamber of Commerce PO Box 324 Pelham AL 35124 205-663-4542 663-4524
Web: www.shelbychamber.org
Phenix City-Russell County Chamber of Commerce
1107 Broad St Phenix City AL 36867 334-298-3639 298-3846
TF: 800-892-2248 ■ *Web:* www.pc-rcchamber.com
Franklin County Chamber of Commerce 103 N Jackson AVe Russellville AL 35653 256-332-1760 332-1740
Web: www.franklincountychamber.org
Greater Jackson County Chamber of Commerce
PO Box 973 Scottsboro AL 35768 256-259-5500 259-4447
TF: 800-259-5508 ■ *Web:* www.jacksoncountychamber.com
Selma-Dallas County Chamber of Commerce 912 Selma Ave Selma AL 36701 334-875-7241 875-7142
TF: 800-457-3562 ■ *Web:* www.selmaalabama.com
Greater Talladega Area Chamber of Commerce 210 East St S Talladega AL 35160 256-362-9075 362-9093
Web: www.talladegachamber.com
Pike County Chamber of Commerce 300 US Hwy 231 N Troy AL 36079 334-566-2294 566-2298
Web: www.pikecountychamber.com
Chamber of Commerce of West Alabama PO Box 020410 Tuscaloosa AL 35402 205-758-7588 391-0565
Web: www.tuscaloosachamber.com

Alaska

Phone | Fax

Anchorage Chamber of Commerce
1016 W 6th Ave Suite 303 Anchorage AK 99501 907-272-2401 272-4117
Web: www.anchoragechamber.org
Chugiak-Eagle River Chamber of Commerce
11401 Old Glenn Hwy Suite 105 Eagle River AK 99577 907-694-4702 694-1205
Web: www.cer.org
Fairbanks Chamber of Commerce 800 Cushman St Suite 114 Fairbanks AK 99701 907-452-1105 456-6968
Web: www.fairbankschamber.org
Juneau Chamber of Commerce 3100 Channel Dr Suite 300 Juneau AK 99801 907-463-3488 463-3489
Web: www.juneauchamber.com

Arizona

Phone | Fax

Apache Junction Chamber of Commerce
567 W Apache Trail Apache Junction AZ 85220 480-982-3141 982-3234
TF: 800-252-3141 ■ *Web:* www.apachejunctioncoc.com
Bullhead Area Chamber of Commerce 1251 Hwy 95 Bullhead City AZ 86429 928-754-4121 754-5514
TF: 800-987-7457 ■ *Web:* www.bullheadchamber.com
Chandler Chamber of Commerce 25 S Arizona Pl Suite 201 Chandler AZ 85225 480-963-4571 963-0188
TF: 800-963-4571 ■ *Web:* www.chandlerchamber.com
Cottonwood Chamber of Commerce 1010 S Main St Cottonwood AZ 86326 928-634-7593 634-7594
Web: cottonwood.verdevalley.com
Flagstaff Chamber of Commerce 101 W Rt 66 Flagstaff AZ 86001 928-774-4505 779-1209
Web: www.flagstaffchamber.com
Gilbert Chamber of Commerce 118 N Gilbert Rd Suite 101 Gilbert AZ 85234 480-892-0056 250-5735*
*Fax Area Code: 602 ■ *Web:* www.gilbertaz.com
Glendale Chamber of Commerce PO Box 249 Glendale AZ 85311 623-937-4754 937-3333
TF: 800-437-8669 ■ *Web:* www.glendaleazchamber.org
Southwest Valley Chamber of Commerce 289 N Litchfield Rd Goodyear AZ 85338 623-932-2260 932-9057
Web: www.southwestvalleychamber.org
Kingman Area Chamber of Commerce
120 W Andy Devine Ave Kingman AZ 86401 928-753-6253 753-1049
Web: www.kingmanchamber.org
Lake Havasu Area Chamber of Commerce
314 London Bridge Rd Lake Havasu City AZ 86403 928-855-4115 680-0010
Web: www.havasuchamber.com
Mesa Chamber of Commerce 120 N Center St Mesa AZ 85201 480-969-1307 827-0727
Web: www.mesachamber.org
Nogales Chamber of Commerce 123 W Kino Park Nogales AZ 85621 520-287-3685 287-3688
Web: www.nogaleschamber.com
Rim Country Regional Chamber of Commerce 100 W Main St Payson AZ 85547 928-474-4515 474-8812
TF: 800-672-9766 ■ *Web:* www.rimcountrychamber.com
Peoria Chamber of Commerce 10601 N 83rd Dr Peoria AZ 85345 623-979-3601 486-4729
TF: 800-580-2645 ■ *Web:* www.peoriachamber.com
Greater Phoenix Chamber of Commerce
201 N Central Ave Suite 2700 Phoenix AZ 85073 602-254-5521 495-8913
Web: www.phoenixchamber.com
North Phoenix Chamber of Commerce PO Box 7225 Phoenix AZ 85050 602-482-3344 482-2261
Web: www.northphoenixchamber.com
Prescott Chamber of Commerce 117 W Goodwin St Prescott AZ 86303 928-445-2000 445-0068
TF: 800-266-7534 ■ *Web:* www.prescott.org
Prescott Valley Chamber of Commerce
3001 N Main St Suite 2A Prescott Valley AZ 86314 928-772-8857 772-4267
Web: www.pvchamber.org
Graham County Chamber of Commerce 1111 Thatcher Blvd Safford AZ 85546 928-428-2511 428-0744
TF: 888-837-1841 ■ *Web:* www.graham-chamber.com
Scottsdale Area Chamber of Commerce
7343 Scottsdale Mall Scottsdale AZ 85251 480-945-8481 947-4523
Web: www.scottsdalechamber.com
Greater Sierra Vista Area Chamber of Commerce
21 E Wilcox Dr Sierra Vista AZ 85635 520-458-6940 452-0878
Web: www.sierravistachamber.org

Phone | Fax

Northwest Valley Chamber of Commerce
12801 W Bell Rd Suite 14 Surprise AZ 85374 623-583-0692 583-0694
Web: www.northwestvalley.com
Tempe Chamber of Commerce PO Box 28500 Tempe AZ 85285 480-967-7891 966-5365
Web: www.tempechamber.org
Tucson Metropolitan Chamber of Commerce
465 W St Mary's Rd Tucson AZ 85701 520-792-2250 882-5704
Web: www.tucsonchamber.org
Yuma County Chamber of Commerce 180 W 1st St Suite A Yuma AZ 85364 928-782-2567 343-0038
Web: www.yumachamber.org

Arkansas

Phone | Fax

Bentonville/Bella Vista Chamber of Commerce
412 S Main St Bentonville AR 72712 479-273-2841 273-2180
Web: www.bentonvillebellavistachamber.com
Berryville Chamber of Commerce PO Box 402 Berryville AR 72616 870-423-3704
Web: www.berryvillear.com
Conway Area Chamber of Commerce 900 Oak St Conway AR 72032 501-327-7788 327-7790
Web: www.conwayarkcc.org
El Dorado Chamber of Commerce 111 W Main St El Dorado AR 71730 870-863-6113 863-6115
Web: www.boomtown.org/chamber.aspx
Fayetteville Chamber of Commerce 123 W Mountain St Fayetteville AR 72701 479-521-1710 521-1791
Web: www.fayettevillear.com
Fort Smith Chamber of Commerce 612 Garrison Ave Fort Smith AR 72901 479-783-6118 783-6110
Web: www.fschamber.com
Phillips County Chamber of Commerce
111 Hickory Hill Dr PO Box 447 Helena AR 72342 870-338-8327 338-8882
Web: www.phillipscountychamber.com
Greater Hot Springs Chamber of Commerce
659 Ouachita Ave Hot Springs AR 71901 501-321-1700 321-3551
TF: 800-467-4636 ■ *Web:* www.hotspringschamber.com
Jacksonville Chamber of Commerce 200 Dupree Dr Jacksonville AR 72076 501-982-1511 982-1464
Web: www.jacksonville-arkansas.com
Jonesboro Regional Chamber of Commerce
1709 E Nettleton St Jonesboro AR 72401 870-932-6691 933-5758
Web: www.jonesborochamber.org
Little Rock Regional Chamber of Commerce
1 Chamber Plaza Little Rock AR 72201 501-374-2001 374-6018
Web: www.littlerockchamber.com
Magnolia-Columbia County Chamber of Commerce
621 E North St Magnolia AR 71753 870-234-4352 234-7937
Web: www.magnoliachamber.com
Mountain Home Area Chamber of Commerce
1023 Hwy 62 E Mountain Home AR 72653 870-425-5111 425-4446
TF: 800-822-3536 ■ *Web:* www.enjoymountainhome.com
North Little Rock Chamber of Commerce 100 Main St North Little Rock AR 72114 501-372-5959 372-5955
Web: www.nlrchamber.org
Paragould Regional Chamber of Commerce 300 W Court St Paragould AR 72450 870-236-7684 236-1517
Web: www.paragould.org
Greater Pine Bluff Chamber of Commerce 510 S Main St Pine Bluff AR 71601 870-535-0110 535-1643
Web: www.pinebluffchamber.com
Rogers-Lowell Area Chamber of Commerce 317 W Walnut St Rogers AR 72756 479-636-1240 636-5485
TF: 800-364-1240 ■ *Web:* www.rogerslowell.com
Russellville Chamber of Commerce 708 W Main St Russellville AR 72801 479-968-2530 968-5894
Web: www.russellvillechamber.org
Springdale Chamber of Commerce 202 W Emma Springdale AR 72765 479-872-2222 751-4699
TF: 800-972-7261 ■ *Web:* www.springdale.com
West Memphis Chamber of Commerce 108 W Broadway West Memphis AR 72301 870-735-1134 735-6283
Web: www.wmcoc.com

California

Phone | Fax

Alameda Chamber of Commerce 1416 Park Ave Alameda CA 94501 510-522-0414 522-7677
Web: www.alamedachamber.com
Alhambra Chamber of Commerce 104 S 1st St Alhambra CA 91801 626-282-8481 282-5596
Web: www.alhambrachamber.org
Altadena Chamber of Commerce 730 E Altadena Dr Altadena CA 91001 626-794-3988 794-6015
Web: www.abacus-es.com/altadena
Anaheim Chamber of Commerce 201 E Center St Anaheim CA 92805 714-758-0222 758-0468
Web: anaheimchamber.org
Calaveras County Chamber of Commerce PO Box 1145 Angels Camp CA 95222 209-736-2580 736-2576
Web: www.chamber@calaveras.org
Antioch Chamber of Commerce 324 G St Antioch CA 94509 925-757-1800 757-5286
Web: www.antiochchamber.com
Apple Valley Chamber of Commerce
16010 Apple Valley Rd Apple Valley CA 92307 760-242-2753 242-0303
Web: www.avchamber.org
Aptos Chamber of Commerce 7605-A Old Dominion Ct Aptos CA 95003 831-688-1467 688-6961
Web: www.aptoschamber.com
Arcadia Chamber of Commerce 388 W Huntington Dr Arcadia CA 91007 626-447-2159 445-0273
Web: www.arcadiachamber.com
Atascadero Chamber of Commerce 6550 El Camino Real Atascadero CA 93422 805-466-2044 466-9218
TF: 800-756-5592 ■ *Web:* www.atascaderochamber.org
Atwater Chamber of Commerce 1181 3rd St Atwater CA 95301 209-358-4251 358-0934
Web: www.atwater-chamber.com
Auburn Area Chamber of Commerce 601 Lincoln Way Auburn CA 95603 530-885-5616 885-5854
Web: www.auburnchamber.net
Azusa Chamber of Commerce 240 W Foothill Blvd Azusa CA 91702 626-334-1507 334-5217
Web: www.azusachamber.org
Greater Bakersfield Chamber of Commerce 1725 Eye St Bakersfield CA 93301 661-327-4421 327-8751
Web: www.bakersfieldchamber.org
Kern County Board of Trade 2101 Oak St Bakersfield CA 93301 661-868-5376 868-5376
TF: 800-500-5376 ■ *Web:* www.visitkern.com
Baldwin Park Chamber of Commerce 14327 Ramona Blvd Baldwin Park CA 91706 626-960-4848 960-2990
Web: www.bpchamber.com
Beaumont Chamber of Commerce 726 Beaumont Ave Beaumont CA 92223 951-845-9541 769-9080
Web: www.beaumontcachamber.com
Bell Chamber of Commerce 4401 E Gage Ave PO Box 294 Bell CA 90201 323-560-8755 560-2060
Bell Gardens Chamber 6006 Shull St Bell Gardens CA 90201 562-806-2355 806-1585
Web: www.bellgardenschamber.org
Bellflower Chamber of Commerce 16730 Bellflower Blvd Bellflower CA 90706 562-867-1744 866-7545
Belmont Chamber of Commerce 1625 El Camino Real Suite 2 Belmont CA 94002 650-595-8696 595-8731
Web: www.belmontchamber.org
Benicia Chamber of Commerce 601 1st St Suite 100 Benicia CA 94510 707-745-2120 745-2275
Web: www.beniciachamber.com
Berkeley Chamber of Commerce 1834 University Ave Berkeley CA 94703 510-549-7000
Web: www.berkeleychamber.com
Beverly Hills Chamber of Commerce 239 S Beverly Dr Beverly Hills CA 90212 310-248-1000 248-1020
TF: 800-345-2210 ■ *Web:* www.beverlyhillschamber.com
Blythe Chamber of Commerce 201 S Broadway Blythe CA 92225 760-922-8166 922-4010
Web: www.blytheareachamberofcommerce.com

California (Cont'd)

	City	State	ZIP	Phone	Fax
Brea Chamber of Commerce 1 Civic Ctr Cir	Brea	CA	92821	714-529-4938	529-6103
Web: www.breachamber.com					
Buena Park Chamber of Commerce 6601 Beach Blvd	Buena Park	CA	90621	714-521-0261	521-1851
Web: www.buenaparkchamber.org					
Burbank Chamber of Commerce 200 W Magnolia Blvd	Burbank	CA	91502	818-846-3111	846-0109
Web: www.burbankchamber.org					
Burlingame Chamber of Commerce 290 California Dr	Burlingame	CA	94010	650-344-1735	344-1763
Web: burlingamechamber.org					
Camarillo Chamber of Commerce 2400 E Ventura Blvd	Camarillo	CA	93010	805-484-4383	484-1395
Web: www.camarillochamber.org					
Campbell Chamber of Commerce 1628 W Campbell Ave	Campbell	CA	95008	408-378-6252	378-0192
Web: www.campbellchamber.com					
Canoga Park/West Hills Chamber of Commerce					
7248 Owensmouth Ave	Canoga Park	CA	91303	818-884-4222	884-4604
Web: www.cpwhchamber.com					
Carlsbad Chamber of Commerce 5934 Priestly Dr	Carlsbad	CA	92008	760-931-8400	931-9153
Web: www.carlsbad.org					
Carmichael Chamber of Commerce					
6825 Fair Oaks Blvd Suite 100	Carmichael	CA	95608	916-481-1002	481-1003
Web: www.carmichaelchamber.com					
Carson Chamber of Commerce 530 E Del Amo Blvd	Carson	CA	90746	310-217-4590	217-4591
Web: www.carsonchamber.com					
Castro Valley Chamber of Commerce					
3467 Castro Valley Blvd	Castro Valley	CA	94546	510-537-5300	537-5335
Web: www.mycastrovalley.com/chamber_of_commerce					
Cathedral City Chamber of Commerce					
68950 Hwy 115 Perez Rd Suite 6 Suite 106	Cathedral City	CA	92234	760-328-1213	321-0659
Web: www.cathedralcitycc.com					
Ceres Chamber of Commerce 2908 E Whitmore Ave Box H-213	Ceres	CA	95307	209-537-2601	537-2699
Web: www.cereschamber.org					
Cerritos Chamber of Commerce 13259 E South St	Cerritos	CA	90703	562-467-0800	467-0840
Web: www.cerritos.org					
Chatsworth Chamber of Commerce					
10038 Old Depot Plaza Rd	Chatsworth	CA	91311	818-341-2428	341-4930
Web: www.chatsworthchamber.com					
Chico Chamber of Commerce 300 Salem St	Chico	CA	95928	530-891-5556	891-3613
TF: 800-852-8570 ■ *Web:* www.chicochamber.com					
Chino Valley Chamber of Commerce 13150 7th St	Chino	CA	91710	909-627-6177	627-4180
Web: www.chinovalleychamber.com					
Chula Vista Chamber of Commerce 233 4th Ave	Chula Vista	CA	91910	619-420-6602	420-1269
Web: www.chulavistachamber.org					
Citrus Heights Chamber of Commerce					
7115-A Greenback Ln	Citrus Heights	CA	95621	916-722-4545	722-4543
Web: www.chchamber.com					
Claremont Chamber of Commerce 205 Yale Ave	Claremont	CA	91711	909-624-1681	624-6629
Web: www.claremontchamber.org					
Clovis Chamber of Commerce 325 Pollasky Ave	Clovis	CA	93612	559-299-7363	299-2969
Web: www.clovischamber.com					
Colton Chamber of Commerce 655 N La Cadena Dr	Colton	CA	92324	909-825-2222	824-1650
Web: www.coltonchamber.com					
Compton Chamber of Commerce					
310 N Willowbrook Ave Suite 4A	Compton	CA	90220	310-631-8611	631-2066
Greater Concord Chamber of Commerce					
2280 Diamond Blvd Suite 200	Concord	CA	94520	925-685-1181	685-5623
Web: www.concordchamber.com					
Corona Chamber of Commerce 904 E 6th St	Corona	CA	92879	951-737-3350	737-3531
Web: www.coronachamber.org					
Coronado Chamber of Commerce 875 Orange Ave Suite 102	Coronado	CA	92118	619-435-9260	522-6577
Web: www.coronadochamber.com					
Costa Mesa Chamber of Commerce					
1700 Adams Ave Suite 101	Costa Mesa	CA	92626	714-885-9092	885-9094
Web: www.costamesachamber.com					
Covina Chamber of Commerce 935 W Badillo St Suite 100	Covina	CA	91722	626-967-4191	966-9660
Web: www.covina.org					
Culver City Chamber of Commerce 4249 Overland Ave	Culver City	CA	90230	310-287-3850	287-1350
Web: www.culvercitychamber.com					
Cupertino Chamber of Commerce 20455 Silverado Ave	Cupertino	CA	95014	408-252-7054	252-0638
Web: www.cupertino-chamber.org					
Cypress Chamber of Commerce 5550 Cerritos Ave Suite D	Cypress	CA	90630	714-827-2430	827-1229
Web: www.cypresschamber.org					
Daly City-Colma Chamber of Commerce					
355 Gellert Blvd Suite 138	Daly City	CA	94015	650-755-3900	755-5160
Web: www.dalycity-colmachamber.org					
Dana Point Chamber of Commerce					
24681 La Plaza Suite 115	Dana Point	CA	92629	949-496-1555	496-5321
Web: www.danapoint-chamber.com					
Davis Chamber of Commerce 130 G St Suite B	Davis	CA	95616	530-756-5160	756-5190
Web: www.davischamber.com					
Del Mar Regional Chamber of Commerce					
1104 Camino Del Mar Suite 1	Del Mar	CA	92014	858-755-4844	793-5293
Web: www.delmarchamber.org					
Regional Chamber of Commerce San Gabriel Valley					
21845 E Copley Dr Suite 1170	Diamond Bar	CA	91765	909-860-1904	860-6064
Web: www.regionalchambersgv.com					
Downey Chamber of Commerce 11131 Brookshire Ave	Downey	CA	90241	562-923-2191	869-0461
Web: www.downeychamber.com					
Dublin Chamber of Commerce 7080 Donlon Way Suite 110	Dublin	CA	94568	925-828-6200	828-4247
Web: www.dublinchamberofcommerce.org					
San Diego East County Chamber of Commerce					
201 S Magnolia Ave	El Cajon	CA	92020	619-440-6161	440-6164
Web: www.eastcountychamber.org					
El Centro Chamber of Commerce & Visitors Bureau					
1095 S 4th St	El Centro	CA	92243	760-352-3681	352-3246
Web: www.elcentrochamber.org					
El Monte/South El Monte Chamber of Commerce					
10505 Valley Blvd Suite 312	El Monte	CA	91731	626-443-0180	443-0463
Web: www.emsem.com					
Elk Grove Chamber of Commerce					
9280 W Stockton Blvd Suite 104	Elk Grove	CA	95758	916-691-3760	691-3810
Web: www.elkgroveca.com					
Encinitas Chamber of Commerce 138 Encinitas Blvd	Encinitas	CA	92024	760-753-6041	753-6270
TF: 800-953-6041 ■ *Web:* www.encinitaschamber.com					
Encino Chamber of Commerce 4933 Balboa Blvd	Encino	CA	91316	818-789-4711	789-2485
Web: www.encinochamber.org					
Escondido Chamber of Commerce 720 N Broadway	Escondido	CA	92025	760-745-2125	745-1183
Web: www.escondidochamber.org					
Greater Eureka Chamber of Commerce 2112 Broadway	Eureka	CA	95501	707-442-3738	442-0079
TF: 800-356-6381 ■ *Web:* www.eurekachamber.com					
Fair Oaks Chamber of Commerce					
10224 Fair Oaks Blvd PO Box 352	Fair Oaks	CA	95628	916-967-2903	967-8536
Web: www.fairoakschamber.com					
Fairfield-Suisun Chamber of Commerce 1111 Webster St	Fairfield	CA	94533	707-425-4625	425-0826
Web: www.ffsc-chamber.com					
Fallbrook Chamber of Commerce 233 E Mission Rd	Fallbrook	CA	92028	760-728-5845	728-4031
Web: www.fallbrookca.org					
Folsom Chamber of Commerce 200 Wool St	Folsom	CA	95630	916-985-2698	985-4117
Web: www.folsomchamber.com					
Fontana Chamber of Commerce 8491 Sierra Ave	Fontana	CA	92335	909-822-4433	822-6238
Web: www.fontanachamber.com					
Mendocino Coast Chamber of Commerce					
332 N Main St PO Box 1141	Fort Bragg	CA	95437	707-961-6300	964-2056
TF: 800-726-2780 ■ *Web:* www.mendocinocoast.com					
Foster City Chamber of Commerce					
1031 E Hillsdale Blvd Suite F	Foster City	CA	94404	650-573-7600	573-5201
Web: www.fostercitychamber.com					
Fountain Valley Chamber of Commerce					
11100 Warner Ave Suite 204	Fountain Valley	CA	92708	714-668-0542	668-9164
Web: www.fvchamber.com					
Fremont Chamber of Commerce 39488 Stevenson Pl Suite 100	Fremont	CA	94539	510-795-2244	795-2240
Web: www.fremontbusiness.com					
Fresno Chamber of Commerce 2331 Fresno St	Fresno	CA	93721	559-495-4800	495-4811
Web: www.fresnochamber.com					
Fullerton Chamber of Commerce 444 N Harbor Blvd Suite 200	Fullerton	CA	92832	714-871-3100	871-2871
Web: www.fullertonchamber.com					
Garden Grove Chamber of Commerce					
12866 Main St Suite 102	Garden Grove	CA	92840	714-638-7950	636-6672
TF: 800-959-5560 ■ *Web:* www.gardengrovechamber.org					
Gardena Valley Chamber of Commerce					
1204 W Gardena Blvd Suite E	Gardena	CA	90247	310-532-9905	329-7307
Web: www.gardenachamber.com					
Gilroy Chamber of Commerce 7471 Monterey St	Gilroy	CA	95020	408-842-6437	842-6010
Web: www.gilroy.org					
Glendale Chamber of Commerce 200 S Louise St	Glendale	CA	91205	818-240-7870	240-2872
Web: www.glendalechamber.com					
Glendora Chamber of Commerce 131 E Foothill Blvd	Glendora	CA	91741	626-963-4128	914-4822
Web: www.glendora-chamber.org					
Goleta Valley Chamber of Commerce					
271 N Fairview Ave Suite 104	Goleta	CA	93117	805-967-2500	967-4615
TF: 800-646-5382 ■ *Web:* www.goletavalley.com					
Granada Hills Chamber of Commerce 17723 Chatworth St	Granada Hills	CA	91344	818-368-3235	366-7425
Web: www.granadachamber.com					
Hanford Chamber of Commerce 200 Santa Fe Ave Suite D	Hanford	CA	93230	559-582-0483	582-0960
Web: www.hanfordchamber.com					
Hawthorne Chamber of Commerce 4444 S El Segundo Blvd	Hawthorne	CA	90250	310-676-1163	676-7661
Web: www.hawthorne-chamber.com					
Hayward Chamber of Commerce 22561 Main St	Hayward	CA	94541	510-537-2424	537-2730
Web: www.hayward.org					
Hemet Jacinto Valley Chamber of Commerce					
615 N San Jacinto St	Hemet	CA	92543	951-658-3211	766-5013
TF: 800-334-9344 ■ *Web:* hemetsanjacintochamber.com					
Hesperia Chamber of Commerce 16816 Main St Suite D	Hesperia	CA	92345	760-244-2135	244-1333
Web: www.hesperiachamber.org					
Highland Chamber of Commerce 7750 Palm Ave Suite N	Highland	CA	92346	909-864-4073	864-4583
Web: www.highlandchamber.org					
San Benito County Chamber of Commerce					
650 San Benito St Suite 130	Hollister	CA	95023	831-637-5315	637-1008
Web: www.sanbenitocountychamber.com					
Hollywood Chamber of Commerce 7018 Hollywood Blvd	Hollywood	CA	90028	323-469-8311	469-2805
Web: www.hollywoodchamber.net					
Huntington Beach Chamber of Commerce					
19891 Beach Blvd Suite 140	Huntington Beach	CA	92648	714-536-8888	960-7654
Web: www.hbchamber.org					
Greater Huntington Park Area Chamber of Commerce					
6330 Pacific Blvd Suite 208	Huntington Park	CA	90255	323-585-1155	585-2176
Web: www.hpchamber1.com					
Imperial Beach Chamber of Commerce & Visitors Bureau					
702 Seacoast Dr	Imperial Beach	CA	91932	619-424-3151	424-3008
Web: www.ib-chamber.com					
Indio Chamber of Commerce 82921 Indio Blvd	Indio	CA	92201	760-347-0676	347-6069
TF: 800-775-8440 ■ *Web:* www.indiochamber.org					
Inglewood Chamber of Commerce 330 E Queen St	Inglewood	CA	90301	310-677-1121	677-1001
Web: www.inglewoodchamber.com					
Irvine Chamber of Commerce 2485 McCabe Way Suite 150	Irvine	CA	92614	949-660-9112	660-0829
TF: 800-558-4262 ■ *Web:* www.irvinechamber.com					
Orange County Business Council 2 Park Plaza Suite 100	Irvine	CA	92614	949-476-2242	476-9240
Web: www.ocbc.org					
Amador County Chamber of Commerce PO Box 596	Jackson	CA	95642	209-223-0350	223-4425
TF: 800-649-4988 ■ *Web:* www.amadorcountychamber.com					
Crescenta Valley Chamber of Commerce					
3131 Foothill Blvd Suite D	La Crescenta	CA	91214	818-248-4957	248-9625
Web: www.lacrescenta.org					
La Habra Area Chamber of Commerce 321 E La Habra Blvd	La Habra	CA	90631	562-697-1704	697-8359
Web: www.lahabrachamber.com					
La Jolla Town Council PO Box 1101	La Jolla	CA	92038	858-454-1444	454-1848
Web: www.lajollatowncouncil.com					
La Mirada Chamber of Commerce 11900 La Mirada Blvd	La Mirada	CA	90638	562-902-1970	902-1218
Web: lmchamber.org					
La Verne Chamber of Commerce 2078 Bonita Ave	La Verne	CA	91750	909-593-5265	596-0579
Web: www.lavernechamber.org					
Laguna Beach Chamber of Commerce 357 Glenneyre	Laguna Beach	CA	92651	949-494-1018	376-8916
Web: www.lagunabeachchamber.org					
Laguna Niguel Chamber of Commerce					
30011 Ivy Glenn Dr Suite 125	Laguna Niguel	CA	92677	949-363-0136	363-9026
Web: www.lagunaniguelchamber.net					
Lake Elsinore Valley Chamber of Commerce					
132 W Graham Ave	Lake Elsinore	CA	92530	951-245-8848	245-9127
Web: www.lakeelsinorechamber.com					
Lakeport Regional Chamber of Commerce					
875 Lakeport Blvd PO Box 295	Lakeport	CA	95453	707-263-5092	263-5104
TF: 866-525-3767 ■ *Web:* www.lakeportchamber.com					
Lakeside Chamber of Commerce 9924 Vine St	Lakeside	CA	92040	619-561-1031	561-7951
Web: www.lakesideca.com					
Lakewood Chamber of Commerce PO Box 160	Lakewood	CA	90714	562-920-2120	920-9191
Web: www.lakewoodchamber.com					
Antelope Valley Board of Trade					
548 W Lancaster Blvd Suite 103	Lancaster	CA	93534	661-942-9581	723-9279
Web: www.avbot.org					
Antelope Valley Chambers of Commerce					
554 W Lancaster Blvd	Lancaster	CA	93534	661-948-4518	949-1212
Web: www.avchambers.com					
South Orange County Regional Chambers of Commerce					
26111 Antonio Pkwy Suite 400	Las Flores	CA	92688	949-635-5800	635-1635
Web: www.socchambers.com					
Lemon Grove Chamber of Commerce 3443 Main St	Lemon Grove	CA	91945	619-469-9621	469-0035
Web: www.lemongrovechamber.com					
Livermore Chamber of Commerce 2157 1st St	Livermore	CA	94550	925-447-1606	447-1641
Web: www.livermorechamber.org					
Lodi District Chamber of Commerce 35 S School St	Lodi	CA	95240	209-367-7840	334-0528
Web: www.lodichamber.com					

	City	State	Zip	Phone	Fax
Lompoc Valley Chamber of Commerce & Visitors Bureau PO Box 626	Lompoc	CA	93438	805-736-4567	737-0453
TF: 800-240-0999 ■ *Web:* www.lompoc.com					
Long Beach Area Chamber of Commerce 1 World Trade Center Suite 206	Long Beach	CA	90831	562-436-1251	436-7099
Web: www.lbchamber.com					
Los Altos Chamber of Commerce 321 University Ave	Los Altos	CA	94022	650-948-1455	948-6238
Web: www.losaltoschamber.org					
Century City Chamber of Commerce 2029 Century Park E Concourse Level	Los Angeles	CA	90067	310-553-2222	553-4623
Web: www.centurycitycc.com					
Eagle Rock Chamber of Commerce 4771 Eagle Rock Blvd PO Box 41354	Los Angeles	CA	90041	323-257-2197	255-5466
Web: www.eaglerockchamberofcommerce.com					
East Los Angeles Chamber of Commerce PO Box 63220	Los Angeles	CA	90063	323-722-2005	722-2405
Lincoln Heights Chamber of Commerce 2716 N Broadway Suite 210	Los Angeles	CA	90031	323-221-6571	221-1513
Los Angeles Area Chamber of Commerce 350 S Bixel St	Los Angeles	CA	90017	213-580-7500	580-7511
Web: www.lachamber.org					
Westchester/LAX- Marina del Rey Chamber of Commerce 9100 S Sepulveda Blvd Suite 210	Los Angeles	CA	90045	310-645-5151	645-0130
Web: www.wlaxmdrchamber.com					
Los Gatos Chamber of Commerce 349 N Santa Cruz Ave	Los Gatos	CA	95030	408-354-9300	399-1594
Web: www.losgatosweb.com					
Lynwood Chamber of Commerce 3651 E Imperial Hwy	Lynwood	CA	90262	310-537-6484	537-8143
Web: www.lynwoodchamber.org					
Madera District Chamber of Commerce 120 N 'E' St	Madera	CA	93638	559-673-3563	673-5009*
**Fax:* Acctg ■ *Web:* www.maderachamber.com					
Malibu Chamber of Commerce 23805 Stuart Ranch Rd Suite 100	Malibu	CA	90265	310-456-9025	456-0195
Web: www.malibu.org					
Manhattan Beach Chamber of Commerce 425 15th St	Manhattan Beach	CA	90266	310-545-5313	545-7203
Web: www.manhattanbeachchamber.net					
Manteca Chamber of Commerce 107 N Lincoln Ave	Manteca	CA	95336	209-823-6121	823-9959
Web: www.manteca.org					
Marina Chamber of Commerce PO Box 425	Marina	CA	93933	831-384-9155	883-9077
Web: www.marinachamber.com					
Martinez Area Chamber of Commerce 603 Marina Vista	Martinez	CA	94553	925-228-2345	228-2356
Web: www.martinezchamber.com					
Yuba-Sutter Chamber of Commerce 429 10th St	Marysville	CA	95901	530-743-6501	741-8645
Web: www.yubasutterchamber.com					
Menlo Park Chamber of Commerce 1100 Merrill St	Menlo Park	CA	94025	650-325-2818	325-0920
Web: www.menloparkchamber.com					
Greater Merced Chamber of Commerce 690 W 16th St	Merced	CA	95340	209-384-7092	384-8472
Web: www.merced-chamber.com					
Merced County Chamber of Commerce 646 S Hwy 59 PO Box 1112	Merced	CA	95341	209-722-3864	722-2406
Web: www.mercedcountychamber.com					
Milpitas Chamber of Commerce 828 N Hillview Dr	Milpitas	CA	95035	408-262-2613	262-2823
Web: www.milpitas-chamber.com					
Modesto Chamber of Commerce PO Box 844	Modesto	CA	95353	209-577-5757	577-2673
Web: www.modchamber.org					
Monrovia Chamber of Commerce 620 S Myrtle Ave	Monrovia	CA	91016	626-358-1159	357-6036
Web: www.monroviacc.com					
Montclair Chamber of Commerce 5220 Benito St	Montclair	CA	91763	909-624-4569	625-2009
Web: www.montclairchamber.com					
Montebello Chamber of Commerce 817 W Whittier Blvd Suite 200	Montebello	CA	90640	323-721-1153	721-7946
Web: www.montebellochamber.org					
Monterey Peninsula Chamber of Commerce 380 Alvarado St	Monterey	CA	93940	831-648-5360	649-3502
Web: www.mpcc.com					
Monterey Park Chamber of Commerce 700 El Mercado Ave	Monterey Park	CA	91754	626-570-9429	570-9491
Moorpark Chamber of Commerce 225 W Los Angeles Ave	Moorpark	CA	93021	805-529-0322	529-5304
Web: www.moorparkchamber.com					
Moreno Valley Chamber of Commerce 22500 Town Cir Suite 2090	Moreno Valley	CA	92553	951-697-4404	697-0995
Web: www.movalchamber.org					
Morgan Hill Chamber of Commerce 17450 Monterey Rd	Morgan Hill	CA	95037	408-779-9444	779-5405
Web: www.morganhill.org					
Chamber of Commerce Mountain View 580 Castro St	Mountain View	CA	94041	650-968-8378	968-5668
Web: www.chambermv.org					
Murrieta Chamber of Commerce 41870 Kalmia St Suite 135	Murrieta	CA	92562	951-677-7916	677-9976
Web: www.murrietachamber.org					
Napa Chamber of Commerce 1556 1st St	Napa	CA	94559	707-226-7455	226-1171
Web: www.napachamber.org					
National City Chamber of Commerce 901 National City Blvd	National City	CA	91950	619-477-9339	477-5018
TF: 800-292-4624 ■ *Web:* www.nationalcitychamber.org					
Newark Chamber of Commerce 6066 Civic Terrace Ave Suite 8	Newark	CA	94560	510-744-1000	744-1003
Web: www.newark-chamber.com					
Newport Beach Chamber of Commerce 1470 Jamboree Rd	Newport Beach	CA	92660	949-729-4400	729-4417
Web: www.newportbeach.com					
Universal City-North Hollywood Chamber of Commerce 6369 Bellingham Ave	North Hollywood	CA	91606	818-508-5155	508-5156
Web: www.noho.org					
Northridge/Porter Ranch Chamber of Commerce 9401 Reseda Blvd Suite 100	Northridge	CA	91324	818-349-5676	349-4343
Web: www.nchamber.org					
Norwalk Chamber of Commerce 12040 Foster Rd	Norwalk	CA	90650	562-864-7785	864-8539
Web: www.norwalkchamber.com					
Novato Chamber of Commerce 807 DeLong Ave	Novato	CA	94945	415-897-1164	898-9097
TF: 800-897-1164 ■ *Web:* www.novatochamber.com					
Oakhurst Area Chamber of Commerce 49074 Civic Cir	Oakhurst	CA	93644	559-683-7766	658-2942
Web: www.oakhurstchamber.com					
Oakland Metropolitan Chamber of Commerce 475 14th St Suite 100	Oakland	CA	94612	510-874-4800	839-8817
Web: www.oaklandchamber.com					
Oceanside Chamber of Commerce 928 N Coast Hwy	Oceanside	CA	92054	760-722-1534	722-8336
Web: www.oceansidechamber.com					
Ojai Valley Chamber of Commerce 201 S Signal St	Ojai	CA	93023	805-646-8126	646-9762
Web: www.ojaichamber.org					
Ontario Chamber of Commerce 500 East E St Suite 200	Ontario	CA	91764	909-984-2458	984-6439
Web: www.ontario.org					
Orange Chamber of Commerce 439 E Chapman Ave	Orange	CA	92866	714-538-3581	532-1675
TF: 800-938-0073 ■ *Web:* www.orangechamber.com					
Orangevale Chamber of Commerce 9267 Greenback Ln Suite B-91	Orangevale	CA	95662	916-988-0175	988-1049
Web: www.orangevalechamber.com					
Oroville Area Chamber of Commerce 1789 Montgomery St	Oroville	CA	95965	530-538-2542	538-2546
TF: 800-655-4653 ■ *Web:* www.orovillechamber.net					
Oxnard Chamber of Commerce 400 E Esplanade Dr Suite 302	Oxnard	CA	93036	805-983-6118	604-7331
Web: www.oxnardchamber.org					
Pacifica Chamber of Commerce 225 Rockaway Beach Ave Suite 1	Pacifica	CA	94044	650-355-4122	355-6949
Web: www.pacificachamber.com					

	City	State	Zip	Phone	Fax
Palm Desert Chamber of Commerce 73710 Fred Waring Dr Suite 114	Palm Desert	CA	92260	760-346-6111	346-3263
Web: www.pdcc.org					
Palm Springs Chamber of Commerce 190 W Amado Rd	Palm Springs	CA	92262	760-325-1577	325-8549
Web: www.pschamber.org					
Palmdale Chamber of Commerce 817 East Ave Q-9	Palmdale	CA	93550	661-273-3232	273-8508
Web: www.palmdalechamber.org					
Palo Alto Chamber of Commerce 122 Hamilton Ave	Palo Alto	CA	94301	650-324-3121	324-1215
Web: www.paloaltochamber.com					
Paradise Chamber of Commerce 5550 Sky Way Suite 1	Paradise	CA	95969	530-877-9356	877-1865
TF: 888-845-2769 ■ *Web:* www.paradisechamber.com					
Paramount Chamber of Commerce 15357 Paramount Blvd	Paramount	CA	90723	562-634-3980	634-0891
Web: www.paramountchamber.org					
Pasadena Chamber of Commerce & Civic Assn 865 E Del Mar Blvd	Pasadena	CA	91101	626-795-3355	795-5603
Web: www.pasadena-chamber.org					
Petaluma Area Chamber of Commerce 6 Petaluma Blvd N Suite A-2	Petaluma	CA	94952	707-762-2785	762-4721
Web: www.petalumachamber.com					
Pico Rivera Chamber of Commerce PO Box 901	Pico Rivera	CA	90660	562-949-2473	949-8320
Web: www.picoriverachamber.org					
Pittsburg Chamber of Commerce 485 Railroad Ave	Pittsburg	CA	94565	925-432-7301	427-5555
Web: www.pittsburg.org					
Placentia Chamber of Commerce 201 E Yorba Linda Blvd Suite C	Placentia	CA	92870	714-528-1873	528-1879
Web: www.placentiachamber.com					
El Dorado County Chamber of Commerce 542 Main St	Placerville	CA	95667	530-621-5885	642-1624
TF: 800-457-6279 ■ *Web:* www.eldoradocounty.org					
Pleasant Hill Chamber of Commerce 91 Gregory Ln Suite 11	Pleasant Hill	CA	94523	925-687-0700	676-7422
Web: www.pleasanthillchamber.com					
Pleasanton Chamber of Commerce 777 Peters Ave	Pleasanton	CA	94566	925-846-5858	846-9697
Web: www.pleasanton.org					
Pomona Chamber of Commerce 101 W Mission Blvd Suite 223	Pomona	CA	91766	909-622-1256	620-5986
Web: pomonachamberofcommerce.homestead.com					
Porterville Chamber of Commerce 93 N Main St Suite A	Porterville	CA	93257	559-784-7502	784-0770
Web: www.chamber.porterville.com					
Poway Chamber of Commerce 13381 Poway Rd	Poway	CA	92064	858-748-0016	748-1710
Web: www.poway.com					
Ramona Chamber of Commerce 960 Main St	Ramona	CA	92065	760-789-1311	789-1317
Web: www.ramonachamber.com					
Rancho Cordova Chamber of Commerce 2728 Prospect Park Dr Suite 117	Rancho Cordova	CA	95670	916-273-5688	273-5727
Web: www.ranchocordova.org					
Rancho Cucamonga Chamber of Commerce 7945 Vineyard Ave Suite D5	Rancho Cucamonga	CA	91730	909-987-1012	987-5917
Web: www.ranchochamber.org					
Greater Redding Chamber of Commerce 747 Auditorium Dr	Redding	CA	96001	530-225-4433	225-4398
Web: www.reddingchamber.com					
Redlands Chamber of Commerce 1 E Redlands Blvd	Redlands	CA	92373	909-793-2546	335-6388
Web: www.redlandschamber.org					
Redondo Beach Chamber of Commerce & Visitors Bureau 200 N Pacific Coast Hwy	Redondo Beach	CA	90277	310-376-6911	374-7373
Web: www.redondochamber.org					
Redwood City-San Mateo County Chamber of Commerce 1450 Veterans Blvd Suite 125	Redwood City	CA	94063	650-364-1722	364-1729
Web: www.redwoodcitychamber.com					
Reseda Chamber of Commerce 18210 Sherman Way Suite 107	Reseda	CA	91335	818-345-1920	345-1925
Rialto Chamber of Commerce 120 N Riverside Ave	Rialto	CA	92376	909-875-5364	875-6790
Web: www.rialtochamber.org					
Richmond Chamber of Commerce 3925 Macdonald Ave	Richmond	CA	94805	510-234-3512	234-3540
Web: www.rcoc.com					
Ridgecrest Chamber of Commerce 128 E California Ave Suite B	Ridgecrest	CA	93555	760-375-8331	375-0365
Web: www.ridgecrestchamber.com					
Greater Riverside Chambers of Commerce 3985 University Ave	Riverside	CA	92501	951-683-7100	683-2670
Web: www.riverside-chamber.com					
Jurupa Chamber of Commerce 7920 Limonite Ave Suite C	Riverside	CA	92509	951-681-9242	681-2720
Rocklin Area Chamber of Commerce 3700 Rocklin Rd	Rocklin	CA	95677	916-624-2548	624-5743
Web: www.rocklinchamber.com					
Rohnert Park Chamber of Commerce 6050 Commerce Blvd Suite 211	Rohnert Park	CA	94928	707-584-1415	584-2945
Web: www.rohnertparkchamber.org					
Palos Verdes Peninsula Chamber of Commerce 707 Silver Spur Rd Suite 100	Rolling Hills Estates	CA	90274	310-377-8111	377-0614
Web: www.palosverdeschamber.com					
Rosemead Chamber of Commerce 3953 N Muscatel Ave	Rosemead	CA	91770	626-288-0811	288-2514
Roseville Chamber of Commerce 650 Douglas Blvd	Roseville	CA	95678	916-783-8136	783-5261
Web: www.rosevillechamber.com					
Sacramento Metro Chamber of Commerce 1 Capital Mall Suite 300	Sacramento	CA	95814	916-552-6800	443-2672
Web: www.metrochamber.org					
Salinas Valley Chamber of Commerce 119 E Alisal St	Salinas	CA	93901	831-424-7611	424-8639
Web: www.salinaschamber.com					
San Bernardino Area Chamber of Commerce PO Box 658	San Bernardino	CA	92402	909-885-7515	384-9979
Web: www.sbachamber.org					
San Bruno Chamber of Commerce 618 San Mateo Ave	San Bruno	CA	94066	650-588-0180	588-6473
Web: www.sanbrunochamber.com					
San Carlos Chamber of Commerce 1500 Laurel St Suite B	San Carlos	CA	94070	650-593-1068	593-9108
Web: www.sancarloschamber.org					
San Clemente Chamber of Commerce 1100 N El Camino Real	San Clemente	CA	92672	949-492-1131	492-3764
Web: www.scchamber.com					
Peninsula Chamber of Commerce PO Box 6015	San Diego	CA	92166	619-225-6665	225-1294
Web: www.peninsulachamber.com					
San Diego North Chamber of Commerce 11650 Iberia Pl Suite 220	San Diego	CA	92128	858-487-1767	487-8051
Web: www.sdncc.com					
San Diego Regional Chamber of Commerce 402 W Broadway Suite 1000	San Diego	CA	92101	619-544-1300	
Web: sdchamber.org					
San Dimas Chamber of Commerce 246 E Bonita Ave	San Dimas	CA	91773	909-592-3818	592-8178
Web: www.sandimaschamber.com					
Northeast San Fernando Valley Chamber of Commerce 225 N Maclay Ave	San Fernando	CA	91340	818-361-1184	898-1986
Web: www.sanfernando.com					
San Francisco Chamber of Commerce 235 Montgomery St 12th Fl	San Francisco	CA	94104	415-392-4520	392-0485
Web: www.sfchamber.com					
San Francisco Hispanic Chamber of Commerce 703 Market St Suite 611	San Francisco	CA	94103	415-278-9611	
Web: www.sfhcc.com					
San Gabriel Chamber of Commerce 620 W Santa Anita St	San Gabriel	CA	91776	626-576-2525	289-2901
Web: www.sangabrielchamber.com					

California (Cont'd)

Phone Fax

San Jose Silicon Valley Chamber of Commerce 310 S 1st St ..... San Jose CA 95113 408-291-5250 286-5019
Web: www.sjchamber.com
San Juan Capistrano Chamber of Commerce
31421 La Matanza St ..... San Juan Capistrano CA 92675 949-493-4700 489-2695
Web: www.sanjuanchamber.com
San Leandro Chamber of Commerce 262 Davis St ..... San Leandro CA 94577 510-351-1481 351-6740
Web: www.sanleandrochamber.com
San Luis Obispo Chamber of Commerce
1039 Chorro St ..... San Luis Obispo CA 93401 805-781-2777 543-1255
Web: www.slochamber.org
San Marcos Chamber of Commerce 939 Grand Ave ..... San Marcos CA 92078 760-744-1270 744-5230
Web: www.sanmarcoschamber.com
San Mateo Area Chamber of Commerce 385 1st Ave ..... San Mateo CA 94401 650-401-2440 401-2446
Web: www.sanmateoca.org
San Pablo Chamber of Commerce PO Box 6204 ..... San Pablo CA 94806 510-234-2067 234-0604
San Pedro Peninsula Chamber of Commerce 390 W 7th St ..... San Pedro CA 90731 310-832-7272 832-0685
TF: 888-447-3376 ■ *Web:* www.sanpedrochamber.com
San Rafael Chamber of Commerce 817 Mission Ave ..... San Rafael CA 94901 415-454-4163 454-7039
TF: 800-454-4163 ■ *Web:* sanrafaelchamber.com
San Ramon Chamber of Commerce
12667 Alcosta Blvd Suite 160 ..... San Ramon CA 94583 925-242-0600 242-0603
Web: www.sanramon.org
San Ysidro Chamber of Commerce 663 E San Ysidro Blvd ..... San Ysidro CA 92173 619-428-1281 428-1294
Web: www.sanysidrochamber.org
Santa Ana Chamber of Commerce PO Box 205 ..... Santa Ana CA 92702 714-541-5353 541-2238
Web: www.santaanachamber.com
Santa Barbara Region Chamber of Commerce
924 Anacapa St Suite 1 ..... Santa Barbara CA 93101 805-965-3023 966-5954
Web: www.sbchamber.org
Santa Clara Chamber of Commerce 1850 Warburton Ave ..... Santa Clara CA 95050 408-244-8244 244-7830
TF: 800-272-6822 ■ *Web:* www.santaclarachamber.org
Santa Clarita Valley Chamber of Commerce
28460 Ave Stanford Suite 100 ..... Santa Clarita CA 91355 661-702-6977 702-6980
Web: www.scvchamber.com
Santa Cruz Chamber of Commerce 611 Ocean St Suite 1 ..... Santa Cruz CA 95060 831-457-3713 423-1847
Web: www.santacruzchamber.org
Santa Maria Valley Chamber of Commerce
614 S Broadway ..... Santa Maria CA 93454 805-925-2403 928-7559
TF: 800-331-3779 ■ *Web:* www.santamaria.com
Santa Monica Chamber of Commerce
1234 6th St Suite 100 ..... Santa Monica CA 90401 310-393-9825 394-1868
Web: www.smchamber.com
Santa Paula Chamber of Commerce 200 N 10th St ..... Santa Paula CA 93060 805-525-5561 525-8950
Web: www.santapaulachamber.com
Santa Rosa Chamber of Commerce 637 1st St ..... Santa Rosa CA 95404 707-545-1414 545-6914
Web: www.santarosachamber.com
Santee Chamber of Commerce 10315 Mission Gorge Rd ..... Santee CA 92071 619-449-6572 562-7906
Web: www.santee-chamber.org
Saratoga Chamber of Commerce 14485 Big Basin Way ..... Saratoga CA 95070 408-867-0753 867-5213
Web: www.saratogachamber.org
Seal Beach Chamber & Business Assn 201 8th St Suite 120 ..... Seal Beach CA 90740 562-799-0179 795-5637
Web: www.sealbeachchamber.org
Seaside-Sand City Chamber of Commerce 505 Broadway Ave ..... Seaside CA 93955 831-394-6501 394-1977
Web: www.seaside-sandcity.com
Sebastopol Area Chamber of Commerce 265 S Main St ..... Sebastopol CA 95472 707-823-3032 823-8439
TF: 877-828-4748 ■ *Web:* www.sebastopol.org
Greater Sherman Oaks Chamber of Commerce
14827 Ventura Blvd Suite 207 ..... Sherman Oaks CA 91403 818-906-1951 783-3100
Web: www.shermanoakschamber.org
Simi Valley Chamber of Commerce
40 W Cochran St Suite 100 ..... Simi Valley CA 93065 805-526-3900 526-6234
Web: www.simivalleychamber.org
Sonoma Valley Chamber of Commerce 651A Broadway ..... Sonoma CA 95476 707-996-1033 996-9402
Web: www.sonomachamber.com
Tuolumne County Chamber of Commerce 222 S Shepherd St ..... Sonora CA 95370 209-532-4212 532-8068
Web: www.tcchamber.com
South Gate Chamber of Commerce 3350 Tweedy Blvd ..... South Gate CA 90280 323-567-1203 567-1204
Web: www.southgatechamber.com
South Lake Tahoe Chamber of Commerce
3066 Lake Tahoe Blvd ..... South Lake Tahoe CA 96150 530-541-5255 541-7121
Web: www.tahoeinfo.com
South San Francisco Chamber of Commerce
213 Linden Ave ..... South San Francisco CA 94080 650-588-1911 588-2534
Web: www.ssfchamber.com
Spring Valley Chamber of Commerce
3322 Sweetwater Springs Blvd Suite 202 ..... Spring Valley CA 91977 619-670-9902 670-9924
Web: www.springvalleychamber.org
Stanton Chamber of Commerce 8381 Katella Ave Suite H ..... Stanton CA 90680 714-995-1485 995-1184
Web: www.stanton-chamber.org
Greater Stockton Chamber of Commerce
445 W Weber Ave Suite 220 ..... Stockton CA 95203 209-547-2770 466-5271
Web: www.stocktonchamber.org
Studio City Chamber of Commerce
4024 Radford Ave Edit 2 Suite F ..... Studio City CA 91604 818-769-3213 655-8392
Web: www.studiocitychamber.com
Greater Menifee Valley Chamber of Commerce
27070 Sun City Blvd Suite B ..... Sun City CA 92586 951-672-1991 672-4022
Web: menifeevalleychamber.com
Sun Valley Area Chamber of Commerce
8133 San Fernando Rd Suite A ..... Sun Valley CA 91352 818-768-2014 767-1947
Web: www.chambersunvalleyca.org
Sunland-Tujunga Chamber of Commerce
8250 Foothill Blvd Suite A ..... Sunland CA 91040 818-352-4433 353-7551
Web: www.stchamber.com
Sunnyvale Chamber of Commerce 101 W Olive Ave ..... Sunnyvale CA 94086 408-736-4971 736-1919
Web: www.svcoc.org
Lassen County Chamber of Commerce 84 N Lassen St ..... Susanville CA 96130 530-257-4323 251-2561
Web: www.lassencountychamber.org
Sylmar Chamber of Commerce 13867 Foothill Blvd Suite 104 ..... Sylmar CA 91342 818-367-1177 367-1633
Greater Tehachapi Chamber of Commerce PO Box 401 ..... Tehachapi CA 93581 661-822-4180 822-9036
TF: 866-822-4180 ■ *Web:* www.tehachapi.com
Temecula Valley Chamber of Commerce 26790 Ynez Ct ..... Temecula CA 92591 951-676-5090 694-0201
TF: 866-676-5090 ■ *Web:* www.temecula.org
Temple City Chamber of Commerce 9050 E Las Tunas Dr ..... Temple City CA 91780 626-286-3101 286-2590
Web: www.templecitychamber.org
Harbor City-Harbor Gateway Chamber of Commerce
19401 S Vermont Ave Suite G104 ..... Torrance CA 90502 310-516-7933 516-7734
Web: www.hchgchamber.com
Torrance Area Chamber of Commerce
3400 Torrance Blvd Suite 100 ..... Torrance CA 90503 310-540-5858 540-7662
Web: www.torrancechamber.com
Tracy Chamber of Commerce 223 E 10th St ..... Tracy CA 95376 209-835-2131 833-9526
Web: www.tracychamber.org

Phone Fax

Greater Tulare Chamber of Commerce 220 E Tulare Ave ..... Tulare CA 93274 559-686-1547 686-4915
Web: www.tularechamber.org
Turlock Chamber of Commerce 115 S Golden State Blvd ..... Turlock CA 95380 209-632-2221 632-5289
Web: www.turlockchamber.org
Tustin Chamber of Commerce 399 El Camino Real ..... Tustin CA 92780 714-544-5341 544-2083
Web: www.tustinchamber.org
Twentynine Palms Chamber of Commerce
73660 Civic Center Dr Suite D ..... Twentynine Palms CA 92277 760-367-3445 367-3366
Web: www.29chamber.com
Ukiah Chamber of Commerce 200 S School St ..... Ukiah CA 95482 707-462-4705 462-2088
Web: www.ukiahchamber.com
Union City Chamber of Commerce 33412 Alvarado-Niles Rd ..... Union City CA 94587 510-471-3115 471-6011
Web: www.unioncitychamber.com
Upland Chamber of Commerce 433 N 2nd Ave ..... Upland CA 91786 909-931-4108 931-4184
Web: www.uplandchamber.org
Vacaville Chamber of Commerce 300 Main St ..... Vacaville CA 95688 707-448-6424 448-0424
Web: www.vacavillechamber.com
Vallejo Chamber of Commerce 427 York St ..... Vallejo CA 94590 707-644-5551 644-5590
Web: www.vallejochamber.com
Mid Valley Chamber of Commerce
7120 Hayvenhurst Ave Suite 114 ..... Van Nuys CA 91406 818-989-0300 989-3836
Web: www.midvalleychamber.com
Venice Chamber of Commerce
327 Washington Blvd PO Box 202 ..... Venice CA 90294 310-822-5425 248-3837
Web: www.venicechamber.net
Ventura Chamber of Commerce 801 S Victoria Ave Suite 200 ..... Ventura CA 93003 805-676-7500 650-1414
Web: www.venturachamber.org
Victorville Chamber of Commerce 14174 Green Tree Blvd ..... Victorville CA 92395 760-245-6506 245-6505
Web: www.vvchamber.com
Visalia Chamber of Commerce 220 N Santa Fe St ..... Visalia CA 93292 559-734-5876 734-7479
TF: 877-847-2542 ■ *Web:* www.visaliachamber.org
Vista Chamber of Commerce 201 Washington St ..... Vista CA 92084 760-726-1122 726-8654
Web: www.vistachamber.org
Walnut Creek Chamber of Commerce
1777 Botelho Dr Suite 103 ..... Walnut Creek CA 94596 925-934-2007 934-2404
Web: www.walnut-creek.com
Pajaro Valley Chamber of Commerce 444 Main St ..... Watsonville CA 95076 831-724-3900 728-5300
Web: www.pajarovalleychamber.com
West Covina Chamber of Commerce 811 S Sunset Ave ..... West Covina CA 91790 626-338-8496 960-0511
Web: www.westcovinachamber.com
West Hollywood Chamber of Commerce
8272 Santa Monica Blvd ..... West Hollywood CA 90046 323-650-2688 650-2689
Web: www.wehochamber.com
West Sacramento Chamber of Commerce
1414 Merkley Ave Suite 1 ..... West Sacramento CA 95691 916-371-7042 371-7007
Web: www.westsacramentochamber.com
Thousand Oaks/Westlake Village Regional Chamber of Commerce 600 Hampshire Rd Suite 200 ..... Westlake Village CA 91361 805-370-0035 370-1083
Web: www.towlvchamber.org
Westminster Chamber of Commerce 14491 Beach Blvd ..... Westminster CA 92683 714-898-9648 373-1499
Web: www.westminsterchamber.org
Whittier Area Chamber of Commerce 8158 Painter Ave ..... Whittier CA 90602 562-698-9554 693-2700
Web: www.whittierchamber.com
Willows Chamber of Commerce 118 W Sycamore ..... Willows CA 95988 530-934-8150 934-8710
TF: 888-799-4254 ■ *Web:* www.willowschamber.org
Wilmington Chamber of Commerce
544 N Avalon Blvd Suite 104 ..... Wilmington CA 90744 310-834-8586 834-8887
Web: www.wilmington-chamber.com
Woodland Chamber of Commerce 307 1st St ..... Woodland CA 95695 530-662-7327 662-4086
TF: 888-843-2636 ■ *Web:* www.woodlandchamber.org
Woodland Hills Chamber of Commerce
20121 Ventura Blvd Suite 309 ..... Woodland Hills CA 91364 818-347-4737 347-3321
Web: www.woodlandhillscc.net
Yorba Linda Chamber of Commerce
17670 Yorba Linda Blvd ..... Yorba Linda CA 92886 714-993-9537 993-7764
Web: www.yorbalindachamber.org
Yucaipa Valley Chamber of Commerce 35139 Yucaipa Blvd ..... Yucaipa CA 92399 909-790-1841 790-3484
Web: www.yucaipachamber.com
Yucca Valley Chamber of Commerce
56711 29 Palms Hwy ..... Yucca Valley CA 92284 760-365-6323 365-0763
Web: www.yuccavalley.org

Colorado

Phone Fax

Arvada Chamber of Commerce 7305 Grandview Ave ..... Arvada CO 80002 303-424-0313 424-5370
Web: www.arvadachamber.org
Aspen Chamber Resort Assn 425 Rio Grande Pl ..... Aspen CO 81611 970-925-1940 920-1173
TF: 800-670-0792 ■ *Web:* www.aspenchamber.org
Aurora Chamber of Commerce 562 Sable Blvd Suite 200 ..... Aurora CO 80011 303-344-1500 344-1564
Web: www.aurorachamber.org
Boulder Chamber of Commerce 2440 Pearl St ..... Boulder CO 80302 303-442-1044 938-8837
Web: www.boulderchamber.com
Broomfield Chamber of Commerce
350 Interlocken Blvd Suite 250 ..... Broomfield CO 80021 303-466-1775 466-4481
Web: www.broomfieldchamber.com
Cañon City Chamber of Commerce 403 Royal Gorge Blvd ..... Canon City CO 81212 719-275-2331 275-2332
TF: 800-876-7922 ■ *Web:* www.canoncitychamber.com
South Metro Denver Chamber of Commerce
6840 S University Blvd ..... Centennial CO 80122 303-795-0142 795-7520
Web: www.bestchamber.com
Colorado Springs Chamber of Commerce
6 S Tejon St Suite 700 ..... Colorado Springs CO 80903 719-635-1551 635-1571
Web: www.coloradospringschamber.org
Delta Area Chamber of Commerce 301 Main St ..... Delta CO 81416 970-874-8616 874-8618
Web: www.deltacolorado.org
Denver Metro Chamber of Commerce 1445 Market St ..... Denver CO 80202 303-534-8500 534-3200
Web: www.denverchamber.org
MetroNorth Chamber of Commerce
2921 W 120th Ave Suite 210 ..... Denver CO 80234 303-288-1000 227-1050
Web: www.metronorthchamber.com
Durango Area Chamber of Commerce
111 S Camino del Rio PO Box 2587 ..... Durango CO 81303 970-247-0312 385-7884
TF: 888-414-0835 ■ *Web:* www.durangobusiness.org
Fort Collins Area Chamber of Commerce
225 S Meldrum St ..... Fort Collins CO 80521 970-482-3746 482-3774
Web: www.fcchamber.org
Fort Morgan Area Chamber of Commerce 300 Main St ..... Fort Morgan CO 80701 970-867-6702 867-6121
TF: 800-354-8660 ■ *Web:* www.fortmorganchamber.org
Greater Golden Chamber of Commerce 1010 Washington Ave ..... Golden CO 80401 303-279-3113 279-0332
Web: www.goldencochamber.org
West Chamber of Commerce 1667 Cole Blvd Bldg 19 Suite 400 ..... Golden CO 80401 303-233-5555 237-7633
Web: www.westchamber.org
Grand Junction Area Chamber of Commerce
360 Grand Ave ..... Grand Junction CO 81501 970-242-3214 242-3694
TF: 800-352-5286 ■ *Web:* www.gjchamber.org

	City	State	ZIP	Phone	Fax
Greeley-Weld Chamber of Commerce 902 7th Ave *Web:* www.greeleychamber.com	Greeley	CO	80631	970-352-3566	352-3572
La Veta/Cuchara Chamber of Commerce PO Box 32 *TF:* 866-615-3676 ■ *Web:* www.lavetacucharachamber.com	La Veta	CO	81055	719-742-3676	
Longmont Area Chamber of Commerce 528 Main St. *Web:* www.longmontchamber.org	Longmont	CO	80501	303-776-5295	776-5657
Loveland Chamber of Commerce 5400 Stone Creek Cir Suite 200 *Web:* www.loveland.org	Loveland	CO	80538	970-667-6311	667-5211
Montrose Chamber of Commerce 1519 E Main St. *TF:* 800-923-5515 ■ *Web:* www.montrosechamber.com	Montrose	CO	81401	970-249-5000	249-2907
Parker Chamber of Commerce 19751 E Main st Unit R-12 *Web:* www.parkerchamber.com	Parker	CO	80134	303-841-4268	841-8061
Greater Pueblo Chamber of Commerce 302 N Santa Fe Ave. *TF:* 800-233-3446 ■ *Web:* www.pueblochamber.org	Pueblo	CO	81003	719-542-1704	542-1624
Vail Valley Chamber of Commerce 100 E Meadow Dr Suite 34 *TF:* 800-525-3875 ■ *Web:* www.visitvailvalley.com	Vail	CO	81657	970-476-1000	476-6008

Connecticut

	City	State	ZIP	Phone	Fax
Branford Chamber of Commerce 239 N Main St PO Box 375 *Web:* www.branfordct.com	Branford	CT	06405	203-488-5500	488-5046
Bridgeport Regional Business Council 10 Middle St 14th Fl. *Web:* www.brbc.org	Bridgeport	CT	06604	203-335-3800	366-0105
Greater Bristol Chamber of Commerce 200 Main St. *Web:* www.bristol-chamber.org	Bristol	CT	06010	860-584-4718	584-4722
Cheshire Chamber of Commerce 195 S Main St *Web:* www.cheshirechamber.com	Cheshire	CT	06410	203-272-2345	271-3044
Greater Danbury Chamber of Commerce 39 West St *Web:* www.danburychamber.com	Danbury	CT	06810	203-743-5565	794-1439
Northeastern Connecticut Chamber of Commerce 3 Central St *Web:* www.newenglanditgroup.com/nectcc	Danielson	CT	06239	860-774-8001	774-4299
East Hartford Chamber of Commerce 1137 Main St. *Web:* www.ehcoc.com	East Hartford	CT	06108	860-289-0239	289-0230
East Haven Chamber of Commerce 157 Main St. *Web:* www.ehchamber.org	East Haven	CT	06512	203-467-4305	469-2299
Fairfield Chamber of Commerce 1597 Post Rd. *Web:* www.fairfieldctchamber.com	Fairfield	CT	06824	203-255-1011	256-9990
Chamber of Commerce of Eastern Connecticut Inc PO Box 726 *Web:* www.chamberect.com	Gales Ferry	CT	06335	860-464-7373	464-7374
Glastonbury Chamber of Commerce 2400 Main St *Web:* www.glastonburychamber.org	Glastonbury	CT	06033	860-659-3587	659-0102
Greenwich Chamber of Commerce 45 E Putnam Ave Suite 121 *Web:* www.greenwichchamber.com	Greenwich	CT	06830	203-869-3500	869-3502
Hamden Chamber of Commerce 2969 Whitney Ave. *Web:* www.hamdenchamber.com	Hamden	CT	06518	203-288-6431	288-4499
MetroHartford Alliance 31 Pratt St Suite 5 *Web:* www.metrohartford.com	Hartford	CT	06103	860-525-4451	293-2592
Greater Manchester Chamber of Commerce 20 Hartford Rd *Web:* www.manchesterchamber.com	Manchester	CT	06040	860-646-2223	646-5871
Greater Meriden Chamber of Commerce 3 Colony St Suite 301 *Web:* www.meridenchamber.com	Meriden	CT	06451	203-235-7901	686-0172
Middlesex County Chamber of Commerce 393 Main St *Web:* middlesexchamber.com	Middletown	CT	06457	860-347-6924	346-1043
Milford Chamber of Commerce 5 Broad St *Web:* www.milfordct.com	Milford	CT	06460	203-878-0681	876-8517
Mystic Chamber of Commerce 14 Holmes St PO Box 143 *TF:* 866-572-9578 ■ *Web:* www.mysticchamber.org	Mystic	CT	06355	860-572-9578	572-9273
Waterbury/Naugatuck Chamber of Commerce 195 Water St.	Naugatuck	CT	06770	203-729-4511	729-4512
New Britain Chamber of Commerce 1 Court St 4th Fl. *Web:* www.newbritainchamber.com	New Britain	CT	06051	860-229-1665	223-8341
Greater New Haven Chamber of Commerce 900 Chapel St 10th Fl *Web:* www.gnhcc.com	New Haven	CT	06510	203-787-6735	782-4329
Greater New Milford Chamber of Commerce 11 Railroad St *Web:* www.newmilford-chamber.com	New Milford	CT	06776	860-354-6080	354-8526
Greater Norwalk Chamber of Commerce 101 East Ave *Web:* www.norwalkchamberofcommerce.com	Norwalk	CT	06851	203-866-2521	852-0583
Old Saybrook Chamber of Commerce 665 Boston Post Rd Community Policing Office *Web:* oldsaybrookchamber.com	Old Saybrook	CT	06475	860-388-3266	388-9433
Greater Valley Chamber of Commerce 900 Bridgeport Ave 2nd Fl. *Web:* www.greatervalleychamber.com	Shelton	CT	06484	203-925-4981	925-4984
Greater Southington Chamber of Commerce 37 W Center St Suite 201 *Web:* www.southingtoncoc.com	Southington	CT	06489	860-628-8036	276-9696
Business Council of Fairfield County (SACIA) 1 Landmark Sq Suite 230 *Web:* www.sacia.org	Stamford	CT	06901	203-359-3220	967-8294
Stamford Chamber of Commerce 733 Summer St Suite 101 *Web:* www.stamfordchamber.com	Stamford	CT	06901	203-359-4761	363-5069
Chamber of Commerce of Northwest Connecticut 333 Kennedy Dr Suite R 101 *Web:* www.northwestchamber.org	Torrington	CT	06790	860-482-6586	489-8851
Tolland County Chamber of Commerce 30 Lafayette Sq *Web:* www.tollandcountychamber.org	Vernon	CT	06066	860-872-0587	872-0588
Quinnipiac Chamber of Commerce 350 Center St *Web:* www.quinncham.com	Wallingford	CT	06492	203-234-0332	269-1358
Greater Waterbury Chamber of Commerce 83 Bank St PO Box 1469 *Web:* www.waterburychamber.org	Waterbury	CT	06721	203-757-0701	756-3507
West Hartford Chamber of Commerce 948 Farmington Ave. *Web:* www.whchamber.com	West Hartford	CT	06107	860-521-2300	521-1996
West Haven Chamber of Commerce 334 Main St *Web:* www.westhavenchamber.com	West Haven	CT	06516	203-933-1500	931-1940
Windham Region Chamber of Commerce 1010 Main St *Web:* www.windhamchamber.com	Willimantic	CT	06226	860-423-6389	423-8235
Windsor Chamber of Commerce 261 Broad St. *Web:* www.windsorcc.org	Windsor	CT	06095	860-688-5165	688-0809

Delaware

	City	State	ZIP	Phone	Fax
Central Delaware Economic Development Council 435 N DuPont Hwy *TF:* 800-624-2522 ■ *Web:* www.cdedc.org	Dover	DE	19901	302-678-3028	678-0189
Rehoboth Beach-Dewey Beach Chamber of Commerce 501 Rehoboth Ave *TF:* 800-441-1329 ■ *Web:* www.beach-fun.com	Rehoboth Beach	DE	19971	302-227-2233	227-8351

Florida

	City	State	ZIP	Phone	Fax
Amelia Island-Fernandina Beach-Yulee Chamber of Commerce 961687 Gateway Blvd Suite 101-G *TF:* 800-226-3542 ■ *Web:* www.islandchamber.com	Amelia Island	FL	32034	904-261-3248	261-6997
Apalachicola Bay Chamber of Commerce 122 Commerce St *Web:* www.apalachicolabay.org	Apalachicola	FL	32320	850-653-9419	653-8219
DeSoto County Chamber of Commerce 16 S Volusia Ave *Web:* www.desotochamber.net	Arcadia	FL	34266	863-494-4033	494-3312
Florida Gold Coast Chamber of Commerce 1100 Kane Concourse Suite 210 *Web:* www.flgoldcc.org	Bay Harbor Islands	FL	33154	305-866-6020	866-0635
Belleview-South Marion Chamber of Commerce 5301 SE Abshier Blvd *Web:* www.bsmcc.org	Belleview	FL	34420	352-245-2178	245-7673
Lower Keys Chamber of Commerce 31020 Overseas Hwy. *TF:* 800-872-3722 ■ *Web:* www.lowerkeyschamber.com	Big Pine Key	FL	33043	305-872-2411	872-0752
Greater Boca Raton Chamber of Commerce 1800 N Dixie Hwy *Web:* www.bocaratonchamber.com	Boca Raton	FL	33432	561-395-4433	392-3780
Bonita Springs Area Chamber of Commerce 25071 Chamber of Commerce Dr *TF:* 800-226-2943 ■ *Web:* www.bonitaspringschamber.com	Bonita Springs	FL	34135	239-992-2943	992-5011
Greater Boynton Beach Chamber of Commerce 639 E Ocean Ave Suite 108 *Web:* www.boyntonbeach.org	Boynton Beach	FL	33435	561-732-9501	734-4304
Manatee Chamber of Commerce 222 10th St W. *Web:* www.manateechamber.com	Bradenton	FL	34205	941-748-3411	745-1877
Greater Brandon Chamber of Commerce 330 Pauls Dr Suite 100 *Web:* www.brandonchamber.com	Brandon	FL	33511	813-689-1221	689-9440
Greater Hernando County Chamber of Commerce 101 E Fort Dade Ave *Web:* www.hernandochamber.com	Brooksville	FL	34601	352-796-0697	796-3704
Flagler County Chamber of Commerce 20 Palm Coast Rd *TF:* 800-881-1022 ■ *Web:* www.flaglerpcchamber.org	Bunnell	FL	32164	386-437-0106	437-5700
Cape Coral Chamber of Commerce 2051 Cape Coral Pkwy E *TF:* 800-226-9609 ■ *Web:* capecoralchamber.com	Cape Coral	FL	33904	239-549-6900	549-9609
Clearwater Regional Chamber of Commerce 1130 Cleveland St *TF:* 888-425-3279 ■ *Web:* www.clearwaterflorida.org	Clearwater	FL	33755	727-461-0011	449-2889
Coral Gables Chamber of Commerce 224 Catalonia *Web:* cg.wliinc2.com	Coral Gables	FL	33134	305-446-1657	446-9900
Coral Springs Chamber of Commerce 11805 Heron Bay Blvd *Web:* www.cschamber.com	Coral Springs	FL	33076	954-752-4242	827-0543
Crestview Area Chamber of Commerce 502 S Main St. *Web:* www.crestviewchamber.com	Crestview	FL	32536	850-682-3212	682-7413
Citrus County Chamber of Commerce 28 NW Hwy 19 *Web:* www.citruscountychamber.com	Crystal River	FL	34428	352-795-3149	795-4260
Davie-Cooper City Chamber of Commerce 4185 Davie Rd *Web:* www.davie-coopercity.org	Davie	FL	33314	954-581-0790	581-9684
Daytona Beach-Halifax Area Chamber of Commerce 126 E Orange Ave *Web:* www.daytonachamber.com	Daytona Beach	FL	32114	386-255-0981	258-5104
Greater Deerfield Beach Chamber of Commerce 1601 E Hillsboro Blvd *Web:* www.deerfieldchamber.com	Deerfield Beach	FL	33441	954-427-1050	427-1056
DeLand Area Chamber of Commerce 336 N Woodland Blvd *Web:* www.delandchamber.org	DeLand	FL	32720	386-734-4331	734-4333
Greater Delray Beach Chamber of Commerce 64-A SE 5th Ave. *Web:* www.delraybeach.com	Delray Beach	FL	33483	561-278-0424	278-0555
Destin Area Chamber of Commerce 4484 Legendary Dr Suite A *Web:* www.destinchamber.com	Destin	FL	32541	850-837-6241	654-5612
Dunedin Chamber of Commerce 301 Main St *Web:* www.dunedin-fl.com	Dunedin	FL	34698	727-733-3197	734-8942
Dunnellon Area Chamber of Commerce PO Box 868 *TF:* 800-830-2087 ■ *Web:* www.dunnellonchamber.org	Dunnellon	FL	34430	352-489-2320	489-6846
Englewood/Cape Haze Chamber of Commerce 601 S Indiana Ave *TF:* 800-603-7198 ■ *Web:* www.englewoodchamber.com	Englewood	FL	34223	941-474-5511	475-9257
Broward County Chamber of Commerce 1640 W Oakland Park Blvd *Web:* www.browardbiz.com	Fort Lauderdale	FL	33311	954-565-5750	566-3398
Greater Fort Lauderdale Chamber of Commerce 512 NE 3rd Ave *Web:* www.ftlchamber.com	Fort Lauderdale	FL	33301	954-462-6000	527-8766
Chamber of Southwest Florida 1520 Royal Palm Sq Blvd Suite 210 *Web:* www.chamber-swflorida.com	Fort Myers	FL	33919	239-278-4001	278-3319
Greater Fort Myers Chamber of Commerce 2310 Edwards Dr *TF:* 800-366-3622 ■ *Web:* www.fortmyers.org	Fort Myers	FL	33902	239-332-3624	332-7276
Fort Myers Beach Chamber of Commerce 17200 San Carlos Blvd *TF:* 800-782-9283 ■ *Web:* www.fmbchamber.com	Fort Myers Beach	FL	33931	239-454-7500	454-7910
Greater Fort Walton Beach Chamber of Commerce PO Box 640 *Web:* www.fwbchamber.org	Fort Walton Beach	FL	32549	850-244-8191	244-1935
Gainesville Area Chamber of Commerce 300 E University Ave Suite 100 *Web:* www.gainesvillechamber.com	Gainesville	FL	32601	352-334-7100	334-7141
Hallandale Pembroke Park Chamber of Commerce 1117 E hallandale Blvd Suite 5 *Web:* www.hallandalebeachchamber.com	Hallandale	FL	33009	954-454-0541	454-0930
Camara de Comercio Hispana de Hialeah 4410 W 16th Ave Suite 62	Hialeah	FL	33012	305-557-5060	556-7333
Hialeah Chamber of Commerce & Industries 240 E 1st Ave. *Web:* www.hialeahchamber.org	Hialeah	FL	33010	305-888-7780	888-7804
Greater Hollywood Chamber of Commerce 330 N Federal Hwy. *TF:* 800-231-5562 ■ *Web:* www.hollywoodchamber.org	Hollywood	FL	33020	954-923-4000	923-8737
Greater Homestead/Florida City Chamber of Commerce 43 N Krome Ave. *TF:* 888-352-4891 ■ *Web:* www.chamberinaction.com	Homestead	FL	33030	305-247-2332	246-1100
Citrus County Chamber of Commerce 3495 S Suncoast Blvd *Web:* www.citruscountychamber.com	Homosassa Springs	FL	34447	352-628-2666	621-0920

Florida (Cont'd)

Chamber	City	State	Zip	Phone	Fax
Citrus County Chamber of Commerce 401 W Tompkins St *Web:* www.citruscountychamber.com	Inverness	FL	34450	352-726-2801	637-6498
Islamorada Chamber of Commerce PO Box 915 *TF:* 800-322-5397 ■ *Web:* www.islamoradachamber.com	Islamorada	FL	33036	305-664-4503	664-4289
Jacksonville Chamber of Commerce 3 Independent Dr *Web:* www.myjaxchamber.com	Jacksonville	FL	32202	904-366-6600	632-0617
Jacksonville Chamber of Commerce Beaches Div 325 Jacksonville Dr *Web:* www.myjaxchamber.com	Jacksonville Beach	FL	32250	904-249-3868	241-7556
Jupiter Tequesta Juno Beach Chamber of Commerce 800 N US Hwy 1 *TF:* 800-616-7402 ■ *Web:* www.jupiterfl.org	Jupiter	FL	33477	561-746-7111	746-7715
Key Largo Chamber of Commerce 106000 Overseas Hwy *Web:* www.keylargo.org	Key Largo	FL	33037	305-451-1414	451-4726
Key West Chamber of Commerce 402 Wall St *TF:* 800-527-8539 ■ *Web:* www.keywestchamber.org	Key West	FL	33040	305-294-2587	294-7806
Kissimmee/Osceola County Chamber of Commerce 1425 E Vine St *Web:* www.kissimmeechamber.com	Kissimmee	FL	34744	407-847-3174	870-8607
Lake City/Columbia County Chamber of Commerce 162 S Marion Ave *Web:* www.lakecitychamber.com	Lake City	FL	32025	386-752-3690	755-7744
Seminole County/Lake Mary Regional Chamber of Commerce 725 Primera Blvd Suite 100 *Web:* www.seminolebusiness.org	Lake Mary	FL	32746	407-333-4748	829-2100
Greater Lake Placid Chamber of Commerce 10 N Oak Ave *Web:* www.lpfla.com	Lake Placid	FL	33852	863-465-4331	465-2588
Lake Wales Area Chamber of Commerce 340 W Central Ave *Web:* www.lakewaleschamber.com	Lake Wales	FL	33859	863-676-3445	676-3446
Greater Lake Worth Chamber of Commerce 807 Lucerne Ave *Web:* www.lwchamber.com	Lake Worth	FL	33460	561-582-4401	547-8300
Lakeland Area Chamber of Commerce 35 Lake Morton Dr *Web:* www.lakelandchamber.com	Lakeland	FL	33801	863-688-8551	683-7454
Central Pasco Chamber of Commerce 2810 Land O' Lakes Blvd *Web:* www.centralpascochamber.com	Land O' Lakes	FL	34639	813-909-2722	909-0827
Greater Largo Chamber of Commerce 151 3rd St NW *Web:* www.largochamber.com	Largo	FL	33770	727-584-2321	586-3112
Lehigh Acres Chamber of Commerce 4100 Lee Blvd *Web:* www.lehighacreschamber.org	Lehigh Acres	FL	33971	239-369-3322	368-0500
Suwannee County Chamber of Commerce PO Box 4 C *Web:* www.suwanneechamber.com	Live Oak	FL	32064	386-362-3071	362-4758
Palms West Chamber of Commerce PO Box 1062 *TF:* 800-790-2364 ■ *Web:* www.palmswest.com	Loxahatchee	FL	33470	561-790-6200	791-2069
Maitland Area Chamber of Commerce 110 N Maitland Ave *Web:* www.maitlandchamber.com	Maitland	FL	32751	407-644-0741	539-2529
Greater Marathon Chamber of Commerce 12222 Overseas Hwy *TF:* 800-262-7284 ■ *Web:* www.floridakeysmarathon.com	Marathon	FL	33050	305-743-5417	289-0183
Marco Island Chamber of Commerce 1102 N Collier Blvd *TF:* 800-788-6272 ■ *Web:* www.marcoislandchamber.org	Marco Island	FL	34145	239-394-7549	394-3061
Jackson County Chamber of Commerce PO Box 130 *Web:* jacksoncounty.com	Marianna	FL	32447	850-482-8061	482-8002
Melbourne-Palm Bay Area Chamber of Commerce 1005 E Strawbridge Ave *TF:* 800-771-9922 ■ *Web:* www.melpb-chamber.org	Melbourne	FL	32901	321-724-5400	725-2093
Cocoa Beach Area Chamber of Commerce 400 Fortenberry Rd *TF:* 877-321-8474 ■ *Web:* www.cocoabeachchamber.com	Merritt Island	FL	32952	321-459-2200	459-2232
Greater Miami Chamber of Commerce 1601 Biscayne Blvd *TF:* 888-660-5955 ■ *Web:* www.greatermiami.com	Miami	FL	33132	305-350-7700	374-6902
Miami-Dade Chamber of Commerce 11380 NW 27th Ave Suite 1328 *Web:* www.m-dcc.org	Miami	FL	33167	305-751-8648	758-3839
North Dade Regional Chamber of Commerce 1300 NW 167th St Suite 1 *Web:* www.thechamber.cc	Miami	FL	33169	305-690-9123	690-9124
Miami Beach Chamber of Commerce 1920 Meridian Ave 3rd Fl *Web:* www.miamibeachchamber.com	Miami Beach	FL	33139	305-672-1270	538-4336
Santa Rosa County Chamber of Commerce 5247 Stewart St *Web:* www.srcchamber.com	Milton	FL	32570	850-623-2339	623-4413
Naples Area Chamber of Commerce 2390 Tamiami Trail N *Web:* www.napleschamber.org	Naples	FL	34103	239-262-6141	435-9910
West Pasco Chamber of Commerce 5443 Main St *Web:* westpasco.com	New Port Richey	FL	34652	727-842-7651	848-0202
Southeast Volusia Chamber of Commerce 115 Canal St *TF:* 877-460-8410 ■ *Web:* www.sevchamber.com	New Smyrna Beach	FL	32168	386-428-2449	423-3512
Niceville-Valparaiso Bay Area Chamber of Commerce 1055 E John Sims Pkwy *Web:* www.nicevillechamber.com	Niceville	FL	32578	850-678-2323	678-2602
North Fort Myers Chamber of Commerce 3323 N Key Dr Suite 1 *Web:* www.northfortmyerschamber.org	North Fort Myers	FL	33903	239-997-9111	997-4026
Greater North Miami Chamber of Commerce 13100 W Dixie Hwy *Web:* www.northmiamichamber.com	North Miami	FL	33161	305-891-7811	893-8522
North Miami Beach Chamber of Commerce 1870 NE 171st St *Web:* www.nmbchamber.com	North Miami Beach	FL	33162	305-944-8500	944-8191
Sunny Isles Beach Resort Assn 16701 Collins Ave Suite 219 *Web:* www.sunnyislesfla.com	North Miami Beach	FL	33160	305-947-5826	956-9527
Ocala-Marion County Chamber of Commerce 110 E Silver Springs Blvd *TF:* 888-629-8051 ■ *Web:* www.ocalacc.com	Ocala	FL	34470	352-629-8051	629-7651
Okeechobee Chamber of Commerce 55 S Parrott Ave *Web:* www.okeechobeechamberofcommerce.com	Okeechobee	FL	34972	863-763-6464	763-3531
Upper Tampa Bay Regional Chamber of Commerce 163 SR 580 W *Web:* www.utbchamber.com	Oldsmar	FL	34677	813-855-4233	854-1237
Clay County Chamber of Commerce 1734 Kingsley Ave *Web:* www.claychamber.org	Orange Park	FL	32073	904-264-2651	264-0070
East Orlando Chamber of Commerce 10111 E Colonial Dr *Web:* www.eocc.org	Orlando	FL	32817	407-277-5951	381-1720
Orlando Regional Chamber of Commerce PO Box 1234 *Web:* www.orlando.org	Orlando	FL	32802	407-425-1234	835-2500
Ormond Beach Chamber of Commerce 165 W Granada Blvd *Web:* www.ormondchamber.com	Ormond Beach	FL	32174	386-677-3454	677-4363

Chamber	City	State	Zip	Phone	Fax
Putnam County Chamber of Commerce 1100 Reid St *Web:* www.putnamcountychamber.org	Palatka	FL	32177	386-328-1503	328-7076
North Palm Beach County Chamber of Commerce 3970 RCA Blvd Suite 7010 *Web:* www.npbchamber.com	Palm Beach Gardens	FL	33410	561-694-2300	694-0126
Greater Palm Harbor Area Chamber of Commerce 1151 Nebraska Ave *Web:* www.palmharborcc.org	Palm Harbor	FL	34683	727-784-4287	786-2336
Bay County Chamber of Commerce 235 W 5th St *Web:* www.panamacity.org	Panama City	FL	32401	850-785-5206	763-6229
Panama City Beaches Chamber of Commerce 415 Beckrich Rd Suite 200 *Web:* www.pcbeach.org	Panama City Beach	FL	32407	850-234-3193	235-2301
Miramar-Pembroke Pines Regional Chamber of Commerce 10100 Pines Blvd 4th Fl *Web:* www.miramarpembrokepines.org	Pembroke Pines	FL	33026	954-432-9808	432-9193
Pensacola Area Chamber of Commerce 117 W Garden St *Web:* www.pensacolachamber.com	Pensacola	FL	32502	850-438-4081	438-6369
Pinellas Park Mid-County Chamber of Commerce 5851 Park Blvd *Web:* www.pinellasparkchamber.com	Pinellas Park	FL	33781	727-544-4777	209-0837
Greater Plant City Chamber of Commerce 106 N Evers St *TF:* 800-760-2315 ■ *Web:* www.plantcity.org	Plant City	FL	33563	813-754-3707	752-8793
Greater Plantation Chamber of Commerce 7401 NW 4th St *Web:* www.plantationchamber.org	Plantation	FL	33317	954-587-1410	587-1886
Greater Pompano Beach Chamber of Commerce 2200 E Atlantic Blvd *Web:* www.pompanobeachchamber.com	Pompano Beach	FL	33062	954-941-2940	785-8358
Charlotte County Chamber of Commerce 2702 Tamiami Trail *Web:* www.charlottecountychamber.org	Port Charlotte	FL	33952	941-627-2222	627-9730
Port Orange-South Daytona Chamber of Commerce 3431 Ridgewood Ave *Web:* www.pschamber.com	Port Orange	FL	32129	386-761-1601	788-9165
Charlotte County Chamber of Commerce 311 W Retta Esplanade *Web:* www.charlottecountychamber.org	Punta Gorda	FL	33950	941-639-2222	639-6330
Gadsden County Chamber of Commerce 208 N Adams St *TF:* 800-627-9231 ■ *Web:* www.gadsdencc.com	Quincy	FL	32351	850-627-9231	875-3299
Greater Riverview Chamber of Commerce PO Box 128 *Web:* www.riverviewchamber.com	Riverview	FL	33569	813-234-5944	234-5945
Ruskin Chamber of Commerce 315 S Tamiami Tr *Web:* www.ruskinchamber.org	Ruskin	FL	33570	813-645-3808	645-2099
Saint Augustine & Saint Johns County Chamber of Commerce 1 Riberia St *Web:* www.staugustinechamber.com	Saint Augustine	FL	32084	904-829-5681	829-6477
Saint Cloud/Greater Osceola Chamber of Commerce 1200 New York Ave *Web:* stcloudflchamber.com	Saint Cloud	FL	34769	407-892-3671	892-5289
Tampa Bay Beaches Chamber of Commerce 6990 Gulf Blvd *TF:* 800-944-1847 ■ *Web:* www.tampabaybeaches.com	Saint Pete Beach	FL	33706	727-360-6957	360-2233
Saint Petersburg Area Chamber of Commerce 100 2nd Ave N Suite 150 *Web:* www.stpete.com	Saint Petersburg	FL	33701	727-821-4069	895-6326
Sanford Seminole County Chamber of Commerce 400 E 1st St *Web:* www.sanfordchamber.com	Sanford	FL	32771	407-322-2212	322-8160
Sanibel & Captiva Islands Chamber of Commerce 1159 Causeway Rd *Web:* www.sanibel-captiva.org	Sanibel	FL	33957	239-472-1080	472-1070
Walton County Chamber of Commerce 63 South Ctr Trail *Web:* www.waltoncountychamber.com	Santa Rosa Beach	FL	32459	850-267-0683	267-0603
Greater Sarasota Chamber of Commerce 1945 Fruitville Rd *Web:* www.sarasotachamber.org	Sarasota	FL	34236	941-955-8187	366-5621
Sebastian River Area Chamber of Commerce 700 Main St *TF:* 888-881-7568 ■ *Web:* www.sebastianchamber.com	Sebastian	FL	32958	772-589-5969	589-5993
Greater Sebring Chamber of Commerce 309 Circle Park Dr *TF:* 877-844-6007 ■ *Web:* www.sebringflchamber.com	Sebring	FL	33870	863-385-8448	385-8810
Greater Seffner Area Chamber of Commerce 11816 US Hwy 92 E PO Box 1920 *Web:* www.seffnerchamber.com	Seffner	FL	33583	813-627-8686	627-8699
Greater Seminole Area Chamber of Commerce 8400 113th St N *Web:* www.seminolechamber.net	Seminole	FL	33772	727-392-3245	397-7753
Chamber South 6410 SW 80th St *Web:* www.chambersouth.com	South Miami	FL	33143	305-661-1621	666-0508
Stuart-Martin County Chamber of Commerce 1650 S Kanner Hwy *Web:* www.goodnature.org	Stuart	FL	34994	772-287-1088	220-3437
Sumter County Chamber of Commerce 225 N US 301 *Web:* www.gosumter.com	Sumterville	FL	33585	352-793-3099	793-2120
Sunrise Chamber of Commerce 12801 W Sunrise Blvd Suite 101 *Web:* www.greatersunrisechamber.org	Sunrise	FL	33323	954-835-2428	835-2431
Tallahassee Chamber of Commerce PO Box 1639 *Web:* www.talchamber.com/	Tallahassee	FL	32302	850-224-8116	561-3860
Tamarac Chamber of Commerce 8525 W McNab Rd *Web:* www.tamaracchamber.org	Tamarac	FL	33321	954-722-1520	721-2725
Greater Tampa Chamber of Commerce PO Box 420 *TF:* 800-298-2672 ■ *Web:* www.tampachamber.com	Tampa	FL	33601	813-228-7777	223-7899
North Tampa Chamber of Commerce PO Box 82043 *Web:* www.northtampachamber.com	Tampa	FL	33682	813-961-2420	961-2903
Ybor City Chamber of Commerce 1800 E 9th Ave *Web:* www.ybor.org	Tampa	FL	33605	813-248-3712	247-1764
Tarpon Springs Chamber of Commerce 11 E Orange St *Web:* www.tarponsprings.com	Tarpon Springs	FL	34689	727-937-6109	937-2879
Titusville Area Chamber of Commerce 2000 S Washington Ave *Web:* www.titusville.org	Titusville	FL	32780	321-267-3036	264-0127
Venice Area Chamber of Commerce 597 Tamiami Trail S *Web:* www.venicechamber.com	Venice	FL	34285	941-488-2236	484-5903
Indian River County Chamber of Commerce 1216 21st St *Web:* www.indianriverchamber.com	Vero Beach	FL	32960	772-567-3491	778-3181
Chamber of Commerce of the Palm Beaches 401 N Flagler Dr *Web:* www.palmbeaches.org	West Palm Beach	FL	33401	561-833-3711	833-5582
Weston Area Chamber of Commerce 1290 Weston Rd Suite 200 *Web:* www.westonchamber.com	Weston	FL	33326	954-389-0600	384-6133
West Orange Chamber of Commerce 12184 W Colonial Dr *Web:* www.wochamber.com	Winter Garden	FL	34787	407-656-1304	656-0221
Greater Winter Haven Area Chamber of Commerce 401 Ave 'B' NW *TF:* 800-871-7027 ■ *Web:* www.winterhavenfl.com	Winter Haven	FL	33881	863-293-2138	297-5818

	City	State	Zip	Phone	Fax
Goldenrod Area Chamber of Commerce 4755 Palmetto Ave *Web:* www.goldenrodchamber.com	Winter Park	FL	32792	407-677-5980	677-4928
Winter Park Chamber of Commerce 150 N New York Ave *TF:* 877-972-4262 ■ *Web:* www.winterpark.org	Winter Park	FL	32789	407-644-8281	644-7826
Zephyrhills Chamber of Commerce 38550 5th Ave *Web:* www.lschamber.com	Zephyrhills	FL	33542	813-782-1913	783-6060

Georgia

	City	State	Zip	Phone	Fax
Albany Area Chamber of Commerce 225 W Broad Ave *TF:* 800-475-8700 ■ *Web:* www.albanyga.com	Albany	GA	31701	229-434-8700	434-8716
Greater North Fulton Chamber of Commerce 11605 Haynes Bridge Rd Suite 100 *Web:* www.gnfcc.com	Alpharetta	GA	30004	770-993-8806	594-1059
Americus-Sumter County Chamber of Commerce 400 W Lamar St PO Box 724 *Web:* www.americus-sumterchamber.com	Americus	GA	31709	229-924-2646	924-8784
Athens Area Chamber of Commerce 246 W Hancock Ave *Web:* www.athenschamber.net	Athens	GA	30601	706-549-6800	549-5636
Cobb Chamber of Commerce 240 Interstate N Pkwy *Web:* www.cobbchamber.org	Atlanta	GA	30339	770-980-2000	980-9510
Metro Atlanta Chamber of Commerce 235 Andrew Young International Blvd NW *Web:* www.metroatlantachamber.com	Atlanta	GA	30303	404-880-9000	586-8426
Augusta Metro Chamber of Commerce PO Box 1837 *Web:* www.augustagausa.com	Augusta	GA	30903	706-821-1300	821-1330
Bainbridge-Decatur County Chamber of Commerce PO Box 755 *TF:* 800-243-4774 ■ *Web:* www.bainbridgega.com/chamber/chamber.shtml	Bainbridge	GA	39818	229-246-4774	243-7633
Brunswick-Golden Isles Chamber of Commerce 4 Glynn Ave *Web:* brunswick-georgia.com/chamber	Brunswick	GA	31520	912-265-0620	265-0629
Gordon County Chamber of Commerce 300 S Wall St *TF:* 800-887-3811 ■ *Web:* www.gordonchamber.org	Calhoun	GA	30701	706-625-3200	625-5062
Cherokee County Chamber of Commerce 3605 Marietta Hwy *Web:* www.cherokee-chamber.com	Canton	GA	30114	770-345-0400	345-0030
Carroll County Chamber of Commerce 200 Northside Dr *Web:* www.carroll-ga.org	Carrollton	GA	30117	770-832-2446	832-1300
Cartersville-Bartow County Chamber of Commerce 122 W Main St PO Box 307 *Web:* www.cartersvillechamber.com	Cartersville	GA	30120	770-382-1466	382-2704
Chatsworth-Murray County Chamber of Commerce 126 N 3rd Ave *TF:* 800-969-9490 ■ *Web:* www.murraycountychamber.com	Chatsworth	GA	30705	706-695-6060	517-0198
White County Chamber of Commerce 122 N Main St *TF:* 800-392-8279 ■ *Web:* www.whitecountychamber.org	Cleveland	GA	30528	706-865-5356	865-0758
Greater Columbus Chamber of Commerce 1200 6th Ave PO Box 1200 *TF:* 800-360-8552 ■ *Web:* www.columbusgachamber.com	Columbus	GA	31902	706-327-1566	327-7512
Conyers-Rockdale Chamber of Commerce 1186 Scott St *Web:* www.conyers-rockdale.com	Conyers	GA	30012	770-483-7049	922-8415
Habersham County Chamber of Commerce PO Box 366 *TF:* 800-835-2559 ■ *Web:* www.habershamchamber.com	Cornelia	GA	30531	706-778-4654	776-1416
Newton County Chamber of Commerce 2100 Washington St *Web:* www.newtonchamber.com	Covington	GA	30014	770-786-7510	786-1294
Cumming-Forsyth County Chamber of Commerce 212 Kelly Mill Rd *Web:* www.cummingforsythchamber.org	Cumming	GA	30040	770-887-6461	781-8800
Paulding County Chamber of Commerce 455 Jimmy Campbell Pkwy *Web:* www.pauldingcountygeorgia.com	Dallas	GA	30132	770-445-6016	445-3050
Dalton-Whitfield Chamber of Commerce 890 College Dr *Web:* www.daltonchamber.org	Dalton	GA	30720	706-278-7373	226-8739
DeKalb Chamber of Commerce 150 E Ponce de Leon Ave Suite 400 *Web:* www.dekalbchamber.org	Decatur	GA	30030	404-378-8000	378-3397
Douglas-Coffee County Chamber of Commerce 211 S Gaskin Ave *TF:* 888-426-3334 ■ *Web:* www.douglasga.org	Douglas	GA	31533	912-384-1873	383-6304
Douglas County Chamber of Commerce 6658 Church St *Web:* www.douglascountygeorgia.com	Douglasville	GA	30134	770-942-5022	942-5876
Dublin-Laurens County Chamber of Commerce 1200 Bellvue *Web:* www.dublin-georgia.com	Dublin	GA	31021	478-272-5546	275-0811
Gwinnett Chamber of Commerce 6500 Sugarloaf Pkwy *Web:* www.gwinnettchamber.org	Duluth	GA	30097	770-232-3000	232-8807
Columbia County Chamber of Commerce 4424 Evans to Locks Rd *Web:* www.columbiacountychamber.com	Evans	GA	30809	706-651-0018	651-0023
Fayette County Chamber of Commerce 200 Courthouse Sq *Web:* www.fayettechamber.org	Fayetteville	GA	30214	770-461-9983	461-9622
Greater Hall Chamber of Commerce 230 EE Butler Pkwy *Web:* www.ghcc.com	Gainesville	GA	30501	770-532-6206	535-8419
Griffin-Spalding Chamber of Commerce 143 N Hill St *Web:* www.griffinchamber.com	Griffin	GA	30223	770-228-8200	228-8031
Liberty County Chamber of Commerce 500 E Oglethorpe Hwy *Web:* www.libertycounty.org	Hinesville	GA	31313	912-368-4445	368-4677
Jackson County Area Chamber of Commerce 270 Athens St *Web:* www.jacksoncountyga.com	Jefferson	GA	30549	706-387-0300	387-0304
Clayton County Chamber of Commerce 2270 Mt Zion Rd *Web:* www.claytonchamber.org	Jonesboro	GA	30236	678-610-4021	610-4025
LaGrange-Troup County Chamber of Commerce PO Box 636 *Web:* www.lagrangechamber.com	LaGrange	GA	30241	706-884-8671	882-8012
Greater Macon Chamber of Commerce 305 Coliseum Dr *Web:* www.maconchamber.com	Macon	GA	31217	478-621-2000	621-2021
Henry County Chamber of Commerce 1709 Hwy 20 W West Ridge Business Ctr *TF:* 800-436-7926 ■ *Web:* www.henrycounty.com	McDonough	GA	30253	770-957-5786	957-8030
Milledgeville-Baldwin County Chamber of Commerce 130 S Jefferson St *Web:* www.milledgevillega.com	Milledgeville	GA	31061	478-453-9311	453-0051
Walton County Chamber of Commerce 132 E Spring St *Web:* www.waltonchamber.org	Monroe	GA	30655	770-267-6594	267-0961
Moultrie-Colquitt County Chamber of Commerce 116 1st Ave SE *TF:* 888-408-4748 ■ *Web:* www.moultriechamber.com	Moultrie	GA	31768	229-985-2131	890-2638
Newnan-Coweta Chamber of Commerce 23 Bullsboro Dr *Web:* www.newnancowetachamber.org	Newnan	GA	30263	770-253-2270	253-2271
Catoosa County Area Chamber of Commerce 264 Catoosa Cir *TF:* 877-965-5201 ■ *Web:* www.gatewaytogeorgia.com	Ringgold	GA	30736	706-965-5201	965-8224
Walker County Chamber of Commerce 10052 N Hwy 27 *Web:* www.walkercochamber.com	Rock Spring	GA	30739	706-375-7702	375-7797
Polk County Chamber of Commerce/Development Authority 604 Goodyear St *TF:* 800-226-2517 ■ *Web:* polk.ofgeorgia.org	Rockmart	GA	30153	770-684-8760	684-9155
Greater Rome Chamber of Commerce 1 Riverside Pkwy *TF:* 800-234-3154 ■ *Web:* www.romega.com	Rome	GA	30161	706-291-7663	232-5755
Camden-Kings Bay Area Chamber of Commerce 2603 Osborne Rd Suite R *Web:* www.camdenchamber.com	Saint Marys	GA	31558	912-729-5840	576-7924
Savannah Area Chamber of Commerce 101 E Bay St *TF:* 877-728-2662 ■ *Web:* www.savannahchamber.com	Savannah	GA	31401	912-644-6400	644-6499
Effingham County Chamber of Commerce 520 W 3rd St PO Box 1078 *TF:* 866-754-3301 ■ *Web:* www.effinghamcounty.com	Springfield	GA	31329	912-754-3301	754-1236
Statesboro-Bulloch Chamber of Commerce 102 S Main St *Web:* www.statesboro-chamber.org	Statesboro	GA	30458	912-764-6111	489-3108
Thomaston-Upson Chamber of Commerce 213 E Gordon St *Web:* www.thomastonchamber.com	Thomaston	GA	30286	706-647-9686	647-1703
Thomasville-Thomas County Chamber of Commerce 401 S Broad St *Web:* www.thomasvillechamber.com	Thomasville	GA	31792	229-226-9600	226-9603
Tifton-Tift County Chamber of Commerce 100 Central Ave *TF:* 800-550-8438 ■ *Web:* www.tiftonchamber.org	Tifton	GA	31794	229-382-6200	386-2232
Toccoa-Stephens County Chamber of Commerce 160 N Alexander St *Web:* www.toccoagachamber.com	Toccoa	GA	30577	706-886-2132	886-2133
South Fulton Chamber of Commerce 6400 Shannon Pkwy *Web:* www.sfcoc.org	Union City	GA	30291	770-964-1984	969-1969
Valdosta-Lowndes County Chamber of Commerce 416 N Ashley St *Web:* www.valdostachamber.com	Valdosta	GA	31601	229-247-8100	245-0071
Warner Robins Area Chamber of Commerce 1420 Watson Blvd *Web:* www.warner-robins.com	Warner Robins	GA	31093	478-922-8585	328-7745
Waycross-Ware County Chamber of Commerce 315 Plant Ave Suite B *Web:* www.waycrosschamber.org	Waycross	GA	31501	912-283-3742	283-0121
Barrow County Chamber of Commerce PO Box 456 *Web:* www.barrowchamber.com	Winder	GA	30680	770-867-9444	867-6366

Hawaii

	City	State	Zip	Phone	Fax
Hawaii Island Chamber of Commerce 106 Kamehameha Ave	Hilo	HI	96720	808-935-7178	961-4435
Maui Chamber of Commerce 313 Ano St *Web:* www.mauichamber.com	Kahului	HI	96732	808-871-7711	871-0706
Kailua Chamber of Commerce 600 Kailua Rd Suite 107 *Web:* www.visitkailua.com	Kailua	HI	96734	808-261-2727	
Kona-Kohala Chamber of Commerce 75-5737 Kuakini Hwy Suite 208 *Web:* www.kona-kohala.com	Kailua-Kona	HI	96740	808-329-1758	329-8564
Kaua'i Chamber of Commerce PO Box 1969 *Web:* www.kauaichamber.org	Lihue	HI	96766	808-245-7363	245-8815

Idaho

	City	State	Zip	Phone	Fax
Boise Metro Chamber of Commerce PO Box 2368 *Web:* www.boisechamber.org	Boise	ID	83701	208-472-5205	472-5201
Caldwell Chamber of Commerce 704 Blaine St *Web:* chamber.cityofcaldwell.com/index.v3page?p=32790	Caldwell	ID	83605	208-459-7493	454-1284
Coeur d'Alene Area Chamber of Commerce 1621 N 3rd St Suite 100 *TF:* 877-782-9232 ■ *Web:* www.cdachamber.com	Coeur d'Alene	ID	83814	208-664-3194	667-9338
Mini-Cassia Chamber of Commerce 1177 7th St *Web:* www.minicassiachamber.org	Heyburn	ID	83336	208-679-4793	679-4794
Greater Idaho Falls Chamber of Commerce 630 W Broadway *TF:* 866-365-6943 ■ *Web:* www.idahofallschamber.com	Idaho Falls	ID	83402	208-523-1010	523-2255
Lewiston Chamber of Commerce 111 Main St Suite 120 *TF:* 800-473-3543 ■ *Web:* www.lewistonchamber.org	Lewiston	ID	83501	208-743-3531	743-2176
Meridian Chamber of Commerce PO Box 7 *Web:* www.meridianchamber.org	Meridian	ID	83680	208-888-2817	888-2682
Moscow Chamber of Commerce 411 S Main St *TF:* 800-380-1801 ■ *Web:* www.moscowchamber.com	Moscow	ID	83843	208-882-1800	882-6186
Nampa Chamber of Commerce 312 13th Ave S *Web:* www.nampa.com	Nampa	ID	83651	208-466-4641	466-4677
Greater Pocatello Chamber of Commerce 324 S Main St *Web:* www.pocatelloidaho.com	Pocatello	ID	83204	208-233-1525	233-1527
Sun Valley/Ketchum Chamber & Visitors Bureau PO Box 2420 *TF:* 800-634-3347 ■ *Web:* www.visitsunvalley.com	Sun Valley	ID	83353	208-726-3423	726-4533
Twin Falls Area Chamber of Commerce 858 Blue Lakes Blvd N *TF:* 866-894-6325 ■ *Web:* www.twinfallschamber.com	Twin Falls	ID	83301	208-733-3974	733-9216

Illinois

	City	State	Zip	Phone	Fax
Addison Chamber of Commerce & Industry 777 W Army Trail Rd Suite D *Web:* www.addisonchamber.org	Addison	IL	60101	630-543-4300	543-4355
Algonquin/Lake in the Hills Chamber of Commerce 106 S Main St *Web:* www.algonquin-lith-chamber.com	Algonquin	IL	60102	847-658-5300	658-6546
Arlington Heights Chamber of Commerce 311 S Arlington Heights Rd Suite 20 *Web:* www.arlingtonhtschamber.com	Arlington Heights	IL	60005	847-253-1703	253-9133
Greater Aurora Chamber of Commerce 43 W Galena Blvd *Web:* www.aurorachamber.com	Aurora	IL	60506	630-897-9214	897-7002
Barrington Area Chamber of Commerce 325 N Hough St *Web:* www.barringtonchamber.com	Barrington	IL	60010	847-381-2525	381-2540
Bartlett Chamber of Commerce 138 S Oak Ave *Web:* www.bartlettchamber.com	Bartlett	IL	60103	630-830-0324	830-9724
Belvidere Area Chamber of Commerce 200 S State St *Web:* www.belviderechamber.com	Belvidere	IL	61008	815-544-4357	547-7654
Berwyn Development Corp 3322 S Oak Pk Ave 2nd Fl *Web:* www.berwyn.net	Berwyn	IL	60402	708-788-8100	788-0966
McLean County Chamber of Commerce 210 S East St *Web:* www.mcleancochamber.org	Bloomington	IL	61702	309-829-6344	827-3940
Bolingbrook Chamber of Commerce & Industry 375 W Briarcliff Rd *Web:* www.bolingbrookchamber.org	Bolingbrook	IL	60440	630-226-8420	759-9937
Bradley-Bourbonnais Chamber of Commerce 1690 Newtown Dr *Web:* www.bbchamber.com	Bourbonnais	IL	60914	815-932-2222	932-3294
Buffalo Grove Area Chamber of Commerce 50 1/2 Raupp Blvd *Web:* www.bgacc.org	Buffalo Grove	IL	60089	847-541-7799	541-7819

Illinois (Cont'd)

Phone | Fax

Calumet City Chamber of Commerce
80 River Oaks Center Westwood Bldg ARC 6 ... Calumet City IL 60409 708-891-5888 891-8877
Web: www.calumetcitychamber.com/
Carbondale Chamber of Commerce 131 S Illinois Ave ... Carbondale IL 62901 618-549-2146 529-5063
Web: www.carbondalechamber.com
Northern Kane County Chamber of Commerce
2429 Randall Rd Suite B ... Carpentersville IL 60110 847-426-8565 426-1098
Web: www.nkcchamber.com
Champaign County Chamber of Commerce
1817 S Neil St Suite 201 ... Champaign IL 61820 217-359-1791 359-1809
Web: www.ccchamber.org
Charleston Area Chamber of Commerce 501 Jackson Ave ... Charleston IL 61920 217-345-7041 345-7042
Web: www.charlestonchamber.com
Albany Park Chamber of Commerce 4745 N Kedzie Ave ... Chicago IL 60625 773-478-0202 478-0282
Web: www.kacm.com/albanypchamber.html
Business Partners the Chamber for Uptown
4753 N Broadway Suite 822 ... Chicago IL 60640 773-878-1184 878-3678
Web: www.uptownbusinesspartners.com
Chicagoland Chamber of Commerce
200 E Randolph St Suite 2200 ... Chicago IL 60601 312-494-6700 494-0660
Web: www.chicagolandchamber.org
Cosmopolitan Chamber of Commerce 560 W Lake St 5th Fl ... Chicago IL 60661 312-786-0212 243-9847
Web: www.cchamber.org
East Side Chamber of Commerce 3658 E 106th St ... Chicago IL 60617 773-721-7948 721-7446
Web: www.eastsidechamber.com
Hyde Park Chamber of Commerce 5211-D S Harper Ave ... Chicago IL 60615 773-288-0124 288-0464
Web: www.hpchamber.com
Jefferson Park Chamber of Commerce
4849 N Milwaukee Ave Suite 305 ... Chicago IL 60630 773-736-6697 736-3508
Web: www.jeffersonpark.net
Lincoln Park Chamber of Commerce
1925 N Clybourn Ave Suite 301 ... Chicago IL 60614 773-880-5200 880-0266
Web: www.lincolnparkchamber.com
Portage Park Chamber of Commerce 4849-A W Irving Park Rd ... Chicago IL 60641 773-777-2020 777-0202
Web: www.portageparkchamber.org
Cicero Chamber of Commerce & Industry 5801 Cermak Rd ... Cicero IL 60804 708-863-6000 863-8981
Web: www.cicerochamber.org
Collinsville Chamber of Commerce 221 W Main St ... Collinsville IL 62234 618-344-2884 344-7499
Web: www.discovercollinsville.com
Crete Area Chamber of Commerce 1182 Main St PO Box 263 ... Crete IL 60417 708-672-9216 672-7640
Web: www.cretechamber.com
Crystal Lake Chamber of Commerce 427 Virginia St ... Crystal Lake IL 60014 815-459-1300
Web: www.clchamber.com
Danville Area Chamber of Commerce 28 W North St ... Danville IL 61832 217-442-1887 442-6228
TF: 800-373-6201
Chamber of Commerce for Decatur & Macon County
243 S Water St Suite 100 ... Decatur IL 62523 217-422-2200 422-4576
Web: www.decaturchamber.com
Deerfield Bannockburn & Riverwoods Chamber of Commerce
601 Deerfield Rd Suite 200 ... Deerfield IL 60015 847-945-4660 940-0381
Web: www.dbrchamber.com
DeKalb Chamber of Commerce 164 E Lincoln Hwy ... DeKalb IL 60115 815-756-6306 756-5164
Web: www.dekalb.org
Des Plaines Chamber of Commerce & Industry
1401 E Oakton St ... Des Plaines IL 60018 847-824-4200 824-7932
Web: www.dpchamber.com
Dolton Chamber of Commerce 1515 E 154th St Suite 121 ... Dolton IL 60419 708-841-4810 841-4833
Downers Grove Area Chamber of Commerce & Industry
1015 Curtiss St ... Downers Grove IL 60515 630-968-4050 968-8368
Web: www.downersgrove.org
Greater East Saint Louis Chamber of Commerce
327 Missouri Ave Suite 602 ... East Saint Louis IL 62201 618-271-2855 271-4622
Elgin Area Chamber of Commerce 31 S Grove Ave ... Elgin IL 60120 847-741-5660 741-5677
Web: www.elginchamber.com
Greater O'Hare Assn of Industry & Commerce
PO Box 1516 ... Elk Grove Village IL 60009 630-350-2944 350-2979
TF: 877-355-4768 ■ *Web:* www.greater-ohare.com
Elmhurst Chamber of Commerce & Industry 113 Adell Pl ... Elmhurst IL 60126 630-834-6060 834-6002
Web: www.elmhurstchamber.org
Mont Clare-Elmwood Park Chamber of Commerce
11 Conti Pkwy ... Elmwood Park IL 60707 708-456-8000 456-8680
Web: www.mcepchamber.org
Evanston Chamber of Commerce
1560 Sherman Ave Suite 860 ... Evanston IL 60201 847-328-1500 328-1510
Web: www.evchamber.com
Evergreen Park Chamber of Commerce
3960 W 95 St 3rd Fl ... Evergreen Park IL 60805 708-423-1118 423-1859
Web: www.evergreenparkchamber.org
Freeport Area Chamber of Commerce 27 W Stephenson St ... Freeport IL 61032 815-233-1350 235-4038
Web: www.freeportilchamber.com
Galesburg Area Chamber of Commerce 311 E Waters St ... Galesburg IL 61401 309-343-1194 343-1195
Web: www.galesburg.org
Glen Ellyn Chamber of Commerce
800 Roosevelt Rd Bldg D Suite 108 ... Glen Ellyn IL 60137 630-469-0907 469-0426
Web: www.glenellynchamber.com
Glenview Chamber of Commerce 2320 Glenview Rd ... Glenview IL 60025 847-724-0900 724-0202
Web: www.glenviewchamber.com
Growth Assn of Southwestern Illinois
5800 Godfrey Rd Alden Hall ... Godfrey IL 62035 618-467-2280 466-8289
Web: www.growthassociation.com
Chamber of Commerce of Southwestern Madison County
3600 Nameoki Rd Suite 202 ... Granite City IL 62040 618-876-6400 876-6448
Web: www.chamberswmadisoncounty.com
Lake County Chamber of Commerce 5221 W Grand Ave ... Gurnee IL 60031 847-249-3800 249-3892
Web: www.lakecountychamber.com
Chicago Southland Chamber of Commerce
1916 W 174th St ... Hazel Crest IL 60429 708-957-6950 957-6968
Web: www.chicagosouthland.com
Highland Park Chamber of Commerce
508 Central Ave Suite 206 ... Highland Park IL 60035 847-432-0284 432-2802
Web: www.ehighlandpark.com
Hoffman Estates Chamber of Commerce
2200 W Higgins Rd Suite 201 ... Hoffman Estates IL 60169 847-781-9100 781-9172
Web: www.hechamber.com
Jacksonville Area Chamber of Commerce
155 W Morton Ave ... Jacksonville IL 62650 217-245-2174 245-0661
Web: www.jacksonvilleil.org
Joliet Region Chamber of Commerce & Industry 63 N Chicago St ... Joliet IL 60432 815-727-5371 727-5374
Web: www.jolietchamber.com
Joliet/Will County Center for Economic Development
116 N Chicago St Suite 101 ... Joliet IL 60432 815-723-1800 723-6972
Web: www.willcountyced.com
Kankakee Regional Chamber of Commerce PO Box 905 ... Kankakee IL 60901 815-933-7721 933-7675
Web: www.kankakee.org

Phone | Fax

West Suburban Chamber of Commerce
9440 Joliet Rd Suite B ... La Grange IL 60525 708-387-7550 387-7556
Web: www.westsuburbanchamber.org
Illinois Valley Area Chamber of Commerce & Economic Development 300 Bucklin St ... La Salle IL 61301 815-223-0227 223-4827
Web: www.ivaced.org
Lake Zurich Area Chamber of Commerce
1st Bank Plaza Suite 308 ... Lake Zurich IL 60047 847-438-5572 438-5574
Web: www.lzacc.com
Lansing Chamber of Commerce 3404 Lake St ... Lansing IL 60438 708-474-4170 474-7393
Green Oaks/Libertyville/Mundelein/Vernon Hills Area Chamber of Commerce & Industry 1123 S Milwaukee Ave ... Libertyville IL 60048 847-680-0750 680-0760
Web: www.glmvchamber.org
Lincoln/Logan County Chamber of Commerce 1555 5th St ... Lincoln IL 62656 217-735-2385 735-9205
Web: www.lincolnillinois.com
Lombard Area Chamber of Commerce 225 W St Charles Rd ... Lombard IL 60148 630-627-5040 627-5519
Web: www.lombardchamber.com
Parks Chamber of Commerce 100 Heart Blvd ... Loves Park IL 61111 815-633-3999 633-4057
Web: www.parkschamber.com
Macomb Area Chamber of Commerce & Downtown Development Corp 214 N Lafayette St ... Macomb IL 61455 309-837-4855 837-4857
Web: www.macombareachamber.com
Greater Marion Area Chamber of Commerce 2305 W Main St ... Marion IL 62959 618-997-6311 997-4665
TF: 800-699-1760 ■ *Web:* www.marionillinois.com
McHenry Area Chamber of Commerce 1257 N Green St ... McHenry IL 60050 815-385-4300 385-9142
Web: www.mchenrychamber.com
Illinois Quad City Chamber of Commerce 622 19th St ... Moline IL 61265 309-757-5416 757-5435
Web: www.quadcitychamber.com
Grundy County Chamber of Commerce & Industry
909 N Liberty St ... Morris IL 60450 815-942-0113 942-0117
Web: www.grundychamber.com
Mount Prospect Chamber of Commerce 107 S Main St ... Mount Prospect IL 60056 847-398-6616 398-6780
Web: www.mountprospectchamber.org
Jefferson County Chamber of Commerce PO Box 1047 ... Mount Vernon IL 62864 618-242-5725 242-5130
Web: www.southernillinois.com
Naperville Area Chamber of Commerce
55 S Main St Suite 351 ... Naperville IL 60540 630-355-4141 355-8335
Web: www.naperville.net
Niles Chamber of Commerce 8060 W Oakton St Suite 101 ... Niles IL 60714 847-268-8180 268-8186
Web: www.nileschamber.org
Northbrook Chamber of Commerce & Industry
2002 Walters Ave ... Northbrook IL 60062 847-498-5555 498-5510
Web: www.northbrookchamber.org
Oak Forest Chamber of Commerce 15440 S Central Ave ... Oak Forest IL 60452 708-687-4600 687-7878
Web: www.oakforestchamber.org
Oak Lawn Chamber of Commerce 5314 W 95th St ... Oak Lawn IL 60453 708-424-8300 229-2236
Web: www.oaklawnchamber.com
Oak Park-River Forest Chamber of Commerce
1110 North Blvd ... Oak Park IL 60301 708-848-8151 848-8182
Web: www.oprfchamber.org
Orland Park Area Chamber of Commerce 8799 W 151 St ... Orland Park IL 60462 708-349-2972 349-7454
Web: www.orlandparkchamber.org
Palatine Area Chamber of Commerce
625 N North Ct Suite 320 ... Palatine IL 60067 847-359-7200 359-7246
Web: www.palatinechamber.com
Paris Area Chamber of Commerce & Tourism 105 N Central Ave ... Paris IL 61944 217-465-4179 465-4170
Web: www.parisilchamber.com
Matteson Area Chamber of Commerce 298 Main St ... Park Forest IL 60466 708-747-6000 747-6054
Web: www.macclink.com
Park Ridge Chamber of Commerce 32 Main St Suite F ... Park Ridge IL 60068 847-825-3121 825-3122
Web: www.parkridgeilchamber.com
Pekin Area Chamber of Commerce 402 Court St ... Pekin IL 61554 309-346-2106 346-2104
Web: www.pekin.net
Peoria Area Chamber of Commerce 124 SW Adams St Suite 300 ... Peoria IL 61602 309-676-0755 676-7534
Web: www.peoriachamber.org
Quincy Area Chamber of Commerce
300 Civic Ctr Plaza Suite 245 ... Quincy IL 62301 217-222-7980 222-3033
Web: www.quincychamber.org
Rockford Regional Chamber of Commerce
308 W State St Suite 190 ... Rockford IL 61101 815-987-8100 987-8122
Web: www.rockfordchamber.com
Rolling Meadows Chamber of Commerce
2775 Algonquin Rd Suite 230 ... Rolling Meadows IL 60008 847-398-3730 398-3745
Web: www.rmchamber.com
Round Lake Area Chamber of Commerce & Industry
2007 Civic Center Way ... Round Lake Beach IL 60073 847-546-2002 546-2254
Web: www.rlchamber.org
Skokie Chamber of Commerce 5002 Oakton St PO Box 106 ... Skokie IL 60077 847-673-0240 673-0249
Web: www.skokiechamber.org
Greater Springfield Chamber of Commerce
3 S Old State Capitol Plaza ... Springfield IL 62701 217-525-1173 525-8768
Web: www.gscc.org
Illinois Assn of Chamber of Commerce Executives
215 E Adams St ... Springfield IL 62701 217-522-5512 522-5518
Web: www.iacce.org
Streamwood Chamber of Commerce
22 W Streamwood Blvd PO Box 545 ... Streamwood IL 60107 630-837-5200 837-5251
Web: www.streamwoodchamber.com
Streator Area Chamber of Commerce & Industry
320 E Main St PO Box 360 ... Streator IL 61364 815-672-2921 672-1768
Web: www.streatorchamber.com
Tinley Park Chamber of Commerce 17316 S Oak Park Ave ... Tinley Park IL 60477 708-532-5700 532-1475
Web: www.tinleychamber.org
Wheaton Chamber of Commerce 108 E Wesley St ... Wheaton IL 60187 630-668-6464 668-2744
Web: www.ewheaton.com
Wheeling/Prospect Heights Area Chamber of Commerce & Industry 395 E Dundee Rd Suite 300 ... Wheeling IL 60090 847-541-0170 541-0296
Web: www.wphchamber.com
Wilmette Chamber of Commerce 1150 Wilmette Ave Suite A ... Wilmette IL 60091 847-251-3800 251-6321
Web: www.wilmettechamber.org
Woodridge Chamber of Commerce 5 Plaza Dr Suite 212 ... Woodridge IL 60517 630-960-7080 852-2316
Web: www.woodridgechamber.org
Woodstock Chamber of Commerce & Industry 136 Cass St ... Woodstock IL 60098 815-338-2436 338-2927
Web: www.woodstockilchamber.com
Chicago Ridge-Worth Chamber of Commerce PO Box 356 ... Worth IL 60482 708-923-2050 728-7887

Indiana

Phone | Fax

Chamber of Commerce for Anderson & Madison County
205 W 11th St ... Anderson IN 46016 765-642-0264 642-0266
Web: www.andersoninchamber.com
Angola Area Chamber of Commerce 211 E Maumee St Suite B ... Angola IN 46703 260-665-3512 665-7418
Web: www.angolachamber.org
Auburn Chamber of Commerce 208 S Jackson St ... Auburn IN 46706 260-925-2100 925-2199
Web: www.chamberinauburn.com

	City	State	ZIP	Phone	Fax
Greater Bloomington Chamber of Commerce 400 W 7th St Suite 102 *Web:* www.chamberbloomington.org	Bloomington	IN	47404	812-336-6381	336-0651
Warrick County Chamber of Commerce 224 W Main St *Web:* www.warrickcounty.us	Boonville	IN	47601	812-897-2340	897-2360
Carmel-Clay Chamber of Commerce 41 E Main St *Web:* www.carmelchamber.com	Carmel	IN	46032	317-846-1049	844-6843
Columbia City Area Chamber of Commerce 201 N Line St *Web:* www.columbiacity.org	Columbia City	IN	46725	260-248-8131	248-8162
Columbus Area Chamber of Commerce 500 Franklin St *Web:* www.columbusareachamber.com	Columbus	IN	47201	812-379-4457	378-7308
Connersville/Fayette County Chamber of Commerce 115 E 6th St	Connersville	IN	47331	765-825-2561	825-4613
Chamber of Commerce of Harrison County 310 N Elm St *Web:* www.harrisonchamber.org	Corydon	IN	47112	812-738-2137	738-6438
Crawfordsville-Montgomery County Chamber of Commerce 309 N Green St *Web:* www.crawfordsvillechamber.com	Crawfordsville	IN	47933	765-362-6800	362-6900
Greater Elkhart Chamber of Commerce 418 S Main St *Web:* www.elkhart.org	Elkhart	IN	46516	574-293-1531	294-1859
Metropolitan Evansville Chamber of Commerce 100 NW 2nd St Suite 100 *Web:* www.evansvillechamber.com	Evansville	IN	47708	812-425-8147	421-5883
Greater Fort Wayne Chamber of Commerce 826 Ewing St *Web:* www.fwchamber.org	Fort Wayne	IN	46802	260-424-1435	426-7232
Clinton County Chamber of Commerce 259 E Walnut St *Web:* www.ccinchamber.org	Frankfort	IN	46041	765-654-5507	654-9592
Gary Chamber of Commerce 504 Broadway Suite 328 *Web:* www.garychamber.com	Gary	IN	46402	219-885-7407	885-7408
Goshen Chamber of Commerce 232 S Main St *TF:* 800-307-4204 ■ *Web:* www.goshen.org	Goshen	IN	46526	574-533-2102	533-2103
Greencastle Chamber of Commerce 16 S Jackson St *Web:* www.gogreencastle.com	Greencastle	IN	46135	765-653-4517	653-6385
Greater Greenwood Chamber of Commerce 550 US 31 S *Web:* www.greenwood-chamber.com	Greenwood	IN	46142	317-888-4856	865-2609
Lakeshore Chamber of Commerce 5246 Hohman Ave Suite 100 *Web:* www.lakeshorechamber.com	Hammond	IN	46320	219-931-1000	937-8778
Greater Lawrence Township Chamber of Commerce 9120 Otis Ave Suite 100 *Web:* www.lawrencechamberofcommerce.org	Indianapolis	IN	46216	317-541-9876	546-5106
Indianapolis Chamber of Commerce 111 Monument Cir Suite 1950 *Web:* www.indychamber.com	Indianapolis	IN	46204	317-464-2200	464-2217
Kokomo/Howard County Chamber of Commerce 325 N Main St *Web:* www.kokomochamber.com	Kokomo	IN	46901	765-457-5301	452-4564
Lafayette-West Lafayette Chamber of Commerce 337 Columbia St *Web:* www.lafayettechamber.com	Lafayette	IN	47901	765-742-4041	742-6276
LaGrange County Chamber of Commerce 901 S Detroit St Suite A *Web:* www.lagrangechamber.org	LaGrange	IN	46761	260-463-2443	463-2683
Dearborn County Chamber of Commerce 320 Walnut St *TF:* 800-322-8198 ■ *Web:* www.dearborncountychamber.org	Lawrenceburg	IN	47025	812-537-0814	537-0845
Boone County Chamber of Commerce 221 N Lebanon St *Web:* www.boonechamber.org	Lebanon	IN	46052	765-482-1320	482-3114
Logansport/Cass County Chamber of Commerce 300 E Broadway Suite 103 *TF:* 800-425-2071 ■ *Web:* www.logan-casschamber.com	Logansport	IN	46947	574-753-6388	735-0909
Madison Area Chamber of Commerce 975 Industrial Dr Suite 1 *Web:* www.madisonchamber.org	Madison	IN	47250	812-265-3135	265-9784
Marion-Grant County Chamber of Commerce 215 S Adams St *Web:* www.marionchamber.org	Marion	IN	46952	765-664-5107	668-5443
Merrillville Chamber of Commerce 255 W 80th Pl *Web:* www.merrillvillecoc.org	Merrillville	IN	46410	219-769-8180	736-6223
Michigan City Area Chamber of Commerce 200 E Michigan Blvd *Web:* www.michigancitychamber.com	Michigan City	IN	46360	219-874-6221	873-1204
Greater Monticello Chamber of Commerce PO Box 657 *Web:* www.monticelloin.com	Monticello	IN	47960	574-583-7220	583-3399
Posey County Chamber of Commerce 915 E 4th St *Web:* www.mtvernonposeycochamber.com	Mount Vernon	IN	47620	812-838-3639	838-6358
Muncie-Delaware County Chamber of Commerce 401 S High St *TF:* 800-336-1373 ■ *Web:* www.muncie.com	Muncie	IN	47305	765-288-6681	751-9151
One Southern Indiana 4100 Charlestown Rd *Web:* www.1si.org/	New Albany	IN	47150	812-945-0266	948-4664
Noblesville Chamber of Commerce 54 N 9th St Suite 100 *Web:* www.noblesvillechamber.com	Noblesville	IN	46060	317-773-0086	773-1966
Jennings County Chamber of Commerce 524 N State St PO Box 340 *Web:* www.jenningscountychamber.org	North Vernon	IN	47265	812-346-2339	346-2065
Peru/Miami County Chamber of Commerce 13 E Main St *Web:* www.miamicochamber.com	Peru	IN	46970	765-472-1923	472-7099
Greater Portage Chamber of Commerce 2642 Eleanor St *Web:* www.portageinchamber.com	Portage	IN	46368	219-762-3300	763-2450
Richmond-Wayne County Chamber of Commerce 33 S 7th St Suite 2 *Web:* www.rwchamber.org	Richmond	IN	47374	765-962-1511	966-0882
Schererville Chamber of Commerce 105 E Joliet St *Web:* www.scherervillechamber.com	Schererville	IN	46375	219-322-5412	322-0598
Shelby County Chamber of Commerce 501 N Harrison St *TF:* 800-318-4083 ■ *Web:* www.shelbychamber.net	Shelbyville	IN	46176	317-398-6647	392-3901
Chamber of Commerce of Saint Joseph County 401 E Colfax Ave Suite 310 *Web:* www.sjchamber.org	South Bend	IN	46617	574-234-0051	289-0358
Winchester Area Chamber of Commerce 112 W Washington St *Web:* www.winchesterchamber.org	Winchester	IN	47394	765-584-3731	584-5544

Iowa

	City	State	ZIP	Phone	Fax
Ames Chamber of Commerce 1601 Golden Aspen Dr Suite 110 *Web:* www.chamber.ames.ia.us	Ames	IA	50010	515-232-2310	232-6716
Bettendorf Chamber of Commerce 2117 State St *Web:* www.bettendorfchamber.com	Bettendorf	IA	52722	563-355-4753	344-4203
Burlington/West Burlington Area Chamber of Commerce 610 N 4th St Suite 200 *TF:* 800-827-4837 ■ *Web:* www.growburlington.com	Burlington	IA	52601	319-752-6365	752-6454
Cedar Falls Chamber of Commerce 10 Main St *Web:* www.cedarfalls.org	Cedar Falls	IA	50613	319-266-3593	277-4325
Cedar Rapids Area Chamber of Commerce 424 1st Ave NE *Web:* www.cedarrapids.org	Cedar Rapids	IA	52401	319-398-5317	398-5228
Clinton Area Chamber of Commerce 721 S 2nd St *TF:* 800-828-5702 ■ *Web:* www.clintonia.com	Clinton	IA	52732	563-242-5702	242-5803
Council Bluffs Area Chamber of Commerce 7 N 6th St *TF:* 800-228-6878 ■ *Web:* www.councilbluffsiowa.com	Council Bluffs	IA	51503	712-325-1000	322-5698
DavenportOne 130 W 2nd St *Web:* www.davenportone.com	Davenport	IA	52801	563-322-1706	322-7804
Greater Des Moines Partnership 700 Locust St Suite 100 *TF:* 800-376-9059 ■ *Web:* www.desmoinesmetro.com	Des Moines	IA	50309	515-286-4950	286-4974
Dubuque Area Chamber of Commerce 300 Main St Suite 200 *TF:* 800-798-4748 ■ *Web:* www.dubuquechamber.com	Dubuque	IA	52001	563-557-9200	557-1591
Fort Dodge Chamber of Commerce 1406 Central Ave *Web:* www.fortdodgechamber.com	Fort Dodge	IA	50501	515-955-5500	955-3245
Iowa City Area Chamber of Commerce 325 E Washington St Suite 100 *Web:* www.iowacityarea.com	Iowa City	IA	52240	319-337-9637	338-9958
Keokuk Area Chamber of Commerce 329 Main St	Keokuk	IA	52632	319-524-5055	524-5016
Marion Chamber of Commerce 790 11th St *Web:* www.cedarrapids.org/region/marion.asp	Marion	IA	52302	319-377-6316	377-1576
Marshalltown Area Chamber of Commerce 709 S Center St PO Box 1000 *Web:* www.marshalltown.org	Marshalltown	IA	50158	641-753-6645	752-8373
Mason City Area Chamber of Commerce 25 W State St *Web:* www.masoncityia.com	Mason City	IA	50401	641-423-5724	423-5725
Ottumwa Area Chamber of Commerce 217 E Mian St *TF:* 800-564-5274 ■ *Web:* www.ottumwaiowa.com	Ottumwa	IA	52501	641-682-3465	682-3466
Siouxland Chamber of Commerce 101 Pierce St *Web:* www.siouxlandchamber.com	Sioux City	IA	51101	712-255-7903	258-7578
Urbandale Chamber of Commerce 3600 86th St *Web:* www.urbandalechamber.com	Urbandale	IA	50322	515-331-6855	278-3927
Waterloo Chamber of Commerce 315 E 5th St *Web:* www.waterloochamber.org	Waterloo	IA	50703	319-233-8431	233-4580
West Des Moines Chamber of Commerce 4200 Mills Civic Pkwy Suite E100 *Web:* www.wdmchamber.org	West Des Moines	IA	50265	515-225-6009	225-7129

Kansas

	City	State	ZIP	Phone	Fax
Arkansas City Area Chamber of Commerce PO Box 795 *Web:* www.arkcity.org	Arkansas City	KS	67005	620-442-0230	441-0048
Dodge City Area Chamber of Commerce 311 W Spruce St *Web:* www.dodgechamber.com	Dodge City	KS	67801	620-227-3119	227-2957
Emporia Area Chamber of Commerce 719 Commercial St *Web:* www.emporia.com	Emporia	KS	66801	620-342-1600	342-3223
Garden City Area Chamber of Commerce 1511 E Fulton Terr *Web:* www.gardencity.net/chamber	Garden City	KS	67846	620-276-3264	276-3290
Hutchinson/Reno County Chamber of Commerce 117 N Walnut St *TF:* 800-691-4262 ■ *Web:* www.hutchchamber.com	Hutchinson	KS	67501	620-662-3391	662-2168
Junction City Area Chamber of Commerce 814 N Washington St *Web:* www.junctioncitychamber.org	Junction City	KS	66441	785-762-2632	762-3353
Kansas City Kansas Area Chamber of Commerce PO Box 171337 *Web:* www.kckchamber.com	Kansas City	KS	66117	913-371-3070	371-3732
Women's Chamber of Commerce PO Box 171337	Kansas City	KS	66117	913-371-3165	371-3732
Leavenworth-Lansing Area Chamber of Commerce 518 Shawnee St *TF:* 800-844-4114 ■ *Web:* www.leavenworth-lansingareachamberofcommerce.com	Leavenworth	KS	66048	913-682-4112	682-8170
Lenexa Chamber of Commerce 11180 Lackman Rd *TF:* 800-950-7867 ■ *Web:* www.lenexa.org	Lenexa	KS	66219	913-888-1414	888-3770
Liberal Area Chamber of Commerce PO Box 676 *Web:* www.liberalkschamber.com	Liberal	KS	67905	620-624-3855	624-8851
Manhattan Area Chamber of Commerce 501 Poyntz Ave *TF:* 800-759-0134 ■ *Web:* www.manhattan.org	Manhattan	KS	66502	785-776-8829	776-0679
Olathe Chamber of Commerce 142 N Cherry St *TF:* 800-921-5678 ■ *Web:* www.olathe.com	Olathe	KS	66061	913-764-1050	782-4636
Overland Park Chamber of Commerce 9001 W 110th St Suite 150 *Web:* www.opks.org	Overland Park	KS	66210	913-491-3600	491-0393
Pittsburg Area Chamber of Commerce 117 W 4th St *TF:* 800-879-1112 ■ *Web:* www.pittsburgkschamber.com	Pittsburg	KS	66762	620-231-1000	231-3178
Salina Area Chamber of Commerce 120 W Ash St *Web:* www.salinakansas.org	Salina	KS	67401	785-827-9301	827-9758
Shawnee Area Chamber of Commerce 15100 W 67th St Suite 202 *TF:* 888-550-7282 ■ *Web:* www.shawneekschamber.com	Shawnee	KS	66217	913-631-6545	631-9628
Greater Topeka Chamber of Commerce 120 SE 6th St Suite 110 *Web:* www.topekachamber.org	Topeka	KS	66603	785-234-2644	234-8656
Wichita Area Chamber of Commerce 350 W Douglas Ave *Web:* www.wichitachamber.org	Wichita	KS	67202	316-265-7771	265-7502

Kentucky

	City	State	ZIP	Phone	Fax
Ashland Alliance Chamber of Commerce PO Box 830 *TF:* 888-524-6860 ■ *Web:* www.ashlandalliance.com	Ashland	KY	41105	606-324-5111	325-4607
Knox County Chamber of Commerce 196 Daniel Boone Dr Suite 205 *Web:* www.knoxcochamber.com	Barbourville	KY	40906	606-546-4300	
Bardstown-Nelson County Chamber of Commerce 1 Court Sq *TF:* 866-894-9545 ■ *Web:* www.bardstownchamber.com	Bardstown	KY	40004	502-348-9545	348-6478
Marshall County Chamber of Commerce 17 US Hwy 68 W *Web:* www.marshallcounty.net	Benton	KY	42025	270-527-7665	527-9193
Bowling Green Area Chamber of Commerce 812 State St *Web:* www.bgchamber.com	Bowling Green	KY	42101	270-781-3200	843-0458
Danville-Boyle County Chamber of Commerce 304 S 4th St Suite 102 *Web:* www.danville-ky.com	Danville	KY	40422	859-236-2361	236-3197
Elizabethtown-Hardin County Chamber of Commerce 111 W Dixie Ave *Web:* www.elizabethtownchamber.org	Elizabethtown	KY	42701	270-765-4334	737-0690
Northern Kentucky Chamber of Commerce 300 Buttermilk Pike Suite 330 *Web:* www.nkychamber.com	Fort Mitchell	KY	41017	859-578-8800	578-8802
Frankfort Area Chamber of Commerce 100 Capitol Ave *Web:* www.frankfortky.org	Frankfort	KY	40601	502-223-8261	223-5942
Georgetown-Scott County Chamber of Commerce 160 E Main St *Web:* www.gtown.org	Georgetown	KY	40324	502-863-5424	863-5756

Kentucky (Cont'd)

Chamber	City	State	ZIP	Phone	Fax
Glasgow-Barren County Chamber of Commerce 118 E Public Sq *TF:* 800-264-3161 ■ *Web:* www.glasgowbarrenchamber.com	Glasgow	KY	42141	270-651-3161	651-3122
Greenville-Muhlenberg County Chamber of Commerce PO Box 313	Greenville	KY	42345	270-338-5422	338-5440
Harlan County Chamber of Commerce PO Box 268	Harlan	KY	40831	606-573-4717	573-4717
Henderson-Henderson County Chamber of Commerce 201 N Main St *Web:* www.hendersonky.com	Henderson	KY	42420	270-826-9531	827-4461
Hopkinsville-Christian County Chamber of Commerce 2800 Port Campbell Blvd *TF:* 800-842-9959 ■ *Web:* www.commercecenter.org/chamber	Hopkinsville	KY	42240	270-885-9096	886-2059
Jeffersontown Chamber of Commerce 10434 Watterson Tr *Web:* www.jtownchamber.com	Jeffersontown	KY	40299	502-267-1674	267-6874
Oldham County Chamber of Commerce 412 E Main ST *TF:* 800-813-9953 ■ *Web:* www.oldhamcountychamber.com	LaGrange	KY	40031	502-222-1635	222-3159
Greater Lexington Chamber of Commerce 330 E Main St Suite 100 *Web:* www.lexchamber.com	Lexington	KY	40507	859-254-4447	233-3304
Greater Louisville Inc 614 W Main St *TF:* 800-500-1066 ■ *Web:* www.greaterlouisville.com	Louisville	KY	40202	502-625-0000	625-0010
Madisonville-Hopkins County Chamber of Commerce 15 E Center St *Web:* www.hopkinschamber.com	Madisonville	KY	42431	270-821-3435	821-9190
Mayfield-Graves County Chamber of Commerce 201 E College St *Web:* www.mayfieldchamber.com	Mayfield	KY	42066	270-247-6101	247-6101
Bell County Chamber of Commerce PO Box 788 *Web:* www.bellcountyworks.com	Middlesboro	KY	40965	606-248-1075	248-8851
Murray-Calloway County Chamber of Commerce 805 N 12th St *TF:* 800-900-5171 ■ *Web:* www.murraylink.com	Murray	KY	42071	270-753-5171	753-0948
Jessamine County Chamber of Commerce 508 N Main St Sutie A	Nicholasville	KY	40356	859-887-4351	887-1211
Greater Owensboro Chamber of Commerce 200 W 3rd St PO Box 825 *Web:* www.owensboro.com	Owensboro	KY	42303	270-926-1860	926-3364
Paducah Area Chamber of Commerce 401 Kentucky Ave *Web:* www.paducahchamber.org	Paducah	KY	42003	270-443-1746	442-9152
Pike County Chamber of Commerce 787 Hambley Blvd *Web:* www.pikecountychamber.org	Pikeville	KY	41501	606-432-5504	432-7295
Radcliff Hardin County Chamber of Commerce 306 N Wilson Rd *Web:* www.radcliffchamber.org	Radcliff	KY	40160	270-351-4450	352-4449
Logan County Chamber of Commerce 116 S Main St *Web:* www.loganchamber.com	Russellville	KY	42276	270-726-2206	726-2237
Shelby County Chamber of Commerce 316 Main St *Web:* www.shelbycountykychamber.com	Shelbyville	KY	40065	502-633-1636	633-7501
Bullitt County Chamber of Commerce 505 Buffalo Run Rd Suite 101 *Web:* www.bullittcounty.org	Shepherdsville	KY	40165	502-543-6727	543-1765
Somerset-Pulaski County Chamber of Commerce 445 S Hwy 27 Suite 301 *Web:* www.spcchamber.com	Somerset	KY	42501	606-679-7323	679-1744
Winchester-Clark County Chamber of Commerce 2 S Maple St *Web:* www.winchesterkychamber.com	Winchester	KY	40391	859-744-6420	744-9229

Louisiana

Chamber	City	State	ZIP	Phone	Fax
Central Louisiana Chamber of Commerce 1118 3rd St PO Box 992 *Web:* www.cenlachamber.org	Alexandria	LA	71309	318-442-6671	442-6734
Bastrop-Morehouse Parish Chamber of Commerce 110 N Franklin St *Web:* www.bastrop-morehouse.com	Bastrop	LA	71220	318-281-3794	281-3781
Greater Baton Rouge Chamber of Commerce 564 Laurel St *Web:* www.brchamber.org	Baton Rouge	LA	70801	225-381-7125	336-4306
Bossier Chamber of Commerce 710 Benton Rd *Web:* www.bossierchamber.com	Bossier City	LA	71111	318-746-0252	746-0357
Saint Tammany West Chamber of Commerce 610 Hollycrest Blvd *Web:* www.sttammanychamber.org	Covington	LA	70433	985-892-3216	893-4244
Greater Denham Springs Chamber of Commerce PO Box 591 *Web:* www.denhamspringschamber.com	Denham Springs	LA	70726	225-665-8155	665-2411
Greater Beauregard Chamber of Commerce PO Box 309 *Web:* www.beauparish.org/chamber/	DeRidder	LA	70634	337-463-5533	463-2244
Ascension Chamber of Commerce PO Box 1204 *Web:* www.ascensionchamber.com	Gonzales	LA	70707	225-647-7487	647-5124
Houma-Terrebonne Chamber of Commerce 6133 Hwy 311 *Web:* www.houmachamber.com	Houma	LA	70360	985-876-5600	876-5611
Greater Jennings Chamber of Commerce 246 N Main St *Web:* www.jenningschamber.com	Jennings	LA	70546	337-824-0933	824-0934
Greater Lafayette Chamber of Commerce 804 E St Mary Blvd *Web:* www.lafchamber.org	Lafayette	LA	70503	337-233-2705	234-8671
Chamber/Southwest Louisiana 120 W Pujo St *Web:* www.chamberswla.org	Lake Charles	LA	70601	337-433-3632	436-3727
Chamber of Commerce of Lafourche & the Bayou Region 107 W 26th St *Web:* www.lafourchechamber.com	Larose	LA	70373	985-693-6700	693-6702
Greater Vernon Chamber of Commerce PO Box 1228 *Web:* www.chambervernonparish.com	Leesville	LA	71496	337-238-0349	238-0340
DeSoto Parish Chamber of Commerce 101 N Washington St *Web:* desotoparishchamber.net	Mansfield	LA	71052	318-872-1310	871-1875
Jefferson Chamber of Commerce 3421 N Causeway Blvd Suite 203 *Web:* www.jeffersonchamber.org	Metairie	LA	70002	504-835-3880	835-3828
Monroe Chamber of Commerce 212 Walnut St Suite 100 *TF:* 888-531-9535 ■ *Web:* www.monroe.org	Monroe	LA	71201	318-323-3461	322-7594
Saint Mary Parish Chamber of Commerce 7332 Hwy 182 *Web:* www.stmarychamberofcommerce.com	Morgan City	LA	70380	985-384-3830	384-0771
Natchitoches Area Chamber of Commerce 550 2nd St *Web:* www.natchitocheschamber.com	Natchitoches	LA	71457	318-352-6894	352-5385
Greater Iberia Chamber of Commerce 111 W Main St	New Iberia	LA	70560	337-364-1836	367-7405
New Orleans Chamber of Commerce 1515 Poydras St Suite 1010 *Web:* www.neworleanschamber.org	New Orleans	LA	70112	504-522-7226	522-1355
Iberville Parish Chamber of Commerce 23675 Church St *TF:* 888-687-3560 ■ *Web:* www.ibervillechamber.com	Plaquemine	LA	70764	225-687-3560	687-3575
Ruston/Lincoln Chamber of Commerce 104 E Mississippi Ave *TF:* 800-392-9032 ■ *Web:* www.rustonlincoln.org	Ruston	LA	71270	318-255-2031	255-3481
Greater Shreveport Chamber of Commerce 400 Edwards St *TF:* 800-448-5432 ■ *Web:* www.shreveportchamber.org	Shreveport	LA	71101	318-677-2500	677-2541
Greater Slidell Area Chamber of Commerce 118 W Hall Ave *TF:* 800-471-3758 ■ *Web:* www.slidellchamber.com	Slidell	LA	70460	985-643-5678	649-2460
Thibodaux Chamber of Commerce 318 E Bayou Rd PO Box 467 *Web:* www.thibodauxchamber.com	Thibodaux	LA	70302	985-446-1187	446-1191

Maine

Chamber	City	State	ZIP	Phone	Fax
Kennebec Valley Chamber of Commerce 21 University Dr *Web:* www.augustamaine.com	Augusta	ME	04330	207-623-4559	626-9342
Bangor Region Chamber of Commerce 519 Main St *Web:* www.bangorregion.com	Bangor	ME	04401	207-947-0307	990-1427
Bar Harbor Chamber of Commerce 93 Cottage St PO Box 158 *TF:* 888-540-9990 ■ *Web:* www.barharborinfo.com	Bar Harbor	ME	04609	207-288-5103	288-2565
Belfast Area Chamber of Commerce PO Box 58 *Web:* www.belfastmaine.org	Belfast	ME	04915	207-338-5900	338-3808
Southern Midcoast Maine Chamber 59 Pleasant St *TF:* 800-725-8797 ■ *Web:* www.midcoastmaine.com	Brunswick	ME	04011	207-725-8797	725-9787
Calais Regional Chamber of Commerce 39 Union St *TF:* 888-422-3112 ■ *Web:* www.visitcalais.com	Calais	ME	04619	207-454-2308	454-2308
Ellsworth Area Chamber of Commerce 163 High St *Web:* www.ellsworthchamber.org	Ellsworth	ME	04605	207-667-5584	667-2617
Androscoggin County Chamber of Commerce PO Box 59 *Web:* www.androscoggincounty.com	Lewiston	ME	04243	207-783-2249	783-4481
Greater Lincoln Lakes Region Chamber of Commerce 256 W Broadway *TF:* 888-794-8065 ■ *Web:* www.lincolnmechamber.org	Lincoln	ME	04457	207-794-8065	794-2606
Portland Regional Chamber 60 Pearl St *Web:* www.portlandregion.com	Portland	ME	04101	207-772-2811	772-1179
Biddeford-Saco Chamber of Commerce & Industry 110 Main St Suite 1202 *Web:* www.biddefordsacochamber.org	Saco	ME	04072	207-282-1567	282-3149
Sanford-Springvale Chamber of Commerce & Economic Development 917 Main St Suite B *Web:* www.sanfordchamber.org	Sanford	ME	04073	207-324-4280	324-8290
Oxford Hills Chamber of Commerce 213 Main ST *Web:* www.oxfordhillsmaine.com	South Paris	ME	04281	207-743-2281	743-0687
Mid-Maine Chamber of Commerce 1 Post Office Sq *Web:* www.midmainechamber.com	Waterville	ME	04901	207-873-3315	877-0087

Maryland

Chamber	City	State	ZIP	Phone	Fax
Annapolis & Anne Arundel County Chamber of Commerce 49 Old Solomons Island Rd Suite 204 *Web:* www.annapolischamber.com	Annapolis	MD	21401	410-266-3960	266-8270
Baltimore City Chamber of Commerce 312 N ML King Blvd *Web:* www.baltimorecitychamber.com	Baltimore	MD	21201	410-837-7101	837-7104
Harford County Chamber of Commerce 108 S Bond St *TF:* 800-682-8536 ■ *Web:* www.harfordchamber.org	Bel Air	MD	21014	410-838-2020	893-4715
Greater Bethesda-Chevy Chase Chamber of Commerce 7910 Woodmont Ave Suite 1204 *Web:* www.bccchamber.org	Bethesda	MD	20814	301-652-4900	657-1973
Greater Bowie Chamber of Commerce 6911 Laurel Bowie Rd Suite 302 *Web:* www.bowiechamber.org	Bowie	MD	20715	301-262-0920	262-0921
Saint Mary's County Chamber of Commerce 44200 Airport Rd Suite B *Web:* www.smcchamber.com	California	MD	20619	301-737-3001	737-0089
Dorchester Chamber of Commerce 528 Poplar St *Web:* www.dorchesterchamber.org	Cambridge	MD	21613	410-228-3575	228-6848
Queen Anne's County Chamber of Commerce 1561 Postal Rd *Web:* www.qacchamber.com	Chester	MD	21619	410-643-8530	643-8477
Howard County Chamber of Commerce 5560 Sterrett Pl Suite 105 *Web:* www.howardchamber.com	Columbia	MD	21044	410-730-4111	730-4584
Greater Crofton Chamber of Commerce PO Box 4146 *Web:* www.croftonchamber.com	Crofton	MD	21114	410-721-9131	721-0785
Allegany County Chamber of Commerce 24 Frederick St *Web:* www.alleganycountychamber.com	Cumberland	MD	21502	301-722-2820	722-5995
Caroline County Chamber of Commerce PO Box 494	Denton	MD	21629	410-479-4638	479-5551
Talbot County Chamber of Commerce 101 Marlboro Ave Suite 53 *Web:* www.talbotchamber.org	Easton	MD	21601	410-822-4606	822-7922
Cecil County Chamber of Commerce 233 E Main St PO Box 96 *Web:* www.cecilchamber.com	Elkton	MD	21922	410-392-3833	392-6225
Essex-Middle River-White Marsh Chamber of Commerce 435C Eastern Blvd *Web:* www.emrchamber.org	Essex	MD	21221	410-686-2233	687-9081
Frederick County Chamber of Commerce 43A S Market St *Web:* frederickchamber.org	Frederick	MD	21701	301-662-4164	846-4427
Gaithersburg-Germantown Chamber of Commerce 4 Professional Dr Suite 132 *Web:* www.ggchamber.org	Gaithersburg	MD	20879	301-840-1400	963-3918
Northern Anne Arundel County Chamber of Commerce 7477 Baltimore-Annapolis Blvd Suite 203 *Web:* www.naaccc.com	Glen Burnie	MD	21061	410-766-8282	766-5722
Hagerstown-Washington County Chamber of Commerce 28 W Washington St *Web:* www.hagerstown.org	Hagerstown	MD	21740	301-739-2015	739-1278
Charles County Chamber of Commerce 101 Centennial St Suite A *Web:* www.charlescountychamber.org	La Plata	MD	20646	301-932-6500	932-3945
Prince George's Chamber of Commerce 4640 Forbes Blvd Suite 130 *Web:* www.pgcoc.org	Lanham	MD	20706	301-731-5000	731-5013
Baltimore/Washington Corridor Chamber of Commerce 312 Marshall Ave Suite 104 *Web:* www.baltwashchamber.org	Laurel	MD	20707	301-725-4000	725-0776
Garrett County Chamber of Commerce 15 Visitors Ctr Dr *TF:* 800-387-5237 ■ *Web:* www.garrettchamber.com	McHenry	MD	21541	301-387-4386	387-2080
Ocean City Chamber of Commerce 12320 Ocean Gateway *TF:* 888-626-3386 ■ *Web:* www.oceancity.org	Ocean City	MD	21842	410-213-0144	213-7521
West Anne Arundel County Chamber of Commerce 8373 Piney Orchard Pkwy Suite 100 *Web:* www.waaccc.org	Odenton	MD	21113	410-672-3422	672-3475
Olney Chamber of Commerce PO Box 550 *Web:* www.olneymd.org	Olney	MD	20830	301-924-3555	774-4944

	City	State	Zip	Phone	Fax
Reisterstown-Owings Mills-Glyndon Chamber of Commerce 66 Painters Mill Rd Suite 1 *Web:* www.romgchamber.org	Owings Mills	MD	21117	410-356-2888	356-5112
Pikesville Chamber of Commerce 7 Church Ln Suite 14 *Web:* www.pikesvillechamber.org	Pikesville	MD	21208	410-484-2337	484-4151
Calvert County Chamber of Commerce PO Box 9 *Web:* www.calvertchamber.org	Prince Frederick	MD	20678	410-535-2577	257-3140
Montgomery County Chamber of Commerce 51 Monroe St Suite 1800 *Web:* www.montgomery-chamber.com	Rockville	MD	20850	301-738-0015	738-8792
Rockville Chamber of Commerce 255 Rockville Pike Suite L10 *Web:* www.rockvillechamber.org	Rockville	MD	20850	301-424-9300	762-7599
Salisbury Area Chamber of Commerce 144 E Main St *Web:* www.salisburyarea.com	Salisbury	MD	21801	410-749-0144	860-9925
Greater Severna Park Chamber of Commerce 1 Holly Ave *Web:* www.severnaparkchamber.com	Severna Park	MD	21146	410-647-3900	647-3999
Greater Silver Spring Chamber of Commerce 8601 Georgia Ave Suite 203 *Web:* www.silverspringchamber.com	Silver Spring	MD	20910	301-565-3777	565-3377
Snow Hill Chamber of Commerce PO Box 176 *Web:* www.snowhillmd.com	Snow Hill	MD	21863	410-632-0809	632-3158
Baltimore County Chamber of Commerce 102 W Pennsylvania Ave Suite 101 *Web:* www.baltcountycc.com	Towson	MD	21204	410-825-6200	821-9901
Eastern Baltimore Area Chamber of Commerce 102 W Pennsylvania Ave Suite 101 *Web:* www.baltcountycc.com	Towson	MD	21204	410-825-6200	821-9901
Carroll County Chamber of Commerce 700 Corporate Ctr Ct Suite L *Web:* www.carrollcountychamber.org	Westminster	MD	21158	410-876-7212	876-1023
Wheaton-Kensington Chamber of Commerce 2401 Blueridge Ave Suite 101 *Web:* www.wkchamber.org	Wheaton	MD	20902	301-949-0080	949-0081

Massachusetts

	City	State	Zip	Phone	Fax
Middlesex West Chamber of Commerce 77 Great Rd Suite 214 *Web:* www.mwcoc.com	Acton	MA	01720	978-263-0010	264-0303
Amherst Area Chamber of Commerce 28 Amity St *Web:* www.amherstarea.com	Amherst	MA	01002	413-253-0700	256-0771
Arlington Chamber of Commerce 1 Whittemore Pk *Web:* www.arlcc.org	Arlington	MA	02474	781-643-4600	646-5581
North Quabbin Chamber of Commerce 512 Main St *Web:* www.northquabbinchamber.com	Athol	MA	01331	978-249-3849	249-7151
Chamber of Commerce of the Attleboro Area 42 Union St *Web:* www.attleborochamber.com	Attleboro	MA	02703	508-222-0801	222-1498
Beverly Chamber of Commerce 28 Cabot St *Web:* www.beverlychamber.com	Beverly	MA	01915	978-232-9559	232-9372
Billerica Chamber of Commerce 574 Boston Rd Unit 1 *Web:* www.billericachamberofcommerce.com/	Billerica	MA	01821	978-663-0036	670-1020
Greater Boston Chamber of Commerce 265 Franklin St 12th Fl *Web:* www.bostonchamber.com	Boston	MA	02110	617-227-4500	227-7505
Metro South Chamber of Commerce 60 School St *Web:* www.metrosouthchamber.com	Brockton	MA	02301	508-586-0500	587-1340
Brookline Chamber of Commerce 251 Harvard St Suite 1 *Web:* www.brooklinechamber.com	Brookline	MA	02446	617-739-1330	739-1200
Cape Cod Canal Regional Chamber of Commerce 70 Main St *Web:* www.capecodcanalchamber.org	Buzzards Bay	MA	02532	508-759-6000	759-6965
Cambridge Chamber of Commerce 859 Massachusetts Ave *Web:* www.cambridgechamber.org	Cambridge	MA	02139	617-876-4100	354-9874
Cape Cod Chamber of Commerce 5 Shoot Flying Hill Road *TF:* 888-332-2732 ■ *Web:* www.capecodchamber.org	Centerville	MA	02632	508-362-3225	362-3698
Chicopee Chamber of Commerce 264 Exchange St *Web:* www.chicopeechamber.org	Chicopee	MA	01013	413-594-2101	594-2103
Wachusett Chamber of Commerce 167 Church St PO Box 703 *Web:* www.wachusettchamber.com	Clinton	MA	01510	978-368-7687	368-7689
North Shore Chamber of Commerce 5 Cherry Hill Dr Suite 100 *Web:* www.northshorechamber.org	Danvers	MA	01923	978-774-8565	774-3418
Nashoba Valley Chamber of Commerce 100 Sherman Ave *Web:* www.nvcoc.com	Devens	MA	01434	978-772-6976	772-3503
East Boston Chamber of Commerce 296 Bennington St 2nd Fl *Web:* www.eastbostonchamber.com	East Boston	MA	02128	617-569-5000	569-1945
Everett Chamber of Commerce 467 Broadway *Web:* www.everettmachamber.org	Everett	MA	02149	617-387-9100	389-6655
Fall River Area Chamber of Commerce & Industry 200 Pocasset St *Web:* www.fallriverchamber.com	Fall River	MA	02721	508-676-8226	675-5932
Falmouth Chamber of Commerce 20 Academy Ln *TF:* 800-526-8532 ■ *Web:* www.falmouth-capecod.com	Falmouth	MA	02540	508-548-8500	548-8521
North Central Massachusetts Chamber of Commerce 860 South St *Web:* www.northcentralmass.com	Fitchburg	MA	01420	978-353-7600	353-4896
Metro West Chamber of Commerce 1671 Worcester Rd Suite 201 *Web:* www.metrowest.org	Framingham	MA	01701	508-879-5600	875-9325
United Chamber of Commerce 620 Old West Central St *Web:* www.unitedchamber.org	Franklin	MA	02038	508-528-2800	520-7864
Greater Gardner Chamber of Commerce 210 Main St *Web:* www.gardnerma.com	Gardner	MA	01440	978-632-1780	630-1767
Cape Ann Chamber of Commerce 33 Commercial St *Web:* www.capeannchamber.com	Gloucester	MA	01930	978-283-1601	283-4740
Franklin County Chamber of Commerce 395 Main St *Web:* www.co.franklin.ma.us	Greenfield	MA	01301	413-773-5463	773-7008
Greater Haverhill Chamber of Commerce 87 Winter St *Web:* www.haverhillchamber.com	Haverhill	MA	01830	978-373-5663	373-8060
Greater Holyoke Chamber of Commerce 177 High St *Web:* www.holycham.com	Holyoke	MA	01040	413-534-3376	534-3385
Assabet Valley Chamber of Commerce 18 Church St PO Box 578 *Web:* www.assabetvalleychamber.org	Hudson	MA	01749	978-568-0360	562-4118
Hyannis Area Chamber of Commerce 397 Main St *TF:* 800-449-6647 ■ *Web:* www.hyannis.com	Hyannis	MA	02601	508-775-2201	362-9499
Merrimack Valley Chamber of Commerce 264 Essex St *Web:* www.merrimackvalleychamber.com	Lawrence	MA	01840	978-686-0900	794-9953
Lexington Chamber of Commerce 1875 Massachusetts Ave *Web:* www.lexingtonchamber.org	Lexington	MA	02420	781-862-2480	862-5995
Greater Lowell Chamber of Commerce 144 Merrimack St Suite 203 *Web:* www.glcc.biz	Lowell	MA	01852	978-459-8154	452-4145
Lynn Area Chamber of Commerce 100 Oxford St *Web:* www.lynnchamber.com	Lynn	MA	01901	781-592-2900	592-2903
Malden Chamber of Commerce 200 Pleasant St Suite 416 *Web:* www.maldenchamber.org	Malden	MA	02148	781-322-4500	322-4866
Marlborough Regional Chamber of Commerce 11 Florence St *Web:* www.marlboroughchamber.org	Marlborough	MA	01752	508-485-7746	481-1819
Medford Chamber of Commerce 1 Shipyard Way Suite G-01 *Web:* www.medfordchamberma.com	Medford	MA	02155	781-396-1277	396-1278
Melrose Chamber of Commerce 1 W Foster St *Web:* www.melrosechamber.org	Melrose	MA	02176	781-665-3033	665-5595
Cranberry Country Chamber of Commerce 40 N Main St *Web:* www.cranberrycountry.org	Middleboro	MA	02346	508-947-1499	947-1446
Milford Area Chamber of Commerce 258 Main St PO Box 621 *Web:* www.milfordchamber.org	Milford	MA	01757	508-473-6700	473-8467
New Bedford Area Chamber of Commerce 794 Purchase St *Web:* www.newbedfordchamber.com	New Bedford	MA	02740	508-999-5231	999-5237
Newton-Needham Chamber of Commerce 281 Needham St *Web:* www.nnchamber.com	Newton	MA	02464	617-244-5300	244-5302
North Attleboro & Plainville Chamber of Commerce PO Box 1071 *Web:* www.napcc.org	North Attleboro	MA	02761	508-695-6011	695-6096
Greater Northampton Chamber of Commerce 99 Pleasant St *Web:* www.northamptonuncommon.com	Northampton	MA	01060	413-584-1900	584-1934
Neponset Valley Chamber of Commerce 190 Vanderbilt Ave *Web:* www.nvcc.com	Norwood	MA	02062	781-769-1126	769-0808
Quaboag Valley Chamber of Commerce 3 Converse St Suite 103 *Web:* www.quaboagvalley.org	Palmer	MA	01069	413-283-2418	289-1355
Peabody Chamber of Commerce 24 Main St Suite 28 *Web:* www.peabody-chamber.com	Peabody	MA	01960	978-531-0384	532-7227
Berkshire Chamber of Commerce 75 North St Suite 360 *Web:* www.berkshirechamber.com	Pittsfield	MA	01201	413-499-4000	447-9641
Plymouth Area Chamber of Commerce 10 Cordage Park Cir Suite 231 *Web:* www.plymouthchamber.com	Plymouth	MA	02360	508-830-1620	830-1621
South Shore Chamber of Commerce 36 Miller Stile Rd *Web:* www.southshorechamber.org	Quincy	MA	02169	617-479-1111	479-9274
Reading-North Reading Chamber of Commerce PO Box 771 *Web:* www.readingnreadingchamber.org	Reading	MA	01867	781-944-8824	944-6125
Revere Chamber of Commerce 270 Broadway Suite 10 *Web:* www.reverechamber.org	Revere	MA	02151	781-289-8009	289-2166
Salem Chamber of Commerce 265 Essex St *Web:* salem-chamber.org	Salem	MA	01970	978-744-0004	745-3855
Saugus Chamber of Commerce 394 Lincoln Ave *Web:* www.sauguschamber.org	Saugus	MA	01906	781-233-8407	231-1145
Somerville Chamber of Commerce 2 Alpine St *Web:* www.somervillechamber.org	Somerville	MA	02144	617-776-4100	776-1157
Agawam Chamber of Commerce 1441 Main St *Web:* www.myonlinechamber.com	Springfield	MA	01003	413-787-1555	731-8530
Greater Springfield Chamber of Commerce 1441 Main St Suite 136	Springfield	MA	01103	413-787-1555	731-8530
West Springfield Chamber of Commerce 1441 Main St *Web:* www.myonlinechamber.com	Springfield	MA	01103	413-787-1555	731-8530
Tri-Community Area Chamber of Commerce 380 Main St *TF:* 888-788-7274 ■ *Web:* www.sturbridge.org	Sturbridge	MA	01566	508-347-2761	347-5218
Taunton Area Chamber of Commerce 12 Taunton Green Suite 201 *Web:* www.tauntonareachamber.org	Taunton	MA	02780	508-824-4068	884-8222
Wakefield Chamber of Commerce 467 Main St Americal Civic Ctr *Web:* www.wakefieldma.org/chamber_page2.html	Wakefield	MA	01880	781-245-0741	
Waltham/West Suburban Chamber of Commerce 84 South St *Web:* www.walthamchamber.com	Waltham	MA	02453	781-894-4700	894-1708
Watertown-Belmont Chamber of Commerce PO Box 45 *Web:* www.wbcc.org	Watertown	MA	02471	617-926-1017	926-2322
Wellesley Chamber of Commerce 1 Hollis St Suite 111 *Web:* www.wellesleychamber.org	Wellesley	MA	02482	781-235-2446	235-7326
Greater Westfield Chamber of Commerce 53 Court St *Web:* www.westfieldchamber.org	Westfield	MA	01085	413-568-1618	731-8530
Blackstone Valley Chamber of Commerce 110 Church St *TF:* 800-841-0919 ■ *Web:* www.blackstonevalley.org	Whitinsville	MA	01588	508-234-9090	234-5152
North Suburban Chamber of Commerce 76-R Winn St Suite 3D *Web:* www.northsuburbanchamber.com	Woburn	MA	01801	781-933-3499	933-1071
Worcester Regional Chamber of Commerce 339 Main St *Web:* www.worcesterchamber.org	Worcester	MA	01608	508-753-2924	754-8560

Michigan

	City	State	Zip	Phone	Fax
Lenawee County Chamber of Commerce 202 N Main St Suite A *Web:* www.lenaweechamber.com	Adrian	MI	49221	517-265-5141	263-6065
Allen Park Chamber of Commerce 6543 Allen Rd *Web:* www.allenparkchamber.org	Allen Park	MI	48101	313-382-7303	382-4409
Gratiot Area Chamber of Commerce 110 W Superior St PO Box 516 *Web:* www.gratiot.org/chamber	Alma	MI	48801	989-463-5525	463-6588
Alpena Area Chamber of Commerce 235 W Chisholm St PO Box 65 *TF:* 800-425-7362 ■ *Web:* www.alpenachamber.com	Alpena	MI	49707	989-354-4181	356-3999
Ann Arbor Area Chamber of Commerce 115 W Heron 3rd Fl *Web:* www.annarborchamber.org	Ann Arbor	MI	48104	734-665-4433	665-4191
Battle Creek Area Chamber of Commerce 77 E Michigan Ave Suite 80 *Web:* www.battlecreek.org/chamber	Battle Creek	MI	49017	269-962-4076	962-6309
Bay Area Chamber of Commerce 901 Saginaw St *Web:* www.baycityarea.com	Bay City	MI	48708	989-893-4567	895-5594
Belleville Area Chamber of Commerce 248 Main St *Web:* www.bellevillech.org	Belleville	MI	48111	734-697-7151	697-1415
Cornerstone Alliance Chamber Services 38 W Wall St *Web:* www.cstonealliance.org	Benton Harbor	MI	49022	269-925-6100	925-4471
Mecosta County Area Chamber of Commerce 246 N State St *Web:* www.mecostacounty.com	Big Rapids	MI	49307	231-796-7649	796-1625
Birmingham-Bloomfield Chamber of Commerce 124 W Maple Rd *Web:* www.bbcc.com	Birmingham	MI	48009	248-644-1700	644-0286
Greater Brighton Area Chamber of Commerce 131 Hyne St *Web:* www.brightoncoc.org	Brighton	MI	48116	810-227-5086	227-5940
Brooklyn-Irish Hills Chamber of Commerce 221 N Main St PO Box 805 *Web:* www.brooklynmi.com	Brooklyn	MI	49230	517-592-8907	
Cadillac Area Chamber of Commerce 222 Lake St *Web:* www.cadillac.org	Cadillac	MI	49601	231-775-9776	775-1440
Canton Chamber of Commerce 45525 Hanford Rd *Web:* www.cantonchamber.com	Canton	MI	48187	734-453-4040	453-4503
Clarkston Area Chamber of Commerce 5856 S Main St *Web:* www.clarkston.org	Clarkston	MI	48346	248-625-8055	625-8041

Michigan (Cont'd)

Phone Fax

Branch County Area Chamber of Commerce 20 Division St Coldwater MI 49036 517-278-5985 278-8369
Web: www.branch-county.com
Davison Area Chamber of Commerce 709-A S State Rd Davison MI 48423 810-653-6266 653-0669
Web: www.davisonchamberofcommerce.com
Dearborn Chamber of Commerce 15544 Michigan Ave Dearborn MI 48126 313-584-6100 584-9818
Web: www.dearbornchamber.org
Dearborn Heights Chamber of Commerce
24624 W Warren Ave Dearborn Heights MI 48127 313-274-7480 565-0913
Web: www.dearbornheightschamber.com
Detroit Regional Chamber
PO Box 33840 1 Woodward Ave Suite 1900 Detroit MI 48232 313-964-4000 964-0183
Web: www.detroitchamber.com
Eastpointe Chamber of Commerce PO Box 24 Eastpointe MI 48021 586-776-5520 776-7808
Web: www.epchamber.com
Delta County Area Chamber of Commerce 230 Ludington St Escanaba MI 49829 906-786-2192 786-8830
TF: 888-335-8264 ■ *Web:* www.deltami.org
Farmington/Farmington Hills Chamber of Commerce
30903-B W 10-Mile Rd Farmington Hills MI 48336 248-474-3440 474-9235
Web: www.ffhchamber.com
Ferndale Chamber of Commerce 407 E 9-Mile Rd Ferndale MI 48220 248-542-2160 542-8979
Web: www.ferndalechamber.com
Genesee Regional Chamber of Commerce
519 S Saginaw St Suite 200 Flint MI 48502 810-232-7101 233-7437
Web: www.thegrcc.org
Garden City Chamber of Commerce 30120 Ford Rd Suite D Garden City MI 48135 734-422-4448 422-1601
Web: www.gardencity.org
Grand Blanc Chamber of Commerce 512 E Grand Blanc Rd Grand Blanc MI 48439 810-695-4222 695-0053
Web: www.grandblancchamber.org
Chamber of Commerce - Grand Haven-Spring Lake-Ferrysburg 1 S Harbor Dr Grand Haven MI 49417 616-842-4910 842-0379
Web: www.grandhavenchamber.org
Grand Rapids Area Chamber of Commerce
111 Pearl St NW Grand Rapids MI 49503 616-771-0300 771-0318
Web: www.grandrapids.org
Hillsdale County Chamber of Commerce 22 N Manning St Hillsdale MI 49242 517-437-6401 437-6408
Web: www.hillsdalecountychamber.com
Holland Area Chamber of Commerce 272 E 8th St Holland MI 49423 616-392-2389 392-7379
Web: www.hollandchamber.org
Keweenaw Peninsula Chamber of Commerce
902 College Ave Houghton MI 49931 906-482-5240 482-5241
TF: 866-304-5722 ■ *Web:* www.keweenaw.org
Howell Area Chamber of Commerce 123 E Washington St Howell MI 48843 517-546-3920 546-4115
Web: www.howell.org
Dickinson Area Partnership 600 S Stephenson Ave Iron Mountain MI 49801 906-774-2002 774-2004
TF: 800-236-2447 ■ *Web:* www.dickinsonchamber.com
Greater Jackson Chamber of Commerce
1 Jackson Sq Suite 1100 Jackson MI 49201 517-782-8221 782-0061
Web: www.gjcc.org
Kalamazoo Regional Chamber of Commerce
346 W Michigan Ave Kalamazoo MI 49007 269-381-4000 343-0430
Web: www.kazoochamber.com
Orion Area Chamber of Commerce PO Box 484 Lake Orion MI 48361 248-693-6300 693-9227
Web: orion.lib.mi.us/orion
Lansing Regional Chamber of Commerce
300 E Michigan Ave Suite 300 Lansing MI 48933 517-487-6340 484-6910
Web: www.lansingchamber.org
Lapeer Area Chamber of Commerce 108 W Park St Lapeer MI 48446 810-664-6641 664-4349
Web: www.lapeerareachamber.org
Lincoln Park Chamber of Commerce
1335 Southfield Rd PO Box 382 Lincoln Park MI 48146 313-386-0140 386-0140
Livonia Chamber of Commerce 33233 5 Mile Rd Livonia MI 48154 734-427-2122 427-6055
Web: www.livonia.org
Madison Heights-Hazel Park Chamber of Commerce
724 W 11-Mile Rd Madison Heights MI 48071 248-542-5010 542-6821
Web: www.madisonheightschamber.org
Midland Area Chamber of Commerce 300 Rodd St Suite 101 Midland MI 48640 989-839-9901 835-3701
Web: www.macc.org
Huron Valley Chamber of Commerce 317 Union St Milford MI 48381 248-685-7129 685-9047
Web: huronvcc.com
Monroe County Chamber of Commerce 1122 W Front St Monroe MI 48161 734-242-3366 242-7253
Web: monroemi.usachamber.com
Central Macomb County Chamber of Commerce
49 Macomb St Mount Clemens MI 48043 586-493-7600 493-7602
Web: www.central-macomb.com
Mount Pleasant Area Chamber of Commerce
114 E Broadway Mount Pleasant MI 48858 989-772-2396 773-2656
Web: www.mt-pleasant.net
Muskegon Area Chamber of Commerce
900 3rd St Suite 200 Muskegon MI 49440 231-722-3751 728-7251
Web: www.muskegon.org
Anchor Bay Chamber of Commerce
35054 23-Mile Rd Suite 110 New Baltimore MI 48047 586-725-5148 725-5369
Web: www.anchorbaychamber.com
Four Flags Area Chamber of Commerce 321 E Main St Niles MI 49120 269-683-3720 683-3722
TF: 888-683-8361 ■ *Web:* www.nilesmi.com
Novi Chamber of Commerce 43700 Expo Ctr Dr Suite 100 Novi MI 48375 248-349-3743 349-4523
Web: www.novichamber.com
Petoskey Regional Chamber of Commerce 401 E Mitchell St Petoskey MI 49770 231-347-4150 348-1810
Web: www.petoskey.com
Plymouth Community Chamber of Commerce
850 W Ann Arbor Trail Plymouth MI 48170 734-453-1540 453-1724
Web: www.plymouthchamber.org
Greater Pontiac Area Chamber of Commerce
402 N Telegraph Rd Pontiac MI 48341 248-335-9600 335-9601
Web: www.pontiacchamber.com
Greater Port Huron Area Chamber of Commerce
920 Pine Grove Ave Port Huron MI 48060 810-985-7101 985-7311
TF: 800-361-0526 ■ *Web:* www.porthuron-chamber.org
Redford Township Chamber of Commerce 26050 5-Mile Rd Redford MI 48239 313-535-0960 535-6356
Web: www.redfordchamber.org
Greater Rochester Chamber of Commerce
71 Walnut Blvd Suite 110 Rochester MI 48307 248-651-6700 651-5270
Web: www.rochesterregionalchamber.com
Rockford Area Chamber of Commerce PO Box 520 Rockford MI 49341 616-866-2000 866-2141
Web: www.rockfordmichamber.com
Romeo-Washington Chamber of Commerce
228 N Main St PO Box 175 Romeo MI 48065 586-752-4436 752-2835
Web: www.rwchamber.com
Greater Royal Oak Chamber of Commerce
200 S Washington Ave Royal Oak MI 48067 248-547-4000 547-0504
Web: www.virtualroyaloak.com
Saginaw County Chamber of Commerce
515 N Washington Ave 2nd Fl Saginaw MI 48607 989-752-7161 752-9055
Web: www.saginawchamber.org

Phone Fax

Metro East Chamber of Commerce
27601 Jefferson Ave Saint Clair Shores MI 48081 586-777-2741 777-4811
Web: www.metroeastchamber.com
Sault Area Chamber of Commerce
2581 I-75 Business Spur Sault Sainte Marie MI 49783 906-632-3301 632-2331
Web: www.saultstemarie.org
South Lyon Area Chamber of Commerce 125 N Lafayette St South Lyon MI 48178 248-437-3257 437-4116
Web: www.southlyonchamber.com
Southfield Chamber of Commerce
17515 W 9-Mile Rd Suite 750 Southfield MI 48075 248-557-6661 557-3931
Web: www.southfieldchamber.com
Sterling Heights Area Chamber of Commerce
12900 Hall Rd Suite 190 Sterling Heights MI 48313 586-731-5400 731-3521
Web: www.suscc.com
Southern Wayne County Regional Chamber
20600 Eureka Rd Suite 315 Taylor MI 48180 734-284-6000 284-0198
Web: www.swccc.org
Traverse City Area Chamber of Commerce
202 E Grandview Pkwy Traverse City MI 49684 231-947-5075 946-2565
Web: www.tcchamber.org
Troy Chamber of Commerce 4555 Investment Dr Suite 300 Troy MI 48098 248-641-8151 641-0545
Web: www.troychamber.com
Lakes Area Chamber of Commerce
305 N Pontiac Trail Suite B Walled Lake MI 48390 248-624-2826 624-2892
Web: www.lakesareachamber.com
Macomb Chamber 31201 Chicago Rd Suite C-102 Warren MI 48093 586-268-6430 268-6397
Web: www.macombchamber.com
West Bloomfield Chamber of Commerce
6668 Orchard Lake Rd Suite 207 West Bloomfield MI 48322 248-626-3636 626-4218
Web: www.westbloomfieldchamber.com
Westland Chamber of Commerce 36900 Ford Rd Westland MI 48185 734-326-7222 326-6040
Web: www.westlandchamber.com
Wyoming-Kentwood Area Chamber of Commerce
590 32nd St SE Wyoming MI 49548 616-531-5990 531-0252
Web: www.southkent.org
Ypsilanti Area Chamber of Commerce
301 W Michigan Ave Suite 101 Ypsilanti MI 48197 734-482-4920 482-2021
Web: www.ypsichamber.org

Minnesota

Phone Fax

Albert Lea-Freeborn County Chamber of Commerce
701 Marshall St Albert Lea MN 56007 507-373-3938 373-0344
Web: www.albertlea.org
Alexandria Lakes Area Chamber of Commerce
206 Broadway Alexandria MN 56308 320-763-3161 763-6857
TF: 800-235-9441 ■ *Web:* www.alexandriamn.org
Anoka Area Chamber of Commerce 12 Bridge Sq Anoka MN 55303 763-421-7130 421-0577
Web: www.anokaareachamber.com
Apple Valley Chamber of Commerce
14800 Galaxy Ave W Suite 301 Apple Valley MN 55124 952-432-8422 432-7964
TF: 800-301-9435 ■ *Web:* www.applevalleychamber.com
Bemidji Area Chamber of Commerce 300 Bemidji Ave Bemidji MN 56601 218-444-3541 444-4276
TF: 800-458-2223 ■ *Web:* www.bemidji.org
Brainerd Lakes Area Chamber of Commerce PO Box 356 Brainerd MN 56401 218-829-2838 829-8199
TF: 800-450-2838 ■ *Web:* www.explorebrainerdlakes.com
Burnsville Chamber of Commerce
101 W Burnsville Pkwy Suite 150 Burnsville MN 55337 952-435-6000 435-6972
Web: www.burnsvillechamber.com
Cloquet Area Chamber of Commerce 225 Sunnyside Dr Cloquet MN 55720 218-879-1551 878-0223
TF: 800-554-4350 ■ *Web:* www.cloquet.com
Detroit Lakes Regional Chamber of Commerce
700 Summit Ave Detroit Lakes MN 56501 218-847-9202 847-9082
TF: 800-542-3992 ■ *Web:* www.visitdetroitlakes.com
Duluth Area Chamber of Commerce 5 W 1st St Suite 101 Duluth MN 55802 218-722-5501 722-3223
Web: www.duluthchamber.com
Northern Dakota County Chambers of Commerce
1121 Town Center Dr Suite 102 Eagan MN 55123 651-452-9872 452-8978
Web: www.ndcchambers.com
Eden Prairie Chamber of Commerce
11455 Viking Dr Suite 270 Eden Prairie MN 55344 952-944-2830 944-0229
Web: www.epchamber.org
Forest Lake Area Chamber of Commerce
56 E Broadway Ave Forest Lake MN 55025 651-464-3200 464-3201
Web: www.flacc.org
Grand Rapids Area Chamber of Commerce 1 NW 3rd St Grand Rapids MN 55744 218-326-6619 326-4825
TF: 800-472-6366 ■ *Web:* www.grandmn.com
Hastings Area Chamber of Commerce & Tourism Bureau
111 E 3rd St Hastings MN 55033 651-437-6775 437-2697
TF: 888-612-6122 ■ *Web:* www.hastingsmn.org
River Heights Chamber of Commerce
5782 Blackshire Path Inver Grove Heights MN 55076 651-451-2266 451-0846
Web: www.riverheights.com
Lakeville Area Chamber of Commerce & Convention & Visitors Bureau PO Box 12 Lakeville MN 55044 952-469-2020 469-2028
TF: 888-525-3845 ■ *Web:* www.lakevillechamber.org
Minneapolis Regional Chamber of Commerce
81 S 9th St Suite 200 Minneapolis MN 55402 612-370-9100 370-9195
Web: www.minneapolischamber.org
Chamber of Commerce of Fargo Moorhead 202 1st Ave N Moorhead MN 56560 218-233-1100 233-1200
Web: www.fmchamber.com
Lake Minnetonka Chamber of Commerce 2323 Commerce Blvd Mound MN 55364 952-472-5622 472-5624
Web: www.lakeminnetonkachamber.com
Twin Cities North Chamber of Commerce
5394 Edgewood Dr Suite 100 Mounds View MN 55112 763-571-9781 572-7950
Web: www.twincitiesnorth.org
North Hennepin Chamber of Commerce 229 1st Ave NE Osseo MN 55369 763-424-6744 424-6927
Web: www.nhachamber.com
Owatonna Area Chamber of Commerce & Tourism
320 Hoffman Dr Owatonna MN 55060 507-451-7970 451-7972
TF: 800-423-6466 ■ *Web:* www.owatonna.org
TwinWest Chamber of Commerce 10700 Old County Rd 15 Plymouth MN 55441 763-450-2220 450-2221
Web: www.twinwest.com
Richfield Chamber of Commerce
6601 Lyndale Ave S Suite 106 Richfield MN 55423 612-866-5100 861-8302
Web: www.richfieldchambercvb.org
Rochester Area Chamber of Commerce
220 S Broadway Suite 100 Rochester MN 55904 507-288-1122 282-8960
Web: www.rochestermnchamber.com
Saint Cloud Area Chamber of Commerce 110 6th Ave S Saint Cloud MN 56301 320-251-2940 251-0081
TF: 800-264-2040 ■ *Web:* stc.stcloudareachamber.com
Minnesota Chamber of Commerce
400 Robert St N Suite 1500 Saint Paul MN 55101 651-292-4650 292-4656
TF: 800-821-2230 ■ *Web:* www.mnchamber.com

	City	State	Zip	Phone	Fax
Saint Paul Area Chamber of Commerce 401 N Robert St Suite 150 Web: www.saintpaulchamber.com	Saint Paul	MN	55101	651-223-5000	223-5119
Greater Stillwater Chamber of Commerce 106 S Main St. Web: www.ilovestillwater.com	Stillwater	MN	55082	651-439-4001	439-4035
Leech Lake Area Chamber of Commerce PO Box 1089 TF: 800-833-1118 ■ Web: www.leech-lake.com	Walker	MN	56484	218-547-1313	547-1338
White Bear Lake Area Chamber of Commerce 4801 Hwy 61 Suite 109 Web: www.whitebearchamber.com	White Bear Lake	MN	55110	651-429-8593	429-8592
Willmar Lakes Area Chamber of Commerce 2104 E Hwy 12 Web: www.willmarareachamber.com	Willmar	MN	56201	320-235-0300	231-1948
Winona Area Chamber of Commerce 67 Main St PO Box 870 Web: www.winonachamber.com	Winona	MN	55987	507-452-2272	454-8814

Mississippi

	City	State	Zip	Phone	Fax
Monroe County Chamber of Commerce 124 W Commerce St. Web: www.gomonroe.org	Aberdeen	MS	39730	662-369-6488	369-6489
Panola Partnership Inc 150-A Public Sq TF: 888-872-6652	Batesville	MS	38606	662-563-3126	563-0704
Hancock County Chamber of Commerce 412 Hwy 90 Suite 6 Web: www.hancockchamber.org	Bay Saint Louis	MS	39520	228-467-9048	467-1573
Rankin County Chamber of Commerce 101 Service Dr Web: www.rankinchamber.com	Brandon	MS	39043	601-825-2268	825-1977
Brookhaven-Lincoln County Chamber of Commerce 230 S Whitworth Ave TF: 800-613-4667 ■ Web: www.brookhavenchamber.com	Brookhaven	MS	39601	601-833-1411	833-1412
Clarksdale-Coahoma County Chamber of Commerce & Industrial Foundation 1540 DeSoto Ave TF: 800-626-3764 ■ Web: www.clarksdale.com	Clarksdale	MS	38614	662-627-7337	627-1313
Cleveland-Bolivar County Chamber of Commerce 600 3rd St TF: 800-295-7473 ■ Web: www.clevelandmschamber.com	Cleveland	MS	38732	662-843-2712	843-2718
Marion County Development Partnership 412 Courthouse Sq Web: www.marionpartnership.org	Columbia	MS	39429	601-736-6385	736-6392
Alliance The PO Box 1089 TF: 877-347-0545 ■ Web: www.corinth.ms/Chamber.htm	Corinth	MS	38835	662-287-5269	287-5260
Greenville Area Chamber of Commerce 915 Washington Ave. Web: www.greenvilleareachamber.com	Greenville	MS	38702	662-378-3141	378-3143
Greenwood-Leflore County Chamber of Commerce 402 Hwy 82 Web: www.greenwoodms.com	Greenwood	MS	38930	662-453-4152	453-8003
Gulfport Chamber of Commerce 1197-E Seaway Rd	Gulfport	MS	39503	228-604-0014	604-0105
Mississippi Gulf Coast Chamber of Commerce 11975-E Seaway Rd Web: www.mscoastchamber.com	Gulfport	MS	39503	228-604-0014	604-0105
Area Development Partnership 1 Convention Center Plaza TF: 800-238-4288 ■ Web: www.theadp.com	Hattiesburg	MS	39401	601-296-7500	296-7505
Horn Lake Chamber of Commerce 3040 Goodman Rd W Suite 2-A Web: www.hornlakechamber.com	Horn Lake	MS	38637	662-393-9897	393-2942
MetroJackson Chamber of Commerce PO Box 22548 Web: www.metrochamber.com	Jackson	MS	39225	601-948-7575	352-5539
Jones County Chamber of Commerce PO Box 527 TF: 800-392-9629	Laurel	MS	39441	601-428-0574	428-2047
Pike County Chamber of Commerce & Economic Development District 112 N Railroad Blvd TF: 800-399-4404 ■ Web: www.pikeinfo.com	McComb	MS	39648	601-684-2291	684-4899
East Mississippi Business Development Corp 1901 Front St Union Station Suite A Web: www.embdc.org	Meridian	MS	39302	601-693-1306	693-5638
Natchez-Adams County Chamber of Commerce 108 S Commerce Web: www.natchezchamber.com	Natchez	MS	39121	601-445-4611	445-9361
Olive Branch Chamber of Commerce 9123 Pigeon Roost PO Box 608 Web: www.olivebranchms.com	Olive Branch	MS	38654	662-895-2600	895-2625
Oxford-Lafayette County Chamber of Commerce 299 W Jackson Ave TF: 800-880-6967 ■ Web: www.oxfordms.com	Oxford	MS	38655	662-234-4651	234-4655
Jackson County Chamber of Commerce 720 Krebs Ave Web: www.jcchamber.com	Pascagoula	MS	39567	228-762-3391	769-1726
Philadelphia-Neshoba County Chamber of Commerce 410 Poplar Ave PO Box 330 TF: 877-752-2643 ■ Web: www.neshoba.org	Philadelphia	MS	39350	601-656-1000	656-1066
Madison County Chamber of Commerce 618 Crescent Blvd Suite 101 Web: www.madisoncountychamber.com	Ridgeland	MS	39157	601-605-2554	605-2260
Sardis Chamber of Commerce 120 S Main St PO Box 377	Sardis	MS	38666	662-487-3451	
Southaven Chamber of Commerce 8700 Northwest Dr Suite 100 TF: 800-272-6551 ■ Web: www.southavenchamber.com	Southaven	MS	38671	662-342-6114	342-6365
Starkville Area Chamber of Commerce 200 E Main St TF: 800-649-8687 ■ Web: www.starkville.org	Starkville	MS	39759	662-323-3322	323-5815
Vicksburg-Warren County Chamber of Commerce 2020 Mission 66 TF: 888-842-5728 ■ Web: www.vicksburg.org	Vicksburg	MS	39180	601-636-1012	636-4422
Yazoo County Chamber of Commerce 212 E Broadway PO Box 172 TF: 800-748-8875 ■ Web: www.yazoochamber.org	Yazoo City	MS	39194	662-746-1273	746-7238

Missouri

	City	State	Zip	Phone	Fax
Affton Chamber of Commerce 10203 Gravois Rd Web: www.afftonchamber.com	Affton	MO	63123	314-849-6499	849-6399
West Saint Louis County Chamber of Commerce 14811 Manchester Rd Suite 100 Web: www.westcountychamber.com	Ballwin	MO	63011	636-230-9900	230-9912
Blue Springs Chamber of Commerce 1000 SW Main St Web: www.bluespringschamber.com	Blue Springs	MO	64015	816-229-8558	229-1244
Branson/Lakes Area Chamber of Commerce PO Box 1897 TF: 800-214-3661 ■ Web: www.bransonchamber.com	Branson	MO	65615	417-334-4136	334-4139
Northwest Chamber of Commerce 11965 St Charles Rock Rd Suite 203 Web: northwestchamber.com	Bridgeton	MO	63044	314-291-2131	291-2153
Cape Girardeau Chamber of Commerce 1267 N Mt Auburn Rd Web: www.capechamber.com	Cape Girardeau	MO	63701	573-335-3312	335-4686
Cassville Area Chamber of Commerce 504 Main St TF: 866-847-2814 ■ Web: www.cassville.com	Cassville	MO	65625	417-847-2814	847-0804
Chesterfield Chamber of Commerce 101 Chesterfield Business Pkwy TF: 888-242-4262 ■ Web: www.chesterfieldmochamber.com	Chesterfield	MO	63005	636-532-3399	532-7446
Columbia Chamber of Commerce 300 S Providence Rd Web: chamber.columbia.mo.us	Columbia	MO	65203	573-874-1132	443-3986
North County Chamber of Commerce 119 Church St Suite 135	Ferguson	MO	63135	314-521-6000	521-2897
Twin City Area Chamber of Commerce 114 Main St. Web: www.twincity.org	Festus	MO	63028	636-931-7697	937-0925
Florissant Valley Chamber of Commerce 420 W Washington St Web: www.florissantvalleycc.com	Florissant	MO	63031	314-831-3500	831-9682
Kingdom of Callaway Chamber of Commerce 409 Court St TF: 800-257-3554 ■ Web: www.callawaychamber.com	Fulton	MO	65251	573-642-3055	642-5182
Gladstone Area Chamber of Commerce 6504 N Oak Traffic Way Web: www.gladstonechamber.com	Gladstone	MO	64118	816-436-4523	436-4352
Grandview Area Chamber of Commerce 12500 S 71 Hwy Web: www.grandview.org	Grandview	MO	64030	816-761-6505	763-8460
Independence Chamber of Commerce 210 W Truman Rd Web: www.independencechamber.com	Independence	MO	64050	816-252-4745	252-4917
Jefferson City Area Chamber of Commerce 213 Adams St Web: www.jcchamber.org	Jefferson City	MO	65101	573-634-3616	634-3805
Joplin Area Chamber of Commerce 320 E 4th St Web: www.joplincc.com	Joplin	MO	64801	417-624-4150	624-4303
Greater Kansas City Chamber of Commerce 911 Main St Suite 2600 Web: www.kcchamber.com	Kansas City	MO	64105	816-221-2424	221-7440
Northland Regional Chamber of Commerce 634 NW Englewood Rd Web: www.northlandchamber.com	Kansas City	MO	64118	816-455-9911	455-9933
South Kansas City Chamber of Commerce 5908 E Bannister Rd Web: www.southkcchamber.com	Kansas City	MO	64134	816-761-7660	761-7340
Kirkwood Area Chamber of Commerce 108 W Adams Ave Web: www.kirkwoodarea.com	Kirkwood	MO	63122	314-821-4161	821-5229
Lebanon Area Chamber of Commerce 186 N Adams St TF: 888-588-5710 ■ Web: www.lebanonmissouri.com	Lebanon	MO	65536	417-588-3256	588-3251
Lee's Summit Chamber of Commerce 220 SE Main St TF: 888-816-5757 ■ Web: www.lschamber.com	Lee's Summit	MO	64063	816-524-2424	524-5246
Neosho Area Chamber of Commerce 308 W Spring St Web: www.neoshocc.com	Neosho	MO	64850	417-451-1925	451-8097
O'Fallon Chamber of Commerce 2897 Hwy K Suite 200 Web: www.ofallonmochamber.com	O'Fallon	MO	63368	636-240-1818	281-8288
Park Hills Chamber of Commerce 5 Municipal Dr Web: parkhillscoc.brick.net	Park Hills	MO	63601	573-431-1051	431-2327
Crossroads Chamber-Raytown Area Chamber of Commerce 5909 Raytown Trafficway Web: www.raytownchamber.com	Raytown	MO	64133	816-353-8500	353-8525
Rolla Area Chamber of Commerce 1301 Kingshighway TF: 888-809-3817 ■ Web: www.rollachamber.org	Rolla	MO	65401	573-364-3577	364-5222
Saint Charles Chamber of Commerce 2201 First Capitol Dr Web: www.stcharleschamber.org	Saint Charles	MO	63301	636-946-0633	946-0301
Saint Joseph Area Chamber of Commerce 3003 Frederick Ave TF: 800-748-7856 ■ Web: www.saintjoseph.com	Saint Joseph	MO	64506	816-232-4461	364-4873
Maryland Heights Chamber of Commerce 545 W Port Plaza Web: www.mhcc.com	Saint Louis	MO	63146	314-576-6603	576-6855
Saint Louis Regional Commerce & Growth Assn 1 Metropolitan Sq Suite 1300 TF: 877-785-7242 ■ Web: www.stlrcga.org	Saint Louis	MO	63102	314-231-5555	444-1122
South County Chamber of Commerce 6921 S Lindburg Blvd Web: www.scountychamber.org	Saint Louis	MO	63125	314-894-6800	894-6888
Saint Peters Chamber of Commerce 1236 Jungermann Rd Suite C Web: www.stpeterschamber.com	Saint Peters	MO	63376	636-447-3336	447-9575
Waynesville-Saint Robert Area Chamber of Commerce 137 St Robert Blvd Web: www.waynesville-strobertchamber.com	Saint Robert	MO	65584	573-336-5121	336-5472
Sedalia Area Chamber of Commerce 600 E 3rd St TF: 800-827-5295 ■ Web: www.sedaliachamber.com	Sedalia	MO	65301	660-826-2222	826-2223
Springfield Area Chamber of Commerce 202 S John Q Hammons Pkwy TF: 800-879-7504 ■ Web: www.springfieldchamber.com	Springfield	MO	65806	417-862-5567	862-1611
Washington Area Chamber of Commerce 323 W Main St. TF: 888-792-7466 ■ Web: www.washmo.org	Washington	MO	63090	636-239-2715	239-1381

Montana

	City	State	Zip	Phone	Fax
Billings Area Chamber of Commerce 815 S 27th St TF: 800-735-2635	Billings	MT	59101	406-245-4111	245-7333
Bozeman Area Chamber of Commerce 2000 Commerce Way Web: www.bozemanchamber.com	Bozeman	MT	59715	406-586-5421	586-8286
Butte-Silver Bow Chamber of Commerce 1000 George St TF: 800-735-6814 ■ Web: www.butteinfo.org	Butte	MT	59701	406-723-3177	723-1215
Great Falls Area Chamber of Commerce 710 1st Ave N TF: 800-735-8535 ■ Web: www.greatfallschamber.org	Great Falls	MT	59401	406-761-4434	761-6129
Bitterroot Valley Chamber of Commerce 105 E Main St. Web: www.bvchamber.com	Hamilton	MT	59840	406-363-2400	363-2402
Helena Area Chamber of Commerce 225 Cruse Ave TF: 800-743-5362 ■ Web: www.helenachamber.com	Helena	MT	59601	406-442-4120	447-1532
Kalispell Area Chamber of Commerce 15 Depot Park Web: www.kalispellchamber.com	Kalispell	MT	59901	406-758-2800	758-2805
Missoula Area Chamber of Commerce 825 E Front St Web: www.missoulachamber.com	Missoula	MT	59802	406-543-6623	543-6625

Nebraska

	City	State	Zip	Phone	Fax
Bellevue Chamber of Commerce 204 W Mission Ave Web: www.bellevuenebraska.com	Bellevue	NE	68005	402-898-3000	291-8729
Grand Island Area Chamber of Commerce 309 W 2nd St. Web: www.gichamber.com	Grand Island	NE	68802	308-382-9210	382-1154
Kearney Area Chamber of Commerce 1007 2nd Ave. TF: 800-652-9435 ■ Web: www.kearneycoc.org	Kearney	NE	68847	308-237-3101	237-3103
Lincoln Chamber of Commerce PO Box 83006 Web: www.lcoc.com	Lincoln	NE	68501	402-436-2350	436-2360
North Platte Area Chamber of Commerce 502 S Dewey St Web: www.northplattechamber.com	North Platte	NE	69101	308-532-4966	532-4827
Greater Omaha Chamber of Commerce 1301 Harney St Web: www.omahachamber.org/	Omaha	NE	68102	402-346-5000	346-7050

Nebraska (Cont'd)

				Phone	Fax
Sarpy County Chamber of Commerce 501 Olson Dr Suite 4 *Web:* www.sarpychamber.org	Papillion	NE	68046	402-339-3050	339-9968

Nevada

				Phone	Fax
Carson City Area Chamber of Commerce 1900 S Carson St Suite 200 *Web:* www.carsoncitychamber.com	Carson City	NV	89701	775-882-1565	882-4179
Elko Area Chamber of Commerce 1405 Idaho St *TF:* 800-428-7143 ■ *Web:* www.elkonevada.com	Elko	NV	89801	775-738-7135	738-7136
Greater Fallon Area Chamber of Commerce 85 N Taylor St *Web:* www.fallonchamber.com	Fallon	NV	89406	775-423-2544	423-0540
Carson Valley Chamber of Commerce & Visitors Authority 1477 Hwy 395 N Suite A *TF:* 800-727-7677 ■ *Web:* www.carsonvalleynv.org	Gardnerville	NV	89410	775-782-8144	782-1025
Henderson Chamber of Commerce 590 S Boulder Hwy *Web:* www.hendersonchamber.com	Henderson	NV	89015	702-565-8951	565-3115
Las Vegas Chamber of Commerce 3720 Howard Hughes Pkwy *Web:* www.lvchamber.com	Las Vegas	NV	89169	702-735-1616	735-2011
Latin Chamber of Commerce 300 N 13th St *Web:* www.lvlcc.com	Las Vegas	NV	89101	702-385-7367	385-2614
North Las Vegas Chamber of Commerce 3345 W Craig Rd Suite B *Web:* www.nlvchamber.org	North Las Vegas	NV	89032	702-642-9595	642-0439
Sparks Chamber of Commerce 831 Victorian Ave *Web:* www.sparkschamber.org	Sparks	NV	89431	775-358-1976	358-1992
Lake Tahoe Chamber of Commerce PO Box 7139 *Web:* www.tahoechamber.org	Stateline	NV	89449	775-588-1728	588-1941
Tonopah Chamber of Commerce PO Box 869 *Web:* www.tonopahnevada.com	Tonopah	NV	89049	775-482-3859	

New Hampshire

				Phone	Fax
Souhegan Valley Chamber of Commerce 89 SR 101A *Web:* www.souhegan.net	Amherst	NH	03031	603-673-4360	673-5018
Greater Concord Chamber of Commerce 40 Commercial St *Web:* www.concordnhchamber.com	Concord	NH	03301	603-224-2508	224-8128
Greater Derry Chamber of Commerce 29 W Broadway *Web:* www.derry-chamber.org	Derry	NH	03038	603-432-8205	432-7938
Greater Dover Chamber of Commerce 299 Central Ave *Web:* www.dovernh.org	Dover	NH	03820	603-742-2218	749-6317
Exeter Area Chamber of Commerce 120 Water St *Web:* www.exeterarea.org	Exeter	NH	03833	603-772-2411	772-9965
Hampton Area Chamber of Commerce 1 Layfayette Rd *Web:* www.hamptonchamber.com	Hampton	NH	03842	603-926-8718	926-9977
Hanover Area Chamber of Commerce PO Box 5105 *Web:* www.hanoverchamber.org	Hanover	NH	03755	603-643-3115	643-5606
Greater Keene Chamber of Commerce 48 Central Sq *Web:* www.keenechamber.com	Keene	NH	03431	603-352-1303	358-5341
Greater Laconia-Weirs Beach Chamber of Commerce 383 S Main St *Web:* www.laconia-weirs.org	Laconia	NH	03246	603-524-5531	524-5534
Greater Manchester Chamber of Commerce 889 Elm St *Web:* www.manchester-chamber.org	Manchester	NH	03101	603-666-6600	626-0910
Greater Nashua Chamber of Commerce 151 Main St *Web:* www.nashuachamber.com	Nashua	NH	03060	603-881-8333	881-7323
Greater Portsmouth Chamber of Commerce 500 Market St PO Box 239 *Web:* www.portsmouthchamber.org	Portsmouth	NH	03802	603-436-1118	436-5118
Greater Rochester Chamber of Commerce 18 S Main St *Web:* www.rochesternh.org	Rochester	NH	03867	603-332-5080	332-5216
Greater Salem Chamber of Commerce 224 N Broadway 1st Fl *Web:* www.salemnhchamber.org	Salem	NH	03079	603-893-3177	894-5158

New Jersey

				Phone	Fax
Asbury Park Chamber of Commerce PO Box 649 *Web:* www.asburyparkchamber.com	Asbury Park	NJ	07712	732-775-7676	775-7675
Atlantic City Regional Chamber of Commerce 1125 Atlantic Ave Suite 105 *Web:* www.atlanticcitychamber.com	Atlantic City	NJ	08401	609-345-5600	345-1666
Bayonne Chamber of Commerce 621 Ave C *Web:* www.bayonnenj.org/commerce.htm	Bayonne	NJ	07002	201-436-4333	436-8546
Bergenfield Chamber of Commerce 35 S Washington Ave *Web:* www.bergenfieldboro.com	Bergenfield	NJ	07621	201-387-8300	387-8302
Brick Township Chamber of Commerce 270 Chambers Bridge Rd *Web:* www.brickchamber.org	Brick	NJ	08723	732-477-4949	477-5788
Bridgeton Area Chamber of Commerce PO Box 1063 *Web:* www.baccnj.com	Bridgeton	NJ	08302	856-455-1312	453-9795
Somerset County Business Partnership 360 Grove St *Web:* www.somersetbusinesspartnership.com	Bridgewater	NJ	08807	908-218-4300	722-7823
Mount Olive Area Chamber of Commerce PO Box 197 *Web:* www.mtolivechambernj.com	Budd Lake	NJ	07828	973-691-0109	691-0110
Cape May County Chamber of Commerce PO Box 74 *Web:* www.capemaycountychamber.com	Cape May Court House	NJ	08210	609-465-7181	465-5017
Salem County Chamber of Commerce 91-A S Virginia Ave *Web:* www.salemnjchamber.homestead.com	Carneys Point	NJ	08069	856-299-6699	299-0299
Cherry Hill Regional Chamber of Commerce 1060 Kings Hwy N Suite 200 *Web:* www.cherryhillregional.com	Cherry Hill	NJ	08034	856-667-1600	667-1464
North Jersey Regional Chamber of Commerce 1033 Rt 46 E *Web:* www.njrcc.org	Clifton	NJ	07013	973-470-9300	470-9245
East Brunswick Regional Chamber of Commerce 21 Brunswick Woods Dr PO Box 56 *Web:* www.ebnjchamber.org	East Brunswick	NJ	08816	732-257-3009	257-0949
Edison Chamber of Commerce 336 Raritan Center Pkwy *Web:* www.edisonchamber.com	Edison	NJ	08837	732-738-9482	738-9485
Gateway Regional Chamber of Commerce 135 Jefferson Ave PO Box 300 *Web:* www.gatewaychamber.com	Elizabeth	NJ	07207	908-352-0900	352-0865
Englewood Chamber of Commerce 2-10 N Van Brunt St *Web:* www.englewood-chamber.com	Englewood	NJ	07631	201-567-2381	871-4549
Fair Lawn Chamber of Commerce 18-00 Fairmont Ave *Web:* www.fairlawnchamber.org	Fair Lawn	NJ	07410	201-796-7050	475-0619
Greater Fort Lee Chamber of Commerce 210 Whiteman St *Web:* www.fortleenj.com	Fort Lee	NJ	07024	201-944-7575	944-5168
Western Monmouth Chamber of Commerce 17 Broad St *Web:* www.wmchamber.com	Freehold	NJ	07728	732-462-3030	462-2123
Greater Hackensack Chamber of Commerce 5 University Plaza Dr *Web:* www.hackensackchamber.org	Hackensack	NJ	07601	201-489-3700	489-1741
Greater Hammonton Chamber of Commerce 10 S Egg Harbor Rd PO Box 554 *Web:* www.hammontonnj.us	Hammonton	NJ	08037	609-561-9080	561-9411
Howell Chamber of Commerce PO Box 196 *Web:* www.howellchamber.com	Howell	NJ	07731	732-363-4114	363-8747
Irvington Chamber of Commerce PO Box 323 *Web:* www.irvington-nj.com/ICC.html	Irvington	NJ	07111	973-372-4100	673-5828
Hudson County Chamber of Commerce 660 Newark Ave Suite 220 *Web:* www.hudsonchamber.org	Jersey City	NJ	07306	201-386-0699	386-8480
Parsippany Area Chamber of Commerce 12-14 N Beverwyck Rd *Web:* www.parsippanychamber.org	Lake Hiawatha	NJ	07034	973-402-6400	206-5856
Lakewood Chamber of Commerce 395 Hwy 70 W Suite 125 *Web:* www.mylakewoodchamber.com	Lakewood	NJ	08701	732-363-0012	367-4453
Hunterdon County Chamber of Commerce 2200 Rt 31 Suite 15 *Web:* www.hunterdon-chamber.org	Lebanon	NJ	08833	908-735-5955	730-6580
Greater Long Branch Chamber of Commerce PO Box 628 *Web:* www.longbranchchamber.org	Long Branch	NJ	07740	732-222-0400	571-3385
Matawan-Aberdeen Chamber of Commerce PO Box 522	Matawan	NJ	07747	732-290-1125	290-1125
Mercer Regional Chamber of Commerce 1A Quakerbridge Plaza Dr Suite 2 *Web:* www.mercerchamber.org	Mercerville	NJ	08619	609-689-9960	586-9989
Millville Chamber of Commerce 4 City Park Dr *Web:* www.millville-nj.com	Millville	NJ	08332	856-825-2600	825-5333
Middlesex County Regional Chamber of Commerce 1 Distribution Way *Web:* www.mcrcc.org	Monmouth Junction	NJ	08852	732-821-1700	821-5852
Morris County Chamber of Commerce 25 Lindsley Dr Suite 105 *Web:* www.morrischamber.org	Morristown	NJ	07960	973-539-3882	539-3960
Randolph Area Chamber of Commerce PO Box 391 *Web:* www.randolphchamber.org	Mount Freedom	NJ	07970	973-361-3462	895-3297
Burlington County Chamber of Commerce 900 Briggs Rd Suite 110 *Web:* www.bccoc.com	Mount Laurel	NJ	08054	856-439-2520	439-2523
Northern Monmouth Chamber of Commerce 1041 Hwy 36 Suite 206 *Web:* www.northernmonmouth.org	Navesink	NJ	07752	732-291-7870	291-7871
Newark Regional Business Partnership 744 Broad St 26th Fl *Web:* www.newarkrbp.org	Newark	NJ	07102	973-522-0099	824-6587
Sussex County Chamber of Commerce 120 Hampton House Rd *Web:* www.sussexcountychamber.org	Newton	NJ	07860	973-579-1811	579-3031
Nutley Chamber of Commerce 299 Franklin Ave *Web:* www.nutleychamber.com	Nutley	NJ	07110	973-667-5300	
Orange Chamber of Commerce PO Box 1178 *Web:* www.orangechamber.biz	Orange	NJ	07050	973-676-8725	673-5828
Commerce & Industry Assn of New Jersey S 61 Paramus Rd *Web:* new.cianj.org	Paramus	NJ	07652	201-368-2100	368-3438
Paramus Chamber of Commerce 58 E Midland Ave *Web:* www.paramuschamber.com	Paramus	NJ	07652	201-261-3344	261-3346
Greater Paterson Chamber of Commerce 100 Hamilton Plaza Suite 1201 *Web:* www.greaterpatersoncc.org	Paterson	NJ	07505	973-881-7300	881-8233
Perth Amboy Chamber of Commerce 69-A Smith St *Web:* www.perthamboychamber.com	Perth Amboy	NJ	08861	732-442-7400	442-7450
Piscataway/Middlesex/South Plainfield Area Chamber of Commerce 1315 Stelton Rd *Web:* www.pmspcoc.org	Piscataway	NJ	08854	732-394-0220	394-0223
Point Pleasant Beach Chamber of Commerce 517-A Arnold Ave *Web:* www.pointpleasantbeachnj.com	Point Pleasant Beach	NJ	08742	732-899-2424	899-0103
Princeton Regional Chamber of Commerce 9 Vandeventer Ave *Web:* www.princetonchamber.org	Princeton	NJ	08542	609-924-1776	924-5776
Eastern Monmouth Area Chamber of Commerce 170 Broad St *Web:* www.emacc.org	Red Bank	NJ	07701	732-741-0055	741-6778
Ridgewood Chamber of Commerce 199 Dayton St *Web:* www.webridgewood.com	Ridgewood	NJ	07450	201-445-2600	251-1958
Meadowlands Regional Chamber of Commerce 201 Rt 17 N *Web:* www.meadowlands.org	Rutherford	NJ	07070	201-939-0707	939-0522
Southern Ocean County Chamber of Commerce 265 W 9th St *TF:* 800-292-6372 ■ *Web:* www.discoversouthernocean.com	Ship Bottom	NJ	08008	609-494-7211	494-5807
Chamber of Commerce of Franklin Township 675 Franklin Blvd *Web:* www.franklinchamber.com	Somerset	NJ	08873	732-545-7044	545-7043
Suburban Chambers of Commerce 71 Summit Ave *Web:* www.suburbanchambers.org	Summit	NJ	07901	908-522-1700	522-9252
Toms River-Ocean County Chamber of Commerce 1200 Hooper Ave *Web:* www.oc-chamber.com	Toms River	NJ	08753	732-349-0220	349-1252
Union Township Chamber of Commerce 355 Chestnut St 2nd Fl *Web:* www.unionchamber.com	Union	NJ	07083	908-688-2777	688-0338
Greater Vineland Chamber of Commerce 2115 S Delsea Dr *TF:* 800-309-0019 ■ *Web:* www.vinelandchamber.org	Vineland	NJ	08360	856-691-7400	691-2113
Chamber of Commerce of Southern New Jersey 6014 Main St *Web:* www.chambersnj.com	Voorhees	NJ	08043	856-424-7776	424-8180
Southern Monmouth Area Chamber of Commerce 2510 Belmar Blvd Unit I-20 PO Box 1305 *Web:* www.southernmonmouthchamber.com	Wall	NJ	07719	732-280-8800	280-8505
Warren County Regional Chamber of Commerce 10 Brasscastle Rd *Web:* www.warrencountychamber.org	Washington	NJ	07882	908-835-9200	835-9296
Tri-County Chamber of Commerce 2055 Hamburg Tpke *Web:* www.tricounty.org	Wayne	NJ	07470	973-831-7788	831-9112
North Essex Chamber of Commerce 3 Fairfield Ave *Web:* www.northessexchamber.com	West Caldwell	NJ	07006	973-226-5500	403-9335
West Milford Chamber of Commerce PO Box 234 *Web:* www.westmilford.com	West Milford	NJ	07480	973-728-3150	697-5177
Westfield Area Chamber of Commerce 173 Elm St 3rd Fl *Web:* westfieldchamber.com	Westfield	NJ	07090	908-233-3021	654-8183
Woodbridge Metro Chamber of Commerce 52 Main St *Web:* www.woodbridgechamber.org	Woodbridge	NJ	07095	732-636-4040	636-3492

New Mexico

Chamber	City	State	ZIP	Phone	Fax
Alamogordo Chamber of Commerce 1301 N White Sands Blvd *TF:* 800-826-0294 ■ *Web:* www.alamogordo.com	Alamogordo	NM	88310	505-437-6120	437-6334
Greater Albuquerque Chamber of Commerce PO Box 25100 *Web:* abqchamber.com	Albuquerque	NM	87125	505-764-3700	764-3714
Carlsbad Chamber of Commerce 302 S Canal St *TF:* 800-221-1224 ■ *Web:* www.chamber.caverns.com	Carlsbad	NM	88220	505-887-6516	885-1455
Clovis/Curry County Chamber of Commerce 105 E Grant *TF:* 800-261-7656 ■ *Web:* www.clovisnm.org	Clovis	NM	88101	505-763-3435	763-7266
Espanola Valley Chamber of Commerce 710 Paseo de Onate *Web:* www.espanolanmchamber.com	Espanola	NM	87532	505-753-2831	753-1252
Farmington Chamber of Commerce 100 W Broadway *TF:* 888-325-0279 ■ *Web:* www.gofarmington.com	Farmington	NM	87401	505-325-0279	327-7556
Grants/Cibola County Chamber of Commerce 100 N Iron Ave *TF:* 800-748-2142 ■ *Web:* www.grants.org	Grants	NM	87020	505-287-4802	287-8224
Hobbs Chamber of Commerce 400 N Marland Blvd *TF:* 800-658-6291 ■ *Web:* www.hobbschamber.org	Hobbs	NM	88240	505-397-3202	397-1689
Greater Las Cruces Chamber of Commerce 760 W Picacho Ave *Web:* lascruces.org	Las Cruces	NM	88005	505-524-1968	527-5546
Las Vegas-San Miguel Chamber of Commerce PO Box 128 *TF:* 800-832-5947 ■ *Web:* www.lasvegasnm.org	Las Vegas	NM	87701	505-425-8631	425-3057
Rio Rancho Chamber of Commerce 4001 Southern Blvd SE *Web:* www.rrchamber.org	Rio Rancho	NM	87124	505-892-1533	892-6157
Roswell Chamber of Commerce 131 W 2nd St *TF:* 877-849-7679 ■ *Web:* www.roswellnm.org	Roswell	NM	88202	505-623-5695	624-6870
Santa Fe Chamber of Commerce 8380 Cerrillos Rd Suite 302 *Web:* www.santafechamber.com	Santa Fe	NM	87507	505-988-3279	984-2205
Silver City-Grant County Chamber of Commerce 201 N Hudson St *TF:* 800-548-9378 ■ *Web:* www.silvercity.org	Silver City	NM	88061	505-538-3785	538-3786

New York

Chamber	City	State	ZIP	Phone	Fax
Albany-Colonie Regional Chamber of Commerce 107 Washington Ave *Web:* www.ac-chamber.org	Albany	NY	12210	518-434-1214	434-1339
Guilderland Chamber of Commerce 2021 Western Ave Suite 105 *Web:* www.guilderlandchamber.com	Albany	NY	12203	518-456-6611	456-6690
Orleans County Chamber of Commerce 121 N Main St Suite 110 *Web:* www.orleanschamber.com	Albion	NY	14411	585-589-7727	589-7326
Montgomery County Chamber of Commerce 366 W Main St PO Box 309 *TF:* 800-743-7337 ■ *Web:* www.montgomerycountyny.com	Amsterdam	NY	12010	518-842-8200	843-8327
Cayuga County Chamber of Commerce 36 South St *Web:* www.cayugacountychamber.com	Auburn	NY	13021	315-252-7291	255-3077
Greater Baldwinsville Chamber of Commerce 50 Oswego St *Web:* www.baldwinsvillechamber.com	Baldwinsville	NY	13027	315-638-0550	
Genesee County Chamber of Commerce 210 E Main St *TF:* 800-622-2686 ■ *Web:* www.geneseeny.com	Batavia	NY	14020	585-343-7440	343-7487
Greater Bath Area Chamber of Commerce 10 Pulteney Sq W *Web:* www.bathnychamber.com	Bath	NY	14810	607-776-7122	776-7122
Bay Shore Chamber of Commerce 77 E Main St PO Box 5110 *Web:* www.bayshorecommerce.com	Bay Shore	NY	11706	631-665-7003	665-5204
Chamber of Commerce of the Bellmores PO Box 861 *Web:* www.bellmorechamber.com	Bellmore	NY	11710	516-679-1875	409-0544
Greater Binghamton Chamber of Commerce 49 Court St *TF:* 800-836-6740 ■ *Web:* www.greaterbinghamtonchamber.com	Binghamton	NY	13902	607-772-8860	722-4513
New Bronx Chamber of Commerce Inc 1200 Waters Pl Suite 305 *Web:* www.bronxmall.com/com/chamber	Bronx	NY	10461	718-828-3900	409-3748
Brooklyn Chamber of Commerce 25 Elm Pl Suite 200 *Web:* www.ibrooklyn.com	Brooklyn	NY	11201	718-875-1000	237-4274
Coney Island Chamber of Commerce 1015 Surf Ave	Brooklyn	NY	11224	718-266-1234	714-0379
Buffalo Niagara Partnership 665 Main St Suite 200 *TF:* 800-241-0474 ■ *Web:* www.thepartnership.org	Buffalo	NY	14203	716-852-7100	852-2761
Saint Lawrence County Chamber of Commerce 101 Main St *TF:* 877-228-7810 ■ *Web:* www.northcountryguide.com/slc-chamber	Canton	NY	13617	315-386-4000	379-0134
Greene County Chamber of Commerce 1 Bridge St 2nd Fl *Web:* www.greenecounty-chamber.com	Catskill	NY	12414	518-943-4222	943-1700
Cheektowaga Chamber of Commerce 2875 Union Rd Suite 50 *Web:* www.cheektowaga.org	Cheektowaga	NY	14227	716-684-5838	684-5571
Southern Saratoga County Chamber of Commerce 15 Park Ave Suite 7-B *Web:* www.ssccc.org	Clifton Park	NY	12065	518-371-7748	371-5025
Corning Area Chamber of Commerce 1 W Market St Suite 302 *TF:* 866-463-6264 ■ *Web:* www.corningny.com	Corning	NY	14830	607-936-4686	936-4685
Cortland County Chamber of Commerce 37 Church St *Web:* www.cortlandchamber.com	Cortland	NY	13045	607-756-2814	756-4698
Delaware County Chamber of Commerce 5 1/2 Main St *TF:* 800-642-4443 ■ *Web:* www.delawarecounty.org	Delhi	NY	13753	607-746-2281	746-3571
Bethlehem Chamber of Commerce 318 Delaware Ave *Web:* www.bethlehemchamber.com	Delmar	NY	12054	518-439-0512	475-0910
Chautauqua County Chamber of Commerce 10785 Bennett Rd *Web:* www.chautauquachamber.org	Dunkirk	NY	14048	716-366-6200	366-4276
Greater East Aurora Chamber of Commerce 431 Main St *TF:* 800-441-2881 ■ *Web:* www.eanycc.com	East Aurora	NY	14052	716-652-8444	652-8384
Chemung County Chamber of Commerce 400 E Church St *TF:* 800-627-5892 ■ *Web:* www.chemungchamber.org	Elmira	NY	14901	607-734-5137	734-4490
Livingston County Chamber of Commerce 4635 Millennium Dr *TF:* 800-538-7365 ■ *Web:* www.fingerlakeswest.com	Geneseo	NY	14454	585-243-2222	243-4824
Adirondack Regional Chambers of Commerce 5 Warren St *TF:* 888-516-7247 ■ *Web:* www.adirondackchamber.org	Glens Falls	NY	12801	518-798-1761	792-4147
Fulton County Regional Chamber of Commerce 2 N Main St *TF:* 800-676-3858 ■ *Web:* www.fultoncountyny.org	Gloversville	NY	12078	518-725-0641	725-0643
Hamburg Chamber of Commerce 8 S Buffalo St *TF:* 877-322-6890 ■ *Web:* www.hamburg-chamber.org	Hamburg	NY	14075	716-649-7917	649-6362
Hempstead Village Chamber of Commerce 1776 Denton Green *Web:* www.hempsteadchamber.com	Hempstead	NY	11550	516-483-2000	483-2000
Hicksville Chamber of Commerce 10 W Marie St *Web:* www.hicksvillechamber.com	Hicksville	NY	11801	516-931-7170	931-8546
Southern Ulster County Chamber of Commerce 33 Main St *Web:* www.southernulsterchamber.org	Highland	NY	12528	845-691-6070	691-9194
Columbia County Chamber of Commerce 507 Warren St *Web:* www.columbiachamber-ny.com	Hudson	NY	12534	518-828-4417	822-9539
Huntington Township Chamber of Commerce 164 Main St *TF:* 888-361-5710 ■ *Web:* www.huntingtonchamber.com	Huntington	NY	11743	631-423-6100	351-8276
Hyde Park Chamber of Commerce PO Box 17 *Web:* www.hydeparkchamber.org	Hyde Park	NY	12538	845-229-8612	229-8638
Tompkins County Chamber of Commerce 904 E Shore Dr *Web:* www.tompkinschamber.org	Ithaca	NY	14850	607-273-7080	272-7617
Chamber of Commerce of Borough of Queens 75-20 Astoria Blvd Suite 140 *Web:* www.queenschamber.org	Jackson Heights	NY	11370	718-898-8500	898-8599
Jamaica Chamber of Commerce 90-25 161st St Suite 505 *Web:* www.jccnewyork.net	Jamaica	NY	11432	718-657-4800	658-4642
Chautauqua County Chamber of Commerce 101 W 5th St *Web:* www.chautauquachamber.org	Jamestown	NY	14701	716-484-1101	487-0785
Kenmore-Town of Tonawanda Chamber of Commerce 3411 Delaware Ave *TF:* 888-281-1680 ■ *Web:* www.ken-ton.org	Kenmore	NY	14217	716-874-1202	874-3151
Chamber of Commerce of Ulster County 55 Albany Ave *Web:* www.ulsterchamber.org	Kingston	NY	12401	845-338-5100	338-0968
Lake Placid/Essex County Visitors Bureau 2610 Main St Suite 2 Olympic Ctr *TF:* 800-447-5224 ■ *Web:* www.lakeplacid.com	Lake Placid	NY	12946	518-523-2445	523-2605
Latham Area Chamber of Commerce 950 New Loudon Rd *Web:* www.lathamchamber.org	Latham	NY	12110	518-785-6995	785-7173
Greater Liverpool Chamber of Commerce 314 2nd St *Web:* www.liverpoolchamber.com	Liverpool	NY	13088	315-457-3895	234-3226
Long Beach Chamber of Commerce 350 National Blvd *TF:* 866-563-3275 ■ *Web:* www.longbeachnychamber.com	Long Beach	NY	11561	516-432-6000	432-0273
Lewis County Chamber of Commerce 7383-C Utica Blvd *TF:* 800-724-0242 ■ *Web:* www.lewiscountychamber.org	Lowville	NY	13367	315-376-2213	376-0326
Greater Mahopacs-Carmel Chamber of Commerce 953 S Lake Blvd PO Box 160 *Web:* www.mahopaccarmelchamber.com/	Mahopac	NY	10541	845-628-5553	628-5962
Chamber of Commerce of the Massapequas Inc 674 Broadway *Web:* www.massapequachamber.com	Massapequa	NY	11758	516-541-1443	541-8625
Long Island Assn 300 Broadhollow Rd Suite 110-W *Web:* www.longislandassociation.org	Melville	NY	11747	631-499-4400	499-2194
Herkimer County Chamber of Commerce 28 W Main St *TF:* 877-984-4636 ■ *Web:* www.herkimercountychamber.com	Mohawk	NY	13407	315-866-7820	866-7833
Sullivan County Chamber of Commerce 452 Broadway *Web:* www.catskills.com	Monticello	NY	12701	845-791-4200	791-4220
Mount Vernon Chamber of Commerce 22 W 1st St Suite 210 *Web:* www.mvnycoc.org	Mount Vernon	NY	10550	914-667-7500	699-0139
Chamber of Commerce of New Rochelle 459 Main St *Web:* www.newrochellechamber.org	New Rochelle	NY	10801	914-632-5700	632-0708
Greater New York Chamber of Commerce 172 Madison Ave 7th Fl *Web:* nyc.chamber.com	New York	NY	10016	212-244-0003	686-7232
Manhattan Chamber of Commerce 1375 Broadway 3rd F *Web:* www.manhattancc.org	New York	NY	10018	212-479-7772	473-8074
New York City Partnership & Chamber of Commerce Inc 1 Battery Park Plaza 5th Fl *Web:* www.nycp.org	New York	NY	10004	212-493-7500	344-3344
West Side Chamber of Commerce 1841 Broadway Suite 701 *Web:* www.westsidechamber.org	New York	NY	10023	212-541-8880	541-8883
Orange County Chamber of Commerce 11 Racquet Rd *Web:* www.orangeny.com	Newburgh	NY	12550	845-567-6229	567-6271
Chamber of Commerce of the Tonawandas 15 Webster St *Web:* www.the-tonawandas.com	North Tonawanda	NY	14120	716-692-5120	692-1867
Chenango County Chamber of Commerce 19 Eaton Ave *TF:* 800-556-8596 ■ *Web:* www.chenangony.org	Norwich	NY	13815	607-334-1400	336-6963
Oceanside Chamber of Commerce PO Box 1 *Web:* www.oceansidechamber.com	Oceanside	NY	11572	516-763-9177	
Greater Olean Area Chamber of Commerce 120 N Union St *Web:* www.oleanny.com	Olean	NY	14760	716-372-4433	372-7912
Otsego County Chamber 12 Carbon St *TF:* 877-568-7346 ■ *Web:* www.otsegocountychamber.com	Oneonta	NY	13820	607-432-4500	432-4506
Orchard Park Chamber of Commerce 4211 N Buffalo St Suite 14 *Web:* www.orchardparkchamber.com	Orchard Park	NY	14127	716-662-3366	662-5946
Greater Oswego Chamber of Commerce 156 W 2nd St *Web:* www.oswegochamber.com	Oswego	NY	13126	315-343-7681	342-0831
Tioga County Chamber of Commerce 188 Front St *Web:* www.tiogachamber.com	Owego	NY	13827	607-687-2020	687-9028
Hudson Valley Gateway Chamber of Commerce 1 S Division St *Web:* www.hvgatewaychamber.com	Peekskill	NY	10566	914-737-3600	737-0541
Plattsburgh North Country Chamber of Commerce 7061 Rt 9 *Web:* www.northcountrychamber.com	Plattsburgh	NY	12901	518-563-1000	563-1028
Port Chester-Rye Brook Chamber of Commerce 122 N Ridge St PO Box 629 *Web:* www.portchesterryebrookchamber.com	Port Chester	NY	10573	914-939-1900	
Tri-State Chamber of Commerce 5 S Broome St *Web:* www.tristatechamber.org	Port Jervis	NY	12771	845-856-6694	856-6695
Port Washington Chamber of Commerce 329 Main St *Web:* www.pwguide.com	Port Washington	NY	11050	516-883-6566	883-6591
Poughkeepsie Area Chamber of Commerce 1 Civic Ctr Plaza Suite 400 *Web:* www.pokchamb.org	Poughkeepsie	NY	12601	845-454-1700	454-1702
Rochester Business Alliance 150 State St *Web:* www.rochesterbusinessalliance.com	Rochester	NY	14614	585-454-2220	263-3679
Chamber of Commerce of the Rockaways 253 Beach 116th St *Web:* www.rockawaychamberofcommerce.com	Rockaway Park	NY	11694	718-634-1300	634-9623
Rome Area Chamber of Commerce 139 W Dominick St *Web:* www.romechamber.com	Rome	NY	13440	315-337-1700	337-1715
Niagara USA Chamber of Commerce 6311 Inducon Corporate Dr Suite 2 *Web:* www.niagarachamber.org	Sanborn	NY	14132	716-285-9141	285-0941
Saratoga County Chamber of Commerce 28 Clinton St *TF:* 800-526-8970 ■ *Web:* www.saratoga.org	Saratoga Springs	NY	12866	518-584-3255	587-0318
Chamber of Schenectady County 306 State St *TF:* 800-962-8007 ■ *Web:* www.schenectadychamber.net	Schenectady	NY	12305	518-372-5656	370-3217
Schoharie County Chamber of Commerce 113 Park Pl Suite 2 *TF:* 800-418-4748 ■ *Web:* www.schohariechamber.com	Schoharie	NY	12157	518-295-6550	295-7453
Seneca County Chamber of Commerce 2020 Rt 5 & 20 W *Web:* www.senecachamber.org	Seneca Falls	NY	13148	315-568-2906	568-1730
Smithtown Chamber of Commerce 79 E Main St Suite E *Web:* www.smithtownchamber.org	Smithtown	NY	11787	631-979-8069	979-2206
Southampton Chamber of Commerce 76 Main St *Web:* www.southamptonchamber.com	Southampton	NY	11968	631-283-0402	283-8707
Staten Island Chamber of Commerce 130 Bay St *Web:* www.sichamber.com	Staten Island	NY	10301	718-727-1900	727-2295
Greater Syracuse Chamber of Commerce 572 S Salina St *Web:* www.syracusechamber.com	Syracuse	NY	13202	315-470-1800	471-8545

New York (Cont'd)

Phone | Fax

Rensselaer County Regional Chamber of Commerce 255 River St. ... Troy NY 12180 518-274-7020 272-7729
Web: www.renscochamber.com
Mohawk Valley Chamber of Commerce 520 Seneca St. ... Utica NY 13502 315-724-3151 724-3177
Web: www.mvchamber.org
Greater Southern Dutchess Chamber of Commerce
2582 South Ave ... Wappingers Falls NY 12590 845-296-0001 296-0006
Web: gsdcc.org
Warwick Valley Chamber of Commerce PO Box 202 ... Warwick NY 10990 845-986-2720 986-6982
Web: www.warwickcc.org
Greater Watertown-North Country Chamber of Commerce
1241 Coffeen St ... Watertown NY 13601 315-788-4400 788-3369
Web: www.watertownny.com
Webster Chamber of Commerce 26 E Main St ... Webster NY 14580 585-265-3960 265-3702
Web: www.websterchamber.com
West Seneca Chamber of Commerce
950-A Union Rd Suite 5 ... West Seneca NY 14224 716-674-4900 674-5846
Web: www.westseneca.org
Business Council of Westchester
108 Corporate Pk Dr Suite 101 ... White Plains NY 10604 914-948-2110 948-0122
Web: www.westchesterny.org
Amherst Chamber of Commerce 325 Essjay Rd Suite 200 ... Williamsville NY 14221 716-632-6905 632-0548
Web: www.amherst.org
Yonkers Chamber of Commerce 20 S Broadway Suite 1205 ... Yonkers NY 10701 914-963-0332 963-0455
Web: www.yonkerschamber.com

North Carolina

Phone | Fax

Ahoskie Chamber of Commerce PO Box 7 ... Ahoskie NC 27910 252-332-2042 332-8617
Stanly County Chamber of Commerce 116 E North St ... Albemarle NC 28001 704-982-8116 983-5000
Web: www.stanlychamber.org
Archdale-Trinity Chamber of Commerce 213 Balfour Dr ... Archdale NC 27263 336-434-2073 431-5845
Web: www.archdaletrinitychamber.com
Asheboro/Randolph Chamber of Commerce 317 E Dixie Dr ... Asheboro NC 27203 336-626-2626 626-7077
Web: chamber.asheboro.com
Asheville Area Chamber of Commerce 36 Montford Ave ... Asheville NC 28801 828-258-6101 251-0926
TF: 800-257-1300 ■ *Web:* www.ashevillechamber.org
Black Mountain-Swannanoa Chamber of Commerce
201 E State St ... Black Mountain NC 28711 828-669-2300 669-1407
TF: 800-669-2301 ■ *Web:* www.blackmountain.org
Blowing Rock Chamber of Commerce 7738 Valley Blvd ... Blowing Rock NC 28605 828-295-7851 295-4643
TF: 800-295-7851 ■ *Web:* www.blowingrock.com
Brevard-Transylvania Chamber of Commerce 35 W Main St ... Brevard NC 28712 828-883-3700 883-8550
TF: 800-648-4523 ■ *Web:* www.brevardncchamber.org
Alamance County Area Chamber of Commerce PO Box 450 ... Burlington NC 27216 336-228-1338 228-1330
Web: www.alamancechamber.com
Cary Chamber of Commerce 307 N Academy St ... Cary NC 27513 919-467-1016 469-2375
TF: 800-919-2279 ■ *Web:* www.carychamber.com
Chapel Hill-Carrboro Chamber of Commerce 104 S Estes Dr ... Chapel Hill NC 27515 919-967-7075 968-6874
Web: www.carolinachamber.org
Charlotte Chamber of Commerce PO Box 32785 ... Charlotte NC 28232 704-378-1300 374-1903
Web: www.charlottechamber.com
Lake Norman Chamber of Commerce 19900 W Catawba Ave ... Cornelius NC 28031 704-987-3300 892-5313
TF: 800-305-2508 ■ *Web:* www.lakenormanchamber.org
Greater Durham Chamber of Commerce
300 W Morgan St Suite 1400 ... Durham NC 27701 919-682-2133 688-8351
Web: www.durhamchamber.org
Elizabeth City Area Chamber of Commerce
502 E Ehringhaus St ... Elizabeth City NC 27909 252-335-4365 335-5732
TF: 888-258-4832 ■ *Web:* www.elizcity.com
Yadkin Valley Chamber of Commerce
116 E Market St PO Box 496 ... Elkin NC 28621 336-526-1111 526-1879
Web: www.yadkinvalley.org
Cumberland County Business Council 201 Hay St 4th Fl ... Fayetteville NC 28301 910-483-8133 483-0263
Web: www.ccbusinesscouncil.org
Fuquay-Varina Area Chamber of Commerce
121 N Main St ... Fuquay-Varina NC 27526 919-552-4947 552-1029
Web: www.fuquay-varina.com
Gaston Chamber of Commerce 601 W Franklin Blvd ... Gastonia NC 28052 704-864-2621 854-8723
TF: 800-348-8461 ■ *Web:* www.gastonchamber.com
Chamber of Commerce of Wayne County 308 N Williams St ... Goldsboro NC 27530 919-734-2241 734-2247
Web: www.waynecountychamber.com
Greensboro Area Chamber of Commerce 342 N Elm St ... Greensboro NC 27401 336-275-8675 275-9299
Web: www.greensborochamber.com
Greenville-Pitt County Chamber of Commerce
302 S Greene St ... Greenville NC 27834 252-752-4101 752-5934
Web: www.greenvillenc.org
Henderson-Vance County Chamber of Commerce
PO Box 1302 ... Henderson NC 27536 252-438-8414 492-8989
Web: www.hendersonvance.org
Greater Hendersonville Chamber of Commerce
330 N King St ... Hendersonville NC 28792 828-692-1413 693-8802
Web: www.hendersonvillechamber.org
Catawba County Chamber of Commerce
1055 Southgate Corporate Pk SW PO Box 1828 ... Hickory NC 28603 828-328-6111 328-1175
Web: www.catawbachamber.org
High Point Chamber of Commerce 1101 N Main St ... High Point NC 27262 336-889-8151 889-9499
Web: www.highpointchamber.org
Jacksonville/Onslow Chamber of Commerce
1099 Gum Branch Rd ... Jacksonville NC 28541 910-347-3141 347-4705
Web: www.jacksonvilleonline.org
Cabarrus Regional Chamber of Commerce
3003 Dale Earnhardt Blvd ... Kannapolis NC 28083 704-782-4000 782-4050
Web: www.cabarruschamber.org
Outer Banks Chamber of Commerce 101 Town Hall Dr ... Kill Devil Hills NC 27948 252-441-8144 441-0338
Web: www.outerbankschamber.com
Kinston-Lenoir County Chamber of Commerce 301 N Queen St ... Kinston NC 28501 252-527-1131 527-1914
Web: www.kinstonchamber.com
Laurinburg/Scotland County Area Chamber of Commerce
PO Box 1025 ... Laurinburg NC 28353 910-276-7420 277-8785
Web: www.laurinburgchamber.org
Caldwell County Chamber of Commerce 1909 Hickory Blvd SE ... Lenoir NC 28645 828-726-0616 726-0385
Web: www.caldwellcochamber.org
Lincolnton-Lincoln County Chamber of Commerce
PO Box 1617 ... Lincolnton NC 28093 704-735-3096 735-5449
Web: www.lincolnchambernc.org
Franklin County Chamber of Commerce
112 E Nash St PO Box 62 ... Louisburg NC 27549 919-496-3056 496-0422
Web: www.franklin-chamber.org
Lumberton Area Chamber of Commerce 800 N Chestnut St ... Lumberton NC 28358 910-739-4750 671-9722
Web: www.lumbertonchamber.com

Phone | Fax

Western Rockingham Chamber of Commerce
112 W Murphy St ... Madison NC 27025 336-548-6248 548-4466
Web: www.westernrockinghamchamber.com
McDowell Chamber of Commerce 1170 W Tate St ... Marion NC 28752 828-652-4240 659-9620
Web: www.mcdowellchamber.com
Davie County Chamber of Commerce 135 S Salisbury St ... Mocksville NC 27028 336-751-3304 751-5697
Web: www.daviecounty.com/commerce
Union County Chamber of Commerce 903 Skyway Dr ... Monroe NC 28110 704-289-4567 282-0122
Web: www.unioncountycoc.com
Mooresville-South Iredell Chamber of Commerce
149 E Iredell Ave ... Mooresville NC 28115 704-664-3898 664-2549
Web: www.mooresvillenc.org
Carteret County Chamber of Commerce
801 Arendell St Suite 1 ... Morehead City NC 28557 252-726-6350 726-3505
TF: 800-622-6278 ■ *Web:* www.nccoastchamber.com
Burke County Chamber of Commerce 110 E Meeting St ... Morganton NC 28655 828-437-3021 437-1613
Web: www.burkecounty.org
Greater Mount Airy Chamber of Commerce 200 N Main St ... Mount Airy NC 27030 336-786-6116 786-1488
TF: 800-948-0949 ■ *Web:* www.mtairyncchamber.org
Mount Olive Area Chamber of Commerce 123 N Center St ... Mount Olive NC 28365 919-658-3113 658-3125
Web: www.moachamber.com
Cherokee County Chamber of Commerce 805 W US 64 ... Murphy NC 28906 828-837-2242 837-6012
Web: www.cherokeecountychamber.org
New Bern Area Chamber of Commerce 316 S Front St ... New Bern NC 28560 252-637-3111 637-7541
Web: www.newbernchamber.com
Wilkes Chamber of Commerce 717 Main St ... North Wilkesboro NC 28659 336-838-8662 838-3728
Web: www.wilkesnc.org
Granville County Chamber of Commerce 124 Hillsboro St ... Oxford NC 27565 919-693-6125 693-6126
Web: www.granville-chamber.com
Raeford/Hoke Chamber of Commerce 101 N Main St ... Raeford NC 28376 910-875-5929 875-1010
Web: www.hoke-raeford.com/chamber.htm
Greater Raleigh Chamber of Commerce PO Box 2978 ... Raleigh NC 27602 919-664-7000 664-7099
Web: www.raleighchamber.org
Roanoke Valley Chamber of Commerce
1640 Julian Allsbrook Hwy ... Roanoke Rapids NC 27870 252-537-3513 535-5767
Web: www.rvchamber.com
Richmond County Chamber of Commerce
505 Rockingham Rd ... Rockingham NC 28380 910-895-9058 895-9056
TF: 800-858-1688 ■ *Web:* www.richmondcountychamber.com
Rocky Mount Area Chamber of Commerce PO Box 392 ... Rocky Mount NC 27802 252-446-0323 446-5103
Web: www.rockymountchamber.org
Roxboro Area Chamber of Commerce 211 N Main St ... Roxboro NC 27573 336-599-8333 599-8335
Web: www.roxboronc.com
Rutherford County Chamber of Commerce 162 N Main St ... Rutherfordton NC 28139 828-287-3090 287-0799
Web: www.rutherfordcoc.org
Rowan County Chamber of Commerce
204 E Innes St Suite 110 ... Salisbury NC 28144 704-633-4221 639-1200
Web: www.rowanchamber.com
Sanford Area Chamber of Commerce
143 Charlotte Ave Suite 101 ... Sanford NC 27330 919-775-7341 776-6244
Web: www.sanford-nc.com
Brunswick County Chamber of Commerce PO Box 1185 ... Shallotte NC 28459 910-754-6644 754-6539
TF: 800-426-6644 ■ *Web:* www.brunswickcountychamber.org
Cleveland County Chamber of Commerce 200 S Layfayette St ... Shelby NC 28150 704-487-8521 487-7458
Web: www.clevelandchamber.org
Chatham County United Chamber of Commerce
1609 E 11th St ... Siler City NC 27344 919-742-3333 742-1333
Web: www.ccucc.net
Greater Smithfield-Selma Area Chamber of Commerce
PO Box 467 ... Smithfield NC 27577 919-934-9166 934-1337
Web: www.smithfieldselma.com
Moore County Chamber of Commerce
10677 Hwy 15-501 ... Southern Pines NC 28387 910-692-3926 692-0619
Web: www.moorecountychamber.com
Jackson County Chamber of Commerce 773 W Main St ... Sylva NC 28779 828-586-2155 586-4887
TF: 800-962-1911 ■ *Web:* www.mountainlovers.com
Tarboro Edgecombe Chamber of Commerce 325 N Main St ... Tarboro NC 27886 252-823-7241 823-1499
Web: www.tarborochamber.com
Alexander County Chamber of Commerce 16 W Main Ave ... Taylorsville NC 28681 828-632-8141 632-1096
Web: www.alexandercountychamber.com
Thomasville Area Chamber of Commerce 6 W Main St ... Thomasville NC 27360 336-475-6134 475-4802
Web: www.thomasvillechamber.net
Polk County Chamber of Commerce 2753 Lynn Rd Suite A ... Tryon NC 28782 828-859-6236 859-2301
Web: www.polkchamber.org
Washington-Beaufort County Chamber of Commerce
102 Stewart Pkwy ... Washington NC 27889 252-946-9168 946-9169
Web: www.wbcchamber.com
Haywood County Chamber of Commerce
591 N Main St PO Box 600 ... Waynesville NC 28786 828-456-3021 452-7265
TF: 877-456-3073 ■ *Web:* www.haywood-nc.com
Martin County Chamber of Commerce 419 East Blvd ... Williamston NC 27892 252-792-4131 792-1013
Web: www.martincountync.com
Greater Wilmington Chamber of Commerce 1 Estell Lee Pl ... Wilmington NC 28401 910-762-2611 762-9765
Web: www.wilmingtonchamber.org
Wilson Chamber of Commerce 200 W Nash St ... Wilson NC 27893 252-237-0165 243-7931
Web: www.wilsonncchamber.com
Windsor-Bertie Area Chamber of Commerce 102 N York St ... Windsor NC 27983 252-794-4277 794-5070
Web: www.albemarle-nc.com/windsor/chamber
Greater Winston-Salem Chamber of Commerce
PO Box 1408 ... Winston-Salem NC 27102 336-725-2361 721-2209
Web: www.winstonsalem.com
Yadkin County Chamber of Commerce 205 S Jackson St ... Yadkinville NC 27055 336-679-2200 679-3034
Web: www.yadkinchamber.org

North Dakota

Phone | Fax

Bismarck Mandan Chamber of Commerce 1640 Burnt Boat Dr ... Bismarck ND 58502 701-223-5660 255-6125
Web: www.bismarckmandan.com
Grand Forks Chamber of Commerce 202 N 3rd St ... Grand Forks ND 58203 701-772-7271 772-9238
Web: www.gfchamber.com
Jamestown Area Chamber of Commerce 120 2nd St SE ... Jamestown ND 58401 701-252-4830 952-4837
Web: www.jamestownchamber.com
Minot Area Chamber of Commerce 1020 20th Ave SW ... Minot ND 58701 701-852-6000 838-2488
Web: www.minotchamber.org

Ohio

Phone | Fax

Greater Akron Chamber 1 Cascade Plaza 17th Fl ... Akron OH 44308 330-376-5550 379-3164
TF: 800-621-8001 ■ *Web:* www.greaterakronchamber.org
Alliance Area Chamber of Commerce 210 E Main St ... Alliance OH 44601 330-823-6260 823-4434
Web: www.allianceohiochamber.org
Ashtabula Area Chamber of Commerce 4536 Main Ave ... Ashtabula OH 44004 440-998-6998 992-8216
Web: www.ashtabulachamber.net

				Phone	Fax
Athens Area Chamber of Commerce 449 E State St	Athens	OH	45701	740-594-2251	594-2252
Web: www.athenschamber.com					
Barberton South Summitt Chamber of Commerce 503 W Park Ave	Barberton	OH	44203	330-745-3141	745-4559
Web: www.southsummitchamber.org					
Beavercreek Chamber of Commerce 3299 Kemp Rd	Beavercreek	OH	45431	937-426-2202	426-2204
Web: www.beavercreekchamber.org					
Logan County Chamber of Commerce 100 S Main St	Bellefontaine	OH	43311	937-599-5121	599-2411
Web: www.logancountyohio.com					
Muskingum Valley Area Chamber of Commerce PO Box 837	Beverly	OH	45715	740-984-8259	
Web: www.mvacc.com					
Bowling Green Chamber of Commerce 163 N Main St	Bowling Green	OH	43402	419-353-7945	
Web: www.bowlinggreen-oh.com					
Brunswick Area Chamber of Commerce 3511 Center Rd Suite A-B	Brunswick	OH	44212	330-225-8411	273-8172
Web: www.brunswickareachamber.org					
Cambridge Area Chamber of Commerce 918 Wheeling Ave	Cambridge	OH	43725	740-439-6688	439-6689
Web: www.cambridgeohiochamber.com					
Canton Regional Chamber of Commerce 222 Market Ave N	Canton	OH	44702	330-456-7253	452-7786
TF: 800-533-4302 ■ *Web:* www.cantonchamber.org					
Carroll County Chamber of Commerce & Economic Development 61 N Lisbon St	Carrollton	OH	44615	330-627-4811	627-3647
TF: 800-956-4684 ■ *Web:* www.carrollohchamber.com					
Celina-Mercer County Chamber of Commerce 226 N Main St	Celina	OH	45822	419-586-2219	586-8645
Web: www.celinamercer.com					
Chagrin Valley Chamber of Commerce 16 S Main St	Chagrin Falls	OH	44022	440-247-6607	247-6503
Web: www.cvcc.org					
Chillicothe-Ross Chamber of Commerce 45 E Main St	Chillicothe	OH	45601	740-702-2722	702-2727
Web: www.chillicotheohio.com					
Anderson Area Chamber of Commerce 8072-B Beechmont Ave	Cincinnati	OH	45255	513-474-4802	474-4857
Web: www.andersonareachamber.com					
Cincinnati USA Regional Chamber 441 Vine St Suite 300	Cincinnati	OH	45202	513-579-3100	579-3102
Web: www.gccc.com					
Pickaway County Chamber of Commerce 325 W Main St	Circleville	OH	43113	740-474-4923	477-6800
Web: www.pickaway.com					
Greater Cleveland Partnership 50 Public Sq Suite 200	Cleveland	OH	44113	216-621-3300	621-6013
TF: 800-562-7121 ■ *Web:* www.gcpartnership.com					
Greater Columbus Chamber of Commerce 37 N High St	Columbus	OH	43215	614-221-1321	221-9360
TF: 800-950-1321 ■ *Web:* www.columbus.org					
Coshocton County Chamber of Commerce 101 N Whitewoman St	Coshocton	OH	43812	740-622-5411	622-9902
TF: 800-589-2430 ■ *Web:* www.coshoctonchamber.com					
Cuyahoga Falls Chamber of Commerce 2020 Front St Suite 103	Cuyahoga Falls	OH	44221	330-929-6756	
Web: www.cuyahogafallschamberofcommerce.com					
Dayton Area Chamber of Commerce 1 Chamber Plaza Suite 200	Dayton	OH	45402	937-226-1444	226-8254
Web: www.daytonchamber.org					
South Metro Regional Chamber of Commerce 7887 Washington Village Dr Suite 265	Dayton	OH	45459	937-433-2032	433-6881
Web: www.smrcoc.org					
Defiance Area Chamber of Commerce 615 W 3rd St	Defiance	OH	43512	419-782-7946	782-0111
Web: www.defiancechamber.com					
East Liverpool Area Chamber of Commerce 529 Market St PO Box 94	East Liverpool	OH	43920	330-385-0845	385-0581
Web: www.elchamber.com					
Eaton-Preble County Chamber of Commerce 110 W Main St PO Box 303	Eaton	OH	45320	937-456-4949	456-4949
Web: www.preblecountyohio.com					
Lorain County Chamber of Commerce 226 Middle Ave	Elyria	OH	44035	440-328-2550	328-2557
Web: www.loraincountychamber.com					
Englewood-Northmont Chamber of Commerce PO Box 62	Englewood	OH	45322	937-836-2550	836-2485
Web: www.englewood-northmontcoc.com					
Euclid Chamber of Commerce 21935 Lake Shore Blvd	Euclid	OH	44123	216-731-9322	731-8354
Web: www.euclidchamberofcommerce.com					
Fairborn Area Chamber of Commerce 12 N Central Ave	Fairborn	OH	45324	937-878-3191	878-3197
Web: www.fairborn.com					
Fairfield Chamber of Commerce 670 Wessel Dr	Fairfield	OH	45014	513-881-5500	881-5503
Web: www.fairfieldchamber.com					
Findlay-Hancock County Chamber of Commerce 123 E Main Cross St	Findlay	OH	45840	419-422-3313	422-9508
TF: 800-424-3326 ■ *Web:* www.findlayhancockchamber.com					
Fostoria Area Chamber of Commerce 121 N Main St	Fostoria	OH	44830	419-435-0486	435-0936
Web: www.fostoriaoh.org					
Chamber of Commerce of Sandusky County 101 S Front St	Fremont	OH	43420	419-332-1591	332-8666
Web: www.scchamber.org					
Gahanna Area Chamber of Commerce 94 N High St	Gahanna	OH	43230	614-471-0451	471-5122
Web: www.gahannaareachamber.com					
Gallia County Chamber of Commerce 16 State St PO Box 465	Gallipolis	OH	45631	740-446-0596	446-7031
Web: www.galliacounty.org					
Garfield Heights Chamber of Commerce 5284 Transportation Blvd	Garfield Heights	OH	44125	216-475-7775	475-2237
Web: www.garfieldchamber.com					
Geneva Area Chamber of Commerce 866 E Main St	Geneva	OH	44041	440-466-8694	466-0823
Web: www.genevachamber.org					
Brown County Chamber of Commerce 110 E State St	Georgetown	OH	45121	937-378-4784	378-1634
TF: 888-276-9664 ■ *Web:* www.browncountyohio.org					
Darke County Chamber of Commerce 622 S Broadway	Greenville	OH	45331	937-548-2102	548-5608
Web: www.darkecountyohio.com					
Greater Hamilton Chamber of Commerce 201 Dayton St	Hamilton	OH	45011	513-844-1500	844-1999
Web: www.hamilton-ohio.com					
Highland County Chamber of Commerce 1575 N High St Suite 400	Hillsboro	OH	45133	937-393-1111	393-9604
Web: www.highlandcountychamber.com					
Huber Heights Chamber of Commerce 4756 Fishburg Rd	Huber Heights	OH	45424	937-233-5700	233-5769
Web: www.huberheightschamber.com					
Jackson Area Chamber of Commerce 234 Broadway St	Jackson	OH	45640	740-286-2722	286-8443
Web: www.jacksonohio.org					
Jackson-Beldon Chamber of Commerce 5735 Wales Ave NW	Jackson Township	OH	44646	330-833-4400	833-4456
Web: www.jbcc.org					
Kent Area Chamber of Commerce 138 E Main St	Kent	OH	44240	330-673-9855	673-9860
Web: www.kentbiz.com					
Hardin County Chamber of Commerce 225 S Detroit St	Kenton	OH	43326	419-673-4131	674-4876
Web: www.hardinohio.org					
Kettering-Moraine-Oakwood Area Chamber of Commerce 2977 Far Hills Ave	Kettering	OH	45419	937-299-3852	299-3851
Web: www.kmo-coc.org					
Lakewood Chamber of Commerce 14701 Detroit Ave Suite 130	Lakewood	OH	44107	216-226-2900	226-1340
Web: www.lakewoodchamber.org					
Lancaster-Fairfield County Chamber of Commerce PO Box 2450	Lancaster	OH	43130	740-653-8251	653-7074
Web: www.lancoc.org					
Lima/Allen County Chamber of Commerce 147 N Main St	Lima	OH	45801	419-222-6045	229-0266
Web: www.limachamber.com					
Logan-Hocking Chamber of Commerce PO Box 838	Logan	OH	43138	740-385-6836	385-7259
TF: 800-414-6731 ■ *Web:* www.logan-hockingchamber.com					
Madison-Perry Area Chamber of Commerce 5965 N Ridge Rd	Madison	OH	44057	440-428-3760	428-6668
Web: www.mpacc.org					
Mansfield-Richland Area Chamber of Commerce 55 N Mulberry St	Mansfield	OH	44902	419-522-3211	526-6853
Web: www.mrachamber.com					
Marietta Area Chamber of Commerce 100 Front St Suite 200	Marietta	OH	45750	740-373-5176	373-7808
Web: www.mariettachamber.com					
Marion Area Chamber of Commerce 205 W Center St Suite 100	Marion	OH	43302	740-382-2181	387-7722
Web: www.marionareachamber.org					
Union County Chamber of Commerce 227 E 5th St	Marysville	OH	43040	937-642-6279	644-0422
TF: 800-642-0087 ■ *Web:* www.unioncounty.org					
Massillon Area Chamber of Commerce 137 Lincoln Way E	Massillon	OH	44646	330-833-3146	833-8944
Web: www.massillonohchamber.com					
Mentor Chamber of Commerce 6972 Spinach Dr	Mentor	OH	44060	440-255-1616	255-1717
Web: www.mentorchamber.org					
Chamber of Commerce serving Middletown Monroe & Trenton 1500 Central Ave	Middletown	OH	45044	513-422-4551	422-6831
Web: www.mmvchamber.org					
Clermont Chamber of Commerce 553 Chamber Dr	Milford	OH	45150	513-576-5000	576-5001
Web: www.clermontchamber.com					
Milford-Miami Township Chamber of Commerce 983 Liala Ave	Milford	OH	45150	513-831-2411	831-3547
Web: www.milfordmiamitownship.com					
Holmes County Chamber of Commerce 35 N Monroe St	Millersburg	OH	44654	330-674-3975	674-3976
Web: www.holmescountychamber.com					
Morrow County Chamber of Commerce 17 1/2 W High St PO Box 174	Mount Gilead	OH	43338	419-946-2821	946-3861
Web: www.morrowcochamber.com					
Mount Vernon-Knox County Chamber of Commerce 7 E Ohio Ave	Mount Vernon	OH	43050	740-393-1111	393-1590
Web: www.knoxchamber.com					
Napoleon/Henry County Chamber of Commerce 611 N Perry St	Napoleon	OH	43545	419-592-1786	592-4945
Web: www.ohiohenrycounty.com					
Perry County Chamber of Commerce 103 W Brown St	New Lexington	OH	43764	740-342-3547	342-3704
Web: www.perrycountyohiocofc.com					
Tuscarawas County Chamber of Commerce 1323 4th St NW	New Philadelphia	OH	44663	330-343-4474	343-6526
Web: www.tuschamber.com					
Licking County Chamber of Commerce 50 W Locust St	Newark	OH	43055	740-345-9757	345-5141
Web: www.lickingcountychamber.com					
North Canton Area Chamber of Commerce 121 S Main St	North Canton	OH	44720	330-499-5100	499-7181
Web: www.northcantonchamber.org					
North Olmsted Chamber of Commerce 25045 Lorain Rd	North Olmsted	OH	44070	440-777-3368	777-9361
Web: www.nolmstedchamber.org					
North Royalton Chamber of Commerce 13737 State Rd	North Royalton	OH	44133	440-237-6180	237-6181
Web: www.nroyaltonchamber.com					
Eastern Maumee Bay Chamber of Commerce 2448 Navaree Ave	Oregon	OH	43616	419-693-5580	693-9990
Web: www.embchamber.org					
Painesville Area Chamber of Commerce 391 W Washington St	Painesville	OH	44077	440-357-7572	357-8752
Web: www.painesvilleohchamber.org					
Parma Area Chamber of Commerce 7908 Day Dr	Parma	OH	44129	440-886-1700	886-1770
Web: www.parmaareachamber.org					
Perrysburg Area Chamber of Commerce 105 W Indiana Ave	Perrysburg	OH	43551	419-874-9147	872-9347
Web: www.perrysburgchamber.com					
Portsmouth Area Chamber of Commerce 342 2nd St PO Box 509	Portsmouth	OH	45662	740-353-7647	353-5824
TF: 800-648-2574 ■ *Web:* www.portsmouth.org					
Reynoldsburg Area Chamber of Commerce 1580 Brice Rd	Reynoldsburg	OH	43068	614-866-4753	866-7313
Web: www.reynoldsburgchamber.com					
Salem Area Chamber of Commerce 713 E State St	Salem	OH	44460	330-337-3473	337-3474
Web: www.salemohio.com/chamber					
Erie County Chamber of Commerce 225 W Washington Row	Sandusky	OH	44870	419-625-6421	625-7914
Web: www.eriecountyohiocofc.com					
Shelby Chamber of Commerce 142 N Gamble St Suite A	Shelby	OH	44875	419-342-2426	342-2189
TF: 888-245-2426 ■ *Web:* www.shelbyoh.com					
Sidney-Shelby County Chamber of Commerce 101 S Ohio Ave 2nd Fl	Sidney	OH	45365	937-492-9122	498-2472
Web: www.sidneyshelbychamber.com					
Greater Lawrence County Area Chamber of Commerce PO Box 488	South Point	OH	45680	740-377-4550	377-2091
TF: 800-408-1334 ■ *Web:* www.lawrencecountyohio.org					
Springfield-Clark County Chamber of Commerce 333 N Limestone St Suite 201	Springfield	OH	45503	937-325-7621	325-8765
TF: 800-803-1553 ■ *Web:* www.springfieldnet.com					
Jefferson County Chamber of Commerce 630 Market St PO Box 278	Steubenville	OH	43952	740-282-6226	282-6285
Web: www.jeffersoncountychamber.com					
Stow-Munroe Falls Chamber of Commerce 4381 Hudson Dr Suite K2	Stow	OH	44224	330-688-1579	688-6234
Web: www.smfcc.com					
Strongsville Chamber of Commerce 18829 Royalton Rd	Strongsville	OH	44136	440-238-3366	238-7010
Web: www.strongsvillecofc.com					
Sylvania Area Chamber of Commerce 6616 Monroe St Suite 8	Sylvania	OH	43560	419-882-2135	885-7740
Web: www.sylvaniachamber.org					
Tiffin Area Chamber of Commerce 62 S Washington St	Tiffin	OH	44883	419-447-4141	447-5141
TF: 800-253-3314 ■ *Web:* www.tiffinchamber.com					
Toledo Regional Chamber of Commerce 300 Madison Ave Suite 200	Toledo	OH	43604	419-243-8191	241-8302
Web: www.toledochamber.com					
Trotwood Chamber of Commerce 4000 Lake Center Dr	Trotwood	OH	45426	937-837-1484	837-1508
Web: www.trotwoodchamber.org					
Upper Arlington Area Chamber of Commerce 2120 Tremont Ctr	Upper Arlington	OH	43221	614-481-5710	481-5711
Web: www.uachamber.org					
Champaign County Chamber of Commerce 113 Miami St	Urbana	OH	43078	937-653-5764	652-1599
TF: 877-873-5764 ■ *Web:* www.ccchamber.org					
Van Wert Area Chamber of Commerce 118 W Main St	Van Wert	OH	45891	419-238-4390	238-4589
Web: www.vanwertchamber.com					
Vandalia-Butler Chamber of Commerce 76 Ford Way Dr	Vandalia	OH	45377	937-898-5351	898-5491
Web: www.vandaliabutlerchamber.com					
Fayette County Chamber of Commerce 101 E East St	Washington Court House	OH	43160	740-335-0761	335-0762
Web: www.fayettecountychamberoh.com					
West Chester Chamber Alliance 7617 Voice of America Centre Dr	West Chester	OH	45069	513-777-3600	777-0188
TF: 877-924-3783 ■ *Web:* www.westchesterchamberalliance.com					
Adams County Chamber of Commerce PO Box 398	West Union	OH	45693	937-544-5454	544-6957
TF: 877-232-6764 ■ *Web:* www.adamscountyohchamber.org					
Westerville Area Chamber of Commerce 99-B Commerce Pk Dr	Westerville	OH	43082	614-882-8917	882-2085
Web: www.westervillechamber.com					

Ohio (Cont'd)

Phone Fax

West Shore Chamber of Commerce
24600 Center Ridge Rd Suite 480 .... Westlake OH 44145 440-835-8787 835-8798
Web: www.westshorechamber.org
Willougby Area Chamber of Commerce 28 Public Sq .... Willoughby OH 44094 440-942-1632 942-0586
Web: www.wacoc.com
Wilmington Clinton County Chamber of Commerce
40 N South St .... Wilmington OH 45177 937-382-2737 383-2316
Web: www.wcchamber.com
Wooster Area Chamber of Commerce 377 W Liberty St .... Wooster OH 44691 330-262-5735 262-5745
Web: www.wooster-wayne.com
Worthington Area Chamber of Commerce
25 W New England Ave .... Worthington OH 43085 614-888-3040 841-4842
Web: www.worthington.org/business/chamber.htm
Xenia Area Chamber of Commerce 334 W Market St .... Xenia OH 45385 937-372-3591 372-2192
Web: www.xacc.com
Youngstown Warren Regional Chamber
11 Federal Plaza Center Suite 1600 .... Youngstown OH 44503 330-744-2131 746-0330
Web: www.regionalchamber.com
Zanesville-Muskingum County Chamber of Commerce
205 N 5th St .... Zanesville OH 43701 740-455-8282 454-2963
TF: 800-743-2303 ■ *Web:* www.zmchamber.com

Oklahoma

Phone Fax

Ada Area Chamber of Commerce PO Box 248 .... Ada OK 74820 580-332-2506 332-3265
Web: www.adachamber.com
Ardmore Chamber of Commerce 410 W Main St .... Ardmore OK 73401 580-223-7765 223-7825
Web: www.ardmore.org
Bartlesville Area Chamber of Commerce PO Box 2366 .... Bartlesville OK 74005 918-336-8708 337-0216
TF: 800-364-8708 ■ *Web:* www.bartlesville.com
Broken Arrow Chamber of Commerce 123 N Main St .... Broken Arrow OK 74012 918-251-1518 251-1777
Web: www.brokenarrow.org
Del City Chamber of Commerce PO Box 15642 .... Del City OK 73115 405-677-1910 677-2275
Durant Area Chamber of Commerce 215 N 4th St .... Durant OK 74701 580-924-0848 924-0348
Web: www.durantchamber.org
Edmond Area Chamber of Commerce 825 E 2nd St .... Edmond OK 73034 405-341-2808 340-5512
Web: www.edmondchamber.com
Greater Enid Chamber of Commerce PO Box 907 .... Enid OK 73702 580-237-2494 237-2497
TF: 888-229-2443 ■ *Web:* www.enidchamber.com
Lawton Chamber of Commerce & Industry
629 SW 'C' Ave Suite A .... Lawton OK 73501 580-355-3541 357-3642
TF: 800-872-4540 ■ *Web:* lawtonfortsillchamber.com
Midwest City Chamber of Commerce PO Box 10980 .... Midwest City OK 73140 405-733-3801 733-5633
Web: www.midwestcityok.com/chamber.html
Moore Chamber of Commerce 305 W Main St PO Box 6305 .... Moore OK 73160 405-794-3400 794-8555
Web: www.moorechamber.com
Greater Muskogee Area Chamber of Commerce PO Box 797 .... Muskogee OK 74402 918-682-2401 682-2403
Web: www.muskogeechamber.org
Norman Chamber of Commerce 115 E Gray .... Norman OK 73069 405-321-7260 360-4679
Web: www.normanok.org
Greater Oklahoma City Chamber of Commerce
123 Park Ave .... Oklahoma City OK 73102 405-297-8900 297-8916
TF: 800-616-1114 ■ *Web:* www.okcchamber.com
South Oklahoma City Chamber of Commerce
701 SW 74th St .... Oklahoma City OK 73139 405-634-1436 634-1462
Web: www.southokc.com
Owasso Chamber of Commerce 315 S Cedar St .... Owasso OK 74055 918-272-2141 272-8564
Web: www.owassochamber.com
Ponca City Area Chamber of Commerce 420 E Grand Ave .... Ponca City OK 74601 580-765-4400 765-2798
Web: www.poncacitychamber.com
Poteau Chamber of Commerce 201 S Broadway .... Poteau OK 74953 918-647-9178 647-4099
Web: poteau.org
Sallisaw Chamber of Commerce 301 E Cherokee Ave .... Sallisaw OK 74955 918-775-2558 775-4021
Web: www.sallisawchamber.com
Greater Shawnee Area Chamber of Commerce PO Box 1613 .... Shawnee OK 74801 405-273-6092 275-9851
Web: www.shawneechamber.com
Stillwater Chamber of Commerce 409 S Main St .... Stillwater OK 74076 405-372-5573 372-4316
TF: 800-593-5573 ■ *Web:* www.stillwaterchamber.org
Tulsa Metro Chamber
2 W 2nd St Suite 150 Williams Center Tower II .... Tulsa OK 74103 918-585-1201 585-8016*
*Fax: Hum Res ■ *Web:* www.tulsachamber.com
Yukon Chamber of Commerce 510 Elm St .... Yukon OK 73099 405-354-3567 350-0724
Web: www.yukoncc.com

Oregon

Phone Fax

Albany Area Chamber of Commerce 435 W 1st Ave W .... Albany OR 97321 541-926-1517 926-7064
Web: www.albanychamber.com
Beaverton Area Chamber of Commerce
12655 SW Center St Suite 140 .... Beaverton OR 97005 503-644-0123 526-0349
Web: www.beaverton.org
Bend Chamber of Commerce 777 NW Wall St Suite 200 .... Bend OR 97701 541-382-3221 385-9929
TF: 800-905-2363 ■ *Web:* www.bendchamber.org
Bay Area Chamber of Commerce 50 Central Ave .... Coos Bay OR 97420 541-269-0215 269-2861
TF: 800-824-8486 ■ *Web:* www.oregonsbayareachamber.com
Corvallis Area Chamber of Commerce 420 NW 2nd St .... Corvallis OR 97330 541-757-1505 766-2996
Web: www.corvallischamber.com
Cottage Grove Area Chamber of Commerce
700 E Gibbs Ave Suite C .... Cottage Grove OR 97424 541-942-2411 767-0783
Web: www.cgchamber.com
Eugene Chamber of Commerce 1401 Willamette St .... Eugene OR 97401 541-484-1314 484-4942
Web: www.eugenechamber.com
Florence Area Chamber of Commerce 290 Hwy 101 .... Florence OR 97439 541-997-3128 997-4101
TF: 800-524-4864 ■ *Web:* www.florencechamber.com
Grants Pass Chamber of Commerce
1995 NW Vine St PO Box 970 .... Grants Pass OR 97528 541-476-7717 476-9574
TF: 800-547-5927 ■ *Web:* www.grantspasschamber.org
Gresham Area Chamber of Commerce PO Box 1768 .... Gresham OR 97030 503-665-1131 666-1041
Web: www.greshamchamber.org
Hermiston Chamber of Commerce
415 S Hwy 395 PO box 185 .... Hermiston OR 97838 541-567-6151 564-9109
Web: www.hermistonchamber.com
Hillsboro Chamber of Commerce 334 SE 5th Ave .... Hillsboro OR 97123 503-648-1102 681-0535
Web: www.hillchamber.org
Keizer Chamber of Commerce 980 Chemawa Rd NE .... Keizer OR 97303 503-393-9111 393-1003
Web: www.keizerchamber.com
Klamath County Chamber of Commerce 706 Main St .... Klamath Falls OR 97601 541-884-5193 884-5195
TF: 877-552-6284 ■ *Web:* www.klamath.org

Phone Fax

La Grande-Union County Chamber of Commerce 102 Elm St .... La Grande OR 97850 541-963-8588 963-3936
Web: www.unioncountychamber.org
Lake Oswego Chamber of Commerce 242 B Ave .... Lake Oswego OR 97034 503-636-3634 636-7427
Web: www.lake-oswego.com
Chamber of Medford/Jackson County 101 E 8th St .... Medford OR 97501 541-779-4847 776-4808
Web: www.medfordchamber.com
North Clackamas County Chamber of Commerce
7740 SE Harmony Rd .... Milwaukie OR 97222 503-654-7777 653-9515
Web: www.yourchamber.com
Greater Newport Chamber of Commerce 555 SW Coast Hwy .... Newport OR 97365 541-265-8801 265-5589
TF: 800-262-7844 ■ *Web:* www.newportchamber.org
Oregon City Chamber of Commerce 1201 Washington St .... Oregon City OR 97045 503-656-1619 656-2274
Web: www.oregoncity.org
Portland Business Alliance 200 SW Market St Suite 1717 .... Portland OR 97201 503-224-8684 323-9186
Web: www.portlandalliance.com
Salem Area Chamber of Commerce 1110 Commercial St NE .... Salem OR 97301 503-581-1466 581-0972
Web: www.salemchamber.org
Springfield Chamber of Commerce 101 S 'A' St PO Box 155 .... Springfield OR 97477 541-746-1651 726-4727
TF: 866-346-1651 ■ *Web:* www.springfield-chamber.org
Tigard Area Chamber of Commerce 12345 SW Main St .... Tigard OR 97223 503-639-1656 639-6302
Web: www.tigardchamber.com

Pennsylvania

Phone Fax

Greater Lehigh Valley Chamber of Commerce
840 W Hamilton St .... Allentown PA 18101 610-841-5800 437-4907
Web: www.lehighvalleychamber.org
Altoona-Blair County Chamber of Commerce
3900 Industrial Pk Dr Suite 12 .... Altoona PA 16602 814-943-8151 943-5239
Web: www.blairchamber.com
Beaver County Chamber of Commerce
300 S Walnut Ln Suite 202 .... Beaver PA 15009 724-775-3944 728-9737
TF: 888-832-7591 ■ *Web:* www.bcchamber.com
Bedford County Chamber of Commerce 137 E Pitt St .... Bedford PA 15522 814-623-2233 623-6089
Web: www.bedfordcountychamber.org
Bellefonte Intervalley Chamber of Commerce 320 W High St .... Bellefonte PA 16823 814-355-2917 355-2761
Web: www.bellefonte.com/bellefontechamber
Berwick Area Chamber of Commerce 206 Mulberry St .... Berwick PA 18603 570-752-3601 752-3602
Web: www.berwickpa.org
Lehigh Valley Chamber of Commerce 509 Main St .... Bethlehem PA 18018 610-867-3788 758-9533
Web: www.lehighvalleychamber.org/
Bloomsburg Area Chamber of Commerce 238 Market St .... Bloomsburg PA 17815 570-784-2522 784-2661
Web: www.bloomsburg.org
Allegheny Valley Chamber of Commerce
1030 Broadview Blvd .... Brackenridge PA 15014 724-224-3400 224-3442
Web: www.alleghenyvalleychamber.com
Butler County Chamber of Commerce PO Box 1082 .... Butler PA 16003 724-283-2222 283-0224
Web: www.butlercountychamber.com
West Shore Chamber of Commerce 4211 Trindle Rd .... Camp Hill PA 17011 717-761-0702 761-4315
Web: www.wschamber.org
Greater Chambersburg Chamber of Commerce
100 Lincoln Way E Suite A .... Chambersburg PA 17201 717-264-7101 267-0399
Web: www.chambersburg.org
Clarion Area Chamber of Business & Industry 21 N 6th Ave .... Clarion PA 16214 814-226-9161 226-4903
Web: www.clarionpa.com
Perkiomen Valley Chamber of Commerce 351 E Main St .... Collegeville PA 19426 610-489-6660 454-1270
Web: www.pvchamber.net
Greater Connellsville Chamber of Commerce
923 W Crawford Ave .... Connellsville PA 15425 724-628-5500 628-5676
Web: www.greaterconnellsville.org
Central Bucks Chamber of Commerce
252 W Swamp Rd Suite 23 .... Doylestown PA 18901 215-348-3913 348-7154
Web: www.centralbuckschamber.com
Two Rivers Area Chamber of Commerce 158 A Northampton St .... Easton PA 18042 610-841-4582 330-9177
Web: www.eastonareachamber.org
Erie Regional Chamber & Growth Partnership 208 E Bayfront Pkwy .... Erie PA 16507 814-454-7191 459-0241
TF: 800-524-3743 ■ *Web:* www.eriechamber.com
Exton Region Chamber of Commerce 233 W Lincoln Hwy .... Exton PA 19341 610-363-7746 363-2374
Web: www.ercc.net
Lower Bucks County Chamber of Commerce
409 Hood Blvd .... Fairless Hills PA 19030 215-943-7400 943-7404
Web: www.lbccc.org
Franklin Area Chamber of Commerce 1259 Liberty St .... Franklin PA 16323 814-432-5823 437-2453
TF: 888-547-2377 ■ *Web:* www.franklin-pa.org
Gettysburg-Adams County Area Chamber of Commerce
18 Carlisle St Suite 203 .... Gettysburg PA 17325 717-334-8151 334-3368
Web: www.gettysburg-chamber.org
Westmoreland Chamber of Commerce 241 Tollgate Hill Rd .... Greensburg PA 15601 724-834-2900 837-7635
Web: www.westmorelandchamber.com
Hanover Area Chamber of Commerce 146 Carlisle St .... Hanover PA 17331 717-637-6130 637-9127
Web: www.hanoverchamber.com
Harrisburg Regional Chamber 3211 N Front St Suite 201 .... Harrisburg PA 17110 717-232-4099 232-5184
Web: www.harrisburgregionalchamber.org
Wayne County Chamber of Commerce 32 Commercial St .... Honesdale PA 18431 570-253-1960 253-1517
TF: 800-433-9008 ■ *Web:* www.waynecountycc.com
Suburban Horsham Willow Grove Chamber of Commerce
PO Box 100 .... Horsham PA 19090 215-657-2227 657-8564
Web: www.suburbanchamber.org
Huntingdon County Business & Industry 419 14th St .... Huntingdon PA 16652 814-643-4322 506-1283
Web: www.hcbi.com
Indiana County Chamber of Commerce 1019 Philadelphia St .... Indiana PA 15701 724-465-2511 465-3706
Web: www.indianapa.com/chamber
Norwin Chamber of Commerce 321 Main St .... Irwin PA 15642 724-863-0888 863-5133
Web: www.norwinchamber.com
Greater Johnstown/Cambria County Chamber of Commerce
245 Market St Suite 100 .... Johnstown PA 15901 814-536-5107 539-5800
TF: 800-790-4522 ■ *Web:* www.johnstownchamber.com
Southern Chester County Chamber of Commerce
206 E State St .... Kennett Square PA 19348 610-444-0774 444-5105
Web: www.scccc.com
King of Prussia Chamber of Commerce
101 Bill Smith Blvd .... King of Prussia PA 19406 610-265-1776 265-0473
Web: www.gvfcc.com
Armstrong County Chamber of Commerce 124 Market St .... Kittanning PA 16201 724-543-1305 548-2951
Web: www.armstrongchamber.org
Lancaster Chamber of Commerce & Industry
100 S Queen St PO Box 1558 .... Lancaster PA 17608 717-397-3531 293-3159
Web: www.lcci.com
North Penn Chamber of Commerce 229 S Broad St .... Lansdale PA 19446 215-362-9200 362-0393
Web: www.northpenn.org
Latrobe Area Chamber of Commerce
326 McKinley Ave Suite 102 .... Latrobe PA 15650 724-537-2671 537-2690
Web: www.latrobearea.com
Lebanon Valley Chamber of Commerce
728 Walnut St PO Box 899 .... Lebanon PA 17042 717-273-3727 273-7940
Web: www.lvchamber.org

Organization	City	State	ZIP	Phone	Fax
Juniata Valley Area Chamber of Commerce 1 W Market St Suite 119 *TF:* 877-568-9739 ■ *Web:* www.juniatavalleychamber.org	Lewistown	PA	17044	717-248-6713	248-6714
Clinton County Economic Partnership 212 N Jay St *TF:* 888-388-6991 ■ *Web:* www.clintoncountyinfo.com	Lock Haven	PA	17745	570-748-5782	893-0433
Meadville-Western Crawford County Chamber of Commerce 211 Chestnut St *Web:* www.meadvillechamber.com	Meadville	PA	16335	814-337-8030	337-8022
Delaware County Chamber of Commerce 602 E Baltimore Pike *Web:* www.delcochamber.org	Media	PA	19063	610-565-3677	565-1606
Pike County Chamber of Commerce 209 E Hartford St PO Box 883 *Web:* www.pikechamber.com	Milford	PA	18337	570-296-8700	296-3921
Monroeville Area Chamber of Commerce 4268 Northern Pike *TF:* 888-753-5522 ■ *Web:* www.monroevillechamber.com	Monroeville	PA	15146	412-856-0622	856-1030
Pittsburgh Airport Area Chamber of Commerce 850 Beaver Grade Rd *Web:* www.paacc.com	Moon Township	PA	15108	412-264-6270	264-1575
Laurel Highlands Chamber of Commerce 537 W Main St *Web:* www.laurelhighlandschamber.com	Mount Pleasant	PA	15666	724-547-7521	547-5530
Nazareth Area Chamber of Commerce 201 N Main St PO Box 173 *Web:* www.nazarethchamber.com	Nazareth	PA	18064	610-759-9188	759-5262
Lawrence County Chamber of Commerce 138 W Washington St *Web:* www.lawrencecountychamber.com	New Castle	PA	16101	724-654-5593	654-3330
MONTCO Chamber of Commerce 1341 Sandy Hill Rd *Web:* www.montcocc.org	Norristown	PA	19401	610-277-9500	277-2659
Pennridge Chamber of Commerce 538 W Market St *Web:* www.pennridge.com	Perkasie	PA	18944	215-257-5390	257-6840
Greater Northeast Philadelphia Chamber of Commerce 8601 E Roosevelt Blvd *Web:* www.gnpcc.org	Philadelphia	PA	19152	215-332-3400	332-6050
Greater Philadelphia Chamber of Commerce 200 S Broad St Suite 700 *Web:* www.greaterphilachamber.com	Philadelphia	PA	19102	215-545-1234	790-3600
Moshannon Valley Economic Development Partnership 200 Shady Ln *Web:* www.mvedp.org	Philipsburg	PA	16866	814-342-2260	342-2878
Phoenixville Regional Chamber of Commerce 171 E Bridge St *Web:* www.phoenixvillechamber.org	Phoenixville	PA	19460	610-933-3070	917-0503
East Liberty Quarter Chamber of Commerce 5907 Penn Ave Suite 305 *Web:* www.eastlibertychamber.org	Pittsburgh	PA	15206	412-661-9660	661-9661
Greater Pittsburgh Chamber of Commerce 425 6th Ave Suite 1100 *TF:* 800-843-8772 ■ *Web:* www.alleghenyconference.org/Chamber/	Pittsburgh	PA	15219	412-392-4500	392-1040
North Side Chamber of Commerce 809 Middle St *Web:* www.northsidechamberofcommerce.com	Pittsburgh	PA	15212	412-231-6500	321-6760
Penn Hills Chamber of Commerce 13049 Frankstown Rd *Web:* www.pennhillschamber.org	Pittsburgh	PA	15235	412-795-8741	795-7993
South Hills Chamber of Commerce 1910 Cochran Rd Suite 140 *Web:* www.shchamber.org	Pittsburgh	PA	15220	412-833-1177	833-1354
South Side Chamber of Commerce PO Box 42380	Pittsburgh	PA	15203	412-431-3360	
Greater Pittston Chamber of Commerce PO Box 704 *Web:* www.pittstonchamber.org	Pittston	PA	18640	570-655-1424	655-0336
Tri County Area Chamber of Commerce 152 High St Suite 360 *Web:* www.tricountyareachamber.com	Pottstown	PA	19464	610-326-2900	970-9705
Schuylkill Chamber of Commerce 91 S Progress Ave *TF:* 800-755-1942 ■ *Web:* www.schuylkillchamber.com	Pottsville	PA	17901	570-622-1942	622-1638
Upper Bucks Chamber of Commerce 2170 Portzer Rd *Web:* www.ubcc.org	Quakertown	PA	18951	215-536-3211	536-7767
Greater Reading Chamber of Commerce & Industry 601 Penn St Suite 101 *Web:* www.greaterreadingchamber.org/	Reading	PA	19601	610-376-6766	376-4135
Greater Scranton Chamber of Commerce 222 Mulberry St *Web:* www.scrantonchamber.com	Scranton	PA	18503	570-342-7711	347-6262
Greater Susquehanna Valley Chamber of Commerce 2859 N Susquehanna Trail PO Box 10 *TF:* 800-410-2880 ■ *Web:* www.gsvcc.org	Shamokin Dam	PA	17876	570-743-4100	743-1221
Shenango Valley Chamber of Commerce 41 Chestnut St *Web:* www.svchamber.com	Sharon	PA	16146	724-981-5880	981-5480
Shippensburg Area Chamber of Commerce 22 E King St *Web:* www.shippensburg.org	Shippensburg	PA	17257	717-532-5509	532-7501
Somerset County Chamber of Commerce 601 N Center Ave *Web:* www.somersetcntypachamber.org	Somerset	PA	15501	814-445-6431	443-4313
Chamber of Business & Industry of Centre County 200 Innovation Blvd Suite 150 *Web:* www.cbicc.org	State College	PA	16803	814-234-1829	234-5869
Pocono Mountains Chamber of Commerce 556 Main St *Web:* www.poconochamber.net	Stroudsburg	PA	18360	570-421-4433	424-7281
Indian Valley Chamber of Commerce 100 Penn Ave *Web:* www.indianvalleychamber.com	Telford	PA	18969	215-723-9472	723-2490
Fayette Chamber of Commerce 65 W Main St *TF:* 800-916-9365 ■ *Web:* www.faycham.org	Uniontown	PA	15401	724-437-4571	438-3304
StrongLand Chamber of Commerce 1129 Industrial Pk Rd Box 10 Suite 108 *Web:* www.strongland.org	Vandergrift	PA	15690	724-845-5426	845-5428
Warren County Chamber of Commerce 308 Market St *Web:* www.warrenpachamber.com	Warren	PA	16365	814-723-3050	723-6024
Washington County Chamber of Commerce 20 E Beau St *Web:* www.washcochamber.com	Washington	PA	15301	724-225-3010	228-7337
Main Line Chamber of Commerce 175 Strafford Ave Suite 130 *Web:* www.mlcc.org	Wayne	PA	19087	610-687-6232	687-8085
Greater Waynesboro Chamber of Commerce 5 Roadside Ave *Web:* www.waynesboro.org	Waynesboro	PA	17268	717-762-7123	762-7124
Greater West Chester Chamber of Commerce 119 N High St *Web:* www.greaterwestchester.com	West Chester	PA	19380	610-696-4046	696-9110
Mon-Yough Chamber of Commerce 3001 Jacks Run Rd *Web:* www.rba-pa.com/monyough.htm	White Oak	PA	15131	412-678-2450	678-2451
Greater Wilkes-Barre Chamber of Business & Industry 2 Public Sq PO Box 5340 *TF:* 800-331-0912 ■ *Web:* www.wilkes-barre.org	Wilkes-Barre	PA	18710	570-823-2101	822-5951
Williamsport/Lycoming Chamber of Commerce 100 W 3rd St *Web:* www.williamsport.org	Williamsport	PA	17701	570-326-1971	321-1208
York County Chamber of Commerce 96 S George St Suite 300 *TF:* 888-878-9675 ■ *Web:* www.yorkchamber.com	York	PA	17401	717-848-4000	843-6737

Rhode Island

Organization	City	State	ZIP	Phone	Fax
Greater Cranston Chamber of Commerce 48A Rolfe Sq *Web:* www.cranstonchamber.com	Cranston	RI	02910	401-785-3780	785-3782
East Providence Chamber of Commerce 850 Waterman Ave *Web:* www.eastprovchamber.com	East Providence	RI	02914	401-438-1212	435-4581
North Central Chamber of Commerce 255 Greenville Ave *Web:* www.ncrichamber.com	Johnston	RI	02919	401-349-4674	349-4676
Northern Rhode Island Chamber of Commerce 6 Blackstone Valley Pl Suite 301 *Web:* www.nrichamber.com	Lincoln	RI	02865	401-334-1000	334-1009
Newport County Chamber of Commerce 45 Valley Rd *Web:* www.newportchamber.com	Middletown	RI	02842	401-847-1600	849-5848
North Kingstown Chamber of Commerce 8045 Post Rd *Web:* www.northkingstown.com	North Kingstown	RI	02852	401-295-5566	295-5582
Greater Providence Chamber of Commerce 30 Exchange Terr 4th Fl *Web:* www.provchamber.com	Providence	RI	02903	401-521-5000	751-2434
South Kingstown Chamber of Commerce 382 Main St PO Box 289 *Web:* www.skchamber.com	Wakefield	RI	02880	401-783-2801	789-3120
East Bay Chamber of Commerce 16 Cutler St Suite 102 *TF:* 888-278-9948 ■ *Web:* www.eastbaychamberri.org	Warren	RI	02885	401-245-0750	245-0110
Central Rhode Island Chamber of Commerce 3288 Post Rd *Web:* www.centralrichamber.com	Warwick	RI	02886	401-732-1100	732-1107
Pawtuxet Valley Chamber of Commerce 1192 Main St	West Warwick	RI	02893	401-823-3349	823-8162

South Carolina

Organization	City	State	ZIP	Phone	Fax
Greater Abbeville Chamber of Commerce 107 Court Sq *Web:* www.abbevillecitysc.com/chamberdev/	Abbeville	SC	29620	864-366-4600	366-4068
Greater Aiken Chamber of Commerce PO Box 892 *TF:* 800-542-4536 ■ *Web:* www.aikenchamber.net	Aiken	SC	29802	803-641-1111	641-4174
Anderson Area Chamber of Commerce 907 N Main St Suite 200 *Web:* www.andersonscchamber.com	Anderson	SC	29621	864-226-3454	226-3300
Bennettsville Chamber of Commerce 304 W Main St	Bennettsville	SC	29512	843-479-3941	479-4859
Kershaw County Chamber of Commerce 607 S Broad St *TF:* 800-968-4037 ■ *Web:* www.camden-sc.org	Camden	SC	29020	803-432-2525	432-4181
West Metro Chamber of Commerce 1006 12th St *Web:* www.westmetrochamber.com	Cayce	SC	29033	803-794-6504	794-6505
Chester County Chamber of Commerce 109 Gadsden St *Web:* www.chesterchamber.com	Chester	SC	29706	803-581-4142	581-2431
Laurens County Chamber of Commerce 291 Professional Park Rd *Web:* www.laurenscounty.org	Clinton	SC	29325	864-833-2716	833-6935
Greater Columbia Chamber of Commerce 930 Richland St *Web:* www.columbiachamber.com	Columbia	SC	29201	803-733-1110	733-1149
Conway Area Chamber of Commerce 203 Main St *Web:* www.conwayscchamber.com	Conway	SC	29526	843-248-2273	248-0003
Greater Darlington Chamber of Commerce 38 Public Sq *Web:* www.darlingtonchamber.com	Darlington	SC	29532	843-393-2641	393-8059
Dillon County Chamber of Commerce 100 N MacArthur Ave *TF:* 800-444-6838	Dillon	SC	29536	843-774-8551	774-0114
Greater Easley Chamber of Commerce PO Box 241 *Web:* www.easleychamber.org	Easley	SC	29641	864-859-2693	859-1941
Greater Florence Chamber of Commerce 610 W Palmetto St *Web:* www.florencescchamber.com	Florence	SC	29501	843-665-0515	662-2010
Cherokee County Chamber of Commerce 225 S Limestone St *Web:* www.cherokeechamber.org	Gaffney	SC	29340	864-489-5721	487-3399
Georgetown County Chamber of Commerce 1001 Front St *TF:* 800-777-7705 ■ *Web:* www.georgetownchamber.com	Georgetown	SC	29442	843-546-8436	520-4876
Greater Greenville Chamber of Commerce 24 Cleveland St *Fax: PR ■ *Web:* www.greenvillechamber.org	Greenville	SC	29601	864-242-1050	282-8509*
Greenwood Chamber of Commerce PO Box 980 *Web:* www.greenwoodscchamber.org	Greenwood	SC	29648	864-223-8431	229-9785
Greater Hartsville Chamber of Commerce 214 N 5th St *Web:* www.hartsvillechamber.org	Hartsville	SC	29550	843-332-6401	332-8017
Hilton Head Island-Bluffton Chamber of Commerce 1 Chamber Dr *TF:* 800-523-3373 ■ *Web:* www.hiltonheadisland.org	Hilton Head Island	SC	29928	843-785-3673	785-7110
Williamsburg Hometown Chamber of Commerce 130 E Main St *Web:* www.williamsburgsc.org	Kingstree	SC	29556	843-355-6431	354-3343
Lancaster County Chamber of Commerce PO Box 430 *Web:* www.lancasterchambersc.org	Lancaster	SC	29721	803-283-4105	286-4360
Lexington Chamber of Commerce PO Box 44 *Web:* www.lexingtonsc.org	Lexington	SC	29071	803-359-6113	359-0634
Clarendon County Chamber of Commerce 19 N Brooks St *TF:* 800-731-5253 ■ *Web:* www.clarendoncounty.com	Manning	SC	29102	803-435-4405	435-4406
Berkeley County Chamber of Commerce PO Box 968 *TF:* 800-882-0337 ■ *Web:* www.bcoc.com	Moncks Corner	SC	29461	843-761-8238	899-6491
Myrtle Beach Area Chamber of Commerce 1200 N Oak St *TF:* 800-356-3016 ■ *Web:* www.myrtlebeachinfo.com/chamber/	Myrtle Beach	SC	29577	843-626-7444	626-0009
Newberry County Chamber of Commerce 1109 Main St PO Box 396 *Web:* www.newberrycounty.org	Newberry	SC	29108	803-276-4274	276-4373
North Augusta Chamber of Commerce 302 Georgia Ave *Web:* www.northaugusta.net/chamber	North Augusta	SC	29841	803-279-2323	279-0003
Charleston Metro Chamber of Commerce 2750 Speissegger Dr Suite 100 *Web:* www.charlestonchamber.net	North Charleston	SC	29405	843-577-2510	723-4853
Orangeburg County Chamber of Commerce 155 Riverside Dr *TF:* 800-545-6153 ■ *Web:* www.orangeburgsc.net/chamber/chamber.html	Orangeburg	SC	29116	803-534-6821	531-9435
York County Regional Chamber of Commerce 116 E Main St *Web:* www.yorkcountychamber.com	Rock Hill	SC	29731	803-324-7500	324-1889
Spartanburg Area Chamber of Commerce 105 N Pine St *Web:* www.spartanburgchamber.com	Spartanburg	SC	29302	864-594-5000	594-5055
Greater Summerville-Dorchester County Chamber of Commerce 402 N Main St *Web:* www.gsdcchamber.org	Summerville	SC	29483	843-873-2931	875-4464
Greater Sumter Chamber of Commerce 32 E Calhoun St *Web:* www.sumterchamber.com	Sumter	SC	29150	803-775-1231	775-0915
Union County Chamber of Commerce 135 W Main St *TF:* 877-202-8755 ■ *Web:* www.unionsc.com	Union	SC	29379	864-427-9039	427-9030
Walterboro-Colleton Chamber of Commerce 109 Benson St *Web:* www.walterboro.org	Walterboro	SC	29488	843-549-9595	549-5775

South Dakota

Chamber	City	State	ZIP	Phone	Fax
Aberdeen Area Chamber of Commerce 516 S Main St *TF:* 800-874-9038 ■ *Web:* www.aberdeen-chamber.com	Aberdeen	SD	57401	605-225-2860	225-2437
Brookings Area Chamber of Commerce 2308 6th St E *TF:* 800-699-6125	Brookings	SD	57006	605-692-6125	697-8109
Pierre Area Chamber of Commerce 800 W Dakota Ave *TF:* 800-962-2034 ■ *Web:* pierre.org	Pierre	SD	57501	605-224-7361	224-6485
Rapid City Area Chamber of Commerce 444 Mt Rushmore Rd N *Web:* www.rapidcitychamber.com	Rapid City	SD	57701	605-343-1744	343-6550
Sioux Falls Area Chamber of Commerce 200 N Phillips Ave Suite 102 *Web:* www.siouxfalls.com	Sioux Falls	SD	57104	605-336-1620	336-6499

Tennessee

Chamber	City	State	ZIP	Phone	Fax
Cheatham County Chamber of Commerce 106 Duke St *Web:* www.cheathamchamber.org	Ashland City	TN	37015	615-792-6722	792-5001
Bartlett Area Chamber of Commerce 2969 Elmore Pk Rd *Web:* www.bartlettchamber.org	Bartlett	TN	38134	901-372-9457	372-9488
Bristol Chamber of Commerce 20 Volunteer Pkwy *Web:* www.bristolchamber.org	Bristol	TN	37620	423-989-4850	989-4867
Chattanooga Area Chamber of Commerce 811 Broad St *Web:* www.chattanoogachamber.com	Chattanooga	TN	37402	423-756-2121	267-7242
Clarksville Area Chamber of Commerce 25 Jefferson St Suite 300 *TF:* 800-530-2487 ■ *Web:* www.clarksvillechamber.com	Clarksville	TN	37040	931-647-2331	645-1574
Cleveland/Bradley Chamber of Commerce 225 Keith St *TF:* 800-472-6588 ■ *Web:* www.clevelandchamber.com	Cleveland	TN	37320	423-472-6587	472-2019
Anderson County Chamber of Commerce 245 N Main St Suite 200 *Web:* www.andersoncountychamber.org	Clinton	TN	37716	865-457-2559	463-7480
Collierville Chamber of Commerce 485 Halle Park Dr *TF:* 888-853-1949 ■ *Web:* www.colliervillechamber.com	Collierville	TN	38017	901-853-1949	853-2399
Maury Alliance 106 W 6th St *Web:* www.mauryalliance.com	Columbia	TN	38401	931-388-2155	380-0335
Cookeville Area-Putnam County Chamber of Commerce 1 W 1st St *TF:* 800-264-5541 ■ *Web:* www.cookevillechamber.com	Cookeville	TN	38501	931-526-2211	526-4023
Covington-Tipton County Chamber of Commerce 106 W Liberty St *Web:* www.covington-tiptoncochamber.com	Covington	TN	38019	901-476-9727	476-0056
Crossville Cumberland County Chamber of Commerce 34 S Main St *TF:* 877-465-3861 ■ *Web:* www.crossville-chamber.com	Crossville	TN	38555	931-484-8444	484-7511
Jefferson County Chamber of Commerce PO Box 890 *TF:* 877-237-3847 ■ *Web:* www.jefferson-tn-chamber.org	Dandridge	TN	37725	865-397-9642	397-0164
Dayton Chamber of Commerce 107 Main St	Dayton	TN	37321	423-775-0361	570-0105
Dickson County Chamber of Commerce 119 Hwy 70 E *TF:* 877-718-4967 ■ *Web:* www.dicksoncountychamber.com	Dickson	TN	37055	615-446-2349	441-3112
Weakley County Chamber of Commerce 114 W Maple St PO Box 67 *Web:* www.weakleycountychamber.com	Dresden	TN	38225	731-364-3787	364-2099
Dyersburg/Dyer County Chamber of Commerce 2000 Commerce Ave *Web:* ddcc.dyercountychamber.com	Dyersburg	TN	38024	731-285-3433	286-4926
Elizabethton/Carter County Chamber of Commerce 500 Veterans Memorial Pkwy	Elizabethton	TN	37644	423-547-3850	547-3854
Fayetteville-Lincoln County Chamber of Commerce 208 S Elk Ave *TF:* 888-433-1238 ■ *Web:* www.vallnet.com/chamberofcommerce	Fayetteville	TN	37334	931-433-1234	433-9087
Williamson County-Franklin Chamber of Commerce PO Box 156 *TF:* 800-356-3445 ■ *Web:* www.williamson-franklinchamber.com	Franklin	TN	37065	615-794-1225	790-5337
Germantown Area Chamber of Commerce 2195 S Germantown Rd *Web:* www.germantownchamber.com	Germantown	TN	38138	901-755-1200	755-9168
Greene County Partnership & Chamber of Commerce 115 Academy St *Web:* www.greenecountypartnership.com	Greeneville	TN	37743	423-638-4111	638-5345
Hendersonville Area Chamber of Commerce 101 Wessington Pl *Web:* www.hendersonvillechamber.com	Hendersonville	TN	37075	615-824-2818	822-7498
Carroll County Chamber of Commerce 20740 E Main St PO Box 726 *Web:* www.carrollcounty-tn-chamber.com	Huntingdon	TN	38344	731-986-4664	986-2029
Jackson Area Chamber of Commerce 197 Auditorium St *TF:* 800-858-5596 ■ *Web:* www.jacksontn.com	Jackson	TN	38302	731-423-2200	424-4860
Johnson City/Jonesborough/Washington County Chamber of Commerce 603 E Market St *TF:* 800-852-3392 ■ *Web:* www.johnsoncitytn.com	Johnson City	TN	37601	423-461-8000	461-8047
Kingsport Area Chamber of Commerce 151 E Main St *Web:* www.kingsportchamber.org	Kingsport	TN	37660	423-392-8800	246-7234
Roane County Chamber of Commerce 1209 N Kentucky St *Web:* www.roanealliance.org	Kingston	TN	37763	865-376-5572	376-4978
Knoxville Area Chamber Partnership 17 Market Sq Suite 201 *Web:* www.knoxvillechamber.com	Knoxville	TN	37902	865-637-4550	523-2071
Lawrence County Chamber of Commerce 1609 N Locust Ave PO Box 86 *TF:* 877-388-4911 ■ *Web:* www.chamberofcommerce.lawrence.tn.us	Lawrenceburg	TN	38464	931-762-4911	762-3153
Lebanon-Wilson County Chamber of Commerce 149 Public Sq *Web:* www.lebanonwilsontnchamber.org	Lebanon	TN	37087	615-444-5503	443-0596
Loudon County Chamber of Commerce 318 Angel Row *Web:* www.loudoncountychamber.com	Loudon	TN	37774	865-458-2067	458-1206
Madison Rivergate Area Chamber of Commerce 301 Madison St *Web:* www.madisonrivergatechamber.com	Madison	TN	37115	615-865-5400	865-0448
Monroe County Chamber of Commerce 520 Cook St Suite A *Web:* www.monroecountychamber.org	Madisonville	TN	37354	423-442-4588	442-9016
Blount County Chamber of Commerce 201 S Washington St *Web:* www.blountchamber.com	Maryville	TN	37804	865-983-2241	984-1386
McMinnville-Warren County Chamber of Commerce 110 S Court Sq *Web:* www.warrentn.com	McMinnville	TN	37111	931-473-6611	473-4741
Memphis Regional Chamber of Commerce 22 N Front St Suite 200 *Web:* www.memphischamber.com	Memphis	TN	38103	901-543-3500	543-3510
Morristown Area Chamber of Commerce 825 W 1st North St *Web:* www.morristownchamber.com	Morristown	TN	37814	423-586-6382	586-6576
Mount Juliet/West Wilson County Chamber of Commerce 46 W Caldwell St *Web:* www.mtjulietchamber.com	Mount Juliet	TN	37122	615-758-3478	754-8595
Rutherford County Chamber of Commerce 501 Memorial Blvd *TF:* 800-716-7560 ■ *Web:* www.rutherfordchamber.org	Murfreesboro	TN	37129	615-893-6565	890-7600
Donelson-Hermitage Chamber of Commerce PO Box 140200	Nashville	TN	37214	615-883-7896	391-4880
Nashville Chamber of Commerce 211 Commerce St Suite 100 *Web:* www.nashvillechamber.com	Nashville	TN	37201	615-743-3000	256-3074
Newport/Cocke County Chamber of Commerce 433-B Prospect Ave *Web:* cockecounty.org	Newport	TN	37821	423-623-7201	623-7216
Oak Ridge Chamber of Commerce 1400 Oak Ridge Tpke *Web:* www.orcc.org	Oak Ridge	TN	37830	865-483-1321	483-1678
Paris-Henry County Chamber of Commerce 2508 Eastwood St *TF:* 800-345-1103 ■ *Web:* www.paris.tn.org	Paris	TN	38242	731-642-3431	642-3454
Giles County Chamber of Commerce 110 N 2nd St *Web:* www.gilescountychamber.com	Pulaski	TN	38478	931-363-3789	363-7279
Rogersville/Hawkins County Chamber of Commerce 107 E Main St Suite 100 *Web:* www.welcome.to/hawkinscounty	Rogersville	TN	37857	423-272-2186	272-2186
Shelbyville-Bedford County Chamber of Commerce 100 N Cannon Blvd *TF:* 888-662-2525 ■ *Web:* www.shelbyvilletn.com	Shelbyville	TN	37160	931-684-3482	684-3483
Fayette County Chamber of Commerce 107 W Court Sq PO Box 411 *Web:* fayettecountychamber.com	Somerville	TN	38068	901-465-8690	465-6497
Springfield-Robertson County Chamber of Commerce 100 5th Ave W *Web:* www.sprobchamber.org	Springfield	TN	37172	615-384-3800	384-1260
Claiborne County Chamber of Commerce 3222 Hwy 25 E Suite 1 *TF:* 800-332-8164 ■ *Web:* www.claibornecounty.com	Tazewell	TN	37879	423-626-4149	626-1611
Greater Gibson County Area Chamber of Commerce PO Box 464 *Web:* www.gibsoncountytn.com	Trenton	TN	38382	731-855-0973	855-0979
Obion County Chamber of Commerce 214 E Church St *TF:* 877-885-0211 ■ *Web:* www.obioncounty.com	Union City	TN	38261	731-885-0211	885-7155
Franklin County Chamber of Commerce 44 Chamber Way PO Box 280 *Web:* www.franklincountychamber.com	Winchester	TN	37398	931-967-6788	967-9418

Texas

Chamber	City	State	ZIP	Phone	Fax
Abilene Chamber of Commerce 174 Cypress St Suite 200 *Web:* www.abilenechamber.com/	Abilene	TX	79601	325-677-7241	677-0622
Alice Chamber of Commerce 612 E Main St *TF:* 877-992-5423 ■ *Web:* www.alicetx.org	Alice	TX	78332	361-664-3454	664-2291
Allen Chamber of Commerce 210 W McDermott Dr *Web:* www.allenchamber.com	Allen	TX	75013	972-727-5585	727-9000
Alvin-Manvel Area Chamber of Commerce 105 W Willis St *TF:* 800-331-4063 ■ *Web:* www.alvinmanvelchamber.org	Alvin	TX	77511	281-331-3944	585-8662
Amarillo Chamber of Commerce 1000 S Polk St *Web:* www.amarillo-chamber.org	Amarillo	TX	79101	806-373-7800	373-3909
Arlington Chamber of Commerce 505 E Border St *TF:* 800-834-3928 ■ *Web:* www.arlingtontx.com	Arlington	TX	76010	817-275-2613	261-7535
Atlanta Area Chamber of Commerce PO Box 29 *Web:* www.atlantatexas.org/Chamber/index.htm	Atlanta	TX	75551	903-796-3296	796-5711
Greater Austin Chamber of Commerce 210 Barton Springs Rd Suite 400 *TF:* 800-856-5602 ■ *Web:* www.austinchamber.org	Austin	TX	78704	512-478-9383	478-6389
Bastrop Chamber of Commerce 927 Main St *Web:* www.bastropchamber.com	Bastrop	TX	78602	512-321-2419	303-0305
Baytown Chamber of Commerce 4721 Garth Rd Suite C *Web:* www.baytownchamber.com	Baytown	TX	77521	281-422-8359	428-1758
Beaumont Chamber of Commerce 1110 Park St *Web:* www.bmtcoc.org	Beaumont	TX	77701	409-838-6581	833-6718
Hurst-Euless-Bedford Chamber of Commerce PO Box 969 *Web:* www.heb.org	Bedford	TX	76095	817-283-1521	267-5111
Bee County Chamber of Commerce 1705 N Saint Mary's St *Web:* www.beecountychamber.org	Beeville	TX	78102	361-358-3267	358-3966
Greater Southwest Houston Chamber of Commerce PO Box 788 *Web:* www.gswhcc.org	Bellaire	TX	77402	713-666-1521	666-1523
Bonham Area Chamber of Commerce 327 N Main St *Web:* www.bonhamchamber.com	Bonham	TX	75418	903-583-4811	583-7972
Washington County Chamber of Commerce 314 S Austin St *TF:* 888-273-6426 ■ *Web:* www.brenhamtexas.com	Brenham	TX	77833	979-836-3695	836-2540
Brownsville Chamber of Commerce 1600 University Blvd *Web:* www.brownsvillechamber.com	Brownsville	TX	78520	956-542-4341	504-3348
Brownwood Area Chamber of Commerce 600 E Depot St *Web:* www.brownwoodchamber.org	Brownwood	TX	76801	325-646-9535	643-6686
Bryan-College Station Chamber of Commerce 4001 E 29th St Suite 175 *TF:* 800-777-8292 ■ *Web:* www.bcschamber.org	Bryan	TX	77802	979-260-5200	260-5208
Burleson Area Chamber of Commerce 1044 SW Wilshire Blvd *Web:* www.burleson.org	Burleson	TX	76028	817-295-6121	295-6192
Canyon Chamber of Commerce 1518 5th Ave *TF:* 800-999-9481 ■ *Web:* www.canyonchamber.org	Canyon	TX	79015	806-655-7815	655-4608
Metrocrest Chamber of Commerce 1204 Metrocrest Dr *Web:* www.metrocrestchamber.com	Carrollton	TX	75006	972-416-6600	416-7874
Panola County Chamber of Commerce 300 W Panola St *Web:* www.carthagetexas.com	Carthage	TX	75633	903-693-6634	693-8578
Cleburne Chamber of Commerce PO Box 701 *Web:* www.cleburnechamber.com	Cleburne	TX	76033	817-645-2455	641-3069
Greater Conroe-Lake Conroe Area Chamber of Commerce 505 W Davis St *TF:* 800-283-6645 ■ *Web:* www.conroe.org	Conroe	TX	77301	936-756-6644	756-6462
Greater Conroe/Lake Conroe Area Chamber of Commerce PO Box 2347 *TF:* 800-283-6645 ■ *Web:* www.conroe.org	Conroe	TX	77305	936-756-6644	756-6462
Coppell Chamber of Commerce 509 W Bethel Rd Suite 200 *Web:* www.coppellchamber.org	Coppell	TX	75019	972-393-2829	393-0659
Copperas Cove Chamber of Commerce 204 E Robertson Ave *Web:* www.copperascove.com	Copperas Cove	TX	76522	254-547-7571	547-5015
Corpus Christi Chamber of Commerce 1201 N Shoreline Blvd *Web:* www.corpuschristichamber.org	Corpus Christi	TX	78401	361-881-1800	882-4256
Corsicana Area Chamber of Commerce 120 N 12th St *TF:* 877-376-7477 ■ *Web:* www.corsicana.org	Corsicana	TX	75110	903-874-4731	874-4187
Dallas Northeast Chamber of Commerce 6260 E Mockingbird Ln Suite 250 *Web:* www.dallasnortheastchamber.net	Dallas	TX	75214	214-828-1400	828-9994
Greater Dallas Chamber of Commerce 700 N Pearl St Suite 1200 *Web:* www.dallaschamber.org	Dallas	TX	75201	214-746-6600	746-6799
North Dallas Chamber of Commerce 10707 Preston Rd *Web:* www.ndcc.org	Dallas	TX	75230	214-368-6485	691-5584

Organization	City	State	Zip	Phone	Fax
Oak Cliff Chamber of Commerce 400 S Zang Blvd Suite 110 *Web:* www.oakcliffchamber.org	Dallas	TX	75208	214-943-4567	943-4582
Southeast Dallas Chamber of Commerce 1515 S Buckner Blvd Suite 357 *Web:* www.sedcc.org	Dallas	TX	75217	214-398-9590	398-9591
Deer Park Chamber of Commerce 110 Center St. *Web:* www.deerpark.org	Deer Park	TX	77536	281-479-1559	476-4041
Del Rio Chamber of Commerce 1915 Veterans Blvd *TF:* 800-889-8149 ■ *Web:* www.drchamber.com	Del Rio	TX	78840	830-775-3551	774-1813
Denton Chamber of Commerce 414 Parkway St *TF:* 888-381-1818 ■ *Web:* www.denton-chamber.org	Denton	TX	76202	940-382-9693	382-0040
DeSoto Chamber of Commerce 205 E Pleasant Run Rd *Web:* www.desotochamber.org	DeSoto	TX	75115	972-224-3565	224-7228
North Galveston County Chamber of Commerce 2718 FM 517 E *Web:* www.northgalvestoncountychamber.com	Dickinson	TX	77539	281-337-3434	337-0641
Duncanville Chamber of Commerce 300 E Wheatland Rd *Web:* www.duncanvillechamber.org	Duncanville	TX	75116	972-780-4990	298-9370
Eagle Pass Chamber of Commerce 400 Garrison St *TF:* 888-355-3224 ■ *Web:* www.eaglepasstexas.com	Eagle Pass	TX	78852	830-773-3224	773-8844
Edinburg Chamber of Commerce 602 W University Dr *TF:* 800-800-7214 ■ *Web:* www.edinburg.com	Edinburg	TX	78540	956-383-4974	383-6942
Greater El Paso Chamber of Commerce 10 Civic Center Plaza *TF:* 800-651-8065 ■ *Web:* www.elpaso.org	El Paso	TX	79901	915-534-0500	534-0510
Farmers Branch Chamber of Commerce 12875 Josey Ln Suite 150 *Web:* www.fbchamber.com	Farmers Branch	TX	75234	972-243-8966	243-8968
Flower Mound Chamber of Commerce 700 Parker Sq Suite 100 *Web:* www.flowermoundchamber.com	Flower Mound	TX	75028	972-539-0500	539-4307
Fort Worth Chamber of Commerce 777 Taylor St Suite 900 *Web:* www.fortworthcoc.org	Fort Worth	TX	76102	817-336-2491	877-4034
Friendswood Chamber of Commerce 1100 S Friendswood Dr Suite A *Web:* www.friendswood-chamber.com	Friendswood	TX	77546	281-482-3329	482-3911
Gainesville Area Chamber of Commerce 101 S Culberson St. *TF:* 888-585-4468 ■ *Web:* www.gainesvilletexas.org	Gainesville	TX	76240	940-665-2831	665-2833
Galveston Chamber of Commerce 519 25th St *Web:* www.galvestonchamber.com	Galveston	TX	77550	409-763-5326	763-8271
Garland Chamber of Commerce 914 S Garland Ave *Web:* www.garlandchamber.com	Garland	TX	75040	972-272-7551	276-9261
Georgetown Chamber of Commerce 100 Stadium Dr PO Box 346 *Web:* www.georgetownchamber.org	Georgetown	TX	78626	512-930-3535	930-3587
Gilmer Area Chamber of Commerce 106 Buffalo St. *Web:* www.gilmerareachamber.com	Gilmer	TX	75644	903-843-2413	843-3759
Lake Granbury Area Chamber of Commerce 3408 E Hwy 377 *Web:* www.granburychamber.com	Granbury	TX	76049	817-573-1622	573-0805
Grapevine Chamber of Commerce PO Box 368 *Web:* www.grapevinechamber.org	Grapevine	TX	76099	817-481-1522	424-5208
Northeast Tarrant Chamber of Commerce 5001 Denton Hwy *Web:* www.netarrant.org	Haltom City	TX	76117	817-281-9376	281-9379
Harlingen Area Chamber of Commerce 311 E Tyler St *TF:* 800-531-7346 ■ *Web:* www.harlingen.com	Harlingen	TX	78550	956-423-5440	425-3870
Henderson Area Chamber of Commerce 201 N Main St *Web:* www.hendersontx.com	Henderson	TX	75652	903-657-5528	657-9454
Clear Lake Area Chamber of Commerce 1201 NASA Pkwy. *Web:* www.clearlakearea.com	Houston	TX	77058	281-488-7676	488-8981
Cy-Fair Houston Chamber of Commerce 11050 FM 1960 W Suite 100 *Web:* www.cyfairchamber.com	Houston	TX	77065	281-955-1100	955-0138
Galleria Area Chamber of Commerce 5075 Westheimer Rd Suite 660 *Web:* www.galleriachamber.com	Houston	TX	77056	713-629-5555	629-6403
Greater Heights Area Chamber of Commerce 545 W 19th St 2nd Fl *Web:* www.heightschamber.com	Houston	TX	77008	713-861-6735	861-9310
Greater Houston Partnership 1200 Smith St Suite 700 *Web:* www.houston.org	Houston	TX	77002	713-844-3600	844-0200
Houston Northwest Chamber of Commerce 14511 Falling Creek Suite 205 *Web:* www.hnwcc.com	Houston	TX	77014	281-440-4160	440-5302
Houston West Chamber of Commerce 10777 Westheimer St Suite 916 *Web:* www.hwcoc.org	Houston	TX	77042	713-785-4922	785-4944
North Channel Area Chamber of Commerce 13301 I-10 E Suite 100 *Web:* www.northchannelarea.com	Houston	TX	77015	713-450-3600	450-0700
North Houston-Greenspoint Chamber of Commerce 15600 John F Kennedy Blvd Suite 150 *Web:* www.nhgcc.org	Houston	TX	77032	281-442-8701	442-8713
South Belt-Ellington Chamber of Commerce 10500 Scarsdale Blvd. *Web:* www.southbeltchamber.com	Houston	TX	77089	281-481-5516	922-7045
Humble Area Chamber of Commerce 110 W Main St *Web:* www.humbleareachamber.org	Humble	TX	77338	281-446-2128	446-7483
Huntsville-Walker County Chamber of Commerce 1327 11th St *TF:* 800-289-0389 ■ *Web:* www.chamber.huntsville.tx.us	Huntsville	TX	77340	936-295-8113	295-0571
Greater Irving & Las Colinas Chamber of Commerce 5221 N O'Connor Blvd Suite 100 *Web:* www.irvingchamber.com	Irving	TX	75039	214-217-8484	389-2513
Kerrville Area Chamber of Commerce 1700 Sidney Baker St Suite 100 *Web:* www.kerrvilletx.com	Kerrville	TX	78028	830-896-1155	896-1175
Greater Killeen Chamber of Commerce 1 Santa Fe Plaza *TF:* 800-869-8265 ■ *Web:* www.gkcc.com	Killeen	TX	76540	254-526-9551	526-6090
Kingsville Chamber of Commerce PO Box 1030 *Web:* www.kingsville.org	Kingsville	TX	78364	361-592-6438	592-0866
La Porte-Bayshore Chamber of Commerce PO Box 996 *Web:* www.laportechamber.org	La Porte	TX	77572	281-471-1123	471-1710
Brazosport Area Chamber of Commerce 300 Abner Jackson Pkwy *TF:* 888-477-2505 ■ *Web:* www.brazosport.org	Lake Jackson	TX	77566	979-285-2501	285-2505
Laredo-Webb County Chamber of Commerce 2310 San Bernardo Ave *TF:* 800-292-2122 ■ *Web:* www.laredochamber.com	Laredo	TX	78042	956-722-9895	791-4503
Lewisville Chamber of Commerce 551 N Valley Pkwy. *Web:* www.lewisville-chamber.org	Lewisville	TX	75067	972-436-9571	436-5949
Liberty-Dayton Area Chamber of Commerce PO Box 1270 *Web:* www.libertydaytonchamber.com	Liberty	TX	77575	936-336-5736	336-1159
Polk County Chamber of Commerce PO Box 600 *TF:* 800-918-1305 ■ *Web:* www.lpcchamber.com	Livingston	TX	77351	936-327-4929	327-2660
Longview Partnership 410 N Center St. *Web:* www.longviewchamber.com	Longview	TX	75601	903-237-4000	237-4049
Lubbock Chamber of Commerce 1301 Broadway Suite 101 *TF:* 800-321-5822 ■ *Web:* www.lubbockchamber.com	Lubbock	TX	79403	806-761-7000	761-7010
Lufkin/Angelina County Chamber of Commerce 1615 S Chestnut St *TF:* 800-409-5659 ■ *Web:* www.lufkintexas.org	Lufkin	TX	75901	936-634-6644	634-8726
Greater Cedar Creek Lake Area Chamber of Commerce 604 S 3rd St Suite E *TF:* 877-222-5253 ■ *Web:* www.cclake.net	Mabank	TX	75147	903-887-3152	887-3695
Greater Marshall Chamber of Commerce 213 W Austin St. *TF:* 800-953-7868 ■ *Web:* www.marshall-chamber.com	Marshall	TX	75670	903-935-7868	935-9982
McAllen Chamber of Commerce 1200 Ash Ave *TF:* 877-622-5536 ■ *Web:* www.mcallenchamber.com	McAllen	TX	78505	956-682-2871	687-2917
McKinney Chamber of Commerce 1650 W Virginia St Suite 110 *Web:* www.mckinneytx.org	McKinney	TX	75069	972-542-0163	548-0876
Mesquite Chamber of Commerce 617 N Ebrite St. *TF:* 800-541-2355 ■ *Web:* www.mesquitechamber.com	Mesquite	TX	75149	972-285-0211	285-3535
Midland Chamber of Commerce 109 N Main St *TF:* 800-624-6435 ■ *Web:* www.midlandtxchamber.com	Midland	TX	79701	432-683-3381	682-9205
Mineral Wells Area Chamber of Commerce 511 E Hubbard St *TF:* 800-252-6989 ■ *Web:* www.mineralwellstx.com	Mineral Wells	TX	76067	940-325-2557	328-0850
Mission Chamber of Commerce 220 E 9th St *TF:* 800-580-2700 ■ *Web:* www.missionchamber.com	Mission	TX	78572	956-585-2727	585-3044
Mount Pleasant-Titus County Chamber of Commerce 1604 N Jefferson Ave *Web:* www.mtpleasanttx.com	Mount Pleasant	TX	75455	903-572-8567	572-0613
Nacogdoches County Chamber of Commerce 2516 North St *Web:* www.nacogdoches.org	Nacogdoches	TX	75965	936-560-5533	560-3920
New Braunfels Chamber of Commerce 390 S Seguin St. *TF:* 800-572-2626 ■ *Web:* www.nbcham.org	New Braunfels	TX	78130	830-625-2385	625-7918
Odessa Chamber of Commerce 700 N Grant Suite 200 *TF:* 800-780-4678 ■ *Web:* www.odessachamber.com	Odessa	TX	79761	432-332-9111	333-7858
Greater Orange Area Chamber of Commerce 1012 Green Ave *Web:* www.goacc.org	Orange	TX	77630	409-883-3536	886-3247
Lamar County Chamber of Commerce 1125 Bonham St *TF:* 800-727-4789 ■ *Web:* www.paristexas.com	Paris	TX	75460	903-784-2501	784-2503
Pasadena Chamber of Commerce 4334 Fairmont Pkwy *Web:* www.pasadenachamber.org	Pasadena	TX	77504	281-487-7871	487-5530
Pearland Area Chamber of Commerce 3501 Liberty Dr. *Web:* www.pearlandchamber.com	Pearland	TX	77581	281-485-3634	485-2420
Greater Pflugerville Chamber of Commerce 101 S 3rd St PO Box 483 *Web:* www.pfchamber.com	Pflugerville	TX	78691	512-251-7799	251-7802
Pharr Chamber of Commerce 308 W Park St. *Web:* www.visitpharr.com	Pharr	TX	78577	956-787-1481	787-7972
Plainview Chamber of Commerce 710 W 5th St *TF:* 800-658-2685 ■ *Web:* www.plainviewtex.com	Plainview	TX	79072	806-296-7431	296-0819
Plano Chamber of Commerce 1200 E 15th St *Web:* www.planocc.org	Plano	TX	75074	972-424-7547	422-5182
Greater Port Arthur Chamber of Commerce 4749 Twin City Hwy Suite 300 *Web:* www.portarthurtexas.com	Port Arthur	TX	77642	409-963-1107	963-3322
Quinlan Area Chamber of Commerce 711 E Quinlan Pkwy *Web:* www.quinlanchamber.com	Quinlan	TX	75474	903-356-4703	356-4208
Richardson Chamber of Commerce 411 Belle Grove Dr *Web:* www.telecomcorridor.com	Richardson	TX	75080	972-792-2800	792-2825
Rockwall County Chamber of Commerce 697 E I-30 PO Box 92 *Web:* www.rockwallchamber.org	Rockwall	TX	75087	972-771-5733	772-3642
Rosenberg-Richmond Area Chamber of Commerce 4120 Ave H *Web:* www.roserichchamber.org	Rosenberg	TX	77471	281-342-5464	342-2990
Round Rock Chamber of Commerce 212 E Main St *TF:* 800-747-3479 ■ *Web:* www.roundrockchamber.org	Round Rock	TX	78664	512-255-5805	255-3345
Rowlett Chamber of Commerce 3910 Main St. *TF:* 800-796-8644 ■ *Web:* www.rowlettchamber.com	Rowlett	TX	75088	972-475-3200	463-1699
San Angelo Chamber of Commerce 418 W Avenue B *TF:* 800-375-1206 ■ *Web:* www.sanangelo.org/chamber.php	San Angelo	TX	76903	325-655-4136	658-1110
Greater San Antonio Chamber of Commerce PO Box 1628 *Web:* www.sachamber.org	San Antonio	TX	78296	210-229-2100	229-1600
North San Antonio Chamber of Commerce 12930 Country Pkwy *Web:* www.northsachamber.com	San Antonio	TX	78216	210-344-4848	525-8207
South San Antonio Chamber of Commerce 3319 Sidney Brooks Bldg 510 Brooks City-Base *Web:* www.southsachamber.org	San Antonio	TX	78235	210-533-1600	533-1611
San Benito Chamber of Commerce 401 Sam Houston Blvd *Web:* www.sanbenitochamber.org	San Benito	TX	78586	956-399-5321	399-5421
San Marcos Area Chamber of Commerce 202 N CM Allen Pkwy *TF:* 888-200-5620 ■ *Web:* www.sanmarcostexas.com	San Marcos	TX	78667	512-393-5900	393-5912
Seguin Area Chamber of Commerce 427 N Austin St *TF:* 800-580-7322 ■ *Web:* www.seguinchamber.com	Seguin	TX	78155	830-379-6382	379-6971
Sherman Area Chamber of Commerce 121 N Rush St *TF:* 888-893-1188 ■ *Web:* www.shermantexas.com	Sherman	TX	75090	903-893-1184	893-4266
Springtown Chamber of Commerce PO Box 296 *Web:* www.springtowntexas.com	Springtown	TX	76046	817-220-7828	523-3268
Fort Bend Chamber of Commerce 445 Commerce Green Blvd *Web:* www.visitfortbend.com	Sugar Land	TX	77478	281-491-0800	491-0112
Hopkins County Chamber of Commerce 1200 Houston St *Web:* www.sulphursprings-tx.com	Sulphur Springs	TX	75482	903-885-6515	885-6516
Temple Chamber of Commerce 2 N 5th St *TF:* 800-374-9123 ■ *Web:* www.temple-tx.org	Temple	TX	76501	254-773-2105	773-0661
Texarkana Chamber of Commerce 819 State Line Ave *TF:* 877-275-5289 ■ *Web:* www.texarkanachamber.com	Texarkana	TX	75501	903-792-7191	793-4304
Texas City-La Marque Chamber of Commerce 8419 Emmett F Lowry *Web:* www.texascitychamber.com	Texas City	TX	77591	409-935-1408	935-5186
The Colony Chamber of Commerce 6900 Main St. *Web:* www.thecolonychamber.com	The Colony	TX	75056	972-625-4916	625-8027
South Montgomery County Woodlands Chamber of Commerce 1400 Woodloch Forest Dr Suite 500 *Web:* www.smcwcc.org	The Woodlands	TX	77380	281-367-5777	292-1655
Tyler Area Chamber of Commerce 315 N Broadway Ave. *TF:* 800-235-5712 ■ *Web:* www.tylertexas.com	Tyler	TX	75702	903-592-1661	593-2746
Randolph Metrocom Chamber of Commerce 1001 Pat Booker Rd Suite 206 *Web:* www.randolphmetrocomchamber.org	Universal City	TX	78148	210-658-8322	658-1817
Victoria Chamber of Commerce 700 N Main Suite 100 *Web:* www.victoriachamber.org	Victoria	TX	77901	361-573-5277	573-5911
Greater Waco Chamber of Commerce 900 Washington St 1st Fl *Web:* www.wacochamber.com	Waco	TX	76703	254-752-6551	752-6618

Texas (Cont'd)

Chamber	City	State	Zip	Phone	Fax
Weatherford Chamber of Commerce 401 Fort Worth St *TF:* 888-594-3801 ■ *Web:* www.weatherford-chamber.com	Weatherford	TX	76086	817-596-3801	613-9216
Rio Grande Valley Chamber of Commerce 322 S Missouri St *Web:* www.valleychamber.com	Weslaco	TX	78596	956-968-3141	968-0210
Weslaco Area Chamber of Commerce 205 W Railroad *TF:* 888-968-2102 ■ *Web:* www.weslaco.com	Weslaco	TX	78596	956-968-2102	968-6451
Wichita Falls Board of Commerce & Industry 900 8th St Suite 218 *Web:* www.wichitafallscommerce.com	Wichita Falls	TX	76301	940-723-2741	723-8773

Utah

Chamber	City	State	Zip	Phone	Fax
Davis Chamber of Commerce 450 S Simmons Way *Web:* www.davischamberofcommerce.com	Kaysville	UT	84037	801-593-2200	593-2212
Cache Chamber of Commerce 160 N Main St *Web:* www.cachechamber.com	Logan	UT	84321	435-752-2161	753-5825
Murray Area Chamber of Commerce 5250 S Commerce Dr Suite 180 *Web:* www.murraychamber.net	Murray	UT	84107	801-263-2632	263-8262
Chamber Ogden/Weber 2484 Washington Blvd Suite 400 *TF:* 866-990-1299 ■ *Web:* www.echamber.cc/	Ogden	UT	84401	801-621-8300	392-7609
Commission for Economic Development in Orem 777 S State St *Web:* www.cedo.org	Orem	UT	84058	801-226-1538	226-2678
Provo/Orem Chamber of Commerce 51 S University Ave Suite 215 *Web:* thechamber.org	Provo	UT	84601	801-379-2555	379-2557
Saint George Area Chamber of Commerce 97 E Saint George Blvd *Web:* www.stgeorgechamber.com	Saint George	UT	84770	435-628-1658	673-1587
Salt Lake City Chamber of Commerce 175 E 400 South Suite 600 *Web:* www.saltlakechamber.org	Salt Lake City	UT	84111	801-364-3631	328-5098
Sandy Area Chamber of Commerce 8807 S 700 E *Web:* www.sandychamber.com	Sandy	UT	84070	801-566-0344	566-0346
South Salt Lake Chamber of Commerce 2880 S Main St Suite 208 *Web:* www.southsaltlakechamber.com	South Salt Lake	UT	84115	801-466-3377	467-3322
Tooele County Chamber of Commerce 201 N Main PO Box 460 *TF:* 800-378-0690 ■ *Web:* www.tooelechamber.com	Tooele	UT	84074	435-882-0690	833-0946
West Jordan Chamber of Commerce 8000 S Redwood Rd *Web:* www.westjordanchamber.com	West Jordan	UT	84088	801-569-5151	569-5153
ChamberWest 1241 W Village Main Dr Suite B *Web:* www.chamberwest.com	West Valley City	UT	84119	801-977-8755	977-8329

Vermont

Chamber	City	State	Zip	Phone	Fax
Great Falls Region Chamber of Commerce 17 Depot St PO Box 554 *Web:* www.gfrcc.org	Bellows Falls	VT	05101	802-463-4280	463-9882
Bennington Area Chamber of Commerce 100 Veterans Memorial Dr *TF:* 800-229-0252 ■ *Web:* www.bennington.com	Bennington	VT	05201	802-447-3311	447-1163
Central Vermont Chamber of Commerce 33 Stewart Rd *TF:* 877-887-3678 ■ *Web:* www.central-vt.com/chamber/index.html	Berlin	VT	05602	802-229-5711	229-5713
Brattleboro Area Chamber of Commerce 180 Main St *TF:* 877-254-4565 ■ *Web:* www.brattleborochamber.org	Brattleboro	VT	05301	802-254-4565	254-5675
Lake Champlain Regional Chamber of Commerce 60 Main St Suite 100 *TF:* 877-686-5253 ■ *Web:* www.vermont.org	Burlington	VT	05401	802-863-3489	863-1538
Addison County Chamber of Commerce 2 Court St *TF:* 800-733-8376 ■ *Web:* www.midvermont.com	Middlebury	VT	05753	802-388-7951	388-8066
Vermont's North Country Chamber of Commerce 246 The Causeway *TF:* 800-635-4643 ■ *Web:* www.vtnorthcountry.com	Newport	VT	05855	802-334-7782	
Franklin County Regional Chamber of Commerce 2 N Main St Suite 101 *Web:* www.stalbanschamber.com	Saint Albans	VT	05478	802-524-2444	527-2256
Northeast Kingdom Chamber of Commerce 51 Depot Sq Suite 3 *TF:* 800-639-6379 ■ *Web:* www.nekchamber.com	Saint Johnsbury	VT	05819	802-748-3678	748-0731

Virginia

Chamber	City	State	Zip	Phone	Fax
Washington County Chamber of Commerce 179 E Main St *Web:* www.washingtonvachamber.org/area.htm	Abingdon	VA	24210	276-628-8141	628-3984
Alexandria Chamber of Commerce 801 N Fairfax St Suite 402 *Web:* www.alexchamber.com	Alexandria	VA	22314	703-549-1000	739-3805
Mount Vernon-Lee Chamber of Commerce 8804-D Pear Tree Village Ct *Web:* www.mtvernon-leechamber.org	Alexandria	VA	22309	703-360-6925	360-6928
Amherst County Chamber of Commerce PO Box 560 *Web:* www.amherstvachamber.com	Amherst	VA	24521	434-946-0990	946-0879
Annandale Chamber of Commerce 7263 Maple Pl Suite 207 *Web:* www.annandalechamber.com	Annandale	VA	22003	703-256-7232	256-7233
Arlington Chamber of Commerce 2009 14th St N Suite 111 *Web:* www.arlingtonchamber.org	Arlington	VA	22201	703-525-2400	522-5273
Hanover Assn of Businesses & Chamber of Commerce PO Box 16 *Web:* www.habcc.com	Ashland	VA	23005	804-798-8130	798-0014
Bedford Area Chamber of Commerce 305 E Main St *TF:* 800-933-9535 ■ *Web:* www.bedfordareachamber.com	Bedford	VA	24523	540-586-9401	587-6650
Danville Pittsylvania County Chamber of Commerce 8653 US Hwy 29 PO Box 99 *Web:* www.dpchamber.org	Blairs	VA	24527	434-836-6990	836-6955
Charlottesville Regional Chamber of Commerce 209 5th St NE *Web:* www.cvillechamber.com	Charlottesville	VA	22902	434-295-3141	295-3144
Hampton Roads Chamber of Commerce-Chesapeake 400 Volvo Pkwy *Web:* www.hamptonroadschamber.com	Chesapeake	VA	23320	757-622-2312	548-1835
Montgomery County Chamber of Commerce 612 New River Rd *Web:* www.montgomerycc.org	Christiansburg	VA	24073	540-382-4010	382-4390
Culpeper County Chamber of Commerce & Visitors Center 109 S Commerce St *TF:* 888-285-7373 ■ *Web:* www.culpepervachamber.com	Culpeper	VA	22701	540-825-8628	825-1449
Pulaski County Chamber of Commerce 4440 Cleburne Blvd Suite B *Web:* www.pulaskichamber.info	Dublin	VA	24084	540-674-1991	674-4163
Central Fairfax Chamber of Commerce 11166 Fairfax Blvd Suite 407 *Web:* www.cfcc.org	Fairfax	VA	22030	703-591-2450	591-2820
Botetourt County Chamber of Commerce PO Box 81 *Web:* www.bot-co-chamber.com	Fincastle	VA	24090	540-473-8280	473-8365
Greater Augusta Regional Chamber of Commerce 30 Ladd Rd PO Box 1107 *Web:* www.augustachamber.org	Fishersville	VA	22939	540-949-8203	949-7740
Franklin-Southampton Area Chamber of Commerce 108 W 3rd Ave PO Box 531 *Web:* www.fsachamber.com	Franklin	VA	23851	757-562-4900	562-6138
Fredericksburg Regional Chamber of Commerce 2300 Fall Hill Ave Suite 240 *Web:* www.fredericksburgchamber.org	Fredericksburg	VA	22401	540-373-9400	373-9570
Front Royal-Warren County Chamber of Commerce 104 E Main St *Web:* www.frontroyalchamber.com	Front Royal	VA	22630	540-635-3185	635-9758
Galax-Carroll-Grayson Chamber of Commerce 405 N Main St *Web:* www.gcgchamber.com	Galax	VA	24333	276-236-2184	236-1338
Gloucester County Chamber of Commerce 6688 Main St PO Box 296 *Web:* www.gloucestervacc.com	Gloucester	VA	23061	804-693-2425	693-7193
Buchanan County Chamber of Commerce Main St PO Box 2818	Grundy	VA	24614	276-935-4147	935-5458
Virginia Peninsula Chamber of Commerce 21 Enterprise Pkwy Suite 100 *TF:* 800-556-1822 ■ *Web:* www.vpcc.org	Hampton	VA	23666	757-262-2000	262-2009
Harrisonburg-Rockingham Chamber of Commerce 800 Country Club Rd *Web:* www.hrchamber.org	Harrisonburg	VA	22802	540-434-3862	434-4508
Carroll County Chamber of Commerce 515 N Main St *Web:* www.thecarrollchamber.com	Hillsville	VA	24343	276-728-5397	728-7825
Hopewell-Prince George Chamber of Commerce PO Drawer 1297 *Web:* www.hpgchamber.org	Hopewell	VA	23860	804-458-5536	458-0041
Russell County Chamber of Commerce 331 W Main St	Lebanon	VA	24266	276-889-8041	889-8002
Loudoun County Chamber of Commerce 101 Blue Seal Dr Suite 100 *TF:* 800-578-5222 ■ *Web:* www.loudounchamber.org	Leesburg	VA	20177	703-777-2176	777-1392
Lexington-Rockbridge County Chamber of Commerce 100 E Washington St *Web:* www.lexrockchamber.com	Lexington	VA	24450	540-463-5375	463-3567
Lynchburg Regional Chamber of Commerce 2015 Memorial Ave *Web:* www.lynchburgchamber.org	Lynchburg	VA	24501	434-845-5966	522-9592
Prince William County-Greater Manassas Chamber of Commerce 8963 Center St *Web:* www.pwcgmcc.org	Manassas	VA	20110	703-368-6600	368-4733
Chamber of Commerce of Smyth County 214 W Main St *Web:* www.smythchamber.org	Marion	VA	24354	276-783-3161	783-8003
Martinsville-Henry County Chamber of Commerce 115 Broad St *TF:* 866-632-3378 ■ *Web:* www.martinsville.com	Martinsville	VA	24112	276-632-6401	632-5059
Eastern Shore of Virginia Chamber of Commerce PO Box 460 *Web:* www.esvachamber.org	Melfa	VA	23410	757-787-2460	787-8687
Hampton Roads Chamber of Commerce 420 Bank St *Web:* www.hamptonroadschamber.com	Norfolk	VA	23510	757-622-2312	622-5563
Wise County Chamber of Commerce 765 Park Ave *Web:* www.wisecountychamber.org	Norton	VA	24273	276-679-0961	679-2655
Petersburg Chamber of Commerce 325 E Washington St *Web:* www.petersburg-va.org/chamber	Petersburg	VA	23804	804-733-8131	733-9891
Hampton Roads Chamber of Commerce Portsmouth 200 High St TowneBank Financial Ctr Suite 305	Portsmouth	VA	23704	757-664-2561	397-4483
Prince William Regional Chamber of Commerce 4320 Ridgewood Ctr Dr *Web:* www.regionalchamber.org	Prince William	VA	22192	703-590-5000	590-9815
Greater Reston Chamber of Commerce 1763 Fountain Dr *Web:* www.restonchamber.org	Reston	VA	20190	703-707-9045	707-9049
Greater Richmond Chamber of Commerce 600 E Main St 7th Fl *Web:* www.grcc.com	Richmond	VA	23219	804-648-1234	783-9366
Roanoke Regional Chamber of Commerce 212 S Jefferson St *Web:* www.roanokechamber.org	Roanoke	VA	24011	540-983-0700	983-0723
Franklin County Chamber of Commerce 261 Franklin St PO Box 158 *Web:* www.franklincounty.org	Rocky Mount	VA	24151	540-483-9542	483-0653
Salem/Roanoke County Chamber of Commerce 611 E Main St *Web:* www.s-rcchamber.org	Salem	VA	24153	540-387-0267	387-4110
Halifax County Chamber of Commerce 515 Broad St *Web:* www.halifaxchamber.net	South Boston	VA	24592	434-572-3085	572-1733
Greater Springfield Chamber of Commerce 6434 Brandon Ave Suite 3A *Web:* www.springfieldchamber.org	Springfield	VA	22150	703-866-3500	866-3501
Hampton Roads Chamber of Commerce-Suffolk 127 E Washington St Suite 100	Suffolk	VA	23434	757-622-2312	925-1281
Tazewell Area Chamber of Commerce Tazewell Mall Box 6 *Web:* www.tazewellchamber.org	Tazewell	VA	24651	276-988-5091	988-5093
Fairfax County Chamber of Commerce 8230 Old Courthouse Rd Suite 350 *Web:* www.fccc.org	Vienna	VA	22182	703-749-0400	749-9075
Vienna-Tysons Regional Chamber of Commerce 513 Maple Ave W 2nd Fl *Web:* www.vtrcc.org	Vienna	VA	22180	703-281-1333	242-1482
Fauquier County Chamber of Commerce 183-A Keith St *Web:* www.fauquierchamber.org	Warrenton	VA	20186	540-347-4414	347-7510
Williamsburg Area Chamber of Commerce PO Box 3495 *TF:* 800-368-6511 ■ *Web:* www.williamsburgcc.com	Williamsburg	VA	23185	757-229-6511	229-2047
Winchester-Frederick County Chamber of Commerce 2 N Cameron St Suite 200 *Web:* www.winchesterva.org	Winchester	VA	22601	540-662-4118	722-6365
Wytheville-Wythe-Bland Chamber of Commerce Inc 150 E Monroe St *Web:* chamber.wytheville.com	Wytheville	VA	24382	276-223-3365	223-3412

Washington

Chamber	City	State	Zip	Phone	Fax
Grays Harbor Chamber of Commerce 506 Duffy St *TF:* 800-321-1924 ■ *Web:* www.graysharbor.org	Aberdeen	WA	98520	360-532-1924	533-7945
Auburn Area Chamber of Commerce 108 S Division St Suite B *Web:* www.auburnareawa.org	Auburn	WA	98001	253-833-0700	735-4091
Bellevue Chamber of Commerce 302 Bellevue Sq *Web:* www.bellevuechamber.org	Bellevue	WA	98004	425-454-2464	462-4660

Phone Fax

Bellingham/Whatcom Chamber of Commerce & Industry
1201 Cornwall Ave Suite 100 Bellingham WA 98225 360-734-1330 734-1332
Web: www.bellingham.com
Bremerton Area Chamber of Commerce 301 Pacific Ave. Bremerton WA 98337 360-479-3579 479-1033
Web: www.bremertonchamber.org
Camas-Washougal Chamber of Commerce PO Box 919 Camas WA 98607 360-834-2472 834-9171
Web: www.cwchamber.com
Centralia-Chehalis Chamber of Commerce
500 NW Chamber of Commerce Way Chehalis WA 98532 360-748-8885 748-8763
Web: www.chamberway.com
Greater Edmonds Chamber of Commerce PO Box 146 Edmonds WA 98020 425-670-1496 712-1808
Web: www.edmondswa.com
Enumclaw Area Chamber of Commerce 1421 Cole St. Enumclaw WA 98022 360-825-7666 825-8369
Web: chamber.enumclaw.wa.us
Everett Area Chamber of Commerce 2000 Hewitt Ave Suite 205 Everett WA 98201 425-257-3222 257-2074
Web: www.everettchamber.com
Greater Federal Way Chamber of Commerce
1230 S 336th St Suite F Federal Way WA 98003 253-838-2605 661-9050
Web: www.federalwaychamber.com
Gig Harbor/Peninsula Area Chamber of Commerce
3311 Harborview Dr Suite 101 Gig Harbor WA 98332 253-851-6865 851-6881
Web: www.gigharborchamber.com
Greater Issaquah Chamber of Commerce 155 NW Gilman Blvd Issaquah WA 98027 425-392-7024 392-8101
Web: www.issaquahchamber.com
Tri-City Area Chamber of Commerce
3180 W Clearwater Ave Suite F Kennewick WA 99336 509-736-0510 783-1733
Web: www.tcacc.com
Kent Chamber of Commerce 524 W Meeker St Suite 1 Kent WA 98032 253-854-1770 854-8567
Web: www.kentchamber.com
Greater Kirkland Chamber of Commerce 401 Park Pl Suite 102 Kirkland WA 98033 425-822-7066 827-4878
Web: www.kirklandchamber.org
Lacey-Thurston County Chamber of Commerce
4804 Lacey Blvd SE Suite A Lacey WA 98503 360-491-4141 491-9403
Web: www.laceychamber.com
Lakewood Chamber of Commerce
4650 Steilacoom Blvd Bldg 19 Suite 109 Lakewood WA 98499 253-582-9400 581-5241
Web: www.lakewood-wa.com
Kelso Longview Chamber of Commerce 1563 Olympia Way Longview WA 98632 360-423-8400 423-0432
Web: www.kelsolongviewchamber.org
South Snohomish County Chamber of Commerce
3815 196th St SW Suite 136 Lynnwood WA 98036 425-774-0507 774-4636
Web: www.sscchamber.org
Greater Maple Valley-Black Diamond Chamber of Commerce
22035 SE Wax Rd Suite 4 Maple Valley WA 98038 425-432-0222 413-8017
Web: www.maplevalley.com
Moses Lake Area Chamber of Commerce
324 S Pioneer Way Moses Lake WA 98837 509-765-7888 765-7891
TF: 800-992-6234 ■ *Web:* www.moseslake.com
Greater Oak Harbor Chamber of Commerce 32630 SR 20 Oak Harbor WA 98277 360-675-3755 679-1624
Web: www.oakharborchamber.org
Olympia/Thurston County Chamber of Commerce
809 Legion Way Olympia WA 98501 360-357-3362 357-3376
Web: www.thurstonchamber.com
Greater Pasco Area Chamber of Commerce
2705 St Andrews Loop Suite C Pasco WA 99301 509-547-9755 547-9756
Web: www.pascochamber.org
Port Orchard Chamber of Commerce 1014 Bay St Suite 8 Port Orchard WA 98366 360-876-3505 895-1920
TF: 800-982-8139 ■ *Web:* www.portorchard.com
Pullman Chamber of Commerce 415 N Grand Ave Pullman WA 99163 509-334-3565 332-3232
TF: 800-365-6948 ■ *Web:* www.pullmanchamber.com
Eastern Pierce County Chamber of Commerce
417 Eastern Pioneer St Puyallup WA 98372 253-845-6755 848-6164
Web: www.puyallupchamber.com
Redmond Chamber of Commerce 16210 NE 80th St Redmond WA 98052 425-885-4014 882-0996
Web: www.redmondchamber.org
Greater Renton Chamber of Commerce 300 Rainier Ave N Renton WA 98057 425-226-4560 226-4287
Web: www.renton-chamber.com
Richland Chamber of Commerce
710-A George Washington Way Richland WA 99352 509-946-1651 943-6187
TF: 877-218-7729 ■ *Web:* richlandwa.usachamber.com
Ballard Chamber of Commerce 2208 NW Market St Suite 100 Seattle WA 98107 206-784-9705 783-8154
Web: www.ballardchamber.com
Greater Seattle Chamber of Commerce
1301 5th Ave Suite 2500 Seattle WA 98101 206-389-7200 389-7288
Web: www.seattlechamber.com
Greater University Chamber of Commerce
4710 University Way NE Suite 212 Seattle WA 98105 206-547-4417 547-5266
Web: www.udistrictchamber.org
Lake City Chamber of Commerce 12345 30th Ave NE Suite FG Seattle WA 98125 206-363-3287 363-6456
Web: www.lakecitychamber.org
White Center Chamber of Commerce 1327 SW 102nd St. Seattle WA 98146 206-763-4196 763-1042
Shelton-Mason County Chamber of Commerce
221 W Railroad Ave Shelton WA 98584 360-426-2021 426-8678
TF: 800-576-2021 ■ *Web:* www.sheltonchamber.org
Shoreline Chamber of Commerce 18560 1st Ave NE Shoreline WA 98155 206-361-2260 361-2268
Web: shorecham.org
Spokane Regional Chamber of Commerce
801 W Riverside Ave Suite 100 Spokane WA 99201 509-624-1393 747-0077
Web: www.spokanechamber.org
Spokane Valley Chamber of Commerce
9507 E Sprague Ave Spokane Valley WA 99206 509-924-4994 924-4992
Web: www.spokanevalleychamber.org
Tacoma-Pierce County Chamber of Commerce
950 Pacific Ave Suite 300 Tacoma WA 98402 253-627-2175 597-7305
Web: www.tacomachamber.org
Southwest King County Chamber of Commerce
14220 Interurban Ave S Tukwila WA 98168 206-575-1633 575-2007
TF: 800-638-8613 ■ *Web:* www.swkcc.org
Greater Vancouver Chamber of Commerce
1101 Broadway Suite 100 Vancouver WA 98660 360-694-2588 693-8279
Web: www.vancouverusa.com
Walla Walla Valley Chamber of Commerce
29 E Sumach St Walla Walla WA 99362 509-525-0850 522-2038
TF: 877-998-4748 ■ *Web:* www.wwvchamber.com
Wenatchee Valley Chamber of Commerce
300 S Columbia St 3rd Fl Wenatchee WA 98801 509-662-2116 663-2022
Web: www.wenatchee.org
Greater Yakima Chamber of Commerce 10 N 9th St. Yakima WA 98901 509-248-2021 248-0601
Web: www.yakima.org

West Virginia

Phone Fax

Beckley-Raleigh County Chamber of Commerce
245 N Kanawha St Beckley WV 25801 304-252-7328 252-7373
TF: 800-718-1474 ■ *Web:* www.brccc.com
Buckhannon-Upshur Chamber of Commerce
16 S Kanawha St Buckhannon WV 26201 304-472-1722 472-4938
Web: www.buchamber.com
Jefferson County Chamber of Commerce PO Box 426 Charles Town WV 25414 304-725-2055 728-8307
TF: 800-624-0577 ■ *Web:* www.jeffersoncounty.com
Charleston Regional Chamber of Commerce 1116 Smith St. Charleston WV 25301 304-340-4253 340-4275
Web: www.charlestonwvchamber.org
Harrison County Chamber of Commerce
168 W Main St Suite 100 Clarksburg WV 26301 304-624-6331 624-5190
Web: www.harrisoncountychamber.com
Elkins-Randolph County Chamber of Commerce
200 Executive Plaza Elkins WV 26241 304-636-2717 636-8046
TF: 800-422-3304 ■ *Web:* www.randolphcountywv.com
Marion County Chamber of Commerce 110 Adams St Fairmont WV 26554 304-363-0442 363-0480
TF: 800-296-3379 ■ *Web:* www.marionchamber.com
Huntington Regional Chamber of Commerce 720 4th Ave Huntington WV 25716 304-525-5131 525-5158
Web: www.huntingtonchamber.org
Mineral County Chamber of Commerce
Grand Central Business Ctr Suite 2011 Keyser WV 26726 304-788-2513 788-3887
Web: mineralcounty.info
Preston County Chamber of Commerce 200 1/2 W Main St Kingwood WV 26537 304-329-0576 329-1407
Web: www.prestonchamber.com
Greater Greenbrier Chamber of Commerce
540 N Jefferson St Box 17 Suite N Lewisburg WV 24901 304-645-1000 647-3001
TF: 800-833-2068
Logan County Chamber of Commerce 214 Stratton St Logan WV 25601 304-752-1324 752-5988
Web: www.chamber.logan.wv.us
Martinsburg-Berkeley County Chamber of Commerce
198 Viking Way Martinsburg WV 25401 304-267-4841 263-4695
TF: 800-332-9007 ■ *Web:* www.berkeleycounty.org
Upper Kanawha Valley Chamber of Commerce
PO Box 831 Montgomery WV 25136 304-442-5756 442-3052
Morgantown Area Chamber of Commerce
1009 University Ave Morgantown WV 26507 304-292-3311 296-6619
TF: 800-618-2525 ■ *Web:* www.morgantownchamber.com
Marshall County Chamber of Commerce 609 Jefferson Ave Moundsville WV 26041 304-845-2773 845-2773
Web: www.marshallcountychamber.com
Greater New Martinsville Development Corp
201 Main St New Martinsville WV 26155 304-455-3825 455-3637
Web: www.gnmdc.com
Fayette County Chamber of Commerce 310 Oyler Ave Oak Hill WV 25901 304-465-5617 465-5618
TF: 800-927-0263 ■ *Web:* www.fayettecounty.com
Chamber of Commerce of Mid-Ohio Valley 214 8th St Parkersburg WV 26101 304-422-3588 422-3580
Web: www.parkersburgchamber.com
Mason County Area Chamber of Commerce 305 Main St Point Pleasant WV 25550 304-675-1050 675-2838
Web: www.masoncountychamber.org
Princeton-Mercer County Chamber of Commerce
1522 N Walker St. Princeton WV 24740 304-487-1502 425-0227
Web: www.pmccc.com
Wheeling Area Chamber of Commerce 1310 Market St Wheeling WV 26003 304-233-2575 233-1320
Web: www.wheelingchamber.com
Tug Valley Chamber of Commerce PO Box 376 Williamson WV 25661 304-235-5240 235-4509
Web: www.tugvalleychamberofcommerce.com
Putnam County Chamber of Commerce 5664 SR 34 N Winfield WV 25213 304-757-6510 757-6562
Web: www.putnamcounty.org

Wisconsin

Phone Fax

Fox Cities Chamber of Commerce & Industry
125 N Superior St Appleton WI 54911 920-734-7101 734-7161
TF: 800-999-3224 ■ *Web:* www.foxcitieschamber.com
Greater Beloit Chamber of Commerce 520 E Grand Ave. Beloit WI 53511 608-365-8835 365-9345
TF: 800-683-2774 ■ *Web:* www.greaterbeloitchamber.com
Greater Brookfield Chamber of Commerce
1305 N Barker Rd Suite 5 Brookfield WI 53045 262-786-1886 786-1959
Web: www.brookfieldchamber.com
Chippewa Falls Area Chamber of Commerce
10 S Bridge St Chippewa Falls WI 54729 715-723-0331 723-0332
TF: 888-723-0024 ■ *Web:* www.chippewachamber.org
Eau Claire Area Chamber of Commerce
101 N Farwell St Suite 101 Eau Claire WI 54703 715-834-1204 834-1956
Web: www.eauclairechamber.org
Fond du Lac Area Assn of Commerce 207 N Main St Fond du Lac WI 54935 920-921-9500 921-9559
Web: www.fdlac.com
Green Bay Area Chamber of Commerce
400 S Washington St Green Bay WI 54301 920-437-8704 437-1024
Web: www.titletown.org
Greenfield Chamber of Commerce 4818 S 76th St Suite 129 Greenfield WI 53220 414-327-8500 421-6797
Web: greenfieldchamber.org
Heart of the Valley Chamber of Commerce
101 E Wisconsin Ave Kaukauna WI 54130 920-766-1616 766-5504
Web: www.heartofthevalleychamber.com
Kenosha Area Chamber of Commerce 715 56th St Kenosha WI 53140 262-654-1234 654-4655
Web: www.kenoshaareachamber.com
Greater La Crosse Area Chamber of Commerce 712 Main St La Crosse WI 54601 608-784-4880 784-4919
TF: 800-889-0539 ■ *Web:* www.lacrossechamber.com
Greater Madison Chamber of Commerce PO Box 71 Madison WI 53701 608-256-8348 256-0333
Web: www.greatermadisonchamber.com
Manitowoc-Two Rivers Area Chamber of Commerce
1515 Memorial Dr PO Box 903 Manitowoc WI 54221 920-684-5575 684-1915
TF: 800-262-7892 ■ *Web:* www.manitowocchamber.com
Menomonee Falls Chamber of Commerce
N 88 W 16621 Appleton Ave PO Box 73 Menomonee Falls WI 53051 262-251-2430 251-0969
Web: www.menomoneefallschamber.com
Greater Menomonie Area Chamber of Commerce
342 E Main St Menomonie WI 54751 715-235-9087 235-2824
TF: 800-283-1862 ■ *Web:* www.menomoniechamber.org
Merrill Area Chamber of Commerce 705 N Center Ave. Merrill WI 54452 715-536-9474 539-2043
TF: 877-907-2757 ■ *Web:* www.merrillchamber.com
Metropolitan Milwaukee Assn of Commerce
756 N Milwaukee St Milwaukee WI 53202 414-287-4100 271-7753
Web: www.mmac.org
Monroe Chamber of Commerce & Industry 1505 9th St Monroe WI 53566 608-325-7648 325-7710
Web: www.monroechamber.org
New Berlin Chamber of Commerce 2140 S Calhoun Rd New Berlin WI 53151 262-786-5280 786-9165
Web: www.nb-chamber.org
SECUB-Southeastern Chamber United in Business
8580 S Howell Ave. Oak Creek WI 53154 414-768-5845 768-5848
Web: www.secub.net
Oconomowoc Area Chamber of Commerce
152 E Wisconsin Ave Oconomowoc WI 53066 262-567-2666 567-3477
Web: www.oconomowoc.org
Oshkosh Chamber of Commerce 120 Jackson St. Oshkosh WI 54901 920-303-2266 303-2263
Web: www.oshkoshchamber.com

Wisconsin (Cont'd)

Organization	City	State	ZIP	Phone	Fax
Racine Area Mfg & Commerce 300 5th St. *Web:* www.racinechamber.com	Racine	WI	53403	262-634-1931	634-7422
Ripon Area Chamber of Commerce 127 Jefferson St *Web:* www.ripon-wi.com	Ripon	WI	54971	920-748-6764	748-6784
Shawano Country Chamber of Commerce 213 E Green Bay St. *TF:* 800-235-8528 ■ *Web:* www.shawanocountry.com	Shawano	WI	54166	715-524-2139	524-3127
Sheboygan County Chamber of Commerce 712 Riverfront Dr Suite 101 *TF:* 800-457-9497 ■ *Web:* www.sheboygan.org	Sheboygan	WI	53081	920-457-9491	457-6269
Portage County Business Council 5501 Vern Holmes Dr *Web:* www.portagecountybiz.com	Stevens Point	WI	54481	715-344-1940	344-4473
Superior-Douglas County Chamber of Commerce 205 Belknap St. *Web:* www.superiorchamber.org	Superior	WI	54880	715-394-7716	394-3810
Waukesha County Chamber of Commerce 223 Wisconsin Ave *Web:* www.waukesha.org	Waukesha	WI	53186	262-542-4249	542-8068
Wausau Area Chamber of Commerce 200 Washington St Suite 120 *Web:* www.wausauchamber.com	Wausau	WI	54403	715-845-6231	845-6235
West Suburban Chamber of Commerce 2421 N Mayfair Rd Suite 17 *Web:* www.westsuburbanchamber.com	Wauwatosa	WI	53226	414-453-2330	453-2336
West Allis-West Milwaukee Chamber of Commerce 7149 W Greenfield Ave *Web:* www.wawmchamber.com	West Allis	WI	53214	414-302-9901	302-9918
West Bend Area Chamber of Commerce 548 S Main St. *TF:* 888-338-8666 ■ *Web:* www.wbachamber.org	West Bend	WI	53095	262-338-2666	338-1771
Heart of Wisconsin Business & Economic Alliance 1120 Lincoln St *Web:* www.heartofwi.com	Wisconsin Rapids	WI	54494	715-423-1830	423-1865

Wyoming

Organization	City	State	ZIP	Phone	Fax
Casper Area Chamber of Commerce 500 N Center St. *TF:* 866-234-5311 ■ *Web:* www.casperwyoming.org	Casper	WY	82601	307-234-5311	265-2643
Greater Cheyenne Chamber of Commerce 121 W 15th St Suite 204 *Web:* www.cheyennechamber.org	Cheyenne	WY	82001	307-638-3388	778-1407
Campbell County Chamber of Commerce 314 S Gillette Ave. *Web:* www.gillettechamber.com	Gillette	WY	82716	307-682-3673	682-0538
Jackson Hole Chamber of Commerce 990 W Broadway St. *Web:* www.jacksonholechamber.com	Jackson	WY	83001	307-733-3316	733-5585
Laramie Area Chamber of Commerce 800 S 3rd St *TF:* 866-876-1012 ■ *Web:* www.laramie.org	Laramie	WY	82070	307-745-7339	745-4624
Rock Springs Chamber of Commerce 1897 Dewar Dr. *TF:* 800-463-8637 ■ *Web:* www.rockspringswyoming.net	Rock Springs	WY	82901	307-362-3771	362-3838
Sheridan County Chamber of Commerce PO Box 707 *TF:* 800-453-3650 ■ *Web:* www.sheridanwyomingchamber.org	Sheridan	WY	82801	307-672-2485	672-7321

140 CHAMBERS OF COMMERCE - US - STATE

Organization	City	State	ZIP	Phone	Fax
US Chamber of Commerce 1615 H St NW *TF:* 800-638-6582 ■ *Web:* www.uschamber.com	Washington	DC	20062	202-659-6000	463-5836
Alaska State Chamber of Commerce 217 2nd St Suite 201 *Web:* www.alaskachamber.com	Juneau	AK	99801	907-586-2323	463-5515
Arizona Chamber of Commerce & Industry 1850 N Central Ave Suite 1433 *TF:* 800-498-6973 ■ *Web:* www.azchamber.com	Phoenix	AZ	85004	602-248-9172	265-1262
Arkansas State Chamber of Commerce PO Box 3645 *Web:* www.statechamber-aia.dina.org	Little Rock	AR	72203	501-372-2222	372-2722
Business Council of Alabama PO Box 76 *TF:* 800-665-9647 ■ *Web:* www.bcatoday.org	Montgomery	AL	36101	334-834-6000	241-5984
California Chamber of Commerce PO Box 1736 *Web:* www.calchamber.com	Sacramento	CA	95812	916-444-6670	325-1272
Colorado Assn of Commerce & Industry 1600 Broadway Suite 1000 *Web:* www.cochamber.com	Denver	CO	80202	303-831-7411	860-1439
Connecticut Business & Industry Assn 350 Church St. *Web:* www.cbia.com	Hartford	CT	06103	860-244-1900	278-8562
Delaware State Chamber of Commerce PO Box 671 *TF:* 800-292-9507 ■ *Web:* www.dscc.com	Wilmington	DE	19899	302-655-7221	654-0691
District of Columbia Chamber of Commerce 1213 K St NW *Web:* www.dcchamber.org	Washington	DC	20005	202-347-7201	638-6762
Florida Chamber of Commerce 136 S Bronough St. *TF:* 877-521-1200 ■ *Web:* www.flchamber.com	Tallahassee	FL	32301	850-521-1200	521-1219
Georgia Chamber of Commerce 233 Peachtree St NE Suite 2000 *TF:* 800-241-2286 ■ *Web:* www.gachamber.com	Atlanta	GA	30303	404-223-2264	223-2290
Hawaii Chamber of Commerce 1132 Bishop St Suite 402 *TF:* 800-464-2924 ■ *Web:* www.cochawaii.com	Honolulu	HI	96813	808-545-4300	545-4369
Idaho Assn of Commerce & Industry PO Box 389 *Web:* www.iaci.org	Boise	ID	83701	208-343-1849	338-5623
Illinois State Chamber of Commerce 311 S Wacker Dr Suite 1500 *Web:* www.ilchamber.org	Chicago	IL	60606	312-983-7100	983-7101
Indiana State Chamber of Commerce 115 W Washington St Suite 850-S *Web:* www.indianachamber.com	Indianapolis	IN	46204	317-264-3110	264-6855
Iowa Assn of Business & Industry 904 Walnut St Suite 100 *TF:* 800-383-4224 ■ *Web:* www.iowaabi.org	Des Moines	IA	50309	515-280-8000	244-8907
Kansas Chamber of Commerce & Industry 835 SW Topeka Blvd *Web:* www.kansaschamber.org	Topeka	KS	66612	785-357-6321	357-4732
Kentucky Chamber of Commerce 464 Chenault Rd *Web:* www.kychamber.com	Frankfort	KY	40601	502-695-4700	695-6824
Louisiana Assn of Business & Industry 3113 Valley Creek Dr PO Box 80258 *TF:* 888-816-5224 ■ *Web:* www.labi.org	Baton Rouge	LA	70898	225-928-5388	929-6054
Maine State Chamber of Commerce 7 University Dr. *Web:* www.mainechamber.org	Augusta	ME	04330	207-623-4568	622-7723
Maryland Chamber of Commerce 60 West St Suite 100 *Web:* www.mdchamber.org	Annapolis	MD	21401	410-269-0642	269-5247
Michigan Chamber of Commerce 600 S Walnut St. *TF:* 800-748-0266 ■ *Web:* www.michamber.com	Lansing	MI	48933	517-371-2100	371-7224
Minnesota Chamber of Commerce 400 Robert St N Suite 1500 *TF:* 800-821-2230 ■ *Web:* www.mnchamber.com	Saint Paul	MN	55101	651-292-4650	292-4656
Mississippi Economic Council PO Box 23276 *TF:* 800-748-7626 ■ *Web:* www.msmec.com	Jackson	MS	39225	601-969-0022	353-0247
Missouri Chamber of Commerce PO Box 149 *Web:* www.mochamber.org	Jefferson City	MO	65102	573-634-3511	634-8855
Montana Chamber of Commerce PO Box 1730 *Web:* www.montanachamber.com	Helena	MT	59624	406-442-2405	442-2409
Nebraska Chamber of Commerce & Industry PO Box 95128 *Web:* www.nechamber.com	Lincoln	NE	68509	402-474-4422	474-5681
New England Council Inc 98 N Washington St Suite 201 *Web:* www.newenglandcouncil.com	Boston	MA	02114	617-723-4009	723-3943
New Hampshire Business & Industry Assn 122 N Main St 3rd Fl *Web:* www.nhbia.org	Concord	NH	03301	603-224-5388	224-2872
New Jersey State Chamber of Commerce 216 W State St *Web:* www.njchamber.com	Trenton	NJ	08608	609-989-7888	989-9696
New Mexico Assn of Commerce & Industry PO Box 9706 *Web:* www.aci.nm.org	Albuquerque	NM	87119	505-842-0644	842-0734
[New York] Business Council of New York State Inc 152 Washington Ave *TF:* 800-358-1202 ■ *Web:* www.bcnys.org	Albany	NY	12210	518-465-7511	465-4389
North Carolina Chamber 701 Corporate Center Dr Suite 400 *Web:* www.nccbi.org	Raleigh	NC	27607	919-836-1400	836-1425
North Dakota (Greater) Assn PO Box 2639 *TF:* 800-382-1405 ■ *Web:* www.gnda.com	Bismarck	ND	58502	701-222-0929	222-1611
Ohio Chamber of Commerce 230 E Town St *TF:* 800-622-1893 ■ *Web:* www.ohiochamber.com	Columbus	OH	43215	614-228-4201	228-6403
Oklahoma State Chamber 330 NE 10th St *TF:* 800-364-6465 ■ *Web:* www.okstatechamber.com	Oklahoma City	OK	73104	405-235-3669	235-3670
Pennsylvania Chamber of Business & Industry 417 Walnut St *TF:* 800-225-7224 ■ *Web:* www.pachamber.org	Harrisburg	PA	17101	717-255-3252	255-3298
Puerto Rico Chamber of Commerce PO Box 9024033 *Web:* camarapr.org	San Juan	PR	00902	787-721-6060	721-6060
Rhode Island Economic Development Corp 315 Iron Horse Way Suite 101 *Web:* www.riedc.com	Providence	RI	02908	401-278-9100	273-8270
South Carolina Chamber of Commerce 1201 Main St Suite 1700 *TF:* 800-799-4601 ■ *Web:* www.scchamber.net	Columbia	SC	29201	803-799-4601	779-6043
South Dakota Chamber of Commerce & Industry 108 N Euclid Ave *Web:* www.sdchamber.biz	Pierre	SD	57501	605-224-6161	224-7198
Tennessee Chamber of Commerce & Industry 611 Commerce St Suite 3030 *Web:* www.tnchamber.org	Nashville	TN	37203	615-256-5141	256-6726
Texas Assn of Business DBA javascript:SaveChanges() 1209 Nueces St *Web:* www.tabcc.org	Austin	TX	78701	512-477-6721	477-0836
Vermont Chamber of Commerce PO Box 37 *Web:* www.vtchamber.com	Montpelier	VT	05601	802-223-3443	223-4257
Virginia Chamber of Commerce 9 S 5th St *TF:* 800-477-7682 ■ *Web:* www.vachamber.com	Richmond	VA	23219	804-644-1607	783-6112
[Washington] Association of Washington Business PO Box 658 *TF:* 800-521-9325 ■ *Web:* www.awb.org	Olympia	WA	98507	360-943-1600	943-5811
West Virginia Chamber of Commerce PO Box 2789 *Web:* www.wvchamber.com	Charleston	WV	25330	304-342-1115	342-1130
Wisconsin Manufacturers & Commerce PO Box 352 *Web:* www.wmc.org	Madison	WI	53701	608-258-3400	258-3413

141 CHECK CASHING SERVICES

Organization	City	State	ZIP	Phone	Fax
ACE Cash Express Inc 1231 Greenway Dr Suite 800 *NASDAQ: AACE* ■ *TF Sales:* 800-713-3338 ■ *Web:* www.acecashexpress.com	Irving	TX	75038	972-550-5000	550-5150
Advance America Cash Advance Centers Inc 135 N Church St *NYSE: AEA* ■ *TF:* 866-640-4227 ■ *Web:* www.advanceamerica.net	Spartanburg	SC	29306	864-342-5600	342-5612
America's Cash Express 1231 Greenway Dr Suite 800 *NASDAQ: AACE* ■ *TF Sales:* 800-713-3338 ■ *Web:* www.acecashexpress.com	Irving	TX	75038	972-550-5000	550-5150
Cash Plus Inc 3002 Dow Ave Suite 120 *TF:* 888-707-2274 ■ *Web:* www.cashplusinc.com	Tustin	CA	92780	714-731-2274	731-2099
CashZone Check Cashing Service 365 7th Ave *Web:* www.cashzoneusa.com	New York	NY	10001	212-564-4705	268-7312
Check Cashing Store 6340 NW 5th Way *Web:* www.thecheckcashingstore.com	Fort Lauderdale	FL	33309	954-731-4086	731-8452
Dollar Financial Corp 1436 Lancaster Ave Suite 300 *NASDAQ: DLLR* ■ *Web:* www.dfg.com	Berwyn	PA	19312	610-296-3400	296-7844
eFunds Corp 8501 N Scottsdale Rd Gainey Center II Suite 300 *NYSE: EFD* ■ *Web:* www.efunds.com	Scottsdale	AZ	85253	480-629-7700	
First Cash Financial Services Inc 690 E Lamar Blvd Suite 400 *NASDAQ: FCFS* ■ *Web:* www.firstcash.com	Arlington	TX	76011	817-460-3947	461-7019
Mister Money USA 2057 Vermont Dr *TF:* 800-827-7296 ■ *Web:* www.mistermoney.com	Fort Collins	CO	80525	970-493-0574	490-2099
Mr Payroll Check Cashing 1600 W 7th St *TF:* 800-322-3250 ■ *Web:* www.cashamerica.com	Fort Worth	TX	76102	817-335-1100	570-1738
Nix Check Cashing 17019 Kingsview Ave *Web:* www.nixcheckcashing.com	Carson	CA	90746	310-538-2242	538-0131
Pay-O-Matic Corp 160 Oak Dr *TF:* 888-729-3773 ■ *Web:* www.payomatic.com	Syosset	NY	11791	516-496-4900	496-2282
QC Holdings Inc 2812 W 47th Ave *NASDAQ: QCCO* ■ *Web:* www.qcholdings.com	Kansas City	KS	66103	913-439-1100	439-1170
TeleCheck International Inc 5251 Westheimer Rd *TF:* 800-835-3243 ■ *Web:* www.telecheck.com	Houston	TX	77056	713-331-7600	331-7740
United Financial Services Group 400 Market St Suite 1030 *TF:* 800-826-0787 ■ *Web:* www.unitedfsg.com	Philadelphia	PA	19106	215-238-0300	238-9056

142 CHECKS - PERSONAL & BUSINESS

Organization	City	State	ZIP	Phone	Fax
Artistic Checks Inc 11501 Otter Creek Rd S PO Box 1000 **Fax Area Code:* 866 ■ *TF:* 800-243-2577 ■ *Web:* www.artisticchecks.com	Mabelvale	AR	72103	410-679-3300	567-5560*
Check Printers Inc 1530 Antioch Pike *TF:* 800-766-1217 ■ *Web:* www.check-printers.com	Antioch	TN	37013	615-277-7100	831-0153
CheckCrafters Inc PO Box 100 *TF:* 888-404-5245 ■ *Web:* www.checkcrafters.com	Edgewood	MD	21040	410-679-3300	679-4658
Checks In The Mail Inc 2435 Goodwin Ln. **Fax Area Code:* 877 ■ *TF:* 888-325-3614 ■ *Web:* secure.checksinthemail.com	New Braunfels	TX	78135	830-609-5500	397-1541*

Company	City	State	ZIP	Phone	Fax
Checks Unlimited 8245 N Union Blvd PO Box 35630	Colorado Springs	CO	80935	800-565-8332	231-7024*
**Fax Area Code:* 866 ■ *Web:* www.checksunlimited.com					
Clarke American Checks Inc 10931 Laureate Dr	San Antonio	TX	78249	210-697-8888	696-1676
TF: 800-382-0818 ■ *Web:* www.clarkeamerican.com					
Classic Checks Inc PO Box 2	Edgewood	MD	21040	410-679-3300	676-1510
TF: 800-354-3588 ■ *Web:* www.classicchecks.com					
Custom Direct LLC 1802 Fashion Ct	Joppa	MD	21085	410-679-3300	676-0950
TF: 800-354-3540 ■ *Web:* www.cdi-us.com					
Deluxe Business Forms 3680 Victoria St N	Shoreview	MN	55126	651-483-7111	447-1407*
**Fax Area Code:* 800 ■ **Fax:* Sales ■ *TF Cust Svc:* 800-328-7205 ■ *Web:* www.deluxe.com					
Deluxe Paper Payment Systems LLC 3660 Victoria St N	Saint Paul	MN	55126	651-490-8000	490-8569
Harland John H Co 2939 Miller Rd	Decatur	GA	30035	770-981-9460	593-5347
NYSE: JH ■ *TF:* 800-723-3690 ■ *Web:* www.harland.net					
Image Checks Inc PO Box 548	Little Rock	AR	72203	501-455-1600	455-4299
TF: 800-562-8768 ■ *Web:* www.imagechecks.com					
John H Harland Co 2939 Miller Rd	Decatur	GA	30035	770-981-9460	593-5347
NYSE: JH ■ *TF:* 800-723-3690 ■ *Web:* www.harland.net					
Printegra Inc 403 Westpark Ct Suite A	Peachtree City	GA	30269	770-631-6070	631-6188
TF: 800-422-6070 ■ *Web:* www.printegra.com					
Safeguard Business Systems Inc					
8585 N Stemmons Fwy Suite 600 N	Dallas	TX	75247	214-905-3935	630-6821
TF: 800-338-0636 ■ *Web:* www.safeguard.org					
Wilmer Service Line 515 W Sycamore St	Coldwater	OH	45828	888-494-5637	553-4849*
**Fax Area Code:* 800 ■ *Web:* www.4wilmer.com					

CHEMICALS - AGRICULTURAL

SEE Fertilizers & Pesticides p. 1635

143 CHEMICALS - INDUSTRIAL (INORGANIC)

Company	City	State	ZIP	Phone	Fax
Air Liquide America LP 2700 Post Oak Blvd Suite 1800	Houston	TX	77056	713-624-8000	624-8793*
**Fax:* Mktg ■ *TF:* 877-855-9533 ■ *Web:* www.airliquide.com					
Air Products & Chemicals Inc 7201 Hamilton Blvd	Allentown	PA	18195	610-481-4911	481-3855*
NYSE: APD ■ **Fax:* Sales ■ *TF Prod Info:* 800-345-3148 ■ *Web:* www.airproducts.com					
Akzo Nobel Inc 525 W Van Buren St	Chicago	IL	60607	312-544-7000	544-7198
TF Cust Svc: 800-227-7070 ■ *Web:* www.akzonobelusa.com					
Almatis Inc 501 W Park Rd	Leetsdale	PA	15056	412-630-2800	630-2900
TF: 800-643-8771 ■ *Web:* www.almatis.com					
American Chemet Corp 740 Waukegan Rd	Deerfield	IL	60015	847-948-0800	948-0811
Web: www.chemet.com					
Americhem Inc 225 Broadway St E	Cuyahoga Falls	OH	44221	330-929-4213	929-4144
TF: 800-228-3476 ■ *Web:* www.americhem.com					
Ampacet Corp 660 White Plains Rd	Tarrytown	NY	10591	914-631-6600	631-7197
TF Cust Svc: 800-888-4267 ■ *Web:* www.ampacet.com					
Arkema Inc 2000 Market St	Philadelphia	PA	19103	215-419-7000	419-7591
TF: 800-533-5552					
Ashta Chemicals Inc 3509 Middle Rd	Ashtabula	OH	44004	440-997-5221	992-0151
TF Cust Svc: 800-492-5082 ■ *Web:* www.ashtachemicals.com					
Astaris LLC 622 Emerson Rd Suite 500	Saint Louis	MO	63141	314-983-7500	
Web: www.astaris.com					
BASF Canada 100 Milverton Dr 5th Fl	Mississauga	ON	L5R4H1	289-360-1300	360-6000
TF Cust Svc: 800-267-2955 ■ *Web:* www.basf.ca					
BASF Corp 100 Campus Dr	Florham Park	NJ	07932	973-245-6000	895-8002
NYSE: BF ■ *TF:* 800-526-1072 ■ *Web:* www.basf.com					
Bio-Lab Inc 1735 N Brown Rd	Lawrenceville	GA	30043	678-502-4000	502-4702
TF: 800-859-7946					
BOC Gases America 575 Mountain Ave	Murray Hill	NJ	07974	908-464-8100	771-1701
TF Cust Svc: 800-262-4273 ■ *Web:* www.boc.com/gases					
BOC Group 575 Mountain Ave	Murray Hill	NJ	07974	908-665-2400	464-9015
TF: 800-932-0803 ■ *Web:* www.boc.com					
BWX Technologies Inc 1570 Mt Athos Rd	Lynchburg	VA	24504	434-522-6000	522-5922
Web: www.bwxt.com					
Cabot Corp 2 Seaport Ln Suite 1300	Boston	MA	02210	617-345-0100	342-6103
NYSE: CBT ■ *TF:* 800-853-5407 ■ *Web:* w1.cabot-corp.com					
Calgon Carbon Corp 500 Calgon Carbon Dr	Pittsburgh	PA	15205	412-787-6700	787-6737
NYSE: CCC ■ *TF Cust Svc:* 800-422-7266 ■ *Web:* www.calgoncarbon.com					
Carus Corp 315 5th St	Peru	IL	61354	815-223-1500	224-6697
TF: 800-435-6856 ■ *Web:* www.caruschem.com					
CDR Pigments & Dispersions 305 Ring Rd	Elizabethtown	KY	42701	270-737-1700	737-0318
TF: 800-898-3421 ■ *Web:* www.cdrpigments.com					
Chemical Products Corp 102 Old Mill Rd	Cartersville	GA	30120	770-382-2144	386-6053
Web: www.chemicalproductscorp.com					
Cormetech Inc 5000 International Dr	Durham	NC	27712	919-620-3000	620-3001
Web: www.cormetech.com					
Criterion Catalysts & Technologies					
16825 Northchase Dr Suite 1000	Houston	TX	77060	281-874-2600	874-2641
TF: 800-777-2650 ■ *Web:* www.criterioncatalysts.com					
Dow Chemical Co 2030 Dow Ctr	Midland	MI	48674	989-636-1000	636-3518
NYSE: DOW ■ *TF Cust Svc:* 800-331-6451 ■ *Web:* www.dow.com					
DuPont Titanium Technologies 1007 Market St	Wilmington	DE	19898	302-774-1000	999-5166
TF: 800-441-7515 ■ *Web:* www.titanium.dupont.com					
Elementis Chromium 3800 Buddy Lawrence Dr	Corpus Christi	TX	78407	361-883-6421	883-5145
TF Cust Svc: 800-531-3188 ■ *Web:* www.elementis.com/divisions/chromium.html					
Elementis Pigments Inc 2051 Lynch Ave	East Saint Louis	IL	62204	618-646-2110	646-2178
TF Cust Svc: 800-323-7796 ■ *Web:* www.elementis.com/divisions/pigments.html					
EMD Chemicals Inc 480 S Democrat Rd	Gibbstown	NJ	08027	856-423-6300	423-4389
TF Cust Svc: 800-222-0342 ■ *Web:* www.emdchemicals.com					
Enersul LP 7210 Blackfood Tr SE	Calgary	AB	T2H1M5	403-253-5969	259-2771
Web: www.enersul.com					
Engelhard Corp 101 Wood Ave	Iselin	NJ	08830	732-205-5000	321-1161
NYSE: EC ■ *TF:* 800-631-9505 ■ *Web:* www.engelhard.com					
Erachem Comilog Inc 610 Pittman Rd	Baltimore	MD	21226	410-789-8800	636-7134
TF: 800-789-2686 ■ *Web:* www.erachem-comilog.com					
Ethyl Corp 330 S 4th St	Richmond	VA	23219	804-788-5600	788-5688
TF: 800-403-0044 ■ *Web:* www.ethyl.com					
ExxonMobil Chemical Co 13501 Katy Fwy	Houston	TX	77079	281-870-6000	870-6661
Web: www.exxonmobilchemical.com					
Ferro Corp Color Div 251 W Wylie Ave PO Box 519	Washington	PA	15301	724-223-5900	223-5901
Ferro Corp Electronic Materials Div 4150 E 56th St	Cleveland	OH	44105	216-641-8580	750-7339
FMC Corp 1735 Market St	Philadelphia	PA	19103	215-299-6000	299-5998
NYSE: FMC ■ *Web:* www.fmc.com					
FMC Corp Industrial Chemicals Group 1735 Market St	Philadelphia	PA	19103	215-299-6000	299-6728
TF: 800-323-7107 ■ *Web:* www.fmcchemicals.com					
General Chemical Group Inc 90 E Halsey Rd	Parsippany	NJ	07054	973-515-0900	515-3232
TF Cust Svc: 800-631-8050 ■ *Web:* www.genchem.com					
Georgia Gulf Corp 115 Parimeter Center Pl Suite 460	Atlanta	GA	30346	770-395-4500	395-4529
NYSE: GGC ■ *Web:* www.ggc.com					
Giles Chemical Corp PO Box 370	Waynesville	NC	28786	828-452-4784	452-4786
Web: www.gileschemical.com					
Hammond Lead Products Inc 1414 Field St Bldg B	Hammond	IN	46320	219-931-9360	931-2140
Web: www.hammondlead.com					
Hawkins Inc 3100 E Hennepin Ave	Minneapolis	MN	55413	612-331-6910	331-5304
NASDAQ: HWKN ■ *TF:* 800-328-5460 ■ *Web:* www.hawkinschemical.com					
Henkel Corp 2200 Renaissance Blvd Suite 200	Gulph Mills	PA	19406	610-270-8100	270-8102
TF: 800-521-5317 ■ *Web:* www.henkel.com					
Heucotech Ltd 99 Newbold Rd	Fairless Hills	PA	19030	215-736-0712	736-2249
TF: 800-438-2224					
Horsehead Corp 300 Frankfort Rd	Monaca	PA	15061	724-774-1020	773-2299
TF Cust Svc: 800-648-8897 ■ *Web:* www.horsehead.net					
INEOS Silicas Americas 111 Ingalls Ave	Joliet	IL	60435	815-727-3651	727-5312
TF: 800-775-3651 ■ *Web:* www.ineossilicas.com					
Interstate Chemical Co Inc 2797 Freedland Rd	Hermitage	PA	16148	724-981-3771	981-8383
TF: 800-422-2436 ■ *Web:* www.interstatechemical.com					
JCI Jones Chemicals Inc 100 Sunny Sol Blvd	Caledonia	NY	14423	585-538-2314	538-2362
TF: 800-255-3789 ■ *Web:* www.jcichemicals.com					
Johnson Matthey Inc Catalysts & Chemicals Div					
2001 Nolte Dr	West Deptford	NJ	08066	856-853-8000	384-7282
TF: 800-444-1411 ■ *Web:* www.chemicals.matthey.com					
Jones Hamilton Co 30354 Tracy Rd	Walbridge	OH	43465	419-666-9838	662-5049
TF: 877-797-5426 ■ *Web:* www.jones-hamilton.com					
Kemira Chemicals Inc 245 TownPark Dr Suite 200	Kennesaw	GA	30144	770-436-1542	436-3432
TF: 800-347-1542 ■ *Web:* kc.kemira.com					
LSB Industries Inc 16 S Pennsylvania Ave	Oklahoma City	OK	73107	405-235-4546	235-5067
AMEX: LXU ■ *Web:* www.lsb-okc.com					
Martin Marietta Magnesia Specialties Inc					
195 Chesapeake Park Plaza Suite 200	Baltimore	MD	21220	410-780-5500	780-5777
TF: 800-648-7400 ■ *Web:* www.magspecialties.com					
Matheson Tri-Gas Inc 959 Rt 46 E	Parsippany	NJ	07054	973-257-1100	257-9393
Web: www.mathesongas.com					
Minerals Technologies Inc 405 Lexington Ave 20th Fl	New York	NY	10174	212-878-1800	878-1801
NYSE: MTX ■ *Web:* www.mineralstech.com					
National Welders Supply Co Inc 810 Gesco St	Charlotte	NC	28208	704-333-5475	342-0260
TF: 800-866-4422 ■ *Web:* www.nwsco.com					
Nevada Chemicals Inc 9149 S Monroe Plaza Suite B	Sandy	UT	84070	801-984-0228	984-0231
NASDAQ: NCEM ■ *Web:* www.nevadachemicals.com					
NL Industries Inc 16825 Northchase Dr Suite 1200	Houston	TX	77060	281-423-3300	423-3216
NYSE: NL ■ *Web:* www.nl-ind.com					
Norit Americas Inc 3200 W University Ave PO Box 790	Marshall	TX	75671	903-923-1000	938-9701
TF: 800-641-9245 ■ *Web:* www.norit.com					
Noveon Hilton-Davis Inc 2235 Langdon Farm Rd	Cincinnati	OH	45237	513-841-4000	841-3808
TF Cust Svc: 800-477-1022					
Nuclear Fuel Services Inc 1205 Banner Hill Rd	Erwin	TN	37650	423-743-9141	743-9025
Web: www.atnfs.com					
Occidental Chemical Corp 5005 LBJ Fwy	Dallas	TX	75244	972-404-3300	404-3669
TF: 800-570-8880 ■ *Web:* www.oxychem.com					
Occidental Petroleum Corp 10889 Wilshire Blvd	Los Angeles	CA	90024	310-208-8800	443-6690
NYSE: OXY ■ *Web:* www.oxy.com					
Olin Chlor Alkali Products Div Olin Corp 490 Stuart Rd NE	Cleveland	TN	37312	423-336-4850	336-4830
Web: www.chloralkali.com					
Olin Corp Olin Chlor Alkali Products Div 490 Stuart Rd NE	Cleveland	TN	37312	423-336-4850	336-4830
Web: www.chloralkali.com					
Omni Oxide Corp 5929 Lakeside Blvd	Indianapolis	IN	46278	317-290-5000	290-5011
OMYA Inc 100 North Point Ctr E Suite 310	Alpharetta	GA	30022	770-751-7030	751-8629
TF: 800-749-6692 ■ *Web:* www.omya.com					
OMYA Inc 61 Main St	Proctor	VT	05765	802-459-3311	459-6327
TF: 800-451-4468 ■ *Web:* www.omya-na.com					
Phibro Animal Health Corp 65 Challenger Rd 3rd Fl	Ridgefield Park	NJ	07660	201-329-7300	329-7399
TF: 800-223-0434 ■ *Web:* www.phibrochem.com					
Pioneer Cos Inc 700 Louisiana St Suite 4300	Houston	TX	77002	713-570-3200	225-6475
NASDAQ: PONR ■ *TF:* 800-423-4117 ■ *Web:* www.piona.com					
Potash Corp 1101 Skokie Blvd	Northbrook	IL	60062	847-849-4200	849-4695
TF: 800-645-2183 ■ *Web:* www.potashcorp.com					
Potash Corp of Saskatchewan Inc 122 1st Ave S Suite 500	Saskatoon	SK	S7K7G3	306-933-8500	933-8844
NYSE: POT ■ *TF:* 800-667-3930 ■ *Web:* www.potashcorp.com					
PQ Corp 1200 W Swedes Ford Rd	Berwyn	PA	19312	610-651-4200	651-4504
TF Cust Svc: 800-944-7411 ■ *Web:* www.pqcorp.com					
Praxair Inc 39 Old Ridgebury Rd	Danbury	CT	06810	203-837-2000	837-2731
NYSE: PX ■ *TF:* 800-772-9247 ■ *Web:* www.praxair.com					
Reheis Inc 235 Snyder Ave	Berkeley Heights	NJ	07922	908-464-1500	464-7726
Web: www.reheis.com					
Rutgers Organics Corp 201 Struble Rd	State College	PA	16801	814-238-2424	238-1567
TF: 800-458-3434 ■ *Web:* www.ruetgers-organics-corp.com					
Schlenk-Both Metallic Pigments 40 Nickerson Rd	Ashland	MA	01721	508-881-4100	881-1278
TF: 800-288-2684 ■ *Web:* www.schlenkboth.com					
Sensient Colors Inc 2526 Baldwin St	Saint Louis	MO	63106	314-889-7600	658-7318
TF: 800-325-8110					
Shepherd Chemical Co 4900 Beech St	Cincinnati	OH	45212	513-731-1110	731-1532
Web: www.shepchem.com					
Silberline Mfg Co Inc 130 Lincoln Dr PO Box B	Tamaqua	PA	18252	570-668-6050	668-0197
TF: 800-348-4824 ■ *Web:* www.silberline.com					
Solutia Inc 575 Maryville Centre Dr	Saint Louis	MO	63141	314-674-1000	674-1585*
**Fax:* Hum Res ■ *TF:* 800-325-4330 ■ *Web:* www.solutia.com					
Solvay America Inc 3333 Richmond Ave	Houston	TX	77098	713-525-6000	525-7887
TF: 800-231-6313 ■ *Web:* www.solvay.com					
Solvay Interox Inc 3333 Richmond Ave	Houston	TX	77098	713-525-6500	524-9032
TF: 800-468-3769 ■ *Web:* www.solvayinterox.com					
Sud-Chemie Inc 1600 W Hill St	Louisville	KY	40210	502-634-7200	637-3732
TF: 800-626-5355 ■ *Web:* www.sud-chemieinc.com					
Synalloy Corp 2155 W Croft Cir	Spartanburg	SC	29302	864-585-3605	596-1501
NASDAQ: SYNL ■ *TF Orders:* 800-763-1001 ■ *Web:* www.synalloy.com					
Tanner Systems Inc PO Box 488	Saint Joseph	MN	56374	320-363-1800	362-1812
TF: 800-461-6454 ■ *Web:* www.tannersystems.com					
TETRA Technologies Inc 25025 I-45 N	The Woodlands	TX	77380	281-367-1983	364-4306
NYSE: TTI ■ *TF:* 800-327-7817 ■ *Web:* www.tetratec.com					
Texas United Corp 4800 San Felipe St	Houston	TX	77056	713-877-1793	877-2664
TF: 800-554-8658					
TOR Minerals International Inc 722 Burleson St	Corpus Christi	TX	78302	361-882-5175	883-7619
NASDAQ: TORM ■ *TF:* 888-464-0147 ■ *Web:* www.torminerals.com					
Tronox Inc 211 N Robinson St 1 Leadership Sq	Oklahoma City	OK	73102	405-775-5000	775-5155
NYSE: TRX ■ *TF:* 866-775-5009 ■ *Web:* www.tronox.com					
UOP LLC 25 E Algonquin Rd	Des Plaines	IL	60017	847-391-2000	391-2253
TF: 800-877-6184 ■ *Web:* www.uop.com					
US Borax Inc 26877 Tourney Rd	Valencia	CA	91355	661-287-5400	287-5495
TF: 800-533-4872 ■ *Web:* www.borax.com					
USEC Inc 6903 Rockledge Dr 4th Fl	Bethesda	MD	20817	301-564-3200	564-3201
NYSE: USU ■ *TF:* 800-273-7754 ■ *Web:* www.usec.com					
Vulcan Materials Co					
1200 Urban Center Dr PO Box 385014	Birmingham	AL	35238	205-298-3000	298-2942
NYSE: VMC ■ *Web:* www.vulcanmaterials.com					
Westlake Chemical Corp 2801 Post Oak Blvd Suite 600	Houston	TX	77056	713-960-9111	963-1562
NYSE: WLK ■ *Web:* www.westlakechemical.com					

144 CHEMICALS - INDUSTRIAL (ORGANIC)

Company	City	State	Zip	Phone	Fax
Altair Nanotechnologies Inc 204 Edison Way *NASDAQ: ALTI* ■ *Web:* www.altairinc.com	Reno	NV	89502	775-856-2500	856-1619
American Natural Soda Ash Corp 15 Riverside Ave *Web:* www.ansac.com	Westport	CT	06880	203-226-9056	227-1484
Ampacet Corp 660 White Plains Rd *TF Cust Svc:* 800-888-4267 ■ *Web:* www.ampacet.com	Tarrytown	NY	10591	914-631-6600	631-7197
Arizona Chemical Co Inc PO Box 550850 **Fax:* Cust Svc ■ *Web:* www.arizonachemical.com	Jacksonville	FL	32255	904-928-8700	928-8778*
Arkema Inc 2000 Market St *TF:* 800-533-5552	Philadelphia	PA	19103	215-419-7000	419-7591
ATOFINA Petrochemicals Inc 15710 JFK Blvd **Fax:* Sales	Houston	TX	77032	281-227-5000	227-5200*
BASF Canada 100 Milverton Dr 5th Fl *TF Cust Svc:* 800-267-2955 ■ *Web:* www.basf.ca	Mississauga	ON	L5R4H1	289-360-1300	360-6000
BASF Corp 100 Campus Dr *NYSE: BF* ■ *TF:* 800-526-1072 ■ *Web:* www.basf.com	Florham Park	NJ	07932	973-245-6000	895-8002
Bayer Corp 100 Bayer Rd *NYSE: BAY* ■ *TF:* 800-662-2927 ■ *Web:* www.bayerus.com	Pittsburgh	PA	15205	412-777-2000	778-4430
Bayer Corp Chemicals Div 100 Bayer Rd *TF:* 800-662-2927 ■ *Web:* www.bayerus.com/industrial	Pittsburgh	PA	15205	412-777-2000	777-7626
Bayer Inc 77 Belfield Rd **Fax:* Hum Res ■ *TF:* 800-622-2937 ■ *Web:* bayer.ca	Toronto	ON	M9W1G6	416-248-0771	248-1297*
Blackman Uhler LLC 2155 W Croft Cir *TF:* 800-832-8985 ■ *Web:* www.blackmanuhler.com	Spartanburg	SC	29302	864-585-3661	596-1501
BP Plc 28100 Torch Pkwy *NYSE: BP* ■ **Fax Area Code:* 281 ■ *TF:* 866-427-6947 ■ *Web:* www.bp.com	Warrenville	IL	60555	630-420-5111	298-0738*
Cambrex Corp 1 Meadowlands Plaza 15th Fl *NYSE: CBM* ■ *TF:* 800-638-8174 ■ *Web:* www.cambrex.com	East Rutherford	NJ	07073	201-804-3000	804-9852
Celanese Corp 1601 W LBJ Fwy *NYSE: CE* ■ *Web:* www.celanese.com	Dallas	TX	75234	972-443-4000	443-8557
ChemDesign Corp 99 Development Rd *Web:* www.chemdesigncorp.com	Fitchburg	MA	01420	978-345-9999	342-9769
Chemical Exchange Industries Inc 900 Clinton Dr PO Box 67 *Web:* www.cxi.com	Galena Park	TX	77547	713-526-8291	455-8959
Chemstar Products Co 3915 Hiawatha Ave *TF:* 800-328-5037 ■ *Web:* www.chemstar.com	Minneapolis	MN	55406	612-722-0079	722-2473
Chevron Phillips Chemical Co LP 10001 Six Pines Dr *TF:* 800-231-1212 ■ *Web:* www.cpchem.com	The Woodlands	TX	77380	832-813-4100	
Clariant Corp 4000 Monroe Rd *TF Cust Svc:* 800-631-8077 ■ *Web:* www.clariant-northamerica.com	Charlotte	NC	28205	704-331-7000	377-1063
Cognis Corp 5051 Estecreek Dr *TF Cust Svc:* 800-254-1029 ■ *Web:* www.na.cognis.com	Cincinnati	OH	45232	513-482-3000	482-5503
Colgate-Palmolive Co Institutional Products Div 191 E Hanover Ave **Fax:* Hum Res ■ *TF:* 888-276-0783	Morristown	NJ	07962	973-630-1500	292-6172*
Colorcon Inc 415 Moyer Blvd *Web:* www.colorcon.com	West Point	PA	19486	215-699-7733	661-2605
Corsicana Technologies Inc 2733 E Hwy 31 *TF:* 800-477-5353 ■ *Web:* www.corsicanatech.com	Corsicana	TX	75110	903-874-9500	874-9595
CP Hall Co 120 S Riverside Plaza Suite 1620 *TF:* 800-762-6198 ■ *Web:* www.cphall.com	Chicago	IL	60606	312-554-7400	554-7499
Dow Chemical Canada Inc 450 1st St SW Suite 2100 *TF:* 800-433-4398 ■ *Web:* www.dowcanada.com	Calgary	AB	T2P5H1	403-267-3500	267-3597
Dow Chemical Co 2030 Dow Ctr *NYSE: DOW* ■ *TF Cust Svc:* 800-331-6451 ■ *Web:* www.dow.com	Midland	MI	48674	989-636-1000	636-3518
Dow Corning Corp PO Box 994 **Fax:* Hum Res ■ *TF Cust Svc:* 800-248-2481 ■ *Web:* www.dowcorning.com	Midland	MI	48686	989-496-4000	496-1886*
DSM Chemicals North America Inc 1 Columbia Nitrogen Rd **Fax:* Cust Svc ■ *TF:* 800-825-4376 ■ *Web:* www.dsm.com	Augusta	GA	30901	706-849-6600	849-6760*
Eastman Chemical Co 200 S Wilcox Dr *NYSE: EMN* ■ **Fax:* Mktg ■ *TF Cust Svc:* 800-327-8626 ■ *Web:* www.eastman.com	Kingsport	TN	37660	423-229-2000	229-1194*
Elan Chemical Co 268 Doremus Ave *Web:* www.elan-chemical.com	Newark	NJ	07105	973-344-8014	344-1948
EMD Chemicals Inc 480 S Democrat Rd *TF Cust Svc:* 800-222-0342 ■ *Web:* www.emdchemicals.com	Gibbstown	NJ	08027	856-423-6300	423-4389
Equistar Chemicals LP PO Box 2583 *Web:* www.equistarchem.com	Houston	TX	77252	713-652-7300	
Ferro Corp Grant Chemical Div 111 W Irene Rd *TF:* 800-325-3578 ■ *Web:* www.ferro.com	Zachary	LA	70791	225-654-6801	654-3268
Ferro Corp Polymer Additives Div 7050 Krick Rd **Fax Area Code:* 440 ■ *TF:* 800-321-9946	Walton Hills	OH	44146	216-641-8580	439-7686*
First Chemical Corp 1001 Industrial Rd *Web:* www.firstchem.com	Pascagoula	MS	39581	228-762-0870	769-5355
GE Advanced Materials 1 Plastics Ave *Web:* www.geadvancedmaterials.com	Pittsfield	MA	01201	413-448-7110	448-5573
GE Petrochemicals Inc SR 892 *TF Cust Svc:* 800-643-4346 ■ *Web:* www.geplastics.com/petrochemicals	Washington	WV	26181	304-863-7778	863-7791
GE Silicones 260 Hudson River Rd *TF Cust Svc:* 800-332-3390 ■ *Web:* www.gesilicones.com	Waterford	NY	12188	518-237-3330	233-2307
Georgia-Pacific Corp 133 Peachtree St NE *Web:* www.gp.com	Atlanta	GA	30303	404-652-4000	230-5774
Grant Chemical Div Ferro Corp 111 W Irene Rd *TF:* 800-325-3578 ■ *Web:* www.ferro.com	Zachary	LA	70791	225-654-6801	654-3268
Hall CP Co 120 S Riverside Plaza Suite 1620 *TF:* 800-762-6198 ■ *Web:* www.cphall.com	Chicago	IL	60606	312-554-7400	554-7499
Hercules Inc 1313 N Market St Hercules Plaza *NYSE: HPC* ■ *TF:* 800-441-7600 ■ *Web:* www.herc.com	Wilmington	DE	19894	302-594-5000	594-5400
Heucotech Ltd 99 Newbold Rd *TF:* 800-438-2224	Fairless Hills	PA	19030	215-736-0712	736-2249
Huntsman Corp 500 Huntsman Way *NYSE: HUN* ■ *TF:* 800-421-2411 ■ *Web:* www.huntsman.com	Salt Lake City	UT	84108	801-584-5700	584-5781
ICC Industries Inc 460 Park Ave *TF:* 800-422-1720 ■ *Web:* www.iccchem.com	New York	NY	10022	212-521-1700	521-1794
Indspec Chemical Corp 411 7th Ave Suite 300 *Web:* www.indspec-chem.com	Pittsburgh	PA	15219	412-765-1200	765-0439
Innospec Inc 200 Executive Dr *NYSE: IOP* ■ *Web:* www.octel-corp.com	Newark	DE	19702	302-454-8100	451-1380
Inolex Chemical Co 2101 S Swanson St **Fax:* Cust Svc ■ *TF Cust Svc:* 800-521-9891 ■ *Web:* www.inolex.com	Philadelphia	PA	19148	215-271-0800	271-6282*
International Flavors & Fragrances Inc 521 W 57th St *NYSE: IFF* ■ *Web:* www.iff.com	New York	NY	10019	212-765-5500	708-7132
International Specialty Products Inc 1361 Alps Rd *TF:* 800-365-7353 ■ *Web:* www.ispcorp.com	Wayne	NJ	07470	973-628-4000	628-3311
JLM Industries Inc 8675 Hidden River Pkwy *TF:* 800-457-3743 ■ *Web:* www.jlmgroup.com	Tampa	FL	33637	813-632-3300	632-3301
Kingsford Products Co PO Box 24305 *Web:* www.kingsford.com	Oakland	CA	94623	510-271-7000	832-1463
Lyondell Chemical Co 1221 McKinney St *NYSE: LYO* ■ *Web:* www.lyondell.com	Houston	TX	77010	713-652-7200	652-4686
Magruder Color Co Inc 1029 Newark Ave *TF:* 800-631-4461 ■ *Web:* www.magruder.com	Elizabeth	NJ	07208	973-242-1300	242-4087
Merichem Co 5455 Old Spanish Trail *Web:* www.merichem.com	Houston	TX	77023	713-428-5000	926-3634
Methanex Corp 200 Burrard St Suite 1800 *NASDAQ: MEOH* ■ *TF:* 800-900-6384 ■ *Web:* www.methanex.com	Vancouver	BC	V6C3M1	604-661-2600	661-2676
Millennium Chemicals Inc 20 Wight Ave Suite 100 *TF:* 866-225-5642 ■ *Web:* www.millenniumchem.com	Hunt Valley	MD	21030	410-229-4400	229-5003
Mitsubishi Chemical America Inc 1 N Lexington Ave 16th Fl *Web:* www.mitsubishichemical.com	White Plains	NY	10601	914-286-3600	286-3677
Mitsui Chemicals America Inc 800 Westchester Ave **Fax:* PR ■ *TF:* 800-682-2377 ■ *Web:* mitsuichemicals.com	Rye Brook	NY	10573	914-253-0777	253-0790*
Morflex Inc 2110 High Point Rd *Web:* www.morflex.com	Greensboro	NC	27403	336-292-1781	854-4058
Niacet Corp 400 47th St *TF:* 800-828-1207 ■ *Web:* www.niacet.com	Niagara Falls	NY	14304	716-285-1474	285-1497
Perstorp Polyols Inc 600 Matzinger Rd *TF Cust Svc:* 800-537-0280 ■ *Web:* www.perstorppolyols.com	Toledo	OH	43612	419-729-5448	729-3291
PMC Specialties Group Inc 501 Murray Rd *TF:* 800-543-2466 ■ *Web:* www.pmcsg.com	Cincinnati	OH	45217	513-242-3300	482-7315
PPG Industries Inc 1 PPG Pl *NYSE: PPG* ■ **Fax:* Hum Res ■ *Web:* www.ppg.com	Pittsburgh	PA	15272	412-434-3131	434-2011*
Rhodia Inc 8 Cedar Brook Dr CN 7500 **Fax:* Cust Svc ■ *TF Cust Svc:* 888-776-7337 ■ *Web:* www.us.rhodia.com	Cranbury	NJ	08512	609-860-4000	860-0138*
RT Vanderbilt Co Inc 30 Winfield St *TF Cust Svc:* 800-243-6064 ■ *Web:* www.rtvanderbilt.com	Norwalk	CT	06855	203-853-1400	853-1452
Sasol North America Inc 900 Threadneedle St Suite 100 *Web:* www.sasolnorthamerica.com	Houston	TX	77079	281-588-3000	588-3144
Sensient Colors Inc 2526 Baldwin St *TF:* 800-325-8110	Saint Louis	MO	63106	314-889-7600	658-7318
Shell Chemical Co 910 Louisiana St *Web:* www.shellchemicals.com	Houston	TX	77002	713-241-6161	241-4044
Shin-Etsu Silicones of America 1150 Damar Dr *TF:* 800-544-1745 ■ *Web:* www.shinetsusilicones.com	Akron	OH	44305	330-630-9860	630-9855
Sloss Industries Corp 3500 35th Ave N **Fax:* Sales ■ *Web:* www.sloss.com	Birmingham	AL	35207	205-808-7806	808-7715*
Solutia Inc 575 Maryville Centre Dr **Fax:* Hum Res ■ *TF:* 800-325-4330 ■ *Web:* www.solutia.com	Saint Louis	MO	63141	314-674-1000	674-1585*
Sun Chemical Corp 35 Waterview Blvd *Web:* www.sunchemical.com	Parsippany	NJ	07054	973-404-6000	404-6001
Sunoco Chemicals 1735 Market St Suite LL *TF:* 800-786-6261 ■ *Web:* www.sunocochem.com	Philadelphia	PA	19103	215-977-3321	977-3470
Sunoco Inc 1735 Market St Suite LL *NYSE: SUN* ■ *TF:* 800-786-6261 ■ *Web:* www.sunocoinc.com	Philadelphia	PA	19103	215-977-3000	977-3409
Synalloy Corp 2155 W Croft Cir *NASDAQ: SYNL* ■ *TF Orders:* 800-763-1001 ■ *Web:* www.synalloy.com	Spartanburg	SC	29302	864-585-3605	596-1501
Texas Petrochemicals LP 3 Riverway Suite 1500 *TF:* 877-584-3256 ■ *Web:* www.txpetrochem.com	Houston	TX	77056	713-627-7474	626-3650
Vanderbilt Chemical Corp 30 Winfield St *TF:* 800-243-6064	Norwalk	CT	06855	203-853-1400	853-1452
Vanderbilt RT Co Inc 30 Winfield St *TF Cust Svc:* 800-243-6064 ■ *Web:* www.rtvanderbilt.com	Norwalk	CT	06855	203-853-1400	853-1452
Velsicol Chemical Corp 10400 W Higgins Rd Suite 600 *TF Cust Svc:* 800-843-7759 ■ *Web:* www.velsicol.com	Rosemont	IL	60018	847-298-9000	298-9018
Vulcan Materials Co 1200 Urban Center Dr PO Box 385014 *NYSE: VMC* ■ *Web:* www.vulcanmaterials.com	Birmingham	AL	35238	205-298-3000	298-2942
Wacker Chemical Corp DBA Wacker Silicones 3301 Sutton Rd *TF:* 800-248-0063 ■ *Web:* www.wackersilicones.com	Adrian	MI	49221	517-264-8500	264-8246
Wausau Chemical Corp 2001 N River Dr *TF:* 800-950-6656 ■ *Web:* www.wausauchemical.com	Wausau	WI	54403	715-842-2285	842-9059
Western Polymer Corp 32 Rd 'R' SE *Web:* www.westernpolymer.com	Moses Lake	WA	98837	509-765-1803	765-0327

CHEMICALS - MEDICINAL

SEE Medicinal Chemicals & Botanical Products p. 1957

145 CHEMICALS - SPECIALTY

Company	City	State	Zip	Phone	Fax
ADA-ES Inc 8100 Southpark Way Suite B *NASDAQ: ADES* ■ *TF:* 888-822-8617 ■ *Web:* www.adaes.com	Littleton	CO	80120	303-734-1727	734-0330
Afton Chemical Corp 330 S 4th St *Web:* www.aftonchemical.com	Richmond	VA	23219	804-788-5800	788-5184
Airosol Co Inc 1101 Illinois St PO Box 120 *TF:* 800-633-9576 ■ *Web:* www.airosol.com	Neodesha	KS	66757	620-325-2666	325-2602
Albemarle Corp 330 S 4th St *NYSE: ALB* ■ *Web:* www.albemarle.com	Richmond	VA	23219	804-788-6000	788-6020
Alex C Fergusson Inc 5000 Letterkenny Rd Suite 220 *TF:* 800-345-1329 ■ *Web:* www.afco.net	Chambersburg	PA	17201	717-264-9147	264-9182
Alfa Aesar Co 26 Parkridge Rd 2nd Fl **Fax Area Code:* 800 ■ *TF:* 800-343-0660 ■ *Web:* www.alfa.com	Ward Hill	MA	01835	978-521-6300	322-4757*
Allied Diagnostic Imaging Resources Inc 5440-A Oakbrook Pkwy *TF:* 800-262-9333 ■ *Web:* www.alliedautex.com	Norcross	GA	30093	770-448-0250	448-0257
Altana Inc 60 Baylis Rd *Web:* www.altana.com	Melville	NY	11747	631-454-7677	756-7017
AM Todd Co 1717 Douglas Ave *TF:* 800-968-2603 ■ *Web:* www.amtodd.com	Kalamazoo	MI	49007	269-343-2603	343-3399
American Pacific Corp (AMPAC) 3770 Howard Hughes Pkwy Suite 300 *NASDAQ: APFC* ■ *Web:* www.american-pacific-corp.com	Las Vegas	NV	89169	702-735-2200	735-4876
American Polywater Corp 5630 Memorial Ave Suite 2 *TF:* 800-328-9384 ■ *Web:* www.polywater.com/	Stillwater	MN	55082	651-430-2270	430-3634
American Vanguard Corp 4695 MacArthur Ct Suite 1250 *AMEX: AVD* ■ *Web:* www.amvac-chemical.com	Newport Beach	CA	92660	949-260-1200	
Ameron International Corp 245 S Los Robles Ave *NYSE: AMN* ■ *Web:* www.ameron.com	Pasadena	CA	91101	626-683-4000	683-4060
Ameron/PPG Industries 1200 Bluegrass Lakes Pkwy Suite 100 **Fax:* PR ■ *TF:* 800-926-3766 ■ *Web:* www.ppg.com	Alpharetta	GA	30004	678-393-0653	393-2699*
AMJAY Chemicals PO Box 218786	Houston	TX	77218	281-492-2000	
AMPAC (American Pacific Corp) 3770 Howard Hughes Pkwy Suite 300 *NASDAQ: APFC* ■ *Web:* www.american-pacific-corp.com	Las Vegas	NV	89169	702-735-2200	735-4876
AMPAC Fine Chemicals Hwy 50 Aerojet Rd PO Box 1718 MS 1007 *Web:* www.ampacfinechemicals.com	Rancho Cordova	CA	95741	916-355-4000	355-5045
AMREP Inc 990 Industrial Park Dr *TF Cust Svc:* 800-241-7766 ■ *Web:* www.amrep.com	Marietta	GA	30062	770-422-2071	422-1737

Phone Fax

Anderson Chemical Co 325 S Davis Ave PO Box 1041 .... Litchfield MN 55355 320-693-2477 693-8238
TF: 800-366-2477 ■ *Web:* www.andersonchemco.com
Anderson Development Co 1415 E Michigan St.................. Adrian MI 49221 517-263-2121 263-1000
Web: www.andersondevelopment.com
Angstrom Technologies Inc
1895 Airport Exchange Blvd Suite 110 .... Erlanger KY 41018 859-282-0020 282-8577
TF Cust Svc: 800-543-7358 ■ *Web:* www.angstromtechnologies.com
Anzon Co Inc 12326 Denholm Dr .... El Monte CA 91732 626-443-8861 444-7005
Web: www.anzon.com
Apollo Chemical Co LLC 1105 Southerland St.................. Graham NC 27253 336-226-1161 226-7494
TF: 800-374-3827 ■ *Web:* www.apollochemical.com
Arch Chemicals Inc 501 Merritt Seven PO Box 5204 .... Norwalk CT 06856 203-229-2900 229-2880
NYSE: ARJ ■ *Web:* www.archchemicals.com
Ashland Specialty Chemical Co 5200 Blazer Pkwy .... Dublin OH 43017 614-790-3333 357-3344*
**Fax Area Code: 859* ■ *Web:* www.ashchem.com
Athea Laboratories Inc 7855 N Faulkner Rd PO Box 240014 ..... Milwaukee WI 53224 414-354-6417 354-9219
TF: 800-743-6417 ■ *Web:* www.athea.com
Atlas Refinery Inc 142 Lockwood St .... Newark NJ 07105 973-589-2002 589-7377
Web: www.atlasrefinery.com
Atotech USA Inc 1750 Overview Dr .... Rock Hill SC 29730 803-817-3500 817-3666
TF: 800-752-8464 ■ *Web:* www.atotechusa.com
Baker Hughes Inc Baker Petrolite Div
12645 W Airport Blvd .... Sugar Land TX 77478 281-276-5400 275-7392*
**Fax: Hum Res* ■ *TF:* 800-231-3606 ■ *Web:* www.bakerhughes.com/bakerpetrolite
Baker Petrolite Div Baker Hughes Inc
12645 W Airport Blvd .... Sugar Land TX 77478 281-276-5400 275-7392*
**Fax: Hum Res* ■ *TF:* 800-231-3606 ■ *Web:* www.bakerhughes.com/bakerpetrolite
Barclay Water Management Inc 150 Coolidge Ave .... Watertown MA 02472 617-926-3400 924-5467
Web: www.barclaywm.com
Baroid Drilling Fluids 3000 N Sam Houston Pkwy E Bldg J .... Houston TX 77032 281-871-5900 871-5565*
**Fax: Hum Res* ■ *Web:* www.baroid.com
BASF Admixture Systems 23700 Chagrin Blvd .... Beachwood OH 44122 216-839-7500 839-8821
TF: 800-628-9990 ■ *Web:* www.basf-admixtures.com
BASF Wall Systems 3550 St Johns Bluff Rd S............... Jacksonville FL 32224 904-996-6000 996-6300
TF: 800-221-9255 ■ *Web:* www.basfwallsystems.com
Benchmark Inc 4660 13th St .... Wyandotte MI 48192 734-285-0900 285-4236
TF: 800-521-9107 ■ *Web:* www.thebenchmarkprocess.com
Bercen Inc 1381 Cranston St .... Cranston RI 02920 401-943-7400 943-2640
TF: 800-525-0595 ■ *Web:* www.bercen.com
BG Products Inc 740 S Wichita St PO Box 1282 .... Wichita KS 67201 316-265-2686 265-1082
TF: 800-961-6228 ■ *Web:* www.bgprod.com
Birchwood Laboratories Inc 7900 Fuller Rd................ Eden Prairie MN 55344 952-937-7900 937-7979
TF: 800-328-6156 ■ *Web:* www.birchwoodcasey.com
Blue Grass Chemical Specialties LP 895 Industrial Blvd........ New Albany IN 47150 812-948-1115 948-1561
TF: 800-638-7197
Brewster Foods Inc 7121 Candy Ave PO Box 306................ Reseda CA 91335 818-881-4268 881-6370
Web: www.testlabinc.com
Brulin & Co Inc 2920 Dr AJ Brown Ave.................... Indianapolis IN 46205 317-923-3211 925-4596
TF: 800-776-7149 ■ *Web:* www.brulin.com
Buckman Laboratories Inc 1256 N McLean Blvd................ Memphis TN 38108 901-278-0330 276-5343
TF: 800-282-5626 ■ *Web:* www.buckman.com
Cabot Corp 2 Seaport Ln Suite 1300 .... Boston MA 02210 617-345-0100 342-6103
NYSE: CBT ■ *TF:* 800-853-5407 ■ *Web:* w1.cabot-corp.com
Cabot Microelectronics Corp 870 N Commons Dr .... Aurora IL 60504 630-375-6631 375-5539
NASDAQ: CCMP ■ *TF:* 800-811-2756 ■ *Web:* www.cabotcmp.com
Cabot Specialty Fluids
10001 Woodlock Forest Dr Suite 275 .... The Woodlands TX 77380 281-298-9955 298-6190
TF: 888-273-7455 ■ *Web:* www.cabot-corp.com/csf
Cal-Pac Chemical Co Inc 6231 Maywood Ave............ Huntington Park CA 90255 323-585-2178 585-3087
Champion Technologies Inc 3200 Southwest Fwy Suite 2700 ...... Houston TX 77027 713-627-3303 627-7603
Web: www.champ-tech.com
Chem Lab Products Inc 5160 E Airport Dr....................... Ontario CA 91761 909-390-9912 390-9911
TF: 800-745-4536 ■ *Web:* www.kem-tek.com
Chemetall Oakite 50 Valley Rd...................... Berkeley Heights NJ 07922 908-464-6900 464-4658
TF: 800-526-4473 ■ *Web:* www.oakite.com
Chemical Packaging Corp 2700 SW 14th St............. Pompano Beach FL 33069 954-974-5440 977-7513
TF Cust Svc: 800-327-1835 ■ *Web:* www.cpcaerosols.com
Chemtool Inc 8200 Ridgefield Rd......................... Crystal Lake IL 60039 815-459-1250 459-1955
Web: www.chemtool.com
Chemtura Corp 199 Benson Rd.............................. Middlebury CT 06749 203-573-2000 573-3323
NYSE: CEM ■ *Web:* www.chemtura.com
CHT R Beitlich Corp 5046 Old Pineville Rd .... Charlotte NC 28217 704-523-4242 522-8142
TF: 800-277-4941 ■ *Web:* www.cht-group.com
Ciba Specialty Chemicals 540 White Plains Rd................. Tarrytown NY 10591 914-785-2000 785-4535*
**Fax: Cust Svc* ■ *TF:* 800-431-1900 ■ *Web:* www.cibasc.com
Citrus & Allied Essences Ltd 3000 Marcus Ave Ste 3E11...... Lake Success NY 11042 516-354-1200 354-1262
Web: www.citrusandallied.com
Claire Mfg Co 500 Vista Ave.............................. Addison IL 60101 630-543-7600 543-4310
TF Sales: 800-252-4731 ■ *Web:* www.clairemfg.com
Clariant Corp 4000 Monroe Rd.............................. Charlotte NC 28205 704-331-7000 377-1063
TF Cust Svc: 800-631-8077 ■ *Web:* www.clariant-northamerica.com
Cognis Corp 5051 Estecreek Dr.......................... Cincinnati OH 45232 513-482-3000 482-5503
TF Cust Svc: 800-254-1029 ■ *Web:* www.na.cognis.com
Columbian Chemicals Co 1800 W Oak Commons Ct............. Marietta GA 30062 770-792-9400 792-9623
TF: 800-235-4003 ■ *Web:* www.columbianchemicals.com
Contact Industries Inc 641 Dowd Ave .... Elizabeth NJ 07201 908-351-5900 351-6037
Coral Chemical Co 1915 Industrial Blvd.......................... Zion IL 60099 847-246-6666 246-6667
TF: 800-228-4646 ■ *Web:* www.coral.com
Cortec Corp 4119 White Bear Pkwy .... Saint Paul MN 55110 651-429-1100 429-1122
TF: 800-426-7832 ■ *Web:* www.cortecvci.com
CPAC Inc 2364 Leicester Rd .... Leicester NY 14481 585-382-3223 382-3031
NASDAQ: CPAK ■ *TF Cust Svc:* 800-828-6011 ■ *Web:* www.cpac-fuller.com
CRC Industries Inc 885 Louis Dr .... Warminster PA 18974 215-674-4300 674-2196
TF Cust Svc: 800-556-5074 ■ *Web:* www.crcindustries.com
Croda Inc 300-A Columbus Cir.............................. Edison NJ 08837 732-417-0800 417-0804
TF: 888-252-7632 ■ *Web:* www.croda.com
Crystal Inc 601 W 8th St .... Lansdale PA 19446 215-368-1661 368-3205
TF: 800-525-3842
Cytec Industries Inc 5 Garret Mountain Plaza .... West Paterson NJ 07424 973-357-3100 357-3060
NYSE: CYT ■ *Web:* www.cytec.com
Degussa Corp 379 Interpace Pkwy Bldg 2 .... Parsippany NJ 07054 973-541-8000 541-8013
TF: 800-334-8772 ■ *Web:* www.degussa.com
Delta Chemical Corp 2601 Cannery Ave....................... Baltimore MD 21226 410-354-0100 354-1021
TF: 800-282-5322 ■ *Web:* www.deltachemical.com
Detrex Corp 24901 Northwestern Hwy Suite 410............... Southfield MI 48075 248-358-5800 799-7192
Web: www.detrex.com
Dexter Chemical LLC 845 Edgewater Rd .... Bronx NY 10474 718-542-7700 991-7684
TF: 800-339-9111 ■ *Web:* www.dexterchem.com
Diversified Chemical Technologies Inc
15477 Woodrow Wilson St .... Detroit MI 48238 313-867-5444 867-3831
TF: 800-243-1424 ■ *Web:* www.diversifiedchemicalinc.com
Dober Chemical Group 11230 Katherine Crossing .... Woodridge IL 60517 630-410-7300 410-7444
TF: 800-323-4983 ■ *Web:* www.dobergroup.com
Dover Chemical Corp 3000 Sheffield Ave .... Hammond IN 46327 219-931-2630 853-9703
TF: 800-426-3042 ■ *Web:* www.doverchem.com
DSM Desotech Inc 1122 Saint Charles St........................ Elgin IL 60120 847-697-0400 468-7785*
**Fax: Sales* ■ *TF:* 800-223-7191 ■ *Web:* www.desotech.com

DuPont Canada Inc 7070 Mississauga Rd .... Mississauga ON L5N5M8 905-821-3300 821-5110
Web: ca.dupont.com
DuPont Chemical Solutions 1007 Market St .... Wilmington DE 19898 302-774-1000
Eastman Gelatine Corp 227 Washington St .... Peabody MA 01960 978-573-3700 573-3880
Web: www.eastmangelatine.com
EKC Technology Inc 2520 Barrington Ct......................... Hayward CA 94545 510-784-9105 784-9181
Web: www.ekctech.com
ELANTAS PDG INC 5200 N 2nd St........................... Saint Louis MO 63147 314-621-5700 436-1030
TF: 800-325-7492 ■ *Web:* www.elantas.com/pdg
Elementis Specialities Inc
329 Wyckoffs Mill Rd PO Box 700 .... Hightstown NJ 08520 609-443-2500 443-2323
TF: 800-418-5196 ■ *Web:* www.elementisspecialities.com
Eltech Systems Corp 100 7th Ave Suite 300 .... Chardon OH 44024 440-285-0300 285-0302
TF: 800-795-6832 ■ *Web:* www.eltechsystems.com
Enthone Inc 350 Frontage Rd .... West Haven CT 06516 203-934-8611 932-5061
TF: 800-496-8326 ■ *Web:* www.enthone.com
Eureka Chemical Co 234 Lawrence Ave.............. South San Francisco CA 94080 650-761-3536 589-1943
TF: 888-387-3522 ■ *Web:* www.eurekafluidfilm.com
Excelda Mfg Co 12785 Emerson Dr .... Brighton MI 48116 248-486-3800 486-3810
TF: 800-550-4062 ■ *Web:* www.excelda.com
Fabric Chemical Corp 61 Cornelison Ave.................... Jersey City NJ 07304 201-432-0440 432-7997
Fergusson Alex C Inc 5000 Letterkenny Rd Suite 220........ Chambersburg PA 17201 717-264-9147 264-9182
TF: 800-345-1329 ■ *Web:* www.afco.net
Flotek Industries Inc 7030 Empire Central Dr .... Houston TX 77040 713-849-9911 896-4511
AMEX: FTK ■ *Web:* www.flotekind.com
FMC Corp Specialty Chemicals Group 1735 Market St......... Philadelphia PA 19103 215-299-6000 299-5998
Web: www.fmc.com
Foseco Metallurgical Inc 20200 Sheldon Rd................... Cleveland OH 44142 440-826-4548 826-3434
TF: 800-321-3132 ■ *Web:* www.fosecomet.com
Frank Miller & Sons Inc 13831 S Emerald Ave .... Riverdale IL 60827 708-201-7200 841-8073
TF: 800-423-6358 ■ *Web:* www.icemelt.com
Freezetone Products Inc 7986 NW 14th St .... Miami FL 33126 305-640-0414 640-0454
Web: www.freezetone-usa.com
Fremont Industries Inc
4400 Valley Industrial Blvd N PO Box 67 .... Shakopee MN 55379 952-445-4121 496-3027
TF: 800-436-1238 ■ *Web:* www.fremontind.com
GE Betz 4636 Somerton Rd................................... Trevose PA 19053 866-755-5936 422-5878*
**Fax Area Code: 888* ■ *TF Cust Svc:* 866-439-8372
GE Infrastructure 187 Danbury Rd .... Wilton CT 06897 203-761-1900 761-1924
Web: www.geinfrastructure.com
Genieco Inc 200 N Laflin St .... Chicago IL 60607 312-421-2383 421-3042
TF: 800-223-8217 ■ *Web:* www.gonesh.net
GenTek Inc 90 E Hasley Rd..................................... Parsippany NJ 07054 973-515-1977 515-1997
NASDAQ: GETI ■ *TF:* 800-631-8050 ■ *Web:* www.gentek-global.com
GEO Specialty Chemicals Inc 401 S Earl Suite 3-A .... Lafayette IN 47904 765-448-9412 448-6728
Web: www.geosc.com
Gold Eagle Co 4400 S Kildare Ave .... Chicago IL 60632 773-376-4400 376-3245
TF: 800-621-1251 ■ *Web:* www.goldeagleco.com
Goulston Technologies Inc 700 N Johnson St...................... Monroe NC 28110 704-289-6464 296-6400
Web: www.goulston.com
Grace Construction Products 62 Whittemore Ave .... Cambridge MA 02140 617-876-1400 498-4311
Web: www.na.graceconstruction.com
Grace Davison 7500 Grace Dr................................. Columbia MD 21044 410-531-4000 531-4367
TF: 800-638-6014 ■ *Web:* www.gracedavison.com
Grace WR & Co 7500 Grace Dr................................ Columbia MD 21044 410-531-4000 531-4367
NYSE: GRA ■ *TF:* 888-398-4646 ■ *Web:* www.grace.com
H Krevit & Co Inc 73 Welton St .... New Haven CT 06511 203-772-3350 776-0730
Web: www.hkrevit.com
Hanson-Loran Chemical Co 6700 Caballero Blvd .... Buena Park CA 90620 714-522-5700 522-5834
Web: www.hansonloran.com
Harcros Chemicals Inc 5200 Speaker Rd.................... Kansas City KS 66106 913-321-3131 621-7718
TF: 800-765-4748 ■ *Web:* www.harcroschem.com
Henkel Corp 32100 Stephenson Hwy .... Madison Heights MI 48071 248-583-9300 583-2976
TF: 800-521-6895 ■ *Web:* www.henkel.com
Hercules Inc 1313 N Market St Hercules Plaza .... Wilmington DE 19894 302-594-5000 594-5400
NYSE: HPC ■ *TF:* 800-441-7600 ■ *Web:* www.herc.com
Hercules Inc Pulp & Paper Div 1313 N Market St............. Wilmington DE 19894 302-594-5000 594-5400
Hexion Specialty Chemicals Inc 180 E Broad St................ Columbus OH 43215 614-225-4000 220-6693*
**Fax: Hum Res* ■ *Web:* www.hexionchem.com
Hickman Williams & Co 595 Forest Ave Suite 1-B............... Plymouth MI 48170 734-414-9575 414-9725
TF: 800-862-1890 ■ *Web:* www.hicwilco.com
Hitachi Chemical Co America Ltd
10080 N Wolfe Rd Suite SW3-200 .... Cupertino CA 95014 408-873-2200 873-2284
Web: www.hitachi-chemical.com
Honeywell Fluorine Products 101 Columbia Rd............... Morristown NJ 07962 973-455-2000 458-9073*
**Fax Area Code: 800* ■ *TF:* 800-631-8138 ■ *Web:* www.genetron.com
Honeywell Specialty Chemicals 101 Columbia Rd .... Morristown NJ 07962 973-455-2145 455-6154
TF: 800-222-0094 ■ *Web:* www.specialtychem.com
Houghton Chemical Corp 52 Cambridge St .... Boston MA 02134 617-254-1010 254-2713
TF: 800-777-2466 ■ *Web:* www.houghtonchemical.com
Huber JM Corp 333 Thornall St.................................. Edison NJ 08837 732-549-8600 549-2239*
**Fax: Hum Res* ■ *Web:* www.huber.com
Hydrite Chemical Co 300 N Patrick Blvd .... Brookfield WI 53045 262-792-1450 792-8721
TF: 800-545-4560 ■ *Web:* www.hydrite.com
I-K-I Mfg Co Inc 116 N Swift St................................ Edgerton WI 53534 608-884-3411 884-4712
Web: www.ikimfg.com
ICI Americas Inc 10 Finderne Ave.......................... Bridgewater NJ 08807 908-203-5000 685-5005
TF: 800-998-9986 ■ *Web:* www.ici.com/UnitedStatesofAmerica
Intercontinental Chemical Corp 4660 Spring Grove Ave......... Cincinnati OH 45232 513-541-7100 541-6880
TF: 800-543-2075 ■ *Web:* www.icc-chemicals.com
International Chemical Co 2628 N Mascher St .... Philadelphia PA 19133 215-739-2313 423-7171
TF: 800-541-2504 ■ *Web:* www.e-icc.com
ITW Chemtronics Inc 8125 Cobb Centre Dr.................... Kennesaw GA 30152 770-424-4888 423-0748
TF: 800-645-5244 ■ *Web:* www.chemtronics.com
ITW Texwipe 300-B Rt 17 S .... Mahwah NJ 07430 201-327-9100 684-1803
TF: 800-839-9473 ■ *Web:* www.texwipe.com
JM Huber Corp 333 Thornall St.................................. Edison NJ 08837 732-549-8600 549-2239*
**Fax: Hum Res* ■ *Web:* www.huber.com
Jordan Industries Inc Flavor & Fragrance Group
1751 Lake Cook Rd ArborLake Ctr Suite 550..................... Deerfield IL 60015 847-945-5591 945-3645
Kao Specialties Americas LLC
243 Woodline St PO Box 2316 .... High Point NC 27261 336-884-2214 884-4390
TF: 800-727-2214 ■ *Web:* www.ksallc.com
Kester Solder Co 800 W Thorndale Ave .... Kenilworth IL 60043 847-297-1600 699-5689
TF: 800-253-7837 ■ *Web:* www.kester.com
Kik Custom Products 1919 Superior St .... Elkhart IN 46515 574-295-0000 296-1711
Web: www.kikcorp.com
King Industries Inc 1 Science Rd .... Norwalk CT 06852 203-866-5551 866-1268
TF: 800-431-7900 ■ *Web:* www.kingindustries.com
Kolene Corp 12890 Westwood Ave................................. Detroit MI 48223 313-273-9220 273-5207
TF: 800-521-4182 ■ *Web:* www.kolene.com
Koppers Inc 436 7th Ave.................................... Pittsburgh PA 15219 412-227-2001 227-2333
NYSE: KOP ■ *TF:* 800-321-9876 ■ *Web:* www.koppers.com
Kronos Worldwide Inc 5430 LBJ Pkwy Suite 1700................. Dallas TX 75240 972-233-1700 448-1445
NYSE: KRO ■ *Web:* www.kronostio2.com
Lloyd Laboratories Inc 24 Fitch Ct PO Box 256................. Wakefield MA 01880 781-224-0083 245-1557

Company	City	State	Zip	Phone	Fax
Lonza Inc 90 Boroline Rd *Fax: Cust Svc ■ TF Cust Svc: 800-631-3647 ■ Web: www.lonzagroup.com	Allendale	NJ	07401	201-316-9200	785-9989*
LPS Laboratories 4647 Hugh Howell Rd *Fax Area Code: 800 ■ TF: 800-241-8334 ■ Web: www.lpslabs.com	Tucker	GA	30084	770-934-7800	543-1563*
Lubrizol Corp 29400 Lakeland Blvd NYSE: LZ ■ TF: 800-522-4125 ■ Web: www.lubrizol.com	Wickliffe	OH	44092	440-943-4200	347-3583
Lucas-Milhaupt Inc 5656 S Pennsylvania Ave TF: 800-558-3856 ■ Web: www.lucas-milhaupt.com	Cudahy	WI	53110	414-769-6000	769-1093
MacDermid Inc 1401 Blake St NYSE: MRD ■ TF: 800-325-4158 ■ Web: www.macdermid.com	Denver	CO	80202	720-479-3060	479-3086
McGean 2910 Harvard Ave TF Orders: 800-932-7006 ■ Web: www.mcgean.com	Cleveland	OH	44105	216-441-4900	441-1377
McGean-Rohco Inc DBA McGean 2910 Harvard Ave TF Orders: 800-932-7006 ■ Web: www.mcgean.com	Cleveland	OH	44105	216-441-4900	441-1377
MeadWestvaco Chemical Div PO Box 118005 Web: www.meadwestvaco.com/chemicals.nsf	Charleston	SC	29423	843-745-3000	740-2147
Michelman Inc 9080 Shell Rd TF: 800-477-0498 ■ Web: www.michem.com	Cincinnati	OH	45236	513-793-7766	793-2504
Micro Powders Inc 580 White Plains Rd Web: www.micropowders.com	Tarrytown	NY	10591	914-793-4058	472-7098
Milacron Inc 2090 Florence Ave NYSE: MZ ■ Web: www.milacron.com	Cincinnati	OH	45206	513-487-5000	487-5615
Millennium Specialty Chemicals 601 Crestwood St TF: 800-231-6728	Jacksonville	FL	32208	904-768-5800	768-2200
Miller Frank & Sons Inc 13831 S Emerald Ave TF: 800-423-6358 ■ Web: www.icemelt.com	Riverdale	IL	60827	708-201-7200	841-8073
Miller-Stephenson Chemical Co 55 Backus Ave TF Tech Supp: 800-992-2424 ■ Web: www.miller-stephenson.com	Danbury	CT	06810	203-743-4447	791-8702
Mitsubishi Chemical America Inc 1 N Lexington Ave 16th Fl Web: www.mitsubishichemical.com	White Plains	NY	10601	914-286-3600	286-3677
Momar Inc 1830 Ellsworth Industrial Dr TF: 800-556-3967 ■ Web: www.momar.com	Atlanta	GA	30318	404-355-4580	355-8284
Monroe Fluid Technology Inc 36 Draffin Rd Box 810 TF: 800-828-6351 ■ Web: www.monroefluid.com	Hilton	NY	14468	585-392-3434	392-2691
Montello Inc 6106 E 32nd Pl Suite 100 TF: 800-331-4628 ■ Web: www.montelloinc.com	Tulsa	OK	74135	918-665-1170	665-1480
Mount Pulaski Products Inc 908 N Vine St TF: 800-577-2627 ■ Web: www.mtpulaski.com	Mount Pulaski	IL	62548	217-792-3211	792-5040
Multisorb Technologies Inc 325 Harlem Rd TF Cust Svc: 800-445-9890 ■ Web: www.multisorb.com	West Seneca	NY	14224	716-824-8900	824-4091
Nalco Co 1601 W Diehl Rd NYSE: NLC ■ TF: 800-288-0879 ■ Web: www.nalco.com	Naperville	IL	60563	630-305-1000	305-2900
Nalco Co Energy Services Div 7705 Hwy 90-A Web: www.nalcoenergyservices.com	Sugar Land	TX	77478	281-263-7000	263-7900
Nanophase Technologies Corp 1319 Marquette Dr NASDAQ: NANX ■ Web: www.nanophase.com	Romeoville	IL	60446	630-771-6708	771-0825
National Starch & Chemical Co 10 Finderne Ave TF: 800-797-4992 ■ Web: www.nationalstarch.com	Bridgewater	NJ	08807	908-685-5000	685-5005
Northern Technologies International Corp (NTIC) 4201 Woodland Rd AMEX: NTI ■ TF: 800-328-2433 ■ Web: www.ntic.com	Circle Pines	MN	55014	763-225-6600	225-6645
Noveon Inc 9911 Brecksville Rd TF: 800-380-5397 ■ Web: www.noveon.com	Cleveland	OH	44141	216-447-5000	447-5238
Nox-Crete Inc 1444 S 20th St TF: 800-369-9800 ■ Web: www.nox-crete.com	Omaha	NE	68108	402-341-2080	341-9752
NTIC (Northern Technologies International Corp) 4201 Woodland Rd AMEX: NTI ■ TF: 800-328-2433 ■ Web: www.ntic.com	Circle Pines	MN	55014	763-225-6600	225-6645
O2Diesel Corp 100 Commerce Dr Suite 301 AMEX: OTD ■ Web: www.o2diesel.net	Newark	DE	19713	302-266-6000	266-7076
Octagon Process Inc 450 Raritan Ctr Pkwy Suite F Web: www.octagonprocess.com	Edison	NJ	08837	732-346-8000	346-8010
Oil Chem Inc 711 W 12th St Web: www.oilcheminc.com	Flint	MI	48503	810-235-3040	238-5260
OM Group Inc 811 Sharon Dr NYSE: OMG ■ TF: 800-321-9696 ■ Web: www.omgi.com	Westlake	OH	44145	440-899-2950	808-7114
OMNOVA Solutions Inc 175 Ghent Rd NYSE: OMN ■ Web: www.omnova.com	Fairlawn	OH	44333	330-869-4200	869-4288
OMNOVA Solutions Inc Performance Chemicals Div 165 S Cleveland Ave *Fax: Cust Svc ■ TF Cust Svc: 888-353-4173 ■ Web: www.omnova.com/pc.htm	Mogadore	OH	44260	330-628-9925	628-6500*
Ortec Inc 505 Gentry Memorial Hwy PO Box 1469 Web: www.ortecinc.com	Easley	SC	29641	864-859-1471	859-8580
Pacific Ethanol Corp 5711 N West Ave NASDAQ: PEIX ■ Web: www.pacificethanol.net	Fresno	CA	93711	559-435-1771	435-1478
Pavco Inc 1935 John Crosland Jr Dr TF Orders: 800-321-7735 ■ Web: www.pavco.com	Charlotte	NC	28208	704-496-6800	496-6810
Peach State Labs Inc 180 Burlington Rd PO Box 1087 TF: 800-634-1653 ■ Web: www.peachstatelabs.com	Rome	GA	30162	706-291-8743	291-4888
Penford Corp 7094 S Revere Pkwy NASDAQ: PENX ■ TF: 800-204-7369 ■ Web: www.penx.com	Centennial	CO	80112	303-649-1900	649-1700
Penray Cos Inc 440 Denniston Ct TF: 800-373-6729 ■ Web: www.penray.com	Wheeling	IL	60090	847-459-5000	459-5043
Phelps Dodge Industries 1 N Central Ave Web: www.phelpsdodge.com	Phoenix	AZ	85004	602-366-8100	366-7300
Pilot Chemical Co 11756 Burke St TF: 800-707-4568 ■ Web: www.pilotchemical.com	Santa Fe Springs	CA	90670	562-698-6778	945-1877
PMC Global Inc 12243 Branford St TF: 800-423-5632 ■ Web: www.pmcglobalinc.com	Sun Valley	CA	91352	818-896-1101	686-2531
Polarome International Inc 200 Theodore Conrad Dr Web: www.polarome.com	Jersey City	NJ	07305	201-309-4500	433-0638
Precision Laboratories Inc 1429 S Shields Dr TF: 800-323-6280 ■ Web: www.precisionlab.com	Waukegan	IL	60085	847-596-3001	596-3017
Prime Leather Finishes Co Inc 205 S 2nd St TF: 800-558-7285	Milwaukee	WI	53204	414-276-1668	276-9462
PVS Chemicals Inc 10900 Harper Ave TF: 800-787-6659 ■ Web: www.pvschemicals.com	Detroit	MI	48213	313-921-1200	921-1378
Quaker Chemical Corp 901 Hector St NYSE: KWR ■ TF: 800-523-7010 ■ Web: www.quakerchem.com	Conshohocken	PA	19428	610-832-4000	832-8682
Radiator Specialty Co 1900 Wilkinson Blvd TF: 877-464-4865 ■ Web: www.gunk.com	Charlotte	NC	28208	704-377-6555	688-2383
Rentech Inc 1331 17th St Suite 720 AMEX: RTK ■ Web: www.rentechinc.com	Denver	CO	80202	303-298-8008	298-8010
Rhein Chemie Corp 1014 Whitehead Rd Ext TF Cust Svc: 800-289-2436 ■ Web: www.rheinchemieus.com	Trenton	NJ	08638	609-771-9100	771-0409
Richardson Sid Carbon & Energy Cos 201 Main St Web: www.sidrich.com	Fort Worth	TX	76102	817-390-8600	
Rochester Midland Corp 333 Hollenbeck St TF: 800-836-1627 ■ Web: www.rochestermidland.com	Rochester	NY	14621	585-336-2200	467-4406
Rockwood Specialties Group Inc 100 Overlook Center Web: www.rockwoodspecialties.com	Princeton	NJ	08540	609-514-0300	514-8722
Roebic Laboratories Inc 25 Connair Rd PO Box 927 Web: www.roebic.com	Orange	CT	06477	203-795-1283	795-5227
Rohm & Haas Co 100 Independence Mall W NYSE: ROH ■ *Fax: Hum Res ■ Web: www.rohmhaas.com	Philadelphia	PA	19106	215-592-3000	592-3377*
Rohm & Haas Electronic Materials 455 Forest St TF: 800-832-6200 ■ Web: electronicmaterials.rohmhaas.com	Marlborough	MA	01752	508-481-7950	485-9113
Rohm Haas Electronic Materials 272 Buffalo Ave Web: electronicmaterials.rohmhaas.com	Freeport	NY	11520	516-868-8800	868-4781
Ronson Corp Campus Dr Corporate Pk 3 NASDAQ: RONC ■ TF: 800-526-4281 ■ Web: www.ronsoncorp.com	Somerset	NJ	08875	732-469-8300	469-6079
Rycoline Products Inc 5540 N Northwest Hwy TF: 800-621-1003 ■ Web: www.rycoline.com	Chicago	IL	60630	773-775-6755	775-9414
SA Day Mfg Co Inc 1489 Niagara St Web: www.saday.com	Buffalo	NY	14213	716-881-3030	881-4353
Scholler Inc 95 James Way Suite 100 TF: 800-220-1504 ■ Web: www.schollerinc.com	Southampton	PA	18966	215-942-0200	942-0255
Senomyx Inc 4767 Nexus Centre Dr NASDAQ: SNMX ■ Web: www.senomyx.com	San Diego	CA	92121	858-646-8300	404-0752
Sid Richardson Carbon & Energy Cos 201 Main St Web: www.sidrich.com	Fort Worth	TX	76102	817-390-8600	
Sigma-Aldrich Corp 3050 Spruce St NASDAQ: SIAL ■ *Fax Area Code: 800 ■ TF: 800-325-3010 ■ Web: www.sigmaaldrich.com	Saint Louis	MO	63103	314-771-5765	325-5052*
Sika Corp 201 Polito Ave *Fax: Acctg ■ TF: 800-933-7452 ■ Web: www.sikacorp.com	Lyndhurst	NJ	07071	201-933-8800	933-9379*
Solutek Corp 94 Shirley St TF: 800-403-0770 ■ Web: www.solutekcorporation.com	Boston	MA	02119	617-445-5335	445-9623
Spartan Chemical Co Inc 1110 Spartan Dr TF: 800-537-8990 ■ Web: www.spartanchemical.com	Maumee	OH	43537	419-531-5551	536-8423
Specco Industries Inc 13087 Main St TF: 800-441-6646 ■ Web: www.specco.com	Lemont	IL	60439	630-257-5060	257-9006
Sprayway Inc 500 S Vista Ave TF: 800-332-9000 ■ Web: www.spraywayinc.com	Addison	IL	60101	630-628-3000	543-7797
Standard Tar Products Co Inc 2456 W Cornell St TF: 800-825-7650 ■ Web: www.standardtar.com	Milwaukee	WI	53209	414-873-7650	873-7737
Stapleton Technologies Inc 1350 W 12th St TF: 800-266-0541 ■ Web: www.stapletontech.com	Long Beach	CA	90813	562-437-0541	437-8632
Stepan Co 22 W Frontage Rd NYSE: SCL ■ TF Cust Svc: 800-745-7837 ■ Web: www.stepan.com	Northfield	IL	60093	847-446-7500	501-2284
STP Products Mfg Co 1221 Broadway TF: 888-464-7871 ■ Web: www.stp.com	Oakland	CA	94612	510-271-7000	832-1463
SulphCo Inc 850 Spice Islands Dr AMEX: SUF ■ Web: www.sulphco.com	Sparks	NV	89431	775-829-1310	829-1351
Sunland Chemical & Research Corp 5447 San Fernando Rd W Web: www.sunlandchemical.com	Los Angeles	CA	90039	818-244-9600	246-0478
Sweetwater Technologies PO Box 1473 TF: 888-711-7575 ■ Web: www.sweetwatertech.com	Temecula	CA	92593	951-303-0999	344-8388
Sybron Chemicals Inc 200 Birmingham Rd PO Box 66 TF: 800-678-0020 ■ Web: www.sybronchemicals.com	Birmingham	NJ	08011	609-893-1100	726-0049
Symons Corp 200 E Touhy Ave TF: 800-800-7601 ■ Web: www.symons.com	Des Plaines	IL	60018	847-298-3200	635-9287
Symrise Inc 300 North St TF: 800-422-1559 ■ Web: www.symrise.com	Teterboro	NJ	07608	201-288-3200	288-0843
Technic Inc 1170 Hawk Cir Web: www.technic.com	Anaheim	CA	92807	714-632-0200	632-1056
Technical Chemical Co 3327 Pipeline Rd TF: 800-527-0885 ■ Web: www.technicalchemical.com	Cleburne	TX	76033	817-645-6088	556-0694
Texas Refinery Corp 840 N Main St TF: 800-827-0711 ■ Web: www.texasrefinery.com	Fort Worth	TX	76106	817-332-1161	336-8441
Thatcher Co 1905 Fortune Rd PO Box 27407 TF: 800-348-0034 ■ Web: www.thatchercompany.com	Salt Lake City	UT	84127	801-972-4587	972-4606
Todd AM Co 1717 Douglas Ave TF: 800-968-2603 ■ Web: www.amtodd.com	Kalamazoo	MI	49007	269-343-2603	343-3399
Tronox Inc 211 N Robinson St 1 Leadership Sq NYSE: TRX ■ TF: 866-775-5009 ■ Web: www.tronox.com	Oklahoma City	OK	73102	405-775-5000	775-5155
Uniqema 4650 S Racine Ave *Fax Area Code: 973 ■ Web: www.uniqema.com	Chicago	IL	60609	773-376-9000	345-3527*
United Laboratories Inc 320 37th Ave *Fax: Sales ■ TF: 800-323-2594 ■ Web: www.beearthsmart.com	Saint Charles	IL	60174	630-377-0900	443-2087*
United Salt Corp 4800 San Felipe St TF: 800-554-8658 ■ Web: www.unitedsalt.com	Houston	TX	77056	713-877-2600	877-2604
Univertical Corp 203 Weatherhead St Web: www.univertical.com	Angola	IN	46703	260-665-1500	665-1400
Vertellus Specialties Inc 300 N Meridian St Suite 1500 Web: www.vertellus.com	Indianapolis	IN	46204	317-247-8141	248-6472
Watcon Inc 2215 S Main St TF: 800-492-8266 ■ Web: www.watcon-inc.com	South Bend	IN	46613	574-287-3397	287-2427
WR Grace & Co 7500 Grace Dr NYSE: GRA ■ TF: 888-398-4646 ■ Web: www.grace.com	Columbia	MD	21044	410-531-4000	531-4367
Wynn's Oil Co 1050 W 5th St TF: 800-989-8363 ■ Web: www.wynnsusa.com	Azusa	CA	91702	626-334-0231	
XL Brands 4284 S Dixie Hwy TF: 800-367-4583 ■ Web: www.xlbrands.com	Resaca	GA	30735	706-625-0025	226-9210

146 CHEMICALS & RELATED PRODUCTS - WHOL

Company	City	State	Zip	Phone	Fax
Aceto Corp 1 Hollow Ln Suite 201 NASDAQ: ACET ■ Web: www.aceto.com	Lake Success	NY	11042	516-627-6000	627-6093
AEP Colloids Div SARCOM Inc 6299 Rt 9 N TF: 800-848-0658 ■ Web: www.aepcolloids.com	Hadley	NY	12835	518-696-9900	696-9997
Airgas Inc 259 N Radnor-Chester Rd Suite 100 NYSE: ARG ■ TF: 800-255-2165 ■ Web: www.airgas.com	Radnor	PA	19087	610-687-5253	687-1052
Andrews Paper & Chemical Co 1 Channel Dr PO Box 509	Port Washington	NY	11050	516-767-2800	767-1632
Ashland Distribution Co 5200 Blazer Pkwy PO Box 2219 Web: www.ashchem.com/adc	Columbus	OH	43216	614-790-3333	790-4119
Astro Chemicals Inc 126 Memorial Dr TF: 800-223-0776 ■ Web: www.astrochemicals.com	Springfield	MA	01104	413-781-7240	781-7246
Barton Solvents Inc 1920 NE Broadway Ave TF: 800-383-6488 ■ Web: www.barsol.com	Des Moines	IA	50313	515-265-7998	265-0259
Basic Chemicals Solutions LLC (BCS) 525 Seaport Blvd TF: 888-810-4787 ■ Web: www.basicchem.com	Redwood City	CA	94063	650-363-1661	363-0713
Becker DB Co Inc 46 Leigh St TF: 800-394-3991 ■ Web: www.dbbecker.com	Clinton	NJ	08809	908-730-6010	730-9118
Brenntag Great Lakes LLC PO Box 444 *Fax: Sales ■ TF: 800-558-8501 ■ Web: www.brenntaggreatlakes.com	Butler	WI	53007	262-252-3550	252-5250*
Brenntag Mid-South 3111 N Post Rd TF: 800-844-8632 ■ Web: brenntagmid-south.com	Indianapolis	IN	46226	317-898-8632	895-0614
Brenntag Mid-South Inc 1405 Hwy 136 W *Fax: Hum Res ■ TF: 800-950-1727 ■ Web: www.brenntagmid-south.com	Henderson	KY	42419	270-830-1200	827-3990*
Brenntag North America Inc 5083 Pottsville Pike PO Box 13786 Web: www.brenntag.com	Reading	PA	19612	610-926-6100	926-0411
Brenntag Northeast Inc PO Box 13788 Web: www.brenntagnortheast.com	Reading	PA	19612	610-926-4151	926-4160

				Phone	Fax
Brenntag Pacific 4545 Ardine St	South Gate	CA	90280	323-832-5000	773-0909
Brenntag Southeast Inc 2000 E Pedigree St	Durham	NC	27703	919-596-0681	598-0681
TF: 800-849-7000 ■ *Web:* www.brenntagsoutheast.com					
Brenntag Southwest Inc 610 Fisher Rd	Longview	TX	75604	903-759-7151	759-3145
TF: 800-945-1858 ■ *Web:* www.brenntagsouthwest.com					
Budenheim USA 245 Newtown Rd Suite 305	Plainview	NY	11803	516-683-6900	683-6990
TF: 800-645-3044 ■ *Web:* www.gallard.com					
Cachat MF Co 14600 Detroit Ave Suite 600	Lakewood	OH	44107	216-228-8900	228-9916
TF: 800-729-8900 ■ *Web:* www.mfcachat.com					
Callahan Chemical Co 200 Industrial Ave	Richfield Park	NJ	07660	201-440-9000	440-5441
TF: 800-526-7000 ■ *Web:* www.calchem.com					
Canada Colors & Chemicals Ltd 80 Scarsdale Rd	Don Mills	ON	M3B2R7	416-449-7750	449-6282
TF: 800-387-8006 ■ *Web:* www.canadacolors.com					
Canpotex Ltd 111 2nd Ave S Suite 400	Saskatoon	SK	S7K1K6	306-931-2200	653-5505
Web: www.canpotex.com					
Charkit Chemical Corp 32 Haviland St Unit 1	Norwalk	CT	06854	203-299-3230	299-1355
Web: www.charkit.com					
Chemcentral Corp 7050 W 71st St	Bedford Park	IL	60499	708-594-7000	594-7022
TF: 800-331-6174 ■ *Web:* www.chemcentral.com					
Chemicals Inc 270 Osborne Dr	Fairfield	OH	45014	513-682-2000	682-2008
Web: www.chemgroup.com					
Chemroy Canada Inc 106 Summerlea Rd	Brampton	ON	L6T4X3	905-789-0701	789-7170
TF: 888-243-6769 ■ *Web:* www.chemroy.ca					
Chemsolv Inc 1140 Industry Ave SE	Roanoke	VA	24103	540-427-4000	427-3207
TF: 800-523-3099 ■ *Web:* www.chemsolv.com					
Coastal Chemical Co Inc 3520 Veterans Memorial	Abbeville	LA	70510	337-893-3862	892-1185
TF Cust Svc: 800-535-3862 ■ *Web:* www.coastalchem.com					
Cole Chemical & Distributing Inc					
900 Threadneedle St Suite 350	Houston	TX	77079	713-465-2653	461-3462
Web: www.colechem.com					
Connell Brothers Co Ltd 345 California St 27th Fl	San Francisco	CA	94104	415-772-4000	772-4011
Web: www.connellbrothers.com					
Coyne George S Chemical Co 3015 State Rd	Croydon	PA	19021	215-785-3000	785-1585
TF: 800-523-1230 ■ *Web:* www.coynechemical.com					
Dar-tech Inc 16485 Rockside Rd	Cleveland	OH	44137	216-663-7600	663-8007
TF: 800-228-7347 ■ *Web:* www.dar-tech.com					
DB Becker Co Inc 46 Leigh St	Clinton	NJ	08809	908-730-6010	730-9118
TF: 800-394-3991 ■ *Web:* www.dbbecker.com					
DH Litter Co Inc 565 Taxter Rd Suite 610	Elmsford	NY	10523	914-592-1077	592-1499
TF: 800-551-1039 ■ *Web:* www.dhlitter.com					
DIC International USA Inc					
500 Frank W Burr Blvd Glenpointe Center W	Teaneck	NJ	07666	201-836-4097	836-4962
Dorsett & Jackson Inc 3800 Noakes St	Los Angeles	CA	90023	323-268-1815	268-9082
Web: www.dorsettandjackson.com					
Durr Marketing Assoc Inc PO Box 17600	Pittsburgh	PA	15235	412-829-2300	829-7680
TF: 800-937-3877 ■ *Web:* durrmktg.com					
EMCO Chemical Distributors Inc					
2100 Commonwealth Ave	North Chicago	IL	60064	847-689-2200	689-8470
Web: www.emcochem.com					
ET Horn Co 16141 Heron Ave	La Mirada	CA	90638	714-523-8050	670-6851
TF: 800-442-4676 ■ *Web:* www.ethorn.com					
EW Kaufmann Co 1320 Industrial Hwy	Southampton	PA	18966	215-364-0240	364-4397
TF: 800-635-5358 ■ *Web:* www.ewkaufmann.com					
Fitz Chem Corp 450 E Devon Ave Suite 175	Itasca	IL	60143	630-467-8383	467-1183
Web: www.fitzchem.com					
Gallade Chemical Inc 1230 E St Gertrude Pl	Santa Ana	CA	92707	714-546-9901	546-2501
TF: 800-325-8431 ■ *Web:* www.galladechem.com					
George S Coyne Chemical Co 3015 State Rd	Croydon	PA	19021	215-785-3000	785-1585
TF: 800-523-1230 ■ *Web:* www.coynechemical.com					
GJ Chemical Co 370-376 Adams St	Newark	NJ	07114	973-589-1450	589-5786
Web: www.gjchemical.com					
GS Robins & Co 126 Chouteau Ave	Saint Louis	MO	63102	314-621-5165	621-1216
TF: 800-777-5155 ■ *Web:* www.gsrobins.com					
Harcros Chemicals Inc 5200 Speaker Rd	Kansas City	KS	66106	913-321-3131	621-7718
TF: 800-765-4748 ■ *Web:* www.harcroschem.com					
Haviland Enterprises Inc 421 Ann St NW	Grand Rapids	MI	49504	616-361-6691	361-9772
TF: 800-456-1134 ■ *Web:* www.havilandusa.com					
Helm US Chemical Corp 1110 Centennial Ave	Piscataway	NJ	08854	732-981-1116	981-0528
Web: www.helmusa.com					
Hess John R & Co Inc 400 Station St PO Box 3615	Cranston	RI	02910	401-785-9300	785-2510
TF: 800-828-4377 ■ *Web:* www.jrhess.com					
Hill Brothers Chemical Co 1675 N Main St	Orange	CA	92867	714-998-8800	998-6310
TF: 800-994-8801 ■ *Web:* www.hillbrothers.com					
HM Royal Inc 689 Pennington Ave	Trenton	NJ	08618	609-396-9176	396-3185
TF: 800-257-9452 ■ *Web:* www.hmroyal.com					
Horn ET Co 16141 Heron Ave	La Mirada	CA	90638	714-523-8050	670-6851
TF: 800-442-4676 ■ *Web:* www.ethorn.com					
Hubbard-Hall Inc 563 S Leonard St	Waterbury	CT	06708	203-756-5521	756-9017
TF: 800-331-6871 ■ *Web:* www.hubbardhall.com					
Hydrite Chemical Co 300 N Patrick Blvd	Brookfield	WI	53045	262-792-1450	792-8721
TF: 800-545-4560 ■ *Web:* www.hydrite.com					
ICC Chemical Corp 460 Park Ave	New York	NY	10022	212-521-1700	521-1794
TF: 800-422-1720 ■ *Web:* www.iccchem.com					
Ideal Chemical & Supply Co 4025 Air Park St	Memphis	TN	38118	901-363-7720	366-0864
TF: 800-232-6776 ■ *Web:* www.idealchemical.com					
Independent Chemical Corp 79-51 Cooper Ave	Glendale	NY	11385	718-894-0700	894-9224
TF: 800-892-2578 ■ *Web:* www.independentchemical.com					
Industrial Chemicals Inc 2042 Montreat Dr	Birmingham	AL	35216	205-823-7330	978-0485
TF: 800-476-2042					
JLM Industries Inc 8675 Hidden River Pkwy	Tampa	FL	33637	813-632-3300	632-3301
TF: 800-457-3743 ■ *Web:* www.jlmgroup.com					
JLM Marketing Inc 8675 Hidden River Pkwy	Tampa	FL	33637	813-632-3300	632-3301
TF: 800-457-3743 ■ *Web:* www.jlmgroup.com					
John R Hess & Co Inc 400 Station St PO Box 3615	Cranston	RI	02910	401-785-9300	785-2510
TF: 800-828-4377 ■ *Web:* www.jrhess.com					
KA Steel Chemicals Inc 15185 Main St PO Box 729	Lemont	IL	60439	630-257-3900	257-3922
TF: 800-677-8335 ■ *Web:* www.kasteelchemicals.com					
Kaufmann EW Co 1320 Industrial Hwy	Southampton	PA	18966	215-364-0240	364-4397
TF: 800-635-5358 ■ *Web:* www.ewkaufmann.com					
Kraft Chemical Co 1975 N Hawthorne Ave	Melrose Park	IL	60160	708-345-5200	345-4005
TF: 800-345-5200 ■ *Web:* www.kraftchemical.com					
LCI Ltd 415 Pablo Ave N	Jacksonville Beach	FL	32240	904-241-1200	241-1220
TF: 800-578-7891 ■ *Web:* www.lci-ltd.com					
LidoChem Inc 20 Village Ct	Hazlet	NJ	07730	732-888-8000	264-2751
Web: www.lidochem.com					
Litter DH Co Inc 565 Taxter Rd Suite 610	Elmsford	NY	10523	914-592-1077	592-1499
TF: 800-551-1039 ■ *Web:* www.dhlitter.com					
Lomas LV Ltd 99 Summerlea Rd	Brampton	ON	L6T4V2	905-458-1555	458-0722
TF: 800-575-3382 ■ *Web:* www.lvlomas.com					
LV Lomas Ltd 99 Summerlea Rd	Brampton	ON	L6T4V2	905-458-1555	458-0722
TF: 800-575-3382 ■ *Web:* www.lvlomas.com					
Mays Chemical Co 5611 E 71st St	Indianapolis	IN	46220	317-842-8722	576-9630
TF: 800-525-4803 ■ *Web:* www.mayschem.com					
McCullough & Assoc 1746 NE Expy PO Box 29803	Atlanta	GA	30329	404-325-1606	329-0208
TF: 800-969-1606 ■ *Web:* www.mccanda.com					
MF Cachat Co 14600 Detroit Ave Suite 600	Lakewood	OH	44107	216-228-8900	228-9916
TF: 800-729-8900 ■ *Web:* www.mfcachat.com					
Mitsubishi International Corp 655 3rd Ave	New York	NY	10017	212-605-2000	
Web: www.micusa.com					
Mitsui & Co (Canada) Ltd 20 Adelaide St E Suite 1400	Toronto	ON	M5C2T6	416-947-3899	865-1486
Web: www.mitsui.ca					
Mozel 1900 W Gate Dr	Columbia	IL	62236	618-281-3040	281-9176
TF: 800-260-5348 ■ *Web:* www.mozel.com					
NuCo2 Inc 2800 SE Marketplace	Stuart	FL	34997	772-221-1754	221-1690
NASDAQ: NUCO ■ *TF:* 800-472-2855 ■ *Web:* www.nuco2.com					
Palmer Holland Inc 24950 Country Club Blvd Suite 400	North Olmsted	OH	44070	440-686-2300	686-2180
TF: 800-635-4822 ■ *Web:* www.palmerholland.com					
Plaza Group Inc 10375 Richmond Ave Suite 1620	Houston	TX	77042	713-266-0707	266-8660
TF: 800-876-3738 ■ *Web:* www.theplazagrp.com					
Pride Solvents & Chemical Co of New York Inc					
6 Long Island Ave	Holtsville	NY	11742	631-758-0200	758-0290
TF: 800-645-5255 ■ *Web:* www.pridesol.com					
Quadra Chemicals Ltd 370 Joseph Carrier Blvd	Vaudreuil-Dorion	QC	J7V5V5	450-424-0161	424-9458*
**Fax:* Hum Res ■ *TF:* 800-665-6553 ■ *Web:* www.quadra.ca					
Recordati Corp 502 Centennial Ave	Cranford	NJ	07016	908-272-7220	272-2272
Ribelin Sales Inc 3857 Miller Park Dr	Garland	TX	75042	972-272-1594	474-2354*
**Fax Area Code:* 877 ■ *TF:* 877-742-3546 ■ *Web:* www.ribelin.com					
Robins GS & Co 126 Chouteau Ave	Saint Louis	MO	63102	314-621-5165	621-1216
TF: 800-777-5155 ■ *Web:* www.gsrobins.com					
Rockwood Specialties Group Inc 100 Overlook Center	Princeton	NJ	08540	609-514-0300	514-8722
Web: www.rockwoodspecialties.com					
Rosen's Inc 1120 Lake Ave	Fairmont	MN	56031	507-238-4201	238-9966
TF: 800-798-2000					
Rowell Chemical Corp 15 Salt Creek Ln Suite 205	Hinsdale	IL	60521	630-920-8833	920-8994
Web: www.rowellchemical.com					
Royal HM Inc 689 Pennington Ave	Trenton	NJ	08618	609-396-9176	396-3185
TF: 800-257-9452 ■ *Web:* www.hmroyal.com					
Saint Lawrence Chemicals Inc 35 Vulcan St	Rexdale	ON	M9W1L3	416-243-9615	243-9731
Web: www.stlawrencechem.com					
SARCOM Inc AEP Colloids Div 6299 Rt 9 N	Hadley	NY	12835	518-696-9900	696-9997
TF: 800-848-0658 ■ *Web:* www.aepcolloids.com					
Sasol Wax Americas Inc 2 Corporate Dr Suite 434	Shelton	CT	06484	203-925-4300	926-9844
TF: 800-423-7071 ■ *Web:* www.sasolwax.com					
Solvents & Chemicals Inc 4704 Shank Rd PO Box 490	Pearland	TX	77581	281-485-5377	485-6129
TF: 800-622-3990 ■ *Web:* www.solvchem.com					
Stochem Inc 62 Arrow Rd	North York	ON	M9M2L9	416-740-5300	740-2227
Web: www.stochem.com					
Sumitomo Chemical America Inc 335 Madison Ave Suite 830	New York	NY	10017	212-572-8200	572-8234
Web: www.sumitomo-chem.co.jp					
Superior Solvents & Chemicals					
1402 N Capitol Ave Suite 100	Indianapolis	IN	46204	317-781-4400	781-4401
TF: 800-553-5480 ■ *Web:* www.superioroil.com/solv					
Tanner Industries Inc 735 Davisville Rd 3rd Fl	Southampton	PA	18966	215-322-1238	322-7791*
**Fax:* Sales ■ *TF:* 800-643-6226 ■ *Web:* www.tannerind.com					
Tarr LLC 2429 N Borthwick St	Portland	OR	97227	503-288-5294	288-0421
TF: 800-422-5069 ■ *Web:* www.tarr-inc.com					
TCR Industries 26 Centerpointe Dr Suite 120	La Palma	CA	90623	714-521-5222	521-1636
Web: www.tcrindustries.com					
Tilley Chemical Co Inc 501 Chesapeake Park Plaza	Baltimore	MD	21220	410-574-4500	391-6665
TF: 800-638-6968 ■ *Web:* www.tilleychem.com					
TR International Trading Co Inc 1218 3rd Ave Suite 2100	Seattle	WA	98101	206-505-3500	505-3501
Web: www.tritrading.com					
TransChemical Inc 419 E DeSoto Ave	Saint Louis	MO	63147	314-231-6905	231-5851
TF: 888-873-6481 ■ *Web:* www.transchemical.com					
United Mineral & Chemical Corp 1100 Valley Brook Ave	Lyndhurst	NJ	07071	201-507-3300	507-1506
TF: 800-777-0505 ■ *Web:* www.umccorp.com					
Univar Canada Ltd PO box 2009	Richmond	BC	V6B3R2	604-273-1441	273-2046
Web: www.univarcanada.com					
Univar USA Inc PO Box 34325	Seattle	WA	98124	425-889-3400	889-4100
TF: 800-234-4588 ■ *Web:* www.vopakusa.com					
Valley National Gases LLC 67 43rd St PO Box 6628	Wheeling	WV	26003	304-232-1541	233-2812
AMEX: VLG ■ *Web:* vngas.com					
Van Horn Metz & Co 201 E Elm St	Conshohocken	PA	19428	610-828-4500	828-0936
TF: 800-523-0424 ■ *Web:* www.vanhornmetz.com					
Walsh & Assoc Inc 1400 Macklind Ave	Saint Louis	MO	63110	314-781-2520	781-9424
TF: 800-949-2574 ■ *Web:* www.walsh-assoc.com					
Webb Chemical Service Corp 2708 Jarman St	Muskegon	MI	49444	231-733-2181	739-5454
Web: www.webbchemical.com					
Wego Chemical & Mineral Corp 239 Great Neck Rd	Great Neck	NY	11021	516-487-3510	487-3794
TF: 877-489-6645 ■ *Web:* www.wegochem.com					
Whitaker Oil Co 1557 Marietta Rd NW	Atlanta	GA	30318	404-355-8220	355-8217
TF: 000-221-0521 ■ *Web:* www.whitakeroil.com					
Wilson Industrial Sales Co Inc 201 S Wilson St PO Box 425	Brook	IN	47922	219-275-7333	275-9622
TF: 800-633-5427 ■ *Web:* www.wilsonindustrial.com					
Young Chemical Co 6465 Eastland Rd	Brook Park	OH	44142	440-234-3200	234-3255
TF: 800-248-3009 ■ *Web:* www.youngchemical.com					

147 CHILD CARE MONITORING SYSTEMS - INTERNET

				Phone	Fax
Kids-World.net c/o SecurityBase.com PO Box 52282	Irvine	CA	92619	877-801-0354	505-1511*
**Fax Area Code:* 714 ■ *Web:* www.kids-world.net					
KinderCam Inc 5500 Peachtree Pkwy	Norcross	GA	30092	678-966-3000	966-3002
TF: 888-522-6123 ■ *Web:* kindercam.com					
ParentWatch Inc 45 Kensico Dr	Mount Kisco	NY	10549	914-919-1700	919-0495
TF: 800-696-2664 ■ *Web:* www.parentwatch.com					
WatchMeGrow LLC 4405 7th Ave SE Suite 201	Lacey	WA	98503	800-483-5597	528-2536*
**Fax Area Code:* 360 ■ *Web:* www.watchmegrow.com					

148 CHILDREN'S LEARNING CENTERS

				Phone	Fax
Abrakadoodle Inc 1800 Robert Fulton Dr	Reston	VA	22191	703-860-6570	860-6574
Web: www.abrakadoodle.com					
Bright Horizons Family Solutions Inc 200 Talcott Ave S	Watertown	MA	02472	617-673-8000	673-8001
NASDAQ: BFAM ■ *TF:* 800-324-4386 ■ *Web:* www.brighthorizons.com					
Childcare Network Inc 1501-D 13th St	Columbus	GA	31901	706-562-8600	562-0600
TF: 877-424-4530 ■ *Web:* www.childcarenetwork.net					
Children's World Learning Centers					
650 NE Holladay St Suite 1400	Portland	OR	97232	503-872-1300	872-1349
Web: www.childrensworld.com					
Computertots/Computer Explorers 12715 Telge Rd	Cypress	TX	77429	281-256-4100	373-4450
TF: 800-531-5053 ■ *Web:* www.computertots.com					
Educate Inc 1001 Fleet St	Baltimore	MD	21202	410-843-8000	843-8717
NASDAQ: EEEE ■ *TF:* 888-338-2283 ■ *Web:* www.educate-inc.com					

	City	State	Zip	Phone	Fax
FasTracKids International Ltd 6900 E Belleview Ave Suite 100 *TF:* 888-576-6888 ■ *Web:* www.fastrackids.com	Greenwood Village	CO	80111	303-224-0200	224-0222
Goddard Systems Inc 1016 W Ninth Ave *TF:* 800-463-3273 ■ *Web:* www.goddardschool.com	King of Prussia	PA	19406	610-265-8510	265-6931
Gymboree Corp Play & Music Program 500 Howard St *TF:* 800-520-7529 ■ *Web:* www.gymboree.com	San Francisco	CA	94105	415-278-7000	278-7100
Honors Learning Center 5959 Shallowford Rd Suite 515 *Web:* honorslearningcenter.com	Chattanooga	TN	37421	423-892-1800	892-1800
Huntington Learning Centers Inc 23 Jefferson Ave *TF:* 800-226-5327 ■ *Web:* www.huntingtonlearning.com	Westwood	NJ	07675	201-261-8600	
Kiddie Academy International Inc 108 Wheel Rd Suite 200 *TF:* 800-554-3343 ■ *Web:* www.kiddieacademy.com	Bel Air	MD	21015	410-515-0788	569-2729
KinderCare Learning Centers Inc 650 NE Holladay St Suite 1400 **Fax:* Cust Svc ■ *TF:* 800-633-1488 ■ *Web:* www.kindercare.com	Portland	OR	97232	503-872-1300	872-1345*
Knowledge Learning Corp 650 NE Holladay St Suite 1400 *TF:* 888-525-2780 ■ *Web:* www.knowledgelearning.com	Portland	OR	97228	503-872-1300	872-1349
Kumon North America Inc 300 Frank W Burr Blvd Glenpointe Ctr E 5th Fl *TF:* 877-586-6673 ■ *Web:* www.kumon.com	Teaneck	NJ	07666	201-928-0444	928-0044
La Petite Academy Inc 130 S Jefferson *TF:* 800-527-3848 ■ *Web:* www.lapetite.com	Chicago	IL	60661	312-798-1200	382-1776
Learning Care Group Inc 21333 Haggerty Rd Suite 300 **Fax Area Code:* 248 ■ *TF:* 800-425-1212 ■ *Web:* www.childtime.com	Novi	MI	48375	866-244-5384	697-9001*
Mathnasium LLC 5120 W Goldleaf Cir Suite 130 **Fax Area Code:* 310 ■ *Web:* www.mathnasium.com	Los Angeles	CA	90056	877-531-6284	943-2111*
New Horizon Kids Quest Inc 16355 36th Ave N Suite 700 *TF:* 800-941-1007 ■ *Web:* www.kidsquest.com	Plymouth	MN	55446	763-557-1111	383-6101
Oxford Learning Centers Inc 97B S Livingston Ave *TF:* 888-559-2212 ■ *Web:* www.oxfordlearning.com	Livingston	NJ	07039	973-597-4300	
Primrose School Franchising Co 3660 Cedarcrest Rd *TF:* 800-745-0677 ■ *Web:* www.primroseschools.com	Acworth	GA	30101	770-529-4100	529-1551
SCORE! Educational Centers 66 Franklin St Suite 300 **Fax Area Code:* 212 ■ *TF:* 800-497-2673 ■ *Web:* www.escore.com	Oakland	CA	94607	510-817-3700	997-5790*
Tutor Time Child Care/Learning Centers 21333 Haggerty Rd Suite 300 *TF:* 800-275-1235 ■ *Web:* www.tutortime.com	Novi	MI	48375	248-697-9000	697-9001

149 CIRCUS, CARNIVAL, FESTIVAL OPERATORS

	City	State	Zip	Phone	Fax
Big Apple Circus 505 8th Ave 19th Fl *TF:* 800-899-2775 ■ *Web:* www.bigapplecircus.org	New York	NY	10018	212-268-2500	268-3163
Carson & Barnes Circus PO Box J *Web:* www.carsonbarnescircus.com	Hugo	OK	74743	580-326-3173	326-7466
Cirque du Soleil Inc 8400 2nd Ave *TF:* 800-678-2119 ■ *Web:* www.cirquedusoleil.com	Montreal	QC	H1Z4M6	514-722-2324	722-3692
Clyde Beatty Cole Brothers Circus 1038 Martin St *Web:* www.colebroscircus.com	DeLand	FL	32720	386-736-0071	738-7860
Culpepper & Merriweather Circus PO Box 813 *Web:* www.cmcircus.com	Hugo	OK	74743	580-326-8833	326-8866
Feld Entertainment Inc 8607 Westwood Center Dr *TF:* 800-298-3858 ■ *Web:* www.feldentertainment.com	Vienna	VA	22182	703-448-4000	448-4100
International Renaissance Festivals Ltd PO Box 315 *TF:* 800-296-7304 ■ *Web:* www.rennfest.com	Crownsville	MD	21032	410-266-7304	573-1508
Renaissance Entertainment Corp 275 Century Cir Suite 102 *Web:* www.recfair.com	Louisville	CO	80027	303-664-0300	664-0303
Ringling Brothers & Barnum & Bailey Circus 8607 Westwood Ctr Dr *Web:* www.ringling.com	Vienna	VA	22182	703-448-4000	448-4100

150 CLAY PRODUCTS - STRUCTURAL

SEE ALSO Construction Materials - Brick, Stone, Related Materials p. 1549

	City	State	Zip	Phone	Fax
Acme Brick Co 3101 S Bryant Irvin Rd *TF:* 800-433-5650 ■ *Web:* www.acmebrick.com	Fort Worth	TX	76109	817-332-4101	390-2404
Belden Brick Co Inc 700 W Tuscarawas Ave *Web:* www.beldenbrick.com	Canton	OH	44702	330-456-0031	456-2694
Boral Bricks Inc 1630 Arthern Rd *TF:* 800-580-3842 ■ *Web:* www.boralbricks.com	Augusta	GA	30903	706-823-8802	724-0302
Bowerston Shale Co 515 Main St *Web:* www.bowerstonshale.com	Bowerston	OH	44695	740-269-2921	269-5456
Brampton Brick Ltd 225 Wanless Dr *Web:* www.bramptonbrick.com	Brampton	ON	L7A1E9	905-840-1011	840-1535
Brick & Tile Corp of Lawrenceville 16024 Governor Harrison Pkwy *TF:* 877-274-2582 ■ *Web:* www.lawrencevillebrick.com	Lawrenceville	VA	23868	434-848-3151	848-4000
Castaic Brick Inc 32201 Castaic Lake Dr *TF:* 800-227-8242 ■ *Web:* www.castaicbrick.com	Castaic	CA	91384	661-259-3066	257-1253
Cherokee Brick & Tile Co Inc 3250 Waterville Rd *TF:* 800-277-2745 ■ *Web:* www.cherokeebrick.com	Macon	GA	31206	478-781-6800	781-8964
Colloid Environmental Technologies Co (CETCO) 1500 W Shure Dr *TF:* 800-527-9948 ■ *Web:* www.cetco.com	Arlington Heights	IL	60004	847-392-5800	577-6150
Cunningham Brick Co Inc 701 N Main St *TF:* 800-672-6181 ■ *Web:* www.cunninghambrick.com	Lexington	NC	27292	336-248-8541	224-0002
Elgin-Butler Brick Co 1007 E 40th St *Web:* www.elginbutler.com	Austin	TX	78751	512-453-7366	453-7473
Endicott Clay Products Co 57120 707 Rd *TF:* 800-927-9179 ■ *Web:* www.endicott.com	Endicott	NE	68350	402-729-3315	729-5804
Endicott Tile LLC 57120 707 Rd *TF:* 800-927-9179 ■ *Web:* www.endicott.com	Endicott	NE	68350	402-729-3315	729-5804
General Shale Products LLC 3211 N Roan St *TF Cust Svc:* 800-414-4661 ■ *Web:* www.generalshale.com	Johnson City	TN	37601	423-282-4661	952-4104
Glen-Gery Corp 1166 Spring St PO Box 7001 *Web:* www.glengerybrick.com	Wyomissing	PA	19610	610-374-4011	374-1622
Hanson Brick & Tile 15720 John J Delany Dr *TF:* 877-426-7668 ■ *Web:* na.hansonbrick.com	Charlotte	NC	28277	704-341-8750	341-8735
Henry Brick Co Inc 3409 Water Ave *TF:* 800-548-7576 ■ *Web:* www.henrybrick.com	Selma	AL	36703	334-875-2600	875-7842
I-XL Industries Ltd 612 Porcelain Ave SE *Web:* www.ixlbrick.com	Medicine Hat	AB	T1A8S4	403-526-5901	526-7680
International Chimney Corp 55 S Long St *TF:* 800-828-1446 ■ *Web:* www.internationalchimney.com	Williamsville	NY	14221	716-634-3967	634-3983
Interstate Brick Co 9780 S 5200 West *TF:* 800-233-8654 ■ *Web:* interstatebrick.paccoast.com	West Jordan	UT	84088	801-280-5200	280-5220
Irvins Interstate Brick & Block Co Inc 2301 N Hawthorne Ln *TF:* 800-837-3384 ■ *Web:* www.irvinsblock.com	Indianapolis	IN	46218	317-547-9511	543-3385
Jenkins Brick Co Inc 201 N 6th St PO Box 91 *TF:* 888-215-5700 ■ *Web:* www.jenkinsbrick.com	Montgomery	AL	36104	334-834-2210	262-6817
Kansas Brick & Tile Inc PO Box 450 *TF Cust Svc:* 800-999-0480 ■ *Web:* www.kansasbrick.com	Hoisington	KS	67544	620-653-2157	653-7609
Kinney Brick Co 100 Prosperity Rd *TF:* 800-464-4605 ■ *Web:* www.kinneybrick.com	Albuquerque	NM	87105	505-877-4550	877-4557
Lee Brick & Tile Co 3704 Hawkins Ave *TF:* 800-672-7559 ■ *Web:* www.leebrick.com	Sanford	NC	27330	919-774-4800	774-7557
Logan Clay Products Co 201 S Walnut St *TF:* 800-848-2141 ■ *Web:* www.loganclaypipe.com	Logan	OH	43138	740-385-2184	385-9336
Ludowici Roof Tile Inc 4757 Tile Plant Rd PO Box 69 *TF Cust Svc:* 800-945-8453 ■ *Web:* www.ludowici.com	New Lexington	OH	43764	740-342-1995	342-0025
Marion Ceramics Inc PO Box 1134 *TF:* 800-845-4010 ■ *Web:* www.marionceramics.com	Marion	SC	29571	843-423-1311	423-1515
McNear Brick & Block 1 McNear Brickyard Rd *TF:* 888-442-6811 ■ *Web:* www.mcnear.com	San Rafael	CA	94901	415-454-6811	257-6833
MCP Industries Inc Mission Clay Products Div 708 S Temescal St Suite 101 *TF:* 800-795-6067 ■ *Web:* www.no-dig-pipe.com	Corona	CA	92879	951-736-1881	549-8280
Mission Clay Products Div MCP Industries Inc 708 S Temescal St Suite 101 *TF:* 800-795-6067 ■ *Web:* www.no-dig-pipe.com	Corona	CA	92879	951-736-1881	549-8280
Morin Brick Co 130 Morin Brick Rd *Web:* www.morinbrick.com	Auburn	ME	04210	207-784-9375	784-2013
Mutual Materials Co 605 119th Ave NE *TF:* 800-477-3008 ■ *Web:* www.mutualmaterials.com	Bellevue	WA	98005	425-452-2300	454-7732
Ochs Brick Co 801 E Rock St PO Box 106 *Web:* www.ochsbrick.com	Springfield	MN	56087	507-723-4221	723-4223
Old Virginia Brick Co 2500 W Main St *TF:* 800-879-8227 ■ *Web:* www.oldvirginiabrick.com	Salem	VA	24153	540-389-2357	389-4716
Pacific Clay Products Inc 14741 Lake St *Web:* www.pacificclay.com	Lake Elsinore	CA	92530	951-674-2131	674-4909
Palmetto Brick Co 3501 Brickyard Rd *TF:* 800-922-4423 ■ *Web:* www.palmettobrick.com	Wallace	SC	29596	843-537-7861	537-4802
Phoenix Brick Yard Corp 1814 S 7th Ave *Web:* www.phxbrickyard.com	Phoenix	AZ	85007	602-258-7158	258-1751
Pine Hall Brick Co 2701 Shorefair Dr *TF:* 800-952-7425 ■ *Web:* www.pinehallbrick.com	Winston-Salem	NC	27116	336-721-7536	725-3940
Potomac Valley Brick & Supply Co 15810 Indianola Dr Suite 100 *Web:* www.pvbrick.com	Rockville	MD	20855	301-309-9600	309-0929
Redland Brick Inc 15718 Clear Spring Rd *TF:* 800-366-2742 ■ *Web:* www.redlandbrick.com	Williamsport	MD	21795	301-223-7700	223-6675
Richards Brick Co 234 Springer Ave *Web:* www.richardsbrick.com	Edwardsville	IL	62025	618-656-0230	656-0944
Riverside Brick & Supply Co 12th & Maury St *TF:* 800-666-0444	Richmond	VA	23224	804-232-6786	231-3708
Robinson Brick Co 1845 W Dartmouth Ave *TF:* 800-477-9002 ■ *Web:* www.robinsonbrick.com	Denver	CO	80110	303-783-3000	781-1818
Sioux City Brick & Tile Co 310 S Floyd Blvd *Web:* www.siouxcitybrick.com	Sioux City	IA	51101	712-258-6571	252-3215
Stark Ceramics Inc 600 W Church St *TF:* 800-321-0662 ■ *Web:* www.starkceramics.com	East Canton	OH	44730	330-488-1211	488-0333
Statesville Brick Co 391 Brickyard Rd *TF:* 800-522-4716 ■ *Web:* www.statesvillebrick.com	Statesville	NC	28677	704-872-4123	872-4125
Summitville Tiles Inc SR-644 *Web:* www.summitville.com	Summitville	OH	43962	330-223-1511	223-1414
Superior Clay Corp 6566 Superior Rd SE *TF:* 800-848-6166 ■ *Web:* www.superiorclay.com	Uhrichsville	OH	44683	740-922-4122	922-6626
Taylor Clay Products Co 185 Peeler Rd PO Box 2128 *Web:* www.taylorclay.com	Salisbury	NC	28145	704-636-2411	636-2413
Tri-State Brick & Tile Co Inc 2050 Forest Ave *TF:* 800-962-2101 ■ *Web:* www.tristatebrickandtile.com	Jackson	MS	39286	601-981-1410	366-2205
Triangle Brick Co 6523 Hwy 55 *TF:* 800-672-8547 ■ *Web:* www.trianglebrick.com	Durham	NC	27713	919-544-1796	544-3904
US Tile Co Inc 909 W Railroad St *TF:* 800-252-9548 ■ *Web:* www.ustile.com	Corona	CA	92882	951-737-0200	734-9591
Whitacre Greer Fireproofing Inc 1400 S Mahoning Ave *TF:* 800-947-2837 ■ *Web:* www.wgpaver.com	Alliance	OH	44601	330-823-1610	823-5502
Yankee Hill Brick & Tile 3705 S Coddington Ave *Web:* www.yankeehillbrick.com	Lincoln	NE	68522	402-477-6663	477-2832

151 CLEANING PRODUCTS

SEE ALSO Brushes & Brooms p. 1397; Mops, Sponges, Wiping Cloths p. 1975

	City	State	Zip	Phone	Fax
3M Automotive Aftermarket Div 3M Center Bldg 223-6N-01 **Fax Area Code:* 800 ■ *TF:* 800-364-3577 ■ *Web:* www.3m.com/us/auto_marine_aero/aad	Saint Paul	MN	55144	651-737-6515	699-7840*
3M Commercial Care Div 3M Center *TF:* 800-847-3021 ■ *Web:* www.3m.com/us/mfg_industrial/commcare	Saint Paul	MN	55144	800-626-8578	
3M Consumer & Office Div 3M Ctr *TF:* 800-364-3577	Saint Paul	MN	55144	651-733-1110	736-2133
3M Safety Security & Protection Services Div 3M Center *TF:* 800-364-3577 ■ *Web:* www.3m.com	Saint Paul	MN	55144	651-733-1110	
3M Transportation Div 3M Center *TF:* 888-364-3577	Saint Paul	MN	55144	651-733-1110	
ABC Compounding Co Inc & Acme Wholesale 6970 Jonesboro Rd *TF:* 800-795-9222 ■ *Web:* www.abccompounding.com	Morrow	GA	30260	770-968-9222	968-7281
Abso-Clean Industries Inc 199 Wales Ave *TF:* 800-837-5000	Tonawanda	NY	14150	716-693-2111	693-2155
Adco Inc 900 W Main St *TF:* 800-821-7556 ■ *Web:* www.adco-inc.com	Sedalia	MO	65301	660-826-3300	826-1361
Advanced Sterilization Products 33 Technology Dr *TF:* 800-595-0200 ■ *Web:* www.cidex.com	Irvine	CA	92618	949-581-5799	450-6800
AJ Funk & Co 1471 Timber Dr *TF:* 877-225-3865 ■ *Web:* www.glasscleaner.com	Elgin	IL	60123	847-741-6760	741-6767
American Cleaning Co 39-30 Review Ave *TF:* 888-929-7587 ■ *Web:* www.cleaning-solutions.com	Long Island City	NY	11101	718-392-8080	482-9366
Angelus Shoe Polish Co 13500 Excelsior Dr *TF:* 800-722-4848 ■ *Web:* www.angelusshoepolish.com	Santa Fe Springs	CA	90670	562-229-0521	229-0702
Armor All Products Corp 1221 Broadway PO Box 24305 *TF:* 800-222-7784 ■ *Web:* www.armorall.com	Oakland	CA	94623	510-271-7000	832-1463
Arrow-Magnolia International 2646 Rodney Ln *TF:* 800-527-2101 ■ *Web:* www.arrowmagnolia.com	Dallas	TX	75229	972-247-7111	484-2896
Austin James Co 115 Downieville Rd PO Box 827 *TF:* 800-245-1942 ■ *Web:* www.jamesaustin.com	Mars	PA	16046	724-625-1535	625-3288
Aztec International Inc 5225 Middlebrook Pike *TF:* 800-369-5357 ■ *Web:* www.buywax.com	Knoxville	TN	37921	865-588-5357	558-6214

Phone Fax

BAF Industries Inc 1910 S Yale St — Santa Ana CA 92704 714-540-3850 545-2367
TF: 800-437-9893 ■ *Web:* www.prowax.com

Blue Cross Laboratories 20950 Center Pointe Pkwy — Santa Clarita CA 91350 661-255-0955 255-3628
Web: www.bc-labs.com

Brulin & Co Inc 2920 Dr AJ Brown Ave — Indianapolis IN 46205 317-923-3211 925-4596
TF: 800-776-7149 ■ *Web:* www.brulin.com

Buckeye International Inc 2700 Wagner Pl — Maryland Heights MO 63043 314-291-1900 298-2850
TF: 800-321-2583 ■ *Web:* www.buckeyeinternational.com

Bullen Cos 1640 Delmar Dr PO Box 37 — Folcroft PA 19032 610-534-8900 534-8912
TF: 800-444-8900 ■ *Web:* www.bullenairx.com

Butcher Co 8310 16th St — Sturtevant WI 53177 800-795-9550 786-7337
Web: www.butchers.com

C & H Chemical Inc 222 Starkey St — Saint Paul MN 55107 651-227-4343 227-2485
TF: 800-966-2909 ■ *Web:* www.chchemical.com

Camco Chemical Co 8150 Holton Dr — Florence KY 41042 859-727-3200 727-1508
TF Cust Svc: 800-354-1001 ■ *Web:* www.camco-chem.com

Car Brite Inc 1910 S State Ave — Indianapolis IN 46203 317-788-9925 781-3292
TF: 800-347-2439 ■ *Web:* www.carbrite.com

Car-Freshner Corp 21205 Little Tree Dr — Watertown NY 13601 315-788-6250 788-7467
TF: 800-545-5454 ■ *Web:* www.little-trees.com

Carroll Co 2900 W Kingsley Rd — Garland TX 75041 972-278-1304 840-0678
TF: 800-527-5722 ■ *Web:* carrollco.com

Cello Professional Products 1354 Old Post Rd — Havre de Grace MD 21078 410-939-1234 939-3028
TF: 800-638-4850 ■ *Web:* www.cello-online.com

Champion Chemical Co 8319 S Greenleaf Ave — Whittier CA 90602 562-945-1456 898-8064*
**Fax Area Code:* 800 ■ *TF:* 800-621-7868 ■ *Web:* www.championchemical.com

Chemetall Oakite 50 Valley Rd — Berkeley Heights NJ 07922 908-464-6900 464-4658
TF: 800-526-4473 ■ *Web:* www.oakite.com

Chemical Specialties Mfg Corp (Chemspec)
901 N Newkirk St — Baltimore MD 21205 410-675-4800 675-0038
TF Sales: 800-638-7370 ■ *Web:* www.chemspecworld.com

Chemspec (Chemical Specialties Mfg Corp)
901 N Newkirk St — Baltimore MD 21205 410-675-4800 675-0038
TF Sales: 800-638-7370 ■ *Web:* www.chemspecworld.com

Church & Dwight Co Inc 469 N Harrison St — Princeton NJ 08543 609-683-5900
NYSE: CHD ■ *Web:* www.churchdwight.com

Clorox Co 1221 Broadway — Oakland CA 94612 510-271-7000 832-1463
NYSE: CLX ■ *TF Cust Svc:* 800-292-2808 ■ *Web:* www.thecloroxcompany.com

Colgate-Palmolive Co 300 Park Ave — New York NY 10022 212-310-2000 310-2595
NYSE: CL ■ *Web:* www.colgate.com

Concord Chemical Co 1700 Federal St — Camden NJ 08105 856-966-1526 963-0246
TF: 800-282-2436 ■ *Web:* www.concordchemical.com

Continental Commercial Products 305 Rock Industrial Park — Bridgeton MO 63044 314-739-8585 327-5492*
**Fax Area Code:* 800 ■ *TF:* 800-325-1051 ■
Web: www.continentalcommercialproducts.com

Copper Brite Inc 1482 E Valley Rd Suite 29 — Santa Barbara CA 93108 805-565-1566 565-1394
Web: www.copperbrite.com

Correlated Products Inc 5616 Progress Rd — Indianapolis IN 46242 317-243-3248 244-8461
TF: 800-428-3266 ■ *Web:* www.cpicorrelated.com

CR Brands Inc 141 Venture Blvd PO Box 2708 — Spartanburg SC 29304 864-587-9308 574-1495
TF: 800-835-3712

Crain Chemical Co 2624 Andjon Dr — Dallas TX 75220 214-358-3301 358-3304

Damon Industries Inc 12435 Rockhill Ave NE PO Box 2120 — Alliance OH 44601 330-821-5310 821-6355
TF: 800-362-9850 ■ *Web:* www.damonq.com

Delta Carbona LP 376 Hollywood Ave Suite 208 — Fairfield NJ 07004 973-808-6260 808-5661
TF: 888-746-5599 ■ *Web:* www.carbona.com

DeSoto LLC 900 Washington St PO Box 609 — Joliet IL 60433 815-727-4931 727-4333

Dial Corp 15501 N Dial Blvd — Scottsdale AZ 85260 480-754-3425
TF Cust Svc: 800-258-3425 ■ *Web:* www.dialcorp.com

Diamond Chemical Co Inc Union Ave & Dubois St — East Rutherford NJ 07073 201-935-4300 935-6997
TF: 800-654-7627 ■ *Web:* www.diamondchem.com

Dubois Chemicals Inc 200 Crowne Point Place — Sharonville OH 45241 513-326-8800 543-1720*
**Fax Area Code:* 800 ■ *TF:* 800-543-4906 ■ *Web:* www.duboischemicals.com

Dura Wax Co 4101 W Albany St — McHenry IL 60050 815-385-5000 344-8056
TF: 800-435-5705 ■ *Web:* www.janitorialsuppliesandequipment.com

Ecolab Inc 370 N Wabasha St — Saint Paul MN 55102 651-293-2233 293-2069
NYSE: ECL ■ *TF:* 800-392-3392 ■ *Web:* www.ecolab.com

Empire Cleaning Supply 12821 S Figueroa St — Los Angeles CA 90061 310-715-6500 715-1166
Web: www.empirecleaningsupply.com

Emulso Corp 301 Ellicott St — Buffalo NY 14203 716-854-2889 854-2809
TF: 800-724-7667 ■ *Web:* www.emulso.com

Falcon Safety Products Inc 25 Chubb Way — Somerville NJ 08876 908-707-4900 707-8855
Web: www.falconsafety.com

Faultless Starch/Bon Ami Co 1025 W 8th St — Kansas City MO 64101 816-842-1230 842-3417
TF Cust Svc: 800-821-5565 ■ *Web:* www.bonami.com

Fine Organics Corp 420 Kuller Rd PO Box 2277 — Clifton NJ 07015 973-478-1000 478-6120
TF: 800-526-7480 ■ *Web:* www.fineorganicscorp.com

Frank B Ross Co 970-H New Brunswick Ave — Rahway NJ 07065 732-669-0810 669-0814
Web: www.frankbross.com

Frank Miller & Sons Inc 13831 S Emerald Ave — Riverdale IL 60827 708-201-7200 841-8073
TF: 800-423-6358 ■ *Web:* www.icemelt.com

Funk AJ & Co 1471 Timber Dr — Elgin IL 60123 847-741-6760 741-6767
TF: 877-225-3865 ■ *Web:* www.glasscleaner.com

Glissen Chemical Co Inc 1321 58th St — Brooklyn NY 11219 718-436-4200
TF: 800-356-9922

Goodwin Co 12102 Industry St — Garden Grove CA 92841 714-894-0531 897-7673
Web: www.goodwininc.com

Granitize Products Inc 11022 Vulcan St — South Gate CA 90280 562-923-5438 861-3475
TF: 800-553-6866 ■ *Web:* www.granitize.com

Guardian Chemical Co 694- Jefferson St PO Box 93667 — Atlanta GA 30377 404-873-1692 873-1695
TF: 800-241-6742

Hill Mfg Co Inc 1500 Jonesboro Rd SE — Atlanta GA 30315 404-522-8364 789-1754*
**Fax Area Code:* 800 ■ *TF:* 800-445-5123 ■ *Web:* www.soap.com

Hillyard Chemical Co Inc 302 N 4th St — Saint Joseph MO 64501 816-233-1321 861-0256*
**Fax Area Code:* 800 ■ *TF:* 800-365-1555 ■ *Web:* www.hillyard.com

ITW Dymon 805 E Old 56 Hwy — Olathe KS 66061 913-397-9889 397-8761
TF: 800-443-9536 ■ *Web:* www.dymon.com

James Austin Co 115 Downieville Rd PO Box 827 — Mars PA 16046 724-625-1535 625-3288
TF: 800-245-1942 ■ *Web:* www.jamesaustin.com

Johnson SC & Son Inc 1525 Howe St — Racine WI 53403 262-260-2000 260-2632
TF: 800-494-4855 ■ *Web:* www.scjohnson.com

JohnsonDiversey Inc 8310 16th St — Sturtevant WI 53177 262-631-4001 631-4282
Web: www.johnsondiversey.com

Kay Chemical Co 8300 Capital Dr — Greensboro NC 27409 336-668-7290 668-9763
TF: 800-333-4300 ■ *Web:* www.ecolab.com/Businesses/Kay

KozaK Auto DryWash Inc 6 Lyon St PO Box 910 — Batavia NY 14021 585-343-8111 343-3732
TF: 800-237-9927 ■ *Web:* www.kozak.com

Lincoln Industrial Chemicals Co 600 S 9th St PO Box 381 — Reading PA 19603 610-375-4596 375-3557

Lincoln Shoe Polish Co 172 Commercial St — Sunnyvale CA 94086 408-732-5120 732-0659
Web: www.lincolnshoepolish.com

LPS Laboratories 4647 Hugh Howell Rd — Tucker GA 30084 770-934-7800 543-1563*
**Fax Area Code:* 800 ■ *TF:* 800-241-8334 ■ *Web:* www.lpslabs.com

Luseaux Laboratories Inc 16816 S Gramercy Pl — Gardena CA 90247 310-324-1555

M-Chem Technologies Inc 1607 Derwent Way — Delta BC V3M6K8 800-663-9925 526-1618*
**Fax Area Code:* 604 ■ *Web:* www.mchem.com

Madison Chemical Co Inc 3141 Clifty Dr — Madison IN 47250 812-273-6000 273-6002
TF: 800-345-1915 ■ *Web:* www.madchem.com

Phone Fax

Magic American Corp 26901 Cannon Rd Suite 190 — Bedford Heights OH 44146 440-786-3100 786-3101
TF Cust Svc: 800-321-6330 ■ *Web:* www.magicamerican.com

Malco Products Inc 361 Fairview Ave PO Box 892 — Barberton OH 44203 330-753-0361 753-2025
TF: 800-253-2526 ■ *Web:* www.malcopro.com

Matchless Metal Polish Co 840 W 49th Pl — Chicago IL 60609 773-924-1515 924-5513
Web: www.matchlessmetal.com

Meguiar's Inc 17991 Mitchell S — Irvine CA 92614 949-752-8000 752-5784
TF Cust Svc: 800-347-5700 ■ *Web:* www.meguiars.com

Micro Care Corp 595 John Downey Dr — New Britain CT 06051 860-827-0626 827-8105
TF: 800-638-0125 ■ *Web:* www.microcare.com

Miller Frank & Sons Inc 13831 S Emerald Ave — Riverdale IL 60827 708-201-7200 841-8073
TF: 800-423-6358 ■ *Web:* www.icemelt.com

Mission Kleensweep Products Inc 2433 Birkdale St — Los Angeles CA 90031 323-223-1405 223-9968
TF: 888-201-8866 ■ *Web:* www.missionlabs.net

Mother's Polishes Waxes & Cleaners
5456 Industrial Dr — Huntington Beach CA 92649 714-891-3364 893-1827
TF: 800-221-8257 ■ *Web:* www.mothers.com

National Chemical Laboratories 401 N 10th St — Philadelphia PA 19123 215-922-1200 922-5517
TF: 800-628-2436 ■ *Web:* www.nclonline.com

National Chemicals Inc 105 Liberty St PO box 32 — Winona MN 55987 507-454-5640 454-5641
TF Cust Svc: 800-533-0027 ■ *Web:* www.natlchem.com

Navico Inc DBA Navy Brand Mfg Co 3670 Scarlet Oak Blvd — Saint Louis MO 63122 636-861-5500 861-5509
TF: 800-325-3312 ■ *Web:* www.navybrand.com

Navy Brand Mfg Co 3670 Scarlet Oak Blvd — Saint Louis MO 63122 636-861-5500 861-5509
TF: 800-325-3312 ■ *Web:* www.navybrand.com

NCH Corp 2727 Chemsearch Blvd — Irving TX 75062 972-438-0226 438-0707
TF: 800-527-9919 ■ *Web:* www.nch.com

New Pig Corp 1 Pork Ave — Tipton PA 16684 814-684-0101 621-7447*
**Fax Area Code:* 800 ■ *TF:* 800-468-4647 ■ *Web:* www.newpig.com

Nord-Viscount Corp PO Box 300166 — Brooklyn NY 11230 718-854-5586 660-7000*
**Fax Area Code:* 866 ■ *TF:* 866-278-7674 ■ *Web:* nord-viscount.com

Northern Labs Inc 5800 West Dr PO Box 850 — Manitowoc WI 54221 920-684-7137 684-6573
TF: 800-558-7621 ■ *Web:* www.northernlabs.com

Nuvite Chemical Compounds Corp 213 Freeman St — Brooklyn NY 11222 718-383-8351 383-0008
TF: 800-394-8351 ■ *Web:* www.nuvitechemical.com

Ocean Bio-Chem Inc 4041 SW 47th Ave — Fort Lauderdale FL 33314 954-587-6280 587-2813
NASDAQ: OBCI ■ *TF:* 800-327-8583 ■ *Web:* www.oceanbiochem.com

Oil Chem Inc 711 W 12th St — Flint MI 48503 810-235-3040 238-5260
Web: www.oilcheminc.com

Peck's Products Co 1220 Switzer Ave — Saint Louis MO 63147 314-385-5454 385-0744
TF: 800-325-8891

Prestige Brands International Inc 90 N Broadway — Irvington NY 10533 914-524-6810 524-6815
NYSE: PBH ■ *Web:* www.prestigebrands.com

Procter & Gamble Mfg Co 1 Procter & Gamble Plaza — Cincinnati OH 45202 513-983-1100
Web: www.pg.com

Reckitt Benckiser Inc 399 Interpace Pkwy PO Box 225 — Parsippany NJ 07054 973-404-2600 404-5700
TF Cust Svc: 800-333-3899 ■ *Web:* www.reckitt.com

Ross Frank B Co 970-H New Brunswick Ave — Rahway NJ 07065 732-669-0810 669-0814
Web: www.frankbross.com

Safeguard Chemical Corp 411 Wales Ave — Bronx NY 10454 718-585-3170 585-3657
TF: 800-536-3170 ■ *Web:* www.safeguardchemical.com

SC Johnson & Son Inc 1525 Howe St — Racine WI 53403 262-260-2000 260-2632
TF: 800-494-4855 ■ *Web:* www.scjohnson.com

Scot Laboratories Div Scott Fetzer Co
16841 Park Circle Dr — Chagrin Falls OH 44023 440-543-3033 543-1825
TF: 800-486-7268 ■ *Web:* www.scotlabs.com

Scott Fetzer Co Scot Laboratories Div
16841 Park Circle Dr — Chagrin Falls OH 44023 440-543-3033 543-1825
TF: 800-486-7268 ■ *Web:* www.scotlabs.com

Scott's Liquid Gold Inc 4880 Havana St — Denver CO 80239 303-373-4860
TF: 800-447-1919 ■ *Web:* www.scottsliquidgold.com

Selig Chemical Industries Inc 115 Kendall Park Ln — Atlanta GA 30336 800-447-3544 999-3566
Web: www.seligind.com

Seventh Generation Inc 60 Lake St — Burlington VT 05401 802-658-3773 658-1771
TF: 800-456-1191 ■ *Web:* www.seventhgeneration.com

Share Corp 7821 N Faulkner Rd — Milwaukee WI 53224 414-355-4000 355-0516
TF: 800-776-7192 ■ *Web:* www.sharecorp.com

Simoniz USA 201 Boston Tpke — Bolton CT 06043 860-646-0172 645-6070
TF: 800-227-5536 ■ *Web:* www.simonizusa.com

Snyder Mfg Corp 1541 W Cowles St — Long Beach CA 90813 562-432-2038 432-1603
Web: www.snydermanufacturing.com

State Industrial Products 3100 Hamilton Ave — Cleveland OH 44114 216-861-7114 771-9670*
**Fax Area Code:* 888 ■ *TF:* 800-782-2436 ■ *Web:* www.stateindustrial.com

Stearns Packaging Corp 4200 Sycamore Ave — Madison WI 53714 608-246-5150 246-5149
TF: 800-655-5008 ■ *Web:* www.stearnspkg.com

STP Products Mfg Co 1221 Broadway — Oakland CA 94612 510-271-7000 832-1463
TF: 888-464-7871 ■ *Web:* www.stp.com

Summit Industries Inc 839 Pickens Industrial Dr — Marietta GA 30062 770-590-0600 590-0714
TF: 800-241-6996 ■ *Web:* www.summitinds.com

Sunshine Makers Inc 15922 Pacific Coast Hwy — Huntington Harbour CA 92649 562-795-6000 592-3034
TF: 800-228-0709 ■ *Web:* www.simplegreen.com

Turtle Wax Inc 625 Willowbrook Centre Pkwy — Willowbrook IL 60527 630-455-3700 789-9343
TF: 800-323-9883 ■ *Web:* www.turtlewax.com

Unit Chemical Corp 7360 Commercial Way — Henderson NV 89011 702-564-6454 564-6629
TF: 800-879-8648 ■ *Web:* www.unitchemical.com

UNX Inc 707 E Arlington Blvd PO Box 7206 — Greenville NC 27835 252-756-8616 756-2764
Web: www.unxinc.com

Venus Laboratories Inc 855 Lively Blvd — Wood Dale IL 60191 630-595-1902 595-3252
TF: 800-592-1900 ■ *Web:* www.venuslabs.com

Warsaw Chemical Co Inc 390 Argonne Rd — Warsaw IN 46580 574-267-3251 267-3884
TF: 800-548-3396 ■ *Web:* www.warsaw-chem.com

WD-40 Co 1061 Cudahy Pl — San Diego CA 92110 619-275-1400 275-5823
NASDAQ: WDFC ■ *TF:* 800-448-9340 ■ *Web:* www.wd40.com

Webco Chemical Corp 420 W Main St — Dudley MA 01571 508-943-2337 987-0366
Web: www.webcochemical.com

West Penetone Corp 700 Gotham Pkwy — Carlstadt NJ 07072 201-567-3000 510-3973
TF: 800-631-1652 ■ *Web:* www.west-penetone.com

Willert Home Products Inc 4044 Park Ave — Saint Louis MO 63110 314-772-2822 772-3506
TF: 800-325-9680 ■ *Web:* www.willert.com

ZEP Inc 1310 Seaboard Industrial Blvd NW — Atlanta GA 30318 404-355-3120 603-7958
NYSE: ZEP ■ *Web:* www.zepinc.com

Zep Mfg Co 1310 Seaboard Industrial Blvd NW — Atlanta GA 30318 404-352-1680
TF: 877-428-9937 ■ *Web:* www.zepmfg.com

152 CLEANING SERVICES

SEE ALSO Bio-Recovery Services p. 1380; Building Maintenance Services p. 1398

Phone Fax

1-800-Water Damage 1167 Mercer St — Seattle WA 98109 206-381-3047 381-3052
TF: 800-940-9745 ■ *Web:* www.1800waterdamage.com

ABM Janitorial Services 420 Taylor St Suite 200 — San Francisco CA 94102 415-351-4450 351-4445
Web: www01.abm.com

Company	City	State	Zip	Phone	Fax
Amtech Lighting Services 2390 E Orangewood Ave Suite 100 *TF:* 800-423-4481 ■ *Web:* www01.abm.com	Anaheim	CA	92806	714-940-4000	940-4090
Anago Franchising Inc 3111 N University Dr Suite 625 *TF:* 800-213-5857 ■ *Web:* www.anagousa.com	Coral Springs	FL	33065	954-752-3111	752-1200
BearCom Building Services 7022 South 400 W *TF:* 888-569-9533 ■ *Web:* www.bearcomservices.com	Midvale	UT	84047	801-569-9500	569-8400
BG Service Solutions 730 W Sexton Rd	Columbia	MO	65203	573-874-8000	449-0338
Bonus of America Inc Rt 2 Box 132-C *TF:* 800-931-1102 ■ *Web:* www.bonusbuildingcare.com	McAlester	OK	74501	918-823-4990	823-4994
Bonus Building Care Inc 14331 Proton Rd *TF:* 800-931-1102 ■ *Web:* www.bonusbuildingcare.com	Dallas	TX	75244	972-789-9400	789-9399
Boston's Best Chimney Sweep 80 Rear Bacon St *TF:* 800-660-6708 ■ *Web:* www.bestchimney.com	Waltham	MA	02451	781-893-6611	893-1132
Braco Window Cleaning Service Inc 1 Braco International Blvd *TF:* 877-878-7091 ■ *Web:* bracowindowcleaning.com	Wilder	KY	41076	859-442-6000	442-6001
BuildingStars Inc 11489 Page Service Dr *Web:* www.buildingstars.com	Saint Louis	MO	63146	314-991-3356	991-3198
Chem-Dry 1530 N 1000 West *TF:* 800-243-6379 ■ *Web:* www.chemdry.com	Logan	UT	84321	435-755-0099	755-0021
Clean-Tech Co 2815 Olive St **Fax Area Code:* 800 ■ *TF:* 800-852-2388	Saint Louis	MO	63103	314-652-2388	762-7910*
Cleaning Authority 6994 Columbia Gateway Dr Suite 100 **Fax Area Code:* 866 ■ *TF:* 800-783-6243 ■ *Web:* www.thecleaningauthority.com	Columbia	MD	21046	410-740-1900	685-6243*
CleanNet USA 9861 Brokenland Pkwy Suite 208 *TF:* 800-735-8838 ■ *Web:* www.cleannetusa.com	Columbia	MD	21046	410-720-6444	720-5307
Cleanol Services Inc 60 Norelco Dr *TF:* 800-263-9430 ■ *Web:* www.cleanol.com	North York	ON	M9L2X6	416-745-5221	745-5209
Clola Enterprises LP 2324 Ridgepoint Dr Suite A *TF:* 800-833-2923	Austin	TX	78754	512-615-3400	615-3509
Coverall Cleaning Concepts 5201 Congress Ave Suite 275 *TF:* 800-537-3371 ■ *Web:* www.coverall.com	Boca Raton	FL	33487	561-922-2500	922-2423
Deluxe Carpet Cleaning Co Inc 5907 High Grove Rd *Web:* www.deluxecarpetcleaning.com	Grandview	MO	64030	816-763-3331	765-5984
Duraclean International Inc 220 Campus Dr *TF Cust Svc:* 800-251-7070 ■ *Web:* www.duraclean.com	Arlington Heights	IL	60004	847-704-7100	704-7101
Fish Window Cleaning Services Inc 200 Enchanted Pkwy *TF:* 877-707-3474 ■ *Web:* www.fishwindowcleaning.com	Saint Louis	MO	63021	636-530-7334	530-7856
GCA Services Group 300 Conshohocken State Rd Suite 650 *TF:* 800-422-8760 ■ *Web:* www.gcaservices.com	West Conshohocken	PA	19428	610-834-7555	834-9727
Healthcare Services Group Inc 3220 Tillman Dr Suite 300 *NASDAQ: HCSG* ■ *TF:* 800-523-2248 ■ *Web:* www.hcsgcorp.com	Bensalem	PA	19020	215-639-4274	
Heaven's Best Carpet & Upholstery Cleaning PO Box 607 *TF:* 800-359-2095 ■ *Web:* www.heavensbest.com	Rexburg	ID	83440	208-359-1106	359-1236
Hospital Housekeeping Systems 322 Congress Ave 2nd Fl *TF:* 800-229-2028 ■ *Web:* www.hhs1.com	Austin	TX	78701	512-478-1888	478-1971
HydroChem Industrial Services Inc 900 Georgia Ave *TF:* 800-934-9376 ■ *Web:* www.hydrochem.com	Deer Park	TX	77536	713-393-5600	393-5950
Jan-Pro International Inc 11605 Haynes Bridge Rd Suite 425 *TF:* 800-668-1001 ■ *Web:* www.jan-pro.com	Alpharetta	GA	30004	678-336-1780	336-1781
Jani-King International Inc 16885 Dallas Pkwy **Fax Area Code:* 800 ■ *TF:* 800-552-5264 ■ *Web:* www.janiking.com	Addison	TX	75001	972-991-0900	526-4546*
Maid Brigade USA/Minimaid Canada 4 Concourse Pkwy Suite 200 *TF:* 800-722-6243 ■ *Web:* www.maidbrigade.com	Atlanta	GA	30328	770-551-9630	391-9092
Maid to Perfection Corp 1101 Opal Ct 2nd Fl *TF:* 800-648-6243 ■ *Web:* www.maidtoperfectioncorp.com	Hagerstown	MD	21740	301-790-7900	790-3949
MaidPro Corp 180 Canal St *TF:* 888-624-3776 ■ *Web:* www.maidpro.com	Boston	MA	02114	617-742-8787	720-0700
Maids Home Services 4820 Dodge St *TF:* 800-843-6243 ■ *Web:* www.maids.com	Omaha	NE	68132	402-558-5555	558-4112
Maids International DBA Maids Home Services 4820 Dodge St *TF:* 800-843-6243 ■ *Web:* www.maids.com	Omaha	NE	68132	402-558-5555	558-4112
Merry Maids 3839 Forrest Hill-Irene Rd *TF:* 800-798-8000 ■ *Web:* www.merrymaids.com	Memphis	TN	38125	901-597-8100	597-8140
Molly Maid Inc 3948 Ranchero Dr *TF:* 800-665-5962 ■ *Web:* www.mollymaid.com	Ann Arbor	MI	48108	734-822-6800	822-6888
MPW Industrial Services Group Inc 9711 Lancaster Rd SE PO Box 10 *NASDAQ: MPWG* ■ *TF:* 800-827-8790 ■ *Web:* www.mpwgroup.com	Hebron	OH	43025	740-927-8790	928-8140
OctoClean Franchising Systems 5225 Canyon Crest Dr Suite 71-339 *Web:* www.octoclean.com	Riverside	CA	92507	951-683-5859	779-0270
OpenWorks 4742 N 24th St Suite 300 *TF:* 800-777-6736 ■ *Web:* www.openworksweb.com	Phoenix	AZ	85016	602-224-0440	468-3788
Patriarch Inc 2011 N Smallwood St	Baltimore	MD	21216	410-225-9122	728-4256
Paul Davis Restoration Inc 1 Independent Dr Suite 2300 *TF:* 800-722-1818 ■ *Web:* www.pdrestoration.com	Jacksonville	FL	32202	904-737-2779	737-4204
Professional Carpet Systems Inc (PCS) 4211 Atlantic Ave *TF:* 800-925-5055 ■ *Web:* www.procarpetsys.com	Raleigh	NC	27604	919-875-8871	875-9855
Rainbow International 1010 N University Park Dr *TF:* 800-583-9100 ■ *Web:* www.rainbowintl.com	Waco	TX	76707	254-745-2444	745-2592
Rentokil Initial 4067 Industrial Pk Dr Bldg 3 *Web:* www.rentokil-initial.com	Norcross	GA	30071	770-476-2590	497-3350
Serv-U-Clean Ltd 207 Edgeley Blvd Unit 5 *Web:* www.serv-u-clean.com	Concord	ON	L4K4B5	905-660-0899	660-0550
ServiceMaster Clean 3839 Forrest Hill Irene Rd *TF:* 800-633-5703 ■ *Web:* www.servicemasterclean.com	Memphis	TN	38125	901-597-7500	597-7600
Servpro Industries Inc 801 Industrial Blvd *TF:* 800-826-9586 ■ *Web:* www.servpro.com	Gallatin	TN	37066	615-451-0600	451-4861
Sharian Inc 368 W Ponce de Leon Ave	Decatur	GA	30030	404-373-2274	370-1812
Sparkle International Inc 26851 Richmond Rd *TF:* 800-321-0770 ■ *Web:* www.sparklewash.com	Cleveland	OH	44146	216-464-4212	464-8869
Stanley Steemer International Inc 5500 Stanley Steemer Pkwy *TF:* 800-848-7496 ■ *Web:* www.stanleysteemer.com	Dublin	OH	43016	614-764-2007	764-1506
Steam Brothers Inc 2124 E Sweet Ave *TF:* 800-767-5064 ■ *Web:* www.steambrothers.com	Bismarck	ND	58504	701-222-1263	222-1372
Steamatic Inc 303 Arthur St *TF:* 800-544-1303 ■ *Web:* www.steamatic.com	Fort Worth	TX	76107	817-332-1575	332-5349
Swisher Hygiene Co 6849 Fairview Rd **Fax Area Code:* 800 ■ *TF:* 800-444-4138 ■ *Web:* www.swisheronline.com	Charlotte	NC	28210	704-364-7707	444-4565*
System4 10060 Brecksville Rd *Web:* www.system4usa.com	Brecksville	OH	44141	440-746-0440	746-9544
Vanguard Cleaning Systems Inc 655 Mariners Island Blvd Suite 303 *TF:* 800-564-6422 ■ *Web:* www.vanguardcleaning.com	San Mateo	CA	94404	650-594-1500	591-1545
Window Gang 405 Arendell St *TF:* 877-946-4264 ■ *Web:* www.windowgang.com	Morehead City	NC	28557	252-726-1463	726-2837

153 CLOCKS, WATCHES, RELATED DEVICES, PARTS

Company	City	State	Zip	Phone	Fax
Baume & Mercier Inc 645 5th Ave *TF:* 800-683-2286 ■ *Web:* www.baume-et-mercier.com	New York	NY	10022	212-593-0444	755-3138
Benrus Watch Co Inc 2976 Northern Blvd **Fax:* Cust Svc ■ *TF:* 800-221-0131	Long Island City	NY	11101	718-472-7500	472-7661*
Berger MZ & Co Inc 2976 Northern Blvd *TF:* 800-221-0131 ■ *Web:* www.mzberger.com	Long Island City	NY	11101	718-472-7500	610-2745
Borg Indak Inc 701 Enterprise Dr *Web:* www.borgindak.com	Delavan	WI	53115	262-728-5531	728-3788
Bulova Corp 1 Bulova Ave *TF:* 800-228-5682 ■ *Web:* www.bulova.com	Woodside	NY	11377	718-204-3300	204-3546
Casio Inc 570 Mt Pleasant Ave **Fax:* Hum Res ■ *TF Cust Svc:* 800-634-1895 ■ *Web:* www.casio.com	Dover	NJ	07801	973-361-5400	537-8910*
Citizen Watch Co of America Inc 1200 Wall St W *TF:* 800-321-1023 ■ *Web:* www.citizenwatch.com	Lyndhurst	NJ	07071	201-438-8150	438-4161
Colibri/Park Lane Assoc Inc Linden Div 100 Niantic Ave *TF Sales:* 800-556-7354	Providence	RI	02907	401-943-2100	943-4230
E Gluck Corp 29-10 Thompson Ave *TF:* 800-937-0051 ■ *Web:* www.armitron.com	Long Island City	NY	11101	718-784-0700	482-2702
Elgin Watch Co 2976 Northern Blvd *TF:* 800-221-0131	Long Island City	NY	11101	718-472-7500	361-1705
Emperor Clock LLC 340 Industrial Park Dr **Fax Area Code:* 434 ■ *TF:* 800-642-0011 ■ *Web:* www.emperorclock.com	Amherst	VA	24521	800-642-0011	946-7747*
Fossil Inc 2280 N Greenville Ave *NASDAQ: FOSL* ■ *TF:* 800-969-0900 ■ *Web:* www.fossil.com	Richardson	TX	75082	972-234-2525	699-2169
Gluck E Corp 29-10 Thompson Ave *TF:* 800-937-0051 ■ *Web:* www.armitron.com	Long Island City	NY	11101	718-784-0700	482-2702
Hamilton Watch Co Inc 1200 Harbor Blvd *TF Cust Svc:* 800-456-5354 ■ *Web:* www.hamiltonwatch.com	Weehawken	NJ	07086	201-271-1400	271-4633
Howard Miller Clock Co 860 E Main Ave *Web:* www.howardmiller.com	Zeeland	MI	49464	616-772-9131	772-1670
Jules Jurgensen Helbros International 101 W City Ave *TF:* 800-220-1233 ■ *Web:* www.jjwatch.com	Bala Cynwyd	PA	19004	610-667-3500	667-3522
LVMH Watch & Jewelry USA 966 S Springfield Ave *TF:* 800-321-4832	Springfield	NJ	07081	973-467-1890	467-5495
Marcel Watch Corp 200 Meadowland Pkwy **Fax:* Cust Svc ■ *TF:* 800-422-6053 ■ *Web:* marcelwatch.com	Secaucus	NJ	07094	201-330-5600	330-0218*
Miller Howard Clock Co 860 E Main Ave *Web:* www.howardmiller.com	Zeeland	MI	49464	616-772-9131	772-1670
Movado Group Inc 650 From Rd *NYSE: MOV* ■ *TF:* 800-810-2311 ■ *Web:* www.movadogroupinc.com	Paramus	NJ	07652	201-267-8000	267-8070
MZ Berger & Co Inc 2976 Northern Blvd *TF:* 800-221-0131 ■ *Web:* www.mzberger.com	Long Island City	NY	11101	718-472-7500	610-2745
Pyramid Technologies Inc 48 Elm St *TF:* 888-479-7264 ■ *Web:* www.pyramid-technologies.com	Meriden	CT	06450	203-238-0550	634-1696
RADO USA 1200 Harbor Blvd *TF:* 877-839-5223 ■ *Web:* www.rado.ch	Weehawken	NJ	07086	201-271-1400	271-4633
Ridgeway Clock Co 1131 Mica Rd PO Box 407 *TF Cust Svc:* 800-828-4441 ■ *Web:* www.ridgewayclocks.com	Ridgeway	VA	24148	276-956-3116	956-2033
Rolex Watch USA Inc 665 5th Ave *Web:* www.rolex.com	New York	NY	10022	212-758-7700	371-0371
Seiko Corp of America 1111 MacArthur Blvd **Fax:* Cust Svc ■ *TF Cust Svc:* 800-782-2510 ■ *Web:* www.seikousa.com	Mahwah	NJ	07430	201-529-5730	529-5985*
Seiko Instruments USA Inc 12301 Technology Blvd *TF:* 800-358-0880 ■ *Web:* www.seikoinstruments.com	Austin	TX	78727	512-349-3800	349-3000
Skagen Designs Inc 640 Maestro Dr Suite 100 *TF:* 800-791-6784 ■ *Web:* www.skagen.com	Reno	NV	89511	775-850-5500	850-5530
Sligh Furniture Co 217 E 24th St Suite 102 *TF:* 866-277-0258 ■ *Web:* www.sligh.com	Holland	MI	49423	616-392-7101	392-9495
Speidel Corp 25 Fairmount Ave *TF:* 800-441-2200 ■ *Web:* www.speidel.com	East Providence	RI	02914	401-519-2000	519-2019
Swatch Group 1200 Harbor Blvd 7th Fl *TF:* 800-456-5354 ■ *Web:* www.swatchgroup.com	Weehawken	NJ	07087	201-271-1400	271-4633
Swiss Army Brands Inc 1 Research Dr PO Box 874 *TF Cust Svc:* 800-243-4057 ■ *Web:* www.swissarmy.com	Shelton	CT	06484	203-929-6391	929-3786
Telechron Inc 2025 Trade St *Web:* www.telechrontimers.com	Leland	NC	28451	910-371-1132	371-1133
Timex Corp 555 Christian Rd *TF:* 800-367-8463 ■ *Web:* www.timex.com	Middlebury	CT	06762	203-346-5000	346-5139
Verdin Co 444 Reading Rd *TF:* 800-543-0488 ■ *Web:* www.verdin.com	Cincinnati	OH	45202	513-241-4010	241-1855
Vulcan Inc 410 E Berry Ave *TF:* 800-633-6845 ■ *Web:* www.vulcaninc.com	Foley	AL	36535	251-943-1541	943-9270
Wittnauer International Co 26-15 Brooklyn Queens Expy *TF Orders:* 800-228-5682 ■ *Web:* www.wittnauer.com	Woodside	NY	11377	718-204-3300	204-3373
World of Watches 14051 NW 14th St Bay 6 *TF:* 800-222-0077 ■ *Web:* www.worldofwatches.com	Sunrise	FL	33323	954-453-2821	453-2950

154 CLOSURES - METAL OR PLASTICS

Company	City	State	Zip	Phone	Fax
Alcoa Closure Systems International Inc 6625 Network Way Suite 200 *Web:* www.alcoa.com/csi	Indianapolis	IN	46278	317-390-5000	390-5137
Alliance Plastics Inc 3123 Station Rd *TF:* 877-728-9227 ■ *Web:* www.allianceplastics.com	Erie	PA	16510	814-899-7671	898-1638
AptarGroup Inc 475 W Terra Cotta Ave Suite E *NYSE: ATR* ■ *Web:* www.aptargroup.com	Crystal Lake	IL	60014	815-477-0424	477-0481
Caplugs LLC 2150 Elmwood Ave *TF:* 888-227-5847 ■ *Web:* www.caplugs.com	Buffalo	NY	14207	716-876-9855	874-1680
Captive Plastics Inc 251 Circle Dr N *Web:* www.caplas.com	Piscataway	NJ	08854	732-469-7900	271-5200
Carpin Mfg Inc 411 Austin Rd *TF:* 800-227-7461 ■ *Web:* www.carpin.com	Waterbury	CT	06705	203-574-2556	753-8771
Champion Container Corp 180 Essex Ave PO Box 90 *Web:* www.championcontainer.com	Avenel	NJ	07001	732-636-6700	855-8663
Danbury Plastics Inc 87 Beaver Brook Rd *Web:* www.danburyplastics.com	Danbury	CT	06810	203-743-6745	790-6801
Magenta Corp 3800 N Milwaukee Ave *TF:* 800-387-4378 ■ *Web:* www.magentacorp.com	Chicago	IL	60641	773-777-5050	777-4055
MeadWestvaco Calmar 2300-B Pellissier Rd *TF:* 800-841-4112 ■ *Web:* www.calmar.com	City of Industry	CA	90601	562-463-3500	463-3591
New High Glass Inc 12713 SW 125th Ave *TF:* 800-452-7787 ■ *Web:* www.newhigh.com	Miami	FL	33186	305-232-0840	251-4622
Niagara Plastics Co 7090 Edinboro Rd *TF Sales:* 800-458-0465 ■ *Web:* www.niagaraplastics.com	Erie	PA	16509	814-868-3671	864-7584
Penn-Wheeling Metal Closure & Caps 1701 Wheeling Ave *TF:* 800-999-2567 ■ *Web:* www.penn-wheeling.com	Glen Dale	WV	26038	304-845-3402	843-5475
Phoenix Closures Inc 1899 High Grove Ln *Web:* www.phoenixclosures.com	Naperville	IL	60540	630-420-4750	420-4774
Polytop Corp 110 Graham Dr *Web:* www.polytop.com	Slatersville	RI	02876	401-767-2400	765-2694
Portola Packaging Inc 97 E Brokaw Rd Suite 250 *TF:* 800-767-8652 ■ *Web:* www.portpack.com	San Jose	CA	95112	408-454-4961	454-4969
Portola Tech International Inc 85 Fairmount St *TF:* 800-556-7630 ■ *Web:* www.portolatech.com	Woonsocket	RI	02895	401-765-0600	766-8324

Phone Fax

Rexam Closures & Containers 3245 Kansas Rd ... Evansville IN 47725 812-867-6671 867-6861
Web: www.rexamclosures.com

Rieke Corp 500 W 7th St ... Auburn IN 46706 260-925-3700 925-2493
Web: www.riekepackaging.com

Seaquist Closures LLC 711 Fox St ... Mukwonago WI 53149 262-363-7191 363-9418
Web: www.seaquistclosures.com

Silgan Holdings Inc 4 Landmark Sq Suite 400 ... Stamford CT 06901 203-975-7110 975-7902
NASDAQ: SLGN ■ *Web:* www.silganholdings.com

StockCap 123 Manufacturers Dr ... Arnold MO 63010 636-282-6800 282-6888
TF: 800-827-2277 ■ *Web:* www.stockcap.com

Stull Technologies Inc 17 Veronica Ave ... Somerset NJ 08873 732-873-5000 873-1295
Web: www.stulltech.com

Tipper Tie Inc 2000 Lufkin Rd ... Apex NC 27502 919-362-8811 362-7058
TF: 800-331-2905 ■ *Web:* www.tippertie.com

Top-Seal Corp 2236 E University Dr ... Phoenix AZ 85034 602-629-9000 629-9002
TF: 800-452-8677 ■ *Web:* www.top-seal.com

Tri-Sure Closures North America 290 E Fullerton Ave ... Carol Stream IL 60188 630-665-7900 665-7720
Web: www.tri-sure.com

Van Blarcom Closures Inc 156 Sandford St ... Brooklyn NY 11205 718-855-3810 935-9855
Web: www.vbcpkg.com

Weatherchem Corp 2222 Highland Rd ... Twinsburg OH 44087 330-425-4206 425-1385
Web: www.weatherchem.com

West Penn Plastic Inc 4117 Pulaski Rd ... New Castle PA 16101 724-654-2081 654-5126
Web: www.westpennplastic.com

155 CLOTHING & ACCESSORIES - MFR

SEE ALSO Baby Products p. 1366; Clothing & Accessories - Whol p. 1455; Fashion Design Houses p. 1634; Footwear p. 1665; Leather Goods - Personal p. 1889; Personal Protective Equipment & Clothing p. 2105

155-1 Athletic Apparel

Phone Fax

Ashworth Inc 2765 Loker Ave W ... Carlsbad CA 92010 760-438-6610 476-8417
NASDAQ: ASHW ■ *TF:* 800-800-8443 ■ *Web:* www.ashworthinc.com

Betlin Inc 4411 Marketing Pl ... Groveport OH 43125 614-443-0248 788-1233*
**Fax Area Code: 800* ■ *TF:* 800-923-8546 ■ *Web:* www.betlin.com

Bike Athletic Co 3303 Cumberland Blvd ... Atlanta GA 30339 678-742-8255 742-3182
Web: www.bikeathletic.com

Bogner of America Inc 172 Bogner Dr ... Newport VT 05855 802-334-6507 334-6870
TF: 800-415-4477 ■ *Web:* www.bogner.com

Bristol Products Corp 700 Shelby St ... Bristol TN 37620 423-968-4140 968-2084
TF Orders: 800-336-8775 ■ *Web:* www.bristolproducts.com

Capezio/Ballet Makers Inc 1 Campus Rd ... Totowa NJ 07512 973-595-9000 595-9120
TF: 800-595-9002 ■ *Web:* www.capeziodance.com

Champion Athletic Wear 1000 E Hanes Mill Rd ... Winston-Salem NC 27105 336-519-4400 519-6501
TF: 800-999-2249 ■ *Web:* www.championforwomen.com

Choi Brothers Inc 3401 W Division St ... Chicago IL 60651 773-489-2800 489-3030
TF: 800-524-2464 ■ *Web:* www.choibrothers.com

Columbia Sportswear Co 14375 NW Science Park Dr ... Portland OR 97229 503-985-4000 985-5800
NASDAQ: COLM ■ *TF:* 800-547-8066 ■ *Web:* www.columbia.com

CranBarry Inc 330 C Lynnway ... Lynn MA 01901 781-586-0111 586-0122
TF: 800-992-2021 ■ *Web:* www.cranbarry.com

Cutter & Buck Inc 701 N 34th St Suite 400 ... Seattle WA 98103 206-622-4191 448-0589
NASDAQ: CBUK ■ *TF:* 800-929-9299 ■ *Web:* www.cutterbuck.com

Darbo Mfg Co Inc 182 N Cypress St ... Pomona CA 91768 909-622-0321 622-0192
Web: www.dancewearforyou.com

DeLong Sportswear Inc 821 5th Ave ... Grinnell IA 50112 641-236-3106 236-4891
TF: 800-733-5664 ■ *Web:* www.delong-sportswear.com

Dodger Industries 1702 21st St ... Eldora IA 50627 641-939-5464 939-5185
TF: 800-247-7879 ■ *Web:* www.dodgerindustries.com

Elite Sportswear LP 2136 N 13th St ... Reading PA 19604 610-921-1469 921-0208
TF Cust Svc: 800-345-4087 ■ *Web:* www.gk-elitesportswear.com

Everlast Worldwide Inc 1350 Broadway Suite 2300 ... New York NY 10018 212-239-0990 239-4261
NASDAQ: EVST ■ *Web:* www.everlast.com

Fila USA Inc 1 Fila Way ... Sparks MD 21152 410-773-3000 773-1073
TF: 800-787-3452 ■ *Web:* www.fila.com

Gear for Sports Inc 9700 Commerce Pkwy ... Lenexa KS 66219 913-693-3200 693-3908
TF: 800-423-5044 ■ *Web:* www.gearforsports.com

Hanesbrands Inc 1000 E Hanes Mill Rd ... Winston-Salem NC 27105 336-519-4400 519-8746
NYSE: HBI ■ *Web:* www.hanesbrands.com

Hilton Apparel Group 510 Maryville University Dr Suite 110 ... Saint Louis MO 63141 314-819-2800 819-2988
TF: 800-323-5590 ■ *Web:* www.hiltoncc.com

Jantzen Inc 424 NE 18th Ave ... Portland OR 97232 503-238-5000 238-5930
TF: 800-626-0215 ■ *Web:* www.jantzen.com

King Louie International Inc 13500 15th St ... Grandview MO 64030 816-765-5212 765-3228
TF: 800-521-5212 ■ *Web:* www.kinglouie.com/home

Marika Group Inc 8960 Carroll Way ... San Diego CA 92121 858-537-5300 537-5400
TF: 800-666-2927 ■ *Web:* www.marika.com

Marker International 1070 W 2300 South ... Salt Lake City UT 84119 801-972-2100 972-1011
TF: 800-453-3862 ■ *Web:* www.markerusa.com

MJ Soffe Co 1 Soffe Dr ... Fayetteville NC 28312 910-483-2500 486-9030
TF: 800-723-4223 ■ *Web:* www.mjsoffe.com

Moving Comfort Inc 4500 Southgate Pl Suite 800 ... Chantilly VA 20151 703-631-1000 631-1001
TF: 800-763-6000 ■ *Web:* www.movingcomfort.com

No Fear 2251 Faraday Ave ... Carlsbad CA 92008 760-931-9550 931-9741
TF: 800-266-3327 ■ *Web:* www.nofear.com

Onfield Apparel Group LLC 8677 LogoAthletic Ct ... Indianapolis IN 46219 317-895-7000 895-7250
TF: 800-955-6467

Pacific Trail Inc 1700 Westlake Ave N Suite 200 ... Seattle WA 98109 206-270-5300 270-5301
TF: 800-877-8878 ■ *Web:* www.pacifictrail.com

Powers Mfg Co 1340 Sycamore St PO Box 2157 ... Waterloo IA 50704 319-233-6118 234-8048
Web: www.powersathletic.com

Race Face Components Inc 100 Braid St Unit 100 ... New Westminster BC V3L3P4 604-527-9996 527-9959
TF: 800-527-9244 ■ *Web:* www.raceface.com

Royal Textile Mills Inc 929 Firetower Rd ... Yanceyville NC 27379 336-694-4121 694-9084
TF: 800-334-9361 ■ *Web:* www.dukeathletic.com

Russell Corp 755 Lee St ... Alexander City AL 35010 256-500-4000 500-5045
NYSE: RML ■ *TF:* 800-729-2905 ■ *Web:* www.russellcorp.com

Russell Corp Russell Athletic Div 755 Lee St ... Alexander City AL 35010 256-500-4000 500-5045
TF: 800-729-2905 ■ *Web:* www.russellathletic.com

Salomon North America 5055 N Greeley Ave ... Portland OR 97217 971-234-2300 234-2450
TF: 877-272-5666 ■ *Web:* www.salomonsports.com

Scotty's Fashions Inc 636 Pen Argyl St ... Pen Argyl PA 18072 610-863-6454 863-6495
Web: www.scottysfashions.com

Shaffer Sportswear Mfg Inc 224 N Washington St ... Neosho MO 64850 417-451-9444 451-6451
TF Orders: 800-643-3300

Southland Athletic Mfg Co 714 E Grove St ... Terrell TX 75160 972-563-3321 563-0943
TF: 800-527-7637 ■ *Web:* www.southland-athletic.com

Speedline Athletic Wear 1804 N Habana Ave ... Tampa FL 33607 813-876-1375 873-8714
Web: www.propakspeedline.com

Sports Belle Inc 6723 Pleasant Ridge Rd ... Knoxville TN 37921 865-938-2063 947-4466
TF Sales: 800-888-2063 ■ *Web:* www.sportsbelle.com

Stone International LLC 317 Neely Ferry Rd ... Mauldin SC 29662 864-288-4822 288-1478
TF Cust Svc: 800-762-2637 ■ *Web:* www.stonellc.com

Tighe Industries Inc 333 E 7th Ave ... York PA 17404 717-252-1578 852-6982
TF: 800-839-1039 ■ *Web:* www.tighe.com

Under Armour Inc 1020 Hull St 3rd Fl ... Baltimore MD 21230 410-454-6428 468-2516
NASDAQ: UARM ■ *TF:* 888-427-6687 ■ *Web:* www.underarmour.com

Volcom Inc 1740 Monrovia Ave ... Costa Mesa CA 92627 949-646-2175 646-5247
NASDAQ: VCLM ■ *Web:* www.volcom.com

155-2 Belts (Leather, Plastics, Fabric)

Phone Fax

Chambers Belt Co Inc 3230 E Broadway Rd Suite A-200 ... Phoenix AZ 85040 602-276-0016 276-0210
TF: 800-528-1388 ■ *Web:* www.chambersbelt.com

Circa Corp 1330 Fitzgerald Ave ... San Francisco CA 94124 415-822-1600 822-1700
Web: www.circacorp.com

French Craft Leather Goods Co Inc 234 W 24th St ... Los Angeles CA 90007 213-746-6771 746-4610
TF: 800-541-0088

Gem Dandy Inc 200 W Academy St ... Madison NC 27025 336-548-9624 427-7105
TF: 800-334-5101 ■ *Web:* www.gem-dandy.com

Humphreys Inc 2009 W Hastings St ... Chicago IL 60608 312-997-2358 997-2147
TF Cust Svc: 800-621-8541 ■ *Web:* www.humphreysinc.com

L Chessler Inc 5301 Tacony St Bldg 208 ... Philadelphia PA 19137 215-288-4403 288-4633

Leegin Creative Leather Co 14022 Nelson Ave ... City of Industry CA 91746 626-961-9381 369-1771
TF: 800-235-8748 ■ *Web:* www.brighton.com

M Aron Corp 350 5th Ave Suite 3005 ... New York NY 10118 212-643-8883 643-8884
TF: 800-899-2766

Max Leather Group Inc 14-15 Redfern Ave ... Far Rockaway NY 11691 718-471-3300 471-3707

Swank Inc 90 Park Ave 13th Fl ... New York NY 10016 212-867-2600 370-1039
Web: www.swankinc.com

Tandy Brands Accessories Inc 690 E Lamar Blvd Suite 200 ... Arlington TX 76011 817-548-0090 548-1144
NASDAQ: TBAC ■ *TF:* 800-570-7443 ■ *Web:* www.tandybrands.com

TGL 300 Wilson Ave ... Norwalk CT 06854 203-853-4747 853-0070

Trafalgar Ghurka Ltd 300 Wilson Ave ... Norwalk CT 06854 203-853-4747 853-0070

155-3 Casual Wear (Men's & Women's)

Phone Fax

Alps Sportswear Mfg Co 15 Union St ... Lawrence MA 01840 978-683-2438 686-8051
TF: 800-262-7010 ■ *Web:* www.alps-sportswear.com

Attraction Inc 672 rue du Parc ... Lac-Drolet QC G0Y1C0 819-549-2477 549-2734
TF: 800-567-6095 ■ *Web:* www.attraction.com

Badger Sportswear Inc 850 Meacham Rd ... Statesville NC 28677 704-876-4648 871-0521
TF: 800-868-0105 ■ *Web:* www.badgersportswear.com

Beltex Corp 130 Knitcraft Access Rd ... Belmont NC 28012 704-825-3381 825-4260

Big Dog Holdings Inc 121 Gray Ave ... Santa Barbara CA 93101 805-963-8727 962-9460
NASDAQ: BDOG ■ *TF Sales:* 800-244-3647 ■ *Web:* www.bigdogs.com

Big Dog Sportswear 121 Gray Ave ... Santa Barbara CA 93101 805-963-8727 899-2917*
**Fax: Hum Res* ■ *TF Orders:* 800-642-3647 ■ *Web:* www.bigdogs.com

Bobby Jones Retail Corp 1155 N Clinton Ave ... Rochester NY 14621 585-467-7021 987-8953*
**Fax Area Code: 800* ■ **Fax: Sales* ■ *TF Cust Svc:* 888-603-8968 ■
Web: www.bobbyjonesshop.com

California Mfg Co 2270 Weldon Pkwy ... Saint Louis MO 63146 314-567-4404 567-5062
TF: 888-567-7004 ■ *Web:* www.californiamfg.com

Champion Products Inc 1000 E Hanes Mill Rd ... Winston-Salem NC 27105 336-519-6500 519-6501*
**Fax: Hum Res* ■ *TF:* 800-999-2249 ■ *Web:* www.saralee.com

Cherokee Inc 6835 Valjean Ave ... Van Nuys CA 91406 818-908-9868 908-9191
NASDAQ: CHKE ■ *Web:* www.cherokeegroup.com

Columbia Sportswear Co 14375 NW Science Park Dr ... Portland OR 97229 503-985-4000 985-5800
NASDAQ: COLM ■ *TF:* 800-547-8066 ■ *Web:* www.columbia.com

Crazy Shirts Inc 99-969 Iwaena St ... Aiea HI 96701 808-487-9919 486-1276
TF: 800-771-2720 ■ *Web:* www.crazyshirts.com

Cross Creek Apparel LLC 3330 Cumberland Blvd Suite 1000 ... Atlanta GA 30339 678-742-8000 742-8300
TF: 800-321-1138 ■ *Web:* www.crosscreek.com

Deckers Outdoor Corp 495-A S Fairview Ave ... Goleta CA 93117 805-967-7611 967-9722
NASDAQ: DECK ■ *TF:* 800-858-5342 ■ *Web:* www.deckers.com

Delta Apparel Inc 2750 Premier Pkwy Suite 100 ... Duluth GA 30097 678-775-6900 775-6992
AMEX: DLA ■ *TF:* 800-285-4456 ■ *Web:* www.deltaapparel.com

Eddie Bauer Inc 15010 NE 36th St ... Redmond WA 98052 425-755-6100 414-6110*
**Fax Area Code: 800* ■ *TF Orders:* 800-426-8020 ■ *Web:* www.eddiebauer.com

Fortune Dogs Inc DBA Big Dog Sportswear 121 Gray Ave ... Santa Barbara CA 93101 805-963-8727 899-2917*
**Fax: Hum Res* ■ *TF Orders:* 800-642-3647 ■ *Web:* www.bigdogs.com

Fortune Fashions Industries LLC 4700 S Boyle Ave ... Vernon CA 90058 323-277-7740 277-7745
TF: 800-788-6550

Fruit of the Loom Inc 1 Fruit of the Loom Dr ... Bowling Green KY 42103 270-781-6400 438-1197
Web: www.fruit.com

Fun-Tees Inc 209 S Chestnut St ... Lumberton NC 28358 910-738-6231 739-1753
Web: www.funtees.com

Garan Inc 350 5th Ave 19th Fl ... New York NY 10118 212-563-2000 971-2250
TF: 800-326-0225

Gildan 600 Maisonneuve ... Montreal QC H3A3J2 514-735-2023 735-6810
NYSE: GSE ■ *TF:* 866-755-2023 ■ *Web:* gildan.com

Hamrick Industries 742 Peachoid Rd ... Gaffney SC 29341 864-489-6095 489-9514
TF: 800-487-5411 ■ *Web:* www.hamricks.com

Harper Industries Inc 52 Virginia St ... Lucedale MS 39452 601-947-2746 947-4739

Hilfiger Tommy Sportswear Inc 25 W 39th St ... New York NY 10018 212-840-8888
TF: 800-888-8802 ■ *Web:* www.tommy.com

IC Isaacs & Co Inc 3840 Bank St ... Baltimore MD 21224 410-342-8200 276-4087
TF: 800-537-5995 ■ *Web:* www.icisaacs.com

JanSport Inc N 850 County Hwy CB ... Appleton WI 54914 920-734-5708 735-1933
TF Cust Svc: 800-346-8239 ■ *Web:* www.jansport.com

Kellwood New England 300 Manley St ... Brockton MA 02303 508-588-7200 513-3013
TF Cust Svc: 800-225-6987 ■ *Web:* www.kellwood.com

L & L Mfg Co 815 N Nash St ... El Segundo CA 90245 310-615-0000 615-4549

Mossimo Inc 2016 Broadway ... Santa Monica CA 90404 310-460-0040
NASDAQ: MOSS

Nemanco Inc 1028 Hopewell Rd ... Philadelphia MS 39350 601-656-7361 656-7645

North Face Inc 2013 Farallon Dr ... San Leandro CA 94577 510-618-3500 618-3571*
**Fax: Sales* ■ *TF:* 800-535-3331 ■ *Web:* www.thenorthface.com

Ocean Pacific Apparel Corp 3 Studebaker ... Irvine CA 92618 949-580-1888 580-1870
TF: 800-562-3269 ■ *Web:* www.op.com

Phat Fashions LLC 512 7th Ave 43rd Fl ... New York NY 10018 212-391-9443 391-9448
Web: www.phatfarm.com

Pomare Ltd 700 N Nimitz Hwy ... Honolulu HI 96817 808-524-3966 533-6809
TF: 800-233-8912

Casual Wear (Men's & Women's) (Cont'd)

Phone Fax

Quiksilver Inc 15202 Graham St .... Huntington Beach CA 92649 714-889-2200 889-3700
NYSE: ZQK ■ *TF:* 800-576-4004 ■ *Web:* www.quiksilver.com
Quitman Mfg Co Inc 604 N Highland Rd .... Quitman GA 31643 229-263-7573 263-7903
Rothschild & Co Inc 500 7th Ave .... New York NY 10018 212-354-8550 382-1187
Russell Corp Jerzees Div 755 Lee St .... Alexander City AL 35010 256-500-4000 500-5045
TF: 800-729-2905 ■ *Web:* www.jerzees.com
Seattle Pacific Industries 21216 72nd Ave S .... Kent WA 98032 253-872-2940 872-2949
Sherry Mfg Co Inc 3287 NW 65th St .... Miami FL 33147 305-693-7000 691-6132
TF: 800-741-4750 ■ *Web:* www.sherrymfg.com
Sport-Haley Inc 4600 E 48th Ave .... Denver CO 80216 303-320-8800 320-8822
NASDAQ: SPOR ■ *TF:* 800-627-9211 ■ *Web:* www.sporthaley.com
Stussy Inc 17426 Daimler St .... Irvine CA 92614 949-474-9255 474-8229
Web: www.stussy.com
Surf Line Hawaii Ltd 1451 Kalani St .... Honolulu HI 96817 808-847-5985 841-5254
Web: www.jamsworld.com/jamsworld/
Tommy Hilfiger USA Inc 25 W 39th St .... New York NY 10018 212-840-8888
TF: 800-888-8802 ■ *Web:* www.tommy.com
Val D'Or Inc 475 Park Ave S 9th Fl .... New York NY 10016 212-594-7050 564-0043
VF Activewear 4408 W Linebaugh Ave .... Tampa FL 33624 813-963-6153 969-6509*
**Fax:* Hum Res ■ *TF:* 800-444-5574
VF Corp 105 Corporate Center Blvd .... Greensboro NC 27408 336-424-6000 424-7634
NYSE: VFC ■ *Web:* www.vfc.com
VF Imagewear Inc 3375 Joseph Martin Hwy .... Martinsville VA 24115 276-632-7200 956-7826*
**Fax:* Sales ■ *TF:* 800-832-6469 ■ *Web:* www.vfc.com
Wex-Tex Industries Inc 814 6th Ave .... Ashford AL 36312 334-899-5116 899-4546
TF: 866-456-6843
Whisper Knits Ltd 10195 Hwy 211 E .... Aberdeen NC 28315 910-944-2005 944-2094
Web: www.whisperknits.com
Wolf Mfg Co 1801 W Waco Dr .... Waco TX 76707 254-753-7301 753-8919*
**Fax Area Code:* 257 ■ *TF:* 800-437-0940 ■ *Web:* www.wolfmfg.com
Wright's Knitwear Corp 10 E 34th St .... New York NY 10016 212-779-2600 779-2661
TF: 800-952-8788

155-4 Children's & Infants' Clothing

Phone Fax

Alexis Playsafe 999 Chestnut St SE .... Gainesville GA 30503 770-535-3000 535-2429
TF: 800-253-9476
Baby Togs Inc 460 W 34th St 15th Fl .... New York NY 10001 212-868-2100 947-2039
Web: www.babytogs.com
Bentex Group Inc 34 W 33rd St 2nd Fl .... New York NY 10001 212-594-4250 967-9328
TF: 800-451-0285
Boscorale 112 W 34th St Suite 1618 .... New York NY 10120 212-279-6542 967-6446
Byer California 66 Potrero Ave .... San Francisco CA 94103 415-626-7844 626-7865
TF: 800-998-2937 ■ *Web:* www.byer.com
Candlesticks Inc 112 W 34th St Suite 911 .... New York NY 10120 212-947-8900 643-9653
Carter's Inc 1170 Peachtree St NE Suite 900 .... Atlanta GA 30309 404-745-2700 892-0968
NYSE: CRI ■ *TF:* 888-782-9548 ■ *Web:* www.carters.com
Chocolate Soup Inc 905 NE Colbern Rd .... Lee's Summit MO 64086 816-525-2222 525-7514
Devil Dog Mfg Co Inc 400 E Gannon Ave .... Zebulon NC 27597 919-269-7485 269-5962
Donegal Industries Inc 860 Anderson Ferry Rd .... Mount Joy PA 17552 717-653-1486 653-6658
Eiseman Co LLC 342 N Water St .... Milwaukee WI 53202 414-272-3222 272-4274
Web: www.florenceeiseman.com
Garan Inc 350 5th Ave 19th Fl .... New York NY 10118 212-563-2000 971-2250
TF: 800-326-0225
Gerber Childrenswear Inc 7005 Pelham Rd Suite D .... Greenville SC 29602 864-987-5200 987-5264
TF: 800-642-4452 ■ *Web:* gerberchildrenswear.com
Gerson & Gerson Inc 112 W 34th St 17th Fl .... New York NY 10120 212-244-6775 244-6794
Web: bonniejean.com
Good Lad Apparel 431 E Tioga St .... Philadelphia PA 19134 215-739-0200 739-5150
Web: www.goodlad.com
Happy Kids Inc 100 W 33rd St Suite 1100 .... New York NY 10001 212-695-1151 736-0397
Herzman & Co Inc 145 N Franklin Tpke .... Ramsey NJ 07446 201-236-1212 236-1252
IFG Corp 100 W 33rd St .... New York NY 10001 212-629-9600 629-6699
TF: 800-873-5511
Irwin Mfg Corp 398 Fitzgerald Hwy .... Ocilla GA 31774 229-468-9481 468-9484
Isfel Co Inc 900 Hart St .... Rahway NJ 07065 732-382-3100 388-0587
TF: 800-927-8760
Kahn Lucas Lancaster Inc 100 W 33rd St Suite 921 .... New York NY 10001 212-244-4500 643-1345
Web: www.kahnlucas.com
Lollytogs Ltd 100 W 33rd St Suite 1012 .... New York NY 10001 212-594-4740 268-5160
TF: 800-262-5437 ■ *Web:* www.lollytogs.com
Mayfair Co Absorba Div 100 W 33rd St Suite 813 .... New York NY 10001 212-279-3211 714-0401
Mayfair Infant Wear Co 100 Wesley White Rd .... Carteret NJ 07008 732-382-4055 381-4020
Mini Togs Inc 3030 Aurora Ave .... Monroe LA 71211 318-388-4916 323-1899
TF: 800-588-6227
My Michelle 13071 E Temple Ave .... City of Industry CA 91746 626-934-4166 934-4165
New ICM LP 112 W 34th St Suite 1108 .... New York NY 10020 212-695-8554 268-0422
TF: 800-978-9008 ■ *Web:* www.newicm.com
OshKosh B'Gosh Inc 112 Otter Ave .... Oshkosh WI 54901 920-231-8800 231-8621
TF: 800-282-4674 ■ *Web:* www.oshkoshbgosh.com
Robin International (USA) Inc 131 W 33rd St Suite 408 .... New York NY 10001 212-967-6800 967-6840
Royal Park Uniforms Co 14139 Hwy 86 S .... Prospect Hill NC 27314 336-562-3345 562-3832
Web: www.royal-park.com
S Schwab Co Inc 12101 Upper Potomac Industrial Park ST .... Cumberland MD 21502 301-729-4488 729-4057
TF: 800-533-5437 ■ *Web:* www.sschwab.com
Samara Brothers Inc 112 W 34th St Suite 1101 .... New York NY 10120 212-695-0210 695-0267
Spencers Inc 238 Willow St .... Mount Airy NC 27030 336-789-9111 789-6824
TF: 800-633-9111 ■ *Web:* www.spencers.com
Star Children's Dress Co Inc 100 W 33rd St Suite 1005 .... New York NY 10001 212-279-1524 967-4915
Tawil Assoc Inc 100 Wesley White Rd .... Carteret NJ 07008 732-382-4055 381-4020
Warren Featherbone Co DBA Alexis Playsafe
999 Chestnut St SE .... Gainesville GA 30503 770-535-3000 535-2429
TF: 800-253-9476
Waterbury Garment LLC 1669 Thomaston Ave .... Waterbury CT 06704 203-574-3811 575-0169

155-5 Coats (Overcoats, Jackets, Raincoats, etc)

Phone Fax

Alpha Industries Inc 14155 Sullyfield Cir Suite G .... Chantilly VA 20151 703-378-1420 378-4910
Web: www.alphaindustries.com
Bradley-Scott Clothes Inc PO Box 326 .... Fall River MA 02724 508-676-1078 676-0339
Essex Mfg Inc 350 5th Ave Suite 501 .... New York NY 10118 212-239-0080 714-2958
TF: 800-648-6010 ■ *Web:* www.baum-essex.com
Forecaster of Boston 1 Ace St .... Fall River MA 02720 508-676-6200 676-1118
TF: 800-760-7000
G-III Apparel Group Ltd 512 7th Ave 35th Fl .... New York NY 10018 212-403-0600 403-0551
NASDAQ: GIII ■ *Web:* www.g-iii.com
Helly Hansen US Inc
3326 160th Ave SE Kenyon Center Suite 200 .... Bellevue WA 98008 425-378-8700 649-3740
TF: 800-435-5901 ■ *Web:* www.hellyhansen.com

Phone Fax

High Sierra Sport Co 880 Corporate Woods Pkwy .... Vernon Hills IL 60061 847-913-1100 913-1145
TF: 800-323-9590 ■ *Web:* www.hssc.com
Holloway Sportswear Inc 2633 Campbell Rd .... Sidney OH 45365 937-596-7575 497-1555*
**Fax:* Cust Svc ■ *TF:* 800-331-5156 ■ *Web:* www.hollowayusa.com
Item House Inc 2920 S Steele St .... Tacoma WA 98409 253-627-7168 627-1070
TF: 800-426-8990
La Cross/Rainfair Inc 18550 NE Riverside Pkwy .... Portland OR 97230 503-766-1005 558-0188*
**Fax Area Code:* 800 ■ *TF:* 800-558-5990
Levy Group Inc 512 7th Ave 3rd Fl .... New York NY 10018 212-398-0707 944-7857
TF: 800-223-2073
London Fog Industries 1700 Westlake Ave N Suite 200 .... Seattle WA 98109 206-270-5300 270-5301
TF: 800-877-8878 ■ *Web:* www.londonfog.com
MECA Sportswear Inc 3499 Lexington Ave N Suite 205 .... Arden Hills MN 55126 651-638-3800
TF: 800-729-6322 ■ *Web:* www.mecasportswear.com
Pacific Trail Inc 1700 Westlake Ave N Suite 200 .... Seattle WA 98109 206-270-5300 270-5301
TF: 800-877-8878 ■ *Web:* www.pacifictrail.com
Pendleton Woolen Mills Inc 220 NW Broadway .... Portland OR 97209 503-226-4801 535-5502
TF: 800-760-4844 ■ *Web:* www.pendleton-usa.com
Perfect Petite Coat Co 463 7th Ave 12th Fl .... New York NY 10018 212-239-2025 239-8823
RefrigiWear Inc 54 Breakstone Dr .... Dahlonega GA 30533 706-864-5757 864-5898
TF Cust Svc: 800-645-3744 ■ *Web:* www.refrigiwear.com
Rennoc Corp 3501 Southeast Blvd .... Vineland NJ 08360 856-327-5400 327-0197
TF Cust Svc: 800-252-2538 ■ *Web:* www.rennoc.com
Sport-Haley Inc 4600 E 48th Ave .... Denver CO 80216 303-320-8800 320-8822
NASDAQ: SPOR ■ *TF:* 800-627-9211 ■ *Web:* www.sporthaley.com
Sport Obermeyer Ltd USA Inc 115 AABC .... Aspen CO 81611 970-925-5060 925-9203
TF: 800-525-4203 ■ *Web:* www.obermeyer.com
Standard Mfg Co Inc 750 2nd Ave .... Troy NY 12182 518-235-2200 235-2668
TF Cust Svc: 800-227-1056
Whaling Mfg Co 451 Quarry St .... Fall River MA 02723 508-678-9061 678-9726
TF: 800-225-8554 ■ *Web:* www.newportharboronline.com
Woolrich Inc 2 Mill St .... Woolrich PA 17779 570-769-6464 769-6470
TF: 800-995-1299 ■ *Web:* www.woolrich.com

155-6 Costumes

Phone Fax

Art Stone Enterprises 1795 Express Dr N .... Smithtown NY 11787 631-582-9500 582-9541
TF: 800-522-8897 ■ *Web:* www.artstonecostumes.com
Bevan Mfg Co 4451 Rt 130 .... Burlington NJ 08016 609-386-6501 386-0677
TF: 800-222-8125 ■ *Web:* www.costumegallery.net
Cleveland Costume & Display 18489 Pearl Rd .... Strongsville OH 44136 440-846-9292 846-9294
Costume Specialists Inc 211 N 5th St .... Columbus OH 43215 614-464-2115 464-2114
TF: 800-596-9357 ■ *Web:* www.costumespecialists.com
Curtain Call Costumes 333 E 7th Ave .... York PA 17404 717-852-6910 839-1039*
**Fax Area Code:* 800 ■ *TF:* 888-808-0801 ■ *Web:* www.curtaincallcostumes.com
Disguise 11906 Tech Ctr Ct .... Poway CA 92064 858-391-3600 391-3601
TF: 800-786-4864 ■ *Web:* www.disguise.com
Morris Costumes Inc 4300 Monroe Rd .... Charlotte NC 28205 704-333-4653 348-3032
Rubie's Costume Co Inc 1 Rubie Plaza .... Richmond Hill NY 11418 718-846-1008 846-6174
Web: www.rubies.com
Sew Biz Industries 174 Cross St .... Central Falls RI 02863 401-724-8410 726-9845
Stagecraft Costuming Inc 3950 Spring Grove Ave .... Cincinnati OH 45223 513-541-7150 541-7159
Web: www.stagecraftinc.com

155-7 Fur Goods

Phone Fax

American Legend Cooperative PO Box 58308 .... Seattle WA 98138 425-251-3200 251-3222
Web: www.americanlegend.com
Blum & Fink Inc 158 W 29th St 12th Fl .... New York NY 10001 212-695-2606 967-8123
Corn Furs Inc 337 7th Ave .... New York NY 10001 212-695-3914 473-1380*
**Fax Area Code:* 646
Corniche Furs Inc 345 7th Ave 20th Fl .... New York NY 10001 212-239-8655 239-1811
Web: www.cornichefurs.com
Goodman Couture 224 W 30 St Suite 902 .... New York NY 10001 212-244-7422 594-0657
Group Panache 345 7th Ave 19th Fl .... New York NY 10001 212-594-4415
HBA Fur Corp 345 7th Ave 20th Fl .... New York NY 10001 212-564-1080 239-1811
Jerry Sorbara Furs Inc 12 W 32nd St 11th Fl .... New York NY 10001 212-594-3897 643-9098
Kaitery Furs Ltd 25-29 49th St .... Long Island City NY 11103 718-204-1396 204-0721
Web: www.kaitery.com
LA Rockler Fur Co 16 N 4th St .... Minneapolis MN 55401 612-332-8643 332-2926
Michaels Furs 301 N Canon Dr Suite G .... Beverly Hills CA 90210 310-285-0832 273-7270
Mohl Fur Co Inc 345 7th Ave 3rd Fl .... New York NY 10001 212-736-7676
Rockler LA Fur Co 16 N 4th St .... Minneapolis MN 55401 612-332-8643 332-2926
Sekas International Ltd 345 7th Ave 4th Fl .... New York NY 10001 212-629-6095 629-6097
Sorbara Jerry Furs Inc 12 W 32nd St 11th Fl .... New York NY 10001 212-594-3897 643-9098
Steve's Original Furs Inc 150 W 30th St 8th Fl .... New York NY 10001 212-967-8007 967-3871
Web: www.stevesoriginalfurs.com

155-8 Gloves & Mittens

Phone Fax

Ansell Occupational Healthcare 1300 Walnut St .... Coshocton OH 43812 740-622-4311 623-3556
TF Cust Svc: 800-800-0444 ■ *Web:* www.ansellpro.com
Berlin Glove Co Inc 150 W Franklin St .... Berlin WI 54923 920-361-5050 361-5055
TF: 800-236-3367 ■ *Web:* www.berlingloveco.com
Boss Mfg Co 221 W 1st St .... Kewanee IL 61443 309-852-2131 852-0848
TF Cust Svc: 800-447-4581 ■ *Web:* www.bossgloves.com
Brookville Glove Mfg Co Inc 5-15 Western Ave .... Brookville PA 15825 814-849-7324 849-6874
TF: 800-322-7324 ■ *Web:* www.brookvilleglove.com
Carolina Glove Co Inc PO Drawer 820 .... Newton NC 28658 828-464-1132 464-1710
TF: 800-438-6888 ■ *Web:* www.carolinaglove.com
Fairfield Line Inc 605 W Stone PO Box 500 .... Fairfield IA 52556 641-472-3191 472-3194
TF: 800-247-3383
Fownes Brothers & Co Inc 16 E 34th St .... New York NY 10016 212-683-0150 683-2832
TF: 800-345-6837
Gloves Inc 50 Suffolk Rd .... Mansfield MA 02048 508-339-2590 339-3181
TF: 800-225-6076
Grandoe Corp PO Box 713 .... Gloversville NY 12078 518-725-8641 725-9088
TF: 800-472-6363 ■ *Web:* www.grandoe.com
Guard-Line Inc 215 S Louise St PO Box 1030 .... Atlanta TX 75551 903-796-4111 796-7262*
**Fax:* Orders ■ *TF:* 800-527-8822 ■ *Web:* www.guardline.com
Illinois Glove Co 3701 Commercial Ave .... Northbrook IL 60062 847-291-1700 291-7722
TF: 800-342-5458 ■ *Web:* www.illinoisglove.com
Kinco International 4286 NE 185th Ave .... Portland OR 97230 503-674-9002 674-3513
TF: 800-547-8410 ■ *Web:* www.kinco.com
Magid Glove & Safety Mfg Co 2060 N Kolmar Ave .... Chicago IL 60639 773-384-2070 384-6677
TF: 800-444-8010 ■ *Web:* www.magidglove.com
Manzella Productions 80 Sonwil Dr .... Buffalo NY 14225 716-681-8880 681-6888
TF: 800-645-6837 ■ *Web:* www.manzella.com
MCR Safety 5321 E Shelby Dr .... Memphis TN 38118 901-795-5810 999-3908*
**Fax Area Code:* 800 ■ **Fax:* Sales ■ *TF:* 800-955-6887 ■ *Web:* www.mcrsafety.com

Phone Fax

Midwest Quality Gloves Inc 835 Industrial Rd. Chillicothe MO 64601 660-646-2165 646-6933
TF: 800-821-3028 ■ *Web:* www.midwestglove.com
Montpelier Glove & Safety Co Inc 129 N Main St PO Box 7 Montpelier IN 47359 765-728-2481 728-5239
TF: 800-645-3931 ■ *Web:* www.montpeliergsp.com
Nationwide Glove Co 924 Bauman Ln PO Box K Harrisburg IL 62946 618-252-6303 252-4497
North Star Glove Co 2916 S Steele St Tacoma WA 98409 253-627-7107 627-0597
TF: 800-423-1616 ■ *Web:* www.northstarglove.com
Perfect Fit Glove Co Inc 85 Innsbruck Dr Buffalo NY 14227 716-668-2000 668-3224
TF: 800-245-6837 ■ *Web:* www.perfectfitglove.com
Saranac Glove Co 999 LOmbardi Ave Green Bay WI 54304 920-435-3737 435-7618
TF: 800-727-2622 ■ *Web:* www.saranacglove.com
Seal Glove Mfg Inc 525 North St Millersburg PA 17061 717-692-4747 692-5442
TF: 800-992-5444 ■ *Web:* www.sealglove.com
Slate Springs Glove Co 148 Vance St. Calhoun City MS 38916 662-637-2222 637-2515
Southern Glove Mfg Co Inc 749 AC Little Dr Newton NC 28658 828-464-4884 464-7968
TF Cust Svc: 800-222-1113 ■ *Web:* www.southernglove.com
Swany America Corp 115 Corp Dr Johnstown NY 12095 518-725-3333 725-2026
TF: 800-237-9269 ■ *Web:* www.swanyamerica.com
Totes Isotoner Corp 9655 International Blvd Cincinnati OH 45246 513-682-8200 682-8600
TF: 800-762-8712 ■ *Web:* www.totes-isotoner.com/ecommerce/control/main
Wells Lamont Corp 6640 W Touhy Ave Niles IL 60714 847-647-8200 647-6943
TF: 800-323-2830 ■ *Web:* www.wellslamont.com
Wells Lamont Industry Group 6640 W Touhy Ave Niles IL 60714 800-247-3295 647-6943*
**Fax Area Code:* 847 ■ *Web:* www.wellslamontindustry.com

155-9 Hats & Caps

Phone Fax

180s Inc 701 E Pratt St Baltimore MD 21202 410-534-6320 534-6321
TF: 877-725-4386 ■ *Web:* www.180s.com
Ahead 270 Samuel Barnet Blvd New Bedford MA 02745 508-999-4466 985-3091*
**Fax:* Cust Svc ■ *TF:* 800-282-2246 ■ *Web:* www.aheadweb.com
American Needle Inc 1275 Bush Pkwy Buffalo Grove IL 60089 847-215-0011 215-0013
TF: 800-356-7589 ■ *Web:* www.americanneedle.com
Arlington Hat Co Inc 4725 34th St Long Island City NY 11101 718-361-3000 361-8713
Ashworth Inc 2765 Loker Ave W Carlsbad CA 92010 760-438-6610 476-8417
NASDAQ: ASHW ■ *TF:* 800-800-8443 ■ *Web:* www.ashworthinc.com
Bancroft Cap Co Inc 1122 S 2nd St Cabot AR 72023 501-843-6561 843-8996
TF: 800-345-8784 ■ *Web:* www.bancroftcaps.com
Bayly Inc 4151 N 29th Ave Hollywood FL 33020 954-923-0255 923-9596
TF: 800-882-0255 ■ *Web:* www.baylyinc.com
Bollman Hat Co 110 E Main St Adamstown PA 19501 717-484-4361 484-2139
TF: 800-451-4287 ■ *Web:* www.bollman@bollmanhats.com
Drew Pearson Marketing Inc 15006 Beltway Dr Addison TX 75001 972-702-8055 702-0143
TF: 800-879-0880 ■ *Web:* www.drewpearson.com
F & M Hat Co Inc 103 Walnut St PO Box 40 Denver PA 17517 717-336-5505 336-0501
TF: 800-953-4287 ■ *Web:* www.fmhat.com
Greg Norman Collection 110 W 57th St 4th Fl New York NY 10023 646-840-5200
Hatco Inc 601 Marion Dr Garland TX 75042 972-494-0511 494-2369
TF: 800-288-6579
Imperial Headwear Inc 5200 E Evans Ave Denver CO 80222 303-757-1166 757-8543*
**Fax Area Code:* 800 ■ **Fax:* Cust Svc ■ *TF Cust Svc:* 800-933-9444 ■
Web: www.imperialheadwear.com
Julie Hat Co Inc 5948 Industrial Blvd PO Box 518 Patterson GA 31557 912-647-2031 647-2605
TF: 800-841-2592 ■ *Web:* www.juliehat.com
Korber Hats Inc 394 Kilburn St Fall River MA 02724 508-672-7033 673-0762
TF Cust Svc: 800-428-9911
Kraft Hat Mfg Inc 725 Whittier St Bronx NY 10474 718-620-6100 620-0127
Web: www.krafthat.com
M & B Headwear Co Inc 2323 E Main St PO Box 8180 Richmond VA 23223 804-648-1603 648-1613
MPC Promotions Inc 2026 Shepherdsville Rd Louisville KY 40218 502-451-4900 451-5075
TF: 800-331-0989 ■ *Web:* www.mpcpromotions.com
New Era Cap Co Inc 8061 Erie Rd Derby NY 14047 716-549-0445 549-5424
TF: 800-989-0445 ■ *Web:* www.neweracap.com
Onfield Apparel Group LLC 8677 LogoAthletic Ct. Indianapolis IN 46219 317-895-7000 895-7250
TF: 800-955-6467
Paramount Apparel International Inc
1 Paramount Dr PO Box 98 Bourbon MO 65441 573-732-4411 732-5211
TF: 800-255-4287 ■ *Web:* www.paramountheadwear.com
Pearson Drew Marketing Inc 15006 Beltway Dr Addison TX 75001 972-702-8055 702-0143
TF: 800-879-0880 ■ *Web:* www.drewpearson.com
Pro-Line Cap Co 1332 N Main St Fort Worth TX 76106 817-246-1978 367-1585
TF: 800-227-2456 ■ *Web:* www.prolinecap.com
Stetson Hat Co 4500 Stetson Trail Saint Joseph MO 64503 816-233-8031 233-8032
Web: www.stetsonhat.com
Stratton Hats Inc 3200 Randolph St. Bellwood IL 60104 708-544-5220 544-5243
Web: www.strattonhats.com
Texace Corp 5405 Vandera Rd Suite 121 San Antonio TX 78238 210-227-7551 227-4237
TF: 800-835-8973 ■ *Web:* www.texace.com
Town Talk Inc 6310 Cane Run Rd PO Box 58157 Louisville KY 40268 502-933-7575 933-7599
TF: 800-626-2220 ■ *Web:* www.ttcaps.com

155-10 Hosiery & Socks

Phone Fax

Acme-McCrary Corp 159 North St Asheboro NC 27203 336-625-2161 629-2263
Web: www.acme-mccrary.com
Americal Corp 389 Americal Rd PO Box 1419 Henderson NC 27536 252-762-2000 762-0439
TF: 800-633-9707
Auburn Hosiery Mills Inc 113 E Main St PO Box 95 Auburn KY 42206 270-542-4175 542-7120
Bossong Hosiery Mills Inc 840 W Salisbury St Asheboro NC 27203 336-625-2175 626-6607
TF: 800-833-8895
Candor Hosiery Mills Inc 2235 NC Hwy 2427-E Biscoe NC 27209 910-428-1242 428-2918
Carolina Hosiery Mills Inc 710 Plantation Dr PO Box 850 Burlington NC 27216 336-226-5581 226-9721
Charleston Hosiery Inc 855 Raider Dr Cleveland TN 37311 423-472-5095 479-5522
Web: www.charlestonhosiery.com
Cherokee Hosiery Mills Inc 208 NE 35th St Fort Payne AL 35967 256-845-0004 845-0892
Clayson Knitting Co 734 S Main St PO Box 39 Star NC 27356 910-428-2171 428-1133
Commonwealth Hosiery Mills Inc 4964 Island Ford Rd Randleman NC 27317 336-498-2621 498-5560
Web: www.commonwealth-hosiery.com
Cooper Hosiery Mills Inc 4005 Gault Ave N PO Box 680909 Fort Payne AL 35968 256-845-1491 845-3554
Crescent Inc 527 Willson St PO Box 669 Niota TN 37826 423-568-2101 568-2104
TF: 877-807-7625 ■ *Web:* www.crescenthosiery.com
Danskin Inc 530 7th Ave M 1 Fl New York NY 10018 212-764-4630 930-9138
Web: www.danskin.com
DeSoto Mills Inc 3850 Sand Valley Rd PO Box 680228 Fort Payne AL 35968 256-845-6700 845-9658
TF: 800-551-7625
Emby Hosiery Corp 3905 2nd Ave. Brooklyn NY 11232 718-499-6300 499-7156
TF: 800-287-6916 ■ *Web:* www.embyhosiery.com
Fox River Mills Inc 227 Poplar Stq PO Box 298 Osage IA 50461 641-732-3798 732-3375
TF: 800-247-1815 ■ *Web:* www.foxsox.com
Gold Toe Brands Inc 661 Plaid St. Burlington NC 27215 336-229-3700 229-3710
TF Cust Svc: 800-523-8265 ■ *Web:* www.goldtoebrands.com
Hampshire Group Ltd PO Box 2667 Anderson SC 29622 864-225-6232 225-4421
NASDAQ: HAMP ■ *TF:* 800-275-3520 ■ *Web:* www.hamp.com

Phone Fax

Hanesbrands Inc 1000 E Hanes Mill Rd Winston-Salem NC 27105 336-519-4400 519-8746
NYSE: HBI ■ *Web:* www.hanesbrands.com
Harriss & Covington Hosiery Mills Inc
1250 Hickory Chapel Rd High Point NC 27260 336-882-6811 889-2412
HCI Direct Inc 3050 Tillman Dr Bensalem PA 19020 215-244-9600 244-0328
TF: 800-989-3695 ■ *Web:* www.silkies.com
Highland Mills Inc 340 E 16th St Charlotte NC 28206 704-375-3333 342-0391
Web: www.highlandmills.com
Holt Hosiery Mills Inc 733 Koury Dr PO Box 1757 Burlington NC 27216 336-227-1431 227-8614
Jefferies Socks LLC 1176 N Church St Burlington NC 27217 336-226-7315 226-8217
TF Cust Svc: 800-334-6831 ■ *Web:* www.jefferiessocks.com
Jockey International Inc 2300 60th St PO Box 1417 Kenosha WI 53140 262-658-8111 658-1942
TF: 800-562-5391 ■ *Web:* www.jockey.com
Johnson Hosiery Mills Inc 3395 Young Ave NE Fort Payne AL 35968 256-845-1561 845-5958
Johnson Hosiery Mills Inc 2808 Main Ave NW Hickory NC 28601 828-322-6185 322-6539
TF: 800-438-1511 ■ *Web:* www.johnsonhosiery.com
Kayser-Roth Corp 102 Corporate Ctr Blvd Greensboro NC 27408 336-852-2030 632-1921*
**Fax:* Acctg ■ *Web:* www.kayser-roth.com
Keepers International Inc 20720 Marilla St Chatsworth CA 91311 818-882-5000 700-1152
TF: 800-797-6257 ■ *Web:* www.keepers.com
Kentucky Derby Hosiery Co Inc 123 W 7th St PO Box 550 Hopkinsville KY 42241 270-886-0131 887-6426
Lavitt Paul Mills Inc 1517 'F' Ave SE Hickory NC 28602 828-328-2463 328-5908
TF: 800-825-7285 ■ *Web:* www.paullavittmills.com
Lemco Mills Inc 766 Koury Dr PO Box 2098 Burlington NC 27216 336-226-5548 226-6356
Mauney Hosiery Mills Inc PO Box 1279 Kings Mountain NC 28086 704-739-3621 734-0608
Mayer Berkshire Corp 25 Edison Dr Wayne NJ 07470 973-696-6200 696-6203
TF: 800-245-6789 ■ *Web:* www.berkshirestore.com
Mayo Knitting Mills Inc 2204 Austin St PO Box 160 Tarboro NC 27886 252-823-3101 823-0368
Menzies Southern Hosiery Mills Inc 953 Central Ave SE Hickory NC 28601 828-328-5201 328-2896
Web: www.southernhosiery.com
Moretz Inc 514 W 21st St Newton NC 28658 828-464-0751 465-4203
TF: 800-438-9127 ■ *Web:* www.moretzsports.com
Mountain High Hosiery Ltd 675 Gateway Center Dr San Diego CA 92102 619-262-9202 262-9682
TF: 800-528-5355 ■ *Web:* www.mtnhighinc.com
Neuville Industries Inc 9451 Neuville Ave PO Box 286 Hildebran NC 28637 828-397-5566 397-2377
TF: 800-334-2587
Parker Hosiery Co Inc 78 Catawba Ave Old Fort NC 28762 828-668-7628 668-2081
Paul Lavitt Mills Inc 1517 'F' Ave SE Hickory NC 28602 828-328-2463 328-5908
TF: 800-825-7285 ■ *Web:* www.paullavittmills.com
Premiere Direct/Legwear Express 227 Avery Ave Morganton NC 28655 828-439-8724 439-8571
TF Orders: 800-280-1222 ■ *Web:* www.legwearexpress.com
Prewitt Hosiery Mills Inc 208 NE 35th St PO Box 708 Fort Payne AL 35967 256-845-0004 845-0892
Web: www.prewettmills.com
Renfro Corp 661 Linville Rd Mount Airy NC 27030 336-719-8000 719-8215
TF: 800-334-9091 ■ *Web:* www.renfro.com
Robinson Hosiery Mill Inc 113 Robinson St PO Box 730 Valdese NC 28690 828-874-2228 879-1660
Royce Hosiery Mills Inc 350 5th Ave Suite 300 New York NY 10118 212-695-5113 629-8150
Shogren Hosiery Mfg Co 225 Wilshire Ave SW Concord NC 28025 704-786-5617 788-8614
TF: 888-206-0002
Slane Hosiery Mills Inc 313 S Centennial St High Point NC 27261 336-883-4138 886-4543
Web: slanehosiery.com
Tefron USA Inc 720 W Main St Valdese NC 28690 828-879-6500 879-6579
TF: 800-554-5541 ■ *Web:* www.tefron.com
Thor-Lo Inc 2210 Newton Dr Statesville NC 28677 704-872-6522 838-7010
TF: 888-846-7567 ■ *Web:* www.thorlo.com
Trimfit Inc 1900 Frost Rd Suite 111 Bristol PA 19007 215-781-0600 781-1803
TF: 800-347-7697 ■ *Web:* www.trimfit.com
Twin City Knitting Co Inc 104 Rock Barn Rd NE PO Box 1179 Conover NC 28613 828-464-4830 497-6257*
**Fax Area Code:* 800 ■ *TF Cust Svc:* 800-438-6884 ■ *Web:* www.twincityknitting.com
US Textile Corp 1197 Silkies Blvd PO Box 1179 Lancaster SC 29721 803-283-6800 286-5306
Wigwam Mills Inc 3402 Crocker Ave Sheboygan WI 53082 920-457-5551 457-0311
TF: 800-558-7760 ■ *Web:* www.wigwam.com
WY Shugart & Sons Inc 405 Beeson Gap Rd NE Fort Payne AL 35968 256-845-1251 845-4502
Web: www.wyshugart.com

155-11 Jeans

Phone Fax

Aalfs Mfg Co 1005 4th St Sioux City IA 51101 712-252-1877 252-5205
TF: 888-412-2537
Baxter International 1931 Myrtle Ave. El Paso TX 79901 915-532-4481 534-7189
Ditto Apparel of California Inc Hwy 8 E PO Box 226 Colfax LA 71417 318-627-3264 627-3446
Elk Brand Mfg Co 1601 County Hospital Rd Nashville TN 37218 615-264-1300 242-3137
Web: www.elkbrand.com
Flynn Enterprises Inc 2203 Walnut St PO Box 1047 Hopkinsville KY 42241 270-886-0223 886-0573
Guess? Inc 1444 S Alameda St Los Angeles CA 90021 213-765-3100 765-3226
NYSE: GES ■ *TF:* 800-394-8377 ■ *Web:* www.guess.com
Innovo Group Inc 2633 Kingston Pike Suite 100 Knoxville TN 37919 865-546-1110 546-9277
NASDAQ: INNO ■ *TF:* 800-627-2621 ■ *Web:* www.innovogroup.com
Jordache Enterprises 1400 Broadway 15th Fl New York NY 10018 212-643-8400 629-9223
TF: 888-295-3267 ■ *Web:* www.jordache.com
Kayo of California Inc 161 W 39th St Los Angeles CA 90037 323-233-6107 231-4828
TF: 800-233-6140
Lee Jeans 1 Lee Dr Merriam KS 66202 913-384-4000 384-0190
TF: 800-453-3348 ■ *Web:* www.leejeans.com
Levi Strauss & Co 1155 Battery St San Francisco CA 94111 415-501-6000 501-3161
TF: 800-872-5384 ■ *Web:* www.levistrauss.com
Miller International Inc Rocky Mountain Clothing Co Div
8500 Zuni St Denver CO 80260 303-428-5696 430-1130
TF: 800-688-4449 ■ *Web:* www.rockymountainclothing.com
Reed Mfg Co Inc 1321 S Veterans Blvd Tupelo MS 38801 662-842-4472 680-9644
TF: 800-647-1280 ■ *Web:* www.reedmanufacturing.com
Rocky Mountain Clothing Co Div Miller International Inc
8500 Zuni St Denver CO 80260 303-428-5696 430-1130
TF: 800-688-4449 ■ *Web:* www.rockymountainclothing.com
Spencer Industries 475 Wall St Princeton NJ 08540 609-252-0111 252-0060
VF Imagewear Inc 3375 Joseph Martin Hwy Martinsville VA 24115 276-632-7200 956-7826*
**Fax:* Sales ■ *TF:* 800-832-6469 ■ *Web:* www.vfc.com
VF Jeanswear LP 335 Church Ct PO Box 21488 Greensboro NC 27420 336-332-3400 283-3113*
**Fax Area Code:* 800 ■ *TF Orders:* 800-888-8010 ■ *Web:* www.vfc.com
Vintage Blue 13087 E Temple Ave City of Industry CA 91746 626-934-4144 934-4145

155-12 Men's Clothing

Phone Fax

After Six Inc 240 Collins Industrial Dr Athens GA 30601 706-543-5286 549-5430
TF Cust Svc: 800-554-8212 ■ *Web:* www.aftersix.com
American Apparel LLC 747 Warehouse St Los Angeles CA 90021 213-488-0226 488-0334
Web: www.americanapparel.net
American Trouser Inc 605 17th St S Columbus MS 39701 662-328-1556 329-8115
Anniston Sportswear Corp 919 W 9th St Anniston AL 36201 256-237-9411 237-7569
Antigua Sportswear Inc 16651 N 84 Ave Peoria AZ 85382 623-523-6000 523-6001
TF: 800-528-3133 ■ *Web:* www.antigua.com
Arrow Shirt Co 200 Madison Ave 10th Fl New York NY 10016 212-381-3500 381-3950
Web: www.arrowshirt.com

Men's Clothing (Cont'd)

				Phone	Fax
Asher Winer Co 208 Lurgan Ave	Shippensburg	PA	17257	717-532-4146	532-6836
TF: 800-556-8001					
Barrow Mfg Co Inc 83 Horton St	Winder	GA	30680	770-867-2121	867-1129
TF: 800-476-0047					
Barry Better Menswear 309 McLaws Cir Suite D	Williamsburg	VA	23185	757-345-0971	345-6224
Web: www.bettermenswear.com					
Berle Mfg Co 1411 Folly Rd	Charleston	SC	29412	843-762-7150	762-7151
TF: 800-845-4503					
Black Corp 901 S Main St	Amory	MS	38821	662-256-2606	256-2673
Boss Hugo Fashions Inc 601 W 26th St Suite 845	New York	NY	10001	212-940-0600	940-0616
TF: 800-484-6207 ■ *Web:* www.hugo.com					
Bowdon Mfg Co 127 N Carrol St	Bowdon	GA	30108	770-258-7201	258-9416
TF: 800-937-7242 ■ *Web:* www.bowdonmfgco.com					
Calvin Klein Inc 205 W 39th St 3rd Fl	New York	NY	10018	212-719-2600	730-4818
Web: www.pvh.com					
Capital Mercury Apparel 1359 Broadway 19th Fl	New York	NY	10018	212-704-4800	704-4996
Carabella Corp 17662 Armstrong Ave	Irvine	CA	92614	949-263-2300	263-2323
TF Cust Svc: 800-227-2235 ■ *Web:* www.carabella.com					
Charles Navasky & Co Inc 124 Walton St	Philipsburg	PA	16866	814-342-1160	342-1920
Chesterfield Mfg Corp 1815 Coffee Pointe Dr Suite 103	Charlotte	NC	28217	704-283-0001	289-2158
TF: 800-322-1746					
Christian Dior 712 5th Ave 37th Fl	New York	NY	10019	212-582-0500	582-1063
TF: 800-929-3467 ■ *Web:* www.dior.com					
Cluett American Group 48 W 38th St 8th Fl	New York	NY	10018	212-984-8900	984-8925
Corbin Ltd 208 Lurgan Ave	Shippensburg	PA	17257	717-532-4146	532-9301
TF: 800-950-3330					
Crown Clothing Corp 340 Vanderbilt Ave	Norwood	MA	02062	781-769-0001	769-7337
TF: 800-225-8950 ■ *Web:* www.crownclothingcorp.com					
Daniel John H Co Inc 120 W Jackson Ave	Knoxville	TN	37902	865-637-6441	523-6435
Web: www.johnhdaniel.com					
David Peyser Sportswear Inc 8890 Spence St	Bay Shore	NY	11706	631-231-7788	435-8018
TF: 800-367-7900					
Dior Christian 712 5th Ave 37th Fl	New York	NY	10019	212-582-0500	582-1063
TF: 800-929-3467 ■ *Web:* www.dior.com					
Ely & Walker Co 208 Hartmann Dr	Lebanon	TN	37087	615-443-1878	443-2214
English American Tailoring Co 411 N Cranberry Rd	Westminster	MD	21157	410-857-5774	386-0417
Web: www.englishamericanco.com					
Fishman & Tobin Inc 625 Ridge Pike Bldg E Suite 320	Conshohocken	PA	19428	610-828-8400	828-4426
TF: 800-367-2772					
Forsythe of Canada Inc 301 Harris St	Cordele	GA	31015	229-273-5694	273-5695
Freeman H & Son Inc 411 N Cranberry Rd	Westminster	MD	21157	410-857-5774	857-1560
TF: 800-468-0689 ■ *Web:* www.hfreemanco.com					
Gitman Brothers Shirt Co Inc 641 Lexington Ave 19th Fl	New York	NY	10019	212-581-6968	581-6960
TF Cust Svc: 800-526-3929 ■ *Web:* www.gitmanco.com					
Gitman & Co 2309 Chestnut St	Ashland	PA	17921	570-875-3100	875-2841
TF: 800-526-3929					
GK Teamwear 3150 N Elm St Suite 200	Greensboro	NC	27408	336-545-9990	545-9989
Gordon Kenneth IAG 1209 Distributors Row	New Orleans	LA	70123	504-734-1433	733-1625
TF Cust Svc: 800-234-1433					
Granite Knitwear Inc 805 S Salberry Ave Hwy 52S	Granite Quarry	NC	28072	704-279-5526	279-8205
TF: 800-476-9944					
Greg Norman Collection 110 W 57th St 4th Fl	New York	NY	10023	646-840-5200	
H Freeman & Son Inc 411 N Cranberry Rd	Westminster	MD	21157	410-857-5774	857-1560
TF: 800-468-0689 ■ *Web:* www.hfreemanco.com					
Haggar Clothing Co 11511 Luna Rd Two Colinas Crossing	Dallas	TX	75234	214-352-8481	
TF: 800-942-4427 ■ *Web:* www.haggar.com					
Hardwick Clothes Inc 3800 Old Tasso Rd NE	Cleveland	TN	37312	423-476-6534	442-7394*
**Fax Area Code:* 800 ■ *TF:* 800-251-6392					
Hartmarx Inc 101 N Wacker Dr	Chicago	IL	60606	312-372-6300	444-2710
TF: 800-327-4466 ■ *Web:* www.hartschaffnermarx.com					
Hartz & Co 1341 Hughes Ford Rd	Frederick	MD	21701	301-662-7500	662-0800
TF: 800-638-8170					
Harve Benard Ltd Inc 125 Delawanna Ave	Clifton	NJ	07014	201-319-0909	249-1665*
**Fax Area Code:* 973 ■ **Fax:* Acctg					
Hickey-Freeman Co Inc 1155 N Clinton Ave	Rochester	NY	14621	585-467-7240	467-1236
TF Cust Svc: 800-295-2000 ■ *Web:* www.hickeyfreeman.com					
HMXTailored Co 2020 Elmwood Ave	Buffalo	NY	14207	716-874-5000	874-5844
TF: 800-874-5000 ■ *Web:* www.ibahartmarx.com					
HR Kaminsky & Sons Inc 136 Bowen's Mill Hwy	Fitzgerald	GA	31750	229-423-4396	423-4390
Hubbard Co Inc 208 Lurgan Ave	Shippensburg	PA	17257	717-532-4146	884-1390*
**Fax Area Code:* 800 ■ *TF:* 800-241-1226					
Hugo Boss Fashions Inc 601 W 26th St Suite 845	New York	NY	10001	212-940-0600	940-0616
TF: 800-484-6207 ■ *Web:* www.hugo.com					
Indiana Knitwear Corp 230 E Osage St	Greenfield	IN	46140	317-462-4413	462-0994
Individualized Shirts Co 581 Cortland St	Perth Amboy	NJ	08861	732-826-8400	826-6382
TF: 888-474-4787					
James Tom Co 424 S Lynn Riggs Blvd	Claremore	OK	74017	918-341-3773	343-1711
TF: 800-237-2140 ■ *Web:* www.tomjamesco.com					
John H Daniel Co Inc 120 W Jackson Ave	Knoxville	TN	37902	865-637-6441	523-6435
Web: www.johnhdaniel.com					
Jos A Bank Clothiers 500 Hanover Pike	Hampstead	MD	21074	410-239-2700	239-5700
NASDAQ: JOSB ■ *TF Cust Svc:* 800-999-7472 ■ *Web:* www.josbank.com					
Kaminsky HR & Sons Inc 136 Bowen's Mill Hwy	Fitzgerald	GA	31750	229-423-4396	423-4390
Kenneth Gordon IAG Inc 1209 Distributors Row	New Orleans	LA	70123	504-734-1433	733-1625
TF Cust Svc: 800-234-1433					
Klein Calvin Inc 205 W 39th St 3rd Fl	New York	NY	10018	212-719-2600	730-4818
Web: www.pvh.com					
Lanier Clothes 1031 S Green St	Tupelo	MS	38804	662-842-5252	841-2281
Merrill-Sharpe Ltd 250 Clearbrook Rd	Elmsford	NY	10523	914-347-8686	347-8861
TF: 800-832-0159 ■ *Web:* www.merrillsharpe.com					
Nautica Enterprises Inc 40 W 57th St 3rd Fl	New York	NY	10019	212-541-5990	245-4724*
**Fax:* Cust Svc ■ *Web:* www.nautica.com					
Navasky Charles & Co Inc 124 Walton St	Philipsburg	PA	16866	814-342-1160	342-1920
Nitches Inc 10280 Camino Santa Fe	San Diego	CA	92121	858-625-2633	625-0746
NASDAQ: NICH ■ *Web:* www.nitches.com					
Northern Isles 300 Manley St	Brockton	MA	02303	508-513-3013	583-1702
TF: 800-666-5105					
Nu-Look Fashions Inc 5080 Sinclair Rd Suite 200	Columbus	OH	43229	614-885-4936	885-4193
TF: 800-800-4500					
Oxford Industries Inc 222 Piedmont Ave NE	Atlanta	GA	30308	404-659-2424	525-3650
NYSE: OXM ■ *Web:* www.oxfordinc.com					
Oxxford Clothes Inc 1220 W Van Buren St	Chicago	IL	60607	312-829-3600	829-6075
TF: 888-469-9367 ■ *Web:* www.oxxfordclothes.com					
Palm Beach Co 2020 Elmwood Ave	Buffalo	NY	14207	716-874-5000	
TF: 800-543-1919 ■ *Web:* www.hartmarx.com					
Perry Ellis International Inc 3000 NW 107th Ave	Miami	FL	33172	305-592-2830	594-2307
NASDAQ: PERY ■ *TF:* 800-327-7587 ■ *Web:* www.perryelliscorporate.com					
Peyser David Sportswear Inc 8890 Spence St	Bay Shore	NY	11706	631-231-7788	435-8018
TF: 800-367-7900					
Phillips-Van Heusen Corp 200 Madison Ave	New York	NY	10016	212-381-3500	381-3950
NYSE: PVH ■ *TF:* 800-777-1726 ■ *Web:* www.pvh.com					
PremiumWear Inc 5500 Feltl Rd	Minnetonka	MN	55343	952-979-1700	979-1717
TF Cust Svc: 800-347-6098 ■ *Web:* www.premiumwear.com					
R Siskind & Co Inc 1385 Broadway 24th Fl	New York	NY	10018	212-840-0880	
Savane International Div 4902 W Waters Ave	Tampa	FL	33634	813-249-4900	
TF: 800-327-2464 ■ *Web:* www.savane.com					
Scotty's Fashions Inc 636 Pen Argyl St	Pen Argyl	PA	18072	610-863-6454	863-6495
Web: www.scottysfashions.com					
Seitchik Industries Inc 920 E Lycoming St	Philadelphia	PA	19124	215-743-0400	743-5914
TF: 800-523-0814					
Sewell Clothing Co Inc 115 Pacific Ave	Bremen	GA	30110	770-537-3862	537-4799
TF: 800-241-1221					
Sewell Warren Clothing Co 126 Hamilton Ave	Bremen	GA	30110	770-537-2391	537-6898
TF: 800-876-9722 ■ *Web:* www.warrensewell.com					
Smart Apparel US Inc 1400 Broadway 10th Fl	New York	NY	10018	212-329-3400	329-3486
Southwick Clothing LLC 50 Island St	Lawrence	MA	01840	978-686-3833	738-0802
Web: www.southwickclothing.com					
State-O-Maine 1372 Broadway Suite 1800	New York	NY	10018	212-302-1070	302-1370
TF: 866-456-6843					
Thorngate Ltd 1507 Independence St	Cape Girardeau	MO	63703	573-334-7723	
Web: www.thorngate.com					
Tom James Co 424 S Lynn Riggs Blvd	Claremore	OK	74017	918-341-3773	343-1711
TF: 800-237-2140 ■ *Web:* www.tomjamesco.com					
Trans-Apparel Group 5000 S Ohio St	Michigan City	IN	46360	219-879-7341	879-0388
Warnaco Inc 501 7th Ave	New York	NY	10018	212-287-8250	
Web: www.warnaco.com					
Warren Sewell Clothing Co 126 Hamilton Ave	Bremen	GA	30110	770-537-2391	537-6898
TF: 800-876-9722 ■ *Web:* www.warrensewell.com					
Weatherproof Garment Co 1071 Ave of the Americas 12th Fl	New York	NY	10018	212-695-7716	239-9786
TF: 800-645-7788 ■ *Web:* www.weatherproofco.com					

155-13 Neckwear

				Phone	Fax
Bost Neckwear Co Inc 503 Industrial Pk PO Box 1065	Asheboro	NC	27204	336-625-6650	626-7667
TF: 800-334-8441					
Burma Bibas Inc 597 5th Ave 10th Fl	New York	NY	10017	212-750-2500	750-2834
TF: 800-362-0037					
Carter & Holmes 3645 W Irving Park Rd	Chicago	IL	60618	773-588-2626	588-3092
TF: 800-621-4646 ■ *Web:* www.carterholmes.com					
Cornell of California Inc 4340 Bond St	Oakland	CA	94601	510-261-2204	261-0957
Echo Design Group 10 E 40th St 16th Fl	New York	NY	10016	212-686-8771	686-5017
TF: 800-331-3246 ■ *Web:* www.echodesign.com					
Fendrich Industries Inc 7025 Augusta Rd	Greenville	SC	29605	864-299-0600	299-0603
TF: 800-845-2744					
Handcraft Mfg Corp 10 E 34th St 2nd Fl	New York	NY	10016	212-251-0022	251-0076
Isaco International Corp 5980 Miami Lakes Dr	Miami	FL	33014	305-594-4455	594-4496
Web: www.isaco.com					
Mallory & Church LLC 676 S Industrial Way	Seattle	WA	98108	206-587-2100	587-2971
TF: 800-255-8437 ■ *Web:* www.malloryandchurch.com					
Marlin Ralph & Co 1814 Dolphin Dr Suite A	Waukesha	WI	53186	262-549-5100	549-5122
TF: 800-922-8437 ■ *Web:* www.ralphmarlin.com					
MMG Corp 1717 Olive St	Saint Louis	MO	63103	314-421-2182	421-4912
TF: 800-264-8437					
New York Accessories Group Inc 411 5th Ave 4th Fl	New York	NY	10016	212-532-7911	213-4347
TF: 800-366-7254					
Paris Accessories Inc 350 5th Ave 70th Fl	New York	NY	10118	212-868-0500	967-4936
TF: 800-223-7557					
Ralph Marlin & Co 1814 Dolphin Dr Suite A	Waukesha	WI	53186	262-549-5100	549-5122
TF: 800-922-8437 ■ *Web:* www.ralphmarlin.com					
Randa Corp 120 W 45th St 38th Fl	New York	NY	10036	212-768-8800	768-8585
TF: 800-632-5843 ■ *Web:* www.randa.net					
Robert Talbott Inc 2901 Monterey Salinas Hwy PO Box 996	Monterey	CA	93940	831-649-6000	
Web: www.roberttalbott.com					
Superba Inc 1735 S Santa Fe Ave	Los Angeles	CA	90021	213-688-7970	623-3226
Web: www.superbainc.com					
Talbott Robert Inc 2901 Monterey Salinas Hwy PO Box 996	Monterey	CA	93940	831-649-6000	
Web: www.roberttalbott.com					
Tie King Inc 243 44th St	Brooklyn	NY	11232	718-768-8484	768-0355
TF: 800-852-9261					
White Mountain Traders 100 Factory St	Nashua	NH	03060	603-889-5115	889-3126
TF: 800-648-6505 ■ *Web:* www.whitemountaintraders.com					
Wolfmark 1026 W Van Buren St	Chicago	IL	60607	312-563-5510	563-0280
TF Cust Svc: 800-621-3435 ■ *Web:* www.wolfmarkties.com					
Zanzara International Ltd 1160 S Rogers Cir Suite 1	Boca Raton	FL	33487	561-998-8898	998-9711

155-14 Robes (Ceremonial)

				Phone	Fax
Academic Apparel 20644 Superior St	Chatsworth	CA	91311	818-886-8697	886-8743
TF: 800-626-5000 ■ *Web:* www.academicapparel.com					
CM Almy Inc 1 Ruth Rd	Pittsfield	ME	04967	207-487-3232	487-3240
TF: 800-225-2569 ■ *Web:* www.almy.com					
Herff Jones Inc 4501 W 62nd St	Indianapolis	IN	46268	317-297-3740	329-3308*
**Fax:* Hum Res ■ *TF:* 800-427-3393 ■ *Web:* www.herff-jones.com					
Jostens Inc 3601 Minnesota Ave Suite 400	Minneapolis	MN	55435	952-830-3300	830-3309*
**Fax:* Hum Res ■ *TF:* 800-235-4774 ■ *Web:* www.jostens.com					
Oak Hall Industries 840 Union St	Salem	VA	24153	540-387-0000	387-2034
TF: 800-456-7623 ■ *Web:* www.oakhalli.com					
Robert Gaspard Co Inc 200 N Janacek Rd	Brookfield	WI	53045	262-784-6800	784-7567
TF: 800-784-6868 ■ *Web:* www.robertgaspardco.com					
Thomas Creative Apparel Inc 1 Harmony Pl	New London	OH	44851	419-929-1506	929-0122
TF: 800-537-2575 ■ *Web:* www.thomasrobes.com					
Willsie Cap & Gown Co 1220 S 13th St	Omaha	NE	68108	402-341-6536	341-6551
TF: 800-234-4696 ■ *Web:* www.willsieco.com					

155-15 Sleepwear

				Phone	Fax
Bernstein Sidney & Son Lingerie Inc 1115 Broadway	New York	NY	10010	212-679-4270	689-3152
Charles Komar & Sons Inc 16 E 34th St 10th Fl	New York	NY	10016	212-725-1500	889-1408
Eileen West 525 Brannan St Suite 410	San Francisco	CA	94107	415-957-9378	495-8628
TF: 800-421-0731 ■ *Web:* www.eileenwest.com					
Faris Brothers of California Inc 12801 Arroyo St	Sylmar	CA	91342	818-898-2377	361-2812
TF: 800-433-2747 ■ *Web:* www.farislingerie.com					
Isaco International Corp 5980 Miami Lakes Dr	Miami	FL	33014	305-594-4455	594-4496
Web: www.isaco.com					
Komar Charles & Sons Inc 16 E 34th St 10th Fl	New York	NY	10016	212-725-1500	889-1408
LSC LLC DBA Eileen West 525 Brannan St Suite 410	San Francisco	CA	94107	415-957-9378	495-8628
TF: 800-421-0731 ■ *Web:* www.eileenwest.com					
Magnolia Garment Corp 101 Ostrover Dr	Tower Town	MS	39667	601-876-6524	876-6069
Milco Industries Inc 550 E 5th St	Bloomsburg	PA	17815	570-784-0400	387-8433
TF: 800-867-0288					
Miss Elaine Inc 8430 Valcour Ave	Saint Louis	MO	63123	314-631-1900	631-7577
TF: 800-458-1422 ■ *Web:* www.misselaine.com					
Movie Star Inc 1115 Broadway 11th Fl	New York	NY	10010	212-684-3400	684-3295
AMEX: MSI ■ *Web:* www.moviestarinc.com					

Phone Fax

NAP Inc 171 Madison Ave Suite 600 New York NY 10016 212-481-5000 481-7498

O'Bryan Brothers Inc 4220 W Belmont Ave Chicago IL 60641 773-283-3000 283-2470
TF: 800-627-9262

Rice Mills Inc 110 Rice Rd PO Box 98 Belton SC 29627 864-338-6761 338-8029

Roytex Inc 16 E 34th St 17th Fl New York NY 10016 212-686-3500 686-4336
Web: www.roytex.com

Russell-Newman Ltd 600 N Loop 288 Denton TX 76209 940-898-8888 382-6453
Web: www.russellnewman.com

Sidney Bernstein & Son Lingerie Inc 1115 Broadway New York NY 10010 212-679-4270 689-3152

Universal Mfg Corp 318 Gidney St Shelby NC 28150 704-487-4359 482-0723
TF: 800-553-8648

VF Intimates 3025 Windward Plaza Suite 600 Alpharetta GA 30005 770-753-0900 753-5050
TF: 800-366-8339 ■ *Web:* www.vanityfairlingerie.com

Wormser Co 820 W Jackson Blvd Suite 400 Chicago IL 60607 312-525-2670 525-0108
Web: www.wormser.com

155-16 Sweaters (Knit)

Phone Fax

AM Knitwear Corp 681 Grand Blvd Deer Park NY 11729 631-586-3200 586-3657

Binghamton Knitting Co Inc 11 Alice St PO Box 1646 Binghamton NY 13902 607-722-6941 722-4621
Web: www.brimwick.com

Designers Knitting Mills 119 W 40th St 22nd Fl New York NY 10018 212-840-5666 840-5670
TF: 800-275-3520

Hampshire Group Ltd PO Box 2667 Anderson SC 29622 864-225-6232 225-4421
NASDAQ: HAMP ■ *TF:* 800-275-3520 ■ *Web:* www.hamp.com

Mamiye Brothers Inc Group 112 W 34th St Suite 1000 New York NY 10120 212-279-4150 279-4115
Web: www.mamiye.com

Oakdale Mills Inc 1670 Weirfield St Ridgewood NY 11385 718-417-8880 417-4570

155-17 Swimwear

Phone Fax

A & H Sportswear Co Inc 500 Williams St Pen Argyl PA 18072 610-863-4176 863-7838

AH Schreiber Co 460 W 34th St 10th Fl New York NY 10001 212-564-2700 594-7234
TF: 800-724-1612

Apparel Ventures Inc 13809 S Figueroa St Los Angeles CA 90061 310-538-4980 538-0515
TF: 800-289-7946

Baltex Swimsuits 5555 Cypihot St Ville Saint-Laurent QC H4S1R3 514-383-1850 383-7589
TF: 888-225-8391 ■ *Web:* www.baltex.com

Blue Sky Swimwear 729 E International Speedway Blvd Daytona Beach FL 32118 386-255-9009 253-5938
TF Orders: 800-799-6445 ■ *Web:* blueskyswimwear.com

Carabella Corp 17662 Armstrong Ave Irvine CA 92614 949-263-2300 263-2323
TF Cust Svc: 800-227-2235 ■ *Web:* www.carabella.com

Christina America Inc 5555 Cypihot St Ville Saint-Laurent QC H4S1R3 514-381-2365 381-8202
TF Cust Svc: 800-463-7946 ■ *Web:* www.christina.ca

Jantzen Inc 424 NE 18th Ave Portland OR 97232 503-238-5000 238-5930
TF: 800-626-0215 ■ *Web:* www.jantzen.com

Manhattan Beachwear Inc 6600 Katella Ave Cypress CA 90630 714-892-7354 799-5381
TF: 800-279-2987 ■ *Web:* www.manhattanbeachwear.com

Ocean Pacific Apparel Corp 3 Studebaker Irvine CA 92618 949-580-1888 580-1870
TF: 800-562-3269 ■ *Web:* www.op.com

Quiksilver Inc 15202 Graham St Huntington Beach CA 92649 714-889-2200 889-3700
NYSE: ZQK ■ *TF:* 800-576-4004 ■ *Web:* www.quiksilver.com

Robby Len Fashions 460 W 34th St 10th Fl New York NY 10001 212-564-2700 594-7234

Schreiber AH Co 460 W 34th St 10th Fl New York NY 10001 212-564-2700 594-7234
TF: 800-724-1612

TYR Sport 15391 Springdale St Huntington Beach CA 92649 714-897-0799 897-6420
TF: 800-252-7878 ■ *Web:* www.tyr.com

Venus Swimwear 11711 Marco Beach Dr 1 Venus Plaza Jacksonville FL 32224 904-645-6000 648-0411*
**Fax Area Code:* 800 ■ *TF:* 800-366-7946 ■ *Web:* www.venusswimwear.com

Warnaco Inc 501 7th Ave New York NY 10018 212-287-8250
Web: www.warnaco.com

Warnaco Swimwear Group Inc 6040 Bandini Blvd Los Angeles CA 90040 323-726-1262 721-3613*
**Fax:* Mktg ■ *TF Cust Svc:* 800-547-8770 ■ *Web:* www.warnaco.com

155-18 Undergarments

Phone Fax

Alpha Mills Corp 122 Margaretta Ct Schuylkill Haven PA 17972 570-385-0511 385-0467

Biflex Intimates Group 180 Madison Ave 6th Fl New York NY 10016 212-532-8340 696-3485
TF: 888-532-8340 ■ *Web:* www.kellwood.com

Burlen Corp 1904 McCormick Dr Tifton GA 31793 229-382-4100 387-8622

Carolina Underwear Co 110 W Guilford St Thomasville NC 27361 336-472-7788 472-8839
TF: 888-664-5211

Carter's Inc 1170 Peachtree St NE Suite 900 Atlanta GA 30309 404-745-2700 892-0968
NYSE: CRI ■ *TF:* 888-782-9548 ■ *Web:* www.carters.com

Champion Athletic Wear 1000 E Hanes Mill Rd Winston-Salem NC 27105 336-519-4400 519-6501
TF: 800-999-2249 ■ *Web:* www.championforwomen.com

Cupid Foundations Inc 475 Park Ave S 17th Fl New York NY 10016 212-686-6224 481-9357

Delta Galil USA 150 Meadowland Pkwy Secaucus NJ 07094 201-902-0055 902-0070
TF: 800-645-4461 ■ *Web:* www.deltagalil.com

Eveden Ltd 65 Sprague St Hyde Park MA 02136 617-361-7559 361-7527
TF: 800-733-8964 ■ *Web:* www.eveden.com

Gelmart Industries Inc 136 Madison Ave 4th Fl New York NY 10016 212-743-6900 725-7248
TF: 800-746-0014 ■ *Web:* www.gelmart.com

Glamorise Foundations Inc 135 Madison Ave New York NY 10016 212-684-5025 689-7793

Hanesbrands Inc 1000 E Hanes Mill Rd Winston-Salem NC 27105 336-519-4400 519-8746
NYSE: HBI ■ *Web:* www.hanesbrands.com

Indera Mills Co 350 W Maple St PO Box 309 Yadkinville NC 27055 336-679-4440 679-4475
TF: 800-334-8605 ■ *Web:* www.inderamills.com

International Intimates Inc 180 Madison Ave 7th Fl New York NY 10016 212-213-4848 213-4120

Isaco International Corp 5980 Miami Lakes Dr Miami FL 33014 305-594-4455 594-4496
Web: www.isaco.com

JE Morgan Knitting Mills Inc 143 Mahanoy Ave PO Box 390 Tamaqua PA 18252 570-668-3330 668-9016
TF: 800-448-8240

Jockey International Inc 2300 60th St PO Box 1417 Kenosha WI 53140 262-658-8111 658-1942
TF: 800-562-5391 ■ *Web:* www.jockey.com

KP Sports Inc 1020 Hull St Baltimore MD 21230 410-468-2512 927-6687*
**Fax Area Code:* 866 ■ *TF:* 888-427-6687 ■ *Web:* www.underarmour.com

Leading Lady Cos 24050 Commerce Park Beachwood OH 44122 216-464-5490 464-9365
TF Cust Svc: 800-321-4804 ■ *Web:* www.leadinglady.com

Maidenform Inc 154 Ave 'E' Bayonne NJ 07002 201-436-9200 436-8322
NYSE: MFB ■ *TF:* 800-496-8727 ■ *Web:* www.maidenform.com

Movie Star Inc 1115 Broadway 11th Fl New York NY 10010 212-684-3400 684-3295
AMEX: MSI ■ *Web:* www.moviestarinc.com

New Age Intimates Inc 21-07 41st Ave Long Island City NY 11101 718-392-6600 392-5342

Playtex Apparel Inc 1000 E Hanes Mill Rd Winston-Salem NC 27105 336-519-6053 519-4400
TF: 800-225-4872 ■ *Web:* www.playtexnet.com

Reliable of Milwaukee Inc 233 E Chicago St PO Box 563 Milwaukee WI 53201 414-272-5084 272-6443
TF: 800-336-6876 ■ *Web:* www.reliableofmilwaukee.com

Robinson Mfg Co Inc 798 Market St PO Box 338 Dayton TN 37321 423-775-2212 775-0489
TF: 800-251-7286 ■ *Web:* www.robinsonmfg.com

Phone Fax

Russell-Newman Ltd 600 N Loop 288 Denton TX 76209 940-898-8888 382-6453
Web: www.russellnewman.com

Shadowline Inc 550 Lenoir Rd Morganton NC 28655 828-437-3821 437-8423
Web: www.shadowline-lingerie.com

Spencers Inc 238 Willow St Mount Airy NC 27030 336-789-9111 789-6824
TF: 800-633-9111 ■ *Web:* www.spencers.com

Spirite Industries Inc 150 S Dean St Englewood NJ 07631 201-871-4910 871-9790
TF: 800-272-6897 ■ *Web:* www.spirite.com

Tefron USA Inc 720 W Main St Valdese NC 28690 828-879-6500 879-6579
TF: 800-554-5541 ■ *Web:* www.tefron.com

Under Armour Performance Apparel DBA KP Sports Inc
1020 Hull St Baltimore MD 21230 410-468-2512 927-6687*
**Fax Area Code:* 866 ■ *TF:* 888-427-6687 ■ *Web:* www.underarmour.com

United Retail Group Inc 365 W Passaic St Rochelle Park NJ 07662 201-845-0880 909-2114
NASDAQ: URGI ■ *TF:* 877-708-8740 ■ *Web:* www.unitedretail.com

VF Corp 105 Corporate Center Blvd Greensboro NC 27408 336-424-6000 424-7634
NYSE: VFC ■ *Web:* www.vfc.com

VF Intimates 3025 Windward Plaza Suite 600 Alpharetta GA 30005 770-753-0900 753-5050
TF: 800-366-8339 ■ *Web:* www.vanityfairlingerie.com

Wacoal America 1 Wacoal Plaza Lyndhurst NJ 07071 201-933-8400 635-0208
TF: 800-526-6286 ■ *Web:* www.wacoal-america.com

Warnaco Inc 501 7th Ave New York NY 10018 212-287-8250
Web: www.warnaco.com

Windsong Allegiance Group LLC 1599 Post Rd E Westport CT 06880 203-319-3600 319-3610
Web: www.windsongallegiance.com

155-19 Uniforms & Work Clothes

Phone Fax

Action Sports Systems Inc 617 Carbon City Rd Morganton NC 28655 828-584-8000 584-8440
TF: 800-631-1091

Algy Costume & Uniform Co 440 NE 1st Ave Hallandale FL 33009 954-457-8100 928-2282*
**Fax Area Code:* 888 ■ *TF:* 800-458-2549 ■ *Web:* www.algyteam.com

All-Bilt Uniform Fashion 4545 Malsbary Rd Cincinnati OH 45242 866-638-5390 793-2725*
**Fax Area Code:* 513 ■ *TF:* 800-221-2980 ■ *Web:* www.allbilt.com

American Apparel Inc 107 Selma Bypass PO Box 1310 Selma AL 36702 334-872-6337 872-2449

American Uniform Co 4363 N Ocoee St Suite 300-W Cleveland TN 37312 423-476-6561 559-3855
Web: www.amuniform.com

Anson Shirt Co 620 Anson Shirt Apparel Rd PO Box 311 Wadesboro NC 28170 704-694-5148 694-6679

Barco Uniforms Inc 350 W Rosecrans Ave Gardena CA 90248 310-323-7315 324-5274*
**Fax:* Cust Svc ■ *TF:* 800-421-1874 ■ *Web:* www.barcouniforms.com

Berne Apparel Co 2210 Summit St New Haven IN 46774 260-469-3136 469-8193
TF: 800-843-7657 ■ *Web:* www.berneapparel.com

Best Mfg Group LLC 10 Exchange Pl 22nd Fl Jersey City NJ 07302 201-356-3800 356-3815
TF: 800-843-3233 ■ *Web:* www.bestmfg.com

Blauer Mfg Co Inc 20 Aberdeen St Boston MA 02215 617-536-6606 536-6948
TF: 800-225-6715 ■ *Web:* www.blauer.com

Blue Generation Div of M Rubin & Sons Inc
34-01 38th Ave Long Island City NY 11101 718-361-2800 361-2680
Web: www.bluegeneration.com

Carhartt Inc 5750 Mercury Dr Dearborn MI 48126 313-271-8460 271-3455
TF: 800-358-3825 ■ *Web:* www.carhartt.com

Choi Brothers Inc 3401 W Division St Chicago IL 60651 773-489-2800 489-3030
TF: 800-524-2464 ■ *Web:* www.choibrothers.com

Cintas Corp PO Box 625737 Cincinnati OH 45262 513-459-1200
NASDAQ: CTAS ■ *TF:* 800-786-4367 ■ *Web:* www.cintas-corp.com

City Shirt Co Inc 242 Frackville Industrial Park Rd Frackville PA 17931 570-874-4251 874-0593

DeMoulin Brothers & Co Inc 1025 S 4th St Greenville IL 62246 618-664-2000 664-1712
TF: 800-228-8134 ■ *Web:* www.demoulin.com

Dennis Uniform Mfg Co Inc 714 NE Hancock St Portland OR 97212 503-238-7123 238-2529
TF Orders: 800-544-7123 ■ *Web:* www.dennisuniform.com

Dickson Industries Inc 2425 Dean Ave Des Moines IA 50317 515-262-8061 262-1844
Web: www.dicksonindustries.com

Earl's Apparel Inc 908 S 4th St PO Box 939 Crockett TX 75835 936-544-5521 544-7973
TF: 800-527-3148 ■ *Web:* www.stanray.us

Elbeco Inc 4203 Pottsville Pike Reading PA 19605 610-921-0651 921-8651
TF: 800-468-4654 ■ *Web:* elbeco.com

Elder Mfg Co Inc 999 Executive Pkwy Suite 300 Saint Louis MO 63141 314-469-1120
TF: 800-829-8880 ■ *Web:* www.elderwearwecare.com

Encompass Group LLC 615 Macon Rd McDonough GA 30253 770-957-3981 957-8728
TF: 800-284-4540 ■ *Web:* www.encompassgroup.net

Euclid Garment Mfg Co 333 Martinel Dr Kent OH 44240 330-673-7413 673-0228
Web: www.euclidgarment.com

Eudora Garment 304 Superior Dr Eudora AR 71640 870-355-8381 355-2676

Fechheimer Brothers Co Inc 4545 Malsbary Rd Cincinnati OH 45242 513-793-5400 793-7819
TF: 800-543-1939 ■ *Web:* www.fechheimer.com

Fechheimer Martin Plant Co 1445 Main St Martin TN 38237 731-587-3861 587-9292
Web: www.fechheimer.com

French Toast 100 W 33rd St Suite 1012 New York NY 10001 212-594-4740 268-5160
TF: 800-262-5437 ■ *Web:* frenchtoast.com

Galion Mfg 7916 Millsboro Rd Galion OH 44833 419-468-6100 468-5400

Garment Corp of America 801 W 41st St 3rd Fl Miami Beach FL 33140 305-531-4040 777-1015*
**Fax Area Code:* 800 ■ **Fax:* Cust Svc ■ *TF Cust Svc:* 800-944-4500 ■
Web: www.gcauniforms.com

Gibson & Barnes 1675 Pioneer Way El Cajon CA 92020 619-440-6976 748-6694*
**Fax Area Code:* 800 ■ *TF:* 800-748-6693 ■ *Web:* www.gibson-barnes.com

Globe Corp 490 E McMillan St Cincinnati OH 45206 513-961-0200 961-0101

Golden Mfg Co Inc 125 Hwy 366 PO Box 390 Golden MS 38847 662-454-3428 454-9240
Web: www.goldenmfg.com

Herzman & Co Inc 145 N Franklin Tpke Ramsey NJ 07446 201-236-1212 236-1252

Howard Uniform Co 313 W Baltimore St Baltimore MD 21201 410-727-3086 727-3142
TF: 800-628-8299 ■ *Web:* www.howarduniform.com

I Spiewak & Sons Inc 469 7th Ave 10th Fl New York NY 10018 212-695-1620 629-4803
TF Cust Svc: 800-223-6850 ■ *Web:* www.spiewak.com

Integrated Textile Solutions Inc 865 Cleveland Ave Salem VA 24153 540-389-8113 387-5855
Web: www.intextile.com

Key Industries Inc 400 Marble Rd Fort Scott KS 66701 620-223-2000 223-5822
TF: 800-835-0365 ■ *Web:* www.keyindustriesinc.com

King LC Mfg Co Inc 24 7th St PO Box 367 Bristol TN 37620 423-764-5188 764-6809
TF: 800-826-2510 ■ *Web:* www.pointerbrand.com

Landau Uniforms Inc 8410 W Sandidge Rd Olive Branch MS 38654 662-895-7200 895-5099
TF: 800-238-7513 ■ *Web:* www.landau.com

LC King Mfg Co Inc 24 7th St PO Box 367 Bristol TN 37620 423-764-5188 764-6809
TF: 800-826-2510 ■ *Web:* www.pointerbrand.com

Leventhal Ltd 1295 Northern Blvd Manhasset NY 11030 516-365-9540 365-9547
TF: 800-847-4095 ■ *Web:* www.leventhalltd.com

Lion Apparel Inc 6450 Poe Ave Dayton OH 45414 937-898-1949 898-2848*
**Fax:* Hum Res ■ *TF:* 800-548-6614 ■ *Web:* www.lionapparel.com

M Rubin & Sons Inc Blue Generation Div
34-01 38th Ave Long Island City NY 11101 718-361-2800 361-2680
Web: www.bluegeneration.com

National Spirit Group Ltd 2010 Merritt Dr Garland TX 75041 972-840-1233 840-4077
TF: 800-527-4366 ■ *Web:* www.nationalspirit.com

Nationwide Uniform Corp 235 Shepherdsville Rd Hodgenville KY 42748 270-358-4173 358-8255

OshKosh B'Gosh Inc 112 Otter Ave Oshkosh WI 54901 920-231-8800 231-8621
TF: 800-282-4674 ■ *Web:* www.oshkoshbgosh.com

Uniforms & Work Clothes (Cont'd)

	City	State	Zip	Phone	Fax
Polkton Mfg Co Inc 6713 E Marshville Blvd PO Box 220	Marshville	NC	28103	704-624-3200	624-6128
TF: 800-445-0044 ■ *Web:* www.seafarer.com					
Protexall Inc 77 S Henderson St PO Box 1287	Galesburg	IL	61402	309-342-3106	342-4320
TF: 800-334-8939 ■ *Web:* www.protexallinc.com					
Regent Apparel 255 Utah Ave	South San Francisco	CA	94080	415-552-2065	552-8622
TF: 800-326-2065 ■ *Web:* www.regentapparel.com					
Riverside Mfg Co 301 Riverside Dr	Moultrie	GA	31768	229-985-5210	890-2932
TF: 800-841-8677 ■ *Web:* www.riversideuniforms.com					
Royal Park Uniforms Co 14139 Hwy 86 S	Prospect Hill	NC	27314	336-562-3345	562-3832
Web: www.royal-park.com					
Rubin Brothers Inc 2241 S Halsted St	Chicago	IL	60608	312-942-1111	942-1871
TF: 800-632-2308					
School Apparel Inc 1099 Sneath Ln	San Bruno	CA	94066	650-827-7400	277-2272*
**Fax Area Code:* 800 ■ *TF:* 888-628-9020 ■ *Web:* www.schoolapparel.com					
SCORE American Soccer Co Inc 726 E Anaheim St	Wilmington	CA	90744	310-830-6161	426-1222*
**Fax Area Code:* 800 ■ *TF:* 800-626-7774 ■ *Web:* www.scoresports.com					
Scotty's Fashions Inc 636 Pen Argyl St	Pen Argyl	PA	18072	610-863-6454	863-6495
Web: www.scottysfashions.com					
Spiewak I & Sons Inc 469 7th Ave 10th Fl	New York	NY	10018	212-695-1620	629-4803
TF Cust Svc: 800-223-6850 ■ *Web:* www.spiewak.com					
Stanbury Uniforms Inc 108 Stanbury Industrial Dr PO Box 100	Brookfield	MO	64628	660-258-2246	258-5781
TF: 800-826-2246 ■ *Web:* www.stanbury.com					
Standard Textile Co Inc 1 Knollcrest Dr	Cincinnati	OH	45237	513-761-9255	761-0467
TF: 800-888-5000 ■ *Web:* www.standardtextile.com					
Superior Uniform Group Inc 10055Seminole Blvd	Seminole	FL	33772	727-397-9611	391-5401
AMEX: SGC ■ *TF Cust Svc:* 800-727-8643 ■ *Web:* www.superiorsurgicalmfg.com					
Tennessee Apparel Corp 401 N Atlantic St	Tullahoma	TN	37388	931-455-3468	455-1209
Topps Safety Apparel Inc 2516 E State Rd 14	Rochester	IN	46975	574-223-4311	223-8622
TF: 800-348-2990 ■ *Web:* www.toppssafetyapparel.com					
Union Line Inc 2241 S Halsted St	Chicago	IL	60608	312-942-1111	942-1871
TF: 800-632-2308 ■ *Web:* www.unionmadeclothing.com					
Universal Overall Co 1060 W Van Buren St	Chicago	IL	60607	312-226-3336	226-1986
TF Cust Svc: 800-621-3344 ■ *Web:* www.universaloverall.com					
Varsity Spirit Div Varsity Brands Inc 6745 Lenox Center Ct Suite 300	Memphis	TN	38115	901-387-4370	387-4357
Web: www.varsity.com					
VF Imagewear Inc 3375 Joseph Martin Hwy	Martinsville	VA	24115	276-632-7200	956-7826*
**Fax:* Sales ■ *TF:* 800-832-6469 ■ *Web:* www.vfc.com					
Walls Industries Inc 1905 N Main St	Cleburne	TX	76033	817-645-4366	645-4366
TF: 800-433-1765					
Wenaas AGS Inc 202 E Larkspur St	Victoria	TX	77904	361-576-2668	576-2674
TF: 888-576-2668 ■ *Web:* www.wenaasusa.com					
White Swan Meta 14 Douglas St	Rome	GA	30161	706-295-2882	295-3436
TF: 800-247-0388					
Williamson-Dickie Mfg Co 509 W Vickery Blvd	Fort Worth	TX	76104	817-336-7201	336-8643*
**Fax Area Code:* 800 ■ *TF:* 800-336-7201 ■ *Web:* www.dickies.com					

155-20 Western Wear (Except Hats & Boots)

	City	State	Zip	Phone	Fax
Darwood Mfg Co 620 W Railroad St S PO Box 625	Pelham	GA	31779	229-294-4932	294-9323
Web: www.darwoodmfg.com					
Karman Inc DBA Roper Apparel & Footwear 14707 E 2nd Ave 3rd Fl	Aurora	CO	80011	303-893-2320	571-2248
TF: 800-825-6555 ■ *Web:* www.roperusa.com					
Miller International Inc Rocky Mountain Clothing Co Div 8500 Zuni St	Denver	CO	80260	303-428-5696	430-1130
TF: 800-688-4449 ■ *Web:* www.rockymountainclothing.com					
Niver Western Wear Inc PO Box 10122	Fort Worth	TX	76185	817-924-4299	924-4296
TF: 800-433-5752					
Rockmount Ranch Wear Mfg Co 1626 Wazee St	Denver	CO	80202	303-629-7777	629-5836
TF: 800-776-2566 ■ *Web:* www.rockmount.com					
Rocky Mountain Clothing Co Div Miller International Inc 8500 Zuni St	Denver	CO	80260	303-428-5696	430-1130
TF: 800-688-4449 ■ *Web:* www.rockymountainclothing.com					
Sidran Inc 14280 Gillis Rd	Farmers Branch	TX	75244	214-352-7979	352-0439
TF Cust Svc: 800-969-5015 ■ *Web:* www.sidraninc.com					

155-21 Women's Clothing

	City	State	Zip	Phone	Fax
Adrianna Papell Ltd 512 7th Ave	New York	NY	10018	212-695-5244	714-1871
Web: www.adriannapapell.com					
Alfred Angelo Inc 1301 Virginia Dr Suite 110	Fort Washington	PA	19034	215-659-5300	659-1532
TF: 800-504-7263 ■ *Web:* www.alfredangelo.com					
American Apparel LLC 747 Warehouse St	Los Angeles	CA	90021	213-488-0226	488-0334
Web: www.americanapparel.net					
Anne Klein & Co 1411 Broadway 15th Fl	New York	NY	10018	212-536-9000	777-9354*
**Fax Area Code:* 917 ■ *Web:* www.anneklein.com					
Bari-Jay Fashions Inc 225 W 37th St 7th Fl	New York	NY	10018	212-921-1551	391-0165
Web: www.barijay.com					
Basham Industries Hwy 56 & Industrial Dr	Coalmont	TN	37313	931-692-3218	692-3481
bebe stores Inc 400 Valley Dr	Brisbane	CA	94005	415-715-3900	715-3939
NASDAQ: BEBE ■ *TF:* 877-232-3777 ■ *Web:* www.bebe.com					
Bernard Chaus Inc 530 7th Ave 18th Fl	New York	NY	10018	212-354-1280	768-2954
Web: www.bernardchaus.com					
Bill Blass Ltd 550 7th Ave 12th Fl	New York	NY	10018	212-221-6660	398-5545
Web: www.billblass.com					
Blass Bill Ltd 550 7th Ave 12th Fl	New York	NY	10018	212-221-6660	398-5545
Web: www.billblass.com					
Bleyle Inc 67 Liberty Church Rd	Carrollton	GA	30116	678-853-0023	853-0029
TF Cust Svc: 800-241-3437 ■ *Web:* www.bleyle.com					
Bowdon Mfg Co 127 N Carrol St	Bowdon	GA	30108	770-258-7201	258-9416
TF: 800-937-7242 ■ *Web:* www.bowdonmfgco.com					
Byer California 66 Potrero Ave	San Francisco	CA	94103	415-626-7844	626-7865
TF: 800-998-2937 ■ *Web:* www.byer.com					
Calvin Klein Inc 205 W 39th St 3rd Fl	New York	NY	10018	212-719-2600	730-4818
Web: www.pvh.com					
Carabella Corp 17662 Armstrong Ave	Irvine	CA	92614	949-263-2300	263-2323
TF Cust Svc: 800-227-2235 ■ *Web:* www.carabella.com					
Carole Wren Inc 30-00 47th Ave 5th Fl	Long Island City	NY	11101	718-552-3800	937-5812
Web: www.carolewren.com					
Christian Dior 712 5th Ave 37th Fl	New York	NY	10019	212-582-0500	582-1063
TF: 800-929-3467 ■ *Web:* www.dior.com					
Claiborne Liz Inc 1441 Broadway 22nd Fl	New York	NY	10018	212-354-4900	626-1800
NYSE: LIZ ■ *Web:* www.lizclaiborneinc.com					
Crown Clothing Corp 340 Vanderbilt Ave	Norwood	MA	02062	781-769-0001	769-7337
TF: 800-225-8950 ■ *Web:* www.crownclothingcorp.com					
Crystal Springs Apparel 206 W Railroad Ave	Crystal Springs	MS	39059	601-892-4551	892-4014
TF: 800-633-4635 ■ *Web:* www.csapparel.com					
Darue of California Inc 14102 S Broadway	Los Angeles	CA	90061	310-323-1350	323-8133
TF: 800-733-3375 ■ *Web:* www.darue.com					
David Dart 13083 E Temple Ave	City of Industry	CA	91746	626-934-4133	934-6498
Dawn Joy Fashion Inc 1400 Broadway 16th Fl	New York	NY	10018	212-354-9840	944-7853
Depeche Mode Inc 520 8th Ave 11th Fl	New York	NY	10018	212-643-6633	643-1184
Web: www.depecheco.com					
Dior Christian 712 5th Ave 37th Fl	New York	NY	10019	212-582-0500	582-1063
TF: 800-929-3467 ■ *Web:* www.dior.com					
Donna Karan International Inc 550 7th Ave 15th Fl	New York	NY	10018	212-789-1500	789-1821
TF: 800-231-0884 ■ *Web:* www.donnakaran.com					
Dorby Group 1400 Broadway	New York	NY	10018	212-695-6211	354-3747
Double Z Mfg 1410 Broadway 16th Fl	New York	NY	10018	212-391-8510	730-1363
Web: www.zum-zum.com					
ENC 13071 E Temple Ave	City of Industry	CA	91746	626-934-4111	
Evan-Picone Dress Div Jones Apparel Group Inc 250 Rittenhouse Cir	Bristol	PA	19007	215-785-4000	785-1795
TF: 800-848-8668					
Evans Tracy Ltd 530 7th Ave Suite 1901	New York	NY	10018	212-869-3619	869-5237
Web: www.tracyevans.com					
Gator of Florida Inc 5002 N Howard Ave	Tampa	FL	33603	813-877-8267	876-3372
Graff Californiawear 1515 E 15th St	Los Angeles	CA	90021	213-749-0171	746-5754
TF: 800-421-8692 ■ *Web:* www.graffwear.com					
Halmode Apparel Inc 1400 Broadway 11th Fl	New York	NY	10018	212-564-7800	398-6462
TF: 800-388-0938					
Harve Benard Ltd Inc 125 Delawanna Ave	Clifton	NJ	07014	201-319-0909	249-1665*
**Fax Area Code:* 973 ■ **Fax:* Acctg					
Jessica McClintock Inc 1400 16th St	San Francisco	CA	94103	415-553-8200	553-8329
TF: 800-333-5301 ■ *Web:* www.jessicamcclintock.com					
JLM Couture Inc 225 W 37th St 5th Fl	New York	NY	10018	212-921-7058	921-7608
TF: 800-924-6475 ■ *Web:* www.jlmcouture.com					
Jones Apparel Group Inc 250 Rittenhouse Cir	Bristol	PA	19007	215-785-4000	785-1795
NYSE: JNY ■ *Web:* www.jny.com					
Jones Apparel Group Inc Evan-Picone Dress Div 250 Rittenhouse Cir	Bristol	PA	19007	215-785-4000	785-1795
TF: 800-848-8668					
Jones Apparel Group Inc Jones New York Career Div 250 Rittenhouse Cir	Bristol	PA	19007	215-785-4000	785-1795*
**Fax:* Hum Res ■ *TF:* 800-848-8668					
Jones Apparel Group Inc Jones New York Dress Div 250 Rittenhouse Cir	Bristol	PA	19007	215-785-4000	785-1795*
**Fax:* Hum Res ■ *TF:* 800-848-8668					
Jones Apparel Group Inc Lauren/Ralph Lauren Div 250 Rittenhouse Cir	Bristol	PA	19007	215-785-4000	785-1795*
**Fax:* Hum Res ■ *TF:* 800-848-8668					
Jones Apparel Group Inc Rena Rowan for Saville Div 250 Rittenhouse Cir	Bristol	PA	19007	215-785-4000	785-1795*
**Fax:* Hum Res ■ *TF:* 800-848-8668					
Karan Donna International Inc 550 7th Ave 15th Fl	New York	NY	10018	212-789-1500	789-1821
TF: 800-231-0884 ■ *Web:* www.donnakaran.com					
Kellwood Co 600 Kellwood Pkwy	Chesterfield	MO	63017	314-576-3100	576-3462
NYSE: KWD ■ *Web:* www.kellwood.com					
Klein Anne & Co 1411 Broadway 15th Fl	New York	NY	10018	212-536-9000	777-9354*
**Fax Area Code:* 917 ■ *Web:* www.anneklein.com					
Klein Calvin Inc 205 W 39th St 3rd Fl	New York	NY	10018	212-719-2600	730-4818
Web: www.pvh.com					
Koret Co 505 14th St	Oakland	CA	94612	510-622-7000	622-7294
TF: 800-468-6006 ■ *Web:* www.koretcompany.com					
Land N Sea Inc 1375 Broadway 2nd Fl	New York	NY	10018	212-444-6000	444-6019
Lauren/Ralph Lauren Div Jones Apparel Group Inc 250 Rittenhouse Cir	Bristol	PA	19007	215-785-4000	785-1795*
**Fax:* Hum Res ■ *TF:* 800-848-8668					
Leon Levin Inc 250 W 39th St 5th Fl	New York	NY	10018	212-575-1900	944-1482
TF: 800-822-3363 ■ *Web:* www.leonlevin.com					
Leon Max Inc 3100 New York Dr	Pasadena	CA	91107	626-797-6886	797-8555
TF: 800-345-3813 ■ *Web:* www.maxstudio.com					
Liz Claiborne Inc 1441 Broadway 22nd Fl	New York	NY	10018	212-354-4900	626-1800
NYSE: LIZ ■ *Web:* www.lizclaiborneinc.com					
Maggy London International Ltd 530 7th Ave 16th Fl	New York	NY	10018	212-944-7199	840-2483
Marisa Christina Inc 8101 Tonnelle Ave	North Bergen	NJ	07047	201-758-9800	861-9767
Web: www.marisachristina.com					
McClintock Jessica Inc 1400 16th St	San Francisco	CA	94103	415-553-8200	553-8329
TF: 800-333-5301 ■ *Web:* www.jessicamcclintock.com					
My Michelle 13071 E Temple Ave	City of Industry	CA	91746	626-934-4166	934-4165
Nitches Inc 10280 Camino Santa Fe	San Diego	CA	92121	858-625-2633	625-0746
NASDAQ: NICH ■ *Web:* www.nitches.com					
Northern Isles 300 Manley St	Brockton	MA	02303	508-513-3013	583-1702
TF: 800-666-5105					
Paquette Alfred Inc 1201 Rio Vista Ave	Los Angeles	CA	90023	323-266-4561	267-1086
TF: 800-585-2937					
Perry Mfg Co 100 Woltz St	Mount Airy	NC	27030	336-786-6171	719-6301
TF: 800-922-8384 ■ *Web:* www.perrymfg.com					
Polo Ralph Lauren Corp 650 Madison Ave	New York	NY	10022	212-318-7000	888-5780
NYSE: RL ■ *TF:* 800-377-7656 ■ *Web:* www.polo.com					
Rena Rowan for Saville Div Jones Apparel Group Inc 250 Rittenhouse Cir	Bristol	PA	19007	215-785-4000	785-1795*
**Fax:* Hum Res ■ *TF:* 800-848-8668					
S & S Mfg Co 175 Old Airport Rd	Roebuck	SC	29376	864-574-5807	574-3694
Sag Harbor 1407 Broadway	New York	NY	10018	212-391-8666	730-2040
Web: www.sag-harbor.com					
Saint John Knits Inc 17522 Armstrong Ave	Irvine	CA	92614	949-863-1171	261-9585
TF: 877-755-8463 ■ *Web:* www.stjohnknits.com					
Sally Lou Fashions Corp 1400 Broadway 6th Fl	New York	NY	10018	212-354-9670	819-0166
TF: 800-258-1540					
Scotty's Fashions Inc 636 Pen Argyl St	Pen Argyl	PA	18072	610-863-6454	863-6495
Web: www.scottysfashions.com					
Tahari Ltd Inc 11 W 42nd St	New York	NY	10036	212-763-2000	763-2299
Web: www.elietahari.com					
Tama Mfg Co Inc 100A Cascade Dr	Allentown	PA	18109	610-231-3100	231-3180
Web: www.tamamfg.com					
Tanner Cos LLC 581Rock Rd	Rutherfordton	NC	28139	828-287-4205	286-2072
TF: 800-669-3662					
Tarrant Apparel Group 3151 E Washington Blvd	Los Angeles	CA	90023	323-780-8250	780-0751
NASDAQ: TAGS ■ *TF:* 800-780-8250 ■ *Web:* www.tags.com					
Taylor Togs Inc 621 Micaville Loop PO Box 180	Micaville	NC	28755	828-675-4153	675-9602
TF: 800-872-4290 ■ *Web:* www.taylortogs.com					
Tracy Evans Ltd 530 7th Ave Suite 1901	New York	NY	10018	212-869-3619	869-5237
Web: www.tracyevans.com					
United Retail Group Inc 365 W Passaic St	Rochelle Park	NJ	07662	201-845-0880	909-2114
NASDAQ: URGI ■ *TF:* 877-708-8740 ■ *Web:* www.unitedretail.com					
Ursula of Switzerland Inc 31 Mohawk Ave	Waterford	NY	12188	518-237-2580	237-3038
TF: 800-826-4041 ■ *Web:* www.ursula.com					
Warnaco Inc 501 7th Ave	New York	NY	10018	212-287-8250	
Web: www.warnaco.com					
Young Stuff Apparel Group Inc 1359 Broadway 16th Fl	New York	NY	10018	646-839-7000	846-7001
Z Cavaricci 5807 Smithway St	City of Commerce	CA	90040	323-271-3285	724-8082
Web: www.zcavaricci.com					

156 CLOTHING & ACCESSORIES - WHOL

Company	City	State	Zip	Phone	Fax
Alpha Shirt Co 401 E Hunting Park Ave *Fax Area Code: 800 ■ TF: 800-523-4585 ■ Web: www.alphashirt.com	Philadelphia	PA	19124	215-291-0300	845-4970*
Bounty Trading Corp 1370 Broadway 14th Fl TF: 800-526-8689 ■ Web: www.bountytrading.com	New York	NY	10018	212-279-5900	564-5950
Broder Bros Co 45555 Port St TF: 800-521-0850 ■ Web: www.broderbros.com	Plymouth	MI	48170	734-454-4800	454-8971
Coleman William B Co Inc 4001 Earhart Blvd	New Orleans	LA	70125	504-822-1000	822-3152
Crew Outfitters 579 W High St *Fax Area Code: 417 ■ Web: www.crewoutfitters.com	Aurora	MO	65605	888-567-2739	678-6277*
Herman's Inc 2820 Blackhawk Rd TF Cust Svc: 800-447-1295 ■ Web: www.hermansinc.com	Rock Island	IL	61201	309-788-9568	786-8296
Intercontinental Importers Inc 25992 W Eight-Mile Rd	Southfield	MI	48034	248-355-1770	355-3873
International Women's Apparel 610 Uhler Rd TF Cust Svc: 800-735-7848 ■ Web: www.iwainc.com	Easton	PA	18040	610-258-9143	258-4978
Jacob Ash Co Inc 301 Munson Ave TF: 800-245-6111 ■ Web: www.jacobash.com	McKees Rocks	PA	15136	412-331-6660	331-6347
Marmaxx Group 770 Cochituate Rd	Framingham	MA	01701	508-390-1000	390-3132
Mast Industries Inc 3425 Morse Crossing Web: www.mast.com	Columbus	OH	43219	614-337-5600	337-5080
Mid-Continent Imports Inc 12920 Metcalf Ave Suite 170	Overland Park	KS	66213	913-681-0090	681-0091
Nike Team Sports 15550 SW Milikan Way Web: www.niketeam.com	Beaverton	OR	97006	503-532-6874	532-6704
Noamex Inc 625 Wortman Ave Web: www.noamex.com	Brooklyn	NY	11208	718-342-2278	342-2258
Prewitt Hosiery Mills Inc 208 NE 35th St PO Box 708 Web: www.prewettmills.com	Fort Payne	AL	35967	256-845-0004	845-0892
Romerovski Corp 450 W Westfield Ave TF: 800-852-9944 ■ Web: www.romerovski.com	Roselle Park	NJ	07204	908-241-3000	241-6662
Scope Imports Inc 8020 Blankenship Dr	Houston	TX	77055	713-688-0077	688-8768
South Carolina Tees Inc PO Box 66 TF: 800-829-5000	Columbia	SC	29202	803-256-1393	771-7635
Sussex Co Inc PO Box 749 TF: 800-537-5995	Milford	DE	19963	302-422-8037	422-8244
TSC Apparel LLC 12080 Mosteller Rd *Fax Area Code: 800 ■ TF: 800-543-7230 ■ Web: www.tscapparel.com	Cincinnati	OH	45241	513-771-1138	248-1069*
Tucker Rocky Distributing Inc 4900 Alliance Gateway Fwy *Fax Area Code: 800 ■ *Fax: Cust Svc ■ TF: 800-283-8787 ■ Web: www.tuckerrocky.com	Fort Worth	TX	76177	817-258-9000	304-1020*
William B Coleman Co Inc 4001 Earhart Blvd	New Orleans	LA	70125	504-822-1000	822-3152
World Wide Dreams LLC 350 5th Ave Suite 2101 TF: 800-221-8828	New York	NY	10118	212-273-9200	273-9599
WS Emerson Co Inc 15 Acme Rd TF: 800-789-6120 ■ Web: www.wsemerson.com	Brewer	ME	04412	207-989-3410	989-8540

157 CLOTHING STORES

SEE ALSO Department Stores p. 1586

157-1 Children's Clothing Stores

Company	City	State	Zip	Phone	Fax
Babies 'R' Us 545 Rt 17 S Web: www.babiesrus.com	Paramus	NJ	07652	201-251-3191	251-2469
Children's Place Retail Stores Inc 915 Secaucus Rd NASDAQ: PLCE ■ *Fax: Cust Svc ■ TF: 877-752-2387 ■ Web: www.childrensplace.com	Secaucus	NJ	07094	201-558-2400	558-2819*
GapKids 1 Harrison St *Fax: Hum Res ■ TF: 800-333-7899 ■ Web: www.gap.com	San Francisco	CA	94105	650-952-4400	874-7815*
Gymboree Corp 500 Howard St NASDAQ: GYMB ■ TF: 800-222-7758 ■ Web: www.gymboree.com	San Francisco	CA	94105	415-278-7000	278-7100
Hang Up Shoppes for Juniors 5745 W 80th St	Indianapolis	IN	46278	317-337-2121	337-2127
Kid to Kid 452 E 500 South TF: 888-543-2543 ■ Web: www.kidtokid.com	Salt Lake City	UT	84111	801-359-0071	359-3207
Limited Too 8323 Walton Pkwy *Fax: Mktg ■ TF: 800-934-4496 ■ Web: www.limitedtoo.com	New Albany	OH	43054	614-775-3500	775-3949*
Once Upon A Child 4200 Dahlberg Dr Suite 100 TF: 800-433-2540 ■ Web: www.ouac.com	Minneapolis	MN	55422	763-520-8500	520-8510
Rainbow Apparel Cos 1000 Pennsylvania Ave TF: 877-695-9858 ■ Web: www.rainbowshops.com	Brooklyn	NY	11207	718-485-3000	
Tween Brands Inc 8323 Walton Pkwy NYSE: TWB ■ TF: 800-934-4496 ■ Web: www.tooinc.com	New Albany	OH	43054	614-775-3500	775-3938
Winmark Corp 4200 Dahlberg Dr Suite 100 NASDAQ: WINA ■ TF: 800-433-2540 ■ Web: www.winmarkcorporation.com	Minneapolis	MN	55422	763-520-8500	520-8410

157-2 Family Clothing Stores

Company	City	State	Zip	Phone	Fax
Abdalla's Lafayette Inc 900 E St Mary Blvd Web: www.abdallas.com	Lafayette	LA	70503	337-262-7100	262-7199
Benetton USA Corp 601 5th Ave Web: www.benetton.com	New York	NY	10017	212-593-0290	371-1438
Benos Family Fashions 1512 S Santee St	Los Angeles	CA	90015	213-748-2222	741-2329
Bob's Stores Inc 160 Corporate Ct TF: 866-333-2627 ■ Web: www.bobstores.com	Meriden	CT	06450	203-235-5775	634-1185
Burlington Coat Factory Warehouse Corp 1830 Rt 130 N NYSE: BCF ■ *Fax: Cust Svc ■ Web: www.burlingtoncoatfactory.com	Burlington	NJ	08016	609-387-7800	239-1923*
Citi Trends Inc 102 Fahm St NASDAQ: CTRN ■ Web: www.cititrends.com	Savannah	GA	31401	912-236-1561	443-3674
Cohn MM Co Inc 300 S University Ave	Little Rock	AR	72205	501-664-5501	664-2582
Daffy's Inc Daffy's Way Web: www.daffys.com	Secaucus	NJ	07094	201-902-0800	902-9016
Dawahares Inc 1845 Alexandria Dr TF: 800-677-9108 ■ Web: www.dawahares.com	Lexington	KY	40504	859-278-0422	514-3298
De Byles Inc PO Box 128	Rhinelander	WI	54501	715-362-4406	362-1772
Decelle Inc 1525 Washington St Web: www.decelle.com	Braintree	MA	02184	781-849-1480	848-2292
Eblens Casual Clothing 299 Industrial Ln TF: 800-464-2898 ■ Web: www.eblens.com	Torrington	CT	06790	860-489-3073	496-7446
Foursome Inc 841 Lake St E TF: 888-368-7766 ■ Web: www.thefoursome.com	Wayzata	MN	55391	952-473-4667	473-9731
Goody's Family Clothing Inc PO Box 22000 *Fax: Hum Res ■ TF: 800-224-3114 ■ Web: www.goodysonline.com	Knoxville	TN	37933	865-966-2000	777-4220*
Hammer's 102 1st Ave SE	Winchester	TN	37398	931-967-3787	962-0717
Hamrick Industries 742 Peachoid Rd TF: 800-487-5411 ■ Web: www.hamricks.com	Gaffney	SC	29341	864-489-6095	489-9514
Jake's Department Store 509 Saint Mary St Suite A	Thibodaux	LA	70301	985-447-4663	448-2282
Kittery Trading Post 301 US Rt 1 TF: 888-587-6246 ■ Web: www.kitterytradingpost.com	Kittery	ME	03904	207-439-2700	439-8001
Lanai Sportswear Ltd PO Box 88003	Honolulu	HI	96830	808-522-1872	522-0777
Marshalls Inc 770 Cochituate Rd *Fax: Hum Res ■ Web: www.marshallsonline.com	Framingham	MA	01701	508-390-1000	390-3147*
McCaulou's Inc 3512 Mt Diablo Blvd *Fax: Acctg	Lafayette	CA	94549	925-283-3380	283-5780*
MM Cohn Co Inc 300 S University Ave	Little Rock	AR	72205	501-664-5501	664-2582
National Stores Inc 15001 S Figueroa St	Gardena	CA	90248	310-324-9962	
Old Navy Clothing Co 1 Harrison St *Fax Area Code: 415 ■ TF Cust Svc: 800-653-6289 ■ Web: www.oldnavy.com	San Francisco	CA	94105	650-952-4400	427-5488*
Palais Royal 10201 S Main St TF: 800-324-3244 ■ Web: www.palaisroyal.com	Houston	TX	77025	713-667-5601	669-2709
Peter Harris Clothes 952 Troy-Schenectady Rd TF: 800-444-1650	Latham	NY	12110	518-785-1650	785-0100
Puritan of Cape Cod 408 Main St TF: 800-924-0606 ■ Web: www.puritancapecod.com	Hyannis	MA	02601	508-775-2400	771-3277
Reynolds Bros Inc 1720 Hwy 34	Wall	NJ	07719	732-282-9750	282-0370
Rogers Department Store Inc 1001 28th St SW TF: 800-727-7643 ■ Web: www.rogersdepartmentstore.com	Grand Rapids	MI	49509	616-538-6000	538-0613
Rolane Factory Outlet Inc PO Box 19866	Greensboro	NC	27419	336-315-8596	855-1253
Ross Stores Inc 4440 Rosewood Dr NASDAQ: ROST ■ TF: 800-289-7677 ■ Web: www.rossstores.com	Pleasanton	CA	94588	925-965-4400	965-4388
Sealfons Inc 410 Springfield Ave Web: www.sealfons.com	Summit	NJ	07901	908-277-1777	277-3054
Sharpe Dry Goods Co Inc 200 N Broadway St TF: 800-238-6491 ■ Web: www.sharpeclothing.com	Checotah	OK	74426	918-473-2233	473-2755
Syms Corp 1 Syms Way NYSE: SYM ■ TF: 800-322-7967 ■ Web: www.syms.com	Secaucus	NJ	07094	201-902-9600	902-9874
TJ Maxx 770 Cochituate Rd *Fax: Mktg ■ TF Cust Svc: 800-926-6299 ■ Web: www.tjmaxx.com	Framingham	MA	01701	508-390-1000	390-2366*
Wakefield's Inc 1212 Quintard Ave TF: 800-333-1552 ■ Web: www.wakefields.com	Anniston	AL	36201	256-237-9521	236-9253
Zellers Inc 8925 Torbram Rd TF Cust Svc: 888-226-2225 ■ Web: www.hbc.com/zellers	Brampton	ON	L6T4G1	905-792-4400	792-6399
Zumiez Inc 6300 Merrill Creek Pkwy Suite B NASDAQ: ZUMZ ■ TF: 877-828-6929 ■ Web: www.zumiez.com	Everett	WA	98203	425-551-1500	551-1555

157-3 Men's Clothing Stores

Company	City	State	Zip	Phone	Fax
Bachrach Clothing Inc 1 Bachrach Ct TF: 800-222-4722 ■ Web: www.bachrach.com	Decatur	IL	62526	217-875-1020	875-0030
Barry Mfg Better Men's Wear Inc 2303 John Glenn Dr Web: www.bettermenswear.com	Chamblee	GA	30341	770-451-5476	451-8095
Boyd's 1818 Chestnut St Web: www.boydsphila.com	Philadelphia	PA	19103	215-564-9000	564-2876
Brooks Brothers Inc 346 Madison Ave TF: 800-444-1613 ■ Web: www.brooksbrothers.com	New York	NY	10017	212-682-8800	309-7273
C & R Clothiers Inc 5803 Glenmont Dr *Fax: Hum Res ■ TF: 800-447-8487	Houston	TX	77081	713-295-7200	592-7008*
Caplan's Mens Shops Inc 916 3rd St	Alexandria	LA	71301	318-487-4231	443-8816
Carroll & Co 425 N Canon Dr TF: 800-238-9400 ■ Web: www.carrollandco.com	Beverly Hills	CA	90210	310-273-9060	273-7974
Casual Male Inc 555 Turnpike St *Fax: Hum Res ■ TF: 800-767-0319 ■ Web: www.casualmale.com	Canton	MA	02021	781-828-9300	828-5059*
Casual Male Retail Group Inc 555 Turnpike St NASDAQ: CMRG ■ Web: www.casualmale.com	Canton	MA	02021	781-828-9300	821-1366
Culwell & Son Inc 6319 Hillcrest Ave Web: www.culwell.com	Dallas	TX	75205	214-522-7000	521-7329
Dahle Management Corp 4065 S Commerce Dr Suite 300-W Web: www.dahles-bigandtall.com	Murray	UT	84107	801-892-2555	892-2556
Express 2 Limited Pkwy *Fax: Hum Res ■ TF Cust Svc: 800-477-8844 ■ Web: www.limitedexpress.com	Columbus	OH	43230	614-415-4000	415-5805*
Fine's Men's Shops Inc 1164 Azalea Garden Rd	Norfolk	VA	23502	757-857-6013	857-4603
Fredrick Paul Menstyle 223 W Poplar St TF: 800-247-1417 ■ Web: www.paulfredrick.com	Fleetwood	PA	19522	610-944-0909	944-6452
Gushner Brothers Inc DBA Boyd's 1818 Chestnut St Web: www.boydsphila.com	Philadelphia	PA	19103	215-564-9000	564-2876
H & M Hennes & Mauritz Corp 1328 Broadway 3rd Fl Web: www.hm.com	New York	NY	10001	646-473-1165	473-1165
Harold's Men's Wear 350 W 19th St	Houston	TX	77008	713-864-2647	864-9830
Hugestore.com 427 S Illinois St TF: 800-259-7283 ■ Web: www.hugestore.com	Indianapolis	IN	46225	317-321-9999	321-9988
Hyman M & Son Inc 425 Huehl Rd Suite 11A	Northbrook	IL	60062	847-205-5556	205-1011
International Male 741 F St TF: 800-293-9333 ■ Web: www.internationalmale.com	San Diego	CA	92101	619-544-9900	881-3940
Jos A Bank Clothiers 500 Hanover Pike NASDAQ: JOSB ■ TF Cust Svc: 800-999-7472 ■ Web: www.josbank.com	Hampstead	MD	21074	410-239-2700	239-5700
Joseph Davidson Inc 412 S Jefferson St	Roanoke	VA	24011	540-343-2441	345-6021
K & G Men's Center Inc 1225 Chattahoochee Ave NW TF: 800-351-7987 ■ Web: www.kgmens.com	Atlanta	GA	30318	404-351-7987	351-8038
Kramer Corp PO Box 3617	Honolulu	HI	96811	808-845-3737	845-3812
Louis Boston 234 Berkeley St TF: 800-225-5135 ■ Web: www.louisboston.com	Boston	MA	02116	617-262-6100	266-4586
Lourie's Inc 1601 Main St Web: www.louries.com	Columbia	SC	29201	803-765-9200	256-1906
Marsh's Men's Shop 270 Main St	Huntington	NY	11743	631-423-1660	423-1670
Men's Wearhouse Inc 40650 Encyclopedia Cir NYSE: MW ■ *Fax Area Code: 877 ■ TF: 800-777-8580 ■ Web: www.menswearhouse.com	Fremont	CA	94538	510-723-8200	586-9669*
Miltons Inc 250 Granite St TF: 800-645-8667 ■ Web: www.miltons.com	Braintree	MA	02184	781-848-1880	848-1090
Norton Ditto Co Inc 2425 W Alabama St Web: www.nortonditto.com	Houston	TX	77098	713-688-9800	621-3875
Patrick James Inc 3457 W Shaw Ave TF: 888-427-6003 ■ Web: www.patrickjames.com	Fresno	CA	93711	559-275-4300	275-0137
Paul Fredrick Menstyle 223 W Poplar St TF: 800-247-1417 ■ Web: www.paulfredrick.com	Fleetwood	PA	19522	610-944-0909	944-6452
Repp Ltd Big & Tall Stores 555 Turnpike St TF: 800-690-7377 ■ Web: www.reppbigandtall.com	Canton	MA	02021	781-828-9300	575-9866
Richards of Greenwich 359 Greenwich Ave Web: www.richardsonline.com	Greenwich	CT	06830	203-622-0551	622-7352
Rochester Big & Tall 700 Mission St TF: 800-282-8200 ■ Web: www.rochesterclothing.com	San Francisco	CA	94103	415-982-6455	227-0727
Rubenstein Brothers Inc 102 St Charles Ave TF: 800-725-7823	New Orleans	LA	70130	504-581-6666	582-6982
S & K Famous Brands Inc 11100 W Broad St Web: www.skmenswear.com	Glen Allen	VA	23060	804-346-2500	346-2627

157-4 Men's & Women's Clothing Stores

Company	City	State	Zip	Phone	Fax
Abercrombie & Fitch Co 6301 Fitch Pass NYSE: ANF ■ TF: 800-666-2595 ■ Web: www.abercrombie.com	New Albany	OH	43054	614-283-6500	283-6565

Men's & Women's Clothing Stores (Cont'd)

				Phone	Fax
American Apparel LLC 747 Warehouse St	Los Angeles	CA	90021	213-488-0226	488-0334
Web: www.americanapparel.net					
American Eagle Outfitters 150 Thorn Hill Dr	Warrendale	PA	15086	724-776-4857	779-5740
NASDAQ: AEOS ■ *TF Cust Svc:* 888-232-4535 ■ *Web:* www.ae-outfitters.com					
Banana Republic 1 Harrison St	San Francisco	CA	94105	650-952-4400	874-7803*
**Fax:* Hum Res ■ *TF:* 800-333-7899 ■ *Web:* www.bananarepublic.com					
Barneys New York Inc 575 5th Ave	New York	NY	10017	212-450-8700	450-8489*
**Fax:* Hum Res ■ *Web:* www.barneys.com					
Bergdorf Goodman Inc 754 5th Ave	New York	NY	10019	212-753-7300	872-8616*
**Fax:* Sales ■ *TF Cust Svc:* 800-558-1855 ■ *Web:* www.bergdorfgoodman.com					
Bruhn Dick Inc 300 Main St	Salinas	CA	93901	831-758-4684	422-2620
Buckle Inc 2407 W 24th St	Kearney	NE	68845	308-236-8491	236-4493
NYSE: BKE ■ *TF:* 800-626-1255 ■ *Web:* www.buckle.com					
Burberry Ltd (New York) 9 E 57th St	New York	NY	10022	212-407-7100	355-9870
Web: www.burberry.com					
Canal Jean Co 2236 Nostrand Ave	Brooklyn	NY	11210	718-421-7590	421-7580
Web: www.canaljean.com					
Cohoes Fashions Inc 43 Mohawk St	Cohoes	NY	12047	518-237-0524	237-0234
TF: 800-736-8765 ■ *Web:* www.cohoesfashions.com					
Eddie Bauer Inc 15010 NE 36th St	Redmond	WA	98052	425-755-6100	414-6110*
**Fax Area Code:* 800 ■ *TF Orders:* 800-426-8020 ■ *Web:* www.eddiebauer.com					
Forever 21 Inc 2001 S Alameda St	Los Angeles	CA	90058	213-741-5100	741-5161
TF Cust Svc: 800-966-1355 ■ *Web:* www.forever21.com					
Gap Inc 2 Folsom St	San Francisco	CA	94105	650-952-4400	874-7803
NYSE: GPS ■ *TF:* 800-333-7899 ■ *Web:* www.gapinc.com					
GapBody 1 Harrison St	San Francisco	CA	94105	650-952-4400	874-7803*
**Fax:* Hum Res ■ *Web:* www.gap.com					
Harold's Stores Inc 5919 Maple Ave	Dallas	TX	75235	214-366-0600	366-1061
AMEX: HLD ■ *TF:* 800-949-3533 ■ *Web:* www.harolds.com					
Henry Jack Clothing Co Inc 612 W 47th St	Kansas City	MO	64112	816-753-3800	753-0284
Hirshleifer J & Son Inc 2080 Northern Blvd	Manhasset	NY	11030	516-627-3566	627-3579
TF: 800-401-9313 ■ *Web:* www.hirshleifers.com					
J Crew Group Inc 770 Broadway	New York	NY	10003	212-209-2500	209-2666
TF: 800-932-0043 ■ *Web:* www.jcrew.com					
J Hirshleifer & Son Inc 2080 Northern Blvd	Manhasset	NY	11030	516-627-3566	627-3579
TF: 800-401-9313 ■ *Web:* www.hirshleifers.com					
J McLaughlin 1008 Lexington Ave	New York	NY	10021	212-879-9565	879-0066
Jack Henry Clothing Co Inc 612 W 47th St	Kansas City	MO	64112	816-753-3800	753-0284
James Davis 400 S Grove Park Rd	Memphis	TN	38117	901-767-4640	682-3338
John B Malouf Inc 8201 Quaker Ave Suite 106	Lubbock	TX	79424	806-794-9500	798-3428
Web: www.maloufs.com					
Korshak Stanley 500 Crescent Ct Suite 100	Dallas	TX	75201	214-871-3600	871-3617
TF: 800-972-5959 ■ *Web:* www.stanleykorshak.com					
Limited Brands Inc 3 Limited Pkwy	Columbus	OH	43230	614-415-7000	415-2491*
NYSE: LTD ■ **Fax:* Mail Rm ■ *TF:* 800-945-9000 ■ *Web:* www.limitedbrands.com					
Malouf John B Inc 8201 Quaker Ave Suite 106	Lubbock	TX	79424	806-794-9500	798-3428
Web: www.maloufs.com					
Mark Fore & Strike Inc 6500 Park of Commerce Blvd	Boca Raton	FL	33487	561-241-1700	241-1055
TF Orders: 800-327-3627 ■ *Web:* www.markforeandstrike.com					
Mark Shale 10441 Beaudin Blvd Suite 100	Woodridge	IL	60517	630-427-1100	427-1200
TF: 800-488-2686 ■ *Web:* www.markshale.com					
Maurices Inc 105 W Superior St	Duluth	MN	55802	218-727-8431	720-2102
Web: maurices.com					
McLaughlin J 1008 Lexington Ave	New York	NY	10021	212-879-9565	879-0066
Modecraft 263 W 38th St	New York	NY	10018	212-221-0010	391-0074
Oak Hall Inc 6150 Poplar Ave Suite 146	Memphis	TN	38119	901-761-3580	761-5731
Pacific Sunwear of California Inc 3450 E Miraloma Ave	Anaheim	CA	92806	714-414-4000	
NASDAQ: PSUN ■ *TF:* 800-444-6770 ■ *Web:* www.pacificsunwear.com					
Patagonia Inc 259 W Santa Clara Dr PO Box 150	Ventura	CA	93001	805-643-8616	653-6355
TF Cust Svc: 800-638-6464 ■ *Web:* www.patagonia.com					
Paul Stuart Inc Madison Ave & 45th St	New York	NY	10017	212-682-0320	983-2742
TF Orders: 800-678-8278 ■ *Web:* www.paulstuart.com					
Plato's Closet 4200 Dahlberg Dr Suite 100	Minneapolis	MN	55422	763-520-8500	520-8410
Web: www.platoscloset.com					
Rodes Apparel 4938 Brownsboro Rd	Louisville	KY	40222	502-584-3112	584-8840
TF: 800-950-7633 ■ *Web:* www.rodes.com					
Shale Mark Co 10441 Beaudin Blvd Suite 100	Woodridge	IL	60517	630-427-1100	427-1200
TF: 800-488-2686 ■ *Web:* www.markshale.com					
Stage Stores Inc 10201 S Main St	Houston	TX	77025	713-667-5601	663-9780*
NASDAQ: STGS ■ **Fax:* Hum Res ■ *TF:* 800-324-3244 ■ *Web:* www.stagestoresinc.com					
Stanley Korshak 500 Crescent Ct Suite 100	Dallas	TX	75201	214-871-3600	871-3617
TF: 800-972-5959 ■ *Web:* www.stanleykorshak.com					
TJX Cos Inc 770 Cochituate Rd	Framingham	MA	01701	508-390-3000	390-5391*
NYSE: TJX ■ **Fax:* Hum Res ■ *Web:* www.tjx.com					
Town & County Inc 2660 S Glenstone Ave	Springfield	MO	65804	417-883-6131	883-7271
Up Against the Wall 1420 Wisconsin Ave NW	Washington	DC	20007	202-337-6610	333-1246
Web: www.upagainstthewall.com					
Urban Outfitters Inc 5000 S Broad St	Philadelphia	PA	19112	215-564-2313	568-1691
NASDAQ: URBN ■ *Web:* www.urbanoutfitters.com					

157-5 Specialty Clothing Stores

Specialty clothing stores are those which sell a specific type of clothing, such as Western wear, uniforms, etc.

				Phone	Fax
Aeropostale Inc 112 W 34th St 22nd Fl	New York	NY	10120	646-485-5410	485-5440
NYSE: ARO ■ *Web:* www.aeropostale.com					
Cavender's 2025 SW Loop 323	Tyler	TX	75701	903-561-4992	561-4849
Web: www.cavenders.com					
Corral West Ranchwear 4519 Frontier Mall Dr	Cheyenne	WY	82009	307-632-0951	632-4032
Web: www.corralwest.com					
Dunham's Sports 5000 Dixie Hwy	Waterford	MI	48329	248-674-4991	674-1407
Web: www.dunhamssports.com					
Hat World Corp DBA Lids 8142 Woodland Dr	Indianapolis	IN	46278	317-334-9428	337-1428
Web: www.lids.com					
Hilo Hattie 700 N Nimitz Hwy	Honolulu	HI	96817	808-524-3966	533-6809
TF: 800-233-8912 ■ *Web:* www.hilohattie.com					
Hot Topic Inc 18305 E San Jose Ave	City of Industry	CA	91748	626-839-4681	839-4686
NASDAQ: HOTT ■ *Web:* www.hottopic.com					
Libertyville Saddle Shop Inc PO Box M	Libertyville	IL	60048	847-362-0570	680-3200
Web: www.saddleshop.com					
Life Uniform Co 2132 Kratky Rd	Saint Louis	MO	63114	314-824-2900	327-8070*
**Fax Area Code:* 800 ■ *TF:* 800-325-8033 ■ *Web:* www.lifeuniform.com					
Luskey's/Ryon's Western Stores Inc 2601 N Main St	Fort Worth	TX	76106	817-625-2391	625-0457
TF: 800-725-7966 ■ *Web:* www.luskeys.com					
Mark's Work Warehouse 30-1035 64th Ave SE	Calgary	AB	T2H2J7	403-255-9220	255-6005
TF: 800-663-6275 ■ *Web:* www.marks.com					
Modell's Sporting Goods 498 7th Ave 20th Fl	New York	NY	10018	212-822-1000	822-1090
TF: 800-250-7405 ■ *Web:* www.modells.com					
Niver Western Wear Inc PO Box 10122	Fort Worth	TX	76185	817-924-4299	924-4296
TF: 800-433-5752					
Post & Nickel 144 N 14th St	Lincoln	NE	68508	402-476-3432	476-3454
Web: www.postandnickel.com					
Pro Image Franchise LC 233 N 1250 West Suite 200	Centerville	UT	84014	801-296-9999	296-1319
TF: 888-477-6326 ■ *Web:* www.proimage.net					
Sheplers Inc 6501 W Kellogg Dr	Wichita	KS	67209	316-946-3838	946-3778
Web: www.sheplers.com					
Warnaco Swimwear Group Inc 6040 Bandini Blvd	Los Angeles	CA	90040	323-726-1262	721-3613*
**Fax:* Mktg ■ *TF Cust Svc:* 800-547-8770 ■ *Web:* www.warnaco.com					
Watumull Brothers Ltd 307 Lewers St Suite 600	Honolulu	HI	96815	808-971-8800	971-8824
Western Warehouse 1130 Dragon St Suite 190	Dallas	TX	75207	972-788-1301	573-8797*
**Fax Area Code:* 214 ■ *TF:* 800-532-4888 ■ *Web:* www.westernwarehouse.com					
Wilsons The Leather Experts Inc 7401 Boone Ave N	Brooklyn Park	MN	55428	763-391-4000	391-4535
NASDAQ: WLSN ■ *TF:* 800-967-6270 ■ *Web:* www.wilsonsleather.com					
Women's Health Boutique Franchise System Inc 12715 Telge Rd	Cypress	TX	77429	281-256-4100	373-4450
TF: 888-280-2053 ■ *Web:* www.w-h-b.com					
Work 'n Gear Stores 293 Libby Industrial Pkwy	Weymouth	MA	02189	781-746-0100	746-0180
Web: www.workngear.com					

157-6 Women's Clothing Stores

				Phone	Fax
5-7-9 Shops 1000 Pennsylvania Ave	Brooklyn	NY	11207	718-485-3000	485-3807
TF: 877-695-9858 ■ *Web:* www.579.com					
A & E Stores Inc 1000 Huyler St	Teterboro	NJ	07608	201-393-0600	393-0233
Web: www.aestores.com					
A Nose For Clothes 13100 SW 128th St	Miami	FL	33186	305-253-8631	235-4370
TF: 877-870-6673 ■ *Web:* www.anoseforclothes.com					
ABS by Allan Schwartz 1231 Long Beach Ave	Los Angeles	CA	90021	213-895-4400	891-2812*
**Fax:* Hum Res ■ *TF:* 800-499-5534 ■ *Web:* www.absstyle.com					
Albrechts Co 3930 W 50th St	Edina	MN	55424	612-333-8104	
AnnTaylor Inc 7 Times Sq	New York	NY	10036	212-541-3300	541-3379
TF: 800-677-6788 ■ *Web:* www.anntaylor.com					
AnnTaylor Stores Corp 7 Times Sq	New York	NY	10036	212-541-3300	541-3379
NYSE: ANN ■ *TF:* 800-677-6788					
Anthony's Inc 5000 Georgia Ave	West Palm Beach	FL	33405	561-588-7336	588-4325
TF: 800-324-1380 ■ *Web:* www.anthonysfla.com					
Avenue Stores Inc 365 W Passaic St	Rochelle Park	NJ	07662	201-845-0880	909-2216*
**Fax:* Mktg ■ *TF:* 877-708-8740 ■ *Web:* www.avenue.com					
B Moss Clothing Co Ltd 550 Meadowland Pkwy	Secaucus	NJ	07094	201-866-6677	866-0387
TF: 800-524-0639					
Balliet's Inc 1900 NW Expy	Oklahoma City	OK	73118	405-848-7811	848-9632
TF: 877-841-8078 ■ *Web:* www.balliets.com					
Ben Thylan Furs Corp 345 7th Ave 5th Fl	New York	NY	10001	212-753-7700	643-2082
Web: www.benthylanfurs.com					
Bifano Furs 4205 Sigma Rd	Dallas	TX	75244	972-458-1111	458-1197
Big M Inc 12 Vreeland Ave	Totowa	NJ	07512	973-890-0021	890-1923
Bluefly Inc 42 W 39th St 9th Fl	New York	NY	10018	212-944-8000	354-3400
NASDAQ: BFLY ■ *TF Cust Svc:* 877-258-3359 ■ *Web:* www.bluefly.com					
Body Shops of America Inc 6225 Powers Ave	Jacksonville	FL	32217	904-737-0811	737-6509
Web: www.bodyc.com					
Cache Inc 1440 Broadway 5th Fl	New York	NY	10018	212-575-3200	575-3225
NASDAQ: CACH ■ *TF:* 800-788-2224 ■ *Web:* www.cache.com					
Cargoland Inc 153 W Orangethorpe Ave	Placentia	CA	92870	714-524-1301	524-1302
Catherines Stores Corp 3742 Lamar Ave	Memphis	TN	38118	901-363-3900	794-8459*
**Fax:* Hum Res ■ *TF:* 800-289-6372 ■ *Web:* catherines.charmingshoppes.com					
Cato Corp 8100 Denmark Rd	Charlotte	NC	28273	704-554-8510	
NYSE: CTR ■ *TF:* 800-488-0619 ■ *Web:* www.catofashions.com					
Charlotte Russe 4645 Morena Blvd	San Diego	CA	92117	858-587-9900	875-0336
TF: 877-266-9327 ■ *Web:* www.charlotte-russe.com					
Charming Shoppes Inc 450 Winks Ln	Bensalem	PA	19020	215-245-9100	633-4748
NASDAQ: CHRS ■ *Web:* www.charmingshoppes.com					
Chico's FAS Inc 11215 Metro Pkwy	Fort Myers	FL	33912	239-277-6200	267-4259
NYSE: CHS ■ *TF:* 888-855-4986 ■ *Web:* www.chicos.com					
Christopher & Banks Corp 2400 Xenium Ln N	Plymouth	MN	55441	763-551-5000	551-5198
NYSE: CBK ■ *Web:* www.christopherandbanks.com					
Claire's Accessories 2400 W Central Rd	Hoffman Estates	IL	60195	847-765-1100	765-4676
TF: 800-252-4737 ■ *Web:* www.claires.com					
Country Casuals 311 E Mitchell St	Petoskey	MI	49770	231-347-6501	
Daffodil 163 Pearl St	Essex Junction	VT	05452	802-879-0212	872-3221
TF: 800-795-1305					
David's Bridal Inc 1001 Washington St	Conshohocken	PA	19428	610-943-5000	943-5020*
**Fax:* Cust Svc ■ *TF:* 800-823-2403 ■ *Web:* www.davidsbridal.com					
Deb Shops Inc 9401 Blue Grass Rd	Philadelphia	PA	19114	215-676-6000	969-2830
NASDAQ: DEBS ■ *TF:* 800-676-6700 ■ *Web:* www.debshops.com					
Dittrich EC & Co 7373 3rd Ave	Detroit	MI	48202	313-873-8300	873-3762
Web: www.dittrichfurs.com					
Drapers & Damons 9 Pasteur St	Irvine	CA	92618	949-784-3000	784-3300
TF: 800-843-1174 ■ *Web:* www.drapers.com					
Dress Barn Inc 30 Dunnigan Dr	Suffern	NY	10901	845-369-4500	369-8010*
NASDAQ: DBRN ■ **Fax:* Mktg ■ *TF Cust Svc:* 800-373-7722 ■ *Web:* www.dressbarn.com					
Dress Code Inc 1778 Ellsworth Industrial Blvd	Atlanta	GA	30318	404-351-1777	355-7029
EC Dittrich & Co 7373 3rd Ave	Detroit	MI	48202	313-873-8300	873-3762
Web: www.dittrichfurs.com					
EM Scarbrough & Sons Inc DBA Scarbroughs 4001 N Lamar Blvd Bldg 400	Austin	TX	78756	512-452-4220	452-6608
Web: www.scarbroughs.com					
Embry's & Co 3363 Tates Creek Rd Suite 212	Lexington	KY	40502	859-266-9785	266-9618
TF: 800-236-2797 ■ *Web:* www.embrysfurs.com					
Express 1 Limited Pkwy	Columbus	OH	43230	614-415-4000	415-4340*
**Fax:* Hum Res ■ *TF:* 800-945-9000 ■ *Web:* www.expressfashion.com					
Fashion Bug 450 Winks Ln	Bensalem	PA	19020	215-245-9100	633-4640*
**Fax:* Hum Res					
Fashion Shops of Kentucky Inc 11008 Decimal Dr	Louisville	KY	40299	502-267-5415	267-0480
Fendi NA Inc 720 5th Ave 5th Fl	New York	NY	10019	212-920-8100	767-0545
TF: 800-336-3469 ■ *Web:* www.fendi.com					
Flemington Fur Co 8 Spring St	Flemington	NJ	08822	908-782-2212	782-2773
Web: www.flemingtonfurs.com					
Forever 21 Inc 2001 S Alameda St	Los Angeles	CA	90058	213-741-5100	741-5161
TF Cust Svc: 800-966-1355 ■ *Web:* www.forever21.com					
Frederick's of Hollywood Inc 6255 Sunset Blvd Suite 600	Hollywood	CA	90028	323-466-5151	962-9935
TF: 800-323-9525 ■ *Web:* www.fredericks.com					
Gartenhaus Furs 6950 Wisconsin Ave	Chevy Chase	MD	20815	301-656-2800	656-2819
Girlshop Inc 154 W 14th St 9th Fl	New York	NY	10011	212-645-6240	645-5554
TF: 888-450-7467 ■ *Web:* www.girlshop.com					
Gucci Group Inc 50 Hartz Way	Secaucus	NJ	07094	201-867-8800	617-2398*
**Fax:* Hum Res ■ *Web:* www.guccigroup.com					
GWK Enterprises 120 S State St	Geneseo	IL	61254	309-944-6516	944-8262
H & M Hennes & Mauritz Corp 1328 Broadway 3rd Fl	New York	NY	10001	646-473-1165	473-1165
Web: www.hm.com					
Henig Inc 4135 Carmichael Rd	Montgomery	AL	36106	334-277-7610	272-3562
TF: 800-521-2037 ■ *Web:* www.henigfurs.com					
Henri Bendel Inc 712 5th Ave	New York	NY	10019	212-247-1100	
TF: 800-423-6335 ■ *Web:* www.limitedbrands.com					
Irresistibles 7 Hawkes St	Marblehead	MA	01945	781-631-1248	631-8965
TF: 800-555-9865 ■ *Web:* www.irresistibles.com					

	City	State	Zip	Phone	Fax
Johnny Appleseed's Inc 30 Tozer Rd	Beverly	MA	01915	978-922-2040	922-7001
TF Cust Svc: 800-767-6666 ■ *Web:* www.appleseeds.com					
Joyce Leslie Inc 135 W Commercial Ave	Moonachie	NJ	07074	201-804-7800	804-8841
TF: 800-526-6216 ■ *Web:* www.joyceleslie.com					
Kaye Louise 3121 W Hallandale Beach Blvd Suite 110	Pembroke Park	FL	33009	954-989-2448	989-8716
Lady Grace Stores Inc 61 Exchange St	Malden	MA	02148	781-322-1721	321-8476
TF: 800-922-0504 ■ *Web:* www.ladygrace.com					
Lane Bryant Inc 3344 Morse Crossing	Columbus	OH	43219	614-463-5200	463-5240*
**Fax:* Mktg ■ *TF:* 800-876-8728 ■ *Web:* www.lanebryant.com					
Limited The 3 Limited Pkwy	Columbus	OH	43230	614-415-2000	415-2491*
**Fax:* Mail Rm ■ *TF:* 800-945-9000 ■ *Web:* www.limitedbrands.com					
Limited Brands Inc 3 Limited Pkwy	Columbus	OH	43230	614-415-7000	415-2491*
NYSE: LTD ■ **Fax:* Mail Rm ■ *TF:* 800-945-9000 ■ *Web:* www.limitedbrands.com					
Loehmann's Holdings Inc 2500 Halsey St	Bronx	NY	10461	718-409-2000	518-2766
Web: www.loehmanns.com					
Louis Vuitton NA Inc 19 E 57th St	New York	NY	10022	212-931-2000	931-2097*
**Fax:* Mktg ■ *TF Cust Svc:* 866-884-8866 ■ *Web:* www.vuitton.com					
Maison Weiss 4500 I-55 at Highland Village	Jackson	MS	39211	601-981-4621	981-4671
Mandee Shop 12 Vreeland Ave	Totowa	NJ	07512	973-890-0021	890-1923
TF: 800-969-2446 ■ *Web:* www.mandee.com					
Marshall Retail Group LLC 5385 Wynn Rd	Las Vegas	NV	89118	702-385-5233	385-2842
Web: www.marshallretailgroup.com					
Max Rave 317 Madison Ave Suite 1010	New York	NY	10018	212-297-0005	297-0215
Motherhood Maternity 456 N 5th St	Philadelphia	PA	19123	215-873-2200	625-3843*
**Fax:* Cust Svc ■ *TF:* 800-291-7800 ■ *Web:* www.motherhood.com					
Mothers Work Inc 456 N 5th St	Philadelphia	PA	19123	215-873-2200	625-3843*
NASDAQ: MWRK ■ **Fax:* Cust Svc ■ *TF:* 800-291-7800 ■ *Web:* www.motherswork.com					
New York & Co 450 W 33rd St 5th Fl	New York	NY	10001	212-736-1222	884-2698
NYSE: NWY ■ *TF:* 800-723-5333 ■ *Web:* www.nyandcompany.com					
Orva Stores Inc 155 E 86th St	New York	NY	10028	212-369-3448	722-6904
Petite Sophisticate 100 Phoenix Ave	Enfield	CT	06082	860-741-0771	
Web: www.securerba.com					
Rainbow Apparel Cos 1000 Pennsylvania Ave	Brooklyn	NY	11207	718-485-3000	
TF: 877-695-9858 ■ *Web:* www.rainbowshops.com					
Right On Casuals 2496 Central Ave	Yonkers	NY	10710	914-337-7300	337-5266
rue21 Inc 800 Commonwealth Dr Suite 100	Warrendale	PA	15086	724-776-9780	776-4111
TF: 888-871-2744 ■ *Web:* www.rue21.com					
Saks Jandel 5510 Wisconsin Ave	Chevy Chase	MD	20815	301-652-2250	652-2044
Scarbroughs 4001 N Lamar Blvd Bldg 400	Austin	TX	78756	512-452-4220	452-6608
Web: www.scarbroughs.com					
Schweser's Stores Inc 630 N Park Ave	Fremont	NE	68025	402-721-1700	727-4925
Silver Fox Inc 1207 3rd St S Suite 7	Naples	FL	34102	239-262-7598	262-5382
Styles for Less 12728 S Shoemaker Ave	Santa Fe Springs	CA	90670	562-229-3400	229-3401
TF: 800-929-3466 ■ *Web:* www.stylesforless.com					
Swim 'n Sport Retail Inc 2396 NW 96th Ave	Miami	FL	33172	305-593-5071	593-2669
TF: 800-497-2111 ■ *Web:* www.swimnsport.com					
Talbots Inc 1 Talbots Dr	Hingham	MA	02043	781-749-7600	741-4369
NYSE: TLB ■ *TF:* 800-225-8200 ■ *Web:* www1.talbots.com					
Thylan Ben Furs Corp 345 7th Ave 5th Fl	New York	NY	10001	212-753-7700	643-2082
Web: www.benthylanfurs.com					
Tootsies 4045 Westheimer Rd	Houston	TX	77027	713-629-9990	960-0470
TF: 800-580-2220 ■ *Web:* www.tootsies.com					
Twigland Fashions Ltd 12460 Network Blvd Suite 106	San Antonio	TX	78249	210-377-3393	377-1546
TF: 866-362-4224 ■ *Web:* www.agacitoo.com					
United Retail Group Inc 365 W Passaic St	Rochelle Park	NJ	07662	201-845-0880	909-2114
NASDAQ: URGI ■ *TF:* 877-708-8740 ■ *Web:* www.unitedretail.com					
Vanity Shop of Grand Forks Inc 1001 25th St N	Fargo	ND	58102	701-237-3330	237-4692
Web: www.vanityshops.com					
Victoria's Secret Stores 4 Limited Pkwy	Reynoldsburg	OH	43068	614-577-7000	577-7047
TF: 800-411-5116 ■ *Web:* www.victoriassecret.com					
Wet Seal Inc 26972 Burbank Ave	Foothill Ranch	CA	92610	949-699-3900	699-4722
NASDAQ: WTSLA ■ *Web:* www.wetseal.com					
White House/Black Market 11215 Metro Pkwy	Fort Meyers	FL	33966	239-277-9426	277-0259
TF: 888-669-4911 ■ *Web:* www.whiteandblack.com					
Willow Tree 2944 Biddle Ave	Wyandotte	MI	48192	734-285-7020	285-0895
Web: www.willowtreefashions.com					
Windsor Fashions Inc 4533 Pacific Blvd	Vernon	CA	90058	323-282-9000	973-4379
TF: 888-494-6376 ■ *Web:* www.windsorfashions.com					

158 COAST GUARD INSTALLATIONS

	City	State	Zip	Phone	Fax
Astoria Coast Guard Air Station 2285 SE Airport Rd	Warrenton	OR	97146	503-861-6220	861-6358
Web: www.uscg.mil/d13/units/gruastoria					
Atlantic City Coast Guard Air Station					
Atlantic City International Airport Bldg 350	Atlantic City	NJ	08505	609-677-2222	677-2228
Barbers Point Coast Guard Air Station 1 Coral Sea Rd	Kapolei	HI	96707	808-682-2771	
Web: www.uscg.mil/d14/units/asbp/uscgasbp					
Borinquen Coast Guard Air Station 260 Guard Rd	Aguadilla	PR	00604	787-890-8400	890-8407
Web: www.uscg.mil/d7/units/as-borinquen					
Cape Cod Coast Guard Air Station Bldg 3172	Cape Cod	MA	02542	508-968-6305	968-6315
Web: www.uscg.mil/d1/units/ascapecod					
Charleston Coast Guard Base 196 Tradd St	Charleston	SC	29401	843-724-7600	724-7633
Web: www.uscg.mil/d7/units/gruchasn					
Clearwater Coast Guard Air Station 15100 Rescue Way	Clearwater	FL	33762	727-535-1437	
Web: www.uscg.mil/d7/units/as-clearwater					
Corpus Christi Coast Guard Air Station 8930 Ocean Dr	Corpus Christi	TX	78419	361-939-6200	939-6377
Web: www.uscg.mil/d8/group/corpus					
Detroit Coast Guard Air Station Selfridge ANGB	Selfridge	MI	48045	586-307-6700	307-6705
Web: www.uscg.mil/d9/asdet/asdet.htm					
Detroit Coast Guard Base 110 Mt Elliott Ave	Detroit	MI	48207	313-568-9600	568-9469
Web: www.uscg.mil/d9/grudet					
Elizabeth City Coast Guard Air Station	Elizabeth City	NC	27909	252-335-6000	335-6185
Web: www.uscg.mil/d5/airstation/ecity					
Galveston Coast Guard Base PO Box 1943	Galveston	TX	77553	409-766-5620	766-4702
Honolulu Integrated Support Command 400 Sand Island Pkwy	Honolulu	HI	96819	808-541-2121	
Web: www.uscg.mil/d14					
Houston Coast Guard Air Station 1178 Ellington Field	Houston	TX	77034	281-481-0025	481-9628
Web: www.uscg.mil/d8/airstahouston					
Humboldt Bay Coast Guard Air Station 1001 Lyconing Ave	McKinleyville	CA	95519	707-839-6113	839-6198
Web: www.uscg.mil/d11/humboldt/home.htm					
Ketchikan Integrated Support Command 1300 Stedman St	Ketchikan	AK	99901	907-228-0340	228-0342
Web: www.uscg.mil/d17/iscketch/ketchpages					
Kodiak Coast Guard Air Station PO Box 190033	Kodiak	AK	99619	907-487-5733	487-5033
Los Angeles Coast Guard Air Station 7159 World Way W	Los Angeles	CA	90045	310-215-2204	215-1348
Web: www.uscg.mil/d11/airstationla					
Mayport Coast Guard Base 4200 Ocean St	Atlantic Beach	FL	32233	904-564-7521	564-7533
Web: www.uscg.mil/d7/units/grumayport					
Miami Beach Integrated Support Command					
100 MacArthur Cswy	Miami Beach	FL	33139	305-535-4300	535-4520
Web: www.uscg.mil/mlclant/iscmiami					
Miami Coast Guard Air Station					
Opa Locka Airport 14750 NW 44th	Opa Locka	FL	33054	305-953-2130	953-2348
Milwaukee Coast Guard Base 2420 S Lincoln Memorial Dr	Milwaukee	WI	53207	414-747-7100	747-7108
Web: www.uscg.mil/d9/grumil/unit					
Mobile Coast Guard Base S Broad St	Mobile	AL	36615	251-441-6217	639-6115
Web: www.uscg.mil/d8/group/mobile					
New Orleans Coast Guard Air Station 400 Russell Ave	New Orleans	LA	70143	504-393-6005	393-6016
North Bend Coast Guard Air Station 2000 Connecticut Ave	North Bend	OR	97459	541-756-9220	756-9203
Web: www.uscg.mil/d13/units/grunbend					
Port Angeles Coast Guard Air Station Ediz Hook Rd	Port Angeles	WA	98362	360-417-5840	457-5849
Web: www.uscg.mil/d13/units/grupangeles					
Sacramento Coast Guard Air Station 6037 Price Ave	McClellan	CA	95652	916-643-7659	643-7700
Web: www.uscg.mil/d11/airstationsac					
San Diego Coast Guard Air Station 2710 N Harbor Dr	San Diego	CA	92101	619-683-6470	683-6474
Web: www.uscg.mil/d11/sandiego					
San Francisco Coast Guard Air Station					
SFO International Airport Bldg 1020	San Francisco	CA	94128	650-808-2900	808-2916
Web: www.uscg.mil/d11/airstationsf					
San Juan Coast Guard Base 5 La Puntilla Final	San Juan	PR	00901	787-729-6800	729-1017
Sault Saint Marie Coast Guard Base 337 Water St	Sault Sainte Marie	MI	49783	906-635-3217	635-3216
Web: www.uscg.mil/d9/sault/home.html					
Savannah Coast Guard Air Station					
Hunter AAF 1297 N Lightning Rd	Savannah	GA	31409	912-652-4646	652-4661
Web: www.uscg.mil/d7/units/as-savannah					
Sitka Coast Guard Air Station 611 Airport Rd	Sitka	AK	99835	907-966-5434	966-5514
Traverse City Coast Guard Air Station					
1175 Airport Access Rd	Traverse City	MI	49686	231-922-8300	922-8213
Web: www.uscg.mil/d9/astc/astc.htm					

159 COFFEE & TEA STORES

	City	State	Zip	Phone	Fax
Ahh-Some Gourmet Coffee Inc 900 Elm St	Manchester	NH	03101	603-665-9487	669-7040
Bad Ass Coffee Co of Hawaii Inc 155 W Malvern Ave	Salt Lake City	UT	84115	801-463-1966	463-2606
TF: 888-422-3277 ■ *Web:* www.badasscoffee.com					
Barnie's Coffee & Tea Co Inc 2126 Landstreet Rd Suite 300	Orlando	FL	32809	407-854-6600	854-6601
TF: 800-854-1416 ■ *Web:* www.barniescoffee.com					
Brewster's Coffee Co Inc 500 Lake Cook Rd Suite 475	Deerfield	IL	60015	847-948-7520	405-8140
TF: 800-251-6101 ■ *Web:* www.babcorp.com					
Bucks County Coffee Co 2250 W Cabot Blvd	Langhorne	PA	19047	215-741-1855	741-1799
TF Sales: 800-844-8790 ■ *Web:* www.buckscountycoffee.com					
Caribou Coffee Co Inc 3900 Lakebreeze Ave N	Brooklyn Center	MN	55429	763-592-2200	592-2300
NASDAQ: CBOU ■ *TF Cust Svc:* 888-227-4268 ■ *Web:* www.cariboucoffee.com					
Coffee Bean & Tea Leaf 1945 S La Cienega Blvd	Los Angeles	CA	90034	310-237-2326	842-7902
TF: 800-832-5323 ■ *Web:* www.coffeebean.com					
Coffee Beanery Ltd 3429 Pierson Pl	Flushing	MI	48433	810-733-1020	733-1536
TF: 800-728-2326 ■ *Web:* www.coffeebeanery.com					
Coffee People Inc 28 Executive Park Suite 200	Irvine	CA	92614	949-260-1600	260-1610
TF: 800-354-5282 ■ *Web:* www.coffeepeople.com					
Diedrich Coffee Inc 28 Executive Park Suite 200	Irvine	CA	92614	949-260-1600	260-1610*
NASDAQ: DDRX ■ **Fax:* Cust Svc ■ *TF:* 800-354-5282 ■ *Web:* www.diedrich.com					
Dunkin' Donuts 130 Royall St	Canton	MA	02021	781-737-3000	737-4000
TF Cust Svc: 800-859-5339 ■ *Web:* www.dunkindonuts.com					
International Coffee & Tea Inc 1945 S La Cienega Blvd	Los Angeles	CA	90034	310-237-2326	815-2520
TF: 800-854-6252 ■ *Web:* www.coffeebean.com					
It's A Grind Inc 6272 E Pacific Coast Hwy Suite E	Long Beach	CA	90803	562-594-5600	594-4100
TF: 866-424-5282 ■ *Web:* www.itsagrind.com					
McNulty's Tea & Coffee Co Inc 109 Christopher St	New York	NY	10014	212-242-5351	
TF: 800-356-5200 ■ *Web:* www.mcnultys.com					
Moxie Java International LLC 4990 W Chinden Blvd	Boise	ID	83714	208-322-7773	321-0279
TF: 800-659-6963 ■ *Web:* www.moxiejava.com					
New World Coffee 100 Horizon Ctr Blvd	Hamilton	NJ	08691	609-631-7000	631-7068
TF: 800-308-2457 ■ *Web:* www.nwcb.com					
Pannikin Coffee & Tea 675 G St	San Diego	CA	92101	619-239-7891	
TF: 888-290-1996					
Peet's Coffee & Tea Inc 1400 Park Ave	Emeryville	CA	94608	510-594-2100	594-2180*
NASDAQ: PEET ■ **Fax:* Orders ■ *TF Orders:* 800-999-2132 ■ *Web:* www.peets.com					
PJ's Coffee Franchises LLC 1801 Peachtree Rd Suite 160	Atlanta	GA	30309	678-999-0513	
Web: www.pjscoffee.com					
Seattle's Best Coffee Co 2401 Utah Ave S	Seattle	WA	98134	800-611-7793	318-0772*
**Fax Area Code:* 206 ■ *Web:* www.seattlesbest.com					
Second Cup Ltd 6303 Airport Rd	Mississauga	ON	L4V1R8	905-405-6700	405-6479
TF: 800-338-2610 ■ *Web:* www.secondcup.com					
Shefield Group 2265 W Railway St	Abbotsford	BC	V2S2E3	604-859-1014	859-1711
Web: www.shefieldgourmet.com					
Starbucks Coffee Co 2401 Utah Ave S	Seattle	WA	98134	206-447-1575	318-3432
NASDAQ: SBUX ■ *TF:* 800-782-7282 ■ *Web:* www.starbucks.com					
Tully's Coffee Corp 3100 Airport Way S	Seattle	WA	98134	206-233-2070	233-2077
TF: 800-968-8559 ■ *Web:* www.tullys.com					

160 COLLECTION AGENCIES

	City	State	Zip	Phone	Fax
ABC-Amega Inc 1100 Main St	Buffalo	NY	14209	716-885-4444	878-2872
Web: abc-amega.com					
Alden Curtis & Michaels Ltd 1170 Broadway Suite 316	New York	NY	10001	212-532-7996	213-6731
TF: 800-569-3877 ■ *Web:* www.aldencurtis.com					
Alexander & Hamilton Inc 2721 Division St	Metairie	LA	70002	504-887-9153	887-8620
TF: 800-627-2539 ■ *Web:* www.alhamco.com					
Allen Daniel Assoc Inc 411 Waverly Oaks Rd Bldg 1 Suite 113	Waltham	MA	02454	781-647-7722	
TF: 800-882-2100					
Alliance One Inc 4797 Ruffner St	San Diego	CA	92111	858-560-6000	560-0250
TF: 866-855-0727 ■ *Web:* www.allianceoneinc.com					
Allied International Credit Corp 16635 Young St Suite 26	Newmarket	ON	L3X1V6	905-470-8181	470-8155
TF: 888-478-8181 ■ *Web:* www.aiccorp.com					
American Accounts & Advisors Inc 3904 Cedarvale Dr	Eagan	MN	55122	651-405-9760	405-9846
TF: 800-732-9115					
American Agencies Co Inc 21 E Ogden Ave Suite 201	Westmont	IL	60559	630-493-1776	493-1781
Asset Acceptance Capital Corp					
28405 Van Dyke Ave PO Box 2036	Warren	MI	48090	586-939-9600	446-7837
NASDAQ: AACC ■ *TF:* 800-545-9931 ■ *Web:* www.assetacceptance.com					
Associated Creditors Exchange Inc					
3443 N Central Ave Suite 1100	Phoenix	AZ	85012	602-954-6554	650-5949
TF: 800-280-3800 ■ *Web:* www.ace-collects.com					
Atlantic Credit & Finance Inc 3353 Orange Ave	Roanoke	VA	24012	540-772-7800	
TF: 800-888-9419 ■ *Web:* www.atlanticcreditfinance.com					
Barry Jon & Associates Inc 216 LePhillip Ct	Concord	NC	28025	704-723-4200	334-3612*
**Fax Area Code:* 800 ■ *TF:* 800-264-0384					
Bonneville Billing & Collection Inc					
1186 E 4600 South Suite 100	Ogden	UT	84403	801-621-7880	393-5808
TF: 800-660-6138 ■ *Web:* www.bonncoll.com					

	City	State	Zip	Phone	Fax
Capital Asset Research Corp Ltd 3980 RCA Blvd Suite 8012 *Fax: Cust Svc ■ TF: 800-888-8293 ■ Web: www.carc.com	Palm Beach Gardens	FL	33410	561-776-5000	776-5030*
Collectcorp Corp 415 Yonge St Suite 700 *Fax Area Code: 888 ■ TF: 800-900-4238	Toronto	ON	M5B2E7	416-961-9622	432-2923*
Collection Co of America 700 Longwater Dr TF: 800-886-9177 ■ Web: www.collecto.com	Norwell	MA	02061	781-681-4300	681-4340
Collecto Inc DBA Collection Co of America 700 Longwater Dr TF: 800-886-9177 ■ Web: www.collecto.com	Norwell	MA	02061	781-681-4300	681-4340
Communications Credit & Recovery Corp 100 Garden City Plaza Suite 222 TF: 800-327-3618 ■ Web: www.ccrcollect.com	Garden City	NY	11530	516-294-6800	294-5682
Computer Credit Inc 640 W 4th St TF: 800-942-2995	Winston-Salem	NC	27101	336-761-1524	761-8852
Credit Collections Inc 2915 N Classen Blvd Suite 100 TF: 866-723-2455 ■ Web: www.cciokc.com	Oklahoma City	OK	73106	405-290-2000	290-2043
Credit Control Services Inc 2 Wells Ave Suite 1 TF: 800-998-5000 ■ Web: www.ccsusa.com	Newton	MA	02459	617-965-2000	762-3311
Credit Management LP 4200 International Pkwy TF: 800-377-7723 ■ Web: www.thecmigroup.com	Carrollton	TX	75007	972-862-4200	862-4355
Diversified Account Systems of Georgia Inc 1331 Citizens Pkwy Suite 110 TF: 800-226-1464	Morrow	GA	30287	770-961-5400	
Diversified Adjustment Service Inc 600 Coon Rapids Blvd TF: 800-279-3733 ■ Web: www.diversifiedadjustment.com	Coon Rapids	MN	55433	763-780-1042	780-9338
Diversified Collection Services Inc 333 N Canyons Pkwy Suite 100 TF: 800-327-9467	Livermore	CA	94551	925-960-4800	960-4880
Dun & Bradstreet Receivable Management Services 899 Eaton Ave TF: 800-999-3867 ■ Web: www.dnbcollections.com	Bethlehem	PA	18025	610-882-7000	882-6005
Dynamic Recovery Services Inc 4101 McEwen Rd Suite 150 TF: 800-886-8088 ■ Web: www.dynamicrecoveryservices.com	Farmers Branch	TX	75244	972-241-5611	241-9552
Encore Capital Group Inc 8875 Aero Dr Suite 200 NASDAQ: ECPG ■ *Fax Area Code: 800 ■ TF: 877-445-4581 ■ Web: www.mcmcg.com	San Diego	CA	92123	858-560-2600	306-4443*
Fidelity National Credit Services 2411 N Glassell St TF: 800-648-9341	Orange	CA	92865	714-921-0271	921-8693
GC Services LP 6330 Gulfton St TF: 800-756-6524 ■ Web: www.gcserv.com	Houston	TX	77081	713-777-4441	776-6558
General Revenue Corp 11501 Northlake Dr TF: 800-234-1472 ■ Web: www.generalrevenue.com	Cincinnati	OH	45249	513-469-1472	469-7428
Gulf Coast Collection Bureau Inc 5630 Marquesas Cir TF: 888-839-6999 ■ Web: www.gulfcoastcollection.com	Sarasota	FL	34233	941-927-6999	684-4023
Hill Top Collections Inc 38 W 32nd St Suite 1510 TF: 800-564-2322	New York	NY	10001	212-564-2322	564-4322
Hospital Billing & Collection Service Ltd 118 Lukens Dr TF: 877-254-9580 ■ Web: www.hbcs.org	New Castle	DE	19720	302-552-8000	254-3750
IntelliRisk Management Corp 3000 Corporate Exchange Dr 6th FL TF: 800-260-5170 ■ Web: www.irmc.com	Columbus	OH	43231	614-865-2800	
JJ MacIntyre Co 1801 California Ave TF: 800-777-9929 ■ Web: www.jjmac.com	Corona	CA	92881	951-898-4300	898-4399
Jon Barry & Associates Inc 216 LePhillip Ct *Fax Area Code: 800 ■ TF: 800-264-0384	Concord	NC	28025	704-723-4200	334-3612*
LC Financial Inc 66111 Valjean Ave Suite 109 TF: 800-800-4523 ■ Web: www.lcf.net	Van Nuys	CA	91406	818-780-9300	780-3112
Leland Scott & Assoc Inc 1600 E Pioneer Pkwy Suite 550 TF: 800-808-5061 ■ Web: www.lelandscott.com	Arlington	TX	76010	817-460-7100	460-7135
LTD Financial Services LP 7322 Southwest Fwy Suite 1600 TF: 800-414-2101	Houston	TX	77074	713-414-2100	414-2120
MacIntyre JJ Co 1801 California Ave TF: 800-777-9929 ■ Web: www.jjmac.com	Corona	CA	92881	951-898-4300	898-4399
National Revenue Corp 4000 E 5th Ave *Fax: Cust Svc ■ TF: 800-789-7862 ■ Web: www.nationalrevenue.com	Columbus	OH	43219	614-829-7500	827-7873*
Nationwide Credit Inc 2015 Vaughn Rd Bldg 400 TF: 800-456-4729 ■ Web: www.nationcredit.com	Kennesaw	GA	30144	770-644-7400	612-7340
Nationwide Recovery Systems Inc 2304 Tarpley Rd Suite 134 TF: 800-458-6357 ■ Web: www.nationwide-recovery.com	Carrollton	TX	75006	972-798-1000	798-1020
NCO Financial Systems Inc 507 Prudential Rd TF: 800-220-2274 ■ Web: www.ncogroup.com	Horsham	PA	19044	215-441-3000	442-8470
NCO Group Inc 507 Prudential Rd NASDAQ: NCOG ■ TF: 800-220-2274 ■ Web: www.ncogroup.com	Horsham	PA	19044	215-441-3000	441-3929
Outsourcing Solutions Inc 390 S Woods Mill Rd Suite 350 Web: www.osioutsourcing.com	Chesterfield	MO	63017	314-576-0022	576-1867
Portfolio Recovery Assoc LLC 140 Corporate Blvd NASDAQ: PRAA ■ TF: 888-772-7326 ■ Web: www.portfoliorecovery.com	Norfolk	VA	23502	757-519-9300	321-2504
Preferred Collection Management Services Inc 1 Davis Blvd Suite 703 Web: www.preferredcms.com	Tampa	FL	33606	813-251-0802	254-7026
Recovery's Unlimited Inc 225 Broadhollow Rd Suite 405-E TF: 800-356-7402 ■ Web: www.ruicreditservices.com	Melville	NY	11747	516-222-1200	222-1144
Richmond North Assoc Inc 4232 Ridge Lea Rd Suite 12 TF: 888-228-9112 ■ Web: www.rnacollects.com	Amherst	NY	14226	716-832-5668	832-4236
Sterling Phillips & Assoc Inc 4739 Utica St Suite 212 TF: 800-375-5773 ■ Web: www.s-p-a.com	Metairie	LA	70006	504-887-0202	887-0701
Transworld Systems Inc 2235 Mercury Way Suite 275 TF: 800-435-1526 ■ Web: www.transworldsystems.com	Santa Rosa	CA	95407	707-236-3800	
Twenty-First Century Assoc 266 Summit Ave Web: www.tfc-associates.com	Hackensack	NJ	07601	201-678-1144	678-9088
United Recovery Systems LP 5800 N Course Dr TF: 800-568-0399 ■ Web: www.ursi.com	Houston	TX	77072	713-977-1234	977-0119
United Resource Systems Inc 10075 W Colfax Ave TF: 800-441-7364 ■ Web: www.urs-inc.com	Lakewood	CO	80215	303-205-0152	205-0153
Van Ru Credit Corp 1350 E Touhy Ave Suite 300E TF: 800-337-8331 ■ Web: www.vanru.com	Des Plaines	IL	60018	847-824-2414	824-0769
Vengroff Williams & Assoc Inc 7441 Lincoln Way TF: 888-374-2600 ■ Web: www.vwainc.com	Garden Grove	CA	92841	714-889-6200	889-6300

161 COLLEGES - BIBLE

SEE ALSO Colleges & Universities - Christian p. 1474

	City	State	Zip	Phone	Fax
Alaska Bible College PO Box 289 TF: 800-478-7884 ■ Web: www.akbible.edu	Glennallen	AK	99588	907-822-3201	822-5027
Allegheny Wesleyan College 2161 Woodsdale Rd TF: 800-292-3153 ■ Web: www.awc.edu	Salem	OH	44460	330-337-6403	337-6255
American Baptist College 1800 Baptist World Center Dr Web: www.abcnash.edu	Nashville	TN	37207	615-256-1463	226-7855
Appalachian Bible College PO Box ABC TF: 800-678-9222 ■ Web: www.abc.edu	Bradley	WV	25818	304-877-6428	877-5082
Baptist Bible College 628 E Kearney St *Fax: Admissions ■ TF: 800-228-5754 ■ Web: www.baptist.edu	Springfield	MO	65803	417-268-6060	268-6694*
Baptist Bible College 538 Venard Rd TF: 800-451-8668 ■ Web: www.bbc.edu	Clarks Summit	PA	18411	570-586-2400	585-9400
Baptist University of the Americas 8019 S Pan Am Expy TF: 800-721-1396 ■ Web: www.bua.edu	San Antonio	TX	78224	210-924-4338	924-2701
Barclay College 607 N Kingman St TF: 800-862-0226 ■ Web: www.barclaycollege.edu	Haviland	KS	67059	620-862-5252	862-5403
Bethesda Christian University 730 N Euclid Web: www.bcu.edu	Anaheim	CA	92801	714-517-1945	563-0623
Beulah Heights Bible College 892 Berne St SE PO Box 18145 *Fax: Admissions ■ TF: 888-777-2422 ■ Web: www.beulah.org	Atlanta	GA	30316	404-627-2681	627-0702*
Boise Bible College 8695 W Marigold St TF: 800-893-7755 ■ Web: www.boisebible.edu	Boise	ID	83714	208-376-7731	376-7743
Calvary Bible College & Theological Seminary 15800 Calvary Rd *Fax: Admissions ■ TF: 800-326-3960 ■ Web: www.calvary.edu	Kansas City	MO	64147	816-322-3960	331-4474*
Central Bible College 3000 N Grant Ave TF: 800-831-4222 ■ Web: www.cbcag.edu	Springfield	MO	65803	417-833-2551	833-5478
Central Christian College of the Bible 911 E Urbandale Dr TF: 888-263-3900 ■ Web: www.cccb.edu	Moberly	MO	65270	660-263-3900	263-3936
Cincinnati Christian University 2700 Glenway Ave TF: 800-949-4228 ■ Web: www.ccuniversity.edu	Cincinnati	OH	45204	513-244-8100	244-8140
Circleville Bible College PO Box 458 TF: 800-701-0222 ■ Web: www.hocking.edu/universitycenter/circleville_bible_college.htm	Circleville	OH	43113	740-474-8896	477-7755
Clear Creek Baptist Bible College 300 Clear Creek Rd Web: www.ccbbc.edu	Pineville	KY	40977	606-337-3196	337-2372
College of Biblical Studies-Houston 7000 Regency Square Blvd Suite 110 Web: www.cbshouston.edu	Houston	TX	77036	713-785-5995	532-8150
Columbia International University 7435 Monticello Rd TF: 800-777-2227 ■ Web: www.ciu.edu	Columbia	SC	29203	803-754-4100	786-4209
Crossroads Bible College 601 N Shortridge Rd TF: 800-822-3119 ■ Web: www.crossroads.edu	Indianapolis	IN	46219	317-352-8736	352-9145
Crossroads College 920 Mayowood Rd SW TF: 800-456-7651 ■ Web: www.crossroadscollege.edu	Rochester	MN	55902	507-288-4563	288-9046
Crown College 8700 College View Dr TF: 800-682-7696 ■ Web: www.crown.edu	Saint Bonifacius	MN	55375	952-446-4100	446-4149
Dallas Christian College 2700 Christian Pkwy TF: 800-688-1029 ■ Web: www.dallas.edu	Dallas	TX	75234	972-241-3371	241-8021
Davis College 400 Riverside Dr TF: 800-331-4137 ■ Web: www.davisny.edu	Johnson City	NY	13790	607-729-1581	729-2962
Ecclesia College 9653 Nations Dr TF: 800-735-9926 ■ Web: www.ecclesiacollege.org	Springdale	AR	72762	479-248-7236	248-1455
Emmaus Bible College 2570 Asbury Rd TF: 800-397-2425 ■ Web: www.emmaus.edu	Dubuque	IA	52001	563-588-8000	588-1216
Eugene Bible College 2155 Bailey Hill Rd *Fax: Admissions ■ TF: 800-322-2638 ■ Web: www.ebc.edu	Eugene	OR	97405	541-485-1780	343-5801*
Faith Baptist Bible College 1900 NW 4th St TF: 888-324-8448 ■ Web: www.faith.edu	Ankeny	IA	50023	515-964-0601	964-1638
Florida Christian College 1011 Bill Beck Blvd *Fax Area Code: 321 ■ TF: 888-468-6322 ■ Web: www.fcc.edu	Kissimmee	FL	34744	407-847-8966	206-2007*
Free Will Baptist Bible College 3606 West End Ave TF: 800-763-9222 ■ Web: www.fwbbc.edu	Nashville	TN	37205	615-383-1340	269-6028
God's Bible School & College 1810 Young St TF: 800-486-4637 ■ Web: www.gbs.edu	Cincinnati	OH	45202	513-721-7944	721-1357
Grace Bible College 1011 Aldon St SW PO Box 910 TF: 800-968-1887 ■ Web: www.gbcol.edu	Wyoming	MI	49509	616-538-2330	538-0599
Grace University 1311 S 9th St TF: 800-383-1422 ■ Web: www.graceuniversity.edu	Omaha	NE	68108	402-449-2800	341-9587
Great Lakes Christian College 6211 W Willow Hwy TF Admissions: 800-937-4522 ■ Web: www.glcc.edu	Lansing	MI	48917	517-321-0242	321-5902
Heritage Christian University 3625 Helton Dr PO Box HCU TF: 800-367-3565 ■ Web: www.hcu.edu	Florence	AL	35630	256-766-6610	760-0981
Hobe Sound Bible College PO Box 1065 TF: 800-881-5534 ■ Web: www.hsbc.edu	Hobe Sound	FL	33475	772-546-5534	545-1422
John Wesley College 2314 N Centennial St Web: www.johnwesley.edu	High Point	NC	27265	336-889-2262	889-2261
Johnson Bible College 7900 Johnson Dr TF: 800-827-2122 ■ Web: www.jbc.edu	Knoxville	TN	37998	865-251-2309	251-2336
Kentucky Mountain Bible College 855 Hwy 541 PO Box 10 TF: 800-879-5622 ■ Web: www.kmbc.edu	Vancleve	KY	41385	606-693-5000	693-4884
King's College & Seminary 14800 Sherman Way Web: www.kingscollege.edu	Los Angeles	CA	91405	818-779-8040	779-8429
Kuyper College 3333 East Beltline Ave NE TF: 800-511-3749 ■ Web: www.kuyper.edu	Grand Rapids	MI	49525	616-222-3000	222-3045
Lancaster Bible College 901 Eden Rd PO Box 83403 TF: 800-544-7335 ■ Web: www.lbc.edu	Lancaster	PA	17608	717-569-7071	560-8213
Life Pacific College 1100 Covina Blvd TF: 877-886-5433 ■ Web: www.lifepacific.edu	San Dimas	CA	91773	909-599-5433	599-6690
Lincoln Christian College Seminary 100 Campus View Dr TF: 888-522-5228 ■ Web: www.lccs.edu	Lincoln	IL	62656	217-732-3168	732-4078
Manhattan Christian College 1415 Anderson Ave Web: www.mccks.edu	Manhattan	KS	66502	785-539-3571	776-9251
Moody Bible Institute 820 N La Salle St *Fax: Admissions ■ TF: 800-967-4624 ■ Web: www.moody.edu	Chicago	IL	60610	312-329-4400	329-8955*
Multnomah Bible College & Biblical Seminary 8435 NE Glisan St TF: 800-275-4672 ■ Web: www.multnomah.edu	Portland	OR	97220	503-255-0332	254-1268
Nazarene Bible College 1111 Academy Park Loop TF: 800-873-3873 ■ Web: www.nbc.edu	Colorado Springs	CO	80910	719-884-5000	884-5199
Nebraska Christian College 1800 Syracuse Ave Web: www.nechristian.edu	Norfolk	NE	68701	402-379-5000	379-5100
Oak Hills Christian College 1600 Oak Hills Rd SW TF: 888-751-8670 ■ Web: www.oakhills.edu	Bemidji	MN	56601	218-751-8670	751-8825
Ozark Christian College 1111 N Main St TF: 800-299-4622 ■ Web: www.occ.edu	Joplin	MO	64801	417-624-2518	624-0090
Philadelphia Biblical University 200 Manor Ave *Fax: Admissions ■ TF: 800-366-0049 ■ Web: www.pbu.edu	Langhorne	PA	19047	215-752-5800	702-4248*
Pillsbury Baptist Bible College 315 S Grove Ave TF: 800-747-4557 ■ Web: www.pillsbury.edu	Owatonna	MN	55060	507-451-2710	451-0156
Puget Sound Christian College 2610 Wetmore Ave TF: 888-775-8699 ■ Web: www.pscc.edu	Everett	WA	98201	425-257-3090	258-1488
Rio Grande Bible Institute 4300 S Business Hwy 281 Web: www.nbc.edu	Edinburg	TX	78539	956-380-8100	380-8101
Roanoke Bible College 715 N Poindexter St TF: 800-722-8980 ■ Web: www.roanokebible.edu	Elizabeth City	NC	27909	252-334-2070	334-2071
Rosedale Bible College 2270 Rosedale Rd *Fax Area Code: 877 ■ Web: www.rosedale.edu	Irwin	OH	43029	740-857-1311	857-1312*
Saint Louis Christian College 1360 Grandview Dr TF Admissions: 800-887-7522 ■ Web: www.slcconline.edu	Florissant	MO	63033	314-837-6777	837-8291
Somerset Christian College 10 Liberty Sq TF: 800-234-9305 ■ Web: www.somerset.edu	Zarephath	NJ	08890	732-356-1595	356-4846
Southeastern Baptist College 4229 Hwy 15 N Web: www.southeasternbaptist.edu	Laurel	MS	39440	601-426-6346	426-6347
Southwestern College 2625 E Cactus Rd TF: 800-247-2697 ■ Web: www.swcaz.edu	Phoenix	AZ	85032	602-489-5300	404-2159
Toccoa Falls College 328 Chappel Dr TF: 800-868-3257 ■ Web: www.tfc.edu	Toccoa Falls	GA	30598	706-886-6831	282-6012

	City	State	Zip	Phone	Fax
Tri-State Bible College 506 Margaret St	South Point	OH	45680	740-377-2520	377-0001
TF: 800-261-2947 ■ *Web:* www.tsbc.edu					
Trinity Bible College 50 S 6th Ave	Ellendale	ND	58436	701-349-3621	349-5786
TF: 800-523-1603 ■ *Web:* www.trinitybiblecollege.edu					
Trinity College of Florida 2430 Welbilt Blvd	Trinity	FL	34655	727-376-6911	569-1410
TF: 800-388-0869 ■ *Web:* www.trinitycollege.edu					
Vennard College 2300 8th Ave E PO Box 29	University Park	IA	52595	641-673-8391	673-8365
TF: 800-686-8391 ■ *Web:* www.vennard.edu					
Washington Bible College/Capital Bible Seminary					
6511 Princess Garden Pkwy	Lanham	MD	20706	301-552-1400	552-2775
TF: 877-793-7227 ■ *Web:* www.bible.edu					
Zion Bible College 27 Middle Hwy	Barrington	RI	02806	401-246-0900	246-0906
TF: 800-356-4014 ■ *Web:* www.zbc.edu					

162 COLLEGES - COMMUNITY & JUNIOR

SEE ALSO Colleges & Universities - Four-Year p. 1475; Colleges - Fine Arts p. 1472; Colleges - Tribal p. 1473; Vocational & Technical Schools p. 2406

Institutions that offer academic degrees that can be transferred to a four-year college or university.

Alabama

	City	State	Zip	Phone	Fax
Alabama Southern Community College					
2800 S Alabama Ave	Monroeville	AL	36460	251-575-3156	575-5356
Web: www.ascc.edu					
Alabama Southern Community College					
30755 Hwy 43 S PO Box 2000	Thomasville	AL	36784	334-636-9642	636-1380
Web: www.ascc.edu					
Bevill State Community College 2631 Temple Ave N	Fayette	AL	35555	205-932-3221	932-3294*
*Fax: Admissions ■ *Web:* www.bscc.edu					
Jasper 1411 Indiana Ave	Jasper	AL	35501	205-387-0511	387-5191*
*Fax: Admissions ■ *Web:* www.bscc.edu/mainjasper.asp					
Bishop State Community College 351 N Broad St	Mobile	AL	36603	251-690-6412	438-5403*
*Fax: Admissions ■ *Web:* www.bishop.edu					
Baker-Gaines Central 1365 Dr ML King Jr Ave	Mobile	AL	36603	251-405-4400	405-4427
Web: www.bishop.edu/centralcp.htm					
Carver 414 Stanton St	Mobile	AL	36617	251-473-8692	473-7915*
*Fax: Admissions ■ *Web:* www.bishop.edu/carvercp.htm					
Southwest 925 Dauphin Island Pkwy	Mobile	AL	36605	251-665-4100	478-5170*
*Fax: Admissions ■ *Web:* www.bishop.edu/sw_camp.htm					
Calhoun Community College PO Box 2216	Decatur	AL	35609	256-306-2500	306-2941
TF: 800-626-3628 ■ *Web:* www.calhoun.cc.al.us					
Huntsville 102B Wynn Dr	Huntsville	AL	35805	256-890-4701	890-4775*
*Fax: Admissions ■ *Web:* www.calhoun.edu					
Redstone Arsenal PO Box 2216	Decatur	AL	35609	256-876-7431	306-2941*
*Fax: Admissions ■ *Web:* www.calhoun.edu					
Central Alabama Community College 1675 Cherokee Rd	Alexander City	AL	35010	256-215-4255	234-0384*
*Fax: Admissions ■ *TF:* 800-643-2657 ■ *Web:* www.cacc.cc.al.us					
Childersburg 34091 US Hwy 280	Childersburg	AL	35044	256-378-5576	378-5281
Web: www.cacc.edu					
Chattahoochee Valley Community College 2602 College Dr	Phenix City	AL	36869	334-291-4900	291-4994*
*Fax: Admissions ■ *Web:* www.cv.edu					
Community College of the Air Force					
CCAF/RRA 130 W Maxwell Blvd	Maxwell AFB	AL	36112	334-953-8409	953-3621
Web: www.au.af.mil/au/ccaf/					
Enterprise-Ozark Community College					
600 Plaza Dr PO Box 1300	Enterprise	AL	36331	334-393-3752	393-6223
Web: www.eocc.edu					
Faulkner State Community College					
Bay Minette 1900 US Hwy 31 S	Bay Minette	AL	36507	251-580-2100	580-2285*
*Fax: Admissions ■ *TF:* 800-231-3752 ■ *Web:* www.faulkner.cc.al.us					
Fairhope 440 Fairhope Ave	Fairhope	AL	36532	251-990-0420	580-2285*
*Fax: Admissions ■ *TF:* 800-231-3752 ■ *Web:* www.faulkner.cc.al.us/locations/fairhope					
Gulf Shores 3301 Gulf Shores Pkwy	Gulf Shores	AL	36542	251-968-3101	968-3120
TF: 800-231-3752 ■ *Web:* www.faulkner.cc.al.us/locations/gulfshores					
Gadsden State Community College					
1001 George Wallace Dr PO Box 227	Gadsden	AL	35902	256-549-8200	549-8205*
*Fax: Admissions ■ *TF:* 800-226-5563 ■ *Web:* www.gadsdenst.cc.al.us					
Jefferson Davis Community College					
Atmore PO Box 1119	Atmore	AL	36504	251-368-8118	368-8211*
*Fax: Admissions ■ *Web:* www.jeffdavis.cc.al.us					
Brewton PO Box 958	Brewton	AL	36427	251-867-4832	809-1596*
*Fax: Admissions ■ *Web:* www.jdcc.edu					
Jefferson State Community College 2601 Carson Rd	Birmingham	AL	35215	205-853-1200	856-6070*
*Fax: Admissions ■ *TF:* 800-239-5900 ■ *Web:* www.jeffstateonline.com					
Lurleen B Wallace Community College Andalusia					
1000 Dannelly Blvd PO Box 1418	Andalusia	AL	36420	334-222-6591	881-2201*
*Fax: Admissions ■ *Web:* www.lbwcc.edu					
Marion Military Institute 1101 Washington St	Marion	AL	36756	334-683-2306	683-2383
TF: 800-664-1842 ■ *Web:* www.marionmilitary.edu					
Northeast Alabama Community College PO Box 159	Rainsville	AL	35986	256-228-6001	228-6861
Web: www.nacc.edu					
Northwest-Shoals Community College					
Muscle Shoals 800 George Wallace Blvd	Muscle Shoals	AL	35661	256-331-5200	331-5366*
*Fax: Admissions ■ *Web:* www.nwscc.edu					
Phil Campbell 2080 College Rd	Phil Campbell	AL	35581	256-331-6200	331-6272*
*Fax: Admissions ■ *Web:* www.nwscc.edu					
Shelton State Community College 9500 Old Greensboro Rd	Tuscaloosa	AL	35405	205-759-1541	391-3910*
*Fax: Admissions ■ *Web:* www.sheltonstate.edu					
Snead State Community College 220 N Walnut St PO Box 734	Boaz	AL	35957	256-593-5120	593-7180*
*Fax: Admissions ■ *Web:* www.snead.edu					
Southern Union State Community College					
750 Roberts St PO Box 1000	Wadley	AL	36276	256-395-2211	745-6368*
*Fax Area Code: 334 ■ *Fax: Admissions ■ *Web:* www.suscc.edu					
Opelika 1701 Lafayette Pkwy	Opelika	AL	36801	334-745-6437	742-9418*
*Fax: Admissions ■ *Web:* www.suscc.edu					
Valley 321 Fob James Dr	Valley	AL	36854	334-756-4151	756-5183*
*Fax: Admissions ■ *Web:* www.suscc.edu					
Wallace Community College 1141 Wallace Dr	Dothan	AL	36303	334-983-3521	983-6066*
*Fax: Admissions ■ *TF:* 800-543-2426 ■ *Web:* www.wallace.edu					
Wallace State Community College PO Box 2000	Hanceville	AL	35077	256-352-8000	352-8129*
*Fax: Admissions ■ *Web:* www.wallacestate.edu					

Alaska

	City	State	Zip	Phone	Fax
Kenai Peninsula College 34820 College Dr	Soldotna	AK	99669	907-262-5801	262-0322
Web: www.kpc.alaska.edu					
Kodiak College 117 Benny Benson Dr	Kodiak	AK	99615	907-486-4161	486-1264
TF: 800-486-7660 ■ *Web:* www.koc.alaska.edu					
Matanuska-Susitna College PO Box 2889	Palmer	AK	99645	907-745-9774	745-9747
Web: www.matsu.alaska.edu					
Prince William Sound Community College PO Box 97	Valdez	AK	99686	907-834-1600	834-1691
Web: www.pwscc.edu					
University of Alaska Prince William Sound Community College					
PO Box 97	Valdez	AK	99686	907-834-1600	834-1691
Web: www.pwscc.edu					
University of Alaska Anchorage					
Kenai Peninsula College 34820 College Dr	Soldotna	AK	99669	907-262-5801	262-0322
Web: www.kpc.alaska.edu					
Kodiak College 117 Benny Benson Dr	Kodiak	AK	99615	907-486-4161	486-1264
TF: 800-486-7660 ■ *Web:* www.koc.alaska.edu					
Matanuska-Susitna College PO Box 2889	Palmer	AK	99645	907-745-9774	745-9747
Web: www.matsu.alaska.edu					
University of Alaska Fairbanks Northwest					
400 E Front St Pouch 400	Nome	AK	99762	907-443-2201	443-5602
Web: www.nwc.uaf.edu					
University of Alaska Southeast					
Ketchikan 2600 7th Ave	Ketchikan	AK	99901	907-225-6177	225-3624
Web: www.ketch.alaska.edu					
Sitka 1332 Seward Ave	Sitka	AK	99835	907-747-6653	747-7768
TF: 800-478-6653 ■ *Web:* www.uas.alaska.edu/sitka/					

Arizona

	City	State	Zip	Phone	Fax
Arizona Western College PO Box 929	Yuma	AZ	85366	928-317-6000	344-7543*
*Fax: Admissions ■ *TF:* 888-293-0392 ■ *Web:* www.azwestern.edu					
Central Arizona College 8470 N Overfield Rd	Coolidge	AZ	85228	520-494-5444	494-5083*
*Fax: Admissions ■ *TF:* 800-237-9814 ■ *Web:* www.centralaz.edu					
Chandler-Gilbert Community College					
Pecos 2626 E Pecos Rd	Chandler	AZ	85225	480-732-7000	732-7099*
*Fax: Admissions ■ *Web:* www.cgc.maricopa.edu/campuses.shtml					
Williams 7360 E Tahoe Ave	Mesa	AZ	85212	480-988-8000	988-8993
Web: www.cgc.maricopa.edu/campuses.shtml					
Cochise College 4190 W Hwy 80	Douglas	AZ	85607	520-364-7943	417-4006*
*Fax: Admissions ■ *TF:* 800-966-7943 ■ *Web:* www.cochise.edu					
Sierra Vista 901 N Colombo Ave	Sierra Vista	AZ	85635	520-515-0500	515-5452*
*Fax: Admissions ■ *TF:* 800-966-7943 ■ *Web:* www.cochise.edu					
Coconino Community College Lonetree 2800 S Lone Tree Rd	Flagstaff	AZ	86001	928-527-1222	226-4110*
*Fax: Admissions ■ *TF:* 800-350-7122 ■ *Web:* www.coconino.edu					
Dine College PO Box 67	Tsaile	AZ	86556	928-724-6600	724-3327*
*Fax: Admissions ■ *TF:* 877-988-3463 ■ *Web:* www.dinecollege.edu					
Eastern Arizona College 615 N Stadium Ave	Thatcher	AZ	85552	928-428-8472	428-8462*
*Fax: Admissions ■ *TF:* 800-678-3808 ■ *Web:* www.easternarizona.com					
Estrella Mountain Community College 3000 N Dysart Rd	Avondale	AZ	85323	623-935-8000	935-8870*
*Fax: Admissions ■ *Web:* www.emc.maricopa.edu					
GateWay Community College 108 N 40th St	Phoenix	AZ	85034	602-392-5000	286-8072*
*Fax: Admissions ■ *Web:* www.gatewaycc.edu					
Glendale Community College 6000 W Olive Ave	Glendale	AZ	85302	623-845-3000	845-3303*
*Fax: Admissions ■ *Web:* www.gc.maricopa.edu					
North 5727 W Happy Valley Rd	Glendale	AZ	85310	623-845-4000	845-4010
Web: www.gc.maricopa.edu/gccnorth					
Mesa Community College 1833 W Southern Ave	Mesa	AZ	85202	480-461-7000	461-7321*
*Fax: Admissions ■ *TF:* 866-532-4983 ■ *Web:* www.mc.maricopa.edu					
Red Mountain 7110 E McKellips Rd	Mesa	AZ	85207	480-654-7200	654-7379
Web: www.mc.maricopa.edu/other/redmountain					
Mohave Community College					
Bullhead City 3400 Hwy 95	Bullhead City	AZ	86442	928-758-3926	704-9460
TF: 866-664-2832 ■ *Web:* www.mohave.edu					
Kingman 1971 Jagerson Ave	Kingman	AZ	86409	928-757-0879	757-0808*
*Fax: Admissions ■ *TF:* 866-664-2832 ■ *Web:* www.mohave.edu					
Lake Havasu 1977 W Acoma Blvd	Lake Havasu City	AZ	86403	928-855-7812	680-5955*
*Fax: Admissions ■ *TF:* 866-664-2832 ■ *Web:* www.mohave.edu					
North Mohave PO Box 980	Colorado City	AZ	86021	928-875-2799	875-2831*
*Fax: Admissions ■ *TF:* 800-678-3992 ■ *Web:* www.mohave.edu					
Northland Pioneer College PO Box 610	Holbrook	AZ	86025	928-532-6111	536-3382*
*Fax: Admissions ■ *TF:* 800-266-7845 ■ *Web:* www.npc.edu					
Paradise Valley Community College 18401 N 32nd St	Phoenix	AZ	85032	602-787-6500	787-7025*
*Fax: Admissions ■ *Web:* www.pvc.maricopa.edu					
Phoenix College 1202 W Thomas Rd	Phoenix	AZ	85013	602-264-2492	285-7813*
*Fax: Admissions ■ *Web:* www.pc.maricopa.edu					
Pima Community College 401 N Bonita Ave Suite B-220	Tucson	AZ	85709	520-206-2733	206-4790*
*Fax: Admissions ■ *TF:* 800-860-7462 ■ *Web:* www.pima.edu					
Desert Vista 5901 S Calle Santa Cruz	Tucson	AZ	85709	520-206-5000	206-5050*
*Fax: Admissions ■ *Web:* dv.pima.edu					
East 8181 E Irvington Rd	Tucson	AZ	85709	520-206-7000	206-7875*
*Fax: Admissions ■ *Web:* ecc.pima.edu					
West 2202 W Anklam Rd	Tucson	AZ	85709	520-206-6600	206-6728*
*Fax: Admissions ■ *TF:* 800-860-7462 ■ *Web:* wc.pima.edu					
Rio Salado College 2323 W 14th St	Tempe	AZ	85281	480-517-8540	517-8199
TF: 800-729-1197 ■ *Web:* www.riosalado.edu					
Scottsdale Community College 9000 E Chaparral Rd	Scottsdale	AZ	85256	480-423-6000	423-6200*
*Fax: Admissions ■ *Web:* www.scottsdalecc.edu					
South Mountain Community College 7050 S 24th St	Phoenix	AZ	85042	602-243-8000	243-8199*
*Fax: Admissions ■ *Web:* www.southmountaincc.edu					
Tohono O'odham Community College PO Box 3129	Sells	AZ	85634	520-383-8401	383-8403
Web: www.tocc.cc.az.us					
Yavapai College 1100 E Sheldon St	Prescott	AZ	86301	928-445-7300	776-2151*
*Fax: Admissions ■ *TF:* 800-922-6787 ■ *Web:* www2.yc.edu					
Verde Valley 601 Black Hills Dr	Clarkdale	AZ	86324	928-634-7501	634-6549*
*Fax: Admissions ■ *TF:* 800-922-6787 ■ *Web:* www2.yc.edu					

Arkansas

	City	State	Zip	Phone	Fax
Arkansas Northeastern College					
2501 S Division St PO Box 1109	Blytheville	AR	72316	870-762-1020	763-1654*
*Fax: Admissions ■ *Web:* www.anc.edu					
Arkansas State University					
Beebe 1000 Iowa St	Beebe	AR	72012	501-882-6452	882-8295*
*Fax: Admissions ■ *TF:* 800-632-9985 ■ *Web:* www.asub.edu/					
Mountain Home 1600 S College St	Mountain Home	AR	72653	870-508-6100	508-6287
Web: www.asumh.edu					
Newport 7648 Victory Blvd	Newport	AR	72112	870-512-7800	512-7825*
*Fax: Admissions ■ *TF:* 800-976-1676 ■ *Web:* www.asun.edu					
Black River Technical College 1410 Hwy 304 E	Pocahontas	AR	72455	870-248-4000	248-4100
Web: www.blackrivertech.org					
Crowley's Ridge College 100 College Dr	Paragould	AR	72450	870-236-6901	236-7748*
*Fax: Admissions ■ *TF:* 800-264-1096 ■ *Web:* www.crowleysridgecollege.edu					
East Arkansas Community College 1700 Newcastle Rd	Forrest City	AR	72335	870-633-4480	633-3840*
*Fax: Admissions ■ *TF:* 877-797-3222 ■ *Web:* www.eacc.edu					

Arkansas (Cont'd)

				Phone	Fax
Mid-South Community College 2000 W Broadway	West Memphis	AR	72301	870-733-6722	733-6719*
*Fax: Admissions ■ Web: www.midsouthcc.edu					
National Park Community College 101 College Dr	Hot Springs	AR	71913	501-760-4222	760-4236*
*Fax: Admissions ■ TF: 800-760-1825 ■ Web: npcc.edu					
North Arkansas College 1515 Pioneer Dr	Harrison	AR	72601	870-743-3000	391-3339
TF: 800-679-6622 ■ Web: www.northark.edu					
NorthWest Arkansas Community College 1 College Dr	Bentonville	AR	72712	479-636-9222	619-2229*
*Fax: Admissions ■ TF: 800-995-6922 ■ Web: www.nwacc.edu					
Ouachita Technical College 1 College Cir	Malvern	AR	72104	501-337-5000	337-9382
Web: www.otcweb.edu					
Ozarka College PO Box 10	Melbourne	AR	72556	870-368-7371	368-2091
TF: 800-821-4335 ■ Web: www.ozarka.edu					
Phillips Community College PO Box 785	Helena	AR	72342	870-338-6474	338-7542
Web: www.pccua.edu					
Pulaski Technical College 3000 W Scenic Dr	North Little Rock	AR	72118	501-812-2200	771-2844
Web: www.pulaskitech.edu					
Rich Mountain Community College 1100 College Dr	Mena	AR	71953	479-394-7622	394-2760*
*Fax: Admissions ■ Web: www.rmcc.edu					
Shorter College 604 N Locust St	North Little Rock	AR	72114	501-374-6305	374-9333*
*Fax: Admissions ■ Web: www.shortercollege.4t.com					
South Arkansas Community College PO Box 7010	El Dorado	AR	71731	870-862-8131	864-7134*
*Fax: Admissions ■ TF: 800-955-2289 ■ Web: www.southark.edu					
Southeast Arkansas College 1900 Hazel St	Pine Bluff	AR	71603	870-543-5900	543-5956
Web: www.seark.org					
University of Arkansas Fort Smith PO Box 3649	Fort Smith	AR	72913	479-788-7000	788-7016
TF: 888-512-5466 ■ Web: www.uafortsmith.edu					

California

				Phone	Fax
Allan Hancock College 800 S College Dr	Santa Maria	CA	93454	805-922-6966	922-3477*
*Fax: Admissions ■ Web: www.hancockcollege.edu					
Lompoc Valley 1 Hancock Dr	Lompoc	CA	93436	805-735-3366	736-9368
Web: www.hancock.cc.ca.us					
American River College 4700 College Oak Dr	Sacramento	CA	95841	916-484-8011	484-8864*
*Fax: Admissions ■ Web: www.arc.losrios.edu					
Antelope Valley College 3041 W Ave K	Lancaster	CA	93536	661-722-6300	722-6531*
*Fax: Admissions ■ Web: www.avc.edu					
Bakersfield College 1801 Panorama Dr	Bakersfield	CA	93305	661-395-4011	395-4500*
*Fax: Admissions ■ Web: www.bakersfieldcollege.edu					
Barstow College 2700 Barstow Rd	Barstow	CA	92311	760-252-2411	252-6754
TF: 877-336-6868 ■ Web: www.barstow.cc.ca.us					
Berkeley City College 2050 Center St	Berkeley	CA	94704	510-981-2800	841-7333
Web: berkeley.peralta.edu					
Butte College 3536 Butte Campus Dr	Oroville	CA	95965	530-895-2511	879-4313*
*Fax: Admissions ■ TF Hum Res: 800-933-8322 ■ Web: www.butte.edu					
Cabrillo College 6500 Soquel Dr	Aptos	CA	95003	831-479-6100	479-5782*
*Fax: Admitting ■ Web: www.cabrillo.edu					
Canada College 4200 Farm Hill Blvd	Redwood City	CA	94061	650-306-3100	306-3113*
*Fax: Admissions ■ Web: canadacollege.edu					
Cerritos College 11110 Alondra Blvd	Norwalk	CA	90650	562-860-2451	467-5068*
*Fax: Admitting ■ Web: www.cerritos.edu					
Cerro Coso Community College					
Bishop 4090 W Line St	Bishop	CA	93514	760-872-1565	872-5319*
*Fax: Admissions ■ TF: 888-537-6932 ■ Web: www.cerrocoso.edu/escc/bishop					
Indian Wells Valley 3000 College Heights Blvd	Ridgecrest	CA	93555	760-384-6100	384-6377*
*Fax: Admissions ■ TF: 888-537-6932 ■ Web: www.cerrocoso.edu/iwv					
Kern River Valley 5520 Lake Isabella Blvd	Lake Isabella	CA	93240	760-379-5501	379-5547*
*Fax: Admissions ■ TF: 888-537-6932 ■ Web: www.cerrocoso.edu/krv					
Mammoth 101 College Pkwy PO Box 1865	Mammoth Lakes	CA	93546	760-934-2875	924-1613*
*Fax: Admissions ■ TF: 888-537-6932 ■ Web: www.cerrocoso.edu/escc/mammoth					
South Kern 140 Methusa Ave	Edwards AFB	CA	93524	661-258-8644	258-0651*
*Fax: Admissions ■ Web: www.cerrocoso.edu/sk					
Chaffey College 5885 Haven Ave	Rancho Cucamonga	CA	91737	909-987-1737	466-2875*
*Fax: Admissions ■ Web: www.chaffey.edu					
Citrus College 1000 W Foothill Blvd	Glendora	CA	91741	626-963-0323	914-8613*
*Fax: Admissions ■ Web: www.citruscollege.edu					
City College of San Francisco 50 Phelan Ave	San Francisco	CA	94112	415-239-3000	239-3936*
*Fax: Admissions ■ Web: www.ccsf.edu					
Coastline Community College 11460 Warner Ave	Fountain Valley	CA	92708	714-546-7600	241-6288*
*Fax: Admissions ■ Web: coastline.edu					
College of Alameda 555 Atlantic Ave	Alameda	CA	94501	510-522-7221	769-6019
Web: alameda.peralta.edu					
College of the Canyons 26455 Rockwell Canyon Rd	Santa Clarita	CA	91355	661-259-7800	362-5566*
*Fax: Admissions ■ Web: www.canyons.edu					
College of the Desert 43-500 Monterey Ave	Palm Desert	CA	92260	760-346-8041	862-1379*
*Fax: Admissions ■ Web: www.collegeofthedesert.edu					
College of Marin 835 College Ave	Kentfield	CA	94904	415-457-8811	460-0773*
*Fax: Admissions ■ Web: www.marin.cc.ca.us					
Indian Valley 1800 Ignacio Blvd	Novato	CA	94949	415-883-2211	884-0429*
*Fax: Admissions ■ Web: www.marin.cc.ca.us					
College of the Redwoods 7351 Tompkins Hill Rd	Eureka	CA	95501	707-476-4100	476-4406*
*Fax: Admissions ■ TF: 800-641-0400 ■ Web: www.redwoods.edu					
Del Norte 883 W Washington Blvd	Crescent City	CA	95531	707-465-2300	464-6867*
*Fax: Admissions ■ TF: 800-641-0400 ■ Web: www.redwoods.edu/delnorte					
Mendocino Coast 1211 Del Mar Dr	Fort Bragg	CA	95437	707-962-2600	961-0943*
*Fax: Admissions ■ TF: 800-641-0400 ■ Web: www.redwoods.edu/mendocino					
College of San Mateo 1700 W Hillsdale Blvd	San Mateo	CA	94402	650-574-6161	574-6506*
*Fax: Admissions ■ Web: www.collegeofsanmateo.edu					
College of the Sequoias 915 S Mooney Blvd	Visalia	CA	93277	559-730-3700	737-4820*
*Fax: Admissions ■ Web: www.cos.edu					
College of the Siskiyous 800 College Ave	Weed	CA	96094	530-938-4461	938-5367*
*Fax: Admissions ■ TF: 888-397-4339 ■ Web: www.siskiyous.edu					
Columbia College 11600 Columbia College Dr	Sonora	CA	95370	209-588-5100	588-5104
Web: columbia.yosemite.cc.ca.us					
Contra Costa College 2600 Mission Bell	San Pablo	CA	94806	510-235-7800	412-0769
Web: www.contracosta.cc.ca.us					
Copper Mountain College 6162 Rotary Way PO Box 1398	Joshua Tree	CA	92252	760-366-3791	366-5257*
*Fax: Admissions ■ TF: 866-366-3791 ■ Web: www.cmccd.cc.ca.us					
Cosumnes River College 8401 Center Pkwy	Sacramento	CA	95823	916-691-7410	691-7467*
*Fax: Admissions ■ Web: crc.losrios.edu					
Crafton Hills College 11711 Sand Canyon Rd	Yucaipa	CA	92399	909-794-2161	389-9141*
*Fax: Admissions ■ Web: www.craftonhills.edu					
Cuesta College PO Box 8106	San Luis Obispo	CA	93403	805-546-3100	546-3975*
*Fax: Admissions ■ Web: www.cuesta.edu					
North County 2800 Buena Vista Dr	Paso Robles	CA	93446	805-591-6200	591-6370
Web: academic.cuesta.edu/norco					
Cuyamaca College 900 Rancho San Diego Pkwy	El Cajon	CA	92019	619-660-4000	660-4575*
*Fax: Admissions ■ Web: www.cuyamaca.net					
Cypress College 9200 Valley View St	Cypress	CA	90630	714-484-7000	484-7446*
*Fax: Admissions ■ Web: www.cypresscollege.edu					
DeAnza College 21250 Stevens Creek Blvd	Cupertino	CA	95014	408-864-5678	864-8329*
*Fax: Admissions ■ Web: www.deanza.edu					
Diablo Valley College 321 Golf Club Rd	Pleasant Hill	CA	94523	925-685-1230	609-8085*
*Fax: Admissions ■ Web: www.dvc.edu					
East Los Angeles College 1301 Avenida Cesar Chavez	Monterey Park	CA	91754	323-265-8650	265-8688*
*Fax: Admissions ■ Web: www.elac.edu					
El Camino College 16007 Crenshaw Blvd	Torrance	CA	90506	310-532-3670	660-3818
Web: www.elcamino.edu					
Compton Center 1111 E Artesia Blvd	Compton	CA	90221	310-637-2660	900-1662*
*Fax: Admissions ■ Web: www.compton.cc.ca.us					
Evergreen Valley College 3095 Yerba Buena Rd	San Jose	CA	95135	408-274-7900	223-9351*
*Fax: Admissions ■ Web: www.evc.edu					
Feather River College 570 Golden Eagle Ave	Quincy	CA	95971	530-283-0202	283-9961*
*Fax: Admissions ■ TF: 800-442-9799 ■ Web: www.frc.edu					
Foothill College 12345 El Monte Rd	Los Altos Hills	CA	94022	650-949-7777	949-7048*
*Fax: Admissions ■ Web: www.foothill.edu					
Fresno City College 1101 E University Ave	Fresno	CA	93741	559-442-4600	237-4232*
*Fax: Admissions ■ TF: 866-245-3276 ■ Web: www.fresnocitycollege.edu					
Fullerton College 321 E Chapman Ave	Fullerton	CA	92832	714-992-7000	870-7751*
*Fax: Admissions ■ Web: www.fullcoll.edu					
Gavilan College 5055 Santa Teresa Blvd	Gilroy	CA	95020	408-847-1400	846-4940*
*Fax: Admissions ■ Web: www.gavilan.edu					
Glendale Community College 1500 N Verdugo Rd	Glendale	CA	91208	818-240-1000	551-5255*
*Fax: Admissions ■ Web: www.glendale.edu					
Golden West College					
15744 Golden West St PO Box 2748	Huntington Beach	CA	92647	714-892-7711	895-8960*
*Fax: Admissions ■ Web: www.gwc.info					
Grossmont College 8800 Grossmont College Dr	El Cajon	CA	92020	619-644-7000	644-7933*
*Fax: Admissions ■ TF: 866-476-7766 ■ Web: www.grossmont.edu					
Hartnell College 156 Homestead Ave	Salinas	CA	93901	831-755-6700	759-6014*
*Fax: Admissions ■ Web: www.hartnell.edu					
Imperial Valley College 380 E Atten Rd PO Box 158	Imperial	CA	92251	760-352-8320	355-2663*
*Fax: Admissions ■ Web: www.imperial.cc.ca.us					
Irvine Valley College 5500 Irvine Center Dr	Irvine	CA	92618	949-451-5100	451-5443*
*Fax: Admissions ■ Web: www.ivc.edu					
Lake Tahoe Community College 1 College Dr	South Lake Tahoe	CA	96150	530-541-4660	542-1781*
*Fax: Admissions ■ Web: www.ltcc.edu					
Laney College 900 Fallon St	Oakland	CA	94607	510-834-5740	466-7394*
*Fax: Admissions ■ Web: www.peralta.cc.ca.us/laney					
Las Positas College 3033 Collier Canyon Rd	Livermore	CA	94551	925-424-1000	443-0742
Web: www.laspositascollege.edu					
Lassen Community College 478-200 Hwy 139 PO Box 3000	Susanville	CA	96130	530-257-6181	251-8802*
*Fax: Admissions ■ TF: 800-461-9389 ■ Web: www.lassen.cc.ca.us					
Long Beach City College 4901 E Carson St	Long Beach	CA	90808	562-938-4111	938-4858*
*Fax: Admissions ■ Web: www.lbcc.edu					
Los Angeles City College 855 N Vermont Ave	Los Angeles	CA	90029	323-953-4000	953-4013*
*Fax: Admissions ■ Web: www.lacitycollege.edu					
Los Angeles Harbor College 1111 Figueroa Pl	Wilmington	CA	90744	310-233-4000	233-4223
Web: www.lahc.cc.ca.us					
Los Angeles Mission College 13356 Eldridge Ave	Sylmar	CA	91342	818-364-7600	364-7806*
*Fax: Admissions ■ Web: www.lamission.edu					
Los Angeles Southwest College 1600 W Imperial Hwy	Los Angeles	CA	90047	323-241-5225	
Web: www.lasc.edu					
Los Angeles Trade Technical College					
400 W Washington Blvd	Los Angeles	CA	90015	213-763-7000	763-5386*
*Fax: Admissions ■ Web: www.lattc.cc.ca.us					
Los Angeles Valley College 5800 Fulton Ave	Valley Glen	CA	91401	818-947-2600	947-2501*
*Fax: Admissions ■ Web: www.lavc.cc.ca.us					
Los Medanos College 2700 E Leland Rd	Pittsburg	CA	94565	925-439-2181	427-1599
Web: www.losmedanos.edu					
Marymount College Palos Verdes					
30800 Palos Verdes Dr E	Rancho Palos Verdes	CA	90275	310-377-5501	265-0962*
*Fax: Admissions ■ Web: www.marymountpv.edu					
Mendocino College 1000 Hensley Creek Rd	Ukiah	CA	95482	707-468-3000	468-3430*
*Fax: Admissions ■ Web: www.mendocino.edu					
Merced College 3600 M St	Merced	CA	95348	209-384-6000	384-6339*
*Fax: Admissions ■ Web: www.merced.cc.ca.us					
Merritt College 12500 Campus Dr	Oakland	CA	94619	510-531-4911	436-2405*
*Fax: Admissions ■ Web: www.merritt.edu					
MiraCosta College					
Oceanside 1 Barnard Dr	Oceanside	CA	92056	760-757-2121	795-6626*
*Fax: Admissions ■ TF: 888-201-8480 ■ Web: www.miracosta.edu					
San Elijo 3333 Manchester Ave	Cardiff	CA	92007	760-944-4449	634-7875
TF: 888-201-8480 ■ Web: www.miracosta.cc.ca.us					
Mission College 3000 Mission College Blvd	Santa Clara	CA	95054	408-988-2200	980-8980*
*Fax: Admissions ■ Web: www.missioncollege.org					
Modesto Junior College 435 College Ave	Modesto	CA	95350	209-575-6550	575-6859*
*Fax: Admissions ■ Web: www.mjc.edu					
Monterey Peninsula College 980 Fremont St	Monterey	CA	93940	831-646-4000	646-4015*
*Fax: Admissions ■ Web: www.mpc.edu					
Moorpark College 7075 Campus Rd	Moorpark	CA	93021	805-378-1400	378-1583*
*Fax: Admissions ■ Web: www.moorpark.cc.ca.us					
Mount Saint Mary's College Doheny 10 Chester Pl	Los Angeles	CA	90007	213-477-2561	477-2569*
*Fax: Admissions ■ TF Admissions: 800-999-9893 ■ Web: www.msmc.la.edu					
Mount San Antonio College 1100 N Grand Ave	Walnut	CA	91789	909-594-5611	468-4068*
*Fax: Admissions ■ Web: www.mtsac.edu					
Mount San Jacinto College 1499 N State St	San Jacinto	CA	92583	951-487-6752	654-6738*
*Fax: Admissions ■ TF: 800-624-5561 ■ Web: www.msjc.edu					
Menifee Valley 28237 La Piedra Rd	Menifee	CA	92584	951-672-6752	
Web: www.msjc.edu					
Napa Valley College 2277 Napa-Vallejo Hwy	Napa	CA	94558	707-253-3005	253-3064
TF: 800-826-1077 ■ Web: www.napavalley.edu					
Ohlone College 43600 Mission Blvd	Fremont	CA	94539	510-659-6000	659-7321*
*Fax: Admissions ■ Web: www.ohlone.edu					
Orange Coast College 2701 Fairview Rd PO Box 5005	Costa Mesa	CA	92628	714-432-5735	432-5957*
*Fax: Admissions ■ Web: www.orangecoastcollege.com					
Oxnard College 4000 S Rose Ave	Oxnard	CA	93033	805-986-5800	986-5943*
*Fax: Admissions ■ Web: www.oxnardcollege.edu					
Palo Verde College 1 College Dr	Blythe	CA	92225	760-921-5500	921-3608*
*Fax: Admissions ■ Web: www.paloverde.edu					
Palomar College 1140 W Mission Rd	San Marcos	CA	92069	760-744-1150	744-8123*
*Fax: Admissions ■ Web: www.palomar.edu					
Pasadena City College 1570 E Colorado Blvd	Pasadena	CA	91106	626-585-7123	585-7915*
*Fax: Admissions ■ Web: www.pasadena.edu					
Pierce College 6201 Winnetka Ave	Woodland Hills	CA	91371	818-347-0551	716-1087*
*Fax: Admissions ■ Web: www.piercecollege.com					
Pierce College 6201 Winnetka Ave	Woodland Hills	CA	91371	818-719-6401	710-9844
Web: www.piercecollege.edu					
Porterville College 100 E College Ave	Porterville	CA	93257	559-791-2200	791-2349*
*Fax: Admissions ■ Web: www.pc.cc.ca.us					
Queen of the Holy Rosary College 43326 Mission Blvd	Fremont	CA	94539	510-657-2468	657-1734*
*Fax: Admissions ■ Web: www.msjdominicans.org/QHRC					
Reedley College 995 N Reed Ave	Reedley	CA	93654	559-638-3641	638-5040
Web: www.reedleycollege.edu					
Rio Hondo College 3600 Workman Mill Rd	Whittier	CA	90601	562-692-0921	692-8318
Web: www.riohondo.edu					

	City	State	Zip	Phone	Fax
Riverside Community College					
Moreno Valley 16130 Lasselle St.	Moreno Valley	CA	92551	951-571-6100	571-6188*
**Fax:* Admissions ■ *Web:* www.rcc.edu/morenovalley					
Norco 2001 3rd St	Norco	CA	92860	951-372-7000	372-7054*
**Fax:* Admissions ■ *Web:* www.rcc.edu/norco					
Riverside 4800 Magnolia Ave.	Riverside	CA	92506	951-222-8000	328-3503*
**Fax:* Admissions ■ *Web:* www.rcc.edu/riverside					
Sacramento City College 3835 Freeport Blvd.	Sacramento	CA	95822	916-558-2351	558-2190*
**Fax:* Admissions ■ *Web:* www.scc.losrios.edu					
Saddleback College 28000 Marguerite Pkwy	Mission Viejo	CA	92692	949-582-4500	347-8315*
**Fax:* Admissions ■ *Web:* www.saddleback.edu					
San Bernardino Valley College 701 S Mt Vernon Ave.	San Bernardino	CA	92410	909-888-6511	889-4988
Web: www.valleycollege.edu					
San Diego City College 1313 Park Blvd	San Diego	CA	92101	619-230-2400	388-3505*
**Fax:* Admissions ■ *Web:* www.sdcity.edu					
San Diego Mesa College 7250 Mesa College Dr	San Diego	CA	92111	619-388-2600	388-2960
Web: www.sandiegomesacollege.net					
San Diego Miramar College 10440 Black Mountain Rd	San Diego	CA	92126	619-388-7844	388-7915*
**Fax:* Admissions ■ *Web:* www.miramarcollege.net					
San Joaquin Delta College 5151 Pacific Ave	Stockton	CA	95207	209-954-5151	954-5769*
**Fax:* Admissions ■ *Web:* www.deltacollege.edu					
San Jose City College 2100 Moorpark Ave	San Jose	CA	95128	408-298-2181	298-1935*
**Fax:* Admissions ■ *Web:* www.sjcc.edu					
Santa Ana College 1530 W 17th St	Santa Ana	CA	92706	714-564-6000	564-6455*
**Fax:* Admissions ■ *Web:* www.sac.edu					
Santa Barbara City College 721 Cliff Dr.	Santa Barbara	CA	93109	805-965-0581	963-7222*
**Fax:* Admissions ■ *Web:* www.sbcc.edu					
Santa Monica College 1900 Pico Blvd	Santa Monica	CA	90405	310-434-4000	434-3645*
**Fax:* Admissions ■ *Web:* www.smc.edu					
Santa Rosa Junior College 1501 Mendocino Ave	Santa Rosa	CA	95401	707-527-4011	527-4798
TF: 800-564-7752 ■ *Web:* www.santarosa.edu					
Petaluma 680 Sonoma Mountain Pkwy	Petaluma	CA	95954	707-778-3801	778-3910*
**Fax:* Admissions ■ *Web:* www.santarosa.edu/petaluma					
Santiago Canyon College 8045 E Chapman Ave	Orange	CA	92869	714-628-4900	628-4723*
**Fax:* Admissions ■ *Web:* www.sccollege.edu					
Sierra College Nevada County 250 Sierra College Dr	Grass Valley	CA	95945	530-274-5300	274-5324*
**Fax:* Admissions ■ *Web:* www.sierra.cc.ca.us/AboutUs/campuses/ncc					
Sierra Community College 5000 Rocklin Rd	Rocklin	CA	95677	916-624-3333	781-0403*
**Fax:* Admissions ■ *Web:* www.sierra.cc.ca.us					
Skyline College 3300 College Dr	San Bruno	CA	94066	650-738-4100	738-4222*
**Fax:* Admissions ■ *Web:* www.skylinecollege.edu					
Solano Community College 4000 Suisun Valley Rd	Fairfield	CA	94534	707-864-7171	864-7175*
**Fax:* Admissions ■ *Web:* www.solano.edu					
Southwestern College 900 Otay Lakes Rd	Chula Vista	CA	91910	619-421-6700	482-6489*
**Fax:* Admissions ■ *Web:* www.swc.cc.ca.us					
Taft College 29 Emmons Park Dr	Taft	CA	93268	661-763-7700	763-7758*
**Fax:* Admissions ■ *TF:* 800-379-6784 ■ *Web:* www.taftcollege.edu					
Ventura College 4667 Telegraph Rd	Ventura	CA	93003	805-654-6400	654-6357*
**Fax:* Admissions ■ *Web:* www.venturacollege.edu					
Victor Valley Community College 18422 Bear Valley Rd.	Victorville	CA	92392	760-245-4271	245-9745
Web: www.vvc.edu					
West Hills College					
Coalinga 300 Cherry Ln	Coalinga	CA	93210	559-934-2000	935-3788*
**Fax:* Admissions ■ *TF:* 800-266-1114 ■ *Web:* www.westhillscollege.com/coalinga					
Lemoore 555 College Ave	Lemoore	CA	93245	559-925-3000	924-1539
Web: www.westhillscollege.com/lemoore					
West Los Angeles College 9000 Overland Ave.	Culver City	CA	90230	310-287-4200	287-4327*
**Fax:* Admissions ■ *Web:* www.wlac.edu					
West Valley College 14000 Fruitvale Ave	Saratoga	CA	95070	408-867-2200	867-5033*
**Fax:* Admissions ■ *Web:* www.westvalley.edu					

Colorado

	City	State	Zip	Phone	Fax
Aims Community College 5401 W 20th St	Greeley	CO	80634	970-330-8008	506-6958*
**Fax:* Admissions ■ *TF:* 800-301-5388 ■ *Web:* www.aims.edu					
Fort Lupton 260 College Ave	Fort Lupton	CO	80621	303-857-4022	352-5443*
**Fax Area Code:* 970 ■ *Web:* www.aims.edu/fort_lupton					
Arapahoe Community College 5900 S Santa Fe Dr	Littleton	CO	80160	303-794-1550	797-5970*
**Fax:* Admissions ■ *Web:* www.arapahoe.edu					
Colorado Mountain College					
Alpine 1330 Bob Adams Dr	Steamboat Springs	CO	80487	970-870-4444	870-4535*
**Fax:* Admissions ■ *TF:* 800-621-8559 ■ *Web:* www.coloradomtn.edu					
Aspen 0255 Sage Way	Aspen	CO	81611	970-925-7740	925-6045
Web: www.coloradomtn.edu/campus_asp					
Roaring Fork-Spring Valley 3000 County Rd 114	Glenwood Springs	CO	81601	970-945-7481	928-9668
TF: 800-621-8559 ■ *Web:* www.coloradomtn.edu/campus_rfc/springvalley					
Timberline 901 S Hwy 24	Leadville	CO	80461	719-486-2015	486-3212*
**Fax:* Admissions ■ *Web:* www.coloradomtn.edu/campus_tmb					
Colorado Northwestern Community College 500 Kennedy Dr	Rangely	CO	81648	970-675-2261	675-3343*
**Fax:* Admissions ■ *TF:* 800-562-1105 ■ *Web:* www.cncc.edu					
Craig 50 College Dr	Craig	CO	81625	970-824-7071	824-1134*
**Fax:* Admissions ■ *TF:* 800-562-1105 ■ *Web:* www.cncc.edu/craig					
Community College of Aurora 16000 E Centretech Pkwy	Aurora	CO	80011	303-360-4700	361-7432*
**Fax:* Admissions ■ *Web:* www.ccaurora.edu					
Community College of Denver PO Box 173363 CB 201	Denver	CO	80217	303-556-2600	556-2431
Web: www.ccd.edu					
Front Range Community College					
Boulder County 2190 Miller Dr	Longmont	CO	80501	303-678-3722	678-3699*
**Fax:* Admissions ■ *Web:* www.frontrange.edu					
Larimer 4616 S Shields St.	Fort Collins	CO	80526	970-226-2500	204-8484
TF: 800-289-3722 ■ *Web:* www.frontrange.edu					
Westminster 3645 W 112th Ave	Westminster	CO	80031	303-466-8811	466-1623*
**Fax:* Admissions ■ *Web:* www.frontrange.edu					
Lamar Community College 2401 S Main St	Lamar	CO	81052	719-336-2248	336-2400*
**Fax:* Admissions ■ *TF:* 800-968-6920 ■ *Web:* www.lcc.cccoes.edu					
Morgan Community College 920 Barlow Rd.	Fort Morgan	CO	80701	970-542-3100	867-6608
TF: 800-622-0216 ■ *Web:* www.morgancc.edu					
Northeastern Junior College 100 College Ave	Sterling	CO	80751	970-521-6600	522-4664
TF: 800-626-4637 ■ *Web:* www.njc.edu					
Otero Junior College 1802 Colorado Ave	La Junta	CO	81050	719-384-6831	384-6933*
**Fax:* Admissions ■ *Web:* www.ojc.edu					
Pikes Peak Community College					
Centennial 5675 S Academy Blvd	Colorado Springs	CO	80906	719-576-7711	540-7092*
**Fax:* Claims ■ *TF:* 800-456-6847 ■ *Web:* www.ppcc.edu					
Downtown Studio 100 W Pikes Peak Ave	Colorado Springs	CO	80903	719-527-6000	527-6010
TF: 800-456-6847 ■ *Web:* www.ppcc.edu/ourcampuses/thedowntownstudio					
Rampart Range 11195 Hwy 83	Colorado Springs	CO	80921	719-538-5000	538-5144
Web: www.ppcc.edu					
Pueblo Community College 900 W Orman Ave	Pueblo	CO	81004	719-549-3200	543-7566*
**Fax:* Admissions ■ *TF:* 888-642-6017 ■ *Web:* www.pueblocc.edu					
Red Rocks Community College 13300 W 6th Ave	Lakewood	CO	80228	303-914-6600	914-6666
Web: www.rrcc.edu					
Trinidad State Junior College 600 Prospect St	Trinidad	CO	81082	719-846-5011	846-5620*
**Fax:* Admissions ■ *TF:* 800-621-8752 ■ *Web:* www.trinidadstate.edu					

Connecticut

	City	State	Zip	Phone	Fax
Asnuntuck Community College 170 Elm St	Enfield	CT	06082	860-253-3000	253-3014*
**Fax:* Admissions ■ *TF:* 800-501-3967 ■ *Web:* www.acc.commnet.edu					
Capital Community College 950 Main St	Hartford	CT	06103	860-906-5000	906-5129
TF: 800-894-6126 ■ *Web:* www.ccc.commnet.edu					
Gateway Community College 60 Sargent Dr	New Haven	CT	06510	203-285-2000	285-2260*
**Fax:* Admissions ■ *Web:* www.gwcc.commnet.edu					
Housatonic Community College 900 Lafayette Blvd	Bridgeport	CT	06604	203-332-5000	332-5123*
**Fax:* Admissions ■ *Web:* www.hctc.commnet.edu					
Manchester Community College PO Box 1046	Manchester	CT	06045	860-646-4900	512-3221*
**Fax:* Admissions ■ *Web:* www.mcc.commnet.edu					
Middlesex Community College 100 Training Hill Rd	Middletown	CT	06457	860-343-5800	344-7488*
**Fax:* Admissions ■ *Web:* www.mxctc.commnet.edu					
Naugatuck Valley Community College 750 Chase Pkwy	Waterbury	CT	06708	203-575-8078	596-8766*
**Fax:* Admissions ■ *Web:* www.nvcc.commnet.edu					
Northwestern Connecticut Community College Park Place E	Winsted	CT	06098	860-738-6300	738-6437*
**Fax:* Admissions ■ *Web:* www.nwctc.commnet.edu					
Norwalk Community College 188 Richards Ave	Norwalk	CT	06854	203-857-7060	857-3335*
**Fax:* Admissions ■ *Web:* www.ncc.commnet.edu					
Quinebaug Valley Community College 742 Upper Maple St	Danielson	CT	06239	860-774-1130	779-2998*
**Fax:* Admissions ■ *Web:* www.qvctc.commnet.edu					
Three Rivers Community College					
Mohegan 7 Mahan Dr	Norwich	CT	06360	860-885-2300	885-1684*
**Fax:* Admissions ■ *Web:* www.trcc.commnet.edu					
Thames Valley 7 Mahan Drive	Norwich	CT	06360	860-886-0177	892-5753*
**Fax:* Admissions ■ *Web:* www.trcc.commnet.edu					
Tunxis Community College 271 Scott Swamp Rd	Farmington	CT	06032	860-677-7701	676-8906
Web: www.tunxis.commnet.edu					
University of Connecticut					
Avery Point 1084 Shennecossett Rd	Groton	CT	06340	860-405-9019	405-9018
Web: www.averypoint.uconn.edu					
Greater Hartford 85 Lawler Rd.	West Hartford	CT	06117	860-570-9214	570-9210
Web: www.hartford.uconn.edu					
Torrington 855 University Dr	Torrington	CT	06790	860-626-6800	626-6847
Web: www.torrington.uconn.edu					
Waterbury 99 E Main St.	Waterbury	CT	06702	203-236-9800	236-9805
Web: www.waterbury.uconn.edu					

Florida

	City	State	Zip	Phone	Fax
Brevard Community College					
Cocoa 1519 Clearlake Rd	Cocoa	FL	32922	321-632-1111	433-7357*
**Fax:* Admissions ■ *TF:* 888-747-2802 ■ *Web:* www.brevard.cc.fl.us					
Melbourne 3865 N Wickham Rd	Melbourne	FL	32935	321-632-1111	433-5770*
**Fax:* Admissions ■ *TF:* 888-747-2802 ■ *Web:* www.brevardcc.edu					
Palm Bay 250 Community College Pkwy	Palm Bay	FL	32909	321-632-1111	433-5325*
**Fax:* Admissions ■ *TF:* 888-747-2802 ■ *Web:* www.brevardcc.edu					
Titusville 1311 N US 1	Titusville	FL	32796	321-632-1111	433-5115*
**Fax:* Admissions ■ *TF:* 888-747-2802 ■ *Web:* www.brevardcc.edu					
Broward Community College					
Central 3501 SW Davie Rd	Davie	FL	33314	954-201-6500	201-6954
Web: www.broward.edu					
Downtown Center 111 E Las Olas Blvd	Fort Lauderdale	FL	33301	954-201-7350	201-7466*
**Fax:* Admissions ■ *Web:* www.broward.edu					
North 1000 Coconut Creek Blvd	Coconut Creek	FL	33066	954-201-2240	201-2242*
**Fax:* Admissions ■ *Web:* www.broward.edu					
Pines 16957 Sheridan St	Pembroke Pines	FL	33331	954-201-3601	201-3614
Web: www.broward.edu/locations/pines					
South 7200 Hollywood/Pines Blvd	Pembroke Pines	FL	33024	954-201-8835	201-8060*
**Fax:* Admissions ■ *Web:* www.broward.edu					
Central Florida Community College					
Citrus County 3800 S Lecanto Hwy	Lecanto	FL	34461	352-746-6721	249-1218
Web: www.cf.edu					
Levy County 114 Rodgers Blvd	Chiefland	FL	32626	352-493-9533	493-9994
Web: www.cf.edu/departments/levy					
Ocala PO Box 1388	Ocala	FL	34478	352-237-2111	291-4450
Web: www.gocfcc.com					
Daytona Beach Community College					
1200 W International Speedway Blvd	Daytona Beach	FL	32114	386-506-3222	
Web: www.dbcc.edu					
Edison College					
Charlotte 26300 Airport Rd	Punta Gorda	FL	33950	941-637-5629	637-3538*
**Fax:* Admissions ■ *TF:* 800-749-2322 ■ *Web:* www.edison.edu/charlotte					
Collier County 7007 Lely Cultural Pkwy.	Naples	FL	34113	239-732-3701	732-3761*
**Fax:* Admissions ■ *TF:* 800-749-2322 ■ *Web:* www.edison.edu/collier					
Lee County 8099 College Pkwy SW	Fort Myers	FL	33919	239-489-9054	489-9372*
**Fax:* Admissions ■ *TF:* 800-749-2322 ■ *Web:* www.edison.edu/lee					
Florida Community College at Jacksonville					
Downtown 101 W State St.	Jacksonville	FL	32202	904-633-8100	633-8400
TF: 877-633-5950 ■ *Web:* www.fccj.org/campuses/downtown					
Kent 3939 Roosevelt Blvd	Jacksonville	FL	32205	904-381-3400	381-3771*
**Fax:* Admissions ■ *Web:* www.fccj.org/campuses/kent					
North 4501 Capper Rd	Jacksonville	FL	32218	904-766-6500	713-6002
Web: www.fccj.org/campuses/north					
South 11901 Beach Blvd	Jacksonville	FL	32246	904-646-2111	646-2124*
**Fax:* Admissions ■ *Web:* www.fccj.org/campuses/south					
Florida Keys Community College 5901 College Rd	Key West	FL	33040	305-296-9081	292-5155*
**Fax:* Admissions ■ *Web:* www.fkcc.edu					
Florida National College 4425 W 20th Ave	Hialeah	FL	33012	305-821-3333	362-0595*
**Fax:* Acctg ■ *Web:* www.florida-national.edu					
Gulf Coast Community College 5230 W Hwy 98	Panama City	FL	32401	850-769-1551	913-3308*
**Fax:* Admissions ■ *TF:* 800-311-3685 ■ *Web:* www.gc.cc.fl.us					
Hillsborough Community College					
Brandon 10414 E Columbus Dr	Tampa	FL	33619	813-253-7801	
Web: www.hccfl.edu/campus/br					
Dale Mabry 4001 Tampa Bay Blvd.	Tampa	FL	33614	813-253-7000	253-7400*
**Fax:* Admissions ■ *Web:* www.hccfl.edu/campus/dm/					
Plant City 1206 N Park Rd	Plant City	FL	33566	813-757-2102	757-2187
Web: www.hccfl.edu/campus/pc					
Ybor City 2112 N 15th St	Tampa	FL	33675	813-253-7602	
Web: www.hccfl.edu/campus/yb					
Indian River Community College 3209 Virginia Ave.	Fort Pierce	FL	34981	772-462-4700	462-4699*
**Fax:* Admissions ■ *TF:* 866-866-4722 ■ *Web:* www.ircc.edu					
Lake City Community College 149 SE College Pl.	Lake City	FL	32025	386-752-1822	754-4581*
**Fax:* Admissions ■ *Web:* www.lakecitycc.edu					
Lake-Sumter Community College 9501 US Hwy 441	Leesburg	FL	34788	352-787-3747	365-3553*
**Fax:* Admissions ■ *Web:* www.lscc.edu					
South Lake 1250 N Hancock Rd	Clermont	FL	34711	352-243-5722	243-0117
Web: www.lscc.edu/southlakecampus					
Sumter 1405 CR 526A	Sumterville	FL	33585	352-568-0001	568-7515
Web: www.lscc.edu/sumtercampus					
Manatee Community College 5840 26th St W	Bradenton	FL	34207	941-752-5000	727-6380
Web: www.mccfl.edu					

Florida (Cont'd)

	City	State	Zip	Phone	Fax
South 8000 S Tamiami Trail **Fax:* Admissions ■ *Web:* www.mccfl.edu	Venice	FL	34293	941-408-1300	727-6380*
Miami Dade College					
Homestead 500 College Terr **Fax:* Admissions ■ *Web:* www.mdc.edu/homestead	Homestead	FL	33030	305-237-5555	237-5019*
Kendall 11011 SW 104th St. **Fax:* Admissions ■ *Web:* www.mdc.edu/kendall	Miami	FL	33176	305-237-2000	237-2964*
Medical Center 950 NW 20th St *Web:* www.mdc.edu/medical/	Miami	FL	33127	305-237-4100	237-4339
North 11380 NW 27th Ave. **Fax:* Admissions ■ *Web:* www.mdc.edu/north	Miami	FL	33167	305-237-1000	237-8070*
North-Hialeah Center 1776 W 49th St. **Fax:* Admissions ■ *Web:* www.mdc.edu/north/hialeah	Hialeah	FL	33012	305-237-8700	237-8771*
Wolfson 300 NE 2nd Ave. **Fax:* Admissions ■ *Web:* www.mdc.edu/wolfson	Miami	FL	33132	305-237-3000	237-3669*
North Florida Community College 321 NW Turner Davis Dr *Web:* www.nfcc.edu	Madison	FL	32340	850-973-2288	973-1696
Okaloosa-Walton Community College 100 College Blvd *Web:* www.owcc.cc.fl.us/	Niceville	FL	32578	850-678-5111	729-5273
Palm Beach Community College					
Belle Glade 1977 College Dr **Fax:* Admissions ■ *Web:* www.pbcc.edu	Belle Glade	FL	33430	561-993-1121	993-1129*
Boca Raton 3000 St Lucie Ave *Web:* www.pbcc.edu	Boca Raton	FL	33431	561-862-4340	862-4350
Lake Worth 4200 Congress Ave **Fax:* Admissions ■ *TF:* 866-576-7222 ■ *Web:* www.pbcc.edu	Lake Worth	FL	33461	561-868-3350	868-3584*
Palm Beach Gardens 3160 PGA Blvd *TF:* 866-576-7222 ■ *Web:* www.pbcc.edu	Palm Beach Gardens	FL	33410	561-207-5300	207-5315
Pasco-Hernando Community College 10230 Ridge Rd **Fax:* Admissions ■ *TF:* 877-879-7422 ■ *Web:* www.phcc.edu	New Port Richey	FL	34654	727-847-2727	816-3389*
East 36727 Blanton Rd *Web:* www.pasco-hernandocc.com	Dade City	FL	33523	352-567-6701	518-1225
North 11415 Ponce de Leon Blvd *Web:* www.pasco-hernandocc.com	Brooksville	FL	34601	352-796-6726	797-5133
Pensacola Junior College 1000 College Blvd. **Fax:* Admissions ■ *TF:* 888-897-3605 ■ *Web:* www.pjc.edu	Pensacola	FL	32504	850-484-1000	484-1829*
Warrington 5555 W Hwy 98 *Web:* www.pjc.edu	Pensacola	FL	32507	850-484-2200	484-2375
Polk Community College 999 Ave H NE **Fax:* Admissions ■ *Web:* www.polk.edu	Winter Haven	FL	33881	863-297-1000	297-1060*
Lakeland 999 Ave H NE *Web:* www.polk.edu	Winter Haven	FL	33881	863-297-1000	297-1023
Saint Johns River Community College 5001 Saint Johns Ave. **Fax:* Admissions ■ *Web:* www.sjrcc.edu/palcamp.html	Palatka	FL	32177	386-312-4200	312-4048*
Orange Park 283 College Dr **Fax:* Admissions ■ *Web:* www.sjrcc.edu/opcamp.html	Orange Park	FL	32065	904-276-6800	276-6888*
Saint Augustine 2990 College Dr. **Fax:* Admissions ■ *Web:* www.sjrcc.edu/staugcamp.html	Saint Augustine	FL	32084	904-808-7400	808-7420*
Saint Petersburg College					
Clearwater 2465 Drew St. *Web:* www.spcollege.edu/clw	Clearwater	FL	33765	727-791-2473	791-2423
Gibbs 6605 5th Ave N *Web:* www.spcollege.edu	Saint Petersburg	FL	33710	727-341-3239	341-4792
Seminole 9200 113th St N. *Web:* www.spjc.edu/se	Seminole	FL	33772	727-394-6134	394-6132
Santa Fe Community College 3000 NW 83rd St **Fax:* Admissions ■ *Web:* www.sfcc.edu	Gainesville	FL	32606	352-395-5000	395-4118*
Seminole Community College 100 Weldon Blvd **Fax:* Admissions ■ *Web:* www.scc-fl.edu	Sanford	FL	32773	407-328-4722	328-2395*
Oviedo 2505 Lockwood Blvd *Web:* www.scc-fl.edu/oviedo	Oviedo	FL	32765	407-971-5000	971-5012
South Florida Community College 600 W College Dr **Fax:* Admissions ■ *Web:* www.southflorida.edu	Avon Park	FL	33825	863-453-6661	453-2365*
Tallahassee Community College 444 Appleyard Dr. **Fax:* Admissions ■ *Web:* www.tcc.fl.edu	Tallahassee	FL	32304	850-201-6200	201-8474*
Valencia Community College PO Box 3028 *Web:* www.valenciacc.edu	Orlando	FL	32802	407-299-5000	582-1450
East 701 N Econlockhatchee Trail *Web:* valenciacc.edu/east	Orlando	FL	32825	407-299-5000	582-2621
Osceola 1800 Denn John Ln *Web:* valenciacc.edu/osceola	Kissimmee	FL	34744	407-847-9496	

Georgia

	City	State	Zip	Phone	Fax
Abraham Baldwin Agricultural College 2802 Moore Hwy ABAC 3 **Fax:* Admissions ■ *TF:* 800-733-3653 ■ *Web:* www.abac.edu	Tifton	GA	31793	229-386-3236	391-5002*
Andrew College 413 College St. *TF:* 800-664-9250 ■ *Web:* www.andrewcollege.edu	Cuthbert	GA	39840	229-732-2171	732-2176
Atlanta Metropolitan College 1630 Metropolitan Pkwy SW **Fax:* Admissions ■ *Web:* www.atlm.edu	Atlanta	GA	30310	404-756-4000	756-4407*
Bainbridge College 2500 E Shotwell St *Web:* www.bainbridge.edu	Bainbridge	GA	39819	229-248-2505	248-2513
Coastal Georgia Community College 3700 Altama Ave **Fax:* Admissions ■ *TF:* 800-675-7235 ■ *Web:* www.cgcc.edu	Brunswick	GA	31520	912-264-7235	262-3072*
Darton College 2400 Gillionville Rd **Fax:* Admissions ■ *TF:* 866-775-1214 ■ *Web:* www.darton.edu	Albany	GA	31707	229-430-6742	317-6607*
East Georgia College 131 College Cir. **Fax:* Admissions ■ *Web:* www.ega.edu	Swainsboro	GA	30401	478-289-2000	289-2140*
Emory University Oxford College 100 Hamill St PO Box 1418 *TF:* 800-723-8328 ■ *Web:* www.emory.edu/OXFORD	Oxford	GA	30054	770-784-8328	784-8359
Gainesville State College 3820 Mundy Mill Rd PO Box 1358 **Fax:* Admissions ■ *Web:* www.gsc.edu	Gainesville	GA	30566	770-718-3639	718-3751*
Georgia Highlands College					
Cartersville 5441 Hwy 20 SE *Web:* www.highlands.edu/about/campuses	Cartersville	GA	30121	678-872-8000	872-8013
Floyd 3175 Cedartown Hwy SE **Fax:* Admissions ■ *TF:* 800-332-2406 ■ *Web:* www.highlands.edu/about/campuses	Rome	GA	30161	706-802-5000	295-6341*
Georgia Military College 201 E Green St. **Fax:* Admissions ■ *TF:* 800-342-0413 ■ *Web:* www.gmc.cc.ga.us	Milledgeville	GA	31061	478-445-2700	445-6520*
Georgia Perimeter College					
Clarkston 555 N Indian Creek Dr. *Web:* www.gpc.edu/gpccla	Clarkston	GA	30021	678-891-3200	
Decatur 3251 Panthersville Rd. *Web:* www.gpc.edu	Decatur	GA	30034	678-891-2300	
Dunwoody 2101 Womack Rd *Web:* www.gpc.edu/gpcdun	Dunwoody	GA	30338	770-274-5000	551-3148
Gordon College 419 College Dr. **Fax:* Admissions ■ *Web:* www.gdn.edu	Barnesville	GA	30204	770-358-5000	358-5080*
Middle Georgia College 1100 2nd St SE **Fax:* Admissions ■ *Web:* www.mgc.edu	Cochran	GA	31014	478-934-6221	934-3403*
Oxford College 100 Hamill St PO Box 1418 *TF:* 800-723-8328 ■ *Web:* www.emory.edu/OXFORD	Oxford	GA	30054	770-784-8328	784-8359
South Georgia College 100 W College Park Dr **Fax:* Admissions ■ *TF:* 800-342-6364 ■ *Web:* www.sga.edu	Douglas	GA	31533	912-389-4510	389-4388*
Waycross College 2001 S Georgia Pkwy **Fax:* Admissions ■ *Web:* www.waycross.edu	Waycross	GA	31503	912-285-6130	285-6158*
Young Harris College PO Box 116 **Fax:* Admissions ■ *TF:* 800-241-3754 ■ *Web:* www.yhc.edu	Young Harris	GA	30582	706-379-3111	379-3108*

Hawaii

	City	State	Zip	Phone	Fax
Hawaii Community College 200 W Kawili St **Fax:* Admissions ■ *Web:* www.hawcc.hawaii.edu	Hilo	HI	96720	808-974-7662	974-7692*
Honolulu Community College 874 Dillingham Blvd **Fax:* Admissions ■ *Web:* honolulu.hawaii.edu	Honolulu	HI	96817	808-845-9129	847-9829*
Kauai Community College 3-1901 Kaumualii Hwy *Web:* www.kauai.hawaii.edu	Lihue	HI	96766	808-245-8311	245-8220
Leeward Community College 96-045 Ala Ike **Fax:* Admissions ■ *Web:* www.lcc.hawaii.edu	Pearl City	HI	96782	808-455-0011	454-8804*
Maui Community College 310 W Kaahumanu Ave **Fax:* Admissions ■ *TF:* 800-479-6692 ■ *Web:* www.maui.hawaii.edu	Kahului	HI	96732	808-984-3267	242-9618*
University of Hawaii					
Honolulu Community College 874 Dillingham Blvd **Fax:* Admissions ■ *Web:* honolulu.hawaii.edu	Honolulu	HI	96817	808-845-9129	847-9829*
Kapiolani Community College 4303 Diamond Head Rd *Web:* www.kcc.hawaii.edu	Honolulu	HI	96816	808-734-9000	734-9896
Leeward Community College 96-045 Ala Ike St **Fax:* Admissions ■ *Web:* www.lcc.hawaii.edu	Pearl City	HI	96782	808-455-0001	454-8804*
Windward Community College 45-720 Keaahala Rd **Fax:* Admissions ■ *Web:* www.wcc.hawaii.edu	Kaneohe	HI	96744	808-235-7400	235-9148*

Idaho

	City	State	Zip	Phone	Fax
College of Southern Idaho PO Box 1238 **Fax:* Admissions ■ *Web:* www.csi.edu	Twin Falls	ID	83303	208-733-9554	736-3014*
North Idaho College 1000 W Garden Ave. **Fax:* Library ■ *TF:* 877-404-4536 ■ *Web:* www.nic.edu	Coeur d'Alene	ID	83814	208-769-3300	769-3399*

Illinois

	City	State	Zip	Phone	Fax
Black Hawk College					
East 1501 Illinois Hwy 78 **Fax:* Admissions ■ *TF:* 800-233-5671 ■ *Web:* www.bhc.edu	Kewanee	IL	61443	309-852-5671	856-6005*
Quad Cities 6600 34th Ave **Fax:* Admissions ■ *TF:* 800-334-1311 ■ *Web:* www.bhc.edu	Moline	IL	61265	309-796-5000	796-5209*
Carl Sandburg College 2400 Tom L Wilson Blvd *TF:* 877-236-1862 ■ *Web:* www.sandburg.edu	Galesburg	IL	61401	309-344-2518	344-3291
College of DuPage 425 Fawell Blvd **Fax:* Admissions ■ *Web:* www.cod.edu	Glen Ellyn	IL	60137	630-858-2800	790-2686*
College of Lake County					
Grayslake 19351 W Washington St **Fax:* Admissions ■ *Web:* www.clcillinois.edu	Grayslake	IL	60030	847-223-6601	543-3061*
Lakeshore 33 N Genessee St **Fax:* Admissions ■ *Web:* www.clcillinois.edu/aboutclc/fac_lakeshore.asp	Waukegan	IL	60085	847-623-8686	543-2170*
Danville Area Community College 2000 E Main St **Fax:* Hum Res ■ *TF:* 888-455-3222 ■ *Web:* www.dacc.cc.il.us	Danville	IL	61832	217-443-3222	443-8560*
Elgin Community College 1700 Spartan Dr **Fax:* Admissions ■ *Web:* www.elgin.edu	Elgin	IL	60123	847-697-1000	608-5458*
Fountain Square 51 S Spring St **Fax:* Admissions ■ *Web:* www.elgin.edu	Elgin	IL	60120	847-214-6900	608-5458*
Frontier Community College 2 Frontier Dr **Fax:* Admissions ■ *TF:* 877-464-3687 ■ *Web:* www.iecc.cc.il.us/fcc	Fairfield	IL	62837	618-842-3711	842-3412*
Harold Washington College 30 E Lake St. **Fax:* Admissions ■ *Web:* hwashington.ccc.edu	Chicago	IL	60601	312-553-6000	553-3075*
Harper College 1200 W Algonquin Rd **Fax:* Admissions ■ *Web:* www.harpercollege.edu	Palatine	IL	60067	847-925-6000	925-6044*
Harry S Truman College 1145 W Wilson Ave **Fax:* Admissions ■ *Web:* www.trumancollege.cc	Chicago	IL	60640	773-878-1700	907-4464*
Heartland Community College 1500 W Raab Rd *Web:* www.hcc.cc.il.us	Normal	IL	61761	309-268-8000	268-7992
Highland Community College 2998 W Pearl City Rd **Fax:* Admissions ■ *Web:* www.highland.cc.il.us	Freeport	IL	61032	815-235-6121	235-6130*
Illinois Central College 1 College Dr **Fax:* Admissions ■ *Web:* www.icc.edu	East Peoria	IL	61635	309-694-5011	694-8461*
Illinois Valley Community College 815 N Orlando Smith Ave. **Fax:* Admissions ■ *Web:* www.ivcc.edu	Oglesby	IL	61348	815-224-2720	224-3033*
John A Logan College 700 Logan College Rd **Fax:* Admissions ■ *Web:* www.jal.cc.il.us	Carterville	IL	62918	618-985-3741	985-4433*
John Wood Community College 1301 S 48th St **Fax:* Admissions ■ *Web:* www.jwcc.edu	Quincy	IL	62305	217-224-6500	641-4192*
Pittsfield 1308 W Washington St. *Web:* www.jwcc.edu/about/pec.asp	Pittsfield	IL	62363	217-285-5319	641-4192
Joliet Junior College 1215 Houbolt Rd **Fax:* Admissions ■ *TF:* 800-636-9886 ■ *Web:* www.jjc.edu	Joliet	IL	60431	815-729-9020	280-2493*
North 1125 135th St *TF:* 800-636-9886 ■ *Web:* www.jjc.edu/north/	Romeoville	IL	60446	815-886-3000	886-4331
Kankakee Community College 100 College Dr. **Fax:* Admissions ■ *Web:* www.kcc.edu	Kankakee	IL	60901	815-933-0345	802-8101*
Kennedy-King College 6800 S Wentworth Ave. **Fax:* Admissions ■ *Web:* kennedyking.ccc.edu	Chicago	IL	60621	773-602-5000	602-5247*
Kishwaukee College 21193 Malta Rd *Web:* www.kishwaukeecollege.edu	Malta	IL	60150	815-825-2086	825-2306
Lake Land College 5001 Lake Land Blvd **Fax:* Admissions ■ *Web:* www.lakeland.cc.il.us	Mattoon	IL	61938	217-234-5253	234-5390*
Lewis & Clark Community College 5800 Godfrey Rd **Fax:* Admissions ■ *Web:* www.lc.edu	Godfrey	IL	62035	618-466-3411	468-2310*
Lincoln College 300 Keokuk St. *Web:* www.lincolncollege.edu	Lincoln	IL	62656	217-732-3155	732-8859
Lincoln Land Community College					
5250 Shepherd Rd PO Box 19256 *TF:* 800-727-4161 ■ *Web:* www.llcc.edu	Springfield	IL	62794	217-786-2200	786-2468
Lincoln Trail College 11220 State Hwy 1 **Fax:* Admissions ■ *TF:* 866-582-4322 ■ *Web:* www.iecc.cc.il.us/ltc	Robinson	IL	62454	618-544-8657	544-4705*
Malcolm X College 1900 W Van Buren St *Web:* malcolmx.ccc.edu	Chicago	IL	60612	312-850-7000	850-7092
McHenry County College 8900 US Hwy 14 *Web:* www.mchenry.edu	Crystal Lake	IL	60012	815-455-3700	455-3766
Moraine Valley Community College 10900 S 88th Ave. **Fax:* Admissions ■ *Web:* www.morainevalley.edu	Palos Hills	IL	60465	708-974-4300	974-0974*
Morton College 3801 S Central Ave **Fax:* Admitting ■ *Web:* www.morton.edu	Cicero	IL	60804	708-656-8000	656-9592*
Oakton Community College 1600 E Golf Rd. **Fax:* Admissions ■ *Web:* www.oakton.edu	Des Plaines	IL	60016	847-635-1600	635-1890*

	City	State	ZIP	Phone	Fax
Ray Hartstein 7701 N Lincoln Ave	Skokie	IL	60077	847-635-1400	635-1497
Web: www.oakton.edu/visitor/rhc					
Olive-Harvey College 10001 S Woodlawn Ave	Chicago	IL	60628	773-291-6100	291-6185*
*Fax: Admissions ■ *Web:* oliveharvey.ccc.edu					
Olney Central College 305 N West St	Olney	IL	62450	618-395-4351	395-1261*
*Fax: Admissions ■ *TF:* 866-622-4322 ■ *Web:* www.iecc.cc.il.us/occ					
Parkland College 2400 W Bradley Ave	Champaign	IL	61821	217-351-2200	353-2640*
*Fax: Admissions ■ *Web:* www.parkland.edu					
Prairie State College 202 S Halsted St	Chicago Heights	IL	60411	708-709-3500	709-3951*
*Fax: Admissions ■ *Web:* www.prairiestate.edu					
Rend Lake College 468 N Ken Gray Pkwy	Ina	IL	62846	618-437-5321	437-5677*
*Fax: Admitting ■ *Web:* www.rlc.cc.il.us					
Richard J Daley College 7500 S Pulaski Rd	Chicago	IL	60652	773-838-7500	838-7605*
*Fax: Admissions ■ *Web:* daley.ccc.edu					
Richland Community College 1 College Park	Decatur	IL	62521	217-875-7200	875-6965*
*Fax: Hum Res ■ *Web:* www.richland.edu					
Rock Valley College 3301 N Mulford Rd	Rockford	IL	61114	815-921-7821	921-4269*
*Fax: Admissions ■ *TF:* 800-973-7821 ■ *Web:* www.rockvalleycollege.edu					
Saint Augustine College 1333-1345 W Argyle St	Chicago	IL	60640	773-878-8756	878-0937*
*Fax: Admissions ■ *Web:* www.staugustinecollege.edu					
Sauk Valley Community College 173 Illinois Rt 2	Dixon	IL	61021	815-288-5511	288-3190*
*Fax: Admissions ■ *Web:* www.svcc.cc.il.us					
Shawnee Community College 8364 Shawnee College Rd	Ullin	IL	62992	618-634-3200	634-3300*
*Fax: Admitting ■ *Web:* www.shawneecc.edu					
South Suburban College 15800 S State St	South Holland	IL	60473	708-596-2000	225-5806*
*Fax: Admissions ■ *Web:* www.southsuburbancollege.edu					
Southeastern Illinois College 3575 College Rd	Harrisburg	IL	62946	618-252-6376	252-3062*
*Fax: Admissions ■ *TF:* 866-338-2742 ■ *Web:* www.sic.edu					
Southwestern Illinois College 2500 Carlyle Ave	Belleville	IL	62221	618-235-2700	222-9768*
*Fax: Admissions ■ *TF:* 800-222-5131 ■ *Web:* www.southwestern.cc.il.us					
Granite City 4950 Maryville Rd	Granite City	IL	62040	618-931-0600	931-1598
Web: www.southwestern.cc.il.us/granitecity					
Red Bud 500 W South 4th St	Red Bud	IL	62278	618-282-6682	282-6568
Web: www.southwestern.cc.il.us/redbud					
Spoon River College 23235 N County 22	Canton	IL	61520	309-647-4645	649-6393*
*Fax: Admissions ■ *TF:* 800-334-7337 ■ *Web:* www.spoonrivercollege.net					
Springfield College in Illinois - Benedictine University					
1500 N 5th St	Springfield	IL	62702	217-525-1420	525-1497
TF: 800-635-7289 ■ *Web:* www.sci.edu					
Triton College 2000 N 5th Ave	River Grove	IL	60171	708-456-0300	583-3147*
*Fax: Admissions ■ *TF:* 800-942-7404 ■ *Web:* www.triton.edu					
Wabash Valley College 2200 College Dr	Mount Carmel	IL	62863	618-262-8641	262-8641*
*Fax: Admissions ■ *TF:* 866-982-4322 ■ *Web:* www.iecc.cc.il.us/wvc					
Waubonsee Community College Rt 47 At Waubonsee Dr	Sugar Grove	IL	60554	630-466-4811	466-4964*
*Fax: Admissions ■ *Web:* www.waubonsee.edu					
Wilbur Wright College 4300 N Narragansett Ave	Chicago	IL	60634	773-777-7900	481-8185
Web: wright.ccc.edu					

Indiana

	City	State	ZIP	Phone	Fax
Ancilla College PO Box 1	Donaldson	IN	46513	574-936-8898	935-1773*
*Fax: Admissions ■ *Web:* www.ancilla.edu					
Vincennes University 1002 N 1st St	Vincennes	IN	47591	812-888-4313	888-5707*
*Fax: Admissions ■ *TF:* 800-742-9198 ■ *Web:* www.vinu.edu					
Jasper 850 College Ave	Jasper	IN	47546	812-482-3030	481-5960*
*Fax: Admissions ■ *TF:* 800-809-8852 ■ *Web:* vujc.vinu.edu					

Iowa

	City	State	ZIP	Phone	Fax
Clinton Community College 1000 Lincoln Blvd	Clinton	IA	52732	563-244-7001	244-7107*
*Fax: Library ■ *Web:* www.eicc.edu/ccc					
Des Moines Area Community College					
Ankeny 2006 S Ankeny Blvd	Ankeny	IA	50021	515-964-6200	964-6391*
*Fax: Admissions ■ *TF:* 800-362-2127 ■ *Web:* www.dmacc.edu					
Boone 1125 Hancock Dr	Boone	IA	50036	515-432-7203	433-5033*
*Fax: Admissions ■ *TF:* 800-362-2127 ■ *Web:* www.dmacc.edu/boone					
Carroll 906 N Grant Rd	Carroll	IA	51401	712-792-1755	792-6358
TF: 800-622-3334 ■ *Web:* www.dmacc.edu/carroll					
Urban/Des Moines 1100 7th St	Des Moines	IA	50314	515-244-4226	248-7253
TF: 800-622-3334 ■ *Web:* www.dmacc.edu/urban					
Ellsworth Community College 1100 College Ave	Iowa Falls	IA	50126	641-648-4611	648-3128*
*Fax: Admissions ■ *TF:* 800-322-9235 ■ *Web:* iavalley.cc.ia.us/ecc					
Hawkeye Community College 1501 E Orange Rd	Waterloo	IA	50704	319-296-2320	296-2874*
*Fax: Admissions ■ *TF:* 800-670-4769 ■ *Web:* www.hawkeye.cc.ia.us					
Indian Hills Community College 623 Indian Hills Dr	Ottumwa	IA	52501	641-683-5111	683-5741*
*Fax: Admitting ■ *TF:* 800-726-2585 ■ *Web:* www.ihcc.cc.ia.us					
Iowa Central Community College 330 Ave M	Fort Dodge	IA	50501	515-576-7201	576-7724*
*Fax: Admissions ■ *TF:* 800-362-2793 ■ *Web:* www.iccc.cc.ia.us					
Iowa Lakes Community College 300 S 18th St	Estherville	IA	51334	712-362-2604	362-8363*
*Fax: Admissions ■ *TF:* 800-242-5106 ■ *Web:* www.iowalakes.edu					
Iowa Western Community College					
Clarinda 923 E Washington St	Clarinda	IA	51632	712-542-5117	542-4608*
*Fax: Admissions ■ *TF:* 800-521-2073 ■ *Web:* www.iwcc.cc.ia.us					
Council Bluffs 2700 College Rd Box 4-C	Council Bluffs	IA	51502	712-325-3200	325-3720*
*Fax: Admissions ■ *TF:* 800-432-5852 ■ *Web:* iwcc.cc.ia.us					
Kirkwood Community College 6301 Kirkwood Blvd SW	Cedar Rapids	IA	52404	319-398-5411	398-1244*
*Fax: Admissions ■ *TF:* 800-332-2055 ■ *Web:* www.kirkwood.edu					
Marshalltown Community College 3700 S Center St	Marshalltown	IA	50158	641-752-7106	752-8149
TF: 866-622-4748 ■ *Web:* www.iavalley.cc.ia.us/mcc					
Muscatine Community College 152 Colorado St	Muscatine	IA	52761	563-288-6001	288-6104*
*Fax: Admissions ■ *TF:* 888-336-3907 ■ *Web:* www.eicc.edu/mcc					
North Iowa Area Community College 500 College Dr	Mason City	IA	50401	641-423-1264	422-4385*
*Fax: Admissions ■ *TF:* 888-466-4222 ■ *Web:* www.niacc.cc.ia.us					
Northeast Iowa Community College					
Calmar 1625 Hwy 150 S PO Box 400	Calmar	IA	52132	563-562-3263	562-4369*
*Fax: Admissions ■ *TF:* 800-728-2256 ■ *Web:* www.nicc.edu					
Peosta 10250 Sundown Rd	Peosta	IA	52068	563-556-5110	557-0347*
*Fax: Admissions ■ *TF:* 800-728-7367 ■ *Web:* www.nicc.edu					
Northwest Iowa Community College 603 W Park St	Sheldon	IA	51201	712-324-5061	324-4136
TF: 800-352-4907 ■ *Web:* www.nwicc.edu					
Scott Community College 500 Belmont Rd	Bettendorf	IA	52722	563-441-4001	441-4131*
*Fax: Admissions ■ *TF:* 888-336-3907 ■ *Web:* www.eicc.edu/scc					
Southeastern Community College					
North 1500 W Agency Rd	West Burlington	IA	52655	319-752-2731	758-6725*
*Fax: Admissions ■ *Web:* www.secc.cc.ia.us					
South 335 Messenger Rd	Keokuk	IA	52632	319-524-3221	524-8621*
*Fax: Admissions ■ *Web:* www.secc.cc.ia.us					
Southwestern Community College 1501 W Townline St	Creston	IA	50801	641-782-7081	782-3312*
*Fax: Admissions ■ *TF:* 800-247-4023 ■ *Web:* www.swcciowa.edu					

Kansas

	City	State	ZIP	Phone	Fax
Allen County Community College 1801 N Cottonwood St	Iola	KS	66749	620-365-5116	365-7406*
*Fax: Admissions ■ *Web:* www.allencc.edu					
Barton County Community College 245 NE 30th Rd	Great Bend	KS	67530	620-792-2701	786-1160*
*Fax: Admissions ■ *TF:* 800-722-6842 ■ *Web:* www.bartonccc.edu					
Butler Community College 901 S Haverhill Rd	El Dorado	KS	67042	316-321-2222	322-3316*
*Fax: Admissions ■ *Web:* www.butlercc.edu					
Cloud County Community College 2221 Campus Dr	Concordia	KS	66901	785-243-1435	243-1040*
*Fax: Admissions ■ *TF:* 800-729-5101 ■ *Web:* www.cloud.edu					
Coffeyville Community College 400 W 11th St	Coffeyville	KS	67337	620-251-7700	252-7010*
*Fax: Admissions ■ *TF:* 800-782-4732 ■ *Web:* www.coffeyville.edu					
Colby Community College 1255 S Range Ave	Colby	KS	67701	785-462-3984	460-4691*
*Fax: Admissions ■ *TF:* 888-634-9350 ■ *Web:* colbycc.edu					
Cowley County Community College & Area Vocational-Technical School PO Box 1147	Arkansas City	KS	67005	620-442-0430	441-5350
TF: 800-593-2222 ■ *Web:* www.cowley.edu					
Dodge City Community College 2501 N 14th Ave	Dodge City	KS	67801	620-225-1321	227-9277*
*Fax: Admissions ■ *TF:* 800-367-3222 ■ *Web:* www.dc3.edu					
Donnelly College 608 N 18th St	Kansas City	KS	66102	913-621-6070	621-8734*
*Fax: Admissions ■ *Web:* www.donnelly.edu					
Fort Scott Community College 2108 S Horton St	Fort Scott	KS	66701	620-223-2700	223-6530*
*Fax: Admissions ■ *TF:* 800-874-3722 ■ *Web:* www.fortscott.edu					
Garden City Community College 801 Campus Dr	Garden City	KS	67846	620-276-7611	276-9573*
*Fax: Admissions ■ *TF:* 800-658-1696 ■ *Web:* www.gcccks.edu					
Hesston College 325 S College Dr PO Box 3000	Hesston	KS	67062	620-327-4221	327-8300
TF: 800-995-2757 ■ *Web:* www.hesston.edu					
Highland Community College 606 W Main St	Highland	KS	66035	785-442-6000	442-6106*
*Fax: Admissions ■ *Web:* www.highlandcc.edu					
Hutchinson Community College & Area Vocational School					
1300 N Plum St	Hutchinson	KS	67501	620-665-3500	728-8199*
*Fax: Admissions ■ *TF:* 800-289-3501 ■ *Web:* www.hutchcc.edu					
Independence Community College					
1057 W College Ave PO Box 708	Independence	KS	67301	620-331-4100	331-0946*
*Fax: Admissions ■ *TF:* 800-842-6063 ■ *Web:* www.indy.cc.ks.us					
Johnson County Community College 12345 College Blvd	Overland Park	KS	66210	913-469-8500	469-2524*
*Fax: Admissions ■ *TF:* 866-896-5893 ■ *Web:* www.jccc.net					
Kansas City Kansas Community College 7250 State Ave	Kansas City	KS	66112	913-334-1100	288-7648*
*Fax: Admissions ■ *Web:* www.kckcc.edu					
Labette Community College 200 S 14th St	Parsons	KS	67357	620-421-6700	421-0180*
*Fax: Admissions ■ *TF:* 888-522-3883 ■ *Web:* www.labette.cc.ks.us					
Neosho County Community College 800 W 14th St	Chanute	KS	66720	620-431-2820	431-6056*
*Fax: Admissions ■ *Web:* www.neosho.edu					
Ottawa 226 S Beech St	Ottawa	KS	66067	785-242-2067	242-2068*
*Fax: Admissions ■ *Web:* www.neosho.edu					
Pratt Community College 348 NE SR-61	Pratt	KS	67124	620-672-5641	672-5288*
*Fax: Admissions ■ *Web:* www.prattcc.edu					
Seward County Community College					
1801 N Campus Ave PO Box 1137	Liberal	KS	67905	620-624-1951	629-2725
TF: 800-373-9951 ■ *Web:* www.sccc.edu					

Kentucky

	City	State	ZIP	Phone	Fax
Ashland Community & Technical College 1400 College Dr	Ashland	KY	41101	606-329-2999	326-2192*
*Fax: Admissions ■ *TF:* 800-928-4256 ■ *Web:* www.ashland.kctcs.edu					
Big Sandy Community & Technical College					
1 Bert T Combs Dr	Prestonsburg	KY	41653	606-886-3863	886-6943*
*Fax: Admissions ■ *TF:* 888-641-4132 ■ *Web:* www.bigsandy.kctcs.edu					
Mayo 513 3rd St	Paintsville	KY	41240	606-789-5321	789-9753
Web: www.kctcs.net/bigsandy					
Bluegrass Community & Technical College Cooper Campus					
Cooper Dr 203 Oswald Bldg	Lexington	KY	40506	859-246-6200	246-4666*
*Fax: Admissions ■ *TF:* 866-774-4872 ■ *Web:* www.bluegrass.kctcs.edu					
Elizabethtown Community & Technical College					
600 College Street Rd	Elizabethtown	KY	42701	270-769-2371	769-0736
TF: 877-246-2322 ■ *Web:* www.elizabethtown.kctcs.edu					
Hazard Community & Technical College 101 Votech Dr	Hazard	KY	41701	606-436-5721	439-2988*
*Fax: Admissions ■ *TF:* 800-246-7521 ■ *Web:* www.hazcc.kctcs.edu					
Hazard Campus 1 Community College Dr	Hazard	KY	41701	606-435-6101	487-8417*
*Fax: Admissions ■ *TF:* 800-246-7521 ■ *Web:* www.hazcc.kctcs.edu					
Lees Campus 601 Jefferson Ave	Jackson	KY	41339	606-666-7521	666-4312
TF: 800-246-7521 ■ *Web:* www.hazard.kctcs.edu					
Henderson Community College 2660 S Green St	Henderson	KY	42420	270-827-1867	831-9612*
*Fax: Admissions ■ *Web:* www.hencc.kctcs.net					
Hopkinsville Community College 720 North Dr	Hopkinsville	KY	42240	270-886-3921	886-0237*
*Fax: Admissions ■ *Web:* www.hopcc.kctcs.net					
Jefferson Community & Technical College 109 E Broadway	Louisville	KY	40202	502-584-0181	213-2540*
*Fax: Admissions ■ *Web:* www.jefferson.kctcs.edu					
Madisonville Community College 2000 College Dr	Madisonville	KY	42431	270-821-2250	824-1864*
*Fax: Admissions ■ *TF:* 866-227-4812 ■ *Web:* www.madisonville.kctcs.edu					
Maysville Community & Technical College 1755 US 68	Maysville	KY	41056	606-759-7141	759-5818
Web: www.maysville.kctcs.edu					
Saint Catharine College 2735 Bardstown Rd	Saint Catharine	KY	40061	859-336-5082	336-5031*
*Fax: Admissions ■ *Web:* www.sccky.edu					
Somerset Community College 808 Monticello St	Somerset	KY	42501	606-679-8501	676-9065
TF: 877-629-9722 ■ *Web:* www.somerset.kctcs.edu					
Southeast Kentucky Community & Technical College					
Cumberland 700 College Rd	Cumberland	KY	40823	606-589-2145	589-3175*
*Fax: Admissions ■ *TF:* 888-274-7322 ■ *Web:* www.secc.kctcs.edu					
Middlesboro 1300 Chichester Ave	Middlesboro	KY	40965	606-242-2145	248-3233
TF: 888-274-7322 ■ *Web:* www.secc.kctcs.edu					
Whitesburg 2 Long Ave	Whitesburg	KY	41858	606-633-0279	589-3377
TF: 888-274-7322 ■ *Web:* www.secc.kctcs.edu					
West Kentucky Community & Technical College					
4810 Alben Barkley Dr PO Box 7380	Paducah	KY	42002	270-554-9200	554-6203*
*Fax: Admissions ■ *Web:* www.westkentucky.kctcs.edu					

Louisiana

	City	State	ZIP	Phone	Fax
Baton Rouge Community College 5310 Florida Blvd	Baton Rouge	LA	70806	225-216-8000	216-8010*
*Fax: Admissions ■ *TF:* 800-601-4558 ■ *Web:* www.brcc.cc.la.us					
Bossier Parish Community College 6220 E Texas St	Bossier City	LA	71111	318-678-6000	678-6390
Web: www.bpcc.edu					
Elaine P Nunez Community College 3710 Paris Rd	Chalmette	LA	70043	504-278-7497	278-7480
TF: 866-825-1954 ■ *Web:* www.nunez.edu					
Louisiana Delta Community College 1201 Bayou Dr	Monroe	LA	71203	318-342-3700	342-3747
TF: 866-500-5322 ■ *Web:* www.ladelta.cc.la.us					
Louisiana State University Eunice PO Box 1129	Eunice	LA	70535	337-457-7311	550-1306*
*Fax: Admissions ■ *Web:* www.lsue.edu					
Southern University Shreveport 3050 ML King Jr Dr	Shreveport	LA	71107	318-674-3300	674-3344*
*Fax: Admissions ■ *TF:* 800-458-1472 ■ *Web:* www.susla.edu					

Maine

				Phone	Fax
Kennebec Valley Community College 92 Western Ave	Fairfield	ME	04937	207-453-5000	453-5010
TF: 800-528-5882 ■ *Web:* www.kvcc.me.edu					
Washington County Community College 1 College Dr	Calais	ME	04619	207-454-1000	454-1092
Web: www.wccc.me.edu					
York County Community College 112 College Dr	Wells	ME	04090	207-646-9282	641-0837
TF: 800-580-3820 ■ *Web:* www.yccc.edu					

Maryland

				Phone	Fax
Allegany College of Maryland 12401 Willowbrook Rd SE	Cumberland	MD	21502	301-784-5000	784-5027*
**Fax:* Admissions ■ *Web:* www.allegany.edu					
Anne Arundel Community College 101 College Pkwy	Arnold	MD	21012	410-647-7100	777-2827*
**Fax:* Admissions ■ *Web:* www.aacc.edu					
Baltimore City Community College 2901 Liberty Heights Ave	Baltimore	MD	21215	410-462-8000	462-8345*
**Fax:* Admissions ■ *TF:* 888-203-1261 ■ *Web:* www.bccc.edu					
Carroll Community College 1601 Washington Rd	Westminster	MD	21157	410-386-8000	386-8431*
**Fax:* Admissions ■ *Web:* www.carrollcc.edu					
Cecil Community College 1 Seahawk Dr	North East	MD	21901	410-287-6060	287-1001*
**Fax:* Admissions ■ *Web:* www.cecilcc.edu					
Chesapeake College PO Box 8	Wye Mills	MD	21679	410-758-1537	827-5878*
**Fax:* Admissions ■ *Web:* www.chesapeake.edu					
College of Southern Maryland					
La Plata 8730 Mitchell Rd PO Box 910	La Plata	MD	20646	301-934-2251	870-3008
Web: www.csmd.edu/about					
Leonardtown 22950 Hollywood Rd	Leonardtown	MD	20650	240-725-5300	725-5400*
**Fax:* Admissions ■ *TF:* 800-933-9177 ■ *Web:* www.csmd.edu					
Prince Frederick 115 Williams Rd	Prince Frederick	MD	20678	443-550-6000	550-6100
TF: 800-933-9177 ■ *Web:* www.csmd.edu					
Community College of Baltimore County					
Catonsville 800 S Rolling Rd	Catonsville	MD	21228	410-455-6050	719-6546*
**Fax:* Admissions ■ *Web:* www.ccbcmd.edu					
Dundalk 7200 Sollers Point Rd	Baltimore	MD	21222	410-282-6700	285-9903
Web: www.ccbcmd.edu					
Essex 7201 Rossville Blvd	Baltimore	MD	21237	410-682-6000	686-9503*
**Fax:* Admissions ■ *TF:* 800-832-0262 ■ *Web:* www.ccbcmd.edu					
Hunt Valley 11101 McCormick Rd	Hunt Valley	MD	21031	410-771-6835	527-0993
Web: www.ccbcmd.edu					
Owings Mills 110 Painters Mill Rd	Owings Mills	MD	21117	410-363-4111	363-6575
Web: www.ccbcmd.edu					
Frederick Community College 7932 Opossumtown Pike	Frederick	MD	21702	301-846-2400	846-2498
Web: www.frederick.edu					
Garrett College 687 Mosser Rd	McHenry	MD	21541	301-387-3000	387-3038*
**Fax:* Admissions ■ *Web:* www.garrettcollege.edu					
Hagerstown Community College 11400 Robinwood Dr	Hagerstown	MD	21742	301-790-2800	791-9165*
**Fax:* Admissions ■ *Web:* www.hagerstowncc.edu					
Harford Community College 401 Thomas Run Rd	Bel Air	MD	21015	410-879-8920	836-4169*
**Fax:* Admissions ■ *Web:* www.harford.edu					
Howard Community College 10901 Little Patuxent Pkwy	Columbia	MD	21044	410-772-4800	772-4589*
**Fax:* Admissions ■ *TF:* 800-234-9981 ■ *Web:* www.howardcc.edu					
Montgomery College					
Germantown 20200 Observation Dr	Germantown	MD	20876	301-353-7700	353-7815*
**Fax:* Admissions ■ *Web:* www.montgomerycollege.edu/gthome					
Rockville 51 Mannakee St	Rockville	MD	20850	301-279-5000	279-5037*
**Fax:* Admissions ■ *Web:* www.montgomerycollege.edu/rvhome					
Takoma Park/Silver Spring 7600 Takoma Ave	Takoma Park	MD	20912	301-650-1501	650-1497*
**Fax:* Admissions ■ *Web:* www.montgomerycollege.edu/tphome					
Prince George's Community College 301 Largo Rd	Largo	MD	20774	301-336-6000	322-0119*
**Fax:* Admissions ■ *Web:* www.pgcc.edu					
Wor-Wic Community College 32000 Campus Dr	Salisbury	MD	21804	410-334-2800	334-2954*
**Fax:* Admissions ■ *Web:* www.worwic.edu					

Massachusetts

				Phone	Fax
Berkshire Community College 1350 West St	Pittsfield	MA	01201	413-499-4660	447-7840
Web: www.berkshirecc.edu					
Bristol Community College 777 Elsbree St	Fall River	MA	02720	508-678-2811	730-3255*
**Fax:* Admissions ■ *Web:* www.bristol.mass.edu					
Attleboro 135 County St	Attleboro	MA	02703	508-226-2484	222-7638
TF: 888-710-8999 ■ *Web:* srvweb.bristol.mass.edu					
New Bedford 188 Union St	New Bedford	MA	02740	508-984-8226	730-3264
Web: srvweb.bristol.mass.edu					
Bunker Hill Community College					
Charlestown 250 New Rutherford Ave	Boston	MA	02129	617-228-2000	228-2082*
**Fax:* Admissions ■ *Web:* www.bhcc.mass.edu					
Chelsea 175 Hawthorne St Bellingham Sq	Chelsea	MA	02150	617-228-2101	228-2106
Web: www.bhcc.mass.edu					
Cape Cod Community College 2240 Iyanough Rd	West Barnstable	MA	02668	508-362-2131	375-4089*
**Fax:* Admissions ■ *TF:* 877-846-3672 ■ *Web:* www.capecod.edu					
Dean College 99 Main St	Franklin	MA	02038	508-541-1508	541-8726*
**Fax:* Admissions ■ *TF:* 877-879-3326 ■ *Web:* www.dean.edu					
Fisher College 118 Beacon St	Boston	MA	02116	617-236-8800	236-5473*
**Fax:* Admissions ■ *TF:* 800-446-1226 ■ *Web:* www.fisher.edu					
Greenfield Community College 1 College Dr	Greenfield	MA	01301	413-775-1837	775-1838*
**Fax:* Admissions ■ *Web:* www.gcc.mass.edu					
Holyoke Community College 303 Homestead Ave	Holyoke	MA	01040	413-538-7000	552-2192*
**Fax:* Admissions ■ *Web:* www.hcc.edu					
Marian Court College 35 Littles Pt Rd	Swampscott	MA	01907	781-595-6768	595-3560*
**Fax:* Admissions ■ *TF:* 800-418-9868 ■ *Web:* www.mariancourt.edu					
Massachusetts Bay Community College					
Framingham 19 Flagg Dr	Framingham	MA	01702	508-270-4000	872-4067
Web: www.massbay.edu					
Wellesley Hills 50 Oakland St	Wellesley Hills	MA	02481	781-239-3000	239-1047
Web: www.massbay.edu					
Massasoit Community College 1 Massasoit Blvd	Brockton	MA	02302	508-588-9100	427-1255*
**Fax:* Admissions ■ *Web:* www.massasoit.mass.edu					
Middlesex Community College 590 Springs Rd	Bedford	MA	01730	781-275-8910	280-3603
Web: www.middlesex.mass.edu					
Mount Wachusett Community College 444 Green St	Gardner	MA	01440	978-632-6600	630-9554*
**Fax:* Admissions ■ *Web:* www.mwcc.mass.edu					
North Shore Community College 1 Ferncroft Rd	Danvers	MA	01923	978-762-4000	762-4015*
**Fax:* Admissions ■ *Web:* www.northshore.edu					
Northern Essex Community College 100 Elliott St	Haverhill	MA	01830	978-556-3000	556-3729*
**Fax:* Admissions ■ *Web:* www.necc.mass.edu					
Quincy College 34 Coddington St	Quincy	MA	02169	617-984-1600	984-1794
TF: 800-698-1700 ■ *Web:* www.quincycollege.edu					
Plymouth 385 Court St	Plymouth	MA	02369	508-747-0400	747-8168*
**Fax:* Admissions ■ *Web:* www.quincycollege.edu/qc/about/p_campus.htm					
Quinsigamond Community College 670 W Boylston St	Worcester	MA	01606	508-853-2300	854-4357*
**Fax:* Admissions ■ *Web:* www.qcc.edu					
Roxbury Community College 1234 Columbus Ave	Roxbury Crossing	MA	02120	617-541-5310	427-5316*
**Fax:* Admitting ■ *Web:* www.rcc.mass.edu					
Springfield Technical Community College					
1 Armory Sq PO Box 900	Springfield	MA	01102	413-781-7822	746-0344*
**Fax:* Admissions ■ *Web:* www.stcc.edu					

Michigan

				Phone	Fax
Alpena Community College 666 Johnson St	Alpena	MI	49707	989-356-9021	358-7561
TF: 888-468-6222 ■ *Web:* www.alpena.cc.mi.us					
Bay Mills Community College 12214 W Lakeshore Dr	Brimley	MI	49715	906-248-3354	248-3351
TF: 800-844-2622 ■ *Web:* www.bmcc.edu					
Bay de Noc Community College 2001 N Lincoln Rd	Escanaba	MI	49829	906-786-5802	786-8515*
**Fax:* Admissions ■ *TF:* 800-221-2001 ■ *Web:* www.baydenoc.cc.mi.us					
Bay De Noc Community College West					
1401 S Carpenter Ave	Iron Mountain	MI	49801	906-774-8547	774-1910
Web: www.baydenoc.cc.mi.us/newdickin.html					
Charles Stewart Mott Community College 1401 E Court St	Flint	MI	48503	810-762-0200	762-5611
Web: www.mcc.edu					
Delta College 1961 Delta Rd	University Center	MI	48710	989-686-9000	667-2202*
**Fax:* Admissions ■ *Web:* www.delta.edu					
Glen Oaks Community College 62249 Shimmel Rd	Centreville	MI	49032	269-467-9945	467-9068*
**Fax:* Admissions ■ *TF:* 888-994-7818 ■ *Web:* www.glenoaks.edu					
Gogebic Community College E 4946 Jackson Rd	Ironwood	MI	49938	906-932-4231	932-0868*
**Fax:* Admissions ■ *TF:* 800-682-5910 ■ *Web:* www.gogebic.cc.mi.us					
Grand Rapids Community College 143 Bostwick Ave NE	Grand Rapids	MI	49503	616-234-4000	234-4107*
**Fax:* Admissions ■ *Web:* www.grcc.edu					
Henry Ford Community College 5101 Evergreen Rd	Dearborn	MI	48128	313-845-9600	845-9891*
**Fax:* Admissions ■ *TF:* 800-585-4322 ■ *Web:* www.hfcc.edu					
Jackson Community College 2111 Emmons Rd	Jackson	MI	49201	517-787-0800	796-8631*
**Fax:* Admissions ■ *TF:* 888-522-7344 ■ *Web:* www.jccmi.edu					
Hillsdale 3120 W Carleton Rd PO Box 712	Hillsdale	MI	49242	517-437-3343	437-0232
Web: www.jccmi.edu/hillsdale					
Kalamazoo Valley Community College					
Arcadia Commons 202 N Rose St	Kalamazoo	MI	49003	269-373-7800	373-7892
Web: puma.kvcc.edu/accweb					
Texas Township 6767 W 'O' Ave	Kalamazoo	MI	49003	269-488-4400	488-4161*
**Fax:* Admissions ■ *Web:* www.kvcc.edu					
Kellogg Community College 450 North Ave	Battle Creek	MI	49017	269-965-3931	966-4089*
**Fax:* Admissions ■ *Web:* www.kellogg.cc.mi.us					
Keweenaw Bay Ojibwa Community College 111 Beartown Rd	Baraga	MI	49908	906-353-4600	353-8107
Web: www.kbocc.org					
Kirtland Community College 10775 N St Helen Rd	Roscommon	MI	48653	989-275-5121	275-6789
Web: www.kirtland.edu					
Lake Michigan College 2755 E Napier Ave	Benton Harbor	MI	49022	269-927-3571	927-6875*
**Fax:* Admissions ■ *Web:* www.lakemichigancollege.edu					
Bertrand Crossing 1905 Foundation Dr	Niles	MI	49120	269-695-1391	695-2999
TF: 800-252-1562 ■ *Web:* www.lakemichigancollege.edu					
South Haven 125 Veterans Blvd	South Haven	MI	49090	269-639-8442	637-7515
TF: 800-252-1562 ■ *Web:* www.lakemichigancollege.edu					
Lansing Community College 520 N Washington Sq	Lansing	MI	48901	517-483-1957	483-9668*
**Fax:* Admissions ■ *TF:* 800-644-4522 ■ *Web:* www.lansing.cc.mi.us					
Macomb Community College					
Center 44575 Garfield Rd	Clinton Township	MI	48038	586-286-2000	286-4787*
**Fax:* Admissions ■ *TF:* 866-622-6624 ■ *Web:* www.macomb.edu					
South 14500 E 12-Mile Rd	Warren	MI	48088	586-445-7000	445-7140*
**Fax:* Admissions ■ *TF:* 866-622-6624 ■ *Web:* www.macomb.edu					
Mid Michigan Community College 1375 S Clare Ave	Harrison	MI	48625	989-386-6622	386-6613*
**Fax:* Admissions ■ *Web:* www.midmich.cc.mi.us					
Mount Pleasant 5805 E Pickard Ave	Mount Pleasant	MI	48858	989-773-6622	772-2386
Web: www.midmich.cc.mi.us					
Monroe County Community College 1555 S Raisinville Rd	Monroe	MI	48161	734-242-7300	242-9711*
**Fax:* Admissions ■ *TF:* 877-937-6222 ■ *Web:* www.monroeccc.edu					
Montcalm Community College 2800 College Dr	Sidney	MI	48885	989-328-2111	328-2950*
**Fax:* Admissions ■ *Web:* www.montcalm.edu					
Mott Community College 1401 E Court St	Flint	MI	48503	810-762-0200	762-5611
Web: www.mcc.edu					
Muskegon Community College 221 S Quarterline Rd	Muskegon	MI	49442	231-773-9131	777-0255*
**Fax:* Admissions ■ *TF:* 866-711-4622 ■ *Web:* www.muskegon.cc.mi.us					
North Central Michigan College 1515 Howard St	Petoskey	MI	49770	231-348-6605	348-6672*
**Fax:* Admissions ■ *TF:* 888-298-6605 ■ *Web:* www.ncmich.edu					
Northwestern Michigan College 1701 E Front St	Traverse City	MI	49686	231-995-1000	995-1339*
**Fax:* Admissions ■ *TF:* 800-748-0566 ■ *Web:* www.nmc.edu					
Oakland Community College 2480 Opdyke Rd	Bloomfield Hills	MI	48304	248-341-2000	341-2199
Web: www.oaklandcc.edu					
Auburn Hills 2900 Featherstone Rd	Auburn Hills	MI	48326	248-232-4100	
Web: www.oaklandcc.edu/campuses/ah.htm					
Highland Lakes 7350 Cooley Lake Rd	Waterford	MI	48327	248-942-3100	942-3113
Web: www.oaklandcc.edu/campuses/hl.htm					
Orchard Ridge 27055 Orchard Lake Rd	Farmington Hills	MI	48334	248-522-3400	522-3530*
**Fax:* Library ■ *Web:* www.oaklandcc.edu/campuses/or.htm					
Royal Oak 739 S Washington Ave	Royal Oak	MI	48067	248-246-2400	246-2520*
**Fax:* Library ■ *Web:* www.oaklandcc.edu/campuses/ro.htm					
Southfield 22322 Rutland Dr	Southfield	MI	48075	248-233-2700	233-2828*
**Fax:* Library ■ *Web:* www.oaklandcc.edu/campuses/sf.htm					
Saginaw Chippewa Tribal College 2274 Enterprise Dr	Mount Pleasant	MI	48858	989-775-4123	775-4528
Web: www.sagchip.org/tribalcollege					
Saint Clair County Community College					
323 Erie St PO Box 5015	Port Huron	MI	48061	810-984-3881	989-5541
Web: www.sc4.edu					
Schoolcraft College 18600 Haggerty Rd	Livonia	MI	48152	734-462-4400	462-4553*
**Fax:* Admissions ■ *Web:* www.schoolcraft.edu					
Southwestern Michigan College 58900 Cherry Grove Rd	Dowagiac	MI	49047	269-782-1000	782-1331*
**Fax:* Admissions ■ *TF:* 800-456-8675 ■ *Web:* www.smc.cc.mi.us					
Niles Area 2229 US 12 E	Niles	MI	49120	269-687-1600	684-2281
TF: 800-456-8675 ■ *Web:* www.smc.cc.mi.us					
Washtenaw Community College					
4800 E Huron River Dr PO Box 1610	Ann Arbor	MI	48106	734-973-3300	677-5408*
**Fax:* Admissions ■ *Web:* www.wccnet.edu					
Wayne County Community College					
Downriver 21000 Northline Rd	Taylor	MI	48180	734-946-3500	374-0240
Web: www.wcccd.edu/campus_information					
Downtown 1001 W Fort St	Detroit	MI	48226	313-496-2758	961-9648
Web: www.wcccd.edu					
Eastern 5901 Conner	Detroit	MI	48213	313-922-3311	922-1104
Web: www.wcccd.edu/campus_information					
Northwest 8551 Greenfield Rd	Detroit	MI	48228	313-943-4000	943-4025
Web: www.wcccd.edu/campus_information					
Western 9555 Haggerty Rd	Belleville	MI	48111	734-699-7008	699-7152
Web: www.wcccd.edu/campus_information					
West Shore Community College PO Box 277	Scottville	MI	49454	231-845-6211	845-3944*
**Fax:* Admissions ■ *TF:* 800-848-9722 ■ *Web:* www.westshore.edu					

Minnesota

Phone Fax

Alexandria Technical College 1601 Jefferson St. .... Alexandria MN 56308 320-762-0221 762-4501
TF: 888-234-1222 ■ *Web:* www.alextech.org
Anoka-Ramsey Community College
11200 Mississippi Blvd NW.... Coon Rapids MN 55433 763-433-1100 433-1521
Web: www.anokaramsey.edu
Cambridge 300 Polk St S.... Cambridge MN 55008 763-689-7000 433-1841*
*Fax: Admissions ■ *Web:* www.anokaramsey.edu
Central Lakes College
Brainerd 501 W College Dr .... Brainerd MN 56401 218-855-8000 855-8057*
*Fax: Admissions ■ *TF:* 800-933-0346 ■ *Web:* www.clcmn.edu
Staples 1830 Airport Rd.... Staples MN 56479 218-894-5100 894-5185
TF: 800-247-6836 ■ *Web:* www.clcmn.edu
Century College 3300 Century Ave N .... White Bear Lake MN 55110 651-779-3200 773-1796*
*Fax: Admissions ■ *TF:* 800-228-1978 ■ *Web:* www.century.cc.mn.us
Fond du Lac Tribal & Community College 2101 14th St.... Cloquet MN 55720 218-879-0800 879-0814
TF: 800-657-3712 ■ *Web:* www.fdltcc.edu
Hibbing Community College 1515 E 25th St .... Hibbing MN 55746 218-262-6700 262-6717*
*Fax: Admissions ■ *TF:* 800-224-4422 ■ *Web:* www.hcc.mnscu.edu
Inver Hills Community College 2500 80th St E .... Inver Grove Heights MN 55076 651-450-8500 450-8677*
*Fax: Admissions ■ *Web:* www.inverhills.edu
Itasca Community College 1851 E Hwy 169 .... Grand Rapids MN 55744 218-327-4460 327-4350*
*Fax: Admissions ■ *TF:* 800-996-6422 ■ *Web:* www.itascacc.edu
Lake Superior College 2101 Trinity Rd.... Duluth MN 55811 218-733-7600 733-5945*
*Fax: Admissions ■ *TF:* 800-432-2884 ■ *Web:* www.lsc.cc.mn.us
Leech Lake Tribal College PO Box 180 .... Cass Lake MN 56633 218-335-4200 335-4209
TF: 800-627-3529 ■ *Web:* www.lltc.org
Mesabi Range Community & Technical College
1100 Industrial Park Dr PO Box 648.... Eveleth MN 55734 218-741-3095 744-7466
TF: 800-657-3860 ■ *Web:* www.mr.mnscu.edu
Minneapolis Community & Technical College
1501 Hennepin Ave .... Minneapolis MN 55403 612-659-6200 659-6210*
*Fax: Admissions ■ *TF:* 800-247-0911 ■ *Web:* www.minneapolis.edu
Minnesota State Community & Technical College
Detroit Lakes 900 Hwy 34E .... Detroit Lakes MN 56501 218-846-3700 846-3794
TF: 800-492-4836 ■ *Web:* www.minnesota.edu/campuses/detroit_lakes
Fergus Falls 1414 College Way .... Fergus Falls MN 56537 218-736-1500 736-1510*
*Fax: Admissions ■ *TF:* 877-450-3322 ■
Web: www.minnesota.edu/campuses/fergus_falls
Moorhead 1900 28th Ave S.... Moorhead MN 56560 218-299-6500 299-6584*
*Fax: Admissions ■ *TF:* 800-426-5603 ■ *Web:* www.minnesota.edu/campuses/moorhead
Minnesota West Community & Technical College
1450 Collegeway .... Worthington MN 56187 507-372-3400 372-5803*
*Fax: Admissions ■ *TF:* 800-657-3966 ■ *Web:* www.mnwest.edu
Normandale Community College 9700 France Ave S.... Bloomington MN 55431 952-487-8200 487-8230*
*Fax: Admissions ■ *TF:* 866-880-8740 ■ *Web:* www.normandale.edu
North Hennepin Community College 7411 85th Ave N .... Brooklyn Park MN 55445 763-424-0702 424-0929*
*Fax: Admissions ■ *TF:* 800-818-0395 ■ *Web:* www.nhcc.edu
Northland Community & Technical College
1101 US Hwy 1 E .... Thief River Falls MN 56701 218-681-0701 681-0774*
*Fax: Admissions ■ *TF:* 800-959-6282 ■ *Web:* www.northlandcollege.edu
East Grand Forks 2022 Central Ave NE.... East Grand Forks MN 56721 218-773-3441 773-4502
TF: 800-451-3441 ■ *Web:* www.northlandcollege.edu
Rainy River Community College 1501 Hwy 71.... International Falls MN 56649 218-285-7722 285-2239*
*Fax: Admissions ■ *TF:* 800-456-3996 ■ *Web:* www.rrcc.mnscu.edu
Riverland Community College 1900 8th Ave NW.... Austin MN 55912 507-433-0600 433-0515
TF: 800-247-5039 ■ *Web:* www.riverland.edu
Rochester Community & Technical College 851 30th Ave SE .... Rochester MN 55904 507-285-7210 280-3529*
*Fax: Admissions ■ *TF:* 800-247-1296 ■ *Web:* www.rctc.edu
South Central College
Faribault 1225 3rd St SW .... Faribault MN 55021 507-332-5800 332-5888
TF: 800-422-0391 ■ *Web:* www.southcentral.edu
Mankato 1920 Lee Blvd.... North Mankato MN 56003 507-389-7200 388-9951
TF: 800-722-9359 ■ *Web:* www.southcentral.edu
Vermilion Community College 1900 E Camp St.... Ely MN 55731 218-365-7200 365-7218
TF: 800-657-3608 ■ *Web:* www.vcc.edu
White Earth Tribal & Community College
210 Main St S PO Box 478.... Mahnomen MN 56557 218-935-0417 936-5736
Web: www.wetcc.org

Mississippi

Phone Fax

Coahoma Community College 3240 Friars Point Rd .... Clarksdale MS 38614 662-667-2571 621-4297*
*Fax: Admissions ■ *Web:* www.coahomacc.edu
Copiah-Lincoln Community College
1028 JC Redd Dr PO Box 649.... Wesson MS 39191 601-643-5101 643-8225*
*Fax: Admissions ■ *Web:* www.colin.edu
Natchez 11 Co-Lin Cir .... Natchez MS 39120 601-442-9111 446-1222*
*Fax: Admissions ■ *Web:* www.colin.edu/natchez
East Central Community College PO Box 129 .... Decatur MS 39327 601-635-2126 635-4060*
*Fax: Admissions ■ *TF:* 877-462-3222 ■ *Web:* www.eccc.cc.ms.us
East Mississippi Community College
1512 Kemper St PO Box 158.... Scooba MS 39358 662-476-8442 476-5038*
*Fax: Admissions ■ *Web:* www.emcc.cc.ms.us
Hinds Community College 501 E Main St PO Box 1100 .... Raymond MS 39154 601-857-5261 857-3539*
*Fax: Admissions ■ *TF:* 800-446-3722 ■ *Web:* www.hindscc.edu/
Rankin 3805 Hwy 80 E .... Pearl MS 39208 601-932-5237 936-1833*
*Fax: Admissions ■ *Web:* www.hindscc.edu/rankin
Utica Hwy 18 W.... Utica MS 39175 601-354-2327 885-6026*
*Fax: Admissions ■ *TF:* 800-446-3722 ■ *Web:* www.hindscc.edu/utica
Holmes Community College PO Box 369 .... Goodman MS 39079 662-472-2312 472-9152*
*Fax: Admissions ■ *TF:* 800-465-6374 ■ *Web:* www.holmescc.edu
Itawamba Community College
Fulton 602 W Hill St.... Fulton MS 38843 662-862-8000 862-8234*
*Fax: Admissions ■ *Web:* www.iccms.edu
Tupelo 2176 S Eason Blvd.... Tupelo MS 38804 662-620-5000 620-5315*
*Fax: Admissions ■ *Web:* www.iccms.edu
Jones County Junior College 900 S Court St.... Ellisville MS 39437 601-477-4000 477-4258*
*Fax: Admissions ■ *Web:* www.jcjc.cc.ms.us
Meridian Community College 910 Hwy 19 N.... Meridian MS 39307 601-483-8241 484-8838*
*Fax: Admissions ■ *TF:* 800-622-8431 ■ *Web:* www.mcc.cc.ms.us
Mississippi Delta Community College PO Box 668.... Moorhead MS 38761 662-246-6322 246-6288
Web: www.msdelta.edu
Mississippi Gulf Coast Community College
51 Main St PO Box 548.... Perkinston MS 39573 601-928-5211 928-6345*
*Fax: Admitting ■ *TF:* 866-735-1122 ■ *Web:* www.mgccc.edu
Jackson County PO Box 100.... Gautier MS 39553 228-497-9602 497-7873
TF: 866-735-1122 ■ *Web:* www.mgccc.edu
Jefferson Davis 2226 Switzer Rd.... Gulfport MS 39507 228-896-3355 896-2520*
*Fax: Admissions ■ *TF:* 866-735-1122 ■ *Web:* www.mgccc.edu
Northeast Mississippi Community College
101 Cunningham Blvd .... Booneville MS 38829 662-728-7751 720-7405*
*Fax: Admissions ■ *TF:* 800-555-2154 ■ *Web:* www.nemcc.edu

Phone Fax

Northwest Mississippi Community College 4975 Hwy 51 N.... Senatobia MS 38668 662-562-3200 562-3221
Web: www.northwestms.edu
Pearl River Community College 101 Highway 11 N.... Poplarville MS 39470 601-403-1000 403-1339*
*Fax: Admissions ■ *Web:* www.prcc.edu
Southwest Mississippi Community College 1156 College Dr .... Summit MS 39666 601-276-2000 276-3888
Web: www.smcc.edu

Missouri

Phone Fax

Cottey College 1000 W Austin Blvd .... Nevada MO 64772 417-667-8181 667-8103*
*Fax: Admissions ■ *TF:* 888-526-8839 ■ *Web:* www.cottey.edu
Crowder College 601 Laclede Ave.... Neosho MO 64850 417-451-3223 455-5731*
*Fax: Admissions ■ *TF:* 866-238-7788 ■ *Web:* www.crowder.edu
Watley Center 504 E 13th St .... Cassville MO 65625 417-847-1706 847-1367
Web: www.crowder.edu/locations/cassville
East Central College 1964 Prairie Dell Rd .... Union MO 63084 636-583-5193 583-1897*
*Fax: Admissions ■ *Web:* www.eastcentral.edu
Jefferson College 1000 Viking Dr.... Hillsboro MO 63050 636-789-3951 789-5103*
*Fax: Admissions ■ *Web:* www.jeffco.edu
Maple Woods Community College 2601 NE Barry Rd .... Kansas City MO 64156 816-437-3000 437-3351*
*Fax: Admissions ■ *Web:* mcckc.edu
Metropolitan Community College
Blue River 20301 E 78 Hwy.... Independence MO 64057 816-220-6500 220-6577*
*Fax: Admissions ■ *Web:* mcckc.edu
Longview 500 SW Longview Rd .... Lee's Summit MO 64081 816-672-2000 672-2378*
*Fax: Admissions ■ *Web:* mcckc.edu
Penn Valley 3201 SW Trafficway.... Kansas City MO 64111 816-759-4000 759-4161
Web: mcckc.edu
Mineral Area College 5270 Frat River Rd PO Box 1000 .... Park Hills MO 63601 573-431-4593 518-2166*
*Fax: Admissions ■ *Web:* www.mineralarea.edu
Moberly Area Community College 101 College Ave.... Moberly MO 65270 660-263-4110 263-2406
TF: 800-622-2070 ■ *Web:* www.macc.edu
North Central Missouri College 1301 Main St.... Trenton MO 64683 660-359-3948 359-2211*
*Fax: Admissions ■ *TF:* 800-880-6180 ■ *Web:* www.ncmc.cc.mo.us
Ozarks Technical Community College 1001 E Chestnut Expy .... Springfield MO 65802 417-447-7500 447-6906*
*Fax: Admissions ■ *Web:* www.otc.edu
Saint Charles Community College 4601 Mid Rivers Mall Dr.... Saint Peters MO 63376 636-922-8000 922-8236
Web: www.stchas.edu
Saint Louis Community College 300 S Broadway .... Saint Louis MO 63102 314-539-5000 539-5170*
*Fax: Admissions ■ *Web:* www.stlcc.edu
Florissant Valley 3400 Pershall Rd .... Saint Louis MO 63135 314-595-4200 595-2224*
*Fax: Admissions ■ *Web:* www.stlcc.edu/fv
Forest Park 5600 Oakland Ave.... Saint Louis MO 63110 314-644-9100 644-9375*
*Fax: Admissions ■ *Web:* www.stlcc.edu/fp
Meramec 11333 Big Bend Blvd .... Kirkwood MO 63122 314-984-7500 984-7051*
*Fax: Admissions ■ *Web:* www.stlcc.edu/mc
State Fair Community College 3201 W 16th St.... Sedalia MO 65301 660-530-5800 596-7472*
*Fax: Admissions ■ *Web:* www.sfcc.cc.mo.us
Three Rivers Community College 2080 Three Rivers Blvd.... Poplar Bluff MO 63901 573-840-9600 840-9058*
*Fax: Admissions ■ *TF:* 877-879-8722 ■ *Web:* www.trcc.edu

Montana

Phone Fax

Blackfeet Community College PO Box 819 .... Browning MT 59417 406-338-5421 338-3272*
*Fax: Admissions ■ *TF:* 800-549-7457 ■ *Web:* www.bfcc.org
Chief Dull Knife College PO Box 98.... Lame Deer MT 59043 406-477-6215 477-6219
Web: www.cdkc.edu
Dawson Community College PO Box 421.... Glendive MT 59330 406-377-3396 377-8132*
*Fax: Admissions ■ *TF:* 800-821-8320 ■ *Web:* www.dawson.cc.mt.us
Flathead Valley Community College 777 Grandview Dr .... Kalispell MT 59901 406-756-3822 756-3815
TF: 800-313-3822 ■ *Web:* www.fvcc.edu
Libby 225 Commerce Way.... Libby MT 59923 406-293-2721 293-5112*
*Fax: Admissions ■ *Web:* www.fvcc.edu
Fort Belknap College PO Box 159 .... Harlem MT 59526 406-353-2607 353-2898*
*Fax: Admissions ■ *Web:* www.fbcc.edu
Fort Peck Community College PO Box 398 .... Poplar MT 59255 406-768-6300 768-6301
Web: www.fpcc.edu
Little Big Horn College 1 Forestry Ln PO Box 370 .... Crow Agency MT 59022 406-638-3104 638-3169
Web: www.lbhc.cc.mt.us
Miles Community College 2715 Dickinson St .... Miles City MT 59301 406-874-6100 874-6283*
*Fax: Admissions ■ *TF:* 800-541-9281 ■ *Web:* www.milescc.edu
Salish Kootenai College PO Box 70.... Pablo MT 59855 406-275-4800 275-4801*
*Fax: Admissions ■ *TF:* 877-752-6553 ■ *Web:* www.skc.edu
Stone Child College RR 1 Box 1082 .... Box Elder MT 59521 406-395-4313 395-4836*
*Fax: Admissions ■ *Web:* www.montana.edu/wwwscc

Nebraska

Phone Fax

Central Community College
Columbus 4500 63rd St PO Box 1027 .... Columbus NE 68602 402-564-7132 562-1201*
*Fax: Admissions ■ *Web:* www.cccneb.edu
Grand Island 3134 W Hwy 34 .... Grand Island NE 68802 308-398-7410 398-7531*
*Fax: Admissions ■ *Web:* www.cccneb.edu
Hastings PO Box 1024.... Hastings NE 68902 402-463-9811 461-2454*
*Fax: Admissions ■ *Web:* www.cccneb.edu
Little Priest Tribal College PO Box 270.... Winnebago NE 68071 402-878-2380 878-2355
Web: www.lptc.bia.edu
McCook Community College 1205 E 3rd St.... McCook NE 69001 308-345-8100 345-8180*
*Fax: Admissions ■ *TF:* 800-658-4348 ■ *Web:* www.mpcc.edu
Metropolitan Community College PO Box 3777 .... Omaha NE 68103 402-457-2400 457-2788*
*Fax: Admissions ■ *TF:* 800-228-9553 ■ *Web:* www.mccneb.edu
Elkhorn Valley 829 N 204th .... Elkhorn NE 68022 402-289-1200
Web: www.mccneb.edu
Nebraska Indian Community College PO Box 428.... Macy NE 68039 402-837-5078 837-4183*
*Fax: Admissions ■ *Web:* www.thenicc.edu/
North Platte Community College
North 1101 Halligan Dr .... North Platte NE 69101 308-535-3601 534-5767*
*Fax: Admissions ■ *TF:* 800-658-4308 ■ *Web:* www.mpcc.edu
South 601 W State Farm Rd .... North Platte NE 69101 308-535-3700 535-3794
TF: 800-658-4308 ■ *Web:* www.mpcc.edu
Northeast Community College 801 E Benjamin Ave PO Box 469 .... Norfolk NE 68702 402-371-2020 844-7396*
*Fax: Admissions ■ *Web:* www.northeastcollege.com
Southeast Community College
Beatrice 4771 W Scott Rd.... Beatrice NE 68310 402-228-3468 228-2218*
*Fax: Admissions ■ *TF:* 800-233-5027 ■ *Web:* www.southeast.edu
Lincoln 8800 'O' St .... Lincoln NE 68520 402-471-3333 437-2404*
*Fax: Admissions ■ *TF:* 800-642-4075 ■ *Web:* www.southeast.edu
Western Nebraska Community College 1601 E 27th St.... Scottsbluff NE 69361 308-635-3606 635-6732
TF: 800-348-4435 ■ *Web:* www.wncc.net

Nevada

				Phone	Fax
Community College of Southern Nevada					
Cheyenne 3200 E Cheyenne Ave	North Las Vegas	NV	89030	702-651-4000	651-4811*
**Fax:* Admissions ■ *TF:* 800-492-5728 ■ *Web:* www.ccsn.nevada.edu/cy					
Henderson 700 College Dr	Henderson	NV	89002	702-651-3000	651-3509*
**Fax:* Admissions ■ *Web:* www.ccsn.nevada.edu/hn					
West Charleston 6375 W Charleston Blvd	Las Vegas	NV	89146	702-651-5610	651-7495*
**Fax:* Admissions ■ *Web:* www.ccsn.nevada.edu/wc					
Truckee Meadows Community College					
7000 Dandini Blvd Red Mountain Bldg Rm 319	Reno	NV	89512	775-673-7042	673-7028*
**Fax:* Admissions ■ *Web:* www.tmcc.edu					
Western Nevada Community College 2201 W College Pkwy	Carson City	NV	89703	775-445-3000	445-3151
TF: 800-748-5690 ■ *Web:* www.wncc.edu					
Douglas 1680 Bently Pkwy S	Minden	NV	89423	775-782-2413	782-2415
Web: www.wncc.edu/location/douglascampus.php					
Fallon 160 Campus Way	Fallon	NV	89406	775-423-7565	423-8029
Web: www.wncc.edu/fallon					

New Hampshire

				Phone	Fax
New Hampshire Community Technical College					
Berlin 2020 Riverside Dr	Berlin	NH	03570	603-752-1113	752-6335
TF: 800-445-4525 ■ *Web:* www.berlin.nhctc.edu					
Claremont 1 College Dr	Claremont	NH	03743	603-542-7744	543-1844
TF: 800-837-0658 ■ *Web:* www.claremont.nhctc.edu					
Laconia 379 Belmont Rd	Laconia	NH	03246	603-524-3207	524-8084
TF: 800-357-2992 ■ *Web:* www.laconia.nhctc.edu					
Manchester 1066 Front St	Manchester	NH	03102	603-668-6706	668-5354
TF: 800-924-3445 ■ *Web:* www.ms.nhctc.edu					
Nashua 505 Amherst St	Nashua	NH	03063	603-882-6923	882-8690
TF: 800-247-3420 ■ *Web:* www.nashua.nhctc.edu					
Stratham 277 Portsmouth Ave	Stratham	NH	03885	603-772-1194	772-1198*
**Fax:* Admissions ■ *Web:* ms.nhctc.edu					
New Hampshire Technical Institute 31 College Dr	Concord	NH	03301	603-271-6484	271-7139*
**Fax:* Admissions ■ *TF:* 800-247-0179 ■ *Web:* www.nhti.edu					

New Jersey

				Phone	Fax
Assumption College for Sisters					
Mallinckrodt Convent 350 Bernardsville Rd	Mendham	NJ	07945	973-543-6528	543-9459*
**Fax:* Admissions ■ *Web:* www.acscollegeforsisters.org					
Atlantic Cape Community College 5100 Black Horse Pike	Mays Landing	NJ	08330	609-343-4900	343-4921*
**Fax:* Admissions ■ *Web:* www.atlantic.edu					
Bergen Community College 400 Paramus Rd	Paramus	NJ	07652	201-447-7200	670-7973*
**Fax:* Admissions ■ *Web:* www.bergen.edu					
Brookdale Community College 765 Newman Springs Rd	Lincroft	NJ	07738	732-842-1900	224-2271*
**Fax:* Admissions ■ *Web:* www.brookdalecc.edu					
Burlington County College					
Rt 530 Pemberton Browns Mills Rd	Pemberton	NJ	08068	609-894-9311	726-0401*
**Fax:* Admissions ■ *Web:* www.bcc.edu					
Camden County College PO Box 200 College Dr	Blackwood	NJ	08012	856-227-7200	374-4917
TF: 888-228-2466 ■ *Web:* www.camdencc.edu					
Camden City 601 Cooper St	Camden	NJ	08102	856-338-1817	968-1399*
**Fax:* Admissions ■ *Web:* www.camdencc.edu/camdencampus					
County College of Morris 214 Center Grove Rd	Randolph	NJ	07869	973-328-5000	328-5199*
**Fax:* Admissions ■ *TF:* 888-226-8001 ■ *Web:* www.ccm.edu					
Cumberland County College 3322 College Dr	Vineland	NJ	08360	856-691-8600	691-6157*
**Fax:* Admissions ■ *Web:* www.cccnj.net					
Essex County College 303 University Ave	Newark	NJ	07102	973-877-3000	877-3446*
**Fax:* Admissions ■ *Web:* www.essex.edu					
West Essex 730 Bloomfield Ave	West Caldwell	NJ	07006	973-877-3000	364-0881*
**Fax:* Admissions ■ *Web:* www.essex.edu/westessex					
Gloucester County College 1400 Tanyard Rd	Sewell	NJ	08080	856-468-5000	468-8498*
**Fax:* Admissions ■ *Web:* www.gccnj.edu					
Hudson County Community College 162 Sip Ave	Jersey City	NJ	07306	201-714-7200	714-2136*
**Fax:* Admissions ■ *Web:* www.hccc.edu					
Mercer County Community College PO Box B	Trenton	NJ	08690	609-586-4800	586-6944
TF: 800-392-6222 ■ *Web:* www.mccc.edu					
Kerney Center N Broad & Academy St	Trenton	NJ	08608	609-586-4800	570-3106
TF: 800-392-6222 ■ *Web:* www.mccc.edu/welcome_kerney.shtml					
West Windsor 1200 Old Trenton Rd	West Windsor	NJ	08550	609-586-4800	570-3861*
**Fax:* Admissions ■ *TF:* 800-392-6222 ■ *Web:* www.mccc.edu					
Middlesex County College 2600 Woodbridge Ave PO Box 3050	Edison	NJ	08818	732-548-6000	906-7728*
**Fax:* Admissions ■ *Web:* www.middlesex.cc.nj.us					
Ocean County College PO Box 2001	Toms River	NJ	08754	732-255-0400	255-0444
Web: www.ocean.edu					
Passaic County Community College 1 College Blvd	Paterson	NJ	07505	973-684-6800	684-6778*
**Fax:* Admissions ■ *Web:* www.pccc.cc.nj.us					
Raritan Valley Community College PO Box 3300	Somerville	NJ	08876	908-526-1200	704-3442*
**Fax:* Admissions ■ *Web:* www.raritanval.edu					
Salem Community College 460 Hollywood Ave	Carneys Point	NJ	08069	856-299-2100	351-2763*
**Fax:* Admissions ■ *Web:* www.salemcc.edu					
Sussex County Community College 1 College Hill Rd	Newton	NJ	07860	973-300-2100	579-5226*
**Fax:* Admissions ■ *Web:* www.sussex.edu					
Union County College 1033 Springfield Ave	Cranford	NJ	07016	908-709-7000	709-7125*
**Fax:* Admissions ■ *Web:* www.ucc.edu					
Warren County Community College 475 Rt 57 W	Washington	NJ	07882	908-835-9222	689-5824*
**Fax:* Admissions ■ *Web:* www.warren.edu					

New Mexico

				Phone	Fax
Clovis Community College 417 Schepps Blvd	Clovis	NM	88101	505-769-2811	769-4027*
**Fax:* Admissions ■ *Web:* www.clovis.edu					
Doña Ana Branch Community College					
Box 30001 Dept 3DA	Las Cruces	NM	88003	505-527-7500	527-7763*
**Fax:* Admissions ■ *TF:* 800-903-7503 ■ *Web:* dabcc.nmsu.edu					
Eastern New Mexico University Roswell					
52 University Blvd PO Box 6000	Roswell	NM	88202	505-624-7000	624-7144*
**Fax:* Admissions ■ *TF:* 800-243-6687 ■ *Web:* www.roswell.enmu.edu					
Luna Community College 366 Luna Dr	Las Vegas	NM	87701	505-454-2500	454-2519
TF: 800-588-7232 ■ *Web:* www.luna.cc.nm.us					
Mesalands Community College 911 S 10th St	Tucumcari	NM	88401	505-461-4413	461-1901
Web: www.mesalands.edu					
New Mexico Junior College 5317 Lovington Hwy	Hobbs	NM	88240	505-392-4510	392-0322*
**Fax:* Admissions ■ *TF:* 800-657-6260 ■ *Web:* www.nmjc.edu					
New Mexico Military Institute 101 W College Blvd	Roswell	NM	88201	505-624-8050	624-8058*
**Fax:* Admissions ■ *TF Admitting:* 800-421-5376 ■ *Web:* www.nmmi.cc.nm.us					
New Mexico State University					
Alamogordo 2400 N Scenic Dr	Alamogordo	NM	88310	505-439-3700	439-3760*
**Fax:* Admissions ■ *Web:* alamo.nmsu.edu					
Carlsbad 1500 University Dr	Carlsbad	NM	88220	505-234-9200	885-4951*
**Fax:* Admissions ■ *TF:* 888-888-2199 ■ *Web:* artemis.nmsu.edu					
Grants 1500 3rd St	Grants	NM	87020	505-287-7981	287-2329*
**Fax:* Admissions ■ *Web:* www.grants.nmsu.edu					
Northern New Mexico College 921 Paseo de Onate	Espanola	NM	87532	505-747-2100	747-5449
Web: www.nnmc.edu					
San Juan College 4601 College Blvd	Farmington	NM	87402	505-326-3311	566-3500*
**Fax:* Admissions ■ *Web:* www.sanjuancollege.edu					
Santa Fe Community College 6401 Richards Ave	Santa Fe	NM	87508	505-428-1000	428-1237
Web: www.sfccnm.edu					
University of New Mexico					
Los Alamos 4000 University Dr	Los Alamos	NM	87544	505-662-5919	661-4698*
**Fax:* Admissions ■ *TF:* 800-225-5866 ■ *Web:* www.la.unm.edu					
Valencia 280 La Entrada	Los Lunas	NM	87031	505-925-8580	925-8563*
**Fax:* Admissions ■ *TF:* 800-225-5866 ■ *Web:* www.unm.edu/unmvc					

New York

				Phone	Fax
Adirondack Community College 640 Bay Rd	Queensbury	NY	12804	518-743-2200	745-1433
Web: www.sunyacc.edu					
Alfred State College 10 Upper College Dr	Alfred	NY	14802	607-587-4215	587-4299*
**Fax:* Admissions ■ *TF:* 800-425-3733 ■ *Web:* www.alfredstate.edu					
Borough of Manhattan Community College					
199 Chambers St Rm S-300	New York	NY	10007	212-220-1265	220-2366
TF: 877-669-2622 ■ *Web:* www.bmcc.cuny.edu					
Bronx Community College W 181st St & University Ave	Bronx	NY	10453	718-289-5100	289-6003*
**Fax:* Admissions ■ *Web:* www.bcc.cuny.edu					
Broome Community College 901 Upper Front St	Binghamton	NY	13905	607-778-5000	778-5442*
**Fax:* Admissions ■ *TF:* 800-836-0689 ■ *Web:* www.sunybroome.edu					
Cayuga Community College 197 Franklin St	Auburn	NY	13021	315-255-1743	255-2117
Web: www.cayuga-cc.edu					
Clinton Community College 136 Clinton Point Dr	Plattsburgh	NY	12901	518-562-4200	562-4158
TF: 800-552-1160 ■ *Web:* clintoncc.suny.edu					
Columbia-Greene Community College 4400 Rt 23	Hudson	NY	12534	518-828-4181	828-8543
Web: www.sunycgcc.edu					
Corning Community College 1 Academic Dr	Corning	NY	14830	607-962-9011	962-9582*
**Fax:* Admissions ■ *Web:* www.corning-cc.edu					
Dutchess Community College 53 Pendell Rd	Poughkeepsie	NY	12601	845-431-8010	431-8605
TF: 800-763-3933 ■ *Web:* www.sunydutchess.edu					
Erie Community College 121 Ellicott St	Buffalo	NY	14203	716-842-2770	851-1129
TF: 800-836-0981 ■ *Web:* www.ecc.edu					
North 6205 Main St	Williamsville	NY	14221	716-634-0800	851-1429
Web: www.ecc.edu					
South 4041 Southwestern Blvd	Orchard Park	NY	14127	716-851-1003	851-1687*
**Fax:* Admissions ■ *TF:* 800-836-0983 ■ *Web:* www.ecc.edu					
Finger Lakes Community College 4355 Lakeshore Dr	Canandaigua	NY	14424	585-394-3500	394-5005
Web: www.fingerlakes.edu					
Fulton-Montgomery Community College 2805 Hwy 67	Johnstown	NY	12095	518-762-4651	762-4334
Web: fmcc.suny.edu					
Genesee Community College 1 College Rd	Batavia	NY	14020	585-343-0068	345-6810
Web: www.genesee.edu					
Herkimer County Community College 100 Reservoir Rd	Herkimer	NY	13350	315-866-0300	866-0062*
**Fax:* Admissions ■ *Web:* www.herkimer.edu					
Hostos Community College 500 Grand Concourse	Bronx	NY	10451	718-518-4444	518-4256*
**Fax:* Admissions ■ *Web:* www.hostos.cuny.edu					
Hudson Valley Community College 80 Vandenburgh Ave	Troy	NY	12180	518-629-4822	629-4576*
**Fax:* Admissions ■ *TF:* 877-325-4822 ■ *Web:* www.hvcc.edu					
Jamestown Community College 525 Faulkner St	Jamestown	NY	14702	716-665-5220	338-1466
TF: 800-388-8557 ■ *Web:* www.sunyjcc.edu					
Cattaraugus County 260 N Union St PO Box 5901	Olean	NY	14760	716-376-7500	376-7020*
**Fax:* Admissions ■ *TF:* 800-388-9776 ■					
Web: www.sunyjcc.edu/cattaraugus/cattaraugus.html					
Jefferson Community College 1220 Coffeen St	Watertown	NY	13601	315-786-2200	786-2459
TF: 888-435-6522 ■ *Web:* www.sunyjefferson.edu					
Kingsborough Community College 2001 Oriental Blvd	Brooklyn	NY	11235	718-368-5000	368-5356*
**Fax:* Admissions ■ *Web:* www.kbcc.cuny.edu					
LaGuardia Community College 31-10 Thomson Ave	Long Island City	NY	11101	718-482-5000	609-2033*
**Fax:* Admissions ■ *Web:* www.lagcc.cuny.edu					
Maria College 700 New Scotland Ave	Albany	NY	12208	518-438-1368	453-1366
Web: www.mariacollege.edu					
Mohawk Valley Community College 1101 Sherman Dr	Utica	NY	13501	315-792-5400	792-5527
Web: www.mvcc.edu					
Monroe Community College 1000 E Henrietta Rd	Rochester	NY	14623	585-292-2000	292-3860
Web: www.monroecc.edu					
Nassau Community College 1 Education Dr	Garden City	NY	11530	516-572-7500	572-9743
Web: www.ncc.edu					
Niagara County Community College					
3111 Saunders Settlement Rd	Sanborn	NY	14132	716-614-6222	614-6820*
**Fax:* Admissions ■ *Web:* www.niagaracc.suny.edu					
North Country Community College 23 Santanoni Ave	Saranac Lake	NY	12983	518-891-2915	891-2915
TF: 888-879-6222 ■ *Web:* www.nccc.edu					
Onondaga Community College 4941 Onondaga Rd	Syracuse	NY	13215	315-498-2622	498-2107
Web: www.sunyocc.edu					
Orange County Community College 115 South St	Middletown	NY	10940	845-344-6222	342-8662
Web: www.sunyorange.edu					
Queensborough Community College 222-05 56th Ave	Bayside	NY	11364	718-631-6262	281-5189*
**Fax:* Admissions ■ *Web:* www.qcc.cuny.edu					
Rockland Community College 145 College Rd	Suffern	NY	10901	845-574-4000	574-4433
TF: 800-722-7666 ■ *Web:* www.sunyrockland.edu					
Schenectady County Community College					
78 Washington Ave	Schenectady	NY	12305	518-381-1200	381-1477
Web: www.sunysccc.edu					
State University of New York					
Canton 34 Cornell Dr	Canton	NY	13617	315-386-7011	386-7929
TF: 800-388-7123 ■ *Web:* www.canton.edu					
College of Technology at Alfred 10 Upper College Dr	Alfred	NY	14802	607-587-4215	587-4299*
**Fax:* Admissions ■ *TF:* 800-425-3733 ■ *Web:* www.alfredstate.edu					
Delhi 2 Main St	Delhi	NY	13753	607-746-4000	746-4104
TF: 800-963-3544 ■ *Web:* www.delhi.edu					
Suffolk County Community College					
Ammerman 533 College Rd	Selden	NY	11784	631-451-4110	451-4094
Web: www.sunysuffolk.edu					
Eastern 121 Speonk-Riverhead Rd	Riverhead	NY	11901	631-548-2513	548-2504*
**Fax:* Admissions ■ *Web:* www.sunysuffolk.edu					
Grant 1001 Crooked Hill Rd	Brentwood	NY	11717	631-851-6700	851-6819*
**Fax:* Admissions ■ *Web:* www.sunysuffolk.edu					
Sullivan County Community College 112 College Rd	Loch Sheldrake	NY	12759	845-434-5750	434-0923*
**Fax:* Admissions ■ *Web:* www.sullivan.suny.edu					
SUNY Canton 34 Cornell Dr	Canton	NY	13617	315-386-7011	386-7929
TF: 800-388-7123 ■ *Web:* www.canton.edu					
SUNY Delhi 2 Main St	Delhi	NY	13753	607-746-4000	746-4104
TF: 800-963-3544 ■ *Web:* www.delhi.edu					

				Phone	Fax
SUNY Orange 115 South St	Middletown	NY	10940	845-344-6222	342-8662
Web: www.sunyorange.edu					
SUNY Rockland 145 College Rd	Suffern	NY	10901	845-574-4000	574-4433
TF: 800-722-7666 ■ *Web:* www.sunyrockland.edu					
SUNY Ulster Cottekill Rd	Stone Ridge	NY	12484	845-687-5000	687-5090
TF: 800-724-0833 ■ *Web:* www.sunyulster.edu					
Tompkins Cortland Community College 170 North St	Dryden	NY	13053	607-844-8211	844-6541*
**Fax:* Admissions ■ *TF:* 888-567-8211 ■ *Web:* www.tc3.edu					
Trocaire College 360 Choate Ave	Buffalo	NY	14220	716-826-1200	828-6107*
**Fax:* Admissions ■ *Web:* www.trocaire.edu					
Ulster County Community College Cottekill Rd	Stone Ridge	NY	12484	845-687-5000	687-5090
TF: 800-724-0833 ■ *Web:* www.sunyulster.edu					
Villa Maria College 240 Pine Ridge Rd	Buffalo	NY	14225	716-896-0700	896-0705
Web: www.villa.edu					
Westchester Community College 75 Grasslands Rd	Valhalla	NY	10595	914-606-6600	785-6540*
**Fax:* Admissions ■ *Web:* www.sunywcc.edu					

North Carolina

				Phone	Fax
Alamance Community College PO Box 8000	Graham	NC	27253	336-578-2002	578-3964*
**Fax:* Acctg ■ *Web:* www.alamance.cc.nc.us					
Asheville-Buncombe Technical Community College 340 Victoria Rd	Asheville	NC	28801	828-254-1921	251-6718*
**Fax:* Admissions ■ *Web:* www.abtech.edu					
Madison 4646 US Hwy 25-70	Marshall	NC	28753	828-649-2947	281-9859
Web: www.abtech.edu/madison					
Beaufort County Community College 5337 Hwy 264 E	Washington	NC	27889	252-946-6194	940-6393*
**Fax:* Admissions ■ *Web:* www.beaufort.cc.nc.us					
Bladen Community College PO Box 266	Dublin	NC	28332	910-862-2164	879-5564
Web: www.bladen.cc.nc.us					
Blue Ridge Community College 180 W Campus Dr	Flat Rock	NC	28731	828-694-1700	694-1690
Web: www.blueridge.edu					
Transylvania 45 Old Park Dr	Brevard	NC	28712	828-883-2520	884-5725
Web: www.blueridge.edu					
Brunswick Community College PO Box 30	Supply	NC	28462	910-754-6900	754-9609*
**Fax:* Admissions ■ *TF:* 800-754-1050 ■ *Web:* www.brunswick.cc.nc.us					
Caldwell Community College & Technical Institute 2855 Hickory Blvd	Hudson	NC	28638	828-726-2200	726-2216*
**Fax:* Admissions ■ *Web:* www.caldwell.cc.nc.us					
Watauga 294 Community College Dr PO Box 3318	Boone	NC	28607	828-297-3811	297-4174
Web: www.caldwell.cc.nc.us					
Cape Fear Community College 411 N Front St	Wilmington	NC	28401	910-362-7000	362-7080*
**Fax:* Admissions ■ *Web:* cfcc.edu					
Carteret Community College 3505 Arendell St	Morehead City	NC	28557	252-222-6000	222-6265
Web: www.carteret.edu					
Catawba Valley Community College 2550 Hwy 70 SE	Hickory	NC	28602	828-327-7000	327-7276*
**Fax:* Admissions ■ *Web:* www.cvcc.edu					
Central Carolina Community College 1105 Kelly Dr	Sanford	NC	27330	919-775-5401	718-7380*
**Fax:* Admissions ■ *Web:* www.cccc.edu					
Central Piedmont Community College 1201 Elizabeth Ave	Charlotte	NC	28204	704-330-2722	330-6136*
**Fax:* Admissions ■ *Web:* www.cpcc.edu					
Cato 8120 Grier Rd PO Box 35009	Charlotte	NC	28235	704-330-4801	330-4884*
**Fax:* Admissions ■ *Web:* www1.cpcc.edu/campuses/cato					
Harper PO Box 35009	Charlotte	NC	28273	704-330-4400	330-4444
Web: www.cpcc.edu/southwest					
Levine 2800 Campus Ridge Rd	Matthews	NC	28105	704-330-4242	330-4210
Web: www1.cpcc.edu/campuses/levine					
North 11930 Verhoeff Dr	Huntersville	NC	28078	704-330-4100	330-4113*
**Fax:* Admissions ■ *Web:* www1.cpcc.edu/campuses/north					
Cleveland Community College 137 S Post Rd	Shelby	NC	28152	704-484-4000	484-5305*
**Fax:* Admissions ■ *Web:* www.cleveland.cc.nc.us					
Coastal Carolina Community College 444 Western Blvd	Jacksonville	NC	28546	910-455-1221	455-7027*
**Fax:* Admissions ■ *Web:* www.coastal.cc.nc.us					
College of the Albemarle PO Box 2327	Elizabeth City	NC	27906	252-335-0821	335-2011*
**Fax:* Admissions ■ *Web:* www.albemarle.edu					
Craven Community College 800 College Ct	New Bern	NC	28562	252-638-4131	638-4649*
**Fax:* Admissions ■ *Web:* www.cravencc.edu					
Davidson County Community College PO Box 1287	Lexington	NC	27293	336-249-8186	224-0240*
**Fax:* Admissions ■ *Web:* www.davidson.cc.nc.us					
Durham Technical Community College 1637 E Lawson St	Durham	NC	27703	919-686-3300	686-3669*
**Fax:* Admissions ■ *Web:* www.durhamtech.edu					
Edgecombe Community College 2009 W Wilson St	Tarboro	NC	27886	252-823-5166	823-6817*
**Fax:* Admissions ■ *Web:* www.edgecombe.cc.nc.us					
Fayetteville Technical Community College PO Box 35236	Fayetteville	NC	28303	910-678-8400	678-8407*
**Fax:* Admissions ■ *Web:* www.faytechcc.edu					
Gaston College 201 Hwy 321-S	Dallas	NC	28034	704-922-6200	922-2344*
**Fax:* Admissions ■ *Web:* www.gaston.cc.nc.us					
Guilford Technical Community College 601 Highpoint Rd PO Box 309	Jamestown	NC	27282	336-334-4822	819-2022*
**Fax:* Admissions ■ *Web:* www.gtcc.edu					
Halifax Community College 200 College Dr	Weldon	NC	27890	252-536-2551	536-4144*
**Fax:* Admissions ■ *Web:* www.halifaxcc.edu					
Haywood Community College 185 Freedlander Dr	Clyde	NC	28721	828-627-2821	627-4513*
**Fax:* Admissions ■ *Web:* www.haywood.edu					
Isothermal Community College 806 ICC Loop Rd PO Box 804	Spindale	NC	28160	828-286-3636	286-8109*
**Fax:* Admissions ■ *Web:* www.isothermal.edu					
James Sprunt Community College 133 James Sprunt Dr	Kenansville	NC	28349	910-296-2400	296-1636*
**Fax:* Admissions ■ *Web:* www.sprunt.com					
Johnston Community College 245 College Rd	Smithfield	NC	27577	919-934-3051	989-7862*
**Fax:* Admissions ■ *Web:* www.johnston.cc.nc.us					
Lenoir Community College PO Box 188	Kinston	NC	28502	252-527-6223	233-6879
TF: 800-848-5497 ■ *Web:* www.lenoir.cc.nc.us					
Louisburg College 501 N Main St	Louisburg	NC	27549	919-496-2521	496-1788*
**Fax:* Admissions ■ *TF:* 800-775-0208 ■ *Web:* www.louisburg.edu					
Martin Community College 1161 Kehukee Park Rd	Williamston	NC	27892	252-792-1521	792-0826
Web: www.martin.cc.nc.us					
Mayland Community College 200 Mayland Dr PO Box 547	Spruce Pine	NC	28777	828-765-7351	765-0728*
**Fax:* Admissions ■ *TF:* 800-462-9526 ■ *Web:* www.mayland.edu					
McDowell Technical Community College 54 College Dr	Marion	NC	28752	828-652-6021	652-1014*
**Fax:* Admissions ■ *Web:* www.mcdowelltech.cc.nc.us					
Mitchell Community College 500 W Broad St	Statesville	NC	28677	704-878-3200	878-0872
Web: www.mitchellcc.edu					
Montgomery Community College 1011 Page St	Troy	NC	27371	910-576-6222	576-2176
TF: 800-839-6222 ■ *Web:* www.montgomery.cc.nc.us					
Nash Community College PO Box 7488	Rocky Mount	NC	27804	252-443-4011	443-0828*
**Fax:* Admissions ■ *Web:* www.nashcc.edu					
Pamlico Community College PO Box 185	Grantsboro	NC	28529	252-249-1851	249-2377*
**Fax:* Library ■ *Web:* www.pamlico.cc.nc.us					
Piedmont Community College PO Box 1197	Roxboro	NC	27573	336-599-1181	598-9283*
**Fax:* Admissions ■ *Web:* www.piedmont.cc.nc.us					
Caswell County 331 Piedmont Dr PO Box 1150	Yanceyville	NC	27379	336-694-5707	694-7086
Web: www.piedmont.cc.nc.us					
Pitt Community College PO Drawer 7007	Greenville	NC	27835	252-321-4200	321-4209*
**Fax:* Admissions ■ *Web:* www.pitt.cc.nc.us					
Randolph Community College 629 Industrial Park Ave PO Box 1009	Asheboro	NC	27204	336-633-0200	629-4695*
**Fax:* Admissions ■ *Web:* www.randolph.cc.nc.us					
Richmond Community College PO Box 1189	Hamlet	NC	28345	910-582-7000	582-7102*
**Fax:* Admissions ■ *Web:* www.richmondcc.edu					
Roanoke-Chowan Community College 109 Community College Rd	Ahoskie	NC	27910	252-862-1200	862-1355*
**Fax:* Admissions ■ *Web:* www.roanoke.cc.nc.us					
Robeson Community College PO Box 1420	Lumberton	NC	28359	910-272-3700	272-3328*
**Fax:* Admissions ■ *Web:* www.robeson.cc.nc.us/					
Rockingham Community College PO Box 38	Wentworth	NC	27375	336-342-4261	342-1809
Web: www.rockinghamcc.edu					
Rowan-Cabarrus Community College					
North 1333 Jake Alexander Blvd PO Box 1595	Salisbury	NC	28145	704-637-0760	633-6804*
**Fax:* Admissions ■ *Web:* www.rowancabarrus.edu					
South 1531 Trinity Church Rd	Concord	NC	28027	704-788-3197	788-2168*
**Fax:* Admissions ■ *Web:* www.rowancabarrus.edu					
Sampson Community College PO Box 318	Clinton	NC	28329	910-592-8081	592-8048*
**Fax:* Admissions ■ *Web:* www.sampson.cc.nc.us					
Sandhills Community College 3395 Airport Rd	Pinehurst	NC	28374	910-692-6185	695-3981*
**Fax:* Admissions ■ *TF:* 800-338-3944 ■ *Web:* www.sandhills.edu					
South Piedmont Community College 129 Ledbetter St PO Box 126	Polkton	NC	28135	704-272-7635	272-5303*
**Fax:* Admissions ■ *TF:* 800-766-0319 ■ *Web:* www.spcc.edu					
Southeastern Community College PO Box 151	Whiteville	NC	28472	910-642-7141	642-1267*
**Fax:* Admissions ■ *Web:* www.sccnc.edu					
Southwestern Community College 447 College Dr	Sylva	NC	28779	828-586-4091	586-3129*
**Fax:* Admissions ■ *TF:* 800-447-4091 ■ *Web:* www.southwest.cc.nc.us					
Surry Community College 630 S Main St	Dobson	NC	27017	336-386-8121	386-3690*
**Fax:* Admissions ■ *Web:* www.surry.cc.nc.us					
Tri-County Community College 4600 E US 64	Murphy	NC	28906	828-837-6810	837-3266
Web: www.tricountycc.edu					
Vance-Granville Community College PO Box 917	Henderson	NC	27536	252-492-2061	430-0460*
**Fax:* Admissions ■ *Web:* www.vgcc.edu					
Franklin PO Box 777	Louisburg	NC	27549	919-496-1567	496-6604*
**Fax:* Admissions ■ *Web:* www.vgcc.edu					
South PO Box 39	Creedmoor	NC	27522	919-528-4737	528-1201*
**Fax:* Admissions ■ *Web:* www.vgcc.edu					
Warren County PO Box 207	Warrenton	NC	27536	252-257-1900	257-3612*
**Fax:* Admissions ■ *Web:* www.vgcc.edu					
Wake Technical Community College 9101 Fayetteville Rd	Raleigh	NC	27603	919-662-3500	661-0117*
**Fax:* Admissions ■ *Web:* www.waketech.edu					
Wayne Community College 3000 Wayne Memorial Dr Box 8002	Goldsboro	NC	27533	919-735-5151	736-9425*
**Fax:* Admissions ■ *TF:* 866-414-5064 ■ *Web:* www.waynecc.edu					
Western Piedmont Community College 1001 Burkemont Ave	Morganton	NC	28655	828-438-6000	
Web: www.wpcc.edu					
Wilkes Community College 1328 S Collegiate Dr PO Box 120	Wilkesboro	NC	28697	336-838-6100	838-6547
Web: www.wilkes.cc.nc.us					
Wilson Technical Community College PO Box 4305	Wilson	NC	27893	252-291-1195	246-1384
Web: www.wilsontech.cc.nc.us					

North Dakota

				Phone	Fax
Bismarck State College 1500 Edwards Ave	Bismarck	ND	58501	701-224-5400	224-5643*
**Fax:* Admissions ■ *TF:* 800-445-5073 ■ *Web:* www.bismarckstate.edu					
Cankdeska Cikana Community College 214 1st Ave PO Box 269	Fort Totten	ND	58335	701-766-4415	766-4077
TF: 888-783-1463 ■ *Web:* www.littlehoop.cc					
Fort Berthold Community College PO Box 490	New Town	ND	58763	701-627-3665	627-3609*
**Fax:* Admissions ■ *Web:* www.fbcc.bia.edu					
Lake Region State College 1801 College Dr N	Devils Lake	ND	58301	701-662-1514	662-1581*
**Fax:* Admissions ■ *TF:* 800-443-1313 ■ *Web:* www.lrsc.nodak.edu					
Minot State University Bottineau 105 Simrall Blvd	Bottineau	ND	58318	701-228-5451	228-5499*
**Fax:* Admissions ■ *TF:* 800-542-6866 ■ *Web:* www.misu-b.nodak.edu					
North Dakota State College of Science 800 6th St N	Wahpeton	ND	58076	701-671-2401	671-2201*
**Fax:* Admissions ■ *TF:* 800-342-4325 ■ *Web:* www.ndscs.nodak.edu					
Sitting Bull College 1341 92nd St	Fort Yates	ND	58538	701-854-3864	854-3861*
**Fax:* Admissions ■ *Web:* www.sittingbull.edu					
Turtle Mountain Community College PO Box 340	Belcourt	ND	58316	701-477-7862	477-7892*
**Fax:* Admissions ■ *Web:* www.tm.edu					
Williston State College 1410 University Ave PO Box 1326	Williston	ND	58802	701-774-4200	774-4211*
**Fax:* Admissions ■ *TF:* 888-863-9455 ■ *Web:* www.wsc.nodak.edu					

Ohio

				Phone	Fax
Agricultural Technical Institute 1328 Dover Rd	Wooster	OH	44691	330-287-1331	287-1333*
**Fax:* Admissions ■ *Web:* www.ati.osu.edu					
Bowling Green State University Firelands 1 University Dr	Huron	OH	44839	419-433-5560	433-9696*
**Fax:* Admissions ■ *Web:* www.firelands.bgsu.edu					
Chatfield College 20918 SR-251	Saint Martin	OH	45118	513-875-3344	875-3912*
**Fax:* Admissions ■ *Web:* www.chatfield.edu					
Cincinnati State Technical & Community College 3520 Central Pkwy	Cincinnati	OH	45223	513-569-1500	569-1562*
**Fax:* Admissions ■ *TF:* 877-569-0115 ■ *Web:* www.cincinnatistate.edu					
Clark State Community College PO Box 570	Springfield	OH	45501	937-325-0691	328-6097*
**Fax:* Admissions ■ *Web:* www.clarkstate.edu					
Clermont College 4200 Clermont College Dr	Batavia	OH	45103	513-732-5200	732-5303*
**Fax:* Admissions ■ *TF:* 866-446-2822 ■ *Web:* www.clc.uc.edu					
Columbus State Community College 550 E Spring St	Columbus	OH	43215	614-287-2400	287-6019*
**Fax:* Admissions ■ *TF:* 800-621-6407 ■ *Web:* www.cscc.edu					
Cuyahoga Community College					
Eastern 4250 Richmond Rd	Highland Hills	OH	44122	216-987-2024	987-2214*
**Fax:* Admissions ■ *TF:* 800-954-8742 ■ *Web:* www.tri-c.edu/east					
Metropolitan 2900 Community College Ave	Cleveland	OH	44115	216-987-4200	696-2567*
**Fax:* Admitting ■ *TF:* 800-954-8742 ■ *Web:* www.tri-c.edu/metro					
Western 11000 Pleasant Valley Rd	Parma	OH	44130	216-987-5000	987-5071*
**Fax:* Admissions ■ *TF:* 800-954-8742 ■ *Web:* www.tri-c.edu/west					
Edison Community College 1973 Edison Dr	Piqua	OH	45356	937-778-8600	778-1920
TF: 800-922-3722 ■ *Web:* www.edisonohio.edu					
Kent State University					
Ashtabula 3300 Lake Rd W	Ashtabula	OH	44004	440-964-3322	964-4269*
**Fax:* Admissions ■ *Web:* www.ashtabula.kent.edu					
Geauga 14111 Claridon-Troy Rd	Burton	OH	44021	440-834-4187	834-8846*
**Fax:* Admissions ■ *Web:* www.geauga.kent.edu					
Kettering College of Medical Arts 3737 Southern Blvd	Kettering	OH	45429	937-395-8601	395-8338*
**Fax:* Admissions ■ *TF:* 800-433-5262 ■ *Web:* www.kcma.edu					
Lakeland Community College 7700 Clocktower Dr	Kirtland	OH	44094	440-525-7000	525-7651*
**Fax:* Admissions ■ *TF:* 800-589-8520 ■ *Web:* www.lakeland.cc.oh.us					
Lorain County Community College 1005 N Abbe Rd	Elyria	OH	44035	440-365-5222	366-4167
TF: 800-995-5222 ■ *Web:* www.lorainccc.edu					

Ohio (Cont'd)

Phone Fax

Miami University Hamilton 1601 University Blvd . . . . . Hamilton OH 45011 513-785-3000 785-3148*
*Fax: Admissions ■ *Web:* www.ham.muohio.edu
Ohio State University Agricultural Technical Institute
1328 Dover Rd . . . . . Wooster OH 44691 330-287-1331 287-1333*
*Fax: Admissions ■ *Web:* www.ati.osu.edu
Owens Community College
Findlay 3200 Bright Rd . . . . . Findlay OH 45840 419-429-3500 424-5194
TF: 800-346-3529 ■ *Web:* www.owens.edu
Toledo 30335 Oregon Rd . . . . . Perrysburg OH 43551 419-661-7000 661-7734*
*Fax: Admissions ■ *TF:* 800-466-9367 ■ *Web:* www.owens.edu
Raymond Walters College 9555 Plainfield Rd . . . . . Cincinnati OH 45236 513-745-5600 745-5768*
*Fax: Admissions ■ *Web:* www.rwc.uc.edu
Sinclair Community College 444 W 3rd St . . . . . Dayton OH 45402 937-512-2500 512-2393*
*Fax: Admissions ■ *Web:* www.sinclair.edu
Southern State Community College
North 1850 Davids Dr . . . . . Wilmington OH 45177 937-382-6645 383-1206*
*Fax: Admissions ■ *Web:* www.sscc.edu
South 12681 US Rt 62 . . . . . Sardinia OH 45171 937-695-0751 695-8093*
*Fax: Admissions ■ *Web:* www.sscc.edu
Terra Community College 2830 Napoleon Rd . . . . . Fremont OH 43420 419-334-8400 334-9035
TF: 800-334-3886 ■ *Web:* www.terra.edu
University of Akron Wayne College 1901 Smucker Rd . . . . . Orrville OH 44667 330-683-2010 684-8989
TF: 800-221-8308 ■ *Web:* www.wayne.uakron.edu
University of Cincinnati Clermont College
4200 Clermont College Dr . . . . . Batavia OH 45103 513-732-5200 732-5303*
*Fax: Admissions ■ *TF:* 866-446-2822 ■ *Web:* www.clc.uc.edu
University of Rio Grande Rio Grande Community College
218 N College Ave . . . . . Rio Grande OH 45674 740-245-5353 245-7260*
*Fax: Admissions ■ *TF:* 800-282-7201 ■ *Web:* www.urgrgcc.edu
Washington State Community College 710 Colegate Dr . . . . . Marietta OH 45750 740-374-8716 376-0257
Web: www.wscc.edu
Wayne College 1901 Smucker Rd . . . . . Orrville OH 44667 330-683-2010 684-8989
TF: 800-221-8308 ■ *Web:* www.wayne.uakron.edu
Wright State University Lake 7600 SR-703 . . . . . Celina OH 45822 419-586-2365 586-0358*
*Fax: Admissions ■ *Web:* www.wright.edu/lake

Oklahoma

Phone Fax

Carl Albert State College 1507 S McKenna St . . . . . Poteau OK 74953 918-647-1300 647-1306
Web: www.carlalbert.edu
Comanche Nation College 1608 SW 9th St . . . . . Lawton OK 73501 580-591-0203 353-7075
TF: 877-591-0203 ■ *Web:* www.cnc.cc.ok.us
Connors State College Rt 1 Box 1000 . . . . . Warner OK 74469 918-463-2931 463-6324
Web: www.connors.cc.ok.us
Eastern Oklahoma State College 1301 W Main St . . . . . Wilburton OK 74578 918-465-2361 465-4417
Web: www.eosc.edu
Murray State College 1 Murray Campus . . . . . Tishomingo OK 73460 580-371-2371 371-9844*
*Fax: Admissions ■ *TF:* 800-342-0698 ■ *Web:* www.mscok.edu
Northeastern Oklahoma A&M College 200 I St NE . . . . . Miami OK 74354 918-542-8441 540-6946*
*Fax: Admissions ■ *Web:* www.neoam.edu
Northern Oklahoma College 1220 E Grand St PO Box 310 . . . . . Tonkawa OK 74653 580-628-6200 628-6371*
*Fax: Admissions ■ *TF:* 888-429-5715 ■ *Web:* www.north-ok.edu
Oklahoma City Community College 7777 S May Ave . . . . . Oklahoma City OK 73159 405-682-1611 682-7521*
*Fax: Admissions ■ *Web:* www.occc.edu
Oklahoma State University Oklahoma City
900 N Portland Ave . . . . . Oklahoma City OK 73107 405-947-4421 945-9120*
*Fax: Admissions ■ *TF:* 800-560-4099 ■ *Web:* www.osuokc.edu
Redlands Community College 1300 S Country Club Rd . . . . . El Reno OK 73036 405-262-2552 422-1200*
*Fax: Admissions ■ *TF:* 866-415-6367 ■ *Web:* www.redlandscc.edu
Rogers State University
Bartlesville 401 E Adams Rd . . . . . Bartlesville OK 74003 918-335-3500 338-8095*
*Fax: Admissions ■ *TF:* 800-256-7511 ■ *Web:* www.rsu.edu/bville
Pryor 421 S Elliott St . . . . . Pryor OK 74361 918-825-6117 825-6135*
*Fax: Admissions ■ *Web:* www.rsu.edu/pryor
Rose State College 6420 SE 15th St . . . . . Midwest City OK 73110 405-733-7311 736-0309*
*Fax: Admissions ■ *Web:* www.rose.edu
Seminole State College 2701 Boren Blvd PO Box 351 . . . . . Seminole OK 74818 405-382-9950 382-9524*
*Fax: Admissions ■ *Web:* www.ssc.cc.ok.us
Southwestern Oklahoma State University Sayre
409 E Mississippi St . . . . . Sayre OK 73662 580-928-5533 928-1140*
*Fax: Admissions ■ *Web:* www.swosu.edu/sayre/
Tulsa Community College
Metro 909 S Boston Ave . . . . . Tulsa OK 74119 918-595-7000 595-7347*
*Fax: Admissions ■ *Web:* www.tulsacc.edu
Northeast 3727 E Apache St . . . . . Tulsa OK 74115 918-595-7000 595-7594
Web: www.tulsacc.edu
Southeast 10300 E 81st St . . . . . Tulsa OK 74133 918-595-7000 595-7748
Web: www.tulsacc.edu
West 7505 W 41st St . . . . . Tulsa OK 74107 918-595-7000 595-8130
Web: www.tulsacc.edu
Western Oklahoma State College 2801 N Main St . . . . . Altus OK 73521 580-477-2000 477-7723
Web: www.wosc.edu

Oregon

Phone Fax

Blue Mountain Community College
2411 NW Carden Ave PO Box 100 . . . . . Pendleton OR 97801 541-276-1260 278-5871*
*Fax: Admissions ■ *Web:* www.bluecc.edu
Central Oregon Community College 2600 NW College Way . . . . . Bend OR 97701 541-383-7700 383-7506*
*Fax: Admissions ■ *Web:* www.cocc.edu
Chemeketa Community College
4000 Lancaster Dr NE PO Box 14007 . . . . . Salem OR 97309 503-399-5006 399-3918*
*Fax: Admissions ■ *Web:* www.chemek.cc.or.us
Clackamas Community College 19600 S Molalla Ave . . . . . Oregon City OR 97045 503-657-8400 722-5864*
*Fax: Admissions ■ *Web:* www.clackamas.edu
Clatsop Community College 1653 Jerome Ave . . . . . Astoria OR 97103 503-325-0910 325-5738
TF: 866-252-8767 ■ *Web:* www.clatsopcc.edu
Klamath Community College 7390 S 6th St . . . . . Klamath Falls OR 97603 541-882-3521 885-7758
Web: www.kcc.cc.or.us
Lane Community College 4000 E 30th Ave . . . . . Eugene OR 97405 541-463-3000 463-3995*
*Fax: Admissions ■ *Web:* lanecc.edu
Cottage Grove 1275 S River Rd PO Box 96 . . . . . Cottage Grove OR 97424 541-463-4202 942-5186
Web: www.lanecc.edu/cotgrove
Florence 3149 Oak St . . . . . Florence OR 97439 541-997-8444 997-8448
Web: www.lanecc.edu/florence
Linn-Benton Community College 6500 Pacific Blvd SW . . . . . Albany OR 97321 541-917-4999 917-4838*
*Fax: Admissions ■ *Web:* www.linnbenton.edu
Mount Hood Community College 26000 SE Stark St . . . . . Gresham OR 97030 503-491-6422 491-7388*
*Fax: Admissions ■ *Web:* www.mhcc.edu

Phone Fax

Portland Community College Sylvania 12000 SW 49th Ave . . . . . Portland OR 97219 503-244-6111 977-4740*
*Fax: Admissions ■ *Web:* www.pcc.edu/about/locations/sylvania
Rogue Community College 3345 Redwood Hwy . . . . . Grants Pass OR 97527 541-956-7500 471-3585*
*Fax: Admissions ■ *TF:* 800-411-6508 ■ *Web:* www.roguecc.edu
Riverside 117 S Central . . . . . Medford OR 97501 541-245-7500 245-7648
Web: www.roguecc.edu/campus/rvc.asp
Southwestern Oregon Community College 1988 Newmark Ave . . . . . Coos Bay OR 97420 541-888-2525 888-1513
TF: 800-962-2838 ■ *Web:* www.socc.edu
Tillamook Bay Community College 2510 1st St . . . . . Tillamook OR 97141 503-842-8222 842-2214
TF: 888-306-8222 ■ *Web:* www.tbcc.cc.or.us
Treasure Valley Community College 650 College Blvd . . . . . Ontario OR 97914 541-881-8822 881-2721*
*Fax: Admissions ■ *Web:* www.tvcc.cc.or.us
Umpqua Community College
1140 Umpqua College Rd PO Box 967 . . . . . Roseburg OR 97470 541-440-4600 440-4612
Web: www.umpqua.edu

Pennsylvania

Phone Fax

Bucks County Community College 275 Swamp Rd . . . . . Newtown PA 18940 215-968-8000 968-8110*
*Fax: Admissions ■ *Web:* www.bucks.edu
Bristol 1280 New Rodgers Rd . . . . . Bristol PA 19007 215-781-3939 781-3928
Web: www.bucks.edu
Upper County 1 Hillendale Dr . . . . . Perkasie PA 18944 215-258-7700 258-7749
Web: www.bucks.edu
Butler County Community College PO Box 1203 . . . . . Butler PA 16003 724-287-8711 285-6047*
*Fax: Admissions ■ *TF:* 888-826-2829 ■ *Web:* www.bc3.edu
Community College of Allegheny County
Allegheny 808 Ridge Ave . . . . . Pittsburgh PA 15212 412-237-2525 237-4581*
*Fax: Admissions ■ *Web:* www.ccac.edu
Boyce 595 Beatty Rd . . . . . Monroeville PA 15146 724-325-6614 325-6859*
*Fax: Admissions ■ *Web:* www.ccac.edu
North 8701 Perry Hwy . . . . . Pittsburgh PA 15237 412-366-7000 369-3635*
*Fax: Admissions ■ *Web:* www.ccac.edu
South 1750 Clairton Rd Rt 885 . . . . . West Mifflin PA 15122 412-469-1100 469-6291*
*Fax: Admissions ■ *Web:* www.ccac.edu
Community College of Beaver County 1 Campus Dr . . . . . Monaca PA 15061 724-775-8561 728-7599*
*Fax: Admissions ■ *TF:* 800-335-0222 ■ *Web:* www.ccbc.edu
Community College of Philadelphia 1700 Spring Garden St . . . . . Philadelphia PA 19130 215-751-8000 751-8001*
*Fax: Admissions ■ *Web:* www.ccp.edu
Delaware County Community College 901 S Media Line Rd . . . . . Media PA 19063 610-359-5000 359-5343*
*Fax: Admissions ■ *TF:* 800-543-0146 ■ *Web:* www.dccc.edu
Downingtown 100 Bond Dr . . . . . Downingtown PA 19335 484-237-6200 237-6305
Web: www.dccc.edu/locations/about_dtown
Southeast 2000 Elmwood Ave . . . . . Sharon Hill PA 19079 610-957-5700 957-5787
Web: www.dccc.edu/sec
Harcum College 750 Montgomery Ave . . . . . Bryn Mawr PA 19010 610-525-4100 526-6147*
*Fax: Admissions ■ *TF:* 800-345-2600 ■ *Web:* www.harcum.edu
Harrisburg Area Community College 1 HACC Dr . . . . . Harrisburg PA 17110 717-780-2300 231-7674*
*Fax: Admissions ■ *TF:* 800-222-4222 ■ *Web:* www.hacc.edu
Gettysburg 731 Old Harrisburg Rd . . . . . Gettysburg PA 17325 717-337-3855 337-3015*
*Fax: Admissions ■ *TF:* 800-222-4222 ■ *Web:* www.hacc.edu/gettysburg
Lebanon 735 Cumberland St . . . . . Lebanon PA 17042 717-270-4222 270-6385
TF: 800-222-4222 ■ *Web:* www.hacc.edu/college/tour/lebanon
Lackawanna College 501 Vine St . . . . . Scranton PA 18509 570-961-7810 961-7843*
*Fax: Admissions ■ *TF:* 877-346-3552 ■ *Web:* www.lackawanna.edu
Lehigh Carbon Community College 4525 Education Park Dr . . . . . Schnecksville PA 18078 610-799-2121 799-1527
TF: 800-414-3975 ■ *Web:* www.lccc.edu
Morgan Center 234 High St . . . . . Tamaqua PA 18252 570-668-6880 668-7296
TF: 888-414-3975 ■ *Web:* www.lccc.edu/schuylkill
Luzerne County Community College 1333 S Prospect St . . . . . Nanticoke PA 18634 570-740-0200 740-0238*
*Fax: Admissions ■ *TF:* 800-377-5222 ■ *Web:* www.luzerne.edu
Manor College 700 Fox Chase Rd . . . . . Jenkintown PA 19046 215-885-2360 576-6564*
*Fax: Admissions ■ *Web:* www.manor.edu
Montgomery County Community College
Central 340 DeKalb Pike . . . . . Blue Bell PA 19422 215-641-6300 619-7188*
*Fax: Admitting ■ *Web:* www.mc3.edu
Pottstown 101 College Dr . . . . . Pottstown PA 19464 610-718-1800 718-1999
Web: www.mc3.edu/aa/west/west-campus.htm
Northampton Community College 3835 Green Pond Rd . . . . . Bethlehem PA 18020 610-861-5300 861-4560*
*Fax: Admissions ■ *TF:* 877-543-0998 ■ *Web:* www.northampton.edu
Monroe 3 Old Mill Rd PO Box 530 . . . . . Tannersville PA 18372 570-620-9221 620-9317
TF: 877-543-0998 ■ *Web:* www.northampton.edu/monroe
Penn State Berks PO Box 7009 . . . . . Reading PA 19610 610-396-6000 396-6077
Web: www.bk.psu.edu
Penn State DuBois 1 College Pl . . . . . Du Bois PA 15801 814-375-4700 375-4784*
*Fax: Admissions ■ *TF:* 800-346-7627 ■ *Web:* www.ds.psu.edu
Penn State Fayette Rt 119 N PO Box 519 . . . . . Uniontown PA 15401 724-430-4100 430-4175*
*Fax: Admissions ■ *TF:* 877-568-4130 ■ *Web:* www.fe.psu.edu
Penn State Hazleton 76 University Dr . . . . . Hazleton PA 18202 570-450-3000 450-3182*
*Fax: Admissions ■ *TF:* 800-279-8495 ■ *Web:* www.hn.psu.edu
Penn State Lehigh Valley 8380 Mohr Ln . . . . . Fogelsville PA 18051 610-285-5000 285-5220*
*Fax: Admissions ■ *Web:* www.lv.psu.edu
Penn State McKeesport 4000 University Dr . . . . . McKeesport PA 15132 412-675-9000 675-9056*
*Fax: Admissions ■ *Web:* www.mk.psu.edu
Penn State Mont Alto 1 Campus Dr . . . . . Mont Alto PA 17237 717-749-6000 749-6132*
*Fax: Admissions ■ *TF:* 800-392-6173 ■ *Web:* www.ma.psu.edu
Penn State New Kensington 3550 7th Street Rd Rt 780 . . . . . New Kensington PA 15068 724-334-6000 334-6111
Web: www.nk.psu.edu
Penn State Schuylkill 200 University Dr . . . . . Schuylkill Haven PA 17972 570-385-6000 385-6272*
*Fax: Admissions ■ *Web:* www.sl.psu.edu
Penn State Shenango 147 Shenango Ave . . . . . Sharon PA 16146 724-983-2814 983-2839*
*Fax: Admissions ■ *Web:* www.shenango.psu.edu
Penn State Wilkes-Barre PO Box PSU . . . . . Lehman PA 18627 570-675-2171 675-9113*
*Fax: Admissions ■ *Web:* www.wb.psu.edu
Penn State Worthington Scranton 120 Ridge View Dr . . . . . Dunmore PA 18512 570-963-2500 963-2524*
*Fax: Admissions ■ *Web:* www.sn.psu.edu
Penn State York 1031 Edgecomb Ave . . . . . York PA 17403 717-771-4000 771-4005*
*Fax: Admissions ■ *TF:* 800-778-6227 ■ *Web:* www.yk.psu.edu
Pennsylvania Highlands Community College
881 Hills Plaza Dr Suite 450 . . . . . Ebensburg PA 15931 814-262-6446 262-6420
Web: www.pennhighlands.edu
Pennsylvania State University
Beaver 100 University Dr . . . . . Monaca PA 15061 724-773-3500 773-3578*
*Fax: Admissions ■ *TF:* 877-564-6778 ■ *Web:* www.br.psu.edu
Berks PO Box 7009 . . . . . Reading PA 19610 610-396-6000 396-6077
Web: www.bk.psu.edu
DuBois 1 College Pl . . . . . Du Bois PA 15801 814-375-4700 375-4784*
*Fax: Admissions ■ *TF:* 800-346-7627 ■ *Web:* www.ds.psu.edu
Fayette Rt 119 N PO Box 519 . . . . . Uniontown PA 15401 724-430-4100 430-4175*
*Fax: Admissions ■ *TF:* 877-568-4130 ■ *Web:* www.fe.psu.edu
Hazleton 76 University Dr . . . . . Hazleton PA 18202 570-450-3000 450-3182*
*Fax: Admissions ■ *TF:* 800-279-8495 ■ *Web:* www.hn.psu.edu
Lehigh Valley 8380 Mohr Ln . . . . . Fogelsville PA 18051 610-285-5000 285-5220*
*Fax: Admissions ■ *Web:* www.lv.psu.edu
McKeesport 4000 University Dr . . . . . McKeesport PA 15132 412-675-9000 675-9056*
*Fax: Admissions ■ *Web:* www.mk.psu.edu

	City	State	ZIP	Phone	Fax
Mont Alto 1 Campus Dr	Mont Alto	PA	17237	717-749-6000	749-6132*
Fax: Admissions ■ *TF:* 800-392-6173 ■ *Web:* www.ma.psu.edu					
New Kensington 3550 7th Street Rd Rt 780	New Kensington	PA	15068	724-334-6000	334-6111
Web: www.nk.psu.edu					
Schuylkill 200 University Dr	Schuylkill Haven	PA	17972	570-385-6000	385-6272*
Fax: Admissions ■ *Web:* www.sl.psu.edu					
Shenango 147 Shenango Ave	Sharon	PA	16146	724-983-2814	983-2839*
Fax: Admissions ■ *Web:* www.shenango.psu.edu					
Wilkes-Barre PO Box PSU	Lehman	PA	18627	570-675-2171	675-9113*
Fax: Admissions ■ *Web:* www.wb.psu.edu					
Worthington Scranton 120 Ridge View Dr	Dunmore	PA	18512	570-963-2500	963-2524*
Fax: Admissions ■ *Web:* www.sn.psu.edu					
York 1031 Edgecomb Ave	York	PA	17403	717-771-4000	771-4005*
Fax: Admissions ■ *TF:* 800-778-6227 ■ *Web:* www.yk.psu.edu					
Reading Area Community College 10 S 2nd St PO Box 1706	Reading	PA	19603	610-372-4721	607-6290*
Fax: Admissions ■ *TF:* 800-626-1665 ■ *Web:* www.racc.edu					
University of Pittsburgh Titusville 504 E Main St	Titusville	PA	16354	814-827-5668	827-4519*
Fax: Admissions ■ *TF:* 888-878-0462 ■ *Web:* www.upt.pitt.edu					
Valley Forge Military Academy & College 1001 Eagle Rd	Wayne	PA	19087	610-989-1300	688-1545*
Fax: Admissions ■ *TF:* 800-234-8362 ■ *Web:* www.vfmac.edu					
Westmoreland County Community College 145 Pavilion Ln	Youngwood	PA	15697	724-925-4000	925-5802*
Fax: Admissions ■ *TF:* 800-262-2103 ■ *Web:* www.wccc-pa.edu					

Rhode Island

	City	State	ZIP	Phone	Fax
Community College of Rhode Island					
Flanagan 1762 Louisquisset Pike	Lincoln	RI	02865	401-333-7000	333-7122*
Fax: Admissions ■ *Web:* www.ccri.edu					
Knight 400 East Ave	Warwick	RI	02886	401-825-1000	825-2394*
Fax: Admissions ■ *Web:* www.ccri.edu					
Liston 1 Hilton St	Providence	RI	02905	401-455-6000	455-6014
Web: www.ccri.edu					

South Carolina

	City	State	ZIP	Phone	Fax
Aiken Technical College					
2276 Jefferson Davis Pkwy PO Drawer 696	Graniteville	SC	29829	803-593-9231	593-6526*
Fax: Admissions ■ *Web:* www.atc.edu					
Clinton Junior College 1029 Crawford Rd	Rock Hill	SC	29730	803-327-7402	327-3261*
Fax: Admissions ■ *Web:* www.clintonjuniorcollege.edu					
Greenville Technical College					
Barton 506 S Pleasantburg Dr	Greenville	SC	29606	864-250-8000	250-8534*
Fax: Admissions ■ *TF:* 800-723-0673 ■ *Web:* greenvilletech.com/barton					
Brashier PO Box 5616	Greenville	SC	29606	864-228-5000	228-5009
TF: 800-723-0673 ■ *Web:* greenvilletech.com/locations/brashier					
Greer 2522 Locust Hill Rd	Taylors	SC	29607	864-848-2000	848-2982*
Fax: Admissions ■ *TF:* 800-723-0673 ■ *Web:* greenvilletech.com/locations/greer					
Midlands Technical College PO Box 2408	Columbia	SC	29202	803-738-1400	790-7524*
Fax: Admissions ■ *TF:* 800-922-8038 ■ *Web:* www.midlandstech.edu					
North Greenville University 7801 N Tigerville Rd PO Box 1892	Tigerville	SC	29688	864-977-7000	977-7177*
Fax: Admissions ■ *TF:* 800-468-6642 ■ *Web:* www.ngu.edu					
Northeastern Technical College PO Drawer 1007	Cheraw	SC	29520	843-921-6900	921-1476*
Fax: Admissions ■ *Web:* www.netc.edu					
Orangeburg-Calhoun Technical College					
3250 St Matthews Rd NE	Orangeburg	SC	29118	803-536-0311	535-1368*
Fax: Admissions ■ *Web:* www.octech.org					
Spartanburg Methodist College 1000 Powell Mill Rd	Spartanburg	SC	29301	864-587-4000	587-4355*
Fax: Admissions ■ *Web:* www.smcsc.edu					
University of South Carolina					
Lancaster PO Box 889	Lancaster	SC	29721	803-313-7471	313-7106*
Fax: Admissions ■ *Web:* usclancaster.sc.edu					
Salkehatchie PO Box 617	Allendale	SC	29810	803-584-3446	584-5038
TF: 800-922-5500 ■ *Web:* uscsalkehatchie.sc.edu					
Union PO Box 729	Union	SC	29379	864-429-8728	427-3682*
Fax: Admissions ■ *TF:* 800-768-5566 ■ *Web:* uscunion.sc.edu					
Williamsburg Technical College 601 MLK Jr Ave	Kingstree	SC	29556	843-355-4110	355-4289*
Fax: Admissions ■ *TF:* 800-768-2021 ■ *Web:* www.williamsburgtech.com					
York Technical College 452 S Anderson Rd	Rock Hill	SC	29730	803-327-8000	327-8059
TF: 800-922-8324 ■ *Web:* www.yorktech.com					

South Dakota

	City	State	ZIP	Phone	Fax
Kilian Community College 300 E 6th St	Sioux Falls	SD	57103	605-221-3100	336-2606*
Fax: Admissions ■ *TF:* 800-888-1147 ■ *Web:* www.kilian.edu					
Lake Area Technical Institute 230 11th St NE PO Box 730	Watertown	SD	57201	605-882-5284	882-6299
TF: 800-657-4344 ■ *Web:* lati.tec.sd.us					
Mitchell Technical Institute 821 N Capital St	Mitchell	SD	57301	605-995-3024	996-3299
TF: 800-952-0042 ■ *Web:* www.mitchelltech.com					
Sisseton Wahpeton College					
Agency Village CPO BIA Road 700 PO Box 689	Sisseton	SD	57262	605-698-3966	742-0394
Web: www.swc.tc					

Tennessee

	City	State	ZIP	Phone	Fax
Chattanooga State Technical Community College					
4501 Amnicola Hwy	Chattanooga	TN	37406	423-697-4400	697-3115*
Fax: Admissions ■ *TF:* 866-547-3733 ■ *Web:* www.chattanoogastate.edu					
Cleveland State Community College PO Box 3570	Cleveland	TN	37320	423-472-7141	478-6255*
Fax: Admissions ■ *Web:* www.clevelandstatecc.edu					
Columbia State Community College PO Box 1315	Columbia	TN	38402	931-540-2722	540-2830*
Fax: Admissions ■ *Web:* www.columbiastate.edu					
Clifton 795 Main St	Clifton	TN	38425	931-676-6966	676-6941
Web: www.columbiastate.edu/locations					
Dyersburg State Community College 1510 Lake Rd	Dyersburg	TN	38024	731-286-3200	286-3325*
Fax: Admissions ■ *Web:* www.dscc.edu					
Hiwassee College 225 Hiwassee College Dr	Madisonville	TN	37354	423-442-2001	442-8521*
Fax: Admissions ■ *TF:* 800-356-2187 ■ *Web:* www.hiwassee.edu					
Jackson State Community College 2046 North Pkwy	Jackson	TN	38301	731-424-3520	425-9559*
Fax: Admissions ■ *Web:* www.jscc.edu					
Lexington-Henderson County 932 E Church St	Lexington	TN	38351	731-968-5722	968-1539
Web: www.jscc.edu/lexington					
Motlow State Community College PO Box 8500	Lynchburg	TN	37352	931-393-1500	393-1971*
Fax: Admissions ■ *TF:* 800-654-4877 ■ *Web:* www.mscc.cc.tn.us					
Pellissippi State Technical Community College					
10915 Hardin Valley Rd	Knoxville	TN	37933	865-694-6400	539-7217*
Fax: Admissions ■ *Web:* www.pstcc.edu					
Roane State Community College 276 Patton Ln	Harriman	TN	37748	865-354-3000	882-4562*
Fax: Admitting ■ *TF:* 800-343-9104 ■ *Web:* www.rscc.cc.tn.us					
Southwest Tennessee Community College PO Box 780	Memphis	TN	38101	901-333-5000	333-4473
TF: 877-717-7822 ■ *Web:* www.southwest.tn.edu					
Volunteer State Community College 1480 Nashville Pike	Gallatin	TN	37066	615-452-8600	230-4875*
Fax: Admissions ■ *TF:* 888-335-8722 ■ *Web:* www.volstate.edu					
Walters State Community College 500 S Davy Crockett Pkwy	Morristown	TN	37813	423-585-2600	585-6786*
Fax: Admissions ■ *TF:* 800-225-4770 ■ *Web:* www.ws.edu					

Texas

	City	State	ZIP	Phone	Fax
Alvin Community College 3110 Mustang Rd	Alvin	TX	77511	281-331-6111	756-3843*
Fax: Admissions ■ *Web:* www.alvincollege.edu					
Amarillo College PO Box 447	Amarillo	TX	79178	806-371-5000	371-5066
Web: www.actx.edu					
Angelina College PO Box 1768	Lufkin	TX	75902	936-639-1309	633-5455*
Fax: Admissions ■ *Web:* www.angelina.cc.tx.us					
Austin Community College 5930 Middle Fiskville Rd	Austin	TX	78752	512-223-7000	223-7665*
Fax: Admissions ■ *Web:* www.austincc.edu					
Cypress Creek 1555 Cypress Creek Rd	Cedar Park	TX	78613	512-223-2000	223-2048*
Fax: Admissions ■ *Web:* www.austincc.edu/cyp					
Eastview 3401 Webberville Rd	Austin	TX	78702	512-223-5100	223-5900*
Fax: Admissions ■ *Web:* www.austincc.edu/evc					
Northridge 11928 Stonehollow Dr	Austin	TX	78758	512-223-4000	223-4651*
Fax: Admissions ■ *Web:* www.austincc.edu/nrg					
Pinnacle 7748 Hwy 290 W	Austin	TX	78736	512-223-8001	223-8122*
Fax: Admissions ■ *Web:* www.austincc.edu/pin					
Rio Grande 1212 Rio Grande St	Austin	TX	78701	512-223-3000	223-3444*
Fax: Admissions ■ *Web:* www.austincc.edu/rgc					
Riverside 1020 Grove Blvd	Austin	TX	78741	512-223-6000	223-6767*
Fax: Admissions ■ *Web:* www.austincc.edu/rvs					
Blinn College 902 College Ave	Brenham	TX	77833	979-830-4000	830-4110*
Fax: Admissions ■ *Web:* www.blinn.edu					
Brazosport College 500 College Dr	Lake Jackson	TX	77566	979-230-3000	230-3443*
Fax: Admissions ■ *Web:* www.brazosport.edu					
Brookhaven College 3939 Valley View Ln	Farmers Branch	TX	75244	972-860-4700	860-4886*
Fax: Admitting ■ *Web:* www.brookhavencollege.edu					
Cedar Valley College 3030 N Dallas Ave	Lancaster	TX	75134	972-860-8200	860-8001*
Fax: Admissions ■ *Web:* www.dcccd.edu/cvc/cvc.htm					
Central Texas College 6200 W Central Texas Expy	Killeen	TX	76549	254-526-1696	526-1111*
Fax: Admissions ■ *TF:* 800-792-3348 ■ *Web:* online.ctcd.edu					
Cisco Junior College 101 College Heights	Cisco	TX	76437	254-442-2567	442-5100*
Fax: Admissions ■ *Web:* www.cisco.cc.tx.us					
Abilene 717 E Industrial Blvd	Abilene	TX	79602	325-794-4400	442-5100*
Fax Area Code: 254 ■ *Web:* www.cisco.cc.tx.us					
Clarendon College 1122 College Dr PO Box 968	Clarendon	TX	79226	806-874-3571	874-5080*
Fax: Admissions ■ *TF:* 800-687-9737 ■ *Web:* www.clarendoncollege.edu					
Coastal Bend College Beeville 3800 Charco Rd	Beeville	TX	78102	361-358-2838	354-2254*
Fax: Admissions ■ *TF:* 866-722-2838 ■ *Web:* vct.coastalbend.edu					
College of the Mainland 1200 Amburn Rd	Texas City	TX	77591	409-938-1211	938-1306*
Fax: Admissions ■ *Web:* www.com.edu					
Collin County Community College					
Central Park 2200 W University Dr	McKinney	TX	75070	972-548-6790	548-6702*
Fax: Admissions ■ *Web:* www.cccd.edu/campuses/central					
Preston Ridge 9700 Wade Blvd	Frisco	TX	75035	972-377-1790	377-1723*
Fax: Admissions ■ *Web:* www.cccd.edu/campuses/prestonridge					
Spring Creek 2800 E Spring Creek Pkwy	Plano	TX	75074	972-881-5790	881-5174*
Fax: Admissions ■ *Web:* www.cccd.edu/campuses/SCC					
Del Mar College East 101 Baldwin Blvd	Corpus Christi	TX	78404	361-698-1200	698-1595*
Fax: Admissions ■ *TF:* 800-652-3357 ■ *Web:* www.delmar.edu					
Eastfield College 3737 Motley Dr	Mesquite	TX	75150	972-860-7100	860-8306
Web: www.eastfieldcollege.com					
El Centro College 801 Main St	Dallas	TX	75202	214-860-2037	860-2233*
Fax: Admissions ■ *Web:* www.ecc.dcccd.edu					
El Paso Community College					
Mission Del Paso 10700 Gateway E	El Paso	TX	79927	915-831-7017	
Web: www.epcc.edu					
Northwest 6701 S Desert Blvd	El Paso	TX	79932	915-831-8803	831-8926
Web: www.epcc.edu					
Rio Grande 100 W Rio Grande Ave	El Paso	TX	79902	915-831-4000	831-4409*
Fax: Admissions ■ *Web:* www.epcc.edu					
Transmountain 9570 Gateway Blvd N	El Paso	TX	79924	915-831-5030	831-5209*
Fax: Admissions ■ *Web:* www.epcc.edu					
Valle Verde 919 Hunter Dr	El Paso	TX	79915	915-831-2000	831-2161*
Fax: Admissions ■ *Web:* www.epcc.edu					
Frank Phillips College PO Box 5118	Borger	TX	79008	806-457-4200	273-7642*
Fax: Admissions ■ *TF:* 800-687-2056 ■ *Web:* www.fpc.cc.tx.us					
Galveston College 4015 Ave Q	Galveston	TX	77550	409-763-6551	944-1501*
Fax: Admissions ■ *Web:* www.gc.edu					
Grayson County College 6101 Grayson Dr	Denison	TX	75020	903-465-6030	463-5284*
Fax: Admissions ■ *Web:* www.grayson.edu					
Hill College PO Box 619	Hillsboro	TX	76645	254-582-2555	582-7591*
Fax: Admissions ■ *Web:* www.hillcollege.edu					
Houston Community College					
Central College 1300 Holman	Houston	TX	77004	713-718-6000	718-6112
Web: ccollege.hccs.edu					
Northeast College 555 Community College Dr	Houston	TX	77013	713-718-8100	
Web: www.hccs.edu/necollege					
Southwest College 9910 Cash Rd	Stafford	TX	77477	713-718-7802	718-7793
Web: swc2.hccs.edu					
Howard College 1001 Birdwell Ln	Big Spring	TX	79720	432-264-5000	264-5082*
Fax: Admissions ■ *Web:* www.howardcollege.edu					
Southwest Collegiate Institute for the Deaf 3200 Ave C	Big Spring	TX	79720	432-264-3700	264-3707*
Fax: Admissions ■ *Web:* www.howardcollege.edu/swcid					
Jacksonville College 105 BJ Albritton Dr	Jacksonville	TX	75766	903-586-2518	586-0743*
Fax: Admissions ■ *TF:* 800-256-8522 ■ *Web:* www.jacksonville-college.edu					
Kilgore College 1100 Broadway	Kilgore	TX	75662	903-984-8531	988-7531*
Fax: Admissions ■ *Web:* www.kilgore.edu					
Kingwood College 20000 Kingwood Dr	Kingwood	TX	77339	281-312-1600	312-1477*
Fax: Admissions ■ *TF:* 800-883-7939 ■ *Web:* kcweb.nhmccd.edu					
Lamar State College					
Orange 410 Front St	Orange	TX	77630	409-883-7750	882-3055*
Fax: Admissions ■ *Web:* www.orange.lamar.edu					
Port Arthur PO Box 310	Port Arthur	TX	77641	409-983-4921	984-6025*
Fax: Admissions ■ *TF:* 800-477-5872 ■ *Web:* www.pa.lamar.edu					
Laredo Community College West End Washington St	Laredo	TX	78040	956-722-0521	721-5493*
Fax: Admissions ■ *Web:* www.laredo.cc.tx.us					
Lee College 511 S Whiting St	Baytown	TX	77520	281-427-5611	425-6831*
Fax: Admissions ■ *Web:* www.lee.edu					
Lon Morris College 800 College Ave Administrative Bldg	Jacksonville	TX	75766	903-589-4000	589-4006*
Fax: Admissions ■ *TF:* 800-259-5753 ■ *Web:* www.lonmorris.edu					
McLennan Community College 1400 College Dr	Waco	TX	76708	254-299-8000	299-8694*
Fax: Admissions ■ *Web:* www.mclennan.edu					
Midland College 3600 N Garfield St	Midland	TX	79705	432-685-4500	685-4623*
Fax: Admissions ■ *Web:* www.midland.edu					
Montgomery College 3200 College Park Dr	Conroe	TX	77384	936-273-7000	273-7234*
Fax: Admissions ■ *Web:* www.montgomery-college.com					

Texas (Cont'd)

Phone Fax

Mountain View College 4849 W Illinois Ave ... Dallas TX 75211 214-860-8600 860-8570*
*Fax: Admissions ■ *Web:* www.mvc.dcccd.edu

Navarro College 3200 W 7th Ave ... Corsicana TX 75110 903-874-6501 875-7353*
*Fax: Admissions ■ *TF:* 800-628-2776 ■ *Web:* www.navarrocollege.edu

North Central Texas College 1525 W California St ... Gainesville TX 76240 940-668-7731 665-7075*
*Fax: Admissions ■ *Web:* www.nctc.edu
Bowie 810 S Mill St ... Bowie TX 76230 940-872-4002 872-3065
Web: www.nctc.edu

North Harris College 2700 WW Thorne Rd ... Houston TX 77073 281-618-5400 618-7141*
*Fax: Admissions ■ *Web:* www.northharriscollege.com

North Lake College 5001 N MacArthur Blvd ... Irving TX 75038 972-273-3000 273-3112*
*Fax: Admissions ■ *Web:* www.northlakecollege.edu

Northeast Texas Community College 1735 Chapel Hill Rd ... Mount Pleasant TX 75455 903-572-1911 572-6712*
*Fax: Admissions ■ *TF:* 800-870-0142 ■ *Web:* www.ntcc.edu

Odessa College 201 W University Blvd ... Odessa TX 79764 432-335-6400 335-6824
Web: www.odessa.edu

Palo Alto College 1400 W Villaret Blvd ... San Antonio TX 78224 210-921-5000 921-5310*
*Fax: Admissions ■ *Web:* www.accd.edu/pac

Panola College 1109 W Panola St ... Carthage TX 75633 903-693-2000 693-2031*
*Fax: Admissions ■ *Web:* www.panola.edu

Paris Junior College 2400 Clarksville St ... Paris TX 75460 903-785-7661 782-0427*
*Fax: Admissions ■ *TF:* 800-232-5804 ■ *Web:* www.parisjc.edu

Ranger College 1100 College Cir ... Ranger TX 76470 254-647-3234 647-3739*
*Fax: Admissions ■ *Web:* www.ranger.cc.tx.us

Richland College 12800 Abrams Rd ... Dallas TX 75243 972-238-6100 238-6346*
*Fax: Admissions ■ *Web:* www.rlc.dcccd.edu

Saint Philip's College 1801 ML King Dr ... San Antonio TX 78203 210-531-3200 531-3235*
*Fax: Admissions ■ *TF:* 866-493-3940 ■ *Web:* www.accd.edu/spc

San Antonio College 1300 San Pedro Ave ... San Antonio TX 78212 210-733-2000 733-2579*
*Fax: Admissions ■ *Web:* www.accd.edu/sac/

San Jacinto College
Central 8060 Spencer Hwy ... Pasadena TX 77505 281-476-1501 478-2720
Web: www.sjcd.edu
North 5800 Uvalde Rd ... Houston TX 77049 281-458-4050 459-7688*
*Fax: Admissions ■ *Web:* www.sjcd.edu
South 13735 Beamer Rd ... Houston TX 77089 281-922-3431 922-3485
Web: www.sjcd.edu

South Plains College 1401 S College Ave ... Levelland TX 79336 806-894-9611 897-3167*
*Fax: Admissions ■ *Web:* www.southplainscollege.edu

Southwest Texas Junior College 2401 Garner Field Rd ... Uvalde TX 78801 830-278-4401 591-7396*
*Fax: Admissions ■ *Web:* www.swtjc.net

Tarrant County College
Northeast 828 Harwood Rd ... Hurst TX 76054 817-515-6100 515-6988*
*Fax: Admissions ■ *Web:* www.tccd.edu
Northwest 4801 Marine Creek Pkwy ... Fort Worth TX 76179 817-515-7100 515-7732*
*Fax: Admissions ■ *Web:* www.tccd.edu
South 5301 Campus Dr ... Fort Worth TX 76119 817-515-4100 515-4110*
*Fax: Admissions ■ *Web:* www.tccd.edu/campus/
Southeast 2100 Southeast Pkwy ... Arlington TX 76018 817-515-3100 515-3182*
*Fax: Admissions ■ *Web:* www.tccd.edu

Temple College 2600 S 1st St ... Temple TX 76504 254-298-8300 298-8288*
*Fax: Admissions ■ *TF Admissions:* 800-460-4636 ■ *Web:* www.templejc.edu

Texarkana College 2500 N Robison Rd ... Texarkana TX 75599 903-838-4541 832-5030*
*Fax: Admissions ■ *Web:* www.texarkanacollege.edu

Texas Southmost College 80 Fort Brown St ... Brownsville TX 78520 956-882-8200 882-8832
TF: 800-850-0160 ■ *Web:* www.utb.edu

Texas State Technical College
Abilene 650 E Hwy 80 ... Abilene TX 79601 325-672-7091 734-3658
Web: www.westtexas.tstc.edu
Harlingen 1902 N Loop 499 ... Harlingen TX 78550 956-364-4000 364-5117
TF: 800-852-8784 ■ *Web:* www.harlingen.tstc.edu
Sweetwater 300 Homer K Taylor Dr ... Sweetwater TX 79556 325-235-7300 235-7443
Web: www.westtexas.tstc.edu
Waco 3801 Campus Dr ... Waco TX 76705 254-799-3611 867-3044
TF: 800-792-8784 ■ *Web:* www.waco.tstc.edu

Tomball College 30555 Tomball Pkwy ... Tomball TX 77375 281-351-3300 351-3384*
*Fax: Admissions ■ *Web:* www.tomballcollege.com

Trinity Valley Community College
Athens 100 Cardinal Dr ... Athens TX 75751 903-675-6200 675-6209*
*Fax: Admissions ■ *TF:* 866-882-2937 ■ *Web:* www.tvcc.edu/centers/athens
Palestine PO Box 2530 ... Palestine TX 75802 903-729-0256 729-2325
Web: www.tvcc.edu/centers/palestine
Terrell 1200 E I-20 ... Terrell TX 75160 972-563-9573 563-1667
Web: www.tvcc.edu/centers/terrell

Tyler Junior College PO Box 9020 ... Tyler TX 75711 903-510-2523 510-2161*
*Fax: Admissions ■ *TF:* 800-687-5680 ■ *Web:* www.tjc.edu

Vernon College 4400 College Dr ... Vernon TX 76384 940-552-6291 553-1753
Web: www.vernoncollege.edu

Victoria College 2200 E Red River St ... Victoria TX 77901 361-573-3291 582-2525
Web: www.vc.cc.tx.us

Weatherford College 225 College Park Dr ... Weatherford TX 76086 817-594-5471 598-6205*
*Fax: Admissions ■ *TF:* 800-287-5471 ■ *Web:* www.wc.edu

Western Texas College 6200 College Ave ... Snyder TX 79549 325-573-8511 573-9321*
*Fax: Admissions ■ *TF:* 888-468-6982 ■ *Web:* www.wtc.edu

Wharton County Junior College 911 Boling Hwy ... Wharton TX 77488 979-532-4560 532-6494*
*Fax: Admissions ■ *TF:* 800-561-9252 ■ *Web:* www.wcjc.edu
Sugar Land 550 Julie Rivers Dr ... Sugar Land TX 77478 281-243-8410 243-8432*
*Fax: Admissions ■ *TF:* 800-561-9252 ■ *Web:* www.wcjc.edu

Utah

Phone Fax

College of Eastern Utah 451 E 400 North ... Price UT 84501 435-637-2120 613-5814*
*Fax: Admissions ■ *TF:* 800-336-2381 ■ *Web:* www.ceu.edu
San Juan 639 W 100 S ... Blanding UT 84511 435-678-2201 678-2220*
*Fax: Admissions ■ *TF:* 800-395-2969 ■ *Web:* sjc.ceu.edu

Salt Lake Community College
Jordan 3491 W 9000 South ... West Jordan UT 84088 801-957-2600 957-2688
Web: www.slcc.edu
Redwood 4600 S Redwood Rd ... Salt Lake City UT 84130 801-957-4111 957-4444
Web: www.slcc.edu
South City 1575 S State St ... Salt Lake City UT 84115 801-957-3413 957-3150
Web: www.slcc.edu

Snow College 150 E College Ave ... Ephraim UT 84627 435-283-7000 283-7157*
*Fax: Admissions ■ *Web:* www.snow.edu

Stevens Henager College 1890 S 1350 West ... Ogden UT 84401 801-394-7791 621-0853
Web: www.stevenshenager.edu

Utah Valley State College 800 W University Pkwy ... Orem UT 84058 801-863-8000 225-4677*
*Fax: Admissions ■ *Web:* www.uvsc.edu

Vermont

Phone Fax

Community College of Vermont
Bennington 324 Main St ... Bennington VT 05201 802-447-2361 447-3246*
*Fax: Admissions ■ *Web:* www.ccv.edu/locations/bennington
Brattleboro 70 Landmark Hill Suite 101 ... Brattleboro VT 05301 802-254-6370 257-2593
Web: www.ccv.edu/locations/brattleboro
Burlington 119 Pearl St ... Burlington VT 05401 802-865-4422 865-3323*
*Fax: Admissions ■ *Web:* www.ccv.edu/locations/burlington
Middlebury 10 Merchants Row Suite 223 ... Middlebury VT 05753 802-388-3032 388-4686*
*Fax: Admissions ■ *Web:* www.ccv.edu/locations/montpelier
Montpelier 32 College St ... Montpelier VT 05602 802-828-4060 828-2801*
*Fax: Admissions ■ *Web:* www.ccv.edu/locations/montpelier
Morrisville 197 Harrell St Suite 2 ... Morrisville VT 05661 802-888-4258 888-2554*
*Fax: Admissions ■ *Web:* www.ccv.edu/locations/morrisville
Newport 100 Main St Suite 150 ... Newport VT 05855 802-334-3387 334-5373*
*Fax: Admissions ■ *Web:* www.ccv.edu/locations/newport
Rutland 24 Evelyn St ... Rutland VT 05701 802-786-6996 786-4980*
*Fax: Admissions ■ *Web:* www.ccv.edu/locations/rutland
Saint Albans 142 S Main St Suite 2 ... Saint Albans VT 05478 802-524-6541 524-5216*
*Fax: Admissions ■ *Web:* www.ccv.edu/locations/st_albans
Saint Johnsbury 1197 Main St Suite 3 ... Saint Johnsbury VT 05819 802-748-6673 748-5014*
*Fax: Admissions ■ *Web:* www.ccv.edu/locations/st_johnsbury
Springfield 307 South St ... Springfield VT 05156 802-885-8360 885-8373
Web: www.ccv.edu/locations/springfield
Upper Valley 145 Billings Farm Rd ... White River Junction VT 05001 802-295-8822 295-8862*
*Fax: Admissions ■ *Web:* www.ccv.edu/locations/upper_valley
Waterbury 103 S Main St ... Waterbury VT 05676 802-241-3535 241-3526*
*Fax: Admissions ■ *Web:* www.ccv.vsc.edu

Landmark College River Road S PO Box 820 ... Putney VT 05346 802-387-6718 387-6868*
*Fax: Admissions ■ *Web:* www.landmarkcollege.org

Virginia

Phone Fax

Blue Ridge Community College 1 College Ln PO Box 80 ... Weyers Cave VA 24486 540-234-9261 453-2437*
*Fax: Admissions ■ *Web:* www.brcc.edu
Harrisonburg 160C N Mason St ... Harrisonburg VA 22802 540-432-3690
Web: www.brcc.edu

Central Virginia Community College 3506 Wards Rd ... Lynchburg VA 24502 434-832-7600 832-7793*
*Fax: Admissions ■ *Web:* www.cv.cc.va.us

Dabney S Lancaster Community College
PO Box 1000 1000 Dabney Dr ... Clifton Forge VA 24422 540-863-2800 863-2915
Web: www.dl.vccs.edu

Danville Community College 1008 S Main St ... Danville VA 24541 434-797-2222 797-8541*
*Fax: Admissions ■ *Web:* www.dcc.vccs.edu

Eastern Shore Community College 29300 Lankford Hwy ... Melfa VA 23410 757-787-5900 789-1737*
*Fax: Admissions ■ *Web:* www.es.vccs.edu

Germanna Community College
Fredericksburg 10000 Germanna Point Dr ... Fredericksburg VA 22408 540-891-3000 891-3092*
*Fax: Admissions ■ *Web:* www.germanna.edu
Locust Grove 2130 Germanna Hwy ... Locust Grove VA 22508 540-423-9030 727-3207
Web: www.germanna.edu

J Sargeant Reynolds Community College 1701 E Parham Rd ... Richmond VA 23228 804-371-3000 371-3650*
*Fax: Admissions ■ *Web:* www.reynolds.edu
Downtown 700 E Jackson St ... Richmond VA 23219 804-523-5455 371-3650
Web: www.jsr.vccs.edu

John Tyler Community College 13101 Jefferson Davis Hwy ... Chester VA 23831 804-796-4000 796-4362*
*Fax: Admissions ■ *Web:* www.jtcc.edu
Midlothian 800 Charter Colony Pkwy ... Midlothian VA 23114 804-594-1400
Web: www.jt.cc.va.us

Lord Fairfax Community College
Fauquier 6480 College St ... Warrenton VA 20187 540-351-1505 351-1530*
*Fax: Admissions ■ *Web:* www.lfcc.edu
Middletown 173 Skirmisher Ln ... Middletown VA 22645 540-868-7000 868-7005*
*Fax: Admissions ■ *TF:* 800-906-5322 ■ *Web:* www.lfcc.edu

Mountain Empire Community College
3441 Mountain Empire Rd ... Big Stone Gap VA 24219 276-523-2400 523-8297*
*Fax: Admissions ■ *Web:* www.me.cc.va.us

New River Community College 5251 College PO Box 1127 ... Dublin VA 24084 540-674-3600 674-3644*
*Fax: Admissions ■ *TF:* 866-462-6722 ■ *Web:* www.nr.edu

Northern Virginia Community College
Alexandria 3001 N Beauregard St ... Alexandria VA 22311 703-845-6200 845-6046*
*Fax: Admissions ■ *Web:* www.nvcc.edu/alexandria
Annandale 8333 Little River Tpke ... Annandale VA 22003 703-323-3401 323-3367*
*Fax: Admissions ■ *Web:* www.nvcc.edu/annandale
Loudoun 1000 Harry Flood Byrd Hwy ... Sterling VA 20164 703-450-2500 450-2536
Web: www.nvcc.edu/loudoun
Manassas 6901 Sudley Rd ... Manassas VA 20109 703-257-6600 257-6565*
*Fax: Admitting ■ *Web:* www.nvcc.edu/manassas
Woodbridge 15200 Neabsco Mills Rd ... Woodbridge VA 22191 703-878-5700 878-5692*
*Fax: Admissions ■ *Web:* www.nvcc.edu/woodbridge

Patrick Henry Community College 645 Patriot Ave PO Box 5311 ... Martinsville VA 24115 276-638-8777 656-0352*
*Fax: Admissions ■ *Web:* www.ph.vccs.edu

Paul D Camp Community College PO Box 737 ... Franklin VA 23851 757-569-6700 569-6795*
*Fax: Admissions ■ *Web:* www.pc.vccs.edu
Hobbs Suffolk 271 Kenyon Rd PO Box 500 ... Suffolk VA 23439 757-925-6300 925-6370*
*Fax: Admissions ■ *Web:* www.pc.vccs.edu

Piedmont Virginia Community College 501 College Dr ... Charlottesville VA 22902 434-977-3900 961-5425*
*Fax: Admissions ■ *Web:* www.pvcc.edu

Rappahannock Community College
Glenns 12745 College Dr ... Glenns VA 23149 804-758-6700 758-5819*
*Fax: Admissions ■ *Web:* www.rcc.vccs.edu
Warsaw 52 Campus Dr ... Warsaw VA 22572 804-333-6700 333-0106*
*Fax: Admissions ■ *Web:* www.rcc.vccs.edu

Richard Bland College 11301 Johnson Rd ... Petersburg VA 23805 804-862-6100 862-6490*
*Fax: Admissions ■ *Web:* www.rbc.edu

Southside Virginia Community College 109 Campus Dr ... Alberta VA 23821 434-949-1000 949-7863*
*Fax: Admissions ■ *TF:* 888-220-7822 ■ *Web:* www.sv.vccs.edu

Southwest Virginia Community College PO Box SVCC ... Richlands VA 24641 276-964-2555 964-9307*
*Fax: Admissions ■ *Web:* www.sw.vccs.edu

Thomas Nelson Community College 99 Thomas Nelson Dr ... Hampton VA 23666 757-825-2700 825-2763*
*Fax: Admissions ■ *Web:* www.tncc.vccs.edu

Tidewater Community College
Chesapeake 1428 Cedar Rd ... Chesapeake VA 23322 757-822-5100 822-5122
TF: 800-371-0898 ■ *Web:* www.tcc.edu/welcome/locations/chesapeake
Norfolk 315 Granby St ... Norfolk VA 23510 757-822-1110 822-1154
TF: 800-371-0898 ■ *Web:* www.tcc.edu/welcome/locations/norfolk
Portsmouth 7000 College Dr ... Portsmouth VA 23703 757-822-2124 822-2002*
*Fax: Admissions ■ *TF:* 800-371-0898 ■
Web: www.tcc.edu/welcome/locations/portsmouth
Virginia Beach 1700 College Crescent ... Virginia Beach VA 23453 757-822-7100 822-7350
TF: 800-371-0898 ■ *Web:* www.tcc.edu/welcome/locations/vabeach

Virginia Highlands Community College 100 VHCC Dr PO Box 828 ... Abingdon VA 24212 276-739-2400 739-2591*
*Fax: Admissions ■ *Web:* www.vhcc.edu

	City	State	Zip	Phone	Fax
Virginia Western Community College 3094 Colonial Ave PO Box 14007 *Fax: Admissions ■ Web: www.virginiawestern.edu	Roanoke	VA	24038	540-857-7231	857-6102*
Wytheville Community College 1000 E Main St *Fax: Admissions ■ Web: www.wcc.vccs.edu	Wytheville	VA	24382	276-223-4700	223-4860*

Washington

	City	State	Zip	Phone	Fax
Bates Technical College 1101 S Yakima Ave *Fax: Admissions ■ Web: www.bates.ctc.edu	Tacoma	WA	98405	253-680-7000	680-7001*
Bellevue Community College 3000 Landerholm Cir SE *Fax: Admissions ■ Web: www.bcc.ctc.edu	Bellevue	WA	98007	425-564-1000	564-4065*
Big Bend Community College 7662 Chanute St *Fax: Admissions ■ Web: www.bigbend.edu	Moses Lake	WA	98837	509-762-5351	762-6243*
Centralia College 600 W Locust St *Fax: Admissions ■ Web: www.centralia.ctc.edu	Centralia	WA	98531	360-736-9391	330-7503*
Clark College 1800 E McLoughlin Blvd *Fax: Admissions ■ Web: www.clark.edu	Vancouver	WA	98663	360-992-2000	992-2876*
Clover Park Technical College 4500 Steilacoom Blvd SW Web: www.cptc.edu	Lakewood	WA	98499	253-589-5800	589-5750
Columbia Basin College 2600 N 20th Ave Web: www.columbiabasin.edu	Pasco	WA	99301	509-547-0511	546-0401
Edmonds Community College 20000 68th Ave W Web: www.edcc.edu	Lynnwood	WA	98036	425-640-1500	640-1159
Everett Community College 2000 Tower St *Fax: Admissions ■ Web: www.everettcc.edu	Everett	WA	98201	425-388-9100	388-9129*
Grays Harbor College 1620 Edward P Smith Dr *Fax: Admissions ■ Web: ghc.ctc.edu	Aberdeen	WA	98520	360-532-9020	538-4293*
Green River Community College 12401 SE 320th St *Fax: Admissions ■ Web: www.greenriver.edu	Auburn	WA	98092	253-833-9111	288-3454*
Lower Columbia College 1600 Maple St PO Box 3010 *Fax: Admissions ■ Web: lowercolumbia.edu	Longview	WA	98632	360-442-2301	442-2379*
North Seattle Community College 9600 College Way N Web: www.northseattle.edu	Seattle	WA	98103	206-527-3600	527-3671
Northwest Indian College 2522 Kwina Rd *Fax: Admissions ■ TF: 866-676-2772 ■ Web: www.nwic.edu/	Bellingham	WA	98226	360-676-2772	392-4333*
Olympic College 1600 Chester Ave *Fax: Admissions ■ TF: 800-259-6718 ■ Web: www.olympic.edu	Bremerton	WA	98337	360-792-6050	475-7202*
Shelton 937 W Alpine Way *Fax: Admissions ■ TF: 800-259-6718 ■ Web: www.olympic.edu/shelton	Shelton	WA	98584	360-427-2119	432-5412*
Peninsula College 1502 E Lauridsen Blvd *Fax: Admissions ■ Web: www.pc.ctc.edu	Port Angeles	WA	98362	360-452-9277	417-6581*
Pierce College 9401 Farwest Dr SW *Fax: Admissions ■ Web: www.pierce.ctc.edu	Lakewood	WA	98498	253-964-6500	964-6427*
Puyallup 1601 39th Ave SE *Fax: Admissions ■ Web: www.pierce.ctc.edu	Puyallup	WA	98374	253-840-8400	840-8449*
Renton Technical College 3000 NE 4th St Web: www.rtc.edu	Renton	WA	98056	425-235-2352	235-7832
Seattle Central Community College 1701 Broadway *Fax: Admissions ■ Web: seattlecentral.org	Seattle	WA	98122	206-587-3800	587-6321*
Shoreline Community College 16101 Greenwood Ave N Web: www.shoreline.edu	Shoreline	WA	98133	206-546-4101	546-5835
Skagit Valley College 2405 E College Way *Fax: Admissions ■ TF: 877-385-5360 ■ Web: www.skagit.edu	Mount Vernon	WA	98273	360-416-7600	416-7890*
Whidbey Island 1900 SE Pioneer Way *Fax: Admissions ■ Web: www.skagit.edu	Oak Harbor	WA	98277	360-679-5330	679-5375*
South Puget Sound Community College 2011 Mottman Rd SW *Fax: Admissions ■ Web: www.spscc.ctc.edu	Olympia	WA	98512	360-754-7711	596-5709*
South Seattle Community College 6000 16th Ave SW Web: www.southseattle.edu	Seattle	WA	98106	206-764-5300	764-7947
Spokane Community College 1810 N Greene St TF: 800-248-5644 ■ Web: www.scc.spokane.edu	Spokane	WA	99217	509-533-7000	533-8181
Spokane Falls Community College 3410 W Fort George Wright Dr *Fax: Admissions ■ TF: 888-509-7944 ■ Web: www.spokanefalls.edu	Spokane	WA	99224	509-533-3500	533-3237*
Tacoma Community College 6501 S 19th St *Fax: Admissions ■ Web: www.tacomacc.edu	Tacoma	WA	98466	253-566-5000	566-6011*
Walla Walla Community College 500 Tausick Way *Fax: Admissions ■ TF: 877-992-9922 ■ Web: www.wwcc.edu	Walla Walla	WA	99362	509-522-2500	527-3661*
Wenatchee Valley College 1300 5th St *Fax: Admissions ■ TF: 877-982-4968 ■ Web: www.wvc.edu	Wenatchee	WA	98801	509-682-6800	682-6801*
Omak 116 W Apple Ave PO Box 2058 *Fax: Admissions ■ Web: www.wvc.edu/directory/departments/wvcomak	Omak	WA	98841	509-422-7803	422-7801*
Whatcom Community College 237 W Kellogg Rd Web: www.whatcom.ctc.edu	Bellingham	WA	98226	360-676-2170	676-2171
Yakima Valley Community College PO Box 22520 *Fax: Admissions ■ Web: www.yvcc.edu	Yakima	WA	98907	509-574-4600	574-4649*
Grandview 500 W Main St Web: www.yvcc.edu/grandview	Grandview	WA	98930	509-882-7000	882-7012

West Virginia

	City	State	Zip	Phone	Fax
Eastern West Virginia Community & Technical College 1929 SR 55 TF: 877-982-2322 ■ Web: www.eastern.wvnet.edu	Moorefield	WV	26836	304-434-8000	434-7000
Potomac State College 101 Fort Ave *Fax: Admissions ■ TF: 800-262-7332 ■ Web: www.potomacstatecollege.edu	Keyser	WV	26726	304-788-6800	788-6939*
Southern West Virginia Community & Technical College Logan PO Box 2900 *Fax: Admissions ■ Web: www.southern.wvnet.edu	Mount Gay	WV	25637	304-792-7098	792-7056*
West Virginia Northern Community College 1704 Market St Web: www.northern.wvnet.edu	Wheeling	WV	26003	304-233-5900	232-8187
West Virginia University Parkersburg 300 Campus Dr *Fax: Admissions ■ Web: www.wvup.edu	Parkersburg	WV	26104	304-424-8000	424-8332*

Wisconsin

	City	State	Zip	Phone	Fax
College of Menominee Nation PO Box 1179 *Fax: Admissions ■ TF: 800-567-2344 ■ Web: www.menominee.edu	Keshena	WI	54135	715-799-5600	799-4392*
Lac Courte Oreilles Ojibwa Community College 13466 W Trepania Rd *Fax: Admissions ■ TF: 888-526-6221 ■ Web: www.lco.edu	Hayward	WI	54843	715-634-4790	634-5049*
Nicolet Area Technical College PO Box 518 *Fax: Admissions ■ TF: 800-544-3039 ■ Web: www.nicolet.tec.wi.us	Rhinelander	WI	54501	715-365-4410	365-4901*
University of Wisconsin					
Baraboo/Sauk County 1006 Connie Rd *Fax: Admissions ■ Web: www.baraboo.uwc.edu	Baraboo	WI	53913	608-355-5200	356-0752*
Barron County 1800 College Dr Web: www.barron.uwc.edu	Rice Lake	WI	54868	715-234-8176	234-1975
Fond du Lac 400 University Dr *Fax: Admissions ■ Web: www.fdl.uwc.edu	Fond du Lac	WI	54935	920-929-3600	929-3626*
Fox Valley 1478 Midway Rd Web: www.uwfox.uwc.edu	Menasha	WI	54952	920-832-2600	832-2674
Manitowoc 705 Viebahn St Web: www.uwmanitowoc.uwc.edu	Manitowoc	WI	54220	920-683-4700	683-4776
Marathon County 518 S 7th Ave TF: 888-367-8962 ■ Web: www.marathon.uwc.edu	Wausau	WI	54401	715-261-6100	261-6331
Marinette 750 W Bay Shore St *Fax: Admissions ■ Web: www.marinette.uwc.edu	Marinette	WI	54143	715-735-4300	735-4304*
Marshfield/Wood County 2000 W 5th St Web: www.marshfield.uwc.edu	Marshfield	WI	54449	715-389-6530	384-1718
Richland 1200 Hwy 14 W *Fax: Admissions ■ Web: richland.uwc.edu	Richland Center	WI	53581	608-647-6186	647-2275*
Rock County 2909 Kellogg Ave Web: rock.uwc.edu	Janesville	WI	53546	608-758-6523	758-6579
Sheboygan 1 University Dr *Fax: Admissions ■ Web: sheboygan.uwc.edu	Sheboygan	WI	53081	920-459-6600	459-6662*
Washington County 400 S University Dr Web: washington.uwc.edu	West Bend	WI	53095	262-335-5200	335-5251
Waukesha 1500 N University Dr *Fax: Admissions ■ Web: waukesha.uwc.edu	Waukesha	WI	53188	262-521-5210	521-5530*

Wyoming

	City	State	Zip	Phone	Fax
Casper College 125 College Dr *Fax: Admissions ■ TF: 800-442-2963 ■ Web: www.caspercollege.edu	Casper	WY	82601	307-268-2110	268-2611*
Central Wyoming College 2660 Peck Ave TF: 800-735-8418 ■ Web: www.cwc.edu	Riverton	WY	82501	307-855-2000	855-2092
Eastern Wyoming College 3200 W 'C' St *Fax: Admissions ■ TF: 800-658-3195 ■ Web: www.ewc.wy.edu	Torrington	WY	82240	307-532-8200	532-8222*
Laramie County Community College 1400 E College Dr *Fax: Admissions ■ TF: 800-522-2993 ■ Web: www.lccc.cc.wy.us	Cheyenne	WY	82007	307-778-5222	778-1350*
Albany County 1125 Boulder Dr TF: 800-522-2993 ■ Web: www.lccc.wy.edu/acc	Laramie	WY	82070	307-721-5138	772-4266
Northwest College 231 W 6th St *Fax: Admissions ■ TF: 800-560-4692 ■ Web: www.northwestcollege.edu	Powell	WY	82435	307-754-6000	754-6249*
Sheridan College 3059 Coffeen Ave PO Box 1500 TF: 800-913-9139 ■ Web: www.sheridan.edu	Sheridan	WY	82801	307-674-6446	674-7205
Gillette 300 W Sinclair St *Fax: Admissions ■ Web: www.sheridan.edu	Gillette	WY	82718	307-686-0254	686-0339*
Western Wyoming Community College 2500 College Dr *Fax: Admissions ■ TF: 800-226-1181 ■ Web: www.wwcc.wy.edu	Rock Springs	WY	82901	307-382-1600	382-1636*

163 • COLLEGES - CULINARY ARTS

	City	State	Zip	Phone	Fax
Arizona Culinary Institute 10585 N 114th St Suite 401 TF: 866-294-2433 ■ Web: www.azculinary.com	Scottsdale	AZ	85259	480-603-1066	603-1067
Atlantic Culinary Academy at McIntosh College 181 Silver St TF: 877-628-1222	Dover	NH	03820	603-743-3523	749-0837
Baltimore International College 17 Commerce St *Fax: Admissions ■ TF: 800-624-9926 ■ Web: www.bic.edu	Baltimore	MD	21202	410-752-4710	752-3730*
California Culinary Academy Inc 625 Polk St *Fax: Admissions ■ TF: 800-229-2433 ■ Web: www.baychef.com	San Francisco	CA	94102	415-771-3500	771-2194*
California School of the Culinary Arts 521 E Green St TF: 866-230-9450 ■ Web: www.csca.edu	Pasadena	CA	91101	626-229-1300	403-8494
Cambridge School of Culinary Arts 2020 Massachusetts Ave Web: www.cambridgeculinary.com	Cambridge	MA	02140	617-354-2020	576-1963
Capital Culinary Institute of Keiser College					
Melbourne 900 S Babcock St Web: www.keisercollege.edu/culinary.html	Melbourne	FL	32901	321-255-2255	725-3766
Sarasota 6151 Lake Osprey Dr TF: 866-534-7372 ■ Web: www.keisercollege.edu/culinary.html	Sarasota	FL	34240	941-907-3900	907-2016
Capital Culinary Institute of Keiser Institute Tallahassee 1700 Halstead Blvd Bldg 4 TF: 877-243-3123 ■ Web: www.capitalculinaryinstitute.com	Tallahassee	FL	32309	850-906-9494	906-0069
Cascade Culinary Institute 2600 NW College Way Web: culinary.cocc.edu	Bend	OR	97701	541-383-7700	
Center for Culinary Arts 106 Sebethe Dr Web: www.centerforculinaryarts.com	Cromwell	CT	06416	860-613-3350	613-3353
Chef John Folse Culinary Institute PO Box 2099 Web: www.nicholls.edu/jfolse	Thibodaux	LA	70310	985-449-7100	449-7089
Connecticut Culinary Institute 85 Sigourney St TF: 800-762-4337 ■ Web: www.ctculinary.edu	Hartford	CT	06105	860-895-6100	895-6101
Suffield 1760 Mapleton Ave TF: 866-672-4337 ■ Web: www.ctculinary.com	Suffield	CT	06032	860-668-3500	668-3518
Cook Street School of Fine Cooking 1937 Market St Web: www.cookstreet.com	Denver	CO	80202	303-308-9300	308-9400
Cooking & Hospitality Institute of Chicago 361 W Chestnut St TF: 888-295-7222 ■ Web: www.chic.edu	Chicago	IL	60610	312-944-0882	944-8557
Culinard-the Culinary Institute of Virginia College 65 Bagby Dr TF: 877-812-8428 ■ Web: www.culinard.com	Birmingham	AL	35209	205-802-1200	943-3940
Culinary Academy of Long Island 125 Michael Dr Web: www.culinaryacademyli.com	Syosset	NY	11791	516-364-4344	364-1894
Manhattan 154 W 14th St 11th Fl Web: www.culinaryacademyli.com	New York	NY	10011	212-675-6655	463-9194
Culinary Institute Alain & Marie LeNotre 7070 Allensby TF: 888-536-6873 ■ Web: www.lenotre-alain-marie.com	Houston	TX	77022	713-692-0077	692-7399
Culinary Institute of America 1946 Campus Dr TF Admissions: 800-285-4627 ■ Web: www.ciachef.edu	Hyde Park	NY	12538	845-452-9430	451-1068
Culinary Institute of America at Greystone 2555 Main St Web: www.ciachef.edu/california	Saint Helena	CA	94574	707-967-2350	
Culinary Institute of Charleston 7000 Rivers Ave TF: 877-349-7184 ■ Web: www.tridenttech.edu/culinary_institute_of_charleston.htm	Charleston	SC	29406	843-574-6111	820-5060
Florida Culinary Institute 2410 Metro Centre Blvd TF: 800-262-9986 ■ Web: www.floridaculinary.com	West Palm Beach	FL	33407	561-688-2001	688-9882
French Culinary Institute 462 Broadway *Fax: Admissions ■ TF: 888-324-2433 ■ Web: www.frenchculinary.com	New York	NY	10013	212-219-8890	431-3065*
Institute of Culinary Education 50 W 23rd St TF: 800-522-4610 ■ Web: www.iceculinary.com	New York	NY	10010	212-847-0700	847-0723
International Institute of Culinary Arts 215 Bank St Web: www.iicaculinary.com	Fall River	MA	02720	508-675-9305	678-5214
JNA Institute of Culinary Arts 1212 S Broad St Web: www.culinaryarts.com	Philadelphia	PA	19146	215-468-8800	468-8838
Kendall College 900 N North Branch St *Fax: Admissions ■ TF: 866-667-3344 ■ Web: www.kendall.edu	Chicago	IL	60622	312-752-2000	752-2010*
Kitchen Academy 6370 W Sunset Blvd TF: 866-548-2223 ■ Web: www.kitchenacademy.com	Los Angeles	CA	90028	323-203-3967	460-4198

Phone | Fax

L'Academie de Cuisine Inc 16006 Industrial Dr. Gaithersburg MD 20877 301-670-8670 670-0450
TF: 800-664-2433 ■ *Web:* www.lacademie.com

Le Cordon Bleu College of Culinary Arts
Atlanta 1927 Lakeside Pkwy Tucker GA 30084 770-938-4711 938-4571
TF: 866-315-2433 ■ *Web:* www.atlantaculinary.com
Las Vegas 1451 Center Crossing Rd Las Vegas NV 89144 702-365-7690 365-7911
Web: www.vegasculinary.com
Miami 3221 Enterprise Way Miramar FL 33025 954-628-4400 438-9519
TF: 866-762-2433 ■ *Web:* www.miamiculinary.com

L'Ecole de Cuisine 3050 Hempland Rd Lancaster PA 17601 717-295-1100 295-1135
TF: 866-984-2433 ■ *Web:* chefs.yti.edu

Lincoln Tech Center for Culinary Arts 8 Progress Dr Shelton CT 06484 203-929-0592 929-0763
Web: www.centerforculinaryarts.com

Louisiana Culinary Institute 5837 Essen Ln Baton Rouge LA 70810 225-769-8820 769-8792*
**Fax:* Admissions ■ *TF:* 877-769-8820 ■ *Web:* www.louisianaculinary.com

New England Culinary Institute 56 College St Montpelier VT 05602 802-223-6324 225-3280
TF: 877-223-6324 ■ *Web:* www.neci.edu

Oregon Coast Culinary Institute 1988 Newmark Ave Coos Bay OR 97420 541-888-2525 888-7247
TF: 877-895-2433 ■ *Web:* www.occi.net

Orlando Culinary Academy 8511 Commodity Cir Suite 100 Orlando FL 32819 407-888-4000 888-4019
TF: 800-622-2433 ■ *Web:* www.orlandoculinary.com

Pennsylvania Culinary Institute 717 Liberty Ave Pittsburgh PA 15222 412-566-2433 566-2434
TF: 800-432-2433 ■ *Web:* www.pci.edu

Restaurant School at Walnut Hill College 4207 Walnut St Philadelphia PA 19104 215-222-4200 222-2811*
**Fax:* Admissions ■ *Web:* www.walnuthillcollege.com

Robert Morris University Institute of Culinary Arts
401 S State St Chicago IL 60605 312-935-4100 935-4182*
**Fax:* Admissions ■ *TF:* 800-762-5960 ■ *Web:* www.robertmorris.edu/culinary
Dupage 905 Meridian Lake Dr Aurora IL 60504 800-762-5960 375-8020*
**Fax Area Code:* 630 ■ *Web:* www.robertmorris.edu/culinary

San Diego Culinary Institute 8024 La Mesa Blvd La Mesa CA 91941 619-644-2100 644-2106
Web: www.sdci-inc.com

Sclafani's Cooking School Inc 107 Gennaro Pl Metairie LA 70001 504-833-7861 833-7872
TF: 800-583-1282 ■ *Web:* www.sclafanicookingschool.com

Scottsdale Culinary Institute
8100 E Camelback Rd Suite 1001 Scottsdale AZ 85251 480-990-3773 990-0351
TF: 800-848-2433 ■ *Web:* www.chefs.edu

Stratford University School of Culinary Arts
7777 Leesburg Pike Falls Church VA 22043 703-821-8570 734-5336
TF: 800-444-0804 ■ *Web:* www.stratford.edu/?page=home_culinary

Sullivan University National Center for Hospitality Studies
3101 Bardstown Rd Louisville KY 40205 502-456-6505 456-0040
TF: 800-844-1354 ■ *Web:* www.sullivan.edu/nchs

Tante Marie's Cooking School 271 Francisco St San Francisco CA 94133 415-788-6699 788-8924
Web: www.tantemarie.com

Texas Culinary Academy 11400 Burnet Rd Suite 2100 Austin TX 78758 512-837-2665 977-7753*
**Fax:* Admissions ■ *TF:* 888-553-2433 ■ *Web:* www.tca.edu

Western Culinary Institute 921 SW Morrison St Suite 400 Portland OR 97205 503-223-2245 223-5554*
**Fax:* Admissions ■ *TF:* 888-848-3202 ■ *Web:* www.wci.edu

164 COLLEGES - FINE ARTS

SEE ALSO Colleges & Universities - Four-Year p. 1475; Vocational & Technical Schools p. 2406

Phone | Fax

American Academy of Art 332 S Michigan Ave 3rd Fl Chicago IL 60604 312-461-0600 294-9570
TF: 888-461-0600 ■ *Web:* www.aaart.edu

American Academy of Dramatic Arts 1336 N La Brea Ave Hollywood CA 90028 323-464-2777 464-1250
TF: 800-222-2867 ■ *Web:* www.aada.org

American Academy of Dramatic Arts 120 Madison Ave New York NY 10016 212-686-9244 545-7934
TF: 800-463-8990 ■ *Web:* www.aada.org

Antonelli Institute 300 Montgomery Ave Erdenheim PA 19038 215-836-2222 836-2794
TF: 800-722-7871 ■ *Web:* www.antonelli.org

Art Academy of Cincinnati 1212 Jackson St Cincinnati OH 45202 513-562-6262 562-8778
TF: 800-323-5692 ■ *Web:* www.artacademy.edu

Art Center College of Design 1700 Lida St Pasadena CA 91103 626-396-2200 795-0578
Web: www.artcenter.edu

Art Institute of Atlanta
6600 Peachtree Dunwoody Rd NE 100 Embassy Row Atlanta GA 30328 770-394-8300 394-0008
TF: 800-275-4242 ■ *Web:* www.artinstitutes.edu/atlanta

Art Institute of Boston at Lesley 700 Beacon St Suite 202 Boston MA 02215 617-585-6600 585-6721
TF: 800-773-0494 ■ *Web:* web.lesley.edu/aib

Art Institute of California
Inland Empire 630 E Brier Dr San Bernardino CA 92408 909-915-2100
TF: 800-353-0812 ■ *Web:* www.artinstitutes.edu/inlandempire/
Los Angeles 2900 31st St Santa Monica CA 90405 310-752-4700 752-4708
TF: 888-646-4610 ■ *Web:* www.artinstitutes.edu/losangeles
Orange County 3601 W Sunflower Ave Santa Ana CA 92704 714-830-0200 556-1923
TF: 888-549-3055 ■ *Web:* www.artinstitutes.edu/orangecounty
San Diego 7650 Mission Valley Rd San Diego CA 92108 858-598-1200 291-3206*
**Fax Area Code:* 619 ■ *TF:* 800-591-2422 ■ *Web:* www.artinstitutes.edu/sandiego
San Francisco 1170 Market St San Francisco CA 94102 415-865-0198 863-6344
TF: 888-493-3261 ■ *Web:* www.artinstitutes.edu/sanfrancisco

Art Institute of Charlotte
2110 Water Ridge Pkwy 3 LakePointe Plaza Charlotte NC 28217 704-357-8020 357-1133
TF: 800-872-4417 ■ *Web:* www.artinstitutes.edu/charlotte

Art Institute of Colorado 1200 Lincoln St Denver CO 80203 303-837-0825 860-8520
TF: 800-275-2420 ■ *Web:* www.artinstitutes.edu/denver

Art Institute of Dallas 8080 Park Ln Suite 100 Dallas TX 75231 214-692-8080 750-9460
TF: 800-275-4243 ■ *Web:* www.artinstitutes.edu/dallas

Art Institute of Fort Lauderdale 1799 SE 17th St Fort Lauderdale FL 33316 954-463-3000 728-8637
TF: 800-275-7603 ■ *Web:* www.artinstitutes.edu/fortlauderdale

Art Institute of Houston 1900 Yorktown St Houston TX 77056 713-623-2040 966-2700
TF: 800-275-4244 ■ *Web:* www.artinstitutes.edu/houston

Art Institute of Indianapolis 3500 Depauw Blvd Indianapolis IN 46268 317-613-4800 613-4808
TF: 866-441-9031 ■ *Web:* www.artinstitutes.edu/indianapolis

Art Institute of Las Vegas 2350 Corporate Cir Henderson NV 89074 702-369-9944 992-8458
TF: 800-833-2678 ■ *Web:* www.artinstitutes.edu/lasvegas

Art Institute of New York City 75 Varick St 16th Fl New York NY 10013 212-226-5500 625-6065
Web: www.artinstitutes.edu/newyork

Art Institute of Ohio Cincinnati
8845 Governor's Hill Dr Suite 100 Cincinnati OH 45249 513-833-2400 833-2411
TF: 866-613-5184 ■ *Web:* www.artinstitutes.edu/cincinnati

Art Institute of Philadelphia 1622 Chestnut St Philadelphia PA 19103 215-567-7080 405-6398
TF: 800-275-2474 ■ *Web:* www.artinstitutes.edu/philadelphia

Art Institute of Phoenix 2233 W Dunlap Ave Phoenix AZ 85021 602-678-4300 331-5301
TF: 800-474-2479 ■ *Web:* www.artinstitutes.edu/phoenix

Phone | Fax

Art Institute of Pittsburgh 420 Blvd of the Allies Pittsburgh PA 15219 412-263-6600 263-6667
TF: 800-275-2470 ■ *Web:* www.artinstitutes.edu/pittsburgh/galleries

Art Institute of Portland 1122 NW Davis St Portland OR 97209 503-228-6528 227-1945*
**Fax:* Admissions ■ *TF:* 888-228-6528 ■ *Web:* www.artinstitutes.edu/portland

Art Institute of Seattle 2323 Elliott Ave Seattle WA 98121 206-448-0900 448-2501
TF: 800-275-2471 ■ *Web:* www.artinstitutes.edu/seattle

Art Institute of Tampa 4401 N Himes Ave Suite 150 Tampa FL 33614 813-873-2112 873-2171
TF: 866-703-3277 ■ *Web:* www.artinstitutes.edu/tampa

Art Institute of Washington 1820 N Fort Myer Dr Arlington VA 22209 703-358-9550 358-9759
TF: 877-303-3771 ■ *Web:* www.artinstitutes.edu/arlington

Art Institutes International Minnesota 15 S 9th St Minneapolis MN 55402 612-332-3361 332-3934
TF: 800-777-3643 ■ *Web:* www.artinstitutes.edu/minneapolis

Bradley Academy for the Visual Arts 1409 Williams Rd York PA 17402 717-755-2300 840-1951
TF: 800-864-7725 ■ *Web:* www.artinstitutes.edu/york

Brooks College 4825 E Pacific Coast Hwy Long Beach CA 90804 562-498-2441 597-2661
TF: 800-421-3775 ■ *Web:* www.brookscollege.edu

California College of the Arts
Oakland 5212 Broadway Oakland CA 94618 510-594-3600 594-3601
TF: 800-447-1278 ■ *Web:* www.cca.edu
San Francisco 1111 8th St San Francisco CA 94107 415-703-9500 703-9539
TF: 800-447-1278 ■ *Web:* www.cca.edu

California Design College 3440 Wilshire Blvd 10th Fl Los Angeles CA 90010 213-251-3636 385-3545
TF: 877-468-6232 ■ *Web:* www.artinstitutes.edu/cdc

California Institute of the Arts 24700 McBean Pkwy Valencia CA 91355 661-255-1050 253-7710
TF: 800-545-2787 ■ *Web:* www.calarts.edu

Cleveland Institute of Art 11141 East Blvd Cleveland OH 44106 216-421-7400 754-3634
TF: 800-754-3355 ■ *Web:* www.cia.edu

College for Creative Studies 201 E Kirby St Detroit MI 48202 313-664-7425 872-2739
TF: 800-952-2787 ■ *Web:* www.ccscad.edu

Columbus College of Art & Design 107 N 9th St Columbus OH 43215 614-224-9101 222-4040
Web: www.ccad.edu

Corcoran College of Art & Design 500 17th St NW Washington DC 20006 202-639-1800 639-1802
TF: 888-267-2672 ■ *Web:* www.corcoran.edu

Cornish College of the Arts 1000 Lenora St Seattle WA 98121 206-323-1400 720-1011
TF: 800-726-2787 ■ *Web:* www.cornish.edu

Fashion Institute of Design & Merchandising
Los Angeles 919 S Grand Ave Los Angeles CA 90015 213-624-1200 624-4777
TF Admissions: 800-624-1200 ■ *Web:* www.fidm.com
Orange County 17590 Gillette Ave Irvine CA 92614 949-851-6200 851-6808
TF: 888-974-3436 ■ *Web:* www.fidm.com
San Diego 1010 2nd Ave Suite 200 San Diego CA 92101 619-235-2049 232-4322
TF: 800-243-3436 ■ *Web:* www.fidm.com
San Francisco 55 Stockton St San Francisco CA 94108 415-675-5200 296-7299
TF: 800-422-3436 ■ *Web:* www.fidm.com

Fashion Institute of Technology 227 W 27th St New York NY 10001 212-217-7650 217-7481
TF: 800-999-9923 ■ *Web:* www.fitnyc.edu

Florida School of the Arts
St Johns River Community College 5001 St Johns Ave Palatka FL 32177 386-312-4300 312-4306
Web: floarts.org

Hussian School of Art 1118 Market St Philadelphia PA 19107 215-981-0900 864-9115
Web: www.hussianart.edu

Illinois Institute of Art
Chicago 350 N Orleans St Suite 136-L Chicago IL 60654 312-280-3500 280-8562
TF: 800-351-3450 ■ *Web:* www.ilia.aii.edu
Schaumburg 1000 N Plaza Dr Schaumburg IL 60173 847-619-3450 619-3064
TF: 800-314-3450 ■ *Web:* www.artinstitutes.edu/schaumburg

Institute of American Indian Arts 83 Avan Nu Po Rd Santa Fe NM 87508 505-424-2300 424-4500
TF Admissions: 800-804-6422 ■ *Web:* www.iaiancad.org

International Academy of Design & Technology
Chicago 1 N State St Suite 500 Chicago IL 60602 312-980-9200 541-3929
TF: 888-318-6111 ■ *Web:* www.iadtchicago.com
Las Vegas 2495 Village View Dr Henderson NV 89074 702-990-0150 990-0161
TF: 866-400-4238 ■ *Web:* www.iadtvegas.com
Tampa 5104 Eisenhower Blvd Tampa FL 33634 813-881-0007 881-0008
TF: 800-222-3369 ■ *Web:* www.academy.edu

Kansas City Art Institute 4415 Warwick Blvd Kansas City MO 64111 816-474-5224 802-3309
TF: 800-522-5224 ■ *Web:* www.kcai.edu

Maine College of Art 97 Spring St Portland ME 04101 207-775-3052 772-5069
TF: 800-639-4808 ■ *Web:* www.meca.edu

Maryland Institute College of Art 1300 W Mt Royal Ave Baltimore MD 21217 410-669-9200 225-2337
Web: www.mica.edu

Memphis College of Art 1930 Poplar Ave Memphis TN 38104 901-272-5100 272-5158
TF: 800-727-1088 ■ *Web:* www.mca.edu

Miami International University of Art & Design
1501 Biscayne Blvd Miami FL 33132 305-428-5700 374-5933
TF: 800-225-9023 ■ *Web:* www.artinstitutes.edu/miami

Minneapolis College of Art & Design 2501 Stevens Ave Minneapolis MN 55404 612-874-3760 874-3701
TF: 800-874-6223 ■ *Web:* www.mcad.edu

Moore College of Art & Design 1940 Race St Philadelphia PA 19103 215-965-4014 568-3547
TF: 800-523-2025 ■ *Web:* www.moore.edu

New England Institute of Art 10 Brookline Pl W Brookline MA 02245 617-739-1700 582-4500
TF: 800-903-4425 ■ *Web:* www.artinstitutes.edu/boston

New Hampshire Institute of Art 148 Concord St Manchester NH 03104 603-623-0313 647-0658
TF: 866-241-4918 ■ *Web:* www.nhia.edu

North Carolina School of the Arts 1533 S Main St Winston-Salem NC 27127 336-770-3399 770-3370
Web: www.ncarts.edu

Otis College of Art & Design 9045 Lincoln Blvd Los Angeles CA 90045 310-665-6820 665-6821
TF: 800-527-6847 ■ *Web:* www.otis.edu

Pennsylvania Academy of the Fine Arts School of Fine Arts
128 N Broad St Philadelphia PA 19102 215-972-7600 569-0153
Web: www.pafa.org/schoolFineArts.jsp

Pennsylvania College of Art & Design
204 N Prince St PO Box 59 Lancaster PA 17608 717-396-7833 396-1339
Web: www.pcad.edu

Rhode Island School of Design 2 College St Providence RI 02903 401-454-6100 454-6309
TF: 800-364-7473 ■ *Web:* www.risd.edu

Ringling College of Art & Design 2700 N Tamiami Trail Sarasota FL 34234 941-351-5100 359-7517
TF: 800-255-7695 ■ *Web:* www.ringling.edu

San Francisco Art Institute 800 Chestnut St San Francisco CA 94133 415-771-7020 749-1951
TF: 800-345-7324 ■ *Web:* www.sfai.edu

Savannah College of Art & Design 342 Bull St PO Box 2072 Savannah GA 31402 912-525-5100 525-5983
TF: 800-869-7223 ■ *Web:* www.scad.edu
Atlanta 1600 Peachtree St PO Box 77300 Atlanta GA 30357 404-253-2700 253-3466
TF: 877-722-3285 ■ *Web:* www.scad.edu/scadatlanta

School of Visual Arts 209 E 23rd St New York NY 10010 212-592-2000 592-2116
TF: 800-436-4204 ■ *Web:* www.schoolofvisualarts.edu

University of the Arts 320 S Broad St Philadelphia PA 19102 215-717-6049 717-6000
TF: 800-616-2787 ■ *Web:* www.uarts.edu

Virginia Marti College of Art & Design 11724 Detroit Ave Lakewood OH 44107 216-221-8584 221-2311
TF: 800-473-4350 ■ *Web:* www.virginiamarticollege.com

Watkins College of Art & Design 2298 Rose Parks Blvd Nashville TN 37228 615-383-4848 383-4849
TF: 866-877-6395 ■ *Web:* www.watkins.edu

165 COLLEGES - TRIBAL

SEE ALSO Colleges - Community & Junior p. 1459

Tribal Colleges generally serve geographically isolated American Indian populations that have no other means of accessing education beyond the high school level. They are unique institutions that combine personal attention with cultural relevance.

Phone *Fax*

Bay Mills Community College 12214 W Lakeshore Dr ....Brimley MI 49715 906-248-3354 248-3351
TF: 800-844-2622 ■ *Web:* www.bmcc.edu

Blackfeet Community College PO Box 819 ....Browning MT 59417 406-338-5421 338-3272*
*Fax: Admissions ■ *TF:* 800-549-7457 ■ *Web:* www.bfcc.org

Cankdeska Cikana Community College 214 1st Ave PO Box 269 ... Fort Totten ND 58335 701-766-4415 766-4077
TF: 888-783-1463 ■ *Web:* www.littlehoop.cc

Chief Dull Knife College PO Box 98.........................Lame Deer MT 59043 406-477-6215 477-6219
Web: www.cdkc.edu

College of Menominee Nation PO Box 1179...................Keshena WI 54135 715-799-5600 799-4392*
*Fax: Admissions ■ *TF:* 800-567-2344 ■ *Web:* www.menominee.edu

Comanche Nation College 1608 SW 9th St.....................Lawton OK 73501 580-591-0203 353-7075
TF: 877-591-0203 ■ *Web:* www.cnc.cc.ok.us

Crownpoint Institute of Technology PO Box 849 .... Crownpoint NM 87313 505-786-4100 786-5644
Web: www.cit.cc.nm.us

Dine College PO Box 67 ....Tsaile AZ 86556 928-724-6600 724-3327*
*Fax: Admissions ■ *TF:* 877-988-3463 ■ *Web:* www.dinecollege.edu

Fond du Lac Tribal & Community College 2101 14th St...........Cloquet MN 55720 218-879-0800 879-0814
TF: 800-657-3712 ■ *Web:* www.fdltcc.edu

Fort Belknap College PO Box 159 ....Harlem MT 59526 406-353-2607 353-2898*
*Fax: Admissions ■ *Web:* www.fbcc.edu

Fort Berthold Community College PO Box 490 .... New Town ND 58763 701-627-3665 627-3609*
*Fax: Admissions ■ *Web:* www.fbcc.bia.edu

Fort Peck Community College PO Box 398 .... Poplar MT 59255 406-768-6300 768-6301
Web: www.fpcc.edu

Haskell Indian Nations University 155 Indian Ave Box 5031 ...... Lawrence KS 66046 785-749-8454 749-8429*
*Fax: Admissions ■ *Web:* www.haskell.edu

Institute of American Indian Arts 83 Avan Nu Po Rd............Santa Fe NM 87508 505-424-2300 424-4500
TF Admissions: 800-804-6422 ■ *Web:* www.iaiancad.org

Keweenaw Bay Ojibwa Community College 111 Beartown Rd .... Baraga MI 49908 906-353-4600 353-8107
Web: www.kbocc.org

Lac Courte Oreilles Ojibwa Community College
13466 W Trepania Rd ....Hayward WI 54843 715-634-4790 634-5049*
*Fax: Admissions ■ *TF:* 888-526-6221 ■ *Web:* www.lco.edu

Leech Lake Tribal College PO Box 180 .... Cass Lake MN 56633 218-335-4200 335-4209
TF: 800-627-3529 ■ *Web:* www.lltc.org

Little Big Horn College 1 Forestry Ln PO Box 370 .... Crow Agency MT 59022 406-638-3104 638-3169
Web: www.lbhc.cc.mt.us

Little Priest Tribal College PO Box 270.....................Winnebago NE 68071 402-878-2380 878-2355
Web: www.lptc.bia.edu

Nebraska Indian Community College PO Box 428.................. Macy NE 68039 402-837-5078 837-4183*
*Fax: Admissions ■ *Web:* www.thenicc.edu/

Northwest Indian College 2522 Kwina Rd ....Bellingham WA 98226 360-676-2772 392-4333*
*Fax: Admissions ■ *TF:* 866-676-2772 ■ *Web:* www.nwic.edu/

Oglala Lakota College PO Box 629 .... Martin SD 57551 605-685-6407 685-6887
Web: www.olc.edu

Saginaw Chippewa Tribal College 2274 Enterprise Dr ...... Mount Pleasant MI 48858 989-775-4123 775-4528
Web: www.sagchip.org/tribalcollege

Salish Kootenai College PO Box 70............................ Pablo MT 59855 406-275-4800 275-4801*
*Fax: Admissions ■ *TF:* 877-752-6553 ■ *Web:* www.skc.edu

Sinte Gleska University 101 Antelope Lake Cir Dr PO Box 105...... Mission SD 57535 605-856-8100 856-4194
Web: www.sinte.edu

Sisseton Wahpeton College
Agency Village CPO BIA Road 700 PO Box 689.................Sisseton SD 57262 605-698-3966 742-0394
Web: www.swc.tc

Sitting Bull College 1341 92nd St .... Fort Yates ND 58538 701-854-3864 854-3861*
*Fax: Admissions ■ *Web:* www.sittingbull.edu

Southwestern Indian Polytechnic Institute
9169 Coors Rd NW PO Box 10146.......................Albuquerque NM 87184 505-346-2346 346-2373
TF: 800-586-7474 ■ *Web:* www.sipi.bia.edu

Stone Child College RR 1 Box 1082 ....Box Elder MT 59521 406-395-4313 395-4836*
*Fax: Admissions ■ *Web:* www.montana.edu/wwwscc

Tohono O'odham Community College PO Box 3129 ....Sells AZ 85634 520-383-8401 383-8403
Web: www.tocc.cc.az.us

Turtle Mountain Community College PO Box 340...............Belcourt ND 58316 701-477-7862 477-7892*
*Fax: Admissions ■ *Web:* www.tm.edu

United Tribes Technical College 3315 University Dr............ Bismarck ND 58504 701-255-3285 530-0640
Web: www.uttc.edu

White Earth Tribal & Community College
210 Main St S PO Box 478.............................Mahnomen MN 56557 218-935-0417 936-5736
Web: www.wetcc.org

Wind River Tribal College PO Box 8300 ....Ethete WY 82520 307-335-8243 335-8148
TF: 866-701-8385 ■ *Web:* www.wrtribalcollege.com

166 COLLEGES - WOMEN'S (FOUR-YEAR)

Phone *Fax*

Agnes Scott College 141 E College Ave........................ Decatur GA 30030 404-471-6000 471-6414*
*Fax: Admissions ■ *TF:* 800-868-8602 ■ *Web:* www.agnesscott.edu

Alverno College PO Box 343922.......................... Milwaukee WI 53234 414-382-6100 382-6055
TF: 800-933-3401 ■ *Web:* www.alverno.edu

Barnard College Columbia University 3009 Broadway............New York NY 10027 212-854-2014 854-6220*
*Fax: Admissions ■ *Web:* www.barnard.edu

Bay Path College 588 Longmeadow St ....Longmeadow MA 01106 413-567-0621 565-1105
TF: 800-782-7284 ■ *Web:* www.baypath.edu

Bennett College 900 E Washington St..................... Greensboro NC 27401 336-370-8624 517-2166*
*Fax: Admissions ■ *TF Admissions:* 800-413-5323 ■ *Web:* www.bennett.edu

Blue Mountain College PO Box 160..................... Blue Mountain MS 38610 662-685-4161 685-4776*
*Fax: Admissions ■ *TF:* 800-235-0136 ■ *Web:* www.bmc.edu

Brenau University 500 Washington St .... Gainesville GA 30501 770-534-6299 538-4701*
*Fax: Admissions ■ *TF:* 800-252-5119 ■ *Web:* www.brenau.edu

Phone *Fax*

Bryn Mawr College 101 N Merion Ave ....Bryn Mawr PA 19010 610-526-5000 526-7471*
*Fax: Admissions ■ *TF Admissions:* 800-262-1885 ■ *Web:* www.brynmawr.edu

Carlow University 3333 5th Ave .... Pittsburgh PA 15213 412-578-6000 578-6689
TF: 800-333-2275 ■ *Web:* www.carlow.edu

Cedar Crest College 100 College Dr.........................Allentown PA 18104 610-437-4471 606-4647*
*Fax: Admissions ■ *TF Admissions:* 800-360-1222 ■ *Web:* www.cedarcrest.edu

Chatham University Woodland Rd .... Pittsburgh PA 15232 412-365-1100 365-1609*
*Fax: Admissions ■ *TF:* 800-837-1290 ■ *Web:* www.chatham.edu

College of New Rochelle 29 Castle Pl ....New Rochelle NY 10805 914-654-5452 654-5464
TF: 800-933-5923 ■ *Web:* www.cnr.edu

College of Notre Dame of Maryland 4701 N Charles St .... Baltimore MD 21210 410-435-0100 532-6287*
*Fax: Admissions ■ *TF Admissions:* 800-435-0300 ■ *Web:* www.ndm.edu

College of Saint Benedict 37 S College Ave .... Saint Joseph MN 56374 320-363-5011 363-3206*
*Fax: Admissions ■ *TF:* 800-249-9840 ■ *Web:* www.csbsju.edu

College of Saint Catherine 2004 Randolph Ave................ Saint Paul MN 55105 651-690-6000 690-6024*
*Fax: Admissions ■ *TF:* 800-945-4599 ■ *Web:* www.stkate.edu
Minneapolis 601 25th Ave S .... Minneapolis MN 55454 651-690-7700 690-7849*
*Fax: Admissions ■ *TF:* 800-945-4599 ■ *Web:* www.stkate.edu

College of Saint Elizabeth 2 Convent Rd.................... Morristown NJ 07960 973-290-4700 290-4710*
*Fax: Admissions ■ *TF Admissions:* 800-210-7900 ■ *Web:* www.cse.edu

College of Saint Mary 7000 Mercy Rd.............................Omaha NE 68106 402-399-2400 399-2412*
*Fax: Admissions ■ *TF:* 800-926-5534 ■ *Web:* www.csm.edu

Columbia College 1301 Columbia College Dr.................. Columbia SC 29203 803-786-3012 786-3674
TF: 800-277-1301 ■ *Web:* www.columbiacollegesc.edu

Converse College 580 E Main St ....Spartanburg SC 29302 864-596-9000 596-9225*
*Fax: Admissions ■ *TF Admissions:* 800-766-1125 ■ *Web:* www.converse.edu

Douglass College 125 George St .... New Brunswick NJ 08901 732-932-9500 932-8877
Web: www.douglass.rutgers.edu

Georgian Court University 900 Lakewood Ave.................Lakewood NJ 08701 732-987-2760 987-2000*
*Fax: Admissions ■ *TF:* 800-458-8422 ■ *Web:* www.georgian.edu

Hollins University 7916 Williamson Rd........................Roanoke VA 24020 540-362-6401 362-6218*
*Fax: Admissions ■ *TF Admissions:* 800-456-9595 ■ *Web:* www.hollins.edu

Judson College 302 Bibb St ....Marion AL 36756 334-683-5110 683-5282*
*Fax: Admissions ■ *TF Admissions:* 800-447-9472 ■ *Web:* www.judson.edu

Mary Baldwin College 318 Prospect St .... Staunton VA 24401 540-887-7019 887-7292*
*Fax: Admissions ■ *TF Admissions:* 800-468-2262 ■ *Web:* www.mbc.edu

Marymount College of Fordham University 100 Marymount Ave.....Tarrytown NY 10591 914-332-8295 332-7442
TF: 800-724-4312 ■ *Web:* www.fordham.edu

Meredith College 3800 Hillsborough St.........................Raleigh NC 27607 919-760-8581 760-2348*
*Fax: Admissions ■ *TF:* 800-637-3348 ■ *Web:* www.meredith.edu

Midway College 512 E Stephens St .... Midway KY 40347 859-846-5346 846-5787*
*Fax: Admissions ■ *TF:* 800-755-0031 ■ *Web:* www.midway.edu

Mills College 5000 MacArthur Blvd .... Oakland CA 94613 510-430-2135 430-3298*
*Fax: Admissions ■ *TF Admissions:* 800-876-4557 ■ *Web:* www.mills.edu

Moore College of Art & Design 1940 Race St................Philadelphia PA 19103 215-965-4014 568-3547
TF: 800-523-2025 ■ *Web:* www.moore.edu

Mount Holyoke College 50 College St .... South Hadley MA 01075 413-538-2000 538-2409
Web: www.mtholyoke.edu

Mount Mary College 2900 N Menomonee River Pkwy........... Milwaukee WI 53222 414-256-1219 256-0180*
*Fax: Admissions ■ *TF Admissions:* 800-321-6265 ■ *Web:* www.mtmary.edu

Mount Saint Mary's College 12001 Chalon Rd ....Los Angeles CA 90049 310-954-4250 954-4259*
*Fax: Admissions ■ *TF Admissions:* 800-999-9893 ■ *Web:* www.msmc.la.edu

Newcomb College Institute for Women 43 Newcomb Pl....... New Orleans LA 70118 504-865-5422 862-8589
TF: 888-862-8589 ■ *Web:* www.newcomb.tulane.edu

Peace College 15 E Peace St..................................Raleigh NC 27604 919-508-2000 508-2326*
*Fax: Admissions ■ *TF:* 800-732-2347 ■ *Web:* www.peace.edu

Pine Manor College 400 Heath St .... Chestnut Hill MA 02467 617-731-7104 731-7102
TF: 800-762-1357 ■ *Web:* www.pmc.edu

Randolph College 2500 Rivermont Ave .... Lynchburg VA 24503 434-947-8000 947-8996*
*Fax: Admissions ■ *TF Admissions:* 800-745-7692 ■ *Web:* www.randolphcollege.edu

Regis College 235 Wellesley St ....Weston MA 02493 781-768-7000 768-7071
TF: 866-438-7344 ■ *Web:* www.regiscollege.edu

Rosemont College 1400 Montgomery Ave .... Rosemont PA 19010 610-527-0200 520-4399*
*Fax: Admissions ■ *TF Admissions:* 800-331-0708 ■ *Web:* www.rosemont.edu

Russell Sage College 45 Ferry St..................................Troy NY 12180 518-244-2217 244-6880*
*Fax: Admissions ■ *TF Admissions:* 888-837-9724 ■ *Web:* www.sage.edu/rsc

Saint Joseph College 1678 Asylum Ave................... West Hartford CT 06117 860-232-4571 231-5744*
*Fax: Admissions ■ *TF Admissions:* 866-442-8753 ■ *Web:* www.sjc.edu

Saint Mary-of-the-Woods College
3301 St Mary Rd .... Saint Mary-of-the-Woods IN 47876 812-535-5106 535-5010*
*Fax: Admissions ■ *TF:* 800-926-7692 ■ *Web:* www.smwc.edu

Saint Mary's College Le Mans Hall Rm 122 .... Notre Dame IN 46556 574-284-4587 284-4841*
*Fax: Admissions ■ *TF Admissions:* 800-551-7621 ■ *Web:* www.saintmarys.edu

Salem College 601 S Church St......................... Winston-Salem NC 27101 336-721-2600 917-5572*
*Fax: Admissions ■ *TF Admissions:* 800-327-2536 ■ *Web:* www.salem.edu

Scripps College 1030 Columbia Ave........................ Claremont CA 91711 909-621-8149 607-7508*
*Fax: Admissions ■ *TF:* 800-770-1333 ■ *Web:* www.scrippscol.edu

Simmons College 300 The Fenway ....Boston MA 02115 617-521-2000 521-3190*
*Fax: Admissions ■ *TF:* 800-345-8468 ■ *Web:* www.simmons.edu

Smith College 7 College Ln.......................... Northampton MA 01063 413-584-2700 585-2527
TF: 800-383-3232 ■ *Web:* www.smith.edu

Spelman College 350 Spelman Ln SW......................... Atlanta GA 30314 404-681-3643 270-5201*
*Fax: Admissions ■ *TF Admissions:* 800-982-2411 ■ *Web:* www.spelman.edu

Stephens College 1200 E Broadway Box 2121.................Columbia MO 65215 573-876-7207 876-7237*
*Fax: Admissions ■ *TF Admissions:* 800-876-7207 ■ *Web:* www.stephens.edu

Stern College for Women of Yeshiva University
245 Lexington Ave...................................New York NY 10016 212-340-7701 340-7837*
*Fax: Admissions ■ *Web:* www.yu.edu/stern

Sweet Briar College 134 Chappel Rd .... Sweet Briar VA 24595 434-381-6100 381-6152*
*Fax: Admissions ■ *TF Admissions:* 800-381-6142 ■ *Web:* www.sbc.edu

Texas Woman's University
304 Administration Dr PO Box 425589.........................Denton TX 76204 940-898-3188 898-3081*
*Fax: Admissions ■ *TF:* 866-809-6130 ■ *Web:* www.twu.edu

Trinity University Trinity College 125 Michigan Ave NE .... Washington DC 20017 202-884-9000 884-9403*
*Fax: Admissions ■ *TF Admissions:* 800-492-6882 ■ *Web:* www.trinitydc.edu

University of Richmond Westhampton College
The Deanery 28 Westhampton Way..............University of Richmond VA 23173 804-289-8640 287-6003
TF: 800-700-1662 ■ *Web:* oncampus.richmond.edu/student/affairs

Ursuline College 2550 Lander Rd..........................Pepper Pike OH 44124 440-449-4200 684-6138*
*Fax: Admissions ■ *TF:* 888-877-8546 ■ *Web:* www.ursuline.edu

Wellesley College 106 Central St.......................... Wellesley MA 02481 781-283-1000 283-3678*
*Fax: Admissions ■ *Web:* www.wellesley.edu

Wesleyan College 4760 Forsyth Rd ....Macon GA 31210 478-477-1110 757-4030*
*Fax: Admissions ■ *TF:* 800-447-6610 ■ *Web:* www.wesleyancollege.edu

Westhampton College
The Deanery 28 Westhampton Way.............University of Richmond VA 23173 804-289-8640 287-6003
TF: 800-700-1662 ■ *Web:* oncampus.richmond.edu/student/affairs

Wilson College 1015 Philadelphia Ave .... Chambersburg PA 17201 717-264-4141 264-1578*
*Fax: Admissions ■ *TF Admissions:* 800-421-8402 ■ *Web:* www.wilson.edu

Women's College of the University of Denver 1901 E Asbury Ave...... Denver CO 80208 303-871-6848 871-6897
Web: www.womenscollege.du.edu

167 COLLEGES & UNIVERSITIES - CHRISTIAN

SEE ALSO Colleges & Universities - Jesuit p. 1498; Colleges - Bible p. 1458

The institutions listed here are members of the Council for Christian Colleges & Universities (CCCU). Although many other colleges and universities describe themselves as "religiously affiliated," members of CCCU are intentionally Christ-centered. Among the criteria for membership in CCCU, schools must have curricular and extra-curricular programs that reflect the integration of scholarship, biblical faith, and service.

				Phone	Fax
Abilene Christian University 1705 Campus Ct	Abilene	TX	79601	325-674-2000	674-2130*
*Fax: Admissions ■ *TF Admissions:* 800-460-6228 ■ *Web:* www.acu.edu					
Anderson University 1100 E 5th St	Anderson	IN	46012	765-649-9071	641-4091*
*Fax: Admissions ■ *TF Admissions:* 800-428-6414 ■ *Web:* www.anderson.edu					
Asbury College 1 Macklem Dr	Wilmore	KY	40390	859-858-3511	858-3921*
*Fax: Admissions ■ *TF Admissions:* 800-888-1818 ■ *Web:* www.asbury.edu					
Azusa Pacific University 901 E Alosta Ave PO Box 7000	Azusa	CA	91702	626-969-3434	812-3096
TF: 800-825-5278 ■ *Web:* www.apu.edu					
Belhaven College 1500 Peachtree St Box 153	Jackson	MS	39202	601-968-5940	968-8946*
*Fax: Admissions ■ *TF:* 800-960-5940 ■ *Web:* www.belhaven.edu					
Bethel College 1001 W McKinley Ave	Mishawaka	IN	46545	574-257-3339	257-3335*
*Fax: Admissions ■ *TF Admissions:* 800-422-4101 ■ *Web:* www.bethelcollege.edu					
Bethel University 3900 Bethel Dr	Saint Paul	MN	55112	651-638-6400	635-1490*
*Fax: Admissions ■ *TF:* 800-255-8706 ■ *Web:* www.bethel.edu					
Biola University 13800 Biola Ave	La Mirada	CA	90639	562-903-6000	903-4709*
*Fax: Admissions ■ *TF Admissions:* 800-652-4652 ■ *Web:* www.biola.edu					
Bluffton University 1 University Dr	Bluffton	OH	45817	419-358-3000	358-3081*
*Fax: Admissions ■ *TF:* 800-488-3257 ■ *Web:* www.bluffton.edu					
Bryan College 721 Bryan Dr PO Box 7000	Dayton	TN	37321	423-775-2041	775-7199
TF: 800-277-9522 ■ *Web:* www.bryan.edu					
California Baptist University 8432 Magnolia Ave	Riverside	CA	92504	951-689-5771	343-4525*
*Fax: Admissions ■ *TF:* 877-228-8866 ■ *Web:* www.calbaptist.edu					
Calvin College 3201 Burton St SE	Grand Rapids	MI	49546	616-526-6000	526-6777*
*Fax: Admissions ■ *TF:* 800-688-0122 ■ *Web:* www.calvin.edu					
Campbellsville University 1 University Dr	Campbellsville	KY	42718	270-789-5000	789-5071*
*Fax: Admissions ■ *TF Admissions:* 800-264-6014 ■ *Web:* www.campbellsville.edu					
Carson-Newman College 1646 Russell Ave	Jefferson City	TN	37760	865-475-9061	471-3502*
*Fax: Admissions ■ *TF:* 800-678-9061 ■ *Web:* www.cn.edu					
Cedarville University 251 N Main St	Cedarville	OH	45314	937-766-7700	766-7575*
*Fax: Admissions ■ *TF:* 800-233-2784 ■ *Web:* www.cedarville.edu					
College of the Ozarks 1 Industrial Dr PO Box 17	Point Lookout	MO	65726	417-334-6411	335-2618*
*Fax: Admissions ■ *TF Admissions:* 800-222-0525 ■ *Web:* www.cofo.edu					
Colorado Christian University 8787 W Alameda Ave	Lakewood	CO	80226	303-963-3200	963-3201
TF: 800-443-2484 ■ *Web:* www.ccu.edu					
Corban College 5000 Deer Park Dr SE	Salem	OR	97317	503-581-8600	585-4316
TF: 800-845-3005 ■ *Web:* www.corban.edu					
Cornerstone University 1001 E Beltline Ave NE	Grand Rapids	MI	49525	616-222-1426	222-1418*
*Fax: Admissions ■ *TF Admissions:* 800-787-9778 ■ *Web:* www.cornerstone.edu					
Covenant College 14049 Scenic Hwy	Lookout Mountain	GA	30750	706-820-1560	419-1044*
*Fax: Admissions ■ *TF:* 888-451-2683 ■ *Web:* www.covenant.edu					
Crichton College 255 N Highland Ave	Memphis	TN	38111	901-320-9797	320-9791*
*Fax: Admissions ■ *TF:* 800-960-9777 ■ *Web:* www.crichton.edu					
Crown College 8700 College View Dr	Saint Bonifacius	MN	55375	952-446-4100	446-4149
TF: 800-682-7696 ■ *Web:* www.crown.edu					
Dallas Baptist University 3000 Mountain Creek Pkwy	Dallas	TX	75211	214-333-7100	333-5447*
*Fax: Admissions ■ *TF:* 800-460-1328 ■ *Web:* www.dbu.edu					
Dordt College 498 4th Ave NE	Sioux Center	IA	51250	712-722-6080	722-1198
TF: 800-343-6738 ■ *Web:* www.dordt.edu					
East Texas Baptist University 1209 N Grove St	Marshall	TX	75670	903-935-7963	923-2001*
*Fax: Admissions ■ *TF:* 800-804-3828 ■ *Web:* www.etbu.edu					
Eastern Mennonite University 1200 Park Rd	Harrisonburg	VA	22802	540-432-4118	432-4444*
*Fax: Admissions ■ *TF Admissions:* 800-368-2665 ■ *Web:* www.emu.edu					
Eastern Nazarene College 23 E Elm Ave	Quincy	MA	02170	617-745-3000	745-3929
TF: 800-883-6288 ■ *Web:* www.enc.edu					
Eastern University 1300 Eagle Rd	Saint Davids	PA	19087	610-341-5800	341-1723*
*Fax: Admissions ■ *TF Admissions:* 800-452-0996 ■ *Web:* www.eastern.edu					
Erskine College PO Box 176	Due West	SC	29639	864-379-2131	379-3048*
*Fax: Admissions ■ *TF Admissions:* 800-241-8721 ■ *Web:* www.erskine.edu					
Evangel University 1111 N Glenstone Ave	Springfield	MO	65802	417-865-2815	865-9599
TF: 800-382-6435 ■ *Web:* www.evangel.edu					
Fresno Pacific University 1717 S Chestnut Ave Box 2005	Fresno	CA	93702	559-453-2039	453-2007*
*Fax: Admissions ■ *TF:* 800-660-6089 ■ *Web:* www.fresno.edu					
Geneva College 3200 College Ave	Beaver Falls	PA	15010	724-847-6500	847-6776*
*Fax: Admissions ■ *TF:* 800-847-8255 ■ *Web:* www.geneva.edu					
George Fox University 414 N Meridian St	Newberg	OR	97132	503-538-8383	554-3110*
*Fax: Admissions ■ *TF:* 800-765-4369 ■ *Web:* www.georgefox.edu					
Gordon College 255 Grapevine Rd	Wenham	MA	01984	978-927-2300	867-4682*
*Fax: Admissions ■ *TF:* 800-343-1379 ■ *Web:* www.gordon.edu					
Goshen College 1700 S Main St	Goshen	IN	46526	574-535-7000	535-7609*
*Fax: Admissions ■ *TF:* 800-348-7422 ■ *Web:* www.goshen.edu					
Grace College 200 Seminary Dr	Winona Lake	IN	46590	574-372-5100	372-5120*
*Fax: Admissions ■ *TF:* 800-544-7223 ■ *Web:* www.grace.edu					
Greenville College 315 E College Ave	Greenville	IL	62246	618-664-7100	664-9841*
*Fax: Admissions ■ *TF:* 800-345-4440 ■ *Web:* www.greenville.edu					
Hardin-Simmons University 2200 Hickory St	Abilene	TX	79698	325-670-1206	671-2115*
*Fax: Admissions ■ *TF:* 877-464-7889 ■ *Web:* www.hsutx.edu					
Hope International University 2500 E Nutwood Ave	Fullerton	CA	92831	714-879-3901	526-0231*
*Fax: Admissions ■ *TF:* 866-722-4673 ■ *Web:* www.hiu.edu					
Houghton College 1 Willard Ave PO Box 128	Houghton	NY	14744	585-567-9200	567-9522*
*Fax: Admissions ■ *TF:* 800-777-2556 ■ *Web:* www.houghton.edu					
Houston Baptist University 7502 Fondren Rd	Houston	TX	77074	281-649-3000	649-3217*
*Fax: Admissions ■ *TF Admissions:* 800-969-3210 ■ *Web:* www.hbu.edu					
Howard Payne University 1000 Fisk Ave	Brownwood	TX	76801	325-646-2502	649-8901*
*Fax: Admissions ■ *TF:* 800-950-8465 ■ *Web:* www.hputx.edu					
Huntington University 2303 College Ave	Huntington	IN	46750	260-356-6000	358-3699*
*Fax: Admissions ■ *TF Admissions:* 800-642-6493 ■ *Web:* www.huntington.edu					
Indiana Wesleyan University 4201 S Washington St	Marion	IN	46953	765-677-2138	677-2333*
*Fax: Admissions ■ *TF:* 800-332-6901 ■ *Web:* www.indwes.edu					
John Brown University 2000 W University St	Siloam Springs	AR	72761	479-524-3131	524-4196*
*Fax: Admissions ■ *TF Admissions:* 877-528-4636 ■ *Web:* www.jbu.edu					
Judson College 302 Bibb St	Marion	AL	36756	334-683-5110	683-5282*
*Fax: Admissions ■ *TF Admissions:* 800-447-9472 ■ *Web:* www.judson.edu					
Judson College 1151 N State St	Elgin	IL	60123	847-628-2500	628-2526*
*Fax: Admissions ■ *TF Admissions:* 800-879-5376 ■ *Web:* www.judsoncollege.edu					
Kentucky Christian University 100 Academic Pkwy	Grayson	KY	41143	606-474-3000	474-3155*
*Fax: Admissions ■ *TF Admissions:* 800-522-3181 ■ *Web:* www.kcu.edu					
King College 1350 King College Rd	Bristol	TN	37620	423-652-4861	968-4456
TF Admissions: 800-362-0014 ■ *Web:* www.king.edu					
King's University College 9125 50th St	Edmonton	AB	T6B2H3	780-465-3500	465-3534
TF: 800-661-8582 ■ *Web:* www.kingsu.ab.ca					
Lee University 1120 N Ocoee St	Cleveland	TN	37311	423-614-8000	614-8533*
*Fax: Admissions ■ *TF:* 800-533-9930 ■ *Web:* www.leeuniversity.edu					
LeTourneau University 2100 S Mobberly Ave	Longview	TX	75602	903-753-0231	233-4301*
*Fax: Admissions ■ *TF:* 800-759-8811 ■ *Web:* www.letu.edu					
Lipscomb University 3901 Granny White Pike	Nashville	TN	37204	615-966-1000	966-1804*
*Fax: Admissions ■ *TF:* 800-333-4358 ■ *Web:* www.lipscomb.edu					
Louisiana College 1140 College Dr	Pineville	LA	71359	318-487-7011	487-7550*
*Fax: Admissions ■ *TF:* 800-487-1906 ■ *Web:* www.lacollege.edu					
Malone College 515 25th St NW	Canton	OH	44709	330-471-8100	471-8149*
*Fax: Admissions ■ *TF:* 800-521-1146 ■ *Web:* www.malone.edu					
Master's College 21726 Placerita Canyon Rd	Santa Clarita	CA	91321	661-259-3540	288-1037*
*Fax: Admissions ■ *TF:* 800-568-6248 ■ *Web:* www.masters.edu					
Messiah College Box 3005	Grantham	PA	17027	717-691-6000	796-5374*
*Fax: Admissions ■ *TF:* 800-233-4220 ■ *Web:* www.messiah.edu					
MidAmerica Nazarene University 2030 E College Way	Olathe	KS	66062	913-782-3750	791-3481*
*Fax: Admissions ■ *TF:* 800-800-8887 ■ *Web:* www.mnu.edu					
Milligan College PO Box 500	Milligan College	TN	37682	423-461-8730	461-8982*
*Fax: Admissions ■ *TF:* 800-262-8337 ■ *Web:* www.milligan.edu					
Mississippi College 200 S Capitol St PO Box 4026	Clinton	MS	39058	601-925-3000	925-3950*
*Fax: Admissions ■ *TF:* 800-738-1236 ■ *Web:* www.mc.edu					
Missouri Baptist University 1 College Park Dr	Saint Louis	MO	63141	314-434-1115	434-7596
TF: 877-434-1115 ■ *Web:* www.mobap.edu					
Montreat College 310 Gaither Cir PO Box 1267	Montreat	NC	28757	828-669-8011	669-0120
TF: 800-622-6968 ■ *Web:* www.montreat.edu					
Mount Vernon Nazarene University 800 Martinsburg Rd	Mount Vernon	OH	43050	740-392-6868	
TF Admissions: 866-782-2435 ■ *Web:* www.mvnu.edu					
North Greenville University 7801 N Tigerville Rd PO Box 1892	Tigerville	SC	29688	864-977-7000	977-7177*
*Fax: Admissions ■ *TF:* 800-468-6642 ■ *Web:* www.ngu.edu					
North Park University 3225 W Foster Ave	Chicago	IL	60625	773-244-5500	244-4953
TF: 800-888-6728 ■ *Web:* www.northpark.edu					
Northwest Christian College 828 E 11th Ave	Eugene	OR	97401	541-684-7201	684-7317*
*Fax: Admissions ■ *TF:* 877-463-6622 ■ *Web:* www.nwcc.edu					
Northwest Nazarene University 623 Holly St	Nampa	ID	83686	208-467-8000	467-8645*
*Fax: Admissions ■ *TF Admissions:* 877-668-4968 ■ *Web:* www.nnu.edu					
Northwest University 5520 108th Ave NE	Kirkland	WA	98033	425-822-8266	889-5224*
*Fax: Admissions ■ *TF Admissions:* 800-669-3781 ■ *Web:* www.northwestu.edu					
Northwestern College 101 7th St SW	Orange City	IA	51041	712-707-7000	707-7164*
*Fax: Admissions ■ *TF:* 800-747-4757 ■ *Web:* www.nwciowa.edu					
Northwestern College 3003 Snelling Ave N	Saint Paul	MN	55113	651-631-5100	631-5680
TF Admissions: 800-827-6827 ■ *Web:* nwc.nwc.edu					
Nyack College 1 South Blvd	Nyack	NY	10960	845-358-1710	358-3047*
*Fax: Admissions ■ *TF Admissions:* 800-336-9225 ■ *Web:* www.nyackcollege.edu					
Oklahoma Baptist University 500 W University St	Shawnee	OK	74804	405-275-2850	878-2068*
*Fax: Admissions ■ *TF:* 800-654-3285 ■ *Web:* www.okbu.edu					
Oklahoma Christian University PO Box 11000	Oklahoma City	OK	73136	405-425-5000	425-5069*
*Fax: Admissions ■ *TF:* 800-877-5010 ■ *Web:* www.oc.edu					
Oklahoma Wesleyan University 2201 Silver Lake Rd	Bartlesville	OK	74006	918-333-6200	335-6229*
*Fax: Admissions ■ *TF:* 800-468-6292 ■ *Web:* www.okwu.edu					
Olivet Nazarene University 1 University Ave	Bourbonnais	IL	60914	815-939-5011	935-4998*
*Fax: Admissions ■ *TF:* 800-648-1463 ■ *Web:* www.olivet.edu					
Oral Roberts University 7777 S Lewis Ave	Tulsa	OK	74171	918-495-6161	495-6222*
*Fax: Admissions ■ *TF:* 800-678-8876 ■ *Web:* www.oru.edu					
Palm Beach Atlantic University PO Box 24708	West Palm Beach	FL	33416	561-803-2000	803-2115*
*Fax: Admissions ■ *TF:* 888-468-6722 ■ *Web:* www.pba.edu					
Point Loma Nazarene University 3900 Lomaland Dr	San Diego	CA	92106	619-849-2200	849-2601*
*Fax: Admissions ■ *TF Admissions:* 800-733-7770 ■ *Web:* www.pointloma.edu					
Redeemer University College 777 Garner Rd E	Ancaster	ON	L9K1J4	905-648-2131	648-2134
TF: 877-779-0913 ■ *Web:* www.redeemer.on.ca					
Roberts Wesleyan College 2301 Westside Dr	Rochester	NY	14624	585-594-6000	594-6371*
*Fax: Admissions ■ *TF Admissions:* 800-777-4792 ■ *Web:* www.roberts.edu					
Seattle Pacific University 3307 3rd Ave W	Seattle	WA	98119	206-281-2000	281-2544*
*Fax: Admissions ■ *TF:* 800-366-3344 ■ *Web:* www.spu.edu					
Simpson University 2211 College View Dr	Redding	CA	96003	530-226-4606	226-4861*
*Fax: Admissions ■ *TF:* 888-974-6776 ■ *Web:* www.simpsonuniversity.edu					
Southeastern University 1000 Longfellow Blvd	Lakeland	FL	33801	863-667-5000	667-5200*
*Fax: Admissions ■ *TF Admissions:* 800-500-8760 ■ *Web:* www.seuniversity.edu					
Southern Nazarene University 6729 NW 39th Expy	Bethany	OK	73008	405-789-6400	491-6320*
*Fax: Admissions ■ *TF:* 800-648-9899 ■ *Web:* www.snu.edu					
Southern Wesleyan University 907 Wesleyan Dr	Central	SC	29630	864-644-5000	644-5972*
*Fax: Admissions ■ *TF:* 800-282-8798 ■ *Web:* www.swu.edu					
Southwest Baptist University 1600 University Ave	Bolivar	MO	65613	417-326-5281	328-1808*
*Fax: Admissions ■ *TF:* 800-526-5859 ■ *Web:* www.sbuniv.edu					
Spring Arbor University 106 E Main St	Spring Arbor	MI	49283	517-750-1200	750-6620*
*Fax: Admissions ■ *TF Admissions:* 800-968-0011 ■ *Web:* www.spring.arbor.edu					
Sterling College 125 W Cooper	Sterling	KS	67579	620-278-2173	278-4418
TF: 800-346-1017 ■ *Web:* www.sterling.edu					
Tabor College 400 S Jefferson St	Hillsboro	KS	67063	620-947-3121	947-6276*
*Fax: Admissions ■ *TF Admissions:* 800-822-6799 ■ *Web:* www.tabor.edu					
Taylor University 236 W Reade Ave	Upland	IN	46989	765-998-2751	998-4925*
*Fax: Admissions ■ *TF:* 800-882-3456 ■ *Web:* www.taylor.edu					
Trevecca Nazarene University 333 Murfreesboro Rd	Nashville	TN	37210	615-248-1200	248-7406*
*Fax: Admissions ■ *TF:* 888-210-4868 ■ *Web:* www.trevecca.edu					
Trinity Christian College 6601 W College Dr	Palos Heights	IL	60463	866-874-6463	239-4826*
*Fax Area Code: 708 ■ *TF:* 800-748-0085 ■ *Web:* www.trnty.edu					
Trinity International University 2065 Half Day Rd	Deerfield	IL	60015	847-317-7000	317-8097
TF: 800-822-3225 ■ *Web:* www.tiu.edu					
Trinity Western University 7600 Glover Rd	Langley	BC	V2Y1Y1	604-888-7511	513-2064*
*Fax: Admissions ■ *TF:* 888-468-6898 ■ *Web:* www.twu.ca					
Union University 1050 Union University Dr	Jackson	TN	38305	731-661-5210	661-5589*
*Fax: Admissions ■ *TF:* 800-338-6466 ■ *Web:* www.uu.edu					
University of Sioux Falls 1101 W 22nd St	Sioux Falls	SD	57105	605-331-6600	331-6615
TF: 800-888-1047 ■ *Web:* www.thecoo.edu					
Vanguard University of Southern California 55 Fair Dr	Costa Mesa	CA	92626	714-556-3610	966-5471*
*Fax: Admissions ■ *TF Admissions:* 800-722-6279 ■ *Web:* www.vanguard.edu					
Warner Pacific College 2219 SE 68th Ave	Portland	OR	97215	503-517-1020	517-1352
TF: 800-804-1510 ■ *Web:* www1.warnerpacific.edu					
Warner Southern College 13895 Hwy 27	Lake Wales	FL	33859	863-638-1426	638-7290*
*Fax: Admissions ■ *TF:* 800-949-7248 ■ *Web:* www.warner.edu					
Wayland Baptist University 1900 W 7th St	Plainview	TX	79072	806-291-1000	291-1973*
*Fax: Admissions ■ *TF:* 800-588-1928 ■ *Web:* www.wbu.edu					
Waynesburg College 51 W College St	Waynesburg	PA	15370	724-627-8191	627-8124*
*Fax: Admissions ■ *TF Admissions:* 800-225-7393 ■ *Web:* www.waynesburg.edu					
Westmont College 955 La Paz Rd	Santa Barbara	CA	93108	805-565-6000	565-6234*
*Fax: Admissions ■ *TF Admissions:* 800-777-9011 ■ *Web:* www.westmont.edu					
Wheaton College 501 College Ave	Wheaton	IL	60187	630-752-5000	752-5285
TF: 800-222-2419 ■ *Web:* www.wheaton.edu					
Whitworth College 300 W Hawthorne Rd	Spokane	WA	99251	509-777-3212	777-3758*
*Fax: Admissions ■ *TF Admissions:* 800-533-4668 ■ *Web:* www.whitworth.edu					
Williams Baptist College 60 W Fulbright St	Walnut Ridge	AR	72476	870-886-6741	886-3924*
*Fax: Admissions ■ *TF:* 800-722-4434 ■ *Web:* www.wbcoll.edu					

168 COLLEGES & UNIVERSITIES - FOUR-YEAR

SEE ALSO Colleges & Universities - Christian p. 1474; Colleges & Universities - Graduate & Professional Schools p. 1492; Colleges & Universities - Historically Black p. 1497; Colleges & Universities - Jesuit p. 1498; Colleges - Community & Junior p. 1459; Colleges - Fine Arts p. 1472; Colleges - Women's (Four-Year) p. 1473; Military Service Academies p. 1970; Universities - Canadian p. 2392; Vocational & Technical Schools p. 2406

Alabama

				Phone	Fax
Alabama Agricultural & Mechanical University					
4900 Meridian St	Huntsville	AL	35810	256-851-5000	372-5249*
*Fax: Admissions ■ TF: 800-553-0816 ■ Web: www.aamu.edu					
Alabama State University 915 S Jackson St	Montgomery	AL	36104	334-229-4291	229-4984*
*Fax: Admissions ■ TF Admissions: 800-253-5037 ■ Web: www.alasu.edu					
Auburn University 202 Mary Martin Hall	Auburn University	AL	36849	334-844-6425	844-6436*
*Fax: Admissions ■ TF Admissions: 800-282-8769 ■ Web: www.auburn.edu					
Montgomery PO Box 244023	Montgomery	AL	36124	334-244-3000	244-3795*
*Fax: Admissions ■ TF: 800-227-2649 ■ Web: www.aum.edu					
Birmingham-Southern College 900 Arkadelphia Rd	Birmingham	AL	35254	205-226-4600	226-3074*
*Fax: Admissions ■ TF: 800-523-5793 ■ Web: www.bsc.edu					
Concordia College Selma PO Box 2470	Selma	AL	36703	334-874-5700	874-5755*
*Fax: Admissions ■ Web: www.concordiaselma.edu					
Faulkner University 5345 Atlanta Hwy	Montgomery	AL	36109	334-272-5820	260-6137*
*Fax: Admissions ■ TF: 800-879-9816 ■ Web: www.faulkner.edu					
Huntingdon College 1500 E Fairview Ave	Montgomery	AL	36106	334-833-4497	833-4497*
*Fax: Admissions ■ TF Admissions: 800-763-0313 ■ Web: www.huntingdon.edu					
Jacksonville State University 700 Pelham Rd N	Jacksonville	AL	36265	256-782-5781	782-5953*
*Fax: Admissions ■ TF: 800-231-5291 ■ Web: www.jsu.edu					
Judson College 302 Bibb St	Marion	AL	36756	334-683-5110	683-5282*
*Fax: Admissions ■ TF Admissions: 800-447-9472 ■ Web: www.judson.edu					
Miles College 5500 Myron Massey Blvd	Fairfield	AL	35064	205-929-1000	929-1627*
*Fax: Admissions ■ TF Admissions: 800-445-0708 ■ Web: www.miles.edu					
Oakwood College 7000 Adventist Blvd	Huntsville	AL	35896	256-726-7356	726-7154*
*Fax: Admissions ■ TF: 800-824-5312 ■ Web: www.oakwood.edu					
Regions University 1200 Taylor Rd	Montgomery	AL	36117	334-387-3877	387-3878
TF: 888-790-8080 ■ Web: www.amridgeuniversity.edu					
Samford University 800 Lakeshore Dr	Birmingham	AL	35229	205-726-3673	726-2171*
*Fax: Admissions ■ TF Admissions: 800-888-7218 ■ Web: www.samford.edu					
Selma University 1501 Lapsley St	Selma	AL	36701	334-872-2533	872-7746
South University Montgomery 5355 Vaughn Rd	Montgomery	AL	36116	334-395-8800	395-8859*
*Fax: Admissions ■ TF: 866-629-2962 ■ Web: www.southuniversity.edu					
Spring Hill College 4000 Dauphin St	Mobile	AL	36608	251-380-4000	460-2186*
*Fax: Admissions ■ TF Admissions: 800-742-6704 ■ Web: www.shc.edu					
Stillman College PO Box 1430	Tuscaloosa	AL	35403	205-349-4240	366-8941*
*Fax: Admissions ■ TF Admissions: 800-841-5722 ■ Web: www.stillman.edu					
Talladega College 627 W Battle St	Talladega	AL	35160	256-362-0206	362-0274*
*Fax: Admissions ■ Web: www.talladega.edu					
Troy University 600 University Ave	Troy	AL	36082	334-670-3100	670-3733*
*Fax: Admissions ■ TF: 800-551-9716 ■ Web: www.troy.edu					
Dothan PO Box 8368	Dothan	AL	36304	334-983-6556	556-1040*
*Fax: Admissions ■ TF: 866-291-0317 ■ Web: dothan.troy.edu					
Montgomery PO Drawer 4419	Montgomery	AL	36103	334-241-9500	241-5448*
*Fax: Admissions ■ TF Admissions: 800-355-8786 ■ Web: montgomery.troy.edu					
Phenix City 1 University Pl	Phenix City	AL	36869	334-297-1007	448-5229*
*Fax: Admissions ■ Web: phenix.troy.edu					
Tuskegee University 102 Old Admissions Blvd	Tuskegee	AL	36088	334-727-8011	727-5750*
*Fax: Admissions ■ TF Admissions: 800-622-6531 ■ Web: www.tuskegee.edu					
University of Alabama Box 870132	Tuscaloosa	AL	35487	205-348-6010	348-9046*
*Fax: Admissions ■ TF Admissions: 800-933-2262 ■ Web: www.ua.edu					
Birmingham 1530 3rd Ave S HUC260	Birmingham	AL	35294	205-934-8221	975-7114*
*Fax: Admissions ■ TF: 800-421-8743 ■ Web: www.uab.edu					
Huntsville 301 Sparkman Dr	Huntsville	AL	35899	256-824-2733	824-7780*
*Fax: Admissions ■ TF: 800-824-2255 ■ Web: www.uah.edu					
University of Mobile 5735 College Pkwy	Mobile	AL	36613	251-675-5990	442-2498*
*Fax: Admissions ■ TF: 800-946-7267 ■ Web: www.umobile.edu					
University of Montevallo Station 6030	Montevallo	AL	35115	205-665-6000	665-6032*
*Fax: Admissions ■ TF Admissions: 800-292-4349 ■ Web: www.montevallo.edu					
University of North Alabama 1 Harrison Plaza	Florence	AL	35632	256-765-4100	765-4960*
*Fax: Admissions ■ TF: 800-825-5862 ■ Web: www.una.edu					
University of South Alabama 2500 Meisler Hall	Mobile	AL	36688	251-460-6141	460-7876
TF: 800-872-5247 ■ Web: www.usouthal.edu					
University of West Alabama Station 4 UWA	Livingston	AL	35470	205-652-3400	652-3522*
*Fax: Admissions ■ TF Admissions: 800-621-8044 ■ Web: www.uwa.edu					

Alaska

				Phone	Fax
Alaska Pacific University 4101 University Dr	Anchorage	AK	99508	907-564-8248	567-8317*
*Fax: Admissions ■ TF: 800-252-7528 ■ Web: www.alaskapacific.edu					
Sheldon Jackson College 801 Lincoln St	Sitka	AK	99835	907-747-5221	747-6366*
*Fax: Admissions ■ TF Admissions: 800-478-4556 ■ Web: www.sj-alaska.edu					
University of Alaska Anchorage 3211 Providence Dr	Anchorage	AK	99508	907-786-1800	786-4888*
*Fax: Admissions ■ Web: www.uaa.alaska.edu					
University of Alaska Fairbanks PO Box 757480	Fairbanks	AK	99775	907-474-7500	474-5379*
*Fax: Admissions ■ TF: 800-478-1823 ■ Web: www.uaf.edu					
Bristol Bay 527 Seward St PO Box 1070	Dillingham	AK	99576	907-842-5109	842-5692*
*Fax: Admissions ■ TF: 800-478-5109 ■ Web: www.uaf.edu/bbc					
Kuskokwim PO Box 368	Bethel	AK	99559	907-543-4500	543-4527
Web: www.kuskokwim.bethel.alaska.edu					
University of Alaska Southeast 11120 Glacier Hwy	Juneau	AK	99801	907-796-6000	796-6365
TF: 877-465-4827 ■ Web: www.jun.alaska.edu					
Wayland Baptist University Anchorage 7801 E 32 Ave	Anchorage	AK	99504	907-333-2277	337-8122
Web: www.wbu.edu					

Arizona

				Phone	Fax
American Indian College of the Assemblies of God					
10020 N 15th Ave	Phoenix	AZ	85021	602-944-3335	943-8299
TF: 800-933-3828 ■ Web: www.aicag.edu					
Arizona State University 1151 S Forest Ave PO Box 870312	Tempe	AZ	85281	480-965-9011	727-6453
Web: www.asu.edu					
East 7001 E Williams Field Rd	Mesa	AZ	85212	480-727-3278	965-3610
Web: www.poly.asu.edu					
West PO Box 37100	Phoenix	AZ	85069	602-543-5500	543-8312*
*Fax: Admissions ■ Web: www.west.asu.edu					
Embry-Riddle Aeronautical University Prescott					
3700 Willow Creek Rd	Prescott	AZ	86301	928-777-3728	777-6606*
*Fax: Admissions ■ TF: 800-888-3728 ■ Web: www.erau.edu/pr					
Grand Canyon University 3300 W Camelback Rd	Phoenix	AZ	85017	602-639-7500	639-7835*
*Fax: Library ■ TF: 800-800-9776 ■ Web: www.gcu.edu					
Indian Bible College 2918 N Aris Ave	Flagstaff	AZ	86004	928-774-3890	774-2655
Web: www.indianbible.org					
International Baptist College 2150 E Southern Ave	Tempe	AZ	85282	480-838-7070	505-3299
TF: 800-422-4858 ■ Web: www.tricityministries.org/ibc					
Northern Arizona University PO Box 4084	Flagstaff	AZ	86011	928-523-5511	523-6023*
*Fax: Admissions ■ TF Admissions: 888-628-2968 ■ Web: www.nau.edu					
Ottawa University Phoenix 10020 N 25th Ave	Phoenix	AZ	85021	602-371-1188	371-0035
TF: 800-235-9586 ■ Web: www.ottawa.edu					
Prescott College 220 Grove Ave	Prescott	AZ	86301	928-778-2090	776-5242*
*Fax: Admissions ■ TF: 877-350-2100 ■ Web: www.prescott.edu					
University of Arizona 1401 E University Blvd	Tucson	AZ	85721	520-621-2211	621-9799*
*Fax: Admissions ■ Web: www.arizona.edu					
University of Phoenix 4605 E Elwood St	Phoenix	AZ	85040	480-966-7400	
TF: 800-366-9699 ■ Web: www.phoenix.edu					
Western International University 9215 N Black Canyon Hwy	Phoenix	AZ	85021	602-943-2311	371-8637
TF: 866-948-4636 ■ Web: www.wintu.edu					

Arkansas

				Phone	Fax
Arkansas Baptist College 1621 ML King Dr	Little Rock	AR	72202	501-374-7856	372-7992
Web: www.arkansasbaptist.edu					
Arkansas State University PO Box 1630	State University	AR	72467	870-972-3024	972-3406
TF: 800-382-3030 ■ Web: www.astate.edu					
Arkansas Tech University 1605 Coliseum Dr	Russellville	AR	72801	479-968-0389	964-0522*
*Fax: Admissions ■ TF Admissions: 800-582-6953 ■ Web: www.atu.edu					
Harding University 915 E Market Ave	Searcy	AR	72149	501-279-4000	279-4129*
*Fax: Admissions ■ TF Admissions: 800-477-4407 ■ Web: www.harding.edu					
Henderson State University 1100 Henderson St	Arkadelphia	AR	71999	870-230-5000	230-5066*
*Fax: Admissions ■ TF: 800-228-7333 ■ Web: www.hsu.edu					
Hendrix College 1600 Washington Ave	Conway	AR	72032	501-329-6811	450-3843*
*Fax: Admissions ■ TF: 800-277-9017 ■ Web: www.hendrix.edu					
John Brown University 2000 W University St	Siloam Springs	AR	72761	479-524-3131	524-4196*
*Fax: Admissions ■ TF Admissions: 877-528-4636 ■ Web: www.jbu.edu					
Lyon College PO Box 2317	Batesville	AR	72503	870-698-4250	793-1791*
*Fax: Admissions ■ TF: 800-423-2542 ■ Web: www.lyon.edu					
Ouachita Baptist University 410 Ouachita St	Arkadelphia	AR	71998	870-245-5000	245-5500*
*Fax: Admissions ■ TF Admissions: 800-342-5628 ■ Web: www.obu.edu					
Philander Smith College 1 Trudie Kibbe Reed Dr	Little Rock	AR	72202	501-375-9845	370-5225*
*Fax: Admissions ■ Web: www.philander.edu					
Southern Arkansas University 100 E University St	Magnolia	AR	71753	870-235-4000	235-5005*
*Fax: Admissions ■ TF: 800-332-7286 ■ Web: www.saumag.edu					
University of Arkansas 232 Silas Hunt Hall	Fayetteville	AR	72701	479-575-5346	575-7515*
*Fax: Admissions ■ TF: 800-377-8632 ■ Web: www.uark.edu					
Little Rock 2801 S University Ave	Little Rock	AR	72204	501-569-3000	569-8956
Web: www.ualr.edu					
Monticello PO Box 3600	Monticello	AR	71656	870-460-1026	460-1926*
*Fax: Admissions ■ TF: 800-844-1826 ■ Web: www.uamont.edu					
Pine Bluff 1200 N University Dr	Pine Bluff	AR	71601	870-575-8000	575-4608*
*Fax: Admissions ■ TF Admissions: 800-264-6585 ■ Web: www.uapb.edu					
University of Central Arkansas 201 Donaghey Ave	Conway	AR	72035	501-450-5000	450-5228*
*Fax: Admissions ■ TF Admissions: 800-243-8245 ■ Web: www.uca.edu					
University of the Ozarks 415 N College Ave	Clarksville	AR	72830	479-979-1227	979-1417*
*Fax: Admissions ■ TF Admissions: 800-264-8636 ■ Web: www.ozarks.edu					
Williams Baptist College 60 W Fulbright St	Walnut Ridge	AR	72476	870-886-6741	886-3924*
*Fax: Admissions ■ TF: 800-722-4434 ■ Web: www.wbcoll.edu					

California

				Phone	Fax
Academy of Art University 79 New Montgomery St	San Francisco	CA	94105	415-274-2200	618-6287
TF: 800-544-2787 ■ Web: www.academyart.edu					
Alliant International University 10455 Pomerado Rd	San Diego	CA	92131	858-635-4772	635-4739*
*Fax: Admissions ■ TF: 866-825-5426 ■ Web: www.alliant.edu					
American InterContinental University Los Angeles					
12655 W Jefferson Blvd	Los Angeles	CA	90066	310-302-2000	302-2001*
*Fax: Admissions ■ TF: 000-594-9000 ■ Web: la.aiuniv.edu					
Azusa Pacific University 901 E Alosta Ave PO Box 7000	Azusa	CA	91702	626-969-3434	812-3096
TF: 800-825-5278 ■ Web: www.apu.edu					
Bethany University of the Assemblies of God					
800 Bethany Dr	Scotts Valley	CA	95066	831-438-3800	438-6104*
*Fax: Admissions ■ TF Admissions: 800-843-9410 ■ Web: www.bethany.edu					
Biola University 13800 Biola Ave	La Mirada	CA	90639	562-903-6000	903-4709*
*Fax: Admissions ■ TF Admissions: 800-652-4652 ■ Web: www.biola.edu					
Brooks Institute of Photography 801 Alston Rd	Santa Barbara	CA	93108	805-966-3888	565-1386*
*Fax: Admissions ■ TF: 888-304-3456 ■ Web: www.brooks.edu					
California Baptist University 8432 Magnolia Ave	Riverside	CA	92504	951-689-5771	343-4525*
*Fax: Admissions ■ TF: 877-228-8866 ■ Web: www.calbaptist.edu					
California Christian College 4881 E University Ave	Fresno	CA	93703	559-251-4215	251-4231*
*Fax: Admissions ■ Web: www.calchristiancollege.org					
California Institute of Technology 1200 E California Blvd	Pasadena	CA	91125	626-395-6811	683-3026*
*Fax: Admissions ■ TF: 800-568-8324 ■ Web: www.caltech.edu					
California International University 3130 Wilshire Blvd	Los Angeles	CA	90010	213-381-3719	381-6990*
*Fax: Admissions ■ Web: www.ciula.edu					
California Lutheran University 60 W Olsen Rd	Thousand Oaks	CA	91360	805-493-3135	493-3114
TF: 877-258-3678 ■ Web: www.callutheran.edu					
California Maritime Academy 200 Maritime Academy Dr	Vallejo	CA	94590	707-654-1330	654-1336*
*Fax: Admissions ■ TF: 800-561-1945 ■ Web: www.csum.edu					
California Pacific University 1017 E Grand Ave	Escondido	CA	92025	760-739-7730	
TF: 800-458-9667 ■ Web: www.cpu.edu					
California Polytechnic State University	San Luis Obispo	CA	93407	805-756-1111	756-5400
Web: www.calpoly.edu					
California State Polytechnic University Pomona					
3801 W Temple Ave	Pomona	CA	91768	909-869-7659	869-4529*
*Fax: Admissions ■ Web: www.csupomona.edu					
California State University					
Bakersfield 9001 Stockdale Hwy	Bakersfield	CA	93311	661-654-2011	654-3389*
*Fax: Admissions ■ Web: www.csubak.edu					
Channel Islands 1 University Dr	Camarillo	CA	93012	805-437-8400	437-8509*
*Fax: Admissions ■ Web: www.csuci.edu					
Chico CSU Chico	Chico	CA	95929	530-898-6321	898-6456*
*Fax: Admissions ■ TF Admissions: 800-542-4426 ■ Web: www.csuchico.edu					
Dominguez Hills 1000 E Victoria St	Carson	CA	90747	310-243-3300	516-4573*
*Fax: Admissions ■ TF: 888-278-3448 ■ Web: www.csudh.edu					
East Bay 25800 Carlos Bee Blvd	Hayward	CA	94542	510-885-3000	885-4059
Web: www.csueastbay.edu					
Fresno 5241 N Maple Ave	Fresno	CA	93740	559-278-4240	278-4812*
*Fax: Admissions ■ Web: www.csufresno.edu					
Fullerton PO Box 6900	Fullerton	CA	92834	714-278-2011	278-2300
Web: www.fullerton.edu					

California (Cont'd)

	City	State	Zip	Phone	Fax
Long Beach 1250 Bellflower Blvd *Fax: Admissions ■ *Web:* www.csulb.edu	Long Beach	CA	90840	562-985-4111	985-4973*
Los Angeles 5151 State University Dr *Fax: Admissions ■ *Web:* www.calstatela.edu	Los Angeles	CA	90032	323-343-3000	343-6306*
Monterey Bay 100 Campus Center *Fax: Admissions ■ *Web:* csumb.edu	Seaside	CA	93955	831-582-3518	582-3087*
Northridge 18111 Nordhoff St *Web:* www.csun.edu	Northridge	CA	91330	818-677-1200	677-3766
Sacramento 6000 J St *Web:* www.csus.edu	Sacramento	CA	95819	916-278-3901	278-7473
San Bernardino 5500 University Pkwy *Web:* www.csusb.edu	San Bernardino	CA	92407	909-537-5188	537-7034
San Marcos 333 S Twin Oaks Valley Rd *Fax: Admissions ■ *Web:* www.csusm.edu	San Marcos	CA	92096	760-750-4000	750-3248*
Stanislaus 1 University Cir *Web:* www.csustan.edu	Turlock	CA	95382	209-667-3152	667-3788
California State University Stanislaus Stockton Center 612 E Magnolia St *Web:* stockton.csustan.edu	Stockton	CA	95202	209-467-5300	467-5333
Chapman University 1 University Dr *Fax: Admissions ■ *TF:* 888-282-7759 ■ *Web:* www.chapman.edu	Orange	CA	92866	714-997-6815	997-6713*
University College Irvine 7545 Irvine Center Dr Suite 150 *Web:* www1.chapman.edu/univcoll/ac/irvine	Irvine	CA	92618	949-753-4774	753-7875
University College Modesto 5222 Pirrone Ct *Web:* www1.chapman.edu/univcoll	Salida	CA	95368	209-545-1234	545-0596
Charles R Drew University of Medicine & Science 1731 E 120th St *Fax: Admissions ■ *Web:* www.cdrewu.edu	Los Angeles	CA	90059	323-563-4800	563-4957*
City University Los Angeles PO Box 45227 *Fax Area Code: 323 ■ *Fax: Admissions ■ *Web:* www.cula.edu	Los Angeles	CA	90045	310-671-0783	293-1691*
Claremont McKenna College 890 Columbia Ave *Fax: Admissions ■ *Web:* www.claremontmckenna.edu	Claremont	CA	91711	909-621-8088	621-8516*
Cogswell Polytechnical College 1175 Bordeaux Dr *Fax: Admissions ■ *TF:* 800-264-7955 ■ *Web:* www.cogswell.edu	Sunnyvale	CA	94089	408-541-0100	747-0764*
Coleman College 8888 Balboa Ave *Web:* www.coleman.edu	San Diego	CA	92123	858-499-0202	499-0233
Columbia College Hollywood 18618 Oxnard St *TF:* 800-785-0585 ■ *Web:* www.columbiacollege.edu	Tarzana	CA	91356	818-345-8414	345-9053
Concordia University Irvine 1530 Concordia W *TF:* 800-229-1200 ■ *Web:* www.cui.edu	Irvine	CA	92612	949-854-8002	854-6894
Design Institute of San Diego 8555 Commerce Ave *Web:* www.disd.edu	San Diego	CA	92121	858-566-1200	566-2711
Dominican University of California 50 Acacia Ave *Fax: Admissions ■ *TF Admissions:* 888-323-6763 ■ *Web:* www.dominican.edu	San Rafael	CA	94901	415-457-4440	485-3214*
Escondido Bible College 927 Idaho Ave *Web:* www.cotvbiblecollege.edu	Escondido	CA	92025	760-745-9826	
Fresno Pacific University 1717 S Chestnut Ave Box 2005 *Fax: Admissions ■ *TF:* 800-660-6089 ■ *Web:* www.fresno.edu	Fresno	CA	93702	559-453-2039	453-2007*
Harvey Mudd College 301 Platt Blvd Kingston Hall *Fax: Admissions ■ *Web:* www.hmc.edu	Claremont	CA	91711	909-621-8011	607-7046*
Hebrew Union College Los Angeles 3077 University Ave *Fax: Admissions ■ *TF:* 800-899-0925 ■ *Web:* www.huc.edu/about/center-la.shtml	Los Angeles	CA	90007	213-749-3424	747-6128*
Holy Names University 3500 Mountain Blvd *Fax: Admissions ■ *TF:* 800-430-1321 ■ *Web:* www.hnu.edu	Oakland	CA	94619	510-436-1000	436-1325*
Hope International University 2500 E Nutwood Ave *Fax: Admissions ■ *TF:* 866-722-4673 ■ *Web:* www.hiu.edu	Fullerton	CA	92831	714-879-3901	526-0231*
Humboldt State University 1 Harpst St *Fax: Admissions ■ *TF:* 866-850-9556 ■ *Web:* www.humboldt.edu	Arcata	CA	95521	707-826-3011	826-6190*
Humphreys College 6650 Inglewood Ave *Web:* www.humphreys.edu	Stockton	CA	95207	209-478-0800	478-8721
John F Kennedy University 100 Ellinwood Way *Fax: Admissions ■ *TF:* 800-696-5358 ■ *Web:* www.jfku.edu	Pleasant Hill	CA	94523	925-969-3300	969-3101*
La Sierra University 4500 Riverwalk Pkwy *TF:* 800-874-5587 ■ *Web:* www.lasierra.edu	Riverside	CA	92515	951-785-2000	785-2901
Laguna College of Art & Design 2222 Laguna Canyon Rd *Fax: Admissions ■ *TF:* 800-255-0762 ■ *Web:* www.lagunacollege.edu	Laguna Beach	CA	92651	949-376-6000	376-6009*
Lincoln University 401 15th St *Fax: Admissions ■ *TF:* 888-810-9998 ■ *Web:* www.lincolnuca.edu	Oakland	CA	94612	510-628-8010	628-8012*
Loma Linda University 11234 Anderson St *Web:* www.llu.edu	Loma Linda	CA	92354	909-558-1000	
Loyola Marymount University 1 LMU Dr *TF:* 800-568-4636 ■ *Web:* www.lmu.edu	Los Angeles	CA	90045	310-338-2700	338-2797
Master's College 21726 Placerita Canyon Rd *Fax: Admissions ■ *TF:* 800-568-6248 ■ *Web:* www.masters.edu	Santa Clarita	CA	91321	661-259-3540	288-1037*
Menlo College 1000 El Camino Real *TF:* 800-556-3656 ■ *Web:* www.menlo.edu	Atherton	CA	94027	650-543-3753	543-4496
Mills College 5000 MacArthur Blvd *Fax: Admissions ■ *TF Admissions:* 800-876-4557 ■ *Web:* www.mills.edu	Oakland	CA	94613	510-430-2135	430-3298*
Mount Saint Mary's College 12001 Chalon Rd *Fax: Admissions ■ *TF Admissions:* 800-999-9893 ■ *Web:* www.msmc.la.edu	Los Angeles	CA	90049	310-954-4250	954-4259*
National Hispanic University 14271 Story Rd *Fax: Admissions ■ *Web:* www.nhu.edu	San Jose	CA	95127	408-254-6900	254-1369*
National University 11255 N Torrey Pines Rd *TF:* 800-628-8648 ■ *Web:* www.nu.edu	La Jolla	CA	92037	858-642-8000	642-8709
New College of California 777 Valencia St *Fax: Admissions ■ *TF:* 888-437-3460 ■ *Web:* www.newcollege.edu	San Francisco	CA	94110	415-437-3400	437-3470*
Northwestern Polytechnic University 47671 Westinghouse Dr *Web:* www.npu.edu	Fremont	CA	94539	510-657-5913	657-8975
Notre Dame de Namur University 1500 Ralston Ave *Fax: Admissions ■ *TF:* 800-263-0545 ■ *Web:* www.ndnu.edu	Belmont	CA	94002	650-508-3600	508-3426*
Occidental College 1600 Campus Rd *Fax: Admissions ■ *TF Admissions:* 800-825-5262 ■ *Web:* www.oxy.edu	Los Angeles	CA	90041	323-259-2700	341-4875*
Pacific Union College 1 Angwin Ave *Fax: Admissions ■ *TF:* 800-862-7080 ■ *Web:* www.puc.edu	Angwin	CA	94508	707-965-6336	965-6432*
Patten University 2433 Coolidge Ave *Fax: Admissions ■ *TF:* 877-472-8836 ■ *Web:* www.patten.edu	Oakland	CA	94601	510-261-8500	534-4344*
Pepperdine University 24255 Pacific Coast Hwy *Fax: Admissions ■ *Web:* www.pepperdine.edu	Malibu	CA	90263	310-506-4000	506-4861*
Pitzer College 1050 N Mills Ave *Fax: Admissions ■ *TF:* 800-748-9371 ■ *Web:* www.pitzer.edu	Claremont	CA	91711	909-621-8129	621-8770*
Point Loma Nazarene University 3900 Lomaland Dr *Fax: Admissions ■ *TF Admissions:* 800-733-7770 ■ *Web:* www.pointloma.edu	San Diego	CA	92106	619-849-2200	849-2601*
Pomona College 333 N College Way *Fax: Admissions ■ *Web:* www.pomona.edu	Claremont	CA	91711	909-621-8134	621-8952*
Ryokan College 11965 Venice Blvd Suite 304 *Fax: Admissions ■ *TF:* 866-796-5261 ■ *Web:* www.ryokan.edu	Los Angeles	CA	90066	310-390-7560	391-9756*
Saint Mary's College of California 1928 St Mary's Rd *Fax: Admissions ■ *TF:* 800-800-4762 ■ *Web:* www.stmarys-ca.edu	Moraga	CA	94575	925-631-4000	376-7193*
Samuel Merritt College 370 Hawthorne Ave *Fax: Admissions ■ *TF Admissions:* 800-607-6377 ■ *Web:* www.samuelmerritt.edu	Oakland	CA	94609	510-869-6576	869-6525*
San Diego Christian College 2100 Greenfield Dr *Fax: Admissions ■ *TF:* 800-676-2242 ■ *Web:* www.sdcc.edu	El Cajon	CA	92019	619-441-2200	590-1739*
San Diego State University 5500 Campanile Dr *Fax: Admissions ■ *Web:* www.sdsu.edu	San Diego	CA	92182	619-594-5200	594-1250*
Imperial Valley 720 Heber Ave *Fax: Admissions ■ *Web:* www.ivcampus.sdsu.edu	Calexico	CA	92231	760-768-5520	768-5589*
San Francisco Conservatory of Music 50 Oak St *Web:* www.sfcm.edu	San Francisco	CA	94102	415-864-7326	503-6299
San Francisco State University 1600 Holloway Ave *Fax: Admissions ■ *Web:* www.sfsu.edu	San Francisco	CA	94132	415-338-1111	338-7196*
San Jose State University 1 Washington Sq *Web:* www.sjsu.edu	San Jose	CA	95192	408-924-1000	924-2050
Santa Clara University 500 El Camino Real *Web:* www.scu.edu	Santa Clara	CA	95053	408-554-4764	554-5255
Scripps College 1030 Columbia Ave *Fax: Admissions ■ *TF:* 800-770-1333 ■ *Web:* www.scrippscol.edu	Claremont	CA	91711	909-621-8149	607-7508*
Simpson University 2211 College View Dr *Fax: Admissions ■ *TF:* 888-974-6776 ■ *Web:* www.simpsonuniversity.edu	Redding	CA	96003	530-226-4606	226-4861*
Sonoma State University 1801 E Cotati Ave *Fax: Admissions ■ *Web:* www.sonoma.edu	Rohnert Park	CA	94928	707-664-2880	664-2060*
South Baylo University 1126 N Brookhurst St *TF:* 888-642-2956 ■ *Web:* southbaylo.edu	Anaheim	CA	92801	714-533-1495	533-6040
Southern California Institute of Architecture 960 E 3rd St *Fax: Admissions ■ *Web:* www.sciarc.edu	Los Angeles	CA	90013	213-613-2200	613-2260*
Southern California Seminary 2075 E Madison Ave *Web:* www.socalsem.edu	El Cajon	CA	92019	619-442-9841	442-4510
Stanford University 355 Valdez St *Web:* www.stanford.edu	Stanford	CA	94305	650-725-5294	725-2846
Thomas Aquinas College 10000 N Ojai Rd *TF:* 800-634-9797 ■ *Web:* www.thomasaquinas.edu	Santa Paula	CA	93060	805-525-4417	525-9342
Trinity Life Bible College 5225 Hillsdale Blvd *Fax: Admissions ■ *Web:* www.tlbc.edu	Sacramento	CA	95842	916-348-4689	334-2315*
University of California					
Berkeley *Web:* www.berkeley.edu	Berkeley	CA	94720	510-642-6000	643-7333
Davis 1 Shields Ave *Web:* www.ucdavis.edu	Davis	CA	95616	530-752-2971	752-1280
Irvine 204 Administration Bldg *Web:* www.uci.edu	Irvine	CA	92697	949-824-5011	824-2711
Merced PO Box 2039 *Fax: Admissions ■ *TF:* 866-270-7301 ■ *Web:* www.ucmerced.edu	Merced	CA	95344	209-724-4400	724-4244*
Riverside 900 University Ave 1120 Hinderaker Hall *Web:* www.ucr.edu	Riverside	CA	92521	951-827-3411	827-6344
San Diego 9500 Gilman Dr *Fax: Admissions ■ *Web:* www.ucsd.edu	La Jolla	CA	92093	858-534-2230	534-4831*
San Francisco 505 Parnassus Ave *Web:* www.ucsf.edu	San Francisco	CA	94122	415-353-1553	353-3925
Santa Barbara *Web:* www.ucsb.edu	Santa Barbara	CA	93106	805-893-8000	893-2676
Santa Cruz 1156 High St Hahn Bldg Rm 150 *Web:* www.ucsc.edu	Santa Cruz	CA	95064	831-459-2131	459-4163
University of California (UCLA) Los Angeles 405 Hilgard Ave *Fax: Admissions ■ *Web:* www.ucla.edu	Los Angeles	CA	90095	310-825-4321	206-1206*
University of California Irvine College of Health Sciences 244 Irvine Hall *Web:* www.cohs.uci.edu	Irvine	CA	92697	949-824-0174	824-2118
University of Judaism 15600 Mulholland Dr *Fax: Admissions ■ *TF:* 877-862-5852 ■ *Web:* www.ajula.edu	Bel Air	CA	90077	310-476-9777	471-3657*
University of the Pacific 3601 Pacific Ave *TF:* 800-959-2867 ■ *Web:* web.pacific.edu	Stockton	CA	95211	209-946-2211	946-2413
University of Redlands 1200 E Colton Ave PO Box 3080 *Fax: Admissions ■ *TF:* 800-455-5064 ■ *Web:* www.redlands.edu	Redlands	CA	92374	909-335-4074	335-4089*
University of San Diego 5998 Alcala Park *TF:* 800-248-4873 ■ *Web:* www.sandiego.edu	San Diego	CA	92110	619-260-4506	260-6836
University of San Francisco 2130 Fulton St *Fax: Admissions ■ *TF Admissions:* 800-225-5873 ■ *Web:* www.usfca.edu	San Francisco	CA	94117	415-422-5555	422-2217*
University of Southern California (USC) University Park *Fax: Admissions ■ *Web:* www.usc.edu	Los Angeles	CA	90089	213-740-2311	821-3716*
University of La Verne 1950 3rd St *Fax: Admissions ■ *TF Admissions:* 800-876-4858 ■ *Web:* www.ulv.edu	La Verne	CA	91750	909-593-3511	392-2714*
Vanguard University of Southern California 55 Fair Dr *Fax: Admissions ■ *TF Admissions:* 800-722-6279 ■ *Web:* www.vanguard.edu	Costa Mesa	CA	92626	714-556-3610	966-5471*
Weimar College 20601 W Paoli Ln PO Box 486 *TF:* 800-525-9192 ■ *Web:* www.weimarcollege.com	Weimar	CA	95736	530-637-4111	422-7949
Westmont College 955 La Paz Rd *Fax: Admissions ■ *TF Admissions:* 800-777-9011 ■ *Web:* www.westmont.edu	Santa Barbara	CA	93108	805-565-6000	565-6234*
Whittier College 13406 E Philadelphia St *Fax: Admissions ■ *Web:* www.whittier.edu	Whittier	CA	90608	562-907-4200	907-4870*
William Jessup University 333 Sunset Blvd *Fax: Admissions ■ *TF:* 800-355-7522 ■ *Web:* www.jessup.edu	Rocklin	CA	95765	916-577-2200	577-2220*
Woodbury University 7500 Glenoaks Blvd *TF:* 800-784-9663 ■ *Web:* www.woodbury.edu	Burbank	CA	91510	818-767-0888	767-7520
World University 107 N Ventura St PO Box 1567 *Web:* www.worldu.edu	Ojai	CA	93024	805-646-1444	646-1217

Colorado

	City	State	Zip	Phone	Fax
Adams State College 208 Edgemont Blvd *TF:* 800-824-6494 ■ *Web:* www.adams.edu	Alamosa	CO	81102	719-587-7712	587-7522
Auraria Higher Education Center 1201 5th St *Web:* www.ahec.edu	Denver	CO	80204	303-556-3291	
Beth-El College of Nursing & Health Sciences 3955 Craigwood Dr *Web:* web.uccs.edu/bethel	Colorado Springs	CO	80918	719-262-4422	262-4416
Colorado Baptist College 3615 Vickers Dr	Colorado Springs	CO	80918	719-593-7887	593-1798
Colorado Christian University 8787 W Alameda Ave *TF:* 800-443-2484 ■ *Web:* www.ccu.edu	Lakewood	CO	80226	303-963-3200	963-3201
Loveland 1750 Foxtail Dr Suite 100 *Fax: Admissions ■ *TF:* 800-443-2484 ■ *Web:* www.ccu.edu	Loveland	CO	80538	970-669-8700	669-8701*
Colorado College 14 E Cache La Poudre St *Fax: Admissions ■ *TF:* 800-542-7214 ■ *Web:* www.coloradocollege.edu	Colorado Springs	CO	80903	719-389-6344	389-6816*
Colorado School of Mines 1600 Maple St *TF:* 800-446-9488 ■ *Web:* www.mines.edu	Golden	CO	80401	303-273-3000	273-3509
Colorado State University 200 W Lake St *Fax: Admissions ■ *Web:* www.colostate.edu	Fort Collins	CO	80523	970-491-1101	491-7799*
Pueblo 2200 Bonforte Blvd *Web:* www.colostate-pueblo.edu	Pueblo	CO	81001	719-549-2100	549-2419
Colorado Technical University 4435 N Chestnut St *Fax: Admissions ■ *TF:* 800-559-9287 ■ *Web:* www.ctucoloradosprings.com	Colorado Springs	CO	80907	719-598-0200	590-6825*
Fort Lewis College 1000 Rim Dr *Fax: Admissions ■ *Web:* www.fortlewis.edu	Durango	CO	81301	970-247-7010	247-7179*
Johnson & Wales University Denver 7150 Montview Blvd *Fax: Admissions ■ *TF:* 877-598-3368 ■ *Web:* www.jwu.edu/denver	Denver	CO	80220	303-256-9300	256-9333*
Mesa State College 1100 North Ave *Fax: Admissions ■ *TF:* 800-982-6372 ■ *Web:* www.mesastate.edu	Grand Junction	CO	81501	970-248-1020	248-1973*
Metropolitan State College of Denver Campus Box 44 PO Box 173362 *Fax: Admissions ■ *Web:* www.mscd.edu	Denver	CO	80217	303-556-3058	556-6345*

				Phone	Fax
Naropa University 2130 Arapahoe Ave	Boulder	CO	80302	303-444-0202	546-3536
TF: 800-772-6951 ■ Web: www.naropa.edu					
National American University					
Colorado Springs 5125 N Academy Blvd	Colorado Springs	CO	80918	719-277-0588	590-8305
Web: www.national.edu/ColoradoSpringsCampus/Index.htm					
Denver 1325 S Colorado Blvd Bldg B Suite 100	Denver	CO	80222	303-758-6700	876-7105*
*Fax: Admissions ■ Web: www.national.edu/DenverCampus/Index.htm					
Regis University 3333 Regis Blvd	Denver	CO	80221	303-458-4100	964-5534
TF Admissions: 800-568-8932 ■ Web: www.regis.edu					
Colorado Springs 7450 Campus Dr	Colorado Springs	CO	80920	800-568-8932	264-7095*
*Fax Area Code: 719 ■ TF: 800-568-8932 ■ Web: www.regis.edu					
Fort Collins 1501 Academy Ct	Fort Collins	CO	80524	970-472-2208	472-2201*
*Fax: Admissions ■ TF: 800-390-0891 ■ Web: www.regis.edu					
University of Colorado					
Boulder Campus Box 552	Boulder	CO	80309	303-492-1411	492-7115*
*Fax: Admissions ■ Web: www.colorado.edu					
Colorado Springs PO Box 7150	Colorado Springs	CO	80933	719-262-3000	262-3116*
*Fax: Admissions ■ TF: 800-990-8227 ■ Web: www.uccs.edu					
University of Colorado at Denver					
Campus Box 167 PO Box 173364	Denver	CO	80217	303-556-2704	556-4838*
*Fax: Admissions ■ Web: www.cudenver.edu					
University of Denver 2197 S University Blvd	Denver	CO	80208	303-871-2036	871-3301*
*Fax: Admissions ■ TF: 800-525-9495 ■ Web: www.du.edu					
University of Northern Colorado 501 20th St CB 10	Greeley	CO	80639	970-351-2881	351-2984*
*Fax: Admissions ■ TF Admissions: 888-700-4862 ■ Web: www.unco.edu					
US Air Force Academy					
Dept of the Air Force Headquarters USAFA	USAF Academy	CO	80840	719-333-1110	333-3012
TF: 800-443-9266 ■ Web: www.usafa.af.mil					
Western State College of Colorado 600 N Adams St	Gunnison	CO	81231	970-943-2119	943-2363*
*Fax: Admissions ■ TF Admissions: 800-876-5309 ■ Web: www.western.edu					
Women's College of the University of Denver					
1901 E Asbury Ave	Denver	CO	80208	303-871-6848	871-6897
Web: www.womenscollege.du.edu					
Yeshiva Toras Chaim Talmudical Seminary					
1555 Stuart St PO Box 40067	Denver	CO	80204	303-629-8200	623-5949

Connecticut

				Phone	Fax
Albertus Magnus College 700 Prospect St	New Haven	CT	06511	203-773-8550	773-5248*
*Fax: Admissions ■ TF Admissions: 800-578-9160 ■ Web: www.albertus.edu					
Briarwood College 2279 Mount Vernon Rd	Southington	CT	06489	860-628-4751	628-6444*
*Fax: Admissions ■ TF: 800-952-2444 ■ Web: www.briarwood.edu					
Central Connecticut State University 1615 Stanley St	New Britain	CT	06050	860-832-3200	
Web: www.ccsu.edu					
Connecticut College 270 Mohegan Ave	New London	CT	06320	860-439-2000	439-4301*
*Fax: Admissions ■ TF: 888-553-8760 ■ Web: www.connecticutcollege.edu					
Eastern Connecticut State University 83 Windham St	Willimantic	CT	06226	860-465-5000	465-5544*
*Fax: Admissions ■ TF Admissions: 877-353-3278 ■ Web: www.easternct.edu					
Fairfield University 1073 N Benson Rd	Fairfield	CT	06824	203-254-4000	254-4199*
*Fax: Admissions ■ Web: www.fairfield.edu					
Hartford Seminary 77 Sherman St	Hartford	CT	06105	860-509-9500	509-9509*
*Fax: Admissions ■ Web: www.hartsem.edu					
Mitchell College 437 Pequot Ave	New London	CT	06320	860-701-5000	444-1209*
*Fax: Admissions ■ TF Admitting: 800-443-2811 ■ Web: www.mitchell.edu					
Paier College of Art Inc 20 Gorham Ave	Hamden	CT	06514	203-287-3031	287-3021
Web: www.paiercollegeofart.edu					
Post University 800 Country Club Rd	Waterbury	CT	06723	203-596-4500	756-5810*
*Fax: Admissions ■ TF: 800-345-2562 ■ Web: www.post.edu					
Quinnipiac University 275 Mt Carmel Ave	Hamden	CT	06518	203-582-8600	582-8906*
*Fax: Admissions ■ TF Admissions: 800-462-1944 ■ Web: www.quinnipiac.edu					
Sacred Heart University 5151 Park Ave	Fairfield	CT	06825	203-371-7999	365-7609
Web: www.sacredheart.edu					
Saint Joseph College 1678 Asylum Ave	West Hartford	CT	06117	860-232-4571	231-5744*
*Fax: Admissions ■ TF Admissions: 866-442-8753 ■ Web: www.sjc.edu					
Southern Connecticut State University 501 Crescent St	New Haven	CT	06515	203-392-5200	392-5727
TF: 888-500-7278 ■ Web: www.southernct.edu					
Trinity College 300 Summit St	Hartford	CT	06106	860-297-2180	297-2287*
*Fax: Admissions ■ Web: www.trincoll.edu					
University of Bridgeport 126 Park Ave	Bridgeport	CT	06604	203-576-4000	576-4941*
*Fax: Admissions ■ TF: 800-392-3582 ■ Web: www.bridgeport.edu					
University of Connecticut 2131 Hillside Rd Unit 3088	Storrs	CT	06269	860-486-2000	486-1476*
*Fax: Admissions ■ Web: www.uconn.edu					
Stamford 1 University Pl	Stamford	CT	06901	203-251-8400	251-8556
Web: www.stamford.uconn.edu					
University of Hartford 200 Bloomfield Ave	West Hartford	CT	06117	860-768-4296	768-4961
TF: 800-947-4303 ■ Web: www.hartford.edu					
University of New Haven 300 Boston Post Rd	West Haven	CT	06516	203-932-7319	931-6093*
*Fax: Admissions ■ TF: 800-342-5864 ■ Web: www.newhaven.edu					
US Coast Guard Academy 15 Mohegan Ave	New London	CT	06320	860-444-8500	
TF: 800-883-8724 ■ Web: www.cga.edu					
Wesleyan University 70 Wyllys Ave	Middletown	CT	06459	860-685-3000	685-3001*
*Fax: Admissions ■ Web: www.wesleyan.edu					
Western Connecticut State University 181 White St	Danbury	CT	06810	203-837-8200	837-8338
TF: 877-837-9278 ■ Web: www.wcsu.ctstateu.edu					
Yale University					
3800 Hill House Ave PO Box 208234 Yale Stn	New Haven	CT	06520	203-432-4771	432-9392*
*Fax: Admissions ■ Web: www.yale.edu					

Delaware

				Phone	Fax
Delaware State University 1200 N DuPont Hwy	Dover	DE	19901	302-857-6351	857-6352*
*Fax: Admissions ■ TF Admissions: 800-845-2544 ■ Web: www.desu.edu					
Goldey Beacom College 4701 Limestone Rd	Wilmington	DE	19808	302-998-8814	996-5408*
*Fax: Admissions ■ TF: 800-833-4877 ■ Web: goldey.gbc.edu					
University of Delaware Hullihen Hall Rm 116	Newark	DE	19716	302-831-2000	831-6905*
*Fax: Admissions ■ Web: www.udel.edu					
Wesley College 120 N State St	Dover	DE	19901	302-736-2300	736-2382
TF: 800-937-5398 ■ Web: www.wesley.edu					
Wilmington University 320 N DuPont Hwy	New Castle	DE	19720	302-356-6739	328-5902*
*Fax: Admissions ■ TF: 877-967-5464 ■ Web: www.wilmcoll.edu					

District of Columbia

				Phone	Fax
American University 4400 Massachusetts Ave NW	Washington	DC	20016	202-885-1000	885-2558
Web: www.american.edu					
Catholic University of America 620 Michigan Ave NE	Washington	DC	20064	202-319-5000	319-6533
Web: www.cua.edu					
Gallaudet University 800 Florida Ave NE	Washington	DC	20002	202-651-5000	651-5744
Web: www.gallaudet.edu					
George Washington University 2121 'I' St NW	Washington	DC	20052	202-994-1000	994-9619
Web: www.gwu.edu					
Mount Vernon College 2100 Foxhall Rd NW	Washington	DC	20007	202-242-6672	994-0325*
*Fax: Admissions ■ TF: 800-447-3765 ■ Web: www.gwu.edu					
Georgetown University 37th & 'O' Sts NW	Washington	DC	20057	202-687-3600	687-5084
Web: www.georgetown.edu					
Howard University 2400 6th St NW	Washington	DC	20059	202-806-6100	806-4465*
*Fax: Admissions ■ TF: 800-822-6363 ■ Web: www.howard.edu					
Mount Vernon College 2100 Foxhall Rd NW	Washington	DC	20007	202-242-6672	994-0325*
*Fax: Admissions ■ TF: 800-447-3765 ■ Web: www.gwu.edu					
Southeastern University 501 'I' St SW	Washington	DC	20024	202-265-5343	488-8093*
*Fax: Admissions ■ Web: www.seu.edu					
Strayer University 1133 15th St NW	Washington	DC	20005	202-408-2400	419-1425*
*Fax: Admissions ■ TF: 888-360-1588 ■ Web: www.strayer.edu					
Takoma Park 6830 Laurel St NW	Washington	DC	20012	202-722-8100	722-8108*
*Fax: Admissions ■ TF: 888-360-1588 ■ Web: www.strayer.edu					
Trinity University Trinity College 125 Michigan Ave NE	Washington	DC	20017	202-884-9000	884-9403*
*Fax: Admissions ■ TF Admissions: 800-492-6882 ■ Web: www.trinitydc.edu					
University of the District of Columbia					
4200 Connecticut Ave NW	Washington	DC	20008	202-274-5000	274-5552
Web: www.udc.edu					

Florida

				Phone	Fax
American Intercontinental University South Florida					
2250 N Commerce Pkwy	Weston	FL	33326	954-446-6100	
TF: 866-248-4723 ■ Web: www.aiufl.edu					
Ave Maria University 5050 Ave Maria Blvd	Naples	FL	34119	239-280-2500	280-2556*
*Fax: Admissions ■ TF: 877-283-8648 ■ Web: www.naples.avemaria.edu					
Baptist College of Florida 5400 College Dr	Graceville	FL	32440	850-263-3261	263-7506*
*Fax: Admissions ■ TF: 800-328-2660 ■ Web: www.baptistcollege.edu					
Barry University 11300 NE 2nd Ave	Miami Shores	FL	33161	305-899-3000	899-2971*
*Fax: Admissions ■ TF: 800-756-6000 ■ Web: www.barry.edu					
Boynton Beach 1501 Corporate Dr Suite 230	Boynton Beach	FL	33426	561-364-8220	364-8113
Orlando 1650 Sandlake Rd Suite 390	Orlando	FL	32809	407-438-4150	438-9774*
*Fax: Admissions					
Tallahassee 325 John Knox Rd Bldg A	Tallahassee	FL	32303	850-385-2279	385-7576*
*Fax: Admissions					
Bethune-Cookman College					
640 Dr Mary McLeod Bethune Blvd	Daytona Beach	FL	32114	386-255-1401	481-2601*
*Fax: Admissions ■ TF Admissions: 800-448-0228 ■ Web: www.cookman.edu					
Chipola College 3094 Indian Cir	Marianna	FL	32446	850-526-2761	718-2287*
*Fax: Admissions ■ Web: www.chipola.edu					
Clearwater Christian College 3400 Gulf to Bay Blvd	Clearwater	FL	33759	727-726-1153	726-8597*
*Fax: Admissions ■ TF Admissions: 800-348-4463 ■ Web: www.clearwater.edu					
Columbia College Orlando 2600 Technology Dr Suite 100	Orlando	FL	32804	407-293-9911	293-8530*
*Fax: Admissions ■ Web: www.ccis.edu					
Eckerd College 4200 54th Ave S	Saint Petersburg	FL	33711	727-867-1166	866-2304*
*Fax: Admissions ■ TF Admissions: 800-456-9009 ■ Web: www.eckerd.edu					
Edward Waters College 1658 Kings Rd	Jacksonville	FL	32209	904-470-8200	470-8048*
*Fax: Admissions ■ TF Admissions: 888-898-3191 ■ Web: www.ewc.edu					
Embry-Riddle Aeronautical University Daytona Beach					
600 S Clyde Morris Blvd	Daytona Beach	FL	32114	386-226-6000	226-7070*
*Fax: Admissions ■ TF: 800-862-2416 ■ Web: www.erau.edu/db					
Flagler College 74 King St	Saint Augustine	FL	32084	904-829-6481	819-6466*
*Fax: Admissions ■ TF Admissions: 800-304-4208 ■ Web: www.flagler.edu					
Florida A & M University 1601 ML King Blvd	Tallahassee	FL	32307	850-599-3000	561-2152
Web: www.famu.edu					
Florida Atlantic University 777 Glades Rd	Boca Raton	FL	33431	561-297-3000	297-2758*
*Fax: Admissions ■ TF Admissions: 800-299-4328 ■ Web: www.fau.edu					
Davie 2912 College Ave	Davie	FL	33314	954-236-1012	236-1184*
*Fax: Admissions ■ TF: 800-764-2222 ■ Web: www.broward.fau.edu/davie.html					
Fort Lauderdale 111 E Las Olas Blvd	Fort Lauderdale	FL	33301	954-762-5200	762-5673*
*Fax: Admissions ■ TF: 800-764-2222 ■ Web: www.broward.fau.edu/tower.html					
MacArthur 5353 Parkside Dr	Jupiter	FL	33458	561-799-8500	799-8721*
*Fax: Admissions ■ Web: www.fau.edu/jupiter					
Treasure Coast 500 NW California Blvd	Port Saint Lucie	FL	34986	772-873-3300	873-3304*
*Fax: Admissions ■ Web: www.fau.edu/northern/psl					
Florida College 119 N Glen Arven Ave	Temple Terrace	FL	33617	813-988-5131	899-6772*
*Fax: Admissions ■ TF: 800-326-7655 ■ Web: www.floridacollege.edu					
Florida Gulf Coast University 10501 FGCU Blvd S	Fort Myers	FL	33965	239-590-1000	590-7894*
*Fax: Admissions ■ TF Admissions: 800-590-3428 ■ Web: www.fgcu.edu					
Florida Institute of Technology 150 W University Blvd	Melbourne	FL	32901	321-674-8000	674-8004*
*Fax: Admissions ■ TF: 800-888-4348 ■ Web: www.fit.edu					
Florida International University 11200 SW 8th St	Miami	FL	33199	305-348-2000	348-3648
Web: www.fiu.edu					
Florida Memorial University 15800 NW 42nd Ave	Miami	FL	33054	305-626-3600	623-1462*
*Fax: Admissions ■ TF: 800-822-1362 ■ Web: www.fmuniv.edu					
Florida Southern College 111 Lake Hollingsworth Dr	Lakeland	FL	33801	863-680-4131	680-4120*
*Fax: Admissions ■ TF Admissions: 800-274-4131 ■ Web: www.flsouthern.edu					
Florida State University 600 W College Ave	Tallahassee	FL	32306	850-644-2525	645-4670
Web: www.fsu.edu					
Hodges University 2655 Northbrooke Dr	Naples	FL	34119	239-513-1122	598-6254*
*Fax: Admissions ■ TF: 800-466-8017 ■ Web: www.hodges.edu					
Fort Myers 4501 Colonial Blvd	Fort Myers	FL	33966	239-482-0019	938-7891*
*Fax: Admissions ■ TF: 800-466-0019 ■ Web: www.internationalcollege.edu					
Jacksonville University 2800 University Blvd N	Jacksonville	FL	32211	904-256-8000	256-7012*
*Fax: Admissions ■ TF: 800-225-2027 ■ Web: www.ju.edu					
Johnson & Wales University North Miami					
1701 NE 127th St	North Miami	FL	33181	305-892-7551	892-7020
TF: 866-598-3567 ■ Web: www.jwu.edu/florida					
Jones College 5353 Arlington Expy	Jacksonville	FL	32211	904-743-1122	371-1182*
*Fax: Admissions ■ TF: 800-331-0176 ■ Web: www.jones.edu					
Logos Christian College 9000 Regency Sq Blvd	Jacksonville	FL	32211	904-745-3311	743-8866*
*Fax: Admissions ■ TF: 800-252-4253 ■ Web: www.logos.edu					
Lynn University 3601 N Military Trail	Boca Raton	FL	33431	561-237-7900	237-7100*
*Fax: Admissions ■ TF Admissions: 800-544-8035 ■ Web: www.lynn.edu					
New College of Florida 5800 Bay Shore Rd	Sarasota	FL	34243	941-487-5000	487-5010*
*Fax: Admissions ■ Web: www.ncf.edu					
Northwood University Florida 2600 N Military Trail	West Palm Beach	FL	33409	561-478-5500	640-3328*
*Fax: Admissions ■ TF Admissions: 800-458-8325 ■ Web: www.northwood.edu/fl					
Nova Southeastern University 3301 College Ave	Fort Lauderdale	FL	33314	954-262-8000	262-3811*
*Fax: Admissions ■ TF: 800-541-6682 ■ Web: www.nova.edu					
Palm Beach Atlantic University PO Box 24708	West Palm Beach	FL	33416	561-803-2000	803-2115*
*Fax: Admissions ■ TF: 888-468-6722 ■ Web: www.pba.edu					
Pensacola Christian College 250 Brent Ln	Pensacola	FL	32503	850-478-8496	722-3355*
*Fax Area Code: 800 ■ TF: 800-722-4636 ■ Web: www.pcci.edu					
Rollins College 1000 Holt Ave	Winter Park	FL	32789	407-646-2000	646-1502*
*Fax: Admissions ■ Web: www.rollins.edu					
Saint Leo University 33701 State Rd 52	Saint Leo	FL	33574	352-588-8200	588-8257*
*Fax: Admissions ■ TF: 800-334-5532 ■ Web: www.saintleo.edu					
Key West Center 718 Essex Ct Bldg A	Key West	FL	33040	305-293-2847	296-7296*
*Fax: Admissions					
Palatka Center 5001 St Johns Ave Box 28	Palatka	FL	32177	386-325-1477	325-6522*
*Fax: Admissions ■ Web: www.saintleo.edu					

Florida (Cont'd)

Phone | Fax

Saint Thomas University 16401 NW 37th Ave .... Miami Gardens FL 33054 305-628-6546 628-6591
TF: 800-367-9010 ■ Web: www.stu.edu
South University West Palm Beach
1760 N Congress Ave .... West Palm Beach FL 33409 561-697-9200 697-9944*
*Fax: Admissions ■ TF: 866-629-2902 ■ Web: www.southuniversity.edu
Southeastern University 1000 Longfellow Blvd .... Lakeland FL 33801 863-667-5000 667-5200*
*Fax: Admissions ■ TF Admissions: 800-500-8760 ■ Web: www.seuniversity.edu
Stetson University 421 N Woodland Blvd Unit 8378 .... DeLand FL 32723 386-822-7100 822-7112*
*Fax: Admissions ■ TF Admissions: 800-688-0101 ■ Web: www.stetson.edu
Trinity International University South Florida 8190 W SR 84 .... Davie FL 33324 954-382-6400 382-6420
TF: 877-392-3586 ■ Web: www.tiu.edu
University of Central Florida 4000 Central Florida Blvd............ Orlando FL 32816 407-823-2000 823-5625*
*Fax: Admissions ■ Web: www.ucf.edu
University of Florida PO Box 114000............ Gainesville FL 32611 352-392-3261 392-2115*
*Fax: Admissions ■ Web: www.ufl.edu
University of Miami 1252 Memorial Dr .... Coral Gables FL 33146 305-284-4323 284-2507
Web: www.miami.edu
University of North Florida 4567 St Johns Bluff Rd S.......... Jacksonville FL 32224 904-620-1000 620-2414
Web: www.unf.edu
University of South Florida
Lakeland 3433 Winter Lake Rd .... Lakeland FL 33803 863-667-7000 667-7096*
*Fax: Admissions ■ TF: 800-873-5636 ■ Web: www.lklnd.usf.edu
Saint Petersburg 140 7th Ave S .... Saint Petersburg FL 33701 727-553-1142 553-4525
Web: www1.stpt.usf.edu
Sarasota-Manatee 8350 N Tamiami Trail............ Sarasota FL 34243 941-359-4200 359-4236*
*Fax: Admissions ■ TF: 877-873-2855 ■ Web: www.sarasota.usf.edu
Tampa 4202 E Fowler Ave............ Tampa FL 33620 813-974-2011 974-4346
TF: 877-873-2855 ■ Web: www.usf.edu
University of Tampa 401 W Kennedy Blvd............ Tampa FL 33606 813-253-6228 258-7398
TF: 800-733-4773 ■ Web: www.ut.edu
University of West Florida 11000 University Pkwy .... Pensacola FL 32514 850-474-2230 474-3360*
*Fax: Admissions ■ TF: 800-263-1074 ■ Web: www.uwf.edu
Warner Southern College 13895 Hwy 27............ Lake Wales FL 33859 863-638-1426 638-7290*
*Fax: Admissions ■ TF: 800-949-7248 ■ Web: www.warner.edu
Webber International University 1201 N Scenic Hwy .... Babson Park FL 33827 863-638-2910 638-1591*
*Fax: Admissions ■ TF: 800-741-1844 ■ Web: www.webber.edu

Georgia

Phone | Fax

Agnes Scott College 141 E College Ave............ Decatur GA 30030 404-471-6000 471-6414*
*Fax: Admissions ■ TF: 800-868-8602 ■ Web: www.agnesscott.edu
Albany State University 504 College Dr............ Albany GA 31705 229-430-4646 430-4105*
*Fax: Admissions ■ Web: asuweb.asurams.edu/asu
American InterContinental University Atlanta
3330 Peachtree Rd NE............ Atlanta GA 30326 404-965-5700 965-5858*
*Fax: Admissions ■ TF: 877-252-5221 ■ Web: www.aiuniv.edu
American Intercontinental University Dunwoody
6600 Peachtree-Dunwoody Rd 500 Embassy Row............ Atlanta GA 30328 404-965-6500 604-9650*
*Fax Area Code: 770 ■ *Fax: Admissions ■ TF: 800-353-1744 ■
Web: www.aiudunwoody.com
Armstrong Atlantic State University 11935 Abercorn St.......... Savannah GA 31419 912-927-5275 921-5462
TF: 800-633-2349 ■ Web: www.armstrong.edu
Atlanta Christian College 2605 Ben Hill Rd............ East Point GA 30344 404-761-8861 460-2451*
*Fax: Admissions ■ TF: 800-776-1222 ■ Web: www.acc.edu
Augusta State University 2500 Walton Way............ Augusta GA 30904 706-737-1632 667-4355
TF: 800-341-4373 ■ Web: www.aug.edu
Berry College 2277 Martha Berry Hwy PO Box 490159......... Mount Berry GA 30149 706-232-5374 290-2178*
*Fax: Admissions ■ TF: 800-237-7942 ■ Web: www.berry.edu
Brenau University 500 Washington St .... Gainesville GA 30501 770-534-6299 538-4701*
*Fax: Admissions ■ TF: 800-252-5119 ■ Web: www.brenau.edu
Brewton-Parker College
201 David-Eliza Fountain Circle Hwy 280 PO Box 197...... Mount Vernon GA 30445 912-583-2241 583-4498*
*Fax: Admissions ■ TF: 800-342-1087 ■ Web: www.bpc.edu
Carver Bible College 3870 Cascade Rd .... Atlanta GA 30331 404-527-4520 527-4524
Web: www.carver.edu
Clark Atlanta University 223 James P Brawley Dr SW .... Atlanta GA 30314 404-880-8000 880-6174*
*Fax: Admissions ■ TF Admissions: 800-688-3228 ■ Web: www.cau.edu
Clayton State University 200 Clayton State Blvd .... Morrow GA 30260 678-466-4000 466-4149*
*Fax: Admissions ■ Web: www.clayton.edu
Columbus State University 4225 University Ave .... Columbus GA 31907 706-507-8800 568-5091
TF: 866-264-2035 ■ Web: www.colstate.edu
Covenant College 14049 Scenic Hwy............ Lookout Mountain GA 30750 706-820-1560 419-1044*
*Fax: Admissions ■ TF: 888-451-2683 ■ Web: www.covenant.edu
Dalton State College 650 N College Dr .... Dalton GA 30720 706-272-4436 272-2530*
*Fax: Admissions ■ TF: 800-829-4436 ■ Web: www.daltonstate.edu
Emmanuel College PO Box 129 .... Franklin Springs GA 30639 706-245-7226 245-2876*
*Fax: Admissions ■ TF: 800-860-8800 ■ Web: www.emmanuelcollege.edu
Emory University 200 B Jones Center............ Atlanta GA 30322 404-727-6036 727-4303
TF Admissions: 800-727-6036 ■ Web: www.emory.edu
Fort Valley State University 1005 State University Dr........... Fort Valley GA 31030 478-825-6211 825-6169*
*Fax: Admissions ■ TF: 877-462-3878 ■ Web: www.fvsu.edu
Georgia College & State University
231 W Hancock St CB 23 .... Milledgeville GA 31061 478-445-5004 445-3653*
*Fax: Admissions ■ TF: 800-342-0471 ■ Web: www.gcsu.edu
Macon 433 Cherry St............ Macon GA 31206 478-752-4278 752-1064
TF: 800-342-0471 ■ Web: www.gcsu.edu/macon
Georgia Institute of Technology 225 North Ave NW............ Atlanta GA 30332 404-894-2000 894-9511*
*Fax: Admissions ■ Web: www.gatech.edu
Georgia Southern University PO Box 8024............ Statesboro GA 30460 912-681-5391 486-7240
Web: www.georgiasouthern.edu/
Georgia Southwestern State University
800 Georgia Southwestern State University Dr............ Americus GA 31709 229-928-1273 931-2983
TF Admissions: 800-338-0082 ■ Web: www.gsw.edu
Georgia State University PO Box 3965............ Atlanta GA 30302 404-413-2000 413-2002*
*Fax: Admissions ■ Web: www.gsu.edu
Kennesaw State University 1000 Chastain Rd............ Kennesaw GA 30144 770-423-6000 420-4435*
*Fax: Admissions ■ Web: www.kennesaw.edu
LaGrange College 601 Broad St............ LaGrange GA 30240 706-880-8005 880-8010*
*Fax: Admissions ■ TF Admissions: 800-593-2885 ■ Web: www.lagrange.edu
Macon State College 100 College Station Dr............ Macon GA 31206 478-471-2700 471-5343*
*Fax: Admissions ■ TF: 800-272-7619 ■ Web: www.maconstate.edu
Warner Robins 100 University Blvd............ Warner Robins GA 31093 478-929-6700 929-6726
Web: www.maconstate.edu/about/wrinfo.aspx
Medical College of Georgia 1120 15th St............ Augusta GA 30912 706-721-0211 721-7028
TF: 800-736-2273 ■ Web: www.mcg.edu
Mercer University 1400 Coleman Ave............ Macon GA 31207 478-301-2650 301-2828*
*Fax: Admissions ■ TF: 800-637-2378 ■ Web: www.mercer.edu
Cecil B Day 3001 Mercer University Dr............ Atlanta GA 30341 678-547-6089 547-6367
TF: 800-840-8577 ■ Web: www2.mercer.edu
Morehouse College 830 Westview Dr SW .... Atlanta GA 30314 404-681-2800 572-3668*
*Fax: Admissions ■ Web: www.morehouse.edu

Phone | Fax

North Georgia College & State University 82 College Cir........ Dahlonega GA 30597 706-864-1800 864-1478*
*Fax: Admissions ■ TF: 800-498-9581 ■ Web: www.ngcsu.edu
Oglethorpe University 4484 Peachtree Rd NE .... Atlanta GA 30319 404-364-8307 364-8491*
*Fax: Admissions ■ TF: 800-428-4484 ■ Web: www.oglethorpe.edu
Paine College 1235 15th St .... Augusta GA 30901 706-821-8200 821-8293*
*Fax: Admissions ■ TF: 800-476-7703 ■ Web: www.paine.edu
Piedmont College 165 Central Ave............ Demorest GA 30535 706-776-0103 776-6635*
*Fax: Admissions ■ TF: 800-277-7020 ■ Web: www.piedmont.edu
Reinhardt College 7300 Reinhardt College Cir............ Waleska GA 30183 770-720-5526 720-5899*
*Fax: Admissions ■ TF: 877-346-4273 ■ Web: www.reinhardt.edu
Savannah State University 3219 College St............ Savannah GA 31404 912-356-2186 356-2256*
*Fax: Admissions ■ TF Admissions: 800-788-0478 ■ Web: www.savstate.edu
Shorter College 315 Shorter Ave .... Rome GA 30165 706-233-7319 233-7224*
*Fax: Admissions ■ TF: 800-868-6980 ■ Web: www.shorter.edu
South University Savannah 709 Mall Blvd .... Savannah GA 31406 912-691-6000 201-8117*
*Fax: Admissions ■ TF: 866-629-2901 ■ Web: www.southuniversity.edu
Southern Polytechnic State University 1100 S Marietta Pkwy ...... Marietta GA 30060 678-915-4188 915-7292*
*Fax: Admissions ■ TF Admissions: 800-635-3204 ■ Web: www.spsu.edu
Spelman College 350 Spelman Ln SW............ Atlanta GA 30314 404-681-3643 270-5201*
*Fax: Admissions ■ TF Admissions: 800-982-2411 ■ Web: www.spelman.edu
Thomas University 1501 Millpond Rd............ Thomasville GA 31792 229-226-1621 226-1653*
*Fax: Admissions ■ TF: 800-538-9784 ■ Web: www.thomasu.edu
Truett-McConnell College 100 Alumni Dr .... Cleveland GA 30528 706-865-2134 865-7615*
*Fax: Admissions ■ TF: 800-226-8621 ■ Web: www.truett.edu
University of Georgia 212 Terrell Hall............ Athens GA 30602 706-542-3000 542-1466
TF: 866-423-2947 ■ Web: www.uga.edu
University of West Georgia 1601 Maple St .... Carrollton GA 30118 678-839-5000 839-4747*
*Fax: Admissions ■ Web: www.westga.edu
Valdosta State University 1500 N Patterson St............ Valdosta GA 31698 229-333-5800 333-5482*
*Fax: Admissions ■ TF: 800-618-1878 ■ Web: www.valdosta.edu
Wesleyan College 4760 Forsyth Rd .... Macon GA 31210 478-477-1110 757-4030*
*Fax: Admissions ■ TF: 800-447-6610 ■ Web: www.wesleyancollege.edu

Hawaii

Phone | Fax

Brigham Young University Hawaii 55-220 Kulanui St .... Laie HI 96762 808-293-3211 293-3741*
*Fax: Admissions ■ Web: www.byuh.edu
Chaminade University 3140 Waialae Ave .... Honolulu HI 96816 808-735-4711 739-4647*
*Fax: Admissions ■ TF: 800-735-3733 ■ Web: www.chaminade.edu
Hawaii Pacific University 1164 Bishop St Suite 200............ Honolulu HI 96813 808-544-0200 544-1136*
*Fax: Admissions ■ TF: 866-225-5478 ■ Web: www.hpu.edu
Windward Hawaii Loa 45-045 Kamehameha Hwy............ Kaneohe HI 96744 808-236-3500 544-1136
TF Admissions: 866-225-5478
University of Hawaii
Hilo 200 W Kawili St .... Hilo HI 96720 808-974-7414 933-0861*
*Fax: Admissions ■ TF Admissions: 800-897-4456 ■ Web: www.uhh.hawaii.edu
Manoa 2600 Campus Rd Rm 001............ Honolulu HI 96822 808-956-8975 956-4148*
*Fax: Admissions ■ TF Admissions: 800-823-9771 ■ Web: manoa.hawaii.edu
West Oahu 96-129 Ala Ike............ Pearl City HI 96782 808-454-4700 453-6075
TF: 866-299-8656 ■ Web: www.uhwo.hawaii.edu

Idaho

Phone | Fax

Boise State University 1910 University Dr............ Boise ID 83725 208-426-1156 426-3765
TF: 800-824-7017 ■ Web: www.idbsu.edu
Brigham Young University Idaho 525 S Center .... Rexburg ID 83460 208-496-2011 496-1220*
*Fax: Admissions ■ Web: www.byui.edu
College of Idaho 2112 Cleveland Blvd .... Caldwell ID 83605 208-459-5011 459-5757*
*Fax: Admissions ■ TF Admissions: 800-224-3246 ■ Web: www.collegeofidaho.edu
Idaho State University 921 S 8th Ave .... Pocatello ID 83209 208-236-0211 282-4511*
*Fax: Admissions ■ Web: www.isu.edu
Lewis-Clark State College 500 8th Ave............ Lewiston ID 83501 208-792-5272 792-2210*
*Fax: Admissions ■ TF: 800-933-5272 ■ Web: www.lcsc.edu
Northwest Nazarene University 623 Holly St............ Nampa ID 83686 208-467-8000 467-8645*
*Fax: Admissions ■ TF Admissions: 877-668-4968 ■ Web: www.nnu.edu
University of Idaho 709 Deakin Ave PO Box 444264............ Moscow ID 83844 208-885-6111 885-9119*
*Fax: Admissions ■ TF: 888-884-3246 ■ Web: www.uihome.uidaho.edu
Boise 322 E Front St Suite 190............ Boise ID 83702 208-334-2999 364-4035
TF: 866-264-7384 ■ Web: www.boise.uidaho.edu

Illinois

Phone | Fax

American Islamic College 640 W Irving Park Rd .... Chicago IL 60613 773-281-4700 281-8552*
*Fax: Admissions ■ Web: www.aicusa.edu
Augustana College 639 38th St .... Rock Island IL 61201 309-794-7000 794-7174*
*Fax: Admissions ■ TF: 800-798-8100 ■ Web: www.augustana.edu
Aurora University 347 S Gladstone Ave .... Aurora IL 60506 630-844-5533 844-5535
TF: 800-742-5281 ■ Web: www.aurora.edu
Benedictine University 5700 College Rd .... Lisle IL 60532 630-829-6300 829-6301
TF: 888-829-6363 ■ Web: www.ben.edu
Blackburn College 700 College Ave............ Carlinville IL 62626 217-854-3231 854-3713*
*Fax: Admissions ■ TF: 800-233-3550 ■ Web: www.blackburn.edu
Bradley University 1501 W Bradley Ave............ Peoria IL 61625 309-676-7611 677-2797
TF Admissions: 800-447-6460 ■ Web: www.bradley.edu
Chicago State University 9501 S King Dr .... Chicago IL 60628 773-995-2513 995-3820*
*Fax: Admissions ■ Web: www.csu.edu
Christian Life College 400 E Gregory St .... Mount Prospect IL 60056 847-259-1840 259-3888
Web: www.christianlifecollege.edu
Columbia College 600 S Michigan Ave 3rd Fl .... Chicago IL 60605 312-663-1600 344-8024*
*Fax: Admissions ■ Web: www.colum.edu
Concordia University Chicago 7400 Augusta St .... River Forest IL 60305 708-771-8300 209-3347
TF: 800-285-2668 ■ Web: www.cuchicago.edu
DePaul University 1 E Jackson Blvd Suite 9100............ Chicago IL 60614 312-362-8300 362-5749
TF: 800-433-7285 ■ Web: www.depaul.edu
Dominican University 7900 W Division St............ River Forest IL 60305 708-366-2490 524-6864*
*Fax: Admissions ■ TF: 800-828-8475 ■ Web: www.dom.edu
East-West University 816 S Michigan Ave............ Chicago IL 60605 312-939-0111 939-0083*
*Fax: Admissions ■ TF: 877-398-9376 ■ Web: www.eastwest.edu
Eastern Illinois University 600 Lincoln Ave............ Charleston IL 61920 217-581-2223 581-7060*
*Fax: Admissions ■ TF Admissions: 800-252-5711 ■ Web: www.eiu.edu
Elmhurst College 190 Prospect Ave............ Elmhurst IL 60126 630-617-3400 617-5501
TF: 800-697-1871 ■ Web: www.elmhurst.edu
Eureka College 300 E College Ave............ Eureka IL 61530 309-467-6350 467-6576*
*Fax: Admissions ■ TF Admissions: 888-438-7352 ■ Web: www.eureka.edu
Governors State University 1 University Pkwy............ University Park IL 60466 708-534-5000 534-1640*
*Fax: Admissions ■ TF: 800-478-8478 ■ Web: www.govst.edu
Greenville College 315 E College Ave............ Greenville IL 62246 618-664-7100 664-9841*
*Fax: Admissions ■ TF: 800-345-4440 ■ Web: www.greenville.edu
Harrington College of Design 200 W Madison St 2nd Fl............ Chicago IL 60606 312-939-4975 697-8032*
*Fax: Admissions ■ TF: 877-939-4975 ■ Web: www.interiordesign.edu

				Phone	Fax
Illinois College 1101 W College Ave.	Jacksonville	IL	62650	217-245-3030	245-3034*
*Fax: Admissions ■ *TF Admissions:* 800-464-5265 ■ *Web:* www.ic.edu					
Illinois Institute of Technology 10 W 33rd St.	Chicago	IL	60616	312-567-3025	567-6939*
*Fax: Admissions ■ *TF:* 800-448-2329 ■ *Web:* www.iit.edu					
Rice 201 E Loop Rd.	Wheaton	IL	60187	630-682-6000	682-6010*
*Fax: Admissions ■ *Web:* www.rice.iit.edu					
Illinois State University Campus Box 2200 Hovey Hall 201	Normal	IL	61790	309-438-2181	438-3932*
*Fax: Admissions ■ *TF Admissions:* 800-366-2478 ■ *Web:* www.ilstu.edu					
Illinois Wesleyan University 1312 Park ST	Bloomington	IL	61701	309-556-3031	556-3820*
*Fax: Admissions ■ *TF Admissions:* 800-332-2498 ■ *Web:* www.iwu.edu					
Judson College 1151 N State St.	Elgin	IL	60123	847-628-2500	628-2526*
*Fax: Admissions ■ *TF Admissions:* 800-879-5376 ■ *Web:* www.judsoncollege.edu					
Knox College 2 E South St	Galesburg	IL	61401	309-341-7100	341-7070*
*Fax: Admissions ■ *TF Admissions:* 800-678-5669 ■ *Web:* www.knox.edu					
Lake Forest College 555 N Sheridan Rd	Lake Forest	IL	60045	847-234-3100	735-6271
TF: 800-828-4751 ■ *Web:* www.lakeforest.edu					
Lewis University 1 University Pkwy Unit 297	Romeoville	IL	60446	815-836-5250	836-5002
TF: 800-897-9000 ■ *Web:* www.lewisu.edu					
Loyola University Chicago					
Lake Shore 6525 N Sheridan Rd	Chicago	IL	60626	773-508-3075	508-8926
Web: www.luc.edu					
Water Tower 820 N Michigan Ave.	Chicago	IL	60611	312-915-6500	915-7216*
*Fax: Admissions ■ *TF Admissions:* 800-262-2373 ■ *Web:* www.luc.edu					
MacMurray College 447 E College Ave.	Jacksonville	IL	62650	217-479-7056	291-0702*
*Fax: Admissions ■ *TF:* 800-252-7485 ■ *Web:* www.mac.edu					
McKendree College 701 College Rd	Lebanon	IL	62254	618-537-4481	537-6496*
*Fax: Admissions ■ *TF:* 800-232-7228 ■ *Web:* www.mckendree.edu					
Millikin University 1184 W Main St	Decatur	IL	62522	217-424-6211	425-4669*
*Fax: Admissions ■ *TF:* 800-373-7733 ■ *Web:* www.millikin.edu					
Monmouth College 700 E Broadway Ave	Monmouth	IL	61462	309-457-2311	457-2310
TF: 888-827-8268 ■ *Web:* www.monm.edu					
NAES College 2838 W Peterson Ave.	Chicago	IL	60659	773-761-5000	761-3808
Web: www.naes.edu					
National-Louis University 100 Capitol Dr	Wheeling	IL	60090	847-947-5718	465-5659*
*Fax: Admissions ■ *TF:* 800-443-5522 ■ *Web:* www.nl.edu/campuses/wheeling.cfm					
Chicago 122 S Michigan Ave.	Chicago	IL	60603	312-261-3096	465-5730*
*Fax Area Code: 847 ■ *TF:* 800-443-5522 ■ *Web:* www.nl.edu/campuses/chicago.cfm					
National University of Health Sciences 200 E Roosevelt Rd	Lombard	IL	60148	630-629-2000	889-6554
TF: 800-826-6285 ■ *Web:* www.nuhs.edu					
North Central College 30 N Brainard St.	Naperville	IL	60540	630-637-5800	637-5819*
*Fax: Admissions ■ *TF:* 800-411-1861 ■ *Web:* www.noctrl.edu					
North Park University 3225 W Foster Ave	Chicago	IL	60625	773-244-5500	244-4953
TF: 800-888-6728 ■ *Web:* www.northpark.edu					
Northeastern Illinois University 5500 N St Louis Ave.	Chicago	IL	60625	773-442-4050	442-4020*
*Fax: Admissions ■ *Web:* www.neiu.edu					
Northern Illinois University PO Box 3001	DeKalb	IL	60115	815-753-1000	753-8312*
*Fax: Admissions ■ *TF:* 800-892-3050 ■ *Web:* www.niu.edu					
Northwestern University 1801 Hinman Ave	Evanston	IL	60208	847-491-7271	467-2331*
*Fax: Admissions ■ *Web:* www.northwestern.edu					
Olivet Nazarene University 1 University Ave	Bourbonnais	IL	60914	815-939-5011	935-4998*
*Fax: Admissions ■ *TF:* 800-648-1463 ■ *Web:* www.olivet.edu					
Principia College 1 Maybeck Pl	Elsah	IL	62028	618-374-2131	374-4000*
*Fax: Admissions ■ *TF:* 800-277-4648 ■ *Web:* www.prin.edu/college					
Quincy University 1800 College Ave	Quincy	IL	62301	217-228-5210	228-5479*
*Fax: Admissions ■ *TF:* 800-688-4295 ■ *Web:* www.quincy.edu					
Robert Morris College					
Chicago 401 S State St	Chicago	IL	60605	312-935-6800	935-4182
TF: 800-762-5960 ■ *Web:* www.robertmorris.edu					
DuPage 905 Meridian Lake Dr	Aurora	IL	60504	630-375-8100	375-8020*
*Fax: Admissions ■ *TF Admissions:* 800-762-5960 ■ *Web:* www.robertmorris.edu/dupage					
Orland Park 43 Orland Sq Dr.	Orland Park	IL	60462	708-226-3800	226-5350
TF: 800-225-1520 ■ *Web:* www.robertmorris.edu/orlandpark/					
Springfield 3101 Montvale Dr	Springfield	IL	62704	217-793-2500	793-4210*
*Fax: Admitting ■ *TF:* 800-762-5960 ■ *Web:* www.robertmorris.edu/springfield					
Rockford College 5050 E State St	Rockford	IL	61108	815-226-4000	226-2822*
*Fax: Admissions ■ *TF:* 800-892-2984 ■ *Web:* www.rockford.edu					
Roosevelt University 430 S Michigan Ave	Chicago	IL	60605	312-341-3500	341-3523*
*Fax: Admissions ■ *TF Admissions:* 877-277-5978 ■ *Web:* www.roosevelt.edu					
Albert A Robin 1400 N Roosevelt Blvd	Schaumburg	IL	60173	847-619-8600	619-8636*
*Fax: Admissions ■ *TF Admissions:* 877-277-5978 ■ *Web:* www.roosevelt.edu/schaumburg					
Rush University 600 S Paulina St Rm 440	Chicago	IL	60612	312-942-7100	942-2219*
*Fax: Admissions ■ *Web:* www.rushu.rush.edu					
Saint Xavier University 3700 W 103rd St	Chicago	IL	60655	773-298-3000	298-3076*
*Fax: Admissions ■ *TF:* 800-462-9288 ■ *Web:* www.sxu.edu					
School of the Art Institute of Chicago 36 S Wabash Ave.	Chicago	IL	60603	312-629-6100	629-6101*
*Fax: Admissions ■ *TF Admissions:* 800-232-7242 ■ *Web:* www.artic.edu/saic					
Shimer College 3424 S State St	Chicago	IL	60616	800-215-7173	235-3501*
*Fax Area Code: 312 ■ *Fax: Admissions ■ *TF:* 800-215-7173 ■ *Web:* www.shimer.edu					
Southern Illinois University					
Carbondale 425 Clock Tower Dr MC 4710	Carbondale	IL	62901	618-453-2121	453-3250*
*Fax: Admissions ■ *Web:* www.siuc.edu					
Edwardsville SR 157	Edwardsville	IL	62026	618-650-2000	650-5013*
*Fax: Admissions ■ *TF:* 888-328-5168 ■ *Web:* www.siue.edu					
Trinity Christian College 6601 W College Dr.	Palos Heights	IL	60463	866-874-6463	239-4826*
*Fax Area Code: 708 ■ *TF:* 800-748-0085 ■ *Web:* www.trnty.edu					
Trinity International University 2065 Half Day Rd.	Deerfield	IL	60015	847-317-7000	317-8097
TF: 800-822-3225 ■ *Web:* www.tiu.edu					
University of Chicago 5801 S Ellis Ave	Chicago	IL	60637	773-702-1234	702-4199*
*Fax: Admissions ■ *Web:* www.uchicago.edu					
University of Illinois					
Chicago 1200 W Harrison St.	Chicago	IL	60607	312-996-7000	413-7628*
*Fax: Admissions ■ *Web:* www.uic.edu					
Springfield 1 University Plaza MS UHB 1080	Springfield	IL	62703	217-206-4847	206-6620*
*Fax: Admissions ■ *TF:* 888-977-4847 ■ *Web:* www.uis.edu					
Urbana-Champaign 901 W Illinois St.	Urbana	IL	61801	217-333-0302	244-4614*
*Fax: Admissions ■ *TF Admissions:* 800-252-1352 ■ *Web:* www.uiuc.edu					
VanderCook College of Music 3140 S Federal St	Chicago	IL	60616	312-225-6288	225-5211*
*Fax: Admissions ■ *Web:* www.vandercook.edu					
West Suburban College of Nursing 3 Erie Ct.	Oak Park	IL	60302	708-763-6530	763-1531*
*Fax: Admissions ■ *Web:* www.wscn.edu					
Western Illinois University 1 University Cir	Macomb	IL	61455	309-298-1414	298-3111*
*Fax: Admissions ■ *TF Admissions:* 877-742-5948 ■ *Web:* www.wiu.edu					
Quad Cities 3561 60th St.	Moline	IL	61265	309-762-9481	764-7172*
*Fax: Admissions ■ *Web:* www.wiu.edu/qc					
Wheaton College 501 College Ave	Wheaton	IL	60187	630-752-5000	752-5285
TF: 800-222-2419 ■ *Web:* www.wheaton.edu					

Indiana

				Phone	Fax
American Conservatory of Music 252 Wildwood Rd	Hammond	IN	46324	219-931-6000	931-6089*
*Fax: Admissions ■ *Web:* www.americanconservatory.edu					
Anderson University 1100 E 5th St.	Anderson	IN	46012	765-649-9071	641-4091*
*Fax: Admissions ■ *TF Admissions:* 800-428-6414 ■ *Web:* www.anderson.edu					
Ball State University	Muncie	IN	47306	765-285-8300	285-1632*
*Fax: Admissions ■ *TF:* 800-482-4278 ■ *Web:* www.bsu.edu					
Bethel College 1001 W McKinley Ave	Mishawaka	IN	46545	574-257-3339	257-3335*
*Fax: Admissions ■ *TF Admissions:* 800-422-4101 ■ *Web:* www.bethelcollege.edu					
Butler University 4600 Sunset Ave	Indianapolis	IN	46208	317-940-8100	940-8150*
*Fax: Admissions ■ *TF:* 800-368-6852 ■ *Web:* www.butler.edu					
Calumet College of Saint Joseph 2400 New York Ave	Whiting	IN	46394	219-473-4215	473-4336*
*Fax: Admissions ■ *TF:* 877-700-9100 ■ *Web:* www.ccsj.edu					
DePauw University 101 E Seminary St	Greencastle	IN	46135	765-658-4006	658-4007*
*Fax: Admissions ■ *TF:* 800-447-2495 ■ *Web:* www.depauw.edu					
Earlham College 801 National Rd W	Richmond	IN	47374	765-983-1600	983-1560*
*Fax: Admissions ■ *TF:* 800-327-5426 ■ *Web:* www.earlham.edu					
Franklin College 101 Branigin Blvd	Franklin	IN	46131	317-738-8000	738-8274*
*Fax: Admissions ■ *TF:* 800-852-0232 ■ *Web:* www.franklincollege.edu					
Goshen College 1700 S Main St	Goshen	IN	46526	574-535-7000	535-7609*
*Fax: Admissions ■ *TF:* 800-348-7422 ■ *Web:* www.goshen.edu					
Grace College 200 Seminary Dr	Winona Lake	IN	46590	574-372-5100	372-5120*
*Fax: Admissions ■ *TF:* 800-544-7223 ■ *Web:* www.grace.edu					
Hanover College PO Box 108	Hanover	IN	47243	812-866-7000	866-7098
TF: 800-213-2178 ■ *Web:* www.hanover.edu					
Holy Cross College 54515 SR 933 N	Notre Dame	IN	46556	574-239-8400	239-8323*
*Fax: Admissions ■ *Web:* www.hcc-nd.edu					
Huntington University 2303 College Ave.	Huntington	IN	46750	260-356-6000	358-3699*
*Fax: Admissions ■ *TF Admissions:* 800-642-6493 ■ *Web:* www.huntington.edu					
Indiana Institute of Technology 1600 E Washington Blvd	Fort Wayne	IN	46803	260-422-5561	422-7696*
*Fax: Admissions ■ *TF:* 800-937-2448 ■ *Web:* www.indianatech.edu					
Indiana State University 210 N 7th St	Terre Haute	IN	47809	812-237-2121	237-8023
TF: 800-742-0891 ■ *Web:* www.indstate.edu					
Indiana University 300 N Jordan Ave	Bloomington	IN	47405	812-855-0661	855-5102
Web: www.indiana.edu					
East 2325 Chester Blvd	Richmond	IN	47374	765-973-8208	973-8288*
*Fax: Admissions ■ *TF:* 800-959-3278 ■ *Web:* www.iue.edu					
Kokomo 2300 S Washington St PO Box 9003	Kokomo	IN	46904	765-455-9217	455-9537*
*Fax: Admissions ■ *TF:* 888-875-4485 ■ *Web:* www.iuk.edu					
Northwest 3400 Broadway	Gary	IN	46408	219-980-6500	981-4219*
*Fax: Admissions ■ *TF:* 888-968-7486 ■ *Web:* www.iun.edu					
South Bend 1700 Mishawaka Ave Box 7111	South Bend	IN	46634	574-520-4870	237-4834*
*Fax: Admissions ■ *TF:* 877-462-4872 ■ *Web:* www.iusb.edu					
Southeast 4201 Grant Line Rd.	New Albany	IN	47150	812-941-2212	941-2595
Web: www.ius.edu					
Indiana University-Purdue University					
Columbus 4601 Central Ave.	Columbus	IN	47203	812-348-7311	348-7257
Web: www.columbus.iupui.edu					
Fort Wayne 2101 E Coliseum Blvd	Fort Wayne	IN	46805	260-481-6100	481-6880*
*Fax: Hum Res ■ *TF:* 800-324-4739 ■ *Web:* www.ipfw.edu					
Indianapolis 425 University Blvd	Indianapolis	IN	46202	317-274-5555	278-1862
Web: www.iupui.edu					
Indiana Wesleyan University 4201 S Washington St.	Marion	IN	46953	765-677-2138	677-2333*
*Fax: Admissions ■ *TF:* 800-332-6901 ■ *Web:* www.indwes.edu					
Manchester College 604 E College Ave	North Manchester	IN	46962	260-982-5000	982-5239*
*Fax: Admissions ■ *TF Admissions:* 800-852-3648 ■ *Web:* www.manchester.edu					
Marian College 3200 Cold Spring Rd	Indianapolis	IN	46222	317-955-6000	955-6401*
*Fax: Admissions ■ *TF Admissions:* 800-772-7264 ■ *Web:* www.marian.edu					
Martin University 2171 Avondale Pl	Indianapolis	IN	46218	317-543-3235	543-4790
TF: 866-344-3114 ■ *Web:* www.martin.edu					
Oakland City University 138 N Lucretia St	Oakland City	IN	47660	812-749-4781	749-1433
TF: 800-737-5125 ■ *Web:* www.oak.edu					
Purdue University Schleman Hall 475 Stadium Mall Dr	West Lafayette	IN	47907	765-494-1776	494-0544*
*Fax: Admissions ■ *Web:* www.purdue.edu					
Calumet 2200 169th St	Hammond	IN	46323	219-989-2400	989-2775*
*Fax: Admissions ■ *TF:* 800-447-8738 ■ *Web:* www.calumet.purdue.edu					
North Central 1401 S US Hwy 421	Westville	IN	46391	219-872-0527	785-5538*
*Fax: Admissions ■ *Web:* www.pnc.edu					
Rose-Hulman Institute of Technology 5500 Wabash Ave	Terre Haute	IN	47803	812-877-1511	877-8941
TF Admissions: 800-248-7448 ■ *Web:* www.rose-hulman.edu					
Saint Mary-of-the-Woods College					
3301 St Mary Rd	Saint Mary-of-the-Woods	IN	47876	812-535-5106	535-5010*
*Fax: Admissions ■ *TF:* 800-926-7692 ■ *Web:* www.smwc.edu					
Saint Mary's College Le Mans Hall Rm 122	Notre Dame	IN	46556	574-284-4587	284-4841*
*Fax: Admissions ■ *TF Admissions:* 800-551-7621 ■ *Web:* www.saintmarys.edu					
Taylor University 236 W Reade Ave	Upland	IN	46989	765-998-2751	998-4925*
*Fax: Admissions ■ *TF:* 800-882-3456 ■ *Web:* www.taylor.edu					
Fort Wayne 1025 W Rudisill Blvd	Fort Wayne	IN	46807	260-744-8689	744-8850
TF: 800-233-3922 ■ *Web:* fw.taylor.edu					
Tri-State University 1 University Blvd.	Angola	IN	46703	260-665-4100	665-4578*
*Fax: Admissions ■ *TF:* 800-347-4878 ■ *Web:* www.tristate.edu					
University of Evansville 1800 Lincoln Ave	Evansville	IN	47722	812-488-2000	488-4076*
*Fax: Admissions ■ *TF:* 800-423-8633 ■ *Web:* www.evansville.edu					
University of Indianapolis 1400 E Hanna Ave	Indianapolis	IN	46227	317-788-3368	788-3300*
*Fax: Admissions ■ *TF:* 800-232-8634 ■ *Web:* www.uindy.edu					
University of Notre Dame 220 Main Bldg	Notre Dame	IN	46556	574-631-7505	631-8665*
*Fax: Admissions ■ *Web:* www.nd.edu					
University of Saint Francis 2701 Spring St	Fort Wayne	IN	46808	260-434-3100	434-7526*
*Fax: Admissions ■ *TF:* 800-729-4732 ■ *Web:* www.sfc.edu					
University of Southern Indiana 8600 University Blvd.	Evansville	IN	47712	812-464-1765	465-7154
TF: 800-467-1965 ■ *Web:* www.usi.edu					
Valparaiso University 1700 Chapel Dr	Valparaiso	IN	46383	219-464-5011	464-6898*
*Fax: Admissions ■ *TF:* 888-468-2576 ■ *Web:* www.valpo.edu					
Wabash College 410 W Wabash Ave PO Box 352	Crawfordsville	IN	47933	765-361-6225	361-6437*
*Fax: Admissions ■ *TF:* 800-345-5385 ■ *Web:* www.wabash.edu					

Iowa

				Phone	Fax
Ashford University 400 N Bluff Blvd	Clinton	IA	52732	563-242-4023	243-6102*
*Fax: Admissions ■ *TF:* 800-242-4153 ■ *Web:* www.ashford.edu					
Briar Cliff University 3303 Rebecca St.	Sioux City	IA	51104	712-279-5321	279-1632*
*Fax: Admissions ■ *TF:* 800-662-3303 ■ *Web:* www.briarcliff.edu					
Buena Vista University 610 W 4th St.	Storm Lake	IA	50588	712-749-2235	749-2035
TF: 800-383-9600 ■ *Web:* www.bvu.edu					
Central College 812 University St CB 5100	Pella	IA	50219	641-628-5285	628-5983
TF: 877-462-3687 ■ *Web:* www.central.edu					
Clarke College 1550 Clarke Dr	Dubuque	IA	52001	563-588-6316	588-6789*
*Fax: Admissions ■ *TF:* 888-825-2753 ■ *Web:* www.clarke.edu					
Coe College 1220 1st Ave NE	Cedar Rapids	IA	52402	319-399-8500	399-8816
TF: 877-225-5263 ■ *Web:* www.coe.edu					
Cornell College 600 1st St SW	Mount Vernon	IA	52314	319-895-4215	895-4451*
*Fax: Admissions ■ *TF Admissions:* 800-747-1112 ■ *Web:* www.cornellcollege.edu					
Divine Word College 102 Jacoby Dr SW	Epworth	IA	52045	563-876-3353	876-3407*
*Fax: Admissions ■ *Web:* www2.dwci.edu					
Dordt College 498 4th Ave NE	Sioux Center	IA	51250	712-722-6080	722-1198
TF: 800-343-6738 ■ *Web:* www.dordt.edu					
Drake University 2507 University Ave	Des Moines	IA	50311	515-271-3181	271-2831
TF: 800-443-7253 ■ *Web:* www.drake.edu					
Graceland University 1 University Pl	Lamoni	IA	50140	641-784-5000	784-5480*
*Fax: Admissions ■ *Web:* www.graceland.edu					

Iowa (Cont'd)

	City	State	ZIP	Phone	Fax
Grand View College 1200 Grandview Ave *Fax: Admissions ■ TF: 800-444-6083 ■ Web: www.gvc.edu	Des Moines	IA	50316	515-263-2800	263-2974*
Grinnell College 1103 Park St TF: 800-247-0113 ■ Web: www.grinnell.edu	Grinnell	IA	50112	641-269-3600	269-4800
Iowa State University 100 Alumni Hall *Fax: Admissions ■ TF Admissions: 800-262-3810 ■ Web: www.iastate.edu	Ames	IA	50011	515-294-4111	294-2592*
Iowa Wesleyan College 601 N Main St *Fax: Admissions ■ TF: 800-582-2383 ■ Web: www.iwc.edu	Mount Pleasant	IA	52641	319-385-8021	385-6240*
Loras College 1450 Alta Vista St *Fax: Admissions ■ TF: 800-245-6727 ■ Web: www.loras.edu	Dubuque	IA	52001	563-588-7100	588-7119*
Luther College 700 College Dr *Fax: Admissions ■ TF: 800-458-8437 ■ Web: www.luther.edu	Decorah	IA	52101	563-387-2000	387-2159*
Maharishi University of Management 1000 N 4th St TF: 800-369-6480 ■ Web: www.mum.edu	Fairfield	IA	52557	641-472-1110	472-1179
Morningside College 1501 Morningside Ave *Fax: Admissions ■ TF: 800-831-0806 ■ Web: www.morningside.edu	Sioux City	IA	51106	712-274-5000	274-5101*
Mount Mercy College 1330 Elmhurst Dr NE TF: 800-248-4504 ■ Web: www2.mtmercy.edu	Cedar Rapids	IA	52402	319-368-6460	861-2390
Northwestern College 101 7th St SW *Fax: Admissions ■ TF: 800-747-4757 ■ Web: www.nwciowa.edu	Orange City	IA	51041	712-707-7000	707-7164*
Saint Ambrose University 518 W Locust St *Fax: Admissions ■ TF Admissions: 800-383-2627 ■ Web: www.sau.edu	Davenport	IA	52803	563-333-6000	333-6243*
Simpson College 701 N 'C' St *Fax: Admissions ■ TF: 800-362-2454 ■ Web: www.simpson.edu	Indianola	IA	50125	515-961-6251	961-1870*
University of Dubuque 2000 University Ave *Fax: Admissions ■ TF: 800-722-5583 ■ Web: www.dbq.edu	Dubuque	IA	52001	563-589-3000	589-3690*
University of Iowa 107 Calvin Hall TF: 800-553-4692 ■ Web: www.uiowa.edu	Iowa City	IA	52242	319-335-3847	335-1535
University of Northern Iowa 1222 W 27th St *Fax: Admissions ■ TF Admissions: 800-772-2037 ■ Web: www.uni.edu	Cedar Falls	IA	50614	319-273-2281	273-2885*
Upper Iowa University 605 Washington St PO Box 1857 *Fax: Admissions ■ TF Admissions: 800-553-4150 ■ Web: www.uiu.edu	Fayette	IA	52142	563-425-5200	425-5323*
Waldorf College 106 S 6th St *Fax: Admissions ■ TF: 800-292-1903 ■ Web: www.waldorf.edu	Forest City	IA	50436	641-585-2450	585-8184*
Wartburg College 100 Wartburg Blvd *Fax: Admissions ■ TF: 800-772-2085 ■ Web: www.wartburg.edu	Waverly	IA	50677	319-352-8264	352-8579*
William Penn University 201 Trueblood Ave *Fax: Admissions ■ TF: 800-779-7366 ■ Web: www.wmpenn.edu	Oskaloosa	IA	52577	641-673-1001	673-2113*

Kansas

	City	State	ZIP	Phone	Fax
Baker University 618 8th St *Fax: Admissions ■ TF: 800-873-4282 ■ Web: www.bakeru.edu	Baldwin City	KS	66006	785-594-6451	594-8372*
Benedictine College 1020 N 2nd St *Fax: Admissions ■ TF: 800-467-5340 ■ Web: www2.benedictine.edu	Atchison	KS	66002	913-367-5340	367-5462*
Bethany College 421 N 1st St *Fax: Admissions ■ TF Admissions: 800-826-2281 ■ Web: www.bethanylb.edu	Lindsborg	KS	67456	785-227-3311	227-8993*
Bethel College 300 E 27th St *Fax: Admissions ■ TF: 800-522-1887 ■ Web: www.bethelks.edu	North Newton	KS	67117	316-283-2500	284-5286*
Central Christian College PO Box 1403 *Fax: Admissions ■ TF: 800-835-0078 ■ Web: www.centralchristian.edu	McPherson	KS	67460	620-241-0723	241-6032*
Emporia State University 1200 Commercial St Campus Box 4034 TF: 877-468-6378 ■ Web: www.emporia.edu	Emporia	KS	66801	620-341-1200	341-5599
Fort Hays State University 600 Park St *Fax: Admissions ■ TF Admissions: 800-628-3478 ■ Web: www.fhsu.edu	Hays	KS	67601	785-628-4000	628-4187*
Friends University 2100 University St *Fax: Admissions ■ TF: 800-794-6945 ■ Web: www.friends.edu	Wichita	KS	67213	316-295-5000	295-5701*
Haskell Indian Nations University 155 Indian Ave Box 5031 *Fax: Admissions ■ Web: www.haskell.edu	Lawrence	KS	66046	785-749-8454	749-8429*
Kansas State University 114 Anderson Hall *Fax: Admissions ■ TF Admissions: 800-432-8270 ■ Web: www.k-state.edu	Manhattan	KS	66506	785-532-6250	532-6393*
Kansas State University-Salina College of Technology & Aviation 2310 Centennial Rd *Fax: Admissions ■ Web: www.sal.ksu.edu	Salina	KS	67401	785-826-2640	826-2938*
Kansas University Edwards 12600 Quivira Rd *Fax: Admissions ■ Web: edwardscampus.ku.edu	Overland Park	KS	66213	913-897-8400	897-8490*
Kansas Wesleyan University 100 E Claflin Ave *Fax: Admissions ■ TF: 800-874-1154 ■ Web: www.kwu.edu	Salina	KS	67401	785-827-5541	827-0927*
McPherson College PO Box 1402 *Fax: Admissions ■ TF: 800-365-7402 ■ Web: www.mcpherson.edu	McPherson	KS	67460	620-241-0731	241-8443*
MidAmerica Nazarene University 2030 E College Way *Fax: Admissions ■ TF: 800-800-8887 ■ Web: www.mnu.edu	Olathe	KS	66062	913-782-3750	791-3481*
Newman University 3100 McCormick Ave *Fax: Admissions ■ TF: 877-639-6268 ■ Web: www.newmanu.edu	Wichita	KS	67213	316-942-4291	942-4483*
Ottawa University 1001 S Cedar St *Fax: Admissions ■ TF Admissions: 800-755-5200 ■ Web: www.ottawa.edu	Ottawa	KS	66067	785-242-5200	229-1008*
Pittsburg State University 1701 S Broadway St *Fax: Admissions ■ TF: 800-854-7488 ■ Web: www.pittstate.edu	Pittsburg	KS	66762	620-235-4251	235-6003*
Southwestern College 100 College St *Fax: Admissions ■ TF: 800-846-1543 ■ Web: www.sckans.edu	Winfield	KS	67156	620-229-6236	229-6344*
Sterling College 125 W Cooper TF: 800-346-1017 ■ Web: www.sterling.edu	Sterling	KS	67579	620-278-2173	278-4418
Tabor College 400 S Jefferson St *Fax: Admissions ■ TF Admissions: 800-822-6799 ■ Web: www.tabor.edu	Hillsboro	KS	67063	620-947-3121	947-6276*
University of Kansas 1502 Iowa St Web: www.ku.edu	Lawrence	KS	66045	785-864-2700	864-5017
University of Saint Mary 4100 S 4th St *Fax: Admissions ■ TF: 800-752-7043 ■ Web: www.stmary.edu	Leavenworth	KS	66048	913-682-5151	758-6140*
Washburn University 1700 SW College Ave TF: 800-332-0291 ■ Web: www.washburn.edu	Topeka	KS	66621	785-670-1010	670-1113
Wichita State University 1845 Fairmount St *Fax: Admissions ■ TF Admissions: 800-362-2594 ■ Web: www.wichita.edu	Wichita	KS	67260	316-978-3456	978-3174*

Kentucky

	City	State	ZIP	Phone	Fax
Alice Lloyd College 100 Purpose Rd *Fax: Admissions ■ TF Admissions: 888-280-4252 ■ Web: www.alc.edu	Pippa Passes	KY	41844	606-368-2101	368-6215*
Asbury College 1 Macklem Dr *Fax: Admissions ■ TF Admissions: 800-888-1818 ■ Web: www.asbury.edu	Wilmore	KY	40390	859-858-3511	858-3921*
Bellarmine University 2001 Newburg Rd TF: 800-274-4723 ■ Web: www.bellarmine.edu	Louisville	KY	40205	502-452-8000	452-8002
Berea College 101 Chestnut St *Fax: Admissions ■ TF: 800-326-5948 ■ Web: www.berea.edu	Berea	KY	40403	859-985-3500	985-3512*
Brescia University 717 Frederica St *Fax: Admissions ■ TF Admissions: 877-273-7242 ■ Web: brescia.edu	Owensboro	KY	42301	270-685-3131	686-4314*
Campbellsville University 1 University Dr *Fax: Admissions ■ TF Admissions: 800-264-6014 ■ Web: www.campbellsville.edu	Campbellsville	KY	42718	270-789-5000	789-5071*
Centre College 600 W Walnut St TF: 800-423-6236 ■ Web: www.centre.edu	Danville	KY	40422	859-238-5350	238-5373
Eastern Kentucky University 521 Lancaster Ave TF: 800-465-9191 ■ Web: www.eku.edu	Richmond	KY	40475	859-622-2106	622-8024
Georgetown College 400 E College St *Fax: Admissions ■ TF Admissions: 800-788-9985 ■ Web: www.georgetowncollege.edu	Georgetown	KY	40324	502-863-8000	868-7733*
Kentucky Christian University 100 Academic Pkwy *Fax: Admissions ■ TF Admissions: 800-522-3181 ■ Web: www.kcu.edu	Grayson	KY	41143	606-474-3000	474-3155*
Kentucky State University 400 E Main St *Fax: Admissions ■ TF Admissions: 800-325-1716 ■ Web: www.kysu.edu	Frankfort	KY	40601	502-597-6000	597-5814*
Kentucky Wesleyan College 3000 Frederica St *Fax: Admissions ■ TF Admissions: 800-999-0592 ■ Web: www.kwc.edu	Owensboro	KY	42301	270-852-3120	852-3133*
Lindsey Wilson College 210 Lindsey Wilson St *Fax: Admissions ■ TF: 800-264-0138 ■ Web: www.lindsey.edu	Columbia	KY	42728	270-384-2126	384-8591*
Louisville Bible College PO Box 91046 TF: 888-676-7458 ■ Web: louisvillebiblecollege.org	Louisville	KY	40291	502-231-5221	231-5222
Mid-Continent University 99 Powell Rd E *Fax: Admissions ■ Web: www.midcontinent.edu	Mayfield	KY	42066	270-247-8521	247-3115*
Midway College 512 E Stephens St *Fax: Admissions ■ TF: 800-755-0031 ■ Web: www.midway.edu	Midway	KY	40347	859-846-5346	846-5787*
Morehead State University 100 Admissions Center *Fax: Admissions ■ TF: 800-585-6781 ■ Web: www.morehead-st.edu	Morehead	KY	40351	606-783-2000	783-5038*
Murray State University 100 Sparks Hall *Fax: Admissions ■ TF: 800-272-4678 ■ Web: www.murraystate.edu	Murray	KY	42071	270-809-3741	809-3780*
Hopkinsville 5305 Fort Campbell Blvd *Fax: Admissions	Hopkinsville	KY	42240	270-707-1525	707-1535*
Northern Kentucky University Nunn Dr *Fax: Admissions ■ TF Admissions: 800-637-9948 ■ Web: www.nku.edu	Highland Heights	KY	41099	859-572-5220	572-6665*
Pikeville College 147 Sycamore St *Fax: Admissions ■ TF: 866-232-7700 ■ Web: www.pc.edu	Pikeville	KY	41501	606-218-5250	218-5255*
Spalding University 851 S 4th St TF: 800-896-8941 ■ Web: www.spalding.edu	Louisville	KY	40203	502-585-9911	585-7158
Sullivan University 3101 Bardstown Rd TF: 800-844-1354 ■ Web: www.sullivan.edu	Louisville	KY	40205	502-456-6505	456-0040
Thomas More College 333 Thomas More Pkwy TF: 800-825-4557 ■ Web: www.thomasmore.edu	Crestview Hills	KY	41017	859-344-3332	344-3444
Transylvania University 300 N Broadway TF: 800-872-6798 ■ Web: www.transy.edu	Lexington	KY	40508	859-233-8242	233-8797
Union College 310 College St *Fax: Admissions ■ TF: 800-489-8646 ■ Web: www.unionky.edu	Barbourville	KY	40906	606-546-4151	546-1667*
University of the Cumberlands 816 Walnut St *Fax: Admissions ■ TF: 800-343-1609 ■ Web: www.cumberlandcollege.edu	Williamsburg	KY	40769	606-549-2200	539-4303*
University of Kentucky 800 Rose St TF: 866-900-4685 ■ Web: www.uky.edu	Lexington	KY	40536	859-257-9000	257-3823
University of Louisville 2301 S 3rd St *Fax: Admissions ■ TF: 800-334-8635 ■ Web: louisville.edu	Louisville	KY	40292	502-852-5555	852-6526*
Western Kentucky University 1906 College Heights Blvd *Fax: Admissions ■ TF Admissions: 800-495-8463 ■ Web: www.wku.edu	Bowling Green	KY	42101	270-745-0111	745-6133*

Louisiana

	City	State	ZIP	Phone	Fax
Centenary College of Louisiana 2911 Centenary Blvd *Fax: Admissions ■ TF Admissions: 800-234-4448 ■ Web: www.centenary.edu	Shreveport	LA	71104	318-869-5131	869-5005*
Grambling State University 403 Main St TF: 800-569-4714 ■ Web: www.gram.edu	Grambling	LA	71245	318-247-3811	
Louisiana College 1140 College Dr *Fax: Admissions ■ TF: 800-487-1906 ■ Web: www.lacollege.edu	Pineville	LA	71359	318-487-7011	487-7550*
Louisiana State University					
Alexandria 8100 US Hwy 71 S *Fax: Admissions ■ TF Admissions: 888-473-6417 ■ Web: www.lsua.edu	Alexandria	LA	71302	318-445-3672	473-6418*
Baton Rouge 110 Thomas Boyd Hall *Fax: Admissions ■ Web: www.lsu.edu	Baton Rouge	LA	70803	225-578-3202	578-4433*
Shreveport 1 University Pl *Fax: Admissions ■ Web: www.lsus.edu	Shreveport	LA	71115	318-797-5000	797-5286*
Louisiana Tech University 305 Wisteria St *Fax: Admissions ■ TF Admissions: 800-528-3241 ■ Web: www.latech.edu	Ruston	LA	71272	318-257-0211	257-2499*
Loyola University New Orleans 6363 St Charles Ave Campus Box 18 *Fax: Admissions ■ TF Admissions: 800-456-9652 ■ Web: www.loyno.edu	New Orleans	LA	70118	504-865-3240	865-3383*
McNeese State University 4205 Ryan St *Fax: Admissions ■ TF: 800-622-3352 ■ Web: www.mcneese.edu	Lake Charles	LA	70609	337-475-5000	475-5151*
Newcomb College Institute for Women 43 Newcomb Pl TF: 888-862-8589 ■ Web: www.newcomb.tulane.edu	New Orleans	LA	70118	504-865-5422	862-8589
Nicholls State University 906 E 1st St *Fax: Admissions ■ TF Admissions: 877-642-4655 ■ Web: www.nicholls.edu	Thibodaux	LA	70301	985-448-4507	448-4929*
Northwestern State University 200 Central Ave TF: 800-767-8115 ■ Web: www.nsula.edu	Natchitoches	LA	71497	318-357-6361	357-4660
Our Lady of Holy Cross College 4123 Woodland Dr TF: 800-259-7744 ■ Web: www.olhcc.edu	New Orleans	LA	70131	504-394-7744	394-1182
Our Lady of the Lake College 7434 Perkins Rd *Fax: Admissions ■ TF Admissions: 877-242-3509 ■ Web: www.ololcollege.edu	Baton Rouge	LA	70808	225-768-1700	768-1726*
Southeastern Louisiana University 752 University Stn *Fax: Admissions ■ TF: 800-222-7358 ■ Web: www.selu.edu	Hammond	LA	70402	985-549-2062	549-5632*
Southern University & A & M College Branch Post Office *Fax: Admissions ■ TF Admissions: 800-256-1531 ■ Web: www.subr.edu	Baton Rouge	LA	70813	225-771-4500	771-2500*
Tulane University 6823 St Charles Ave *Fax: Admissions ■ TF Admissions: 800-873-9283 ■ Web: www.tulane.edu	New Orleans	LA	70118	504-865-5000	862-8715*
University of Louisiana					
Lafayette 104 University Cir *Fax: Admissions ■ TF: 800-752-6553 ■ Web: www.louisiana.edu	Lafayette	LA	70503	337-482-1000	482-1317*
Monroe 700 University Ave *Fax: Admissions ■ TF Admissions: 800-372-5127 ■ Web: www.ulm.edu	Monroe	LA	71209	318-342-5430	342-1953*
University of New Orleans Administrative Bldg Rm 103 Lakefront TF Admissions: 800-256-5866 ■ Web: www.uno.edu	New Orleans	LA	70148	504-280-6000	280-5522
Xavier University of Louisiana 1 Drexel Dr *Fax: Admissions ■ TF Admissions: 877-928-4378 ■ Web: www.xula.edu	New Orleans	LA	70125	504-486-7411	485-7941*

Maine

	City	State	ZIP	Phone	Fax
Bates College 2 Andrews Rd Lane Hall *Fax: Admissions ■ Web: www.bates.edu	Lewiston	ME	04240	207-786-6255	786-6025*
Bowdoin College 5000 College Station *Fax: Admissions ■ Web: www.bowdoin.edu	Brunswick	ME	04011	207-725-3000	725-3101*
Colby College 4800 Mayflower Hill *Fax: Admissions ■ TF Admissions: 800-723-3032 ■ Web: www.colby.edu	Waterville	ME	04901	207-859-4800	859-4828*
College of the Atlantic 105 Eden St *Fax: Admissions ■ TF Admissions: 800-528-0025 ■ Web: www.coa.edu	Bar Harbor	ME	04609	207-288-5015	288-4126*
Husson College 1 College Cir *Fax: Admissions ■ TF: 800-448-7766 ■ Web: www.husson.edu	Bangor	ME	04401	207-941-7000	941-7935*
Maine Maritime Academy 66 Pleasant St *Fax: Admissions ■ TF Admissions: 800-227-8465 ■ Web: www.mainemaritime.edu	Castine	ME	04420	207-326-4311	326-2515*
New England Bible College 879 Sawyer St PO Box 2886 *Fax: Admissions ■ TF: 800-286-1859 ■ Web: www.nebc.edu	South Portland	ME	04116	207-799-5979	799-6586*

Institution	City	State	Zip	Phone	Fax
Saint Joseph's College of Maine 278 Whites Bridge Rd *Fax: Admissions ■ TF Admissions: 800-338-7057 ■ Web: www.sjcme.edu	Standish	ME	04084	207-893-7746	893-7862*
Thomas College 180 W River Rd *Fax: Admissions ■ TF Admissions: 800-339-7001 ■ Web: www.thomas.edu	Waterville	ME	04901	207-859-1111	859-1114*
Unity College 90 Quaker Hill Rd *Fax: Admissions ■ TF: 800-624-1024 ■ Web: www.unity.edu	Unity	ME	04988	207-948-3131	948-2928*
University of Maine 5713 Chadbourne Hall *Fax: Admissions ■ TF Admissions: 877-486-2364 ■ Web: www.umaine.edu	Orono	ME	04469	207-581-1110	581-1213*
Augusta 46 University Dr *Fax: Admissions ■ Web: www.uma.edu	Augusta	ME	04330	207-621-3000	621-3333*
Farmington 111 South St *Fax: Admissions ■ Web: www.umf.maine.edu	Farmington	ME	04938	207-778-7000	778-8182*
Fort Kent 23 University Dr *Fax: Admissions ■ TF Admissions: 888-879-8635 ■ Web: www.umfk.maine.edu	Fort Kent	ME	04743	207-834-7500	834-7609*
Machias 9 O'Brien Ave *Fax: Admissions ■ TF Admissions: 888-468-6866 ■ Web: www.umm.maine.edu	Machias	ME	04654	207-255-1200	255-1363*
Presque Isle 181 Main St *Fax: Admissions ■ Web: www.umpi.maine.edu	Presque Isle	ME	04769	207-768-9400	768-9777*
University of New England 11 Hills Beach Rd *Fax: Admissions ■ TF Admissions: 800-477-4863 ■ Web: www.une.edu	Biddeford	ME	04005	207-283-0171	602-5900*
Westbrook College 716 Stevens Ave *Fax: Admissions ■ TF Admissions: 800-477-4863 ■ Web: www.une.edu	Portland	ME	04103	207-797-7261	878-4889*
University of Southern Maine PO Box 9300 *Fax: Admissions ■ TF: 800-800-4876 ■ Web: www.usm.maine.edu	Portland	ME	04104	207-780-4141	780-5640*
Gorham 37 College Ave *Fax: Admissions ■ TF: 800-800-4876 ■ Web: www.usm.maine.edu	Gorham	ME	04038	207-780-5670	780-5640*
Lewiston-Auburn College 51 Westminster St *Fax: Admissions ■ TF: 800-800-4876 ■ Web: www.usm.maine.edu/lac	Lewiston	ME	04240	207-753-6500	753-6555*
Westbrook College 716 Stevens Ave *Fax: Admissions ■ TF Admissions: 800-477-4863 ■ Web: www.une.edu	Portland	ME	04103	207-797-7261	878-4889*

Maryland

Institution	City	State	Zip	Phone	Fax
Baltimore Hebrew University 5800 Park Heights Ave TF: 888-248-7420 ■ Web: www.bhu.edu	Baltimore	MD	21215	410-578-6900	578-6940
Bowie State University 14000 Jericho Park Rd TF: 877-772-6943 ■ Web: www.bowiestate.edu	Bowie	MD	20715	301-860-4000	860-3518
Capitol College 11301 Springfield Rd *Fax: Admissions ■ TF: 800-950-1992 ■ Web: www.capitol-college.edu	Laurel	MD	20708	301-369-2800	953-1442*
College of Notre Dame of Maryland 4701 N Charles St *Fax: Admissions ■ TF Admissions: 800-435-0300 ■ Web: www.ndm.edu	Baltimore	MD	21210	410-435-0100	532-6287*
Columbia Union College 7600 Flower Ave TF: 800-835-4212 ■ Web: www.cuc.edu	Takoma Park	MD	20912	301-891-4000	891-4167
Coppin State University 2500 W North Ave *Fax: Admissions ■ TF Admissions: 800-635-3674 ■ Web: www.coppin.edu	Baltimore	MD	21216	410-951-3600	523-7351*
Frostburg State University 101 Braddock Rd *Fax: Admissions ■ Web: www.frostburg.edu	Frostburg	MD	21532	301-687-4000	687-7074*
Goucher College 1021 Dulaney Valley Rd *Fax: Admissions ■ TF: 800-468-2437 ■ Web: www.goucher.edu	Baltimore	MD	21204	410-337-6000	337-6354*
Hood College 401 Rosemont Ave *Fax: Admissions ■ TF: 800-922-1599 ■ Web: www.hood.edu	Frederick	MD	21701	301-696-3400	696-3819*
Johns Hopkins University 3400 N Charles St Web: www.jhu.edu	Baltimore	MD	21218	410-516-8000	516-6025
Loyola College 4501 N Charles St *Fax: Admissions ■ TF: 800-221-9107 ■ Web: www.loyola.edu	Baltimore	MD	21210	410-617-5012	617-2176*
McDaniel College 2 College Hill *Fax: Admissions ■ TF Admissions: 800-638-5005 ■ Web: www.mcdaniel.edu	Westminster	MD	21157	410-857-2230	857-2757*
Morgan State University 1700 E Cold Spring Ln *Fax: Admissions ■ TF: 800-319-4678 ■ Web: www.morgan.edu	Baltimore	MD	21251	443-885-3333	885-8260*
Mount Saint Mary's University 16300 Old Emmitsburg Rd *Fax: Admissions ■ TF Admissions: 800-448-4347 ■ Web: www.msmary.edu	Emmitsburg	MD	21727	301-447-5214	447-5860*
Peabody Conservatory of Music 1 E Mt Vernon Pl TF: 800-368-2521 ■ Web: www.peabody.jhu.edu	Baltimore	MD	21202	410-659-8110	659-8102
Peabody Institute of the Johns Hopkins University Peabody Conservatory of Music 1 E Mt Vernon Pl TF: 800-368-2521 ■ Web: www.peabody.jhu.edu	Baltimore	MD	21202	410-659-8110	659-8102
Saint John's College 60 College Ave *Fax: Admissions ■ TF Admissions: 800-727-9238 ■ Web: www.sjca.edu	Annapolis	MD	21401	410-263-2371	269-7916*
Saint Mary's College of Maryland 18952 E Fisher Rd *Fax: Admissions ■ TF Admissions: 800-492-7181 ■ Web: www.smcm.edu	Saint Mary's City	MD	20686	240-895-2000	895-5001*
Salisbury University 1200 Camden Ave *Fax: Admissions ■ TF: 888-543-0148 ■ Web: www.salisbury.edu	Salisbury	MD	21801	410-543-6000	546-6016*
Sojourner-Douglass College 200 N Central Ave TF: 800-732-2630 ■ Web: www.sdc.edu	Baltimore	MD	21202	410-276-0306	675-1810
Strayer University Prince George's 4710 Auth Pl Suite 100 *Fax: Admissions ■ TF: 866-344-3297 ■ Web: www.strayer.edu	Suitland	MD	20746	301-423-3600	423-3999*
Towson University 8000 York Rd TF: 888-486-9766 ■ Web: www.towson.edu	Towson	MD	21252	410-704-2113	704-3030
University of Baltimore 1420 N Charles St TF Admitting: 888-661-5622 ■ Web: www.ubalt.edu	Baltimore	MD	21201	410-837-4200	837-4793
University of Maryland 7050 Baltimore Ave *Fax: Admissions ■ TF Admissions: 800-422-5867 ■ Web: www.umd.edu	College Park	MD	20742	301-405-1000	314-9693*
Baltimore County 1000 Hilltop Cir TF: 800-862-2482 ■ Web: www.umbc.edu	Baltimore	MD	21250	410-455-1000	455-1094
Eastern Shore 30665 Student Services Center Ln Web: www.umes.edu	Princess Anne	MD	21853	410-651-2200	651-7922
University of Maryland University College 3501 University Blvd E *Fax: Admissions ■ TF: 800-888-8682 ■ Web: www.umuc.edu	Adelphi	MD	20783	301-985-7000	985-7978*
US Naval Academy 121 Blake Rd *Fax: Admissions ■ TF Admissions: 888-249-7707 ■ Web: www.usna.edu	Annapolis	MD	21402	410-293-1000	293-4348*
Villa Julie College 1525 Green Spring Valley Rd *Fax Area Code: 443 ■ TF: 877-468-6852 ■ Web: www.vjc.edu	Stevenson	MD	21153	410-486-7001	352-4440*
Washington College 300 Washington Ave TF: 800-422-1782 ■ Web: www.washcoll.edu	Chestertown	MD	21620	410-778-2800	778-7287

Massachusetts

Institution	City	State	Zip	Phone	Fax
American International College 1000 State St *Fax: Admissions ■ TF Admissions: 800-242-3142 ■ Web: www.aic.edu	Springfield	MA	01109	413-205-3201	205-3051*
Amherst College 220 S Pleasant St *Fax: Admissions ■ Web: www.amherst.edu	Amherst	MA	01002	413-542-2000	542-2040*
Anna Maria College 50 Sunset Ln *Fax: Admissions ■ TF: 800-344-4586 ■ Web: www.annamaria.edu	Paxton	MA	01612	508-849-3365	849-3362*
Assumption College 500 Salisbury St TF: 888-882-7786 ■ Web: www.assumption.edu	Worcester	MA	01609	508-767-7000	799-4412
Atlantic Union College 338 Main St TF: 800-282-2030 ■ Web: auc.edu	South Lancaster	MA	01561	978-368-2000	368-2517
Babson College 231 Forest St *Fax: Admissions ■ TF Admissions: 800-488-3696 ■ Web: www3.babson.edu	Babson Park	MA	02457	781-235-1200	239-4006*
Bay Path College 588 Longmeadow St TF: 800-782-7284 ■ Web: www.baypath.edu	Longmeadow	MA	01106	413-567-0621	565-1105
Becker College 61 Sever St *Fax: Admissions ■ TF: 877-523-2537 ■ Web: www.becker.edu	Worcester	MA	01609	508-791-9241	890-1500*
Bentley College 175 Forest St *Fax: Admissions ■ TF Admissions: 800-523-2354 ■ Web: www.bentley.edu	Waltham	MA	02452	781-891-2244	891-3414*
Berklee College of Music 1140 Boylston St *Fax: Admissions ■ TF: 800-421-0084 ■ Web: www.berklee.edu	Boston	MA	02215	617-747-2221	747-2047*
Boston College 140 Commonwealth Ave TF: 800-360-2522 ■ Web: www.bc.edu	Chestnut Hill	MA	02467	617-552-3100	552-0798
Boston Conservatory of Music Dance & Theater 8 The Fenway *Fax: Admissions ■ Web: www.bostonconservatory.edu	Boston	MA	02215	617-536-6340	247-3159*
Boston University 1 Sherborn St *Fax: Admissions ■ Web: web.bu.edu	Boston	MA	02215	617-353-2000	353-9695*
Brandeis University 415 South St TF: 800-622-0622 ■ Web: www.brandeis.edu	Waltham	MA	02454	781-736-3500	736-3536
Bridgewater State College 131 Summer St *Fax: Admissions ■ Web: www.bridgew.edu	Bridgewater	MA	02325	508-531-1000	531-1746*
Clark University 950 Main St TF: 800-462-5275 ■ Web: www.clarku.edu	Worcester	MA	01610	508-793-7711	793-8821
College of the Holy Cross 1 College St TF: 800-442-2421 ■ Web: www.holycross.edu	Worcester	MA	01610	508-793-2011	793-3888
Curry College 1071 Blue Hill Ave TF: 800-669-0686 ■ Web: www.curry.edu	Milton	MA	02186	617-333-2210	333-2114
Eastern Nazarene College 23 E Elm Ave TF: 800-883-6288 ■ Web: www.enc.edu	Quincy	MA	02170	617-745-3000	745-3929
Elms College 291 Springfield St *Fax: Admissions ■ TF Admissions: 800-255-3567 ■ Web: www.elms.edu	Chicopee	MA	01013	413-592-3189	594-2781*
Emerson College 120 Boylston St *Fax: Admissions ■ Web: www.emerson.edu	Boston	MA	02116	617-824-8500	824-8609*
Emmanuel College 400 The Fenway *Fax: Admissions ■ Web: www.emmanuel.edu	Boston	MA	02115	617-277-9340	735-9801*
Endicott College 376 Hale St *Fax: Admissions ■ TF Admissions: 800-325-1114 ■ Web: www.endicott.edu	Beverly	MA	01915	978-232-2021	232-2520*
Fitchburg State College 160 Pearl St *Fax: Admissions ■ Web: www.fsc.edu	Fitchburg	MA	01420	978-345-2151	665-4540*
Framingham State College 100 State St PO Box 9101 *Fax: Admissions ■ Web: www.framingham.edu	Framingham	MA	01701	508-620-1220	626-4017*
Franklin W Olin College of Engineering Olin Way *Fax: Admissions ■ Web: www.olin.edu	Needham	MA	02492	781-292-2300	292-2210*
Gordon College 255 Grapevine Rd *Fax: Admissions ■ TF: 800-343-1379 ■ Web: www.gordon.edu	Wenham	MA	01984	978-927-2300	867-4682*
Hampshire College 893 West St *Fax: Admissions ■ TF Admissions: 877-937-4267 ■ Web: www.hampshire.edu	Amherst	MA	01002	413-549-4600	559-5631*
Harvard University 8 Garden St *Fax: Admissions ■ Web: www.harvard.edu	Cambridge	MA	02138	617-495-1000	495-8821*
Hebrew College 160 Herrick Rd TF: 800-866-4814 ■ Web: www.hebrewcollege.edu	Newton Center	MA	02459	617-559-8610	559-8601
Hellenic College-Holy Cross School of Theology 50 Goddard Ave *Fax: Admissions ■ Web: www.hchc.edu	Brookline	MA	02445	617-731-3500	850-1460*
Lasell College 1844 Commonwealth Ave *Fax: Admissions ■ TF Admissions: 888-527-3554 ■ Web: www.lasell.edu	Newton	MA	02466	617-243-2225	243-2380*
Lesley University 29 Everett St TF: 800-999-1959 ■ Web: www.lesley.edu	Cambridge	MA	02138	617-868-9600	349-8313
Massachusetts College of Art 621 Huntington Ave Web: www.massart.edu	Boston	MA	02115	617-879-7222	879-7250
Massachusetts College of Liberal Arts 375 Church St Web: www.mcla.edu	North Adams	MA	01247	413-662-5000	662-5179
Massachusetts College of Pharmacy & Health Sciences 179 Longwood Ave TF: 800-225-5506 ■ Web: www.mcphs.edu	Boston	MA	02115	617-732-2850	732-2118
Massachusetts Institute of Technology (MIT) 77 Massachusetts Ave Bldg 3 Rm 108 Web: web.mit.edu	Cambridge	MA	02139	617-253-1000	258-8304
Massachusetts Maritime Academy 101 Academy Dr *Fax: Admissions ■ TF Admissions: 800-544-3411 ■ Web: www.maritime.edu	Buzzards Bay	MA	02532	508-830-5000	830-5077*
Merrimack College 315 Turnpike St *Fax: Admissions ■ Web: www.merrimack.edu	North Andover	MA	01845	978-837-5000	837-5133*
MIT (Massachusetts Institute of Technology) 77 Massachusetts Ave Bldg 3 Rm 108 Web: web.mit.edu	Cambridge	MA	02139	617-253-1000	258-8304
Montserrat College of Art 23 Essex St PO Box 26 *Fax: Admissions ■ TF: 800-836-0487 ■ Web: www.montserrat.edu	Beverly	MA	01915	978-921-4242	921-4241*
Mount Holyoke College 50 College St Web: www.mtholyoke.edu	South Hadley	MA	01075	413-538-2000	538-2409
Mount Ida College 777 Dedham St *Fax: Admissions ■ Web: www.mountida.edu	Newton Center	MA	02459	617-928-4500	928-4507*
New England Conservatory 290 Huntington Ave *Fax: Admissions ■ Web: www.newenglandconservatory.edu	Boston	MA	02115	617-585-1100	585-1115*
Newbury College 129 Fisher Ave *Fax: Admitting ■ TF: 800-639-2879 ■ Web: www.newbury.edu	Brookline	MA	02445	617-730-7000	731-9618*
Nichols College 124 Center Rd TF: 800-470-3379 ■ Web: www.nichols.edu	Dudley	MA	01571	508-218-1560	943-9885
Northeastern University 360 Huntington Ave *Fax: Admissions ■ Web: www.northeastern.edu	Boston	MA	02115	617-373-2000	373-8780*
Olin College of Engineering Olin Way *Fax: Admissions ■ Web: www.olin.edu	Needham	MA	02492	781-292-2300	292-2210*
Pine Manor College 400 Heath St TF: 800-762-1357 ■ Web: www.pmc.edu	Chestnut Hill	MA	02467	617-731-7104	731-7102
Regis College 235 Wellesley St TF: 866-438-7344 ■ Web: www.regiscollege.edu	Weston	MA	02493	781-768-7000	768-7071
Salem State College 352 Lafayette St Web: www.salemstate.edu	Salem	MA	01970	978-542-6000	542-6893
School of the Museum of Fine Arts 230 The Fenway *Fax: Admissions ■ TF Admissions: 800-643-6078 ■ Web: www.smfa.edu	Boston	MA	02115	617-369-3626	369-4264*
Simmons College 300 The Fenway *Fax: Admissions ■ TF: 800-345-8468 ■ Web: www.simmons.edu	Boston	MA	02115	617-521-2000	521-3190*
Simon's Rock College of Bard 84 Alford Rd *Fax: Admissions ■ Web: www.simons-rock.edu	Great Barrington	MA	01230	413-528-0771	528-7380*
Smith College 7 College Ln TF: 800-383-3232 ■ Web: www.smith.edu	Northampton	MA	01063	413-584-2700	585-2527
Springfield College 263 Alden St *Fax: Admissions ■ TF Admissions: 800-343-1257 ■ Web: www.spfldcol.edu	Springfield	MA	01109	413-748-3136	748-3694*
Stonehill College 320 Washington St *Fax: Admissions ■ Web: www.stonehill.edu	Easton	MA	02357	508-565-1000	565-1545*
Suffolk University 8 Ashburton Pl TF: 800-678-3365 ■ Web: www.suffolk.edu	Boston	MA	02108	617-573-8460	557-1574
Tufts University Web: www.tufts.edu	Medford	MA	02155	617-628-5000	627-4079
University of Massachusetts					
Amherst 181 Presidents Dr *Fax: Admissions ■ Web: umass.edu	Amherst	MA	01003	413-545-0111	545-4312*
Boston 100 Morrissey Blvd Campus Center *Fax: Admitting ■ Web: www.umb.edu	Boston	MA	02125	617-287-6100	287-5999*
Dartmouth 285 Old Westport Rd *Fax: Admissions ■ Web: www.umassd.edu	North Dartmouth	MA	02747	508-999-8000	999-8755*
Lowell 1 University Ave *Fax: Admissions ■ Web: www.uml.edu	Lowell	MA	01854	978-934-4000	934-3086*

Massachusetts (Cont'd)

Institution	City	State	ZIP	Phone	Fax
Wellesley College 106 Central St	Wellesley	MA	02481	781-283-1000	283-3678*
*Fax: Admissions ■ Web: www.wellesley.edu					
Wentworth Institute of Technology 550 Huntington Ave	Boston	MA	02115	617-989-4590	989-4010*
*Fax: Admissions ■ TF: 800-556-0610 ■ Web: www.wit.edu					
Western New England College 1215 Wilbraham Rd	Springfield	MA	01119	413-782-3111	782-1777*
*Fax: Admissions ■ TF: 800-325-1122 ■ Web: www.wnec.edu					
Westfield State College 577 Western Ave	Westfield	MA	01086	413-568-3311	572-0520*
*Fax: Admissions ■ Web: www.wsc.mass.edu					
Wheaton College 26 Main St	Norton	MA	02766	508-286-8200	286-8271
TF Admissions: 800-394-6003 ■ Web: www.wheatonma.edu					
Wheelock College 200 The Riverway	Boston	MA	02215	617-879-2206	879-2449
TF: 800-734-5212 ■ Web: www.wheelock.edu					
Williams College 33 Stetson Ct	Williamstown	MA	01267	413-597-3131	597-4052*
*Fax: Admissions ■ Web: www.williams.edu					
Worcester Polytechnic Institute 100 Institute Rd	Worcester	MA	01609	508-831-5000	831-5875*
*Fax: Admissions ■ Web: www.wpi.edu					
Worcester State College 486 Chandler St	Worcester	MA	01602	508-793-8000	929-8193
TF: 866-972-2255 ■ Web: www.worcester.edu					

Michigan

Institution	City	State	ZIP	Phone	Fax
Adrian College 110 S Madison St	Adrian	MI	49221	517-265-5161	264-3331*
*Fax: Admissions ■ TF Admissions: 800-877-2246 ■ Web: www.adrian.edu					
Albion College 611 E Porter St	Albion	MI	49224	517-629-1000	629-0569
TF: 800-858-6770 ■ Web: www.albion.edu					
Alma College 614 W Superior St	Alma	MI	48801	989-463-7139	463-7057
TF: 800-321-2562 ■ Web: www.alma.edu					
Andrews University 100 US 31	Berrien Springs	MI	49104	269-471-7771	471-2670*
*Fax: Admissions ■ TF: 800-253-2874 ■ Web: www.andrews.edu					
Aquinas College 1607 Robinson Rd SE	Grand Rapids	MI	49506	616-632-2900	732-4469*
*Fax: Admissions ■ TF: 800-678-9593 ■ Web: www.aquinas.edu					
Baker College					
Auburn Hills 1500 University Dr	Auburn Hills	MI	48326	248-340-0600	340-0608*
*Fax: Admissions ■ TF: 888-429-0410 ■ Web: www.baker.edu/campusresources/Auburn%20Hills/ahcinfo.cfm					
Cadillac 9600 E 13th St	Cadillac	MI	49601	231-876-3100	876-3440
TF: 888-313-3463 ■ Web: www.baker.edu					
Clinton Township 34950 Little Mack Ave	Clinton Township	MI	48035	586-791-6610	791-5790*
*Fax: Admissions ■ TF: 888-272-2842 ■ Web: www.baker.edu					
Flint 1050 W Bristol Rd	Flint	MI	48507	810-767-7600	766-4255*
*Fax: Admissions ■ TF: 800-964-4299 ■ Web: www.baker.edu					
Jackson 2800 Springport Rd	Jackson	MI	49202	517-788-7800	788-6187
TF: 888-343-3683 ■ Web: www.baker.edu					
Muskegon 1903 Marquette Ave	Muskegon	MI	49442	231-777-8800	777-5201*
*Fax: Admissions ■ TF: 800-937-0337 ■ Web: www.baker.edu/campusresources/Muskegon/mucinfo.cfm					
Owosso 1020 S Washington St	Owosso	MI	48867	989-729-3300	729-3359*
*Fax: Admissions ■ TF: 800-879-3797 ■ Web: www.baker.edu					
Port Huron 3403 Lapeer Rd	Port Huron	MI	48060	810-985-7000	985-7066
TF: 888-262-2442 ■ Web: www.baker.edu					
Calvin College 3201 Burton St SE	Grand Rapids	MI	49546	616-526-6000	526-6777*
*Fax: Admissions ■ TF: 800-688-0122 ■ Web: www.calvin.edu					
Central Michigan University 102 Warriner Hall	Mount Pleasant	MI	48859	989-774-4000	774-7267*
*Fax: Admissions ■ TF Admissions: 888-292-5366 ■ Web: www.cmich.edu					
Concordia University Ann Arbor 4090 Geddes Rd	Ann Arbor	MI	48105	734-995-7322	995-4610
TF: 800-253-0680 ■ Web: www.cuaa.edu					
Cornerstone University 1001 E Beltline Ave NE	Grand Rapids	MI	49525	616-222-1426	222-1418*
*Fax: Admissions ■ TF Admissions: 800-787-9778 ■ Web: www.cornerstone.edu					
Davenport University					
Dearborn 4801 Oakman Blvd	Dearborn	MI	48126	313-581-4400	581-4480
TF: 800-585-1479 ■ Web: www.davenport.edu					
Flint 4318 Miller Rd Suite A	Flint	MI	48507	810-732-9977	732-9128*
*Fax: Admissions ■ TF: 800-727-1443 ■ Web: www.davenport.edu					
Lansing 220 E Kalamazoo St	Lansing	MI	48933	517-484-2600	484-1132*
*Fax: Admissions ■ TF: 800-686-1600 ■ Web: www.davenport.edu					
Lettinga Campus 6191 Kraft Ave SE	Grand Rapids	MI	49512	616-698-7111	554-5214
TF: 866-925-3884 ■ Web: www.davenport.edu					
Saginaw 5300 Bay Rd	Saginaw	MI	48604	989-799-7800	799-9696*
*Fax: Admissions ■ TF: 800-968-8133 ■ Web: www.davenport.edu					
Warren 27650 Dequindre Rd	Warren	MI	48092	586-558-8700	558-7868*
*Fax: Admissions ■ TF: 800-724-7708 ■ Web: www.davenport.edu					
Eastern Michigan University	Ypsilanti	MI	48197	734-487-3060	487-6559*
*Fax: Admissions ■ TF: 800-468-6368 ■ Web: www.emich.edu					
Ferris State University 1201 S State St	Big Rapids	MI	49307	231-591-2000	591-3944*
*Fax: Admissions ■ TF: 800-433-7747 ■ Web: www.ferris.edu					
Traverse City 2200 Dendrinos Dr Suite 200H	Traverse City	MI	49684	231-995-1734	995-1736*
*Fax: Admissions ■ TF: 866-857-1954 ■ Web: www.ferris.edu/ucel/					
Finlandia University 601 Quincy St	Hancock	MI	49930	906-482-5300	487-7383*
*Fax: Admissions ■ TF: 800-682-7604 ■ Web: www.finlandia.edu					
Grand Valley State University 1 Campus Dr	Allendale	MI	49401	616-331-5000	331-2000
TF: 800-748-0246 ■ Web: www.gvsu.edu					
Hillsdale College 33 E College St	Hillsdale	MI	49242	517-607-2327	607-2223*
*Fax: Admissions ■ Web: www.hillsdale.edu					
Hope College 69 E 10th St PO Box 9000	Holland	MI	49422	616-395-7850	395-7130*
*Fax: Admissions ■ TF Admissions: 800-968-7850 ■ Web: www.hope.edu					
Kalamazoo College 1200 Academy St	Kalamazoo	MI	49006	269-337-7166	337-7390*
*Fax: Admissions ■ TF Admissions: 800-253-3602 ■ Web: www.kzoo.edu					
Kendall College of Art & Design of Ferris State University 17 Fountain St NW	Grand Rapids	MI	49503	616-451-2787	831-9689
TF: 800-676-2787 ■ Web: www.kcad.edu					
Kettering University 1700 W 3rd Ave	Flint	MI	48504	810-762-9500	762-9837
TF: 800-955-4464 ■ Web: www.kettering.edu					
Lake Superior State University 650 W Easterday Ave	Sault Sainte Marie	MI	49783	906-632-6841	635-6696*
*Fax: Admissions ■ TF Admissions: 888-800-5778 ■ Web: www.lssu.edu					
Lawrence Technological University 21000 W 10-Mile Rd	Southfield	MI	48075	248-204-3160	204-3188*
*Fax: Admissions ■ TF: 800-225-5588 ■ Web: www.ltu.edu					
Madonna University 36600 Schoolcraft Rd	Livonia	MI	48150	734-432-5339	432-5424
TF: 800-852-4951 ■ Web: www.madonna.edu					
Marygrove College 8425 W McNichols Rd	Detroit	MI	48221	313-927-1200	927-1399*
*Fax: Admissions ■ TF Admissions: 866-313-1927 ■ Web: www.marygrove.edu					
Michigan State University 250 Hannah Administration Bldg	East Lansing	MI	48824	517-355-1855	353-1647
Web: www.msu.edu					
Michigan Technological University 1400 Townsend Dr	Houghton	MI	49931	906-487-2335	487-2125*
*Fax: Admissions ■ TF: 888-688-1885 ■ Web: www.mtu.edu					
Northern Michigan University 1401 Presque Isle Ave	Marquette	MI	49855	906-227-2650	227-1747*
*Fax: Admissions ■ TF: 800-682-9797 ■ Web: www.nmu.edu					
Northwood University Michigan 4000 Whiting Dr	Midland	MI	48640	989-837-4200	837-4490*
*Fax: Admissions ■ TF: 800-457-7878 ■ Web: www.northwood.edu/mi					
Oakland University 2200 Squirrel Rd	Rochester	MI	48309	248-370-2100	370-4462*
*Fax: Admissions ■ TF Admissions: 800-625-8648 ■ Web: www3.oakland.edu					
Olivet College 320 S Main St	Olivet	MI	49076	269-749-7000	749-6617*
*Fax: Admissions ■ TF: 800-456-7189 ■ Web: www.olivetcollege.edu					
Rochester College 800 W Avon Rd	Rochester Hills	MI	48307	248-218-2011	218-2025*
*Fax: Admissions ■ TF: 800-521-6010 ■ Web: www.rc.edu					
Saginaw Valley State University 7400 Bay Rd	University Center	MI	48710	989-964-4200	790-0180
TF: 800-968-9500 ■ Web: www.svsu.edu					
Siena Heights University 1247 E Siena Heights Dr	Adrian	MI	49221	517-263-0731	264-7745*
*Fax: Admissions ■ TF: 800-521-0009 ■ Web: www.sienahts.edu					
Spring Arbor University 106 E Main St	Spring Arbor	MI	49283	517-750-1200	750-6620*
*Fax: Admissions ■ TF Admissions: 800-968-0011 ■ Web: www.spring.arbor.edu					
University of Detroit Mercy 4001 W McNichols Rd	Detroit	MI	48221	313-993-1000	993-3326*
*Fax: Admissions ■ TF Admissions: 800-635-5020 ■ Web: www.udmercy.edu					
University of Detroit Mercy School of Dentistry Corktown Campus 2700 MLK Dr	Detroit	MI	48219	313-494-6611	
Web: www.udmercy.edu					
University of Michigan 515 E Jefferson St	Ann Arbor	MI	48109	734-764-1817	
Web: www.umich.edu					
Dearborn 4901 Evergreen Rd	Dearborn	MI	48128	313-593-5100	436-9167*
*Fax: Admissions ■ Web: www.umd.umich.edu					
Flint 303 E Kearsley St	Flint	MI	48502	810-762-3000	762-3272
TF: 800-942-5636 ■ Web: www.flint.umich.edu					
Wayne State University 42 W Warren	Detroit	MI	48202	313-577-3577	577-7536*
*Fax: Admissions ■ TF: 877-978-4636 ■ Web: www.wayne.edu					
Western Michigan University 1903 W Michigan Ave	Kalamazoo	MI	49008	269-387-1000	387-2096*
*Fax: Admissions ■ Web: www.wmich.edu					

Minnesota

Institution	City	State	ZIP	Phone	Fax
Apostolic Bible Institute Inc 6944 Hudson Blvd N	Saint Paul	MN	55128	651-739-7686	730-8669*
*Fax: Admissions ■ Web: www.apostolic.org					
Argosy University 1515 Central Pkwy	Eagan	MN	55121	651-846-2882	994-7956*
*Fax: Admissions ■ TF: 888-844-2004 ■ Web: www.argosyu.edu					
Augsburg College 2211 Riverside Ave S CB 143	Minneapolis	MN	55454	612-330-1000	330-1590*
*Fax: Admissions ■ TF: 800-788-5678 ■ Web: www.augsburg.edu					
Bemidji State University 1500 Birchmont Dr NE	Bemidji	MN	56601	218-755-2001	755-4048
TF Admissions: 800-475-2001 ■ Web: www.bemidjistate.edu					
Bethany Lutheran College 700 Luther Dr	Mankato	MN	56001	507-344-7000	344-7376*
*Fax: Admissions ■ TF: 800-944-3066 ■ Web: www.blc.edu					
Bethel University 3900 Bethel Dr	Saint Paul	MN	55112	651-638-6400	635-1490*
*Fax: Admissions ■ TF: 800-255-8706 ■ Web: www.bethel.edu					
Carleton College 100 S College St	Northfield	MN	55057	507-646-4000	646-4526*
*Fax: Admissions ■ TF Admissions: 800-995-2275 ■ Web: www.carleton.edu					
College of Saint Benedict 37 S College Ave	Saint Joseph	MN	56374	320-363-5011	363-3206*
*Fax: Admissions ■ TF: 800-249-9840 ■ Web: www.csbsju.edu					
College of Saint Catherine 2004 Randolph Ave	Saint Paul	MN	55105	651-690-6000	690-6024*
*Fax: Admissions ■ TF: 800-945-4599 ■ Web: www.stkate.edu					
Minneapolis 601 25th Ave S	Minneapolis	MN	55454	651-690-7700	690-7849*
*Fax: Admissions ■ TF: 800-945-4599 ■ Web: www.stkate.edu					
College of Saint Scholastica 1200 Kenwood Ave	Duluth	MN	55811	218-723-6046	723-5991*
*Fax: Admissions ■ TF: 800-447-5444 ■ Web: www.css.edu					
Concordia College 901 S 8th St	Moorhead	MN	56562	218-299-4000	299-4720*
*Fax: Admissions ■ TF Admissions: 800-699-9897 ■ Web: www.cord.edu					
Concordia University Saint Paul 275 Syndicate St N	Saint Paul	MN	55104	651-641-8278	603-6320*
*Fax: Admissions ■ TF: 800-333-4705 ■ Web: www.csp.edu					
Gustavus Adolphus College 800 W College Ave	Saint Peter	MN	56082	507-933-8000	933-7474*
*Fax: Admissions ■ TF: 800-487-8288 ■ Web: www.gustavus.edu					
Hamline University 1536 Hewitt Ave	Saint Paul	MN	55104	651-523-2207	523-2458
TF: 800-753-9753 ■ Web: www.hamline.edu					
Macalester College 1600 Grand Ave	Saint Paul	MN	55105	651-696-6357	696-6724*
*Fax: Admissions ■ TF Admissions: 800-231-7974 ■ Web: www.macalester.edu					
Martin Luther College 1995 Luther Ct	New Ulm	MN	56073	507-354-8221	354-8225*
*Fax: Admissions ■ TF: 877-652-1995 ■ Web: www.mlc-wels.edu					
Metropolitan State University 700 E 7th St	Saint Paul	MN	55106	651-793-1200	793-1310*
*Fax: Admissions ■ Web: www.metrostate.edu					
Minnesota State University					
Mankato 122 Taylor Ctr	Mankato	MN	56001	507-389-1822	389-1511
TF Admissions: 800-722-0544 ■ Web: www.mnsu.edu					
Moorhead 1104 7th Ave S	Moorhead	MN	56563	218-477-2161	477-4374*
*Fax: Admissions ■ TF: 800-593-7246 ■ Web: www.mnstate.edu					
National American University Roseville 1550 W Hwy 36	Roseville	MN	55113	651-644-1265	855-6305*
*Fax: Admissions ■ TF: 800-843-8892 ■ Web: www.national.edu/RosevilleCampus/Index.htm					
North Central University 910 Elliot Ave S	Minneapolis	MN	55404	612-343-4460	343-4146*
*Fax: Admissions ■ TF Admissions: 800-289-6222 ■ Web: www.northcentral.edu					
Northwestern College 3003 Snelling Ave N	Saint Paul	MN	55113	651-631-5100	631-5680
TF Admissions: 800-827-6827 ■ Web: nwc.nwc.edu					
Saint Cloud State University 720 4th Ave S	Saint Cloud	MN	56301	320-308-2244	308-2243*
*Fax: Admissions ■ TF: 877-654-7278 ■ Web: www.stcloudstate.edu					
Saint John's University	Collegeville	MN	56321	320-363-2196	363-3206*
*Fax: Admissions ■ TF Admissions: 800-544-1489 ■ Web: www.csbsju.edu					
Saint Mary's University of Minnesota 700 Terrace Heights	Winona	MN	55987	507-452-4430	457-1722*
*Fax: Admissions ■ TF: 800-635-5987 ■ Web: www.smumn.edu					
Saint Olaf College 1520 St Olaf Ave	Northfield	MN	55057	507-646-3025	646-3832*
*Fax: Admissions ■ TF Admissions: 800-800-3025 ■ Web: www.stolaf.edu					
Southwest Minnesota State University 1501 State St	Marshall	MN	56258	507-537-6286	537-7145*
*Fax: Admissions ■ TF: 800-642-0684 ■ Web: www.southwest.msus.edu					
University of Minnesota					
Crookston 2900 University Ave 170 Owen Hall	Crookston	MN	56716	218-281-8569	281-8575*
*Fax: Admissions ■ TF: 800-862-6466 ■ Web: www.crk.umn.edu					
Duluth 1049 University Dr	Duluth	MN	55812	218-726-8000	726-6394*
*Fax: Admissions ■ TF: 800-232-1339 ■ Web: www.d.umn.edu					
Morris 600 E 4th St	Morris	MN	56267	320-589-6035	589-1673*
*Fax: Admissions ■ TF: 800-992-8863 ■ Web: www.morris.umn.edu					
Rochester 111 S Broadway	Rochester	MN	55904	507-280-2838	280-2820
TF: 800-947-0117 ■ Web: www.r.umn.edu					
Twin Cities 231 Pillsbury Dr SE Williamson Hall	Minneapolis	MN	55455	612-625-5000	626-1692*
*Fax: Hum Res ■ TF: 800-752-1000 ■ Web: www1.umn.edu/twincities					
University of Saint Thomas 2115 Summit Ave	Saint Paul	MN	55105	651-962-5000	962-6160*
*Fax: Admissions ■ TF: 800-328-6819 ■ Web: www.stthomas.edu					
Winona State University 175 W Mark St	Winona	MN	55987	507-457-5000	457-5620*
*Fax: Admissions ■ TF: 800-342-5978 ■ Web: www.winona.edu					

Mississippi

Institution	City	State	ZIP	Phone	Fax
Alcorn State University 1000 ASU Dr	Alcorn State	MS	39096	601-877-6100	877-6347*
*Fax: Admissions ■ TF Admissions: 800-222-6790 ■ Web: www.alcorn.edu					
Belhaven College 1500 Peachtree St Box 153	Jackson	MS	39202	601-968-5940	968-8946*
*Fax: Admissions ■ TF: 800-960-5940 ■ Web: www.belhaven.edu					
Blue Mountain College PO Box 160	Blue Mountain	MS	38610	662-685-4161	685-4776*
*Fax: Admissions ■ TF: 800-235-0136 ■ Web: www.bmc.edu					
Delta State University 1003 W Sunflower Rd	Cleveland	MS	38733	662-846-4020	846-4684*
*Fax: Admissions ■ TF: 800-468-6378 ■ Web: www.deltastate.edu					

Phone Fax

Jackson State University 1400 John R Lynch St.......Jackson MS 39217 601-979-2121 979-3445*
*Fax: Admissions ■ TF: 800-848-6817 ■ Web: www.jsums.edu
Magnolia Bible College 822 S Huntington St.......Kosciusko MS 39090 662-289-2896 289-1850*
*Fax: Admissions ■ TF: 800-748-8655 ■ Web: www.magnolia.edu
Millsaps College 1701 N State St.......Jackson MS 39210 601-974-1000 974-1335*
*Fax: Admissions ■ TF Admissions: 800-352-1050 ■ Web: www.millsaps.edu
Mississippi College 200 S Capitol St PO Box 4026.......Clinton MS 39058 601-925-3000 925-3950*
*Fax: Admissions ■ TF: 800-738-1236 ■ Web: www.mc.edu
Mississippi State University PO Box 6305.......Mississippi State MS 39762 662-325-2224 325-7360*
*Fax: Admissions ■ Web: www.msstate.edu
Mississippi University for Women
1100 College St MUW-1613.......Columbus MS 39701 662-329-4750 241-7481*
*Fax: Admissions ■ TF: 877-462-8439 ■ Web: www.muw.edu
Mississippi Valley State University
14000 Hwy 82 W Box 7222.......Itta Bena MS 38941 662-254-9041 254-3759*
*Fax: Admissions ■ TF Admissions: 800-844-6885 ■ Web: www.mvsu.edu
Rust College 150 Rust Ave.......Holly Springs MS 38635 662-252-8000 252-2258*
*Fax: Admissions ■ TF: 888-806-8492 ■ Web: www.rustcollege.edu
Tougaloo College 500 W County Line Rd.......Tougaloo MS 39174 601-977-7700 977-4501*
*Fax: Admissions ■ TF Admissions: 888-424-2566 ■ Web: www.tougaloo.edu
University of Mississippi PO Box 1848.......University MS 38677 662-915-7211 915-5869*
*Fax: Admissions ■ Web: www.olemiss.edu
Tupelo 1918 Briar Ridge Rd.......Tupelo MS 38804 662-844-5622 844-5625*
*Fax: Admissions ■ Web: www.outreach.olemiss.edu/tupelo
University of Southern Mississippi 118 College Dr.......Hattiesburg MS 39406 601-266-1000 266-5148*
*Fax: Admissions ■ Web: www.usm.edu
Gulf Park 730 E Beach Blvd.......Long Beach MS 39560 228-865-4500 865-4587*
*Fax: Admissions ■ Web: www.usm.edu/gulfcoast/
Wesley College PO Box 1070.......Florence MS 39073 601-845-5746 845-2266*
*Fax: Admissions ■ TF: 800-748-9972 ■ Web: www.wesleycollege.edu
William Carey University 498 Tuscan Ave.......Hattiesburg MS 39401 601-318-6051 318-6454*
*Fax: Admissions ■ TF: 800-962-5991 ■ Web: www.wmcarey.edu

Missouri

Phone Fax

Avila University 11901 Wornall Rd.......Kansas City MO 64145 816-501-2400 501-2453
TF: 800-462-8452 ■ Web: www.avila.edu
Central Methodist University 411 Central Methodist Sq.......Fayette MO 65248 660-248-3391 248-1872*
*Fax: Admissions ■ TF: 877-268-1854 ■ Web: www.centralmethodist.edu
Chamberlain College of Nursing 6150 Oakland Ave.......Saint Louis MO 63139 314-768-7501 768-5673*
*Fax: Admissions ■ TF: 800-942-4310 ■ Web: www.chamberlain.edu
College of the Ozarks 1 Industrial Dr PO Box 17.......Point Lookout MO 65726 417-334-6411 335-2618*
*Fax: Admissions ■ TF Admissions: 800-222-0525 ■ Web: www.cofo.edu
Columbia College 1001 Rogers St.......Columbia MO 65216 573-875-8700 875-7506*
*Fax: Admissions ■ TF: 800-231-2391 ■ Web: www.ccis.edu
Jefferson City 3314 Emerald Ln.......Jefferson City MO 65109 573-634-3250 634-8507*
*Fax: Admissions ■ Web: ccis.edu/jeffcity
Lake of the Ozarks 900 College Blvd.......Osage Beach MO 65065 573-348-6463 348-1791
Web: www.ccis.edu
Culver-Stockton College 1 College Hill.......Canton MO 63435 573-288-6000 288-6618*
*Fax: Admissions ■ TF Admissions: 800-537-1883 ■ Web: www.culver.edu
Drury University 900 N Benton Ave.......Springfield MO 65802 417-873-7879 866-3873
TF: 800-922-2274 ■ Web: www.drury.edu
Evangel University 1111 N Glenstone Ave.......Springfield MO 65802 417-865-2815 865-9599
TF: 800-382-6435 ■ Web: www.evangel.edu
Fontbonne University 6800 Wydown Blvd.......Saint Louis MO 63105 314-862-3456 889-1451*
*Fax: Admissions ■ TF: 800-205-5862 ■ Web: www.fontbonne.edu
Graceland University Independence 1401 W Truman Rd.......Independence MO 64050 816-833-0524 833-2990*
*Fax: Admissions ■ TF: 800-833-0524 ■ Web: www.graceland.edu
Hannibal-LaGrange College 2800 Palmyra Rd.......Hannibal MO 63401 573-221-3675 221-6594
TF Admissions: 800-454-1119 ■ Web: www.hlg.edu
Harris-Stowe State University 3026 Laclede Ave.......Saint Louis MO 63103 314-340-3366 340-3555
Web: www.hssu.edu
Lincoln University 820 Chestnut St B-7 Young Hall.......Jefferson City MO 65102 573-681-5599 681-5889*
*Fax: Admissions ■ TF Admissions: 800-521-5052 ■ Web: www.lincolnu.edu
Lindenwood University 209 S Kingshighway.......Saint Charles MO 63301 636-949-2000 949-4989*
*Fax: Admissions ■ Web: www.lindenwood.edu
Maryville University 650 Maryville University Dr.......Saint Louis MO 63141 314-529-9300 529-9927*
*Fax: Admissions ■ TF: 800-627-9855 ■ Web: www.maryville.edu
Missouri Baptist University 1 College Park Dr.......Saint Louis MO 63141 314-434-1115 434-7596
TF: 877-434-1115 ■ Web: www.mobap.edu
Troy/Wentzville Extension 75 College Campus Dr.......Moscow Mills MO 63362 636-366-4363 356-4119*
*Fax: Admissions ■ Web: www.mobap.edu/info/campus/troywentz
Missouri Southern State University 3950 E Newman Rd.......Joplin MO 64801 417-625-9300 659-4429*
*Fax: Admissions ■ TF: 866-818-6778 ■ Web: www.mssu.edu
Missouri State University 901 S National Ave.......Springfield MO 65897 417-836-5000 836-6334
TF: 800-492-7900 ■ Web: www.missouristate.edu
Missouri University of Science & Technology Rolla
1870 Miner Cir G2 Parker Hall.......Rolla MO 65409 573-341-4111 341-4082*
*Fax: Admissions ■ TF: 800-522-0938 ■ Web: www.mst.edu
Missouri Valley College 500 E College St.......Marshall MO 65340 660-831-4000 831-4233*
*Fax: Admissions ■ Web: www.moval.edu
Missouri Western State University 4525 Downs Dr.......Saint Joseph MO 64507 816-271-4266 271-5833
TF: 800-662-7041 ■ Web: www.missouriwestern.edu
National American University Independence
3620 Arrowhead Ave.......Independence MO 64057 816-412-7700 412-7705
TF: 866-628-1288 ■ Web: www.national.edu/IndependenceCampus/Index.htm
Northwest Missouri State University 800 University Dr.......Maryville MO 64468 660-562-1148 562-1821*
*Fax: Admissions ■ TF: 800-633-1175 ■ Web: www.nwmissouri.edu
Ozark Bible Institute & College 906 Summit St PO Box 398.......Neosho MO 64850 417-451-2057 451-2059*
*Fax: Admissions ■ Web: www.obiweb.org
Park University 8700 NW River Park Dr.......Parkville MO 64152 816-741-2000 741-9668
TF: 800-745-7275 ■ Web: www.park.edu
Parks College of Engineering, Aviation & Technology
3450 Lindell Blvd.......Saint Louis MO 63103 314-977-8283 977-8403
Web: parks.slu.edu
Rockhurst University 1100 Rockhurst Rd.......Kansas City MO 64110 816-501-4000 501-4241*
*Fax: Admissions ■ TF: 800-842-6776 ■ Web: www.rockhurst.edu
Saint Louis College of Pharmacy 4588 Parkview Pl.......Saint Louis MO 63110 314-367-8700 446-8304*
*Fax: Admissions ■ TF: 800-278-5267 ■ Web: www.stlcop.edu
Saint Louis University 221 N Grand Blvd.......Saint Louis MO 63103 314-977-2100 977-7136*
*Fax: Admissions ■ TF: 800-758-3678 ■ Web: www.slu.edu
Parks College of Engineering, Aviation & Technology
3450 Lindell Blvd.......Saint Louis MO 63103 314-977-8283 977-8403
Web: parks.slu.edu
Southeast Missouri State University
1 University Plaza MS 3550.......Cape Girardeau MO 63701 573-651-2000 651-5936*
*Fax: Admissions ■ Web: www.semo.edu
Southwest Baptist University 1600 University Ave.......Bolivar MO 65613 417-326-5281 328-1808*
*Fax: Admissions ■ TF: 800-526-5859 ■ Web: www.sbuniv.edu
Stephens College 1200 E Broadway Box 2121.......Columbia MO 65215 573-876-7207 876-7237*
*Fax: Admissions ■ TF Admissions: 800-876-7207 ■ Web: www.stephens.edu
Truman State University 100 E Normal St.......Kirksville MO 63501 660-785-4000 785-7456*
*Fax: Admissions ■ TF: 800-892-7792 ■ Web: www.truman.edu

Phone Fax

University of Central Missouri PO Box 800.......Warrensburg MO 64093 660-543-4111 543-8517*
*Fax: Admissions ■ TF: 877-729-8266 ■ Web: www.ucmo.edu
University of Missouri
Columbia 230 Jesse Hall.......Columbia MO 65211 573-882-7786 882-7887*
*Fax: Admissions ■ Web: www.missouri.edu
Kansas City 5100 Rockhill Rd.......Kansas City MO 64110 816-235-1000 235-5544
TF: 800-775-8652 ■ Web: www.umkc.edu
Saint Louis 1 University Blvd.......Saint Louis MO 63121 314-516-5000 516-5310*
*Fax: Admissions ■ TF Admissions: 888-462-8675 ■ Web: www.umsl.edu
Washington University in Saint Louis 1 Brookings Dr.......Saint Louis MO 63130 314-935-6000 935-4290
TF: 800-638-0700 ■ Web: www.wustl.edu
Webster University 470 E Lockwood Ave.......Saint Louis MO 63119 314-968-6900 968-7115*
*Fax: Admissions ■ TF Admissions: 800-753-6765 ■ Web: www.webster.edu
Westminster College 501 Westminster Ave.......Fulton MO 65251 573-592-5251 592-5255
TF Admissions: 800-475-3361 ■ Web: www.wcmo.edu
William Jewell College 500 College Hill WJC Box 1002.......Liberty MO 64068 816-781-7700 415-5040
TF: 888-253-9355 ■ Web: www.jewell.edu
William Woods University 1 University Ave.......Fulton MO 65251 573-592-2251 592-1146*
*Fax: Admissions ■ TF Admissions: 800-995-3159 ■ Web: www.williamwoods.edu

Montana

Phone Fax

Carroll College 1601 N Benton Ave.......Helena MT 59625 406-447-4300 447-4533
TF: 800-992-3648 ■ Web: www.carroll.edu
Montana State University
Billings 1500 University Dr.......Billings MT 59101 406-657-2011 657-2302*
*Fax: Admissions ■ Web: www.msubillings.edu
Bozeman PO Box 172190.......Bozeman MT 59717 406-994-2452 994-7360*
*Fax: Admissions ■ TF Admissions: 888-678-2287 ■ Web: www.montana.edu
Northern PO Box 7751.......Havre MT 59501 406-265-3700 265-3792*
*Fax: Admissions ■ TF: 800-662-6132 ■ Web: www.montana.edu
Montana Tech of the University of Montana 1300 W Park St.......Butte MT 59701 406-496-4718 496-4710*
*Fax: Admissions ■ TF Admissions: 800-445-8324 ■ Web: www.mtech.edu
Rocky Mountain College 1511 Poly Dr.......Billings MT 59102 406-657-1000 657-1189*
*Fax: Admissions ■ TF: 800-877-6259 ■ Web: www.rocky.edu
University of Great Falls 1301 20th St S.......Great Falls MT 59405 406-761-8210 791-5209*
*Fax: Admissions ■ TF Admissions: 800-856-9544 ■ Web: www.ugf.edu
University of Montana 32 Campus Dr.......Missoula MT 59812 406-243-6266 243-5711*
*Fax: Admissions ■ TF Admissions: 800-462-8636 ■ Web: www.umt.edu
Western 710 S Atlantic St.......Dillon MT 59725 406-683-7011 683-7493*
*Fax: Admissions ■ TF Admissions: 877-683-7331 ■ Web: www.umwestern.edu
Yellowstone Baptist College 1515 S Shiloh Rd.......Billings MT 59106 406-656-9950 656-3737*
*Fax: Admissions ■ TF: 800-487-9950 ■ Web: www.yellowstonebaptist.edu/

Nebraska

Phone Fax

Bellevue University 1000 Galvin Rd S.......Bellevue NE 68005 402-291-8100 293-2020*
*Fax: Admissions ■ TF: 800-756-7920 ■ Web: www.bellevue.edu
Chadron State College 1000 Main St.......Chadron NE 69337 308-432-6263 432-6229
TF: 800-242-3766 ■ Web: www.csc.edu
Clarkson College 101 S 42nd St.......Omaha NE 68131 402-552-3100 552-6057*
*Fax: Admissions ■ TF: 800-647-5500 ■ Web: www.clarksoncollege.edu
College of Saint Mary 7000 Mercy Rd.......Omaha NE 68106 402-399-2400 399-2412*
*Fax: Admissions ■ TF: 800-926-5534 ■ Web: www.csm.edu
Lincoln 4600 Valley Rd Suite 403.......Lincoln NE 68510 402-489-2900 489-4306*
*Fax: Admissions ■ TF: 800-727-6546 ■ Web: www.csm.edu/lincoln_campus
Concordia University Nebraska 800 N Columbia Ave.......Seward NE 68434 402-643-3651 643-4073*
*Fax: Admissions ■ TF: 800-535-5494 ■ Web: www.cune.edu
Creighton University 2500 California Plaza.......Omaha NE 68178 402-280-2700 280-2685*
*Fax: Admissions ■ TF: 800-282-5835 ■ Web: www2.creighton.edu
Dana College 2848 College Dr.......Blair NE 68008 402-426-9000 426-7225*
*Fax: Admissions ■ TF Admissions: 800-444-3262 ■ Web: www.dana.edu
Doane College 1014 Boswell Ave.......Crete NE 68333 402-826-2161 826-8600
TF: 800-333-6263 ■ Web: www.doane.edu
Grand Island 3180 W US Hwy 34.......Grand Island NE 68801 308-398-0800 398-7279
Web: www.doane.edu/GI
Lincoln 303 N 52nd St.......Lincoln NE 68504 402-466-4774 466-4228
TF: 888-803-6263 ■ Web: www.doane.edu/lincoln
Hastings College 710 N Turner Ave.......Hastings NE 68901 402-463-2402 461-7490*
*Fax: Admissions ■ TF: 800-532-7642 ■ Web: www.hastings.edu
Midland Lutheran College 900 N Clarkson St.......Fremont NE 68025 402-721-5480 941-6513*
*Fax: Admissions ■ TF: 800-642-8382 ■ Web: www.mlc.edu
Nebraska Wesleyan University 5000 St Paul Ave.......Lincoln NE 68504 402-466-2371 465-2177*
*Fax: Admissions ■ TF: 800-541-3818 ■ Web: www.nebrwesleyan.edu
Peru State College 600 Hoyt St Box 10.......Peru NE 68421 402-872-3815 872-2296*
*Fax: Admissions ■ TF: 800-742-4412 ■ Web: www.peru.edu
Summit Christian College 2025 21st St.......Gering NE 69341 308-632-6933 632-8599
TF: 888-305-8083 ■ Web: www.summitcc.net
Union College 3800 S 48th St.......Lincoln NE 68506 402-486-2504 486-2566*
*Fax: Admissions ■ TF Admissions: 800-228-4600 ■ Web: www.ucollege.edu
University of Nebraska
Kearney 905 W 25th St.......Kearney NE 68849 308-865-8441 865-8987*
*Fax: Admissions ■ TF: 800-532-7639 ■ Web: www.unk.edu
Lincoln 1410 Q St.......Lincoln NE 68588 402-472-2023 472-0607*
*Fax: Admissions ■ TF: 800-742-8800 ■ Web: www.unl.edu
Omaha 6001 Dodge St.......Omaha NE 68182 402-554-2200 554-3472*
*Fax: Admissions ■ TF: 800-858-8648 ■ Web: www.unomaha.edu
Wayne State College 1111 Main St.......Wayne NE 68787 402-375-7000 375-7180*
*Fax: Admissions ■ TF: 800-228-9972 ■ Web: www.wsc.edu
York College 1125 E 8th St.......York NE 68467 402-362-4441 363-5623*
*Fax: Admissions ■ TF: 800-950-9675 ■ Web: www.york.edu

Nevada

Phone Fax

Great Basin College 1500 College Pkwy.......Elko NV 89801 775-738-8493 753-2311*
*Fax: Admissions ■ Web: www.gbcnv.edu
Morrison University 10315 Professional Cir Suite 201.......Reno NV 89521 775-850-0700 850-0711
Web: www.morrison.neumont.edu
Sierra Nevada College 999 Tahoe Blvd.......Incline Village NV 89451 775-831-1314 831-1347*
*Fax: Admissions ■ TF: 866-412-4636 ■ Web: www.sierranevada.edu
University of Nevada
Las Vegas 4505 S Maryland Pkwy.......Las Vegas NV 89154 702-895-3011 895-1118*
*Fax: Admissions ■ Web: www.unlv.edu
Reno 1664 N Virginia St.......Reno NV 89557 775-784-1110 784-4283*
*Fax: Admissions ■ Web: www.unr.edu

New Hampshire

Phone Fax

Chester College of New England 40 Chester St.......Chester NH 03036 603-887-4401 887-1777*
*Fax: Admissions ■ TF: 800-974-6372 ■ Web: www.chestercollege.edu

New Hampshire (Cont'd)

	City	State	Zip	Phone	Fax
Colby-Sawyer College 541 Main St.	New London	NH	03257	603-526-3700	526-3452*
*Fax: Admissions ■ *TF Admissions:* 800-272-1015 ■ *Web:* www.colby-sawyer.edu					
Daniel Webster College 20 University Dr.	Nashua	NH	03063	603-577-6000	577-6001
TF: 800-325-6876 ■ *Web:* www.dwc.edu					
Dartmouth College 6016 McNutt Hall	Hanover	NH	03755	603-646-1110	646-1216
Web: www.dartmouth.edu					
Franklin Pierce College					
Concord 5 Chenell Dr.	Concord	NH	03301	603-228-1155	899-1067*
*Fax: Admissions ■ *TF:* 800-437-0048 ■ *Web:* www.fpc.edu					
Keene 17 Bradco St	Keene	NH	03431	603-357-0079	899-1062*
*Fax: Admissions ■ *TF:* 800-325-1090 ■ *Web:* www.fpc.edu					
Lebanon 24 Airport Rd Suite 19	West Lebanon	NH	03784	603-298-5549	899-1065*
*Fax: Admissions ■ *TF:* 800-325-1090 ■ *Web:* www.fpc.edu					
Manchester 670 N Commercial St.	Manchester	NH	03101	603-626-4972	626-4815
TF Admissions: 800-437-0048 ■ *Web:* www.fpc.edu					
Portsmouth 73 Corporate Dr	Portsmouth	NH	03801	603-433-2000	899-1067*
*Fax: Admissions ■ *TF:* 800-325-1090					
Rindge 20 College Rd Box 60	Rindge	NH	03461	603-899-4000	899-4394*
*Fax: Admissions ■ *TF Admissions:* 800-437-0048 ■ *Web:* www.fpc.edu					
Granite State College 8 Old Suncook Rd.	Concord	NH	03301	603-228-3000	513-1389
TF: 888-228-3000 ■ *Web:* www.granite.edu					
Berlin 2020 Riverside Dr Rm 144	Berlin	NH	03570	603-752-2479	752-6335
Web: www.granite.edu/locations/berlin.htm					
Portsmouth 51 International Dr.	Portsmouth	NH	03801	603-334-6060	334-6313
Web: www.granite.edu/locations/portsmouth.htm					
Hesser College 3 Sundial Ave	Manchester	NH	03103	603-668-6660	621-8994*
*Fax: Admissions ■ *TF:* 800-526-9231 ■ *Web:* www.hesser.edu					
Keene State College 229 Main St	Keene	NH	03435	603-352-1909	358-2767*
*Fax: Admissions ■ *TF:* 800-572-1909 ■ *Web:* www.keene.edu					
Magdalen College 511 Kearsarge Mountain Rd	Warner	NH	03278	603-456-2656	456-2660
TF: 877-498-1723 ■ *Web:* www.magdalen.edu					
New England College 26 Bridge St.	Henniker	NH	03242	603-428-2223	428-3155*
*Fax: Admissions ■ *TF Admissions:* 800-521-7642 ■ *Web:* www.nec.edu					
Plymouth State University 17 High St	Plymouth	NH	03264	603-535-2237	535-2714*
*Fax: Admissions ■ *TF:* 800-842-6900 ■ *Web:* www.plymouth.edu					
Rivier College 420 S Main St	Nashua	NH	03060	603-888-1311	891-1799*
*Fax: Admissions ■ *TF:* 800-447-4843 ■ *Web:* www.rivier.edu					
Saint Anselm College 100 St Anselm Dr	Manchester	NH	03102	603-641-7500	641-7550
TF: 888-426-7356 ■ *Web:* www.anselm.edu					
Southern New Hampshire University 2500 N River Rd	Manchester	NH	03106	603-668-2211	645-9693
TF: 800-642-4968 ■ *Web:* www.snhu.edu					
University of New Hampshire 4 Garrison Ave Grant House	Durham	NH	03824	603-862-1234	862-0077*
*Fax: Admissions ■ *Web:* www.unh.edu					
Manchester 400 Commercial St.	Manchester	NH	03101	603-641-4321	641-4125
Web: www.unhm.unh.edu					

New Jersey

	City	State	Zip	Phone	Fax
Beth Medrash Govoha 601 Private Way	Lakewood	NJ	08701	732-367-1060	367-7487
Bloomfield College 467 Franklin St	Bloomfield	NJ	07003	973-748-9000	748-0916
TF: 800-848-4555 ■ *Web:* www.bloomfield.edu					
Caldwell College 9 Ryerson Ave.	Caldwell	NJ	07006	973-618-3500	618-3600*
*Fax: Admissions ■ *TF Admissions:* 888-864-9516 ■ *Web:* www.caldwell.edu					
Centenary College 400 Jefferson St.	Hackettstown	NJ	07840	908-852-1400	852-3454*
*Fax: Admissions ■ *TF Admissions:* 800-236-8679 ■ *Web:* www.centenarycollege.edu					
College of New Jersey 2000 Pennington Rd PO Box 7718	Ewing	NJ	08628	609-771-1855	637-5174*
*Fax: Admissions ■ *Web:* www.tcnj.edu					
College of Saint Elizabeth 2 Convent Rd.	Morristown	NJ	07960	973-290-4700	290-4710*
*Fax: Admissions ■ *TF Admissions:* 800-210-7900 ■ *Web:* www.cse.edu					
Douglass College 125 George St	New Brunswick	NJ	08901	732-932-9500	932-8877
Web: www.douglass.rutgers.edu					
Drew University 36 Madison Ave	Madison	NJ	07940	973-408-3000	408-3068*
*Fax: Admissions ■ *Web:* www.drew.edu					
Fairleigh Dickinson University 285 Madison Ave	Madison	NJ	07940	973-593-8500	443-8088*
*Fax: Admissions ■ *TF:* 800-338-8803 ■ *Web:* www.fdu.edu					
Metropolitan 1000 River Rd.	Teaneck	NJ	07666	201-692-2000	692-2560
TF: 800-338-8803 ■ *Web:* www.fdu.edu					
Felician College 262 S Main St	Lodi	NJ	07644	201-559-6000	559-6138*
*Fax: Admissions ■ *Web:* www.felician.edu					
Rutherford 223 Montross Ave	Rutherford	NJ	07070	201-559-6000	559-3578
Web: www.felician.edu					
Georgian Court University 900 Lakewood Ave	Lakewood	NJ	08701	732-987-2760	987-2000*
*Fax: Admissions ■ *TF:* 800-458-8422 ■ *Web:* www.georgian.edu					
Kean University 1000 Morris Ave Kean Hall	Union	NJ	07083	908-737-7100	737-7105*
*Fax: Admissions ■ *Web:* www.kean.edu					
Monmouth University 400 Cedar Ave	West Long Branch	NJ	07764	732-571-3456	263-5166*
*Fax: Admissions ■ *TF:* 800-543-9671 ■ *Web:* www.monmouth.edu					
Montclair State University 1 Normal Ave.	Upper Montclair	NJ	07043	973-655-4000	655-7700*
*Fax: Admissions ■ *TF Admissions:* 800-331-9205 ■ *Web:* www.montclair.edu					
New Jersey City University 2039 JFK Blvd.	Jersey City	NJ	07305	201-200-2000	200-2044
TF: 888-441-6528 ■ *Web:* www.njcu.edu					
New Jersey Institute of Technology University Heights	Newark	NJ	07102	973-596-3000	596-3461
TF: 800-926-6548 ■ *Web:* www.njit.edu					
Princeton University	Princeton	NJ	08544	609-258-3000	258-6743*
*Fax: Admissions ■ *Web:* www.princeton.edu					
Rabbinical College of America					
226 Sussex Ave PO Box 1996	Morristown	NJ	07962	973-267-9404	267-5208
Web: www.rca.edu					
Ramapo College of New Jersey 505 Ramapo Valley Rd	Mahwah	NJ	07430	201-684-7500	684-7964*
*Fax: Admissions ■ *Web:* www.ramapo.edu					
Richard Stockton College of New Jersey PO Box 195	Pomona	NJ	08240	609-652-1776	748-5541*
*Fax: Admissions ■ *Web:* www.stockton.edu					
Rider University 2083 Lawrenceville Rd	Lawrenceville	NJ	08648	609-896-5000	895-6645*
*Fax: Admissions ■ *TF:* 800-257-9026 ■ *Web:* www.rider.edu					
Westminster Choir College 101 Walnut Ln	Princeton	NJ	08540	609-921-7100	921-2538*
*Fax: Admissions ■ *TF:* 800-962-4647 ■ *Web:* westminster.rider.edu					
Rowan University 201 Mullica Hill Rd.	Glassboro	NJ	08028	856-256-4200	256-4430*
*Fax: Admissions ■ *TF Admissions:* 877-787-6926 ■ *Web:* www.rowan.edu					
Rutgers The State University of New Jersey					
Camden 406 Penn St.	Camden	NJ	08102	856-225-6104	225-6498*
*Fax: Admissions ■ *Web:* www.camden.rutgers.edu					
New Brunswick/Piscataway 65 Davison Rd Rm 202	Piscataway	NJ	08854	732-932-1766	445-0237
Web: nbp.rutgers.edu					
Newark 249 University Ave	Newark	NJ	07102	973-353-5205	353-1440*
*Fax: Admissions ■ *Web:* www.newark.rutgers.edu					
Saint Peter's College 2641 JFK Blvd	Jersey City	NJ	07306	201-915-9000	761-7105*
*Fax: Admissions ■ *TF:* 888-772-9933 ■ *Web:* www.spc.edu					
Seton Hall University 400 S Orange Ave	South Orange	NJ	07079	973-761-9332	275-2321*
*Fax: Admissions ■ *TF:* 800-738-6648 ■ *Web:* www.shu.edu					
Stevens Institute of Technology Castle Point on the Hudson	Hoboken	NJ	07030	201-216-5194	216-8348*
*Fax: Admissions ■ *TF:* 800-458-5323 ■ *Web:* www.stevens.edu					
Thomas Edison State College 101 W State St.	Trenton	NJ	08608	609-984-1102	984-8447*
*Fax: Admissions ■ *TF:* 888-442-8372 ■ *Web:* www.tesc.edu					
Westminster Choir College of Rider University					
101 Walnut Ln	Princeton	NJ	08540	609-921-7100	921-2538*
*Fax: Admissions ■ *TF:* 800-962-4647 ■ *Web:* westminster.rider.edu					
William Paterson University 300 Pompton Rd.	Wayne	NJ	07470	973-720-2000	720-2910*
*Fax: Admissions ■ *TF:* 877-978-3923 ■ *Web:* ww2.wpunj.edu					

New Mexico

	City	State	Zip	Phone	Fax
College of Santa Fe 1600 St Michaels Dr	Santa Fe	NM	87505	505-473-6011	473-6129*
*Fax: Admissions ■ *TF:* 800-456-2673 ■ *Web:* www.csf.edu					
Albuquerque 4501 Indian School Rd NE Suite 100	Albuquerque	NM	87110	505-855-7260	262-5595*
*Fax: Admissions ■ *Web:* www.csf.edu/abq					
College of the Southwest 6610 N Lovington Hwy	Hobbs	NM	88240	505-392-6561	392-6006*
*Fax: Admissions ■ *TF:* 800-530-4400 ■ *Web:* www.csw.edu					
Eastern New Mexico University 1500 S Ave K Station 7	Portales	NM	88130	505-562-2178	562-2118*
*Fax: Admissions ■ *TF:* 800-367-3668 ■ *Web:* www.enmu.edu					
National American University Albuquerque					
4775 Indian School Rd NE Suite 200	Albuquerque	NM	87110	505-265-7517	348-3705
Web: www.national.edu/AlbuquerqueCampus/Index.htm					
New Mexico Highlands University 1005 Diamond Ave	Las Vegas	NM	87701	505-425-7511	454-3552*
*Fax: Admissions ■ *TF:* 877-850-9064 ■ *Web:* www.nmhu.edu					
New Mexico Institute of Mining & Technology 801 Leroy Pl.	Socorro	NM	87801	505-835-5424	835-5989*
*Fax: Admissions ■ *TF Admissions:* 800-428-8324 ■ *Web:* www.nmt.edu					
New Mexico State University PO Box 30001 MSC-3A	Las Cruces	NM	88003	505-646-3121	646-6330*
*Fax: Admissions ■ *TF Admissions:* 800-662-6678 ■ *Web:* www.nmsu.edu					
Saint John's College Santa Fe 1160 Camino Cruz Blanca	Santa Fe	NM	87505	505-984-6060	984-6162*
*Fax: Admissions ■ *TF Admissions:* 800-331-5232 ■ *Web:* www.sjcsf.edu					
University of New Mexico 1 University of New Mexico	Albuquerque	NM	87131	505-277-0111	277-6686
TF: 800-225-5866 ■ *Web:* www.unm.edu					
Gallup 200 College Rd	Gallup	NM	87301	505-863-7500	863-7610
TF: 800-225-5866 ■ *Web:* www.gallup.unm.edu					
Western New Mexico University 1000 W College Ave.	Silver City	NM	88061	505-538-6011	538-6155
TF: 800-872-9668 ■ *Web:* www.wnmu.edu					

New York

	City	State	Zip	Phone	Fax
Adelphi University PO Box 701	Garden City	NY	11530	516-877-3050	877-3039*
*Fax: Admissions ■ *TF:* 800-233-5744 ■ *Web:* www.adelphi.edu					
Manhattan Center 75 Varick St 2nd Fl.	New York	NY	10013	212-965-8340	431-5161
TF: 800-233-5744 ■ *Web:* www.adelphi.edu/manhattan					
Albany College of Pharmacy 106 New Scotland Ave.	Albany	NY	12208	518-694-7221	694-7322*
*Fax: Admissions ■ *TF:* 888-203-8010 ■ *Web:* www.acp.edu					
Albert A List College of Jewish Studies 3080 Broadway	New York	NY	10027	212-678-8832	280-6022*
*Fax: Admissions ■ *Web:* www.jtsa.edu/list					
Alfred University 1 Saxon Dr	Alfred	NY	14802	607-871-2111	871-2198*
*Fax: Admissions ■ *TF Admissions:* 800-541-9229 ■ *Web:* www.alfred.edu					
Bard College PO Box 5000	Annandale-on-Hudson	NY	12504	845-758-7472	758-5208
Web: www.bard.edu					
Barnard College Columbia University 3009 Broadway.	New York	NY	10027	212-854-2014	854-6220*
*Fax: Admissions ■ *Web:* www.barnard.edu					
Baruch College 1 Bernard Baruch Way Box H 720	New York	NY	10010	646-312-1000	312-1362*
*Fax: Admissions ■ *Web:* www.baruch.cuny.edu					
Binghamton University PO Box 6000	Binghamton	NY	13902	607-777-2000	777-4445*
*Fax: Admissions ■ *Web:* www.binghamton.edu					
Boricua College 3755 Broadway	New York	NY	10032	212-694-1000	694-1015*
*Fax: Admissions ■ *Web:* www.boricuacollege.edu					
Brooklyn College 2900 Bedford Ave	Brooklyn	NY	11210	718-951-5000	951-4506*
*Fax: Admissions ■ *Web:* www.brooklyn.cuny.edu					
Buffalo State College 1300 Elmwood Ave	Buffalo	NY	14222	716-878-4000	878-6100*
*Fax: Admissions ■ *Web:* www.buffalostate.edu					
Canisius College 2001 Main St.	Buffalo	NY	14208	716-888-2200	888-3230*
*Fax: Admissions ■ *TF:* 800-843-1517 ■ *Web:* www.canisius.edu					
Cazenovia College 22 Sullivan St	Cazenovia	NY	13035	315-655-7208	655-4860*
*Fax: Admissions ■ *TF:* 800-654-3210 ■ *Web:* www.cazenovia.edu					
City College of New York 138th St & Convent Ave	New York	NY	10031	212-650-6448	650-6417*
*Fax: Admissions ■ *TF Admissions:* 800-286-9937 ■ *Web:* www.ccny.cuny.edu					
Clarkson University 10 Clarkson Ave	Potsdam	NY	13699	315-268-6480	268-7647*
*Fax: Admissions ■ *TF Admissions:* 800-527-6577 ■ *Web:* www.clarkson.edu					
Colgate University 13 Oak Dr	Hamilton	NY	13346	315-228-1000	228-7544*
*Fax: Admissions ■ *Web:* www.colgate.edu					
College of Mount Saint Vincent 6301 Riverdale Ave.	Riverdale	NY	10471	718-405-3304	549-7945*
*Fax: Admissions ■ *TF:* 800-665-2678 ■ *Web:* www.mountsaintvincent.edu					
College of New Rochelle 29 Castle Pl	New Rochelle	NY	10805	914-654-5452	654-5464
TF: 800-933-5923 ■ *Web:* www.cnr.edu					
College of Saint Rose 432 Western Ave.	Albany	NY	12203	518-454-5150	454-2013*
*Fax: Admissions ■ *TF:* 800-637-8556 ■ *Web:* www.strose.edu					
College of Staten Island 2800 Victory Blvd	Staten Island	NY	10314	718-982-2000	982-2500
Web: www.csi.cuny.edu					
Columbia University 2960 Broadway	New York	NY	10027	212-854-1754	
Web: www.columbia.edu					
Concordia College New York 171 White Plains Rd	Bronxville	NY	10708	914-337-9300	395-4636*
*Fax: Admissions ■ *TF Admissions:* 800-937-2655 ■ *Web:* www.concordia-ny.edu					
Cooper Union for the Advancement of Science & Art					
30 Cooper Sq	New York	NY	10003	212-353-4120	353-4342*
*Fax: Admissions ■ *Web:* www.cooper.edu					
Cornell University 410 Thurston Ave	Ithaca	NY	14850	607-255-5241	254-5175*
*Fax: Admissions ■ *Web:* www.cornell.edu					
Daemen College 4380 Main St	Amherst	NY	14226	716-839-8225	839-8229*
*Fax: Admissions ■ *TF:* 800-462-7652 ■ *Web:* www.daemen.edu					
Dominican College 470 Western Hwy.	Orangeburg	NY	10962	845-359-7800	365-3150*
*Fax: Admissions ■ *TF:* 866-432-4636 ■ *Web:* www.dc.edu					
Dowling College 150 Idle Hour Blvd.	Oakdale	NY	11769	631-244-3000	244-1059*
*Fax: Admissions ■ *TF:* 800-369-5464 ■ *Web:* www.dowling.edu					
D'Youville College 320 Porter Ave	Buffalo	NY	14201	716-829-7600	829-7900*
*Fax: Admissions ■ *TF:* 800-777-3921 ■ *Web:* www.dyc.edu					
Elmira College 1 Park Place	Elmira	NY	14901	607-735-1724	735-1718*
*Fax: Admissions ■ *TF Admissions:* 800-935-6472 ■ *Web:* www.elmira.edu					
Empire State College 1 Union Ave	Saratoga Springs	NY	12866	518-587-2100	587-9759*
*Fax: Admissions ■ *TF:* 800-847-3000 ■ *Web:* www.esc.edu					
Eugene Lang College 65 W 11th St	New York	NY	10011	212-229-5665	229-5355*
*Fax: Admissions ■ *Web:* www.newschool.edu/lang					
Excelsior College 7 Columbia Cir	Albany	NY	12203	518-464-8500	464-8833*
*Fax: Admissions ■ *TF:* 888-647-2388 ■ *Web:* www.excelsior.edu					
Farmingdale State University of New York					
2350 Broadhollow Rd	Farmingdale	NY	11735	631-420-2000	420-2633
TF: 877-432-7646 ■ *Web:* www.farmingdale.edu					
Fordham University 441 E Fordham Rd	Bronx	NY	10458	718-817-5067	367-9404*
*Fax: Admissions ■ *TF:* 800-367-3426 ■ *Web:* www.fordham.edu					
College at Lincoln Center 113 W 60th St	New York	NY	10023	212-636-6710	636-7002
TF: 800-367-3426 ■ *Web:* www.fordham.edu					

				Phone	Fax
Hamilton College 198 College Hill Rd	Clinton	NY	13323	315-859-4421	859-4457*
*Fax: Admissions ■ TF Admissions: 800-843-2655 ■ Web: www.hamilton.edu					
Hartwick College 1 Hartwick Dr	Oneonta	NY	13820	607-431-4150	431-4154*
*Fax: Admissions ■ TF: 888-427-8942 ■ Web: www.hartwick.edu					
Hebrew Union College Jewish Institute of Religion					
1 W 4th St	New York	NY	10012	212-824-2207	388-1720*
*Fax: 800-424-1336 ■ Web: www.huc.edu					
Hilbert College 5200 S Park Ave	Hamburg	NY	14075	716-649-7900	649-1152
TF: 800-649-8003 ■ Web: www.hilbert.edu					
Hobart & William Smith Colleges 300 Pulteney St	Geneva	NY	14456	315-781-3000	781-3914*
*Fax: Admissions ■ TF Admissions: 800-852-2256 ■ Web: www.hws.edu					
Hofstra University 100 Hofstra University	Hempstead	NY	11549	516-463-6700	463-5100*
*Fax: Admissions ■ TF: 800-463-7872 ■ Web: www.hofstra.edu					
Houghton College 1 Willard Ave PO Box 128	Houghton	NY	14744	585-567-9200	567-9522*
*Fax: Admissions ■ TF: 800-777-2556 ■ Web: www.houghton.edu					
West Seneca 810 Union Rd	West Seneca	NY	14224	716-674-6363	674-0250
TF: 800-247-6448					
Hunter College 695 Park Ave North Bldg Rm 203	New York	NY	10065	212-772-4490	650-3472
Web: www.hunter.cuny.edu					
Iona College 715 North Ave	New Rochelle	NY	10801	914-633-2502	633-2642
TF: 800-231-4662 ■ Web: www.iona.edu					
Ithaca College 953 Danby Rd	Ithaca	NY	14850	607-274-3124	274-1900*
*Fax: Admissions ■ TF Admissions: 800-429-4274 ■ Web: www.ithaca.edu					
Jewish Theological Seminary 3080 Broadway	New York	NY	10027	212-678-8832	678-6022
Web: www.jtsa.edu					
John Jay College of Criminal Justice 899 10th Ave	New York	NY	10019	212-237-8000	237-8777
Web: www.jjay.cuny.edu					
Juilliard School 60 Lincoln Center Plaza	New York	NY	10023	212-799-5000	769-6420*
*Fax: Admissions ■ Web: www.juilliard.edu					
Keuka College 141 Central Ave	Keuka Park	NY	14478	315-279-5254	536-5386*
*Fax: Admissions ■ TF Admissions: 800-335-3852 ■ Web: www.keuka.edu					
Laboratory Institute of Merchandising 12 E 53rd St	New York	NY	10022	212-752-1530	832-6708*
*Fax: Admissions ■ TF: 800-677-1323 ■ Web: www.limcollege.edu					
Le Moyne College 1419 Salt Springs Rd	Syracuse	NY	13214	315-445-4100	445-4711*
*Fax: Admissions ■ TF Admissions: 800-333-4733 ■ Web: www.lemoyne.edu					
Lehman College 250 Bedford Park Blvd W	Bronx	NY	10468	718-960-8000	960-8712*
*Fax: Admissions ■ Web: www.lehman.cuny.edu					
Long Island University					
Brentwood 100 2nd Ave	Brentwood	NY	11717	631-273-5112	273-3155
Web: www.liunet.edu/cwis/brent					
Brooklyn 1 University Plaza	Brooklyn	NY	11201	718-488-1011	797-2399*
*Fax: Admissions ■ TF: 800-548-7526 ■ Web: www.brooklyn.liu.edu					
CW Post 720 Northern Blvd	Greenvale	NY	11548	516-299-2000	299-2137*
*Fax: Admissions ■ TF: 800-548-7526 ■ Web: www.cwpost.liu.edu/cwis/cwp					
Manhattan College 4513 Manhattan College Pkwy	Bronx	NY	10471	718-862-8000	862-8019*
*Fax: Admissions ■ TF: 800-622-9235 ■ Web: www.manhattan.edu					
Manhattan School of Music 120 Claremont Ave	New York	NY	10027	212-749-2802	749-3025*
*Fax: Admissions ■ Web: www.msmnyc.edu					
Manhattanville College 2900 Purchase St	Purchase	NY	10577	914-323-5464	694-1732
TF: 800-328-4553 ■ Web: www.mville.edu					
Mannes College of Music 150 W 85th St	New York	NY	10024	212-580-0210	580-1738*
*Fax: Admissions ■ Web: www.mannes.edu					
Marist College 3399 North Rd	Poughkeepsie	NY	12601	845-575-3000	575-3215
TF: 800-436-5483 ■ Web: www.marist.edu					
Marymount College of Fordham University					
100 Marymount Ave	Tarrytown	NY	10591	914-332-8295	332-7442
TF: 800-724-4312 ■ Web: www.fordham.edu					
Marymount Manhattan College 221 E 71st St	New York	NY	10021	212-517-0400	517-0448
TF: 800-627-9668 ■ Web: marymount.mmm.edu					
Medaille College 18 Agassiz Cir	Buffalo	NY	14214	716-880-2200	880-2007*
*Fax: Admissions ■ TF: 800-292-1582 ■ Web: www.medaille.edu					
Medgar Evers College 1650 Bedford Ave	Brooklyn	NY	11225	718-270-4900	270-6411*
*Fax: Admissions ■ Web: www.mec.cuny.edu					
Mercy College 555 Broadway	Dobbs Ferry	NY	10522	914-674-2324	674-7382*
*Fax: Admissions ■ TF: 800-637-2969 ■ Web: www.mercy.edu					
Bronx 1200 Waters Pl	Bronx	NY	10461	718-678-8899	678-8664*
*Fax: Admissions ■ TF: 800-637-2969 ■ Web: www.mercy.edu/bronx/campus.cfm					
Manhattan 66 W 35th St	New York	NY	10001	212-615-3313	967-2993
TF: 800-637-2969 ■ Web: www.mercy.edu/mercymanhattan					
White Plains 277 Martine Ave	White Plains	NY	10601	914-948-3666	948-6732
TF: 800-637-2969 ■ Web: www.mercy.edu/whiteplains/campus.cfm					
Yorktown Heights 2651 Strang Blvd	Yorktown Heights	NY	10598	914-245-6100	962-0931*
*Fax: Admissions ■ TF: 800-637-2969 ■ Web: www.mercy.edu/yorktown/campus.cfm					
Metropolitan College of New York 431 Canal St	New York	NY	10013	212-343-1234	343-7399*
*Fax: Admissions ■ TF: 800-338-4465 ■ Web: www.metropolitan.edu					
Molloy College 1000 Hempstead Ave PO Box 5002	Rockville Centre	NY	11571	516-678-5000	256-2247*
*Fax: Admissions ■ TF Admissions: 888-466-5569 ■ Web: www.molloy.edu					
Morrisville State College 80 Eaton St PO Box 901	Morrisville	NY	13408	315-684-6000	684-6427*
*Fax: Admissions ■ TF Admissions: 800-258-0111 ■ Web: www.morrisville.edu					
Mount Saint Mary College 330 Powell Ave	Newburgh	NY	12550	845-569-3248	562-6762
TF: 888-937-6762 ■ Web: www.msmc.edu					
Nazareth College of Rochester 4245 East Ave	Rochester	NY	14618	585-389-2860	389-2826
TF: 800-462-3944 ■ Web: www.naz.edu					
New School 66 W 12th St	New York	NY	10011	212-229-5600	989-3887*
*Fax: Admissions ■ Web: www.newschool.edu					
New York City College of Technology 300 Jay St	Brooklyn	NY	11201	718-260-5000	260-5504*
*Fax: Admissions ■ Web: www.citytech.cuny.edu					
New York Institute of Technology					
New York Institute of Technology Northern Blvd PO Box 8000	Old Westbury	NY	11568	516-686-1000	686-7613*
*Fax: Admissions ■ TF: 800-345-6948 ■ Web: www.nyit.edu					
Islip PO Box 9029	Central Islip	NY	11722	631-348-3200	348-0912*
*Fax: Admissions ■ TF: 800-345-6948 ■ Web: www.nyit.edu					
Manhattan 1855 Broadway	New York	NY	10023	212-261-1500	261-1505*
*Fax: Admissions ■ TF: 800-345-6948 ■ Web: www.nyit.edu					
New York School of Interior Design 170 E 70th St	New York	NY	10021	212-472-1500	472-1867*
*Fax: Admissions ■ TF: 800-336-9743 ■ Web: www.nysid.edu					
New York University 22 Washington Sq N	New York	NY	10011	212-998-4500	995-4902*
*Fax: Admissions ■ Web: www.nyu.edu					
Niagara University 5795 Lewiston Rd PO Box 2011	Niagara University	NY	14109	716-286-8700	286-8710*
*Fax: Admissions ■ TF: 800-462-2111 ■ Web: www.niagara.edu					
Nyack College 1 South Blvd	Nyack	NY	10960	845-358-1710	358-3047*
*Fax: Admissions ■ TF Admissions: 800-336-9225 ■ Web: www.nyackcollege.edu					
Pace University 1 Pace Plaza	New York	NY	10038	212-346-1200	346-1040*
*Fax: Admissions ■ TF: 866-874-7223 ■ Web: www.pace.edu					
Pleasantville/Briarcliff 861 Bedford Rd	Pleasantville	NY	10570	914-773-3200	773-3851*
*Fax: Admissions ■ TF: 866-722-3338 ■ Web: www.pace.edu					
Parsons New School for Design 65 5th Ave Rm 103	New York	NY	10003	212-229-8989	229-8975*
*Fax: Admissions ■ TF Admissions: 800-252-0852 ■ Web: www.parsons.edu					
Paul Smith's College Rt 30 & 86 PO Box 265	Paul Smiths	NY	12970	518-327-6227	327-6016*
*Fax: Admissions ■ TF Admissions: 800-421-2605 ■ Web: www.paulsmiths.edu					
Plattsburgh State 101 Broad St	Plattsburgh	NY	12901	518-564-2040	564-2045*
*Fax: Admissions ■ TF Admissions: 888-673-0012 ■ Web: www.plattsburgh.edu					
Polytechnic University 6 Metrotech Center	Brooklyn	NY	11201	718-637-5955	260-3446*
*Fax: Admissions ■ TF: 800-765-9832 ■ Web: www.poly.edu					
Long Island 105 Maxess Rd	Melville	NY	11747	631-755-4300	755-4404*
*Fax: Admissions ■ TF Admissions: 800-765-9832 ■ Web: www.poly.edu/li					
Pratt Institute 200 Willoughby Ave	Brooklyn	NY	11205	718-636-3669	636-3670
TF: 800-331-0834 ■ Web: www.pratt.edu					
Purchase College 735 Anderson Hill Rd	Purchase	NY	10577	914-251-6000	251-6314*
*Fax: Admissions ■ Web: www.purchase.edu					
Queens College 65-30 Kissena Blvd	Flushing	NY	11367	718-997-5000	997-5617
Web: www.qc.cuny.edu					
Rensselaer Polytechnic Institute 110 8th St	Troy	NY	12180	518-276-6216	276-4072*
*Fax: Admissions ■ TF: 800-448-6562 ■ Web: www.rpi.edu					
Roberts Wesleyan College 2301 Westside Dr	Rochester	NY	14624	585-594-6000	594-6371*
*Fax: Admissions ■ TF Admissions: 800-777-4792 ■ Web: www.roberts.edu					
Rochester Institute of Technology 1 Lomb Memorial Dr	Rochester	NY	14623	585-475-2411	475-7424*
*Fax: Admissions ■ Web: www.rit.edu					
Russell Sage College 45 Ferry St	Troy	NY	12180	518-244-2217	244-6880*
*Fax: Admissions ■ TF Admissions: 888-837-9724 ■ Web: www.sage.edu/rsc					
Sage College of Albany 140 New Scotland Ave	Albany	NY	12208	518-292-1730	292-1912*
*Fax: Admissions ■ TF Admissions: 888-837-9724 ■ Web: www.sage.edu/sca					
Saint Bonaventure University PO Box D	Saint Bonaventure	NY	14778	716-375-2400	375-4005*
*Fax: Admissions ■ TF: 800-462-5050 ■ Web: www.sbu.edu					
Saint Francis College 180 Remsen St 3rd Fl	Brooklyn Heights	NY	11201	718-522-2300	802-0453*
*Fax: Admissions ■ Web: www.stfranciscollege.edu					
Saint John Fisher College 3690 East Ave	Rochester	NY	14618	585-385-8064	385-8386*
*Fax: Admissions ■ TF Admissions: 800-444-4640 ■ Web: www.sjfc.edu					
Saint John's University 8000 Utopia Pkwy	Jamaica	NY	11439	718-990-2000	990-2096*
*Fax: Admissions ■ TF: 888-978-5646 ■ Web: www.stjohns.edu					
Staten Island 300 Howard Ave	Staten Island	NY	10301	718-447-4343	390-4298*
*Fax: Admissions ■ Web: www.stjohns.edu/campus/si					
Saint Joseph's College					
Brooklyn 245 Clinton Ave	Brooklyn	NY	11205	718-636-6800	636-8303*
*Fax: Admissions ■ Web: www.sjcny.edu					
Suffolk 155 W Roe Blvd	Patchogue	NY	11772	631-447-3200	447-1731*
*Fax: Admissions ■ Web: www.sjcny.edu					
Saint Lawrence University 23 Romoda Dr	Canton	NY	13617	315-229-5261	229-5818*
*Fax: Admissions ■ TF Admissions: 800-285-1856 ■ Web: www.stlawu.edu					
Saint Thomas Aquinas College 125 Rt 340	Sparkill	NY	10976	845-398-4000	398-4114
TF: 800-999-7822 ■ Web: www.stac.edu					
Sarah Lawrence College 1 Meadway	Bronxville	NY	10708	800-888-2858	395-2515*
*Fax Area Code: 914 ■ *Fax: Admissions ■ TF: 800-888-2858 ■ Web: www.slc.edu					
Siena College 515 Loudon Rd	Loudonville	NY	12211	518-783-2200	783-2436*
*Fax: Admissions ■ TF Admissions: 888-287-4362 ■ Web: www.siena.edu					
Skidmore College 815 N Broadway	Saratoga Springs	NY	12866	518-580-5000	580-5584*
*Fax: Admissions ■ TF: 800-867-6007 ■ Web: www.skidmore.edu					
State University of New York					
Brockport 350 New Campus Dr	Brockport	NY	14420	585-395-2751	395-5452
Web: www.brockport.edu					
College of Agriculture & Technology at Cobleskill Rt 7	Cobleskill	NY	12043	518-255-5525	255-6769*
*Fax: Admissions ■ TF: 800-295-8988 ■ Web: www.cobleskill.edu					
College of Environmental Science & Forestry 1 Forestry Dr	Syracuse	NY	13210	315-470-6500	470-6933*
*Fax: Admissions ■ TF Admissions: 800-777-7373 ■ Web: www.esf.edu					
College at Old Westbury 223 Store Hill Rd PO Box 307	Old Westbury	NY	11568	516-876-3023	876-3307*
*Fax: Admissions ■ Web: www.oldwestbury.edu					
College at Oneonta Ravine Pkwy	Oneonta	NY	13820	607-436-3500	436-3074*
*Fax: Admissions ■ TF: 800-786-9123 ■ Web: www.oneonta.edu					
Cortland PO Box 2000	Cortland	NY	13045	607-753-2011	753-5998*
*Fax: Admissions ■ Web: www.cortland.edu					
Empire State College 1 Union Ave	Saratoga Springs	NY	12866	518-587-2100	587-9759*
*Fax: Admissions ■ TF: 800-847-3000 ■ Web: www.esc.edu					
Fredonia 178 Central Ave	Fredonia	NY	14063	716-673-3251	673-3249*
*Fax: Admissions ■ TF: 800-252-1212 ■ Web: www.fredonia.edu					
Geneseo 1 College Cir	Geneseo	NY	14454	585-245-5571	245-5550*
*Fax: Admitting ■ TF Admitting: 866-245-5211 ■ Web: www.geneseo.edu					
Institute of Technology PO Box 3050	Utica	NY	13504	315-792-7500	792-7837*
*Fax: Admissions ■ TF: 800-786-9832 ■ Web: www.sunyit.edu					
Maritime College 6 Pennyfield Ave Fort Schuyler	Bronx	NY	10465	718-409-7200	409-7465
Web: www.sunymaritime.edu					
New Paltz 1 Hawk Dr	New Paltz	NY	12561	845-257-3212	257-3209*
*Fax: Admissions ■ TF: 888-639-7589 ■ Web: www.newpaltz.edu					
Oswego 7060 SR 104	Oswego	NY	13126	315-312-2500	312-3260*
*Fax: Admissions ■ Web: www.oswego.edu					
Plattsburgh 101 Broad St	Plattsburgh	NY	12901	518-564-2040	564-2045*
*Fax: Admissions ■ TF Admissions: 888-673-0012 ■ Web: www.plattsburgh.edu					
Potsdam 44 Pierrpont Ave	Potsdam	NY	13676	315-267-2180	267-2163*
*Fax: Admissions ■ TF Admissions: 877-768-7326 ■ Web: www.potsdam.edu					
University at Buffalo 12 Capen Hall	Buffalo	NY	14260	716-645-2450	645-6411*
*Fax: Admissions ■ TF: 888-822-3648 ■ Web: www.buffalo.edu					
Stern College for Women of Yeshiva University					
245 Lexington Ave	New York	NY	10016	212-340-7701	340-7837*
*Fax: Admissions ■ Web: www.yu.edu/stern					
Stony Brook University 100 Nicolls Rd	Stony Brook	NY	11794	631-689-6000	632-9898
Web: www.sunysb.edu					
SUNY Brockport 350 New Campus Dr	Brockport	NY	14420	585-395-2751	395-5452
Web: www.brockport.edu					
SUNY College of Agriculture & Technology at Cobleskill					
Rt 7	Cobleskill	NY	12043	518-255-5525	255-6769*
*Fax: Admissions ■ TF: 800-295-8988 ■ Web: www.cobleskill.edu					
SUNY College of Environmental Science & Forestry					
1 Forestry Dr	Syracuse	NY	13210	315-470-6500	470-6933*
*Fax: Admissions ■ TF Admissions: 800-777-7373 ■ Web: www.esf.edu					
SUNY College at Old Westbury					
223 Store Hill Rd PO Box 307	Old Westbury	NY	11568	516-876-3023	876-3307*
*Fax: Admissions ■ Web: www.oldwestbury.edu					
SUNY College at Oneonta Ravine Pkwy	Oneonta	NY	13820	607-436-3500	436-3074*
*Fax: Admissions ■ TF: 800-786-9123 ■ Web: www.oneonta.edu					
SUNY Cortland PO Box 2000	Cortland	NY	13045	607-753-2011	753-5998*
*Fax: Admissions ■ Web: www.cortland.edu					
SUNY Fredonia 178 Central Ave	Fredonia	NY	14063	716-673-3251	673-3249*
*Fax: Admissions ■ TF: 800-252-1212 ■ Web: www.fredonia.edu					
SUNY Geneseo 1 College Cir	Geneseo	NY	14454	585-245-5571	245-5550*
*Fax: Admitting ■ TF Admitting: 866-245-5211 ■ Web: www.geneseo.edu					
SUNY Institute of Technology PO Box 3050	Utica	NY	13504	315-792-7500	792-7837*
*Fax: Admissions ■ TF: 800-786-9832 ■ Web: www.sunyit.edu					
SUNY Maritime College 6 Pennyfield Ave Fort Schuyler	Bronx	NY	10465	718-409-7200	409-7465
Web: www.sunymaritime.edu					
SUNY New Paltz 1 Hawk Dr	New Paltz	NY	12561	845-257-3212	257-3209*
*Fax: Admissions ■ TF: 888-639-7589 ■ Web: www.newpaltz.edu					
SUNY Oswego 7060 SR 104	Oswego	NY	13126	315-312-2500	312-3260*
*Fax: Admissions ■ Web: www.oswego.edu					
SUNY Potsdam 44 Pierrpont Ave	Potsdam	NY	13676	315-267-2180	267-2163*
*Fax: Admissions ■ TF Admissions: 877-768-7326 ■ Web: www.potsdam.edu					
Syracuse University 900 S Crouse Ave	Syracuse	NY	13244	315-443-3611	443-4226*
*Fax: Admissions ■ Web: www.syr.edu					
Touro College 27-33 W 23rd St	New York	NY	10010	212-463-0400	627-9144
Web: www.touro.edu					
Lander College for Men 75-31 150th St	Kew Gardens Hills	NY	11367	718-820-4884	820-4838
Web: www.touro.edu/landercollege					
Union College 807 Union St	Schenectady	NY	12308	518-388-6112	388-6986*
*Fax: Admissions ■ TF Admissions: 888-843-6688 ■ Web: www.union.edu					

New York (Cont'd)

Institution	City	State	ZIP	Phone	Fax
University at Albany 1400 Washington Ave *Fax: Admissions ■ TF: 800-293-7869 ■ Web: www.albany.edu	Albany	NY	12222	518-442-3300	442-5383*
University at Buffalo 12 Capen Hall *Fax: Admissions ■ TF: 888-822-3648 ■ Web: www.buffalo.edu	Buffalo	NY	14260	716-645-2450	645-6411*
University of Rochester Wallace Hall PO Box 270251 *Fax: Admissions ■ TF Admissions: 888-822-2256 ■ Web: www.rochester.edu	Rochester	NY	14627	585-275-2121	461-4595*
US Merchant Marine Academy 300 Steamboat Rd *Fax: Admissions ■ TF: 866-546-4778 ■ Web: www.usmma.edu	Kings Point	NY	11024	516-773-5000	773-5390*
US Military Academy Admissions Bldg 606 TF: 800-822-8762 ■ Web: www.usma.edu	West Point	NY	10996	845-938-5746	938-8121
Utica College 1600 Burrstone Rd *Fax: Admissions ■ TF Admissions: 800-782-8884 ■ Web: www.utica.edu/	Utica	NY	13502	315-792-3111	792-3003*
Vassar College 124 Raymond Ave TF: 800-827-7270 ■ Web: www.vassar.edu	Poughkeepsie	NY	12604	845-437-7000	437-7063
Vaughn College of Aeronautics & Technology 86-01 23rd Ave *Fax: Admissions ■ TF: 800-776-2376 ■ Web: www.vaughn.edu	East Elmhurst	NY	11369	718-429-6600	779-2231*
Wagner College 1 Campus Rd TF Admissions: 800-221-1010 ■ Web: www.wagner.edu	Staten Island	NY	10301	718-390-3411	390-3105
Webb Institute 298 Crescent Beach Rd *Fax: Admissions ■ TF: 866-708-9322 ■ Web: www.webb-institute.edu	Glen Cove	NY	11542	516-671-2213	674-9838*
Wells College 170 Main St PO Box 500 *Fax: Admissions ■ TF Admissions: 800-952-9355 ■ Web: www.wells.edu	Aurora	NY	13026	315-364-3370	364-3227*
Yeshiva University 500 W 185th St *Fax: Admissions ■ Web: www.yu.edu	New York	NY	10033	212-960-5400	960-0086*
York College 94-20 Guy R Brewer Blvd *Fax: Admissions ■ Web: www.york.cuny.edu	Jamaica	NY	11451	718-262-2000	262-2601*

North Carolina

Institution	City	State	ZIP	Phone	Fax
Appalachian State University 287 Rivers St Web: www.appstate.edu	Boone	NC	28608	828-262-2000	262-3296
Barton College PO Box 5000 TF: 800-345-4973 ■ Web: www.barton.edu	Wilson	NC	27893	252-399-6300	399-6572
Belmont Abbey College 100 Belmont-Mt Holly Rd *Fax: Admissions ■ TF: 888-222-0110 ■ Web: belmontabbeycollege.edu	Belmont	NC	28012	704-825-6700	825-6220*
Bennett College 900 E Washington St *Fax: Admissions ■ TF Admissions: 800-413-5323 ■ Web: www.bennett.edu	Greensboro	NC	27401	336-370-8624	517-2166*
Brevard College 1 Brevard College Dr *Fax: Admissions ■ TF: 800-527-9090 ■ Web: www.brevard.edu	Brevard	NC	28712	828-883-8292	884-3790*
Campbell University 56 Main St PO Box 546 *Fax: Admissions ■ TF: 800-334-4111 ■ Web: www.campbell.edu	Buies Creek	NC	27506	910-893-1290	893-1288*
Catawba College 2300 W Innes St *Fax: Admissions ■ TF: 800-228-2922 ■ Web: www.catawba.edu	Salisbury	NC	28144	704-637-4111	637-4222*
Chowan University 1 University Pl *Fax: Admissions ■ TF Admissions: 800-488-4101 ■ Web: www.chowan.edu	Murfreesboro	NC	27855	252-398-6500	398-1190*
Davidson College Box 7156 *Fax: Admissions ■ TF: 800-768-0380 ■ Web: www.davidson.edu	Davidson	NC	28035	704-894-2000	894-2016*
Duke University 2138 Campus Dr Box 90586 *Fax: Admissions ■ Web: www.duke.edu	Durham	NC	27708	919-684-3214	681-8941*
East Carolina University E 5th St Web: www.ecu.edu	Greenville	NC	27858	252-328-6131	328-6640
Elizabeth City State University 1704 Weeksville Rd CB 901 *Fax: Admissions ■ TF Admissions: 800-347-3278 ■ Web: www.ecsu.edu	Elizabeth City	NC	27909	252-335-3305	335-3537*
Elon University Campus Box 2700 *Fax: Admissions ■ TF Admissions: 800-334-8448 ■ Web: www.elon.edu	Elon	NC	27244	336-278-2000	278-7699*
Fayetteville State University 1200 Murchison Rd *Fax: Admissions ■ TF Admissions: 800-222-2594 ■ Web: www.uncfsu.edu	Fayetteville	NC	28301	910-672-1371	672-1414*
Gardner-Webb University PO Box 817 *Fax: Admissions ■ TF: 800-253-6472 ■ Web: www.gardner-webb.edu	Boiling Springs	NC	28017	704-406-4498	406-4488*
Greensboro College 815 W Market St *Fax: Admissions ■ TF: 800-346-8226 ■ Web: www.gborocollege.edu	Greensboro	NC	27401	336-272-7102	378-0154*
Guilford College 5800 W Friendly Ave *Fax: Admissions ■ TF Admissions: 800-992-7759 ■ Web: www.guilford.edu	Greensboro	NC	27410	336-316-2000	316-2954*
Heritage Bible College PO Box 1628 *Fax: Admissions ■ TF: 800-297-6351 ■ Web: www.heritagebiblecollege.org	Dunn	NC	28335	910-892-4268	891-1660*
High Point University 833 Montlieu Ave *Fax: Admissions ■ TF: 800-345-6993 ■ Web: www.highpoint.edu	High Point	NC	27262	336-841-9216	888-6382*
Johnson C Smith University 100 Beatties Ford Rd *Fax: Admissions ■ TF Admissions: 800-782-7303 ■ Web: www.jcsu.edu	Charlotte	NC	28216	704-378-1000	378-1242*
Johnson & Wales University Charlotte 801 W Trade St *Fax: Admissions ■ TF: 866-598-2427 ■ Web: www.jwu.edu/charlotte	Charlotte	NC	28202	980-598-1100	598-1111*
Lee University Charlotte Center 1209 Little Rock Rd *Fax: Admissions	Charlotte	NC	28214	704-394-2307	393-3689*
Lees-McRae College PO Box 128 TF: 800-280-4562 ■ Web: www.lmc.edu	Banner Elk	NC	28604	828-898-5241	898-8707
Lenoir-Rhyne College 510 7th Ave NE PO Box 7227 TF: 800-277-5721 ■ Web: www.lrc.edu	Hickory	NC	28603	828-328-7300	328-7378
Livingstone College 701 W Monroe St TF: 800-835-3435 ■ Web: www.livingstone.edu	Salisbury	NC	28144	704-216-6000	216-6215
Mars Hill College 100 Athletics St *Fax: Admissions ■ TF: 866-642-4968 ■ Web: www.mhc.edu	Mars Hill	NC	28754	828-689-1201	689-1473*
Meredith College 3800 Hillsborough St *Fax: Admissions ■ TF: 800-637-3348 ■ Web: www.meredith.edu	Raleigh	NC	27607	919-760-8581	760-2348*
Methodist College 5400 Ramsey St *Fax: Admissions ■ TF: 800-488-7110 ■ Web: www.methodist.edu	Fayetteville	NC	28311	910-630-7000	630-7285*
Montreat College 310 Gaither Cir PO Box 1267 TF: 800-622-6968 ■ Web: www.montreat.edu	Montreat	NC	28757	828-669-8011	669-0120
Mount Olive College 634 Henderson St *Fax: Admissions ■ TF: 800-653-0854 ■ Web: www.moc.edu	Mount Olive	NC	28365	919-658-2502	658-9816*
North Carolina A & T State University 1601 E Market St *Fax: Admissions ■ TF Admissions: 800-443-8964 ■ Web: www.ncat.edu	Greensboro	NC	27411	336-334-7946	334-7478*
North Carolina Central University 1801 Fayetteville St *Fax: Admissions ■ TF Admissions: 877-667-7533 ■ Web: www.nccu.edu	Durham	NC	27707	919-530-6100	530-7625*
North Carolina State University 2200 Hillsborough St *Fax: Admissions ■ Web: www.ncsu.edu	Raleigh	NC	27695	919-515-2011	515-5039*
North Carolina Wesleyan College 3400 N Wesleyan Blvd *Fax: Admissions ■ TF Admissions: 800-488-6292 ■ Web: ncwc.edu	Rocky Mount	NC	27804	252-985-5100	985-5295*
Peace College 15 E Peace St *Fax: Admissions ■ TF: 800-732-2347 ■ Web: www.peace.edu	Raleigh	NC	27604	919-508-2000	508-2326*
Pfeiffer University 48380 Hwy 52 N *Fax: Admissions ■ TF: 800-338-2060 ■ Web: www.pfeiffer.edu	Misenheimer	NC	28109	704-463-1360	463-1363*
Piedmont Baptist College 420 S Broad St *Fax: Admissions ■ TF Admissions: 800-937-5097 ■ Web: www.pbc.edu	Winston-Salem	NC	27101	336-725-8344	725-5522*
Queens University of Charlotte 1900 Selwyn Ave *Fax: Admissions ■ TF: 800-849-0202 ■ Web: www.queens.edu	Charlotte	NC	28274	704-337-2212	337-2403*
Saint Andrews Presbyterian College 1700 Dogwood Mile *Fax: Admissions ■ TF: 800-763-0198 ■ Web: www.sapc.edu	Laurinburg	NC	28352	910-277-5000	277-5087*
Saint Augustine's College 1315 Oakwood Ave *Fax: Admissions ■ TF Admissions: 800-948-1126 ■ Web: www.st-aug.edu	Raleigh	NC	27610	919-516-4016	516-5805*
Salem College 601 S Church St *Fax: Admissions ■ TF Admissions: 800-327-2536 ■ Web: www.salem.edu	Winston-Salem	NC	27101	336-721-2600	917-5572*
Shaw University 118 E South St *Fax: Admissions ■ TF Admissions: 800-214-6683 ■ Web: www.shawu.edu	Raleigh	NC	27601	919-546-8275	546-8271*
University of North Carolina					
Asheville 1 University Heights CPO 1320 *Fax: Admissions ■ TF: 800-531-9842 ■ Web: www.unca.edu	Asheville	NC	28804	828-251-6481	251-6482*
Chapel Hill 2200 Jackson Hall CB 2200 *Fax: Admissions ■ Web: www.unc.edu	Chapel Hill	NC	27599	919-966-3621	962-3045*
Charlotte 9201 University City Blvd Web: www.uncc.edu	Charlotte	NC	28223	704-687-2000	687-6483
Greensboro 1000 Spring Garden St PO Box 26170 TF: 800-346-8226 ■ Web: www.uncg.edu	Greensboro	NC	27402	336-334-5000	334-4180
Pembroke PO Box 1510 *Fax: Admissions ■ TF: 800-949-8627 ■ Web: www.uncp.edu	Pembroke	NC	28372	910-521-6000	521-6497*
Wilmington 601 S College Rd *Fax: Admissions ■ TF: 800-228-5571 ■ Web: www.uncwil.edu	Wilmington	NC	28403	910-962-3000	962-3038*
Wake Forest University 1834 Wake Forest Rd *Fax: Admissions ■ Web: www.wfu.edu	Winston-Salem	NC	27106	336-758-5255	758-4324*
Warren Wilson College 701 Warren Wilson Rd *Fax: Admissions ■ TF Admissions: 800-934-3536 ■ Web: www.warren-wilson.edu	Swannanoa	NC	28778	828-298-3325	298-1440*
Western Carolina University Web: www.wcu.edu	Cullowhee	NC	28723	828-227-7211	227-7317
Wingate University 220 N Camden St TF: 800-755-5550 ■ Web: www.wingate.edu	Wingate	NC	28174	704-233-8000	233-8110
Winston-Salem State University 601 S ML King Jr Dr 206 Thompson Center *Fax: Admissions ■ TF Admissions: 800-257-4052 ■ Web: www.wssu.edu	Winston-Salem	NC	27110	336-750-2000	750-2079*

North Dakota

Institution	City	State	ZIP	Phone	Fax
Dickinson State University 291 Campus Dr *Fax: Admissions ■ TF: 800-279-4295 ■ Web: www.dickinsonstate.com	Dickinson	ND	58601	701-483-2331	483-9959*
Jamestown College 6088 College Ln *Fax: Admissions ■ TF: 800-336-2554 ■ Web: www.jc.edu	Jamestown	ND	58405	701-252-3467	253-4318*
Mayville State University 330 3rd St NE *Fax: Admissions ■ TF: 800-437-4104 ■ Web: www.masu.nodak.edu	Mayville	ND	58257	701-788-2301	788-4748*
Minot State University 500 University Ave W TF: 800-777-0750 ■ Web: www.minotstateu.edu	Minot	ND	58707	701-858-3000	858-3888
North Dakota State University 1301 12th Ave N *Fax: Admissions ■ TF: 800-488-6378 ■ Web: www.ndsu.edu	Fargo	ND	58105	701-231-8643	231-8802*
University of Mary 7500 University Dr *Fax: Admissions ■ TF Admissions: 800-288-6279 ■ Web: www.umary.edu	Bismarck	ND	58504	701-255-7500	255-7687*
University of North Dakota PO Box 8357 *Fax: Admissions ■ TF: 800-225-5863 ■ Web: www.und.nodak.edu	Grand Forks	ND	58202	701-777-2011	777-2721*
Valley City State University 101 College St SW TF: 800-532-8641 ■ Web: www.vcsu.edu	Valley City	ND	58072	701-845-7990	845-7299

Ohio

Institution	City	State	ZIP	Phone	Fax
Antioch College 795 Livermore St *Fax: Admissions ■ TF: 800-543-9436 ■ Web: www.antioch-college.edu	Yellow Springs	OH	45387	937-769-1100	769-1111*
Ashland University 401 College Ave TF: 800-882-1548 ■ Web: www.ashland.edu	Ashland	OH	44805	419-289-4142	289-5999
Baldwin-Wallace College 275 Eastland Rd *Fax: Admissions ■ TF: 877-292-7759 ■ Web: www.bw.edu	Berea	OH	44017	440-826-2222	826-3830*
Bluffton University 1 University Dr *Fax: Admissions ■ TF: 800-488-3257 ■ Web: www.bluffton.edu	Bluffton	OH	45817	419-358-3000	358-3081*
Bowling Green State University *Fax: Admissions ■ TF Admissions: 866-246-6732 ■ Web: www.bgsu.edu	Bowling Green	OH	43403	419-372-2531	372-6955*
Capital University College & Main St *Fax: Admissions ■ TF: 800-289-6289 ■ Web: www.capital.edu	Columbus	OH	43209	614-236-6101	236-6926*
Case Western Reserve University 10900 Euclid Ave *Fax: Admissions ■ TF Admissions: 800-967-8898 ■ Web: www.case.edu	Cleveland	OH	44106	216-368-2000	368-5111*
Cedarville University 251 N Main St *Fax: Admissions ■ TF: 800-233-2784 ■ Web: www.cedarville.edu	Cedarville	OH	45314	937-766-7700	766-7575*
Central State University 1400 Brush Row Rd PO Box 1004 *Fax: Admissions ■ TF: 800-388-2781 ■ Web: www.centralstate.edu	Wilberforce	OH	45384	937-376-6011	376-6648*
Cleveland Institute of Music 11021 East Blvd Web: www.cim.edu	Cleveland	OH	44106	216-791-5000	791-3063
Cleveland State University 2121 Euclid Ave *Fax: Admissions ■ TF: 888-278-6446 ■ Web: www.csuohio.edu	Cleveland	OH	44115	216-687-2000	687-9210*
College of Mount Saint Joseph 5701 Delhi Rd TF: 800-654-9314 ■ Web: www.msj.edu	Cincinnati	OH	45233	513-244-4200	244-4601
College of Wooster 847 College Ave *Fax: Admissions ■ TF Admissions: 800-877-9905 ■ Web: www.wooster.edu	Wooster	OH	44691	330-263-2000	263-2621*
Defiance College 701 N Clinton St *Fax: Admissions ■ TF: 800-520-4632 ■ Web: www.defiance.edu	Defiance	OH	43512	419-784-4010	783-2468*
Denison University 100 Chapel St *Fax: Admissions ■ TF: 800-336-4766 ■ Web: www.denison.edu	Granville	OH	43023	740-587-0810	587-6306*
Franklin University 201 S Grant Ave *Fax: Admissions ■ TF: 877-341-6300 ■ Web: www.franklin.edu	Columbus	OH	43215	614-797-4700	224-8027*
Hebrew Union College Cincinnati 3101 Clifton Ave Web: www.huc.edu/about/center-cn.shtml	Cincinnati	OH	45220	513-221-1875	221-0321*
Heidelberg College 310 E Market St *Fax: Admissions ■ TF Admissions: 800-434-3352 ■ Web: www.heidelberg.edu	Tiffin	OH	44883	419-448-2000	448-2334*
Hiram College PO Box 67 *Fax: Admissions ■ TF Admissions: 800-362-5280 ■ Web: www.hiram.edu	Hiram	OH	44234	330-569-5169	569-5944*
John Carroll University 20700 N Park Blvd *Fax: Admissions ■ TF: 888-335-6800 ■ Web: www.jcu.edu	University Heights	OH	44118	216-397-1886	397-4981*
Kent State University 1500 Summit St PO Box 5190 *Fax: Admissions ■ TF: 800-988-5368 ■ Web: www.kent.edu	Kent	OH	44242	330-672-2121	672-2499*
Ashtabula 3300 Lake Rd W *Fax: Admissions ■ Web: www.ashtabula.kent.edu	Ashtabula	OH	44004	440-964-3322	964-4269*
East Liverpool 400 E 4th St *Fax: Admissions ■ Web: www.kenteliv.kent.edu	East Liverpool	OH	43920	330-385-3805	382-7566*
Salem 2491 SR-45 S *Fax: Admissions ■ Web: www.salem.kent.edu	Salem	OH	44460	330-332-0361	337-4122*
Stark 6000 Frank Ave NW *Fax: Admissions ■ Web: www.stark.kent.edu	North Canton	OH	44720	330-499-9600	499-0301*
Trumbull Campus 4314 Mahoning Ave NW *Fax: Admissions ■ Web: www.trumbull.kent.edu	Warren	OH	44483	330-847-0571	675-8888*
Tuscarawas 330 University Dr NE *Fax: Admissions ■ Web: www.tusc.kent.edu	New Philadelphia	OH	44663	330-339-3391	339-3321*
Kenyon College 106 College Park St Ranson Hall *Fax: Admissions ■ TF Admissions: 800-848-2468 ■ Web: www.kenyon.edu	Gambier	OH	43022	740-427-5000	427-5770*
Lake Erie College 391 W Washington St *Fax: Admissions ■ TF: 800-533-4996 ■ Web: www.lec.edu	Painesville	OH	44077	440-375-7050	375-7005*
Lourdes College 6832 Convent Blvd *Fax: Admissions ■ TF: 800-878-3210 ■ Web: www.lourdes.edu	Sylvania	OH	43560	419-885-5291	882-3987*
Malone College 515 25th St NW *Fax: Admissions ■ TF: 800-521-1146 ■ Web: www.malone.edu	Canton	OH	44709	330-471-8100	471-8149*

Phone | Fax

Marietta College 215 5th St ... Marietta OH 45750 740-376-4000 376-8888*
*Fax: Admissions ■ TF Admissions: 800-331-7896 ■ Web: www.marietta.edu

Miami University 501 E High St ... Oxford OH 45056 513-529-1809 529-1550*
*Fax: Admissions ■ Web: www.miami.muohio.edu

Middletown 4200 E University Blvd ... Middletown OH 45042 513-727-3200 727-3223
TF: 866-426-4643 ■ Web: www.mid.muohio.edu

Mount Union College 1972 Clark Ave ... Alliance OH 44601 330-823-2590 823-5097*
*Fax: Admissions ■ TF Admissions: 800-334-6682 ■ Web: www.muc.edu

Mount Vernon Nazarene University 800 Martinsburg Rd ... Mount Vernon OH 43050 740-392-6868
TF Admissions: 866-782-2435 ■ Web: www.mvnu.edu

Muskingum College 163 Stormont St ... New Concord OH 43762 740-826-8211 826-8100*
*Fax: Admissions ■ TF Admissions: 800-752-6082 ■ Web: www.muskingum.edu

Myers University 3921 Chester Ave ... Cleveland OH 44114 216-391-6937 361-9274*
*Fax: Admissions ■ TF: 877-366-9377 ■ Web: www.myers.edu

Notre Dame College of Ohio 4545 College Rd ... South Euclid OH 44121 216-381-1680 373-5278*
*Fax: Admissions ■ TF: 877-632-6446 ■ Web: www.ndc.edu

Oberlin College 173 W Lorain St ... Oberlin OH 44074 440-775-8121 775-6905*
*Fax: Admissions ■ Web: www.oberlin.edu

Ohio Dominican University 1216 Sunbury Rd ... Columbus OH 43219 614-251-4500 251-0156*
*Fax: Admissions ■ TF: 800-955-6446 ■ Web: www.ohiodominican.edu

Ohio Northern University 525 S Main St ... Ada OH 45810 419-772-2000 772-2313*
*Fax: Admissions ■ TF Admissions: 888-408-4668 ■ Web: www.onu.edu

Ohio State University 154 W 12th Ave ... Columbus OH 43210 614-292-3980 292-4818*
*Fax: Admissions ■ Web: www.osu.edu

Lima 4240 Campus Dr ... Lima OH 45804 419-995-8600 995-8483
Web: lima.osu.edu/

Mansfield 1760 University Dr ... Mansfield OH 44906 419-755-4011 755-3091*
*Fax: Admissions ■ Web: mansfield.osu.edu

Marion 1465 Mt Vernon Ave ... Marion OH 43302 614-292-9133 725-6258*
*Fax: Admissions ■ Web: www.marion.ohio-state.edu

Newark 1179 University Dr ... Newark OH 43055 740-366-3321 364-9645*
*Fax: Admissions ■ Web: newark.osu.edu

Ohio University 120 Chubb Hall ... Athens OH 45701 740-593-1000 593-0560*
*Fax: Admissions ■ Web: www.ohio.edu

Chillicothe 101 University Dr ... Chillicothe OH 45601 740-774-7200 774-7214*
*Fax: Admissions ■ TF: 877-462-6824 ■ Web: oucweb.chillicothe.ohiou.edu

Eastern 45425 National Rd ... Saint Clairsville OH 43950 740-695-1720 695-7079*
*Fax: Admissions ■ TF: 800-648-3331 ■ Web: www.eastern.ohiou.edu

Lancaster 1570 Granville Pike ... Lancaster OH 43130 740-654-6711 687-9497*
*Fax: Admissions ■ Web: www.lancaster.ohiou.edu

Southern 1804 Liberty Ave ... Ironton OH 45638 740-533-4600 533-4632*
*Fax: Admissions ■ TF: 800-626-0513 ■ Web: www.southern.ohiou.edu

Zanesville 1425 Newark Rd ... Zanesville OH 43701 740-453-0762 453-6161
Web: www.zanesville.ohiou.edu

Ohio Wesleyan University 61 S Sandusky St Slocum Hall ... Delaware OH 43015 740-368-3020 368-3314*
*Fax: Admissions ■ Web: web.owu.edu

Otterbein College 1 Otterbein College ... Westerville OH 43081 614-823-1500 823-1200*
*Fax: Admissions ■ TF Admissions: 800-488-8144 ■ Web: www.otterbein.edu

Shawnee State University 940 2nd St ... Portsmouth OH 45662 740-351-3221 351-3111
TF: 800-959-2778 ■ Web: www.shawnee.edu

Tiffin University 155 Miami St ... Tiffin OH 44883 419-447-6442 443-5006
TF: 800-968-6446 ■ Web: www.tiffin.edu

Union Institute & University 440 E McMillan St ... Cincinnati OH 45206 513-861-6400 861-0779*
*Fax: Admissions ■ TF: 800-486-3116 ■ Web: www.tui.edu

University of Akron 277 E Buchtel Ave ... Akron OH 44325 330-972-7100 972-7022
TF Admissions: 800-655-4884 ■ Web: www.uakron.edu

University of Cincinnati 2600 Clifton Ave ... Cincinnati OH 45221 513-556-6000 556-1105*
*Fax: Admissions ■ Web: www.uc.edu

University of Dayton 300 College Park ... Dayton OH 45469 937-229-4411 229-4729*
*Fax: Admissions ■ TF: 800-837-7433 ■ Web: www.udayton.edu

University of Findlay 1000 N Main St ... Findlay OH 45840 419-422-8313 434-4822
TF: 800-472-9502 ■ Web: www.findlay.edu

University of Rio Grande 218 N College Ave ... Rio Grande OH 45674 740-245-5353 245-7260*
*Fax: Admissions ■ TF: 800-282-7201 ■ Web: www.rio.edu

University of Toledo 2801 W Bancroft St ... Toledo OH 43606 419-530-4636 530-5745*
*Fax: Admissions ■ TF: 800-586-5336 ■ Web: www.utoledo.edu

Urbana University 579 College Way ... Urbana OH 43078 937-484-1400 652-6871*
*Fax: Admissions ■ TF: 800-787-2262 ■ Web: www.urbana.edu

Ursuline College 2550 Lander Rd ... Pepper Pike OH 44124 440-449-4200 684-6138*
*Fax: Admissions ■ TF: 888-877-8546 ■ Web: www.ursuline.edu

Walsh University 2020 E Maple St ... North Canton OH 44720 330-499-7090 490-7165*
*Fax: Admissions ■ TF Admissions: 800-362-9846 ■ Web: www.walsh.edu

Wilberforce University 1055 N Bickett Rd PO Box 1001 ... Wilberforce OH 45384 937-376-2911 376-4751*
*Fax: Admissions ■ TF Admissions: 800-367-8568 ■ Web: www.wilberforce.edu

Wilmington College of Ohio 251 Ludovic St ... Wilmington OH 45177 937-382-6661 383-8542*
*Fax: Admissions ■ TF: 800-341-9318 ■ Web: www.wilmington.edu

Wittenberg University 200 W Ward St PO Box 720 ... Springfield OH 45501 937-327-6314 327-6379*
*Fax: Admissions ■ TF: 800-677-7558 ■ Web: www.wittenberg.edu

Wright State University 3640 Colonel Glenn Hwy ... Dayton OH 45435 937-775-5740 775-5795*
*Fax: Admissions ■ TF Admissions: 800-247-1770 ■ Web: www.wright.edu

Xavier University 3800 Victory Pkwy ... Cincinnati OH 45207 513-745-3000 745-4319*
*Fax: Admissions ■ TF: 800-344-4698 ■ Web: www.xavier.edu

Youngstown State University 1 University Plaza ... Youngstown OH 44555 330-941-3000 941-3694*
*Fax: Admissions ■ TF Admissions: 877-468-6978 ■ Web: www.ysu.edu

Oklahoma

Phone | Fax

Bacone College 2299 Old Bacone Rd ... Muskogee OK 74403 918-683-4581 781-7416*
*Fax: Admissions ■ TF Admissions: 888-682-5514 ■ Web: www.bacone.edu

Cameron University 2800 W Gore Blvd ... Lawton OK 73505 580-581-2289 581-5514*
*Fax: Admissions ■ TF Admissions: 888-454-7600 ■ Web: www.cameron.edu

East Central University 1100 E 14th St ... Ada OK 74820 580-332-8000 310-5432*
*Fax: Admissions ■ Web: www.ecok.edu

Hillsdale Free Will Baptist College PO Box 7208 ... Moore OK 73153 405-912-9000 912-9050*
*Fax: Admissions ■ Web: www.hc.edu

Langston University Hwy 33 PO Box 1500 ... Langston OK 73050 405-466-3428 466-3391
TF: 877-466-2231 ■ Web: www.lunet.edu

Mid-America Christian University 3500 SW 119th St ... Oklahoma City OK 73170 405-691-3800 692-3165*
*Fax: Admissions ■ Web: www.macu.edu

Northeastern State University

Broken Arrow 3100 E New Orleans ... Broken Arrow OK 74014 918-449-6000 449-6147*
*Fax: Admissions ■ TF: 800-772-9614 ■ Web: www.nsuba.edu

Muskogee 2400 W Shawnee ... Muskogee OK 74401 918-683-0040 458-2106
TF: 800-722-9614 ■ Web: www.nsuok.edu/muskogee

Tahlequah 601 N Grand Ave ... Tahlequah OK 74464 918-456-5511 458-2342*
*Fax: Admissions ■ TF: 800-722-9614 ■ Web: www.nsuok.edu

Northwestern Oklahoma State University 709 Oklahoma Blvd ... Alva OK 73717 580-327-1700 327-8699
Web: www.nwalva.edu

Oklahoma Baptist University 500 W University St ... Shawnee OK 74804 405-275-2850 878-2068*
*Fax: Admissions ■ TF: 800-654-3285 ■ Web: www.okbu.edu

Oklahoma Christian University PO Box 11000 ... Oklahoma City OK 73136 405-425-5000 425-5069*
*Fax: Admissions ■ TF: 800-877-5010 ■ Web: www.oc.edu

Oklahoma City University 2501 N Blackwelder Ave ... Oklahoma City OK 73106 405-208-5050 208-5916*
*Fax: Admissions ■ TF Admissions: 800-633-7242 ■ Web: www.okcu.edu

Phone | Fax

Oklahoma Panhandle State University 323 Eagle Blvd ... Goodwell OK 73939 580-349-2611 349-2302*
*Fax: Admitting ■ TF: 800-664-6778 ■ Web: www.opsu.edu

Oklahoma State University 219 Student Union Bldg ... Stillwater OK 74078 405-744-5000 744-7092
TF: 800-852-1255 ■ Web: www.okstate.edu

Tulsa 700 N Greenwood Ave ... Tulsa OK 74106 918-594-8000 594-8202
TF: 800-364-0710 ■ Web: www.osu-tulsa.okstate.edu

Oklahoma Wesleyan University 2201 Silver Lake Rd ... Bartlesville OK 74006 918-333-6200 335-6229*
*Fax: Admissions ■ TF: 800-468-6292 ■ Web: www.okwu.edu

Oral Roberts University 7777 S Lewis Ave ... Tulsa OK 74171 918-495-6161 495-6222*
*Fax: Admissions ■ TF: 800-678-8876 ■ Web: www.oru.edu

Rogers State University 1701 W Will Rogers Blvd ... Claremore OK 74017 918-343-7546 343-7595*
*Fax: Admissions ■ TF: 800-256-7511 ■ Web: www.rsu.edu

Saint Gregory's University 1900 W MacArthur St ... Shawnee OK 74804 405-878-5100 878-5198
TF Admissions: 888-784-7347 ■ Web: www.stgregorys.edu

Southeastern Oklahoma State University 1405 N 4th St ... Durant OK 74701 580-745-2000 745-7502*
*Fax: Admissions ■ TF: 800-435-1327 ■ Web: www.sosu.edu

Southern Nazarene University 6729 NW 39th Expy ... Bethany OK 73008 405-789-6400 491-6320*
*Fax: Admissions ■ TF: 800-648-9899 ■ Web: www.snu.edu

Southwestern Christian University 7210 NW 39th Expy ... Bethany OK 73008 405-789-7661 495-0078*
*Fax: Admissions ■ Web: www.swcu.edu

Southwestern Oklahoma State University 100 Campus Dr ... Weatherford OK 73096 580-772-6611 774-3795
Web: www.swosu.edu

University of Central Oklahoma 100 N University Dr ... Edmond OK 73034 405-974-2000 974-3841*
*Fax: Admissions ■ Web: www.ucok.edu

University of Oklahoma 1000 Asp Ave ... Norman OK 73019 405-325-0311 325-7124
TF: 877-522-0772 ■ Web: www.ou.edu

University of Sciences & Arts of Oklahoma
1727 W Alabama Ave ... Chickasha OK 73018 405-224-3140 574-1220*
*Fax: Admissions ■ TF: 800-933-8726 ■ Web: www.usao.edu

University of Tulsa 600 S College Ave ... Tulsa OK 74104 918-631-2307 631-5003*
*Fax: Admissions ■ TF: 800-331-3050 ■ Web: www.utulsa.edu

Oregon

Phone | Fax

Cascade College 9101 E Burnside St ... Portland OR 97216 503-255-7060 257-1222*
*Fax: Admissions ■ TF Admissions: 800-550-7678 ■ Web: www.cascade.edu

Concordia University Portland 2811 NE Holman St ... Portland OR 97211 503-288-9371 280-8531*
*Fax: Admissions ■ TF: 800-321-9371 ■ Web: www.cu-portland.edu

Corban College 5000 Deer Park Dr SE ... Salem OR 97317 503-581-8600 585-4316
TF: 800-845-3005 ■ Web: www.corban.edu

Eastern Oregon University 1 University Blvd ... La Grande OR 97850 541-962-3393 962-3418*
*Fax: Admissions ■ TF: 800-452-8639 ■ Web: www.eou.edu

George Fox University 414 N Meridian St ... Newberg OR 97132 503-538-8383 554-3110*
*Fax: Admissions ■ TF: 800-765-4369 ■ Web: www.georgefox.edu

Gutenberg College 1883 University St ... Eugene OR 97403 541-683-5141 683-6997
Web: www.gutenberg.edu

Lewis & Clark College 0615 SW Palatine Hill Rd ... Portland OR 97219 503-768-7040 768-7055*
*Fax: Admissions ■ TF Admissions: 800-444-4111 ■ Web: www.lclark.edu

Linfield College 900 SE Baker St ... McMinnville OR 97128 503-883-2213 883-2472*
*Fax: Admissions ■ TF Admissions: 800-640-2287 ■ Web: www.linfield.edu

Marylhurst University 17600 Pacific Hwy 43 PO Box 261 ... Marylhurst OR 97036 503-636-8141 635-6585*
*Fax: Admissions ■ TF: 800-634-9982 ■ Web: www.marylhurst.edu

Northwest Christian College 828 E 11th Ave ... Eugene OR 97401 541-684-7201 684-7317*
*Fax: Admissions ■ TF: 877-463-6622 ■ Web: www.nwcc.edu

Oregon Health & Science University Hospital
3181 SW Sam Jackson Park Rd ... Portland OR 97239 503-494-8311 494-3400
Web: www.ohsu.edu

Oregon Institute of Technology 3201 Campus Dr ... Klamath Falls OR 97601 541-885-1150 885-1024*
*Fax: Admissions ■ TF: 800-422-2017 ■ Web: www.oit.edu

Oregon State University 104 Kerr Administration Bldg ... Corvallis OR 97331 541-737-4411 737-2482
TF: 800-291-4192 ■ Web: oregonstate.edu

Pacific Northwest College of Art 1241 NW Johnson St ... Portland OR 97209 503-226-4391 821-8978
TF: 888-390-7499 ■ Web: www.pnca.edu

Pacific University 2043 College Way ... Forest Grove OR 97116 503-352-2794 352-2975*
*Fax: Admissions ■ TF Admissions: 800-677-6712 ■ Web: www.pacificu.edu

Portland State University 724 SW Harrison St ... Portland OR 97201 503-725-3000 725-5525*
*Fax: Admissions ■ TF: 800-547-8887 ■ Web: www.pdx.edu

Reed College 3203 SE Woodstock Blvd ... Portland OR 97202 503-777-7511 777-7553
TF Admissions: 800-547-4750 ■ Web: www.reed.edu

Southern Oregon University 1250 Siskiyou Blvd ... Ashland OR 97520 541-552-7672 552-6614*
*Fax: Admissions ■ Web: www.sou.edu

University of Oregon 1585 E 13th Ave ... Eugene OR 97403 541-346-1000 346-5815*
*Fax: Admissions ■ TF Admissions: 800-232-3825 ■ Web: www.uoregon.edu

University of Portland 5000 N Willamette Blvd ... Portland OR 97203 503-943-7147 943-7315*
*Fax: Admissions ■ TF: 888-627-5601 ■ Web: www.up.edu

Warner Pacific College 2219 SE 68th Ave ... Portland OR 97215 503-517-1020 517-1352
TF: 800-804-1510 ■ Web: www1.warnerpacific.edu

Western Oregon University 345 Monmouth Ave N ... Monmouth OR 97361 503-838-8000 838-8067
TF Admissions: 877-877-1593 ■ Web: www.wou.edu

Willamette University 900 State St ... Salem OR 97301 503-370-6303 375-5363*
*Fax: Admissions ■ TF: 877-542-2787 ■ Web: www.willamette.edu

Pennsylvania

Phone | Fax

Albright College PO Box 15234 ... Reading PA 19612 610-921-2381 921-7294*
*Fax: Admissions ■ TF Admissions: 800-252-1856 ■ Web: www.albright.edu

Allegheny College 520 N Main St ... Meadville PA 16335 814-332-4351 337-0431
TF: 800-521-5293 ■ Web: www.allegheny.edu

Alvernia College 400 Saint Bernadine St ... Reading PA 19611 610-796-8200 796-8336*
*Fax: Admissions ■ TF: 888-258-3764 ■ Web: www.alvernia.edu

Arcadia University 450 S Easton Rd ... Glenside PA 19038 215-572-2900 881-8767*
*Fax: Admissions ■ TF: 877-272-2342 ■ Web: www.arcadia.edu

Bloomsburg University 400 E 2nd St ... Bloomsburg PA 17815 570-389-3900 389-4741*
*Fax: Admissions ■ TF: 800-745-7320 ■ Web: www.bloomu.edu

Bryn Athyn College of the New Church
2965 College Dr PO Box 717 ... Bryn Athyn PA 19009 267-502-2543 502-2658
Web: www.brynathyn.edu

Bryn Mawr College 101 N Merion Ave ... Bryn Mawr PA 19010 610-526-5000 526-7471*
*Fax: Admissions ■ TF Admissions: 800-262-1885 ■ Web: www.brynmawr.edu

Bucknell University ... Lewisburg PA 17837 570-577-2000 577-1345*
*Fax: Admissions ■ Web: www.bucknell.edu

Cabrini College 610 King of Prussia Rd ... Radnor PA 19087 610-902-8552 902-8508*
*Fax: Acctg ■ TF: 800-848-1003 ■ Web: www.cabrini.edu

California University of Pennsylvania 250 University Ave ... California PA 15419 724-938-4000 938-4564
Web: www.cup.edu

Carlow University 3333 5th Ave ... Pittsburgh PA 15213 412-578-6000 578-6689
TF: 800-333-2275 ■ Web: www.carlow.edu

Carnegie Mellon University 5000 Forbes Ave ... Pittsburgh PA 15213 412-268-2000 268-7838*
*Fax: Admissions ■ Web: www.cmu.edu

Cedar Crest College 100 College Dr ... Allentown PA 18104 610-437-4471 606-4647*
*Fax: Admissions ■ TF Admissions: 800-360-1222 ■ Web: www.cedarcrest.edu

Chatham University Woodland Rd ... Pittsburgh PA 15232 412-365-1100 365-1609*
*Fax: Admissions ■ TF: 800-837-1290 ■ Web: www.chatham.edu

Pennsylvania (Cont'd)

	City	State	ZIP	Phone	Fax
Chestnut Hill College 9601 Germantown Ave	Philadelphia	PA	19118	215-248-7001	248-7082*
**Fax:* Admissions ■ *TF:* 800-248-0052 ■ *Web:* www.chc.edu					
Cheyney University of Pennsylvania					
1837 University Cir PO Box 200	Cheyney	PA	19319	610-399-2275	399-2099*
**Fax:* Admissions ■ *TF:* 800-243-9639 ■ *Web:* www.cheyney.edu					
Clarion University of Pennsylvania 840 Wood St	Clarion	PA	16214	814-393-2306	393-2030*
**Fax:* Admissions ■ *TF:* 800-672-7171 ■ *Web:* www.clarion.edu					
Venango 1801 W 1st St	Oil City	PA	16301	814-676-6591	676-1348
TF: 800-672-7171 ■ *Web:* www.clarion.edu/academic/venango					
College Misericordia 301 Lake St	Dallas	PA	18612	570-674-6400	675-2441*
**Fax:* Admissions ■ *TF:* 866-262-6363					
Curtis Institute of Music 1726 Locust St	Philadelphia	PA	19103	215-893-5252	893-9065
Web: www.curtis.edu					
Delaware Valley College 700 E Butler Ave	Doylestown	PA	18901	215-489-2211	230-2968
TF Admissions: 800-233-5825 ■ *Web:* www.devalcol.edu					
DeSales University 2755 Station Ave	Center Valley	PA	18034	610-282-1100	282-0131
TF: 877-433-7253 ■ *Web:* www.desales.edu					
Dickinson College PO Box 1773	Carlisle	PA	17013	717-245-1231	245-1442*
**Fax:* Admissions ■ *TF:* 800-644-1773 ■ *Web:* www.dickinson.edu					
Drexel University 3141 Chestnut St	Philadelphia	PA	19104	215-895-2000	895-5939*
**Fax:* Admissions ■ *TF Admissions:* 800-237-3935 ■ *Web:* www.drexel.edu					
Duquesne University 600 Forbes Ave	Pittsburgh	PA	15282	412-396-6000	396-6223*
**Fax:* Admissions ■ *TF:* 800-456-0590 ■ *Web:* www.duq.edu					
East Stroudsburg University 200 Prospect St	East Stroudsburg	PA	18301	570-422-3542	422-3933*
**Fax:* Admissions ■ *TF Admissions:* 877-230-5547 ■ *Web:* www.esu.edu					
Eastern University 1300 Eagle Rd	Saint Davids	PA	19087	610-341-5800	341-1723*
**Fax:* Admissions ■ *TF Admissions:* 800-452-0996 ■ *Web:* www.eastern.edu					
Edinboro University of Pennsylvania 148 Meadville St	Edinboro	PA	16444	814-732-2761	732-2420*
**Fax:* Admissions ■ *TF:* 888-846-2676 ■ *Web:* www.edinboro.edu					
Elizabethtown College 1 Alpha Dr	Elizabethtown	PA	17022	717-361-1000	361-1365*
**Fax:* Admissions ■ *Web:* www.etown.edu					
Franklin & Marshall College PO Box 3003	Lancaster	PA	17604	717-291-3951	291-4389*
**Fax:* Admissions ■ *TF:* 877-678-9111 ■ *Web:* www.fandm.edu					
Gannon University 109 University Sq	Erie	PA	16541	814-871-7000	871-5803
TF Admissions: 800-426-6668 ■ *Web:* www.gannon.edu					
Geneva College 3200 College Ave	Beaver Falls	PA	15010	724-847-6500	847-6776*
**Fax:* Admissions ■ *TF:* 800-847-8255 ■ *Web:* www.geneva.edu					
Gettysburg College 300 N Washington St	Gettysburg	PA	17325	717-337-6000	337-6145*
**Fax:* Admissions ■ *TF:* 800-431-0803 ■ *Web:* www.gettysburg.edu					
Gratz College 7605 Old York Rd	Melrose Park	PA	19027	215-635-7300	635-7320*
**Fax:* Admissions ■ *TF:* 800-475-4635 ■ *Web:* www.gratz.edu					
Grove City College 100 Campus Dr	Grove City	PA	16127	724-458-2000	458-3395*
**Fax:* Admissions ■ *Web:* www.gcc.edu					
Gwynedd-Mercy College					
1325 Sumneytown Pike PO Box 901	Gwynedd Valley	PA	19437	215-646-7300	641-5556*
**Fax:* Admissions ■ *TF Admissions:* 800-342-5462 ■ *Web:* www.gmc.edu					
Haverford College 370 W Lancaster Ave	Haverford	PA	19041	610-896-1000	896-1338*
**Fax:* Admissions ■ *Web:* www.haverford.edu					
Holy Family University 9801 Frankford Ave	Philadelphia	PA	19114	215-637-7700	281-1022*
**Fax:* Admissions ■ *TF:* 877-438-4643 ■ *Web:* www.hfc.edu					
Immaculata University 1145 King Rd	Immaculata	PA	19345	610-647-4400	640-0836*
**Fax:* Admissions ■ *TF:* 877-428-6329 ■ *Web:* www.immaculata.edu					
Indiana University of Pennsylvania					
Sutton Hall 1011 South Dr Suite 117	Indiana	PA	15705	724-357-2230	357-6281*
**Fax:* Admissions ■ *TF:* 800-442-6830 ■ *Web:* www.iup.edu					
Juniata College 1700 Moore St	Huntingdon	PA	16652	814-641-3000	641-3100*
**Fax:* Admissions ■ *TF:* 877-586-4282 ■ *Web:* www.juniata.edu					
Keystone College 1 College Green	La Plume	PA	18440	570-945-8111	945-7916*
**Fax:* Admissions ■ *TF:* 877-426-5534 ■ *Web:* www.keystone.edu					
King's College 133 N River St	Wilkes-Barre	PA	18711	570-208-5858	208-5971*
**Fax:* Admissions ■ *TF:* 800-955-5777 ■ *Web:* www.kings.edu					
Kutztown University PO Box 730	Kutztown	PA	19530	610-683-4000	683-1375*
**Fax:* Admissions ■ *TF:* 877-628-1915 ■ *Web:* www.kutztown.edu					
La Roche College 9000 Babcock Blvd	Pittsburgh	PA	15237	412-367-9300	536-1048*
**Fax:* Admissions ■ *TF Admissions:* 800-838-4572 ■ *Web:* www.laroche.edu					
La Salle University 1900 W Olney Ave	Philadelphia	PA	19141	215-951-1500	951-1656*
**Fax:* Admissions ■ *TF:* 800-328-1910 ■ *Web:* www.lasalle.edu					
Lafayette College 118 Markle Hall	Easton	PA	18042	610-330-5000	330-5355*
**Fax:* Admissions ■ *Web:* www.lafayette.edu					
Lebanon Valley College 101 N College Ave	Annville	PA	17003	717-867-6181	867-6026*
**Fax:* Admissions ■ *TF:* 866-582-4236 ■ *Web:* www.lvc.edu					
Lehigh University 27 Memorial Dr W	Bethlehem	PA	18015	610-758-3000	758-4361*
**Fax:* Admissions ■ *Web:* www3.lehigh.edu					
Lincoln University					
1570 Old Baltimore Pike PO Box 179	Lincoln University	PA	19352	610-932-8300	932-1209*
**Fax:* Admissions ■ *TF Admissions:* 800-790-0191 ■ *Web:* www.lincoln.edu					
Lock Haven University	Lock Haven	PA	17745	570-893-2011	893-2201*
**Fax:* Admissions ■ *TF:* 800-233-8978 ■ *Web:* www.lhup.edu					
Lycoming College 700 College Pl	Williamsport	PA	17701	570-321-4000	321-4317*
**Fax:* Admissions ■ *TF:* 800-345-3920 ■ *Web:* www.lycoming.edu					
Mansfield University Alumni Hall	Mansfield	PA	16933	570-662-4000	662-4121
TF Admissions: 800-577-6826 ■ *Web:* www.mansfield.edu					
Marywood University 2300 Adams Ave	Scranton	PA	18509	570-348-6234	961-4763*
**Fax:* Admissions ■ *TF:* 866-279-9663 ■ *Web:* www.marywood.edu					
Mercyhurst College 501 E 38th St	Erie	PA	16546	814-824-2202	824-2071*
**Fax:* Admissions ■ *TF:* 800-825-1926 ■ *Web:* www.mercyhurst.edu					
Messiah College Box 3005	Grantham	PA	17027	717-691-6000	796-5374*
**Fax:* Admissions ■ *TF:* 800-233-4220 ■ *Web:* www.messiah.edu					
Millersville University of Pennsylvania PO Box 1002	Millersville	PA	17551	717-872-3011	871-2147*
**Fax:* Admissions ■ *TF:* 800-682-3648 ■ *Web:* muweb.millersville.edu					
Moravian College 1200 Main St	Bethlehem	PA	18018	610-861-1300	625-7930*
**Fax:* Admissions ■ *Web:* www.moravian.edu					
Mount Aloysius College 7373 Admiral Perry Hwy	Cresson	PA	16630	814-886-6383	886-6441
TF: 888-823-2220 ■ *Web:* www.mtaloy.edu					
Muhlenberg College 2400 Chew St	Allentown	PA	18104	484-664-3100	664-3234
Web: www.muhlberg.edu					
Neumann College 1 Neumann Dr	Aston	PA	19014	610-459-0905	459-1370*
**Fax:* Admissions ■ *TF:* 800-963-8626 ■ *Web:* www.neumann.edu					
Peirce College 1420 Pine St	Philadelphia	PA	19102	215-545-6400	670-9366*
**Fax:* Admissions ■ *TF:* 888-467-3472 ■ *Web:* www.peirce.edu					
Penn State 201 Shields Bldg Office of Admissions	University Park	PA	16802	814-865-4700	863-7590
Web: www.psu.edu					
Penn State Abington 1600 Woodland Rd	Abington	PA	19001	215-881-7300	881-7412*
**Fax:* Admissions ■ *Web:* www.abington.psu.edu					
Penn State Altoona 3000 Ivyside Pk	Altoona	PA	16601	814-949-5466	949-5564*
**Fax:* Admissions ■ *TF:* 800-848-9843 ■ *Web:* www.aa.psu.edu					
Penn State Delaware County 25 Yearsley Mill Rd	Media	PA	19063	610-892-1200	863-9419*
**Fax Area Code:* 814 ■ **Fax:* Admissions ■ *Web:* www.brandywine.psu.edu					
Penn State Erie 5091 Station Rd	Erie	PA	16563	814-898-6000	898-6044*
**Fax:* Admissions ■ *Web:* www.pserie.psu.edu					
Pennsylvania State University					
201 Shields Bldg Office of Admissions	University Park	PA	16802	814-865-4700	863-7590
Web: www.psu.edu					
Abington College 1600 Woodland Rd	Abington	PA	19001	215-881-7300	881-7412*
**Fax:* Admissions ■ *Web:* www.abington.psu.edu					
Altoona 3000 Ivyside Pk	Altoona	PA	16601	814-949-5466	949-5564*
**Fax:* Admissions ■ *TF:* 800-848-9843 ■ *Web:* www.aa.psu.edu					
Brandywine 25 Yearsley Mill Rd	Media	PA	19063	610-892-1200	863-9419*
**Fax Area Code:* 814 ■ *Web:* www.brandywine.psu.edu					
Harrisburg 777 W Harrisburg Pike	Middletown	PA	17057	717-948-6250	948-6325*
**Fax:* Admissions ■ *TF:* 800-222-2056 ■ *Web:* www.hbg.psu.edu					
Pennsylvania State University at Erie Behrend College					
5091 Station Rd	Erie	PA	16563	814-898-6000	898-6044*
**Fax:* Admissions ■ *Web:* www.pserie.psu.edu					
Philadelphia University 4201 Henry Ave	Philadelphia	PA	19144	215-951-2800	951-2907*
**Fax:* Admissions ■ *TF Admissions:* 800-951-7287 ■ *Web:* www.philau.edu					
Point Park University 201 Wood St	Pittsburgh	PA	15222	412-391-4100	392-3902*
**Fax:* Admissions ■ *TF Admissions:* 800-321-0129 ■ *Web:* www.pointpark.edu					
Robert Morris University 6001 University Blvd	Moon Township	PA	15108	412-262-8200	397-2425
TF: 800-762-0097 ■ *Web:* www.rmu.edu					
Rosemont College 1400 Montgomery Ave	Rosemont	PA	19010	610-527-0200	520-4399*
**Fax:* Admissions ■ *TF Admissions:* 800-331-0708 ■ *Web:* www.rosemont.edu					
Saint Francis University 167 Lakeview Dr	Loretto	PA	15940	814-472-3000	472-3335*
**Fax:* Admissions ■ *TF:* 866-342-5738 ■ *Web:* www.saintfrancisuniversity.edu					
Saint Joseph's University 5600 City Ave	Philadelphia	PA	19131	610-660-1000	660-1314*
**Fax:* Admissions ■ *TF:* 888-232-4295 ■ *Web:* www.sju.edu					
Saint Vincent College 300 Fraser Purchase Rd	Latrobe	PA	15650	724-532-6600	805-2953*
**Fax:* Admissions ■ *TF:* 800-782-5549 ■ *Web:* www.stvincent.edu					
Seton Hill University 1 Seton Hill Dr	Greensburg	PA	15601	724-838-4255	830-1294*
**Fax:* Admissions ■ *TF:* 800-826-6234 ■ *Web:* www.setonhill.edu					
Shippensburg University 1871 Old Main Dr	Shippensburg	PA	17257	717-532-9121	477-4016*
**Fax:* Admissions ■ *Web:* www.ship.edu					
Slippery Rock University 1 Morrow Way	Slippery Rock	PA	16057	724-738-9000	738-2913*
**Fax:* Admissions ■ *TF:* 800-929-4778 ■ *Web:* www.sru.edu					
Susquehanna University 514 University Ave	Selinsgrove	PA	17870	570-374-0101	372-2722
TF: 800-326-9672 ■ *Web:* www.susqu.edu					
Swarthmore College 500 College Ave	Swarthmore	PA	19081	610-328-8300	328-8580*
**Fax:* Admissions ■ *TF Admissions:* 800-667-3110 ■ *Web:* www.swarthmore.edu					
Temple University 1801 N Broad St	Philadelphia	PA	19122	215-204-7000	204-5694
Web: www.temple.edu					
Ambler 580 Meetinghouse Rd	Ambler	PA	19002	267-468-8100	468-8110*
**Fax:* Admissions ■ *TF:* 888-462-6253 ■ *Web:* www.ambler.temple.edu					
Thiel College 75 College Ave	Greenville	PA	16125	724-589-2000	589-2013*
**Fax:* Admissions ■ *TF:* 800-248-4435 ■ *Web:* www.thiel.edu					
Thomas Jefferson University 1020 Walnut St	Philadelphia	PA	19107	215-955-6000	955-5151
Web: www.jefferson.edu					
University of Pennsylvania 1 College Hall Rm 1	Philadelphia	PA	19104	215-898-7507	898-9670*
**Fax:* Admissions ■ *Web:* www.upenn.edu					
University of Pittsburgh 4227 5th Ave	Pittsburgh	PA	15260	412-624-4141	648-8815*
**Fax:* Admissions ■ *Web:* www.pitt.edu					
Bradford 300 Campus Dr	Bradford	PA	16701	814-362-7555	362-5150
TF: 800-872-1787 ■ *Web:* www.upb.pitt.edu					
Greensburg 150 Finoli Dr	Greensburg	PA	15601	724-837-7040	836-7160*
**Fax:* Admissions ■ *Web:* www.upg.pitt.edu					
Johnstown 157 Blackington Hall	Johnstown	PA	15904	814-269-7050	269-7044
TF: 800-765-4875 ■ *Web:* www.upj.pitt.edu					
University of the Sciences in Philadelphia 600 S 43rd St	Philadelphia	PA	19104	215-596-8800	596-8821*
**Fax:* Admissions ■ *TF:* 866-304-8747 ■ *Web:* www.usip.edu					
University of Scranton 800 Linden St St Thomas Hall	Scranton	PA	18510	570-941-7400	941-5928*
**Fax:* Admissions ■ *TF:* 888-727-2686 ■ *Web:* matrix.scranton.edu					
Ursinus College 601 E Main St PO Box 1000	Collegeville	PA	19426	610-409-3200	409-3662*
**Fax:* Admissions ■ *Web:* www.ursinus.edu					
Valley Forge Christian College 1401 Charlestown Rd	Phoenixville	PA	19460	610-935-0450	917-2069*
**Fax:* Admissions ■ *TF:* 800-432-8322 ■ *Web:* www.vfcc.edu					
Villanova University 800 Lancaster Ave	Villanova	PA	19085	610-519-4500	519-6450
TF: 800-634-8773 ■ *Web:* www.villanova.edu					
Washington & Jefferson College 60 S Lincoln St	Washington	PA	15301	724-222-4400	223-6534*
**Fax:* Admissions ■ *TF:* 888-926-3529 ■ *Web:* www.washjeff.edu					
Waynesburg College 51 W College St	Waynesburg	PA	15370	724-627-8191	627-8124*
**Fax:* Admissions ■ *TF Admissions:* 800-225-7393 ■ *Web:* www.waynesburg.edu					
West Chester University 700 S High St	West Chester	PA	19383	610-436-1000	436-2907*
**Fax:* Admissions ■ *TF:* 877-315-2165 ■ *Web:* www.wcupa.edu					
Westminster College 319 S Market St	New Wilmington	PA	16172	724-946-8761	946-6171*
**Fax:* Admissions ■ *TF:* 800-942-8033 ■ *Web:* www.westminster.edu					
Widener University 1 University Pl	Chester	PA	19013	610-499-4000	499-4676*
**Fax:* Admissions ■ *TF Admissions:* 888-943-3637 ■ *Web:* www.widener.edu					
Wilkes University 84 W South St	Wilkes-Barre	PA	18766	570-824-4651	408-4904*
**Fax:* Admissions ■ *TF:* 800-945-5378 ■ *Web:* www.wilkes.edu					
Wilson College 1015 Philadelphia Ave	Chambersburg	PA	17201	717-264-4141	264-1578*
**Fax:* Admissions ■ *TF Admissions:* 800-421-8402 ■ *Web:* www.wilson.edu					
York College of Pennsylvania 441 Country Club Rd	York	PA	17403	717-846-7788	
Web: www.ycp.edu					

Rhode Island

	City	State	ZIP	Phone	Fax
Brown University 45 Prospect St	Providence	RI	02912	401-863-2378	863-9300*
**Fax:* Admissions ■ *Web:* www.brown.edu					
Bryant University 1150 Douglas Pike	Smithfield	RI	02917	401-232-6000	232-6741*
**Fax:* Admissions ■ *TF Admissions:* 800-622-7001 ■ *Web:* www.bryant.edu					
Johnson & Wales University Providence 8 Abbott Park Pl	Providence	RI	02903	401-598-1000	598-4641
TF: 800-342-5598 ■ *Web:* www.jwu.edu					
Providence College 549 River Ave	Providence	RI	02918	401-865-1000	865-2826*
**Fax:* Admissions ■ *TF Admissions:* 800-721-6444 ■ *Web:* www.providence.edu					
Rhode Island College 600 Mt Pleasant Ave	Providence	RI	02908	401-456-8000	456-8817
TF: 800-669-5760 ■ *Web:* www.ric.edu					
Roger Williams University 1 Old Ferry Rd	Bristol	RI	02809	401-254-3500	254-3557*
**Fax:* Admissions ■ *TF:* 800-458-7144 ■ *Web:* www.rwu.edu					
Salve Regina University 100 Ochre Point Ave	Newport	RI	02840	401-847-6650	848-2823*
**Fax:* Admissions ■ *TF:* 888-467-2583 ■ *Web:* www.salve.edu					
University of Rhode Island 12 Upper College Rd	Kingston	RI	02881	401-874-7100	874-5523*
**Fax:* Admissions ■ *Web:* www.uri.edu					
Feinstein Providence 80 Washington St	Providence	RI	02903	401-277-5000	277-5168
Web: www.uri.edu/prov.htm					

South Carolina

	City	State	ZIP	Phone	Fax
Allen University 1530 Harden St	Columbia	SC	29204	803-376-5700	376-5733*
**Fax:* Mail Rm ■ *TF:* 877-625-5368 ■ *Web:* www.allenuniversity.edu					
Anderson University 316 Blvd	Anderson	SC	29621	864-231-2030	231-2033
TF: 800-542-3594 ■ *Web:* www.ac.edu					
Benedict College 1600 Harden St	Columbia	SC	29204	803-256-5000	
TF: 800-868-6598 ■ *Web:* www.benedict.edu					
Bob Jones University 1700 Wade Hampton Blvd	Greenville	SC	29614	864-242-5100	232-9258*
**Fax Area Code:* 800 ■ **Fax:* Admissions ■ *TF Admissions:* 800-252-6363 ■ *Web:* www.bju.edu					
Cathedral Bible College 803 Howard Pkwy	Myrtle Beach	SC	29577	843-477-1503	477-1627

	City	State	Zip	Phone	Fax
Charleston Southern University 9200 University Blvd TF: 800-947-7474 ■ Web: www.csuniv.edu	Charleston	SC	29406	843-863-7050	863-7070
Citadel The 171 Moultrie St TF: 800-868-1842 ■ Web: www.citadel.edu	Charleston	SC	29409	843-953-5230	953-7036
Claflin University 400 Magnolia St TF: 800-922-1276 ■ Web: www.claflin.edu	Orangeburg	SC	29115	803-535-5000	535-5385
Clemson University 105 Sikes Hall *Fax: Admissions ■ Web: www.clemson.edu	Clemson	SC	29634	864-656-3311	656-2464*
Coastal Carolina University PO Box 261954 TF: 800-277-7000 ■ Web: www.coastal.edu	Conway	SC	29528	843-349-2170	349-2127
Coker College 300 E College Ave *Fax: Admissions ■ TF: 800-950-1908 ■ Web: www.coker.edu	Hartsville	SC	29550	843-383-8000	383-8056*
College of Charleston 66 George St Web: www.cofc.edu	Charleston	SC	29424	843-805-5507	953-6322
Columbia College 1301 Columbia College Dr TF: 800-277-1301 ■ Web: www.columbiacollegesc.edu	Columbia	SC	29203	803-786-3012	786-3674
Converse College 580 E Main St *Fax: Admissions ■ TF Admissions: 800-766-1125 ■ Web: www.converse.edu	Spartanburg	SC	29302	864-596-9000	596-9225*
Erskine College PO Box 176 *Fax: Admissions ■ TF Admissions: 800-241-8721 ■ Web: www.erskine.edu	Due West	SC	29639	864-379-2131	379-3048*
Francis Marion University PO Box 100547 *Fax: Admissions ■ TF: 800-368-7551 ■ Web: www.fmarion.edu	Florence	SC	29501	843-661-1231	661-4635*
Furman University 3300 Poinsett Hwy *Fax: Admissions ■ Web: www.furman.edu	Greenville	SC	29613	864-294-2000	294-2018*
Lander University 320 Stanley Ave *Fax: Admissions ■ TF Admissions: 888-452-6337 ■ Web: www.lander.edu	Greenwood	SC	29649	864-388-8307	388-8125*
Limestone College 1115 College Dr *Fax: Admissions ■ TF: 800-795-7151 ■ Web: www.limestone.edu	Gaffney	SC	29340	864-489-7151	488-8206*
Medical University of South Carolina 171 Ashley Ave *Fax: Admissions ■ TF: 800-424-6872 ■ Web: www.musc.edu	Charleston	SC	29425	843-792-9241	792-3126*
Morris College 100 W College St *Fax: Admissions ■ TF Admissions: 866-853-1345 ■ Web: www.morris.edu	Sumter	SC	29150	803-934-3200	773-8241*
Newberry College 2100 College St *Fax: Admissions ■ TF: 800-845-4955 ■ Web: www.newberry.edu	Newberry	SC	29108	803-276-5010	321-5138*
Presbyterian College 503 S Broad St *Fax: Admissions ■ TF: 800-476-7272 ■ Web: www.presby.edu	Clinton	SC	29325	864-833-2820	833-8481*
South Carolina State University 300 College St NE PO Box 7127 TF Admissions: 800-260-5956 ■ Web: www.scsu.edu	Orangeburg	SC	29117	803-536-7000	536-8990
South University Columbia 3810 Main St *Fax: Admissions ■ TF: 866-629-3031 ■ Web: www.southuniversity.edu	Columbia	SC	29203	803-799-9082	935-4382*
Southern Wesleyan University 907 Wesleyan Dr *Fax: Admissions ■ TF: 800-282-8798 ■ Web: www.swu.edu	Central	SC	29630	864-644-5000	644-5972*
University of South Carolina *Fax: Admissions ■ TF: 800-868-5872 ■ Web: www.sc.edu	Columbia	SC	29208	803-777-7000	777-0101*
Aiken 471 University Pkwy *Fax: Admissions ■ TF: 888-969-8722 ■ Web: www.usca.edu	Aiken	SC	29801	803-648-6851	641-3727*
Beaufort 801 Carteret St *Fax: Admissions ■ Web: www.sc.edu/beaufort	Beaufort	SC	29902	843-521-4100	521-4198*
Sumter 200 Miller Rd *Fax: Admissions ■ TF: 888-872-7868 ■ Web: www.uscsumter.edu	Sumter	SC	29150	803-775-8727	938-3901*
Upstate 800 University Way *Fax: Admissions ■ TF: 800-277-8727 ■ Web: www.uscupstate.edu	Spartanburg	SC	29303	864-503-5246	503-5727*
Voorhees College 213 Wiggins Dr PO Box 678 TF Admissions: 800-446-6250 ■ Web: www.voorhees.edu	Denmark	SC	29042	803-793-3351	753-9077
Winthrop University 701 Oakland Ave *Fax: Admissions ■ Web: www.winthrop.edu	Rock Hill	SC	29733	803-323-2211	323-2137*
Wofford College 429 N Church St *Fax: Admissions ■ Web: www.wofford.edu	Spartanburg	SC	29303	864-597-4000	597-4149*

South Dakota

	City	State	Zip	Phone	Fax
Augustana College 2001 S Summit Ave *Fax: Admissions ■ TF: 800-727-2844 ■ Web: www.augie.edu	Sioux Falls	SD	57197	605-274-0770	274-5518*
Black Hills State University 1200 University St Unit 9502 TF: 800-255-2478 ■ Web: www.bhsu.edu	Spearfish	SD	57799	605-642-6011	642-6254
Dakota State University 820 N Washington Ave TF: 888-378-9988 ■ Web: www.dsu.edu	Madison	SD	57042	605-256-5139	256-5020
Dakota Wesleyan University 1200 W University Ave TF: 800-333-8506 ■ Web: www.dwu.edu	Mitchell	SD	57301	605-995-2600	995-2699
Mount Marty College 1105 W 8th St *Fax: Admissions ■ TF Admissions: 800-658-4552 ■ Web: www.mtmc.edu	Yankton	SD	57078	605-668-1545	668-1508*
National American University 321 Kansas City St *Fax: Admissions ■ TF: 800-843-8892 ■ Web: www.national.edu	Rapid City	SD	57701	605-394-4800	394-4871*
Sioux Falls 2801 S Kiwanis Ave Suite 100 *Fax: Admissions ■ TF: 800-388-5430 ■ Web: www.national.edu/SiouxFallsCampus/Index.htm	Sioux Falls	SD	57105	605-336-4600	336-4605*
Northern State University 1200 S Jay St *Fax: Admissions ■ TF: 800-678-5330 ■ Web: www.northern.edu	Aberdeen	SD	57401	605-626-3011	626-2587*
Oglala Lakota College PO Box 629 Web: www.olc.edu	Martin	SD	57551	605-685-6407	685-6887
Presentation College 1500 N Main St TF: 800-437-6060 ■ Web: www.presentation.edu	Aberdeen	SD	57401	605-225-1634	229-8425
Sinte Gleska University 101 Antelope Lake Cir Dr PO Box 105 Web: www.sinte.edu	Mission	SD	57535	605-856-8100	856-4194
South Dakota School of Mines & Technology 501 E Saint Joseph St TF: 800-544-8162 ■ Web: www.hpcnet.org/sdsmt	Rapid City	SD	57701	605-394-2414	394-1268
South Dakota State University PO Box 2201 TF: 800-952-3541 ■ Web: www3.sdstate.edu	Brookings	SD	57007	605-688-4121	688-6891
University of Sioux Falls 1101 W 22nd St TF: 800-888-1047 ■ Web: www.thecoo.edu	Sioux Falls	SD	57105	605-331-6600	331-6615
University of South Dakota 414 E Clark St *Fax: Admissions ■ TF: 877-269-6837 ■ Web: www.usd.edu	Vermillion	SD	57069	605-677-5341	677-6323*

Tennessee

	City	State	Zip	Phone	Fax
Aquinas College 4210 Harding Rd *Fax: Admissions ■ TF Admissions: 800-649-9956 ■ Web: www.aquinas-tn.edu	Nashville	TN	37205	615-297-7545	297-7970*
Austin Peay State University 601 College St *Fax: Admissions ■ TF Admissions: 800-844-2778 ■ Web: www.apsu.edu	Clarksville	TN	37044	931-221-7661	221-6168*
Belmont University 1900 Belmont Blvd *Fax: Admissions ■ TF: 800-563-6765 ■ Web: www.belmont.edu	Nashville	TN	37212	615-460-6000	460-5434*
Bethel College 325 Cherry Ave *Fax: Admissions ■ Web: www.bethel-college.edu	McKenzie	TN	38201	731-352-4000	352-4241*
Bryan College 721 Bryan Dr PO Box 7000 TF: 800-277-9522 ■ Web: www.bryan.edu	Dayton	TN	37321	423-775-2041	775-7199
Carson-Newman College 1646 Russell Ave *Fax: Admissions ■ TF: 800-678-9061 ■ Web: www.cn.edu	Jefferson City	TN	37760	865-475-9061	471-3502*
Christian Brothers University 650 East Pkwy S *Fax: Admissions ■ TF Admissions: 800-288-7576 ■ Web: www.cbu.edu	Memphis	TN	38104	901-321-3000	321-3494*
Crichton College 255 N Highland Ave *Fax: Admissions ■ TF: 800-960-9777 ■ Web: www.crichton.edu	Memphis	TN	38111	901-320-9797	320-9791*
Cumberland University 1 Cumberland Sq TF: 800-467-0562 ■ Web: www.cumberland.edu	Lebanon	TN	37087	615-444-2562	444-2569
East Tennessee State University PO Box 70731 TF: 800-462-3878 ■ Web: www.etsu.edu	Johnson City	TN	37614	423-439-4213	439-4630
Fisk University 1000 17th Ave N TF: 800-443-3475 ■ Web: www.fisk.edu	Nashville	TN	37208	615-329-8500	329-8774
Freed-Hardeman University 158 E Main St TF: 800-630-3480 ■ Web: www.fhu.edu	Henderson	TN	38340	731-989-6651	989-6047
King College 1350 King College Rd TF Admissions: 800-362-0014 ■ Web: www.king.edu	Bristol	TN	37620	423-652-4861	968-4456
Lambuth University 705 Lambuth Blvd *Fax: Admissions ■ TF: 800-526-2884 ■ Web: www.lambuth.edu	Jackson	TN	38301	731-425-2500	425-3496*
Lane College 545 Lane Ave *Fax: Admissions ■ TF Admissions: 800-960-7532 ■ Web: www.lanecollege.edu	Jackson	TN	38301	731-426-7500	426-7559*
Lee University 1120 N Ocoee St *Fax: Admissions ■ TF: 800-533-9930 ■ Web: www.leeuniversity.edu	Cleveland	TN	37311	423-614-8000	614-8533*
LeMoyne-Owen College 807 Walker Ave *Fax: Admissions ■ TF Admissions: 800-737-7778 ■ Web: www.loc.edu	Memphis	TN	38126	901-435-1000	435-1524*
Lincoln Memorial University 6965 Cumberland Gap Pkwy TF: 800-325-0900 ■ Web: www.lmunet.edu	Harrogate	TN	37752	423-869-3611	869-6444
Lipscomb University 3901 Granny White Pike *Fax: Admissions ■ TF: 800-333-4358 ■ Web: www.lipscomb.edu	Nashville	TN	37204	615-966-1000	966-1804*
Martin Methodist College 433 W Madison St *Fax: Admissions ■ TF: 800-467-1273 ■ Web: www.martinmethodist.edu	Pulaski	TN	38478	931-363-9804	363-9803*
Maryville College 502 E Lamar Alexander Pkwy *Fax: Admissions ■ TF: 800-597-2687 ■ Web: www.maryvillecollege.edu	Maryville	TN	37804	865-981-8000	981-8005*
Middle Tennessee State University 1301 E Main St *Fax: Admissions ■ TF Admissions: 800-433-6878 ■ Web: www.mtsu.edu	Murfreesboro	TN	37132	615-898-2111	898-5478*
Milligan College PO Box 500 *Fax: Admissions ■ TF: 800-262-8337 ■ Web: www.milligan.edu	Milligan College	TN	37682	423-461-8730	461-8982*
O'More College of Design 423 S Margin St TF: 888-662-1970 ■ Web: www.omorecollege.edu	Franklin	TN	37064	615-794-4254	790-1662
Rhodes College 2000 North Pkwy *Fax: Admissions ■ TF: 800-844-5969 ■ Web: www.rhodes.edu	Memphis	TN	38112	901-843-3700	843-3631*
Sewanee 735 University Ave *Fax: Admissions ■ TF: 800-522-2234 ■ Web: www.sewanee.edu	Sewanee	TN	37383	931-598-1238	598-3248*
Southern Adventist University 4881 Taylor Cir TF: 800-768-8437 ■ Web: www.southern.edu	Collegedale	TN	37315	423-236-2000	236-1000
Tennessee State University 3500 John A Merritt Blvd PO Box 9609 TF Admissions: 888-463-6878 ■ Web: www.tnstate.edu	Nashville	TN	37209	615-963-5000	963-5108
Tennessee Technological University PO Box 5006 *Fax: Admissions ■ TF: 800-255-8881 ■ Web: www.tntech.edu	Cookeville	TN	38505	931-372-3888	372-6250*
Tennessee Temple University 1815 Union Ave *Fax: Admissions ■ TF: 800-553-4050 ■ Web: www.tntemple.edu	Chattanooga	TN	37404	423-493-4100	493-4497*
Tennessee Wesleyan College 204 E College St PO Box 40 TF: 800-742-5892 ■ Web: www.twcnet.edu	Athens	TN	37371	423-745-7504	744-9968
Trevecca Nazarene University 333 Murfreesboro Rd *Fax: Admissions ■ TF: 888-210-4868 ■ Web: www.trevecca.edu	Nashville	TN	37210	615-248-1200	248-7406*
Tusculum College 60 Shiloh Rd Hwy 107 *Fax: Admissions ■ TF: 800-729-0256 ■ Web: www.tusculum.edu	Greeneville	TN	37743	423-636-7300	798-1622*
Union University 1050 Union University Dr *Fax: Admissions ■ TF: 800-338-6466 ■ Web: www.uu.edu	Jackson	TN	38305	731-661-5210	661-5589*
University of Memphis Wilder Tower Rm 101 *Fax: Admissions ■ TF: 800-669-2678 ■ Web: www.memphis.edu	Memphis	TN	38152	901-678-2101	678-3053*
University of the South 735 University Ave *Fax: Admissions ■ TF: 800-522-2234 ■ Web: www.sewanee.edu	Sewanee	TN	37383	931-598-1238	598-3248*
University of Tennessee 1331 Cir Park Dr 320 Student Services Bldg *Fax: Admissions ■ Web: www.utk.edu	Knoxville	TN	37996	865-974-1000	974-3851*
Chattanooga 615 McCallie Ave *Fax: Admissions ■ TF: 800-882-6627 ■ Web: www.utc.edu	Chattanooga	TN	37403	423-425-4111	425-4157*
Health Science Center 800 Madison Ave Web: www.utmem.edu	Memphis	TN	38163	901-448-5000	448-7772
Martin 544 University St TF: 800-829-8861 ■ Web: www.utm.edu	Martin	TN	38238	731-881-7020	881-7029
Vanderbilt University 2305 W End Ave *Fax: Admissions ■ TF Admissions: 800-288-0432 ■ Web: www.vanderbilt.edu	Nashville	TN	37203	615-322-7311	343-7765*

Texas

	City	State	Zip	Phone	Fax
Abilene Christian University 1705 Campus Ct *Fax: Admissions ■ TF Admissions: 800-460-6228 ■ Web: www.acu.edu	Abilene	TX	79601	325-674-2000	674-2130*
Angelo State University 2601 West Ave N ASU Station 11014 *Fax: Admissions ■ TF: 800-946-8627 ■ Web: www.angelo.edu	San Angelo	TX	76909	325-942-2041	942-2078*
Arlington Baptist College 3001 W Division St *Fax: Admissions ■ Web: www.abconline.edu	Arlington	TX	76012	817-461-8741	274-1138*
Austin College 900 N Grand Ave *Fax: Admissions ■ TF: 800-442-5363 ■ Web: www.austincollege.edu	Sherman	TX	75090	903-813-3000	813-3198*
Austin Graduate School of Theology 7640 Guadalupe St TF: 866-287-4723 ■ Web: www.austingrad.edu	Austin	TX	78752	512-476-2772	476-3919
Baylor University 1311 S 5th St *Fax: Admissions ■ TF: 800-229-5678 ■ Web: www.baylor.edu	Waco	TX	76798	254-710-1011	710-3436*
Concordia University Austin 3400 IH-35 N TF: 800-865-4282 ■ Web: www.concordia.edu	Austin	TX	78705	512-486-2000	486-1350
Criswell College 4010 Gaston Ave *Fax: Admissions ■ TF: 800-899-0012 ■ Web: www.criswell.edu	Dallas	TX	75246	214-821-5433	818-1310*
Dallas Baptist University 3000 Mountain Creek Pkwy *Fax: Admissions ■ TF: 800-460-1328 ■ Web: www.dbu.edu	Dallas	TX	75211	214-333-7100	333-5447*
East Texas Baptist University 1209 N Grove St *Fax: Admissions ■ TF: 800-804-3828 ■ Web: www.etbu.edu	Marshall	TX	75670	903-935-7963	923-2001*
Hardin-Simmons University 2200 Hickory St *Fax: Admissions ■ TF: 877-464-7889 ■ Web: www.hsutx.edu	Abilene	TX	79698	325-670-1206	671-2115*
Houston Baptist University 7502 Fondren Rd *Fax: Admissions ■ TF Admissions: 800-969-3210 ■ Web: www.hbu.edu	Houston	TX	77074	281-649-3000	649-3217*
Howard Payne University 1000 Fisk Ave *Fax: Admissions ■ TF: 800-950-8465 ■ Web: www.hputx.edu	Brownwood	TX	76801	325-646-2502	649-8901*
Huston-Tillotson University 900 Chicon St *Fax: Admissions ■ TF: 877-505-3028 ■ Web: www.htu.edu	Austin	TX	78702	512-505-3000	505-3192*
Jarvis Christian College PO Box 1470 *Fax: Admissions ■ Web: www.jarvis.edu	Hawkins	TX	75765	903-769-5700	769-1282*
Lamar University 4400 ML King Jr Pkwy Web: www.lamar.edu	Beaumont	TX	77710	409-880-7011	880-8463
LeTourneau University 2100 S Mobberly Ave *Fax: Admissions ■ TF: 800-759-8811 ■ Web: www.letu.edu	Longview	TX	75602	903-753-0231	233-4301*
Lubbock Christian University 5601 19th St *Fax: Admissions ■ TF: 800-933-7601 ■ Web: www.lcu.edu	Lubbock	TX	79407	806-720-7151	720-7162*
McMurry University S 14 St & Sayles Blvd TF: 800-460-2395 ■ Web: www.mcm.edu	Abilene	TX	79697	325-793-4700	793-4701
Midwestern State University 3410 Taft Blvd *Fax: Admissions ■ TF Admissions: 800-842-1922 ■ Web: www.mwsu.edu	Wichita Falls	TX	76308	940-397-4000	397-4672*
Northwood University Texas 1114 W FM 1382 TF: 800-927-9663 ■ Web: www.northwood.edu/tx	Cedar Hill	TX	75104	972-291-1541	291-3824

Texas (Cont'd)

	City	State	ZIP	Phone	Fax
Our Lady of the Lake University 411 SW 24th St	San Antonio	TX	78207	210-434-6711	431-4036*
*Fax: Admissions ■ TF: 800-436-6558 ■ Web: www.ollusa.edu					
Paul Quinn College 3837 Simpson Stuart Rd	Dallas	TX	75241	214-376-1000	302-3648*
*Fax: Admissions ■ TF: 800-237-2648 ■ Web: www.pqc.edu					
Prairie View A & M University PO Box 519 MS 1009	Prairie View	TX	77446	936-857-2626	857-2699*
*Fax: Admissions ■ TF: 800-787-7826 ■ Web: www.pvamu.edu					
Rice University 6100 Main St	Houston	TX	77005	713-348-0000	348-5323*
*Fax: Admissions ■ TF: 800-527-6957 ■ Web: www.rice.edu					
Saint Edward's University 3001 S Congress Ave	Austin	TX	78704	512-448-8500	464-8877
TF: 800-555-0164 ■ Web: www.stedwards.edu					
Saint Mary's University 1 Camino Santa Maria	San Antonio	TX	78228	210-436-3126	431-6742*
*Fax: Admissions ■ TF Admissions: 800-367-7868 ■ Web: www.stmarytx.edu					
Sam Houston State University 1903 University Ave	Huntsville	TX	77340	936-294-1111	294-3758*
*Fax: Admissions ■ TF: 866-232-7528 ■ Web: www.shsu.edu					
Schreiner University 2100 Memorial Blvd	Kerrville	TX	78028	830-792-7217	792-7226*
*Fax: Admissions ■ TF: 800-343-4919 ■ Web: www.schreiner.edu					
Southern Methodist University 6425 Boaz Ln	Dallas	TX	75205	214-768-2000	768-0202*
*Fax: Admissions ■ TF: 800-323-0672 ■ Web: www.smu.edu					
Southwestern Adventist University 100 W Hillcrest Dr PO Box 567	Keene	TX	76059	817-645-3921	556-4753
TF Admissions: 888-732-7928 ■ Web: www.swau.edu					
Southwestern Assemblies of God University 1200 Sycamore St	Waxahachie	TX	75165	972-937-4010	923-0006*
*Fax: Admissions ■ TF: 888-937-7248 ■ Web: www.sagu.edu					
Southwestern Christian College PO Box 10	Terrell	TX	75160	972-524-3341	563-7133
TF: 800-925-9357 ■ Web: www.swcc.edu					
Southwestern University PO Box 770	Georgetown	TX	78627	512-863-1200	863-9601*
*Fax: Admissions ■ TF: 800-252-3166 ■ Web: www.southwestern.edu					
Stephen F Austin State University 1936 North St	Nacogdoches	TX	75962	936-468-2504	468-3149*
*Fax: Admissions ■ Web: www.sfasu.edu					
Sul Ross State University E Hwy 90	Alpine	TX	79832	432-837-8011	837-8431*
*Fax: Admissions ■ TF: 888-722-7778 ■ Web: www.sulross.edu					
Tarleton State University PO Box T-0030	Stephenville	TX	76402	254-968-9125	968-9951*
*Fax: Admissions ■ TF: 800-687-8236 ■ Web: www.tarleton.edu					
Texas A & M International University 5201 University Blvd	Laredo	TX	78041	956-326-2001	326-2199
Web: www.tamiu.edu					
Texas A & M University PO Box 30014	College Station	TX	77843	979-845-3211	458-0434*
*Fax: Admissions ■ Web: www.tamu.edu					
Commerce PO Box 3011	Commerce	TX	75428	903-886-5081	468-8685
TF: 888-868-2682 ■ Web: www.tamu-commerce.edu					
Corpus Christi 6300 Ocean Dr	Corpus Christi	TX	78412	361-825-7024	825-5887*
*Fax: Admissions ■ Web: www.tamucc.edu					
Galveston 200 Seawolf Pkwy Bldg 3026	Galveston	TX	77553	409-740-4428	740-4731
TF: 877-322-4443 ■ Web: www.tamug.edu					
Kingsville 700 University Blvd Campus Box 128	Kingsville	TX	78363	361-593-2111	593-2195*
*Fax: Admissions ■ Web: www.tamuk.edu					
Texarkana PO Box 5518	Texarkana	TX	75505	903-223-3000	223-3140*
*Fax: Admissions ■ Web: www.tamut.edu					
Texas Christian University TCU Box 297013	Fort Worth	TX	76129	817-257-7490	257-7268
TF: 800-828-3764 ■ Web: www.tcu.edu					
Texas College 2404 N Grand Ave	Tyler	TX	75702	903-593-8311	536-0001*
*Fax: Admissions ■ TF: 800-306-6299 ■ Web: www.texascollege.edu					
Texas Lutheran University 1000 W Court St	Seguin	TX	78155	830-372-8000	372-8096
TF: 800-771-8521 ■ Web: www.tlu.edu					
Texas Southern University 3100 Cleburne St	Houston	TX	77004	713-313-7011	313-1859
Web: www.tsu.edu					
Texas State University San Marcos 601 University Dr	San Marcos	TX	78666	512-245-2340	245-8044*
*Fax: Admissions ■ TF Admissions: 866-798-2287 ■ Web: www.txstate.edu					
Texas Tech University PO Box 45005	Lubbock	TX	79409	806-742-1480	742-0062*
*Fax: Admissions ■ TF: 888-270-3369 ■ Web: www.ttu.edu					
Texas Wesleyan University 1201 Wesleyan St	Fort Worth	TX	76105	817-531-4422	531-7515*
*Fax: Admissions ■ TF: 800-580-8980 ■ Web: www.txwesleyan.edu					
Texas Woman's University					
304 Administration Dr PO Box 425589	Denton	TX	76204	940-898-3188	898-3081*
*Fax: Admissions ■ TF: 866-809-6130 ■ Web: www.twu.edu					
Trinity University 1 Trinity Pl	San Antonio	TX	78212	210-999-7011	999-8164*
*Fax: Admissions ■ TF: 800-874-6489 ■ Web: www.trinity.edu					
University of Dallas 1845 E Northgate Dr	Irving	TX	75062	972-721-5266	721-5017*
*Fax: Admissions ■ TF Admissions: 800-628-6999 ■ Web: www.udallas.edu					
University of Houston 4800 Calhoun Rd	Houston	TX	77004	713-743-1000	743-9665
Web: www.uh.edu					
Clear Lake 2700 Bay Area Blvd	Houston	TX	77058	281-283-7600	283-2522*
*Fax: Admissions ■ Web: www.cl.uh.edu					
Downtown 1 Main St	Houston	TX	77002	713-221-8000	221-8157*
*Fax: Admissions ■ Web: www.dt.uh.edu					
Victoria 3007 N Ben Wilson St	Victoria	TX	77901	361-570-4848	570-4114*
*Fax: Admissions ■ TF: 877-970-4848 ■ Web: www.uhv.edu					
University of the Incarnate Word 4301 Broadway St	San Antonio	TX	78209	210-829-6000	829-3921*
*Fax: Admissions ■ TF Admissions: 800-749-9673 ■ Web: www.uiw.edu					
University of Mary Hardin-Baylor					
900 College St UMHB Box 8004	Belton	TX	76513	254-295-8642	295-5049*
*Fax: Admissions ■ TF: 800-727-8642 ■ Web: www.umhb.edu					
University of North Texas PO Box 311277	Denton	TX	76203	940-565-2681	565-2408*
*Fax: Admissions ■ TF: 800-868-8211 ■ Web: www.unt.edu					
University of Saint Thomas 3800 Montrose Blvd	Houston	TX	77006	713-522-7911	525-3558*
*Fax: Admissions ■ TF: 800-856-8565 ■ Web: www.stthom.edu					
University of Texas					
Allied Health Sciences School 5323 Harry Hines Blvd	Dallas	TX	75390	214-648-3111	648-3289
Web: www3.utsouthwestern.edu					
Arlington 701 S Nedderman Dr Box 19111	Arlington	TX	76019	817-272-6287	272-3435*
*Fax: Admissions ■ Web: www.uta.edu					
Austin 2400 Inner Campus Dr Mail Bldg Rm 7	Austin	TX	78712	512-475-7399	475-7399*
*Fax: Admissions ■ Web: www.utexas.edu					
Brownsville 80 Fort Brown St	Brownsville	TX	78520	956-882-8200	882-7694*
*Fax: Admissions ■ TF: 800-892-3348 ■ Web: www.utb.edu					
Dallas PO Box 830688	Richardson	TX	75083	972-883-2111	883-6803*
*Fax: Admissions ■ TF Admissions: 800-889-2443 ■ Web: www.utdallas.edu					
El Paso 500 W University Ave	El Paso	TX	79968	915-747-5000	747-8893*
*Fax: Admissions ■ TF Admissions: 877-746-4637 ■ Web: www.utep.edu					
Pan American 1201 W University Dr	Edinburg	TX	78541	956-381-2011	381-2212
TF: 866-441-8872 ■ Web: www.panam.edu					
Permian Basin 4901 E University Blvd	Odessa	TX	79762	432-552-2000	552-3605*
*Fax: Admissions ■ TF Admissions: 866-552-8872 ■ Web: www.utpb.edu					
San Antonio 6900 North Loop 1604 W	San Antonio	TX	78249	210-458-4011	458-7716*
*Fax: Admissions ■ TF: 800-669-0919 ■ Web: www.utsa.edu					
Tyler 3900 University Blvd	Tyler	TX	75799	903-566-7000	566-7068*
*Fax: Admissions ■ TF: 800-888-9537 ■ Web: www.uttyler.edu					
Wayland Baptist University 1900 W 7th St	Plainview	TX	79072	806-291-1000	291-1973*
*Fax: Admissions ■ TF: 800-588-1928 ■ Web: www.wbu.edu					
West Texas A & M University 2501 4th Ave	Canyon	TX	79016	806-651-2020	651-5285*
*Fax: Admissions ■ TF: 800-999-8268 ■ Web: www.wtamu.edu					
Wiley College 711 Wiley Ave	Marshall	TX	75670	903-927-3311	927-3366*
*Fax: Admissions ■ TF Admissions: 800-658-6889 ■ Web: www.wileyc.edu					

Utah

	City	State	ZIP	Phone	Fax
Brigham Young University D-238 ASB A-153	Provo	UT	84602	801-422-4636	422-0005*
*Fax: Admissions ■ Web: home.byu.edu					
Dixie State College of Utah 225 S 700 East	Saint George	UT	84770	435-652-7500	656-4005*
*Fax: Admissions ■ TF: 888-324-2998 ■ Web: new.dixie.edu					
Southern Utah University 351 W Center St	Cedar City	UT	84720	435-586-7700	865-8223*
*Fax: Admissions ■ Web: www.suu.edu					
University of Utah 201 S 1460 East	Salt Lake City	UT	84112	801-581-7200	581-7880*
*Fax: Admissions ■ Web: www.utah.edu					
Utah State University 1600 Old Main Hill	Logan	UT	84322	435-797-1000	797-3708*
*Fax: Admissions ■ Web: www.usu.edu					
Weber State University 3850 University Cir	Ogden	UT	84408	801-626-6000	626-6747*
*Fax: Admissions ■ TF: 800-848-7770 ■ Web: www.weber.edu					
Davis 2750 N University Park Blvd	Layton	UT	84041	801-395-3473	395-3538*
*Fax: Admissions ■ TF: 800-848-7770 ■ Web: weber.edu/wsudavis					
Westminster College 1840 S 1300 East	Salt Lake City	UT	84105	801-832-2200	832-3101*
*Fax: Admissions ■ TF: 800-748-4753 ■ Web: www.westminstercollege.edu					

Vermont

	City	State	ZIP	Phone	Fax
Bennington College 1 College Dr	Bennington	VT	05201	802-442-5401	447-4269
TF: 800-833-6845 ■ Web: www.bennington.edu					
Burlington College 95 North Ave	Burlington	VT	05401	802-862-9616	660-4331
TF: 800-862-9616 ■ Web: www.burlingtoncollege.edu					
Castleton State College 86 Seminary St	Castleton	VT	05735	802-468-5611	468-1476*
*Fax: Admissions ■ TF: 800-639-8521 ■ Web: www.csc.vsc.edu					
Champlain College PO Box 670	Burlington	VT	05402	802-860-2700	860-2767*
*Fax: Admissions ■ TF: 800-570-5858 ■ Web: www.champlain.edu					
College of Saint Joseph in Vermont 71 Clement Rd	Rutland	VT	05701	802-773-5900	776-5258*
*Fax: Admissions ■ TF Admissions: 877-270-9998 ■ Web: www.csj.edu					
Goddard College 123 Pitkin Rd	Plainfield	VT	05667	802-454-8311	454-1029*
*Fax: Admissions ■ TF: 800-468-4888 ■ Web: www.goddard.edu					
Green Mountain College 1 College Cir	Poultney	VT	05764	802-287-8000	287-8099
TF Admissions: 800-776-6675 ■ Web: www.greenmtn.edu					
Johnson State College 337 College Hill	Johnson	VT	05656	802-635-2356	635-1230*
*Fax: Admissions ■ TF: 800-635-2356 ■ Web: www.jsc.vsc.edu					
Lyndon State College 1001 College Rd PO Box 919	Lyndonville	VT	05851	802-626-6413	626-6335
TF: 800-225-1998 ■ Web: www.lyndonstate.edu					
Marlboro College 2582 South Rd PO Box A	Marlboro	VT	05344	802-257-4333	451-7555
TF: 800-343-0049 ■ Web: www.marlboro.edu					
Middlebury College 131 S Main St	Middlebury	VT	05753	802-443-3000	443-2056*
*Fax: Admissions ■ Web: www.middlebury.edu					
Norwich University 158 Harmon Dr	Northfield	VT	05663	802-485-2001	485-2032
TF: 800-468-6679 ■ Web: www.norwich.edu					
Saint Michael's College 1 Winooski Park	Colchester	VT	05439	802-654-2000	654-2591
TF: 800-762-8000 ■ Web: www.smcvt.edu					
Southern Vermont College 982 Mansion Dr	Bennington	VT	05201	802-442-5427	447-4695*
*Fax: Admissions ■ TF: 800-378-2782 ■ Web: www.svc.edu					
Union Institute & University Vermont College 36 College St	Montpelier	VT	05602	802-828-8500	828-8855*
*Fax: Admissions ■ TF: 800-336-6794 ■ Web: www.tui.edu/VC					
University of Vermont Waterman Bldg 194 S Prospect St	Burlington	VT	05405	802-656-3131	656-8611*
*Fax: Admissions ■ Web: www.uvm.edu					

Virginia

	City	State	ZIP	Phone	Fax
Averett University 420 W Main St	Danville	VA	24541	434-791-4996	797-2784*
*Fax: Admissions ■ TF: 800-283-7388 ■ Web: www.averett.edu					
Bluefield College 3000 College Dr	Bluefield	VA	24605	276-326-3682	326-4395*
*Fax: Admissions ■ TF: 800-872-0175 ■ Web: www.bluefield.edu					
Bridgewater College 402 E College St	Bridgewater	VA	22812	540-828-5375	828-5481
TF: 800-759-8328 ■ Web: www.bridgewater.edu					
Christendom College 134 Christendom Dr	Front Royal	VA	22630	540-636-2900	636-1655*
*Fax: Admissions ■ TF: 800-877-5456 ■ Web: www.christendom.edu					
Christopher Newport University 1 University Pl	Newport News	VA	23606	757-594-7015	594-7333*
*Fax: Admissions ■ TF Admissions: 800-333-4268 ■ Web: www.cnu.edu					
College of William & Mary PO Box 8795	Williamsburg	VA	23187	757-221-4000	221-1242*
*Fax: Admissions ■ Web: www.wm.edu					
Eastern Mennonite University 1200 Park Rd	Harrisonburg	VA	22802	540-432-4118	432-4444*
*Fax: Admissions ■ TF Admissions: 800-368-2665 ■ Web: www.emu.edu					
Emory & Henry College PO Box 10	Emory	VA	24327	276-944-4121	944-6935*
*Fax: Admissions ■ TF Admissions: 800-848-5493 ■ Web: www.ehc.edu					
Ferrum College PO Box 1000	Ferrum	VA	24088	540-365-2121	365-4266
TF: 800-868-9797 ■ Web: www.ferrum.edu					
George Mason University 4400 University Dr MS N3A4	Fairfax	VA	22030	703-993-1000	993-2392
TF: 888-627-6612 ■ Web: www.gmu.edu					
Prince William 10900 University Blvd	Manassas	VA	20110	703-993-8350	993-8378
Web: princewilliam.gmu.edu					
Hampden-Sydney College PO Box 667	Hampden-Sydney	VA	23943	434-223-6120	223-6120*
*Fax: Admissions ■ TF Admissions: 800-755-0733 ■ Web: www.hsc.edu					
Hampton University 100 E Queen St	Hampton	VA	23668	757-727-5000	727-5095*
*Fax: Admissions ■ TF Admissions: 800-624-3328 ■ Web: www.hamptonu.edu					
Hollins University 7916 Williamson Rd	Roanoke	VA	24020	540-362-6401	362-6218*
*Fax: Admissions ■ TF Admissions: 800-456-9595 ■ Web: www.hollins.edu					
James Madison University 800 S Main St	Harrisonburg	VA	22807	540-568-6211	568-3332*
*Fax: Admissions ■ Web: www.jmu.edu					
Liberty University 1971 University Blvd	Lynchburg	VA	24502	434-582-2000	542-2311*
*Fax Area Code: 800 ■ *Fax: Admissions ■ TF: 800-543-5317 ■ Web: www.liberty.edu					
Longwood University 201 High St	Farmville	VA	23909	434-395-2060	395-2332*
*Fax: Admissions ■ TF: 800-281-4677 ■ Web: www.longwood.edu					
Lynchburg College 1501 Lakeside Dr	Lynchburg	VA	24501	434-544-8100	544-8653*
*Fax: Admissions ■ TF: 800-426-8101 ■ Web: www.lynchburg.edu					
Mary Baldwin College 318 Prospect St	Staunton	VA	24401	540-887-7019	887-7292*
*Fax: Admissions ■ TF Admissions: 800-468-2262 ■ Web: www.mbc.edu					
Marymount University 2807 N Glebe Rd	Arlington	VA	22207	703-522-5600	522-0349
TF: 800-548-7638 ■ Web: www.marymount.edu					
Norfolk State University 700 Park Ave	Norfolk	VA	23504	757-823-8600	823-2078*
*Fax: Admissions ■ TF: 800-274-1821 ■ Web: www.nsu.edu					
Old Dominion University Rollins Hall	Norfolk	VA	23529	757-683-3685	683-3255*
*Fax: Admissions ■ TF: 800-348-7926 ■ Web: www.odu.edu					
Radford University 801 E Main St	Radford	VA	24142	540-831-5371	831-5038*
*Fax: Admissions ■ TF Admissions: 800-890-4265 ■ Web: www.radford.edu					
Randolph College 2500 Rivermont Ave	Lynchburg	VA	24503	434-947-8000	947-8996*
*Fax: Admissions ■ TF Admissions: 800-745-7692 ■ Web: www.randolphcollege.edu					
Randolph-Macon College PO Box 5005	Ashland	VA	23005	804-752-7200	752-4707*
*Fax: Admissions ■ TF: 800-888-1762 ■ Web: www.rmc.edu					
Roanoke College 221 College Ln	Salem	VA	24153	540-375-2270	375-2267*
*Fax: Admissions ■ TF Admissions: 800-388-2276 ■ Web: www.roanoke.edu					
Saint Paul's College 115 College Dr	Lawrenceville	VA	23868	434-848-3111	848-1846*
*Fax: Admissions ■ TF: 800-678-7071 ■ Web: www.saintpauls.edu					
Shenandoah University 1460 University Dr	Winchester	VA	22601	540-665-4581	665-4627*
*Fax: Admissions ■ TF: 800-432-2266 ■ Web: www.su.edu					

	City	State	ZIP	Phone	Fax
Southern Virginia University 1 University Hill Dr	Buena Vista	VA	24416	540-261-8400	261-8559*
*Fax: Admissions ■ TF: 800-229-8420 ■ Web: www.southernvirginia.edu					
Strayer University					
Alexandria 2730 Eisenhower Ave	Alexandria	VA	22314	703-329-9100	329-9602*
*Fax: Admissions ■ TF: 888-478-7293 ■ Web: www.strayer.edu					
Arlington 2121 15th St N	Arlington	VA	22201	703-892-5100	769-2677*
*Fax: Admissions ■ TF: 888-478-7293 ■ Web: www.strayer.edu					
Fredericksburg 150 Riverside Pkwy Jefferson Bldg	Fredericksburg	VA	22406	540-374-4300	374-4330*
*Fax: Admissions ■ TF: 800-765-8680 ■ Web: www.strayer.edu					
Loudoun 45150 Russell Branch Pkwy Suite 200	Ashburn	VA	20147	703-729-8800	729-8820
Web: www.strayer.edu					
Manassas 9990 Battleview Pkwy	Manassas	VA	20109	703-330-8400	330-8135*
*Fax: Admissions ■ Web: www.strayer.edu					
Woodbridge 13385 Minnieville Rd	Woodbridge	VA	22192	703-878-2800	878-2993
Web: www.strayer.edu					
Sweet Briar College 134 Chappel Rd	Sweet Briar	VA	24595	434-381-6100	381-6152*
*Fax: Admissions ■ TF Admissions: 800-381-6142 ■ Web: www.sbc.edu					
Tabernacle Baptist Bible College & Theological Seminary 717 N Whitehurst Landing Rd	Virginia Beach	VA	23464	757-420-5476	424-3014*
*Fax: Admissions ■ Web: www.tabernacle-vb.org					
University of Mary Washington 1301 College Ave	Fredericksburg	VA	22401	540-654-2000	654-1857*
*Fax: Admissions ■ TF Admissions: 800-468-5614 ■ Web: www.umw.edu					
University of Richmond 28 Westhampton Way	Richmond	VA	23173	804-289-8000	287-6003
TF: 800-700-1662 ■ Web: www.richmond.edu					
Westhampton College The Deanery 28 Westhampton Way	University of Richmond	VA	23173	804-289-8640	287-6003
TF: 800-700-1662 ■ Web: oncampus.richmond.edu/student/affairs					
University of Virginia Peabody Hall McCormick Rd	Charlottesville	VA	22903	434-982-3200	924-3587*
*Fax: Admissions ■ Web: www.virginia.edu					
University of Virginia's College at Wise 1 College Ave	Wise	VA	24293	276-328-0102	328-0251*
*Fax: Admissions ■ TF Admissions: 888-282-9324 ■ Web: www.uvawise.edu					
Virginia Commonwealth University 821 W Franklin St PO Box 842526	Richmond	VA	23284	804-828-0100	828-1899*
*Fax: Admissions ■ TF Admissions: 800-841-3638 ■ Web: www.vcu.edu					
Virginia Intermont College 1013 Moore St	Bristol	VA	24201	276-669-6101	466-7855*
*Fax: Admissions ■ TF: 800-451-1842 ■ Web: www.vic.edu					
Virginia Military Institute 319 Letcher Ave	Lexington	VA	24450	540-464-7211	464-7746*
*Fax: Admissions ■ TF: 800-767-4207 ■ Web: www.vmi.edu					
Virginia Polytechnic Institute & State University 201 Burruss Hall	Blacksburg	VA	24061	540-231-6000	231-3242*
*Fax: Admissions ■ Web: www.vt.edu					
Virginia State University 1 Hayden Dr	Petersburg	VA	23806	804-524-5000	524-5055
TF Admissions: 800-871-7611 ■ Web: www.vsu.edu					
Virginia Tech 201 Burruss Hall	Blacksburg	VA	24061	540-231-6000	231-3242*
*Fax: Admissions ■ Web: www.vt.edu					
Virginia Union University 1500 N Lombardy St	Richmond	VA	23220	804-342-3570	342-3511*
*Fax: Admissions ■ TF: 800-368-3227 ■ Web: www.vuu.edu					
Virginia Wesleyan College 1584 Wesleyan Dr	Norfolk	VA	23502	757-455-3208	461-5238*
*Fax: Admissions ■ TF: 800-737-8684 ■ Web: www.vwc.edu					
Washington & Lee University 204 W Washington St	Lexington	VA	24450	540-458-8710	458-8062*
*Fax: Admissions ■ Web: www2.wlu.edu					
Westhampton College The Deanery 28 Westhampton Way	University of Richmond	VA	23173	804-289-8640	287-6003
TF: 800-700-1662 ■ Web: oncampus.richmond.edu/student/affairs					

Washington

	City	State	ZIP	Phone	Fax
Antioch University 2326 6th Ave	Seattle	WA	98121	206-441-5352	268-4242
TF: 888-268-4477 ■ Web: www.antiochsea.edu					
Central Washington University 400 E University Way	Ellensburg	WA	98926	509-963-1111	963-3022*
*Fax: Admissions ■ TF Admissions: 866-298-4968 ■ Web: www.cwu.edu					
City University 11900 NE 1st St	Bellevue	WA	98005	425-637-1010	709-5361
TF Admissions: 800-426-5596 ■ Web: www.cityu.edu					
Eastern Washington University 526 5th St	Cheney	WA	99004	509-359-6200	359-6692*
*Fax: Admissions ■ Web: www.ewu.edu					
Evergreen State College 2700 Evergreen Pkwy NW	Olympia	WA	98505	360-867-6000	867-5114
Web: www.evergreen.edu					
Gonzaga University 502 E Boone Ave	Spokane	WA	99258	509-323-6572	323-5780*
*Fax: Admissions ■ TF: 800-986-9585 ■ Web: www.gonzaga.edu					
Heritage University 3240 Fort Rd	Toppenish	WA	98948	509-865-8500	865-8659*
*Fax: Admissions ■ TF: 888-272-6190 ■ Web: www.heritage.edu					
Northwest University 5520 108th Ave NE	Kirkland	WA	98033	425-822-8266	889-5224*
*Fax: Admissions ■ TF Admissions: 800-669-3781 ■ Web: www.northwestu.edu					
Pacific Lutheran University 1010 122nd St S	Tacoma	WA	98444	253-531-6900	536-5136*
*Fax: Admissions ■ TF: 800-274-6758 ■ Web: www.plu.edu					
Saint Martin's University 5300 Pacific Ave SE	Lacey	WA	98503	360-438-4311	412-6189*
*Fax: Admissions ■ TF Admissions: 800-368-8803 ■ Web: www.stmartin.edu					
Seattle Bible College 11625 Airport Rd Suite B	Everett	WA	98204	425-212-3530	212-3532*
*Fax: Admissions ■ TF: 877-722-9673 ■ Web: www.seattlebiblecollege.edu/					
Seattle Pacific University 3307 3rd Ave W	Seattle	WA	98119	206-281-2000	281-2544*
*Fax: Admissions ■ TF: 800-366-3344 ■ Web: www.spu.edu					
Seattle University 901 12th Ave	Seattle	WA	98122	206-296-6000	296-5656*
*Fax: Admissions ■ TF: 800-426-7123 ■ Web: www.seattleu.edu					
University of Puget Sound 1500 N Warner St	Tacoma	WA	98416	253-879-3611	879-3993*
*Fax: Admissions ■ TF: 800-396-7191 ■ Web: www.ups.edu					
University of Washington Box 355852	Seattle	WA	98195	206-543-2100	685-3655*
*Fax: Admissions ■ Web: www.washington.edu					
Walla Walla University 103 SW 4th St	College Place	WA	99324	509-527-2327	527-2397*
*Fax: Admissions ■ TF: 800-541-8900 ■ Web: www.wallawalla.edu					
Washington State University	Pullman	WA	99164	509-335-3564	335-4902*
*Fax: Admitting ■ TF: 888-468-6978 ■ Web: www.wsu.edu					
Spokane Health Science Bldg 310 Riverpoint Blvd PO Box 1495	Spokane	WA	99210	509-358-7978	358-7538
Web: www.spokane.wsu.edu					
Vancouver 14204 NE Salmon Creek Ave	Vancouver	WA	98686	360-546-9779	546-9030*
*Fax: Admissions ■ Web: www.vancouver.wsu.edu					
Western Washington University 516 High St	Bellingham	WA	98225	360-650-3000	650-7369
Web: www.wwu.edu					
Whitman College 345 Boyer Ave	Walla Walla	WA	99362	509-527-5111	527-4967*
*Fax: Admissions ■ TF Admissions: 877-462-9448 ■ Web: www.whitman.edu					
Whitworth College 300 W Hawthorne Rd	Spokane	WA	99251	509-777-3212	777-3758*
*Fax: Admissions ■ TF Admissions: 800-533-4668 ■ Web: www.whitworth.edu					

West Virginia

	City	State	ZIP	Phone	Fax
Alderson-Broaddus College 101 College Hill Rd CB 2003	Philippi	WV	26416	304-457-1700	457-6239*
*Fax: Admissions ■ TF Admissions: 800-263-1549 ■ Web: www.ab.edu					
Bethany College Main St	Bethany	WV	26032	304-829-7000	829-7142*
*Fax: Admissions ■ TF: 800-922-7611 ■ Web: www.bethanywv.edu					
Bluefield State College 219 Rock St	Bluefield	WV	24701	304-327-4000	325-7747*
*Fax: Admissions ■ TF: 800-654-7798 ■ Web: www.bluefield.wvnet.edu					
Concord University PO Box 1000	Athens	WV	24712	304-384-3115	384-3218*
*Fax: Admissions ■ TF: 800-344-6679 ■ Web: www.concord.edu					
Davis & Elkins College 100 Campus Dr	Elkins	WV	26241	304-637-1900	637-1800*
*Fax: Admissions ■ TF: 800-624-3157 ■ Web: www.davisandelkins.edu/					
Fairmont State University 1201 Locust Ave	Fairmont	WV	26554	304-367-4892	367-4789*
*Fax: Admissions ■ TF Admissions: 800-641-5678 ■ Web: www.fairmontstate.edu					
Glenville State College 200 High St	Glenville	WV	26351	304-462-7361	462-8619*
*Fax: Admissions ■ TF Admissions: 800-924-2010 ■ Web: www.glenville.edu					
Marshall University 1 John Marshall Dr	Huntington	WV	25755	304-696-3170	696-3135*
*Fax: Admissions ■ TF: 877-642-3463 ■ Web: www.marshall.edu					
Mountain State University 609 S Kanawha St	Beckley	WV	25801	304-253-7351	253-5072*
*Fax: Admissions ■ TF: 800-766-6067 ■ Web: www.mountainstate.edu					
Martinsburg 214 Viking Way	Martinsburg	WV	25401	304-263-4381	263-4674*
*Fax: Admissions ■ TF: 888-612-7800 ■ Web: www.martinsburg.mountainstate.edu					
Ohio Valley University 1 Campus View Dr	Vienna	WV	26105	304-865-6000	865-6175*
*Fax: Admissions ■ TF Admissions: 877-446-8668 ■ Web: www.ovu.edu					
Salem International University 223 W Main St	Salem	WV	26426	304-326-1109	326-1592*
*Fax: Admissions ■ TF: 800-283-4562 ■ Web: www.salemiu.edu					
Shepherd University 301 N King St	Shepherdstown	WV	25443	304-876-5000	876-5165*
*Fax: Admissions ■ TF: 800-344-5231 ■ Web: www.shepherd.edu					
University of Charleston 2300 MacCorkle Ave SE	Charleston	WV	25304	304-357-4800	357-4715*
*Fax: Admissions ■ TF Admissions: 800-995-4682 ■ Web: www.ucwv.edu					
West Liberty State College PO Box 295	West Liberty	WV	26074	304-336-5000	336-8403*
*Fax: Admissions ■ TF: 866-937-8542 ■ Web: www.westliberty.edu					
West Virginia State University Barron Dr Rt 25 E PO Box 1000	Institute	WV	25112	304-766-3000	766-5182*
*Fax: Admissions ■ TF: 800-987-2112 ■ Web: www.wvstateu.edu					
West Virginia University PO Box 6009	Morgantown	WV	26506	304-293-2121	293-3080
TF: 800-344-9881 ■ Web: www.wvu.edu					
Institute of Technology 405 Fayette Pike	Montgomery	WV	25136	304-442-3032	442-3737*
*Fax: Admissions ■ TF: 888-554-8324 ■ Web: www.wvutech.edu					
West Virginia Wesleyan College 59 College Ave	Buckhannon	WV	26201	304-473-8000	473-8108*
*Fax: Admissions ■ TF Admitting: 800-722-9933 ■ Web: www.wvwc.edu					
Wheeling Jesuit University 316 Washington Ave	Wheeling	WV	26003	304-243-2000	243-2397*
*Fax: Admissions ■ TF: 800-624-6992 ■ Web: www.wju.edu					

Wisconsin

	City	State	ZIP	Phone	Fax
Alverno College PO Box 343922	Milwaukee	WI	53234	414-382-6100	382-6055
TF: 800-933-3401 ■ Web: www.alverno.edu					
Bellin College of Nursing PO Box 23400	Green Bay	WI	54305	920-433-3560	433-7416
TF: 800-236-8707 ■ Web: www.bcon.edu					
Beloit College 700 College St	Beloit	WI	53511	608-363-2500	363-2075*
*Fax: Admissions ■ TF Admissions: 800-356-0751 ■ Web: www.beloit.edu					
Cardinal Stritch University 6801 N Yates Rd	Milwaukee	WI	53217	414-410-4000	410-4058*
*Fax: Admissions ■ TF: 800-347-8822 ■ Web: www.stritch.edu					
Carroll College 100 N East Ave	Waukesha	WI	53186	262-547-1211	951-3037*
*Fax: Admissions ■ TF: 800-227-7655 ■ Web: www.cc.edu					
Carthage College 2001 Alford Park Dr	Kenosha	WI	53140	262-551-8500	551-5762*
*Fax: Admissions ■ TF Admissions: 800-351-4058 ■ Web: www.carthage.edu					
Columbia College of Nursing 2121 E Newport Ave	Milwaukee	WI	53211	414-961-3530	961-4205
Web: www.ccon.edu					
Concordia University Wisconsin 12800 N Lake Shore Dr	Mequon	WI	53097	262-243-5700	243-4545*
*Fax: Admissions ■ TF Admissions: 888-628-9472 ■ Web: www.cuw.edu					
Edgewood College 1000 Edgewood College Dr	Madison	WI	53711	608-663-2294	663-2214
TF: 800-444-4861 ■ Web: www.edgewood.edu					
Lakeland College W 3718 South Dr	Plymouth	WI	53073	920-565-2111	565-1215*
*Fax: Admissions ■ TF: 800-569-2166 ■ Web: www.lakeland.edu					
Lawrence University PO Box 599	Appleton	WI	54912	920-832-7000	832-6782*
*Fax: Admissions ■ TF Admissions: 888-201-6017 ■ Web: www.lawrence.edu					
Maranatha Baptist Bible College 745 W Main St	Watertown	WI	53094	920-261-2327	261-9109*
*Fax: Admissions ■ TF: 800-622-2947 ■ Web: www.mbbc.edu					
Marian College of Fond du Lac 45 S National Ave	Fond du Lac	WI	54935	920-923-7650	923-8755*
*Fax: Admissions ■ TF: 800-262-7426 ■ Web: www.mariancollege.edu					
Marquette University 1217 W Wisconsin Ave	Milwaukee	WI	53233	414-288-7302	288-3764*
*Fax: Admissions ■ TF Admissions: 800-222-6544 ■ Web: www.marquette.edu					
Milwaukee Institute of Art & Design 273 E Erie St	Milwaukee	WI	53202	414-276-7889	291-8077*
*Fax: Admissions ■ TF: 888-749-6423 ■ Web: www.miad.edu					
Milwaukee School of Engineering 1025 N Broadway St	Milwaukee	WI	53202	414-277-6763	277-7475*
*Fax: Admissions ■ TF: 800-332-6763 ■ Web: www.msoe.edu					
Mount Mary College 2900 N Menomonee River Pkwy	Milwaukee	WI	53222	414-256-1219	256-0180*
*Fax: Admissions ■ TF Admissions: 800-321-6265 ■ Web: www.mtmary.edu					
Northland Baptist Bible College W10085 Pike Plains Rd	Dunbar	WI	54119	715-324-6900	324-6133*
*Fax: Admissions ■ TF Admissions: 888-466-7845 ■ Web: www.nbbc.edu					
Northland College 1411 Ellis Ave	Ashland	WI	54806	715-682-1224	682-1258*
*Fax: Admissions ■ TF: 800-753-1840 ■ Web: www.northland.edu					
Ripon College 300 Seward St	Ripon	WI	54971	920-748-8337	748-8335*
*Fax: Admissions ■ TF Admissions: 800-947-4766 ■ Web: www.ripon.edu					
Saint Norbert College 100 Grant St	De Pere	WI	54115	920-403-3005	403-4072*
*Fax: Admissions ■ TF Admissions: 800-236-4878 ■ Web: www.snc.edu					
Silver Lake College 2406 S Alverno Rd	Manitowoc	WI	54220	920-686-6175	684-7082*
*Fax: Admissions ■ TF: 800-236-4752 ■ Web: www.sl.edu					
University of Wisconsin					
Eau Claire 105 Garfield Ave PO Box 4004	Eau Claire	WI	54701	715-836-2637	836-2409*
*Fax: Admissions ■ Web: www.uwec.edu					
Green Bay 2420 Nicolet Dr	Green Bay	WI	54311	920-465-2000	465-5754*
*Fax: Admissions ■ Web: www.uwgb.edu					
La Crosse 1725 State St 115 Graff Main Hall	La Crosse	WI	54601	608-785-8000	785-6695
Web: www.uwlax.edu					
Madison 716 Langdon St	Madison	WI	53706	608-262-3961	262-7706*
*Fax: Admissions ■ Web: www.wisc.edu					
Milwaukee PO Box 413	Milwaukee	WI	53201	414-229-1122	229-6940*
*Fax: Admissions ■ Web: www.uwm.edu					
Oshkosh 800 Algoma Blvd PO Box 2423	Oshkosh	WI	54903	920-424-0202	424-1207*
*Fax: Admissions ■ Web: www.uwosh.edu					
Parkside 900 Wood Rd	Kenosha	WI	53141	262-595-2345	595-2008*
*Fax: Admissions ■ Web: www.uwp.edu					
Platteville 1 University Plaza	Platteville	WI	53818	608-342-1125	342-1122*
*Fax: Admissions ■ TF: 800-362-5515 ■ Web: www.uwplatt.edu					
River Falls 410 S 3rd St	River Falls	WI	54022	715-425-3911	425-0676*
*Fax: Admissions ■ Web: www.uwrf.edu					
Stevens Point 2100 Main St	Stevens Point	WI	54481	715-346-0123	346-3296*
*Fax: Admissions ■ Web: www.uwsp.edu					
Stout 802 S Broadway	Menomonie	WI	54751	715-232-1232	232-1667*
*Fax: Admissions ■ TF Admissions: 800-447-8688 ■ Web: www.uwstout.edu					
Superior Belknap St & Caitlin Ave PO Box 2000	Superior	WI	54880	715-394-8101	394-8407
TF: 800-442-6459 ■ Web: www.uwsuper.edu					
Whitewater 800 W Main St	Whitewater	WI	53190	262-472-1440	472-1515*
*Fax: Admissions ■ Web: www.uww.edu					
Viterbo University 900 Viterbo Dr	La Crosse	WI	54601	608-796-3000	796-3020*
*Fax: Admissions ■ TF: 800-848-3726 ■ Web: www.viterbo.edu					
Wisconsin Lutheran College 8800 W Bluemound Rd	Milwaukee	WI	53226	414-443-8800	443-8514*
*Fax: Admissions ■ TF: 888-947-5884 ■ Web: www.wlc.edu					

Wyoming

	City	State	ZIP	Phone	Fax
University of Wyoming 1000 E University Ave Dept 3435	Laramie	WY	82071	307-766-5160	766-4042*
*Fax: Admissions ■ TF Admissions: 800-342-5996 ■ Web: www.uwyo.edu					

169 COLLEGES & UNIVERSITIES - GRADUATE & PROFESSIONAL SCHOOLS

169-1 Law Schools

Law schools listed here are approved by the American Bar Association.

				Phone	Fax
Albany Law School of Union University 80 New Scotland Ave *Web:* www.als.edu	Albany	NY	12208	518-445-2326	445-2369
American University Washington College of Law 4801 Massachusetts Ave NW *Web:* www.wcl.american.edu	Washington	DC	20016	202-274-4101	274-4107
Appalachian School of Law Rt 83 Slate Creek Rd PO Box 2825 *TF:* 800-895-7411 ■ *Web:* www.asl.edu	Grundy	VA	24614	276-935-4349	935-8261
Arizona State University Sandra Day O'Connor College of Law PO Box 877906 *Web:* www.law.asu.edu	Tempe	AZ	85287	480-965-6181	727-7930
Ave Maria University School of Law 3475 Plymouth Rd *Web:* www.avemarialaw.edu	Ann Arbor	MI	48105	734-827-8040	622-0123
Barry University Dwayne O Andreas School of Law 6441 E Colonial Dr *Web:* www.barry.edu/law	Orlando	FL	32807	321-206-5600	206-5662
Baylor University School of Law 1114 S University Parks Dr 1 Bear Pl 97288 *Web:* law.baylor.edu	Waco	TX	76798	254-710-1911	710-2316
Benjamin N Cardozo School of Law Yeshiva University 55 5th Ave Brookdale Center *Web:* www.cardozo.yu.edu	New York	NY	10003	212-790-0200	790-0256
Boston College Law School 885 Centre St *Web:* www.bc.edu/schools/law	Newton	MA	02459	617-552-8550	552-2615
Boston University School of Law 765 Commonwealth Ave *Web:* www.bu.edu/law	Boston	MA	02215	617-353-3100	353-0578
Brigham Young University J Reuben Clark Law School JRCB Bldg PO Box 28000 **Fax:* Admissions ■ *Web:* www.law.byu.edu	Provo	UT	84602	801-422-2414	422-0389*
Brooklyn Law School 250 Joralemon St **Fax:* Admissions ■ *Web:* www.brooklaw.edu	Brooklyn	NY	11201	718-780-7906	780-0395*
California Western School of Law 225 Cedar St *TF:* 800-255-4252 ■ *Web:* www.cwsl.edu	San Diego	CA	92101	619-525-1401	615-1401
Campbell University Norman Adrian Wiggins School of Law 113 Main St *TF:* 800-334-4111 ■ *Web:* law.campbell.edu	Buies Creek	NC	27506	910-893-1750	893-1780
Capital University Law School 303 E Broad St *Web:* www.law.capital.edu	Columbus	OH	43215	614-236-6500	236-6972
Case Western Reserve University School of Law 11075 East Blvd **Fax:* Admissions ■ *TF:* 800-756-0036 ■ *Web:* lawwww.cwru.edu	Cleveland	OH	44106	216-368-3600	368-1042*
Catholic University of America Columbus School of Law 3600 John McCormack Rd NE *Web:* law.edu	Washington	DC	20064	202-319-5140	319-4459
Chapman University School of Law 1 University Dr Kennedy Hall **Fax:* Admissions ■ *TF:* 888-242-1913 ■ *Web:* www.chapman.edu/law	Orange	CA	92866	714-628-2500	628-2501*
Chicago-Kent College of Law Illinois Institute of Technology 565 W Adams St *Web:* www.kentlaw.edu	Chicago	IL	60661	312-906-5000	906-5280
City University of New York School of Law 65-21 Main St **Fax:* Admissions ■ *Web:* www.law.cuny.edu	Flushing	NY	11367	718-340-4200	340-4435*
Cleveland State University Cleveland-Marshall College of Law 1801 Euclid Ave LB 138 *Web:* www.law.csuohio.edu	Cleveland	OH	44115	216-687-2344	687-6881
Columbia University School of Law 435 W 116th St *Web:* www.law.columbia.edu	New York	NY	10027	212-854-2640	854-1109
Cornell Law School 226 Myron Taylor Hall *Web:* www.lawschool.cornell.edu	Ithaca	NY	14853	607-255-5141	255-7193
Creighton University School of Law 2133 California St **Fax:* Admissions ■ *Web:* culaw2.creighton.edu	Omaha	NE	68178	402-280-2872	280-3161*
CUNY School of Law 65-21 Main St **Fax:* Admissions ■ *Web:* www.law.cuny.edu	Flushing	NY	11367	718-340-4200	340-4435*
DePaul University College of Law 25 E Jackson Blvd **Fax:* Admissions ■ *Web:* www.law.depaul.edu	Chicago	IL	60604	312-362-8701	362-5280*
Drake University School of Law 2507 University Ave *TF:* 800-443-7253 ■ *Web:* www.law.drake.edu	Des Moines	IA	50311	515-271-2824	271-1958
Duke University School of Law Science Dr & Towerview Rd Box 90393 *TF:* 888-529-2586 ■ *Web:* www.law.duke.edu	Durham	NC	27708	919-613-7001	613-7231
Duquesne University School of Law 600 Forbes Ave *Web:* www.law.duq.edu	Pittsburgh	PA	15282	412-396-6300	396-1073
Emory University School of Law 1301 Clifton Rd **Fax:* Admissions ■ *Web:* www.law.emory.edu	Atlanta	GA	30322	404-727-6816	727-6802*
Florida Coastal School of Law 8787 Bay Pine Rd **Fax:* Admissions ■ *TF:* 877-210-2591 ■ *Web:* www.fcsl.edu	Jacksonville	FL	32256	904-680-7700	680-7692*
Florida State University College of Law 425 W Jefferson St *Web:* www.law.fsu.edu	Tallahassee	FL	32306	850-644-3400	644-5487
Fordham University School of Law 140 W 62nd St **Fax:* Admissions ■ *Web:* law.fordham.edu	New York	NY	10023	212-636-6810	636-7984*
Franklin Pierce Law Center 2 White St **Fax:* Admissions ■ *Web:* www.fplc.edu	Concord	NH	03301	603-228-1541	228-1074*
George Mason University School of Law 3301 N Fairfax Dr New Bldg A01 *Web:* www.gmu.edu/departments/law	Arlington	VA	22201	703-993-8000	993-8088
George Washington University Law School 2000 H St NW **Fax:* Admissions ■ *Web:* www.law.gwu.edu	Washington	DC	20052	202-994-6261	994-7230*
Georgetown University Law Center 600 New Jersey Ave NW **Fax:* Admissions ■ *Web:* www.law.georgetown.edu	Washington	DC	20001	202-662-9000	662-9439*
Georgia State University College of Law 140 Decatur St **Fax:* Admissions ■ *Web:* law.gsu.edu	Atlanta	GA	30303	404-651-2048	651-1244*
Golden Gate University School of Law 536 Mission St *TF:* 800-448-4968 ■ *Web:* www.ggu.edu/school_of_law	San Francisco	CA	94105	415-442-6600	442-6609
Gonzaga University School of Law 721 N Cincinnati St **Fax:* Admissions ■ *TF Admissions:* 800-986-9585 ■ *Web:* www.law.gonzaga.edu	Spokane	WA	99258	509-328-4220	323-5532*
Hamline University School of Law 1536 Hewitt Ave **Fax:* Admissions ■ *TF:* 800-388-3688 ■ *Web:* www.hamline.edu/law	Saint Paul	MN	55104	651-523-2461	523-3064*
Harvard Law School 1515 Massachusetts Ave *Web:* www.law.harvard.edu	Cambridge	MA	02138	617-495-3109	
Hofstra University School of Law 121 Hofstra University **Fax:* Admissions ■ *TF:* 800-463-7872 ■ *Web:* www.hofstra.edu/Academics/Law	Hempstead	NY	11549	516-463-5916	463-5100*
Howard University School of Law 2900 Van Ness St NW **Fax:* Admissions ■ *Web:* www.law.howard.edu	Washington	DC	20008	202-806-8000	806-8162*
Indiana University School of Law Bloomington 211 S Indiana Ave *Web:* www.law.indiana.edu	Bloomington	IN	47405	812-855-7995	855-0555
Indiana University School of Law Indianapolis Lawrence W Inlow Hall 530 W New York St *Web:* indylaw.indiana.edu	Indianapolis	IN	46202	317-274-8523	274-3955
Inter American University School of Law PO Box 70351 *Web:* www.derecho.inter.edu	San Juan	PR	00936	787-751-1912	
John Marshall Law School 315 S Plymouth Ct **Fax:* Admissions ■ *Web:* www.jmls.edu	Chicago	IL	60604	312-427-2737	427-5136*
Lewis & Clark Law School 10015 SW Terwilliger Blvd **Fax:* Admissions ■ *Web:* www.lclark.edu/LAW	Portland	OR	97219	503-768-6600	768-6793*
Louis D Brandeis School of Law at the Univeristy of Louisville 2301 S 3rd St *Web:* louisville.edu/brandeislaw	Louisville	KY	40208	502-852-6358	852-0862
Louisiana State University Paul M Hebert Law Center Paul M Hebert Law Center *Web:* www.law.lsu.edu	Baton Rouge	LA	70803	225-578-8646	578-8647
Loyola Marymount Law School 919 Albany St *Web:* www.lls.edu	Los Angeles	CA	90015	213-736-1000	736-6523
Loyola University Chicago School of Law 25 E Pearson St *Web:* www.luc.edu/law	Chicago	IL	60611	312-915-7120	915-7201
Loyola University New Orleans College of Law 7214 St Charles Ave Box 901 *Web:* law.loyno.edu	New Orleans	LA	70118	504-861-5550	
Marquette University Law School 1103 W Wisconsin Ave Sensenbrenner Hall **Fax:* Admissions ■ *Web:* law.marquette.edu	Milwaukee	WI	53233	414-288-7090	288-6403*
Mercer University Walter F George School of Law 1021 Georgia Ave **Fax:* Admissions ■ *TF:* 800-637-2378 ■ *Web:* www.law.mercer.edu	Macon	GA	31207	478-301-2605	301-2989*
Michigan State University College of Law 368 Law College Bldg **Fax:* Admissions ■ *TF:* 800-844-9352 ■ *Web:* www.law.msu.edu	East Lansing	MI	48824	517-432-6810	432-0098*
Mississippi College School of Law 151 E Griffith St **Fax:* Admissions ■ *Web:* law.mc.edu	Jackson	MS	39201	601-925-7100	925-7166*
New England School of Law 154 Stuart St **Fax:* Admissions ■ *Web:* www.nesl.edu	Boston	MA	02116	617-451-0010	457-3033*
New York Law School 57 Worth St **Fax:* Admissions ■ *TF:* 877-937-6957 ■ *Web:* www.nyls.edu	New York	NY	10013	212-431-2100	966-1522*
New York University School of Law 110 W 3rd St **Fax:* Admissions ■ *Web:* www.law.nyu.edu	New York	NY	10012	212-998-6100	995-4527*
North Carolina Central University School of Law 1512 S Alston Ave *Web:* www.nccu.edu/law	Durham	NC	27707	919-530-6333	530-6339
Northeastern University School of Law 400 Huntington Ave *Web:* www.slaw.neu.edu	Boston	MA	02115	617-373-2395	373-8865
Northern Illinois University College of Law 1425 W Lincoln Hwy *TF:* 800-892-3050 ■ *Web:* law.niu.edu	DeKalb	IL	60115	815-753-8559	753-4501
Northern Kentucky University Salmon P Chase College of Law 1 Nunn Dr **Fax:* Admissions ■ *Web:* chaselaw.nku.edu	Highland Heights	KY	41099	859-572-5340	572-5342*
Northwestern University School of Law 357 E Chicago Ave **Fax:* Admissions ■ *Web:* www.law.northwestern.edu	Chicago	IL	60611	312-503-3100	503-0178*
Notre Dame Law School University of Notre Dame 103 Law School *Web:* law.nd.edu	Notre Dame	IN	46556	574-631-6627	631-4197
Nova Southeastern University Shepard Broad Law Center 3305 College Ave **Fax:* Admissions ■ *TF:* 800-986-6529 ■ *Web:* www.nsulaw.nova.edu	Fort Lauderdale	FL	33314	954-262-6100	262-3844*
Ohio Northern University Claude W Pettit College of Law 525 S Main St *TF:* 888-452-9668 ■ *Web:* www.law.onu.edu	Ada	OH	45810	419-772-2211	772-3042
Ohio State University Moritz College of Law 55 W 12th Ave *Web:* moritzlaw.osu.edu	Columbus	OH	43210	614-292-2631	292-1492
Oklahoma City University School of Law 2501 N Blackwelder Ave *TF:* 800-230-3012 ■ *Web:* www.okcu.edu/law	Oklahoma City	OK	73106	405-208-5000	521-5802
Pace University School of Law 78 N Broadway **Fax:* Admissions ■ *Web:* www.law.pace.edu	White Plains	NY	10603	914-422-4210	989-8714*
Penn State Dickinson School of Law 150 S College St **Fax:* Admissions ■ *TF:* 800-840-1122 ■ *Web:* www.dsl.psu.edu	Carlisle	PA	17013	717-240-5000	241-3503*
Pennsylvania State University Dickinson School of Law 150 S College St **Fax:* Admissions ■ *TF:* 800-840-1122 ■ *Web:* www.dsl.psu.edu	Carlisle	PA	17013	717-240-5000	241-3503*
Pepperdine University School of Law 24255 Pacific Coast Hwy **Fax:* Admissions ■ *Web:* law.pepperdine.edu	Malibu	CA	90263	310-506-4631	506-7668*
Pontifical Catholic University of Puerto Rico School of Law 2250 Ave Las Americas *Web:* www.pucpr.edu/derecho	Ponce	PR	00717	787-651-2000	
Quinney SJ College of Law 332 S 1400 East Rm 101 *Web:* www.law.utah.edu	Salt Lake City	UT	84112	801-581-6833	581-6897
Quinnipiac University School of Law 275 Mt Carmel Ave *TF:* 800-462-1944 ■ *Web:* law.quinnipiac.edu	Hamden	CT	06518	203-582-3400	582-3339
Regent University School of Law 1000 Regent University Dr Regent Hall 239 **Fax:* Admissions ■ *TF:* 877-267-5072 ■ *Web:* www.regent.edu/acad/schlaw	Virginia Beach	VA	23464	757-226-4584	226-4139*
Roger Williams University Ralph R Papitto School of Law 10 Metacom Ave **Fax:* Admissions ■ *TF:* 800-633-2727 ■ *Web:* law.rwu.edu	Bristol	RI	02809	401-254-4500	254-4516*
Rutgers The State University of New Jersey School of Law Camden 217 N 5th St **Fax:* Admissions ■ *TF:* 800-466-7561 ■ *Web:* www-camlaw.rutgers.edu	Camden	NJ	08102	856-225-6375	225-6537*
Rutgers University School of Law Newark 123 Washington St Center for Law & Justice **Fax:* Admissions ■ *Web:* law.newark.rutgers.edu	Newark	NJ	07102	973-353-5557	353-3459*
Saint John's University School of Law 8000 Utopia Pkwy *TF:* 888-978-5646 ■ *Web:* new.stjohns.edu/academics/graduate/law	Jamaica	NY	11439	718-990-6611	990-2526
Saint Louis University School of Law 3700 Lindell Blvd *Web:* law.slu.edu	Saint Louis	MO	63108	314-977-2766	977-3333
Saint Mary's University School of Law 1 Camino Santa Maria **Fax:* Admissions ■ *TF:* 866-639-5831 ■ *Web:* www.stmarytx.edu/law	San Antonio	TX	78228	210-436-3523	431-4202*
Saint Thomas University School of Law 16401 NW 37th Ave **Fax:* Admissions ■ *TF:* 800-245-4569 ■ *Web:* www.stu.edu/lawschool	Miami Gardens	FL	33054	305-623-2310	623-2357*
Samford University Cumberland School of Law 800 Lakeshore Dr *Web:* cumberland.samford.edu/cumberland1.asp?ID=2	Birmingham	AL	35229	205-726-2400	726-2057
Santa Clara University School of Law 500 El Camino Real **Fax:* Admissions ■ *Web:* www.scu.edu/law	Santa Clara	CA	95053	408-554-4361	554-5095*
Seattle University School of Law 901 12th Ave Sullivan Hall **Fax:* Admissions ■ *Web:* www.law.seattleu.edu	Seattle	WA	98122	206-398-4000	398-4058*
Seton Hall University School of Law 1 Newark Center **Fax:* Admissions ■ *TF:* 888-415-7271 ■ *Web:* law.shu.edu	Newark	NJ	07102	973-642-8747	642-8876*
SJ Quinney College of Law 332 S 1400 East Rm 101 *Web:* www.law.utah.edu	Salt Lake City	UT	84112	801-581-6833	581-6897
South Texas College of Law 1303 San Jacinto St **Fax:* Admissions ■ *Web:* www.stcl.edu	Houston	TX	77002	713-659-8040	646-2906*

				Phone	Fax
Southern Illinois University School of Law 1209 W Chautauqua Rd	Carbondale	IL	62901	618-453-8858	453-8921*
*Fax: Admissions ■ TF: 800-739-9187 ■ Web: www.law.siu.edu					
Southern Methodist University Dedman School of Law 3300 University Blvd	Dallas	TX	75205	214-768-2550	768-2549*
*Fax: Admissions ■ TF: 888-768-5291 ■ Web: www.law.smu.edu					
Southern University Law Center 2 Roosevelt Steptoe Dr PO Box 9294	Baton Rouge	LA	70813	225-771-6297	771-2121
TF: 800-537-1135 ■ Web: www.sulc.edu					
Southwestern University School of Law 3050 Wilshire Blvd	Los Angeles	CA	90010	213-738-6700	738-6899
Web: www.swlaw.edu					
Stanford University Law School 559 Nathan Abbott Way Crown Quadrangle	Stanford	CA	94305	650-723-2465	723-0838*
*Fax: Admissions ■ Web: www.law.stanford.edu					
Stetson University College of Law 1401 61st St S	Gulfport	FL	33707	727-562-7800	343-0136*
*Fax: Admissions ■ Web: www.law.stetson.edu					
Suffolk University Law School 120 Tremont St	Boston	MA	02108	617-573-8144	523-1367*
*Fax: Admissions ■ Web: www.law.suffolk.edu					
Syracuse University College of Law 340 White Hall	Syracuse	NY	13244	315-443-1962	443-9568*
*Fax: Admissions ■ Web: www.law.syr.edu					
Temple University James E Beasley School of Law 1719 N Broad St	Philadelphia	PA	19122	215-204-7861	204-1185
Web: www2.law.temple.edu					
Texas Southern University Thurgood Marshall School of Law 3100 Cleburne St	Houston	TX	77004	713-313-4455	313-1049*
*Fax: Admissions ■ Web: www.tsu.edu/academics/law					
Texas Tech University School of Law 1802 Hartford Ave	Lubbock	TX	79409	806-742-3990	742-1629
Web: www.law.ttu.edu					
Texas Wesleyan University School of Law 1515 Commerce St	Fort Worth	TX	76102	817-212-4000	212-4141*
*Fax: Admissions ■ TF: 800-733-9529 ■ Web: law.txwes.edu					
Thomas Jefferson School of Law 2121 San Diego Ave	San Diego	CA	92110	619-297-9700	294-4713*
*Fax: Admissions ■ TF: 800-956-5070 ■ Web: www.tjsl.edu					
Thomas M Cooley Law School 300 S Capitol Ave	Lansing	MI	48933	517-371-5140	334-5752
Web: www.cooley.edu					
Touro College Jacob D Fuchsberg Law Center 225 Eastview Dr	Central Islip	NY	11722	631-421-2244	421-2675
Web: www.tourolaw.edu					
Tulane University Law School 6329 Freret St Weinmann Hall	New Orleans	LA	70118	504-865-5939	865-6710*
*Fax: Admissions ■ TF: 800-734-6031 ■ Web: www.law.tulane.edu					
University of Akron School of Law 150 University Ave	Akron	OH	44325	330-972-7331	258-2343
Web: www.uakron.edu/law					
University of Alabama School of Law 101 Bryant Dr E	Tuscaloosa	AL	35401	205-348-5440	348-3971
Web: www.law.ua.edu					
University of Arizona James E Rogers College of Law 1201 E Speedway Blvd PO Box 210176	Tucson	AZ	85721	520-621-1373	626-1839
Web: www.law.arizona.edu					
University of Arkansas at Little Rock William H Bowen School of Law 1201 McMath Ave	Little Rock	AR	72202	501-324-9903	324-9909
Web: www.law.ualr.edu					
University of Arkansas School of Law 1045 W Maple St	Fayetteville	AR	72701	479-575-5601	575-3937*
*Fax: Admissions ■ Web: law.uark.edu					
University of Baltimore School of Law 1415 Maryland Ave	Baltimore	MD	21201	410-837-4468	837-4450
TF: 877-277-5982 ■ Web: law.ubalt.edu					
University at Buffalo Law School John Lord O'Brian Hall	Buffalo	NY	14260	716-645-2052	645-2064
Web: www.law.buffalo.edu					
University of California Berkeley School of Law 2600 Bancroft Way 5 Boalt Hall	Berkeley	CA	94720	510-642-2274	643-6222*
*Fax: Admissions ■ Web: www.law.berkeley.edu					
University of California Davis School of Law 400 Mrak Hall Dr	Davis	CA	95616	530-752-0243	754-8371
TF: 866-752-6622 ■ Web: www.law.ucdavis.edu					
University of California Hastings College of the Law 200 McAllister St	San Francisco	CA	94102	415-565-4600	581-8946*
*Fax: Admissions ■ Web: www.uchastings.edu					
University of California Los Angeles School of Law 71 Dodd Hall PO Box 951445	Los Angeles	CA	90095	310-825-4841	
Web: www.law.ucla.edu					
University of Chicago Law School 1111 E 60th St	Chicago	IL	60637	773-702-9494	834-0942
Web: www.law.uchicago.edu					
University of Cincinnati College of Law Clifton & Calhoun St PO Box 210040	Cincinnati	OH	45221	513-556-6805	556-2391*
*Fax: Admissions ■ Web: www.law.uc.edu					
University of Colorado School of Law 4050 Kittredge Loop Dr	Boulder	CO	80309	303-492-7203	492-1757
Web: www.colorado.edu/law					
University of Connecticut School of Law 45 Elizabeth St	Hartford	CT	06105	860-570-5100	570-5153*
*Fax: Admissions ■ Web: www.law.uconn.edu					
University of Dayton School of Law 300 College Park	Dayton	OH	45469	937-229-3211	229-4194*
*Fax: Admissions ■ Web: www.law.udayton.edu					
University of Denver College of Law 2255 E Evans Ave	Denver	CO	80208	303-871-6000	871-6378
Web: www.law.du.edu					
University of Detroit Mercy School of Law 651 E Jefferson Ave	Detroit	MI	48226	313-596-0264	596-0280*
*Fax: Admissions ■ TF: 866-428-1610 ■ Web: www.law.udmercy.edu					
University of the District of Columbia David A Clarke School of Law 4200 Connecticut Ave NW	Washington	DC	20008	202-274-7341	274-5583
Web: www.law.udc.edu					
University of Florida Fredric G Levin College of Law 2500 SW 2nd Ave	Gainesville	FL	32611	352-273-0890	392-4087*
*Fax: Admissions ■ TF: 877-429-1297 ■ Web: www.law.ufl.edu					
University of Georgia School of Law 120 Herty Dr	Athens	GA	30602	706-542-5191	542-5556
Web: www.lawsch.uga.edu					
University of Hawaii at Manoa William S Richardson School of Law 2515 Dole St	Honolulu	HI	96822	808-956-7966	956-6402*
*Fax: Admissions ■ Web: www.hawaii.edu/law					
University of Houston Law Center 100 Law Center	Houston	TX	77204	713-743-2100	743-2194*
*Fax: Admissions ■ Web: www.law.uh.edu					
University of Idaho College of Law 6th & Rayburn St PO Box 442321	Moscow	ID	83844	208-885-4977	885-5709
TF: 888-884-3246 ■ Web: www.law.uidaho.edu					
University of Illinois College of Law 504 E Pennsylvania Ave	Champaign	IL	61820	217-333-0930	244-1478
Web: www.law.uiuc.edu					
University of Iowa College of Law 131 Byington Rd	Iowa City	IA	52242	319-335-9034	335-9019
TF: 800-553-4692 ■ Web: www.law.uiowa.edu					
University of Kansas School of Law 1535 W 15th St	Lawrence	KS	66045	785-864-4550	864-5054
Web: www.law.ku.edu					
University of Kentucky College of Law 620 S Limestone St	Lexington	KY	40506	859-257-1678	323-1061
Web: www.uky.edu/Law					
University of Maine School of Law 246 Deering Ave	Portland	ME	04102	207-780-4355	780-4239
Web: mainelaw.maine.edu					
University of Maryland School of Law 500 W Baltimore St	Baltimore	MD	21201	410-706-3492	706-1793*
*Fax: Admissions ■ Web: www.law.umaryland.edu					
University of Memphis Cecil C Humphreys School of Law 3715 Central Ave	Memphis	TN	38152	901-678-2421	678-5210
Web: www.law.memphis.edu					
University of Miami School of Law 1311 Miller Dr	Coral Gables	FL	33146	305-284-2339	284-3084*
*Fax: Admissions ■ Web: www.law.miami.edu					
University of Michigan Law School 625 S State St	Ann Arbor	MI	48109	734-764-1358	647-3218*
*Fax: Admissions ■ Web: www.law.umich.edu					
University of Minnesota Law School 229 19th Ave S Walter F Mondale Hall	Minneapolis	MN	55455	612-625-1000	626-1874*
*Fax: Admissions ■ Web: www.law.umn.edu					
University of Mississippi School of Law 301 Grove Loop	University	MS	38677	662-915-7361	915-1289*
*Fax: Admissions ■ Web: www.olemiss.edu/depts/law_school					
University of Missouri Columbia School of Law 203 Hulston Hall	Columbia	MO	65211	573-882-6487	882-4984
Web: www.law.missouri.edu					
University of Missouri Kansas City School of Law 500 E 52nd St	Kansas City	MO	64110	816-235-1644	235-5276*
*Fax: Admissions ■ Web: www.law.umkc.edu					
University of Montana School of Law 32 Campus Dr	Missoula	MT	59812	406-243-4311	243-2576*
*Fax: Admissions ■ Web: www.umt.edu/law					
University of Nebraska College of Law 1875 N 42nd St	Lincoln	NE	68583	402-472-2161	472-5185
Web: www.unl.edu/lawcoll					
University of Nevada Las Vegas William S Boyd School of Law 4505 Maryland Pkwy	Las Vegas	NV	89154	702-895-3671	895-1095
Web: www.law.unlv.edu					
University of New Mexico School of Law 1 University of New Mexico MSC 11-6070	Albuquerque	NM	87131	505-277-2146	277-0068
Web: lawschool.unm.edu					
University of North Carolina School of Law 100 Ridge Rd	Chapel Hill	NC	27599	919-962-5106	843-7939*
*Fax: Admissions ■ Web: www.law.unc.edu					
University of North Dakota School of Law 2901 University Ave	Grand Forks	ND	58202	701-777-2104	777-2721*
*Fax: Admissions ■ TF: 800-225-5863 ■ Web: www.law.und.nodak.edu					
University of Oklahoma College of Law 300 Timberdell Rd Andrew M Coats Hall	Norman	OK	73019	405-325-4699	325-7474
Web: www.law.ou.edu					
University of Oregon School of Law 1515 Agate St	Eugene	OR	97403	541-346-3852	346-1564
Web: www.law.uoregon.edu					
University of the Pacific McGeorge School of Law 3200 5th Ave	Sacramento	CA	95817	916-739-7105	739-7134*
*Fax: Admissions ■ Web: www.mcgeorge.edu					
University of Pennsylvania Law School 3400 Chestnut St	Philadelphia	PA	19104	215-898-7483	573-2025
Web: www.law.upenn.edu					
University of Pittsburgh School of Law 3900 Forbes Ave	Pittsburgh	PA	15260	412-648-1400	648-2647
Web: www.law.pitt.edu					
University of Richmond School of Law 28 W Hampton Way	University of Richmond	VA	23173	804-289-8740	289-8992
Web: law.richmond.edu					
University of Saint Thomas School of Law 1000 LaSalle Ave	Minneapolis	MN	55403	651-962-4892	962-4876*
*Fax: Admissions ■ TF: 800-328-6819 ■ Web: www.stthomas.edu/law					
University of San Diego School of Law 5998 Alcala Park	San Diego	CA	92110	619-260-4528	260-2218*
*Fax: Admissions ■ TF: 800-248-4873 ■ Web: www.sandiego.edu/usdlaw					
University of San Francisco School of Law 2130 Fulton St	San Francisco	CA	94117	415-422-6586	422-5442*
*Fax: Admissions ■ Web: www.usfca.edu/law					
University of South Carolina School of Law 701 S Main St	Columbia	SC	29208	803-777-6605	777-7751*
*Fax: Admissions ■ Web: www.law.sc.edu					
University of South Dakota School of Law 414 E Clark St	Vermillion	SD	57069	605-677-5443	677-5417
TF: 877-269-6837 ■ Web: www.usd.edu/law					
University of Southern California Law School 699 Exposition Blvd	Los Angeles	CA	90089	213-740-2523	740-4570*
*Fax: Admissions ■ Web: lawweb.usc.edu					
University of Tennessee College of Law 1505 W Cumberland Ave	Knoxville	TN	37996	865-974-2521	974-6595
Web: www.law.utk.edu					
University of Texas School of Law 727 E Dean Keeton St	Austin	TX	78705	512-471-5151	471-6988
Web: www.utexas.edu/law					
University of Toledo College of Law 2801 W Bancroft St	Toledo	OH	43606	419-530-4131	530-4345*
*Fax: Admissions ■ Web: www.utlaw.edu					
University of Tulsa College of Law 3120 E 4th Pl	Tulsa	OK	74104	918-631-2401	631-3126
Web: www.law.utulsa.edu					
University of Utah SJ Quinney College of Law 332 S 1400 East Rm 101	Salt Lake City	UT	84112	801-581-6833	581-6897
Web: www.law.utah.edu					
University of Virginia School of Law 580 Massie Rd	Charlottesville	VA	22903	434-924-7354	924-7536
Web: www.law.virginia.edu					
University of Washington School of Law William H Gates Hall Box 353020	Seattle	WA	98195	206-543-4078	543-5671
Web: www.law.washington.edu					
University of Wisconsin Law School 975 Bascom Mall	Madison	WI	53706	608-262-2240	262-5485
Web: law.wisc.edu					
University of Wyoming College of Law 1000 E University Ave Dept 3035	Laramie	WY	82071	307-766-6416	766-6417
Web: uwadmnweb.uwyo.edu/law					
Valparaiso University School of Law 656 S Greenwich St	Valparaiso	IN	46383	219-465-7829	465-7808
TF: 888-825-7652 ■ Web: www.valpo.edu/law					
Vanderbilt University Law School 131 21st Ave S	Nashville	TN	37203	615-322-2615	322-6631
Web: law.vanderbilt.edu					
Vermont Law School 168 Chelsea St PO Box 96	South Royalton	VT	05068	802-831-1001	763-7071
TF: 800-227-1395 ■ Web: www.vermontlaw.edu					
Villanova University School of Law 299 N Spring Mill Rd	Villanova	PA	19085	610-519-7000	519-6291*
*Fax: Admissions ■ Web: www.law.villanova.edu					
Wake Forest University School of Law Worrell Professional Center Wake Forest Rd	Winston-Salem	NC	27109	336-758-5435	758-3930*
*Fax: Admissions ■ Web: www.law.wfu.edu					
Washburn University School of Law 1700 SW College Ave	Topeka	KS	66621	785-231-1060	670-1024
Web: www.washburnlaw.edu					
Washington & Lee University School of Law Sydney Lewis Hall 4th Fl	Lexington	VA	24450	540-458-8502	458-8586*
*Fax: Admissions ■ Web: law.wlu.edu					
Washington University School of Law 1 Brookings Dr Anheuser-Busch Hall	Saint Louis	MO	63130	314-935-6400	935-8778*
*Fax: Admissions ■ Web: www.wulaw.wustl.edu					
Wayne State University Law School 471 W Palmer St	Detroit	MI	48202	313-577-3937	993-8129*
*Fax: Admissions ■ Web: www.law.wayne.edu					
West Virginia University College of Law 101 Law Center Dr	Morgantown	WV	26506	304-293-5301	293-6891
Web: www.wvu.edu/law					
Western New England College School of Law 1215 Wilbraham Rd	Springfield	MA	01119	413-782-1412	796-2067*
*Fax: Admissions ■ Web: www1.law.wnec.edu					
Western State University College of Law 1111 N State College Blvd	Fullerton	CA	92831	714-738-1000	441-1748*
*Fax: Admissions ■ TF: 800-978-4529 ■ Web: www.wsulaw.edu					
Whittier Law School 3333 Harbor Blvd	Costa Mesa	CA	92626	714-444-4141	444-0250*
*Fax: Admissions ■ TF: 800-808-8188 ■ Web: www.law.whittier.edu					
Widener University School of Law Harrisburg 3800 Vartan Way	Harrisburg	PA	17110	717-541-3900	541-3999
TF: 888-943-3637 ■ Web: www.law.widener.edu					

Law Schools (Cont'd)

				Phone	Fax
Widener University School of Law Wilmington 4601 Concord Pike *Fax: Admissions ■ TF: 888-943-3637 ■ Web: www.law.widener.edu	Wilmington	DE	19803	302-477-2100	477-2224*
Willamette University College of Law 245 Winter St SE *Fax: Admissions ■ Web: www.willamette.edu/wucl	Salem	OR	97301	503-370-6282	370-6087*
William & Mary Law School 613 S Henry St *Fax: Admissions ■ Web: www.wm.edu/law	Williamsburg	VA	23185	757-221-3800	221-3261*
William Mitchell College of Law 875 Summit Ave TF: 888-962-5529 ■ Web: www.wmitchell.edu	Saint Paul	MN	55105	651-227-9171	290-6414
Yale Law School 127 Wall St Web: www.law.yale.edu	New Haven	CT	06511	203-432-4992	432-2112

169-2 Medical Schools

Medical schools listed here are accredited, MD-granting members of the Association of American Medical Colleges. Accredited Canadian schools that do not offer classes in English are not included among these listings.

				Phone	Fax
Albany Medical College 47 New Scotland Ave MC 3 Web: www.amc.edu	Albany	NY	12208	518-262-5521	262-5887
Albert Einstein College of Medicine of Yeshiva University 1300 Morris Park Ave Web: www.aecom.yu.edu	Bronx	NY	10461	718-430-2000	430-4098
Baylor College of Medicine 1 Baylor Plaza MS BCM365 Web: www.bcm.edu	Houston	TX	77030	713-798-7766	798-1518
Boston University School of Medicine 715 Albany St *Fax: Admissions ■ Web: www.bumc.bu.edu	Boston	MA	02118	617-638-8000	638-5258*
Brody School of Medicine at East Carolina University 600 Moye Blvd *Fax: Admissions ■ TF: 800-722-3281 ■ Web: www.ecu.edu/med	Greenville	NC	27834	252-744-1020	744-1926*
Brown Medical School 97 Waterman St *Fax: Admissions ■ Web: bms.brown.edu	Providence	RI	02912	401-863-2149	863-2660*
Burns John A School of Medicine 651 Ilalo St Medical Education Bldg Web: jabsom.hawaii.edu	Honolulu	HI	96813	808-692-1000	692-1251
Case Western Reserve University School of Medicine 10900 Euclid Ave *Fax: Admissions ■ Web: mediswww.meds.cwru.edu	Cleveland	OH	44106	216-368-3450	368-6011*
Cincinnati Children's Hospital Medical Center 3333 Burnet Ave *Fax: Admitting ■ TF: 800-344-2462 ■ Web: www.cincinnatichildrens.org	Cincinnati	OH	45229	513-636-4200	636-3733*
Columbia University College of Physicians & Surgeons 630 W 168th St *Fax: Admissions ■ Web: cpmcnet.columbia.edu	New York	NY	10032	212-305-3806	305-3601*
Creighton University School of Medicine 2500 California Plaza *Fax: Admissions ■ TF: 800-325-4405 ■ Web: medicine.creighton.edu	Omaha	NE	68178	402-280-2799	280-1241*
Dalhousie University Faculty of Medicine CRC Bldg Rm C-132 *Fax: Admissions ■ Web: www.medicine.dal.ca	Halifax	NS	B3H4H7	902-494-1874	494-6369*
Dartmouth Medical School 1 Rope Ferry Rd TF: 877-367-1797 ■ Web: dms.dartmouth.edu	Dartmouth	NH	03755	603-650-1200	650-1202
David Geffen School of Medicine at UCLA Center for Health Sciences 10833 Leconte Ave Web: dgsom.healthsciences.ucla.edu	Los Angeles	CA	90095	310-825-6081	
Drexel University College of Medicine 2900 Queen Ln Web: www.drexelmed.edu	Philadelphia	PA	19129	215-991-8202	843-1766
Duke University School of Medicine Office of Medical School Admissions DUMC 3710 Duke University Medical Center *Fax: Admissions ■ TF: 877-684-2985 ■ Web: medschool.duke.edu	Durham	NC	27710	919-684-2985	668-3714*
East Tennessee State University James H Quillen College of Medicine PO Box 70580 Web: com.etsu.edu	Johnson City	TN	37614	423-439-2033	439-2110
Eastern Virginia Medical School 700 W Olney Rd PO Box 1980 *Fax: Admissions ■ Web: www.evms.edu	Norfolk	VA	23501	757-446-5812	446-5896*
Emory University School of Medicine 1440 Clifton Rd NE Rm 115 *Fax: Admissions ■ Web: www.med.emory.edu	Atlanta	GA	30322	404-727-5660	727-5456*
Florida State University College of Medicine 1115 W Call St *Fax: Admissions ■ Web: www.med.fsu.edu	Tallahassee	FL	32306	850-644-1855	645-2846*
George Washington University School of Medicine & Health Sciences 2300 'I' St NW Ross Hall 716 Web: www.gwumc.edu	Washington	DC	20037	202-994-3506	994-1753
Georgetown University School of Medicine 13900 Reservoir Rd NW *Fax: Admissions ■ Web: som.georgetown.edu	Washington	DC	20007	202-687-1154	687-3079*
Harvard Medical School 25 Shattuck St *Fax: Admissions ■ Web: hms.harvard.edu/hms	Boston	MA	02115	617-432-1550	432-3307*
Howard University College of Medicine 520 'W' St NW Web: www.med.howard.edu	Washington	DC	20059	202-806-6270	806-7934
Indiana University School of Medicine 1120 South Dr Fessler Hall Rm 213 Web: www.medicine.iu.edu	Indianapolis	IN	46202	317-274-3772	278-0211
JABSOM (University of Hawaii at Manoa) John A Burns School of Medicine 651 Ilalo St Medical Education Bldg Web: jabsom.hawaii.edu	Honolulu	HI	96813	808-692-1000	692-1251
Jefferson Medical College of Thomas Jefferson University 1015 Walnut St Web: www.jefferson.edu/JMC	Philadelphia	PA	19107	215-955-6983	955-5151
Joan C Edwards School of Medicine at Marshall University 1600 Medical Center Dr TF: 877-691-1600 ■ Web: musom.marshall.edu	Huntington	WV	25701	304-691-1700	691-1726
Joan & Sanford Weill Medical College of Cornell University 445 E 69th St *Fax: Admissions ■ Web: www.med.cornell.edu	New York	NY	10021	212-746-5454	746-8052*
Johns Hopkins University School of Medicine 733 N Broadway Suite 147 Web: www.hopkinsmedicine.org/som/index.html	Baltimore	MD	21205	410-955-3080	955-0826
Keck School of Medicine of the University of Southern California 1975 Zonal Ave KAM 100 *Fax: Admissions ■ Web: www.usc.edu/schools/medicine/ksom	Los Angeles	CA	90089	323-442-1100	442-2433*
Loma Linda University School of Medicine 11175 Campus St TF: 800-422-4558 ■ Web: www.llu.edu/llu/medicine	Loma Linda	CA	92350	909-558-4467	558-0359
Louisiana State University School of Medicine in New Orleans 433 Bolivar St Web: www.medschool.lsuhsc.edu	New Orleans	LA	70112	504-568-6262	568-7701
Louisiana State University School of Medicine in Shreveport 1501 Kings Hwy PO Box 33932 Web: www.sh.lsuhsc.edu	Shreveport	LA	71130	318-675-5069	675-5000
Loyola University Chicago Stritch School of Medicine 2160 S 1st Ave Bldg 120 Rm 200 *Fax: Admissions ■ Web: www.meddean.luc.edu	Maywood	IL	60153	708-216-3229	216-9160*
Mayo Medical School 200 1st St SW Web: www.mayo.edu/mms	Rochester	MN	55905	507-284-3671	284-2634
McGill University Faculty of Medicine 3655 Promenade Sir-William-Osler 6th Fl *Fax: Admissions ■ Web: www.med.mcgill.ca	Montreal	QC	H3G1Y6	514-398-3517	398-4631*
McMaster University School of Medicine 1200 Main St W Health Sciences Center Rm 1B7 Web: www.fhs.mcmaster.ca	Hamilton	ON	L8N3Z5	905-525-9140	546-0349
Medical College of Georgia School of Medicine 1120 15th St *Fax: Admissions ■ TF: 800-736-2273 ■ Web: www.mcg.edu	Augusta	GA	30912	706-721-0211	721-7279*
Medical College of Wisconsin 8701 Watertown Plank Rd Web: www.mcw.edu	Milwaukee	WI	53226	414-456-8296	456-6506
Medical College of Wisconsin 8701 Watertown Plank Rd Web: www.mcw.edu	Milwaukee	WI	53226	414-456-8296	456-6506
Medical University of South Carolina College of Medicine 96 Jonathan Lucas St *Fax: Admissions ■ Web: find.musc.edu	Charleston	SC	29425	843-792-2300	792-3126*
Meharry Medical College School of Medicine 1005 DB Todd Jr Blvd Web: www.mmc.edu	Nashville	TN	37203	615-327-6111	327-6228
Memorial University of Newfoundland Faculty of Medicine 300 Prince Phillip Dr Rm 1751 Health Sciences Center Web: www.med.mun.ca/med	Saint John's	NL	A1B3V6	709-777-6615	777-8422
Mercer University School of Medicine 1550 College St TF: 800-342-0841 ■ Web: medicine.mercer.edu	Macon	GA	31207	478-301-2542	301-2547
Michigan State University College of Human Medicine A-239 Life Sciences Bldg Web: humanmedicine.msu.edu	East Lansing	MI	48824	517-353-9620	432-0021
Morehouse School of Medicine 720 Westview Dr SW *Fax: Admissions ■ Web: www.msm.edu	Atlanta	GA	30310	404-752-1500	752-1512*
Mount Sinai School of Medicine 1 Gustave L Levy Pl *Fax: Admissions ■ Web: www.mssm.edu	New York	NY	10029	212-241-6696	828-4135*
New Jersey Medical School 185 S Orange Ave Rm C-653 PO Box 1709 Web: njms.umdnj.edu	Newark	NJ	07101	973-972-4631	972-7986
New York Medical College Administration Bldg *Fax: Admissions ■ Web: www.nymc.edu	Valhalla	NY	10595	914-594-4507	594-4976*
New York University School of Medicine 560 1st Ave Web: www.med.nyu.edu	New York	NY	10016	212-263-7300	263-0720
Northeastern Ohio Universities College of Medicine 4209 State Rt 44 PO Box 95 *Fax: Admissions ■ TF: 800-686-2511 ■ Web: www.neoucom.edu	Rootstown	OH	44272	330-325-2511	325-8372*
Northwestern University Feinberg School of Medicine 303 E Chicago Ave Web: www.medschool.northwestern.edu	Chicago	IL	60611	312-503-8649	503-6978
Ohio State University College of Medicine & Public Health 370 W 9th Ave 155 Meiling Hall *Fax: Admitting ■ Web: medicine.osu.edu	Columbus	OH	43210	614-292-2220	247-7959*
Oregon Health & Science University School of Medicine 3181 SW Sam Jackson Park Rd L-109 TF: 800-775-5460 ■ Web: www.ohsu.edu	Portland	OR	97239	503-494-7800	494-4629
Penn State College of Medicine 500 University Dr Rm C1805 PO Box 850 *Fax: Admissions ■ Web: www.hmc.psu.edu/college	Hershey	PA	17033	717-531-8755	531-6225*
Pennsylvania State University College of Medicine 500 University Dr Rm C1805 PO Box 850 *Fax: Admissions ■ Web: www.hmc.psu.edu/college	Hershey	PA	17033	717-531-8755	531-6225*
Queen's University Faculty of Health Sciences School of Medicine 68 Barrie St Web: meds.queensu.ca	Kingston	ON	K7L3N6	613-533-2542	533-3190
Robert Wood Johnson Medical School 675 Hoes Ln Web: rwjms.umdnj.edu	Piscataway	NJ	08854	732-235-4576	235-5078
Rosalind Franklin University of Medicine & Science 3333 Green Bay Rd Web: www.rosalindfranklin.edu	North Chicago	IL	60064	847-578-3205	578-3284
Rush Medical College of Rush University 600 S Paulina St *Fax: Admissions ■ Web: www.rushu.rush.edu/medcol	Chicago	IL	60612	312-942-6913	942-2333*
Saint Louis University School of Medicine 1402 S Grand Blvd Rm 226 Web: www.slu.edu/colleges/med	Saint Louis	MO	63104	314-977-9870	977-9825
Schulich School of Medicine & Dentistry Health Sciences Addition Rm HSA 110 *Fax: Admissions ■ Web: www.med.uwo.ca	London	ON	N6A5C1	519-661-3459	661-3797*
Southern Illinois University School of Medicine 801 N Rutledge St TF: 800-342-5748 ■ Web: www.siumed.edu	Springfield	IL	62794	217-545-8000	
Stanford University School of Medicine 300 Pasteur Dr Web: med-www.stanford.edu	Stanford	CA	94305	650-725-3900	725-7368
State University of New York Downstate Medical Center 450 Clarkson Ave Box 60M Web: www.downstate.edu	Brooklyn	NY	11203	718-270-1000	270-7592
State University of New York Upstate Medical University 766 Irving Ave TF: 800-736-2171 ■ Web: www.upstate.edu	Syracuse	NY	13210	315-464-4570	464-8867
Stony Brook University Health Sciences Center School of Medicine Nichols Rd Health Sciences Center Level 4 Rm 158 *Fax: Admissions ■ Web: www.hsc.stonybrook.edu/som	Stony Brook	NY	11794	631-444-2113	444-6032*
SUNY Downstate Medical Center 450 Clarkson Ave Box 60M Web: www.downstate.edu	Brooklyn	NY	11203	718-270-1000	270-7592
SUNY Upstate Medical University 766 Irving Ave TF: 800-736-2171 ■ Web: www.upstate.edu	Syracuse	NY	13210	315-464-4570	464-8867
Temple University School of Medicine 3340 N Broad St SFC Ste 305 Web: www.temple.edu/medicine	Philadelphia	PA	19140	215-707-3656	707-6932
Texas A & M University System Health Science Center 301 Tarrow St 7th Fl Web: www.tamhsc.edu	College Station	TX	77840	979-458-7200	458-7202
College of Medicine 159 Joe H Reynolds Medical Bldg Web: medicine.tamu.edu	College Station	TX	77843	979-845-7743	845-5533
Texas Tech University Health Sciences Center School of Medicine 3601 4th St MS 6207 Web: www.ttuhsc.edu	Lubbock	TX	79430	806-743-3000	743-3021
Tufts University School of Medicine 136 Harrison Ave Web: www.tufts.edu/med	Boston	MA	02111	617-636-7000	636-3805
Tulane University School of Medicine 1555 Poydras St Suite 1000 Web: www.som.tulane.edu	New Orleans	LA	70118	504-988-5462	988-2945
Uniformed Services University of the Health Sciences 4301 Jones Bridge Rd *Fax: Admissions ■ TF Admissions: 800-772-1743 ■ Web: www.usuhs.mil	Bethesda	MD	20814	301-295-3770	295-3545*
University of Alabama at Birmingham School of Medicine 1670 University Blvd Volker Hall Web: www.uab.edu/uasom	Birmingham	AL	35294	205-934-2330	934-8724

Phone Fax

University of Alberta Faculty of Medicine & Dentistry
2-45 Medical Sciences Bldg . . . Edmonton AB T6G2H7 780-492-6350 492-9531
Web: www.med.ualberta.ca

University of Arizona College of Medicine
1501 N Campbell Ave . . . Tucson AZ 85724 520-626-4555 626-6252
Web: www.medicine.arizona.edu

University of Arkansas for Medical Sciences College of Medicine 4301 W Markham St Slot 551 . . . Little Rock AR 72205 501-686-5354 686-5873*
**Fax:* Admissions ■ *Web:* www.uams.edu/com

University of British Columbia Faculty of Medicine
317-2194 Health Sciences Mall . . . Vancouver BC V6T1Z3 604-822-2421 822-6061
Web: www.med.ubc.ca

University at Buffalo School of Medicine & Biomedical Sciences
131 Biomedical Education Bldg . . . Buffalo NY 14214 716-829-3466 829-3849*
**Fax:* Admissions ■ *Web:* wings.buffalo.edu/smbs

University of Calgary Faculty of Medicine
3330 Hospital Dr NW Health Sciences Center Rm G331 . . . Calgary AB T2N4N1 403-220-7448 270-0178
Web: faculty.med.ucalgary.ca

University of California Davis School of Medicine
4610 X St Suite 1202 . . . Sacramento CA 95817 916-734-4800 734-4050*
**Fax:* Admissions ■ *Web:* som.ucdavis.edu

University of California Irvine School of Medicine
Medical Education Bldg 802 . . . Irvine CA 92697 949-824-5388 824-2485
TF: 800-824-5388 ■ *Web:* www.ucihs.uci.edu

University of California San Diego School of Medicine
9500 Gilman Dr Rm 180 Medical Teaching Facility . . . La Jolla CA 92093 858-534-3880 534-5282*
**Fax:* Admissions ■ *Web:* medicine.ucsd.edu

University of California San Francisco School of Medicine
521 Parnassus Ave . . . San Francisco CA 94143 415-476-4044
Web: medschool.ucsf.edu

University of Chicago Pritzker School of Medicine
924 E 57th St . . . Chicago IL 60637 773-702-1939 702-2598
Web: pritzker.uchicago.edu

University of Cincinnati College of Medicine
231 Albert Sabin Way PO Box 670552 . . . Cincinnati OH 45267 513-558-5575 558-1100
Web: www.med.uc.edu

University of Colorado at Denver
Campus Box 167 PO Box 173364 . . . Denver CO 80217 303-556-2704 556-4838*
**Fax:* Admissions ■ *Web:* www.cudenver.edu

University of Connecticut School of Medicine
263 Farmington Ave Rm AG036 MC 3906 . . . Farmington CT 06030 860-679-4306 679-1899*
**Fax:* Admissions ■ *Web:* medicine.uchc.edu

University of Florida College of Medicine
1600 SW Archer Rd Rm M-108 . . . Gainesville FL 32610 352-392-4569 392-1307
Web: www.med.ufl.edu

University of Hawaii at Manoa (JABSOM) John A Burns School of Medicine 651 Ilalo St Medical Education Bldg . . . Honolulu HI 96813 808-692-1000 692-1251
Web: jabsom.hawaii.edu

University of Illinois College of Medicine
808 S Wood St Rm 165 . . . Chicago IL 60612 312-996-5635 996-6693*
**Fax:* Admissions ■ *Web:* www.uic.edu/depts/mcam

University of Iowa Roy J & Lucille A Carver College of Medicine 200 CMAB . . . Iowa City IA 52242 319-335-6707 335-8318
Web: www.medicine.uiowa.edu

University of Kansas School of Medicine
3901 Rainbow Blvd 3030 Murphy MS1049 . . . Kansas City KS 66160 913-588-5200 588-5259
Web: www.kumc.edu/som

University of Kentucky College of Medicine
Office of Medical Education MN 104 UKMC . . . Lexington KY 40536 859-323-6161 323-2076
Web: www.mc.uky.edu/medicine

University of Louisville School of Medicine
323 E Chestnut St Abell Bldg Rm 413 . . . Louisville KY 40202 502-852-5193 852-0302
TF: 800-334-8635 ■ *Web:* www.louisville.edu/medschool

University of Manitoba Faculty of Medicine
727 McDermot Ave Rm 260 . . . Winnipeg MB R3E3P5 204-789-3557 789-3928
Web: www.umanitoba.ca/faculties/medicine

University of Maryland School of Medicine
685 W Baltimore St 1-005 Bressler Research Bldg . . . Baltimore MD 21201 410-706-7478 706-0467*
**Fax:* Admissions ■ *Web:* medschool.umaryland.edu

University of Medicine & Dentistry of New Jersey Graduate School of Biomedical Sciences 30 Bergen St ADMC 110 . . . Newark NJ 07107 973-972-4511 972-7148
Web: gsbs.umdnj.edu

University of Minnesota Medical School Twin Cities
420 Delaware St SE Mayo MC 293 . . . Minneapolis MN 55455 612-624-1188 626-4911
Web: www.ahc.umn.edu/ahc_content/colleges/med_school

University of Mississippi School of Medicine 2500 N State St . . . Jackson MS 39216 601-984-1080 984-1079
Web: som.umc.edu

University of Missouri-Columbia School of Medicine
1 Hospital Dr Rm MA 215 . . . Columbia MO 65212 573-882-2923 884-2988
Web: www.muhealth.org/%7Emedicine

University of Missouri-Kansas City School of Medicine
2411 Holmes St . . . Kansas City MO 64108 816-235-1111 235-5277
TF: 800-735-2466 ■ *Web:* research.med.umkc.edu

University of Nebraska School of Medicine
986585 Nebraska Medical Center . . . Omaha NE 68198 402-559-2259 559-6840*
**Fax:* Admissions ■ *TF:* 800-626-8431 ■ *Web:* www.unmc.edu/UNCOM

University of Nevada School of Medicine
1664 N Virginia St Pennington Medical Education Bldg 357 . . . Reno NV 89557 775-784-6063 784-6194
Web: www.unr.edu/med

University of New Mexico School of Medicine
1 University of New Mexico BMB Rm 177 MSC08-4720 . . . Albuquerque NM 87131 505-272-2321 272-6581
Web: hsc.unm.edu/som

University of North Dakota School of Medicine & Health Sciences 501 N Columbia Rd . . . Grand Forks ND 58203 701-777-5046 777-4942*
**Fax:* Admissions ■ *Web:* www.med.und.nodak.edu

University of Oklahoma College of Medicine
PO Box 26901 BMSB 357 . . . Oklahoma City OK 73190 405-271-2265 271-3032
Web: www.medicine.ouhsc.edu

University of Ottawa Faculty of Medicine 451 Smyth Rd . . . Ottawa ON K1H8M5 613-562-5700 562-5323
TF: 877-868-8292 ■ *Web:* www.uottawa.ca/academic/med

University of Pennsylvania School of Medicine
3450 Hamilton Walk Stemmler Hall Suite 100 . . . Philadelphia PA 19104 215-898-8004 573-6645*
**Fax:* Admissions ■ *Web:* www.med.upenn.edu

University of Pittsburgh School of Medicine
3550 Terrace St 518 Scaife Hall . . . Pittsburgh PA 15261 412-648-9891 648-8768*
**Fax:* Admissions ■ *Web:* www.medschool.pitt.edu

University of Rochester School of Medicine & Dentistry
601 Elmwood Ave . . . Rochester NY 14642 585-275-0017 756-5479*
**Fax:* Admissions ■ *Web:* www.urmc.rochester.edu/SMD

University of Saskatchewan College of Medicine
107 Wiggins Rd B103 Health Sciences Bldg . . . Saskatoon SK S7N5E5 306-966-6135 966-6164
Web: www.usask.ca/medicine

University of South Alabama College of Medicine
307 N University Blvd . . . Mobile AL 36688 251-460-6101 460-6278
Web: www.southalabama.edu

University of South Carolina School of Medicine
6439 Garners Ferry Rd . . . Columbia SC 29209 803-733-3210 733-3335
Web: www.med.sc.edu

University of South Dakota School of Medicine
414 E Clark St South Dakota Union Bldg 17 . . . Vermillion SD 57069 605-677-5233 677-5109
Web: www.usd.edu/med

University of South Florida College of Medicine
12901 Bruce B Downs Blvd MDC Box 3 . . . Tampa FL 33612 813-974-2229 974-4990*
**Fax:* Admissions ■ *Web:* www.med.usf.edu/medicine

University of Tennessee Health Science Center College of Medicine 800 Medicine Ave . . . Memphis TN 38163 901-448-5529 448-1430*
**Fax:* Admissions ■ *Web:* www.utmem.edu

University of Texas Medical Branch 301 University Blvd . . . Galveston TX 77555 409-772-2618 747-2909*
**Fax:* Admissions ■ *TF:* 800-228-1841 ■ *Web:* www.utmb.edu

University of Texas Medical School at Houston
6431 Fannin St . . . Houston TX 77030 713-500-3333 500-3356
Web: www.med.uth.tmc.edu

University of Texas Medical School at San Antonio
7703 Floyd Curl Dr . . . San Antonio TX 78229 210-567-4420 567-6962*
**Fax:* Admissions ■ *Web:* som.uthscsa.edu

University of Texas Southwestern Medical Center Dallas Southwestern Medical School 5323 Harry Hines Blvd . . . Dallas TX 75390 214-648-3111 648-3289
Web: www.utsouthwestern.edu/home/education/medicalschool/index.html

University of Toledo College of Medicine
3045 Arlington Ave Mulford Library Bldg . . . Toledo OH 43614 419-383-4229 383-4229
Web: hsc.utoledo.edu/smed/smedmain.html

University of Toronto Faculty of Medicine
500 University Ave 2nd Fl . . . Toronto ON M5G1V7 416-978-6976 978-7144
Web: www.facmed.utoronto.ca

University of Utah School of Medicine 50 N Medical Dr . . . Salt Lake City UT 84132 801-581-7201 585-3300
Web: uuhsc.utah.edu/som

University of Vermont College of Medicine
89 Beaumont Ave E-126 Given Bldg . . . Burlington VT 05405 802-656-2156 656-8577
Web: www.med.uvm.edu

University of Virginia School of Medicine
415 Jefferson Park Ave PO Box 800725 . . . Charlottesville VA 22908 434-924-5571 982-2586
Web: www.healthsystem.virginia.edu/education-research/medschl.cfm

University of Washington School of Medicine
A-300 Health Sciences Bldg Box 356340 . . . Seattle WA 98195 206-543-5560 616-3341
Web: www.uwmedicine.org

University of Wisconsin Medical School
750 Highland Ave Rm 2130 . . . Madison WI 53705 608-263-4925 262-4226*
**Fax:* Admissions ■ *Web:* www.med.wisc.edu

Vanderbilt University School of Medicine 215 Light Hall . . . Nashville TN 37232 615-322-2145 343-8397
Web: www.mc.vanderbilt.edu/medschool

Virginia Commonwealth University School of Medicine
1101 E Marshall St PO Box 980565 . . . Richmond VA 23298 804-828-9629 828-1246*
**Fax:* Admissions ■ *Web:* www.medschool.vcu.edu

Wake Forest University School of Medicine
Medical Center Blvd . . . Winston-Salem NC 27157 336-716-4264 716-9593
Web: www1.wfubmc.edu

Washington University in Saint Louis School of Medicine
660 Euclid Ave CB 8107 . . . Saint Louis MO 63110 314-362-6858 362-4658*
**Fax:* Admissions ■ *Web:* medinfo.wustl.edu

Wayne State University School of Medicine
540 E Canfield St 1310 Scott Hall . . . Detroit MI 48201 313-577-1466 577-9420*
**Fax:* Admitting ■ *Web:* www.med.wayne.edu

West Virginia University School of Medicine
Medical Center Dr Health Sciences Center N Rm 1146 . . . Morgantown WV 26506 304-293-2408 293-7814
TF: 800-543-5650 ■ *Web:* www.hsc.wvu.edu/som

Wright State University Boonshoft School of Medicine
3640 Col Glenn Hwy PO Box 1751 . . . Dayton OH 45401 937-775-2934 775-3322*
**Fax:* Admissions ■ *Web:* www.med.wright.edu

Yale University School of Medicine 367 Cedar St . . . New Haven CT 06510 203-785-2643 785-3234
Web: info.med.yale.edu/ysm

169-3 Theological Schools

Theological schools listed here are members of the Association of Theological Schools (ATS), an organization of graduate schools in the U.S. and Canada that conduct post-baccalaureate professional and academic degree programs to educate persons for the practice of ministry and for teaching and research in the theological disciplines. Listings include ATS accredited member schools, candidates for accredited membership, and associate member schools.

Phone Fax

Abilene Christian University 1705 Campus Ct . . . Abilene TX 79601 325-674-2000 674-2130*
**Fax:* Admissions ■ *TF Admissions:* 800-460-6228 ■ *Web:* www.acu.edu

Acadia Divinity College 31 Horton Ave . . . Wolfville NS B4P2R6 902-585-2210 585-2233
TF: 866-875-8975 ■ *Web:* adc.acadiau.ca

Alliance Theological Seminary 350 N Highland Ave . . . Nyack NY 10960 845-353-2020 358-2651
TF: 800-541-6891 ■ *Web:* www.alliance.edu

American Baptist Seminary of the West 2606 Dwight Way . . . Berkeley CA 94704 510-841-1905 841-2446
Web: www.absw.edu

Anderson University 1100 E 5th St . . . Anderson IN 46012 765-649-9071 641-4091*
**Fax:* Admissions ■ *TF Admissions:* 800-428-6414 ■ *Web:* www.anderson.edu

Andover Newton Theological School 210 Herrick Rd . . . Newton Centre MA 02459 617-964-1100 965-9756
TF: 800-964-2687 ■ *Web:* www.ants.edu

Andrews University Seventh-day Adventist Theological Seminary . . . Berrien Springs MI 49104 269-471-3537 471-6202
TF: 800-253-2874 ■ *Web:* www.andrews.edu/SEM

Aquinas Institute of Theology 23 S Spring Ave . . . Saint Louis MO 63108 314-256-8800 256-8888
TF: 800-977-3869 ■ *Web:* www.ai.edu

Asbury Theological Seminary 204 N Lexington Ave . . . Wilmore KY 40390 859-858-3581 858-2173
TF: 800-227-2879 ■ *Web:* www.asburyseminary.edu

Ashland Theological Seminary 910 Center St . . . Ashland OH 44805 419-289-5161 289-5969
Web: www.ashland.edu/seminary

Assemblies of God Theological Seminary
1435 N Glenstone Ave . . . Springfield MO 65802 417-268-1000 268-1001
TF: 800-467-2487 ■ *Web:* www.agts.edu

Associated Mennonite Biblical Seminary 3003 Benham Ave . . . Elkhart IN 46517 574-295-3726 295-0092
TF: 800-964-2627 ■ *Web:* www.ambs.edu

Athenaeum of Ohio 6616 Beechmont Ave . . . Cincinnati OH 45230 513-231-2223 231-3254
Web: www.mtsm.org

Atlantic School of Theology 660 Francklyn St . . . Halifax NS B3H3B5 902-423-6939 492-4048
Web: astheology.ns.ca

Austin Presbyterian Theological Seminary 100 E 27th St . . . Austin TX 78705 512-472-6736 479-0738
Web: www.austinseminary.edu

Azusa Pacific University 901 E Alosta Ave PO Box 7000 . . . Azusa CA 91702 626-969-3434 812-3096
TF: 800-825-5278 ■ *Web:* www.apu.edu

Bangor Theological Seminary 1 College Cir . . . Bangor ME 04401 207-942-6781 990-1267
TF: 800-287-6781 ■ *Web:* www.bts.edu

Baptist Missionary Assn Theological Seminary
1530 E Pine St . . . Jacksonville TX 75766 903-586-2501 586-0378
TF: 800-259-5673 ■ *Web:* www.bmats.edu

Theological Schools (Cont'd)

				Phone	Fax
Baptist Theological Seminary at Richmond 3400 Brook Rd	Richmond	VA	23227	804-355-8135	355-8182
TF: 888-345-2877 ■ *Web:* www.btsr.edu					
Barry University 11300 NE 2nd Ave	Miami Shores	FL	33161	305-899-3000	899-2971*
**Fax:* Admissions ■ *TF:* 800-756-6000 ■ *Web:* www.barry.edu					
Berkeley Divinity School 409 Prospect St	New Haven	CT	06511	203-432-9285	432-9353
Web: research.yale.edu/berkeleydivinity					
Bethany Theological Seminary 615 National Rd W	Richmond	IN	47374	765-983-1800	983-1840
TF: 800-287-8822 ■ *Web:* www.bethanyseminary.edu					
Bethel Seminary 3900 Bethel Dr	Saint Paul	MN	55112	651-638-6400	638-6002
TF: 800-225-8706 ■ *Web:* seminary.bethel.edu					
Bexley Hall Seminary 26 Broadway St	Rochester	NY	14607	585-546-2160	546-1969
Web: www.bexley.edu					
Biblical Theological Seminary 200 N Main St	Hatfield	PA	19440	215-368-5000	368-2301
TF: 800-235-4021 ■ *Web:* www.biblical.edu					
Biola University 13800 Biola Ave	La Mirada	CA	90639	562-903-6000	903-4709*
**Fax:* Admissions ■ *TF Admissions:* 800-652-4652 ■ *Web:* www.biola.edu					
Blessed John XXIII National Seminary 558 South Ave	Weston	MA	02493	781-899-5500	899-5500
Web: www.blessedjohnxxiii.edu					
Briercrest College & Seminary 510 College Dr	Caronport	SK	S0H0S0	306-756-3200	756-5500
TF: 888-232-0531 ■ *Web:* www.briercrest.ca					
Byzantine Catholic Seminary of SS Cyril & Methodius					
3605 Perrysville Ave	Pittsburgh	PA	15214	412-321-8383	321-9936
Web: www.byzcathsem.org					
Calvin Theological Seminary 3233 Burton St SE	Grand Rapids	MI	49546	616-957-6036	957-8621
TF: 800-388-6034 ■ *Web:* www.calvinseminary.edu					
Campbell University 56 Main St PO Box 546	Buies Creek	NC	27506	910-893-1290	893-1288*
**Fax:* Admissions ■ *TF:* 800-334-4111 ■ *Web:* www.campbell.edu					
Canadian Southern Baptist Seminary 200 Seminary View	Cochrane	AB	T4C2G1	403-932-6622	932-7049
TF: 877-922-2727 ■ *Web:* www.csbs.ca					
Canadian Theological Seminary 630-833 4th Ave SW	Calgary	AB	T2P3T5	403-410-2000	571-2556
TF: 800-461-1222 ■ *Web:* www.auc-nuc.ca					
Carey Theological College 5920 Iona Dr	Vancouver	BC	V6T1J6	604-224-4308	224-5014
Web: www.careytheologicalcollege.ca					
Carolina Evangelical Divinity School					
1208 Eastchester Dr Suite 101	High Point	NC	27265	336-882-3370	882-3370
Web: www.carolinadivinity.org					
Catholic Theological Union 5416 S Cornell Ave	Chicago	IL	60615	773-324-8000	324-4360
Web: www.ctu.edu					
Catholic University of America 620 Michigan Ave NE	Washington	DC	20064	202-319-5000	319-6533
Web: www.cua.edu					
Central Baptist Theological Seminary 6601 Monticello Rd	Shawnee	KS	66226	913-667-5700	371-5110
TF: 800-677-2287 ■ *Web:* www.cbts.edu					
Chicago Theological Seminary 5757 S University Ave	Chicago	IL	60637	773-752-5757	752-0905
Web: www.chgosem.edu					
Christ The King Seminary 711 Knox Rd	East Aurora	NY	14052	716-652-8900	652-8903
Web: www.cks.edu					
Christian Theological Seminary 1000 W 42nd St	Indianapolis	IN	46208	317-924-1331	923-1961
TF: 800-585-0108 ■ *Web:* www.cts.edu					
Christian Witness Theological Seminary 1040 Oak Grove Rd	Concord	CA	94518	925-676-5002	676-5220
Web: www.cwts.edu					
Church Divinity School of the Pacific 2451 Ridge Rd	Berkeley	CA	94709	510-204-0700	644-0712
TF: 800-353-2377 ■ *Web:* www.cdsp.edu					
Church of God Theological Seminary 900 Walker St NE	Cleveland	TN	37311	423-478-1131	478-7711
TF: 800-228-9126 ■ *Web:* www.cogts.edu					
Cincinnati Christian University 2700 Glenway Ave	Cincinnati	OH	45204	513-244-8100	244-8140
TF: 800-949-4228 ■ *Web:* www.ccuniversity.edu					
Claremont School of Theology 1325 N College Ave	Claremont	CA	91711	909-626-3521	447-6290*
**Fax:* Admissions ■ *TF:* 866-274-6500 ■ *Web:* www.cst.edu					
Colgate Rochester Crozer Divinity School					
1100 S Goodman St	Rochester	NY	14620	585-271-1320	271-8013
TF: 888-937-3732 ■ *Web:* www.crcds.edu					
Columbia International University 7435 Monticello Rd	Columbia	SC	29203	803-754-4100	786-4209
TF: 800-777-2227 ■ *Web:* www.ciu.edu					
Columbia Theological Seminary 701 Columbia Dr PO Box 520	Decatur	GA	30031	404-378-8821	377-9696
Web: www.ctsnet.edu					
Concordia Lutheran Seminary 7040 Ada Blvd	Edmonton	AB	T5B4E3	780-474-1468	479-3067
Web: www.concordiasem.ab.ca					
Concordia Lutheran Theological Seminary					
470 Glenridge Ave	Saint Catharines	ON	L2T4C3	905-688-2362	688-9744
Web: www.concordia-seminary.ca					
Concordia Seminary 801 Seminary Pl	Saint Louis	MO	63105	314-505-7000	505-7001
TF: 800-822-9545 ■ *Web:* www.csl.edu					
Concordia Theological Seminary 6600 N Clinton St	Fort Wayne	IN	46825	260-452-2100	452-2121
TF: 800-481-2155 ■ *Web:* www.ctsfw.edu					
Cornerstone University 1001 E Beltline Ave NE	Grand Rapids	MI	49525	616-222-1426	222-1418*
**Fax:* Admissions ■ *TF Admissions:* 800-787-9778 ■ *Web:* www.cornerstone.edu					
Covenant Theological Seminary 12330 Conway Rd	Saint Louis	MO	63141	314-434-4044	434-4819
TF: 800-264-8064 ■ *Web:* www.covenantseminary.edu					
Dallas Theological Seminary 3909 Swiss Ave	Dallas	TX	75204	214-824-3094	841-3664
TF: 800-992-0998 ■ *Web:* www.dts.edu					
Denver Seminary 6399 S Santa Fe Dr	Littleton	CO	80120	303-761-2482	761-8060
TF: 800-922-3040 ■ *Web:* www.denverseminary.edu					
Dominican House of Studies 487 Michigan Ave NE	Washington	DC	20017	202-529-5300	636-1700
Web: www.dhs.edu					
Dominican School of Philosophy & Theology 2301 Vine St	Berkeley	CA	94708	510-849-2030	849-1372
TF: 888-450-3778 ■ *Web:* www.dspt.edu					
Drew University Theological School 36 Madison Ave	Madison	NJ	07940	973-408-3258	408-3068
Web: www.drew.edu/theo					
Duke University Divinity School 2 Chapel Dr Box 90968	Durham	NC	27708	919-660-3400	660-3535
TF: 888-246-3853 ■ *Web:* www.divinity.duke.edu					
Earlham School of Religion 228 College Ave	Richmond	IN	47374	765-983-1423	983-1688
TF: 800-432-1377 ■ *Web:* esr.earlham.edu					
Eastern Mennonite University 1200 Park Rd	Harrisonburg	VA	22802	540-432-4118	432-4444*
**Fax:* Admissions ■ *TF Admissions:* 800-368-2665 ■ *Web:* www.emu.edu					
Ecumenical Theological Seminary (ETS) 2930 Woodward Ave	Detroit	MI	48201	313-831-5200	831-1353
Web: www.etseminary.org					
Eden Theological Seminary 475 E Lockwood Ave	Saint Louis	MO	63119	314-961-3627	918-2626
TF: 800-969-3627 ■ *Web:* www.eden.edu					
Emmanuel School of Religion 1 Walker Dr	Johnson City	TN	37601	423-926-1186	926-6198
Web: www.esr.edu					
Episcopal Divinity School 99 Brattle St	Cambridge	MA	02138	617-868-3450	864-5385
TF: 800-433-7669 ■ *Web:* www.eds.edu					
Episcopal Theological Seminary of the Southwest					
606 Rathervue Pl	Austin	TX	78705	512-472-4133	472-3098
Web: www.etss.edu					
Erskine Theological Seminary 210 S Main St	Due West	SC	29639	864-379-8885	379-2171
TF: 877-811-8117 ■ *Web:* www.erskine.edu/seminary					
ETS (Ecumenical Theological Seminary) 2930 Woodward Ave	Detroit	MI	48201	313-831-5200	831-1353
Web: www.etseminary.org					
Evangelical School of Theology 121 S College St	Myerstown	PA	17067	717-866-5775	866-4667
TF: 800-532-5775 ■ *Web:* www.evangelical.edu					
Franciscan School of Theology 1712 Euclid Ave	Berkeley	CA	94709	510-848-5232	549-9466
TF: 800-793-1378 ■ *Web:* www.fst.edu					

				Phone	Fax
Fuller Theological Seminary 135 N Oakland Ave	Pasadena	CA	91182	626-584-5200	795-8767
TF: 800-235-2222 ■ *Web:* www.fuller.edu					
Gardner-Webb University M Christopher White School of Divinity 110 S Main St Noel Hall	Boiling Springs	NC	28017	704-406-4400	406-4734
TF: 800-619-3761 ■ *Web:* www.divinity.gardner-webb.edu					
Garrett-Evangelical Theological Seminary 2121 Sheridan Rd	Evanston	IL	60201	847-866-3900	866-3957
TF: 800-736-4627 ■ *Web:* www.garrett.northwestern.edu					
General Theological Seminary 175 9th Ave	New York	NY	10011	212-243-5150	727-3907
TF: 888-487-5649 ■ *Web:* www.gts.edu					
George Fox Evangelical Seminary 12753 SW 68th Ave	Portland	OR	97223	503-554-6150	554-6111
TF: 800-493-4937 ■ *Web:* www.georgefox.edu/seminary					
Golden Gate Baptist Theological Seminary 201 Seminary Dr	Mill Valley	CA	94941	415-380-1300	380-1302
TF: 888-444-8701 ■ *Web:* www.ggbts.edu					
Gordon-Conwell Theological Seminary 130 Essex St	South Hamilton	MA	01982	978-468-7111	468-6691
TF: 800-428-7329 ■ *Web:* www.gordonconwell.edu					
Grace Theological Seminary 200 Seminary Dr	Winona Lake	IN	46590	574-372-5100	372-5113
TF: 800-544-7223 ■ *Web:* gts.grace.edu					
Graduate Theological Union 2400 Ridge Rd	Berkeley	CA	94709	510-649-2400	649-1730
TF: 800-826-4488 ■ *Web:* www.gtu.edu					
Harding University Graduate School of Religion					
1000 Cherry Rd	Memphis	TN	38117	901-761-1352	761-1358
TF: 800-680-0809 ■ *Web:* www.hugsr.edu					
Hartford Seminary 77 Sherman St	Hartford	CT	06105	860-509-9500	509-9509*
**Fax:* Admissions ■ *Web:* www.hartsem.edu					
Hellenic College-Holy Cross School of Theology					
50 Goddard Ave	Brookline	MA	02445	617-731-3500	850-1460*
**Fax:* Admissions ■ *Web:* www.hchc.edu					
Hood Theological Seminary 1810 Lutheran Synod Dr	Salisbury	NC	28144	704-636-7611	636-7699
Web: www.hoodseminary.edu					
Houston Graduate School of Theology 2501 Central Pkwy	Houston	TX	77092	713-942-9505	942-9506
Web: www.hgst.edu					
Howard University School of Divinity 1400 Shepherd St NE	Washington	DC	20017	202-806-0500	806-0711
Web: www.howard.edu/schooldivinity					
Iliff School of Theology 2201 S University Blvd	Denver	CO	80210	303-744-1287	777-0164
TF: 800-678-3360 ■ *Web:* www.iliff.edu					
Interdenominational Theological Center 700 ML King Jr Dr SW	Atlanta	GA	30314	404-527-7700	527-0901
Web: www.itc.edu					
Jesuit School of Theology at Berkeley 1735 LeRoy Ave	Berkeley	CA	94709	510-549-5000	841-8536
TF: 800-824-0122 ■ *Web:* www.jstb.edu					
Kenrick-Glennon Seminary 5200 Glennon Dr	Saint Louis	MO	63119	314-792-6100	792-6500
Web: www.kenrick.edu					
Knox College 59 Saint George St	Toronto	ON	M5S2E6	416-978-4500	971-2133
Web: www.utoronto.ca/knox					
La Sierra University 4500 Riverwalk Pkwy	Riverside	CA	92515	951-785-2000	785-2901
TF: 800-874-5587 ■ *Web:* www.lasierra.edu					
Lancaster Theological Seminary 555 W James St	Lancaster	PA	17603	717-393-0654	393-4254
TF: 800-393-0654 ■ *Web:* www.lancasterseminary.edu					
Lexington Theological Seminary 631 S Limestone St	Lexington	KY	40508	859-252-0361	281-6042
TF: 866-296-6087 ■ *Web:* www.lextheo.edu					
Lincoln Christian College Seminary 100 Campus View Dr	Lincoln	IL	62656	217-732-3168	732-4078
TF: 888-522-5228 ■ *Web:* www.lccs.edu					
Lipscomb University 3901 Granny White Pike	Nashville	TN	37204	615-966-1000	966-1804*
**Fax:* Admissions ■ *TF:* 800-333-4358 ■ *Web:* www.lipscomb.edu					
Logos Evangelical Seminary 9358 Telstar Ave	El Monte	CA	91731	626-571-5110	571-5119
Web: www.logos-seminary.edu					
Louisville Presbyterian Theological Seminary					
1044 Alta Vista Rd	Louisville	KY	40205	502-895-3411	895-1096
TF: 800-264-1839 ■ *Web:* www.lpts.edu					
Luther Seminary 2481 Como Ave	Saint Paul	MN	55108	651-641-3456	641-3425
Web: www.luthersem.edu					
Lutheran School of Theology at Chicago 1100 E 55th St	Chicago	IL	60615	773-256-0700	256-0782
TF: 800-635-1116 ■ *Web:* www.lstc.edu					
Lutheran Theological Seminary 114 Seminary Crescent	Saskatoon	SK	S7N0X3	306-966-7850	966-7852
Web: www.usask.ca/stu/luther					
Lutheran Theological Seminary at Gettysburg					
61 Seminary Ridge	Gettysburg	PA	17325	717-334-6286	334-3469
TF: 800-658-8437 ■ *Web:* www.ltsg.edu					
Lutheran Theological Seminary at Philadelphia					
7301 Germantown Ave	Philadelphia	PA	19119	215-248-4616	248-4577
TF: 800-286-4616 ■ *Web:* www.ltsp.edu					
Lutheran Theological Southern Seminary 4201 N Main St	Columbia	SC	29203	803-786-5150	786-6499
TF: 800-804-5233 ■ *Web:* www.ltss.edu					
McCormick Theological Seminary 5460 S University Ave	Chicago	IL	60615	773-947-6300	288-2612
TF: 800-228-4687 ■ *Web:* www.mccormick.edu					
Meadville Lombard Theological School 5701 S Woodlawn Ave	Chicago	IL	60637	773-256-3000	256-3007
Web: www.meadville.edu					
Memphis Theological Seminary 168 East Pkwy S	Memphis	TN	38104	901-458-8232	452-4051
TF: 800-822-0687 ■ *Web:* www.memphisseminary.edu					
Mennonite Brethren Biblical Seminary 4824 E Butler Ave	Fresno	CA	93727	559-251-8628	251-7212
TF: 800-251-6227 ■ *Web:* www.mbseminary.com					
Methodist Theological School in Ohio 3081 Columbus Pike	Delaware	OH	43015	740-363-1146	362-3135
TF: 800-333-6876 ■ *Web:* www.mtso.edu					
Michigan Theological Seminary 41550 E Ann Arbor Trail	Plymouth	MI	48170	734-207-9581	207-9582
TF: 888-687-2737 ■ *Web:* www.mts.edu					
Mid-America Reformed Seminary 229 Seminary Dr	Dyer	IN	46311	219-864-2400	864-2410
TF: 888-440-6277 ■ *Web:* www.midamerica.edu					
Midwestern Baptist Theological Seminary					
5001 N Oak Trafficway	Kansas City	MO	64118	816-414-3700	414-3799
TF: 877-414-3720 ■ *Web:* www.mbts.edu					
Moravian Theological Seminary 1200 Main St	Bethlehem	PA	18018	610-861-1516	861-1569
Web: www.moravianseminary.edu					
Mount Angel Seminary 1 Abbey Dr	Saint Benedict	OR	97373	503-845-3951	845-3126
Web: www.mtangel.edu					
Mount Saint Mary's University 16300 Old Emmitsburg Rd	Emmitsburg	MD	21727	301-447-5214	447-5860*
**Fax:* Admissions ■ *TF Admissions:* 800-448-4347 ■ *Web:* www.msmary.edu					
Multnomah Bible College & Biblical Seminary					
8435 NE Glisan St	Portland	OR	97220	503-255-0332	254-1268
TF: 800-275-4672 ■ *Web:* www.multnomah.edu					
Nashotah House 2777 Mission Rd	Nashotah	WI	53058	262-646-6500	646-6504
TF: 800-627-4682 ■ *Web:* www.nashotah.edu					
Nazarene Theological Seminary 1700 E Meyer Blvd	Kansas City	MO	64131	816-333-6254	333-6271
TF: 800-831-3011 ■ *Web:* www.nts.edu					
New Brunswick Theological Seminary 17 Seminary Pl	New Brunswick	NJ	08901	732-247-5241	249-5412
TF: 800-445-6287 ■ *Web:* www.nbts.edu					
New Orleans Baptist Theological Seminary					
3939 Gentilly Blvd	New Orleans	LA	70126	504-282-4455	816-8023
TF: 800-662-8701 ■ *Web:* www.nobts.edu					
New York Theological Seminary 475 Riverside Dr Suite 500	New York	NY	10115	212-870-1211	870-1236
Web: www.nyts.edu					
Newman Theological College 15611 St Albert Trail	Edmonton	AB	T6V1H3	780-447-2993	447-2685
Web: www.newman.edu					
North American Baptist Seminary 1525 S Grange Ave	Sioux Falls	SD	57105	605-336-6588	335-9090
TF: 800-440-6227 ■ *Web:* www.nabs.edu					
North Park Theological Seminary 3225 W Foster Ave	Chicago	IL	60625	773-244-6210	244-6244
TF: 800-964-0101 ■ *Web:* www.northpark.edu/sem					
Northern Seminary 660 E Butterfield Rd	Lombard	IL	60148	630-620-2100	620-2190
TF: 800-937-6287 ■ *Web:* www.seminary.edu					

	City	State	ZIP	Phone	Fax
Notre Dame Seminary 2901 S Carrollton Ave	New Orleans	LA	70118	504-866-7426	866-3119
Web: www.nds.edu					
Oakland City University 138 N Lucretia St	Oakland City	IN	47660	812-749-4781	749-1433
TF: 800-737-5125 ■ *Web:* www.oak.edu					
Oblate School of Theology 285 Oblate Dr	San Antonio	TX	78216	210-341-1366	341-4519
Web: www.ost.edu					
Oral Roberts University 7777 S Lewis Ave	Tulsa	OK	74171	918-495-6161	495-6222*
**Fax:* Admissions ■ *TF:* 800-678-8876 ■ *Web:* www.oru.edu					
Pacific Lutheran Theological Seminary 2770 Marin Ave	Berkeley	CA	94708	510-524-5264	524-2408
TF: 800-235-7587 ■ *Web:* www.plts.edu					
Pacific School of Religion 1798 Scenic Ave	Berkeley	CA	94709	510-848-0528	845-8948
TF: 800-999-0528 ■ *Web:* www.psr.edu					
Palmer Theological Seminary 6 Lancaster Ave	Wynnewood	PA	19096	610-896-5000	649-3834
TF: 800-220-3287 ■ *Web:* www.palmerseminary.edu					
Payne Theological Seminary 1230 Wilberforce Clifton Rd	Wilberforce	OH	45384	937-376-2946	376-3330
TF: 888-816-8933 ■ *Web:* www.payne.edu					
Phillips Theological Seminary 901 N Mingo Rd	Tulsa	OK	74116	918-610-8303	610-8404
TF: 800-843-4675 ■ *Web:* www.ptstulsa.edu					
Phoenix Seminary 4222 E Thomas Rd Suite 400	Phoenix	AZ	85018	602-850-8000	850-8080
TF: 888-443-1020 ■ *Web:* www.phoenixseminary.edu					
Pittsburgh Theological Seminary 616 N Highland Ave	Pittsburgh	PA	15206	412-362-5610	363-3260
TF: 800-451-4194 ■ *Web:* www.pts.edu					
Pontifical College Josephinum 7625 N High St	Columbus	OH	43235	614-885-5585	885-2307
TF: 888-252-5812 ■ *Web:* www.pcj.edu					
Princeton Theological Seminary 64 Mercer St	Princeton	NJ	08540	609-921-8300	924-2973
TF: 800-622-6767 ■ *Web:* www.ptsem.edu					
Protestant Episcopal Theological Seminary in Virginia					
3737 Seminary Rd	Alexandria	VA	22304	703-370-6600	370-6234
TF: 800-941-0083 ■ *Web:* www.vts.edu					
Providence College & Seminary 10 College Crescent	Otterburne	MB	R0A1G0	204-433-7488	433-3046
TF: 800-668-7768 ■ *Web:* prov.ca					
Queen's College Faculty of Theology					
210 Prince Philip Dr Suite 3000	Saint John's	NL	A1B3R6	709-753-0116	753-1214
TF: 888-753-0116 ■ *Web:* www.mun.ca/queens					
Queen's Theological College					
Theological Hall 99 University Ave Rm 212	Kingston	ON	K7L3N6	613-533-2110	533-6879
Web: www.queensu.ca/theology					
Reformed Episcopal Seminary 826 2nd Ave	Blue Bell	PA	19422	610-292-9852	292-9853
Web: www.reseminary.edu					
Reformed Presbyterian Theological Seminary					
7418 Penn Ave	Pittsburgh	PA	15208	412-731-8690	731-4834
TF: 866-778-7338 ■ *Web:* www.rpts.edu					
Reformed Theological Seminary 5422 Clinton Blvd	Jackson	MS	39209	601-923-1600	923-1654
TF: 800-543-2703 ■ *Web:* www.rts.edu					
Regent College 5800 University Blvd	Vancouver	BC	V6T2E4	604-224-3245	224-3097
TF: 800-663-8664 ■ *Web:* www.regent-college.edu					
Regent University School of Divinity					
1000 Regent University Dr Robertson Hall 303	Virginia Beach	VA	23464	757-226-4537	226-4597
TF: 800-723-6162 ■ *Web:* www.regent.edu/acad/schdiv					
Regis College 15 Saint Mary St	Toronto	ON	M4Y2R5	416-922-5474	922-2898
Web: www.regiscollege.ca					
Roberts Wesleyan College 2301 Westside Dr	Rochester	NY	14624	585-594-6000	594-6371*
**Fax:* Admissions ■ *TF Admissions:* 800-777-4792 ■ *Web:* www.roberts.edu					
Sacred Heart Major Seminary 2701 Chicago Blvd	Detroit	MI	48206	313-883-8501	868-6440
Web: www.aodonline.org/SHMS					
Sacred Heart School of Theology 7335 S Hwy 100	Franklin	WI	53132	414-425-8300	529-6999
Web: www.shst.edu					
Saint Andrew's College 1121 College Dr	Saskatoon	SK	S7N0W3	306-966-8970	644-8981
TF: 877-664-8970 ■ *Web:* www.usask.ca/stu/standrews					
Saint Augustine's Seminary of Toronto 2661 Kingston Rd	Toronto	ON	M1M1M3	416-261-7207	261-2529
Web: www.staugustines.on.ca					
Saint Bernard's School of Theology & Ministry					
120 French Rd	Rochester	NY	14618	585-271-3657	271-2045
Web: www.stbernards.edu					
Saint Charles Borromeo Seminary 100 E Wynnewood Rd	Wynnewood	PA	19096	610-667-3394	
Web: www.scs.edu					
Saint Francis Seminary 3257 S Lake Dr	Saint Francis	WI	53235	414-747-6400	747-6442
Web: www.sfs.edu					
Saint John Vianney Theological Seminary 1300 S Steele St	Denver	CO	80210	303-282-3427	282-3453
Web: www.sjvdenver.org					
Saint John's Seminary 5012 Seminary Rd	Camarillo	CA	93012	805-482-2755	484-4074
Web: www.stjohnsem.edu					
Saint John's Seminary 127 Lake St	Brighton	MA	02135	617-254-2610	787-2336
Web: www.sjs.edu					
Saint John's University	Collegeville	MN	56321	320-363-2196	363-3206*
**Fax:* Admissions ■ *TF Admissions:* 800-544-1489 ■ *Web:* www.csbsju.edu					
Saint Joseph's Seminary 201 Seminary Ave	Yonkers	NY	10704	914-968-6200	376-2019
Web: archny.org/seminary					
Saint Mary Seminary & Graduate School of Theology					
28700 Euclid Ave	Wickliffe	OH	44092	440-943-7600	943-7577
Web: www.stmarysem.edu					
Saint Mary's Seminary & University 5400 Roland Ave	Baltimore	MD	21210	410-864-4000	864-4278
Web: www.stmarys.edu					
Saint Meinrad School of Theology 200 Hill Dr	Saint Meinrad	IN	47577	812-357-6611	357-6964
Web: www.saintmeinrad.edu					
Saint Patrick's Seminary & University 320 Middlefield Rd	Menlo Park	CA	94025	650-325-5621	323-5447
Web: www.stpatricksseminary.org					
Saint Paul School of Theology 5123 Truman Rd	Kansas City	MO	64127	816-483-9600	483-9605
TF: 800-825-0378 ■ *Web:* www.spst.edu					
Saint Peter's Seminary 1040 Waterloo St N	London	ON	N6A3Y1	519-432-1824	432-0964
Web: www.stpeterseminary.ca/seminary					
Saint Tikhon's Orthodox Theological Seminary					
St Tikhon's Rd PO Box 130	South Canaan	PA	18459	570-937-4411	937-3100
Web: www.stots.edu					
Saint Vincent de Paul Regional Seminary					
10701 S Military Trail	Boynton Beach	FL	33436	561-732-4424	737-2205
Web: www.svdp.edu					
Saint Vincent Seminary 300 Fraser Purchase Rd	Latrobe	PA	15650	724-537-4592	532-5052
Web: benedictine.stvincent.edu/seminary					
Saint Vladimir's Orthodox Theological Seminary					
575 Scarsdale Rd	Crestwood	NY	10707	914-961-8313	961-4507
Web: www.svots.edu					
Samford University 800 Lakeshore Dr	Birmingham	AL	35229	205-726-3673	726-2171*
**Fax:* Admissions ■ *TF Admissions:* 800-888-7218 ■ *Web:* www.samford.edu					
San Francisco Theological Seminary 105 Seminary Rd	San Anselmo	CA	94960	415-451-2800	451-2851
TF: 800-447-8820 ■ *Web:* www.sfts.edu					
Seabury-Western Theological Seminary 2122 Sheridan Rd	Evanston	IL	60201	847-328-9300	328-9624
TF: 800-275-8235 ■ *Web:* www.seabury.edu					
Seminary of the Immaculate Conception 440 W Neck Rd	Huntington	NY	11743	631-423-0483	423-2346
Web: www.icseminary.edu					
Seton Hall University Immaculate Conception Seminary					
400 S Orange Ave	South Orange	NJ	07079	973-761-9575	761-9577
Web: theology.shu.edu					
Shaw University 118 E South St	Raleigh	NC	27601	919-546-8275	546-8271*
**Fax:* Admissions ■ *TF Admissions:* 800-214-6683 ■ *Web:* www.shawu.edu					
Southeastern Baptist Theological Seminary					
120 S Wingate St	Wake Forest	NC	27587	919-556-3101	556-0998
TF: 800-284-6317 ■ *Web:* www.sebts.edu					
Southern Baptist Theological Seminary 2825 Lexington Rd	Louisville	KY	40280	502-897-4011	897-4723*
**Fax:* Admitting ■ *TF:* 800-626-5525 ■ *Web:* www.sbts.edu					
Southwestern Baptist Theological Seminary					
2001 W Seminary Dr	Fort Worth	TX	76115	817-923-1921	923-0610
Web: www.swbts.edu					
SS Cyril & Methodius Seminary 3535 Indian Trail	Orchard Lake	MI	48324	248-683-0310	738-6735
Web: orchardlakeseminary.org					
Starr King School for the Ministry 2441 LeConte Ave	Berkeley	CA	94709	510-845-6232	845-6273
Web: www.sksm.edu					
Taylor University College & Seminary 11525 23rd Ave	Edmonton	AB	T6J4T3	780-431-5200	436-9416
TF: 800-567-4988 ■ *Web:* www.taylor-edu.ca					
Toronto School of Theology 47 Queen's Park Crescent E	Toronto	ON	M5S2C3	416-978-4039	978-7821
Web: www.tst.edu					
Trinity Episcopal School for Ministry 311 11th St	Ambridge	PA	15003	724-266-3838	266-4617
TF: 800-874-8754 ■ *Web:* www.tesm.edu					
Trinity International University 2065 Half Day Rd	Deerfield	IL	60015	847-317-7000	317-8097
TF: 800-822-3225 ■ *Web:* www.tiu.edu					
Trinity Lutheran Seminary 2199 E Main St	Columbus	OH	43209	614-235-4136	238-0263
TF: 866-610-8571 ■ *Web:* www.trinitylutheranseminary.edu					
Trinity Western University 7600 Glover Rd	Langley	BC	V2Y1Y1	604-888-7511	513-2064*
**Fax:* Admissions ■ *TF:* 888-468-6898 ■ *Web:* www.twu.ca					
Tyndale University College & Seminary 25 Ballyconnor Ct	Toronto	ON	M2M4B3	416-226-6380	226-6746
TF: 877-896-3253 ■ *Web:* www.tyndale.ca					
Union Theological Seminary 3041 Broadway	New York	NY	10027	212-662-7100	280-1416
Web: www.uts.columbia.edu					
Union Theological Seminary & Presbyterian School of Christian Education 3401 Brook Rd	Richmond	VA	23227	804-355-0671	355-3919
TF: 800-229-2990 ■ *Web:* www.union-psce.edu					
United Theological Seminary 4501 Denlinger Rd	Trotwood	OH	45426	937-529-2201	529-2292*
**Fax:* Admissions ■ *Web:* www.united.edu					
United Theological Seminary of the Twin Cities					
3000 5th St NW	New Brighton	MN	55112	651-633-4311	633-4315
TF: 800-937-1316 ■ *Web:* www.unitedseminary-mn.org					
University of Dubuque Theological Seminary					
2000 University Ave	Dubuque	IA	52001	563-589-3122	589-3110
TF: 800-369-8387 ■ *Web:* udts.dbq.edu					
University of Notre Dame 220 Main Bldg	Notre Dame	IN	46556	574-631-7505	631-8665*
**Fax:* Admissions ■ *Web:* www.nd.edu					
University of Saint Mary of the Lake Mundelein Seminary					
1000 E Maple Ave	Mundelein	IL	60060	847-566-6401	566-7330
Web: www.usml.edu					
University of Saint Michael's College Faculty of Theology					
81 Saint Mary St	Toronto	ON	M5S1J4	416-926-1300	926-7276
Web: www.utoronto.ca/stmikes					
University of Saint Thomas 2115 Summit Ave	Saint Paul	MN	55105	651-962-5000	962-6160*
**Fax:* Admissions ■ *TF:* 800-328-6819 ■ *Web:* www.stthomas.edu					
University of Saint Thomas School of Theology					
9845 Memorial Dr	Houston	TX	77024	713-686-4345	683-8673
Web: www.stthom.edu					
University of the South 735 University Ave	Sewanee	TN	37383	931-598-1238	598-3248*
**Fax:* Admissions ■ *TF:* 800-522-2234 ■ *Web:* www.sewanee.edu					
Urshan Graduate School of Theology 704 Howder Shell Rd	Florissant	MO	63031	314-921-9290	921-9203
Web: www.ugst.org					
Vancouver School of Theology 6000 Iona Dr	Vancouver	BC	V6T1L4	604-822-9031	822-9212
TF: 866-822-9031 ■ *Web:* www.vst.edu					
Virginia Union University 1500 N Lombardy St	Richmond	VA	23220	804-342-3570	342-3511*
**Fax:* Admissions ■ *TF:* 800-368-3227 ■ *Web:* www.vuu.edu					
Wartburg Theological Seminary 333 Wartburg Pl	Dubuque	IA	52003	563-589-0200	589-0333
TF: 800-225-5987 ■ *Web:* www.wartburgseminary.edu					
Washington Baptist University 4300 Evergreen Ln	Annandale	VA	22003	703-333-5904	333-5906
Web: www.wbcs.edu					
Washington Bible College/Capital Bible Seminary					
6511 Princess Garden Pkwy	Lanham	MD	20706	301-552-1400	552-2775
TF: 877-793-7227 ■ *Web:* www.bible.edu					
Washington Theological Union 6896 Laurel St NW	Washington	DC	20012	202-726-8800	726-1716
TF: 800-334-9922 ■ *Web:* www.wtu.edu					
Waterloo Lutheran Seminary 75 University Ave W	Waterloo	ON	N2L3C5	519-884-1970	884-8826*
**Fax:* Admissions ■ *Web:* info.wlu.ca/wwwsem					
Wesley Biblical Seminary 787 E Northside Dr	Jackson	MS	39206	601-366-8880	366-8832
TF: 800-788-9571 ■ *Web:* www.wbs.edu					
Wesley Theological Seminary 4500 Massachusetts Ave NW	Washington	DC	20016	202-885-8600	885-8605
TF: 800-882-4987 ■ *Web:* www.wesleysem.edu					
Western Seminary 5511 SE Hawthorne Blvd	Portland	OR	97215	503-517-1800	517-1801
TF: 877-517-1800 ■ *Web:* www.westernseminary.edu					
Western Theological Seminary 101 E 13th St	Holland	MI	49423	616-392-8555	392-7717
TF: 800-392-8554 ■ *Web:* www.westernsem.edu					
Westminster Theological Seminary 2960 W Church Rd	Glenside	PA	19038	215-887-5511	887-5404
TF: 800-373-0119 ■ *Web:* www.wts.edu					
Westminster Theological Seminary in California					
1725 Bear Valley Pkwy	Escondido	CA	92027	760-480-8474	480-0252
Web: www.wscal.edu					
Weston Jesuit School of Theology 3 Phillips Pl	Cambridge	MA	02138	617-492-1960	492-5833
Web: www.wjst.edu					
Winebrenner Theological Seminary 950 N Main St	Findlay	OH	45840	419-434-4200	434-4267
TF: 800-992-4987 ■ *Web:* www.winebrenner.edu					

170 COLLEGES & UNIVERSITIES - HISTORICALLY BLACK

Historically Black Colleges & Universities (HBCUs) are colleges or universities that were established before 1964 with the intention of serving the African-American community. (Prior to 1964, African-Americans were almost always excluded from higher education opportunities at the predominantly white colleges and universities.)

	City	State	ZIP	Phone	Fax
Alabama Agricultural & Mechanical University					
4900 Meridian St	Huntsville	AL	35810	256-851-5000	372-5249*
**Fax:* Admissions ■ *TF:* 800-553-0816 ■ *Web:* www.aamu.edu					
Alabama State University 915 S Jackson St	Montgomery	AL	36104	334-229-4291	229-4984*
**Fax:* Admissions ■ *TF Admissions:* 800-253-5037 ■ *Web:* www.alasu.edu					
Albany State University 504 College Dr	Albany	GA	31705	229-430-4646	430-4105*
**Fax:* Admissions ■ *Web:* asuweb.asurams.edu/asu					
Alcorn State University 1000 ASU Dr	Alcorn State	MS	39096	601-877-6100	877-6347*
**Fax:* Admissions ■ *TF Admissions:* 800-222-6790 ■ *Web:* www.alcorn.edu					
Allen University 1530 Harden St	Columbia	SC	29204	803-376-5700	376-5733*
**Fax:* Mail Rm ■ *TF:* 877-625-5368 ■ *Web:* www.allenuniversity.edu					
Arkansas Baptist College 1621 ML King Dr	Little Rock	AR	72202	501-374-7856	372-7992
Web: www.arkansasbaptist.edu					

	City	State	Zip	Phone	Fax
Benedict College 1600 Harden St. *TF:* 800-868-6598 ■ *Web:* www.benedict.edu	Columbia	SC	29204	803-256-5000	
Bennett College 900 E Washington St **Fax:* Admissions ■ *TF Admissions:* 800-413-5323 ■ *Web:* www.bennett.edu	Greensboro	NC	27401	336-370-8624	517-2166*
Bethune-Cookman College 640 Dr Mary McLeod Bethune Blvd **Fax:* Admissions ■ *TF Admissions:* 800-448-0228 ■ *Web:* www.cookman.edu	Daytona Beach	FL	32114	386-255-1401	481-2601*
Bishop State Community College 351 N Broad St **Fax:* Admissions ■ *Web:* www.bishop.edu	Mobile	AL	36603	251-690-6412	438-5403*
Bluefield State College 219 Rock St **Fax:* Admissions ■ *TF:* 800-654-7798 ■ *Web:* www.bluefield.wvnet.edu	Bluefield	WV	24701	304-327-4000	325-7747*
Bowie State University 14000 Jericho Park Rd *TF:* 877-772-6943 ■ *Web:* www.bowiestate.edu	Bowie	MD	20715	301-860-4000	860-3518
Central State University 1400 Brush Row Rd PO Box 1004 **Fax:* Admissions ■ *TF:* 800-388-2781 ■ *Web:* www.centralstate.edu	Wilberforce	OH	45384	937-376-6011	376-6648*
Charles R Drew University of Medicine & Science 1731 E 120th St **Fax:* Admissions ■ *Web:* www.cdrewu.edu	Los Angeles	CA	90059	323-563-4800	563-4957*
Cheyney University of Pennsylvania 1837 University Cir PO Box 200 **Fax:* Admissions ■ *TF:* 800-243-9639 ■ *Web:* www.cheyney.edu	Cheyney	PA	19319	610-399-2275	399-2099*
Claflin University 400 Magnolia St *TF:* 800-922-1276 ■ *Web:* www.claflin.edu	Orangeburg	SC	29115	803-535-5000	535-5385
Clark Atlanta University 223 James P Brawley Dr SW **Fax:* Admissions ■ *TF Admissions:* 800-688-3228 ■ *Web:* www.cau.edu	Atlanta	GA	30314	404-880-8000	880-6174*
Clinton Junior College 1029 Crawford Rd **Fax:* Admissions ■ *Web:* www.clintonjuniorcollege.edu	Rock Hill	SC	29730	803-327-7402	327-3261*
Coahoma Community College 3240 Friars Point Rd **Fax:* Admissions ■ *Web:* www.coahomacc.edu	Clarksdale	MS	38614	662-667-2571	621-4297*
Concordia College Selma PO Box 2470 **Fax:* Admissions ■ *Web:* www.concordiaselma.edu	Selma	AL	36703	334-874-5700	874-5755*
Coppin State University 2500 W North Ave **Fax:* Admissions ■ *TF Admissions:* 800-635-3674 ■ *Web:* www.coppin.edu	Baltimore	MD	21216	410-951-3600	523-7351*
Delaware State University 1200 N DuPont Hwy **Fax:* Admissions ■ *TF Admissions:* 800-845-2544 ■ *Web:* www.desu.edu	Dover	DE	19901	302-857-6351	857-6352*
Denmark Technical College 500 Solomon Blatt Blvd **Fax:* Admissions ■ *Web:* www.denmarktech.edu	Denmark	SC	29042	803-793-5175	793-5942*
Edward Waters College 1658 Kings Rd **Fax:* Admissions ■ *TF Admissions:* 888-898-3191 ■ *Web:* www.ewc.edu	Jacksonville	FL	32209	904-470-8200	470-8048*
Elizabeth City State University 1704 Weeksville Rd CB 901 **Fax:* Admissions ■ *TF Admissions:* 800-347-3278 ■ *Web:* www.ecsu.edu	Elizabeth City	NC	27909	252-335-3305	335-3537*
Fayetteville State University 1200 Murchison Rd **Fax:* Admissions ■ *TF Admissions:* 800-222-2594 ■ *Web:* www.uncfsu.edu	Fayetteville	NC	28301	910-672-1371	672-1414*
Fisk University 1000 17th Ave N *TF:* 800-443-3475 ■ *Web:* www.fisk.edu	Nashville	TN	37208	615-329-8500	329-8774
Florida A & M University 1601 ML King Blvd *Web:* www.famu.edu	Tallahassee	FL	32307	850-599-3000	561-2152
Florida Memorial University 15800 NW 42nd Ave **Fax:* Admissions ■ *TF:* 800-822-1362 ■ *Web:* www.fmuniv.edu	Miami	FL	33054	305-626-3600	623-1462*
Fort Valley State University 1005 State University Dr **Fax:* Admissions ■ *TF:* 877-462-3878 ■ *Web:* www.fvsu.edu	Fort Valley	GA	31030	478-825-6211	825-6169*
Grambling State University 403 Main St *TF:* 800-569-4714 ■ *Web:* www.gram.edu	Grambling	LA	71245	318-247-3811	
H Councill Trenholm State Technical College 1225 Air Base Blvd *Web:* www.trenholmtech.cc.al.us	Montgomery	AL	36108	334-832-9000	420-4206
Hampton University 100 E Queen St **Fax:* Admissions ■ *TF Admissions:* 800-624-3328 ■ *Web:* www.hamptonu.edu	Hampton	VA	23668	757-727-5000	727-5095*
Harris-Stowe State University 3026 Laclede Ave *Web:* www.hssu.edu	Saint Louis	MO	63103	314-340-3366	340-3555
Hinds Community College 501 E Main St PO Box 1100 **Fax:* Admissions ■ *TF:* 800-446-3722 ■ *Web:* www.hindscc.edu/	Raymond	MS	39154	601-857-5261	857-3539*
Howard University 2400 6th St NW **Fax:* Admissions ■ *TF:* 800-822-6363 ■ *Web:* www.howard.edu	Washington	DC	20059	202-806-6100	806-4465*
Huston-Tillotson University 900 Chicon St **Fax:* Admissions ■ *TF:* 877-505-3028 ■ *Web:* www.htu.edu	Austin	TX	78702	512-505-3000	505-3192*
Interdenominational Theological Center 700 ML King Jr Dr SW *Web:* www.itc.edu	Atlanta	GA	30314	404-527-7700	527-0901
Jackson State University 1400 John R Lynch St **Fax:* Admissions ■ *TF:* 800-848-6817 ■ *Web:* www.jsums.edu	Jackson	MS	39217	601-979-2121	979-3445*
Jarvis Christian College PO Box 1470 **Fax:* Admissions ■ *Web:* www.jarvis.edu	Hawkins	TX	75765	903-769-5700	769-1282*
JF Drake State Technical College 3421 Meridian St N *TF:* 888-413-7253 ■ *Web:* www.drakestate.edu	Huntsville	AL	35811	256-539-8161	539-6439
Johnson C Smith University 100 Beatties Ford Rd **Fax:* Admissions ■ *TF Admissions:* 800-782-7303 ■ *Web:* www.jcsu.edu	Charlotte	NC	28216	704-378-1000	378-1242*
Kentucky State University 400 E Main St **Fax:* Admissions ■ *TF Admissions:* 800-325-1716 ■ *Web:* www.kysu.edu	Frankfort	KY	40601	502-597-6000	597-5814*
Lane College 545 Lane Ave **Fax:* Admissions ■ *TF Admissions:* 800-960-7532 ■ *Web:* www.lanecollege.edu	Jackson	TN	38301	731-426-7500	426-7559*
Langston University Hwy 33 PO Box 1500 *TF:* 877-466-2231 ■ *Web:* www.lunet.edu	Langston	OK	73050	405-466-3428	466-3391
Lawson State Community College 3060 Wilson Rd SW **Fax:* Admissions ■ *Web:* www.ls.cc.al.us	Birmingham	AL	35221	205-925-2515	923-7106*
LeMoyne-Owen College 807 Walker Ave **Fax:* Admissions ■ *TF Admissions:* 800-737-7778 ■ *Web:* www.loc.edu	Memphis	TN	38126	901-435-1000	435-1524*
Lewis College of Business 17370 Meyers Rd **Fax:* Admissions ■ *Web:* www.lewiscollege.edu	Detroit	MI	48235	313-862-6300	862-1027*
Lincoln University 820 Chestnut St B-7 Young Hall **Fax:* Admissions ■ *TF Admissions:* 800-521-5052 ■ *Web:* www.lincolnu.edu	Jefferson City	MO	65102	573-681-5599	681-5889*
Lincoln University 1570 Old Baltimore Pike PO Box 179 **Fax:* Admissions ■ *TF Admissions:* 800-790-0191 ■ *Web:* www.lincoln.edu	Lincoln University	PA	19352	610-932-8300	932-1209*
Livingstone College 701 W Monroe St *TF:* 800-835-3435 ■ *Web:* www.livingstone.edu	Salisbury	NC	28144	704-216-6000	216-6215
Meharry Medical College School of Medicine 1005 DB Todd Jr Blvd *Web:* www.mmc.edu	Nashville	TN	37203	615-327-6111	327-6228
Miles College 5500 Myron Massey Blvd **Fax:* Admissions ■ *TF Admissions:* 800-445-0708 ■ *Web:* www.miles.edu	Fairfield	AL	35064	205-929-1000	929-1627*
Mississippi Valley State University 14000 Hwy 82 W Box 7222 **Fax:* Admissions ■ *TF Admissions:* 800-844-6885 ■ *Web:* www.mvsu.edu	Itta Bena	MS	38941	662-254-9041	254-3759*
Morehouse College 830 Westview Dr SW **Fax:* Admissions ■ *Web:* www.morehouse.edu	Atlanta	GA	30314	404-681-2800	572-3668*
Morehouse School of Medicine 720 Westview Dr SW **Fax:* Admissions ■ *Web:* www.msm.edu	Atlanta	GA	30310	404-752-1500	752-1512*
Morgan State University 1700 E Cold Spring Ln **Fax:* Admissions ■ *TF:* 800-319-4678 ■ *Web:* www.morgan.edu	Baltimore	MD	21251	443-885-3333	885-8260*
Morris College 100 W College St **Fax:* Admissions ■ *TF Admissions:* 866-853-1345 ■ *Web:* www.morris.edu	Sumter	SC	29150	803-934-3200	773-8241*
Norfolk State University 700 Park Ave **Fax:* Admissions ■ *TF:* 800-274-1821 ■ *Web:* www.nsu.edu	Norfolk	VA	23504	757-823-8600	823-2078*
North Carolina A & T State University 1601 E Market St **Fax:* Admissions ■ *TF Admissions:* 800-443-8964 ■ *Web:* www.ncat.edu	Greensboro	NC	27411	336-334-7946	334-7478*
North Carolina Central University 1801 Fayetteville St **Fax:* Admissions ■ *TF Admissions:* 877-667-7533 ■ *Web:* www.nccu.edu	Durham	NC	27707	919-530-6100	530-7625*
Oakwood College 7000 Adventist Blvd **Fax:* Admissions ■ *TF:* 800-824-5312 ■ *Web:* www.oakwood.edu	Huntsville	AL	35896	256-726-7356	726-7154*
Paine College 1235 15th St **Fax:* Admissions ■ *TF:* 800-476-7703 ■ *Web:* www.paine.edu	Augusta	GA	30901	706-821-8200	821-8293*
Paul Quinn College 3837 Simpson Stuart Rd **Fax:* Admissions ■ *TF:* 800-237-2648 ■ *Web:* www.pqc.edu	Dallas	TX	75241	214-376-1000	302-3648*
Philander Smith College 1 Trudie Kibbe Reed Dr **Fax:* Admissions ■ *Web:* www.philander.edu	Little Rock	AR	72202	501-375-9845	370-5225*
Prairie View A & M University PO Box 519 MS 1009 **Fax:* Admissions ■ *TF:* 800-787-7826 ■ *Web:* www.pvamu.edu	Prairie View	TX	77446	936-857-2626	857-2699*
Rust College 150 Rust Ave **Fax:* Admissions ■ *TF:* 888-806-8492 ■ *Web:* www.rustcollege.edu	Holly Springs	MS	38635	662-252-8000	252-2258*
Saint Augustine's College 1315 Oakwood Ave **Fax:* Admissions ■ *TF Admissions:* 800-948-1126 ■ *Web:* www.st-aug.edu	Raleigh	NC	27610	919-516-4016	516-5805*
Saint Paul's College 115 College Dr **Fax:* Admissions ■ *TF:* 800-678-7071 ■ *Web:* www.saintpauls.edu	Lawrenceville	VA	23868	434-848-3111	848-1846*
Savannah State University 3219 College St **Fax:* Admissions ■ *TF Admissions:* 800-788-0478 ■ *Web:* www.savstate.edu	Savannah	GA	31404	912-356-2186	356-2256*
Selma University 1501 Lapsley St	Selma	AL	36701	334-872-2533	872-7746
Shaw University 118 E South St **Fax:* Admissions ■ *TF Admissions:* 800-214-6683 ■ *Web:* www.shawu.edu	Raleigh	NC	27601	919-546-8275	546-8271*
Shelton State Community College 9500 Old Greensboro Rd **Fax:* Admissions ■ *Web:* www.sheltonstate.edu	Tuscaloosa	AL	35405	205-759-1541	391-3910*
Shorter College 604 N Locust St **Fax:* Admissions ■ *Web:* www.shortercollege.4t.com	North Little Rock	AR	72114	501-374-6305	374-9333*
South Carolina State University 300 College St NE PO Box 7127 *TF Admissions:* 800-260-5956 ■ *Web:* www.scsu.edu	Orangeburg	SC	29117	803-536-7000	536-8990
Southern University Shreveport 3050 ML King Jr Dr **Fax:* Admissions ■ *TF:* 800-458-1472 ■ *Web:* www.susla.edu	Shreveport	LA	71107	318-674-3300	674-3344*
Southern University & A & M College Branch Post Office **Fax:* Admissions ■ *TF Admissions:* 800-256-1531 ■ *Web:* www.subr.edu	Baton Rouge	LA	70813	225-771-4500	771-2500*
Southwestern Christian College PO Box 10 *TF:* 800-925-9357 ■ *Web:* www.swcc.edu	Terrell	TX	75160	972-524-3341	563-7133
Spelman College 350 Spelman Ln SW **Fax:* Admissions ■ *TF Admissions:* 800-982-2411 ■ *Web:* www.spelman.edu	Atlanta	GA	30314	404-681-3643	270-5201*
Stillman College PO Box 1430 **Fax:* Admissions ■ *TF Admissions:* 800-841-5722 ■ *Web:* www.stillman.edu	Tuscaloosa	AL	35403	205-349-4240	366-8941*
Talladega College 627 W Battle St **Fax:* Admissions ■ *Web:* www.talladega.edu	Talladega	AL	35160	256-362-0206	362-0274*
Tennessee State University 3500 John A Merritt Blvd PO Box 9609 *TF Admissions:* 888-463-6878 ■ *Web:* www.tnstate.edu	Nashville	TN	37209	615-963-5000	963-5108
Texas College 2404 N Grand Ave **Fax:* Admissions ■ *TF:* 800-306-6299 ■ *Web:* www.texascollege.edu	Tyler	TX	75702	903-593-8311	536-0001*
Texas Southern University 3100 Cleburne St *Web:* www.tsu.edu	Houston	TX	77004	713-313-7011	313-1859
Tougaloo College 500 W County Line Rd **Fax:* Admissions ■ *TF Admissions:* 888-424-2566 ■ *Web:* www.tougaloo.edu	Tougaloo	MS	39174	601-977-7700	977-4501*
Trenholm State Technical College 1225 Air Base Blvd *Web:* www.trenholmtech.cc.al.us	Montgomery	AL	36108	334-832-9000	420-4206
Tuskegee University 102 Old Admissions Blvd **Fax:* Admissions ■ *TF Admissions:* 800-622-6531 ■ *Web:* www.tuskegee.edu	Tuskegee	AL	36088	334-727-8011	727-5750*
University of Arkansas Pine Bluff 1200 N University Dr **Fax:* Admissions ■ *TF Admissions:* 800-264-6585 ■ *Web:* www.uapb.edu	Pine Bluff	AR	71601	870-575-8000	575-4608*
University of the District of Columbia 4200 Connecticut Ave NW *Web:* www.udc.edu	Washington	DC	20008	202-274-5000	274-5552
University of Maryland Eastern Shore 30665 Student Services Center Ln *Web:* www.umes.edu	Princess Anne	MD	21853	410-651-2200	651-7922
University of Texas El Paso 500 W University Ave **Fax:* Admissions ■ *TF Admissions:* 877-746-4637 ■ *Web:* www.utep.edu	El Paso	TX	79968	915-747-5000	747-8893*
Virginia State University 1 Hayden Dr *TF Admissions:* 800-871-7611 ■ *Web:* www.vsu.edu	Petersburg	VA	23806	804-524-5000	524-5055
Virginia Union University 1500 N Lombardy St **Fax:* Admissions ■ *TF:* 800-368-3227 ■ *Web:* www.vuu.edu	Richmond	VA	23220	804-342-3570	342-3511*
Voorhees College 213 Wiggins Dr PO Box 678 *TF Admissions:* 800-446-6250 ■ *Web:* www.voorhees.edu	Denmark	SC	29042	803-793-3351	753-9077
West Virginia State University Barron Dr Rt 25 E PO Box 1000 **Fax:* Admissions ■ *TF:* 800-987-2112 ■ *Web:* www.wvstateu.edu	Institute	WV	25112	304-766-3000	766-5182*
Wilberforce University 1055 N Bickett Rd PO Box 1001 **Fax:* Admissions ■ *TF Admissions:* 800-367-8568 ■ *Web:* www.wilberforce.edu	Wilberforce	OH	45384	937-376-2911	376-4751*
Wiley College 711 Wiley Ave **Fax:* Admissions ■ *TF Admissions:* 800-658-6889 ■ *Web:* www.wileyc.edu	Marshall	TX	75670	903-927-3311	927-3366*
Winston-Salem State University 601 S ML King Jr Dr 206 Thompson Center **Fax:* Admissions ■ *TF Admissions:* 800-257-4052 ■ *Web:* www.wssu.edu	Winston-Salem	NC	27110	336-750-2000	750-2079*
Xavier University of Louisiana 1 Drexel Dr **Fax:* Admissions ■ *TF Admissions:* 877-928-4378 ■ *Web:* www.xula.edu	New Orleans	LA	70125	504-486-7411	485-7941*

171 COLLEGES & UNIVERSITIES - JESUIT

The institutions listed here are members of the Association of Jesuit Colleges & Universities.

	City	State	Zip	Phone	Fax
Boston College 140 Commonwealth Ave *TF:* 800-360-2522 ■ *Web:* www.bc.edu	Chestnut Hill	MA	02467	617-552-3100	552-0798
Canisius College 2001 Main St **Fax:* Admissions ■ *TF:* 800-843-1517 ■ *Web:* www.canisius.edu	Buffalo	NY	14208	716-888-2200	888-3230*
College of the Holy Cross 1 College St *TF:* 800-442-2421 ■ *Web:* www.holycross.edu	Worcester	MA	01610	508-793-2011	793-3888
Creighton University 2500 California Plaza **Fax:* Admissions ■ *TF:* 800-282-5835 ■ *Web:* www2.creighton.edu	Omaha	NE	68178	402-280-2700	280-2685*
Fairfield University 1073 N Benson Rd **Fax:* Admissions ■ *Web:* www.fairfield.edu	Fairfield	CT	06824	203-254-4000	254-4199*
Fordham University 441 E Fordham Rd **Fax:* Admissions ■ *TF:* 800-367-3426 ■ *Web:* www.fordham.edu	Bronx	NY	10458	718-817-5067	367-9404*
College at Lincoln Center 113 W 60th St *TF:* 800-367-3426 ■ *Web:* www.fordham.edu	New York	NY	10023	212-636-6710	636-7002
Georgetown University 37th & 'O' Sts NW *Web:* www.georgetown.edu	Washington	DC	20057	202-687-3600	687-5084
Gonzaga University 502 E Boone Ave **Fax:* Admissions ■ *TF:* 800-986-9585 ■ *Web:* www.gonzaga.edu	Spokane	WA	99258	509-323-6572	323-5780*
John Carroll University 20700 N Park Blvd **Fax:* Admissions ■ *TF:* 888-335-6800 ■ *Web:* www.jcu.edu	University Heights	OH	44118	216-397-1886	397-4981*
Le Moyne College 1419 Salt Springs Rd **Fax:* Admissions ■ *TF Admissions:* 800-333-4733 ■ *Web:* www.lemoyne.edu	Syracuse	NY	13214	315-445-4100	445-4711*
Loyola College 4501 N Charles St **Fax:* Admissions ■ *TF:* 800-221-9107 ■ *Web:* www.loyola.edu	Baltimore	MD	21210	410-617-5012	617-2176*

	City	State	Zip	Phone	Fax
Loyola Marymount University 1 LMU Dr *TF:* 800-568-4636 ■ *Web:* www.lmu.edu	Los Angeles	CA	90045	310-338-2700	338-2797
Loyola University New Orleans 6363 St Charles Ave Campus Box 18 **Fax:* Admissions ■ *TF Admissions:* 800-456-9652 ■ *Web:* www.loyno.edu	New Orleans	LA	70118	504-865-3240	865-3383*
Loyola University Chicago					
Lake Shore 6525 N Sheridan Rd *Web:* www.luc.edu	Chicago	IL	60626	773-508-3075	508-8926
Water Tower 820 N Michigan Ave **Fax:* Admissions ■ *TF Admissions:* 800-262-2373 ■ *Web:* www.luc.edu	Chicago	IL	60611	312-915-6500	915-7216*
Marquette University 1217 W Wisconsin Ave **Fax:* Admissions ■ *TF Admissions:* 800-222-6544 ■ *Web:* www.marquette.edu	Milwaukee	WI	53233	414-288-7302	288-3764*
Regis University 3333 Regis Blvd *TF Admissions:* 800-568-8932 ■ *Web:* www.regis.edu	Denver	CO	80221	303-458-4100	964-5534
Rockhurst University 1100 Rockhurst Rd **Fax:* Admissions ■ *TF:* 800-842-6776 ■ *Web:* www.rockhurst.edu	Kansas City	MO	64110	816-501-4000	501-4241*
Saint Joseph's University 5600 City Ave **Fax:* Admissions ■ *TF:* 888-232-4295 ■ *Web:* www.sju.edu	Philadelphia	PA	19131	610-660-1000	660-1314*
Saint Louis University 221 N Grand Blvd **Fax:* Admissions ■ *TF:* 800-758-3678 ■ *Web:* www.slu.edu	Saint Louis	MO	63103	314-977-2100	977-7136*
Saint Peter's College 2641 JFK Blvd **Fax:* Admissions ■ *TF:* 888-772-9933 ■ *Web:* www.spc.edu	Jersey City	NJ	07306	201-915-9000	761-7105*
Santa Clara University 500 El Camino Real *Web:* www.scu.edu	Santa Clara	CA	95053	408-554-4764	554-5255
Seattle University 901 12th Ave **Fax:* Admissions ■ *TF:* 800-426-7123 ■ *Web:* www.seattleu.edu	Seattle	WA	98122	206-296-6000	296-5656*
Spring Hill College 4000 Dauphin St **Fax:* Admissions ■ *TF Admissions:* 800-742-6704 ■ *Web:* www.shc.edu	Mobile	AL	36608	251-380-4000	460-2186*
University of Detroit Mercy 4001 W McNichols Rd **Fax:* Admissions ■ *TF Admissions:* 800-635-5020 ■ *Web:* www.udmercy.edu	Detroit	MI	48221	313-993-1000	993-3326*
University of Detroit Mercy School of Dentistry Corktown Campus 2700 MLK Dr *Web:* www.udmercy.edu	Detroit	MI	48219	313-494-6611	
University of San Francisco 2130 Fulton St **Fax:* Admissions ■ *TF Admissions:* 800-225-5873 ■ *Web:* www.usfca.edu	San Francisco	CA	94117	415-422-5555	422-2217*
University of Scranton 800 Linden St St Thomas Hall **Fax:* Admissions ■ *TF:* 888-727-2686 ■ *Web:* matrix.scranton.edu	Scranton	PA	18510	570-941-7400	941-5928*
Wheeling Jesuit University 316 Washington Ave **Fax:* Admissions ■ *TF:* 800-624-6992 ■ *Web:* www.wju.edu	Wheeling	WV	26003	304-243-2000	243-2397*
Xavier University 3800 Victory Pkwy **Fax:* Admissions ■ *TF:* 800-344-4698 ■ *Web:* www.xavier.edu	Cincinnati	OH	45207	513-745-3000	745-4319*

172 COMMODITY CONTRACTS BROKERS & DEALERS

SEE ALSO Investment Advice & Management p. 1873; Securities Brokers & Dealers p. 2307

	City	State	Zip	Phone	Fax
ADM Investor Services Inc 141 W Jackson Blvd 1600A Board of Trade Bldg *Web:* www.admis.com	Chicago	IL	60604	312-435-7000	435-7045
Barclays Capital Futures 200 Cedar Knolls Rd *Web:* www.barcap.com/futures	Whippany	NJ	07981	973-576-3000	
Basic Commodities Inc 863 S Orlando Ave *TF:* 800-338-7006 ■ *Web:* www.basiccommodities.com	Winter Park	FL	32789	407-629-2000	740-0200
Bear Stearns Securities Corp 1 Metrotech Ctr N *Web:* www.bearstearns.com	Brooklyn	NY	11201	212-272-1000	
Calyon Financial Inc 550 W Jackson Blvd 5th Fl *Web:* www.calyonfinancial.com	Chicago	IL	60661	312-441-4200	762-1001
Cargill Investor Services Inc 233 S Wacker Dr Suite 2300 *Web:* www.cis.cargill.com	Chicago	IL	60606	312-460-4000	460-4015
Commerzbank Capital Markets Corp 2 World Financial Center 31st Fl *Web:* www.commerzbank.com	New York	NY	10281	212-703-4000	266-7235
Connell & Co 55 Shurman Blvd Suite 600 *Web:* www.connellco.com/CNC.htm	Naperville	IL	60563	630-210-7400	579-9120
Country Hedging Inc PO Box 64089 *TF:* 800-328-6530 ■ *Web:* www.countryhedging.com	Saint Paul	MN	55164	651-355-5151	355-3723
Goldman Sachs & Co 85 Broad St **Fax:* Mail Rm ■ *TF:* 800-323-5678 ■ *Web:* www.gs.com	New York	NY	10004	212-902-1000	902-1512*
Imperial Commodities Corp 17 Battery Pl Suite 636	New York	NY	10004	212-837-9400	269-9878
Keeley Investment Corp 401 S La Salle St Suite 1201 *TF:* 800-533-5344 ■ *Web:* www.keeleyfunds.com	Chicago	IL	60605	312-786-5000	786-5002
Koch Mineral Services LLC 4111 E 37th St N	Wichita	KS	67220	316-828-5500	
Koch Supply & Trading LP 4111 E 37th St N *TF:* 800-245-2243 ■ *Web:* www.kochoil.com	Wichita	KS	67220	316-828-5500	828-5752
LFG 550 W Jackson Blvd Suite 1300 *Web:* www.lfgfutures.com	Chicago	IL	60661	312-788-2000	788-2073
Lind-Waldock 550 W Jackson Blvd Suite 1300 *TF:* 800-327-3562 ■ *Web:* www.lind-waldock.com	Chicago	IL	60661	312-788-2800	788-2815
Louis Dreyfus Group 20 Westport Rd *Web:* www.louisdreyfus.com	Wilton	CT	06897	203-761-2000	761-2375
Man Financial Inc 440 S La Salle St **Fax:* Cust Svc ■ *Web:* www.manfinancial.com	Chicago	IL	60605	312-663-7500	902-6811*
Marubeni America Corp 450 Lexington Ave 35th Fl *Web:* www.marubeni-usa.com	New York	NY	10017	212-450-0100	450-0701
Marubeni Canada Ltd 40 University Ave Suite 600	Toronto	ON	M5J1T1	416-368-1171	947-9004
Morgan Stanley 1585 Broadway *NYSE: MWD* ■ *TF:* 800-223-2440 ■ *Web:* www.morganstanley.com	New York	NY	10036	212-761-4000	
optionsXpress Inc 39 S LaSalle St Suite 220 *NASDAQ: OXPS* ■ *TF:* 888-280-8020 ■ *Web:* www.optionsxpress.com	Chicago	IL	60603	312-630-3300	629-5256
Orion Futures 1905 W Busch Blvd *TF:* 888-769-9399 ■ *Web:* www.orionfutures.com	Tampa	FL	33612	813-876-9662	876-5530
Paragon Investments 9941 NW Hwy 24 Suite 3 **Fax Area Code:* 785 ■ *TF:* 888-452-8751 ■ *Web:* www.paragoninvestments.com	Silver Lake	KS	66539	758-582-5494	582-0121*
PS International Ltd 1414 Raleigh Rd Suite 205 *Web:* www.psinternational.net	Chapel Hill	NC	27517	919-933-7400	933-7441
Rand Financial Services Inc 141 W Jackson Blvd Suite 1950 *TF:* 800-842-7263 ■ *Web:* www.rand-usa.com	Chicago	IL	60604	312-559-8800	559-8801
RJ O'Brien & Assoc 222 S Riverside Plaza Suite 900 *TF:* 800-621-0757 ■ *Web:* www.askrjo.com	Chicago	IL	60606	312-373-5000	373-5350
Rosenthal Collins Group LLC (RCG) 216 W Jackson Blvd Suite 400 **Fax:* Hum Res ■ *Web:* www.rcgdirect.com	Chicago	IL	60606	312-460-9200	795-7887*
XPRESStrade LLC 10 S Wacker Dr Suite 2550 *TF:* 800-947-6228 ■ *Web:* www.xpresstrade.com	Chicago	IL	60606	312-715-6228	715-6177
Zaner Group LLC 150 S Wacker Dr Suite 2350 *TF:* 800-621-1414 ■ *Web:* www.zaner.com	Chicago	IL	60606	312-277-0050	277-0150

173 COMMUNICATIONS TOWER OPERATORS

SEE ALSO Construction - Heavy Construction Contractors - Communications Lines & Towers Construction p. 1533

Listed here are companies that own, operate, lease, maintain, and/or manage towers used by telecommunications services and radio broadcast companies, including free-standing towers as well as antenna systems mounted on monopoles or rooftops. Many of these companies also build their communications towers, but companies that only do the building are classified as heavy construction contractors.

	City	State	Zip	Phone	Fax
Alternative Networking Inc DBA ANI Site Development 1300 Riverland Rd *TF:* 800-733-9929 ■ *Web:* www.anisite.com	Fort Lauderdale	FL	33312	954-581-9929	581-4743
American Tower Corp 116 Huntington Ave 11th Fl *NYSE: AMT* ■ *TF:* 877-282-7483 ■ *Web:* www.americantower.com	Boston	MA	02116	617-375-7500	375-7575
ANI Site Development 1300 Riverland Rd *TF:* 800-733-9929 ■ *Web:* www.anisite.com	Fort Lauderdale	FL	33312	954-581-9929	581-4743
Atlantic Tower Corp 10197 Maple Leaf Ct *TF:* 800-826-8616 ■ *Web:* www.atlantic-tower.com	Ashland	VA	23005	804-550-7490	550-7493
Centerpointe Communications 2106 W Pioneer Pkwy Suite 131 *TF:* 877-277-6811 ■ *Web:* www.cencom.com	Arlington	TX	76013	817-277-6811	277-6768
Central Tower Inc 2855 Hwy 261 *TF:* 800-664-8222 ■ *Web:* www.centraltower.com/centraltower/	Newburgh	IN	47630	812-853-0595	853-6652
CLS Group 1015 Waterwood Pkwy Suite D *TF:* 800-580-5460 ■ *Web:* www.clsgroup.com	Edmond	OK	73034	405-348-5460	341-6334
Crown Castle International Corp 510 Bering Dr Suite 600 *NYSE: CCI* ■ *Web:* www.crowncastle.com	Houston	TX	77057	713-570-3000	570-3100
Crown Communication Inc 2000 Corporate Dr	Canonsburg	PA	15317	724-416-2000	416-2200
DukeNet Communications Inc 400 S Tryon St *TF:* 800-873-3853 ■ *Web:* www.dc.duke-energy.com	Charlotte	NC	28285	704-382-7111	
Fiberless Net Inc PO Box 65960 *Web:* www.fiberlessnet.com	Washington	DC	20035	202-371-6650	659-1931
Global Signal Inc 301 N Cattleman Rd Suite 300 *NYSE: GSL* ■ *TF:* 888-748-3482 ■ *Web:* www.gsignal.com	Sarasota	FL	34232	941-364-8886	364-8761
LTS Wireless Inc 311 S LHS Dr *TF:* 800-255-5471 ■ *Web:* www.ltswireless.com	Lumberton	TX	77657	409-755-4038	755-7409
Millennium Telecom LLC 320 60th St NW *TF:* 877-720-6249 ■ *Web:* www.millenniumtelcomm.com	Sauk Rapids	MN	56379	320-253-5489	654-9226
Mountain Union Telecom 301 N Fairfax St Suite 101 *Web:* www.mountainuniontelecom.com	Alexandria	VA	22314	703-535-3009	535-3051
SBA Communications Corp 5900 Broken Sound Pkwy NW *NASDAQ: SBAC* ■ *TF:* 800-487-7483 ■ *Web:* www.sbasite.com	Boca Raton	FL	33487	561-995-7670	995-7626
SCANA Communications Inc 1426 Main St MC 107 *TF Cust Svc:* 800-679-5463 ■ *Web:* www.scana.com/SCANA+Communications	Columbia	SC	29201	803-217-7383	217-9721
Shaffer Communications Group Inc 8584 Katy Fwy Suite 300 *TF:* 800-243-7525 ■ *Web:* www.shafcomm.com	Houston	TX	77024	713-463-0022	647-0045
SpectraSite Inc 100 Regency Forest Dr Suite 400 *TF:* 888-468-0112 ■ *Web:* www.spectrasite.com	Cary	NC	27511	919-468-0112	468-8522
Spectrum Resources Tower LP 6400 Arlington Blvd Suite 1000 *TF:* 888-508-6937 ■ *Web:* www.spectrumresources.com	Falls Church	VA	22042	703-533-1312	533-1399
Spectrum Site Management Corp 6060 N Central Expy Suite 642 *TF:* 800-966-8885 ■ *Web:* www.spectrumsitemanagement.com	Dallas	TX	75206	214-540-0359	237-1198
US RealTel Inc 15 Piedmont Ctr NE Suite 100 *Web:* www.usrealtel.com	Atlanta	GA	30305	404-442-0126	869-2525

174 COMMUNITIES - ONLINE

SEE ALSO Internet Service Providers (ISPs) p. 1872

	City	State	Zip	Phone	Fax
Allnurses.com Inc 0930 177th St W **Fax Area Code:* 419 ■ *Web:* allnurses.com	Lakeville	MN	55044	612-816-8773	844-2416*
Alloy Inc 151 W 26th St 11th Fl *NASDAQ: ALOY* ■ *TF Cust Svc:* 888-452-5569 ■ *Web:* www.alloy.com	New York	NY	10001	212-244-4307	244-4311
America Online Inc (AOL) 22000 AOL Way *TF Orders:* 888-265-8002 ■ *Web:* www.aol.com	Dulles	VA	20166	703-265-1000	265-5769
AOL (America Online Inc) 22000 AOL Way *TF Orders:* 888-265-8002 ■ *Web:* www.aol.com	Dulles	VA	20166	703-265-1000	265-5769
AOL Black Voices 435 N Michigan Ave Suite L2 *TF:* 877-765-1350 ■ *Web:* blackvoices.aol.com	Chicago	IL	60611	312-222-4326	222-4502
AsianAvenue.com 205 Hudson St 6th Fl *Web:* www.asianavenue.com	New York	NY	10013	212-431-4477	505-3478
Beliefnet Inc 115 E 23rd St Suite 400 *Web:* www.beliefnet.com	New York	NY	10010	212-533-1400	
BET.com LLC 1235 W St NE *Web:* www.bet.com/community	Washington	DC	20018	202-608-2000	533-1999
BlackPlanet.com 205 Hudson St 6th Fl *Web:* www.blackplanet.com	New York	NY	10013	212-431-4477	505-3478
Children with Diabetes 5689 Chancery Pl *Web:* www.childrenwithdiabetes.com	Hamilton	OH	45011	513-755-0186	755-9963
Christianity.com Inc 1423 Powhatan St Suite 1 2nd Fl *Web:* www.christianity.com	Alexandria	VA	22314	703-548-8900	548-8940
Gay.com c/o PlanetOut Inc PO Box 500 *Web:* www.gay.com	San Francisco	CA	94104	415-834-6500	834-6502
Internet World 18 S Main St *Web:* www.iw.com	Norwalk	CT	06854	203-945-2070	945-2078
Internet.com c/o Jupitermedia 23 Old Kings Hwy S *Web:* www.internet.com	Darien	CT	06820	203-662-2800	655-4686
iVillage 500 7th Ave 14th Fl *TF:* 800-977-1436 ■ *Web:* www.ivillage.com	New York	NY	10018	212-664-4444	600-6100
Knot Inc The 462 Broadway 6th Fl *NASDAQ: KNOT* ■ *Web:* www.theknot.com	New York	NY	10013	212-219-8555	219-1929
lawyers.com Martindale-Hubbell 121 Chanlon Rd *TF:* 800-526-4902 ■ *Web:* www.lawyers.com	New Providence	NJ	07974	908-464-6800	464-3553
MaMaMedia Inc 110 Greene St Suite 708 *Web:* www.mamamedia.com	New York	NY	10012	212-334-3277	
MiGente.com 205 Hudson St 6th Fl *Web:* www.migente.com	New York	NY	10013	212-431-4477	
Military Advantage Inc 799 Market St 7th Fl *Web:* www.military.com	San Francisco	CA	94103	415-820-3434	820-0552
OnePlace LLC 9401 Courthouse Rd Suite 300 *Web:* www.oneplace.com	Chesterfield	VA	23832	804-768-9404	768-9359
Open Source Technology Group (OSTG) 46939 Bayside Pkwy *TF:* 877-825-4689 ■ *Web:* www.ostg.com	Fremont	CA	94538	510-687-7000	687-7155

				Phone	Fax
OSTG (Open Source Technology Group) 46939 Bayside Pkwy	Fremont	CA	94538	510-687-7000	687-7155
TF: 877-825-4689 ■ *Web:* www.ostg.com					
PlanetOut Inc 1355 Sansome St.	San Francisco	CA	94111	415-834-6500	834-6502
NASDAQ: LGBT ■ *Web:* www.planetoutinc.com					
Salon.com 101 Spear St Suite 203	San Francisco	CA	94105	415-645-9200	645-9204
Web: www.salon.com					
SeniorNet 900 Lafayette St Suite 604	Santa Clara	CA	95050	408-615-0699	615-0928
TF: 800-747-6848 ■ *Web:* www.seniornet.org					
SHRM Global Forum 1800 Duke St	Alexandria	VA	22314	703-548-3440	535-6490
TF: 800-283-7476 ■ *Web:* www.shrm.org/global					
Spark Networks plc 8383 Wilshire Blvd Suite 800	Beverly Hills	CA	90211	323-836-3000	836-3333
AMEX: LOV ■ *Web:* www.spark.net					
ThirdAge Inc 25 Stillman St Suite 102	San Francisco	CA	94105	415-267-4400	908-6909
Web: www.thirdage.com					
WELL The c/o Salon.com 101 Spear St Suite 203	San Francisco	CA	94105	415-645-9300	645-9309
Web: www.well.com					
Yahoo! GeoCities 701 1st Ave	Sunnyvale	CA	94089	408-349-3300	349-3301
Web: geocities.yahoo.com					

COMPRESSORS - AIR CONDITIONING & REFRIGERATION

SEE Air Conditioning & Heating Equipment - Commercial/Industrial p. 1267

175 COMPRESSORS - AIR & GAS

				Phone	Fax
Airtek Inc PO Box 466	Irwin	PA	15642	724-863-1350	864-7853
TF: 800-424-7835 ■ *Web:* www.airtek-inc.com					
American Air Compressor Services 185 Lackawanna Ave	West Paterson	NJ	07424	201-865-4848	890-5991*
**Fax Area Code:* 973					
Atlas Copco Compressors LLC 94 N Elm St 4th Fl.	Westfield	MA	01085	413-536-0600	536-0091
Web: www.atlascopco.com					
Bauer Compressors Inc 1328 Azalea Garden Rd	Norfolk	VA	23502	757-855-6006	855-6224
Web: www.bauercomp.com					
Blackmer 1809 Century Ave	Grand Rapids	MI	49503	616-241-1611	241-3752
Web: www.blackmer.com					
Cameron Compression Systems 16250 Port Northwest Dr	Houston	TX	77041	713-354-1900	354-1923
TF: 888-423-7463 ■ *Web:* www.c-a-m.com					
Cameron Turbocompressor 3101 Broadway	Buffalo	NY	14225	716-896-6600	896-1233
TF: 877-805-7911 ■ *Web:* www.c-a-m.com					
Champion A Gardner Denver Co 1301 N Euclid Ave	Princeton	IL	61356	815-875-3321	872-0421
Web: www.gardnerdenver.com					
Chapin International Inc 700 Ellicott St	Batavia	NY	14021	585-343-3140	344-1775
Web: www.chapinmfg.com					
Coleman Powermate Inc 3901 Liberty Street Rd	Aurora	IL	60504	630-585-7332	585-7534
Web: www.colemanpowermate.com					
CompAir 130 Fox Dr	Piqua	OH	45356	937-778-2500	778-4123
Web: www.compair.com					
Compressor Engineering Corp (CECO) 5440 Alder Dr.	Houston	TX	77081	713-664-7333	664-6444
TF: 800-879-2326 ■ *Web:* www.compressor-engineering.com					
Corken Inc 3805 NW 36th St	Oklahoma City	OK	73112	405-946-5576	948-6664
TF: 800-631-4929 ■ *Web:* www.corken.com					
CSI Compressor Systems Inc 3809 S FM 1788 PO Box 60760	Midland	TX	79711	432-563-1170	563-0820
TF: 800-365-1170 ■ *Web:* www.compressor-systems.com					
Curtis Dyna-Fog Ltd 17335 US Hwy 31 N	Westfield	IN	46074	317-896-2561	896-3788
TF: 800-544-8990 ■ *Web:* www.dynafog.com					
Curtis-Toledo Inc 1905 Kienlen Ave	Saint Louis	MO	63133	314-383-1300	381-1439
TF: 800-925-5431 ■ *Web:* www.curtistoledo.com					
Delavan Spray Technologies Div Goodrich Corp					
4334 Main Hwy PO Box 969	Bamberg	SC	29003	803-245-4347	245-4146
TF: 800-621-9357 ■ *Web:* www.delavan.com					
Dresser-Rand Co Paul Clark Dr PO Box 560	Olean	NY	14760	716-375-3000	375-3178
Web: www.dresser-rand.com					
Dresser-Rand Co Reciprocating Products Div 100 Chemung St	Painted Post	NY	14870	607-937-2011	937-2204
Web: www.dresser-rand.com/recip					
Elliott Turbomachinery Co 901 N 4th St	Jeannette	PA	15644	724-527-2811	600-8442
TF: 800-635-2208 ■ *Web:* www.elliott-turbo.com					
Federal Equipment Co 928 Low Ave.	Waukegan	IL	60085	847-775-1300	775-1310
Web: www.speedysprayer.com					
Fountainhead Group Inc 23 Garden St	New York Mills	NY	13417	315-736-0037	768-4220
TF: 800-311-9903 ■ *Web:* www.thefountainheadgroup.com					
Gardner Denver Compressor Div 1800 Gardner Expwy	Quincy	IL	62301	217-222-5400	223-5897
TF: 800-682-9868 ■ *Web:* www.gardnerdenver.com					
Gardner Denver Inc 1800 Gardner Expy	Quincy	IL	62305	217-222-5400	223-5897
NYSE: GDI ■ *TF:* 800-682-9868 ■ *Web:* www.gardnerdenver.com					
Gardner Denver Nash 1800 Gardner Expy.	Quincy	IL	62301	217-222-5400	223-5897
TF: 800-682-9868 ■ *Web:* www.gardnerdenver.com					
Gardner Denver Water Jetting Systems Inc					
12300 N Houston Rosslyn Rd	Houston	TX	77086	281-448-5800	448-7500*
**Fax:* Sales ■ *TF:* 800-231-3628 ■ *Web:* www.gardnerdenver.com					
Gast Mfg Inc 2300 M-139 Hwy PO Box 97	Benton Harbor	MI	49023	269-926-6171	925-8288
TF: 800-952-4278 ■ *Web:* www.gastmfg.com					
Goodrich Corp Delavan Spray Technologies Div					
4334 Main Hwy PO Box 969	Bamberg	SC	29003	803-245-4347	245-4146
TF: 800-621-9357 ■ *Web:* www.delavan.com					
Grimmer Industries Inc DBA GrimmerSchmidt Compressors					
1015 N Hurricane Rd	Franklin	IN	46131	317-736-8416	736-3831
TF: 800-428-9703 ■ *Web:* www.grimmerschmidt.com					
GrimmerSchmidt Compressors 1015 N Hurricane Rd	Franklin	IN	46131	317-736-8416	736-3831
TF: 800-428-9703 ■ *Web:* www.grimmerschmidt.com					
Guardair Corp 54 2nd Ave.	Chicopee	MA	01020	413-594-4400	594-4884
TF: 800-482-7324 ■ *Web:* www.guardaircorp.com					
Gusmer Corp 8400 Port Jackson Ave NW	North Canton	OH	44720	732-616-6210	494-5383*
**Fax Area Code:* 330 ■ *TF:* 800-367-4767 ■ *Web:* www.graco.com					
Hamworthy Inc 1418 Edwards Ave Suite B	New Orleans	LA	70123	504-734-5525	734-5716
Web: www.hamworthy.com					
Ingersoll-Rand Co 155 Chestnut Ridge Rd	Montvale	NJ	07645	201-573-0123	573-3172
NYSE: IR ■ *Web:* www.irco.com					
Ingersoll-Rand Co Air Solutions Group 800-D Beaty St.	Davidson	NC	28036	704-896-4000	896-4459
Web: www.air.ingersoll-rand.com					
ITW Automotive Refinishing 1724 Indian Wood Cir.	Maumee	OH	43537	419-891-8100	891-8110
TF: 800-445-3988					
ITW Industrial Finishing 195 International Blvd	Glendale Heights	IL	60139	630-237-5000	246-5012*
**Fax Area Code:* 888 ■ **Fax:* Sales ■ *TF:* 800-992-4657					
ITW Ransburg 320 Phillips Ave	Toledo	OH	43612	419-470-2000	470-2270
TF Cust Svc: 800-726-8097 ■ *Web:* www.itwransburg.com					
Magnum Venus Plastech 5148 113th Ave N	Clearwater	FL	33760	727-573-2955	571-3636
Web: www.mvpind.com					
Master Mfg Co 747 N Yale Ave	Villa Park	IL	60181	630-833-7060	833-7094
Mattson Spray Equipment 230 W Coleman St	Rice Lake	WI	54868	715-234-1617	236-7032
TF: 800-877-4857 ■ *Web:* www.mattsonspray.com					
NEAC Compressor Service USA Inc 191 Howard St	Franklin	PA	16323	814-437-3711	432-3334
TF: 800-458-0453					
Norwalk Compressor Co 1650 Stratford Ave	Stratford	CT	06815	203-386-1234	386-1300
TF: 800-556-5001 ■ *Web:* www.norwalkcompressor.com					
Oerlikon Leybold Vacuum USA 5700 Mellon Rd.	Export	PA	15632	724-327-5700	325-4585*
**Fax:* Hum Res ■ *TF:* 800-764-6369 ■ *Web:* www.leyboldvacuum.com					
Quincy Compressor 3501 Wismann Ln.	Quincy	IL	62305	217-222-7700	222-5109
Web: www.quincycompressor.com					
Saylor Beall Mfg Co Inc 400 N Kibbee St	Saint Johns	MI	48879	989-224-2371	224-8788
TF: 800-248-9001 ■ *Web:* www.saylor-beall.com					
Scales Air Compressor Corp 110 Voice Rd	Carle Place	NY	11514	516-248-9096	248-9639
TF: 800-777-9096 ■ *Web:* www.scales-air.com					
SIHI Pumps Inc 303 Industrial Blvd.	Grand Island	NY	14072	716-773-6450	773-2330
Web: www.sihi-pumps.com					
Spencer Turbine Co 600 Day Hill Rd	Windsor	CT	06095	860-688-8361	688-0098
TF: 800-232-4321 ■ *Web:* www.spencerturbine.com					
Squire Cogswell/Aeros Instruments Inc 1111 Lakeside Dr	Gurnee	IL	60031	847-855-0500	855-6300
TF: 800-448-0770 ■ *Web:* www.squire-cogswell.com					
Sullair Corp 3700 E Michigan Blvd	Michigan City	IN	46360	219-879-5451	874-1273*
**Fax:* Mktg ■ *TF:* 800-785-5247 ■ *Web:* www.sullair.com					
Sullivan-Palatek Inc 386 River Rd	Claremont	NH	03743	603-543-3131	543-0014
TF: 800-334-5022 ■ *Web:* www.sullivanind.com					
Sulzer Metco US Inc 1101 Prospect Ave	Westbury	NY	11590	516-334-1300	338-2342*
**Fax:* Sales ■ *TF:* 800-638-2699 ■ *Web:* www.sulzermetco.com					
Tafa Inc 146 Pembroke Rd	Concord	NH	03301	603-224-9585	225-4342
Web: www.praxair.com/thermalspray					
Tecumseh Products Co 100 E Patterson St	Tecumseh	MI	49286	517-423-8411	423-8760
NASDAQ: TECUA ■ *Web:* www.tecumseh.com					
Thermionics Laboratory Inc PO Box 3711	Hayward	CA	94540	510-538-3304	538-2889
Web: www.thermionics.com					
Thomas Products Div 1419 Illinois Ave	Sheboygan	WI	53081	920-457-4891	451-4237
Web: www.rtpumps.com					
Tuthill Vacuum Systems 4840 W Kearney St	Springfield	MO	65803	417-865-8715	865-2950
TF: 800-225-3810 ■ *Web:* www.tuthill.com					
Varian Vacuum Technologies 121 Hartwell Ave.	Lexington	MA	02421	781-861-7200	860-5437
TF Cust Svc: 800-882-7426 ■ *Web:* www.varianinc.com					
Wagner Spray Tech Corp 1770 Fernbrook Ln.	Plymouth	MN	55447	763-553-0759	553-7288
TF: 800-328-8251 ■ *Web:* www.wagnerspraytech.com					
Wittemann Co LLC 1 Industry Dr Suite A	Palm Coast	FL	32137	386-445-4200	445-7042
Web: www.wittemann.com					
Zeks Compressed Air Solutions 1302 Goshen Pkwy	West Chester	PA	19380	610-692-9100	692-9192
TF: 800-888-2323 ■ *Web:* www.zeks.com					

176 COMPUTER EQUIPMENT

SEE ALSO Automatic Teller Machines (ATMs) p. 1358; Business Machines - Mfr p. 1402; Calculators - Electronic p. 1404; Computer Equipment - Modems p. 1502; Computer Networking Products & Systems p. 1505; Flash Memory Devices p. 1639; Point-of-Sale (POS) & Point-of-Information (POI) Systems p. 2127

176-1 Computer Input Devices

				Phone	Fax
3M Touch Systems 300 Griffin Brook Dr	Methuen	MA	01844	978-659-9000	659-9103
TF: 866-407-6666 ■ *Web:* www.3m.com/3MTouchSystems					
Advanced Input Devices Inc 600 W Wilbur Ave	Coeur d'Alene	ID	83815	208-765-8000	
TF: 800-444-5923 ■ *Web:* www.advanced-input.com					
Altek Corp 12210 Plum Orchard Dr	Silver Spring	MD	20904	301-572-2555	572-2510
Web: www.altek.com					
Andrea Electronics Corp 65 Orville Dr Suite 1	Bohemia	NY	11716	631-719-1800	719-1998
AMEX: AND ■ *TF:* 800-442-7787 ■ *Web:* www.andreaelectronics.com					
BenQ America Corp 53 Discovery	Irvine	CA	92618	949-255-9500	255-9600
TF: 866-600-2367 ■ *Web:* www.benq.com					
CH Products 970 Park Center Dr.	Vista	CA	92081	760-598-2518	598-2524
Web: www.chproducts.com					
Chicony America Inc 53 Parker	Irvine	CA	92618	949-380-0928	380-9204
Web: www.chicony.com.tw					
Cirque Corp 2463 S 3850 West Suite A	Salt Lake City	UT	84120	801-467-1100	467-0208
TF: 800-454-3375 ■ *Web:* www.cirque.com					
Cortron Inc 1 Aegean Dr	Methuen	MA	01844	978-975-5445	975-0357
Web: www.cortroninc.com					
Digit Professional Inc 3926 Varsity Dr.	Ann Arbor	MI	48108	734-677-0840	677-3027
TF: 877-767-8862 ■ *Web:* www.digitprofessional.com					
Electronics for Imaging Inc 303 Velocity Way	Foster City	CA	94404	650-357-3500	357-3907
NASDAQ: EFII ■ *TF:* 800-568-1917 ■ *Web:* www.efi.com					
Elo TouchSystems Inc 301 Constitution Dr	Menlo Park	CA	94025	510-739-4600	361-4731*
**Fax Area Code:* 650 ■ *TF:* 800-557-1458 ■ *Web:* www.elotouch.com					
Fellowes Inc 1789 Norwood Ave	Itasca	IL	60143	630-893-1600	893-1718*
**Fax:* Cust Svc ■ *TF:* 800-945-4545 ■ *Web:* www.fellowes.com					
Fujitsu Components America Inc 250 E Caribbean Dr.	Sunnyvale	CA	94089	408-745-4900	745-4970
Web: www.fujitsu.com/us					
GTCO CalComp Inc 7125 Riverwood Dr	Columbia	MD	21046	410-381-6688	290-9065
TF: 800-344-4723 ■ *Web:* www.gtco.com					
Guillemot North America 5800 rue Saint-Denis Suite 1001	Montreal	QC	H2S3L5	514-279-9960	279-4954
Web: us.guillemot.com					
Gyration Inc 12930 Saratoga Ave	Saratoga	CA	95070	408-973-7070	255-9075
TF: 888-340-0033 ■ *Web:* www.gyration.com					
Immersion Corp 801 Fox Ln	San Jose	CA	95131	408-467-1900	467-1901
NASDAQ: IMMR ■ *TF:* 888-467-1900 ■ *Web:* www.immersion.com					
Innovative Global Solutions Co LLC 511 5th St Unit F	San Fernando	CA	91340	818-837-9495	837-9526
Web: www.igsco.net					
Interlink Electronics Inc 546 Flynn Rd	Camarillo	CA	93012	805-484-8855	484-8726
NASDAQ: LINKE ■ *TF:* 800-340-1331 ■ *Web:* www.interlinkelec.com					
iScribe 101 Redwood Shores Pkwy Suite 101	Redwood City	CA	94065	650-381-2076	
TF: 800-326-3784 ■ *Web:* www.iscribe.com					
Kensington Technology Group 333 Twin Dolphin Dr 6th Fl	Redwood Shores	CA	94065	650-572-2700	267-2800
TF: 800-243-2972 ■ *Web:* www.kensington.com					
Key Tronic Corp DBA KeyTronicEMS 4424 N Sullivan Rd	Spokane	WA	99214	509-928-8000	927-5383
NASDAQ: KTCC ■ *Web:* www.keytronic.com					
KeyTronicEMS 4424 N Sullivan Rd	Spokane	WA	99214	509-928-8000	927-5383
NASDAQ: KTCC ■ *Web:* www.keytronic.com					
Kinesis Corp 22121 17th Ave SE Suite 112	Bothell	WA	98021	425-402-8100	402-8181
TF: 800-454-6374 ■ *Web:* www.kinesis.com					
KYE Systems Corp 1301 NW 84th Ave Suite 127	Miami	FL	33126	305-468-9250	468-9251
Web: www.genius-kye.com					
Lite-On Trading USA Inc 720 S Hillview Dr	Milpitas	CA	95035	408-946-4873	941-4597
Web: www.us.liteon.com					

Phone Fax

Logitech Inc 6505 Kaiser Dr ... Fremont CA 94555 510-795-8500 792-8901
TF Sales: 800-231-7717 ■ *Web:* www.logitech.com

Mace Group Inc 4601 E Airport Dr ... Ontario CA 91761 909-230-6888 230-6889
TF: 800-644-1132 ■ *Web:* www.macally.com

Mad Catz Interactive Inc 7480 Mission Valley Rd Suite 101 ... San Diego CA 92108 619-683-9830 683-9839
AMEX: MCZ ■ *TF:* 800-659-2287 ■ *Web:* www.madcatz.com

Memtron Technologies Inc 530 N Franklin St ... Frankenmuth MI 48734 989-652-2656 652-2659
TF Cust Svc: 800-234-7525 ■ *Web:* www.memtron.com

NaturalPoint Inc 33872 Eastgate Cir SE ... Corvallis OR 97333 541-753-6645 753-6689
Web: www.naturalpoint.com

NMB Technologies Corp 9730 Independence Ave ... Chatsworth CA 91311 818-341-3355 341-8207
Web: www.nmbtech.com

Numonics Corp 101 Commerce Dr ... Montgomeryville PA 18936 215-362-2766 361-0167
TF: 800-523-6716 ■ *Web:* www.numonics.com

PolyVision Corp 3970 Johns Creek Ct Suite 325 ... Suwanee GA 30024 678-542-3100 542-3200
TF: 800-620-7659 ■ *Web:* www.polyvision.com

SCM Microsystems Inc 466 Kato Terr ... Fremont CA 94539 510-360-2300 360-0211
NASDAQ: SCMM ■ *Web:* www.scmmicro.com

Seiko Instruments USA Inc Business & Home Office Products Div 2990 Lomita Blvd ... Torrance CA 90505 310-517-7050 517-7051
Web: www.seikosmart.com

Sejin America Inc 2004 Martin Ave ... Santa Clara CA 95050 408-980-7550 980-7562
Web: www.sejin.com

SMART Modular Technologies Inc 4211 Starboard Dr ... Fremont CA 94538 510-623-1231 623-1434
NASDAQ: SMOD ■ *TF:* 800-956-7627 ■ *Web:* www.smartm.com

SMART Technologies Inc 1207 11th Ave SW Suite 300 ... Calgary AB T3C0M5 403-245-0333 245-0366
TF: 888-427-6278 ■ *Web:* www.smarttech.com

Synaptics Inc 3120 Scott Blvd Suite 130 ... Santa Clara CA 95054 408-454-5100 454-5200
NASDAQ: SYNA ■ *Web:* www.synaptics.com

Think Outside Inc 85 Saratoga Ave Suite 200 ... Santa Clara CA 95051 408-551-4545 551-0660
Web: www.thinkoutside.com

TouchSystems Corp 220 Tradesmen Dr ... Hutto TX 78634 512-846-2424 846-2425
TF: 800-320-5944 ■ *Web:* www.touchsystems.com

Ultra Electronics Measurement Systems Inc
50 Barnes Park N Suite 102 ... Wallingford CT 06492 203-949-3500 949-3598
Web: www.ultra-msi.com

Virtual Ink Corp 150 CambridgePark Dr ... Cambridge MA 02140 617-902-2040 902-2041
TF: 877-696-4646 ■ *Web:* www.mimio.com

Wacom Technology Corp 1311 SE Cardinal Ct ... Vancouver WA 98683 360-896-9833 896-9724
TF: 800-922-9348 ■ *Web:* www.wacom.com

176-2 Computers

Phone Fax

Aberdeen LLC 9130 Norwalk Blvd ... Santa Fe Springs CA 90670 562-699-6998 695-5570*
**Fax:* Sales ■ *Web:* www.aberdeeninc.com

ABS Computer Technologies Inc 9997 E Rosehills Rd ... Whittier CA 90601 562-695-8823 695-8923*
**Fax:* Sales ■ *TF Sales:* 800-876-8088 ■ *Web:* www.buyabs.com

Acer America Corp 2641 Orchard Pkwy Bldg 1 ... San Jose CA 95134 408-432-6200 922-2933*
**Fax:* Sales ■ *TF:* 800-733-2237 ■ *Web:* aac.acer.com

ACMA Computers Inc 1505 Reliance Way ... Fremont CA 94539 510-623-1212 651-0629
TF Sales: 800-786-6888 ■ *Web:* www.acma.com

ACME Portable Machines Inc 1330 Mountain View Cir ... Azusa CA 91702 626-610-1888 610-1881
Web: www.acmeportable.com

Advanced Processing Laboratories Inc 10864 Thornmint Rd ... San Diego CA 92127 858-674-2850 674-2869
TF: 800-822-7522 ■ *Web:* www.sd.aplabs.com

AlphaSmart Inc 973 University Ave ... Los Gatos CA 95032 408-355-1000 355-1055
Web: www3.alphasmart.com

Amax Engineering Corp 1565 Reliance Way ... Fremont CA 94539 510-651-8886 651-0629
TF Cust Svc: 800-889-2629 ■ *Web:* www.amax.com

Apple Inc 1 Infinite Loop ... Cupertino CA 95014 408-996-1010 996-0275*
NASDAQ: AAPL ■ **Fax:* Mail Rm ■ *TF Cust Svc:* 800-275-2273 ■ *Web:* www.apple.com

Aries Research Inc 4121 Clipper Ct ... Fremont CA 94538 510-413-0288 226-0781
TF: 800-282-7437 ■ *Web:* www.ariesresearch.com

ASUSTeK Computer International 44370 Nobel Dr ... Fremont CA 94538 510-739-3777 797-3579
Web: www.asus.com

Au Optronics Corp 9720 Cypresswood Dr Suite 241 ... Houston TX 77070 281-807-2630 807-2642
NYSE: AUO ■ *Web:* www.auo.com

Boundless Corp 50 Engineers Ln Unit 2 ... Farmingdale NY 11735 631-962-1500 962-1505
TF: 800-342-7400 ■ *Web:* www.boundless.com

Chem USA Corp 38507 Cherry St ... Newark CA 94560 510-608-8818 608-8828
TF: 800-866-2436 ■ *Web:* www.chemusa.com

Cognex Corp 1 Vision Dr ... Natick MA 01760 508-650-3000 650-3333
NASDAQ: CGNX ■ *TF:* 877-926-4639

Comark Corp 93 West St ... Medfield MA 02052 508-359-8161 359-2267
TF: 800-280-8522 ■ *Web:* www.comarkcorp.com

Computer Management Corp 260 Lackland Dr ... Middlesex NJ 08846 732-356-3500 356-3501
Web: www.cmcusa.com

Corvallis Microtechnology Inc 413 SW Jefferson Ave ... Corvallis OR 97333 541-752-5456 752-4117
Web: www.cmtinc.com

Cray Inc 411 1st Ave S Suite 600 ... Seattle WA 98104 206-701-2000 701-2500
NASDAQ: CRAY ■ *Web:* www.cray.com

CSP Inc 43 Manning Rd ... Billerica MA 01821 978-663-7598 663-0150
NASDAQ: CSPIE ■ *TF:* 800-325-3110 ■ *Web:* www.cspi.com

CSS Laboratories Inc 1641 McGaw Ave ... Irvine CA 92614 949-852-8161 852-0410
TF: 800-852-2680 ■ *Web:* www.csslabs.com

CTC Parker Automation 50 W TechneCenter Dr Suite H ... Milford OH 45150 513-831-2340 831-5042
TF Cust Svc: 800-233-3329 ■ *Web:* www.ctcusa.com

Cyberchron Corp 2700 Rt 9 Pro Box 160 ... Cold Spring NY 10516 845-265-3700 265-4154
Web: www.cyberchron.com

Cytec Corp 1017 William D Tate Ave Suite 107 ... Grapevine TX 76051 214-349-8881
TF: 888-349-8881 ■ *Web:* www.cytecsys.com

Datalux Corp 155 Aviation Dr ... Winchester VA 22602 540-662-1500 662-1682
TF: 800-328-2589 ■ *Web:* www.datalux.com

Dedicated Computing N26 W23880 Commerce Cir ... Waukesha WI 53188 262-951-7200 523-2222
TF: 877-523-3301 ■ *Web:* www.dedicatedcomputing.com

Dell Inc 1 Dell Way ... Round Rock TX 78682 512-338-4400 283-6161
NASDAQ: DELL ■ *TF:* 800-854-6214 ■ *Web:* www.dell.com

Diamond Flower Electric Instrument Co USA Inc (DFI)
732-C Striker Ave ... Sacramento CA 95834 916-568-1234 568-1233
TF: 800-909-4334 ■ *Web:* www.dfiusa.com

Diversified Technology Inc 476 Highland Colony Pkwy ... Ridgeland MS 39157 601-856-4121 856-2888
TF: 800-443-2667 ■ *Web:* www.dtims.com

DRS Tactical Systems Inc 1110 W Hibiscus Blvd ... Melbourne FL 32901 321-727-3672 725-0496
Web: www.drs-ts.com

Ectaco Inc 31-21 31st St ... Long Island City NY 11106 718-728-6110 728-4023
TF: 800-710-7920 ■ *Web:* www.ectaco.com

Electrovaya Inc 2645 Royal Windsor Dr ... Mississauga ON L5J1K9 905-855-4610 822-7953
TSX: EFL ■ *TF:* 800-388-2865 ■ *Web:* www.electrovaya.com

EliteGroup Computer Systems Inc 45401 Research Ave ... Fremont CA 94539 510-226-7333 226-7350
TF: 800-829-8890 ■ *Web:* www.ecsusa.com

eMachines Inc 14350 Myford Rd Bldg 100 ... Irvine CA 92606 714-481-2828 368-9896
TF: 877-566-3463 ■ *Web:* www.e4me.com

Encore Real Time Computing Inc 105 East Dr ... Melbourne FL 32904 321-727-2211 727-7009
TF Cust Svc: 800-936-2673 ■ *Web:* www.encore.com

ENGlobal Corp 600 Century Plaza Dr Suite 140 ... Houston TX 77073 281-821-3200 821-5488
AMEX: ENG ■ *TF:* 800-411-6040 ■ *Web:* www.englobal.com

Phone Fax

Franklin Electronic Publishers Inc 1 Franklin Plaza ... Burlington NJ 08016 609-386-2500 239-5948
AMEX: FEP ■ *TF:* 800-266-5626 ■ *Web:* www.franklin.com

Fujitsu America Inc 1250 E Arques Ave ... Sunnyvale CA 95085 408-746-6200 746-6260
TF: 800-538-8460 ■ *Web:* www.fujitsu.com

Gateway Inc 7565 Irvine Center Dr ... Irvine CA 92618 949-471-7000 471-7001
NYSE: GTW ■ *TF:* 800-846-2000 ■ *Web:* www.gateway.com

General Dynamics Itronix Corp 12825 E Mirabeau Pkwy ... Spokane Valley WA 99216 509-624-6600 626-4203*
**Fax:* Sales ■ *TF:* 800-441-1309 ■ *Web:* www.gd-itronix.com

Granite Communications Inc 13 Columbia Dr Suite 12 ... Amherst NH 03031 603-881-8666 881-4042
Web: www.gcicom.com

Hand Held Products Inc 700 Vision Dr ... Skaneateles Falls NY 13153 315-685-4100 685-0049
TF: 800-782-4263 ■ *Web:* www.handheld.com

Hewlett-Packard (Canada) Ltd 5150 Spectrum Way ... Mississauga ON L4W5G1 905-206-4725 206-4739
TF: 888-447-4636 ■ *Web:* www.hp.com/country/ca/eng/welcome.html

Hewlett-Packard Co 3000 Hanover St ... Palo Alto CA 94304 650-857-1501 857-5518
NYSE: HPQ ■ *TF Sales:* 800-752-0900 ■ *Web:* www.hp.com

HyperData Technology USA Corp 817 S Lemon Ave ... Walnut CA 91789 909-468-2933 468-2961
TF: 800-786-3343 ■ *Web:* www.hyperdatadirect.com

IBM Canada Ltd 3600 Steeles Ave E ... Markham ON L3R9Z7 905-316-5000 316-2150
Web: www.ibm.com/ca/en

Immecor Corp 2351 Circadian Way ... Santa Rosa CA 95407 707-636-2550 636-2565
Web: www.immecor.com

International Business Machines Corp (IBM)
1 New Orchard Rd ... Armonk NY 10504 914-766-1900
NYSE: IBM ■ *TF:* 800-426-4968 ■ *Web:* www.ibm.com/us

Keydata International Inc 201 Circle Dr N Suite 101 ... Piscataway NJ 08854 732-868-0588 868-6536
TF: 800-486-4800 ■ *Web:* www.keydata-pc.com

Kontron Mobile Computing Inc 7631 Anagram Dr ... Eden Prairie MN 55344 952-974-7000 949-2791
TF: 888-343-5396 ■ *Web:* www.kontronmobile.com

LXE Inc 125 Technology Pkwy ... Norcross GA 30092 770-447-4224 447-4405
TF: 800-664-4593 ■ *Web:* www.lxe.com

MaxVision Corp 495 Production Ave ... Madison AL 35758 256-772-3058 772-3078
TF: 800-533-5805 ■ *Web:* www.maxvision.com

Mercury Computer Systems Inc 199 Riverneck Rd ... Chelmsford MA 01824 978-256-1300 256-3599
NASDAQ: MRCY ■ *TF:* 800-229-2006 ■ *Web:* www.mc.com

Micro Center Online 2701 Charter St Suite A ... Columbus OH 43228 614-334-1496
TF: 800-468-1633 ■ *Web:* www.microcenter.com

Micro Electronics Inc 4119 Leap Rd ... Hilliard OH 43026 614-850-3000 850-3001
TF: 800-634-3478 ■ *Web:* www.microelectronics.com

Micro Express Inc 8 Hammond Dr Suite 105 ... Irvine CA 92618 800-989-9900 460-9974*
**Fax Area Code:* 949 ■ *Web:* www.microexpress.net

Microtech Computers Inc 4921 Legends Dr ... Lawrence KS 66049 785-841-9513 841-1809
TF Tech Supp: 800-828-9533 ■ *Web:* www.microtechcomp.com

Microway Inc 12 Richards Rd ... Plymouth MA 02360 508-746-7341 746-4678
Web: www.microway.com

Miltope Corp 500 Richardson Rd S ... Hope Hull AL 36043 334-284-8665 613-6302
TF: 800-645-8673 ■ *Web:* www.miltope.com

MPC Corp (MPC) 906 E Karcher Rd ... Nampa ID 83687 208-893-3434 893-7248
TF: 888-464-2766 ■ *Web:* www.mpccorp.com

Neoware Systems Inc 3200 Horizon Dr ... King of Prussia PA 19406 610-277-8300 275-5739
NASDAQ: NWRE ■ *TF:* 800-437-1551 ■ *Web:* www.neoware.com

Palm Inc 950 W Maude Ave ... Sunnyvale CA 94085 408-617-7000 617-0100
NASDAQ: PALM ■ *TF:* 800-881-7256 ■ *Web:* www.palm.com

Panasonic Communications & Systems Co 1 Panasonic Way ... Secaucus NJ 07094 201-348-7000 392-6007*
**Fax:* Hum Res ■ *TF Cust Svc:* 800-211-7262 ■ *Web:* www.panasonic.com

Panasonic Computer Solutions Co 1 Panasonic Way ... Secaucus NJ 07094 201-348-7000
TF: 800-662-3537 ■ *Web:* www.panasonic.com/computer/notebook

Pinnacle Data Systems Inc 6600 Port Rd Suite 100 ... Groveport OH 43125 614-748-1150 748-1209
AMEX: PNS ■ *TF:* 800-882-8282 ■ *Web:* www.pinnacle.com

QEI Inc 60 Fadem Rd ... Springfield NJ 07081 973-379-7400 379-2138
Web: www.qeiinc.com

Quantum3D Inc 6330 San Ignacio Ave ... San Jose CA 95119 408-361-9999 361-9980
TF: 888-747-1020 ■ *Web:* www.quantum3d.com

Radix International Corp 4855 Wiley Post Way ... Salt Lake City UT 84116 801-537-1717 328-3401
TF: 800-367-9256 ■ *Web:* www.radix-intl.com

Recortec Inc 1620 Berryessa Rd Suite A ... San Jose CA 95133 408-928-1480 729-3661
TF: 888-732-6783 ■ *Web:* www.recortec.com

Research In Motion Ltd 295 Phillip St ... Waterloo ON N2L3W8 519-888-7465 888-7884
NASDAQ: RIMM ■ *Web:* www.rim.net

Roper Mobile Technology 7450 S Priest Dr ... Tempe AZ 85283 480-705-4200 705-4216
Web: www.ropermobile.com

Roper Mobile Technology 875 Charest Blvd W Suite 200 ... Quebec City QC G1N2C9 418-681-9394 681-7734
TF: 800-363-1993 ■ *Web:* www.daptech.com

Royal Consumer Information Products Inc
379 Campus Dr 2nd Fl ... Somerset NJ 08875 732-627-9977 667-1556
TF Sales: 888-261-4555 ■ *Web:* www.royal.com

SBS Technologies Inc 7401 Snaproll NE ... Albuquerque NM 87109 505-875-0600 875-0400
NASDAQ: SBSE ■ *TF:* 800-727-1553 ■ *Web:* www.sbs.com

Sharp Electronics Corp 1 Sharp Plaza ... Mahwah NJ 07430 201-529-8200 529-8413
TF: 800-237-4277 ■ *Web:* www.sharpusa.com

Sony of Canada Ltd 115 Gordon Baker Rd ... Toronto ON M2H3R6 416-499-1414 499-1774
Web: www.sony.ca

Sony Electronics Inc 1 Sony Dr ... Park Ridge NJ 07656 201-930-1000 358-4058*
**Fax:* Hum Res ■ *TF Cust Svc:* 800-222-7669 ■ *Web:* www.sony.com

Stealth Computer Corp 530 Rowntree Dairy Rd Bldg 4 ... Woodbridge ON L4L8H2 905-264-9000 264-7440
TF: 888-783-2584 ■ *Web:* www.stealth.ca

Symbol Technologies Inc 1 Symbol Plaza ... Holtsville NY 11742 631-738-2400 738-5990
NYSE: SBL ■ *TF:* 800-722-6234 ■ *Web:* www.symbol.com

Sys Technology Inc 17358 Railroad St ... City of Industry CA 91748 714-952-8767
TF: 888-797-7248 ■ *Web:* www.sys.com

Systemax Inc 11 Harbor Park Dr ... Port Washington NY 11050 516-625-3663 608-7744*
NYSE: SYX ■ **Fax:* Sales ■ *TF:* 800-845-6225 ■ *Web:* www.systemaxpc.com

Tadpole Computer Inc 20450 Stevens Creek Blvd 3rd Fl ... Cupertino CA 95014 408-973-9944 973-9593
TF: 800-734-5483 ■ *Web:* www.tadpolecomputer.com

Tangent Computer Inc 197 Airport Blvd ... Burlingame CA 94010 650-342-9388 342-0615
TF: 800-342-9388 ■ *Web:* www.tangent.com

TeleVideo Inc 2345 Harris Way ... San Jose CA 95131 408-954-8333 954-0622
Web: www.televideo.com

Toshiba America Inc 1251 Ave of the Americas Suite 4100 ... New York NY 10020 212-596-0600 593-3875
TF: 800-457-7777 ■ *Web:* www.toshiba.com

Toshiba America Information Systems Inc 9740 Irvine Blvd ... Irvine CA 92618 949-583-3000
TF Cust Svc: 800-457-7777 ■ *Web:* www.tais.com

Total Control Products Inc 2500 Austin Dr ... Charlottesville VA 22911 434-978-5000 984-2213*
**Fax Area Code:* 800 ■ *TF:* 800-263-6041 ■
Web: www.geindustrial.com/cwc/gefanuc/totalcontrol

TouchStar Solutions LLC 5147 S Garnett Rd Suite D ... Tulsa OK 74146 918-307-7100 307-7111
Web: www.touchstarsolutions.com

Transource Computers Corp 2405 W Utopia Rd ... Phoenix AZ 85027 623-879-8882 879-8887
TF: 800-486-3715 ■ *Web:* www.transource.com

Twinhead Corp 48303 Fremont Blvd ... Fremont CA 94538 510-492-0828 492-0820
TF Sales: 800-995-8946 ■ *Web:* www.twinhead.com

Ultradata Systems Inc 1240 Dielman Industrial Ct ... Saint Louis MO 63132 314-997-2250 997-1281
TF: 800-747-2605 ■ *Web:* www.ultradatasystems.com

Wyse Technology Inc 3471 N 1st St ... San Jose CA 95134 408-473-1200 473-2080
TF: 800-800-9973 ■ *Web:* www.wyse.com

Xybernaut Corp 12701 Fair Lakes Cir Suite 550 ... Fairfax VA 22033 703-631-6925 631-6734
TF: 888-992-3777 ■ *Web:* www.xybernaut.com

Computers (Cont'd)

	City	State	Zip	Phone	Fax
Xycom Automation Inc 750 N Maple Rd **Fax: Sales* ■ *TF:* 800-289-9266 ■ *Web:* www.xycom.com	Saline	MI	48176	734-429-4971	429-1010*

176-3 Modems

	City	State	Zip	Phone	Fax
3Com Corp 350 Campus Dr. *NASDAQ: COMS* ■ *Web:* www.3com.com	Marlborough	MA	01752	508-323-5000	323-1111
ActionTec Electronics Inc 760 N Mary Ave. *TF:* 800-752-7820 ■ *Web:* www.actiontec.com	Sunnyvale	CA	94085	408-752-7700	541-9003
Ai-Logix Inc 27 World's Fair Dr. *TF:* 800-648-3647 ■ *Web:* www.ai-logix.com	Somerset	NJ	08873	732-469-0880	469-2298
Arescom Inc 47338 Fremont Blvd *TF:* 800-575-4736 ■ *Web:* www.arescom.com	Fremont	CA	94538	510-445-3638	445-3636
Avocent Corp 4991 Corporate Dr *NASDAQ: AVCT* ■ *TF:* 800-932-9239 ■ *Web:* www.avocent.com	Huntsville	AL	35805	256-430-4000	430-4030
Aztech Labs Inc 4005 Clipper Ct. *TF:* 800-886-8859 ■ *Web:* www.aztech.com	Fremont	CA	94538	510-683-9800	683-9803
Best Data Products Inc 9650 DeSoto Ave *Web:* www.bestdata.com	Chatsworth	CA	91311	818-773-9600	773-9619
Biscom Inc 321 Billerica Rd *TF:* 800-477-2472 ■ *Web:* www.biscom.com	Chelmsford	MA	01824	978-250-1800	250-4449
Canoga Perkins Corp 20600 Prairie St *Web:* www.canoga.com	Chatsworth	CA	91311	818-718-6300	718-6312
Castelle 855 Jarvis Dr Suite 100 *NASDAQ: CSTL* ■ *TF:* 800-289-7555 ■ *Web:* www.castelle.com	Morgan Hill	CA	95037	408-852-8000	852-8100
Cermetek Microelectronics Inc 1390 Borregas Ave *TF:* 800-882-6271 ■ *Web:* www.cermetek.com	Sunnyvale	CA	94089	408-752-5000	752-5004
Circuit Research Corp 5 Northern Blvd Suite 12 *Web:* www.circuitr.com	Amherst	NH	03031	603-880-4000	880-8297
Cirronet Inc 3079 Premiere Pkwy Suite 140 *Web:* www.cirronet.com	Duluth	GA	30097	678-684-2000	684-2001
Comspec Digital Products Inc 2205 Bass Hollow PO Box 178 **Fax Area Code: 903* ■ *TF:* 800-490-6893 ■ *Web:* www.comspecdpi.com	Jacksonville	TX	75766	832-443-4487	586-7944*
Connecticut microComputer Inc 150 Pocono Rd *TF:* 800-426-2872 ■ *Web:* www.2cmc.com	Brookfield	CT	06804	203-740-9890	775-4595
Connexperts 660 Preston Forest Center Suite 214 *Web:* www.connexperts.com	Dallas	TX	75230	214-221-4224	340-5717
Copia International Ltd 1220 Iroquois Dr Suite 180 **Fax: Sales* ■ *TF Sales:* 800-689-8898 ■ *Web:* www.copia.com	Naperville	IL	60563	630-778-8898	778-8848*
CXR Larus Corp 894 Faulstich Ct *TF:* 800-999-9946 ■ *Web:* www.cxrlarus.com	San Jose	CA	95112	408-573-2700	573-2708
Data-Linc Group 3535 Factoria Blvd SE Suite 100 *Web:* www.data-linc.com	Bellevue	WA	98006	425-882-2206	867-0865
Dataforth Corp 3331 E Hemisphere Loop *TF:* 800-444-7644 ■ *Web:* www.dataforth.com	Tucson	AZ	85706	520-741-1404	741-0762
Dataradio Corp 6160 Peachtree Dunwoody Rd Suite C-200 *Web:* www.dataradio.com	Atlanta	GA	30328	770-392-0002	392-9199
Dataradio Inc 5500 Royalmount Ave Suite 200 *Web:* www.dataradio.com	Montreal	QC	H4P1H7	514-737-0020	737-7883
Eiger Technology Inc 144 Front St W Suite 700 *TSX: AXA* ■ *Web:* www.eigertechnology.com	Toronto	ON	M5J2L7	416-216-8659	216-1164
Electronic Systems Technology Inc 415 N Quay St Bldg B-1 *Web:* www.esteem.com	Kennewick	WA	99336	509-735-9092	783-5475
Encore Networks Inc 45472 Holiday Dr Suite 3 *Web:* www.encorenetworks.com	Dulles	VA	20166	703-318-7750	787-4625
Engage Communications Inc 9565 Soquel Dr *Web:* www.engagecom.com	Aptos	CA	95003	831-688-1021	688-1421
FreeWave Technologies Inc 1880 S Flatiron Ct Suite F *Web:* www.freewave.com	Boulder	CO	80301	303-444-3862	786-9948
Gallantry Technologies Inc 5255 Stevens Creek Blvd Suite 234 *Web:* www.gallantry.com	Santa Clara	CA	95051	408-369-1359	377-3277
Global Communication Technologies Inc 14455 Webb Chapel	Dallas	TX	75234	972-620-1670	620-1672
GRE America Inc 425 Harbor Blvd *TF:* 800-233-5973 ■ *Web:* www.greamerica.com	Belmont	CA	94002	650-591-1400	591-2001
Internet Commerce Corp 129 Bankhead Ave *NASDAQ: ICCA* ■ *TF:* 888-422-4401 ■ *Web:* www.icc.net	Carrolton	GA	30117	770-834-6469	834-2945
Jaton Corp 556 S Milpitas Blvd. **Fax: Sales* ■ *Web:* www.jaton.com	Milpitas	CA	95035	408-942-9888	942-9888*
Konexx 5550 Oberlin Dr. *TF:* 800-275-6354 ■ *Web:* www.konexx.com	San Diego	CA	92121	858-622-1400	550-7330
Motorola Canada Ltd 8133 Warden Ave. *TF:* 800-268-3395 ■ *Web:* www.motorola.ca/	Markham	ON	L6G1B3	905-948-5200	948-5250
Motorola Inc 1301 E Algonquin Rd. *NYSE: MOT* ■ **Fax: Hum Res* ■ *TF:* 800-331-6456 ■ *Web:* www.motorola.com	Schaumburg	IL	60196	847-576-5000	538-3617*
Multi-Tech Systems 2205 Woodale Dr *TF Cust Svc:* 800-328-9717 ■ *Web:* www.multitech.com	Mounds View	MN	55112	763-785-3500	785-9874
Nayna Networks Inc 4699 Old Ironsides Dr Suite 420 *Web:* www.nayna.com	Santa Clara	CA	95054	408-956-8000	956-8730
NEC USA Inc 101 E 52nd St *TF Hum Res:* 800-338-9549 ■ *Web:* www.necus.com	New York	NY	10022	212-326-2400	326-2419
Novatel Wireless Inc 9255 Towne Centre Dr Suite 205 *NASDAQ: NVTL* ■ *TF:* 888-888-9231 ■ *Web:* www.novatelwireless.com	San Diego	CA	92121	858-320-8800	812-3419
Phoebe Micro Inc 47606 Kato Rd *Web:* www.phoebemicro.com	Fremont	CA	94538	510-360-0800	360-0818
Radyne Corp 3138 E Elwood St *NASDAQ: RADN* ■ *Web:* www.radynecomstream.com	Phoenix	AZ	85034	602-437-9620	437-4811
Research In Motion Ltd 295 Phillip St *NASDAQ: RIMM* ■ *Web:* www.rim.net	Waterloo	ON	N2L3W8	519-888-7465	888-7884
Siemens Subscriber Networks Inc 4849 Alpha Rd. *Web:* www.efficient.com	Dallas	TX	75244	972-852-1000	852-1001
Sierra Wireless Inc 13811 Wireless Way *NASDAQ: SWIR* ■ *Web:* www.sierrawireless.com	Richmond	BC	V6V3A4	604-231-1100	231-1109
Teldat Corp 1001 Brickell Bay Dr Suite 2810 *Web:* www.teldat.com	Miami	FL	33131	305-372-3480	372-8759
Telenetics Corp 39 Parker *Web:* www.telenetics.com	Irvine	CA	92618	949-455-4000	455-4010
Teletronics International Inc 2 Choke Cherry Rd *Web:* www.teletronics.com	Rockville	MD	20850	301-309-8500	309-8851
Terayon Communication Systems Inc 4988 Great America Pkwy *NASDAQ: TERNE* ■ *TF:* 888-783-7296 ■ *Web:* www.terayon.com	Santa Clara	CA	95054	408-235-5500	235-5501
Toshiba America Information Systems Inc 9740 Irvine Blvd. *TF Cust Svc:* 800-457-7777 ■ *Web:* www.tais.com	Irvine	CA	92618	949-583-3000	
Unlimited Systems Corp Inc DBA Konexx 5550 Oberlin Dr *TF:* 800-275-6354 ■ *Web:* www.konexx.com	San Diego	CA	92121	858-622-1400	550-7330
US Robotics Corp 935 National Pkwy *TF:* 877-710-0884 ■ *Web:* www.usr.com	Schaumburg	IL	60173	847-874-2000	874-2001
Wavecom Inc 4810 Eastgate Mall Rd 2nd Fl *Web:* www.wavecom.com	San Diego	CA	92121	858-362-0101	558-5485
Western Datacom Co Inc 959 Bassett Rd Unit B *TF:* 800-262-3311 ■ *Web:* www.western-data.com	Westlake	OH	44145	440-835-1510	835-9146
Western Telematic Inc 5 Sterling *TF:* 800-854-7226 ■ *Web:* www.wti.com	Irvine	CA	92618	949-586-9950	583-9514
Wi-LAN Inc 11 Holland Ave Suite 608 *Web:* www.wi-lan.com	Ottawa	ON	K1Y4S1	613-688-4900	688-4894
Xecom Inc 374 Turquoise St. *Web:* www.xecom.com	Milpitas	CA	95035	408-945-6640	942-1346
Zoom Technologies Inc 207 South St. *NASDAQ: ZOOM* ■ *TF:* 800-666-6191 ■ *Web:* www.zoomtel.com	Boston	MA	02111	617-423-1072	423-5536
Zypcom Inc 2301 Industrial Pkwy W Bldg 8 *Web:* www.zypcom.com	Hayward	CA	94545	510-783-2501	783-2414
ZyXEL Communications Inc 1130 N Miller St. *TF:* 800-255-4101 ■ *Web:* www.zyxel.com	Anaheim	CA	92806	714-632-0882	632-0858

176-4 Monitors & Displays

	City	State	Zip	Phone	Fax
3M Display & Graphics Div 3M Ctr *TF:* 800-364-3577	Saint Paul	MN	55144	651-733-1110	733-9973
Barco Folsom LLC 11101 Trade Center Dr *TF:* 888-414-7226 ■ *Web:* www.folsom.com	Rancho Cordova	CA	95670	916-859-2500	859-2515
Barco Media & Entertainment LLC 11101-A Trade Center Dr **Fax: Sales* ■ *TF:* 800-543-7904 ■ *Web:* www.barco.com/media	Rancho Cordova	CA	95670	916-859-2500	859-2515*
BarcoView LLC 3059 Premiere Pkwy **Fax: Hum Res* ■ *Web:* www.barco.com	Duluth	GA	30097	678-475-8000	475-8160*
BenQ America Corp 53 Discovery *TF:* 866-600-2367 ■ *Web:* www.benq.com	Irvine	CA	92618	949-255-9500	255-9600
Clarity Visual Systems Inc 27350 SW 95th Ave Suite 3038 *Web:* www.clarityvisual.com	Wilsonville	OR	97070	503-570-0700	682-9441
Computron Display Systems Inc 1697 W Imperial Ct *Web:* www.computrondisplay.com	Mount Prospect	IL	60056	847-952-8800	952-0832
Conrac Inc 5124 Commerce Dr. *Web:* www.conrac.com	Baldwin Park	CA	91706	626-480-0095	480-0077
CopyTele Inc 900 Walt Whitman Rd *Web:* www.copytele.com	Melville	NY	11747	631-549-5900	549-5974
CTX Technology Corp 16728 E Gale Ave **Fax: Cust Svc* ■ *TF Cust Svc:* 877-688-3288 ■ *Web:* www.ctxintl.com	City of Industry	CA	91745	626-363-9328	363-9390*
Daktronics Inc 331 32nd Ave *NASDAQ: DAKT* ■ *TF:* 800-843-9878 ■ *Web:* www.daktronics.com	Brookings	SD	57006	605-697-4300	697-4700
Delta Products Corp 4405 Cushing Pkwy. *Web:* www.deltaww.com	Fremont	CA	94538	510-668-5100	668-0696
Dotronix Inc 160 1st St SE *TF:* 800-720-7218 ■ *Web:* www.dotronix.com	New Brighton	MN	55112	651-633-1742	633-7025
Eizo Nanao Technologies Inc 5710 Warland Dr. *TF:* 800-800-5202 ■ *Web:* www.eizo.com	Cypress	CA	90630	562-431-5011	431-4811
eMagin Corp 2070 Rt 52 Bldg 334 *AMEX: EMA* ■ *Web:* www.emagin.com	Hopewell Junction	NY	12533	845-838-7900	838-7901
Envision Peripherals Inc 47490 Seabridge Dr *TF Tech Supp:* 888-838-6388 ■ *Web:* www.aocmonitor.com/epius	Fremont	CA	94538	510-770-9988	770-1088
Futaba Corp of America 711 E State Pkwy *Web:* www.futaba.com	Schaumburg	IL	60173	847-884-1444	884-1635
General Digital Corp 8 Nutmeg Rd S *TF:* 800-952-2535 ■ *Web:* www.gendig.com	South Windsor	CT	06074	860-282-2900	282-2244
Gunze USA 2113 Wells Branch Pkwy Bldg 5400 *Web:* www.gunzeusa.com	Austin	TX	78728	512-990-3400	990-1912
Hantronix Inc 10080 Bubb Rd. *Web:* www.hantronix.com	Cupertino	CA	95014	408-252-1100	252-1123
Hitachi America Ltd Monitor Div 2000 Sierra Point Pkwy. *TF:* 800-562-2552 ■ *Web:* www.hitachidisplays.com	Brisbane	CA	94005	650-589-8300	583-4207
Iiyama North America Inc 65 West St Rd Suite 101-B *TF:* 800-394-4335 ■ *Web:* www.iiyama.com	Warminster	PA	18974	215-682-9050	682-9066
Image Systems Corp 6103 Blue Circle Dr. *Web:* www.imagesystemscorp.com	Minnetonka	MN	55343	952-935-1171	935-1386
KDS USA 7373 Hunt Ave *TF:* 800-237-9988 ■ *Web:* www.kdsusa.com	Garden Grove	CA	92841	714-379-5599	379-5591
La Cie Ltd 22985 NW Evergreen Pkwy **Fax: Mktg* ■ *Web:* www.lacie.com	Hillsboro	OR	97124	503-844-4500	844-4508*
LG Electronics USA Inc 1000 Sylvan Ave *TF Tech Supp:* 800-243-0000 ■ *Web:* us.lge.com/index.do	Englewood Cliffs	NJ	07632	201-816-2000	816-0636
Lite-On Trading USA Inc 720 S Hillview Dr *Web:* www.us.liteon.com	Milpitas	CA	95035	408-946-4873	941-4597
NEC Corp of America 10850 Gold Center Dr Suite 200 *TF:* 800-632-4636 ■ *Web:* www.necam.com	Rancho Cordova	CA	95670	916-463-7000	636-5656
NEC Display Solutions of America Inc 500 Park Blvd Suite 1100 **Fax: Sales* ■ *TF Cust Svc:* 800-632-4662 ■ *Web:* www.necdisplay.com	Itasca	IL	60143	630-467-3000	467-3050*
OSRAM Sylvania Inc 100 Endicott St *Web:* www.sylvania.com	Danvers	MA	01923	978-777-1900	750-2152
Pioneer Electronics (USA) Inc 2265 E 220th St. *TF Cust Svc:* 800-421-1404 ■ *Web:* www.pioneerelectronics.com	Long Beach	CA	90810	310-952-2000	952-2402
Planar Systems Inc 1195 NW Compton Dr *NASDAQ: PLNR* ■ *TF:* 866-475-2627 ■ *Web:* www.planar.com	Beaverton	OR	97006	503-748-1100	748-1244
Princeton Graphics Systems Inc 3300 Irvine Ave Suite 120 *TF Cust Svc:* 800-747-6249 ■ *Web:* www.princetongraphics.com	Newport Beach	CA	92660	949-777-3379	777-3370
Proview Technology 7373 Hunt Ave *TF:* 800-776-8439 ■ *Web:* www.proview.net	Garden Grove	CA	92841	714-799-3899	379-6290
Sampo Technology 5550 Peachtree Industrial Blvd Suite 100 *Web:* www.sampotech.com	Norcross	GA	30071	770-449-6220	447-1109
Samsung Electronics America Inc 105 Challenger Rd. *TF:* 800-726-7864 ■ *Web:* www.samsungusa.com	Ridgefield Park	NJ	07660	201-229-4000	229-4029
Sharp Electronics Corp 1 Sharp Plaza *TF:* 800-237-4277 ■ *Web:* www.sharpusa.com	Mahwah	NJ	07430	201-529-8200	529-8413
Sharp Microelectronics of the Americas 5700 NW Pacific Rim Blvd. *Web:* www.sharpsma.com	Camas	WA	98607	360-834-2500	834-8903
Sony of Canada Ltd 115 Gordon Baker Rd. *Web:* www.sony.ca	Toronto	ON	M2H3R6	416-499-1414	499-1774
Sony Electronics Inc 1 Sony Dr **Fax: Hum Res* ■ *TF Cust Svc:* 800-222-7669 ■ *Web:* www.sony.com	Park Ridge	NJ	07656	201-930-1000	358-4058*
SpatiaLight Inc 5 Hamilton Landing Suite 100 *NASDAQ: HDTV* ■ *Web:* www.spatialight.com	Novato	CA	94949	415-883-1693	883-3363
Tatung Co of America Inc 2850 El Presidio St *TF:* 800-827-2850 ■ *Web:* www.tatungusa.com	Long Beach	CA	90810	310-637-2105	
Three-Five Systems Inc 1600 N Desert Dr. *Web:* www.35sys.com	Tempe	AZ	85281	602-389-8600	389-8989
Trans-Lux Corp 110 Richards Ave. *AMEX: TLX* ■ **Fax: Sales* ■ *TF:* 800-243-5544 ■ *Web:* www.trans-lux.com	Norwalk	CT	06854	203-853-4321	854-6891*
Trans-Lux Fair-Play Inc 1700 Delaware Ave. *TF:* 800-247-0265 ■ *Web:* www.fair-play.com	Des Moines	IA	50317	515-265-5305	265-3364
Video Display Corp 1868 Tucker Industrial Rd. *NASDAQ: VIDE* ■ *TF Cust Svc:* 800-241-5005 ■ *Web:* www.videodisplay.com	Tucker	GA	30084	770-938-2080	493-3903
ViewSonic Corp 381 Brea Canyon Rd *TF:* 800-888-8583 ■ *Web:* www.viewsonic.com	Walnut	CA	91789	909-444-8800	468-1202
Wells-Gardner Electronics Corp 9500 W 55th St Suite A *AMEX: WGA* ■ *TF:* 800-336-6630 ■ *Web:* www.wellsgardner.com	McCook	IL	60525	708-290-2100	290-2200
Xycom Automation Inc 750 N Maple Rd **Fax: Sales* ■ *TF:* 800-289-9266 ■ *Web:* www.xycom.com	Saline	MI	48176	734-429-4971	429-1010*

176-5 Multimedia Equipment & Supplies

Company	City	State	Zip	Phone	Fax
2Wire Inc 1704 Automation Pkwy *Web:* www.2wire.com	San Jose	CA	95131	408-428-9500	428-9590
AIPTEK Inc 51 Discovery Suite 100 *Web:* www.aiptek.com	Irvine	CA	92618	949-585-9600	585-9345
Altec Lansing Technologies Inc 535 Rt 6 & 209 *TF:* 800-258-3288 ■ *Web:* www.altecmm.com	Milford	PA	18337	570-296-6444	296-1222
Boston Acoustics Inc 300 Jubilee Dr *TF:* 800-288-6148 ■ *Web:* www.bostonacoustics.com	Peabody	MA	01960	978-538-5000	538-5199
Cambridge Soundworks Inc 100 Brickstone Sq 5th Fl *TF:* 800-945-4434 ■ *Web:* www.cambridgesoundworks.com	Andover	MA	01810	978-623-4400	475-7219
Creative Labs Inc 1901 McCarthy Blvd *TF Cust Svc:* 800-998-1000 ■ *Web:* us.creative.com	Milpitas	CA	95035	408-428-6600	428-6611
Cyber Acoustics LLC 11700 NE 60th Way Suite D4 *Web:* www.cyber-acoustics.com	Vancouver	WA	98682	360-883-0333	883-4888
Faroudja 180 Baytech Dr Suite 110 *Web:* www.faroudja.com	San Jose	CA	95134	408-635-4241	957-0364
FOCUS Enhancements Inc 1370 Dell Ave *NASDAQ: FCSE* ■ *TF:* 800-338-3348 ■ *Web:* www.focusinfo.com	Campbell	CA	95008	408-866-8300	866-4859
Guillemot North America 5800 rue Saint-Denis Suite 1001 *Web:* us.guillemot.com	Montreal	QC	H2S3L5	514-279-9960	279-4954
Kinyo Co Inc 14235 Lomitas Ave *TF:* 800-735-4696 ■ *Web:* www.kinyo.com	La Puente	CA	91746	626-333-3711	961-9114
Matrox Electronic Systems Ltd 1055 St Regis Blvd *Web:* www.matrox.com	Dorval	QC	H9P2T4	514-822-6000	822-6000
NMB Technologies Corp 9730 Independence Ave *Web:* www.nmbtech.com	Chatsworth	CA	91311	818-341-3355	341-8207
Pinnacle Systems Inc 280 N Bernardo Ave *TF Sales:* 800-522-8783 ■ *Web:* www.pinnaclesys.com	Mountain View	CA	94043	650-526-1600	526-1601
SCM Microsystems Inc 466 Kato Terr *NASDAQ: SCMM* ■ *Web:* www.scmmicro.com	Fremont	CA	94539	510-360-2300	360-0211
Vocollect Inc 703 Rodi Rd *Web:* www.vocollect.com	Pittsburgh	PA	15235	412-829-8145	829-0972

176-6 Printers

Company	City	State	Zip	Phone	Fax
Addmaster Corp 225 E Huntington Dr *Web:* www.addmaster.com	Monrovia	CA	91016	626-358-2395	358-2784
AMT Datasouth Corp 4765 Calle Quetzal *TF:* 800-215-9192 ■ *Web:* www.amtdatasouth.com	Camarillo	CA	93012	805-388-5799	484-5282
Astro-Med Inc 600 E Greenwich Ave *NASDAQ: ALOT* ■ *TF:* 877-757-7978 ■ *Web:* www.astro-med.com	West Warwick	RI	02893	401-828-4000	822-2430
Avery Dennison Printer Systems Div 7722 Dungan Rd *TF:* 800-395-2282 ■ *Web:* www.machines.averydennison.com	Philadelphia	PA	19111	215-725-4700	725-6850
Brother International Corp 100 Somerset Corporate Blvd *TF Cust Svc:* 800-276-7746 ■ *Web:* www.brother-usa.com	Bridgewater	NJ	08807	908-704-1700	704-8235
Canon USA Inc 1 Canon Plaza *NYSE: CAJ* ■ **Fax:* Hum Res ■ *TF:* 800-828-4040 ■ *Web:* www.usa.canon.com	Lake Success	NY	11042	516-488-6700	328-4669*
Casio Inc 570 Mt Pleasant Ave **Fax:* Hum Res ■ *TF Cust Svc:* 800-634-1895 ■ *Web:* www.casio.com	Dover	NJ	07801	973-361-5400	537-8910*
Citizen Systems America Corp 363 Van Ness Way Suite 404 **Fax:* Sales ■ *TF:* 800-421-6516 ■ *Web:* www.cbma.com	Torrance	CA	90501	310-781-1460	781-9152*
Craden Peripherals Corp 7860 Airport Hwy *Web:* www.craden.com	Pennsauken	NJ	08109	856-488-0700	488-0925
Datamax Corp 4501 Parkway Commerce Blvd *TF:* 800-321-2233 ■ *Web:* www.datamaxcorp.com	Orlando	FL	32808	407-578-8007	578-8377
Digital Design Inc 67 Sand Park Rd *TF:* 800-967-7746 ■ *Web:* www.genesisinkjet.com/ddiworldwide	Cedar Grove	NJ	07009	973-857-0900	857-9375
Eastman Kodak Co 343 State St *NYSE: EK* ■ *Web:* www.kodak.com	Rochester	NY	14650	800-698-3324	
Encad Inc A Kodak Co 6059 Cornerstone Ct W *TF:* 877-362-2387 ■ *Web:* www.encad.com	San Diego	CA	92121	858-452-0882	452-0891
Epson America Inc 3840 Kilroy Airport Way *TF Cust Svc:* 800-533-3731 ■ *Web:* www.epson.com	Long Beach	CA	90806	562-981-3840	290-5220
Fargo Electronics Inc 6533 Flying Cloud Dr *NASDAQ: FRGO* ■ *TF:* 800-327-4622 ■ *Web:* www.fargo.com	Eden Prairie	MN	55344	952-941-9470	941-7836
Fuji Photo Film USA Inc 200 Summit Lake Dr *TF:* 800-755-3854 ■ *Web:* www.fujifilm.com	Valhalla	NY	10595	914-789-8100	789-8295
Fujitsu Components America Inc 250 E Caribbean Dr *Web:* www.fujitsu.com/us	Sunnyvale	CA	94089	408-745-4900	745-4970
GCC Printers USA 209 Burlington Rd *TF Sales:* 800-422-7777 ■ *Web:* gccprinters.com	Bedford	MA	01730	781-275-5800	275-1115
Hewlett-Packard (Canada) Ltd 5150 Spectrum Way *TF:* 888-447-4636 ■ *Web:* www.hp.com/country/ca/eng/welcome.html	Mississauga	ON	L4W5G1	905-206-4725	206-4739
Hewlett-Packard Co 3000 Hanover St *NYSE: HPQ* ■ *TF Sales:* 800-752-0900 ■ *Web:* www.hp.com	Palo Alto	CA	94304	650-857-1501	857-5518
Imaging Technologies Corp (ITEC) 9449 Balboa Ave Suite 211 *Web:* www.itec.net	San Diego	CA	92123	858-277-5300	277-3448
Imaje Co 1650 Airport Rd Suite 101 *TF:* 800-462-5302 ■ *Web:* www.imaje.com	Kennesaw	GA	30144	770-421-7700	421-7702
International Business Machines Corp (IBM) 1 New Orchard Rd *NYSE: IBM* ■ *TF:* 800-426-4968 ■ *Web:* www.ibm.com/us	Armonk	NY	10504	914-766-1900	
ITEC (Imaging Technologies Corp) 9449 Balboa Ave Suite 211 *Web:* www.itec.net	San Diego	CA	92123	858-277-5300	277-3448
Kodak Co 343 State St *NYSE: EK* ■ *Web:* www.kodak.com	Rochester	NY	14650	800-698-3324	
Konica Minolta Business Solutions USA Inc 100 Williams Dr *Web:* www.kmbs.konicaminolta.us	Ramsey	NJ	07446	201-825-4000	
Konica Minolta Printing Solutions USA Inc 101 Williams Dr *TF:* 800-523-2696 ■ *Web:* printer.konicaminolta.net/usa	Ramsey	NJ	07446	201-316-8200	
Kroy LLC 3830 Kelley Ave *TF:* 888-888-5769 ■ *Web:* www.kroy.com	Cleveland	OH	44114	216-426-5600	426-5601
Kyocera Mita America Inc 225 Sand Rd PO Box 40008 *Web:* www.kyoceramita.com	Fairfield	NJ	07004	973-808-8444	882-4418
Lexmark International Inc 740 W New Circle Rd *NYSE: LXK* ■ *TF Cust Svc:* 800-539-6275 ■ *Web:* www.lexmark.com	Lexington	KY	40550	859-232-2000	
Mutoh America Inc 2602 S 47th St Suite 102 *TF:* 800-999-0097 ■ *Web:* www.mutoh.com	Phoenix	AZ	85034	480-968-7772	968-7990
NEC Corp of America 10850 Gold Center Dr Suite 200 *TF:* 800-632-4636 ■ *Web:* www.necam.com	Rancho Cordova	CA	95670	916-463-7000	636-5656
Oce-USA Inc 5450 N Cumberland Ave 6th Fl *TF:* 800-877-6232 ■ *Web:* www.oceusa.com	Chicago	IL	60656	773-714-8500	693-7634
Oki America Inc 785 N Mary Ave *TF:* 800-654-3282 ■ *Web:* www.oki.com	Sunnyvale	CA	94085	408-720-1900	720-1918
Oki Data Americas Inc 2000 Bishops Gate Blvd *TF Cust Svc:* 800-654-3282 ■ *Web:* www.okidata.com	Mount Laurel	NJ	08054	856-235-2600	222-5320
O'Neil Product Development Inc 8 Mason *Web:* www.oneilprinters.com	Irvine	CA	92618	949-458-0500	458-0708
Paxar Corp 105 Corporate Park Dr *NYSE: PXR* ■ *TF:* 888-447-2927 ■ *Web:* www.paxar.com	White Plains	NY	10604	914-697-6800	696-4128
Pentax Imaging Co 600 12th St Suite 300 *TF:* 800-877-0155 ■ *Web:* www.pentaximaging.com	Golden	CO	80401	303-799-8000	728-0217
Plastic Card Systems Inc 31 Pierce St PO Box 1070 *TF:* 800-742-2273 ■ *Web:* www.plasticard-systems.com	Northborough	MA	01532	508-351-6210	351-6211
Practical Automation Inc 45 Woodmont Rd *Web:* www.practicalautomation.com	Milford	CT	06460	203-882-5640	882-5648
Primera Technology Inc 2 Carlson Pkwy Suite 375 *TF:* 800-797-2772 ■ *Web:* www.primeratechnology.com	Plymouth	MN	55447	763-475-6676	475-6677
Printek Inc 1517 Townline Rd *TF:* 800-368-4636 ■ *Web:* www.printek.com	Benton Harbor	MI	49022	269-925-3200	925-8539
Printronix Inc 14600 Myford Rd *NASDAQ: PTNX* ■ *TF:* 800-665-6210 ■ *Web:* www.printronix.com	Irvine	CA	92606	714-368-2300	368-2600
Responsive Terminal Systems Inc 2801 West Loop 820 S *TF:* 800-522-6331 ■ *Web:* www.remoteprint.com	Fort Worth	TX	76116	817-244-5907	244-3555
Ricoh Corp 5 Dedrick Pl **Fax:* Mail Rm ■ *TF:* 800-637-4264 ■ *Web:* www.ricoh-usa.com	West Caldwell	NJ	07006	973-882-2000	244-2605*
Ricoh Printing Systems America Inc 2635-A Park Center Dr *TF Cust Svc:* 800-887-8848 ■ *Web:* www.rpsa.ricoh.com	Simi Valley	CA	93065	805-578-4000	578-4001
RISO Inc 300 Rosewood Dr Suite 210 *TF:* 800-876-7476 ■ *Web:* www.riso.com	Danvers	MA	01923	978-777-7377	777-2517
Roland DGA Corp 15363 Barranca Pkwy *TF:* 800-542-2307 ■ *Web:* www.rolanddga.com	Irvine	CA	92618	949-727-2100	727-2112
Samsung Electronics America Inc 105 Challenger Rd *TF:* 800-726-7864 ■ *Web:* www.samsungusa.com	Ridgefield Park	NJ	07660	201-229-4000	229-4029
Sato America Inc 10350A Nations Ford Rd *TF:* 888-871-8741 ■ *Web:* www.satoamerica.com	Charlotte	NC	28273	704-644-1650	644-1662
Seiko Instruments USA Inc 12301 Technology Blvd *TF:* 800-358-0880 ■ *Web:* www.seikoinstruments.com	Austin	TX	78727	512-349-3800	349-3000
Seiko Instruments USA Inc Business & Home Office Products Div 2990 Lomita Blvd *Web:* www.seikosmart.com	Torrance	CA	90505	310-517-7050	517-7051
Seiko Instruments USA Inc Micro Printer Div 2990 Lomita Blvd *TF:* 800-553-6570 ■ *Web:* www.siibusinessproducts.com	Torrance	CA	90505	310-517-7778	517-8154
Sharp Electronics Corp 1 Sharp Plaza *TF:* 800-237-4277 ■ *Web:* www.sharpusa.com	Mahwah	NJ	07430	201-529-8200	529-8413
SiPix Imaging Inc 47485 Seabridge Dr *Web:* www.sipix.com	Fremont	CA	94538	510-743-2849	
Star Micronics America Inc 1150 King George's Post Rd **Fax:* Sales ■ *TF:* 800-782-7636 ■ *Web:* www.starmicronics.com	Edison	NJ	08837	732-623-5500	623-5590*
Stratix Corp 4920 Avalon Ridge Pkwy Suite 600 *TF:* 800-883-8300 ■ *Web:* www.stratixcorp.com	Norcross	GA	30071	770-326-7580	326-7593
TallyGenicom 4500 Daly Dr Suite 100 *TF:* 800-436-4266 ■ *Web:* www.tallygenicom.com	Chantilly	VA	20151	703-633-8700	222-7629
Telpar Inc 19111 N Dallas Pakwy Suite 100 *TF:* 800-872-4886 ■ *Web:* www.telpar.com	Lewisville	TX	75287	972-532-2513	407-7391
Toshiba America Inc 1251 Ave of the Americas Suite 4100 *TF:* 800-457-7777 ■ *Web:* www.toshiba.com	New York	NY	10020	212-596-0600	593-3875
Toshiba TEC America 4401-A Bankers Cir *Web:* www.toshibatecusa.com	Atlanta	GA	30360	770-449-3040	449-1152
TransAct Technologies Inc 7 Laser Ln *NASDAQ: TACT* ■ *TF:* 800-243-8941 ■ *Web:* www.transact-tech.com	Wallingford	CT	06492	203-269-1198	949-9048
TROY Group Inc 2331 S Pullman St *TF:* 800-633-2266 ■ *Web:* www.troygroup.com	Santa Ana	CA	92705	949-250-3280	250-8972
Unimark Products 10556 Lackman Rd *TF Cust Svc:* 800-255-6356 ■ *Web:* www.unimark.com	Lenexa	KS	66219	913-649-2424	649-5795
Xante Corp 2800 Dauphin St Suite 100 *TF:* 800-926-8839 ■ *Web:* www.xante.com	Mobile	AL	36606	251-473-6502	473-6503
Xerox Corp 800 Long Ridge Rd *NYSE: XRX* ■ **Fax:* Mail Rm ■ *TF:* 800-842-0024 ■ *Web:* www.xerox.com	Stamford	CT	06904	203-968-3000	968-3508*
Zebra Technologies Corp 333 Corporate Woods Pkwy *NASDAQ: ZBRA* ■ *TF:* 800-423-0422 ■ *Web:* www.zebra.com	Vernon Hills	IL	60061	847-634-6700	913-8766

176-7 Scanning Equipment

Company	City	State	Zip	Phone	Fax
Accu-Sort Systems Inc 511 School House Rd *TF:* 800-227-2633 ■ *Web:* www.accusort.com	Telford	PA	18969	215-723-0981	721-5551
AirClic Inc 411 S State St 3rd Fl *Web:* www.airclic.com	Newtown	PA	18940	215-504-0560	504-0565
Altek Corp 12210 Plum Orchard Dr *Web:* www.altek.com	Silver Spring	MD	20904	301-572-2555	572-2510
BenQ America Corp 53 Discovery *TF:* 866-600-2367 ■ *Web:* www.benq.com	Irvine	CA	92618	949-255-9500	255-9600
BOWE Bell + Howell 760 S Wolf Rd *TF:* 800-327-4608 ■ *Web:* www.bowebellhowell.com	Wheeling	IL	60090	847-675-7600	423-7503
Canon USA Inc 1 Canon Plaza *NYSE: CAJ* ■ **Fax:* Hum Res ■ *TF:* 800-828-4040 ■ *Web:* www.usa.canon.com	Lake Success	NY	11042	516-488-6700	328-4669*
CardScan Inc 25 First St Suite 107 *TF:* 800-942-6739 ■ *Web:* www.cardscan.com	Cambridge	MA	02141	617-492-4200	492-6659
Computerwise Inc 302 N Winchester Ln *TF:* 800-255-3739 ■ *Web:* www.computerwise.com	Olathe	KS	66062	913-829-0600	829-0810
Eastman Kodak Co 343 State St *NYSE: EK* ■ *Web:* www.kodak.com	Rochester	NY	14650	800-698-3324	
Epson America Inc 3840 Kilroy Airport Way *TF Cust Svc:* 800-533-3731 ■ *Web:* www.epson.com	Long Beach	CA	90806	562-981-3840	290-5220
Fujitsu Computer Products of America Inc 1255 E Arques Ave *TF:* 800-626-4686 ■ *Web:* www.fcpa.com	Sunnyvale	CA	94085	408-746-7000	746-6910
GTCO CalComp Inc 7125 Riverwood Dr *TF:* 800-344-4723 ■ *Web:* www.gtco.com	Columbia	MD	21046	410-381-6688	290-9065
Hand Held Products Inc 700 Vision Dr *TF:* 800-782-4263 ■ *Web:* www.handheld.com	Skaneateles Falls	NY	13153	315-685-4100	685-0049
Hewlett-Packard Co 3000 Hanover St *NYSE: HPQ* ■ *TF Sales:* 800-752-0900 ■ *Web:* www.hp.com	Palo Alto	CA	94304	650-857-1501	857-5518
Hitachi Canada Ltd 2495 Meadowpine Blvd *TF:* 800-906-4482 ■ *Web:* www.hitachi.ca	Mississauga	ON	L5N6C3	905-821-4545	821-9435
iCAD Inc 4 Townsend W Suite 17 *NASDAQ: ICAD* ■ *TF:* 866-280-2239 ■ *Web:* www.icadmed.com	Nashua	NH	03063	603-882-5200	880-3843
Indala 6850-B Santa Teresa Blvd *TF Sales:* 800-779-8663 ■ *Web:* www.indala.info	San Jose	CA	95119	408-361-4700	361-4701
InPath Devices 3610 Dodge St Suite 200 **Fax Area Code:* 888 ■ *TF:* 800-988-1914 ■ *Web:* www.inpath.com	Omaha	NE	68131	402-345-9200	526-5920*
Intelli-Check Inc 246 Crossways Park W *AMEX: IDN* ■ *TF:* 800-444-9542 ■ *Web:* www.intellicheck.com	Woodbury	NY	11797	516-992-1900	992-1919
I/O Magic Corp 4 Marconi *Web:* www.iomagic.com	Irvine	CA	92618	949-707-4800	855-3550
Kodak Co 343 State St *NYSE: EK* ■ *Web:* www.kodak.com	Rochester	NY	14650	800-698-3324	
KYE Systems Corp 1301 NW 84th Ave Suite 127 *Web:* www.genius-kye.com	Miami	FL	33126	305-468-9250	468-9251
Maniabarco Inc 30 S Satellite Rd *Web:* www.maniagroup.com	South Windsor	CT	06074	860-291-7000	291-7021
Metrologic Instruments Inc 90 Coles Rd *NASDAQ: MTLG* ■ **Fax:* Sales ■ *TF Sales:* 800-436-3876 ■ *Web:* www.metrologic.com	Blackwood	NJ	08012	856-228-8100	228-6673*

Scanning Equipment (Cont'd)

				Phone	Fax
Microtek Lab Inc 16941 Keegan Ave Web: www.microtekusa.com	Carson	CA	90746	310-687-5800	687-5950
Mustek Inc 15271 Barranca Pkwy TF: 800-308-7226 ■ Web: www.mustek.com	Irvine	CA	92618	949-790-3800	788-3670
NCR Corp 1700 S Patterson Blvd NYSE: NCR ■ *Fax: Cust Svc ■ TF Cust Svc: 800-531-2222 ■ Web: www.ncr.com	Dayton	OH	45479	937-445-5000	445-5617*
Oce-USA Inc 5450 N Cumberland Ave 6th Fl TF: 800-877-6232 ■ Web: www.oceusa.com	Chicago	IL	60656	773-714-8500	693-7634
Peripheral Dynamics Inc 5150 Campus Dr Whitemarsh Industrial Pk TF: 800-523-0253 ■ Web: www.pdiscan.com	Plymouth Meeting	PA	19462	610-825-7090	834-7708
PSC Inc 959 Terry St TF: 800-695-5700 ■ Web: www.psc.com	Eugene	OR	97402	541-683-5700	345-7140
Ricoh Corp 5 Dedrick Pl *Fax: Mail Rm ■ TF: 800-637-4264 ■ Web: www.ricoh-usa.com	West Caldwell	NJ	07006	973-882-2000	244-2605*
Roland DGA Corp 15363 Barranca Pkwy TF: 800-542-2307 ■ Web: www.rolanddga.com	Irvine	CA	92618	949-727-2100	727-2112
Scan-Optics Inc 169 Progress Dr TF: 800-543-8681 ■ Web: www.scanoptics.com	Manchester	CT	06043	860-645-7878	645-7995
Scantron Corp 34 Parker TF: 800-722-6876 ■ Web: www.scantron.com	Irvine	CA	92618	949-639-7500	639-7710
Scion Corp 82 Wormans Mill Ct Suite H Web: www.scioncorp.com	Frederick	MD	21701	301-695-7870	695-0035
Siemens Logistics & Assembly Systems Inc Postal Automation Div 1401 Nolan Ryan Expy TF: 800-433-5175 ■ Web: www.logistics-assembly.siemens.com	Arlington	TX	76011	817-436-7000	436-7476
Socket Communications Inc 37400 Central Ct NASDAQ: SCKT ■ TF: 800-552-3300 ■ Web: www.socketcom.com	Newark	CA	94560	510-744-2700	744-2727
SPYRUS Inc 2355 Oakland Rd Suite 1 TF: 800-277-9787 ■ Web: www.spyrus.com	San Jose	CA	95131	408-953-0700	953-9835
Stratix Corp 4920 Avalon Ridge Pkwy Suite 600 TF: 800-883-8300 ■ Web: www.stratixcorp.com	Norcross	GA	30071	770-326-7580	326-7593
Symbol Technologies Inc 1 Symbol Plaza NYSE: SBL ■ TF: 800-722-6234 ■ Web: www.symbol.com	Holtsville	NY	11742	631-738-2400	738-5990
UMAX Technologies Inc 10460 Brockwood Rd Web: www.umax.com	Dallas	TX	75238	214-342-9799	342-9046
Videx Inc 1105 NE Circle Blvd Web: www.videx.com	Corvallis	OR	97330	541-758-0521	752-5285
Visioneer Inc 5673 Gibraltar Dr Suite 150 TF Cust Svc: 888-229-4172 ■ Web: www.visioneer.com	Pleasanton	CA	94588	925-251-6300	416-8600
Wizcom Technologies Inc 257 Great Rd TF: 888-777-0552 ■ Web: www.wizcomtech.com	Acton	MA	01720	978-635-5357	929-9228
ZBA Inc 94 Old Camplain Rd TF: 866-468-6912 ■ Web: www.zbausa.com	Hillsborough	NJ	08844	908-359-2070	359-1272

176-8 Storage Devices

				Phone	Fax
Addonics Technologies Corp 2466 Kruse Dr Web: www.addonics.com	San Jose	CA	95131	408-433-3899	433-3898
Ampex Data Systems Corp 1228 Douglas Ave Web: www.ampexdata.com	Redwood City	CA	94063	650-367-2011	367-3536
Apricorn Inc 12191 Kirkham Rd TF: 800-458-5448 ■ Web: www.apricorn.com	Poway	CA	92064	858-513-2000	513-2020
Archos Technology Inc 3-A Goodyear Web: www.archos.com	Irvine	CA	92618	949-609-1483	609-1414
BenQ America Corp 53 Discovery TF: 866-600-2367 ■ Web: www.benq.com	Irvine	CA	92618	949-255-9500	255-9600
Castlewood Systems Inc 7060 Koll Ctr Pkwy Suite 318	Pleasanton	CA	94566	925-417-2000	417-2070
CMS Peripherals Inc 3095 Redhill Ave TF Sales: 800-327-5773 ■ Web: www.cmsproducts.com	Costa Mesa	CA	92626	714-424-5520	435-9504
Creative Labs Inc 1901 McCarthy Blvd TF Cust Svc: 800-998-1000 ■ Web: us.creative.com	Milpitas	CA	95035	408-428-6600	428-6611
Cybernetics Inc 111 Cybernetics Way Web: www.cybernetics.com	Yorktown	VA	23693	757-833-9100	833-9300
DataDirect Networks 9320 Lurline Ave TF: 800-837-2298 ■ Web: www.datadirectnet.com	Chatsworth	CA	91311	818-700-7600	700-7601
Datalink Corp 8170 Upland Cir NASDAQ: DTLK ■ TF: 800-448-6314 ■ Web: www.datalink.com	Chanhassen	MN	55317	952-944-3462	944-7869
Digital Peripheral Solutions Inc 8015 E Crystal Dr *Fax Area Code: 714 ■ TF: 800-559-4777 ■ Web: www.qps-inc.com	Anaheim	CA	92807	877-998-3440	692-5516*
Engenio Information Technologies Inc 1621 Barber Ln TF Tech Supp: 866-625-3993 ■ Web: www.engenio.com	Milpitas	CA	95035	408-433-8000	433-8323
Exabyte Corp 2108 55th St *Fax: Mktg ■ TF Cust Svc: 800-445-7736 ■ Web: www.exabyte.com	Boulder	CO	80301	303-442-4333	417-7501*
EXP Computer Inc 920 S Oyster Bay Rd Unit B TF Sales: 800-397-6922 ■ Web: www.expnet.com	Hicksville	NY	11801	516-942-0507	942-5646
Fujitsu Computer Products of America Inc 1255 E Arques Ave TF: 800-626-4686 ■ Web: www.fcpa.com	Sunnyvale	CA	94085	408-746-7000	746-6910
Genica Corp 1890 Ord Way Web: www.genicacorporation.com	Oceanside	CA	92056	760-726-7700	726-7723
Greystone Data Systems Inc 40800 Encyclopedia Cir Web: www.greystoneds.com	Fremont	CA	94538	510-661-2101	661-2105
Hewlett-Packard (Canada) Ltd 5150 Spectrum Way TF: 888-447-4636 ■ Web: www.hp.com/country/ca/eng/welcome.html	Mississauga	ON	L4W5G1	905-206-4725	206-4739
Hewlett-Packard Co 3000 Hanover St NYSE: HPQ ■ TF Sales: 800-752-0900 ■ Web: www.hp.com	Palo Alto	CA	94304	650-857-1501	857-5518
Hitachi America Ltd Computer Div 2000 Sierra Pt Pkwy TF: 800-225-1741 ■ Web: www.maxell.com	Brisbane	CA	94005	650-589-8300	583-4207
Hitachi Data Systems Corp 750 Central Expy TF: 800-227-1930 ■ Web: www.hds.com	Santa Clara	CA	95050	408-970-1000	727-8036
Imation Corp 1 Imation Pl NYSE: IMN ■ TF: 888-466-3456 ■ Web: www.imation.com	Oakdale	MN	55128	651-704-4000	704-7100
Interactive Media Corp DBA Kanguru Solutions 1360 Main St TF Sales: 888-526-4878 ■ Web: www.kanguru.com	Millis	MA	02054	508-376-4245	376-4462
International Business Machines Corp (IBM) 1 New Orchard Rd NYSE: IBM ■ TF: 800-426-4968 ■ Web: www.ibm.com/us	Armonk	NY	10504	914-766-1900	
I/O Magic Corp 4 Marconi Web: www.iomagic.com	Irvine	CA	92618	949-707-4800	855-3550
Iomega Corp 1821 W Iomega Way NYSE: IOM ■ *Fax: Hum Res ■ Web: www.iomega.com	Roy	UT	84067	801-332-1000	332-4210*
ITCN Inc 591 Congress Pk Dr Web: www.itcninc.com	Dayton	OH	45459	937-439-9223	439-9173
La Cie Ltd 22985 NW Evergreen Pkwy *Fax: Mktg ■ Web: www.lacie.com	Hillsboro	OR	97124	503-844-4500	844-4508*
LG Electronics USA Inc 1000 Sylvan Ave TF Tech Supp: 800-243-0000 ■ Web: us.lge.com/index.do	Englewood Cliffs	NJ	07632	201-816-2000	816-0636
Luminex Software Inc 871 Marlborough Ave TF: 888-586-4639 ■ Web: www.luminex.com	Riverside	CA	92506	951-781-4100	781-4105
Mace Group Inc 4601 E Airport Dr TF: 800-644-1132 ■ Web: www.macally.com	Ontario	CA	91761	909-230-6888	230-6889
Maxtor Corp 500 McCarthy Blvd NYSE: MXO ■ TF: 800-262-9867 ■ Web: www.maxtor.com	Milpitas	CA	95035	408-894-5000	952-3600
Microboards Technology LLC 8150 Mallory Ct PO Box 846 TF: 800-646-8881 ■ Web: www.microboards.com	Chanhassen	MN	55317	952-556-1600	556-1620
Mitsumi Electronics Corp 5808 W Campus Circle Dr TF Tech Supp: 800-648-7864 ■ Web: www.mitsumi.com	Irving	TX	75063	972-550-7300	550-7424
NEC Corp of America 10850 Gold Center Dr Suite 200 TF: 800-632-4636 ■ Web: www.necam.com	Rancho Cordova	CA	95670	916-463-7000	636-5656
nStor Technologies Inc 6190 Corte del Sedro AMEX: NSO ■ Web: www.nstor.com	Carlsbad	CA	92009	760-683-2500	683-2599
Phoenix International 812 W Southern Ave TF: 800-203-4800 ■ Web: www.phenxint.com	Orange	CA	92865	714-283-4800	283-1169
Pioneer Electronics (USA) Inc 2265 E 220th St TF Cust Svc: 800-421-1404 ■ Web: www.pioneerelectronics.com	Long Beach	CA	90810	310-952-2000	952-2402
Plasmon Plc 4425 Arrows West Dr *Fax Area Code: 719 ■ TF: 800-451-6845 ■ Web: www.plasmon.com	Colorado Springs	CO	80907	720-873-2500	593-4271*
Plextor Corp 48383 Fremont Blvd Suite 120 TF: 800-886-3935 ■ Web: www.plextor.com	Fremont	CA	94538	510-440-2000	651-9755
Procom Technology Inc 58 Discovery TF: 800-800-8600 ■ Web: www.procom.com	Irvine	CA	92618	949-852-1000	852-1221
Qualstar Corp 3990-B Heritage Oak Ct NASDAQ: QBAK ■ TF: 800-468-0680 ■ Web: www.qualstar.com	Simi Valley	CA	93063	805-583-7744	583-7749
Quantum Corp 1650 Technology Dr Suite 800 NYSE: DSS ■ TF Tech Supp: 800-826-8022 ■ Web: www.quantum.com	San Jose	CA	95110	408-944-4000	944-4040
Quantum/ATL PO Box 57100 TF: 800-677-6268 ■ Web: www.quantum.com	Irvine	CA	92619	949-856-7800	856-7799
Rimage Corp 7725 Washington Ave S NASDAQ: RIMG ■ TF: 800-445-8288 ■ Web: www.rimage.com	Minneapolis	MN	55439	952-944-8144	944-7808
Samsung Electronics America Inc 105 Challenger Rd TF: 800-726-7864 ■ Web: www.samsungusa.com	Ridgefield Park	NJ	07660	201-229-4000	229-4029
Seagate Technology Holdings 920 Disc Dr NYSE: STX ■ Web: www.seagate.com	Scotts Valley	CA	95066	831-438-6550	438-7528
Shaffstall Corp 8531 Bash St TF: 800-923-8439 ■ Web: www.shaffstall.com	Indianapolis	IN	46250	317-842-2077	915-9045
SmartDisk Corp 12780 Westlinks Dr Web: www.smartdisk.com	Fort Myers	FL	33913	239-425-4000	425-4009
Sony Electronics Inc 1 Sony Dr *Fax: Hum Res ■ TF Cust Svc: 800-222-7669 ■ Web: www.sony.com	Park Ridge	NJ	07656	201-930-1000	358-4058*
Storage Computer Corp 11 Riverside St Web: www.storage.com	Nashua	NH	03062	603-880-3005	889-7232
Storage Technology Corp 1 StorageTek Dr TF: 800-877-9220 ■ Web: www.stortek.com	Louisville	CO	80028	303-673-5151	673-4945
TDK USA Corp 901 Franklin Ave PO Box 9302 *Fax: Sales ■ TF: 800-835-8273 ■ Web: www.tdk.com	Garden City	NY	11530	516-535-2600	294-7751*
TEAC America Inc 7733 Telegraph Rd Web: www.teac.com	Montebello	CA	90640	323-726-0303	727-7656
Toshiba America Inc 1251 Ave of the Americas Suite 4100 TF: 800-457-7777 ■ Web: www.toshiba.com	New York	NY	10020	212-596-0600	593-3875
Western Digital Corp 20511 Lake Forest Dr NYSE: WDC ■ TF: 800-832-4778 ■ Web: www.westerndigital.com	Lake Forest	CA	92630	949-672-7000	672-5498

177 COMPUTER EQUIPMENT & SOFTWARE - WHOL

SEE ALSO Business Machines - Whol p. 1402; Electrical & Electronic Equipment & Parts - Whol p. 1604

				Phone	Fax
Agilysys Inc 6065 Parkland Blvd NASDAQ: AGYS ■ TF: 800-362-9127 ■ Web: www.agilysys.com	Cleveland	OH	44124	440-720-8500	
Ahearn & Soper Inc 100 Woodbine Downs Blvd TF: 800-263-4258 ■ Web: www.ahearn.com	Rexdale	ON	M9W5S6	416-675-3999	675-6589
American Micro Computer Center Inc 6073 NW 167th St Suite C-27 Web: www.ammicro.com	Miami	FL	33015	305-825-5565	825-7774
Analytical Computer Services 11500 Northwest Fwy Suite 320 TF: 888-744-9451 ■ Web: www.acstexas.com	Houston	TX	77092	713-681-0039	681-0057
Arrow Electronics Components 7459 S Lima St	Englewood	CO	80112	303-824-4000	
Arrow Electronics Inc 60 Marcus Dr NYSE: ARW ■ TF Sales: 800-777-2776 ■ Web: www.arrow.com	Melville	NY	11747	631-847-2000	847-2222
Arrow Electronics Inc SBM Div 11455 Lakefield Dr TF: 888-228-2101 ■ Web: www.arrowecs.com/sbm	Duluth	GA	30097	770-623-3430	623-3429
Arrow Enterprise Computing Solutions 4400 W 96th St *Fax Area Code: 317 ■ TF: 800-786-3425 ■ Web: www.arrowecs.com	Indianapolis	IN	46268	800-255-3390	735-0201*
Arrow Enterprise Storage Solutions 7629 Anagram Dr TF: 800-229-3475 ■ Web: www.arrownacp.com/arrowess	Eden Prairie	MN	55344	952-949-0053	949-0453
ASI Corp 48289 Fremont Blvd *Fax: Sales ■ TF: 800-210-0274 ■ Web: www.asipartner.com	Fremont	CA	94538	510-226-8000	226-8858*
Atlantix Global Systems 1 Sun Ct TF: 888-786-2727 ■ Web: www.atlantixglobal.com	Norcross	GA	30092	770-248-7700	448-7726
Avnet Inc 2211 S 47th St NYSE: AVT ■ TF: 888-822-8638 ■ Web: www.avnet.com	Phoenix	AZ	85034	480-643-2000	
Avnet Technology Solutions 8700 S Price Rd TF: 800-409-1483 ■ Web: www.ats.avnet.com	Tempe	AZ	85284	480-794-6900	
Azerty Inc 13 Centre Dr TF: 800-888-8080 ■ Web: www.azerty.com	Orchard Park	NY	14127	716-662-0200	662-7616
Bell Microproducts Inc 1941 Ringwood Ave NASDAQ: BELM ■ TF: 800-800-1513 ■ Web: www.bellmicro.com	San Jose	CA	95131	408-451-9400	451-1600
Best Computer Supplies 895 E Patriot Blvd Suite 110 TF: 800-544-3472 ■ Web: www.theschoolsupplier.com	Reno	NV	89511	775-850-2600	850-2610
Champion Solutions Group 791 Park of Commerce Blvd Suite 200 TF: 800-771-7000 ■ Web: www.championsg.com	Boca Raton	FL	33487	561-997-2900	997-4043
Comstor Inc 14850 Conference Ctr Dr Suite 200 *Fax: Sales ■ TF: 800-955-9590 ■ Web: www.comstor.com	Chantilly	VA	20151	703-345-5100	345-5572*
Crown Micro 48351 Fremont Blvd Web: www.crownmicro.com	Fremont	CA	94538	510-490-8187	490-8068
D & H Distributing Co Inc 2525 N 7th St *Fax: Mail Rm ■ TF: 800-877-1200 ■ Web: www.dandh.com	Harrisburg	PA	17110	717-236-8001	255-7838*
Data Impressions Inc 13180 Paramount Blvd TF: 800-677-3031 ■ Web: www.dataimpressions.com	South Gate	CA	90280	562-630-8788	634-5033
Data Sales Co Inc 3450 W Burnsville Pkwy TF: 800-328-2730 ■ Web: www.datasales.com	Burnsville	MN	55337	952-890-8838	895-3369
Digital Storage Inc 7611 Green Meadows Dr *Fax Area Code: 800 ■ TF: 800-232-3475 ■ Web: www.digitalstorage.com	Lewis Center	OH	43035	740-548-7179	803-8030*
Electrograph Systems Inc 50 Marcus Blvd TF: 800-632-9877 ■ Web: www.electrograph.com	Hauppauge	NY	11788	631-436-2088	435-2113

Phone Fax

En Pointe Technologies Inc 100 N Sepulveda Blvd 19th Fl. El Segundo CA 90245 310-725-5200 725-1141
NASDAQ: ENPT ■ *TF:* 800-800-4214 ■ *Web:* www.enpointe.com
GE Access 11300 Westmoor Cir Westminster CO 80021 303-545-1000 544-6508
TF Sales: 800-733-9333 ■ *Web:* www.geaccess.com
General Data Co Inc 4354 Ferguson Dr Cincinnati OH 45245 513-752-7978 752-6947*
**Fax:* Sales ■ *TF:* 800-733-5252 ■ *Web:* www.general-data.com
Global Computer Supplies 11 Harbor Pk Dr. Port Washington NY 11050 516-625-6200 787-7595*
**Fax Area Code:* 888 ■ *TF Sales:* 800-845-6225 ■ *Web:* www.globalcomputer.com
GST/E-Systems 2929 E Imperial Hwy Suite 170 Brea CA 92821 714-572-8020 572-8030
TF: 800-833-0128 ■ *Web:* www.gstmc.com
GTSI Corp 3901 Stonecroft Blvd Chantilly VA 20151 703-502-2000 222-5212
NASDAQ: GTSI ■ *TF:* 800-999-4874 ■ *Web:* www.gtsi.com
Infotel Distributing 6990 SR 36 Fletcher OH 45326 937-368-2650 262-6622*
**Fax Area Code:* 800 ■ **Fax:* Cust Svc ■ *TF:* 800-682-0422 ■
Web: www.infoteldistributing.com
Ingram Micro Inc 1600 E St Andrew Pl Santa Ana CA 92705 714-566-1000 565-8899*
NYSE: IM ■ **Fax Area Code:* 716 ■ **Fax:* Cust Svc ■ *TF Sales:* 800-456-8000 ■
Web: www.ingrammicro.com
INTCOMEX Holdings LLC 9835 NW 14th St Miami FL 33172 305-477-6230 477-5694
Web: www.intcomex.com
KeyLink Systems Group 6675 Parkland Blvd Solon OH 44139 440-498-6900 498-5520*
**Fax:* Hum Res ■ *TF:* 800-539-5465 ■ *Web:* www.agilysys.com/agilysys/keylink
LA Computer Center 463 N Oak St Inglewood CA 90302 310-671-4444 671-9565
TF: 800-689-3933 ■ *Web:* www.lacc.com
MA Laboratories Inc 2075 N Capitol Ave San Jose CA 95132 408-941-0808 941-0909
Web: www.malabs.com
Max Group Corp 17011 Green Dr City of Industry CA 91745 626-935-0050 935-0056
TF: 800-256-9040 ■ *Web:* www.maxgroup.com
Media Sciences International Inc 8 Allerman Rd Oakland NJ 07436 201-677-9311 677-1440
AMEX: GFX ■ *TF:* 888-376-8348 ■ *Web:* www.mediasciences.com
Merisel Inc 127 W 30th St 5th Fl New York NY 10001 212-594-4800
Web: www.merisel.com
Micro Technology Concepts Inc (MTC)
17837 Rowland St City of Industry CA 91748 626-839-6800 839-6899
Web: www.mtcdirect.com
Navarre Corp 7400 49th Ave N New Hope MN 55428 763-535-8333 533-2156
NASDAQ: NAVR ■ *TF:* 800-728-4000 ■ *Web:* www.navarre.com
Optical Laser Inc 5702 Bolsa Ave Suite 100 Huntington Beach CA 92649 714-379-4400 903-1247
TF: 800-776-9215 ■ *Web:* www.opticallaser.com
PC Wholesale 444 Scott Dr. Bloomingdale IL 60108 630-307-1700 307-2450*
**Fax:* Sales ■ *TF:* 800-525-4727 ■ *Web:* www.pcwholesale.com
PCNet Inc 100 Technology Dr. Trumbull CT 06611 203-452-8500 452-8644
Web: www.pcnet-inc.com
Peak Technologies Inc 9200 Berger Rd. Columbia MD 21046 410-312-6000 312-7381
TF: 800-950-6372 ■ *Web:* www.peaktech.com
Phoenix Computer Assoc Inc 10 Sasco Hill Rd Fairfield CT 06824 203-319-3060 319-3069
TF: 800-432-1815 ■ *Web:* www.phoenixcomputer.com
Programmer's Paradise Inc 1157 Shrewsbury Ave Suite C Shrewsbury NJ 07702 732-389-8950 389-0010
NASDAQ: PROG ■ *TF:* 800-445-7899 ■ *Web:* www.pparadise.com
Provantage Corp 7249 Whipple Ave NW North Canton OH 44720 330-494-3781 494-5260
TF: 800-336-1166 ■ *Web:* www.provantage.com
SBM Div Arrow Electronics 11455 Lakefield Dr. Duluth GA 30097 770-623-3430 623-3429
TF: 888-228-2101 ■ *Web:* www.arrowecs.com/sbm
ScanSource Inc 6 Logue Ct. Greenville SC 29615 864-288-2432 288-1165*
NASDAQ: SCSC ■ **Fax:* Sales ■ *TF:* 800-944-2432 ■ *Web:* www.scansource.com
SED International Inc 4916 N Royal Atlanta Dr Tucker GA 30084 770-491-8962 938-2814
TF Sales: 800-444-8962 ■ *Web:* www.sedonline.com
SHI (Software House International) 2 Riverview Dr. Somerset NJ 08873 732-764-8888 764-8889
TF: 888-764-8888 ■ *Web:* www.shi.com
Softmart Inc 450 Acorn Ln Downingtown PA 19335 610-518-4000 518-3014
TF Cust Svc: 800-328-1319 ■ *Web:* www.softmart.com
Software House International (SHI) 2 Riverview Dr. Somerset NJ 08873 732-764-8888 764-8889
TF: 888-764-8888 ■ *Web:* www.shi.com
Software Spectrum Inc 3480 Lotus Dr. Plano TX 75075 469-443-3900 567-0111*
**Fax Area Code:* 720 ■ *TF:* 800-624-0503 ■ *Web:* www.softwarespectrum.com
Solarcom Holdings Inc 1 Sun Ct. Norcross GA 30092 770-449-6116 448-7726
TF: 888-786-3282 ■ *Web:* www.solarcom.net
SYNNEX Canada 200 Ronson Dr Etobicoke ON M9W5Z9 416-240-7012 240-2622*
**Fax:* Hum Res ■ *Web:* www.synnex.ca
SYNNEX Corp 44201 Nobel Dr. Fremont CA 94538 510-656-3333 668-3777
NYSE: SNX ■ *TF Cust Svc:* 800-756-1888 ■ *Web:* www.synnex.com
Tech Data Corp 5350 Tech Data Dr Clearwater FL 33760 727-539-7429 538-7054*
NASDAQ: TECD ■ **Fax:* Hum Res ■ *TF:* 800-237-8931 ■ *Web:* www.techdata.com
TigerDirect Inc 7795 W Flagler St Suite 35 Miami FL 33144 305-415-2200 415-2177
TF: 800-800-8300 ■ *Web:* www.tigerdirect.com
Vistamax Inc 6723 Mowry Ave Newark CA 94560 510-578-0001 791-1378
TF: 866-758-4782 ■ *Web:* www.vistamaxinc.com
Voda One Corp 1010 S 120th St Suite 100 Omaha NE 68154 877-642-7750 334-4537*
**Fax Area Code:* 402 ■ *Web:* www.vodaone.com
Wareforce.com Inc 19 Morgan St Irvine CA 92618 949-639-8934 452-1413
Web: www.wareforce.com
WDL Systems 220 Chatham Business Dr Pittsboro NC 27312 919-545-2500 545-2559
TF Sales: 800-548-2319 ■ *Web:* www.wdlsystems.com
Westcon Group Inc 520 White Plains Rd 2nd Fl Tarrytown NY 10591 914-829-7747 829-7183
TF: 800-527-9516 ■ *Web:* www.westcongroup.com
Westwood Computer Corp 11 Diamond Rd Springfield NJ 07081 973-376-4242 376-8846
TF: 800-800-8805 ■ *Web:* www.westcomp.com
Wintec Industries Inc 4280 Technology Dr Fremont CA 94538 510-360-6300 770-9338*
**Fax:* Tech Supp ■ *Web:* www.wintecindustries.com
Zones Inc 1102 15th St SW Auburn WA 98001 253-205-3000 205-3500
NASDAQ: ZONS ■ *TF:* 800-258-2088 ■ *Web:* www.zones.com

COMPUTER & INTERNET TRAINING PROGRAMS

SEE Training & Certification Programs - Computer & Internet p. 2376

178 COMPUTER MAINTENANCE & REPAIR

Phone Fax

Advanced Microelectronics Inc 6001 E Old Hwy 50 Vincennes IN 47591 812-726-4500 726-4551
TF: 800-264-8851 ■ *Web:* www.advancedmicro.com
ATCI Consultants 11720 Chairman Dr Suite 108 Dallas TX 75243 214-343-0600 343-0716
Web: www.dallas.net/~atci
Cera Services 10960 E Crystal Falls Pkwy Suite 300 Leander TX 78641 512-259-5151 597-0810
TF: 800-966-3070 ■ *Web:* www.ceraservices.com
Computer Repair & Sales 2930 W Main St Rapid City SD 57702 605-399-0278 342-6141
Web: www.computerrepair.org
Computer Resource Visions Inc
3407 Northeast Pkwy Suite 170 San Antonio TX 78218 210-828-8552 828-5042
Web: www.crvinc.com
Computer Specialists Inc 904 Wind River Ln Suite 100 Gaithersburg MD 20878 301-921-8860 921-4679
TF: 800-505-4365 ■ *Web:* www.csi-csi.com
Computer Troubleshooters USA 755 Commerce Dr Suite 412 Decatur GA 30030 404-477-1300 234-6162*
**Fax Area Code:* 770 ■ *TF:* 877-704-1702 ■ *Web:* www.comptroub.com/us
Computing Concepts Inc 187 E Union Ave. East Rutherford NJ 07073 201-935-4100 935-3150
Web: www.computingconceptsinc.com
Comtek Computer Systems
2751 Mercantile Dr Suite 100 Rancho Cordova CA 95742 916-859-7000 859-7012
TF: 800-823-4450 ■ *Web:* www.comtekcomsys.com
CPT of South Florida Inc 2699 Stirling Rd Suite A 101 Fort Lauderdale FL 33312 954-963-2775 963-5781
Web: www.cpt-florida.com
CRV Inc 3407 Northeast Pkwy Suite 170 San Antonio TX 78218 210-828-8552 828-5042
Web: www.crvinc.com
Data Exchange Corp 3600 Via Pescador Camarillo CA 93012 805-388-1711 482-4856
TF: 800-237-7911 ■ *Web:* www.dex.com
Data Service Center 324 Remington St Fort Collins CO 80524 970-282-7000 484-0693
Web: www.dataservicecenter.com
Datatech Depot 11390 Knott St Garden Grove CA 92841 714-908-5370 908-5380
TF: 800-888-8181 ■ *Web:* www.dtdi.com
DBK Concepts Inc 12905 SW 129 Ave Miami FL 33186 305-596-7226 596-7222
TF: 800-725-7226 ■ *Web:* www.dbk.com
DecisionOne Corp 426 W Lancaster Ave. Devon PA 19355 610-296-6000 296-6045
TF: 800-767-2876 ■ *Web:* www.decisiononecorporate.com
Essential Technologies Inc 805 Virginia Dr Orlando FL 32803 407-896-8155 897-6603
Web: www.acsisupport.com
Everprint International Inc 18021 Cortney Ct City of Industry CA 91748 626-913-2888 913-5702
TF: 800-984-5777 ■ *Web:* www.everprint.com
Ex-Cel Solutions Inc 14618 Grover St Omaha NE 68144 402-333-6541 333-3124*
**Fax:* Cust Svc ■ *Web:* www.excels.com
Expetic Technology Service 12 2nd Ave SW Aberdeen SD 57401 605-225-4122 225-5176
TF: 888-297-2292 ■ *Web:* www.expetec.biz
Friendly Computers 3440 W Cheyenne Suite 100 North Las Vegas NV 89032 702-458-2780 869-2780
TF: 800-656-3115 ■ *Web:* www.friendlycomputers.com
Geeks On Call America Inc 814 Kempsville Rd Suite 106 Norfolk VA 23502 757-466-3448 466-3457
TF: 800-905-4335 ■ *Web:* www.geeksoncall.com
Genesis Computer Repair & Sales 121 F Grafton Station Ln Yorktown VA 23692 757-833-6262 833-8757
Web: buygenesiscomputers.com/repair.html
ICM Corp 4025 Steve Reynolds Blvd Suite 120 Norcross GA 30093 770-381-2947 279-6036
TF Cust Svc: 800-654-8013 ■ *Web:* www.icmcorp.com
Interactive Services Group Inc 600 Delran Pkwy Suite C Delran NJ 08075 800-566-3310 824-9415*
**Fax Area Code:* 856 ■ *Web:* www.isg-service.com
Jaguar Computer Systems Inc 4135 Indus Way Riverside CA 92503 951-273-7950 734-5615
Web: www.jaguar.net
Just Service Inc 2940 N Clark St Chicago IL 60657 773-871-7171
Web: www.justservice.com
Matthijssen Inc 14 Rt 10 East Hanover NJ 07936 973-887-1100 887-2453
TF: 800-845-2200 ■ *Web:* www.mattnj.com
MCPconnect 21555 Drake Rd Strongsville OH 44149 440-238-0102 238-4546
TF: 800-486-0060 ■ *Web:* www.mcpc.com
Media Sciences International Inc 8 Allerman Rd Oakland NJ 07436 201-677-9311 677-1440
AMEX: GFX ■ *TF:* 888-376-8348 ■ *Web:* www.mediasciences.com
Midwest Computer Support 3315 N Centennial Rd Sylvania OH 43560 419-843-9410 843-9411
Web: www.callmcs.com
Nations First Office Repair 1555 E Flamingo Rd Suite 202 Las Vegas NV 89119 702-699-5657 699-5468
Web: www.laptoprepairs.com
NCE Computer Group 1973 Friendship Dr Suite B El Cajon CA 92020 619-212-3000 212-3036
TF Cust Svc: 800-767-2587 ■ *Web:* www.ncegroup.com
Nexicore 3949 Heritage Oak Ct Simi Valley CA 93063 805-306-2500 306-2599
TF: 800-644-4494 ■ *Web:* www.nexicore.com
Ockers Co 1340 Belmont St Brockton MA 02301 508-586-4642 584-9180
Web: www.ockers.com
PCHero Digital Imaging 2055 Jeff Davis Hwy Stafford VA 22554 540-657-9555 659-6291
Web: www.pchero.biz
Rescuecom Corp 2560 Burnet Ave Syracuse NY 13206 800-737-2837 433-5228*
**Fax Area Code:* 315 ■ *Web:* www.rescuecom.com
Scantron Service Group 2020 S 156th Cir Omaha NE 68130 402-697-3000 697-3350
TF: 800-228-3628 ■ *Web:* www.scantronservicegroup.com
Sierra Inc 2635 Golf Ave Racine WI 53404 262-638-1851 638-1852
TF: 800-722-7263 ■ *Web:* www.sierrainc.com
Sun Valley Technical Repair Inc 15555 Concord Cir Morgan Hill CA 95037 408-779-4115 825-1690
TF: 800-250-5858 ■ *Web:* www.svtr.com
Technology Innovations Inc 555 E Easy St Simi Valley CA 93065 805-426-1000 579-9588
TF: 800-286-0651 ■ *Web:* www.tsli.com

179 COMPUTER NETWORKING PRODUCTS & SYSTEMS

SEE ALSO Computer Equipment - Modems p. 1502; Computer Software - Systems & Utilities Software p. 1518; Telecommunications Equipment & Systems p. 2343

Phone Fax

3Com Corp 350 Campus Dr. Marlborough MA 01752 508-323-5000 323-1111
NASDAQ: COMS ■ *Web:* www.3com.com
Accton Technology Corp 1362 Borregas Ave. Sunnyvale CA 94089 408-747-0994 747-0982
Web: www.accton.com
Alcatel-Lucent 600 Mountain Ave. Murray Hill NJ 07974 908-508-8080 508-2576
Web: www.alcatel-lucent.com
Allied Telesyn International Corp
19800 North Creek Pkwy Suite 200 Bothell WA 98011 425-487-8880 481-3899*
**Fax:* Sales ■ *TF:* 800-424-4284 ■ *Web:* www.allied-telesyn.com
Alvarion Ltd 2495 Leghorn St Mountain View CA 94043 650-314-2500 967-3966
NASDAQ: ALVR ■ *Web:* www.alvarion.com
Am Networks Inc 1900 AM Dr Quakertown PA 18951 215-538-8700 538-8779
TF: 800-248-9004 ■ *Web:* www.amcomm.com
American Megatrends Inc 6145-F Northbelt Pkwy. Norcross GA 30071 770-263-8181 246-8791
TF: 800-828-9264 ■ *Web:* www.ami.com
American Research Corp 602 Monterey Pass Rd Monterey Park CA 91754 626-284-1904 281-0767
TF: 888-462-3899 ■ *Web:* www.800findarc.com
Applied Innovation Inc 5800 Innovation Dr Dublin OH 43016 614-798-2000 798-1770
NASDAQ: AINN ■ *TF:* 800-247-9482 ■ *Web:* www.aiinet.com
Archtek America Corp 1300 John Reed Ct Unit B City of Industry CA 91745 626-330-3600 330-3900
Web: www.archtek.com
Arcom Control Systems 7500 W 161st St Overland Park KS 66085 913-549-1000 549-1001
TF: 888-941-2224 ■ *Web:* www.arcom.com
ASA Computers Inc 2354 Calle del Mundo Santa Clara CA 95054 408-654-2901 654-2910
TF: 800-732-5727 ■ *Web:* www.asacomputers.com
Asante Technologies Inc 673 S Milpitas Blvd Suite 100 Milpitas CA 95035 408-435-8388 719-8594
TF: 800-303-9121 ■ *Web:* www.asante.com
ASUSTeK Computer International 44370 Nobel Dr Fremont CA 94538 510-739-3777 797-3579
Web: www.asus.com
Avaya Inc 211 Mt Airy Rd Basking Ridge NJ 07920 908-953-6000 953-7609
NYSE: AV ■ *TF:* 800-784-6104 ■ *Web:* www.avaya.com

Company / Address	City	State	ZIP	Phone	Fax
Avici Systems Inc 101 Billerica Ave *NASDAQ: AVCI* ■ *TF:* 877-292-8424 ■ *Web:* www.avici.com	North Billerica	MA	01862	978-964-2000	964-2100
Axis Communications Inc 100 Apollo Dr *TF:* 800-444-2947 ■ *Web:* www.axis.com	Chelmsford	MA	01824	978-614-2000	614-2100
Belkin Corp 501 W Walnut St *TF:* 800-223-5546 ■ *Web:* world.belkin.com	Compton	CA	90220	310-898-1100	898-1100
Belobox Networks Inc 18 Technology Dr Suite 103 *TF:* 800-235-6269 ■ *Web:* www.belobox.com	Irvine	CA	92618	949-727-4115	727-2149
Black Box Corp 1000 Park Dr *NASDAQ: BBOX* ■ **Fax Area Code:* 800 ■ *TF:* 877-877-2269 ■ *Web:* www.blackbox.com	Lawrence	PA	15055	724-746-5500	321-0746*
Blue Coat Systems Inc 420 N Mary Ave *NASDAQ: BCSI* ■ *TF:* 888-462-3569 ■ *Web:* www.bluecoat.com	Sunnyvale	CA	94085	408-220-2200	220-2250
Brocade Communications Systems Inc 1745 Technology Dr *NASDAQ: BRCD* ■ *Web:* www.brocade.com	San Jose	CA	95110	408-333-8000	333-8101
Bytex Corp 113 Cedar St 495 Commerce Park Suite S6 *TF:* 800-227-1145 ■ *Web:* www.bytex.com	Milford	MA	01757	508-422-9422	422-9410
CalAmp Corp 1401 N Rice Ave *TF:* 888-554-2024 ■ *Web:* calamp.com	Oxnard	CA	93030	805-987-9000	419-8498
Cambex Corp 115 Flanders Rd *TF:* 800-325-5565 ■ *Web:* www.cambex.com	Westborough	MA	01581	508-983-1200	983-0255
Cantata Technology Inc 15 Crawford St *Web:* www.cantata.com	Needham	MA	02494	781-449-4100	449-9009
Chatsworth Products Inc 31425 Agoura Rd *TF:* 800-834-4969 ■ *Web:* www.chatsworth.com	Westlake Village	CA	91361	818-735-6100	735-6199
CIENA Corp Metro Transport Div 1185 Sanctuary Pkwy	Alpharetta	GA	30004	678-867-5100	867-5101
Ciprico Inc 17400 Medina Rd Suite 800 *NASDAQ: CPCI* ■ *TF:* 800-727-4669 ■ *Web:* www.ciprico.com	Plymouth	MN	55447	763-551-4000	551-4002
Cisco Systems Inc 170 W Tasman Dr *NASDAQ: CSCO* ■ *TF:* 800-553-6387 ■ *Web:* www.cisco.com	San Jose	CA	95134	408-526-4000	526-4100
CNet Technology Inc 1455 McCandless Dr *TF:* 800-486-2638 ■ *Web:* www.cnet.com.tw	Milpitas	CA	95035	408-934-0800	934-0900
Communication Devices Inc 1 Forstmann Ct *TF:* 800-359-8561 ■ *Web:* www.commdevices.com	Clifton	NJ	07011	973-772-6997	772-0747
Compex Inc 840 Columbia St Suite B **Fax:* Sales ■ *TF:* 800-279-8891 ■ *Web:* www.cpx.com	Brea	CA	92821	714-482-0333	482-0332*
Compsee Inc 400 N Main St *TF:* 800-768-5248 ■ *Web:* www.compsee.com	Mount Gilead	NC	27306	910-439-6141	439-1344
CompuCom 7171 Forest Ln *TF Cust Svc:* 800-597-0555 ■ *Web:* www.compucom.com	Dallas	TX	75230	972-856-3600	856-5210
Comtrol Corp 6655 Wedgewood Rd Suite 120 *TF:* 800-926-6876 ■ *Web:* www.comtrol.com	Maple Grove	MN	55311	763-494-4100	494-4199
Comverse Technology Inc 100 Quannapowitt Pkwy *NASDAQ: CMVT* ■ *Web:* www.cmvt.com	Wakefield	MA	01880	781-246-9000	224-8135
Contemporary Control Systems Inc 2431 Curtiss St *Web:* www.ccontrols.com	Downers Grove	IL	60515	630-963-7070	963-0109
Continental Resources Inc 175 Middlesex Tpke *TF:* 800-937-4688 ■ *Web:* www.conres.com	Bedford	MA	01730	781-275-0850	275-6563
Converged Access Inc 305 Foster St *TF:* 888-748-2720 ■ *Web:* www.convergedaccess.com	Littleton	MA	01460	978-742-1400	742-1493
Crossroads Systems Inc 8300 N MoPac Expy *TF:* 800-643-7148 ■ *Web:* www.crossroads.com	Austin	TX	78759	512-349-0300	795-8309
Crystal Group Inc 850 Kacena Rd *TF:* 800-378-1636 ■ *Web:* www.crystalpc.com	Hiawatha	IA	52233	319-378-1636	393-2338
Cubix Corp 2800 Lockheed Way *TF Sales:* 800-829-0554 ■ *Web:* www.cubix.com	Carson City	NV	89706	775-883-7611	888-1002
Cyberdata Corp 2555 Garden Rd *TF:* 800-292-3738 ■ *Web:* www.cyberdata.net	Monterey	CA	93940	831-373-2601	373-4193
D-Link Systems Inc 17595 Mt Herrmann St **Fax Area Code:* 866 ■ *TF:* 800-326-1688 ■ *Web:* www.dlink.com	Fountain Valley	CA	92708	714-885-6000	743-4905*
Daly Computers Inc 22521 Gateway Center Dr *TF:* 800-955-3259 ■ *Web:* www.daly.com	Clarksburg	MD	20871	301-670-0381	963-1516
Datacomm Management Sciences Inc 25 Van Zant St	East Norwalk	CT	06855	203-838-7183	838-1751
Dell Inc 1 Dell Way *NASDAQ: DELL* ■ *TF:* 800-854-6214 ■ *Web:* www.dell.com	Round Rock	TX	78682	512-338-4400	283-6161
Digi International Inc 11001 Bren Rd E *NASDAQ: DGII* ■ *TF:* 877-912-3444 ■ *Web:* www.digi.com	Minnetonka	MN	55343	952-912-3444	912-4991
Digilog Inc 2360 Maryland Rd *TF Cust Svc:* 800-344-4564 ■ *Web:* www.digilog.com	Willow Grove	PA	19090	215-830-9400	830-9444
Dot Hill Systems Corp 2200 Faraday Ave Suite 100 *NASDAQ: HILL* ■ *TF:* 800-872-2783 ■ *Web:* www.dothill.com	Carlsbad	CA	92008	760-931-5500	931-5527
Echelon Corp 550 Meridian Ave *NASDAQ: ELON* ■ *TF:* 800-324-3566 ■ *Web:* www.echelon.com	San Jose	CA	95126	408-938-5200	790-3800
Egenera Inc 165 Forest St *TF:* 800-316-3976 ■ *Web:* www.egenera.com	Marlborough	MA	01752	508-858-2600	481-3114
Electronics for Imaging Inc 303 Velocity Way *NASDAQ: EFII* ■ *TF:* 800-568-1917 ■ *Web:* www.efi.com	Foster City	CA	94404	650-357-3500	357-3907
Eltek Energy LLC 115 Erick St *TF:* 800-447-3484 ■ *Web:* www.eltekenergy.com/americas	Crystal Lake	IL	60014	815-459-9090	459-9118
EMC Corp 176 South St *NYSE: EMC* ■ *TF:* 877-362-6973 ■ *Web:* www.emc.com	Hopkinton	MA	01748	508-435-1000	497-6912
Emulex Corp 3333 Susan St *NYSE: ELX* ■ *TF:* 800-854-7112 ■ *Web:* www.emulex.com	Costa Mesa	CA	92626	714-662-5600	241-0792
Enterasys Networks Inc 50 Minuteman Rd *Web:* www.enterasys.com	Andover	MA	01810	978-684-1000	684-1658
eSoft Inc 295 Interlocken Blvd Suite 500 *TF:* 888-903-7638 ■ *Web:* www.esoft.com	Broomfield	CO	80021	303-444-1600	444-1640
Extreme Networks Inc 3585 Monroe St *NASDAQ: EXTR* ■ *TF:* 888-257-3000 ■ *Web:* www.extremenetworks.com	Santa Clara	CA	95051	408-579-2800	579-3000
Ezenia! Inc 14 Celina Ave Unit 17 **Fax Area Code:* 603 ■ *TF:* 800-966-2301 ■ *Web:* www.ezenia.com	Nashua	NH	03063	781-505-2100	880-4978*
F5 Networks Inc 401 Elliott Ave W *NASDAQ: FFIV* ■ *TF:* 888-882-4447 ■ *Web:* www.f5.com	Seattle	WA	98119	206-272-5555	272-5556
Finisar Corp 1389 Moffett Park Dr *NASDAQ: FNSR* ■ *Web:* www.finisar.com	Sunnyvale	CA	94089	408-548-1000	541-6129
Forsythe Technology Inc 7770 Frontage Rd *TF:* 800-843-4488 ■ *Web:* www.forsythe.com	Skokie	IL	60077	847-675-8000	213-7770
Foundry Networks Inc 2100 Gold St *NASDAQ: FDRY* ■ *TF:* 888-887-2652 ■ *Web:* www.foundrynet.com	Alviso	CA	95002	408-240-5100	240-5109
Fujitsu Computer Systems Corp 1250 E Arques Ave *TF:* 800-831-3183 ■ *Web:* www.computers.us.fujitsu.com	Sunnyvale	CA	94085	408-746-6000	
FusionWare Corp 409 Granville St Suite 1155 *TF:* 866-266-2326 ■ *Web:* www.fusionware.net	Vancouver	BC	V6C1T2	604-633-9891	633-9892
Futurex Inc 864 Old Boerne Rd *TF:* 800-251-5112 ■ *Web:* www.futurex.com	Bulverde	TX	78163	830-980-9782	438-8782
General DataComm Inc 6 Rubber Ave *Web:* www.gdc.com	Naugatuck	CT	06770	203-729-0271	729-2883
GenTek Inc 90 E Hasley Rd *NASDAQ: GETI* ■ *TF:* 800-631-8050 ■ *Web:* www.gentek-global.com	Parsippany	NJ	07054	973-515-1977	515-1997
GlassHouse Technologies Inc 200 Crossing Blvd *Web:* www.glasshouse.com	Framingham	MA	01702	508-879-5729	879-7319
High Point Solutions Inc 5 Gail Ct *Web:* www.highpt.com	Sparta	NJ	07871	973-940-0040	940-0041
Hitachi America Ltd Internetworking Group 2000 Sierra Point Pkwy *TF:* 800-927-9070 ■ *Web:* www.internetworking.hitachi.com	Brisbane	CA	94005	650-244-7759	244-7815
Houston Assoc Inc 4601 N Fairfax Dr Suite 1200 *Web:* www.hai.com	Arlington	VA	22203	703-284-8700	527-0396
iLinc Communications Inc 2999 N 44th St Suite 650 *AMEX: ILC* ■ *TF:* 877-736-8347 ■ *Web:* www.ilinc.com	Phoenix	AZ	85018	602-952-1200	952-0544
IMC Networks Corp 19772 Pauling *TF:* 800-624-1070 ■ *Web:* www.imcnetworks.com	Foothill Ranch	CA	92610	949-465-3000	465-3020
Informer Computer Systems Inc 12711 Western Ave *TF:* 800-650-4636 ■ *Web:* www.informer911.com	Garden Grove	CA	92841	714-891-1112	898-2624
Interphase Corp 2901 N Dallas Pkwy Suite 200 *NASDAQ: INPH* ■ *TF:* 800-327-8638 ■ *Web:* www.iphase.com	Plano	TX	75093	214-654-5000	654-5500
ISDN*Tek 3000 Hwy 84 PO Box 3000 *Web:* www.isdntek.com	San Gregorio	CA	94074	650-712-3000	712-3003
Juniper Networks Inc 1194 N Mathilda Ave *NASDAQ: JNPR* ■ *TF:* 888-586-4737 ■ *Web:* www.juniper.net	Sunnyvale	CA	94089	408-745-2000	745-2100
LGC Wireless Inc 2540 Junction Ave *TF:* 800-530-9960 ■ *Web:* www.lgcwireless.com	San Jose	CA	95134	408-952-2400	952-2410
LightSand Communications Inc 3931 Coronado Way *Web:* www.lightsand.com	San Bruno	CA	94066	650-355-0677	355-7633
Linksys 120 Theory *TF:* 800-326-7114 ■ *Web:* www.linksys.com	Irvine	CA	92612	949-823-3000	660-9515
Logista 327 Yorkville Rd E *TF:* 800-844-2035 ■ *Web:* www.logistasolutions.com	Columbus	MS	39702	662-327-5410	329-4062
Mace Group Inc 4601 E Airport Dr *TF:* 800-644-1132 ■ *Web:* www.macally.com	Ontario	CA	91761	909-230-6888	230-6889
MAPSYS Inc 920 Michigan Ave *Web:* www.mapsysinc.com	Columbus	OH	43215	614-224-5193	224-6048
Marathon Technologies Corp 295 Foster St *TF:* 800-884-6425 ■ *Web:* www.marathontechnologies.com	Littleton	MA	01460	978-489-1100	489-1101
Marvell Semiconductor Inc 5488 Marvell Ln *TF:* 800-752-3334 ■ *Web:* www.marvell.com	Santa Clara	CA	95054	408-222-2500	752-9028
Micro Design International Inc 45 Skyline Dr Suite 1017 *TF:* 800-228-0891 ■ *Web:* www.mdi.com	Lake Mary	FL	32746	407-472-6000	472-6100
Mobility Electronics Inc 17800 N Perimeter Dr Suite 200 *NASDAQ: MOBE* ■ *Web:* www.mobilityelectronics.com	Scottsdale	AZ	85255	480-596-0061	596-0349
MTI Technology Corp 17595 Cartwright Rd *NASDAQ: MTIC* ■ *TF:* 800-999-9684 ■ *Web:* www.mti.com	Irvine	CA	92614	949-251-1101	251-1102
MTM Technologies Inc 1200 High Ridge Rd *NASDAQ: MTMC* ■ *Web:* www.mtm.com	Stamford	CT	06905	203-975-3700	975-3701
NEC America Inc 6555 N State Hwy 161 *TF Cust Svc:* 800-338-9549 ■ *Web:* www.necus.com/necam	Irving	TX	75039	214-262-2000	262-2114
NEC Corp of America 10850 Gold Center Dr Suite 200 *TF:* 800-632-4636 ■ *Web:* www.necam.com	Rancho Cordova	CA	95670	916-463-7000	636-5656
NETGEAR Inc 4500 Great America Pkwy *NASDAQ: NTGR* ■ *TF Cust Svc:* 888-638-4327 ■ *Web:* www.netgear.com	Santa Clara	CA	95054	408-907-8000	907-8097
Netopia Inc 6001 Shellmound St 4th Fl *Web:* www.netopia.com	Emeryville	CA	94608	510-420-7400	420-7601
Network Appliance Inc 495 E Java Dr *NASDAQ: NTAP* ■ *TF Sales:* 800-443-4537 ■ *Web:* www.netapp.com	Sunnyvale	CA	94089	408-822-6000	822-4422
Network Engines Inc 25 Dan Rd *NASDAQ: NENG* ■ *Web:* www.networkengines.com	Canton	MA	02021	781-332-1000	770-2000
Network Equipment Technologies Inc 6900 Paseo Padre Pkwy *NYSE: NWK* ■ *TF:* 888-828-8080 ■ *Web:* www.net.com	Fremont	CA	94555	510-713-7300	574-4000
Newman Group 7400 Newman Blvd *Web:* www.newman.com	Dexter	MI	48130	734-426-3200	426-0777
Nortel Networks Corp 8200 Dixie Rd Suite 100 *NYSE: NT* ■ *TF Cust Svc:* 800-466-7835 ■ *Web:* www.nortel.com	Brampton	ON	L6T5P6	905-863-7000	863-9166
Nortel Networks Corp 2221 Lakeside Blvd *Web:* www.nortelnetworks.com	Richardson	TX	75082	972-684-1000	684-3801
Overland Storage Inc 4820 Overland Ave *NASDAQ: OVRL* ■ *TF:* 800-729-8725 ■ *Web:* www.overlandstorage.com	San Diego	CA	92123	858-571-5555	571-0982
OvisLink Technologies Corp 1301 John Reed Ct *TF:* 888-605-6847 ■ *Web:* www.ovislink.com	City of Industry	CA	91745	626-854-1805	854-0835
Packeteer Inc 10201 N De Anza Blvd *NASDAQ: PKTR* ■ *TF:* 800-697-2253 ■ *Web:* www.packeteer.com	Cupertino	CA	95014	408-873-4400	873-4410
Patton Electronics Co 7622 Rickenbacker Dr *Web:* www.patton.com	Gaithersburg	MD	20879	301-975-1000	869-9293
Peak 10 733 Barret Ave *TF:* 866-732-5836 ■ *Web:* www.peak10.com	Louisville	KY	40204	502-315-6000	315-6035
Performance Technologies Inc 205 Indigo Creek Dr *NASDAQ: PTIX* ■ *Web:* www.pt.com	Rochester	NY	14626	585-256-0200	256-0791
Plaintree Systems Inc 90 Decosta St *TF:* 800-461-0062 ■ *Web:* www.plaintree.com	Arnprior	ON	K7S3X1	613-623-3434	623-4647
Polycom Inc 4750 Willow Rd *NASDAQ: PLCM* ■ **Fax:* Hum Res ■ *TF:* 866-476-5926 ■ *Web:* www.polycom.com	Pleasanton	CA	94588	925-924-6000	924-6101*
PrimeArray Systems Inc 127 Riverneck Rd *TF:* 800-433-5133 ■ *Web:* www.primearray.com	Chelmsford	MA	01824	978-654-6250	654-6249
Quantum Corp 11431 Willows Rd NE *TF:* 800-336-1233 ■ *Web:* www.quantum.com	Redmond	WA	98052	425-881-8004	881-2296
Rackable Systems Inc 46600 Landing Pkwy *NASDAQ: RACK* ■ *Web:* www.rackable.com	Freemont	CA	94538	408-240-8300	321-0293
Racore Technology Corp 4125 S 6000 West *TF:* 877-252-9779 ■ *Web:* www.racore.com	West Valley City	UT	84128	801-973-9779	973-2005
RADVISION Inc 17-17 State Hwy 208 Suite 300 *NASDAQ: RVSN* ■ *Web:* www.radvision.com	Fair Lawn	NJ	07410	201-689-6300	689-6301
Raytheon Computer Products 1001 Boston Post Rd *Web:* www.raytheon-computers.com	Marlborough	MA	01752	508-490-1600	490-1815
Richards Network Solutions Inc 2700 Van Buren St *Web:* www.rnsi.com	Bellwood	IL	60104	708-547-6000	547-6044
Ringdale Technologies Inc 101 Halmar Cove *TF:* 888-288-9080 ■ *Web:* www.ringdale.com	Georgetown	TX	78628	512-869-1018	869-2621
Safari Circuits Inc 411 Washington St *TF:* 888-694-7230 ■ *Web:* www.safaricircuits.com	Otsego	MI	49078	269-694-9471	692-2651
SafeNet Inc 4690 Millennium Dr *NASDAQ: SFNT* ■ *TF Sales:* 800-533-3958 ■ *Web:* www.safenet-inc.com	Belcamp	MD	21017	410-931-7500	931-7524
SARCOM Inc 8337 Green Meadows Dr N Suite A **Fax:* Sales ■ *TF:* 800-326-3962 ■ *Web:* www.sarcom.com	Lewis Center	OH	43035	614-854-1300	854-1800*
Secure Computing Corp 350 SW 12th Ave *NASDAQ: SCUR* ■ *TF:* 800-666-4273 ■ *Web:* www.securecomputing.com	Deerfield Beach	FL	33442	954-375-3500	375-3501
segNET Technologies Inc 325 Mt Support Rd *TF:* 800-763-5556 ■ *Web:* www.segnet.com	Lebanon	NH	03766	603-643-5883	643-9854
Server Technology Inc 1040 Sandhill Dr *TF:* 800-835-1515 ■ *Web:* www.servertech.com	Reno	NV	89521	775-284-2000	284-2065
Siemens Subscriber Networks Inc 4849 Alpha Rd *Web:* www.efficient.com	Dallas	TX	75244	972-852-1000	852-1001
SIGCOM 4230 Beechwood Dr *TF:* 877-474-4266 ■ *Web:* www.sigcom.net	Greensboro	NC	27410	336-547-9700	547-1449
Silicon Graphics Inc (SGI) 1140 E Arques Ave *Web:* www.sgi.com	Sunnyvale	CA	94085	650-960-1980	933-0908
SMC Networks Inc 20 Mason *TF:* 800-762-4968 ■ *Web:* www.smc.com	Irvine	CA	92620	949-679-8000	502-3400
SOHOware Inc 3050 Coronado Dr *TF:* 800-632-1118 ■ *Web:* www.sohoware.com	Santa Clara	CA	95054	408-565-9888	565-9889
Solectek Corp 6370 Nancy Ridge Dr Suite 109 *TF:* 800-437-1518 ■ *Web:* www.solectek.com	San Diego	CA	92121	858-450-1220	457-2681
SonicWALL Inc 1143 Borregas Ave *NASDAQ: SNWL* ■ *TF:* 888-557-6642 ■ *Web:* www.sonicwall.com	Sunnyvale	CA	94089	408-745-9600	745-9300
Spectrum Communications Cabling Services Inc 226 N Lincoln Ave *TF:* 800-319-8711 ■ *Web:* www.spectrumccsi.com	Corona	CA	92882	951-371-0549	270-3833

Phone Fax

Stampede Technologies Inc 80 Rhoads Center Dr Dayton OH 45458 937-291-5035 291-5040
TF: 800-763-3423 ■ *Web:* www.stampede.com

SteelCloud Inc 14040 Park Center Rd Herndon VA 20171 703-674-5500 674-9266
NASDAQ: SCLD ■ *TF:* 800-296-3866 ■ *Web:* www.steelcloud.com

Storage Engine Inc 1 Sheila Dr Bldg 6A Tinton Falls NJ 07724 732-747-6995 747-6542
TF: 866-734-8899 ■ *Web:* www.storageengine.com

Sun Microsystems Inc 4150 Network Cir Santa Clara CA 95054 650-960-1300 856-2114
NASDAQ: SUNW ■ *TF:* 800-786-0404 ■ *Web:* www.sun.com

Sycamore Networks Inc 220 Mill Rd Chelmsford MA 01824 978-250-2900 256-3434
NASDAQ: SCMR ■ *TF:* 877-792-2667 ■ *Web:* www.sycamorenet.com

Symon Communications Inc 500 N Central Expy Suite 175 Plano TX 75074 972-578-8484 422-1680
TF: 800-827-9666 ■ *Web:* www.symon.com

Sys Technology Inc 17358 Railroad St City of Industry CA 91748 714-952-8767
TF: 888-797-7248 ■ *Web:* www.sys.com

Systech Corp 16510 Via Esprillo San Diego CA 92127 858-674-6500 613-2400
TF: 800-800-8970 ■ *Web:* www.systech.com

Systemax Inc 11 Harbor Park Dr Port Washington NY 11050 516-625-3663 608-7744*
NYSE: SYX ■ **Fax:* Sales ■ *TF:* 800-845-6225 ■ *Web:* www.systemaxpc.com

TalkPoint Communications Inc 100 William St 9th Fl New York NY 10038 212-909-2900 909-2901
Web: www.talkpointcommunications.com

Technology Integration Group (TIG) 7810 Trade St San Diego CA 92121 858-566-1900 566-8794
TF: 800-858-0549 ■ *Web:* www.tig.com

Telebyte Inc 355 Marcus Blvd Hauppauge NY 11788 631-423-3232 385-8184
TF: 800-835-3298 ■ *Web:* www.telebyteusa.com

TeleSoft International Inc
4029 S Capital of Texas Hwy Suite 220 Austin TX 78704 512-373-4224 373-4181
Web: www.telesoft-intl.com

Telkonet Inc 20374 Seneca Meadows Pkwy Germantown MD 20876 240-912-1800 912-1839
AMEX: TKO ■ *TF:* 866-375-8446 ■ *Web:* www.telkonet.com

Transition Networks Inc 6103 City West Pkwy Eden Prairie MN 55344 952-941-7600 941-2322
TF: 800-526-9267 ■ *Web:* www.transition.com

TransNet Corp 45 Columbia Rd Somerville NJ 08876 908-253-0500 253-0600
TF: 800-526-4965 ■ *Web:* www.transnet.com

Transource Computers Corp 2405 W Utopia Rd Phoenix AZ 85027 623-879-8882 879-8887
TF: 800-486-3715 ■ *Web:* www.transource.com

Trendware International Inc 20675 Manhattan Pl Torrance CA 90501 310-961-5500 961-5511
TF: 888-326-6061 ■ *Web:* www.trendware.com

Ultera Systems Inc 26052 Merit Cir Suite 106 Laguna Hills CA 92653 949-367-8800 367-0758
Web: www.ultera.com

UNICOM Electric Inc 908 Canada Ct City of Industry CA 91748 626-964-7873 964-7880*
**Fax:* Mktg ■ *TF:* 800-346-6668 ■ *Web:* www.unicomlink.com

Unimark Products 10556 Lackman Rd Lenexa KS 66219 913-649-2424 649-5795
TF Cust Svc: 800-255-6356 ■ *Web:* www.unimark.com

Unisys Corp Township LIne & Union Meeting Rd Blue Bell PA 19424 215-986-4011 986-0540*
NYSE: UIS ■ **Fax:* Hum Res ■ *TF:* 800-874-8647 ■ *Web:* www.unisys.com

US Robotics Corp 935 National Pkwy Schaumburg IL 60173 847-874-2000 874-2001
TF: 877-710-0884 ■ *Web:* www.usr.com

ViewCast Corp 3701 W Plano Pkwy Suite 300 Plano TX 75075 972-488-7200 488-7199
TF: 800-540-4119 ■ *Web:* www.viewcast.com

Visara International Inc 2700 Gateway Centre Blvd Suite 600 Morrisville NC 27560 919-882-0200 882-0163
TF: 888-334-4380 ■ *Web:* www.visara.com

WatchGuard Technologies Inc 505 5th Ave S Suite 500 Seattle WA 98104 206-521-8340 521-8342
NASDAQ: WGRD ■ *TF Sales:* 800-734-9905 ■ *Web:* www.watchguard.com

WAV Inc 2380 Prospect Dr Aurora IL 60504 630-818-1000 818-4450
TF: 800-678-2419 ■ *Web:* www.wavonline.com

WideBand Corp 401 W Grand St Gallatin MO 64640 660-663-3000 663-3736
TF: 888-663-3050 ■ *Web:* www.wband.com

Winchester Systems Inc 149 Middlesex Tpke Burlington MA 01803 781-265-0200 265-0201
TF Cust Svc: 800-325-3700 ■ *Web:* www.winsys.com

Xyratex International 2031 Concourse Dr San Jose CA 95131 408-894-0800 894-0880
Web: www.xyratex.com

ZT Group International Inc 350 Meadowlands Pkwy Secaucus NJ 07094 201-559-1000 559-1004
Web: www.ztgroup.com

180 COMPUTER PROGRAMMING SERVICES - CUSTOM

SEE ALSO Computer Software p. 1507; Computer Systems Design Services p. 1520

Phone Fax

Access Innovations Inc 131 Adams St NE Albuquerque NM 87108 505-265-3591 256-1080
TF: 800-926-8328 ■ *Web:* www.accessinn.com

Acxiom Corp 301 Industrial Blvd Conway AR 72032 501-336-1000
NASDAQ: ACXM ■ *Web:* www.acxiom.com

Aegis Software Inc 225 W 34th St Suite 806 New York NY 10122 212-268-3100 244-4119
Web: www.aegisoft.com

Alliance Consulting 2001 Market St 8th Fl Philadelphia PA 19103 215-569-8722 500-0808*
**Fax Area Code:* 800 ■ *TF:* 800-706-3339 ■ *Web:* www.alliance-consulting.com

Atlantic Internet Technologies Inc 628 Shrewsbury Ave Red Bank NJ 07701 732-758-0505 758-0869
Web: www.aitcorp.net

Big Creek Software LLC 201 N 3rd St Suite E Polk City IA 50226 515-984-6243
Web: www.bigcreek.com

C-Sharp Technologies Inc 5837 Karric Square Dr Suite 340 Dublin OH 43016 614-529-2393
Web: www.c-sharp.com

CareerCast Inc 5963 La Place Ct Suite 100 Carlsbad CA 92008 760-602-9502 602-9260
Web: www.careercast.com

Construx Software 11820 Northup Way Suite E-200 Bellevue WA 98005 425-636-0100 636-0159
TF: 866-296-6300 ■ *Web:* www.construx.com

Control Systems International Inc 8040 Nieman Rd Lenexa KS 66214 913-599-5010 599-5013
Web: www.csiks.com

Digital ChoreoGraphics PO Box 8268 Newport Beach CA 92658 949-548-1969
Web: www.dcgfx.com

Dime Soft Business Solutions Inc
20710 Havenhurst Dr PO Box 1089 Nuevo CA 92567 951-928-1990 928-1171
Web: www.dimesoftinc.com

Documation Inc PO Box 5265 Coeur d'Alene ID 83814 208-665-1410 350-8198*
**Fax Area Code:* 845 ■ *Web:* www.documationinc.com

eCybersuite 9330 Eton Ave Chatsworth CA 91311 818-610-0505 610-0509
Web: www.ecybersuite.com

Edge Systems LLC 1805 High Point Dr Suite 103 Naperville IL 60563 630-810-9669 810-9228
TF Tech Supp: 800-352-3343 ■ *Web:* www.edge.com

Full Spectrum Software 1661 Worcester Rd Suite 504 Framingham MA 01701 508-620-6400
Web: www.fullspectrumsw.com

GDI Infotech Inc 3775 Varsity Dr Ann Arbor MI 48108 734-477-6900 477-7100
TF: 800-608-7682 ■ *Web:* www.gdii.com

Global Solutions Network Inc 7686 Richmond Hwy Suite 107 Alexandria VA 22306 703-768-5200 768-5222
Web: www.gsnhome.com

Human Factors International Inc 410 W Lowe Ave Fairfield IA 52556 641-472-4480 472-5412
TF: 800-242-4480 ■ *Web:* www.humanfactors.com

Inforonics LLC 25 Porter Rd Littleton MA 01460 978-698-7300 698-7500
Web: www.inforonics.com

Integrated Data Services Inc 700 Veterans Hwy Suite 35 Hauppauge NY 11788 631-265-7162 366-4317
Web: www.idserve.com

Phone Fax

Logikos Systems & Software 2914 Independence Dr Fort Wayne IN 46808 260-483-3638 484-5268
Web: www.logikos.com

Paladin Data Systems Corp 19362 Powder Hill Pl NE Poulsbo WA 98370 360-779-2400 779-2600
TF: 800-532-8448 ■ *Web:* www.paladindata.com

Performance Software 2095 W Pinnacle Peak Rd Phoenix AZ 85027 623-337-8003 580-4873
Web: www.psware.com

Prenia Corp 16625 Redmond Way Suite M-418 Redmond WA 98052 425-898-8300 898-8301
Web: www.prenia.com

Progeny Linux Systems Inc
8335 Allison Pointe Trail Suite 160 Indianapolis IN 46250 317-578-8882 578-8920
Web: www.progeny.com

Programming Concepts Inc 640 Johnson Ave Suite 5 Bohemia NY 11716 631-563-3800 563-3898
Web: www.programmingconcepts.com

RDA Corp 303 International Cir Suite 340 Hunt Valley MD 21030 410-308-9300 308-9600
Web: www.rdacorp.com

SEI Information Technology 1420 Kensington Rd Suite 102 Oak Brook IL 60523 630-413-5050
TF: 888-734-7343 ■ *Web:* www.sei-it.com

SingleTap Inc PO Box 178586 San Diego CA 92117 800-536-1256 794-8213*
**Fax Area Code:* 858 ■ *Web:* www.singletap.com

Susquehanna Technologies DBA SusQtech
600 Pegasus Ct Suite 100 Winchester VA 22602 540-723-8700 722-9547
TF: 888-603-0304 ■ *Web:* www.susqtech.com

Tallan Inc 628 Hebron Ave Bldg 2 Suite 502 Glastonbury CT 06033 860-633-3693 633-5361
TF: 800-677-3693 ■ *Web:* www.tallan.com

Vision Systems Group Inc 101 Durham Ave Suite 300 South Plainfield NJ 07080 732-537-9000 537-9990
Web: www.vsginc.com

Youngsoft Inc 49197 Wixom Tech Dr Suite B Wixom MI 48393 248-675-1200 675-1201
TF: 888-470-4553 ■ *Web:* www.youngsoft.com

COMPUTER RESELLERS

SEE Computer Equipment & Software - Whol p. 1504

181 COMPUTER SOFTWARE

SEE ALSO Application Service Providers (ASPs) p. 1281; Computer Equipment & Software - Whol p. 1504; Computer Networking Products & Systems p. 1505; Computer Programming Services - Custom p. 1507; Computer Stores p. 1520; Computer Systems Design Services p. 1520; Educational Materials & Supplies p. 1594

181-1 Business Software (General)

Companies listed here make general-purpose software products that are designed for use by all types of businesses, professionals, and, to some extent, personal users.

Phone Fax

1MAGE Software Inc 6025 S Quebec St Suite 300 Englewood CO 80111 303-773-1424 796-0587
Web: www.1mage.com

4D Inc 3031 Tisch Way Suite 900 San Jose CA 95128 408-557-4600 557-4645
TF: 800-785-3303 ■ *Web:* www.4d.com

ACI Worldwide 4965 Preston Pk Blvd Suite 100 Plano TX 75093 972-599-5600 599-5610
TF: 800-527-4131 ■ *Web:* www.aciworldwide.com

ACL Services Ltd 1550 Alberni St Vancouver BC V6G1A5 604-669-4225 669-3557
Web: www.blackpearl.com

ACOM Solutions Inc 2850 E 29th St Long Beach CA 90806 562-424-7899 424-8662
TF: 800-347-3638 ■ *Web:* www.acom.com

Action Technologies Inc 10970 International Blvd 2nd Fl Oakland CA 94603 510-638-8300 638-8115
TF: 800-967-5356 ■ *Web:* www.actiontech.com

Actuate Corp 701 Gateway Blvd 6th Fl South San Francisco CA 94080 650-837-2000 827-1560
NASDAQ: ACTU ■ *TF Sales:* 800-914-2259 ■ *Web:* www.actuate.com

Aderant North America 3525 Piedmont Rd Bldg 6 Suite 620 Atlanta GA 30305 404-720-3600 720-3001
TF: 877-608-4369 ■ *Web:* www.aderant.com

Adexa Inc 5933 W Century Blvd 12th Fl Los Angeles CA 90045 310-338-8444 338-9878
Web: www.adexa.com

Adobe Systems Inc 345 Park Ave San Jose CA 95110 408-536-6000 537-6000
NASDAQ: ADBE ■ *TF:* 800-833-6687 ■ *Web:* www.adobe.com

Adonix 2200 Georgetowne Dr 5th Fl Sewickley PA 15143 724-933-1377 933-1379
Web: www.adonix.com

AdStar Inc 4553 Glencoe Ave Suite 300 Marina del Rey CA 90292 310-577-8255 577-8266
NASDAQ: ADST ■ *TF:* 800-752-5187 ■ *Web:* www.adstar.com

Advent Software Inc 600 Townsend St Suite 500 Box 20 San Francisco CA 94103 415-543-7696 556-0607
NASDAQ: ADVS ■ *TF:* 800-727-0605 ■ *Web:* www.advent.com

Agile Software Corp 6373 San Ignacio Ave San Jose CA 95119 408-284-4000 284-4002
NASDAQ: AGIL ■ *TF:* 888-594-5736 ■ *Web:* www.agile.com

AgilQuest Corp 9407 Hull St Rd Richmond VA 23236 804-745-0467 745-6243
TF: 888-745-7455 ■ *Web:* www.agilquest.com

Agresso 4420 Chatterton Way Suite 201 Victoria BC V8X5J2 250-704-4450 704-4492
TF: 888-848-3776 ■ *Web:* www.agresso.com

Alpha Software Inc 70 Blanchard Rd Suite 206 Burlington MA 01803 781-229-4500 272-4876
Web: www.alphasoftware.com

Alterian Inc 35 E Wacker Dr Suite 200 Chicago IL 60601 312-704-1700 704-1701
Web: www.alterian.com

American Business Systems Inc 315 Littleton Rd Chelmsford MA 01824 978-250-9600 250-8027
TF: 800-356-4034 ■ *Web:* www.abs-software.com

American Software Inc 470 E Paces Ferry Rd Atlanta GA 30305 404-264-5296 264-5206
NASDAQ: AMSWA ■ *TF:* 800-726-2946 ■ *Web:* www.amsoftware.com

Appian Corp 8000 Towers Crescent Dr 16th Fl Vienna VA 22182 703-442-8844 442-8919
Web: www.appiancorp.com

Applix Inc 289 Turnpike Rd Westborough MA 01581 508-870-0300 366-2278
NASDAQ: APLX ■ *TF:* 800-827-7549 ■ *Web:* www.applix.com

APPX Software Inc 11363 San Jose Blvd Suite 301 Jacksonville FL 32223 904-880-5560 880-6635
TF: 800-879-2779 ■ *Web:* www.appx.com

AquiTec International 547 W Jackson Blvd 9th Fl Chicago IL 60661 312-264-1900 264-1991
Web: www.aquitecintl.com

Art Technology Group Inc 1 Main St 6th Fl Cambridge MA 02142 617-386-1000 386-1111
NASDAQ: ARTG ■ *TF:* 800-746-4284 ■ *Web:* www.atg.com

Artemis International Solutions Corp 6011 W Courtyard Dr Austin TX 78730 512-874-3030 874-8900
TF: 800-477-8900 ■ *Web:* www.aisc.com

AskSam Systems Inc 121 S Jefferson St Perry FL 32347 850-584-6590 584-7481
TF: 800-800-1997 ■ *Web:* www.asksam.com

Astea International Inc 240 Gibraltar Rd Suite 300 Horsham PA 19044 215-682-2500 682-2515
NASDAQ: ATEA ■ *TF:* 800-878-4657 ■ *Web:* www.astea.com

Atos Origin 5599 San Felipe St Suite 300 Houston TX 77056 713-513-3000 403-7204
TF: 866-875-8902 ■ *Web:* www.na.atosorigin.com

Business Software (General) (Cont'd)

Company	City	State	Zip	Phone	Fax
AttachmateWRQ 1500 Dexter Ave N *TF Sales:* 800-872-2829 ■ *Web:* www.attachmate.com	Seattle	WA	98109	206-217-7500	217-7515
Attunity Inc 70 Blanchard Rd 2nd Fl *NASDAQ: ATTU* ■ *Web:* www.attunity.com	Burlington	MA	01803	781-213-5200	213-5240
Autonomy e-talk 4040 W Royal Ln Suite 100 *TF:* 888-258-1528 ■ *Web:* www.e-talkcorp.com	Irving	TX	75063	972-819-3100	819-3300
Avolent Inc 444 De Haro St Suite 100 *TF:* 800-553-5505 ■ *Web:* www.avolent.com	San Francisco	CA	94107	415-553-6400	553-6499
Avue Technologies Corp 1145 Broadway Plaza Suite 800 *Web:* www.avuetech.com	Tacoma	WA	98402	253-573-1877	573-1876
AXS-One Inc 301 Rt 17 N *AMEX: AXO* ■ *TF Sales:* 800-828-7660 ■ *Web:* www.axsone.com	Rutherford	NJ	07070	201-935-3400	935-6355
Baudville Inc 5380 52nd St SE *TF Orders:* 800-728-0888 ■ *Web:* www.baudville.com	Grand Rapids	MI	49512	616-698-0888	698-0554
Blackbaud Inc 2000 Daniel Island Dr *NASDAQ: BLKB* ■ *TF:* 800-468-8996 ■ *Web:* www.blackbaud.com	Charleston	SC	29492	843-216-6200	216-6100
BMC Software Inc 2101 City West Blvd *NYSE: BMC* ■ *TF:* 800-841-2031 ■ *Web:* www.bmc.com	Houston	TX	77042	713-918-8800	918-8000
Borland Software Corp 20450 Stevens Creek Blvd Suite 500 *TF:* 800-287-1329 ■ *Web:* www.borland.com	Cupertino	CA	95014	408-863-2800	
Bottomline Technologies 325 Corporate Dr *NASDAQ: EPAY* ■ *TF:* 800-243-2528 ■ *Web:* www.bottomline.com	Portsmouth	NH	03801	603-436-0700	436-0300
Bradmark Technologies Inc 4265 San Felipe St Suite 800 *TF:* 800-621-2808 ■ *Web:* www.bradmark.com	Houston	TX	77027	713-621-2808	621-1639
Brady Identification Solutions 6555 W Good Hope Rd **Fax Area Code:* 800 ■ **Fax:* Cust Svc ■ *TF Cust Svc:* 800-537-8791 ■ *Web:* www.bradyid.com	Milwaukee	WI	53223	414-358-6600	292-2289*
Bull HN Information Systems Inc 296 Concord Rd *Web:* www.bull.com/us	Billerica	MA	01821	978-294-6000	294-7999
Business Computer Design International Inc 950 York Rd Suite 206 *Web:* www.bcdsoftware.com	Hinsdale	IL	60521	630-986-0800	986-0926
Business Objects SA 3030 Orchard Pkwy *NASDAQ: BOBJ* ■ *TF:* 800-527-0580 ■ *Web:* www.businessobjects.com	San Jose	CA	95134	408-953-6000	953-6001
CA Inc 1 CA Plaza *NYSE: CA* ■ *Web:* www.ca.com	Islandia	NY	11749	631-342-6000	342-6800
Callidus Software Inc 160 W Santa Clara St Suite 1500 *NASDAQ: CALD* ■ *Web:* www.callidussoftware.com	San Jose	CA	95113	408-808-6400	271-2662
Captiva Software Corp 10145 Pacific Heights Blvd *Web:* www.captivasoftware.com	San Diego	CA	92121	858-320-1000	320-1010
Catuity Inc 300 Preston Ave Suite 302 *NASDAQ: CTTY* ■ **Fax Area Code:* 734 ■ *Web:* www.catuity.com	Charlottesville	VA	22902	434-979-0724	943-6850*
Champs Software Inc 1255 N Vantage Pt Dr *TF:* 800-322-6647 ■ *Web:* www.champsinc.com	Crystal River	FL	34429	352-795-2362	795-9100
Cicero Inc 8000 Regency Pkwy *TF:* 866-538-3588 ■ *Web:* www.level8.com	Cary	NC	27511	919-380-5000	380-5121
Cincom Systems Inc 55 Merchant St *TF:* 800-888-0115 ■ *Web:* www.cincom.com	Cincinnati	OH	45246	513-612-2300	612-2000
Claritas Inc 1525 Wilson Blvd Suite 1200 *TF:* 800-234-5973 ■ *Web:* www.claritas.com	Arlington	VA	22209	703-812-2700	812-2701
Clarity Systems Ltd 2 Sheppard Ave E Suite 800 *TF:* 877-410-5070 ■ *Web:* www.claritysystems.com	Toronto	ON	M2N5Y7	416-250-5500	250-5533
ClearStory Systems Inc 1 Research Dr Suite 200-B *TF:* 800-298-9795 ■ *Web:* www.clearstorysystems.com	Westborough	MA	01581	508-870-4000	870-5585
Click Commerce Inc 233 N Michigan Ave 22nd Fl *NASDAQ: CKCM* ■ *TF:* 800-899-2641 ■ *Web:* www.clickcommerce.com	Chicago	IL	60601	312-482-9006	482-8557
Cognos Corp 15 Wayside Rd *TF Orders:* 800-426-4667 ■ *Web:* www.cognos.com	Burlington	MA	01803	781-229-6600	229-9844
Cognos Inc 3755 Riverside Dr PO Box 9707 Stn T *NASDAQ: COGN* ■ *TF:* 800-637-7447 ■ *Web:* www.cognos.com	Ottawa	ON	K1G4K9	613-738-1440	738-0002
Commence Corp 200 Tornillo Way Suite 200 *TF:* 800-933-9069 ■ *Web:* www.commence.com	Tinton Falls	NJ	07712	732-380-9100	380-9170
Computer Corp of America 500 Old Connecticut Path *TF:* 800-488-3444 ■ *Web:* www.cca-int.com	Framingham	MA	01701	508-270-6666	270-6688
Computershare Plans Software 2 Enterprise Dr *TF:* 888-340-4267 ■ *Web:* www.transcentive.com	Shelton	CT	06484	203-944-7300	944-7325
Compuware Corp 1 Campus Martius St *NASDAQ: CPWR* ■ *TF:* 800-292-7432 ■ *Web:* www.compuware.com	Detroit	MI	48226	313-227-7300	
Comsquared Systems Inc 5125 Peachtree Industrial Blvd *TF:* 800-592-3766 ■ *Web:* www.comsquared.com	Norcross	GA	30092	770-734-5300	734-5379
Concur Technologies Inc 18400 NE Union Hill Rd *NASDAQ: CNQR* ■ *TF:* 800-358-0610 ■ *Web:* www.concur.com	Redmond	WA	98052	425-702-8808	702-8828
CorVu Corp 3400 W 66th St Suite 445 *TF:* 800-610-0769 ■ *Web:* www.corvu.com	Edina	MN	55435	952-944-7777	944-7447
Cyma Systems Inc 2330 W University Dr Suite 4 *TF:* 800-292-2962 ■ *Web:* www.cyma.com	Tempe	AZ	85281	480-303-2962	303-2969
D & B Sales & Marketing Solutions 460 Totten Pond Rd 7th Fl *TF Prod Info:* 800-590-0065 ■ *Web:* www.b2bsalesandmarketing.com	Waltham	MA	02451	781-672-9200	672-9290
Data Direct Technologies 14100 SW Fwy Suite 500 *TF:* 800-505-6366 ■ *Web:* www.datadirect.com	Sugar Land	TX	77478	281-491-4200	242-3880
Data Pro Accounting Software Inc 111 2nd Ave NE Suite 1200 *TF:* 800-237-6377 ■ *Web:* www.dpro.com	Saint Petersburg	FL	33701	727-803-1500	803-1535
Datalogics Inc 101 N Wacker Dr Suite 1800 *Web:* www.datalogics.com	Chicago	IL	60606	312-853-8200	853-8282
Datamatics Management Services Inc 330 New Brunswick Ave *TF:* 800-673-0366 ■ *Web:* www.datamaticsinc.com	Fords	NJ	08863	732-738-9600	738-9603
Deltek Corp 15990 N Barkers Landing Rd Suite 350 *Web:* www.deltek.com	Houston	TX	77079	281-558-0514	584-7828
Deltek Systems Inc 13880 Dulles Corner Ln *TF:* 800-456-2009 ■ *Web:* www.deltek.com	Herndon	VA	20171	703-734-8606	734-0346
DemandTec Inc 1 Circle Star Way Suite 200 *Web:* www.demandtec.com	San Carlos	CA	94070	650-226-4600	556-1190
Deploy Solutions Inc 275 Grove St Suite 2-200 *TF:* 877-463-3756 ■ *Web:* www.deploy.com	Auburndale	MA	02466	617-641-2100	641-2101
DeskNet Inc 10 Exchange Pl 20th Fl **Fax Area Code:* 201 ■ *Web:* www.desknetinc.com	Jersey City	NJ	07302	212-343-9800	946-7081*
DLGL Ltd 850 Michele-Bohec Blvd *Web:* www.dlgl.com	Blainville	QC	J7C5E2	450-979-4646	979-4650
Document Sciences Corp 5958 Priestly Dr *NASDAQ: DOCX* ■ *TF:* 877-372-8500 ■ *Web:* www.docscience.com	Carlsbad	CA	92008	760-602-1400	602-1450
Documentum Div EMC Corp 6801 Koll Ctr Pkwy *TF:* 800-611-4829 ■ *Web:* www.documentum.com	Pleasanton	CA	94566	925-600-6800	600-6850
DST Systems Inc 333 W 11th St *NYSE: DST* ■ *Web:* www.dstsystems.com	Kansas City	MO	64105	816-435-1000	435-8630
Dynalogic Inc 1110 N 175th St Suite 216 *TF:* 800-735-0433 ■ *Web:* www.dynalogicinc.com	Shoreline	WA	98133	206-533-1050	542-1326
E*Trade Financial Corp Corporate Services 4500 Bohannon Dr *TF:* 800-786-2575 ■ *Web:* corpservices.etrade.com	Menlo Park	CA	94025	650-331-6000	331-6801
eCopy Inc 1 Oracle Dr *Web:* www.ecopy.com	Nashua	NH	03062	603-881-4450	881-4399
eCredit.com Inc 20 CareMatrix Dr *TF:* 800-276-2321 ■ *Web:* www.ecredit.com	Dedham	MA	02026	781-752-1200	752-1400
Edge Technologies Inc 3702 Pender Dr Suite 420 *TF:* 888-771-3343 ■ *Web:* www.edge-technologies.com	Fairfax	VA	22030	703-691-7900	691-4020
Elcom International Inc 10 Oceana Way *TF:* 800-713-3993 ■ *Web:* www.elcominternational.com	Norwood	MA	02062	781-501-4000	501-4070
EMC Corp Documentum Div 6801 Koll Ctr Pkwy *TF:* 800-611-4829 ■ *Web:* www.documentum.com	Pleasanton	CA	94566	925-600-6800	600-6850
Emerging Technology Solutions Inc 10698 Deerfield Rd Suite 100 PO Box 1024 *Web:* www.etsgroup.com	Franktown	CO	80116	303-688-1987	484-5080
Empagio Inc 225 E Robinson St Suite 240 *Web:* empagio.com	Orlando	FL	32801	407-488-1500	488-1505
Emptoris Inc 200 Wheeler Rd *Web:* www.emptoris.com	Burlington	MA	01803	781-993-9212	993-9213
EntComm Inc 879 W 190th St 12th Fl *Web:* www.entcomm.com	Gardena	CA	90248	310-436-3800	436-3700
Enterprise Informatics Inc 10052 Mesa Ridge Ct Suite 100 *TF:* 800-992-6784 ■ *Web:* www.enterpriseinformatics.com	San Diego	CA	92121	858-625-3000	625-3010
Enterworks Inc 19886 Ashburn Rd *TF:* 888-242-8356 ■ *Web:* www.enterworks.com	Ashburn	VA	20147	703-723-6740	724-3868
Entrade Inc 500 Central Ave	Northfield	IL	60093	847-441-6650	441-6959
ePartners Inc 6565 N MacArthur Blvd Suite 950 *TF:* 888-883-9797 ■ *Web:* www.epartnersolutions.com	Irving	TX	75039	469-587-5660	587-5661
Epicor Software Corp 18200 Von Karman Dr Suite 1000 *NASDAQ: EPIC* ■ *TF:* 800-999-1809 ■ *Web:* www.epicor.com	Irvine	CA	92612	949-585-4000	585-4091
Epsilon Inc 4301 Regent Blvd *TF:* 800-309-0505 ■ *Web:* www.epsilon.com	Irving	TX	75063	972-582-9600	582-9700
Equitrac Corp 1000 S Pine Island Rd Suite 900 *Web:* www.equitrac.com	Plantation	FL	33324	954-888-7800	475-7295
Escalate Inc 9890 Towne Center Suite 100 **Fax Area Code:* 858 ■ *TF:* 800-854-2263 ■ *Web:* www.escalate.com	San Diego	CA	92121	800-854-2263	457-2145*
Escalate Retail 1615 S Congress Ave Suite 200 *Web:* www.escalateretail.com/	Delray Beach	FL	33445	561-265-2700	454-4800
eSignal 3955 Point Eden Way *TF Sales:* 800-367-4670 ■ *Web:* www.esignal.com	Hayward	CA	94545	510-266-6000	266-6100
Essex Corp 1235 Evans Rd *TF:* 800-289-2923 ■ *Web:* www.essexcorp.com	Melbourne	FL	32904	321-837-7000	837-7001
eTEK International Inc 5445 DTC Pkwy PH-4 **Fax Area Code:* 866 ■ *TF:* 800-888-6894 ■ *Web:* www.etek.net	Greenwood Village	CO	80111	303-488-3499	743-5254*
ETS Inc 1115 E Brigadoon Ct *TF:* 800-387-7003 ■ *Web:* www.protext.com	Salt Lake City	UT	84117	801-265-2497	
Evolutionary Technologies International Inc 816 Congress Ave Suite 1450 *TF:* 800-856-8800 ■ *Web:* www.eti.com	Austin	TX	78701	512-383-3000	383-3300
eWorkplace Solutions Inc 24461 Ridge Route Dr Suite 210 *Web:* www.eworkplace.com	Laguna Hills	CA	92653	949-583-1646	598-8144
Exact Software North America 8800 Lyra Dr Suite 350 **Fax Area Code:* 866 ■ *TF:* 800-468-0834 ■ *Web:* www.macola.com	Columbus	OH	43240	614-410-2600	544-5456*
FileMaker Inc 5201 Patrick Henry Dr **Fax:* Cust Svc ■ *TF Cust Svc:* 800-325-2747 ■ *Web:* www.filemaker.com	Santa Clara	CA	95054	408-987-7000	987-3932*
FirePond Inc 181 Wells Ave *TF:* 866-826-6344 ■ *Web:* www.firepond.com	Newton	MA	02459	617-928-6001	
Fischer International Systems Corp 3073 Horseshoe Dr S Suite 104 *TF:* 800-776-7258 ■ *Web:* www.fisc.com	Naples	FL	34104	239-643-1500	643-3772
FlexiInternational Software Inc 2 Enterprise Dr *TF:* 800-353-9492 ■ *Web:* www.flexi.com	Shelton	CT	06484	203-925-3040	925-3044
Formscan Inc 517 E Lancaster Ave Suite 101 **Fax Area Code:* 610 ■ *Web:* www.formscan.com	Downingtown	PA	19355	484-696-4200	269-5247*
FrontRange Solutions Inc 1150 Kelly Johnson Blvd *TF:* 800-776-7889 ■ *Web:* www.frontrange.com	Colorado Springs	CO	80920	719-531-5007	536-0620
Gemmar Systems International Inc 11450 Cote de Liesse *Web:* www.gsi.ca	Dorval	QC	H9P1A9	514-631-3336	631-7722
Gemstone Systems Inc 1260 NW Waterhouse Ave Suite 200 *Web:* www.gemstone.com	Beaverton	OR	97006	503-533-3000	629-8556
Genesys Software Systems Inc 5 Branch St **Fax Area Code:* 801 ■ *Web:* www.genesys-soft.com	Methuen	MA	01844	978-685-5400	761-2015*
Gensym Corp 52 2nd Ave *Web:* www.gensym.com	Burlington	MA	01803	781-265-7100	265-7101
Global Shop Solutions Inc 975 Evergreen Cir *TF Sales:* 800-364-5958 ■ *Web:* www.globalshopsolutions.com	The Woodlands	TX	77380	281-681-1959	681-2663
Global Software Inc 3200 Atlantic Ave Suite 200 *TF Mktg:* 800-326-3444 ■ *Web:* www.glbsoft.com	Raleigh	NC	27604	919-872-7800	876-8205
Glovia International Inc 1940 E Mariposa Ave Suite 200 *TF:* 888-245-6842 ■ *Web:* www.glovia.com	El Segundo	CA	90245	310-563-7000	563-7300
Goodwin Systems Inc 1403 Princeton Ave *TF:* 800-203-1358	Silverton	OR	97381	503-873-8695	
Grandite Inc 1220 Lebourgneuf Blvd Suite 120 *TF:* 800-361-0528 ■ *Web:* www.grandite.com	Quebec	QC	G2K2G4	418-622-4892	622-7001
GSE Systems Inc 7133 Rutherford Rd Suite 200 *AMEX: GVP* ■ *TF Cust Svc:* 800-638-7912 ■ *Web:* www.gses.com	Baltimore	MD	21244	410-277-3740	277-5287
GWI Software 10000 NE 7th Ave Suite 401 *Web:* www.gwi.com	Vancouver	WA	98685	360-397-1000	397-1007
Halogen Software 495 March Rd Suite 500 *TF:* 866-566-7778 ■ *Web:* www.halogensoftware.com	Kanata	ON	K2K3G1	613-270-1011	270-8311
HarrisData 13555 Bishops Ct Suite 300 *TF:* 800-225-0585 ■ *Web:* www.harrisdata.com	Brookfield	WI	53005	262-784-9099	784-5994
Hewlett-Packard 19447 Pruneridge Ave	Cupertino	CA	95014	408-477-6353	
HighJump Software 6455 City West Pkwy *TF:* 800-328-3271 ■ *Web:* www.highjumpsoftware.com	Eden Prairie	MN	55344	952-947-4088	947-0440
HK Systems Inc 2855 S James Dr *TF:* 800-424-7365 ■ *Web:* www.hksystems.com	New Berlin	WI	53151	262-860-7000	860-7014
Hyperion Solutions Corp 5450 Great American Pkwy *NASDAQ: HYSL* ■ *TF:* 800-858-1666 ■ *Web:* www.hyperion.com	Sunnyvale	CA	95054	408-744-9500	588-8500
I-many Inc 399 Thornall St 12th Fl *NASDAQ: IMNY* ■ *TF:* 800-832-0228 ■ *Web:* www.imany.com	Edison	NJ	08837	732-452-1515	
i2 Technologies Inc One i2 Pl 11701 Luna Rd *NASDAQ: ITWO* ■ *TF:* 800-800-3288 ■ *Web:* www.i2.com	Dallas	TX	75234	469-357-1000	357-1798
IBM WebSphere Information Integration 50 Washington St *Web:* ibm.ascential.com	Westborough	MA	01581	508-366-3888	366-3669
iCIMS Inc 1301 Hwy 36 Bldg 1 Suite 102 *TF:* 800-889-4422 ■ *Web:* www.icims.com	Hazlet	NJ	07730	732-847-1941	876-0422
iEmployee 699 Fall River Ave *TF:* 800-884-6504 ■ *Web:* www.iemployee.com	Seekonk	MA	02771	508-336-4441	336-5894
IFS North America Inc 1010 N Finance Center Dr *TF:* 800-807-7610 ■ *Web:* www.ifsworld.com/us	Tucson	AZ	85710	520-512-2000	512-2001
Image Process Design 36800 Woodward Ave Suite 300 *TF:* 888-842-0455 ■ *Web:* www.ipdsolution.com	Bloomfield Hills	MI	48304	248-723-9733	203-2566
Info Directions Inc 833 Phillips Rd *TF:* 888-924-4110 ■ *Web:* www.infodirections.com	Victor	NY	14564	585-924-4110	924-1821
Infoglide Software Corp 6300 Bridge Point Pkwy Bldg 3 Suite 200 *TF:* 800-338-2441 ■ *Web:* www.infoglidesoftware.com	Austin	TX	78730	512-532-3500	532-3505

Company	City	State	ZIP	Phone	Fax
Informatica Corp 100 Cardinal Way *NASDAQ: INFA* ■ *TF:* 800-653-3871 ■ *Web:* www.informatica.com	Redwood City	CA	94063	650-385-5000	385-5500
Inforte Corp 500 N Dearborn St Suite 1200 *NASDAQ: INFT* ■ *Web:* www.inforte.com	Chicago	IL	60610	312-540-0900	540-0855
Infospectrum 5412 Clareton Cr Suite 260 *Web:* www.info-spectrum.com	Agoura Hills	CA	91301	818-874-9226	874-9227
Infosys Technologies Ltd 1 Spectrum Pointe Suite 350 *Web:* www.infosys.com	Lake Forest	CA	92630	949-206-8400	206-8499
InfoVista Corp 12950 Worldgate Dr Suite 250 *Web:* www.infovista.com	Herndon	VA	20170	703-435-2435	435-5122
Innovative Systems Inc 790 Holiday Dr Bldg 11 *TF:* 800-622-6390 ■ *Web:* www.innovativesystems.com	Pittsburgh	PA	15220	412-937-9300	937-9309
iNOVA Solutions 110 Avon St *TF:* 800-637-1077 ■ *Web:* www.inovasolutions.com	Charlottesville	VA	22902	434-817-8000	817-8002
Inspiration Software Inc 7412 SW Beaverton-Hillsdale Hwy Suite 300 *TF:* 800-877-4292 ■ *Web:* www.inspiration.com	Beaverton	OR	97005	503-297-3004	297-4676
Integrated Business Systems & Services Inc 1601 Shop Rd Suite E *Web:* www.ibss.net	Columbia	SC	29201	803-736-5595	736-5639
Intellicorp Inc 2900 Lakeside Dr Suite 221 **Fax Area Code:* 408 ■ *Web:* www.intellicorp.com	Santa Clara	CA	95054	650-965-5500	454-3647*
InterAmerica Technologies Inc 8150 Leesburg Pike Suite 1400 *TF:* 800-945-8329 ■ *Web:* www.interamerica.com	Vienna	VA	22182	703-893-3514	893-1741
International Business Machines Corp (IBM) 1 New Orchard Rd *NYSE: IBM* ■ *TF:* 800-426-4968 ■ *Web:* www.ibm.com/us	Armonk	NY	10504	914-766-1900	
InterraTech Corp 11 Federal St *TF:* 888-589-4889 ■ *Web:* www.interratech.com	Camden	NJ	08103	856-854-5100	854-5102
InterSystems Corp 1 Memorial Dr *Web:* www.intersys.com	Cambridge	MA	02142	617-621-0600	494-1631
Intraware Inc 25 Orinda Way Suite 101 *NASDAQ: ITRA* ■ *TF:* 888-446-8729 ■ *Web:* www.intraware.com	Orinda	CA	94563	925-253-4500	253-4599
Intuit Inc 2632 Marine Way PO Box 7850 *NASDAQ: INTU* ■ **Fax:* Hum Res ■ *TF Cust Svc:* 800-446-8848 ■ *Web:* www.intuit.com	Mountain View	CA	94039	650-944-6000	944-2788*
Intuitive Mfg Systems Inc 12131 113th Ave NE Suite 200 *TF:* 877-549-2149 ■ *Web:* www.intuitivemfg.com	Kirkland	WA	98034	425-821-0740	814-0195
Intuitive Research & Technology Corp 6767 Old Madison Pike Bldg 2 Suite 240 *Web:* www.irtc-hq.com	Huntsville	AL	35806	256-922-9300	922-1122
Invensys Process Systems 33 Commercial St *TF:* 866-746-6477 ■ *Web:* www.invensys.com	Foxboro	MA	02035	508-543-8750	
ISG Novasoft 7901 Stoneridge Dr Suite 499 *Web:* www.isgn.com	Pleasanton	CA	94588	925-847-9090	847-0800
ISYS Search Software Inc 8775 E Orchard Rd Suite 811 *TF:* 800-992-4797 ■ *Web:* www.isysusa.com	Englewood	CO	80111	303-689-9998	689-9997
ITT Visual Information Solutions 4990 Pearl E Cir *Web:* www.ittvis.com/	Boulder	CO	80301	303-786-9900	786-9909
K-Systems Inc 5060 Ritter Rd Suite 2-A *TF:* 800-221-0204 ■ *Web:* www.ksystemsinc.com	Mechanicsburg	PA	17055	717-795-7711	795-7715
Kalido 1 Wayside Rd *Web:* www.kalido.com	Burlington	MA	01803	781-202-3200	202-3299
KNOVA Software Inc 10201 Torre Ave Suite 350 *TF:* 800-572-5748 ■ *Web:* www.knova.com	Cupertino	CA	95014	408-863-5800	863-5810
Lawson Software 1700 E Golf Rd 2 Century Ctr Suite 900 *Web:* www.lawson.com	Schaumburg	IL	60173	847-762-0900	762-0901
Lawson Software Inc 380 Saint Peter St *NASDAQ: LWSN* ■ *TF:* 800-477-1357 ■ *Web:* www.lawson.com	Saint Paul	MN	55102	651-767-7000	767-4929
Levi Ray & Shoup Inc 2401 W Monroe St *Web:* www.lrs.com	Springfield	IL	62704	217-793-3800	787-3286
Liant Software Corp 354 Waverley St *TF:* 800-818-4754 ■ *Web:* www.liant.com	Framingham	MA	01702	508-416-1614	278-3841
Logical Apps 15420 Laguna Canyon Rd Suite 150 *Web:* www.logicalapps.com	Irvine	CA	92618	949-453-9101	753-1841
Logility Inc 470 E Paces Ferry Rd *NASDAQ: LGTY* ■ *TF:* 800-762-5207 ■ *Web:* www.logility.com	Atlanta	GA	30305	404-261-9777	264-5206
Longview Solutions 161 Washington St Suite 750 *TF:* 888-456-6484 ■ *Web:* www.longview.com	Conshohocken	PA	19428	610-325-3295	828-7916
Lotus Development Corp 55 Cambridge Pkwy *TF Sales:* 800-465-6887 ■ *Web:* www-306.ibm.com/software/lotus	Cambridge	MA	02142	617-577-8500	
Macro 4 Inc 35 Waterview Blvd *TF Cust Svc:* 800-866-6224 ■ *Web:* www.macro4.com	Parsippany	NJ	07054	973-402-8000	402-5656
Made2Manage Systems Inc 450 E 96th St Suite 300 *TF:* 800-626-0220 ■ *Web:* www.made2manage.com	Indianapolis	IN	46240	317-249-1200	249-1999
Malvern Systems Inc 81 Lancaster Ave Suite 216 *TF:* 800-296-9642 ■ *Web:* www.malvernsys.com	Malvern	PA	19355	610-206-0612	880-2264
ManageSoft Corp 101 Federal St 25th Fl *TF:* 800-441-4330 ■ *Web:* www.managesoft.com	Boston	MA	02109	617-532-1600	532-1605
Maverick Technologies 504 DD Rd *Web:* www.mavtech.cc	Columbia	IL	62236	618-281-9100	281-9191
MBS Technologies Inc 6600 France Ave S Suite 425 *Web:* www.mbstechnologies.com	Minneapolis	MN	55435	952-844-2626	844-2670
Mediagrif Interactive Technologies Inc 1010 De Serigny St Suite 800 *TSX: MDF* ■ *Web:* www.mediagrif.com	Longueuil	QC	J4K5G7	450-677-8797	677-4612
Mediaplex Inc 177 Steuart St 6th Fl *TF:* 866-417-1271 ■ *Web:* www.mediaplex.com	San Francisco	CA	94105	415-808-1900	348-0374
Meridian Systems 1180 Iron Point Rd Suite 300 *TF:* 800-850-2660 ■ *Web:* www.meridiansystems.com	Folsom	CA	95630	916-294-2000	294-2001
Micro Planning International Inc 9866 E 27 *Web:* www.microplanning.com	Denver	CO	80238	800-852-7526	
MicroBiz Corp 1 Park Way *TF:* 800-385-0072 ■ *Web:* www.microbiz.com	Upper Saddle River	NJ	07458	201-785-1311	785-1568
Microsoft 500 S 10th St *TF:* 877-576-9798 ■ *Web:* www.proclarity.com	Boise	ID	83702	208-344-1630	
Microsoft Corp 4700 S Syracuse Pkwy Suite 150 *TF:* 800-379-8733 ■ *Web:* www.frxsoftware.com	Denver	CO	80237	303-741-8000	741-3335
Microsoft Corp 1 Microsoft Way *NASDAQ: MSFT* ■ *Web:* www.microsoft.com	Redmond	WA	98052	425-882-8080	936-7329
Microsoft Great Plains Business Solutions 1 Lone Tree Rd *TF:* 888-477-7877	Fargo	ND	58104	701-281-6500	
Microsystems 377 E Butterfield Rd Suite 910 *Web:* www.microsystems.com	Lombard	IL	60148	630-598-1100	598-9520
Motive Inc 12515 Research Blvd Bldg 5 *NASDAQ: MOTVE* ■ *Web:* www.motive.com	Austin	TX	78759	512-339-8335	339-9040
Multi-Ad Services Inc 1720 W Detweiller Dr *TF:* 800-348-6485 ■ *Web:* www.multi-ad.com	Peoria	IL	61615	309-692-1530	692-6566
MYOB US Inc 300 Roundhill Dr *TF Cust Svc:* 800-322-6962 ■ *Web:* www.myob.com	Rockaway	NJ	07866	973-586-2200	586-2229
Nakoma Group 16735 Von Karman Ave Suite 225 *TF:* 877-891-2811 ■ *Web:* www.nakomagroup.com	Irvine	CA	92606	949-222-0244	222-0144
Necho Systems Corp 895 Don Mills Rd Suite 401 *TF:* 800-632-4672 ■ *Web:* www.necho.com	Toronto	ON	M3C1W3	416-644-2744	644-2755
Newport Wave Inc 15 McLean *TF:* 800-999-2611 ■ *Web:* www.newportwave.com	Irvine	CA	92620	949-651-1099	786-0167
NexPrise Inc 5963 La Place Ct Suite 302 *Web:* www.nexprise.com	Carlsbad	CA	92008	760-804-1333	804-1331

Company	City	State	ZIP	Phone	Fax
North Atlantic Publishing Systems Inc 66 Commonwealth Ave *Web:* www.napsys.com	Concord	MA	01742	978-371-8989	371-8989
Novell Inc 1800 S Novell Pl *NASDAQ: NOVL* ■ **Fax:* Sales ■ *TF:* 800-453-1267 ■ *Web:* www.novell.com	Provo	UT	84606	801-861-7000	373-6798*
NSB Group 2800 Trans-Canada Hwy *Web:* www.nsbgroup.com	Pointe-Claire	QC	H9R1B1	514-426-0822	426-0824
NuView Systems Inc 155 West Street Suite 8 *Web:* www.nuviewinc.com	Wilmington	MA	01887	978-988-7884	988-1263
OAO Technology Solutions Inc 7500 Greenway Ctr Dr 16th Fl *TF:* 800-720-9030 ■ *Web:* www.oaot.com	Greenbelt	MD	20770	301-486-0400	486-0415
Object/FX Corp 10 2nd St NE Suite 400 *TF:* 866-900-2002 ■ *Web:* www.objectfx.com	Minneapolis	MN	55413	612-312-2002	312-2555
Objectivity Inc 640 W California Ave Suite 210 *TF:* 800-767-6259 ■ *Web:* www.objectivity.com	Sunnyvale	CA	94086	408-992-7100	992-7171
OMD Corp 3705 Missouri Blvd *TF:* 866-440-8664 ■ *Web:* www.omdcorp.com	Jefferson City	MO	65109	573-893-8930	893-3487
Onyx Software 1100 112th Ave NE Suite 100 *NASDAQ: ONXS* ■ *TF:* 888-275-6699 ■ *Web:* www.onyx.com	Bellevue	WA	98004	425-451-8060	990-3343
Open Systems Inc 4301 Dean Lakes Blvd *TF Sales:* 800-328-2276 ■ *Web:* www.osas.com	Shakopee	MN	55379	952-496-2465	403-5870
OpenLink Software Inc 10 Burlington Mall Rd Suite 265 *TF:* 800-495-6322 ■ *Web:* www.openlinksw.com	Burlington	MA	01803	781-273-0900	229-8030
Optio Software Inc 3015 Windward Plaza Windward Fairways 2 *Web:* www.optiosoftware.com	Alpharetta	GA	30005	770-576-3500	576-3699
Oracle 1515 Arapahoe St Suite 1311 **Fax:* Sales ■ *TF:* 800-289-2550 ■ *Web:* www.decisioneering.com	Denver	CO	80202	303-534-1515	534-4818*
Oracle Corp 500 Oracle Pkwy *NASDAQ: ORCL* ■ *TF Sales:* 800-672-2531 ■ *Web:* www.oracle.com	Redwood Shores	CA	94065	650-506-7000	506-7200
Oracle Information Rights Management 500 Oracle Pkwy *Web:* www.oracle.com	Redwood Shores	CA	94065	650-506-0024	
Oracle USA 500 Oracle Pkwy *Web:* www.oracle.com	Redwood Shores	CA	94065	800-392-2999	
Palisade Corp 798 Cascadilla St *TF:* 800-432-7475 ■ *Web:* www.palisade.com	Ithaca	NY	14850	607-277-8000	277-8001
Paperclip Software Inc 1 University Plaza **Fax:* Hum Res ■ *TF:* 800-929-3503 ■ *Web:* www.paperclip.com	Hackensack	NJ	07601	201-525-1221	525-1511*
Passport Corp 85 Chestnut Ridge Rd *TF:* 800-926-6736 ■ *Web:* www.passportcorp.com	Montvale	NJ	07645	201-573-0038	573-0082
Pegasystems Inc 101 Main St *NASDAQ: PEGA* ■ *Web:* www.pegasystems.com	Cambridge	MA	02142	617-374-9600	374-9620
PeopleClick.com Inc 2 Hannover Sq 7th Fl *TF:* 877-820-4400 ■ *Web:* www.peopleclick.com	Raleigh	NC	27601	919-645-2800	645-2801
Percussion Software Inc 600 Unicorn Park Dr *TF:* 800-283-0800 ■ *Web:* www.percussion.com	Woburn	MA	01801	781-438-9900	438-9955
Performance Solutions Technology LLC 1198 Pacific Coast Hwy Suite D515 **Fax Area Code:* 800 ■ *Web:* www.managepro.com	Seal Beach	CA	90740	562-430-7096	645-6618*
Personnel Data Systems Inc (PDS) 650 Sentry Pkwy Suite 200 *TF:* 800-243-8737 ■ *Web:* www.pdssoftware.com	Blue Bell	PA	19422	610-238-4600	238-4550
Pilgrim Software 2807 W Busch Blvd Suite 200 *Web:* www.pilgrimsoftware.com	Tampa	FL	33618	813-915-1663	915-1948
Pilot Software 1 Canal Pk *Web:* www.pilotsoftware.com	Cambridge	MA	02141	617-374-9400	374-1110
Pitney Bowes Group 1 Software 4200 Parliament Pl Suite 600 *TF:* 800-368-5806 ■ *Web:* www.g1.com	Lanham	MD	20706	301-731-2300	731-0360
Planview Inc 8300 N Mopac Suite 100 *TF:* 800-856-8600 ■ *Web:* www.planview.com/	Austin	TX	78759	512-346-8600	346-9180
Platform Computing Inc 3760 14th Ave *TF:* 877-528-3676 ■ *Web:* www.platform.com	Markham	ON	L3R3T7	905-948-8448	948-9975
Portrait Software Inc 125 Summer St 16th Fl *TF:* 800-821-8031 ■ *Web:* www.portraitsoftware.com	Boston	MA	02110	617-457-5200	457-5299
Powerway Inc 429 N Pennsylvania Ave Suite 400-D *TF:* 800-964-9004 ■ *Web:* www.powerwayinc.com	Indianapolis	IN	46204	317-624-4000	624-4040
Primavera Systems Inc 3 Bala Plaza W Suite 700 **Fax:* Sales ■ *TF Sales:* 800-423-0245 ■ *Web:* www.primavera.com	Bala Cynwyd	PA	19004	610-667-8600	667-7894*
Princeton Softech Inc 111 Campus Dr *TF:* 800-457-7060 ■ *Web:* www.princetonsoftech.com	Princeton	NJ	08540	609-627-5500	627-7799
Progress Software Corp 14 Oak Pk *NASDAQ: PRGS* ■ *TF:* 800-477-6473 ■ *Web:* www.progress.com	Bedford	MA	01730	781-280-4000	280-4095
Provue Development Corp 18685-A Main St PMB 356 *TF:* 800-966-7878 ■ *Web:* www.provue.com	Huntington Beach	CA	92648	714-841-7779	
QAD Inc 6450 Via Real *NASDAQ: QADI* ■ *Web:* www.qad.com	Carpinteria	CA	93013	805-566-6000	
QNX Software Sytems 175 Terence Matthews Crescent *TF:* 800-363-9001 ■ *Web:* www.qnx.com	Kanata	ON	K2M1W8	613-591-0931	591-3579
Quest Software Inc 5 Polairis Way *NASDAQ: QSFT* ■ *TF:* 800-306-9329 ■ *Web:* www.quest.com	Aliso Viejo	CA	92656	949-754-8000	754-8999
Quicken 2632 Marine Way PO Box 7850 *NASDAQ: INTU* ■ **Fax:* Hum Res ■ *TF Cust Svc:* 800-446-8848 ■ *Web:* www.intuit.com	Mountain View	CA	94039	650-944-6000	944-2788*
Realtime Software Corp 24 Deane Rd *TF:* 866-418-0590 ■ *Web:* www.realtimesw.com	Bernardston	MA	01337	847-803-1100	954-4764
Red Wing Software Inc 491 Hwy 19 *TF:* 800-732-9464 ■ *Web:* www.redwingsoftware.com	Red Wing	MN	55066	651-388-1106	388-7950
RedPrairie Corp 20700 Swenson Dr Suite 400 *TF:* 800-990-9632 ■ *Web:* www.redprairie.com	Waukesha	WI	53186	262-317-2000	317-2001
Relavis Corp 40 Wall St 33rd Fl *Web:* www.relavis.com	New York	NY	10005	212-995-2900	995-2206
Rentrak Corp 7700 NE Ambassador Pl 3rd Fl 1 Airport Ctr *NASDAQ: RENT* ■ *TF:* 800-929-5656 ■ *Web:* www.rentrak.com	Portland	OR	97220	503-284-7581	331-2746
Rockwell Software Inc 2424 S 102nd St *Web:* www.software.rockwell.com	West Allis	WI	53227	414-328-2000	321-2211
Ross Systems Inc 2 Concourse Pkwy Suite 800 *Web:* www.rossinc.com	Atlanta	GA	30328	770-351-9600	351-0036
royalblue technologies corp 17 State St 42nd Fl *Web:* www.royalblue.com	New York	NY	10004	212-269-9000	785-4327
Sage Accpac 6700 Koll Center Pkwy 3rd Fl **Fax Area Code:* 925 ■ *Web:* www.accpac.com	Pleasanton	CA	94566	800-873-7282	461-5806*
Sage Software Inc 8800 N Gainey Ctr Dr Suite 200 *TF:* 800-643-6400 ■ *Web:* www.sagesoftware.com	Scottsdale	AZ	85258	480-368-3700	368-3799
Sage Software Inc Nonprofit & Government Div 12301 Research Blvd Bldg 4 Suite 350 *TF:* 800-647-3863 ■ *Web:* www.sagesoftware.com	Austin	TX	78759	512-454-5004	454-1246
Sage Software Inc Small Business Div 1715 N Brown Rd *TF Sales:* 800-285-0999 ■ *Web:* www.sagesoftware.com	Lawrenceville	GA	30043	770-724-4000	
Sage Software Inc Specialized Business Div 2325 Dulles Corner Blvd Suite 800 *TF:* 800-368-2405 ■ *Web:* www.bestsoftware.com	Herndon	VA	20171	703-793-2700	793-2770
Sand Technology Inc 215 Redfern St Westmount Suite 410 *TF:* 877-468-2538 ■ *Web:* www.sandtechnology.ca	Westmount	QC	H3Z3L5	514-939-3477	939-2042
SAP America Inc 3999 W Chester Pike *Web:* www.sap.com/usa/	Newtown Square	PA	19073	610-661-1000	
SAP Triversity 3550 Victoria Pk Ave Suite 400 *TF:* 888-287-4629 ■ *Web:* www.sap.com	Toronto	ON	M2H2N5	416-791-7100	791-7101
Sapphire International 101 Merritt Blvd Suite 107 *Web:* www.dataease.com	Trumbull	CT	06611	203-375-8668	375-1965

Business Software (General) (Cont'd)

				Phone	Fax
SAS Institute Inc 100 SAS Campus Dr	Cary	NC	27513	919-677-8000	677-4444
TF: 800-707-0025 ■ *Web:* www.sas.com					
Satori Software Inc 2815 2nd Ave Suite 500	Seattle	WA	98121	206-357-2900	357-2901
TF: 800-553-6477 ■ *Web:* www.satorisoftware.com					
SchoolDESX Technologies LLC 4150 S 100 East Ave Suite 1000	Tulsa	OK	74146	918-664-8383	665-1999
TF: 800-324-9393 ■ *Web:* www.schooldesx.com					
Sciforma Corp 985 University Ave Suite 5	Los Gatos	CA	95032	408-354-0144	354-0122
TF Sales: 800-533-9876 ■ *Web:* www.sciforma.com					
SCO Group Inc 355 S 520 West Suite 100	Lindon	UT	84042	801-765-4999	765-1313
NASDAQ: SCOX ■ *TF:* 888-553-3305 ■ *Web:* www.sco.com					
SDL International 1292 Hammerwood Ave	Sunnyvale	CA	94089	408-743-3500	743-3600
TF: 888-487-2367 ■ *Web:* www.sdl.com					
SEEC Inc 2730 Sidney St Suite 200	Pittsburgh	PA	15203	412-297-0050	297-0052
TF: 800-682-7332 ■ *Web:* www.seec.com					
Select Business Solutions 6260 Lookout Rd	Boulder	CO	80301	303-305-4115	305-4116
TF: 888-472-7347 ■ *Web:* www.selectbs.com					
Selectica Inc 1740 Technology Dr Suite 450	San Jose	CA	95110	408-570-9700	570-9705
NASDAQ: SLTC ■ *TF:* 877-712-9560 ■ *Web:* www.selectica.com					
SERENA Software Inc 2755 Campus Dr 3rd Fl	San Mateo	CA	94403	650-522-6600	522-6699
NASDAQ: SRNA ■ *Web:* www.serena.com					
Sierra Atlantic Inc 6522 Kaiser Dr	Fremont	CA	94555	510-742-4100	742-4101
Web: www.sierraatlantic.com					
Silvon Software Inc 900 Oakmont Lane Suite 400	Westmont	IL	60559	630-655-3313	655-3377
TF: 800-874-5866 ■ *Web:* www.silvon.com					
SmartDB Corp 4600 Bohannon Dr Suite 230	Menlo Park	CA	94025	650-328-9798	328-9774
Web: www.smartdbcorp.com					
SMARTS (System Management ARTS Inc)					
44 S Broadway 7th Fl	White Plains	NY	10601	914-948-6200	
TF: 877-276-2787 ■ *Web:* www.smarts.com					
Soffront Software Inc 45437 Warm Springs Blvd	Fremont	CA	94539	510-413-9000	413-9027
TF: 800-763-3766 ■ *Web:* www.soffront.com					
SoftBrands Inc 2 Meridian Crossings Suite 800	Minneapolis	MN	55423	612-851-1500	851-1560
AMEX: SBN ■ *Web:* www.softbrands.com					
Software AG USA 11700 Plaza America Dr Suite 700	Reston	VA	20190	703-860-5050	391-6975
TF: 800-525-7859 ■ *Web:* www.softwareagusa.com					
Source Technologies 2910 Whitehall Pk Dr	Charlotte	NC	28273	704-969-7500	969-7595
TF: 800-922-8501 ■ *Web:* www.sourcetech.com					
SourceForge Inc 46939 Bayside Pkwy	Fremont	CA	94538	510-687-7000	687-7155
TF: 877-825-4689 ■ *Web:* web.sourceforge.com					
SP Systems Inc 7500 Greenway Ctr Dr Suite 850	Greenbelt	MD	20770	301-614-1322	614-1328
Web: www.sp-systems.com					
Speedware Corp 6380 Cote de Liesse Suite 110	Saint-Laurent	QC	H4T1E3	514-747-7007	747-3380
TF: 800-361-6782 ■ *Web:* www.speedware.com					
SPSS Inc 233 S Wacker Dr 11th Fl	Chicago	IL	60606	312-651-3000	651-3668*
NASDAQ: SPSS ■ **Fax:* Sales ■ *TF:* 800-543-2185 ■ *Web:* www.spss.com					
SRA International Inc 4300 Fair Lakes Ct	Fairfax	VA	22033	703-803-1500	803-1509
NYSE: SRX ■ *Web:* www.sra.com					
Stamps.com Inc 3420 Ocean Park Blvd Suite 1040	Santa Monica	CA	90405	888-434-0055	581-7500*
NASDAQ: STMP ■ **Fax Area Code:* 310 ■ *TF:* 888-434-0055 ■ *Web:* www.stamps.com					
Sterling Commerce Inc 4600 Lakehurst Ct PO Box 8000	Dublin	OH	43016	614-793-7000	793-4040
TF: 800-876-9772 ■ *Web:* www.sterlingcommerce.com					
Sybase Inc 1 Sybase Dr	Dublin	CA	94568	925-236-5000	236-4321
NYSE: SY ■ *TF:* 800-879-2273 ■ *Web:* www.sybase.com					
SYSPRO 959 S Coast Dr Suite 100	Costa Mesa	CA	92626	714-437-1000	437-1407
TF: 800-369-8649 ■ *Web:* www.syspro.com					
Systar Inc 8618 Westwood Center Dr Suite 240	Vienna	VA	22182	703-556-8400	556-8430
Web: www.systar.com					
System Management ARTS Inc (SMARTS)					
44 S Broadway 7th Fl	White Plains	NY	10601	914-948-6200	
TF: 877-276-2787 ■ *Web:* www.smarts.com					
Taleo Corp 575 Market St 8th Fl	San Francisco	CA	94105	415-538-9068	538-9069
NASDAQ: TLEO ■ *TF:* 888-836-3669 ■ *Web:* www.taleo.com					
TECSYS Inc 87 Prince St 5th Fl	Montreal	QC	H3C2M7	514-866-0001	866-1805
TF: 800-922-8649 ■ *Web:* www.tecsys.com					
Telelogic North America Inc 9401 Jeronimo Rd	Irvine	CA	92618	949-830-8022	830-8023
TF Sales: 877-275-4777 ■ *Web:* www.telelogic.com					
TenFold Corp 698 W 10000 S Suite 200	South Jordan	UT	84095	801-495-1010	495-0353
TF: 800-836-3653 ■ *Web:* www.tenfold.com					
Tenrox 3452 E Foothill Blvd Suite 720	Pasadena	CA	91107	626-796-6640	796-6662
Web: www.tenrox.com					
Thomson Tax & Accounting 7322 Newman Blvd	Dexter	MI	48130	734-426-5860	426-3750
TF Cust Svc: 800-968-0600 ■ *Web:* cs.thomson.com					
TIBCO Software Inc 3303 Hillview Ave	Palo Alto	CA	94304	650-846-5000	846-1005
NASDAQ: TIBX ■ *Web:* www.tibco.com					
Tomax Corp 224 S 200 West	Salt Lake City	UT	84101	801-990-0909	924-3400
TF: 800-255-8120 ■ *Web:* www.tomax.com					
TreeAge Software Inc 1075 Main St	Williamstown	MA	01267	413-458-0104	458-0105
TF: 800-254-1911 ■ *Web:* www.treeage.com					
TREEV LLCMetavante Image Solutions					
13454 Sunrise Valley Dr Suite 400	Herndon	VA	20171	703-478-2260	481-6920
TF: 800-254-0994 ■ *Web:* www.metavanteimage.com					
Trilogy Software Inc 6011 W Courtyard Dr Suite 300	Austin	TX	78730	512-874-3100	874-8900
Web: www.trilogy.com					
Trintech Inc 15851 Dallas Pkwy Suite 900	Addison	TX	75001	972-701-9802	701-9337
NASDAQ: TTPA ■ *TF:* 800-416-0075 ■ *Web:* www.trintech.com					
Ultimate Software Group Inc 2000 Ultimate Way	Weston	FL	33326	954-331-7000	331-7306
NASDAQ: ULTI ■ *TF:* 800-432-1729 ■ *Web:* www.ultimatesoftware.com					
Unica Corp 170 Tracer Ln	Waltham	MA	02451	781-839-8000	890-0012
NASDAQ: UNCA ■ *Web:* www.unicacorp.com					
Unz & Co 201 Circle Dr N Suite 104	Piscataway	NJ	08854	732-868-0706	868-0607
TF: 800-631-3098 ■ *Web:* www.unzco.com					
Valiant 110 Crossways Park Dr	Woodbury	NY	11797	516-390-1100	390-1111
TF: 800-521-4555 ■ *Web:* www.valiant.com					
Validar 801 1st Ave S Suite 200	Seattle	WA	98134	206-855-8494	223-8455
TF: 888-784-8455 ■ *Web:* www.validar.com					
Ventyx 3301 Windy Ridge Pkwy	Atlanta	GA	30339	770-952-8444	989-4231
NASDAQ: IINT ■ *TF:* 800-554-6387 ■ *Web:* www.ventyx.com					
Versant Corp 255 Shoreline Dr Suite 450	Redwood City	CA	94065	650-232-2400	232-2401
NASDAQ: VSNT ■ *TF:* 800-837-7268 ■ *Web:* www.versant.com					
Versata Inc 6011 W Courtyard Dr	Austin	TX	87830	512-874-3000	874-8900
TF: 800-984-7638 ■ *Web:* www.versata.com					
Vertex Inc 1041 Old Cassatt Rd	Berwyn	PA	19312	610-640-4200	640-5892
TF: 800-355-3500 ■ *Web:* www.vertexinc.com					
VFA Inc 266 Summer St	Boston	MA	02210	617-451-5100	350-7087
TF: 800-693-3132 ■ *Web:* www.vfa.com					
Viador Inc 505 N Mathilda Ave Suite 200	Sunnyvale	CA	94085	408-992-6000	992-6001
Web: www.viador.com					
Vignette Corp 1301 S Mopac Expy Suite 100	Austin	TX	78746	512-741-4300	741-1537
NASDAQ: VIGN ■ *TF:* 888-608-9900 ■ *Web:* www.vignette.com					
ViryaNet Inc 2 Willow St	Southborough	MA	01745	508-490-8600	490-8666
NASDAQ: VRYA ■ *TF:* 800-661-7096 ■ *Web:* www.viryanet.com					
Visible Systems Corp 201 Spring St	Lexington	MA	02421	781-778-0200	778-0208
TF Sales: 800-684-7425 ■ *Web:* www.visible.com					
Visual Numerics Inc 2500 Wilcrest Dr Suite 200	Houston	TX	77042	713-784-3131	954-6795
TF: 800-222-4675 ■ *Web:* www.vni.com					
Visual Sciences LLC 10182 Telesis Ct 6th Fl	San Diego	CA	92121	858-546-0040	546-0480
NASDAQ: WSSI ■ *Web:* www.websidestory.com					
Vitria Technology Inc 945 Stewart Dr	Sunnyvale	CA	94085	408-212-2700	212-2720
NASDAQ: VITR ■ *TF:* 877-365-5935 ■ *Web:* www.vitria.com					
Volunteer Software 628 S 2nd Ave W	Missoula	MT	59801	406-721-0113	265-9288*
**Fax Area Code:* 303 ■ *TF:* 800-391-9446 ■ *Web:* www.volsoft.com					
Wave Systems Corp 480 Pleasant St	Lee	MA	01238	413-243-1600	243-0045
NASDAQ: WAVX ■ *TF:* 888-669-9283 ■ *Web:* www.wavesys.com					
Web Base Inc 133 E De La Guerra St Suite 223	Santa Barbara	CA	93101	805-275-4505	564-7188
TF: 888-225-8885 ■ *Web:* www.webbase.com					
webMethods Inc 3877 Fairfax Ridge Rd	Fairfax	VA	22030	703-460-2500	460-2599
NASDAQ: WEBM ■ *Web:* www.webmethods.com					
Witness Systems Inc 300 Colonial Center Pkwy Suite 600	Roswell	GA	30076	770-754-1900	754-1888
NASDAQ: WITS ■ *TF:* 888-394-8637 ■ *Web:* www.witness.com					
Wizdom Systems Inc 1300 Iroquois Ave	Naperville	IL	60563	630-357-3000	357-3059
Web: www.wizdom.com					
Xign Corp 7077 Koll Center Pkwy	Pleasanton	CA	94566	925-469-9446	469-9447
Web: www.xign.com					
ZyLAB North America LLC 1577 Spring Hill Rd Suite 420	Vienna	VA	22182	703-448-1420	991-2508
Web: www.zylab.com					

181-2 Computer Languages & Development Tools

				Phone	Fax
Altiris Inc 588 W 400 South	Lindon	UT	84042	801-226-8500	226-8506
NASDAQ: ATRS ■ *TF:* 888-252-5551 ■ *Web:* www.altiris.com					
Amzi! inc 47 Redwood Rd	Asheville	NC	28804	828-350-0350	
Web: www.amzi.com					
Applied Dynamics International Inc 3800 Stone School Rd	Ann Arbor	MI	48108	734-973-1300	668-0012
Web: www.adi.com					
ARC International 3590 N 1st St Suite 2000	San Jose	CA	95134	408-437-3400	437-3401
TF: 866-272-3344 ■ *Web:* www.arc.com					
Borland Software Corp 2450 Stevens Creek Blvd	Cupertino	CA	95014	408-863-7000	
NASDAQ: BORL ■ *TF Cust Svc:* 800-331-0877 ■ *Web:* www.borland.com					
BSQUARE Corp 110 110th Ave NE Suite 200	Bellevue	WA	98004	425-519-5900	519-5999
NASDAQ: BSQR ■ *TF:* 888-820-4500 ■ *Web:* www.bsquare.com					
BulletProof Corp 2400 E Las Olas Blvd Suite 332	Fort Lauderdale	FL	33301	800-505-0105	337-0768*
**Fax Area Code:* 954 ■ *TF:* 800-505-0105 ■ *Web:* www.bulletproof.com					
Data Access Corp 14000 SW 119th Ave	Miami	FL	33186	305-238-0012	238-0017
TF: 800-451-3539 ■ *Web:* www.daccess.com					
DDC-I Inc 1825 E Northern Ave Suite 125	Phoenix	AZ	85020	602-275-7172	252-6054
TF: 800-221-8643 ■ *Web:* www.ddci.com					
Diamond Edge Inc 184 South 300 W	Lindon	UT	84042	801-785-8473	
Web: www.diamondedge.com					
Embarcadero Technologies Inc 100 California St Suite 12	San Francisco	CA	94111	415-834-3131	536-0845
NASDAQ: EMBT ■ *Web:* www.embarcadero.com					
Empress Software Inc 11785 Beltsville Dr	Beltsville	MD	20705	301-220-1919	220-1997
Web: www.empress.com					
FMS Inc 8150 Leesburg Pike Suite 600	Vienna	VA	22182	703-356-4700	448-3861
TF: 866-367-7801 ■ *Web:* www.fmsinc.com					
Forth Inc 5155 W Rosecrans Ave Suite 1018	Hawthorne	CA	90250	310-491-3356	978-9454
TF: 800-553-6784 ■ *Web:* www.forth.com					
Green Hills Software Inc 30 W Sola St	Santa Barbara	CA	93101	805-965-6044	965-6343
TF: 800-765-4733 ■ *Web:* www.ghs.com					
ILOG Inc 1195 W Freemont Ave	Sunnyvale	CA	94084	408-991-7000	991-7001
TF: 800-367-4564 ■ *Web:* www.ilog.com					
Infinite Software 28202 Cabot Rd	Laguna Niguel	CA	92677	949-498-9300	498-9201
TF: 800-474-4047 ■ *Web:* www.infinitesoftware.com					
Integrated Computer Solutions Inc 54 Middlesex Tpke	Bedford	MA	01730	617-621-0060	621-9555
TF: 800-800-4271 ■ *Web:* www.ics.com					
LANSA Inc 3010 Highland Pkwy Suite 275	Downers Grove	IL	60515	630-874-7000	874-7001
Web: www.lansa.com					
Lattice Inc 1751 S Naperville Rd Suite 100	Wheaton	IL	60187	630-949-3250	949-3299
TF Sales: 800-444-4309 ■ *Web:* www.lattice.com					
Mix Software Inc 1203 Berkeley Dr	Richardson	TX	75081	972-231-0949	
TF: 800-333-0330 ■ *Web:* www.mixsoftware.com					
MKS Inc 410 Albert St	Waterloo	ON	N2L3V3	519-884-2251	884-8861
TF Sales: 800-265-2797 ■ *Web:* www.mks.com					
NIS Inc 12995 Thomas Creek Rd	Reno	NV	89511	775-852-0640	852-0640
Web: www.nis.com					
Numara Software Inc 2202 NW Shore Blvd Suite 650	Tampa	FL	33607	813-227-4500	227-4501
TF Sales: 800-557-6970 ■ *Web:* www.numarasoftware.com					
Object/FX Corp 10 2nd St NE Suite 400	Minneapolis	MN	55413	612-312-2002	312-2555
TF: 866-900-2002 ■ *Web:* www.objectfx.com					
Prolifics 22 Courtland St 18th Fl	New York	NY	10007	212-267-7722	608-6753
TF: 800-458-3313 ■ *Web:* www.prolifics.com					
Recital Corp 100 Cummings Center Suite 318J	Beverly	MA	01915	978-921-5594	921-4005
TF: 800-873-7443 ■ *Web:* www.recital.com					
Revelation Software 99 Kinderkamack Rd	Westwood	NJ	07675	201-594-1422	722-9815
TF: 800-262-4747 ■ *Web:* www.revelation.com					
Rogue Wave Software Inc 5500 Flatiron Pkwy	Boulder	CO	80301	303-473-9118	473-9137
TF: 800-487-3217 ■ *Web:* www.roguewave.com					
Savitar Corp 3000 Kent Ave	West Lafayette	IN	47906	765-742-5400	742-5432
Web: www.savitar.com					
SemWare Corp 730 Elk Cove Ct	Kennesaw	GA	30152	678-355-9810	355-9812
Web: www.semware.com					
SlickEdit Inc 3000 Aerial Center Pkwy Suite 120	Morrisville	NC	27560	919-473-0070	473-0080
TF: 800-934-3348 ■ *Web:* www.slickedit.com					
Sunbelt Computer Systems Inc 13090 Swan Lake Rd CR 468	Tyler	TX	75704	903-881-0400	
TF Sales: 800-359-5907 ■ *Web:* www.sunbelt-plb.com					
Thoroughbred Software International Inc					
285 Davidson Ave Suite 302	Somerset	NJ	08873	732-560-1377	560-1594
TF: 800-524-0430 ■ *Web:* www.tbred.com					
Zortec International 209 10th Ave S Suite 501	Nashville	TN	37203	615-361-7000	361-3800
TF: 800-361-7005 ■ *Web:* www.zortec.com					

181-3 Educational & Reference Software

				Phone	Fax
Allen Communication Learning Services					
175 W 200 South Suite 100	Salt Lake City	UT	84101	801-537-7800	537-7805
TF: 866-310-7800 ■ *Web:* www.allencomm.com					
American Education Corp					
7506 N Broadway Ext Suite 505	Oklahoma City	OK	73116	405-840-6031	848-3960
TF Sales: 800-222-2811 ■ *Web:* www.amered.com					
Atari Inc 417 5th Ave 8th Fl	New York	NY	10016	212-726-6500	252-8603
NASDAQ: ATAR ■ *TF:* 800-898-1438 ■ *Web:* www.atari.com					
Authoria Inc 300 5th Ave	Waltham	MA	02451	781-530-2000	530-2001
TF: 877-628-8467 ■ *Web:* www.authoria.com					
Automated Training Systems Corp					
4545 E Industrial St Suite 5B	Simi Valley	CA	93063	805-520-1509	520-1067
TF: 800-426-8737 ■ *Web:* www.ibmuser.com					

Company	City	State	ZIP	Phone	Fax
Blackboard Inc 1899 L St NW 5th Fl *NASDAQ: BBBB* ■ *TF:* 800-424-9299 ■ *Web:* www.blackboard.com	Washington	DC	20036	202-463-4860	463-4863
CBT Direct LLC 25400 US Hwy 19N Suite 285 *TF Orders:* 800-653-4933 ■ *Web:* www.cbtdirect.com	Clearwater	FL	33763	727-724-8994	726-6922
CompassLearning Inc 203 Colorado St *TF:* 800-232-9556 ■ *Web:* www.compasslearning.com	Austin	TX	78701	512-478-9600	492-6193
Cosmi Corp 1351 Charles Willard St *Web:* www.cosmi.com	Carson	CA	90746	310-603-5800	886-3500
Deep River Interactive 7 Custom House St 2nd Fl *Web:* www.cowlesdeepriver.com	Portland	ME	04101	207-775-6405	775-6408
Electronic Courseware Systems Inc 1713 S State St *TF Orders:* 800-832-4965 ■ *Web:* www.ecsmedia.com	Champaign	IL	61820	217-359-7099	359-6578
Gamco Industries Inc 325 N Kirkwood Rd Suite 200 *TF:* 888-726-8100 ■ *Web:* www.gamco.com	Saint Louis	MO	63122	314-909-1670	984-8063
Individual Software Inc 4255 Hopyard Rd Suite 2 *TF:* 800-822-3522 ■ *Web:* www.individualsoftware.com	Pleasanton	CA	94588	925-734-6767	734-8337
Insightful Corp 1700 Westlake Ave N Suite 500 *NASDAQ: IFUL* ■ *TF:* 800-569-0123 ■ *Web:* www.insightful.com	Seattle	WA	98109	206-283-8802	283-8691
Inspiration Software Inc 7412 SW Beaverton-Hillsdale Hwy Suite 300 *TF:* 800-877-4292 ■ *Web:* www.inspiration.com	Beaverton	OR	97005	503-297-3004	297-4676
Language Engineering Co 135 Beaver St Suite 204 *Web:* www.lec.com	Waltham	MA	02452	781-642-8900	642-8904
LJ Technical Systems Inc 85 Corporate Dr *TF:* 800-237-3482 ■ *Web:* www.lj-tech.com	Holtsville	NY	11742	631-758-1616	758-1788
MedTech USA 6310 San Vicente Blvd Suite 404 *TF:* 800-640-8000 ■ *Web:* www.medtech.com	Los Angeles	CA	90048	323-964-1000	964-1001
Milliken Publishing Co Inc 3190 Rider Trail S *TF:* 800-325-4136 ■ *Web:* www.millikenpub.com	Earth City	MO	63045	314-991-4220	991-4807
MindPlay Educational Software 440 S Williams Blvd Suite 206 *TF:* 800-221-7911 ■ *Web:* www.mindplay.com	Tucson	AZ	85711	520-888-1800	888-7904
NCS Pearson Inc 5601 Green Valley Dr Suite 220 *TF:* 800-431-1421 ■ *Web:* www.ncspearson.com	Bloomington	MN	55437	952-681-3000	681-3580
Nordic Software Inc 917 Carlos Dr PO Box 5403 *TF:* 800-306-6502 ■ *Web:* www.nordicsoftware.com	Lincoln	NE	68505	402-489-1557	489-1560
Optimum Resource Inc 18 Hunter Rd *TF:* 888-784-2592 ■ *Web:* www.stickybear.com	Hilton Head Island	SC	29926	843-689-8000	689-8008
PLATO Learning Inc 10801 Nesbitt Ave S *NASDAQ: TUTR* ■ *TF:* 800-869-2000 ■ *Web:* www.plato.com	Bloomington	MN	55437	952-832-1000	832-1200
Queue Inc 1 Controls Dr **Fax Area Code:* 800 ■ *TF:* 800-232-2224 ■ *Web:* www.queueinc.com	Shelton	CT	06484	203-446-8100	775-2729*
Quicksilver Software Inc 18261 McDermott *Web:* www.quicksilver.com	Irvine	CA	92614	949-474-2150	
Renaissance Learning Inc 2911 Peach St *NASDAQ: RLRN* ■ *TF:* 800-338-4204 ■ *Web:* www.renlearn.com	Wisconsin Rapids	WI	54494	715-424-3636	424-4242
Riverdeep Inc LLC 100 Pine St Suite 1900 *TF:* 888-242-6747 ■ *Web:* www.riverdeep.net	San Francisco	CA	94111	415-659-2000	659-2020
Saba Software Inc 2400 Bridge Pkwy *NASDAQ: SABA* ■ *TF:* 877-803-1900 ■ *Web:* www.saba.com	Redwood Shores	CA	94065	650-696-3840	696-1773
Scientific Learning Corp 300 Frank H Ogawa Plaza Suite 600 *NASDAQ: SCIL* ■ *TF:* 888-665-9707 ■ *Web:* www.scilearn.com	Oakland	CA	94612	510-444-3500	444-3580
Siboney Corp 325 N Kirkwood Rd Suite 300 PO Box 221029 *TF:* 888-726-8100 ■ *Web:* www.siboney.com	Saint Louis	MO	63122	314-822-3163	822-3197
Simon & Schuster Interactive 1230 Ave of the Americas **Fax Area Code:* 800 ■ *TF:* 800-223-2348 ■ *Web:* www.simonsays.com	New York	NY	10020	212-698-7000	943-9831*
Snyder Tom Productions Inc 100 Talcott Ave *TF:* 800-342-0236 ■ *Web:* www.tomsnyder.com	Watertown	MA	02472	617-926-6000	926-6222
SumTotal Systems Inc 1808 Shoreline Blvd *NASDAQ: SUMT* ■ *TF:* 866-768-6825 ■ *Web:* www.sumtotalsystems.com	Mountain View	CA	94043	650-934-9500	962-9411
Sunburst Technology 1550 Executive Dr *TF:* 800-321-7511 ■ *Web:* www.sunburst.com	Elgin	IL	60123	888-492-8817	800-3028
Thompson ISI ResearchSoft 2141 Palomar Airport Rd Suite 350 *TF:* 800-722-1227 ■ *Web:* www.isiresearchsoft.com	Carlsbad	CA	92009	760-438-5526	438-5573
Tom Snyder Productions Inc 100 Talcott Ave *TF:* 800-342-0236 ■ *Web:* www.tomsnyder.com	Watertown	MA	02472	617-926-6000	926-6222
Transparent Language Inc 12 Murphy Dr *TF:* 800-567-9619 ■ *Web:* www.transparent.com	Nashua	NH	03062	603-262-6300	262-6476
True BASIC Inc 245 Main St PO Box 500 *TF:* 800-436-2111 ■ *Web:* www.truebasic.com	Bethel	VT	05032	802-705-1403	234-6378
VCampus Corp 1850 Centennial Pk Dr Suite 200 *NASDAQ: VCMP* ■ *TF:* 800-915-9298 ■ *Web:* www2.vcampus.com	Reston	VA	20191	703-893-7800	893-1905
Ventura Educational Systems PO Box 1622 **Fax Area Code:* 800 ■ *TF:* 800-336-1022 ■ *Web:* www.venturaes.com	Arroyo Grande	CA	93421	805-473-7387	493-7380*
Wright Group/McGraw-Hill 19201 120th Ave NE Suite 100 *Web:* www.wrightgroup.com	Bothell	WA	98011	425-486-8011	486-7868
Zane Publishing PO Box 1697 *Web:* www.zane.com	Woodstock	GA	30188	770-795-9195	795-8495

181-4 Electronic Purchasing & Procurement Software

Company	City	State	ZIP	Phone	Fax
1SYNC 10 S Riverside Plaza Suite 2000 *TF:* 877-872-5984 ■ *Web:* www.1sync.org	Chicago	IL	60606	312-463-4000	466-1405
Apptis Inc 4800 Westfields Blvd *TF:* 800-338-8866 ■ *Web:* www.apptis.com	Chantilly	VA	20151	703-279-3000	691-4911
Ariba Inc 807 11th Ave *NASDAQ: ARBA* ■ *TF:* 888-237-3131 ■ *Web:* www.ariba.com	Sunnyvale	CA	94089	650-390-1000	390-1100
BroadVision Inc 585 Broadway *NASDAQ: BVSN* ■ *Web:* www.broadvision.com	Redwood City	CA	94063	650-542-5100	542-5900
CA Inc 1 CA Plaza *NYSE: CA* ■ *Web:* www.ca.com	Islandia	NY	11749	631-342-6000	342-6800
Chase Paymentech Inc 14221 Dallas Pkwy Bldg 2 **Fax:* Hum Res ■ *TF:* 800-280-7061 ■ *Web:* www.chasepaymentech.com	Dallas	TX	75254	214-849-2000	849-2015*
Covisint One Campus Martius *TF:* 888-222-1700 ■ *Web:* www.covisint.com	Detroit	MI	48226	313-227-7300	
Epylon Corp 3675 Mt Diablo Blvd Suite 110 *TF:* 888-211-7438 ■ *Web:* www.epylon.com	Lafayette	CA	94549	925-407-1020	407-1021
Fiserv Credit Processing Services 901 International Pkwy Suite 100 **Fax:* Hum Res ■ *TF:* 800-846-5127	Lake Mary	FL	32746	407-829-4200	829-3258*
Fiserv Lending Solutions 455 S Gulph Rd Suite 125 *Web:* www.fiservlemans.com	King of Prussia	PA	19406	610-337-8686	337-7206
GXS Inc 100 Edison Park Dr *TF:* 800-560-4347 ■ *Web:* www.gxs.com	Gaithersburg	MD	20878	301-340-4000	340-5840
i2 Technologies Inc One i2 Pl 11701 Luna Rd *NASDAQ: ITWO* ■ *TF:* 800-800-3288 ■ *Web:* www.i2.com	Dallas	TX	75234	469-357-1000	357-1798
International Business Machines Corp (IBM) 1 New Orchard Rd *NYSE: IBM* ■ *TF:* 800-426-4968 ■ *Web:* www.ibm.com/us	Armonk	NY	10504	914-766-1900	
MarketAxess Holdings Inc 140 Broadway 42nd Fl *NASDAQ: MKTX* ■ *TF:* 877-638-0037 ■ *Web:* www.marketaxess.com	New York	NY	10005	212-813-6000	813-6340
NOVA Information Systems 1 Concourse Pkwy Suite 300 *TF:* 800-725-1243 ■ *Web:* www.novainfo.com	Atlanta	GA	30328	770-396-1456	
PayNet Merchant Services Inc 950 S Old Woodward Suite 220 *TF:* 888-855-8644 ■ *Web:* www.visa-master.com	Birmingham	MI	48009	248-723-5760	723-5761
SciQuest Inc 6501 Weston Pkwy Suite 200 *TF:* 888-638-7322 ■ *Web:* www.sciquest.com	Cary	NC	27513	919-659-2100	659-2199
Vercuity Solutions Inc 5889 S Greenwood Plaza Blvd Suite 300 *TF:* 888-372-8489 ■ *Web:* www.vercuity.com	Greenwood Village	CO	80111	303-218-5300	218-5301
Verian Technologies Inc 8701 Mallard Creek Rd *TF:* 800-672-8776 ■ *Web:* www.procureit.com	Charlotte	NC	28262	704-547-7301	547-7304

181-5 Engineering Software

Company	City	State	ZIP	Phone	Fax
Accelrys Inc 10188 Telesis Ct Suite 100 *NASDAQ: ACCL* ■ *TF:* 888-249-2284 ■ *Web:* www.accelrys.com	San Diego	CA	92121	858-799-5000	799-5100
Advanced Visual Systems Inc 300 5th Ave *TF Sales:* 800-728-1600 ■ *Web:* www.avs.com	Waltham	MA	02451	781-890-4300	890-8287
Algor Inc 150 Beta Dr *TF:* 800-482-5467 ■ *Web:* www.algor.com	Pittsburgh	PA	15238	412-967-2700	967-2781
Altium Inc 3207 Grey Hawk Ct Suite 100 *TF:* 800-488-0680 ■ *Web:* www.acceltech.com	Carlsbad	CA	92010	760-231-0760	231-0761
Ansoft Corp 225 W Station Sq Dr Suite 200 *NASDAQ: ANST* ■ *Web:* www.ansoft.com	Pittsburgh	PA	15219	412-261-3200	471-9427
ANSYS Inc 275 Technology Dr *NASDAQ: ANSS* ■ *TF:* 800-937-3321 ■ *Web:* www.ansys.com	Canonsburg	PA	15317	724-746-3304	514-9494
Ashlar Inc 12710 Research Blvd Suite 308 *TF:* 800-877-2745 ■ *Web:* www.ashlar.com	Austin	TX	78759	512-250-2186	250-5811
Aspen Technology Inc 10 Canal Pk *NASDAQ: AZPN* ■ *Web:* www.aspentec.com	Cambridge	MA	02141	617-949-1000	949-1030
Autodesk Inc 111 McInnis Pkwy *NASDAQ: ADSK* ■ *TF Prod Info:* 800-964-6432 ■ *Web:* www.autodesk.com	San Rafael	CA	94903	415-507-5000	507-5100
Bentley Systems Inc 685 Stockton Dr *TF:* 800-236-8539 ■ *Web:* www.bentley.com	Exton	PA	19341	610-458-5000	458-1060
Bohannan Huston Inc 7500 Jefferson St NE Courtyard 1 *TF:* 800-877-5332 ■ *Web:* www.bhinc.com	Albuquerque	NM	87109	505-823-1000	798-7988
CACI MTL Systems Inc 3481 Dayton-Xenia Rd *Web:* www.caci.com/mtl/	Dayton	OH	45432	937-426-3111	426-8301
Cadence Design Systems Inc 555 River Oaks Pkwy *NASDAQ: CDNS* ■ *TF Cust Svc:* 800-746-6223 ■ *Web:* www.cadence.com	San Jose	CA	95134	408-943-1234	428-5001
CambridgeSoft Corp 100 CambridgePark Dr *TF:* 800-315-7300 ■ *Web:* www.camsoft.com	Cambridge	MA	02140	617-588-9100	588-9190
Citect Inc 30000 Mill Creek Ave Suite 300 *TF:* 888-248-3281 ■ *Web:* www.citect.com	Alpharetta	GA	30022	770-521-7511	521-7512
CoCreate Software Inc 3801 Automation Way Suite 110 *Web:* www.cocreate.com	Fort Collins	CO	80525	970-267-8000	267-8001
Comarco Inc 25541 Commerce Center Dr *NASDAQ: CMRO* ■ *Web:* www.comarco.com	Lake Forest	CA	92630	949-599-7400	599-1415
CSA Inc 450 Franklin Rd Suite 130 *Web:* www.csaatl.com	Marietta	GA	30067	770-955-3518	956-8748
Data Description Inc 840 Hanshaw Rd 2nd Fl **Fax:* Sales ■ *TF:* 800-573-5121 ■ *Web:* www.datadesk.com	Ithaca	NY	14850	607-257-1000	257-4146*
Disk Software Inc 205 Ridgestone Dr *TF:* 800-635-7760 ■ *Web:* www.disksoft.com	Murphy	TX	75094	972-423-7288	633-0718
Engineered Software Inc 615 Guilford Jamestown Rd *Web:* www.engsw.com	Greensboro	NC	27409	336-299-4843	852-2067
Enovia MatrixOne 900 Chelmsford St Crosspoint Towers Tower 2 5th Fl *NASDAQ: MONE* ■ *Web:* www.matrixone.com	Lowell	MA	01851	978-442-2500	442-1000
Evolution Computing 7000 N 16th St Suite 120 #514 *TF:* 800-874-4028 ■ *Web:* www.fastcad.com	Phoenix	AZ	85020	480-659-5658	
Geocomp Corp 1145 Massachusetts Ave *TF Cust Svc:* 800-822-2669 ■ *Web:* www.geocomp.com	Boxborough	MA	01719	978-635-0012	635-0266
Gibbs & Assoc 323 Science Dr *TF:* 800-654-9399 ■ *Web:* www.gibbsnc.com	Moorpark	CA	93021	805-523-0004	523-0006
IDC Digital Solutions 111 E 1st St *Web:* www.geneseo.com	Geneseo	IL	61254	309-944-4115	944-9475
Infinite Graphics Inc 4611 E Lake St *TF:* 800-679-0676 ■ *Web:* www.igi.com	Minneapolis	MN	55406	612-721-6283	721-3802
Intergraph Corp 170 Graphics Dr *NASDAQ: INGR* ■ *TF:* 800-345-4856 ■ *Web:* www.intergraph.com	Madison	AL	35758	256-730-2000	730-2048
Kubotek USA 100 Locke Dr *TF:* 800-372-3872 ■ *Web:* www.kubotekusa.com	Marlborough	MA	01752	508-229-2020	229-2121
LINDO Systems Inc 1415 N Dayton St *TF Sales:* 800-441-2378 ■ *Web:* www.lindo.com	Chicago	IL	60622	312-988-7422	988-9065
Magma Design Automation Inc 1650 Technology Dr *NASDAQ: LAVA* ■ *Web:* www.magma-da.com	San Jose	CA	95110	408-565-7500	565-7501
Manufacturing & Consulting Services Inc 401-B W Main St *TF:* 800-932-9329 ■ *Web:* www.mcsaz.com	Payson	AZ	85541	480-991-8700	991-8732
Mentor Graphics Corp 8005 SW Boeckman Rd *NASDAQ: MENT* ■ *TF:* 800-592-2210 ■ *Web:* www.mentor.com	Wilsonville	OR	97070	503-685-7000	685-1204
Moldflow Corp 492 Old Connecticut Pass Suite 401 *NASDAQ: MFLO* ■ *TF:* 800-284-6653 ■ *Web:* www.moldflow.com	Framingham	MA	01701	508-358-5848	358-5868
MSC.Software Corp 2 MacArthur Pl *TF:* 800-345-2078 ■ *Web:* www.mscsoftware.com	Santa Ana	CA	92707	714-444-5112	784-4056
National Instruments Corp 11500 N Mopac Expy *NASDAQ: NATI* ■ *TF Cust Svc:* 800-433-3488 ■ *Web:* www.ni.com	Austin	TX	78759	512-794-0100	683-8411
Numerical Control Computer Sciences 4685 MacArthur Ct Suite 200 *Web:* www.nccs.com	Newport Beach	CA	92660	949-553-1077	553-1911
Parametric Technology Corp 140 Kendrick St *NASDAQ: PMTCD* ■ *Web:* www.ptc.com	Needham	MA	02494	781-370-5000	370-6000
Planit Solutions Inc 3800 Palisades Dr *TF:* 800-280-6932 ■ *Web:* www.planitsolutions.com	Tuscaloosa	AL	35405	205-556-9199	556-9210
PMS Systems Corp 2800 28th St Suite 109 *Web:* www.assetsmart.com	Santa Monica	CA	90405	310-450-2566	450-1311
SAIC (Science Application International Corp) 4600 Powder Mill Rd Suite 400 *Web:* www.saic.com	Beltsville	MD	20705	301-931-2900	931-3797
Science Application International Corp (SAIC) 4600 Powder Mill Rd Suite 400 *Web:* www.saic.com	Beltsville	MD	20705	301-931-2900	931-3797
Siemens UGS PLM 10824 Hope St *Web:* www.ugs.com	Cypress	CA	90630	714-952-0311	952-6600
SimSci-Esscor 26561 Rancho Pkwy S *TF:* 800-746-7241 ■ *Web:* www.simsci-esscor.com	Lake Forest	CA	92630	949-455-8150	455-8151
SofTech Inc 2 Highwood Dr Suite 200 *TF:* 800-800-3702 ■ *Web:* www.softech.com	Tewksbury	MA	01876	978-640-6222	858-0440
Synplicity Inc 600 W California Ave *NASDAQ: SYNP* ■ *TF:* 888-617-0400 ■ *Web:* www.synplicity.com	Sunnyvale	CA	94086	408-215-6000	222-0263
Tripos Inc 1699 S Hanley Rd *NASDAQ: TRPS* ■ *TF:* 800-323-2960 ■ *Web:* www.tripos.com	Saint Louis	MO	63144	314-647-1099	647-9241
Zuken USA 238 Littleton Rd Suite 100 *TF:* 800-447-7332 ■ *Web:* www.zuken.com	Westford	MA	01886	978-692-4900	692-4725

181-6 Games & Entertainment Software

Phone Fax

Abacus Software Inc 5130 Patterson St SE .... Grand Rapids MI 49512 616-698-0330 698-0325
TF Sales: 800-451-4319 ■ *Web:* www.abacuspub.com

Activision Inc 3100 Ocean Park Blvd .... Santa Monica CA 90405 310-255-2000 255-2100
NASDAQ: ATVI ■ *Web:* www.activision.com

Alienware Corp 14591 SW 120th St .... Miami FL 33186 305-251-9797 388-5719*
**Fax Area Code:* 786 ■ *TF:* 866-287-6727 ■ *Web:* www.alienware.com

Apogee Software Inc 1999 S Bascom Ave Suite 325 .... Campbell CA 95008 408-369-9001 369-9018
TF: 800-854-6705 ■ *Web:* www.apogee1.com

Atari Inc 417 5th Ave 8th Fl .... New York NY 10016 212-726-6500 252-8603
NASDAQ: ATAR ■ *TF:* 800-898-1438 ■ *Web:* www.atari.com

Bethesda Softworks LLC 1370 Piccard Dr Suite 120 .... Rockville MD 20850 301-926-8300 926-8010
TF: 800-677-0700 ■ *Web:* www.bethsoft.com

Buena Vista Game Entertainment Studio 601 Circle 7 Dr .... Glendale CA 91201 818-553-5000 567-0284
TF: 800-228-0988

Buena Vista Games 500 S Buena Vista St .... Burbank CA 91521 800-228-0988 567-0284*
**Fax Area Code:* 818 ■ *Web:* disney.go.com/DisneyInteractive

Capcom USA Inc 800 Concar Dr Suite 300 .... San Mateo CA 94406 650-350-6500 350-6655
Web: www.capcom.com

Crystal Dynamics Inc 64 Willow Pl .... Menlo Park CA 94025 650-473-3400 473-3410

Cyan Worlds Inc 14617 N Newport Hwy .... Mead WA 99021 509-468-0807 467-2209
TF: 800-219-4119 ■ *Web:* www.cyan.com

Disney Consumer Products 500 S Buena Vista St .... Burbank CA 91521 818-560-1000 560-1930*
**Fax:* Cust Svc ■ *TF PR:* 800-723-4763

EA (Electronic Arts Inc) 209 Redwood Shores Pkwy .... Redwood City CA 94065 650-628-1500 628-1414
NASDAQ: ERTS ■ *TF Sales:* 877-324-2637 ■ *Web:* www.ea.com

Eidos Inc 1300 Seaport Blvde .... Redwood City CA 94063 650-421-7600 421-6701
Web: www.eidos.com

Electronic Arts Inc (EA) 209 Redwood Shores Pkwy .... Redwood City CA 94065 650-628-1500 628-1414
NASDAQ: ERTS ■ *TF Sales:* 877-324-2637 ■ *Web:* www.ea.com

Gemstar-TV Guide International Inc 6922 Hollywood Blvd .... Hollywood CA 90028 323-817-4600 817-4629
NASDAQ: GMST ■ *Web:* www.gemstartvguide.com

Her Interactive Inc 1150 114th Ave SE Suite 200 .... Bellevue WA 98004 425-460-8787 460-8788
TF Orders: 800-561-0908 ■ *Web:* www.herinteractive.com

iEntertainment Network Inc 124 Quade Dr .... Cary NC 27513 919-678-8301 678-8302
TF: 800-438-4263 ■ *Web:* www.ient.com

Jim Henson Co 1416 N La Brea Ave .... Hollywood CA 90028 323-802-1500 802-1825
Web: www.henson.com

LucasArts Entertainment Div Lucasfilm Ltd
1110 Gorgas St .... San Francisco CA 94129 415-746-8000 746-8923
Web: www.lucasarts.com

Lucasfilm Ltd LucasArts Entertainment Div
1110 Gorgas St .... San Francisco CA 94129 415-746-8000 746-8923
Web: www.lucasarts.com

MakeMusic! Inc 7615 Golden Triangle Dr Suite M .... Eden Prairie MN 55344 952-937-9611 937-9760
NASDAQ: MMUS ■ *TF:* 800-843-2066 ■ *Web:* www.makemusic.com

Midway Games Inc 2704 W Roscoe St .... Chicago IL 60618 773-961-2222 961-2099
NYSE: MWY ■ *Web:* www.midway.com

Mythic Entertainment Inc 4035 Ridge Top Rd Suite 800 .... Fairfax VA 22030 703-934-0169 934-0447
Web: www.mythicentertainment.com

Nintendo of America Inc 4820 150th Ave NE .... Redmond WA 98052 425-882-2040 882-3585
TF Cust Svc: 800-255-3700 ■ *Web:* www.nintendo.com

NovaLogic Inc 27489 Agoura Rd .... Agoura Hills CA 91301 818-880-1997 865-6405
Web: www.novalogic.com

Quicksilver Software Inc 18261 McDermott .... Irvine CA 92614 949-474-2150
Web: www.quicksilver.com

SEGA of America Inc 650 Townsend St Suite 650 .... San Francisco CA 94103 415-701-6000 701-6018
Web: www.sega.com

Simon & Schuster Interactive 1230 Ave of the Americas .... New York NY 10020 212-698-7000 943-9831*
**Fax Area Code:* 800 ■ *TF:* 800-223-2348 ■ *Web:* www.simonsays.com

Sony Computer Entertainment America Inc
919 E Hillsdale Blvd 2nd Fl .... Foster City CA 94404 650-655-8000 655-8001
Web: www.playstation.com

Take-Two Interactive Software Inc 622 Broadway 4th Fl .... New York NY 10012 646-536-2842 334-6644*
NASDAQ: TTWO ■ **Fax Area Code:* 212 ■ *Web:* www.take2games.com

Take-Two Licensing Inc 8550 Balboa Blvd .... Northridge CA 91325 818-707-7063 672-8040
Web: www.tdk-mediactive.com

THQ Inc 29903 Agoura Rd .... Agoura Hills CA 91301 818-871-5000 871-7400
NASDAQ: THQI ■ *Web:* www.thq.com

Vivendi Games Inc 6060 Center Dr 5th Fl .... Los Angeles CA 90045 310-431-4000
Web: www.sierra.com

Walt Disney Interactive 601 Circle 7 Dr .... Glendale CA 91201 818-553-5000 547-9035
TF: 800-228-0988 ■ *Web:* disney.go.com/DisneyInteractive/index.html

ZeniMax Media Inc 1370 Piccard Dr Suite 120 .... Rockville MD 20850 301-948-2200 926-8010
TF: 800-677-0700 ■ *Web:* www.zenimax.com

181-7 Internet & Communications Software

Phone Fax

@Comm Corp 2041 Pioneer Ct Suite 204 .... San Mateo CA 94403 650-375-8188 342-1139
Web: www.atcomm.com

180solutions 3600 136th Pl SE .... Bellevue WA 98006 425-279-1200 279-1199
Web: www.180solutions.com

ACE*COMM Corp 704 Quince Orchard Rd Suite 100 .... Gaithersburg MD 20878 301-721-3000 721-3001
NASDAQ: ACEC ■ *TF:* 800-989-5566 ■ *Web:* www.acecomm.com

Active Voice LLC 2033 6th Ave Suite 500 .... Seattle WA 98121 206-441-4700 441-4784
TF Sales: 877-864-8948 ■ *Web:* www.activevoice.com

Activeworlds Inc 95 Parker St .... Newburyport MA 01950 978-499-0222 499-0221
Web: www.activeworlds.com

Adaptive Micro Systems Inc 7840 N 86th St .... Milwaukee WI 53224 414-357-2020 357-2029
TF: 800-558-7022 ■ *Web:* www.ams-i.com

Akamai Technologies Inc 8 Cambridge Center .... Cambridge MA 02142 617-444-3000 444-3001
NASDAQ: AKAM ■ *TF:* 877-425-2624 ■ *Web:* www.akamai.com

Alexa Internet PO Box 29141 .... San Francisco CA 94129 415-561-6900 561-6795
Web: www.alexa.com

Amcom Software Inc 5555 W 78th St .... Minneapolis MN 55439 952-829-7445 946-7700
TF: 800-852-8935 ■ *Web:* www.amcomsoft.com

Anonymizer Inc 6755 Mira Mesa Blvd .... San Diego CA 92121 858-866-1300 866-0164
TF: 888-270-0141 ■ *Web:* www.anonymizer.com

Answers Corp 237 W 35th St Suite 1101 .... New York NY 10001 646-502-4777 502-4778
NASDAQ: ANSW ■ *Web:* www.answers.com

AnyDoc Software Inc 1 Tampa City Center Suite 800 .... Tampa FL 33602 813-222-0414 222-0018
TF: 800-775-3222 ■ *Web:* www.anydocsoftware.com

Apex Voice Communications Inc
21031 Ventura Blvd 2nd Fl .... Woodland Hills CA 91364 818-379-8400 379-8410
TF: 800-727-3970 ■ *Web:* www.apexvoice.com

Apropos Technology Inc 1 Tower Ln 28th Fl .... Oakbrook Terrace IL 60181 630-472-9600 472-9745
TF: 877-277-6767 ■ *Web:* www.apropos.com

Arel Communications & Software Inc
1200 Ashwood Pkwy Suite 550 .... Atlanta GA 30338 770-396-8105 396-1755
NASDAQ: ARLC ■ *Web:* www.arel.net

Ariba Inc 807 11th Ave .... Sunnyvale CA 94089 650-390-1000 390-1100
NASDAQ: ARBA ■ *TF:* 888-237-3131 ■ *Web:* www.ariba.com

AsiaInfo Holdings Inc 5201 Great American Pkwy Suite 429 .... Santa Clara CA 95054 408-970-9788 970-9366
NASDAQ: ASIA ■ *Web:* www.asiainfo.com

Phone Fax

AttachmateWRQ 1500 Dexter Ave N .... Seattle WA 98109 206-217-7500 217-7515
TF Sales: 800-872-2829 ■ *Web:* www.attachmate.com

Authorize.Net Corp 915 S 500 East Suite 200 .... American Fork UT 84003 801-492-6450 818-3312
TF Tech Supp: 877-447-3938 ■ *Web:* www.authorizenet.com

Automation Technology Inc 2001 Gateway Pl Suite 100 .... San Jose CA 95110 408-350-7020 350-7021
Web: www.atinet.com

Autonomy Inc One Market Plaza Spear Tower Suite 19 .... San Francisco CA 94105 415-243-9955 243-9984
Web: www.autonomy.com

Avanquest Software USA 1333 W 120th Ave Suite 314 .... Denver CO 80234 720-330-1400 450-1154*
**Fax Area Code:* 303 ■ *Web:* www.bvrp.com

AvantGo Inc 1 Sybase Dr .... Dublin CA 94568 519-883-6898 747-4971
TF: 800-792-2735 ■ *Web:* avantgo.com

Avistar Communications Corp 1875 S Grant St 10th Fl .... San Mateo CA 94402 650-525-3300 525-1360
NASDAQ: AVSR ■ *TF:* 800-803-0153 ■ *Web:* www.avistar.com

Axeda Systems Inc 25 Forbes Blvd .... Mansville MA 02035 508-337-9200 337-9201
TF: 800-700-0362 ■ *Web:* www.axeda.com

BackWeb Technologies Inc 2077 Gateway Pl Suite 500 .... San Jose CA 95110 408-933-1700 933-1800
NASDAQ: BWEB ■ *TF:* 800-863-0100 ■ *Web:* www.backweb.com

Big Sky Technologies 9325 Sky Park Ct Suite 120 .... San Diego CA 92123 858-715-5000 715-5010
TF: 800-736-2751 ■ *Web:* www.bigskytech.com

Blast Inc 220 Chatham Business Dr .... Pittsboro NC 27312 919-545-2535 542-5955
TF: 800-242-5278 ■ *Web:* www.blast.com

BuzzMetrics 770 Broadway 7th Fl .... New York NY 10003 646-253-1900
TF: 877-999-7335 ■ *Web:* www.nielsenbuzzmetrics.com

Callware Technologies Inc
2755 E Cottonwood Pkwy 4th Fl .... Salt Lake City UT 84121 801-937-6800 937-6820
TF: 800-888-4226 ■ *Web:* www.callware.com

Captaris Inc 10885 NE 4th St Suite 400 .... Bellevue WA 98004 425-455-6000 638-1500
NASDAQ: CAPA ■ *TF:* 800-443-0806 ■ *Web:* www.captaris.com

Century Software 6465 S 3000 East Suite 104 .... Salt Lake City UT 84121 801-268-3088 268-2772
TF: 800-877-3088 ■ *Web:* www.censoft.com

Certeon Inc 4 Van de Graaff Dr .... Burlington MA 01803 781-425-5200 425-5210
Web: www.certeon.com

CertifiedMail.com Inc 35 Airport Rd Suite 120 .... Morristown NJ 07960 973-455-1245 455-0750
TF: 800-672-7233 ■ *Web:* www.certifiedmail.com

Chordiant Software Inc 20400 Stevens Creek Blvd Suite 400 .... Cupertino CA 95014 408-517-6100 517-0270
NASDAQ: CHRD ■ *Web:* www.chordiant.com

ClearCommerce Corp 11921 N Mopac Expy Suite 400 .... Austin TX 78759 512-832-0132 832-8901
TF: 888-725-9345 ■ *Web:* www.clearcommerce.com

Clickmarks Inc 718 University Ave Suite 202 .... Los Gatos CA 95032 408-399-6120 395-5404
Web: www.clickmarks.com

ClickSoftware Inc 35 Corporate Dr Suite 140 .... Burlington MA 01803 781-272-5903 272-6409
NASDAQ: CKSW ■ *TF:* 888-438-3308 ■ *Web:* www.clicksoftware.com

CoCreate Software Inc 3801 Automation Way Suite 110 .... Fort Collins CO 80525 970-267-8000 267-8001
Web: www.cocreate.com

CommTouch Software Ltd 1300 Crittenden Ln Suite 103 .... Mountain View CA 94043 650-864-2000 864-2002
NASDAQ: CTCH ■ *TF:* 800-638-6824 ■ *Web:* www.commtouch.com

Comspec Digital Products Inc
2205 Bass Hollow PO Box 178 .... Jacksonville TX 75766 832-443-4487 586-7944*
**Fax Area Code:* 903 ■ *TF:* 800-490-6893 ■ *Web:* www.comspecdpi.com

Concerto Software 6 Technology Pk Dr .... Westford MA 01886 978-952-0200 952-0201
TF: 800-999-4458 ■ *Web:* www.concerto.com

Conquest Systems Inc 7617 Arlington Rd .... Bethesda MD 20814 800-719-8817 556-2454*
**Fax Area Code:* 301 ■ *TF:* 800-719-8817 ■ *Web:* www.conquestsystems.com

Continuous Computing Corp 9450 Carroll Park Dr .... San Diego CA 92121 858-882-8800 777-3388
Web: www.ccpu.com

Copernic Technologies Inc 360 rue Franquet Suite 60 .... Sainte-Foy QC G1P4N3 418-527-0528 527-1751
Web: www.copernic.com

Corillian Corp 3400 NW John Olsen Pl .... Hillsboro OR 97124 503-629-3500 617-0291
NASDAQ: CORI ■ *TF:* 800-863-6445 ■ *Web:* www.corillian.com

Cothern Computer Systems Inc 1640 Lelia Dr Suite 200 .... Jackson MS 39216 601-969-1155 969-1184
TF: 800-844-1155 ■ *Web:* www.ccslink.com

Cybernetics InfoTech Inc 15245 Shady Grove Road Suite 190 .... Rockville MD 20850 301-590-1233 590-0359
Web: www.cybit.com

CyberSource Corp 1295 Charleston Rd .... Mountain View CA 94043 650-965-6000 625-9145
NASDAQ: CYBS ■ *TF:* 800-709-7779 ■ *Web:* www.cybersource.com

Cykic Software Inc 3739 29th St .... San Diego CA 92104 619-459-8799
Web: www.cykic.com

DealerTrack Holdings Inc 1111 Marcus Ave Suite M04 .... Lake Success NY 11042 516-734-3600
NASDAQ: TRAK ■ *Web:* www.dealertrack.com

Deerfield.com 4241 Old US 27 S .... Gaylord MI 49735 989-732-8856 731-9299
TF: 800-599-8856 ■ *Web:* www.deerfield.com

Digisoft 9 E 40th St .... New York NY 10016 212-687-1810 687-1781
Web: www.digisoft.com

Digital Insight Corp 26025 Mureau Rd .... Calabasas CA 91302 818-871-0000 878-7555
NASDAQ: DGIN ■ *TF:* 888-344-4674 ■ *Web:* www.diginsite.com

Dynamic Instruments Inc 3860 Calle Fortunada .... San Diego CA 92123 858-278-4900 278-6700
TF: 800-793-3358 ■ *Web:* www.dynamicinst.com

eAcceleration Corp 1050 NE Hostmark St Suite 100-B .... Poulsbo WA 98370 360-697-9260 598-2450
TF: 800-811-1485 ■ *Web:* www.eacceleration.com

eGain Communications Corp 345 E Middlefield Rd .... Mountain View CA 94043 650-230-7500 230-7600
TF: 888-603-4246 ■ *Web:* www.egain.com

Enterprise Messaging Services 10 Mystic Ln .... Malvern PA 19355 610-701-7002 653-1070*
**Fax Area Code:* 484 ■ *TF:* 877-367-5050 ■ *Web:* www.emessages.com

Eolas Technologies 330 S Naperville Rd .... Wheaton IL 60187 630-871-3343 653-7341
Web: www.eolas.com

eSpeed Inc 110 E 59th St .... New York NY 10022 212-938-5000 829-5280
NASDAQ: ESPD ■ *Web:* www.espeed.com

EXTOL International Inc 474 N Centre St PO Box 1010 .... Pottsville PA 17901 570-628-5500 628-6983
TF: 888-334-3986 ■ *Web:* www.extol.com

Fast Search & Transfer Inc 117 Kendrick St Suite 100 .... Needham MA 02494 781-304-2400 304-2410
TF: 888-871-3839 ■ *Web:* www.fastsearch.com

FileNet an IBM Co 3565 Harbor Blvd .... Costa Mesa CA 92626 714-327-3400
NASDAQ: FILE ■ *TF:* 800-345-3638 ■ *Web:* www.filenet.com

Forgent Networks Inc 108 Wild Basin Rd .... Austin TX 78746 512-437-2700 437-2792
NASDAQ: FORG ■ *TF:* 888-323-8835 ■ *Web:* www.forgent.com

fusionOne Inc 1 Almaden Blvd 11th Fl .... San Jose CA 95113 408-282-1200 282-1233
Web: www.fusionone.com

FutureSoft Inc 12012 Wickchester Ln Suite 600 .... Houston TX 77079 281-496-9400 496-1090
TF: 800-989-8908 ■ *Web:* www.futuresoft.com

GeoTrust Inc 311 Arsenal St .... Watertown MA 02472 781-820-4100 444-3961
TF: 800-944-0492 ■ *Web:* www.geotrust.com

Grassroots Enterprise Inc
120 Montgomery St Suite 1970 .... San Francisco CA 94104 415-633-1100 633-1101
Web: www.grassroots.com

Hilgraeve Inc 115 E Elm Ave .... Monroe MI 48162 734-243-0576 243-0645
TF Sales: 800-826-2760 ■ *Web:* www.hilgraeve.com

HtmlGear.com 100 5th Ave .... Waltham MA 02451 781-370-2700 370-3415*
**Fax:* Hum Res ■ *Web:* htmlgear.lycos.com

Hyland Software Inc 28500 Clemens Rd .... Westlake OH 44145 440-788-5000 788-5100
Web: www.onbase.com

iAnywhere Solutions Inc 5777 N Meeker Ave .... Boise ID 83713 208-322-7575 327-5004
TF: 800-235-7576 ■ *Web:* www.ianywhere.com

ICQ Inc 22000 AOL Way .... Dulles VA 20166 703-265-1000
TF: 800-827-6364 ■ *Web:* www.icq.com

Idearc Media Corp 4 Clock Tower Pl Suite 300 .... Maynard MA 01754 978-298-1525 298-1535
Web: www.idearcsearch.com

Company	City	State	Zip	Phone	Fax
Imecom Group 8 Governor Wentworth Hwy *TF:* 800-329-9099 ■ *Web:* www.imecominc.com	Wolfeboro	NH	03894	603-569-0600	569-0609
InfoNow Corp 1875 Lawrence St Suite 1100 *Web:* www.infonow.com	Denver	CO	80202	303-293-0212	293-0213
Information Builders Inc 2 Penn Plaza *TF:* 800-969-4636 ■ *Web:* www.informationbuilders.com	New York	NY	10121	212-736-4433	967-6406
Infowave Software Inc 4664 Lougheed Hwy Suite 200 *TF:* 800-463-6928 ■ *Web:* www.infowave.com	Burnaby	BC	V5C5T5	604-473-3600	473-3699
IntelliNet Technologies Inc 1990 W New Haven Ave Suite 303 *TF:* 888-726-0686 ■ *Web:* www.intellinet-tech.com	Melbourne	FL	32904	321-726-0686	726-0683
IntelliReach Corp 690 Canton St *TF:* 800-219-9838 ■ *Web:* www.intellireach.com	Westwood	MA	02090	781-410-3000	407-0084
Interact Inc 1225 L St Suite 600 *TF:* 800-242-8649 ■ *Web:* www.iivip.com	Lincoln	NE	68508	402-476-8786	476-7473
Interactive Intelligence Inc 7601 Interactive Way *NASDAQ: ININ* ■ *TF:* 800-267-1364 ■ *Web:* www.inter-intelli.com	Indianapolis	IN	46278	317-872-3000	872-3000
Intershop Communications Inc 650 Townsend St Suite 285 *Web:* www.intershop.com	San Francisco	CA	94103	415-844-1500	844-3800
Interwoven Inc 160 E Tasman Dr *NASDAQ: IWOV* ■ *Web:* www.interwoven.com	San Jose	CA	95134	408-774-2000	774-2002
Intrinsyc Software International Inc 700 W Pender St 10th Fl *TF:* 800-474-7644 ■ *Web:* www.intrinsyc.com	Vancouver	BC	V6C1G8	604-801-6461	801-6417
Ion Networks Inc 120 Corporate Blvd Suite A *TF:* 800-722-8986 ■ *Web:* www.ion-networks.com	South Plainfield	NJ	07080	908-546-3900	546-3901
IONA Technologies Inc 200 West St 4th Fl *NASDAQ: IONA* ■ *TF:* 800-672-4948 ■ *Web:* www.iona.com	Waltham	MA	02451	781-902-8000	902-8001
Jabber Inc 1899 Wynkoop St Suite 600 *Web:* www.jabber.com	Denver	CO	80202	303-308-3231	308-3219
Jones Cyber Solutions Ltd 9697 E Mineral Ave *TF:* 800-525-7002 ■ *Web:* www.jonescyber.com	Englewood	CO	80112	303-784-3600	784-8928
Jones International Ltd 9697 E Mineral Ave **Fax: Hum Res* ■ *TF:* 800-525-7002 ■ *Web:* www.jones.com	Englewood	CO	80112	303-792-3111	784-8928*
KANA Software Inc 181 Constitution Dr *Web:* www.kana.com	Menlo Park	CA	94025	650-614-8300	614-8301
Keynote Systems Inc 777 Mariners Island Blvd *NASDAQ: KEYN* ■ *TF:* 888-539-7978 ■ *Web:* www.keynote.com	San Mateo	CA	94404	650-403-2400	403-5500
Knexa 1600-409 Granville St *Web:* www.knexa.com	Vancouver	BC	V6C1T2	604-682-2421	682-7576
Language Automation Inc 1670 S Amphlett Blvd Suite 214 *Web:* www.lai.com	San Mateo	CA	94402	650-571-7877	378-8542
LassoSoft LLC PO Box 33 *TF:* 888-286-7753 ■ *Web:* www.lassosoft.com	Manchester	WA	98353	954-302-3526	302-3526
LINK2GOV Corp 1 Burton Hills Blvd Suite 300 *TF:* 800-483-7072 ■ *Web:* www.link2gov.com	Nashville	TN	37215	615-297-2770	234-4376
LOGIKA Corp 3717 N Ravenswood Ave Suite 244 *Web:* www.logika.net	Chicago	IL	60613	773-529-3482	529-3483
Mark/Space Softworks 654 N Santa Cruz Ave Suite 300 *TF:* 800-799-1718 ■ *Web:* www.markspace.com	Los Gatos	CA	95030	408-293-7299	293-7298
Metric Stream 3000 Bridge Pkwy *Web:* www.zaplet.com	Redwood Shores	CA	94065	650-620-2900	632-1953
Mindbridge Software 2546 General Armistead Ave *Web:* www.mindbridge.com	Norristown	PA	19403	610-666-5262	666-5331
Mindmaker Inc 100 Century Center Ct Suite 800 *Web:* www.mindmaker.com	San Jose	CA	95112	408-467-9200	467-9202
Mirror Image Internet Inc 2 Highwood Dr *TF:* 800-353-2923 ■ *Web:* www.mirror-image.com	Tewksbury	MA	01876	781-376-1100	376-1110
Mize Houser & Co 534 S Kansas Ave Suite 700 *Web:* www.mizehouser.com	Topeka	KS	66603	785-233-0536	233-1078
Moai Technologies Inc 100 1st Ave Suite 900 *Web:* www.moai.com	Pittsburgh	PA	15222	412-454-5550	454-5555
MODCOMP Inc 1500 S Powerline Rd *TF:* 800-940-1111 ■ *Web:* www.modcomp.com	Deerfield Beach	FL	33442	954-571-4600	571-4700
Momentum Systems Ltd 41 Twosome Dr Suite 9 *TF:* 800-279-1384 ■ *Web:* www.momsys.com	Moorestown	NJ	08057	856-727-0777	273-3765
Muze Inc 304 Hudson St 8th Fl *TF:* 800-935-4848 ■ *Web:* www.muze.com	New York	NY	10013	212-824-0300	741-1246
NetDIVE Inc 41 Sutter St Suite 1142 **Fax Area Code: 843* ■ *Web:* www.netdive.com	San Francisco	CA	94104	415-378-8200	216-6843*
NetResults Corp 444 High St Suite 250 *Web:* www.netresultscorp.com	Palo Alto	CA	94301	650-473-3933	473-1492
Netrics Inc 707 State Rd Suite 212 *Web:* www.netrics.com	Princeton	NJ	08540	609-683-4002	651-4809
Netscape Communications Corp 475 Ellis St *TF Tech Supp:* 800-411-0707 ■ *Web:* www.netscape.com	Mountain View	CA	94043	650-254-1900	528-4124
NetScout Systems Inc 310 Littleton Rd *NASDAQ: NTCT* ■ *TF:* 800-999-5946 ■ *Web:* www.netscout.com	Westford	MA	01886	978-614-4000	614-4004
netVillage.com LLC 342 Main St *Web:* www.netvillage.com	Laurel	MD	20707	301-498-7797	498-8110
netViz Corp 1 CA Plaza *TF:* 800-827-1856 ■ *Web:* www.netviz.com	Islandia	NY	11749	631-342-6000	342-4854
Nexgenix Inc 320 Commerce *Web:* www.nexgenix.com	Irvine	CA	92602	714-665-6200	669-8848
NICE Systems Inc 301 Rt 17 N 10th Fl *TF:* 888-577-6423 ■ *Web:* www.nice.com	Rutherford	NJ	07070	201-964-2600	964-2610
Northcore Technologies Inc 302 East Mall Suite 300 *TF:* 888-287-7467 ■ *Web:* www.northcore.com	Etobicoke	ON	M9B6C7	416-640-0400	640-0412
Norton-Lambert Corp PO Box 4085 *Web:* www.norton-lambert.com	Santa Barbara	CA	93140	805-964-6767	683-5679
Novell Inc 30 Lafayette St *TF:* 800-262-3877 ■ *Web:* www.novell.com	Lebanon	NH	03766	603-643-1300	643-9366
Nuance Communications Inc 1 Wayside Rd *NASDAQ: NUAN* ■ *TF:* 800-654-1187 ■ *Web:* www.nuance.com	Burlington	MA	01803	781-565-5000	565-5012
OmTool Ltd 6 Riverside Dr *NASDAQ: OMTL* ■ *TF:* 800-886-7845 ■ *Web:* www.omtool.com	Andover	MA	01810	978-327-5700	659-1323
One Touch Systems Inc 40 Airport Pkwy *TF:* 888-777-9677 ■ *Web:* www.onetouch.com	San Jose	CA	95110	408-436-4600	436-4699
Open Text Corp 275 Frank Tompa Dr *NASDAQ: OTEX* ■ *TF Sales:* 888-450-2547 ■ *Web:* www.opentext.com	Waterloo	ON	N2L0A1	519-888-7111	888-0677
Open Text Corp (USA) 100 Tri-State International Pkwy 3rd Fl *TF Sales:* 800-507-5777 ■ *Web:* www.opentext.com	Lincolnshire	IL	60069	847-267-9330	267-9332
OpenCon Systems Inc 377 Hoes Ln 2nd Fl *Web:* www.opencon.com	Piscataway	NJ	08854	732-463-3131	699-0295
OpenConnect Systems Inc 2711 LBJ Fwy Suite 700 *TF:* 800-551-5881 ■ *Web:* www.oc.com	Dallas	TX	75234	972-484-5200	484-6100
OpenTV Corp 275 Sacramento St *NASDAQ: OPTV* ■ *TF:* 800-962-5000 ■ *Web:* www.opentv.com	San Francisco	CA	94111	415-962-5000	962-5300
Openwave Systems Inc 2100 Seaport Blvd *NASDAQ: OPWV* ■ *Web:* www.openwave.com	Redwood City	CA	94063	650-480-8000	480-8100
Oz Communicatons Inc 1100 de la Gauchetiere St W Suite 150 *Web:* www.oz.com	Montreal	QC	H3B2S2	514-390-1333	390-0011
Paloma Systems Inc 11250 Waples Mill Rd *Web:* www.palomasys.com	Fairfax	VA	22030	703-563-2060	591-0985
Path 1 Network Technologies Inc 6215 Ferris Sq Suite 140 *AMEX: PNO* ■ *TF:* 877-663-7284 ■ *Web:* www.path1.com	San Diego	CA	92121	858-450-4220	450-4203
PCTEL Inc 8725 W Higgins Rd Suite 400 *NASDAQ: PCTI* ■ *Web:* www.pctel.com	Chicago	IL	60631	773-243-3000	243-3049
Phoenix Technologies Ltd 915 Murphy Ranch Rd *NASDAQ: PTEC* ■ *TF:* 800-677-7305 ■ *Web:* www.phoenix.com	Milpitas	CA	95035	408-570-1000	570-1001
Planetweb Inc 300 Twin Dolphin Dr Suite 600 *Web:* www.planetweb.com	Redwood Shores	CA	94065	650-632-4356	632-4328
Powersteering Software Inc 141 Portland St *Web:* www.psteering.com	Cambridge	MA	02139	617-492-0707	492-9444
Pragmatech Software Inc 15 Trafalgar Sq *TF:* 800-401-9580 ■ *Web:* www.pragmatech.com	Nashua	NH	03063	603-249-1400	249-1401
Prescient Applied Intelligence 13355 Noel Rd Suite 1015 *TF:* 888-610-1800 ■ *Web:* www.prescient.com	Dallas	TX	75240	972-934-5500	934-5555
Propel Software Corp 1010 Rincon Cir *Web:* www.propel.com	San Jose	CA	95131	408-571-6300	577-1070
QSA ToolWorks LLC 64 W 48th St 9th Fl **Fax Area Code: 570* ■ *TF:* 800-784-7018 ■ *Web:* www.qsatoolworks.com	New York	NY	10036	516-935-9151	662-2636*
Quadbase Systems Inc 275 Saratoga Ave Suite 203 *Web:* www.quadbase.com	Santa Clara	CA	95050	408-982-0835	982-0838
Qualcomm Inc 5775 Morehouse Dr *NASDAQ: QCOM* ■ *Web:* www.qualcomm.com	San Diego	CA	92121	858-587-1121	658-2100
Quigo Technologies Inc 90 Park Ave 10th Fl **Fax Area Code: 917* ■ *TF:* 866-333-7932 ■ *Web:* www.quigo.com	New York	NY	10016	212-213-2363	213-2872*
RADVISION Inc 17-17 State Hwy 208 Suite 300 *NASDAQ: RVSN* ■ *Web:* www.radvision.com	Fair Lawn	NJ	07410	201-689-6300	689-6301
Raindance Communications Inc 1157 Century Dr *NASDAQ: RNDC* ■ *TF:* 800-878-7326 ■ *Web:* www.raindance.com	Louisville	CO	80027	303-928-2400	928-2832
Resonate Inc 2883 Junction Ave *TF:* 877-737-6628 ■ *Web:* www.resonate.com	San Jose	CA	95134	408-545-5500	545-5516
RuleSpace LLC 1925 NW AmberGlen Pkwy Suite 210 *TF:* 800-387-8373 ■ *Web:* www.rulespace.com	Beaverton	OR	97006	503-290-5100	290-5200
S4F Inc 10203-B East 61st St *TF:* 866-743-5196 ■ *Web:* www.s4f.com	Tulsa	OK	74133	918-524-1010	524-1011
Saba Software 430 Bedford St *TF:* 877-722-2101 ■ *Web:* www.saba.com	Lexington	MA	02420	781-861-7000	862-2453
Saqqara Systems Inc 3155 Kearney St Suite 220 *Web:* www.saqqara.com	Fremont	CA	94538	510-360-5361	413-0079
Security Software Systems Inc 1998 Bucktail Ln *TF:* 888-835-7278 ■ *Web:* www.securitysoft.com	Sugar Grove	IL	60554	630-466-1038	466-7678
Selectica Inc 1740 Technology Dr Suite 450 *NASDAQ: SLTC* ■ *TF:* 877-712-9560 ■ *Web:* www.selectica.com	San Jose	CA	95110	408-570-9700	570-9705
Sendmail Inc 6475 Christie Ave Suite 350 *TF:* 888-594-3150 ■ *Web:* www.sendmail.com	Emeryville	CA	94608	510-594-5400	594-5429
SER Solutions Inc 45925 Horseshoe Dr Suite 150 *TF Sales:* 800-274-5676 ■ *Web:* www.sersolutions.com	Dulles	VA	20166	703-948-5500	430-7738
SKY Mobilemedia 11975 El Camino Real Suite 300 *Web:* www.skymobilemedia.com	San Diego	CA	92130	858-259-0415	259-0417
Smith Micro Software Inc 51 Columbia St Suite 200 *NASDAQ: SMSI* ■ *TF:* 800-964-7674 ■ *Web:* www.smithmicro.com	Aliso Viejo	CA	92656	949-362-5800	362-2300
Smith Micro Software Internet & Software Solutions Div 51 Columbia Suite 200 *Web:* www.smithmicro.com	Aliso Viejo	CA	92656	949-362-5800	362-2300
SnapTrack 675 Campbell Technology Pkwy Suite 200 *Web:* www.snaptrack.com	Campbell	CA	95008	408-626-0500	626-0550
Software 602 Inc 500 Oceola Ave *TF:* 888-468-6602 ■ *Web:* www.software602.com	Jacksonville Beach	FL	32250	904-642-5400	565-6024
Soliton Inc 44 Victoria St Suite 820 *TF:* 888-327-9457 ■ *Web:* www.soliton.com	Toronto	ON	M5C1Y2	416-364-9355	364-6159
Sterling Commerce 900 Chelmsford St *TF:* 888-292-6872 ■ *Web:* www.sterlingcommerce.com	Lowell	MA	01851	978-513-6000	513-6006
SupportSoft Inc 575 Broadway *NASDAQ: SPRT* ■ *TF:* 877-493-2778 ■ *Web:* www.support.com	Redwood City	CA	94063	650-556-9440	556-1195
Surety LLC 12020 Sunrise Valley Dr Suite 250 *TF:* 800-298-3115 ■ *Web:* www.surety.com	Reston	VA	20191	571-748-5800	748-5810
SurfControl USA 5550 Scotts Valley Dr *TF:* 800-368-3366 ■ *Web:* www.surfcontrol.com	Scotts Valley	CA	95066	831-440-2500	440-2740
Sybase Inc 1 Sybase Dr *NYSE: SY* ■ *TF:* 800-879-2273 ■ *Web:* www.sybase.com	Dublin	CA	94568	925-236-5000	236-4321
Symantec Corp 20330 Stevens Creek Blvd *NASDAQ: SYMC* ■ *TF Cust Svc:* 800-441-7234 ■ *Web:* www.symantec.com	Cupertino	CA	95014	408-517-8000	517-8186
Symbian Inc 390 Bridge Pkwy Suite 201 *Web:* www.symbian.com	Redwood Shores	CA	94065	650-551-0240	551-0241
Symphony SMS 14881 Quorum Dr Suite 800 *Web:* www.symphonysms.com	Dallas	TX	75254	972-581-7300	581-7301
Syniverse Holdings Inc 8125 Highwoods Palm Way *NYSE: SVR* ■ *TF:* 800-543-6741 ■ *Web:* www.syniverse.com	Tampa	FL	33647	813-637-5000	
SyVox 1850 I-30 *TF:* 866-436-3782 ■ *Web:* www.syvox.com	Rockwall	TX	75087	972-771-1653	722-1179
Teknowledge Corp 1800 Embarcadero Rd *TF:* 800-285-0500 ■ *Web:* www.teknowledge.com	Palo Alto	CA	94303	650-424-0500	493-2645
Telogy Networks 20450 Century Blvd *Web:* www.telogy.com	Germantown	MD	20874	301-515-8580	515-7954
Tenebril Inc 959 Concord St *TF:* 800-722-7770 ■ *Web:* www.tenebril.com	Framingham	MA	01701	508-879-6994	879-0042
Timecruiser Computing Corp 9 Law Dr 2rd Fl *TF:* 877-450-9482 ■ *Web:* www.timecruiser.com	Fairfield	NJ	07004	973-244-7856	244-7859
Transend Corp 225 Emerson St *Web:* www.transend.com	Palo Alto	CA	94301	650-324-5370	324-5377
Transware 7901 Stoneridge Dr Suite 500 *TF:* 800-205-8877 ■ *Web:* www.transware.com	Pleasanton	CA	94588	925-734-3000	224-8642
Tumbleweed Communications Corp 700 Saginaw Dr *NASDAQ: TMWD* ■ *TF:* 800-696-1978 ■ *Web:* www.tumbleweed.com	Redwood City	CA	94063	650-216-2000	216-2001
UmeVoice Inc 20C Pimentel Ct Suite 1 *TF:* 888-230-3300 ■ *Web:* www.umevoice.com	Novato	CA	94949	415-883-1500	883-1711
UNET 80 E 11th St *Web:* www.unet.net	New York	NY	10003	212-777-5463	777-5534
Unify Corp 2101 Arena Blvd Suite 100 *TF:* 800-248-6439 ■ *Web:* www.unify.com	Sacramento	CA	95834	916-928-6400	928-6404
Vendio Services Inc 2800 Campus Dr Suite 150 *Web:* www.vendio.com	San Mateo	CA	94403	650-293-3500	
Verint Systems Inc 9 Polito Ave 9th Fl *TF:* 888-637-2661 ■ *Web:* www.verint.com	Lyndhurst	NJ	07071	201-507-8800	507-5554
Vertical Communications Inc 1 Memorial Dr 10th Fl *TF Sales:* 800-914-9985 ■ *Web:* www.vertical.com	Cambridge	MA	02142	617-354-0600	452-9158
VillageEDOCS Inc 1401 N Tustin Ave Suite 230 *TF:* 800-866-0883 ■ *Web:* www.villageedocs.com	Santa Ana	CA	92705	714-734-1030	734-1040
Visto Corp 101 Redwood Shores Pkwy 4th Fl *Web:* www.visto.com	Redwood Shores	CA	94065	650-486-6000	622-9591
VoiceWorld Inc 383 Kingston Ave Suite 257 *TF:* 800-283-4759 ■ *Web:* www.voiceworld.com	Brooklyn	NY	11213	718-252-3153	467-9899
Vovici Corp 45365 Vintage Park Plaza Suite 250 **Fax Area Code: 703* ■ *TF:* 800-787-8755 ■ *Web:* www.vovici.com	Dulles	VA	20166	571-521-0592	783-0069*
Voxware Inc 168 Franklin Corner Rd *Web:* www.voxware.com	Lawrenceville	NJ	08648	609-514-4100	514-4101
Wave Three Software Inc 1770 N Research Pkwy Suite 140 *TF:* 888-408-8422 ■ *Web:* www.wave3software.com	Logan	UT	84341	435-787-0555	787-0516

Internet & Communications Software (Cont'd)

Phone | Fax

WaveLink Corp 1011 Western Ave Suite 601 ... Seattle WA 98104 206-274-4280 652-2329
TF Tech Supp: 888-699-9283 ■ *Web:* www.wavelink.com

WebBalanced Technologies LLC 6206 Discount Dr ... Fort Wayne IN 46818 866-331-3465
Web: www.webbalanced.com

WebEx Communications Inc 3979 Freedom Cir ... Santa Clara CA 95054 408-435-7000 435-7004
NASDAQ: WEBX ■ *TF:* 877-509-3239 ■ *Web:* www.webex.com

Websense Inc 10240 Sorrento Valley Rd ... San Diego CA 92121 858-320-8000 458-2950
NASDAQ: WBSN ■ *TF:* 800-723-1166 ■ *Web:* www.websense.com

Wexcel Inc 10 S Riverside Plaza Suite 1800 ... Chicago IL 60606 312-347-0955 347-0908
Web: www.wexcel.com

Wind River Systems Inc 500 Wind River Way ... Alameda CA 94501 510-748-4100 749-2010
NASDAQ: WIND ■ *TF:* 800-545-9463 ■ *Web:* www.windriver.com

Witness Systems Inc 300 Colonial Center Pkwy Suite 600 ... Roswell GA 30076 770-754-1900 754-1888
NASDAQ: WITS ■ *TF:* 888-394-8637 ■ *Web:* www.witness.com

WorldFlash Software Inc 3853 Marcasel Ave ... Los Angeles CA 90066 310-745-0632
Web: www.worldflash.com

XAP Corp 3534 Hayden Ave ... Culver City CA 90232 310-842-9800 842-9898
Web: www.xap.com

Xtend Communications Corp 171 Madison Ave ... New York NY 10016 212-951-7600 951-7683
TF Cust Svc: 800-342-5910 ■ *Web:* www.xtend.com

YellowBrix Inc 44 Canal Center Plaza Suite 110 ... Alexandria VA 22314 703-548-3300 548-9151
TF: 888-325-9366 ■ *Web:* www.yellowbrix.com

Yodlee Inc 3600 Bridge Pkwy Suite 200 ... Redwood City CA 94065 650-980-3600 980-3602
Web: corporate.yodlee.com

Zone Alarm 800 Bridge Pkwy ... Redwood City CA 94065 415-633-4500 633-4501
TF: 877-966-5221 ■ *Web:* www.zonealarm.com

181-8 Multimedia & Design Software

Phone | Fax

3D Systems Inc 333 Three D Systems Circle ... Rock Hill SC 29730 803-326-3900 324-4311
NASDAQ: TDSC ■ *TF:* 800-653-1993 ■ *Web:* www.3dsystems.com

ACD Systems International Inc 200-1312 Blanshard St ... Victoria BC V8W2J1 250-419-6700 419-6742
TSX: ASA ■ *TF:* 800-579-5309 ■ *Web:* www.acdsystems.com

Adobe Systems Inc 345 Park Ave ... San Jose CA 95110 408-536-6000 537-6000
NASDAQ: ADBE ■ *TF:* 800-833-6687 ■ *Web:* www.adobe.com

Animation Factory Inc 2000 W 42nd St Suite C ... Sioux Falls SD 57105 605-339-4722 335-1554
TF: 800-525-2475 ■ *Web:* www.animationfactory.com

Apple Inc 1 Infinite Loop ... Cupertino CA 95014 408-996-1010 996-0275*
NASDAQ: AAPL ■ **Fax:* Mail Rm ■ *TF Cust Svc:* 800-275-2273 ■ *Web:* www.apple.com

Arts & Letters Corp 2201 Midway Rd Suite 106 ... Carolton TX 75006 972-661-8960 934-2333
TF: 888-853-9292 ■ *Web:* www.arts-letters.com

Auto FX Software 141 Village St Suite 2 ... Birmingham AL 35242 205-980-0056 980-1121
TF: 800-839-2008 ■ *Web:* www.autofx.com

Autodesk 210 King St E ... Toronto ON M5A1J7 416-362-9181 369-6140
TF: 800-447-2542 ■ *Web:* usa.autodesk.com

Autodessys Inc 2011 Riverside Dr ... Columbus OH 43221 614-488-8838 488-0848
Web: www.formz.com

Avid Technology Inc 1 Park W Metropolitan Technology Park ... Tewksbury MA 01876 978-640-6789 640-3366
NASDAQ: AVID ■ *TF:* 800-949-2843 ■ *Web:* www.avid.com

Bitstream Inc 245 1st St ... Cambridge MA 02142 617-497-6222 868-0784
NASDAQ: BITS ■ *TF:* 800-522-3668 ■ *Web:* www.bitstream.com

Blue Zone Inc 329 Railway St 4th Fl ... Vancouver BC V6A1A4 604-685-4310 685-4391
Web: www.bluezone.net

Brilliant Digital Entertainment Inc
14011 Ventura Blvd Suite 501 ... Sherman Oaks CA 91423 818-386-2180 615-0995
Web: www.brilliantdigital.com

Caligari Corp 1959 Landings Dr ... Mountain View CA 94043 650-390-9600 390-9755
TF: 800-351-7620 ■ *Web:* www.caligari.com

Chyron Corp 5 Hub Dr ... Melville NY 11747 631-845-2000 845-3895*
**Fax:* Sales ■ *Web:* www.chyron.com

Concurrent 4375 River Green Pkwy Suite 100 ... Duluth GA 30096 678-258-4000 258-4300
NASDAQ: CCUR ■ *TF:* 877-978-7363 ■ *Web:* www.ccur.com

Corel Corp 1600 Carling Ave ... Ottawa ON K1Z8R7 613-728-8200 761-9176
TF Orders: 800-772-6735 ■ *Web:* www.corel.ca

cVideo Inc 7745 Business Park Ave ... San Diego CA 92131 858-790-7200 790-7210
TF Tech Supp: 800-724-8562 ■ *Web:* www.cvideo.com

Cybernetics InfoTech Inc 15245 Shady Grove Road Suite 190 ... Rockville MD 20850 301-590-1233 590-0359
Web: www.cybit.com

DeLorme 2 DeLorme Dr ... Yarmouth ME 04096 207-846-7000 575-2244*
**Fax Area Code:* 800 ■ **Fax:* Sales ■ *TF Sales:* 800-452-5931 ■ *Web:* www.delorme.com

EI Technology Group LLC 10860 Gulfdale ... San Antonio TX 78216 210-377-2525 579-6668
Web: www.eitechnologygroup.com

Equilibrium Inc 3 Harbor Dr ... Sausalito CA 94965 415-332-4343 331-8374
Web: www.equilibrium.com

eWorkplace Solutions Inc
24461 Ridge Route Dr Suite 210 ... Laguna Hills CA 92653 949-583-1646 598-8144
Web: www.eworkplace.com

Fonthead Design 3210 Lansdowne Dr ... Wilmington DE 19810 302-479-7922 806-1006*
**Fax Area Code:* 866 ■ *Web:* www.fonthead.com

Global 360 2911 Turtle Creek Blvd Suite 1100 ... Dallas TX 75219 214-520-1660 219-0476
Web: www.global360.com/us/

HydroCAD Software Solutions LLC
216 Chocorua Mountain Hwy ... Chocorua NH 03817 603-323-8666 323-7467
TF: 800-927-7246 ■ *Web:* www.hydrocad.net

Image Labs International 2304 N 7th Ave Suite P ... Bozeman MT 59715 406-585-7225 586-0641
TF: 800-785-5995 ■ *Web:* www.imagelabs.com

Imaging Technologies Corp (ITEC)
9449 Balboa Ave Suite 211 ... San Diego CA 92123 858-277-5300 277-3448
Web: www.itec.net

Infowave Software Inc 4664 Lougheed Hwy Suite 200 ... Burnaby BC V5C5T5 604-473-3600 473-3699
TF: 800-463-6928 ■ *Web:* www.infowave.com

Inmagic Inc 200 Unicorn Pk Dr 4th Fl ... Woburn MA 01801 781-938-4442 938-4446
TF Sales: 800-229-8398 ■ *Web:* www.inmagic.com

Innovatv 12730 High Bluff Dr Suite 120 ... San Diego CA 92130 858-259-4120 259-4104

International Microcomputer Software Inc
100 Rowland Way Suite 300 ... Novato CA 94945 415-878-4000 897-2544
TF: 800-833-8082 ■ *Web:* www.imsisoft.com

ITEC (Imaging Technologies Corp)
9449 Balboa Ave Suite 211 ... San Diego CA 92123 858-277-5300 277-3448
Web: www.itec.net

Kofax Image Products 16245 Laguna Canyon Rd ... Irvine CA 92618 949-727-1733 727-3144
Web: www.kofax.com

La Cie Ltd 22985 NW Evergreen Pkwy ... Hillsboro OR 97124 503-844-4500 844-4508*
**Fax:* Mktg ■ *Web:* www.lacie.com

Liquid Digital Media Inc 999 Main St ... Redwood City CA 94063 650-549-2000 549-2001
TF: 800-222-8132 ■ *Web:* www.liquidaudio.com

MapFrame Corp 5420 LBJ Fwy Suite 1250 ... Dallas TX 75240 214-741-2264 741-2283
Web: www.mapframe.com

MapInfo Corp 1 Global View ... Troy NY 12180 518-285-6000 285-7033
NASDAQ: MAPS ■ *TF:* 800-327-8627 ■ *Web:* www.mapinfo.com

Media 100 Inc 260 Cedar Hill St ... Marlborough MA 01752 703-462-1640 481-8627*
**Fax Area Code:* 508 ■ *TF:* 800-922-3220 ■ *Web:* www.media100.com

Phone | Fax

MicroVision Development Inc 5541 Fermi Ct Suite 120 ... Carlsbad CA 92008 760-438-7781 438-7406
TF: 800-998-4555 ■ *Web:* www.mvd.com

Minds-Eye-View Inc 48 Western Ave ... Cohoes NY 12047 518-237-1975
NASDAQ: IPIX ■ *Web:* www.ipix.com

Mitek Systems Inc 8911 Balboa Ave Suite B ... San Diego CA 92123 858-503-7810 503-7820
Web: www.miteksys.com

Monotype Imaging Inc 500 Unicorn Park Dr ... Woburn MA 01801 781-970-6000 970-6001
Web: www.monotypeimaging.com

Nemetschek North America 7150 Riverwood Dr ... Columbia MD 21046 410-290-5114 290-8050
TF: 888-646-4223 ■ *Web:* www.nemetschek.net

NewSoft America Inc 500 Yosemite Dr Suite 100 ... Milpitas CA 95035 408-503-1200 503-1201
Web: www.newsoftinc.com

NewTek Inc 5131 Beckwith Blvd ... San Antonio TX 78249 210-370-8000 370-8001
TF Cust Svc: 800-862-7837 ■ *Web:* www.newtek.com

Octopus Media LLC 259 W 30th St ... New York NY 10001 212-967-5191 967-5199
Web: www.hypercd.com

On2 Technologies Inc 21 Corporate Dr Suite 103 ... Clifton Park NY 12065 518-348-0099 348-2098
AMEX: ONT ■ *Web:* www.on2.com

Onyx Computing 10 Avon St ... Cambridge MA 02138 617-876-3876 868-8033
Web: www.onyxtree.com

Optio Software Inc
3015 Windward Plaza Windward Fairways 2 ... Alpharetta GA 30005 770-576-3500 576-3699
Web: www.optiosoftware.com

Overwatch Geospatial Operations 103A Carpenter Dr ... Sterling VA 20164 703-437-7651 437-0039
Web: www.geospatial.overwatch.com

Overwatch Systems - Boston Operations
400 W Cummings Park Suite 3050 ... Woburn MA 01801 781-937-9800 937-9877
TF: 800-937-6881 ■ *Web:* www.paragon.com

PaceWorks Inc 16780 Lark Ave ... Los Gatos CA 95032 408-354-5711 884-2281
Web: www.paceworks.com

Patton & Patton Software Corp 1796 W Wimbledon Way ... Oro Valley AZ 85737 520-888-6500 888-2937
TF: 800-525-0082 ■ *Web:* www.patton-patton.com

PC/Nametag 124 Horizon Dr ... Verona WI 53593 877-626-3824 233-9787*
**Fax Area Code:* 800 ■ *TF:* 800-233-9767 ■ *Web:* www.pcnametag.com

Peerless Systems Corp 2381 Rosecrans Ave ... El Segundo CA 90245 310-536-0908 536-0058
NASDAQ: PRLS ■ *TF:* 800-362-5738 ■ *Web:* www.peerless.com

Pegasus Imaging Corp 4001 N Riverside Dr ... Tampa FL 33603 813-875-7575 875-7705
TF Sales: 800-875-7009 ■ *Web:* www.jpg.com

Prediction Systems Inc 309 Morris Ave Suite G ... Spring Lake NJ 07762 732-449-6800 449-0897
Web: www.predictsys.com

Presagis 1301 W George Bush Freeway Suite 120 ... Richardson TX 75080 972-943-2400 467-4563*
**Fax Area Code:* 469 ■ *TF:* 800-361-6424 ■ *Web:* www.presagis.com

Pulse Entertainment Inc 900 Kearny St ... San Francisco CA 94133 415-348-4000 348-4001
Web: www.pulseentertainment.com

Quark Inc 1800 Grant St ... Denver CO 80203 303-894-8888 894-3399
TF Cust Svc: 800-676-4575 ■ *Web:* www.quark.com

RealNetworks Inc 2601 Elliott Ave Suite 1000 ... Seattle WA 98121 206-674-2700 674-2699
NASDAQ: RNWK ■ *TF Cust Svc:* 888-768-3248 ■ *Web:* www.realnetworks.com

Scan-Optics Inc 169 Progress Dr ... Manchester CT 06043 860-645-7878 645-7995
TF: 800-543-8681 ■ *Web:* www.scanoptics.com

Sigma Design 5521 Jackson St ... Alexandria LA 71303 318-449-9900 449-9901
TF Sales: 888-990-0900 ■ *Web:* www.arriscad.com

Silicon Graphics Inc (SGI) 1140 E Argues Ave ... Sunnyvale CA 94085 650-960-1980 933-0908
Web: www.sgi.com

Skywire Software 2401 Internet Blvd Suite 201 ... Frisco TX 75034 972-377-1110 377-1109
TF: 800-735-6620 ■ *Web:* www.skywiresoftware.com

SoftPress Systems Ltd 3020 Bridgeway Suite 408 ... Sausalito CA 94965 415-331-4820 331-4824
TF: 800-853-6454 ■ *Web:* www.softpress.com

Sonic Solutions 101 Rowland Way ... Novato CA 94945 415-893-8000 893-8008
NASDAQ: SNIC ■ *TF:* 888-766-4248 ■ *Web:* www.sonic.com

Strata Inc 3013 Santa Clara Dr ... Santa Clara UT 84765 435-628-5218 628-9756
TF Sales: 800-678-7282 ■ *Web:* www.strata.com

Superscape Inc 131 Calle Iglesia Suite 200 ... San Clemente CA 92672 800-965-7411 940-2841*
**Fax Area Code:* 949 ■ *Web:* www.superscape.com

TechSmith Corp 2405 Woodlake Dr ... Okemos MI 48864 517-381-2300 381-2336
TF: 800-517-3001 ■ *Web:* www.techsmith.com

think3 Inc 7723 Tylers Place Blvd Suite 106 ... West Chester OH 45069 800-323-6770 263-6777*
**Fax Area Code:* 513 ■ *TF:* 800-323-6770 ■ *Web:* www.think3.com

Three D Graphics Inc 11340 W Olympic Blvd Suite 352 ... Los Angeles CA 90064 310-231-3330 231-3303
TF: 800-913-0008 ■ *Web:* www.threedgraphics.com

URW America Inc 93 Canaan Back Rd ... Barrington NH 03825 603-664-2130 664-2295

Videotex Systems Inc 10255 Miller Rd ... Dallas TX 75238 972-231-9200 231-2420
TF: 800-888-4336 ■ *Web:* www.videotexsystems.com

Viewpoint Corp 498 7th Ave 18th Fl ... New York NY 10018 212-201-0800 201-0801
NASDAQ: VWPT ■ *TF:* 866-843-9764 ■ *Web:* www.viewpoint.com

Virage Inc 1 Market St Spear Tower 19th Fl ... San Francisco CA 94105 415-243-9955 243-9984*
**Fax Area Code:* 650 ■ *Web:* www.virage.com

Worlds.com Inc 11 Royal Rd ... Brookline MA 02445 617-725-8900 975-3888
Web: www.worlds.com

Xaos Tools Inc 582 San Luis Rd ... Berkeley CA 94707 510-525-5465 527-9217
TF: 800-833-9267 ■ *Web:* www.xaostools.com

XyEnterprise 101 Edgewater Dr ... Wakefield MA 01880 781-756-4400 756-4300
TF: 800-925-1269 ■ *Web:* www.xyenterprise.com

XyEnterprise 101 Edgewater Dr ... Wakefield MA 01880 781-756-4400 756-4300
TF: 800-925-1269 ■ *Web:* www.xyenterprise.com

181-9 Personal Software

Phone | Fax

Actioneer Inc 56 John F Kennedy St 3rd Fl ... Cambridge MA 02138 617-864-1400 864-1401
Web: www.actioneer.com

Avery Dennison Corp 150 N Orange Grove Blvd ... Pasadena CA 91103 626-304-2000 304-2192
NYSE: AVY ■ *TF Cust Svc:* 800-252-8379 ■ *Web:* www.averydennison.com

Block Financial Corp 10 Fawcett St 1st Fl ... Cambridge MA 02138 617-491-1800 491-9981
Web: www.blocksoft.com

Corel Corp 1600 Carling Ave ... Ottawa ON K1Z8R7 613-728-8200 761-9176
TF Orders: 800-772-6735 ■ *Web:* www.corel.ca

Cosmi Corp 1351 Charles Willard St ... Carson CA 90746 310-603-5800 886-3500
Web: www.cosmi.com

Deep River Interactive 7 Custom House St 2nd Fl ... Portland ME 04101 207-775-6405 775-6408
Web: www.cowlesdeepriver.com

Equis International 90 S 400 West Suite 620 ... Salt Lake City UT 84101 801-265-9996 265-3999
TF Sales: 800-882-3040 ■ *Web:* www.equis.com

HowardSoft 7852 Ivanhoe Ave ... La Jolla CA 92037 858-454-0121 454-7559
Web: www.howardsoft.com

Intuit Inc 2632 Marine Way PO Box 7850 ... Mountain View CA 94039 650-944-6000 944-2788*
NASDAQ: INTU ■ **Fax:* Hum Res ■ *TF Cust Svc:* 800-446-8848 ■ *Web:* www.intuit.com

Mark of the Unicorn Inc 1280 Massachusetts Ave ... Cambridge MA 02138 617-576-2760 576-3609
Web: www.motu.com

Micro Logic Corp 666 Godwin Ave ... Midland Park NJ 07432 201-447-6991 447-6921
Web: www.miclog.com

Microsoft Corp 1 Microsoft Way ... Redmond WA 98052 425-882-8080 936-7329
NASDAQ: MSFT ■ *Web:* www.microsoft.com

Musicam USA 670 N Beers St Bldg 4 ... Holmdel NJ 07733 732-739-5600 739-1818
Web: www.musicamusa.com

Company	City	State	Zip	Phone	Fax
Nolo.com 950 Parker St	Berkeley	CA	94710	510-549-1976	548-5902
TF Cust Svc: 800-728-3555 ■ *Web:* www.nolo.com					
PhotoSpin Inc 100 Oceangate Suite 1200	Long Beach	CA	90802	562-628-5551	628-5556
TF: 888-246-1313 ■ *Web:* www.photospin.com					
Quicken 2632 Marine Way PO Box 7850	Mountain View	CA	94039	650-944-6000	944-2788*
NASDAQ: INTU ■ **Fax:* Hum Res ■ *TF Cust Svc:* 800-446-8848 ■ *Web:* www.intuit.com					
Radialpoint 2050 Bleury St Suite 300	Montreal	QC	H3A2J5	514-286-2636	286-0558
TF: 866-286-2636 ■ *Web:* www.radialpoint.com					
Smyth Systems Inc 101 Greenwood Ave	Jenkintown	PA	19046	800-767-6984	887-9871*
**Fax Area Code:* 215 ■ *TF:* 800-767-6984 ■ *Web:* www.smythsystems.com					
Sony Creative Software 1617 Sherman Ave	Madison	WI	53704	608-256-3133	250-1745
TF: 800-577-6642 ■ *Web:* www.sonycreativesoftware.com					
Stevens Creek Software LLC PO Box 2126	Cupertino	CA	95015	408-725-0424	366-1954
TF: 800-823-4279 ■ *Web:* www.stevenscreek.com					
Symantec Corp 20330 Stevens Creek Blvd	Cupertino	CA	95014	408-517-8000	517-8186
NASDAQ: SYMC ■ *TF Cust Svc:* 800-441-7234 ■ *Web:* www.symantec.com					

181-10 Professional Software (Industry-Specific)

Companies listed here manufacture software designed for specific professions or business sectors (i.e., architecture, banking, investment, physical sciences, real estate, etc.).

Company	City	State	Zip	Phone	Fax
3M Manufacturing & Industry Solutions 3M Ctr	Saint Paul	MN	55144	651-733-1110	733-9973
TF: 888-364-3577 ■ *Web:* www.3m.com/US/mfg_industrial					
a4 Health Systems 5501 Dillard Dr	Cary	NC	27511	919-851-6177	851-5991
Web: www.a4healthsys.com					
Access International Group Inc 248 Columbia Tpk	Florham Park	NJ	07932	973-360-0750	360-0710
Web: www.accessig.com					
ACE*COMM Corp 704 Quince Orchard Rd Suite 100	Gaithersburg	MD	20878	301-721-3000	721-3001
NASDAQ: ACEC ■ *TF:* 800-989-5566 ■ *Web:* www.acecomm.com					
Activant Solutions Inc 804 Las Cimas Pkwy	Austin	TX	78746	512-328-2300	278-5005
TF: 800-678-5266 ■ *Web:* www.activant.com					
Adacel Systems Inc 6200 Lee Vista Blvd	Orlando	FL	32822	407-581-1560	581-1581
Web: www.adacelinc.com					
Advantage Credit International 15 W Strong St Suite 20A	Pensacola	FL	32501	850-470-9336	600-2508*
**Fax Area Code:* 800 ■ *TF:* 800-600-2510 ■ *Web:* www.advantagecredit.com					
Affinity Technology Group Inc 1122 Lady St Suite 1145	Columbia	SC	29201	803-758-2511	758-2560
Web: www.affi.net					
AGRIS Corp 1600 N Lorraine St	Hutchinson	KS	67501	620-669-9811	694-4450
TF: 800-795-7995 ■ *Web:* www.agris.com					
Algorithmics Inc 185 Spadina Ave	Toronto	ON	M5T2C6	416-217-1500	971-6100
Web: www.algorithmics.com					
Allscripts Healthcare Solutions 2401 Commerce Ave	Libertyville	IL	60048	847-680-3515	680-3573
NASDAQ: MDRX ■ *TF:* 800-654-0889 ■ *Web:* www.allscripts.com					
Alogent Corp 4005 Windward Plaza 2nd Fl	Alpharetta	GA	30005	770-752-6400	752-6500
TF: 888-333-6030 ■ *Web:* www.alogent.com					
Alternative System Concepts Inc 22 Haverhill Rd	Windham	NH	03087	603-437-2234	437-2722
Web: www.ascinc.com					
Amdocs Ltd 1390 Timberlake Manor Pkwy	Chesterfield	MO	63017	314-212-7000	212-7500
NYSE: DOX ■ *Web:* www.amdocs.com					
AMICAS Inc 239 Ethan Allen Hwy	Ridgefield	CT	06877	203-438-3654	438-6741
NASDAQ: AMCS ■ *TF:* 800-278-0037 ■ *Web:* www.amicas.com					
AMS Services Inc 3 Waterside Crossing	Windsor	CT	06095	860-602-6000	602-6006*
**Fax:* PR ■ *TF Sales:* 800-444-4813 ■ *Web:* www.ams-services.com					
Anchor Computer Inc 1900 New Hwy	Farmingdale	NY	11735	631-293-6100	293-0891
TF: 800-728-6262 ■ *Web:* www.anchorcomputer.com					
Applied Information Management Sciences Inc PO Box 2970	Monroe	LA	71207	318-323-2467	322-3472
TF: 800-729-2467 ■ *Web:* www.aims1.com					
ARI Network Services Inc 11425 W Lake Pk Dr Suite 900	Milwaukee	WI	53224	414-278-7676	283-4357
TF: 800-233-6997 ■ *Web:* www.arinet.com					
ASI DataMyte Inc 2800 Campus Dr Suite 60	Plymouth	MN	55441	763-553-1040	553-1041
TF: 800-207-5631 ■ *Web:* www.asidatamyte.com					
Aspyra Inc 26115-A Mureau Rd	Calabasas	CA	91302	818-880-6700	880-4398
AMEX: APY ■ *TF:* 800-437-9000 ■ *Web:* www.aspyra.com					
Atex Media Command Inc 24 Crosby Dr	Bedford	MA	01730	781-275-2323	266-1654
TF: 800-872-2839 ■ *Web:* www.atex.com					
Audiotel Corp 15510 Wright Bros Dr	Addison	TX	75001	972-279-4486	239-4511
TF: 800-854-6861 ■ *Web:* www.audiotel.com					
Automated Systems Inc 3900 W 12th St	Sioux Falls	SD	57107	605-335-3636	332-7302
Avicis Inc 21670 Ridgetop Cir	Sterling	VA	20166	703-480-3000	450-7767
TF: 888-591-9985 ■ *Web:* www.avicis.com					
BancTec Inc 4435 Spring Valley Rd	Dallas	TX	75244	972-960-1666	579-6448
TF: 800-226-2832 ■ *Web:* www.banctec.com					
Banta Integrated Media - Cambridge Inc					
150 Cambridge Park Dr	Cambridge	MA	02140	617-914-3100	914-3300
Barra Inc 2100 Milvia St	Berkeley	CA	94704	510-548-5442	548-4374
Web: www.barra.com					
BatchMaster Software Inc					
24461 Ridge Route Dr Suite 210	Laguna Hills	CA	92653	949-583-1646	598-8144
TF: 800-999-5711 ■ *Web:* www.batchmaster.com					
BNA Software Div Tax Management Inc 1250 23rd St NW	Washington	DC	20037	202-728-7962	728-7964
TF: 800-424-2938 ■ *Web:* www.bnasoftware.com					
BNS Co 200 Frenchtown Rd Precision Pk	North Kingstown	RI	02852	401-886-2000	886-2762
TF: 800-283-3600					
Brodart Co 500 Arch St	Williamsport	PA	17701	570-326-2461	326-6769
TF: 800-233-8467 ■ *Web:* www.brodart.com					
C & S Marketing 10360 Old Placerville Rd Suite 100	Sacramento	CA	95827	916-362-9609	455-3851
TF: 888-288-2009 ■ *Web:* www.csmarketing.net					
C-Solutions Inc 1900 Folsom St Suite 205	Boulder	CO	80302	303-786-9461	786-9469
Web: www.gmsworks.com					
CACI MTL Systems Inc 3481 Dayton-Xenia Rd	Dayton	OH	45432	937-426-3111	426-8301
Web: www.caci.com/mtl/					
CAM Commerce Solutions Inc					
17075 Newhope St Suite A	Fountain Valley	CA	92708	714-241-9241	241-9893
NASDAQ: CADA ■ *TF:* 800-726-3282 ■ *Web:* www.camcommerce.com					
Capital Management Sciences 2901 28th St Suite 300	Santa Monica	CA	90405	310-479-9715	479-6333
Capital Technology Information Services Inc					
1 Research Ct Suite 200	Rockville	MD	20850	301-948-3033	948-2242
Web: www.ctisinc.com					
CareCentric Inc 2625 Cumberland Pkwy Suite 310	Atlanta	GA	30339	678-264-4400	384-1650*
**Fax Area Code:* 770 ■ *TF Sales:* 800-254-9872 ■ *Web:* www.carecentric.com					
Cash Technologies Inc 1434 W 11th St	Los Angeles	CA	90015	213-745-2000	745-2005
AMEX: TQ ■ *Web:* www.cashtechnologies.com					
Castek Software Factory Inc 438 University Ave Suite 700	Toronto	ON	M5G2K8	416-777-2550	777-2551
TF: 866-922-7835 ■ *Web:* www.castek.com					
Catalyst International Inc 8989 N Deerwood Dr	Milwaukee	WI	53223	414-362-6800	377-6263*
**Fax Area Code:* 262 ■ *TF:* 800-236-4600 ■ *Web:* www.catalystwms.com					
Cedara Software Corp 6509 Airport Rd	Mississauga	ON	L4V1S7	905-672-2100	672-2307
TF: 800-724-5970 ■ *Web:* www.cedara.com					
Cerner DHT Inc 2800 Rockcreek Pkwy	Kansas City	MO	64117	816-221-1024	
TF: 866-221-8877					
CEVA Inc 2033 Gateway Pl Suite 150	San Jose	CA	95110	408-514-2900	514-2995
NASDAQ: CEVA ■ *Web:* www.parthusceva.com					
Charles River Development Inc					
7 New England Executive Park	Burlington	MA	01803	781-238-0099	238-0088
Web: www.crd.com					
Circa Information Technologies Inc					
12001 Woodruff Ave Suite H	Downey	CA	90241	562-803-1594	803-5898
TF: 877-992-4722 ■ *Web:* www.circausa.com					
City Photo Group 2635 Hampton Ave	Saint Louis	MO	63139	314-645-9999	645-7476
Web: www.cityphoto.com					
CliniComp International 9655 Towne Ctr Dr	San Diego	CA	92121	858-546-8202	546-1801
TF: 800-350-8202 ■ *Web:* www.clinicomp.com					
Cobalt Group Inc 2200 1st Ave S Suite 400	Seattle	WA	98134	206-269-6363	269-6350
TF: 800-909-8244 ■ *Web:* www.cobaltgroup.com					
Coconut Code Inc 673 S Federal Hwy	Deerfield Beach	FL	33441	954-481-9331	481-9360
CodeCorrect Inc 1200 Chesterly Dr Suite 260	Yakima	WA	98902	509-453-0400	
TF: 877-937-3600 ■ *Web:* www.codecorrect.com/home					
Command Alkon Inc 1800 International Park Dr Suite 400	Birmingham	AL	35243	205-879-3282	870-1405
TF: 800-624-1872 ■ *Web:* www.commandalkon.com					
Commerx Inc 555 11th Ave SW Suite 200	Calgary	AB	T2R1P6	403-301-3884	294-1664
Web: www.commerx.com					
Compumedics USA Ltd 7850 Paseo del Norte Suite 101	El Paso	TX	79912	915-845-5600	845-0355
TF: 877-717-3975 ■ *Web:* www.compumedics.com					
Computac Inc 162 N Main St	West Lebanon	NH	03784	603-298-5721	298-6189
Web: www.computac.com					
Computer Sciences Corp Financial Services Group					
2100 E Grand Ave	El Segundo	CA	90245	310-615-0311	643-6185
Web: www.csc-fs.com					
Construction Software Technologies Inc DBA IsqFt					
4430 Carver Woods Dr	Cincinnati	OH	45242	513-645-8004	645-8005
Web: www.isqft.com					
Construction Systems Software Inc 494 Covered Bridge	Schertz	TX	78154	210-979-6494	979-0007
TF: 800-979-6494					
Continental Computer Corp 2200 East Matthews Ave	Jonesboro	AR	72401	870-932-0081	931-1273
TF: 800-874-1413 ■ *Web:* www.continentalcomputers.com					
CoStar Group Inc 2 Bethesda Metro Ctr 10th Fl	Bethesda	MD	20814	301-215-8300	218-2444
NASDAQ: CSGP ■ *Web:* www.costar.com					
CryptoLogic Inc 55 St Claire Ave W 3rd Fl	Toronto	ON	M4V2Y7	416-545-1455	545-1454
NASDAQ: CRYP ■ *Web:* www.cryptologic.com					
CSG Systems International Inc					
7887 E Belleview Ave Suite 1000	Englewood	CO	80111	303-804-4000	796-2872
NASDAQ: CSGS ■ *TF:* 800-366-2744 ■ *Web:* www.csgsystems.com					
CSSC Inc 130 Campus Dr	Edison	NJ	08837	732-225-5555	417-0482
Web: www.csscinc.com					
DataCert Inc 3100 Timmons Suite 310	Houston	TX	77027	713-572-3282	572-3286
TF: 800-770-5121 ■ *Web:* www.datacert.com					
Datastream Systems Inc 50 Datastream Plaza	Greenville	SC	29605	864-422-5001	422-5000
TF: 800-955-6775 ■ *Web:* www.datastream.net					
Datatel Inc 4375 Fair Lakes Ct	Fairfax	VA	22033	703-968-9000	968-4625
TF: 800-328-2835 ■ *Web:* www.datatel.com					
DataTRAK International Inc 6150 Parkland Blvd	Cleveland	OH	44124	440-443-0082	442-3482
NASDAQ: DATA ■ *Web:* www.datatrak.net					
De La Rue Retail Payment Solutions 25 Rockwood Pl	Englewood	NJ	07631	201-894-1700	894-0958
TF: 800-526-0494 ■ *Web:* www.delarue.com					
DealerTrack Holdings Inc 1111 Marcus Ave Suite M04	Lake Success	NY	11042	516-734-3600	
NASDAQ: TRAK ■ *Web:* www.dealertrack.com					
Deltagen Inc 1031 Bing St	San Carlos	CA	94070	650-569-5100	569-5280
Web: www.deltagen.com					
Demand Management Inc 165 N Meramec Ave Suite 300	Saint Louis	MO	63105	314-727-4448	727-4782
Dendrite International Inc 1405-1425 Rt 206 S	Bedminster	NJ	07921	908-443-2000	470-9900
NASDAQ: DRTE ■ *Web:* www.drte.com					
Dentrix Dental Systems Inc					
727 E Utah Valley Dr Suite 500	American Fork	UT	84003	801-763-9300	763-9336
TF: 800-336-8749 ■ *Web:* www.dentrix.com					
Digineer 600 S Hwy 169 Suite 1640	Saint Louis Park	MN	55426	763-544-3400	544-3402
Web: www.digineer.com					
Digital Insight Corp 26025 Mureau Rd	Calabasas	CA	91302	818-871-0000	878-7555
NASDAQ: DGIN ■ *TF:* 888-344-4674 ■ *Web:* www.diginsite.com					
Digital Technology International					
1180 N Mountain Springs Pkwy	Springville	UT	84663	801-853-5000	853-5001*
**Fax:* Sales ■ *Web:* www.dtint.com					
Dimensions International Inc					
2800 Eisenhower Ave Suite 300	Alexandria	VA	22314	703-998-0098	379-1695
Web: www.dimen-intl.com					
DIS Corp 1315 Cornwall Ave	Bellingham	WA	98225	360-733-7610	647-6921
TF Cust Svc: 800-426-8870 ■ *Web:* www.dis-corp.com					
Document Security Systems Inc 28 E Main St Suite 1525	Rochester	NY	14614	585-325-3610	325-2977
AMEX: DMC ■ *TF:* 877-276-0293 ■ *Web:* www.documentsecurity.com					
Domania Inc 63 Pleasant St Suite 210	Watertown	MA	02472	617-926-4442	926-4515
Web: www.domania.com					
Dynix Corp 400 W Dynix Dr	Provo	UT	84604	801-223-5200	223-5202
TF: 800-288-8020 ■ *Web:* www.dynix.com					
DynTek Inc 19700 Fairchild Rd Suite 230	Irvine	CA	92612	949-271-6700	271-0801
Web: www.dyntek.com					
Eagle Point Software Corp 4131 Westmark Dr	Dubuque	IA	52002	563-556-8392	556-5321
TF: 800-678-6565 ■ *Web:* www.eaglepoint.com					
Eastpoint Technology Inc 436 S River Rd	Bedford	NH	03110	603-647-2030	669-8620
Web: www.eastpoint.com					
Eclipsys Corp 1750 Clint Moore Rd	Boca Raton	FL	33487	561-322-4321	322-4320
NASDAQ: ECLP ■ *TF:* 888-325-4779 ■ *Web:* www.eclipsys.com					
Electronics for Imaging Inc 303 Velocity Way	Foster City	CA	94404	650-357-3500	357-3907
NASDAQ: EFII ■ *TF:* 800-568-1917 ■ *Web:* www.efi.com					
Emdeon Corp 669 River Dr Center 2	Elmwood Park	NJ	07407	201-703-3400	703-3401
NASDAQ: HLTH ■ *TF:* 877-469-3263 ■ *Web:* www.emdeon.com					
eMed Technologies Corp 76 Blanchard Rd	Burlington	MA	01803	781-862-0000	272-4333
TF: 800-883-8989 ■ *Web:* www.emed.com					
eMerge Interactive Inc 10305 102nd Terr	Sebastian	FL	32958	772-581-9700	581-0204
NASDAQ: EMRG ■ *TF:* 800-945-5310 ■ *Web:* www.emergeinteractive.com					
Emerging Information Systems Inc 500 - 330 Saint Mary Ave	Winnipeg	MB	R3C3Z5	204-943-3474	942-5100
TF: 888-692-3474 ■ *Web:* www.naviplan.com					
Enghouse Systems Ltd 80 Tiverton Ct Suite 800	Markham	ON	L3R0G4	905-946-3200	946-3201
Web: www.enghouse.com					
Entivity Inc 935 Technology Dr Suite 200	Ann Arbor	MI	48108	734-205-5000	205-5100
TF: 800-888-7388 ■ *Web:* www.entivity.com					
Environmental Systems Research Institute Inc					
380 New York St	Redlands	CA	92373	909-793-2853	793-5953
TF Sales: 800-447-9778 ■ *Web:* www.esri.com					
Envision Telephony Inc 520 Pike St Suite 1600	Seattle	WA	98101	206-225-0800	225-0801
Web: www.envisioninc.com					
EPIQ Systems Inc 501 Kansas Ave	Kansas City	KS	66105	913-621-9500	321-1243
NASDAQ: EPIQ ■ *Web:* www.epiqsystems.com					
EPOS Corp 177 Technology Pkwy	Auburn	AL	36830	334-321-3767	321-7440
Web: www.epos.com					
Equis International 90 S 400 West Suite 620	Salt Lake City	UT	84101	801-265-9996	265-3999
TF Sales: 800-882-3040 ■ *Web:* www.equis.com					
eResearch Technology Inc 30 S 17th St 8th Fl	Philadelphia	PA	19103	215-972-0420	972-0414
NASDAQ: ERES ■ *TF:* 800-704-9698 ■ *Web:* www.ert.com					
Experior Corp 5710 Coventry Ln	Fort Wayne	IN	46804	260-432-2020	432-4753
Web: www.experior.com					

Professional Software (Industry-Specific) (Cont'd)

Company / Address	City	State	ZIP	Phone	Fax
Fidelity Information Services Inc 601 Riverside Avenue	Jacksonville	FL	32204	800-874-7359	854-4282*
*Fax Area Code: 904 ■ Web: www.fidelityinfoservices.com					
Final Draft Inc 26707 W Agoura Rd Suite 205	Calabasas	CA	91302	818-995-8995	995-4422
TF: 800-231-4055 ■ Web: www.finaldraft.com					
Financial Engines Inc 1804 Embarcadero Rd	Palo Alto	CA	94303	650-565-4900	565-4905
TF: 888-443-8577 ■ Web: www.financialengines.com					
Financial Fusion Inc 561 Virginia Rd Bldg 5	Concord	MA	01742	978-287-1975	287-2315
TF: 800-842-0885 ■ Web: www.financialfusion.com					
First DataBank Inc 1111 Bayhill Dr Suite 350	San Bruno	CA	94066	650-588-5454	588-4003
TF: 800-633-3453 ■ Web: www.firstdatabank.com					
Follett Software Co 1391 Corporate Dr	McHenry	IL	60050	815-344-8700	344-8774
TF: 800-323-3397 ■ Web: www.fsc.follett.com					
Gannett Media Technologies International					
151 W 4th St Suite 201	Cincinnati	OH	45202	513-665-3777	241-7219
TF Sales: 800-801-3771 ■ Web: www.gmti.com					
Gene Logic Inc 610 Professional Dr	Gaithersburg	MD	20879	301-987-1700	987-1701
NASDAQ: GLGC ■ Web: www.genelogic.com					
General Dynamics C4 Systems					
400 John Quincy Adams Rd Bldg 80	Taunton	MA	02780	508-880-4000	880-4800
TF: 888-483-2472 ■ Web: www.gdc4s.com					
Genomic Solutions Inc 4355 Varsity Dr Suite E	Ann Arbor	MI	48108	734-975-4800	975-4808
TF: 877-436-6642 ■ Web: www.genomicsolutions.com					
GeoFocus Inc 3651 FAU Blvd Suite 215	Boca Raton	FL	33431	561-955-1480	955-1481
Web: www.geofocus.com					
GeoGraphix 1805 Shea Ctr Dr Suite 400	Highlands Ranch	CO	80129	303-779-8080	796-0807
TF: 800-296-0596 ■ Web: www.geographix.com					
Global Turnkey Systems Inc 2001 Rt 46 Suite 203	Parsippany	NJ	07054	973-331-1010	331-0042
TF Help Line: 800-221-1746 ■ Web: www.gtsystems.com					
GoldenSource Corp 22 Cortlandt St 22nd Fl	New York	NY	10007	212-798-7100	798-7275
Web: www.ftintl.com					
gomembers Inc 11720 Sunrise Valley Dr Suite 300	Reston	VA	20191	703-620-9600	620-4858
TF: 888-288-4634 ■ Web: www.gomembers.com					
Guidance Software Inc 215 N Marengo Ave 2nd Fl	Pasadena	CA	91101	626-229-9191	229-9199
Web: www.guidancesoftware.com					
Heartlab Inc 1 Crosswind Rd	Westerly	RI	02891	401-596-0592	596-8562
TF: 800-959-3205 ■ Web: www.heartlab.com					
HRsmart 2929 N Central Expwy Suite 110	Richardson	TX	75080	214-432-3456	853-5319
Web: www.hrsmart.com					
HyperSpace Communications Inc					
116 Inverness Dr E Suite 265	Englewood	CO	80112	303-566-6500	566-6514
AMEX: HCO ■ TF: 866-888-9578 ■ Web: www.ehyperspace.com					
Hyphen Solutions Inc 5055 Keller Springs Rd Suite 200	Addison	TX	75001	972-728-8100	386-0992
TF Cust Svc: 877-508-2547 ■ Web: www.hyphensolutions.com					
I-Trax Inc 4 Helman Dr Suite 130	Chadds Ford	PA	19317	610-459-2405	459-4705
AMEX: DMX ■ Web: www.i-trax.com					
iHealth Technologies 6666 Powers Ferry Rd Suite 200	Atlanta	GA	30339	770-379-2800	379-2803*
*Fax: Hum Res ■ Web: www.ihealthtechnologies.com					
IHS Energy Group 15 Inverness Way E	Englewood	CO	80112	303-736-3000	397-2923*
*Fax: Hum Res ■ TF: 800-645-3282 ■ Web: www.ihsenergy.com					
ImageWare Systems Inc 10883 Thornmint Rd	San Diego	CA	92127	858-673-8600	673-1770
AMEX: IW ■ TF: 800-842-4199 ■ Web: www.iwsinc.com					
IMPAC Medical Systems Inc 100 W Evelyn Ave	Mountain View	CA	94041	650-623-8800	428-0721
TF: 888-464-6722 ■ Web: www.impac.com					
Incyte Corp Rt 141 & Henry Clay Rd Bldg E-336	Wilmington	DE	19880	302-498-6700	425-2750
NASDAQ: INCY ■ Web: www.incyte.com					
Infor Global Solutions 13560 Morris Rd Suite 4100	Alpharetta	GA	30004	678-319-8000	319-8682
TF: 866-244-5479 ■ Web: www.infor.com					
Inmagic Inc 200 Unicorn Pk Dr 4th Fl	Woburn	MA	01801	781-938-4442	938-4446
TF Sales: 800-229-8398 ■ Web: www.inmagic.com					
Innovative Technologies Corp 1020 Woodman Dr Suite 100	Dayton	OH	45432	937-252-2145	254-6853
TF: 800-745-8050 ■ Web: www.itc-1.com					
Insurance Information Technologies Inc (INSTEC)					
1811 Centre Point Cir Suite 115	Naperville	IL	60563	630-955-9200	955-9240
Web: www.instec-corp.com					
InterAct Public Safety Systems Inc 45 Patton Ave	Asheville	NC	28801	828-254-9876	254-0768
TF: 800-768-3911 ■ Web: www.interactsys.com					
Interactive Market Systems Inc 770 Broadway	New York	NY	10003	646-654-5900	654-5901
TF: 800-223-7942 ■ Web: www.imsms.com					
Intercim Corp 501 E Hwy 13	Burnsville	MN	55337	952-894-9010	894-0399
TF: 800-343-3734 ■ Web: www.intercim.com					
IPC Information Systems Inc 88 Pine St 15th Fl	New York	NY	10005	212-825-9060	344-5106
Web: www.ipc.com					
Island Pacific Inc 19800 MacArthur Blvd Suite 1200	Irvine	CA	92612	949-476-2212	476-0199
TF: 800-944-3847 ■ Web: www.islandpacific.com					
IsqFt 4430 Carver Woods Dr	Cincinnati	OH	45242	513-645-8004	645-8005
Web: www.isqft.com					
JDA Software Group Inc 14400 N 87th St	Scottsdale	AZ	85260	480-308-3000	308-3001
NASDAQ: JDAS ■ Web: www.jda.com					
Jenzabar Inc 5 Cambridge Ctr 11th Fl	Cambridge	MA	02142	617-492-9099	492-9081
TF: 877-536-0222 ■ Web: www.jenzabar.net					
JPMorgan Chase Vastera 45025 Aviation Dr Suite 200	Dulles	VA	20166	703-661-9006	742-4580
TF: 800-275-1374 ■ Web: www.vastera.com					
Kaba Benzing America 5753 Miami Lakes Dr	Miami Lakes	FL	33014	305-819-4000	819-4001
Web: www.kaba-benzing-usa.com					
Kewill Systems PLC 100 Nickerson Rd	Marlborough	MA	01752	508-229-4400	229-4404
TF: 877-872-2379 ■ Web: www.kewill.com					
Khimetrics 4343 N Scottsdale Rd Suite 345	Scottsdale	AZ	85251	480-609-2833	609-4022
Web: www.khimetrics.com					
Kinaxis 700 Silver Seven Rd	Ottawa	ON	K2V1C3	613-592-5780	592-0584
TF: 877-546-2947 ■ Web: www.kinaxis.com					
Knovalent Inc 3135 S State St Suite 300	Ann Arbor	MI	48108	734-996-8300	996-2754
Web: www.knovalent.com					
Knowlagent 3157 Royal Dr	Alpharetta	GA	30022	678-356-3500	
Web: www.knowlagent.com					
Koyosha Graphics of America Inc					
465 California St Suite 610	San Francisco	CA	94104	415-283-1800	283-1801
Web: www.koyosha.com					
Lacerte Software Corp 5601 Headquarters Dr	Plano	TX	75024	800-765-4065	387-2689*
*Fax Area Code: 214 ■ Web: www.lacertesoftware.com					
Land & Legal Solutions Inc 300 S Hamilton Ave	Greensburg	PA	15601	724-853-8992	853-3221
TF: 800-245-7900 ■ Web: www.landlegal.com					
Landacorp Inc 900 Fortress St Suite 100	Chico	CA	95973	530-891-0853	891-8428
Web: www.landacorp.com					
Landmark Graphics Corp 2101 CityWest Blvd Bldg 2	Houston	TX	77242	713-839-2000	839-2015
TF: 800-207-3098 ■ Web: www.lgc.com					
Library Corp The 3801 E Florida Ave Suite 300	Denver	CO	80210	303-758-3030	758-0606
TF: 888-439-2275 ■ Web: www.tlcdelivers.com					
Lilly Software Assoc Inc (LSA) 500 Lafayette Rd	Hampton	NH	03842	603-926-9696	926-9698
Web: www.lillysoftware.com					
LMS Medical Systems Inc 5252 de Maisonneuve W Suite 314	Montreal	QC	H4A3S5	514-488-3461	488-1880
AMEX: LMZ ■ Web: www.lmsmedical.com					
Logic Trends Inc 1050 Crown Pointe Pkwy Suite 295	Atlanta	GA	30338	770-551-5050	551-5055
Web: www.logictrends.com					
Logiplex Corp 4855 N Lagoon	Portland	OR	97217	503-978-6726	285-1355
TF: 800-735-0555 ■ Web: www.logiplex.net					
MAI Systems Corp 26110 Enterprise Way	Lake Forest	CA	92630	949-598-6000	598-6391
Web: www.maisystems.com					
Management Information Control Systems Inc (MICS)					
2025 9th St	Los Osos	CA	93402	805-543-7000	543-0373
TF: 800-838-6427 ■ Web: www.micsonline.com					
Managing Editor Inc 610 Old York Rd Suite 250	Jenkintown	PA	19046	215-886-5662	886-5681
Web: www.maned.com					
Manhattan Assoc Inc 2300 Windy Ridge Pkwy 7th Fl	Atlanta	GA	30339	770-955-7070	955-0302
NASDAQ: MANH ■ Web: www.manhattanassociates.com					
Market Scan Information Systems Inc					
31416 Agoura Rd Suite 110	Westlake Village	CA	91361	818-575-2000	707-8339
TF: 800-658-7226 ■ Web: www.marketscan.com					
Marshall & Swift 911 Wilshire Blvd Suite 1600	Los Angeles	CA	90017	213-683-9000	683-9010
TF: 800-544-2678 ■ Web: www.marshallswift.com					
MAXxess Systems Inc 1515 S Manchester Ave	Anaheim	CA	92802	714-772-1000	780-7999
TF: 800-842-0221 ■ Web: www.maxxesssystems.com					
McDonald Bradley Inc 2250 Corporate Park Dr Suite 500	Herndon	VA	20171	703-326-1000	326-1004
Web: www.mcdonaldbradley.com					
McKesson Information Solutions 5995 Windward Pkwy	Alpharetta	GA	30005	404-338-6000	338-5116*
*Fax: Sales ■ TF: 800-981-8601 ■ Web: infosolutions.mckesson.com					
MEDecision Inc 601 Lee Rd Chesterbrook Corp Ctr	Wayne	PA	19087	610-540-0202	540-0270
Web: www.medecision.com					
Media Cybernetics LP 8484 Georgia Ave Suite 200	Silver Spring	MD	20910	301-495-3305	495-5964
TF Sales: 800-992-4256 ■ Web: www.mediacy.com					
Medical Information Technology Inc 1 Meditech Cir	Westwood	MA	02090	781-821-3000	821-2199
Web: www.meditech.com					
Medical Manager Health Systems					
2202 N West Shore Blvd Suite 300	Tampa	FL	33607	813-287-2990	289-6420
TF: 800-330-3612 ■ Web: www.medicalmanager.com					
MedPlus Inc 4690 Parkway Dr	Mason	OH	45040	513-229-5500	229-5505
TF: 800-444-6235 ■ Web: www.medplus.com					
Merrick Systems Inc 4801 Woodway Suite 100E	Houston	TX	77056	713-355-6800	355-7202
TF: 800-842-8389 ■ Web: www.merricksystems.com					
MetalWare Inc 5022 Campbell Blvd Suite L	Baltimore	MD	21236	443-461-1070	461-1071
Web: www.metalwareinc.com					
MetaSolv Inc 5556 Tennyson Pkwy	Plano	TX	75024	972-403-8300	403-8333
NASDAQ: MSLV ■ TF: 800-925-2940 ■ Web: www.metasolv.com					
MicroBilt Corp 1640 Airport Rd Suite 115	Kennesaw	GA	30144	800-884-4747	
Web: www.microbilt.com					
MICS (Management Information Control Systems Inc)					
2025 9th St	Los Osos	CA	93402	805-543-7000	543-0373
TF: 800-838-6427 ■ Web: www.micsonline.com					
Moody's KMV Co 1350 Treat Blvd Suite 400	Walnut Creek	CA	94597	925-945-1005	945-1162
Web: www.moodyskmv.com					
MSGI Security Solutions Inc 575 Madison Ave 10th Fl	New York	NY	10022	917-339-7100	339-7111
NASDAQ: MSGI ■ Web: www.msgisecurity.com					
NaviSys Inc 499 Thornall St	Edison	NJ	08837	732-549-3663	549-5445
TF: 800-775-3592 ■ Web: www.navisys.com					
Navtech Inc 175 Columbia St W Suite 102	Waterloo	ON	N2L5Z5	519-747-1170	747-1003
Web: www.navtechinc.com					
Nestor Inc 400 Massasoit Ave Suite 200	East Providence	RI	02914	401-434-5522	434-5809
NASDAQ: NEST ■ Web: www.nestor.com					
net-linx Publishing Solutions Inc 1740 N Market Blvd	Sacramento	CA	95834	916-830-2400	830-2413
TF: 800-445-4744					
netGuru Inc 22700 Savi Ranch Pkwy	Yorba Linda	CA	92887	714-974-2500	974-4771
NASDAQ: NGRU ■ Web: www.netguru.com					
Netsol Technologies Inc 23901 Calabasas Rd Suite 2072	Calabasas	CA	91302	818-222-9195	222-9197
NASDAQ: NTWK ■ Web: www.netsoltek.com					
New England Computer Services Inc					
168 Boston Post Rd Suites 6 & 7	Madison	CT	06443	203-245-3999	245-4513
TF Sales: 800-766-6327 ■ Web: www.necs.com					
NIC Inc 10540 S Ridgeview Rd	Olathe	KS	66061	913-498-3468	498-3472
NASDAQ: EGOV ■ TF: 877-234-3468 ■ Web: www.nicusa.com					
OpenTable Inc 799 Market St 4th Fl	San Francisco	CA	94103	415-344-4200	267-0944
TF: 800-673-6822 ■ Web: www.opentable.com					
OSI Software Inc 777 Davis St Suite 250	San Leandro	CA	94577	510-297-5800	357-8136
Web: www.osisoft.com					
OverDrive Inc 8555 Sweet Valley Dr Unit C	Cleveland	OH	44125	216-573-6886	573-6888
Web: www.overdrive.com					
Pacer/CATS 355 Inverness Dr S	Englewood	CO	80112	303-649-9818	414-7805
Web: www.pacercats.com					
Packet Design Inc 3400 Hillview Ave Bldg 3	Palo Alto	CA	94304	650-739-1850	739-0090
Web: www.packetdesign.com					
Pason Systems Inc 6130 3rd St SE	Calgary	AB	T2H1K4	403-301-3400	301-3499
TSX: PSI ■ Web: www.pason.com					
Patient Infosystems Inc 46 Prince St 1st Fl	Rochester	NY	14607	585-242-7200	244-1367
TF: 800-276-2575 ■ Web: www.ptisys.com					
PCi Services Inc 30 Winter St 12th Fl	Boston	MA	02108	617-535-3000	535-3155
TF: 800-261-3111 ■ Web: www.pciwiz.com					
PDF Solutions Inc 333 W San Carlos St Suite 700	San Jose	CA	95110	408-280-7900	280-7915
NASDAQ: PDFS ■ Web: www.pdf.com					
Peace Software Inc 6205 Blue Lagoon Dr Suite 500	Miami	FL	33126	305-341-2400	341-2403
TF: 866-407-3223 ■ Web: www.peacesoftware.com					
Peopleware Inc 110 110th Ave NE Suite 590	Bellevue	WA	98004	425-454-6444	454-7634
TF: 800-869-7166 ■ Web: www.peopleware.com					
Pharsight Corp 800 W El Camino Real Suite 200	Mountain View	CA	94040	650-314-3800	314-3810
Web: www.pharsight.com					
Phase Forward Inc 880 Winter St	Waltham	MA	02451	781-890-7878	890-4848
NASDAQ: PFWD ■ TF: 888-703-1122 ■ Web: www.phaseforward.com					
ProCard Inc 1819 Denver W Dr Bldg 26 Suite 265	Golden	CO	80401	303-279-2255	279-1044
TF: 800-469-6578 ■ Web: www.procard.com					
Promodel Corp 3400 Bath Pike Suite 200	Bethlehem	PA	18017	801-223-4600	
TF: 888-900-3090 ■ Web: www.promodel.com					
ProSight Inc 9600 SW Barnes Rd Suite 300	Portland	OR	97255	503-889-4800	
TF: 877-531-9121 ■ Web: www.prosight.com					
QS/1 Data Systems PO Box 6052	Spartanburg	SC	29304	864-253-8600	253-8690
TF: 800-845-7558 ■ Web: www.qs1.com					
QuadraMed Corp 22 Pelican Way	San Rafael	CA	94901	415-482-2100	482-2110
AMEX: QD ■ TF: 800-473-7633 ■ Web: www.quadramed.com					
Quality Systems Inc 18191 Von Karman Ave Suite 450	Irvine	CA	92612	949-255-2600	255-2605
NASDAQ: QSII ■ TF Cust Svc: 800-888-7955 ■ Web: www.qsii.com					
QUMAS 325 Columbia Tpke	Florham Park	NJ	07932	973-377-8750	377-8687
Web: www.qumas.com					
Quovadx Inc 6400 S Fiddler's Green Cir Suite 1000	Englewood	CO	80111	303-488-2019	488-9738
NASDAQ: QVDX ■ TF: 800-723-3033 ■ Web: www.quovadx.com					
RainMaker Software Inc 475 Sentry Pkwy E Suite 4000	Blue Bell	PA	19422	610-567-3400	567-3449
TF Cust Svc: 800-341-4012 ■ Web: www.rainmakerlegal.com					
Ramesys Hospitality Inc 1 Cragwood Rd Suite 202	South Plainfield	NJ	07080	908-941-1300	941-1312
TF: 800-888-8819 ■ Web: www.us.ramesys.com					
Ramp Corp 33 Maiden Ln 5th Fl	New York	NY	10038	212-440-1500	480-4952
Web: www.ramp.com					
Random Walk Computing Inc 11 Broadway 16th Fl	New York	NY	10004	212-480-5820	480-9541
Web: www.randomwalk.com					
Realigent Inc 2800 Saturn Ave Suite 200	Brea	CA	92821	714-993-4295	572-0588
TF: 800-704-9302 ■ Web: www.realigent.com					

Company	City	State	ZIP	Phone	Fax
RealLegal.com 3025 S Parker Rd 12th Fl	Aurora	CO	80014	303-584-9988	584-8984
TF: 888-584-9988 ■ *Web:* www.reallegal.com					
Red Wing Software Inc 491 Hwy 19	Red Wing	MN	55066	651-388-1106	388-7950
TF: 800-732-9464 ■ *Web:* www.redwingsoftware.com					
RESUMate Inc 135 E Bennett St Suite 5	Saline	MI	48176	734-429-8510	429-4228
TF Cust Svc: 800-530-9310 ■ *Web:* www.resumate.com					
Retek Inc 950 Nicollet Mall	Minneapolis	MN	55403	612-587-5000	587-5100
TF: 877-517-3835 ■ *Web:* www.retek.com					
Reynolds & Reynolds Co 1 Reynolds Way	Dayton	OH	45430	937-485-2000	485-2529*
NYSE: REY ■ **Fax:* Sales ■ *Web:* www.reyrey.com					
Risk Management Solutions Inc 7015 Gateway Blvd	Newark	CA	94560	510-505-2500	505-2501
Web: www.rms.com					
RiskWatch Inc 2568A Riva Rd Suite 300	Annapolis	MD	21401	410-224-4773	224-4995
TF: 800-448-4666 ■ *Web:* www.riskwatch.com					
S1 Corp 3500 Lenox Rd Suite 200	Atlanta	GA	30326	404-923-3500	923-6727
NASDAQ: SONE ■ *TF:* 888-457-2237 ■ *Web:* www.s1.com					
SalesLink Corp 425 Medford St	Charlestown	MA	02129	617-886-4800	886-4916
TF: 888-231-2568 ■ *Web:* www.saleslink.com					
Sapiens International Corp 2000 CentreGreen Way Suite 240	Cary	NC	27513	919-405-1500	405-1700
NASDAQ: SPNS ■ *Web:* www.sapiens.com					
Scantron Corp 34 Parker	Irvine	CA	92618	949-639-7500	639-7710
TF: 800-722-6876 ■ *Web:* www.scantron.com					
Schlumberger Information Solutions					
5599 San Felipe St Suite 1700	Houston	TX	77056	713-513-2000	513-2050
Web: www.oilfield.slb.com					
Scott Studios Corp 13375 Stemmons Fwy Suite 400	Dallas	TX	75234	972-620-2211	620-8811
TF: 888-438-7268 ■ *Web:* www.scottstudios.com					
Serendipity Systems Inc PO Box 10477	Sedona	AZ	86339	928-282-6831	282-4383
Web: www.serendipsys.com					
Siemens Logistics & Assembly Systems					
507 Plymouth Ave	Grand Rapids	MI	49505	616-913-6200	913-5339*
**Fax:* Hum Res ■ *TF:* 877-725-7500 ■ *Web:* www.logistics-assembly.siemens.com					
Simulation Systems Technologies Inc					
520 Fellowship Rd Unit A-110	Mount Laurel	NJ	08054	856-231-7711	231-4663
Web: www.s-s-t-i.com					
Simulations Plus Inc 42505 10th St W	Lancaster	CA	93534	661-723-7723	723-5524
AMEX: SLP ■ *TF:* 888-266-9294 ■ *Web:* www.simulations-plus.com					
Sirsi Corp 101 Washington St SE	Huntsville	AL	35801	256-704-7000	704-7007
TF Sales: 800-917-4774 ■ *Web:* www.sirsi.com					
SM & A 4695 MacArthur Ct 8th Fl	Newport Beach	CA	92660	949-975-1550	975-1624
NASDAQ: WINS ■ *Web:* www.smawins.com					
Softrax Corp 45 Shawmut Rd	Canton	MA	02021	781-830-9200	830-9345
TF: 888-476-3872 ■ *Web:* www.softrax.com					
Software Consulting Services LLC 630 Selvaggio Dr Suite 420	Nazareth	PA	18064	610-746-7700	746-7900
Web: www.newspapersystems.com					
SolidWorks Corp 300 Baker Ave	Concord	MA	01742	978-371-5011	371-7303
TF: 800-693-9000 ■ *Web:* www.solidworks.com					
Solucient 1007 Church St Suite 700	Evanston	IL	60201	847-424-4400	332-1768
TF: 800-366-7526 ■ *Web:* www.solucient.com					
SQN Signature Systems 65 Indel Ave 2nd Fl	Rancocas	NJ	08073	609-261-5500	265-9517
TF: 888-744-7226 ■ *Web:* www.sqnsigs.com					
StatSoft Inc 2300 E 14th St	Tulsa	OK	74104	918-749-1119	749-2217
Web: www.statsoftinc.com					
Stok Software Inc 373 Nesconset Hwy Suite 287	Hauppauge	NY	11788	631-232-2228	
TF: 888-448-8668 ■ *Web:* www.stok.com					
Studio Systems Inc 520 Broadway Suite 230	Santa Monica	CA	90401	310-393-9999	393-7799
TF: 800-858-3669 ■ *Web:* www.studiosystem.com					
SunGard Collegis Inc 2300 Maitland Center Pkwy Suite 340	Maitland	FL	32751	407-660-1199	660-8008
TF: 800-800-1874 ■ *Web:* www.sungardcollegis.com					
SunGard Energy Systems 825 3rd Ave 28th Fl	New York	NY	10022	212-888-3600	888-0691
TF: 877-230-6551 ■ *Web:* www.energy.sungard.com					
SunGard HTE Inc 1000 Business Center Dr	Lake Mary	FL	32746	407-304-3235	304-1005*
**Fax:* Mktg ■ *TF:* 800-727-8088 ■ *Web:* www.sungard.com/hte					
SunGard Portfolio Solutions Inc 7-10 Kingsbridge Rd	Fairfield	NJ	07004	973-882-0011	808-9319
TF: 800-825-2518					
SunGard SCT Inc 4 Country View Rd	Malvern	PA	19355	610-647-5930	578-5102
TF: 800-223-7036 ■ *Web:* www.sctcorp.com					
SunGard Shareholder Systems Inc					
951 Mariners Island Blvd Suite 500	San Mateo	CA	94404	650-377-3700	571-1468
SunGard Trust Systems Inc 5510 77 Center Dr	Charlotte	NC	28217	704-527-6300	527-9617
Web: www.sungardtrust.com					
Symphoni Interactive LLC 580 California St 5th Fl	San Francisco	CA	94104	415-543-2939	391-4985
Web: www.symphoni.com					
Symyx Technologies Inc 3100 Central Expy	Santa Clara	CA	95051	408-764-2000	748-0175
NASDAQ: SMMX ■ *Web:* www.symyx.com					
Synopsys Inc 700 E Middlefield Rd	Mountain View	CA	94043	650-584-5000	965-8637
NASDAQ: SNPS ■ *TF:* 800-541-7737 ■ *Web:* www.synopsys.com					
System Innovators Inc					
10550 Deerwood Park Blvd Suite 700	Jacksonville	FL	32256	904-281-9090	281-0075
TF: 800-963-5000 ■ *Web:* www.systeminnovators.com					
Systems Xcellence Inc 555 Industrial Dr	Milton	ON	L9T5E1	905-876-4741	878-8869
TSX: SXC ■ *Web:* www.sxc.com					
T2 Systems Inc 7835 Woodland Dr Suite 250	Indianapolis	IN	46278	317-524-5500	524-5501
TF: 800-434-1502 ■ *Web:* www.t2systems.com					
Tax Management Inc BNA Software Div 1250 23rd St NW	Washington	DC	20037	202-728-7962	728-7964
TF: 800-424-2938 ■ *Web:* www.bnasoftware.com					
Telcordia Technologies Inc 1 Telcordia Dr	Piscataway	NJ	08854	732-699-2000	336-2844
TF Sales: 800-521-2673 ■ *Web:* www.telcordia.com					
Telos OK 111 SW 'C' Ave	Lawton	OK	73501	580-355-9280	355-9381
Web: www.telosok.com					
Thomson Elite 5100 W Goldleaf Cir Suite 100	Los Angeles	CA	90056	323-642-5200	642-5400
TF Cust Svc: 800-274-9287 ■ *Web:* www.elite.com					
Tm Bioscience Corp 439 University Ave Suite 1050	Toronto	ON	M5G1Y8	416-593-4323	593-1066
Web: www.tmbioscience.com					
Track Data Corp 95 Rockwell Pl	Brooklyn	NY	11217	212-943-4555	612-2014
NASDAQ: TRAC ■ *TF:* 800-223-0113 ■ *Web:* www.trackdata.com					
TradeStation Group Inc 8050 SW 10th St Suite 2000	Plantation	FL	33324	954-652-7000	652-7899
NASDAQ: TRAD ■ *TF:* 800-871-3577 ■ *Web:* www.tradestation.com					
Transaction Systems Architects Inc 330 S 108th Ave	Omaha	NE	68154	402-334-5101	390-8077
NASDAQ: TSAI ■ *Web:* www.tsainc.com					
Transentric 1400 Douglas St Suite 0840	Omaha	NE	68179	402-544-2984	501-2984
Web: www.transentric.com					
TransWorks 9910 Dupont Circle Dr E Suite 200	Fort Wayne	IN	46825	260-487-4400	
TF: 800-435-4691 ■ *Web:* www.trnswrks.com					
TRX Inc 6 W Druid Hills Dr	Atlanta	GA	30329	404-929-6100	929-5270*
NASDAQ: TRXI ■ **Fax:* Hum Res ■ *Web:* www.trx.com					
Tyler Technologies Inc 5949 Sherry Ln Suite 1400	Dallas	TX	75225	972-713-3700	713-3741
NYSE: TYL ■ *Web:* www.tylerworks.com					
Ulticom Inc 1020 Briggs Rd	Mount Laurel	NJ	08054	856-787-2700	866-2033
NASDAQ: ULCM ■ *TF Sales:* 888-295-6664 ■ *Web:* www.ulticom.com					
Universal Tax Systems 6 Mathis Dr	Rome	GA	30165	706-232-7757	236-9168
TF Sales: 800-755-9473 ■ *Web:* www.taxwise.com					
Urchin Software Corp 2165 India St	San Diego	CA	92101	619-233-1400	374-2478
TF Sales: 888-887-2446 ■ *Web:* www.urchin.com					
US Dataworks Inc 5301 Hollister Rd Suite 250	Houston	TX	77040	713-934-3855	
AMEX: UDW ■ *Web:* www.usdataworks.com					
US Digital Corp 11100 NE 34th Cir	Vancouver	WA	98682	360-260-2468	260-2469
TF: 800-736-0194 ■ *Web:* www.usdigital.com					
VantageMed Corp 3017 Kilgore Rd Suite 180	Rancho Cordova	CA	95670	916-638-4744	638-0504
TF: 877-879-8633 ■ *Web:* www.vantagemed.net					
Verint Systems Inc 330 S Service Rd	Melville	NY	11747	631-962-9600	962-9300
NASDAQ: VRNT ■ *TF:* 800-967-1028 ■ *Web:* www.verintsystems.com					
VersaForm Systems Corp 591 W Hamilton Ave Suite 201	Campbell	CA	95008	408-370-2662	370-3393
TF Sales: 800-678-1111 ■ *Web:* www.versaform.com					
Viewlocity Inc 3475 Piedmont Rd Suite 1700	Atlanta	GA	30305	404-267-6400	267-6500
TF: 877-512-8900 ■ *Web:* www.viewlocity.com					
Viisage Technology Inc 296 Concord Rd 3rd Fl	Billerica	MA	01821	978-932-2200	932-2225
NASDAQ: VISG ■ *Web:* www.viisage.com					
ViPS Inc 1 W Pennsylvania Ave Suite 700	Baltimore	MD	21204	410-832-8300	832-8315
TF: 888-289-8477 ■ *Web:* www.vips.com					
Visicu Inc 217 E Redwood St Suite 1900	Baltimore	MD	21202	410-276-1960	276-1970
NASDAQ: EICU ■ *Web:* www.visicu.com					
Vital Images Inc 5850 Opus Pkwy Suite 300	Minnetonka	MN	55343	763-852-4100	852-4110
NASDAQ: VTAL ■ *Web:* www.vitalimages.com					
Viziqor Solutions 902 Clint Moore Rd Suite 230	Boca Raton	FL	33487	561-999-8000	999-8001
Web: www.viziqor.com					
VoltDelta Resources Inc 560 Lexington Ave 14th Fl	New York	NY	10022	212-827-2600	827-2650
Web: www.voltdelta.com					
Votenet Solutions Inc 1629 K St NW	Washington	DC	20006	202-737-2277	737-2283
Web: www.votenet.com					
Weather Services International 400 Minuteman Rd	Andover	MA	01810	978-983-6300	983-6400
Web: www.wsi.com					
Wonderware Corp 26561 Rancho Pkwy S	Lake Forest	CA	92630	949-727-3200	727-3270
Web: www.wonderware.com					
X-Rite Inc 3100 44th St SW	Grandville	MI	49418	616-534-7664	534-0723
NASDAQ: XRIT ■ *TF:* 800-248-9748 ■ *Web:* www.xrite.com					
Xybernet Inc 10640 Scripps Ranch Blvd	San Diego	CA	92131	858-530-1900	530-1419
TF Cust Svc: 800-228-9026 ■ *Web:* www.xyber.net					

181-11 Service Software

Company	City	State	ZIP	Phone	Fax
Aleri Inc 2 Prudential Plaza 41st Fl	Chicago	IL	60601	312-540-0100	540-0118
Web: www.aleri.com					
Alorica Inc 14726 Ramona Ave 3rd Fl	Chino	CA	91710	909-606-3600	606-7708
Web: www.alorica.com					
American HealthNet 2110 S 169th Plaza Suite 100	Omaha	NE	68130	402-733-2700	733-2288
TF: 800-745-4712 ■ *Web:* www.americanhealthnet.com					
Applied Systems Inc 200 Applied Pkwy	University Park	IL	60466	708-534-5575	534-5943*
**Fax:* Hum Res ■ *TF:* 800-999-5368 ■ *Web:* www.appliedsystems.com					
Aptech Computer Systems Inc 135 Delta Dr	Pittsburgh	PA	15238	412-963-7440	963-9799
TF: 800-245-0720 ■ *Web:* www.aptech-inc.com					
ARINC Inc 2551 Riva Rd	Annapolis	MD	21401	410-266-4000	266-4040
TF: 800-492-2182 ■ *Web:* www.arinc.com					
Aristotle Inc 205 Pennsylvania Ave SE	Washington	DC	20003	202-543-8345	543-6407*
**Fax:* Sales ■ *TF Sales:* 800-296-2747 ■ *Web:* www.aristotle.com					
ASA International Ltd 10 Speen St	Framingham	MA	01701	508-626-2727	626-0645
Web: www.asaint.com					
Automated Financial Systems Inc 123 Summit Dr	Exton	PA	19341	610-524-0400	524-7977
Web: www.afsvision.com					
Bankers Systems Inc 6815 Saukview Dr	Saint Cloud	MN	56303	320-251-3060	251-8110
TF: 800-397-2341 ■ *Web:* www.bankerssystems.com					
Barrister Global Services Network Inc PO Box 11253	Jefferson	LA	70181	504-734-9260	734-9812
TF: 800-846-4260 ■ *Web:* www.barrister.com					
CACTUS Software 4900 College Blvd	Overland Park	KS	66211	913-677-0092	677-0185
TF: 800-776-2305 ■ *Web:* www.visualcactus.com					
Camstar Systems Inc 2815 Coliseum Ventre Dr Suite 600	Charlotte	NC	28217	704-227-6600	227-6780
TF: 800-237-2841 ■ *Web:* www.camstar.com					
CaseSoft Div DecisionQuest Inc					
5000 Sawgrass Village Cir Suite 21	Ponte Vedra Beach	FL	32082	904-273-5000	273-5001
Web: www.casesoft.com					
Cerner Corp 2800 Rockcreek Pkwy	Kansas City	MO	64117	816-221-1024	474-1742
NASDAQ: CERN ■ *TF Hum Res:* 800-255-1024 ■ *Web:* www.cerner.com					
CGI Information Systems 600 Federal St	Andover	MA	01810	978-946-3000	686-0130
TF: 800-637-3799 ■ *Web:* www.cgiusa.com					
Computer Technology Corp DBA CACTUS Software					
4900 College Blvd	Overland Park	KS	66211	913-677-0092	677-0185
TF: 800-770-2305 ■ *Web:* www.visualcactus.com					
Convera Corp 1921 Gallows Rd Suite 200	Vienna	VA	22182	703-761-3700	761-1990
NASDAQ: CNVR ■ *TF:* 800-755-7005 ■ *Web:* www.convera.com					
Datamann Inc 1994 Hartford Ave	Wilder	VT	05088	802-295-6600	296-3623
TF: 800-451-4263 ■ *Web:* www.datamann.com					
DecisionQuest Inc CaseSoft Div					
5000 Sawgrass Village Cir Suite 21	Ponte Vedra Beach	FL	32082	904-273-5000	273-5001
Web: www.casesoft.com					
Digital Solutions Inc 4200 Industrial Park Dr	Altoona	PA	16602	814-944-0405	949-3307
TF Cust Svc: 888-222-3081 ■ *Web:* www.dsicdi.com					
DPSI Inc 4905 Koger Blvd Suite 101	Greensboro	NC	27407	336-854-7700	854-7715*
**Fax:* Hum Res ■ *TF:* 800-897-7233 ■ *Web:* www.dpsi.com					
Dr Schueler's Health Informatics Inc 703 Rockledge Dr	Rockledge	FL	32955	321-637-0321	637-0021
Web: www.dshisystems.com					
Ebix Inc 5 Concourse Pkwy Suite 3200	Atlanta	GA	30328	678-281-2020	281-2019
NASDAQ: EBIX ■ *Web:* www.ebix.com					
eMeta Corp 81 Franklin St Suite 500	New York	NY	10013	800-804-0103	925-7462*
**Fax Area Code:* 212 ■ *Web:* www.emeta.com					
EOS International 2382 Faraday Ave Suite 350	Carlsbad	CA	92008	760-431-8400	431-8448
TF Tech Supp: 888-728-8746 ■ *Web:* www.eosintl.com					
First Advantage Recruiting Solutions 10029 E 126th St Suite D	Fishers	IN	46038	317-813-0500	813-0501
TF: 888-547-4472 ■ *Web:* www.fadv.com					
First Data International Inc 6200 S Quebec St	Greenwood Village	CO	80111	303-488-8000	551-3610*
**Fax Area Code:* 407 ■ *TF:* 800-735-3362 ■ *Web:* www.paysys.com					
Firstwave Technologies Inc 2859 Paces Ferry Rd Suite 1000	Atlanta	GA	30339	770-431-1200	431-1201
NASDAQ: FSTW ■ *TF:* 800-540-6061 ■ *Web:* www.firstwave.net					
Fiserv Insurance Solutions 2110 Wiley Blvd SW	Cedar Rapids	IA	52404	319-398-1800	398-1872
TF: 800-943-2851 ■ *Web:* www.fiservinsurance.com					
Fiserv Mortgage Products 3575 Moreau Ct Suite 2	South Bend	IN	46628	574-282-3300	282-3366
Galaxy Hotel Systems LLC 15621 Red Hill Ave Suite 100	Tustin	CA	92780	714-258-5800	258-5880
Web: www.galaxyhotelsystems.com					
Gallagher Financial Systems 7301 SW 57th Ct Suite 570	South Miami	FL	33143	305-665-5099	665-0547
TF: 800-989-9998 ■ *Web:* www.gogallagher.com					
H & M Systems Software Inc					
600 E Crescent Ave Suite 203	Upper Saddle River	NJ	07458	201-934-3414	934-9206
TF Cust Svc: 800-367-3366 ■ *Web:* www.hm-software.com					
Henry Jack & Assoc Inc 663 W Hwy 60	Monett	MO	65708	417-235-6652	235-8406
NASDAQ: JKHY ■ *TF:* 800-299-4222 ■ *Web:* www.jackhenry.com					
I Levy & Assoc Inc 645 Maryville Centre Dr Suite 200	Saint Louis	MO	63141	314-744-7300	744-7399
TF: 800-297-6717 ■ *Web:* www.ilevy.com					
IDX Systems Corp 40 IDX Dr	South Burlington	VT	05403	802-862-1022	862-9591*
NASDAQ: IDXC ■ **Fax:* Mktg ■ *Web:* www.idx.com					
IHS Group 15 Inverness Way E	Englewood	CO	80112	303-790-0600	397-2599*
**Fax:* Cust Svc ■ *TF:* 800-525-7052 ■ *Web:* www.ihs.com					

Service Software (Cont'd)

Phone Fax

Information Handling Services Group Inc
15 Inverness Way E Englewood CO 80112 303-790-0600 397-2599*
*Fax: Cust Svc ■ *TF:* 800-525-7052 ■ *Web:* www.ihs.com

Information Technology Inc 1345 Old Cheney Rd Lincoln NE 68512 402-423-2682 421-4236
Web: www.itiwnet.com

Inmass/MRP PO Box 41000 Tucson AZ 85717 520-795-6800 323-2505
Web: www.inmass.com

Insurance Data Processing Inc 1 Washington Sq Wyncote PA 19095 215-885-2150 884-1947
TF: 800-523-6745 ■ *Web:* www.idpnet.com

Intelligent Health Systems 4275 Executive Sq Suite 550 La Jolla CA 92037 858-453-3600 597-8220
TF: 800-487-5772 ■ *Web:* ihshealthcare.com

Inxight Software Inc 500 Macara Ave Sunnyvale CA 94085 408-738-6200 738-6203
Web: www.inxight.com

Jack Henry & Assoc Inc 663 W Hwy 60 Monett MO 65708 417-235-6652 235-8406
NASDAQ: JKHY ■ *TF:* 800-299-4222 ■ *Web:* www.jackhenry.com

Jobscope Corp PO Box 6767 Greenville SC 29606 864-458-3100 234-4852
TF: 800-443-5794 ■ *Web:* www.jobscope.com

Keane Care Inc 8383 158th Ave NE Suite 100 Redmond WA 98052 425-307-2200 307-2220
TF: 800-426-2675 ■ *Web:* www.keanecare.com

Kirchman Corp PO Box 2269 Orlando FL 32802 407-831-3001 831-2572
TF Cust Svc: 800-327-1892 ■ *Web:* www.kirchman.com

Kronos Inc 297 Billerica Rd Chelmsford MA 01824 978-250-9800 367-5900
NASDAQ: KRON ■ *Web:* www.kronos.com

LegalEdge Software 175 Stratford Ave Suite 1 Wayne PA 19087 610-975-5888 975-5884
Web: www.legaledge.com

Liquent Inc 101 Gibraltar Rd Suite 200 Horsham PA 19044 215-328-4444 328-4445
TF: 800-515-3777 ■ *Web:* www.liquent.com

Management Technology America Ltd
4742 N 24th St Suite 410 Phoenix AZ 85016 602-381-5100 251-0903
TF: 800-366-6633 ■ *Web:* www.mtanet.com

Manatron Inc 510 E Milham Ave Portage MI 49002 269-567-2900 567-2930
NASDAQ: MANA ■ *TF Cust Svc:* 800-666-5300 ■ *Web:* www.manatron.com

McKesson Pharmacy Systems 30881 Schoolcraft Rd Livonia MI 48150 734-427-2000 523-9633
TF: 800-521-1758 ■ *Web:* www.mckhboc-rxsystems.com

MDL Information Systems Inc
2440 Camino Ramon Suite 300 San Ramon CA 94583 925-543-5400 543-5401
TF Cust Svc: 800-326-3002 ■ *Web:* www.mdl.com

Medical Manager MacHealth 210 Gateway Mall Suite 102 Lincoln NE 68505 800-777-4344 466-9044*
*Fax Area Code: 402 ■ *TF:* 800-888-4344 ■ *Web:* www.mmmachealth.com

Mediware Information Systems Inc 11711 W 79th St Lenexa KS 66214 913-307-1000 307-1111
NASDAQ: MEDW ■ *TF:* 800-255-0026 ■ *Web:* www.mediware.com

Meta Health Technology Inc 330 7th Ave 14th Fl New York NY 10001 212-695-5870 643-2913
TF: 800-334-6840 ■ *Web:* www.metahealth.com

Metafile Information Systems Inc 2900 43rd St NW Rochester MN 55901 507-286-9232 286-9065
TF Sales: 800-638-2445 ■ *Web:* www.metafile.com

MicroMass Communications Inc 11000 Regency Pkwy Suite 300 Cary NC 27511 919-851-3182 851-3188
Web: www.micromass.com

MicroStrategy Inc 1861 International Dr McLean VA 22102 703-848-8600 848-8610
NASDAQ: MSTR ■ *TF:* 866-966-6787 ■ *Web:* www.strategy.com

Mincron Software Systems
333 N Sam Houston Pkwy E Suite 1100 Houston TX 77060 281-999-7010 999-6329
Web: www.mincron.com

Misys Healthcare Systems LLC 8529 Six Forks Rd Raleigh NC 27615 919-847-8102 847-7099
TF: 800-334-8534 ■ *Web:* www.misyshealthcare.com

Mortgage Computer Applications Inc
2650 Washington Blvd Suite 203 Ogden UT 84401 801-621-3900 627-2537
TF Cust Svc: 800-421-3277 ■ *Web:* www.mcoffice.com

MPSI Systems Inc 4343 S 118th East Ave Tulsa OK 74146 918-877-6774 877-6960
TF Cust Svc: 800-727-6774 ■ *Web:* www.mpsisys.com

Newmarket International Inc 135 Commerce Way Portsmouth NH 03801 603-436-7500 436-1826
Web: www.newmarketinc.com

Online Resources Corp 4795 Meadow Wood Ln Suite 300 Chantilly VA 20151 703-653-3100 653-3105
NASDAQ: ORCC ■ *Web:* www.orcc.com

Optimal Group Inc 3500 de Maisonneuve Suite 1700 Montreal QC H3Z3C1 514-738-8885 738-8355
NASDAQ: OPMR ■ *Web:* www.opmr.com

PMS Systems Corp 2800 28th St Suite 109 Santa Monica CA 90405 310-450-2566 450-1311
Web: www.assetsmart.com

Private Business Inc 9020 Overlook Blvd PO Box 1603 Brentwood TN 37024 800-235-5584 565-7425*
NASDAQ: PBIZ ■ *Fax Area Code: 615 ■ *Web:* www.privatebusiness.com

Proscape Technologies Inc 1155 Business Ctr Dr Suite 180 Horsham PA 19044 215-441-0300 441-0600
TF: 800-459-9300 ■ *Web:* www.proscape.com

Retalix Ltd USA 6100 Tennyson Pkwy Suite 150 Plano TX 75024 469-241-8400 241-0771
TF: 866-893-7722 ■ *Web:* www.retalix.com

Right On Computer Software 778 New York Ave Huntington NY 11743 631-424-7777 424-7207
Web: www.rightonprograms.com

Sandata Technologies Inc 26 Harbor Park Dr Port Washington NY 11050 516-484-4400 484-6084
TF Sales: 800-544-7263 ■ *Web:* www.sandata.com

Saratoga Systems Inc 900 E Hamilton Ave 6th Fl Campbell CA 95008 408-558-9600 558-9690
Web: www.saratogasystems.com

Settlement Services Corp 1004 W Taft Ave Orange CA 92865 714-998-1111 282-9602*
*Fax: Hum Res ■ *TF Sales:* 800-767-7832 ■ *Web:* www.smscorp.com

Ship Analytics Inc
183 Providence New London Tpke North
Stonington Professional Ctr North Stonington CT 06359 860-535-3092 535-0560
Web: www.shipanalytics.com

SS & C Technologies Inc 80 Lamberton Rd Windsor CT 06095 860-298-4500 298-4900
Web: www.ssctech.com

SunGard Insurance Systems 2000 S Dixie Hwy Suite 200 Miami FL 33133 305-858-8200 854-6305*
*Fax: Sales ■ *TF:* 800-337-2677 ■ *Web:* www.insurance.sungard.com

SunGard Pentamation Inc 3 W Broad St Suite 1 Bethlehem PA 18018 610-691-3616 691-1031
TF Cust Svc: 800-333-3619 ■ *Web:* www.pentamation.com

Synergistics Inc 9 Tech Cir Natick MA 01760 508-655-1340 651-2902
Web: www.synergisticsinc.com

Technical Services Assoc Inc (TSA) 2 Kacey Ct Mechanicsburg PA 17055 717-691-5691 691-5690
TF: 800-388-1415 ■ *Web:* www.pox.com

Thermeon Corp 12241 Newport Ave Suite 111 Santa Ana CA 92705 714-731-9191 731-5938
Web: www.thermeon.com

TimeValue Software 4 Jenner St Suite 100 Irvine CA 92618 949-727-1800 727-3268
TF Sales: 800-426-4741 ■ *Web:* www.timevalue.com

TSA (Technical Services Assoc Inc) 2 Kacey Ct Mechanicsburg PA 17055 717-691-5691 691-5690
TF: 800-388-1415 ■ *Web:* www.pox.com

United Data Systems 959 Broad St Augusta GA 30901 706-823-9723 823-9709
TF Sales: 800-241-2404 ■ *Web:* www.udsnet.com

Velos Inc 2201 Walnut Ave Suite 208 Fremont CA 94538 510-739-4010 739-4018
Web: www.velos.com

181-12 Systems & Utilities Software

Phone Fax

Accelr8 Technology Corp 7000 Broadway Bldg 3-307 Denver CO 80221 303-863-8088 863-1218
AMEX: AXK ■ *TF:* 800-582-8898 ■ *Web:* www.accelr8.com

ACCESS Systems Americas Inc 1188 E Arques Ave Sunnyvale CA 94085 408-400-3000 400-1500
Web: www.access-company.com

Phone Fax

ActivCard Inc 6623 Dumbarton Cir Fremont CA 94555 510-574-0100 574-0101
NASDAQ: ACTI ■ *TF:* 800-529-9499 ■ *Web:* www.activcard.com

activePDF Inc 27405 Puerta Real Suite 100 Mission Viejo CA 92691 949-582-9002 582-9004
TF: 866-468-6733 ■ *Web:* www.activepdf.com

Adaptive Solutions Inc 1301 Azalea Rd Suite 101 Mobile AL 36619 251-666-3045 660-1788
TF: 800-299-3045 ■ *Web:* www.talksight.com

Advantage IQ Inc 1313 N Atlantic St 5th Fl Spokane WA 99201 509-329-7600
TF: 877-828-8208 ■ *Web:* www.advantageiq.com

AEP Networks 347 Elizabeth Ave Suite 100 Somerset NJ 08873 732-652-5200 764-8862
TF: 877-638-4552 ■ *Web:* www.aepnetworks.com

Aladdin Knowledge Systems Ltd
601 Campus Dr Suite C-1 Arlington Heights IL 60004 847-818-3800 818-3810
NASDAQ: ALDN ■ *TF:* 800-562-2543 ■ *Web:* www.aladdin.com

Allen Systems Group Inc (ASG) 1333 3rd Ave S Naples FL 34102 239-435-2200 325-2555*
*Fax Area Code: 800 ■ *TF:* 800-932-5536 ■ *Web:* www.asg.com

Allume Systems Inc 185 Westridge Dr Watsonville CA 95076 831-761-6200 761-6206
TF: 800-732-8881 ■ *Web:* www.allume.com

Altiris Inc 588 W 400 South Lindon UT 84042 801-226-8500 226-8506
NASDAQ: ATRS ■ *TF:* 888-252-5551 ■ *Web:* www.altiris.com

Aonix North America Inc 5040 Shoreham Pl Suite 100 San Diego CA 92122 858-457-2700 824-0212
TF: 800-972-6649 ■ *Web:* www.aonix.com

Apex CoVantage LLC 200 Van Buren St 120 Presidents Plaza Herndon VA 20170 703-709-3000 709-0333
TF: 800-628-2739 ■ *Web:* www.apexcovantage.com

Ardence Inc 266 2nd Ave Waltham MA 02451 781-647-3000 647-3999
TF: 800-334-8649 ■ *Web:* www.vci.com

AREVA T & D 1 International Plaza Suite 300 Philadelphia PA 19113 484-766-8100 766-8150
Web: www.areva-td.com

Argus Systems Group Inc 1809 Woodfield Dr Savoy IL 61874 217-355-6308 355-1433
Web: www.argus-systems.com

ASG (Allen Systems Group Inc) 1333 3rd Ave S Naples FL 34102 239-435-2200 325-2555*
*Fax Area Code: 800 ■ *TF:* 800-932-5536 ■ *Web:* www.asg.com

Aspect Business Solutions 7550 IH-10 W 14th Fl San Antonio TX 78229 210-256-8300 682-2137
TF: 800-609-8113 ■ *Web:* 4aspect.com

Atos Origin 5599 San Felipe St Suite 300 Houston TX 77056 713-513-3000 403-7204
TF: 866-875-8902 ■ *Web:* www.na.atosorigin.com

Authentium Inc 7121 Fairway Dr Suite 102 Palm Beach Gardens FL 33418 561-575-3200 575-3026
TF: 800-423-9147 ■ *Web:* www.authentium.com

Auto-trol Technology Corp 12500 N Washington St Denver CO 80241 303-452-4919 252-2249
TF: 800-233-2882 ■ *Web:* www.auto-trol.com

Avanquest Publishing USA Inc 7031 Koll Ctr Pkwy Suite 150 Pleasanton CA 94566 925-474-1700 474-1800
Web: www.avanquestusa.com

Avatier Corp 12647 Alcosta Blvd Suite 140 San Ramon CA 94583 925-217-5170 275-0853
TF: 800-609-8610 ■ *Web:* www.avatier.com

Aventail Corp 808 Howell St 2nd Fl Seattle WA 98101 206-215-1111 215-1120
TF: 877-283-6824 ■ *Web:* www.aventail.com

BakBone Software Inc 9540 Town Centre Dr Suite 100 San Diego CA 92121 858-450-9009 450-9929
TF: 877-939-2663 ■ *Web:* www.bakbone.com

Basis International Ltd 5901 Jefferson St NE Albuquerque NM 87109 505-345-5232 345-5082
TF Orders: 800-423-1394 ■ *Web:* www.basis.com

BEA Systems Inc 2315 N 1st St San Jose CA 95131 408-570-8000 570-8901
NASDAQ: BEAS ■ *TF:* 800-817-4232 ■ *Web:* www.beasys.com

BenchmarkQA Inc 3800 American Blvd W Suite 1580 Minneapolis MN 55431 952-392-2381 392-2382
TF: 877-425-2581 ■ *Web:* www.benchmarkqa.com

Beta Systems Software Inc 2201 Cooperative Way Suite 350 Herndon VA 20171 703-889-1240 889-1241
TF: 800-475-1168 ■ *Web:* www.betasystems.com

Blue Lance Inc 1401 McKinney St Suite 950 Houston TX 77010 713-255-4800 590-0040
TF: 800-856-2583 ■ *Web:* www.bluelance.com

bNimble Technologies 45987 Paseo Padre Pkwy Suite 7 Fremont CA 94539 510-870-2312 445-0625
Web: www.bnimbletech.com

CA Inc 1 CA Plaza Islandia NY 11749 631-342-6000 342-6800
NYSE: CA ■ *Web:* www.ca.com

CardLogix 16 Hughes Suite 100 Irvine CA 92618 949-380-1312 380-1428
Web: www.cardlogix.com

Certicom Corp 5520 Explorer Dr 4th Fl Mississauga ON L4W5L1 905-507-4220 507-4230
TF: 800-561-6100 ■ *Web:* www.certicom.com

Check Point Software Technologies Ltd
800 Bridge Pkwy Redwood City CA 94065 650-628-2000 654-4233
NASDAQ: CHKP ■ *TF:* 800-429-4391 ■ *Web:* www.checkpoint.com

Cincom Systems Inc 55 Merchant St Cincinnati OH 45246 513-612-2300 612-2000
TF: 800-888-0115 ■ *Web:* www.cincom.com

Citrix Systems Inc 851 W Cypress Creek Rd Fort Lauderdale FL 33309 954-267-3000 267-9319
NASDAQ: CTXS ■ *TF:* 800-393-1888 ■ *Web:* www.citrix.com

Claria Corp 555 Broadway St Redwood City CA 94063 650-980-1500 980-1599
Web: www.claria.com

Cognetics Corp PO Box 386 Princeton Junction NJ 08550 609-799-5005
Web: www.cognetics.com

Columbia Data Products Inc
925 Sunshine Ln Suite 1080 Altamonte Springs FL 32714 407-869-6700 862-4725
TF Sales: 800-613-6288 ■ *Web:* www.cdpi.com

Communication Intelligence Corp
275 Shoreline Dr Suite 500 Redwood Shores CA 94065 650-802-7888 802-7777
TF Sales: 800-888-8242 ■ *Web:* www.cic.com

ComponentOne LLC 4516 Henry St Suite 500 Pittsburgh PA 15213 412-681-4343 681-4384
TF: 800-858-2739 ■ *Web:* www.component1.com

Configuresoft Inc 4390 Arrowswest Dr Colorado Springs CO 80907 719-447-4600 447-4601
Web: www.configuresoft.com

CSI International Inc 8120 State Rt 138 Williamsport OH 43164 740-420-5400 986-6022
TF: 800-795-4914 ■ *Web:* www.e-vse.com

CSP Inc 43 Manning Rd Billerica MA 01821 978-663-7598 663-0150
NASDAQ: CSPIE ■ *TF:* 800-325-3110 ■ *Web:* www.cspi.com

CT Holdings Enterprises Inc 5420 LBJ Fwy Suite 1600 Dallas TX 75240 214-520-9292 520-9293
TF: 800-962-0701 ■ *Web:* www.ct-holdings.com

CYA Technologies Inc 4 Research Dr Shelton CT 06484 203-513-3111 513-3139
Web: www.cya.com

CyberTeams Inc 6910 E Bowers Rd Frederick MD 21702 301-473-7778 473-9751
TF: 888-449-5575 ■ *Web:* www.cyberteams.com

Cybertrust Corp 13650 Dulles Technology Dr Suite 500 Herndon VA 20171 703-480-8200 480-8740
TF: 888-627-2281 ■ *Web:* www.cybertrust.com

DataDirect Technologies 3202 Tower Oaks Blvd Suite 300 Rockville MD 20852 301-468-8501 468-8592
TF: 800-876-3101 ■ *Web:* www.datadirect.com

DataMirror Corp 3100 Steeles Ave E Suite 1100 Markham ON L3R8T3 905-415-0310 415-0340
TF: 800-362-5955 ■ *Web:* www.datamirror.com

DataPath Inc 3095 Satellite Blvd Bldg 800 Suite 600 Duluth GA 30096 678-597-0300 252-4101
TF: 866-855-3800 ■ *Web:* www.datapath.com

DataViz Inc 612 Wheelers Farms Rd Milford CT 06460 203-874-0085 874-4345
TF: 800-733-0030 ■ *Web:* www.dataviz.com

Datawatch Corp 271 Mill Rd Chelmsford MA 01824 978-441-2200 441-1114
NASDAQ: DWCH ■ *TF:* 800-445-3311 ■ *Web:* www.datawatch.com

Descartes Systems Group Inc 120 Randall Dr Waterloo ON N2V1C6 519-746-8110 747-0082
NASDAQ: DSGX ■ *TF:* 800-419-8495 ■ *Web:* www.descartes.com

Digicomp Research Corp 930 Danby Rd Ithaca NY 14850 607-273-5900 273-8779
TF Cust Svc: 800-457-6000 ■ *Web:* www.digicomp.com

Digimarc Corp 9405 SW Gemini Dr Beaverton OR 97008 503-469-4800 469-4780
NASDAQ: DMRC ■ *TF:* 800-344-4627 ■ *Web:* www.digimarc.com

Digital Persona Inc 720 Bay Rd Suite 100 Redwood City CA 94063 650-474-4000 298-8313
TF: 877-378-2738 ■ *Web:* www.digitalpersona.com

Company	City	State	Zip	Phone	Fax
Direct Insite Corp 80 Orville Dr Suite 100	Bohemia	NY	11716	631-244-1500	563-8085
TF: 800-619-0757 ■ *Web:* www.directinsite.com					
Diskeeper Corp 7590 N Glenoaks Blvd	Burbank	CA	91504	818-771-1600	252-5514
TF Sales: 800-829-6468 ■ *Web:* www.execsoft.com					
Distinct Corp 3315 Almaden Expy Suite 10	San Jose	CA	95118	408-445-3270	445-3274
Web: www.distinct.com					
Diversified International Sciences Corp					
4550 Forbes Blvd Suite 300	Lanham	MD	20706	301-731-9070	731-9074
Web: www.discmd.com					
Diversinet Corp 2225 Sheppard Ave E Suite 1700	Toronto	ON	M2J5B5	416-756-2324	756-7346
Web: www.diversinet.com					
Double-Take Software Inc 257 Turnpike Rd	Southborough	MA	01772	508-229-8483	229-0866
TF Tech Supp: 800-775-8674 ■ *Web:* www.doubletake.com					
E-Net Corp 300 Valley St Suite 204	Sausalito	CA	94965	415-332-6200	339-9592
Web: www.enet.com					
EasyLink Services Corp 33 Knightbridge Rd	Piscataway	NJ	08854	732-652-3500	652-3810
NASDAQ: EASY ■ *TF:* 800-624-5266 ■ *Web:* www.easylink.com					
Electronic Scriptorium Ltd 26 Fairfax St SE Suite K	Leesburg	VA	20175	703-779-0376	779-0378
Web: www.electronicscriptorium.com					
eMag Solutions LLC					
3495 Piedmont Rd 11 Piedmont Ctr Suite 500	Atlanta	GA	30305	404-995-6060	872-8247
TF: 800-364-9838 ■ *Web:* www.emaglink.com					
EMC Corp 176 South St	Hopkinton	MA	01748	508-435-1000	497-6912
NYSE: EMC ■ *TF:* 877-362-6973 ■ *Web:* www.emc.com					
EMC Legato 2831 Mission College Blvd	Santa Clara	CA	95054	408-566-2000	566-2701
TF Tech Supp: 877-534-2867 ■ *Web:* software.emc.com					
Empirix Inc 20 Crosby Dr	Bedford	MA	01730	781-266-3200	266-3201
Web: www.empirix.com					
Entegrity Solutions Corp 410 Amherst St Suite 150	Nashua	NH	03063	603-882-1306	882-6092
TF: 800-525-4343 ■ *Web:* www.entegrity.com					
Entrust Inc 16633 Dallas Pkwy Suite 800	Addison	TX	75001	972-713-5800	713-5805
NASDAQ: ENTU ■ *TF Sales:* 888-690-2424 ■ *Web:* www.entrust.com					
Esker Inc 1212 Deming Way	Madison	WI	53717	608-828-6000	828-6001
TF: 800-368-5283 ■ *Web:* www.esker.com					
Expert Choice Inc 1501 Lee Hwy Suite 302	Arlington	VA	22209	703-243-5595	243-5587
TF: 888-259-6400 ■ *Web:* www.expertchoice.com					
F-Secure Inc 100 Century Center Ct Suite 700	San Jose	CA	95112	408-938-6700	938-6701
Web: www.f-secure.com					
FalconStor Software Inc 2 Huntington Quad Suite 2S01	Melville	NY	11747	631-777-5188	501-7633
NASDAQ: FALC ■ *Web:* www.falconstor.com					
FileStream Inc 333 Glen Head Rd	Glen Head	NY	11545	516-759-4100	759-3011
Web: www.filestream.com					
Finjan Software Inc 2025 Gateway Pl Suite 180	San Jose	CA	95110	408-452-9700	452-9701
TF: 888-346-5268 ■ *Web:* www.finjan.com					
Forvus Research Inc 742-200 McKnight Dr	Knightdale	NC	27545	919-954-0063	954-9254
TF: 888-323-4887 ■ *Web:* www.forvus.com					
Fujitsu Computer Systems Corp 1250 E Arques Ave	Sunnyvale	CA	94085	408-746-6000	
TF: 800-831-3183 ■ *Web:* www.computers.us.fujitsu.com					
Greenwald Industries 212 Middlesex Ave	Chester	CT	06412	860-526-0800	526-4205
TF: 800-221-0982 ■ *Web:* www.greenwaldindustries.com					
GroupSystems.com 520 Zang St Suite 211	Broomfield	CO	80021	303-468-8680	468-8681
TF: 800-368-6338 ■ *Web:* www.groupsystems.com					
Heroix Corp 57 Wells Ave	Newton	MA	02459	617-527-1550	527-6132
TF: 800-229-6500 ■ *Web:* www.heroix.com					
Hitachi Data Systems Corp 750 Central Expy	Santa Clara	CA	95050	408-970-1000	727-8036
TF: 800-227-1930 ■ *Web:* www.hds.com					
HyperSpace Communications Inc					
116 Inverness Dr E Suite 265	Englewood	CO	80112	303-566-6500	566-6514
AMEX: HCO ■ *TF:* 866-888-9578 ■ *Web:* www.ehyperspace.com					
Information Security Corp 1141 Lake Cook Rd Suite D	Deerfield	IL	60015	847-405-0500	405-0506
TF: 800-203-5563 ■ *Web:* www.infoseccorp.com					
Infosystems Technology Inc 7700 Leesburg Pike Suite 402	Falls Church	VA	22043	703-448-0002	448-9898
Web: www.rubix.com					
Innodata Isogen Inc 3 University Plaza Dr Suite 506	Hackensack	NJ	07601	201-488-1200	488-3341
NASDAQ: INOD ■ *TF:* 800-567-4784 ■ *Web:* www.inod.com					
Innovative Security Systems Inc DBA Argus Systems Group Inc					
1809 Woodfield Dr	Savoy	IL	61874	217-355-6308	355-1433
Web: www.argus-systems.com					
Integralis US 111 Founders Plaza 13th Fl	East Hartford	CT	06108	860-291-0851	291-0847
TF: 877-557-1475 ■ *Web:* www.us.integralis.com					
International Business Machines Corp (IBM)					
1 New Orchard Rd	Armonk	NY	10504	914-766-1900	
NYSE: IBM ■ *TF:* 800-426-4968 ■ *Web:* www.ibm.com/us					
Internet Security Systems Inc 6303 Barfield Rd	Atlanta	GA	30328	404-236-2600	236-2626
NASDAQ: ISSX ■ *TF:* 888-901-7477 ■ *Web:* www.iss.net					
InterTrust Technologies Corp 955 Stewart Dr	Sunnyvale	CA	94085	408-616-1600	616-1626
Web: www.intertrust.com					
Intrusion Inc 1101 E Arapaho Rd	Richardson	TX	75081	972-234-6400	234-1467
TF: 800-862-6637 ■ *Web:* www.intrusion.com					
I/O Software Inc 6711 Lee Hwy Suite 214	Arlington	VA	22205	703-738-9267	852-7914
Web: www.iosoftware.com					
Ipswitch Inc 10 Maguire Rd Suite 220	Lexington	MA	02421	781-676-5700	676-5710
TF: 800-793-4825 ■ *Web:* www.ipswitch.com					
Kroll Ontrack Inc 9023 Columbine Rd	Eden Prairie	MN	55347	952-937-1107	937-5815
TF Sales: 800-872-2599 ■ *Web:* www.krollontrack.com					
Lakeview Technology Inc					
1901 S Meyers Rd Suite 600	Oakbrook Terrace	IL	60181	630-282-8100	282-8500
TF: 800-536-8308 ■ *Web:* www.lakeviewtech.com					
LapLink Software Inc 14335 NE 24th St Suite 201	Bellevue	WA	98007	425-952-6000	952-6002
TF: 800-343-8080 ■ *Web:* www.laplink.com					
Lattice Inc 1751 S Naperville Rd Suite 100	Wheaton	IL	60187	630-949-3250	949-3299
TF Sales: 800-444-4309 ■ *Web:* www.lattice.com					
Lenel System International Inc 1212 Pittsford-Victor Rd	Pittsford	NY	14534	585-248-9720	248-9185
Web: www.lenel.com					
Linspire Inc 5960 Cornorstone Ct W Suite 200	San Diego	CA	92121	858-587-6700	587-8095
Web: www.linspire.com					
Luminex Software Inc 871 Marlborough Ave	Riverside	CA	92506	951-781-4100	781-4105
TF: 888-586-4639 ■ *Web:* www.luminex.com					
Macrovision Corp 2830 De La Cruz Blvd	Santa Clara	CA	95050	408-743-8600	567-1800
NASDAQ: MVSN ■ *TF:* 866-891-6876 ■ *Web:* www.macrovision.com					
Magic Software Enterprises Inc					
23046 Avenida de la Carlotta Suite 300	Laguna Hills	CA	92653	949-250-1718	250-7404
NASDAQ: MGIC ■ *TF:* 800-345-6244 ■ *Web:* www.magic-sw.com					
Mainsoft Corp 226 Airport Pkwy Suite 250	San Jose	CA	95110	408-200-4000	200-4044
TF: 800-624-6946 ■ *Web:* www.mainsoft.com					
Mainstay 1320 Flynn Rd Suite 401	Camarillo	CA	93012	805-484-9400	484-9428
TF Orders: 800-362-2605 ■ *Web:* www.mstay.com					
Management Science Assoc Inc 6565 Penn Ave	Pittsburgh	PA	15206	412-362-2000	363-8878
TF: 800-672-4636 ■ *Web:* www.msa.com					
Mandarin Library Automation Inc 1100 Holland Dr	Boca Raton	FL	33487	561-995-4010	995-4065
TF: 800-426-7477 ■ *Web:* www.mlasolutions.com					
Mangosoft Inc 29 Riverside St Suite A box 8	Nashua	NH	03062	603-324-0400	324-0400
TF: 888-886-2646 ■ *Web:* www.mangosoft.com					
MARX Software Security Inc					
2900 Chamblee-Tucker Rd Bldg 9 Suite 100	Atlanta	GA	30341	770-986-8887	986-8891
TF: 800-627-9468 ■ *Web:* www.marx.com					

Company	City	State	Zip	Phone	Fax
Maxum Development Corp PO Box 315	Crystal Lake	IL	60039	815-444-0100	444-0301*
**Fax:* Sales ■ *TF:* 800-813-3410 ■ *Web:* www.maxum.com					
McAfee Inc 3965 Freedom Cir	Santa Clara	CA	95054	408-988-3832	970-9727
NYSE: MFE ■ *TF:* 888-847-8766 ■ *Web:* www.mcafee.com					
McCabe & Assoc Inc 9730 Patuxent Dr Suite 400	Columbia	MD	21045	410-381-3710	381-7912
TF: 800-638-6316 ■ *Web:* www.mccabe.com					
Mercury Interactive Corp 379 N Whisman Rd	Mountain View	CA	94043	650-603-5200	603-5300
TF: 800-837-8911 ■ *Web:* www.mercury.com					
Micro 2000 Inc 600 N Brand Blvd 2nd Fl	Glendale	CA	91203	818-547-0125	543-7092
TF: 800-864-8008 ■ *Web:* www.micro2000.com					
Micro Logic Corp 666 Godwin Ave	Midland Park	NJ	07432	201-447-6991	447-6921
Web: www.miclog.com					
Microsoft Corp 1 Microsoft Way	Redmond	WA	98052	425-882-8080	936-7329
NASDAQ: MSFT ■ *Web:* www.microsoft.com					
Mitem Corp 640 Menlo Ave	Menlo Park	CA	94025	650-323-1500	323-1511
TF Sales: 800-826-4836 ■ *Web:* www.mitem.com					
Neon Software Inc 244 Lafayette Cir	Lafayette	CA	94549	925-283-9771	283-6507
TF Sales: 800-334-6366 ■ *Web:* www.neon.com					
NetIQ Corp DBA Attachmate 1233 W Loop South	Houston	TX	77027	713-548-1700	548-1771
TF Sales: 888-323-6768 ■ *Web:* www.netiq.com					
NetManage Inc 20883 Stevens Creek Blvd	Cupertino	CA	95014	408-973-7171	257-6405
NASDAQ: NETM ■ *TF:* 800-558-7656 ■ *Web:* www.netmanage.com					
NetPro Computing Inc 4747 N 22 St Suite 400	Phoenix	AZ	85016	602-346-3600	346-3610
TF: 800-998-5090 ■ *Web:* www.netpro.com					
Network Appliance Inc 495 E Java Dr	Sunnyvale	CA	94089	408-822-6000	822-4422
NASDAQ: NTAP ■ *TF Sales:* 800-443-4537 ■ *Web:* www.netapp.com					
Norman Data Defense Systems Inc 9302 Lee Hwy Suite 950A	Fairfax	VA	22031	703-267-6109	934-6368
TF: 888-466-6762 ■ *Web:* www.norman.com					
Northrop Grumman Information Technology					
2101 Gaither Rd Suite 600	Rockville	MD	20850	301-527-6400	527-6401
Web: www.it.northropgrumman.com/index.asp					
NovaStor Corp 80-B W Cochran St	Simi Valley	CA	93065	805-579-6700	579-6710*
**Fax:* Sales ■ *TF:* 800-668-2786 ■ *Web:* www.novastor.com					
Novell Inc 30 Lafayette St	Lebanon	NH	03766	603-643-1300	643-9366
TF: 800-262-3877 ■ *Web:* www.novell.com					
NSTL Inc 670 Sentry Pkwy 2nd Fl	Blue Bell	PA	19422	610-832-8400	941-9952
Web: www.nstl.com					
NTP Software 427-3 Amherst St Suite 381	Nashua	NH	03063	603-622-4400	263-2375
TF: 800-226-2755 ■ *Web:* www.ntpsoftware.com					
Numara Software Inc 2202 NW Shore Blvd Suite 650	Tampa	FL	33607	813-227-4500	227-4501
TF Sales: 800-557-6970 ■ *Web:* www.numarasoftware.com					
Open Door Networks Inc 110 S Laurel St	Ashland	OR	97520	541-488-4127	
Web: www.opendoor.com					
Open Systems Management Inc 1511 3rd Ave Suite 905	Seattle	WA	98101	206-583-8373	583-8374
TF: 866-601-8011 ■ *Web:* www.osmcorp.com					
OPNET Technologies Inc 7255 Woodmont Ave	Bethesda	MD	20814	240-497-3000	497-3001
NASDAQ: OPNT ■ *Web:* www.opnet.com					
Oracle Corp 500 Oracle Pkwy	Redwood Shores	CA	94065	650-506-7000	506-7200
NASDAQ: ORCL ■ *TF Sales:* 800-672-2531 ■ *Web:* www.oracle.com					
Panda Software 230 N Maryland Ave Suite 303 PO Box 10578	Glendale	CA	91209	818-553-0599	543-6910
Web: www.pandasoftware.com					
Peoplesmith Software Inc 50 Cole Pkwy Suite 34	Scituate	MA	02066	781-545-7300	545-7717
TF Sales: 800-777-2460 ■ *Web:* www.peoplesmith.com					
Perceptics Corp 9737 Cogdill Rd Suite 200	Knoxville	TN	37932	865-966-9200	966-9330
TF: 800-448-8544 ■ *Web:* www.perceptics.com					
Pervasive Software Inc 12365 Riata Trace Pkwy Bldg B	Austin	TX	78727	512-231-6000	231-6010
NASDAQ: PVSW ■ *TF:* 800-287-4383 ■ *Web:* www.pervasive.com					
Phoenix Technologies Ltd 915 Murphy Ranch Rd	Milpitas	CA	95035	408-570-1000	570-1001
NASDAQ: PTEC ■ *TF:* 800-677-7305 ■ *Web:* www.phoenix.com					
PKWare Inc 648 N Plankinton Ave Suite 220	Milwaukee	WI	53203	414-354-8699	289-9789
Web: www.pkware.com/company					
Pragma Systems Inc 13708 Research Blvd Suite 675	Austin	TX	78750	512-219-7270	219-7110
TF Sales: 800-224-1675 ■ *Web:* www.pragmasys.com					
Process Software Corp 959 Concord St	Framingham	MA	01701	508-879-6994	879-0042
TF: 800-722-7770 ■ *Web:* www.process.com					
Proginet Corp 200 Garden City Plaza Suite 220	Garden City	NY	11530	516-535-3600	535-3601
Web: www.proginet.com					
Quick Eagle Networks Inc 830 Maude Ave	Mountain View	CA	94043	650-962-8282	962-7950
TF: 888-280-5465 ■ *Web:* www.quickeagle.com					
RadView Software Inc 111 Deerwood Rd Suite 200	San Ramon	CA	94583	925-831-4808	831-4807
TF: 888-723-8439 ■ *Web:* www.radview.com					
Raining Data Corp 25-A Technology Dr	Irvine	CA	92618	949-442-4400	250-8187
NASDAQ: RDTA ■ *TF:* 800-367-7425 ■ *Web:* www.rainingdata.com					
Raxco Software Inc 6 Montgomery Village Ave Suite 500	Gaithersburg	MD	20879	301-527-0803	519-7711
TF Tech Supp: 800-546-9728 ■ *Web:* www.raxco.com					
RDKS Inc DBA Litronic 17861 Cartwright Rd	Irvine	CA	92614	949-622-3632	851-8588
Web: www.litronic.com					
Red Hat Inc 1801 Varsity Dr	Raleigh	NC	27606	919-754-3700	754-3701
NASDAQ: RHAT ■ *TF:* 888-733-4281 ■ *Web:* www.redhat.com					
Relais International 1690 Woodward Dr Suite 215	Ottawa	ON	K2C3R8	613-226-5571	226-0998
TF: 888-294-5244 ■ *Web:* www.relais-intl.com					
Rhintek Inc 8835 Columbia 100 Pkwy Suite C	Columbia	MD	21045	410-730-2575	730-5960
Web: www.rhintek.com					
Rockwell Software Inc 2424 S 102nd St	West Allis	WI	53227	414-328-2000	321-2211
Web: www.software.rockwell.com					
RSA Security Inc 174 Middlesex Tpke	Bedford	MA	01730	781-515-5000	515-5010
NASDAQ: RSAS ■ *TF:* 800-301-5000 ■ *Web:* www.rsasecurity.com					
SAFLINK Corp 777 108th Ave NE Suite 2100	Bellevue	WA	98004	425-278-1100	278-1300
NASDAQ: SFLK ■ *TF:* 800-762-9595 ■ *Web:* www.saflink.com					
Seagull Software 3340 Peachtree Rd NE	Atlanta	GA	30326	404-760-1560	760-0061
Web: www.seagullsoftware.com					
Secure Computing Corp 4810 Hardwood Rd	San Jose	CA	95124	408-979-6100	979-6501
NASDAQ: SCUR ■ *TF:* 800-692-5625 ■ *Web:* www.securecomputing.com					
Securify Inc 20425 Stevens Creek Blvd Suite 200	Cupertino	CA	95014	408-343-4300	343-4301
Web: www.securify.com					
Sensory Inc 1991 Russell Ave	Santa Clara	CA	95054	408-327-9000	727-4748
Web: www.sensoryinc.com					
Serengeti Systems Inc 812 W 11th St 3rd Fl	Austin	TX	78701	512-345-2211	480-8729
TF: 800-634-3122 ■ *Web:* www.serengeti.com					
ShowCase Div SPSS Inc 233 S Wacker Dr 11th Fl	Chicago	IL	60606	312-651-3000	
TF: 800-259-1028 ■ *Web:* www.spss.com					
Silicon Graphics Inc (SGI) 1140 E Argues Ave	Sunnyvale	CA	94085	650-960-1980	933-0908
Web: www.sgi.com					
Simtrol Inc 2200 Norcross Pkwy Suite 255	Norcross	GA	30071	770-242-7566	441-1823
TF: 800-423-0769 ■ *Web:* www.simtrol.com					
Smart Card Integrators Inc 5250 W Century Blvd Suite 442	Los Angeles	CA	90045	310-215-1234	215-1237
Web: www.sci-s.com					
Smart Card Solutions LLC 229 E Capitol Dr	Hartland	WI	53029	262-369-3400	369-3401
TF: 888-225-6442 ■ *Web:* www.sc-solutions.com					
Smart Dynamics LLC 3601 Wilson Blvd Suite 500	Arlington	VA	22201	703-312-7383	812-5190
Web: www.smartdynamics.com					
SNMP Research International Inc 3001 Kimberlin Heights Rd	Knoxville	TN	37920	865-579-3311	579-6565
Web: www.snmp.com					
Software Engineering of America Inc					
1230 Hempstead Tpke	Franklin Square	NY	11010	516-328-7000	354-4015
TF: 800-272-7322 ■ *Web:* www.seasoft.com					

Systems & Utilities Software (Cont'd)

Company	City	State	ZIP	Phone	Fax
Software Pursuits Inc 1500 Fashion Island Blvd Suite 205 *TF:* 800-367-4823 ■ *Web:* www.softwarepursuits.com	San Mateo	CA	94404	650-372-0900	372-2912
Soliton Inc 44 Victoria St Suite 820 *TF:* 888-327-9457 ■ *Web:* www.soliton.com	Toronto	ON	M5C1Y2	416-364-9355	364-6159
Sophos Inc 6 Kimball Ln Suite 400 *TF:* 888-767-4679 ■ *Web:* www.sophos.com	Lynnfield	MA	01940	781-973-0110	245-8620
SPSS Inc ShowCase Div 233 S Wacker Dr 11th Fl *TF:* 800-259-1028 ■ *Web:* www.spss.com	Chicago	IL	60606	312-651-3000	
SPYRUS Inc 2355 Oakland Rd Suite 1 *TF:* 800-277-9787 ■ *Web:* www.spyrus.com	San Jose	CA	95131	408-953-0700	953-9835
Stalker Software Inc 655 Redwood Hwy Suite 275 *TF:* 800-262-4722 ■ *Web:* www.stalker.com	Mill Valley	CA	94941	415-383-7164	383-7461
Stirling Networks Inc 2751 Currier Ave *Web:* www.businessbasic.com	Simi Valley	CA	93065	805-579-8998	579-8190
Stratus Technologies 111 Powdermill Rd *TF:* 800-787-2887 ■ *Web:* www.stratus.com	Maynard	MA	01754	978-461-7000	461-5210
Sun Microsystems Inc 4150 Network Cir *NASDAQ: SUNW* ■ *TF:* 800-786-0404 ■ *Web:* www.sun.com	Santa Clara	CA	95054	650-960-1300	856-2114
Sunbelt Software USA 33 N Garden Ave Suite 1200 *TF:* 888-688-8457 ■ *Web:* www.sunbelt-software.com	Clearwater	FL	33755	727-562-0101	562-5199
Symantec Corp 20330 Stevens Creek Blvd *NASDAQ: SYMC* ■ *TF Cust Svc:* 800-441-7234 ■ *Web:* www.symantec.com	Cupertino	CA	95014	408-517-8000	517-8186
Symark Software 30401 Agoura Rd Suite 200 *TF:* 800-234-9072 ■ *Web:* www.symark.com	Agoura Hills	CA	91301	818-575-4000	889-1894
Syncsort Inc 50 Tice Blvd *Web:* www.syncsort.com	Woodcliff Lake	NJ	07677	201-930-9700	930-8290
SystemSoft Corp 275 Grove St Suite I-300 *TF:* 800-796-0088 ■ *Web:* www.systemsoft.com	Newton	MA	02466	617-614-4315	614-4601
TeamQuest Corp 1 TeamQuest Way *TF:* 800-551-8326 ■ *Web:* www.teamquest.com	Clear Lake	IA	50428	641-357-2700	357-2778
TechSmith Corp 2405 Woodlake Dr *TF:* 800-517-3001 ■ *Web:* www.techsmith.com	Okemos	MI	48864	517-381-2300	381-2336
Tecsec Inc 1953 Gallows Rd Suite 220 *Web:* www.tecsec.com	Vienna	VA	22182	703-506-9069	506-1484
Telesensory Inc 38083 Cherry St *Web:* www.telesensory.com	Newark	CA	94560	510-793-3075	793-2017
Tenebril Inc 959 Concord St *TF:* 800-722-7770 ■ *Web:* www.tenebril.com	Framingham	MA	01701	508-879-6994	879-0042
Thales e-Security Inc 2200 N Commerce Pkwy Suite 200 *TF:* 888-744-4976 ■ *Web:* www.thales-esecurity.com	Weston	FL	33326	954-888-6200	888-6211
TouchStone Software Corp 1538 Turnpike St *TF:* 800-800-2467 ■ *Web:* www.touchstonesoftware.com	North Andover	MA	01845	978-686-6468	683-1630
TrendMicro Inc 10101 N De Anza Blvd Suite 200 *TF:* 800-228-5651 ■ *Web:* www.trendmicro.com	Cupertino	CA	95014	408-257-1500	257-2003
Tripwire Inc 326 SW Broadway 3rd Fl *TF:* 800-874-7947 ■ *Web:* www.tripwire.com	Portland	OR	97205	503-276-7500	223-0182
Trust Digital Inc 1600 International Dr Suite 100 *TF:* 888-760-9401 ■ *Web:* www.trustdigital.com	McLean	VA	22102	703-760-9400	760-9415
TurboLinux Inc 600 Townsend St Suite 120E *Web:* www.turbolinux.com	San Francisco	CA	94103	415-503-4330	437-2892
UltraBac Software 15015 Main St Suite 200 *Web:* www.ultrabac.com	Bellevue	WA	98007	425-644-6000	644-8222
UniSoft Corp 10 Rollins Rd Suite 118 *Web:* www.unisoft.com	Millbrae	CA	94030	650-259-1290	259-1299
US Design Corp 9075 Guilford Rd *Web:* www.usdesign.com	Columbia	MD	21046	410-381-3000	381-3235
VanDyke Software Inc 4848 Tramway Ridge Dr NE Suite 101 *Web:* www.vandyke.com	Albuquerque	NM	87111	505-332-5700	332-5701
Vendant Inc 26 Parker St *TF:* 800-714-4900 ■ *Web:* www.vedanthealth.com	Newburyport	MA	01950	978-462-0737	462-4755
Vision Solutions Inc 17911 Von Karman Ave 5th Fl *TF:* 800-683-4667 ■ *Web:* www.visionsolutions.com	Irvine	CA	92614	949-253-6500	253-6501
Visiphor Corp 4710 Kingsway Suite 1100 *Web:* www.imagistechnologies.com	Bernaby	BC	V5H4M2	604-684-2449	684-9314
Visual Automation Inc 403 S Clinton St Suite 4 *Web:* www.visualautomation.com	Grand Ledge	MI	48837	517-622-1850	622-1761
Watchfire Corp 880 Winter St *Web:* www.watchfire.com	Watham	MA	02451	781-810-1450	890-2087
WatchGuard Technologies Inc 505 5th Ave S Suite 500 *NASDAQ: WGRD* ■ *TF Sales:* 800-734-9905 ■ *Web:* www.watchguard.com	Seattle	WA	98104	206-521-8340	521-8342
Webroot Software Inc PO Box 19816 *TF:* 800-772-9383 ■ *Web:* www.webroot.com	Boulder	CO	80308	303-442-3813	442-3846
WildPackets Inc 1340 Treat Blvd Suite 500 *TF:* 800-466-2447 ■ *Web:* www.wildpackets.com	Walnut Creek	CA	94597	925-937-3200	937-3211
Wilson WindowWare Inc 5421 California Ave SW *TF:* 800-762-8383 ■ *Web:* www.windowware.com	Seattle	WA	98136	206-938-1740	935-7129
Wind River Systems Inc 500 Wind River Way *NASDAQ: WIND* ■ *TF:* 800-545-9463 ■ *Web:* www.windriver.com	Alameda	CA	94501	510-748-4100	749-2010
WinZip Computing Inc PO Box 540 *Web:* www.winzip.com	Mansfield	CT	06268	860-429-3539	429-3542
Wipro Technologies 75 Federal St 14th Fl *NYSE: WIT* ■ *TF:* 866-449-4776 ■ *Web:* www.wipro.com	Boston	MA	02110	617-850-6000	850-4399
Xinet Inc 2560 9th St Suite 312 *Web:* www.xinet.com	Berkeley	CA	94710	510-845-0555	644-2680
XIOtech Corp 6455 Flying Cloud Dr *TF:* 866-472-6764 ■ *Web:* www.xiotech.com	Eden Prairie	MN	55344	952-983-3000	983-2330
Yrrid Software Inc 507 Monroe St *TF:* 800-443-0065 ■ *Web:* www.yrrid.com	Chapel Hill	NC	27516	919-968-7858	968-7856
Zix Corp 2711 N Haskell Ave Suite 2300-LB *NASDAQ: ZIXI* ■ *TF:* 888-771-4049 ■ *Web:* www.zixcorp.com	Dallas	TX	75204	214-370-2000	370-2070
Zone Alarm 800 Bridge Pkwy *TF:* 877-966-5221 ■ *Web:* www.zonealarm.com	Redwood City	CA	94065	415-633-4500	633-4501

182 COMPUTER STORES

SEE ALSO Appliance & Home Electronics Stores p. 1279

Company	City	State	ZIP	Phone	Fax
A Matter of Fax 105 Harrison Ave *TF:* 800-433-3329 ■ *Web:* www.amatteroffax.com	Harrison	NJ	07029	973-482-3700	485-8900
Aberdeen LLC 9130 Norwalk Blvd **Fax:* Sales ■ *Web:* www.aberdeeninc.com	Santa Fe Springs	CA	90670	562-699-6998	695-5570*
CDW Corp 200 N Milwaukee Ave *NASDAQ: CDWC* ■ *TF:* 800-828-4239 ■ *Web:* www.cdw.com	Vernon Hills	IL	60061	847-465-6000	465-6800
ClubMac Inc 19 Morgan St *TF:* 800-258-2622 ■ *Web:* www.clubmac.com	Irvine	CA	92618	949-768-8130	707-4085
CompUSA Inc 14951 N Dallas Pkwy *TF:* 800-278-4685 ■ *Web:* www.compusa.com	Dallas	TX	75254	972-982-4000	
Computer Renaissance 500 S Florida Ave Suite 400 **Fax Area Code:* 800 ■ *Web:* www.compren.com	Lakeland	FL	33801	863-669-1155	665-6324*
Cyberian Outpost Inc 25 N Main St *TF:* 877-688-7678 ■ *Web:* www.outpost.com	Kent	CT	06757	860-927-2050	927-8600
GameStop Corp 625 Westport Pkwy *NYSE: GME* ■ *TF:* 800-288-9020 ■ *Web:* www.gamestop.com	Grapevine	TX	76051	817-424-2000	424-2002
Gateway Inc 7565 Irvine Center Dr *NYSE: GTW* ■ *TF:* 800-846-2000 ■ *Web:* www.gateway.com	Irvine	CA	92618	949-471-7000	471-7001
Geeks.com 1890 Ord Way *Web:* www.geeks.com	Oceanside	CA	92056	760-726-7700	726-7723
Hartco LP 9393 boul Louis H Lafontaine *Web:* www.hartco.com	Ville d'Anjou	QC	H1J1Y8	514-354-3810	354-2299
Insight Enterprises Inc 6820 S Harl Ave *NASDAQ: NSIT* ■ *TF:* 800-467-4448 ■ *Web:* www.insight.com	Tempe	AZ	85283	480-333-3000	760-3330
MacConnection 730 Milford Rd Rt 101A *TF:* 800-800-0014 ■ *Web:* www.macconnection.com	Merrimack	NH	03054	603-683-2000	683-5766
Micrologistix Technologies Inc 221 N 1st St *Web:* www.chumbo.com	Minneapolis	MN	55401	612-486-1234	204-0499
PC Club Inc 18537 E Gale Ave Suite B *TF:* 800-839-8080 ■ *Web:* www.pcclub.com	City of Industry	CA	91748	626-839-8080	839-8088
PC Connection Inc 730 Milford Rd Rt 101A *NASDAQ: PCCC* ■ *TF:* 800-800-1111 ■ *Web:* www.pcconnection.com	Merrimack	NH	03054	603-683-2000	683-5766
PC Connection Inc MacConnection Div DBA MacConnection 730 Milford Rd Rt 101A *TF:* 800-800-0014 ■ *Web:* www.macconnection.com	Merrimack	NH	03054	603-683-2000	683-5766
PC Mall Inc 2555 W 190th St *NASDAQ: MALL* ■ **Fax:* Mktg ■ *TF:* 800-413-3833 ■ *Web:* www.pcmall.com	Torrance	CA	90504	310-354-5600	353-7475*
Tech Depot 6 Cambridge Dr **Fax:* Cust Svc ■ *TF Cust Svc:* 800-585-4080 ■ *Web:* www.4sure.com	Trumbull	CT	06611	203-615-7000	615-7005*

183 COMPUTER SYSTEMS DESIGN SERVICES

SEE ALSO Web Site Design Services p. 2414

Companies that plan and design computer systems that integrate hardware, software, and communication technologies.

Company	City	State	ZIP	Phone	Fax
3t Systems Inc 999 18th St Suite 2100 *TF:* 800-485-1180 ■ *Web:* www.3tsystems.com	Denver	CO	80202	303-858-8800	790-9784
Abacus Technology Corp 5454 Wisconsin Ave Suite 1100 *TF:* 800-225-2135 ■ *Web:* www.abacustech.com	Chevy Chase	MD	20815	301-907-8500	907-8508
Acumen Solutions Inc 8614 Westwood Center Dr Suite 700 *Web:* www.acumensolutions.com	Vienna	VA	22182	703-600-4000	600-4001
Advanced Information Systems Group Inc 11315 Corporate Blvd Suite 210 *Web:* www.aisg.com	Orlando	FL	32817	407-581-2929	581-2935
Advanced Resource Technologies Inc 1555 King St Suite 400 *TF:* 800-796-9936 ■ *Web:* www.team-arti.com	Alexandria	VA	22314	703-682-4740	682-4820
AETEA Information Technology Inc 1445 Research Blvd Suite 300 *TF:* 888-772-3832 ■ *Web:* www.aetea.com	Rockville	MD	20850	301-721-4200	721-1730
AGSI 3390 Peachtree Rd NE Suite 350 *TF:* 800-768-2474 ■ *Web:* www.agsi.com	Atlanta	GA	30326	404-816-7577	816-7578
Allied Technology Inc 1803 Research Blvd Suite 601 *Web:* www.alliedtech.com	Rockville	MD	20850	301-309-1234	309-0978
Allin Corp 381 Mansfield Ave Suite 400 *Web:* www.allin.com	Pittsburgh	PA	15220	412-928-8800	928-0887
AlphaSoft Services Corp 2121 N California Blvd Suite 345 *Web:* www.alphasoftservices.com	Walnut Creek	CA	94596	925-952-6300	932-3743
American Systems Corp 13990 Parkeast Cir *TF:* 800-733-2721 ■ *Web:* www.2asc.com	Chantilly	VA	20151	703-968-6300	968-5151
Analex Corp 2677 Prosperity Ave Suite 400 *AMEX: NLX* ■ *Web:* www.analex.com	Fairfax	VA	22031	703-329-9400	852-2206
Analysts International Corp 3601 W 76th St *NASDAQ: ANLY* ■ *TF:* 800-800-5044 ■ *Web:* www.analysts.com	Minneapolis	MN	55435	952-835-5900	897-4555
Apogen Technologies 7450B Boston Blvd	Springfield	VA	22153	703-644-6433	644-6435
Arlington Computer Products Inc 851 Commerce Ct *TF Orders:* 800-548-5105 ■ *Web:* www.arlingtoncp.com	Buffalo Grove	IL	60089	847-541-6333	541-6881
Arrow Strategies LLC 2851 Charlevoix Dr Suite 221 *Web:* arrowweb3.irun.com	Grand Rapids	MI	49546	616-885-1126	885-1135
Atos Origin 5599 San Felipe St Suite 300 *TF:* 866-875-8902 ■ *Web:* www.na.atosorigin.com	Houston	TX	77056	713-513-3000	403-7204
Automation Image Inc 2650 Valley View Ln Suite 100 *Web:* www.ccentrix.com	Dallas	TX	75234	972-247-8816	243-2814
Bay State Computers Inc 4201 Northview Dr Suite 408 *TF:* 800-266-3783 ■ *Web:* www.bayst.com	Bowie	MD	20716	301-352-7878	352-6925
BearingPoint Inc 1676 International Dr *NYSE: BE* ■ *TF:* 866-276-4768 ■ *Web:* www.bearingpoint.com	McLean	VA	22102	703-747-3000	747-8500
Bell Industries Inc 1960 E Grand Ave Suite 560 *AMEX: BI* ■ *TF:* 800-782-2355 ■ *Web:* www.bellind.com	El Segundo	CA	90245	310-563-2355	648-7280
Bell Industries Inc Tech.logix Group 8888 Keystone Crossing Suite 1700 *TF:* 800-722-1599 ■ *Web:* www.belltechlogix.com	Indianapolis	IN	46241	317-227-6700	704-0064
Berbee Information Networks Corp 5520 Research Park Dr *TF:* 888-888-8835 ■ *Web:* www.berbee.com	Madison	WI	53711	608-288-3000	288-3007
Bull HN Information Systems Inc 300 Concord Rd *Web:* www.bull.com/us/usa.html	Billerica	MA	01821	978-294-6000	294-7999
CACI International Inc 1100 N Glebe Rd *NYSE: CAI* ■ *Web:* www.caci.com	Arlington	VA	22201	703-841-7800	841-7882
Calence Inc 1620 W Fountainhead Pkwy Suite 400 *TF:* 877-225-3623 ■ *Web:* www.calence.com	Tempe	AZ	85282	480-889-9500	889-9599
Camber Corp 635 Discovery Dr NW *TF:* 800-998-7988 ■ *Web:* www.camber.com	Huntsville	AL	35806	256-922-0200	922-3599
Capgemini US LLC 750 7th Ave Suite 1800 *Web:* www.us.capgemini.com	New York	NY	10036	917-934-8000	934-8001
Carreker Corp 4055 Valley View Ln Suite 1000 *NASDAQ: CANI* ■ *TF:* 800-486-1981 ■ *Web:* www.carreker.com	Dallas	TX	75244	972-458-1981	701-0758
CCSI Technology Solutions Corp 2480 Meadowvale Blvd *TF:* 800-268-2106	Mississauga	ON	L5N7Y1	905-816-3000	
CellExchange Inc 101 Main St *Web:* www.cellexchange.com	Cambridge	MA	02142	617-528-2100	
Cexec Inc 11440 Commerce Pk Dr Suite 600 *Web:* www.cexec.com	Reston	VA	20191	703-435-0099	766-8539
CGI Group Inc 1130 Sherbrooke St W 7th Fl *NYSE: GIB* ■ *Web:* www.cgi.ca	Montreal	QC	H3A2M8	514-841-3200	841-3299
Cherokee Information Services Inc 1225 S Clark St Suite 1300 *Web:* www.cherokee-inc.com	Arlington	VA	22202	703-416-0720	416-1045
CIBER Inc 5251 DTC Pkwy Suite 1400 *NYSE: CBR* ■ *TF:* 800-242-3799 ■ *Web:* www.ciber.com	Greenwood Village	CO	80111	303-220-0100	220-7100

Phone | Fax

Clarkston Consulting 1007 Slater Rd Suite 400 ... Durham NC 27703 919-484-4400 484-4450
TF: 800-652-4274 ■ *Web:* www.clarkstonpotomac.com

Clever Devices Ltd 137 Commercial St ... Plainview NY 11803 516-433-6100 433-5088
TF: 800-872-6129 ■ *Web:* www.cleverdevices.com

CodeSoft International Inc 6470 E Johns Crossing Suite 450 ... Duluth GA 30097 770-913-0101 913-0611
Web: www.codesoft.net

Cognizant Technology Solutions Corp
500 Glenpointe Ctr W 7th Fl ... Teaneck NJ 07666 201-801-0233 678-2782*
NASDAQ: CTSH ■ **Fax:* Mktg ■ *TF:* 888-937-3277 ■ *Web:* www.cognizant.com

COLSA Corp 6726 Odyssey Dr ... Huntsville AL 35806 256-964-5555 964-5418
Web: www.colsa.com

ComGlobal Systems Inc 4250 Pacific Hwy Suite 225 ... San Diego CA 92110 619-321-6000 294-8748
Web: www.comglobal.com

Compri Consulting Inc 1580 Lincoln St Suite 860 ... Denver CO 80203 303-860-1533 860-1557
Web: www.compri.com

CompuCom Systems Inc Excell Data Div
1756 114th Ave SE Suite 220 ... Bellevue WA 98004 425-974-2000 974-2001
TF: 800-539-2355 ■ *Web:* www.excell.com

Computer Analytical Systems Inc (CASI) 1418 S 3rd St ... Louisville KY 40208 502-635-2019 636-9157
TF: 800-977-3475 ■ *Web:* www.c-a-s-i.com

Computer Horizons Corp 49 Old Bloomfield Ave ... Mountain Lakes NJ 07046 973-299-4000 402-7988
NASDAQ: CHRZ ■ *TF:* 800-321-2421 ■ *Web:* www.computerhorizons.com

Computer Methods Corp 525 Rt 73 S Suite 300 ... Marlton NJ 08053 856-596-4360 596-4362
TF: 800-969-4360 ■ *Web:* www.computermethods.com

Computer Sciences Corp 2100 E Grand Ave ... El Segundo CA 90245 310-615-0311 640-2648
NYSE: CSC ■ *TF:* 800-342-5272 ■ *Web:* www.csc.com

Computer Task Group Inc (CTG) 800 Delaware Ave ... Buffalo NY 14209 716-882-8000 887-7456
NYSE: CTG ■ *TF:* 800-992-5350 ■ *Web:* www.ctg.com

Computer Technology Assoc (CTA)
12530 Parklawn Dr Suite 300 ... Rockville MD 20852 301-581-3200 581-3201
TF: 800-753-9201 ■ *Web:* www.cta.com

Covansys Corp 32605 W 12 Mile Rd Suite 250 ... Farmington Hills MI 48334 248-488-2088 488-2089
NASDAQ: CVNS ■ *Web:* www.covansys.com

Custom Computer Specialists Inc 70 Suffolk Ct ... Hauppauge NY 11788 631-864-6699 543-2512
TF: 800-735-1775 ■ *Web:* www.customonline.com

Cybertech Systems & Software Inc
1250 E Diehl Rd Suite 403 ... Naperville IL 60563 630-472-3200 472-3299
TF: 800-874-1985 ■ *Web:* www.cybertech.com

Data Return LLC 222 W Las Colinas Blvd Suite 350E ... Irving TX 75039 972-869-0770 869-0150
TF: 800-767-1514 ■ *Web:* www.datareturn.com

Data Systems Analysts Inc 8 Neshaminy Interplex Suite 209 ... Trevose PA 19053 215-245-4800 245-4375
Web: www.dsainc.com

Datashare Corp 9485 Priority Way W Dr ... Indianapolis IN 46240 317-569-7485 569-7481
TF: 800-228-5465 ■ *Web:* www.datashare.com

DataSource Inc 7500 Greenway Center Dr Suite 420 ... Greenbelt MD 20770 301-441-2357 441-3678
TF: 800-330-4752 ■ *Web:* www.jetsonj2ee.com

Delta CompuTec Inc 900 Huyler St ... Teterboro NJ 07608 201-440-8585 440-3985
TF: 800-477-8586 ■ *Web:* www.dcis.com

Delta Corporate Services Inc 129 Littleton Rd ... Parsippany NJ 07054 973-334-6260 331-0144
TF: 800-335-8220 ■ *Web:* www.deltacorp.com

Design Strategy Corp 600 3rd Ave 25th Fl ... New York NY 10016 212-370-0000 949-3648
TF: 800-331-8726 ■ *Web:* www.designstrategy.com

DPE Systems Inc 425 Pontius Ave N Suite 430 ... Seattle WA 98109 206-223-3737 223-0859
TF: 800-541-6566 ■ *Web:* www.dpes.com

DRS Technical Services Inc 4041 Powder Mill Rd Suite 700 ... Calverton MD 20705 301-595-0710 937-5236
TF: 800-282-6727 ■ *Web:* www.drs.com

Dynamic Decisions Inc 31 Suttons Ln ... Piscataway NJ 08854 732-819-3946 819-4570
TF: 800-689-9908 ■ *Web:* www.ddidynex.com

Dynamics Research Corp 60 Frontage Rd ... Andover MA 01810 978-475-9090 470-0201
NASDAQ: DRCO ■ *TF:* 800-522-4321 ■ *Web:* www.drc.com

ea inc 1130 Iron Point Rd Suite 288 ... Folsom CA 95630 916-357-6588 200-0368
TF: 800-399-2828 ■ *Web:* www.ea-inc.com

Edgewater Technology Inc 20 Harvard Mill Sq ... Wakefield MA 01880 781-246-3343 246-5903
NASDAQ: EDGW ■ *TF:* 800-233-7924 ■ *Web:* www.edgewater.com

EDO Professional Services 2800 Shirlington Rd 12th Fl ... Arlington VA 22206 703-824-5000 824-5003
Web: www.edo-services.com

EDS (Electronic Data Systems Corp) 5400 Legacy Dr ... Plano TX 75024 972-605-6000 605-2643
NYSE: EDS ■ *Web:* www.eds.com

EDS Canada 33 Yonge St Suite 500 ... Toronto ON M5E1G4 416-814-4500 814-4600
TF: 800-814-9038 ■ *Web:* www.eds.com/canada

Electronic Warfare Assoc Inc (EWA Inc)
13873 Park Center Rd Suite 500 ... Herndon VA 20171 703-904-5700 904-5779
TF: 888-392-0002 ■ *Web:* www.ewa.com

EMC Microsoft Practice 98 Inverness Dr E Suite 150 ... Englewood CO 80112 303-542-7100 790-0908
Web: www.emc.com/mspractice/

ePartners Inc 6565 N MacArthur Blvd Suite 950 ... Irving TX 75039 469-587-5660 587-5661
TF: 888-883-9797 ■ *Web:* www.epartnersolutions.com

Everdream Corp 6591 Dumbarton Cir ... Fremont CA 94555 510-818-5500 818-5510
TF: 877-437-3264 ■ *Web:* www.everdream.com

EWA Inc (Electronic Warfare Assoc Inc)
13873 Park Center Rd Suite 500 ... Herndon VA 20171 703-904-5700 904-5779
TF: 888-392-0002 ■ *Web:* www.ewa.com

Excell Data Div CompuCom Systems Inc
1756 114th Ave SE Suite 220 ... Bellevue WA 98004 425-974-2000 974-2001
TF: 800-539-2355 ■ *Web:* www.excell.com

Facilite Informatique Canada Inc
1010 Sherbrooke St W Suite 2510 ... Montreal QC H3A2R7 514-284-5636 284-9529
Web: www.facilite.com

Force 3 Inc 2151 Priest Bridge Dr Suite 7 ... Crofton MD 21114 301-261-0204 721-5624*
**Fax Area Code:* 410 ■ *TF:* 800-391-0204 ■ *Web:* www.force3.com

Fujitsu Consulting 1450 E American Ln Suite 1700 ... Schaumburg IL 60173 847-706-4000 706-4020
TF: 800-453-0347 ■ *Web:* www.fujitsu.com/us/

General Dynamics Information Technology
3211 Jermantown Rd ... Fairfax VA 22030 703-246-0200 246-0351*
NYSE: ANT ■ **Fax:* Mktg ■ *TF:* 888-483-0022 ■ *Web:* www.gdit.com/

General Dynamics Network Systems 77 A St ... Needham Heights MA 02494 781-449-2000
TF: 888-483-0022 ■ *Web:* www.gd-ns.com

GeoLogics Corp 5285 Shawnee Rd Suite 300 ... Alexandria VA 22312 703-750-4000 750-4010
TF: 800-684-3455 ■ *Web:* www.geologics.com

Getronics 290 Concord Rd ... Billerica MA 01821 978-625-5000
TF: 800-225-0654 ■ *Web:* www.getronics.com

Global Consultants Inc 25 Airport Rd ... Morristown NJ 07960 973-889-5200 292-1643
TF: 877-264-6424 ■ *Web:* www.g-c-i.com

Global Management Systems Inc (GMSI)
2201 Wisconsin Ave NW Suite 300 ... Washington DC 20007 202-471-4674 625-9016
Web: www.gmsi.com

Government Micro Resources Inc 7403 Gateway Ct ... Manassas VA 20109 703-330-1199 330-7833
TF Cust Svc: 800-220-4672 ■ *Web:* www.gmri.com

GramTel USA PO Box 720 ... South Bend IN 46601 574-472-4726 472-0904
TF: 866-481-7622 ■ *Web:* www.gramtel.com

Harris Information Technology Services
13665 Dulles Technology Dr Suite 250 ... Herndon VA 20171 703-480-2607 480-2610
TF: 800-339-8828 ■ *Web:* www.multimax.com

Hartford Computer Group Inc 3949 Heritage Oak Ct ... Simi Valley CA 93063 805-306-2500 836-3600*
**Fax Area Code:* 224 ■ *TF:* 800-680-4424 ■ *Web:* www.hcgi.com

Helios & Matheson North America Inc
200 Park Ave S Suite 901 ... New York NY 10003 732-499-8229 979-2517*
**Fax Area Code:* 212 ■ *Web:* www.tact.com

Howard Systems International 290 Harbor Dr 1st Fl ... Stamford CT 06901 203-324-4600 358-0193*
**Fax Area Code:* 888 ■ **Fax:* Hum Res ■ *TF:* 800-326-4860 ■
Web: www.howardsystems.com

Iconixx Corp 5301 Hollister Suite 400 ... Houston TX 77040 713-934-0200 934-7744
TF: 877-426-6499 ■ *Web:* www.iconixx.com

Ikon Office Solutions Inc 5100 W Lemon St Suite 250 ... Tampa FL 33609 813-261-2000 261-2500
Web: www.ikon.com/

Indotronix International Corp 331 Main St ... Poughkeepsie NY 12601 845-473-1137 473-1197
TF: 800-800-8442 ■ *Web:* www.iic.com

Infinite Technology Group Inc 1055 Stewart Ave Suite 3 ... Bethpage NY 11714 516-349-5824 349-5827

Infinity Software Development Inc
3522 Thomasville Rd Suite 200 ... Tallahassee FL 32309 850-383-1011 383-1015
Web: www.infinity-software.com

Information Analysis Inc 11240 Waples Mill Rd Suite 400 ... Fairfax VA 22030 703-383-3000 293-7979
TF: 800-829-7614 ■ *Web:* www.infoa.com

Information Systems & Networks Corp (ISN)
10411 Motor City Dr 7th Fl ... Bethesda MD 20817 301-469-0400 469-0767
Web: www.isncorp.com

InfoTech USA Inc 7 Kingsbridge Rd ... Fairfield NJ 07004 973-227-8772 227-6120
TF: 800-305-8201 ■ *Web:* www.infotechusa.com

INNOLOG (Innovative Logistics Techniques Inc)
1751 Pinnacle Dr Suite 600 ... McLean VA 22102 703-506-1555 506-4559
TF: 800-466-6564 ■ *Web:* www.innolog.com

Innovative Logistics Techniques Inc (INNOLOG)
1751 Pinnacle Dr Suite 600 ... McLean VA 22102 703-506-1555 506-4559
TF: 800-466-6564 ■ *Web:* www.innolog.com

Integrated Systems Analysts Inc
2001 N Beauregard St Suite 600 ... Alexandria VA 22311 703-824-0700 379-6321
TF: 800-929-3436 ■ *Web:* www.isa.com

Integro Inc 7670 S Chester St Suite 180 ... Englewood CO 80112 303-575-9300 575-9633
TF: 888-575-9300 ■ *Web:* www.integro.com

Intermedia Group Inc 5 Hanover Sq 15th Fl ... New York NY 10004 212-248-0100 248-0600
Web: www.intermediagroup.com

Inventa Technologies Inc 10000 Midlantic Dr Suite 301 ... Mount Laurel NJ 08054 856-914-5200 608-7970
Web: www.inventa.com

Iris Software Inc 200 Metroplex Dr Suite 300 ... Edison NJ 08817 732-393-0034 393-0035
Web: www.irissoftinc.com

James River Technical Inc 4439 Cox Rd ... Glen Allen VA 23060 804-935-0150 935-0165
Web: www.jrti.com

Keane Inc 100 City Sq ... Boston MA 02129 617-241-9200 241-9507
NYSE: KEA ■ *TF:* 800-365-3263 ■ *Web:* www.keane.com

KForce Government Soultions 2750 Prosperity Ave Suite 300 ... Fairfax VA 22031 703-245-7350 245-7560
Web: www.pcci.com

L-3 Communications Government Services Inc
3750 Centerview Dr ... Chantilly VA 20151 703-708-1400 708-5700
Web: www.l-3gsi.com

Levanta Inc 1825 S Grant St Suite 350 ... San Mateo CA 94402 650-403-7200 403-7206
TF: 888-546-4878 ■ *Web:* www.levanta.com

Lighthouse Computer Services Inc
6 Blackstone Valley Pl Suite 205 ... Lincoln RI 02865 401-334-0799 334-0719
TF: 888-542-8030 ■ *Web:* www.lighthousecs.com

LogicaCMG 10375 Richmond Ave ... Houston TX 77042 713-954-7000 785-0880
Web: www.logicacmg.com

Logicalis 1750 S Telegraph Rd Suite 300 ... Bloomfield Hills MI 48302 248-745-5400 335-8715
TF: 866-456-4422 ■ *Web:* www.us.logicalis.com

Maden Technologies 2110 Washington Blvd Suite 200 ... Arlington VA 22204 703-769-4440 769-4424
TF: 800-601-5112 ■ *Web:* www.madentech.com

Mainline Information Systems Inc 1700 Summit Lake Dr ... Tallahassee FL 32317 850-219-5000 219-5050
TF: 800-811-4429 ■ *Web:* www.mainline.com

Maintech Div Volt Information Sciences Inc
39 Paterson Ave ... Wallington NJ 07057 973-330-3200 330-3187*
**Fax:* Sales ■ *TF:* 800-426-8324 ■ *Web:* www.maintech.com

MANDEX Inc 12500 Fair Lakes Cir Suite 125 ... Fairfax VA 22033 703-227-0900 227-0910
TF: 888-662-6339 ■ *Web:* www.mandex.com

ManTech International Corp 12015 Lee Jackson Hwy ... Fairfax VA 22033 703-218-6000 218-6005
NASDAQ: MANT ■ *Web:* www.mantech.com

Maryville Technologies 540 Maryville Center Suite 300 ... Saint Louis MO 63141 636-519-4100 519-4141
Web: www.maryville.com

Meridian Group 9 Parkway N Suite 500 ... Deerfield IL 60015 847-940-1200 964-2662
TF: 800-811-2674 ■ *Web:* www.onlinemeridian.com

Metters Industries Inc 8200 Greensboro Dr Suite 500 ... McLean VA 22102 703-821-3300 821-3996
TF: 800-638-8377 ■ *Web:* www.metters.com

NCI Inc 11730 Plaza America Dr Suite 700 ... Reston VA 20190 703-707-6900 707-6901
NASDAQ: NCIT ■ *Web:* www.nciinc.com

NCI Information Systems Inc 11730 Plaza America Dr ... Reston VA 20190 703-707-6900 707-6901
TF: 888-409-5457 ■ *Web:* www.nciinc.com

New Technologies Inc 133386 International Pkwy ... Jacksonville FL 32218 800-773-8294 588-0399
Web: www.forensics-intl.com

NewAgeSys Inc 231 Clarksville Rd Suite 200 ... Princeton Junction NJ 08550 609-919-9800 919-9830
TF: 888-863-9243 ■ *Web:* www.newagesys.com

Niteo Partners Inc 379 Thornall St 5th Fl ... Edison NJ 08837 732-767-0400 767-0401
Web: www.niteo.com

Nortel Government Solutions Inc 12730 Fair Lakes Cir ... Fairfax VA 22033 703-679-4900 679-4901
Web: nortelgov.com

NuWare Technology Corp Inc 120 Wood Ave S Suite 404 ... Iselin NJ 08830 732-494-0550 494-4586
Web: www.nuware.com

OAO Technology Solutions Inc 7500 Greenway Ctr Dr 16th Fl ... Greenbelt MD 20770 301-486-0400 486-0415
TF: 800-720-9030 ■ *Web:* www.oaot.com

Omicron Systems Inc 1700 Market St ... Philadelphia PA 19103 215-854-3400 854-0079
Web: www.omicron.com

Open Systems Solutions Inc 2325 Maryland Rd Suite 100 ... Willow Grove PA 19090 215-659-4440 659-4550
TF: 866-483-9827 ■ *Web:* www.ossi.net

PacificNet Inc 655 N Central Ave 17th Fl ... Glendale CA 91203 888-250-6478 349-1096*
NASDAQ: PACT ■ **Fax Area Code:* 646 ■ *Web:* www.pacificnet.com

Paradigm Solutions 9715 Key West Ave 3rd Fl ... Rockville MD 20850 301-468-1200 468-1201
Web: www.paradigmsolutions.com

Paragon Computer Professionals Inc 11 Commerce Dr 3rd Fl ... Cranford NJ 07016 908-709-6767 709-8071
TF: 800-462-5582 ■ *Web:* www.paracomp.com

Perficient Inc 1120 S Capital of Texas Hwy Bldg 3 ... Austin TX 78746 512-531-6000 531-6011
NASDAQ: PRFT ■ *Web:* www.perficient.com

Perot Systems Corp 12320 Racetrack Rd ... Tampa FL 33626 813-891-6084 891-6138
TF: 800-872-2992 ■ *Web:* www.perotsystems.com

Perot Systems Corp 2300 W Plano Pkwy ... Plano TX 75075 972-577-0000 455-4100
NYSE: PER ■ *TF:* 888-317-3768 ■ *Web:* www.perotsystems.com

Perot Systems Government Services
4500 Forbes Blvd Suite 200 ... Lanham MD 20706 301-577-0700 918-4822
Web: www.perotsystems.com/government/

Pointe Technology Group Inc 8201 Corporate Dr Suite 700 ... Landover MD 20785 301-306-4400 306-4421
TF: 800-730-6171 ■ *Web:* www.pointetech.com

Pomeroy IT Solutions Inc 1020 Petersburg Rd ... Hebron KY 41048 859-586-1515 586-4414
NASDAQ: PMRY ■ *TF:* 800-846-8727 ■ *Web:* www.pomeroy.com

Preferred Systems Solutions Inc 3040 Williams Dr Suite 505 ... Fairfax VA 22031 703-663-2777 663-2780
Web: www.pssfed.com

Company	City	State	ZIP	Phone	Fax
Presidio Corp 7601 Ora Glen Dr Suite 100 *TF:* 800-452-6926 ■ *Web:* www.presidio.com	Greenbelt	MD	20770	301-313-2000	313-2400
Professional Software Engineering Inc DBA Prosoft 477 Viking Dr Suite 400 *TF:* 800-951-5161 ■ *Web:* www.prosoft-eng.com	Virginia Beach	VA	23452	757-431-2400	463-1071
Proxicom Inc 11600 Sunrise Valley Dr Suite 200 *Web:* www.proxicom.com	Reston	VA	20191	703-262-3200	262-3201
RCG Information Technology Inc 379 Thornall St 14th Fl *TF:* 800-333-7816 ■ *Web:* www.rcgit.com	Edison	NJ	08837	732-744-3500	744-3501
Remtech Services Inc (RSI) 804 Middle Ground Blvd Suite A *Web:* www.remtech.com	Newport News	VA	23606	757-873-8733	873-8403
Resource One Computer Systems Inc 1159 Dublin Rd *Web:* www.rocs.com	Columbus	OH	43215	614-485-4800	485-4848
RiverPoint Group LLC 2200 E Devon Ave Unit 385 *TF:* 800-297-5601 ■ *Web:* www.riverpoint.com	Des Plains	IL	60018	847-233-9600	233-9602
RS Information Systems Inc 1651 Old Meadow Rd 1st Fl *Web:* www.rsis.com	McLean	VA	22102	703-734-7800	734-7808
RWD Technologies 5521 Research Park Dr *TF:* 877-952-8301 ■ *Web:* www.rwd.com	Baltimore	MD	21228	410-869-1000	869-3001
San Vision Technology Inc 50 Broadway *Web:* www.svtinc.com	New York	NY	10004	212-571-6904	571-3588
Satyam Computer Services Ltd 1 Gatehall Dr Suite 301 *TF:* 800-450-7605 ■ *Web:* www.satyam.com	Parsippany	NJ	07054	973-656-0650	656-0653
Sayers Group LLC 1150 Feehanville Dr *TF:* 800-323-5357 ■ *Web:* www.sayers.com	Mount Prospect	IL	60056	847-391-4040	294-0750
SecureInfo Corp 211 North Loop 1604 E Suite 200 *TF:* 888-677-9351 ■ *Web:* www.secureinfo.com	San Antonio	TX	78232	210-403-5600	403-5702
SI International Inc 12012 Sunset Hills Rd Suite 800 *NASDAQ: SINT* ■ *Web:* www.si-intl.com	Reston	VA	20190	703-234-7000	234-7500
Siemens IT Solutions & Services Inc 101 Merritt 7 *Web:* www.sbs-usa.siemens.com	Norwalk	CT	06851	203-642-2300	642-2399
Siemens Logistics & Assembly Systems 507 Plymouth Ave **Fax:* Hum Res ■ *TF:* 877-725-7500 ■ *Web:* www.logistics-assembly.siemens.com	Grand Rapids	MI	49505	616-913-6200	913-5339*
SM Consulting Inc 1306 Concourse Dr Suite 200 *TF:* 888-476-2937 ■ *Web:* www.smcteam.com	Linthicum	MD	21090	410-691-5200	691-0303
SMS Data Products Group Inc 1501 Farm Credit Dr Suite 2000 *TF:* 800-331-1767 ■ *Web:* www.sms.com	McLean	VA	22102	703-709-9898	356-4831
Social & Scientific Systems Inc 8757 Georgia Ave 12th Fl *Web:* www.s-3.com	Silver Spring	MD	20910	301-628-3000	628-3001
Software Information Systems Inc 455 Park Pl Suite 301 *Web:* www.thinksis.com	Lexington	KY	40511	859-977-4747	977-4750
Software Technology Group 555 S 300 East *TF:* 888-595-1001 ■ *Web:* www.swtg.com	Salt Lake City	UT	84111	801-595-1000	595-1080
Solutions Consulting LLC 370 Southpointe Blvd 4th Fl *Web:* www.scglobal.com	Canonsburg	PA	15317	724-514-5000	514-5050
SRA International Inc 4300 Fair Lakes Ct *NYSE: SRX* ■ *Web:* www.sra.com	Fairfax	VA	22033	703-803-1500	803-1509
Stanley Assoc Inc 3101 Wilson Blvd Suite 700 *TF:* 866-774-0577 ■ *Web:* www.stanleyassociates.com	Arlington	VA	22201	703-684-1125	683-0039
Starpoint Solutions 115 Broadway 2nd Fl *Web:* www.starpoint.com	New York	NY	10006	212-962-1550	967-7175
Strategic Technologies Inc 301 Gregson Dr *Web:* www.stratech.com	Cary	NC	27511	919-379-8000	379-8100
Sumaria Systems Inc 99 Rosewood Dr Suite 140 *TF:* 888-245-9810 ■ *Web:* www.sumariasystems.com	Danvers	MA	01923	978-739-4200	739-4850
Sykes Enterprises Inc 400 N Ashley Dr Suite 2800 *NASDAQ: SYKE* ■ *TF:* 800-867-9537 ■ *Web:* www.sykes.com	Tampa	FL	33602	813-274-1000	273-0148
Syntel Inc 525 E Big Beaver Rd Suite 300 *NASDAQ: SYNT* ■ *Web:* www.syntelinc.com	Troy	MI	48083	248-619-2800	619-2888
Sysorex Federal Inc 13921 Park Center Rd Suite 2204 *Web:* www.sysorex.com	Herndon	VA	20171	703-356-2900	734-4825
Sytel Inc 6430 Rockledge Dr Suite 400 *TF:* 888-866-0881 ■ *Web:* www.sytel.com	Bethesda	MD	20817	301-530-1000	530-1032
TASC Inc 4801 Stonecroft Blvd *Web:* www.tasc.com	Chantilly	VA	20151	703-633-8300	449-3400
Tech.logix Group of Bell Industries Inc 8888 Keystone Crossing Suite 1700 *TF:* 800-722-1599 ■ *Web:* www.belltechlogix.com	Indianapolis	IN	46241	317-227-6700	704-0064
Technica Corp 45245 Business Ct Suite 300 *Web:* www.technicacorp.com	Dulles	VA	20166	703-662-2000	662-2001
Technology Infrastructure Solutions Inc 701 Park of Commerce Blvd Suite 101 *TF:* 800-667-6506 ■ *Web:* www.deploytis.com	Boca Raton	FL	33487	561-998-9847	314-0660
Technology Solutions Co (TSC) 55 E Monroe St Suite 2600 *NASDAQ: TSCC* ■ *TF:* 800-819-2250 ■ *Web:* www.techsol.com	Chicago	IL	60603	312-228-4500	228-4501
TechTeam Global Inc 27335 W Eleven-Mile Rd *NASDAQ: TEAM* ■ *TF:* 800-522-4451 ■ *Web:* www.techteam.com	Southfield	MI	48034	248-357-2866	357-2570
Telesciences Inc 2000 Midlantic Dr Suite 410 *Web:* www.telesciences.com	Mount Laurel	NJ	08054	856-866-1000	866-0185
Thaumaturgix Inc 19 W 44th St Suite 810 *Web:* www.tgix.com	New York	NY	10036	212-918-5000	918-5001
ThruPoint Inc 1372 Broadway 6th Fl *Web:* www.thrupoint.net	New York	NY	10018	646-562-6000	562-6100
Tier Technologies Inc 10780 Parkridge Blvd Suite 400 *NASDAQ: TIERE* ■ *TF:* 800-789-8437 ■ *Web:* www.tier.com	Reston	VA	20191	571-382-1000	382-1002
TRI-COR Industries Inc 4600 Forbes Blvd Suite 205 *Web:* www.tricorind.com	Lanham	MD	20706	301-731-6140	306-6740
Unisys Corp Township LIne & Union Meeting Rd *NYSE: UIS* ■ **Fax:* Hum Res ■ *TF:* 800-874-8647 ■ *Web:* www.unisys.com	Blue Bell	PA	19424	215-986-4011	986-0540*
UNITECH (Universal Systems & Technology Inc) 5870 Trinity Pkwy Suite 400 *TF:* 800-243-7027 ■ *Web:* www.unitech1.com	Centreville	VA	20110	703-502-9600	502-9300
Universal Systems & Technology Inc (UNITECH) 5870 Trinity Pkwy Suite 400 *TF:* 800-243-7027 ■ *Web:* www.unitech1.com	Centreville	VA	20110	703-502-9600	502-9300
Ventera Corp 8444 Westpark Dr Suite 800 *TF:* 877-836-8372 ■ *Web:* www.ventera.com	McLean	VA	22102	703-760-4600	760-9494
Visionary Integration Professionals Inc 80 Iron Point Cir Suite 100 *Web:* www.vipincorp.com	Folsom	CA	95630	916-985-9625	985-9632
Vistronix Inc 8401 Greensboro Dr Suite 500 *TF:* 800-483-2434 ■ *Web:* www.vistronix.com	McLean	VA	22102	703-734-2270	734-2271
Volt Information Sciences Inc Maintech Div 39 Paterson Ave **Fax:* Sales ■ *TF:* 800-426-8324 ■ *Web:* www.maintech.com	Wallington	NJ	07057	973-330-3200	330-3187*
Washington Consulting Group Inc 4915 Auburn Ave Suite 301 *Web:* www.washcg.com	Bethesda	MD	20814	301-656-2330	656-1996
WidePoint Corp 18W140 Butterfield Rd Suite 1100 1 Lincoln Center *Web:* www.widepoint.com	Oakbrook Terrace	IL	60181	630-629-0003	629-7559
Wolcott Systems Group LLC 3700 Embassy Pkwy Suite 430 *Web:* www.wolcottgroup.com	Fairlawn	OH	44333	330-666-5900	666-5600
Xtria 2435 N Central Expy Suite 700 *TF:* 866-769-2987 ■ *Web:* www.xtria.com	Richardson	TX	75080	972-301-4000	699-4025
ZyQuest Inc 1385 W Main Ave *TF:* 800-992-0533 ■ *Web:* www.zyquest.com	De Pere	WI	54115	920-499-0533	490-3218

184 CONCERT, SPORTS, OTHER LIVE EVENT PRODUCERS & PROMOTERS

Company	City	State	ZIP	Phone	Fax
ACME Special Events Inc. 7095 Hollywood Blvd Suite 838 *Web:* www.acme-events.com	Los Angeles	CA	90028	818-559-8788	
AMS Entertainment 226 E Cannon Perdido Suite H *TF:* 800-267-3548 ■ *Web:* www.amsentertainment.com	Santa Barbara	CA	93101	805-899-4000	899-4184
Capital Sports & Entertainment 98 San Jacinto Blvd Suite 430 *Web:* www.planetcse.com	Austin	TX	78701	512-370-1919	470-1920
Clear Channel Entertainment Inc 220 W 42nd St 17th Fl *Web:* cc.com	New York	NY	10036	917-421-4000	421-5624
Contemporary Productions LLC 190 Carondelet Plaza Suite 1111 *Web:* www.contemporaryproductions.com	Saint Louis	MO	63105	314-721-9090	721-9091
Don King Productions Inc 501 Fairway Dr *Web:* www.donking.com	Deerfield Beach	FL	33441	954-418-5800	418-0166
Executive Visions Inc 7000 Miller Ct E *Web:* www.executivevisions.com	Norcross	GA	30071	770-416-6100	416-6300
Gilmore Entertainment Group 8901-A Business 17 N PO Box 7576 *TF:* 800-843-6779 ■ *Web:* www.cgp.net	Myrtle Beach	SC	29572	843-449-4444	913-1441
Harlem Globetrotters International Inc 400 E Van Buren St Suite 300 *TF:* 800-641-4667 ■ *Web:* www.harlemglobetrotters.com	Phoenix	AZ	85004	602-258-0000	258-5925
House of Blues Entertainment Inc 6255 Sunset Blvd 16th Fl *TF:* 800-843-2583 ■ *Web:* www.hob.com	Hollywood	CA	90028	323-769-4600	769-4792
IMG Inc 1360 E 9th St IMG Center Suite 100 *Web:* www.imgworld.com	Cleveland	OH	44114	216-522-1200	522-1145
JAM Productions Ltd 207 W Goethe St *Web:* www.jamusa.com	Chicago	IL	60610	312-266-6262	266-9568
Live Nation Inc 9348 Civic Center Dr *NYSE: LYV* ■ *Web:* www.livenation.com	Beverly Hills	CA	90210	310-867-7000	867-7001
Miss America Organization 2 Miss America Way Suite 1000 *TF:* 800-282-6477 ■ *Web:* www.missamerica.org	Atlantic City	NJ	08401	609-345-7571	347-6079
Miss Universe LP 1370 Ave of the Americas 16th Fl *Web:* www.missuniverse.com	New York	NY	10019	212-373-4999	315-5378
Nocturne Productions 3000 Harvestore Dr *Web:* www.nocturneprods.com	DeKalb	IL	60115	815-756-9600	756-9377
Northwest Sports & Entertainment Inc 835 W Warner Rd Suite 101-445 *Web:* www.northwestsports.org	Gilbert	AZ	85233	480-635-8720	699-4190
On Stage Entertainment Inc 333 Orville Wright Ct *Web:* onst.com	Las Vegas	NV	89119	702-253-1333	253-1122
Radio City Entertainment LLC 1260 6th Ave **Fax:* PR ■ *Web:* www.radiocity.com	New York	NY	10020	212-485-7200	472-0603*
Shubert Organization Inc 225 W 44th St	New York	NY	10036	212-944-3700	944-3841
Speedway Motorsports Inc 5555 Concord Pkwy *NYSE: TRK* ■ *TF:* 800-455-7267 ■ *Web:* www.speedwaymotorsports.com	Concord	NC	28027	704-455-3239	455-2168
Threshold Sports LLC 2650 Eisenhower Ave Suite 100A *Web:* www.thresholdsports.com	Norristown	PA	19403	610-676-0390	676-0391
Top Rank Inc 3980 Howard Hughes Pkwy Suite 580 *Web:* www.toprank.com	Las Vegas	NV	89109	702-732-2717	733-8232
Walt Disney Theatrical Productions 500 S Buena Vista St *Web:* disney.go.com/disneytheatrical	Burbank	CA	91521	818-553-5342	
Willy Bietak Productions Inc 1404 3rd St Promenade Suite 200 *Web:* www.iceshows.com	Santa Monica	CA	90401	310-576-2400	576-2405
World Wrestling Entertainment Inc 1241 E Main St *NYSE: WWE* ■ *Web:* corporate.wwe.com	Stamford	CT	06902	203-352-8600	352-8699

185 CONCRETE - READY-MIXED

Company	City	State	ZIP	Phone	Fax
A Teichert & Son Inc 3500 American River Dr *TF:* 888-554-5627 ■ *Web:* www.teichert.com	Sacramento	CA	95864	916-484-3011	484-6506
AJ Walker Construction Co 421 S 21st St	Mattoon	IL	61938	217-235-5647	235-5939
Alamo Concrete Products Ltd PO Box 34210	San Antonio	TX	78265	210-208-1880	208-1501
American Materials LLC 717 Short St PO Box 1246 *TF:* 866-421-7625	Eau Claire	WI	54702	715-835-2251	835-3324
Anderson Concrete Corp 400 Frank Rd *Web:* www.andersonconcrete.com	Columbus	OH	43207	614-443-0123	443-4001
Antioch Building Materials Co PO Box 870	Antioch	CA	94509	925-432-0171	432-9441
AVR Inc 14698 Galaxy Ave *Web:* www.avrconcrete.com	Apple Valley	MN	55124	952-432-7132	432-7530
AVR Inc AME Ready Mix PO Box 307 *TF Cust Svc:* 800-374-8544	Elk River	MN	55330	763-441-2800	441-2827
Baccala Concrete Corp 100 Armento St *TF:* 866-705-2382 ■ *Web:* www.baccalaconcrete.com	Johnston	RI	02919	401-231-8300	232-3965
BARD Concrete 2021 325th Ave PO Box 246	Dyersville	IA	52040	563-875-7145	875-7860
Bennett Thomas & Hunter Inc 70 John St *Web:* www.tbhconcrete.com	Westminster	MD	21157	410-848-9030	876-0733
Berks Products Corp 965 Berkshire Blvd *TF:* 800-282-2375 ■ *Web:* www.berksproducts.com	Reading	PA	19610	610-374-5131	375-1469
Big Horn Redi-Mix Inc 600 Industrial Park PO Box 672	Greybull	WY	82426	307-765-4610	765-4462
Binkley & Ober Inc 2742 Lancaster Rd PO Box 7 *TF:* 800-860-0441 ■ *Web:* www.binkleyandober.com	East Petersburg	PA	17520	717-569-0441	569-5066
Block WG Co 1414 Mississippi Blvd PO Box 280 *TF:* 800-397-1651 ■ *Web:* www.wgblock.com	Bettendorf	IA	52722	563-823-2080	823-2071
Blue Rock Industries 58 Main St *TF:* 800-439-2561 ■ *Web:* www.bluerockmaine.com	Westbrook	ME	04092	207-854-2561	854-2539
Bode Concrete 450 Amador St *Web:* www.bodegravel.com	San Francisco	CA	94124	415-920-7100	920-7106
Bonded Concrete Inc 303 Rt 155 *TF:* 800-252-8589 ■ *Web:* www.bondedconcrete.com	Watervliet	NY	12189	518-273-5800	273-0848
Bornhoft Concrete Products Inc 150 County Rd 8 *TF:* 800-257-5576 ■ *Web:* www.bornhoftconcrete.com	Tyler	MN	56178	507-247-5575	247-5576
Bosshart Co Inc 217 N 1st Ave W *Web:* www.bosshartconcrete.com	Truman	MN	56088	507-776-2081	776-2001
Boston Sand & Gravel Co Inc 100 N Washington St PO Box 9187 *TF:* 800-624-2724 ■ *Web:* www.bostonsand.com	Boston	MA	02114	617-227-9000	523-7947
Brown Joe Co Inc 20 3rd St NE PO Box 1669 *TF:* 800-444-4293	Ardmore	OK	73402	580-223-4555	223-2546
Builders Redi-Mix Inc 1384 Lake Lansing Rd *Web:* www.buildersredimix.com	Lansing	MI	48912	517-372-9765	372-0222

Company	City	State	ZIP	Phone	Fax
Builders Supply Co Inc 1400 Marshall St PO Box 295	Shreveport	LA	71162	318-222-5721	429-8200
Building Products Corp 950 Freeburg Ave	Belleville	IL	62220	618-233-4427	233-2031
TF: 800-233-1996 ■ *Web:* www.buildingproductscorp.com					
Cadman Inc 7554 185th Ave NE Suite 100 PO Box 97038	Redmond	WA	98073	425-868-1234	961-7390
TF: 888-322-6847 ■ *Web:* www.cadman.com					
Campbell Concrete & Materials LP 105 E Boothe St PO Box 1147	Cleveland	TX	77328	281-592-5201	592-1785
TF: 800-749-1843 ■ *Web:* www.campbell-lp.com					
Campbell Concrete & Materials LP 9500 Harwin Dr	Houston	TX	77036	713-783-4761	784-1745
Web: www.campbell-lp.com					
Capitol Aggregates Ltd 11551 Nacogdoches Rd	San Antonio	TX	78217	210-655-3010	599-0560
TF: 800-292-5315 ■ *Web:* www.capaggltd.com					
Carlo Ditta Inc 1445 MacArthur Ave	Harvey	LA	70058	504-347-3785	347-3787
CB Concrete Co PO Box 11767	Reno	NV	89510	775-329-8841	329-2803
Cemex Inc PO Box 3004	Florida City	FL	33034	305-247-3011	248-9112
Web: www.cemexusa.com					
Cemex Puerto Rico Inc RT 165 KM 2.7 Industrial Amelia Park	Bucahna Guaynabo	PR	00968	787-783-3000	781-8850
Web: www.cemex.com					
Cemex USA 840 Gessner Suite 1400	Houston	TX	77024	713-650-6200	722-5105
NYSE: CX ■ *TF:* 800-999-8529 ■ *Web:* www.cemex.com					
Cemstone Products Co 2025 Centre Pointe Blvd Suite 300	Mendota Heights	MN	55120	651-688-9292	688-0124
TF: 800-236-7866 ■ *Web:* www.cemstone.com					
Centex Materials Inc 3801 S Capital of Texas Hwy Suite 250	Austin	TX	78704	512-460-3003	444-9809
Central Builders Supply Co Inc 125 Bridge Ave PO Box 152	Sunbury	PA	17801	570-286-6461	286-5108
TF: 800-326-9361					
Central Concrete Supermix Inc 4300 SW 74th Ave	Miami	FL	33155	305-262-3250	267-0698
Web: www.supermix.com					
Central Concrete Supply Co Inc 755 Stockton Ave	San Jose	CA	95126	408-293-6272	294-3162
TF: 866-404-1000 ■ *Web:* www.centralconcrete.com					
Central Ready-Mix Concrete Inc 12005 W Hampton Ave	Milwaukee	WI	53208	414-258-7000	258-4960
TF: 800-258-0010					
Centre Concrete Co 2280 E College Ave PO Box 859	State College	PA	16804	814-238-2471	238-2914
Century Ready-Mix Corp 3250 Armand St PO Box 4420	Monroe	LA	71211	318-322-4444	322-7299
TF: 800-732-3969					
Champion Inc 180 Traders Mine Rd PO Box 490	Iron Mountain	MI	49801	906-779-2300	779-2326
TF: 800-962-5615 ■ *Web:* www.championinc.com					
Chandler Concrete Co Inc 1006 S Church St PO Box 131	Burlington	NC	27216	336-226-1181	226-2969
TF: 800-237-1259 ■ *Web:* www.chandlerconcrete.com					
Chaney Enterprises 12480 Mattawoman Dr PO Box 548	Waldorf	MD	20604	301-932-5000	843-9123*
**Fax:* Sales ■ *TF:* 800-492-3495 ■ *Web:* www.chaney-ent.com					
Chapman Concrete Products Inc PO Box 4275	Spartanburg	SC	29305	864-585-8133	583-5638
Web: www.chapmancp.com					
CJ Horner Co Inc 105 W Grand Ave	Hot Springs	AR	71901	501-321-9600	321-9623
Clayton Cos The PO Box 3015	Lakewood	NJ	08701	732-905-3154	751-7623
TF: 800-905-3154 ■ *Web:* www.claytonco.com					
Collinwood Shale Brick & Supply Co 12400 Broadway Ave	Cleveland	OH	44125	216-587-2700	587-2711
Conco Cos 431 S Jefferson St Suite 2508	Springfield	MO	65806	417-831-7622	831-7236
Web: www.concocompanies.com					
Concrete Materials Corp 106 Industry Rd	Richmond	KY	40475	859-623-4238	623-4255
TF: 877-623-4238 ■ *Web:* www.concretematerialscompany.com					
Concrete Nor'West Inc 663 Pease Rd	Burlington	WA	98233	360-757-3121	757-3816
Concrete Supply Co 3823 Raleigh St	Charlotte	NC	28206	704-372-2930	334-8650
Web: www.concretesupplyco.com					
Cornejo & Sons Inc 2060 E Tulsa	Wichita	KS	67216	316-522-5100	522-8187
Web: www.cornejocorp.com					
Cranesville Block Co Inc 774 State Hwy 5 S PO Box 430	Amsterdam	NY	12010	518-887-5560	887-2560
Web: www.cranesville.com					
Cumberland Concrete Corp Narrows Park Rt 40 PO Box 3369	LaVale	MD	21504	301-724-2000	724-6416
Delta Concrete Products Co Inc 425 Florida Blvd PO Box 1589	Denham Springs	LA	70727	225-665-6103	665-3854
Web: www.deltaconcreteinc.com					
Devcon International Corp 1350 E Newport Ctr Dr Suite 201	Deerfield Beach	FL	33442	954-429-1500	429-1506
NASDAQ: DEVC ■ *Web:* www.devc.com					
Devine Brothers Inc 38 Commerce St	Norwalk	CT	06850	203-866-4421	857-4609
Web: www.devinebioheat.com					
Dickey DW & Son Inc 7896 Dickey Dr PO Box 189	Lisbon	OH	44432	330-424-1441	424-1481
Web: www.dwdickey.com/dwdickey					
Ditta Carlo Inc 1445 MacArthur Ave	Harvey	LA	70058	504-347-3785	347-3787
Doan Cos 3670 Carpenter Rd	Ypsilanti	MI	48197	734-971-4678	971-4415
TF: 866-266-2738 ■ *Web:* www.doancompanies.com					
Dolese Brothers Co 20 NW 13th St	Oklahoma City	OK	73103	405-235-2311	297-8329
TF: 800-375-2311					
Dragon Products Co 38 Preble St	Portland	ME	04101	207-774-6355	761-5694
TF: 800-828-8352 ■ *Web:* www.dragonproducts.com					
DuBrook Inc 40 Hoover Ave PO Box 388	Du Bois	PA	15801	814-371-3113	375-9054
Web: www.dubrook.com					
Dunham Price Inc 210 Mike Hooks Rd PO Box 760	Westlake	LA	70669	337-433-3900	433-8895
Web: www.dunhamprice.com					
DW Dickey & Son Inc 7896 Dickey Dr PO Box 189	Lisbon	OH	44432	330-424-1441	424-1481
Web: www.dwdickey.com/dwdickey					
Eagle Materials Inc 3811 Turtle Creek Blvd Suite 1100	Dallas	TX	75219	214-432-2000	432-2100
NYSE: EXP ■ *TF:* 800-759-7625 ■ *Web:* www.eaglematerials.com					
Eastern Concrete Materials Inc 475 Market St	Elmwood Park	NJ	07407	201-797-7979	791-9631*
**Fax:* Sales ■ *TF:* 800-822-7242 ■ *Web:* www.us-concrete.com					
Eastern Industries Inc 4401 Camp Meeting Rd Suite 200	Center Valley	PA	18034	610-866-0932	867-1886
Web: www.eastern-ind.com					
Elkins Builders Supply Co 5 11th St	Elkins	WV	26241	304-636-2640	636-8078
Web: www.wvbuilders.com					
Elsinore Ready-Mix Co Inc 16960 Lakeshore Dr PO Box 959	Lake Elsinore	CA	92531	951-674-2127	674-0450
Ernst Enterprises Inc 3361 Successful Way	Dayton	OH	45414	937-233-5555	233-9203
TF: 800-353-1555 ■ *Web:* ernstconcrete.com					
Federal Materials Concrete 2425 Wayne Sullivan Dr	Paducah	KY	42003	270-442-5496	443-6484
Web: www.fmc1.com					
Flemington Block & Supply Co 207 Everitts Rd PO Box 2050	Flemington	NJ	08822	908-782-8545	782-2378
Florida Rock Industries Inc 155 E 21st St	Jacksonville	FL	32206	904-355-1781	791-1807
NYSE: FRK ■ *TF:* 800-874-8382 ■ *Web:* www.flarock.com					
Foley Products Co 5526 Schatulga Rd PO Box 7877	Columbus	GA	31908	706-563-7882	563-1869
TF: 800-762-6773 ■ *Web:* www.theconcretecompany.com					
G & B Ready-Mix 6701 E Flamingo Ave	Nampa	ID	83687	208-466-6688	463-8786
Gallup Sand & Gravel Co 601 W Roundhouse Rd PO Box 1119	Gallup	NM	87305	505-863-3818	863-4720
TF: 800-257-3818 ■ *Web:* www.gallupsand-gravel.com					
Geneva Rock Products Inc 1565 W 400 North PO Box 538	Orem	UT	84059	801-765-7800	765-7830
TF: 800-464-2003 ■ *Web:* www.genevarock.com					
Glacier Northwest Inc 5050 1st Ave Suite 102 PO Box 1730	Seattle	WA	98111	206-764-3000	764-3012
TF: 800-750-0123 ■ *Web:* www.glaciernw.com					
Griswold ST & Co Inc 193 Industrial Ave PO Box 849	Williston	VT	05495	802-658-0201	658-6869
TF: 800-339-4565 ■ *Web:* www.stgriswold.com					
Hanson Aggregates North America 8505 Freeport Pkwy Suite 500	Irving	TX	75063	972-621-0345	621-0506
TF: 800-687-6549 ■ *Web:* www.hanson-america.com					
Hardaway Concrete Co Inc 2001 Taylor St PO Box 4128	Columbia	SC	29240	803-254-4350	343-2408
Web: www.hardawayconcrete.com					
Hawaiian Cement 99-1300 Halawa Valley St	Aiea	HI	96701	808-532-3400	532-3490
Web: www.hawaiiancement.com					
Hempt Brothers Inc 205 Creek Rd	Camp Hill	PA	17011	717-737-3411	761-5019
Hilltop Basic Resources Inc 1 W 4th St Suite 1100	Cincinnati	OH	45202	513-651-5000	684-8222
Web: www.hilltopbasicresources.com					
Horner CJ Co Inc 105 W Grand Ave	Hot Springs	AR	71901	501-321-9600	321-9623
Hunterdon Concrete Inc Rt 202 & 31 PO Box 2050	Flemington	NJ	08822	908-782-3619	782-2378
Illini Concrete Inc 1300 East A St	Belleville	IL	62221	618-235-4141	235-7599
Ingram Enterprises LP PO Box 1166	Brownwood	TX	76804	325-646-6518	646-3415
Web: www.ingramconcrete.com					
Irving Materials Inc 8032 N SR-9	Greenfield	IN	46140	317-326-3101	326-3105
Web: www.irvmat.com					
Irving Ready-Mix Inc 13415 Coldwater Rd	Fort Wayne	IN	46845	260-637-3101	637-3104
TF: 888-637-3101					
Jackson Ready Mix Concrete Inc 100 W Woodrow Wilson Dr	Jackson	MS	39213	601-354-3801	292-3924
Janesville Sand & Lycon Co 1110 Harding St	Janesville	WI	53547	608-754-7701	754-8555
TF: 800-955-7702 ■ *Web:* www.jsandg.com					
Joe Brown Co Inc 20 3rd St NE PO Box 1669	Ardmore	OK	73402	580-223-4555	223-2546
TF: 800-444-4293					
Joe's Ready Mix Inc 1140 N Main St PO Box 168	Sioux Center	IA	51250	712-722-1646	722-4040
TF: 800-888-2649					
Ken-Crete Products Co 7900 75th St	Kenosha	WI	53142	262-694-3737	697-1560
Kienstra Inc 201 W Ferguson Ave	Wood River	IL	62095	618-254-4366	254-7429
TF: 888-543-6787 ■ *Web:* www.kienstra.com					
King's Material Inc 650 12th Ave SW PO Box 368	Cedar Rapids	IA	52406	319-363-0233	366-0249
TF: 800-332-5298 ■ *Web:* www.kingsmaterial.com					
Kirkpatrick Concrete Co 2000-A Southbridge Pkwy Suite 610	Birmingham	AL	35209	205-423-2630	423-2626
TF: 800-489-0205					
Kloepfer Concrete & Paving Inc 505 E Ellis St PO Box 840	Paul	ID	83347	208-438-4525	438-5030
Web: www.kloepfer.com					
Knife River Corp 1150 W Century Ave	Bismarck	ND	58503	701-530-1400	530-1451
TF: 800-982-5339 ■ *Web:* www.kniferiver.com					
Koenig Fuel & Supply Co 500 E Seven-Mile Rd	Detroit	MI	48203	313-368-1870	368-3040
Krehling Industries Inc 1425 E Wiggins Pass Rd	Naples	FL	34108	239-597-3162	254-7322
TF: 800-226-3162 ■ *Web:* www.krehling.com					
Kuert Concrete Inc 3402 Lincoln Way W	South Bend	IN	46628	574-232-9911	232-9977
TF: 866-465-8378 ■ *Web:* www.kuert.com					
Kuhlman Corp 1845 Indian Woods Cir	Maumee	OH	43537	419-897-6000	897-6061
TF: 800-669-3309 ■ *Web:* www.kuhlman-corp.com					
L Suzio Concrete Co Inc 975 Westfield Rd	Meriden	CT	06450	203-237-8421	238-9177
TF: 888-789-4626 ■ *Web:* www.suzioyorkhill.com					
Lafarge North America Inc 12950 Worldgate Dr Suite 600	Herndon	VA	20170	703-480-3600	796-2214
NYSE: LAF ■ *Web:* www.lafargenorthamerica.com					
Loveland Ready Mix Concrete Inc 644 N County Rd 19 E	Loveland	CO	80539	970-667-1108	667-0092
LTM Inc PO Box 1145	Medford	OR	97501	541-770-2960	664-4567
Web: www.ltminc.com					
Lycon Inc 110 Harding St PO Box 427	Janesville	WI	53547	608-754-7701	754-8555
TF: 800-955-8758 ■ *Web:* www.lyconinc.com					
Manitou Construction Co Inc 1260 Jefferson Rd	Rochester	NY	14623	585-424-6410	424-1846
Marshall Concrete Products Inc 1088 Industrial Ave	Danville	VA	24541	434-792-1233	792-1145
TF: 800-537-5884 ■ *Web:* www.marshallconcrete.com					
McCabe Sand & Gravel Co 120 Berkley St	Taunton	MA	02780	508-823-0771	823-7305
Metromont Materials Corp PO Box 1292	Spartanburg	SC	29304	864-585-4241	582-8435*
**Fax:* Sales ■ *Web:* www.metromontmaterials.com					
Meyer Material Co 1819 N Dot St PO Box 511	McHenry	IL	60051	815-331-7200	331-5050
Web: www.meyermaterial.com					
Mid-Continent Concrete Co 431 W 23rd St	Tulsa	OK	74107	918-582-8111	560-4601*
**Fax:* Sales ■ *TF:* 800-771-7334 ■ *Web:* www.midcoconcrete.com					
MMC Materials Inc 1052 Highland Colony Pkwy Suite 201	Ridgeland	MS	39157	601-898-4000	898-4030
Web: www.mmcmaterials.com					
Moraine Materials Co Inc 1400 Commerce Center Dr	Franklin	OH	45005	937-743-0650	743-0651
TF: 888-667-2463 ■ *Web:* www.mormat.com					
National Cement Co of California Inc 15821 Ventura Blvd Suite 475	Encino	CA	91436	818-728-5200	788-0615
Web: www.vicat.com					
New Holland Concrete 828 E Earl Rd PO Box 218	New Holland	PA	17557	717-354-1200	428-7538*
**Fax Area Code:* 888 ■ *TF:* 800-543-3860 ■ *Web:* www.newhollandconcrete.com					
Pacific Concrete Industries 4170 Holz Rd PO Box J	Bellingham	WA	98227	360-734-0910	354-5677
Paramount Ready Mix Concrete Inc 13949 E Stage Rd PO Box 2823	Santa Fe Springs	CA	90670	562-404-4125	802-3792
TF: 888-404-4125 ■ *Web:* www.paramountreadymix.com					
Pennsy Supply Inc 1001 Paxton St	Harrisburg	PA	17104	717-233-4511	238-7312
Web: www.pennsysupply.com					
Pfaff & Smith Builders Supply Co 1009 Bullitt St PO Box 2508	Charleston	WV	25329	304-342-4171	342-4170
Pine Bluff Sand & Gravel Inc 1501 Port Rd	Pine Bluff	AR	71601	870-534-7120	534-2980
Prairie Group Inc 7601 W 79th St	Bridgeview	IL	60455	708-458-0400	458-6007
TF Sales: 800-649-3690 ■ *Web:* www.prairiegroup.com					
PRM Concrete Corp 775 School St PO Box 2190	Pawtucket	RI	02861	401-727-0400	723-6880
Web: www.prmconcrete.com					
Ready Mix Concrete Co 3610 Bush St PO Box 27326	Raleigh	NC	27611	919-790-1520	981-7475
TF: 800-849-0668 ■ *Web:* www.rmcc.info					
Ready Mix Concrete Co of Knoxville 1104 Spring Hill Rd PO Box 6509	Knoxville	TN	37914	865-524-3331	524-3337
Ready Mix Inc 3430 E Flamingo Rd Suite 100	Las Vegas	NV	89121	702-433-2090	433-0189
AMEX: RMX ■ *Web:* www.readymixinc.com					
Ready Mixed Concrete Co 4395 Washington St	Denver	CO	80216	303-292-1771	295-0470
Ready Mixed Concrete Co 4315 Cuming St	Omaha	NE	68131	402-556-3600	556-5171
Rinker Materials Corp 1501 Belvedere Rd	West Palm Beach	FL	33406	561-833-5555	820-8666
TF: 800-226-5521 ■ *Web:* www.rinker.com					
RiverStone Group Inc 1701 5th Ave	Moline	IL	61265	309-757-8250	757-8257
TF: 800-906-2489 ■ *Web:* www.riverstonegrp.com					
Rockville Fuel & Feed Co Inc 14901 S Lawn Ln PO Box 1707	Rockville	MD	20849	301-762-3988	309-3894
Rosenfeld Concrete Corp 75 Plain St	Hopedale	MA	01747	508-473-7200	478-4250
TF: 800-982-2284					
S & G Concrete Co 2110 Philadelphia Rd	Edgewood	MD	21040	410-679-0500	679-3293
Saint Lawrence Cement Group Inc 1945 Graham Blvd	Mont-Royal	QC	H3R1H1	514-340-1881	342-8154
TSX: STa ■ *Web:* www.stlawrencecement.com					
Sequatchie Concrete Service Inc 406 Cedar Ave	South Pittsburg	TN	37380	423-837-7913	837-7479
TF: 800-824-0824 ■ *Web:* www.seqconcrete.com					
Shamrock Materials Inc 548 DuBois St	San Rafael	CA	94901	415-455-1576	453-6429
TF: 800-779-5777 ■ *Web:* www.shamrockmat.com					
Shelby Materials Inc 157 E Rampart Rd PO Box 280	Shelbyville	IN	46176	317-398-4485	398-2727
TF: 800-548-9516 ■ *Web:* www.shelbymaterials.com					
Silver State Materials LLC 4005 Dean Martin Dr	Las Vegas	NV	89103	702-893-6557	893-2953
Web: www.ssmaterials.com					
Silvi Concrete Products Inc 355 Newbold Rd	Fairless Hills	PA	19030	215-295-0777	295-0630
TF: 800-367-2667 ■ *Web:* www.silvi.com					
Smith Ready Mix Inc 251 W Lincolnway	Valparaiso	IN	46383	219-462-3191	465-4025
TF: 888-632-5656 ■ *Web:* www.smithreadymix.com					
Southern Concrete Materials Inc 35 Meadow Rd	Asheville	NC	28803	828-253-6421	254-3024
TF: 800-288-6421 ■ *Web:* www.scmusa.com					
Speedway Redi Mix Inc 1201 N Taylor Rd	Garrett	IN	46783	260-357-6885	357-0238
TF: 800-227-5649 ■ *Web:* www.speedwayredimix.com					
ST Griswold & Co Inc 193 Industrial Ave PO Box 849	Williston	VT	05495	802-658-0201	658-6869
TF: 800-339-4565 ■ *Web:* www.stgriswold.com					

Company	City	State	Zip	Phone	Fax
Staker & Parson Cos 2350 S 1900 W *TF:* 800-748-4100 ■ *Web:* www.stakerparson.com	Ogden	UT	84401	801-731-1111	731-8800
Starvaggi Industries Inc 401 Pennsylvania Ave *Web:* www.starvaggi.com	Weirton	WV	26062	304-748-1400	797-5208
Stocker Concrete Co 7574 US Rt 36 PO Box 176 *Web:* www.stockerconcrete.com	Gnadenhutten	OH	44629	740-254-4626	254-9108
Stoneway Concrete Co 9125 10th Ave S	Seattle	WA	98108	206-762-9125	763-4178
Superior Ready Mix Concrete LP 1508 W Mission Rd *Web:* www.superiorrm.com/	Escondido	CA	92029	760-745-0556	740-9557
Suzio L Concrete Co Inc 975 Westfield Rd *TF:* 888-789-4626 ■ *Web:* www.suzioyorkhill.com	Meriden	CT	06450	203-237-8421	238-9177
TCS Materials Inc 5423 Airport Rd *TF:* 800-874-8382	Williamsburg	VA	23188	757-591-9340	591-0947
Teichert A & Son Inc 3500 American River Dr *TF:* 888-554-5627 ■ *Web:* www.teichert.com	Sacramento	CA	95864	916-484-3011	484-6506
Texas Industries Inc 1341 W Mockingbird Ln Suite 700W *NYSE:* TXI ■ *Web:* www.txi.com	Dallas	TX	75247	972-647-6700	647-3878
Thomas Bennett & Hunter Inc 70 John St *Web:* www.tbhconcrete.com	Westminster	MD	21157	410-848-9030	876-0733
Thomas Concrete Inc 2500 Cumberland Pkwy Suite 200 *TF:* 800-633-4661 ■ *Web:* www.thomasconcrete.com	Atlanta	GA	30339	770-431-3300	431-3305
Tilcon Connecticut Inc PO Box 1357 *Web:* www.tilconct.com	New Britain	CT	06050	860-224-6005	225-1865
Titan America Inc 1151 Azalea Garden Rd *TF:* 800-468-7622 ■ *Web:* www.titanamerica.com	Norfolk	VA	23502	757-858-6500	855-7707
Transit Mix Concrete & Materials Co 505 Orleans St *TF:* 800-835-4933 ■ *Web:* www.transitmixconcrete.com	Beaumont	TX	77726	409-835-4933	981-1364
Tucker Concrete Co Inc 2201 Moon St *Web:* www.tuckerconcrete.com	Tucker	GA	30084	770-938-4208	491-3198
Union Sand & Supply Corp 1037 Banks St PO Box 1457	Painesville	OH	44077	440-354-4347	354-0847
United Cos of Mesa County Inc 2273 River Rd	Grand Junction	CO	81505	970-243-4900	243-5945
United Materials LLC 561 Pavement Rd *Web:* www.umconcrete.com	Lancaster	NY	14086	716-683-1432	683-0270
US Concrete Inc 2925 Briarpark Dr Suite 1050 *NASDAQ:* RMIX ■ *Web:* www.us-concrete.com	Houston	TX	77042	713-499-6200	499-6201
Valco Inc 200 S 17th St PO Box 550 *Web:* www.valco-inc.com	Rocky Ford	CO	81067	719-254-7464	254-7468
Van Der Vaart Inc 1436 S 15th St	Sheboygan	WI	53081	920-459-2400	459-2410
Varmicon Industries Inc 2301 Industrial Crossway PO Box 531808	Harlingen	TX	78550	956-423-6380	425-3336
Vulcan Materials Co Western Div 3200 San Fernando Rd *TF:* 800-225-6280 ■ *Web:* www.vulcanmaterials.com	Los Angeles	CA	90065	323-258-2777	258-1583
Walker AJ Construction Co 421 S 21st St	Mattoon	IL	61938	217-235-5647	235-5939
Westroc Inc 670 W 220 S *Web:* www.westrocinc.com	Pleasant Grove	UT	84062	801-785-5600	785-7408
WG Block Co 1414 Mississippi Blvd PO Box 280 *TF:* 800-397-1651 ■ *Web:* www.wgblock.com	Bettendorf	IA	52722	563-823-2080	823-2071
Wingra Stone Co 2975 Kapec Rd PO Box 44284 *TF:* 800-249-6908 ■ *Web:* www.wingrastone.com	Madison	WI	53744	608-271-5555	271-3142
Yohn Ready Mix Concrete Inc 320 Hwy 18 W	Garner	IA	50438	641-923-2601	923-2471

186 CONCRETE PRODUCTS - MFR

Company	City	State	Zip	Phone	Fax
A Duchini Inc 2550 McKinley Ave *TF:* 800-937-7317 ■ *Web:* www.duchini.com	Erie	PA	16503	814-456-7027	454-0737
AC Miller Concrete Products Inc 312 E Bridge St PO Box 199 *TF:* 800-229-2922 ■ *Web:* www.acmiller.com	Spring City	PA	19475	610-948-4600	948-9750
Accord Industries 4001 Forsyth Rd *TF:* 800-477-7675 ■ *Web:* www.accordindustries.com	Winter Park	FL	32792	407-671-5200	679-2297
Adams Products Co 5701 McCrimmon Pkwy PO Box 189 *TF:* 800-672-3131 ■ *Web:* www.adamsproducts.com	Morrisville	NC	27560	919-467-2218	469-0509
Alamo Concrete Products Ltd PO Box 34210	San Antonio	TX	78265	210-208-1880	208-1501
Amcor Precast 801 W 12th St *TF:* 800-776-8760 ■ *Web:* www.amcorogden.com	Ogden	UT	84404	801-399-1171	392-7849
American Concrete Pipe Co Inc 2448 Century Rd PO Box 10508 *Web:* www.spancrete.com	Green Bay	WI	54307	920-494-3436	494-3472
Americast Div Valley Blox Inc 11352 Virginia Precast Rd *TF:* 800-999-2279 ■ *Web:* www.americastusa.com	Ashland	VA	23005	804-798-6068	798-3426
Ameron International Corp 245 S Los Robles Ave *NYSE:* AMN ■ *Web:* www.ameron.com	Pasadena	CA	91101	626-683-4000	683-4060
Ameron International Water Transmission Group 10681 Foothill Blvd Suite 450 *Web:* www.ameronpipe.com	Rancho Cucamonga	CA	91730	909-944-4100	944-4113
Angelus Block Co Inc 11374 Tuxford St *Web:* www.angelusblock.com	Sun Valley	CA	91352	818-767-8576	768-3124
Arkansas Precast Corp 2601 Cory Dr PO Box 425 *Web:* www.arkansasprecast.com	Jacksonville	AR	72078	501-982-1547	982-4001
Atlantic Concrete Products Inc 8900 Old Rt 13 *Web:* www.atlanticconcrete.com	Tullytown	PA	19007	215-945-5600	946-3102
Basalite Concrete Products LLC 605 Industrial Way *TF:* 800-776-6690 ■ *Web:* basalite.paccoast.com	Dixon	CA	95620	707-678-1901	678-6268
Bayshore Concrete Products Corp 1134 Bayshore Rd PO Box 230 *Web:* www.usacivil.skanska.com	Cape Charles	VA	23310	757-331-2300	331-2501
Beavertown Block Co Inc 3612 Paxtonville Rd PO Box 337 *TF Cust Svc:* 800-597-2565 ■ *Web:* www.beavertownblock.com	Middleburg	PA	17842	570-837-1744	837-1591
Bend Industries Inc 2200 S Main St *TF:* 800-686-2363 ■ *Web:* www.bendindustries.com	West Bend	WI	53095	262-338-5700	306-8257
Best Block Co PO Box 13707 *TF:* 800-782-7708 ■ *Web:* www.bestblock.com	Milwaukee	WI	53213	262-781-7200	781-7253
Betco Block & Products Inc 5400 Butler Rd *TF:* 800-486-2312	Bethesda	MD	20816	301-654-2312	654-0525
Binkley & Ober Inc 2742 Lancaster Rd PO Box 7 *TF:* 800-860-0441 ■ *Web:* www.binkleyandober.com	East Petersburg	PA	17520	717-569-0441	569-5066
Blakeslee Construction 200 N Branford Rd *TF:* 800-922-6203	Branford	CT	06405	203-488-2500	488-4538
Blakeslee Prestress Inc Rt 139 McDermott Rd PO Box 510 *Web:* www.blakesleeprestress.com	Branford	CT	06405	203-481-5306	488-3307
Block USA 327 Fiberglass Rd *TF:* 888-942-5625 ■ *Web:* www.specblockusa.com	Jackson	TN	38301	731-421-4624	421-4625
Blocklite Corp 1201 Golden State Blvd PO Noc 540 *Web:* www.blocklite.com	Selma	CA	93662	559-896-0753	896-9652
BNZ Materials Inc 6901 S Pierce St Suite 260 *TF:* 800-999-0890 ■ *Web:* www.bnzmaterials.com	Littleton	CO	80128	303-978-1199	978-0308
Bonsal American Inc 8201 Arrowridge Blvd PO Box 241148 *TF:* 800-738-1621 ■ *Web:* www.bonsal.com	Charlotte	NC	28224	704-525-1621	529-5261
Buehner Block Co 2800 S West Temple *TF:* 800-999-2565 ■ *Web:* www.buehnerblock.com	Salt Lake City	UT	84115	801-467-5456	467-0866
Building Products Corp 950 Freeburg Ave *TF:* 800-233-1996 ■ *Web:* www.buildingproductscorp.com	Belleville	IL	62220	618-233-4427	233-2031
Burtco Inc Rt 123 PO Box 40 *TF:* 800-451-4401	Westminster Station	VT	05159	802-722-3358	722-9088
Cary Concrete Products Inc 211 Dean St Suite 1D *Web:* www.caryconcrete.com	Woodstock	IL	60098	815-338-2301	337-5801
Cement Industries Inc 2709 Jeffcott St *TF:* 800-332-1440 ■ *Web:* www.cementindustries.com	Fort Myers	FL	33901	239-332-1440	332-0370
Cement Products & Supply Co Inc 516 W Main St	Lakeland	FL	33815	863-686-5141	683-2034
Century Group Inc 1106 W Napoleon St PO Box 228 *TF:* 800-527-5232 ■ *Web:* www.centurygrp.com	Sulphur	LA	70664	337-527-5266	527-8028
Chandler Materials Co 5805 E 15th St	Tulsa	OK	74112	918-836-9151	836-2002
Chaney Enterprises 12480 Mattawoman Dr PO Box 548 **Fax:* Sales ■ *TF:* 800-492-3495 ■ *Web:* www.chaney-ent.com	Waldorf	MD	20604	301-932-5000	843-9123*
Christy Concrete Products Inc 5236 Arboga Rd *TF:* 800-370-8882 ■ *Web:* www.christyconcrete.com	Marysville	CA	95901	530-742-8368	742-9421
Cinder & Concrete Block Corp 10111 Beaver Dam Rd PO Box 9	Cockeysville	MD	21030	410-666-2350	666-8781
Clayton Block Co 515 Lakewood New Egypt Rd *TF Orders:* 800-662-3044 ■ *Web:* www.claytonco.com/block/block.asp	Lakewood	NJ	08701	732-751-7600	751-7618
Clayton Cos The PO Box 3015 *TF:* 800-905-3154 ■ *Web:* www.claytonco.com	Lakewood	NJ	08701	732-905-3154	751-7623
Con Forms PO Box 308 *TF:* 800-223-3676 ■ *Web:* www.conforms.com	Port Washington	WI	53074	262-268-6800	268-6868
Concrete Technology Corp 1123 Port of Tacoma Rd PO Box 2259 *Web:* www.concretetech.com	Tacoma	WA	98401	253-383-3545	572-9386
Concrete Tie Corp 130 Oris St PO Box 5406 *Web:* www.concretetie.net	Compton	CA	90224	310-886-1000	638-8363
Construction Products Inc 1631 Ashport Rd *TF:* 800-238-8226 ■ *Web:* www.cpi-tn.com	Jackson	TN	38305	731-668-7305	668-1361
Continental Florida Materials 13450 W Sunrise Blvd Suite 430 *TF:* 888-969-9100	Sunrise	FL	33323	954-858-0780	858-0821
Cook Concrete Products Inc 5461 Eastside Rd *Web:* www.cookconcreteproducts.com	Redding	CA	96001	530-243-2562	243-6881
Coreslab International 332 Jones Rd Unit 8 *Web:* www.coreslab.com	Stoney Creek	ON	L8E5N2	905-643-0220	643-0233
Coreslab Structures Inc 150 W Placentia Ave *Web:* www.coreslab.com	Perris	CA	92571	951-943-9119	943-7571
County Concrete Corp 1111 Menomonie St *Web:* www.countyconcrete.com	Eau Claire	WI	54703	715-834-7701	834-5583
Cranesville Block Co Inc 774 State Hwy 5 S PO Box 430 *Web:* www.cranesville.com	Amsterdam	NY	12010	518-887-5560	887-2560
Cretex Cos Inc 311 Lowell Ave *Web:* www.cretexinc.com	Elk River	MN	55330	763-441-2121	441-3585
Crom Corp 250 SW 36th Terr *TF:* 800-289-2766 ■ *Web:* www.cromgnv.com	Gainesville	FL	32607	352-372-3436	372-6209
Cumberland Concrete Corp Narrows Park Rt 40 PO Box 3369	LaVale	MD	21504	301-724-2000	724-6416
Dakota Block Co 3292 Lien St PO Box 440	Rapid City	SD	57709	605-342-6070	394-7239
Devcon International Corp 1350 E Newport Ctr Dr Suite 201 *NASDAQ:* DEVC ■ *Web:* www.devc.com	Deerfield Beach	FL	33442	954-429-1500	429-1506
Dickey DW & Son Inc 7896 Dickey Dr PO Box 189 *Web:* www.dwdickey.com/dwdickey	Lisbon	OH	44432	330-424-1441	424-1481
Dillon E & Co Rt 1 Box 800 PO Box 160 *TF:* 800-234-8970 ■ *Web:* www.edillon.com	Swords Creek	VA	24649	276-873-6816	873-4208
Dolese Brothers Co 20 NW 13th St *TF:* 800-375-2311	Oklahoma City	OK	73103	405-235-2311	297-8329
Domine Builders Supply Corp 100 E Highland Dr *TF:* 800-836-2565 ■ *Web:* www.domineblock.com	Rochester	NY	14610	585-271-6330	271-2053
Duchini A Inc 2550 McKinley Ave *TF:* 800-937-7317 ■ *Web:* www.duchini.com	Erie	PA	16503	814-456-7027	454-0737
Dura-Stress Inc 11325 CR 44 E PO Box 490779 *TF:* 800-342-9239 ■ *Web:* www.durastress.com	Leesburg	FL	34749	352-787-1422	787-0080
DW Dickey & Son Inc 7896 Dickey Dr PO Box 189 *Web:* www.dwdickey.com/dwdickey	Lisbon	OH	44432	330-424-1441	424-1481
DYK Inc 351 Cypress Ln *TF:* 800-227-8181 ■ *Web:* www.dyk.com	El Cajon	CA	92020	619-440-8181	440-8653
E Dillon & Co Rt 1 Box 800 PO Box 160 *TF:* 800-234-8970 ■ *Web:* www.edillon.com	Swords Creek	VA	24649	276-873-6816	873-4208
Echo Rock Ventures 13620 Lincoln Way Suite 380	Auburn	CA	95603	530-823-9600	823-9650
Egyptian Concrete Co 749 W Commercial St PO Box 488 *Web:* www.egyptianconcrete.com	Salem	IL	62881	618-548-1190	548-1294
Elk River Concrete Products Co 6550 Wedgwood Rd *TF:* 800-557-7473 ■ *Web:* www.ercp.com	Maple Grove	MN	55311	763-545-7473	545-8399
EP Henry Corp 201 Park Ave *TF:* 800-444-3679 ■ *Web:* www.ephenry.com	Woodbury	NJ	08096	856-845-6200	845-0023
Ernest Maier Inc 4700 Annapolis Rd *Web:* www.emcoblock.com	Bladensburg	MD	20710	301-927-8300	779-8924
Fabcon Inc 6111 Hwy 13 W *TF:* 800-727-4444 ■ *Web:* www.fabcon-usa.com	Savage	MN	55378	952-890-4444	890-6657
Featherlite Building Products Corp 508 McNeil St *Web:* www.featherlitetexas.com	Round Rock	TX	78681	512-255-2573	255-2572
Federal Block Corp 247 Walsh Ave *TF:* 800-724-1999 ■ *Web:* www.montfortgroup.com	New Windsor	NY	12553	845-561-4108	561-5344
Fendt Builders Supply Inc 22005 Gill Rd *TF:* 888-706-9974 ■ *Web:* www.fendtbuilderssupply.com	Farmington Hills	MI	48335	248-474-3211	474-8110
Fizzano Brothers Concrete Products Inc 1776 Chester Pike *Web:* www.fizzano.com	Crum Lynne	PA	19022	610-833-1100	833-5347
Florida Rock Industries Inc 155 E 21st St *NYSE:* FRK ■ *TF:* 800-874-8382 ■ *Web:* www.flarock.com	Jacksonville	FL	32206	904-355-1781	791-1807
Foley Products Co 5526 Schatulga Rd PO Box 7877 *TF:* 800-762-6773 ■ *Web:* www.theconcretecompany.com	Columbus	GA	31908	706-563-7882	563-1869
Fritz Industries Inc PO Box 170040 *TF:* 800-955-1323 ■ *Web:* www.fritztile.com	Dallas	TX	75217	972-285-5471	270-0179
Frontier Precast LLC 2633 Waterford Rd *TF:* 800-633-9969 ■ *Web:* www.frontierprecast.com	Marietta	OH	45750	740-373-3211	373-5678
General Shale Products LLC 3211 N Roan St *TF Cust Svc:* 800-414-4661 ■ *Web:* www.generalshale.com	Johnson City	TN	37601	423-282-4661	952-4104
Glacier Northwest Inc 5050 1st Ave Suite 102 PO Box 1730 *TF:* 800-750-0123 ■ *Web:* www.glaciernw.com	Seattle	WA	98111	206-764-3000	764-3012
Glen-Gery Corp 1166 Spring St PO Box 7001 *Web:* www.glengerybrick.com	Wyomissing	PA	19610	610-374-4011	374-1622
Goria Enterprises 108 Buchanan Church Rd PO Box 14489 *TF:* 800-828-5879	Greensboro	NC	27415	336-375-5821	375-8259
Grand Blanc Cement Products 10709 S Center Rd *TF:* 800-875-7500 ■ *Web:* www.grandblanccement.com	Grand Blanc	MI	48439	810-694-7500	694-2995
Grand River Infrastructure Inc 2701 Chicago Dr SW *TF:* 800-968-2662	Grand Rapids	MI	49519	616-534-9645	534-8010
Greensburg Concrete Block Co 1011 Green St PO Box 729	Greensburg	PA	15601	724-834-5210	834-8873
Griswold ST & Co Inc 193 Industrial Ave PO Box 849 *TF:* 800-339-4565 ■ *Web:* www.stgriswold.com	Williston	VT	05495	802-658-0201	658-6869
Hancock Concrete Products Inc 17 Atlantic Ave *TF:* 800-992-8982 ■ *Web:* www.hancockconcrete.com	Hancock	MN	56244	320-392-5207	392-5155
Hanson Aggregates North America 8505 Freeport Pkwy Suite 500 *TF:* 800-687-6549 ■ *Web:* www.hanson-america.com	Irving	TX	75063	972-621-0345	621-0506
Hanson Building Products North America 3500 Maple Ave *TF:* 800-527-2362 ■ *Web:* www.hanson-america.com	Dallas	TX	75219	214-525-5500	525-5563

Phone Fax

Hanson Pipe & Products PO Box 368 ....Green Cove Springs FL 32043 904-284-3213 284-9865
TF: 800-432-0030 ■ *Web:* www.hansonpipeandproducts.com
Hartford Concrete Products Inc
1400 N Walbash Ave PO Box 660 .... Hartford City IN 47348 765-348-3506 348-3121
TF: 800-662-8788 ■ *Web:* www.hartfordconcrete.com
Hastings Pavement Co LLC PO Box 178 .... Islip NY 11751 631-669-4900 669-0559
TF: 800-669-9294 ■ *Web:* www.hastingspavers.com
Henry EP Corp 201 Park Ave .... Woodbury NJ 08096 856-845-6200 845-0023
TF: 800-444-3679 ■ *Web:* www.ephenry.com
High Concrete Structures Inc 125 Denver Rd .... Denver PA 17517 717-336-9300 336-9301*
**Fax:* Sales ■ *TF:* 800-773-2278 ■ *Web:* www.highconcrete.com
High Industries Inc PO Box 10008 .... Lancaster PA 17605 717-293-4444 293-4416*
**Fax:* Mktg ■ *Web:* www.high.net
Hunterdon Concrete Inc Rt 202 & 31 PO Box 2050 ....Flemington NJ 08822 908-782-3619 782-2378
Illinois Concrete Co Inc PO Box 3096 ....Champaign IL 61826 217-352-4181 352-9601
Web: www.illinois-concrete.com
Independent Concrete Pipe Co
3701 Kramers Ln PO Box 16098 .... Louisville KY 40256 502-448-2920 448-3134
Iowa Prestressed Concrete Inc 601 SW 9th St Suite B .... Des Moines IA 50309 515-243-5118 243-5502
TF: 800-826-0464
Jensen Precast 625 Bergin Way .... Sparks NV 89431 775-359-6200 359-1038
TF: 800-648-1134 ■ *Web:* www.jensenprecast.com
JW Peters Inc 500 W Market St .... Burlington WI 53105 262-763-2401 763-2779
TF: 800-877-9040 ■ *Web:* www.jwpeters.com
K & S Contractors Supply Co Inc 1971 Gunnville Rd .... Lancaster NY 14086 716-759-6911 759-2129
Kerr Concrete Pipe Co Inc 1920 12th St PO Box 312 ....Hammonton NJ 08037 609-561-3400 561-5786*
**Fax Area Code:* 877 ■ *TF:* 800-642-3755 ■ *Web:* www.kerrpipe.com
Kieft Brothers Inc 837 S Riverside Dr .... Elmhurst IL 60126 630-832-8090 834-5765
Web: www.kieftbros.com
Kienstra Inc 201 W Ferguson Ave .... Wood River IL 62095 618-254-4366 254-7429
TF: 888-543-6787 ■ *Web:* www.kienstra.com
King's Material Inc 650 12th Ave SW PO Box 368 ....Cedar Rapids IA 52406 319-363-0233 366-0249
TF: 800-332-5298 ■ *Web:* www.kingsmaterial.com
Kistner Concrete Products Inc 8713 Read Rd ....East Pembroke NY 14056 585-762-8216 762-8315
TF: 800-809-2801 ■ *Web:* www.kistner.com
Krehling Industries Inc 1425 E Wiggins Pass Rd .... Naples FL 34108 239-597-3162 254-7322
TF: 800-226-3162 ■ *Web:* www.krehling.com
Lafarge North America Inc 12950 Worldgate Dr Suite 600 ....Herndon VA 20170 703-480-3600 796-2214
NYSE: LAF ■ *Web:* www.lafargenorthamerica.com
Lakelands Concrete Products Inc 7520 E Main St ....Lima NY 14485 585-624-1990 624-2102
Web: www.lakelandsconcrete.com
Lampus RI Co 816 RI Lampus Ave .... Springdale PA 15144 724-274-5035 274-2181
TF: 800-872-7310 ■ *Web:* www.lampus.com
Landis Block Co 711 N County Line Rd PO Box 64418 .... Souderton PA 18964 215-723-5506 723-5500
Web: www.landisbc.com
Lombard Co 4245 W 123rd St ....Alsip IL 60803 708-389-1060 389-7120
Louisiana Industries PO Box 5396 .... Bossier City LA 71171 318-742-3111 742-4047
TF: 800-894-5422
Maier Ernest Inc 4700 Annapolis Rd ....Bladensburg MD 20710 301-927-8300 779-8924
Web: www.emcoblock.com
Marshall Concrete Products Inc 1088 Industrial Ave .... Danville VA 24541 434-792-1233 792-1145
TF: 800-537-5884 ■ *Web:* www.marshallconcrete.com
Martin Fireproofing Corp 2200 Military Rd ....Tonawanda NY 14150 716-692-3680 693-3402
TF: 800-766-3969 ■ *Web:* www.martinfireproofing.com
Mathis-Akins Concrete Block Co Inc 130 Lower Elm St .... Macon GA 31202 478-746-5154 746-3030
TF: 888-469-0680 ■ *Web:* www.mathisakinsconcreteblock.com
Metro Supply Co 4950 White Lake Rd .... Clarkston MI 48346 248-625-8080 625-7820
Metromont Corp PO Box 2486 ....Greenville SC 29602 864-295-0295 269-8183
TF: 888-295-0383 ■ *Web:* www.metromontusa.com
Metromont Materials Corp PO Box 1292 ....Spartanburg SC 29304 864-585-4241 582-8435*
**Fax:* Sales ■ *Web:* www.metromontmaterials.com
Midwest Tile & Concrete Products Inc 4309 Webster Rd .... Woodburn IN 46797 260-749-5173 493-2477
TF: 800-359-4701 ■ *Web:* www.midwesttile.net
Miller AC Concrete Products Inc
312 E Bridge St PO Box 199 ....Spring City PA 19475 610-948-4600 948-9750
TF: 800-229-2922 ■ *Web:* www.acmiller.com
MMC Materials Inc 1052 Highland Colony Pkwy Suite 201 ....Ridgeland MS 39157 601-898-4000 898-4030
Web: www.mmcmaterials.com
Modern Building Materials Inc 8011 Green Bay Rd ....Kenosha WI 53142 262-694-3166 694-9185
TF Cust Svc: 800-622-3166
Modern Concrete Septic Tank Co 210 Durham Rd .... Ottsville PA 18942 610-847-5112 847-1046
Web: www.modcon.com
Molin Concrete Products Co 415 Lilac St ....Lino Lakes MN 55014 651-786-7722 786-0229
TF: 800-336-6546 ■ *Web:* www.molin.com
MonierLifetile Inc 7575 Irvine Center Dr Suite 100 .... Irvine CA 92618 949-756-1605 756-2401
TF: 800-224-2024 ■ *Web:* www.monierlifetile.com
Montfort Bros Inc 44 Elm St .... Fishkill NY 12524 845-896-6225 896-0021
TF: 800-724-1777 ■ *Web:* www.montfortgroup.com/mb_f.htm
Montfort Group The 44 Elm St .... Fishkill NY 12524 845-896-6225 896-0021
TF: 800-724-1777 ■ *Web:* www.montfortgroup.com
Mutual Materials Co 605 119th Ave NE .... Bellevue WA 98005 425-452-2300 454-7732
TF: 800-477-3008 ■ *Web:* www.mutualmaterials.com
National Concrete Products Co 939 S Mill St .... Plymouth MI 48170 734-453-8448 453-1890
NC Products Corp 920 Withers Rd PO Box 27077 ....Raleigh NC 27611 919-772-6301 772-1209
TF: 800-662-1983 ■ *Web:* www.ncproducts.com
New Holland Concrete 828 E Earl Rd PO Box 218 .... New Holland PA 17557 717-354-1200 428-7538*
**Fax Area Code:* 888 ■ *TF:* 800-543-3860 ■ *Web:* www.newhollandconcrete.com
New Milford Block & Supply 574 Danbury Rd ....New Milford CT 06776 860-355-1101 355-3772
Web: www.montfortgroup.com
Nitterhouse Concrete Products Inc
2655 Molly Pitcher Hwy S ....Chambersburg PA 17201 717-264-6154 267-4518
Web: www.nitterhouse.com
O & G Industries Inc 112 Wall St .... Torrington CT 06790 860-489-9261 496-4286
Web: www.ogindustries.com
Oldcastle Inc 375 N Ridge Rd Suite 350 ....Atlanta GA 30350 770-804-3363 804-3369
TF: 800-899-8455 ■ *Web:* www.oldcastle.com
Oldcastle Precast Group 2820 'A' St SE ....Auburn WA 98002 253-833-2777 939-9126
Web: www.oldcastle-precast.com
Orco Block Co Inc 11100 Beach Blvd .... Stanton CA 90680 714-527-2239 889-1280
TF: 800-473-6726 ■ *Web:* www.orco.com
Owatonna Construction Co 900 30th Pl PO Box 246 ....Owatonna MN 55060 507-451-8950 451-0575
Web: www.owatonnaconstruction.com
Pavestone Plus Inc RR 1 1081 Rife Rd ....Cambridge ON N1R5S3 519-740-6000 740-2543
TF: 800-265-6496 ■ *Web:* www.pavestoneplus.com
Pomeroy Corp PO Box 411 .... Petaluma CA 94953 707-763-1918 763-2227
Web: www.pomeroycorp.com
Pontchartrain Materials Corp 3819 France Rd .... New Orleans LA 70126 504-949-7571 944-3338
TF: 800-255-9848
Preload Inc 60 Commerce Dr .... Hauppauge NY 11788 631-231-8100 231-8881
Web: www.preload.com
Prestress Engineering Corp 2220 Rt 176 ....Prairie Grove IL 60014 815-459-4545 459-6855
Web: www.pre-stress.com
Prestress Services Inc PO Box 111 .... Decatur IN 46733 260-724-7117 724-3349
Web: www.prestressservices.com
Price Brothers Co 333 W 1st St Suite 700 PO Box 825 .... Dayton OH 45401 937-226-8700 226-8936
TF: 800-543-5147

Phone Fax

QUIKRETE Cos 3490 Piedmont Rd Suite 1300 .... Atlanta GA 30305 404-634-9100 842-1424
TF: 800-282-5828 ■ *Web:* www.quikrete.com
Rancho Building Materials Co 4701 Wible Rd .... Bakersfield CA 93313 661-831-0831 831-0244
RCP Block & Brick Inc 8240 Broadway ....Lemon Grove CA 91945 619-460-7250 460-3926
TF: 800-732-7425 ■ *Web:* www.rcpblock.com
Reading Rock Inc 4600 Devitt Dr ....Cincinnati OH 45246 513-874-2345 874-2520
TF: 800-482-6466 ■ *Web:* www.readingrock.com
RI Lampus Co 816 RI Lampus Ave .... Springdale PA 15144 724-274-5035 274-2181
TF: 800-872-7310 ■ *Web:* www.lampus.com
Rinker Materials Corp 1501 Belvedere Rd .... West Palm Beach FL 33406 561-833-5555 820-8666
TF: 800-226-5521 ■ *Web:* www.rinker.com
Rinker Materials Corp Concrete Pipe Div 8311 W Carder Ct .... Littleton CO 80125 303-791-1600 791-1710
TF: 800-285-2902 ■ *Web:* www.rinkermaterials.com/ProdsServices/ConcretePipe/
Rockwood Retaining Walls Inc 7200 Hwy 63 N ....Rochester MN 55906 507-288-8850 288-3810
TF: 800-535-2375 ■ *Web:* www.rockwoodwalls.com
Schuster's Building Products Inc 901 E Troy Ave .... Indianapolis IN 46203 317-787-3201 788-5906
TF: 800-424-0190 ■ *Web:* www.schusters.com
Schuylkill Products Inc 121 River St .... Cressona PA 17929 570-385-2352 385-2404
Web: www.spibeams.com
Sequatchie Concrete Service Inc 406 Cedar Ave ....South Pittsburg TN 37380 423-837-7913 837-7479
TF: 800-824-0824 ■ *Web:* www.seqconcrete.com
Sherman Industries 250 Palmer Rd PO Box 646 ....Madison AL 35758 256-772-7490 772-3220
TF: 800-239-7490
Sherman International Corp 1400 Urban Ctr Dr Suite 200 ...... Birmingham AL 35242 205-970-7500 970-7555
TF: 800-277-6920 ■ *Web:* www.shermaninternational.com
Smith-Midland Corp 5119 Catlett Rd PO Box 300 .... Midland VA 22728 540-439-3266 439-1232
Web: www.smithmid.com
Southern Concrete Construction Co Inc
733 Liberty Expy PO Box 711 .... Albany GA 31702 229-435-0786 434-4755
Spancrete Industries Inc
N 16 W 23415 Stone Ridge Dr PO Box 828 .... Waukesha WI 53187 414-290-9000 290-9125*
**Fax:* Sales ■ *Web:* www.spancrete.com
Speed Fab-Crete Corp International PO Box 15580 ....Fort Worth TX 76119 817-478-1137 561-2544
TF: 800-758-1137 ■ *Web:* www.speedfab-crete.com
ST Griswold & Co Inc 193 Industrial Ave PO Box 849 ....Williston VT 05495 802-658-0201 658-6869
TF: 800-339-4565 ■ *Web:* www.stgriswold.com
Stanley Hardware 480 Myrtle St .... New Britain CT 06053 860-225-5111 529-4254*
**Fax Area Code:* 877 ■ **Fax:* Cust Svc ■ *TF Cust Svc:* 800-337-4393 ■
Web: www.stanleyhardware.com
Stoneway Concrete Co 9125 10th Ave S .... Seattle WA 98108 206-762-9125 763-4178
Stresscon Corp 3210 Astrozon Blvd ....Colorado Springs CO 80910 719-390-5041 390-5564
Web: www.stresscon.com
Superior Concrete Co Inc 982 Minot Ave PO Box 1996 ....Auburn ME 04211 207-784-9144 784-9647
Web: www.superiorconcrete.com
Superlite Block Co Inc 4150 W Turney Ave .... Phoenix AZ 85019 602-269-3561 352-3813
TF: 800-366-7877 ■ *Web:* www.superliteblock.com
Texas Concrete Co 4702 N Vine St ....Victoria TX 77904 361-573-9145 578-5859
TF: 800-242-3511
Thomas Concrete Inc 2500 Cumberland Pkwy Suite 200 .... Atlanta GA 30339 770-431-3300 431-3305
TF: 800-633-4661 ■ *Web:* www.thomasconcrete.com
Tindall Corp PO Box 1778 ....Spartanburg SC 29304 864-576-3230 587-8828
TF: 800-849-4521 ■ *Web:* www.tindallcorp.com
Trenwyth Industries Inc 1 Connely Rd PO Box 438 ....Emigsville PA 17318 717-767-6868 767-4023
TF Cust Svc: 800-233-1924 ■ *Web:* www.trenwyth.com
TXI Operations LP DBA Louisiana Industries PO Box 5396 ...... Bossier City LA 71171 318-742-3111 742-4047
TF: 800-894-5422
Unistress Corp 550 Cheshire Rd PO Box 1145 ....Pittsfield MA 01202 413-499-1441 499-9930
TF: 800-927-9468 ■ *Web:* www.unistresscorp.com
United Building Centers Masonry Products Div
1514 E Fulton St PO Box 599 .... Garden City KS 67846 620-276-8294 276-8299
TF: 800-545-7411
Universal Concrete Products Corp
400 Old Reading Pike Suite 200 ....Stowe PA 19464 610-323-0700 323-4046
Web: www.universalconcrete.com
Valley Blox Inc 210 Stone Spring Rd .... Harrisonburg VA 22801 540-434-6725 434-6514*
**Fax:* Acctg ■ *TF:* 800-648-6725
Valley Blox Inc Americast Div 11352 Virginia Precast Rd .... Ashland VA 23005 804-798-6068 798-3426
TF: 800-999-2279 ■ *Web:* www.americastusa.com
Walters & Wolf Precast 41777 Boyce Rd .... Fremont CA 94538 510-226-9800 226-0360
Web: www.waltersandwolf.com
Wieser Concrete Products Inc W3716 US Hwy 10 .... Maiden Rock WI 54750 715-647-2311 647-5181
TF: 800-325-8456 ■ *Web:* www.wieserconcrete.com
Wilbert Inc PO Box 147 .... Forest Park IL 60130 708-865-1600 865-1646
TF: 800-323-7188
Willamette Graystone Inc 3700 Franklin Blvd ....Eugene OR 97403 541-726-7666 744-8953
Web: www.willamettegraystone.com
Wingra Stone Co 2975 Kapec Rd PO Box 44284 ....Madison WI 53744 608-271-5555 271-3142
TF: 800-249-6908 ■ *Web:* www.wingrastone.com
Wisconsin Brick & Block Corp 6399 Nesbitt Rd ....Madison WI 53719 608-845-8636 845-8630
TF: 800-601-2889
WPC Florida PO Box 35189 ....Panama City FL 32412 850-763-2811 785-1413*
**Fax:* Sales ■ *TF:* 800-763-2811
Wyoming Concrete Products Co 725 Bryan Stock Trail .... Casper WY 82609 307-265-3100 265-0013
York Building Products Co Inc 950 Smile Way PO Box 1708 .... York PA 17405 717-848-2831 854-9156
TF: 800-673-2408 ■ *Web:* www.yorkbuilding.com

187 CONFERENCE & EVENTS COORDINATORS

Phone Fax

Accent on Cincinnati 915 W 8th St ....Cincinnati OH 45203 513-721-8687 721-1542
Web: www.accentcinti.com
Accenting Chicago Events & Tours Inc
333 N Michigan Ave Suite 425 .... Chicago IL 60601 312-819-5363 819-5366
Web: www.accentingchicago.com
Action Motivation 465 Forbes Blvd .... South San Francisco CA 94080 650-416-2400 416-2499
Web: www.amotive.com
Advanstar Communications Inc 7500 Old Oak Blvd ....Cleveland OH 44130 440-243-8100 891-2651
TF: 800-225-4569 ■ *Web:* web.advanstar.com
AJ Babkow & Assoc 520 E 76th St ....New York NY 10021 212-988-2756 535-0927
Ambassadors International Inc 1071 Camelback St .... Newport Beach CA 92660 949-759-5900 759-5901
NASDAQ: AMIE ■ *TF:* 800-325-7103 ■ *Web:* www.ambassadors.com
Ann Becker & Assoc Inc 1416 E 56th St ....Chicago IL 60637 773-377-2480 955-0164
Web: www.abecker.com
ASD/AMD Merchandise Group
11835 W Olympic Blvd Suite 550-E ....Los Angeles CA 90064 310-481-7300 481-1900
TF: 800-421-4511 ■ *Web:* www.merchandisegroup.com
At Your Service of the Low Country Inc 355 E Broad St ....Savannah GA 31401 912-232-6866 234-8437
TF: 800-868-6867 ■ *Web:* www.savannah.com/atyourservice
Babkow AJ & Assoc 520 E 76th St ....New York NY 10021 212-988-2756 535-0927
Bayliss Gene Productions 208 Goodhill Rd ....Weston CT 06883 203-227-7521 454-1032
Bixel & Co 8721 Sunset Blvd Suite 101 ....Los Angeles CA 90069 310-854-3828 854-0115
Web: www.bixelco.com

Phone Fax

Brede Exposition Services Div Casey & Hayes Exhibits Inc
100 Industrial Pk Rd Hingham MA 02043 781-741-5900 741-5902
TF: 800-835-3976 ■ *Web:* www.brede.com
Briggs Inc 1501 Broadway Suite 406 New York NY 10036 212-354-9440 382-1560
Web: www.briggsnyc.com
CA Larsen & Assoc 309 E Rand Rd Suite 365 Arlington Heights IL 60004 847-255-3003 577-7276
Cappa & Graham Inc 401 Terry A Francois Blvd Suite 200 San Francisco CA 94158 415-512-6967 512-6982
Web: www.cappa-graham.com
Carden Convention Service Co
2500 Sweetwater Spring Blvd Suite 105 Spring Valley CA 91978 619-670-8211 670-7242
Web: www.cardenconvention.com
Casey & Hayes Exhibits Inc Brede Exposition Services Div
100 Industrial Pk Rd Hingham MA 02043 781-741-5900 741-5902
TF: 800-835-3976 ■ *Web:* www.brede.com
Celebrity International Entertainment Inc
1800 Century Park E Suite 600 Los Angeles CA 90067 323-848-2300 848-2303*
*Fax Area Code: 310 ■ *Web:* www.celebrityinternational.com
Centennial Conferences 901 Front St Suite 130 Louisville CO 80027 303-499-2299 499-2599
Web: www.centennialconferences.com
CMP Inc 3641 Pebble Beach Northbrook IL 60062 847-564-8160 564-8536
TF: 888-848-6700
COMCOR Event & Meeting Production
5353 N Federal Hwy Suite 402 Fort Lauderdale FL 33308 954-491-3233 491-6466
Web: www.comcorevents.com
Complete Conference 1540 River Park Dr Suite 111 Sacramento CA 95815 916-922-7032 922-7379
Web: www.completeconference.com
Conference Connection 8338 E Buena Terra Way Scottsdale AZ 85250 480-949-8472 949-2894
Web: www.conferenceconnection.org
Conference Consultants 445 El Escarpado Stanford CA 94305 650-324-1653 326-7751
Conference Group Inc 1580 Fishinger Rd Columbus OH 43221 614-488-2030 488-5747
Conference Hotels Unlimited 51 Harborview Rd Hull MA 02045 781-925-4000 925-2474
Conference & Logistics Consultants 31 Old Solomans Island Rd Annapolis MD 21401 410-571-0590 571-0592
Web: www.gomeeting.com
Conference Management Assoc Inc 45 Lyme Rd Suite 304 Hanover NH 03755 603-643-2325 643-1444
Conference Management Services PO Box 2506 Monterey CA 93942 831-622-7772 622-0711
TF: 800-882-1891 ■ *Web:* www.conferencemanagement.net
Conference Solutions Inc
2545 SW Spring Garden St Suite 150 Portland OR 97219 503-244-4294 244-2401
Web: www.conferencesolutionsinc.com
Conference & Travel 5701 Coventry Ln Fort Wayne IN 46804 260-434-6600 436-3177
TF: 800-346-9807 ■ *Web:* www.conftvl.com
Convention Consultants Historic Savannah Foundation Special Tours & Meeting Services 117 W Perry St Savannah GA 31401 912-234-4088
TF: 800-627-5030 ■ *Web:* www.savtours.com
Convention Planning Services Inc 2453 Orlando Central Pkwy Orlando FL 32809 407-851-5122 851-8313
TF: 800-777-5333 ■ *Web:* www.cpsorlando.com
Convention & Show Management Co Inc
6175 Barfield Rd NE Suite 220 Atlanta GA 30328 404-252-2454 252-0215
Courtesy Assoc 2025 M St NW Suite 800 Washington DC 20036 202-331-2000 331-0111
Web: www.courtesyassociates.com
Creative Convention Services 1300 6th Ave Beaver Falls PA 15010 724-843-7501 843-7613
TF: 800-365-8501 ■ *Web:* www.creativeconventions.com
Creative Impact Group Inc 155 Revere Dr Suite 1 Northbrook IL 60062 847-945-7401 945-7405
TF: 800-445-2171 ■ *Web:* www.creativeimpactgroup.com
Crescent City Consultants 210 Baronne St Suite 1108 New Orleans LA 70112 504-561-1191 561-5894
TF: 800-899-1191 ■ *Web:* www.ccc-nola.com
David Price & Assoc Inc 8410 SW 156 St Palmetto Bay FL 33157 305-259-7903 259-7416
Web: www.dprice.com
Destination Resources 5435 Balboa Blvd Suite 206 Encino CA 91316 818-995-7915 990-6129
TF: 800-234-7027 ■ *Web:* www.destinationresources.com
Destination Services of Colorado Inc 0020 Eagle Rd Bldg 1 Avon CO 81620 970-476-6565 476-6768
TF: 800-372-7686 ■ *Web:* www.dmc-colorado.com
Diversified Conference Management Inc 1878 Cypress Point Ct Ann Arbor MI 48108 734-665-2535 665-4541
TF: 800-458-2535 ■ *Web:* mywebpages.comcast.net/dcmi/
Eisenstodt Assoc 770 5th St NW Suite 1105 Washington DC 20001 202-543-7971 543-4619
Elite Show Services Inc 2878 Camino Del Rio S Suite 260 San Diego CA 92108 619-574-1589 574-1588
Web: www.eliteshowservices.com
Event Planning International Corp 10900 Granite St Charlotte NC 28273 980-233-3777 233-3800
TF: 800-940-2164 ■ *Web:* www.epicreg.com
Events Organization 10480 Little Patuxent Pkwy Suite 400 Columbia MD 21044 301-596-2003 854-0280
Web: www.eventsorg.com
Executive Arrangements Inc 24800 Chagrin Blvd Suite 200 Cleveland OH 44122 216-595-2950 595-2951
Web: www.executivearrangements.com
Experient Inc 2500 Enterprise Pkwy E Twinsburg OH 44087 330-425-8333 425-3299
Web: www.experient-inc.com
Expo Group 1740 Hurd Dr Irving TX 75038 972-580-9000 550-7877
TF: 800-736-7775 ■ *Web:* www.theexpogroup.com
Freeman Cos 1600 Viceroy Suite 100 Dallas TX 75235 214-445-1000 445-0200
Web: www.freemanco.com
Gavel International Corp 300 Tri State International Suite 320 Lincolnshire IL 60069 847-945-8150 945-6569
TF: 800-544-2835 ■ *Web:* www.gavelintl.com
Gene Bayliss Productions 208 Goodhill Rd Weston CT 06883 203-227-7521 454-1032
George P Johnson Cos 3600 Giddings Rd Auburn Hills MI 48326 248-475-2500 475-2325
Web: www.gpjco.com
GES Exposition Services 7050 Lindell Rd Las Vegas NV 89118 702-515-5500 329-1437*
*Fax Area Code: 866 ■ *TF:* 800-443-9767 ■ *Web:* www.ges.com
Great Events & TEAMS Inc 2170 S Parker Rd Suite 290 Denver CO 80231 303-394-2022 394-3450
Web: www.geteams.com
GT Consultants Inc 3050 Eagle Watch Dr Woodstock GA 30189 770-591-1343 591-1559
TF: 800-659-0345 ■ *Web:* www.gtconsultantsinc.com
Henry V Events 6360 ML King Blvd Portland OR 97211 503-232-6666 239-8556
TF: 877-463-3846 ■ *Web:* www.henryvevents.com
Holiday Convention Service Group 5830 W Flamingo Rd Suite 229 Las Vegas NV 89103 702-735-7353 796-5676
Web: www.holidaymodels.com
Host Communications Inc 546 E Main St Lexington KY 40508 859-226-4678 226-4221
TF: 888-484-4678 ■ *Web:* www.hostcommunications.com
Hughes Production 875 W Broadway Jackson WY 83001 307-733-6505 733-0542
Web: www.hughesproduction.com
IDG World Expo 3 Speen St Suite 320 Framingham MA 01701 508-879-6700 620-6668
Web: www.idgworldexpo.com
Incentive Travel & Meetings (ITM) 970 Clementstone Dr Suite 100 Atlanta GA 30342 404-252-2728 252-8328
Web: www.usaitm.com
Incentive Travel Services Inc 805 Peachtree St NE Suite 602 Atlanta GA 30308 404-872-6165 872-6695
Web: www.itstravel.com
Individualized Events Inc 34893 Staccato St Palm Desert CA 92211 760-200-8700 200-8770
Web: www.individualizedevents.com
International Destinations Inc 2025 M St NW Suite 500 Washington DC 20036 202-797-1222 265-5930
TF: 800-833-5254 ■ *Web:* www.meetingsworldwide.com
International Meeting Managers Inc 4550 Post Oak Pl Suite 342 Houston TX 77027 713-965-0566 960-0488
TF: 800-423-7175 ■ *Web:* www.meetingmanagers.com
International Meeting Planners Ltd 4863 Hampshire Ct Suite 303 Naples FL 34112 239-775-1467 775-1472
Web: www.internationalplanners.com
International Trade Information Inc
23241 Ventura Blvd Suite 308 Woodland Hills CA 91364 818-591-2255 591-2289
Web: www.internationaltradeinformation.com

ITM (Incentive Travel & Meetings)
970 Clementstone Dr Suite 100 Atlanta GA 30342 404-252-2728 252-8328
Web: www.usaitm.com
Jack Morton Worldwide 498 7th Ave 7th Fl New York NY 10018 212-401-7270 401-7016
Web: www.jackmorton.com
Key Event & Helen Moskovitz Group
95 White Bridge Rd Suite 500 Nashville TN 37205 615-352-6900 356-9285
Web: www.nashvilledmc.com
Kraus-Anderson Communications Group 523 S 8th St Minneapolis MN 55404 612-375-1080 342-2239
Web: www.kacommunications.com
Krebs Convention Management Services 657 Carolina St San Francisco CA 94107 415-920-7000 920-7001
Larsen CA & Assoc 309 E Rand Rd Suite 365 Arlington Heights IL 60004 847-255-3003 577-7276
LMS Meetings & Incentives 300 Corporate Pointe Suite 310 Culver City CA 90230 310-641-4222 641-5222
Web: www.thelmscorp.com
Lydon Co 143 St Clair Dr Saint Simons Island GA 31522 912-638-0901 638-2451
Lyons Co Inc 158-D Manchester Dr Basking Ridge NJ 07920 908-953-0202
Management International Inc 1828 SE 1st Ave Fort Lauderdale FL 33316 954-763-8811 425-1995*
*Fax Area Code: 800 ■ *Web:* www.currentreviews.com
Maritz Travel Co 1395 N Highway Dr Fenton MO 63099 636-827-4000
TF: 800-253-7562 ■ *Web:* www.maritztravel.com
Maxcel Co 6600 LBJ Fwy Suite 109 Dallas TX 75240 972-644-0880 680-2488
Web: www.maxcel.net
Mayer Motivations Inc 2434 E Las Olas Blvd Fort Lauderdale FL 33301 954-523-0074 523-0076
TF: 888-611-4376 ■ *Web:* www.mayermotivations.com
MC2 10601 Baur Blvd Saint Louis MO 63132 314-569-0333 569-1204
TF: 800-826-3977 ■ *Web:* www.mc-2online.com
McNabb Roick & Assoc Inc 234 W 44th St Suite 1005 New York NY 10036 212-944-7784 944-7786
Web: www.mcnabbroick.com
Meeting Connection 893 High St Suite J Worthington OH 43085 614-888-2568 888-1684
Web: www.the-meeting-connection.com
Meeting Consultants Inc 1350 Center Dr Bldg 1350 Suite 100 Atlanta GA 30338 770-399-3190 399-3170
Web: www.meetingconsultants.com
Meeting & Event Design Inc 5010 Dodge St Omaha NE 68132 402-554-4422 554-4433
Meeting Services Unlimited 135 S Mitthoeffer Rd Indianapolis IN 46229 317-841-7171 578-0621
Web: www.conventionmanagers.com
Meetings & Incentives Group 21760 Stevens Creek Blvd Cupertino CA 95014 408-973-1915 973-9712
TF: 800-752-9202 ■ *Web:* www.migr.com
Meetings & Media 4730 W 72nd St Indianapolis IN 46268 317-254-0316 872-1480
Web: www.meetingsandmedia.net
Morton Jack Worldwide 498 7th Ave 7th Fl New York NY 10018 212-401-7270 401-7016
Web: www.jackmorton.com
Moshman Assoc Inc
4340 East West Hwy South Tower Suite 1105 Bethesda MD 20814 301-229-3000 654-6940
TF: 888-223-9958 ■ *Web:* www.moshmanassociates.com
National Trade Productions Inc 313 S Patrick St Alexandria VA 22314 703-683-8500 836-4486
TF: 800-687-7469 ■ *Web:* www.ntpshow.com
Navigant Performance Group 86 Pleasant St Marlborough MA 01752 508-460-1900 460-9996
Web: npg.navigant.com
On the Scene 500 N Dearborn St Suite 550 Chicago IL 60610 312-661-1440 661-1182
TF: 800-621-5327 ■ *Web:* www.onthescenechicago.com
Pacific Agenda PO Box 10142 Portland OR 97296 503-223-8633
Pearson Group Inc 904 Princess Anne St Suite 103 Fredericksburg VA 22401 540-373-4493 373-8893
Web: www.pearsonplanners.com
Pearson & Pipkin Inc 1101 Pennsylvania Ave SE Suite 201 Washington DC 20003 202-547-7177 546-3091
Phillips International Inc 9420 Key West Ave 4th Fl Rockville MD 20850 301-279-4200
Web: www.phillips.com
Planning Experts Ltd 10732 S Emerald Ave Chicago IL 60628 773-928-7200 928-7526
Premier Meetings & Incentives 2150 S Washburn St Oshkosh WI 54903 920-236-8030 236-8006
TF: 800-236-5095 ■ *Web:* www.gopmi.com
Presenting Baltimore 3501 Century Ave Baltimore MD 21227 410-539-1344 461-9994
Web: www.presentingbaltimore.com
Prestige Accommodations International
1231 E Dyer Rd Suite 240 Santa Ana CA 92705 714-957-9100 957-9112
TF: 800-321-6338 ■ *Web:* www.meetingplanners.com
Price David & Assoc Inc 8410 SW 156 St Palmetto Bay FL 33157 305-259-7903 259-7416
Web: www.dprice.com
Productions USA 1960 N Lincoln Park W Suite 1704 Chicago IL 60614 773-296-6200 296-6333
Web: www.productionsusa.com
Professional Meeting Organizers Inc 7990 SW 64th St Miami FL 33143 305-630-9414
Web: www.pmoinc.com
Professional Meetings International Inc
130 Spruce St Penn's Landing Sq Suite 16B Philadelphia PA 19106 215-922-3222 922-5282
Web: www.pmimeetings.com
Publicis Meetings USA 340 N Primrose Dr Orlando FL 32803 407-513-3700 513-3705
TF: 800-944-9797 ■ *Web:* www.publicismeetingsusa.com
R/A Performance Group 135 Main St Suite 1120 San Francisco CA 94105 415-869-6500 495-7080
TF: 800-235-1446 ■ *Web:* www.raevents.com
Reed Exhibitions 225 Wyman St Waltham MA 02451 617-630-2260 630-2197
TF: 800-732-2914 ■ *Web:* www.reedexpo.com
Resource Connection Inc 161 S Main St Middleton MA 01949 978-777-9333 777-3360
TF: 800-649-5228 ■ *Web:* www.resource-connection.com
Robustelli Event Services 30 Spring St Stamford CT 06902 888-258-9398
Web: www.robustelli.com/eventservices
Rosenberg & Risinger Meeting Professionals
5855 Green Valley Cir Suite 101 Culver City CA 90230 310-216-6772 216-7327
Web: www.meetingsrr.com
Rx Worldwide Meetings Inc
3060 Communications Pkwy Suite 200 Plano TX 75093 214-291-2920 291-2930
TF: 800-562-1713 ■ *Web:* www.rx-worldwide.net
Sand Assoc 3560 Green St Harrisburg PA 17110 717-238-5558 238-4626
Web: www.sandassociates.com
Schneider Group 5400 Bosque Blvd Suite 680 Waco TX 76710 254-776-3550 776-3767
TF: 800-375-7363 ■ *Web:* www.sgmeet.com
Seattle Hospitality Group 1500 4th Ave Suite 200 Seattle WA 98101 206-623-2090 623-2540
Web: www.seattlehospitality.com
Secretariat PO Box 3509 Wilmington DE 19805 302-654-4479 654-4117
Web: www.secevents.com
Shepard Exposition Services 1531 Carroll Dr NW Atlanta GA 30318 404-720-8600 720-8750
Web: www.shepardes.com
Showcase Assoc Inc 911 Cypress Ave Elkins Park PA 19027 215-884-6205 884-2306
Web: www.showcasephilly.com
Sociometrics Inc 1325 Jonquil St NW Washington DC 20012 202-882-2118 882-8589
Southwest Events Etc 3200 N Hayden Rd Suite 280 Scottsdale AZ 85251 480-947-6800 947-6888
Web: www.swevents.com
Star Meetings & Events 1025 Acuff Rd Bloomington IN 47404 812-331-8800 331-6669
TF: 866-546-1687 ■ *Web:* www.starmeetingsandevents.com
TBA Global Events 21700 Oxnard St Suite 1430 Woodland Hills CA 91367 818-226-2800 226-2801
Web: www.tbaglobal.com
Transeair Travel LLC 2813 McKinley Pl NW Washington DC 20015 202-362-6100 362-7411
Travel Meetings & Leisure Services
1152 Brantley Estates Dr Altamonte Springs FL 32714 407-774-6474
Travizon Meeting Management 10 State St 2nd Fl Woburn MA 01801 781-994-1200 343-6128
TF: 888-625-6338 ■ *Web:* www.meetingmakers.com
Universal Odyssey Inc 1601 Dove St Suite 260 Newport Beach CA 92660 949-263-1222 263-0983
Web: www.universalodyssey.com
Vega Group 7220 Washington Ave New Orleans LA 70125 504-488-5222 488-5214
TF: 800-771-2979 ■ *Web:* www.vegagroup.com

	City	State	Zip	Phone	Fax
Wedgewood Productions Inc 1015 Generals Hwy	Crownsville	MD	21032	301-621-9600	621-7825
Weston Assoc 110 Thomas St Web: www.westoninc.com	Winston-Salem	NC	27101	336-725-1147	725-0551
Wings Unlimited Inc 397 Boston Post Rd Suite 104 Web: www.wingsunlimited.net	Darien	CT	06820	203-656-9591	656-1141

188 CONGLOMERATES

SEE ALSO Holding Companies p. 1776

A business conglomerate is defined here as a corporation that consists of many business units in different industries.

	City	State	Zip	Phone	Fax
3M Co 3M Center *NYSE: MMM* ■ **Fax:* Mail Rm ■ *TF:* 800-364-3577 ■ *Web:* www.3m.com	Saint Paul	MN	55144	651-733-1110	733-9973*
Alberto-Culver Co 2525 W Armitage Ave *NYSE: ACV* ■ **Fax:* Hum Res ■ *TF:* 800-333-0005 ■ *Web:* www.alberto.com	Melrose Park	IL	60160	708-450-3000	450-3419*
Alexander & Baldwin Inc 822 Bishop St *NASDAQ: ALEX* ■ *Web:* www.alexanderbaldwin.com	Honolulu	HI	96813	808-525-6611	525-6652
Alleghany Corp 7 Times Sq Tower *NYSE: Y* ■ *Web:* www.alleghany.com	New York	NY	10036	212-752-1356	759-8149
Alticor Inc 7575 Fulton St E **Fax:* Hum Res ■ *Web:* www.alticor.com	Ada	MI	49355	616-787-6000	787-4195*
Altria Group Inc 120 Park Ave *NYSE: MO* ■ *Web:* www.altria.com	New York	NY	10017	917-663-4000	663-2167
AMERCO 1325 Airmotive Way Suite 100 *NASDAQ: UHAL* ■ *Web:* www.amerco.com	Reno	NV	89502	775-688-6300	688-6338
Andersons Inc 480 W Dussel Dr *NASDAQ: ANDE* ■ **Fax:* Hum Res ■ *TF:* 800-537-3370 ■ *Web:* www.andersonsinc.com	Maumee	OH	43537	419-893-5050	891-6393*
Anheuser-Busch Cos Inc 1 Busch Pl *NYSE: BUD* ■ *TF:* 800-342-5283 ■ *Web:* www.anheuser-busch.com	Saint Louis	MO	63118	314-577-2000	577-2900
APi Group Inc 2366 Rose Pl *Web:* www.apigroupinc.com	Saint Paul	MN	55113	651-636-4320	636-0312
ARAMARK Corp 1101 Market St Aramark Tower *NYSE: RMK* ■ *TF:* 800-999-8989 ■ *Web:* www.aramark.com	Philadelphia	PA	19107	215-238-3000	238-3333
Archer Daniels Midland Co (ADM) 4666 E Faries Pkwy *NYSE: ADM* ■ **Fax:* PR ■ *TF:* 800-637-5824 ■ *Web:* www.admworld.com	Decatur	IL	62526	217-424-5200	424-5580*
Ashland Inc 50 E River Ctr Blvd *NYSE: ASH* ■ *Web:* www.ashland.com	Covington	KY	41012	859-815-3333	815-5053
Ball Corp 10 Longs Peak Dr *NYSE: BLL* ■ **Fax:* Sales ■ *Web:* www.ball.com	Broomfield	CO	80021	303-469-3131	460-5256*
Berkshire Hathaway Inc 1440 Kiewit Plaza *NYSE: BRKa* ■ *Web:* www.berkshirehathaway.com	Omaha	NE	68131	402-346-1400	346-3375
Berwind Group 1500 Market St 3000 Centre Sq W *Web:* www.berwind.com	Philadelphia	PA	19102	215-563-2800	575-2314
BFC Financial Corp 2100 W Cypress Creek Rd *NASDAQ: BFCF* ■ *Web:* www.bfcfinancial.com	Fort Lauderdale	FL	33309	954-940-4994	760-5210
Block H & R Inc 4400 Main St *NYSE: HRB* ■ *TF:* 800-829-7733 ■ *Web:* hrblock.com	Kansas City	MO	64111	816-753-6900	753-5346
Brink's Co 1801 Bayberry Ct PO Box 18100 *NYSE: BCO* ■ **Fax:* Mail Rm ■ *TF:* 877-877-9119 ■ *Web:* www.brinkscompany.com	Richmond	VA	23226	804-289-9600	289-9770*
Broe Cos Inc 252 Clayton St 4th Fl *Web:* www.broe.com	Denver	CO	80206	303-393-2966	393-0041
Brown-Forman Corp PO Box 1080 *NYSE: BFA* ■ *Web:* www.brown-forman.com	Louisville	KY	40201	502-585-1100	
Canadian Tire Corp Ltd PO Box 770 Stn K *TSX: CTR* ■ *TF:* 800-387-8803 ■ *Web:* www2.canadiantire.ca	Toronto	ON	M4P2V8	416-480-3000	544-7715
Carlson Cos Inc PO Box 59159 **Fax:* Hum Res ■ *Web:* www.carlson.com	Minneapolis	MN	55459	763-212-1000	212-1135*
Ceridian Corp 3311 E Old Shakopee Rd *NYSE: CEN* ■ *TF:* 800-767-4969 ■ *Web:* www.ceridian.com	Minneapolis	MN	55425	952-853-8100	
Chemed Corp 255 E 5th St Chemed Ctr Suite 2600 *NYSE: CHE* ■ *TF:* 800-224-3633 ■ *Web:* www.chemed.com	Cincinnati	OH	45202	513-762-6900	762-6919
Clear Channel Communications Inc 200 E Basse Rd *NYSE: CCU* ■ *TF:* 888-937-6131 ■ *Web:* www.clearchannel.com	San Antonio	TX	78209	210-822-2828	822-2299
Clorox Co 1221 Broadway *NYSE: CLX* ■ *TF Cust Svc:* 800-292-2808 ■ *Web:* www.thecloroxcompany.com	Oakland	CA	94612	510-271-7000	832-1463
Colgate-Palmolive Co 300 Park Ave *NYSE: CL* ■ *Web:* www.colgate.com	New York	NY	10022	212-310-2000	310-2595
Connell Co 1 Connell Dr *TF:* 800-233-3240 ■ *Web:* www.connellco.com	Berkeley Heights	NJ	07922	908-673-3700	673-3800
Continental Grain Co 277 Park Ave *Web:* www.contigroup.com	New York	NY	10172	212-207-5100	207-5181
Cook Group Inc PO Box 1608 *TF:* 800-457-4500 ■ *Web:* www.cookgroup.com	Bloomington	IN	47402	812-331-1025	331-8990
Cox Enterprises Inc 1400 Lake Hearn Dr **Fax:* PR ■ *Web:* www.coxenterprises.com	Atlanta	GA	30319	404-843-5000	843-5775*
CSX Corp 500 Water St 15th Fl *NYSE: CSX* ■ *Web:* www.csx.com	Jacksonville	FL	32202	904-359-3100	359-1899
Deere & Co 1 John Deere Pl *NYSE: DE* ■ *Web:* www.deere.com	Moline	IL	61265	309-765-8000	765-4609
Delaware North Cos Inc 40 Fountain Plaza *TF:* 800-828-7240 ■ *Web:* www.delawarenorth.com	Buffalo	NY	14202	716-858-5000	858-5266
Deseret Management Corp 60 E South Temple St Suite 575 *Web:* www.deseretmanagement.com	Salt Lake City	UT	84111	801-538-0651	538-0655
Disney Walt Co 500 S Buena Vista St *NYSE: DIS* ■ **Fax:* Mail Rm ■ *Web:* corporate.disney.go.com	Burbank	CA	91521	818-560-1000	843-5346*
Dover Corp 280 Park Ave 34th Fl *NYSE: DOV* ■ *Web:* www.dovercorporation.com	New York	NY	10017	212-922-1640	922-1656
Dyson-Kissner-Moran Corp (DKM) 565 5th Ave 4th Fl *Web:* www.dkmcorp.com	New York	NY	10017	212-661-4600	986-7169
EBSCO Industries Inc 5724 Hwy 280 E *TF:* 800-527-5901 ■ *Web:* www.ebscoind.com	Birmingham	AL	35242	205-991-6600	995-1636
ElkCorp 14911 Quorum Dr Suite 600 *NYSE: ELK* ■ *Web:* www.elkcorp.com	Dallas	TX	75254	972-851-0500	851-0543
Empire Co Ltd 115 King St *TSX: EMP.a* ■ *Web:* www.empireco.ca	Stellarton	NS	B0K1S0	902-755-4440	755-6477
Ergon Inc 2829 Lakeland Dr **Fax:* Hum Res ■ *TF:* 800-824-2626 ■ *Web:* www.ergon.com	Jackson	MS	39232	601-933-3000	933-3373*
Everett Smith Group Ltd 800 N Marshall St *Web:* www.esmithgroup.com	Milwaukee	WI	53202	414-273-3421	273-1058
Federal Signal Corp 1415 W 22nd St Suite 1100 *NYSE: FSS* ■ *Web:* www.federalsignal.com	Oak Brook	IL	60523	630-954-2000	954-2030
FirstService Corp 1140 Bay St FirstService Bldg Suite 4000 *NASDAQ: FSRV* ■ *Web:* www.firstservice.com	Toronto	ON	M5S2B4	416-960-9500	960-5333
Fortune Brands Inc 520 Lake Cook Rd *NYSE: FO* ■ *TF:* 800-225-2719 ■ *Web:* www.fortunebrands.com	Deerfield	IL	60015	847-484-4400	478-0073
GE (General Electric Co) 3135 Easton Tpke *NYSE: GE* ■ *TF Cust Svc:* 800-626-2000 ■ *Web:* www.ge.com	Fairfield	CT	06828	203-373-2211	373-3131
GenCorp Inc PO Box 537012 *NYSE: GY* ■ *Web:* www.gencorp.com	Sacramento	CA	95853	916-355-4000	355-3626
General Electric Co (GE) 3135 Easton Tpke *NYSE: GE* ■ *TF Cust Svc:* 800-626-2000 ■ *Web:* www.ge.com	Fairfield	CT	06828	203-373-2211	373-3131
Griffon Corp 100 Jericho Quadrangle Suite 224 *NYSE: GFF* ■ *Web:* www.griffoncorp.com	Jericho	NY	11753	516-938-5544	938-5644
H & R Block Inc 4400 Main St *NYSE: HRB* ■ *TF:* 800-829-7733 ■ *Web:* hrblock.com	Kansas City	MO	64111	816-753-6900	753-5346
Hackney HT Co 502 S Gay St *TF:* 800-406-1291 ■ *Web:* www.hthackney.com	Knoxville	TN	37902	865-546-1291	546-1501
Halliburton Co 1401 McKinney Ave *NYSE: HAL* ■ *Web:* www.halliburton.com	Houston	TX	77010	713-759-2600	676-4414
Hallwood Group Inc 3710 Rawlins St Suite 1500 *AMEX: HWG* ■ *TF:* 800-225-0135 ■ *Web:* www.hallwood.com	Dallas	TX	75219	214-528-5588	528-8855
Harsco Corp 350 Poplar church Rd *NYSE: HSC* ■ *Web:* www.harsco.com	Camp Hill	PA	17011	717-763-7064	763-6424
Hawaiian Electric Industries Inc 900 Richards St *NYSE: HE* ■ *Web:* www.hei.com	Honolulu	HI	96813	808-543-5662	543-7966
Hillenbrand Industries Inc 700 SR-46 E *NYSE: HB* ■ *Web:* www.hillenbrand.com	Batesville	IN	47006	812-934-7000	934-7364
Hitachi America Ltd 50 Prospect Ave *TF:* 800-448-2244 ■ *Web:* www.hitachi.com	Tarrytown	NY	10591	914-332-5800	332-5555
HNI Corp 408 E 2nd St PO Box 1109 *NYSE: HNI* ■ *TF:* 800-336-8398 ■ *Web:* www.hnicorp.com	Muscatine	IA	52761	563-264-7400	264-7217
Holiday Cos 4567 American Blvd W *TF:* 800-745-7411	Bloomington	MN	55437	952-830-8700	832-8551
Honeywell International Inc 101 Columbia Rd *NYSE: HON* ■ *TF Cust Svc:* 800-707-4555 ■ *Web:* www.honeywell.com	Morristown	NJ	07962	973-455-2000	455-4807
HT Hackney Co 502 S Gay St *TF:* 800-406-1291 ■ *Web:* www.hthackney.com	Knoxville	TN	37902	865-546-1291	546-1501
IAC/InterActiveCorp 152 W 57th St 42nd Fl *NASDAQ: IACI* ■ *Web:* www.iac.com	New York	NY	10019	212-314-7300	314-7309
Ilitch Holdings Inc 2211 Woodward Ave *TF:* 800-722-3727 ■ *Web:* www.ilitchholdings.com	Detroit	MI	48201	313-983-6000	983-6494
Ingram Industries Inc 1 Belle Meade Pl 4400 Harding Rd **Fax:* Hum Res ■ *TF:* 800-876-2047	Nashville	TN	37205	615-298-8200	298-8352*
Intermec Inc 6001 36th Ave W *NYSE: IN* ■ *TF:* 800-829-8959 ■ *Web:* www.intermec.com	Everett	WA	98203	425-265-2400	265-2425
Jim Pattison Group 1067 W Cordova St Suite 1800 *Web:* www.jimpattison.com	Vancouver	BC	V6C1C7	604-688-6764	687-2601
Johnson & Johnson 1 Johnson & Johnson Plaza *NYSE: JNJ* ■ *TF:* 800-635-6789 ■ *Web:* www.jnj.com	New Brunswick	NJ	08933	732-524-0400	214-0332
Jordan Industries Inc 1751 Lake Cook Rd Suite 550 *Web:* www.jordanindustries.com	Deerfield	IL	60015	847-945-5591	945-5698
Kaman Corp PO Box 2 *NASDAQ: KAMN* ■ *Web:* www.kaman.com	Bloomfield	CT	06002	860-243-7100	243-7354
Katy Industries Inc 2461 S Clark St Suite 630 *NYSE: KT* ■ *Web:* www.katyindustries.com	Arlington	VA	22202	703-236-4300	236-3170
Kimball International Inc 1600 Royal St *NASDAQ: KBALB* ■ **Fax:* Hum Res ■ *TF:* 800-482-1616 ■ *Web:* www.kimball.com	Jasper	IN	47549	812-482-1600	482-8803*
Koch Enterprises Inc 14 S 11th Ave *Web:* www.kochenterprises.com	Evansville	IN	47744	812-465-9800	465-9613
Koch Industries Inc 4111 E 37th St N *Web:* www.kochind.com	Wichita	KS	67220	316-828-5500	828-5327
Kohler Co Inc 444 Highland Dr **Fax:* Mktg ■ *TF:* 800-456-4537 ■ *Web:* www.kohlerco.com	Kohler	WI	53044	920-457-4441	459-1796*
Kraus-Anderson Inc 525 S 8th St *Web:* www.krausanderson.com	Minneapolis	MN	55404	612-332-7281	332-8739
Lancaster Colony Corp 37 W Broad St Suite 500 *NASDAQ: LANC* ■ *Web:* www.lancastercolony.com	Columbus	OH	43215	614-224-7141	469-8219
Lane Industries Inc 1200 Shermer Rd	Northbrook	IL	60062	847-498-6789	498-2104
Larry H Miller Group 9350 S 150 East Suite 1000 *Web:* www.lhm.com	Sandy	UT	84070	801-563-4100	563-4198
LDI Ltd 54 Monument Cir Suite 800 *Web:* www.ldiltd.com	Indianapolis	IN	46204	317-237-2251	237-2280
Leucadia National Corp 315 Park Ave S 20th Fl *NYSE: LUK* ■ *Web:* www.leucadia.com	New York	NY	10010	212-460-1900	598-4869
LGL Group Inc 2525 Shader Rd *AMEX: LGL* ■ *Web:* www.lynchcorp.com	Orlando	FL	32804	407-298-2000	
Loews Corp 667 Madison Ave *NYSE: LTR* ■ **Fax:* Mktg ■ *TF:* 800-235-6397 ■ *Web:* www.loews.com	New York	NY	10021	212-521-2000	521-2379*
MacAndrews & Forbes Holdings Inc 35 E 62nd St *Web:* www.macandrewsandforbes.com	New York	NY	10065	212-572-8600	572-8400
Marmon Group Inc 225 W Washington St 19th Fl *TF:* 800-621-0386 ■ *Web:* www.marmon.com	Chicago	IL	60606	312-372-9500	845-5305
Mars Inc 6885 Elm St *Web:* www.mars.com	McLean	VA	22101	703-821-4900	448-9678
MAXXAM Inc 1330 Post Oak Blvd Suite 2000 *AMEX: MXM* ■ **Fax:* Hum Res ■ *Web:* www.maxxaminc.com	Houston	TX	77056	713-975-7600	267-3701*
McRae Industries Inc PO Box 1239 *TF:* 800-768-5248 ■ *Web:* www.mcraeindustries.com	Mount Gilead	NC	27306	910-439-6147	439-4190
MDFC Holding Co 10900 Wilshire Blvd Suite 1600	Los Angeles	CA	90024	310-208-3636	824-7756
MDU Resources Group Inc 1200 W Century Ave PO Box 5650 *NYSE: MDU* ■ *Web:* www.mdu.com	Bismarck	ND	58506	701-530-1000	530-1698
Metromedia Co 810 7th Ave 29th Fl *TF:* 800-461-8368	New York	NY	10019	212-606-4400	397-3802
Midcontinent Media Inc 3600 Minnesota Dr Suite 700 *Web:* www.mmi.net	Minneapolis	MN	55435	952-844-2600	844-2660
Miller Larry H Group 9350 S 150 East Suite 1000 *Web:* www.lhm.com	Sandy	UT	84070	801-563-4100	563-4198
NACCO Industries Inc 5875 Landerbrook Dr Suite 300 *NYSE: NC* ■ *TF:* 800-531-3964 ■ *Web:* www.nacco.com	Cleveland	OH	44124	440-449-9600	
National Service Industries Inc 4111 Pleasantdale Rd *Web:* www.nationalservice.com	Doraville	GA	30340	770-510-5700	510-5910
NESCO Inc 6140 Parkland Blvd	Mayfield Heights	OH	44124	440-461-6000	449-3111
Newell Rubbermaid Inc 10-B Glenlake Pkwy Suite 600 *NYSE: NWL* ■ *Web:* www.newellco.com	Atlanta	GA	30328	770-407-3800	407-3970
Nicor Inc PO Box 2020 *NYSE: GAS* ■ **Fax:* Hum Res ■ *Web:* www.nicor.com	Aurora	IL	60507	630-305-9500	983-9296*
Norfolk Southern Corp 3 Commercial Pl *NYSE: NSC* ■ **Fax:* Mktg ■ *TF Cust Svc:* 800-635-5768 ■ *Web:* www.nscorp.com	Norfolk	VA	23510	757-629-2600	533-4824*
Olin Corp 190 Carondelet Plaza Suite 1530 *NYSE: OLN* ■ *Web:* www.olin.com	Clayton	MO	63105	314-480-1400	862-7406
Onex Corp 161 Bay St 49th Fl *Web:* www.onex.com	Toronto	ON	M5J2S1	416-362-7711	362-5765
Oxbow Corp 1601 Forum Pl Suite 1400 **Fax:* Hum Res ■ *Web:* www.oxbow.com	West Palm Beach	FL	33401	561-697-4300	640-8727*
Pamplin RB Corp 805 SW Broadway Suite 2400 *Web:* www.pamplin.org	Portland	OR	97205	503-248-1133	248-1175
Pattison Jim Group 1067 W Cordova St Suite 1800 *Web:* www.jimpattison.com	Vancouver	BC	V6C1C7	604-688-6764	687-2601
PepsiCo Inc 700 Anderson Hill Rd *NYSE: PEP* ■ *TF PR:* 800-433-2652 ■ *Web:* www.pepsico.com	Purchase	NY	10577	914-253-2000	253-2070
Power Corp of Canada 751 Victoria Sq *TSX: POW* ■ *TF:* 800-890-7440 ■ *Web:* www.powercorp.ca	Montreal	QC	H2Y2J3	514-286-7400	286-7424

	City	State	ZIP	Phone	Fax
Procter & Gamble Co 1 Procter & Gamble Plaza *NYSE: PG* ■ *Web:* www.pg.com	Cincinnati	OH	45202	513-983-1100	
Raleigh Enterprises 100 Wilshire Blvd 8th Fl *TF:* 866-669-7685 ■ *Web:* www.raleighenterprises.com	Santa Monica	CA	90401	310-899-8900	899-8910
Raytheon Co 870 Winter St *NYSE: RTN* ■ *Web:* www.raytheon.com	Waltham	MA	02451	781-522-3000	522-3001
RB Pamplin Corp 805 SW Broadway Suite 2400 *Web:* www.pamplin.org	Portland	OR	97205	503-248-1133	248-1175
Renco Group 30 Rockefeller Plaza Suite 4225 *Web:* www.rencogroup.net	New York	NY	10112	212-541-6000	541-6197
Roll International Corp 11444 W Olympic Blvd 10th Fl	Los Angeles	CA	90064	310-966-5700	914-4747
Rowan Cos Inc 2800 Postoak Blvd Suite 5450 *NYSE: RDC* ■ *Web:* www.rowancompanies.com	Houston	TX	77056	713-621-7800	960-7560
Ruddick Corp 301 S Tryon St Suite 1800 *NYSE: RDK* ■ *Web:* www.ruddickcorp.com	Charlotte	NC	28202	704-372-5404	372-6409
Sammons Enterprises Inc 5949 Sherry Ln Suite 1900 *Web:* www.sammonsenterprises.com	Dallas	TX	75225	214-210-5000	210-5099
Seaboard Corp 9000 W 67th St *AMEX: SEB* ■ *TF:* 800-388-4647 ■ *Web:* www.seaboardcorp.com	Shawnee Mission	KS	66202	913-676-8800	676-8872
Sequa Corp 200 Park Ave 44th Fl *NYSE: SQAa* ■ *Web:* www.sequa.com	New York	NY	10166	212-986-5500	370-1969
ServiceMaster Co 3250 Lacey Rd Suite 600 *NYSE: SVM* ■ *TF:* 866-782-6787 ■ *Web:* corporate.servicemaster.com	Downers Grove	IL	60515	630-663-2000	663-2001
Services Group of America 4025 Delridge Way SW Suite 500	Seattle	WA	98106	206-933-5225	933-5247
Siemens Corp 153 E 53rd St 56th Fl **Fax: Mktg* ■ *TF:* 800-743-6367 ■ *Web:* www.usa.siemens.com	New York	NY	10022	212-258-4000	258-4099*
Smith Everett Group Ltd 800 N Marshall St *Web:* www.esmithgroup.com	Milwaukee	WI	53202	414-273-3421	273-1058
Sotheby's Holdings Inc 1334 York Ave *NYSE: BID* ■ *Web:* www.sothebys.com	New York	NY	10021	212-606-7000	606-7107
SPX Corp 13515 Ballantyne Corporate Pl *NYSE: SPW* ■ *TF:* 800-446-2617 ■ *Web:* www.spx.com	Charlotte	NC	28277	704-752-4400	752-4505
Standex International Corp 6 Manor Pkwy *NYSE: SXI* ■ *Web:* www.standex.com	Salem	NH	03079	603-893-9701	893-7324
Steiner Corp 505 E South Temple *TF:* 800-408-0208	Salt Lake City	UT	84102	801-328-8831	363-5680
Sten Corp 13828 Lincoln St NE *NASDAQ: STEN* ■ *TF:* 800-328-7958 ■ *Web:* www.stencorporation.com	Ham Lake	MN	55304	763-755-9516	755-9466
Susquehanna Pfaltzgraff Co 140 E Market St **Fax: Mktg* ■ *TF:* 800-999-2811 ■ *Web:* www.suspfz.com	York	PA	17401	717-848-5500	852-2398*
Tang Industries Inc 3773 Howard Hughes Pkwy Suite 350N *Web:* www.tangindustries.com	Las Vegas	NV	89109	702-734-3700	734-6766
TECO Energy Inc 702 N Franklin St *NYSE: TE* ■ *Web:* www.tecoenergy.com	Tampa	FL	33602	813-228-1111	228-1545
Teleflex Inc 155 S Limerick Rd *NYSE: TFX* ■ *Web:* www.teleflex.com	Limerick	PA	19468	610-948-5100	948-0811
Temple-Inland Inc 1300 S Mopac Expy *NYSE: TIN* ■ *TF:* 800-826-8807 ■ *Web:* www.temple-inland.com	Austin	TX	78746	512-434-5800	434-8723
Textron Inc 40 Westminster St *NYSE: TXT* ■ *Web:* www.textron.com	Providence	RI	02903	401-421-2800	421-2878
Time Warner Inc 1 Time Warner Center *NYSE: TWX* ■ *Web:* www.timewarner.com	New York	NY	10019	212-484-8000	
Topa Equities Ltd 1800 Ave of the Stars Suite 1400	Los Angeles	CA	90067	310-203-9199	557-1837
Trinity Industries Inc 2525 Stemmons Fwy *NYSE: TRN* ■ *TF:* 800-631-4420 ■ *Web:* www.trin.net	Dallas	TX	75207	214-631-4420	589-8501
TRT Holdings Inc 420 Decker Dr Suite 100	Irving	TX	75062	972-730-6664	871-9240
Tyco International (US) Ltd 9 Roszel Rd *NYSE: TYC* ■ *TF:* 800-320-2350 ■ *Web:* www.tyco.com	Princeton	NJ	08540	609-720-4200	720-4208
United Services Automobile Assn (USAA) 9800 Fredericksburg Rd *TF:* 800-531-8222 ■ *Web:* www.usaa.com	San Antonio	TX	78288	210-498-2211	498-9940
United Technologies Corp 755 Main St *NYSE: UTX* ■ **Fax: Hum Res* ■ *Web:* www.utc.com	Hartford	CT	06103	860-728-7000	728-7028*
Universal Corp 1501 N Hamilton St *NYSE: UVV* ■ *Web:* www.universalcorp.com	Richmond	VA	23230	804-359-9311	254-3582
Valhi Inc 5430 LBJ Fwy Suite 1700 3 Lincoln Ctr *NYSE: VHI* ■ **Fax: Acctg* ■ *Web:* www.valhi.net	Dallas	TX	75240	972-233-1700	448-1444*
Viacom Inc 1515 Broadway 28th Fl *NYSE: VIA* ■ *Web:* www.viacom.com	New York	NY	10036	212-258-6000	258-6100
Viad Corp 1850 N Central Ave Suite 800 *NYSE: VVI* ■ **Fax: Hum Res* ■ *Web:* www.viad.com	Phoenix	AZ	85004	602-207-4000	207-5455*
Volt Information Sciences Inc 560 Lexington Ave *NYSE: VOL* ■ *Web:* www.volt.com	New York	NY	10022	212-704-2400	704-2417
Walt Disney Co 500 S Buena Vista St *NYSE: DIS* ■ **Fax: Mail Rm* ■ *Web:* corporate.disney.go.com	Burbank	CA	91521	818-560-1000	843-5346*
Walter Industries Inc 4211 W Boy Scout Blvd *NYSE: WLT* ■ *TF:* 800-888-9258 ■ *Web:* www.walterind.com	Tampa	FL	33607	813-871-4811	871-4644
Washington Post Co 1150 15th St NW *NYSE: WPO* ■ *TF:* 800-627-1150 ■ *Web:* www.washpostco.com	Washington	DC	20071	202-334-6000	
Watkins Associated Industries 1958 Monroe Dr NE	Atlanta	GA	30324	404-872-3841	
Wesco Financial Corp 301 E Colorado Blvd Suite 300 *AMEX: WSC* ■ *Web:* wescofinancial.com	Pasadena	CA	91101	626-585-6700	449-1455
Weyerhaeuser Co 33663 Weyerhaeuser Way S *NYSE: WY* ■ *TF:* 800-525-5440 ■ *Web:* www.weyerhaeuser.com	Federal Way	WA	98003	253-924-2345	924-2685
Wirtz Corp 680 N Lake Shore Dr Suite 1900	Chicago	IL	60611	312-943-7000	943-9017

189 CONSTRUCTION - BUILDING CONTRACTORS - NON-RESIDENTIAL

	City	State	ZIP	Phone	Fax
Abrams Construction Inc 1945 The Exchange Suite 350 *TF:* 800-935-9350 ■ *Web:* www.aciatl.com	Atlanta	GA	30339	770-952-3555	952-4010
Absher Construction Co Inc PO Box 280 *Web:* www.abshernw.com	Puyallup	WA	98371	253-845-9544	841-0925
ACI Construction Services 601 N Ashley Dr Suite 1100	Tampa	FL	33602	813-490-4300	490-4301
Adolfson & Peterson Inc 6701 W 23rd St *Web:* www.adolfsonpeterson.com	Saint Louis Park	MN	55426	952-544-1561	525-2333
Alberici Constructors 8800 Page Ave *Web:* www.alberici.com	Saint Louis	MO	63114	314-733-2000	733-2001
Albert M Higley Co 2926 Chester Ave *Web:* www.amhigley.com	Cleveland	OH	44114	216-861-2050	861-0038
Alvin H Butz Inc PO Box 509 *Web:* www.butz.com	Allentown	PA	18105	610-395-6871	395-3363
AMEC Construction Management 1979 Lakeside Pkwy *Web:* www.amec.com	Atlanta	GA	30084	770-688-2500	
Andersen Construction Co Inc PO Box 6712 *Web:* www.andersen-const.com	Portland	OR	97228	503-283-6712	283-3607
Anderson Roy Corp 11400 Reichold Rd *TF:* 800-688-4003 ■ *Web:* www.rac.com	Gulfport	MS	39503	228-896-4000	896-4086
Armada/Hoffler Construction Co 222 Central Pk Ave Suite 2100 *TF:* 800-766-0543 ■ *Web:* www.armadahoffler.com	Virginia Beach	VA	23462	757-366-4000	523-0782
Auchter Co 4804 Kernan Blvd S *Web:* www.auchter.com	Jacksonville	FL	32224	904-355-3536	353-0234
Austin Co 6095 Parkland Blvd *Web:* www.theaustin.com	Cleveland	OH	44124	440-544-2600	544-2661
Austin Commercial Inc 3535 Travis Suite 300 **Fax: Acctg* ■ *Web:* www.austin-ind.com	Dallas	TX	75204	214-443-5700	443-5791*
Baldwin & Shell Construction Co Inc PO Box 1750 *Web:* www.baldwinshell.com	Little Rock	AR	72203	501-374-8677	375-7649
Barlovento LLC 165 Hostdale Dr Suite 1 *TF:* 877-498-6039 ■ *Web:* www.barlovento8a.com	Dothan	AL	36303	334-983-9979	983-9983
Barney Skanska Construction Co Inc 136 Madison Ave 11th Fl *Web:* www.skanskausa.com	New York	NY	10016	212-301-0200	301-0299
Barnhart Douglas E Inc 10760 Thornmint Rd *Web:* www.debinc.com	San Diego	CA	92127	858-385-8200	385-8201
Barnhill Contracting Co PO Box 1529 *Web:* www.barnhillcontracting.com	Tarboro	NC	27886	252-823-1021	823-0137
Barr & Barr Inc 460 W 34th St 16th Fl *Web:* www.barrandbarr.com	New York	NY	10001	212-563-2330	967-2297
Barton Malow Enterprises Inc 26500 American Dr *Web:* www.bmco.com	Southfield	MI	48034	248-351-4500	436-5001
Batson-Cook Co Inc 817 4th Ave PO Box 151 *Web:* www.batson-cook.com	West Point	GA	31833	706-643-2500	643-2199
Bayley Construction Co PO Box 9004 *TF:* 800-598-8884 ■ *Web:* www.bayley.net	Mercer Island	WA	98040	206-621-8884	343-7728
BBL Construction Services Inc 302 Washington Ave Ext *Web:* www.bblinc.com	Albany	NY	12203	518-452-8200	452-2897
BE & K Building Group 201 E McBee Ave Suite 400 *TF:* 800-388-2724 ■ *Web:* www.bekbuildinggroup.com	Greenville	SC	29601	864-250-5000	250-5037
Beacon Skanska Inc 253 Summer St	Boston	MA	02210	617-574-1400	574-1399
Beck Group Inc 1807 Ross Ave Suite 500 *Web:* www.beckgroup.com	Dallas	TX	75201	214-303-6200	303-6300
Becker Bros Inc 401 Main St Suite 110	Peoria	IL	61602	309-674-1200	674-5454
Beers Skanska Inc 70 Ellis St NE	Atlanta	GA	30303	404-659-1970	656-1665
Bellows WS Construction Corp PO Box 2132 *Web:* www.wsbellows.com	Houston	TX	77252	713-680-2132	680-2614
Big-D Construction Corp 404 W 400 South *TF:* 877-415-6009 ■ *Web:* www.big-d.com	Salt Lake City	UT	84101	801-415-6000	415-6900
BL Harbert International Inc PO Box 531390 *Web:* www.bharbert.com	Birmingham	AL	35253	205-802-2800	802-2801
Blaine Construction Corp PO Box 10147 *TF:* 800-424-0426 ■ *Web:* www.blaineconstruction.com	Knoxville	TN	37939	865-693-8900	691-7606
Boldt Oscar J Construction Co 2525 N Roemer Rd *Web:* www.theboldtcompany.com	Appleton	WI	54911	920-739-6321	739-4409
Bor-Son Construction Inc 2001 Killebrew Dr Suite 400 *Web:* www.borson.com	Bloomington	MN	55425	952-854-8444	854-8910
Boran Craig Barber Engel Construction Co Inc 3606 Enterprise Ave *Web:* www.bcbe.com	Naples	FL	34104	239-643-3343	643-4548
Bovis Lend Lease 200 Park Ave 9th Fl *Web:* www.bovis.com	New York	NY	10166	212-592-6700	592-6988
Bradbury & Stamm Construction Co Inc 3701 Paseo del Norte NE *Web:* www.bradburystamm.com	Albuquerque	NM	87113	505-765-1200	842-5419
Branch Group Inc PO Box 40004 *Web:* www.branch-associates.com	Roanoke	VA	24022	540-982-1678	982-4127
Brasfield & Gorrie LLC 3021 7th Ave S *TF:* 800-239-8017 ■ *Web:* www.brasfieldgorrie.com	Birmingham	AL	35233	205-328-4000	251-1304
Brice Building Co Inc 2311 Highland Ave S Suite 200 *Web:* www.bricebuilding.com	Birmingham	AL	35205	205-930-9911	918-1850
Brode WM Co 100 Elizabeth St PO Box 299 *TF:* 800-848-9217 ■ *Web:* www.wmbrode.com	Newcomerstown	OH	43832	740-498-5121	498-8553
BSI Constructors Inc 6767 Southwest Ave *TF:* 800-769-8090 ■ *Web:* www.bsistl.com	Saint Louis	MO	63143	314-781-7820	781-1354
BT Mancini Co Inc 876 S Milpitas Blvd *TF:* 800-488-4286 ■ *Web:* www.btmancini.com	Milpitas	CA	95036	408-942-7900	945-1360
BT Mancini Co Inc Brookman Div 876 S Milpitas Blvd *TF:* 800-488-4286 ■ *Web:* www.btmancini.com	Milpitas	CA	95035	408-942-7900	945-1360
BUCON Inc DBA Butler Construction 6601 Executive Dr *Web:* www.bucon.com	Kansas City	MO	64120	816-245-6000	245-6099
Bulley & Andrews LLC 1755 W Armitage Ave *Web:* www.bulley.com	Chicago	IL	60622	773-235-2433	235-2471
Butler Construction 6601 Executive Dr *Web:* www.bucon.com	Kansas City	MO	64120	816-245-6000	245-6099
Butler Construction Co 6601 Executive Dr *Web:* www.bucon.com	Kansas City	MO	64120	816-245-6000	245-6099
Butz Alvin H Inc PO Box 509 *Web:* www.butz.com	Allentown	PA	18105	610-395-6871	395-3363
C Overaa & Co Inc 200 Parr Blvd *Web:* www.overaa.com	Richmond	CA	94801	510-234-0926	237-2435
Caddell Construction Co Inc PO Box 210099 *Web:* www.caddell.com	Montgomery	AL	36121	334-272-7723	394-0189
Careage Inc PO Box 1969 *Web:* www.careage.com	Gig Harbor	WA	98335	253-853-4457	853-5280
Carothers Construction Inc PO Box 687 *Web:* www.carothersconstruction.com	Water Valley	MS	38965	662-473-2525	473-4666
CD Moody Construction Co Inc 6017 Redan Rd *Web:* www.cdmoodyconstruction.com	Lithonia	GA	30058	770-482-7778	482-7727
CD Smith Construction Inc PO Box 1006 *Web:* www.cd-smith.com	Fond du Lac	WI	54936	920-924-2900	924-2910
CDI Contractors LLC 3000 Cantrell Rd *Web:* www.cdicon.com	Little Rock	AR	72202	501-666-4300	666-4741
Centex Construction Co Inc 3100 McKinnon St 7th Fl *Web:* www.centexconstruction.com	Dallas	TX	75201	214-468-4700	468-4357
Centex Construction Group Inc PO Box 199000 *Web:* centex-construction.com	Dallas	TX	75219	214-981-5000	981-6888
Centex Construction Inc 2636 Elm Hill Pike Suite 120 *Web:* www.centexconstruction.com	Nashville	TN	37214	615-889-4400	872-1107
Centex Rooney Construction Co Inc 7901 SW 6th Ct *Web:* www.centexconstruction.com	Plantation	FL	33324	954-585-4000	585-4501
CF Jordan Inc 7700 CF Jordan Dr *Web:* www.cfjordan.com	El Paso	TX	79912	915-877-3333	877-3999
CG Schmidt Inc 11777 W Lake Pk Dr *TF:* 800-248-1254 ■ *Web:* www.cgschmidt.com	Milwaukee	WI	53224	414-577-1177	577-1155
Charles N White Construction Co 613 Crescent Cir Suite 100 *Web:* www.whiteconst.com	Ridgeland	MS	39157	601-898-5180	989-5190
Charles Pankow Builders Ltd 3280 E Foothill Blvd Suite 100 *Web:* www.pankow.com	Pasadena	CA	91107	626-304-1190	696-1782
Choate Construction Co 8200 Roberts Dr Suite 600 *Web:* www.choateco.com	Atlanta	GA	30350	678-892-1200	892-1202
Christman Co Inc 408 Kalamazoo Plaza *Web:* www.christmanco.com	Lansing	MI	48933	517-482-1488	482-3520
Ciminelli Louis P Construction Corp 369 Franklin St *Web:* www.lpciminelli.com	Buffalo	NY	14202	716-855-1200	854-6655
Clancy & Theys Construction Co PO Box 27608 *Web:* www.clancytheys.com	Raleigh	NC	27611	919-834-3601	834-2439
Clark Construction Group LLC 7500 Old Georgetown Rd *TF:* 800-827-4422 ■ *Web:* www.clarkconstruction.com	Bethesda	MD	20814	301-272-8100	272-8414

				Phone	Fax
Clark John S Co Inc PO Box 1468	Mount Airy	NC	27030	336-789-1000	789-7609
Web: www.jsclark.com					
Clark Sports Inc 7500 Old Georgetown Rd.	Bethesda	MD	20814	301-272-8259	272-1922
Clayco Construction Co 2199 Innerbelt Business Ctr Dr	Saint Louis	MO	63114	314-429-5100	429-3137
TF: 888-429-3330 ■ Web: www.claycorp.com					
Codina Construction Corp 355 Alhambra Cir Suite 900	Coral Gables	FL	33134	305-520-2403	520-2422
Web: www.codina.com/construction.home.aspx					
Corna/Kokosing Construction Co 6235 Westerville Rd	Westerville	OH	43081	614-901-8844	212-5599
Web: www.corna.com					
CR Meyer & Sons Co 895 W 20th Ave	Oshkosh	WI	54902	920-235-3350	235-3419
Web: www.crmeyer.com					
Crossland Construction Co Inc PO Box 45	Columbus	KS	66725	620-429-1414	429-1416
Web: www.crosslandconstruction.com					
CW Driver General Contractors Inc 468 N Rosemead Blvd	Pasadena	CA	91107	626-351-8800	351-8880
Web: www.cwdriver.com					
Dalmac Construction 111 W Spring Valley Rd Suite 200	Richardson	TX	75081	972-725-3400	725-3700
Web: www.dalmac.com					
Davis James G Construction Corp					
12530 Parklawn Dr Suite 100	Rockville	MD	20852	301-881-2990	468-3918
Web: www.davisconstruction.com					
Daw Inc 12552 S 125 West	Draper	UT	84020	801-553-9111	553-2345
TF Sales: 800-748-4778 ■ Web: www.dawinc.com					
Deerfield Construction Co Inc 8960 Glendale Milford Rd	Loveland	OH	45140	513-984-4096	984-3035
Web: www.deerfieldconstruction.com					
Deig Brothers Lumber & Construction Inc PO Box 6429	Evansville	IN	47719	812-423-4201	421-5058
Web: www.deigbros.com					
DeMaria Building Co Inc PO Box 8018	Novi	MI	48376	248-348-8710	348-6251
Web: www.demariabldgco.com					
Devcon Construction Inc 690 Gibraltar Dr	Milpitas	CA	95035	408-942-8200	262-2342
Web: www.devconconstruction.com					
DiCarlo Construction Co 33 E 2nd St	Kansas City	MO	64106	816-471-3300	471-3311
Web: www.dicarlo.com					
Dick Corp 1900 Rt 51	Large	PA	15025	412-384-1000	384-1150
TF: 800-245-6577 ■ Web: www.dickcorp.com/dickcorp					
Dick Pacific Construction Co Ltd 707 Richards St Suite 400	Honolulu	HI	96813	808-533-5000	533-5320
Web: www.dickpacific.com					
Dick PJ Inc PO Box 98100	Pittsburgh	PA	15227	412-462-9300	462-2588
Web: www.pjdick.com					
Diffenbaugh Inc 6865 Airport Dr	Riverside	CA	92504	951-351-6865	351-6880
TF: 800-394-5334 ■ Web: www.diffenbaugh.com					
Dimeo Construction Co 75 Chapman St	Providence	RI	02905	401-781-9800	461-4580
Web: www.dimeo.com					
DL Withers Construction LC 3220 E Harbour Dr	Phoenix	AZ	85034	602-438-9500	438-9600
Web: www.dlwithers.com					
Donohoe Cos Inc 2101 Wisconsin Ave NW	Washington	DC	20007	202-333-0880	342-3924
TF: 877-366-6463 ■ Web: www.donohoe.com					
Doster Construction Co 2100 International Park Dr	Birmingham	AL	35243	205-956-5902	951-2612
Web: www.dosterconstruction.com					
Douglas E Barnhart Inc 10760 Thornmint Rd	San Diego	CA	92127	858-385-8200	385-8201
Web: www.debinc.com					
DPR Construction Inc 1450 Veterans Blvd	Redwood City	CA	94063	650-474-1450	474-2571*
*Fax: Hum Res ■ Web: www.dprinc.com					
Drees Co 211 Grandview Dr	Fort Mitchell	KY	41017	859-578-4200	341-5854
TF: 800-647-1711 ■ Web: www.dreeshomes.com					
Driscoll LF Co Inc 9 Presidential Blvd	Bala Cynwyd	PA	19004	610-668-0950	668-9425
Web: www.lfdriscoll.com					
Driver CW General Contractors Inc 468 N Rosemead Blvd	Pasadena	CA	91107	626-351-8800	351-8880
Web: www.cwdriver.com					
Dunn Industries Inc 929 Holmes St	Kansas City	MO	64106	816-474-8600	391-2510
Web: www.jedunn.com					
Dunn JE Construction Co 929 Holmes St	Kansas City	MO	64106	816-474-8600	391-2510
Web: www.jedunn.com					
EE Reed Construction Co 333 Commerce Green Blvd	Sugar Land	TX	77478	281-933-4000	933-4852
Web: www.eereed.com					
EllisDon Corp 2045 Oxford St E	London	ON	N5V2Z7	519-455-6770	455-2944
Web: www.ellisdon.com					
EMJ Corp 2030 Hamilton Pl Blvd Suite 200	Chattanooga	TN	37421	423-855-1550	855-6857
Web: www.emjcorp.com					
EW Howell Co Inc 113 Crossways Pk Dr	Woodbury	NY	11797	516-921-7100	921-0119
Web: www.ewhowell.com					
FA Wilhelm Construction Co Inc 3914 Prospect St	Indianapolis	IN	46203	317-359-5411	359-8346
Web: www.fawilhelm.com					
Facility Group Inc 2233 Lake Pk Dr Suite 100	Smyrna	GA	30080	770-437-2700	437-7554
TF: 800-525-2463 ■ Web: www.facilitygroup.com					
FCI Construction Inc 3901 S Lamar Blvd Suite 200	Austin	TX	78704	512-486-3700	486-3801
Ferguson Construction Co PO Box 726	Sidney	OH	45365	937-498-2381	498-1796
Web: www.ferguson-construction.com					
Findorff JH & Son Inc 300 S Bedford St	Madison	WI	53703	608-257-5321	257-5306
Web: www.findorff.com					
Fisher Development Inc 1485 Bayshore Blvd Suite 126	San Francisco	CA	94124	415-468-1717	468-6241
TF: 800-227-4392 ■ Web: www.fisherinc.com					
Flintco Cos Inc 1624 W 21st St	Tulsa	OK	74107	918-587-8451	586-0648
Web: www.flintco.com					
Flintco Inc 1624 W 21st St	Tulsa	OK	74107	918-587-8451	582-7506
TF: 800-947-2828 ■ Web: www.flintco.com					
Fluor Constructors International Inc 3 Polaris Way	Aliso Viejo	CA	92698	949-349-2000	349-2585
Web: www.fluor.com					
Fluor Daniel Inc 1 Fluor Daniel Dr	Aliso Viejo	CA	92698	949-349-2000	349-2585
Web: www.fluor.com					
Foushee & Assoc Inc 3260 118th Ave SE	Bellevue	WA	98005	425-746-1000	746-3737
Web: www.foushee.com					
Frederick Quinn Corp 103 S Church St	Addison	IL	60101	630-628-8500	628-8595
Web: www.fquinncorp.com					
Fru-Con Construction Corp 15933 Clayton Rd	Ballwin	MO	63011	636-391-6700	391-4563
TF: 800-937-8266 ■ Web: www.fru-con.com					
GE Johnson Construction Co					
25 N Cascade Ave Suite 400	Colorado Springs	CO	80903	719-473-5321	473-5324
Web: www.gejohnson.com					
GE Moore Div MB Kahn Construction Co Inc PO Box 578	Greenwood	SC	29648	864-229-7411	229-1146
Web: www.mbkahn.com					
Gerald H Phipps Inc 1530 W 13th Ave	Denver	CO	80204	303-571-5377	629-7467
Web: www.ghpd.com					
Geupel DeMars Hagerman Inc 7930 Castleway Dr	Indianapolis	IN	46250	317-713-0632	713-0641
Web: www.hagermangc.com/geupel_demars_manage.htm					
Gilbane Building Co 7 Jackson Walkway	Providence	RI	02903	401-456-5800	456-5936
Web: www.gilbaneco.com					
Gilbane Building Co Mid-Atlantic Regional Office					
7901 Sandy Spring Rd Suite 500	Laurel	MD	20707	301-317-6100	317-6155
TF: 800-445-2263 ■ Web: www.gilbaneco.com					
Gilbane Building Co New England Regional Office					
7 Jackson Walkway	Providence	RI	02903	401-456-5800	456-5936
Web: www.gilbaneco.com					
Gilbane Building Co Northeast Regional Office					
3150 Brunswick Pike Suite 300	Lawrenceville	NJ	08648	609-671-4200	671-4255
Web: www.gilbaneco.com					
Gilbane Building Co Southwest Regional Office					
1331 Lamar St Suite 1170	Houston	TX	77010	713-209-1873	651-0541
TF: 800-445-2263 ■ Web: www.gilbaneco.com					
Gilbane Building Co Western Regional Office					
224 Airport Pkwy Suite 630	San Jose	CA	95110	415-591-3400	591-3402
Web: www.gilbaneco.com					
Giordano Construction Co Inc 1155 Main St	Branford	CT	06405	203-488-7264	481-5764
Web: www.giordano-construction.com					
GLY Construction Inc 15 Lake Belview Dr Suite 200	Bellevue	WA	98004	425-451-8877	453-5680
Web: www.gly.com					
Granger Construction Co 6267 Aurelius Rd	Lansing	MI	48911	517-393-1670	393-1382
Web: www.grangerconstruction.com					
Gray James N Construction Co Inc 10 Quality St	Lexington	KY	40507	859-281-5000	252-5300
TF: 800-950-4729 ■ Web: www.jngray.com					
Graycor Inc 1 Graycor Dr	Homewood	IL	60430	708-206-0500	206-0505
Web: www.graycor.com					
Griffin RJ & Co 800 Mount Vernon Hwy Suite 200	Atlanta	GA	30328	770-551-8883	551-8483
Web: www.rjgriffin.com					
Grunley Construction Co 15020 Shady Grove Rd Suite 500	Rockville	MD	20850	301-881-1180	881-6387
Web: www.grunley.com					
H & M Construction Co Inc 50 Security Dr	Jackson	TN	38305	731-664-6300	664-1358
Web: www.hmcompany.com					
H Miller & Sons Inc 700 NW 107th Ave	Miami	FL	33172	305-559-4000	227-7115
Hagerman Construction Corp PO Box 10690	Fort Wayne	IN	46853	260-424-1470	422-3129
Web: www.hagermancorp.com					
Harbert BL International Inc PO Box 531390	Birmingham	AL	35253	205-802-2800	802-2801
Web: www.bharbert.com					
Harbison-Mahony-Higgins Inc 15 Business Pkwy Suite 101	Sacramento	CA	95828	916-383-4825	383-6014
Web: www.hmh.com					
Harbour Contractors Inc 215 W Main St	Plainfield	IL	60544	815-254-5500	254-5505
Web: www.harbour-cm.com					
Hardaway Group 615 Main St	Nashville	TN	37206	615-254-5461	254-4518
Web: www.hardaway.net					
Hardin Construction Group Inc 1380 W Paces Ferry Rd NW	Atlanta	GA	30327	404-264-0404	264-3514
Web: www.hardinconstruction.com					
Harkins Builders Inc 2201 Warwick Way	Marriottsville	MD	21104	410-750-2600	480-4299
TF: 888-224-5697 ■ Web: www.harkinsbuilders.com					
Harrell Construction Group LLC PO Box 12850	Jackson	MS	39236	601-206-7600	206-7601
Web: www.harrellcontracting.com					
Haselden Construction Inc 6950 S Potomac St Suite 100	Centennial	CO	80112	303-751-1478	751-1627
Web: www.haselden.com					
Haskell Co 111 Riverside Ave	Jacksonville	FL	32202	904-791-4500	791-4699
TF: 800-733-4275 ■ Web: www.thehaskellco.com					
Hathaway Dinwiddie Construction Co					
275 Battery St Suite 300	San Francisco	CA	94111	415-986-2718	956-5669
Web: www.hdcco.com					
Hawkins Construction Co 2516 Deer Pk Blvd	Omaha	NE	68105	402-342-1607	342-3221
Web: www.hawkins1.com					
HBE Corp 11330 Olive Blvd	Saint Louis	MO	63141	314-567-9000	567-0602
Web: www.hbecorp.com					
Henderson Corp 575 State Hwy 28	Raritan	NJ	08869	908-685-1300	595-1131
Web: www.henco.com					
Hensel Phelps Construction Co 420 6th Ave PO Box 0	Greeley	CO	80631	970-352-6565	352-9311
TF: 800-826-6309 ■ Web: www.henselphelps.com					
Higley Albert M Co 2926 Chester Ave	Cleveland	OH	44114	216-861-2050	861-0038
Web: www.amhigley.com					
Hitt Contracting Inc 2704 Dorr Ave	Fairfax	VA	22031	703-846-9000	846-9110
Web: www.hitt-gc.com					
HJ Russell & Co 504 Fair St SW	Atlanta	GA	30313	404-330-1000	330-0922
Web: www.hjrussell.com					
Hoar Construction Inc PO Box 660400	Birmingham	AL	35266	205-803-2121	423-2323
Web: www.hoarllc.com					
Hoffman Construction Corp 805 SW Broadway Suite 2100	Portland	OR	97205	503-221-8811	221-8934
Web: www.hoffmancorp.com					
Hoffman Corp 805 SW Broadway Suite 2100	Portland	OR	97205	503-221-8811	221-8934
Web: www.hoffmancorp.com					
Holder Construction Co 3333 Riverwood Pkwy Suite 400	Atlanta	GA	30339	770-988-3000	988-3265
Web: www.holderconstruction.com					
Howell EW Co Inc 113 Crossways Pk Dr	Woodbury	NY	11797	516-921-7100	921-0119
Web: www.ewhowell.com					
HSU Development Co 1335 Rockville Pike Suite 255	Rockville	MD	20852	301-881-3500	881-3505
Web: www.hsubuilders.com					
Hunt Construction Group 2450 S Tibbs Ave	Indianapolis	IN	46241	317-227-7800	227-7810
TF: 800-223-6301 ■ Web: www.huntconstructiongroup.com					
Hunzinger Construction Co 21100 Enterprise Ave	Brookfield	WI	53045	262-797-0797	797-0474
Web: www.hunzinger.com					
Industrial Contractors Inc PO Box 208	Evansville	IN	47702	812-423-7832	464-7255
Web: www.industrialcontractors.com					
Irmscher Inc 1030 Osage St	Fort Wayne	IN	46808	260-422-5572	424-1487
Web: www.irmscherinc.com					
JA Tiberti Construction Co 1806 Industrial Rd	Las Vegas	NV	89102	702-248-4000	382-5361
Web: www.tiberti.com					
Jacobsen Construction Co Inc PO Box 27608	Salt Lake City	UT	84127	801-973-0500	973-7496
Web: www.jacobsen-const.com					
James G Davis Construction Corp					
12530 Parklawn Dr Suite 100	Rockville	MD	20852	301-881-2990	468-3918
Web: www.davisconstruction.com					
James N Gray Co 10 Quality St	Lexington	KY	40507	859-281-5000	252-5300
TF: 800-950-4729 ■ Web: www.jngray.com					
Jansen JP Co Inc 8355 W Bradley Rd	Milwaukee	WI	53223	414-357-8800	357-8830
Web: www.jansengroup.com					
Jaynes Corp 2906 Broadway NE	Albuquerque	NM	87107	505-345-8591	345-8598
TF: 800-432-5204 ■ Web: www.jaynescorp.com					
JE Dunn Construction Co 929 Holmes St	Kansas City	MO	64106	816-474-8600	391-2510
Web: www.jedunn.com					
JESCO Inc 2020 McCullough Blvd	Tupelo	MS	38801	662-842-3240	680-6123
John M Olson Corp 26210 Harper Ave	Saint Clair Shores	MI	48081	586-771-9330	771-2440
Web: www.jmolson.com					
John S Clark Co Inc PO Box 1468	Mount Airy	NC	27030	336-789-1000	789-7609
Web: www.jsclark.com					
Johnson GE Construction Co					
25 N Cascade Ave Suite 400	Colorado Springs	CO	80903	719-473-5321	473-5324
Web: www.gejohnson.com					
Jordan CF Inc 7700 CF Jordan Dr	El Paso	TX	79912	915-877-3333	877-3999
Web: www.cfjordan.com					
Jordan WM Co Inc 11010 Jefferson Ave	Newport News	VA	23601	757-596-6341	596-7425
Web: www.wmjordan.com					
JP Jansen Co Inc 8355 W Bradley Rd	Milwaukee	WI	53223	414-357-8800	357-8830
Web: www.jansengroup.com					
JR Framing Inc PO Box 2709	Corona	CA	92878	951-340-1999	340-9970
JR Roberts Corp 7745 Greenback Ln Suite 300	Citrus Heights	CA	95610	916-729-5600	729-5666
TF: 800-551-1534 ■ Web: www.jrroberts.com					
K3 Construction Group 11307 Sunset Hills Rd	Reston	VA	20190	703-736-1000	736-0736
Web: www.kfoury.com					
Kahn MB Construction Co Inc 101 Flintlake Rd	Columbia	SC	29223	803-736-2950	736-5833
Web: www.mbkahn.com					

				Phone	Fax
Kajima International Inc Group 395 W Passaic St 3rd Fl	Rochelle Park	NJ	07662	201-518-1500	518-1535
Web: kajimausa.com					
Keating Building Corp 1600 Arch St Suite 300	Philadelphia	PA	19103	610-668-4100	668-4060
Web: www.keatingweb.com					
Keene Construction Co Inc 1400 Hope Rd	Maitland	FL	32751	407-740-6116	539-3468
Web: www.keenecon.com					
Kennedy Roger Construction Inc 370 S North Lake Blvd Suite 1028	Altamonte Springs	FL	32701	407-831-1809	831-4594
Web: www.rkcinc.com					
Kickerillo Cos 1306 S Fry Rd	Katy	TX	77450	713-951-0666	492-2018*
*Fax Area Code: 281 ■ *Web:* www.kickerillo.com					
Kiewit Construction Group Inc 1000 Kiewit Plaza	Omaha	NE	68131	402-342-2052	271-2829
Web: www.kiewit.com					
Kinsley Construction Inc 2700 Water St	York	PA	17403	717-741-3841	741-9054
TF: 800-546-7539 ■ *Web:* www.rkinsley.com					
Kitchell Corp 1707 E Highland Ave Suite 100	Phoenix	AZ	85016	602-264-4411	631-6121*
*Fax: Hum Res ■ *Web:* www.kitchell.com					
Kjellstrom & Lee Inc 1607 Ownby Ln	Richmond	VA	23220	804-288-0082	285-4288
Web: www.kjellstrom-lee.com					
Klewin Building Co 40 Connecticut Ave	Norwich	CT	06360	860-886-2491	886-6960
Web: www.klewin.com					
Klinger WA LLC PO Box 8800	Sioux City	IA	51102	712-277-3901	277-5300
Web: www.klinger-const.com					
Knutson Construction Services Inc 5500 Wyzata Blvd Suite 300	Minneapolis	MN	55416	763-546-1400	546-2226
Web: www.knutsonconstruction.com					
Koll Construction LP 4343 Von Karman Ave Suite 150	Newport Beach	CA	92660	949-833-3030	250-4344
Web: www.koll.com					
Koll Development Co 4343 Von Karman Ave	Newport Beach	CA	92660	949-833-3030	250-4344
Web: www.koll.com					
Korte Construction Co 12441 US Hwy 40	Highland	IL	62249	618-654-8611	654-4999
Web: www.korteco.com					
Korte Construction Co 700 Saint Louis Union Stn Suite 200	Saint Louis	MO	63103	314-231-3700	231-4682
Web: www.korteco.com					
Kraemer Brothers Inc 925 Park Ave	Plain	WI	53577	608-546-2411	546-2509
Web: www.kraemerbrothers.com					
Kraus-Anderson Construction Co 525 S 8th St	Minneapolis	MN	55404	612-332-7281	332-8739
Web: kraus-anderson.com/construction/home.html					
Landis Construction LLC 241 Industrial Ave	Jefferson	LA	70121	504-833-6070	833-6662
Web: www.landisllc.com					
Lathrop Co 460 W Dussel Dr	Maumee	OH	43537	419-893-7000	893-1741
Web: www.turnerconstruction.com/lathrop/					
Law Co Inc 345 Riverview St Suite 300	Wichita	KS	67203	316-268-0200	268-0210
Web: www.law-co.com					
Layton Construction Co Inc 9090 S Sandy Pkwy	Sandy	UT	84070	801-568-9090	569-5450
Web: www.layton-const.com					
Lease Crutcher Lewis 107 Spring St	Seattle	WA	98104	206-622-0500	343-6541
Web: www.lcl.com					
Lee Lewis Construction Inc 7810 Orlando Ave	Lubbock	TX	79423	806-797-8400	797-8492
Web: www.leelewis.com					
Leonard Construction Co Inc PO Box 14547	Saint Louis	MO	63178	314-275-5814	275-5998
Leopardo Cos Inc 5200 Prairie Stone Pkwy	Hoffman Estates	IL	60192	847-783-3000	783-3001
Web: www.leopardo.com					
Lewis Cos 30500 Northwestern Hwy Suite 525	Farmington Hills	MI	48334	248-354-9005	354-6809
TF: 800-968-6808 ■ *Web:* www.lewiscompanies.com					
Lewis Lee Construction Inc 7810 Orlando Ave	Lubbock	TX	79423	806-797-8400	797-8492
Web: www.leelewis.com					
LF Driscoll Co Inc 9 Presidential Blvd	Bala Cynwyd	PA	19004	610-668-0950	668-9425
Web: www.lfdriscoll.com					
Linbeck Construction Corp PO Box 22500	Houston	TX	77227	713-621-2350	840-7525*
*Fax: Mktg ■ *Web:* www.linbeck.com					
Lincoln Property Co 500 N Akard St Suite 3300	Dallas	TX	75201	214-740-3300	740-3313
Web: www.lincolnproperty.com					
Louis P Ciminelli Construction Corp 369 Franklin St	Buffalo	NY	14202	716-855-1200	854-6655
Web: www.lpciminelli.com					
Loving TA Co Inc PO Box 919	Goldsboro	NC	27533	919-734-8400	731-7538
Web: www.taloving.com					
Lusardi Construction Co Inc 1570 Linda Vista Dr	San Marcos	CA	92078	760-744-3133	744-9064
Web: www.lusardi.com					
Lyda Builders Inc 12400 Hwy 281 N Suite 200	San Antonio	TX	78216	210-684-1770	684-1859
TF: 800-846-7026 ■ *Web:* www.lydabuilders.com					
Lydig Construction Inc 11001 E Montgomery St	Spokane	WA	99206	509-534-0451	535-6622
Web: www.lydig.com					
MA Mortenson Co 700 Meadow Ln N	Minneapolis	MN	55422	763-522-2100	287-5430
Web: www.mortenson.com					
Magnum Construction Inc 6201 SW 70th St 2nd Fl	Miami	FL	33143	305-541-0000	541-9771
Web: www.mcmcorp.com					
Mancini BT Co Inc 876 S Milpitas Blvd	Milpitas	CA	95036	408-942-7900	945-1360
TF: 800-488-4286 ■ *Web:* www.btmancini.com					
Mancini BT Co Inc Brookman Div 876 S Milpitas Blvd	Milpitas	CA	95035	408-942-7900	945-1360
TF: 800-488-4286 ■ *Web:* www.btmancini.com					
Manhattan Construction Co 5601 S 122nd East Ave	Tulsa	OK	74146	918-583-6900	592-4334
Web: www.mccbuilds.com					
Marnell Corrao Assoc Inc 222 Via Marnell Way	Las Vegas	NV	89119	702-739-2000	739-2005
Web: www.marnellcorrao.com					
Martin-Harris Construction Co 3030 S Highland Dr	Las Vegas	NV	89109	702-385-5257	387-6934
Web: www.martinharris.com					
MB Kahn Construction Co Inc 101 Flintlake Rd	Columbia	SC	29223	803-736-2950	736-5833
Web: www.mbkahn.com					
MB Kahn Construction Co Inc Moore GE Div PO Box 578	Greenwood	SC	29648	864-229-7411	229-1146
Web: www.mbkahn.com					
McCarthy Building Cos Inc 1341 N Rock Hill Rd	Saint Louis	MO	63124	314-968-3300	968-4642*
*Fax: Mktg ■ *Web:* www.mccarthy.com					
McGough Construction Co Inc 2737 Fairview Ave N	Saint Paul	MN	55113	651-633-5050	633-5673
Web: www.mcgough.com					
Messer Construction Co 5158 Fishwick Dr	Cincinnati	OH	45216	513-242-1541	242-6467
Web: www.messer.com					
Meyer CR & Sons Co 895 W 20th Ave	Oshkosh	WI	54902	920-235-3350	235-3419
Web: www.crmeyer.com					
MGM Mirage Design Group Inc 3260 Industrial Rd	Las Vegas	NV	89109	702-792-4600	792-4790
TF: 800-477-5110					
Midwest Titan Inc 11865 S Conley St	Olathe	KS	66061	913-782-6700	829-2785
Web: www.titanbuilt.com					
Miller H & Sons Inc 700 NW 107th Ave	Miami	FL	33172	305-559-4000	227-7115
Miller/Davis Co 1029 Portage St	Kalamazoo	MI	49001	269-345-3561	345-1372
Millie & Severson Inc PO Box 3601	Los Alamitos	CA	90720	562-493-3611	598-6871
Web: www.mandsinc.com					
Miron Construction Co Inc 1471 McMahon Dr	Neenah	WI	54956	920-969-7000	969-7393
Web: www.mironconst.com					
Monarch Construction Co Inc PO Box 12249	Cincinnati	OH	45212	513-351-6900	351-0979
Web: www.monarchconstruction.cc					
Moody CD Construction Co Inc 6017 Redan Rd	Lithonia	GA	30058	770-482-7778	482-7727
Web: www.cdmoodyconstruction.com					
Morganti Group Inc 100 Mill Plain Rd 4th Fl	Danbury	CT	06811	203-743-2675	792-8066*
*Fax: Sales ■ *Web:* www.morganti.com					
Morley Group 2901 28th St Suite 100	Santa Monica	CA	90405	310-399-1600	314-7347
Web: www.morleybuilders.com					
Mortenson MA Co 700 Meadow Ln N	Minneapolis	MN	55422	763-522-2100	287-5430
Web: www.mortenson.com					
Mosser Group Inc 122 S Wilson Ave	Fremont	OH	43420	419-334-3801	332-1534
Web: www.mossergrp.com					
Murnane Building Contractors Inc 99 Boynton Ave	Plattsburgh	NY	12901	518-561-4010	561-5926
Web: www.murnanebuilding.com					
Nabholz Construction Corp PO Box 2090	Conway	AR	72033	501-327-7781	327-8231
Web: www.nabholz.com					
Neenan Co 2620 E Prospect Rd Suite 100	Fort Collins	CO	80525	970-493-8747	493-5869
Web: www.neenan.com					
Nibbi Brothers Inc 180 Hubbell St	San Francisco	CA	94107	415-863-1820	863-7488
Web: www.nibbi.com					
North Texas Construction Co Inc 4100 N Frisco Rd	Sherman	TX	75090	903-893-4362	893-0159
Norwood Co 530 Brandywine Pkwy	West Chester	PA	19380	610-431-3500	431-7197
Web: www.norwdco.com					
O & G Industries Inc 112 Wall St	Torrington	CT	06790	860-489-9261	496-4286
Web: www.ogindustries.com					
Oakview Construction Inc PO Box 450	Red Oak	IA	51566	712-623-4927	623-9402
Web: www.oakviewconst.com					
Obayashi Construction Inc 420 E 3rd St Suite 906-D	Los Angeles	CA	90013	213-687-8700	687-3700
Web: www.ocac.com					
O'Connor Constructors Inc 45 Industrial Dr	Canton	MA	02021	781-828-0271	828-8248
Odebrecht Construction Inc 201 Alhambra Cir Suite 1400	Coral Gables	FL	33134	305-341-8800	569-1500
Web: www.odebrecht.com.br					
Okland Construction Co Inc 1978 S West Temple	Salt Lake City	UT	84115	801-486-0144	486-7570
Web: www.okland.com					
Olson John M Corp 26210 Harper Ave	Saint Clair Shores	MI	48081	586-771-9330	771-2440
Web: www.jmolson.com					
Olson RD Construction 2955 Main St 3rd Fl	Irvine	CA	92614	949-474-2001	474-1534
Web: www.rdolson.com					
Oltmans Construction Co 10005 Mission Mill Rd	Whittier	CA	90601	562-948-4242	699-3128
Web: www.oltmans.com					
O'Neil WE Construction Co Inc 2751 N Clybourn Ave	Chicago	IL	60614	773-755-1611	327-4784
Web: www.weoneil.com					
Opus East LLC 2099 Gaither Rd Suite 100	Rockville	MD	20850	301-354-4444	354-3199
Web: www.opuscorp.com					
Opus Group of Cos 10350 Bren Rd W	Minnetonka	MN	55343	952-656-4444	656-4529
Web: www.opuscorp.com					
Opus National 10350 Bren Rd W	Minnetonka	MN	55343	952-656-4444	656-4529
Web: www.opuscorp.com					
Opus North Corp 9700 W Higgins Rd Suite 900	Rosemont	IL	60018	847-692-4444	318-1618
Web: www.opuscorp.com					
Opus Northwest LLC 10350 Bren Rd W	Minnetonka	MN	55343	952-656-4444	656-4529
Web: www.opuscorp.com					
Opus South Corp 4200 W Cypress St Suite 444	Tampa	FL	33607	813-877-4444	877-1222
Web: www.opuscorp.com					
Opus West Corp 2555 E Camelback Rd Suite 800	Phoenix	AZ	85016	602-468-7000	468-7045
Web: www.opuscorp.com					
Osborne Construction Co Inc PO Box 97010	Kirkland	WA	98083	425-827-4221	828-4314
TF: 888-270-8221 ■ *Web:* www.osborne.cc					
Oscar J Boldt Construction Co 2525 N Roemer Rd	Appleton	WI	54911	920-739-6321	739-4409
Web: www.theboldtcompany.com					
Overaa C & Co Inc 200 Parr Blvd	Richmond	CA	94801	510-234-0926	237-2435
Web: www.overaa.com					
Owen-Ames-Kimball Co 300 Ionia Ave NW	Grand Rapids	MI	49503	616-456-1521	458-0770
Web: www.owen-ames-kimball.com					
Ozanne Construction Co Inc 1635 E 25th St	Cleveland	OH	44114	216-696-2876	696-8613
Web: www.ozanne.com					
Pankow Charles Builders Ltd 3280 E Foothill Blvd Suite 100	Pasadena	CA	91107	626-304-1190	696-1782
Web: www.pankow.com					
PCL Construction Group Inc 5400 99th St	Edmonton	AB	T6E3N7	780-435-9600	435-9654
Web: www.pcl.ca					
PCL Enterprises Inc 2000 S Colorado Blvd Tower 2 Suite 2-500	Denver	CO	80222	303-365-6500	365-6515
Web: www.pcl.com					
Pence Kelly Construction LLC 2747 Pence Loop SE	Salem	OR	97302	503-399-7223	585-7477
Web: www.pencekelly.com					
Pepper Cos Inc 643 N Orleans St	Chicago	IL	60610	312-266-4703	266-2792
Web: www.pepperconstruction.com					
Performance Contracting Inc 6621 E Mission Ave	Spokane	WA	99212	509-535-4814	534-5921
TF: 800-541-4323 ■ *Web:* www.pcg.com					
Perini Corp 73 Mt Wayte Ave	Framingham	MA	01701	508-628-2000	
NYSE: PCR ■ *Web:* www.perini.com					
Perley-Halladay Assoc Inc 1442 Phoenixville Pike	West Chester	PA	19380	610-296-5800	647-1711
TF: 800-248-5800 ■ *Web:* www.perleyhalladay.com					
Phipps Gerald H Inc 1530 W 13th Ave	Denver	CO	80204	303-571-5377	629-7467
Web: www.ghpd.com					
Pike Co 1 Circle St	Rochester	NY	14607	585-271-5256	271-3101
Web: www.pikeco.com/home.cfm					
Pinkerton & Laws Inc 1165 N Chase Pkwy Suite 100	Marietta	GA	30067	770-956-9000	618-8688
Pioneer Construction Co Inc 550 Kirtland St SW	Grand Rapids	MI	49507	616-247-6966	247-0186
Web: www.pioneerinc.com					
Pizzagalli Construction Co 50 Joy Dr	South Burlington	VT	05403	802-658-4100	651-1360
TF: 800-760-7607 ■ *Web:* www.pizzagalli.com					
PJ Dick Inc PO Box 98100	Pittsburgh	PA	15227	412-462-9300	462-2588
Web: www.pjdick.com					
Plant Process Equipment Inc 280 Reynolds Ave	League City	TX	77573	281-332-2589	332-6280
Web: www.plant-process.com					
Power Construction Co LLC 2360 Palmer Dr	Schaumburg	IL	60173	847-925-1300	925-1372
TF: 800-307-4048 ■ *Web:* www.powerconstruction.net					
Powers & Sons Construction Co Inc 2636 W 15th Ave	Gary	IN	46404	219-949-3100	949-5906
Web: www.powersandsons.com					
Quandel Group Inc 4755 Linglestown Rd Bldg 200	Harrisburg	PA	17112	717-657-0909	652-6282
Web: www.quandel.com					
R & L Brosamer Co Inc 1777 Oakland Blvd Suite 300	Walnut Creek	CA	94591	925-837-5600	627-1700
Web: www.brosamer.com					
RD Olson Construction 2955 Main St 3rd Fl	Irvine	CA	92614	949-474-2001	474-1534
Web: www.rdolson.com					
Reed EE Construction Co 333 Commerce Green Blvd	Sugar Land	TX	77478	281-933-4000	933-4852
Web: www.eereed.com					
Rentenbach Constructors Inc 2400 Sutherland Ave	Knoxville	TN	37919	865-546-2440	546-3414
Web: www.rentenbach.com					
River City Construction LLC 101 Hoffer Ln	East Peoria	IL	61611	309-694-3120	435-2457
Web: www.rccllc.com					
RJ Griffin & Co 800 Mount Vernon Hwy Suite 200	Atlanta	GA	30328	770-551-8883	551-8483
Web: www.rjgriffin.com					
RM Shoemaker Co 100 Front St 13th Fl	West Conshohocken	PA	19428	610-941-5500	941-5526
Web: www.shoemakerco.com					
Roberts JR Corp 7745 Greenback Ln Suite 300	Citrus Heights	CA	95610	916-729-5600	729-5666
TF: 800-551-1534 ■ *Web:* www.jrroberts.com					
Robins & Morton Group 400 Shades Creek Pkwy Suite 200	Birmingham	AL	35209	205-870-1000	871-0906
Web: www.robinsmorton.com					
Roche Constructors Inc 361 71st Ave	Greeley	CO	80634	970-356-3611	356-3619
Web: www.rocheconstructors.com					
Roebbelen Construction Inc 1241 Hawks Flight Ct	El Dorado Hills	CA	95762	916-939-4000	939-4028
Web: www.krcon.com					
Roel Construction Co Inc 3366 Kurtz St	San Diego	CA	92110	619-297-4156	297-1522
TF: 800-662-7635 ■ *Web:* www.roel.com					

Phone Fax

Roger Kennedy Construction Inc
370 S North Lake Blvd Suite 1028 Altamonte Springs FL 32701 407-831-1809 831-4594
Web: www.rkcinc.com
Rooney Holdings 5601 S 122nd East Ave Tulsa OK 74146 918-583-6900 592-4334
Web: www.rooneyholdings.com
Roy Anderson Corp 11400 Reichold Rd Gulfport MS 39503 228-896-4000 896-4086
TF: 800-688-4003 ■ *Web:* www.rac.com
Rudolph & Sletten Inc 1600 Seaport Blvd Suite 350 Redwood City CA 94063 650-216-3600 599-9030
Web: www.rsconstruction.com
Rudolph/Libbe Inc 6494 Latcha Rd Walbridge OH 43465 419-241-5000 837-9373
Web: www.rlcos.com
Ruhlin Co Inc PO Box 190 Sharon Center OH 44274 330-239-2800 239-1828
Web: www.ruhlin.com
Ruscilli Construction Co Inc 2041 Arlingate Ln Columbus OH 43228 614-876-9484 771-2634
Web: www.ruscilli.com
Russell HJ & Co 504 Fair St SW Atlanta GA 30313 404-330-1000 330-0922
Web: www.hjrussell.com
Ryan Cos US Inc 50 S 10th St Suite 300 Minneapolis MN 55403 612-492-4000 492-3000
Web: www.ryancompanies.com
Saunders Construction Inc 6950 S Jordan Rd Centennial CO 80112 303-699-9000 680-7448
Web: www.saundersci.com
Schmidt CG Inc 11777 W Lake Pk Dr Milwaukee WI 53224 414-577-1177 577-1155
TF: 800-248-1254 ■ *Web:* www.cgschmidt.com
Sellen Construction Co Inc 227 Westlake Ave N Seattle WA 98109 206-682-7770 623-5206
Web: www.sellen.com
Service Products Buildings Inc 460 W Duffel Dr Maumee OH 43537 419-897-0708 897-0938
Servidyne Inc 1945 The Exchange Suite 300 Atlanta GA 30339 770-933-4200 953-9922
NASDAQ: SERV ■ *TF:* 800-241-8996 ■ *Web:* www.servidyne.com
Shaw Construction Co LLC 300 Kalamath St Denver CO 80223 303-825-4740 825-6403
Web: www.shawconstruction.net
Shawmut Design & Construction 560 Harrison Ave Boston MA 02118 617-622-7000 622-7001
Web: www.shawmut.com
Shiel Sexton Co Inc 902 N Capitol Ave Indianapolis IN 46204 317-423-6000 423-6300
Web: www.shielsexton.com
Shioi Construction Inc 98-724 Kuaho Pl Pearl City HI 96782 808-487-2441 487-2445
Shoemaker RM Co 100 Front St 13th Fl West Conshohocken PA 19428 610-941-5500 941-5526
Web: www.shoemakerco.com
Sigal Construction Corp 2231 Crystal Dr Arlington VA 22202 703-302-1500 302-1520
Web: www.sigal.com
Skanska USA Building Inc 1633 Littleton Rd Parsippany NJ 07054 973-334-5300 334-5376
Web: www.skanskausa.com
Skanska USA Building Inc 516 Township Line Rd Blue Bell PA 19422 267-470-1000 470-1010
Web: www.skanskausa.com
Skanska USA Inc 16-16 Whitestone Expy Whitestone NY 11357 718-767-2600 767-2663
Web: www.skanska.com
Sletten Construction Co Inc 1000 25th St N Great Falls MT 59401 406-761-7920 761-0923
Web: www.slettencompanies.com
SM Wilson & Co PO Box 5210 Saint Louis MO 63139 314-645-9595 645-1700
Web: www.smwilson.com
Smith CD Construction Inc PO Box 1006 Fond du Lac WI 54936 920-924-2900 924-2910
Web: www.cd-smith.com
Snyder Langston Inc 17962 Cowan St Irvine CA 92614 949-863-9200 863-1087
Web: www.snyder-langston.com
Solo Construction Corp 3855 Commerce Pkwy Miramar FL 33025 954-447-2800 447-6768
Soltek of San Diego 2424 Congress St Suite A San Diego CA 92110 619-296-6247 296-0730*
**Fax:* Mktg ■ *Web:* www.soltekpacific.com
Sordoni Construction Services Inc 45 Owen St Forty Fort PA 18704 570-287-3161 287-0298
Web: www.sordoni-construction.com
Speed Fab-Crete Corp International PO Box 15580 Fort Worth TX 76119 817-478-1137 561-2544
TF: 800-758-1137 ■ *Web:* www.speedfab-crete.com
Stellar Group 2900 Hartley Rd Jacksonville FL 32257 904-260-2900 268-4932*
**Fax:* Sales ■ *TF:* 800-488-2900 ■ *Web:* www.tsgjax.com
Sterling Construction Co Inc 20810 Fernbush Ln Houston TX 77073 281-821-9091 821-2995
NASDAQ: STRL ■ *Web:* www.sterlingconstructionco.com
Stiles Construction Co 300 SE 2nd St Fort Lauderdale FL 33301 954-627-9300 627-9305
Web: www.stiles.com/construction_about_us.htm
Structure Tone Inc 770 Broadway 9th Fl New York NY 10003 212-481-6100 685-9267
Web: www.structuretone.com
Suffolk Construction Co Inc 65 Allerton St Boston MA 02119 617-445-3500 445-9234
Web: www.suffolk-construction.com
Sundt Construction Inc 4101 E Irvington Rd Tucson AZ 85714 520-748-7555 750-6266*
**Fax:* Mktg ■ *TF:* 800-467-5544 ■ *Web:* www.sundt.com
Swinerton Builders 260 Townsend St San Francisco CA 94107 415-421-2980 984-1384
Web: www.swinerton.com
Swinerton Inc 260 Townsend St San Francisco CA 94107 415-421-2980 984-1306*
**Fax:* Hum Res ■ *Web:* www.swinerton.com
TA Loving Co Inc PO Box 919 Goldsboro NC 27533 919-734-8400 731-7538
Web: www.taloving.com
Tarlton Corp 5500 W Park Ave Saint Louis MO 63110 314-633-3300 647-1940
TF: 888-827-5866 ■ *Web:* www.tarltoncorp.com
Taylor Construction Group Inc
6100 Thornton Ave Suite 200 Des Moines IA 50321 515-471-4700 471-4701
TF: 800-373-0330 ■ *Web:* www.taylorconstrgrp.com
TCM Construction Inc 3801 Portland Ave S Minneapolis MN 55407 612-822-2121 822-5851
Web: www.tcmconstruction.com
Tesoro Corp 5250 Challedon Dr Virginia Beach VA 23462 757-518-8491 518-8589
TF: 800-645-2059 ■ *Web:* www.tesorocorp.com
Thomas S Byrne Ltd 900 Summit Ave Fort Worth TX 76102 817-429-0452 877-5507
Web: www.tsbyrne.com
Tiberti JA Construction Co 1806 Industrial Rd Las Vegas NV 89102 702-248-4000 382-5361
Web: www.tiberti.com
Tishman Realty & Construction Co Inc 666 5th Ave New York NY 10103 212-399-3600 957-9791
TF: 800-609-8474 ■ *Web:* www.tishman.com
Titan Global Technologies Ltd 5005 3rd Ave S Seattle WA 98134 206-832-8165 832-8161
Web: www.titanglobal.com
TN Ward Co 129 Coulter Ave PO Box 191 Ardmore PA 19003 610-649-0400 649-1790
Web: www.tnward.com
Torcon Inc 328 Newman Springs Rd Red Bank NJ 07701 732-704-9800 704-9810
Web: www.torcon.com
Turner Construction Co 375 Hudson St New York NY 10014 212-229-6000 229-6185*
**Fax:* Mktg ■ *Web:* www.turnerconstruction.com
Turner International LLC 375 Hudson St New York NY 10014 212-229-6000 229-6390
Turner Universal 336 James Record Rd Huntsville AL 35824 256-461-0568 461-6731
Web: www.turneruniversal.com
Tutor-Saliba Corp 15901 Olden St Sylmar CA 91342 818-362-8391 367-5379
Web: www.tutorsaliba.com
Ukpeagvik Inupiat Corp 1250 Agvik St PO Box 890 Barrow AK 99723 907-852-4460 852-4459
Web: www.ukpik.com
Universal Construction Co Inc 11200 W 79th St Lenexa KS 66214 913-342-1150 342-1151
Web: www.universalconstruction.net
Vegas General Construction Co 5795 Rogers St Las Vegas NV 89118 702-873-9450 873-9568
Vratsinas Construction PO Box 2596 Little Rock AR 72203 501-376-0017 376-4145
Web: www.vccconstruction.com
VRH Construction Corp 320 Grand Ave Englewood NJ 07631 201-871-4422 871-6727
Web: www.vrhcorp.com
WA Klinger LLC PO Box 8800 Sioux City IA 51102 712-277-3901 277-5300
Web: www.klinger-const.com
Walbridge Aldinger Co 613 Abbott St Detroit MI 48226 313-963-8000 963-8129
Web: www.walbridge.com
Wallick Construction Co Inc PO Box 1023 Columbus OH 43216 614-863-4640 863-1725
Web: www.wallickcos.com
Walsh Construction Co 2905 SW 1st Ave Portland OR 97201 503-222-4375 274-7676
Web: www.walshconstructionco.com
Walsh Group Inc 929 W Adams St Chicago IL 60607 312-563-5400 563-5466
TF: 800-759-2574 ■ *Web:* www.walshgroup.com
Walton Construction Co 3252 Roanoke Rd Kansas City MO 64111 816-753-2121 753-6161
Web: www.waltoncci.com
WE O'Neil Construction Co Inc 2751 N Clybourn Ave Chicago IL 60614 773-755-1611 327-4784
Web: www.weoneil.com
Webcor Builders Inc 951 Mariners Island Blvd 7th Fl San Mateo CA 94404 650-349-2727 578-8158
Web: www.webcor.com
Wehr Constructors Inc 2517 Plantside Dr Louisville KY 40299 502-491-9250 491-3540
Web: www.wehrconstructors.com
Weis Builders Inc 2227 7th St NW Rochester MN 55901 507-288-2041 288-7979
Web: www.weisbuilders.com
Weitz Co Inc 5901 Thornton Ave Des Moines IA 50321 515-246-4700 246-4799
Web: www.weitz.com
Weitz/Cohen Construction Co 4725 S Monaco St Suite 100 Denver CO 80237 303-860-6600 860-6698
Web: www.weitz.com
Wentz Group 555 Twin Dolphin Dr Suite 160 Redwood Shores CA 94065 650-592-3950 593-5632
Web: www.wentzgroup.com
WG Yates & Sons Construction Co Inc
1 Gulley Ave PO Box 456 Philadelphia MS 39350 601-656-5411 656-8958
Web: www.wgyates.com
White Charles N Construction Co 613 Crescent Cir Suite 100 Ridgeland MS 39157 601-898-5180 989-5190
Web: www.whiteconst.com
Whiting-Turner Contracting Co 300 E Joppa Rd 8th Fl Baltimore MD 21286 410-821-1100 337-5770
TF: 800-638-4279 ■ *Web:* www.whiting-turner.com
Wilhelm FA Construction Co Inc 3914 Prospect St Indianapolis IN 46203 317-359-5411 359-8346
Web: www.fawilhelm.com
William Blanchard Co 199 Mountain Ave Springfield NJ 07081 973-376-9100 376-9154
Williams Co of Orlando Inc 2301 Silver Star Rd Orlando FL 32804 407-295-2530 297-0459
Web: www.williamsco.com
Williams Service Group Inc 2076 West Park Pl Stone Mountain GA 30087 770-879-4000 469-0251*
**Fax:* Acctg ■ *TF:* 800-892-0992 ■ *Web:* www.wmsgrpintl.com
Wilson SM & Co PO Box 5210 Saint Louis MO 63139 314-645-9595 645-1700
Web: www.smwilson.com
Winter Construction Co 1330 Spring St NW Atlanta GA 30309 404-588-3300 223-1146
Web: www.wintercompanies.com
Winter Group of Cos 1330 Spring St NW Atlanta GA 30309 404-588-3300 223-1146*
**Fax:* Acctg ■ *Web:* www.wintercompanies.com
Winter Park Construction Co 221 Circle Dr Maitland FL 32751 407-644-8923 645-1972
Web: www.wpc.com
Withers DL Construction LC 3220 E Harbour Dr Phoenix AZ 85034 602-438-9500 438-9600
Web: www.dlwithers.com
WM Brode Co 100 Elizabeth St PO Box 299 Newcomerstown OH 43832 740-498-5121 498-8553
TF: 800-848-9217 ■ *Web:* www.wmbrode.com
WM Jordan Co Inc 11010 Jefferson Ave Newport News VA 23601 757-596-6341 596-7425
Web: www.wmjordan.com
Worth Construction Co Inc 24 Taylor Ave Bethel CT 06801 203-797-8788 791-2515
Web: www.worthconstruction.com
Wright Construction Corp 5811 Youngquist Rd Fort Myers FL 33912 239-481-5000 481-2448
Web: www.wrightconstructioncorp.com
WS Bellows Construction Corp PO Box 2132 Houston TX 77252 713-680-2132 680-2614
Web: www.wsbellows.com
Yates WG & Sons Construction Co
1 Gulley Ave PO Box 456 Philadelphia MS 39350 601-656-5411 656-8958
Web: www.wgyates.com

190 CONSTRUCTION - BUILDING CONTRACTORS - RESIDENTIAL

Phone Fax

AG Spanos Cos 10100 Trinity Pkwy 5th Fl Stockton CA 95219 209-478-7954 478-3309
Web: www.agspanos.com
Albert D Seeno Construction Co Inc 4021 Port Chicago Hwy Concord CA 94520 925-671-7711 689-7752
Web: www.seenohomes.com
Apartment House Builders Inc PO Box 959 North Little Rock AR 72115 501-758-2842 758-1903
Arthur Rutenberg Homes Inc 13922 58th St N Clearwater FL 33760 727-536-5900 538-9089
TF: 800-274-6637 ■ *Web:* www.arthurrutenberghomes.com
Ashton Woods Homes Inc
11375 W Sam Houston Pkwy S Suite 100 Houston TX 77031 281-561-7773 561-7774
Web: www.ashtonwoods.com
Ball Homes LLC 3609 Walden Dr Lexington KY 40517 859-268-1191 268-9093
TF: 888-268-1101 ■ *Web:* www.ballhomes.com
Barbour & Short Inc PO Box 6509 Norman OK 73070 405-321-0482 360-8950
Blandford Development Corp 3321 E Baseline Rd Gilbert AZ 85234 480-892-4492 892-5106
Bob Schmitt Homes Inc 8501 Woodbridge Ct North Ridgeville OH 44039 440-327-9495 327-7540
Web: www.bobschmitthomes.com
Bozzuto Group 7850 Walker Dr Suite 400 Greenbelt MD 20770 301-220-0100 220-3738
TF: 800-718-0200 ■ *Web:* www.bozzuto.com
Breeden Homes Inc 366 E 40th Ave Eugene OR 97405 541-686-9431 686-0918
TF Sales: 800-322-3198 ■ *Web:* www.breedenhomes.com
Brookfield Homes Corp 12865 Pointe Del Mar Suite 200 Del Mar CA 92014 858-481-8500 481-9375
NYSE: BHS ■ *Web:* www.brookfieldhomes.com
Burnstead Construction Co 1215 120th Ave NE Suite 201 Bellevue WA 98005 425-454-1900 454-4543
Web: www.burnstead.com
Bush Construction Corp 4029 Ironbound Rd Suite 200 Williamsburg VA 23188 757-220-2874 229-2542
Calton Inc 2050 40th Ave Suite 1 Vero Beach FL 32960 772-794-1414 794-2828
Web: www.caltoninc.com
Capital Pacific Holdings Inc
4100 MacArthur Blvd Suite 150 Newport Beach CA 92660 949-622-8400 622-8404
Web: www.capitalpacifichomes.com/corp
Case Group 855 E Bell Rd Suite 104 Scottsdale AZ 85260 602-955-5800 505-9335*
**Fax Area Code:* 480
Centex Construction Co Inc 3100 McKinnon St 7th Fl Dallas TX 75201 214-468-4700 468-4357
Web: www.centexconstruction.com
Centex Corp 2728 N Harwood St Dallas TX 75201 214-981-5000 981-6859*
NYSE: CTX ■ **Fax:* Investor Rel ■ *TF:* 888-847-5130 ■ *Web:* www.centex.com
Centex Rooney Construction Co Inc 7901 SW 6th Ct Plantation FL 33324 954-585-4000 585-4501
Web: www.centexconstruction.com
Century-Crowell Communities Inc
1535 S 'D' St Suite 200 San Bernardino CA 92408 909-381-6007 381-0041
Web: www.centuryvintagehomes.com
Coastal Contractors Inc PO Box 759 Beaufort SC 29901 843-524-3191 524-8468
Web: www.coastalcontractors.net
Colson & Colson Construction Co PO Box 14111 Salem OR 97309 503-370-7070 370-4205
Web: www.colson-colson.com
Continental Homes Inc 7001 N Scottsdale Rd Suite 2050 Scottsdale AZ 85253 480-483-0006 566-4956*
**Fax:* Cust Svc
Craft Homes USA Inc 2649 Breckenridge Ctr Dr Suite 104 Monroe NC 28110 704-238-1229 238-1150
Web: www.crafthomesusa.com

	City	State	Zip	Phone	Fax
Crossgates Inc 3555 Washington Rd *Web:* www.crossgatesinc.com	McMurray	PA	15317	724-941-9240	941-4339
Dick Pacific Construction Co Ltd 707 Richards St Suite 400 *Web:* www.dickpacific.com	Honolulu	HI	96813	808-533-5000	533-5320
DL Horton Torrey Homes 8200 Roberts Dr Suite 400	Atlanta	GA	30350	770-730-7900	730-7901
Drees Co 211 Grandview Dr *TF:* 800-647-1711 ■ *Web:* www.dreeshomes.com	Fort Mitchell	KY	41017	859-578-4200	341-5854
Edward Rose Building Enterprises Inc 30057 Orchard Lake Rd PO Box 9070 *Web:* www.edwardrose.com	Farmington Hills	MI	48334	248-539-2255	539-2125
Eid-Co Buildings Inc 1701 32nd Ave S *Web:* www.eid-co.com	Fargo	ND	58103	701-237-0510	239-4702
Eyde Construction Co PO Box 4218 *TF:* 800-442-3933 ■ *Web:* www.eyde.com	East Lansing	MI	48826	517-351-2480	351-3946
FH Martin Construction Co 28740 Mound Rd *Web:* www.fhmartin.com	Warren	MI	48092	586-558-2100	558-2921
Fischer Henry Builder Inc 2670 Chancellor Dr Suite 300 *Web:* www.fischerhomesinc.com	Crestview Hills	KY	41017	859-341-4709	344-5900
Forbes Homes Inc PO Box 597 *Web:* www.forbeshomes.com	Getzville	NY	14068	716-688-5597	688-6674
Fulton Homes Corp 9140 S Kyrene Rd Suite 202 *Web:* www.fultonhomes.com	Tempe	AZ	85284	480-753-6789	753-5554
Galaxy Builders Ltd 4729 College Pk *Web:* www.galaxybuilders.com	San Antonio	TX	78249	210-493-0550	493-1238
Glen Construction Co Inc 9801 Washington Blvd Suite 650 *Web:* www.glencon.com	Gaithersburg	MD	20878	301-258-2700	977-1212
Godley Builders Inc 415 Minuet Ln Suite D *Web:* www.godleybuilders.com	Charlotte	NC	28217	704-522-6146	525-4657
Gottfried Robert W Inc 340 Royal Poinciana Way Suite 315	Palm Beach	FL	33480	561-655-7107	833-8889
Green Valley Corp 777 N 1st St 5th Fl *Web:* www.barryswensonbuilder.com	San Jose	CA	95112	408-287-0246	998-1737
Grupe Co 3255 W March Ln Suite 400 *Web:* www.grupe.com	Stockton	CA	95219	209-473-6000	473-6001
H Miller & Sons Inc 700 NW 107th Ave	Miami	FL	33172	305-559-4000	227-7115
Hardaway Group 615 Main St *Web:* www.hardaway.net	Nashville	TN	37206	615-254-5461	254-4518
Harkins Builders Inc 2201 Warwick Way *TF:* 888-224-5697 ■ *Web:* www.harkinsbuilders.com	Marriottsville	MD	21104	410-750-2600	480-4299
Henry Fischer Builder Inc 2670 Chancellor Dr Suite 300 *Web:* www.fischerhomesinc.com	Crestview Hills	KY	41017	859-341-4709	344-5900
Hernandez Cos Inc 3734 E Anne St *Web:* www.hernandezcompanies.com	Phoenix	AZ	85040	602-438-7825	438-6558
Hitt Contracting Inc 2704 Dorr Ave *Web:* www.hitt-gc.com	Fairfax	VA	22031	703-846-9000	846-9110
House Doctors 575 Chamber Dr *TF:* 800-319-3359 ■ *Web:* www.housedoctors.com	Milford	OH	45150	513-831-0100	831-6010
HRH Construction LLC 50 Main St 15th Fl *Web:* www.hrhconstruction.com	White Plains	NY	10606	212-616-3100	696-5458
JA Jones/Tompkins Builders 1333 H St NW Suite 200 *Web:* www.tompkinsbuilders.com	Washington	DC	20005	202-789-0770	898-2531
Jacobs Facilities 1527 Cole Blvd *Web:* www.jacobs.com	Golden	CO	80401	303-462-7000	462-7001
JB Sandlin Cos 5137 Davis Blvd *TF:* 800-821-4663 ■ *Web:* www.sandlinhomes.com	Fort Worth	TX	76180	817-281-3509	656-0719
Jim Walter Homes Inc PO Box 31601 *TF:* 800-492-5837 ■ *Web:* www.jimwalterhomes.com	Tampa	FL	33631	813-871-4811	
John Laing Homes 895 Dove St Suite 200 *Web:* www.johnlainghomes.com	Newport Beach	CA	92660	949-265-2400	265-2500
Jones Co 16640 Chesterfield Grove Rd Suite 200 *TF:* 866-675-6637 ■ *Web:* www.thejonesco.com	Chesterfield	MO	63005	636-537-7000	537-9952
Kara Homes 197 Rt 18 Suite 235S *Web:* www.karahomes.com	New Brunswick	NJ	08816	732-565-0720	565-0569
Keith Waters & Assoc Inc 6216 Baker Rd Suite 110 *Web:* www.keithwaters.com	Eden Prairie	MN	55346	952-974-0004	974-0005
Kickerillo Cos 1306 S Fry Rd **Fax Area Code:* 281 ■ *Web:* www.kickerillo.com	Katy	TX	77450	713-951-0666	492-2018*
Kopf Builders Inc 420 Avon Belden Rd *TF:* 800-242-8913 ■ *Web:* www.kopf.net	Avon Lake	OH	44012	440-933-6908	933-6956
Kraft Construction Co Inc 2606 S Horseshoe Dr *Web:* www.kraftconstruction.com	Naples	FL	34104	239-643-6000	643-1988
Landstar Homes Inc 550 Biltmore Way Suite 1110 *Web:* www.landstarhomes.com	Coral Gables	FL	33134	305-461-2440	461-3190
Lane Realty Construction Corp 11390 Old Roswell Rd Suite 100 *Web:* www.lanecompany.com	Alpharetta	GA	30004	770-777-7500	663-3403
LAS Enterprises Inc 2413 L & A Rd *TF:* 800-264-1527 ■ *Web:* www.lasenterprises.com	Metairie	LA	70001	504-887-1515	832-0036
Lease Crutcher Lewis 107 Spring St *Web:* www.lcl.com	Seattle	WA	98104	206-622-0500	343-6541
Lennar Corp 700 NW 107th Ave Suite 400 *NYSE:* LEN ■ *TF:* 800-741-4663 ■ *Web:* www.lennar.com	Miami	FL	33172	305-559-4000	226-4158
Levitt & Sons Corp 7777 Glades Rd Suite 410 *TF:* 800-741-5110 ■ *Web:* www.levittandsons.com	Boca Raton	FL	33434	561-482-5100	488-9188
Lewis Builders Inc 54 Sawyer Ave *Web:* www.lewisbuilders.com	Atkinson	NH	03811	603-362-5333	362-4936
Lincoln Property Co 500 N Akard St Suite 3300 *Web:* www.lincolnproperty.com	Dallas	TX	75201	214-740-3300	740-3313
Lowder Construction Co Inc 2000 Interstate Park Dr Suite 401 *Web:* www.lowder-construction.com	Montgomery	AL	36109	334-270-6524	270-6540
Lyon William Homes 4490 Von Karman Ave *NYSE:* WLS ■ *Web:* www.lyonhomes.com	Newport Beach	CA	92660	949-833-3600	476-2178
Martin FH Construction Co 28740 Mound Rd *Web:* www.fhmartin.com	Warren	MI	48092	586-558-2100	558-2921
Mayer Homes Inc 755 S New Ballas Rd Suite 210 *Web:* www.mayerhomes.com	Saint Louis	MO	63141	314-997-2300	997-3322
McBride & Son Inc 1 McBride & Son Ctr Dr *Web:* www.mcbrideandson.com	Chesterfield	MO	63005	636-537-2000	537-2546
McCarty Corp 13496 Pond Springs Rd	Austin	TX	78729	512-258-6611	258-7915
Meritage Homes Corp 17851 N 85th St Suite 300 *NYSE:* MTH ■ *Web:* www.meritagecorp.com	Scottsdale	AZ	85255	480-515-8100	515-7904
Michaels Group LLC 10 Blacksmith Dr Suite 1 *Web:* www.michaelsgroup.com	Malta	NY	12020	518-899-6311	899-6260
Miller H & Sons Inc 700 NW 107th Ave	Miami	FL	33172	305-559-4000	227-7115
Miller WC & AN Cos 4701 Sangamore Rd Suite LL-1 *TF:* 800-599-4711 ■ *Web:* www.wcanmiller.com	Bethesda	MD	20816	301-229-4000	229-4015
Morgan Group Inc 5606 S Rice Ave *Web:* www.morgangroup.com	Houston	TX	77081	713-361-7200	361-7299
Morris General Building Co PO Box 3632	Chatsworth	CA	91313	818-341-5135	
Nordaas American Homes Co Inc 10091 State Hwy 22 PO Box 116 *TF:* 800-658-7076 ■ *Web:* www.nordaashomes.com	Minnesota Lake	MN	56068	507-462-3331	462-3211
NVR Inc 11700 Plaza America Dr Suite 500 *AMEX:* NVR ■ *Web:* www.nvrinc.com	Reston	VA	20190	703-956-4000	956-4750
Obayashi Construction Inc 420 E 3rd St Suite 906-D *Web:* www.ocac.com	Los Angeles	CA	90013	213-687-8700	687-3700
Pardee Homes 10880 Wilshire Blvd Suite 1900 *Web:* www.pardeehomes.com	Los Angeles	CA	90024	310-475-3525	446-1291
Pasquinelli Construction Co Inc 6880 N Frontage Rd Suite 100 *Web:* www.pasquinelli.com	Burr Ridge	IL	60527	630-455-5400	
Paul H Schwendener Inc 1000 Vandustrial Dr **Fax Area Code:* 773 ■ *Web:* www.schwendener.com	Westmont	IL	60559	630-971-3303	242-4025*
Prestige Builders Partners LLC 14160 Palmetto Frontage Rd Suite 21 *Web:* www.prestigebuildersgroup.net	Miami Lakes	FL	33016	305-827-5665	827-6263
Purcell Construction Co 1550 Starkey Rd **Fax Area Code:* 727	Largo	FL	33771	888-568-1555	587-6560*
Pyramid Construction Inc 275 N Franklin Tpke	Ramsey	NJ	07446	201-327-1919	327-0054
Realen Homes LP 1040 Stoney Hill Rd Suite 100 **Fax:* Cust Svc ■ *TF:* 800-732-5368 ■ *Web:* www.realenhomes.com	Yardley	PA	19067	215-497-0600	497-9550*
Regency Homes Inc 2840 University Dr *Web:* www.regency-homes.net	Coral Springs	FL	33065	954-755-1775	341-8873
Reimers & Jolivette Inc 2344 NW 24th Ave	Portland	OR	97210	503-228-7691	228-2721
Rio Verde Development Inc 18815 E Four Peaks Blvd *TF:* 800-233-7103 ■ *Web:* www.rioverdeaz.com	Rio Verde	AZ	85263	480-471-3350	471-0107
Robert W Gottfried Inc 340 Royal Poinciana Way Suite 315	Palm Beach	FL	33480	561-655-7107	833-8889
Rohde Construction Co Inc 4087 Brockton Dr	Kentwood	MI	49512	616-698-0880	698-1850
Rose Edward Building Enterprises Inc 30057 Orchard Lake Rd PO Box 9070 *Web:* www.edwardrose.com	Farmington Hills	MI	48334	248-539-2255	539-2125
Rutenberg Arthur Homes Inc 13922 58th St N *TF:* 800-274-6637 ■ *Web:* www.arthurrutenberghomes.com	Clearwater	FL	33760	727-536-5900	538-9089
Ryan Homes Corp 11460 Cronridge Dr Suite 128 *Web:* www.ryanhomes.com	Owings Mills	MD	21117	410-654-5720	654-0069
S & A Custom Built Homes 2121 Old Gatesburg Rd Suite 200 *Web:* www.sahomebuilder.com	State College	PA	16803	814-231-4780	272-8821
Schmitt Bob Homes Inc 8501 Woodbridge Ct *Web:* www.bobschmitthomes.com	North Ridgeville	OH	44039	440-327-9495	327-7540
Schuck & Sons Construction Co Inc 8205 N 67th Ave *Web:* www.schuckaz.com	Glendale	AZ	85302	623-931-3661	937-3435
Schwendener Paul H Inc 1000 Vandustrial Dr **Fax Area Code:* 773 ■ *Web:* www.schwendener.com	Westmont	IL	60559	630-971-3303	242-4025*
Seeno Albert D Construction Co Inc 4021 Port Chicago Hwy *Web:* www.seenohomes.com	Concord	CA	94520	925-671-7711	689-7752
Shaw Construction Co LLC 300 Kalamath St *Web:* www.shawconstruction.net	Denver	CO	80223	303-825-4740	825-6403
Shreve Land Co Inc 666 Travis St Suite 100 *TF:* 800-259-0056 ■ *Web:* www.shreveland.com	Shreveport	LA	71101	318-226-0056	226-0064
Simpson Housing Solutions LLC 320 Golden Shore Suite 200 *Web:* www.simpsonsolutions.com	Long Beach	CA	90802	562-256-2000	256-2001
Skogman Construction Co Inc 411 1st Ave Suite 500 *Web:* www.skogman.com	Cedar Rapids	IA	52401	319-363-8285	366-7257
Spanos AG Cos 10100 Trinity Pkwy 5th Fl *Web:* www.agspanos.com	Stockton	CA	95219	209-478-7954	478-3309
SS Steele & Co Inc 4951 Government Blvd *Web:* steelehomes.cc	Mobile	AL	36693	251-661-9600	
Stabile Cos Inc 20 Cotton Rd Suite 200 *TF:* 800-432-4892 ■ *Web:* www.stabilecompanies.com	Nashua	NH	03063	603-889-0318	595-2571
Standard Pacific Corp 15326 Alton Pkwy *NYSE:* SPF ■ *Web:* www.standardpacifichomes.com	Irvine	CA	92618	949-789-1600	789-1708
Stanmar Inc 130 Boston Post Rd *Web:* www.stanmar-inc.com	Sudbury	MA	01776	978-443-9922	443-0479
Suffolk Construction Co Inc 65 Allerton St *Web:* www.suffolk-construction.com	Boston	MA	02119	617-445-3500	445-9234
Sunset Development Co 1 Annabel Ln Suite 201 *Web:* www.bishopranch.com	San Ramon	CA	94583	925-866-0100	866-1330
Technical Olympic USA Inc 4000 Hollywood Blvd Suite 500N *NYSE:* TOA ■ *Web:* www.tousa.com	Hollywood	FL	33021	954-364-4000	364-4030
TH Properties 345 Main St *TF Sales:* 800-225-5847 ■ *Web:* www.thproperties.com	Harleysville	PA	19438	215-513-4270	513-0700
Tishman Realty & Construction Co Inc 666 5th Ave *TF:* 800-609-8474 ■ *Web:* www.tishman.com	New York	NY	10103	212-399-3600	957-9791
Turner Construction Co 375 Hudson St **Fax:* Mktg ■ *Web:* www.turnerconstruction.com	New York	NY	10014	212-229-6000	229-6185*
Turner Universal 336 James Record Rd *Web:* www.turneruniversal.com	Huntsville	AL	35824	256-461-0568	461-6731
United-Bilt Homes Inc PO Box 4346 *TF:* 800-551-8955 ■ *Web:* www.ubh.com	Shreveport	LA	71134	318-861-4572	869-0132
Village Green Cos 30833 Northwestern Hwy Suite 300 *Web:* www.villagegreen.com	Farmington Hills	MI	48334	248-851-9600	851-6161
Wagoner Construction Co Inc PO Box 1127 *TF:* 800-222-1027	Salisbury	NC	28145	704-633-1431	637-7091
Wallick Construction Co Inc PO Box 1023 *Web:* www.wallickcos.com	Columbus	OH	43216	614-863-4640	863-1725
Walsh Group Inc 929 W Adams St *TF:* 800-759-2574 ■ *Web:* www.walshgroup.com	Chicago	IL	60607	312-563-5400	563-5466
Walter Jim Homes Inc PO Box 31601 *TF:* 800-492-5837 ■ *Web:* www.jimwalterhomes.com	Tampa	FL	33631	813-871-4811	
Waters Keith & Assoc Inc 6216 Baker Rd Suite 110 *Web:* www.keithwaters.com	Eden Prairie	MN	55346	952-974-0004	974-0005
Wayne Homes LLC 3777 Boettler Oaks Dr *TF:* 800-686-5354 ■ *Web:* www.wayne-homes.com	Uniontown	OH	44685	330-896-7611	896-7622
WC & AN Miller Cos 4701 Sangamore Rd Suite LL-1 *TF:* 800-599-4711 ■ *Web:* www.wcanmiller.com	Bethesda	MD	20816	301-229-4000	229-4015
Wesseln Construction Co Inc 292 N Wilshire Ave Suite 103 *Web:* www.wesseln.com	Anaheim	CA	92801	714-772-0888	772-7697
Wexford Homes 135 Keveling Dr *Web:* www.wexfordbuilders.com	Saline	MI	48176	734-429-5300	429-3358
Wheeler Construction Inc PO Box 310 *Web:* www.citrusbuilder.com	Inverness	FL	34451	352-726-0973	637-4959
Whittaker Builders Inc DBA Whittaker Homes 355A Mid Rivers Mall Dr *Web:* www.whittakerhomes.com	Saint Peters	MO	63376	636-970-1511	397-4894
Whittaker Homes 355A Mid Rivers Mall Dr *Web:* www.whittakerhomes.com	Saint Peters	MO	63376	636-970-1511	397-4894
Wildish Land Co Inc 3600 Wildish Ln PO Box 7428 *Web:* www.wildish.com	Eugene	OR	97401	541-485-1700	683-7722
William Lyon Homes 4490 Von Karman Ave *NYSE:* WLS ■ *Web:* www.lyonhomes.com	Newport Beach	CA	92660	949-833-3600	476-2178
WL Homes DBA John Laing Homes 895 Dove St Suite 200 *Web:* www.johnlainghomes.com	Newport Beach	CA	92660	949-265-2400	265-2500
Wohlsen Construction Co 548 Steel Way *Web:* www.wohlsen.com	Lancaster	PA	17601	717-299-2500	299-3419
Woodside Homes Corp 39 Eagle Ridge Dr Suite 100 *Web:* www.woodsidegroupinc.com	Salt Lake City	UT	84054	801-299-6700	
World Development Inc 44600 Village Ct *Web:* www.world-development.com	Palm Desert	CA	92260	760-568-2955	568-4335

191 CONSTRUCTION - HEAVY CONSTRUCTION CONTRACTORS

191-1 Communications Lines & Towers Construction

Phone | Fax

Allied Tower Co 4646 Mandale Rd ... Alvin TX 77511 281-331-9627 332-0325
TF: 800-207-4623 ■ *Web:* www.alliedtower.com
Barlovento LLC 165 Hostdale Dr Suite 1 ... Dothan AL 36303 334-983-9979 983-9983
TF: 877-498-6039 ■ *Web:* www.barlovento8a.com
Bechtel Telecommunications 5275 Westview Dr ... Frederick MD 21703 301-228-6000 228-2200
Web: www.bechtel.com
Black & Veatch 8400 Ward Pkwy ... Kansas City MO 64114 913-458-2000 458-3730
Web: www.bv.com
Cellcom Services Inc 11301 W 218th St ... Peculiar MO 64078 816-779-5660 779-5120
CLS Group 1015 Waterwood Pkwy Suite D ... Edmond OK 73034 405-348-5460 341-6334
TF: 800-580-5460 ■ *Web:* www.clsgroup.com
CommStructures Inc 101 E Roberts Rd ... Pensacola FL 32534 850-968-9293 968-9289
Web: www.commstructures.com
Contemporary Constructors Inc 19240 Red Land Rd ... San Antonio TX 78259 210-496-1926 491-0932
Web: www.ccitele.com
Davidson Engineering Co 296 Covered Bridge Rd ... Rogue River OR 97537 541-582-8074 582-0072
Web: www.tower-structures.com
Fluor Daniel Inc 1 Fluor Daniel Dr ... Aliso Viejo CA 92698 949-349-2000 349-2585
Web: www.fluor.com
Malouf Engineering International Inc
17950 Preston Rd Suite 720 ... Dallas TX 75252 972-783-2578 783-2583
Web: www.maloufengineering.com
MasTec Inc 800 Douglas Rd 12th Fl ... Coral Gables FL 33134 305-599-1800 599-1900
NYSE: MTZ ■ *Web:* www.mastec.com
NAT-COM Inc 2622 Audubon Rd ... Audubon PA 19403 610-666-7947 666-7136
TF: 800-486-7947 ■ *Web:* www.nat-com.com
NEESCom Inc 25 Research Dr ... Westborough MA 01582 508-389-3300 389-3001
Web: www.neescom.com
Orius Corp 829 Pk Lamar Dr ... Villa Ridge MO 63089 636-451-0055 742-4990
Web: www.oriuscorp.com
Quanta Services Inc 1360 Post Oak Blvd Suite 2100 ... Houston TX 77056 713-629-7600 629-7676
NYSE: PWR ■ *Web:* www.quantaservices.com
Radian Communications Services Corp
461 Cornwall Rd PO Box 880 ... Oakville ON L6J5C5 905-844-1242 844-8837
TF: 866-472-3126 ■ *Web:* www.radiancorp.com
Seacomm Erectors Inc 32527 SR 2 ... Sultan WA 98294 360-793-6564 793-4402
TF: 800-497-8320 ■ *Web:* www.seacomm.com
Swager Communications Inc 501 E Swager Dr ... Fremont IN 46737 260-495-5165 495-4205
TF: 800-968-5601 ■ *Web:* www.swager.com
T-Cubed Inc 3 Commercial Pl ... Norfolk VA 23510 757-629-2600 533-4884
Web: www.t3inc.com
Thoroughbred Technology & Telecommunications Inc
3 Commercial Pl ... Norfolk VA 23510 757-629-2600 533-4884
Web: www.t3inc.com
Tower 2000 Inc 310 60th St NW ... Sauk Rapids MN 56379 320-253-5489 654-9226
TF: 877-720-6249 ■ *Web:* www.tower2000.net
Tyco Telecommunications 60 Columbia Rd ... Morristown NJ 07960 973-656-8000 656-8990
Web: www.tycotelecom.com
Utility Services Inc 400 N 4th St ... Bismarck ND 58501 701-222-7900 222-7607
TF: 800-638-3278 ■
Web: www.montana-dakota.com/mdu_docs/company_profile/UTILITY_SERVICES.html

191-2 Foundation Drilling & Pile Driving

Phone | Fax

Barcus LG & Sons Inc 1430 State Ave ... Kansas City KS 66102 913-621-1100 621-3288
TF: 800-255-0180 ■ *Web:* www.barcus.com
Berkel & Co Contractors Inc PO Box 335 ... Bonner Springs KS 66012 913-422-5125 422-2013
Web: www.berkelandcompany.com
Brode WM Co 100 Elizabeth St PO Box 299 ... Newcomerstown OH 43832 740-498-5121 498-8553
TF: 800-848-9217 ■ *Web:* www.wmbrode.com
Case Foundation Co 1325 W Lake St ... Roselle IL 60172 630-529-2911 529-2995
Web: www.casefoundation.com
Coastal Caisson Corp 12290 US Hwy 19 N ... Clearwater FL 33764 727-536-4748 530-1571
TF: 800 723 0015 ■ *Web:* www.coastalcaisson.com
Kiewit Construction Group Inc 1000 Kiewit Plaza ... Omaha NE 68131 402-342-2052 271-2829
Web: www.kiewit.com
Lawrence Construction Co Inc 9002 N Moore Rd ... Littleton CO 80125 303-791-5642 791-5647
LG Barcus & Sons Inc 1430 State Ave ... Kansas City KS 66102 913-621-1100 621-3288
TF: 800-255-0180 ■ *Web:* www.barcus.com
Malcolm Drilling Co Inc 3503 Breakwater Ct ... Hayward CA 94545 510-780-9181 780-9167
Web: www.malcolmdrilling.com
WM Brode Co 100 Elizabeth St PO Box 299 ... Newcomerstown OH 43832 740-498-5121 498-8553
TF: 800-848-9217 ■ *Web:* www.wmbrode.com

191-3 Golf Course Construction

Phone | Fax

Barbaron Inc 4411 E Arlington St ... Inverness FL 34453 352-344-9100 344-9510
Web: www.barbaron.com
Bruce Co of Wisconsin Inc Golf Div 2830 W Beltline Hwy ... Middleton WI 53562 608-836-7041 831-4236
Web: www.brucegolf.com
Buky Golf Inc 522 Bethel Church Rd ... Mount Washington KY 40047 502-538-4494 538-3193
DBI Golf 408 6th St ... Prinsburg MN 56281 320-978-6011 978-4978
TF: 800-328-8949 ■ *Web:* www.dbigolf.com
Formost Construction Co 41220 Guava St ... Murrieta CA 92562 951-698-7270 698-6170
TF: 800-247-7532 ■ *Web:* www.formostconstruction.com
Furness Golf Construction Inc PO Box 2752 ... Kailua Kona HI 96745 808-930-1361 930-1360
Golf Course Construction Inc 1150 Victory Dr ... Howell MI 48843 517-545-3681 545-3798
Golf Development Construction Inc
2843 Brownsboro Rd Suite 106 ... Louisville KY 40206 502-894-8916 893-1932
Web: www.golfdev.com
Golf Visions LLC 344 E Lyndale Ave ... Northlake IL 60164 708-562-5247 562-7497
Golf Works Inc 3660 Stone Ridge Rd Suite F102 ... Austin TX 78746 512-327-8089 327-8169
Web: www.golfworksinc.com
Harris Miniature Golf 141 W Burk Ave ... Wildwood NJ 08260 609-522-4200 729-0100
TF: 888-294-6530 ■ *Web:* www.harrisminigolf.com
Johnson Golf Course Builders 499 Golf Rd ... South Sioux City NE 68776 402-494-4687 494-0816
Landscapes Unlimited Inc 1201 Aries Dr ... Lincoln NE 68512 402-423-6653 423-4487
Web: www.landscapesunlimited.com
MacCurrach Golf Construction Inc 3501 Faye Rd ... Jacksonville FL 32226 904-646-1581
TF: 800-646-1581 ■ *Web:* www.maccurrachgolf.com
Niebur Golf Inc 1330 Quail Lake Loop Suite 200 ... Colorado Springs CO 80906 719-527-0313 527-0337
Web: www.nieburgolf.com
Prince Contracting Co Inc 5411 Willis Rd ... Palmetto FL 34221 941-722-7707 722-4641
Web: www.princeinc.com
Ryan Inc Central 2700 E Racine St ... Janesville WI 53545 608-754-2291 754-3290
Web: www.ryancentral.com
Shapemasters Inc 5003 O'Quinn Blvd Suite J ... Southport NC 28461 910-278-1434 278-1944
Web: www.shapemasters.com
Total Golf Construction Inc 4045 43rd Ave ... Vero Beach FL 32960 772-562-1177 562-2773
Web: www.totalgolfconstruction.com
Wadsworth Golf Construction Co 1901 Van Dyke Rd ... Plainfield IL 60544 815-436-8400 436-8404
Web: www.wadsworthgolf.com
Weitz Golf International 11780 US Hwy 1 Suite 302 ... North Palm Beach FL 33408 561-626-3352 799-7850
Web: www.weitzgolf.com

191-4 Highway, Street, Bridge, Tunnel Construction

Phone | Fax

A Teichert & Son Inc 3500 American River Dr ... Sacramento CA 95864 916-484-3011 484-6506
TF: 888-554-5627 ■ *Web:* www.teichert.com
Abrams JD LP 111 Congress Ave Suite 2400 ... Austin TX 78701 512-322-4000 322-4018
Web: www.jdabrams.com
Ace Asphalt & Paving Co 115 Averill Ave ... Flint MI 48506 810-238-1737 238-4326
ACI Construction Services 601 N Ashley Dr Suite 1100 ... Tampa FL 33602 813-490-4300 490-4301
Adams Construction Co 523 Rutherford Ave NE ... Roanoke VA 24016 540-982-2366 982-2942
TF: 800-523-4417 ■ *Web:* www.adamspaving.com
AFC Enterprises Inc 88-43 76th Ave ... Glendale NY 11385 718-275-1100 275-4602
Ajax Paving Industries Inc PO Box 7058 ... Troy MI 48007 248-244-3300 244-0800
Web: www.ajaxpaving.com
AL Blades & Sons Inc PO Box 590 ... Hornell NY 14843 607-324-3636 324-0998
Allan A Myers Inc PO Box 98 ... Worcester PA 19490 610-584-6020 584-4280*
**Fax:* Hum Res ■ *Web:* www.americaninfrastructure.com
Allen Co Inc PO Box 537 ... Winchester KY 40392 859-744-3361 744-3961
TF: 888-744-3361 ■ *Web:* www.theallen.com
Alpha Construction Co 1340 W 171st St ... Hazel Crest IL 60429 708-335-2323 335-0760
American Bridge Co 1000 American Bridge Way ... Coraopolis PA 15108 412-631-1000 631-2000
Web: www.americanbridge.net
American Civil Constructors Inc 4901 S Windemere St ... Littleton CO 80120 303-795-2582 347-1844
TF: 800-725-5699 ■ *Web:* www.acconstructors.com
American Paving Co Inc PO Box 4348 ... Fresno CA 93744 559-268-9886 268-0662
Web: www.americanpavingco.com
Amon BR & Sons Inc W 2950 Hwy 11 ... Elkhorn WI 53121 262-723-2547 723-2666
Web: www.bramon.com
Anderson Brothers Construction Co Inc PO Box 668 ... Brainerd MN 56401 218-829-1768 829-7607
Web: www.andersonbrothers.com
Anderson Columbia Co Inc 871 NW Guerdon St PO Box 1829 ... Lake City FL 32056 386-752-7585 755-5430
Web: www.andersoncolumbia.com
Angelo Iafrate Construction Co 26300 Sherwood Ave ... Warren MI 48091 586-756-1070 756-0467*
**Fax:* Hum Res ■ *Web:* www.iafrate.com
Angelo Tony Cement Construction Co 46850 Grand River Ave ... Novi MI 48374 248-344-4000 344-4048
Web: www.tonyangelo.com
APAC Inc 900 Ashwood Pkwy Suite 700 ... Atlanta GA 30338 770-392-5300 392-5393
TF: 800-241-7074 ■ *Web:* www.apac.com
APAC Kansas Inc Shears Div 819 W 1st St ... Hutchinson KS 67501 620-662-2112 662-9505
Arrow Road Construction Co PO Box 334 ... Mount Prospect IL 60056 847-437-0700 437-0779
Web: www.arrowroad.com
Ashmore Brothers Inc PO Box 529 ... Greer SC 29652 864-879-7311 879-7315
TF: 800-601-5884 ■ *Web:* www.ashmorebros.com
Atkinson Guy F Construction LLC
600 Naches Ave SW Suite 1201 ... Renton WA 98057 425-255-7551 255-7325
Web: www.atkn.com
Austin Bridge & Road Inc 6330 Commerce Dr Suite 150 ... Irving TX 75063 214-596-7300 596-7396
Web: www.austin-ind.com
Autostrade International of Virginia
45305 Catalina Ct Suite 102 ... Sterling VA 20166 703-707-8870 904-8004
Web: www.autostradeint.com
Bacco Construction Co PO Box 458 ... Iron Mountain MI 49801 906-774-2616 774-1160
Web: www.baccoconstruction.com
Baker Michael Corp 100 Airsite Dr Airsite Business Pk ... Moon Township PA 15108 412-269-6300 375-3977
AMEX: BKR ■ *TF:* 800-553-1153 ■ *Web:* www.mbakercorp.com
Baldwin Contracting Co Inc 1764 Skyway ... Chico CA 95928 530-891-6555 894-6220
TF: 800-682-5726
Balfour Beatty Inc 999 Peachtree St NE Suite 200 ... Atlanta GA 30309 404-875-0356 607-1784
Web: www.balfourbeatty.com
Barber Brothers Contracting Co LLC 2636 Dougherty Dr ... Baton Rouge LA 70805 225-355-5611 355-5615
Web: www.barber-brothers.com
Barcus LG & Sons Inc 1430 State Ave ... Kansas City KS 66102 913-621-1100 621-3288
TF: 800-255-0180 ■ *Web:* www.barcus.com
Barnhart Douglas E Inc 10760 Thornmint Rd ... San Diego CA 92127 858-385-8200 385-8201
Web: www.debinc.com
Barnhill Contracting Co PO Box 1529 ... Tarboro NC 27886 252-823-1021 823-0137
Web: www.barnhillcontracting.com
Barrett Industries Corp 3 Becker Farm Rd ... Roseland NJ 07068 973-533-1001 533-1020
Web: www.barrettpaving.com
Barriere Construction Co LLC 1 Galleria Blvd Suite 1650 ... Metairie LA 70001 504-581-7283 581-2270
Web: www.barriere.com
Bay Cities Paving & Grading Inc 5029 Forni Dr ... Concord CA 94520 925-687-6666 687-2122
Bechtel Corp 50 Beale St ... San Francisco CA 94105 415-768-1234 768-9038
Web: www.bechtel.com
Becon Construction Co Inc 3000 Post Oak Blvd ... Houston TX 77056 713-235-2089 235-1699
Web: www.beconconstruction.com
Bell Ray Construction Co Inc PO Box 363 ... Brentwood TN 37024 615-373-4343 373-9224
Web: www.raybellconstruction.com
Bizzack Inc 2265 Executive Dr ... Lexington KY 40505 859-299-8001 299-0480
TF: 800-599-0424
Blades AL & Sons Inc PO Box 590 ... Hornell NY 14843 607-324-3636 324-0998
Blain WE & Sons Inc PO Box 1208 ... Mount Olive MS 39119 601-797-4551 797-4777
Blalock Charles & Sons Inc 1225 Parkway Dr ... Sevierville TN 37862 865-546-2641 429-5909
Blattner DH & Sons Inc 400 CR 50 ... Avon MN 56310 320-356-7351 356-7392
TF: 800-877-2866 ■ *Web:* www.dhblattner.com
Blue Rock Industries 58 Main St ... Westbrook ME 04092 207-854-2561 854-2539
TF: 800-439-2561 ■ *Web:* www.bluerockmaine.com
Blythe Construction Inc PO Box 31635 ... Charlotte NC 28231 704-375-8474 375-7814
Web: www.blytheconstruction.com/blythe
Boh Brothers Construction Co LLC 730 S Tonti St ... New Orleans LA 70119 504-821-2400 821-0714
TF: 800-284-3377 ■ *Web:* www.bohbros.com
Border States Paving Inc 4101 N 32nd St ... Fargo ND 58102 701-237-4860 237-0233
Borderland Construction Co Inc 400 E 38 St ... Tucson AZ 85713 520-623-0900 623-0232
BR Amon & Sons Inc W 2950 Hwy 11 ... Elkhorn WI 53121 262-723-2547 723-2666
Web: www.bramon.com
Bramble David A Inc PO Box 419 ... Chestertown MD 21620 410-778-3023 778-3427
Web: www.davidabrambleinc.com
Branch Group Inc PO Box 40004 ... Roanoke VA 24022 540-982-1678 982-4127
Web: www.branch-associates.com
Branch Highways Inc PO Box 40004 ... Roanoke VA 24022 540-982-1678 982-4217
Web: www.branchhighways.com
Brechan Enterprises Inc 2705 Mill Bay Rd ... Kodiak AK 99615 907-486-3215 486-4889
Broce Construction Co Inc 2821 N Flood Ave ... Norman OK 73069 405-321-1076 321-4996
Brode WM Co 100 Elizabeth St PO Box 299 ... Newcomerstown OH 43832 740-498-5121 498-8553
TF: 800-848-9217 ■ *Web:* www.wmbrode.com

Highway, Street, Bridge, Tunnel Construction (Cont'd)

Company	City	State	ZIP	Phone	Fax
Brox Industries Inc 1471 Methuen St	Dracut	MA	01826	978-454-9105	805-9720
Web: www.broxindustries.com					
Brutoco Engineering & Construction Inc PO Box 429	Fontana	CA	92334	909-350-3535	822-9661
Web: www.brutoco.net					
CA Meyer Paving & Construction Co 807 S Orlando Ave Suite N	Winter Park	FL	32789	407-647-9900	647-9811
CA Rasmussen Inc 2320 Shasta Way Suite F	Simi Valley	CA	93065	805-581-2275	581-2265
TF: 800-479-2888					
Cardi Corp 400 Lincoln Ave	Warwick	RI	02888	401-739-8300	736-2977
Web: www.cardi.com					
Carlo John Inc 45000 River Ridge Dr	Clinton Township	MI	48038	586-416-4500	226-5664
TF: 800-465-6234 ■ *Web:* www.carlocompanies.com					
CC Mangum Co LLC 6105 Chapel Hill Rd	Raleigh	NC	27607	919-783-5700	783-6072
Web: www.ccmangum.com					
CC Myers Inc 3286 Fitzgerald Rd	Rancho Cordova	CA	95742	916-635-9370	635-8961
Web: www.ccmyers.com					
Central Allied Enterprises Inc 1243 Raff Rd SW	Canton	OH	44710	330-477-6751	477-1660
TF: 800-862-6011 ■ *Web:* www.central-allied.com					
Cessford Construction Co PO Box 160	Le Grand	IA	50142	641-479-2695	479-2003
Charles Blalock & Sons Inc 1225 Parkway Dr	Sevierville	TN	37862	865-546-2641	429-5909
Cherry Hill Construction Inc 8211 Washington Blvd	Jessup	MD	20794	410-799-3577	799-5483
TF: 800-262-2606 ■ *Web:* cherryhillconstruction.com					
Cianbro Corp PO Box 1000	Pittsfield	ME	04967	207-487-3311	679-2422
Web: www.cianbro.com					
Civil Constructors Inc 2283 Rt 20 E	Freeport	IL	61032	815-235-2200	235-2219
Web: www.helmgroup.com					
CJ Mahan Construction Co 3400 Southwest Blvd	Grove City	OH	43123	614-875-8200	875-1175
Web: www.cjmahan.com					
Clark Construction Group LLC 7500 Old Georgetown Rd	Bethesda	MD	20814	301-272-8100	272-8414
TF: 800-827-4422 ■ *Web:* www.clarkconstruction.com					
Clarkson Construction Co 4133 Gardner Ave	Kansas City	MO	64120	816-483-8800	241-6823
Web: www.clarksonconstruction.com					
Colas Inc 10 Madison Ave 4th Fl	Morristown	NJ	07960	973-290-9082	290-9088
Web: www.colas.com/home.asp					
Collet Construction Co Inc PO Box 2207	Woodland	CA	95776	530-662-9383	661-1554
Collins DA Construction Co Inc PO Box 191	Mechanicville	NY	12118	518-664-9855	664-9609
Web: www.dacollins.com					
Concrete General Inc 8000 Beechcraft Ave	Gaithersburg	MD	20879	301-948-4450	948-8273
Concrete Materials Inc 1201 W Russell St	Sioux Falls	SD	57118	605-357-6000	334-6221
Web: www.concretematerialscompany.com					
Constructors Inc 1815 Y St	Lincoln	NE	68508	402-434-1764	434-1799
Web: www.constructorslincoln.com					
Cornejo & Sons Inc 2060 E Tulsa	Wichita	KS	67216	316-522-5100	522-8187
Web: www.cornejocorp.com					
Coxwell JB Contracting Inc 6741 Lloyd Rd W	Jacksonville	FL	32254	904-786-1120	783-2970
Web: www.jbcoxwell.com					
Crowder Construction Co Inc PO Box 30007	Charlotte	NC	28230	704-372-3541	376-3573
TF: 800-849-2966 ■ *Web:* www.crowdercc.com					
CS McCrossan Inc PO Box 1240	Maple Grove	MN	55311	763-425-4167	425-1255
Cummins Construction Co Inc PO Box 748	Enid	OK	73702	580-233-6000	233-9858
TF: 800-375-6001					
Curran Contracting Co Inc 7502 S Main St	Crystal Lake	IL	60014	815-455-5100	455-7894
Web: www.currancontracting.com					
Curran Group Inc 7502 S Main St	Crystal Lake	IL	60014	815-455-5100	455-7894
Web: www.currangroup.com					
CW Matthews Contracting Co Inc 1600 Kenview Dr	Marietta	GA	30061	770-422-7520	422-1068
Web: www.cwmatthews.com					
DA Collins Construction Co Inc PO Box 191	Mechanicville	NY	12118	518-664-9855	664-9609
Web: www.dacollins.com					
D'Ambra Construction Co Inc 800 Jefferson Blvd	Warwick	RI	02887	401-737-1300	732-4725
Web: www.d-ambra.com					
David A Bramble Inc PO Box 419	Chestertown	MD	21620	410-778-3023	778-3427
Web: www.davidabrambleinc.com					
David Nelson Construction Co 3483 Alternate 19	Palm Harbor	FL	34683	727-784-7624	786-8894
Web: www.nelson-construction.com					
Dawson Bridge Co PO Box 28	Lexington	KY	40588	859-269-4644	266-7378
Dean Word Co Ltd 1245 River Rd PO Box 310330	New Braunfels	TX	78131	830-625-2365	606-5008
TF: 800-683-3926 ■ *Web:* www.deanword.com					
DeFoe Corp 800 S Columbus Ave	Mount Vernon	NY	10550	914-699-7440	699-6734
Delta Cos Inc PO Box 880	Cape Girardeau	MO	63702	573-334-5261	334-9576
Web: www.deltacos.com					
Dement Construction Co PO Box 1812	Jackson	TN	38302	731-424-6306	424-5308
TF: 800-821-5778 ■ *Web:* www.dementconstruction.com					
Denton Enterprises Inc 22003 Harper Ave	Saint Clair Shores	MI	48080	586-777-9444	777-7523
DH Blattner & Sons Inc 400 CR 50	Avon	MN	56310	320-356-7351	356-7392
TF: 800-877-2866 ■ *Web:* www.dhblattner.com					
Dick Corp 1900 Rt 51	Large	PA	15025	412-384-1000	384-1150
TF: 800-245-6577 ■ *Web:* www.dickcorp.com/dickcorp					
Dickerson Florida Inc PO Box 910	Fort Pierce	FL	34954	772-429-4444	429-4445
TF: 800-772-6246					
Dondlinger & Sons Construction Co Inc PO Box 398	Wichita	KS	67201	316-945-0555	945-9009
Web: www.dondlinger.biz					
Douglas E Barnhart Inc 10760 Thornmint Rd	San Diego	CA	92127	858-385-8200	385-8201
Web: www.debinc.com					
Drew James H Corp 8701 Zionsville Rd	Indianapolis	IN	46268	317-876-3739	876-3829
TF: 800-772-7342					
Driggs Co LLC 8700 Ashwood Dr	Capitol Heights	MD	20743	301-336-6700	336-0004
Web: www.driggs.net					
Duininck Brothers Inc PO Box 208	Prinsburg	MN	56281	320-978-6011	978-4978
TF: 800-328-8949 ■ *Web:* www.dbimn.com					
Dunn Roadbuilders LLC PO Drawer 6560	Laurel	MS	39441	601-649-4111	425-4644
Web: www.dunnroadbuilders.com					
Eby Corp PO Box 1679	Wichita	KS	67201	316-268-3500	268-3664
Web: www.ebycorp.com					
ECCO III Enterprises Inc 201 Saw Mill River Rd	Yonkers	NY	10701	914-963-3600	963-3989
Edward Kraemer & Sons Inc PO Box 220	Plain	WI	53577	608-546-2311	546-2130
Web: www.edkraemer.com					
Elam Construction Inc 1225 S 7th St	Grand Junction	CO	81501	970-242-5370	245-7716
Web: www.elamconstruction.com					
Ellis WA Construction Co Inc PO Box 1095	Independence	MO	64051	816-257-2300	257-2450
Elmo Greer & Sons Inc PO Box 730	London	KY	40743	606-843-6136	843-7825
English Construction Co Inc 615 Church St	Lynchburg	VA	24504	434-845-0301	845-0306
Web: www.englishconst.com					
Evans & Assoc Construction Co Inc PO Box 30	Ponca City	OK	74602	580-765-6693	765-2298
Facchina Construction Co Inc 102 Centennial St Suite 201	La Plata	MD	20646	240-776-7000	776-7001
Web: www.facchina.com					
FCI Constructors Inc PO Box 1767	Grand Junction	CO	81502	970-434-9093	434-7583
Web: www.fciol.com					
Flanigan P & Sons Inc 2444 Loch Raven Rd	Baltimore	MD	21218	410-467-5900	467-3127
Web: www.pflanigan.com					
Flatiron Constructors Inc 10090 I-25 Frontage Rd	Longmont	CO	80504	303-485-4050	485-3922
TF: 800-333-1760 ■ *Web:* www.flatironcorp.com					
Fluor Constructors International Inc 3 Polaris Way	Aliso Viejo	CA	92698	949-349-2000	349-2585
Web: www.fluor.com					
FNF Construction Inc 115 S 48th St	Tempe	AZ	85281	480-784-2910	829-8607
TF: 800-542-9490 ■ *Web:* www.fnfinc.com					
Francis O Day Construction Co Inc 850 E Gude Dr	Rockville	MD	20850	301-652-2400	340-6592
Web: www.foday.com					
Frank W Whitcomb Construction Corp PO Box 1000	Walpole	NH	03608	603-445-5555	445-5307
TF: 800-238-7283					
Fred Weber Inc 2320 Creve Coeur Mill Rd	Maryland Heights	MO	63043	314-344-0070	344-0970
TF: 800-808-0980 ■ *Web:* www.fredweberinc.com					
Frehner Construction Co Inc 4040 Frehner Rd	North Las Vegas	NV	89030	702-649-6250	642-2213
GA & FC Wagman Inc 3290 Susquehanna Trail N	York	PA	17406	717-764-8521	764-2799
Web: www.wagman.com					
Gallagher Asphalt Corp 18100 S Indiana Ave	Thornton	IL	60476	708-877-7160	877-5222
TF: 800-536-7160 ■ *Web:* www.gallagherasphalt.com					
Gallagher & Burk Inc 344 High St	Oakland	CA	94601	510-261-0466	261-3806
Garey Construction Ltd 11607 N Lamar Blvd	Austin	TX	78753	512-837-5916	837-5934
Gary Merlino Construction Co Inc 9125 10th Ave S	Seattle	WA	98108	206-762-9125	763-4178
George Harms Construction Co Inc PO Box 817	Farmingdale	NJ	07727	732-938-4004	938-2782
Web: www.ghcci.com					
George & Lynch Inc 150 Lafferty Ln	Dover	DE	19901	302-736-3031	734-9743
Web: www.geolyn.com					
Gilbert Southern Corp 1000 Kiewit Plaza	Omaha	NE	68131	402-342-2052	271-2829
Gilvin-Terrill Inc PO Box 9027	Amarillo	TX	79105	806-944-5200	944-5271
Glasgow Inc PO Box 1089	Glenside	PA	19038	215-884-8800	884-1465
TF: 888-222-7570 ■ *Web:* www.glasgowinc.com					
Glover James W Ltd 248 Sand Island Access Rd	Honolulu	HI	96819	808-591-8977	591-9174
Godbersen-Smith Construction Co Inc PO Box 33	Ida Grove	IA	51445	712-364-3388	364-4301
Gohmann Asphalt & Construction Inc PO Box 2428	Clarksville	IN	47131	812-282-1349	288-2168
Web: www.gohmannasphalt.com					
Grace Pacific Corp PO Box 78	Honolulu	HI	96810	808-674-8383	674-1040
Web: www.gracepacificcorp.com					
Granite Construction Inc PO Box 50085	Watsonville	CA	95077	831-724-1011	722-9657
NYSE: GVA ■ *Web:* www.graniteconstruction.com					
Gray & Sons Inc P430 W Padonia Rd	Timonium	MD	21093	410-771-4311	771-8125
TF: 800-254-0752 ■ *Web:* www.graynson.com					
Great Lakes Construction Co 2608 Great Lakes Way	Hinckley	OH	44233	330-220-3900	220-7670
Web: www.tglcc.com					
Greggo & Ferrara Inc 4048 New Castle Ave	New Castle	DE	19720	302-658-5241	658-0671
Gulf Asphalt Corp 4116 US Hwy 231	Panama City	FL	32404	850-785-4675	769-3456
TF: 800-300-0177 ■ *Web:* www.gaccontractors.com					
Guy F Atkinson Construction LLC 600 Naches Ave SW Suite 1201	Renton	WA	98057	425-255-7551	255-7325
Web: www.atkn.com					
Guy Pratt Inc 608 Union Ave	Holtsville	NY	11742	631-289-6100	289-6119
H-K Contractors Inc PO Box 51450	Idaho Falls	ID	83405	208-523-6600	524-1426
Hale Jr Contracting Co Inc PO Box 25667	Albuquerque	NM	87125	505-345-6628	345-1145
Halverson Construction Co Inc 620 N 19th St	Springfield	IL	62702	217-753-0027	753-1904
Web: www.halversonconstruction.com					
Hardrives of Delray Inc 2101 S Congress Ave	Delray Beach	FL	33445	561-278-0456	278-2147
Web: www.hardrivespaving.com					
Harms George Construction Co Inc PO Box 817	Farmingdale	NJ	07727	732-938-4004	938-2782
Web: www.ghcci.com					
Harper Co 1648 Petersburg Rd	Hebron	KY	41048	859-586-8890	586-8891
Harper Industries Inc 960 N HC Mathis Dr	Paducah	KY	42001	270-442-2753	443-9154
TF: 800-669-0077 ■ *Web:* www.harper1.com					
Hempt Brothers Inc 205 Creek Rd	Camp Hill	PA	17011	717-737-3411	761-5019
Herzog Contracting Corp PO Box 1089	Saint Joseph	MO	64502	816-233-9001	233-9881
TF: 800-950-1969 ■ *Web:* www.herzogcompanies.com					
Hi-Way Paving Inc PO Box 550	Hilliard	OH	43026	614-876-1700	876-1899
Web: www.hiwaypaving.com					
Hinkle Contracting Corp PO Box 200	Paris	KY	40362	859-987-3670	987-0727
Web: www.hinklecontracting.com					
HRI Inc 1750 W College Ave	State College	PA	16801	814-238-5071	238-0131
Web: www.hrico.com					
Hubbard Construction Co 1936 Lee Rd 3rd Fl	Winter Park	FL	32789	407-645-5500	623-3865
TF: 800-476-1228 ■ *Web:* www.hubbard.com					
Hudson River Construction Co 101 Dunham Dr Port of Albany	Albany	NY	12202	518-434-6677	434-8638
Web: www.hudsonriverconstruction.com					
Hughes Group Inc PO Box 369	Jeffersonville	IN	47131	812-282-4393	283-0142
Hunter Contracting Co 701 N Cooper Rd	Gilbert	AZ	85233	480-892-0521	892-4932
Web: www.huntercontracting.com					
IA Construction Corp 158 Lindsay Rd	Zelienople	PA	16063	724-452-8621	452-0514
Web: www.iaconstruction.com					
Iafrate Angelo Construction Co 26300 Sherwood Ave	Warren	MI	48091	586-756-1070	756-0467*
**Fax:* Hum Res ■ *Web:* www.iafrate.com					
Interstate Highway Construction Inc PO Box 4356	Englewood	CO	80155	303-790-9100	790-8524
Web: www.ihcquality.com					
Jack B Parson Cos 2350 S 1900 West	Ogden	UT	84401	801-731-1111	731-8800
TF: 888-672-7766 ■ *Web:* www.jbparson.com					
Jacobsen KF & Co PO Box 82245	Portland	OR	97282	503-239-5532	235-1350
James D Morrissey Inc 9119 Frankford Ave	Philadelphia	PA	19114	215-333-8000	624-3308
Web: www.jdm-inc.com					
James H Drew Corp 8701 Zionsville Rd	Indianapolis	IN	46268	317-876-3739	876-3829
TF: 800-772-7342					
James Julian Inc 405 S DuPont Rd	Wilmington	DE	19805	302-999-0271	998-8385
James McHugh Construction Co 1737 S Michigan Ave	Chicago	IL	60616	312-986-8000	431-8518
Web: www.mchughconstruction.com					
James W Glover Ltd 248 Sand Island Access Rd	Honolulu	HI	96819	808-591-8977	591-9174
Jay Dee Contractors Inc 38881 Schoolcraft Rd	Livonia	MI	48150	734-591-3400	464-6868
Web: www.jaydeecontr.com					
JB Coxwell Contracting Inc 6741 Lloyd Rd W	Jacksonville	FL	32254	904-786-1120	783-2970
Web: www.jbcoxwell.com					
JD Abrams LP 111 Congress Ave Suite 2400	Austin	TX	78701	512-322-4000	322-4018
Web: www.jdabrams.com					
JD Posillico Inc 1610 New Hwy	Farmingdale	NY	11735	631-249-1872	249-8124
Web: www.jdposillico.com					
Jensen Construction Co Inc PO Box 3345	Des Moines	IA	50316	515-266-5173	266-9857
JF Shea Construction Inc 655 Brea Canyon Rd	Walnut	CA	91789	909-594-9500	594-0935
TF: 800-755-7432 ■ *Web:* www.jfshea.com					
JF White Contracting Co 10 Burr St	Framingham	MA	01701	508-879-4700	558-0460*
**Fax Area Code:* 617 ■ *TF:* 866-539-4400 ■ *Web:* www.jfwhite.com					
JH Lynch & Sons Inc 50 Lynch Pl	Cumberland	RI	02864	401-333-4300	333-2659
Web: www.jhlynch.com					
JLB Contracting LP 7151 Randol Mill Rd	Fort Worth	TX	76120	817-261-2991	261-3044
John Carlo Inc 45000 River Ridge Dr	Clinton Township	MI	48038	586-416-4500	226-5664
TF: 800-465-6234 ■ *Web:* www.carlocompanies.com					
John R Jurgensen Co 11641 Mosteller Rd	Cincinnati	OH	45241	513-771-0820	771-2678
TF: 800-686-9725 ■ *Web:* www.jrjnet.com					
Johnson Brothers Corp 5476 Lithia Pinecrest Rd	Lithia	FL	33547	813-685-5101	685-5939
Web: www.johnson-bros.com					
JR Hale Contracting Co Inc PO Box 25667	Albuquerque	NM	87125	505-345-6628	345-1145
Jurgensen John R Co 11641 Mosteller Rd	Cincinnati	OH	45241	513-771-0820	771-2678
TF: 800-686-9725 ■ *Web:* www.jrjnet.com					
K-Five Construction Corp 13769 Main St	Lemont	IL	60439	630-257-5600	257-6788
Web: www.k-five.net					
Kamminga & Roodvoets Inc 3435 Broadmoor Ave SE	Grand Rapids	MI	49512	616-949-0800	949-1894
TF: 800-632-9755					

Company	City	State	Zip	Phone	Fax
Kankakee Valley Construction Co Inc PO Box 767	Kankakee	IL	60901	815-937-8700	937-0402
Web: www.kvcci.com					
Keating PJ Co Inc 998 Reservoir Rd	Lunenburg	MA	01462	978-582-9931	582-7130
TF: 800-441-4119 ■ *Web:* www.pjkeating.com					
KF Jacobsen & Co PO Box 82245	Portland	OR	97282	503-239-5532	235-1350
Kiewit Construction Group Inc 1000 Kiewit Plaza	Omaha	NE	68131	402-342-2052	271-2829
Web: www.kiewit.com					
Kiska Construction Corp USA 10-34 44th Dr	Long Island City	NY	11101	718-943-0400	943-0401
Web: www.kiskagroup.com					
Knife River Corp 1150 W Century Ave	Bismarck	ND	58503	701-530-1400	530-1451
TF: 800-982-5339 ■ *Web:* www.kniferiver.com					
Kokosing Construction Co Inc 17531 Waterford Rd	Fredericktown	OH	43019	740-694-6315	694-1481
TF: 800-800-6315 ■ *Web:* www.kokosing.biz					
Koss Construction Co 5830 SW Drury Ln	Topeka	KS	66604	785-228-2928	228-2927
Web: www.kossconstruction.com					
Kraemer Edward & Sons Inc PO Box 220	Plain	WI	53577	608-546-2311	546-2130
Web: www.edkraemer.com					
Lacy LH Co Inc PO Box 541297	Dallas	TX	75354	214-357-0146	350-0662
TF: 800-280-2885 ■ *Web:* www.lhlacy.com					
Lake Erie Construction Co Inc 25 S Norwalk Rd	Norwalk	OH	44857	419-668-3302	668-3314
Lakeside Industries Inc PO Box 7016	Issaquah	WA	98027	425-313-2600	313-2620
Web: www.lakesideind.com					
Lambrecht TJ Construction Inc 10 Gougar Rd	Joliet	IL	60432	815-727-9211	727-6421
Web: www.tjlambrecht.com					
Lane Construction Co Inc 1 Indian Rd	Denville	NJ	07834	973-586-2700	586-2965
Web: www.thelanegroup.us					
Lane Construction Corp 965 E Main St	Meriden	CT	06450	203-235-3351	237-4260
Web: www.laneconstruct.com					
Las Vegas Paving Corp 4420 S Decatur Blvd	Las Vegas	NV	89103	702-251-5800	251-1968
Web: www.lasvegaspaving.com					
Lawrence Construction Co Inc 9002 N Moore Rd	Littleton	CO	80125	303-791-5642	791-5647
LC Whitford Co Inc PO Box 663	Wellsville	NY	14895	585-593-3601	593-1876
Web: www.lcwhitford.com					
Lee Construction Co PO Box 7667	Charlotte	NC	28241	704-588-5272	588-1535
TF: 800-849-5272 ■ *Web:* www.leecarolinas.com					
LeGrand Johnson Construction Co Inc PO Box 248	Logan	UT	84323	435-752-2000	752-2968
TF: 800-286-6820					
Lehigh Asphalt Paving & Construction Co Inc PO Box 549	Tamaqua	PA	18252	570-668-4303	668-5910
LG Barcus & Sons Inc 1430 State Ave	Kansas City	KS	66102	913-621-1100	621-3288
TF: 800-255-0180 ■ *Web:* www.barcus.com					
LH Lacy Co PO Box 541297	Dallas	TX	75354	214-357-0146	350-0662
TF: 800-280-2885 ■ *Web:* www.lhlacy.com					
Lionmark Construction Cos 1620 Woodson Rd	Saint Louis	MO	63114	314-991-2180	991-9624
TF: 800-392-4295					
Lunda Construction Co Inc 620 Gebhardt Rd	Black River Falls	WI	54615	715-284-9491	284-9146
Web: www.lundaconstruction.com					
Lynch JH & Sons Inc 50 Lynch Pl	Cumberland	RI	02864	401-333-4300	333-2659
Web: www.jhlynch.com					
MA Mortenson Co 700 Meadow Ln N	Minneapolis	MN	55422	763-522-2100	287-5430
Web: www.mortenson.com					
Madden Contracting Co Inc PO Box 856	Minden	LA	71058	318-377-0928	377-9065
Manatt's Inc 1775 Old Six Rd	Brooklyn	IA	52211	641-522-9206	522-5594
TF: 800-877-1258 ■ *Web:* www.manatts.com					
Markham Contracting Co Inc 22820 N 19th Ave	Phoenix	AZ	85027	623-869-9100	869-9400
Web: www.markhamcontracting.com					
Mashuda Corp 21101 Rt 19	Cranberry Township	PA	16066	724-452-8330	452-5272
Massman Construction Co					
8901 State Line Rd Suite 240 PO Box 8458	Kansas City	MO	64114	816-523-1000	333-2109
Web: www.massman.net					
Mathy Construction Co Inc 920 10th Ave N	Onalaska	WI	54650	608-783-6411	783-4311
Matthews CW Contracting Co Inc 1600 Kenview Dr	Marietta	GA	30061	770-422-7520	422-1068
Web: www.cwmatthews.com					
MCC Inc PO Box 1137	Appleton	WI	54912	920-749-3360	749-3384
TF: 800-236-8132 ■ *Web:* www.mcc-inc.bz					
McCarthy Building Cos Inc 1341 N Rock Hill Rd	Saint Louis	MO	63124	314-968-3300	968-4642*
**Fax:* Mktg ■ *Web:* www.mccarthy.com					
McCarthy Improvement Co Inc 5401 Victoria Ave	Davenport	IA	52807	563-359-0321	344-3740
TF: 800-728-0322 ■ *Web:* www.mccarthy-improvement.com					
McCrossan CS Inc PO Box 1240	Maple Grove	MN	55311	763-425-4167	425-1255
MCM Construction Inc 6413 32nd St	North Highlands	CA	95660	916-334-1221	334-0562
Web: www.mcmconstructioninc.com					
McMurry Ready Mix Co 5684 Old W Yellowstone Hwy	Casper	WY	82604	307-473-9581	235-0144
Web: www.mcmurryreadymix.com					
Meadow Valley Corp 4002 E Thomas	Phoenix	AZ	85018	602-437-5400	437-1681
NASDAQ: MVCO ■ *TF:* 800-428-4119 ■ *Web:* www.meadowvalley.com					
Merco Inc 1117 Rt 31 S	Lebanon	NJ	08833	908-730-8622	730-6472
Web: www.mercoinc.com					
Merlino Gary Construction Co Inc 9125 10th Ave S	Seattle	WA	98108	206-762-9125	763-4178
Meyer CA Paving & Construction Co					
807 S Orlando Ave Suite N	Winter Park	FL	32789	407-647-9900	647-9811
Mica Corp 5750 N Riverside Dr	Fort Worth	TX	76137	817-847-6121	847-6831
Web: www.micacorporation.com					
Michael Baker Corp 100 Airsite Dr Airsite Business Pk	Moon Township	PA	15108	412-269-6300	375-3977
AMEX: BKR ■ *TF:* 800-553-1153 ■ *Web:* www.mbakercorp.com					
Michigan Paving & Materials Co 2575 S Haggerty Rd Suite 100	Canton	MI	48188	734-397-2050	397-8480
Web: www.thompsonmccully.com					
Milestone Contractors LP 3410 S-650 E	Columbus	IN	47203	812-579-5248	579-6703
Web: www.milestonelp.com					
Modern Continental Construction Co 175 Purchase St	Boston	MA	02110	617-864-6300	864-8766
TF: 800-833-6307 ■ *Web:* www.moderncontinental.com					
Morrissey James D Inc 9119 Frankford Ave	Philadelphia	PA	19114	215-333-8000	624-3308
Web: www.jdm-inc.com					
Mortenson MA Co 700 Meadow Ln N	Minneapolis	MN	55422	763-522-2100	287-5430
Web: www.mortenson.com					
Mountain States Constructors Inc					
3601 Pan American Rd NE	Albuquerque	NM	87107	505-292-0108	292-5311
Myers Allan A Inc PO Box 98	Worcester	PA	19490	610-584-6020	584-4280*
**Fax:* Hum Res ■ *Web:* www.americaninfrastructure.com					
Myers CC Inc 3286 Fitzgerald Rd	Rancho Cordova	CA	95742	916-635-9370	635-8961
Web: www.ccmyers.com					
NAB Construction Corp 112-20 14th Ave	College Point	NY	11356	718-762-0001	961-3789
Web: www.nabconstruction.com					
National Engineering & Contracting Co Inc					
8150 E Dow Cir Suite 200	Strongsville	OH	44136	440-243-8533	243-8561
Web: www.natlengr.com					
Nelson David Construction Co 3483 Alternate 19	Palm Harbor	FL	34683	727-784-7624	786-8894
Web: www.nelson-construction.com					
Nesbitt Contracting Co Inc 100 S Price Rd	Tempe	AZ	85281	480-894-2831	423-7680
Web: www.nesbitts.com					
Newell Roadbuilders Inc 13266 US Hwy 31	Hope Hull	AL	36043	334-288-2702	288-2721
Northern Improvement Co 4000 12th Ave NW	Fargo	ND	58102	701-277-1225	277-1516
Web: www.northernimprovement.com					
O & G Industries Inc 112 Wall St	Torrington	CT	06790	860-489-9261	496-4286
Web: www.ogindustries.com					
Oakgrove Construction Inc PO Box 103	Elma	NY	14059	716-652-2200	655-3919
Web: www.oakgroveconst.com					
Odebrecht Construction Inc 201 Alhambra Cir Suite 1400	Coral Gables	FL	33134	305-341-8800	569-1500
Web: www.odebrecht.com.br					
Overstreet Paving Inc 17728 US Hwy 41	Spring Hill	FL	34610	352-796-1631	799-6435
TF: 800-741-1631					
P Flanigan & Sons Inc 2444 Loch Raven Rd	Baltimore	MD	21218	410-467-5900	467-3127
Web: www.pflanigan.com					
Parson Jack B Cos 2350 S 1900 West	Ogden	UT	84401	801-731-1111	731-8800
TF: 888-672-7766 ■ *Web:* www.jbparson.com					
Parsons Corp 100 W Walnut St	Pasadena	CA	91124	626-440-2000	440-2630
TF: 800-883-7300 ■ *Web:* www.parsons.com					
Pavex Inc 4400 Gettysburg Rd	Camp Hill	PA	17011	717-761-1502	761-0329
PCL Enterprises Inc 2000 S Colorado Blvd Tower 2 Suite 2-500	Denver	CO	80222	303-365-6500	365-6515
Web: www.pcl.com					
Peckham Industries Inc 20 Haarlem Ave	White Plains	NY	10603	914-949-2000	949-2075
Web: www.peckham.com					
Perini Corp 73 Mt Wayte Ave	Framingham	MA	01701	508-628-2000	
NYSE: PCR ■ *Web:* www.perini.com					
Perry Engineering Co Inc 1945 Millwood Pike	Winchester	VA	22602	540-667-4310	667-7618
TF: 800-272-4310 ■ *Web:* www.perryeng.com					
Peterson Contractors Inc 104 Blackhawk St PO Box A	Reinbeck	IA	50669	319-345-2713	345-2991
Web: www.petersoncontractors.com					
Petracca & Sons Inc 1802 Petracca Pl	Whitestone	NY	11357	718-746-8000	321-8476
Petricca Industries Inc 550 Cheshire Rd	Pittsfield	MA	01201	413-442-6926	499-9930
Pike Industries Inc 3 Eastgate Park Rd	Belmont	NH	03220	603-527-5100	527-5101
TF: 800-283-7453 ■ *Web:* www.pikeindustries.com					
PJ Keating Co 998 Reservoir Rd	Lunenburg	MA	01462	978-582-9931	582-7130
TF: 800-441-4119 ■ *Web:* www.pjkeating.com					
PKF-Mark III Inc 170 Pheasant Run	Newtown	PA	18940	215-968-5041	968-3829
Web: www.pkfmarkiii.com					
Plote Inc 1100 Brandt Dr	Hoffman Estates	IL	60192	847-695-9300	695-9317
Web: www.plote.com					
Posillico JD Inc 1610 New Hwy	Farmingdale	NY	11735	631-249-1872	249-8124
Web: www.jdposillico.com					
Pratt Guy Inc 608 Union Ave	Holtsville	NY	11742	631-289-6100	289-6119
Prince Contracting Co Inc 5411 Willis Rd	Palmetto	FL	34221	941-722-7707	722-4641
Web: www.princeinc.com					
Professional Construction Services Inc PO Box 2005	Prairieville	LA	70769	225-744-4016	744-4938
TF: 800-562-4318 ■ *Web:* www.professionalconstruction.com					
Progressive Contractors Inc 14123 42nd St NE	Saint Michael	MN	55376	763-497-6100	497-6101
TF: 888-549-1820 ■ *Web:* www.progressivecontractors.com					
Pulice Construction Inc 2033 W Mountain View Rd	Phoenix	AZ	85021	602-944-2241	870-3395
Web: www.pulice.com					
Rados Steve P Inc 2002 E McFadden Ave Suite 200	Santa Ana	CA	92705	714-835-4612	835-2186
Web: www.radoscompanies.com					
Ranger Construction Industries Inc					
101 Sansbury's Way	West Palm Beach	FL	33411	561-793-9400	790-4332
TF: 800-969-9402 ■ *Web:* www.rangerconstruction.com					
Rasmussen CA Inc 2320 Shasta Way Suite F	Simi Valley	CA	93065	805-581-2275	581-2265
TF: 800-479-2888					
Ray Bell Construction Co Inc PO Box 363	Brentwood	TN	37024	615-373-4343	373-9224
Web: www.raybellconstruction.com					
Rea Contracting LLC 6135 Park South Dr Suite 400	Charlotte	NC	28210	704-553-6500	553-6599
Web: www.reaconst.com					
Reeves Construction Co Inc 4931 Riverside Dr Bldg 200 Box 13	Macon	GA	31210	478-474-9092	474-9192
Web: www.reevescc.com					
Reliable Contracting Co Inc 1 Church View Rd	Millersville	MD	21108	410-987-0313	987-8020
Web: www.reliablecontracting.com					
Republic Contracting Corp PO Box 9167	Columbia	SC	29290	803-783-4920	783-1623
Richard F Kline Inc 7700 Grove Rd	Frederick	MD	21704	301-662-8211	662-0041
Web: www.rfkline.com					
Rieth-Riley Construction Co Inc PO Box 477	Goshen	IN	46527	574-875-5183	875-8405
Web: www.rieth-riley.com					
Rifenburg Construction Inc 159 Brick Church Rd	Troy	NY	12180	518-279-3265	279-4260
Web: www.rifenburg.com					
Rockford Blacktop Construction Co Inc 5290 Nimitz Rd	Loves Park	IL	61111	815-654-4700	654-4736
Web: www.rockfordblacktop.com					
Rogers Group Inc 421 Great Circle Rd	Nashville	TN	37228	615-242-0585	
Web: www.rogersgroupinc.com					
Royal Contracting Co Ltd 677 Ahua St	Honolulu	HI	96819	808-839-9006	839-7571
Web: www.royalcontracting.com					
RS Audley Inc 609 Rt 3A	Bow	NH	03304	603-224-7724	225-7614
Web: www.audleyconstruction.com					
Ruhlin Co Inc PO Box 190	Sharon Center	OH	44274	330-239-2800	239-1828
Web: www.ruhlin.com					
Sargent Corp 378 Bennoch Rd	Stillwater	ME	04489	207-827-4435	827-6150
TF: 800-533-1812 ■ *Web:* www.sargent-corp.com					
Schiavone Construction Co Inc					
150 Meadowlands Pkwy 3rd Fl	Secaucus	NJ	07094	201-867-5070	866-6132
Web: www.schiavoneconstruction.com					
Scott Construction Inc PO Box 340	Lake Delton	WI	53940	608-254-2555	254-2249
TF: 800-843-1556 ■ *Web:* www.scottconstruct.com					
Scruggs Co Inc PO Box 2065	Valdosta	GA	31604	229-242-2388	242-7109
TF: 800-230-7263					
Shelly Co 80 Park Dr	Thornville	OH	43076	740-246-6315	246-4715
Web: www.shellyco.com					
Shepherd Construction Co Inc 1800 Briarcliff Rd NE	Atlanta	GA	30329	404-325-9350	633-5585
TF: 800-282-0806					
Sherwood Construction Co Inc 3219 W May St	Wichita	KS	67213	316-943-0211	943-3772
TF: 800-852-6038					
Shirley Contracting Corp 8435 Backlick Rd	Lorton	VA	22079	703-550-8100	550-7897
Web: www.shirleycontracting.com					
Sioux Falls Construction Co Inc PO Drawer F	Sioux Falls	SD	57101	605-336-1640	334-9342
TF: 800-888-1640 ■ *Web:* www.sfconst.com					
Skanska USA Civil Inc 1995 Aqua Mansa Rd	Riverside	CA	92509	951-684-5360	684-1644
TF: 800-222-5360 ■ *Web:* www.usacivil.skanska.com					
Skanska USA Inc 16-16 Whitestone Expy	Whitestone	NY	11357	718-767-2600	767-2663
Web: www.skanska.com					
Sletten Construction Co Inc 1000 25th St N	Great Falls	MT	59401	406-761-7920	761-0923
Web: www.slettencompanies.com					
Sloan Construction Co Inc 250 Plemmons Rd	Duncan	SC	29334	864-416-0200	416-0201
Web: www.sloan-construction.com					
Staker & Parson Cos 2350 S 1900 W	Ogden	UT	84401	801-731-1111	731-8800
TF: 800-748-4100 ■ *Web:* www.stakerparson.com					
Standard Concrete Products PO Box 1360	Columbus	GA	31902	706-322-3274	576-2669
Web: www.standardconcrete.net					
Steve P Rados Inc 2002 E McFadden Ave Suite 200	Santa Ana	CA	92705	714-835-4612	835-2186
Web: www.radoscompanies.com					
Suburban Grading & Utilities Inc 1190 Harmony Rd	Norfolk	VA	23502	757-461-1800	461-0989
Web: www.suburbangrading.com					
Sully-Miller Contracting Co Inc					
1100 E Orangethorpe Ave Suite 200	Anaheim	CA	92801	714-578-9600	578-2850*
**Fax:* Hum Res ■ *TF:* 800-431-9842					
Summers-Taylor Inc 300 W Elk Ave	Elizabethton	TN	37643	423-543-3181	543-6189
Sundt Construction Inc 4101 E Irvington Rd	Tucson	AZ	85714	520-748-7555	750-6266*
**Fax:* Mktg ■ *TF:* 800-467-5544 ■ *Web:* www.sundt.com					
Superior Construction Co Inc 2045 E Dunes Hwy	Gary	IN	46402	219-886-3728	885-4328
Web: www.superior-construction.com					

Highway, Street, Bridge, Tunnel Construction (Cont'd)

Company	City	State	Zip	Phone	Fax
Teichert A & Son Inc 3500 American River Dr *TF:* 888-554-5627 ■ *Web:* www.teichert.com	Sacramento	CA	95864	916-484-3011	484-6506
Tidewater Skanska Inc PO Box 57 *TF:* 877-263-1119 ■ *Web:* www.usacivil.skanska.com	Norfolk	VA	23501	757-420-4140	420-3551
TJ Lambrecht Construction Inc 10 Gougar Rd *Web:* www.tjlambrecht.com	Joliet	IL	60432	815-727-9211	727-6421
Tony Angelo Cement Construction Co 46850 Grand River Ave *Web:* www.tonyangelo.com	Novi	MI	48374	248-344-4000	344-4048
Traylor Brothers Inc 835 N Congress Ave *Web:* www.traylor.com	Evansville	IN	47715	812-477-1542	474-3223
Trumbull Corp 1020 Lebanon Rd *Web:* www.trumbullcorp.com	West Mifflin	PA	15122	412-462-9300	462-1074
United Contractors Midwest Inc PO Box 13420 *Web:* www.ucm.biz	Springfield	IL	62791	217-546-6192	546-1904
Utility Contractors Inc PO Box 2079 *TF:* 888-766-2576 ■ *Web:* www.ucict.com	Wichita	KS	67201	316-265-9506	265-8314
Vecellio & Grogan Inc 2251 Robert C Byrd Dr *TF:* 800-255-6575 ■ *Web:* www.vecelliogrogan.com	Beckley	WV	25802	304-252-6575	252-4131
Viasys Services Inc 2944 Drane Field Rd *Web:* www.viasyscorp.com	Lakeland	FL	33811	863-607-9988	607-9955
WA Ellis Construction Co Inc PO Box 1095	Independence	MO	64051	816-257-2300	257-2450
Wagman GA & FC Inc 3290 Susquehanna Trail N *Web:* www.wagman.com	York	PA	17406	717-764-8521	764-2799
Walsh Group Inc 929 W Adams St *TF:* 800-759-2574 ■ *Web:* www.walshgroup.com	Chicago	IL	60607	312-563-5400	563-5466
Washington Corp PO Box 16630 *TF:* 800-832-7329 ■ *Web:* www.washcorp.com	Missoula	MT	59808	406-523-1300	523-1399
Washington Group International Inc PO Box 73 *NASDAQ: WGII* ■ **Fax:* Mktg ■ *Web:* www.wgint.com	Boise	ID	83729	208-386-5000	386-5658*
Waterland Trucking Service PO Box 9320335	Wixom	MI	48393	248-349-1582	349-5385
WE Blain & Sons Inc PO Box 1208	Mount Olive	MS	39119	601-797-4551	797-4777
Webber Development Inc 44710 Morley Dr	Clinton Township	MI	48036	586-465-3800	465-3808
WG Yates & Sons Construction Co Inc 1 Gulley Ave PO Box 456 *Web:* www.wgyates.com	Philadelphia	MS	39350	601-656-5411	656-8958
Whitcomb Frank W Construction Corp PO Box 1000 *TF:* 800-238-7283	Walpole	NH	03608	603-445-5555	445-5307
White Oak Corp 7 W Main St	Plainville	CT	06062	860-747-1627	793-2119
Whitford LC Co Inc PO Box 663 *Web:* www.lcwhitford.com	Wellsville	NY	14895	585-593-3601	593-1876
Wilder Construction Co Inc 1525 E Marine View Dr *TF:* 800-377-0954 ■ *Web:* www.wilderconstruction.com	Everett	WA	98201	425-551-3100	551-3116
Williams Brothers Construction Co Inc 3800 Milam St *Web:* www.wbctx.com	Houston	TX	77006	713-522-9821	522-9927
Windsor Service 2415 Kutztown Rd	Reading	PA	19605	610-929-0716	929-4825
Winzinger Inc 1704 Marne Hwy PO Box 537 *Web:* www.winzinger.com	Hainesport	NJ	08036	609-267-8600	267-4079
WM Brode Co 100 Elizabeth St PO Box 299 *TF:* 800-848-9217 ■ *Web:* www.wmbrode.com	Newcomerstown	OH	43832	740-498-5121	498-8553
Woodworth & Co Inc 1200 E 'D' St *Web:* www.woodworthandcompany.com	Tacoma	WA	98421	253-383-3585	572-8648
Word Dean Co Ltd 1245 River Rd PO Box 310330 *TF:* 800-683-3926 ■ *Web:* www.deanword.com	New Braunfels	TX	78131	830-625-2365	606-5008
Yantis Co PO Box 17045 *Web:* www.yantiscompany.com	San Antonio	TX	78217	210-655-3780	655-8526
Yates WG & Sons Construction Co 1 Gulley Ave PO Box 456 *Web:* www.wgyates.com	Philadelphia	MS	39350	601-656-5411	656-8958
Yonkers Contracting Co Inc 969 Midland Ave *Web:* www.ycc969midland.com	Yonkers	NY	10704	914-965-1500	378-8885
Zachry Construction Corp 527 Logwood St *Web:* www.zachry.com	San Antonio	TX	78221	210-475-8000	475-8060

191-5 Marine Construction

Company	City	State	Zip	Phone	Fax
Andrie Inc 561 E Western Ave *Web:* www.andrie.com	Muskegon	MI	49442	231-728-2226	726-6747
Atlantic Meeco Inc 1501 E Gene Stipe Blvd *TF:* 800-627-4621 ■ *Web:* www.atlantic-meeco.com	McAlester	OK	74501	918-423-6833	423-3215
Bancroft Construction Co 44 Bancroft Mills *Web:* www.bancroftconstruction.com	Wilmington	DE	19806	302-655-3434	655-4599
Bellingham Marine Industries Inc 1001 C St *TF:* 800-733-5679 ■ *Web:* www.bellingham-marine.com	Bellingham	WA	98225	360-676-2800	734-2417
Choctaw Transportation Co Inc PO Box 585	Dyersburg	TN	38025	731-285-4664	285-4668
Civil Constructors Inc 2283 Rt 20 E *Web:* www.helmgroup.com	Freeport	IL	61032	815-235-2200	235-2219
Corey Delta Inc 610 Industrial Way PO box 637 *TF:* 800-707-2260 ■ *Web:* www.coreydelta.com	Benicia	CA	94510	707-747-7500	745-5619
DeSilva Gates Construction Inc 11555 Dublin Blvd *Web:* www.desilvagates.com	Dublin	CA	94568	925-829-9220	803-4268
Frontier-Kemper Constructors Inc 1695 Allen Rd *Web:* www.frontierkemper.com	Evansville	IN	47710	812-426-2741	428-0337
General Construction Co 19472 Powder Hill Pl *Web:* www.generalconstructionco.com	Poulsbo	WA	98370	360-779-3200	779-3132
Granite Construction Inc PO Box 50085 *NYSE: GVA* ■ *Web:* www.graniteconstruction.com	Watsonville	CA	95077	831-724-1011	722-9657
Great Lakes Dredge & Dock Co 2122 York Rd Suite 200 *TF:* 800-323-7100 ■ *Web:* www.gldd.com	Oak Brook	IL	60523	630-574-3000	574-2981
Hawaiian Dredging & Construction Co 201 Merchant St *Web:* www.hdcc.com	Honolulu	HI	96813	808-735-3211	735-7416
Horizon Offshore Inc 2500 Citywest Blvd Suite 2200 *TF:* 877-361-2600 ■ *Web:* www.horizonoffshore.com	Houston	TX	77042	713-361-2600	361-2690
JR Filanc Construction Co Inc 740 N Andreasen Dr *TF:* 877-225-5428 ■ *Web:* www.filanc.com	Escondido	CA	92029	760-941-7130	941-3969
Kiewit Construction Group Inc 1000 Kiewit Plaza *Web:* www.kiewit.com	Omaha	NE	68131	402-342-2052	271-2829
King Fisher Marine Services Inc 159 Hwy 316 PO Box 108 *TF:* 888-553-6751 ■ *Web:* www.orionmarinegroup.com	Port Lavaca	TX	77979	361-552-6751	552-1200
Lane Construction Corp 965 E Main St *Web:* www.laneconstruct.com	Meriden	CT	06450	203-235-3351	237-4260
Luhr Brothers Inc 250 W Sand Bank Rd *Web:* www.luhr.com	Columbia	IL	62236	618-281-4106	281-4288
Manson Construction Co 5209 E Marginal Way S *TF:* 800-262-6766 ■ *Web:* www.mansonconstruction.com	Seattle	WA	98134	206-762-0850	764-8595
Massman Construction Co 8901 State Line Rd Suite 240 PO Box 8458 *Web:* www.massman.net	Kansas City	MO	64114	816-523-1000	333-2109
McDermott International Inc 757 N Eldridge Pkwy *NYSE: MDR* ■ *Web:* www.mcdermott.com	Houston	TX	77079	281-870-5000	870-5095
McLean Contracting Co 6700 McLean Way *Web:* www.mcleancont.com	Glen Burnie	MD	21060	410-553-6700	553-6718
Misener Marine Construction Inc 5600 W Commerce St *TF:* 866-211-9742 ■ *Web:* www.orionmarinegroup.com/misener.htm	Tampa	FL	33616	813-839-8441	831-7498
Modern Continental Construction Co 175 Purchase St *TF:* 800-833-6307 ■ *Web:* www.moderncontinental.com	Boston	MA	02110	617-864-6300	864-8766
Obayashi Construction Inc 420 E 3rd St Suite 906-D *Web:* www.ocac.com	Los Angeles	CA	90013	213-687-8700	687-3700
P Gioioso & Sons Inc 50 Sprague St *Web:* www.pgioioso.com	Hyde Park	MA	02136	617-364-5800	364-9462
Patton-Tully Transportation LLC 1242 N 2nd St *Web:* www.patton-tully.com	Memphis	TN	38107	901-576-1400	576-1486
PCL Enterprises Inc 2000 S Colorado Blvd Tower 2 Suite 2-500 *Web:* www.pcl.com	Denver	CO	80222	303-365-6500	365-6515
RCI Environmental Inc 1216 140th Ave PO Box 1730 *TF:* 800-848-3777 ■ *Web:* www.rci-group.com	Sumner	WA	98390	253-863-5300	859-5702
Steve P Rados Inc 2002 E McFadden Ave Suite 200 *Web:* www.radoscompanies.com	Santa Ana	CA	92705	714-835-4612	835-2186
Tidewater Skanska Inc PO Box 57 *TF:* 877-263-1119 ■ *Web:* www.usacivil.skanska.com	Norfolk	VA	23501	757-420-4140	420-3551
TL James & Co Inc 300 N Vienna St	Ruston	LA	71270	318-255-7912	255-3129
Washington Corp PO Box 16630 *TF:* 800-832-7329 ■ *Web:* www.washcorp.com	Missoula	MT	59808	406-523-1300	523-1399
Waterland Trucking Service PO Box 9320335	Wixom	MI	48393	248-349-1582	349-5385
Weeks Marine Inc 4 Commerce Dr *Web:* www.weeksmarine.com	Cranford	NJ	07016	908-272-4010	272-4740

191-6 Mining Construction

Company	City	State	Zip	Phone	Fax
AME Inc PO Box 909 *TF:* 800-849-7766 ■ *Web:* www.ameonline.com	Fort Mill	SC	29716	803-548-7766	548-7448
Frontier-Kemper Constructors Inc 1695 Allen Rd *Web:* www.frontierkemper.com	Evansville	IN	47710	812-426-2741	428-0337
Gunther-Nash Mining Construction Co 2 City Place Dr Suite 380 *TF:* 800-261-2611	Saint Louis	MO	63141	314-692-2611	692-4288
Kiewit Construction Group Inc 1000 Kiewit Plaza *Web:* www.kiewit.com	Omaha	NE	68131	402-342-2052	271-2829
Kokosing Construction Co Inc 17531 Waterford Rd *TF:* 800-800-6315 ■ *Web:* www.kokosing.biz	Fredericktown	OH	43019	740-694-6315	694-1481
Sundt Construction Inc 4101 E Irvington Rd **Fax:* Mktg ■ *TF:* 800-467-5544 ■ *Web:* www.sundt.com	Tucson	AZ	85714	520-748-7555	750-6266*
TIC - The Industrial Co 2211 Elk River Rd *TF:* 888-810-9367 ■ *Web:* www.tic-inc.com	Steamboat Springs	CO	80487	970-879-2561	879-2998

191-7 Plant Construction

Company	City	State	Zip	Phone	Fax
AECL (Atomic Energy of Canada Ltd) 2251 Speakman Dr *Web:* www.aecl.ca	Mississauga	ON	L5K1B2	905-823-9040	823-6120
Aker Kvaerner 3600 Briarpark Dr *TF:* 800-859-8691 ■ *Web:* www.akerkvaerner.com/Internet/default.htm	Houston	TX	77042	713-988-2002	772-4673
Amoroso SJ Construction Co Inc 390 Bridge Pkwy *Web:* www.sjamoroso.com	Redwood Shores	CA	94065	650-654-1900	654-9002
Angelo Iafrate Construction Co 26300 Sherwood Ave **Fax:* Hum Res ■ *Web:* www.iafrate.com	Warren	MI	48091	586-756-1070	756-0467*
Atomic Energy of Canada Ltd (AECL) 2251 Speakman Dr *Web:* www.aecl.ca	Mississauga	ON	L5K1B2	905-823-9040	823-6120
Bancroft Construction Co 44 Bancroft Mills *Web:* www.bancroftconstruction.com	Wilmington	DE	19806	302-655-3434	655-4599
Barton Malow Enterprises Inc 26500 American Dr *Web:* www.bmco.com	Southfield	MI	48034	248-351-4500	436-5001
BE & K Building Group 201 E McBee Ave Suite 400 *TF:* 800-388-2724 ■ *Web:* www.bekbuildinggroup.com	Greenville	SC	29601	864-250-5000	250-5037
Bechtel Corp 50 Beale St *Web:* www.bechtel.com	San Francisco	CA	94105	415-768-1234	768-9038
Bechtel North America 3000 Post Oak Blvd *Web:* www.bechtel.com	Houston	TX	77056	713-235-2000	960-9031
Bechtel Petroleum & Chemical 3000 Post Oak Blvd *Web:* www.bechtel.com	Houston	TX	77056	713-235-2000	235-4494
Big-D Construction Corp 404 W 400 South *TF:* 877-415-6009 ■ *Web:* www.big-d.com	Salt Lake City	UT	84101	801-415-6000	415-6900
Black & Veatch 8400 Ward Pkwy *Web:* www.bv.com	Kansas City	MO	64114	913-458-2000	458-3730
Bowen Engineering Corp 10315 Allisonville Rd *TF:* 800-377-2580 ■ *Web:* www.bowenengineering.com	Fishers	IN	46038	317-842-2616	841-4257
Brasfield & Gorrie LLC 3021 7th Ave S *TF:* 800-239-8017 ■ *Web:* www.brasfieldgorrie.com	Birmingham	AL	35233	205-328-4000	251-1304
Brinderson 3330 Harbor Blvd Suite 100 *Web:* www.brinderson.com	Costa Mesa	CA	92626	714-466-7100	466-7320
Burns & Roe Enterprises Inc 800 Kinderkamack Rd *Web:* www.roe.com	Oradell	NJ	07649	201-986-4800	
Butler Construction Co 6601 Executive Dr *Web:* www.bucon.com	Kansas City	MO	64120	816-245-6000	245-6099
Cajun Constructors Inc PO Box 104 **Fax:* Hum Res ■ *Web:* www.cajunusa.com	Baton Rouge	LA	70821	225-753-5857	751-9777*
CCC Group Inc 5797 Dietrich Rd *Web:* www.cccgroupinc.com	San Antonio	TX	78219	210-661-4251	662-1662
Chicago Bridge & Iron Co 14105 S Rt 59 *NYSE: CBI* ■ *TF:* 800-799-8443 ■ *Web:* www.cbi.com	Plainfield	IL	60544	815-439-6000	439-6010
Cianbro Corp PO Box 1000 *Web:* www.cianbro.com	Pittsfield	ME	04967	207-487-3311	679-2422
Ciminelli Louis P Construction Corp 369 Franklin St *Web:* www.lpciminelli.com	Buffalo	NY	14202	716-855-1200	854-6655
Cives Corp 1825 Old Alabama Rd Suite 200 *Web:* www.cives.com	Roswell	GA	30076	770-993-4424	998-2361
Civil Constructors Inc 2283 Rt 20 E *Web:* www.helmgroup.com	Freeport	IL	61032	815-235-2200	235-2219
Clark Construction Co 3535 Moores River Dr *Web:* www.clarkconstructionco.com	Lansing	MI	48911	517-372-0940	372-0668
Clark Construction Group LLC 7500 Old Georgetown Rd *TF:* 800-827-4422 ■ *Web:* www.clarkconstruction.com	Bethesda	MD	20814	301-272-8100	272-8414
Clayco Construction Co 2199 Innerbelt Business Ctr Dr *TF:* 888-429-3330 ■ *Web:* www.claycorp.com	Saint Louis	MO	63114	314-429-5100	429-3137
Congaree Construction Co Inc 1634 Pineview Rd PO Box 90446	Columbia	SC	29290	803-783-7812	783-7816
Day & Zimmermann Group Inc 1818 Market St *TF:* 800-523-0786 ■ *Web:* www.dayzim.com	Philadelphia	PA	19103	215-299-8000	299-8030
Devcon Construction Inc 690 Gibraltar Dr *Web:* www.devconconstruction.com	Milpitas	CA	95035	408-942-8200	262-2342
Dick Corp 1900 Rt 51 *TF:* 800-245-6577 ■ *Web:* www.dickcorp.com/dickcorp	Large	PA	15025	412-384-1000	384-1150
DPR Construction Inc 1450 Veterans Blvd **Fax:* Hum Res ■ *Web:* www.dprinc.com	Redwood City	CA	94063	650-474-1450	474-2571*
English Construction Co Inc 615 Church St *Web:* www.englishconst.com	Lynchburg	VA	24504	434-845-0301	845-0306

	City	State	Zip	Phone	Fax
FCI Construction Inc 3901 S Lamar Blvd Suite 200	Austin	TX	78704	512-486-3700	486-3801
Fluor Daniel Inc 1 Fluor Daniel Dr	Aliso Viejo	CA	92698	949-349-2000	349-2585
Web: www.fluor.com					
Forcum Lannom Contractors LLC 350 US Hwy 51 Bypass S	Dyersburg	TN	38024	731-285-6503	287-4701
Web: www.forcumlannom.com					
ForeRunner Corp 3900 S Wadsworth Blvd Suite 600	Lakewood	CO	80235	303-969-0223	696-0230
Web: www.forerunnercorp.com					
Foster Wheeler Constructors Inc					
53 Frontage Rd Perryville Corporate Park	Clinton	NJ	08809	908-730-4000	730-5315
Web: www.fwc.com					
Foster Wheeler Ltd 53 Frontage Rd Perryville Corporate Park	Clinton	NJ	08809	908-730-4000	730-5315*
NASDAQ: FWLT ■ **Fax:* Hum Res ■ *Web:* www.fwc.com					
Foster Wheeler North America Corp					
53 Frontage Rd Perryville Corporate Park	Clinton	NJ	08809	908-730-4000	730-5315
Web: www.fwc.com					
Fru-Con Construction Corp 15933 Clayton Rd	Ballwin	MO	63011	636-391-6700	391-4563
TF: 800-937-8266 ■ *Web:* www.fru-con.com					
Geupel DeMars Hagerman Inc 7930 Castleway Dr	Indianapolis	IN	46250	317-713-0632	713-0641
Web: www.hagermangc.com/geupel_demars_manage.htm					
Gilbane Building Co 3150 Brunswick Pike Suite 300	Lawrenceville	NJ	08648	609-671-4200	671-4255
Web: www.gilbaneco.com					
Gilbane Building Co 7 Jackson Walkway	Providence	RI	02903	401-456-5800	456-5936
Web: www.gilbaneco.com					
Gray James N Construction Co Inc 10 Quality St	Lexington	KY	40507	859-281-5000	252-5300
TF: 800-950-4729 ■ *Web:* www.jngray.com					
H & M Construction Co Inc 50 Security Dr	Jackson	TN	38305	731-664-6300	664-1358
Web: www.hmcompany.com					
Haskell Co 111 Riverside Ave	Jacksonville	FL	32202	904-791-4500	791-4699
TF: 800-733-4275 ■ *Web:* www.thehaskellco.com					
Hoffman Construction Corp 805 SW Broadway Suite 2100	Portland	OR	97205	503-221-8811	221-8934
Web: www.hoffmancorp.com					
Hunt Construction Group 2450 S Tibbs Ave	Indianapolis	IN	46241	317-227-7800	227-7810
TF: 800-223-6301 ■ *Web:* www.huntconstructiongroup.com					
Hunter Contracting Co 701 N Cooper Rd	Gilbert	AZ	85233	480-892-0521	892-4932
Web: www.huntercontracting.com					
Iafrate Angelo Construction Co 26300 Sherwood Ave	Warren	MI	48091	586-756-1070	756-0467*
**Fax:* Hum Res ■ *Web:* www.iafrate.com					
James N Gray Co 10 Quality St	Lexington	KY	40507	859-281-5000	252-5300
TF: 800-950-4729 ■ *Web:* www.jngray.com					
JF White Contracting Co 10 Burr St	Framingham	MA	01701	508-879-4700	558-0460*
**Fax Area Code:* 617 ■ *TF:* 866-539-4400 ■ *Web:* www.jfwhite.com					
Johnson Brothers Corp 5476 Lithia Pinecrest Rd	Lithia	FL	33547	813-685-5101	685-5939
Web: www.johnson-bros.com					
JR Roberts Corp 7745 Greenback Ln Suite 300	Citrus Heights	CA	95610	916-729-5600	729-5666
TF: 800-551-1534 ■ *Web:* www.jrroberts.com					
Kahn MB Construction Co Inc 101 Flintlake Rd	Columbia	SC	29223	803-736-2950	736-5833
Web: www.mbkahn.com					
Kiewit Construction Group Inc 1000 Kiewit Plaza	Omaha	NE	68131	402-342-2052	271-2829
Web: www.kiewit.com					
Kimmins Corp 1501 2nd Ave E	Tampa	FL	33605	813-248-3878	247-0183
Web: www.kimmins.com					
Koch Specialty Plant Services 12221 E Sam Houston Pkwy N	Houston	TX	77044	713-427-7700	427-7748
TF: 800-497-1789 ■ *Web:* www.kochservices.com					
Kokosing Construction Co Inc 17531 Waterford Rd	Fredericktown	OH	43019	740-694-6315	694-1481
TF: 800-800-6315 ■ *Web:* www.kokosing.biz					
Louis P Ciminelli Construction Corp 369 Franklin St	Buffalo	NY	14202	716-855-1200	854-6655
Web: www.lpciminelli.com					
MA Mortenson Co 700 Meadow Ln N	Minneapolis	MN	55422	763-522-2100	287-5430
Web: www.mortenson.com					
Martin-Harris Construction Co 3030 S Highland Dr	Las Vegas	NV	89109	702-385-5257	387-6934
Web: www.martinharris.com					
MB Kahn Construction Co Inc 101 Flintlake Rd	Columbia	SC	29223	803-736-2950	736-5833
Web: www.mbkahn.com					
MECS Inc 14522 S Outer 40 Rd	Chesterfield	MO	63017	314-275-5700	275-5701
Web: www.mecsglobal.com					
Modern Continental Construction Co 175 Purchase St	Boston	MA	02110	617-864-6300	864-8766
TF: 800-833-6307 ■ *Web:* www.moderncontinental.com					
Mortenson MA Co 700 Meadow Ln N	Minneapolis	MN	55422	763-522-2100	287-5430
Web: www.mortenson.com					
Mosser Group Inc 122 S Wilson Ave	Fremont	OH	43420	419-334-3801	332-1534
Web: www.mossergrp.com					
NAB Construction Corp 112-20 14th Ave	College Point	NY	11356	718-762-0001	961-3789
Web: www.nabconstruction.com					
Neenan Co 2020 E Prospect Rd Suite 100	Fort Collins	CO	80525	970-493-8747	493-5869
Web: www.neenan.com					
Northeast Remsco Construction Inc Rt 34 Bldg B	Farmingdale	NJ	07727	732-557-6100	736-8913
TF: 800-879-8204 ■ *Web:* www.northeastconstruction.org					
O & G Industries Inc 112 Wall St	Torrington	CT	06790	860-489-9261	496-4286
Web: www.ogindustries.com					
Obayashi Construction Inc 420 E 3rd St Suite 906-D	Los Angeles	CA	90013	213-687-8700	687-3700
Web: www.ocac.com					
O'Connor Constructors Inc 45 Industrial Dr	Canton	MA	02021	781-828-0271	828-8248
Parsons Corp 100 W Walnut St	Pasadena	CA	91124	626-440-2000	440-2630
TF: 800-883-7300 ■ *Web:* www.parsons.com					
PCL Enterprises Inc 2000 S Colorado Blvd Tower 2 Suite 2-500	Denver	CO	80222	303-365-6500	365-6515
Web: www.pcl.com					
Performance Contractors Inc 9901 Pecu Ln	Baton Rouge	LA	70810	225-751-4156	751-8409
Web: www.performance-br.com					
Pizzagalli Construction Co 50 Joy Dr	South Burlington	VT	05403	802-658-4100	651-1360
TF: 800-760-7607 ■ *Web:* www.pizzagalli.com					
PKF-Mark III Inc 170 Pheasant Run	Newtown	PA	18940	215-968-5041	968-3829
Web: www.pkfmarkiii.com					
Powell Construction Co Inc 3622 Bristol Hwy	Johnson City	TN	37601	423-282-0111	282-1541
RCI Environmental Inc 1216 140th Ave PO Box 1730	Sumner	WA	98390	253-863-5300	859-5702
TF: 800-848-3777 ■ *Web:* www.rci-group.com					
Ref-Chem LP PO Box 2588	Odessa	TX	79760	432-332-8531	332-3325
Web: www.ref-chem.com					
Roberts JR Corp 7745 Greenback Ln Suite 300	Citrus Heights	CA	95610	916-729-5600	729-5666
TF: 800-551-1534 ■ *Web:* www.jrroberts.com					
Rudolph & Sletten Inc 1600 Seaport Blvd Suite 350	Redwood City	CA	94063	650-216-3600	599-9030
Web: www.rsconstruction.com					
Rudolph/Libbe Inc 6494 Latcha Rd	Walbridge	OH	43465	419-241-5000	837-9373
Web: www.rlcos.com					
Sargent Corp 378 Bennoch Rd	Stillwater	ME	04489	207-827-4435	827-6150
TF: 800-533-1812 ■ *Web:* www.sargent-corp.com					
Shaw Stone & Webster Inc 100 Technology Center Dr	Stoughton	MA	02072	617-589-5111	589-2156
Shook National Corp 4977 Northcutt Pl	Dayton	OH	45414	937-276-6666	276-6675
TF: 800-664-1844 ■ *Web:* www.shookcorp.com					
SJ Amoroso Construction Co Inc 390 Bridge Pkwy	Redwood Shores	CA	94065	650-654-1900	654-9002
Web: www.sjamoroso.com					
Skanska USA Building Inc 1633 Littleton Rd	Parsippany	NJ	07054	973-334-5300	334-5376
Web: www.skanskausa.com					
Skanska USA Building Inc 516 Township Line Rd	Blue Bell	PA	19422	267-470-1000	470-1010
Web: www.skanskausa.com					
Skanska USA Inc 16-16 Whitestone Expy	Whitestone	NY	11357	718-767-2600	767-2663
Web: www.skanska.com					
T E Ibberson Co 828 5th St S	Hopkins	MN	55343	952-938-7007	939-0451
Web: www.ibberson.com					
T Moriarty & Son Inc 63 Creamer St	Brooklyn	NY	11231	718-858-4800	624-4059
Technip USA Corp 11700 Old Katy Rd Suite 150	Houston	TX	77079	281-870-1111	249-8899
Web: www.technip.com					
TIC - The Industrial Co 2211 Elk River Rd	Steamboat Springs	CO	80487	970-879-2561	879-2998
TF: 888-810-9367 ■ *Web:* www.tic-inc.com					
Todd & Sargent Inc 620 Arrasmith Trail	Ames	IA	50010	515-232-0442	232-0682
Web: www.tsargent.com					
Turner Industries Group LLC					
8687 United Plaza Blvd Suite 500	Baton Rouge	LA	70809	225-922-5050	922-5055*
**Fax:* Mail Rm ■ *TF:* 800-288-6503 ■ *Web:* www.turner-industries.com					
US Contractors Inc 622 Commerce St	Clute	TX	77531	979-265-7451	265-4229
TF: 800-897-9882 ■ *Web:* www.us-contractors.com					
Ventech Inc 1149 Ellsworth Dr	Pasadena	TX	77506	713-477-0201	477-2420
Web: www.ventech-eng.com					
Walbridge Aldinger Co 613 Abbott St	Detroit	MI	48226	313-963-8000	963-8129
Web: www.walbridge.com					
Walsh Group Inc 929 W Adams St	Chicago	IL	60607	312-563-5400	563-5466
TF: 800-759-2574 ■ *Web:* www.walshgroup.com					
WG Yates & Sons Construction Co Inc					
1 Gulley Ave PO Box 456	Philadelphia	MS	39350	601-656-5411	656-8958
Web: www.wgyates.com					
Whiting-Turner Contracting Co 300 E Joppa Rd 8th Fl	Baltimore	MD	21286	410-821-1100	337-5770
TF: 800-638-4279 ■ *Web:* www.whiting-turner.com					
Yates WG & Sons Construction Co					
1 Gulley Ave PO Box 456	Philadelphia	MS	39350	601-656-5411	656-8958
Web: www.wgyates.com					
Zachry Construction Corp 527 Logwood St	San Antonio	TX	78221	210-475-8000	475-8060
Web: www.zachry.com					

191-8 Railroad Construction

	City	State	Zip	Phone	Fax
Acme Construction Co Inc 7695 Bond St	Cleveland	OH	44139	440-232-7474	232-7477
TF: 800-938-2263					
Atlas Railroad Construction Co 1253 SR 519 PO Box 8	Eighty Four	PA	15330	724-228-4500	228-3183
TF: 800-245-4980 ■ *Web:* www.atlasrailroad.com					
Bechtel Corp 50 Beale St	San Francisco	CA	94105	415-768-1234	768-9038
Web: www.bechtel.com					
Marta Track Constructors Inc 4390 Imeson Rd	Jacksonville	FL	32219	888-250-5746	378-7298*
**Fax Area Code:* 904 ■ *TF:* 888-250-5746					
Nielsons Skanska Inc 22419 County Rd G PO Box 1660	Cortez	CO	81321	970-565-8000	565-0188
TF: 800-638-5545 ■ *Web:* www.usacivil.skanska.com					
Parsons Corp 100 W Walnut St	Pasadena	CA	91124	626-440-2000	440-2630
TF: 800-883-7300 ■ *Web:* www.parsons.com					
RailWorks Corp 5 Penn Plaza	New York	NY	10001	212-502-7900	
Web: www.railworks.com					
RW Summers Railroad Contractor Inc 3693 E Gandy Rd	Bartow	FL	33830	863-533-8107	533-8100
Web: www.rwsummers.net					
Smith William A Construction Co Inc 6060 Armour Dr	Houston	TX	77020	713-673-6208	672-9614
TF: 800-925-5011					
Snelson Co Inc 601 W State St	Sedro Woolley	WA	98284	360-856-6511	856-5816
TF: 800-624-6536 ■ *Web:* www.snelsonco.com					
Steve P Rados Inc 2002 E McFadden Ave Suite 200	Santa Ana	CA	92705	714-835-4612	835-2186
Web: www.radoscompanies.com					
Summers RW Railroad Contractor Inc 3693 E Gandy Rd	Bartow	FL	33830	863-533-8107	533-8100
Web: www.rwsummers.net					
Swanson Contracting Co 11701 S Mayfield Ave	Alsip	IL	60803	708-388-0623	388-9986
TF: 800-622-6850 ■ *Web:* www.swansoncontracting.com					
Trac-Work Inc 3801 I-45 PO Box 550	Ennis	TX	75120	972-875-6565	875-9552
Tutor-Saliba Corp 15901 Olden St	Sylmar	CA	91342	818-362-8391	367-5379
Web: www.tutorsaliba.com					
WE Yoder Inc 41 S Maple St	Kutztown	PA	19530	610-683-7383	683-8638
TF: 800-889-5149 ■ *Web:* www.weyoderinc.com					
William A Smith Construction Co Inc 6060 Armour Dr	Houston	TX	77020	713-673-6208	672-9614
TF: 800-925-5011					

191-9 Refinery (Petroleum or Oil) Construction

	City	State	Zip	Phone	Fax
ARB Inc 26000 Commercentre Dr	Lake Forest	CA	92630	949-598-9242	454-7190
TF: 800-622-2699 ■ *Web:* www.arbinc.com					
Austin Industrial Inc 8031 Airport Blvd	Houston	TX	77061	713-641-3400	641-2424
TF: 800-460-3402 ■ *Web:* www.austin-ind.com					
BE & K Inc PO Box 2332	Birmingham	AL	35201	205-969-3600	972-6300
Web: www.bek.com					
Bechtel Corp 50 Beale St	San Francisco	CA	94105	415-768-1234	768-9038
Web: www.bechtel.com					
Bechtel North America 3000 Post Oak Blvd	Houston	TX	77056	713-235-2000	960-9031
Web: www.bechtel.com					
Bechtel Petroleum & Chemical 3000 Post Oak Blvd	Houston	TX	77056	713-235-2000	235-4494
Web: www.bechtel.com					
Butler Construction Co 6601 Executive Dr	Kansas City	MO	64120	816-245-6000	245-6099
Web: www.bucon.com					
Fluor Daniel Inc 1 Fluor Daniel Dr	Aliso Viejo	CA	92698	949-349-2000	349-2585
Web: www.fluor.com					
Foster Wheeler Constructors Inc					
53 Frontage Rd Perryville Corporate Park	Clinton	NJ	08809	908-730-4000	730-5315
Web: www.fwc.com					
Foster Wheeler Ltd 53 Frontage Rd Perryville Corporate Park	Clinton	NJ	08809	908-730-4000	730-5315*
NASDAQ: FWLT ■ **Fax:* Hum Res ■ *Web:* www.fwc.com					
McDermott International Inc 757 N Eldridge Pkwy	Houston	TX	77079	281-870-5000	870-5095
NYSE: MDR ■ *Web:* www.mcdermott.com					
Miller & Lents Ltd 1100 Louisiana St 27th Fl	Houston	TX	77002	713-651-9455	654-9914
Web: www.millerandlents.com					
Oscar J Boldt Construction Co 2525 N Roemer Rd	Appleton	WI	54911	920-739-6321	739-4409
Web: www.theboldtcompany.com					
Parsons Corp 100 W Walnut St	Pasadena	CA	91124	626-440-2000	440-2630
TF: 800-883-7300 ■ *Web:* www.parsons.com					
Ref-Chem LP PO Box 2588	Odessa	TX	79760	432-332-8531	332-3325
Web: www.ref-chem.com					
Snelson Co Inc 601 W State St	Sedro Woolley	WA	98284	360-856-6511	856-5816
TF: 800-624-6536 ■ *Web:* www.snelsonco.com					
TIC - The Industrial Co 2211 Elk River Rd	Steamboat Springs	CO	80487	970-879-2561	879-2998
TF: 888-810-9367 ■ *Web:* www.tic-inc.com					
Turner Industries Group LLC					
8687 United Plaza Blvd Suite 500	Baton Rouge	LA	70809	225-922-5050	922-5055*
**Fax:* Mail Rm ■ *TF:* 800-288-6503 ■ *Web:* www.turner-industries.com					
Underground Construction Co Inc 5145 Industrial Way	Benicia	CA	94510	707-746-8800	746-1314
TF: 800-227-2314 ■ *Web:* www.undergrnd.com					
Zachry Construction Corp 527 Logwood St	San Antonio	TX	78221	210-475-8000	475-8060
Web: www.zachry.com					

191-10 Water & Sewer Lines, Pipelines, Power Lines Construction

Phone Fax

AFC Enterprises Inc 88-43 76th Ave. Glendale NY 11385 718-275-1100 275-4602
Affholder Inc 714 Spirit 40 Park Dr Chesterfield MO 63005 636-532-2622 537-2533
TF: 800-325-1159 ■ *Web:* www.insituform.com
Amzak International 12410 NW 39th St. Coral Springs FL 33065 954-323-0624 346-6226
Web: www.amzak.com
Angelo Iafrate Construction Co 26300 Sherwood Ave Warren MI 48091 586-756-1070 756-0467*
**Fax:* Hum Res ■ *Web:* www.iafrate.com
APAC Inc 900 Ashwood Pkwy Suite 700 Atlanta GA 30338 770-392-5300 392-5393
TF: 800-241-7074 ■ *Web:* www.apac.com
ARB Inc 26000 Commercentre Dr Lake Forest CA 92630 949-598-9242 454-7190
TF: 800-622-2699 ■ *Web:* www.arbinc.com
Arcon Construction Co Inc 5973 433 St PO Box 159 Harris MN 55032 651-674-4474 674-2027
Argonaut Constructors Inc 1236 Central Ave Santa Rosa CA 95401 707-542-4862 542-3210
Web: www.argonautconstructors.com
Arthur Brothers Inc 29 Vista Ave San Mateo CA 94403 650-345-3591 572-8522
Aubrey Silvey Enterprises Inc 371 Hamp Jones Rd Carrollton GA 30117 770-834-0738 834-1055
TF: 800-206-3815 ■ *Web:* www.silvey.com
B Frank Joy LLC 5355 Kilmer Pl Hyattsville MD 20781 301-779-9400 699-6013
TF: 800-992-3569 ■ *Web:* www.bfjoy.com
Balfour Beatty Inc 999 Peachtree St NE Suite 200 Atlanta GA 30309 404-875-0356 607-1784
Web: www.balfourbeatty.com
Bancker Construction Corp 218 Blydenburgh Rd Islandia NY 11749 631-582-8880 582-3698
Bancroft Construction Co 44 Bancroft Mills Wilmington DE 19806 302-655-3434 655-4599
Web: www.bancroftconstruction.com
Barbarossa & Sons Inc PO Box 367 Osseo MN 55369 763-425-4146 425-0797
Barnard Construction Co Inc PO Box 99 Bozeman MT 59771 406-586-1995 586-3530
Web: www.barnard-inc.com
Bechtel Corp 50 Beale St San Francisco CA 94105 415-768-1234 768-9038
Web: www.bechtel.com
Bechtel North America 3000 Post Oak Blvd Houston TX 77056 713-235-2000 960-9031
Web: www.bechtel.com
Bechtel Pipeline 3000 Post Oak Blvd Houston TX 77056 713-235-2000 235-3662
Web: www.bechtel.com
Bechtel Power Corp 5275 West View Dr Frederick MD 21703 301-228-6000 620-8586*
**Fax:* Mail Rm
Bechtel Telecommunications 5275 Westview Dr Frederick MD 21703 301-228-6000 228-2200
Web: www.bechtel.com
Berra JH Construction Co Inc 5091 New Baumgartner Rd Saint Louis MO 63129 314-487-5617 487-5817
Web: www.jhberra.com
BRB Contractors Inc PO Box 750940 Topeka KS 66675 785-232-1245 235-8045
Web: www.brbcontractors.com
Cajun Constructors Inc PO Box 104 Baton Rouge LA 70821 225-753-5857 751-9777*
**Fax:* Hum Res ■ *Web:* www.cajunusa.com
Callas Contractors Inc 10549 Downsville Pike Hagerstown MD 21740 301-739-8400 739-7065
Web: www.callascontractors.com
CERBCO Inc 1419 Forrest Dr Suite 209 Annapolis MD 21403 443-482-3374 263-2960*
**Fax Area Code:* 410
Cianbro Corp PO Box 1000 Pittsfield ME 04967 207-487-3311 679-2422
Web: www.cianbro.com
Cives Corp 1825 Old Alabama Rd Suite 200 Roswell GA 30076 770-993-4424 998-2361
Web: www.cives.com
Contractors Northwest Inc 3731 N Ramsey Rd Coeur d'Alene ID 83815 208-667-2456 667-6388
Web: www.contractorsnorthwest.com
Cruz EE & Co Inc 943 Holmdel Rd Holmdel NJ 07733 732-946-9700 946-7592
Web: www.eecruz.com
Cullum Construction Co Inc PO Box 550489 Dallas TX 75355 972-271-9333 271-4881
CW Wright Construction Co Inc PO Box 3810 Chester VA 23831 804-768-1054 768-6057
Dillard Smith Construction Co 4001 Industry Dr Chattanooga TN 37416 423-894-4336 490-2219
Web: www.dillardsmith.com
Eatherly Constructors Inc PO Box 756 Garden City KS 67846 620-276-6611 276-4351
Eby Corp PO Box 1679 Wichita KS 67201 316-268-3500 268-3664
Web: www.ebycorp.com
ECCO III Enterprises Inc 201 Saw Mill River Rd Yonkers NY 10701 914-963-3600 963-3989
EE Cruz & Co Inc 943 Holmdel Rd Holmdel NJ 07733 732-946-9700 946-7592
Web: www.eecruz.com
Elkins Constructors Inc 701 W Adams St Jacksonville FL 32204 904-353-6500 387-1303
Web: www.elkinsconstructors.com
Evans JC Construction Co Inc 8660 183 A Toll Rd Leander TX 78641 512-244-1400 244-1900
Web: www.jcevans.com
Facchina Construction Co Inc 102 Centennial St Suite 201 La Plata MD 20646 240-776-7000 776-7001
Web: www.facchina.com
FCI Constructors Inc PO Box 1767 Grand Junction CO 81502 970-434-9093 434-7583
Web: www.fciol.com
Filanc JR Construction Co Inc 740 N Andreasen Dr Escondido CA 92029 760-941-7130 941-3969
TF: 877-225-5428 ■ *Web:* www.filanc.com
Fishel Co 1810 Arlingate Ln Columbus OH 43228 614-274-8100 274-6794
TF: 800-347-4351 ■ *Web:* www.teamfishel.com
Flint Energy Services Inc 7633 E 63rd Pl Suite 500 Tulsa OK 74133 918-294-3030 307-8960
TF: 800-580-7641 ■ *Web:* www.flintenergy.com
Frontier-Kemper Constructors Inc 1695 Allen Rd Evansville IN 47710 812-426-2741 428-0337
Web: www.frontierkemper.com
Garney Cos Inc 1333 NW Vivion Rd Kansas City MO 64118 816-741-4600 741-4488
Web: www.garney.com
Gioioso P & Sons Inc 50 Sprague St Hyde Park MA 02136 617-364-5800 364-9462
Web: www.pgioioso.com
Global Industries Ltd PO Box 442 Sulphur LA 70664 337-583-5000 583-5100
NASDAQ: GLBL ■ *TF:* 800-525-3483 ■ *Web:* www.globalind.com
Granite Construction Inc PO Box 50085 Watsonville CA 95077 831-724-1011 722-9657
NYSE: GVA ■ *Web:* www.graniteconstruction.com
GSE Construction Co Inc 1020 Shannon Ct Livermore CA 94550 925-447-0292 447-0962
Web: www.gseconstruction.com
Hagerman Construction Corp PO Box 10690 Fort Wayne IN 46853 260-424-1470 422-3129
Web: www.hagermancorp.com
Hailey WL & Co Inc 2971 Kraft Dr Nashville TN 37204 615-255-3161 256-1316
Web: www.wlhailey.com
Hall Contracting Corp 6415 Lakeview Rd Charlotte NC 28269 704-598-0818 598-3855
TF: 800-741-2117 ■ *Web:* www.hallcontracting.com
Henkels & McCoy Inc 985 Jolly Rd Blue Bell PA 19422 215-283-7600 283-7659
TF: 800-523-2568 ■ *Web:* www.henkelsandmccoy.com
Hess Brothers Inc 400 Hartle St Sayreville NJ 08872 732-254-4395 238-0810
Hood Corp PO Box 5716 Norco CA 92860 951-520-4282 520-4385
Web: www.hoodcorp.com
Hubbard Construction Co 1936 Lee Rd 3rd Fl Winter Park FL 32789 407-645-5500 623-3865
TF: 800-476-1228 ■ *Web:* www.hubbard.com
Iafrate Angelo Construction Co 26300 Sherwood Ave Warren MI 48091 586-756-1070 756-0467*
**Fax:* Hum Res ■ *Web:* www.iafrate.com
Inco Inc PO Box 2705 Rocky Mount NC 27802 252-446-1174 977-3039
InfraSource Services Inc 100 W 6th St Suite 300 Media PA 19063 610-480-8000
NYSE: IFS ■ *Web:* www.infrasourceinc.com
Insituform Technologies Inc 17988 Edison Ave Chesterfield MO 63005 636-530-8000 519-8010
NASDAQ: INSU ■ *TF Cust Svc:* 800-234-2992 ■ *Web:* www.insituform.com
Irby Construction Co Inc 817 S State St Jackson MS 39201 601-709-4729 960-7231*
TF: 800-872-0615 ■ *Web:* www.irby.com
Irish Construction Inc 2641 River Ave Rosemead CA 91770 626-288-8530 573-5136
Web: www.irishteam.com

Phone Fax

James White Construction Co Inc 4156 Freedom Way Weirton WV 26062 304-748-8181 748-8183
Jay Dee Contractors Inc 38881 Schoolcraft Rd Livonia MI 48150 734-591-3400 464-6868
Web: www.jaydeecontr.com
JC Evans Construction Co Inc 8660 183 A Toll Rd Leander TX 78641 512-244-1400 244-1900
Web: www.jcevans.com
JF Shea Construction Inc 655 Brea Canyon Rd Walnut CA 91789 909-594-9500 594-0935
TF: 800-755-7432 ■ *Web:* www.jfshea.com
JF White Contracting Co 10 Burr St Framingham MA 01701 508-879-4700 558-0460*
**Fax Area Code:* 617 ■ *TF:* 866-539-4400 ■ *Web:* www.jfwhite.com
JH Berra Construction Co Inc 5091 New Baumgartner Rd Saint Louis MO 63129 314-487-5617 487-5817
Web: www.jhberra.com
John F Otto Inc 1717 2nd St Sacramento CA 95814 916-441-6870 441-6138
Web: www.ottoconstruction.com
Johnson Brothers Corp 5476 Lithia Pinecrest Rd Lithia FL 33547 813-685-5101 685-5939
Web: www.johnson-bros.com
Joy B Frank LLC 5355 Kilmer Pl Hyattsville MD 20781 301-779-9400 699-6013
TF: 800-992-3569 ■ *Web:* www.bfjoy.com
JR Filanc Construction Co Inc 740 N Andreasen Dr Escondido CA 92029 760-941-7130 941-3969
TF: 877-225-5428 ■ *Web:* www.filanc.com
Kankakee Valley Construction Co Inc PO Box 767 Kankakee IL 60901 815-937-8700 937-0402
Web: www.kvcci.com
Kearney Development Co Inc 5115 Joanne Kearney Blvd Tampa FL 33619 813-621-0855 620-0001
Web: www.kearneydev.com
Kiewit Construction Group Inc 1000 Kiewit Plaza Omaha NE 68131 402-342-2052 271-2829
Web: www.kiewit.com
Kimmins Contracting Corp 1501 2nd Ave Tampa FL 33605 813-248-3878 247-0183
Web: www.kimmins.com
Kiska Construction Corp USA 10-34 44th Dr Long Island City NY 11101 718-943-0400 943-0401
Web: www.kiskagroup.com
Koch Specialty Plant Services 12221 E Sam Houston Pkwy N Houston TX 77044 713-427-7700 427-7748
TF: 800-497-1789 ■ *Web:* www.kochservices.com
Lambrecht TJ Construction Inc 10 Gougar Rd Joliet IL 60432 815-727-9211 727-6421
Web: www.tjlambrecht.com
Landmark Structures LP 1665 Harmon Rd Fort Worth TX 76177 817-439-8888 439-9001
Web: www.ldmkusa.com
Lane Construction Corp 965 E Main St Meriden CT 06450 203-235-3351 237-4260
Web: www.laneconstruct.com
Laquila Construction Inc 1590 Troy Ave Brooklyn NY 11234 718-252-0126 421-4061
Latex Construction Co Inc PO Box 917 Conyers GA 30012 770-760-0820 760-0852
TF: 800-241-1101 ■ *Web:* www.latexconstruction.com
Loving TA Co Inc PO Box 919 Goldsboro NC 27533 919-734-8400 731-7538
Web: www.taloving.com
Lyles WM Co 1210 W Olive Ave Fresno CA 93728 559-441-1900 441-1290
Web: www.wmlyles.com
MasTec Energy Services Inc 209 Art Bryan Dr PO Box 1 Asheboro NC 27204 336-672-1244 672-3025
TF: 800-672-5853 ■ *Web:* www.mastec.com
MasTec Inc 800 Douglas Rd 12th Fl Coral Gables FL 33134 305-599-1800 599-1900
NYSE: MTZ ■ *Web:* www.mastec.com
McLean Contracting Co 6700 McLean Way Glen Burnie MD 21060 410-553-6700 553-6718
Web: www.mcleancont.com
Michels Corp 817 W Main St Brownsville WI 53006 920-583-3132 583-3429
Web: www.michels-usa.com
Miller Pipeline Corp 8850 Crawfordsville Rd Indianapolis IN 46234 317-293-0278 293-8502
TF: 800-428-3742 ■ *Web:* www.millerpipeline.com
Miron Construction Co Inc 1471 McMahon Dr Neenah WI 54956 920-969-7000 969-7393
Web: www.mironconst.com
New River Electrical Corp PO Box 70 Cloverdale VA 24077 540-966-1650 966-1699
Web: www.newriverelectrical.com
Northeast Remsco Construction Inc Rt 34 Bldg B Farmingdale NJ 07727 732-557-6100 736-8913
TF: 800-879-8204 ■ *Web:* www.northeastconstruction.org
Northern Pipeline Construction Co Inc
1 W Deer Valley Rd Suite 101 Phoenix AZ 85027 623-582-1235 582-6853
Web: www.nplcc.com
O'Brien & Gere Technical Services Inc PO Box 4873 Syracuse NY 13221 315-437-6400 463-7554
Web: www.obg.com
Otto John F Inc 1717 2nd St Sacramento CA 95814 916-441-6870 441-6138
Web: www.ottoconstruction.com
P Gioioso & Sons Inc 50 Sprague St Hyde Park MA 02136 617-364-5800 364-9462
Web: www.pgioioso.com
PCL Enterprises Inc 2000 S Colorado Blvd Tower 2 Suite 2-500 Denver CO 80222 303-365-6500 365-6515
Web: www.pcl.com
Penn Line Service Inc PO Box 462 Scottdale PA 15683 724-887-9110 887-0545
TF: 800-448-9110 ■ *Web:* www.pennline.com
Progressive Contractors Inc 14123 42nd St NE Saint Michael MN 55376 763-497-6100 497-6101
TF: 888-549-1820 ■ *Web:* www.progressivecontractors.com
Quanta Services Inc 1360 Post Oak Blvd Suite 2100 Houston TX 77056 713-629-7600 629-7676
NYSE: PWR ■ *Web:* www.quantaservices.com
R & L Brosamer Co Inc 1777 Oakland Blvd Suite 300 Walnut Creek CA 94591 925-837-5600 627-1700
Web: www.brosamer.com
Rados Steve P Inc 2002 E McFadden Ave Suite 200 Santa Ana CA 92705 714-835-4612 835-2186
Web: www.radoscompanies.com
RCI Environmental Inc 1216 140th Ave PO Box 1730 Sumner WA 98390 253-863-5300 859-5702
TF: 800-848-3777 ■ *Web:* www.rci-group.com
Reliable Contracting Co Inc 1 Church View Rd Millersville MD 21108 410-987-0313 987-8020
Web: www.reliablecontracting.com
Reynolds Inc 4520 N State Rd 37 Orleans IN 47452 812-865-3232 865-3075
TF: 888-891-8009 ■ *Web:* www.reynoldsinc.com
RH White Construction Co Inc 41 Central St Auburn MA 01501 508-832-3295 832-7084
TF: 800-922-8182 ■ *Web:* www.rhwhite.com
River City Construction LLC 101 Hoffer Ln East Peoria IL 61611 309-694-3120 435-2457
Web: www.rcclc.com
Rockford Blacktop Construction Co Inc 5290 Nimitz Rd Loves Park IL 61111 815-654-4700 654-4736
Web: www.rockfordblacktop.com
Shaw Constructors Inc 36443 Old Perkins Rd Prairieville LA 70769 225-673-4606 744-6202*
**Fax:* Hum Res
Sheehan Pipe Line Construction Co 2431 E 61st St Suite 700 Tulsa OK 74136 918-747-3471 747-9888
Web: www.sheehanpipeline.com
Siciliano Inc 3650 Winchester Rd Springfield IL 62707 217-585-1200 585-1211
Web: www.sicilianoinc.com
Sletten Construction Co Inc 1000 25th St N Great Falls MT 59401 406-761-7920 761-0923
Web: www.slettencompanies.com
Snelson Co Inc 601 W State St Sedro Woolley WA 98284 360-856-6511 856-5816
TF: 800-624-6536 ■ *Web:* www.snelsonco.com
Spiniello Cos 12 E Daniel Rd Fairfield NJ 07004 973-808-8383 808-9591
TF: 800-227-8384 ■ *Web:* www.spiniello.com
Stacy & Witbeck Inc 1320 Harbor Bay Pkwy Suite 240 Alameda CA 94502 510-748-1870 748-1205
Web: www.stacywitbeck.com
Steve P Rados Inc 2002 E McFadden Ave Suite 200 Santa Ana CA 92705 714-835-4612 835-2186
Web: www.radoscompanies.com
Suburban Grading & Utilities Inc 1190 Harmony Rd Norfolk VA 23502 757-461-1800 461-0989
Web: www.suburbangrading.com
Sumter Utilities Inc PO Box 579 Sumter SC 29151 803-469-8585 469-4600
TF: 800-678-8665 ■ *Web:* www.sumter-utilities.com
TA Loving Co Inc PO Box 919 Goldsboro NC 27533 919-734-8400 731-7538
Web: www.taloving.com
TJ Lambrecht Construction Inc 10 Gougar Rd Joliet IL 60432 815-727-9211 727-6421
Web: www.tjlambrecht.com

Phone | Fax

Underground Construction Co Inc 5145 Industrial Way ... Benicia CA 94510 707-746-8800 746-1314
TF: 800-227-2314 ■ *Web:* www.undergrnd.com
Utility Contractors Inc PO Box 2079 ... Wichita KS 67201 316-265-9506 265-8314
TF: 888-766-2576 ■ *Web:* www.ucict.com
Utility Services Inc 400 N 4th St ... Bismarck ND 58501 701-222-7900 222-7607
TF: 800-638-3278 ■
Web: www.montana-dakota.com/mdu_docs/company_profile/UTILITY_SERVICES.html
UTILX Corp PO Box 97009 ... Kent WA 98064 253-395-0200 395-1040
TF: 800-829-3039 ■ *Web:* www.utilx.com
Walbridge Aldinger Co 613 Abbott St ... Detroit MI 48226 313-963-8000 963-8129
Web: www.walbridge.com
Waterland Trucking Service PO Box 9320335 ... Wixom MI 48393 248-349-1582 349-5385
Welded Construction LP 26933 Eckel Rd ... Perrysburg OH 43551 419-874-3548 874-4883
TF: 800-874-3548 ■ *Web:* www.welded-construction.com
West Valley Construction Co Inc 580 McGlincey Ln ... Campbell CA 95008 408-371-5510 371-3604
TF: 800-588-5510 ■ *Web:* www.westvalleyconstruction.com
Wharton-Smith Inc PO Box 471028 ... Lake Monroe FL 32747 407-321-8410 323-1236
TF: 888-393-0068 ■ *Web:* www.whartonsmith.com
White James Construction Co Inc 4156 Freedom Way ... Weirton WV 26062 304-748-8181 748-8183
White RH Construction Co Inc 41 Central St ... Auburn MA 01501 508-832-3295 832-7084
TF: 800-922-8182 ■ *Web:* www.rhwhite.com
Whitesell-Green Inc 3881 N Palafox St ... Pensacola FL 32505 850-434-5311 434-5315
Web: www.whitesell-green.com
Willbros Engineers Inc 2087 E 71st St ... Tulsa OK 74136 918-496-0400 491-9436
TF: 800-434-8970 ■ *Web:* www.willbros.com
WL Hailey & Co Inc 2971 Kraft Dr ... Nashville TN 37204 615-255-3161 256-1316
Web: www.wlhailey.com
WM Lyles Co 1210 W Olive Ave ... Fresno CA 93728 559-441-1900 441-1290
Web: www.wmlyles.com
Wright CW Construction Co Inc PO Box 3810 ... Chester VA 23831 804-768-1054 768-6057
Yantis Co PO Box 17045 ... San Antonio TX 78217 210-655-3780 655-8526
Web: www.yantiscompany.com
Yukon Pacific Corp 1127 W 7th Ave ... Anchorage AK 99501 907-276-1550

192 CONSTRUCTION - SPECIAL TRADE CONTRACTORS

SEE ALSO Swimming Pools p. 2336

192-1 Building Equipment Installation or Erection

Phone | Fax

ACM Elevator Co 2293 S Mount Prospect Rd ... Des Plaines IL 60018 847-390-3720 390-3768
APi Group Inc Specialty Construction Services Group
2366 Rose Pl ... Saint Paul MN 55113 651-636-4320 636-0312
Web: www.apigroupinc.com/construction.html
Auch George W Co 735 S Paddock St PO Box 430719 ... Pontiac MI 48341 248-334-2000 334-3404
Web: www.auchconstruction.com
AWC Commercial Window Coverings Inc
825 W Williamson Way ... Fullerton CA 92832 714-879-3880 879-8419
TF: 800-252-2280 ■ *Web:* www.awc-cwc.com
Aycock LLC 8261 Derry St ... Hummelstown PA 17036 717-566-5066 566-5077
Web: www.aycockrigging.com
Baltimore Rigging Co Inc 7475 Lake Dr ... Baltimore MD 21237 410-866-6701 866-6807
TF: 800-626-2150 ■ *Web:* www.baltimorerigging.com
Bigge Crane & Rigging Co Inc
10700 Bigge St PO Box 1657 ... San Leandro CA 94577 510-638-8100 639-4053
TF: 888-337-2444 ■ *Web:* www.bigge.com
Chicago Elevator Co 3260 W Grand Ave ... Chicago IL 60651 773-227-0737 645-7581
Columbia Elevator Products Co Inc 175 N Main St ... Port Chester NY 10573 914-937-7100 937-9181
TF: 877-265-3538 ■ *Web:* www.columbiaelevator.com
Commercial Contracting Corp 4260 N Atlantic Blvd ... Auburn Hills MI 48326 248-209-0500 209-0501
TF: 800-521-4386 ■ *Web:* www.cccnetwork.com
Don R Fruchey Inc 5608 Old Maumee Rd ... Fort Wayne IN 46803 260-749-8502 749-6337
Web: www.donrfruchey.com
DW Nicholson Corp 24747 Clawiter Rd ... Hayward CA 94545 510-887-0900 783-9948
Web: www.dwnicholson.com
Elward Construction Co 680 Harlan St ... Lakewood CO 80214 303-239-6303 239-8719
TF: 800-933-5339 ■ *Web:* www.elward.com
Fenton Rigging & Contracting Inc 2150 Langdon Farm Rd ... Cincinnati OH 45237 513-631-5500 631-4361
Web: www.fentonrigging.com
Fruchey R Don Inc 5608 Old Maumee Rd ... Fort Wayne IN 46803 260-749-8502 749-6337
Web: www.donrfruchey.com
George W Auch Co 735 S Paddock St PO Box 430719 ... Pontiac MI 48341 248-334-2000 334-3404
Web: www.auchconstruction.com
Hite Crane & Rigging Inc 4323 E Broadway Ave ... Spokane WA 99212 509-535-7738 535-7730
Hoffman Corp 805 SW Broadway Suite 2100 ... Portland OR 97205 503-221-8811 221-8934
Web: www.hoffmancorp.com
KONE Inc 1 Kone Ct ... Moline IL 61265 309-764-6771 743-5474
TF: 800-334-9556 ■ *Web:* www.us.kone.com
Mainco Elevator Services Inc 5-25 51st Ave ... Long Island City NY 11101 718-786-3301 729-7640
TF: 800-464-6487 ■ *Web:* www.mainco-elevator.com
PS Marcato Elevator Co Inc 44-11 11th St ... Long Island City NY 11101 718-392-6400 392-6445
Web: www.psmarcato.com
Sand Steel Building Co 101 Browell St PO Box 129 ... Emerado ND 58228 701-594-4435 594-4438
Schindler Elevator Corp 20 Whippany Rd ... Morristown NJ 07960 973-397-6500 397-6485*
*Fax: Mail Rm ■ *TF:* 800-225-3123 ■ *Web:* www.us.schindler.com
SCI Global Structural Contours Inc PO Box 4970 ... Greenwich CT 06830 203-531-4400 531-4403
Web: www.sciglobal.com
Southern Elevator Co Inc 130 O'Connor St ... Greensboro NC 27416 336-274-2401 333-9928
TF: 800-373-0058 ■ *Web:* www.southernelevator.com
Thyssen Elevator Co 15141 E Whittier Blvd Suite 505 ... Whittier CA 90603 562-693-9491 693-0028
TF: 800-288-3538
W & H Systems Inc 120 Asia Pl ... Carlstadt NJ 07072 201-933-7840 933-2144
TF: 800-966-6993 ■ *Web:* www.whsystems.com
Wyatt Field Services Co 10810 W Little York St Suite 130-A ... Houston TX 77241 713-570-2000 937-1617
TF: 800-324-3000 ■ *Web:* www.wyattfieldservice.com

192-2 Carpentry & Flooring Contractors

Phone | Fax

ACMAT Corp 233 Main St ... New Britain CT 06050 860-229-9000 229-1111
Web: www.acmatcorp.com
Acousti Inc 1550 Southland Cir NW ... Atlanta GA 30318 404-355-1331 355-1338
Web: www.acoustiatlanta.com
Airtite Contractors Inc 343 Carol Ln ... Elmhurst IL 60128 630-530-9001 530-9034
Web: www.air-tite.net
Archadeck 2112 W Laburnum Ave Suite 100 ... Richmond VA 23227 804-353-6999 353-2364
TF: 800-722-4668 ■ *Web:* www.archadeck.com
Arvada Hardwood Floor Co 3301 Lewiston St ... Aurora CO 80011 303-343-9000 363-3699
Web: www.arvadahardwood.com
Bonitz Contracting Co Inc 645 Rosewood Dr ... Columbia SC 29201 803-799-0181 748-9223
TF: 800-452-7281 ■ *Web:* www.bonitz.com
Carpenter Contractors of America 941 SW 12th Ave ... Pompano Beach FL 33069 954-781-2660 786-9016
TF: 800-959-8805 ■ *Web:* www.carpentercontractors.com
Cincinnati Floor Co Inc 5162 Broerman Ave ... Cincinnati OH 45217 513-641-4500 482-4204
TF: 800-886-4501 ■ *Web:* www.cincifloor.com
Conklin Brothers of San Leandro Inc 2999 Teagarden St ... San Leandro CA 94577 510-357-1090 357-3554
Covington Flooring Co Inc 288-A Oxmore Ct ... Birmingham AL 35209 205-328-2330 328-2496
TF: 800-824-1229 ■ *Web:* www.covington.com
Dresser RL Inc 4100 Atlantic Ave ... Raleigh NC 27604 919-876-4141 876-4300
Web: www.rldresserinc.com
Frank Novak & Sons Inc 23940 Miles Rd ... Cleveland OH 44128 216-475-5440 475-2802
Hampshire John H Inc 320 W 24th St ... Baltimore MD 21211 410-366-8900 467-7391
TF: 800-638-0076 ■ *Web:* www.jhhampshire.com
Interior Construction Services Ltd 2930 Market St ... Saint Louis MO 63103 314-534-6664 534-6663
Web: www.ics-stl.com
John H Hampshire Inc 320 W 24th St ... Baltimore MD 21211 410-366-8900 467-7391
TF: 800-638-0076 ■ *Web:* www.jhhampshire.com
Kalman Floor Co Inc 1202 Bergen Pkwy Suite 110 ... Evergreen CO 80439 303-674-2290 674-1238
TF: 800-525-7840 ■ *Web:* www.kalmanfloor.com
Kesseli & Morse Co Inc 242 Canterbury St ... Worcester MA 01603 508-752-1901 753-7078
Web: www.kesseliandmorse.com
M & H Building Specialties Inc 3084 S Highland Dr Suite E ... Las Vegas NV 89109 702-385-3168 385-9042
Web: www.mhbsinc.com
Meyer & Lundahl 2345 W Lincoln St ... Phoenix AZ 85009 602-254-9286 258-6943
TF: 800-264-9286 ■ *Web:* www.meyerandlundahl.com
Novak Frank & Sons Inc 23940 Miles Rd ... Cleveland OH 44128 216-475-5440 475-2802
Overhead Door Co of Sacramento Inc 6756 Franklin Blvd ... Sacramento CA 95823 916-421-3747 399-9485
TF: 800-929-3667 ■ *Web:* www.overheaddoor.com
Partition Specialties Inc 714 C St Suite 3 ... San Rafael CA 94901 415-721-1040 721-1053
TF: 800-982-9255 ■ *Web:* www.partitionspecialties.com
RL Dresser Inc 4100 Atlantic Ave ... Raleigh NC 27604 919-876-4141 876-4300
Web: www.rldresserinc.com
Rock-Tred Corp 3415 W Howard St ... Skokie IL 60076 847-673-8200 679-6665
TF: 800-762-8733 ■ *Web:* www.rocktred.com
Schuck Component Systems Inc 8205 N 67th Ave ... Glendale AZ 85302 623-931-3661 937-3435
TF: 800-666-3661 ■ *Web:* www.schuckaz.com
Tribco Construction Services 200 S Michigan Ave Suite 200 ... Chicago IL 60604 312-341-0303 341-1534
Turner-Brooks Inc 28811 John R Rd ... Madison Heights MI 48071 248-548-3400 548-9213
TF: 800-560-7003

192-3 Concrete Contractors

Phone | Fax

Ahal Contracting Co Inc 3746 Pennridge Dr ... Bridgeton MO 63044 314-739-1142 739-5968
Web: www.ahal.com
Allied Contractors Inc 204 E Preston St ... Baltimore MD 21202 410-539-6727 332-4594
Aurora Blacktop Inc 1065 Sard Ave ... Montgomery IL 60538 630-892-9389 892-3481
B Gentle Concrete Construction Co 5241 NE 89th Ave ... Portland OR 97220 503-236-3902 255-0417
Baker Concrete Construction Inc 900 N Garver Rd ... Monroe OH 45050 513-539-4000 539-4380
TF: 800-359-3935 ■ *Web:* www.bakerconcrete.com
Ballard SB Construction Co 2828 Shipps Corner Rd ... Virginia Beach VA 23453 757-440-5555 451-2873
TF: 800-296-0209 ■ *Web:* www.sbballard.com
Barnard Construction Co Inc PO Box 99 ... Bozeman MT 59771 406-586-1995 586-3530
Web: www.barnard-inc.com
Baum Otto Co Inc 866 N Main St PO Box 161 ... Morton IL 61550 309-266-7114 263-1050
Web: www.ottobaum.com
Berglund Construction 8410 S Chicago Ave ... Chicago IL 60617 773-374-1000 374-8847
Web: www.berglundco.com
Bi-Con Services Inc 10901 Clay Pike Rd ... Derwent OH 43733 740-685-2542 685-3863
Web: www.bsicos.com
Blue Rock Industries 58 Main St ... Westbrook ME 04092 207-854-2561 854-2539
TF: 800-439-2561 ■ *Web:* www.bluerockmaine.com
Bomel Construction Co Inc 8195 E Kaiser Blvd ... Anaheim Hills CA 92808 714-921-1660 921-1943
Web: www.bomelconstruction.com
Bowen Engineering Corp 10315 Allisonville Rd ... Fishers IN 46038 317-842-2616 841-4257
TF: 800-377-2580 ■ *Web:* www.bowenengineering.com
Capform Inc PO Box 111130 ... Carrollton TX 75011 972-245-7292 242-5096
Ceco Concrete Construction LLC
10100 NWAmbassador Dr Suite 400 ... Kansas City MO 64153 816-459-7000 459-7735
TF: 800-237-7096 ■ *Web:* www.cecoconcrete.com
Cleveland Cement Contractors Inc 4823 Van Epps Rd ... Brooklyn Heights OH 44131 216-741-3954 741-9278
Web: www.clevelandcement.com
Colasanti Cos 24500 Wood Ct ... Macomb Township MI 48042 586-598-9700 598-9661
Web: www.colasantigroup.com
Concrete Contractors Interstate Inc 995 Hwy 85 PO Box 8 ... Brighton CO 80601 303-659-2383 659-2387
Culbertson Enterprises Inc 600-A Snyder Ave ... West Chester PA 19382 610-436-6400 436-6309
Daisy Construction Co Inc 3128 New Castle Ave ... New Castle DE 19720 302-658-4417 658-0618
Web: www.daisyconstruction.com
Damon G Douglas Co Inc 245 Birchwood Ave Box 1030 ... Cranford NJ 07016 908-272-0100 272-3949
TF: 800-724-1759 ■ *Web:* www.dgdco.com
Dance Brothers Inc 825C Hammonds Ferry Rd ... Linthicum MD 21090 410-789-8200 636-3663
Donley's Inc 5430 Warner Rd ... Cleveland OH 44125 216-524-6800 642-3216
Web: www.donleyinc.com
Douglas Damon G Co Inc 245 Birchwood Ave Box 1030 ... Cranford NJ 07016 908-272-0100 272-3949
TF: 800-724-1759 ■ *Web:* www.dgdco.com
Dywidag Systems International 320 Marmon Dr ... Bolingbrook IL 60440 630-739-1100 739-5517
Web: www.dywidag-systems.com
Egizii Electric Inc 700 N MacArthur Blvd ... Springfield IL 62702 217-528-4001 528-1677
Web: www.eeiholding.com
Francis O Day Construction Co Inc 850 E Gude Dr ... Rockville MD 20850 301-652-2400 340-6592
Web: www.foday.com
Fricks Co Inc 3000 W Loop 820 S ... Fort Worth TX 76116 817-560-8281 560-8137
Web: www.fricksfloorsystems.com
Frontier Precast LLC 2633 Waterford Rd ... Marietta OH 45750 740-373-3211 373-5678
TF: 800-633-9969 ■ *Web:* www.frontierprecast.com
Goettle Richard Inc 12071 Hamilton Ave ... Cincinnati OH 45231 513-825-8100 825-8107
TF: 800-248-8661 ■ *Web:* www.goettle.com
Harris Companies Inc 909 Montreal Cir ... Saint Paul MN 55102 651-602-6500 602-6699
Web: www.harris-companies.com
Healy Long & Jevin Inc 2000 Rodman Rd ... Wilmington DE 19805 302-654-8039 654-8153
Web: www.healylongjevin.com
Hubbard Construction Co 1936 Lee Rd 3rd Fl ... Winter Park FL 32789 407-645-5500 623-3865
TF: 800-476-1228 ■ *Web:* www.hubbard.com
Inco Inc PO Box 2705 ... Rocky Mount NC 27802 252-446-1174 977-3039
John Rohrer Contracting Co Inc 2820 Roe Lane Bldg S ... Kansas City KS 66103 913-236-5005 236-7291
TF: 800-255-6119 ■ *Web:* www.johnrohrercontracting.com
Kalman Floor Co Inc 1202 Bergen Pkwy Suite 110 ... Evergreen CO 80439 303-674-2290 674-1238
TF: 800-525-7840 ■ *Web:* www.kalmanfloor.com
Kent Cos Inc 130 60th St SW ... Grand Rapids MI 49548 616-534-4909 534-4890
TF: 800-968-2345 ■ *Web:* www.kentcompanies.com
Landavazo Brothers Inc 29280 Pacific St ... Hayward CA 94544 510-581-7104 581-7423
Lindblad Construction Co 717 E Cass St ... Joliet IL 60432 815-726-6251 723-4907
Web: www.lindbladconstruction.com
Manafort Brothers Inc PO Box 99 ... Plainville CT 06062 860-229-4853 229-1878
TF: 888-626-2367 ■ *Web:* www.manafort.com

Concrete Contractors (Cont'd)

Phone Fax

Miller & Long Concrete Construction Inc 4824 Rugby Ave .... Bethesda MD 20814 301-657-8000 652-9242
Web: www.millerandlong.com

Oldcastle Precast Building Systems Div 1401 Trimble Rd .... Edgewood MD 21040 410-612-1213 612-1214
TF: 800-523-9144 ■ Web: www.oldcastle-precast.com

Otto Baum Co Inc 866 N Main St PO Box 161 .... Morton IL 61550 309-266-7114 263-1050
Web: www.ottobaum.com

Perez Interboro Asphalt Co 91 Paidge Ave .... Brooklyn NY 11222 718-383-4100 383-9164

Proshot Concrete Inc 4158 Musgrove Dr PO Box 1636 .... Florence AL 35631 256-764-5941 764-5946
TF: 800-633-3141 ■ Web: www.proshotconcrete.com

RCI Environmental Inc 1216 140th Ave PO Box 1730 .... Sumner WA 98390 253-863-5300 859-5702
TF: 800-848-3777 ■ Web: www.rci-group.com

Richard Goettle Inc 12071 Hamilton Ave .... Cincinnati OH 45231 513-825-8100 825-8107
TF: 800-248-8661 ■ Web: www.goettle.com

Rogele Inc 1025 S 21st St .... Harrisburg PA 17104 717-564-0478 564-5179

Ross Brothers Construction Co Inc 7201 SR 168 .... Catlettsburg KY 41129 606-739-5139 739-8315
TF: 800-910-7222

SB Ballard Construction Co 2828 Shipps Corner Rd .... Virginia Beach VA 23453 757-440-5555 451-2873
TF: 800-296-0209 ■ Web: www.sbballard.com

Smock Fansler Corp 2910 W Minnesota St .... Indianapolis IN 46241 317-248-8371 244-4507
TF: 800-281-6605 ■ Web: www.smockfansler.com

Structural Preservation Systems Inc
7455 New Ridge Rd Suite T .... Hanover MD 21076 410-850-7000 850-4111
TF: 800-899-1016 ■ Web: www.structural.net

Suncoast Post-Tension LP
654 N Sam Houston Pkwy E Suite 110 .... Houston TX 77060 281-668-1840 931-6645
TF: 866-838-3281 ■ Web: www.suncoast-pt.com

Superior Gunite Inc 12306 Van Nuys Blvd .... Lakeview Terrace CA 91342 818-896-9199 896-6699
Web: www.shotcrete.com

TAS Commercial Concrete Construction Inc 20105 Krahn Rd .... Spring TX 77388 281-350-0832 350-6664
TF: 800-652-2227 ■ Web: www.tasconcrete.com

Treviicos Corp 273 Summer St .... Boston MA 02210 617-737-1453 737-5810
Web: www.treviicos.com

UBM Inc 330 S Wells St Suite 1214 .... Chicago IL 60606 312-939-0505 939-0483
Web: www.ubm-inc.com

Western Construction Group 1637 N Warson Rd .... Saint Louis MO 63132 314-427-6733 427-6199
TF Cust Svc: 800-325-2801 ■ Web: www.westerngroup.com

192-4 Electrical Contractors

Phone Fax

Abbett Electric Corp 1850 Bryant St .... San Francisco CA 94110 415-864-7500 864-3140

AC Corp 301 Creek Ridge Rd .... Greensboro NC 27406 336-273-4472 274-6035
TF: 800-582-3073 ■ Web: www.accorporation.com

AC Electric Co PO Box 81977 .... Bakersfield CA 93380 661-410-0000 392-9132
Web: www.a-celectric.com

Acme Electric Inc 412 E Gowan Rd .... North Las Vegas NV 89032 702-876-1116 642-9936

Aldridge Electric Inc 844 E Rockland Rd .... Libertyville IL 60048 847-680-5200 680-5298
Web: www.aldridge-electric.com

Allan Briteway Electrical Contractors Inc
130 Algonquin Pkwy .... Whippany NJ 07981 973-781-0022 781-1744
Web: allanbriteway.com

Allison-Smith Co Inc 2284 Marietta Blvd .... Atlanta GA 30318 404-351-6430 350-1065
Web: www.allison-smith.com

Alterman Nathan Electric Co 14703 Jones Maltsberger St ...... San Antonio TX 78247 210-496-6888 496-7349
Web: www.nalterman.com

Althoff Industries Inc 8001 S Rt 31 .... Crystal Lake IL 60014 815-455-7000 455-9375*
*Fax: Sales ■ TF: 800-225-2443 ■ Web: www.althoffind.com

Anderson Electric Inc PO Box 758 .... Springfield IL 62705 217-529-5471 529-8946
Web: www.anderson-electric.com

Anixter Inc 2301 Patriot Blvd .... Glenview IL 60026 224-521-8000 521-8100
TF: 800-323-8166 ■ Web: www.anixter.com

APi Electric 4330 W 1st St Suite B .... Duluth MN 55807 218-628-3323 624-7485
TF: 866-624-0064 ■ Web: www.apielectric.com

APi Group Inc Specialty Construction Services Group
2366 Rose Pl .... Saint Paul MN 55113 651-636-4320 636-0312
Web: www.apigroupinc.com/construction.html

Arc Electric Inc PO Box 1667 .... Chesapeake VA 23327 757-424-5164 424-7145
TF: 800-989-1053 ■ Web: www.arcelectricinc.com

Arc Electrical Construction Co Inc 739 2nd Ave .... New York NY 10016 212-573-9600 682-0650

Arrow Electric Co Inc 317 Wabasso Ave .... Louisville KY 40209 502-367-0141 361-8613
TF: 888-999-5591 ■ Web: www.arrowelectric.com

Aschinger Electric Co 877 Horan Dr .... Fenton MO 63026 636-343-1211 343-9658
TF: 800-280-4061 ■ Web: www.aschinger.com

B & I Contractors Inc 2701 Prince St .... Fort Myers FL 33916 239-332-4646 332-5928
Web: www.bandicontractors.com

Baker Electric Inc 111 SW Jackson Ave .... Des Moines IA 50315 515-288-6774 288-2226
TF: 800-779-6774 ■ Web: www.bakerelectric.com

Barlovento LLC 165 Hostdale Dr Suite 1 .... Dothan AL 36303 334-983-9979 983-9983
TF: 877-498-6039 ■ Web: www.barlovento8a.com

Barth Electric Co Inc 1934 N Illinois St .... Indianapolis IN 46202 317-924-6226 923-6938
TF: 800-666-6226 ■ Web: www.barthelectric.com

Bell Electrical Contractors Inc 128 Millwell Dr .... Maryland Heights MO 63043 314-739-7744 739-0717
TF: 800-717-2355 ■ Web: www.bellelectrical.com

Bergelectric Corp 5650 W Centinela Ave .... Los Angeles CA 90045 310-337-1377 337-2663
TF: 800-734-2374 ■ Web: www.bergelectric.com

Berger Engineering Co 10900 Shady Trail .... Dallas TX 75220 214-358-4451 351-2954
Web: www.berger-engr.com

Berwick Electric Co 3450 N Nevada Ave Suite 100 .... Colorado Springs CO 80907 719-632-7683 471-9660
Web: www.berwickelectric.com

BK Truland 10233 S Dolfield Rd .... Owings Mills MD 21117 410-363-1200 363-1215
TF: 800-238-8012 ■ Web: www.bktruland.com

Bodine Electric of Decatur Inc PO Box 976 .... Decatur IL 62525 217-423-2593 423-4658
TF: 800-252-3369 ■ Web: www.bodineelectricofdecatur.com

Bolton Corp 919 W Morgan St .... Raleigh NC 27603 919-828-9021 828-8574
TF: 800-438-1098 ■ Web: www.boltoncorp.com

Brink Constructors Inc PO Box 1186 .... Rapid City SD 57709 605-342-6966 342-5905
Web: www.brinkconstructors.com

Broadway Electrical Service Co Inc PO Box 3250 .... Knoxville TN 37927 865-524-1851 546-2104
TF: 800-516-6992

Bruce & Merrilees Electric Co 930 Cass St .... New Castle PA 16101 724-652-5566 652-8290
TF: 800-652-5560 ■ Web: www.bruceandmerrilees.com

Cache Valley Electric Inc 919 N 1000 W .... Logan UT 84321 435-752-6405 787-0534
TF: 800-735-9345 ■ Web: www.cvelectric.com

Cannon & Wendt Electric Co 4020 N 16th St .... Phoenix AZ 85016 602-279-1681 230-8464
Web: www.cannon-wendt.com

Capital Electric Construction Co Inc
600 Broadway Suite 600 .... Kansas City MO 64105 816-472-9500 421-4244
Web: www.capitalelectric.com

Casey Electric Inc 245 Preston St .... Jackson TN 38301 731-424-7741 424-7945
TF: 800-424-0428

Church & Murdock Electric Inc 5709 Wattsburg Rd .... Erie PA 16509 814-825-3456 825-4043
TF: 800-638-4313 ■ Web: www.churchandmurdock.com

Phone Fax

Cleveland Electric Co Inc 1281 Fulton Industrial Blvd NW .... Atlanta GA 30336 404-696-4550 696-2849
TF: 800-282-7150 ■ Web: www.clevelectric.com

Cleveland Group Inc 1281 Fulton Industrial Blvd .... Atlanta GA 30336 404-696-4550 505-7792
TF: 800-282-7150 ■ Web: www.clevelectric.com

Coastal Mechanical Services Ltd 191 N Travis St .... San Benito TX 78586 956-399-5157 399-9770
TF: 800-568-2612

Cochran Electric Co Inc PO Box 33524 .... Seattle WA 98133 206-367-1900 368-3262
Web: www.cochraninc.com

Collins Electric Co Inc 53 2nd Ave .... Chicopee MA 01020 413-592-9221 592-4157
TF: 800-321-4459 ■ Web: www.collinselectricco.com

Collins Electrical Co Inc 611 W Fremont St .... Stockton CA 95203 209-466-3691 466-3146
Web: www.collinselectric.com

Commander Electric Inc PO Box 526 .... Bohemia NY 11716 631-563-3223 563-8322
Web: www.commanderelectric.com

Commonwealth Electric Co of Midwest PO Box 80638 .... Lincoln NE 68501 402-474-1341 474-0114
Web: www.commonwealthelectric.com

Compel Corp 10410 Pioneer Blvd Suite 7 .... Santa Fe Springs CA 90670 562-946-8321 944-9905
TF: 800-553-1162 ■ Web: www.compel-corp.com

Comstock LK & Co Inc 5 Penn Plaza 12th Fl .... New York NY 10001 212-502-7900 502-1865

Continental Electric Co Inc 9501 E 5th Ave PO Box 2710 .... Gary IN 46403 219-938-3460 938-3469
Web: www.continentalelectric.com

Cupertino Electric Inc 1132 N 7th St .... San Jose CA 95112 408-808-8000 275-8575
Web: www.cei.com

Daidone Electric Inc 200 Raymond Blvd .... Newark NJ 07105 973-690-5216 344-3645

Dashiell Corp PO Box 1300 .... Deer Park TX 77536 281-479-7407 479-1815
TF: 800-736-6400 ■ Web: www.dashiellcorp.com

Davis Electrical Constructors Inc PO Box 1907 .... Greenville SC 29602 864-250-2500 250-2555
TF: 800-849-3284 ■ Web: www.daviselectrical.com

Davis H Elliot Co Inc PO Box 12707 .... Roanoke VA 24027 540-992-2865 992-1495
Web: www.davishelliot.com

Decker Electric Co Inc 1282 Folsom St .... San Francisco CA 94103 415-552-1622 861-4257
TF: 800-755-1622

Del Monte Electric Co Inc 6998 Sierra Ct .... Dublin CA 94568 925-829-6000 829-6033
Web: www.delmonteelectric.com

Divane Brothers Electric Co 2424 N 25th Ave .... Franklin Park IL 60131 847-455-7143 455-7899
Web: www.divanebros.com

Dorey Electric Co PO Box 10158 .... Norfolk VA 23513 757-855-3381 857-7835
Web: www.doreyelectric.com

Ducci Electrical Contractors Inc 427 Goshen Rd .... Torrington CT 06790 860-489-9267 489-7980

Dycom Industries Inc 11770 US Hwy 1 Suite 101 ...... Palm Beach Gardens FL 33408 561-627-7171 627-7709
NYSE: DY ■ TF: 877-210-0347 ■ Web: www.dycomind.com

Dynalectric Corp 4462 Corporate Ctr Dr .... Los Alamitos CA 90720 714-828-7000 484-2387*
*Fax: Acctg ■ TF: 800-729-0444 ■ Web: www.kdc-systems.com

E-J Electric Installation Co 4641 Vernon Blvd .... Long Island City NY 11101 718-786-9400 937-9120
TF: 800-660-8658 ■ Web: www.ej1899.com

EC Co PO Box 10286 .... Portland OR 97296 503-224-3623 241-0807
TF: 800-462-3370 ■ Web: www.e-c-co.com

EC Ernst Inc 1420 Ritchie Marlboro Rd .... Capitol Heights MD 20743 301-350-7770 499-0933
TF: 800-683-7770 ■ Web: www.ecernst.com

Edwin L Heim Co 1918 Greenwood St .... Harrisburg PA 17104 717-233-8711 233-8619
TF: 800-692-7317 ■ Web: www.elheim.com

Egizii Electric Inc 700 N MacArthur Blvd .... Springfield IL 62702 217-528-4001 528-1677
Web: www.eeiholding.com

ElDeCo Inc 5751 Augusta Rd .... Greenville SC 29605 864-277-9088 277-2811
Web: www.eldecoinc.com

Electric Machinery Enterprises Inc 2515 E Hanna Ave .... Tampa FL 33610 813-238-5010 238-8490
TF: 800-824-2557 ■ Web: www.e-m-e.com

Electrical Contractors Inc 3510 Main St .... Hartford CT 06120 860-549-2822 549-7948
Web: www.ecincorporated.com

Electrical Corp of America 7320 Arlington Ave .... Raytown MO 64133 816-737-3206 356-0731
TF: 800-426-9453

Elliot Davis H Co Inc PO Box 12707 .... Roanoke VA 24027 540-992-2865 992-1495
Web: www.davishelliot.com

EMCOR Construction Services Inc
1420 Spring Hill Rd Suite 500 .... McLean VA 22102 703-556-8000 556-0890
Web: www.emcorgroup.com

EMCOR Group Inc 301 Merritt 7 6th Fl .... Norwalk CT 06851 203-849-7800 849-7900
NYSE: EME ■ Web: www.emcorgroup.com

EMCOR Hyre Electric Co 2655 Garfield Ave .... Highland IN 46322 219-923-6100 838-3631
TF: 800-272-9659 ■ Web: www.emcorhyre.com

Enterprise Electric Co 4204 Shannon Dr .... Baltimore MD 21213 410-488-8200 488-6639
Web: www.eecompany.com

Ermco Inc 1625 W Thompson Rd .... Indianapolis IN 46217 317-780-2923 780-2853
TF: 800-380-2923 ■ Web: www.ermco.com

Ernst EC Inc 1420 Ritchie Marlboro Rd .... Capitol Heights MD 20743 301-350-7770 499-0933
TF: 800-683-7770 ■ Web: www.ecernst.com

ESI Inc 3400 Kettering Blvd .... Dayton OH 45439 937-293-6138 293-6301
Web: www.esielectrical.com

Ferguson Electric Construction Co Inc 333 Ellicott St .... Buffalo NY 14203 716-852-2010 852-4887

Ferndale Electric Co Inc 915 E Drayton Ave .... Ferndale MI 48220 248-545-4404 545-8140
Web: www.ferndale-electric.com

Ferran Services & Contracting 530 Grand St .... Orlando FL 32805 407-422-3551 648-0961
Web: www.ferran-services.com

Fisk Electric Co 111 TC Jester Blvd .... Houston TX 77007 713-868-6111 868-3749
Web: www.fiskcorp.com

Flowers Construction Co Inc PO Box 1207 .... Hillsboro TX 76645 254-582-2501 582-2510
TF: 800-792-3295

Forest Electric Corp 2 Penn Plaza 4th Fl .... New York NY 10121 212-318-1500 318-1791
Web: www.forestelectric.net

Fox Electric Ltd 1104 Colorado Ln .... Arlington TX 76015 817-461-2571 261-7311
Web: www.foxelectric.com

Frazer HB Co 514 Shoemaker Rd .... King of Prussia PA 19406 610-992-5060 992-5070
Web: www.hbfrazer.com

Fuellgraf Electric Co 245 Pittsburgh Rd Suite 100 .... Butler PA 16001 724-282-4800 282-1926
Web: www.fuellgraf.com

G & M Electrical Contractors Co 1746 N Richmond St .... Chicago IL 60647 773-278-8200 278-8038
TF: 800-546-8050

Gardner-Zemke Co Inc 6100 Indian School Rd NE .... Albuquerque NM 87110 505-881-0555 888-1536

Gaylor Electric 11711 N College Ave Suite 150 .... Carmel IN 46032 317-843-0577 848-0364
TF: 800-878-0577 ■ Web: www.gaylor.com

GEM Industrial Inc 6842 Commodore Dr .... Walbridge OH 43465 419-666-6554 666-7004
TF: 800-837-5909 ■ Web: www.gemindustrial.com

George F Schuler Inc 1650 Report Ave .... Stockton CA 95205 209-462-2398 467-4436

Gibson Electric Co Inc 3100 Woodcreek Dr .... Downers Grove IL 60515 630-288-3800 572-6261
Web: www.gibsonelec.com

Gill-Simpson Inc 2834 Loch Raven Rd .... Baltimore MD 21218 410-467-3335 366-4557
Web: www.gill-simpson.com

Goldfield Corp 1684 W Hibiscus Blvd .... Melbourne FL 32901 321-724-1700 724-1703
AMEX: GV ■ Web: www.goldfieldcorp.com

GR Sponaugle & Sons Inc 4391 Chambers Hill Rd .... Harrisburg PA 17111 717-564-1515 564-3675
TF: 800-866-7036 ■ Web: www.grsponaugle.com

Grand-Kahn Electric 16760 S Richmond Rd .... Hazel Crest IL 60429 708-333-4900 596-2280
Web: www.grandkahn.com

Griffin Wayne J Electric Inc 116 Hopping Brook Rd .... Holliston MA 01746 508-429-8830 429-7825
TF: 800-421-0151 ■ Web: www.waynejgriffin.com

GSL Electric Inc 8540 S Sandy Pkwy .... Sandy UT 84070 801-565-0088 565-0099
TF: 800-221-4135 ■ Web: www.gslelectric.com

Phone Fax

Guarantee Electrical Co 3405 Bent Ave Saint Louis MO 63116 314-772-5400 772-9261
TF: 800-854-4326 ■ *Web:* www.geco.com
Gulf States Inc 6711 E Hwy 332 Freeport TX 77541 979-233-5555 233-3050
TF: 800-231-9849
H & H Group Inc 2801 Syene Rd Madison WI 53713 608-273-3434 273-9654
Web: www.h-hgroup.com
Hargrove Electric Co Inc 1522 Market Center Blvd Dallas TX 75207 214-742-8665 744-0846
Web: www.hargroveelectric.com
Harlan Electric Co 2695 Crooks Rd Rochester Hills MI 48309 248-853-4601 853-4603
Web: www.myrgroup.com
Harry F Ortlip Co Inc 780 Lancaster Ave Bryn Mawr PA 19010 610-527-7000 527-7437
Hatzel & Buehler Inc PO Box 7499 Wilmington DE 19803 302-478-4200 478-2750
Web: www.hatzelandbuehler.com
HB Frazer Co 514 Shoemaker Rd King of Prussia PA 19406 610-992-5060 992-5070
Web: www.hbfrazer.com
Heim Edwin L Co 1918 Greenwood St Harrisburg PA 17104 717-233-8711 233-8619
TF: 800-692-7317 ■ *Web:* www.elheim.com
Helix Electric Inc 8260 Camino Santa Fe Suite A San Diego CA 92121 858-535-0505 623-1241
TF: 800-554-3549 ■ *Web:* www.helixelectric.com
Herre Brothers Inc 4417 Valley Rd Enola PA 17025 717-732-4454 732-8208
Web: www.herrebros.com
Hi-Tech Electric Inc 11116 W Little York Rd Bldg 8 Houston TX 77041 832-243-0345 467-0132
TF: 800-315-6041 ■ *Web:* www.hitechelectric.com
Highlines Construction Co Inc
701 Bridge City Ave PO Box 408 Westwego LA 70096 504-436-3961 436-4939
TF: 800-762-8860 ■ *Web:* www.highlines.com
Hilscher Clarke Electric Co 519 4th St NW Canton OH 44703 330-452-9806 452-5867
Web: www.hilscher-clarke.com
Hoffman Corp 805 SW Broadway Suite 2100 Portland OR 97205 503-221-8811 221-8934
Web: www.hoffmancorp.com
Hooper Corp 2030 Pennsylvania Ave Madison WI 53704 608-249-0451 249-7360
TF: 800-999-0451 ■ *Web:* www.hoopercorp.com
Howe Electric Inc 4682 E Olive Ave Fresno CA 93702 559-255-8992 255-9745
Hunt Electric Corp 2300 Territorial Rd Saint Paul MN 55114 651-646-2911 643-6575
TF: 800-989-4432 ■ *Web:* www.huntelec.com
Hyre Electric Co Inc 2320 W Ogden Ave Chicago IL 60608 312-738-7200 738-4090
Web: www.hyreelectric.com
Industrial Contractors Inc 701 Channel Dr Bismarck ND 58501 701-258-9908 258-9988
Web: www.icinorthdakota.com
Industrial Power & Lighting Corp 701 Seneca St Suite 500 Buffalo NY 14210 716-854-1811 854-1828
TF: 800-639-3702 ■ *Web:* www.iplcorp.com
Industrial Specialty Contractors LLC 20480 Highland Rd Baton Rouge LA 70817 225-756-8001 756-8586
Web: www.iscgrp.com
Inglett & Stubbs LLC 5200 Riverview Rd Mableton GA 30126 404-881-1199 872-3101
Web: www.inglett-stubbs.com
Integrated Electrical Services Inc
1800 West Loop S Suite 500 Houston TX 77027 713-860-1500 860-1599
NYSE: IES ■ *Web:* www.ielectric.com
Intermountain Electric Inc 602 S Lipan St Denver CO 80223 303-733-7248 722-2410
Interstates Construction Services Inc PO Box 260 Sioux Center IA 51250 712-722-1662 722-1667
TF: 800-827-1662 ■ *Web:* www.interstates.com/construction.asp
J & M Brown Co Inc 267 Amory St Jamaica Plain MA 02122 617-522-6800 522-6424
Web: www.jmbco.com
John A Penney Co Inc 270 Sidney St Cambridge MA 02139 617-547-7744 547-4332
John W Tieder Inc PO Box 653 Cambridge MD 21613 410-228-5262 228-6402
Kearney Electric Inc 3609 E Superior Ave Phoenix AZ 85040 602-437-0235 437-2914
Web: www.kearneyelectric.com
Kelso-Burnett Co 5200 Newport Dr Rolling Meadows IL 60008 847-259-0720 259-0839
Web: www.kelso-burnett.com
Kirby Electric Inc 170 Thorn Hill Rd Warrendale PA 15086 724-772-1800 772-2227
Web: www.kirbyelectricinc.com
Klinger Electrical Corp 222 Market Ridge Dr Ridgeland MS 39157 601-956-7774 956-7542
Koontz-Wagner Electric Co Inc 3801 Voorde Dr South Bend IN 46628 574-232-2051 288-8510
TF: 800-345-2051 ■ *Web:* www.koontz-wagner.com
Lake Erie Electric Inc PO Box 450859 Westlake OH 44145 440-835-5565 835-5688
Web: www.leeinc.com
Linder & Assoc Inc 840 N Main St PO Box 1202 Wichita KS 67201 316-265-6691 265-8097
Web: www.linderandassociates.com
LK Comstock & Co Inc 5 Penn Plaza 12th Fl New York NY 10001 212-502-7900 502-1865
Long Electric Co Inc 1310 S Franklin Rd Indianapolis IN 46239 317-356-2455 356-0630
TF: 800-356-2450
Ludvik Electric Co 3900 S Teller St Lakewood CO 80235 303-781-9601 783-6320
Web: www.ludvik.com
Magaw Electric Inc PO Box 510337 New Berlin WI 53151 262-782-7400 797-7550
Web: www.h-hgroup.com
Marine Electric Co 110 S 1st St Louisville KY 40202 502-587-6514 584-1656
Web: www.marine-electric.com
Mass Electric Construction Co 180 Guest St Boston MA 02135 617-254-1015 254-0706
TF: 800-933-6322 ■ *Web:* www.masselec.com
Matco Electric Corp 320 N Jensen Rd Vestal NY 13850 607-729-4921 729-0932
Web: www.matcoelectric.com
Meade Electric Co Inc 9550 W 55th St Suite A McCook IL 60525 708-588-2500 588-2501
Web: www.meadeelectric.com
Merit Electric Co Inc 6520 125th Ave N Largo FL 33773 727-536-5945 536-9014
TF: 800-539-3900 ■ *Web:* www.meritelectricco.com
Merit Electrical Inc 17723 Airline Hwy Prairieville LA 70769 225-673-8850 673-8838
Web: www.merit-electrical.com
Mid-City Electrical Construction 1099 Sullivant Ave Columbus OH 43223 614-221-5153 221-2225
Web: www.midcityelectric.com
Miller Electric Co 2251 Rosselle St Jacksonville FL 32204 904-388-8000 389-8653
TF Sales: 800-554-4761 ■ *Web:* www.mecojax.com
Miller Engineering Co 1616 S Main St Rockford IL 61102 815-963-4878 963-0823
MJ Electric Inc PO Box 686 Iron Mountain MI 49801 906-774-8000 779-4217
Web: www.mjelectric.com
MMR Group Inc 15961 Airline Hwy Baton Rouge LA 70817 225-756-5090 753-7012
Web: www.mmrgrp.com
Mojave Electric Inc 3755 W Hacienda Ave Las Vegas NV 89118 702-798-2970 798-3740
Mona Electric Group Inc 7915 Malcolm Rd Suite 102 Clinton MD 20735 301-868-8400 868-9769
TF: 800-438-6662 ■ *Web:* www.monaelectric.com
Morrow-Meadows Corp 231 Benton Ct Walnut CA 91789 909-598-7700 598-3907
TF: 800-438-6366 ■ *Web:* www.morrow-meadows.com
Morrow-Meadows Corp Northern California
385 Oyster Point Blvd Suite 2 South San Francisco CA 94080 650-634-0682 634-0683
Web: www.morrow-meadowsnc.com
Motor City Electric Co 9440 Grinnell St Detroit MI 48213 313-921-5300 921-5310
TF: 800-860-8020 ■ *Web:* www.mceco.com
Mr Electric Corp 1010 N University Parks Dr Waco TX 76707 800-253-9151 745-5068*
*Fax Area Code: 254 ■ *Web:* www.mrelectric.com
Muska Electric Co 1985 Oakcrest Ave Roseville MN 55113 651-636-5820 636-0916
Web: www.muskaelectric.com
Muth Electric Inc 400 N Rowley St Mitchell SD 57301 605-996-3983 996-2203
Web: www.muthelec.com
MYR Group 1701 W Golf Rd Tower 3 Suite 1012 Rolling Meadows IL 60008 847-290-1891 290-1892
Web: www.myrgroup.com
Nathan Alterman Electric Co Inc 14703 Jones Maltsberger St San Antonio TX 78247 210-496-6888 496-7349
Web: www.nalterman.com

Phone Fax

Newcomb Electric Co 2708 Shenandoah Ave NW Roanoke VA 24017 540-342-5498 342-7512
TF: 800-833-0094 ■ *Web:* www.newcombelectric.com
Newkirk Electric Assoc Inc 1875 Roberts St Muskegon MI 49442 231-722-1691 722-1690
Web: www.newkirk-electric.com
Newtron Group Inc 8183 W El Cajon Dr Baton Rouge LA 70815 225-927-8921 927-8921
TF: 800-644-2752 ■ *Web:* www.thenewtrongroup.com
Nitro Electric Company LLC
500 Corporate Centre Dr 2nd Fl Suite 520 Scott Depot WV 25560 304-722-7700 722-7792*
*Fax: Acctg ■ *Web:* www.nitro-electric.com
O'Connell Electric Co 830 Phillips Rd Victor NY 14564 585-924-2176 924-4973
Web: www.oconnellelectric.com
Ortlip Harry F Co Inc 780 Lancaster Ave Bryn Mawr PA 19010 610-527-7000 527-7437
Ostrow Electric Co Inc 9 Mason St Worcester MA 01609 508-754-2641 757-1645
TF: 800-922-8289
P1 Group Inc 2151 Haskell Ave Bldg 1 Lawrence KS 66046 785-843-2910 843-2884
TF: 800-376-2911 ■ *Web:* www.p1group.com
Palmer Electric & Showcase Lighting 875 Jackson Ave Winter Park FL 32789 407-646-8700 647-8951
Web: www.palmer-electric.com
Parsons Electric LLC 5960 Main St NE Minneapolis MN 55432 763-571-8000 571-7210
Web: www.parsons-electric.com
PayneCrest Electric Inc 10411 Baur Blvd Saint Louis MO 63132 314-996-0400 996-0500
Web: www.payneelectric.com
Penney John A Co Inc 270 Sidney St Cambridge MA 02139 617-547-7744 547-4332
Peoples Electric Co Inc 277 E Fillmore Ave Saint Paul MN 55107 651-227-7711 227-9684
TF: 888-777-3409 ■ *Web:* www.peoplesco.com
Perreca Electric Co 520 Broadway Newburgh NY 12550 845-562-4080 562-0801
TF: 800-973-7732 ■ *Web:* www.perreca.com
Petrocelli Electric Co Inc 2209 Queens Plaza N Long Island City NY 11101 718-752-2200 756-0695
TF: 800-253-2721 ■ *Web:* www.petrocelli.com
Phillips Brothers Electrical Contractors Inc
235 Sweet Spring Rd Glenmoore PA 19343 610-458-8578 458-8438
TF: 800-220-5051
Pieper Electric Inc 5070 N 35th St Milwaukee WI 53209 414-462-7700 462-7711
Web: www.pieperpower.com
Pike Electric Corp 100 Pike Way Mount Airy NC 27030 336-789-2171 719-7453
NYSE: PEC ■ *TF:* 800-343-7453 ■ *Web:* www.pikeelectric.com
Port City Electric Co 2550 Charlotte Hwy Mooresville NC 28117 704-663-4215 663-7184
TF: 877-316-2264 ■ *Web:* www.portcityelectric.com
Power City Electric Inc 3327 E Olive Ave Spokane WA 99202 509-535-8500 535-8598
TF: 800-877-8549 ■ *Web:* www.callsesco.com/powercity.html
Premier Electrical Corp 4401 85th Ave N Brooklyn Park MN 55443 763-424-6551 424-5225
TF: 800-466-8818
Pritchard Electric Co Inc PO Box 2503 Huntington WV 25725 304-529-2566 529-2567
TF: 877-457-8904 ■ *Web:* www.pritchardelectric.com
Professional Construction Services Inc PO Box 2005 Prairieville LA 70769 225-744-4016 744-4938
TF: 800-562-4318 ■ *Web:* www.professionalconstruction.com
Ready Electric Co Inc 2030 Frankfort Ave Louisville KY 40206 502-893-2511 893-2519
Web: www.readyelec.com
Regency Electric 4348 Southpoint Blvd Suite 400 Jacksonville FL 32216 904-281-0600 281-0599
TF: 877-309-0204
Rex Moore Electrical Contractors & Engineers
3601 Parkway Pl West Sacramento CA 95691 916-372-1300 372-4013
TF: 800-266-1922 ■ *Web:* www.rexmoore.com
Riggs Distler Co Inc 9411 Philadelphia Rd Unit P Baltimore MD 21237 410-633-0300 633-2119
Web: www.riggsdistler.com
Riviera Electric 5001 S Zuni St Littleton CO 80120 303-937-9300 922-1421
TF: 800-765-5767 ■ *Web:* www.riviera-electric.com
Roman Electric Co Inc PO Box 14396 Milwaukee WI 53214 414-771-5400 471-8693
TF: 877-772-7760 ■ *Web:* www.romanelectric.com
Romanoff Electric Co LLC 5055 Enterprise Blvd Toledo OH 43612 419-726-2627 726-5406
TF: 800-866-2627
Ronco Communications & Electronics Inc 595 Sheridan Dr Tonawanda NY 14150 716-873-0760 879-8150
TF: 888-879-8011 ■ *Web:* www.ronconet.com
Rosendin Electric Inc 880 N Mabury Rd San Jose CA 95133 408-286-2800 793-5019*
*Fax: Hum Res ■ *TF:* 800-540-4734 ■ *Web:* www.rosendin.com
Salem Electric Co Inc 3933 Westpoint Blvd Winston-Salem NC 27103 336-765-0221 765-7286
Web: www.salemelectriccoinc.com
Sargent Electric Co 2801 Liberty Ave Pittsburgh PA 15222 412-391-0588 394-7535
Web: www.sargent.com
SASCO Electric 12900 Alondra Blvd Cerritos CA 90703 562-926-0900 926-1399
TF: 800-477-4422 ■ *Web:* www.sasco.com
Schoonover Electric Co Inc 1063 Rt 22 Mountainside NJ 07092 908-233-2400 233-8521
Schuler George F Inc 1650 Report Ave Stockton CA 95205 209-462-2398 467-4436
Shambaugh & Son LP 7614 Opportunity Dr Fort Wayne IN 46825 260-487-7777 487-7701
TF: 800-234-9988 ■ *Web:* www.shambaugh.com
Shaw Electric Co 33200 Schoolcraft Rd Livonia MI 48150 734-425-6800 425-6824
Web: www.shawelectric.com
Shawver & Son Inc 144 NE 44th St Oklahoma City OK 73105 405-525-9451 525-6136
TF: 800-320-5121 ■ *Web:* www.shawver.net
Shelley Electric Inc PO Box 12124 Wichita KS 67277 316-945-8311 945-2604
Web: www.shelleyelectric.com
SM Electric Co Inc 601 New Brunswick Ave Rahway NJ 07065 732-388-3540 388-3052
Web: www.smelectric.com
Smith & Keene Electric Service Inc PO Box 1777 Chesapeake VA 23327 757-420-1231 420-5340
Web: www.smithandkeene.com
Southern Air Inc PO Box 4205 Lynchburg VA 24502 434-385-6200 385-9081
TF: 800-743-1214 ■ *Web:* www.southern-air.com
Sponaugle GR & Sons Inc 4391 Chambers Hill Rd Harrisburg PA 17111 717-564-1515 564-3675
TF: 800-866-7036 ■ *Web:* www.grsponaugle.com
Staff Electric Co Inc W 133 N 5030 Campbell Dr Menomonee Falls WI 53051 262-781-8230 781-1680
Starr Electric Co Inc PO Box 9298 Greensboro NC 27429 336-275-0241 273-0734
TF: 800-732-0241 ■ *Web:* www.starrelectric.net
Steiny & Co Inc 221 N Ardmore Ave PO Box 74901 Los Angeles CA 90004 213-382-2331 381-6781
TF: 800-350-2331 ■ *Web:* www.steinyco.com
Sturgeon Electric Co Inc 12150 E 112th Ave Henderson CO 80640 303-286-8000 286-1887
TF: 800-288-5155 ■ *Web:* www.sturgeonelectric.com
Super Electric Construction Co 4300 W Chicago Ave Chicago IL 60651 773-489-4400 235-1455
TF: 800-344-1936 ■ *Web:* www.superelec.com
Syracuse Merit Electric Inc 301 Stoutenger St East Syracuse NY 13057 315-437-1453 437-7431
Web: www.syracusemerit.com
System Electric Co 1278 Montalvo Way Palm Springs CA 92262 760-327-7847 323-7247
TF: 800-998-9017 ■ *Web:* www.systemelectric.com
Taft Electric Co 1694 Eastman Ave Ventura CA 93003 805-642-0121 650-9015
TEC Corp PO Box 207 Sioux City IA 51102 712-252-4275 252-5344
TF: 800-832-2936 ■ *Web:* www.tec-corp.com
TECO Solutions 702 N Franklin St Tampa FL 33602 813-228-1111 228-1527
Web: www.tecosolutions.com
Tennessee Associated Electric Inc 312 W Jackson Ave Knoxville TN 37902 865-524-3686 522-1553
Terry's Electric Inc 600 N Thacker Ave Suite A Kissimmee FL 34741 407-846-4252 846-6607
TF: 888-278-3779 ■ *Web:* www.terryselectric.com
Tieder John W Inc PO Box 653 Cambridge MD 21613 410-228-5262 228-6402
Totem Electric of Tacoma Inc 2332 S Jefferson Ave Tacoma WA 98402 253-383-5022 272-5214
TF: 800-562-8478 ■ *Web:* www.totemelectric.com
Town & Country Electric 2662 American Dr Appleton WI 54915 920-738-1500 738-1515
TF: 800-274-2345
Traffic Control Devices Inc 242 Westmonte Dr Altamonte Springs FL 32714 407-869-5300 682-0076
Web: www.trafficcontroldevices.com

Electrical Contractors (Cont'd)

Company	City	State	ZIP	Phone	Fax
Tri-City Electrical Contractors Inc 430 West Dr	Altamonte Springs	FL	32714	407-788-3500	682-7353
TF: 800-768-2489 ■ *Web:* www.tcelectric.com					
Triangle Electric Co 29787 Stephenson Hwy	Madison Heights	MI	48071	248-399-2200	399-2612
Web: www.trielec.com					
Truland Systems Corp 1900 Oracle Way Suite 700	Reston	VA	20190	703-464-3000	796-1718
Web: www.truland.com					
Van Ert Electric Co Inc 7019 W Stewart Ave	Wausau	WI	54401	715-845-4308	848-3671
Web: www.vanert.com					
WA Chester LLC 4390 Parliament Pl Suite Q	Lanham	MD	20706	240-487-1940	487-1941
Web: www.wachester.com					
Wagner Industrial Electric Inc PO Box 55	Dayton	OH	45401	937-298-7481	298-0268
TF: 800-775-7799 ■ *Web:* www.wagner-ind.com					
Wasa Electrical Services Inc 2908 Kaihikapu St	Honolulu	HI	96819	808-839-2741	839-5461*
**Fax:* Acctg					
Wasatch Electric 1574 S West Temple	Salt Lake City	UT	84115	801-487-4511	487-5032
TF: 800-999-4511 ■ *Web:* www.wasatchelectric.com					
Watson Electrical 1500 Charleston St	Wilson	NC	27893	252-237-7511	243-1607
Web: www.watsonelec.com					
Wayne J Griffin Electric Inc 116 Hopping Brook Rd	Holliston	MA	01746	508-429-8830	429-7825
TF: 800-421-0151 ■ *Web:* www.waynejgriffin.com					
Wellington Power Corp 40th & Butler Sts	Pittsburgh	PA	15201	412-681-0103	681-0109
TF: 800-540-0017 ■ *Web:* www.wellingtonpower.com					
Welsbach Electric Corp 111-01 14th Ave	College Point	NY	11356	718-670-7900	670-7999
Web: www.welsbachelectric.com					
West-Fair Electric Contractors Inc PO Box 298	Hawthorne	NY	10532	914-769-8050	769-7451
TF: 800-525-0585					
West Virginia Electric Corp PO Box 1587	Fairmont	WV	26554	304-363-6900	366-6356
TF: 800-982-3532 ■ *Web:* www.wvelectric.com					
White Electrical Construction Co 1730 Chattahoochee Ave	Atlanta	GA	30318	404-351-5740	355-5823
TF: 888-519-4483 ■ *Web:* www.whitelectric.com					
Williard Limbach 175 Titus Ave Suite 100	Warrington	PA	18976	215-488-9700	488-9699*
**Fax:* Cust Svc ■ *TF:* 800-827-5030 ■ *Web:* www.limbachinc.com					
Windemuller Electric Inc 1176 Electric Ave	Wayland	MI	49348	616-877-8770	877-8700
TF: 800-333-3641 ■ *Web:* www.windemullerelectric.com					
Zwicker Electrical Co Inc 360 Park Ave S 4th Fl	New York	NY	10010	212-477-8400	995-8469
Web: www.zwicker-electric.com					

192-5 Excavation Contractors

Company	City	State	ZIP	Phone	Fax
AGRA Foundations Inc 19324 67th Ave NE	Arlington	WA	98223	360-474-8290	474-8291
Web: www.agrafoundations.com					
Allied Contractors Inc 204 E Preston St	Baltimore	MD	21202	410-539-6727	332-4594
Aman Environmental Construction Inc 614 E Edna Pl	Covina	CA	91723	626-967-4287	332-1877
Web: www.amanenvironmental.com					
Anastasi Trucking & Paving Inc 4430 Walden St	Lancaster	NY	14086	716-683-5003	683-5045
Web: www.anastasitrucking.com					
Andrews Excavating Inc PO Box 249	Willow Street	PA	17584	717-464-3329	464-4963
APAC Inc 900 Ashwood Pkwy Suite 700	Atlanta	GA	30338	770-392-5300	392-5393
TF: 800-241-7074 ■ *Web:* www.apac.com					
B & B Wrecking & Excavating Inc 5801 Train Ave	Cleveland	OH	44102	216-651-9090	651-9095
Web: www.bbwrecking.com					
Barnard Construction Co Inc PO Box 99	Bozeman	MT	59771	406-586-1995	586-3530
Web: www.barnard-inc.com					
Beaver Excavating Co Inc 2000 Beaver Place Ave	Canton	OH	44706	330-478-2151	478-2122
TF: 800-255-3767 ■ *Web:* www.beaverexcavating.com					
Beers JH Inc PO Box 669	Wind Gap	PA	18091	610-759-7628	863-8270
Bencor Corp of America 2315 Southwell Rd	Dallas	TX	75229	972-247-6767	484-5574
Berkel & Co Contractors Inc PO Box 335	Bonner Springs	KS	66012	913-422-5125	422-2013
Web: www.berkelandcompany.com					
Bi-Con Services Inc 10901 Clay Pike Rd	Derwent	OH	43733	740-685-2542	685-3863
Web: www.bsicos.com					
Bolander Carl & Sons Co Inc 251 Starkey St	Saint Paul	MN	55107	651-224-6299	223-8197
TF: 800-676-6504 ■ *Web:* www.bolander.com					
Borderland Construction Co Inc 400 E 38 St	Tucson	AZ	85713	520-623-0900	623-0232
BR Kreider & Son Inc 63 Kreider Ln	Manheim	PA	17545	717-898-7651	898-0759
TF: 800-689-7651 ■ *Web:* www.brkreider.com					
Branscome Inc 4551 John Tyler Hwy	Williamsburg	VA	23185	757-229-2504	220-0390
TF: 888-229-2504 ■ *Web:* www.branscome.com					
CA Rasmussen Inc 2320 Shasta Way Suite F	Simi Valley	CA	93065	805-581-2275	581-2265
TF: 800-479-2888					
Callas Contractors Inc 10549 Downsville Pike	Hagerstown	MD	21740	301-739-8400	739-7065
Web: www.callascontractors.com					
Carl Bolander & Sons Co Inc 251 Starkey St	Saint Paul	MN	55107	651-224-6299	223-8197
TF: 800-676-6504 ■ *Web:* www.bolander.com					
Case Foundation Co 1325 W Lake St	Roselle	IL	60172	630-529-2911	529-2995
Web: www.casefoundation.com					
Corrado American Inc 200 Marsh Ln	New Castle	DE	19720	302-655-6501	655-3214
CP Ward Inc PO Box 900	Scottsville	NY	14546	585-889-8800	889-6008
Web: www.cpward.com					
Creamer J Fletcher & Son Inc 101 E Broadway	Hackensack	NJ	07601	201-488-9800	488-2901
TF: 800-835-9801 ■ *Web:* www.jfcson.com					
Daisy Construction Co Inc 3128 New Castle Ave	New Castle	DE	19720	302-658-4417	658-0618
Web: www.daisyconstruction.com					
Devcon International Corp					
1350 E Newport Ctr Dr Suite 201	Deerfield Beach	FL	33442	954-429-1500	429-1506
NASDAQ: DEVC ■ *Web:* www.devc.com					
Dywidag Systems International 320 Marmon Dr	Bolingbrook	IL	60440	630-739-1100	739-5517
Web: www.dywidag-systems.com					
Ferro PT Construction Co PO Box 156	Joliet	IL	60434	815-726-6284	726-5614
Web: www.ptferro.com					
Feutz Contractors Inc 1120 N Main St PO Box 130	Paris	IL	61944	217-465-8402	463-2256
TF: 800-252-0273 ■ *Web:* www.feutzcontractors.com					
Fisher Contracting Co 614 Jefferson Ave	Midland	MI	48640	989-835-7771	835-8461
Foundation Constructors Inc 81 Big Break Rd PO Box 97	Oakley	CA	94561	925-625-4455	625-5783
TF: 800-841-8740 ■ *Web:* www.foundationpile.com					
Francis O Day Construction Co Inc 850 E Gude Dr	Rockville	MD	20850	301-652-2400	340-6592
Web: www.foday.com					
Geo-Con Inc 4075 Monroeville Blvd Suite 400 Bldg 2	Monroeville	PA	15146	412-856-7700	373-3357
Web: www.geocon.net					
George J Igel & Co Inc 2040 Alum Creek Dr	Columbus	OH	43207	614-445-8421	445-8205
TF: 800-345-4435 ■ *Web:* www.igelco.com					
Glen Rehbein Excavating Inc 8651 Naples St NE	Blaine	MN	55449	763-784-0657	784-6001
Web: www.rehbein.com					
Goettle Richard Inc 12071 Hamilton Ave	Cincinnati	OH	45231	513-825-8100	825-8107
TF: 800-248-8661 ■ *Web:* www.goettle.com					
Hayward Baker Inc 1130 Annapolis Rd Suite 202	Odenton	MD	21113	410-551-8200	551-1900
TF: 800-456-6548 ■ *Web:* www.haywardbaker.com					
HT Sweeney & Son Inc 308 Dutton Mill Rd	Brookhaven	PA	19015	610-872-8896	874-6730
Igel George J & Co Inc 2040 Alum Creek Dr	Columbus	OH	43207	614-445-8421	445-8205
TF: 800-345-4435 ■ *Web:* www.igelco.com					
Inco Inc PO Box 2705	Rocky Mount	NC	27802	252-446-1174	977-3039
Independence Excavating Inc 5720 Schaaf Rd	Independence	OH	44131	216-524-1700	524-1701
TF: 800-524-3478 ■ *Web:* www.indexc.com					
J Fletcher Creamer & Son Inc 101 E Broadway	Hackensack	NJ	07601	201-488-9800	488-2901
TF: 800-835-9801 ■ *Web:* www.jfcson.com					
JH Beers Inc PO Box 669	Wind Gap	PA	18091	610-759-7628	863-8270
Kamminga & Roodvoets Inc 3435 Broadmoor Ave SE	Grand Rapids	MI	49512	616-949-0800	949-1894
TF: 800-632-9755					
Kerns Construction Co Inc PO Box 902	Stillwater	OK	74076	405-372-2750	377-8802
Kreider BR & Son Inc 63 Kreider Ln	Manheim	PA	17545	717-898-7651	898-0759
TF: 800-689-7651 ■ *Web:* www.brkreider.com					
Lambrecht TJ Construction Inc 10 Gougar Rd	Joliet	IL	60432	815-727-9211	727-6421
Web: www.tjlambrecht.com					
Larry's Inc 2020 Schoonover St	Gillette	WY	82718	307-682-5394	686-6523
TF: 800-967-1473					
Lawrence Construction Co Inc 9002 N Moore Rd	Littleton	CO	80125	303-791-5642	791-5647
Luburgh Inc 4174 E Pike	Zanesville	OH	43701	740-452-3668	454-7225
M Rondano Inc 49 East Ave	Norwalk	CT	06851	203-846-1577	846-9564
Web: www.rondano.com					
Maclean Construction Co Inc PO Box 190	Ludington	MI	49431	231-845-6275	843-2303
Manafort Brothers Inc PO Box 99	Plainville	CT	06062	860-229-4853	229-1878
TF: 888-626-2367 ■ *Web:* www.manafort.com					
Mann Brothers Inc PO Box 48	Elkhorn	WI	53121	262-723-5500	723-3463
Web: www.mannbrosinc.com					
Markham Contracting Co Inc 22820 N 19th Ave	Phoenix	AZ	85027	623-869-9100	869-9400
Web: www.markhamcontracting.com					
McAninch Corp 6800 Lake Dr Suite 125	West Des Moines	IA	50266	515-267-2500	267-2550
TF: 800-383-3201 ■ *Web:* www.mcaninchcorp.com					
McGowan-Stauffer Inc PO Box 524	Carnegie	PA	15106	412-279-8846	279-8848
Web: www.mcgowan-stauffer.com					
Merlyn Contractors Inc PO Box 917	Novi	MI	48376	248-349-3800	347-2966
Web: www.merlyn.us					
Millgard Corp 33039 Schoolcraft Rd	Livonia	MI	48150	734-425-8550	425-0624
Moretrench American Corp 100 Stickle Ave PO Box 316	Rockaway	NJ	07866	973-627-2100	627-6078
TF: 800-394-6673 ■ *Web:* www.moretrench.com					
Nicholson Construction Co 12 McClane St	Cuddy	PA	15031	412-221-4500	221-3127
TF: 800-388-2340 ■ *Web:* www.nicholson-rodio.com					
Noralco Corp 1920 Lincoln Rd	Pittsburgh	PA	15235	412-361-6678	361-6535
Web: www.noralco.com					
Ortiz Enterprises Inc 6 Cushing Way Suite 200	Irvine	CA	92618	949-753-1414	753-1477
Web: www.ortizent.com					
Park Construction Co Inc 500 73rd Ave NE Suite 123	Minneapolis	MN	55432	763-786-9800	786-2952
TF: 800-328-2556					
Pavex Inc 4400 Gettysburg Rd	Camp Hill	PA	17011	717-761-1502	761-0329
Perry Engineering Co Inc 1945 Millwood Pike	Winchester	VA	22602	540-667-4310	667-7618
TF: 800-272-4310 ■ *Web:* www.perryeng.com					
Phillips & Jordan Inc 6621 Wilbanks Rd	Knoxville	TN	37912	865-688-8342	688-8369
TF: 800-955-0876 ■ *Web:* www.pandj.com					
Pleasant Excavating Co Inc 24024 Frederick Rd Suite 200	Clarksburg	MD	20871	301-428-0800	428-1736
TF: 800-842-1180					
Professional Construction Services Inc PO Box 2005	Prairieville	LA	70769	225-744-4016	744-4938
TF: 800-562-4318 ■ *Web:* www.professionalconstruction.com					
PT Ferro Construction Co PO Box 156	Joliet	IL	60434	815-726-6284	726-5614
Web: www.ptferro.com					
Railroad Construction Co Inc 75-77 Grove St	Paterson	NJ	07503	973-684-0362	684-1355
Rasmussen CA Inc 2320 Shasta Way Suite F	Simi Valley	CA	93065	805-581-2275	581-2265
TF: 800-479-2888					
Raymond Excavating Co Inc 800 Gratiot Blvd	Marysville	MI	48040	810-364-6881	364-6450
TF: 888-837-6770 ■ *Web:* www.raymondexcavating.com					
Rehbein Glen Excavating Inc 8651 Naples St NE	Blaine	MN	55449	763-784-0657	784-6001
Web: www.rehbein.com					
Richard Goettle Inc 12071 Hamilton Ave	Cincinnati	OH	45231	513-825-8100	825-8107
TF: 800-248-8661 ■ *Web:* www.goettle.com					
Rondano M Inc 49 East Ave	Norwalk	CT	06851	203-846-1577	846-9564
Web: www.rondano.com					
Ruttura & Sons Construction Co Inc 165 Sherwood Ave	Farmingdale	NY	11735	631-454-0291	454-8804
Web: www.ruttura.com					
Ryan Inc Central 2700 E Racine St	Janesville	WI	53545	608-754-2291	754-3290
Web: www.ryancentral.com					
Seubert Excavators Inc PO Box 57	Cottonwood	ID	83522	208-962-3314	962-3392
Sierrita Mining & Ranching Co Inc HC-70 Box 4260	Sahuarita	AZ	85629	520-625-1204	625-3234
Soil Engineering Construction Inc 927 Arguello St	Redwood City	CA	94063	650-367-9595	367-8139
Stevens Painton Corp 7850 Freeway Cir Suite 100	Middleburg Heights	OH	44130	440-234-7888	234-1967
Web: www.spcdmg.com					
Stroer & Graff Inc 1830 Phillips Ln	Antioch	CA	94509	925-778-0200	778-6766
Subsurface Constructors Inc 110 Angelica St	Saint Louis	MO	63147	314-421-2460	421-2479
Web: www.subsurfaceconstructors.com					
Super Excavators Inc N 59 W 14601 Bobolink Ave	Menomonee Falls	WI	53051	262-252-3200	252-3406
Web: www.superexcavators.com					
Sweeney HT & Son Inc 308 Dutton Mill Rd	Brookhaven	PA	19015	610-872-8896	874-6730
Terra Engineering & Construction Corp 2201 Vondron Rd	Madison	WI	53718	608-221-3501	221-4075
TJ Lambrecht Construction Inc 10 Gougar Rd	Joliet	IL	60432	815-727-9211	727-6421
Web: www.tjlambrecht.com					
Union Engineering Co Inc PO Box 1000	Ventura	CA	93002	805-648-3373	648-6634
Urban Foundation/Engineering LLC PO Box 158	East Elmhurst	NY	11369	718-478-3021	397-1917
Velting Contractors Inc 3060 Breton Rd SE	Kentwood	MI	49512	616-949-6660	949-8168
Web: www.velting.com					
Ward CP Inc PO Box 900	Scottsville	NY	14546	585-889-8800	889-6008
Web: www.cpward.com					
Wes Construction Corp 175 Commercial Cir	Dedham	MA	02026	781-326-4030	326-9957

192-6 Glass & Glazing Contractors

Company	City	State	ZIP	Phone	Fax
American Glass & Metals Corp					
15100 Keel St PO Box 701511	Plymouth	MI	48170	734-459-0760	459-0238
Beals Royal Glass & Mirror Co 6420 Arville St	Las Vegas	NV	89118	702-736-8788	736-8362
Benson Industries Inc 1650 NW Naito Pkwy Suite 250	Portland	OR	97209	503-226-7611	226-0070
TF: 800-999-5113 ■ *Web:* www.bensonglobal.com					
Builders Architectural Products Inc					
430 Lake Cook Rd Suite C	Deerfield	IL	60015	847-945-9200	945-9210
Web: www.buildersarch.com					
Building Erection Services Co Inc 15585 S Keeler PO Box 970	Olathe	KS	66051	913-764-5560	764-2317
Carter Glass Co Inc 1608 Locust St	Kansas City	MO	64108	816-471-8288	471-0174
TF: 866-471-8287 ■ *Web:* www.carterglass.net					
Cartner Glass Systems Inc					
2508 Westinghouse Blvd PO Box 7744	Charlotte	NC	28241	704-588-1976	588-9440
TF: 800-968-2818					
Culbertson Enterprises Inc 600-A Snyder Ave	West Chester	PA	19382	610-436-6400	436-6309
Enclos Corp 2770 Blue Water Rd	Eagan	MN	55121	651-796-6100	994-6360
TF: 800-831-1108 ■ *Web:* www.enclos.com					
General Glass Co Inc 5797 MacCorkle Ave SE	Charleston	WV	25304	304-925-2171	925-8915
Giroux Glass Inc 850 W Washington Blvd	Los Angeles	CA	90015	213-747-7406	747-8778
TF: 800-684-5277 ■ *Web:* www.girouxglass.com					
K & M Glass Contractors Inc 500 Production Ave Suite A	Madison	AL	35758	256-461-7222	461-0009
Karas & Karas Glass Co Inc 455 Dorchester Ave	Boston	MA	02127	617-268-8800	269-0536
TF: 800-888-1235 ■ *Web:* www.karasglass.com					

Company	City	State	Zip	Phone	Fax
Lafayette Glass Co Inc 2841 Teal Rd *TF Cust Svc:* 800-382-7862 ■ *Web:* www.lafayetteglass.com	Lafayette	IN	47905	765-474-1402	474-3382
Lee & Cates Glass Inc 142 Madison St *Web:* www.leeandcatesglass.com	Jacksonville	FL	32203	904-354-4643	355-0131
Masonry Arts Inc 2105 3rd Ave N *Web:* www.masonryarts.com	Bessemer	AL	35020	205-428-0780	424-1931
MTH Industries 1 MTH Plaza *TF:* 800-231-9711 ■ *Web:* www.mthindustries.com	Hillside	IL	60162	708-498-1100	498-1101
National Glass & Metal Co Inc 1424 Easton Rd Suite 400 *Web:* www.ngmco.com	Horsham	PA	19044	215-938-8880	938-7028
Reliant Glass & Door Systems LLC 3208 Washington Ave *TF:* 800-234-7432 ■ *Web:* www.reliantglassanddoor.com	Sheboygan	WI	53081	920-458-4611	458-4927
Sashco Inc 720 S Rochester Ave Suite D *TF:* 800-600-3232 ■ *Web:* www.sashcoinc.com	Ontario	CA	91761	909-937-8222	937-8223
Waltek & Co Ltd 2130 Waycorss Rd *Web:* www.walteklt d.com	Cincinnati	OH	45240	513-577-7980	577-7990
Walters & Wolf 41450 Boscell Rd *TF:* 800-969-9653 ■ *Web:* www.waltersandwolf.com	Fremont	CA	94538	510-490-1115	651-7172
Young Group Ltd 1054 Central Industrial Dr *TF:* 800-331-3080 ■ *Web:* www.theyounggroup.net	Saint Louis	MO	63110	314-771-3080	771-4597

192-7 Masonry & Stone Contractors

Company	City	State	Zip	Phone	Fax
Berglund Construction 8410 S Chicago Ave *Web:* www.berglundco.com	Chicago	IL	60617	773-374-1000	374-8847
Boettcher Edgar Mason Contractors Inc 1616 S Airport Rd *TF:* 800-562-3827 ■ *Web:* www.boettchermasonry.com	Traverse City	MI	49686	231-941-5802	941-7627
Brisk Waterproofing Co Inc 720 Grand Ave *TF:* 800-942-9228 ■ *Web:* www.briskwaterproofing.com	Ridgefield	NJ	07657	201-945-0210	945-7841
Brown Dee Inc PO Box 570335 *Web:* www.deebrown.com	Dallas	TX	75357	214-321-6443	328-1039
Bruns-Gutzwiller Inc 309 S John St PO Box 119 *Web:* www.bruns-gutzwiller.com	Batesville	IN	47006	812-934-2105	934-2107
Caretti Inc 4590 Industrial Park Rd PO Box 331 *Web:* www.carettimasonry.com	Camp Hill	PA	17011	717-737-6759	737-6880
Culbertson Enterprises Inc 600-A Snyder Ave	West Chester	PA	19382	610-436-6400	436-6309
Dee Brown Inc PO Box 570335 *Web:* www.deebrown.com	Dallas	TX	75357	214-321-6443	328-1039
DH Johnson Co 320 W Saint Charles Rd	Villa Park	IL	60181	630-832-1021	832-2233
Edgar Boettcher Mason Contractors Inc 1616 S Airport Rd *TF:* 800-562-3827 ■ *Web:* www.boettchermasonry.com	Traverse City	MI	49686	231-941-5802	941-7627
Evans-Mason Inc 1021 S Grand Ave E	Springfield	IL	62703	217-522-3396	522-3190
Fred A Kinateder Masonry Inc 2307 Badger Dr *Web:* www.fkmi.com	Waukesha	WI	53188	262-548-9876	548-0102
Haynes MB Corp 187 Deaverview Rd *Web:* www.mbhaynes.com	Asheville	NC	28806	828-254-6141	253-8136
International Chimney Corp 55 S Long St *TF:* 800-828-1446 ■ *Web:* www.internationalchimney.com	Williamsville	NY	14221	716-634-3967	634-3983
JD Long Masonry Inc 8253 Backlick Rd Suite J *Web:* www.jdlongmasonry.com	Lorton	VA	22079	703-550-8880	550-9567
John J Smith Masonry Co 9200 Green Park Rd *Web:* www.smithmasonry.com	Saint Louis	MO	63123	314-894-9500	894-1172
Kauai Builders Ltd 3988 Halau St	Lihue	HI	96766	808-245-2911	245-1769
Kretschmar & Smith Inc 6293 Pedley Rd	Riverside	CA	92509	951-361-1405	361-1381
Leonard Masonry Inc 5925 Fee Fee Rd *Web:* www.leonardmasonry.com	Hazelwood	MO	63042	314-731-5500	731-3366
Lindblad Construction Co 717 E Cass St *Web:* www.lindbladconstruction.com	Joliet	IL	60432	815-726-6251	723-4907
Long JD Masonry Inc 8253 Backlick Rd Suite J *Web:* www.jdlongmasonry.com	Lorton	VA	22079	703-550-8880	550-9567
Manganaro Corp New England 52 Cummings Park	Woburn	MA	01801	781-937-8880	937-8882
Masonry Arts Inc 2105 3rd Ave N *Web:* www.masonryarts.com	Bessemer	AL	35020	205-428-0780	424-1931
MB Haynes Corp 187 Deaverview Rd *Web:* www.mbhaynes.com	Asheville	NC	28806	828-254-6141	253-8136
Mid-Continental Restoration Co Inc 401 E Hudson Rd PO Box 429 *TF:* 800-835-3700 ■ *Web:* www.midcontinental.com	Fort Scott	KS	66701	620-223-3700	223-5052
Midwest Titan Inc 11865 S Conley St *Web:* www.titanbuilt.com	Olathe	KS	66061	913-782-6700	829-2785
Otto Baum Co Inc 866 N Main St PO Box 161 *Web:* www.ottobaum.com	Morton	IL	61550	309-266-7114	263-1050
Performance Contracting Group Inc 16400 College Blvd *Web:* www.pcg.com	Lenexa	KS	66219	913-888-8600	307-0453
Pettit Construction Inc 450 Partners Ln PO Box 307 *Web:* www.pettitconstruction.com	Roebuck	SC	29376	864-576-4762	576-4766
Pompano Masonry Corp 880 S Andrews Ave *TF:* 800-762-7425 ■ *Web:* www.pompanomasonry.com	Pompano Beach	FL	33069	954-946-3033	941-4857
Pyramid Masonry Contractors Inc 2330 Mellon Ct *TF:* 800-345-4750	Decatur	GA	30035	770-987-4750	981-7142
R & R Masonry Inc 5337 Cahuenga Blvd Bldg A Unit E	North Hollywood	CA	91601	323-877-2118	877-1715
Rock & Waterscape Systems Inc 24400 Sinacola Dr **Fax Area Code:* 949 ■ *TF:* 800-328-9762 ■ *Web:* www.rockandwaterscape.com	Farmington Hills	MI	48335	248-473-0500	458-6331*
RP Carbone Construction Co 5885 Landerbrook Dr Suite 110 *Web:* www.rpcarbone.com	Cleveland	OH	44124	440-449-6750	449-5717
Schiffer Mason Contractors Inc 2190 Delhi NE PO Box 250 *Web:* www.schiffermasonry.com	Holt	MI	48842	517-694-2566	694-1936
Seedorff Masonry Inc 408 W Mission St *Web:* www.seedorff.com	Strawberry Point	IA	52076	563-933-2296	933-4114
Snow Jr & King Inc 2415 Church St *Web:* www.snowjrandking.com	Norfolk	VA	23504	757-627-8621	622-3883
Sun Valley Masonry Inc 10828 N Cave Creek Rd *Web:* www.svmasonry.com	Phoenix	AZ	85020	602-943-6106	997-6857
Treviicos Corp 273 Summer St *Web:* www.treviicos.com	Boston	MA	02210	617-737-1453	737-5810
UBM Inc 330 S Wells St Suite 1214 *Web:* www.ubm-inc.com	Chicago	IL	60606	312-939-0505	939-0483
WASCO Inc 1138 2nd Ave N *TF:* 800-952-8631	Nashville	TN	37208	615-244-9090	726-2643
Western Construction Group 1637 N Warson Rd *TF Cust Svc:* 800-325-2801 ■ *Web:* www.westerngroup.com	Saint Louis	MO	63132	314-427-6733	427-6199

192-8 Painting & Paperhanging Contractors

Company	City	State	Zip	Phone	Fax
Ascher Brothers Co Inc 3033 W Fletcher St *Web:* www.ascherbrothers.com	Chicago	IL	60618	773-588-0001	588-5350
Avalotis Corp 400 Jones St *Web:* www.avalotis.com	Verona	PA	15147	412-242-5825	828-6599
Benise-Dowling & Assoc Inc 5068 Snapfinger Woods Dr *Web:* www.benise-dowling.com	Decatur	GA	30035	770-981-4237	593-0342
Borbon Inc 7312 Walnut Ave *TF:* 800-929-1467	Buena Park	CA	90620	714-994-0170	994-0641
Brock Services Ltd 1670 E Cardinal Dr *TF:* 800-537-7479	Beaumont	TX	77705	409-833-7571	833-3279
Campbell George Painting Corp 31-40 College Pt Blvd	Flushing	NY	11354	718-353-8330	353-4537
Cannon Sline Industrial Inc 10 Industrial Hwy MS 38 *TF:* 800-729-4600 ■ *Web:* www.cannonsline.com	Lester	PA	19113	610-521-2100	521-2178
CB Askins & Co Inc 208 S Blanding St	Lake City	SC	29560	843-394-8555	394-8333
CertaPro Painters Ltd 150 Green Tree Rd Suite 1003 *TF:* 800-462-3782 ■ *Web:* www.certapro.com	Oaks	PA	19456	610-983-9411	650-9997
Certified Coatings of California 1045 Detroit Ave *TF:* 888-686-5551	Concord	CA	94518	925-686-1550	671-7036
E Caligari & Son Inc 1333 Ingleside Rd *Web:* www.ecaligariandson.com	Norfolk	VA	23502	757-853-4511	855-9424
George Campbell Painting Corp 31-40 College Pt Blvd	Flushing	NY	11354	718-353-8330	353-4537
George E Masker Inc 887 71st Ave *Web:* www.maskerpainting.com	Oakland	CA	94621	510-568-1206	638-2530
Goodman Decorating Co 3400 Atlanta Industrial Pkwy *Web:* www.goodman-decorating.com	Atlanta	GA	30318	404-965-3626	965-2558
Hartman-Walsh Painting Co 7144 N Market St *TF:* 800-899-3535 ■ *Web:* www.hartmanwalsh.com	Saint Louis	MO	63133	314-863-1800	863-6964
Hess Sweitzer Inc 2805 160th St *TF:* 800-491-4377 ■ *Web:* www.hesssweitzer.com	New Berlin	WI	53151	262-641-9100	641-6362
JP Carroll Co Inc 310 N Madison Ave *TF:* 800-660-0162	Los Angeles	CA	90004	323-660-9230	660-9238
K2 Industrial Services 5233 Hohman Ave *Web:* www.k2industrial.com	Hammond	IN	46320	219-933-5300	933-5301
King Peter Corp 11040 N 19th Ave	Phoenix	AZ	85029	602-944-4441	943-4876
Long Painting Co 21414 68th Ave S *TF:* 800-678-5664 ■ *Web:* www.longpainting.com	Kent	WA	98032	253-234-8050	234-0034
Madias Brothers Inc 12850 Evergreen Rd	Detroit	MI	48223	313-272-5330	272-5345
Masker George E Inc 887 71st Ave *Web:* www.maskerpainting.com	Oakland	CA	94621	510-568-1206	638-2530
ML McDonald Co 50 Oakland St PO Box 315 *TF:* 800-733-6243 ■ *Web:* www.mlmcdonald.com	Watertown	MA	02471	617-923-0900	923-0597
NLP Enterprises Inc 11422 Fletchers Town Rd PO Box 349 *TF:* 800-962-9380 ■ *Web:* www.nlpentinc.com	Owings Mills	MD	21117	410-356-7500	356-7525
Partition Specialties Inc 714 C St Suite 3 *TF:* 800-982-9255 ■ *Web:* www.partitionspecialties.com	San Rafael	CA	94901	415-721-1040	721-1053
Peter King Corp 11040 N 19th Ave	Phoenix	AZ	85029	602-944-4441	943-4876
Redwood Painting Co Inc 620 W 10th St *TF:* 800-227-0622 ■ *Web:* www.redwoodptg.com	Pittsburg	CA	94565	925-432-4500	432-6129
Specialty Finishes Inc 1545 Marietta Blvd NW *TF:* 800-864-7706 ■ *Web:* www.specialtyfinishes.com	Atlanta	GA	30318	404-351-1062	351-0535
Swanson & Youngdale Inc 6565 W 23rd St *TF:* 800-486-7824 ■ *Web:* www.swansonyoungdale.com	Saint Louis Park	MN	55426	952-545-2541	545-4435
TMI Coatings Inc 3291 Terminal Dr *TF:* 800-328-0229 ■ *Web:* www.tmicoatings.com	Saint Paul	MN	55121	651-452-6100	452-0598
Vulcan Painters Inc PO Box 1010 *Web:* www.vulcan-group.com	Bessemer	AL	35021	205-428-0556	424-2267
Whitehouse-PMC LLC 121 Locus St PO Box 368 *TF:* 800-626-5859 ■ *Web:* www.whitehousepmc.com	Charlestown	IN	47111	812-256-1300	256-1303

192-9 Plastering, Drywall, Acoustical, Insulation Contractors

Company	City	State	Zip	Phone	Fax
Acousti Engineering Co of Florida Inc 4656 34th St SW *Web:* www.acousti.com	Orlando	FL	32811	407-425-3467	422-6502
Airtite Contractors Inc 343 Carol Ln *Web:* www.air-tite.net	Elmhurst	IL	60128	630-530-9001	530-9034
Allied Construction Services & Color Inc 2122 Fleur Dr PO Box 937 *TF:* 800-365-4855 ■ *Web:* www.alliedconst.com	Des Moines	IA	50304	515-288-4855	288-2069
Anning Johnson Co Inc 1959 Anson Dr	Melrose Park	IL	60160	708-681-1300	681-1386
Anson Industries Inc 1959 Anson Dr *Web:* www.ansonindustries.com	Melrose Park	IL	60160	708-681-1300	681-1310
APi Construction Co 2366 Rose Pl *TF:* 800-223-4922	Saint Paul	MN	55113	651-636-4320	636-0312
Baker Drywall Co Inc 415 E Hwy 80 PO Box 38299 *TF:* 800-458-3480 ■ *Web:* www.bakerdrywall.com	Dallas	TX	75238	972-289-5534	289-4580
Bayside Interiors Inc 3220 Darby Common *Web:* www.baysideinteriors.com	Fremont	CA	94539	510-438-9171	438-9375
BHN Corp 435 Madison Ave *TF:* 800-238-9046 ■ *Web:* www.bhncorp.com	Memphis	TN	38103	901-521-9500	521-9507
Bouma Corp 4101 Roger B Chaffee Memorial Blvd SE *TF:* 800-813-9208 ■ *Web:* www.boumacorp.com	Grand Rapids	MI	49548	616-538-3600	538-0143
Burjon Construction Co PO Box 1590	Troy	NY	12181	518-271-7400	271-7412
Cannon Constructors Inc 17000 Ventura Blvd Suite 301 *Web:* www.cannongroup.com	Encino	CA	91316	818-906-6200	906-6220
CE Thurston & Sons Inc 3335 Croft St *TF Cust Svc:* 800-444-7713 ■ *Web:* www.cethurston.com	Norfolk	VA	23513	757-855-7700	855-1214
Central Ceilings Inc 36 Norfolk Ave *TF:* 800-442-2115 ■ *Web:* www.centralceilings.com	South Easton	MA	02375	508-238-6985	238-2191
Chempower Inc 1501 Raff Rd SW *TF:* 800-442-4299 ■ *Web:* www.chempower.com	Canton	OH	44710	330-479-4202	479-1866
Circle B Co Inc 5636 S Meridian St *TF:* 800-775-5640	Indianapolis	IN	46217	317-787-5746	780-2654
Cleveland Construction Inc 8620 Tyler Blvd *Web:* www.clevelandconstruction.com	Mentor	OH	44060	440-255-8000	255-8096
Crane FL & Sons Inc 508 S Spring St PO Box 428 *TF:* 800-748-9523 ■ *Web:* www.flcrane.com	Fulton	MS	38843	662-862-2172	862-2649
Davenport Insulation Inc 7400 Gateway Ct *TF:* 800-328-9485	Manassas	VA	20109	703-631-7744	631-8730
Daw Technologies Inc 1600 W 2200 South Suite 201 *Web:* www.dawtech.com	Salt Lake City	UT	84119	801-977-3100	973-6640
Ecker M & Co 9525 W Bryn Mawr Ave Suite 900 *Web:* www.eckerusa.com	Rosemont	IL	60018	847-994-6000	233-9710
EL Thompson & Assoc LLC 600 Virginia Ave NE *Web:* www.elta-ga.com	Atlanta	GA	30306	404-872-4726	876-4299
Eliason & Knuth Cos Inc 13324 Chandler Rd *TF:* 800-365-5760 ■ *Web:* www.e-kco.com	Omaha	NE	68138	402-896-1614	896-4058
Entrx Corp 800 Nicollet Mall Suite 2690	Minneapolis	MN	55402	612-333-0614	338-7332
FL Crane & Sons Inc 508 S Spring St PO Box 428 *TF:* 800-748-9523 ■ *Web:* www.flcrane.com	Fulton	MS	38843	662-862-2172	862-2649
Group Builders Inc 2020 Democrat St	Honolulu	HI	96819	808-832-0888	832-0890
Henderson-Johnson Co Inc 918 Canal St PO Box 6964 *Web:* www.henderson-johnson.com	Syracuse	NY	13217	315-479-5561	479-5585
Hoge-Warren-Zimmermann Co 40 W Cresentville Rd *TF:* 800-322-3521	Cincinnati	OH	45246	513-671-3300	671-3514
Interior Construction Services Ltd 2930 Market St *Web:* www.ics-stl.com	Saint Louis	MO	63103	314-534-6664	534-6663
Irex Contracting Group 120 N Lime St *TF:* 800-487-7255 ■ *Web:* www.irexcontracting.com	Lancaster	PA	17608	717-397-3633	399-5135
ISI Insulation Specialties Inc 2142 Rheem Dr Suite A *Web:* www.insulspec.com	Pleasanton	CA	94588	925-846-7990	846-7490

Plastering, Drywall, Acoustical, Insulation Contractors (Cont'd)

Phone | Fax

Jacobson & Co Inc 1079 E Grand Ave PO Box 511 Elizabeth NJ 07207 908-355-5200 355-8680
TF: 800-352-2627 ■ *Web:* www.jacobsoncompany.com
KHS & S Contractors Inc 5422 Bay Center Dr Suite 200 Tampa FL 33609 813-628-9330 628-4339
Web: www.khss.com
Land Coast Insulation Inc 4017 2nd St New Iberia LA 70560 337-367-7741 367-7744
TF: 800-333-9424 ■ *Web:* www.landcoast.com
Lotspeich Co 16101 NW 54th Ave Miami FL 33014 305-624-7777 624-4517
Web: www.lotspeich.com
Luse-Stevenson Co 3990 Enterprise Ct Aurora IL 60504 630-862-2600 862-2674
Web: www.luse.com
M Ecker & Co 9525 W Bryn Mawr Ave Suite 900 Rosemont IL 60018 847-994-6000 233-9710
Web: www.eckerusa.com
Manganaro Corp New England 52 Cummings Park Woburn MA 01801 781-937-8880 937-8882
Marek Brothers Co 3701 Piney Woods Dr Houston TX 77018 713-681-9213 681-0446
Web: www.marekbros.com
McCartney TJ Inc 3 Capitol St Suite 1 Nashua NH 03063 603-889-6380 880-0770
TF: 800-889-6380 ■ *Web:* www.tjminc.com
Midwest Drywall Co Inc 1351 S Reca Ct Wichita KS 67209 316-722-9559 722-9682
Web: www.mwdw.com
ML McDonald Co 50 Oakland St PO Box 315 Watertown MA 02471 617-923-0900 923-0597
TF: 800-733-6243 ■ *Web:* www.mlmcdonald.com
Nastasi & Assoc Inc 147 Herricks Rd Garden City Park NY 11040 516-746-1800 746-6796
TF: 800-353-0990
National Acoustics Inc 515 W 36th St New York NY 10018 212-695-1252 695-4539
National Construction Enterprises Inc 5075 Carpenter Rd Ypsilanti MI 48197 734-434-1600 434-6699
Niehaus Construction Services Inc 4151 Sarpy Ave Saint Louis MO 63110 314-533-8434 533-1448
Web: www.ncs-stl.com
P & P Contractors Inc 660 Lofstrand Ln Rockville MD 20850 301-251-6750 251-6777
Web: www.pandpcontractors.com
Padilla Construction Co 1605 N O'Donnell Way Orange CA 92867 714-685-8500 685-8500
Partition Specialties Inc 714 C St Suite 3 San Rafael CA 94901 415-721-1040 721-1053
TF: 800-982-9255 ■ *Web:* www.partitionspecialties.com
Paul J Krez Co 7831 N Nagle Ave Morton Grove IL 60053 847-581-0017 965-7841
Web: www.krezgroup.com/pjkc.html
Performance Contracting Group Inc 16400 College Blvd Lenexa KS 66219 913-888-8600 307-0453
Web: www.pcg.com
Performance Contracting Inc 6621 E Mission Ave Spokane WA 99212 509-535-4814 534-5921
TF: 800-541-4323 ■ *Web:* www.pcg.com
Precision Walls Inc 1230 NE Maynard Rd Cary NC 27513 919-832-0380 839-1402
TF: 800-849-9255 ■ *Web:* www.precisionwalls.com
Professional Construction Services Inc PO Box 2005 Prairieville LA 70769 225-744-4016 744-4938
TF: 800-562-4318 ■ *Web:* www.professionalconstruction.com
RE Kramig Co Inc 323 S Wayne Ave Cincinnati OH 45215 513-761-4010 761-0362
Web: www.kramigco.com
Shields Inc 2625 Hope Church Rd Winston-Salem NC 27103 336-765-9040 765-3715
Web: www.shieldsinc.com
South Valley Drywall Inc 12362 Dumont Way Littleton CO 80125 303-791-7212 470-0116
Web: www.southvalleydrywall.com
Specialty Systems Inc 302 S State Ave Indianapolis IN 46201 317-269-3600 269-3606
Web: www.ssiweb.com
Spectrum Interiors Inc 2652 Crescent Springs Rd Crescent Springs KY 41017 859-331-2696 331-4322
TF: 888-353-2696 ■ *Web:* www.spectruminterior.com
Thompson EL & Assoc LLC 600 Virginia Ave NE Atlanta GA 30306 404-872-4726 876-4299
Web: www.elta-ga.com
Thorne Assoc Inc 1450 W Randolph St Chicago IL 60607 312-738-5230 738-5249
Web: www.thorneassociates.com
Thurston CE & Sons Inc 3335 Croft St Norfolk VA 23513 757-855-7700 855-1214
TF Cust Svc: 800-444-7713 ■ *Web:* www.cethurston.com
TJ McCartney Inc 3 Capitol St Suite 1 Nashua NH 03063 603-889-6380 880-0770
TF: 800-889-6380 ■ *Web:* www.tjminc.com
Turner-Brooks Inc 28811 John R Rd Madison Heights MI 48071 248-548-3400 548-9213
TF: 800-560-7003
United/Anco Industries Inc 15981 Airline Hwy Baton Rouge LA 70817 225-752-2000 756-7686*
**Fax:* Mail Rm ■ *TF:* 800-999-8479 ■ *Web:* www.unitedanco.com
Waco Inc 5450 Lewis Rd Sandston VA 23150 804-222-8440 226-3241
Web: www.wacoinc.com
Western Partitions Inc 8300 SW Hunziker Rd Tigard OR 97223 503-620-1600 624-5781
Web: www.westernpartitions.com
Wyatt Inc 4545 Campbells Run Rd Pittsburgh PA 15205 412-787-5800 787-5845
TF: 800-966-5801 ■ *Web:* www.wyattinc.com

192-10 Plumbing, Heating, Air Conditioning Contractors

Phone | Fax

AC Corp 301 Creek Ridge Rd Greensboro NC 27406 336-273-4472 274-6035
TF: 800-582-3073 ■ *Web:* www.accorporation.com
ACCO Engineered Systems 6265 San Fernando Rd Glendale CA 91201 818-244-6571 247-6533
TF Cust Svc: 800-998-2226 ■ *Web:* www.accoair.com
AD Jacobson Co Inc 16210 W 108th St Lenexa KS 66219 913-529-5000 529-5020
Advance Mechanical Contractors Inc 1456 E Hill St Signal Hill CA 90755 562-426-1725 424-7251
Advance Mechanical Systems Inc 2080 S Carboy Rd Mount Prospect IL 60056 847-593-2510 593-2536
Web: www.jfahern.com
Air Comfort Corp 2550 Braga Dr Broadview IL 60155 708-345-1900 345-2730
TF: 800-466-3779 ■ *Web:* www.aircomfort.com
Air Con Refrigeration & Heating Inc 123 Lake St Waukegan IL 60085 847-336-4128 336-4949
Air Engineering Co Inc 2308 Pahounui Dr Honolulu HI 96819 808-848-1040 841-5193
Air-Rite Heating & Cooling Inc 100 Overland Dr North Aurora IL 60542 630-966-8100 966-8101
Web: www.air-rite.com
Aire Serv Heating & Air Conditioning Inc
1020 N University Parks Dr Waco TX 76707 800-583-2662 745-5098*
**Fax Area Code:* 254 ■ *Web:* www.aireserv.com
Airtrol Inc 3960 North St Baton Rouge LA 70806 225-383-2617 343-7986
Alaka'i Mechanical Corp 2655 Waiwai Loop Honolulu HI 96819 808-834-1085 834-1800
TF: 800-600-1085 ■ *Web:* www.alakaimechanical.com
Aldag Honold Mechanical Inc 3509 S Business Dr Sheboygan WI 53082 920-458-5558 458-3750
TF: 800-967-1712 ■ *Web:* www.aldaghonold.com
Allied Mechanical Services Inc PO Box 2587 Kalamazoo MI 49003 269-344-0191 344-0196
TF: 888-237-3017 ■ *Web:* www.alliedmechanical.com
Althoff Industries Inc 8001 S Rt 31 Crystal Lake IL 60014 815-455-7000 455-9375*
**Fax:* Sales ■ *TF:* 800-225-2443 ■ *Web:* www.althoffind.com
American Leak Detection 888 Research Dr Suite 100 Palm Springs CA 92262 760-320-9991 320-1288
TF: 800-755-6697 ■ *Web:* www.americanleakdetection.com
American Mechanical Services 8039 Laurel Lakes Ct Laurel MD 20707 301-206-5070 206-2520
TF: 888-805-4267 ■ *Web:* www.amsofusa.com
American Residential Services LLC 9010 Maier Rd Suite 105 Laurel MD 20723 301-470-1212 470-3724
TF: 800-822-7332 ■ *Web:* www.ars.com
Anderson Rowe & Buckley Inc 2833 3rd St San Francisco CA 94107 415-282-1625 282-0752
Anron Heating & Air Conditioning Inc
440 Wyandanch Ave North Babylon NY 11704 631-643-3433 491-6983
TF: 800-924-3336
Anthony Mechanical Inc 525 E 40th St Lubbock TX 79404 806-747-4151 747-7733
AO Reed & Co 4777 Ruffner St San Diego CA 92111 858-565-4131 292-6958
Web: www.aoreed.com

Phone | Fax

APi Group Inc Specialty Construction Services Group
2366 Rose Pl Saint Paul MN 55113 651-636-4320 636-0312
Web: www.apigroupinc.com/construction.html
Arden Engineering Constructors LLC 505 Narragansett Pk Dr Pawtucket RI 02861 401-727-3500 727-3540
Web: www.ardeneng.com
Armon Inc 2265 Carlson Dr Northbrook IL 60062 847-498-4800 498-9091
Web: www.femoran.com
Atlantic Constructors Inc 1401 Battery Brooke Pkwy Richmond VA 23237 804-233-7671 233-5970
Web: www.atlanticconstructors.com
Atlas Comfort Systems USA LP 4133 Southerland Rd Houston TX 77092 713-460-7300 460-7301
TF: 800-460-9973 ■ *Web:* www.atlas-air.com
Atlas Welding & Boiler Repair 2960 Webster Ave Bronx NY 10458 718-365-6600 367-5658
TF: 800-476-0556
August Arace & Sons Inc 642 3rd Ave Elizabeth NJ 07202 908-354-1626 354-9124
Web: www.augustarace.com
Azco Inc PO Box 567 Appleton WI 54912 920-734-5791 734-7432
Web: www.azco-inc.com
B-G Mechanical Service Inc 12 2nd Ave Chicopee MA 01020 413-888-1500 594-2983
TF: 800-992-7386 ■ *Web:* www.bgmechanical.com
B & I Contractors Inc 2701 Prince St Fort Myers FL 33916 239-332-4646 332-5928
Web: www.bandicontractors.com
Baker Group 4224 Hubbell Ave Des Moines IA 50317 515-262-4000 266-1025
TF: 800-789-8933 ■ *Web:* www.thebakergroup.com
Ballard SB Construction Co 2828 Shipps Corner Rd Virginia Beach VA 23453 757-440-5555 451-2873
TF: 800-296-0209 ■ *Web:* www.sbballard.com
Benjamin Franklin Plumbing
50 Central Ave Suite 920 Plaza Five Points Sarasota FL 34236 941-366-9692 951-0942
TF: 800-695-3579 ■ *Web:* www.benfranklinplumbing.com
Berg Inc 531 W 61st St Shreveport LA 71106 318-868-8884 868-7408
Web: www.bergind.com
Bernhard Mechanical Contractors Inc 10321 Airline Hwy Baton Rouge LA 70816 225-293-2791 296-0931
TF: 888-773-2791 ■ *Web:* www.bernhardmechanical.com
Beutler Corp 4700 Lang Ave McClellan CA 95652 916-646-2222 646-2200
TF: 800-238-8537 ■ *Web:* www.beutler.com/
BMW Constructors Inc 1740 W Michigan St Indianapolis IN 46222 317-267-0400 267-0572
Web: www.bmwcnstrs.com
Bogot Cos 8137 Austin Ave Morton Grove IL 60053 847-965-8800 965-8805
Web: www.bogot.com
Bolton Corp 919 W Morgan St Raleigh NC 27603 919-828-9021 828-8574
TF: 800-438-1098 ■ *Web:* www.boltoncorp.com
Bosch Mechanical Contractors Inc
3325 Three-Mile Rd NW Grand Rapids MI 49534 616-453-5483 453-7111
Web: www.boschmechanical.com
Bouchard John & Sons Co 1024 Harrison St Nashville TN 37203 615-256-0112 256-2427
TF: 800-842-9156 ■ *Web:* www.jbouchard.com
Brandt Engineering Co Inc 11245 Indian Trail Dallas TX 75229 972-241-9411 484-6013
Web: www.brandteng.com
Butters-Fetting Co Inc 1669 S 1st St Milwaukee WI 53204 414-645-1535 645-7622
Web: www.buttersfetting.com
Butzer Harold G Inc 730 Wicker Ln Jefferson City MO 65109 573-636-4115 636-7053
C & R Mechanical 12825 Pennridge Dr Bridgeton MO 63044 314-739-1800 739-1721
TF: 800-233-3828 ■ *Web:* www.crmechanical.com
Caid TA Industries Inc 2275 E Ganley Rd Tucson AZ 85706 520-294-3126 294-8180
Web: www.tacaid.com
Calvert-Jones Co Inc 5703 Edsall Rd Alexandria VA 22304 703-370-5850 370-6515
Web: www.calvertjones.com
Campito Plumbing & Heating Inc 3 Hemlock St Latham NY 12110 518-785-0994 785-0769
CCI Mechanical Inc 758 S Redwood Rd Salt Lake City UT 84104 801-973-9000 975-7204
TF: 800-521-7600 ■ *Web:* www.ccimech.com
Central Air Conditioning Inc 3435 W Harry St Wichita KS 67213 316-945-0797 945-3174
Web: www.centralairco.com
Central Mechanical Construction Co Inc 631 Pecan Cir Manhattan KS 66502 785-537-2437 537-2491
TF: 800-631-6999 ■ *Web:* www.centralmechanical.com
Champion Industrial Contractors Inc 1420 Coldwell Ave Modesto CA 95350 209-524-6601 524-6931
Web: www.championindustrial.com
Chapman Corp 331 S Main St Washington PA 15301 724-228-1900 228-4311
Web: www.chapmancorp.com
Chas Roberts Heating & Air Conditioning Inc 9828 N 19th Ave Phoenix AZ 85021 602-331-2686 997-0068
Web: www.chasroberts.com
Christianson Air Conditioning & Plumbing
1950 Louis Henna Blvd Round Rock TX 78664 512-246-5200 246-5201
Web: www.christiansonco.com
Cinfab Mechanical Inc 5240 Lester Rd Cincinnati OH 45213 513-396-6100 396-7574
Web: www.cinfab.com
Coastal Mechanical Services LLC 394 East Dr Melbourne FL 32904 321-725-3061 984-0718
TF: 800-391-5757 ■ *Web:* www.coastalmechanical.com
Coastal Mechanical Services Ltd 191 N Travis St San Benito TX 78586 956-399-5157 399-9770
TF: 800-568-2612
Cobb Mechanical Contractors Inc PO Box 6729 Colorado Springs CO 80934 719-471-8958 389-0127
TF: 800-808-2622 ■ *Web:* www.cobbmechanical.com
ColonialWebb Contractors Co 2820 Ackley Ave Richmond VA 23228 804-916-1400 264-5083
TF: 800-849-5504 ■ *Web:* www.colonialwebb.com
Comfort Engineers Inc 4008 Comfort Ln Durham NC 27705 919-383-2502 383-2507
Web: www.comfortengineers.com
Comfort Systems USA Inc 777 Post Oak Blvd Suite 500 Houston TX 77056 713-830-9600 830-9696
NYSE: FIX ■ *TF:* 800-723-8431 ■ *Web:* www.comfortsystemsusa.com
Connelly GF Mechanical Contractors Inc 2515 S Wabash Ave Chicago IL 60616 312-326-4100 326-3780
Continental Mechanical of the Pacific 2146 Puuhale Pl Honolulu HI 96819 808-845-5936 846-4218
Web: www.contmech.com
Corrigan Co 3545 Gratiot St Saint Louis MO 63103 314-771-6200 771-8537
Web: www.corriganco.com
Cox Engineering Co 35 Industrial Dr Canton MA 02021 781-302-3300 302-3444
TF: 800-538-0027
Crabb Inc 4771 Fox St Denver CO 80216 303-295-1152 295-1158
Craft James & Son Inc 2780 York Haven Rd PO Box 8 York Haven PA 17370 717-266-6629 266-6623
TF: 800-673-2519 ■ *Web:* www.jamescraftson.com
Critchfield Mechanical Inc 4085 Campbell Ave Menlo Park CA 94025 650-321-7801 321-1798
Web: www.cmihvac.com
Cullum Mechanical Construction Inc 3325 Pacific Ave North Charleston SC 29418 843-554-6645 747-9964
Web: www.culluminc.com
Danforth John W Co 300 Colvin Woods Pkwy Tonawanda NY 14150 716-832-1940 832-2388
TF: 800-888-6119 ■ *Web:* www.jwdanforth.com
DeBra-Kuempel 3976 Southern Ave Cincinnati OH 45227 513-271-6500 271-4676
TF: 800-395-5741 ■ *Web:* www.debra-kuempel.com
Doody Mechanical Inc 520 Front Ave Saint Paul MN 55117 651-487-1061 487-2637
Web: www.doody-united.com
Dorvin D Leis Co Inc 202 Lalo St Kahului HI 96732 808-877-3902 877-5168
Web: www.leisinc.com
Downey Inc 2203 W Michigan St Milwaukee WI 53233 414-933-3123 933-1552
Web: www.downeyinc.com
Duggan EM Inc 140 Will Dr Canton MA 02021 781-828-2292 828-0991
Dunbar Mechanical Inc 2806 N Reynolds Rd Toledo OH 43615 419-537-1900 537-8840
TF: 800-719-2201 ■ *Web:* www.dunbarmechanical.com/
Egan Companies Inc 7625 Boone Ave N Brooklyn Park MN 55428 763-544-4131 591-5532
TF: 800-275-3426 ■ *Web:* www.eganco.com
EM Duggan Inc 140 Will Dr Canton MA 02021 781-828-2292 828-0991

Company	City	State	Zip	Phone	Fax
EMCOR Group Inc 301 Merritt 7 6th Fl *NYSE:* EME ■ *Web:* www.emcorgroup.com	Norwalk	CT	06851	203-849-7800	849-7900
Engineering & Refrigeration Inc 56 Baldwin Ave *TF:* 800-631-3000	Jersey City	NJ	07306	201-333-4200	333-3051
EW Tompkins Co Inc 124 Sheridan Ave *Web:* www.thetompkinsgroup.com/Tompkins.html	Albany	NY	12210	518-462-6577	462-6570
Fagan Co 3125 Brinkerhoff Rd *TF:* 800-966-1178 ■ *Web:* www.faganco.com	Kansas City	KS	66115	913-621-4444	621-3626
Farmer & Irwin Corp 3300 Ave K *TF:* 800-883-8229 ■ *Web:* www.fandicorp.com	Riviera Beach	FL	33404	561-842-5316	842-5999
FE Moran Inc 2265 Carlson Dr *Web:* www.femoran.com	Northbrook	IL	60062	847-498-4800	498-9091
Ferran Services & Contracting 530 Grand St *Web:* www.ferran-services.com	Orlando	FL	32805	407-422-3551	648-0961
Fisher Container Corp 1111 Busch Pkwy *TF:* 800-837-2247 ■ *Web:* www.fishercontainer.com	Buffalo Grove	IL	60089	847-541-0000	541-0075
Fitzgerald Contractors Inc PO Box 6600 *Web:* www.fitzgeraldcontractors.com	Shreveport	LA	71136	318-869-3262	865-9640
Flaherty MJ Co 1 Gateway Center Suite 450 *TF:* 800-370-2280 ■ *Web:* www.mjflaherty-hvac.com	Newton	MA	02458	617-969-1492	964-0176
Fountain Construction Co 5655 Hwy 18 S *Web:* www.fountainconstruction.com	Jackson	MS	39289	601-373-4162	373-4300
Frank Lill & Son Inc 656 Basket Rd *TF:* 800-756-0490 ■ *Web:* www.franklillandson.com	Webster	NY	14580	585-265-0490	265-1842
Frank M Booth Inc 222 3rd St *TF:* 800-540-9369 ■ *Web:* www.frankbooth.com	Marysville	CA	95901	530-742-7134	742-8109
Fujikawa Assoc DBA Continental Mechanical of the Pacific 2146 Puuhale Pl *Web:* www.contmech.com	Honolulu	HI	96819	808-845-5936	846-4218
FW Spencer & Son Inc 99 S Hill Dr *Web:* www.fwspencersoninc.com	Brisbane	CA	94005	415-468-5000	468-4579
Gay WW Mechanical Contractor Inc 524 Stockton St *Web:* www.wwgmc.com	Jacksonville	FL	32204	904-388-2696	389-4901
GEM Industrial Inc 6842 Commodore Dr *TF:* 800-837-5909 ■ *Web:* www.gemindustrial.com	Walbridge	OH	43465	419-666-6554	666-7004
George F Schuler Inc 1650 Report Ave	Stockton	CA	95205	209-462-2398	467-4436
George H Wilson Inc 250 Harvey West Blvd	Santa Cruz	CA	95060	831-423-9522	423-9903
GF Connelly Mechanical Contractors Inc 2515 S Wabash Ave	Chicago	IL	60616	312-326-4100	326-3780
Gibb Robert & Sons Inc 205 SW 40th St *TF:* 800-842-7366 ■ *Web:* www.robertgibb.com	Fargo	ND	58103	701-282-5900	281-0819
Gowan Inc 5550 Airline Dr *TF:* 888-724-6926 ■ *Web:* www.gowaninc.com	Houston	TX	77076	713-696-5400	695-1726
Goyette Mechanical Co 3842 Gorey Ave *TF:* 877-469-3883 ■ *Web:* www.goyettemechanical.com	Flint	MI	48501	810-743-6883	743-9090
GR Sponaugle & Sons Inc 4391 Chambers Hill Rd *TF:* 800-866-7036 ■ *Web:* www.grsponaugle.com	Harrisburg	PA	17111	717-564-1515	564-3675
Green John E Co 220 Victor Ave *Web:* www.johnegreen.com	Highland Park	MI	48203	313-868-2400	868-0011
Griesemer RE Inc 440 S Hancock St	Indianapolis	IN	46222	317-638-4344	264-1165
Griffith ID Inc 735 S Market St *Web:* www.idgriffith.com	Wilmington	DE	19801	302-656-8253	656-8268
Grodsky Harry & Co Inc 33 Shaws Ln *Web:* www.grodsky.com	Springfield	MA	01104	413-785-1947	737-9870
Gross Mechanical Contractors Inc 3622 Greenwood Blvd *TF:* 800-641-0071 ■ *Web:* www.grossmechanical.com	Saint Louis	MO	63143	314-645-0077	645-0098
Grunau Co Inc 1100 W Anderson Ct *TF:* 800-365-1920 ■ *Web:* www.grunau.com	Oak Creek	WI	53154	414-216-6900	768-7950
Guimarin WB & Co Inc 1124 Bluff Industrial Blvd *Web:* www.wbguimarin.com	Columbia	SC	29202	803-256-0515	988-0733
Gulf States Inc 6711 E Hwy 332 *TF:* 800-231-9849	Freeport	TX	77541	979-233-5555	233-3050
H & H Group Inc 2801 Syene Rd *Web:* www.h-hgroup.com	Madison	WI	53713	608-273-3434	273-9654
HACI Mechanical Contractors Inc 2108 W Shangri La Rd *Web:* www.hacimechanical.com	Phoenix	AZ	85029	602-944-1555	678-0266
Hansen Mechanical Contractors Inc 6325 S Valley View Blvd	Las Vegas	NV	89118	702-361-5111	361-6753
Har-Con Corp 551 N Shepherd Dr Suite 270 *TF:* 800-438-0536 ■ *Web:* www.har-con.com	Houston	TX	77007	713-869-8451	864-1837
Harder Mechanical Contractors Inc PO Box 5118 *TF:* 800-392-3729 ■ *Web:* www.hardercompanies.com	Portland	OR	97208	503-281-1112	287-5284
Hardy Corp 430 12th St S *TF:* 800-289-4822 ■ *Web:* www.hardycorp.com	Birmingham	AL	35233	205-252-7191	326-6268
Harold G Butzer Inc 730 Wicker Ln	Jefferson City	MO	65109	573-636-4115	636-7053
Harris Mechanical Contracting Co 909 Montreal Cir	Saint Paul	MN	55102	651-602-6500	602-6699
Harry Grodsky & Co Inc 33 Shaws Ln *Web:* www.grodsky.com	Springfield	MA	01104	413-785-1947	737-9870
HE Neumann Inc 2100 Middle Creek Rd *TF:* 800-627-5312 ■ *Web:* www.heneumann.com	Triadelphia	WV	26059	304-232-3040	232-7858
Heathorn NV Co 1155 Beecher St *Web:* www.nvheathorn.com	San Leandro	CA	94577	510-569-9100	569-9106
Heating & Plumbing Engineers Inc 407 W Fillmore Pl *TF:* 800-530-8592 ■ *Web:* www.hpeinc.com	Colorado Springs	CO	80907	719-633-5414	633-4031
Heide & Cook Ltd 1714 Kanakanui St *Web:* www.heide-cook.com	Honolulu	HI	96819	808-841-6161	841-4889
Hellwig Ray L Plumbing & Heating Inc 1301 Laurelwood Rd *Web:* www.rlhellwig.com	Santa Clara	CA	95054	408-727-5612	727-4382
Heritage Mechanical Services Inc 305 Suburban Ave *TF:* 800-734-0384 ■ *Web:* www.heritagemech.com	Deer Park	NY	11729	631-667-1044	667-8613
Herre Brothers Inc 4417 Valley Rd *Web:* www.herrebros.com	Enola	PA	17025	717-732-4454	732-8208
Higgins JC Corp 70 Hawes Way *Web:* www.jchigginscorp.com	Stoughton	MA	02072	781-341-1500	344-6075
Hill Mechanical Group 11045 Gage Ave *Web:* www.hillmech.com	Franklin Park	IL	60131	847-451-5000	451-5011
Hill York Corp 2125 S Andrews Ave *TF:* 800-777-2971 ■ *Web:* www.hillyork.com	Fort Lauderdale	FL	33316	954-525-2971	525-2973
HiMEC Inc 1400 7th St NW *TF:* 888-454-4632 ■ *Web:* www.himec.com	Rochester	MN	55901	507-281-4000	281-5206
Hoffman Corp 805 SW Broadway Suite 2100 *Web:* www.hoffmancorp.com	Portland	OR	97205	503-221-8811	221-8934
Holaday-Parks Inc 4600 S 134 Pl PO Box 69208 *Web:* www.holadayparks.com	Seattle	WA	98168	206-248-9700	248-8700
Hooper Corp 2030 Pennsylvania Ave *TF:* 800-999-0451 ■ *Web:* www.hoopercorp.com	Madison	WI	53704	608-249-0451	249-7360
Horwitz Inc 8825 Xylon Ave N *Web:* www.horwitzinc.com	Brooklyn Park	MN	55445	763-425-7566	425-4436
Humphrey Co Ltd 4439 W 12th St *Web:* www.humphreyltd.com	Houston	TX	77055	713-686-8606	686-7619
IHP Industrial Inc 1701 S 8th St	Saint Joseph	MO	64503	816-364-1581	232-4473
IMCOR-Interstate Mechanical Corp 1841 E Washington St *TF:* 800-628-0211 ■ *Web:* www.imcor-az.com	Phoenix	AZ	85034	602-257-1319	271-0674
Independent Mechanical Industries Inc 4155 N Knox Ave *Web:* www.independentmech.com	Chicago	IL	60641	773-282-4500	282-2046
Industrial Air Inc 428 Edwardia Dr PO Box 8769 *Web:* www.industrialairinc.com	Greensboro	NC	27419	336-292-1030	855-7763
Industrial Contractors Inc 701 Channel Dr *Web:* www.icinorthdakota.com	Bismarck	ND	58501	701-258-9908	258-9988
Industrial Piping & Engineering Corp 2215 Meyer Rd *TF:* 800-422-8405 ■ *Web:* www.ipecorp.net	Fort Wayne	IN	46803	260-422-8402	426-0441
Industrial Piping Inc 800 Culp Rd *TF:* 800-951-0988 ■ *Web:* www.goipi.com	Pineville	NC	28134	704-588-1100	588-5614
Interstate Mechanical Contractors Inc 3200 Henson Rd *TF:* 800-556-7072 ■ *Web:* www.interstatemechanical.com	Knoxville	TN	37921	865-588-0180	602-4124
Jackson & Blanc Inc 7929 Arjons Dr *TF:* 800-236-1121 ■ *Web:* www.jacksonandblanc.com	San Diego	CA	92126	858-831-7900	527-1502
Jacobson AD Co Inc 16210 W 108th St	Lenexa	KS	66219	913-529-5000	529-5020
Jamar Co 4701 Mike Colalillo Dr *Web:* www.jamarcompany.com	Duluth	MN	55807	218-628-1027	628-1174
James Craft & Son Inc 2780 York Haven Rd PO Box 8 *TF:* 800-673-2519 ■ *Web:* www.jamescraftson.com	York Haven	PA	17370	717-266-6629	266-6623
Janazzo Services Corp 140 Norton St *Web:* www.janazzo.com	Milldale	CT	06467	860-621-7381	621-7529
JC Higgins Corp 70 Hawes Way *Web:* www.jchigginscorp.com	Stoughton	MA	02072	781-341-1500	344-6075
JF Ahern Co 855 Morris St *TF:* 800-532-0155 ■ *Web:* www.jfahern.com	Fond du Lac	WI	54935	920-921-9020	921-8632
JH Kelly 821 3rd Ave *Web:* www.jhkelly.com	Longview	WA	98632	360-423-5510	423-9170
John Bouchard & Sons Co 1024 Harrison St *TF:* 800-842-9156 ■ *Web:* www.jbouchard.com	Nashville	TN	37203	615-256-0112	256-2427
John E Green Co 220 Victor Ave *Web:* www.johnegreen.com	Highland Park	MI	48203	313-868-2400	868-0011
John W Danforth Co 300 Colvin Woods Pkwy *TF:* 800-888-6119 ■ *Web:* www.jwdanforth.com	Tonawanda	NY	14150	716-832-1940	832-2388
Johnson Contracting Co Inc 2750 Morton Dr *Web:* www.jccinc.com	East Moline	IL	61244	309-755-0601	752-7056
Johnson Controls Inc 12393 Slauson Ave *TF:* 800-222-5247 ■ *Web:* www.johnsoncontrols.com	Whittier	CA	90606	562-698-8301	693-4375
Kaelber Co 2925 61st St	Kenosha	WI	53143	262-654-3589	654-2730
Kelly JH 821 3rd Ave *Web:* www.jhkelly.com	Longview	WA	98632	360-423-5510	423-9170
Kinetics Systems Inc 26055 SW Canyon Creek Rd *TF:* 800-888-7597 ■ *Web:* www.kineticsgroup.com	Wilsonville	OR	97070	503-224-5200	224-8521
Kuhlman Inc N 56 W 16865 Ridgewood Dr Suite 100 *TF:* 800-781-9229 ■ *Web:* www.kuhlmaninc.com	Menomonee Falls	WI	53051	262-252-9400	252-9401
Lawson Mechanical Contractors 6090 S Watt Ave *Web:* www.lawsonmechanical.com	Sacramento	CA	95829	916-381-5000	381-5073
Lee Co Inc 331 Mallory Station Rd *TF:* 888-567-7747 ■ *Web:* www.leecompany.com	Franklin	TN	37067	615-567-1000	567-1027
Leis Dorvin D Co Inc 202 Lalo St *Web:* www.leisinc.com	Kahului	HI	96732	808-877-3902	877-5168
Limbach Facility Services LLC 31 35th St *Web:* www.limbachinc.com	Pittsburgh	PA	15201	412-359-2200	359-2235
Linc Mechanical LLC 37695 Interchange Dr	Farmington Hills	MI	48335	248-471-0600	442-6219
MacDonald-Miller Facility Solutions Inc 7717 Detroit Ave SE *TF:* 800-962-5979 ■ *Web:* www.macmiller.com	Seattle	WA	98106	206-763-9400	767-6773
Mallory & Evans Inc 646 Kentucky St *Web:* www.malloryandevans.com	Scottdale	GA	30079	404-297-1000	297-1075
Manor WD Plumbing & Heating Inc 1838 N 23rd Ave *Web:* www.wdmanor.com	Phoenix	AZ	85009	602-253-0703	253-3659
Martin Petersen Co Inc 9800 55th St *TF:* 800-677-1326 ■ *Web:* www.martin-petersen.com	Kenosha	WI	53144	262-658-1326	658-1048
Masters Inc 7891 Beechcraft Ave *TF:* 800-257-2871	Gaithersburg	MD	20879	301-948-8950	258-7368
McCarl's Inc 1413 9th Ave *TF:* 800-643-5660 ■ *Web:* www.mccarl.com	Beaver Falls	PA	15010	724-843-5660	843-3180
McClure Co 4101 N 6th St *TF:* 800-382-1319 ■ *Web:* www.mcclureco.com	Harrisburg	PA	17110	717-232-9743	236-5239
McCrea Equipment Co Inc 4463 Beech Rd *TF:* 800-597-0091 ■ *Web:* www.mccreaway.com	Temple Hills	MD	20748	301-423-4585	899-9476
McKenney's Inc 1056 Moreland Industrial Blvd SE *TF:* 800-489-5000 ■ *Web:* www.mckenneys.com	Atlanta	GA	30316	404-622-5000	624-8665
McKinstry Co 5005 3rd Ave S *TF:* 800-669-6223 ■ *Web:* www.mckinstry.com	Seattle	WA	98134	206-762-3311	768-7741
Meccon Industries Inc 2703 Bernice Rd *Web:* www.meccon.com	Lansing	IL	60438	708-474-8300	474-9550
Mechanical Construction Co LLC 3001 17th St *Web:* www.mccgroup.com	Metairie	LA	70002	504-833-8291	831-4760
Mechanical Inc 2279 Rt 20 E *TF:* 800-747-1955 ■ *Web:* www.helmgroup.com/mechanical	Freeport	IL	61032	815-962-8050	235-1940
Merit Electrical Inc 17723 Airline Hwy *Web:* www.merit-electrical.com	Prairieville	LA	70769	225-673-8850	673-8838
Metropolitan Mechanical Contractors Inc 7340 Washington Ave S *Web:* www.metromech.com	Eden Prairie	MN	55344	952-941-7010	941-9118
Mid-State Contracting LLC 2001 County Hwy U *TF:* 866-644-6722 ■ *Web:* www.midstatecontracting.com	Wausau	WI	54402	715-675-2388	675-6971
Midwest Mechanical Contractors Inc 4550 W 109th St Suite 100 *Web:* www.mmckc.com	Overland Park	KS	66211	913-469-2200	469-2290
Midwest Mechanical Group 540 Executive Dr *TF Svc:* 800-600-4047 ■ *Web:* www.midwestmech.com	Willowbrook	IL	60527	630-655-4200	655-4201
Miller Engineering Co 1616 S Main St	Rockford	IL	61102	815-963-4878	963-0823
MJ Flaherty Co 1 Gateway Center Suite 450 *TF:* 800-370-2280 ■ *Web:* www.mjflaherty-hvac.com	Newton	MA	02458	617-969-1492	964-0176
MMC Corp 10955 Lowell Suite 350	Overland Park	KS	66210	913-469-0101	469-8780
Modern Piping Inc 210 33rd St Dr SE *Web:* www.modernpiping.com	Cedar Rapids	IA	52403	319-364-0131	364-8368
Mollenberg-Betz Inc 300 Scott St *TF:* 800-368-4998 ■ *Web:* www.mollenbergbetz.com	Buffalo	NY	14204	716-614-7473	614-7465
Monterey Mechanical Co 8275 San Leandro St *Web:* www.montmech.com	Oakland	CA	94621	510-632-3173	632-0732
Moran FE Inc 2265 Carlson Dr *Web:* www.femoran.com	Northbrook	IL	60062	847-498-4800	498-9091
Morrison Construction Co 1834 Summer St *Web:* www.morrison-const.com	Hammond	IN	46320	219-932-5036	933-7302
Mr Rooter Corp 1010 N University Pk Dr *TF:* 800-583-8003 ■ *Web:* www.mrrooter.com	Waco	TX	76707	254-745-2444	745-2501
Murphy Co Mechanical Contractors & Engineers 1233 N Price Rd *TF:* 800-992-6601 ■ *Web:* www.murphynet.com	Saint Louis	MO	63132	314-997-6600	997-4536
Murphy & Miller Inc 600 W Taylor St *Web:* www.murphymiller.com	Chicago	IL	60607	312-427-8900	427-0324
MYR Group 1701 W Golf Rd Tower 3 Suite 1012 *Web:* www.myrgroup.com	Rolling Meadows	IL	60008	847-290-1891	290-1892
Nagelbush Mechanical Inc 1800 NW 49th St Suite 110 *TF:* 800-354-3111 ■ *Web:* www.nagelbush.com	Fort Lauderdale	FL	33309	954-736-3000	748-7881
Neumann HE Inc 2100 Middle Creek Rd *TF:* 800-627-5312 ■ *Web:* www.heneumann.com	Triadelphia	WV	26059	304-232-3040	232-7858
New England Insulation Co 55 North St *TF:* 800-346-6307	Canton	MA	02021	781-828-6600	828-6749

Plumbing, Heating, Air Conditioning Contractors (Cont'd)

Phone / Fax

NewMech Cos Inc 1633 Eustis St. Saint Paul MN 55108 651-645-0451 642-5591
TF: 800-942-4444 ■ Web: www.newmech.com
Nitro Electric Company LLC
500 Corporate Centre Dr 2nd Fl Suite 520 Scott Depot WV 25560 304-722-7700 722-7792*
*Fax: Acctg ■ Web: www.nitro-electric.com
Northern Peabody LLC 25 Depot St Manchester NH 03101 603-669-3601 669-2285
NV Heathorn Co 1155 Beecher St San Leandro CA 94577 510-569-9100 569-9106
Web: www.nvheathorn.com
P1 Group Inc 2151 Haskell Ave Bldg 1 Lawrence KS 66046 785-843-2910 843-2884
TF: 800-376-2911 ■ Web: www.p1group.com
Pace Mechanical Services Inc 6060 Hix Rd Westland MI 48185 734-595-8300 595-4704
Web: www.pacemech.com
Pacific Mechanical Corp 2501 Anna Lisa Dr Concord CA 94520 925-827-4940 827-0519
TF: 800-362-2202
Palmer & Sicard Inc 140 Epping Rd Exeter NH 03833 603-778-1841 778-0119
Par Plumbing Co Inc 60 N Prospect Ave Lynbrook NY 11563 516-887-4000 593-9089
TF: 800-660-4000 ■ Web: www.parplumbing.com
PC Godfrey Inc 1816 Rozzells Ferry Rd Charlotte NC 28208 704-334-8604 376-5186
Penguin Air Conditioning Corp 26 West St Brooklyn NY 11222 718-706-6500 706-2536
Web: www.penguinac.com
Performance Contracting Group Inc 16400 College Blvd Lenexa KS 66219 913-888-8600 492-8723
TF: 800-255-6866 ■ Web: www.pcg.com
Petersburg Plumbing & Heating Co Inc 117 N 7th St Petersburg IL 62675 217-632-2221 632-3117
Petersen Martin Co Inc 9800 55th St Kenosha WI 53144 262-658-1326 658-1048
TF: 800-677-1326 ■ Web: www.martin-petersen.com
Piedmont Mechanical Inc 116 John Dodd Rd Spartanburg SC 29303 864-578-9114 578-5314
TF: 800-849-5724 ■ Web: www.piedmontmechanical.com
Pierce Assoc Inc 4216 Wheeler Ave Alexandria VA 22304 703-751-2400 751-2479
Web: www.pierceassociates.com
Poole & Kent Corp 4530 Hollins Ferry Rd Baltimore MD 21227 410-247-2200 247-2331
Web: www.poole-kent.com
Postler & Jaeckle Corp 615 South Ave Rochester NY 14620 585-546-7450 546-4316
TF: 800-724-4252 ■ Web: www.postler.com
Power Piping Co 436 Butler St Pittsburgh PA 15223 412-323-6200 323-6334
Power Process Piping Inc 45780 Port St PO Box 8100-C Plymouth MI 48170 734-451-0130 451-0763
Web: www.powerprocesspiping.com
Process Construction Inc 1421 Queen City Ave Cincinnati OH 45214 513-251-2211 251-2267
TF: 888-251-2211 ■ Web: www.processconstruction.com
PSF Industries Inc 65 S Horton St Seattle WA 98134 206-622-1252 682-1070
TF: 800-426-1204 ■ Web: www.psfindustries.com
Quality Mechanical Contractors 3175 Westwood Dr Las Vegas NV 89109 702-732-2545 731-5661
Web: www.qualitymechanical.com
Ray L Hellwig Plumbing & Heating Inc
1301 Laurelwood Rd Santa Clara CA 95054 408-727-5612 727-4382
Web: www.rlhellwig.com
Reedy Industries Inc 2440 Ravine Way Suite 200 Glenview IL 60025 847-729-9450 729-0558
Web: www.reedyindustries.com
Riggs Distler Co Inc 9411 Philadelphia Rd Unit P Baltimore MD 21237 410-633-0300 633-2119
Web: www.riggsdistler.com
RK Mechanical Inc 9300 E Smith Rd Denver CO 80207 303-355-9696 355-8666
TF: 800-783-0075 ■ Web: www.rkmi.com
Robert Gibb & Sons Inc 205 SW 40th St Fargo ND 58103 701-282-5900 281-0819
TF: 800-842-7366 ■ Web: www.robertgibb.com
Rock Hill Mechanical Corp 524 Clark Ave Kirkwood MO 63122 314-966-0600 966-3679
Web: www.rhmcorp.com
Rooter-Man 268 Rangeway Rd North Billerica MA 01862 978-667-1144 663-0061
TF: 800-700-8062 ■ Web: www.rooterman.com
Ross Brothers Construction Co Inc 7201 SR 168 Catlettsburg KY 41129 606-739-5139 739-8315
TF: 800-910-7222
Roto-Rooter Inc 255 E 5th St 2500 Chemed Ctr Cincinnati OH 45202 513-762-6690 762-6590
Web: www.rotorooter.com
Russell AC Inc 2425 W Louise Dr Phoenix AZ 85027 623-582-8855 582-8971
Web: www.russellac.com
RW Warner Inc 217 Monroe Ave Frederick MD 21701 301-662-5387 698-0451
TF: 800-854-5387 ■ Web: www.rwwarner.com
Sanders Brothers Inc 1709 Old Georgia Hwy Gaffney SC 29342 864-489-1144 487-6165
TF: 800-527-1684 ■ Web: www.sandersbros.net
Sauer Inc 30 51st St Pittsburgh PA 15201 412-687-4100 687-3576
Web: www.sauer-inc.com
SB Ballard Construction Co 2828 Shipps Corner Rd Virginia Beach VA 23453 757-440-5555 451-2873
TF: 800-296-0209 ■ Web: www.sbballard.com
Schuler George F Inc 1650 Report Ave Stockton CA 95205 209-462-2398 467-4436
Schweizer Dipple Inc 7227 Division St Oakwood Village OH 44146 440-786-8090 786-8099
Web: www.schweizer-dipple.com
Service Experts Inc 2140 Lake Pk Blvd Richardson TX 75080 972-497-5000 497-6948
TF: 877-536-8580 ■ Web: www.serviceexperts.com
Shambaugh & Son LP 7614 Opportunity Dr Fort Wayne IN 46825 260-487-7777 487-7701
TF: 800-234-9988 ■ Web: www.shambaugh.com
Shook & Fletcher Mechanical Contractors Inc
2915 Richard Arrington Jr Blvd N Birmingham AL 35202 205-252-9400 252-9407
SI Goldman Co Inc 799 Bennett Dr Longwood FL 32750 407-830-5000 830-4599
Web: www.sigoldmanco.com
Smith & Oby Co 6107 Carnegie Ave Cleveland OH 44103 216-361-5121 361-1635
Web: www.smithandoby.com
Southeast Mechanical Contractors Inc 2120 SW 57th Terr Hollywood FL 33023 954-981-3600 962-8630
Southern Air Inc PO Box 4205 Lynchburg VA 24502 434-385-6200 385-9081
TF: 800-743-1214 ■ Web: www.southern-air.com
Southern Industrial Constructors Inc 6101 Triangle Dr Raleigh NC 27617 919-782-4600 782-2935
TF: 800-851-0868 ■ Web: www.southernindustrial.com
Southland Industries 7421 Orangewood Ave Garden Grove CA 92841 714-901-5800 901-5811
Web: www.southlandind.com
Speer Mechanical 600 Oakland Park Ave Columbus OH 43214 614-261-6331 261-6330
TF: 800-282-6017 ■ Web: www.speermechanical.com
Spencer FW & Son Inc 99 S Hill Dr Brisbane CA 94005 415-468-5000 468-4579
Web: www.fwspencersoninc.com
Stanley-Carter Co 28702 Wall St Wixom MI 48393 248-349-4944 349-4955
Web: www.stanley-carter.com
Stromberg Sheet Metal Works Inc 6701 Distribution Dr Beltsville MD 20705 301-931-1000 931-1020
TF: 800-348-5778 ■ Web: www.strombergmetals.com
Superior Air Handling Corp 200 E 700 S Clearfield UT 84015 801-776-1997 825-8967
Web: www.sahco.com
TA Caid Industries Inc 2275 E Ganley Rd Tucson AZ 85706 520-294-3126 294-8180
Web: www.tacaid.com
TDIndustries 13850 Diplomat Dr Dallas TX 75234 972-888-9500 888-9338
Web: www.tdindustries.com
TECO Solutions 702 N Franklin St Tampa FL 33602 813-228-1111 228-1527
Web: www.tecosolutions.com
Todd-Ford Inc 1914 Breeden Ave San Antonio TX 78212 210-732-9791 732-9910
Tomko WG & Son Inc 2559 SR 88 Finleyville PA 15332 724-348-2000 348-7001
Web: www.wgtomko.com
Tompkins EW Co Inc 124 Sheridan Ave Albany NY 12210 518-462-6577 462-6570
Web: www.thetompkinsgroup.com/Tompkins.html
Tougher Industries Inc 47 Broadway Albany NY 12204 518-465-3426 465-1030
TF: 800-836-0752 ■ Web: www.tougher.net
Trautman & Shreve Inc 4406 Race St Denver CO 80216 303-295-1414 295-0324
Web: www.trautman-shreve.com
Triad Mechanical Inc 1419 NE Lombard Pl Portland OR 97211 503-289-9000 289-0316
TF: 800-308-7423 ■ Web: www.triadpdx.com
United Industrial Piping Inc 9740 Near Dr Cincinnati OH 45246 513-874-2004 874-7473
TF: 800-633-9690 ■ Web: www.unitedpiping.com
University Mechanical & Engineering Contractors Inc
1168 Fesler St El Cajon CA 92020 619-956-2500 956-2300
Web: www.umec.com
US Engineering Co 3433 Roanoke Rd Kansas City MO 64111 816-753-6969 931-5773
Web: www.usengineering.com
US Home Services 7813 N Dixie Dr Dayton OH 45414 937-898-0826 898-7166
Walter N Yoder & Sons Inc
16200 McMullen Hwy SW PO Box 1337 Cumberland MD 21501 301-729-0610 729-1517
Walter William E Inc 1917 Howard Ave Flint MI 48503 810-232-7459 232-8698
TF: 800-681-3320 ■ Web: www.williamewalter.com
Warner RW Inc 217 Monroe Ave Frederick MD 21701 301-662-5387 698-0451
TF: 800-854-5387 ■ Web: www.rwwarner.com
Warwick Plumbing & Heating Corp 11048 Warwick Blvd Newport News VA 23601 757-599-6111 595-9739
TF: 800-423-6111 ■ Web: www.wphcorp.com
Way Engineering Ltd 5308 Ashbrook Dr Houston TX 77081 713-666-3541 666-8455
Web: www.wayholding.com/wayeng
Wayne Crouse Inc 3370 Stafford St Pittsburgh PA 15204 412-771-5176 771-2357
Web: www.waynecrouse.com
WB Guimarin & Co Inc 1124 Bluff Industrial Blvd Columbia SC 29202 803-256-0515 988-0733
Web: www.wbguimarin.com
WD Manor Mechanical Contractors Inc 1838 N 23rd Ave Phoenix AZ 85009 602-253-0703 253-3659
Web: www.wdmanor.com
Wellington Power Corp 40th & Butler Sts Pittsburgh PA 15201 412-681-0103 681-0109
TF: 800-540-0017 ■ Web: www.wellingtonpower.com
Western Air Limbach LP 15914 S Avalon Blvd Compton CA 90220 310-327-4400 329-1815
TF: 800-927-1331 ■ Web: www.limbachinc.com
Western Allied Corp 12046 E Florence Ave Santa Fe Springs CA 90670 562-944-6341 944-7092
Web: www.westernallied.com
WG Tomko & Son Inc 2559 SR 88 Finleyville PA 15332 724-348-2000 348-7001
Web: www.wgtomko.com
William E Walter Inc 1917 Howard Ave Flint MI 48503 810-232-7459 232-8698
TF: 800-681-3320 ■ Web: www.williamewalter.com
Williard Limbach 175 Titus Ave Suite 100 Warrington PA 18976 215-488-9700 488-9699*
*Fax: Cust Svc ■ TF: 800-827-5030 ■ Web: www.limbachinc.com
Wilson George H Inc 250 Harvey West Blvd Santa Cruz CA 95060 831-423-9522 423-9903
Worth & Co Inc 6263 Kellers Church Rd Pipersville PA 18947 267-362-1100 362-1130
TF: 800-220-5130 ■ Web: www.worthandcompany.com
Yoder Walter N & Sons Inc
16200 McMullen Hwy SW PO Box 1337 Cumberland MD 21501 301-729-0610 729-1517
Young Plumbing & Heating Co PO Box 1077 Waterloo IA 50704 319-234-4411 234-4540
Web: www.youngphc.com

192-11 Remodeling, Refinishing, Resurfacing Contractors

Phone / Fax

American Restoration Services Inc 22 Rutgers Rd Pittsburgh PA 15205 412-351-7100 429-4234
Bathcrest Inc 5195 W 4700 South Salt Lake City UT 84118 801-972-1110 955-6499
TF: 800-826-6790 ■ Web: www.bathcrest.com
California Closet Co 1000 4th St Suite 800 San Rafael CA 94901 415-256-8500 256-8501
TF: 800-873-4264 ■ Web: www.calclosets.com
Closet Factory 12800 S Broadway Los Angeles CA 90061 310-516-7000 516-8065
TF: 800-318-8800 ■ Web: www.closetfactory.com
DreamMaker Bath & Kitchen by Worldwide
1020 N University Parks Dr Waco TX 76707 254-745-2477 745-2588
TF: 800-583-9099 ■ Web: www.dreammaker-remodel.com
Granite Transformations 2700 Biscayne Blvd Miami FL 33137 786-497-3007 438-1578*
*Fax Area Code: 305 ■ TF: 866-685-5300 ■ Web: www.granitetransformations.com
Handyman Connection Inc 9403 Kenwood Rd Suite D-207 Cincinnati OH 45242 513-771-1122 771-2030
TF: 800-466-5530 ■ Web: www.handymanconnection.com
Home Solutions of America Inc 1500 Dragon St Suite B Dallas TX 75207 214-623-8446 333-9435
AMEX: HOM ■ Web: www.homcorp.com
Kitchen Solvers Inc 401 Jay St La Crosse WI 54601 608-791-5516 784-2917
TF: 800-845-6779 ■ Web: www.kitchensolvers.com
Kitchen Tune-Up Inc 813 Circle Dr Aberdeen SD 57401 605-225-4049 225-1371
TF: 800-333-6385 ■ Web: www.kitchentuneup.com
Miracle Method US Corp
4239 N Nevada Ave Suite 115 Colorado Springs CO 80907 719-594-9091 594-9282
TF: 800-444-8827 ■ Web: www.miraclemethodusa.com
Perma-Glaze Inc 1638 Research Loop Rd Suite 160 Tucson AZ 85710 520-722-9718 296-4393
TF: 800-332-7397 ■ Web: www.permaglaze.com
Re-Bath LLC 1055 S Country Club Dr Mesa AZ 85210 480-844-1575 833-7199
TF: 800-426-4573 ■ Web: www.re-bath.com

192-12 Roofing, Siding, Sheet Metal Contractors

Phone / Fax

A Zahner Sheet Metal Co Inc 1400 E 9th St Kansas City MO 64106 816-474-8882 474-7994
Web: www.azahner.com
AC Dellovade Inc 108 Cavasina Dr Canonsburg PA 15317 724-873-8190 873-8186
TF: 800-245-1556 ■ Web: www.acdel.com
All-South Subcontractors Inc 2678 Queenstown Rd Birmingham AL 35210 205-836-8111 836-4227
Web: www.allsouthsub.com
Anning Johnson Co Inc 1959 Anson Dr Melrose Park IL 60160 708-681-1300 681-1386
Anson Industries Inc 1959 Anson Dr Melrose Park IL 60160 708-681-1300 681-1310
Web: www.ansonindustries.com
APi Group Inc Specialty Construction Services Group
2366 Rose Pl Saint Paul MN 55113 651-636-4320 636-0312
Web: www.apigroupinc.com/construction.html
B & M Roofing of Colorado Inc 3768 Eureka Way Frederick CO 80516 303-443-5843 938-9642
Web: www.bmroofing.com
Baker Roofing Co 517 Mercury St Raleigh NC 27603 919-828-2975 828-9352
TF: 800-849-4096 ■ Web: www.bakerroofing.com
BHW Sheet Metal Co 113 Johnson St Jonesboro GA 30236 770-471-9303 478-7923
Birdair Inc 65 Lawrence Bell Dr Amherst NY 14221 716-633-9500 633-9850
TF: 800-622-2246 ■ Web: www.birdair.com
BL Dalsin Roofing Inc 8824 Wentworth Ave S Bloomington MN 55420 952-884-5244 884-4342
Web: www.bldalsinroofing.com
Bonland Industries Inc 50 Newark-Pompton Tpke Wayne NJ 07474 973-694-3211 628-1120
TF: 800-289-7482 ■ Web: www.bonlandhvac.com
Bostwick CG Co Inc 41 Francis Ave Hartford CT 06106 860-523-5249 523-5938
Web: www.bostwickroofing.com
BT Mancini Co Inc 876 S Milpitas Blvd Milpitas CA 95036 408-942-7900 945-1360
TF: 800-488-4286 ■ Web: www.btmancini.com
Campbell John J Co Inc 6012 Resources Dr Memphis TN 38134 901-372-8400 372-8404
TF: 800-274-7663 ■ Web: www.campbellroofing.com
CEI West Roofing Co 1881 W 13th Ave Denver CO 80204 303-573-5953 573-3819
Centimark Corp 12 Grandview Cir Canonsburg PA 15317 724-743-7777 743-7770
TF: 800-558-4100 ■ Web: www.centimark.com

	City	State	Zip	Phone	Fax
CG Bostwick Co 41 Francis Ave	Hartford	CT	06106	860-523-5249	523-5938
Web: www.bostwickroofing.com					
Charles F Evans Co Inc 800 Canal St.	Elmira	NY	14901	607-734-8151	733-5422
Web: www.evans-roofing.com					
Construction Services Inc 2214 S Lincoln St	Amarillo	TX	79109	806-373-1732	373-9472
Cramer Dee Inc 4221 E Baldwin Rd	Holly	MI	48442	810-238-2664	579-2664
TF: 888-342-6995 ■ Web: www.deecramer.com					
Crown Corr Inc 7100 W 21st Ave	Gary	IN	46406	219-949-8080	944-9922
Web: www.crowncorr.com					
Dalsin BL Roofing Inc 8824 Wentworth Ave S	Bloomington	MN	55420	952-884-5244	884-4342
Web: www.bldalsinroofing.com					
DC Taylor Co 312 29th St NE	Cedar Rapids	IA	52402	319-363-2073	363-8311
TF: 800-333-7763 ■ Web: www.dctaylorco.com					
Dee Cramer Inc 4221 E Baldwin Rd	Holly	MI	48442	810-238-2664	579-2664
TF: 888-342-6995 ■ Web: www.deecramer.com					
Dix Corp 4024 S Grove Rd	Spokane	WA	99224	509-838-4455	838-4464
TF: 800-827-8548 ■ Web: www.dixcorp.com					
Douglass Earl F Roofing Co Inc 7281 E 54th Pl	Commerce City	CO	80022	303-288-2635	288-8602
Web: www.douglassroofing.com					
Earl F Douglass Roofing Co Inc 7281 E 54th Pl	Commerce City	CO	80022	303-288-2635	288-8602
Web: www.douglassroofing.com					
Elmsford Sheet Metal Work Inc 23 Arlo Ln	Cortlandt Manor	NY	10567	914-739-6300	739-1285
Web: www.elmsfordsheetmetal.com					
Enterprise Roofing & Sheet Metal Co 1021 Irving St	Dayton	OH	45419	937-298-8664	298-4516
Web: www.enterpriserfg.com					
Evans Charles F Co Inc 800 Canal St.	Elmira	NY	14901	607-734-8151	733-5422
Web: www.evans-roofing.com					
Flynn Canada Ltd 1390 Spruce St	Winnipeg	MB	R3E2V7	204-786-6951	788-4584
TF: 800-304-8751 ■ Web: www.flynn.ca					
Fort Roofing & Sheet Metal Works Inc					
4230 Domino Ave	North Charleston	SC	29405	843-554-9711	554-9708
TF: 800-356-6716 ■ Web: www.fortroofing.com					
Gowan Inc 5550 Airline Dr	Houston	TX	77076	713-696-5400	695-1726
TF: 888-724-6926 ■ Web: www.gowaninc.com					
Hahnel Brothers Co 46 Strawberry Ave	Lewiston	ME	04243	207-784-6477	782-9859
Web: www.hahnelbrosco.com					
Hans Rosenow Roofing Co Inc					
700 Nicholas Blvd Suite 206	Elk Grove Village	IL	60007	847-427-0200	427-0250
Henry C Smither Roofing Co Inc					
6850 E 32nd St PO Box 26057	Indianapolis	IN	46226	317-545-1304	546-4764
Web: www.smitherroofing.com					
Herbert RD & Sons Co Inc 1407 3rd Ave N	Nashville	TN	37208	615-242-3501	256-4056
Web: www.rdherbert.com					
Industrial First Inc 16400 Miles Ave	Cleveland	OH	44128	216-991-8600	991-2139
Web: www.industrialfirst.com					
Jamar Co 4701 Mike Colalillo Dr.	Duluth	MN	55807	218-628-1027	628-1174
Web: www.jamarcompany.com					
John J Campbell Co Inc 6012 Resources Dr	Memphis	TN	38134	901-372-8400	372-8404
TF: 800-274-7663 ■ Web: www.campbellroofing.com					
Johnson Contracting Co Inc 2750 Morton Dr	East Moline	IL	61244	309-755-0601	752-7056
Web: www.jccinc.com					
JP Patti Co Inc 365 Jefferson St PO Box 539	Saddle Brook	NJ	07663	973-478-6200	478-2175
Web: www.jppatti.com					
Ketcher & Co Inc 1717 E 5th	North Little Rock	AR	72119	501-372-5216	372-0949
Kirk & Blum Mfg Co Inc 3120 Forrer St.	Cincinnati	OH	45209	513-458-2600	351-5475
TF: 800-333-5475 ■ Web: www.kirkblum.com					
LE Schwartz & Son Inc 279 Reid St	Macon	GA	31206	478-745-6563	745-2711
Web: www.leschwartz.com					
M Gottfried Inc 89 Research Dr	Stamford	CT	06906	203-323-8173	359-2498
Web: www.mgottfried.com					
Midland Engineering Co 52369 US 33 N	South Bend	IN	46637	574-272-0200	272-7400
Web: www.midlandengineering.com					
Miller-Thomas-Gyekis Inc 3341 Stafford St	Pittsburgh	PA	15204	412-331-4610	331-8871
Mountain Co 166 60th St	Vienna	WV	26105	304-295-3311	295-6991
National International Roofing Corp 11317 Smith Dr	Huntley	IL	60142	847-669-3444	669-3173
TF: 800-221-7663 ■ Web: www.nir.com					
North American Roofing Services Inc 6151 W 80th St	Indianapolis	IN	46278	317-875-5434	872-8253
TF: 800-876-5602 ■ Web: www.naroofing.com					
Olson Bros Inc 2651 St Mary's Ave	Omaha	NE	68105	402-341-2360	341-0877
Olsson Roofing Co Inc 740 S Lake St	Aurora	IL	60506	630-892-0449	892-1556
TF: 888-766-3967 ■ Web: www.olssonroofing.com					
Orndorff & Spaid Inc 11722 Old Baltimore Pike	Beltsville	MD	20705	301-937-5911	937-0310
TF: 800-278-7663 ■ Web: www.osroofing.com					
RD Herbert & Sons Co Inc 1407 3rd Ave N	Nashville	TN	37208	615-242-3501	256-4056
Web: www.rdherbert.com					
Roofing Constructors Inc DBA Western Roofing Service					
2594 Oakdale Ave	San Francisco	CA	94124	415-648-6472	648-5164
Web: www.westroof.com					
Rosenow Contracting Inc 700 Nicholas Blvd Suite 206	Elk Grove Village	IL	60007	847-427-0200	427-0250
Sanders Brothers Inc 1709 Old Georgia Hwy	Gaffney	SC	29342	864-489-1144	487-6165
TF: 800-527-1684 ■ Web: www.sandersbros.net					
Schreiber Corp 2239 Fenkell St.	Detroit	MI	48238	313-864-4900	864-3016
TF: 800-275-3024 ■ Web: www.schreiberroofing.com					
Schust Engineering Inc 2520 Charleston Pl	Fort Wayne	IN	46808	260-482-4820	482-9291
Web: www.schustengineering.com					
Schwartz LE & Son Inc 279 Reid St	Macon	GA	31206	478-745-6563	745-2711
Web: www.leschwartz.com					
Sechrist-Hall Co 102 Omaha	Corpus Christi	TX	78465	361-884-5264	883-3915
Seyforth Roofing Co Inc 2601 Wood Dr.	Garland	TX	75041	972-864-8591	864-8593
TF: 866-870-2800					
SingleSource Roofing Corp 24 Summit Park Dr.	Pittsburgh	PA	15275	412-249-6800	249-6950
TF: 800-777-6610 ■ Web: www.singlesourceroofing.com					
Smither Henry C Roofing Co Inc					
6850 E 32nd St PO Box 26057	Indianapolis	IN	46226	317-545-1304	546-4764
Web: www.smitherroofing.com					
Snyder Roofing & Sheet Metal Inc 12650 SW Hall Blvd.	Tigard	OR	97223	503-620-5252	684-3310
Web: www.snyderroofing.com					
Standard Roofing Co 516 N McDonough St PO Box 1309	Montgomery	AL	36102	334-834-3000	834-3004
TF: 800-239-5705 ■ Web: www.standardtaylor.com					
Superior Roofing & Sheet Metal Co Inc					
3405 S 500 West	Salt Lake City	UT	84115	801-266-1473	266-1522
Taylor DC Co 312 29th St NE	Cedar Rapids	IA	52402	319-363-2073	363-8311
TF: 800-333-7763 ■ Web: www.dctaylorco.com					
TDIndustries 13850 Diplomat Dr.	Dallas	TX	75234	972-888-9500	888-9338
Web: www.tdindustries.com					
Tri-State Roofing & Sheet Metal Co 1001 S Meadville Rd	Davisville	WV	26142	304-485-6593	485-2841
Web: www.tri-stateservicegroup.com					
Universal General Sheet Metal Inc 31 National Rd	Edison	NJ	08817	732-287-3333	287-3328
US Industries Inc 1701 1st Ave	Evansville	IN	47710	812-425-2428	421-4443
TF: 800-264-1501					
Young Group Ltd 1054 Central Industrial Dr.	Saint Louis	MO	63110	314-771-3080	771-4597
TF: 800-331-3080 ■ Web: www.theyounggroup.net					
Zahner A Sheet Metal Co Inc 1400 E 9th St	Kansas City	MO	64106	816-474-8882	474-7994
Web: www.azahner.com					
Zero-Breese Co 4120 Clifton Ave	Cincinnati	OH	45232	513-541-1221	541-1918
Web: www.zerobreese.com					

192-13 Sprinkler System Installation (Fire Sprinklers)

	City	State	Zip	Phone	Fax
Active Fire Sprinkler Corp 63 Flushing Ave Unit 216	Brooklyn	NY	11205	718-834-8300	834-4887
Advance Fire Protection Co Inc 1451 W Lambert Rd	La Habra	CA	90631	562-691-0918	691-5482
All-South Subcontractors Inc 2678 Queenstown Rd	Birmingham	AL	35210	205-836-8111	836-4227
Web: www.allsouthsub.com					
Anson Industries Inc 1959 Anson Dr	Melrose Park	IL	60160	708-681-1300	681-1310
Web: www.ansonindustries.com					
APi Group Inc Fire Protection Group 2366 Rose Pl	Saint Paul	MN	55113	651-636-4320	636-0312
TF: 800-223-4941 ■ Web: www.apigroupinc.com/fire.html					
Armon Inc 2265 Carlson Dr	Northbrook	IL	60062	847-498-4800	498-9091
Web: www.femoran.com					
August Winter & Sons Inc 2323 N Roemer Rd	Appleton	WI	54911	920-739-8881	739-2230
TF: 800-236-8882 ■ Web: www.augustwinter.com					
Brendle Sprinkler Co Inc PO Box 210609	Montgomery	AL	36121	334-270-8571	277-7967
TF: 800-392-8021					
Comunale SA Co Inc 2900 Newpark Dr	Barberton	OH	44203	330-706-3040	861-0860
TF: 800-776-7181 ■ Web: www.comunale.com					
Cosco Fire Protection Inc 321 E Gardena Blvd	Gardena	CA	90248	323-321-5155	323-0761*
*Fax Area Code: 310 ■ TF: 800-827-5612 ■ Web: www.coscofire.com					
Daly MJ & Sons Inc 110 Mattatuck Heights	Waterbury	CT	06705	203-753-5131	597-0227
TF: 800-992-3603 ■ Web: www.mjdalyinc.com					
Davis Joseph Inc 120 W Tupper St	Buffalo	NY	14201	716-842-1500	842-1829
Farmer & Irwin Corp 3300 Ave K	Riviera Beach	FL	33404	561-842-5316	842-5999
TF: 800-883-8229 ■ Web: www.fandicorp.com					
Fire Protection Co 12828 S Ridgeway Ave	Alsip	IL	60803	708-371-4300	371-4340
Fire Protection Systems Inc 22 Industrial Park Dr	Hendersonville	TN	37075	615-822-3600	822-3427
Firetrol Protection Systems Inc					
3696 W 900 South Suite A	Salt Lake City	UT	84104	801-485-6900	485-6902
Web: www.firetrol.net					
Geo M Robinson & Co 852 85th Ave	Oakland	CA	94621	510-632-7017	638-5466
TF: 800-894-8942 ■ Web: www.geomrobinson.com					
High Point Sprinkler Inc 2 Regency Industrial Blvd	Thomasville	NC	27360	336-475-6181	475-4613
JF Ahern Co 855 Morris St	Fond du Lac	WI	54935	920-921-9020	921-8632
TF: 800-532-0155 ■ Web: www.jfahern.com					
John E Green Co 220 Victor Ave.	Highland Park	MI	48203	313-868-2400	868-0011
Web: www.johnegreen.com					
Joseph Davis Inc 120 W Tupper St	Buffalo	NY	14201	716-842-1500	842-1829
Ladew Fire Protection Inc 10440 Markison Rd	Dallas	TX	75238	214-349-1927	341-9553
Martin Fireproofing Corp 2200 Military Rd	Tonawanda	NY	14150	716-692-3680	693-3402
TF: 800-766-3969 ■ Web: www.martinfireproofing.com					
McDaniel Fire Systems 1055 W Joliet Rd	Valparaiso	IN	46385	219-462-0571	611-2907*
*Fax Area Code: 800 ■ TF: 800-348-2632 ■ Web: mcdanielfire.com					
MJ Daly & Sons Inc 110 Mattatuck Heights	Waterbury	CT	06705	203-753-5131	597-0227
TF: 800-992-3603 ■ Web: www.mjdalyinc.com					
National Automatic Sprinkler Industries 8000 Corporate Dr.	Landover	MD	20785	301-577-1700	429-4709
TF: 800-638-2603 ■ Web: www.nasifund.org					
Oliver Sprinkler Co Inc 501 Feheley Dr	King of Prussia	PA	19406	610-277-1331	277-2837
Web: www.oliversprinkler.com					
Patti & Sons Inc 8 Berry St	Brooklyn	NY	11211	718-963-3700	388-8671
SA Comunale Co Inc 2900 Newpark Dr	Barberton	OH	44203	330-706-3040	861-0860
TF: 800-776-7181 ■ Web: www.comunale.com					
Security Fire Protection Co Inc 4495 Mendenhall Rd S	Memphis	TN	38141	901-362-6250	366-7869
TF: 800-362-6256 ■ Web: www.securityfire.com					
Tyco Fire & Security 1 Town Center Rd.	Boca Raton	FL	33486	561-988-7200	
Web: www.tycofireandsecurity.com					
VFP Fire Systems 1301 L'Orient St.	Saint Paul	MN	55117	651-558-3300	558-3310
TF: 800-229-6263 ■ Web: www.vfpfire.com					
VFS Fire Protection Systems 1011 E Lacy Ave	Anaheim	CA	92805	714-778-6070	778-6090
Viking Automatic Sprinkler Co 1301 L'Orient St	Saint Paul	MN	55117	651-558-3300	558-3310
Web: www.vikingsprinkler.com					
Wayne Automatic Fire Sprinklers Inc 222 Capital Ct	Ocoee	FL	34761	407-656-3030	656-8026
Web: www.waynefire.com					
Western States Fire Protection Co					
12150 E Briarwood Ave Suite 202	Centennial	CO	80112	303-768-0456	790-3875
Web: www.wsfp.com					
Wiginton Fire Systems 450 S County Rd 427	Longwood	FL	32750	407-831-3414	831-5740
Web: www.wigintonfiresystems.com					

192-14 Structural Steel Erection

	City	State	Zip	Phone	Fax
Adams & Smith Inc 1300 W Center St	Lindon	UT	84042	801-785-6900	785-6400
Web: www.adamssmithinc.com					
Advance Tank & Construction Co PO Box 219	Wellington	CO	80549	970-568-3444	568-3435
Web: www.advancetank.com					
Albach Co Inc 301 E Prosper St PO Box 1159	Chalmette	LA	70044	504-271-1113	271-1032
Web: www.albachco.com					
Albany Steel Inc 566 Broadway	Albany	NY	12204	518-436-4851	436-1458
TF: 800-342-9317 ■ Web: www.albanysteel.net					
Allstate Steel Co Inc 130 S Jackson Ave	Jacksonville	FL	32220	904-781-6040	693-0255
TF: 888-781-6040 ■ Web: www.allstatesteel.com					
American Bridge Co 1000 American Bridge Way	Coraopolis	PA	15108	412-631-1000	631-2000
Web: www.americanbridge.net					
APi Group Inc Specialty Construction Services Group					
2366 Rose Pl	Saint Paul	MN	55113	651-636-4320	636-0312
Web: www.apigroupinc.com/construction.html					
Arben Corp 175 Marble Ave	Pleasantville	NY	10570	914-741-5459	741-2923
Area Erectors Inc 2323 Harrison Ave	Rockford	IL	61104	815-398-6700	398-6787
Web: www.areaerectors.com					
Ben Hur Construction Co 3783 Rider Trail S	Saint Louis	MO	63045	314-298-8007	298-8565
Web: www.benhurconstruction.com					
Bratton Corp 2801 E 85th St	Kansas City	MO	64132	816-363-1014	361-8021
Web: www.brattonsteel.com					
Buckner CP Steel Erection Inc 4732 NC 54 East PO Box 598	Graham	NC	27253	336-376-8888	376-8855
Web: www.bucknersteel.com					
Building Erection Services Co Inc 15585 S Keeler PO Box 970	Olathe	KS	66051	913-764-5560	764-2317
Caldwell Tanks Alliance LLC 57 E Broad St	Newnan	GA	30263	770-253-2600	251-9253
TF: 800-241-1650					
CBI Services Inc 24 Read's Way	New Castle	DE	19720	302-325-8400	323-0788
TF: 800-642-8675 ■ Web: www.cbi.com					
CE Toland & Son 5300 Industrial Way	Benicia	CA	94510	707-747-1000	747-5300
TF: 800-675-1166					
Central Maintenance & Welding Inc					
2620 E Keysville Rd PO Drawer 777	Lithia	FL	33547	813-737-1402	737-1820
TF: 877-704-7411 ■ Web: www.cmw-inc.com					
Century Steel Erectors Co					
210 Washington Ave PO Box 490	Dravosburg	PA	15034	412-469-8800	469-0813
TF: 888-601-8801 ■ Web: www.centurysteel.com					
Chicago Bridge & Iron Co 14105 S Rt 59	Plainfield	IL	60544	815-439-6000	439-6010
NYSE: CBI ■ TF: 800-799-8443 ■ Web: www.cbi.com					
CP Buckner Steel Erection Inc 4732 NC 54 East PO Box 598	Graham	NC	27253	336-376-8888	376-8855
Web: www.bucknersteel.com					
Davidson JL Co Inc 8663 N Magnolia Ave Suite H	Santee	CA	92071	619-562-2002	562-8453
Derr Construction Co 13400 Trinity Blvd PO Box 637	Euless	TX	76039	817-571-4044	571-4544
Web: www.derrsteel.com					

Structural Steel Erection (Cont'd)

Phone | Fax

Dix Corp 4024 S Grove Rd .... Spokane WA 99224 509-838-4455 838-4464
TF: 800-827-8548 ■ *Web:* www.dixcorp.com
Fenton Rigging & Contracting Inc 2150 Langdon Farm Rd .... Cincinnati OH 45237 513-631-5500 631-4361
Web: www.fentonrigging.com
Fontana Steel Inc 12451 Arrow Rt PO Box 2219 .... Rancho Cucamonga CA 91729 909-899-9993 899-9799
TF: 800-877-8758
Havens National Riggers & Erectors Inc 14650 Jib St .... Plymouth MI 48170 734-459-9515 459-9543
Web: www.havenssteel.com
Higgins Erectors & Haulers Inc 7715 Lockport Rd .... Niagara Falls NY 14304 716-297-2600 205-0159
High Industries Inc PO Box 10008 .... Lancaster PA 17605 717-293-4444 293-4416*
**Fax:* Mktg ■ *Web:* www.high.net
High Steel Structures Inc
1853 William Penn Way PO Box 10008 .... Lancaster PA 17605 717-299-5211 293-4416
Web: www.highsteel.com
Highland Tank & Mfg Co 1 Highland Rd .... Stoystown PA 15563 814-893-5701 893-6126
Web: www.highlandtank.com
JL Davidson Co Inc 8663 N Magnolia Ave Suite H .... Santee CA 92071 619-562-2002 562-8453
Jones & Brown Co Inc 568 W Winthrop Ave .... Addison IL 60101 630-543-0300 543-0341
Web: www.jonesandbrowncompany.com
Keller-Hall Inc 1247 Eastwood Ave .... Tallmadge OH 44278 330-633-6160 633-5773
TF: 800-831-6147 ■ *Web:* www.kellerrigging.com
Kelly Steel Erectors Inc 7220 Division St .... Bedford OH 44146 440-232-9595 232-0272
Koch Skanska Inc 400 Roosevelt Ave .... Carteret NJ 07008 732-969-1700 969-0197
Lafayette Steel Erector Inc 313 Westgate Rd .... Lafayette LA 70506 337-234-9435 234-0217
Web: www.l-s-e.com
Mansfield Structural & Erecting Co 429 Park Ave E .... Mansfield OH 44905 419-522-5911 525-4948
Midwest Steel & Equipment Co Inc 9825 Moers Rd .... Houston TX 77075 713-991-7843 991-4745
Web: www.midwest-steel.com
Midwest Steel Inc 2525 E Grand Blvd .... Detroit MI 48211 313-873-2220 873-2222
TF: 800-578-7880 ■ *Web:* www.midweststeel.com
Patent Construction Systems 1 Mack Centre Dr .... Paramus NJ 07652 201-261-5600 261-5544
TF: 800-969-5600 ■ *Web:* www.pcshd.com
Paxton & Vierling Steel Co 501 Ave H .... Carter Lake IA 51510 712-347-5500 347-6166
TF: 800-831-9252 ■ *Web:* www.pvsteel.com
Pittsburg Tank & Tower Co Inc 1 Watertank Pl .... Henderson KY 42420 270-826-9000 826-1970*
**Fax:* Sales ■ *TF:* 800-499-8265 ■ *Web:* www.watertank.com
Rebar Engineering Inc 10706 Painter Ave .... Santa Fe Springs CA 90670 562-946-2461 941-7740
TF: 800-555-9807
Ryan Iron Works Inc 1830 Broadway .... Raynham MA 02767 508-822-8001 823-1359
Web: www.ryanironworks.net
Schuff Steel Co 420 S 19th Ave .... Phoenix AZ 85009 602-252-7787 452-4466
TF: 800-528-0513 ■ *Web:* www.schuff.com
Shurtleff & Andrews Corp 1875 W 500 South .... Salt Lake City UT 84104 801-973-9096 973-2248
Southeastern Construction & Maintenance Co Inc
1150 Pebbledale Rd PO Box 1055 .... Mulberry FL 33860 863-428-1511 428-1110
TF: 800-511-1600 ■ *Web:* www.southeasternconst.com
Sowles Co 3045 Hwy 13 Suite 100 .... Eagan MN 55121 651-287-9700 287-9710
TF: 888-376-9537 ■ *Web:* www.sowles.com
Steel City Inc 2563 Commerce Clr .... Birmingham AL 35217 205-426-3807 426-3814
TF: 800-264-5075 ■ *Web:* www.steelcitysafe.com
Tampa Steel Erecting Co 5127 Bloomingdale Ave .... Tampa FL 33619 813-677-7184 677-8364
Toland CE & Son 5300 Industrial Way .... Benicia CA 94510 707-747-1000 747-5300
TF: 800-675-1166
Waldinger Corp 2601 Bell Ave .... Des Moines IA 50321 515-284-1911 323-5150
TF: 800-225-0638 ■ *Web:* www.waldinger.com
Washington Ornamental Iron Works Inc 17926 S Broadway .... Gardena CA 90248 310-327-8660 329-4180
TF: 800-332-4766
Williams Industries Inc 8624 JD Reading Dr .... Manassas VA 20109 703-335-7800 335-7802
NASDAQ: WMSI ■ *Web:* www.wmsi.com
WO Grubb Steel Erection Inc 5120 Jefferson Davis Hwy .... Richmond VA 23234 804-271-9471 271-2539
TF: 800-344-6824 ■ *Web:* www.wogrubb.com
Zimkor Industries Inc 7011 Titan Rd .... Littleton CO 80125 303-791-1333 791-1340
Web: www.zimkor.com

192-15 Terrazzo, Tile, Marble, Mosaic Contractors

Phone | Fax

Belfi Brothers & Co Inc 4310-18 Josephine St .... Philadelphia PA 19124 215-289-2766 289-9208
Web: www.belfibrothers.com
DMI Tile & Marble Inc 3012 5th Ave S .... Birmingham AL 35233 205-322-8473 251-9611
TF: 800-322-8449 ■ *Web:* www.dmi-tmt.com
Marblelife Inc 300 Northstar Ct .... Sanford FL 32771 407-302-9297 302-9311
TF: 800-627-4569 ■ *Web:* www.marblelife.com
Tile Trends 1311 Lawrence Dr .... Newbury Park CA 91320 805-497-7471 498-7460

192-16 Water Well Drilling

Phone | Fax

Grosch Irrigation Co Inc 3110 33rd Rd .... Silver Creek NE 68663 308-773-2261 773-2414
TF: 800-509-2261
Kelley Dewatering & Construction Co 5175 Clay Ave SW .... Wyoming MI 49548 616-538-8010 538-0708
Web: www.kelleydewatering.com
Layne Christensen Co 1900 Shawnee Mission Pkwy .... Mission Woods KS 66205 913-362-0510 362-0133
NASDAQ: LAYN ■ *Web:* www.laynechristensen.com
Ohio Drilling Co 2405 Bostic Blvd SW .... Massillon OH 44647 330-832-1521 832-5302
TF: 800-860-2285
Raba-Kistner Consultants Inc 12821 W Golden Ln .... San Antonio TX 78249 210-699-9090 699-6426
TF: 866-722-2547 ■ *Web:* www.rkci.com
RE Chapman Co 30 N Main St .... West Boylston MA 01583 508-835-6231 835-3978
TF: 800-727-6231
Rosencrantz-Bemis Enterprises Inc 1105 281 Bypass .... Great Bend KS 67530 620-793-5512 793-5176
TF: 800-466-2467
Sargent Irrigation Co PO Box 627 .... Broken Bow NE 68822 308-872-6451 872-6912
Web: www.sargentirrigation.com
Tri-State Drilling Inc 16940 Hwy 55 W .... Plymouth MN 55446 763-553-1234 553-9778
TF: 800-383-1033 ■ *Web:* www.tristatedrilling.com
Water Resources International Inc 1100 Alakea St Suite 2900 .... Honolulu HI 96813 808-531-8422 531-7181

192-17 Wrecking & Demolition Contractors

Phone | Fax

Allied Erecting & Dismantling Co Inc 2100 Poland Ave .... Youngstown OH 44502 330-744-0808 744-3218
TF: 800-624-2867 ■ *Web:* www.aed.cc
Barnard Construction Co Inc PO Box 99 .... Bozeman MT 59771 406-586-1995 586-3530
Web: www.barnard-inc.com
Bi-Con Services Inc 10901 Clay Pike Rd .... Derwent OH 43733 740-685-2542 685-3863
Web: www.bsicos.com
Bierlein Cos Inc 2000 Bay City Rd .... Midland MI 48642 989-496-0066 496-0144
TF: 800-336-6626 ■ *Web:* www.bierlein.com
Big Apple Wrecking & Construction Corp 1379 Commerce Ave .... Bronx NY 10461 718-829-8800 829-7210
Web: www.bigapplewrecking.com
Bolander Carl & Sons Co Inc 251 Starkey St .... Saint Paul MN 55107 651-224-6299 223-8197
TF: 800-676-6504 ■ *Web:* www.bolander.com
Callas Contractors Inc 10549 Downsville Pike .... Hagerstown MD 21740 301-739-8400 739-7065
Web: www.callascontractors.com
Carl Bolander & Sons Co Inc 251 Starkey St .... Saint Paul MN 55107 651-224-6299 223-8197
TF: 800-676-6504 ■ *Web:* www.bolander.com
Cherry Demolition 6131 Selinsky Rd .... Houston TX 77048 713-987-0000 987-0629
TF: 800-444-1123 ■ *Web:* www.cherrydemolition.com
Edgerton Contractors Inc 6466 S 13th St .... Oak Creek WI 53154 414-764-4443 764-9788
Web: www.edgertoncontractors.com
Gateway Demolition Corp 134-22 32nd Ave .... Flushing NY 11354 718-359-1400 461-6558
Web: www.gatewaydemolition.com
Geppert Brothers Inc 3101 Trewigtown Rd .... Colmar PA 18915 215-822-0511 822-0635
ICONCO Inc 4700 Coliseum Way .... Oakland CA 94601 510-261-1900 261-2459
Web: www.iconco-inc.com
Invirex Demolition Co PO Box 481 .... Huntington NY 11743 631-368-4485 368-4485
TF: 800-783-2336
James White Construction Co Inc 4156 Freedom Way .... Weirton WV 26062 304-748-8181 748-8183
Kimmins Contracting Corp 1501 2nd Ave .... Tampa FL 33605 813-248-3878 247-0183
Web: www.kimmins.com
Kipin Industries Inc 4194 Green Garden Rd .... Aliquippa PA 15001 724-495-6200 495-2219
Web: www.kipin.com
Manafort Brothers Inc PO Box 99 .... Plainville CT 06062 860-229-4853 229-1878
TF: 888-626-2367 ■ *Web:* www.manafort.com
Mercer Wrecking Recycling Corp 4 Beakes St .... Trenton NJ 08638 609-394-9494 394-6839
Web: www.demolitionrecycle.com/mwr.htm
Midwest Steel & Equipment Co Inc 9825 Moers Rd .... Houston TX 77075 713-991-7843 991-4745
Web: www.midwest-steel.com
National Wrecking Co 2441 N Leavitt St .... Chicago IL 60647 773-384-2800 384-0403
Web: www.nationalwrecking.com
Noralco Corp 1920 Lincoln Rd .... Pittsburgh PA 15235 412-361-6678 361-6535
Web: www.noralco.com
Nuprecon Inc 35131 SE Center St .... Snoqualmie WA 98065 425-881-0623 881-5935
TF: 800-442-2072 ■ *Web:* www.nuprecon.com
O'Rourke Wrecking Co 660 Lunken Park Dr .... Cincinnati OH 45226 513-871-1400 871-1313
TF: 800-354-9850 ■ *Web:* www.orourkewrecking.com
Penhall International Inc 1801 Penhall Way .... Anaheim CA 92803 714-778-6677 778-8437
TF: 800-736-4255 ■ *Web:* www.penhall.com
Plant Reclamation 912 Harbour Way S .... Richmond CA 94804 510-233-6552 237-6739
TF: 800-637-0339 ■ *Web:* www.plantreclamation.com
RCI Environmental Inc 1216 140th Ave PO Box 1730 .... Sumner WA 98390 253-863-5300 859-5702
TF: 800-848-3777 ■ *Web:* www.rci-group.com
Robinette Demolition Inc 0 S 560 Hwy 83 .... Oakbrook Terrace IL 60181 630-833-7997 833-8047
Web: www.rdidemolition.com
Siciliano Inc 3650 Winchester Rd .... Springfield IL 62707 217-585-1200 585-1211
Web: www.sicilianoinc.com
US Dismantlement LLC 2600 S Throop St .... Chicago IL 60608 312-328-1400 328-1477
TF: 800-648-3801 ■ *Web:* www.usdllc.com

193 CONSTRUCTION MACHINERY & EQUIPMENT

SEE ALSO Industrial Machinery, Equipment, & Supplies p. 1854; Material Handling Equipment p. 1949

Phone | Fax

Allied Construction Products LLC 3900 Kelley Ave .... Cleveland OH 44114 216-431-2600 431-2601
TF Cust Svc: 800-321-1046 ■ *Web:* www.alliedcp.com
Altec Industries Inc 210 Inverness Center Dr .... Birmingham AL 35242 205-991-7733 991-9993
Web: www.altec.com
Asphalt Drum Mixers Inc 1 ADM Pkwy .... Huntertown IN 46748 260-637-5729 637-3164
Web: www.admasphaltplants.com
Astec Industries Inc 4101 Jerome Ave .... Chattanooga TN 37407 423-867-4210 827-1485*
NASDAQ: ASTE ■ **Fax:* Hum Res ■ *TF:* 800-468-5938 ■ *Web:* www.astecinc.com
Bandit Industries Inc 6750 Millbrook Rd .... Remus MI 49340 989-561-2270 561-2273
TF: 800-952-0178 ■ *Web:* www.banditchippers.com
Bid-Well Corp PO Box 97 .... Canton SD 57013 605-987-2603 987-2605
TF: 800-843-9824 ■ *Web:* www.bid-well.com
Blount Forestry & Industrial Equipment Div
535 Mack Todd Rd .... Zebulon NC 27597 919-269-7421 269-2406
Web: www.blount-fied.com
Boart Longyear Co 2640 W 1700 South .... Salt Lake City UT 84104 801-972-6430 977-3372
TF Cust Svc: 800-457-5778 ■ *Web:* www.boartlongyear.com
Bomag Americas Inc 2000 Kentville Rd .... Kewanee IL 61443 309-853-3571 852-0350
TF: 800-782-6624 ■ *Web:* www.bomag.com
BradenCarco Gearmatic Paccar Winch Div
800 E Dallas St .... Broken Arrow OK 74012 918-251-8511 259-1575
Web: www.paccarwinch.com
Bucyrus Blades Inc 260 E Beal Ave .... Bucyrus OH 44820 419-562-6015 562-8360
TF: 800-532-5233 ■ *Web:* www.escocorp.com/bucyrus_blades/index.html
Bucyrus International Inc 1100 Milwaukee Ave .... South Milwaukee WI 53172 414-768-4000 768-4006
NASDAQ: BUCY ■ *Web:* www.bucyrus.com
Caterpillar Inc 100 NE Adams St .... Peoria IL 61629 309-675-1000 675-4332*
NYSE: CAT ■ **Fax:* PR ■ *Web:* www.cat.com
Cedarapids Inc 909 17th St NE .... Cedar Rapids IA 52402 319-363-3511 399-4871*
**Fax:* Sales ■ *TF Cust Svc:* 800-821-5600 ■ *Web:* www.cedarapids.com
Central Mine Equipment Co Inc 4215 Rider Trail N .... Earth City MO 63045 314-291-7700 291-4880
TF: 800-325-8827 ■ *Web:* www.cmeco.com
Charles Machine Works Inc PO Box 66 .... Perry OK 73077 580-336-4402 336-3458
TF: 800-654-6481 ■ *Web:* www.ditchwitch.com
Chemgrout Inc 805 E 31st St .... La Grange Park IL 60526 708-354-7125 354-3881
Web: www.chemgrout.com
Cleveland Trencher Co 1755 W Market St .... Akron OH 44313 330-869-2800 869-5200
Web: www.cleveland-trencher.com
CRC Evans Pipeline International Inc 10700 E Independence St .... Tulsa OK 74116 918-438-2100 438-6237
TF: 800-395-5192 ■ *Web:* www.crc-evans.com
Deere & Co John Deere Construction & Forestry Div
1515 5th Ave .... Moline IL 61265 309-765-0227 748-0117*
**Fax:* Cust Svc
Demag Cranes & Components 29201 Aurora Rd .... Cleveland OH 44139 440-248-2400 248-3036
TF: 800-321-6560 ■ *Web:* www.demag-us.com
Eagle Iron Works 129 E Holcomb Ave .... Des Moines IA 50313 515-243-1123 243-8214
Web: www.eagleironworks.com
ED Etnyre & Co 1333 S Daysville Rd .... Oregon IL 61061 815-732-2116 732-7400
TF: 800-995-2116 ■ *Web:* www.etnyre.com
Elgin National Industries Inc
2001 Butterfield Rd Suite 1020 .... Downers Grove IL 60515 630-434-7200 434-7246
Web: www.eni.com
Erie Strayer Co 1851 Rudolph Ave .... Erie PA 16502 814-456-7001 452-3422
Web: www.eriestrayer.com
Esco Corp 2141 NW 25th Ave .... Portland OR 97210 503-228-2141 778-6330
TF: 800-523-3795 ■ *Web:* www.escocorp.com

Company	City	State	Zip	Phone	Fax
Fairchild International 200 Fairchild Ln *Web:* www.fairchildint.com	Glen Lyn	VA	24093	540-726-2380	726-2388
Franklin Equipment Co 33551 Carver Rd *TF:* 800-835-7503 ■ *Web:* www.franklineq.com	Franklin	VA	23851	757-562-6111	229-7152
Gencor Industries Inc 5201 N Orange Blossom Trail **Fax:* Sales ■ *TF:* 800-234-3626 ■ *Web:* www.gencor.com	Orlando	FL	32810	407-290-6000	578-0577*
Gradall Industries Inc 406 Mill Ave SW *Web:* www.gradall.com	New Philadelphia	OH	44663	330-339-2211	339-8468
Group Canam Inc 11505 1st Ave Bureau 500 *TSX:* CAM ■ *TF:* 877-499-6049 ■ *Web:* www.canammanac.com	Saint-Georges	QC	G5Y7X3	418-228-8031	228-1750
Grove Worldwide LLC PO Box 21 *Web:* www.groveworldwide.com	Shady Grove	PA	17256	717-597-8121	597-4062
H & E Equipment Services Inc 11100 Mead Rd Suite 200 *NASDAQ:* HEES ■ *TF:* 877-700-7368 ■ *Web:* www.he-equipment.com	Baton Rouge	LA	70816	225-298-5200	298-5377
Hendrix Mfg Co Inc 816 Jenkins St *Web:* www.hendrixmfg.com	Mansfield	LA	71052	318-872-1660	872-1508
Hensley Industries Inc 2108 Joe Field Rd PO Box 29779 **Fax:* Cust Svc ■ *TF:* 888-406-6262 ■ *Web:* www.hensleyind.com	Dallas	TX	75229	972-241-2321	241-0915*
Highway Equipment Co Inc 1330 76th Ave SW *Web:* www.highwayequipment.com	Cedar Rapids	IA	52404	319-363-8281	632-3084
Hydralift AmClyde Inc 240 E Plato Blvd *Web:* www.amclyde.com	Saint Paul	MN	55107	651-293-4646	293-4648
Ingersoll-Rand Co 155 Chestnut Ridge Rd *NYSE:* IR ■ *Web:* www.irco.com	Montvale	NJ	07645	201-573-0123	573-3172
Jennmar Corp 258 Kappa Dr *Web:* www.jennmar.com	Pittsburgh	PA	15238	412-963-9071	963-6809
JH Fletcher & Co Inc 402 High St *Web:* www.jhfletcher.com	Huntington	WV	25705	304-525-7811	525-3770
JLG Industries Inc 1 JLG Dr *NYSE:* JLG ■ *Web:* www.jlg.com	McConnellsburg	PA	17233	717-485-5161	485-6417
John Deere Construction & Forestry Div Deere & Co 1515 5th Ave **Fax:* Cust Svc	Moline	IL	61265	309-765-0227	748-0117*
Joy Mining Machinery 177 Thorn Hill Rd *Web:* www.joyglobal.com/joymining	Warrendale	PA	15086	724-779-4500	779-4509
Komatsu America Corp 440 N Fairway Dr *Web:* www.komatsuamerica.com	Vernon Hills	IL	60061	847-970-4100	970-4183
Komatsu Forest LLC 1075 Airport Dr PO Box 516 *Web:* www.komatsuforest.com	Shawano	WI	54166	715-524-2820	526-2347
Kress Corp 227 W Illinois St *Web:* www.kresscarrier.com	Brimfield	IL	61517	309-446-3395	446-9625
LeTourneau Inc PO Box 2307 *Web:* www.letourneau-inc.com	Longview	TX	74606	903-237-7000	237-7032
Liebherr-America Inc 4100 Chestnut Ave	Newport News	VA	23607	757-245-5251	928-8700
Link-Belt Construction Equipment Co 2651 Palumbo Dr **Fax:* Sales ■ *Web:* www.linkbelt.com	Lexington	KY	40583	859-263-5200	263-5260*
Manitowoc Co Inc 2400 S 44th St *NYSE:* MTW ■ *Web:* www.manitowoc.com	Manitowoc	WI	54220	920-684-4410	652-9778
Mayville Engineering Co Inc 715 South St *Web:* www.mayvl.com	Mayville	WI	53050	920-387-4500	387-2682
McLellan Equipment Inc 251 Shaw Rd *TF:* 800-848-8449 ■ *Web:* www.mclellanequipment.com	South San Francisco	CA	94080	650-873-8100	589-7398
Metso Dynapac Inc 16435 I-H 35 N PO Box 615 *TF:* 800-867-6060 ■ *Web:* www.dynapac.com	Selma	TX	78154	210-474-5770	474-5780
Metso Minerals Inc 20965 Crossroads Cir *Web:* www.metsominerals.com	Waukesha	WI	53186	262-717-2500	717-2501
Meyer Products 18513 Euclid Ave **Fax:* Sales ■ *Web:* www.meyerproducts.com	Cleveland	OH	44112	216-486-1313	486-1321*
Midwestern Industries Inc 915 Oberlin Rd SW *TF:* 877-474-9464 ■ *Web:* www.midwesternind.com	Massillon	OH	44647	330-837-4203	837-4210
Millcraft Industries Inc 400 Southpointe Blvd Plaza 1 Suite 400 *Web:* www.millcraftindustries.com	Canonsburg	PA	15317	724-743-3400	745-2400
Pengo Corp 500 E Hwy 10 *TF Cust Svc:* 800-599-0211 ■ *Web:* www.pengocorp.com	Laurens	IA	50554	712-845-2540	845-2497
Pennsylvania Crusher Corp 600 Abbott Dr *Web:* penncrusher.com	Broomall	PA	19008	610-544-7200	543-0190
Pettibone Corp 2626 Warrenville Rd Suite 300 *Web:* www.pettibone.com	Downers Grove	IL	60515	630-353-5000	353-5026
Philadelphia Mixers Corp 1221 E Main St *TF Cust Svc:* 800-733-1341 ■ *Web:* www.philadelphiamixers.com	Palmyra	PA	17078	717-832-2800	832-1740
Pierce Pacific Mfg Inc PO Box 30509 *TF:* 800-760-3270 ■ *Web:* www.piercepacific.com	Portland	OR	97294	503-808-9110	808-9111
Precision Husky Corp 850 Markeeta Spur Rd *Web:* www.precisionhusky.com	Moody	AL	35004	205-640-5181	640-1147
Putzmeister America 1733 90th St *TF:* 800-884-7210 ■ *Web:* www.putzmeister.com	Sturtevant	WI	53177	262-886-3200	886-3212
Racine Federated Inc 8635 Washington Ave *Web:* www.racinefederated.com	Racine	WI	53406	262-639-6770	639-2267
Ramsey Winch Co Inc 1600 N Garnett Rd *TF:* 800-777-2760 ■ *Web:* www.ramsey.com	Tulsa	OK	74116	918-438-2760	438-6688
RKI Inc 2301 Central Pkwy *Web:* www.rki-us.com	Houston	TX	77092	713-688-4414	688-5776
Somero Enterprises 82 Fitzgerald Dr *Web:* www.somero.com	Jaffrey	NH	03452	603-532-5900	532-5930
Stone Construction Equipment Inc 8662 Main St *TF:* 800-888-9926 ■ *Web:* www.stone-equip.com	Honeoye	NY	14471	585-229-5141	229-2363
Superwinch Inc 45 Danco Rd *Web:* www.superwinch.com	Putnam	CT	06260	860-928-7787	928-1143
Swenson Spreader Co 127 Walnut St *TF:* 888-825-7323 ■ *Web:* www.swensonspreader.com	Lindenwood	IL	61049	815-393-4455	393-4964
Symons Corp 200 E Touhy Ave *TF:* 800-800-7601 ■ *Web:* www.symons.com	Des Plaines	IL	60018	847-298-3200	635-9287
Telsmith Inc 10910 N Industrial Dr *TF:* 800-765-6601 ■ *Web:* www.telsmith.com	Mequon	WI	53092	262-242-6600	242-5812
Terex Corp 500 Post Rd E Suite 320 *NYSE:* TEX ■ *Web:* www.terex.com	Westport	CT	06880	203-222-7170	222-7976
Terex Corp Crane Div 202 Raleigh St **Fax:* Hum Res ■ *TF:* 800-250-2726 ■ *Web:* www.terex.com	Wilmington	NC	28412	910-395-8500	395-8551*
Terex Roadbuilding PO Box 1985 *Web:* www.terexrb.com	Oklahoma City	OK	73101	405-787-6020	491-2417
Trencor Inc 9600 Corporate Pk Dr *TF:* 800-527-6020 ■ *Web:* www.trencor.com	Loudon	TN	37774	865-408-2100	458-6252
Tulsa Winch Group PO Box 1130 *Web:* www.team-twg.com	Jenks	OK	74037	918-298-8300	298-8301
Varel International 1434 Patton Pl Suite 106 *TF:* 800-827-3526 ■ *Web:* www.varelintl.com	Carrollton	TX	75007	972-242-1160	242-3369
Volvo Construction Equipment of North America Inc 1 Volvo Dr *Web:* www.volvo.com/constructionequipment	Asheville	NC	28803	828-650-2000	650-2501
Wacker Corp N 92 W 15000 Anthony Ave *TF:* 800-770-0957 ■ *Web:* www.wackergroup.com	Menomonee Falls	WI	53051	262-255-0500	255-0550
Western Products Inc 7777 N 73rd St **Fax:* Cust Svc ■ *Web:* www.westernplows.com	Milwaukee	WI	53223	414-354-2310	354-6664*
Young Corp 3231 Utah Ave S *TF:* 800-321-9090 ■ *Web:* www.youngcorp.com	Seattle	WA	98134	206-624-1071	682-6881

194 CONSTRUCTION MATERIALS

SEE ALSO Home Improvement Centers p. 1788

194-1 Brick, Stone, Related Materials

Company	City	State	Zip	Phone	Fax
Alley-Cassetty Cos Inc 2 Oldham St *Web:* www.alley-cassetty.com	Nashville	TN	37213	615-244-0440	254-4553
Arizona Portland Cement Co 2400 N Central Ave *TF:* 800-462-2475	Phoenix	AZ	85004	602-271-0069	254-9027
Block USA 327 Fiberglass Rd *TF:* 888-942-5625 ■ *Web:* www.specblockusa.com	Jackson	TN	38301	731-421-4624	421-4625
Breckenridge Material 2833 Breckenridge Industrial Ct PO Box 19918 *Web:* www.breckenridgematerial.com	Saint Louis	MO	63144	314-962-1234	962-1540
Clay Ingels Co Inc 914 Delaware Ave *TF:* 800-282-9064 ■ *Web:* www.clay-ingels.com	Lexington	KY	40505	859-252-0836	259-0938
Corriveau-Routhier Inc 266 Clay St *Web:* www.corriveaurouthier.com	Manchester	NH	03103	603-627-3805	622-6758
Dayton/Richmond Concrete Accessories 721 Richard St *TF:* 800-745-3700 ■ *Web:* www.daytonrichmond.com	Miamisburg	OH	45342	937-866-0711	866-8027
E Stewart Mitchell Inc 1250 Benhill Ave PO Box 2799 *TF:* 800-870-6365 ■ *Web:* www.estewartmitchell.com	Baltimore	MD	21225	410-354-0600	354-3029
Franklin Industries Inc 612 10th Ave N *TF:* 800-626-8147 ■ *Web:* www.frankmin.com	Nashville	TN	37203	615-259-4222	726-2693
Granite Construction Inc PO Box 50085 *NYSE:* GVA ■ *Web:* www.graniteconstruction.com	Watsonville	CA	95077	831-724-1011	722-9657
Graniterock Co 350 Technology Dr PO Box 50001 *TF:* 800-327-1711 ■ *Web:* www.graniterock.com	Watsonville	CA	95077	831-768-2000	768-2201
Hanson Building Products North America 3500 Maple Ave *TF:* 800-527-2362 ■ *Web:* www.hanson-america.com	Dallas	TX	75219	214-525-5500	525-5563
Hudson Liquid Asphalts Inc 89 Ship St *TF:* 800-556-3406 ■ *Web:* www.hudsoncompanies.com	Providence	RI	02903	401-274-2200	274-2220
Ingram Materials Co 1030 Visco Dr *TF:* 800-421-6998 ■ *Web:* www.ingrammaterials.com	Nashville	TN	37210	615-256-5111	256-8522
Intrepid Enterprises Inc 1848 Industrial Blvd	Harvey	LA	70058	504-348-2861	340-7018
Jack B Parson Cos 2350 S 1900 West *TF:* 888-672-7766 ■ *Web:* www.jbparson.com	Ogden	UT	84401	801-731-1111	731-8800
Jaeckle Wholesale Inc 4101 Owl Creek Dr *TF:* 800-236-7225 ■ *Web:* www.jaecklewholesale.com	Madison	WI	53718	608-838-5400	838-5393
Jenkins Brick Co Inc 201 N 6th St PO Box 91 *TF:* 888-215-5700 ■ *Web:* www.jenkinsbrick.com	Montgomery	AL	36104	334-834-2210	262-6817
Kuhlman Corp 1845 Indian Woods Cir *TF:* 800-669-3309 ■ *Web:* www.kuhlman-corp.com	Maumee	OH	43537	419-897-6000	897-6061
L Thorn Co Inc 6000 Grant Line Rd PO Box 198 *TF:* 800-662-4594 ■ *Web:* www.lthorn.com	New Albany	IN	47151	812-246-4461	246-2678
Lyman-Richey Corp 4315 Cuming St *TF:* 800-727-8432 ■ *Web:* www.lymanrichey.com	Omaha	NE	68131	402-558-2727	556-5171
Rio Grande Co 201 Santa Fe Dr *TF:* 800-864-4280 ■ *Web:* www.riograndeco.com	Denver	CO	80223	303-825-2211	629-0417
Ross Island Sand & Gravel Co 4315 SE McLoughlin Blvd PO Box 82249 *TF:* 800-543-0230	Portland	OR	97282	503-239-5504	235-1350
Vimco Concrete Accessories Inc 300 Hansen Access Rd *TF:* 888-468-4626	King of Prussia	PA	19406	610-768-0500	768-0586
Walker & Zanger Inc 31 Warren Pl *TF:* 800-634-0866 ■ *Web:* www.marblestone.com	Mount Vernon	NY	10550	914-667-1600	667-6244
WF Saunders & Sons Inc PO Box A *Web:* www.saundersconcrete.com	Nedrow	NY	13120	315-469-3217	469-3940
Wildish Land Co Inc 3600 Wildish Ln PO Box 7428 *Web:* www.wildish.com	Eugene	OR	97401	541-485-1700	683-7722

194-2 Construction Materials (Misc)

Company	City	State	Zip	Phone	Fax
Acoustical Material Services Inc 1620 S Maple Ave *TF:* 800-486-3517 ■ *Web:* www.a-m-s.com	Montebello	CA	90640	323-721-9011	721-2476
American Fence Co 2502 N 27th Ave *TF:* 888-691-4565 ■ *Web:* www.americanfence.com	Phoenix	AZ	85009	602-734-0500	734-0573
APi Group Inc Materials Distribution Group 2366 Rose Pl *TF:* 800-223-4922 ■ *Web:* www.apigroupinc.com/materials.html	Saint Paul	MN	55113	651-636-4320	636-0312
Atlantic Service & Supply 16C Overmeyer Way **Fax Area Code:* 800 ■ *TF:* 800-921-0343	Forest Park	GA	30297	404-691-3591	921-0344*
Brown DS Co 300 E Cherry St *TF:* 800-848-1730 ■ *Web:* www.dsbrown.com	North Baltimore	OH	45872	419-257-3561	257-2200
Concrete Materials Inc 1201 W Russell St *Web:* www.concretematerialscompany.com	Sioux Falls	SD	57118	605-357-6000	334-6221
CR Laurence Co Inc 2503 E Vernon Ave PO Box 58923 **Fax Area Code:* 800 ■ *TF:* 800-421-6144 ■ *Web:* www.crlaurence.com	Los Angeles	CA	90058	323-588-1281	262-3299*
DS Brown Co 300 E Cherry St *TF:* 800-848-1730 ■ *Web:* www.dsbrown.com	North Baltimore	OH	45872	419-257-3561	257-2200
E Kinast Distributors Inc 9362 W Grand Ave *Web:* www.ekd.com	Franklin Park	IL	60131	847-451-9300	451-0733
Fargo Glass & Paint Co Inc 1801 7th Ave N *TF:* 800-437-4612	Fargo	ND	58102	701-235-4441	235-3435
Kinast E Distributors Inc 9362 W Grand Ave *Web:* www.ekd.com	Franklin Park	IL	60131	847-451-9300	451-0733
L & W Supply Corp 125 S Franklin St *TF:* 800-621-9622 ■ *Web:* www.lwsupply.com	Chicago	IL	60606	312-606-4000	606-5323
Laurence CR Co Inc 2503 E Vernon Ave PO Box 58923 **Fax Area Code:* 800 ■ *TF:* 800-421-6144 ■ *Web:* www.crlaurence.com	Los Angeles	CA	90058	323-588-1281	262-3299*
Oldcastle Glass Group 2425 Olympic Blvd Suite 525E *TF:* 866-653-2278 ■ *Web:* www.oldcastleglass.com	Santa Monica	CA	90404	310-264-4700	264-4703
Sumitomo Metal USA Corp 25 NW Point Blvd Suite 675	Elk Grove	IL	60007	847-290-2600	290-2666
Tech-Aerofoam Products Inc DBA Tech Products 1264 La Quinta Dr Suite D *TF:* 866-211-7763	Orlando	FL	32809	407-447-6108	447-6115
Tech Products 1264 La Quinta Dr Suite D *TF:* 866-211-7763	Orlando	FL	32809	407-447-6108	447-6115

194-3 Lumber & Building Supplies

Company	City	State	Zip	Phone	Fax
84 Lumber Co 1019 Rte 519 *TF:* 800-664-1984 ■ *Web:* www.84lumber.com	Eighty Four	PA	15330	724-228-8820	228-8820
AC Houston Lumber Co 2912 E La Madre Way *Web:* www.achoustonlumber.com	North Las Vegas	NV	89081	702-633-5100	633-5111

Lumber & Building Supplies (Cont'd)

Company	City	State	Zip	Phone	Fax
Advanced Environmental Recycling Technologies Inc 914 N Jefferson St *NASDAQ: AERTA* ■ *TF:* 800-951-5117 ■ *Web:* www.aertinc.com	Springdale	AR	72764	479-756-7400	756-7410
Aljoma Lumber Inc 10300 NW 121st Way *Web:* www.aljoma.com	Medley	FL	33178	305-556-8003	557-2146
Allied Building Products Corp 15 E Union Ave *TF:* 800-541-2198 ■ *Web:* www.alliedbuilding.com	East Rutherford	NJ	07073	201-507-8400	507-3855
Alpine Lumber Co 1120 W 122nd Ave Suite 301 *TF:* 800-275-2365 ■ *Web:* www.alpinelumber.com	Westminster	CO	80234	303-451-8001	451-5232
American International Forest Products LLC 5560 SW 107th St *TF:* 800-366-1611 ■ *Web:* www.lumber.com	Beaverton	OR	97005	503-641-1611	641-2800
Arnold Lumber Co 251 Fairgrounds Rd *TF:* 800-339-0116 ■ *Web:* www.arnoldlumber.com	West Kingston	RI	02892	401-783-2266	792-3610
Barton EC & Co 2929 Browns Ln *Web:* www.ecbarton.com	Jonesboro	AR	72403	870-932-6673	972-1304
Berks Products Corp 965 Berkshire Blvd *TF:* 800-282-2375 ■ *Web:* www.berksproducts.com	Reading	PA	19610	610-374-5131	375-1469
Birmingham International Forest Products LLC 1800 International Park Dr Suite 200 *TF:* 800-767-2437 ■ *Web:* www.bifp.com	Birmingham	AL	35243	205-972-1500	972-1461
Bison Building Materials Ltd 1445 W Sam Houston Pkwy N *Web:* www.bisonbuilding.com	Houston	TX	77043	713-467-6700	935-1212
BlueLinx Holdings Inc 4300 Wildwood Pkwy *NYSE: BXC* ■ **Fax Area Code: 800* ■ *TF:* 888-502-2583 ■ *Web:* www.bluelinxco.com	Atlanta	GA	30339	770-953-7000	203-3780*
Boise Cascade Building Materials Distribution Div 1111 W Jefferson St *Web:* www.bc.com/bmd/index.jsp	Boise	ID	83728	208-384-6354	384-7291
Bradco Supply Corp 13 Production Way *TF:* 877-427-2320 ■ *Web:* www.bradcosupply.com	Avenel	NJ	07001	732-382-3400	382-6577
Buckeye Pacific LLC 4386 SW Macadam Ave Suite 200 *TF:* 800-767-9191 ■ *Web:* www.buckeyepacific.com	Portland	OR	97207	503-228-3330	274-1039
Builders FirstSource Inc 2001 Bryan St Suite 1600 *NASDAQ: BLDR* ■ *Web:* www.buildersfirstsource.com	Dallas	TX	75201	214-880-3500	880-3599
Builders General Supply Co 15 Sycamore Ave *TF:* 800-570-7227 ■ *Web:* www.buildersgeneral.com	Little Silver	NJ	07739	732-747-0808	741-1095
Canfor USA Corp 4395 Curtis Rd	Bellingham	WA	98226	360-647-2434	647-2437
Carolina Holdings Inc 4403 Bland Rd *TF:* 877-734-6365 ■ *Web:* www.carolinaholdings.com	Raleigh	NC	27609	919-431-1000	431-1199
Causeway Lumber Co 2601 S Andrews Ave *TF:* 800-375-5050 ■ *Web:* www.causewaylumber.com	Fort Lauderdale	FL	33316	954-763-1224	768-5921
Chicago Lumber Co of Omaha 1324 Pierce St *TF:* 800-642-8210 ■ *Web:* www.chicagolumbercompany.com	Omaha	NE	68103	402-342-0840	344-8323
EC Barton & Co 2929 Browns Ln *Web:* www.ecbarton.com	Jonesboro	AR	72403	870-932-6673	972-1304
Edward Hines Lumber Co 1000 Corporate Grove Dr *TF:* 888-334-4637 ■ *Web:* www.hineslumber.com	Buffalo Grove	IL	60089	847-353-7700	353-7891
Fagen's Building Centers Inc 2515 Pebble Ave *Web:* www.fagens.com	Pittsburgh	PA	15233	412-323-2100	323-9509
FE Wheaton & Co 204 W Wheaton Ave *Web:* www.fewheaton.com	Yorkville	IL	60560	630-553-8300	553-8320
Forest City Trading Group LLC 10250 SW Greenburg Rd Suite 200 PO Box 4209 *TF:* 800-767-3284 ■ *Web:* www.fctg.com	Portland	OR	97208	503-246-8500	246-1116
Foxworth-Galbraith Lumber Co 17111 Waterview Pkwy **Fax: Hum Res* ■ *TF:* 800-688-8082 ■ *Web:* www.foxgal.com	Dallas	TX	75252	972-437-6100	454-4238*
Frank Paxton Lumber Co 7455 Dawson Rd **Fax: Sales* ■ *TF:* 800-325-9800 ■ *Web:* www.paxtonwood.com	Cincinnati	OH	45243	513-984-8200	984-9060*
Georgia-Pacific Corp 133 Peachtree St NE *Web:* www.gp.com	Atlanta	GA	30303	404-652-4000	230-5774
Guardian Building Products Distribution 979 Batesville Rd *Web:* www.gbpd.com	Greer	SC	29651	864-297-6101	281-3498
Higgins JE Lumber Co 6999 S Front Rd *TF:* 800-241-1883 ■ *Web:* www.higlum.com	Livermore	CA	94551	925-245-4300	245-4343
Hines Edward Lumber Co 1000 Corporate Grove Dr *TF:* 888-334-4637 ■ *Web:* www.hineslumber.com	Buffalo Grove	IL	60089	847-353-7700	353-7891
Home Lumber 8037 Midway Dr *TF:* 800-211-2571 ■ *Web:* www.homelumber.com	Littleton	CO	80125	303-791-3715	791-4352
Hood Distribution McQuesten Group 600 Iron Horse Pk *TF:* 800-752-0129 ■ *Web:* www.hoodindustries.com/distribution/mcquesten	North Billerica	MA	01862	978-663-3435	667-0934
Hope Lumber & Supply Co 12213 E 61st St *Web:* www.hopelumber.com	Broken Arrow	OK	74012	918-250-9766	252-0727
Houston AC Lumber Co 2912 E La Madre Way *Web:* www.achoustonlumber.com	North Las Vegas	NV	89081	702-633-5100	633-5111
Huttig Building Products Inc 555 Maryville University Dr *NYSE: HBP* ■ **Fax: Mktg* ■ *TF:* 800-325-4466 ■ *Web:* www.huttig.com	Saint Louis	MO	63141	314-216-2600	216-2769*
Idaho Pacific Lumber Co (IdaPac) 370 N Benjamin Ln Suite 120 *TF:* 800-231-2310 ■ *Web:* www.idapac.com	Boise	ID	83704	208-375-8052	375-3054
IdaPac (Idaho Pacific Lumber Co) 370 N Benjamin Ln Suite 120 *TF:* 800-231-2310 ■ *Web:* www.idapac.com	Boise	ID	83704	208-375-8052	375-3054
JE Higgins Lumber Co 6999 S Front Rd *TF:* 800-241-1883 ■ *Web:* www.higlum.com	Livermore	CA	94551	925-245-4300	245-4343
Jewett-Cameron Trading Co Ltd 32275 NW Hillcrest PO Box 1010 *NASDAQ: JCTCF* ■ *TF:* 800-547-5877 ■ *Web:* www.jewettcameron.com	North Plains	OR	97133	503-647-0110	647-2272
Livonia Building Materials Co 33900 Concord Rd *Web:* www.livoniabldg.com	Livonia	MI	48150	734-421-1170	421-5237
Louis & Co 895 Columbia St *TF:* 800-422-4389 ■ *Web:* www.louisandcompany.com	Brea	CA	92821	714-529-1771	990-6184
Lumbermen's Merchandising Corp 137 W Wayne Ave *Web:* www.lmc.net	Wayne	PA	19087	610-293-7000	293-7924
Lyman Lumber Co 300 Morse Ave *Web:* www.lymanlumber.com	Excelsior	MN	55331	952-470-3600	470-3666
Magbee Contractors Supply 1065 Bankhead Hwy *Web:* www.magbee.com	Winder	GA	30680	678-425-2600	425-2602
McCray Lumber Co 10741 El Monte Ln *Web:* www.mccraylumber.com	Overland Park	KS	66211	913-341-6900	341-1881
Mill Creek Lumber & Supply Co 6201 S 129th East Ave PO Box 4770 *TF:* 800-364-6455 ■ *Web:* www.millcreeklumber.com	Tulsa	OK	74159	918-747-2000	747-4625
Modern Builders Supply Inc 302 McClurg Rd *TF:* 800-783-4117 ■ *Web:* www.modernbuilderssupply.com	Youngstown	OH	44512	330-729-2690	729-2696
Moore's Lumber & Building Supplies Inc 3441 Brandon Ave *Web:* www.moores.com	Roanoke	VA	24018	540-982-5900	985-5510
National Lumber Co 24595 Groesbeck Hwy *TF:* 800-462-9712 ■ *Web:* www.nationallumber.com	Warren	MI	48089	586-775-8200	775-4110
North Pacific 2419 Science Pkwy *TF:* 800-942-8220 ■ *Web:* www.northpacific.com	Okemos	MI	48864	517-349-8220	349-8377
North Pacific Group Inc (NOR PAC) 815 NE Davis St **Fax: Hum Res* ■ *TF:* 800-547-8440 ■ *Web:* www.north-pacific.com	Portland	OR	97232	503-231-1166	238-2646*
Palmer-Donavin Mfg Co 1200 Steelwood Rd *TF:* 800-589-4412 ■ *Web:* www.palmerdonavin.com	Columbus	OH	43212	614-486-9657	486-5073
Parr Lumber 5630 NW 5 Oaks Dr *TF:* 877-849-7277 ■ *Web:* www.parr.com	Hillsboro	OR	97124	503-614-2500	614-0500
Ply Mart 4955 Buford Hwy *Web:* www.plymart.com	Norcross	GA	30071	770-447-5338	447-1433
PrimeSource Building Products Inc 2115 E Beltline Rd *TF:* 800-745-3341 ■ *Web:* www.primesourcebp.com	Carrollton	TX	75006	972-416-1976	416-8331
Raymond Building Supply Corp 7751 Bayshore Rd *TF:* 877-731-7272 ■ *Web:* www.rbsc.net	North Fort Myers	FL	33917	239-731-8300	731-3299
Reliable Wholesale Lumber Inc 7600 Redondo Cir *Web:* www.rwli.net	Huntington Beach	CA	92648	714-848-8222	847-1605
Richmond International Forest Products Inc 4050 Innslake Dr Suite 100 *TF:* 800-767-0111 ■ *Web:* www.rifp.com	Glen Allen	VA	23060	804-747-0111	270-4547
Riverhead Building Supply Corp 1093 Pulaski St *TF:* 800-378-3650 ■ *Web:* www.rbscorp.com	Riverhead	NY	11901	631-727-3650	727-7713
RP Lumber Co Inc 514 E Vandalia St *Web:* www.rplumber.com	Edwardsville	IL	62025	618-656-1514	656-6785
Saxonville USA 96 Springfield Rd *TF:* 800-882-2106 ■ *Web:* www.saxonville.com	Charlestown	NH	03603	603-826-4024	826-5205
Seaboard International Forest Products LLC 22 Cotton Rd Suite F PO Box 6059 *TF:* 800-669-6800 ■ *Web:* www.sifp.com	Nashua	NH	03063	603-881-3700	598-2280
Seigle's 1331 Davis Rd *Web:* www.seigles.com	Elgin	IL	60123	847-742-2000	697-6521
Stevenson Lumber 1585 Monroe Tpke PO Box 123 *TF:* 800-972-4260 ■ *Web:* www.stevensonlumber.com	Stevenson	CT	06491	203-261-2555	261-8046
Stock Building Supply 8020 Arco Corporate Dr *TF:* 877-734-6365 ■ *Web:* www.stockbuildingsupply.com	Raleigh	NC	27617	919-431-1000	431-1199
Timber Products Co 305 S 4th St *TF:* 800-547-9520 ■ *Web:* www.timberproducts.com	Springfield	OR	97477	541-747-4577	744-4296
Viking Forest Products LLC 7615 Smetana Ln Suite 140 *TF:* 800-733-3801 ■ *Web:* www.vikingforest.com	Eden Prairie	MN	55344	952-941-6512	941-4633
West Elizabeth Lumber Co 1 Chicago Ave *TF:* 800-289-9352	Elizabeth	PA	15037	412-384-3900	384-3955
White Cap Industries Inc 1723 S Ritchie St *TF:* 800-922-9922 ■ *Web:* www.whitecap.net	Santa Ana	CA	92705	714-258-3300	258-3289
Williams Bros Lumber Co 3165 Pleasant Hill Rd *Web:* www.wmsbros.com	Duluth	GA	30096	770-623-0344	623-0344
Wolohan Lumber Co 1740 Midland Rd *Web:* www.wolohan.com	Saginaw	MI	48603	989-793-4532	793-5066

194-4 Roofing, Siding, Insulation Materials

Company	City	State	Zip	Phone	Fax
ABC Seamless 3001 Fiechtner Dr *TF:* 800-732-6577 ■ *Web:* www.abcseamless.com	Fargo	ND	58103	701-293-5952	293-3107
ABC Supply Co Inc 1 ABC Pkwy *TF:* 800-366-2227 ■ *Web:* www.abc-supply.com	Beloit	WI	53511	608-362-7777	362-6215
Alcoa Home Exteriors 1590 Omega Dr *TF:* 866-496-0370 ■ *Web:* www.alcoahomes.com	Pittsburgh	PA	15205	412-249-6000	249-6059
Bartells EJ Co 700 Powell Ave SW PO Box 4160 *TF:* 800-468-9528 ■ *Web:* www.ejbartells.com	Renton	WA	98057	425-228-4111	228-8807
Beacon Roofing Supply Inc 1 Lakeland Park Dr *NASDAQ: BECN* ■ *TF:* 877-645-7663 ■ *Web:* www.beaconroofingsupply.net	Peabody	MA	01960	978-535-7668	535-7358
Bradco Supply Corp 13 Production Way *TF:* 877-427-2320 ■ *Web:* www.bradcosupply.com	Avenel	NJ	07001	732-382-3400	382-6577
Branton Industries Inc 1101 Edwards Ave *TF:* 800-548-5783 ■ *Web:* www.brantonindustries.com	Harahan	LA	70123	504-733-7770	734-7818
Carlisle Cos Inc 13925 Ballantyne Corporate Pl Suite 400 *NYSE: CSL* ■ *Web:* www.carlisle.com	Charlotte	NC	28277	704-501-1100	501-1190
Carlisle SynTec Inc 1285 Ritner Hwy PO Box 7000 *TF:* 800-479-6832 ■ *Web:* www.carlisle-syntec.com	Carlisle	PA	17013	717-245-7000	245-7053
Co-op Reserve Supply Inc 1100 Iron Horse Pk *TF Cust Svc:* 800-769-2667	North Billerica	MA	01862	978-528-5320	528-5319
Collins Cos 1618 SW 1st Ave Suite 500 *TF:* 800-329-1219 ■ *Web:* www.collinswood.com	Portland	OR	97201	503-227-1219	227-5349
Crane Performance Siding 1441 Universal Rd **Fax Area Code: 800* ■ *TF:* 800-366-8472 ■ *Web:* www.vinyl-siding.com	Columbus	OH	43207	614-443-4841	733-8469*
EJ Bartells Co 700 Powell Ave SW PO Box 4160 *TF:* 800-468-9528 ■ *Web:* www.ejbartells.com	Renton	WA	98057	425-228-4111	228-8807
Gulfeagle Supply 1451 Channelside Dr	Tampa	FL	33605	813-636-9808	
H Verby Co Inc 186-14 Jamaica Ave *Web:* www.hverby.com	Jamaica	NY	11423	718-454-5522	454-6609
Hardie James Building Products 26300 La Alameda Ave Suite 250 *TF:* 888-542-7343 ■ *Web:* www.jameshardie.com	Mission Viejo	CA	92691	949-348-1800	367-1294
Harvey Industries Inc 1400 Main St *TF:* 800-942-7839 ■ *Web:* www.harveyind.com	Waltham	MA	02451	781-899-3500	398-7826
Howred Corp 7887 San Felipe St Suite 122 *Web:* www.howred.com	Houston	TX	77063	713-781-3980	784-3985
James Hardie Building Products 26300 La Alameda Ave Suite 250 *TF:* 888-542-7343 ■ *Web:* www.jameshardie.com	Mission Viejo	CA	92691	949-348-1800	367-1294
JPS Industries Inc 555 N Pleasantburg Dr Suite 202	Greenville	SC	29607	864-239-3900	271-9939
Kemlite Co 23525 W Eames St **Fax: Hum Res* ■ *TF:* 800-435-0080 ■ *Web:* www.kemlite.com	Channahon	IL	60410	815-467-8600	467-8664*
LaPolla Industries Inc 15402 Vantage Pkwy E Suite 322 *AMEX: LPA* ■ *TF:* 800-382-4931 ■ *Web:* www.lapollaindustries.com	Houston	TX	77032	281-219-4100	219-4102
MacArthur Co 2400 Wycliff St *TF:* 800-777-7507 ■ *Web:* www.macarthurco.com	Saint Paul	MN	55114	651-646-2773	642-9630
McClure-Johnston Co 201 Corey Ave *TF:* 800-232-0018 ■ *Web:* www.mcclurejohnston.com	Braddock	PA	15104	412-351-4300	351-1480
Norandex Inc 8450 S Bedford Rd *Web:* www.norandex.com	Macedonia	OH	44056	330-468-2200	468-8117
North Carolina Foam Industries Inc 1515 Carter St *TF:* 800-346-8229 ■ *Web:* www.ncfi.com	Mount Airy	NC	27030	336-789-9161	789-9586
Owens Corning 1 Owens Corning Pkwy *Web:* www.owenscorning.com	Toledo	OH	43659	419-248-8000	325-1538
Pacific Coast Building Products Inc 10600 White Rock Rd Bldg B Suite 100 *Web:* www.paccoast.com	Rancho Cordova	CA	95670	916-631-6500	631-6685
Philadelphia Reserve Supply Co 400 Mack Dr *TF:* 800-347-7726 ■ *Web:* www.prsco.org	Croydon	PA	19021	215-785-3141	785-5806
Roofing Wholesale Co Inc 1918 W Grant St *TF:* 800-782-2116 ■ *Web:* www.rwc.org	Phoenix	AZ	85009	602-258-3794	256-0932

Phone | Fax

Saint-Gobain Corp 750 E Swedesford Rd ... Valley Forge PA 19482 610-341-7000 341-7797
TF: 800-274-8530 ■ *Web:* www.saint-gobain.com/us
SG Wholesale Roofing Supplies Inc 1000 E 6th St ... Santa Ana CA 92701 714-568-1906 568-1915
TF: 888-747-8500 ■ *Web:* www.sgroof.com
Shelter Distribution Inc 1602 Lavon Dr ... McKinney TX 75069 972-369-8000 369-8040
Web: www.shelterdistribution.com
Shook & Fletcher Insulation Co 4625 Valleydale Rd ... Birmingham AL 35242 205-991-7606 991-7745
TF: 888-829-2575 ■ *Web:* www.shookandfletcher.com
Spec Building Materials Inc 4300 West Ave ... San Antonio TX 78213 210-342-2727 340-0688
TF: 800-588-3892
Specialty Products & Insulation Co
1097 Commercial Ave ... East Petersburg PA 17520 717-519-4000 519-4046
TF: 800-788-7764 ■ *Web:* www.spi-co.com
Standard Roofings Inc 100 Park Rd ... Tinton Falls NJ 07724 732-542-3300 542-3807
TF: 800-624-0036
Sunniland Corp 1721 Hwy 1735 ... Sanford FL 32773 407-322-2421 324-5784
TF: 800-432-1130 ■ *Web:* www.sunniland.com
Tallant Industries Inc 4900 Ondura Dr ... Fredericksburg VA 22407 540-898-7000 898-4991
TF: 800-777-7663 ■ *Web:* www.ondura.com
Ted Lansing Corp 8501 Sanford Dr ... Richmond VA 23228 804-266-8771 266-0166
TF: 800-768-5762 ■ *Web:* www.tedlansing.com
Variform Inc 303 W Major St PO Box 559 ... Kearney MO 64060 816-903-6400 903-6942
TF: 800-800-2244 ■ *Web:* www.variform.com
Wesco Cedar Inc 105 E Hilliard Ln PO Box 40847 ... Eugene OR 97404 541-688-5020 688-5024
TF: 800-547-2511 ■ *Web:* www.wescocedar.com

195 CONSULTING SERVICES - ENVIRONMENTAL

SEE ALSO Recyclable Materials Recovery p. 2208; Remediation Services p. 2210; Waste Management p. 2412

Phone | Fax

Ameresco Inc 111 Speen St Suite 410 ... Framingham MA 01701 508-661-2200 661-2201
TF: 800-263-7372 ■ *Web:* www.ameresco.com
Arcadis 630 Plaza Dr Suite 200 ... Highlands Ranch CO 80129 720-344-3500 344-3535
Web: www.arcadis-us.com
ATC Assoc Inc 104 E 25th St 10th Fl ... New York NY 10010 212-353-8280 353-8306
TF: 800-725-3282 ■ *Web:* www.atc-enviro.com
Beck RW Inc 1001 4th Ave Suite 2500 ... Seattle WA 98154 206-695-4700 695-4701
TF: 800-285-2325 ■ *Web:* www.rwbeck.com
CET Services Inc 7032 S Revere Pkwy ... Englewood CO 80112 720-875-9115 875-9112
AMEX: ENV
CH2M Hill Cos Ltd 9191 S Jamica St ... Englewood CO 80112 303-771-0900 286-9250*
**Fax Area Code: 720* ■ *Web:* www.ch2m.com
Conti Cos 3001 S Clinton Ave ... South Plainfield NJ 07080 908-561-7600 754-3283
Web: www.conticorp.com
DPRA Inc 200 Research Dr ... Manhattan KS 66503 785-539-3565 539-5353
Web: www.dpra.com
Earth Systems Inc 895 Aerovista Pl Suite 100 ... San Luis Obispo CA 93401 805-781-0112 781-0180
Web: www.earthsystems.com
Earth Tech 300 Oceangate Suite 700 ... Long Beach CA 90802 562-951-2000 951-2100
Web: www.earthtech.com
Ecology & Environment Inc 368 Pleasant View Dr ... Lancaster NY 14086 716-684-8060 684-0844
AMEX: EEI ■ *Web:* www.ene.com
Energy & Environmental Analysis Inc
1655 N Fort Myer Dr Suite 600 ... Arlington VA 22209 703-528-1900 528-5106
Web: www.eea-inc.com
EnSafe 5724 Summer Trees Dr ... Memphis TN 38134 901-372-7962 372-2454
TF: 800-588-7962 ■ *Web:* www.ensafe.com
ENVIRON International Corp 4350 N Fairfax Dr Suite 300 ... Arlington VA 22203 703-516-2300 516-2345
Web: www.environcorp.com
Environmental Compliance Services Inc (ECS)
7 Island Dock Rd ... Haddam CT 06438 860-345-4578 345-3854
TF: 800-524-9256 ■ *Web:* www.ecsconsult.com
Environmental & Safety Designs Inc DBA EnSafe
5724 Summer Trees Dr ... Memphis TN 38134 901-372-7962 372-2454
TF: 800-588-7962 ■ *Web:* www.ensafe.com
ERM Group Inc 350 Eagle View Blvd ... Exton PA 19341 610-524-3500 524-7335
TF: 800-662-1124 ■ *Web:* www.erm.com
Evans Environmental & Geosciences
14505 Commerce Way Suite 400 ... Miami Lakes FL 33016 305-374-8300 374-9004
TF: 800-486-7458 ■ *Web:* www.eeandg.com
First Environment Inc 91 Fulton St ... Boonton NJ 07005 973-334-0003 334-0928
TF: 800-486-5869 ■ *Web:* www.firstenvironment.com
GZA GeoEnvironmental Inc 1 Edgewater Dr ... Norwood MA 02062 781-278-3700 278-5701
Web: www.gza.com
Heath Consultants Inc 9030 Monroe Rd ... Houston TX 77061 713-844-1300 844-1309
TF: 800-432-8487 ■ *Web:* www.heathus.com
Kemron Environmental Services Inc
8150 Leesburg Pike Suite 1410 ... Vienna VA 22182 703-893-4106 893-5636
TF: 800-777-1042 ■ *Web:* www.kemron.com
KFx Inc 55 Madison St Suite 745 ... Denver CO 80206 303-293-2992 293-8430
AMEX: KFX ■ *TF:* 800-590-4180 ■ *Web:* www.kfx.com
Los Alamos Technical Assoc 99 Central Ave Suite 300 ... Los Alamos NM 87544 505-662-9080 662-1757
Web: www.lata.com
MACTEC Inc 1105 Lakewood Dr Suite 300 ... Alpharetta GA 30004 770-360-0600
Web: www.mactec.com
Metcalf & Eddy Inc 701 Edgewater Dr ... Wakefield MA 01880 781-246-5200 245-6293
Web: www.m-e.aecom.com
Micah Group LLC 274 Southland Dr Suite 201 ... Lexington KY 40503 859-260-7760 260-1256
Web: www.micahgroup.com
MPS Group Inc 2920 Scotten St ... Detroit MI 48210 313-841-7588 843-1479
TF: 800-741-8779 ■ *Web:* www.mpsgrp.com
Normandeau Assoc Inc 25 Nashua Rd ... Bedford NH 03110 603-472-5191 472-7052
Web: www.normandeau.com
Parsons Infrastructure & Technology 100 W Walnut St ... Pasadena CA 91124 626-440-4000 440-6200
TF: 800-883-7300 ■ *Web:* www.parsons.com
Perma-Fix Environmental Services Inc 1940 NW 67th Pl ... Gainesville FL 32653 352-373-4200 372-8963
NASDAQ: PESI ■ *TF:* 800-365-6066 ■ *Web:* www.perma-fix.com
Philip Services Corp (PSC) 51 San Felipe Rd Suite 1600 ... Houston TX 77056 713-623-8777 625-7185
TF: 800-726-1300 ■ *Web:* www.contactpsc.com
Portage Enviromental 1075 S Utah Ave Suite 200 ... Idaho Falls ID 83402 208-528-6608 523-8860
Web: www.portageenv.com
Retec Group 300 Baker Ave Suite 302 ... Concord MA 01742 978-371-1422 371-1448
TF: 877-222-2260 ■ *Web:* www.thermoretec.com
RJN Group Inc 200 W Front St ... Wheaton IL 60187 630-682-4700 682-4754
TF: 800-227-7838 ■ *Web:* www.rjn.com
RW Beck Inc 1001 4th Ave Suite 2500 ... Seattle WA 98154 206-695-4700 695-4701
TF: 800-285-2325 ■ *Web:* www.rwbeck.com
S & ME Inc 3201 Spring Forest Rd ... Raleigh NC 27616 919-872-2660 876-3958
TF Cust Svc: 800-849-2517 ■ *Web:* www.smeinc.com
Shaw Environmental & Infrastructure Inc 4171 Essen Ln ... Baton Rouge LA 70809 225-932-2500 932-2618
TF: 800-747-3322 ■ *Web:* www.shawgrp.com/ShawEandI/

Phone | Fax

Spherix Inc 12051 Indian Creek Ct ... Beltsville MD 20705 301-419-3900 210-4909
NASDAQ: SPEX ■ *TF Mktg:* 800-727-0602 ■ *Web:* www.spherixinc.com
Sullivan International Group Inc
409 Camino Del Rio S Suite 100 ... San Diego CA 92108 619-260-1432 260-1421
TF: 888-744-1432 ■ *Web:* www.onesullivan.com
SWCA Inc 2120 N Central Ave Suite 130 ... Phoenix AZ 85004 602-274-3831 274-3958
TF: 800-828-8517 ■ *Web:* www.swca.com
Tetra Tech EC Inc 1000 The American Rd ... Morris Plains NJ 07950 973-630-8000 630-8165
TF: 800-580-3765 ■ *Web:* www.tteci.com
Tetra Tech Inc 3475 E Foothill Blvd ... Pasadena CA 91107 626-351-4664 351-5291
NASDAQ: TTEK ■ *Web:* www.tetratech.com
TRC Cos Inc 21 Griffin Rd N ... Windsor CT 06095 860-289-8631 298-6399
NYSE: TRR ■ *TF:* 800-365-8254 ■ *Web:* www.trcsolutions.com
TRC Environmental Corp 21 Griffin Rd N ... Windsor CT 06095 860-289-8631 298-6399
TF: 800-365-8254 ■ *Web:* www.trcsolutions.com
US Biosystems Inc 3231 NW 7th Ave ... Boca Raton FL 33431 561-447-7373 447-6136
TF: 888-862-5227 ■ *Web:* www.usbiosystems.com
Vertex Engineering Services Inc 400 Libbey Pkwy ... Weymouth MA 02189 781-952-6000 335-3543
TF: 888-298-5162 ■ *Web:* www.vertexeng.com
Western Technologies Inc 3737 E Broadway Rd ... Phoenix AZ 85040 602-437-3737 470-1341
TF: 800-580-3737 ■ *Web:* www.wt-us.com
Wetlandsbank Inc 814 S Military Trail ... Deerfield Beach FL 33442 954-596-2411 480-6250
TF: 888-301-1707 ■ *Web:* www.wetlandsbank.com
Woolpert Inc 409 E Monument Ave ... Dayton OH 45402 937-461-5660 461-0743
Web: www.woolpert.com
WorleyParsons 5 Greenway Plaza ... Houston TX 77046 713-407-5000 350-1300
Web: www.worleyparsons.com

196 CONSULTING SERVICES - HUMAN RESOURCES

SEE ALSO Professional Employer Organizations (PEOs) p. 2142

Phone | Fax

Abbott Langer & Assoc Inc 548 1st St ... Crete IL 60417 708-672-4200 672-4674
Web: www.abbott-langer.com
Aon Consulting Worldwide 200 E Randolph Suite 1000 ... Chicago IL 60601 312-381-4800 381-0240
Web: www.aon.com
Arthur J Gallagher & Co 2 Pierce Pl ... Itasca IL 60143 630-773-3800 285-4023
NYSE: AJG ■ *Web:* www.ajg.com
BH Careers International 192 Lexington Ave Suite 804 ... New York NY 10016 212-679-3360 532-0059
Web: www.bhcareers.com
CA Short Co Inc 7221 Pineville Matthews Rd Suite 600 ... Charlotte NC 28226 704-752-0119 752-9698
TF: 800-535-5690 ■ *Web:* www.cashort.com
Cambridge Human Resource Group Inc
230 W Monroe St Suite 310 ... Chicago IL 60606 312-251-0400 251-0455
Web: www.cambridgehr.com
Casco International Inc DBA CA Short Co Inc
7221 Pineville Matthews Rd Suite 600 ... Charlotte NC 28226 704-752-0119 752-9698
TF: 800-535-5690 ■ *Web:* www.cashort.com
Challenger Gray & Christmas Inc 150 S Wacker Dr Suite 2700 ... Chicago IL 60606 312-332-5790 332-4843
Web: www.challengergray.com
Clark Consulting 102 S Wynstone Park Dr ... North Barrington IL 60010 847-304-5800 304-7977
NYSE: CLK ■ *TF:* 800-597-7976 ■ *Web:* www.clarkconsulting.com
Cook Frederic W & Co 90 Park Ave 35th Fl ... New York NY 10016 212-986-6330 986-3836
Web: www.fwcook.com
Development Dimensions International
1225 Washington Pike ... Bridgeville PA 15017 412-257-0600 257-3916
TF Mktg: 800-933-4463 ■ *Web:* www.ddiworld.com
Drake Beam Morin Inc 100 Park Ave 11th Fl ... New York NY 10017 212-692-7700 297-0426
Web: www.dbm.com
Findley Davies 300 Madison Ave Suite 1000 ... Toledo OH 43604 419-255-1360 259-5685
Web: www.findleydavies.com
FPMI Solutions Inc 4901 University Sq Suite 3 ... Huntsville AL 35816 256-539-1850 539-0911
Web: www.fpmisolutions.com
Frederic W Cook & Co 90 Park Ave 35th Fl ... New York NY 10016 212-986-6330 986-3836
Web: www.fwcook.com
Gallagher Arthur J & Co 2 Pierce Pl ... Itasca IL 60143 630-773-3800 285-4023
NYSE: AJG ■ *Web:* www.ajg.com
Hay Group Inc 100 Penn Sq E Wanamaker Bldg ... Philadelphia PA 19107 215-861-2000 861-2111
TF: 800-776-1774 ■ *Web:* www.haygroup.com
Hewitt Assoc LLC 100 Half Day Rd ... Lincolnshire IL 60069 847-295-5000 295-7654
NYSE: HEW
Hudson Highland Group Inc 622 3rd Ave ... New York NY 10017 212-351-7300 256-8546*
NASDAQ: HHGP ■ **Fax Area Code: 917* ■ *Web:* www.hhgroup.com
Kenexa Corp 650 Swedesford Rd 2nd Fl ... Wayne PA 19087 610-971-9171 971-9181
NASDAQ: KNXA ■ *Web:* www.kenexa.com
Lee Hecht Harrison LLC 50 Tice Blvd ... Woodcliff Lake NJ 07677 201-782-3704 505-1428
TF: 800-611-4544 ■ *Web:* www.lhh.com
Mercer Human Resource Consulting 777 S Figueroa St ... Los Angeles CA 90017 213-346-2200 346-2680
TF: 866-879-3384 ■ *Web:* www.mercerhr.com
Modern Management Inc 253 Commerce Dr Suite 105 ... Grayslake IL 60030 847-945-7400 543-7710
TF: 800-323-1331 ■ *Web:* www.modernmanagement.com
National Center for Retirement Benefits Inc
666 Dundee Rd Suite 1200 ... Northbrook IL 60062 847-564-1111 564-4944
TF: 800-666-1000 ■ *Web:* www.ncrb.com
Novations Group Inc 10 Guest St Suite 300 ... Boston MA 02135 617-254-7600 254-7117
TF: 888-652-9975 ■ *Web:* www.novations.com
ORC Worldwide 500 5th Ave 5th Fl ... New York NY 10110 212-719-3400 398-1358
Web: www.orcworldwide.com
Outsource Group LLC 1646 N California Blvd Suite 210 ... Walnut Creek CA 94596 925-280-1200 280-1532
Ricklin-Echikson Assoc 374 Millburn Ave ... Millburn NJ 07041 973-376-2020 376-2072
TF: 800-544-2317 ■ *Web:* www.r-e-a.com
Right Management Consultants Inc 1818 Market St 33rd Fl ... Philadelphia PA 19103 215-988-1588 988-9112
TF: 800-237-4448 ■ *Web:* www.right.com
Runzheimer International Runzheimer Pk ... Rochester WI 53167 262-971-2200 971-2254
TF: 800-558-1702 ■ *Web:* www.runzheimer.com
Segal Co 1 Park Ave ... New York NY 10016 212-251-5000 251-5490
Web: www.segalco.com
Sibson Consulting 600 Alexander Pk Suite 208 ... Princeton NJ 08540 609-520-2700 520-0369
TF: 888-233-5837 ■ *Web:* www.sibson.com
Stanley Hunt DuPree & Rhine Inc PO Box 14967 ... Greensboro NC 27415 336-273-9492 273-9491
TF: 888-999-4701 ■ *Web:* www.shdr.com
Stanton Group 3405 Annapolis Ln N Suite 100 ... Plymouth MN 55447 763-278-4000 278-4007*
**Fax: Mktg* ■ *TF:* 800-754-9867 ■ *Web:* www.stanton-group.com
Systema Corp 900 N Shore Dr Suite 166 ... Lake Bluff IL 60044 847-615-0900 615-0901
TF: 800-270-9530 ■ *Web:* www.systema.com
TerraFirma 600 Grant St Suite 700 ... Denver CO 80203 303-861-0388 861-0377
Web: www.exposonline.com/terrafirma
Towers Perrin Inc 335 Madison Ave ... New York NY 10017 212-309-3400 309-3760
Web: www.towersperrin.com
Towers Perrin Inc 175 Bloor St E South Tower Suite 1701 ... Toronto ON M4W3T6 416-960-2700 960-2819
Web: www.towersperrin.com

Phone Fax

Watson Wyatt & Co 901 N Glebe Rd ... Arlington VA 22203 703-258-8000 258-8585
TF: 800-675-7282 ■ *Web:* www.watsonwyatt.com

Watson Wyatt & Co Holdings 1717 H St NW Suite 800 ... Washington DC 20006 202-715-7000 715-7700
NYSE: WW

Watson Wyatt Worldwide 1717 H St NW Suite 800 ... Washington DC 20006 202-715-7000 715-7953
Web: www.watsonwyatt.com

197 CONSULTING SERVICES - MANAGEMENT

SEE ALSO Association Management Companies p. 1287; Management Services p. 1945

Phone Fax

ABB Reliability Engineering & Consulting Services
1701 N Beauregard St Suite 400 ... Alexandria VA 22311 703-671-3800 820-7489
TF: 800-368-3371 ■ *Web:* www.hsbrt.com

Accenture Ltd 161 N Clark St ... Chicago IL 60601 312-693-0161 693-0507
NYSE: ACN ■ *Web:* www.accenture.com

Advisory Board Co 2445 M St NW ... Washington DC 20037 202-672-5600 672-5700
NASDAQ: ABCO ■ *TF:* 800-672-6620 ■ *Web:* www.advisoryboardcompany.com

Agency.com Ltd 488 Madison Ave 22nd Fl ... New York NY 10022 212-358-2600 358-2604
TF: 800-736-4644 ■ *Web:* www.agency.com

AIG Consultants Inc 70 Pine St 10th Fl ... New York NY 10270 212-770-7000 943-1125
Web: www.aigconsultants.com

Albert JH International Advisors Inc 72 River Pk ... Needham MA 02494 781-449-2866 449-5340
Web: www.jhalbert.com

Allen Michael Co 8 Wright St ... Westport CT 06880 203-221-7900 221-1914
Web: www.michaelallencompany.com

Altman Weil Inc PO Box 625 ... Newtown Square PA 19073 610-359-9900 359-0467
TF: 800-947-2875 ■ *Web:* www.altmanweil.com

American Management Services Inc 21 Hickory Dr ... Waltham MA 02451 781-487-0400 890-1660
Web: www.amserv.com

Analysis Group Inc 111 Huntington Ave 10th Fl ... Boston MA 02199 617-425-8400 425-8401
Web: www.analysisgroup.com

Answerthink Inc 1001 Brickell Bay Dr Suite 3000 ... Miami FL 33131 305-375-8005 379-8810
NASDAQ: ANSR ■ *TF:* 888-844-6504 ■ *Web:* www.answerthink.com

APEX Management Group Inc 125-310 Village Blvd ... Princeton NJ 08540 609-452-2488 452-2668
Web: www.apexmgmt.com

AT Kearney Inc 222 W Adams St Suite 2500 ... Chicago IL 60606 312-648-0111 223-6200
Web: www.atkearney.com

Atlantic Data Services Inc 1 Batterymarch Pk ... Quincy MA 02169 617-770-3333 689-1103
TF: 800-729-3334 ■ *Web:* www.atlanticdataservices.com

Austin Co Austin Consulting Div 303 E Wacker Dr Suite 900 ... Chicago IL 60601 312-373-7700 373-7710
Web: www.theaustin.com

Bain & Co 131 Dartmouth St ... Boston MA 02116 617-572-2000 572-2427
TF: 800-800-8338 ■ *Web:* www.bain.com

Banta Global Turnkey Group 6315 West by Northwest Blvd ... Houston TX 77040 713-354-1300 354-1365

Barnett International
1400 N Providence Rd Rose Tree Corporate Center Suite 1050 ... Media PA 19063 610-565-9400 565-5223
TF: 800-856-2556 ■ *Web:* www.barnettinternational.com

Booz Allen Hamilton Inc 8283 Greensboro Dr ... McLean VA 22102 703-902-5000 902-3333
TF: 800-862-4511 ■ *Web:* www.boozallen.com

Bortz Media & Sports Group Inc 4582 S Ulster St Suite 1450 ... Denver CO 80237 303-893-9902 893-9913
Web: www.bortz.com

Boston Consulting Group Inc 53 State St 6th Fl ... Boston MA 02109 617-973-1200 973-1399
TF: 800-367-1989 ■ *Web:* www.bcg.com

Bowne Global Solutions 6500 Wilshire Blvd Suite 700 ... Los Angeles CA 90048 917-339-4700 395-0983*
**Fax Area Code: 310* ■ *TF:* 800-628-4808 ■ *Web:* www.bowne.com/globalsolutions

BrandPartners Group Inc 10 Main St ... Rochester NH 03839 603-335-1400 332-7429
TF: 800-732-3999 ■ *Web:* www.bptr.com

Brooks Group 4731 W Atlantic Ave Suite B10 ... Delray Beach FL 33445 561-865-3800 865-3700
Web: www.tbrooksgroup.com

Business Resource Group 8080 Park Ln Suite 770 ... Dallas TX 75231 214-777-5100 777-5101
Web: www.brg.com

Carmody & Bloom Inc 600 Lake St Suite 600B ... Ramsey NJ 07446 201-670-1700 670-1771
TF: 800-242-9000 ■ *Web:* www.carmodyandbloom.com

CFI Group 625 Avis Dr ... Ann Arbor MI 48108 734-930-9090 930-0911
Web: www.cfigroup.com

Chang Richard Assoc 15265 Alton Pkwy Suite 300 ... Irvine CA 92618 949-727-7477 727-7007
TF: 800-756-8096 ■ *Web:* www.richardchangassociates.com

Checchi & Co Consulting Inc 1899 L St NW Suite 800 ... Washington DC 20036 202-452-9700 466-9070
Web: www.checchiconsulting.com

Circadian Technologies Inc 2 Main St Suite 310 ... Stoneham MA 02180 781-439-6300 439-6399
TF: 800-284-5001 ■ *Web:* www.circadian.com

Concours Group 800 Rockmead Dr Suite 151 ... Kingwood TX 77339 281-359-3464 359-3443
Web: www.concoursgroup.com

Coreval Consulting 6161 Oak Tree Blvd Suite 450 ... Independence OH 44131 216-520-3600
Web: www.corevalconsulting.com

Corporate Dynamics Inc 1560 Wall St Suite 222 ... Naperville IL 60563 630-778-9991 778-9915
TF: 888-267-7396 ■ *Web:* www.corpdyn.com

Corporate Executive Board Co 2000 Pennsylvania Ave NW ... Washington DC 20006 202-777-5000 777-5100
NASDAQ: EXBD ■ *TF:* 888-777-9561 ■ *Web:* www.executiveboard.com

CRA International Inc 200 Clarendon St Suite T-33 ... Boston MA 02116 617-425-3000 425-3132
NASDAQ: CRAI ■ *Web:* www.crai.com

Creative Associates International Inc
5301 Wisconsin Ave NW Suite 700 ... Washington DC 20015 202-966-5804 363-4771
Web: www.caii-dc.com

Crosby Philip Assoc Inc 306 Dartmouth St ... Boston MA 02116 617-716-0218 716-0223*
**Fax: Hum Res* ■ *TF:* 800-223-3932 ■ *Web:* www.philipcrosby.com

CTI Consulting 20410 Observation Dr Suite 203 ... Germantown MD 20876 301-528-8591 528-2037
TF: 800-783-4284 ■ *Web:* www.countertech.com

Cyon Research Corp 8220 Stone Trail Dr ... Bethesda MD 20817 301-365-9085 365-4586
Web: www.cyonresearch.com

Davies Consulting Inc 6935 Wisconsin Ave Suite 600 ... Chevy Chase MD 20815 301-652-4535 907-9355
TF: 800-535-6470 ■ *Web:* www.daviescon.com

Dechert-Hampe & Co 27101 Puerta Real Suite 400 ... Mission Viejo CA 92691 949-282-0035 282-0048
TF: 888-790-6626 ■ *Web:* www.dechert-hampe.com

Deloitte Consulting LLP 25 Broadway Cunard Bldg ... New York NY 10004 212-618-4000
Web: www.deloitte.com

Demos Solutions 600 Cordwainer Dr ... Norwell MA 02061 781-681-1400 681-1499
TF: 800-434-4924 ■ *Web:* www.demossolutions.com

DevTech Systems Inc 1700 N Moore St Suite 1720 ... Arlington VA 22209 703-312-6038 312-6039
Web: www.devtechsys.com

DiamondCluster International Inc
875 N Michigan Ave Suite 3000 ... Chicago IL 60611 312-255-5000 255-6000
NASDAQ: DTPI ■ *TF:* 800-455-5875 ■ *Web:* www.diamondcluster.com

Digitas Inc 33 Arch St 8th Fl ... Boston MA 02110 617-867-1000 867-1111
NASDAQ: DTAS ■ *Web:* www.digitas.com

Earning Performance Group 830 Morris Tpke 3rd Fl ... Short Hills NJ 07078 973-379-7772 379-3639
Web: www.epggroup.com

ECG Management Consultants Inc 1111 3rd Ave Suite 2700 ... Seattle WA 98101 206-689-2200 689-2209
TF: 800-729-7635 ■ *Web:* www.ecgmc.com

Phone Fax

Eckler Ltd 110 Sheppard Ave E Suite 900 ... Toronto ON M2N7A3 416-429-3330 429-3713
Web: www.eckler.ca

EDO Professional Services 2800 Shirlington Rd 12th Fl ... Arlington VA 22206 703-824-5000 824-5003
Web: www.edo-services.com

Eltrex Industries 65 Sullivan St ... Rochester NY 14605 585-454-6100 263-7766
Web: www.eltrex.com

EnerVision Inc 2100 E Exchange Pl ... Tucker GA 30084 770-270-7900 270-7535
TF: 888-999-8840 ■ *Web:* www.enervision-inc.com

Enterprise IG 570 Lexington Ave 5th Fl ... New York NY 10022 212-755-4200 755-9474
Web: www.enterpriseig.com

Excel Partnership Inc 75 Glen Rd ... Sandy Hook CT 06482 203-426-3281 426-7811
TF: 800-374-3818 ■ *Web:* www.xlp.com

First Advantage Corp 100 Carillon Pkwy ... Saint Petersburg FL 33716 727-214-3411 214-3410
TF: 800-321-4473 ■ *Web:* www.fadv.com

First Consulting Group Inc
111 W Ocean Blvd Suite 400 PO Box 90801 ... Long Beach CA 90802 562-624-5200 437-1895*
NASDAQ: FCGI ■ **Fax: Hum Res* ■ *TF:* 800-251-8005 ■ *Web:* www.fcg.com

First Manhattan Consulting Group 90 Park Ave 18th Fl ... New York NY 10016 212-557-0500 338-9296
Web: www.fmcg.com

Fluor Global Services Inc 6700 Las Colinas Blvd ... Irving TX 75039 469-398-7000 398-7255
TF: 800-405-6637 ■ *Web:* www.fluor.com

FMI Corp 5171 Glenwood Ave Suite 200 ... Raleigh NC 27612 919-787-8400 785-9320
TF: 800-669-1364 ■ *Web:* www.fminet.com

Fry Consultants 2100 Powers Ferry Rd Suite 125 ... Atlanta GA 30339 770-226-8888 226-8899
Web: www.fryconsultants.com

Fujitsu Consulting 343 Thornall St Suite 630 ... Edison NJ 08837 732-549-4100
TF: 800-882-3212 ■ *Web:* www.fujitsu.com/us/services/consulting

George S May International Co 303 S Northwest Hwy ... Park Ridge IL 60068 847-825-8806 825-7937
TF: 800-999-3020 ■ *Web:* www.georgesmay.com

Glass & Assoc Inc 4571 Stephen Cir NW Suite 130 ... Canton OH 44718 330-494-3252 494-2420
Web: www.glass-consulting.com

Gordon Rj & Co 6300 Wilshire Blvd Suite 710 ... West Hollywood CA 90048 323-801-0410 801-0406
TF: 800-746-7366 ■ *Web:* www.rjgordon.com

GP Deltapoint 6095 Marshalee Dr ... Elkridge MD 21075 410-379-3600 540-5302
TF: 888-843-4784 ■ *Web:* www.gpworldwide.com

Grant Thornton LLP 175 W Jackson Blvd 20th Fl ... Chicago IL 60604 312-856-0001 602-8099
Web: www.grantthornton.com

Hatch Inc 2800 Speakman Dr ... Mississauga ON L5K2R7 905-855-7600 855-8270
Web: www.hatch.ca

Hay Group Inc 100 Penn Sq E Wanamaker Bldg ... Philadelphia PA 19107 215-861-2000 861-2111
TF: 800-776-1774 ■ *Web:* www.haygroup.com

HB Maynard & Co Inc 7 Parkway Center ... Pittsburgh PA 15220 412-921-2400 921-4575
TF: 888-629-6273 ■ *Web:* www.hbmaynard.com

Hildebrandt International 200 Cottontail Ln ... Somerset NJ 08873 732-560-8888 560-2566
TF: 800-223-0937 ■ *Web:* www.hildebrandt.com

HRB Business Services Inc 4400 Main St ... Kansas City MO 64111 816-753-6900 504-1160

Huron Consulting Group Inc 550 W Van Buren St ... Chicago IL 60607 312-583-8700 583-8701
NASDAQ: HURN ■ *Web:* www.huronconsultinggroup.com

IBM Global Services Rt 100 ... Somers NY 10589 914-766-1900 499-6300
Web: www-1.ibm.com/services

IDS Scheer North America 1055 Westlakes Dr Suite 100 ... Berwyn PA 19312 610-854-6800 854-7382
TF: 800-810-2747 ■ *Web:* www.ids-scheer.com/us

Innovative Resources Consultant Group Inc
1 Park Plaza Suite 600 ... Irvine CA 92614 949-252-0590 252-0592
TF: 800-945-4724 ■ *Web:* www.ircginc.com

Interaction Assoc 625 Mount Auburn St ... Cambridge MA 02138 617-234-2700 234-2727
TF: 888-441-8283 ■ *Web:* www.interactionassociates.com

International Banking Technologies Inc
1770 Indian Trail Rd Suite 300 ... Norcross GA 30093 770-381-2023 381-2123
Web: www.intbantec.com

International Profit Assoc Inc 1250 Barclay Blvd ... Buffalo Grove IL 60089 847-808-5590 808-5599
TF: 800-531-7100 ■ *Web:* www.ipa-iba.com

Jacobs-Sirrine Consultants 1 Concourse Pkwy Suite 600 ... Atlanta GA 30328 770-673-6700 673-6681

JH Albert International Advisors Inc 72 River Pk ... Needham MA 02494 781-449-2866 449-5340
Web: www.jhalbert.com

John Snow Inc 44 Farnsworth St ... Boston MA 02210 617-482-9485 482-0617
Web: www.jsi.com

Julie Morgenstern's Professional Organizers
850 7th Ave Suite 901 ... New York NY 10019 212-544-8722 544-0755
TF: 866-742-6473 ■ *Web:* www.juliemorgenstern.com

Kaiser Assoc 1747 Pennsylvania Ave NW Suite 900 ... Washington DC 20006 202-454-2000 454-2001
Web: www.kaiserassociates.com

Keane Consulting Group 500 Park Blvd ... Itasca IL 60143 630-773-6777 773-8760
Web: www.kcg.keane.com

Kearney AT Inc 222 W Adams St Suite 2500 ... Chicago IL 60606 312-648-0111 223-6200
Web: www.atkearney.com

KEMA Consulting 67 S Bedford St Suite 201 East ... Burlington MA 01803 781-273-5700 229-4867
TF: 800-892-2006 ■ *Web:* www1.kemaconsulting.com

Kepner-Tregoe Inc PO Box 704 ... Princeton NJ 08542 609-921-2806 497-0130
TF: 800-854-2655 ■ *Web:* www.kepner-tregoe.com

Kimley-Horn & Assoc Inc PO Box 33068 ... Raleigh NC 27636 919-677-2000 677-2050
Web: www.kimley-horn.com

Kline & Co Inc 150 Clove Rd 7th Fl ... Little Falls NJ 07424 973-435-6262 435-6291
TF: 800-290-5214 ■ *Web:* www.klinegroup.com

KnowledgePlanet.com 5095 Ritter Rd Suite 400 ... Mechanicsburg PA 17055 717-790-0400 790-0401
TF: 800-869-5763 ■ *Web:* www.knowledgeplanet.com

KPMG LLP 199 Bay St Suite 3300 ... Toronto ON M5L1B2 416-777-8500 777-8818
Web: www.kpmg.ca

KPMG LLP US 3 Chestnut Ridge Rd ... Montvale NJ 07645 201-307-7000 307-7575
Web: www.kpmg.com

Kroll Inc 900 3rd Ave 7th Fl ... New York NY 10022 212-593-1000 593-2631
TF: 800-675-3772 ■ *Web:* www.krollworldwide.com

Kurt Salmon Assoc Inc 1355 Peachtree St NE Suite 900 ... Atlanta GA 30309 404-892-0321 898-9590
TF: 800-637-7403 ■ *Web:* www.kurtsalmon.com

LEK Consulting 28 State St 16th Fl ... Boston MA 02109 617-951-9500 951-9392
TF: 800-929-4535 ■ *Web:* www.lekalcar.com

Lewin Group 3130 Fairview Park Dr Suite 800 ... Falls Church VA 22042 703-269-5500 269-5501
TF: 877-227-5030 ■ *Web:* www.lewin.com

Lochridge & Co 420 Boylston St ... Boston MA 02116 617-267-5959 267-8438
Web: www.lochridge.com

LTD Management 1230 Pottstown Pike Suite 6 ... Glenmoore PA 19343 610-458-3636 458-8039
Web: www.ltdmgmt.com

Marakon Assoc 245 Park Ave 44th Fl ... New York NY 10167 212-377-5000 377-6000
TF: 800-264-3000 ■ *Web:* www.marakon.com

Marasco Newton Group Ltd 2801 Clarendon Blvd ... Arlington VA 22201 703-516-9100 516-9108
TF: 800-486-0220

Mars & Co 124 Mason St ... Greenwich CT 06830 203-629-9292 629-9432
Web: www.marsandco.com

MasiMax Resources Inc 1375 Piccard Dr Suite 175 ... Rockville MD 20850 240-632-0610 632-0519
Web: www.masimax.com

MAXIMUS Inc 11419 Sunset Hills Rd ... Reston VA 20190 703-251-8500 251-8240
NYSE: MMS ■ *Web:* www.maximus.com

May George S International Co 303 S Northwest Hwy ... Park Ridge IL 60068 847-825-8806 825-7937
TF: 800-999-3020 ■ *Web:* www.georgesmay.com

Maynard HB & Co Inc 7 Parkway Center ... Pittsburgh PA 15220 412-921-2400 921-4575
TF: 888-629-6273 ■ *Web:* www.hbmaynard.com

Phone Fax

McKinsey & Co Inc 55 E 52nd St ... New York NY 10022 212-446-7000 446-8575
TF: 800-221-1026 ■ *Web:* www.mckinsey.com

Medical Doctor Assoc Inc 145 Technology Pkwy NW ... Norcross GA 30092 770-246-9191 246-0882
TF: 800-780-3500 ■ *Web:* www.mdainc.com

Mercer Delta Consulting 1166 Ave of the Americas 40th Fl ... New York NY 10036 212-345-0555 221-5882
Web: www.deltacg.com

Mercer Inc 1166 Ave of the Americas ... New York NY 10036 212-345-5000 345-7415
Web: www.mercer.com

Mercer Management Consulting
1166 Ave of the Americas 32 Fl ... New York NY 10036 212-345-8000 345-8075
TF: 800-532-6888 ■ *Web:* www.mercermc.com

MGT of America Inc 2123 Centre Point Blvd ... Tallahassee FL 32308 850-386-3191 385-4501
TF: 800-326-9132 ■ *Web:* www.mgtamer.com

Milliman USA 1301 5th Ave Suite 3800 ... Seattle WA 98101 206-624-7940 340-1380*
**Fax:* Mktg ■ *Web:* www.milliman.com

Modem Media 230 East Ave ... Norwalk CT 06855 203-299-7000 299-7060
Web: www.modemmedia.com

Monitor Group 2 Canal Park ... Cambridge MA 02141 617-252-2000 252-2100
Web: www.monitor.com

Morris-Anderson & Assoc Ltd 1111 E Touhy Ave Suite 286 ... Des Plaines IL 60018 847-768-4400 768-4401
Web: www.morris-anderson.com

Nathan Assoc Inc 2101 Wilson Blvd Suite 1200 ... Arlington VA 22201 703-516-7700 351-6162
Web: www.nathanassoc.com

National Economic Research Assoc Inc
50 Main St 14th Fl ... White Plains NY 10606 914-448-4000 448-4040
Web: www.nera.com

Navigant Consulting Inc 615 N Wabash Ave ... Chicago IL 60611 312-573-5600 573-5678*
NYSE: NCI ■ **Fax:* Mktg ■ *TF:* 800-621-8390 ■ *Web:* www.navigantconsulting.com

Nexant Inc 44 S Broadway 5th Fl ... White Plains NY 10601 914-609-0300 609-0399
Web: www.nexant.com

Nextera Enterprises Inc 10 High St 6th Fl ... Boston MA 02110 617-262-0055 262-7105
Web: www.nextera.com

Nolan Robert E Co Inc 90 Hopmeadow St ... Weatogue CT 06089 860-658-1941 651-3465
TF: 800-653-1941 ■ *Web:* www.renolan.com

Organization Consultants Inc 1949 Park Rd ... Charlotte NC 28203 704-375-6262 375-2217
Web: www.ociofcharlotte.com

Organizational Dynamics Inc 790 Boston Rd Suite 201 ... Billerica MA 01821 978-671-5454 671-5005
TF: 800-634-4636 ■ *Web:* www.orgdynamics.com

Ortloff Engineers Ltd 415 W Wall Ave Suite 2000 ... Midland TX 79701 432-685-0277 685-0258
Web: www.ortloff.com

PA Consulting Group
1750 Pennsylvania Ave NW Suite 1000 ... Washington DC 20006 202-442-2000 442-2001
Web: www.paconsulting.com

Parson Group 333 W Wacker Dr Suite 1010 ... Chicago IL 60606 312-578-1170 578-1355
TF: 800-389-8686 ■ *Web:* www.parsonconsulting.com

Parthenon Group 200 State St 14th Fl ... Boston MA 02109 617-478-2550 478-2555
Web: www.parthenon.com

Perot Systems Corp Government Services Group
8270 Willow Oaks Corporate Dr Suite 300 ... Fairfax VA 22031 703-289-8000 289-8099
TF: 888-560-9477

Philip Crosby Assoc Inc 306 Dartmouth St ... Boston MA 02116 617-716-0218 716-0223*
**Fax:* Hum Res ■ *TF:* 800-223-3932 ■ *Web:* www.philipcrosby.com

Pinnacle Consulting Group Inc 71 Moore Rd ... Wayland MA 01778 508-358-8070 358-8071
TF: 800-693-7466 ■ *Web:* www.pinnaclecg.com

Pittiglio Rabin Todd & McGrath 1050 Winter St ... Waltham MA 02451 781-647-2800 647-2804
Web: www.prtm.com

Power Technologies Inc 1482 Erie Blvd ... Schenectady NY 12305 518-374-1220 346-2777
TF: 800-395-4784 ■ *Web:* www.pti-us.com

Preferred Health Strategies 2 Bellesair Blvd ... Rye Brook NY 10573 914-937-1072 206-4129
Web: www.phsconsult.com

PricewaterhouseCoopers LLP
77 King St W Royal Trust Tower 25th Fl ... Toronto ON M5K1G8 416-863-1133 365-8215
Web: www.pwcglobal.com/ca

Pritchett LLC 13355 Noel Rd Suite 1650 ... Dallas TX 75240 972-731-1500 731-1550
TF: 800-992-5922 ■ *Web:* www.pritchettnet.com

Pro2Serve Professional Project Services Inc
545 Oakridge Tpke Suite 101 ... Oak Ridge TN 37830 865-483-2030 483-2660
TF: 888-243-4150 ■ *Web:* www.p2s.com

Professional Bank Services Inc
6200 Dutchmans Ln Suite 305 ... Louisville KY 40205 502-451-6633 451-6755
TF: 800-523-4778 ■ *Web:* www.probank.com

Progeny Marketing Innovations 801 Crescent Ctr Dr Suite 200 ... Franklin TN 37067 800-251-2148
Web: www.progenymarketing.com

Program Planning Professionals 3923 Ranchero Dr ... Ann Arbor MI 48108 734-741-7770 741-1343
TF: 888-364-1182 ■ *Web:* www.pcubed.com

Proudfoot PLC 11621 Kew Gardens Ave Suite 200 ... Palm Beach Gardens FL 33410 561-624-4377 656-2313
TF: 800-826-5740 ■ *Web:* www.proudfootconsulting.com

Rath & Strong Inc 45 Hayden Ave ... Lexington MA 02421 781-861-1700 861-1424
TF: 800-622-2025 ■ *Web:* www.rathstrong.com

Raytheon Professional Services LLC 1200 South Jupiter Rd ... Dallas TX 75042 972-205-5100 344-5369
Web: www.raytheon.com/businesses/rps

Reden & Anders Ltd 222 S 9th St Suite 1500 ... Minneapolis MN 55402 612-339-7933 349-3788
TF: 800-643-7933 ■ *Web:* www.reden-anders.com

Resource Dynamics International Inc PO Box 70 ... Montvale NY 07645 888-999-1623 999-1624
Web: www.resourcedynamics.com

Revere Group 325 N LaSalle Suite 325 ... Chicago IL 60610 312-873-3400 873-3500
TF: 888-473-8373 ■ *Web:* www.reveregroup.com

RHR International Co 220 Gerry Dr ... Wood Dale IL 60191 630-766-7007 766-9037
TF: 800-892-4496 ■ *Web:* www.rhrinternational.com

Richard Chang Assoc 15265 Alton Pkwy Suite 300 ... Irvine CA 92618 949-727-7477 727-7007
TF: 800-756-8096 ■ *Web:* www.richardchangassociates.com

Rj Gordon & Co 6300 Wilshire Blvd Suite 710 ... West Hollywood CA 90048 323-801-0410 801-0406
TF: 800-746-7366 ■ *Web:* www.rjgordon.com

Robbins-Gioia 11 Canal CenterPlaza Suite 200 ... Alexandria VA 22314 703-548-7006 684-5189
Web: www.rgalex.com

Robert E Nolan Co Inc 90 Hopmeadow St ... Weatogue CT 06089 860-658-1941 651-3465
TF: 800-653-1941 ■ *Web:* www.renolan.com

Robert H Schaffer & Assoc 30 Oak St 3rd Fl ... Stamford CT 06905 203-322-1604 322-3599
Web: www.rhsa.com

Robert Half Management Resources (RHIMR)
2884 Sand Hill Rd Suite 200 ... Menlo Park CA 94025 650-234-6000 234-6999
TF: 888-400-7474 ■ *Web:* www.rhimr.com

Roland Berger & Partners 230 Park Ave 10th Fl ... New York NY 10169 212-651-9660 756-8750
Web: www.rolandberger.com

RSM/McGladrey & Pullen LLP
3600 American Blvd W 3rd Fl ... Bloomington MN 55431 952-835-9930 921-7702
TF: 866-835-9930 ■ *Web:* www.rsmmcgladrey.com

Ryan Group Inc 14110 Dallas Pkwy Suite 270 ... Dallas TX 75254 972-385-7781 385-7884
Web: www.ryangroupinc.com

Salmon Kurt Assoc Inc 1355 Peachtree St NE Suite 900 ... Atlanta GA 30309 404-892-0321 898-9590
TF: 800-637-7403 ■ *Web:* www.kurtsalmon.com

Sandy Corp 1500 W Big Beaver Rd ... Troy MI 48084 248-649-0800 649-3614
TF: 800-733-4739 ■ *Web:* www.sandycorp.com

Sapient Corp 25 1st St 4th Fl ... Cambridge MA 02141 617-621-0200 621-1300
NASDAQ: SAPE ■ *Web:* www.sapient.com

Schaffer Robert H & Assoc 30 Oak St 3rd Fl ... Stamford CT 06905 203-322-1604 322-3599
Web: www.rhsa.com

Phone Fax

Scott Madden & Assoc Inc 2626 Glenwood Ave Suite 480 ... Raleigh NC 27608 919-781-4191 781-2537
TF: 800-321-9774 ■ *Web:* www.scottmadden.com

Sedlak Management Consultants
22901 Millcreek Blvd Suite 600 ... Highland Hills OH 44122 216-206-4700 206-4840
Web: www.jasedlak.com

Sirius Solution LLC 3700 Buffalo Speedway Suite 1100 ... Houston TX 77098 713-888-0488 888-0235
TF: 800-585-1085 ■ *Web:* www.sirsol.com

Solving International 1755 The Exchange Suite 380 ... Atlanta GA 30339 770-988-2600 988-2626
TF: 800-637-4887 ■ *Web:* www.solving-int.com

Strategic Decisions Group 735 Emerson St ... Palo Alto CA 94301 650-475-4400 475-4401
Web: www.sdg.com

Strategic Management Group Inc
181 Washington St 6 Tower Bridge Suite 540 ... Conshohocken PA 19428 484-391-2900 391-2901
TF: 866-874-4899 ■ *Web:* www.smginc.com

Stromberg Consulting 1285 Ave of the Americas ... New York NY 10019 646-935-4300 935-4368
Web: www.scny.com

Superior Consultant Holdings Corp 5225 Auto Club Dr ... Dearborn MI 48126 248-386-8300 386-8301
TF: 800-781-0960 ■ *Web:* www.superiorconsultant.com

SYS Technologies Inc 5050 Murphy Canyon Rd Suite 200 ... San Diego CA 92123 858-715-5500 715-5510
AMEX: SYS ■ *Web:* www.systechnologies.com

Sysorex Consulting Inc 506 Clyde Ave ... Mountain View CA 94043 650-967-2200 967-9327
Web: www.sysorex.com

Systech Solutions Inc 550 N Brand Blvd Suite 1200 ... Glendale CA 91203 818-550-9690 550-9692
Web: www.systechusa.com

Tata Consultancy Services 115 Perimeter Center Pl Suite 1099 ... Atlanta GA 30346 770-396-1223 396-1239
Web: www.tcs.com

Technology & Business Integrators 275 N Franklin Tpke ... Ramsey NJ 07446 201-573-0400 573-9191
TF: 800-676-9470 ■ *Web:* www.tbicentral.com

Technomic Inc 300 S Riverside Plaza Suite 1200 ... Chicago IL 60606 312-876-0004 876-1158
Web: www.technomic.com

Tenera Environmental 971 Dewing Ave Suite 101 ... Lafayette CA 94549 925-962-9769
TF: 800-447-9388 ■ *Web:* www.tenera.com

ThinkFast Consulting Inc 8700 W Bryn Mawr Ave Suite 800 ... Chicago IL 60631 773-714-9999 714-9998

Thomas Group Inc 5221 N O'Connor Blvd Suite 500 ... Irving TX 75039 972-869-3400 443-1701
NASDAQ: TGIS ■ *TF:* 800-826-2057 ■ *Web:* www.thomasgroup.com

Tompkins Assoc 8970 Southall Rd ... Raleigh NC 27616 919-876-3667 872-9666
TF: 800-789-1257 ■ *Web:* www.tompkinsinc.com

Towers Perrin Inc 335 Madison Ave ... New York NY 10017 212-309-3400 309-3760
Web: www.towersperrin.com

Towers Perrin Inc 175 Bloor St E South Tower Suite 1701 ... Toronto ON M4W3T6 416-960-2700 960-2819
Web: www.towersperrin.com

Tunnell Consulting 900 E 8th Ave Suite 106 ... King of Prussia PA 19406 610-337-0820 337-1884
TF: 800-532-2483 ■ *Web:* www.tunnellconsulting.com

UMS Group Inc 20 Waterview Blvd ... Parsippany NJ 07054 973-335-3555 335-7738
Web: www.umsgroup.com

University Research Co LLC 7200 Wisconsin Ave Suite 600 ... Bethesda MD 20814 301-654-8338 941-8427
Web: www.urc-chs.com

Venture Development Corp 1 Apple Hill Dr Suite 206 ... Natick MA 01760 508-653-9000 653-9836
Web: www.vdc-corp.com

Wakely Consulting Group Inc 19321 US Hwy 19 N Suite 515 ... Clearwater FL 33764 727-507-9858 507-9658
Web: www.wakelyconsulting.com

Wohl Assoc 40 Old Lancaster Rd Unit 608 ... Merion Station PA 19066 610-667-4842 664-3955
Web: www.wohl.com

198 CONSULTING SERVICES - MARKETING

Phone Fax

4Kids Entertainment Licensing Inc 1414 Ave of the Americas ... New York NY 10019 212-758-7666 980-0933
Web: www.4kidsentertainment.com

Acosta Sales & Marketing Co 665 W North Ave Suite 300 ... Lombard IL 60148 630-620-7600 620-7698
TF: 800-843-2750 ■ *Web:* www.acosta.com

Alexander Group Inc 14635 N Kierland Blvd Suite 200 ... Scottsdale AZ 85254 480-998-9644 951-8964
TF: 800-327-8525 ■ *Web:* www.alexandergroupinc.com

ANALYTICi 100 W 33rd St 6th Fl ... New York NY 10001 877-568-8032 907-7490*
**Fax Area Code:* 212 ■ *Web:* www.analytici.com

Beverage Marketing Corp 850 3rd Ave 18th Fl ... New York NY 10022 212-688-7640 826-1255
TF: 800-275-4630 ■ *Web:* www.beveragemarketing.com

Busse Design USA Inc 4053 Harlan St Studio 101 ... Emeryville CA 94608 510-596-9422 596-9424
Web: www.bussedesign.com

Cargill AgHorizons PO Box 9300 MS 19 ... Minneapolis MN 55440 952-742-7575 742-7313
TF: 800-227-4455 ■ *Web:* www.cargillaghorizons.com

ChannelAdvisor Corp 5001 Hospitality Ct Suite 100 ... Morrisville NC 27560 919-465-5680 388-9405
TF: 866-264-8594 ■ *Web:* www.channeladvisor.com

CMGI Inc 1100 Winter St Suite 4600 ... Waltham MA 02451 781-663-5001 663-5100
NASDAQ: CMGI ■ *Web:* www.cmgi.com

Competitive Technologies Inc 777 Commerce Dr Suite 100 ... Fairfield CT 06825 203-368-6044 368-5399
AMEX: CTT ■ *Web:* www.competitivetech.net

Corporate Branding 470 West Ave ... Stamford CT 06902 203-327-6333 353-8180
TF: 888-969-2726 ■ *Web:* www.corebrand.com

Creative Good Inc 307 W 38th St Suite 1701 ... New York NY 10018 212-736-2075 736-0697
Web: www.creativegood.com

Crimson Consulting Group 4970 El Camino Real Suite 200 ... Los Altos CA 94022 650-960-3600 960-3737
Web: www.crimson-consulting.com

Crossmark Inc 5100 Legacy Dr ... Plano TX 75024 469-814-1000 814-1355
TF: 888-695-6733 ■ *Web:* www.crossmark.com

Daymon Assoc Inc 700 Fairfield Ave ... Stamford CT 06902 203-352-7500 352-7947
Web: www.daymon.com

DCI Marketing Inc 2727 W Good Hope Rd ... Milwaukee WI 53209 414-228-7000 228-3421
TF: 800-778-4805 ■ *Web:* www.dcimarketing.com

Dynetech Corp 255 S Orange Ave Suite 600 ... Orlando FL 32801 407-206-6500 206-6507
TF: 800-874-0388 ■ *Web:* www.dynetech.com

EBSCO Professional Partnership Group
110 Olmsted St Suite 101 ... Birmingham AL 35242 205-991-1188 980-3830
TF: 800-528-3476 ■ *Web:* www.ebscodas.com

Economic Consulting Services LLC 2001 L St NW ... Washington DC 20036 202-466-7720 466-2710
Web: www.economic-consulting.com

Faith Popcorn's BrainReserve 885 2nd Ave 16th Fl ... New York NY 10017 212-772-7778 772-7787
TF: 800-873-6337 ■ *Web:* www.faithpopcorn.com

Fitch Inc 1266 Manning Pkwy ... Powell OH 43065 614-885-3453 885-4289
Web: www.fitch.com

Frank Lynn & Assoc Inc 150 S Wacker Dr 17th Fl ... Chicago IL 60606 312-263-7888 263-1117
TF: 800-245-5966 ■ *Web:* www.franklynn.com

Frost & Sullivan 7550 W I-10 Suite 400 ... San Antonio TX 78229 210-348-1000 348-1003
TF: 877-463-7678 ■ *Web:* www.frost.com

Fulcrum Analytics 70 W 40th St 10th Fl ... New York NY 10018 212-651-7000 651-7049
TF: 888-421-6655 ■ *Web:* www.fulcrumanalytics.com

Harte-Hanks Market Intelligence 9980 Huennekens St ... San Diego CA 92121 858-450-1667 452-7491
TF: 800-854-8409 ■ *Web:* www.hartehanksmi.com

Hunter Business Group 4650 N Port Washington Rd ... Milwaukee WI 53212 414-203-8060 203-8225
Web: www.hunterbusiness.com

I-F Consulting 28 State St 11th Fl ... Boston MA 02109 617-232-8880 232-2525
Web: www.i-f.com

IdentityWEB Inc 2999 Overland Ave Suite 2112 ... Los Angeles CA 90064 310-559-2476 559-2485
Web: www.identityweb.com

	City	State	Zip	Phone	Fax
Impact Planning Group 10 Winfield St *Web:* www.impactplan.com	Norwalk	CT	06855	203-854-1011	854-4888
Innotrac Corp 6655 Sugarloaf Pkwy *NASDAQ: INOC* ■ *TF:* 800-827-4666 ■ *Web:* www.innotrac.com	Duluth	GA	30097	678-584-4000	475-5840
Intellimar Inc 7560 Main St *Web:* www.intellimar.com	Sykesville	MD	21784	410-552-9940	552-9939
Kuczmarski & Assoc 1165 N Clark St Suite 700 *Web:* www.kuczmarski.com	Chicago	IL	60610	312-988-1500	988-9393
Lexicon Branding Inc 30 Liberty Ship Way Suite 3360 *TF:* 800-783-9713 ■ *Web:* www.lexicon-branding.com	Sausalito	CA	94965	415-332-1811	332-2528
Lippincott Mercer Inc 499 Park Ave *Web:* www.lippincottmercer.com	New York	NY	10022	212-521-0000	308-8952
Lynn Frank & Assoc Inc 150 S Wacker Dr 17th Fl *TF:* 800-245-5966 ■ *Web:* www.franklynn.com	Chicago	IL	60606	312-263-7888	263-1117
MarketBridge 4550 Montgomery Ave 500 N Tower *Web:* www.market-bridge.com	Bethesda	MD	20814	301-907-3800	907-3282
Massini Group 1323 NE Orenco Station Pkwy Suite 300 *Web:* www.massini-group.com	Hillsboro	OR	97124	503-640-9800	640-9888
Mattson Jack Group 11960 Westline Industrial Dr Suite 180 *Web:* www.mattsonjack.com	Saint Louis	MO	63146	314-469-7600	469-6794
Morgan Anderson Consulting 4 Park Ave 22nd Fl **Fax Area Code:* 866 ■ *TF:* 800-850-3550 ■ *Web:* www.morgananderson.com	New York	NY	10016	212-741-0777	851-4883*
National Food Laboratory Inc 6363 Clark Ave *Web:* www.thenfl.com	Dublin	CA	94568	925-828-1440	833-9239
PDI Inc 1 Rt 17 S Saddle River Executive Center *NASDAQ: PDII* ■ *TF:* 800-242-7494 ■ *Web:* www.pdi-inc.com	Upper Saddle River	NJ	07458	201-258-8450	258-8400
Peppers & Rogers Group 20 Glover Ave *Web:* www.1to1.com	Norwalk	CT	06850	203-642-5121	642-5126
Rainmaker Systems Inc 900 E Hamilton Ave Suite 400 *NASDAQ: RMKR* ■ *TF:* 800-631-1545 ■ *Web:* www.rainmakersystems.com	Campbell	CA	95008	408-626-3800	369-0910
RedF 14120 Ballantyne Corp Pl Suite 200 *Web:* www.redf.com	Charlotte	NC	28277	704-971-2300	971-2303
Richmark Group 39 S LaSalle St 5th Fl *Web:* www.richmark.com	Chicago	IL	60603	312-368-0800	368-0832
Ries & Ries 2195 River Cliff Dr *Web:* www.ries.com	Roswell	GA	30076	770-643-0880	643-0051
Ronin Corp 2 Research Way 2nd Fl *TF:* 800-352-2926 ■ *Web:* www.ronin.com	Princeton	NJ	08540	609-452-0060	452-0091
Starmark International Inc 1815 Griffin Rd *Web:* www.starmark.com	Dania Beach	FL	33004	954-874-9000	874-9010
Suss Consulting 801 Old York Rd Noble Plaza Suite 305 *TF:* 888-984-5900 ■ *Web:* www.sussconsulting.com	Jenkintown	PA	19046	215-884-5900	884-1637
Ventiv Health Inc 200 Cottontail Ln *NASDAQ: VTIV* ■ **Fax Area Code:* 732 ■ *Web:* www.ventiv.com	Somerset	NJ	08873	800-416-0555	537-4912*
Weller Co PO Box 8637	Tucson	AZ	85738	520-818-7797	
Wellness International Network Ltd 5800 Democracy Dr *Web:* web.winltd.com	Plano	TX	75024	972-312-1100	943-5260
Worldwide Partners Inc 2280 S Xanadu Way Suite 300	Aurora	CO	80014	303-671-8551	337-9576
WSI Internet 5580 Explorer Dr Suite 600 *TF:* 888-678-7588 ■ *Web:* www.wsicorporate.com	Mississauga	ON	L4W4Y1	905-678-7588	678-7242
Wunderman 285 Madison Ave *Web:* www.wunderman.com	New York	NY	10017	212-941-3000	
Y2Marketing 6363 N State Hwy 161 Suite 600 **Fax Area Code:* 469 ■ *Web:* www.y2marketing.com	Irving	TX	75038	972-823-2000	417-0890*
Young & Assoc Ltd 2625 Butterfield Rd Suite 216 South *TF:* 800-553-2503 ■ *Web:* www.youngltd.com	Oak Brook	IL	60523	630-573-2500	573-2522
ZS Assoc 1800 Sherman Ave Suite 700 *Web:* www.zsassociates.com	Evanston	IL	60201	847-492-3600	864-6280

199 CONSULTING SERVICES - TELECOMMUNICATIONS

	City	State	Zip	Phone	Fax
ACRS (Associated Communications & Research Services Inc) 817 NE 63rd St *TF:* 800-442-3341 ■ *Web:* www.acrsokc.com	Oklahoma City	OK	73105	405-843-9966	843-9852
Adesta Communications Inc 1200 Landmark Ctr Suite 1300 *Web:* www.adestagroup.com	Omaha	NE	68102	402-233-7700	233-7650
Ajilon Communications 970 Peachtree Industrial Blvd Suite 200 **Fax Area Code:* 800 ■ *TF:* 800-843-6910 ■ *Web:* www.ajiloncom.com	Suwanee	GA	30024	678-482-5103	215-4910*
Angus TeleManagement Group Inc 8 Old Kingston Rd *Web:* www.angustel.ca	Ajax	ON	L1T2Z7	905-686-5050	686-2655
Associated Communications & Research Services Inc (ACRS) 817 NE 63rd St *TF:* 800-442-3341 ■ *Web:* www.acrsokc.com	Oklahoma City	OK	73105	405-843-9966	843-9852
Atcom Business Telecom Solutions PO Box 13476 *TF:* 800-891-3917 ■ *Web:* www.atcombts.com	Research Triangle Park	NC	27709	919-314-1001	314-1010
Behr Lawrence Assoc Inc PO Box 8026 *TF:* 800-522-4464 ■ *Web:* www.lbagroup.com/associates	Greenville	NC	27835	252-757-0279	752-9155
BoldTech Systems Inc 1050 17th St Suite 1100 *Web:* www.boldtech.com	Denver	CO	80202	303-629-9206	629-9208
Chasecom LP 3311 W Alabama St *Web:* www.chasecom.net	Houston	TX	77098	713-874-5800	874-5812
Communication Sciences Inc 379 Thornall St Suite 7 *Web:* www.comsci.com	Edison	NJ	08837	732-632-8000	632-1830
DIGICON Corp 9601 Blackwell Rd Suite 250 *Web:* www.digicon.com	Rockville	MD	20850	301-721-6300	869-8081
eLinear Inc 2901 W Sam Houston Pkwy N Suite E-300 *AMEX: ELU* ■ *TF:* 800-896-0501 ■ *Web:* www.elinear.com	Houston	TX	77043	713-896-0500	896-0510
First Communications Inc 3340 W Market St *TF:* 800-860-1261 ■ *Web:* www.firstcommunications.com	Akron	OH	44333	330-835-2323	835-2330
GLA Integrated Network Solutions LLC 17 Research Park Dr Suite 200 *TF:* 800-896-3355 ■ *Web:* www.glai.com	Saint Charles	MO	63304	636-720-0900	720-0913
Infotrends/CAP Ventures Inc 97 Libbey Industrial Pkwy Suite 300 *Web:* www.capv.com	Weymouth	MA	02189	781-616-2100	616-2121
Lawrence Behr Assoc Inc PO Box 8026 *TF:* 800-522-4464 ■ *Web:* www.lbagroup.com/associates	Greenville	NC	27835	252-757-0279	752-9155
Lightbridge Inc 30 Corporate Dr *NASDAQ: LTBG* ■ *Web:* www.lightbridge.com	Burlington	MA	01803	781-359-4000	359-4500
Lucent Technologies Inc NetworkCare Professional Services 1213 Innsbruck Dr	Sunnyvale	CA	94089	650-318-1000	318-1101
Management Network Group Inc 7300 College Blvd Suite 302 *NASDAQ: TMNG* ■ *TF:* 888-480-8664 ■ *Web:* www.tmng.com	Overland Park	KS	66210	913-345-9315	451-1845
QuBX Consulting Inc 660 First Bank Dr *Web:* www.qubxconsulting.com	Palatine	IL	60067	847-776-3400	776-3406
Superior Communications Inc 704 E Gude Dr *Web:* www.scicommo.com	Rockville	MD	20850	301-762-7878	762-6870
Technology Futures Inc 13740 N Research Blvd Bldg C *TF:* 800-835-3887 ■ *Web:* www.tfi.com	Austin	TX	78750	512-258-8898	258-0087
Telcordia Technologies Inc 1 Telcordia Dr *TF Sales:* 800-521-2673 ■ *Web:* www.telcordia.com	Piscataway	NJ	08854	732-699-2000	336-2844
Telwares Inc 7901 Stoneridge Dr *TF:* 888-835-9273 ■ *Web:* www.telwares.com	Pleasanton	CA	94588	925-224-7800	
Vectren Communications Services 421 John St *TF:* 888-326-6782 ■ *Web:* www.vectrencom.com	Evansville	IN	47713	812-437-6700	437-6781
WFI (Wireless Facilities Inc) 4810 Eastgate Mall *NASDAQ: WFII* ■ *TF:* 888-824-0017 ■ *Web:* www.wfinet.com	San Diego	CA	92121	858-228-2000	228-2001
Windfall Assoc 981 Chestnut St *TF:* 877-946-3325 ■ *Web:* www.windfall-assoc.com	Newton Upper Falls	MA	02464	617-969-1790	969-1777
Wireless Facilities Inc (WFI) 4810 Eastgate Mall *NASDAQ: WFII* ■ *TF:* 888-824-0017 ■ *Web:* www.wfinet.com	San Diego	CA	92121	858-228-2000	228-2001

200 CONSUMER INFORMATION RESOURCES - GOVERNMENT

	City	State	Zip	Phone	Fax
ADEAR Center PO Box 8250 **Fax Area Code:* 301 ■ *Web:* www.nia.nih.gov/alzheimers	Silver Spring	MD	20907	800-438-4380	495-3334*
Afterschool.gov Admin for Children & Families 370 L'Enfant Promenade *Web:* www.afterschool.gov	Washington	DC	20447	202-401-9215	401-5450
AIDSinfo PO Box 6303 *TF:* 800-448-0440 ■ *Web:* www.aidsinfo.nih.gov	Rockville	MD	20849	301-519-0459	519-6616
Alzheimer's Disease Education & Referral Center PO Box 8250 **Fax Area Code:* 301 ■ *Web:* www.nia.nih.gov/alzheimers	Silver Spring	MD	20907	800-438-4380	495-3334*
AmeriCorps USA 1201 New York Ave NW *Web:* www.americorps.org	Washington	DC	20525	202-606-5000	
Ask USGS 12201 Sunrise Valley Dr *Web:* ask.usgs.gov	Reston	VA	20192	888-275-8747	
Cancer Information Service National Cancer Institute 9000 Rockville Pike Bldg 31 *Web:* cis.nci.nih.gov	Bethesda	MD	20892	800-422-6237	
Center for Nutrition Policy & Promotion 3101 Park Center Dr *Web:* www.cnpp.usda.gov	Alexandria	VA	22302	703-305-7600	305-3300
Center for Substance Abuse Treatment 1 Choke Cherry Rd *Web:* csat.samhsa.gov	Rockville	MD	20857	240-276-2757	276-1670
Centers for Disease Control & Prevention (CDC NPIN) National Prevention Information Network PO Box 6003 **Fax Area Code:* 888 ■ *TF:* 800-458-5231 ■ *Web:* www.cdcnpin.org	Rockville	MD	20849	919-361-4892	282-7681*
Centers for Disease Control & Prevention (CDC) Travelers' Health 1600 Clifton Rd NE **Fax Area Code:* 888 ■ *Web:* wwwn.cdc.gov/travel	Atlanta	GA	30333	877-394-8747	232-3299*
Child Welfare Information Gateway 1250 Maryland Ave SW 8th Fl *TF:* 800-394-3366 ■ *Web:* www.childwelfare.gov	Washington	DC	20024	703-385-7565	385-3206
Consumer Product Safety Commission (CPSC) 4330 East West Hwy *TF:* 800-638-2772 ■ *Web:* www.cpsc.gov	Bethesda	MD	20814	301-504-7923	504-0051
Consumer.gov *Web:* www.consumer.gov	Pueblo	CO	81009	888-878-3256	
Education Resource Information Center (ERIC) 655 15th St NW Suite 500 *Web:* www.eric.ed.gov	Washington	DC	20005	800-538-3742	
Eldercare Locator 1730 Rhode Island Ave NW Suite 1200 *TF:* 800-677-1116 ■ *Web:* www.eldercare.gov	Washington	DC	20036	202-872-0888	872-0057
Energy Efficiency & Renewable Energy Information Center PO Box 43165 **Fax Area Code:* 360 ■ *Web:* www.eere.energy.gov/consumer	Olympia	WA	98504	877-337-3463	236-2023*
ERIC (Education Resource Information Center) 655 15th St NW Suite 500 *Web:* www.eric.ed.gov	Washington	DC	20005	800-538-3742	
Federal Citizen Information Center *Web:* www.pueblo.gsa.gov	Pueblo	CO	81009	888-878-3256	
Federal Student Aid Information Center PO Box 84 *Web:* studentaid.ed.gov	Washington	DC	20044	800-433-3243	
FedWorld.gov National Technical Information Service 5285 Port Royal Rd *Web:* www.fedworld.gov	Springfield	VA	22161	703-605-6000	
FirstGov en Espanol 1800 F St NW *Web:* www.firstgov.gov/Espanol	Washington	DC	20405	800-333-4636	
FoodSafety.gov 5100 Paint Branch Pkwy *Web:* www.foodsafety.gov	College Park	MD	20740	888-723-3366	
Foster Grandparent Program c/o Senior Corps 1201 New York Ave NW *TF:* 800-424-8867 ■ *Web:* www.seniorcorps.gov/about/programs/fg.asp	Washington	DC	20525	202-606-5000	561-2414
Girl Power! Substance Abuse & Mental Health Services Administration 5600 Fishersn Ln *Web:* www.girlpower.gov	Rockville	MD	20857	800-729-6686	
GovLoans.gov *Web:* www.govloans.gov	Washington	DC	20405	800-333-4636	
Grants.gov Dept of Health & Human Services 200 Independence Ave SW *Web:* www.grants.gov	Washington	DC	20201	800-518-4726	
Healthfinder US Dept of Health & Human Services PO Box 1133 *Web:* www.healthfinder.gov	Washington	DC	20013	301-565-4167	984-4256
Homeland Security Information Center National Technical Information Service 5285 Port Royal Rd *Web:* www.ntis.gov/hs	Springfield	VA	22161	703-605-6000	
Insure Kids Now! Health Resources & Services Administration 5600 Fishers Ln *Web:* www.insurekidsnow.gov	Rockville	MD	20857	877-543-7669	
Learn & Serve America 1201 New York Ave NW *Web:* www.learnandserve.org	Washington	DC	20525	202-606-5000	
Medicare Hotline *Web:* www.medicare.gov	Baltimore	MD	21207	800-633-4227	
MedlinePlus National Library of Medicine 8600 Rockville Pike *TF:* 888-346-3656 ■ *Web:* medlineplus.gov	Bethesda	MD	20894	301-594-5983	402-1384
MedWatch Center for Drug Evaluation & Research 5515 Security Ln Suite 5100 *Web:* www.fda.gov/medwatch	Rockville	MD	20852	888-463-6332	
MyPyramid Center for Nutrition Policy & Promotion 3101 Park Center Dr Rm 1034 *Web:* www.mypyramid.gov	Alexandria	VA	22302	703-305-7600	

Name / Address	City	State	Zip	Phone	Fax
National Center for Immunization & Respiratory Diseases 1600 Clifton Rd NE MS E-05	Atlanta	GA	30333	800-832-4636	
Web: www.cdc.gov/vaccines					
Veterans Health Administration National Center for Post-Traumatic Stress Disorder 215 N Main St	White River Junction	VT	05009	802-296-5132	296-5135
Web: www.ncptsd.va.gov					
National Child Care Information Center (NCCIC) 10530 Rosehaven St Suite 400	Fairfax	VA	22030	800-616-2242	716-2242
Web: nccic.org					
National Clearinghouse for Alcohol & Drug Information PO Box 2345	Rockville	MD	20847	301-468-2600	
TF: 800-729-6686 ■ *Web:* ncadi.samhsa.gov					
National Contact Center	Pueblo	CO	81009	800-333-4636	
Web: www.info.gov					
National Do Not Call Registry	Washington	DC	20580	888-382-1222	
Web: www.ftc.gov/donotcall					
National Health Information Center (NHIC) PO Box 1133	Washington	DC	20013	301-565-4167	984-4256
TF: 800-336-4797 ■ *Web:* www.health.gov/nhic					
National Institute for Literacy (NIFL) 1775 'I' St NW Suite 730	Washington	DC	20006	202-233-2025	233-2050
TF: 800-228-8813 ■ *Web:* www.nifl.gov					
National Mental Health Information Center PO Box 42557	Washington	DC	20015	240-747-5484	747-5470
TF: 800-789-2647 ■ *Web:* mentalhealth.samhsa.gov					
National Passport Information Center	Washington	DC	20520	877-487-2778	
Web: travel.state.gov/passport					
National Prevention Information Network PO Box 6003	Rockville	MD	20849	919-361-4892	282-7681*
**Fax Area Code: 888* ■ *TF:* 800-458-5231 ■ *Web:* www.cdcnpin.org					
National Weather Service (NWS) 1325 East-West Hwy Metro Ctr 2	Silver Spring	MD	20910	301-713-0689	713-0662
Web: www.weather.gov					
National Women's Health Information Center 8270 Willow Oaks Corporate Dr	Fairfax	VA	22031	800-994-9662	
Web: www.womenshealth.gov					
NIH SeniorHealth 9000 Rockville Pike Bldg 31	Bethesda	MD	20892	301-496-1752	496-1072
TF: 800-222-2225 ■ *Web:* nihseniorhealth.gov					
Preserve America c/o Advisory Council on Historic Preservation 1100 Pennsylvania Ave NW Suite 803	Washington	DC	20004	202-606-8503	606-8647
Web: www.preserveamerica.gov					
President's Council on Physical Fitness & Sports Dept W 200 Independence Ave SW Rm 738-H	Washington	DC	20201	202-690-9000	690-5211
Web: www.fitness.gov					
Project Safe Neighborhoods Office of Justice Programs 810 7th St NW	Washington	DC	20531	800-458-0786	
Web: www.psn.gov					
PubMed National Library of Medicine 8600 Rockville Pike	Bethesda	MD	20894	301-594-5983	402-1384
Web: www.pubmed.gov					
Recreation.gov Dept of the Interior MS 5258 MIB 1849 C St NW	Washington	DC	20240	202-208-3171	
Web: www.recreation.gov					
Regulations.gov Government Printing Office	Washington	DC	20401	888-293-6498	
Web: www.regulations.gov					
Retired & Senior Volunteer Program (RSVP) c/o Senior Corps 1201 New York Ave NW	Washington	DC	20525	202-606-5000	
TF: 800-424-8867 ■ *Web:* www.seniorcorps.gov/about/programs/rsvp.asp					
Senior Companion Program 2900 Newton St NE	Washington	DC	20018	202-529-8701	832-0127
Web: www.seniorcorps.gov/home/site_map/index.asp					
Senior Corps 1201 New York Ave NW	Washington	DC	20525	202-606-5000	
Web: www.seniorcorps.org					
Taxpayer Advocate Service 1111 Constitution Ave NW	Washington	DC	20224	202-622-6100	622-7854
TF: 877-777-4778 ■ *Web:* www.irs.gov/advocate					
Tobacco Information & Prevention Source (TIPS) National Ctr for Chronic Disease Prevention & Health Promotion 2900 Woodcock Blvd	Atlanta	GA	30341	800-311-3435	
Web: www.cdc.gov/tobacco					
US Coast Guard (USCG) Boating Safety Office 2100 2nd St SW	Washington	DC	20593	202-372-1051	
Web: www.uscgboating.org					
US Geological Survey (USGS) Ask USGS 12201 Sunrise Valley Dr	Reston	VA	20192	888-275-8747	
Web: ask.usgs.gov					
USA Freedom Corps 1600 Pennsylvania Ave NW West Wing	Washington	DC	20500	877-872-2677	
Web: www.usafreedomcorps.gov					
USA.gov Office of Citizen Services & Communications 1800 F St NW Suite G-142	Washington	DC	20405	800-488-3111	
Web: www.usa.gov					
USAJOBS Office of Personnel Management 1900 'E' St NW	Washington	DC	20415	202-606-1800	
Web: www.usajobs.opm.gov					
Veterans Health Administration Gulf War Veterans Information 50 Irving St NW	Washington	DC	20422	202-745-8000	
TF: 800-749-8387 ■ *Web:* www1.va.gov/gulfwar					
Volunteer.Gov/Gov 736 Jackson Place	Washington	DC	20002	877-872-2677	
Web: www.volunteer.gov/gov					
White House Office 1600 Pennsylvania Ave NW	Washington	DC	20500	202-456-1111	
Web: www.whitehouse.gov					
Wi$e Up Women Dept of Labor Women's Bureau 200 Constitution Ave NW	Washington	DC	20210	800-827-5335	
Web: wiseupwomen.tamu.edu					

201 CONTAINERS - METAL (BARRELS, DRUMS, KEGS)

Name / Address	City	State	Zip	Phone	Fax
Actron Steel Inc PO Box 966	Traverse City	MI	49685	231-947-3981	947-2961
Bakerstown Container Corp PO Box 51	Bakerstown	PA	15007	724-443-7255	443-4090
Berenfield Containers Inc PO Box 350	Mason	OH	45040	513-398-1300	398-3457
Web: www.berenfield.com					
Champion Co 400 Harrison St	Springfield	OH	45505	937-324-5681	324-2397
TF Sales: 800-328-0115 ■ *Web:* www.championspd.com					
Champion Container Corp 180 Essex Ave PO Box 90	Avenel	NJ	07001	732-636-6700	855-8663
Web: www.championcontainer.com					
Chicago Steel Container Corp 1846 S Kilbourn Ave	Chicago	IL	60623	773-277-2244	277-1585
Conco Inc 4000 Oaklawn Dr	Louisville	KY	40219	502-969-1333	962-2190
Web: www.conco.org					
Container Research Corp PO Box 159	Glen Riddle	PA	19037	610-459-2160	358-9297
Web: www.crc-flex.com					
CP Louisiana Inc 6000 Jefferson Hwy	Harahan	LA	70123	504-733-6644	733-4412
CSI Fabricated Metal Bins Inc 6910 W Ridge Rd	Fairview	PA	16415	814-474-9353	474-5797
TF: 800-937-9033 ■ *Web:* www.flo-bin.com					
Erie Engineered Products Inc 908 Niagara Falls Blvd	North Tonawanda	NY	14120	716-694-2020	694-4339
Web: www.containers-cases.com					
Evans Industries Inc 1255 Peters Rd	Harvey	LA	70058	504-374-6000	374-6001
TF: 800-749-6012 ■ *Web:* www.evansind.com					
Greif Inc 425 Winter Rd	Delaware	OH	43015	740-549-6000	549-6100
NYSE: GEF ■ *TF:* 800-354-7343 ■ *Web:* www.greif.com					
Hoover Materials Handling Group Inc 2001 Westside Pkwy Suite 155	Alpharetta	GA	30004	770-664-4047	664-2850
TF: 800-391-3561 ■ *Web:* www.hooveribcs.com					
Imperial Industries Inc 505 Industrial Park Ave	Rothschild	WI	54474	715-359-0200	355-5349
TF: 800-558-2945 ■ *Web:* www.imperialind.com					
Industrial Container Services 7152 1st Ave S	Seattle	WA	98108	206-763-2345	763-2699
TF: 800-451-3471 ■ *Web:* www.iconserv.com					
Innovative Fluid Handling Systems Inc 200 E 3rd St	Rock Falls	IL	61071	815-626-1018	626-1438
TF: 800-435-7003 ■ *Web:* www.ifhgroup.com					
Justrite Mfg Co 2454 Dempster St Suite 300	Des Plaines	IL	60016	847-298-9250	298-3429
TF: 800-469-5382 ■ *Web:* www.justritemfg.com					
Lebus International Inc 25 Industrial Blvd PO Box 2352	Longview	TX	75606	903-758-5521	757-7782
Web: www.lebus-intl.com					
Mid-America Steel Drum Co Inc 8570 S Chicago Rd	Oak Creek	WI	53154	414-762-1114	762-1623
Web: www.midamericasteeldrum.com					
Myers Container Corp 5801 Christie Ave Suite 255	Emeryville	CA	94608	510-652-6847	271-6280
TF: 800-228-7269 ■ *Web:* www.myerscontainer.com					
New England Container Co Inc 455 George Washington Hwy	Smithfield	RI	02917	401-231-2100	231-7960
TF: 800-333-3109					
North Coast Container Corp 8806 Crane Ave	Cleveland	OH	44105	216-441-6214	441-6239
Web: www.ncc-corp.com					
Norton Packaging Inc 20670 Cosair Blvd	Hayward	CA	94545	510-786-3445	782-5329
Web: www.nortonpackaging.com					
Packaging Specialties Inc 300 Lake Rd	Medina	OH	44256	330-723-6000	725-8180
Web: www.packspec.com					
Queen City Barrel Co 1937 South St	Cincinnati	OH	45204	513-921-8811	921-3684
Web: www.qcbarrel.com					
Rayfo Inc 15629 Clayton Ave	Rosemount	MN	55068	651-437-4441	437-2272
TF: 800-624-4764					
Russell-Stanley Corp 685 Rt 202/206	Bridgewater	NJ	08807	908-203-9500	203-1940
Web: www.russell-stanley.com					
Self Industries Inc 3491 Mary Taylor Rd	Birmingham	AL	35235	205-655-3284	655-3288
Southline Metal Products Co PO Box 19526	Houston	TX	77224	713-869-4343	869-5650
Spartanburg Steel Products Inc PO Box 6428	Spartanburg	SC	29304	864-585-5216	583-5641
TF: 800-334-6318					
Stackbin Corp 29 Powderhill Rd	Lincoln	RI	02865	401-333-1600	333-1952
TF Sales: 800-333-1603 ■ *Web:* www.stackbin.com					
Stainless Metals Inc 4349 10th St	Long Island City	NY	11101	718-784-1454	784-4719
Web: www.stainlessmetals.com					
Trilla-Nesco Corp 2391 Cassens Dr	Fenton	MO	63026	636-343-7333	326-2891
TF: 800-966-3786 ■ *Web:* www.trilla-nesco.com					

202 CONTAINERS - PLASTICS (DRUMS, CANS, CRATES, BOXES)

Name / Address	City	State	Zip	Phone	Fax
Akro-Mils Inc 250 Seville Rd	Wadsworth	OH	44281	330-336-6621	334-7100
Web: www.akro-mils.com					
Amherst-Merritt International 5565 Red Bird Ctr Dr Suite 150	Dallas	TX	75237	214-339-0753	339-1313
TF: 800-627-7752 ■ *Web:* amherst-merritt.com					
B & R Specialties Inc 2092 Rt 9G	Staatsburg	NY	12580	845-889-4000	889-4002
Web: www.unifuse.com					
Beden-Baugh Products Inc 105 Lisbon Rd	Laurens	SC	29360	864-682-3136	682-9302
TF: 800-679-9419 ■ *Web:* www.naclsolutions.com					
Belco Mfg Co Inc 2303 Taylors Valley Rd	Belton	TX	76513	254-933-9000	939-2644
TF: 800-251-8265 ■ *Web:* www.belco-mfg.com					
Berry Plastics Corp 101 Oakley St	Evansville	IN	47710	812-424-2904	424-0128
TF: 800-234-1930 ■ *Web:* www.berryplastics.com					
Brentwood Industries Inc 610 Morgantown Rd	Reading	PA	19611	610-374-5109	376-6022
Web: www.brentw.com					
Buckhorn Inc 55 W TechneCenter Dr	Milford	OH	45150	513-831-4402	831-5474
TF: 800-543-4454 ■ *Web:* www.buckhorninc.com					
Captive Plastics Inc 251 Circle Dr N	Piscataway	NJ	08854	732-469-7900	271-5200
Web: www.caplas.com					
Case Design Corp 333 School Ln	Telford	PA	18969	215-703-0130	703-0139
TF: 800-847-4176 ■ *Web:* www.casedesigncorp.com					
Champion Container Corp 180 Essex Ave PO Box 90	Avenel	NJ	07001	732-636-6700	855-8663
Web: www.championcontainer.com					
Chem-Tainer Industries Inc 361 Neptune Ave	North Babylon	NY	11704	631-661-8300	661-8209
TF: 800-275-2436 ■ *Web:* www.chemtainer.com					
Comar Inc 1 Comar Pl	Buena	NJ	08310	856-692-6100	692-9251
Web: www.comar.com					
Continental Mfg Co 305 Rock Industrial Pk Dr	Bridgeton	MO	63044	314-656-4301	770-9938
TF: 800-325-1051 ■ *Web:* www.continental-mfg.com					
Custom-Pak Inc 86 16th Ave N	Clinton	IA	52732	563-242-1801	244-5362
Web: www.custom-pak.com					
EarthShell Corp 1301 York Rd Suite 200	Lutherville	MD	21093	410-847-9420	847-9431
Web: www.earthshell.com					
ECS Composites Inc 3560 Rogue River Hwy	Grants Pass	OR	97527	541-476-8871	474-2479
Web: www.ecscase.com					
Fibrenetics Inc 2 Cutters Dock Rd	Woodbridge	NJ	07095	732-636-5670	636-6624
Web: www.fibglass.com					
Fort Recovery Industries Inc 2440 SR-49	Fort Recovery	OH	45846	419-375-4121	375-4150
TF Sales: 800-445-5695 ■ *Web:* www.fortrecoveryindustries.com					
Handley Industries Inc 2101 Brooklyn Rd	Jackson	MI	49203	517-787-8821	787-3946
TF: 800-870-5088 ■ *Web:* www.handleyind.com					
Hardigg Industries Inc 147 N Main St	South Deerfield	MA	01373	413-665-2163	665-4801
TF: 800-542-7344 ■ *Web:* www.hardigg.com					
Hedwin Corp 1600 Roland Heights Ave	Baltimore	MD	21211	410-467-8209	889-5189*
**Fax:* Cust Svc ■ *TF:* 800-638-1012 ■ *Web:* www.hedwin.com					
HGI Skydyne 100 River Rd	Port Jervis	NY	12771	845-856-6655	856-8378
TF: 800-428-2273 ■ *Web:* www.skydyne.com					
Iroquois Products of Chicago 2220 W 56th St	Chicago	IL	60636	773-436-3900	436-4908
TF: 800-453-3355 ■ *Web:* www.iroquoisproducts.com					
Jewel Case Corp 300 Niantic Ave	Providence	RI	02907	401-943-1400	943-1426
TF: 800-441-4447 ■ *Web:* www.jewelcase.com					
Meese Orbitron Dunne Co 4902 State Rd	Ashtabula	OH	44004	440-998-1202	
TF: 800-829-3230 ■ *Web:* www.meeseinc.com					
Menasha Corp 1645 Bergstrom Rd	Neenah	WI	54956	920-751-1000	751-1236
TF: 800-558-5073 ■ *Web:* www.menasha.com					
Molded Fiber Glass Tray Co 6175 US Hwy 6	Linesville	PA	16424	814-683-4500	683-4504
TF Sales: 800-458-6050 ■ *Web:* www.mfgtray.com					
Myers Industries Inc 1293 S Main St	Akron	OH	44301	330-253-5592	761-6156*
NYSE: MYE ■ **Fax:* Acctg ■ *Web:* myersindustries.com					
North America Packaging Inc 4101 Lake Boone Trail Suite 201	Raleigh	NC	27607	919-791-2380	791-2390
Web: www.nampac.com					
ORBIS Corp 1055 Corporate Center Dr	Oconomowoc	WI	53066	262-560-5000	560-5841
TF: 800-999-8683 ■ *Web:* www.orbiscorporation.com					
Owens-Illinois Inc 1 SeaGate	Toledo	OH	43666	419-247-5000	247-7107
NYSE: OI ■ *Web:* www.o-i.com					
Paragon Mfg Co Inc 2001 N 15th Ave	Melrose Park	IL	60160	708-345-1717	345-1721
Web: www.paragonmanufacturing.com					

				Phone	Fax
Plano Molding Co 431 E South St TF: 800-451-2122 ■ Web: www.planomolding.com	Plano	IL	60545	630-552-3111	552-8989
Plas-Tanks Industries Inc 39 Standen Dr Web: www.plastanks.com	Hamilton	OH	45015	513-942-3800	942-3993
Plastic Enterprises Co Inc 401 SE Thomson Dr Web: www.plasticenterprises.com	Lee's Summit	MO	64082	816-246-8200	246-8119
Plastic Forming Co Inc 20 S Bradley Rd TF: 800-732-2060 ■ Web: www.pfccases.com	Woodbridge	CT	06525	203-397-1338	389-0420
Plastic Packaging Corp 1227 Union St TF Cust Svc: 800-342-2011 ■ Web: www.plasticpkg.com	West Springfield	MA	01090	413-785-1553	731-5952
Plastican Inc 196 Industrial Rd PO Box 868 Web: www.plastican.com	Leominster	MA	01453	978-537-4911	466-6073
Plastics Research Corp 1400 S Campus Ave Web: www.prccal.com	Ontario	CA	91761	909-391-2006	391-2205
PNE Inc 7482 Presidents Dr TF: 800-998-2525	Orlando	FL	32809	407-857-3888	857-0900
Rehrig Pacific Co 4010 E 26th St TF: 800-421-6244 ■ Web: www.rehrigpacific.com	Los Angeles	CA	90023	323-262-5145	269-8506
River Bend Industries 2421 16th Ave S TF: 800-365-3070 ■ Web: www.riverbendind.com	Moorhead	MN	56560	218-236-1818	236-6168
Rocket Box Inc 125 E 144th St TF: 800-762-5521 ■ Web: www.rocketbox.com	Bronx	NY	10451	718-292-5370	402-2021
Ropak Corp 10540 Talbert Ave Suite 200-W TF: 800-367-3779 ■ Web: www.ropakcorp.com	Fountain Valley	CA	92708	714-845-2845	845-2846
Rotonics Mfg Inc 17038 S Figueroa St AMEX: RMI ■ Web: www.rotonics.com	Gardena	CA	90248	310-327-5401	323-9567
RPM Industries Inc 26 Aurelius Ave Web: www.rpmindustriesinc.com	Auburn	NY	13021	315-255-1105	252-1167
Schaefer Systems International Inc 10021 Westlake Dr TF: 800-876-6000 ■ Web: www.ssi.schaefer-us.com	Charlotte	NC	28273	704-944-4500	588-1862
Setco Inc 4875 E Hunter Ave Web: www.setcobottle.com	Anaheim	CA	92817	714-777-5200	777-5234
Shaw-Clayton Corp 123 Carlos Dr TF Cust Svc: 800-537-6712 ■ Web: www.shaw-clayton.com	San Rafael	CA	94903	415-472-1522	472-1599
Snyder Industries Inc 4700 Fremont St Web: www.snydernet.com	Lincoln	NE	68504	402-467-5221	465-1210
Specialty Plastic Fabricators Inc 9658 W 196th St TF: 800-747-9509 ■ Web: www.spfinc.com	Mokena	IL	60448	708-479-5501	479-5598
Stack-On Products Co PO Box 489 TF: 800-323-9601 ■ Web: www.stack-on.com	Wauconda	IL	60084	847-526-1611	526-6599
Toter Inc PO Box 5338 TF: 800-424-0422 ■ Web: www.toter.com	Statesville	NC	28687	704-872-8171	878-0734
Tulip Corp 3125 Highland Ave Web: www.tulipcorp.com	Niagara Falls	NY	14305	716-282-1261	285-6075
Tulip Corp 714 E Keefe Ave Web: www.tulipproducts.com	Milwaukee	WI	53212	414-963-3120	962-1825
US Plastic Corp 1390 Newbrecht Rd TF: 800-537-9724 ■ Web: www.usplastic.com	Lima	OH	45801	419-228-2242	228-5034
Xerxes Corp 7901 Xerxes Ave S Suite 201 Web: www.xerxescorp.com	Minneapolis	MN	55431	952-887-1890	887-1870
Zarn LLC 12700 General Dr TF: 800-227-5885 ■ Web: www.zarn.com	Charlotte	NC	28273	704-588-9191	588-5250

203 CONTAINERS - WOOD

SEE ALSO Pallets & Skids p. 2045

				Phone	Fax
Abbot & Abbot Box Corp 37-11 10th St TF: 800-377-0037 ■ Web: www.abbotbox.com	Long Island City	NY	11101	718-392-2600	392-8439
Bluegrass Cooperage Co Inc PO Box 37210 TF: 800-364-6004 ■ Web: www.bluegrasscooperage.com	Louisville	KY	40233	502-368-1626	364-4567
Calpine Containers Inc 3478 Buskirk Ave Suite 336	Pleasant Hill	CA	94523	925-287-8800	279-1272
Carter Mfg Co Inc 346 S Church St	Lake City	SC	29560	843-394-8123	394-3069
Chick Packaging Inc PO Box 80 TF: 800-258-4692 ■ Web: www.chickpackaging.com	Silver Lake	NH	03875	603-367-8857	367-4329
Container Systems Inc 6863 Hwy 56 E	Franklinton	NC	27525	919-496-6133	496-2873
Corbett Package Co PO Box 210 TF: 800-334-0684	Wilmington	NC	28402	910-763-9991	763-3426
Demptos Napa Cooperage 1050 Soscol Ferry Rd Web: www.demptosusa.com	Napa	CA	94558	707-257-2628	257-1622
Elberta Crate & Box Co 606 Dothan Hwy PO Box 760 Web: www.elberta.net	Bainbridge	GA	39818	229-246-2266	246-0387
Flight Form Cases Inc 5950 192nd St NE TF Cust Svc: 800-657-1199 ■ Web: www.flightform.com	Arlington	WA	98223	360-435-6688	435-5144
Franklin Crates Inc PO Box 279 Web: www.franklincrates.org	Micanopy	FL	32667	352-466-3141	466-0708
Georgia Crate & Basket Co Inc 1200 Parnell St TF: 800-841-0001	Thomasville	GA	31792	229-226-2541	226-6117
Greif Inc 425 Winter Rd NYSE: GEF ■ TF: 800-354-7343 ■ Web: www.greif.com	Delaware	OH	43015	740-549-6000	549-6100
Independent Stave Co Inc PO Box 104 Web: www.independentstavecompany.com	Lebanon	MO	65536	417-588-4151	588-3344
Johnston's Trading Inc 11 N Pioneer Ave Suite 101	Woodland	CA	95776	530-661-6152	661-0566
Martin Brothers Container & Timber Products Corp 747 Lindell St PO Box 87 TF: 800-426-6984	Martin	TN	38237	731-587-3171	587-3174
Mautner Enterprises 155 E 76 St TF: 800-628-8637	New York	NY	10021	212-452-1871	
McGraw Box Co Inc PO Box 547	McGraw	NY	13101	607-836-6465	836-6413
Mele Enterprises Inc 2007 Beechgrove Pl TF: 800-635-6353 ■ Web: www.melejewelrybox.com	Utica	NY	13501	315-733-4600	733-3183
Monte Package Co Inc 3752 Riverside Rd TF: 800-653-2807 ■ Web: www.montepkg.com	Riverside	MI	49084	269-849-1722	849-0185
Peacock Crate Factory 225 Cash St TF Orders: 800-666-5647 ■ Web: www.peacocks.com	Jacksonville	TX	75766	903-586-5321	586-7476
Pomona Box Co 301 W Imperial Hwy *Fax Area Code: 310	La Habra	CA	90631	562-697-6728	871-3483*
Quality Woodworking Corp 260 Butler St	Brooklyn	NY	11217	718-875-3437	875-0036
Smalley Package Co Inc 210 1st St	Berryville	VA	22611	540-955-2550	955-4590
Stearnswood Inc PO Box 50 TF: 800-657-0144 ■ Web: www.stearnswood.com	Hutchinson	MN	55350	320-587-2137	587-7646
Texas Basket Co 100 Myrtle Dr TF: 800-657-2200 ■ Web: www.texasbasket.com	Jacksonville	TX	75766	903-586-8014	586-0988
TKV Containers Inc 4582 E Harvey Ave Web: www.tkvcontainers.com	Fresno	CA	93702	559-251-5551	255-8090
Wisconsin Box Co Inc 929 Townline Rd TF: 800-876-6658 ■ Web: www.wisconsinbox.com	Wausau	WI	54402	715-842-2248	842-2240

204 CONTROLS - INDUSTRIAL PROCESS

				Phone	Fax
ADA-ES Inc 8100 Southpark Way Suite B NASDAQ: ADES ■ TF: 888-822-8617 ■ Web: www.adaes.com	Littleton	CO	80120	303-734-1727	734-0330
ADS Corp 4940 Research Dr TF: 800-633-7246 ■ Web: www.adsenv.com	Huntsville	AL	35805	256-430-3366	430-6633
AeroControlex Group 313 Gillett St Web: www.aerocontrolex.com	Painesville	OH	44077	440-352-6182	354-2912
Alpha Technologies Services LLC 2689 Wingate Ave TF: 800-356-9886 ■ Web: www.alpha-technologies.com	Akron	OH	44314	330-745-1641	848-7326
AMETEK Automation & Process Technologies 1080 N Crooks Rd TF: 800-635-0289 ■ Web: www.ametekapt.com	Clawson	MI	48017	248-435-0700	435-8120
AMETEK Power Instruments 50 Fordham Rd *Fax: Cust Svc ■ Web: www.ametekpower.com	Wilmington	MA	01887	978-988-4101	988-4944*
AMETEK Power Instruments Rochester Instruments Products Div 255 N Union St	Rochester	NY	14605	585-263-7700	262-4777
AMETEK Process & Analytical Instruments Process Instruments Div 455 Corporate Blvd Web: www.ametekpi.com	Newark	DE	19702	302-456-4400	456-4444
AMETEK Process & Analytical Instruments THERMOX Div 150 Freeport Rd Web: www.thermox.com	Pittsburgh	PA	15238	412-828-9040	826-0399
Amot Controls Corp 8824 Fallbrook Dr Web: www.amotusa.com	Houston	TX	77064	281-940-1800	668-8808
Anderson Instrument Co 156 Auriesville Rd TF: 800-833-0081 ■ Web: www.andinst.com	Fultonville	NY	12072	518-922-5315	922-8997
Andros Inc 870 Harbour Way S Web: www.andros.com	Richmond	CA	94804	510-837-3500	837-3600
Athena Controls Inc 5145 Campus Dr TF: 800-782-6776	Plymouth Meeting	PA	19462	610-828-2490	828-7084
Automation Products Group Inc 1025 W 1700 N TF: 888-525-7300 ■ Web: www.apgsensors.com	Logan	UT	84321	435-753-7300	753-7490
Azonix Corp 900 Middlesex Tpke Bldg 6 TF: 800-967-5558 ■ Web: www.azonix.com	Billerica	MA	01821	978-670-6300	670-8855
Bacharach Inc 621 Hunt Valley Cir TF: 800-736-4666 ■ Web: www.bacharach-inc.com	New Kensington	PA	15068	724-334-5000	334-5001
Barksdale Inc 3211 Fruitland Ave TF: 800-835-1060 ■ Web: www.barksdale.com	Los Angeles	CA	90058	323-589-6181	589-3463
Blue-White Industries Ltd 5300 Business Dr Web: www.bluwhite.com	Huntington Beach	CA	92649	714-893-8529	894-9492
Bristol Babcock Inc 1100 Buckingham St TF: 800-395-5497 ■ Web: www.bristolbabcock.com	Watertown	CT	06795	860-945-2200	945-2213
Brookfield Engineering Lab Inc 11 Commerce Blvd TF: 800-628-8139 ■ Web: www.brookfieldengineering.com	Middleboro	MA	02346	508-946-6200	946-6262
Buhler Inc 13105 12th Ave N Web: www.buhlergroup.com/us	Plymouth	MN	55441	763-847-9900	847-9911
Campbell Scientific Inc 815 W 1800 North Web: www.campbellsci.com	Logan	UT	84321	435-753-2342	750-9540
Compressor Controls Corp 4725 121st St Web: www.cccglobal.com	Des Moines	IA	50323	515-270-0857	270-1331
Conax Buffalo Technologies LLC 2300 Walden Ave TF: 800-223-2389 ■ Web: www.conaxbuffalo.com	Buffalo	NY	14225	716-684-4500	684-7433
Cooper Atkins Corp 33 Reeds Gap Rd TF Sales: 800-835-5011 ■ Web: www.cooperinstrument.com	Middlefield	CT	06455	860-349-3473	349-8994
CPM Beta Raven 40 S Corporate Hills Dr *Fax Area Code: 636 ■ Web: www.betaraven.com	Saint Charles	MO	63301	314-291-4504	255-0299*
Crane Co Dynalco Controls Div 3690 NW 53rd St TF: 800-368-6666 ■ Web: www.dynalco.com	Fort Lauderdale	FL	33309	954-739-4300	484-3376
Custom Control Sensors Inc 21111 Plummer St Web: www.ccsdualsnap.com	Chatsworth	CA	91311	818-341-4610	709-0426
Custom Sensors & Technologies 14501 Princeton Avew Web: www.cst.schneider-electric.com	Moorpark	CA	93021	805-552-3599	552-3577
Daniel Measurement & Control Inc 11100 Brittmoore Park Dr PO Box 19097 Web: www.emersonprocess.com/daniel/	Houston	TX	77224	713-467-6000	827-3880
Davis Inotek Instruments LLC 4701 Mt Hope Dr Suite J TF: 800-358-5545 ■ Web: www.davis.com	Baltimore	MD	21215	410-358-3900	358-0252
DICKEY-john Corp 5200 Dickey-john Rd TF: 800-637-2952 ■ Web: www.dickey-john.com	Auburn	IL	62615	217-438-3371	438-6012
Dickson Co 930 S Westwood Ave TF: 800-323-2448 ■ Web: www.dicksonweb.com	Addison	IL	60101	630-543-3747	543-0498
Dresser Instruments 250 E Main St Web: www.dresserinstruments.com	Stratford	CT	06614	203-378-8281	385-0357
Dwyer Instruments Inc 102 Indiana Hwy 212 Web: www.dwyer-inst.com	Michigan City	IN	46360	219-879-8000	872-9057
Dynalco Controls Div Crane Co 3690 NW 53rd St TF: 800-368-6666 ■ Web: www.dynalco.com	Fort Lauderdale	FL	33309	954-739-4300	484-3376
Emerson Process Management 8100 W Florissant Bldg K-Annex PO Box 36911 Web: www.emersonprocess.com	Saint Louis	MO	63136	314-553-1900	553-1880
Encoder Products Co 464276 Hwy 95 S PO box 249 TF: 800-366-5412 ■ Web: www.encoderprod.com	Sagle	ID	83860	208-263-8541	263-0541
Endress+Hauser Inc 2350 Endress Pl TF: 800-428-4344 ■ Web: www.us.endress.com	Greenwood	IN	46143	317-535-7138	535-8498
Environmental Systems Corp 200 Tech Center Dr Web: www.envirosys.com	Knoxville	TN	37912	865-688-7900	687-8977
Environmental Systems Products Inc 11 Kripes Rd TF: 800-446-4708 ■ Web: www.environmental-systems.com	East Granby	CT	06026	860-653-0081	392-2105
Fairchild Industrial Products Co 3920 West Point Blvd *Fax: Sales ■ TF: 800-423-1093 ■ Web: www.fairchildproducts.com	Winston-Salem	NC	27103	336-659-3400	659-9323*
Fast Heat Inc 776 Oaklawn Ave TF: 800-982-4328 ■ Web: www.fastheat.com	Elmhurst	IL	60126	630-833-5400	833-2040
Fluid Components International 1755 La Costa Meadows Dr TF: 800-863-8703 ■ Web: www.fluidcomponents.com	San Marcos	CA	92078	760-744-6950	736-6250
Forney Corp 3405 Wiley Post Rd TF Cust Svc: 800-356-7740 ■ Web: www.forneycorp.com	Carrollton	TX	75006	972-458-6100	458-6650
FW Murphy 5311 S 122nd East Ave PO Box 470248 Web: www.fwmurphy.com	Tulsa	OK	74147	918-317-4100	317-4266
GE Fanuc Automation Corp 2500 Austin Dr TF Cust Svc: 800-432-7521 ■ Web: www.gefanuc.com	Charlottesville	VA	22911	434-978-5000	
GE Infrastructure Sensing 1100 Technology Park Dr Web: www.gesensing.com	Billerica	MA	01821	978-437-1000	437-1031
Gems Sensors Inc 1 Cowles Rd TF: 800-378-1600 ■ Web: www.gemssensors.com	Plainville	CT	06062	860-747-3000	747-4244
Harco Laboratories Inc 186 Cedar St Web: www.harcolabs.com	Branford	CT	06405	203-483-3700	483-0391
Hart Scientific Inc 799 E Utah Valley Dr TF: 800-438-4278 ■ Web: www.hartscientific.com	American Fork	UT	84003	801-763-1600	763-1010
Heraeus Electro-Nite Co 1 Summit Sq Suite 100 Web: www.electro-nite.com	Langhorne	PA	19047	215-464-4200	860-6657
HO Trerice Co 12950 W Eight-Mile Rd TF: 888-873-7423 ■ Web: www.hotrericeco.com	Oak Park	MI	48237	248-399-8000	399-7246

Phone Fax

Honeywell ACS 11 W Spring St ... Freeport IL 61032 815-235-5500
Web: www.honeywell.com/acs
Honeywell Automation & Control Solutions 11 W Spring St ... Freeport IL 61032 815-235-5500
Web: www.honeywell.com/acs
HSQ Technology 26227 Research Rd ... Hayward CA 94545 510-259-1334 259-1391
TF: 800-486-6684 ■ *Web:* www.hsq.com
Industrial Scientific Corp 1001 Oakdale Rd ... Oakdale PA 15071 412-788-4353 788-8353
TF: 800-338-3287 ■ *Web:* www.indsci.com
INFICON Inc 2 Technology Pl ... East Syracuse NY 13057 315-434-1100 437-3803
Web: www.inficon.com
Isco Inc 4700 Superior St PO Box 82531 ... Lincoln NE 68501 402-464-0231 465-3022*
**Fax:* Cust Svc ■ *TF:* 800-228-4250 ■ *Web:* www.isco.com
ITT Conoflow 5154 Hwy 78 PO Box 768 ... Saint George SC 29477 843-563-9281 563-2131*
**Fax:* Cust Svc ■ *Web:* www.ittconoflow.com
ITT Fluid Technology Corp
10 Mountainview Rd 3rd Fl ... Upper Saddle River NJ 07458 201-760-9800 760-9692
Web: www.ittfluidtechnology.com/home.html
ITT Industries Inc 4 W Red Oak Ln ... White Plains NY 10604 914-641-2000 696-2950
NYSE: ITT ■ *Web:* www.itt.com
K-Tron International Inc Rts 55 & 553 ... Pitman NJ 08071 856-589-0500 582-7968
NASDAQ: KTII ■ *TF:* 800-355-8766 ■ *Web:* www.ktron.com
Kinetics Group Inc 33225 Western Ave ... Union City CA 94587 510-675-6000 675-6187
Web: www.kineticsgroup.com
Kistler-Morse Corp 150 Venture Blvd ... Spartanburg SC 29306 864-574-2763 574-8063
TF: 800-426-9010 ■ *Web:* www.kistlermorse.com
Lake Shore Cryotronics 575 McCorkle Blvd ... Westerville OH 43082 614-891-2243 818-1600
TF: 800-394-2243 ■ *Web:* www.lakeshore.com
LaMotte Co 802 Washington Ave ... Chestertown MD 21620 410-778-3100 778-6394
TF: 800-344-3100 ■ *Web:* www.lamotte.com
Linear Laboratories 42025 Osgood Rd ... Fremont CA 94539 510-226-0488 226-1112
Web: www.linearlabs.com
Luxtron Corp 3033 Scott Blvd ... Santa Clara CA 95054 408-727-1600 727-1677
Web: www.luxtron.com
Magnetrol International Inc 5300 Belmont Rd ... Downers Grove IL 60515 630-969-4000 969-9489
TF: 800-624-8765 ■ *Web:* www.magnetrol.com
Mahr Federal Inc 1144 Eddy St ... Providence RI 02905 401-784-3100 784-3251
TF Orders: 800-343-2050 ■ *Web:* www.mahrfederal.com
Marsh Bellofram Corp 8019 Ohio River Blvd ... Newell WV 26050 304-387-1200 387-1212
TF: 800-727-5646 ■ *Web:* www.marshbellofram.com
Maxitrol Co 23555 Telegraph Rd PO Box 2230 ... Southfield MI 48034 248-356-1400 356-0829
Web: www.maxitrol.com
McCrometer Inc 3255 W Stetson Ave ... Hemet CA 92545 951-652-6811 652-3078
TF: 800-220-2279 ■ *Web:* www.mccrometer.com
Mercury Instruments Inc 3940 Virginia Ave ... Cincinnati OH 45227 513-272-1111 272-0211
TF: 800-642-4629 ■ *Web:* www.mercuryinstruments.com
Metron Inc 1505 W 3rd Ave ... Denver CO 80223 303-592-1903 534-1947
Web: www.metroninc.com
Metrosonics 1060 Corporate Center Dr ... Oconomowoc WI 53066 262-567-9157 567-4047
TF: 800-245-0779 ■ *Web:* www.metrosonics.com
Micro Motion Inc 7070 Winchester Cir ... Boulder CO 80301 303-530-8400 530-8242
Web: www.emersonprocess.com/micromotion
Mikron Infrared Inc 16 Thornton Rd ... Oakland NJ 07436 201-405-0900 405-0090
NASDAQ: MIKR ■ *TF:* 800-631-0176 ■ *Web:* www.mikroninfrared.com
Minco Products Inc 7300 Commerce Ln NE ... Minneapolis MN 55432 763-571-3121 571-0927*
**Fax:* Sales ■ *Web:* www.minco.com
MKS Instruments Inc 90 Industrial Way ... Wilmington MA 01887 978-284-4000 284-4088
NASDAQ: MKSI ■ *TF:* 800-227-8766 ■ *Web:* www.mksinst.com
Mocon Inc 7500 Boone Ave N Suite 111 ... Minneapolis MN 55428 763-493-6370 493-6358
NASDAQ: MOCO ■ *Web:* www.mocon.com
Moore Industries International Inc 16650 Schoenborn St ... North Hills CA 91343 818-894-7111 891-2816
TF: 800-999-2900 ■ *Web:* www.miinet.com
NDC Infrared Engineering 5314 N Irwindale Ave ... Irwindale CA 91706 626-960-3300 939-3870
Web: www.ndc.com
Norwich Aero Products Inc 50 O'Hara Dr ... Norwich NY 13815 607-336-7636 336-2610
Web: www.norwichaero.com
NRD LLC 2937 Alt Blvd PO Box 310 ... Grand Island NY 14072 716-773-7634 773-7744
TF: 800-525-8076 ■ *Web:* www.nrdstaticcontrol.com
Omega Engineering Inc 1 Omega Dr PO Box 4047 ... Stamford CT 06907 203-359-1660 359-7700*
**Fax:* Cust Svc ■ *TF:* 800-826-6342 ■ *Web:* www.omega.com
OPW Fuel Management Systems 6900 Santa Fe Dr ... Hodgkins IL 60525 708-485-4200 485-7137
Web: www.opwfms.com
Parker Climate & Industrial Controls Group
6035 Parkland Blvd ... Cleveland OH 44124 216-896-3000 896-4007
Web: www.parker.com/cig
Parker Hannifin Corp Veriflo Div 250 Canal Blvd ... Richmond CA 94804 510-235-9590 232-7396
TF: 800-962-4074 ■ *Web:* www.parker.com/veriflodivision
Portage Electric Products Inc 7700 Freedom Ave NW ... North Canton OH 44720 330-499-2727 499-1853
TF: 888-464-7374 ■ *Web:* www.pepiusa.com
Porter Instrument Co Inc 245 Township Line Rd PO Box 907 ... Hatfield PA 19440 215-723-4000 723-2199
TF: 800-457-2001 ■ *Web:* www.porterinstrument.com
Potter Electric Signal Co Inc 2081 Craig Rd ... Saint Louis MO 63146 314-878-4321 878-7264
TF: 800-325-3936 ■ *Web:* www.pottersignal.com
Precision Energy Services 500 Winscott Rd ... Fort Worth TX 76126 817-249-7200 249-7222
TF: 800-669-9326 ■ *Web:* www.precisiondrilling.com
Pressure Systems Inc 34 Research Dr ... Hampton VA 23666 757-865-1243 766-2644
TF: 800-678-7226 ■ *Web:* www.pressuresystems.com
Projects Inc 65 Sequin Dr PO box 190 ... Glastonbury CT 06033 860-633-4615 633-2231
Web: www.projectsinc.com
Pyromation Inc 5211 Industrial Rd ... Fort Wayne IN 46825 260-484-2580 482-6805
Web: www.pyromation.com
Qualitrol Co LLC 1385 Fairport Rd ... Fairport NY 14450 585-586-1515 377-0220
Web: www.qualitrolcorp.com
Quest Technologies Inc 1060 Corporate Center Dr ... Oconomowoc WI 53066 262-567-9101 567-4047
TF: 800-245-0779 ■ *Web:* www.quest-technologies.com
Racine Federated Inc 8635 Washington Ave ... Racine WI 53406 262-639-6770 639-2267
Web: www.racinefederated.com
RAE Systems 3775 N 1st St ... San Jose CA 95134 408-952-8200 952-8480
AMEX: RAE ■ *TF:* 877-723-2878 ■ *Web:* www.raesystems.com
Raven Industries Inc 205 E 6th St ... Sioux Falls SD 57104 605-336-2750 335-0268
NASDAQ: RAVN ■ *TF:* 800-227-2836 ■ *Web:* www.ravenind.com
Raytheon Commercial Infrared 13532 N Central Expy MS 37 ... Dallas TX 75243 972-344-4000 344-4004
TF: 800-990-3275 ■ *Web:* www.raytheoninfrared.com
Raytheon Network Centric Systems 2501 W University ... McKinney TX 75071 972-952-2000
Renco Encoders Inc 26 Coromar Dr ... Goleta CA 93117 805-968-1525 685-7965
TF: 800-248-6044 ■ *Web:* www.renco.com
Research Inc 7128 Shady Oak Rd ... Eden Prairie MN 55344 952-941-3300 941-3628
Web: www.researchinc.com
Robertshaw Industrial Products 1602 Mustang Dr ... Maryville TN 37801 865-981-3100 981-3168
TF: 800-228-7429 ■ *Web:* www.robertshawindustrial.com
Rochester Gauges Inc of Texas 11616 Harry Hines Blvd ... Dallas TX 75229 972-241-2161 620-1403
TF: 800-821-1829 ■ *Web:* www.rochestergauges.com
Rochester Instruments Products Div AMETEK Power Instruments 255 N Union St ... Rochester NY 14605 585-263-7700 262-4777
Ronan Engineering Co 21200 Oxnard St ... Woodland Hills CA 91367 818-883-5211 992-6435
TF: 800-327-6626 ■ *Web:* www.ronan.com
Roper Industries Inc 2160 Satellite Blvd Suite 200 ... Duluth GA 30097 770-495-5100 495-5150
NYSE: ROP ■ *Web:* www.roperind.com

Phone Fax

Rosemount Analytical Inc Process Analytical Div
6565 P Davis Industrial Pkwy ... Solon OH 44139 330-682-9010 684-4434
TF: 800-433-6076 ■ *Web:* www.emersonprocess.com/proanalytic
Rosemount Analytical Inc Uniloc Div 2400 Barranca Pkwy ... Irvine CA 92606 949-863-1181 474-7250
TF: 800-854-8257 ■ *Web:* www.emersonprocess.com/raihome/liquid
Rosemount Inc 8200 Market Blvd ... Chanhassen MN 55317 952-941-5560 949-7999*
**Fax:* Mktg ■ *TF Cust Svc:* 800-999-9307 ■ *Web:* www.rosemount.com
RTP Corp 1834 SW 2nd St ... Pompano Beach FL 33069 954-974-5500 975-9815
Web: www.rtpcorp.com
Sabina Motors & Controls Inc 1440 N Burton Pl ... Anaheim CA 92806 714-956-0480 956-0486
Web: www.sabinamotors.com
Schmitt Industries Inc 2765 NW Nicolai St ... Portland OR 97210 503-227-7908 223-1258
NASDAQ: SMIT ■ *Web:* www.schmitt-ind.com
Schneider Automation Inc 1 High St ... North Andover MA 01845 978-794-0800 975-9400
TF: 800-468-5342 ■ *Web:* www.modicon.com
Scully Signal Co 70 Industrial Way ... Wilmington MA 01887 617-692-8600 692-8620
TF: 800-272-8559 ■ *Web:* www.scully.com
Sensidyne Inc 16333 Bay Vista Dr ... Clearwater FL 33760 727-530-3602 539-0550
TF: 800-451-9444 ■ *Web:* www.sensidyne.com
Sierra Instruments Inc 5 Harris Ct Bldg L ... Monterey CA 93940 831-373-0200 373-4402
TF: 800-866-0200 ■ *Web:* www.sierrainstruments.com
Signet Scientific Co Inc 3401 Aero Jet Ave ... El Monte CA 91731 626-571-2770 573-2057
Web: www.gfsignet.com
SJE-Rhombus 22650 County Hwy 6 PO Box 1708 ... Detroit Lakes MN 56502 218-847-1317 847-4617
TF: 800-746-6287 ■ *Web:* www.sjerhombus.com
SOR Inc 14685 W 105th St ... Lenexa KS 66215 913-888-2630 888-0767
TF: 800-676-6794 ■ *Web:* www.sorinc.com
Sparton Electronics 8500 Bluewater Rd NW ... Albuquerque NM 87121 505-892-5300 892-5515
TF: 800-772-7866 ■ *Web:* www.sparton.com
Spectronics Corp 956 Brush Hollow Rd ... Westbury NY 11590 800-274-8888 491-6868
Web: www.spectroline.com
Spirax Sarco Inc 1150 Northpoint Blvd ... Blythewood SC 29016 803-714-2000 714-2222
TF: 800-883-4411 ■ *Web:* www.spiraxsarco.com/us
Sterling Inc 2900 S 160th St ... New Berlin WI 53151 262-641-8600 641-8654
TF Cust Svc: 800-783-7835 ■ *Web:* www.sterlco.com
Sutron Corp 21300 Ridgetop Cir ... Sterling VA 20166 703-406-2800 406-2801
NASDAQ: STRN ■ *Web:* www.sutron.com
Taylor Precision Products LLC 2311 W 22nd St Suite 200 ... Oak Brook IL 60523 630-954-1250 954-1275
TF: 800-289-0944 ■ *Web:* www.taylorusa.com
Teledyne Advanced Pollution Instrumentation
9480 Carroll Park Dr ... San Diego CA 92121 858-657-9800 657-9818
Web: www.teledyne-api.com
Teledyne Monitor Labs 35 Inverness Dr E ... Englewood CO 80112 303-792-3300 799-4853
TF: 800-422-1499 ■ *Web:* www.monitorlabs.com
Test Automation & Controls 1036 Destrehan Ave ... Harvey LA 70058 504-371-3000 371-3001
TF: 800-861-6792 ■ *Web:* www.test-us.com
Thermo Electric Co Inc 109 N 5th St ... Saddle Brook NJ 07663 201-843-5800 843-4568
TF Sales: 800-766-4020 ■ *Web:* www.thermo-electric-direct.com
Thermo Fisher Scientific 81 Wyman St PO Box 9046 ... Waltham MA 02454 781-622-1000 622-1207
NYSE: TMO ■ *TF:* 800-678-5599 ■ *Web:* www.thermofisher.com
Thermometrics Inc 808 US Hwy 1 ... Edison NJ 08817 732-287-2870 287-8847
TF: 800-246-7019 ■ *Web:* www.thermometrics.com
THERMOX Div AMETEK Process & Analytical Instruments
150 Freeport Rd ... Pittsburgh PA 15238 412-828-9040 826-0399
Web: www.thermox.com
Transcat Inc 35 Vantage Point Dr ... Rochester NY 14624 585-352-7777 395-0543*
NASDAQ: TRNS ■ **Fax Area Code:* 800 ■ *TF:* 800-828-1470 ■ *Web:* www.transcat.com
Trerice HO Co 12950 W Eight-Mile Rd ... Oak Park MI 48237 248-399-8000 399-7246
TF: 888-873-7423 ■ *Web:* www.hotrericeco.com
Troxler Electronic Laboratories Inc
3008 Cornwallis Rd PO Box 12057 ... Research Triangle Park NC 27709 919-549-8661 549-0761
TF: 877-876-9537 ■ *Web:* www.troxlerlabs.com
TSI Inc 500 Cardigan Rd ... Shoreview MN 55126 651-483-0900 490-3824
TF: 800-874-2811 ■ *Web:* www.tsi.com
Tyco Thermal Controls 2415 Bay Rd ... Redwood City CA 94063 650-216-1526 827-5703*
**Fax Area Code:* 800 ■ *TF:* 800-545-6258 ■ *Web:* www.tycothermal.com
Uniloc Div Rosemount Analytical Inc 2400 Barranca Pkwy ... Irvine CA 92606 949-863-1181 474-7250
TF: 800-854-8257 ■ *Web:* www.emersonprocess.com/raihome/liquid
United Electric Controls Co 180 Dexter Ave ... Watertown MA 02472 617-926-1000 926-2568
TF: 800-545-1416 ■ *Web:* www.ueonline.com
Veeder-Root 125 Powder Forest Dr ... Simsbury CT 06070 860-651-2700 651-2704
TF: 800-879-0301 ■ *Web:* www.veeder.com
Venture Measurement Co LLC 150 Venture Blvd ... Spartanburg SC 29306 864-574-8960 578-7308
Web: www.venturemeasurement.com
Veriflo Div Parker Hannifin Corp 250 Canal Blvd ... Richmond CA 94804 510-235-9590 232-7396
TF: 800-962-4074 ■ *Web:* www.parker.com/veriflodivision
Wika Instrument Corp 1000 Wiegand Blvd ... Lawrenceville GA 30043 770-513-8200 338-5118
TF: 888-945-2872 ■ *Web:* www.ewika.com
Winland Electronics Inc 1950 Excel Dr ... Mankato MN 56001 507-625-7231 387-2488
AMEX: WEX ■ *TF:* 800-635-4269 ■ *Web:* www.winland.com
Yokogawa Corp of America 2 Dart Rd ... Newnan GA 30265 770-253-7000 254-0928
TF: 800-888-6400 ■ *Web:* www.yokogawa.com/us
YSI Inc 1700-1725 Brannum Ln ... Yellow Springs OH 45387 937-767-7241 767-9320
TF Cust Svc: 800-765-4974 ■ *Web:* www.ysi.com

205 CONTROLS - TEMPERATURE - RESIDENTIAL & COMMERCIAL

Phone Fax

APCOM Inc 125 Southeast Pkwy ... Franklin TN 37064 615-794-5574 791-0660
TF: 800-251-3535 ■ *Web:* www.apcom-inc.com
Automated Logic Corp 1150 Roberts Blvd NW ... Kennesaw GA 30144 770-429-3000 429-3001
Web: www.automatedlogic.com
Azonix Corp 900 Middlesex Tpke Bldg 6 ... Billerica MA 01821 978-670-6300 670-8855
TF: 800-967-5558 ■ *Web:* www.azonix.com
CAPP/USA 201 Marple Ave ... Clifton Heights PA 19018 610-394-1100 237-3292*
**Fax Area Code:* 800 ■ **Fax:* Sales ■ *TF:* 800-356-8000 ■ *Web:* www.cappusa.com
Channel Products Inc 7100 Wilson Mills Rd ... Chesterland OH 44026 440-423-0113 423-1502
Web: www.channelproducts.com
Columbus Electric Mfg Co PO Box 4973 ... Johnson City TN 37602 423-477-4131 477-0084
TF: 800-682-3398
Cooper Atkins Corp 33 Reeds Gap Rd ... Middlefield CT 06455 860-349-3473 349-8994
TF Sales: 800-835-5011 ■ *Web:* www.cooperinstrument.com
DeltaTRAK Inc PO Box 398 ... Pleasanton CA 94566 925-249-2250 249-2251
TF: 800-962-6776 ■ *Web:* www.deltatrak.com
Emerson Climate Technologies - Retail Solutions
1640 Airport Rd NW Suite 104 ... Kennesaw GA 30144 770-425-2724 425-9319
TF: 800-829-2724 ■ *Web:* www.emersonretailsolutions.com
Emerson Electric Co White-Rodgers Div
8100 W Florissant Ave ... Saint Louis MO 63136 314-553-3600 553-3706
Web: www.white-rodgers.com
Eurotherm Controls Inc 741-F Miller Dr ... Leesburg VA 20175 703-443-0000 669-1300
Web: www.eurotherm.com

Phone | Fax

FAST (Food Automation-Service Techniques Inc)
905 Honeyspot Rd ... Stratford CT 06615 203-377-4414 377-8187
TF: 800-327-8766 ■ *Web:* www.fastinc.com

Food Automation-Service Techniques Inc (FAST)
905 Honeyspot Rd ... Stratford CT 06615 203-377-4414 377-8187
TF: 800-327-8766 ■ *Web:* www.fastinc.com

Hallcrest Inc 1820 Pickwick Ln ... Glenview IL 60026 847-998-8580 998-6866
TF: 800-527-1419 ■ *Web:* www.hallcrest.com

HSQ Technology 26227 Research Rd ... Hayward CA 94545 510-259-1334 259-1391
TF: 800-486-6684 ■ *Web:* www.hsq.com

Invensys Controls 191 E North Ave ... Carol Stream IL 60188 630-260-3400
Web: www.icca.invensys.com

Ircon Inc 7300 N Natchez Ave ... Niles IL 60714 847-967-5151 647-0948
TF: 800-323-7660 ■ *Web:* www.ircon.com

ITT McDonnell & Miller 8200 N Austin Ave ... Morton Grove IL 60053 847-966-3700 983-5954
Web: www.mcdonnellmiller.com

Johnson Controls Inc 5757 N Green Bay Ave ... Milwaukee WI 53209 414-524-1200 524-3232
NYSE: JCI ■ *TF:* 800-972-8040 ■ *Web:* www.johnsoncontrols.com

Johnson Controls Systems 9410 Bunsen Pkwy Suite 100-B ... Louisville KY 40220 502-671-7300 499-2135
TF: 800-765-7773 ■ *Web:* www.johnsoncontrols.com

Kidde-Fenwal Inc 400 Main St ... Ashland MA 01721 508-881-2000 881-6729
TF: 800-872-6527 ■ *Web:* www.kidde-fenwal.com

KMC Controls Inc 19476 Industrial Dr ... New Paris IN 46553 574-831-5250 831-5252
TF: 877-444-5622 ■ *Web:* www.kmc-controls.com

Liebert Corp 1050 Dearborn Dr ... Columbus OH 43085 614-888-0246 841-6022
TF Tech Supp: 800-543-2778 ■ *Web:* www.liebert.com

Nexus Custom Electronics Inc PO Box 250 ... Brandon VT 05733 802-247-6811 247-3946
Web: www.nexuscei.com

Novar Controls Corp 6060 Rockside Woods Blvd Suite 400 ... Cleveland OH 44118 216-682-1600
TF: 800-348-1235 ■ *Web:* www.novarcontrols.com

PECO Mfg Co Inc PO Box 82189 ... Portland OR 97282 503-233-6401 233-6407
Web: www.peco-sunne.com

Phoenix Controls Corp 75 Discovery Way ... Acton MA 01720 978-795-1285 795-1112
Web: www.phoenixcontrols.com

Portage Electric Products Inc 7700 Freedom Ave NW ... North Canton OH 44720 330-499-2727 499-1853
TF: 888-464-7374 ■ *Web:* www.pepiusa.com

Residential Control Systems
11460 Sunrise Gold Cir Suite A ... Rancho Cordova CA 95742 916-635-6784 635-7668
Web: www.resconsys.com

Robinair Div SPX Corp 655 Eisenhower Dr ... Owatonna MN 55060 507-455-7000
TF: 800-628-6496 ■ *Web:* www.robinair.com

Siemens Building Technologies Inc 1000 Deerfield Pkwy ... Buffalo Grove IL 60089 847-215-1000 215-1093
TF: 800-877-7545 ■ *Web:* www.us.sbt.siemens.com

SPX Corp Robinair Div 655 Eisenhower Dr ... Owatonna MN 55060 507-455-7000
TF: 800-628-6496 ■ *Web:* www.robinair.com

Standard-Thomson Corp 152 Grove St ... Waltham MA 02453 781-894-7310 894-2235

TAC Americas 1650 W Crosby Rd ... Carrollton TX 75006 972-323-1111 242-0026
TF: 800-274-5551 ■ *Web:* www.tac-global.com

Taylor Precision Products LLC 2311 W 22nd St Suite 200 ... Oak Brook IL 60523 630-954-1250 954-1275
TF: 800-289-0944 ■ *Web:* www.taylorusa.com

Therm-O-Disc Inc 1320 S Main St ... Mansfield OH 44907 419-525-8500 525-8344*
**Fax:* Sales ■ *Web:* www.tod.com

WAKO Electronics 3600 Chamberlain Ln Suite 500 ... Louisville KY 40241 502-429-8866 429-8869
Web: wako-usa.com

Watlow Electric Mfg Co 12001 Lackland Rd ... Saint Louis MO 63146 314-878-4600 878-6814
TF: 800-492-8569 ■ *Web:* www.watlow.com

Watlow Winona 1241 Bundy Blvd ... Winona MN 55987 507-454-5300 452-4507
TF: 800-833-7492 ■ *Web:* www.watlow.com

Weiss Instruments Inc 905 Waverly Ave ... Holtsville NY 11742 631-207-1200 207-0900
Web: www.weissinstruments.com

White-Rodgers Div Emerson Electric Co 8100 W Florissant Ave ... Saint Louis MO 63136 314-553-3600 553-3706
Web: www.white-rodgers.com

206 CONTROLS & RELAYS - ELECTRICAL

Phone | Fax

ABB SSAC 8242 Loop Rd ... Baldwinsville NY 13027 315-638-1300 638-0333
TF Tech Supp: 800-377-7722 ■ *Web:* www.ssac.com

Alcoa Fujikura Ltd 830 Crescent Ctr Dr Suite 600 ... Franklin TN 37067 615-778-6000 778-5927
TF: 800-627-7854 ■ *Web:* www.alcoa.com

Allied Controls Inc 150 E Aurora St ... Waterbury CT 06708 203-757-4200 757-4202
TF: 800-648-8871 ■ *Web:* www.alliedcontrols.com

American Relays Inc 10306 Norwalk Blvd ... Santa Fe Springs CA 90670 562-944-0447 944-0590
Web: www.americanrelays.com

American Zettler Inc 75 Columbia ... Aliso Viejo CA 92656 949-831-5000 831-8642
Web: www.azettler.com

AMETEK National Controls Corp 1725 Western Dr ... West Chicago IL 60185 630-231-5900 231-1377
TF: 800-323-2593 ■ *Web:* www.nationalcontrols.com

AMX Corp 3000 Research Dr ... Richardson TX 75082 469-624-8000 624-7153
TF: 800-222-0193 ■ *Web:* www.amx.com

Anaheim Automation 910 E Orangefair Ln ... Anaheim CA 92801 714-992-6990 992-0471
TF Sales: 800-345-9401 ■ *Web:* www.anaheimautomation.com

Arens Controls Co LLC 855 Commerce Pkwy ... Carpentersville IL 60110 847-844-4700 844-4790
Web: www.arenscontrols.com

Basler Electric Co Rt 143 Box 269 ... Highland IL 62249 618-654-2341 654-2351
Web: www.basler.com

Bright Image Corp 4900 Harrison St ... Hillside IL 60162 708-449-5656 449-1155
TF: 800-733-5656 ■ *Web:* www.touchnglow.com

Cleveland Motion Controls Inc 7550 Hub Pkwy ... Cleveland OH 44125 216-524-8800 642-2199
TF: 800-321-8072 ■ *Web:* www.cmccontrols.com

Con-Syst-Int Group Inc 14200 Frazho Rd ... Warren MI 48089 586-779-7914 779-1220

Control Masters Inc 5235 Katrine Ave ... Downers Grove IL 60515 630-968-2390 968-3260
Web: www.controlmasters.com

Converteam Inc 610 Epsilon Dr ... Pittsburgh PA 15238 412-967-6900 967-7660
Web: www.converteam.com

Coto Technology 171 Service Rd Suite 301 ... Warwick RI 02886 401-943-2686 942-0920
Web: www.cotorelay.com

Digi-Data Corp 8920-D Rt 108 ... Columbia MD 21045 410-730-6880 730-7708
Web: www.digidata.com

DST Controls 651 Stone Rd ... Benicia CA 94510 707-745-5117 745-8952
TF: 800-251-0773 ■ *Web:* www.dstcontrols.com

Ducommun Technologies Inc 23301 Wilmington Ave ... Carson CA 90745 310-513-7200 513-7298
TF: 800-421-5032 ■ *Web:* www.ductech.com

Duct-O-Wire Co PO Box 519 ... Corona CA 92882 951-735-8220 735-2372
TF: 800-752-6001 ■ *Web:* www.ductowire.com

Eaton Corp 1111 Superior Ave Eaton Center ... Cleveland OH 44114 216-523-5000 523-4787
NYSE: ETN ■ *Web:* www.eaton.com

Eaton Electrical Inc 811 Greencrest Dr ... Columbus OH 43081 614-882-3282 899-5390
TF: 877-386-2273 ■ *Web:* www.eatonelectrical.com

Electric Regulator Corp 6189 El Camino Real ... Carlsbad CA 92009 760-438-7873 438-0437
TF: 800-458-6566 ■ *Web:* www.electricregulator.com

Electrical Design & Control Co 2200 Stephenson Hwy ... Troy MI 48083 248-743-2400 743-2401
Web: www.edandc.com

Phone | Fax

Electro-Matic Products Co 2235 N Knox Ave ... Chicago IL 60639 773-235-4010 235-7317
Web: www.em-chicago.com

Electroid Co 45 Fadem Rd ... Springfield NJ 07081 973-467-8100 467-2606
TF: 800-242-7184 ■ *Web:* www.electroid.com

Electronic Theatre Controls Inc 3031 Pleasantview Rd ... Middleton WI 53562 608-831-4116 836-1736
TF: 800-688-4116 ■ *Web:* www.etcconnect.com

Enercon Engineering Inc 1 Altorfer Ln ... East Peoria IL 61611 309-694-1418 694-3703
TF: 800-218-8831 ■ *Web:* www.enercon-eng.com

Entron Controls LLC 601 High Tech Port ... Greer SC 29650 864-416-0190 416-0195
Web: www.entroncontrols.com

Fife Corp 222 W Memorial Rd PO Box 26508 ... Oklahoma City OK 73126 405-755-1600 755-8425
TF: 800-333-3433 ■ *Web:* www.fife.com

Fincor Automation Inc 3750 E Market St ... York PA 17402 717-751-4200 751-4372
TF Sales: 800-334-3040 ■ *Web:* www.fincor.net

FSI/Fork Standards Inc 668 E Western Ave ... Lombard IL 60148 630-932-9380 932-0016
TF: 800-468-6009 ■ *Web:* www.fsinet.com

Fujitsu Components America Inc 250 E Caribbean Dr ... Sunnyvale CA 94089 408-745-4900 745-4970
Web: www.fujitsu.com/us

FXC Corp 3410 S Susan St ... Santa Ana CA 92704 714-556-7400 641-5093
Web: www.pia.com/fxc/

GE Multilin 215 Anderson Ave ... Markham ON L6E1B3 905-294-6222 201-2098
TF: 800-547-8629 ■ *Web:* www.geindustrial.com/multilin

GET Engineering Corp 9350 Bond Ave ... El Cajon CA 92021 619-443-8295 443-8613
Web: www.getntds.com

Glendinning Marine Products 740 Century Cir ... Conway SC 29526 843-399-6146 399-5005
TF: 800-500-2380 ■ *Web:* www.glendinningprods.com

Globe Electronic Hardware Inc 34-24 56th St ... Woodside NY 11377 718-457-0303 457-7493
TF: 800-221-1505 ■ *Web:* www.globelectronics.com

Guardian Electric Mfg Co Inc 1425 Lake Ave ... Woodstock IL 60098 815-337-0050 337-0377
TF: 800-762-0369 ■ *Web:* www.guardian-electric.com

Hamlin Electronics Inc 612 E Lake St ... Lake Mills WI 53551 920-648-3000 648-3001
Web: www.hamlin.com

Honeywell ACS 11 W Spring St ... Freeport IL 61032 815-235-5500
Web: www.honeywell.com/acs

Honeywell Automation & Control Solutions 11 W Spring St ... Freeport IL 61032 815-235-5500
Web: www.honeywell.com/acs

Honeywell Sensing & Control 11 W Spring St ... Freeport IL 61032 815-235-5500 235-5574
TF Cust Svc: 800-537-6945 ■ *Web:* www.honeywell.com/sensing

Hubbell Industrial Controls 4301 Cheyenne Dr ... Archdale NC 27263 336-434-2800 434-2803
TF: 800-828-4032 ■ *Web:* www.hubbell-icd.com

IDEC Corp 1175 Elko Dr ... Sunnyvale CA 94089 408-747-0550 744-9055
TF: 800-262-4332 ■ *Web:* www.idec.com

Intermatic Inc 7777 Winn Rd ... Spring Grove IL 60081 815-675-2321 675-7105
Web: www.intermatic.com

Jennings Technology Co 970 McLaughlin Ave ... San Jose CA 95122 408-292-4025 286-1789
Web: www.jenningstech.com

Johnson Controls Inc 5757 N Green Bay Ave ... Milwaukee WI 53209 414-524-1200 524-3232
NYSE: JCI ■ *TF:* 800-972-8040 ■ *Web:* www.johnsoncontrols.com

Jordan Controls 5607 W Douglas Ave ... Milwaukee WI 53218 414-461-9200 461-1024
TF Prod Info: 800-637-5547 ■ *Web:* www.jordancontrols.com

Joslyn Clark Controls 2013 W Meeting St ... Lancaster SC 29720 803-286-8491 285-0885
TF: 800-476-6952 ■ *Web:* www.joslynclark.com

KB Electronics Inc 12095 NW 39th St ... Coral Springs FL 33065 954-346-4900 346-3377
TF: 800-221-6570 ■ *Web:* www.kbelectronics.com

K/E Electric Supply Co 146 N Groesbeck Hwy ... Mount Clemens MI 48043 586-469-3005 469-3006
Web: www.keelectric.com

Keyence Corp of America 50 Tice Blvd ... Woodcliff Lake NJ 07677 201-930-0100 930-0099
TF: 888-539-3623 ■ *Web:* www.keyence.com

Leach International Corp 6900 Orangethorpe Ave ... Buena Park CA 90622 714-736-7598 739-1713
Web: www.leachintl.com

Lutron Electronics Co Inc 7200 Suter Rd ... Coopersburg PA 18036 610-282-3800 282-3691
TF Tech Supp: 800-523-9466 ■ *Web:* www.lutron.com

Mac Products Inc 60 Pennsylvania Ave PO Box 469 ... Kearny NJ 07032 973-344-0700 344-5368
Web: www.macproducts.net

Magnet Schultz of America Inc 401 Plaza Dr ... Westmont IL 60559 630-789-0600 789-0614
TF Cust Svc: 800-635-3778 ■ *Web:* www.magnet-schultz.com

MagneTek Inc N49 W13650 Campbell Dr ... Menomonee Falls WI 53051 262-783-3500 298-3503*
NYSE: MAG ■ **Fax Area Code:* 800 ■ *TF:* 800-288-8178 ■ *Web:* www.magnetek.com

Mallory Automotive Group 2831 Waterfront Pkwy E Dr ... Indianapolis IN 46214 317-328-4000 328-4037

Martin Automatic Inc 1661 Northrock Ct ... Rockford IL 61103 815-654-4800 654-4810
Web: www.martinauto.com

Moeller Electric Corp USA 4140 World Houston Pkwy Suite 100 ... Houston TX 77032 713-933-0999 613-6255*
**Fax Area Code:* 832 ■ *TF:* 866-663-5537 ■ *Web:* www.moellerusa.net

Moog Inc Seneca & Jamison Rd ... East Aurora NY 14052 716-652-2000 687-4457
NYSE: MOG/A ■ *Web:* www.moog.com

Namco Controls Corp 201 W Meeting St ... Lancaster SC 29720 803-286-8491 678-6263*
**Fax Area Code:* 800 ■ *TF:* 800-626-8324 ■ *Web:* www.ncdjsolutions.com/namco

Networks Electronic Co 9750 De Soto Ave ... Chatsworth CA 91311 818-341-0440 718-7133
Web: www.networkselectronic.com

OEM Controls Inc 10 Controls Dr ... Shelton CT 06484 203-929-8431 929-3867
Web: www.oemcontrols.com

Omron Electronics LLC 1 Commerce Dr ... Schaumburg IL 60173 847-843-7900 843-8261
TF: 800-556-6766 ■ *Web:* www.omron247.com

OMRON Scientific Technologies Inc 6550 Dumbarton Cir ... Fremont CA 94555 510-608-3400 744-1440
TF: 888-510-4357 ■ *Web:* www.sti.com

OMRON STI 6550 Dumbarton Cir ... Fremont CA 94555 510-608-3400 744-1440
TF: 888-510-4357 ■ *Web:* www.sti.com

Ormec Systems Corp 19 Linden Pk ... Rochester NY 14625 585-385-3520 385-5999
TF: 800-656-7632 ■ *Web:* www.ormec.com

Panasonic Electric Works Corp of America 629 Central Ave ... New Providence NJ 07974 908-464-3550 464-8513
TF: 800-276-6289 ■ *Web:* pewa.panasonic.com

Parker Hannifin Corp Electromechanical Automation Div
5500 Business Park Dr ... Rohnert Park CA 94928 707-584-7558 584-8015
TF: 800-358-9068 ■ *Web:* www.parkermotion.com

Parker McCrory Mfg Co 2000 Forest Ave ... Kansas City MO 64108 816-221-2000 221-9879
TF: 800-662-1038 ■ *Web:* www.parmakusa.com

Payne Engineering Co Rt 29 Rocky Step Rd PO Box 70 ... Scott Depot WV 25560 304-757-7353 757-7305
TF Orders: 800-331-1345 ■ *Web:* www.payneng.com

Peerless Instrument Co Inc 1966-D Broadhollow Rd ... Farmingdale NY 11735 631-396-6500 396-6555
Web: www.peerlessny.com

Polytron Corp 4400 Wyland Dr ... Elkhart IN 46516 574-522-0246 522-0457
TF: 888-228-0246 ■ *Web:* www.polytron-corp.com

Precision Multiple Controls Inc 33 Greenwood Ave ... Midland Park NJ 07432 201-444-0600 445-8575
Web: www.precisionmulticontrols.com

Rockford Systems Inc 4620 Hydraulic Rd ... Rockford IL 61109 815-874-7891 874-6144*
**Fax:* Sales ■ *TF Cust Svc:* 800-922-7533 ■ *Web:* www.rockfordsystems.com

Rockwell Automation Inc 1201 S 2nd St ... Milwaukee WI 53204 414-382-2000 382-4444
NYSE: ROK ■ *Web:* www.rockwell.com

Rockwell Collins Electromechanical Systems 17000 S Red Hill Ave ... Irvine CA 92614 949-250-1015 250-0497
TF: 800-866-5775 ■ *Web:* www.rockwellcollins.com/electromechanical

Saia-Burgess Inc PO Box 427 ... Vandalia OH 45377 937-898-3621 454-2350
TF: 800-888-9765 ■ *Web:* www.saia-burgess.com

SBE Inc 4000 Excutive Pkwy Suite 200 ... San Ramon CA 94583 925-355-2000 355-2020
NASDAQ: SBEI ■ *Web:* www.sbei.net

Siemens Energy & Automation Inc 3333 Old Milton Pkwy ... Alpharetta GA 30005 770-751-2000 740-2534
TF: 800-964-4114 ■ *Web:* automation.usa.siemens.com

Name / Address	City	State	Zip	Phone	Fax
SMC Electrical Products Inc 6072 Ohio River Rd *Web:* www.smcelectrical.com	Huntington	WV	25702	304-736-8933	736-4541
SOR Inc 14685 W 105th St *TF:* 800-676-6794 ■ *Web:* www.sorinc.com	Lenexa	KS	66215	913-888-2630	888-0767
South/Shore Controls Inc 4823 N Ridge Rd *Web:* www.southshorecontrols.com	Perry	OH	44081	440-259-2500	259-5015
Sprecher & Schuh 15910 International Plaza *Web:* www.ssusa.cc	Houston	TX	77032	281-442-9000	442-1570
Square D Schneider Electric 1415 S Roselle Rd *TF:* 888-778-2733 ■ *Web:* www.squared.com	Palatine	IL	60067	847-397-2600	925-7500
SRC Devices Inc 6295 Ferris Sq Suite D *TF:* 866-772-8668 ■ *Web:* www.srcdevices.com	San Diego	CA	92121	858-729-2650	729-2647
Static Controls Corp 30460 Wixom Rd *Web:* www.scccontrols.com	Wixom	MI	48393	248-926-4400	926-4412
Struthers-Dunn 2295 Hoffmeyer Rd *Web:* www.struthers-dunn.com	Florence	SC	29501	843-664-3303	662-8862
Sturdy Corp 1822 Carolina Beach Rd *TF:* 800-721-3282 ■ *Web:* www.sturdycorp.com	Wilmington	NC	28401	910-763-8261	763-2650
Tech/Ops Sevcon Inc 155 Northboro Rd *AMEX: TO* ■ *Web:* www.sevcon.com	Southborough	MA	01772	508-281-5500	281-5341
Time Mark Corp 11440 E Pine St *TF:* 800-862-2875 ■ *Web:* www.time-mark.com	Tulsa	OK	74116	918-438-1220	437-7584
Time-O-Matic Inc 1015 Maple St *TF:* 800-637-2645 ■ *Web:* www.timeomatic.com	Danville	IL	61832	217-442-0611	442-1020
Tork Inc 1 Grove St *TF:* 888-500-4598 ■ *Web:* www.tork.com	Mount Vernon	NY	10550	914-664-3542	664-5052
Transdyn Inc 5669 Gibraltar Dr *Web:* www.transdyn.com	Pleasanton	CA	94588	925-225-1600	225-1610
Triumph Controls Inc 205 Church Rd PO Box 2100 *Web:* www.triumph-controls.com	North Wales	PA	19454	215-699-4861	699-2595
Tyco Electronics Corp Hartman Div 175 N Diamond St	Mansfield	OH	44902	419-521-9500	526-2749
Unico Inc 3725 Nicholson Rd *TF:* 800-245-1859 ■ *Web:* www.unicous.com	Franksville	WI	53126	262-886-5678	504-7396
Wescon Products Co 2533 S West St *TF:* 800-835-0160 ■ *Web:* www.wesconproducts.com	Wichita	KS	67217	316-942-7266	942-5114
Whittaker Controls Inc 12838 Saticoy St *Web:* www.whittakercontrols.com	North Hollywood	CA	91605	818-765-8160	759-2190
Yaskawa Electric America Inc 2121 Norman Dr S **Fax:* Mktg ■ *TF:* 800-927-5292 ■ *Web:* www.yaskawa.com	Waukegan	IL	60085	847-887-7000	887-7310*

207 CONVENIENCE STORES

SEE ALSO Gas Stations p. 1687; Grocery Stores p. 1767

Name / Address	City	State	Zip	Phone	Fax
7-Eleven Canada Inc 3185 Willingdon Green **Fax:* Mktg ■ *TF:* 800-255-0711	Burnaby	BC	V5G4P3	604-299-0711	293-5634*
7-Eleven Inc 2711 N Haskell Ave PO Box 711 *TF:* 800-255-0711 ■ *Web:* www.7-eleven.com	Dallas	TX	75221	214-828-7011	828-7848
Alimentation Couche-Tard Inc 1600 boul St Martin E Suite 200 Tower B *TSX: ATD* ■ *TF:* 800-361-2612 ■ *Web:* www.couche-tard.qc.ca	Laval	QC	H7G4S7	450-662-3272	662-7537
Allsup's Convenience Stores Inc 2112 Thornton St PO Box 1907	Clovis	NM	88102	505-769-2311	769-2564
Brower CW Inc 413 S Riverside Dr *TF:* 800-400-0477	Modesto	CA	95354	209-523-1828	523-9305
Bull Brothers Inc 401 Herkimer Rd	Utica	NY	13503	315-797-7760	797-1174
Calfee Co of Dalton DBA Favorite Market 1503 N Tibbs Rd *TF:* 800-634-2944 ■ *Web:* www.favmkt.com	Dalton	GA	30720	706-226-4834	275-4417
Casey's General Stores Inc 1 Convenience Blvd *NASDAQ: CASY* ■ *Web:* www.caseys.com	Ankeny	IA	50021	515-965-6100	965-6160
CHS Inc 5500 Cenex Dr *NASDAQ: CHSCP* ■ *TF:* 800-232-3639 ■ *Web:* www.chsinc.com	Inver Grove Heights	MN	55077	651-355-6000	355-6432
Circle K Co 7840 E Broadway Blvd Suite 201 **Fax:* Hum Res ■ *Web:* www.circlek.com	Tucson	AZ	85710	520-722-6434	751-6999*
Convenient Food Mart Inc 467 N State St **Fax Area Code:* 440 ■ *Web:* www.convenientfoodmart.com	Painesville	OH	44077	800-860-4844	639-6526*
Cracker Barrel Convenience Stores Inc 12221 Industriplex Blvd *Web:* www.crackerbarrelstores.com	Baton Rouge	LA	70809	225-753-3200	753-2600
Cumberland Farms Inc 777 Dedham St **Fax:* Hum Res ■ *TF:* 800-225-9702 ■ *Web:* www.cumberlandfarms.com	Canton	MA	02021	781-828-4900	828-9012*
CW Brower Inc 413 S Riverside Dr *TF:* 800-400-0477	Modesto	CA	95354	209-523-1828	523-9305
Dairy Barn Stores Inc 544 Elwood Rd *TF:* 888-320-0246 ■ *Web:* www.dairybarn.com	East Northport	NY	11731	631-368-8050	266-2547
Deweese Enterprises Inc DBA Super Stop Stores 5625 Old Hwy 80 W	Meridian	MS	39307	601-483-8291	693-5410
E-Z Mart Stores Inc 602 W Falvey St *TF:* 800-234-6502 ■ *Web:* www.ezmart.com	Texarkana	TX	75501	903-832-6502	832-7903
Erickson Petroleum Corp 4567 American Blvd W *TF:* 800-745-7411	Bloomington	MN	55437	952-830-8700	830-8864
Farm Stores 5800 NW 74th Ave *TF:* 800-726-3276 ■ *Web:* www.farmstores.com	Miami	FL	33166	305-471-5141	591-4243
Favorite Market 1503 N Tibbs Rd *TF:* 800-634-2944 ■ *Web:* www.favmkt.com	Dalton	GA	30720	706-226-4834	275-4417
FFP Marketing Co Inc DBA Kwik Pantry 2801 Glenda Ave *TF:* 800-695-3282 ■ *Web:* www.ffpmarketing.com	Fort Worth	TX	76117	817-838-4700	838-4799
Gibbs Oil Co LP 90 Everett Ave PO Box 9151 *TF:* 800-352-3558 ■ *Web:* www.gibbsoil.com	Chelsea	MA	02150	617-889-9000	884-6075
Green Valley Aquisition Co 477 E Beaver Ave *TF:* 800-494-1500 ■ *Web:* www.uni-mart.com	State College	PA	16801	814-234-6000	234-8595
Handy Dandy Food Stores Inc 1800 Magnavox Way *TF:* 800-686-2836 ■ *Web:* www.lassus.com	Fort Wayne	IN	46804	260-436-1415	436-0340
Heritage Dairy Stores Inc 376 Jessup Rd *Web:* www.heritages.com	Thorofare	NJ	08086	856-845-2855	845-8392
Holiday Stationstores 4567 American Blvd W *Web:* www.holidaystationstores.com	Bloomington	MN	55437	952-830-8700	
Hollar Co 2012 Rainbow Dr	Gadsden	AL	35901	256-547-1644	547-1494
Jet Food Stores of Georgia 1106 S Harris St *TF:* 800-277-1168	Sandersville	GA	31082	478-552-2588	552-8758
JFM Inc 4276 Lakeland Dr	Flowood	MS	39232	601-664-7177	664-7272
Johnny Quick Food Stores Inc 96 Shaw Ave Suite 240	Clovis	CA	93612	559-297-6830	297-7519
Junior Food Stores of West Florida Inc DBA Tom Thumb 619 8th Ave *TF:* 800-682-8486	Crestview	FL	32536	850-682-5171	689-1055
Krause Gentle Corp DBA Kum & Go 6400 Westown Pkwy *Web:* www.kumandgo.com	West Des Moines	IA	50266	515-226-0128	226-0995
Kum & Go 6400 Westown Pkwy *Web:* www.kumandgo.com	West Des Moines	IA	50266	515-226-0128	226-0995
Kwik Pantry 2801 Glenda Ave *TF:* 800-695-3282 ■ *Web:* www.ffpmarketing.com	Fort Worth	TX	76117	817-838-4700	838-4799
Kwik Shop Inc 734 E 4th Ave	Hutchinson	KS	67501	620-669-8504	694-1820
Kwik Trip Inc 1626 Oak St *Web:* www.kwiktrip.com	La Crosse	WI	54602	608-781-8988	781-8950
Kwik-Way Inc 509 N 24 St W	Billings	MT	59102	406-656-6310	656-0244
Lil' Champ/Jiffy Food Stores Inc 8930 Western Way Suite 4	Jacksonville	FL	32256	904-464-7200	464-7233
Li'l Thrift Food Marts Inc DBA Short Stop Food Marts 1007 Arsenal Ave *Web:* www.shortstopfoodmarts.com	Fayetteville	NC	28305	910-433-4490	433-2691
Loaf N' Jug Mini Mart 442 Keeler Pkwy	Pueblo	CO	81001	719-948-3071	948-2602
Love's Travel Stops & Country Stores Inc 10601 N Pennsylvania Ave *TF:* 800-388-0983 ■ *Web:* www.loves.com	Oklahoma City	OK	73120	405-751-9000	749-9110
Mac's Convenience Stores Inc 305 Milner Ave Suite 300 *TF:* 800-268-5574 ■ *Web:* www.macs.ca	Toronto	ON	M1B3V4	416-291-4441	291-4947
MAPCO Express Inc 7102 Commerce Way *Web:* www.mapcoexpress.com	Brentwood	TN	37027	615-771-6701	771-8098
Marsh Village Pantries Inc 9800 Crosspoint Blvd *Web:* www.marsh.net	Indianapolis	IN	46256	317-594-2100	594-2704
Maverik Country Stores Inc 1014 S Washington St PO Box 8008 *Web:* www.maverik.com	Afton	WY	83110	307-885-3861	885-3832
Mom & Pops Palmer Wasilla Hwy Mile 4.5	Palmer	AK	99645	907-745-0333	745-0342
Norkus Enterprises Inc 505 Richmond Ave *TF:* 800-281-4047 ■ *Web:* www.norkus.com	Point Pleasant Beach	NJ	08742	732-899-4040	899-0752
Ohio Valley AFM Inc 3955 Alexandria Pike *TF:* 800-359-3971	Cold Spring	KY	41076	859-781-3800	781-6821
Okay Food Co Inc 500 Abney Ave *TF:* 800-256-6455	Lufkin	TX	75902	936-634-4648	639-6441
Open Pantry Food Mart 10505 Corporate Dr Suite 101 *Web:* www.openpantry.com	Pleasant Prairie	WI	53158	262-857-1156	857-9667
Pantry Inc 1801 Douglas Dr *NASDAQ: PTRY* ■ *TF:* 800-476-7574 ■ *Web:* www.thepantry.com	Sanford	NC	27330	919-774-6700	776-5303
Plaid Pantries Inc 10025 SW Allen Blvd *TF:* 800-677-5243 ■ *Web:* www.plaidpantry.com	Beaverton	OR	97005	503-646-4246	646-3071
Presto Food Stores Inc 2009 N Airport Rd *TF:* 800-881-3511	Plant City	FL	33563	813-754-3511	752-5494
Quick Chek Food Stores 3 Old Hwy 28 *Web:* www.qchek.com	Whitehouse Station	NJ	08889	908-534-2200	534-7216
Quik Stop Markets Inc 4567 Enterprise St	Fremont	CA	94538	510-657-8500	657-1544
QuikTrip Corp 4705 S 129th East Ave *TF:* 800-544-5749 ■ *Web:* www.quiktrip.com	Tulsa	OK	74134	918-615-7700	615-7615
Red Apple Group Inc 823 11th Ave	New York	NY	10019	212-956-5803	247-4509
Rosenberger's Dairies Inc 847 Forty Foot Rd PO Box 901 *TF:* 800-355-9074 ■ *Web:* www.rosenbergers.com	Hatfield	PA	19440	215-855-9074	855-6486
Sheetz Inc 5700 6th Ave *TF:* 800-487-5444 ■ *Web:* www.sheetz.com	Altoona	PA	16602	814-946-3611	946-4375
Short Stop Food Marts 1007 Arsenal Ave *Web:* www.shortstopfoodmarts.com	Fayetteville	NC	28305	910-433-4490	433-2691
Speedway SuperAmerica LLC 500 Speedway Dr *TF Cust Svc:* 800-643-1948 ■ *Web:* www.speedway.com	Enon	OH	45323	937-864-3000	
Stop-N-Go Inc 1 Valero Way **Fax:* Cust Svc ■ *TF:* 800-333-3377	San Antonio	TX	78249	210-592-2000	592-2306*
Super Stop Stores 5625 Old Hwy 80 W	Meridian	MS	39307	601-483-8291	693-5410
Susser Holdings LLC 4433 Baldwin Blvd *TF:* 800-569-3585 ■ *Web:* www.susser.com	Corpus Christi	TX	78408	361-693-3600	884-2494
Tedeschi Food Shops 14 Howard St *Web:* www.tedeschifoodshops.com	Rockland	MA	02370	781-878-8210	878-0476
Time Saver Inc 7360 Skidaway Rd	Savannah	GA	31406	912-351-6000	351-6018
Tom Thumb 619 8th Ave *TF:* 800-682-8486	Crestview	FL	32536	850-682-5171	689-1055
Tom Thumb Food Stores Inc 97 W Okeechobee Rd *Web:* www.tomthumbfla.com	Hialeah	FL	33010	305-885-5451	885-0144
Valdak Corp 1149 36th Ave S *Web:* www.valleydairy.com	Grand Forks	ND	58201	701-746-8371	780-9286
Wawa Inc 260 W Baltimore Pike **Fax:* Hum Res ■ *TF:* 800-283-9292 ■ *Web:* www.wawa.com	Media	PA	19063	610-358-8000	358-8878*
Weigels Inc 3100 Staffordshire Blvd	Powell	TN	37849	865-938-2042	938-2444
White Hen Pantry Inc 700 E Butterfield Rd Suite 300 *TF:* 800-726-8791 ■ *Web:* www.whitehen.com	Lombard	IL	60148	630-366-3100	366-3447
Worsley Cos Inc 10 Cardinal Dr *TF:* 800-348-3429 ■ *Web:* www.scotchmanstores.com	Wilmington	NC	28403	910-395-5300	395-6691
Xtra Mart 221 Quinebaug Rd *TF:* 800-243-6366 ■ *Web:* www.xtramart.com	North Grosvenordale	CT	06255	860-935-5200	
Yates Enterprises Inc 602 W Falvey St	Texarkana	TX	75501	903-832-6502	832-7903

208 CONVENTION CENTERS

SEE ALSO Performing Arts Facilities p. 2090; Stadiums & Arenas p. 2329

Listings are alphabetized by city names within state groupings.

Alabama

Name / Address	City	State	Zip	Phone	Fax
Birmingham-Jefferson Convention Complex 2100 Richard Arrington Jr Blvd N *TF:* 877-843-2522 ■ *Web:* www.bjcc.org	Birmingham	AL	35203	205-458-8400	458-8437
Von Braun Center 700 Monroe St *Web:* www.vonbrauncenter.com	Huntsville	AL	35801	256-533-1953	551-2203
Arthur R Outlaw Mobile Convention Center 1 S Water St *TF:* 800-566-2453 ■ *Web:* www.mobileconventions.com	Mobile	AL	36602	251-208-2100	208-2150
Montgomery Civic Center 300 Water St Suite 214	Montgomery	AL	36104	334-241-2100	241-2117

Alaska

Name / Address	City	State	Zip	Phone	Fax
William A Egan Civic & Convention Center 555 W 5th Ave *Web:* www.egancenter.com	Anchorage	AK	99501	907-263-2800	263-2858
Carlson Center 2010 2nd Ave *Web:* www.carlson-center.com	Fairbanks	AK	99701	907-451-7800	451-1195
Centennial Hall Convention Center 101 Egan Dr *Web:* www.juneau.org/centennial	Juneau	AK	99801	907-586-5283	586-1135
Valdez Civic & Convention Center 110 Clifton Dr	Valdez	AK	99686	907-835-4440	835-2472

Arizona

Name / Address	City	State	Zip	Phone	Fax
Glendale Civic Center 5750 W Glenn Dr *Web:* www.glendaleciviccenter.com	Glendale	AZ	85301	623-930-4300	930-4319

Arizona (Cont'd)

	City	State	ZIP	Phone	Fax
Mesa Convention Center 263 N Center St *Web:* www.mesaconventioncenter.com	Mesa	AZ	85201	480-644-2178	644-2617
Phoenix Convention Center 100 N 3rd St *TF:* 800-282-4842 ■ *Web:* www.phoenixconventioncenter.com	Phoenix	AZ	85004	602-262-6225	495-3642
Tucson Convention Center 260 S Church Ave *Web:* www.tucsonaz.gov/tcc	Tucson	AZ	85701	520-791-4101	791-5572
Yuma Civic Center 1440 W Desert Hills Dr *Web:* www.yumaconventioncenter.com	Yuma	AZ	85365	928-373-5040	344-9121

Arkansas

	City	State	ZIP	Phone	Fax
Fort Smith Convention Center 55 S 7th St *Web:* www.fortsmith.org	Fort Smith	AR	72901	479-788-8932	788-8930
Hot Springs Convention Center 134 Convention Blvd *TF:* 800-543-2284 ■ *Web:* www.hotsprings.org	Hot Springs	AR	71901	501-321-1705	321-2136
Statehouse Convention Center Markham & Main #1 1 Statehouse Plaza *TF:* 800-844-4781 ■ *Web:* www.littlerockmeetings.com/conv-centers/Statehouse	Little Rock	AR	72201	501-376-4781	376-7833
Pine Bluff Convention Center 1 Convention Center Plaza *TF:* 800-536-7660 ■ *Web:* www.pinebluffonline.com	Pine Bluff	AR	71601	870-536-7600	535-4867

British Columbia

	City	State	ZIP	Phone	Fax
Vancouver Convention & Exposition Centre 999 Canada Pl Suite 200 *TF:* 866-785-8232 ■ *Web:* www.vanconex.com	Vancouver	BC	V6C3C1	604-689-8232	647-7232

California

	City	State	ZIP	Phone	Fax
Anaheim Convention Center 800 W Katella Ave *Web:* www.anaheimconventioncenter.com	Anaheim	CA	92802	714-765-8900	765-8965
Rabobank Arena Theater & Convention Center 1001 Truxtun Ave *Web:* www.rabobankarena.com	Bakersfield	CA	93301	661-852-7300	861-9904
Carson Center 801 E Carson St *Web:* www.carsoncenter.com	Carson	CA	90745	310-835-0212	835-0160
Cow Palace 2600 Geneva Ave *Web:* www.cowpalace.com	Daly City	CA	94014	415-404-4111	469-6111
Fresno Convention Center 848 M St *Web:* www.fresnoconventioncenter.com	Fresno	CA	93721	559-445-8100	445-8110
Bren Events Center 100 Bren Events Ctr *Web:* www.bren.uci.edu	Irvine	CA	92697	949-824-5050	824-5097
Long Beach Convention & Entertainment Center 300 E Ocean Blvd *Web:* www.longbeachcc.com	Long Beach	CA	90802	562-436-3636	436-9491
California Market Center 110 E 9th St *TF:* 800-225-6278 ■ *Web:* www.californiamarketcenter.com	Los Angeles	CA	90079	213-630-3600	630-3708
Los Angeles Convention Center 1201 S Figueroa St *TF:* 800-448-7775 ■ *Web:* www.lacclink.com	Los Angeles	CA	90015	213-741-1151	765-4266
Shrine Auditorium & Exposition Center 665 W Jefferson Blvd *Web:* www.shrineauditorium.com	Los Angeles	CA	90007	213-748-5116	742-9922
Modesto Centre Plaza 1000 L St *Web:* www.modestogov.com/prnd/facilities/cplaza/	Modesto	CA	95354	209-577-6444	544-6729
Monterey Conference Center 1 Portola Plaza *TF:* 800-314-5502 ■ *Web:* www.monterey.org/mcc	Monterey	CA	93940	831-646-3770	646-3777
Oakland Convention Center 1001 Broadway *TF:* 800-228-9290	Oakland	CA	94607	510-451-4000	835-3466
Ontario Convention Center 2000 Convention Center Way *TF:* 800-455-5755 ■ *Web:* www.ontariocc.com	Ontario	CA	91764	909-937-3000	937-3080
Oxnard Performing Arts & Convention Center 800 Hobson Way *Web:* www.oxnardpacc.com	Oxnard	CA	93030	805-486-2424	483-7303
Palm Springs Convention Center 277 N Avenida Caballeros *TF:* 800-333-7535 ■ *Web:* www.palmspringscc.com	Palm Springs	CA	92262	760-325-6611	778-4102
Richmond Memorial Convention Center 403 Civic Center Plaza	Richmond	CA	94804	510-620-6950	620-6583
Riverside Convention Center 3443 Orange St *Web:* www.riversidecb.com	Riverside	CA	92501	951-787-7950	346-4700
Sacramento Convention Center 1400 J St *Web:* www.sacramentoconventioncenter.com	Sacramento	CA	95814	916-808-5291	808-7687
NOS Events Center 689 S 'E' St *Web:* www.nosevents.com	San Bernardino	CA	92408	909-888-6788	889-7666
San Diego Convention Center 111 W Harbor Dr *TF:* 800-525-7322 ■ *Web:* www.sdccc.org	San Diego	CA	92101	619-525-5000	525-5005
Concourse Exhibition Center 635 8th St *TF:* 800-877-8522	San Francisco	CA	94103	415-864-1500	490-5885
Moscone Center 747 Howard St *Web:* www.moscone.com	San Francisco	CA	94103	415-974-4000	974-4073
Nob Hill Masonic Center 1111 California St *Web:* www.sfmasoniccenter.com	San Francisco	CA	94108	415-776-4702	776-3945
San Jose Convention & Cultural Facilities 408 Almaden Blvd *TF:* 800-533-2345 ■ *Web:* www.sjcc.com	San Jose	CA	95110	408-277-5277	277-3535
San Mateo County Expo Center 2495 S Delaware St *TF:* 800-338-3976 ■ *Web:* www.sanmateoexpo.org	San Mateo	CA	94403	650-574-3247	574-3985
Santa Clara Convention Center 5001 Great America Pkwy *Web:* www.santaclara.org/conventioncenter	Santa Clara	CA	95054	408-748-7000	748-7013
Santa Monica Civic Auditorium 1855 Main St *Web:* www.santamonicacivic.org	Santa Monica	CA	90401	310-458-8551	394-3411
Visalia Convention Center 303 E Acequia Ave *Web:* www.visalia.org	Visalia	CA	93291	559-713-4000	713-4804

Colorado

	City	State	ZIP	Phone	Fax
Colorado Springs City Auditorium 221 E Kiowa *Web:* www.springsgov.com	Colorado Springs	CO	80903	719-385-5969	385-6584
Colorado Convention Center 700 14th St *Web:* www.denverconvention.com	Denver	CO	80202	303-228-8000	228-8104
Two Rivers Convention Center 159 Main St *Web:* www.gjcity.org	Grand Junction	CO	81501	970-245-0031	263-5720

Connecticut

	City	State	ZIP	Phone	Fax
Hartford Civic Center 1 Civic Center Plaza *Web:* www.hartfordciviccenter.com	Hartford	CT	06103	860-249-6333	241-4226

District of Columbia

	City	State	ZIP	Phone	Fax
Washington Convention Center 801 Mt Vernon Pl NW *TF:* 800-368-9000 ■ *Web:* www.dcconvention.com	Washington	DC	20001	202-249-3000	249-3116

Florida

	City	State	ZIP	Phone	Fax
Harborview Center 300 Cleveland St *Web:* www.harborv.com	Clearwater	FL	33755	727-462-6778	462-6798
Ocean Center 101 N Atlantic Ave *TF:* 800-858-6444 ■ *Web:* www.oceancenter.com	Daytona Beach	FL	32118	386-254-4500	254-4512
Greater Fort Lauderdale-Broward County Convention Center 1950 Eisenhower Blvd *Web:* www.ftlauderdalecc.com/main.html	Fort Lauderdale	FL	33316	954-765-5900	763-9551
Harborside Event Center 1375 Monroe St *TF:* 800-294-9516 ■ *Web:* www.fmharborside.com	Fort Myers	FL	33901	239-332-6888	332-2241
Prime Osborn Convention Center 1000 Water St *Web:* www.jaxevents.com/primeosbornconventioncenter	Jacksonville	FL	32205	904-630-4000	630-4029
Lakeland Center 701 W Lime St *Web:* www.thelakelandcenter.com	Lakeland	FL	33815	863-834-8100	834-8101
Miami Beach Convention Center 1901 Convention Center Dr *Web:* www.miamibeachconvention.com	Miami Beach	FL	33139	305-673-7311	673-7435
Orange County Convention Center 9800 International Dr *Fax: Mktg ■ *TF:* 800-345-9845 ■ *Web:* www.occc.net	Orlando	FL	32819	407-685-9800	685-9876*
Orlando Expo Center 500 W Livingston St *Web:* www.orlandocentroplex.com	Orlando	FL	32801	407-849-2000	849-2329
Manatee Convention Center 1 Haben Blvd *Web:* www.manateecenter.org	Palmetto	FL	34221	941-722-3244	729-1820
Sarasota Bradenton International Convention Center 8005 15th St E *Web:* www.sbicc.net	Sarasota	FL	34243	941-355-9161	355-9163
Tallahassee-Leon County Civic Center 505 W Pensacola St *TF:* 800-322-3602 ■ *Web:* www.tlccc.org	Tallahassee	FL	32301	850-487-1691	222-6947
Turnbull Conference Center 555 W Pensacola St FSU Center for Professional Development	Tallahassee	FL	32306	850-644-3801	644-2589
Tampa Convention Center 333 S Franklin St *TF:* 800-426-5630 ■ *Web:* www.tampagov.net/dept_Convention_Center/	Tampa	FL	33602	813-274-8511	274-7430
Palm Beach County Convention Center 650 Okeechobee Blvd *Web:* www.palmbeachfl.com	West Palm Beach	FL	33401	561-366-3000	366-3001

Georgia

	City	State	ZIP	Phone	Fax
AmericasMart 240 Peachtree St NW Suite 2200 *TF:* 800-285-6278 ■ *Web:* www.americasmart.com	Atlanta	GA	30303	404-220-3000	220-3030
Cobb Galleria Centre 2 Galleria Pkwy *Web:* www.cobbgalleria.com	Atlanta	GA	30339	770-955-8000	955-7719
Georgia World Congress Center 285 Andrew Young International Blvd NW *Web:* www.gwcc.com	Atlanta	GA	30313	404-223-4000	223-4011
Georgia International Convention Center 2000 Convention Center Concourse *TF:* 888-331-4422 ■ *Web:* www.gicc.com	College Park	GA	30337	770-997-3566	994-8559
Columbus Georgia Convention & Trade Center 801 Front Ave *Web:* www.columbusga.org/TradeCenter	Columbus	GA	31901	706-327-4522	327-0162
Northwest Georgia Trade & Convention Center 2211 Dug Gap Battle Rd *TF:* 800-824-7469 ■ *Web:* www.nwgtcc.com	Dalton	GA	30720	706-272-7676	278-5811
Gwinnett Center 6400 Sugarloaf Pkwy Bldg 100 *TF:* 800-224-6422 ■ *Web:* www.gwinnettcenter.com	Duluth	GA	30097	770-813-7500	813-7501
Georgia Mountains Center 301 Main St SW *Web:* www.gainesville.org	Gainesville	GA	30501	770-534-8420	534-8425
Jekyll Island Convention Center 1 Beachview Dr *TF:* 877-453-5955 ■ *Web:* www.jekyllisland.com	Jekyll Island	GA	31527	912-635-3400	635-4106
Edgar H Wilson Convention Centre 200 Coliseum Dr *TF:* 877-532-6144 ■ *Web:* www.maconcentreplex.com	Macon	GA	31217	478-751-9152	751-9154
Savannah International Trade & Convention Center 1 International Dr PO Box 248 *Fax: Sales ■ *TF:* 888-644-6822 ■ *Web:* www.savtcc.com	Savannah	GA	31402	912-447-4000	447-4722*

Hawaii

	City	State	ZIP	Phone	Fax
Hawaii Convention Center 1801 Kalakaua Ave *TF:* 800-295-6603 ■ *Web:* www.hawaiiconvention.com	Honolulu	HI	96815	808-943-3500	943-3599
Neal S Blaisdell Center 777 Ward Ave *Web:* www.blaisdellcenter.com	Honolulu	HI	96814	808-527-5400	527-5433

Idaho

	City	State	ZIP	Phone	Fax
Boise Centre on the Grove 850 W Front St *Web:* www.boisecentre.com	Boise	ID	83702	208-336-8900	336-8803

Illinois

	City	State	ZIP	Phone	Fax
McCormick Place 2301 S Lake Shore Dr *TF:* 800-263-9170 ■ *Web:* www.mccormickplace.com	Chicago	IL	60616	312-791-7000	791-6543
Merchandise Mart 320 N Wells St *TF:* 800-677-6278 ■ *Web:* www.merchandisemart.com/mmart	Chicago	IL	60654	312-527-7902	527-7998
Navy Pier 600 E Grand Ave *TF:* 877-244-2246 ■ *Web:* www.navypier.com	Chicago	IL	60611	312-595-7437	595-5091
Gateway Center 1 Gateway Dr *TF:* 800-289-2388 ■ *Web:* www.gatewaycenter.com	Collinsville	IL	62234	618-345-8998	345-9024
Exposition Gardens 1601 W Northmoor Rd	Peoria	IL	61614	309-691-6332	691-2372

				Phone	Fax
Oakley-Lindsay Center 300 Civic Center Plaza Suite 237 TF: 800-978-4748 ■ Web: www.quincyciviccenter.com	Quincy	IL	62301	217-223-1000	223-1330
Quad City Conservation Alliance Expo Center 2621 4th Ave Web: www.qccaexpocenter.com	Rock Island	IL	61201	309-788-5912	788-9619
Donald E Stephens Convention Center 5555 N River Rd Web: www.rosemont.com	Rosemont	IL	60018	847-692-2220	696-9700
Prairie Capital Convention Center 1 Convention Center Plaza Web: www.springfield-pccc.com	Springfield	IL	62701	217-788-8800	788-0811

Indiana

				Phone	Fax
Bloomington Convention Center 302 S College Ave Web: www.bloomingtonconvention.com	Bloomington	IN	47403	812-336-3681	349-2981
Evansville Auditorium & Convention Center 715 Locust St Web: www.smgevansville.com/centre/centre.html	Evansville	IN	47708	812-435-5770	435-5500
Grand Wayne Convention Center 120 W Jefferson Blvd Web: www.grandwayne.com	Fort Wayne	IN	46802	260-426-4100	420-9080
Genesis Convention Center 1 Genesis Center Plaza Web: www.genesisarena.com	Gary	IN	46402	219-882-5505	885-3133
Indiana Convention Center & RCA Dome 100 S Capitol Ave Web: www.iccrd.com	Indianapolis	IN	46225	317-262-3400	262-3685
Horizon Convention Center 401 S High St TF: 888-288-8860 ■ Web: www.horizonconvention.com	Muncie	IN	47305	765-288-8860	751-9190
Century Center 120 S Saint Joseph St Web: centurycenter.org	South Bend	IN	46601	574-235-9711	235-9185

Iowa

				Phone	Fax
US Cellular Center 370 1st Ave NE Web: www.uscellularcenter.com	Cedar Rapids	IA	52401	319-398-5211	362-2102
RiverCenter Adler Theatre 136 E 3rd St Web: www.riverctr.com	Davenport	IA	52801	563-326-8500	326-8505
Polk County Convention Complex 501 Grand Ave Web: www.iowaeventscenter.com	Des Moines	IA	50309	515-242-2500	242-2530
Veterans Memorial Auditorium 833 5th Ave Web: www.iowaeventscenter.com	Des Moines	IA	50309	515-323-5400	564-8001
Sioux City Convention Center 801 4th St TF: 800-593-2228 ■ Web: www.siouxcitytourism.com/convention.htm	Sioux City	IA	51101	712-279-4800	279-4900
Tyson Events Center 401 Gordon Dr TF: 800-593-2228 ■ Web: www.tysoncenter.com	Sioux City	IA	51101	712-279-4850	279-4903

Kansas

				Phone	Fax
Kansas Expocentre 1 Expocentre Dr Web: www.ksexpo.com	Topeka	KS	66612	785-235-1986	235-2967
Century II Convention Center 225 W Douglas Ave Web: www.century2.org	Wichita	KS	67202	316-264-9121	303-8688

Kentucky

				Phone	Fax
Frankfort Convention Center 405 Mero St TF: 800-960-7200 ■ Web: www.frankfortconventioncenter.com	Frankfort	KY	40601	502-564-5335	564-3310
Lexington Convention Center 430 W Vine St Web: www.lexingtoncenter.com	Lexington	KY	40507	859-233-4567	253-2718
Kentucky International Convention Center 221 4th St TF: 800-701-5831 ■ Web: www.kyconvention.org	Louisville	KY	40202	502-595-4381	584-9711

Louisiana

				Phone	Fax
Baton Rouge River Center 275 S River Rd Web: www.brrivercenter.com	Baton Rouge	LA	70802	225-389-3030	389-4954
Bossier Civic Center 620 Benton Rd TF: 800-522-4842	Bossier City	LA	71111	318-741-8900	741-8910
Pontchartrain Center 4545 Williams Blvd Web: www.pontchartraincenter.com	Kenner	LA	70065	504-465-9985	468-6692
Cajundome & Convention Center 444 Cajundome Blvd Web: www.cajundome.com	Lafayette	LA	70506	337-265-2100	265-2311
Monroe Civic Center 401 Lea Joyner Expy	Monroe	LA	71201	318-329-2225	329-2548
Ernest N Morial Convention Center 900 Convention Center Blvd Web: www.mccno.com	New Orleans	LA	70130	504-582-3023	582-3088
Shreveport Civic Center Complex 400 Clyde Fant Pkwy	Shreveport	LA	71101	318-673-5100	673-5105
West Monroe Convention Center 901 Ridge Ave Web: www.wmconventioncenter.com	West Monroe	LA	71291	318-396-5000	396-4807

Maine

				Phone	Fax
Augusta Civic Center 76 Community Dr Web: www.augustaciviccenter.org	Augusta	ME	04330	207-626-2405	626-5968
Bangor Civic Center 100 Dutton St Web: www.bangorciviccenter.com	Bangor	ME	04401	207-947-5555	947-5105

Maryland

				Phone	Fax
Baltimore Convention Center 1 W Pratt St Web: www.bccenter.org	Baltimore	MD	21201	410-649-7000	649-7008
Roland E Powell Convention Center 4001 Coastal Hwy TF: 800-626-2326 ■ Web: www.ocean-city.com/convention/	Ocean City	MD	21842	410-289-8311	289-0058

Massachusetts

				Phone	Fax
Bayside Expo Center 200 Mt Vernon St Web: www.baysideexpo.com	Boston	MA	02125	617-474-6534	265-8434
Boston Convention & Exhibition Center 415 Summer St TF: 800-845-8800 ■ Web: www.mccahome.com	Boston	MA	02210	617-954-2000	954-2299
Exchange Conference Center 212 Northern Ave Web: www.exchangeconferencecenter.com	Boston	MA	02210	617-790-1900	790-1922
John B Hynes Veterans Memorial Convention Center 415 Summer St TF: 800-845-8800 ■ Web: www.mccahome.com	Boston	MA	02210	617-954-2000	954-2299
MassMutual Center 1277 Main St TF: 800-639-8602 ■ Web: www.massmutualcenter.com	Springfield	MA	01103	413-787-6610	787-6645
DCU Center 50 Foster St Web: www.centrumcentre.com	Worcester	MA	01608	508-755-6800	929-0111

Michigan

				Phone	Fax
Cobo Conference & Exhibition Center 1 Washington Blvd Web: www.cobocenter.com	Detroit	MI	48226	313-877-8777	877-8577
DeVos Place 303 Monroe Ave Web: www.devosplace.org	Grand Rapids	MI	49503	616-742-6600	742-6590
Lansing Center 333 E Michigan Ave Web: www.lepfa.com	Lansing	MI	48933	517-483-7400	483-7439
Horizons Conference Center 6200 State St Web: www.horizonscenter.com	Saginaw	MI	48603	989-799-4122	799-4188

Minnesota

				Phone	Fax
Duluth Entertainment Convention Center 350 Harbor Dr TF: 800-628-8385 ■ Web: www.decc.org	Duluth	MN	55802	218-722-5573	722-4247
Earle Brown Heritage Center 6155 Earle Brown Dr TF: 800-524-0239 ■ Web: www.earlebrown.com	Minneapolis	MN	55430	763-569-6300	569-6320
Minneapolis Convention Center 1301 2nd Ave S Web: www.minneapolisconventioncenter.com/	Minneapolis	MN	55403	612-335-6000	335-6757
Mayo Civic Center 30 Civic Center Dr SE TF: 800-422-2199 ■ Web: www.mayociviccenter.com	Rochester	MN	55904	507-281-6184	281-6277
Saint Cloud Civic Center 10 4th Ave S TF: 800-450-7272 ■ Web: www.ci.stcloud.mn.us/CivicCenter/	Saint Cloud	MN	56301	320-255-7272	255-9863
Saint Paul RiverCentre 175 W Kellogg Blvd Web: www.rivercentre.org	Saint Paul	MN	55102	651-265-4800	265-4899

Mississippi

				Phone	Fax
Mississippi Coast Coliseum & Convention Center 2350 Beach Blvd TF: 800-726-2781 ■ Web: www.mscoastcoliseum.com	Biloxi	MS	39531	228-594-3700	594-3812
James M Trotter Convention Center 402 2nd Ave N	Columbus	MS	39701	662-328-4164	329-5166
Washington County Convention Center 1040 S Raceway Rd	Greenville	MS	38703	662-332-0488	334-2785
Natchez Convention Center 211 Main St TF: 888-475-9744	Natchez	MS	39120	601-442-5881	442-5998

Missouri

				Phone	Fax
Columbia Expo Center 2200 I-70 Dr SW	Columbia	MO	65203	573-446-3976	446-1159
Jack Lawton Webb Convention Center 5300 S Range Line Rd	Joplin	MO	64804	417-781-4000	623-7400
Kansas City Convention & Entertainment Centers 301 W 13th St TF: 800-821-7060 ■ Web: www.kcconvention.com	Kansas City	MO	64105	816-513-5000	513-5001
America's Center Convention Center 701 Convention Plaza Web: www.explorestlouis.com/americasCenter/public.asp	Saint Louis	MO	63101	314-342-5036	342-5040
Saint Louis Executive Conference Center 701 Convention Plaza America's Center TF: 800-325-7962 ■ Web: www.executiveconferencecenter.com	Saint Louis	MO	63101	314-342-5050	342-5040
Springfield Exposition Center 635 E Saint Louis St	Springfield	MO	65806	417-522-3976	864-3077

Montana

				Phone	Fax
MetraPark 308 6th Ave N PO Box 2514 TF: 800-366-8538 ■ Web: www.metrapark.com	Billings	MT	59103	406-256-2422	256-2479
Mansfield Convention Center 2 Park Dr S Great Falls Civic Center	Great Falls	MT	59401	406-455-8495	
Helena Civic Center 340 Neill Ave Web: www.ci.helena.mt.us/index.php?id=279	Helena	MT	59601	406-447-8492	447-8480

Nebraska

				Phone	Fax
Pershing Center 226 Centennial Mall S Web: www.pershingcenter.com	Lincoln	NE	68508	402-441-8744	441-7913

Nevada

				Phone	Fax
Elko Civic Auditorium & Convention Center 700 Moren Way TF: 800-248-3556 ■ Web: www.elkocva.com	Elko	NV	89801	775-738-4091	738-2420
Henderson Convention Center 200 Water St TF: 877-775-5252 ■ Web: www.visithenderson.com	Henderson	NV	89015	702-267-2171	267-2177
Las Vegas Convention Center 3150 Paradise Rd *Fax: Mktg ■ TF: 800-332-5333 ■ Web: www.lvcva.com	Las Vegas	NV	89109	702-892-0711	892-2824*
Sands Expo & Convention Center 201 Sands Ave Web: www.sandsexpo.com	Las Vegas	NV	89169	702-733-5556	733-5353
Reno-Sparks Convention Center 4590 S Virginia St TF: 800-367-7366 ■ Web: www.visitrenotahoe.com	Reno	NV	89502	775-827-7600	827-7701

New Jersey

				Phone	Fax
Atlantic City Convention Center 1 Miss America Way Web: www.accenter.com	Atlantic City	NJ	08401	609-449-2000	449-2090
Edison Arts Society Conference Center 97 Sunfield Ave Raritan Center Web: www.njexpocenter.com/EB&CC/index.html	Edison	NJ	08837	732-661-1205	417-1414

New Jersey (Cont'd)

	City	State	ZIP	Phone	Fax
New Jersey Convention & Exposition Center 97 Sunfield Ave Raritan Center *Web:* www.njexpocenter.com	Edison	NJ	08837	732-417-1400	417-1414
Meadowlands Exposition Center 355 Plaza Dr *TF:* 888-400-3976 ■ *Web:* www.mecexpo.com	Secaucus	NJ	07094	201-330-7773	330-1172
Garden State Exhibit Center 50 Atrium Dr. *Web:* www.gsec.com	Somerset	NJ	08873	732-469-4000	563-4500
Wildwoods Convention Center 4501 Boardwalk *TF:* 800-992-9732 ■ *Web:* www.wildwoodsnj.com/cc	Wildwood	NJ	08260	609-729-9000	846-2631

New Mexico

	City	State	ZIP	Phone	Fax
Albuquerque Convention Center 401 2nd St NW *TF Mktg:* 800-733-9918 ■ *Web:* www.itsatrip.org/planners/conventioncntr	Albuquerque	NM	87102	505-768-4575	768-3239
LifeWay Glorieta Conference Center PO Box 8 *TF Resv:* 800-797-4222 ■ *Web:* www.lifeway.com/glorieta	Glorieta	NM	87535	505-757-6161	757-6149
Santa Fe Convention Center 60 E San Francisco St *TF:* 800-777-2489 ■ *Web:* www.santafe.org	Santa Fe	NM	87504	505-955-6200	955-6222

New York

	City	State	ZIP	Phone	Fax
Empire State Plaza Convention Center Madison & State St Concorse Level Base of EGG *TF:* 877-659-4377 ■ *Web:* www.ogs.state.ny.us/visiting/cultural/ConventionCtr/intro.html	Albany	NY	12242	518-474-4759	473-2190
Buffalo Niagara Convention Center 153 Franklin St Convention Center Plaza *TF:* 800-995-7570 ■ *Web:* www.buffaloconvention.com/	Buffalo	NY	14202	716-855-5555	855-3158
Jacob K Javits Convention Center 655 W 34th St *Web:* www.javitscenter.com	New York	NY	10001	212-216-2000	216-2588
Rochester Riverside Convention Center 123 E Main St *Web:* www.rrcc.com	Rochester	NY	14604	585-232-7200	232-1510
Saratoga Springs City Center 522 Broadway	Saratoga Springs	NY	12866	518-584-0027	584-0117
Oncenter Complex 800 S State St *TF:* 888-797-6623 ■ *Web:* www.oncenter.org	Syracuse	NY	13202	315-435-8000	435-8099

North Carolina

	City	State	ZIP	Phone	Fax
Asheville Civic Center 87 Haywood St. *Web:* www.ashevilleciviccenter.com	Asheville	NC	28801	828-259-5736	259-5777
Charlotte Convention Center 501 S College St *Web:* www.charlotteconventionctr.com	Charlotte	NC	28202	704-339-6000	339-6111
Charlotte Merchandise Mart 2500 E Independence Blvd. *Web:* www.carolinasmart.com	Charlotte	NC	28205	704-333-7709	375-9410
Metrolina Expo Trade Center 7100 Statesville Rd PO Box 26668 *Web:* www.metrolinaexpotradeshow.com	Charlotte	NC	28221	704-596-4650	295-1983
Crown Center 1960 Coliseum Dr. *Web:* www.crowncoliseum.com	Fayetteville	NC	28306	910-323-5088	323-0489
Greensboro Coliseum Complex 1921 W Lee St *Web:* www.greensborocoliseum.com	Greensboro	NC	27403	336-373-7400	373-2170
International Home Furnishings Center 210 E Commerce Ave *Web:* www.ihfc.com	High Point	NC	27260	336-888-3700	882-1873
Raleigh Convention Center 2 E South St *Web:* www.raleighconvention.com	Raleigh	NC	27601	919-831-6011	831-6013
Benton Convention Center 301 W 5th St *Web:* www.twincityquarter.com/benton.html	Winston-Salem	NC	27101	336-727-2976	727-2879

North Dakota

	City	State	ZIP	Phone	Fax
Bismarck Civic Center 315 S 5th St *Web:* www.bismarckciviccenter.com	Bismarck	ND	58504	701-222-6487	222-6599
Fargo Civic Center 207 N 4th St *Web:* www.cityoffargo.com/civiccenter/	Fargo	ND	58102	701-241-1480	241-1483
Alerus Center 1200 42nd St S *Web:* www.aleruscenter.com	Grand Forks	ND	58201	701-792-1200	746-6511

Ohio

	City	State	ZIP	Phone	Fax
John S Knight Center 77 E Mill St *TF:* 800-245-4254 ■ *Web:* www.johnsknightcenter.org	Akron	OH	44308	330-374-8900	374-8971
Duke Energy Center 525 Elm St *Web:* www.duke-energycenter.com	Cincinnati	OH	45202	513-419-7300	419-7327
Cleveland Convention Center 500 Lakeside Ave *TF:* 800-543-2489 ■ *Web:* www.clevelandconventioncenter.com	Cleveland	OH	44114	216-348-2200	348-2262
International Exposition Center 1-X Center Dr *TF:* 800-492-3683 ■ *Web:* www.ixcenter.com	Cleveland	OH	44135	216-265-2500	265-7300
Franklin County Veterans Memorial 300 W Broad St *Web:* www.fcvm.com/home.htm	Columbus	OH	43215	614-221-4341	221-8422
Greater Columbus Convention Center 400 N High St *TF:* 800-626-0241 ■ *Web:* www.columbusconventions.com	Columbus	OH	43215	614-827-2500	221-7239
Dayton Convention Center 22 E 5th St. *TF:* 800-822-3498 ■ *Web:* www.daytonconventioncenter.com	Dayton	OH	45402	937-333-4700	333-4711
Veterans Memorial Civic & Convention Center 7 Town Sq *TF:* 877-377-0674 ■ *Web:* www.limaciviccenter.com	Lima	OH	45801	419-224-5222	224-6964
Eastwood Expo Center 5555 Youngstown Warren Rd Unit 700 *Web:* www.eastwoodexpo.com	Niles	OH	44446	330-652-6980	743-2902
Sharonville Convention Center 11355 Chester Rd. *Web:* www.sharonvilleconventioncenter.com	Sharonville	OH	45246	513-771-7744	772-5745
SeaGate Convention Centre 401 Jefferson Ave *TF:* 800-243-4667 ■ *Web:* www.toledo-seagate.com	Toledo	OH	43604	419-255-3300	255-7731

Oklahoma

	City	State	ZIP	Phone	Fax
Cherokee Strip Conference Center 123 W Maine St *Web:* www.csccenid.com	Enid	OK	73701	580-234-1919	242-8975
Cox Business Services Convention Center 1 Myriad Gardens *Web:* www.coxconventioncenter.com	Oklahoma City	OK	73102	405-602-8500	602-8505
Expo Square 4145 E 21st St *Web:* www.exposquare.com	Tulsa	OK	74114	918-744-1113	744-8725
Tulsa Convention Center W 7th & S Houston St. *TF:* 800-678-7177 ■ *Web:* www.tulsaconvention.com	Tulsa	OK	74103	918-596-7177	596-7155

Ontario

	City	State	ZIP	Phone	Fax
Metro Toronto Convention Centre 255 Front St W **Fax:* Sales ■ *Web:* www.mtccc.com	Toronto	ON	M5V2W6	416-585-8000	585-8198*

Oregon

	City	State	ZIP	Phone	Fax
Lane Events Center 796 W 13th Ave *Web:* www.atthefair.com	Eugene	OR	97402	541-682-4292	682-3614
Florence Events Center 715 Quince St. *TF:* 888-968-4086 ■ *Web:* www.eventcenter.org	Florence	OR	97439	541-997-1994	902-0991
Pendleton Convention Center 1601 Westgate *TF:* 800-863-9358 ■ *Web:* www.pendleton.or.us	Pendleton	OR	97801	541-276-6569	278-1317
Oregon Convention Center 777 NE ML King Jr Blvd *TF:* 800-791-2250 ■ *Web:* www.oregoncc.org	Portland	OR	97232	503-235-7575	235-7417
Portland Metropolitan Exposition Center 2060 N Marine Dr *Web:* www.expocenter.org	Portland	OR	97217	503-736-5200	736-5201
Oregon State Fair & Expo Center 2330 17th St NE *Web:* www.oregonstatefair.org/expo/index.htm	Salem	OR	97301	503-947-3247	947-3206
Salem Conference Center 200 Commercial St SE *TF Sales:* 877-589-1700 ■ *Web:* www.salemconferencecenter.org	Salem	OR	97301	503-589-1700	589-1715
Seaside Civic & Convention Center 415 1st Ave. *TF:* 800-394-3303 ■ *Web:* www.seasideconvention.com	Seaside	OR	97138	503-738-8585	738-0198

Pennsylvania

	City	State	ZIP	Phone	Fax
Valley Forge Convention Center 1160 1st Ave *TF:* 888-267-1500 ■ *Web:* www.vfconventioncenter.com	King of Prussia	PA	19406	610-337-4000	768-3290
Hampton Inn Philadelphia Center City-Convention Center 1301 Race St *TF:* 800-426-7866 ■ *Web:* hamptoninn1.hilton.com	Philadelphia	PA	19107	215-665-9100	665-9200
Pennsylvania Convention Center 1101 Arch St *TF:* 800-428-9000 ■ *Web:* www.paconvention.com	Philadelphia	PA	19107	215-418-4700	418-4747
David L Lawrence Convention Center 1000 Fort Duquesne Blvd. *Web:* www.pittsburghcc.com	Pittsburgh	PA	15222	412-565-6000	565-6008

Quebec

	City	State	ZIP	Phone	Fax
Palais des Congres de Montreal-Convention Centre 159 Saint-Antoine St W 9th Fl. *TF:* 800-268-8122 ■ *Web:* www.congresmtl.com	Montreal	QC	H2Z1H2	514-871-8122	871-3188

Rhode Island

	City	State	ZIP	Phone	Fax
Rhode Island Convention Center 1 Sabin St *Web:* www.riconvention.com	Providence	RI	02903	401-458-6000	458-6500

South Carolina

	City	State	ZIP	Phone	Fax
Charleston Area Convention Center Complex 5001 Coliseum Dr *Web:* www.charlestonconvention.com	Charleston	SC	29418	843-529-5011	529-5040
Carolina First Center 1 Exposition Ave. *Web:* www.palmettoexpo.com	Greenville	SC	29607	864-233-2562	255-8600
Myrtle Beach Convention Center 2101 N Oak St *TF:* 800-537-1690 ■ *Web:* www.myrtlebeachconventioncenter.com	Myrtle Beach	SC	29577	843-918-1225	918-1243

South Dakota

	City	State	ZIP	Phone	Fax
Rivercenter Convention Center 920 W Sioux Ave	Pierre	SD	57501	605-224-6877	224-1042
Rushmore Plaza Civic Center 444 Mt Rushmore Rd N *TF:* 800-468-6463 ■ *Web:* www.gotmine.com	Rapid City	SD	57701	605-394-4115	394-4119

Tennessee

	City	State	ZIP	Phone	Fax
Chattanooga Convention Center 1150 Carter St *TF:* 800-962-5213 ■ *Web:* www.chattconvention.org	Chattanooga	TN	37402	423-756-0001	267-5291
Gatlinburg Convention Center 234 Historic Nature Trail *TF:* 800-343-1475 ■ *Web:* www.gatlinburg-tennessee.com	Gatlinburg	TN	37738	865-436-2392	436-3704
Carl Perkins Civic Center 400 S Highland Ave *Web:* www.jacksoncentre.com/CivicCenterMain.htm	Jackson	TN	38301	731-425-8580	425-8589
Knoxville Convention Center 701 Henley St. *Web:* www.kccsmg.com	Knoxville	TN	37902	865-522-5669	329-0422
Memphis Cook Convention Center 255 N Main St *TF:* 800-726-0915 ■ *Web:* www.memphisconvention.com	Memphis	TN	38103	901-576-1200	576-1212
Nashville Convention Center 601 Commerce St **Fax:* Mktg ■ *Web:* www.nashvilleconventionctr.com	Nashville	TN	37203	615-742-2000	742-2014*

Texas

	City	State	ZIP	Phone	Fax
Amarillo Civic Center 401 S Buchanan St *Web:* www.civicamarillo.com	Amarillo	TX	79101	806-378-4297	378-4234
Arlington Convention Center 1200 Ballpark Way *Web:* www.arlingtoncc.com	Arlington	TX	76011	817-459-5000	459-5091
Austin Convention Center 500 E Cesar Chavez St *Web:* www.austinconventioncenter.com	Austin	TX	78701	512-404-4000	404-4416
Palmer Events Center 900 Barton Springs Rd *Web:* www.austinconventioncenter.com	Austin	TX	78704	512-404-4500	404-4422

Phone | Fax

Beaumont Civic Center Complex 701 Main St. . . . . Beaumont TX 77701 409-838-3435 838-3715
TF: 800-782-3081 ■ *Web:* www.beaumont-tx-complex.com

Bell County Expo Center 301 W Loop 121. . . . . Belton TX 76513 254-933-5353 933-5354
Web: www.bellcountyexpo.com

American Bank Center 1901 N Shoreline Blvd. . . . . Corpus Christi TX 78401 361-826-4100 826-4905
Web: www.americanbankcenter.com

Dallas Convention Center 650 S Griffin St. . . . . Dallas TX 75202 214-939-2700 939-2795
TF: 877-850-2100 ■ *Web:* www.dallasconventioncenter.com/

Dallas Market Center 2100 Stemmons Fwy Suite MS 150 . . . . . Dallas TX 75207 800-325-6587 749-5479*
**Fax Area Code:* 214 ■ *TF:* 800-325-6587 ■ *Web:* www.dallasmarketcenter.com

Fair Park 1300 Robert B Cullum Blvd. . . . . Dallas TX 75210 214-670-8400 670-8907
Web: www.fairparkdallas.com

El Paso Convention & Performing Arts Center
1 Civic Center Plaza . . . . . El Paso TX 79901 915-534-0600 534-0687
TF: 800-351-6024 ■ *Web:* www.visitelpaso.com/cpac_index.sstg

Fort Worth Convention Center 1201 Houston St. . . . . Fort Worth TX 76102 817-392-6338 392-2756
TF: 866-630-2588 ■ *Web:* www.fortworthgov.org

Moody Gardens Convention Center 1 Hope Blvd . . . . . Galveston TX 77554 409-744-4673 683-4926
TF: 800-582-4673 ■ *Web:* www.moodygardenshotel.com/conventioncenter.htm

Grapevine Convention Center 1209 S Main St. . . . . Grapevine TX 76051 817-410-3459 410-3090
Web: www.grapevineconventioncenter.com

George R Brown Convention Center
1001 Avenida de Las Americas . . . . . Houston TX 77010 713-853-8000 853-8090
TF: 800-427-4697 ■ *Web:* www.houstonconventionctr.com

Maude Cobb Convention Center 100 Grand Blvd. . . . . Longview TX 75604 903-237-1230 236-7845

Lubbock Memorial Civic Center 1501 MacDavis Ln . . . . . Lubbock TX 79401 806-775-2243 775-3240
Web: lmcc.ci.lubbock.tx.us

Plano Centre 2000 E Springcreek Pkwy . . . . . Plano TX 75074 972-422-0296 424-0002
TF: 800-817-5266 ■ *Web:* www.plano.gov/departments/PlanoCentre/

Robert A "Bob" Bowers Civic Center
3401 Cultural Center Dr. . . . . Port Arthur TX 77642 409-985-8801 985-3125
Web: www.portarthur.net/pa_civic_center.cfm

San Angelo Convention Center Coliseum & Auditorium
500 Rio Concho Dr . . . . . San Angelo TX 76903 325-653-9577 659-0900
Web: www.sanangelotexas.org

Henry B Gonzalez Convention Center 200 E Market St . . . . . San Antonio TX 78205 210-207-8500 223-1495
TF: 877-504-8895 ■ *Web:* www.ci.sat.tx.us/convfac

South Padre Island Convention Centre
7355 Padre Blvd. . . . . South Padre Island TX 78597 956-761-3000 761-3024
TF: 800-657-2373

Frank W Mayborn Civic & Convention Center 3303 N 3rd St. . . . . Temple TX 76501 254-298-5720 298-5388
TF: 800-479-0338 ■ *Web:* www.mayborncenter.com

Oil Palace 10408 Hwy 64 E . . . . . Tyler TX 75707 903-566-2122 566-4206
Web: www.oilpalace.com

MPEC (Multi-Purpose Events Center) 1000 5th St . . . . . Wichita Falls TX 76301 940-716-5500 716-5509
TF: 800-799-6732 ■ *Web:* www.wfmpec.com

Utah

Phone | Fax

Golden Spike Event Center 1000 N 1200 West. . . . . Ogden UT 84404 801-399-8544 392-1995
TF: 800-442-7362 ■ *Web:* www.goldenspikeeventcenter.com

Ogden Eccles Conference Center 2415 Washington Blvd. . . . . Ogden UT 84401 801-395-3200 395-3201
TF: 800-337-2690 ■ *Web:* www.oecenter.com

Salt Palace Convention Center 100 S West Temple . . . . . Salt Lake City UT 84101 801-534-4777 534-6383
TF: 877-547-4656 ■ *Web:* www.saltpalace.com

Virginia

Phone | Fax

Greater Richmond Convention Center 403 N 3rd St. . . . . Richmond VA 23219 804-783-7300 225-0508
TF: 800-370-9004 ■ *Web:* www.richmondcenter.com

Washington

Phone | Fax

Meydenbauer Center 11100 NE 6th St. . . . . Bellevue WA 98004 425-637-1020 637-0166
Web: www.meydenbauer.com

Three Rivers Convention Center & Coliseum
7016 W Grandbridge Blvd . . . . . Kennewick WA 99336 509-735-9400 735-9431
Web: www.threeriversconventioncenter.com

Ocean Shores Convention Center 120 Chance A La Mer. . . . . Ocean Shores WA 98569 360-289-4411 289-4412
TF: 800-874-6737 ■ *Web:* www.oceanshoresconventioncenter.com

Bell Harbor International Conference Center
2211 Alaskan Way Pier 66. . . . . Seattle WA 98121 206-441-6666 269-4159
TF: 888-772-4422 ■ *Web:* www.bellharbor.org

Washington State Convention & Trade Center
800 Convention Pl . . . . . Seattle WA 98101 206-694-5000 694-5399
Web: www.wsctc.com

Spokane Center 334 W Spokane Falls Blvd . . . . . Spokane WA 99201 509-353-6500 353-6511
Web: www.spokanecenter.com

Greater Tacoma Convention & Trade Center 1500 Broadway. . . . . Tacoma WA 98402 253-830-6601 573-2363
TF: 888-227-3705 ■ *Web:* www.tacomaconventioncenter.com

Yakima Convention Center 10 N 8th St. . . . . Yakima WA 98901 509-575-6062 575-6252
TF: 800-221-0751 ■ *Web:* www.yakimacenter.com

West Virginia

Phone | Fax

Charleston Civic Center & Coliseum 200 Civic Center Dr. . . . . Charleston WV 25301 304-345-1500 345-3492
Web: www.charlestonwvciviccenter.com

Wisconsin

Phone | Fax

Brown County Veterans Memorial Complex
1901 S Oneida St. . . . . Green Bay WI 54304 920-497-5664 494-9229
TF: 800-895-0071 ■ *Web:* www.pmiwi.com/venues/bcvma/bcvma.php

La Crosse Center 300 Harborview Plaza. . . . . La Crosse WI 54601 608-789-7400 789-7444
Web: www.lacrossecenter.com

Alliant Energy Center of Dane County
1919 Alliant Energy Center Way . . . . . Madison WI 53713 608-267-3976 267-0146
Web: www.alliantenergycenter.com

Monona Terrace Community & Convention Center
1 John Nolen Dr. . . . . Madison WI 53703 608-261-4000 261-4049
Web: www.mononaterrace.com

Midwest Airlines Center 400 W Wisconsin Ave. . . . . Milwaukee WI 53203 414-908-6000 908-6010
Web: www.midwestexpresscenter.com

Sunnyview Exposition Center 500 E County Rd Y. . . . . Oshkosh WI 54901 920-236-4921 303-4707

Wyoming

Phone | Fax

Casper Events Center 1 Events Dr . . . . . Casper WY 82601 307-235-8441 235-8445
TF: 800-442-2256 ■ *Web:* www.caspereventscenter.com

209 CONVENTION & VISITORS BUREAUS

SEE ALSO Travel & Tourism Information - Canadian p. 2384; Travel & Tourism Information - Foreign Travel p. 2384

Listings are alphabetized by city names.

Phone | Fax

Aberdeen Convention & Visitors Bureau
10 Railroad Ave SW PO Box 78 . . . . . Aberdeen SD 57402 605-225-2414 225-3573
TF: 800-645-3851 ■ *Web:* www.aberdeencvb.com

Abilene Convention & Visitors Bureau 201 NW 2nd St . . . . . Abilene KS 67410 785-263-2231 263-4125
TF: 800-569-5915 ■ *Web:* www.abilenekansas.org

Abilene Convention & Visitors Bureau 1101 N 1st St. . . . . Abilene TX 79601 325-676-2556 676-1630
TF: 800-727-7704 ■ *Web:* abilenevisitors.com

Abingdon Convention & Visitors Bureau 335 Cummings St . . . . . Abingdon VA 24210 276-676-2282 676-3076
TF: 800-435-3440 ■ *Web:* www.abingdon.com/tourism

Akron/Summit County Convention & Visitors Bureau 77 E Mill St. . . . . Akron OH 44308 330-374-7560 374-7626
TF: 800-245-4254 ■ *Web:* www.visitakron-summit.org

Albany County Convention & Visitors Bureau
25 Quackenbush Sq. . . . . Albany NY 12207 518-434-1217 434-0887
TF: 800-258-3582 ■ *Web:* www.albany.org

Albany Visitors Assn 250 Broadalbin St SW Suite 110 . . . . . Albany OR 97321 541-928-0911 926-1500
TF: 800-526-2256 ■ *Web:* www.albanyvisitors.com

Albuquerque Convention & Visitors Bureau
20 First Plaza Suite 601. . . . . Albuquerque NM 87102 505-842-9918 247-9101
TF: 800-733-9918 ■ *Web:* www.itsatrip.org/

Alexandria/Pineville Area Convention & Visitors Bureau
707 Main St. . . . . Alexandria LA 71301 318-442-9546 443-1617
TF: 800-551-9546 ■ *Web:* www.louisianafromhere.com

Alexandria Convention & Visitors Assn 221 King St. . . . . Alexandria VA 22314 703-838-4200 838-4683
TF: 800-388-9119 ■ *Web:* www.funside.com

Allegan County Tourist & Recreational Council
3255 122nd Ave Suite 102 . . . . . Allegan MI 49010 269-686-9088 673-0454
TF: 888-425-5342 ■ *Web:* visitallegancounty.com

Lehigh Valley Convention & Visitors Bureau
840 Hamilton St Suite 200. . . . . Allentown PA 18101 610-882-9200 882-0343
TF: 800-747-0561 ■ *Web:* www.lehighvalleypa.org

Alpena Area Convention & Visitors Bureau 235 W Chisholm St . . . . . Alpena MI 49707 989-354-4181 356-3999
TF: 800-425-7362 ■ *Web:* www.oweb.com/upnorth/

Alton Regional Convention & Visitors Bureau 200 Piasa St. . . . . Alton IL 62002 618-465-6676 465-6151
TF: 800-258-6645 ■ *Web:* www.visitalton.com

Alvin Convention & Visitors Bureau 105 W Willis St . . . . . Alvin TX 77511 281-585-3359 585-8662
TF: 800-331-4063 ■ *Web:* www.alvintexas.org

Amana Colonies Convention & Visitors Bureau 622 46th Ave . . . . . Amana IA 52203 319-622-7622 622-6395
TF: 800-579-2294 ■ *Web:* www.iowa-city.com/amanas

Amarillo Convention & Visitor Council
1000 S Polk St PO Box 9480 . . . . . Amarillo TX 79105 806-374-1497 373-3909
TF: 800-692-1338 ■ *Web:* www.visitamarillotx.com

Lorain County Visitors Bureau 8025 Leavitt Rd . . . . . Amherst OH 44001 440-984-5282 984-7363
TF: 800-334-1673 ■ *Web:* www.lcvb.org

Anaheim/Orange County Visitor & Convention Bureau
800 W Katella Ave . . . . . Anaheim CA 92802 714-765-8888 991-8963
TF: 888-598-3200 ■ *Web:* www.anaheimoc.org

Anchorage Convention & Visitors Bureau 524 W 4th Ave . . . . . Anchorage AK 99501 907-276-4118 278-5559
TF: 800-478-1255 ■ *Web:* www.anchorage.net

Anderson/Madison County Visitors & Convention Bureau
6335 S Scatterfield Rd. . . . . Anderson IN 46013 765-643-5633 643-9083
TF: 800-533-6569 ■ *Web:* www.heartlandspirit.com

Steuben County Tourism Bureau 207 S Wayne St. . . . . Angola IN 46703 260-665-5386 665-5461
TF: 800-525-3101 ■ *Web:* www.lakes101.org

Ann Arbor Area Convention & Visitors Bureau
120 W Huron St. . . . . Ann Arbor MI 48104 734-995-7281 995-7283
TF: 800-888-9487 ■ *Web:* www.annarbor.org

Southernmost Illinois Tourism Bureau
1000 N Main St PO Box 378. . . . . Anna IL 62906 618-833-9928 833-9924
TF: 800-248-4373 ■ *Web:* www.southernmostillinois.com

Annapolis & Anne Arundel County Conference & Visitors Bureau 26 West St . . . . . Annapolis MD 21401 410-268-8687 263-9591
TF: 888-302-2852 ■ *Web:* www.visit-annapolis.org

Fox Cities Convention & Visitors Bureau 3433 W College Ave. . . . . Appleton WI 54914 920-734-3358 734-1080
TF: 800-236-6673 ■ *Web:* www.foxcities.org

Arkansas City Convention & Visitors Bureau
106 S Summit St PO Box 795. . . . . Arkansas City KS 67005 620-442-0230 441-0048
Web: www.arkcity.org

Arlington Convention & Visitors Bureau
1905 E Randol Mill Rd. . . . . Arlington TX 76011 817-265-7721 265-5640
TF: 800-433-5374 ■ *Web:* www.newmediagateway.com/

Arlington Convention & Visitors Service
1100 N Glebe Rd Suite 1500. . . . . Arlington VA 22201 703-228-0888 228-0806
TF: 800-296-7996 ■ *Web:* www.stayarlington.com

Asheville Area Convention & Visitors Bureau
36 Montford Ave PO Box 1010. . . . . Asheville NC 28802 828-258-6102 254-6054
TF: 800-257-5583 ■ *Web:* www.exploreasheville.com

Aspen Chamber Resort Assn 425 Rio Grande Pl . . . . . Aspen CO 81611 970-925-1940 920-1173
TF: 800-670-0792 ■ *Web:* www.aspenchamber.org

Athens Convention & Visitors Bureau 300 N Thomas St . . . . . Athens GA 30601 706-357-4430 546-8040
TF: 800-653-0603 ■ *Web:* www.visitathensga.com

Athens County Convention & Visitors Bureau 667 E State St. . . . . Athens OH 45701 740-592-1819 593-7365
TF: 800-878-9767 ■ *Web:* www.athensohio.com

Atlanta Convention & Visitors Bureau
233 Peachtree St NE Suite 1400. . . . . Atlanta GA 30303 404-521-6600 584-6331*
**Fax:* Sales ■ *TF:* 800-285-2682 ■ *Web:* www.atlanta.net

Cobb County Convention & Visitors Bureau 1 Galleria Pkwy . . . . . Atlanta GA 30339 678-303-2622 303-2625
TF: 800-451-3480 ■ *Web:* www.cobbcvb.com

Atlantic City Convention & Visitors Authority
2314 Pacific Ave . . . . . Atlantic City NJ 08401 609-449-7130 348-3426
TF: 888-228-4748 ■ *Web:* www.atlanticcitynj.com

Auburn-Opelika Tourism Bureau 714 E Glenn Ave. . . . . Auburn AL 36830 334-887-8747 821-5500
TF: 800-321-8880 ■ *Web:* www.auburn-opelika.com

Augusta Metropolitan Convention & Visitors Bureau
1450 Greene St Suite 110. . . . . Augusta GA 30901 706-823-6600 823-6609
TF: 800-726-0243 ■ *Web:* www.augustaga.org

Aurora Area Convention & Visitors Bureau 43 W Galena Blvd. . . . . Aurora IL 60506 630-897-5581 897-5589
TF: 800-477-4369 ■ *Web:* www.enjoyaurora.com

Phone Fax

Austin Convention & Visitors Bureau
301 Congress Ave Suite 200 Austin TX 78701 512-474-5171 583-7282
TF: 800-926-2282 ■ *Web:* www.austintexas.org

Catalina Island Visitors Bureau PO Box 217 Avalon CA 90704 310-510-1520 510-7606
Web: www.visitcatalina.org

Baker County Visitors & Convention Bureau
490 Campbell St. Baker City OR 97814 541-523-3356 523-9187
TF: 800-523-1235 ■ *Web:* www.visitbaker.com

Greater Bakersfield Convention & Visitors Bureau
515 Truxtun Ave. Bakersfield CA 93301 661-325-5051 325-7074
TF: 866-425-7353 ■ *Web:* www.bakersfieldcvb.org

Baltimore Area Convention & Visitors Assn
100 Light St 12th Fl. Baltimore MD 21202 410-659-7300 727-2308
TF: 800-343-3468 ■ *Web:* www.baltimore.org

Bandera County Convention & Visitors Bureau
126 State Hwy 16 S PO Box 171 Bandera TX 78003 830-796-3045 796-4121
TF: 800-364-3833 ■ *Web:* www.banderatexas.com

Greater Bangor Convention & Visitors Bureau 40 Harlow Pl Bangor ME 04401 207-947-5205 942-2146
TF: 800-916-6673 ■ *Web:* www.bangorcvb.org

Bardstown-Nelson County Tourist & Convention Commission
1 Court Sq PO Box 867 Bardstown KY 40004 502-348-4877 349-0804
TF: 800-638-4877 ■ *Web:* www.visitbardstown.com

Clermont County Convention & Visitors Bureau
410 E Main St PO Box 100 Batavia OH 45103 513-732-3600 732-2244
TF: 800-796-4282 ■ *Web:* www.clermontcvb-ohio.com

Baton Rouge Convention & Visitors Bureau
730 North Blvd. Baton Rouge LA 70802 225-383-1825 346-1253
TF: 800-527-6843 ■ *Web:* www.visitbatonrouge.com

Battle Creek/Calhoun County Visitors & Convention Bureau
77 E Michigan Ave Suite 100. Battle Creek MI 49017 269-962-2240 962-6917
TF: 800-397-2240 ■ *Web:* www.battlecreekvisitors.org

Beaumont Convention & Visitors Bureau
801 Main St Suite 100 Beaumont TX 77701 409-880-3749 880-3750
TF: 800-392-4401 ■ *Web:* www.beaumontcvb.com

Greene County Convention & Visitors Bureau
1221 Meadowbridge Dr Beavercreek OH 45434 937-429-9100 429-7726
TF: 800-733-9109 ■ *Web:* www.greenecountyohio.org

Washington County Convention & Visitors Bureau
5075 SW Griffith Dr Suite 120. Beaverton OR 97005 503-644-5555 644-9784
TF: 800-537-3149 ■ *Web:* www.wcva.org

Southern West Virginia Convention & Visitors Bureau
1406 Harper Rd Beckley WV 25801 304-252-2244 252-2252
TF: 800-847-4898 ■ *Web:* www.visitwv.org

Bedford County Visitors Bureau 131 S Juliana St Bedford PA 15522 814-623-1771 623-1671
TF: 800-765-3331 ■ *Web:* www.bedfordcounty.net

Bellevue Area Tourism & Visitors Bureau PO Box 63 Bellevue OH 44811 419-483-5359
Web: www.bellevuetourism.org

Gaston County Travel & Tourism 620 N Main St. Belmont NC 28012 704-825-4044 825-4029
TF: 800-849-9994 ■ *Web:* www.gastontourism.com

Beloit Convention & Visitors Bureau 1003 Pleasant St. Beloit WI 53511 608-365-4838 365-6850
TF: 800-423-5648 ■ *Web:* www.visitbeloit.com

Northern Illinois Tourism Development Office 200 S State St Belvidere IL 61008 815-547-3740 547-3749
Web: www.visitnorthernillinois.com

Bucks County Conference & Visitors Bureau 3207 Street Rd Bensalem PA 19020 215-639-0300 642-3277
TF: 800-836-2825 ■ *Web:* www.buckscountycvb.org

Franklin County Tourism Bureau 209 W Main St PO Box 1641 Benton IL 62812 618-439-0608 435-4054
TF: 800-661-9998 ■ *Web:* www.fctb.com

Southwestern Michigan Tourism Council
2300 Pipestone Rd. Benton Harbor MI 49022 269-925-6301 925-7540
Web: www.swmichigan.org

Berkeley Convention & Visitors Bureau 2015 Center St 1st Fl. Berkeley CA 94704 510-549-7040 644-2052
TF: 800-847-4823 ■ *Web:* www.visitberkeley.com

Beverly Hills Conference & Visitors Bureau
239 S Beverly Dr Beverly Hills CA 90212 310-248-1000 248-1020
TF: 800-345-2210 ■ *Web:* www.beverlyhillscvb.com

Greater Big Rapids Convention & Visitors Bureau
246 N State St Big Rapids MI 49307 231-796-7640 796-0832
TF: 888-229-4386 ■ *Web:* www.bigrapids.org

Big Spring Convention & Visitor Bureau 310 Nolan St. Big Spring TX 79720 432-263-8235 264-9111
TF: 866-430-7100 ■ *Web:* www.bigspringtx.com

Billings Convention & Visitors Bureau
815 S 27th St PO Box 31177 Billings MT 59107 406-245-4111 245-7333
TF: 800-735-2635 ■ *Web:* www.billingscvb.visitmt.com

Broome County Convention & Visitors Bureau
49 Court St PO Box 995 Binghamton NY 13902 607-772-8860 722-4513
TF: 800-836-6740 ■ *Web:* www.binghamtoncvb.com

Greater Birmingham Convention & Visitors Bureau
2200 9th Ave N Birmingham AL 35203 205-458-8000 458-8086
TF: 800-458-8085 ■ *Web:* www.sweetbirmingham.com

Bismarck-Mandan Convention & Visitors Bureau
1600 Burnt Boat Dr Bismarck ND 58503 701-222-4308 222-0647
TF: 800-767-3555 ■ *Web:* www.discoverbismarckmandan.com

Bloomington-Normal Area Convention & Visitors Bureau
3201 CIRA Dr Suite 201 Bloomington IL 61704 309-665-0033 661-0743
TF: 800-433-8226 ■ *Web:* www.visitbn.org

Bloomington/Monroe County Convention & Visitors Bureau
2855 N Walnut St Bloomington IN 47404 812-334-8900 334-2344
TF: 800-800-0037 ■ *Web:* www.visitbloomington.com

Bloomington Convention & Visitors Bureau
7900 International Dr Suite 990. Bloomington MN 55425 952-858-8500 858-8854
TF: 800-346-4289 ■ *Web:* www.bloomingtonmn.org

Columbia-Montour Visitors Bureau 121 Papermill Rd. Bloomsburg PA 17815 570-784-8279 784-1166
TF: 800-847-4810 ■ *Web:* www.itourcolumbiamontour.com

Mercer County Convention & Visitors Bureau
704 Bland St PO Box 4088 Bluefield WV 24701 304-325-8438 324-8483
TF: 800-221-3206 ■ *Web:* www.mccvb.com

Boise Convention & Visitors Bureau 312 S 9th St Suite 100. Boise ID 83702 208-344-7777 344-6236
TF: 800-635-5240 ■ *Web:* www.boise.org

Boone Convention & Visitors Bureau 208 Howard St Boone NC 28607 828-262-3516 264-6644
TF: 800-852-9506 ■ *Web:* visitboonenc.com

North Carolina High Country Host 1700 Blowing Rock Rd Boone NC 28607 828-264-1299 265-0550
TF: 800-438-7500 ■ *Web:* www.highcountryhost.com

Greater Boston Convention & Visitors Bureau
2 Copley Pl Suite 105 Boston MA 02116 617-536-4100 424-7664
TF: 888-733-2678 ■ *Web:* www.bostonusa.com

Bottineau Convention & Visitor Bureau 519 Main St Bottineau ND 58318 701-228-3849 228-5130
TF: 800-735-6932 ■ *Web:* www.bottineau.com

Boulder Convention & Visitors Bureau 2440 Pearl St. Boulder CO 80302 303-442-2911 938-2098
TF: 800-444-0447 ■ *Web:* www.bouldercoloradousa.com

Bradenton Area Convention & Visitors Bureau
1 Haven Blvd PO Box 1000 Bradenton FL 34206 941-729-9177 729-1820
TF: 800-822-2017 ■ *Web:* www.floridaislandbeaches.org

Brainerd Lakes Area Convention & Visitors Bureau
7393 State Hwy 371 Brainerd MN 56401 218-829-2838 829-8199
TF: 800-450-2838 ■ *Web:* www.brainerd.com

Branson/Lakes Area Convention & Visitors Bureau
269 State Hwy 248 PO Box 1897 Branson MO 65615 417-334-4136 334-4139
TF: 800-214-3661 ■ *Web:* www.bransonchamber.com

Brenham/Washington County Convention & Visitor Bureau
314 S Austin St Brenham TX 77833 979-836-3695 836-2540
TF: 800-225-3695 ■ *Web:* www.brenhamtx.org

Greater Bridgeport Conference & Vistors Center
164 W Main St. Bridgeport WV 26330 304-842-7272 842-1941
TF: 800-368-4324 ■ *Web:* www.greater-bridgeport.com

Visit Minneapolis North
6200 Shingle Creek Pkwy Suite 248 Brooklyn Center MN 55430 763-566-7722 566-6526
TF: 800-541-4364 ■ *Web:* www.visitminneapolisnorth.com

Northwest Pennsylvania's Great Outdoors Visitors Bureau
175 Main St Brookville PA 15825 814-849-5197 849-1969
TF: 800-348-9393 ■ *Web:* www.pagreatoutdoors.com

Brownsville Convention & Visitors Bureau PO Box 4697 Brownsville TX 78523 956-546-3721 546-3972
TF: 800-626-2639 ■ *Web:* www.brownsville.org

Brunswick & The Golden Isles of Georgia Visitors Bureau
2000 Glynn Ave Brunswick GA 31520 912-264-5337 265-0629
Web: www.bgivb.com

Buckhannon/Upshur Convention & Visitor Bureau
16 S Canal St PO Box 442 Buckhannon WV 26201 304-472-1722 472-4938
Web: www.buchamber.com

Buena Park Convention & Visitors Office
6601 Beach Blvd Suite 200 Buena Park CA 90621 714-562-3560 562-3569
TF: 800-541-3953 ■ *Web:* www.visitbuenapark.com

Buffalo Niagara Convention & Visitors Bureau
617 Main St Suite 200. Buffalo NY 14203 716-852-2356 852-0131
TF: 800-283-3256 ■ *Web:* www.visitbuffaloniagara.com

San Mateo County Convention & Visitors Bureau
111 Anza Blvd Suite 410 Burlingame CA 94010 650-348-7600 348-7687
TF: 800-288-4748 ■ *Web:* www.sanmateocountycvb.com

Burlington/Alamance County Convention & Visitors Bureau
610 S Lexington Ave Burlington NC 27215 336-570-1444 228-1330
TF: 800-637-3804 ■ *Web:* www.burlington-area-nc.org

Burlington Convention & Visitors Bureau
60 Main St Suite 100. Burlington VT 05401 802-863-3489 863-1538
TF: 877-264-3503

Cadillac Area Visitors Bureau 222 N Lake St Cadillac MI 49601 231-775-0657 775-1440
TF: 800-225-2537 ■ *Web:* www.cadillacmichigan.com

Tourism Calgary 238 11th Ave SE Suite 200 Calgary AB T2G0X8 403-263-8510 262-3809
TF: 800-661-1678 ■ *Web:* www.tourismcalgary.com

Finger Lakes Visitors Connection 25 Gorham St Canandaigua NY 14424 585-394-3915 394-4067
TF: 877-386-4669 ■ *Web:* www.ontariony.com

Canton/Stark County Convention & Visitors Bureau
222 Market Ave N Canton OH 44702 330-454-1439 456-3600
TF: 800-533-4302 ■ *Web:* www.visitcantonohio.com

Cape Girardeau Convention & Visitors Bureau
400 Broadway Suite 100 Cape Girardeau MO 63701 573-335-1631 334-6702
TF: 800-777-0068 ■ *Web:* www.capegirardeaucvb.org

Carbondale Convention & Tourism Bureau
1185 E Main St Suite 1046 Carbondale IL 62901 618-529-4451 529-5590
TF: 800-526-1500 ■ *Web:* www.cctb.org

Carlsbad Convention & Visitors Bureau
400 Carlsbad Village Dr Carlsbad CA 92008 760-434-6093 434-6056
TF: 800-227-5722 ■ *Web:* www.carlsbadca.org

Carlsbad Convention & Visitors Bureau 302 S Canal St Carlsbad NM 88220 505-887-6516 885-1455
TF: 800-221-1224 ■ *Web:* www.chamber.caverns.com

Hamilton County Convention & Visitors Bureau 37 E Main St Carmel IN 46032 317-848-3181 848-3191
TF: 800-776-8687 ■ *Web:* www.hccvb.org

Carrington Convention & Visitors Bureau PO Box 439 Carrington ND 58421 701-652-2524 652-2391
TF: 800-641-9668

Carson City Convention & Visitors Bureau
1900 S Carson St Suite 100 Carson City NV 89701 775-687-7410 687-7416
TF: 800-638-2321 ■ *Web:* www.carson-city.org

Cartersville Bartow County Convention & Visitors Bureau
1 Friendship Plaza Suite 1 PO Box 200397 Cartersville GA 30120 770-387-1357 607-3105
TF: 800-733-2280 ■ *Web:* www.notatlanta.org

Casper Area Convention & Visitors Bureau 992 N Poplar St Casper WY 82601 307-234-5362 261-9928
TF: 800-852-1889 ■ *Web:* www.casperwyoming.info

Cedar City-Brian Head Tourism & Convention Bureau
581 N Main St Cedar City UT 84720 435-586-5124 586-4022
TF: 800-354-4849 ■ *Web:* www.scenicsouthernutah.com

Cedar Rapids Area Convention & Visitors Bureau
119 1st Ave SE PO Box 5339 Cedar Rapids IA 52406 319-398-5009 398-5089
TF: 800-735-5557 ■ *Web:* www.cedar-rapids.com

Lewis County Convention & Visitor Bureau 1401 W Mellen St. Centralia WA 98531 360-330-7598 330-7567
TF: 800-525-3323 ■ *Web:* www.tourlewiscounty.com

Brandywine Conference & Visitors Bureau 1 Beaver Valley Rd Chadford PA 19317 610-565-3679 565-0833
TF: 800-343-3983 ■ *Web:* www.brandywinecvb.org

Champaign County Convention & Visitors Bureau
1817 S Neil St Suite 201 Champaign IL 61820 217-351-4133 359-1809
TF: 800-369-6151 ■ *Web:* www.visitchampaigncounty.org

Chapel Hill/Orange County Visitors Bureau
501 W Franklin St Chapel Hill NC 27516 919-968-2060 968-2062
TF: 888-968-2060 ■ *Web:* www.chocvb.org

Charleston Area Convention & Visitors Bureau 423 King St Charleston SC 29403 843-853-8000 853-0444
TF: 800-868-8118 ■ *Web:* www.charlestoncvb.com

Charleston Convention & Visitors Bureau
200 Civic Center Dr Charleston WV 25301 304-344-5075 344-1241
TF: 800-733-5469 ■ *Web:* www.charlestonwv.com

Charlotte Convention & Visitors Bureau
500 S College St Suite 300 Charlotte NC 28202 704-334-2282 342-3972
TF: 800-722-1994 ■ *Web:* www.visitcharlotte.com/Default.asp

Chattanooga Area Convention & Visitors Bureau
2 Broad St Chattanooga TN 37402 423-756-8687 265-1630
TF: 800-322-3344 ■ *Web:* www.chattanoogafun.com

Chautauqua County Visitors Bureau Rt 394 PO Box 1441 Chautauqua NY 14722 716-357-4569 357-2284
TF: 800-242-4569 ■ *Web:* www.tourchautauqua.com

Cherokee Tribal Travel & Promotions 498 Tsali Blvd Cherokee NC 28719 828-497-9195 497-3220
TF: 800-438-1601 ■ *Web:* www.cherokee-nc.com

Chesapeake Conventions & Tourism Bureau
3815 Bainbridge Blvd. Chesapeake VA 23324 757-502-4898 502-4883
TF: 888-889-5551 ■ *Web:* www.visitchesapeake.com

Randolph County Tourism Committee
1 Taylor St Rm 104 Randolph County Courthouse Chester IL 62233 618-826-5000 826-3750
Web: www.randolphco.org

Cheyenne Area Convention & Visitors Bureau
121 W 15th St Suite 202 Cheyenne WY 82001 307-778-3133 778-3190
TF: 800-426-5009 ■ *Web:* www.cheyenne.org

Chicago Convention & Tourism Bureau
2301 S Lake Shore Dr McCormick Complex Lakeside Center Chicago IL 60616 312-567-8500 567-8533
Web: www.choosechicago.com

Chicago Office of Tourism 78 E Washington St 4th Fl Chicago IL 60602 312-744-2400 744-2359
TF: 877-244-2246 ■ *Web:* egov.cityofchicago.org

				Phone	Fax
Chula Vista Convention & Visitors Bureau 233 4th Ave Chamber of Commerce Bldg *Web:* www.chulavistaconvis.org	Chula Vista	CA	91910	619-426-2882	420-1269
Greater Cincinnati Convention & Visitors Bureau 300 W 6th St *TF:* 800-246-2987 ■ *Web:* www.cincyusa.com	Cincinnati	OH	45202	513-621-2142	621-5020
Pickaway County Visitors Bureau 325 W Main St *TF:* 888-770-7425 ■ *Web:* www.pickaway.com	Circleville	OH	43113	740-474-4923	477-6800
Clarksville/Montgomery County Tourist Commission 25 Jefferson St Suite 300-B *TF:* 800-530-2487 ■ *Web:* www.clarksville.tn.us	Clarksville	TN	37040	931-648-0001	645-1574
Clear Lake Convention & Visitors Bureau 205 Main Ave PO Box 188 *TF:* 800-285-5338 ■ *Web:* www.clearlakeiowa.com	Clear Lake	IA	50428	641-357-2159	357-8141
Saint Petersburg/Clearwater Area Convention & Visitors Bureau 13805 58th St N Suite 2-200 *TF:* 800-345-6710 ■ *Web:* www.floridasbeach.com	Clearwater	FL	33760	727-464-7200	464-7222
Convention & Visitors Bureau of Greater Cleveland 100 Public Sq Terminal Tower Suite Suite 100 *TF:* 800-321-1001 ■ *Web:* www.positivelycleveland.com/	Cleveland	OH	44113	216-621-4110	621-5967
Cleveland/Bradley Convention & Visitors Bureau 225 Keith St PO Box 2275 *TF:* 800-472-6588 ■ *Web:* www.clevelandchamber.com	Cleveland	TN	37320	423-472-6587	472-2019
Clinton Convention & Visitors Bureau 721 S 2nd St *TF:* 800-828-5702 ■ *Web:* www.clintonia.com	Clinton	IA	52732	563-242-5702	242-5803
Park County Travel Council 836 Sheridan Ave *TF:* 800-393-2639 ■ *Web:* www.pctc.org	Cody	WY	82414	307-587-2297	527-6228
Coffeyville Convention & Visitors Bureau 807 *TF:* 800-626-3357 ■ *Web:* www.coffeyville.com	Coffeyville	KS	67337	620-251-1194	251-5448
Colby Convention & Visitors Bureau 350 S Range Ave Suite 10 *TF:* 800-611-8835 ■ *Web:* www.colbychamber.com	Colby	KS	67701	785-460-7643	460-4509
Bryan/College Station Convention & Visitors Bureau 715 University Dr E *TF:* 800-777-8292 ■ *Web:* www.bryan-collegestation.org	College Station	TX	77840	979-260-9898	260-9800
Colorado Springs Convention & Visitors Bureau 515 S Cascade Ave *TF:* 800-368-4748 ■ *Web:* www.experiencecoloradosprings.com	Colorado Springs	CO	80903	719-635-7506	635-4968
Columbia Convention & Visitors Bureau 300 S Providence Rd *TF:* 800-652-0987 ■ *Web:* www.visitcolumbiamo.com	Columbia	MO	65203	573-875-1231	443-3986
Columbia Metropolitan Convention & Visitors Bureau PO Box 15 *TF:* 800-264-4884 ■ *Web:* www.columbiacvb.com	Columbia	SC	29201	803-545-0000	545-0013
Columbus Convention & Visitors Bureau 900 Front Ave *TF:* 800-999-1613 ■ *Web:* www.visitcolumbusga.com	Columbus	GA	31901	706-322-1613	322-0701
Columbus Area Visitors Center 506 5th St *TF:* 800-468-6564 ■ *Web:* columbus.in.us	Columbus	IN	47201	812-378-2622	372-7348
Columbus Convention & Visitors Bureau 318 7th St N PO Box 789 *TF:* 800-327-2686 ■ *Web:* www.columbus-ms.org	Columbus	MS	39703	662-329-1191	329-8969
Polk County Travel & Tourism 20 E Mills St *TF:* 800-440-7848 ■ *Web:* www.nc-mountains.org	Columbus	NC	28822	828-894-2324	894-6142
Greater Columbus Convention & Visitors Bureau 277 W Nationwide Blvd Suite 125 *TF:* 800-354-2657 ■ *Web:* www.experiencecolumbus.com	Columbus	OH	43215	614-221-6623	221-5618
New Hampshire Div of Travel & Tourism Development 172 Pembroke Rd PO Box 1856 *TF:* 800-262-6660 ■ *Web:* www.visitnh.gov	Concord	NH	03302	603-271-2666	271-6870
Bay Area Chamber of Commerce/Visitor Bureau 145 Central Ave *TF:* 800-824-8486 ■ *Web:* www.oregonsbayareachamber.com	Coos Bay	OR	97420	541-266-0868	267-6704
Iowa City/Coralville Convention & Visitors Bureau 900 1st Ave *TF:* 800-283-6592 ■ *Web:* www.iowacitycoralville.org	Coralville	IA	52241	319-337-6592	337-9953
Corinth Area Convention & Visitors Bureau PO Box 2158 *TF:* 800-748-9048 ■ *Web:* www.corinth.net	Corinth	MS	38835	662-287-8300	286-0102
Corpus Christi Convention & Visitors Bureau 1201 N Shoreline Blvd *TF:* 800-678-6232 ■ *Web:* www.corpuschristicvb.com	Corpus Christi	TX	78401	361-881-1888	887-9023
Corvallis Tourism 553 NW Harrison Blvd *TF:* 800-334-8118 ■ *Web:* www.visitcorvallis.com	Corvallis	OR	97330	541-757-1544	753-2664
Council Grove/Morris County Chamber of Commerce & Tourism 212 W Main St *TF:* 800-732-9211 ■ *Web:* www.councilgrove.com	Council Grove	KS	66846	620-767-5882	767-5553
Northern Kentucky Convention & Visitors Bureau 50 E RiverCenter Blvd Suite 200 *TF:* 800-447-8489 ■ *Web:* www.nkycvb.com	Covington	KY	41011	859-261-4677	261-5135
Montgomery County Visitors & Convention Bureau 218 E Pike St *TF:* 800-866-3973 ■ *Web:* www.crawfordsville.org	Crawfordsville	IN	47933	765-362-5200	362-5215
Crescent City-Del Norte County Chamber of Commerce 1001 Front St *TF:* 800-343-8300 ■ *Web:* www.northerncalifornia.net	Crescent City	CA	95531	707-464-3174	464-9676
Dallas Convention & Visitors Bureau 325 N Saint Paul St Suite 700 *TF:* 800-232-5527 ■ *Web:* www.dallascvb.com	Dallas	TX	75201	214-571-1000	571-1008
Central Florida Visitors & Convention Bureau 101 Adventure Ct Polk Outpost 27 *TF:* 800-828-7655 ■ *Web:* www.sunsational.org	Davenport	FL	33837	863-298-7565	298-7564
Tucker County Convention & Visitors Bureau William Ave & 4th St PO Box 565 *TF:* 800-782-2775 ■ *Web:* www.canaanvalley.org	Davis	WV	26260	304-259-5315	259-4210
Dayton/Montgomery County Convention & Visitors Bureau 1 Chamber Plaza Suite A *TF:* 800-221-8235 ■ *Web:* www.daytoncvb.com	Dayton	OH	45402	937-226-8211	226-8294
Daytona Beach Area Convention & Visitors Bureau 126 E Orange Ave *TF:* 800-544-0415 ■ *Web:* www.daytonabeachcvb.org	Daytona Beach	FL	32114	386-255-0415	255-5478
Decatur/Morgan County Convention & Visitors Bureau 719 6th Ave SE PO Box 2349 *TF:* 800-524-6181 ■ *Web:* www.decaturcvb.org	Decatur	AL	35601	256-350-2028	350-2054
Decatur Area Convention & Visitors Bureau 202 E North St *TF:* 800-331-4479 ■ *Web:* www.decaturcvb.com	Decatur	IL	62523	217-423-7000	423-7455
Wicomico County Convention & Visitors Bureau 8480 Ocean Hwy *TF:* 800-332-8687 ■ *Web:* www.wicomicotourism.org	Delmar	MD	21875	410-548-4914	341-4996
Denver Metro Convention & Visitors Bureau 1555 California St Suite 300 *TF:* 800-234-6257 ■ *Web:* www.denver.org	Denver	CO	80202	303-892-1112	892-1636
Greater Des Moines Convention & Visitors Bureau 400 Locust St Suite 265 *TF:* 800-451-2625 ■ *Web:* www.seedesmoines.com	Des Moines	IA	50309	515-286-4960	244-9757
Detroit Metropolitan Convention & Visitors Bureau 211 W Fort St Suite 1000 *TF:* 800-225-5389 ■ *Web:* www.visitdetroit.com	Detroit	MI	48226	313-202-1800	202-1808
Dickinson Convention & Visitors Bureau 72 E Museum Dr *TF:* 800-279-7391 ■ *Web:* www.dickinsoncvb.com	Dickinson	ND	58601	701-483-4988	483-9261
Dothan Area Convention & Visitors Bureau 3311 Ross Clark Cir NW PO Box 8765 *TF:* 888-449-0212 ■ *Web:* www.dothanalcvb.com	Dothan	AL	36304	334-794-6622	712-2731
Saugatuck/Douglas Convention & Visitors Bureau 2902 Blue Star Hwy *Web:* www.saugatuck.com	Douglas	MI	49406	269-857-1701	857-2319
Kent County Tourism Corp 435 N DuPont Hwy *TF:* 800-233-5368 ■ *Web:* www.visitdover.com	Dover	DE	19901	302-734-1736	734-0167
Downers Grove Tourism & Events 801 Burlington Ave *TF:* 800-934-0615 ■ *Web:* visitor.downers.us	Downers Grove	IL	60515	630-434-5921	434-5573
Drummond Island Tourism Assn 34974 S Townline Rd PO Box 200 *TF:* 800-737-8666 ■ *Web:* www.drummondislandchamber.com	Drummond Island	MI	49726	906-493-5245	493-6362
Dublin Convention & Visitors Bureau 9 S High St *TF:* 800-245-8387 ■ *Web:* www.dublinvisit.org	Dublin	OH	43017	614-792-7666	760-1818
Dubuque Convention & Visitors Bureau 300 Main St Suite 200 *TF:* 800-798-4748	Dubuque	IA	52001	563-557-9200	557-1591
Atlanta's Gwinnett Convention & Visitors Bureau 6500 Sugarloaf Pkwy Suite 200 *TF:* 888-494-6638 ■ *Web:* www.gcvb.org	Duluth	GA	30097	770-623-3600	623-1667
Duluth Convention & Visitors Bureau 21 W Superior St Suite 100 *TF:* 800-438-5884 ■ *Web:* www.visitduluth.com	Duluth	MN	55802	218-722-4011	722-1322
Duncanville Convention & Visitors Bureau 203 James Collins Blvd	Duncanville	TX	75116	972-780-5086	780-6417
DuQuoin Tourism Commission 20 N Chestnut St PO Box 1037 *TF:* 800-455-9570 ■ *Web:* www.duquoin.org	DuQuoin	IL	62832	618-542-8338	542-2098
Durango Area Tourism Office 111 S Camino del Rio *TF:* 800-525-8855 ■ *Web:* www.durango.org	Durango	CO	81301	970-247-3500	385-7884
Durham Convention & Visitors Bureau 101 E Morgan St *TF:* 800-446-8604 ■ *Web:* www.durham-nc.com/	Durham	NC	27701	919-687-0288	683-9555
Eagan Convention & Visitors Bureau 1501 Central Pkwy *TF:* 800-324-2620 ■ *Web:* www.eaganmn.com	Eagan	MN	55121	651-675-5546	675-5545
Talbot County Tourism Office 11 S Harrison St *Web:* www.tourtalbot.org	Easton	MD	21601	410-770-8000	770-8057
Chippewa Valley Convention & Visitors Bureau 3625 Gateway Dr Suite F *TF:* 888-523-3866 ■ *Web:* www.chippewavalley.net	Eau Claire	WI	54701	715-831-2345	831-2340
Edmonton Tourism 9990 Jasper Ave NW 3rd Fl *TF:* 800-463-4667 ■ *Web:* www.edmonton.com	Edmonton	AB	T5J1P7	780-426-4715	425-5283
Effingham Convention & Visitors Bureau 201 E Jefferson Ave *TF:* 800-772-0750 ■ *Web:* www.effinghamil.com/visitorsbureau	Effingham	IL	62401	217-342-5305	342-2746
El Paso Convention & Visitors Bureau 1 Civic Center Plaza *TF:* 800-351-6024 ■ *Web:* www.elpasocvb.com	El Paso	TX	79901	915-534-0600	534-0687
Elgin Area Convention & Visitors Bureau 77 Riverside Dr *TF:* 800-217-5362 ■ *Web:* www.enjoyelgin.com	Elgin	IL	60120	847-695-7540	695-7668
Elkhart County Convention & Visitors Bureau 219 Caravan Dr *TF:* 800-262-8161 ■ *Web:* www.amishcountry.org	Elkhart	IN	46514	574-262-8161	262-3925
Howard County Tourism Council 8267 Main St *TF:* 800-288-8747 ■ *Web:* www.visithowardcounty.com	Ellicott City	MD	21043	410-313-1900	313-1902
Grays Harbor Tourism 32 Elma McCleary Rd PO Box 1229 *TF:* 800-621-9625 ■ *Web:* www.graysharbortourism.com	Elma	WA	98541	360-482-2651	482-3297
Erie Area Convention & Visitors Bureau 208 E Bayfront Pkwy Suite 103 *TF:* 800-524-3743 ■ *Web:* www.eriepa.com	Erie	PA	16507	814-454-7191	459-0241
Convention & Visitors Assn of Lane County Oregon PO Box 10286 *TF:* 800-547-5445 ■ *Web:* www.visitlanecounty.org	Eugene	OR	97440	541-484-5307	343-6335
Eureka/Humboldt County Convention & Visitors Bureau 1034 2nd St *TF:* 800-346-3482 ■ *Web:* www.redwoodvisitor.org	Eureka	CA	95501	707-443-5097	443-5115
Evansville Convention & Visitors Bureau 401 SE Riverside Dr *TF:* 800-433-3025 ■ *Web:* www.evansvillecvb.org	Evansville	IN	47713	812-425-5402	421-2207
Fairbanks Convention & Visitors Bureau 550 1st Ave *TF:* 800-327-5774 ■ *Web:* www.explorefairbanks.com	Fairbanks	AK	99701	907-456-5774	452-2867
Jefferson County Visitor's Bureau PO Box 274	Fairbury	NE	68352	402-729-3000	729-3076
Fairmont Convention & Visitors Bureau 323 E Blue Earth Ave *TF:* 800-657-3280 ■ *Web:* www.fairmont.org	Fairmont	MN	56031	507-235-8585	235-8411
Convention & Visitors Bureau of Marion County 110 Adams St *TF:* 800-834-7365 ■ *Web:* www.marioncvb.com	Fairmont	WV	26554	304-368-1123	363-0480
Tourism Bureau Southwestern Illinois 10950 Lincoln Trail *TF:* 800-442-1488 ■ *Web:* www.thetourismbureau.org	Fairview Heights	IL	62208	618-397-1488	397-1945
Fargo-Moorhead Convention & Visitors Bureau 2001 44th St SW *TF:* 800-235-7654 ■ *Web:* www.fargomoorhead.org	Fargo	ND	58103	701-282-3653	282-7815
Farmington Convention & Visitors Bureau 3041 E Main St *TF:* 800-448-1240 ■ *Web:* www.farmingtonnm.org	Farmington	NM	87402	505-326-7602	327-0577
Fayetteville Area Convention & Visitors Bureau 245 Person St *TF:* 800-255-8217 ■ *Web:* www.visitfayettevillenc.com	Fayetteville	NC	28301	910-483-5311	484-6632
Flagstaff Convention & Visitors Bureau 323 W Aspen Ave *TF:* 800-217-2367 ■ *Web:* www.flagstaffarizona.org	Flagstaff	AZ	86001	928-779-7611	556-1305
Flint Area Convention & Visitors Bureau 316 Water St *TF Sales:* 800-253-5468 ■ *Web:* flintcommercecenter.com	Flint	MI	48502	810-232-8900	232-1515
Florence Convention & Visitors Bureau 3290 W Radio Dr *TF:* 800-325-9005	Florence	SC	29501	843-664-0330	665-9480
Tropical Everglades Visitor Assn 160 US 1 *TF:* 800-388-9669 ■ *Web:* www.tropicaleverglades.com	Florida City	FL	33034	305-245-9180	247-4335
Fond du Lac Convention & Visitors Bureau 171 S Pioneer Rd *TF:* 800-937-9123 ■ *Web:* www.fdl.com	Fond du Lac	WI	54935	920-923-3010	929-6846
Rutherford County Tourism Development Authority 1990 US Hwy 221 S *TF:* 800-849-5998 ■ *Web:* www.rutherfordtourism.com	Forest City	NC	28043	828-245-1492	247-0499
Fort Collins Convention & Visitors Bureau 19 Old Town Sq Suite 137 *TF:* 800-274-3678 ■ *Web:* www.ftcollins.com	Fort Collins	CO	80524	970-232-3840	232-3841
Greater Fort Lauderdale Convention & Visitors Bureau 100 E Broward Blvd Suite 200 *TF:* 800-227-8669 ■ *Web:* sunny.org	Fort Lauderdale	FL	33301	954-765-4466	765-4467
Fort Madison Convention & Visitors Bureau 614 9th *TF:* 800-210-8687 ■ *Web:* www.visitfortmadison.com	Fort Madison	IA	52627	319-372-5472	372-6404
Lee County Visitors & Convention Bureau 12800 University Dr Suite 550 *TF:* 800-237-6444 ■ *Web:* www.leeislandcoast.com	Fort Myers	FL	33907	239-338-3500	334-1106
Saint Lucie County Tourist Development Council 2300 Virginia Ave *TF:* 800-344-8443 ■ *Web:* www.visitstluciefla.com	Fort Pierce	FL	34982	772-462-1535	462-1579
Fort Smith Convention & Visitors Bureau 2 N 'B' St *TF:* 800-637-1477 ■ *Web:* www.fortsmith.org	Fort Smith	AR	72901	479-783-8888	784-2421
Fort Wayne/Allen County Convention & Visitors Bureau 1021 S Calhoun St *TF:* 800-767-7752 ■ *Web:* www.visitfortwayne.com	Fort Wayne	IN	46802	260-424-3700	424-3914

Phone Fax

Fort Worth Convention & Visitors Bureau
415 Throckmorton St. Fort Worth TX 76102 817-336-8791 336-3282
TF: 800-433-5747 ■ *Web:* www.fortworth.com

Frankenmuth Convention & Visitors Bureau
635 S Main St Frankenmuth MI 48734 989-652-6106 652-6106
TF: 800-386-8696 ■ *Web:* www.frankenmuth.org

Frankfort/Franklin County Tourist & Convention Commission
100 Capitol Ave Frankfort KY 40601 502-875-8687 227-2604
TF: 800-960-7200 ■ *Web:* www.frankfortky.org

Williamson County Convention & Visitors Bureau
109 2nd Ave S Suite 137 Franklin TN 37064 615-794-1225 790-5337
TF: 800-356-3445 ■ *Web:* www.williamsoncvb.org

Fredericksburg Convention & Visitors Bureau
302 E Austin St Fredericksburg TX 78624 830-997-6523 997-8588
TF: 888-997-3600 ■ *Web:* www.fredericksburg-texas.com

Dodge County Convention & Visitors Bureau
1420 E Military Ave Fremont NE 68025 402-753-6414 753-6482
TF: 800-727-8323 ■ *Web:* www.visitdodgecountyne.org

Fremont/Sandusky County Convention & Visitors Bureau
712 North St Suite 102 Fremont OH 43420 419-332-4470 332-4359
TF: 800-255-8070 ■ *Web:* www.sanduskycounty.org

Fresno City & County Convention & Visitors Bureau
848 M St 3rd Fl Fresno CA 93721 559-445-8300 445-0122
TF: 800-788-0836 ■ *Web:* www.fresnocvb.org

Alachua County Visitors & Convention Bureau
30 E University Ave Gainesville FL 32601 352-374-5231 338-3213
TF: 866-778-5002 ■ *Web:* www.visitgainesville.net

Galena/Jo Daviess County Convention & Visitors Bureau
720 Park Ave Galena IL 61036 815-777-3557 777-3566
TF: 800-747-9377 ■ *Web:* www.galena.org

Galesburg Area Convention & Visitors Bureau
2163 East Main St Galesburg IL 61401 309-343-2485 343-2521
TF: 800-916-3330 ■ *Web:* www.visitgalesburg.com

Finney County Convention & Visitors Bureau
1511 E Fulton Terr Garden City KS 67846 620-276-3264 276-3290
TF: 800-879-9803 ■ *Web:* www.gardencity.net/chamber/

Garden Grove Visitors Bureau 12866 Main St Suite 102 Garden Grove CA 92840 714-638-7950 636-6672
Web: www.gardengrovechamber.org

Garland Convention & Visitors Bureau 200 N 5th St Garland TX 75040 972-205-2749 205-2504
Web: www.ci.garland.tx.us

Gatlinburg Dept of Tourism & Convention Center
234 Historic Nature Trail Gatlinburg TN 37738 865-436-2392 436-3704
TF: 800-343-1475 ■ *Web:* www.gatlinburg-tennessee.com

Georgetown Convention & Visitors Bureau
103 W 7th St PO Box 409 Georgetown TX 78627 512-930-3545 930-3697
TF: 800-436-8696 ■ *Web:* visitgeorgetown.com

Gettysburg Convention & Visitors Bureau
571 Middle St PO Box 4117 Gettysburg PA 17325 717-334-6274 334-1166
TF: 800-337-5015 ■ *Web:* www.gettysburg.travel/

Grafton Area Convention & Visitors Bureau 1 W Main St Grafton WV 26354 304-265-1412 265-0119

Greater Grand Forks Convention & Visitors Bureau
4251 Gateway Dr Grand Forks ND 58203 701-746-0444 746-0775
TF: 800-866-4566 ■ *Web:* www.visitgrandforks.com

Grand Junction Visitors & Convention Bureau
740 Horizon Dr Grand Junction CO 81506 970-244-1480 243-7393
TF: 800-962-2547 ■ *Web:* www.visitgrandjunction.com

Grand Rapids/Kent County Convention & Visitors Bureau
171 Monroe Ave NW Suite 700 Grand Rapids MI 49503 616-459-8287 459-7291
TF: 800-678-9859 ■ *Web:* www.visitgrandrapids.org

Grand Rapids Area Convention & Visitors Bureau
501 S Tokegama Ave Grand Rapids MN 55744 218-326-9607 326-8219
TF: 800-355-9740 ■ *Web:* visitgrandrapids.com

Grants Pass Visitors & Convention Bureau
1995 NW Vine St Grants Pass OR 97526 541-476-5510 476-9574
TF: 800-547-5927 ■ *Web:* www.visitgrantspass.org

Grapevine Convention & Visitors Bureau 1 Liberty Park Plaza Grapevine TX 76051 817-410-3185 410-3038
TF: 800-457-6338 ■ *Web:* www.grapevinetexasusa.com

Houma-Terrebonne Tourist Commission 114 Tourist Dr Gray LA 70359 985-868-2732 868-7170
TF: 800-688-2732 ■ *Web:* www.houmatourism.com

Grayling Visitors Bureau 213 N James St Grayling MI 49738 989-348-4945 348-7315
TF: 800-937-8837 ■ *Web:* www.grayling-mi.com

Greeley Convention & Visitors Bureau 902 7th Ave Greeley CO 80631 970-352-3567 352-3572
TF: 800-449-3866 ■ *Web:* www.greeleycvb.com

Packer Country Visitor & Convention Bureau
1901 S Oneida St Green Bay WI 54304 920-494-9507 494-9229
TF: 888-867-3342 ■ *Web:* www.packercountry.com

Putnam County Convention & Visitors Bureau
12 W Washington St Greencastle IN 46135 765-653-8743 653-0851
TF: 800-829-4639 ■ *Web:* www.coveredbridgecountry.com

Greensboro Area Convention & Visitors Bureau
2200 Pinecroft Rd Suite 200 Greensboro NC 27407 336-274-2282 230-1183
TF: 800-344-2282 ■ *Web:* www.greensboronc.org

Greenville-Pitt County Convention & Visitors Bureau
303 SW Greenville Blvd Greenville NC 27834 252-329-4200 329-4205
TF: 800-537-5564 ■ *Web:* www.visitgreenvillenc.com

Greater Greenville Convention & Visitors Bureau
631 S Main St Suite 301 Greenville SC 29601 864-421-0000 421-0005
TF: 800-351-7180 ■ *Web:* www.greatergreenville.com

Greenwood Convention & Visitors Bureau 111 E Market St Greenwood MS 38930 662-453-9197 453-5526
TF: 800-748-9064 ■ *Web:* www.gcvb.com

Alabama Gulf Coast Convention & Visitors Bureau
3150 Gulf Shores Pkwy PO Drawer 457 Gulf Shores AL 36547 251-968-7511 968-6095
TF: 800-745-7263 ■ *Web:* www.gulfshores.com

Mississippi Gulf Coast Convention & Visitors Bureau
PO Box 6128 Gulfport MS 39506 228-896-6699 896-6788
TF: 888-467-4853 ■ *Web:* www.gulfcoast.org

Hagerstown/Washington County Convention & Visitors Bureau
16 Public Sq Ellizabeth Hager Center Hagerstown MD 21740 301-791-3246 791-2601
TF: 888-257-2600 ■ *Web:* www.marylandmemories.org

Haines Visitors Bureau 122 2nd Ave PO Box 530 Haines AK 99827 907-766-2234 766-3155
TF: 800-458-3579 ■ *Web:* www.haines.ak.us

Lake County Convention & Visitors Bureau 7770 Corinne Dr Hammond IN 46323 219-989-7770 989-7777
TF: 800-255-5253 ■ *Web:* www.alllake.org

Hampton Conventions & Visitors Bureau
1919 Commerce Dr Suite 290 Hampton VA 23666 757-722-1222 896-4600
TF: 800-487-8778 ■ *Web:* www.hamptoncvb.com

Hannibal Convention & Visitors Bureau 505 N 3rd St Hannibal MO 63401 573-221-2477 221-6999
TF: 866-263-4825 ■ *Web:* www.visithannibal.com

Jefferson County Convention & Visitors Bureau
37 Washington Ct Harpers Ferry WV 25425 304-535-2627 535-2131
TF: 800-848-8687 ■ *Web:* www.jeffersoncountycvb.com

Hershey Harrisburg Region Visitors Bureau
112 Market St 4th Fl Harrisburg PA 17101 717-231-7788 231-2808
TF: 877-727-8573 ■ *Web:* www.pacapitalregions.com

Greater Hartford Convention & Visitors Bureau
31 Pratt St 4th Fl Hartford CT 06103 860-728-6789 293-2365
Web: www.enjoyhartford.com

Long Island Convention & Visitors Bureau
330 Motor Pkwy Suite 203 Hauppauge NY 11788 631-951-3440 951-3439
TF: 800-441-4601 ■ *Web:* www.licvb.com

Hays Convention & Visitors Bureau 1301 Pine St Suite B Hays KS 67601 785-628-8202 628-1471
TF: 800-569-4505 ■ *Web:* www.haysusa.net

Alpine Helen/White County Convention & Visitors Bureau
PO Box 730 Helen GA 30545 706-878-2181 878-4032
TF: 800-858-8027 ■ *Web:* www.helenga.org

Helena Convention & Visitors Bureau 225 Cruse Ave Helena MT 59601 406-447-1530 447-1532
TF: 800-743-5362 ■ *Web:* helenacvb.visitmt.com

Henderson County Tourist Commission
101 N Water St Suite B Henderson KY 42420 270-826-3128 826-0234
TF: 800-648-3128 ■ *Web:* www.hendersonky.org

Henderson County Travel & Tourism 201 S Main St Hendersonville NC 28792 828-693-9708 697-4996
TF: 800-828-4244 ■ *Web:* www.historichendersonville.org

Huntingdon County Visitors Bureau
7 Points Rd RD 1 Box 222A Hesston PA 16647 814-658-0060 658-0068
TF: 888-729-7869 ■ *Web:* www.raystown.org

Hickory Metro Convention & Visitors Bureau
1960A 13th Ave Dr SE Hickory NC 28602 828-322-1335 322-8983
TF: 800-509-2444 ■ *Web:* www.hickorymetro.com

High Point Convention & Visitors Bureau 300 S Main St High Point NC 27260 336-884-5255 884-5256
TF: 800-720-5255 ■ *Web:* www.highpoint.org

Hilton Head Island Visitors & Convention Bureau
1 Chamber Dr PO Box 5647 Hilton Head Island SC 29938 843-785-3673 785-7110
TF: 800-523-3373 ■ *Web:* www.hiltonheadisland.org

Summers County Convention & Visitors Bureau 206 Temple St Hinton WV 25951 304-466-5420
Web: www.summerscvb.com

Holland Area Convention & Visitors Bureau 76 E 8th St Holland MI 49423 616-394-0000 394-0122
TF: 800-506-1299 ■ *Web:* www.holland.org

Hawaii Visitors & Convention Bureau
2270 Kalakaua Ave Suite 801 Honolulu HI 96815 808-923-1811 924-0290
TF: 800-464-2924 ■ *Web:* www.gohawaii.com

Hot Springs Convention & Visitors Bureau
134 Convention Blvd Hot Springs AR 71901 501-321-2277 321-2136
TF: 800-543-2284 ■ *Web:* www.hotsprings.org

Houghton Lake Area Tourism & Convention Bureau
4482 W Houghton Lake Dr Houghton Lake MI 48629 989-366-8474 366-8395
TF: 800-676-5330 ■ *Web:* www.visithoughtonlake.com

Greater Houston Convention & Visitors Bureau
901 Bagby St Suite 100 Houston TX 77002 713-437-5200 227-6336
TF: 800-446-8786 ■ *Web:* www.visithoustontexas.com

Huntington County Visitors & Convention Bureau
407 N Jefferson St Huntington IN 46750 260-359-8687 359-9754
TF: 800-848-4282 ■ *Web:* www.visithuntington.org

Cabell-Huntington Convention & Visitors Bureau
763 3rd Ave PO Box 347 Huntington WV 25708 304-525-7333 525-7345
TF: 800-635-6329 ■ *Web:* www.wvvisit.org

Huntington Beach Conference & Visitors Bureau
301 Main St Suite 208 Huntington Beach CA 92648 714-969-3492 969-5592
Web: surfcityusa.com

Huntsville/Madison County Convention & Visitor's Bureau
500 Church St Huntsville AL 35801 256-551-2230 551-2324
TF: 800-772-2348 ■ *Web:* www.huntsville.org

Huron Chamber & Visitors Bureau 15 4th St SW Huron SD 57350 605-352-0000 352-8321
TF: 800-487-6673 ■ *Web:* www.huronsd.com

Hurricane Convention & Visitors Bureau
3255 Teays Valley Rd Hurricane WV 25526 304-562-5896 562-5858
Web: www.hurricanewv.com

Greater Hutchinson Convention & Visitors Bureau
117 N Walnut St Hutchinson KS 67501 620-662-3391 662-2168
TF: 800-691-4282 ■ *Web:* www.hutchchamber.com

Incline Village/Crystal Bay Visitors Bureau
969 Tahoe Blvd Incline Village NV 89451 775-832-1606 832-1605
TF: 800-468-2463 ■ *Web:* www.gotahoe.com

Indiana County Tourist Bureau 2334 Oakland Ave Suite 7 Indiana PA 15701 724-463-7505 465-3819
TF: 877-746-3426 ■ *Web:* www.indiana-co-pa-tourism.org

Indianapolis Convention & Visitors Assn
200 S Capitol Ave 1 RCA Dome Suite 100 Indianapolis IN 46225 317-639-4282 639-5273
TF: 800-323-4639 ■ *Web:* www.indy.org

Tourism Assn of the Dickinson County Area
600 S Stephenson Ave Iron Mountain MI 49801 906-774-2945 774-2005
TF: 800-236-2447 ■ *Web:* www.ironmountain.org

Western Upper Peninsula Convention & Visitor Bureau
648 Cloverland Dr PO Box 706 Ironwood MI 49938 906-932-4850 932-3455
TF: 800-522-5657 ■ *Web:* www.westernup.com

Irving Convention & Visitors Bureau
222 W Las Colinas Blvd Suite 1550 Irving TX 75039 972-252-7476 257-3153
TF: 800-247-8464 ■ *Web:* www.irvingtexas.com

Ithaca/Tompkins County Convention & Visitors Bureau
904 E Shore Dr Ithaca NY 14850 607-272-1313 272-7617
TF: 800-284-8422 ■ *Web:* www.visitithaca.com

East Feliciana Parish Tourist Commission
1752 High St PO Box 667 Jackson LA 70748 225-634-7155 634-7155
Web: www.felicianatourism.org

Jackson County Convention & Visitors Bureau
141 S Jackson St Jackson MI 49201 517-764-4440 780-3685
TF: 800-245-5282 ■ *Web:* www.jackson-mich.org

Metro Jackson Convention & Visitors Bureau
111 E Capitol St Suite 102 Jackson MS 39202 601-960-1891 960-1827
TF: 800-354-7695 ■ *Web:* www.visitjackson.com

Visit Jacksonville 550 Water St Suite 1000 Jacksonville FL 32202 904-798-9111 798-9103
TF: 800-733-2668 ■ *Web:* www.visitjacksonville.com

Jacksonville Convention & Visitors Bureau
155 W Morton Ave Jacksonville IL 62650 217-243-5678 245-0661
TF: 800-593-5678 ■ *Web:* www.jacksonvilleil.org/tourism/

Onslow County Tourism 1099 Gum Branch Rd Jacksonville NC 28540 910-455-1113 347-4705
TF: 800-932-2144 ■ *Web:* www.onslowcountytourism.com

Jamestown Promotions & Tourism Center
404 Louis L'Amour Ln PO Box 917 Jamestown ND 58401 701-251-9145 251-9146
TF: 800-222-4766 ■ *Web:* www.jamestownnd.com

Jefferson Convention & Visitors Bureau
1221 Elmwood Park Blvd Suite 300 Jefferson LA 70123 504-731-7083 731-7089
TF: 877-572-7474 ■ *Web:* www.gatewaytoneworleans.com

Jefferson City Convention & Visitors Bureau
213 Adams St Jefferson City MO 65101 573-632-2820 638-4892
TF: 800-769-4183 ■ *Web:* www.visitjeffersoncity.com

Southern Indiana Convention & Tourism Bureau
315 Southern Indiana Ave Jeffersonville IN 47130 812-282-6654 282-1904
TF: 800-552-3842 ■ *Web:* www.sunnysideoflouisville.org

Johnson City Convention & Visitors Bureau
603 E Market St Johnson City TN 37601 423-461-8000 461-8047
TF: 800-852-3392 ■ *Web:* www.johnsoncitytn.com

Greater Johnstown/Cambria County Convention & Visitors Bureau 416 Main St Suite 100 Johnstown PA 15901 814-536-7993 539-3370
TF: 800-237-8590 ■ *Web:* www.visitjohnstownpa.com

	City	State	Zip	Phone	Fax
Heritage Corridor Convention & Visitors Bureau 81 N Chicago St *TF:* 800-926-2262 ■ *Web:* www.heritagecorridorcvb.com	Joliet	IL	60432	815-727-2323	727-2324
Joplin Convention & Visitors Bureau 602 S Main St *TF:* 800-657-2534 ■ *Web:* www.joplincvb.com	Joplin	MO	64801	417-625-4789	624-7948
Juneau Convention & Visitors Bureau One Sealaska Plaza Suite 305 *TF:* 800-587-2201 ■ *Web:* www.traveljuneau.com	Juneau	AK	99801	907-586-1737	586-1449
Kalamazoo County Convention & Visitors Bureau 346 W Michigan Ave *TF:* 800-530-9192 ■ *Web:* www.kalamazoomi.com/conv.htm	Kalamazoo	MI	49007	269-381-4003	343-0430
Flathead Convention & Visitors Bureau 15 Depot Park *TF:* 800-543-3105 ■ *Web:* www.fcvb.org	Kalispell	MT	59901	406-756-9091	257-2500
Cabarrus County Convention & Visitors Bureau 3003 Dale Earnhardt Blvd *TF:* 800-848-3740 ■ *Web:* www.cabarruscvb.com	Kannapolis	NC	28083	704-782-4340	782-4333
Kansas City Kansas/Wyandotte County Convention & Visitors Bureau 727 Minnesota Ave PO Box 171517 *TF:* 800-264-1563 ■ *Web:* www.visitthedot.com	Kansas City	KS	66117	913-321-5800	371-3732
Convention & Visitors Bureau of Greater Kansas City 1100 Main St Suite 2200 *TF:* 800-767-7700 ■ *Web:* www.visitkc.com	Kansas City	MO	64105	816-221-5242	691-3805
Cowlitz County Tourism 105 Minor Rd *Web:* www.cowlitzcounty.org/tourism	Kelso	WA	98626	360-577-3137	578-2660
Tri-Cities Convention & Visitors Bureau 6951 W Grandridge Blvd *TF:* 800-254-5824 ■ *Web:* www.visittri-cities.com	Kennewick	WA	99336	509-735-8486	783-9005
Kenosha Area Convention & Visitors Bureau 812 56th St *TF:* 800-654-7309 ■ *Web:* www.kenoshacvb.com	Kenosha	WI	53140	262-654-7307	654-0882
Kerrville Convention & Visitors Bureau 2108 Sidney Baker St *TF:* 800-221-7958 ■ *Web:* www.ktc.net/kerrcvb	Kerrville	TX	78028	830-792-3535	792-3230
Ketchikan Visitors Bureau 131 Front St *TF:* 800-770-3300 ■ *Web:* www.visit-ketchikan.com	Ketchikan	AK	99901	907-225-6166	225-4250
Key West Visitors Center 402 Wall St *TF:* 800-648-6269 ■ *Web:* www.keywestchamber.org	Key West	FL	33040	305-294-2587	294-7806
Monroe County Tourist Development Council 1201 White St Suite 102 *TF:* 800-648-5510 ■ *Web:* www.fla-keys.com	Key West	FL	33040	305-296-1552	296-0788
Greater Killeen Convention & Visitors Bureau 3601 WS Young PO Box 1329 *Web:* www.killeen-cvb.com	Killeen	TX	76540	254-501-3888	554-3219
Kingsport Convention & Visitors Bureau 151 E Main St *TF:* 800-743-5282 ■ *Web:* www.kcvb.org	Kingsport	TN	37660	423-392-8820	392-8803
Preston County Convention & Visitors Bureau 200 1/2 W Main St *TF:* 800-571-0912	Kingwood	WV	26537	304-329-4660	329-1407
Kinston Convention & Visitors Bureau 301 N Queens St PO Box 157 *TF:* 800-869-0032 ■ *Web:* www.visitkinston.com	Kinston	NC	28502	252-523-2500	527-1914
Kissimmee Convention & Visitors Bureau 1925 E Irlo Bronson Memorial Hwy *TF:* 800-327-9159 ■ *Web:* www.floridakiss.com	Kissimmee	FL	34744	407-847-5000	847-0878
Armstrong County Tourist Bureau 125 Market St Suite 2 *TF:* 888-265-9954 ■ *Web:* www.armstrongcounty.com	Kittanning	PA	16201	724-548-3226	545-3119
Travel Klamath 205 Riverside Dr *TF:* 800-445-6728 ■ *Web:* www.travelklamath.com	Klamath Falls	OR	97601	541-884-0666	884-0219
Knoxville Tourism & Sports Corp 301 S Gay St *TF:* 866-790-5373 ■ *Web:* www.knoxville.org	Knoxville	TN	37902	865-523-7263	673-4400
Lyon County Joint Tourism Commission 82 Days Inn Dr *TF:* 800-355-3885 ■ *Web:* www.lakebarkley.org	Kuttawa	KY	42055	270-388-5300	388-5301
La Crosse Area Convention & Visitors Bureau 410 Veterans Memorial Dr *TF:* 800-658-9424 ■ *Web:* www.explorelacrosse.com	La Crosse	WI	54601	608-782-2366	782-4082
Lafayette-West Lafayette Convention & Visitors Bureau 301 Frontage Rd *TF:* 800-872-6648 ■ *Web:* www.lafayette-in.com	Lafayette	IN	47905	765-447-9999	447-5062
Lafayette Convention & Visitors Commission 1400 NW Evageline Thwy *TF:* 800-346-1958 ■ *Web:* www.lafayettetravel.com	Lafayette	LA	70501	337-232-3737	232-0161
Laguna Beach Visitors & Conference Bureau 252 Broadway *TF:* 800-877-1115 ■ *Web:* www.lagunabeachinfo.org	Laguna Beach	CA	92651	949-497-9229	376-0558
Southwest Louisiana Convention & Visitors Bureau 1205 N Lakeshore Dr *TF:* 800-456-7952 ■ *Web:* www.visitlakecharles.org	Lake Charles	LA	70601	337-436-9588	494-7952
Lake Placid Convention & Visitors Bureau 2610 Main St Olympic Center *TF:* 800-447-5224 ■ *Web:* www.lakeplacid.com	Lake Placid	NY	12946	518-523-2445	523-2605
Pennsylvania Dutch Convention & Visitors Bureau 501 Greenfield Rd *TF:* 800-723-8824 ■ *Web:* www.padutchcountry.com	Lancaster	PA	17601	717-299-8901	299-0470
Chicago Southland Convention & Visitors Bureau 2304 173rd St *TF:* 888-895-8233 ■ *Web:* www.cscvb.com	Lansing	IL	60438	708-895-8200	895-8288
Greater Lansing Convention & Visitors Bureau 1223 Turner St Suite 200 *TF:* 800-648-6630 ■ *Web:* www.lansing.org	Lansing	MI	48906	517-487-0077	487-5151
Prince George's County Conference & Visitors Bureau 9200 Basil Ct Suite 101 *TF:* 888-925-8300 ■ *Web:* www.goprincegeorgescounty.com	Largo	MD	20774	301-925-8300	925-2053
Marin County Visitors Bureau 1013 Larkspur Landing Cir *TF:* 866-925-2060 ■ *Web:* www.visitmarin.org	Larkspur	CA	94939	415-925-2060	925-2063
Las Cruces Convention & Visitors Bureau 211 N Water St *TF:* 800-343-7827 ■ *Web:* www.lascrucescvb.org	Las Cruces	NM	88001	505-541-2444	541-2164
Las Vegas Convention & Visitors Authority 3150 S Paradise Rd *TF:* 800-332-5333 ■ *Web:* www.lvcva.com	Las Vegas	NV	89109	702-892-0711	892-2824
Lawrence Visitor Information Center 402 N 2nd St *TF:* 888-529-5267 ■ *Web:* www.visitlawrence.com	Lawrence	KS	66044	785-865-4499	865-4488
Leavenworth Convention & Visitors Bureau 518 Shawnee St PO Box 44 *TF:* 800-844-4114 ■ *Web:* www.lvarea.com/cvb	Leavenworth	KS	66048	913-682-4113	682-8170
Lenexa Convention & Visitors Bureau 11180 Lackman Rd *TF:* 800-950-7867 ■ *Web:* www.lenexa.org	Lenexa	KS	66219	913-888-1414	888-3770
Greenbrier County Convention & Visitors Bureau 540 N Jefferson St Suite N *TF:* 800-833-2068 ■ *Web:* www.greenbrierwv.com	Lewisburg	WV	24901	304-645-1000	647-3001
Juniata River Valley Visitors Bureau Historic Court House 1 W Market St Suite 103 *TF:* 877-568-9739 ■ *Web:* www.juniatarivervalley.org	Lewistown	PA	17044	717-248-6713	248-6714
Lexington Convention & Visitors Bureau 301 E Vine St *TF:* 800-845-3959 ■ *Web:* www.visitlex.com	Lexington	KY	40507	859-233-7299	254-4555
Laurel Highlands Visitors Bureau 120 E Main St *TF:* 800-333-5661 ■ *Web:* www.laurelhighlands.org	Ligonier	PA	15658	724-238-5661	238-3673
Lima/Allen County Convention & Visitors Bureau 147 N Main St *TF:* 888-222-6075 ■ *Web:* www.allencvb.lima.oh.us	Lima	OH	45801	419-222-6075	222-0134
Abraham Lincoln Tourism Bureau of Logan County 1555 5th St *Web:* www.logancountytourism.org	Lincoln	IL	62656	217-732-8687	735-9205
Lincoln Convention & Visitors Bureau 1135 M St 3rd Fl *TF:* 800-423-8212 ■ *Web:* www.lincoln.org	Lincoln	NE	68508	402-434-5335	436-2360
Lincoln City Visitor & Convention Bureau 801 SW Hwy 101 Suite 1 *TF:* 800-452-2151 ■ *Web:* www.oregoncoast.org	Lincoln City	OR	97367	541-994-8378	994-2408
Lisle Convention & Visitors Bureau 4746 Main St *TF:* 800-733-9811 ■ *Web:* www.lislecvb.com	Lisle	IL	60532	630-769-1000	769-1006
Little Rock Convention & Visitors Bureau 426 W Markham St PO Box 3232 *TF:* 800-844-4781 ■ *Web:* www.littlerock.com	Little Rock	AR	72203	501-376-4781	374-2255
Lodi Conference & Visitors Bureau 115 S School St Suite 9 *TF:* 800-798-1810 ■ *Web:* www.visitlodi.com	Lodi	CA	95240	209-365-1195	365-1191
London/Laurel County Tourist Commission 140 Faith Assembly Church Rd *TF:* 800-348-0095 ■ *Web:* www.laurelkytourism.com	London	KY	40741	606-878-6900	877-1689
Long Beach Convention & Visitors Bureau 1 World Trade Center Suite 300 *TF:* 800-452-7829 ■ *Web:* www.visitlongbeach.com	Long Beach	CA	90831	562-436-3645	435-5653
Seminole County Convention & Visitors Bureau 1230 Douglas Ave Suite 116 *TF:* 800-800-7832 ■ *Web:* www.visitseminole.com	Longwood	FL	32779	407-665-2900	665-2920
Los Angeles Convention & Visitors Bureau 333 S Hope St 18th Fl *TF:* 800-228-2452 ■ *Web:* www.greaterLosAngeles.com/	Los Angeles	CA	90071	213-624-7300	624-9746
Louisville & Jefferson County Convention & Visitors Bureau 401 W Main St Suite 2300 *TF:* 800-792-5595 ■ *Web:* www.gotolouisville.com	Louisville	KY	40202	502-584-2121	584-6697
Greater Merrimack Valley Convention & Visitors Bureau 9 Central St Suite 201 *TF:* 800-443-3332 ■ *Web:* www.lowell.org	Lowell	MA	01852	978-459-6150	459-4595
Lubbock Convention & Visitors Bureau 1301 Broadway St Suite 200 *TF:* 800-692-4035 ■ *Web:* www.visitlubbock.org	Lubbock	TX	79401	806-747-5232	747-1419
Lufkin Visitor & Convention Bureau 1615 S Chestnut St *TF:* 800-409-5659 ■ *Web:* www.visitlufkin.com	Lufkin	TX	75901	936-631-3926	634-8726
Lumberton Area Visitors Bureau 3431 Lackey St *TF:* 800-359-6971 ■ *Web:* www.lumberton-nc.com	Lumberton	NC	28360	910-739-9999	739-9777
Mackinaw Area Visitors Bureau 10800 US 23 *TF:* 800-666-0160 ■ *Web:* www.mackinawcity.com	Mackinaw City	MI	49701	231-436-5664	436-5991
Macomb Area Convention & Visitors Bureau 201 S Lafayette St *Web:* www.makeitmacomb.com	Macomb	IL	61455	309-833-1315	833-3575
Macon-Bibb County Convention/Visitors Bureau 450 ML King Blvd *TF:* 800-768-3401 ■ *Web:* www.maconga.org	Macon	GA	31201	478-743-3401	745-2022
Madison Convention & Visitors Bureau 115 E Jefferson St *TF:* 800-709-7406 ■ *Web:* www.madisonga.org	Madison	GA	30650	706-342-4454	342-4455
Greater Madison Convention & Visitors Bureau 615 E Washington Ave *TF:* 800-373-6376 ■ *Web:* www.visitmadison.com	Madison	WI	53703	608-255-2537	258-4950
Maggie Valley Area Convention & Visitors Bureau 2961 Soco Rd PO Box 279 *TF:* 800-624-4431 ■ *Web:* www.maggievalley.com	Maggie Valley	NC	28751	828-926-1686	926-9398
Manchester Area Convention & Visitors Bureau 889 Elm St 3rd Fl *Web:* www.manchestercvb.com	Manchester	NH	03101	603-666-6600	626-0910
Saint Tammany Parish Tourist & Convention Commission 68099 Hwy 59 *TF:* 800-634-9443 ■ *Web:* www.neworleansnorthshore.com	Mandeville	LA	70471	985-892-0520	892-1441
Manhattan Convention & Visitors Bureau 501 Poyntz Ave *TF:* 800-759-0134 ■ *Web:* www.manhattancvb.org	Manhattan	KS	66502	785-776-8829	776-0679
Manitowoc Visitor & Convention Bureau 4221 Calumet Ave PO Box 966 *TF:* 800-627-4896 ■ *Web:* www.manitowoc.org	Manitowoc	WI	54221	920-683-4388	683-4876
Greater Mankato Chamber & Convention Bureau 112 S Riverfront Dr *TF:* 800-657-4733 ■ *Web:* www.mankato.com	Mankato	MN	56001	507-345-4519	345-4451
Mansfield/Richland County Convention & Visitors Bureau 124 N Main St *TF:* 800-642-8282 ■ *Web:* www.mansfieldtourism.org	Mansfield	OH	44902	419-525-1300	524-7722
Outer Banks Visitors Bureau 1 Visitor Center Cir *TF:* 877-629-4386 ■ *Web:* www.outerbanks.org	Manteo	NC	27954	252-473-2138	473-5106
Williamson County Tourism Bureau 1602 Sioux Dr *TF:* 800-433-7399 ■ *Web:* www.wctb.org	Marion	IL	62959	618-997-3690	997-1874
Marion-Grant County Convention & Visitors Bureau 428 S Washington St *TF:* 800-662-9474 ■ *Web:* www.jamesdeancountry.com	Marion	IN	46953	765-668-5435	668-5424
Marquette Country Convention & Visitors Bureau 337 W Washington St *TF:* 800-544-4321 ■ *Web:* www.marquettecountry.org	Marquette	MI	49855	906-228-7749	228-3642
Marshall Convention & Visitors Bureau 317 W Main St *Web:* www.marshall-mn.org	Marshall	MN	56258	507-537-1865	532-4485
Marshfield Convention & Visitors Bureau 700 S Central Ave *TF:* 800-422-4541 ■ *Web:* www.marshfieldchamber.com	Marshfield	WI	54449	715-384-3454	387-8925
Mason City Convention & Visitors Bureau 25 W State St *TF:* 800-423-5724 ■ *Web:* www.masoncitytourism.com	Mason City	IA	50401	641-422-1663	423-5725
Northeast Pennsylvania Convention & Visitors Bureau 1300 Old Plank Rd *TF:* 800-229-3526 ■ *Web:* www.visitnepa.org	Mayfield	PA	18433	570-963-6363	963-6852
McAllen Convention & Visitors Bureau 1200 Ash St *TF:* 877-622-5536 ■ *Web:* www.mcallenchamber.com	McAllen	TX	78501	956-682-2871	631-8571
Fairfax County Convention & Visitors Corp 7927 Jones Branch Dr Suite 100 *Web:* www.visitfairfax.org	McLean	VA	22102	703-790-0643	893-1269
Melbourne/Palm Bay Area Convention & Visitor Bureau 1005 E Strawbridge Ave *TF:* 800-771-9922 ■ *Web:* www.melpb-chamber.org	Melbourne	FL	32901	321-724-5400	725-2093
Memphis Convention & Visitors Bureau 47 Union Ave *TF:* 800-873-6282 ■ *Web:* www.memphistravel.com	Memphis	TN	38103	901-543-5300	543-5350
Merced Conference & Visitors Bureau 710 W 16th St *TF:* 800-446-5353 ■ *Web:* www.yosemite-gateway.org	Merced	CA	95340	209-384-2791	384-2793
Capital Region Convention & Visitors Bureau 1A Quakerbridge Plaza Dr *Web:* www.trentonnj.com/	Mercerville	NJ	08619	609-689-9964	586-9989
Meridian/Lauderdale County Tourism Bureau 212 Constitution Ave PO Box 5313 *TF:* 888-868-7720 ■ *Web:* www.visitmeridian.com	Meridian	MS	39302	601-482-8001	486-4988
Mesa Convention & Visitors Bureau 120 N Center St *TF:* 800-283-6372 ■ *Web:* www.mesacvb.com	Mesa	AZ	85201	480-827-4700	827-4704
Greater Miami Convention & Visitors Bureau 701 Brickell Ave Suite 2700 *TF:* 800-933-8448 ■ *Web:* www.gmcvb.com	Miami	FL	33131	305-539-3000	530-5859
LaPorte County Convention & Visitors Bureau 1503 S Meer Rd *TF:* 800-634-2650 ■ *Web:* www.visitlaportecounty.com	Michigan City	IN	46360	219-872-5055	872-3660
Middletown Convention & Visitors Bureau PO Box 1245 *TF:* 888-664-3353 ■ *Web:* www.visitmiddletown.org	Middletown	OH	45042	513-422-3030	425-7925

				Phone	Fax
Midland County Convention & Visitors Bureau 300 Rodd St Suite 101	Midland	MI	48640	989-839-9901	835-3701
TF: 888-464-3526 ■ *Web:* www.midlandcvb.org					
Milledgeville-Baldwin County Convention & Visitors Bureau 200 W Hancock St	Milledgeville	GA	31061	478-452-4687	453-4440
TF: 800-653-1804 ■ *Web:* www.milledgevillecvb.com					
Greater Milwaukee Convention & Visitors Bureau 101 W Wisconsin Ave Suite 425	Milwaukee	WI	53203	414-273-3950	273-5596
TF: 800-231-0903 ■ *Web:* www.milwaukee.org					
Greater Minneapolis Convention & Visitors Assn 250 Marquette Ave Suite 1300	Minneapolis	MN	55401	612-767-8000	335-5839
TF: 800-445-7412 ■ *Web:* www.minneapolis.org					
Minot Convention & Visitors Bureau 1020 S Broadway	Minot	ND	58701	701-857-8206	857-8228
TF: 800-264-2626 ■ *Web:* www.visitminot.org					
Missoula Convention & Visitors Bureau 1121 E Broadway Suite 103	Missoula	MT	59802	406-532-3250	532-3252
TF: 800-526-3465 ■ *Web:* www.missoulacvb.org/index.php					
Mobile Bay Convention & Visitors Bureau 1 S Water St	Mobile	AL	36602	251-208-2000	208-2060
TF: 800-566-2453 ■ *Web:* www.mobile.org					
Modesto Convention & Visitors Bureau 1150 9th St Suite C	Modesto	CA	95354	209-526-5588	526-5586
TF: 888-640-8467 ■ *Web:* www.visitmodesto.com					
Quad Cities Convention & Visitors Bureau 2021 River Dr	Moline	IL	61265	563-322-3911	764-9443*
**Fax Area Code: 309 ■ *TF:* 800-747-7800 ■ *Web:* www.visitquadcities.com					
Monterey County Convention & Visitors Bureau 150 Oliver St PO Box 1770	Monterey	CA	93942	831-649-1770	648-5373
TF: 888-221-1010 ■ *Web:* www.montereyinfo.org					
Montgomery Area Chamber of Commerce Convention & Visitor Bureau 300 Water St Union Stn	Montgomery	AL	36104	334-261-1100	261-1111
TF: 800-240-9452 ■ *Web:* www.visitingmontgomery.com					
Greater Montreal Convention & Tourism Bureau 1555 Peel St Bureau 600	Montreal	QC	H3A3L8	514-844-5400	844-5757
TF: 800-363-7777 ■ *Web:* www.tourisme-montreal.org					
Tourisme Montréal 1555 Peel St Bureau 600	Montreal	QC	H3A3L8	514-844-5400	844-5757
TF: 800-363-7777 ■ *Web:* www.tourisme-montreal.org					
Montrose Visitor & Convention Bureau 1519 E Main St	Montrose	CO	81401	970-252-0505	249-2907
TF: 800-873-0244 ■ *Web:* www.visitmontrose.net					
Greater Morgantown Convention & Visitors Bureau 201 High St Suite 3	Morgantown	WV	26505	304-292-5081	291-1354
TF: 800-458-7373 ■ *Web:* www.tourmorgantown.com					
Mount Vernon Convention & Visitors Bureau 200 Potomac Blvd	Mount Vernon	IL	62864	618-242-3151	242-6849
TF: 800-252-5464 ■ *Web:* www.mtvernon.com/Tourism_frame_page.htm					
Knox County Convention & Visitors Bureau 107 S Main St	Mount Vernon	OH	43050	740-392-6102	392-7840
TF: 800-837-5282 ■ *Web:* www.visitknoxohio.org					
Muncie Visitors Bureau 425 N High St	Muncie	IN	47305	765-284-2700	284-3002
TF: 800-568-6862 ■ *Web:* www.munciecvb.org					
Muskegon County Convention & Visitors Bureau 610 W Western Ave	Muskegon	MI	49440	231-724-3100	724-1398
TF: 800-250-9283 ■ *Web:* www.visitmuskegon.org					
Myrtle Beach Area Convention Bureau 1200 N Oak St	Myrtle Beach	SC	29577	843-626-7444	448-3010
TF: 800-356-3016 ■ *Web:* www.myrtlebeachinfo.com					
Nacogdoches Convention & Visitors Bureau 200 E Main St	Nacogdoches	TX	75961	936-564-7351	462-7688
TF: 888-653-3788 ■ *Web:* www.visitnacogdoches.org					
Napa Valley Conference & Visitors Bureau 1310 Napa Town Center	Napa	CA	94559	707-226-7459	255-2066
Web: www.napavalley.org					
Greater Naples Marco Island Everglades Convention & Visitors Bureau 3050 N Horseshoe Dr Suite 218	Naples	FL	34104	239-403-2384	403-2404
TF: 800-688-3600 ■ *Web:* www.paradisecoast.com					
Brown County Convention & Visitors Bureau 10 N Van Buren St PO Box 840	Nashville	IN	47448	812-988-7303	988-1070
TF: 800-753-3255 ■ *Web:* www.browncounty.com					
Nashville Convention & Visitors Bureau 211 Commerce St Suite 100	Nashville	TN	37201	615-259-4700	259-4126
TF: 800-657-6910 ■ *Web:* www.visitmusiccity.com/					
Natchez Convention & Visitors Bureau 640 S Canal St Box C	Natchez	MS	39120	601-446-6345	442-0814
TF: 800-647-6724 ■ *Web:* www.natchez.ms.us					
Craven County Convention & Visitors Bureau 203 S Front St	New Bern	NC	28560	252-637-9400	637-0250
TF: 800-437-5767 ■ *Web:* www.visitnewbern.com					
Greater New Braunfels Chamber of Commerce 171 E Garden St PO Box 311417	New Braunfels	TX	78131	830-625-2385	625-7918
TF: 800-572-2626 ■ *Web:* nbcham.org					
Convention & Visitors Bureau of Henry County 2020 S Memorial Dr Suite I	New Castle	IN	47362	765-593-0764	593-0766
TF: 888-676-4300 ■ *Web:* www.henrycountyin.org					
Lawrence County Tourist Promotion Agency 229 S Jefferson St	New Castle	PA	16101	724-654-8408	654-2044
TF: 888-284-7599 ■ *Web:* www.visitlawrencecounty.com					
Greater New Haven Convention & Visitors Bureau 169 Orange St	New Haven	CT	06510	203-777-8550	782-7755
TF: 800-332-7829 ■ *Web:* www.newhavencvb.org					
Connecticut's Mystic & More! 32 Huntington St	New London	CT	06320	860-444-2206	442-4257
TF: 800-863-6569 ■ *Web:* www.mysticmore.com					
New Orleans Metropolitan Convention & Visitors Bureau 2020 St Charles Ave	New Orleans	LA	70130	504-566-5011	566-5046
TF: 800-672-6124 ■ *Web:* www.neworleanscvb.com					
NYC & Co 810 7th Ave 3rd Fl	New York	NY	10019	212-484-1200	484-1222
TF: 800-692-8474 ■ *Web:* www.nycvisit.com					
Newberry Area Tourism Assn 4947 E County Rd 460	Newberry	MI	49868	906-293-5739	293-5739
TF: 800-831-7292 ■ *Web:* www.exploringthenorth.com					
Newport County Convention & Visitors Bureau 23 America's Cup Ave	Newport	RI	02840	401-849-8048	849-0291
TF: 800-326-6030 ■ *Web:* www.gonewport.com					
Newport Beach Conference & Visitors Bureau 110 Newport Center Dr Suite 120	Newport Beach	CA	92660	949-719-6100	719-6101
TF: 800-942-6278 ■ *Web:* www.newportbeach-cvb.com					
Newport News Tourism Development Office 700 Town Center Dr Suite 320	Newport News	VA	23606	757-926-1400	926-1441
TF: 888-493-7386 ■ *Web:* www.newport-news.org					
Newton Convention & Visitor Bureau 113 1st Ave W	Newton	IA	50208	641-792-5545	791-0879
TF: 800-798-0299 ■ *Web:* www.visitnewton.com					
Niagara Tourism & Convention Corp 345 3rd St Suite 605	Niagara Falls	NY	14303	716-282-8992	285-0809
TF: 800-338-7890 ■ *Web:* niagara-usa.com					
Four Flags Area Council on Tourism 321 E Main St	Niles	MI	49120	269-684-7444	683-3722
Web: www.fourflagsarea.org					
Nome Convention & Visitors Bureau 301 Front St PO Box 240 HP-N	Nome	AK	99762	907-443-6624	443-5832
Web: www.nomealaska.org/vc					
Madison County Convention & Visitors Bureau 405 Madison Ave	Norfolk	NE	68701	402-371-2932	371-0182
TF: 888-371-2932 ■ *Web:* www.norfolk.ne.us					
Norfolk Convention & Visitors Bureau 232 E Main St	Norfolk	VA	23510	757-664-6620	622-3663
TF: 800-368-3097 ■ *Web:* www.norfolkcvb.com					
Norman Convention & Visitors Bureau 223 E Main St	Norman	OK	73069	405-366-8095	366-8096
TF: 800-767-7260 ■ *Web:* www.visitnorman.com					

				Phone	Fax
North Platte/Lincoln County Convention & Visitors Bureau 219 S Dewey St	North Platte	NE	69103	308-532-4729	532-5914
TF: 800-955-4528 ■ *Web:* www.visitnorthplatte.com					
North Ridgeville Visitors Bureau 34845 Lorain Rd	North Ridgeville	OH	44039	440-327-3737	327-1474
Web: www.nrchamber.com					
DuPage Convention & Visitors Bureau 915 Harger Rd Suite 240	Oak Brook	IL	60523	630-575-8070	575-8078
TF: 800-232-0502 ■ *Web:* www.dupagecvb.com					
Oak Park Area Convention and Visitors Bureau 1118 Westgate	Oak Park	IL	60301	708-524-7800	524-7473
TF: 888-625-7275 ■ *Web:* www.visitoakpark.com					
Oak Ridge Convention & Visitors Bureau 302 S Tulane Ave	Oak Ridge	TN	37830	865-482-7821	481-3543
TF: 800-887-3429 ■ *Web:* oakridgevisitor.com					
Yosemite Sierra Visitors Bureau 41969 Hwy 41	Oakhurst	CA	93644	559-683-4636	683-5697
Web: www.yosemite-sierra.org					
Oakland Convention & Visitors Bureau 463 11th St	Oakland	CA	94607	510-839-9000	839-5924
Web: www.oaklandcvb.com					
Oberlin Convention & Tourist Committee 104 S Penn Ave	Oberlin	KS	67749	785-475-3441	475-2128
Ocean City Convention & Visitors Bureau 4001 Coastal Hwy	Ocean City	MD	21842	410-289-8181	723-8655
TF: 800-626-2326 ■ *Web:* www.ococean.com					
Oconomowoc Convention & Visitors Bureau 174 E Wisconsin Ave	Oconomowoc	WI	53066	262-569-2185	569-3238
TF: 800-524-3744 ■ *Web:* www.oconomowocusa.com					
Odessa Convention & Visitors Bureau 700 N Grant Ave Suite 200	Odessa	TX	79761	432-333-7871	333-7858
TF: 800-780-4678 ■ *Web:* www.odessacvb.com					
Ogden/Weber Convention & Visitors Bureau 2501 Wall Ave Union Stn Suite 201	Ogden	UT	84401	801-627-8288	399-0783
TF: 800-255-8824 ■ *Web:* www.ogdencvb.org/					
Oklahoma City Convention & Visitors Bureau 189 W Sheridan St	Oklahoma City	OK	73102	405-297-8912	297-8888
TF: 800-225-5652 ■ *Web:* www.visitokc.com					
McDowell County Tourism Development Authority 25 US 70 W	Old Fort	NC	28762	828-668-4282	668-4928
TF: 888-233-6111 ■ *Web:* www.mcdowellnc.org					
Olympia/Thurston County Visitor & Convention Bureau PO Box 7338	Olympia	WA	98507	360-704-7544	704-7533
TF: 877-704-7500 ■ *Web:* www.visitolympia.com					
Greater Omaha Convention & Visitors Bureau 1001 Farnam St Suite 200	Omaha	NE	68102	402-444-4660	444-4511
TF: 800-332-1819 ■ *Web:* www.visitomaha.com					
Onalaska Center for Commerce & Tourism 1101 Main St	Onalaska	WI	54650	608-781-9570	781-9572
TF: 800-873-1901 ■ *Web:* www.tourism.onalaska.wi.us					
Ontario Convention & Visitors Bureau 2000 E Convention Center Way	Ontario	CA	91764	909-937-3000	937-3080
TF: 800-455-5755 ■ *Web:* www.ontariocvb.com					
Ontario Convention & Visitors Bureau 676 SW 5th Ave	Ontario	OR	97914	541-889-8012	889-8331
TF: 866-889-8012 ■ *Web:* www.ontariochamber.com					
Orange Convention & Visitors Bureau 803 W Green Ave	Orange	TX	77631	409-883-1011	988-7321
TF: 800-528-4906 ■ *Web:* www.org-tx.com/chamber					
Mountainland Travel Region Office 586 E 800 North	Orem	UT	84097	801-229-3800	229-3801
Web: www.mountainland.org					
Orlando/Orange County Convention & Visitors Bureau 6700 Forum Dr Suite 100	Orlando	FL	32821	407-363-5800	370-5000
TF: 800-551-0181 ■ *Web:* www.orlandoinfo.com					
Lake of the Ozarks Convention & Visitors Bureau 5815 Hwy 54	Osage Beach	MO	65065	573-348-1599	348-4292
TF: 800-386-5253 ■ *Web:* www.funlake.com					
Ottawa Visitors Center 100 W Lafayette St	Ottawa	IL	61350	815-434-2737	434-5477
TF: 888-688-2924 ■ *Web:* www.ottawa.il.us					
Ottawa Tourism & Convention Authority 130 Albert St Suite 1800	Ottawa	ON	K1P5G4	613-237-5150	237-7339
TF: 800-363-4465 ■ *Web:* www.ottawatourism.ca					
Overland Park Convention & Visitors Bureau 9001 W 110th St Suite 100	Overland Park	KS	66210	913-491-0123	491-0015
TF: 800-262-7275 ■ *Web:* www.opcvb.org					
Owatonna Area Chamber of Commerce & Tourism 320 Hoffman Dr	Owatonna	MN	55060	507-451-7970	451-7972
TF: 800-423-6466 ■ *Web:* www.owatonna.org					
Owensboro-Davies County Tourist Commission 215 E 2nd St	Owensboro	KY	42303	270-926-1100	926-1161
TF: 800-489-1131 ■ *Web:* www.visitowensboro.com					
Oxford Tourism Council 107 Courthouse Sq Suite 1	Oxford	MS	38655	662-234-4680	234-0355
TF: 800-758-9177 ■ *Web:* www.touroxfordms.com					
Oxnard Convention & Visitors Bureau 200 W 7th St	Oxnard	CA	93030	805-385-7545	385-7571
TF: 800-269-6273 ■ *Web:* www.oxnardtourism.com					
Panama City Beach Convention & Visitors Bureau 17001 Panama City Beach Pkwy	Panama City Beach	FL	32413	850-233-5070	233-5072
TF: 800-722-3224 ■ *Web:* www.thebeachloversbeach.com					
Paris Convention & Visitors Bureau 1125 Bonham St	Paris	TX	75460	903-784-2501	784-2503
TF: 800-727-4789 ■ *Web:* www.paristexas.com					
Park City Chamber of Commerce/Convention & Visitors Bureau 1910 Prospector Ave Suite 103	Park City	UT	84060	435-649-6100	649-4132
TF: 800-453-1360 ■ *Web:* www.parkcityinfo.com					
Parkersburg/Wood County Convention & Visitors Bureau 350 7th St	Parkersburg	WV	26101	304-428-1130	428-8117
TF: 800-752-4982 ■ *Web:* www.greaterparkersburg.com					
Pasadena Convention & Visitors Bureau 171 S Los Robles Ave	Pasadena	CA	91101	626-795-9311	795-9656
TF: 800-307-7977 ■ *Web:* www.pasadenacal.com					
North of Boston Convention & Visitors Bureau 17 Peabody Sq	Peabody	MA	01960	978-977-7760	977-7758
TF: 877-662-9299 ■ *Web:* www.northofboston.org					
Pensacola Convention & Visitors Bureau 1401 E Gregory St	Pensacola	FL	32502	850-434-1234	432-8211
TF: 800-874-1234 ■ *Web:* www.visitpensacola.com					
Peoria Area Convention & Visitors Bureau 456 Fulton St Suite 300	Peoria	IL	61602	309-676-0303	676-8470
TF: 800-747-0302 ■ *Web:* www.peoria.org					
Perry Area Convention & Visitors Bureau 101 Gen Courtney Hodges Blvd	Perry	GA	31069	478-988-8000	988-8005
Web: www.perryga.com					
Petoskey/Harbor Springs/Boyne Country Visitors Bureau 401 E Mitchell St	Petoskey	MI	49770	231-348-2755	348-1810
TF: 800-845-2828 ■ *Web:* www.boynecountry.com					
Philadelphia Convention & Visitors Bureau 1700 Market St Suite 3000	Philadelphia	PA	19103	215-636-3300	636-3327
TF: 800-225-5745 ■ *Web:* www.philadelphiausa.travel/					
Greater Phoenix Convention & Visitors Bureau 400 E Van Buren St 1 Arizona Center Suite 600	Phoenix	AZ	85004	602-254-6500	253-4415
TF: 877-225-5749 ■ *Web:* www.visitphoenix.com					
Pierre Convention & Visitors Bureau 800 W Dakota Ave	Pierre	SD	57501	605-224-7361	224-6485
TF: 800-962-2034 ■ *Web:* pierre.org/					
Pigeon Forge Dept of Tourism 2450 Parkway	Pigeon Forge	TN	37863	865-453-8574	429-7362
TF: 800-251-9100 ■ *Web:* www.mypigeonforge.com					
Pine Bluff Convention & Visitors Bureau 1 Convention Ctr Plaza	Pine Bluff	AR	71601	870-536-7600	535-4867
TF: 800-536-7660 ■ *Web:* www.pinebluff.com					

Phone Fax

Greater Pittsburgh Convention & Visitors Bureau
425 6th Ave 30th Fl Pittsburgh PA 15219 412-281-7711 644-5512
TF: 800-359-0758 ■ *Web:* www.visitpittsburgh.com

Plano Convention & Visitors Bureau 2000 E Spring Creek Pkwy Plano TX 75074 972-422-0296 424-0002
TF: 800-817-5266 ■ *Web:* www.plano.gov/departments/cvb/

Valley Forge Convention & Visitors Bureau
600 W Germantown Pike Suite 130 Plymouth Meeting PA 19462 610-834-1550 834-0202
TF: 800-441-3549 ■ *Web:* www.valleyforge.org

Pocatello Convention & Visitors Bureau
324 S Main St Suite B Pocatello ID 83204 208-235-7659 233-1527
TF: 877-922-7659 ■ *Web:* www.pocatellocvb.com

Ponca City Tourism 420 E Grand Ave Ponca City OK 74601 580-765-4400 765-2798
TF: 866-763-8092 ■ *Web:* www.poncacitytourism.com

North Olympic Peninsula Visitor & Convention Bureau
338 W 1st St Suite 104 Port Angeles WA 98362 360-452-8552 452-7383
TF: 800-942-4042 ■ *Web:* www.olympicpeninsula.org/vcb

Port Arthur Convention & Visitors Bureau
3401 Cultural Ctr Dr Port Arthur TX 77642 409-985-7822 985-5584
TF: 800-235-7822 ■ *Web:* www.portarthurtexas.com

Ottawa County Visitors Bureau 770 SE Catawba Rd Port Clinton OH 43452 419-734-4386 734-9798
TF: 800-441-1271 ■ *Web:* www.lake-erie.com

Blue Water Area Convention & Visitors Bureau
520 Thomas Edison Pkwy Port Huron MI 48060 810-987-8687 987-1441
TF: 800-852-4242 ■ *Web:* www.bluewater.org

Indiana Dunes - The Casual Coast 1420 Munson Rd Porter IN 46304 219-926-2255 929-5395
TF: 800-283-8687 ■ *Web:* www.casualcoast.com

Convention & Visitors Bureau of Greater Portland
245 Commercial St Portland ME 04101 207-772-5800 874-9043
Web: www.visitportland.com

Portland Oregon Visitors Assn 1000 SW Broadway Suite 2300 Portland OR 97205 503-275-9750 275-9774
TF: 800-962-3700 ■ *Web:* www.travelportland.com

Portsmouth Convention & Visitors Bureau
505 Crawford St Suite 2 Portsmouth VA 23704 757-393-5327 393-5330
TF: 800-767-8782 ■ *Web:* www.portsmouthva.gov/tourism

Providence Warwick Convention & Visitors Bureau
1 W Exchange St Providence RI 02903 401-274-1636 351-2090
TF: 800-233-1636 ■ *Web:* www.pwcvb.com

Utah Valley Convention & Visitors Bureau 111 S University Ave Provo UT 84601 801-851-2100 851-2109
TF: 800-222-8824 ■ *Web:* www.utahvalley.org/cvb

Greater Pueblo Chamber of Commerce & Visitors Council
302 N Santa Fe Ave Pueblo CO 81003 719-542-1704 542-1624
TF: 800-233-3446 ■ *Web:* www.pueblo.org

Quebec City Tourism 399 Saint-Joseph St E Quebec QC G1K8E2 418-641-6654 641-6578
Web: www.quebecregion.com/e

Plumas County Visitors Bureau 550 Crescent St Quincy CA 95971 530-283-6345 283-5465
TF: 800-326-2247 ■ *Web:* www.plumascounty.org

Quincy Convention & Visitors Bureau
300 Civic Center Plaza Suite 237 Quincy IL 62301 217-223-1000 223-1330
TF: 800-978-4748 ■ *Web:* www.quincy-cvb.org

Greater Raleigh Convention & Visitors Bureau
421 Fayetteville St Mall Suite 1505 Raleigh NC 27602 919-834-5900 831-2887
TF: 800-849-8499 ■ *Web:* www.visitraleigh.com

Palm Springs Desert Resorts Convention & Visitors Authority 70-100 Hwy 111 Rancho Mirage CA 92270 760-770-9000 770-9001
TF: 800-967-3767 ■ *Web:* www.giveintothedesert.com

Rapid City Convention & Visitors Bureau
444 Mt Rushmore Rd N Rapid City SD 57701 605-343-1744 348-9217
TF: 800-487-3223 ■ *Web:* www.visitrapidcity.com/index.php

Reading & Berks County Visitors Bureau 352 Penn St Reading PA 19602 610-375-4085 375-9606
TF: 800-443-6610 ■ *Web:* www.readingberkspa.com

Redding Convention & Visitors Bureau 777 Auditorium Dr Redding CA 96001 530-225-4100 225-4354
TF: 888-225-4130 ■ *Web:* visitredding.org

Rehoboth Beach Convention Center 229 Rehoboth Ave Rehoboth Beach DE 19971 302-227-4641 227-4643
Web: cityofrehoboth.com

Reno-Sparks Convention & Visitors Authority PO Box 837 Reno NV 89504 775-827-7600 827-7686
TF: 800-443-1482 ■ *Web:* www.visitrenotahoe.com

Richardson Convention & Visitors Services
411 W Arapaho Rd Suite 105 Richardson TX 75080 972-744-4034 744-5834
TF: 888-690-7287 ■ *Web:* www.richardsontexas.org

Richmond/Wayne County Convention & Tourism Bureau
5701 National Rd E Richmond IN 47374 765-935-8687 935-0440
TF: 800-828-8414 ■ *Web:* www.visitrichmond.org

Richmond Metropolitan Convention & Visitors Bureau
401 N 3rd St Richmond VA 23219 804-782-2777 780-2577
TF: 800-370-9004 ■ *Web:* visit.richmond.com/index.aspx

Ridgecrest Area Convention & Visitors Bureau
139 Balsam St Ridgecrest CA 93555 760-375-8202 375-9850
TF: 800-847-4830 ■ *Web:* www.visitdeserts.com

Rising Sun/Ohio County Convention & Tourism Bureau
120 N Walnut St Rising Sun IN 47040 812-438-4933 438-4932
TF: 888-776-4786 ■ *Web:* www.risingsun-in.org

Riverside Convention & Visitors Bureau
3750 University Ave Suite 175 Riverside CA 92501 951-222-4700 222-4712
TF: 888-913-4636 ■ *Web:* www.riversidecvb.com

Roanoke Valley Convention & Visitors Bureau
101 Shenandoah Ave NE Roanoke VA 24016 540-342-6025 342-7119
TF: 800-635-5535 ■ *Web:* www.visitroanokeva.com

Tunica County Convention & Visitors Bureau
13625 Hwy 61 N Robinsonville MS 38664 662-363-3800 363-1493
TF: 888-488-6422 ■ *Web:* www.tunicamiss.org

Rochester Convention & Visitors Bureau
111 S Broadway Suite 301 Rochester MN 55904 507-288-4331 288-9144
TF: 800-634-8277 ■ *Web:* www.rochestercvb.org

Greater Rochester Visitors Assn 45 East Ave Suite 400 Rochester NY 14604 585-546-3070 232-4822
TF: 800-677-7282 ■ *Web:* www.visitrochester.com

Rockhill-York County Convention & Visitors Bureau
452 S Anderson Rd Rock Hill SC 29730 803-329-5200 329-0145
TF: 800-866-5200 ■ *Web:* www.visityorkcounty.com

Rockford Area Convention & Visitors Bureau 102 N Main St Rockford IL 61101 815-963-8111 963-4298
TF: 800-521-0849 ■ *Web:* www.gorockford.com

Conference & Visitors Bureau of Montgomery County
111 Rockville Pike Suite 800 Rockville MD 20850 240-777-2060 777-2065
TF: 800-925-0880 ■ *Web:* www.cvbmontco.com

Nash County Visitors Bureau
107 Gateway Blvd PO Box 7637 Rocky Mount NC 27804 252-972-5080 972-5090
TF: 800-849-6825 ■ *Web:* www.rockymounttravel.com

Greater Rome Convention & Visitors Bureau
402 Civics Center Dr PO Box 5823 Rome GA 30162 706-295-5576 236-5029
TF: 800-444-1834 ■ *Web:* www.romegeorgia.com

Rosemont Convention Bureau 9301 W Bryn Mawr Ave Rosemont IL 60018 847-823-2100 696-9700
Web: www.rosemont.com

Historic Roswell Convention & Visitors Bureau 617 Atlanta St Roswell GA 30075 770-640-3253 640-3252
TF: 800-776-7935 ■ *Web:* www.cvb.roswell.ga.us

Wausau Central Wisconsin Convention & Visitors Bureau
10204 Park Plaza Suite B Rothschild WI 54474 715-355-8788 359-2306
TF: 888-948-4748 ■ *Web:* www.visitwausau.com

Greater Rugby Area Convention & Visitors Bureau
224 Hwy 2 SW Rugby ND 58368 701-776-5846 776-6390

Sacramento Convention & Visitors Bureau 1608 'I' St Sacramento CA 95814 916-808-7777 808-7788
TF: 800-292-2334 ■ *Web:* www.sacramentocvb.org

Saginaw County Convention & Visitors Bureau
515 N Washington Ave 3rd Fl Saginaw MI 48607 989-752-7164 752-6642
TF: 800-444-9979 ■ *Web:* www.saginawcvb.org

Saint Johns County Convention & Visitors Bureau
88 Riberia St Suite 400 Saint Augustine FL 32084 904-829-1711 829-6149
TF: 800-653-2489 ■ *Web:* www.oldcity.com

Greater Saint Charles Convention & Visitors Bureau
230 S Main St Saint Charles MO 63301 636-946-7776 949-3217
TF: 800-366-2427 ■ *Web:* www.historicstcharles.com

Saint Cloud Area Convention & Visitors Bureau
525 Hwy 10 S Suite 1 Saint Cloud MN 56304 320-251-4170 656-0401
TF: 800-264-2940 ■ *Web:* www.granitecountry.com

Saint Joseph Convention & Visitors Bureau 109 S 4th St Saint Joseph MO 64501 816-233-6688 233-9120
TF: 800-785-0360 ■ *Web:* www.stjomo.com

Saint Louis Convention & Visitors Commission
1 Metropolitan Sq Suite 1100 Saint Louis MO 63102 314-421-1023 421-0039
TF: 800-325-7962 ■ *Web:* www.explorestlouis.com

Auglaize & Mercer Counties Convention & Visitors Bureau
900 Edgewater Dr Saint Marys OH 45885 419-394-1294 394-1642
TF: 800-860-4726 ■ *Web:* www.seemore.org

Saint Paul RiverCentre Convention & Visitors Authority
175 W Kellogg Blvd Suite 502 Saint Paul MN 55102 651-265-4900 265-4999
TF: 800-627-6101 ■ *Web:* www.stpaulcvb.org

Salem Tourism Board 101 S Broadway Salem IL 62881 618-548-2222 548-5330
Web: www.ci.salem.il.us

Salem Convention & Visitors Assn 1313 Mill St SE Salem OR 97301 503-581-4325 581-4540
TF: 800-874-7012 ■ *Web:* www.travelsalem.com

Rowan County Convention & Visitors Bureau
204 E Innes St Suite 120 Salisbury NC 28144 704-638-3100 642-2011
TF: 800-332-2343 ■ *Web:* www.visitsalisburync.com

Salt Lake Convention & Visitors Bureau
90 S West Temple Salt Lake City UT 84101 801-521-2822 355-9323
TF: 800-541-4955 ■ *Web:* www.visitsaltlake.com

San Angelo Convention & Visitors Bureau 418 West Ave B San Angelo TX 76903 325-653-1206 658-1110
TF: 800-375-1206 ■ *Web:* www.sanangelo.org/tourism/rtourindex.html

San Antonio Convention & Visitors Bureau
203 S Saint Marys St 2nd Fl San Antonio TX 78205 210-207-6700 207-6768
TF: 800-447-3372 ■ *Web:* www.sanantoniocvb.com

San Bernardino Convention & Visitors Bureau
201 N 'E' St Suite 103 San Bernardino CA 92401 909-889-3980 888-5998
TF: 800-867-8366 ■ *Web:* san-bernardino.org

San Diego Convention & Visitors Bureau 2215 India St San Diego CA 92101 619-232-3101 696-9371
Web: www.sandiego.org

San Francisco Convention & Visitors Bureau
201 3rd St Suite 900 San Francisco CA 94103 415-974-6900 227-2602
Web: www.sfvisitor.org

San Jose Convention & Visitors Bureau 408 Almaden Blvd San Jose CA 95110 408-295-9600 277-3535
TF: 800-726-5673 ■ *Web:* www.sanjose.org

Puerto Rico Convention Bureau 500 Tanca St Suite 402 San Juan PR 00901 787-725-2110 725-2133
TF: 800-875-4765 ■ *Web:* www.meetpuertorico.com

Santa Barbara Visitors Bureau & Film Commission
1601 Anacapa St Santa Barbara CA 93101 805-966-9222 966-1728
TF: 800-927-4688 ■ *Web:* www.santabarbaraca.com

Santa Clara Convention/Visitors Bureau
1850 Warburton Ave Santa Clara CA 95050 408-244-9660 244-9202
TF: 800-272-6822 ■ *Web:* www.santaclara.org

Santa Cruz County Conference & Visitors Council
1211 Ocean St Santa Cruz CA 95060 831-425-1234 425-1260
TF: 800-833-3494 ■ *Web:* www.santacruz.org

Santa Fe Convention & Visitors Bureau 60 E San Francisco St Santa Fe NM 87501 505-955-6200 955-6222
TF: 800-777-2489 ■ *Web:* www.santafe.org

Santa Maria Valley Convention & Visitors Bureau
614 S Broadway Santa Maria CA 93454 805-925-2403 928-7559
TF: 800-331-3779 ■ *Web:* www.santamaria.com

Santa Monica Convention & Visitors Bureau
1920 Main St Suite B Santa Monica CA 90405 310-319-6263 319-6273
TF: 800-544-5319 ■ *Web:* www.santamonica.com

Beaches of South Walton Tourist Development Council
PO Box 1248 Santa Rosa Beach FL 32459 850-267-1216 267-3943
TF: 800-822-6877 ■ *Web:* www.beachesofsouthwalton.com

Sarasota Convention & Visitors Bureau 6701 N Tamiami Trail Sarasota FL 34236 941-957-1877 951-2956
TF: 800-522-9799 ■ *Web:* www.sarasotafl.org

Saratoga Convention & Tourism Bureau
60 Railroad Pl Suite 100 Saratoga Springs NY 12866 518-584-1531 584-2969
Web: www.discoversaratoga.org

Sault Sainte Marie Convention & Visitors Bureau
536 Ashman St Sault Sainte Marie MI 49783 906-632-3366 632-6161
TF: 800-647-2858 ■ *Web:* www.saultstemarie.com

Savannah Area Convention & Visitors Bureau 101 E Bay St Savannah GA 31401 912-644-6401 644-6499
TF: 877-728-2662 ■ *Web:* www.savcvb.com

Hardin County Convention & Visitors Bureau 495 Main St Savannah TN 38372 731-925-2364 925-6987
TF: 800-552-3866 ■ *Web:* www.tourhardincounty.org

Greater Woodfield Convention & Visitors Bureau
1430 N Meacham Rd Suite 1400 Schaumburg IL 60173 847-490-1010 490-1212
TF: 800-847-4849 ■ *Web:* www.chicagonorthwest.com

Scottsdale Convention & Visitors Bureau
4343 N Scottsdale Rd Suite 170 Scottsdale AZ 85251 480-421-1004 421-9733
TF: 800-782-1117 ■ *Web:* www.scottsdalecvb.com

Seattle's Convention & Visitors Bureau
1 Convention Pl 701 Pike St Suite 800 Seattle WA 98101 206-461-5800 461-5855
TF: 866-732-2695 ■ *Web:* www.visitseattle.org/

Seward Convention & Visitors Bureau
2001 Seward Hwy PO Box 749 Seward AK 99664 907-224-8051 224-5353
Web: www.sewardak.org

Southeastern Welcome Center 394 Whiteville Rd NW Shallotte NC 28459 910-754-2505 754-3670

Mercer County Convention & Visitors Bureau 50 N Water Ave Sharon PA 16146 724-346-3771 346-0575
TF: 800-637-2370 ■ *Web:* www.mercercountypa.org

Shelby County Office of Tourism 315 E Main St Shelbyville IL 62565 217-774-2244 774-2224
TF: 800-874-3529 ■ *Web:* www.lakeshelbyville.com

Shepherdsville-Bullitt County Tourist & Convention Commission 395 Paraquet Springs Dr Shepherdsville KY 40165 502-543-8687 543-4889
TF: 800-526-2068 ■ *Web:* www.travelbullitt.org

Sherman Convention & Visitors Council 101 S Travis St Sherman TX 75090 903-957-0310 957-0312
TF: 888-893-1188 ■ *Web:* www.shermantexas.com

LaGrange County Convention & Visitor Bureau
440 1/2 S Van Buren St Shipshewana IN 46565 260-768-4008 768-4091
TF: 800-254-8090 ■ *Web:* www.backroads.org

Shreveport-Bossier Convention & Tourist Bureau
629 Spring St Shreveport LA 71101 318-222-9391 222-0056
TF: 800-551-8682 ■ *Web:* www.shreveport-bossier.org

Sioux City Tourism Bureau 801 4th St Sioux City IA 51101 712-279-4800 279-4900
TF: 800-593-2228 ■ *Web:* www.siouxcitytourism.com

Name / Address	City	State	Zip	Phone	Fax
Sioux Falls Convention & Visitors Bureau 200 N Phillips Ave Suite 102 *TF:* 800-333-2072 ■ *Web:* www.siouxfallscvb.com	Sioux Falls	SD	57104	605-336-1620	336-6499
Sitka Convention & Visitors Bureau 303 Lincoln St Suite 4 *TF:* 800-557-4852 ■ *Web:* www.sitka.org	Sitka	AK	99835	907-747-5940	747-3739
Skagway Convention & Visitors Bureau 245 Broadway PO Box 1029 *TF:* 888-762-1898 ■ *Web:* www.skagway.org	Skagway	AK	99840	907-983-2854	983-3854
Johnston County Visitors Bureau 1525-A Booker Dairy Rd *TF:* 800-441-7829 ■ *Web:* www.johnstonco-cvb.org	Smithfield	NC	27577	919-989-8687	989-6295
South Bend/Mishawaka Convention & Visitors Bureau 401 E Colfax Ave Suite 310 *TF:* 800-828-7881 ■ *Web:* www.livethelegends.org	South Bend	IN	46617	574-234-0051	289-0358
Lake Tahoe Visitors Authority 3066 Lake Tahoe Blvd *TF:* 800-288-2463 ■ *Web:* www.virtualtahoe.com	South Lake Tahoe	CA	96150	530-544-5050	541-7121
South Padre Island Convention & Visitors Bureau 600 Padre Blvd *TF:* 800-767-2373 ■ *Web:* www.sopadre.com	South Padre Island	TX	78597	956-761-6433	761-9462
South Sioux City Convention & Visitors Bureau 3900 Dakota Ave Suite 11 *TF:* 800-793-6327	South Sioux City	NE	68776	402-494-1307	494-5010
Convention & Visitors Bureau-Village of Pinehurst Southern Pines Aberdeen Area 10677 Hwy 15-501 *TF:* 800-346-5362 ■ *Web:* www.homeofgolf.com	Southern Pines	NC	28387	910-692-3330	692-2493
Spokane Convention & Visitors Bureau 201 W Main Suite 301 *TF:* 888-776-5263 ■ *Web:* www.visitspokane.com	Spokane	WA	99201	509-747-3230	623-1297
Central Illinois Tourism Development Office 700 E Adams St *Web:* www.visitcentralillinois.com	Springfield	IL	62701	217-525-7980	525-8004
Springfield Convention & Visitors Bureau 109 N 7th St *TF:* 800-545-7300 ■ *Web:* www.visitspringfieldillinois.com	Springfield	IL	62701	217-789-2360	544-8711
Greater Springfield Convention & Visitors Bureau 1441 Main St Suite 136 *TF:* 800-723-1548 ■ *Web:* www.valleyvisitor.com	Springfield	MA	01103	413-787-1548	781-4607
Springfield Missouri Convention & Visitors Bureau 815 E Saint Louis St *TF:* 800-678-8767 ■ *Web:* www.springfieldmo.org	Springfield	MO	65806	417-881-5300	881-2231
Springfield Area Convention & Visitors Bureau 333 N Limestone St Suite 201 *TF:* 800-803-1553 ■ *Web:* www.springfield-clarkcountyohio.info	Springfield	OH	45503	937-325-7621	325-8765
Centre County Convention & Visitors Bureau 800 E Park Ave *TF:* 800-358-5466 ■ *Web:* www.visitpennstate.org	State College	PA	16803	814-231-1400	231-8123
Stevens Point Area Convention & Visitors Bureau 340 Division St N *TF:* 800-236-4636 ■ *Web:* www.spacvb.com	Stevens Point	WI	54481	715-344-2556	344-5818
Stockton Conference & Visitors Bureau 445 W Webber Ave Suite 220 *Web:* www.visitstockton.org	Stockton	CA	95203	209-547-2770	466-5271
Pocono Mountains Vacation Bureau 1004 Main St *TF:* 800-722-9199 ■ *Web:* www.800poconos.com	Stroudsburg	PA	18360	570-421-5791	421-6927
River Country Tourism Bureau 65984 N M66 *TF:* 800-447-2821 ■ *Web:* www.rivercountry.com	Sturgis	MI	49091	269-659-8811	651-4342
Racine County Convention & Visitors Bureau 14015 Washington Ave *TF:* 800-272-2463 ■ *Web:* www.racine.org	Sturtevant	WI	53177	262-884-6400	884-6404
Superior/Douglas County Convention & Visitors Bureau 205 Belknap St *TF:* 800-942-5313 ■ *Web:* www.visitsuperior.com	Superior	WI	54880	715-394-7716	394-3810
Surfside Tourist Bureau 9301 Collins Ave *TF:* 800-327-4557 ■ *Web:* town.surfside.fl.us	Surfside	FL	33154	305-864-0722	993-5128
Syracuse Convention & Visitors Bureau 572 S Salina St *TF:* 800-234-4797 ■ *Web:* www.visitsyracuse.org	Syracuse	NY	13202	315-470-1910	471-8545
Tacoma Regional Convention & Visitor Bureau 1119 Pacific Ave 5th Fl *TF:* 800-272-2662 ■ *Web:* www.traveltacoma.com	Tacoma	WA	98402	253-627-2836	627-8783
North Lake Tahoe Resort Assn 100 N Lake Blvd *TF:* 800-824-6348 ■ *Web:* www.mytahoevacation.com	Tahoe City	CA	96145	530-583-3494	581-1686
North Lake Tahoe Visitors & Convention Bureau PO Box 1757 *TF:* 800-462-5196 ■ *Web:* www.gotahoenorth.com	Tahoe City	CA	96145	530-581-8703	581-1686
Tallahassee Area Convention & Visitors Bureau 106 E Jefferson St *TF:* 800-628-2866 ■ *Web:* www.visittallahassee.com	Tallahassee	FL	32301	850-606-2305	606-2301
Tampa Bay Convention & Visitors Bureau 400 N Tampa St Suite 2800 *TF:* 800-826-8358 ■ *Web:* www.visittampabay.com	Tampa	FL	33602	813-223-1111	229-6616
Tawas Area Tourism & Convention Bureau PO Box 10 **Fax Area Code: 989* ■ *Web:* www.tawasbay.com	Tawas City	MI	48764	877-868-2927	362-7880*
Tempe Convention & Visitors Bureau 51 W 3rd St Suite 105 *TF:* 800-283-6734 ■ *Web:* www.tempecvb.com	Tempe	AZ	85281	480-894-8158	968-8004
Terre Haute Convention & Visitors Bureau 643 Wabash Ave *TF:* 800-366-3043 ■ *Web:* www.terrehaute.com	Terre Haute	IN	47807	812-234-5555	234-6750
Thief River Falls Convention & Visitors Bureau 2017 Hwy 59 SE *TF:* 800-827-1629 ■ *Web:* www.visitthiefriverfalls.com	Thief River Falls	MN	56701	218-681-3720	681-3739
City of Thomasville Tourism Authority 401 S Broad St *TF:* 866-577-3600 ■ *Web:* www.thomasvillega.com	Thomasville	GA	31799	229-227-7099	228-4188
Three Lakes Information Bureau 1704 Superior St PO Box 268 *TF:* 800-972-6103 ■ *Web:* www.threelakes.com	Three Lakes	WI	54562	715-546-3344	546-2103
Seneca County Convention & Visitors Bureau 114 S Washington St *TF:* 888-736-3221 ■ *Web:* www.senecacounty.com/visitor	Tiffin	OH	44883	419-447-5866	447-6628
Greater Toledo Convention & Visitors Bureau 401 Jefferson Ave *TF:* 800-243-4667 ■ *Web:* www.dotoledo.org	Toledo	OH	43604	419-321-6404	255-7731
Tomah Convention & Visitors Bureau 805 Superior Ave PO Box 625 *TF:* 800-948-6624 ■ *Web:* www.tomahwisconsin.com	Tomah	WI	54660	608-372-2166	372-2167
Travel Industry Assn of Kansas 919 S Kansas Ave *Web:* www.tiak.org	Topeka	KS	66612	785-233-9465	232-5705
Visit Topeka Inc 1275 SW Topeka Blvd *TF:* 800-235-1030 ■ *Web:* www.visittopeka.travel	Topeka	KS	66612	785-234-1030	234-8282
Toronto Convention & Visitors Assn 207 Queen's Quay W Suite 590 *TF:* 800-363-1990 ■ *Web:* www.torontotourism.com/visitor	Toronto	ON	M5J1A7	416-203-2600	203-6753
Smoky Mountain Visitors Bureau 7906 E Lamar Alexander Pkwy *TF:* 800-525-6834 ■ *Web:* www.smokymountains.org	Townsend	TN	37882	865-448-6134	448-9806
Baltimore County Conference & Visitors Bureau 825 Delaney Valley Rd *TF:* 877-782-9636 ■ *Web:* www.visitbacomd.com	Towson	MD	21204	410-296-4886	296-8618
Traverse City Convention & Visitors Bureau 101 W Grandview Pkwy *TF:* 800-940-1120 ■ *Web:* www.mytraversecity.com	Traverse City	MI	49684	231-947-1120	947-2621
Atlanta's DeKalb Convention & Visitors Bureau 1957 Lakeside Pkwy Suite 510 *TF:* 800-999-6055 ■ *Web:* www.dcvb.org	Tucker	GA	30084	770-492-5000	492-5033
Metropolitan Tucson Convention & Visitors Bureau 100 S Church Ave *TF:* 800-638-8350 ■ *Web:* www.visittucson.org	Tucson	AZ	85701	520-624-1817	884-7804
Tulsa Convention & Visitors Bureau 2 W 2nd St Suite 150 Williams Center Tower II *TF:* 800-558-3311 ■ *Web:* www.visittulsa.com	Tulsa	OK	74103	918-585-1201	592-6244
Tupelo Convention & Visitors Bureau 399 E Main St *TF:* 800-533-0611 ■ *Web:* tupelo.net	Tupelo	MS	38804	662-841-6521	841-6558
Turlock Convention & Visitors Bureau 115 S Golden State Blvd *Web:* www.visitturlock.org	Turlock	CA	95380	209-632-2221	632-5289
Tuscaloosa Convention & Visitors Bureau 1305 Greensboro Ave *TF:* 800-538-8696 ■ *Web:* www.tcvb.org	Tuscaloosa	AL	35401	205-391-9200	759-9002
Colbert County Tourism & Convention Bureau 719 Hwy 72 W PO Box 740425 *TF:* 800-344-0783 ■ *Web:* www.colbertcountytourism.org	Tuscumbia	AL	35674	256-383-0783	383-2080
Tyler Convention & Visitors Bureau 315 N Broadway *TF:* 800-235-5712 ■ *Web:* www.tylertexas.com/cvb	Tyler	TX	75702	903-592-1661	592-1268
Oneida County Convention & Visitors Bureau PO Box 551 *TF:* 800-426-3132 ■ *Web:* www.oneidacountycvb.com	Utica	NY	13503	315-724-7221	724-7335
Vail Valley Tourism Bureau 100 E Meadow Dr Suite 34 *TF:* 800-525-3875 ■ *Web:* www.visitvailvalley.com	Vail	CO	81657	970-476-1000	476-6008
Vallejo Convention & Visitors Bureau 289 Mare Island Way *TF:* 800-482-5535 ■ *Web:* www.visitvallejo.com	Vallejo	CA	94590	707-642-3653	644-2206
Greater Vancouver Convention & Visitors Bureau 200 Burrard St *TF:* 800-663-6000 ■ *Web:* www.tourismvancouver.com	Vancouver	BC	V6C3L6	604-683-2000	682-6839
Tourism Vancouver 200 Burrard St *TF:* 800-663-6000 ■ *Web:* www.tourismvancouver.com	Vancouver	BC	V6C3L6	604-683-2000	682-6839
Southwest Washington Convention & Visitors Bureau 101 E 8th St Suite 110 *TF:* 877-600-0800 ■ *Web:* www.southwestwashington.com	Vancouver	WA	98660	360-750-1553	750-1933
Ventura Visitors & Convention Bureau 89 S California St Suite C *TF:* 800-333-2989 ■ *Web:* www.ventura-usa.com	Ventura	CA	93001	805-648-2075	648-2150
Vicksburg Convention & Visitors Bureau 1221 Washington St *TF:* 800-221-3536 ■ *Web:* www.vicksburgcvb.org	Vicksburg	MS	39183	601-636-9421	636-9475
Florida's Space Coast Office of Tourism 2725 Judge Fran Jamieson Way Suite B-105 *TF:* 877-572-3224 ■ *Web:* www.space-coast.com	Viera	FL	32940	321-637-5483	637-5494
Iron Range Tourism Bureau 403 N 1st St *TF:* 800-777-8497 ■ *Web:* www.ironrange.org	Virginia	MN	55792	218-749-8161	749-8055
Virginia Beach Convention & Visitor Bureau 2101 Parks Ave Suite 500 *TF:* 800-700-7702 ■ *Web:* www.vbfun.com	Virginia Beach	VA	23451	757-437-4700	437-4747
Visalia Convention & Visitors Bureau 303 E Acequia Ave *TF:* 800-524-0303 ■ *Web:* www.cvbvisalia.com	Visalia	CA	93291	559-713-4000	713-4804
Waco Convention & Visitors Bureau 100 Washington Ave *TF:* 800-321-9226 ■ *Web:* www.wacocvb.com	Waco	TX	76701	254-750-5810	750-5801
Wahpeton Visitors Bureau 118 N 6th St *TF:* 800-892-6673 ■ *Web:* www.wahpchamber.com	Wahpeton	ND	58075	701-642-8744	642-8745
Northern Alleghenies Vacation Region 2883 Pennsylvania Ave W Ext *TF:* 800-624-7802 ■ *Web:* www.northernalleghenies.com	Warren	PA	16365	814-726-1222	726-7266
Kosciusko County Convention & Visitors Bureau 111 Capital Dr *TF:* 800-800-6090 ■ *Web:* www.koscvb.org	Warsaw	IN	46582	574-269-6090	269-2405
Puerto Rico Convention Bureau 1100 17th St NW Suite 901 *TF:* 800-875-4765 ■ *Web:* www.meetpuertorico.com	Washington	DC	20036	202-457-9262	331-0824
Washington DC Convention & Tourism Corp 901 7th St NW 4th Fl *TF:* 800-422-8644 ■ *Web:* www.washington.org	Washington	DC	20001	202-789-7000	789-7037
Northwest Connecticut Convention & Visitors Bureau 21 Church St *TF:* 888-588-7880 ■ *Web:* www.northwestct.com	Waterbury	CT	06702	203-597-9527	597-8452
Waterloo Convention & Visitor Bureau 313 E 5th St *TF:* 800-728-8431 ■ *Web:* www.waterloocvb.org	Waterloo	IA	50703	319-233-8350	233-2733
Tioga County Visitors Bureau 114 Main St *TF:* 888-846-4228 ■ *Web:* www.visittiogapa.com	Wellsboro	PA	16901	570-724-0635	723-1016
West Branch/Ogemaw County Travelers & Visitors Bureau 422 W Houghton Ave *TF:* 800-755-9091 ■ *Web:* www.wboctvb.com	West Branch	MI	48661	989-345-2821	345-9075
Chester County Tourist Bureau 17 Wilmot Suite 400 *TF:* 800-228-9933 ■ *Web:* www.brandywinevalley.com	West Chester	PA	19380	610-719-1730	719-1736
West Hollywood Convention & Visitors Bureau 8687 Melrose Ave Suite M38 *TF:* 800-368-6020 ■ *Web:* www.visitwesthollywood.com	West Hollywood	CA	90069	310-289-2525	289-2529
Monroe-West Monroe Convention & Visitors Bureau 601 Constitution Dr *TF:* 800-843-1872 ■ *Web:* www.monroe-westmonroe.org	West Monroe	LA	71292	318-387-5691	324-1752
Palm Beach County Convention & Visitors Bureau 1555 Palm Beach Lakes Blvd Suite 800 *TF:* 800-833-5733 ■ *Web:* www.palmbeachfl.com	West Palm Beach	FL	33401	561-233-3000	471-3990
Wheeling Convention & Visitors Bureau 1401 Main St *TF:* 800-828-3097 ■ *Web:* www.wheelingcvb.com	Wheeling	WV	26003	304-233-7709	233-1470
Westchester County Office of Tourism 222 Mamaroneck Ave Suite 100 *TF:* 800-833-9282 ■ *Web:* www.westchestertourism.com	White Plains	NY	10605	914-995-8500	995-8505
Wichita Convention & Visitors Bureau 100 S Main St Suite 100 *TF:* 800-288-9424 ■ *Web:* www.visitwichita.com	Wichita	KS	67202	316-265-2800	265-0162
Wichita Falls Convention & Visitors Bureau 1000 5th St PO Box 76301 *TF:* 800-799-6732 ■ *Web:* www.wichitafalls.org	Wichita Falls	TX	76301	940-716-5500	716-5509
Williamsburg Area Convention & Visitors Bureau 421 N Boundary St *TF:* 800-368-6511 ■ *Web:* www.visitwilliamsburg.com	Williamsburg	VA	23185	757-229-6511	229-2047
Martin County Travel & Tourism Authority 100 E Church St *TF:* 800-776-8566 ■ *Web:* www.visitmartincounty.com	Williamston	NC	27892	252-792-6605	792-8710
Greater Wilmington Convention & Visitors Bureau 100 W 10th St Suite 20 *TF:* 800-422-1181 ■ *Web:* www.wilmcvb.org	Wilmington	DE	19801	302-652-4088	652-4726
Cape Fear Coast Convention & Visitors Bureau 24 N 3rd St *TF:* 800-222-4757 ■ *Web:* www.cape-fear.nc.us	Wilmington	NC	28401	910-341-4030	341-4029
Wilson Visitors Bureau PO Box 2882 *TF:* 800-497-7398 ■ *Web:* www.wilson-nc.com	Wilson	NC	27894	252-243-8440	243-7550
Winnemucca Convention & Visitors Authority 50 W Winnemucca Blvd *TF:* 800-962-2638 ■ *Web:* www.winnemucca.nv.us	Winnemucca	NV	89445	775-623-5071	623-5087
Destination Winnipeg 259 Portage Ave Suite 300 *TF:* 800-665-0204 ■ *Web:* www.destinationwinnipeg.ca	Winnipeg	MB	R3B2A9	204-943-1970	942-4043

				Phone	Fax
Winona Convention & Visitors Bureau 160 Johnson St	Winona	MN	55987	507-452-0735	454-0006
TF: 800-657-4972 ■ *Web:* www.visitwinona.com					
Winston-Salem Convention & Visitors Bureau 200 Brookstown Ave	Winston-Salem	NC	27101	336-728-4200	728-4220
TF: 800-331-7018 ■ *Web:* www.wscvb.com					
Wisconsin Dells Visitors & Convention Bureau 701 Superior St	Wisconsin Dells	WI	53965	608-254-8088	254-4293
TF: 800-223-3557 ■ *Web:* www.wisdells.com					
Wayne County Convention & Visitors Bureau 428 W Liberty St	Wooster	OH	44691	330-264-1800	264-1141
TF: 800-362-6474 ■ *Web:* www.wooster-wayne.com/wccvb/					
Worcester County Convention & Visitors Bureau 30 Worcester Center Blvd	Worcester	MA	01608	508-755-7400	754-2703
TF: 800-231-7557 ■ *Web:* www.worcester.org					
York County Convention & Visitors Bureau 155 W Market St	York	PA	17401	717-852-9675	854-5095
TF: 888-858-9675 ■ *Web:* www.yorkpa.org					
Mahoning County Convention & Visitors Bureau 21 W Boardsman St	Youngstown	OH	44503	330-740-2130	286-0093
TF: 800-447-8201 ■ *Web:* www.visitmahoningcounty.com/					
Ypsilanti Area Visitors & Convention Bureau 106 W Michigan Ave	Ypsilanti	MI	48197	734-483-4444	483-0400
TF: 800-265-9045 ■ *Web:* www.ypsilanti.org					
Yuma Convention & Visitors Bureau 377 S Main St Suite 102	Yuma	AZ	85364	928-783-0071	783-1897
TF: 800-293-0071 ■ *Web:* www.visityuma.com					
Zanesville-Muskingum County Convention & Visitors Bureau 205 N 5th St	Zanesville	OH	43701	740-455-8282	454-2963
TF: 800-743-2303 ■ *Web:* www.zanesville-ohio.com					

210 CONVEYORS & CONVEYING EQUIPMENT

SEE ALSO Material Handling Equipment p. 1949

				Phone	Fax
ACEquip Transact Inc 22 Thorndal Cir	Darien	CT	06820	203-656-0065	
Airfloat LLC 2230 Brush College Rd	Decatur	IL	62526	217-423-6001	422-1049
TF: 800-888-0018 ■ *Web:* www.airfloat.com					
Allor Mfg Inc 12534 Emerson Dr	Brighton	MI	48116	248-486-4500	486-4040
TF: 888-244-4028 ■ *Web:* www.allor.com					
Alloy Wire Belt Co 2318 Tenaya Dr	Modesto	CA	95354	209-575-4900	575-4904
TF: 800-538-7933 ■ *Web:* www.alloywirebelt.com					
Ambec Inc 1320 Wards Ferry Rd	Lynchburg	VA	24502	434-582-1200	582-1284
TF: 800-899-4406					
AMF Bakery Systems 2115 W Laburnum Ave	Richmond	VA	23227	804-355-7961	355-1074
TF: 800-225-3771 ■ *Web:* www.amfbakery.com					
Arrowhead Conveyor Corp Inc 3255 Medalist Dr PO Box 2408	Oshkosh	WI	54903	920-235-5562	235-3638
Web: www.arrowheadconveyor.com					
Automated Conveyor Systems Inc 3850 Southland Dr	West Memphis	AR	72301	870-732-5050	732-5191
Web: www.automatedconveyors.com					
Automatic Systems Inc 9230 E 47th St	Kansas City	MO	64133	816-356-0660	356-5730
TF: 800-366-3488 ■ *Web:* www.asiconveyors.com					
Automotion Inc 11000 S Lavergne Ave	Oak Lawn	IL	60453	708-229-3700	229-3702
Web: www.automotionconveyors.com					
Beltservice Corp 4143 Rider Trail N	Earth City	MO	63045	314-344-8500	344-8511
TF: 800-727-2358 ■ *Web:* www.beltservice.com					
Bilt-Rite Conveyors Inc 141 Lanza Ave	Garfield	NJ	07026	973-546-1000	546-2539
Web: www.bilt-rite.com					
Brake Roller Co 730 E Michigan Ave	Battle Creek	MI	49016	269-968-9311	965-2389
TF: 800-537-9940					
C & M Conveyor 4598 SR 37	Mitchell	IN	47446	812-849-5647	849-6126
TF: 800-551-3195 ■ *Web:* www.cmconveyor.com					
Caddy Corp of America 509 Sharptown Rd	Bridgeport	NJ	08014	856-467-4222	467-5511
Web: www.caddycorp.com					
Cambelt International Corp 2820 W 1100 South	Salt Lake City	UT	84104	801-972-5511	
Web: www.cambelt.com					
Cambridge Inc 105 Goodwill Rd	Cambridge	MD	21613	410-228-3000	901-4905
TF: 800-638-9560 ■ *Web:* www.cambridge-inc.com					
Can Lines Engineering 9839 Downey Norwalk Rd PO Box 7039	Downey	CA	90241	323-773-5676	869-5293*
**Fax Area Code:* 562 ■ *TF:* 800-233-4597 ■ *Web:* www.canlines.com					
Carman Industries Inc 1005 W Riverside Dr PO box 579	Jeffersonville	IN	47131	812-288-4700	288-4707
TF: 800-456-7560 ■ *Web:* www.carmanindustries.com					
Carrier Vibrating Equipment Inc 3400 Fern Valley Rd	Louisville	KY	40213	502-969-3171	969-3172
TF: 800-547-7278 ■ *Web:* www.carriervibrating.com					
Christianson Systems Inc 20421 15th St SE	Blomkest	MN	56216	320-995-6141	995-6145
TF: 800-328-8896 ■ *Web:* www.christianson.com					
CIGNYS 68 Williamson St	Saginaw	MI	48601	989-753-1411	753-4386
TF: 888-424-4697 ■ *Web:* www.cignys.com					
Cinetic Sorting Corp 500 E Burnett Ave	Louisville	KY	40217	502-636-1414	636-1491
TF: 800-926-6839 ■ *Web:* www.sorting.com					
Con-Vey Keystone Inc 526 NE Chestnut St PO Box 1399	Roseburg	OR	97470	541-672-5506	672-2513
TF: 800-668-1425 ■ *Web:* www.con-vey.com					
Continental Conveyor & Equipment Co 438 Industrial Dr	Winfield	AL	35594	205-487-6492	487-4233
Web: www.continentalconveyor.com					
Conveyor Components Co 130 Seltzer Rd	Croswell	MI	48422	810-679-4211	679-4510
TF Cust Svc: 800-233-3233 ■ *Web:* www.conveyorcomponents.com					
Conveyors Inc 620 S 4th Ave	Mansfield	TX	76063	817-473-4645	473-3024
Web: www.conveyorsinc.net					
Daifuku America Corp 6700 Tussing Rd	Reynoldsburg	OH	43068	614-863-1888	863-9997
TF: 800-531-1888 ■ *Web:* www.daifukuamerica.com					
Dearborn Mid-West Conveyor Co 20334 Superior Rd	Taylor	MI	48180	734-288-4400	288-1916
TF: 800-655-5105 ■ *Web:* www.dmwcc.com					
Dematic 507 Plymouth Ave NE	Grand Rapids	MI	49505	616-913-6200	913-7701
TF Cust Svc: 800-530-9153 ■ *Web:* www.dematic.us/					
Dynamic Air Inc 1125 Willow Lake Blvd	Saint Paul	MN	55110	651-484-2900	484-7015
Web: www.dynamicair.com					
Engineered Products Inc 355 Woodruff Rd Suite 204	Greenville	SC	29607	864-234-4888	234-4860
TF: 888-301-1421 ■ *Web:* www.engprod.com					
Essmueller Co 334 Ave A PO Box 1966	Laurel	MS	39440	601-649-2400	649-4320
TF: 800-325-7175 ■ *Web:* www.essmueller.com					
Fame Industries Inc 51100 Grand River Ave	Wixom	MI	48393	248-348-7760	348-2120
Web: www.fameind.com					
Feeco International Inc 3913 Algoma Rd	Green Bay	WI	54311	920-469-5100	469-5110
TF Mktg: 800-373-9347 ■ *Web:* www.feeco.com					
Fenner Dunlop Americas 21 Laredo Dr	Scottdale	GA	30079	404-297-3170	296-5165*
**Fax:* Sales ■ *Web:* www.gaduck.com					
FKI Logistex 9301 Olive Blvd	Saint Louis	MO	63132	314-993-4700	995-2400
TF: 877-935-4565 ■ *Web:* www.fkilogistex.com					
Fleetwood Inc 1305 Lakeview Dr	Romeoville	IL	60446	630-759-6800	759-2299
TF: 800-824-6609 ■ *Web:* www.fleetinc.com/fleetinc/fleetinc.htm					
Fred D Pfening Co 1075 W 5th Ave	Columbus	OH	43212	614-294-5361	294-1633
Web: www.pfening.com					
Frost Inc 2020 Bristol Ave NW	Grand Rapids	MI	49504	616-453-7781	453-2161
TF Cust Svc: 800-783-6633 ■ *Web:* www.frostinc.com					
Garvey Corp 208 S Rt 73	Blue Anchor	NJ	08037	609-561-2450	561-2328
TF: 800-257-8581 ■ *Web:* www.garvey.com					
General Kinematics Corp 5050 Rickert Rd	Crystal Lake	IL	60014	815-455-3222	455-2285
Web: www.generalkinematics.com					
Goodman Conveyor Co 645 Floyd Wright Dr	Belton	SC	29627	864-338-7793	338-8732
Web: www.goodmanconveyor.com					
Grasan Equipment Co 440 S Illinois Ave	Mansfield	OH	44907	419-526-4440	524-2176
TF: 800-526-4602 ■ *Web:* www.grasan.com					
Hapman Conveyors 6002 E Kilgore Rd	Kalamazoo	MI	49048	269-382-8200	349-7770
TF: 800-427-6260 ■ *Web:* www.hapman.com					
Hohl Machine & Conveyor Co Inc 1580 Niagara St	Buffalo	NY	14213	716-882-7210	882-9575
Web: www.hohl.com					
Hytrol Conveyor Co Inc 2020 Hytrol St	Jonesboro	AR	72401	870-935-3700	852-3233*
**Fax Area Code:* 800 ■ *Web:* www.hytrol.com					
Intelligrated Products 475 E High St PO Box 899	London	OH	43140	740-490-0300	490-0281
TF: 888-239-1167 ■ *Web:* www.intelligrated.com					
Interlake Material Handling Inc 1230 E Diehl Rd Suite 400	Naperville	IL	60563	630-245-8800	245-8906
TF Sales: 800-282-8032 ■ *Web:* www.interlake.com					
Interroll Corp 3000 Corporate Dr	Wilmington	NC	28405	910-799-1100	830-9679*
**Fax Area Code:* 800 ■ *TF Sales:* 800-830-9680 ■ *Web:* www.interroll.com					
Intralox LLC 8715 Bollman Pl	Savage	MD	20763	301-575-2200	575-2266
Web: www.mhs-usa.com					
Jervis B Webb Co 34375 W 12-Mile Rd	Farmington Hills	MI	48331	248-553-1220	553-1200
TF: 800-526-9322 ■ *Web:* www.jervisbwebb.com					
Jorgensen Conveyors Inc 10303 N Baehr Rd	Mequon	WI	53092	262-242-3089	242-4382
TF: 800-325-7705 ■ *Web:* www.jorgensenconveyors.com					
K-Tron International Inc Rts 55 & 553	Pitman	NJ	08071	856-589-0500	582-7968
NASDAQ: KTII ■ *TF:* 800-355-8766 ■ *Web:* www.ktron.com					
Kice Industries Inc 5500 Mill Heights Dr	Wichita	KS	67219	316-744-7151	744-7355
Web: www.kice.com					
Krasny-Kaplan Corp 4899 Commerce Pkwy	Cleveland	OH	44128	216-292-6300	831-7948
TF: 800-631-0520 ■ *Web:* www.krasnykaplan.com					
KWS Mfg Co Ltd 3041 Conveyor Dr	Burleson	TX	76028	817-295-2247	447-8528
TF: 800-543-6558 ■ *Web:* www.kwsmfg.com					
Laitram LLC 220 Laitram Ln	Harahan	LA	70123	504-733-6000	733-2143
TF: 800-533-8253 ■ *Web:* www.laitram.com					
Lipe Automation Equipment 7650 Edgecomb Dr	Liverpool	NY	13088	315-457-1052	457-1678
TF: 800-448-7822 ■ *Web:* www.lipeautomation.com					
Mac Equipment Inc 7901 NW 107th Terr	Kansas City	MO	64153	816-891-9300	891-8978
TF: 800-821-2476 ■ *Web:* www.macequipment.com					
MARCO 2275 Cassens Ct Suite 105	Fenton	MO	63026	636-680-2031	680-2037
Web: www.marcoconveyors.com					
Martin Engineering 1 Martin Pl	Neponset	IL	61345	309-594-2384	594-2432
TF: 800-544-2947 ■ *Web:* www.martin-eng.com					
Mayfran International 6650 Beta Dr	Mayfield Village	OH	44143	440-461-4100	461-0147
TF: 800-321-6988 ■ *Web:* www.mayfran.com					
Metzgar Conveyor Co Inc 901 Metzgar Dr NW	Comstock Park	MI	49321	616-784-0930	784-4100
Web: www.metzgarconveyors.com					
Montague Industrial Inc 1236-A Wilson Hall Rd	Sumter	SC	29150	803-905-7676	905-7683
Web: www.montague-ind.com					
Nercon Engineering & Mfg Inc 3972 S US Hwy 45	Oshkosh	WI	54902	920-233-3268	233-3159
Web: www.nercon.com					
Nim-Cor Inc 575 Amherst St	Nashua	NH	03063	603-889-2153	883-6980
TF: 888-464-6267 ■ *Web:* www.nimcor.com					
NKC of America Inc 1584 E Brooks Rd	Memphis	TN	38116	901-396-5353	396-2339
TF: 800-532-6727					
Novi Precision Products Inc 11777 Grand River Rd	Brighton	MI	48116	810-227-1024	227-6160
Web: www.noviprecision.com					
Overhead Conveyor Co 1330 Hilton Rd	Ferndale	MI	48220	248-547-3800	547-8344
TF: 800-396-2554 ■ *Web:* www.occ-conveyor.com					
Pfening Fred D Co 1075 W 5th Ave	Columbus	OH	43212	614-294-5361	294-1633
Web: www.pfening.com					
Prab Inc 5944 E Kilgore Rd	Kalamazoo	MI	49048	269-382-8200	349-2477
TF: 800-968-7722 ■ *Web:* www.prab.com					
Railex Corp 89-02 Atlantic Ave	Ozone Park	NY	11416	718-845-5454	738-1020
TF: 800-352-3244 ■ *Web:* www.railexcorp.com					
Railglide Systems 12995 Hillview St	Detroit	MI	48227	313-834-0100	834-3313
TF: 800-451-5262 ■ *Web:* www.railglide.com					
Ransohoff Inc 4933 Provident Dr	Cincinnati	OH	45246	513-870-0100	870-0105
TF: 800-248-9274 ■ *Web:* www.ransohoff.com					
Rapid Industries Inc 4003 Oaklawn Dr	Louisville	KY	40219	502-968-3645	968-6331
TF: 800-727-4381 ■ *Web:* www.rapidi.com					
Renold Jeffrey 2307 Maden Dr	Morristown	TN	37813	423-586-1951	581-2399
TF: 800-251-9012 ■ *Web:* www.renoldjeffrey.com					
Richards-Wilcox Inc 600 S Lake St	Aurora	IL	60506	630-897-6951	897-6994
TF: 800-253-5668 ■ *Web:* www.richardswilcox.com					
Roll-A-Way Conveyor Inc 2335 N Delaney Rd	Gurnee	IL	60031	847-336-5033	336-6542
Web: www.roll-away.com					
Ryson International Inc 300 Newsome Dr	Yorktown	VA	23692	757-898-1530	898-1580
Web: www.ryson.com					
Schroeder Industries LLC 580 W Park Rd	Leetsdale	PA	15056	724-318-1100	318-1200
TF: 800-722-4810 ■ *Web:* www.schroederindustries.com					
Screw Conveyor Corp 700 Hoffman St	Hammond	IN	46327	219-931-1450	931-0209
Web: www.screwconveyor.com					
Shick Tube Veyor Corp 4346 Clary Blvd	Kansas City	MO	64130	816-861-7224	921-1901
Web: www.shickusa.com					
Shuttleworth Inc 10 Commercial Rd	Huntington	IN	46750	260-356-8500	359-7810
TF: 800-444-7412 ■ *Web:* www.shuttleworth.com					
Southern Systems Inc 4101 Viscount Ave	Memphis	TN	38118	901-362-7340	360-8002
Web: www.ssiconveyors.com					
Spar Aerospace Ltd 7th Ave & Airport Service Rd Edmonton International Airport PO Box 9864	Edmonton	AB	T5J2T2	780-890-6300	890-6652
Web: www.spar.ca					
Stewart Systems 808 Stewart Ave	Plano	TX	75074	972-422-5808	424-5041
TF: 800-966-5808 ■ *Web:* www.stewart-systems.com					
Sweet Mfg Co Inc 2000 E Leffel Ln	Springfield	OH	45505	937-325-1511	322-1963
TF Cust Svc: 800-334-7254 ■ *Web:* www.sweetmfg.com					
Swisslog 10825 E 47th Ave	Denver	CO	80239	303-371-7770	373-7870
TF: 800-525-1841 ■ *Web:* www.swisslog.com					
TGW-Ermanco Inc 6870 Grand Haven Rd	Spring Lake	MI	49456	231-798-4547	798-4146
Web: www.tgw-ermanco.com					
Thomas Conveyor Co 555 Burleson Blvd	Burleson	TX	76028	817-295-7151	447-3840
TF: 800-433-2217 ■ *Web:* www.thomasconveyor.com					
Transco Industries Inc 5534 NE 122nd Ave	Portland	OR	97230	503-256-1955	256-0723
TF: 800-545-9991 ■ *Web:* www.transco-ind.com					
Unex Manufacturing Inc 50 Progress Pl	Jackson	NJ	08527	732-928-2800	928-2828
TF Cust Svc: 800-695-7726 ■ *Web:* www.unex.com					
Uni-Pak Corp 1015 N Ronald Reagan Blvd	Longwood	FL	32750	407-830-9300	830-4106
Web: www.unipak.com					
United Conveyor Corp 2100 Norman Dr W	Waukegan	IL	60085	847-473-5900	473-5959
Web: www.unitedconveyor.com					
Universal Industries Inc 5800 Nordic Dr	Cedar Falls	IA	50613	319-277-7501	277-2318
TF: 800-553-4446 ■ *Web:* www.universalindustries.com					
W & H Systems Inc 120 Asia Pl	Carlstadt	NJ	07072	201-933-7840	933-2144
TF: 800-966-6993 ■ *Web:* www.whsystems.com					
Webb Jervis B Co 34375 W 12-Mile Rd	Farmington Hills	MI	48331	248-553-1220	553-1200
TF: 800-526-9322 ■ *Web:* www.jervisbwebb.com					

Phone | Fax

Webb-Stiles Co 675 Liverpool Dr .... Valley City OH 44280 330-225-7761 225-5532
Web: www.webb-stiles.com
Webster Industries Inc 325 Hall St .... Tiffin OH 44883 419-447-8232 448-1618
TF: 800-243-9327 ■ *Web:* www.websterchain.com
Westfalia Technologies Inc 3655 Sandhurst Dr .... York PA 17406 717-764-1115 764-1118
TF: 800-673-2522 ■ *Web:* www.westfaliausa.com
Westmont Industries 10805 S Painter Ave .... Santa Fe Springs CA 90670 562-944-6137 946-5299
Web: www.westmont.com
Whirl Air Flow Corp 20055 177th St .... Big Lake MN 55309 763-262-1200 262-1212
TF: 800-373-3461 ■ *Web:* www.whirlair.com
White Tool Corp 30 Boright Ave .... Kenilworth NJ 07033 908-272-9380 272-4633
Wire Belt Co of America 154 Harvey Rd .... Londonderry NH 03053 603-644-2500 644-3600
TF Cust Svc: 800-922-2637 ■ *Web:* www.wirebelt.com
Young Industries Inc 16 Painter St .... Muncy PA 17756 570-546-3165 546-1888
TF: 800-546-3165 ■ *Web:* www.younginds.com

211 CORD & TWINE

Phone | Fax

40-Up Tackle Co 16 Union Ave .... Westfield MA 01085 413-562-3629 562-7328
TF: 800-456-4665 ■ *Web:* www.usline.com
Algoma Net Co 1525 Mueller St .... Algoma WI 54201 920-487-5577 487-2852
Web: www.algomanet.com
All Line Inc 31 W 310 91st St .... Naperville IL 60564 630-820-1800 820-1830
TF: 800-843-5733 ■ *Web:* www.alllinerope.com
Ashaway Line & Twine Mfg Co PO Box 549 .... Ashaway RI 02804 401-377-2221 377-9091
TF: 800-556-7260 ■ *Web:* www.ashawayusa.com
Atkins & Pearce Inc 1 Braid Way .... Covington KY 41017 859-356-2001 356-2395
TF: 800-837-7477 ■ *Web:* www.braidway.com
Bridon Cordage LLC 909 16th St .... Albert Lea MN 56007 507-377-1601 377-7221*
**Fax:* Sales ■ *TF:* 800-533-6002 ■ *Web:* www.bridoncordage.com
Brownell & Co Inc 423 E Haddam-Moodus Rd .... Moodus CT 06469 860-873-8625 873-1944
TF: 800-222-4007 ■ *Web:* www.brownellco.com
Carron Net Co Inc 1623 17th St PO Box 177 .... Two Rivers WI 54241 920-793-2217 793-2122
TF: 800-558-7768 ■ *Web:* www.carronnet.com
Columbian Rope Co 145 Towery St .... Guntown MS 38849 662-348-2241 348-5749*
**Fax:* Sales ■ *TF:* 800-692-0151 ■ *Web:* www.columbianrope.com
Cordage Inc 1140 Monticello Hwy PO Box 244 .... Madison GA 30650 706-342-1916 342-1720
TF: 800-221-5054 ■ *Web:* www.wellingtoninc.com
Cordage Source The 70 Dundas St .... Deseronto ON K0K1X0 613-396-6998 396-3996
TF Cust Svc: 800-634-8011 ■ *Web:* www.bridgelineropes.com
Cortland Line Co Inc 3736 Kellogg Rd .... Cortland NY 13045 607-756-2851 753-8835
TF: 800-847-6787 ■ *Web:* www.cortlandline.com
Flow Tek Inc PO Box 2018 .... Boulder CO 80306 303-530-3050
Web: www.monic.com
FNT Industries Inc 927 1st St .... Menominee MI 49858 906-863-5531 863-5777
TF Cust Svc: 800-338-9860 ■ *Web:* www.fnt-victory.net
Forten Corp 7815 Silverton Ave Suite 2-A .... San Diego CA 92126 858-693-9888 673-0888
Web: www.forten.com
Frank W Winne & Son Inc 17175 Von Karman Ave Suite 108 .... Irvine CA 92614 949-756-1335 756-2144
TF: 800-755-6110 ■ *Web:* www.frankwinne.com
Gladding Braided Products LLC 1 Gladding St .... South Otselic NY 13155 315-653-7211 653-4492
James Thompson & Co Inc 475 Park Ave S 9th Fl .... New York NY 10016 212-686-4242 686-9528
Web: www.jamesthompson.com
Lehigh Group 2834 Shoeneck Rd .... Macungie PA 18062 610-966-9702 966-3529
TF: 800-523-9382 ■ *Web:* www.lehighgroup.com
New England Ropes Inc 848 Airport Rd .... Fall River MA 02720 508-678-8200 679-2363
TF: 800-333-6679 ■ *Web:* www.neropes.com
Pacific Fibre & Rope Co Inc 903 Flint Ave Suite 27 .... Wilmington CA 90748 310-834-4567 835-6781
TF: 800-825-7673 ■ *Web:* www.pacificfibre.com
Pelican Rope Works Inc 4001 W Carriage Dr .... Santa Ana CA 92704 714-545-0116 545-7673
TF: 800-464-7673 ■ *Web:* www.pelicanrope.com
PlymKraft Inc 479 Export Cir .... Newport News VA 23601 757-595-0364 595-3993
Web: www.plymkraft.com
Puget Sound Rope Corp 1012 2nd St .... Anacortes WA 98221 360-293-8488 293-8480
TF: 888-525-8488 ■ *Web:* www.psrope.com
Rockford Mfg Co 3901 Little River Rd .... Rockford TN 37853 865-970-3131
Rocky Mount Cord Co 381 N Grace St .... Rocky Mount NC 27804 252-977-9130 977-9123
TF Orders: 800-342-9130 ■ *Web:* www.rmcord.com
Ryan Rope Works 953 Benton Ave .... Winslow ME 04901 207-872-0031 873-4301
TF: 888-537-7673
Samson Rope Technologies Inc 2090 Thornton Rd .... Ferndale WA 98248 360-384-4669 299-9246*
**Fax Area Code:* 800 ■ *TF Cust Svc:* 800-227-7673 ■ *Web:* www.samsonrope.com
Sinco Inc 701 Middle St .... Middletown CT 06457 860-632-0500 632-1509
TF Cust Svc: 800-243-6753 ■ *Web:* www.sinco.com
Thompson James & Co Inc 475 Park Ave S 9th Fl .... New York NY 10016 212-686-4242 686-9528
Web: www.jamesthompson.com
Trio Mfg Co 2 N Jackson St PO Box 270 .... Forsyth GA 31029 478-994-2671 994-0506
Web: www.trioyarn.com
Wall Industries Inc 1615 N Lee St .... Spencer NC 28159 704-637-7414 637-2434
TF: 888-289-9255 ■ *Web:* www.wallrope.com
Winne Frank W & Son Inc 17175 Von Karman Ave Suite 108 .... Irvine CA 92614 949-756-1335 756-2144
TF: 800-755-6110 ■ *Web:* www.frankwinne.com

212 CORK & CORK PRODUCTS

SEE ALSO Office & School Supplies p. 2034

Phone | Fax

American Star Cork Co 33-53 62nd St .... Woodside NY 11377 718-335-3000 335-3037
TF: 800-338-3581 ■ *Web:* www.amstarcork.com
Amorim Industrial Solutions 26112 110th St PO Box 25 .... Trevor WI 53179 262-862-2311 862-2500
TF: 800-558-3206 ■ *Web:* www.amorimsolutions.com
Expanko Cork Co Inc 3135 Lower Valley Rd .... Parkesburg PA 19365 610-593-3000 593-3027
TF Cust Svc: 800-345-6202 ■ *Web:* www.expanko.com
Manton Industrial Cork Products Inc 415 Oser Ave Unit U .... Hauppauge NY 11788 631-273-0700 273-0038
TF: 800-663-1921 ■ *Web:* www.mantoncork.com
Maryland Cork Co Inc 190 Triumph Industrial Pk PO Box 126 .... Elkton MD 21922 410-398-2955 392-9433
TF: 800-662-2675 ■ *Web:* www.marylandcork.com

213 CORPORATE HOUSING

Phone | Fax

Alikar Gardens Apartments 1123 Verde Dr .... Colorado Springs CO 80910 719-475-2564 471-5835
TF: 800-456-1123 ■ *Web:* www.alikar.com
BridgeStreet Worldwide Inc 2242 Pinnacle Pkwy .... Twinsburg OH 44087 330-405-6060 405-6061
TF: 800-278-7338 ■ *Web:* www.bridgestreet.com
Cabernet Corporate Housing PO Box 18281 .... Oklahoma City OK 73154 405-236-0066 285-4379
TF: 888-413-3463 ■ *Web:* www.cabernetsuites.com
Charles E Smith Corporate Living 400 15th St S .... Arlington VA 22202 703-920-9550 271-0190
TF: 888-234-7829 ■ *Web:* www.smithliving.com
Churchill Corporate Services 56 Utter Ave .... Hawthorne NJ 07506 973-636-9400 636-0179
TF: 800-941-7458 ■ *Web:* www.furnishedhousing.com
Coast to Coast Corporate Housing PO Box 1597 .... Cypress CA 90630 562-795-0250 795-0251
TF: 800-451-9466 ■ *Web:* www.ctchousing.com
ExecSuites 702 3rd Ave SW .... Calgary AB T2P3B4 403-294-5800 294-5959
TF: 800-667-4980 ■ *Web:* www.execsuite.ca
ExecuStay Corp 1 Marriott Dr .... Washington DC 20058 301-212-9660 778-1113*
**Fax Area Code:* 888 ■ *TF:* 888-840-7829 ■ *Web:* execustay.com
Gables Corporate Accommodations 100 Asbury Way .... Boynton Beach FL 33426 561-735-6053 735-6052
Web: www.gcarents.com
K & M Corporate Housing Inc 16060 Caputo Dr Suite 120 .... Morgan Hill CA 95037 408-782-1212 782-8744
TF: 800-646-0907 ■ *Web:* www.kmrelo.com
Klein & Co Corporate Housing Services Inc
914 Washington Ave .... Golden CO 80401 303-796-2100 796-2101
TF: 800-208-9826 ■ *Web:* www.kleinandcompany.com
Marriott International Inc ExecuStay Corp 1 Marriott Dr .... Washington DC 20058 301-212-9660 778-1113*
**Fax Area Code:* 888 ■ *TF:* 888-840-7829 ■ *Web:* execustay.com
Oakwood Worldwide 2222 Corinth Ave .... Los Angeles CA 90064 310-478-1021 444-2210
TF: 800-888-0808 ■ *Web:* www.oakwood.com
Preferred Living 88 Upham St .... Malden MA 02148 781-321-5793 321-8353
TF: 800-343-2177 ■ *Web:* www.preferred-living.com
Smith Charles E Corporate Living 400 15th St S .... Arlington VA 22202 703-920-9550 271-0190
TF: 888-234-7829 ■ *Web:* www.smithliving.com
SuiteAmerica 4970 Windplay Dr Suite C-1 .... El Dorado Hills CA 95762 916-367-9501 941-7989
TF: 800-363-9779 ■ *Web:* www.suiteamerica.com
US Suites 8301 Washington St .... Albuquerque NM 87113 505-292-1896 294-2588
TF: 800-877-8483 ■ *Web:* www.us-suites.com
Windsor Corporate Suites 3516 Stearns Hills Rd .... Waltham MA 02451 781-899-5100
TF: 800-888-7368 ■ *Web:* www.windsorcommunities.com/CorporateSuites
Wynne Residential Corporate Housing 2214 Westwood Ave .... Richmond VA 23230 804-359-8534 355-7931
TF: 800-338-8534 ■ *Web:* www.wynneres.com

214 CORRECTIONAL & DETENTION MANAGEMENT (PRIVATIZED)

SEE ALSO Correctional Facilities - Federal p. 1572; Correctional Facilities - State p. 1573; Juvenile Detention Facilities p. 1879

Phone | Fax

Avalon Correctional Services Inc 13401 Railway Dr .... Oklahoma City OK 73114 405-752-8802 752-8852
TF: 800-919-9113 ■ *Web:* www.avaloncorrections.com
Cornell Cos Inc 1700 West Loop S Suite 1500 .... Houston TX 77027 713-623-0790 623-2853
NYSE: CRN ■ *TF:* 888-624-0816 ■ *Web:* www.cornellcompanies.com
Correctional Services Corp 1819 Main St Suite 1000 .... Sarasota FL 34236 941-953-9199 953-9198
NASDAQ: CSCQ ■ *TF:* 800-275-3766 ■ *Web:* www.correctionalservices.com
Corrections Corp of America 10 Burton Hills Blvd .... Nashville TN 37215 615-263-3000 263-3140
NYSE: CXW ■ *TF:* 800-624-2931 ■ *Web:* www.correctionscorp.com
GEO Group Inc 621 NW 53rd St Suite 700 .... Boca Raton FL 33487 561-893-0101 999-7635
NYSE: GGI ■ *TF:* 800-666-5640 ■ *Web:* www.thegeogroupinc.com
Keystone Education & Youth Services
3401 West End Ave Suite 400 .... Nashville TN 37203 615-250-0000 250-1000
TF: 800-726-4032 ■ *Web:* www.keystoneyouth.com
Securicor New Century LLC 9609 Gayton Rd Suite 100 .... Richmond VA 23238 804-754-1100 741-9515
Web: www.securicor.com/us.htm
Youth Services International Inc 1819 Main St Suite 1000 .... Sarasota FL 34236 941-953-9199 953-9198
TF: 800-275-3766 ■ *Web:* www.youthservices.com

215 CORRECTIONAL FACILITIES - FEDERAL

SEE ALSO Correctional & Detention Management (Privatized) p. 1572; Correctional Facilities - State p. 1573; Juvenile Detention Facilities p. 1879

Phone | Fax

Federal Bureau of Prisons 320 1st St NW .... Washington DC 20534 202-307-3250 514-6620
Web: www.bop.gov
Administrative-Maximum US Penitentiary Florence
PO Box 8500 .... Florence CO 81226 719-784-9464 784-5290
Federal Correctional Complex
Beaumont PO Box 26015 .... Beaumont TX 77720 409-727-8187 626-3401
Coleman 846 NE 54th Terr .... Coleman FL 33521 352-689-5000 689-3013
Federal Correctional Institution
Allenwood PO Box 2500 .... White Deer PA 17887 570-547-7950 547-7751
Ashland SR 716 .... Ashland KY 41105 606-928-6414 928-1854
Bastrop 1341 Hwy 95 N PO Box 730 .... Bastrop TX 78602 512-321-3903 304-0117
Beckley 1600 Industrial Pk Rd .... Beaver WV 25813 304-252-9758 256-4956
Big Spring 1900 Simler Ave .... Big Spring TX 79720 432-263-6699 268-6867
Web: www.bop.gov/locations/institutions/big/index.jsp
Butner PO Box 1000 .... Butner NC 27509 919-575-4541 575-6341
Cumberland 14601 Burbridge Rd SE .... Cumberland MD 21502 301-784-1000 784-1008*
**Fax:* Hum Res
Danbury Rt 37 33 1/2 Pembroke Rd .... Danbury CT 06811 203-743-6471 312-5110
Dublin 5701 8th St Camp Parks .... Dublin CA 94568 925-833-7500 833-7599
Edgefield 501 Gary Hill Rd PO Box 723 .... Edgefield SC 29824 803-637-1500 637-9840
El Reno PO Box 1000 .... El Reno OK 73036 405-262-4875 262-6266
Elkton 8730 Scroggs Rd PO Box 89 .... Elkton OH 44415 330-424-7448 424-7075
Englewood 9595 W Quincy Ave .... Littleton CO 80123 303-985-1566 763-2553
Estill 100 Prison Rd PO Box 699 .... Estill SC 29918 803-625-4607 625-5635
Fairton PO Box 280 .... Fairton NJ 08320 856-453-1177 453-4186
Florence 5880 State Hwy 67 S .... Florence CO 81226 719-784-9100 784-9504
Forrest City PO Box 7000 .... Forrest City AR 72336 870-630-6000 630-6250
Fort Dix PO Box 38 .... Fort Dix NJ 08640 609-723-1100 723-6847
Greenville 100 US Rt 40 PO Box 4000 .... Greenville IL 62246 618-664-6200 664-6398
Jesup 2600 Hwy 301 S .... Jesup GA 31599 912-427-0870 427-1125
La Tuna 8500 Doniphan Rd PO Box 1000 .... Anthony TX 88021 915-886-6600 886-4951
Lompoc 3600 Guard Rd .... Lompoc CA 93436 805-736-4154 737-7163
Loretto PO Box 1000 .... Loretto PA 15940 814-472-4140 472-6046
Manchester PO Box 3000 .... Manchester KY 40962 606-598-1900 599-4115
Marianna 3625 FCI Rd .... Marianna FL 32446 850-526-2313 718-2014
McKean PO Box 5000 .... Bradford PA 16701 814-362-8900 363-6821
Memphis 1101 John A Denie Rd .... Memphis TN 38134 901-372-2269 380-2462
Miami 15801 SW 137th Ave .... Miami FL 33177 305-259-2100 259-2160
Milan PO Box 9999 .... Milan MI 48160 734-439-1511 439-0949

Facility	City	State	ZIP	Phone	Fax
Morgantown 446 Greenbag Rd	Morgantown	WV	26505	304-296-4416	284-3613
Oakdale PO Box 5050	Oakdale	LA	71463	318-335-4070	215-2688
Otisville PO Box 600	Otisville	NY	10963	845-386-5855	386-1527
Oxford PO Box 500	Oxford	WI	53952	608-584-5511	584-6371
Pekin 2600 S 2nd St	Pekin	IL	61554	309-346-8588	477-4685
Petersburg PO Box 90042	Petersburg	VA	23804	804-504-7200	504-7204
Phoenix 37900 N 45th Ave	Phoenix	AZ	85086	623-465-9757	465-5199
Ray Brook 128 Ray Brook Rd PO Box 300	Ray Brook	NY	12977	518-897-4000	897-4216
Web: www.bop.gov/locations/institutions/rbk/index.jsp					
Safford PO Box 820	Safford	AZ	85548	928-428-6600	348-1331
Sandstone 2300 County Rd 29	Sandstone	MN	55072	320-245-2262	245-0385
Schuylkill PO Box 700	Minersville	PA	17954	570-544-7100	544-7225
Seagoville 2113 N Hwy 175	Seagoville	TX	75159	972-287-2911	287-5466
Sheridan 27072 Ballston Rd PO Box 8000	Sheridan	OR	97378	503-843-4442	843-3408
Talladega 565 E Renfroe Rd	Talladega	AL	35160	256-315-4100	315-4495
Tallahassee 501 Capital Cir NE	Tallahassee	FL	32301	850-878-2173	216-1299
Terminal Island 1299 Seaside Ave	Terminal Island	CA	90731	310-831-8961	732-5335
Texarkana PO Box 9500	Texarkana	TX	75505	903-838-4587	223-4417
Three Rivers PO Box 4000	Three Rivers	TX	78071	361-786-3576	786-5069
Tucson 8901 S Wilmot Rd	Tucson	AZ	85706	520-574-7100	574-4341
Victorville PO Box 5400	Adelanto	CA	92301	760-246-2400	246-2621
Waseca 1000 University Dr SW PO Box 1731	Waseca	MN	56093	507-835-8972	837-4547
Yazoo City 2225 Haley Barbour Pkwy PO Box 5050	Yazoo City	MS	39194	662-751-4800	751-4958
Federal Detention Center					
Honolulu 351 Elliot St PO Box 30547	Honolulu	HI	96820	808-838-4200	838-4510
Houston 1200 Texas Ave PO Box 52645	Houston	TX	77052	713-221-5400	229-4200
Miami 33 NE 4th St PO Box 019120	Miami	FL	33101	305-577-0010	536-7368
Oakdale PO Box 5060	Oakdale	LA	71463	318-335-4466	215-2046
Philadelphia PO Box 572	Philadelphia	PA	19106	215-521-4000	521-7220
SeaTac PO Box 13901	Seattle	WA	98198	206-870-5700	870-5717
Federal Medical Center					
Butner PO Box 1500	Butner	NC	27509	919-575-3900	575-4801
Carswell J St Bldg 3000 PO Box 271066	Fort Worth	TX	76127	817-782-4000	782-4875
Devens 42 Patton Rd	Ayer	MA	01432	978-796-1000	796-1118
Fort Worth 3150 Horton Rd	Fort Worth	TX	76119	817-534-8400	413-3350
Lexington 3301 Leestown Rd	Lexington	KY	40511	859-255-6812	253-8821
Rochester 2110 E Center St PO Box 4600	Rochester	MN	55903	507-287-0674	287-9601
Federal Prison Camp					
Alderson Glen Ray Rd Box A	Alderson	WV	24910	304-445-3300	445-3320
Bryan 1100 Ursuline Ave PO Box 2197	Bryan	TX	77805	979-823-1879	775-5765
Duluth 6902 Airport Rd PO Box 1400	Duluth	MN	55814	218-722-8634	733-4701
Montgomery Maxwell AFB	Montgomery	AL	36112	334-293-2100	293-2326
Pensacola 110 Raby Ave	Pensacola	FL	32509	850-457-1911	458-7295
Yankton PO Box 680	Yankton	SD	57078	605-665-3262	668-1116
Federal Transfer Center					
7410 S MacArthur Blvd PO Box 898802	Oklahoma City	OK	73189	405-682-4075	682-4055
Medical Center for Federal Prisoners Springfield					
1900 W Sunshine St PO Box 4000	Springfield	MO	65801	417-862-7041	837-1711
Metropolitan Correctional Center					
Chicago 71 W Van Buren St	Chicago	IL	60605	312-322-0567	322-1120
New York 150 Park Row	New York	NY	10007	646-836-6300	836-7751
San Diego 808 Union St	San Diego	CA	92101	619-232-4311	595-0390
Metropolitan Detention Center					
Brooklyn 80 29th St	Brooklyn	NY	11232	718-840-4200	840-5005
Guaynabo PO Box 2146	San Juan	PR	00922	787-749-4480	775-7824
Los Angeles 535 N Alameda St	Los Angeles	CA	90012	213-485-0439	253-9510
US Penitentiary					
Allenwood PO Box 3500	White Deer	PA	17887	570-547-0963	547-9201
Atlanta 601 McDonough Blvd SE	Atlanta	GA	30315	404-635-5100	331-2137
Atwater 1 Federal Way PO Box 019000	Atwater	CA	95301	209-386-4620	386-4719
Florence PO Box 7500	Florence	CO	81226	719-784-9454	784-5150
Leavenworth 1300 Metropolitan Ave	Leavenworth	KS	66048	913-682-8700	578-1026
Lee PO Box 900	Jonesville	VA	24263	276-546-0150	546-9115
Lewisburg 2400 Robert Miller Dr	Lewisburg	PA	17837	570-523-1251	522-7745
Lompoc 3901 Klein Blvd	Lompoc	CA	93436	805-735-2771	737-0295
Marion 4500 Prison Rd PO Box 2000	Marion	IL	62959	618-964-1441	964-1895
Pollock 1000 Airbase Rd PO Box 1000	Pollock	LA	71467	318-561-5300	561-5391
Terre Haute Hwy 63 S	Terre Haute	IN	47808	812-238-1531	238-9873

216 CORRECTIONAL FACILITIES - STATE

SEE ALSO Correctional & Detention Management (Privatized) p. 1572; Correctional Facilities - Federal p. 1572; Juvenile Detention Facilities p. 1879

Alabama

Facility	City	State	ZIP	Phone	Fax
Bibb Correctional Facility 565 Bibb Ln	Brent	AL	35034	205-926-5252	926-9928
Bullock County Correctional Facility					
104 Bullock Dr PO Box 5107	Union Springs	AL	36089	334-738-5625	738-5020
Davis JO Correctional Facility Fountain 4000	Atmore	AL	36503	251-368-8122	368-7472
Donaldson Correctional Facility 100 Warrior Ln	Bessemer	AL	35023	205-436-3681	436-3399
Draper Correctional Facility 2828 Hwy 143 PO Box 1107	Elmore	AL	36025	334-567-2221	567-1519
Elmore Correctional Center 3720 Marion Spillway Rd PO Box 8	Elmore	AL	36025	334-567-1460	567-1804
Web: www.doc.state.al.us					
Holman Correctional Facility PO Box 3700	Atmore	AL	36503	251-368-8173	368-1095
JO Davis Correctional Facility Fountain 4000	Atmore	AL	36503	251-368-8122	368-7472
Kilby Correctional Facility PO Box 150	Mount Meigs	AL	36057	334-215-6600	
Limestone Correctional Facility 28779 Nick Davis Rd	Harvest	AL	35749	256-233-4600	233-1930
Saint Clair Correctional Facility 1000 St Clair Rd	Springville	AL	35146	205-467-6111	467-2474
Staton Correctional Facility PO Box 56	Elmore	AL	36025	334-567-2221	567-0704
Tutwiler Prison for Women 8966 US Hwy 231	Wetumpka	AL	36092	334-567-4369	514-6576
Ventress Correctional Facility PO Box 767	Clayton	AL	36016	334-775-3331	775-8905

Alaska

Facility	City	State	ZIP	Phone	Fax
Anchorage Correctional Complex 1400 E 4th Ave	Anchorage	AK	99501	907-269-4100	269-4208
Web: www.correct.state.ak.us/corrections/institutions/anch/					
Anvil Mountain Correctional Center					
1810 Center Creek Rd PO Box 730	Nome	AK	99762	907-443-2241	443-5195
Web: www.correct.state.ak.us					
Fairbanks Correctional Center 1931 Eagan Ave	Fairbanks	AK	99701	907-458-6700	458-6751
Hiland Mountain Correctional Center 9101 Glenn Hwy	Eagle River	AK	99577	907-694-9511	694-4507
Ketchikan Correctional Center 1201 Schoenbar Rd	Ketchikan	AK	99901	907-225-9429	225-7031
Web: www.correct.state.ak.us/corrections					
Lemon Creek Correctional Center 2000 Lemon Creek Rd	Juneau	AK	99801	907-465-6200	465-6224
Web: www.correct.state.ak.us/corrections					
Palmer Correctional Center PO Box 919	Palmer	AK	99645	907-745-5054	746-1574
Spring Creek Correctional Center PO Box 2109	Seward	AK	99664	907-224-8200	224-8062
Web: www.correct.state.ak.us/corrections					
Wildwood Correctional Center 10 Chugach Ave	Kenai	AK	99611	907-260-7200	260-7208
Web: www.correct.state.ak.us/corrections					
Yukon-Kuskokwim Correctional Center					
1000 Chief Eddie Hoffman Hwy PO Box 400	Bethel	AK	99559	907-543-5245	543-4475
Web: www.correct.state.ak.us/corrections					

Arizona

Facility	City	State	ZIP	Phone	Fax
Arizona State Prison Complex-Douglas					
6911 N BDI Blvd PO Box 3867	Douglas	AZ	85607	520-364-7521	364-7445
Web: www.adc.state.az.us/prison1.htm					
Arizona State Prison Complex-Eyman					
4374 E Butte Ave PO Box 3500	Florence	AZ	85232	520-868-0201	868-0276
Web: www.adc.state.az.us/prison1.htm					
Arizona State Prison Complex-Florence					
915 E Diversion Dam Rd	Florence	AZ	85232	520-868-4251	868-4245
Web: www.adc.state.az.us/prison1.htm					
Arizona State Prison Complex-Florence					
1365 E Butte Ave PO Box 629	Florence	AZ	85232	520-868-4011	868-5333
Web: www.adc.state.az.us/prison1.htm					
Arizona State Prison Complex-Lewis					
26700 S Hwy 85 PO Box 70	Buckeye	AZ	85326	623-386-6160	386-7332
Web: www.adc.state.az.us/prison1.htm					
Arizona State Prison Complex-Perryville					
2014 N Citrus Rd PO Box 3000	Goodyear	AZ	85338	623-853-0304	853-0425
Web: www.adc.state.az.us/prison1.htm					
Arizona State Prison Complex-Phoenix					
2500 E Van Buren PO Box 52109	Phoenix	AZ	85072	602-685-3100	685-3124
Web: www.adc.state.az.us/prison1.htm					
Arizona State Prison Complex-Safford					
896 S Crook Rd PO Box 2222	Safford	AZ	85546	928-428-4698	428-3235
Web: www.adc.state.az.us/prison1.htm					
Arizona State Prison Complex-Winslow 2100 S Hwy 87	Winslow	AZ	86047	928-289-9551	289-2951
Web: www.adc.state.az.us/prison1.htm					
Arizona State Prison Complex-Yuma					
7125 E Juan Sanchez Blvd	San Luis	AZ	85349	928-627-8871	627-5912
Web: www.adc.state.az.us/prison1.htm					

Arkansas

Facility	City	State	ZIP	Phone	Fax
Arkansas Dept of Corrections Cummins Unit					
Hwy 388 PO Box 500	Grady	AR	71644	870-850-8899	850-8862
Web: www.arkansas.gov/doc					
Arkansas Dept of Corrections Delta Regional Unit					
880 E Gaines St	Dermott	AR	71638	870-538-2000	538-2027
Web: www.arkansas.gov/doc					
Arkansas Dept of Corrections East Arkansas Regional Unit					
326 Lee St PO Box 180	Brickeys	AR	72320	870-295-4700	295-6564
Web: www.arkansas.gov/doc					
Arkansas Dept of Corrections Maximum Security Unit					
2501 State Farm Rd	Tucker	AR	72168	501-842-3800	842-1977
Web: www.arkansas.gov/doc					
Arkansas Dept of Corrections North Central Unit					
HC 62 Box 300	Calico Rock	AR	72519	870-297-4311	297-4322
Web: www.arkansas.gov/doc					
Arkansas Dept of Corrections Tucker Unit					
2400 State Farm Rd PO Box 240	Tucker	AR	72168	501-842-2519	842-3958
Web: www.arkansas.gov/doc					
Arkansas Dept of Corrections Varner Unit Hwy 388 PO Box 600	Grady	AR	71644	870-479-3030	479-3803
Web: www.arkansas.gov/doc					
Arkansas Dept of Corrections Wrightsville Unit					
8400 Hwy 386 PO Box 1000	Wrightsville	AR	72183	501-897-5806	897-5716
Web: www.arkansas.gov/doc					
McPherson Ronald Correctional Facility 302 Wackenhut Way	Newport	AR	72701	870-523-2639	523-6202
Ronald McPherson Correctional Facility 302 Wackenhut Way	Newport	AR	72701	870-523-2639	523-6202
Scott Grimes Correctional Facility 300 Wackenhut Way	Newport	AR	72112	870-523-5877	523-8302
Web: www.arkansas.gov/doc					
Texarkana Regional Correction Center 305 E 5th St	Texarkana	AR	71854	870-779-3939	779-1616

California

Facility	City	State	ZIP	Phone	Fax
Avenal State Prison 1 Kings Hwy PO Box 39	Avenal	CA	93204	559-386-0587	386-0907
California Correctional Institution Hwy 202 PO Box 1031	Tehachapi	CA	93581	661-822-4402	823-5020
Web: www.corr.ca.gov					
California Men's Colony Hwy 1 PO Box 8101	San Luis Obispo	CA	93409	805-547-7900	547-7529
California State Prison Corcoran 4001 King Ave PO Box 8800	Corcoran	CA	93212	559-992-8800	992-7354
California State Prison Los Angeles County 44750 60th St W	Lancaster	CA	93536	661-729-2000	729-6930
California State Prison Sacramento 100 Prison Rd	Folsom	CA	95630	916-985-8610	294-3001
California State Prison Solano					
2100 Peabody Rd PO Box 4000	Vacaville	CA	95696	707-451-0182	454-3200
Calipatria State Prison 7018 Blair Rd	Calipatria	CA	92233	760-348-7000	348-7188
Centinela State Prison 2302 Brown Rd PO Box 731	Imperial	CA	92251	760-337-7900	337-7692
Central California Women's Facility PO Box 1501	Chowchilla	CA	93610	559-665-5531	665-7158
Chuckawalla Valley State Prison PO Box 2289	Blythe	CA	92226	760-922-5300	922-6855
Web: www.corr.ca.gov					
Donovan RJ Correctional Facility at Rock Mountain					
480 Alta Rd	San Diego	CA	92179	619-661-6500	661-6253
Folsom State Prison 300 Prison Rd	Represa	CA	95671	916-985-2561	351-3010
High Desert State Prison PO Box 750	Susanville	CA	96127	530-251-5100	
Ironwood State Prison PO Box 2229	Blythe	CA	92226	760-921-3000	921-4331
Mule Creek State Prison 4001 Hwy 104	Ione	CA	95640	209-274-4911	274-4861
Pelican Bay State Prison PO Box 7000	Crescent City	CA	95532	707-465-1000	465-4376
Pleasant Valley State Prison PO Box 8500	Coalinga	CA	93210	559-935-4900	935-4903
RJ Donovan Correctional Facility at Rock Mountain					
480 Alta Rd	San Diego	CA	92179	619-661-6500	661-6253
Salinas Valley State Prison 31625 Hwy 101 N	Soledad	CA	93960	831-678-5500	678-5503
San Quentin State Prison	San Quentin	CA	94974	415-454-1460	454-6288
Valley State Prison for Women PO Box 99	Chowchilla	CA	93610	559-665-6100	665-6102

Colorado

Facility	City	State	ZIP	Phone	Fax
Arkansas Valley Correctional Facility					
12750 Hwy 96 PO Box 1000	Crowley	CO	81034	719-267-3520	267-5024
Web: www.doc.state.co.us					

Colorado (Cont'd)

Facility	City	State	ZIP	Phone	Fax
Buena Vista Correctional Complex 15125 Hwy 24 & 285 PO Box 2017	Buena Vista	CO	81211	719-395-2404	395-7214
Web: www.doc.state.co.us/Facilities/bvcf/bvcf.asp					
Centennial Correctional Facility Hwy 50 PO Box 600	Canon City	CO	81215	719-269-5510	269-5545
Web: www.doc.state.co.us					
Colorado Correctional Center 15445 S Old Golden Rd	Golden	CO	80401	303-273-1620	279-4407
Web: www.doc.state.co.us					
Colorado State Penitentiary 57500 E Hwy 50	Canon City	CO	81212	719-269-5120	269-5125
Web: www.doc.state.co.us					
Colorado Territorial Correctional Facility 275 W Hwy 50	Canon City	CO	81212	719-275-4181	269-4129
Colorado Women's Correctional Facility 3800 Grandview Ave	Canon City	CO	81212	719-269-4715	269-4716
Web: www.doc.state.co.us					
Delta Correctional Center 4102 Saw Mill Mesa Rd	Delta	CO	81416	970-874-7614	874-7614
Denver Women's Correctional Facility 3600 Havana St	Denver	CO	80239	303-307-2500	307-2514
Web: www.doc.state.co.us					
Fremont Correctional Facility Hwy 50 & Evans Blvd PO Box 999	Canon City	CO	81215	719-269-5002	269-5020
Web: www.doc.state.co.us					
Limon Correctional Facility 49030 State Hwy 71	Limon	CO	80826	719-775-9221	775-7607
Rifle Correctional Center 200 County Rd 219	Rifle	CO	81650	970-625-1700	625-1706
Sterling Correctional Facility PO Box 6000	Sterling	CO	80751	970-521-5010	521-8225

Connecticut

Facility	City	State	ZIP	Phone	Fax
Bridgeport Correctional Center 1106 North Ave	Bridgeport	CT	06606	203-579-6131	579-6693
Brooklyn Correctional Institution 59 Hartford Rd	Brooklyn	CT	06234	860-779-2600	779-2394
Cheshire Correctional Institution 900 Highland Ave	Cheshire	CT	06410	203-250-2600	250-2707
Corrigan Correctional Institution 982 Norwich-New London Tpke	Uncasville	CT	06382	860-848-5700	848-5762
Enfield Correctional Institution 289 Shaker Rd	Enfield	CT	06082	860-763-7310	763-7300
Garner Correctional Institution 50 Nunnawauk Rd	Newtown	CT	06470	203-270-2800	270-1826
Gates Correctional Institution 131 N Bridebrook Rd	Niantic	CT	06357	860-691-4700	691-4745
Hartford Correctional Center 177 Weston St	Hartford	CT	06120	860-240-1800	566-2725
MacDougall Correctional Institution 1153 East St S	Suffield	CT	06080	860-627-2100	627-2144
New Haven Correctional Center 245 Whalley Ave	New Haven	CT	06511	203-789-7111	974-4153
Northeast Correctional Institution 251 Middle Tpke	Storrs	CT	06268	860-487-2712	487-2764
Northern Correctional Institution 287 Bilton Rd	Somers	CT	06071	860-763-8600	763-8651
Osborn Correctional Institution 100 Bilton Rd	Somers	CT	06071	860-566-7500	763-0826
Radgowski Correctional Institution 982 Norwich-New London Tpke	Uncasville	CT	06382	860-848-5000	848-5020
Robinson Correctional Institution 285 Shaker Rd	Enfield	CT	06083	860-763-6200	763-6317
Webster Correctional Institution 111 Jarvis St	Cheshire	CT	06410	203-271-5900	271-5909
Willard-Cybulski Correctional Institution 391 Shaker Rd	Enfield	CT	06082	860-763-6100	763-6111
York Correctional Institution 201 W Main St	Niantic	CT	06357	860-691-6700	691-6800

Delaware

Facility	City	State	ZIP	Phone	Fax
Baylor Delores J Women's Correctional Institution 660 Baylor Blvd	New Castle	DE	19720	302-577-3004	577-7099
Delaware Correctional Center 1181 Paddock Rd	Smyrna	DE	19977	302-653-9261	653-5023
Delores J Baylor Women's Correctional Institution 660 Baylor Blvd	New Castle	DE	19720	302-577-3004	577-7099
Gander Hill Correctional Facility 1301 E 12th St	Wilmington	DE	19801	302-429-7700	429-7707
John L Webb Correctional Facility 200 Greenbank Rd	Wilmington	DE	19808	302-995-6120	995-8596
Multi-Purpose Criminal Facility 1301 E 12th St	Wilmington	DE	19801	302-429-7700	429-7707
Sussex Correctional Institution PO Box 500	Georgetown	DE	19947	302-856-5280	856-5103
Webb John L Correctional Facility 200 Greenbank Rd	Wilmington	DE	19808	302-995-6120	995-8596

Florida

Facility	City	State	ZIP	Phone	Fax
Apalachee Correctional Institution 35 Apalachee Dr	Sneads	FL	32460	850-593-6431	593-6445
Web: www.dc.state.fl.us/facilities					
Avon Park Correctional Institution Hwy 64 E PO Box 1100	Avon Park	FL	33826	863-453-3174	453-1511
Baker Correctional Institution 20706 US Hwy 90 W PO Box 500	Sanderson	FL	32087	386-719-4500	758-5759
Web: www.dc.state.fl.us					
Bay Correctional Facility 5400 Bayline Dr	Panama City	FL	32404	850-769-1455	769-1942
Web: www.correctionscorp.com					
Brevard Correctional Institution 855 Camp Rd	Cocoa	FL	32927	321-634-6000	634-6066
Broward Correctional Institution 20421 Sheridan St	Fort Lauderdale	FL	33332	954-252-6500	680-4568
Web: www.dc.state.fl.us					
Calhoun Correctional Institution 19562 SE Institutional Dr Unit 1	Blountstown	FL	32424	850-237-6500	237-6508
Web: www.dc.state.fl.us/facilities/region1					
Century Correctional Institution 400 Tedder Rd	Century	FL	32535	850-256-2600	256-2335
Charlotte Correctional Institution 33123 Oil Well Rd	Punta Gorda	FL	33955	941-833-2300	575-5747
Web: www.dc.state.fl.us/facilities/region4					
Columbia Correctional Institution 216 SE Corrections Way	Lake City	FL	32055	386-754-7600	754-7602
Cross City Correctional Institution 568 NE 255 St	Cross City	FL	32628	352-498-4444	498-1265
Web: www.dc.state.fl.us/facilities/region2/					
Dade Correctional Institution 19000 SW 377th St	Florida City	FL	33034	305-242-1700	242-1881
Dade Correctional Institution-Annex 19000 SW 377th St	Florida City	FL	33034	305-242-1700	242-1881
Desoto Correctional Institution 13617 SE Hwy 70	Arcadia	FL	34266	863-494-3727	494-1740
Everglades Correctional Institution 1601 SW 187th Ave	Miami	FL	33185	305-228-2000	228-2052
Florida State Prison 7819 NW 228 St	Raiford	FL	32026	904-368-2500	368-2732
Gadsden Correctional Facility 6044 Greensboro Hwy	Quincy	FL	32351	850-875-9701	875-9710
Web: www.correctionscorp.com					
Gainesville Correctional Institution 2845 NE 39th Ave	Gainesville	FL	32609	352-955-2001	334-1675
Glades Correctional Institution 500 Orange Avenue Cir	Belle Glade	FL	33430	561-829-1400	992-1355
Gulf Correctional Institution 500 Ike Steele Rd	Wewahitchka	FL	32465	850-639-1000	639-1182
Hamilton Correctional Institution 10650 SW 46th St	Jasper	FL	32052	386-792-5151	792-5159
Web: www.dc.state.fl.us					
Hamilton Correctional Institution Annex 10650 SW 46th St	Jasper	FL	32052	386-792-5151	792-5159
Web: www.dc.state.fl.us					
Hardee Correctional Institution 6901 SR 62	Bowling Green	FL	33834	863-773-2441	773-4310
Hendry Correctional Institution 12551 Wainwright Dr	Immokalee	FL	34142	239-867-2100	867-2255
Web: www.dc.state.fl.us/facilities/region4					
Hernando Correctional Institution 16415 Spring Hill Dr	Brooksville	FL	34604	352-754-6715	544-2307
Hillsborough Correctional Institution 11150 County Rd 672	Riverview	FL	33569	813-671-5022	671-5037
Holmes Correctional Institution 3142 Thomas Dr	Bonifay	FL	32425	850-547-2100	547-0522
Indian River Correctional Institution 7625 17th St SW	Vero Beach	FL	32968	772-564-2812	564-2880
Jackson Correctional Institution 5563 10th St	Malone	FL	32445	850-569-5260	482-9969
Jefferson Correctional Institution 1050 Big Joe Rd	Monticello	FL	32344	850-997-1987	997-0791
Lake City Correctional Facility 7906 E US Hwy 90	Lake City	FL	32055	386-755-3379	752-7202
Lake Correctional Institution 19225 US Hwy 27	Clermont	FL	34711	352-394-6146	394-3504
Lancaster Correctional Institution 3449 SW SR 26	Trenton	FL	32693	352-463-4100	463-3476
Lawtey Correctional Institution 7819 NW 228 St	Raiford	FL	32026	904-782-2000	782-1388
Liberty Correctional Institution 11064 NW Dempsey Barron Rd	Bristol	FL	32321	850-643-9400	643-9412
Web: www.dc.state.fl.us/facilities/region1					
Lowell Correctional Institution-Men's Unit PO Box 158	Lowell	FL	32663	352-401-6400	840-5657
Lowell Correctional Institution-Women's Unit 11120 NW Gainesville Rd	Ocala	FL	34482	352-401-5301	401-5331
Madison Correctional Institution 382 SW MCI Way	Madison	FL	32340	850-973-5300	973-3666
Martin Correctional Institution 1150 SW Allapattah Rd	Indiantown	FL	34956	772-597-3705	597-3742
Mayo Correctional Institution 8784 W US 27	Mayo	FL	32066	386-294-4500	829-4534*
**Fax Area Code:* 904					
Moore Haven Correctional Facility 1990 E SR 78 NW PO Box 718501	Moore Haven	FL	33471	863-946-2420	946-2481
New River East Correctional Institution 7819 NW 228th St	Raiford	FL	32028	904-368-3000	368-3205
New River West Correctional Institution 7819 NW 228th St	Raiford	FL	32028	904-368-3000	368-3205
Okaloosa Correctional Institution 3189 Little Silver Rd	Crestview	FL	32539	850-682-0931	689-7803
Okeechobee Correctional Institution 3420 NE 168th St	Okeechobee	FL	34972	863-462-5400	462-5430
Polk Correctional Institution 10800 Evans Rd	Polk City	FL	33868	863-984-2273	984-3072
Putnam Correctional Institution 128 Yelvington Rd	East Palatka	FL	32131	386-326-6800	312-2219
Quincy Correctional Institution 2225 Pat Thomas Pkwy	Quincy	FL	32351	850-627-5400	875-3572
Santa Rosa Correctional Institution 5850 E Milton Rd	Milton	FL	32583	850-983-5800	983-5907
South Bay Correctional Facility 600 US Hwy 27 S	South Bay	FL	33493	561-992-9505	992-9551
Sumter Correctional Institution 9544 County Rd 476 B	Bushnell	FL	33513	352-793-2525	793-3542
Taylor Correctional Institution 8501 Hampton Springs Rd	Perry	FL	32348	850-838-4136	838-4024
Tomoka Correctional Institution 3950 Tiger Bay Rd	Daytona Beach	FL	32124	386-323-1072	323-1006
Union Correctional Institution 7819 NW 228th St	Raiford	FL	32026	386-431-2000	431-2010
Wakulla Correctional Institution 110 Melaleuca Dr	Crawfordville	FL	32327	850-421-0777	421-7667
Walton Correctional Institution 691 World War II Veterans Ln	De Funiak Springs	FL	32433	850-951-1300	951-1750
Washington Correctional Institution 4455 Sam Mitchell Dr	Chipley	FL	32428	850-773-6100	773-6252
Zephyrhills Correctional Institution 2739 Gall Blvd	Zephyrhills	FL	33540	813-782-5521	782-4954

Georgia

Facility	City	State	ZIP	Phone	Fax
Arrendale Lee State Prison PO Box 709	Alto	GA	30510	706-776-4700	776-4998
Autry State Prison 3178 Mt Zion Church Rd	Pelham	GA	31779	229-294-2940	294-6691
Baldwin State Prison Laying Farm Rd PO Box 218	Hardwick	GA	31034	478-445-5218	445-6507
Bostick State Prison Bostick Cir PO Box 1700	Hardwick	GA	31034	478-445-4623	445-4623
Calhoun State Prison 823 Main St PO Box 24927	Morgan	GA	39866	229-849-5000	849-5017
Central State Prison 4600 Fulton Mill Rd	Macon	GA	31208	478-471-2906	471-2068
Coastal State Prison 200 Gulfstream Rd	Garden City	GA	31418	912-965-6330	966-6799
Dodge State Prison 2971 Old Bethel Church Rd PO Box 276	Chester	GA	31012	478-358-7200	358-7310
Dooly State Prison 1412 Plunkett Rd PO Box 750	Unadilla	GA	31091	478-627-2000	627-2140
Georgia State Prison 300 1st Ave S	Reidsville	GA	30453	912-557-7301	557-7341
Hancock State Prison 701 Prison Blvd PO Box 339	Sparta	GA	31087	706-444-1000	444-1137
Hays State Prison PO Box 668	Trion	GA	30753	706-857-0400	857-0624
Homerville State Prison PO Box 337	Homerville	GA	31634	912-487-3052	487-2902
Lee Arrendale State Prison PO Box 709	Alto	GA	30510	706-776-4700	776-4998
Lee State Prison 153 Pinewood Rd	Leesburg	GA	31763	229-759-6453	759-3065
Macon State Prison PO Box 426	Oglethorpe	GA	31068	478-472-3400	472-3524
Men's State Prison PO Box 396	Hardwick	GA	31034	478-445-4702	445-4223
Metro State Prison 1301 Constitution Rd	Atlanta	GA	30316	404-624-2200	624-2235
Milan State Prison PO Box 410	Milan	GA	31060	229-362-4900	362-4939
Phillips State Prison 2989 W Rock Quarry Rd	Buford	GA	30519	770-932-4500	932-4544
Pulaski State Prison PO Box 839	Hawkinsville	GA	31036	478-783-6000	783-6008
Rivers State Prison PO Box 1500	Hardwick	GA	31034	478-445-4591	445-1391
Rogers State Prison 1978 Georgia Hwy 147	Reidsville	GA	30453	912-557-7771	557-7051
Rutledge State Prison 7175 Manor Rd	Columbus	GA	31907	706-568-2340	568-2126
Scott State Prison PO Box 417	Hardwick	GA	31034	478-445-5375	445-3183
Smith State Prison PO Box 726	Glennville	GA	30427	912-654-5000	654-5131
Telfair State Prison PO Box 549	Helena	GA	31037	229-868-7721	868-6509
Valdosta State Prison PO Box 310	Valdosta	GA	31601	229-333-7900	333-5387
Walker State Prison PO Box 98	Rock Spring	GA	30739	706-764-3600	764-3613
Ware State Prison 3620 N Harris Rd	Waycross	GA	31501	912-285-6400	287-6520
Wayne State Prison 1007 Shed Rd	Odum	GA	31555	912-586-2244	586-2260
West Central State Prison PO Box 589	Zebulon	GA	30295	770-567-0531	567-0257
Wilcox State Prison 470 S Broad St	Abbeville	GA	31001	229-467-3000	467-3017

Hawaii

Facility	City	State	ZIP	Phone	Fax
Halawa Correctional Facility 99-902 Moanalua Rd	Aiea	HI	96701	808-486-2600	483-7275
Kulani Correctional Facility HC 01 Stainback Hwy	Hilo	HI	96720	808-935-2280	969-9107
Waiawa Correctional Facility PO Box 1839	Pearl City	HI	96782	808-677-6150	677-6155

Idaho

Facility	City	State	ZIP	Phone	Fax
Idaho Correctional Institution-Orofino 23 N Hospital Dr	Orofino	ID	83544	208-476-3655	476-4050
Idaho Maximum Security Institution PO Box 51	Boise	ID	83707	208-338-1635	344-9826
Idaho State Correctional Institution PO Box 14	Boise	ID	83707	208-336-0740	334-2748
North Idaho Correctional Institution 236 Radar Rd	Cottonwood	ID	83522	208-962-3276	962-7119
Pocatello Women's Correctional Center 1451 Fore Rd	Pocatello	ID	83204	208-236-6360	236-6362

Illinois

Facility	City	State	ZIP	Phone	Fax
Big Muddy River Correctional Center 251 N Hwy 37 PO Box 1000	Ina	IL	62846	618-437-5300	437-5627
Centralia Correctional Center 9330 Shattuc Rd PO Box 1266	Centralia	IL	62801	618-533-4111	533-4112
Danville Correctional Center 3820 E Main St	Danville	IL	61834	217-446-0441	446-5347
Dixon Correctional Center 2600 N Brinton Ave	Dixon	IL	61021	815-288-5561	288-0118
Dwight Correctional Center 23813 E 3200 North Rd PO Box 5001	Dwight	IL	60420	815-584-2806	584-2889
East Moline Correctional Center 100 Hillcrest Rd	East Moline	IL	61244	309-755-4511	755-2589
Graham Correctional Center RR1 Hwy 185 PO Box 499	Hillsboro	IL	62049	217-532-6961	532-6799
Hill Correctional Center PO Box 1327	Galesburg	IL	61401	309-343-4212	343-3812
Illinois River Correctional Center Rt 9 W PO Box 999	Canton	IL	61520	309-647-7030	647-0353
Jacksonville Correctional Center 2268 E Morton Ave	Jacksonville	IL	62650	217-245-1481	
Joliet Correctional Center 1125 Collins St	Joliet	IL	60432	815-727-6141	727-5314
Lincoln Correctional Center PO Box 549	Lincoln	IL	62656	217-735-5411	735-1361
Logan Correctional Center 1096 1350th St	Lincoln	IL	62656	217-735-5581	735-2339
Menard Correctional Center 711 Kaskaskia St	Menard	IL	62259	618-826-5071	826-4915
Pinckneyville Correctional Center 5835 SR 154	Pinckneyville	IL	62274	618-357-9722	357-2083
Pontiac Correctional Center 700 W Lincoln St	Pontiac	IL	61764	815-842-2816	842-3420
Robinson Correctional Center PO Box 1000	Robinson	IL	62454	618-546-5659	544-2166
Shawnee Correctional Center 6665 SR 146 E	Vienna	IL	62995	618-658-8331	658-8822
Southwestern Correctional Center 950 Kings Hwy	East Saint Louis	IL	62203	618-394-2200	394-2228
Stateville Correctional Center PO Box 112	Joliet	IL	62434	815-727-3607	727-5511
Tamms Correctional Center 200 E Supermax Rd	Tamms	IL	62988	618-747-2042	747-2062
Taylorville Correctional Center PO Box 1000	Taylorville	IL	62568	217-824-4004	824-4371

Facility	City	State	Zip	Phone	Fax
Vandalia Correctional Center PO Box 500	Vandalia	IL	62471	618-283-4170	283-9147
Vienna Correctional Center 6695 SR 146 E	Vienna	IL	62995	618-658-8371	658-3609
Western Illinois Correctional Center RR 4 Box 196	Mount Sterling	IL	62353	217-773-4441	773-2202

Indiana

Facility	City	State	Zip	Phone	Fax
Atterbury Correctional Facility 3856 Hospital Rd PO Box 95	Edinburgh	IN	46124	812-526-9829	526-0406
Branchville Correctional Facility 21390 Old State Rd 37 N	Tell City	IN	47586	812-843-5921	843-4262
Chain O'Lakes Correctional Facility 3516 E-75 S	Albion	IN	46701	260-636-3114	636-2914
Edinburgh Correctional Facility 23 & Schoolhouse Rd	Edinburgh	IN	46124	812-526-8434	526-0406
Henryville Correctional Facility PO Box 148	Henryville	IN	47126	812-294-4372	294-1523
Indiana State Prison PO Box 41	Michigan City	IN	46361	219-874-7258	878-5825
Minimum Security Unit PO Box 9047	Michigan City	IN	46361	219-872-8239	874-8281
Indiana Women's Prison 401 N Randolph St	Indianapolis	IN	46201	317-639-2671	639-8807
Madison Correctional Facility 800 MSH Busstop Dr	Madison	IN	47250	812-265-6154	265-2142
Medaryville Correctional Facility 5426 E 850 N	Medaryville	IN	47957	219-843-4131	843-1211
Miami Correctional Facility PO Box 900	Bunker Hill	IN	46914	765-689-8920	689-7479
Pendleton Correctional Facility 4490 W Reformatory Rd	Pendleton	IN	46064	765-778-2107	778-3395
Plainfield Correctional Facility 727 Moon Rd	Plainfield	IN	46168	317-839-2513	837-1875
Putnamville Correctional Facility 1946 W Hwy 40	Greencastle	IN	46135	765-653-8441	653-8441
Rockville Correctional Facility 811 W 50 North	Rockville	IN	47872	765-569-3178	569-3178
Wabash Valley Correctional Facility PO Box 500	Carlisle	IN	47838	812-398-5050	398-5065

Iowa

Facility	City	State	Zip	Phone	Fax
Anamosa State Penitentiary 406 N High St Box 10	Anamosa	IA	52205	319-462-3504	462-4962
Clarinda Correctional Facility 2000 N 16th St PO Box 1338 *Web:* www.doc.state.ia.us	Clarinda	IA	51632	712-542-5634	542-4844
Fort Dodge Correctional Facility 1550 L St	Fort Dodge	IA	50501	515-574-4700	574-4752
Iowa Correctional Institution for Women 300 Elm Ave SW PO Box 700	Mitchellville	IA	50169	515-967-4236	967-5347
Iowa State Penitentiary PO Box 316	Fort Madison	IA	52627	319-372-5432	372-6967
Newton Correctional Facility 307 S 50th Ave W PO Box 218	Newton	IA	50208	641-792-7552	791-1683
North Central Correctional Facility 313 Lanedale St	Rockwell City	IA	50579	712-297-7521	297-7875

Kansas

Facility	City	State	Zip	Phone	Fax
El Dorado Correctional Facility 1737 SE Hwy 54 PO Box 311 *Web:* docnet.dc.state.ks.us/EDCF	El Dorado	KS	67042	316-321-7284	321-5349
Ellsworth Correctional Facility 1607 State St	Ellsworth	KS	67439	785-472-5501	
Hutchinson Correctional Facility 500 S Reformatory St *Web:* docnet.dc.state.ks.us	Hutchinson	KS	67501	620-662-2321	662-8662
Lansing Correctional Facility PO Box 2 *Web:* www.accesskansas.org/lcf	Lansing	KS	66043	913-727-3235	727-2675
Norton Correctional Facility PO Box 546 *Web:* docnet.dc.state.ks.us	Norton	KS	67654	785-877-3380	877-3972
Topeka Correctional Facility 815 SE Rice Rd	Topeka	KS	66607	785-296-3432	296-0184
Winfield Correctional Facility 1806 Pine Crest Cir	Winfield	KS	67156	620-221-6660	221-0068

Kentucky

Facility	City	State	Zip	Phone	Fax
Blackburn Correctional Complex 3111 Spurr Rd	Lexington	KY	40511	859-246-2366	246-2376
Eastern Kentucky Correctional Complex 200 Road to Justice *Web:* www.corrections.ky.gov/ekcc/	West Liberty	KY	41472	606-743-2800	743-2811
Green River Correctional Complex 1200 River Rd PO Box 9300	Central City	KY	42330	270-754-5415	754-2732
Kentucky Correctional Institution for Women PO Box 337	Pewee Valley	KY	40056	502-241-8454	241-0372
Kentucky State Penitentiary PO Box 128	Eddyville	KY	42038	270-388-2211	388-7753
Kentucky State Reformatory 3001 W Hwy 146	LaGrange	KY	40032	502-222-9441	222-8115
Luckett Luther Correctional Complex PO Box 6	LaGrange	KY	40031	502-222-0363	222-2043
Luther Luckett Correctional Complex PO Box 6	LaGrange	KY	40031	502-222-0363	222-2043
Western Kentucky Correctional Complex 374 New Bethel Rd	Fredonia	KY	42411	270-388-9781	388-0031

Louisiana

Facility	City	State	Zip	Phone	Fax
Allen Correctional Center 3751 Lauderdale Woodyard Rd	Kinder	LA	70648	337-639-2942	639-2944
Avoyelles Correctional Center 1630 Prison Rd	Cottonport	LA	71327	318-876-2891	876-4220
C Paul Phelps Correctional Center 14925 Hwy 27 N PO Box 1056	Dequincy	LA	70633	337-786-7963	786-4524
Catahoula Correctional Center 499 Columbia Rd	Harrisonburg	LA	71340	318-744-2121	744-2126
David Wade Correctional Center 670 Bell Hill Rd	Homer	LA	71040	318-927-9631	927-0443
Dixon Correctional Institute 5568 Hwy 68	Jackson	LA	70748	225-634-1200	634-4543
Elayn Hunt Correctional Center 6925 Hwy 74 PO Box 174	Saint Gabriel	LA	70776	225-642-3306	319-4596
Hunt Elayn Correctional Center 6925 Hwy 74 PO Box 174	Saint Gabriel	LA	70776	225-642-3306	319-4596
Louisiana State Penitentiary Hwy 66	Angola	LA	70712	225-655-4411	655-2319
Phelps C Paul Correctional Center 14925 Hwy 27 N PO Box 1056	Dequincy	LA	70633	337-786-7963	786-4524
Vernon Correctional Facility 2294 Slagle Rd	Leesville	LA	71446	337-238-4522	238-4208
Wade David Correctional Center 670 Bell Hill Rd	Homer	LA	71040	318-927-9631	927-0443
Washington Correctional Institute 27268 Hwy 21	Angie	LA	70426	985-986-5000	986-5159

Maine

Facility	City	State	Zip	Phone	Fax
Charleston Correctional Facility 1202 Dover Rd	Charleston	ME	04422	207-285-0800	285-0815
Downeast Correctional Facility 64 Base Rd	Machiasport	ME	04655	207-255-1100	255-1176
Maine Correctional Center 17 Mallison Falls Rd	Windham	ME	04062	207-893-7000	893-7001
Maine State Prison 200 Main St	Thomaston	ME	04861	207-354-3000	354-3004

Maryland

Facility	City	State	Zip	Phone	Fax
Eastern Correctional Institution 30420 Revells Neck Rd	Westover	MD	21890	410-845-4000	845-4055
Herman L Toulson Correctional Boot Camp PO Box 1425	Jessup	MD	20794	410-799-4040	799-5649
Maryland Correctional Adjustment Center 401 E Madison St	Baltimore	MD	21202	410-539-5445	332-4561
Maryland Correctional Institution-Hagerstown 18601 Roxbury Rd	Hagerstown	MD	21746	301-733-2800	797-2872
Maryland Correctional Institution-Jessup PO Box 549	Jessup	MD	20794	410-799-7610	799-9061
Maryland Correctional Institution for Women PO Box 535	Jessup	MD	20794	410-799-5550	799-6146
Maryland Correctional Training Center 18601 Roxbury Rd	Hagerstown	MD	21746	301-791-7200	797-8574
Maryland House of Correction PO Box 534	Jessup	MD	20794	410-799-0100	799-1025
Maryland House of Correction Annex PO Box 534	Jessup	MD	20794	410-799-0100	799-1025
Roxbury Correctional Institution 18701 Roxbury Rd **Fax Area Code:* 301	Hagerstown	MD	21746	240-420-3000	797-0795*
Toulson Herman L Correctional Boot Camp PO Box 1425	Jessup	MD	20794	410-799-4040	799-5649
Western Correctional Institution 13800 McMullen Hwy	Cumberland	MD	21502	301-729-7000	729-7063

Massachusetts

Facility	City	State	Zip	Phone	Fax
Bay State Correctional Center 28 Clark St	Norfolk	MA	02056	508-668-1687	668-1688
Massachusetts Correctional Institution-Cedar Junction Rt 1 Box 100	South Walpole	MA	02071	508-668-2100	660-8008
Massachusetts Correctional Institution-Concord PO Box 9106	Concord	MA	01742	978-405-6100	405-6133
Massachusetts Correctional Institution-Framingham PO Box 9007	Framingham	MA	01704	508-532-5100	532-5104
Massachusetts Correctional Institution-Norfolk 2 Clark St	Norfolk	MA	02056	508-668-0800	
Massachusetts Correctional Institution-Plymouth PO Box 207	South Carver	MA	02366	508-291-2441	727-3005
North Central Correctional Institution at Gardner 500 Colony Rd	Gardner	MA	01440	978-632-2000	632-2802
Old Colony Correctional Center 1 Administration Rd	Bridgewater	MA	02324	508-279-6000	279-6754
Pondville Correctional Center PO Box 146	Norfolk	MA	02056	508-660-3924	660-7963
South Middlesex Correctional Center 135 Western Ave	Framingham	MA	01701	508-879-1241	
Souza-Baranowski Correctional Center PO Box 8000	Shirley	MA	01464	978-514-6500	514-6529

Michigan

Facility	City	State	Zip	Phone	Fax
Alger Maximum Correctional Facility 6141 Industrial Pk Dr PO Box 600 *Web:* www.michigan.gov/corrections	Munising	MI	49862	906-387-5000	387-5033
Baraga Maximum Correctional Facility 301 Wadaga Rd *Web:* www.michigan.gov/corrections	Baraga	MI	49908	906-353-7070	353-8246
Brooks Earnest C Correctional Facility 2500 S Sheridan Rd *Web:* www.michigan.gov/corrections	Muskegon Heights	MI	49444	231-773-9200	777-2097
Carson City Correctional Facility 10522 Boyer Rd PO Box 5000 *Web:* www.michigan.gov/corrections	Carson City	MI	48811	989-584-3941	
Charles E Egeler Correctional Facility 3855 Cooper St *Web:* www.michigan.gov/corrections	Jackson	MI	49201	517-780-5600	780-5814
Chippewa Correctional Facility 4269 W M-80 *Web:* www.michigan.gov/corrections	Kincheloe	MI	49784	906-495-2275	495-5787
Cooper Street Correctional Facility 3100 Cooper St *Web:* www.michigan.gov/corrections	Jackson	MI	49201	517-780-6175	780-6179
Cotton G Robert Correctional Facility 3500 N Elm Rd *Web:* www.michigan.gov/corrections	Jackson	MI	49201	517-780-5000	780-5100
Earnest C Brooks Correctional Facility 2500 S Sheridan Rd *Web:* www.michigan.gov/corrections	Muskegon Heights	MI	49444	231-773-9200	777-2097
Egeler Charles E Correctional Facility 3855 Cooper St *Web:* www.michigan.gov/corrections	Jackson	MI	49201	517-780-5600	780-5814
Florence Crane Correctional Facility 38 4th St *Web:* www.michigan.gov/corrections	Coldwater	MI	49036	517-279-9165	278-2328
G Robert Cotton Correctional Facility 3500 N Elm Rd *Web:* www.michigan.gov/corrections	Jackson	MI	49201	517-780-5000	780-5100
Gus Harrison Correctional Facility 2727 E Beecher St *Web:* www.michigan.gov/corrections	Adrian	MI	49221	517-265-3900	263-4401
Harrison Gus Correctional Facility 2727 E Beecher St *Web:* www.michigan.gov/corrections	Adrian	MI	49221	517-265-3900	263-4401
Hiawatha Correctional Facility 4533 W Industrial Pk Dr *Web:* www.michigan.gov/corrections	Kincheloe	MI	49786	906-495-5661	495-5291
Huron Valley Correctional Facility 3201 Bemis Rd *Web:* www.michigan.gov/corrections	Ypsilanti	MI	48197	734-572-9900	572-9499
Ionia Maximum Correctional Facility 1576 W Bluewater Hwy *Web:* www.michigan.gov/corrections	Ionia	MI	48846	616-527-6331	527-6863
Kinross Correctional Facility 16770 S Watertower Dr	Kincheloe	MI	49788	906-495-2282	495-5837
Lakeland Correctional Facility 141 1st St	Coldwater	MI	49036	517-278-6942	279-0327
Macomb Correctional Facility 34625 26th Mile Rd	New Haven	MI	48048	586-749-4900	749-4927
Marquette Branch Prison 1960 US Hwy 41 S *Web:* www.michigan.gov/corrections	Marquette	MI	49855	906-226-6531	226-6557
Michigan Reformatory 1727 Bluewater Hwy *Web:* www.michigan.gov/corrections	Ionia	MI	48846	616-527-2500	527-7155
Mid-Michigan Correctional Facility 8201 Croswell Rd *Web:* www.michigan.gov/corrections	Saint Louis	MI	48880	989-681-4361	681-4203
Mound Correctional Facility 17601 Mound Rd *Web:* www.michigan.gov/corrections	Detroit	MI	48212	313-368-8300	368-8972
Muskegon Correctional Facility 2400 S Sheridan Dr *Web:* www.michigan.gov/corrections	Muskegon	MI	49442	231-773-3201	773-3657
Newberry Correctional Facility 3001 S Newberry Ave *Web:* www.michigan.gov/corrections	Newberry	MI	49868	906-293-6200	293-0011
Oaks Correctional Facility 1500 Caberfae Hwy PO Box 38 *Web:* www.michigan.gov/corrections	Eastlake	MI	49626	231-723-8272	728-4278
Richard A Handlon Correctional Facility 1728 Bluewater Hwy *Web:* www.michigan.gov/corrections	Ionia	MI	48846	616-527-3100	527-2991
Riverside Correctional Facility 777 W Riverside Dr *Web:* www.michigan.gov/corrections	Ionia	MI	48846	616-527-0110	527-2936
Saginaw Correctional Facility 9625 Pierce Rd *Web:* www.michigan.gov/corrections	Freeland	MI	48623	989-695-9880	695-6662
Saint Louis Correctional Facility 8585 N Croswell Rd *Web:* www.michigan.gov/corrections	Saint Louis	MI	48880	989-681-6444	681-2425
Standish Maximum Correctional Facility 4713 W M-61 *Web:* www.michigan.gov/corrections	Standish	MI	48658	989-846-7000	846-7017
Thumb Correctional Facility 3225 John Conley Dr *Web:* www.michigan.gov/corrections	Lapeer	MI	48446	810-667-2045	667-2048

Minnesota

Facility	City	State	Zip	Phone	Fax
Minnesota Correctional Facility-Faribault 1101 Linden Ln	Faribault	MN	55021	507-334-0700	334-0730
Minnesota Correctional Facility-Lino Lakes 7525 4th Ave	Lino Lakes	MN	55014	651-717-6100	
Minnesota Correctional Facility-Moose Lake 1000 Lake Shore Dr	Moose Lake	MN	55767	218-485-5000	485-5010
Minnesota Correctional Facility-Park Heights 5329 Osgood Ave N	Stillwater	MN	55082	651-779-1400	779-1385
Minnesota Correctional Facility-Rush City 7600 525th St	Rush City	MN	55069	320-358-0400	358-0538

Minnesota (Cont'd)

Facility	City	State	Zip	Phone	Fax
Minnesota Correctional Facility-Shakopee 1010 W 6th Ave	Shakopee	MN	55379	952-496-4440	496-4476
Minnesota Correctional Facility-Stillwater 970 Picket St N	Bayport	MN	55003	651-779-2700	351-3603

Mississippi

Facility	City	State	Zip	Phone	Fax
Central Mississippi Correctional Facility 3794 Hwy 468	Pearl	MS	39208	601-932-2880	932-6201
Issaquena County Correctional Facility PO Box 220	Mayersville	MS	39113	662-873-2153	873-2956
Jefferson/Franklin Correctional Facility 279 Hwy 33	Fayette	MS	39069	601-786-2284	786-2289
Leake County Correctional Facility 399 CO Brooks St	Carthage	MS	39051	601-298-9003	298-9006
Marion/Walthall Correctional Facility 503 S Main St	Columbia	MS	39429	601-736-3621	736-4473
Marshall County Correctional Facility PO Box 5188	Holly Springs	MS	38634	662-252-7111	252-5777
Mississippi State Penitentiary PO Box 1057	Parchman	MS	38738	662-745-6611	745-8912
South Mississippi Correctional Institution PO Box 1419	Leakesville	MS	39451	601-394-5600	394-6433
Wilkinson County Correctional Center PO Box 1079	Woodville	MS	39669	601-888-3199	888-3235
Winston County Correctional Facility PO Drawer 928	Louisville	MS	39339	662-773-2528	773-4989

Missouri

Facility	City	State	Zip	Phone	Fax
Algoa Correctional Center 8501 No More Victims Rd PO Box 538	Jefferson City	MO	65102	573-751-3911	751-7375
Boonville Correctional Center 1216 E Morgan St	Boonville	MO	65233	660-882-6521	882-7825
Camp Hawthorn 413 Camp Hawthorn Dr PO Box 140	Kaiser	MO	65047	573-348-3194	348-4679
Central Missouri Correctional Center 2600 Hwy 179 PO Box 539	Jefferson City	MO	65102	573-751-2053	751-9037
Chillicothe Correctional Center 1500 W 3rd St	Chillicothe	MO	64601	660-646-4032	646-1217
Farmington Correctional Center 1012 W Columbia St	Farmington	MO	63640	573-218-7100	
Jefferson City Correctional Center 8200 No More Victims Rd	Jefferson City	MO	65101	573-751-3224	751-0355
Missouri Eastern Correctional Center 18701 Old Hwy 66	Pacific	MO	63069	636-257-3322	257-5296
Moberly Correctional Center 201 S Morley St PO Box 7	Moberly	MO	65270	660-263-3778	263-0377
Northeast Correctional Center 13698 Airport Rd	Bowling Green	MO	63334	573-324-9975	324-5183
Ozark Correctional Center 929 Honor Camp Ln	Fordland	MO	65652	417-767-4491	738-2400
Potosi Correctional Center 11593 State Hwy O	Mineral Point	MO	63660	573-438-6000	438-6006
Tipton Correctional Center 619 N Osage Ave	Tipton	MO	65081	660-433-2031	433-2613
Western Missouri Correctional Center 609 E Pence Rd	Cameron	MO	64429	816-632-1390	632-2562

Montana

Facility	City	State	Zip	Phone	Fax
Montana State Prison 400 Conley Lake Rd	Deer Lodge	MT	59722	406-846-1320	846-2951
Montana Women's Prison 701 S 27th St	Billings	MT	59101	406-247-5100	247-5161

Nebraska

Facility	City	State	Zip	Phone	Fax
Lincoln Correctional Center PO Box 22800	Lincoln	NE	68542	402-471-2861	479-6100
Nebraska Correctional Center for Women 1107 Recharge Rd	York	NE	68467	402-362-3317	362-3892
Nebraska State Penitentiary 4201 S 14th St	Lincoln	NE	68502	402-471-3161	471-4326
Omaha Correctional Center 2323 Ave J PO Box 11099	Omaha	NE	68111	402-595-3964	595-2227

Nevada

Facility	City	State	Zip	Phone	Fax
Ely State Prison 4569 N SR 590	Ely	NV	89301	775-289-8800	289-1263
Lovelock Correctional Center 1200 Prison Rd	Lovelock	NV	89419	775-273-1300	273-4277
Nevada State Prison 3301 E 5th St	Carson City	NV	89702	775-887-3406	887-3420
Northern Nevada Correctional Center 1721 Snyder Dr	Carson City	NV	89702	775-882-9203	887-9267
Southern Desert Correctional Center 1 Cold Creek Rd PO Box 208	Indian Springs	NV	89072	702-486-3888	486-3398
Southern Nevada Women's Correctional Facility 4370 Smiley Rd	Las Vegas	NV	89115	702-651-8866	651-0978
Warm Springs Correctional Center PO Box 7007	Carson City	NV	89702	775-684-3000	684-3051

New Hampshire

Facility	City	State	Zip	Phone	Fax
Lakes Region Facility 1 Right Way Path	Laconia	NH	03246	603-528-9203	
New Hampshire State Prison PO Box 14	Concord	NH	03302	603-271-1801	271-4092
New Hampshire State Prison for Women 317 Mast Rd	Goffstown	NH	03045	603-668-6137	666-7109
Northern New Hampshire Correctional Facility 138 E Milan Rd	Berlin	NH	03570	603-752-2906	752-0405

New Jersey

Facility	City	State	Zip	Phone	Fax
Bayside State Prison 4293 Rt 47	Leesburg	NJ	08327	856-785-0040	785-2559
East Jersey State Prison 1100 Woodbridge Ave Lock Bag R	Rahway	NJ	07065	732-499-5010	499-5022
Edna Mahan Correctional Facility for Women 30 County Rd 513 PO Box 4004	Clinton	NJ	08809	908-735-7111	735-5246
Mahan Edna Correctional Facility for Women 30 County Rd 513 PO Box 4004	Clinton	NJ	08809	908-735-7111	735-5246
Mid-State Correctional Facility PO Box 866	Wrightstown	NJ	08562	609-723-4221	723-1091
New Jersey State Prison PO Box 861	Trenton	NJ	08625	609-292-9700	777-1203
Riverfront State Prison PO Box 9104	Camden	NJ	08101	856-225-5700	225-5998
South Woods State Prison 215 Burlington Rd S	Bridgeton	NJ	08302	856-459-7000	459-7140
Southern State Correctional Facility 4295 Rt 47 PO Box 150	Delmont	NJ	08314	856-785-1300	785-1236

New Mexico

Facility	City	State	Zip	Phone	Fax
Central New Mexico Correctional Facility 1525 Morris Rd	Los Lunas	NM	87031	505-865-1622	865-2316
Guadalupe County Correctional Facility S Hwy 54 PO Box 520	Santa Rosa	NM	88435	505-472-1001	472-1006
Lea County Correctional Center 6900 W Millen Dr	Hobbs	NM	88244	505-392-5681	392-6488
New Mexico Women's Correctional Facility PO Box 800	Grants	NM	87020	505-287-2941	285-6828
Penitentiary of New Mexico 4311 Hwy 14	Santa Fe	NM	87505	505-827-8205	827-8220
Roswell Correctional Center 578 W Chickasaw Rd	Hagerman	NM	88232	505-625-3100	625-3190
Southern New Mexico Correctional Facility 1983 Joe R Silva Blvd	Las Cruces	NM	88004	505-523-3200	523-3349
Torrance County Detention Center PO Box 837	Estancia	NM	87016	505-384-2711	384-5184
Western New Mexico Correctional Facility PO Box 250	Grants	NM	87020	505-876-8300	876-8200

New York

Facility	City	State	Zip	Phone	Fax
Adirondack Correctional Facility Old Ray Brooks Rd PO Box 110	Ray Brook	NY	12977	518-891-1343	
Albion Correctional Facility 3595 State School Rd	Albion	NY	14411	585-589-5511	
Altona Correctional Facility 555 Devil Den Rd	Altona	NY	12910	518-236-7841	
Arthur Kill Correctional Facility 2911 Arthur Kill Rd	Staten Island	NY	10309	718-356-7333	
Attica Correctional Facility 639 Exchange St PO Box 149	Attica	NY	14011	585-591-2000	
Auburn Correctional Facility 135 State St Box 618	Auburn	NY	13021	315-253-8401	
Bare Hill Correctional Facility 181 Brand Rd	Malone	NY	12953	518-483-8411	483-8411
Bayview Correctional Facility 550 W 20th St	New York	NY	10011	212-255-7590	
Beacon Correctional Facility 50 Camp Beacon Rd PO Box 780	Beacon	NY	12508	845-831-4200	
Bedford Hills Correctional Facility 247 Harris Rd	Bedford Hills	NY	10507	914-241-3100	
Buffalo Correctional Facility 3052 Wende Rd PO Box 300	Alden	NY	14004	716-937-3786	937-3789
Camp Gabriels Correctional Facility Rt 86 Box 100	Gabriels	NY	12939	518-327-3111	
Camp Georgetown Correctional Facility 3191 Crumbhill Rd	Georgetown	NY	13072	315-837-4446	847-2099
Camp Pharsalia Correctional Facility 496 Center Rd	South Plymouth	NY	13844	607-334-2264	
Cape Vincent Correctional Facility Rt 12E Box 599	Cape Vincent	NY	13618	315-654-4100	654-4103
Cayuga Correctional Facility Rt 38 A PO Box 1150	Moravia	NY	13118	315-497-1110	
Chateaugay Correctional Facility 7874 SR 11 PO Box 320	Chateaugay	NY	12920	518-497-3300	
Clinton Correctional Facility 1156 Cook St PO Box 2000	Dannemora	NY	12929	518-492-2511	
Collins Correctional Facility Middle Rd PO Box 490	Collins	NY	14034	716-532-4588	
Coxsackie Correctional Facility Rt 9 W PO Box 200	Coxsackie	NY	12051	518-731-2781	
Downstate Correctional Facility 121 Red School House Rd	Fishkill	NY	12524	845-831-6600	
Eastern Correctional Facility Institution Rd PO Box 338	Napanoch	NY	12458	845-647-7400	
Edgecombe Correctional Facility 611 Edgecombe Ave	New York	NY	10032	212-923-2575	
Elmira Correctional Facility 1879 Davis St	Elmira	NY	14902	607-734-3901	
Fishkill Correctional Facility PO Box 1245	Beacon	NY	12508	845-831-4800	
Franklin Correctional Facility 62 Bare Hill Rd PO Box 10	Malone	NY	12953	518-483-6040	
Fulton Correctional Facility 1511 Fulton Ave	Bronx	NY	10457	718-583-8000	
Gouverneur Correctional Facility Scott Settlement Rd PO Box 370	Gouverneur	NY	13642	315-287-7351	287-7351
Gowanda Correctional Facility South Rd PO Box 350	Gowanda	NY	14070	716-532-0177	
Great Meadow Correctional Facility 11739 SR 22 PO Box 51	Comstock	NY	12821	518-639-5516	
Green Haven Correctional Facility Rt 554	Stormville	NY	12582	845-221-2711	
Greene Correctional Facility Rt 9 W PO Box 975	Coxsackie	NY	12051	518-731-2741	
Groveland Correctional Facility 7000 Sonyea Rd	Sonyea	NY	14556	585-658-2871	
Hudson Correctional Facility 50 E Court St PO Box 576	Hudson	NY	12534	518-828-4311	
Kill Arthur Correctional Facility 2911 Arthur Kill Rd	Staten Island	NY	10309	718-356-7333	
Lakeview Correctional Facility PO Box T	Brocton	NY	14716	716-792-7100	792-3099
Lincoln Correctional Facility 31-33 W 110th St	New York	NY	10026	212-860-9400	860-2099
Livingston Correctional Facility Rt 36 PO Box 49 Sonyea Rd	Sonyea	NY	14556	585-658-3710	658-3710
Lyon Mountain Correctional Facility 3864 SR 374	Lyon Mountain	NY	12952	518-735-4546	
Marcy Correctional Facility PO Box 5000	Marcy	NY	13403	315-768-1400	
Mid-Orange Correctional Facility 900 Kings Hwy	Warwick	NY	10990	845-986-2291	
Mid-State Correctional Facility PO Box 216	Marcy	NY	13403	315-768-8581	
Mohawk Correctional Facility 6100 School Rd Box 8450	Rome	NY	13440	315-339-5232	
Monterey Shock Incarceration Correctional Facility 2150 Evergreen Hill Rd	Beaver Dams	NY	14812	607-962-3184	
Moriah Shock Incarceration Correctional Facility PO Box 999	Mineville	NY	12956	518-942-7561	
Mount McGregor Correctional Facility 1000 Mt McGregor Rd PO Box 2071	Wilton	NY	12831	518-587-3960	
Ogdensburg Correctional Facility 1 Correctional Way	Ogdensburg	NY	13669	315-393-0281	
Oneida Correctional Facility 6100 School Rd	Rome	NY	13440	315-339-6880	
Orleans Correctional Facility 3531 Gaines Basin Rd	Albion	NY	14411	585-589-6820	
Otisville Correctional Facility PO Box 8	Otisville	NY	10963	845-386-1490	
Queensboro Correctional Facility 47-04 Van Dam St	Long Island City	NY	11101	718-361-8920	
Riverview Correctional Facility PO Box 158	Ogdensburg	NY	13669	315-393-8400	
Rochester Correctional Facility 470 Ford St	Rochester	NY	14608	585-454-2280	454-3412
Shawangunk Correctional Facility 750 Prison Rd	Wallkill	NY	12589	845-895-2081	
Sing Sing Correctional Facility 354 Hunter St	Ossining	NY	10562	914-941-0108	
Southport Correctional Facility PO Box 2000	Pine City	NY	14871	607-737-0850	
Sullivan Correctional Facility 325 Riverside Dr	Fallsburg	NY	12733	845-434-2080	
Summit Shock Incarceration Correctional Facility 137 Eagle Heights Rd	Summit	NY	12175	518-287-1721	
Taconic Correctional Facility 250 Harris Rd	Bedford Hills	NY	10507	914-241-3010	
Ulster Correctional Facility 750 Berme Rd PO Box 800	Napanoch	NY	12458	845-647-1670	
Upstate Correctional Facility PO Box 2000	Malone	NY	12953	518-483-6997	
Wallkill Correctional Facility PO Box G	Wallkill	NY	12589	845-895-2021	
Washington Correctional Facility PO Box 180	Comstock	NY	12821	518-639-4486	
Watertown Correctional Facility 23147 Swan Rd	Watertown	NY	13601	315-782-7490	
Wende Correctional Facility 3040 Wende Rd PO Box 1187	Alden	NY	14004	716-937-4000	
Wyoming Correctional Facility PO Box 501	Attica	NY	14011	585-591-1010	

North Carolina

Facility	City	State	Zip	Phone	Fax
Anson Correctional Center Rt 1 Box 189 *Web:* www.doc.state.nc.us/dop	Polkton	NC	28135	704-694-7500	694-9655
Avery/Mitchell Correctional Center Amity Rd PO Box 608	Spruce Pine	NC	28777	828-765-0229	765-0946
Brown Creek Correctional Institution 248 Prison Camp Rd PO Box 310	Polkton	NC	28135	704-694-2622	694-2709
Buncombe Correctional Center Hwy 251 N PO Box 18089	Asheville	NC	28814	828-645-7630	658-2494
Cabarrus Correctional Center 130 Dutch Rd Box 158	Mount Pleasant	NC	28124	704-436-6519	436-2709
Caldwell Correctional Center 480 Pleasant Hill Rd *Web:* www.doc.state.nc.us	Hudson	NC	28645	828-726-2509	726-2516
Caledonia Correctional Institution 2787 Caledonia Dr PO Box 137	Tillery	NC	27887	252-826-5621	826-5434
Carteret Correctional Facility 1084 Orange St PO Box 220 www.doc.state.nc.us/dop/prisons/Carteret.htm	Newport	NC	28570	252-223-5100	223-3069
Caswell Correctional Center 444 County Home Rd PO Box 217 *Web:* www.doc.state.nc.us	Yanceyville	NC	27379	336-694-4531	694-5098
Catawba Correctional Center 1347 Prison Camp Rd	Newton	NC	28658	828-466-5521	466-5523
Central Prison 1300 Western Blvd	Raleigh	NC	27606	919-733-0800	733-6915
Charlotte Correctional Center 4100 Meadow Oak Dr *Web:* www.doc.state.nc.us	Charlotte	NC	28208	704-357-6030	357-8313
Cleveland Correctional Center 260 Kemper Rd	Shelby	NC	28152	704-480-5428	480-5429
Columbus Correctional Institution 1255 Prison Camp Rd	Brunswick	NC	28424	910-642-3285	642-8456
Craggy Correctional Center 2990 Riverside Dr	Asheville	NC	28804	828-645-5315	658-2183
Davidson Correctional Center 1400 Thomason St *Web:* www.doc.state.nc.us	Lexington	NC	27292	336-249-7528	249-6962
Duplin Correctional Center 364 S Hwy 11 & 903 PO Box 780 *Web:* www.doc.state.nc.us	Kenansville	NC	28349	910-296-0315	296-0165
Durham Correctional Center 3900 Guess Rd	Durham	NC	27705	919-477-2314	471-2257
Eastern Correctional Institution 2821 Hwy 903 N PO Box 215	Maury	NC	28554	252-747-8101	747-8260
Forsyth Correctional Center 307 Craft Dr *Web:* www.doc.state.nc.us	Winston-Salem	NC	27105	336-896-7041	896-7045
Fountain Correctional Center for Women 300 Fountain School Rd PO Box 1435	Rocky Mount	NC	27802	252-442-9712	442-1413

Facility	City	State	ZIP	Phone	Fax
Franklin Correctional Center 5918 NC 39 Hwy S PO Box 155	Bunn	NC	27508	919-496-6119	496-6032
Gaston Correctional Center 520 Justice Ct	Dallas	NC	28034	704-922-3861	922-1491
Web: www.doc.state.nc.us					
Gates Correctional Center 308 US 158 W PO Box 385	Gatesville	NC	27938	252-357-0778	357-2005
Greene Correctional Institution 2699 Hwy 903 N PO Box 39	Maury	NC	28554	252-747-3676	747-4432
Guilford Correctional Center 4250 Camp Burton Rd	McLeansville	NC	27301	336-375-5024	375-0382
Harnett Correctional Institution 1210 McNeil St	Lillington	NC	27546	910-893-2751	893-6432
Haywood Correctional Center 141 Hemlock St	Waynesville	NC	28786	828-452-5141	456-8473
Hoke Correctional Institution PO Box 700	Raeford	NC	28376	910-944-7612	944-4752
Hyde Correctional Center PO Box 278	Swanquarter	NC	27885	252-926-1494	926-2306
Johnston Correctional Institution 2465 US 70 W	Smithfield	NC	27577	919-934-8386	934-9150
Lincoln Correctional Center 464 Roper Dr	Lincolnton	NC	28092	704-735-0485	735-7801
Lumberton Correctional Institution PO Box 1649	Lumberton	NC	28359	910-618-5574	618-5615
Marion Correctional Institution 355 Old Glenwood Rd	Marion	NC	28752	828-659-7810	652-0115
Nash Correctional Institution PO Box 600	Nashville	NC	27856	252-459-4455	459-7728
Neuse Correctional Institution Caller Box 8009	Goldsboro	NC	27533	919-731-2023	731-2033
New Hanover Correctional Center PO Box 240	Wilmington	NC	28402	910-251-2666	251-2670
North Carolina Correctional Institution for Women 1034 Bragg St	Raleigh	NC	27610	919-733-4340	733-8031
North Piedmont Correctional Center for Women PO Box 1227	Lexington	NC	27292	336-242-1259	248-6539
Odom Correctional Institution 485 Odom Prison Rd	Jackson	NC	27845	252-534-5611	534-1852
Orange Correctional Center 2110 Clarence Walters Rd	Hillsborough	NC	27278	919-732-9301	644-1395
Pasquotank Correctional Institution 527 Commerce Dr	Elizabeth City	NC	27906	252-331-4881	331-4866
Pender Correctional Institution PO Box 1058	Burgaw	NC	28425	910-259-8735	259-8760
Piedmont Correctional Institution 1245 Camp Rd	Salisbury	NC	28147	704-639-7540	639-7610
Raleigh Correctional Center for Women 1201 S State St	Raleigh	NC	27610	919-733-4248	733-9737
Randolph Correctional Center 2760 US Hwy 220 PO Box 4128	Asheboro	NC	27203	336-625-2578	625-5717
Robeson Correctional Center PO Box 1979	Lumberton	NC	28356	910-618-5535	618-5539
Rowan Correctional Center PO Box 1207	Salisbury	NC	28145	704-639-7552	639-7558
Rutherford Correctional Center PO Box 127	Spindale	NC	28160	828-286-4121	286-9285
Sampson Correctional Institution PO Box 1109	Clinton	NC	28328	910-592-2151	592-2543
Sanford Correctional Center 417 Prison Camp Rd	Sanford	NC	27330	919-776-4325	774-1866
Southern Correctional Institution PO Box 786	Troy	NC	27371	910-572-3784	576-2145
Tillery Correctional Center PO Box 222	Tillery	NC	27887	252-826-4165	826-3287
Union Correctional Center 200 S Sutherland Ave	Monroe	NC	28112	704-283-6142	283-6832
Wake Correctional Center 1000 Rock Quarry Rd	Raleigh	NC	27610	919-733-7988	733-9166
Warren Correctional Institution 379 Collins Rd PO Box 399	Manson	NC	27553	252-456-3400	456-4300
Wayne Correctional Center 700 Stevens Mill Rd	Goldsboro	NC	27530	919-734-5911	734-5580
Wilkes Correctional Center 404 Statesville Rd	North Wilkesboro	NC	28659	336-667-4533	667-4095

Ohio

Facility	City	State	ZIP	Phone	Fax
Allen Correctional Institution 2238 N West St	Lima	OH	45802	419-224-8000	224-2726
Web: www.drc.state.oh.us					
Belmont Correctional Institution 68318 Bannock Rd	Saint Clairsville	OH	43950	740-695-5169	695-6869
Chillicothe Correctional Institution 15802 SR 104 PO Box 5500	Chillicothe	OH	45601	740-774-7080	773-8296
Dayton Correctional Institution 4104 Germantown St	Dayton	OH	45417	937-263-0058	263-9285
Grafton Correctional Institution 2500 S Avon Beldon Rd	Grafton	OH	44044	440-748-1161	748-2521
Hocking Correctional Facility 16759 Snake Hollow Rd	Nelsonville	OH	45764	740-753-1917	759-4277
Lebanon Correctional Institution PO Box 56	Lebanon	OH	45036	513-932-1211	932-5093
London Correctional Institution 1580 SR 56	London	OH	43140	740-852-2454	852-4854
Lorain Correctional Institution 2075 S Avon Beldon Rd	Grafton	OH	44044	440-748-1049	748-2191
Madison Correctional Institution PO Box 740	London	OH	43140	740-852-9777	852-2017
Mansfield Correctional Institution PO Box 788	Mansfield	OH	44901	419-525-4455	524-8022
Marion Correctional Institution PO Box 57	Marion	OH	43302	740-382-5781	382-0595
Noble Correctional Institution 15708 SR 78	Caldwell	OH	43724	740-732-5188	732-2651
North Central Correctional Institution 670 Marion Williamsport	Marion	OH	43302	740-387-7040	387-5587
Ohio Reformatory for Women 1479 Collins Ave	Marysville	OH	43040	937-642-1065	642-7678
Ohio State Penitentiary 878 Coitsville Hubbard Rd	Youngstown	OH	44505	330-743-0700	742-5144
Pickaway Correctional Camp 1171 SR 762 PO Box 209	Orient	OH	43146	614-877-4367	877-1739
Pickaway Correctional Institution PO Box 209	Orient	OH	43146	614-877-4362	877-4514
Richland Correctional Institution 1001 Olivesburg Rd	Mansfield	OH	44905	419-526-2100	521-2810
Ross Correctional Institution 16149 SR 104 PO Box 7010	Chillicothe	OH	45601	740-774-7050	774-7065
Southeastern Correctional Institution 5900 B I S Rd	Lancaster	OH	43130	740-653-4324	653-0779
Southern Ohio Correctional Facility 1724 SR 728 PO Box 45699	Lucasville	OH	45699	740-259-5544	259-2882
Toledo Correctional Institution 2001 E Central Ave PO Box 80033	Toledo	OH	43608	419-726-7977	726-7157
Trumbull Correctional Institution PO Box 901	Leavittsburg	OH	44430	330-898-0820	898-0848
Warren Correctional Institution 5787 SR 63	Lebanon	OH	45036	513-932-3388	932-0312

Oklahoma

Facility	City	State	ZIP	Phone	Fax
Alford Mack Correctional Center PO Box 220	Stringtown	OK	74569	580-346-7301	346-7214
Bassett Mabel Correctional Center 29501 Kickapoo Rd	McLoud	OK	74851	405-964-3020	964-3014
Web: www.doc.state.ok.us/docs/MBCC.HTM					
Brannon Jackie Correctional Center PO Box 1999	McAlester	OK	74502	918-421-3399	426-0004
Charles E Johnson Correctional Center 1856 Eastland St	Alva	OK	73717	580-327-8000	327-8010
Cimarron Correctional Facility 3700 S Kings Hwy	Cushing	OK	74023	918-225-3336	225-3363
Web: www.correctionscorp.com					
Conner RB Correctional Center PO Box 220	Hominy	OK	74035	918-885-2192	885-4703
Crabtree James Correctional Center Rt 1 Box 8	Helena	OK	73741	580-852-3221	852-3695
Davis Correctional Facility 6888 E 133rd Rd	Holdenville	OK	74848	405-379-6400	379-6496
Web: www.correctionscorp.com					
Diamondback Correctional Facility Rt 2 Box 336	Watonga	OK	73772	580-614-2000	614-2020
Web: www.correctionscorp.com					
Dunn Jess Correctional Center PO Box 316	Taft	OK	74463	918-682-7841	682-4372
Eddie Warrior Correctional Center 400 N Oak St	Taft	OK	74463	918-683-8365	682-4782
Great Plains Correctional Facility 700 Sugar Creek Dr PO Box 1018	Hinton	OK	73047	405-542-3711	542-3710
Harp Joseph Correctional Center PO Box 548	Lexington	OK	73051	405-527-5593	527-4841
Howard McLeod Correctional Center 1970 E Whippoorwill Ln	Atoka	OK	74525	580-889-6651	889-2264
Jackie Brannon Correctional Center PO Box 1999	McAlester	OK	74502	918-421-3399	426-0004
James Crabtree Correctional Center Rt 1 Box 8	Helena	OK	73741	580-852-3221	852-3695
Jess Dunn Correctional Center PO Box 316	Taft	OK	74463	918-682-7841	682-4372
John Lilley Correctional Center PO Box 1908	Boley	OK	74829	918-667-3381	667-3959
Johnson Charles E Correctional Center 1856 Eastland St	Alva	OK	73717	580-327-8000	327-8010
Joseph Harp Correctional Center PO Box 548	Lexington	OK	73051	405-527-5593	527-4841
Key William S Correctional Center PO Box 61	Fort Supply	OK	73841	580-766-2224	766-2266
Lawton Correctional Facility 8607 SE Flower Mound Rd	Lawton	OK	73501	580-351-2778	351-2641
Lilley John Correctional Center PO Box 1908	Boley	OK	74829	918-667-3381	667-3959
Mabel Bassett Correctional Center 29501 Kickapoo Rd	McLoud	OK	74851	405-964-3020	964-3014
Web: www.doc.state.ok.us/docs/MBCC.HTM					
Mack Alford Correctional Center PO Box 220	Stringtown	OK	74569	580-346-7301	346-7214
McLeod Howard Correctional Center 1970 E Whippoorwill Ln	Atoka	OK	74525	580-889-6651	889-2264
Northeast Oklahoma Correctional Center PO Box 887	Vinita	OK	74301	918-256-3392	256-2108
Oklahoma State Penitentiary PO Box 97	McAlester	OK	74502	918-423-4700	423-3862
Oklahoma State Reformatory PO Box 514	Granite	OK	73547	580-480-3700	535-4803
RB Conner Correctional Center PO Box 220	Hominy	OK	74035	918-885-2192	885-4703
Warrior Eddie Correctional Center 400 N Oak St	Taft	OK	74463	918-683-8365	682-4782
William S Key Correctional Center PO Box 61	Fort Supply	OK	73841	580-766-2224	766-2266

Oregon

Facility	City	State	ZIP	Phone	Fax
Coffee Creek Correctional Facility 24499 SW Grahams Ferry Rd	Wilsonville	OR	97070	503-570-6400	570-6417
Web: www.doc.state.or.us					
Columbia River Correctional Institution 9111 NE Sunderland Ave	Portland	OR	97211	503-280-6646	280-6012
Web: www.doc.state.or.us					
Eastern Oregon Correctional Institution 2500 Westgate Ave	Pendleton	OR	97801	541-276-0700	278-1841
Millcreek Correctional Facility 5465 Turner Rd	Salem	OR	97301	503-378-2600	373-7697
Oregon State Correctional Institution 3405 Deer Park Dr SE	Salem	OR	97310	503-373-0101	378-8919
Oregon State Penitentiary 2605 State St	Salem	OR	97310	503-378-2453	378-3897
Powder River Correctional Facility 3600 13th St	Baker City	OR	97814	541-523-6680	523-6678
Santiam Correctional Institution 4005 Aumsville Hwy SE	Salem	OR	97301	503-378-5807	378-3261
Shutter Creek Correctional Institution 95200 Shutters Landing Ln	North Bend	OR	97459	541-756-6666	756-6888
Snake River Correctional Institution 777 Stanton Blvd	Ontario	OR	97914	541-881-5000	881-5460
South Fork Forest Camp 48300 Wilson River Hwy	Tillamook	OR	97141	503-842-2811	842-6572
Two Rivers Correctional Institution 82911 Beach Access Rd	Umatilla	OR	97882	541-922-2001	922-2011

Pennsylvania

Facility	City	State	ZIP	Phone	Fax
Quehanna Motivational Boot Camp HC Box 32	Karthaus	PA	16845	814-263-4125	263-3901
SCI-Albion 10745 Rt 18	Albion	PA	16475	814-756-5778	756-9737
SCI-Cambridge Springs 451 Fullerton Ave	Cambridge Springs	PA	16403	814-398-5400	398-5413
SCI-Chester 500 E 4th St	Chester	PA	19013	610-490-5412	447-3000
SCI-Coal Township 1 Kelley Dr	Coal Township	PA	17866	570-644-7890	644-3410
SCI-Cresson PO Box A	Cresson	PA	16699	814-886-8181	946-6977
SCI-Dallas 1000 Follies Rd	Dallas	PA	18612	570-675-1101	820-4842
SCI-Frackville 1111 Altamont Blvd	Frackville	PA	17931	570-874-4516	794-2013
SCI-Graterford PO Box 246	Graterford	PA	19426	610-489-4151	409-1165
SCI-Greene 169 Progress Dr	Waynesburg	PA	15370	724-852-2902	852-5548
SCI-Greensburg Rt 119 S RD 10 Box 10	Greensburg	PA	15601	724-837-4397	832-5412
SCI-Houtzdale PO Box 1000	Houtzdale	PA	16698	814-378-1000	378-1030
SCI-Huntingdon 1100 Pike St	Huntingdon	PA	16654	814-643-2400	946-7380
SCI-Laurel Highlands PO Box 631	Somerset	PA	15501	814-443-0305	433-0269
SCI-Mahanoy 301 Morea Rd	Frackville	PA	17932	570-773-2158	621-3096
SCI-Muncy PO Box 180	Muncy	PA	17756	570-546-3171	546-8609
SCI-Pine Grove 189 Fyock Rd	Indiana	PA	15701	724-465-9630	464-5139
SCI-Pittsburgh 3001 Beaver Rd	Pittsburgh	PA	15233	412-761-1955	223-2010
SCI-Retreat 660 SR 11	Hunlock Creek	PA	18621	570-735-8754	733-1041
SCI-Rockview PO Box A	Bellefonte	PA	16823	814-355-4874	355-6026
SCI-Smithfield 1120 Pike St	Huntingdon	PA	16652	814-643-6520	946-7339
SCI-Somerset 1590 Walters Mill Rd	Somerset	PA	15510	814-443-8100	443-8137
SCI-Waymart PO Box 256	Waymart	PA	18472	570-488-5811	253-7129

Rhode Island

Facility	City	State	ZIP	Phone	Fax
Donald Price Medium Security Center Goddard Rd PO Box 20983	Cranston	RI	02920	401-462-1202	462-1198
Donald W Wyatt Detention Facility 950 High St	Central Falls	RI	02863	401-729-1190	729-1194
Web: www.wyattdetention.com					
High Security Center PO Box 8200	Cranston	RI	02920	401-462-2028	462-2936
John J Moran Medium Security Center PO Box 8274	Cranston	RI	02920	401-462-3774	
Maximum Security Center PO Box 8273	Cranston	RI	02920	401-462-2054	
Moran John J Medium Security Center PO Box 8274	Cranston	RI	02920	401-462-3774	
Price Donald Medium Security Center Goddard Rd PO Box 20983	Cranston	RI	02920	401-462-1202	462-1198
Women's Facility PO Box 8312	Cranston	RI	02920	401-462-2361	462-1842
Wyatt Donald W Detention Facility 950 High St	Central Falls	RI	02863	401-729-1190	729-1194
Web: www.wyattdetention.com					

South Carolina

Facility	City	State	ZIP	Phone	Fax
Allendale Correctional Institution 1057 Revolutionary Trail PO Box 1151	Fairfax	SC	29827	803-632-2561	632-2498
Broad River Correctional Institution 4460 Broad River Rd	Columbia	SC	29210	803-896-2200	896-2192
Evans Correctional Institution 610 Hwy 9 W	Bennettsville	SC	29512	843-479-4181	896-4977*
Goodman Correctional Institution 4556 Broad River Rd	Columbia	SC	29210	803-896-8565	896-1216
Kershaw Correctional Institution 4848 Gold Mine Hwy	Kershaw	SC	29067	803-896-3300	896-3310
Kirkland Correctional Institution 4344 Broad River Rd	Columbia	SC	29210	803-896-8572	896-8570
Leath Correctional Institution 2809 Airport Rd	Greenwood	SC	29649	864-229-5709	896-1012*
**Fax Area Code: 803*					
Lee Correctional Institution 990 Wisacky Hwy	Bishopville	SC	29010	803-896-2400	896-2405
Lieber Correctional Institution PO Box 205	Ridgeville	SC	29472	843-875-3332	896-3740*
**Fax Area Code: 803*					
MacDougall Correctional Institution 1516 Old Gilliard Rd	Ridgeville	SC	29472	843-688-5251	688-4047
Manning Correctional Institution 502 Beckman Dr	Columbia	SC	29203	803-935-7248	935-6016
McCormick Correctional Institution 386 Redemption Way	McCormick	SC	29899	864-443-2114	443-2114
Northside Correctional Institution PO Box 580	Una	SC	29378	864-594-4915	594-4919
Perry Correctional Institution 430 Oaklawn Rd	Pelzer	SC	29669	864-243-4700	243-4700
Ridgeland Correctional Institution PO Box 2039	Ridgeland	SC	29936	843-726-6888	896-3222*
**Fax Area Code: 803*					
Stevenson Correctional Institution 4546 Broad River Rd	Columbia	SC	29210	803-896-8575	896-1222
Tiger River Correctional Institution 200 Prison Rd	Enoree	SC	29335	864-596-1600	896-3544*
**Fax Area Code: 803*					
Trenton Correctional Institution 84 Greenhouse Rd	Trenton	SC	29847	803-896-3000	896-3013
Turbeville Correctional Institution PO Box 252	Turbeville	SC	29162	843-659-4800	896-3195*
**Fax Area Code: 803*					
Walden Correctional Institution 4340 Broad River Rd	Columbia	SC	29210	803-896-8580	896-1225
Wateree River Correctional Institution PO Box 189	Rembert	SC	29128	803-432-6191	896-3408
Women's Correctional Institution 4450 Broad River Rd	Columbia	SC	29210	803-896-8590	896-1226

South Dakota

Facility	City	State	ZIP	Phone	Fax
Durfee Mike State Prison 1412 Wood St	Springfield	SD	57062	605-369-2201	369-2813
Jameson Annex PO Box 5911	Sioux Falls	SD	57117	605-367-5120	367-5585
Mike Durfee State Prison 1412 Wood St	Springfield	SD	57062	605-369-2201	369-2813
Redfield Trusty Unit 17262 W 6th St	Redfield	SD	57469	605-472-4424	472-4408
South Dakota State Penitentiary PO Box 5911	Sioux Falls	SD	57117	605-367-5051	367-5038

South Dakota (Cont'd)

Facility	City	State	Zip	Phone	Fax
Yankton Trusty Unit 176 Micholson Dr	Yankton	SD	57078	605-668-3354	668-3358

Tennessee

Facility	City	State	Zip	Phone	Fax
Hardeman County Correctional Facility 2520 Union Springs Rd PO Box 549	Whiteville	TN	38075	731-254-6000	
Northeast Correctional Complex PO Box 5000	Mountain City	TN	37683	423-727-7387	727-5415
Northwest Correctional Complex 960 SR 212	Tiptonville	TN	38079	731-253-5000	253-5150
Riverbend Maximum Security Institution 7475 Cockrill Bend Blvd	Nashville	TN	37243	615-350-3100	350-3372
South Central Correctional Facility PO Box 279	Clifton	TN	38425	931-676-5372	676-5104
Southeastern Tennessee State Regional Correctional Facility Rt 4 Box 600	Pikeville	TN	37367	423-881-3251	881-4226
Tennessee Prison for Women 3881 Stewarts Ln	Nashville	TN	37243	615-741-1255	253-5388
Turney Center Industrial Prison & Farm 1499 RW Moore Memorial Hwy	Only	TN	37140	931-729-5161	729-9275
Wayne County Boot Camp PO Box 182	Clifton	TN	38425	931-676-3345	676-3050
West Tennessee State Penitentiary PO Box 1150	Henning	TN	38041	731-738-5044	

Texas

Facility	City	State	Zip	Phone	Fax
Bartlett State Jail 1018 Arnold Dr *Web:* www.correctionscorp.com	Bartlett	TX	76511	254-527-3300	527-4489
Bradshaw State Jail 3900 W Loop 571 N PO Box 9000 *Web:* www.correctionscorp.com	Henderson	TX	75653	903-655-0880	655-0500
Cole State Jail 3801 Silo Rd	Bonham	TX	75418	903-583-1100	583-7903
Dawson State Jail 106 W Commerce St *Web:* www.correctionscorp.com	Dallas	TX	75207	214-744-4422	744-3113
Dominguez State Jail 6535 Cagnon Rd	San Antonio	TX	78252	210-675-6620	677-0316
Formby State Jail 998 County Rd AA	Plainview	TX	79072	806-296-2448	293-4877
Gist State Jail 3295 FM 3514	Beaumont	TX	77705	409-727-8400	722-9569
Hutchins State Jail 1500 E Langdon Rd	Dallas	TX	75241	972-225-1304	225-8355
Kegans State Jail 707 Top St	Houston	TX	77002	713-224-6584	224-6212
Lindsey State Jail 1620 Post Oak Rd	Jacksboro	TX	76458	940-567-2272	567-2292
Lopez State Jail 1203 El Cibolo Rd	Edinburg	TX	78541	956-316-3810	316-3810
Lychner State Jail 2350 Atascocita Rd	Humble	TX	77396	281-454-5036	454-4163
Plane State Jail 904 FM 686	Dayton	TX	77535	936-258-2476	257-0269
Sanchez State Jail 3901 State Jail Rd	El Paso	TX	79938	915-856-0046	
Travis County State Jail 8101 FM 969	Austin	TX	78724	512-926-4482	929-8297
Willacy County State Jail 1695 S Buffalo Dr	Raymondville	TX	78580	956-689-4900	689-4001
Woodman State Jail 1210 Coryell City Rd	Gatesville	TX	76528	254-865-9398	865-2940

Utah

Facility	City	State	Zip	Phone	Fax
Central Utah Correctional Facility 255 E 300 N	Gunnison	UT	84634	435-528-6000	528-6051
Iron County Utah State Correctional Facility 2136 N Main St	Cedar City	UT	84720	435-867-7555	867-7604
Utah State Prison PO Box 250	Draper	UT	84020	801-576-7000	545-5523

Vermont

Facility	City	State	Zip	Phone	Fax
Chittenden Regional Correctional Facility 7 Farrell St *Web:* www.doc.state.vt.us	South Burlington	VT	05403	802-863-7356	863-7473
Marble Valley Regional Correctional Facility 167 State St	Rutland	VT	05701	802-786-5830	786-5843
Northeast Regional Correctional Facility 1270 W Rt 5	Saint Johnsbury	VT	05819	802-748-8151	748-6604
Northern State Correctional Facility 2559 Glen Rd	Newport	VT	05855	802-334-3364	334-3367
Northwest State Correctional Facility 3649 Lower Newton Rd	Swanton	VT	05488	802-524-6771	527-7534
Southeast State Correctional Facility 546 State Farm Rd	Windsor	VT	05089	802-674-6717	674-2243

Virginia

Facility	City	State	Zip	Phone	Fax
Augusta Correctional Center 1821 Estaline Valley Rd	Craigsville	VA	24430	540-997-7000	997-7017
Bland Correctional Center 256 Bland Farm Rd *Web:* www.vadoc.state.va.us/facilities/institutions/bland.htm	Bland	VA	24315	276-688-3341	688-3318
Brunswick Correctional Center 1147 Planters Rd	Lawrenceville	VA	23868	434-848-4131	848-4842
Buckingham Correctional Center Rt 20 N PO Box 430 *Web:* www.vadoc.state.va.us/facilities/institutions/buckingham.htm	Dillwyn	VA	23936	434-391-5980	983-1752
Coffeewood Correctional Center 12352 Coffeewood Dr	Mitchells	VA	22729	540-829-6483	829-7383
Deep Meadow Correctional Center 300 Woods Way	State Farm	VA	23160	804-598-5503	403-3406
Deerfield Correctional Center 21360 Deerfield Dr	Capron	VA	23829	434-658-4368	658-9302
Dillwyn Correctional Center Rt 20 N PO Box 670	Dillwyn	VA	23936	434-983-5034	983-5064
Fluvanna Correctional Center for Women 144 Prison Ln PO Box 1000	Troy	VA	22974	434-984-3700	984-6435
Greensville Correctional Center 901 Corrections Way	Jarratt	VA	23870	434-535-7000	535-7640
Haynesville Correctional Center PO Box 129	Haynesville	VA	22472	804-333-3577	333-0192
Indian Creek Correctional Center 801 Sanderson Rd	Chesapeake	VA	23328	757-421-0095	421-0938
Keen Mountain Correctional Center PO Box 860	Oakwood	VA	24631	276-498-7411	498-3396
Lawrenceville Correctional Center 1607 Planters Rd	Lawrenceville	VA	23868	434-848-9349	848-0232
Lunenburg Correctional Center PO Box Y	Victoria	VA	23974	434-696-2045	696-2155
Mecklenburg Correctional Center PO Box 500	Boydton	VA	23917	434-738-6114	738-0556
Nottoway Correctional Center PO Box 488	Burkeville	VA	23922	434-767-5543	767-4685
Powhatan Correctional Center	State Farm	VA	23160	804-598-4251	598-1974
Red Onion State Prison PO Box 970	Pound	VA	24279	276-796-7510	796-4369
Saint Brides Correctional Center PO Box 16482	Chesapeake	VA	23328	757-421-6600	421-2594
Southampton Correctional Center 14545 Old Belfield Rd	Capron	VA	23829	434-658-4174	658-3960
Sussex I State Prison 24414 Musselwhite Dr	Waverly	VA	23891	804-834-9967	834-9995
Sussex II State Prison 24427 Musselwhite Dr	Waverly	VA	23891	804-834-2678	834-4073
Virginia Correctional Center for Women 2841 River Rd W PO Box 1	Goochland	VA	23063	804-784-3582	784-5037
Wallens Ridge State Prison PO Box 759	Big Stone Gap	VA	24219	276-523-3310	523-9612

Washington

Facility	City	State	Zip	Phone	Fax
Airway Heights Corrections Center 11919 W Sprague Ave PO Box 1899 *Web:* www.doc.wa.gov	Airway Heights	WA	99001	509-244-6700	244-6710
Cedar Creek Correctional Center 12200 Bordeaux Rd	Littlerock	WA	98556	360-753-7278	586-5826
Clallam Bay Corrections Center 1830 Eagle Crest Way	Clallam Bay	WA	98326	360-963-2000	963-3292
Coyote Ridge Corrections Center 1301 N Ephrata St *Web:* www.doc.wa.gov	Connell	WA	99326	509-234-9201	543-5801
Larch Corrections Center 15314 NE Dole Valley Rd	Yacolt	WA	98675	360-260-6300	686-3892
McNeil Island Correctional Center PO Box 88900 MS WT-01	Steilacoom	WA	98388	253-588-5281	512-6603
Olympic Corrections Center 11235 Hoh Mainline	Forks	WA	98331	360-374-6181	374-8336
Twin Rivers Corrections Center PO Box 888	Monroe	WA	98272	360-794-2400	794-2584
Washington Corrections Center for Women 9601 Bujacich Rd NW	Gig Harbor	WA	98332	253-858-4200	858-4289
Washington State Penitentiary 1313 N 13th Ave	Walla Walla	WA	99362	509-525-3610	526-6326
Washington State Reformatory PO Box 777	Monroe	WA	98272	360-794-2600	794-2569

West Virginia

Facility	City	State	Zip	Phone	Fax
Denmar Correctional Center HC 64 Box 125	Hillsboro	WV	24946	304-653-4201	653-4855
Huttonsville Correctional Center PO Box 1	Huttonsville	WV	26273	304-335-2291	335-4680
Mount Olive Correctional Complex 1 Mountainside Way	Mount Olive	WV	25185	304-442-7213	442-7225
Northern Regional Correctional Facility RD 2 Box 1	Moundsville	WV	26041	304-843-4067	843-4089
Ohio County Correctional Center 1501 Eoff St	Wheeling	WV	26003	304-238-1007	238-1009
Pruntytown Correctional Center PO Box 159	Grafton	WV	26354	304-265-6112	265-6120
Saint Mary's Correctional Center 2880 N Pleasants Hwy	Saint Marys	WV	26170	304-684-5500	684-5506

Wisconsin

Facility	City	State	Zip	Phone	Fax
Columbia Correctional Institution 2925 Columbia Dr PO Box 950	Portage	WI	53901	608-742-9100	742-9111
Dodge Correctional Institution 1 W Lincoln St	Waupun	WI	53963	920-324-5577	324-6297
Fox Lake Correctional Institution Lake Emily Rd PO Box 147	Fox Lake	WI	53933	920-928-3151	928-6929
Green Bay Correctional Institution 2833 Riverside Dr	Green Bay	WI	54307	920-432-4877	432-5388
Jackson Correctional Institution PO Box 232	Black River Falls	WI	54615	715-284-4550	284-7335
Kettle Moraine Correctional Institution PO Box 31	Plymouth	WI	53073	920-526-3244	526-3989
Oakhill Correctional Institution 5212 Hwy M	Oregon	WI	53575	608-835-3101	835-9196
Oshkosh Correctional Institution PO Box 3530	Oshkosh	WI	54903	920-231-4010	236-2626
Prairie du Chien Correctional Institution 500 E Parrish St *Web:* www.wi-doc.com/prairie_du_chien.htm	Prairie du Chien	WI	53821	608-326-7828	326-5960
Racine Correctional Institution 2019 Wisconsin St	Sturtevant	WI	53177	262-886-3214	886-3514
Supermax Correctional Institution PO Box 1000	Boscobel	WI	53805	608-375-5656	375-5595
Taycheedah Correctional Institution PO Box 1947	Fond du Lac	WI	54935	920-929-3800	929-2946
Waupun Correctional Institution 200 S Madison St PO Box 351	Waupun	WI	53963	920-324-5571	324-4478

Wyoming

Facility	City	State	Zip	Phone	Fax
Wyoming Honor Conservation Camp & Boot Camp PO Box 160	Newcastle	WY	82701	307-746-4436	746-9316
Wyoming Honor Farm 40 Honor Farm Rd	Riverton	WY	82501	307-856-9578	856-2505
Wyoming State Penitentiary PO Box 400	Rawlins	WY	82301	307-328-1441	328-7464
Wyoming Women's Center PO Box 20	Lusk	WY	82225	307-334-3693	334-2254

217 COSMETICS, SKIN CARE, AND OTHER PERSONAL CARE PRODUCTS

SEE ALSO Perfumes p. 2104

Company	City	State	Zip	Phone	Fax
ABRA Therapeutics Inc PO Box 795185 **Fax:* Orders ■ *TF:* 800-745-0761 ■ *Web:* www.abratherapeutics.com	Dallas	TX	75379	972-818-2860	818-2861*
Access Business Group 7575 Fulton St E *TF Cust Svc:* 800-253-6500 ■ *Web:* www.accessbusinessgroup.com	Ada	MI	49355	616-787-5358	
Advanced Research Laboratories 1063 McGaw Ave Suite 100 *TF:* 800-966-6960 ■ *Web:* www.advreslab.com	Irvine	CA	92614	949-221-8238	794-5508
AHAVA North America 411 5th Ave 4th Fl *TF:* 800-366-7254 ■ *Web:* www.ahavaus.com	New York	NY	10016	212-532-7911	696-9789
Aire-Master of America Inc 1821 N Highway CC PO Box 2310 *TF:* 800-525-0957 ■ *Web:* www.airemaster.com	Nixa	MO	65714	417-725-2691	725-5737
Alberto-Culver Consumer Products Worldwide 2525 Armitage Ave *TF:* 800-333-0005 ■ *Web:* www.alberto.com	Melrose Park	IL	60160	708-450-3000	
Alchemy International Inc 14909 Community St **Fax Area Code:* 714 ■ *TF Orders:* 800-798-4801 ■ *Web:* www.bodyvitals.com	Panorama City	CA	91402	818-830-3374	960-1527*
Alleghany Pharmacal Corp 277 Northern Blvd *TF:* 800-645-6190 ■ *Web:* www.alleghanypharmacal.com	Great Neck	NY	11022	516-466-0660	482-1525
Almay Inc 237 Park Ave **Fax:* Hum Res ■ *TF:* 800-473-8566 ■ *Web:* www.almay.com	New York	NY	10017	212-527-4000	527-4995*
Aloe Vera of America Inc 13745 Jupiter Rd	Dallas	TX	75238	214-343-5700	355-5454
Aloette Cosmetics Inc 4900 Highlands Pkwy *TF:* 800-256-3883 ■ *Web:* www.aloettecosmetics.com	Smyrna	GA	30082	678-444-2563	444-2564
American Safety Razor Co 1 Razor Blade Ln *TF:* 800-445-9284 ■ *Web:* www.asrco.com	Verona	VA	24482	540-248-8000	248-0522
Arizona Natural Resources 2525 E Beardsley Rd *Web:* www.arizonanaturalresources.com	Phoenix	AZ	85050	602-569-6900	569-9697
At Last Naturals Inc 401 Columbus Ave *TF:* 800-527-8123 ■ *Web:* www.atlastnaturals.com	Valhalla	NY	10595	914-747-3599	747-3791
Autumn Harp Inc 61 Pine St *Web:* www.autumnharp.com	Bristol	VT	05443	802-453-4807	453-4903
Avalon Natural Cosmetics Inc 1105 Industrial Ave Suite 200 *TF:* 800-227-5120	Petaluma	CA	94952	707-769-5120	769-0868
Aveda Corp 4000 Pheasant Ridge Dr *TF:* 800-283-3224 ■ *Web:* www.aveda.com	Blaine	MN	55449	763-783-4000	783-4110
Avon Products Inc 1251 Ave of the Americas *NYSE:* AVP ■ *TF Cust Svc:* 800-367-2866 ■ *Web:* www.avon.com	New York	NY	10020	212-282-5000	282-6825
Bassett WE Co 100 Trap Falls Rd Ext *TF:* 800-394-8746 ■ *Web:* www.trim.com	Shelton	CT	06484	203-929-8483	929-8963
Bath & Body Works 7 Limited Pkwy E *TF:* 888-856-1616 ■ *Web:* www.bathandbodyworks.com	Reynoldsburg	OH	43068	614-856-6000	856-6313
Bath-and-Body.com 1073 Exchange St *TF:* 866-667-2284 ■ *Web:* www.bath-and-body.com	Boise	ID	83716	208-345-5136	947-1504
BeautiControl Cosmetics Inc 2121 Midway Rd **Fax:* Sales ■ *TF:* 800-232-8841 ■ *Web:* www.beauticontrol.com	Carrollton	TX	75006	972-458-0601	458-6904*
Beehive Botanicals Inc 16297 W Nursery Rd *TF:* 800-233-4483 ■ *Web:* www.beehive-botanicals.com	Hayward	WI	54843	715-634-4274	634-3523
Beiersdorf North America 187 Danbury Rd **Fax:* Hum Res ■ *TF:* 800-233-2340 ■ *Web:* www.beiersdorf.com	Wilton	CT	06897	203-563-5800	854-8112*
Belcam Inc Delagar Div 27 Montgomery St **Fax Area Code:* 518 ■ *Web:* www.delagar.com	Rouses Point	NY	12979	800-848-9281	297-2943*

Company	City	State	Zip	Phone	Fax
BeneFit Cosmetics 685 Market St 7th Fl	San Francisco	CA	94105	415-781-8153	781-3930
TF Cust Svc: 800-781-2336 ■ *Web:* www.benefitcosmetics.com					
Blissworld LLC 75 Varick St 10th Fl	New York	NY	10013	212-931-6383	931-8257
TF: 888-243-8825 ■ *Web:* www.blissworld.com					
Blue Cross Laboratories 20950 Center Pointe Pkwy	Santa Clarita	CA	91350	661-255-0955	255-3628
Web: www.bc-labs.com					
Bobbi Brown Professional Cosmetics Inc 767 5th Ave	New York	NY	10153	877-310-9222	
Web: www.bobbibrowncosmetics.com					
Body Shop The 5036 One World Way	Wake Forest	NC	27587	919-554-4900	554-4361
TF Cust Svc: 800-747-4827 ■ *Web:* www.thebodyshop.com					
Bonne Bell Inc 18519 Detroit Ave	Lakewood	OH	44107	216-221-0800	
TF: 800-321-1006 ■ *Web:* www.bonnebell.com					
Bronner Brothers Inc 2141 Powers Ferry Rd	Marietta	GA	30067	770-988-0015	953-0848
TF: 800-241-6151 ■ *Web:* www.bronnerbros.com					
Carme Cosmeceutical Sciences 831-A Latour Ct	Napa	CA	94558	707-226-3900	226-3999*
**Fax:* Cust Svc					
Carter-Horner Inc 6600 Kitimat Rd	Mississauga	ON	L5N1L9	905-826-6200	826-0389
TF: 800-387-2130 ■ *Web:* www.carterhorner.com					
Caswell-Massey Co Ltd 121 Fieldcrest Ave	Edison	NJ	08837	732-225-2181	225-2385
TF: 800-326-0500 ■ *Web:* www.caswellmassey.com					
CBI Laboratories 4201 Diplomacy Rd	Fort Worth	TX	76155	972-241-7546	352-1094*
**Fax Area Code:* 800 ■ *TF:* 800-822-7546 ■ *Web:* www.cbiskincare.com					
CCA Industries Inc 200 Murray Hill Pkwy	East Rutherford	NJ	07073	201-330-1400	935-6784*
AMEX: CAW ■ **Fax:* Sales ■ *TF Cust Svc:* 800-524-2720 ■ *Web:* www.ccaindustries.com					
Chattem Inc 1715 W 38th St	Chattanooga	TN	37409	423-821-4571	821-0395
NASDAQ: CHTT ■ *TF:* 800-366-6077 ■ *Web:* www.chattem.com					
Church & Dwight Co Inc 469 N Harrison St	Princeton	NJ	08543	609-683-5900	
NYSE: CHD ■ *Web:* www.churchdwight.com					
Clairol Div Procter & Gamble Co 1 Blachley Rd	Stamford	CT	06922	203-357-5000	357-5930
TF: 800-223-5800 ■ *Web:* www.clairol.com					
Clarins USA Inc 110 E 59th St 36th Fl	New York	NY	10022	212-980-1800	752-5910
Web: us.clarins.com					
Clinique Laboratories Inc 767 5th Ave 37th Fl	New York	NY	10153	212-572-3800	572-4770
TF: 800-723-7310 ■ *Web:* www.clinique.com					
Colgate-Palmolive Co 300 Park Ave	New York	NY	10022	212-310-2000	310-2595
NYSE: CL ■ *Web:* www.colgate.com					
Color Factory The 11312 Penrose St	Sun Valley	CA	91352	818-767-2889	767-4062
Web: www.colorfactoryla.com					
Combe Inc 1101 Westchester Ave	White Plains	NY	10604	914-694-5454	694-6233
TF: 800-873-7400 ■ *Web:* www.combe.com					
Cosmetic Essence Inc 2182 SR-35	Holmdel	NJ	07733	732-888-7788	888-6086
Web: www.onex.com					
Cosmolab Inc 1100 Garrett Pkwy	Lewisburg	TN	37091	931-359-6253	359-8465
TF: 800-359-6254 ■ *Web:* www.cosmolab.com					
Cosmopolitan Cosmetics 909 3rd Ave 20th Fl	New York	NY	10022	212-980-6400	980-6464
TF: 800-589-1412 ■ *Web:* www.cosmopolitan-cosmetics.com					
Cosrich Group Inc 55 LaFrance Ave	Bloomfield	NJ	07003	973-566-6240	566-6241
TF: 888-898-9176 ■ *Web:* www.cosrich.com					
Cover Girl 1 Procter & Gamble Plaza	Cincinnati	OH	45202	513-983-1100	
Web: www.covergirl.com					
Crabtree & Evelyn Ltd 102 Peake Brook Rd	Woodstock	CT	06281	860-928-2761	928-0462
TF: 800-624-5211 ■ *Web:* www.crabtree-evelyn.com					
Deb SBS 1100 Hwy 27 S	Stanley	NC	28164	704-263-4240	263-9601
TF: 800-248-7190 ■ *Web:* www.debsbs.com					
Del Laboratories Inc 726 Reckson Plaza PO Box 9357	Uniondale	NY	11553	516-844-2020	
TF: 800-952-5080 ■ *Web:* www.dellabs.com					
Delagar Div Belcam Inc 27 Montgomery St	Rouses Point	NY	12979	800-848-9281	297-2943*
**Fax Area Code:* 518 ■ *Web:* www.delagar.com					
Dena Corp 825 Nicholas Blvd	Elk Grove Village	IL	60007	847-593-3041	593-3087
Web: www.denacorp.com					
Dial Corp 15501 N Dial Blvd	Scottsdale	AZ	85260	480-754-3425	
TF Cust Svc: 800-258-3425 ■ *Web:* www.dialcorp.com					
Dudley Products Inc 1080 Old Greensboro Rd	Kernersville	NC	27284	336-993-8800	993-1768
TF: 800-334-4150 ■ *Web:* www.dudleyq.com					
Elizabeth Arden Inc 2400 SW 145th Ave	Miramar	FL	33327	954-364-6900	364-6910
NASDAQ: RDEN ■ *TF:* 800-227-2445 ■ *Web:* www.elizabetharden.com					
Estee Lauder Cos Inc 767 5th Ave	New York	NY	10153	212-572-4200	572-3941
NYSE: EL ■ *Web:* www.elcompanies.com					
Estee Lauder International Inc 767 5th Ave	New York	NY	10153	212-572-4200	
Web: www.esteelauder.com					
Estee Lauder USA 767 5th Ave	New York	NY	10153	212-572-4200	572-3941
Web: www.esteelauder.com					
Flents Products Co 5401 S Graham Rd	Saint Charles	MI	48655	989-865-8221	865-8156
TF: 800-262-8221 ■ *Web:* www.flents.com					
Flowery Beauty Products Inc 47 Miry Brook Rd	Danbury	CT	06810	203-205-0686	205-0690
TF: 800-545-5247 ■ *Web:* www.flowery.com					
Forever Living Products International Inc					
7501 E McCormick Pkwy	Scottsdale	AZ	85258	480-998-8888	905-8451
TF: 888-440-2563 ■ *Web:* www.foreverliving.com					
Framesi USA Inc 400 Chess St	Coraopolis	PA	15108	412-269-2950	264-5696
TF: 800-321-9648					
Fuller Brush Co 1 Fuller Way	Great Bend	KS	67530	620-792-1711	792-1906
TF Cust Svc: 800-438-5537 ■ *Web:* www.fuller.com					
Gillette Co Prudential Tower Bldg	Boston	MA	02199	617-421-7000	421-7617
TF Cust Svc: 800-445-5388 ■ *Web:* www.gillette.com					
Gloss.com Inc 767 5th Ave	New York	NY	10153	212-572-4200	
TF Orders: 888-550-4567 ■ *Web:* www.gloss.com					
GOJO Industries Inc PO Box 991	Akron	OH	44309	330-255-6000	329-4656*
**Fax Area Code:* 800 ■ *TF:* 800-321-9647 ■ *Web:* www.gojo.com					
Goody Products Inc 400 Galleria Pkwy Suite 1100	Atlanta	GA	30339	770-615-4700	615-4740
TF: 800-241-4324 ■ *Web:* www.goody.com					
Guest Supply Inc 4301 US Hwy 1 PO Box 902	Monmouth Junction	NJ	08852	609-514-9696	514-2692
TF Cust Svc: 800-221-1457 ■ *Web:* www.guestsupply.com					
H2O Plus Inc 845 W Madison St	Chicago	IL	60607	312-850-9283	633-1470
TF Cust Svc: 800-690-2284 ■ *Web:* www.h2oplus.com					
Hawaiian Tropic 1190 US Hwy 1 N	Ormond Beach	FL	32174	386-677-9559	677-9595
TF: 800-874-4844 ■ *Web:* www.hawaiiantropic.com					
Helene Curtis Industries Inc 205 N Michigan Ave Suite 3200	Chicago	IL	60601	312-661-0222	661-2522
TF: 800-621-2013 ■ *Web:* www.helenecurtis.com					
Henkel Corp 1063 McGraw Ave Suite 100	Irvine	CA	92614	949-794-5500	794-5541
TF: 800-326-2855 ■ *Web:* www.henkel.us					
Henkel Corp Schwartzkopf & Henkel Div					
1063 McGraw Ave Suite 100	Irvine	CA	92614	949-794-5500	794-5541
TF: 800-326-2855 ■ *Web:* www.henkel.us					
Hydron Technologies Inc 4400 34th St N Suite F	Saint Petersburg	FL	33714	727-342-5050	344-3920
TF: 800-449-3766 ■ *Web:* www.hydron.com					
Jafra Cosmetics International 2451 Townsgate Rd	Westlake Village	CA	91361	805-449-3000	449-3254
TF: 800-551-2345 ■ *Web:* www.jafra.com					
Jason Natural Cosmetics Inc 5500 W 83rd St	Los Angeles	CA	90045	310-838-7543	838-9274
TF: 800-527-6605 ■ *Web:* www.jason-natural.com					
John Amico Products 4731 W 136th St	Crestwood	IL	60445	708-824-4000	824-0413
TF: 800-676-5264 ■ *Web:* www.johnamico.com					
John Frieda Professional Hair Care Inc 333 Ludlow St	Stamford	CT	06902	203-762-1233	762-2262
TF Cust Svc: 800-521-3189 ■ *Web:* www.johnfrieda.com					
John Paul Mitchell Systems					
9701 Wilshire Blvd Suite 1205	Beverly Hills	CA	90212	310-248-3888	248-2780
TF Cust Svc: 800-793-8790 ■ *Web:* www.paulmitchell.com					
Johnson & Johnson Consumer Products Co 199 Grandview Rd	Skillman	NJ	08558	908-874-1000	
TF: 800-526-3967 ■ *Web:* www.johnsonsbaby.com					
Johnson & Johnson Inc 7101 Notre-Dame E	Montreal	QC	H1N2G4	514-251-5100	251-6233
TF: 800-361-8990 ■ *Web:* www.jnjcanada.com					
Kao Brands Co 2535 Spring Grove Ave	Cincinnati	OH	45214	513-421-1400	455-7889
TF: 800-742-8798 ■ *Web:* www.kaobrands.com					
Key West Fragrance & Cosmetics Factory Inc 540 Greene St	Key West	FL	33040	305-293-1885	
TF Orders: 800-445-2563 ■ *Web:* www.keywestaloe.com					
Kolmar Laboratories Inc 20 W King St	Port Jervis	NY	12771	845-856-5311	856-2203*
**Fax:* Sales ■ *Web:* www.kolmar.com					
Korex Corp 50000 W Pontiac Trail PO Box 930339	Wixom	MI	48393	248-624-0000	624-3441
TF: 800-678-7627					
Lancome Div L''Oreal USA 575 5th Ave	New York	NY	10017	212-818-1500	984-4776
Web: www.lancome.com					
Lander Co Inc 200 Lenox Dr Suite 202	Lawrenceville	NJ	08648	609-219-0930	219-1238
TF Orders: 800-452-6337 ■ *Web:* www.lander-hba.com					
Lee Pharmaceuticals Inc 1434 Santa Anita Ave	South El Monte	CA	91733	626-442-3141	443-8745
TF: 800-950-5337 ■ *Web:* www.leepharmaceuticals.com					
Limited Brands Inc 3 Limited Pkwy	Columbus	OH	43230	614-415-7000	415-2491*
NYSE: LTD ■ **Fax:* Mail Rm ■ *TF:* 800-945-9000 ■ *Web:* www.limitedbrands.com					
L'Oreal USA 575 5th Ave	New York	NY	10017	212-818-1500	
TF: 800-562-2159 ■ *Web:* www.lorealusa.com					
L'Oreal USA Lancome Div 575 5th Ave	New York	NY	10017	212-818-1500	984-4776
Web: www.lancome.com					
Luster Products Inc 1104 W 43rd St	Chicago	IL	60609	773-579-1800	579-1912
TF: 800-621-4255 ■ *Web:* www.lusterproducts.com					
Luzier Personalized Cosmetics Inc 7910-12 Troost Ave	Kansas City	MO	64131	816-531-8338	531-6979
TF: 800-821-6632 ■ *Web:* www.luzier.com					
MAC Cosmetics 767 5th Ave	New York	NY	10153	212-572-4200	572-3941
TF: 800-723-7310 ■ *Web:* www.maccosmetics.com					
MakeUpMania! of New York 154 Orchard St	New York	NY	10002	212-533-5900	533-5019
TF: 800-711-7182 ■ *Web:* www.makeupmania.com					
Mana Products Inc 32-02 Queens Blvd	Long Island City	NY	11101	718-361-2550	786-3204
TF Cust Svc: 800-221-3071 ■ *Web:* www.manaproducts.com					
Markwins International Corp 22067 Ferrero Pkwy	City of Industry	CA	91789	909-595-8898	595-8820
TF: 800-626-8878 ■ *Web:* www.markwins.com					
Mary Kay Inc 16251 Dallas Pkwy	Addison	TX	75001	972-687-6300	687-1623*
**Fax:* Cust Svc ■ *TF Cust Svc:* 800-627-9529 ■ *Web:* www.marykay.com					
Mary Kay Inc Mfg Group 1330 Regal Row	Dallas	TX	75247	972-687-6300	905-6997*
**Fax Area Code:* 214 ■ **Fax:* Hum Res ■ *TF Cust Svc:* 800-627-9529 ■					
Web: www.marykay.com					
Matrix Essentials Inc 30601 Carter St	Solon	OH	44139	440-248-3700	
TF: 800-282-2822 ■ *Web:* www.matrixbeautiful.com					
Max Factor 1 Procter & Gamble Plaza	Cincinnati	OH	45202	513-983-1100	
TF: 800-526-8787 ■ *Web:* www.maxfactor.com					
Maybelline New York 575 5th Ave	New York	NY	10017	212-818-1500	984-4511*
**Fax:* Mail Rm ■ *TF:* 800-944-0730 ■ *Web:* www.maybelline.com					
Merle Norman Cosmetics Inc 9130 Bellanca Ave	Los Angeles	CA	90045	310-641-3000	641-7144
TF: 800-421-2060 ■ *Web:* www.merlenorman.com					
Neutrogena Corp 5760 W 96th St	Los Angeles	CA	90045	310-642-1150	642-3260
TF Cust Svc: 800-217-1136 ■ *Web:* www.neutrogena.com					
Newell Rubbermaid Inc Home & Family Group					
10B Glenlake Pkwy Suite 300	Atlanta	GA	30328	770-407-3800	407-3970
TF: 800-434-4314 ■ *Web:* www.newellrubbermaid.com					
Nexxus Products Co 82 Coromar Dr	Goleta	CA	93117	805-968-6900	968-6540
TF: 800-444-6399 ■ *Web:* www.nexxusproducts.com					
Norelco Consumer Products Co 1010 Washington Blvd	Stamford	CT	06912	203-973-0200	351-5717*
**Fax:* Cust Svc ■ *TF:* 800-243-7884 ■ *Web:* www.norelco.com					
NutraMax Products Inc 51 Blackburn Dr	Gloucester	MA	01930	978-283-1800	282-3794
Web: www.nutramax.com					
Obagi Medical Products Inc 310 Golden Shore Suite 100	Long Beach	CA	90802	562-628-1007	628-1008
TF: 800-636-7546 ■ *Web:* www.obagi.com					
Original Bradford Soap Works Inc 200 Providence St	West Warwick	RI	02893	401-821-2141	821-1660
Web: www.bradfordsoap.com					
Origins Natural Resources Inc 767 5th Ave	New York	NY	10153	212-572-4200	
TF Cust Svc: 800-723-7310 ■ *Web:* www.origins.com					
Para Laboratories Inc 100 Rose Ave	Hempstead	NY	11550	516-538-4600	538-4751
TF: 800-645-3752 ■ *Web:* www.queenhelene.com					
Paramount Cosmetics Inc 93 Entin Rd Suite 4	Clifton	NJ	07014	973-472-2323	472-5005
TF: 800-522-9880 ■ *Web:* www.paramountcosmetics.net					
Penthouse Mfg Co Inc 225 Buffalo Ave	Freeport	NY	11520	516-379-1300	378-2844
Web: www.thepenthousegroup.com					
Person & Covey Inc 616 Allen Ave	Glendale	CA	91201	818-240-1030	547-9821
TF: 800-423-2341 ■ *Web:* www.personandcovey.com					
Personal Products Co 199 Grandview Rd	Skillman	NJ	08558	908-874-1000	
Web: www.jnj.com/our_company/family_of_companies					
Pfizer Inc 235 E 42nd St	New York	NY	10017	212-573-2323	573-7851
NYSE: PFE ■ *TF Prod Info:* 800-733-4717 ■ *Web:* www.pfizer.com					
Philips Oral Healthcare Inc 35301 SE Center St	Snoqualmie	WA	98065	425-396-2000	396-4824
TF: 800-957-9310 ■ *Web:* www.sonicare.com					
philosophy inc 3809 E Watkins	Phoenix	AZ	85034	602-794-8500	794-8701
TF: 800-568-3151 ■ *Web:* www.philosophy.com					
Playtex Products Inc 300 Nyala Farms Rd	Westport	CT	06880	203-341-4000	341-4027*
NYSE: PYX ■ **Fax:* Hum Res ■ *TF:* 800-999-9700 ■ *Web:* www.playtexproductsinc.com					
Prescriptives Inc 767 5th Ave	New York	NY	10153	212-572-4200	
TF: 800-723-7310 ■ *Web:* www.prescriptives.com					
Prestige Brands International Inc 90 N Broadway	Irvington	NY	10533	914-524-6810	524-6815
NYSE: PBH ■ *Web:* www.prestigebrands.com					
Prestige Cosmetics Corp 1441 W Newport Center Dr	Deerfield Beach	FL	33442	954-480-9202	480-9220
TF: 800-722-7488 ■ *Web:* www.prestigecosmetics.com					
Pro-Line International Inc 2121 Panoramic Cir	Dallas	TX	75212	214-631-4247	634-8155
TF: 800-527-5879 ■ *Web:* www.prolinecorp.com					
Procter & Gamble Co Clairol Div 1 Blachley Rd	Stamford	CT	06922	203-357-5000	357-5930
TF: 800-223-5800 ■ *Web:* www.clairol.com					
Procter & Gamble Cosmetics 11050 York Rd	Hunt Valley	MD	21030	800-851-8262	
TF Cust Svc: 800-638-6204 ■ *Web:* www.pg.com					
Procter & Gamble Mfg Co 1 Procter & Gamble Plaza	Cincinnati	OH	45202	513-983-1100	
Web: www.pg.com					
Qosmedix 150-Q Executive Dr	Edgewood	NY	11717	631-242-3270	242-3291
Web: www.qosmedix.com					
Queen Helene 100 Rose Ave	Hempstead	NY	11550	516-538-4600	538-4751
TF: 800-645-3752 ■ *Web:* www.queenhelene.com					
Reckitt Benckiser Inc 399 Interpace Pkwy PO Box 225	Parsippany	NJ	07054	973-404-2600	404-5700
TF Cust Svc: 800-333-3899 ■ *Web:* www.reckitt.com					
Redken Laboratories Inc 575 5th Ave	New York	NY	10017	212-818-1500	810-1205
TF Cust Svc: 800-423-5280 ■ *Web:* www.redken.com					
Remington Products Co LLC 601 Rayovac Dr	Madison	WI	53711	608-275-3340	275-4969
TF Cust Svc: 800-736-4648 ■ *Web:* www.remington-products.com					
Revlon Consumer Products Corp 237 Park Ave	New York	NY	10017	212-527-4000	527-4995*
**Fax:* Hum Res ■ *TF Cust Svc:* 800-473-8566 ■ *Web:* www.revlon.com					
Revlon Implement Corp 196 Coit St	Irvington	NJ	07111	973-373-5803	416-4985
Rozelle Cosmetics PO Box 70	Westfield	VT	05874	802-744-2270	744-2236
TF: 800-451-4216 ■ *Web:* www.rozelle.com					
Saint Ives Laboratories Inc 2525 Armitage Ave	Melrose Park	IL	60160	708-450-3000	450-3394
TF: 800-333-6666 ■ *Web:* www.stives.com					
Sara Lee Household & Body Care 707 Eagleview Blvd	Exton	PA	19341	610-321-1220	321-1440
TF: 800-879-5494 ■ *Web:* www.saralee.com					

				Phone	Fax
Schering-Plough Corp 2000 Galloping Hill Rd	Kenilworth	NJ	07033	908-298-4000	595-3699*
NYSE: SGP ■ **Fax:* Mktg ■ *TF Mktg:* 888-793-7253 ■ *Web:* www.schering-plough.com					
Schering-Plough HealthCare Products Corp PO Box 377	Memphis	TN	38151	901-320-2011	320-2080
TF Cust Svc: 800-842-4090					
Scolding Locks Corp 1520 W Rogers Ave	Appleton	WI	54914	920-733-5561	733-8800
TF: 800-537-9707 ■ *Web:* www.scoldinglocks.com					
Sebastian International Inc 6109 DeSoto Ave	Woodland Hills	CA	91367	818-999-5112	712-7770
TF Cust Svc: 800-347-4424 ■ *Web:* www.sebastian-intl.com					
Sentinel Consumer Products Inc 7750 Tyler Blvd	Mentor	OH	44060	440-974-8144	974-9268
Web: www.sentinelconsumer.com					
sephora.com Inc 525 Market St First Market Tower 32nd Fl	San Francisco	CA	94105	415-284-3300	284-3427*
**Fax:* Hum Res ■ *TF Cust Svc:* 877-737-4672 ■ *Web:* www.sephora.com					
Sheffield Laboratories 170 Broad St	New London	CT	06320	860-442-4451	442-0356
TF: 800-222-1087 ■ *Web:* www.sheffield-labs.com					
Shiseido Cosmetics America Ltd 900 3rd Ave 15th Fl	New York	NY	10022	212-805-2300	688-0109
TF: 800-906-7503 ■ *Web:* www.sca.shiseido.com					
Softsoap Enterprises Inc 300 Park Ave	New York	NY	10022	212-310-2000	310-3284
Web: www.softsoap.com					
Stahl Soap Corp 1 Branca Rd	East Rutherford	NJ	07073	201-507-5770	507-8868
TF: 800-527-5115 ■ *Web:* www.stahlsoap.com					
Star Nail Products Inc 29120 Ave Paine	Valencia	CA	91355	661-257-7827	257-5856
TF: 800-762-6245 ■ *Web:* www.starnail.com					
Stephan Co 1850 W McNab Rd	Fort Lauderdale	FL	33309	954-971-0600	971-2633
AMEX: TSC ■ *TF:* 800-327-0388 ■ *Web:* www.thestephanco.com					
Stila Cosmetics 551 Madison Ave 12th Fl	New York	NY	10022	646-282-1000	282-1010
TF: 877-565-1299 ■ *Web:* www.stila.net					
Tanning Research Labs Inc DBA Hawaiian Tropic 1190 US Hwy 1 N	Ormond Beach	FL	32174	386-677-9559	677-9595
TF: 800-874-4844 ■ *Web:* www.hawaiiantropic.com					
Tom's of Maine Inc PO Box 710	Kennebunk	ME	04043	207-985-2944	985-2196
TF: 800-367-8667 ■ *Web:* www.toms-of-maine.com					
Twincraft Inc 2 Tigan St	Winooski	VT	05404	802-655-2200	
Web: www.twincraft.com					
Ulta3 Inc 1135 Arbor Dr	Romeoville	IL	60446	630-226-0020	226-8210
TF: 866-304-3704 ■ *Web:* www.ulta.com					
Unilever Home & Personal Care North America 800 Sylvan Ave 1st Fl	Englewood Cliffs	NJ	07632	201-862-2000	862-2108
TF: 800-745-9595					
Unilever of Puerto Rico Inc PO Box 599	Bayamon	PR	00960	787-740-3400	740-3779
TF: 800-981-3405 ■ *Web:* www.unilever.com					
Unilever US Inc 33 Benedict Pl	Greenwich	CT	06830	203-625-1000	625-1602
Web: www.unileverusa.com					
Urban Decay 729 Farad St	Costa Mesa	CA	92627	949-631-4504	631-5986*
**Fax:* Cust Svc ■ *TF:* 800-784-8722 ■ *Web:* www.urbandecay.com					
Vi-Jon Labs Inc 8515 Page Ave	Saint Louis	MO	63114	314-427-1000	427-1010
TF: 800-325-8167 ■ *Web:* www.vijon.com					
Victoria Vogue Inc 90 Southland Dr	Bethlehem	PA	18017	610-865-1500	865-6089
TF: 800-967-7833 ■ *Web:* www.victoriavogue.com					
Vidal Sassoon 1 Procter & Gamble Plaza	Cincinnati	OH	45202	513-983-1100	983-1233
Web: www.vssassoon.com					
Wahl Clipper Corp 2900 Locust St	Sterling	IL	61081	815-625-6525	625-1193
TF: 800-767-9245 ■ *Web:* www.wahlclipper.com					
WE Bassett Co 100 Trap Falls Rd Ext	Shelton	CT	06484	203-929-8483	929-8963
TF: 800-394-8746 ■ *Web:* www.trim.com					
Wella Corp 6109 DeSoto Ave	Woodland Hills	CA	91367	818-999-5112	712-7770
TF: 800-829-4422 ■ *Web:* www.wellausa.com					
White Laboratories Inc 110 Bomar Ct Suite 122	Longwood	FL	32750	407-869-0107	525-6082*
**Fax Area Code:* 800 ■ *TF:* 800-327-2014 ■ *Web:* www.softshave.com					
YSL Boutique 855 Madison Ave	New York	NY	10021	212-988-3821	517-4814
Web: www.ysl.com					
Zia Natural Skincare 8468 Warner Dr	Culver City	CA	90232	800-527-6605	945-4451*
**Fax Area Code:* 310 ■ *TF:* 800-334-7546 ■ *Web:* www.zianatural.com					
Zotos International Inc 100 Tokeneke Rd	Darien	CT	06820	203-655-8911	656-7865
TF: 800-242-9283 ■ *Web:* www.zotos.com					

218 CREDIT CARD PROVIDERS & RELATED SERVICES

Companies listed here include those that issue credit cards as well as companies that provide services to these companies (i.e., rewards programs, theft prevention, etc.).

				Phone	Fax
American Express Co Inc World Financial Center 200 Vesey St	New York	NY	10285	212-640-2000	640-0128
NYSE: AXP ■ *TF:* 800-666-1775 ■ *Web:* home.americanexpress.com					
Applied Card Systems 800 Delaware Ave	Wilmington	DE	19801	302-467-4600	467-4650
TF: 800-334-3180 ■ *Web:* www.appliedcard.com					
AT & T Universal Card Services PO Box 44167	Jacksonville	FL	32231	904-954-7500	954-7816
TF: 800-235-3549 ■ *Web:* www.universalcard.com					
Bank of America Card Services 1 Commercial Pl 2nd Fl	Norfolk	VA	23510	757-441-4770	441-4780
TF: 800-732-9194					
Bloomingdale's Credit Services 9111 Duke Blvd	Mason	OH	45040	513-398-5221	573-2957*
**Fax:* Cust Svc ■ *TF:* 800-456-9529					
BP Amoco Credit Card	Des Moines	IA	50360	800-462-6626	226-4252*
**Fax Area Code:* 515 ■ *TF:* 800-850-6266					
Capital One Financial Corp 1680 Capital One Dr	McLean	VA	22102	703-720-1000	720-1755
NYSE: COF ■ *TF:* 800-801-1164 ■ *Web:* www.capitalone.com					
ChevronTexaco Credit Card Center 2001 Diamond Blvd	Concord	CA	94520	925-842-1000	827-7919
TF: 800-243-8766 ■ *Web:* www.chevrontexacocards.com					
CITGO Petroleum Corp 1293 Eldridge Pkwy	Houston	TX	77077	832-486-4000	
Web: www.spsecurities.com					
CompuCredit Corp 245 Perimeter Center Pkwy Suite 600	Atlanta	GA	30346	770-206-6200	206-6181
NASDAQ: CCRT ■ *Web:* www.compucredit.com					
Credit Card Sentinel Inc PO Box 4401	Carol Stream	IL	60197	847-605-7485	605-7368
TF Cust Svc: 800-423-5166					
Dillard's Credit Services Inc PO Box 960012	Orlando	FL	32896	800-643-8278	
Web: www.dillards.com					
Diners Club Carte Blanche 7958 S Chester St Waterview IV	Englewood	CO	80112	303-799-9000	649-2644*
**Fax:* Cust Svc ■ *TF:* 800-234-6377 ■ *Web:* www.dinersclubnorthamerica.com					
Diners Club International 8430 W Bryn Mawr Ave	Chicago	IL	60631	773-380-5100	380-5532
TF: 800-234-6377 ■ *Web:* www.dinersclubnorthamerica.com					
Discover Financial Services Inc 2500 Lake Cook Rd	Riverwoods	IL	60015	224-405-0900	405-2009
TF Cust Svc: 800-347-2683 ■ *Web:* www.discoverfinancial.com					
ExxonMobil Credit Card Services PO Box 530962	Atlanta	GA	30353	800-344-4355	518-3104*
**Fax Area Code:* 678 ■ *TF:* 800-344-4355 ■ *Web:* www.exxonmobilecard.com					
GE Capital Card Services PO Box 276	Dayton	OH	45401	800-333-1071	
TF: 800-844-6543 ■ *Web:* www.onlinecreditcenter5.com					
Household Retail Services USA Churman's Corporate Ctr 90 Christiana Rd	New Castle	DE	19720	302-327-2400	433-5975*
**Fax Area Code:* 800 ■ *TF:* 800-695-6950					
Intersections Inc 14901 Bogle Dr	Chantilly	VA	20151	703-488-6100	488-6223
NASDAQ: INTX ■ *TF:* 800-695-7536 ■ *Web:* www.intersections.com					
iPayment Inc 40 Burton Hills Blvd Suite 415	Nashville	TN	37215	615-665-1858	665-8434
NASDAQ: IPMT ■ *TF Cust Svc:* 800-324-9825 ■ *Web:* www.ipaymentinc.com					
Macy's Credit Services 5300 Kings Island Dr	Mason	OH	45040	513-459-1500	573-3132*
**Fax:* Cust Svc ■ *TF Cust Svc:* 800-743-6229					
MasterCard Inc 2000 Purchase St	Purchase	NY	10577	914-249-2000	249-4135*
NYSE: MA ■ **Fax:* Hum Res ■ *TF:* 800-247-4623 ■ *Web:* www.mastercard.com					
Rewards Network 2 N Riverside Plaza Suite 950	Chicago	IL	60606	312-521-6767	521-6768
AMEX: IRN ■ *TF:* 800-841-7102 ■ *Web:* www.rewardsnetwork.com					
Saks Inc 3455 Hwy 80 W	Jackson	MS	39209	601-968-4400	592-2925
TF: 800-443-6856					
Shell Credit Card 4300 Westown Pkwy	West Des Moines	IA	50266	877-236-5153	226-4031*
**Fax Area Code:* 515 ■ *TF:* 877-236-5153					
TNS Merchant & Credit Card Services 1939 Roland Clarke Pl	Reston	VA	20191	703-453-8338	453-8460
TF: 800-240-2824 ■ *Web:* www.tnsi.com					
Vesta Corp 11950 SW Garden PL	Portland	OR	97223	503-790-2500	790-2525
Web: www.trustvesta.com					
Visa International PO Box 8999	San Francisco	CA	94128	650-432-3200	
TF: 800-847-2911 ■ *Web:* www.visa.com					
Wright Express Corp 97 Darling Ave	South Portland	ME	04106	207-773-8171	828-5181
NYSE: WXS ■ *TF:* 800-761-7181 ■ *Web:* www.wrightexpress.com					

219 CREDIT & FINANCING - COMMERCIAL

SEE ALSO Banks - Commercial & Savings p. 1368; Credit & Financing - Consumer p. 1581

				Phone	Fax
Advanta Corp Welsh McKean Rd PO Box 844	Spring House	PA	19477	215-657-4000	444-6121
NASDAQ: ADVNA ■ *TF:* 877-250-6245 ■ *Web:* www.advanta.com					
Advanta Leasing Services 40 E Clementon Rd	Gibbsboro	NJ	08026	800-255-0022	782-1110*
**Fax Area Code:* 856 ■ *Web:* www.advantalease.com					
AFCO Credit Corp 110 William St 29th Fl	New York	NY	10038	212-401-4400	401-4436
TF: 800-288-2313 ■ *Web:* www.mellon.com/insurancefinancing					
Agricredit Acceptance LLC 8001 Birchwood Ct Suite C PO Box 2000	Johnston	IA	50131	515-251-2800	334-5825
TF: 800-873-2474 ■ *Web:* www.agricredit.com					
Amada Capital Corp 7025 Firestone Blvd	Buena Park	CA	90621	714-739-2111	739-4099
TF: 800-626-6612 ■ *Web:* amadacapital.com					
American Capital Strategies Ltd 2 Bethesda Metro Ctr 14th Fl	Bethesda	MD	20814	301-951-6122	654-6714
NASDAQ: ACAS ■ *Web:* www.american-capital.com					
American Express Credit Corp 301 N Walnut St 1 Christina Centre Suite 1002	Wilmington	DE	19801	302-594-3350	571-8073
TF: 800-525-5450 ■ *Web:* www.axpcp.com					
Arkansas Capital Corp Group 200 S Commerce St Suite 400	Little Rock	AR	72201	501-374-9247	374-9425
TF: 800-216-7237 ■ *Web:* www.arcapital.com					
ATEL Capital Group 600 California St 6th Fl	San Francisco	CA	94108	415-989-8800	989-3796
TF: 800-543-2835 ■ *Web:* www.atel.com					
Automotive Finance Corp (AFC) 13085 Hamilton Crossing Blvd	Carmel	IN	46032	317-815-9645	815-9650
TF: 888-335-6675 ■ *Web:* www.afcdealer.com					
AutoStar 180 Glastonbury Blvd Suite 201	Glastonbury	CT	06033	860-815-5900	815-5901
Web: www.autostar.com					
Bank of America Business Capital 200 Glastonbury Blvd	Glastonbury	CT	06033	860-659-3200	657-7768
TF: 866-287-4098 ■ *Web:* www.bofabusinesscapital.com					
Bank of America Leasing & Capital Group 555 California St 4th Fl MC CA5-705-04-01	San Francisco	CA	94104	415-765-7300	765-7353*
**Fax:* Hum Res					
Bank of America Leasing Corp 2059 Northlake Pkwy 4th Fl	Tucker	GA	30084	770-270-8400	270-8404
Bombardier Capital Group 261 Mountain View Dr	Colchester	VT	05446	802-654-8100	654-8430*
**Fax:* Sales ■ *TF:* 800-525-5871 ■ *Web:* www.bcgroup.com					
BTM Capital Corp 111 Huntington Ave	Boston	MA	02199	617-573-9000	345-5153
TF: 800-343-6597 ■ *Web:* www.btmcapital.com					
Business Loan Express 645 Madison Ave 19th Fl	New York	NY	10022	212-751-5626	888-3949
TF: 800-690-9089 ■ *Web:* www.blxonline.com					
Capital Lease Funding Inc 1065 Ave of the Americas 19th Fl	New York	NY	10018	212-217-6300	217-6301
NYSE: LSE ■ *Web:* www.caplease.com					
Capital Trust Inc 410 Park Ave 14th Fl	New York	NY	10022	212-655-0220	655-0044
NYSE: CT ■ *Web:* www.capitaltrust.com					
CDC Small Business Finance Corp 2448 Historic Decatur Rd Suite 200	San Diego	CA	92106	619-291-3594	291-6954
TF: 800-611-5170 ■ *Web:* www.cdcloans.com					
Century Business Credit Corp 119 W 40th St 10th Fl	New York	NY	10018	212-703-3500	703-3520
TF: 800-883-3539					
Church Loans & Investment Trust PO Box 8203	Amarillo	TX	79114	806-358-3666	358-1430
TF: 800-692-1111 ■ *Web:* www.churchloans.com					
CIT Group Inc 1 CIT Dr	Livingston	NJ	07039	973-740-5000	
Web: www.cit.com					
CIT Group Inc 505 5th Ave	New York	NY	10017	212-771-0505	382-6871
NYSE: CIT ■ *Web:* www.cit.com					
CitiCapital 450 Mamaroneck Ave	Harrison	NY	10528	914-899-7000	
TF: 800-227-6766 ■ *Web:* www.citicapital.com					
CNH Capital 100 S Saunders Rd Suite 200	Lake Forest	IL	60045	847-735-9200	
Web: www.casecapital.com					
Comerica Leasing Corp 29201 Telegraph Rd 2nd Fl	Southfield	MI	48034	248-948-2950	948-2995
Comfort Financial Services PO Box 1140	Evansville	IN	47706	866-866-1331	866-1334
Web: www.comfortfinancial.com					
Connell Equipment Leasing Co 1 Connell Dr	Berkeley Heights	NJ	07922	908-673-3700	673-3800
Web: www.connellco.com/CEL.htm					
Connell Finance Co Inc 100 Connell Dr Suite 4000	Berkeley Heights	NJ	07922	908-673-3700	673-3800
TF: 800-233-3240 ■ *Web:* www.connellco.com/CFC.htm					
Connell Technologies Co LLC 350 Lindbergh Ave	Livermore	CA	94550	925-455-6790	455-6791
TF: 888-301-0300 ■ *Web:* www.connellco.com/CTL.htm					
ContiInvestments LLC 277 Park Ave	New York	NY	10172	212-207-5142	207-5181
Web: www.contigroup.com/2004_business_ci.html					
Cooperative Finance Assn Inc 10100 N Ambassador Dr Suite 315 PO Box 901532	Kansas City	MO	64190	816-214-4200	214-4221
TF: 877-835-5232 ■ *Web:* www.cfafs.com					
Dana Commercial Credit Corp 6201 Trust Dr	Holland	OH	43528	419-866-7256	
Web: dcc.com					
De Lage Landen Financial Services 1111 Old Eagle School Rd	Wayne	PA	19087	610-386-5000	386-5840
TF: 800-669-9441 ■ *Web:* www.delagelandenus.com					
Deere John Credit Co 6400 NW 86th St	Johnston	IA	50131	515-267-3000	267-4579
TF: 800-275-5322 ■ *Web:* www.deere.com/en_US/jdc					
Dexia CLF 445 Park Ave 7th Fl	New York	NY	10022	212-515-7000	753-5522
Web: www.dexia.com					
Edison Capital 18101 Von Karman Ave Suite 1700	Irvine	CA	92612	949-757-2400	
TF: 800-241-8101					
Farm Credit Leasing 5500 Wayzata Blvd Colonnade Bldg Suite 1600	Minneapolis	MN	55416	763-797-7400	797-3555
TF: 800-328-8863 ■ *Web:* www.fcleasing.com					
Farm Credit Services of Mid-America 1601 UPS Dr	Louisville	KY	40223	502-420-3700	420-3823
TF: 888-444-3276 ■ *Web:* www.farmcredit.com					
Financial Federal Corp 733 3rd Ave 24th Fl	New York	NY	10017	212-599-8000	286-5885
NYSE: FIF ■ *TF:* 800-480-1003 ■ *Web:* www.financialfederal.com					

Company	City	State	Zip	Phone	Fax
First Community Financial Corp 4000 N Central Ave Suite 100 — *TF:* 800-242-3232 ■ *Web:* www.fcfinancial.com	Phoenix	AZ	85012	602-265-7714	265-6827
First Hawaiian Leasing Inc 1580 Kapiolani Blvd PO Box 1240	Honolulu	HI	96807	808-943-4905	943-4975
First South FarmCredit 713 S Pear Orchard Rd Suite 102 — *TF:* 800-955-1722 ■ *Web:* www.firstsouthfarmcredit.com	Ridgeland	MS	39157	601-977-8353	977-8358
Ford Motor Credit Co 1 American Rd PO Box 1732 — *TF:* 800-727-7000 ■ *Web:* www.fordcredit.com	Dearborn	MI	48121	313-322-3000	323-2959
Frost Capital Group 1010 Lamar St Suite 700	Houston	TX	77002	713-759-9070	388-7551
GATX Corp 500 W Monroe St — *NYSE: GMT* ■ **Fax:* Hum Res ■ *TF:* 800-525-4289 ■ *Web:* www.gatx.com	Chicago	IL	60661	312-621-6200	621-6665*
GATX Specialty Finance 4 Embarcadero Ctr Suite 2200 — *TF:* 800-227-4289 ■ *Web:* www.gatx.com	San Francisco	CA	94111	415-955-3200	955-3415
GE Capital Auto Financial Services 540 W Northwest Hwy — **Fax Area Code:* 800 ■ **Fax:* Cust Svc ■ *TF Cust Svc:* 800-488-5208 ■ *Web:* www.ge.com/capital/auto	Barrington	IL	60010	847-277-4000	704-6974*
GE Capital Corp 260 Long Ridge Rd — **Fax:* PR ■ *Web:* www.gecapital.com	Stamford	CT	06927	203-357-4000	357-6226*
GE Capital Public Finance 8400 Normandale Lake Blvd Suite 470 — *TF:* 800-346-3164 ■ *Web:* www.cefcorp.com/publicfinance	Minneapolis	MN	55437	952-897-5649	897-5601
GE Capital Small Business Finance 635 Maryville Ctr Dr Suite 120 — **Fax:* Mktg ■ *TF:* 800-447-2025 ■ *Web:* www.ge.com/capital/smallbiz	Saint Louis	MO	63141	314-205-3500	205-3698*
GE Commercial Distribution Finance 2625 S Plaza Dr Suite 201 — *TF:* 800-289-4488 ■ *Web:* www.gecdf.com	Tempe	AZ	85282	480-449-7100	829-3963
GE Commercial Equipment Financing 44 Old Ridgebury Rd — **Fax Area Code:* 888 ■ *TF:* 800-937-4322 ■ *Web:* www.cefcorp.com/commequip	Danbury	CT	06810	203-796-1000	301-7958*
GE Commercial Finance 260 Long Ridge Rd — **Fax Area Code:* 914 ■ *Web:* www.gecommercialfinance.com	Stamford	CT	06927	203-357-4000	335-8287*
GE Commercial Finance Real Estate 292 Long Ridge Rd — *Web:* usa.gerealestate.com	Stamford	CT	06927	203-961-5400	357-4475
GE Healthcare Financail Services 500 W Monroe — *TF:* 800-598-6201 ■ *Web:* www.gehealthcarefinance.com	Chicago	IL	60661	312-441-7705	441-7770
GE Vendor Financial Services 10 Riverview Dr — *TF:* 800-876-2033 ■ *Web:* www.ge.com/capital/vendor	Danbury	CT	06810	203-749-6000	
Green Tree Servicing LLC 345 Saint Peter St Suite 600 — **Fax:* Hum Res ■ *TF:* 800-423-9527 ■ *Web:* www.gtservicing.com	Saint Paul	MN	55102	651-293-3400	293-3622*
Greystone Metro Financial LP 8144 Walnut Hill Ln Suite 100 — *TF:* 800-327-2274 ■ *Web:* www.metrofinancial.com	Dallas	TX	75221	214-363-4557	987-7381
IBM Credit Corp 1 N Castle Dr	Armonk	NY	10504	914-499-1900	
iStar Financial Inc 1114 Ave of the Americas 39th Fl — *NYSE: SFI* ■ *Web:* www.istarfinancial.com	New York	NY	10036	212-930-9400	930-9494
John Deere Credit Co 6400 NW 86th St — *TF:* 800-275-5322 ■ *Web:* www.deere.com/en_US/jdc	Johnston	IA	50131	515-267-3000	267-4579
Key Equipment Finance 1000 S McCaslin Blvd — *TF:* 888-301-6238 ■ *Web:* www.kefonline.com	Superior	CO	80027	720-304-1500	
Koch Financial Corp 17767 N Perimeter Dr Suite 101 — *TF:* 866-545-2327 ■ *Web:* www.kochfinancial.com	Scottsdale	AZ	85255	480-419-3600	419-3603
Kraus-Anderson Capital Inc 523 S 8th St Suite 523 — *TF:* 888-547-3983 ■ *Web:* www.krausanderson.com/ka-capital.html	Minneapolis	MN	55404	612-305-2934	305-2932
M & I Equipment Finance Co 250 E Wisconsin Ave Suite 1400 — **Fax:* Mktg ■ *TF:* 800-558-9840 ■ *Web:* www.micorp.com	Milwaukee	WI	53202	414-272-2374	272-1765*
MarCap Corp 200 W Jackson Blvd Suite 2000 — *TF:* 800-621-1677 ■ *Web:* www.marcapcorp.com	Chicago	IL	60606	312-641-0233	425-2441
Marquette Commercial Finance Inc 801 Cherry St Suite 3400 — *TF:* 800-711-7557 ■ *Web:* www.marquettecommercial.com	Fort Worth	TX	76102	817-258-6000	258-6107
Marquette Financial Cos 60 S 6th St Suite 3800 — *Web:* www.marquette.com	Minneapolis	MN	55402	612-661-3880	
Medallion Financial Corp 437 Madison Ave 38th Fl — *NASDAQ: TAXI* ■ **Fax:* PR ■ *TF:* 877-633-2554 ■ *Web:* www.medallionfinancial.com	New York	NY	10022	212-328-2100	328-2195*
MicroFinancial Inc 10-M Commerce Way — *AMEX: MFI* ■ *TF:* 800-843-5327 ■ *Web:* www.microfinancial.com	Woburn	MA	01801	781-994-4800	994-4710
NAFCO 3907 Aero Pl Suite 1 — *TF:* 800-999-3712 ■ *Web:* www.airloans.com	Lakeland	FL	33811	863-644-8463	646-1671
National Rural Utilities Cooperative Finance Corp 2201 Cooperative Way Woodland Pk — *TF:* 800-424-2954 ■ *Web:* www.nrucfc.org	Herndon	VA	20171	703-709-6700	709-6777
Navistar Financial Corp 425 N Martingale Rd Suite 1800 — *TF:* 800-233-9121	Schaumburg	IL	60173	630-753-4000	
New York Business Development Corp 50 Beaver St 6th Fl — *TF:* 800-923-2504 ■ *Web:* www.nybdc.com	Albany	NY	12207	518-463-2268	463-0240
Orix Financial Services Inc 600 Town Park Ln — *TF:* 866-674-9112 ■ *Web:* www.orixfinancialservices.com	Kennesaw	GA	30144	770-970-6000	970-6014
ORIX USA Corp 1717 Main St Suite 900 — *Web:* www.orix.com	Dallas	TX	75201	214-237-2000	237-2018
PACCAR Financial Corp 777 106th Ave NE — **Fax:* Mktg ■ *Web:* www.paccarfinancial.com	Bellevue	WA	98004	425-468-7100	468-8220*
PDS Gaming Corp 6280 Annie Oakley Dr — *TF:* 800-479-3612 ■ *Web:* www.pdsgaming.com	Las Vegas	NV	89120	702-736-0700	740-8692
Philip Morris Capital Corp 225 High Ridge Rd Suite 300-W — **Fax Area Code:* 914 ■ *Web:* www.philipmorriscapitalcorp.com	Stamford	CT	06902	203-348-1350	335-8287*
Phoenix American Inc 2401 Kerner Blvd — *TF:* 866-895-5050 ■ *Web:* www.phxa.com	San Rafael	CA	94901	415-485-4500	485-4813
Phoenix Growth Capital Corp 2401 Kerner Blvd — *TF:* 866-895-5050 ■ *Web:* www.phxa.com	San Rafael	CA	94901	415-485-4500	485-4813
Phoenix Leasing Inc 2401 Kerner Blvd — *TF:* 866-895-5050 ■ *Web:* www.phxa.com	San Rafael	CA	94901	415-485-4500	485-4813
Pitney Bowes Credit Corp 27 Waterview Dr — **Fax:* Cust Svc ■ *TF:* 800-243-9506	Shelton	CT	06484	203-922-4000	922-4111*
PMC Commercial Trust 17950 Preston Rd Suite 600 — *AMEX: PCC* ■ *TF:* 800-486-3223 ■ *Web:* www.pmctrust.com	Dallas	TX	75252	972-349-3200	349-3265
PNC Leasing LLC 249 5th Ave — *TF:* 800-762-6260 ■ *Web:* www.pnc.com	Pittsburgh	PA	15222	412-762-4848	762-7575
Premium Financing Specialists Inc 427 W 12th St Suite 100 — *TF:* 800-838-2350 ■ *Web:* web1.premiumfinance.com	Kansas City	MO	64105	816-627-0500	627-0502
Presidential Realty Corp 180 S Broadway — *AMEX: PDL/A* ■ *TF:* 800-948-2977	White Plains	NY	10605	914-948-1300	948-1327
Private Export Funding Corp 280 Park Ave 4th Fl W — *Web:* www.pefco.com	New York	NY	10017	212-916-0300	286-0304
Republic Financial Corp 3300 S Parker Rd Suite 500 — *Web:* www.republic-financial.com	Aurora	CO	80014	303-751-3501	751-4777
Reyna Capital Corp 1 Reynolds Way	Kettering	OH	45430	937-485-2955	485-2569
SBC Capital Services 2000 W SBC Center Dr — *TF:* 800-346-8082	Hoffman Estates	IL	60196	847-290-5000	290-9290
Siemens Financial Services Inc 170 Wood Ave S — *TF:* 800-327-4443 ■ *Web:* www.siemensfinancial.com	Iselin	NJ	08830	732-590-6500	476-3417
Snap-on Credit LLC 950 Technology Way Suite 301 — **Fax Area Code:* 877 ■ *TF:* 877-777-8455 ■ *Web:* www.snaponcredit.com	Libertyville	IL	60048	847-782-7700	777-6866*
Systran Financial Services Div Textron Financial Corp 4949 SW Meadows Rd Suite 500 — *TF:* 800-824-2075 ■ *Web:* www.textronfinancial.com/systran	Oswego	OR	97035	503-675-5700	675-5794
Textron Financial Corp 40 Westminster St — *Web:* www.textronfinancial.com	Providence	RI	02903	401-621-4200	621-5037
Textron Financial Corp Systran Financial Services Div 4949 SW Meadows Rd Suite 500 — *TF:* 800-824-2075 ■ *Web:* www.textronfinancial.com/systran	Oswego	OR	97035	503-675-5700	675-5794
Universal Premium Acceptance Corp (UPAC) 8245 Nieman Rd Suite 100 — *TF:* 800-877-7848 ■ *Web:* www.upac.com	Lenexa	KS	66214	913-894-6150	894-4988
US Bancorp Equipment Finance Inc 13010 SW 68th Pkwy — *TF:* 800-253-3468	Portland	OR	97223	503-797-0200	234-4210
Verizon Credit Inc 201 N Franklin St Suite 3300 — *TF:* 800-483-7988 ■ *Web:* www22.verizon.com/credit	Tampa	FL	33602	813-229-6000	229-4883
Wachovia Capital Finance 1133 Ave of the Americas — **Fax:* Mktg ■ *TF:* 800-223-6352 ■ *Web:* www.wachovia.com/corp_inst	New York	NY	10036	212-840-2000	545-4555*
Wells Fargo Business Credit 109 S 7th St — *TF:* 800-634-6224	Minneapolis	MN	55402	612-673-8500	341-2372
Wells Fargo Equipment Finance Inc 733 Marquette Ave Investors Bldg Suite 700 — *TF:* 800-322-6220	Minneapolis	MN	55402	612-667-9876	667-9711
Wells Fargo Financial Leasing Inc PO Box 4943 — **Fax Area Code:* 866 ■ *TF:* 800-451-3322 ■ *Web:* www.wellsfargoleasing.com	Syracuse	NY	13221	800-451-3322	887-1950*
Wells Fargo Foothill Inc 2450 Colorado Ave Suite 3000W — *TF:* 800-535-1811 ■ *Web:* www.wffoothill.com	Santa Monica	CA	90404	310-453-7300	453-7474
Winthrop Resources Corp 11100 Wayzata Blvd Suite 800 — *TF:* 800-843-8264	Minnetonka	MN	55305	952-936-0226	936-0201
Xerox Financial Services Inc 800 Long Ridge Rd — **Fax Area Code:* 972 ■ *TF:* 800-822-2502	Stamford	CT	06904	203-968-3000	420-3402*

220 CREDIT & FINANCING - CONSUMER

SEE ALSO Banks - Commercial & Savings p. 1368; Credit & Financing - Commercial p. 1580; Credit Unions p. 1582

Company	City	State	Zip	Phone	Fax
American General Financial Services 601 NW 2nd St — *TF:* 800-457-3741 ■ *Web:* www.agfinance.com	Evansville	IN	47701	812-424-8031	468-5682
AmeriCredit Corp 801 Cherry St Suite 3900 — *NYSE: ACF* ■ *TF:* 800-644-2297 ■ *Web:* www.americredit.com	Fort Worth	TX	76102	817-302-7000	302-7934
Ameristar Financial 1795 N Butterfield Rd — *TF:* 800-784-1535 ■ *Web:* www.ameristarfinancial.com	Libertyville	IL	60048	847-247-2600	247-2585
AutoNation Financial Services 110 SE 6th St — *TF:* 888-825-8929 ■ *Web:* www.autonation.com	Fort Lauderdale	FL	33301	954-769-7000	769-8994
BB & T Sales Finance PO Box 1793 — **Fax Area Code:* 703 ■ *TF:* 877-398-4441 ■ *Web:* www.bbandt.com/dealerservices	Charleston	WV	25326	877-398-4441	533-6327*
Central Financial Acceptance Corp 1900 S Main St — *TF:* 800-550-2830	Los Angeles	CA	90007	213-763-4992	763-4895
Chrysler Financial Corp LLC 27777 Franklin Rd — **Fax Area Code:* 877 ■ *TF Cust Svc:* 800-556-8172 ■ *Web:* www.chryslerfinancial.com	Southfield	MI	48034	248-427-6424	230-1382*
CitiFinancial 300 St Paul Pl — *Web:* www.citifinancial.com	Baltimore	MD	21202	410-332-3000	332-3489
CitiFinancial Auto PO Box 1437 — *TF:* 800-486-1750 ■ *Web:* www.citifinancialauto.com	Eden Prairie	MN	55440	952-944-4520	944-0034
Collegiate Funding Services LLC 10304 Spotsylvania Ave Suite 100 — *TF:* 800-762-6441 ■ *Web:* www.cfsloans.com	Fredericksburg	VA	22408	540-374-1600	374-1981
Comfort Financial Services PO Box 1140 — *Web:* www.comfortfinancial.com	Evansville	IN	47706	866-866-1331	866-1334
Credit Acceptance Corp 25505 W 12 Mile Rd — *TF:* 800-634-1506 ■ *Web:* www.credaccept.com	Southfield	MI	48034	248-353-2700	827-8532
Deere John Credit Co 6400 NW 86th St — *TF:* 800-275-5322 ■ *Web:* www.deere.com/en_US/jdc	Johnston	IA	50131	515-267-3000	267-4579
EduCap Inc 1676 International Dr Suite 501 — *TF Cust Svc:* 800-865-3276 ■ *Web:* www.loantolearn.com	McLean	VA	22102	703-442-3000	442-3088
Educational Lending Group Inc 12680 High Bluff Dr Suite 310 — *TF Cust Svc:* 866-311-8060 ■ *Web:* www.edlending.com	San Diego	CA	92130	858-793-4151	617-6079
Finance Factors Ltd 1164 Bishop St — *TF:* 800-648-7136 ■ *Web:* www.financefactors.com	Honolulu	HI	96813	808-548-3311	548-5148
First Investors Financial Services Group Inc 675 Bering Dr Suite 710 — *TF:* 800-722-9112	Houston	TX	77057	713-977-2600	260-0068
Ford Motor Credit Co 1 American Rd PO Box 1732 — *TF:* 800-727-7000 ■ *Web:* www.fordcredit.com	Dearborn	MI	48121	313-322-3000	323-2959
Franklin Credit Management Corp 6 Harrison St — *NASDAQ: FCMC* ■ *TF:* 800-255-5897 ■ *Web:* www.franklincredit.com	New York	NY	10013	212-925-8745	925-1971
GE Capital Auto Financial Services 540 W Northwest Hwy — **Fax Area Code:* 800 ■ **Fax:* Cust Svc ■ *TF Cust Svc:* 800-488-5208 ■ *Web:* www.ge.com/capital/auto	Barrington	IL	60010	847-277-4000	704-6974*
GE Capital Corp 260 Long Ridge Rd — **Fax:* PR ■ *Web:* www.gecapital.com	Stamford	CT	06927	203-357-4000	357-6226*
GE Consumer Finance 260 Long Ridge Rd — *Web:* www.geconsumerfinance.com	Stamford	CT	06927	203-357-4000	
General Motors Acceptance Corp (GMAC) 200 Renaissance Ctr — *TF:* 800-200-4622 ■ *Web:* www.gmacfs.com	Detroit	MI	48265	313-556-5000	556-5108
General Motors Acceptance Corp Canada (GMAC Canada) 3300 Bloor St W Suite 2800 — *TF:* 800-616-4622 ■ *Web:* www.gmcanada.com	Toronto	ON	M8X2X5	416-234-6600	234-6614
GMAC Canada (General Motors Acceptance Corp Canada) 3300 Bloor St W Suite 2800 — *TF:* 800-616-4622 ■ *Web:* www.gmcanada.com	Toronto	ON	M8X2X5	416-234-6600	234-6614
Green Tree Servicing LLC 345 Saint Peter St Suite 600 — **Fax:* Hum Res ■ *TF:* 800-423-9527 ■ *Web:* www.gtservicing.com	Saint Paul	MN	55102	651-293-3400	293-3622*
Harley-Davidson Financial Services 222 W Adams St Suite 200 — *TF:* 800-538-3150	Chicago	IL	60606	312-368-9501	368-4376
Household Finance Corp 2700 Sanders Rd — *Web:* www.householdfinance.com	Prospect Heights	IL	60070	847-564-5000	205-7506
HSBC Finance Corp 2700 Sanders Rd — *Web:* www.hsbcusa.com	Prospect Heights	IL	60070	847-564-5000	205-7452
John Deere Credit Co 6400 NW 86th St — *TF:* 800-275-5322 ■ *Web:* www.deere.com/en_US/jdc	Johnston	IA	50131	515-267-3000	267-4579
Key Corporate Banking & Finance 601 Oakmont Ln Suite 110 — *TF:* 800-877-2860 ■ *Web:* www.key.com	Westmont	IL	60559	630-655-7100	
Mercedes-Benz Credit Corp 2050 Roanoke Rd — *Web:* www.mbcredit.com	Westlake	TX	76262	800-654-6222	873-5468
National Auto Finance Co 12850 W Gran Bay Pkwy — **Fax Area Code:* 877 ■ *TF:* 800-856-6190	Jacksonville	FL	32258	904-886-5200	375-2244*
Nellie Mae Corp 50 Braintree Hill Park Suite 300 — **Fax Area Code:* 800 ■ *TF Cust Svc:* 800-367-8848 ■ *Web:* www.nelliemae.com	Braintree	MA	02184	781-849-1325	338-5626*
Nelnet Inc 121 S 13th St Suite 201 — *NYSE: NNI* ■ *TF:* 888-486-4722 ■ *Web:* www.nelnet.net	Lincoln	NE	68508	402-458-2370	458-2399
Nicholas Financial Inc 2454 McMullen Booth Rd Bldg C — *NASDAQ: NICK* ■ *TF:* 800-237-2721 ■ *Web:* www.nicholasfinancial.com	Clearwater	FL	33759	727-726-0763	726-2140

Phone | Fax

Nissan Motor Acceptance Corp 8900 Freeport Pkwy Irving TX 75063 214-596-4000 607-7658*
*Fax Area Code: 972 ■ TF: 800-842-4949

Prestige Financial 1420 S 500 West Salt Lake City UT 84115 801-844-2100 219-8266*
*Fax Area Code: 800 ■ TF: 866-737-2733 ■ Web: www.prestige-financial.com

Prime Rate Premium Finance Corp
2141 Enterprise Dr PO Box 100507 Florence SC 29501 843-669-0937 677-9850*
*Fax Area Code: 800 ■ TF Cust Svc: 800-777-7458 ■ Web: www.primeratepfc.com

Providian Financial Corp 201 Mission St San Francisco CA 94105 415-543-0404 278-6028*
*Fax: Hum Res ■ TF: 800-525-7557 ■ Web: www.providian.com

Regional Acceptance Corp 1424 E Fire Tower Rd Greenville NC 27858 252-321-7700 353-1852
TF: 877-999-7708 ■ Web: www.regionalacceptance.com

Republic Finance LLC 8427 Kellwood Ave Baton Rouge LA 70806 225-927-0005 927-1063

Sallie Mae 12061 Bluemont Way Reston VA 20190 703-810-3000 848-1949*
*Fax Area Code: 800 ■ TF Cust Svc: 888-272-5543 ■ Web: www.salliemae.com

Search Financial Services LP 32600 Five-Mile Rd Livonia MI 48154 734-425-8774 522-2866*
*Fax: PR

Sears Roebuck Acceptance Corp 3711 Kennett Pike Greenville DE 19807 302-434-3100 434-3150
TF: 800-729-7722 ■ Web: www.sracweb.com

Security Finance Corp 181 Security Pl Spartanburg SC 29307 864-582-8193
TF: 800-395-8195 ■ Web: www.security-finance.com

Select Portfolio Servicing Inc PO Box 65250 Salt Lake City UT 84165 801-293-1883
TF: 800-258-8602 ■ Web: www.spservicing.com

SLM Corp 12061 Bluemont Way Reston VA 20190 703-810-3000 984-5046
NYSE: SLM ■ TF Cust Svc: 888-272-5543 ■ Web: www.salliemae.com

Sotheby's Financial Services Inc 1334 York Ave New York NY 10021 212-894-1140 894-1141

Student Loan Corp 701 E 60th St N PO Box 6191 Sioux Falls SD 57117 605-331-0821 357-2013*
NYSE: STU ■ *Fax: Cust Svc ■ TF: 800-967-2400 ■ Web: www.studentloan.com

Toyota Motor Credit Corp 19001 S Western Ave Torrance CA 90509 310-787-1310 787-3505
TF Cust Svc: 800-392-2968

TranSouth Financial Corp 112 Cherokee Rd Florence SC 29504 843-669-4111 678-3730

United Finance Co 515 E Burnside St Portland OR 97214 503-232-5153 238-6453
Web: www.unitedfinance.com

United Student Aid Funds Inc DBA USA Funds 11100 USA Pkwy Fishers IN 46037 317-849-6510 594-1974*
*Fax: Hum Res ■ TF: 800-824-7044 ■ Web: www.usafunds.org

USA Funds 11100 USA Pkwy Fishers IN 46037 317-849-6510 594-1974*
*Fax: Hum Res ■ TF: 800-824-7044 ■ Web: www.usafunds.org

Wachovia Education Finance 11000 White Rock Rd Rancho Cordova CA 85670 800-338-2243 631-5958*
*Fax Area Code: 916 ■ Web: www.educaid.com

Wells Fargo Education Financial Services PO Box 5185 Sioux Falls SD 57117 800-658-3567 456-0561
Web: www.wellsfargo.com

Wells Fargo Financial 800 Walnut St Des Moines IA 50309 515-243-2131 237-7138*
*Fax: Cust Svc ■ Web: financial.wellsfargo.com

Wells Fargo Financial Acceptance Inc 3101 W 69th St Edina MN 55435 952-920-9270 915-3874
TF: 888-346-4357 ■ Web: financial.wellsfargo.com

WFS Financial Inc 23 Pasteur Irvine CA 92618 949-727-1000 775-2886*
*Fax Area Code: 888 ■ TF: 800-289-8004 ■ Web: www.wfsfinancial.com

World Acceptance Corp PO Box 6429 Greenville SC 29606 864-298-9800 298-9810
NASDAQ: WRLD ■ Web: www.worldacceptance.com

World Omni Financial Corp 120 NW 12th Ave Deerfield Beach FL 33442 954-429-2200 429-2299
TF Cust Svc: 866-663-9663 ■ Web: www.worldomni.com

221 CREDIT REPORTING SERVICES

Phone | Fax

Coface Services North America Inc 900 Chapel St New Haven CT 06510 203-781-3800 929-7779*
*Fax Area Code: 800 ■ TF: 800-929-8374 ■ Web: www.coface-usa.com

Equifax Credit Marketing Services
1525 Windward Concourse Alpharetta GA 30005 404-885-8000 885-8030
TF: 888-869-8413 ■ Web: www.equifax.com

Equifax Inc 1550 Peachtree St NW Atlanta GA 30309 404-885-8000 888-5043
NYSE: EFX ■ TF Sales: 888-202-4025 ■ Web: www.equifax.com

Experian Information Solutions Inc 475 Anton Blvd Costa Mesa CA 92626 714-830-7000
TF: 888-397-3742 ■ Web: www.experian.com

Experian Real Estate Services 4 Executive Campus Cherry Hill NJ 08002 856-532-6500 324-8864*
*Fax Area Code: 800 ■ TF: 800-248-0470 ■ Web: www.cbainfo.com

Fair Isaac Corp 901 Marquette Ave Suite 3200 Minneapolis MN 55402 612-758-5200 758-5201
NYSE: FIC ■ TF Cust Svc: 877-434-7877 ■ Web: www.fairisaac.com

Federal Financial Network 5860 Canton Center Rd Suite 380 Canton MI 48187 734-357-0200 357-0222
Web: icrservices.com

Fitch Ratings Inc 1 State St Plaza New York NY 10004 212-908-0500
TF: 800-753-4824 ■ Web: www.fitchratings.com

Kroll Factual Data Inc 5200 Hahns Peak Dr Loveland CO 80538 970-663-5700 929-3297*
*Fax Area Code: 800 ■ TF: 800-929-3400 ■ Web: www.factualdata.com

Merchants Credit Bureau 955 Green St Augusta GA 30901 706-823-6246 823-6253
TF: 800-426-5265 ■ Web: www.mcbusa.com

Moody's Corp 99 Church St New York NY 10007 212-553-0300 553-5376
NYSE: MCO ■ Web: www.moodys.com

Standard & Poor's Ratings Services 55 Water St New York NY 10041 212-438-2000 438-6738*
*Fax: Hum Res ■ Web: www.standardandpoors.com

Tele-Track 155 Technology Pkwy Suite 800 Norcross GA 30092 770-449-8809 449-6647
TF: 800-729-6981 ■ Web: www.teletrack.com

TransUnion LLC 555 W Adams St Chicago IL 60661 312-258-1717
TF: 800-916-8800 ■ Web: www.transunion.com

222 CREDIT UNIONS

Phone | Fax

Addison Avenue Federal Credit Union 3408 Hillview Ave Palo Alto CA 94304 877-233-4766 855-3703*
*Fax Area Code: 650 ■ *Fax: Hum Res ■ Web: www.addisonavenue.com

AEDC Federal Credit Union
550 William Northern Blvd PO Box 1210 Tullahoma TN 37388 931-455-5441 454-1311
TF: 800-342-3086 ■ Web: www.aedcfcu.org

Affinity Federal Credit Union
73 Mountain View Blvd PO Box 621 Basking Ridge NJ 07920 908-860-7300
TF: 800-325-0808 ■ Web: www.affinityfcu.org

Alaska USA Federal Credit Union 4000 Credit Union Dr Anchorage AK 99503 907-563-4567 561-0773
TF: 800-525-9094 ■ Web: www.alaskausa.org

Allegacy Federal Credit Union 1691 Westbrook Plaza Dr Winston-Salem NC 27103 336-774-3400 844-6464*
*Fax Area Code: 800 ■ TF: 800-782-4670 ■ Web: www.allegacyfcu.org

America First Credit Union 1344 W 4675 South Riverdale UT 84405 801-627-0900 778-8447*
*Fax: Hum Res ■ TF: 800-999-3961 ■ Web: www.americafirst.com

American Airlines Employees Federal Credit Union
PO Box 155489 Fort Worth TX 76155 817-963-6000 963-6108
TF: 800-533-0035 ■ Web: www.aacreditunion.org

American Eagle Federal Credit Union 417 Main St East Hartford CT 06118 860-568-2020 568-1939
TF: 800-842-0145 ■ Web: www.americaneagle.org

Andrews Federal Credit Union PO Box 4000 Clinton MD 20735 301-702-5500 702-5330
TF: 800-487-5500 ■ Web: www.andrewsfcu.org

APCO Employees Credit Union 1608 7th Ave N Birmingham AL 35203 205-257-3601 257-3787
TF: 800-249-2726 ■ Web: www.apcocu.org

Phone | Fax

Arizona Federal Credit Union PO Box 60070 Phoenix AZ 85082 602-683-1000 683-1902
TF: 800-523-4603 ■ Web: www.azfcu.org

Atlanta Postal Credit Union 3900 Crown Rd Atlanta GA 30380 404-768-4126 768-0815*
*Fax: Loans ■ TF: 800-849-8431 ■ Web: www.apcu.com

Bank-Fund Staff Federal Credit Union PO Box 27755 Washington DC 20038 202-458-4300 522-1528
TF: 800-923-7328 ■ Web: www.bfsfcu.org

BECU (Boeing Employees' Credit Union) PO Box 97050 Seattle WA 98124 206-439-5700 439-5806*
*Fax: Mktg ■ TF: 800-233-2328 ■ Web: www.becu.org

Bellco First Federal Credit Union PO Box 6611 Greenwood Village CO 80155 303-689-7800 689-7942
TF: 800-235-5261 ■ Web: www.bellco.org

Bethpage Federal Credit Union 899 S Oyster Bay Rd Bethpage NY 11714 516-349-6700 349-6765
TF: 800-628-7070 ■ Web: www.bethpage.org

Boeing Employees' Credit Union (BECU) PO Box 97050 Seattle WA 98124 206-439-5700 439-5806*
*Fax: Mktg ■ TF: 800-233-2328 ■ Web: www.becu.org

California Credit Union The
3330 Cahuenga Blvd W Suite 115 Los Angeles CA 90068 818-291-6700 436-0255*
*Fax Area Code: 323 ■ TF: 800-334-8788 ■ Web: www.californiacu.org

Chartway Federal Credit Union 160 Newtown Rd Virginia Beach VA 23462 757-552-1000 671-7691*
*Fax: Hum Res ■ TF: 800-678-8765 ■ Web: www.chartway.com

Citizens Equity First Credit Union 5401 W Dirksen Pkwy Peoria IL 61607 309-633-7000 633-3621
TF: 800-633-7077 ■ Web: www.cefcu.com

Coastal Federal Credit Union 1000 St Albans Dr Raleigh NC 27609 919-420-8000
TF: 800-868-4262 ■ Web: www.coastalfcu.org

Community America Credit Union 9777 Ridge Dr Lenexa KS 66219 913-905-7000 905-7070
TF: 800-892-7957 ■ Web: www.cacu.com

Connecticut State Employees Credit Union 84 Wadsworth St Hartford CT 06106 860-249-4839 525-4077
Web: www.csecreditunion.com

Credit Union of Texas PO Box 517028 Dallas TX 75251 972-263-9497 301-1980
TF: 800-314-3828 ■ Web: www.cuoftexas.org

Dearborn Federal Credit Union 400 Town Center Dr Dearborn MI 48126 313-336-2700 322-8287
TF: 888-336-2700 ■ Web: secure.dfcufinancial.com

Delta Employees Credit Union PO Box 20541 Atlanta GA 30320 404-715-4725 677-4776
TF: 800-544-3328 ■ Web: www.deltacommunitycu.com

Desert Schools Federal Credit Union PO Box 2945 Phoenix AZ 85062 602-433-7000 335-3186
TF Mktg: 800-456-9171 ■ Web: www.desertschools.org

Digital Employees' Federal Credit Union
220 Donald Lynch Blvd Marlborough MA 01752 508-263-6700 263-6392
TF: 800-328-8797 ■ Web: www.dcu.org

Dow Chemical Employees' Credit Union 600 E Lyon Rd Midland MI 48640 989-835-7794 832-2622
TF: 800-835-7794 ■ Web: www.dcecu.org

Eastern Financial Florida Credit Union 3700 Lakeside Dr Miramar FL 33027 954-704-5000 704-5380
TF: 800-882-5007 ■ Web: www.effcu.org

Eastman Credit Union PO Box 1989 Kingsport TN 37662 423-229-8200 229-8249
TF: 800-999-2328 ■ Web: www.eastmancu.org

Educational Employees Credit Union PO Box 5242 Fresno CA 93755 559-437-7700 437-7914
TF: 800-538-3328 ■ Web: www.eecufresno.org

Eglin Federal Credit Union 838 Eglin Pkwy NE Fort Walton Beach FL 32547 850-862-0111 862-7120
TF: 800-367-6159 ■ Web: www.eglinfcu.org

Ent Federal Credit Union 7250 Campus Dr Colorado Springs CO 80920 719-574-1100 388-9065
TF: 800-525-9623 ■ Web: www.ent.com

ESL Federal Credit Union 100 Kings Hwy S Suite 1200 Rochester NY 14617 585-336-1000 336-1034
TF: 800-848-2265 ■ Web: www.esl.org

Fairwinds Federal Credit Union 3075 N Alafaya Trail Orlando FL 32826 407-277-5045 281-9216*
*Fax: Acctg ■ TF: 800-443-6887 ■ Web: www.fairwinds.org

First Community Credit Union 15715 Manchester Rd Ellisville MO 63011 636-386-8386 386-8373
TF: 800-843-0769 ■ Web: www.firstcommunity.com

Founders Federal Credit Union 607 N Main St Lancaster SC 29720 803-283-5900 283-5919
TF: 800-845-1614 ■ Web: www.foundersfcu.com

Georgia Telco Credit Union 1155 Peachtree St NE Suite 400 Atlanta GA 30309 404-874-1166 881-2950
TF: 800-533-2062 ■ Web: www.gatelco.org

Golden One Credit Union PO Box 15966 Sacramento CA 95852 916-732-2900 451-3053
TF: 877-465-3361 ■ Web: www.golden1.com

Government Employees Credit Union of El Paso
7227 Viscount Blvd El Paso TX 79925 915-778-9221 774-1798
TF: 800-772-4328 ■ Web: www.gecu-ep.org

GTE Federal Credit Union PO Box 172599 Tampa FL 33672 813-871-2690 414-8441
TF: 800-241-4120 ■ Web: www.gtefcu.org

HarborOne Credit Union 770 Oak St Brockton MA 02301 508-895-1000 895-1674
TF: 800-244-7592 ■ Web: www.harboronecu.com

Hudson Valley Federal Credit Union 159 Barnegat Rd Poughkeepsie NY 12601 845-463-3011 463-3613
TF: 800-468-3011 ■ Web: www.hvfcu.org

Kern Schools Federal Credit Union PO Box 9506 Bakersfield CA 93389 661-833-7900 833-7989
TF: 800-221-3311 ■ Web: www.ksfcu.com

KeyPoint Credit Union 2805 Bowers Ave Santa Clara CA 95051 408-731-4100 731-4485
TF: 888-255-3637 ■ Web: www.keypointcu.com

Kinecta Federal Credit Union 1440 Rosecrans Ave Manhattan Beach CA 90266 310-643-5400 643-5473*
*Fax: Hum Res ■ TF: 800-854-9846 ■ Web: kinecta.org

Langley Federal Credit Union 1055 W Mercury Blvd Hampton VA 23666 757-827-7200 825-7557
TF: 800-826-7490 ■ Web: www.langleyfcu.org

Lockheed Federal Credit Union 2340 Hollywood Way Burbank CA 91505 818-565-2020 846-4379
TF: 800-328-5328 ■ Web: www.lockheedfcu.org

MacDill Federal Credit Union 9927 Delaney Lake Dr Tampa FL 33619 813-837-2451 832-2080
TF: 800-839-6328 ■ Web: www.macdill.org

Mission Federal Credit Union 5785 Oberlin Dr Suite 333 San Diego CA 92121 858-524-2850 546-7637
TF: 800-500-6328 ■ Web: www.missionfcu.org

Mountain America Credit Union PO Box 9001 West Jordan UT 84084 801-325-6228 325-6395
TF: 800-748-4302 ■ Web: www.macu.com

Municipal Credit Union PO Box 3205 New York NY 10007 212-693-4900 416-7051
TF: 800-843-1867 ■ Web: www.nymcu.org

Navy Federal Credit Union PO Box 3000 Merrifield VA 22119 703-255-8500 206-4600
TF: 800-914-9494 ■ Web: www.navyfcu.org

Newport News Shipbuilding Employees Credit Union
3711 Huntington Ave Newport News VA 23607 757-928-8850 245-1019
TF: 800-928-8801 ■ Web: www.nnsecu.org

North Island Financial Credit Union 2300 Boswell Rd Chula Vista CA 91914 619-656-1600 656-4056
TF Cust Svc: 800-752-4419 ■ Web: www.myisland.com/nifcu

Northwest Federal Credit Union 200 Spring St Herndon VA 20170 703-709-8900 709-9510*
*Fax: Acctg ■ TF: 800-336-3384 ■ Web: www.northwestfcu.org

NuUnion Credit Union 501 S Capitol Ave Lansing MI 48933 517-267-7200 267-7095
TF: 800-937-7328 ■ Web: www.nuunion.org

Orange County Teachers Federal Credit Union
2115 N Broadway Santa Ana CA 92706 714-258-4000 258-4219
TF: 800-462-8328 ■ Web: www.octfcu.org

Pacific Service Federal Credit Union 2850 Shadelands Dr Walnut Creek CA 94598 925-296-6200 296-6209
TF: 888-858-6878 ■ Web: www.pacificservice.org

Patelco Credit Union 156 2nd St San Francisco CA 94105 415-442-6200 442-6248
TF: 800-358-8228 ■ Web: www.patelco.org

Pennsylvania State Employees Credit Union
1 Credit Union Pl Harrisburg PA 17110 717-234-8484 772-2272
TF: 800-237-7328 ■ Web: www.psecu.com

Pentagon Federal Credit Union 2930 Eisenhower Ave Alexandria VA 22314 800-247-5626 253-6589
Web: www.penfed.org

Police & Fire Federal Credit Union 901 Arch St Philadelphia PA 19107 215-931-0300 931-2926
TF: 800-228-8801 ■ Web: www.pffcu.org

Polish & Slavic Federal Credit Union 140 Greenpoint Ave Brooklyn NY 11222 718-383-6268 389-8210
TF: 800-297-2181 ■ Web: www.psfcu.com

	City	State	Zip	Phone	Fax
Portland Teachers Credit Union 2701 NW Vaughn Suite 800	Portland	OR	97210	503-228-7077	273-2698
TF: 800-527-3932 ■ *Web:* www.onpointcu.com					
Provident Central Credit Union 303 Twin Dolphin Dr	Redwood City	CA	94065	650-508-0300	508-7202
TF: 800-632-4600 ■ *Web:* www.providentcu.org					
Randolph-Brooks Federal Credit Union PO Box 2097	Universal City	TX	78148	210-945-3300	945-3764
TF: 800-580-3300 ■ *Web:* www.rbfcu.org					
Redstone Federal Credit Union 220 Wynn Dr NW	Huntsville	AL	35893	256-837-6110	722-3655*
**Fax:* Cust Svc ■ *TF:* 800-234-1234 ■ *Web:* www.redfcu.org					
SAFE Credit Union 3720 Madison Ave	North Highlands	CA	95660	916-979-7233	331-7125
TF: 800-733-7233 ■ *Web:* www.safecu.org					
San Antonio Federal Credit Union 6061 IH 10W	San Antonio	TX	78201	210-258-1414	258-1543
TF: 800-234-7228 ■ *Web:* www.sacu.com					
San Diego County Credit Union 6545 Sequence Dr	San Diego	CA	92121	877-732-2848	294-9320*
**Fax Area Code:* 619 ■ *Web:* www.sdccu.com					
Schools Financial Credit Union 5210 Madison Ave	Sacramento	CA	95841	916-569-5400	331-2242
TF: 800-962-0990 ■ *Web:* www.schools.org					
Security Service Federal Credit Union					
16211 La Cantera Pkwy	San Antonio	TX	78256	210-476-4000	444-3000
TF: 800-527-7328 ■ *Web:* www.ssfcu.org					
South Carolina Federal Credit Union PO Box 190012	North Charleston	SC	29419	843-797-8300	
TF: 800-845-0432 ■ *Web:* www.scfederal.org					
Space Coast Credit Union PO Box 419001	Melbourne	FL	32941	321-752-2222	723-3716
TF: 800-447-7228 ■ *Web:* www.sccu.com					
Star One Federal Credit Union 1306 Bordeaux Dr	Sunnyvale	CA	94089	408-543-5202	543-5203
TF: 800-552-1455 ■ *Web:* www.starone.org					
State Employees' Credit Union 1000 Wade Ave	Raleigh	NC	27605	919-839-5000	839-5476
TF: 888-732-8562 ■ *Web:* www.ncsecu.org					
State Employees Credit Union of Maryland Inc					
971 Corporate Blvd	Linthicum	MD	21090	410-487-7328	487-7011
TF: 800-879-7328 ■ *Web:* www.secumd.org					
State Employees Federal Credit Union					
700 Patroon Creek Blvd Patroon Creek Corporate Center	Albany	NY	12206	518-452-8234	464-5363*
**Fax:* Hum Res ■ *TF:* 800-727-3328 ■ *Web:* www.sefcu.com					
Suncoast Schools Federal Credit Union					
6804 E Hillsborough Ave	Tampa	FL	33610	813-621-7511	621-2527
TF: 800-999-5887 ■ *Web:* www.suncoastfcu.org					
Teachers Credit Union 110 S Main St	South Bend	IN	46601	574-232-8012	284-6313*
**Fax:* Hum Res ■ *TF:* 800-333-3828 ■ *Web:* www.tcunet.com					
Teachers Federal Credit Union					
2410 N Ocean Ave PO Box 9029	Farmingville	NY	11738	631-698-7000	698-7004
TF: 800-341-4333 ■ *Web:* www.teachersfcu.org					
Texans Credit Union 777 E Campbell Rd	Richardson	TX	75081	972-348-2000	348-2203
TF: 800-843-5295 ■ *Web:* www.texanscu.org					
Texas Dow Employees Credit Union 1001 FM 2004	Lake Jackson	TX	77566	979-297-1154	299-1462
TF: 800-839-1154 ■ *Web:* www.tdecu.org					
Think Federal Credit Union 5200 Members Pkwy NW	Rochester	MN	55901	507-288-3425	536-5730
TF: 800-288-3425 ■ *Web:* www.thinkcu.com/					
Tinker Federal Credit Union PO Box 45750	Tinker AFB	OK	73145	405-732-0324	946-6251
TF: 800-456-4828 ■ *Web:* www.tinkerfcu.org					
Tower Federal Credit Union 7901 Sandy Spring Rd	Laurel	MD	20707	301-497-7000	497-8930*
**Fax:* Cust Svc ■ *TF:* 800-787-8328 ■ *Web:* www.towerfcu.org					
Travis Federal Credit Union 1 Travis Way	Vacaville	CA	95687	707-449-4000	449-9566
TF: 800-877-8328 ■ *Web:* www.traviscu.org					
Truliant Federal Credit Union 3200 Truliant Way	Winston-Salem	NC	27103	336-659-1955	659-3540
TF: 800-822-0382 ■ *Web:* www.truliantfcu.org					
United Nations Federal Credit Union					
24-01 44th Rd Court Square Pl	Long Island City	NY	11101	347-686-6000	686-6400
TF: 800-891-2471 ■ *Web:* www.unfcu.org					
US Alliance Federal Credit Union 600 Midland Ave	Rye	NY	10580	914-921-0500	881-3464
TF Cust Svc: 800-431-2754 ■ *Web:* www.usalliance.org					
US Central Credit Union 9701 Renner Blvd	Lenexa	KS	66219	913-227-6000	438-1564
TF: 888-872-0440 ■ *Web:* www.uscentral.org					
Virginia Credit Union 7500 Boulders View Dr	Richmond	VA	23225	804-323-6000	608-8619
TF: 800-285-5051 ■ *Web:* www.vacu.org					
Visions Federal Credit Union 24 McKinley Ave	Endicott	NY	13760	607-754-7900	754-3807
TF: 800-242-2120 ■ *Web:* www.visionsfcu.org					
Vystar Credit Union 4949 Blanding Blvd	Jacksonville	FL	32210	904-777-6000	908-2488
TF Cust Svc: 800-445-6289 ■ *Web:* www.vystarcu.org					
Washington State Employees Credit Union 400 E Union Ave	Olympia	WA	98501	360-943-7911	754-1385
TF: 800-562-0999 ■ *Web:* www.wsecu.org					
Wescom Credit Union 123 S Marengo Ave	Pasadena	CA	91101	626-535-1000	535-1366
TF: 888-493-7266 ■ *Web:* www.wescom.org					
WesCorp (Western Corporate Federal Credit Union)					
924 Overland Ct	San Dimas	CA	91773	909-394-6300	592-4545
TF: 000-442-4300 ■ *Web:* www.wescorp.org					
Western Corporate Federal Credit Union (WesCorp)					
924 Overland Ct	San Dimas	CA	91773	909-394-6300	592-4545
TF: 800-442-4366 ■ *Web:* www.wescorp.org					
Wings Financial Credit Union 14985 Glazier Ave Suite 100	Apple Valley	MN	55124	952-997-8000	997-8124
TF: 800-692-2274 ■ *Web:* www.wingsfinancial.com					
Wright-Patt Credit Union 2455 Executive Park Blvd	Fairborn	OH	45324	937-912-7000	912-7012
TF: 800-762-0047 ■ *Web:* www.wrightpattcu.com					

223 CRUISE LINES

SEE ALSO Casinos p. 1409; Cruises - Riverboat p. 1583; Ports & Port Authorities p. 2130; Travel Agencies p. 2380

	City	State	Zip	Phone	Fax
American Canadian Caribbean Line Inc 461 Water St	Warren	RI	02885	401-247-0955	247-2350
TF: 800-556-7450 ■ *Web:* www.accl-smallships.com					
American Safari Cruises Inc 19221 36th Ave W Suite 208	Lynnwood	WA	98036	425-776-4700	776-8889
TF: 888-862-8881 ■ *Web:* www.amsafari.com					
Aquanaut Cruise Line Ltd 241 E Commercial Blvd	Fort Lauderdale	FL	33334	954-491-0333	772-9340
TF: 800-327-8223 ■ *Web:* www.aquanautcruise.com					
Baja Expeditions Inc 2625 Garnet Ave	San Diego	CA	92109	858-581-3311	581-6542
TF: 800-843-6967 ■ *Web:* www.bajaex.com					
Blackbeard Cruises 8346 NW South River Dr Suite G	Medley	FL	33166	305-888-1226	884-4214
TF: 800-327-9600 ■ *Web:* www.blackbeard-cruises.com					
Blue Lagoon Cruises					
2222 Foothill Blvd Suite E-175	La Canada Flintridge	CA	91011	818-424-7550	957-2476
Web: www.bluelagooncruises.com					
Bluewater Adventures Ltd 252 E 1st St Suite 3	North Vancouver	BC	V7L1B3	604-980-3800	980-1800
TF: 888-877-1770 ■ *Web:* www.bluewateradventures.ca					
Carnival Cruise Lines 3655 NW 87th Ave	Miami	FL	33178	305-599-2600	406-4700
TF: 888-227-6482 ■ *Web:* www.carnivalcruises.com					
Celebrity Cruises 1050 Caribbean Way	Miami	FL	33132	305-539-6000	982-4995
TF: 800-256-6649 ■ *Web:* www.celebrity-cruises.com					
Clipper Cruise Line Inc 11969 Westline Industrial Dr	Saint Louis	MO	63146	314-655-6700	655-6670
TF: 800-325-0010 ■ *Web:* www.clippercruise.com					
Costa Cruise Lines 200 S Park Rd Suite 200	Hollywood	FL	33021	954-266-5600	266-2100
TF: 800-462-6782 ■ *Web:* www.costacruises.com					
Cruise West 2301 5th Ave Suite 401	Seattle	WA	98121	206-441-8687	441-4757
TF: 888-851-8133 ■ *Web:* www.cruisewest.com					
Crystal Cruises Inc 2049 Century Pk E Suite 1400	Los Angeles	CA	90067	310-785-9300	785-9201*
**Fax:* Hum Res ■ *TF:* 866-446-6625 ■ *Web:* www.crystalcruises.com					
Cunard Line Ltd 24303 Town Ctr Dr Suite 200	Valencia	CA	91355	661-753-1000	753-1005
TF: 800-223-0764 ■ *Web:* www.cunard.com					
Discovery Cruises Inc 1775 NW 70th Ave	Miami	FL	33126	305-597-0336	477-2867
TF: 800-866-8687 ■ *Web:* www.discoverycruiseline.com					
Disney Cruise Line 210 Celebration Pl	Celebration	FL	34747	407-566-3500	566-3751
TF: 800-511-1333 ■ *Web:* disneycruise.disney.go.com/dcl/en_US/index?bhcp=1					
GlobalQuest Journeys Ltd 185 Willis Ave 2nd Fl	Mineola	NY	11501	516-739-3690	739-8022
TF: 800-221-3254 ■ *Web:* www.globalquesttravel.com					
Great Lakes Cruise Co 3270 Washtenaw Ave	Ann Arbor	MI	48104	734-677-0900	677-1428
TF: 888-891-0203 ■ *Web:* www.greatlakescruising.com					
Holland America Line 300 Elliott Ave W	Seattle	WA	98119	206-281-3535	281-7110
TF: 800-426-0327 ■ *Web:* www.hollandamerica.com					
Hurtigruten 405 Park Ave	New York	NY	10022	212-319-1300	319-1390
TF: 866-257-6071 ■ *Web:* www.hurtigruten.us					
Imperial Majesty Cruise Line 2950 Gateway Dr	Pompano Beach	FL	33069	954-956-9505	971-6678
TF: 800-394-3865 ■ *Web:* www.majestycruise.com					
Lindblad Expeditions 96 Morton St 9th Fl	New York	NY	10014	212-765-7740	265-3770
TF: 800-397-3348 ■ *Web:* www.expeditions.com					
Maine Windjammer Cruises PO Box 617	Camden	ME	04843	207-236-2938	236-3229
TF: 800-736-7981 ■ *Web:* www.mainewindjammercruises.com					
Maui-Molokai Sea Cruises 831 Eha St Suite 101	Wailuku	HI	96793	808-242-8777	244-5890
TF: 800-468-1287 ■ *Web:* www.mvprince.com					
Mediterranean Shipping Co Cruises					
6750 N Andrews Ave Suite 100	Fort Lauderdale	FL	33309	954-772-6262	776-5881
TF: 800-666-9333 ■ *Web:* www.msccruises.com					
MSC Cruises USA Inc 6750 N Andrews Ave Suite 100	Fort Lauderdale	FL	33309	954-772-6262	776-5881
TF: 800-666-9333 ■ *Web:* www.msccruises.com					
Nekton Diving Cruises 520 SE 32nd St	Fort Lauderdale	FL	33316	954-463-9324	463-8938
TF: 800-899-6753 ■ *Web:* www.nektoncruises.com					
Norwegian Cruise Line Ltd 7665 Corporate Ctr Dr	Miami	FL	33126	305-436-4000	436-4124*
**Fax:* PR ■ *TF:* 800-327-7030 ■ *Web:* www.ncl.com					
Oceania Cruises Inc 8300 NW 33rd St Suite 308	Miami	FL	33122	305-514-2300	514-2222
TF: 800-531-5619 ■ *Web:* www.oceaniacruises.com					
Orient Lines Inc 7665 Corporate Ctr Dr	Miami	FL	33126	305-468-2000	436-4118
TF: 800-333-7300 ■ *Web:* www.orientlines.com					
Party Line Cruise Co 301 Broadway Suite 142	Riviera Beach	FL	33404	561-472-9860	841-0472
TF: 866-463-3779 ■ *Web:* www.plcruises.com					
Peter Deilmann Cruises 1800 Diagonal Rd Suite 170	Alexandria	VA	22314	703-549-1741	549-7924
TF: 800-348-8287 ■ *Web:* www.deilmann-cruises.com					
Princess Cruises 24844 Rockefeller Ave	Santa Clarita	CA	91355	661-753-0000	284-4771*
**Fax:* Sales ■ *TF:* 800-872-6779 ■ *Web:* www.princess.com					
Quark Expeditions Inc 1019 Post Rd	Darien	CT	06820	203-656-0499	655-6623
TF: 800-356-5699 ■ *Web:* www.quarkexpeditions.com					
Radisson Seven Seas Cruises					
600 Corporate Dr Suite 410	Fort Lauderdale	FL	33334	954-776-6123	772-3763
TF: 800-477-7500 ■ *Web:* www.rssc.com					
ResidenSea 5200 Blue Lagoon Dr Suite 790	Miami	FL	33139	305-264-9090	269-1058
TF: 800-970-6601 ■ *Web:* www.residensea.com					
Rockport Schooner Cruises PO Box 272	Belfast	ME	04915	207-338-3088	
TF: 866-732-2473 ■ *Web:* www.wanderbirdcruises.com					
Royal Caribbean Cruises Ltd 1050 Caribbean Way	Miami	FL	33132	305-539-6000	374-7354
NYSE: RCL ■ *TF:* 800-398-9819 ■ *Web:* www.royalcaribbean.com					
Royal Caribbean International 1050 Caribbean Way	Miami	FL	33132	305-539-6000	539-6168*
**Fax:* Hum Res ■ *TF:* 800-327-6700 ■ *Web:* www.rccl.com					
Sea Cloud Cruises Inc 32-40 N Dean St	Englewood	NJ	07631	201-227-9404	227-9424
TF: 888-732-2568 ■ *Web:* www.seacloud.com					
Seabourn Cruise Line 6100 Blue Lagoon Dr Suite 400	Miami	FL	33126	305-463-3000	463-3010
TF: 800-929-9595 ■ *Web:* www.seabourn.com					
SeaDream Yacht Club 2601 S Bayshore Dr PH 1B	Coconut Grove	FL	33133	305-631-6100	631-6110
TF: 800-707-4911 ■ *Web:* www.seadreamyachtclub.com					
Silversea Cruises 110 E Broward Blvd	Fort Lauderdale	FL	33301	954-522-4477	522-4499
TF: 800-722-9955 ■ *Web:* www.silversea.com					
Star Clippers Inc 7200 NW 19th St Suite 206	Miami	FL	33126	305-442-0550	442-1611
TF: 800-442-0551 ■ *Web:* www.star-clippers.com					
Star Cruises 7665 Corporate Ctr Dr	Miami	FL	33126	305-436-4000	436-4126
TF: 800-327-9020 ■ *Web:* www.starcruises.com					
Swan Hellenic Cruises 631 Commack Rd Suite 1A	Commack	NY	11725	631-858-1263	858-1279
TF: 877-800-7926 ■ *Web:* www.swanhellenic.com					
Travel Dynamics International 132 E 70th St	New York	NY	10021	212-517-7555	774-1545
TF: 800-257-5767 ■ *Web:* www.traveldynamicsinternational.com					
Windjammer Barefoot Cruises Ltd 1759 Bay Rd	Miami Beach	FL	33139	305-672-6453	674-1219
TF: 800-327-2601 ■ *Web:* www.windjammer.com					
Windstar Cruises 2101 4th Ave Suite 1150	Seattle	WA	98121	206-292-9606	733-2790
TF Resv: 800-258-7245 ■ *Web:* www.windstarcruises.com					

224 CRUISES - RIVERBOAT

SEE ALSO Casinos p. 1409; Cruise Lines p. 1583

	City	State	Zip	Phone	Fax
American Cruise Lines 741 Boston Post Rd Suite 200	Guilford	CT	06437	203-453-6800	453-0417
TF: 800-814-6880 ■ *Web:* americancruiselines.com					
American Rivers Cruise Lines 2101 4th Ave Suite 2200	Seattle	WA	98121	206-388-0444	388-0445
TF: 800-901-9152 ■ *Web:* www.americanriverscruiseline.com					
American West Steamboat Co 2101 4th Ave Suite 1150	Seattle	WA	98121	206-292-9606	340-0975
TF: 800-434-1232 ■ *Web:* www.columbiarivercruise.com					
French Country Waterways Ltd PO Box 2195	Duxbury	MA	02331	781-934-2454	934-9048
TF: 800-222-1236 ■ *Web:* www.fcwl.com					
Gateway Clipper Fleet 350 W Station Sq Dr	Pittsburgh	PA	15219	412-355-7980	355-7987
Web: www.gatewayclipper.com					
Gateway Riverboat Cruises 707 N 1st St	Saint Louis	MO	63102	314-621-4040	622-3049
TF: 877-982-1410 ■ *Web:* www.gatewayarchriverboats.com					
Les Etoiles Barges 3355 Lenox Rd Suite 750	Atlanta	GA	30326	770-394-6565	237-1841*
**Fax Area Code:* 404 ■ *TF:* 800-280-1492 ■ *Web:* www.lesetoilesbarges.com					
Peter Deilmann Cruises 1800 Diagonal Rd Suite 170	Alexandria	VA	22314	703-549-1741	549-7924
TF: 800-348-8287 ■ *Web:* www.deilmann-cruises.com					
RiverBarge Excursion Lines Inc 201 Opelousas Ave	New Orleans	LA	70114	504-365-0022	365-0000
TF: 888-462-2743 ■ *Web:* www.riverbarge.com					
Spirit of Dubuque 400 E 3rd St Ice Harbor	Dubuque	IA	52001	563-583-8093	585-0634
TF: 800-747-8093 ■ *Web:* www.spiritofdubuque.com					
Uniworld 17323 Ventura Blvd	Encino	CA	91316	818-382-7820	382-7829
TF: 800-733-7820 ■ *Web:* www.uniworld.com					
Victoria Cruises Inc 57-08 39th Ave	Woodside	NY	11377	212-818-1680	818-9889
TF: 800-348-8084 ■ *Web:* www.victoriacruises.com					
Viking River Cruises 5700 Canoga Ave Suite 200	Woodland Hills	CA	91367	818-227-1234	227-1237
TF: 877-668-4546 ■ *Web:* www.vikingrivercruises.com					
Wings Nile Cruises 11350 McCormick Rd Suite 703	Hunt Valley	MD	21031	410-771-0925	771-0928
TF: 800-869-4647 ■ *Web:* www.wingsegypt.com					

225 CUTLERY

SEE ALSO Silverware p. 2318

	City	State	Zip	Phone	Fax
Alcas Corp 1116 E State St TF: 800-828-0448	Olean	NY	14760	716-373-6141	
American Safety Razor Co 1 Razor Blade Ln TF: 800-445-9284 ■ Web: www.asrco.com	Verona	VA	24482	540-248-8000	248-0522
Atlanta Cutlery Corp 2147 Gees Mill Rd TF: 800-883-0300 ■ Web: www.atlantacutlery.com	Conyers	GA	30013	770-922-3700	918-2026
Buck Knives Inc 660 S Lochsa St TF: 800-326-2825 ■ Web: www.buckknives.com	Post Falls	ID	83854	208-262-0500	262-0555
Camillus Cutlery Co 54 Main St TF Sales: 800-344-0456 ■ Web: www.camillusknives.com	Camillus	NY	13031	315-672-8111	672-8832
Case WR & Sons Cutlery Co Owens Way TF: 800-523-6350 ■ Web: www.wrcase.com	Bradford	PA	16701	814-368-4123	368-1729
Crescent Mfg Co 1310 Majestic Dr TF: 800-537-1330 ■ Web: www.crescentblades.com	Fremont	OH	43420	419-332-6484	332-6564
Dexter-Russell Inc 44 River St Web: www.dexter-russell.com	Southbridge	MA	01550	508-765-0201	764-2897
Douglas/Quikut Co 118 E Douglas Rd TF: 800-982-5233 ■ Web: www.quikut.com	Walnut Ridge	AR	72476	870-886-6774	886-9162
Excel Group 1 Merrick Ave TF: 800-252-3390 ■ Web: www.lifetimebrands.com	Westbury	NY	11590	516-683-6000	683-6116
Fiskars Brands Inc 2537 Daniels St TF: 800-500-4849 ■ Web: www.fiskars.com	Madison	WI	53718	608-259-1649	294-4790
Gerber Legendary Blades Inc 14200 SW 72nd Ave *Fax: Cust Svc ■ TF: 800-950-6161 ■ Web: www.gerberblades.com	Portland	OR	97224	503-639-6161	684-7008*
Goodell Inc 9440 Science Ctr Dr TF Cust Svc: 800-542-3906 ■ Web: www.goodelltools.com	Minneapolis	MN	55428	763-531-0053	531-0252
KA-BAR Knives Inc 200 Homer St TF: 800-282-0130 ■ Web: www.kabar.com	Olean	NY	14760	716-372-5952	790-7188
Lamson & Goodnow Mfg Co 45 Conway St TF: 800-872-6564 ■ Web: www.lamsonsharp.com	Shelburne Falls	MA	01370	413-625-6331	625-9816
Midwest Tool & Cutlery Co Inc 1210 Progress St PO Box 160 TF: 800-782-4659 ■ Web: www.midwestsnips.com	Sturgis	MI	49091	269-651-2476	651-1811
Millers Forge Inc 1411 Capital Ave TF: 800-527-3474 ■ Web: www.millersforge.com	Plano	TX	75074	972-422-2145	881-0639
Ontario Knife Co 26 Empire St *Fax Area Code: 800 ■ TF: 800-222-5233 ■ Web: www.ontarioknife.com	Franklinville	NY	14737	716-676-5527	299-2618*
Pacific Handy Cutter Inc 2968 Randolph Ave TF Cust Svc: 800-229-2233 ■ Web: www.pacifichandycutter.com	Costa Mesa	CA	92626	714-662-1033	662-7595
Queen Cutlery Co 507 Chestnut St TF Sales: 800-222-5233 ■ Web: www.queencutlery.com	Titusville	PA	16354	814-827-3673	827-9693
Rada Mfg Co 905 Industrial St TF: 800-311-9691 ■ Web: www.radamfg.com	Waverly	IA	50677	319-352-5454	352-3947
Swiss Army Brands Inc 1 Research Dr PO Box 874 TF Cust Svc: 800-243-4057 ■ Web: www.swissarmy.com	Shelton	CT	06484	203-929-6391	929-3786
Taylor Cutlery 1736 N Eastman Rd TF: 800-251-0254 ■ Web: www.taylorcutlery.com	Kingsport	TN	37664	423-247-2406	247-5371
Utica Cutlery Co 820 Noyes St TF: 800-888-4223 ■ Web: www.uticastainless.com	Utica	NY	13502	315-733-4663	733-6602
Wenger North America Inc 15 Corporate Dr TF Cust Svc: 800-431-2996 ■ Web: www.wengerna.com	Orangeburg	NY	10962	845-365-3500	425-4700
WR Case & Sons Cutlery Co Owens Way TF: 800-523-6350 ■ Web: www.wrcase.com	Bradford	PA	16701	814-368-4123	368-1729
Zippo Mfg Co 33 Barbour St Web: www.zippo.com	Bradford	PA	16701	814-368-2700	362-2388

226 CYLINDERS & ACTUATORS - FLUID POWER

SEE ALSO Automotive Parts & Supplies - Mfr p. 1360

	City	State	Zip	Phone	Fax
Actuant Corp 6100 N Baker Rd NYSE: ATU ■ TF: 800-624-5242 ■ Web: www.actuant.com	Milwaukee	WI	53209	414-352-4160	247-5550
Advance Automation Co Inc 3526 N Elston Ave Web: www.advanceautomationco.com	Chicago	IL	60618	773-539-7633	539-7299
American Cylinder Co Inc 481 Governors Hwy Web: www.americancylinder.com	Peotone	IL	60468	708-258-3935	258-3980
ARO Fluid Products Div Ingersoll-Rand Co 1 Aro Ctr PO Box 151 TF Cust Svc: 800-495-0276 ■ Web: www.arozone.com	Bryan	OH	43506	419-636-4242	633-1674
Atlas Cylinder Corp 500 S Wolf Rd Web: www.parker.com/atlas	Des Plaines	IL	60016	847-298-2400	294-2655
Beaver Aerospace & Defense Inc 11850 Mayfield St Web: www.beaver-online.com	Livonia	MI	48150	734-261-9352	853-5043
BEI Technologies Inc Kimco Magnetics Div 2470 Coral St Bldg D Web: www.beikimco.com	Vista	CA	92081	760-597-6322	597-6320
Best Metal Products Co 3570 Raleigh Dr SE PO Box 888440 Web: www.bestmetalproducts.com	Grand Rapids	MI	49588	616-942-7141	942-0949
Bettis Actuators & Controls 18703 GH Cir PO Box 508 Web: www.emersonprocess.com/valveautomation/bettis	Waller	TX	77484	281-727-5300	727-5353
Bimba Mfg Co PO Box 68 *Fax: Cust Svc ■ TF: 800-323-0445 ■ Web: www.bimba.com	Monee	IL	60449	708-534-8544	534-8346*
Bosch Rexroth Corp 5150 Prairie Stone Pkwy TF: 800-860-1055 ■ Web: www.boschrexroth-us.com	Hoffman Estates	IL	60192	847-645-3600	645-6201
Clippard Instrument Lab 7390 Colerain Ave TF: 877-245-6247 ■ Web: www.clippard.com	Cincinnati	OH	45239	513-521-4261	521-4464
Columbus Hydraulics Co PO Box 250 Web: www.columbushydraulics.com	Columbus	NE	68602	402-564-8544	564-0129
Commercial Honing Co Inc 8606 Sultana Ave Web: www.commercialhoning.com	Fontana	CA	92335	909-829-1211	829-7631
Cross Mfg Inc 11011 King St Suite 210 TF: 800-542-7677 ■ Web: www.crossmfg.com	Overland Park	KS	66210	913-451-1233	451-1235
Cunningham Mfg Co 318 S Webster St TF: 800-767-0038 ■ Web: www.cunninghamcylinders.com	Seattle	WA	98108	206-767-3713	762-3457
Dynex Rivett Inc 770 Capitol Dr Web: www.dynexhydraulics.com	Pewaukee	WI	53072	262-691-0300	691-0312
Eckel Mfg Co Inc PO Box 1375 TF: 800-654-4779 ■ Web: www.eckel.com	Odessa	TX	79760	432-362-4336	362-1827
Energy Mfg Co Inc 204 Plastic Ln Web: www.energymfg.com	Monticello	IA	52310	319-465-3537	465-5279
Engineered Valves Div ITT Industries Inc 33 Centerville Rd TF: 800-366-1111 ■ Web: www.engvalves.com	Lancaster	PA	17603	717-291-1901	509-2336
Fabco-Air Inc 3716 NE 49th Ave Web: www.fabco-air.com	Gainesville	FL	32609	352-373-3578	375-8024
Flo-Tork Inc 1701 N Main St PO Box 68 *Fax: Sales ■ Web: www.flo-tork.com	Orrville	OH	44667	330-682-0010	683-6857*
Galland Henning Nopak Inc 1025 S 40th St Web: www.nopak.com	West Milwaukee	WI	53215	414-645-6000	645-6048
General Engineering Co 26485 Hillman Hwy PO Box 549	Abingdon	VA	24212	276-628-6068	628-4311
Great Bend Industries Inc 8701 6th St Web: www.hampton-hydraulics.com/greatbend.htm	Great Bend	KS	67530	620-792-4368	792-3935
Hader/Seitz Inc 156 W Lincoln Ave PO Box 510260 TF: 877-388-2101 ■ Web: www.hader-seitz.com	New Berlin	WI	53151	262-641-6000	641-5310
Hannon Hydraulics Inc 625 N Loop 12 TF: 800-333-4266 ■ Web: www.hannonhydraulics.com	Irving	TX	75061	972-438-2870	554-4047
Hol-Mac Corp 2730-A Hwy 15 PO Box 349 TF: 800-844-3019 ■ Web: www.hol-mac.com	Bay Springs	MS	39422	601-764-4121	764-3438
Humphrey Products Co 5070 East N Ave TF: 800-477-8707 ■ Web: www.humphrey-products.com	Kalamazoo	MI	49048	269-381-5500	381-4113
IMI Norgren Inc 325 Carr Dr Web: www.iminorgren.com	Brookville	OH	45309	937-833-4033	833-4205
Ingersoll-Rand Co ARO Fluid Products Div 1 Aro Ctr PO Box 151 TF Cust Svc: 800-495-0276 ■ Web: www.arozone.com	Bryan	OH	43506	419-636-4242	633-1674
ITT Aerospace Controls 28150 Industry Dr Web: www.ittaerospace.com	Valencia	CA	91355	661-295-4000	295-4155
ITT Industries Inc Engineered Valves Div 33 Centerville Rd TF: 800-366-1111 ■ Web: www.engvalves.com	Lancaster	PA	17603	717-291-1901	509-2336
Jarp Industries Inc 1051 Pine St PO Box 923 Web: www.jarpind.com	Schofield	WI	54476	715-359-4241	355-4960
Jordan Controls 5607 W Douglas Ave TF Prod Info: 800-637-5547 ■ Web: www.jordancontrols.com	Milwaukee	WI	53218	414-461-9200	461-1024
Kaydon Corp 315 E Eisenhower Pkwy Suite 300 NYSE: KDN ■ Web: www.kaydon.com	Ann Arbor	MI	48108	734-747-7025	747-6565
Kimco Magnetics Div BEI Technologies Inc 2470 Coral St Bldg D Web: www.beikimco.com	Vista	CA	92081	760-597-6322	597-6320
Limitorque Corp 5114 Woodall Rd Web: www.limitorque.com	Lynchburg	VA	24502	434-528-4400	845-9736
Lynair Inc 3515 Scheele Dr Web: www.lynair.com	Jackson	MI	49202	517-787-2240	787-4521
Micromatic Textron 525 Berne St Web: www.micromatictextron.com	Berne	IN	46711	260-589-2136	589-8966
Miller Fluid Power Corp 800 N York Rd TF: 800-323-8207	Bensenville	IL	60106	630-766-3400	766-3012
Milwaukee Cylinder 5877 S Pennsylvania Ave PO Box 100498 Web: www.milwaukeecylinder.com	Cudahy	WI	53110	414-769-9700	769-0157
Monarch Hydraulics Inc 1316 Michigan St NE Web: www.monarchhyd.com	Grand Rapids	MI	49503	616-458-1306	458-1616
Motion Systems Corp 600 Industrial Way W Web: www.motionsystem.com	Eatontown	NJ	07724	732-222-1800	389-9191
Norris Cylinder Co 1535 FM 1845 TF: 800-527-8418 ■ Web: www.norriscylinder.com	Longview	TX	75603	903-757-7633	753-3012
Oildyne Div Parker Hannifin Corp 5520 Hwy 169 N Web: www.parker.com/oildyne	Minneapolis	MN	55428	763-533-1600	533-0082
Omhaline Hydraulic Co 106 Freedom Dr PO Box 19	North Sioux City	SD	57049	605-232-9060	232-4652
Parker Hannifin Corp 6035 Parkland Blvd NYSE: PH ■ TF Cust Svc: 800-272-7537 ■ Web: www.parker.com	Cleveland	OH	44124	216-896-3000	896-4000
Parker Hannifin Corp Automation Actuator Div 135 Quadral Dr TF: 866-727-5228 ■ Web: www.parker.com/automation	Wadsworth	OH	44281	330-336-3511	334-3335
Parker Hannifin Corp Cylinder Div 500 S Wolf Rd Web: www.parker.com/cylinder	Des Plaines	IL	60016	847-298-2400	294-2655
Parker Hannifin Corp Oildyne Div 5520 Hwy 169 N Web: www.parker.com/oildyne	Minneapolis	MN	55428	763-533-1600	533-0082
Parker Instrumentation Group 6035 Parkland Blvd TF: 800-272-7537 ■ Web: www.parker.com/instrumentation	Cleveland	OH	44124	216-896-3000	896-4022
PHD Inc 9009 Clubridge Dr TF: 800-624-8511 ■ Web: www.phdinc.com	Fort Wayne	IN	46809	260-747-6151	747-6754
Production Engineering Inc 2330 Brooklyn Rd	Jackson	MI	49203	517-788-6800	788-6705
Quincy Ortman Cylinders 3501 Wismann Ln PO Box C-2 Web: www.quincyortmancylinders.com	Quincy	IL	62305	217-222-7766	222-1773
Roper Pump Co 3475 Old Maysville Rd PO Box 269 TF Sales: 800-944-6769 ■ Web: www.roperpumps.com	Commerce	GA	30529	706-335-5551	335-5490
Sargent Controls & Aerospace 5675 W Burlingame Rd TF: 800-932-5273 ■ Web: www.sargentcontrols.com	Tucson	AZ	85743	520-744-1000	744-9290
Seabee Corp 712 First St NW Web: www.hampton-hydraulics.com/seabeecorp.htm	Hampton	IA	50441	641-456-4871	456-5303
Shafer Valve Co 2500 Park Ave W TF: 800-876-4311 ■ Web: www.emersonprocess.com	Mansfield	OH	44906	419-529-4311	529-3688
Sheffer Corp 6990 Cornell Rd *Fax: Sales ■ TF Sales: 800-387-2191 ■ Web: www.sheffercorp.com	Cincinnati	OH	45242	513-489-9770	489-3034*
Siemens Building Technologies Inc 1000 Deerfield Pkwy TF: 800-877-7545 ■ Web: www.us.sbt.siemens.com	Buffalo Grove	IL	60089	847-215-1000	215-1093
SMC Pneumatics Inc 3011 N Franklin Rd PO Box 26646 TF: 800-762-7621 ■ Web: www.smcusa.com	Indianapolis	IN	46226	317-899-4440	899-3102
Smith Industries Actuation Systems Inc 110 Algonquin Pkwy	Whippany	NJ	07981	973-428-9898	428-8532
Standex International Corp Custom Hoists Div 771 County Rd 30-A West PO Box 98 TF: 800-837-4668 ■ Web: www.customhoists.com	Hayesville	OH	44838	419-368-4721	368-4209
Tactair Fluid Controls Inc 4806 W Taft Rd Web: www.tactair.com	Liverpool	NY	13088	315-451-3928	451-8919
Texas Hydraulics Inc PO Box 1067 Web: www.texashyd.com	Temple	TX	76503	254-778-4701	774-9940
Tol-O-Matic Inc 3800 County Rd 116 TF: 800-328-2174 ■ Web: www.tolomatic.com	Hamel	MN	55340	763-478-8000	478-8080
Wabash Technologies 1375 Swan St PO Box 829 *Fax: Sales ■ Web: www.wabashtech.com	Huntington	IN	46750	260-356-8300	355-4265*

227 DATA COMMUNICATIONS SERVICES FOR WIRELESS DEVICES

Companies listed here deliver data such as customized news or stock information, other personalized content, and/or multimedia, audio, and video from the Internet to wireless devices (cellular phones, Personal Digital Assistants, pagers, laptop computers).

	City	State	Zip	Phone	Fax
@Road Inc 47200 Bayside Pkwy NASDAQ: ARDI ■ TF: 877-428-7623 ■ Web: www.atroad.com	Fremont	CA	94538	510-668-1638	353-6021
724 Solutions Inc 3916 State St NASDAQ: SVNX ■ Web: www.724.com	Santa Barbara	CA	93105	805-884-8308	884-8311
Air2Web Inc 1230 Peachtree St 12th Fl TF: 877-238-3637 ■ Web: www.air2web.com	Atlanta	GA	30309	404-815-7707	815-7708
Antenna Software 111 Pavonia Ave Suite 520 Web: www.antennasoftware.com	Jersey City	NJ	07310	201-217-3800	239-2315
AvantGo Inc 1 Sybase Dr TF: 800-792-2735 ■ Web: avantgo.com	Dublin	CA	94568	519-883-6898	747-4971
BlackBerry 295 Phillip St TF: 877-255-2377 ■ Web: www.blackberry.net	Waterloo	ON	N2L3W8	519-888-7465	888-6906

	City	State	ZIP	Phone	Fax
Broadbeam Inc 2540 Route 130 Suite 116 *Web:* www.broadbeam.com	Cranbury	NJ	08512	609-655-3737	655-1282
Cell-Loc Location Technologies Inc 3015 5th Ave NE Franklin Atrium Suite 220 *Web:* www.cell-loc.com	Calgary	AB	T2A6T8	403-569-5700	569-5701
Dynamic Mobile Data Systems Inc 285 Davidson Ave Suite 501 *TF Tech Supp:* 866-662-4363 ■ *Web:* www.dmdsys.com	Somerset	NJ	08873	732-302-1700	302-9558
e-Travel Inc 1000 Winter St Suite 4200 *Web:* www.e-travel.com	Waltham	MA	02451	781-622-5905	522-9900
Ellipso Inc 4410 Massachusetts Ave NW Suite 385 *Web:* www.ellipso.com	Washington	DC	20016	202-466-4488	466-4493
Everypath Inc 2211 N 1st St Suite 200 *TF Sales:* 800-355-1068 ■ *Web:* www.everypath.com	San Jose	CA	95131	408-562-8000	562-8100
fusionOne Inc 1 Almaden Blvd 11th Fl *Web:* www.fusionone.com	San Jose	CA	95113	408-282-1200	282-1233
GoAmerica Inc 433 Hackensack Ave *NASDAQ: GOAM* ■ *TF:* 888-462-4600 ■ *Web:* www.goamerica.com	Hackensack	NJ	07601	201-996-1717	996-1772
Intermec Technologies Corp 6001 36th Ave W *TF Sales:* 800-934-3163 ■ *Web:* www.intermec.com	Everett	WA	98203	425-348-2600	355-9551
Linx Communications Inc 175 Crossing Blvd Suite 300 *TF:* 888-367-5469 ■ *Web:* www.linxcom.com	Framingham	MA	01702	617-747-4200	747-4203
Meteor Communications Corp 8631 S 212th St *Web:* www.meteorcomm.com	Kent	WA	98031	253-872-2521	872-7662
Metro One Telecommunications Inc 11200 Murray Scholls Pl *NASDAQ: INFO* ■ *TF:* 800-933-4034 ■ *Web:* www.metro1.com	Beaverton	OR	97007	503-643-9500	643-9600
Motricity 2800 Meridian Pkwy Suite 150 *TF:* 800-746-7646 ■ *Web:* www.motricity.com	Durham	NC	27713	919-287-7400	287-7401
MSN Mobile 1 Microsoft Way *Web:* mobile.msn.com	Redmond	WA	98052	425-882-8080	936-7329
MyCorner.com Div NEXAGE.com Inc PO Box 3493 *Web:* www.mycorner.com	Renton	WA	98056	425-985-1020	467-5703
NAVTEQ Corp 222 Merchandise Mart Suite 900 *NYSE: NVT* ■ *TF:* 888-628-6277 ■ *Web:* www.navteq.com	Chicago	IL	60654	312-894-7000	894-7050
NEXAGE.com Inc MyCorner.com Div PO Box 3493 *Web:* www.mycorner.com	Renton	WA	98056	425-985-1020	467-5703
PacketVideo Corp 10350 Science Center Dr Suite 210 *TF:* 877-308-2500 ■ *Web:* www.packetvideo.com	San Diego	CA	92121	858-731-5300	731-5301
Remote Dynamics Inc 1155 Kas Dr Suite 100 *TF:* 800-828-4696 ■ *Web:* www.remotedynamics.com	Richardson	TX	75081	972-301-2000	301-2588
Semotus Solutions Inc 16400 Lark Ave Suite 230 *AMEX: DLK* ■ *TF:* 800-775-1377 ■ *Web:* www.semotus.com	Los Gatos	CA	95032	408-358-7100	358-7110
SmartServ Online Inc 2250 Butler Pike Suite 150 *Web:* www.smartserv.com	Plymouth Meeting	PA	19462	610-397-0689	397-0846
TeleCommunication Systems Inc 275 West St Suite 400 *NASDAQ: TSYS* ■ *TF:* 800-810-0827 ■ *Web:* www.telecomsys.com	Annapolis	MD	21401	410-263-7616	263-7617
Traffic.com Inc 851 Duportail Rd Suite 220 *NASDAQ: TRFC* ■ *Web:* www.traffic.com	Wayne	PA	19087	610-725-9700	725-0530
Vaultus Inc 263 Summer St *TF:* 877-828-5887 ■ *Web:* www.vaultus.com	Boston	MA	02210	617-399-1169	338-9452
Vindigo Inc 500 7th Ave Suite 17-A *Web:* www.vindigo.com	New York	NY	10018	212-590-0500	
Webraska Mobile Technologies 2101 Oregon Pike Suite 201 *Web:* www.webraska.com	Lancaster	PA	17601	717-735-0721	735-0676
Yahoo! Mobile 701 1st Ave *Web:* mobile.yahoo.com	Sunnyvale	CA	94089	408-349-3300	349-3301

228 DATA PROCESSING & RELATED SERVICES

SEE ALSO Electronic Transaction Processing p. 1612; Payroll Services p. 2089

	City	State	ZIP	Phone	Fax
Affiliated Computer Services Inc (ACS) 2828 N Haskell Ave *NYSE: ACS* ■ **Fax:* Hum Res ■ *Web:* www.acs-inc.com	Dallas	TX	75204	214-841-6111	823-9369*
Alliance Data Systems Corp 17655 Waterview Pkwy *NYSE: ADS* ■ **Fax:* Hum Res ■ *Web:* www.alliancedatasystems.com	Dallas	TX	75252	972-348-5100	348-5335*
Automatic Data Processing Inc (ADP) 1 ADP Blvd *NYSE: ADP* ■ *TF:* 800-225-5237 ■ *Web:* www.adp.com	Roseland	NJ	07068	973-994-5000	974-3378
Cass Information Systems Inc 13001 Hollenberg Dr *NASDAQ: CASS* ■ *Web:* www.cassinfo.com	Bridgeton	MO	63044	314-506-5500	506-5560
CCC Information Services Group Inc 444 Merchandise Mart Plaza **Fax Area Code:* 310 ■ **Fax:* Hum Res ■ *TF:* 800-621-8070 ■ *Web:* www.cccis.com	Chicago	IL	60654	312-222-4636	527-5379*
Central Service Assn 93 S Coley Rd *Web:* www.csa1.com	Tupelo	MS	38801	662-842-5962	840-1329
ChoicePoint Inc 1000 Alderman Dr *NYSE: CPS* ■ *TF:* 877-317-5000 ■ *Web:* www.choicepointinc.com	Alpharetta	GA	30005	770-752-6000	
Claimsnet.com Inc 14860 Montfort Dr Suite 250 *TF:* 800-356-1511 ■ *Web:* www.claimsnet.com	Dallas	TX	75254	972-458-1701	458-1737
Commercial Computer Service Inc 2916 W 6th St	Fort Worth	TX	76107	817-335-6411	870-1532
Communication Data Services 1901 Bell Ave *TF:* 800-378-9982 ■ *Web:* www.cdsfulfillment.com	Des Moines	IA	50315	515-247-7500	246-6687
Computer Fulfillment 275 Billerica Rd *Web:* www.computerfulfillment.com	Chelmsford	MA	01824	978-256-9040	256-6597
Computer Services Inc 3901 Technology Dr *TF:* 800-545-4274 ■ *Web:* www.csiweb.com	Paducah	KY	42001	270-442-7361	575-9569
Connecticut On-Line Computer Center Inc 135 Darling Dr *Web:* www.cocc.com	Avon	CT	06001	860-678-0444	677-1169
Continental DataGraphics 222 N Sepulveda Blvd Suite 300 *TF:* 800-862-5691 ■ *Web:* www.cdgnow.com	El Segundo	CA	90245	310-662-2300	662-2310
Continental Graphics Corp DBA Continental DataGraphics 222 N Sepulveda Blvd Suite 300 *TF:* 800-862-5691 ■ *Web:* www.cdgnow.com	El Segundo	CA	90245	310-662-2300	662-2310
Data Lab Corp 7333 N Oak Park Ave *Web:* www.data-lab.com	Niles	IL	60714	847-647-6678	647-6821
DataBank 12000 Baltimore Ave *TF:* 800-873-9426 ■ *Web:* www.databankimx.com	Beltsville	MD	20705	301-837-0197	
Datamark Inc 43 Butterfield Cir Suite C-1 *Web:* www.datamark.net	El Paso	TX	79906	915-774-0856	778-1988
Deposit Computer Services Inc 10 Monument St *Web:* www.4dcsi.com	Deposit	NY	13754	607-467-4600	467-4632
DPF Data Services Group Inc 1990 Swarthmore Ave *TF:* 800-431-4416 ■ *Web:* www.dpfdata.com	Lakewood	NJ	08701	732-370-8840	370-1751
EDS (Electronic Data Systems Corp) 5400 Legacy Dr *NYSE: EDS* ■ *Web:* www.eds.com	Plano	TX	75024	972-605-6000	605-2643
EMSI Data Entry Div 3050 Regent Blvd Suite 500 *TF:* 800-728-2167 ■ *Web:* www.emsinet.com	Irving	TX	75063	214-689-3600	689-3644
Equifax Inc 1550 Peachtree St NW *NYSE: EFX* ■ *TF Sales:* 888-202-4025 ■ *Web:* www.equifax.com	Atlanta	GA	30309	404-885-8000	888-5043
Fair Isaac Corp 901 Marquette Ave Suite 3200 *NYSE: FIC* ■ *TF Cust Svc:* 877-434-7877 ■ *Web:* www.fairisaac.com	Minneapolis	MN	55402	612-758-5200	758-5201
Hartley Data Service Inc 1807 Glenview Rd *TF:* 800-433-2796	Glenview	IL	60025	847-724-9280	729-2199
Health Management Systems Inc 401 Park Ave S **Fax:* Hum Res ■ *Web:* www.hmsy.com	New York	NY	10016	212-685-4545	889-8776*
HMS Holdings Corp 401 Park Ave S *NASDAQ: HMSY*	New York	NY	10016	212-685-4545	889-8776
Inovis Inc 11720 Amberpark Dr Suite 100 *TF:* 877-446-6847 ■ *Web:* www.inovis.com	Alpharetta	GA	30004	404-467-3000	467-3730
MIB Inc 160 University Ave *Web:* www.mib.com	Westwood	MA	02090	781-329-4500	329-3379
National Business Systems Inc 343 Sunnyside Dr	Milton	WI	53563	608-868-3187	868-3075
PRWT Services Inc 1835 Market St 8th Fl *Web:* www.prwt.com	Philadelphia	PA	19103	215-569-8810	569-9893
Resolve Corp 85 The East Mall *TF:* 866-678-6019 ■ *Web:* www.resolvecorporation.com	Toronto	ON	M8Z5W4	416-503-1800	503-8899
Scicom Data Services Ltd 10101 Bren Rd E *TF:* 800-488-9087 ■ *Web:* www.scicom.com	Minnetonka	MN	55343	952-933-4200	936-4132
Securities Industry Automation Corp 2 Metrotech Ctr **Fax:* Hum Res ■ *Web:* www.siac.com	Brooklyn	NY	11201	212-383-4800	479-3755*
SunGard Data Systems Inc 680 E Swedesford Rd **Fax Area Code:* 610 ■ *TF:* 800-523-4970 ■ *Web:* www.sungard.com	Wayne	PA	19087	484-582-2000	225-1120*
SuperComm Inc 5001 LBJ Fwy Suite 550 *TF:* 800-252-9556 ■ *Web:* www.supercomm.com	Dallas	TX	75244	972-726-2000	726-2020
TDEC Inc 7735 Old Georgetown Rd Suite 1010 *TF:* 800-424-8332 ■ *Web:* www.tdec.com	Bethesda	MD	20814	301-718-0703	718-1615
Users Inc 1250 Drummers Ln *TF:* 800-523-7282 ■ *Web:* www.users.com	Valley Forge	PA	19482	610-687-9400	293-4480
Williams Records Management 1925 E Vernon Ave *Web:* www.williamsrecords.com	Los Angeles	CA	90058	323-234-3453	233-5451

229 DATING SERVICES

	City	State	ZIP	Phone	Fax
eharmony.com inc 300 N Lake Ave Suite 1111 *Web:* www.eharmony.com	Pasadena	CA	91101	626-795-4814	585-4040
Friendfinder Network Inc 445 Sherman Ave Suite C *TF:* 800-388-0760 ■ *Web:* www.friendfinder.com	Palo Alto	CA	94306	650-847-3100	324-9379
Great Expectations 14180 Dallas Pkwy Suite 100 *Web:* www.ge-dating.com	Dallas	TX	75254	972-448-7900	448-7969
It's Just Lunch! Inc 101 W Grand Ave Suite 502 *Web:* www.itsjustlunch.com	Chicago	IL	60610	312-644-9999	644-9474
Match.com Inc PO Box 25472 *TF:* 800-926-2824 ■ *Web:* www.match.com	Dallas	TX	75225	214-576-9352	576-9475
Matchmaker International 331 Alberta Dr Suite 102 *Web:* www.matchmakerintl.com	Amherst	NY	14226	716-835-4046	835-1452
Matchmaker.com 100 5th Ave *Web:* www.matchmaker.com	Waltham	MA	02451	781-370-2700	370-2600
Spark Networks plc 8383 Wilshire Blvd Suite 800 *AMEX: LOV* ■ *Web:* www.spark.net	Beverly Hills	CA	90211	323-836-3000	836-3333
Spring Street Networks PO Box 547 *Web:* www.springstreetnetworks.com	New York	NY	10012	212-929-8890	929-9046
Together Dating 5026 Dorsey Hall Dr Suite 205 *Web:* www.togetherdating.com	Ellicott City	MD	21042	410-730-8866	992-6919

230 DENTAL ASSOCIATIONS - STATE

SEE ALSO Associations & Organizations - Professional & Trade - Health & Medical Professionals Associations p. 1326

	City	State	ZIP	Phone	Fax
Alabama 836 Washington Ave *Web:* www.aldaonline.org	Montgomery	AL	36104	334-265-1684	262-6218
Alaska 9170 Jewel Lake Rd Suite 203 *Web:* www.akdental.org	Anchorage	AK	99502	907-563-3003	563-3009
Arizona 3193 N Drinkwater Blvd *TF:* 800-866-2732 ■ *Web:* www.azda.org	Scottsdale	AZ	85251	480-344-5777	344-1442
Arkansas 2501 Crestwood Dr Suite 205 *Web:* www.dental-asda.org	North Little Rock	AR	72116	501-771-7650	
California 1201 K St *TF:* 800-736-7071 ■ *Web:* www.cda.org	Sacramento	CA	95853	916-443-0505	443-2943
Colorado 3690 S Yosemite St Suite 100 *Web:* www.cdaonline.org	Denver	CO	80237	303-740-6900	740-7989
Connecticut 62 Russ St *Web:* www.csda.com	Hartford	CT	06106	860-278-5550	244-8287
Delaware 200 Continental Dr Suite 111 *Web:* www.delawarestatedentalsociety.org	Newark	DE	19713	302-368-7634	368-7669
District of Columbia 502 C St NE *Web:* www.dcdental.org	Washington	DC	20002	202-547-7613	546-1482
Florida 1111 E Tennessee St *TF:* 800-877-9922 ■ *Web:* www.floridadental.org	Tallahassee	FL	32308	850-681-3629	561-0504
Georgia 7000 Peachtree Dunwoody Rd NE Bldg 17 Suite 200 *TF:* 800-432-4357 ■ *Web:* www.gadental.org	Atlanta	GA	30328	404-636-7553	633-3943
Hawaii 1345 S Beretania St Suite 301 *TF:* 800-359-6725 ■ *Web:* www.hawaiidentalassociation.net	Honolulu	HI	96814	808-593-7956	593-7636
Idaho 1220 W Hays St *Web:* www.isdaweb.com	Boise	ID	83702	208-343-7543	343-0775
Illinois 1010 S 2nd St *Web:* www.isds.org	Springfield	IL	62704	217-525-1406	525-8872
Indiana 401 W Michigan St *TF:* 800-562-5646 ■ *Web:* www.indental.org	Indianapolis	IN	46202	317-634-2610	634-2612
Iowa 5530 W Parkway *TF:* 800-828-2181 ■ *Web:* www.iowadental.org	Johnston	IA	50131	515-986-5605	986-5626
Kentucky 1940 Princeton Dr *Web:* www.kyda.org	Louisville	KY	40205	502-459-5373	458-5915
Louisiana 7833 Office Pk Blvd *TF:* 800-388-6642 ■ *Web:* www.ladental.org	Baton Rouge	LA	70809	225-926-1986	926-1886
Maine 29 Association Dr PO Box 215 *Web:* www.medental.org	Manchester	ME	04351	207-622-7900	622-6210
Maryland 6410 Dobbin Rd *Web:* www.msda.com	Columbia	MD	21045	410-964-2880	964-0583
Massachusetts 2 Willow St Suite 200 *TF:* 800-342-8747 ■ *Web:* www.massdental.org	Southborough	MA	01745	508-480-9797	480-0002
Michigan 230 N Washington Sq Suite 208 **Fax:* PR ■ *Web:* www.michigandental.org	Lansing	MI	48933	517-372-9070	372-0008*
Minnesota 2236 Marshall Ave *Web:* www.mndental.org	Saint Paul	MN	55104	651-646-7454	646-8246
Mississippi 2630 Ridgewood Rd *Web:* www.msdental.org	Jackson	MS	39216	601-982-0442	366-3050
Missouri 3340 American Ave *TF:* 800-688-1907 ■ *Web:* www.modental.org	Jefferson City	MO	65109	573-634-3436	635-0764

				Phone	Fax
Montana 17 1/2 S Last Chance Gulch *TF:* 800-257-4988 ■ *Web:* www.mtdental.com	Helena	MT	59601	406-443-2061	443-1546
Nebraska 3120 'O' St. *Web:* www.nedental.org	Lincoln	NE	68510	402-476-1704	476-2641
Nevada 8863 W Flamingo Rd Suite 102 *TF:* 800-962-6710 ■ *Web:* www.nvda.org	Las Vegas	NV	89147	702-255-4211	255-3302
New Hampshire 23 S State St *Web:* www.nhds.org	Concord	NH	03301	603-225-5961	226-4880
New Jersey 1 Dental Plaza PO Box 6020 *Web:* www.njda.org	North Brunswick	NJ	08902	732-821-9400	821-1082
New Mexico 9201 Montgomery Blvd NE Suite 601 *Web:* www.newmexicodental.org	Albuquerque	NM	87111	505-294-1368	294-9958
New York 121 State St *Web:* www.nysdental.org	Albany	NY	12207	518-465-0044	465-3219
North Carolina 1600 Evans Rd *TF:* 800-662-8754 ■ *Web:* www.ncdental.org	Cary	NC	27519	919-677-1396	677-1397
North Dakota 115 N 4th St *Web:* www.nddental.com	Bismarck	ND	58501	701-223-8870	223-0855
Ohio 1370 Dublin Rd *Web:* www.oda.org	Columbus	OH	43215	614-486-2700	486-0381
Oklahoma 317 NE 13th St *TF:* 800-876-8890 ■ *Web:* okda.org	Oklahoma City	OK	73104	405-848-8873	848-8875
Oregon 17898 SW McEwan Rd *TF:* 800-452-5628 ■ *Web:* www.oregondental.org	Portland	OR	97224	503-620-3230	620-4169
Pennsylvania 3501 N Front St *Web:* www.padental.org	Harrisburg	PA	17110	717-234-5941	232-7169
Rhode Island 200 Centerville Rd *Web:* www.ridental.com	Warwick	RI	02886	401-732-6833	732-9351
South Carolina 120 Stonemark Ln *Web:* www.scda.org	Columbia	SC	29210	803-750-2277	750-1644
South Dakota 804 N Euclid Ave Suite 103 *Web:* www.sddental.org	Pierre	SD	57501	605-224-9133	224-9168
Tennessee 2104 Sunset Place *Web:* www.tenndental.org	Nashville	TN	37212	615-383-8962	383-0214
Texas 1946 S IH-35 Suite 400 *Web:* www.tda.org	Austin	TX	78704	512-443-3675	443-3031
Utah 1151 E 3900 South Suite 160	Salt Lake City	UT	84124	801-261-5315	261-1235
Vermont 100 Dorset St Suite 18 *Web:* www.vsds.org	South Burlington	VT	05403	802-864-0115	864-0116
Virginia 7525 Staples Mill Rd *Web:* www.vadental.org	Richmond	VA	23228	804-261-1610	261-1660
Washington 1001 4th Ave Suite 3800 *TF:* 800-448-3368 ■ *Web:* www.wsda.org	Seattle	WA	98154	206-448-1914	443-9266
West Virginia 2003 Quarrier St *Web:* www.wvdental.org	Charleston	WV	25311	304-344-5246	344-5316
Wisconsin 111 E Wisconsin Ave Suite 1300 **Fax Area Code:* 800 ■ *TF:* 800-364-7646 ■ *Web:* www.wda.org	Milwaukee	WI	53202	414-276-4520	864-2997*
Wyoming 1637 S. Spruce St *Web:* www.wyda.org	Casper	WY	82601	307-237-1186	237-1187

231 DENTAL EQUIPMENT & SUPPLIES - MFR

				Phone	Fax
3M ESPE Dental Products Div 3M Ctr Bldg 275-2SE-03 **Fax Area Code:* 800 ■ *Web:* www.3m.com/espe	Saint Paul	MN	55144	888-364-3577	540-7497*
3M Health Care Solutions 3M Ctr *TF Prod Info:* 800-364-3577 ■ *Web:* www.3m.com/US/healthcare	Saint Paul	MN	55144	651-733-1110	
3M Unitek 2724 South Peck Rd *TF:* 800-634-5300 ■ *Web:* www.3m.com/us/healthcare/unitek	Monrovia	CA	91016	626-445-7960	574-4793
A-dec Inc 2601 Crestview Dr *TF Cust Svc:* 800-547-1883 ■ *Web:* www.a-dec.com	Newberg	OR	97132	503-538-9471	538-0276
Align Technology Inc 881 Martin Ave *NASDAQ: ALGN* ■ **Fax Area Code:* 877 ■ *TF:* 888-822-5446 ■ *Web:* www.aligntech.com	Santa Clara	CA	95050	408-470-1000	651-7128*
American Medical Technologies Inc 5655 Bear Ln *TF:* 800-359-1959 ■ *Web:* www.americanmedicaltech.com	Corpus Christi	TX	78405	361-289-1145	289-5554
American Orthodontics Corp 1714 Cambridge Ave *TF:* 800-558-7687 ■ *Web:* www.americanortho.com	Sheboygan	WI	53081	920-457-5051	457-1485
Barnhardt Mfg Co 1100 Hawthorne Ln *TF:* 800-277-0377 ■ *Web:* www.barnhardt.net	Charlotte	NC	28205	704-376-0380	342-1892
Brasseler USA 1 Brasseler Blvd *TF:* 800-841-4522 ■ *Web:* www.brasselerusa.com	Savannah	GA	31419	912-925-8525	927-8671
Closure Medical Corp 5250 Greens Dairy Rd *Web:* www.closuremed.com	Raleigh	NC	27616	919-876-7800	790-1041
Colgate Oral Pharmaceuticals One Colgate Way *TF:* 800-821-2880 ■ *Web:* www.colgateprofessional.com	Canton	MA	02021	781-821-2880	821-2187
Coltene/Whaledent Inc 235 Ascot Pkwy *TF:* 800-221-3046 ■ *Web:* www.coltenewhaledent.com	Cuyahoga Falls	OH	44223	330-916-8800	916-7077
Darby Group Cos Inc 300 Jericho Quad **Fax Area Code:* 800 ■ *TF:* 800-468-1001 ■ *Web:* www.darbygroup.com	Jericho	NY	11753	516-683-1800	957-7362*
Den-Mat Corp 2727 Skyway Dr *TF:* 800-433-6628 ■ *Web:* www.denmat.com	Santa Maria	CA	93455	805-922-8491	922-6933
DEN-TAL-EZ Group Inc 101 Lindenwood Dr Suite 225 *TF:* 866-383-4636 ■ *Web:* www.dentalez.com	Malvern	PA	19355	610-725-8004	725-9898
DEN-TAL-EZ Inc Custom Air Div 2500 Hwy 31 S *TF:* 800-383-4636 ■ *Web:* www.dentalez.com/custom/index.htm	Bay Minette	AL	36507	251-937-6781	937-0461
DEN-TAL-EZ Inc Equipment Div 2500 Hwy 31 S *TF:* 800-383-4636	Bay Minette	AL	36507	251-937-6781	937-0461
Dentsply Caulk 38 W Clarke Ave **Fax:* Acctg ■ *TF:* 800-532-2855 ■ *Web:* www.caulk.com	Milford	DE	19963	302-422-4511	422-3480*
Dentsply Ceramco 6 Terri Ln *TF:* 800-487-0100 ■ *Web:* www.ceramco.com	Burlington	NJ	08016	609-386-8900	386-8282
Dentsply International Inc 221 W Philadelphia St PO Box 872 *NASDAQ: XRAY* ■ *TF:* 800-877-0020 ■ *Web:* www.dentsply.com	York	PA	17405	717-845-7511	849-4762
Dentsply International Inc Rinn Div 1212 Abbott Dr **Fax Area Code:* 800 ■ *TF:* 800-323-0970 ■ *Web:* www.rinncorp.com	Elgin	IL	60123	847-742-1115	544-0787*
Dentsply International Inc Trubyte Div 221 W Philadelphia St PO Box 872 **Fax Area Code:* 800 ■ **Fax:* Cust Svc ■ *TF:* 800-877-0020 ■ *Web:* www.trubyte.com	York	PA	17405	717-845-7511	735-1101*
Dentsply International Inc Tulsa Dental Div 5100 E Skelly Dr Suite 300 *TF:* 800-662-1202 ■ *Web:* www.tulsadental.com	Tulsa	OK	74135	918-493-6598	493-6599
Dentsply Professional 1301 Smile Way **Fax Area Code:* 800 ■ **Fax:* Cust Svc ■ *TF:* 800-989-8825 ■ *Web:* professional.dentsply.com	York	PA	17404	717-767-8500	278-4344*
GC America Inc 3737 W 127th St *TF:* 800-323-3386 ■ *Web:* www.gcamerica.com	Alsip	IL	60803	708-597-0900	371-5103
Heraeus Kulzer Inc 99 Business Pk Dr **Fax Area Code:* 800 ■ **Fax:* Cust Svc ■ *TF:* 800-343-5336 ■ *Web:* www.kulzer.com	Armonk	NY	10504	914-273-8600	522-1545*
Hygenic Corp 1245 Home Ave *TF:* 800-321-2135 ■ *Web:* www.hygenic.com	Akron	OH	44310	330-633-8460	633-9359
Keystone Tube Co 3400 N Wolf Rd *TF Cust Svc:* 800-323-9493	Franklin Park	IL	60131	708-841-2450	841-3724
Lancer Orthodontics Inc 253 Pawnee St *TF Cust Svc:* 800-854-2896 ■ *Web:* www.lancerortho.com	San Marcos	CA	92078	760-744-5585	744-5724
LifeCore Biomedical Inc 3515 Lyman Blvd *NASDAQ: LCBM* ■ *TF Cust Svc:* 800-752-2663 ■ *Web:* www.lifecore.com	Chaska	MN	55318	952-368-4300	368-3411
Matrx by Midmark 145 Mid County Dr *TF:* 800-847-1000 ■ *Web:* www.matrxmedical.com	Orchard Park	NY	14127	716-662-6650	662-8440
Midwest Dental Products Corp 901 W Oakton St *TF Cust Svc:* 800-800-2888 ■ *Web:* www.midwestdental.com	Des Plaines	IL	60018	847-640-4800	640-4806
Nobel Biocare USA Inc 22715 Savi Ranch Pkwy *TF:* 800-993-8100 ■ *Web:* www.nobelbiocare.com	Yorba Linda	CA	92887	714-282-4800	998-9236
ORMCO Corp 1717 W Collins Ave **Fax Area Code:* 800 ■ *TF:* 800-854-1741 ■ *Web:* www.ormco.com	Orange	CA	92867	714-516-7400	317-6012*
Pelton & Crane 11727 Fruehauf Dr *TF Cust Svc:* 800-659-6560 ■ *Web:* www.pelton.net	Charlotte	NC	28273	704-588-2126	587-7204
Premier Dental Products Co 1710 Romano Dr Box 4500 *TF:* 888-773-6872 ■ *Web:* www.premusa.com	Plymouth Meeting	PA	19462	610-239-6000	239-6171
Professional Dental Technologies 267 E Main St *TF:* 800-228-5595 ■ *Web:* www.prodentec.com	Batesville	AR	72501	870-698-2300	793-5554
Rinn Div Dentsply International Inc 1212 Abbott Dr **Fax Area Code:* 800 ■ *TF:* 800-323-0970 ■ *Web:* www.rinncorp.com	Elgin	IL	60123	847-742-1115	544-0787*
Rocky Mountain Orthodontics Inc (RMO Inc) 650 W Colfax Ave **Fax:* Hum Res ■ *TF:* 800-525-6044 ■ *Web:* www.rmortho.com	Denver	CO	80204	303-592-8200	592-8223*
Sunstar Americas Inc DBA Sunstar Butler 4635 W Foster Ave *TF:* 800-528-8537 ■ *Web:* www.jbutler.com	Chicago	IL	60630	773-777-4000	777-5101
Sybron Dental Specialties Inc 1717 W Collins Ave *NYSE: SYD* ■ *TF:* 800-537-7824 ■ *Web:* www.sybrondental.com	Orange	CA	92867	714-516-7400	516-7593
TP Orthodontics Inc 100 Center Plaza *TF:* 800-348-8856 ■ *Web:* www.tportho.com	La Porte	IN	46350	219-785-2591	324-3029
Tulsa Dental Div Dentsply International Inc 5100 E Skelly Dr Suite 300 *TF:* 800-662-1202 ■ *Web:* www.tulsadental.com	Tulsa	OK	74135	918-493-6598	493-6599
Waterpik Technologies Inc/Jandy Pool Products 6000 Condor Dr *NYSE: PIK* ■ **Fax:* Mktg ■ *Web:* www.waterpik.com	Moorpark	CA	93021	805-529-2000	529-5934*

232 DEPARTMENT STORES

				Phone	Fax
Ammar's Inc 710 S College Ave *Web:* www.magicmartstores.com	Bluefield	VA	24605	276-322-4686	326-1060
Ann & Hope Inc 1 Ann & Hope Way *Web:* www.curtainandbathoutlet.com	Cumberland	RI	02864	401-722-1000	495-8218
Apex Inc 100 Main St *TF:* 800-450-2739 ■ *Web:* www.apexstores.com	Pawtucket	RI	02860	401-723-3500	723-9452
Ayres LS & Co 6020 E 82nd St	Indianapolis	IN	46250	317-579-2900	579-2932
BC Moore & Sons Inc 101 S Greene St *Web:* www.mooresonline.com	Wadesboro	NC	28170	704-694-2171	694-6748
Beall's Inc 1806 38th Ave E *Web:* www.beallsinc.com	Bradenton	FL	34208	941-747-2355	746-1171
Belk Inc 2801 W Tyvola Rd *Web:* www.belk.com	Charlotte	NC	28217	704-357-1000	
Bering Home Center Inc DBA Bering's 6102 Westheimer Rd *Web:* www.berings.com	Houston	TX	77057	713-785-6400	785-3697
Bloomingdale's 1000 3rd Ave *TF:* 800-950-0047 ■ *Web:* www.bloomingdales.com	New York	NY	10022	212-705-2000	705-2502
Bob's Merchandise Inc 1111 Hudson St *TF:* 800-292-5551 ■ *Web:* www.bobsmerch.com	Longview	WA	98632	360-425-3870	636-4334
Bon-Ton Stores Inc 2801 E Market St *NASDAQ: BONT* ■ *Web:* www.bonton.com	York	PA	17402	717-757-7660	751-3108
Boscov's Department Stores 4500 Perkiomen Ave *Web:* www.boscovs.com	Reading	PA	19606	610-779-2000	370-3495
Bracker's Department Store 68 N Morley Ave *TF:* 800-635-5431	Nogales	AZ	85621	520-287-3631	287-7137
Capin Co 32 N Marley Ave	Nogales	AZ	85621	520-397-6100	287-4110
Carson Pirie Scott 331 W Wisconsin Ave **Fax:* Hum Res ■ *TF:* 877-627-3006 ■ *Web:* www.carsons.com	Milwaukee	WI	53203	414-347-4141	347-5337*
Century 21 Department Stores 22 Cortlandt St **Fax:* Hum Res ■ *Web:* www.century21deptstores.com	New York	NY	10007	212-227-9092	267-4271*
Dillard's Inc 1600 Cantrell Rd *NYSE: DDS* ■ **Fax:* Acctg ■ *Web:* www.dillards.com	Little Rock	AR	72201	501-376-5200	399-7271*
Doneckers Inc 409 N State St *Web:* www.doneckers.com	Ephrata	PA	17522	717-738-9500	738-9637
Dunlap Co 200 Bailey Ave *TF:* 866-274-0163 ■ *Web:* www.dunlaps.com	Fort Worth	TX	76107	817-336-4985	347-0298
Elder-Beerman Stores Corp 332 W Wisconsin Ave *Web:* www.elderbeerman.com	Milwaukee	WI	53203	414-347-1152	
Federated Department Stores Inc 7 W 7th St *NYSE: FD* ■ *Web:* www.federated-fds.com	Cincinnati	OH	45202	513-579-7000	579-7555
Filene's Basement Corp 25 Corporate Dr Suite 400 *Web:* www.filenesbasement.com	Burlington	MA	01803	617-348-7000	348-7128
Fred's Inc 4300 New Getwell Rd PO Box 18356 *NASDAQ: FRED* ■ *TF:* 800-374-7417 ■ *Web:* www.fredsinc.com	Memphis	TN	38118	901-365-8880	365-8865
Glik Co 3248 Nameoki Rd *TF:* 800-454-5182 ■ *Web:* www.gliks.com	Granite City	IL	62040	618-876-6717	876-7819
Gordman 12100 W Center Rd *TF:* 800-456-7463 ■ *Web:* www.gordmans.com	Omaha	NE	68144	402-691-4000	691-4269
Gottschalks 7 River Park Pl E *NYSE: GOT* ■ **Fax:* Hum Res ■ *Web:* www.gottschalks.com	Fresno	CA	93720	559-434-8000	434-4806*
GR Herberger's Inc 600 W Saint Germain St *TF:* 800-398-7896 ■ *Web:* www.herbergers.com	Saint Cloud	MN	56301	320-251-5351	654-2277
Grigg Enterprises Inc 801 W Columbia St *Web:* www.griggsonline.com	Pasco	WA	99301	509-547-0566	547-4387
Halls Merchandising Inc 200 E 25th St *TF:* 888-545-2121 ■ *Web:* www.halls.com	Kansas City	MO	64108	816-274-8111	274-4471
Herberger's GR Inc 600 W Saint Germain St *TF:* 800-398-7896 ■ *Web:* www.herbergers.com	Saint Cloud	MN	56301	320-251-5351	654-2277
Hudson's Bay Co 401 Bay St Suite 501 *TSX: HBC* ■ **Fax:* Mktg ■ *Web:* www.hbc.com	Toronto	ON	M5H2Y4	416-861-6008	861-4550*
Isetan New York 1411 Broadway Suite 2550	New York	NY	10018	212-767-0300	767-0307
JC Penney Co Inc 6501 Legacy Dr *NYSE: JCP* ■ **Fax:* Cust Svc ■ *TF Orders:* 800-222-6161 ■ *Web:* www.jcpenney.net	Plano	TX	75024	972-431-1000	431-9140*
Jenss Decor 4001 Maple Rd *TF:* 800-536-7710 ■ *Web:* www.jenssdecor.com	Amherst	NY	14226	716-837-1100	837-1132
Jones & Jones Inc 4500 N 10th St Suite 90 *Web:* www.e-jonesandjones.com	McAllen	TX	78504	956-687-1171	631-3345
Kaufmann's 400 5th Ave **Fax:* Cust Svc ■ *TF:* 800-232-2000 ■ *Web:* www.kaufmanns.com	Pittsburgh	PA	15219	412-232-2000	232-9565*
Kohl's Corp N 56 W 17000 Ridgewood Dr *NYSE: KSS* ■ **Fax:* Hum Res ■ *TF:* 800-837-6644 ■ *Web:* www.kohls.com	Menomonee Falls	WI	53051	262-703-7000	703-6373*
Lancaster Sales Co 1375 Old Logan Rd Rt 33S	Lancaster	OH	43130	740-653-5334	653-2783
Langstons Co 2224 Exchange Ave *TF:* 800-658-2831 ■ *Web:* www.langstons.com	Oklahoma City	OK	73108	405-235-9536	235-1645
Lord & Taylor 424 5th Ave *TF:* 800-223-7440 ■ *Web:* www.lordandtaylor.com	New York	NY	10018	212-391-3344	391-3265

Phone Fax

LS Ayres & Co 6020 E 82nd St....Indianapolis IN 46250 317-579-2900 579-2932
Macy's 151 W 34th St....New York NY 10001 212-695-4400 494-1057
TF Cust Svc: 800-526-1202 ■ *Web:* www.macys.com
Macy's Midwest 611 Olive St....Saint Louis MO 63101 314-342-6300 342-3064*
**Fax:* Hum Res ■ *Web:* www.fds.com/
Mansours Department Store Inc 26 W Lafayette Sq....LaGrange GA 30240 706-884-7305 812-5435
Marshall Field & Co 111 N State St....Chicago IL 60602 312-781-1000
Web: www.fields.com
Masters Inc 111 Hempstead Tpke 2nd Fl....West Hempstead NY 11552 516-292-3710 292-3837
May Department Stores International 615 Olive St....Saint Louis MO 63101 314-554-7100 554-7665
McClurkans Department Store 200 Bailey Ave....Fort Worth TX 76107 817-336-4985 877-1302
McRae's 115 N Calderwood St....Alcoa TN 37701 865-983-7000 981-6336
Web: www.mcraes.com
Mervyns 22301 Foothill Blvd....Hayward CA 94541 510-727-3000 727-5760*
**Fax:* Hum Res ■ *TF:* 800-637-8967 ■ *Web:* www.mervyns.com
MH King Co 1032 Idaho Ave PO Box 669....Burley ID 83318 208-678-7181 678-7907
Mitsukoshi USA Inc 286 Madison Ave Suite 1301....New York NY 10017 212-753-5580 355-7161
Moore BC & Sons Inc 101 S Greene St....Wadesboro NC 28170 704-694-2171 694-6748
Web: www.mooresonline.com
Neiman Marcus Group Inc 1618 Main St....Dallas TX 75201 214-741-6911 573-6824
TF: 800-937-9146 ■ *Web:* www.neimanmarcusgroup.com
Neiman Marcus Stores 1618 Main St....Dallas TX 75201 214-741-6911 573-6824
TF: 800-937-9146 ■ *Web:* www.neimanmarcus.com
Nordstrom Inc 1617 6th Ave Suite 500....Seattle WA 98101 206-628-2111 628-1795
NYSE: JWN ■ *TF:* 800-285-5800 ■ *Web:* www.nordstrom.com
OW Houts & Sons Inc 120 N Buckhout St....State College PA 16801 814-238-6701 238-6700
TF Cust Svc: 800-252-3583 ■ *Web:* www.owhouts.com
Pamida Inc 8800 F St....Omaha NE 68127 402-339-2400 596-7330
Web: www.pamida.com
Parisian 3455 Hwy 80 W....Jackson MS 39209 800-832-2455 592-2925*
**Fax Area Code:* 601 ■ *Web:* www.parisian.com
Peebles Inc 1 Peebles St....South Hill VA 23970 434-447-5200 447-5474
TF: 800-723-4548 ■ *Web:* www.peebles.com
Penney JC Co Inc 6501 Legacy Dr....Plano TX 75024 972-431-1000 431-9140*
NYSE: JCP ■ **Fax:* Cust Svc ■ *TF Orders:* 800-222-6161 ■ *Web:* www.jcpenney.net
Phelps Dodge Mercantile Co 172 Plaza Dr....Morenci AZ 85540 928-865-4121 865-2935
Proffitt's 115 N Calderwood St....Alcoa TN 37701 865-983-7000 981-6336
TF Cust Svc: 800-981-3220 ■ *Web:* www.proffitts.com
Reed's 129-131 W Main St....Tupelo MS 38804 662-842-6453 844-8254
TF: 800-627-3337 ■ *Web:* www.reeds.ms
Reitmans (Canada) Ltd 250 Sauve St W....Montreal QC H3L1Z2 514-384-1140
TSX: RET ■ *Web:* www.reitmans.ca
RH Macy & Co Inc DBA Macy's 151 W 34th St....New York NY 10001 212-695-4400 494-1057
TF Cust Svc: 800-526-1202 ■ *Web:* www.macys.com
RH Reny Inc 731 Rt 1....Newcastle ME 04553 207-563-3177 563-5681
Web: www.renys.com
Richard I Spiece Sales Co Inc 1150 Manchester Ave....Wabash IN 46992 260-563-8033 563-0358
TF: 800-824-9622
Rogers 519 W Avalon Ave Suite 7....Muscle Shoals AL 35661 256-383-1828 389-8299
TF: 866-383-8322
RW Reed Co DBA Reed's 129-131 W Main St....Tupelo MS 38804 662-842-6453 844-8254
TF: 800-627-3337 ■ *Web:* www.reeds.ms
Saks Fifth Avenue 12 E 49th St....New York NY 10017 212-940-5305 940-4849
TF: 877-551-7257 ■ *Web:* www.saksfifthavenue.com
Saks Inc 750 Lakeshore Blvd....Birmingham AL 35211 205-940-4000 940-4148*
NYSE: SKS ■ **Fax:* Hum Res ■ *Web:* www.saksincorporated.com
Santa Cruz River Trading Co DBA Capin Co 32 N Marley Ave....Nogales AZ 85621 520-397-6100 287-4110
Sav-Mart Co 1729 N Wenatchee Ave....Wenatchee WA 98801 509-663-1671 662-3788
Schottenstein Stores Corp 1800 Moler Rd....Columbus OH 43207 614-221-9200 449-4880*
**Fax:* Cust Svc ■ *TF:* 800-743-4577
Sears Canada Inc 222 Jarvis St....Toronto ON M5B2B8 416-362-1711 941-2501
TSX: SCC ■ *TF:* 800-973-7579 ■ *Web:* www.sears.ca
Shopko LLC 700 Pilgrim Way....Green Bay WI 54304 920-429-2211
Web: www.shopko.com
Skagway Department Stores 620 State St....Grand Island NE 68801 308-384-8222 384-4308
Web: www.skagwaystores.com
SmartBargains Inc 10 Milk St 10th Fl....Boston MA 02108 617-695-7300 695-7391
Web: www.smartbargains.com
Spiegel Inc 1 Spiegel Ave....Hampton VA 23630 800-345-4500 334-3994*
**Fax Area Code:* 757 ■ *TF:* 800-345-4500 ■ *Web:* www.spiegel.com
Stein Mart Inc 1200 Riverplace Blvd....Jacksonville FL 32207 904-346-1500 398-4341
NASDAQ: SMRT ■ *TF:* 800-634-6915 ■ *Web:* www.steinmart.com
Takashimaya Inc 693 5th Ave....New York NY 10022 212-350-0100 350-0192
TF: 800-753-2038
Target Corp 1000 Nicollett Mall....Minneapolis MN 55403 612-304-6073 370-6675*
NYSE: TGT ■ **Fax:* Hum Res ■ *TF Cust Svc:* 800-440-0680 ■ *Web:* www.targetcorp.com
Target Stores 1000 Nicollet Mall....Minneapolis MN 55403 612-304-6073 307-8870
TF: 800-440-0680 ■ *Web:* www.target.com
Tongass Trading Co 201 Dock St....Ketchikan AK 99901 907-225-5101 225-0481
TF: 800-235-5102 ■ *Web:* www.tongasstrading.com
Trading Union Inc 401 N Nordic Dr....Petersburg AK 99833 907-772-3881 772-9309
TVI Inc DBA Value Village 11400 SE 6th St Suite 220....Bellevue WA 98004 425-462-1515 451-2250
Web: www.valuevillage.com
Valley Fair Corp 260 Bergen Tpke....Little Ferry NJ 07643 201-440-4000 807-0043
Value City 7735 Eastern Ave....Baltimore MD 21224 410-288-1111 285-2150
Web: www.valuecity.com
Value Village 11400 SE 6th St Suite 220....Bellevue WA 98004 425-462-1515 451-2250
Web: www.valuevillage.com
Variety Stores Inc 218 S Garnett St....Henderson NC 27536 252-430-2600 492-4226
Vivre Inc 11 E 26th St 15th Fl....New York NY 10010 212-739-6205 770-3065*
**Fax Area Code:* 800 ■ *TF:* 800-411-6515 ■ *Web:* www.vivre.com
Von Maur Inc 6565 Brady St....Davenport IA 52806 563-388-2200 388-2242
Web: www.vonmaur.com
Wal-Mart Stores Inc 702 SW 8th St....Bentonville AR 72716 479-273-4000 273-4053*
NYSE: WMT ■ **Fax:* PR ■ *TF Cust Svc:* 800-925-6278 ■ *Web:* www.walmartstores.com
Wal-Mart Stores Inc Supercenter Div 702 SW 8th St....Bentonville AR 72716 479-273-4000 273-4053
TF: 800-925-6278 ■ *Web:* www.walmartstores.com
Walmart.com 7000 Marina Blvd....Brisbane CA 94005 650-837-5000
TF: 800-966-6546 ■ *Web:* www.walmart.com
Younkers Inc 701 Walnut St....Des Moines IA 50309 515-244-1112 247-7062*
**Fax:* Sales ■ *TF Acctg:* 800-530-6886 ■ *Web:* www.younkers.com

233 DEVELOPMENTAL CENTERS

Residential facilities for the developmentally disabled.

Phone Fax

Altoona Center 1515 4th St....Altoona PA 16601 814-946-6900 946-6943
TF: 800-398-3202 ■ *Web:* www.altoonacenter.com
Caswell Center 2415 W Vernon Ave....Kinston NC 28504 252-559-5100 208-4288*
**Fax:* Acctg ■ *Web:* www.caswellcenter.org
Central Virginia Training Center 521 Colony Rd....Madison Heights VA 24572 434-947-6000 947-2459*
**Fax:* Hum Res ■ *TF:* 866-897-6095 ■ *Web:* www.cvtc.dmhmrsas.virginia.gov
Devereux Foundation 2012 Renaissance Blvd....King of Prussia PA 19406 610-520-3000 542-3136*
**Fax:* Hum Res ■ *TF:* 800-345-1292 ■ *Web:* www.devereux.org
East Central Regional Hospital Gracewood 100 Myrtle Blvd....Gracewood GA 30812 706-790-2011 790-2047
Web: www.ecrh.dhr.state.ga.us/
Glenwood Resource Center 711 S Vine St....Glenwood IA 51534 712-527-4811 527-2329
Lanterman Developmental Center 3530 Pomona Blvd....Pomona CA 91769 909-595-1221 598-4352
Web: www.dds.ca.gov/DevCtrs/main/Lanterman.cfm
Parsons State Hospital & Training Center 2601 Gabriel St....Parsons KS 67357 620-421-6550 421-3623
Web: www.pshtc.org
Porterville Developmental Center 26501 Avenue 140....Porterville CA 93257 559-782-2222 784-5630
Web: www.dds.cahwnet.gov
Productive Alternatives Inc 1205 N Tower Rd....Fergus Falls MN 56537 218-998-5630 736-2541
TF: 800-477-7246 ■ *Web:* www.paiff.org
Sonoma Developmental Center 15000 Arnold Dr....Eldridge CA 95431 707-938-6000 938-3605*
**Fax:* Admitting ■ *Web:* www.dds.ca.gov/DevCtrs/main/Sonoma.cfm
Woodward Resource Center 1251 334th St....Woodward IA 50276 515-438-2600 438-3176*
**Fax:* Hum Res ■ *Web:* www.dhs.state.ia.us

234 DIAGNOSTIC PRODUCTS

SEE ALSO Biotechnology Companies p. 1380; Medicinal Chemicals & Botanical Products p. 1957; Pharmaceutical Companies p. 2109; Pharmaceutical Companies - Generic Drugs p. 2111

Phone Fax

Abaxis Inc 3240 Whipple Rd....Union City CA 94587 510-675-6500 441-6150
NASDAQ: ABAX ■ *TF:* 800-822-2947 ■ *Web:* www.abaxis.com
Abbott Laboratories 100 Abbott Park Rd....Abbott Park IL 60064 847-937-6100
NYSE: ABT ■ *TF:* 800-323-9100 ■ *Web:* www.abbott.com
Abbott Laboratories Abbott Diagnostics Div
100 Abbott Pk Rd....Abbott Park IL 60064 847-937-6100
TF: 800-323-9100 ■ *Web:* www.abbottdiagnostics.com
Accurate Chemical & Scientific Corp 300 Shames Dr....Westbury NY 11590 516-333-2221 997-4948
TF: 800-645-6264 ■ *Web:* www.accuratechemical.com/accuratechemical
Adeza Biomedical Corp 1240 Elko Dr....Sunnyvale CA 94089 408-745-0975 745-0968
NASDAQ: ADZA ■ *TF Cust Svc:* 877-945-0208 ■ *Web:* www.adeza.com
Advanced Biotechnologies Inc 9108 Guilford Rd Rivers Pk II....Columbia MD 21046 301-470-3220 497-9773
TF: 800-426-0764 ■ *Web:* www.abionline.com
Advanced Magnetics Inc 61 Mooney St....Cambridge MA 02138 617-497-2070 547-2445
AMEX: AVM ■ *Web:* www.advancedmagnetics.com
Aero Pharmaceuticals Inc 3848 FAU Blvd Suite 100....Boca Raton FL 33431 561-208-2200 414-1202*
**Fax Area Code:* 800 ■ *TF:* 800-223-6837 ■ *Web:* www.aeropharmaceuticals.com
Affinity Bioreagents Inc 4620 Technology Dr Suite 600....Golden CO 80403 303-278-4535 278-2424
TF: 800-527-4535 ■ *Web:* www.bioreagents.com
Akorn Inc 2500 Millbrook Dr....Buffalo Grove IL 60089 847-279-6100 279-6123
AMEX: AKN ■ *TF:* 800-932-5676 ■ *Web:* www.akorn.com
ALerCHEK Inc 203 Anderson St....Portland ME 04101 207-775-2574 775-0594
TF: 877-282-9542 ■ *Web:* www.alerchek.com
Allermed Laboratories Inc 7203 Convoy Ct....San Diego CA 92111 858-292-1060 292-5934
TF: 800-221-2748 ■ *Web:* www.allermed.com
Ambion Inc 2130 Woodward St Suite 200....Austin TX 78744 512-651-0200 651-0201
TF: 800-888-8804 ■ *Web:* www.ambion.com
AMDL Inc 2492 Walnut Ave Suite 100....Tustin CA 92780 714-505-4460 505-4464
AMEX: ADL ■ *Web:* www.amdl.com
American Diagnostica Inc 500 West Ave....Stamford CT 06902 203-602-7777 602-2221
TF: 888-234-4435 ■ *Web:* www.americandiagnostica.com
American Qualex International Inc 920-A Calle Negocio....San Clemente CA 92673 949-492-8298 492-6790
TF: 800-772-1776 ■ *Web:* www.americanqualex.com
Amresco Inc 30175 Solon Industrial Pkwy....Solon OH 44139 440-349-1313 349-1182
TF: 800-366-1313 ■ *Web:* www.amresco-inc.com
Anachemia Chemicals Inc 3 Lincoln Blvd....Rouses Point NY 12979 518-297-4444 297-2960
TF: 800-323-1414 ■ *Web:* www.anachemia.com
AnaSpec Inc 2149 O'Toole Ave Suite L....San Jose CA 95131 408-452-5055 452-5059
TF: 800-452-5530 ■ *Web:* www.anaspec.com
Angus Buffers & Biochemicals 2236 Liberty Dr....Niagara Falls NY 14304 716-283-1434 283-1570
TF: 800-648-6689 ■ *Web:* www.angus.com
AntiCancer Inc 7917 Ostrow St....San Diego CA 92111 858-654-2555 268-4175
TF: 800-511-2555 ■ *Web:* www.anticancer.com
Apothecus Pharmaceutical Corp 220 Townsend Sq....Oyster Bay NY 11771 516-624-8200 624-8201
TF: 800-227-2393 ■ *Web:* www.apothecus.com
Applera Corp 301 Merritt 7....Norwalk CT 06856 203-840-2000 841-2014
TF: 800-761-5381 ■ *Web:* www.applera.com
Argonaut Technologies Inc 220 Saginaw Dr....Redwood City CA 94063 650-716-1600 716-1601
NASDAQ: AGNT ■ *TF:* 877-655-4200 ■ *Web:* www.argotech.com
Armor Forensics 13386 International Pkwy....Jacksonville FL 32218 904-485-1836 588-0399*
**Fax Area Code:* 800 ■ *TF:* 800-852-0300 ■ *Web:* www.armorholdings.com
Athena Diagnostics Inc 377 Plantation St 4 Biotech Pk....Worcester MA 01605 508-756-2886 753-5601
TF: 800-394-4493 ■ *Web:* www.athenadiagnostics.com
Bachem-Peninsula Laboratories Inc 305 Old County Rd....San Carlos CA 94070 650-592-5392 595-4071
TF: 800-922-1516 ■ *Web:* www.bachem.com
Bayer Healthcare 511 Benedict Ave....Tarrytown NY 10591 914-631-8000 524-2132
TF: 800-431-1970 ■ *Web:* www.bayerdiag.com
BD Diagnostics 7 Loveton Cir....Sparks MD 21152 410-316-4000 316-4066
TF: 800-666-6433 ■ *Web:* www.bd.com
Becton Dickinson & Co 1 Becton Dr....Franklin Lakes NJ 07417 201-847-6800 847-4882*
NYSE: BDX ■ **Fax:* Cust Svc ■ *TF Cust Svc:* 888-237-2762 ■ *Web:* www.bd.com
Berlex Canada Inc 334 rue Avro....Pointe-Claire QC H9R5W5 514-631-7400 782-2242
Web: www.berlex.ca
Berlex Laboratories Inc 6 W Belt....Wayne NJ 07470 973-694-4100 305-5475
TF: 888-237-2394 ■ *Web:* www.berlex.com
Binax Inc 10 Southgate Rd....Scarborough ME 04074 207-730-5700 730-5710
TF: 800-323-3199 ■ *Web:* www.binax.com
Bio-Rad Laboratories 1000 Alfred Nobel Dr....Hercules CA 94547 510-724-7000 741-5824*
AMEX: BIO ■ **Fax:* Cust Svc ■ *Web:* www.biorad.com
Biodesign International 60 Industrial Pk Rd....Saco ME 04072 207-283-6500 283-4800
TF: 888-530-0140 ■ *Web:* www.biodesign.com
Biofield Corp 1025 Nine N Dr Suite M....Alpharetta GA 30004 770-740-8180 740-9366
Web: www.biofield.com
BioGenex Laboratories Inc 4600 Norris Canyon Rd....San Ramon CA 94583 925-275-0550 275-0580
TF: 800-421-4149 ■ *Web:* www.biogenex.com
Biomeda Corp 1851 Vanderbilt Rd....Texarkana AR 71854 870-779-8787 216-2299
TF: 800-341-8787 ■ *Web:* www.biomeda.com
Biomedical Technologies Inc 378 Page St....Stoughton MA 02072 781-344-9942 341-1451
Web: www.btiinc.com
Biomerica Inc 1533 Monrovia Ave....Newport Beach CA 92663 949-645-2111 722-6674
TF Cust Svc: 800-854-3002 ■ *Web:* www.biomerica.com
BioMerieux Inc 595 Anglum Rd....Hazelwood MO 63042 314-731-8500 325-1598*
**Fax Area Code:* 800 ■ *TF:* 800-638-4835 ■ *Web:* www.biomerieux.com
Bion Enterprises Ltd 455 State St Suite 100....Des Plaines IL 60016 847-544-5044 544-5051
Web: www.bionenterprises.com
Bionostics Inc 7 Jackson Rd....Devens MA 01434 978-772-7070 772-7072
TF: 800-533-6162 ■ *Web:* www.bionostics.com

Company	City	State	Zip	Phone	Fax
Biosite Inc 9975 Summers Ridge Rd	San Diego	CA	92121	858-455-4808	
NASDAQ: BSTE ■ *TF Cust Svc:* 888-246-7483 ■ *Web:* www.biosite.com					
BioSource International Inc 542 Flynn Rd	Camarillo	CA	93012	805-987-0086	383-5379
TF: 800-242-0607 ■ *Web:* www.biosource.com					
BiosPacific Inc 5980 Horton St Suite 225	Emeryville	CA	94608	510-652-6155	652-4531
TF: 800-344-6686 ■ *Web:* www.biospacific.com					
Biotest Diagnostics Corp 66 Ford Rd Suite 220	Denville	NJ	07834	973-625-1300	625-5882
TF: 800-522-0090 ■ *Web:* www.biotest.de					
BioVeris Corp 16020 Industrial Dr	Gaithersburg	MD	20877	301-869-9800	230-0158
NASDAQ: BIOV ■ *TF:* 800-339-4436 ■ *Web:* www.bioveris.com					
Caltag Laboratories Inc 1849 Bayshore Hwy	Burlingame	CA	94010	650-652-0468	652-9030
TF: 800-874-4007 ■ *Web:* www.caltag.com					
Calypte Biomedical Corp 5000 Hopyard Rd Suite 480	Pleasanton	CA	94588	925-730-7200	730-0072
AMEX: HIV ■ *TF:* 877-225-9783 ■ *Web:* www.calypte.com					
CEDARLANE Laboratories Inc 5516 8th Line RR 2	Hornby	ON	L0P1E0	905-878-8891	878-7800
TF: 800-268-5058 ■ *Web:* www.cedarlanelabs.com					
Chematics Inc Hwy 13 S PO Box 293	North Webster	IN	46555	574-834-2406	834-7427
TF: 800-348-5174 ■ *Web:* www.chematics.com					
Cholestech Corp 3347 Investment Blvd	Hayward	CA	94545	510-732-7200	732-7227
NASDAQ: CTEC ■ *TF:* 800-733-0404 ■ *Web:* www.cholestech.com					
Chromaprobe Inc 378 Fee Fee Rd	Maryland Heights	MO	63043	314-738-0001	738-0001
TF: 888-964-1400 ■ *Web:* www.chromaprobe.com					
Cliniqa Corp 1432 S Mission Rd	Fallbrook	CA	92028	760-728-5205	728-2902
TF: 800-728-5205 ■ *Web:* www.cliniqa.com					
Clontech Laboratories Inc 1290 Terra Bella Ave	Mountain View	CA	94043	800-662-2566	424-1350
TF: 877-232-8995 ■ *Web:* www.bdbiosciences.com/clontech					
Cocalico Biologicals Inc 449 Stevens Rd PO Box 265	Reamstown	PA	17567	717-336-1990	336-1993
Web: www.cocalicobiologicals.com					
Cortex Biochem Inc 1933 Davis St Suite 321	San Leandro	CA	94577	510-568-2228	568-2467
TF: 800-888-7713 ■ *Web:* www.cortex-biochem.com					
Covidien Ltd 15 Hampshire St	Mansfield	MA	02048	508-261-8000	261-8062
NYSE: COV ■ *Web:* www.covidien.com					
CST Technologies Inc 55 Northern Blvd Suite 200	Great Neck	NY	11021	516-482-9001	482-0186
TF: 800-448-4407 ■ *Web:* www.cstti.com					
Cytyc Corp 250 Campus Dr	Marlborough	MA	01752	508-263-2900	229-2795
NASDAQ: CYTC ■ *TF:* 800-442-9892 ■ *Web:* www.cytyc.com					
Dade Behring Inc 1717 Deerfield Rd	Deerfield	IL	60015	847-267-5300	236-7298
NASDAQ: DADE ■ *TF:* 800-948-3233 ■ *Web:* www.dadebehring.com					
DakoCytomation 6392 Via Real	Carpinteria	CA	93013	805-566-6655	566-1344
TF Cust Svc: 800-400-3256 ■ *Web:* www.dakocytomation.com					
Diagnostic Chemicals Ltd 16 McCarville St	Charlottetown	PE	C1E2A6	902-566-1396	566-2498
TF: 800-565-0265 ■ *Web:* www.dclchem.com					
Diagnostic Products Corp 5700 W 96th St	Los Angeles	CA	90045	310-645-8200	645-9999
NYSE: DP ■ *TF:* 800-678-6699 ■ *Web:* www.dpcweb.com					
Diagnostic Systems Laboratories Inc 445 Medical Center Blvd	Webster	TX	77598	281-332-9678	338-1895
TF: 800-231-7970 ■ *Web:* www.dslabs.com					
Diagnostic Technology Inc 175 Commerce Dr Suite L	Hauppauge	NY	11788	631-582-4949	582-4694
Diagnostics Biochem Canada Inc 1020 Hargrieve Rd Unit 11	London	ON	N6E1P5	519-681-8731	681-8731
Web: www.dbc-labs.com					
DiaSorin Inc 1951 Northwestern Ave	Stillwater	MN	55082	651-439-9710	351-5669
TF: 800-328-1482 ■ *Web:* www.diasorin.com					
Digene Corp 1201 Clopper Rd	Gaithersburg	MD	20878	301-944-7000	944-7121
NASDAQ: DIGE ■ *TF:* 800-344-3631 ■ *Web:* www.digene.com					
DuPont Agriculture & Nutrition					
1007 Market St DuPont Bldg	Wilmington	DE	19898	302-774-1000	999-4399
TF: 800-441-7515					
DuPont Qualicon Rt 141 Henry Clay Rd Bldg 400	Wilmington	DE	19880	302-695-5300	695-5301
TF: 800-863-6842 ■ *Web:* www.qualicon.com					
E-Z-EM Inc 1111 Marcus Ave Suite LL26	Lake Success	NY	11042	516-333-8230	333-8278
NASDAQ: EZEM ■ *TF:* 800-544-4624 ■ *Web:* www.ezem.com					
EMD Biosciences Inc 10394 Pacific Center Ct	San Diego	CA	92121	858-450-5500	453-3552
TF Cust Svc: 888-854-3417 ■ *Web:* www.emdbiosciences.com					
Enzo Biochem Inc 60 Executive Blvd	Farmingdale	NY	11735	631-755-5500	
NYSE: ENZ ■ *TF:* 800-522-5052 ■ *Web:* www.enzo.com					
EPIX Pharmaceuticals Inc 161 1st St	Cambridge	MA	02142	617-250-6000	250-6031
NASDAQ: EPIX ■ *Web:* www.epixmed.com					
EXACT Sciences Corp 100 Campus Dr	Marlborough	MA	01752	508-683-1200	683-1201
NASDAQ: EXAS ■ *Web:* www.exactlabs.com					
Exalpha Biologicals Inc 5 Clock Tower Pl Suite 255	Maynard	MA	01754	978-461-0435	461-0436
TF: 800-395-1137 ■ *Web:* www.exalpha.com					
Fisher Diagnostics 8365 Valley Pike PO Box 307	Middletown	VA	22645	540-869-3200	869-5249
TF: 800-528-0494 ■ *Web:* www.fisherdiagnostics.com					
Fisher Scientific International Inc 1 Liberty Ln	Hampton	NH	03842	603-926-5911	929-2379
NYSE: FSH ■ *Web:* www.fisherscientific.com					
Fisher Scientific International Inc HealthCare Div					
9999 Veterans Memorial Dr	Houston	TX	77038	281-820-9898	926-1166*
**Fax Area Code:* 800 ■ *TF:* 800-766-7000					
Fortune Biologicals Inc 18919 Premiere Ct	Gaithersburg	MD	20879	301-330-8547	330-8648
Gen-Probe Inc 10210 Genetic Center Dr	San Diego	CA	92121	858-410-8000	410-8625
NASDAQ: GPRO ■ *TF:* 800-523-5001 ■ *Web:* www.gen-probe.com					
GenBio 15222 Ave of Science Suite A	San Diego	CA	92128	858-592-9300	592-9400
TF Tech Supp: 800-288-4368 ■ *Web:* www.genbio.com					
Genzyme Corp 500 Kendall St	Cambridge	MA	02142	617-252-7500	252-7600
NASDAQ: GENZ ■ *TF:* 800-326-7002 ■ *Web:* www.genzyme.com					
Genzyme Diagnostics 500 Kendall Sq	Cambridge	MA	02139	617-252-7500	374-7300
TF: 800-326-7002 ■ *Web:* www.genzymediagnostics.com					
Gibson Laboratories Inc 1040 Manchester St	Lexington	KY	40508	859-254-9500	253-1476
TF: 800-477-4763 ■ *Web:* www.gibsonlabs.com					
Golden Bridge International Inc 9700 Harbour Pl Suite 129	Mukilteo	WA	98275	425-493-1801	672-2027
Web: www.gbi-inc.com					
Goodwin Biotechnology Inc 1850 NW 69th Ave	Plantation	FL	33313	954-321-5300	587-6378
TF: 800-814-8600 ■ *Web:* www.goodwinbio.com					
Harlan Bioproducts for Science Inc 298 S Carroll Rd	Indianapolis	IN	46229	317-353-8810	898-6400
TF: 800-972-4362 ■ *Web:* www.hbps.com					
Harlan Industries Inc 298 S Carroll Rd	Indianapolis	IN	46229	317-894-7521	894-1840
TF: 800-793-7287 ■ *Web:* www.harlan.com					
Helena Laboratories Inc 1530 Lindbergh Dr	Beaumont	TX	77704	409-842-3714	842-3094
TF: 800-231-5663 ■ *Web:* www.helena.com					
Hemagen Diagnostics Inc 9033 Red Branch Rd	Columbia	MD	21045	443-367-5500	997-7812*
**Fax Area Code:* 410 ■ *TF:* 800-436-2436 ■ *Web:* www.hemagen.com					
Hitachi Chemical Diagnostics 630 Clyde Ct	Mountain View	CA	94043	650-961-5501	969-2745
TF: 800-233-6278 ■ *Web:* www.hcdiagnostics.com					
Home Diagnostics Inc 2400 NW 55th Ct	Fort Lauderdale	FL	33309	954-677-9201	739-8506
TF: 800-342-7226 ■ *Web:* www.homediagnosticsinc.com					
Hycor Biomedical Inc 7272 Chapman Ave	Garden Grove	CA	92841	714-933-3000	933-3222
TF Cust Svc: 800-382-2527 ■ *Web:* www.hycorbiomedical.com					
IDEXX Laboratories Inc 1 IDEXX Dr	Westbrook	ME	04092	207-856-0300	856-0346
NASDAQ: IDXX ■ *TF:* 800-932-4399 ■ *Web:* www.idexx.com					
ImmucorGamma Inc 3130 Gateway Dr PO Box 5625	Norcross	GA	30091	770-441-2051	441-3807
NASDAQ: BLUD ■ *TF Cust Svc:* 800-829-2553 ■ *Web:* www.immucor.com					
Immuno-Mycologics Inc 1236 E Redbud Rd	Goldsby	OK	73093	405-288-2383	288-2228
TF: 800-654-3639 ■ *Web:* www.immy.com					
ImmunoDiagnostics Inc 21 F Olympia Ave	Woburn	MA	01801	781-938-6300	938-7300
TF: 800-573-1700 ■ *Web:* www.immunodx.com					
Immunovision Inc 1820 Ford Ave	Springdale	AR	72764	479-751-7005	751-7002
TF: 800-541-0960 ■ *Web:* www.immunovision.com					
InSite Vision Inc 965 Atlantic Ave	Alameda	CA	94501	510-865-8800	865-5700
AMEX: ISV ■ *TF:* 800-726-7483 ■ *Web:* www.insitevision.com					
Interleukin Genetics Inc 135 Beaver St 3rd Fl	Waltham	MA	02452	781-398-0700	398-0720
AMEX: ILI ■ *Web:* www.ilgenetics.com					
International Immunology Corp 25549 Adams Ave	Murrieta	CA	92562	951-677-5629	677-6752
TF: 800-843-2853 ■ *Web:* www.iicsera.com					
International Isotopes Inc 4137 Commerce Circle	Idaho Falls	ID	83401	208-524-5300	524-1411
TF: 800-699-3108 ■ *Web:* www.intisoid.com					
Intracel Resources LLC 93 Monocacy Blvd Unit A 8	Frederick	MD	21701	301-668-8400	668-6317
TF: 877-289-5476 ■ *Web:* www.intracel.com					
Inverness Medical Innovations Inc 51 Sawyer Rd Suite 200	Waltham	MA	02453	781-647-3900	647-3939
AMEX: IMA ■ *TF:* 877-696-2525 ■ *Web:* www.invernessmedicalpd.com					
InVitro International 17751 Sky Park E Suite G	Irvine	CA	92614	949-851-8356	851-4985
TF: 800-246-8487 ■ *Web:* www.invitrointl.com					
Iso-Tex Diagnostics Inc PO Box 909	Friendswood	TX	77549	281-482-1231	482-1070
TF: 800-477-4839 ■ *Web:* www.isotexdiagnostics.com					
IVAX Diagnostics Inc 2140 N Miami Ave	Miami	FL	33127	305-324-2300	324-2395
AMEX: IVD ■ *TF:* 800-327-4565 ■ *Web:* www.ivaxdiagnostics.com					
Jackson ImmunoResearch Laboratories Inc					
872 W Baltimore Pike	West Grove	PA	19390	610-869-4024	869-0171
TF: 800-367-5296 ■ *Web:* www.jacksonimmuno.com					
Kamiya Biomedical Co 12779 Gateway Dr	Seattle	WA	98168	206-575-8068	575-8094
Web: www.kamiyabiomedical.com					
Kirkegaard & Perry Laboratories Inc 910 Clopper Rd	Gaithersburg	MD	20878	301-948-7755	948-0169
TF: 800-638-3167 ■ *Web:* www.kpl.com					
KMI Diagnostics Inc 8201 Central Ave NE Suite P	Minneapolis	MN	55432	763-780-2955	780-2988
TF: 888-523-1246 ■ *Web:* www.kmidiagnostics.com					
Life Sciences Inc 2900 72nd St N	Saint Petersburg	FL	33710	727-345-9371	347-2957
TF: 800-237-4323 ■ *Web:* www.lifesci.com					
LifeScan Inc 1000 Gibraltar Dr	Milpitas	CA	95035	408-263-9789	946-6070
TF: 800-227-8862 ■ *Web:* www.lifescan.com					
Lightning Powder Co Inc 13386 International Pkwy	Jacksonville	FL	32218	904-741-5400	741-5403
Web: www.redwop.com					
LipoScience Inc 2500 Sumner Blvd	Raleigh	NC	27616	919-212-1999	255-3055
TF: 877-547-6837 ■ *Web:* www.liposcience.com					
Maine Biotechnology Services Inc 1037 R Forest Ave	Portland	ME	04103	207-797-5454	797-5595
TF: 800-925-9476 ■ *Web:* www.mainebiotechnology.com					
Mallinckrodt Inc 675 McDonnell Blvd	Hazelwood	MO	63042	314-654-2000	654-6257*
**Fax:* Hum Res ■ *TF:* 888-744-1414 ■ *Web:* www.mallinckrodt.com					
Mallinckrodt Pharmaceutical Products 675 McDonnell Blvd	Hazelwood	MO	63042	314-654-2000	654-6257
TF: 888-744-1414 ■ *Web:* www.mallinckrodt.com					
Matritech Inc 330 Nevada St	Newton	MA	02460	617-928-0820	928-0821
AMEX: MZT ■ *Web:* www.matritech.com					
Medical Analysis Systems Inc 46360 Fremont Blvd	Fremont	CA	94538	510-979-5000	979-5002
TF: 800-232-3342 ■ *Web:* www.mas-inc.com					
MEDTOX Diagnostics Inc 1238 Anthony Rd	Burlington	NC	27215	336-226-6311	229-4471
TF: 800-334-1116 ■ *Web:* www.medtox.com					
Meridian Bioscience Inc 3471 River Hills Dr	Cincinnati	OH	45244	513-271-3700	272-5421
NASDAQ: VIVO ■ *TF Cust Svc:* 800-543-1980 ■ *Web:* www.meridianbioscience.com					
Millipore Corp 290 Concord Rd	Billerica	MA	01821	978-715-4321	645-5439*
NYSE: MIL ■ **Fax Area Code:* 800 ■ *TF:* 800-645-5476 ■ *Web:* www.millipore.com					
Monobind Inc 100 N Point Dr	Lake Forest	CA	92630	949-951-2665	951-3539
TF: 800-854-6265 ■ *Web:* www.monobind.com					
Moss Inc 2605 Cab Over Dr Suite 11	Hanover	MD	21076	410-768-3442	768-3971
TF: 800-932-6677 ■ *Web:* www.mosssubstrates.com					
Nabi Biopharmaceuticals 12276 Wilkins Ave	Rockville	MD	20852	301-770-3099	770-3097
NASDAQ: NABI ■ *TF:* 800-685-5579 ■ *Web:* www.nabi.com					
National Diagnostics Inc 305 Patton Dr	Atlanta	GA	30336	404-699-2121	699-2077
TF: 800-526-3867 ■ *Web:* www.nationaldiagnostics.com					
Neogen Corp 620 Lesher Pl	Lansing	MI	48912	517-372-9200	372-2006
NASDAQ: NEOG ■ *TF:* 800-234-5333 ■ *Web:* www.neogen.com					
New Horizons Diagnostics Corp 9110 Red Branch Rd	Columbia	MD	21045	410-992-9357	992-0328
TF: 800-888-5015 ■ *Web:* www.nhdiag.com					
North American Scientific Inc 20200 Sunburst St	Chatsworth	CA	91311	818-734-8600	734-5200
NASDAQ: NASI ■ *TF:* 800-992-6274 ■ *Web:* www.nasi.net					
Novartis Vaccines & Diagnostics 4560 Horton St	Emeryville	CA	94608	510-655-8730	655-9910
TF: 800-524-4766 ■ *Web:* www.novartis-vaccines.com					
Omega Biologicals Inc 910 Technology Blvd	Bozeman	MT	59718	406-586-3790	586-3792
Oncogene Science 80 Rogers St	Cambridge	MA	02142	617-492-7289	492-8438
TF Sales: 888-674-3424 ■ *Web:* www.oncogene.com					
OraSure Technologies Inc 220 1st St	Bethlehem	PA	18015	610-882-1820	882-1830
NASDAQ: OSUR ■ *TF:* 800-869-3538 ■ *Web:* www.orasure.com					
Ortho-Clinical Diagnostics Inc 1001 US Rt 202 N PO Box 350	Raritan	NJ	08869	908-218-1300	453-3660*
**Fax Area Code:* 585 ■ **Fax:* Cust Svc ■ *TF:* 800-828-6316 ■					
Web: www.orthoclinical.com					
Oxford Biomedical Research Inc					
2165 Avon Industrial Dr	Rochester Hills	MI	48309	248-852-8815	852-4466
TF: 800-692-4633 ■ *Web:* www.oxfordbiomed.com					
Pacific Biometrics Inc 220 W Harrison St	Seattle	WA	98119	206-298-0068	298-9838
TF: 800-767-9151 ■ *Web:* www.pacbio.com					
Panbio Inc 9075 Guilford Rd	Columbia	MD	21046	410-381-8550	381-8984
TF: 800-962-6790 ■ *Web:* www.panbio.com.au					
Peptides International Inc 11621 Electron Dr	Louisville	KY	40299	502-266-8787	267-1329
TF: 800-777-4779 ■ *Web:* www.pepnet.com					
PerkinElmer Inc 45 William St	Wellesley	MA	02481	781-237-5100	237-9386
NYSE: PKI ■ *Web:* www.perkinelmer.com					
PerkinElmer Life & Analytical Sciences Inc 549 Albany St	Boston	MA	02118	617-482-9595	925-4654*
**Fax Area Code:* 203 ■ *TF:* 800-762-4000 ■ *Web:* las.perkinelmer.com					
Pharmaceutical Innovations Inc 897 Frelinghuysen Ave	Newark	NJ	07114	973-242-2900	242-0578
Web: www.pharminnovations.com					
Pierce Biotechnology Inc 3747 N Meridian Rd	Rockford	IL	61101	815-968-0747	968-7316
TF: 800-874-3723 ■ *Web:* www.piercenet.com					
PML Microbiologicals Inc 27120 SW 95th Ave	Wilsonville	OR	97070	503-570-2500	570-2501
TF Cust Svc: 800-628-7014 ■ *Web:* www.pmlmicro.com					
Pointe Scientific Inc 5449 Research Dr	Canton	MI	48188	734-487-8300	483-1592
TF: 800-445-9853 ■ *Web:* www.pointescientific.com					
Polymedco Inc 510 Furnace Dock Rd	Cortlandt Manor	NY	10567	914-739-5400	739-5890
TF: 800-431-2123 ■ *Web:* www.polymedco.com					
Polysciences Inc 400 Valley Rd	Warrington	PA	18976	215-343-6484	343-0214
TF Cust Svc: 800-523-2575 ■ *Web:* www.polysciences.com					
Promega Corp 2800 Woods Hollow Rd	Madison	WI	53711	608-274-4330	277-2516
TF: 800-356-9526 ■ *Web:* www.promega.com					
Protein Sciences Corp 1000 Research Pkwy	Meriden	CT	06450	203-686-0800	686-0268
Web: www.proteinsciences.com					
Prozyme Inc 1933 Davis St Suite 207	San Leandro	CA	94577	510-638-6900	638-6919
TF: 800-457-9444 ■ *Web:* www.prozyme.com					
Quality Biological Inc 7581 Lindbergh Dr	Gaithersburg	MD	20879	301-840-9331	840-0743
TF: 800-443-9331 ■ *Web:* www.qualitybiological.com					
Quantimetrix Corp 2005 Manhattan Beach Blvd	Redondo Beach	CA	90278	310-536-0006	536-9977
TF: 800-624-8380 ■ *Web:* www.4qc.com					
Quidel Corp 10165 McKellar Ct	San Diego	CA	92121	858-552-1100	453-4338
NASDAQ: QDEL ■ *TF:* 800-874-1517 ■ *Web:* www.quidel.com					
R & D Systems Inc 614 McKinley Pl NE	Minneapolis	MN	55413	612-379-2956	656-4400
TF: 800-343-7475 ■ *Web:* www.rndsystems.com					
Remel Inc 12076 Santa Fe Dr	Lenexa	KS	66215	913-888-0939	621-8251*
**Fax Area Code:* 800 ■ *TF:* 800-255-6730 ■ *Web:* www.remelinc.com					

Company	City	State	Zip	Phone	Fax
Research & Diagnostic Antibodies 9030 W Sahara Ave Suite 40-B *Web:* www.rdabs.com	Las Vegas	NV	89117	702-638-7800	
Research Organics Inc 4353 E 49th St *TF:* 800-321-0570 ■ *Web:* www.resorg.com	Cleveland	OH	44125	216-883-8025	883-1576
Roche Diagnostics Corp 9115 Hague Rd *TF Cust Svc:* 800-428-5076 ■ *Web:* www.roche-diagnostics.us	Indianapolis	IN	46250	317-521-2000	521-2090
Roche Diagnostics North America 9115 Hague Rd *TF Cust Svc:* 800-428-5076 ■ *Web:* www.roche-diagnostics.us	Indianapolis	IN	46250	317-521-2000	521-2090
Roche Molecular Systems Inc 4300 Hacienda Dr *TF:* 800-526-1247 ■ *Web:* www.roche-diagnostics.com	Pleasanton	CA	94588	925-730-8000	225-0369
Rockland Immunochemicals Inc 650 Englesville Rd *TF:* 800-656-7625 ■ *Web:* www.rockland-inc.com	Boyertown	PA	19512	610-369-1008	367-7825
Scantibodies Laboratory Inc 9336 Abraham Way *Web:* www.scantibodies.com	Santee	CA	92071	619-258-9300	258-9366
SCIMEDX Corp 100 Ford Rd *TF:* 800-221-5598 ■ *Web:* www.scimedx.com	Denville	NJ	07834	973-625-8822	625-8796
Scripps Laboratories Inc 6838 Flanders Dr *Web:* www.scrippslabs.com	San Diego	CA	92121	858-546-5800	546-5812
Seradyn Inc 7998 Georgetown Rd Suite 1000 *TF:* 800-428-4072 ■ *Web:* www.seradyn.com	Indianapolis	IN	46268	317-610-3800	610-0018
Sigma-Aldrich Corp 3050 Spruce St *NASDAQ: SIAL* ■ **Fax Area Code:* 800 ■ *TF:* 800-325-3010 ■ *Web:* www.sigmaaldrich.com	Saint Louis	MO	63103	314-771-5765	325-5052*
Southern Biotechnology Assoc Inc 160A Oxmoor Blvd *TF:* 800-722-2255 ■ *Web:* www.southernbiotech.com	Birmingham	AL	35209	205-945-1774	945-8768
Stratagene Inc 11011 N Torrey Pines Rd *NASDAQ: STGN* ■ *TF:* 800-894-1304 ■ *Web:* www.stratagene.com	La Jolla	CA	92037	858-535-5400	535-0071
Strategic Diagnostics Inc 111 Pencader Dr *NASDAQ: SDIX* ■ *TF:* 800-544-8881 ■ *Web:* www.sdix.com	Newark	DE	19702	302-456-6789	456-6770
SurModics Inc 9924 W 74th St *NASDAQ: SRDX* ■ *Web:* www.surmodics.com	Eden Prairie	MN	55344	952-829-2700	829-2743
Synergent Biochem Inc 12026 Centralia Rd Suite H *TF:* 800-585-8580 ■ *Web:* www.synergentbiochem.com	Hawaiian Gardens	CA	90716	562-809-3389	809-6191
Techne Corp 614 McKinley Pl NE *NASDAQ: TECH* ■ *TF:* 800-328-2400 ■ *Web:* www.techne-corp.com	Minneapolis	MN	55413	612-379-8854	379-6580
Teco Diagnostics 1268 N Lakeview Ave *TF:* 800-222-9880 ■ *Web:* www.tecodiag.com	Anaheim	CA	92807	714-693-7788	693-3838
Theragenics Corp 5203 Bristol Industrial Way *NYSE: TGX* ■ **Fax Area Code:* 678 ■ *TF:* 800-458-4372 ■ *Web:* www.theragenics.com	Buford	GA	30518	770-271-0233	482-4909*
Trinity Biotech PLC 5919 Farnsworth Ct *NASDAQ: TRIB* ■ *TF:* 800-331-2291 ■ *Web:* www.trinitybiotech.com	Carlsbad	CA	92008	760-929-0500	929-0124
Utak Laboratories Inc 25020 Ave Tibbitts *TF:* 800-235-3442 ■ *Web:* www.utaklabs.com	Valencia	CA	91355	661-294-3935	294-9272
Varian Inc 25200 Commercentre Dr *TF:* 800-854-0277 ■ *Web:* www.varianinc.com	Lake Forest	CA	92630	949-770-9381	768-1050
Wako Chemicals USA Inc 1600 Bellwood Rd *TF:* 800-992-9256 ■ *Web:* www.wakousa.com	Richmond	VA	23237	804-271-7677	271-7791
Worthington Biochemical Corp 730 Vassar Ave *TF:* 800-445-9603 ■ *Web:* www.worthington-biochem.com	Lakewood	NJ	08701	732-942-1660	942-9270
Zepto Metrix Corp 872 Main St *TF Cust Svc:* 800-274-5487 ■ *Web:* www.zeptometrix.com	Buffalo	NY	14202	716-882-0920	882-0959
Zymed Laboratories Inc 561 Eccles Ave *TF:* 800-874-4494 ■ *Web:* www.zymed.com	South San Francisco	CA	94080	650-871-4494	244-8698

235 DISPLAYS - EXHIBIT & TRADE SHOW

Company	City	State	Zip	Phone	Fax
3D Exhibits Inc 2800 Lively Blvd *TF:* 800-471-9617 ■ *Web:* www.3dexhibits.com	Elk Grove Village	IL	60007	847-250-9000	860-8165
CB Displays International 5141 S Procyon Ave *Web:* www.cbdisplay.com	Las Vegas	NV	89118	702-739-9301	739-8154
Charles Mayer Studios Inc 105 E Market St Suite 114	Akron	OH	44308	330-535-6121	434-2016
Derse Exhibits Inc 1234 N 62nd St *TF:* 800-562-2300 ■ *Web:* www.derse.com	Milwaukee	WI	53213	414-257-2000	257-1145
Design & Production Inc 7110 Rainwater Pl *Web:* www.d-and-p.com	Lorton	VA	22079	703-550-8640	339-0296
Downing Displays Inc 550 TechneCenter Dr *TF:* 800-883-1800 ■ *Web:* www.downingdisplays.com	Milford	OH	45150	513-248-9800	248-2605
Exhibitgroup/Giltspur 200 N Gary Ave *TF:* 800-843-3944 ■ *Web:* www.e-g.com	Roselle	IL	60172	630-307-2400	351-7899
Exhibits & More 7615 Omnitech Pl Suite 4 *Web:* www.exhibitsandmore.com	Victor	NY	14564	585-924-4040	924-4056
Expon Exhibits 1902 Channel Dr *TF:* 800-783-9766 ■ *Web:* www.exponexhibits.com	West Sacramento	CA	95691	916-371-1600	371-1665
General Exhibits & Displays Inc 1425 Appleby Rd	Palatine	IL	60067	773-736-6699	736-6699
Group360 Inc 10818 Midwest Industrial Blvd *TF:* 800-666-8243 ■ *Web:* www.group360.com	Saint Louis	MO	63132	314-423-9300	423-6104
Hadley Exhibits Inc 1700 Elmwood Ave *TF:* 866-429-3666 ■ *Web:* www.hadleyexhibits.com	Buffalo	NY	14207	716-874-3666	874-9994
HB Stubbs Co 27027 Mound Rd *TF:* 800-968-2132 ■ *Web:* www.hbstubbs.com	Warren	MI	48092	586-574-9700	574-9741
ICON Exhibits 8333 Clinton Pk Dr *TF:* 800-320-4266 ■ *Web:* www.iconexhibits.com	Fort Wayne	IN	46825	260-483-6441	482-4877
Lynch Exhibits 7 Campus Dr Burlington Business Campus *TF:* 800-343-1666 ■ *Web:* www.lynchindustries.com	Burlington	NJ	08016	609-387-1600	239-1666
Marketechs Exhibit Design Inc 3425 Woodbridge Cir *Web:* www.marketechs.com	York	PA	17406	717-764-2588	764-2930
MG Design Assoc Corp 8778 100th St *TF:* 800-643-9442 ■ *Web:* www.mgdesign.com	Pleasant Prairie	WI	53158	262-947-8890	947-8898
Siegel Display Products 300 6th Ave N **Fax Area Code:* 800 ■ *TF:* 800-626-0322 ■ *Web:* www.siegeldisplay.com	Minneapolis	MN	55401	612-340-1493	230-5598*
Skyline Displays Inc DBA Skyline Exhibits 3355 Discovery Rd *TF:* 800-328-2725 ■ *Web:* www.skycorp.com	Eagan	MN	55121	651-234-6000	234-6001
Sparks Exhibits & Environments 10232 Palm Dr *Web:* www.sparksonline.com	Santa Fe Springs	CA	90670	562-941-0101	941-5551
Structural Display Inc 12-12 33rd Ave *Web:* www.sdiny.com	Long Island City	NY	11106	718-274-1136	278-8212
Tandem Design Inc 1846 Sequoia Ave *Web:* www.tandemdesigninc.com	Orange	CA	92868	714-978-7272	978-7273

236 DISPLAYS - POINT-OF-PURCHASE

SEE ALSO Signs p. 2317

Company	City	State	Zip	Phone	Fax
Acrylic Design Assoc 6050 Nathan Ln N *TF:* 800-445-2167 ■ *Web:* www.acrylicdesign.com	Plymouth	MN	55442	763-559-8395	559-2589
Advance Display Co 1657 N Kostner Ave *Web:* www.advancedisplay.net	Chicago	IL	60639	773-235-0400	235-3633
Alexander Plastics Inc DBA Creations at Dallas 11937 Denton Dr *TF:* 800-421-4171 ■ *Web:* www.creationsatdallas.com	Dallas	TX	75234	972-241-4171	243-3447
AMD Industries Inc 4620 W 19th St *TF:* 800-367-9999 ■ *Web:* www.amdpop.com	Cicero	IL	60804	708-863-8900	863-2065
Apco Products Inc PO Box 236 *Web:* www.apco-products.com	Essex	CT	06426	860-767-2108	767-7259
Archbold Container Corp 800 W Barre Rd PO Box 10 *TF:* 800-446-2520 ■ *Web:* www.archboldcontainer.com	Archbold	OH	43502	419-445-8865	446-2529
Arlington Display Industries 19303 W Davison St *Web:* www.arlingtondisplay.com	Detroit	MI	48223	313-837-1212	837-3425
Array Marketing 45 Progress Ave *TF:* 800-295-4120 ■ *Web:* www.arraymarketing.com	Toronto	ON	M1P2Y6	416-299-4865	
Art-Phyl Creations 16250 NW 48th Ave *TF:* 800-327-8318 ■ *Web:* www.art-phyl.com	Hialeah	FL	33014	305-624-2333	621-4093
Artkraft Strauss LLC 1776 Broadway Suite 1810 *Web:* www.artkraft.com	New York	NY	10019	212-265-5155	265-5262
Blitz USA Inc 404 26th Ave NW *TF Cust Svc:* 800-331-3795 ■ *Web:* www.blitzusa.com	Miami	OK	74354	918-540-1515	542-1380
Cannon Equipment Co 15100 Business Pkwy *TF:* 800-825-8501 ■ *Web:* www.cannonequipment.com	Rosemount	MN	55068	651-322-6300	322-1583
Chicago Display Marketing Corp 2021 West St *TF:* 800-681-4340 ■ *Web:* www.chicagodisplay.com	River Grove	IL	60171	708-842-0001	456-4672
Concept Display & Packaging Corp 250 Hudson St 8th Fl *Web:* www.conceptdisplaycorp.com	New York	NY	10013	212-645-3118	645-3979
Creations at Dallas 11937 Denton Dr *TF:* 800-421-4171 ■ *Web:* www.creationsatdallas.com	Dallas	TX	75234	972-241-4171	243-3447
DAC Products 100 Century Point Dr *TF:* 800-431-1982 ■ *Web:* www.dacproducts.com	East Bend	NC	27018	336-699-2900	699-2231
Display Smart LLC 801 W 27th Terr *TF:* 888-843-1870 ■ *Web:* www.display-smart.com	Lawrence	KS	66046	785-843-1869	843-1874
Display Technologies LLC 111-01 14th Ave 3rd Fl *TF:* 800-424-4220 ■ *Web:* www.display-technologies.com	College Point	NY	11356	718-321-3100	321-1932
Eastern Display 498 Kinsley Ave **Fax:* Orders ■ *TF:* 800-486-3181 ■ *Web:* www.easterndisplaygroup.com	Providence	RI	02909	401-861-1350	274-3988*
Felbro Inc 3666 E Olympic Blvd *TF:* 800-733-5276 ■ *Web:* www.felbro-inc.com	Los Angeles	CA	90023	323-263-8686	263-8874
Frank Mayer & Assoc Inc 1975 Wisconsin Ave *TF:* 800-225-3987 ■ *Web:* www.frankmayer.com	Grafton	WI	53024	262-377-4700	377-3449
Harbor Industries Inc 14130 172nd Ave *TF:* 800-968-6993 ■ *Web:* www.harbor-ind.com	Grand Haven	MI	49417	616-842-5330	842-1385
Hunter Display 14 Hewlett Ave *TF:* 800-767-2110 ■ *Web:* www.hunterdisplays.com	East Patchogue	NY	11772	631-475-5900	475-5950
IDEAL 4800 S Austin Ave *TF:* 800-287-3104 ■ *Web:* www.idealbox.com	Chicago	IL	60638	708-594-3100	594-3109
Ideal Wire Works Inc 820 S Date Ave *Web:* www.idealwireworks.com	Alhambra	CA	91803	626-282-0886	282-2674
International Visual Corp (IVC) 4765 Des Grandes Prairies *TF:* 866-643-0570 ■ *Web:* www.ivcweb.com	Montreal	QC	H1R1A5	514-643-0570	643-4867
IVC (International Visual Corp) 4765 Des Grandes Prairies *TF:* 866-643-0570 ■ *Web:* www.ivcweb.com	Montreal	QC	H1R1A5	514-643-0570	643-4867
Kay Co Inc The 509 W Barner St	Frankfort	IN	46041	765-659-3388	659-2956
Kosakura & Assoc 2215 S Standard Ave *Web:* www.kosakura.com	Santa Ana	CA	92707	714-668-3000	668-3010
Lakeshore Display Co Inc 2031 Washington Ave *Web:* www.lakeshoredisplay.com	Sheboygan	WI	53081	920-457-3695	457-5673
Lingo Mfg Co 7400 Industrial Rd *TF Cust Svc:* 800-354-9771 ■ *Web:* www.lingomfg.com	Florence	KY	41042	859-371-2662	371-0283
Mayer Frank & Assoc Inc 1975 Wisconsin Ave *TF:* 800-225-3987 ■ *Web:* www.frankmayer.com	Grafton	WI	53024	262-377-4700	377-3449
MCA Industries 6811st St SW *Web:* www.mcapop.com	Massillon	OH	44646	330-833-3165	832-9771
MDI Worldwide 38271 W 12-Mile Rd **Fax:* Sales ■ *TF Sales:* 800-228-8925 ■ *Web:* www.mdiworldwide.com	Farmington Hills	MI	48331	248-553-1900	488-5700*
Miller Multiplex Inc 512 Stockton St *TF:* 800-757-1112 ■ *Web:* www.millermultiplex.com	Richmond	VA	23224	804-232-4551	233-0986
Millrock Div Modular Brand Group LLC 405 West St **Fax Area Code:* 617 ■ *TF:* 800-645-7625 ■ *Web:* www.millrock.com	West Bridgewater	MA	02379	508-584-0084	687-7700*
Modular Brand Group LLC Millrock Div 405 West St **Fax Area Code:* 617 ■ *TF:* 800-645-7625 ■ *Web:* www.millrock.com	West Bridgewater	MA	02379	508-584-0084	687-7700*
Nashville Display Mfg Co 306 Hartmann Dr *Web:* www.nashvilledisplay.com	Lebanon	TN	37087	615-255-6331	244-4368
New Dimensions Research Corp 260 Spagnoli Rd *TF:* 800-637-8870 ■ *Web:* www.newdimensionsresearch.com	Melville	NY	11747	631-694-1356	694-6097
Ovation-in-Store 5713 49th Pl *Web:* www.ovationadvantage.com	Maspeth	NY	11378	718-628-2600	628-2637
Rapid Displays 4300 W 47th St *TF:* 800-356-5775 ■ *Web:* www.rapiddisplays.com	Chicago	IL	60632	773-927-5000	927-1091
Rock-Tenn Co 504 Thrasher St PO Box 4098 *NYSE: RKT* ■ *TF:* 800-762-5836 ■ *Web:* www.rocktenn.com	Norcross	GA	30091	770-448-2193	263-4483
Service Products Inc 5900 W 51st St **Fax Area Code:* 708	Chicago	IL	60638	773-767-2360	496-1818*
Sonoco Corrflex Display 701 Rickert St *TF:* 800-334-8384 ■ *Web:* www.corrflexgraphics.com	Statesville	NC	28677	704-872-7777	872-7778
Thorco Industries Inc 1300 E 12th St *TF:* 800-445-3375 ■ *Web:* www.thorco.com	Lamar	MO	64759	417-682-3375	682-3247
Trans World Marketing Corp 360 Murray Hill Pkwy *Web:* www.transworldmarketing.com	East Rutherford	NJ	07073	201-935-5565	559-1888
Unicorr 455 Sackett Point Rd *TF:* 800-229-4269 ■ *Web:* www.unicorr.com	North Haven	CT	06473	203-248-2161	248-0241
United Displaycraft 333 E Touhy Ave *TF:* 877-632-8767 ■ *Web:* www.uniteddisplaycraft.com	Des Plaines	IL	60018	847-375-3800	375-3801
Universal Display & Fixtures Co 726 E Hwy 121 *TF:* 800-235-0701 ■ *Web:* www.udfc.com	Lewisville	TX	75057	972-221-5022	221-6624
Vestcom International Inc 5 Henderson Dr *TF:* 800-865-1821 ■ *Web:* www.vestcom.com	West Caldwell	NJ	07006	973-287-1000	882-9724
Visual Marketing Inc 154 W Erie St *TF:* 800-662-8640 ■ *Web:* www.vmichicago.com	Chicago	IL	60610	312-664-9177	664-9473
Vulcan Industries Inc 300 Display Dr *TF:* 888-444-4417 ■ *Web:* www.vulcanind.com	Moody	AL	35004	205-640-2400	640-2412

DOOR & WINDOW GLASS

SEE Glass - Flat, Plate, Tempered p. 1690

237 DOORS & WINDOWS - METAL

SEE ALSO Shutters - Window (All Types) p. 2316

Company / Address	City	State	Zip	Phone	Fax
Aluma-Glass Industries Inc 909 N Orchard St	Boise	ID	83706	208-375-0326	375-3774
Aluma Shield Industries Inc Butcher Boy Doors Div 725 Summerhill Dr.	DeLand	FL	32724	386-626-6789	626-6884
TF: 888-882-5862					
Amsco Windows Inc 1880 S 1045 West	Salt Lake City	UT	84104	801-978-5000	862-6726*
**Fax Area Code:* 800 ■ *TF:* 800-748-4661 ■ *Web:* www.amscowindows.com					
Anemostat 1220 Watsoncenter Rd	Carson	CA	90745	310-835-7500	835-0448
TF: 800-982-9000 ■ *Web:* www.anemostat.com					
Armaclad Inc 6806 Anthony Hwy	Waynesboro	PA	17268	717-749-3141	749-3712
TF: 800-541-6666 ■ *Web:* www.armaclad.com					
ASSA ABLOY Door Security Solutions 110 Sargent Dr.	New Haven	CT	06511	203-624-5225	777-9042*
**Fax:* Sales ■ *TF:* 800-377-3948 ■ *Web:* www.assaabloydss.com					
Atrium Cos Inc 3890 W Northwest Hwy Suite 500	Dallas	TX	75220	214-630-5757	630-5001
TF: 800-421-6292 ■ *Web:* www.atriumcompanies.com					
Babcock-Davis 9300 73rd Ave N	Brooklyn Park	MN	55428	763-488-9200	488-9248
TF: 888-412-3726 ■ *Web:* www.babcock-davis.com					
Butcher Boy Doors Div Aluma Shield Industries Inc 725 Summerhill Dr.	DeLand	FL	32724	386-626-6789	626-6884
TF: 888-882-5862					
Ceco Door Products 9159 Telecom Dr	Milan	TN	38358	731-686-8345	686-4211
Web: www.cecodoor.com					
Clopay Building Products Inc PO Box 440	Baldwin	WI	54002	715-684-3223	545-0664*
**Fax Area Code:* 800 ■ *TF:* 800-621-3667 ■ *Web:* www.clopaydoor.com					
Columbia Mfg Corp 14400 S San Pedro St	Gardena	CA	90248	310-327-9300	323-9862
TF: 800-729-3667 ■ *Web:* www.columbiamfg.com					
Comprehensive Mfg Services LLC DBA Courion 3044 Lambdin Ave	Saint Louis	MO	63115	314-533-5700	533-5720
TF: 800-533-5760					
Cookson Co 2417 S 50th Ave	Phoenix	AZ	85043	602-272-4244	233-2132
TF: 800-294-4358 ■ *Web:* www.cooksondoor.com					
Cornell Iron Works Inc 100 Elmwood Ave Crestwood Industrial Pk.	Mountain Top	PA	18707	570-474-6773	474-9973
TF Cust Svc: 800-233-8366 ■ *Web:* www.cornelliron.com					
Courion 3044 Lambdin Ave	Saint Louis	MO	63115	314-533-5700	533-5720
TF: 800-533-5760					
Creation Group Inc 53032 County Rd 13 PO Box 1025	Elkhart	IN	46515	574-264-3131	264-6268
TF: 800-862-3131 ■ *Web:* www.creationgroup.com					
Curries Co 1502 12th St SW	Mason City	IA	50401	641-423-1334	424-8305
Web: www.curries.com					
Dawson Metal Co Inc 825 Allen St.	Jamestown	NY	14701	716-664-3815	664-3485
TF: 877-732-9766 ■ *Web:* www.dawsonmetal.com					
Dominion Building Products 6949 Fairbanks N Houston Rd	Houston	TX	77040	713-466-6790	466-8177
Web: www.dominionproducts.com					
Drew Industries Inc 200 Mamaroneck Ave Suite 301	White Plains	NY	10601	914-428-9098	428-4581
NYSE: DW ■ *Web:* www.drewindustries.com					
Dunbarton Corp 868 Murray Rd	Dothan	AL	36303	334-794-0661	793-7022
TF: 800-633-7553 ■ *Web:* www.dunbarton.com					
Eastern Garage Door 417 Canal St	Lawrence	MA	01842	978-683-3158	794-0745
TF: 800-766-6012 ■ *Web:* www.lawrenceplate.com					
EFCO Corp 1000 County Rd.	Monett	MO	65708	417-235-3193	235-7313
TF: 800-221-4169 ■ *Web:* www.efcocorp.com					
Elixir Industries Inc 24800 Chrisanta Dr Suite 210	Mission Viejo	CA	92691	949-860-5000	860-5011
TF: 800-421-1942 ■ *Web:* www.elixirind.com					
Ellison Bronze Co Inc 125 W Main St	Falconer	NY	14733	716-665-6522	665-5552
TF: 800-665-6445 ■ *Web:* www.ellison-bronze.com					
Emco Specialties Inc 2121 E Walnut St.	Des Moines	IA	50317	515-265-6101	299-8765
TF Cust Svc: 800-933-3626 ■ *Web:* www.forever.com					
Empire Pacific Industries 10255 SW Spokane Ct PO Box 4210	Tualatin	OR	97062	503-692-6167	692-3075
TF: 800-473-7013 ■ *Web:* www.empirepacificwindows.com					
Engineered Products Inc 1844 Ardmore Blvd	Pittsburgh	PA	15221	412-242-6900	242-5205
TF: 800-245-4814 ■ *Web:* www.epimetal.com					
Fimbel Architectural Door Specialties LLC PO Box 96	Whitehouse	NJ	08888	908-534-1732	534-9259
Web: www.fimbelarchitecturaldoor.com					
Fleming Door Products Ltd 20 Barr Rd	Ajax	ON	L1S3X9	905-683-3667	427-1668
TF: 800-263-7515 ■ *Web:* www.flemingdoor.com					
GADCO (General American Door Co) 5050 Baseline Rd	Montgomery	IL	60538	630-859-3000	859-8122
TF: 800-323-0813 ■ *Web:* www.gadco.com					
General Aluminum Co of Texas LLP 1001 W Crosby Rd	Carrollton	TX	75006	972-242-5271	242-7322
TF: 800-727-0835 ■ *Web:* www.gactx.com					
General American Door Co (GADCO) 5050 Baseline Rd	Montgomery	IL	60538	630-859-3000	859-8122
TF: 800-323-0813 ■ *Web:* www.gadco.com					
Graef Windows Inc 1750 Indian Woods Cir	Youngstown	OH	44512	330-629-2999	629-2399
TF: 800-877-2911 ■ *Web:* www.graefwindows.com					
Habersham Metal Products Co 264 Stapleton Rd	Cornelia	GA	30531	706-778-2212	778-2769
Web: www.habershammetal.com					
Hehr International Inc 3333 Casitas Ave	Los Angeles	CA	90039	323-663-1261	666-9458
Web: www.hehrintl.com					
Homeshield 7942 N 3350 East Rd	Chatsworth	IL	60921	815-635-3171	635-3551
TF: 800-323-2512 ■ *Web:* www.home-shield.com					
Hope's Windows Inc 84 Hopkins Ave	Jamestown	NY	14701	716-665-5124	665-3365
Web: www.hopeswindows.com					
Hufcor Inc 2101 Kennedy Rd	Janesville	WI	53545	608-756-1241	756-1246
TF: 800-356-6968 ■ *Web:* www.hufcor.com					
Hygrade Metal Moulding Mfg Corp 1990 Highland Ave.	Bethlehem	PA	18020	610-866-2441	866-3761
TF: 800-645-9475 ■ *Web:* www.hygrademetal.com					
International Aluminum Corp 767 Monterey Pass Rd	Monterey Park	CA	91754	323-264-1670	266-3838
NYSE: IAL ■ *Web:* www.intlalum.com					
International Revolving Door Co 2100 N 6th Ave	Evansville	IN	47710	812-425-3311	426-2682
TF Cust Svc: 800-745-4726 ■ *Web:* www.internationalrevolvingdoors.com					
International Window Corp 5625 E Firestone Blvd.	South Gate	CA	90280	562-928-6411	928-3492
TF: 800-477-4032 ■ *Web:* www.intlwindow.com					
Jamison Door Co 55 JV Jamison Dr.	Hagerstown	MD	21740	301-733-3100	791-7339
TF: 800-532-3667 ■ *Web:* www.jamison-door.com					
Jantek Industries 230 Rt 70	Medford	NJ	08055	609-654-1030	654-1083
Jordan Co PO Box 18377	Memphis	TN	38181	901-363-2121	362-5051
TF: 800-888-8848 ■ *Web:* www.jordancompany.com					
Kane Mfg Corp 515 N Fraley St	Kane	PA	16735	814-837-6464	837-6230
TF: 800-952-6399 ■ *Web:* www.kanescreens.com					
Kawneer Co Inc 555 Guthridge Ct	Norcross	GA	30092	770-449-5555	734-1560
Web: www.kawneer.com					
Kewanee Corp 1642 Burlington Ave	Kewanee	IL	61443	309-853-4481	853-5466
TF: 800-666-4481 ■ *Web:* www.kewaneecorp.com					
Kinco Ltd 5245 Old Kings Rd	Jacksonville	FL	32254	904-355-1476	353-0689
TF: 800-342-0244 ■ *Web:* www.kincowindows.com					
Kinro Inc 4381 W Green Oaks Blvd Suite 200	Arlington	TX	76016	817-483-7791	478-8649
Web: www.kinro.com					
Krieger Specialty Products Co 4880 Gregg Rd	Pico Rivera	CA	90660	562-695-0645	692-0146
TF: 866-203-5060 ■ *Web:* www.kriegerproducts.com					
LaForce Inc 1060 W Mason St	Green Bay	WI	54303	920-497-7100	497-4955
TF: 800-236-8858 ■ *Web:* www.laforceinc.com					
Lausell Inc PO Box 938	Bayamon	PR	00960	787-798-7610	740-3415
TF: 800-981-7724 ■ *Web:* www.lausell.com					
Lockheed Window Corp Rt 100 PO Box 166	Pascoag	RI	02859	401-568-3061	568-2273
TF: 800-537-3061 ■ *Web:* www.lockheedwindow.com					
Loxcreen Co Inc 1630 Old Dunbar Rd	West Columbia	SC	29172	803-822-8200	822-8547
TF: 800-394-8667 ■ *Web:* www.loxcreen.com					
M-D Building Products Inc 4041 N Santa Fe Ave	Oklahoma City	OK	73118	405-528-4411	557-3541
TF Cust Svc: 800-654-8454 ■ *Web:* www.mdteam.com					
Mannix Architectural Window Products 345 Crooked Hill Rd.	Brentwood	NY	11717	631-231-0800	231-0571
TF: 800-752-6483 ■ *Web:* www.mannixwindows.com					
Masonite Holdings Inc 1 N Dale Mabry Hwy Suite 950	Tampa	FL	33609	813-877-2726	876-1435
TF: 800-895-2723 ■ *Web:* www.masonite.com					
Masonite International Corp 1600 Britannia Rd E	Mississauga	ON	L4W1J2	905-670-6500	670-6520
Web: www.masonite.com					
McKeon Door Co 95 29th St	Brooklyn	NY	11232	718-965-0700	768-3406
TF: 800-266-9392 ■ *Web:* www.mckeondoor.com					
Mercer Industries Inc 10760 SW Denney Rd.	Beaverton	OR	97008	503-526-3650	643-1992
TF: 800-962-7860 ■ *Web:* www.mercerindustries.com					
MI Windows & Doors Inc 650 W Market St	Gratz	PA	17030	717-365-3300	365-3780
TF: 800-949-3818 ■ *Web:* www.miwd.com					
Milgard Mfg 1010 54th Ave E.	Tacoma	WA	98424	253-922-2030	926-0848
TF: 800-562-8444 ■ *Web:* www.milgard.com					
Milgo Industrial Inc 68 Lombardi St	Brooklyn	NY	11222	718-388-4363	963-0614
Web: www.milgo-bufkin.com					
MM Systems Corp 50 MM Way	Pendergrass	GA	30567	706-824-7500	824-7501
TF: 800-241-3460 ■ *Web:* www.mmsystemscorp.com					
Moss Supply Co Inc PO Box 26338	Charlotte	NC	28221	704-596-8717	598-9012
TF: 800-438-0770 ■ *Web:* www.mosssupply.com					
MW Manufacturers Inc 433 N Main St.	Rocky Mount	VA	24151	540-483-0211	950-3220*
**Fax Area Code:* 800 ■ *TF:* 888-999-8400 ■ *Web:* www.mwwindows.com					
Napco Inc 125 McFann Rd	Valencia	PA	16059	724-898-1511	898-3357
TF: 800-786-2726 ■ *Web:* www.napcobuildingmaterials.com					
Napoleon/Lynx 111 Weires Dr.	Archbold	OH	43502	419-445-1010	446-2616
TF: 800-338-5399 ■ *Web:* www.lynx-nsw.com					
National Guard Products Inc 4985 E Raines Rd	Memphis	TN	38118	901-795-6900	255-7874*
**Fax Area Code:* 800 ■ *TF:* 800-647-7874 ■ *Web:* www.ngpinc.com					
Nu-Air Mfg Co 8105 Anderson Rd	Tampa	FL	33634	813-885-1654	886-9737
TF: 800-282-6627 ■ *Web:* www.nuair.com					
Nystrom Inc 9300 73rd Ave N.	Brooklyn Park	MN	55428	763-488-9200	317-8770*
**Fax Area Code:* 800 ■ *TF:* 800-547-2635 ■ *Web:* www.nystrom.com					
O'Keeffe's Inc 325 Newhall St	San Francisco	CA	94124	415-822-4222	822-5222
TF: 888-653-3333 ■ *Web:* www.okeeffes.com					
Overhead Door Corp 2501 State Hwy 121 Bldg 2.	Louisville	TX	75067	469-549-7100	549-7281
TF: 800-275-3290 ■ *Web:* www.overheaddoor.com					
Overly Mfg Co 574 W Otterman St	Greensburg	PA	15601	724-834-7300	830-2871
TF: 800-979-7300 ■ *Web:* www.overly.com					
Peachtree Doors & Windows Inc 2744 Ramsey Rd.	Gainesville	GA	30501	770-534-8070	538-5331
TF: 800-443-5692 ■ *Web:* www.peachtreedoor.com					
Peelle Co 34 Central Ave.	Hauppauge	NY	11788	631-231-6000	231-6059
TF: 800-645-1056 ■ *Web:* www.peelledoor.com/peelle.htm					
Peerless Products Inc 2403 S Main St	Fort Scott	KS	66701	620-223-4610	224-3107
TF: 800-279-9999 ■ *Web:* www.peerlessproducts.com					
Pemko Mfg Co Inc 4226 Transport St	Ventura	CA	93003	805-642-2600	642-4109
TF: 800-283-9988 ■ *Web:* www.pemko.com					
PGT Industries 1070 Technology Dr	Nokomis	FL	34275	941-480-1600	480-2755
TF: 800-282-6019 ■ *Web:* www.pgtindustries.com					
Philips Products Inc 3221 Magnum Dr	Elkhart	IN	46516	574-296-0000	296-0147*
**Fax Area Code:* 219 ■ *TF:* 800-859-8550 ■ *Web:* www.philipsproducts.com					
Pioneer Industries Inc 171 S Newman St	Hackensack	NJ	07601	201-933-1900	933-9580
Web: www.pioneerindustries.com					
Pipin Industries Inc 6500 W 65th St Suite 200	Chicago	IL	60638	708-458-3440	458-2456
TF: 888-706-8646					
Portal Inc 10 Tracy Dr.	Avon	MA	02322	508-588-3030	580-9943
TF: 800-966-3030 ■ *Web:* www.portal-national.com					
Public Supply Co Inc 1236 NW 4th St	Oklahoma City	OK	73106	405-272-9621	272-9835
TF: 800-259-6355 ■ *Web:* www.publicsupply.com					
Pyramid Mouldings Inc 300 S Magnolia Ave	Green Cove Springs	FL	32043	904-284-5611	284-1705
Web: www.pyramidmouldings.com					
Quaker Window Products Inc 504 S Hwy 63 PO Box 128	Freeburg	MO	65035	573-744-5211	744-5586
TF: 800-347-0438 ■ *Web:* www.quakerwindows.com					
Raynor Garage Doors 1101 E River Rd.	Dixon	IL	61021	815-288-1431	288-3720*
**Fax:* Cust Svc ■ *TF:* 800-472-9667 ■ *Web:* www.raynor.com					
RC Aluminum Industries Inc 2805 NW 75th Ave	Miami	FL	33122	305-592-1515	592-2184
Web: rcalum.com					
Rebco Inc 1171-1225 Madison Ave	Paterson	NJ	07509	973-684-0200	684-0118
TF: 800-777-0787 ■ *Web:* www.rebcoinc.com					
Reese Enterprises Inc 16350 Asher Ave	Rosemount	MN	55068	651-423-1126	423-2662
TF: 800-328-0953 ■ *Web:* www.reeseusa.com					
Republic Windows & Doors Inc 930 W Evergreen Ave	Chicago	IL	60622	312-932-8000	932-8050
TF: 800-248-1775 ■ *Web:* www.republicwindows.com					
Richards-Wilcox Inc 600 S Lake St	Aurora	IL	60506	630-897-6951	897-6994
TF: 800-253-5668 ■ *Web:* www.richardswilcox.com					
Sears Home Improvement Products 1024 Florida Central Pkwy	Longwood	FL	32750	407-767-0990	767-1256
TF: 800-222-5030					
Sellmore Industries Inc 815 Smith St	Buffalo	NY	14206	716-854-1600	856-4509
Web: www.sellmoreind.com					
Silver Line Building Products 1 Silver Line Dr.	North Brunswick	NJ	08902	732-435-1000	418-0190
TF Sales: 800-234-4228 ■ *Web:* www.silverlinewindow.com					
Southeastern Aluminum Products Inc 6701 Suemac Pl	Jacksonville	FL	32254	904-781-8200	224-8068
TF Sales: 800-243-8200 ■ *Web:* www.southeasternaluminum.com					
Southeastern Metals Mfg Co Inc 11801 Industry Dr.	Jacksonville	FL	32218	904-757-4200	696-7542
TF: 800-874-2335 ■ *Web:* www.semetals.com					
Stanley Access Technologies 65 Scott Swamp Rd	Farmington	CT	06032	860-677-2861	679-6436*
**Fax:* Cust Svc ■ *TF:* 800-722-2377 ■ *Web:* www.stanleyworks.com/bu_accesstech.asp					
Stanley Home Decor 480 Myrtle St.	New Britain	CT	06053	860-225-5111	827-3895
TF: 800-782-6539					
State Wide Aluminum 23601 CR 6 E PO Box 987	Elkhart	IN	46515	574-262-2594	262-4125
TF: 800-860-2594 ■ *Web:* www.statewidealum.com					
Steelcraft Mfg Co 9017 Blue Ash Rd	Cincinnati	OH	45242	513-745-6400	745-6300
TF Cust Svc: 800-930-8585 ■ *Web:* www.steelcraft.com					
Steves & Sons Inc 203 Humble Ave	San Antonio	TX	78225	210-924-5111	924-0470*
**Fax:* Sales ■ *TF Sales:* 800-627-5111 ■ *Web:* www.stevesdoors.com					
Stremel Mfg LLC 260 Plymouth Ave N	Minneapolis	MN	55411	612-339-8261	339-2661
Web: www.stremel.com					
Super Sky Products Inc 10301 N Enterprise Dr	Mequon	WI	53092	262-242-2000	242-7409
TF: 800-558-0467 ■ *Web:* www.supersky.com					
Taylor Building Products PO Box 457	West Branch	MI	48661	989-345-5110	345-5116
TF: 800-248-3600 ■ *Web:* www.taylordoor.com					
Therma-Tru Corp 1687 Woodlands Dr	Maumee	OH	43537	419-891-7400	891-7411
TF: 800-537-8827 ■ *Web:* www.thermatru.com					
Thermo-Twin Industries Inc 1155 Allegheny Ave	Oakmont	PA	15139	412-826-1000	826-0455
TF: 800-641-2211 ■ *Web:* www.thermotwin.com					
TKO Dock Doors N56 W24701 N Corporate Cir Suite A	Sussex	WI	53089	262-820-1217	820-1273
TF: 800-575-3366 ■ *Web:* www.tkodoors.com					
TM Window & Door 601 NW 12th Ave	Pompano Beach	FL	33069	954-781-4430	781-3595
TF: 800-511-1746 ■ *Web:* www.floridasbestwindow.com					

Phone | Fax

TRACO 71 Progress Ave. ... Cranberry Township PA 16066 724-776-7000 776-7014
TF: 800-468-7226 ■ *Web:* www.traco.com
Trussbilt LLC 2112 Old Hwy 8 NW ... New Brighton MN 55112 651-633-6100 633-7100
Web: www.trussbilt.com
Tubelite Inc 4878 Mackinaw Trail ... Reed City MI 49677 231-832-2211 832-4392
TF: 800-866-2227 ■ *Web:* www.tubeliteinc.com
Vistawall Architectural Products 803 Airport Rd ... Terrell TX 75160 972-563-2624 551-6323*
*Fax: Cust Svc ■ *TF:* 800-869-4567 ■ *Web:* www.vistawall.com
Wausau Window & Wall Systems 1415 West St ... Wausau WI 54401 715-845-2161 843-4350
TF: 877-678-2983 ■ *Web:* www.wausauwindows.com
Wayne-Dalton Corp 1 Door Dr PO Box 67 ... Mount Hope OH 44660 330-674-7015 763-8047
TF: 800-827-3667 ■ *Web:* www.wayne-dalton.com
West Window Corp PO Drawer 3071 ... Martinsville VA 24115 276-638-2394 638-2300
TF: 800-446-4167 ■ *Web:* www.westwindow.com
Willo Products Co Inc 2115 Veterans Dr SE ... Decatur AL 35601 256-353-7161 350-8436
TF: 800-633-3276 ■ *Web:* www.willoproducts.com
Winco Window Co Inc 6200 Maple Ave ... Saint Louis MO 63130 314-725-8088 725-1419
TF: 800-525-8089 ■ *Web:* www.wincowindow.com
Windowmaster Products inc 1111 Pioneer Way ... El Cajon CA 92020 619-444-6123 442-1994*
*Fax: Orders ■ *TF:* 800-862-7722 ■ *Web:* www.windowmasterproducts.com
Yale Ogron Mfg Co Inc 671 W 18th St ... Hialeah FL 33010 305-887-2646 883-1309
Web: www.yaleogron.com
Young Windows Inc 680 Colwell Ln ... Conshohocken PA 19428 610-828-5422 828-2144
Web: www.youngwindows.com

238 DOORS & WINDOWS - VINYL

Phone | Fax

AlbanyDoor Systems 975A Old Norcross Rd ... Lawrenceville GA 30045 770-962-7997 338-5024
TF: 800-252-2691 ■ *Web:* www.albanydoorsystems.com
Alenco Window Holding LLC 615 Carson St ... Bryan TX 77801 979-779-7770 822-3259
Web: www.alenco.com
Alside Div Associated Materials Inc PO Box 2010 ... Akron OH 44309 330-929-1811 922-2354
TF: 800-922-6009 ■ *Web:* www.alside.com
Amerimax Building Products Inc 5208 Tennyson Pkwy Suite 100 ... Plano TX 75024 469-366-3200 366-3260
TF: 800-258-6295 ■ *Web:* www.amerimaxbp.com
Associated Materials Inc Alside Div PO Box 2010 ... Akron OH 44309 330-929-1811 922-2354
TF: 800-922-6009 ■ *Web:* www.alside.com
Atrium Windows & Doors 9001 Ambassador Rd ... Dallas TX 75247 800-938-2000 424-6730*
*Fax Area Code: 214 ■ *Web:* www.atriumcompanies.com
Benjamin F Rich Co PO Box 6031 ... Newark DE 19714 302-894-0498 894-0499
TF: 800-237-4241 ■ *Web:* www.bfrich.com
CertainTeed Corp 750 E Swedesford Rd ... Valley Forge PA 19482 610-341-7000 341-7797
TF Prod Info: 800-782-8777 ■ *Web:* www.certainteed.com
Chelsea Building Products 565 Cedar Way ... Oakmont PA 15139 412-826-8077 826-0113
Web: www.chelseabuildingproducts.com
Dayton Technologies 351 N Garver Rd ... Monroe OH 45050 513-539-4444 539-5404
TF: 800-432-9560 ■ *Web:* www.daytech.com
Eagle Window & Door Inc 2045 Kerper Blvd ... Dubuque IA 52001 563-556-2270 556-4408
TF: 800-324-5354 ■ *Web:* www.eaglewindow.com
Fortune Brands Home & Hardware Inc 520 Lake Cook Rd ... Deerfield IL 60015 847-484-4400
Web: www.fortunebrands.com
Great Lakes Window Inc 30499 Tracy Rd ... Walbridge OH 43465 419-666-5555 661-2923*
*Fax: Hum Res ■ *Web:* www.greatlakeswindow.com
Harry G Barr Co 6500 S Zero St ... Fort Smith AR 72903 479-646-7891 646-8591
TF: 800-829-2277 ■ *Web:* www.weatherbarr.com
Kensington Windows Inc 1136 Industrial Pk Rd ... Vandergrift PA 15690 724-845-8133 845-9151
TF: 800-444-4972 ■ *Web:* www.kensingtonwindows.com
Larson Mfg Co 2333 Eastbrook Dr ... Brookings SD 57006 605-692-6115 696-6403
TF Cust Svc: 800-352-3360 ■ *Web:* www.larsondoors.com
Mathews Brothers Co PO Box 345 ... Belfast ME 04915 207-338-3360 338-6300
TF: 800-639-7203 ■ *Web:* www.mathewsbrothers.com
Mikron Industries Inc 1034 6th Ave N ... Kent WA 98032 253-854-8020 852-3769
TF: 800-456-8020 ■ *Web:* www.mikronvinyl.com
Moss Supply Co Inc PO Box 26338 ... Charlotte NC 28221 704-596-8717 598-9012
TF: 800-438-0770 ■ *Web:* www.mosssupply.com
PGT Industries 1070 Technology Dr ... Nokomis FL 34275 941-480-1600 480-2755
TF: 800-282-6019 ■ *Web:* www.pgtindustries.com
Philips Products Inc 3221 Magnum Dr ... Elkhart IN 46516 574-296-0000 296-0147*
*Fax Area Code: 219 ■ *TF:* 800-859-8550 ■ *Web:* www.philipsproducts.com
Polybau Windows & Doors 1851 E Paradise Rd ... Tracy CA 95304 209-830-5170 830-5175
TF: 877-765-9228 ■ *Web:* www.polybau.com
Rehau Inc 1501 Edwards Ferry Rd NE ... Leesburg VA 20176 703-777-5255 777-3053
TF: 800-247-9445 ■ *Web:* www.rehau-na.com
Royal Group Technologies Ltd 1 Royal Gate Blvd ... Woodbridge ON L4L8Z7 905-264-0701 264-0702
NYSE: RYG ■ *Web:* www.royplas.com
RubbAir Door Div Eckel Industries Inc 100 Groton Shirley Rd ... Ayer MA 01432 978-772-0480 772-7114
TF: 800-966-7822 ■ *Web:* www.rubbair.com
Slocomb Industries Inc 801 Pencader Dr ... Newark DE 19702 302-266-7101 266-7209
TF: 800-348-6233 ■ *Web:* www.slocombwindows.com
Soft-Lite LLC 10250 Philipp Pkwy ... Streetsboro OH 44241 330-528-3400
TF: 800-551-1953 ■ *Web:* www.softlitewindows.com
Stanley Works 1000 Stanley Dr ... New Britain CT 06053 860-225-5111 827-3895
NYSE: SWK ■ *TF Cust Svc:* 800-262-2161 ■ *Web:* www.stanleyworks.com
Thermal Industries Inc 301 Brushton Ave ... Pittsburgh PA 15221 412-244-6400 244-6496
TF: 800-245-1540 ■ *Web:* www.thermalindustries.com
ThermoView Industries Inc 5611 Fern Valley Rd ... Louisville KY 40228 502-968-2020 968-7798
Web: www.thermoviewinc.com
Weather Shield Mfg Inc 1 Weather Shield Plaza PO Box 309 ... Medford WI 54451 715-748-2100 222-2146*
*Fax Area Code: 800 ■ *TF Prod Info:* 800-222-2995 ■ *Web:* www.weathershield.com
West Window Corp PO Drawer 3071 ... Martinsville VA 24115 276-638-2394 638-2300
TF: 800-446-4167 ■ *Web:* www.westwindow.com
Wilmes Window Mfg Co 234 W 23rd St ... Ferdinand IN 47532 812-367-1811
TF: 800-477-1811
Windsor Windows & Doors 900 S 19th St ... West Des Moines IA 50265 515-223-6660 224-1938*
*Fax: Cust Svc ■ *TF:* 800-218-6186 ■ *Web:* www.windsorwindows.com

239 DOORS & WINDOWS - WOOD

SEE ALSO Millwork p. 1970; Shutters - Window (All Types) p. 2316

Phone | Fax

Algoma Hardwoods Inc 1001 Perry St ... Algoma WI 54201 920-487-5221 487-3636
TF: 800-678-8910 ■ *Web:* www.algomahardwoods.com
Allwood Door Co Inc 6000 3rd St ... San Francisco CA 94124 415-822-8900 822-5832
Andersen Corp 100 4th Ave N ... Bayport MN 55003 651-264-5150 264-5526*
*Fax: Hum Res ■ *TF:* 877-229-2677 ■ *Web:* www.andersencorp.com
Annona Mfg Co PO Box 287 ... Annona TX 75550 903-697-3591 697-3663
Burton Lumber Corp 835 Wilson Rd ... Chesapeake VA 23324 757-545-4613 545-8852
Combination Door Co 1000 Morris St ... Fond du Lac WI 54935 920-922-2050 922-2917
Web: www.combinationdoor.com
Donlin Co Inc 539 E Saint Germain St ... Saint Cloud MN 56302 320-251-3680 251-2722
TF: 800-892-7015 ■ *Web:* www.donlin.com
Eagle Window & Door Inc 2045 Kerper Blvd ... Dubuque IA 52001 563-556-2270 556-4408
TF: 800-324-5354 ■ *Web:* www.eaglewindow.com
General Doors Corp 1 Monroe St PO Box 205 ... Bristol PA 19007 215-788-9277 788-9450
Web: www.general-doors.com
Haley Brothers Inc 6291 Orangethorpe Ave ... Buena Park CA 90620 714-670-2112 994-6971
TF: 800-848-3240 ■ *Web:* www.haleybros.com
Hurd Millwork Co Inc 575 S Whelan Ave ... Medford WI 54451 715-748-2011 748-6043
TF: 800-433-4873 ■ *Web:* www.hurd.com
Jenkins Mfg Co Inc PO Box 249 ... Anniston AL 36202 256-831-7000 261-6116*
*Fax Area Code: 800 ■ *TF:* 800-633-2323
Jordan Millwork Co 1820 E 54th St N ... Sioux Falls SD 57104 605-336-1910 335-1324
TF Cust Svc: 800-843-0076
King Sash & Door Inc PO Box 1029 ... Mocksville NC 27028 336-768-4650 768-4666
TF: 800-642-0886 ■ *Web:* www.kingsashanddoor.com
Larson Mfg Co 2333 Eastbrook Dr ... Brookings SD 57006 605-692-6115 696-6403
TF Cust Svc: 800-352-3360 ■ *Web:* www.larsondoors.com
Lifetime Doors Inc 30700 Northwestern Hwy ... Farmington MI 48334 248-851-7700 851-8534
TF: 800-521-0500 ■ *Web:* www.lifetimedoors.com
Lincoln Wood Products Inc PO Box 375 ... Merrill WI 54452 715-536-2461 536-7090
TF: 800-967-2461 ■ *Web:* www.lincolnwindows.com
Marvin Windows & Doors 104 State Ave N ... Warroad MN 56763 218-386-1430 386-1904
TF: 800-346-5044 ■ *Web:* www.marvin.com
Masonite Holdings Inc 1 N Dale Mabry Hwy Suite 950 ... Tampa FL 33609 813-877-2726 876-1435
TF: 800-895-2723 ■ *Web:* www.masonite.com
Masonite International Corp 1600 Britannia Rd E ... Mississauga ON L4W1J2 905-670-6500 670-6520
Web: www.masonite.com
Mathews Brothers Co PO Box 345 ... Belfast ME 04915 207-338-3360 338-6300
TF: 800-639-7203 ■ *Web:* www.mathewsbrothers.com
McPhillips Mfg Co Inc PO Box 169 ... Mobile AL 36601 251-438-1681 438-1338
TF: 800-348-6274 ■ *Web:* www.mcphillipsmfg.com
Mohawk Flush Doors Inc
980 Point Township Dr PO Box 112 ... Northumberland PA 17857 570-473-3557 473-3737
Web: www.mohawkdoors.com
Norco Windows Inc 811 Factory St PO Box 140 ... Hawkins WI 54530 715-585-6311 585-6357
TF: 800-826-6793 ■ *Web:* www.jeld-wen.com/norco
Peachtree Doors & Windows Inc 2744 Ramsey Rd ... Gainesville GA 30501 770-534-8070 538-5331
TF: 800-443-5692 ■ *Web:* www.peachtreedoor.com
Pella Corp 102 Main St ... Pella IA 50219 641-628-1000 628-6070
TF Cust Svc: 800-288-7281 ■ *Web:* www.pella.com
Quaker Window Products Inc 504 S Hwy 63 PO Box 128 ... Freeburg MO 65035 573-744-5211 744-5586
TF: 800-347-0438 ■ *Web:* www.quakerwindows.com
Semling-Menke Co Inc PO Box 378 ... Merrill WI 54452 715-536-9411 536-3067
TF: 800-333-2206 ■ *Web:* www.semcowindows.com
SNE Enterprises Inc 880 Southview Dr ... Mosinee WI 54455 715-693-7000 693-8505*
*Fax: Hum Res ■ *TF:* 800-826-1707
Steves & Sons Inc 203 Humble Ave ... San Antonio TX 78225 210-924-5111 924-0470*
*Fax: Sales ■ *TF Sales:* 800-627-5111 ■ *Web:* www.stevesdoors.com
Vancouver Door Co Inc PO Box 1418 ... Puyallup WA 98371 253-845-9581 845-3364
TF: 800-999-3667 ■ *Web:* www.vancouverdoorco.com
Weather Shield Mfg Inc 1 Weather Shield Plaza PO Box 309 ... Medford WI 54451 715-748-2100 222-2146*
*Fax Area Code: 800 ■ *TF Prod Info:* 800-222-2995 ■ *Web:* www.weathershield.com
West Coast Door Inc 3102 S Pine St ... Tacoma WA 98409 253-272-4269 572-0385
TF: 800-445-5919
Windsor Windows & Doors 900 S 19th St ... West Des Moines IA 50265 515-223-6660 224-1938*
*Fax: Cust Svc ■ *TF:* 800-218-6186 ■ *Web:* www.windsorwindows.com

240 DRUG STORES

SEE ALSO Health Food Stores p. 1774

Phone | Fax

Aurora Pharmacy Inc 3305 W Forest Home Ave ... Milwaukee WI 53215 414-647-3454
Bartell Drug Co 4727 Denver Ave S ... Seattle WA 98134 206-763-2626 763-2062
TF: 877-227-8355 ■ *Web:* www.bartelldrugs.com
Brooks Pharmacy 50 Service Ave ... Warwick RI 02886 401-825-3900 825-3996
Web: www.brooks-rx.com
Cost Cutters 800 Cottontail Ln ... Somerset NJ 08873 732-748-8900 748-7200
CVS Corp 1 CVS Dr ... Woonsocket RI 02895 401-765-1500 770-6949*
NYSE: CVS ■ *Fax: Cust Svc ■ *TF Cust Svc:* 800-746-7287 ■ *Web:* www.cvs.com
CVS ProCare Pharmacy 695 George Washington Hwy ... Lincoln RI 02865 401-334-0069
Web: www.cvsprocare.com
Discount Drug Mart Inc 211 Commerce Dr ... Medina OH 44256 330-725-2340 722-2990
Web: www.discount-drugmart.com
Doc's Drugs 455 E Reed St ... Braidwood IL 60408 815-458-6104 458-6158
Web: www.docsdrugs.com
Drug Fair 800 Cottontail Ln ... Somerset NJ 08873 732-748-8900 748-7200
Web: www.drugfair.com
drugstore.com inc 411 108th Ave NE Suite 1400 ... Bellevue WA 98004 425-372-3200 372-3800
NASDAQ: DSCM ■ *TF:* 800-378-4786 ■ *Web:* www.drugstore.com
Duane Reade Inc 42 W Broad St ... Mount Vernon NY 10552 914-664-3900 664-7580
Web: www.duanereade.com
Fagen Pharmacy 915 S Halleck St ... Demotte IN 46310 219-987-6468 987-7226
Web: www.fagenpharmacy.com
Familymeds.com Inc 312 Farmington Ave ... Farmington CT 06032 860-676-1222 676-1497
TF: 888-787-2800 ■ *Web:* www.familymeds.com
Feelbest.com 778 Bank St ... Ottawa ON K1S3V6 613-234-4643 234-8432
TF: 888-689-9890 ■ *Web:* www.feelbest.com
Fruth Pharmacy Inc Rt 62 N ... Point Pleasant WV 25550 304-675-1612 675-7338
Web: www.fruthpharmacy.com
Gemmel Pharmacy Group Inc 143 N Euclid Ave ... Ontario CA 91762 909-988-5805 983-2737
Web: www.gemmels.com
Happy Harry's Inc 326 Ruthar Dr ... Newark DE 19711 302-366-0335 453-3167
TF: 866-994-2779 ■ *Web:* www.happy.com
Harmon Stores Inc 650 Liberty Ave ... Union NJ 07083 908-688-7023 688-4876
Web: www.harmondiscount.com
Hartig Drug Co 703 Main St PO Box 709 ... Dubuque IA 52004 563-588-8700 588-8750
Web: www.hartigdrug.com
Hi-School Pharmacy Inc 915 W 11th St ... Vancouver WA 98660 360-693-5879 694-5161
Web: www.hi-schoolpharmacy.com
Hy-Vee Drug Stores 5820 Westown Pkwy ... West Des Moines IA 50266 515-267-2800 327-2162
Web: www.hy-vee.com/pharmacy/pharmacy.asp
Jean Coutu Group (PJC) Inc 530 rue Beriault ... Longueuil QC J4G1S8 450-646-9760 646-5649*
TSX: PJC.A ■ *Fax: PR ■ *Web:* www.jeancoutu.com
Katz Group 10104 103rd Ave Suite 1702 ... Edmonton AB T5J0H8 780-990-0505 425-3980
TF: 800-267-8877 ■ *Web:* www.katzgroup.ca
Keltsch Pharmacy Inc 4118 N Clinton St ... Fort Wayne IN 46805 260-483-9537 484-5034
Kerr Drug Stores Inc 3220 Spring Forest Rd ... Raleigh NC 27616 919-544-3896 544-3796
TF: 800-494-3053 ■ *Web:* www.kerrdrug.com

Phone | Fax

Kinney Drugs Inc 29 E Main St .... Gouverneur NY 13642 315-287-1500 287-4291
TF: 800-552-8044 ■ *Web:* www.kinneys.com

Lewis Drug Inc 2701 S Minnesota Ave Suite 1 .... Sioux Falls SD 57105 605-367-2000 367-2876
TF: 800-658-3620 ■ *Web:* www.lewisdrug.com

Liberty Drug & Surgical Inc 195 Main St .... Chatham NJ 07928 973-635-6200 635-6208
Web: www.libertydrug.com

Longs Drug Stores Corp 141 N Civic Dr .... Walnut Creek CA 94596 925-937-1170 296-5252
NYSE: LDG ■ *Web:* www.longs.com

Love Stores 144 W 72nd St .... New York NY 10023 212-877-5351 877-5135

Mast Drug Co Inc 1910 Ross Mill Rd .... Henderson NC 27537 252-438-3112 492-4096
Web: www.mastdrug.com

Maxi Drug Inc 50 Service Ave .... Warwick RI 02886 401-825-3900 825-3996

Medicap Pharmacies Inc
4350 Westown Pkwy Suite 400 .... West Des Moines IA 50266 515-224-8400 224-8415
TF Cust Svc: 800-445-2244 ■ *Web:* www.medicaprx.com

Medicine Shoppe International Inc 1100 N Lindbergh Blvd .... Saint Louis MO 63132 314-993-6000 872-5500
TF Cust Svc: 800-325-1397 ■ *Web:* www.medshoppe.com

MediServ Inc 3684 Trabue Rd .... Columbus OH 43228 614-481-4272 481-7580

Navarro Discount Pharmacies 5959 NW 37th Ave .... Miami FL 33142 305-633-3000 633-7555
Web: www.navarro.com

Osco Drugs 250 E Park Center Blvd .... Boise ID 83706 208-395-6200 395-6225
TF: 800-541-2863 ■ *Web:* www.savon.com

Price-Less Drugstore Inc 2210 Sunrise Blvd .... Rancho Cordova CA 95670 916-638-0213 638-4160
Web: www.pricelessdrugs.com

Ralston Drug & Discount Liquor 3147 Southmore Blvd .... Houston TX 77004 713-524-3045 524-5981

Reade Duane Inc 42 W Broad St .... Mount Vernon NY 10552 914-664-3900 664-7580
Web: www.duanereade.com

Rite Aid Corp 30 Hunter Ln .... Camp Hill PA 17011 717-761-2633 731-3860*
NYSE: RAD ■ **Fax: Hum Res* ■ *TF:* 800-748-3243 ■ *Web:* www.riteaid.com

Ritzman Pharmacies Inc 8614 Hartman Rd .... Wadsworth OH 44281 330-335-2318 335-3222
Web: www.ritzmanpharmacies.com

Rodman's Discount Food & Drugs 4301 Randolph Rd .... Silver Spring MD 20906 301-230-8930 946-8329
Web: www.rodmans.com

RXD Pharmacies Inc 724 Haddon Ave .... Collingswood NJ 08108 856-858-9292 858-7286

Sav-on Drugs Inc 21118 Bridge St .... Southfield MI 48034 248-357-4550 357-2332
Web: www.sav-ondrugs.com

Sav-Mor Drug Stores 43155 W Nine-Mile Rd .... Novi MI 48376 248-348-1570 348-4316
Web: www.sav-mor.com

Sedano's Pharmacy & Discount Stores Inc
3900 NW 79th Ave Suite 608 .... Miami FL 33166 305-226-2507 227-6058

Shoppers Drug Mart Inc 243 Consumers Rd .... North York ON M2J4W8 416-493-1220
TSX: SC ■ *Web:* www.shoppersdrugmart.ca

Snyder's Drug Stores Inc 14525 Hwy 7 .... Minnetonka MN 55345 952-935-5441 936-2512
Web: www.snyderdrug.com

Stephen L LaFrance Pharmacy Inc DBA USA Drug
3017 N Midland Dr .... Pine Bluff AR 71603 870-535-2411 535-5601
Web: www.usadrug.com

Super D Drugs Inc 7677 Farmington Blvd .... Germantown TN 38138 901-754-0130 754-5586

Thrifty White Stores 6901 E Fish Lake Rd Suite 118 .... Maple Grove MN 55369 763-513-4300 816-2823*
**Fax Area Code: 800* ■ *TF:* 800-816-2887 ■ *Web:* www.thriftywhite.com

USA Drug 3017 N Midland Dr .... Pine Bluff AR 71603 870-535-2411 535-5601
Web: www.usadrug.com

Value Drugs 17 Green St .... Huntington NY 11743 631-271-6663 271-5267

Vitacost.com Inc 2055 High Ridge Rd .... Boynton Beach FL 33426 561-752-8888 752-8900
TF: 800-793-2601 ■ *Web:* www.vitacost.com

Vitamin Shoppe Inc 2101 91st St .... North Bergen NJ 07047 201-868-5959 852-7153*
**Fax Area Code: 800* ■ *TF:* 800-223-1216 ■ *Web:* www.vitaminshoppe.com

Walgreen Co 200 Wilmot Rd .... Deerfield IL 60015 847-940-2500 236-0862
NYSE: WAG ■ *TF Cust Svc:* 800-289-2273 ■ *Web:* www.walgreens.com

DRUGS - MFR

SEE Biotechnology Companies p. 1380; Diagnostic Products p. 1587; Medicinal Chemicals & Botanical Products p. 1957; Pharmaceutical Companies p. 2109; Pharmaceutical Companies - Generic Drugs p. 2111; Vitamins & Nutritional Supplements p. 2405

241 DRUGS & PERSONAL CARE PRODUCTS - WHOL

Companies listed here distribute pharmaceuticals, over-the-counter (OTC) drugs, and/or personal care products typically found in drug stores.

Phone | Fax

American Herbal Products
1440 JFK Causeway Suite 400 .... North Bay Village FL 33141 305-865-2919 865-1538
TF: 888-446-6884 ■ *Web:* www.immuvit.com

AmerisourceBergen Corp 1300 Morris Dr Suite 100 .... Chesterbrook PA 19087 610-727-7000 727-3600
NYSE: ABC ■ *TF:* 800-829-3132 ■ *Web:* www.amerisourcebergen.net

Anderson Wholesale Co PO Box 69 .... Muskogee OK 74402 918-682-5568 687-9567
TF: 800-324-9656 ■ *Web:* www.andersonwholesale.com

ASD Specialty Healthcare 4006 Beltline Rd Suite 200 .... Addison TX 75001 972-490-5551 547-9413*
**Fax Area Code: 800* ■ *TF:* 800-746-6273 ■
Web: www.bergenbrunswig.com/asd/index.cfm

Bellco Health Corp 5500 New Horizons Blvd .... North Amityville NY 11701 631-789-6300 841-6185
TF: 800-645-5314 ■ *Web:* www.bellcoonline.com

Cardinal Health Distribution 7000 Cardinal Pl .... Dublin OH 43017 614-757-5000 757-6000
TF: 800-234-8701 ■ *Web:* www.cardinal.com

Cardinal Health Nuclear Pharmacy Services 7000 Cardinal Pl .... Dublin OH 43017 614-757-5000 757-6000
TF: 800-999-9098 ■ *Web:* nps.cardinal.com

Cardinal Health Specialty Pharmaceutical Distribution
401 Mason Rd .... La Vergne TN 37086 800-879-5569 289-9285
Web: www.cardinal.com/spd

D & K Healthcare Resources Inc 8235 Forsythe Blvd .... Saint Louis MO 63105 314-727-3485 727-5759
TF: 888-727-3485 ■ *Web:* www.dkwd.com

Dakota Drug Inc 28 Main St N .... Minot ND 58703 701-852-2141 857-1134
TF: 800-437-2018 ■ *Web:* www.dakdrug.com

Dohmen F Co W 194 North 11381 McCormick Dr .... Germantown WI 53022 262-255-0022 255-0041
TF: 877-848-4166 ■ *Web:* www.dohmen.com

DrugMax Inc 25400 US Hwy 19 N Suite 137 .... Clearwater FL 33763 727-533-0431 531-1280
NASDAQ: DMAX ■ *Web:* www.drugmax.com

Esscentual Brands LLC 4835 E Cactus Rd Suite 245 .... Scottsdale AZ 85254 602-889-4800 889-4837
Web: www.esscentualbrands.com

F Dohmen Co W 194 North 11381 McCormick Dr .... Germantown WI 53022 262-255-0022 255-0041
TF: 877-848-4166 ■ *Web:* www.dohmen.com

Family Pharmacy 1300 Morris Dr .... Chesterbrook PA 19087 877-892-1254 695-8604*
**Fax Area Code: 610* ■ *Web:* www.familypharmacy.com

HD Smith Wholesale Drug Co 4650 Industrial Dr .... Springfield IL 62703 217-529-0211 529-1546
TF: 800-252-8090 ■ *Web:* www.hdsmith.com

Phone | Fax

Jewett Drug Co Inc 217 E Railroad Ave .... Aberdeen SD 57401 605-225-0870 225-0591
TF: 800-535-0297

JM Smith Corp 9098 Fairforest Rd .... Spartanburg SC 29301 864-582-1216 591-0333
Web: www.cornerdrugstore.com

Kinray Inc 152-35 10th Ave .... Whitestone NY 11357 718-767-1234 767-4706
TF: 800-854-6729 ■ *Web:* www.kinray.com

McKesson Canada 8625 TransCanada Hwy .... Saint-Laurent QC H4S1Z6 514-745-2100 745-2300
TF: 800-363-7139 ■ *Web:* www.mckesson.ca

McKesson Specialty Pharmaceuticals 5712 Jarvis St .... New Orleans LA 70123 504-736-7827 591-8482*
**Fax Area Code: 888* ■ *TF:* 888-456-7274 ■ *Web:* www.mckessonspecialty.com

Medtech Products Inc PO Box 1108 .... Jackson WY 83001 307-733-1680 733-0393
TF: 800-443-4908 ■ *Web:* www.medtechinc.com

Millbrook Distribution Services 88 Huntoon Memorial Hwy .... Leicester MA 01524 508-892-8171 892-4827
TF: 800-225-7398 ■ *Web:* www.millbrookds.com

Morris & Dickson Co Ltd PO Box 51367 .... Shreveport LA 71135 318-797-7900 798-6007
TF: 800-388-3833 ■ *Web:* www.morrisdickson.com

Natural Health Trends Corp 12901 Hutton Dr .... Dallas TX 75234 972-241-4080 243-5430
NASDAQ: BHIP ■ *Web:* www.naturalhealthtrendscorp.com

North Carolina Mutual Wholesale Drug Co 816 Ellis Rd .... Durham NC 27703 919-596-2151 596-1453
TF: 800-800-8551 ■ *Web:* www.mutualdrug.com

Parmed Pharmaceuticals Inc 4220 Hyde Park Blvd .... Niagara Falls NY 14305 716-284-5666 727-6330*
**Fax Area Code: 800* ■ *TF:* 800-727-6331 ■ *Web:* www.parmed.com

Pharmed Group Corp 3075 NW 107th Ave .... Miami FL 33172 305-592-2324 591-9643
TF: 800-683-7342 ■ *Web:* www.pharmed.com

Plantex USA Inc 2 University Plaza .... Hackensack NJ 07601 201-343-4141 343-3833

Procter & Gamble Distributing Co 1 Procter & Gamble Plaza .... Cincinnati OH 45202 513-983-1100 983-1100

Quality King Distributors Inc 2060 9th Ave .... Ronkonkoma NY 11779 631-439-2000 439-2222
TF: 800-676-5554 ■ *Web:* www.qualityking.com

Reese Pharmaceutical Co 10617 Frank Ave .... Cleveland OH 44106 216-231-6441 231-6444
TF: 800-321-7178 ■ *Web:* www.reesechemical.com

Respiratory Distributors Inc 110 E Azalea Ave .... Foley AL 36535 251-943-5844 891-8671*
**Fax Area Code: 800* ■ *TF:* 800-872-8672 ■ *Web:* www.rdiworld.com

RG Shakour Inc 254 Turnpike Rd .... Westborough MA 01581 508-366-8282 898-3212
TF: 800-262-9090 ■ *Web:* www.rgshakour.com

Rochester Drug Co-op Inc PO Box 24389 .... Rochester NY 14624 585-271-7220 271-3551
TF: 800-333-0538 ■ *Web:* www.rdcdrug.com

Shakour RG Inc 254 Turnpike Rd .... Westborough MA 01581 508-366-8282 898-3212
TF: 800-262-9090 ■ *Web:* www.rgshakour.com

Smith HD Wholesale Drug Co 4650 Industrial Dr .... Springfield IL 62703 217-529-0211 529-1546
TF: 800-252-8090 ■ *Web:* www.hdsmith.com

Smith JM Corp 9098 Fairforest Rd .... Spartanburg SC 29301 864-582-1216 591-0333
Web: www.cornerdrugstore.com

Standard Drug Co 1 Westbury Dr Bldg B Suite 270 .... Saint Charles MO 63301 636-946-6557 724-0545
TF: 877-482-5874

Sun Healthcare Group Inc Pharmaceutical Services
101 Sun Ave NE .... Albuquerque NM 87109 505-468-4168 468-4344
TF: 800-729-6600 ■ *Web:* www.sunh.com

Texas Drug Co 1101 W Vickery Blvd .... Fort Worth TX 76104 817-335-5761 334-0310
TF: 888-378-4668

Value In Pharmaceuticals (VIP) 3000 Alt Blvd .... Grand Island NY 14072 716-773-4600 847-3293*
**Fax Area Code: 800* ■ *TF:* 800-724-3784 ■ *Web:* www.vippharm.com

242 DUDE RANCHES

SEE ALSO Resorts & Resort Companies p. 2219

Phone | Fax

7 D Ranch PO Box 100 .... Cody WY 82414 307-587-9885 587-9885
TF: 888-587-9885 ■ *Web:* www.7dranch.com

63 Ranch Box 979 .... Livingston MT 59047 406-222-0570 222-6363
TF: 888-395-5151 ■ *Web:* www.sixtythree.com

Absaroka Ranch PO Box 929 .... Dubois WY 82513 307-455-2275 455-2275
Web: www.absarokaranch.com

Alisal Guest Ranch & Resort 1054 Alisal Rd .... Solvang CA 93463 805-688-6411 688-2510
TF: 800-425-4725 ■ *Web:* www.alisal.com

Aspen Canyon Ranch 13206 County Rd 3 .... Parshall CO 80468 970-725-3600 725-0040
TF: 800-321-1357 ■ *Web:* www.aspencanyon.com

Averill's Flathead Lake Lodge PO Box 248 .... Bigfork MT 59911 406-837-4391 837-6977
Web: www.flatheadlakelodge.com

Bar Lazy J Guest Ranch PO Box N .... Parshall CO 80468 970-725-3437 725-0121
TF: 800-396-6279 ■ *Web:* www.barlazyj.com

Bar M Dude Ranch 58840 Bar M Ln .... Adams OR 97810 541-566-3381 566-0100
TF: 888-824-3381 ■ *Web:* www.barmranch.com

Bellota Ranch 14301 E Speedway .... Tucson AZ 85748 520-623-0203 721-9426
Web: www.bellotaranch.com

Black Mountain Ranch PO Box 219 .... McCoy CO 80463 970-653-4226 653-4227
TF: 800-967-2401 ■ *Web:* www.blackmtnranch.com

Bonanza Creek Country Guest Ranch
523 Bonanza Creek Rd .... Martinsdale MT 59053 406-572-3366 572-3366
TF: 800-476-6045 ■ *Web:* www.bonanzacreekcountry.com

Brooks Lake Lodge & Guest Ranch 458 Brooks Lake Rd .... Dubois WY 82513 307-455-2121 455-2221
Web: www.brookslake.com

Brush Creek Ranch HC 63 Box 10 .... Saratoga WY 82331 307-327-5241 327-5384
TF: 800-726-2499 ■ *Web:* www.brushcreekranch.com

Buffalo Horn Ranch 13825 County Rd 7 .... Meeker CO 81641 970-878-5450
TF: 877-878-5450 ■ *Web:* www.buffalohorn.com

C Lazy U Ranch 3640 Colorado Hwy 125 PO Box 379 .... Granby CO 80446 970-887-3344 887-3917
Web: www.clazyu.com

Cherokee Park Ranch 436 Cherokee Hills Dr .... Livermore CO 80536 970-493-6522 493-5802
TF: 800-628-0949 ■ *Web:* www.cherokeeparkranch.com

Circle Z Ranch PO Box 194 .... Patagonia AZ 85624 520-394-2525 394-2058
TF: 888-854-2525 ■ *Web:* www.circlez.com

CM Ranch 167 Fish Hatchery Rd .... Dubois WY 82513 307-455-2331 455-3984
TF: 800-455-0721 ■ *Web:* www.cmranch.com

Coffee Creek Ranch 4940 Coffee Creek Rd .... Trinity Center CA 96091 530-266-3343 266-3597
TF: 800-624-4480 ■ *Web:* www.coffeecreekranch.com

Colorado Cattle Co & Guest Ranch 70008 County Rd 132 .... New Raymer CO 80742 970-437-5345 437-5432
Web: www.coloradoduderanch.com

Colorado Trails Ranch 12161 County Rd 240 .... Durango CO 81301 970-247-5055 385-7372
TF: 800-323-3833 ■ *Web:* www.coloradotrails.com

Coulter Lake Guest Ranch 80 County Rd 273 .... Rifle CO 81650 970-625-1473 625-2781
TF: 800-858-3046 ■ *Web:* www.coulterlake.com

Crossed Sabres Ranch 829 N Fork Hwy .... Wapiti WY 82450 307-587-3750
TF: 800-535-8944 ■ *Web:* www.crossedsabres.com

David Ranch PO Box 5 .... Daniel WY 83115 307-859-8228
Web: www.davidranch.com

Deer Valley Ranch 16825 County Rd 162 .... Nathrop CO 81236 719-395-2353 395-2394
TF: 800-284-1708 ■ *Web:* www.deervalleyranch.com

Diamond J Ranch PO Box 577 .... Ennis MT 59729 406-682-4867 682-4106
TF: 877-929-4867 ■ *Web:* ranchweb.com/diamondj/

Drowsy Water Ranch PO Box 147 .... Granby CO 80446 970-725-3456 725-3611
TF: 800-845-2292 ■ *Web:* www.drowsywater.com

Phone Fax

Dryhead Schively Ranch 1062 Rd 15 ... Lovell WY 82431 307-548-6688 548-2322
Web: www.dryheadranch.com

Eatons' Ranch 270 Eatons' Ranch Rd ... Wolf WY 82844 307-655-9285 655-9269
TF: 800-210-1049 ■ *Web:* www.eatonsranch.com

Echo Canyon Guest Ranch
12507 Echo Canyon Creek Rd PO Box 328 ... La Veta CO 81055 719-742-5524 742-5525
TF: 800-341-6603 ■ *Web:* www.guestecho.com

Echo Valley Ranch & Spa Clinton PO Box 16 ... Jesmond BC V0K1K0 250-459-2386 459-0086
TF: 800-253-8831 ■ *Web:* www.evranch.com

Elk Mountain Ranch PO Box 910 ... Buena Vista CO 81211 719-539-4430
TF: 800-432-8812 ■ *Web:* www.elkmtn.com

Elkhorn Ranch HC 1 Box 97 ... Tucson AZ 85736 520-822-1040
Web: www.guestranches.com/elkhorn

Elkhorn Ranch Montana 33133 Gallatin Rd ... Gallatin Gateway MT 59730 406-995-4291
Web: www.elkhornranchmt.com

Flying A Ranch 771 Flying A Ranch Rd ... Pinedale WY 82941 307-367-2385
TF: 888-833-3348 ■ *Web:* www.flyinga.com

Flying E Ranch 2801 W Wickenburg Way ... Wickenburg AZ 85390 928-684-2690 684-5304
TF: 888-684-2650 ■ *Web:* www.flyingeranch.com

Focus Ranch Box 52 ... Slater CO 81653 970-583-2410
Web: www.focusranch.com

Fort Ranch PO Box 916 ... Winnemucca NV 89446 775-625-3132
Web: www.wildhorsecountry.com

G Bar M Ranch PO Box 29 ... Clyde Park MT 59018 406-686-4423 686-4423
Web: www.gbarm.com

Grapevine Canyon Ranch Inc PO Box 302 ... Pearce AZ 85625 520-826-3185 826-3636
TF: 800-245-9202 ■ *Web:* www.gcranch.com

Greenhorn Creek Guest Ranch 2116 Greenhorn Ranch Rd ... Quincy CA 95971 530-283-0930 283-4401
TF: 800-334-6939 ■ *Web:* www.greenhornranch.com

Gros Ventre River Ranch PO Box 151 ... Moose WY 83012 307-733-4138 733-4272
Web: www.grosventreriverranch.com

Hawley Mountain Guest Ranch PO Box 4 ... McLeod MT 59052 406-932-5791 932-5715
TF: 877-496-7848 ■ *Web:* www.hawleymountain.com

Heart Six Ranch 16985 Buffalo Valley Rd PO Box 70 ... Moran WY 83013 307-543-2477 543-0918
TF: 888-543-2477 ■ *Web:* www.heartsix.com

Hidden Creek Ranch 11077 E Blue Lake Rd ... Harrison ID 83833 208-689-3209 689-9115
TF: 800-446-3833 ■ *Web:* www.hiddencreek.com

Hideout at Flitner Ranch Resort PO Box 206 ... Shell WY 82441 307-765-2080 765-2681
TF: 800-354-8637 ■ *Web:* www.thehideout.com

High Island Ranch & Cattle Co 346 Amoretti St Suite 10 ... Thermopolis WY 82443 307-867-2374 867-2374
Web: www.highislandranch.com

Historic Pines Ranch PO Box 311 ... Westcliffe CO 81252 719-783-9261 783-2977
TF: 800-446-9462 ■ *Web:* www.historicpines.com

Home Ranch PO Box 822 ... Clark CO 80428 970-879-1780 879-1795
Web: www.homeranch.com

Homeplace Ranch RR 1 Site 2 Box 6 ... Priddis AB T0L1W0 403-931-3245 931-3245
TF: 877-931-3245 ■ *Web:* www.homeplaceranch.com

Horse Prairie Ranch 3300 Bachelor Mountain Rd ... Dillon MT 59725 406-681-3155 719-5312*
**Fax Area Code:* 775 ■ *TF:* 888-726-2454 ■ *Web:* www.ranchlife.com

Horseshoe Canyon Ranch 3900 Lochridge Rd ... North Little Rock AR 72116 501-791-2679
TF: 800-480-9635 ■ *Web:* www.gohcr.com

Hunewill Circle H Ranch PO Box 368 ... Bridgeport CA 93517 760-932-7710 932-1933
Web: www.hunewillranch.com

Kay El Bar Guest Ranch PO Box 2480 ... Wickenburg AZ 85358 928-684-7593 684-4497
TF: 800-684-7583 ■ *Web:* www.kayelbar.com

King Mountain Ranch PO Box 497 ... Granby CO 80446 970-887-2511 887-9511
TF: 800-476-5464 ■ *Web:* www.kingranchresort.com

Lake Mancos Ranch 42688 County Rd 'N' ... Mancos CO 81328 970-533-1190
TF: 800-325-9462 ■ *Web:* www.lakemancosranch.com

Laramie River Dude Ranch 25777 County Rd 103 ... Jelm WY 82063 970-435-5716 435-5731
TF: 800-551-5731 ■ *Web:* www.lrranch.com

Latigo Ranch PO Box 237 ... Kremmling CO 80459 970-724-9008
TF: 800-227-9655 ■ *Web:* www.latigotrails.com

Laughing Water Guest Ranch PO Box 157 ... Fortine MT 59918 406-882-4680 882-4880
TF: 800-847-5095 ■ *Web:* www.lwranch.com

Lazy K Bar Guest Ranch 8401 N Scenic Dr ... Tucson AZ 85743 520-299-7433 744-0350
Web: www.lazykbar.com

Lazy K Bar Ranch PO Box 1550 ... Big Timber MT 59011 406-537-4404 537-4593
Web: www.lazykbar.net

Lazy L & B Ranch 1072 E Fork Rd ... Dubois WY 82513 307-455-2839 455-2849
TF: 800-453-9488 ■ *Web:* www.lazylb.com

Lone Mountain Ranch PO Box 160069 ... Big Sky MT 59716 406-995-4644 995-4670
TF: 800-514-4644 ■ *Web:* www.lmranch.com

Long Hollow Ranch 71105 Holmes Rd ... Sisters OR 97759 541-923-1901 610-1993
TF: 877-923-1901 ■ *Web:* www.lhranch.com

Lost Valley Ranch 29555 Goose Creek Rd ... Sedalia CO 80135 303-647-2311 647-2315
Web: www.ranchweb.com/lost

Lozier's Box R Ranch PO Box 100 ... Cora WY 82925 307-367-4868 367-6260
TF: 800-822-8466 ■ *Web:* www.boxr.com

McGinnis Meadows Cattle & Guest Ranch
6600 McGinnis Meadows Rd ... Libby MT 59923 406-293-5000 293-5005
Web: www.mmgranch.com

Moose Head Ranch Hwy 89 N ... Moose WY 83012 307-733-3141

Mountain Sky Guest Ranch 480 Big Creek Rd PO box 1219 ... Emigrant MT 59027 406-333-4911 333-4537
TF: 800-548-3392 ■ *Web:* www.mtnsky.com

Nine Quarter Circle Ranch 5000 Taylor Fork Rd ... Gallatin Gateway MT 59730 406-995-4276 995-4276
Web: www.ninequartercircle.com

North Fork Ranch 55395 Hwy 285 ... Shawnee CO 80475 303-838-9873 838-1549
TF: 800-843-7895 ■ *Web:* www.northforkranch.com

Paradise Guest Ranch 282 Hunter Creek Rd ... Buffalo WY 82834 307-684-7876 862-2126*
**Fax Area Code:* 720 ■ *Web:* www.paradiseranch.com

Peaceful Valley Ranch 475 Peaceful Valley Rd ... Lyons CO 80540 303-747-2881 747-2167
TF: 800-955-6343 ■ *Web:* www.peacefulvalley.com

Pine Butte Guest Ranch HC 58 Box 34 C ... Choteau MT 59422 406-466-2158 466-5462
Web: nature.org/wherewework/northamerica/states

Price Canyon Ranch PO Box 39 ... Rodeo NM 88056 520-558-2383 558-0024
TF: 800-727-0065 ■ *Web:* www.pricecanyon.com

R Lazy S Ranch PO Box 308 ... Teton Village WY 83025 307-733-2655 734-1120
Web: www.rlazys.com

Rainbow Trout Ranch 1484 FDR 250 ... Antonito CO 81120 719-376-5659 376-5659
TF: 800-633-3397 ■ *Web:* www.rainbowtroutranch.com

Rancho de la Osa Guest Ranch PO Box 1 ... Sasabe AZ 85633 520-823-4257 823-4238
TF: 800-872-6240 ■ *Web:* www.ranchodelaosa.com

Ranger Creek Guest Ranch PO Box 47 ... Shell WY 82441 307-272-5107
TF: 888-817-7787 ■ *Web:* www.rangercreekranch.net

Rawah Ranch 11447 N County Rd 103 ... Jelm WY 82063 800-820-3152 435-5705*
**Fax Area Code:* 970 ■ *Web:* www.rawah.com

Red Rock Ranch PO Box 38 ... Kelly WY 83011 307-733-6288 733-6287
Web: www.theredrockranch.com

Rich Ranch PO Box 495 ... Seeley Lake MT 59868 406-677-2317 677-3530
TF: 800-532-4350 ■ *Web:* www.richranch.com

Rimrock Dude Ranch 2728 Northfork Rt ... Cody WY 82414 307-587-3970 527-5014
TF: 800-208-7468 ■ *Web:* www.rimrockranch.com

Rock Springs Guest Ranch 64201 Tyler Rd ... Bend OR 97701 541-382-1957 382-7774
TF: 800-225-3833 ■ *Web:* www.rocksprings.com

Phone Fax

Scott Valley Resort & Guest Ranch
223 Scott Valley Trail ... Mountain Home AR 72653 870-425-5136
TF: 888-855-7747 ■ *Web:* www.scottvalley.com

Seven Lazy P Guest Ranch PO Box 178 ... Choteau MT 59422 406-466-2044 466-2903
Web: www.sevenlazyp.com

Smith Fork Ranch 45362 Needle Rock Rd ... Crawford CO 81415 970-921-3454 921-3475
Web: www.smithforkranch.com

Spear-O-Wigwam Guest Ranch PO Box 1081 ... Sheridan WY 82801 888-818-3833 673-5609*
**Fax Area Code:* 307 ■ *Web:* www.spear-o-wigwam.com

Sundance Trail Guest Ranch
17931 Red Feather Lakes Rd ... Red Feather Lakes CO 80545 970-224-1222 224-1222
TF: 800-357-4930 ■ *Web:* www.sundancetrail.com

Sweet Grass Ranch 460 Rein Ln ... Big Timber MT 59011 406-537-4477 537-4477
Web: www.sweetgrassranch.com

Sylvan Dale Guest Ranch 2939 N County Rd 31 D ... Loveland CO 80538 970-667-3915 635-9336
TF: 877-667-3999 ■ *Web:* www.sylvandale.com

T Cross Ranch PO Box 638 ... Dubois WY 82513 307-455-2206 455-2720
TF: 877-827-6770 ■ *Web:* www.tcross.com

Tarryall River Ranch 27001.5 County Rd 77 ... Lake George CO 80827 719-748-1214 748-1319
TF: 800-408-8407 ■ *Web:* www.tarryallriverranch.com

Three Bars Cattle & Guest Ranch
9500 Wycliffe Perry Creek Rd ... Cranbrook BC V1C7C7 250-426-5230 426-8240
TF: 877-426-5230 ■ *Web:* www.threebarsranch.com

Trail Creek Ranch Box 10 ... Wilson WY 83014 307-733-2610
Web: www.jacksonholetrailcreekranch.com

Triangle C Ranch 3737 Hwy 26 ... Dubois WY 82513 307-455-2225 455-2031
TF: 800-661-4928 ■ *Web:* www.trianglec.com

Triangle X Ranch 2 Triangle X Ranch Rd ... Moose WY 83012 307-733-2183 733-8685
TF: 888-860-0005 ■ *Web:* www.trianglex.com

Triple J Wilderness Ranch PO Box 310 ... Augusta MT 59410 406-562-3653 562-3836
Web: www.triplejranch.com

Triple R Ranch PO Box 124 ... Keystone SD 57751 605-666-4605
TF: 888-777-2624 ■ *Web:* www.rrrranch.com

Tumbling River Ranch 3715 Park County Rd 62 Box 30 ... Grant CO 80448 303-838-5981 838-5133
TF: 800-654-8770 ■ *Web:* www.tumblingriver.com

Twin Peaks Ranch PO Box 774 ... Salmon ID 83467 208-894-2290 894-2429
TF: 800-659-4899 ■ *Web:* www.twinpeaksranch.com

Two Bars Seven Ranch PO Box 67 ... Tie Siding WY 82084 307-742-6072
Web: www.twobarssevenranch.com

UXU Ranch 1710 Yellowstone Hwy ... Wapiti WY 82450 307-587-2143 587-8307
TF: 800-373-9027 ■ *Web:* www.uxuranch.com

Vee Bar Guest Ranch 2091 State Hwy 130 ... Laramie WY 82070 307-745-7036 745-7433
TF: 800-483-3227 ■ *Web:* www.veebar.com

Vista Verde Guest & Ski Ranch Box 770465 ... Steamboat Springs CO 80477 970-879-3858 879-6814
TF: 800-526-7433 ■ *Web:* www.vistaverde.com

Wapiti Meadow Ranch 1667 Johnson Creek Rd ... Cascade ID 83611 208-633-3217 633-3219
Web: www.wapitimeadowranch.com

Waunita Hot Springs Ranch 8007 County Rd 887 Box 7 D ... Gunnison CO 81230 970-641-1266 641-0650
Web: www.waunita.com

Whistling Acres Guest Ranch
44325 Minnesota Creek Rd PO Box 88 ... Paonia CO 81428 970-527-4560 527-6397
TF: 800-346-1420 ■ *Web:* www.whistlingacres.com

White Stallion Ranch 9251 W Twin Peaks Rd ... Tucson AZ 85743 520-297-0252 744-2786
TF: 888-977-2624 ■ *Web:* www.wsranch.com

Wild Rose Ranch PO Box 181 ... Kimberley BC V1A2Y6 250-422-3403 422-3149
TF: 800-324-6188 ■ *Web:* www.wildrose-ranch.com

Wilderness Trails Ranch 1766 County Rd 302 ... Durango CO 81303 970-247-0722 247-1006
TF: 800-527-2624 ■ *Web:* www.wildernesstrails.com

Wind River Ranch PO Box 3410 ... Estes Park CO 80517 970-586-4212 586-2255
TF: 800-523-4212 ■ *Web:* www.windriverranch.com

Wind Walker Guest Ranch PO Box 7 ... Spring City UT 84662 435-462-0282 462-9212
TF: 888-606-9463 ■ *Web:* www.windwalker.org

243 DUPLICATION & REPLICATION SERVICES

Phone Fax

Adwar Video 303 Sunnyside Blvd ... Plainview NY 11803 516-349-1800 349-1833
Web: www.adwarvideo.com

American Reprographics Co 700 N Central Ave Suite 550 ... Glendale CA 91203 818-500-0225 500-0195
NYSE: ARP ■ *Web:* www.e-arc.com

Andrew T Johnson Co Inc 15 Tremont Pl ... Boston MA 02108 617-742-1610 523-0719
Web: www.andrewtjohnson.com

Avery Dennison Microreplication Div
7590 Auburn Rd MS 16X ... Painesville OH 44077 440-358-4862 358-4835
TF: 866-358-4862 ■ *Web:* www.averydennison.com

Blair Graphics Inc 1740 Stanford St ... Santa Monica CA 90404 310-829-4621 453-0868
Web: www.blairgfx.com

BPS Reprographic Services Inc 945 Bryant St ... San Francisco CA 94103 415-495-8700 495-2773
Web: www.bps.com

Campbell Blueprint & Supply Co Inc PO Box 820344 ... Memphis TN 38182 901-327-7385 327-0917
TF: 800-238-7564 ■ *Web:* www.campbellblueprint.com

Color Film Media Group LLC 28 Thorndale Cir ... Darien CT 06820 203-866-2711 854-3526
TF: 800-882-1120 ■ *Web:* www.colorfilm.com

Consolidated Reprographics 118 E Orangethorpe Ave ... Anaheim CA 92801 714-526-0905 871-8129
Web: www.consrepro.com

Corporate Disk Co 4610 Crime Pkwy ... McHenry IL 60050 815-331-6000 333-6030
TF: 800-634-3475 ■ *Web:* www.disk.com

Denon Digital LLC 1380 Monticello Rd ... Madison GA 30650 706-342-3425 342-0637
Web: www.denondigital.com

Digital Video Services 4592 40th St SE ... Grand Rapids MI 49512 616-975-9911 975-9696
TF: 800-747-8273 ■ *Web:* www.digivid.com

Dunn Blue Print Co 20390 W Eight-Mile Rd ... Southfield MI 48075 248-353-2950 357-5944
Web: www.dunnblue.com

EMI Mfg 1 Capitol Way ... Jacksonville IL 62650 217-245-9631 479-2516

Eva-Tone Soundsheets Inc 4801 Ulmerton Rd ... Clearwater FL 33762 727-572-7000 572-6214
TF Sales: 800-382-8663 ■ *Web:* www.eva-tone.com

Ford Graphics-Northwest 401 NW 14th Ave ... Portland OR 97209 503-227-3424 223-4254
Web: www.fordgraphics.com

Future Media Productions Inc 24811 Rockefeller Ave ... Valencia CA 91355 661-294-5575 294-5583
Web: www.fmpi.com

GlobalWare Solutions Inc 200 Ward Hill ... Haverhill MA 01835 978-469-7500 469-7373
TF: 800-224-6326 ■ *Web:* www.globalwaresolutions.com

Huey Reprographics Co 19 S Wabash Ave 3rd Fl ... Chicago IL 60603 312-782-2226 782-0771
Web: www.hueyrepro.com

Illinois Blueprint Corp 800 SW Jefferson Ave ... Peoria IL 61605 309-676-1300 676-1310
Web: www.illinoisblue.com

Infodisc Technology USA Inc 3535 Hayden Ave ... Culver City CA 90232 310-280-1200 280-1222
Web: www.infodisc.com

Johnson Andrew T Co Inc 15 Tremont Pl ... Boston MA 02108 617-742-1610 523-0719
Web: www.andrewtjohnson.com

Lason Inc 1305 Stephenson Hwy ... Troy MI 48083 248-597-5800 837-7100
Web: www.lason.com

Media Factory Inc 48873 Kato Rd ... Fremont CA 94539 510-438-0373 445-0877
TF: 800-879-9536 ■ *Web:* www.mediafactoryinc.com

				Phone	Fax
MerX City 608 2nd Ave S Suite 167 *TF:* 800-356-6826 ■ *Web:* www.merxcity.com	Minneapolis	MN	55402	612-332-2555	333-4080
Metacom Inc 251 1st Ave N 2nd Fl **Fax Area Code:* 763	Minneapolis	MN	55401	800-236-0289	424-5930*
Music Optical Media 1045 Firestone Pkwy	La Vergne	TN	37086	615-641-2271	641-8555
NBC RT 2000 L St NW Suite B-1 *TF:* 800-231-5758 ■ *Web:* www.repro-tech.com	Washington	DC	20036	202-331-0576	331-0985
Online Copy Corp 48815 Kato Rd *TF:* 800-833-4460 ■ *Web:* www.wecopycds.com	Fremont	CA	94539	510-226-6810	226-7543
Producers & Quantity Photos Inc 6660 Santa Monica Blvd *TF Cust Svc:* 800-843-9259 ■ *Web:* www.pqphoto.com	Hollywood	CA	90038	323-467-6178	466-0939
Rainbo Records & Cassettes 1738 Berkeley St *Web:* www.rainborecords.com	Santa Monica	CA	90404	310-829-3476	828-8765
Reliable Graphics Inc 15013 Califa St *Web:* www.reliablegraphics.com	Van Nuys	CA	91411	818-908-0222	785-9352
Reproduction Systems Inc 1828 Walnut St Suite 900 *TF:* 800-633-6125 ■ *Web:* www.rsi-kc.com	Kansas City	MO	64108	816-471-1414	472-7155
Shaffstall Corp 8531 Bash St *TF:* 800-923-8439 ■ *Web:* www.shaffstall.com	Indianapolis	IN	46250	317-842-2077	915-9045
Smart Document Solutions 120 Bluegrass Valley Pkwy *TF:* 800-367-1500 ■ *Web:* www.smartdocumentsolutions.net	Alpharetta	GA	30005	770-360-1700	360-1740
Standard Digital Imaging 4426 S 108th St *TF:* 800-642-8062 ■ *Web:* www.standarddigital.com	Omaha	NE	68137	402-592-1292	592-8003
T-Square Miami Blueprint Co 998 W Flagler St *TF:* 800-432-3360 ■ *Web:* www.t-square.com	Miami	FL	33130	305-324-1234	547-1556
Thomas Reprographics 600 N Central Expy *TF:* 800-877-3776 ■ *Web:* www.thomasrepro.com	Richardson	TX	75080	972-231-7227	231-0623
Triangle Blueprint Co 2721 Brunswick Pike *TF:* 800-792-8800 ■ *Web:* www.triangleart.com	Lawrenceville	NJ	08648	609-883-3600	883-0011
Universal Reprographics Inc 2706 Wilshire Blvd *Web:* www.reprographics.com	Los Angeles	CA	90057	213-365-7750	365-0287
Victory Studios 2247 15th Ave W *TF:* 888-282-1776 ■ *Web:* www.victorystudios.com	Seattle	WA	98119	206-282-1776	282-3535
WEA Mfg 1400 E Lackawanna Ave *TF:* 800-323-1263	Olyphant	PA	18448	570-383-2471	383-6722

244 DUTY-FREE SHOPS

SEE ALSO Gift Shops p. 1690

				Phone	Fax
Ambassador Duty Free Store 707 Patricia St *Web:* www.ambassadorbridge.com	Windsor	ON	N9B3B8	519-977-9100	977-7811
American Airlines Duty Free 1166 Kane Concourse Suite 301 *TF:* 888-388-9373 ■ *Web:* www.aadutyfree.com	Bay Harbor Islands	FL	33154	305-864-5788	864-5787
Ammex Tax & Duty Free Shops 6100 Hollywood Blvd 7th Fl *Web:* www.dutyfreeamericas.com	Hollywood	FL	33024	954-986-7700	965-6800
Baja Duty Free 4590 Border Village Rd *TF:* 877-438-8937 ■ *Web:* www.bajadutyfree.com	San Ysidro	CA	92173	619-428-6671	428-6673
Colombian Emeralds International PO Box 5868 *TF:* 800-666-3889 ■ *Web:* www.colombianemeralds.com	Fort Lauderdale	FL	33310	954-917-2547	971-7693
DFS Galleria 525 Market St 31st Fl *Web:* www.dfsgalleria.com	San Francisco	CA	94105	415-977-2700	977-4289
DFS Group Ltd DBA DFS Galleria 525 Market St 31st Fl *Web:* www.dfsgalleria.com	San Francisco	CA	94105	415-977-2700	977-4289
Duty Free Americas Inc 6100 Hollywood Blvd 7th Fl *Web:* www.dutyfreeamericas.com	Hollywood	FL	33024	954-986-7700	965-6800
DUTYFREE.COM PO Box 5868 *TF:* 800-666-3889 ■ *Web:* www.dutyfree.com	Fort Lauderdale	FL	33310	954-978-5482	971-7693
Little Switzerland Inc 6800 NW Broken Sound Pkwy Suite 300 *TF:* 888-257-5488 ■ *Web:* www.littleswitzerland.com	Boca Raton	FL	33487	561-206-0080	995-8082
Niagara Duty Free Shop 5726 Falls Ave *TF:* 877-612-4337 ■ *Web:* www.niagaradutyfree.com	Niagara Falls	ON	L2G7T5	905-374-3700	374-7503
Peace Bridge Duty Free Inc Peace Bridge Plaza PO Box 339 *TF:* 800-361-1302 ■ *Web:* www.dutyfree.ca	Fort Erie	ON	L2A5N1	905-871-5400	871-6335
Starboard Cruise Services Inc 8400 NW 36th St *TF:* 800-547-4785 ■ *Web:* www.starboardcruise.com	Miami	FL	33166	786-845-7300	845-1111
Tunnel Duty Free Shop Inc 465 Goyeau St *Web:* www.dutyfreetunnel.com	Windsor	ON	N9A1H1	519-252-2713	252-1688
UETA of Texas Inc 110 International Blvd *Web:* www.ueta.com	Laredo	TX	78045	956-722-7601	

245 EDUCATIONAL INSTITUTION OPERATORS & MANAGERS

				Phone	Fax
Apollo Group Inc 4615 E Elwood St *NASDAQ: APOL* ■ **Fax:* Hum Res ■ *TF:* 800-990-2765 ■ *Web:* www.apollogrp.edu	Phoenix	AZ	85040	480-966-5394	929-7417*
Argosy Education Group 20 S Clark St Suite 2800 *Web:* www.argosyu.edu	Chicago	IL	60603	312-424-7282	201-1907
Capella Education Co 225 S 6th St 9th Fl *TF:* 888-227-3552 ■ *Web:* www.capella.edu	Minneapolis	MN	55402	612-977-5100	977-5058
Career Education Corp 2895 Greenspoint Pkwy Suite 600 *NASDAQ: CECO* ■ *TF:* 888-781-3608 ■ *Web:* www.careered.com	Hoffman Estates	IL	60195	847-781-3600	781-3610
Charter Schools USA 6245 N Federal Hwy 5th Fl *Web:* www.charterschoolsusa.com	Fort Lauderdale	FL	33308	954-202-3500	202-3512
College for Financial Planning Inc 6161 S Syracuse Way **Fax:* Admissions ■ *TF:* 800-237-9990	Greenwood Village	CO	80111	303-220-1200	220-1810*
Corinthian Colleges Inc 6 Hutton Ctr Dr Suite 400 *NASDAQ: COCO* ■ *TF:* 800-611-2101 ■ *Web:* corinthiancolleges.com	Santa Ana	CA	92707	714-427-3000	427-3016
Corinthian Schools Inc 6 Hutton Ctr Dr Suite 400 *Web:* www.cci.edu/corinthianschools.asp	Santa Ana	CA	92707	714-427-3000	427-3016
DeVRY Inc 1 Tower Ln Suite 1000 *NYSE: DV* ■ *TF:* 800-225-8000 ■ *Web:* www.devryinc.com	Oakbrook Terrace	IL	60181	630-571-7700	571-0317
Edison Schools Inc 521 5th Ave 11th Fl *TF:* 877-276-3375 ■ *Web:* www.edisonschools.com	New York	NY	10175	212-419-1600	419-1604
Education Management Corp 210 6th Ave 33rd Fl *NASDAQ: EDMC* ■ *TF:* 800-275-2440 ■ *Web:* www.edumgt.com	Pittsburgh	PA	15222	412-562-0900	562-0934
Excel Education Centers 1040 Whipple St Suite 324 *TF:* 800-417-9036 ■ *Web:* www.exceleducationcenters.org	Prescott	AZ	86305	928-778-5764	445-2989
Imagine Schools 1005 N Glebe Rd Suite 610 *Web:* www.imagineschools.com	Arlington	VA	22201	703-527-2600	527-0038
ITT Educational Services Inc 13000 N Meridian St *NYSE: ESI* ■ *TF:* 800-388-3368 ■ *Web:* www.ittesi.com	Carmel	IN	46032	317-706-9200	706-9327
Kaplan Higher Education 1400 Hembree Rd Suite 100 *Web:* www.khec.com	Roswell	GA	30076	770-510-2000	510-2001
Laureate Education Inc 1001 Fleet St *NASDAQ: LAUR* ■ *TF:* 866-367-5287 ■ *Web:* www.laureate-inc.com	Baltimore	MD	21202	410-843-8000	880-8065
Leona Group LLC 4660 S Hagadorn Rd Suite 500 *TF:* 800-656-6763 ■ *Web:* www.leonagroup.com	East Lansing	MI	48823	517-333-9030	333-4559
Lincoln Educational Services 200 Executive Dr *NASDAQ: LINC* ■ *TF:* 877-693-8887 ■ *Web:* www.lincolneducationalservices.com	West Orange	NJ	07052	973-736-9340	736-1750
Mosaica Education Inc 1050 Northgate Dr Suite 190 *Web:* www.mosaicaeducation.com	San Rafael	CA	94903	415-491-1305	491-1309
National Heritage Academies 3850 Broadmoor Ave SE Suite 201 *TF:* 800-699-9235 ■ *Web:* www.heritageacademies.com	Grand Rapids	MI	49512	616-222-1700	222-1701
Nobel Learning Communities Inc 1615 West Chester Pike Suite 200 *NASDAQ: NLCI* ■ *Web:* www.nobellearning.com	West Chester	PA	19382	484-947-2000	947-2006
Rhodes Colleges Inc 6 Hutton Ctr Dr Suite 400	Santa Ana	CA	92707	714-427-3000	
SABIS Educational Systems Inc 6385 Beach Rd *Web:* www.sabis.net	Eden Prairie	MN	55344	952-918-1850	918-1851
Strayer Education Inc 2121 15th St N *NASDAQ: STRA* ■ *TF:* 877-892-5100 ■ *Web:* www.strayereducation.com	Arlington	VA	22201	703-892-5100	769-2677
Sylvan Learning Centers 1001 Fleet St *TF:* 800-627-4267 ■ *Web:* educate-inc.com	Baltimore	MD	21202	410-843-8000	880-8717
UNext.com 111 N Canal St Suite 455 *TF:* 877-405-4500 ■ *Web:* www.unext.com	Chicago	IL	60606	312-669-5000	669-5005

EDUCATIONAL INSTITUTIONS

SEE Children's Learning Centers p. 1445; Colleges & Universities - Historically Black p. 1497; Colleges & Universities - Jesuit p. 1498; Colleges - Tribal p. 1473; Preparatory Schools - Boarding p. 2135; Preparatory Schools - Non-boarding p. 2137

246 EDUCATIONAL MATERIALS & SUPPLIES

SEE ALSO Computer Software - Educational & Reference Software p. 1510; Office & School Supplies p. 2034

				Phone	Fax
ABC School Supply Inc 1156 Four Star Dr **Fax Area Code:* 800 ■ **Fax:* Mail Rm ■ *TF:* 800-669-4222 ■ *Web:* www.abcschoolsupply.com	Mount Joy	PA	17552	717-653-7500	933-2987*
American Educational Products Inc 401 Hickory St PO Box 2121 *TF:* 800-446-8767 ■ *Web:* www.amep.com	Fort Collins	CO	80522	970-484-7445	484-1198
American Educational Products LLC Hubbard Scientific Div 401 Hickory St *TF Cust Svc:* 800-289-9299 ■ *Web:* www.hubbardscientific.com	Fort Collins	CO	80522	970-484-7445	484-1198
American Educational Products LLC National Teaching Aids Div 401 Hickory St *TF Cust Svc:* 800-289-9299 ■ *Web:* www.shnta.com	Fort Collins	CO	80522	970-484-7445	484-1198
American Educational Products LLC Scott Resources Div 401 Hickory St *TF Cust Svc:* 800-289-9299 ■ *Web:* www.shnta.com	Fort Collins	CO	80522	970-484-7445	484-1198
American Greetings Corp Learning Horizons Div 1 American Rd **Fax Area Code:* 800 ■ *TF:* 800-321-3040 ■ *Web:* www.learninghorizons.com	Cleveland	OH	44144	216-252-7300	941-8693*
American Guidance Service Inc DBA AGS Publishing 4201 Woodland Rd *TF:* 800-471-8457 ■ *Web:* www.agsnet.com	Circle Pines	MN	55014	651-287-7220	287-7223
Carolina Biological Supply Co 2700 York Rd *TF:* 800-334-5551 ■ *Web:* www.carolina.com	Burlington	NC	27215	336-584-0381	584-3399
Carson-Dellosa Publishing Co Inc 7027 Albert Pick Rd *TF:* 800-321-0943 ■ *Web:* www.carsondellosa.com	Greensboro	NC	27409	336-632-0084	808-3271
Center Enterprises Inc 30 Shield St *TF Orders:* 800-542-2214 ■ *Web:* www.centerenterprises.com	West Hartford	CT	06110	860-953-4423	953-2948
Chenille Kraft Co 65 Ambrogio Dr *TF:* 800-621-1261 ■ *Web:* www.chenillekraft.com	Gurnee	IL	60031	847-249-2900	249-2906
Claridge Products & Equipment Inc PO Box 910 *Web:* www.claridgeproducts.com	Harrison	AR	72602	870-743-2200	743-1908
Classroom Connect Inc 8000 Marina Blvd Suite 100 **Fax Area Code:* 888 ■ *TF:* 800-638-1639 ■ *Web:* www.classroom.com	Brisbane	CA	94005	650-589-8326	801-8299*
ClassroomDirect.com PO Box 830677 **Fax Area Code:* 800 ■ *TF:* 800-599-3040 ■ *Web:* www.classroomdirect.com	Birmingham	AL	35283	205-251-9171	628-6250*
Creative Teaching Press Inc 15342 Graham St *TF:* 800-444-4287 ■ *Web:* www.creativeteaching.com	Huntington Beach	CA	92649	714-895-5047	895-6547
Delta Education LLC 80 Northwest Blvd *TF:* 800-258-1302 ■ *Web:* www.delta-education.com	Nashua	NH	03063	603-889-8899	880-6520
Didax Educational Resources Inc 395 Main St *TF:* 800-458-0024 ■ *Web:* www.didax.com	Rowley	MA	01969	978-948-2340	948-2813
E.nopi Daekyo USA Inc 701 E Palisades Ave Suite 201 *TF:* 888-835-1212 ■ *Web:* www.enopi.com	Englewood Cliffs	NJ	07632	201-894-1212	894-8686
Edcon/Imperial/AV 30 Montauk Blvd *TF:* 888-553-3266 ■ *Web:* www.edconpublishing.com	Oakdale	NY	11769	631-567-7227	567-8745
Education Center Inc 3515 W Market St Suite 200 *TF:* 800-714-7991 ■ *Web:* www.theeducationcenter.com	Greensboro	NC	27403	336-854-0309	547-1587
Educational Insights Inc 18730 S Wilmington Ave *TF:* 800-933-3277 ■ *Web:* www.edin.com	Rancho Dominguez	CA	90220	310-884-2000	884-2011
Educational Resources 1550 Executive Dr **Fax:* Orders ■ *TF Orders:* 800-624-2926 ■ *Web:* www.edresources.com	Elgin	IL	60123	847-888-8300	888-8499*
Educational Supplies Inc 1506 S Salisbury Blvd *TF:* 800-797-8775 ■ *Web:* www.educationalsuppliesinc.com	Salisbury	MD	21801	410-543-2519	860-0584
Educators Resource Inc 2575 Schillingers Rd **Fax Area Code:* 800 ■ *TF:* 800-868-8181 ■ *Web:* www.edresource.com	Semmes	AL	36575	251-645-8800	868-6212*
Edupress Inc W 5527 SR 106 *TF:* 800-835-7978 ■ *Web:* www.highsmith.com	Fort Atlinson	WI	53538	920-563-9571	563-7395
Eureka School Div Paper Magic Group Inc 401 Adams Ave *TF Cust Svc:* 800-258-1044 ■ *Web:* www.papermagic.com	Scranton	PA	18510	570-961-3863	961-2628
Evan-Moor Educational Publishers Inc 18 Lower Ragsdale Dr *TF:* 800-777-4489 ■ *Web:* www.evan-moor.com	Monterey	CA	93940	831-649-5901	649-6256
Excelligence Learning Corp 2 Lower Ragsdale Dr Suite 200 **Fax Area Code:* 800 ■ *TF:* 800-627-2829 ■ *Web:* www.excelligencelearning.com	Monterey	CA	93940	831-333-2000	879-3753*
Films for the Humanities & Sciences PO Box 2053 *TF:* 800-257-5126 ■ *Web:* www.films.com	Princeton	NJ	08543	609-671-1000	671-0266
Fisher Scientific International Inc Science Education Div 4500 Turnberry Dr **Fax Area Code:* 800 ■ *TF:* 800-955-1177 ■ *Web:* www.fisheredu.com	Hanover Park	IL	60133	630-259-1200	955-0740*
Frank Schaffer Publications PO Box 141487 **Fax Area Code:* 888 ■ *TF:* 800-253-5469 ■ *Web:* www.schoolspecialtypublishing.com/Frank_Schaffer/?start=0	Grand Rapids	MI	49514	800-417-3261	203-9361*
Frog Street Press Inc 308 E Trunk St **Fax Area Code:* 800 ■ *TF:* 800-884-3764 ■ *Web:* www.frogstreet.com	Crandall	TX	75114	972-472-6896	759-3828*

Phone Fax

Futurekids Inc 1000 N Studebaker Rd Suite 5 . . . Long Beach CA 90815 562-296-1111 296-1110
TF: 800-765-8000 ■ *Web:* www.futurekids.com
Ghent Mfg Inc 2999 Henkle Dr . . . Lebanon OH 45036 513-932-3445 932-9252
TF: 800-543-0550 ■ *Web:* www.ghent.com
Great Source Education Group 181 Ballardvale St . . . Wilmington MA 01887 978-661-1300 289-3994*
**Fax Area Code:* 800 ■ *TF:* 800-289-4490 ■ *Web:* www.greatsource.com
Guidecraft USA 66 Grand Ave Suite 207 . . . Englewood NJ 07631 201-894-5401 894-5405
TF: 800-544-6526 ■ *Web:* www.guidecraft.com
Hayes School Publishing Co Inc 321 Pennwood Ave . . . Pittsburgh PA 15221 412-731-4693 543-8771*
**Fax Area Code:* 800 ■ *TF:* 800-245-6234 ■ *Web:* www.hayespub.com
Highsmith Inc W 5527 SR 106 PO Box 800 . . . Fort Atkinson WI 53538 920-563-9571 563-7395
TF: 800-558-3899 ■ *Web:* www.highsmith.com
Holcomb JR & Co Inc PO Box 94636 . . . Cleveland OH 44101 216-341-3000 341-5151
TF: 800-362-9907 ■ *Web:* www.holcombs.com
Holcomb's Education Resource 3205 Harvard Ave . . . Cleveland OH 44105 216-341-3000 341-5151
TF: 800-362-9907 ■ *Web:* www.holcombs.com
Hubbard Scientific Div American Educational Products LLC
401 Hickory St . . . Fort Collins CO 80522 970-484-7445 484-1198
TF Cust Svc: 800-289-9299 ■ *Web:* www.hubbardscientific.com
Incentive Publications Inc 2400 Crestmoor Dr Suite 211 . . . Nashville TN 37215 615-385-2934 385-2967
TF Mktg: 800-421-2830 ■ *Web:* www.incentivepublications.com
JR Holcomb & Co Inc PO Box 94636 . . . Cleveland OH 44101 216-341-3000 341-5151
TF: 800-362-9907 ■ *Web:* www.holcombs.com
Kaplan Early Learning Co 1310 Lewisville-Clemmons Rd . . . Lewisville NC 27023 336-766-7374 766-6960
TF: 800-334-2014 ■ *Web:* www.kaplanco.com
Kimbo Educational 10 N 3rd Ave . . . Long Branch NJ 07740 732-229-4949 870-3340
TF: 800-631-2187 ■ *Web:* www.kimboed.com
Lauri 51 Magnetic Ave . . . Smethport PA 16749 814-887-6921 887-9272
TF: 800-451-0520
Learning Horizons Div American Greetings Corp 1 American Rd . . . Cleveland OH 44144 216-252-7300 941-8693*
**Fax Area Code:* 800 ■ *TF:* 800-321-3040 ■ *Web:* www.learninghorizons.com
Learning Resources 380 N Fairway Dr . . . Vernon Hills IL 60061 847-573-8400 573-8425
TF: 800-222-3909 ■ *Web:* www.learningresources.com
Learning Works 15342 Graham St . . . Huntington Beach CA 92649 714-895-5047 895-6547
TF: 800-235-5767 ■ *Web:* www.thelearningworks.com
Learning Wrap-Ups Inc 1660 W Gordon Ave Suite 4 . . . Layton UT 84041 801-497-0050 497-0063
TF: 800-992-4966 ■ *Web:* www.learningwrapups.com
Macmillan/McGraw-Hill Div McGraw-Hill Cos Inc 2 Penn Plaza . . . New York NY 10121 212-512-2000 904-6633*
**Fax:* Mktg ■ *TF:* 800-442-9685 ■ *Web:* www.mhschool.com
McDonald Publishing 567 Hanley Industrial Ct . . . Saint Louis MO 63144 314-781-7400 781-7480
TF: 800-722-8080 ■ *Web:* www.mcdonaldpublishing.com
McGraw-Hill Cos Inc Macmillan/McGraw-Hill Div 2 Penn Plaza . . . New York NY 10121 212-512-2000 904-6633*
**Fax:* Mktg ■ *TF:* 800-442-9685 ■ *Web:* www.mhschool.com
McGraw-Hill Cos Inc SRA/McGraw-Hill Div 8787 Orion Pl . . . Columbus OH 43240 614-430-6600 430-6621
TF: 800-468-4850 ■ *Web:* www.sra4kids.com
McGraw-Hill Everyday Learning 1 Prudential Plaza Suite 400 . . . Chicago IL 60601 312-233-7820 233-6730
Web: www.sraonline.com/tlexchange
Milliken Publishing Co Inc 3190 Rider Trail S . . . Earth City MO 63045 314-991-4220 991-4807
TF: 800-325-4136 ■ *Web:* www.millikenpub.com
Monday Morning Books 150 Bayview Dr PO Box 1134 . . . Palo Alto CA 94301 800-255-6049 255-6048
Web: www.mondaymorningbooks.com
National School Products 101 E Broadway . . . Maryville TN 37804 865-984-3960 289-3960*
**Fax Area Code:* 800 ■ *TF:* 800-627-9393 ■ *Web:* www.nationalschoolproducts.com
National Teaching Aids Div American Educational Products LLC 401 Hickory St . . . Fort Collins CO 80522 970-484-7445 484-1198
TF Cust Svc: 800-289-9299 ■ *Web:* www.shnta.com
Paper Magic Group Inc Eureka School Div 401 Adams Ave . . . Scranton PA 18510 570-961-3863 961-2628
TF Cust Svc: 800-258-1044 ■ *Web:* www.papermagic.com
Replogle Globes Inc 2801 S 25th Ave . . . Broadview IL 60155 708-343-0900 343-0923
TF: 800-275-4452 ■ *Web:* www.repologleglobes.com
Rock 'N Learn Inc 105 Commercial Cir . . . Conroe TX 77304 936-539-2731 539-2659
TF: 800-348-8445 ■ *Web:* www.rocknlearn.com
Roylco Inc 3251 Abbeville Hwy PO Box 13409 . . . Anderson SC 29624 864-296-0043 296-6736
TF: 800-362-8656 ■ *Web:* www.roylco.com
Scholastic Corp 557 Broadway . . . New York NY 10012 212-343-6100
NASDAQ: SCHL ■ *TF Cust Svc:* 800-724-6527 ■ *Web:* www.scholastic.com
Scholastic News 557 Broadway . . . New York NY 10012 212-343-6100 343-6930*
**Fax:* PR ■ *TF Orders:* 800-724-6527 ■ *Web:* www.scholastic.com/scholasticnews
School Mate Inc 77 Conalco Dr . . . Jackson TN 38302 731-935-2000 935-2009
TF: 800-264-4108
School Specialty Inc PO Box 1579 . . . Appleton WI 54912 920-734-5712 734-5112
NASDAQ: SCHS ■ *TF:* 888-388-3224 ■ *Web:* www.schoolspecialty.com
School Stuff Inc 7440 Calumet Ave . . . Hammond IN 46324 219-931-6767 931-6727
TF: 877-931-6767 ■ *Web:* www.schoolstuff.net
Scott Resources Div American Educational Products LLC
401 Hickory St . . . Fort Collins CO 80522 970-484-7445 484-1198
TF Cust Svc: 800-289-9299 ■ *Web:* www.shnta.com
SRA/McGraw-Hill Div McGraw-Hill Cos Inc 8787 Orion Pl . . . Columbus OH 43240 614-430-6600 430-6621
TF: 800-468-4850 ■ *Web:* www.sra4kids.com
Teacher Created Resources Inc 6421 Industry Way . . . Westminster CA 92683 714-891-7895 525-1254*
**Fax Area Code:* 800 ■ *TF:* 888-343-4335 ■ *Web:* www.teachercreated.com
Teaching & Learning Co 1204 Buchanan St . . . Carthage IL 62321 217-357-2591 357-6789
TF: 800-852-1234 ■ *Web:* www.teachinglearning.com
Touchstone Applied Science Assoc Inc
4 Hardscrabble Heights PO Box 382 . . . Brewster NY 10509 845-277-8100 277-3548
TF Cust Svc: 800-800-2598 ■ *Web:* www.tasa.com
TREND enterprises Inc 300 9th Ave SW . . . New Brighton MN 55112 651-631-2850 582-3500
TF Cust Svc: 800-328-0818 ■ *Web:* www.trendenterprises.com
Twin Sisters Productions LLC 2680 W Market St . . . Akron OH 44333 330-864-3000 480-8946*
**Fax Area Code:* 800 ■ *TF:* 800-248-8946 ■ *Web:* www.twinsisters.com
Weekly Reader Corp 200 First Stamford Pl 2nd Fl . . . Stamford CT 06912 203-705-3500 705-1665*
**Fax:* Hum Res ■ *TF Cust Svc:* 800-446-3355 ■ *Web:* www.weeklyreader.com
World*Class Learning Materials PO Box 929 . . . Reisterstown MD 21136 443-712-0985 712-0993
TF: 800-638-6470 ■ *Web:* www.wclm.com

247 EDUCATIONAL TESTING SERVICES - ASSESSMENT & PREPARATION

Phone Fax

ACT Inc 500 ACT Dr PO Box 168 . . . Iowa City IA 52243 319-337-1000 339-3020
Web: www.act.org
Alpine Media Corp 560 S State St Suite H-2 . . . Orem UT 84058 801-226-4283 223-9069
Web: www.alpinemedia.com
Applied Measurement Professionals Inc (AMP) 18000 W 105th St . . . Olathe KS 66061 913-895-4600 895-4650
Web: www.goamp.com
Association for Advanced Training in the Behavioral Sciences (AATBS) 5126 Ralston St . . . Ventura CA 93003 805-676-3030 676-3033
TF: 800-472-1931 ■ *Web:* www.aatbs.com
Barron's Educational Series Inc 250 Wireless Blvd . . . Hauppauge NY 11788 631-434-3311 434-3723
TF: 800-645-3476 ■ *Web:* www.barronseduc.com
BISYS Education Services 1100 Circle 75 Pkwy Suite 1300 . . . Atlanta GA 30339 770-659-6000 659-6010
TF: 800-241-9095 ■ *Web:* www.bisyseducation.com
Castle Worldwide Inc 900 Perimeter Park Rd Suite G . . . Morrisville NC 27560 919-572-6880 361-2426
TF: 866-422-7853 ■ *Web:* www.castleworldwide.com
College Board 45 Columbus Ave . . . New York NY 10023 212-713-8000 713-8184*
**Fax:* PR ■ *TF:* 800-927-4302 ■ *Web:* www.collegeboard.com
CTB/McGraw-Hill Div McGraw-Hill Cos Inc 20 Ryan Ranch Rd . . . Monterey CA 93940 831-393-0700 393-6528
TF: 800-538-9547 ■ *Web:* www.ctb.com
Educational Testing Service Rosedale Rd . . . Princeton NJ 08541 609-921-9000 734-5410
Web: www.ets.org
General Educational Development Testing Service
American Council on Education 1 Dupont Cir NW Suite 250 . . . Washington DC 20036 202-939-9490 659-8875
TF: 800-626-9433 ■ *Web:* www.acenet.edu/calec/ged/home.html
H & H Publishing Co Inc 1231 Kapp Drive . . . Clearwater FL 33765 727-442-7760 442-2195
TF: 800-366-4079 ■ *Web:* www.hhpublishing.com
Hale Assoc 9S211 Graceland St . . . Downers Grove IL 60516 630-427-1304 427-1306
Web: www.haleassociates.com
Harcourt Assessment Inc 19500 Bulverde Rd . . . San Antonio TX 78259 210-339-5000 232-1223*
**Fax Area Code:* 800 ■ *TF:* 800-228-0752 ■ *Web:* harcourtassessment.com
Human Resources Research Organization (HumRRO)
66 Canal Ctr Plaza Suite 400 . . . Alexandria VA 22314 703-549-3611 549-9025
Web: www.humrro.org
Kaplan Inc 888 7th Ave 21st Fl . . . New York NY 10106 212-492-5800
TF Cust Svc: 800-527-5268 ■ *Web:* www.kaplan.com
Kaplan Inc Test Preparation & Admissions Div 888 7th Ave 21st Fl . . New York NY 10106 212-492-5800
TF: 888-527-8378 ■ *Web:* www.kaptest.com
Law School Admission Council Inc (LSAC) PO Box 40 . . . Newtown PA 18940 215-968-1101 968-1169
Web: www.lsac.org
McGraw-Hill Cos Inc CTB/McGraw-Hill Div 20 Ryan Ranch Rd . . . Monterey CA 93940 831-393-0700 393-6528
TF: 800-538-9547 ■ *Web:* www.ctb.com
NCS Pearson Inc 5601 Green Valley Dr Suite 220 . . . Bloomington MN 55437 952-681-3000 681-3580
TF: 800-431-1421 ■ *Web:* www.ncspearson.com
Praxis Series Online
Educational Testing Service Teaching & Learning Div
Rosedale Rd . . . Princeton NJ 08541 609-771-7395 530-0581
TF: 800-772-9476 ■ *Web:* www.ets.org/praxis
Princeton Review 2315 Broadway . . . New York NY 10024 212-874-8282 874-0775
NASDAQ: REVU ■ *TF:* 800-333-0369 ■ *Web:* www.princetonreview.com
Professional Assessment for Beginning Teachers
Educational Testing Service Teaching & Learning Div
Rosedale Rd . . . Princeton NJ 08541 609-771-7395 530-0581
TF: 800-772-9476 ■ *Web:* www.ets.org/praxis
Professional Examination Service 475 Riverside Dr 6th Fl . . . New York NY 10115 212-367-4200 367-4266
Web: www.proexam.org
Promissor Inc 1007 Church St Suite 314 . . . Evanston IL 60201 847-866-2001 866-2002
TF: 800-255-1312 ■ *Web:* www.promissor.com
Promissor Inc 3 Bala Plaza W Suite 300 . . . Bala Cynwyd PA 19004 610-617-5093 617-9329*
**Fax:* Cust Svc ■ *TF:* 888-204-6231 ■ *Web:* www.promissor.com
Riverside Publishing Co 425 Spring Lake Dr . . . Itasca IL 60143 630-467-7000 467-7192
TF: 800-323-9540 ■ *Web:* www.riverpub.com
TestTakers 1 Plaza Rd Suite 204 . . . Greenvale NY 11548 516-626-6100 626-6182
Web: www.testtakers.com
Thomson Prometric 1000 Lancaster St . . . Baltimore MD 21202 443-923-8668 751-4997
TF: 866-776-6387 ■ *Web:* www.prometric.com

248 ELECTRIC COMPANIES - COOPERATIVES (RURAL)

SEE ALSO Utility Companies p. 2393

Companies listed here are members of the National Rural Electric Cooperative Association; most are consumer-owned, but some are public power districts. In addition, the companies listed are electricity distribution cooperatives. Companies that generate and/or transmit electricity, but do not distribute it, are not included.

Alabama

Phone Fax

Arab Electric Co-op Inc 331 N Brindlee Mountain Pkwy . . . Arab AL 35016 256-586-3196 586-4943
Baldwin County Electric Membership Corp 19600 Hwy 59 . . . Summerdale AL 36580 251-989-6247 989-0133
TF: 800-837-3374 ■ *Web:* www.baldwinemc.org
Central Alabama Electric Co-op PO Box 681570 . . . Prattville AL 36068 334-365-6762 365-6148
TF: 800-545-5735
Cherokee Electric Co-op 1550 Clarence Chestnut Bypass . . . Centre AL 35960 256-927-5524 927-2278
TF: 800-952-2667 ■ *Web:* www.cherokee-electric.org
Clarke-Washington Electric Membership Corp
1307 College Ave . . . Jackson AL 36545 251-246-9081 246-9822
TF: 800-323-9081 ■ *Web:* www.cwemc.com
Coosa Valley Electric Co-op 69220 Alabama Hwy 77 . . . Talladega AL 35160 256-362-4180 761-2615
TF: 800-273-7210 ■ *Web:* www.coosavalleyec.com
Covington Electric Co-op Inc 18836 US Hwy 84 . . . Andalusia AL 36420 334-222-4121 222-1546
TF: 800-239-4121 ■ *Web:* www.cov-elect.com
Cullman Electric Co-op 1749 Eva Rd NE PO Box 1168 . . . Cullman AL 35055 256-737-3200 737-3218
TF: 800-242-1806 ■ *Web:* www.cullmanec.com
Dixie Electric Co-op PO Box 30 . . . Union Springs AL 36089 334-738-2500 738-2527
TF: 888-349-4332 ■ *Web:* www.dixieec.com
Franklin Electric Co-op Inc PO Box 10 . . . Russellville AL 35653 256-332-2730 332-2753
TF: 800-451-1505
Joe Wheeler Electric Membership Corp PO Box 460 . . . Trinity AL 35673 256-552-2300 552-2388
Web: www.jwemc.org
Marshall DeKalb Electric Co-op PO Box 724 . . . Boaz AL 35957 256-593-4262 840-2211
TF: 800-239-3692 ■ *Web:* mdec.org
North Alabama Electric Co-op PO Box 628 . . . Stevenson AL 35772 256-437-2281 437-2286
TF: 800-572-2900
Pea River Electric Co-op 1311 W Roy Parker Rd PO Box 969 . . . Ozark AL 36361 334-774-2545 774-2548
TF: 800-264-7732
Pioneer Electric Co-op 300 Herbert St . . . Greenville AL 36037 334-382-6636 382-8641
TF: 800-239-3092 ■ *Web:* www.pioneerelectric.com
Sand Mountain Electric Co-op 402 Main St W . . . Rainsville AL 35986 256-638-2153 638-4957
Web: www.sandmtnelectric.com
South Alabama Electric Co-op 13192 Hwy 231 S . . . Troy AL 36081 334-566-2060 566-8949
TF: 800-556-2060 ■ *Web:* www.southaec.com
Southern Pine Electric Co-op 2134 South Blvd PO Box 528 . . . Brewton AL 36427 251-867-5415 867-5219
Web: www.southernpine.org
Tallapoosa River Electric Co-op PO Box 675 . . . Lafayette AL 36862 334-864-9331 864-0817
TF: 800-332-8732 ■ *Web:* www.trec.coop
Tombigbee Electric Co-op Inc PO Box 610 . . . Guin AL 35563 205-468-3325 468-3338
TF: 800-621-8069 ■ *Web:* www2.tombigbee.net
Wheeler Joe Electric Membership Corp PO Box 460 . . . Trinity AL 35673 256-552-2300 552-2388
Web: www.jwemc.org

Alabama (Cont'd)

				Phone	Fax
Wiregrass Electric Co-op Inc PO Box 158 *TF:* 800-239-4602 ■ *Web:* www.wiregrass.coop	Hartford	AL	36344	334-588-2223	588-6192

Alaska

				Phone	Fax
Alaska Village Electric Co-op Inc 4831 Eagle St *Web:* www.avec.org	Anchorage	AK	99503	907-561-1818	562-4086
Barrow Utilities & Electric Co-op 1295 Agvik St PO Box 449 *Web:* www.bueci.org	Barrow	AK	99723	907-852-6166	852-4581
Chugach Electric Assn Inc 5601 Minnesota Dr PO Box 196300 *TF:* 800-478-7494 ■ *Web:* www.chugachelectric.com	Anchorage	AK	99519	907-563-7494	562-0027
Copper Valley Electric Assn Inc Mile 187 Glenn Hwy PO Box 45 *Web:* www.cvea.org	Glennallen	AK	99588	907-822-3211	822-5586
Cordova Electric Co-op Inc 705 2nd St PO Box 20 *Web:* www.cordovaelectric.com	Cordova	AK	99574	907-424-5555	424-5527
Golden Valley Electrical Assn Inc PO Box 71249 *TF:* 800-770-4832 ■ *Web:* www.gvea.com	Fairbanks	AK	99707	907-452-1151	451-5633
Homer Electric Assn Inc 3977 Lake St *Web:* www.homerelectric.com	Homer	AK	99603	907-235-8167	235-3313
Kodiak Electric Assn Inc PO Box 787 *Web:* www.kodiakelectric.com	Kodiak	AK	99615	907-486-7700	486-7717
Kotzebue Electric Assn Inc PO Box 44 *Web:* www.kea.coop	Kotzebue	AK	99752	907-442-3491	442-2482
Matanuska Electric Assn PO Box 1688 **Fax:* Cust Svc ■ *Web:* www.matanuska.com	Palmer	AK	99645	907-745-3231	761-9352*
Naknek Electric Assn Inc PO Box 118 *Web:* www.nea.coop	Naknek	AK	99633	907-246-4261	246-6242
Nushagak Electric Co-op Inc 557 Kenny Wren Rd *Web:* www.nushtel.com	Dillingham	AK	99576	907-842-5251	842-2799
Tlingit-Haida Regional Electrical Authority PO Box 210149	Auke Bay	AK	99821	907-789-3196	790-8517
Unalakleet Valley Electric Co-op PO Box 186	Unalakleet	AK	99684	907-624-3474	624-3009
Yakutat Power Inc PO Box 129	Yakutat	AK	99689	907-784-3248	784-3922

Arizona

				Phone	Fax
Duncan Valley Electric Co-op Inc PO Box 440 *TF:* 800-669-2503 ■ *Web:* www.dvec.org	Duncan	AZ	85534	928-359-2503	359-2370
Farmers Electric Co-op Inc PO Box 80094 *TF:* 800-541-2662 ■ *Web:* www.fecelectric.com	Prescott	AZ	86304	903-455-1715	455-8125
Graham County Electric Co-op Inc PO Drawer B *TF:* 800-577-9266	Pima	AZ	85543	928-485-2451	485-9491
Mohave Electric Co-op Inc 1999 Arena Dr *TF:* 800-685-4251 ■ *Web:* www.mohaveaz.com	Bullhead City	AZ	86442	928-763-4115	763-6094
Navajo Tribal Utility Authority (NTVA) PO Box 170 *Web:* www.ntua.com	Fort Defiance	AZ	86504	928-729-5721	729-2135
Navopache Electric Co-op Inc 1878 W White Mountain Blvd *TF:* 800-543-6324 ■ *Web:* www.navopache.org	Lakeside	AZ	85929	928-368-5118	368-6038
Sulphur Springs Valley Electric Co-op Inc PO Box 820 *TF:* 800-422-9288 ■ *Web:* www.ssvec.org	Willcox	AZ	85644	520-384-2221	384-5223
Tohono O'odham Utility Authority PO Box 816 *Web:* www.toua.net	Sells	AZ	85634	520-383-2236	383-2218
Trico Electric Co-op Inc 8600 W Tangerine Rd *Web:* www.trico.org	Marana	AZ	85653	520-744-2944	744-2329

Arkansas

				Phone	Fax
Arkansas Valley Electric Co-op Corp 1811 W Commercial St PO Box 47 *TF:* 800-468-2176 ■ *Web:* www.avecc.com	Ozark	AR	72949	479-667-2176	667-5238
Ashley-Chicot Electric Co-op Inc 307 E Jefferson St *TF:* 800-281-5212 ■ *Web:* www.ashley-chicot.com	Hamburg	AR	71646	870-853-5212	853-2531
C & L Electric Co-op Corp 900 Church St PO Box 9 *Web:* www.clelectric.com	Star City	AR	71667	870-628-4221	628-4676
Carroll Electric Co-op Corp 920 Hwy 62 Spur *TF:* 800-432-9720 ■ *Web:* www.carrollecc.com	Berryville	AR	72616	870-423-2161	423-4815
Clay County Electric Co-op Corp 300 N Missouri Ave *Web:* www.claycountyelectric.com	Corning	AR	72422	870-857-3661	857-3523
Craighead Electric Co-op Corp 4314 Stadium Blvd *TF:* 800-794-5012 ■ *Web:* www.cecc-ark.com	Jonesboro	AR	72403	870-932-8301	972-5674
Farmers Electric Co-op Corp PO Box 708 *TF:* 800-834-9055 ■ *Web:* www.farmersecc.com	Newport	AR	72112	870-523-3691	523-6853
First Electric Co-op Corp 1000 S JP Wright Loop Rd *TF:* 800-489-7405 ■ *Web:* www.firstelectric.coop	Jacksonville	AR	72076	501-982-4545	982-8450
Mississippi County Electric Co-op PO Box 7 *TF:* 800-439-4563 ■ *Web:* www.mceci.com	Blytheville	AR	72316	870-763-4563	763-0513
North Arkansas Electric Co-op Inc PO Box 1000 *Web:* www.naeci.com	Salem	AR	72576	870-895-3221	895-6279
Ouachita Electric Co-op Corp 700 Bradley Ferry Rd PO Box 877 *Web:* www.oecc.com	Camden	AR	71711	870-836-5791	836-5794
Ozarks Electric Co-op Corp PO Box 848 *TF:* 800-521-6144 ■ *Web:* www.ozarksecc.com	Fayetteville	AR	72702	479-521-2900	444-0943
Petit Jean Electric Co-op 270 Quality Dr PO Box 37 *TF:* 800-786-7618 ■ *Web:* www.pjecc.com	Clinton	AR	72031	501-745-2493	745-4150
Rich Mountain Electric Co-op Inc PO Box 897 *TF:* 877-828-4074 ■ *Web:* www.rmec.com	Mena	AR	71953	479-394-4140	394-1211
South Central Arkansas Electric Co-op PO Box 476 *TF:* 800-814-2931 ■ *Web:* www.scaec.com	Arkadelphia	AR	71923	870-246-6701	246-8223
Southwest Arkansas Electric Co-op Corp PO Box 1807 *TF:* 800-782-2743 ■ *Web:* www.swrea.com	Texarkana	AR	75504	870-772-2743	773-2161
Woodruff Electric Co-op Corp PO Box 1619 *Web:* www.woodruffelectric.com	Forrest City	AR	72336	870-633-2262	633-0629

California

				Phone	Fax
Anza Electric Co-op Inc 58470 Hwy 371 PO Box 391909 *Web:* www.anzaelectric.org	Anza	CA	92539	951-763-4333	763-5297
Plumas-Sierra Rural Electric Co-op 73233 Hwy 70 Suite A *TF:* 800-555-2207 ■ *Web:* www.psln.com/psrec	Portola	CA	96122	530-832-4261	832-5761
Surprise Valley Electric Co-op PO Box 691 *TF:* 866-843-2667	Alturas	CA	96101	530-233-3511	233-2190
Trinity Public Utility District PO Box 1216 *TF:* 800-968-7783	Weaverville	CA	96093	530-623-5536	623-5549
Truckee Donner Public Utility District PO Box 309 *Web:* www.tdpud.org	Truckee	CA	96160	530-587-3896	587-5056

Colorado

				Phone	Fax
Delta-Montrose Electric Assn 11925 6300 Rd *Web:* www.dmea.com	Montrose	CO	81401	970-249-4572	240-6801
Empire Electric Assn Inc PO Drawer K *TF:* 800-709-3726 ■ *Web:* www.eea.coop	Cortez	CO	81321	970-565-4444	565-9198
Grand Valley Rural Power Lines Inc PO Box 190 *Web:* www.gvp.org	Grand Junction	CO	81502	970-242-0040	242-0612
Gunnison County Electric Assn PO Box 180 *TF:* 800-726-3523 ■ *Web:* www.gcea.coop	Gunnison	CO	81230	970-641-3520	641-5302
Highline Electric Assn PO Box 57 *Web:* www.hea.coop	Holyoke	CO	80734	970-854-2236	854-3652
Holy Cross Energy PO Box 2150 *TF:* 888-347-4425 ■ *Web:* www.holycross.com	Glenwood Springs	CO	81602	970-945-5491	945-4081
Intermountain Rural Electric Assn PO Box A *TF:* 800-332-9540 ■ *Web:* www.intermountain-rea.com	Sedalia	CO	80135	303-688-3100	688-7431
KC Electric Assn PO Box 8 *TF:* 800-700-3123	Hugo	CO	80821	719-743-2431	743-2396
La Plata Electric Assn Inc PO Box 2750 *TF:* 888-839-5732 ■ *Web:* www.lpea.com	Durango	CO	81302	970-247-5786	247-2674
Morgan County Rural Electric Assn PO Box 738 *Web:* www.mcrea.org	Fort Morgan	CO	80701	970-867-5688	867-3277
Mountain Parks Electric Inc PO Box 170 *TF:* 877-887-3378 ■ *Web:* www.mpei.com	Granby	CO	80446	970-887-3378	887-3996
Mountain View Electric Assn Inc PO Box 1600 *TF:* 800-388-9881 ■ *Web:* www.mvea.org	Limon	CO	80828	719-775-2861	775-9513
Poudre Valley Rural Electric Assn Inc 7649 Rea Pkwy *TF:* 800-432-1012 ■ *Web:* www.pvrea.com	Fort Collins	CO	80528	970-226-1234	226-2123
San Isabel Electric Assn 893 E Enterprise Dr *TF:* 800-279-7432 ■ *Web:* www.siea.com	Pueblo	CO	81002	719-547-2160	547-2229
San Luis Valley Rural Electric Co-op 3625 US Hwy 160 W *TF:* 800-332-7634 ■ *Web:* www.slvrec.com	Monte Vista	CO	81144	719-852-3538	852-4333
San Miguel Power Assn Inc PO Box 817 *TF:* 800-864-7256 ■ *Web:* www.smpa.com	Nucla	CO	81424	970-864-7311	864-7257
Sangre de Cristo Electric Assn 29780 N US Hwy 24 PO Box 2013 *TF:* 800-933-3823 ■ *Web:* www.sdcea.com	Buena Vista	CO	81211	719-395-2412	395-8742
Southeast Colorado Power Assn 901 W 3rd *TF:* 800-332-8634 ■ *Web:* www.secpa.com	La Junta	CO	81050	719-384-2551	384-7320
United Power Inc PO Box 929 *TF:* 800-468-8809 ■ *Web:* www.unitedpower.com	Brighton	CO	80601	303-659-0551	659-2172
White River Electric Assn Inc PO Box 958 *Web:* www.wrea.org	Meeker	CO	81641	970-878-5041	878-5766
Y-W Electric Assn Inc PO Box Y *TF:* 800-660-2291 ■ *Web:* www.ywelectric.com	Akron	CO	80720	970-345-2291	345-2154
Yampa Valley Electric Assn Inc PO Box 771218 *TF:* 888-873-9832 ■ *Web:* www.yvea.com	Steamboat Springs	CO	80477	970-879-1160	879-7270

Delaware

				Phone	Fax
Delaware Electric Co-op Inc PO Box 600 *TF:* 800-282-8595 ■ *Web:* www.delelect.com	Greenwood	DE	19950	302-349-4571	349-5891

Florida

				Phone	Fax
Central Florida Electric Co-op Inc 1124 N Young Blvd *TF:* 800-227-1302 ■ *Web:* www.cfec.com	Chiefland	FL	32644	352-493-2511	493-4499
Choctawhatchee Electric Co-op Inc 1350 W Baldwin Ave *TF:* 800-342-0990 ■ *Web:* www.chelco.com	De Funiak Springs	FL	32435	850-892-2111	892-9243
Clay Electric Co-op Inc 225 W Walker Dr PO Box 308 *TF Cust Svc:* 800-224-4917 ■ *Web:* clayelectric.com	Keystone Heights	FL	32656	352-473-8000	473-1403
Escambia River Electric Co-op Inc PO Box 428 *TF:* 800-235-3848 ■ *Web:* www.erec.net	Jay	FL	32565	850-675-4521	675-8415
Florida Keys Electric Co-op Assn 91605 Overseas Hwy PO Box 377 *TF:* 800-858-8845 ■ *Web:* www.fkec.com	Tavernier	FL	33070	305-852-2431	853-5381
Glades Electric Co-op Inc PO Box 519 *TF:* 800-226-4024 ■ *Web:* www.gladesec.com	Moore Haven	FL	33471	863-946-0061	946-0824
Gulf Coast Electric Co-op Inc PO Box 220 *TF:* 800-333-9392 ■ *Web:* www.gcec.com	Wewahitchka	FL	32465	850-639-2216	639-5061
Lee County Electric Co-op Inc PO Box 3455 *TF:* 800-282-1643 ■ *Web:* www.lcec.net	North Fort Myers	FL	33918	239-995-2121	995-7904
Peace River Electric Co-op Inc 1499 US Hwy 17 N PO Box 1310 *TF:* 800-282-3824 ■ *Web:* www.preco.org	Wauchula	FL	33873	863-773-4116	773-3737
Sumter Electric Co-op Inc PO Box 301 **Fax:* Mktg ■ *Web:* www.secoenergy.com	Sumterville	FL	33585	352-793-3801	793-6603*
Suwannee Valley Electric Co-op PO Box 160 *Web:* suwanneevalleyemc.com	Live Oak	FL	32064	386-362-2226	364-5008
Talquin Electric Co-op Inc 1640 W Jefferson St *Web:* www.talquinelectric.com	Quincy	FL	32351	850-627-7651	627-2553
Tri-County Electric Co-op Inc PO Box 208 *TF:* 800-999-2285 ■ *Web:* www.tcec.com	Madison	FL	32341	850-973-2285	973-1209
West Florida Electric Co-op PO Box 127 *TF:* 800-342-7400 ■ *Web:* www.wfeca.net	Graceville	FL	32440	850-263-3231	263-3726
Withlacoochee River Electric Co-op PO Box 278 *Web:* www.wrec.net	Dade City	FL	33526	352-567-5133	521-5971

Georgia

				Phone	Fax
Altamaha Electric Membership Corp 611 W Liberty St *TF:* 800-822-4563 ■ *Web:* www.altamahaemc.com	Lyons	GA	30436	912-526-8181	526-4235
Amicalola Electric Membership Corp 544 Hwy 515 S *TF:* 800-992-6471 ■ *Web:* www.amicalolaemc.com	Jasper	GA	30143	706-253-5200	253-5251
Blue Ridge Mountain Electric Membership Corp 1360 Main St *TF:* 800-292-6456 ■ *Web:* www.brmemc.com	Young Harris	GA	30582	706-379-3121	379-4834
Canoochee Electric Membership Corp 342 E Brazell St *TF:* 800-342-0134 ■ *Web:* www.canoocheeemc.com	Reidsville	GA	30453	912-557-4391	557-4396
Carroll Electric Membership Corp 155 N Hwy 113 *Web:* www.cemc.com	Carrollton	GA	30117	770-832-3552	832-0240

				Phone	Fax
Central Georgia Electric Membership Corp 923 S Mulberry St *Fax: Cust Svc ■ TF: 800-222-4877 ■ Web: www.cgemc.com	Jackson	GA	30233	770-775-7857	504-7877*
Coastal Electric Co-op 1265 S Coastal Hwy PO Box 109 TF: 800-421-2343 ■ Web: www.coastalemc.com	Midway	GA	31320	912-884-3311	884-2362
Cobb Electric Membership Corp 1000 EMC Pkwy PO Box 369 *Fax Area Code: 678 ■ *Fax: Hum Res ■ Web: www.cobbemc.com	Marietta	GA	30061	770-429-2100	355-3363*
Colquitt Electric Membership Corp 15 Rowland Dr TF: 800-342-8694 ■ Web: www.colquittemc.com	Moultrie	GA	31768	229-985-3620	985-6705
Coweta-Fayette Electric Membership Corp 807 Collinsworth Rd TF: 877-746-4362 ■ Web: www.utility.org	Palmetto	GA	30268	770-502-0226	251-9788
Diverse Power Inc PO Box 160 TF: 800-845-8362 ■ Web: www.diversepower.com	LaGrange	GA	30241	706-845-2000	845-2020
Excelsior Electric Membership Corp PO Box 297 Web: www.excelsioremc.com	Metter	GA	30439	912-685-2115	685-5782
Flint Energies PO Box 308 TF: 800-342-3616 ■ Web: www.flintenergies.com	Reynolds	GA	31076	478-847-3415	847-5181
Grady Electric Membership Corp 1499 38th Blvd NW PO Box 270 TF: 800-942-4362 ■ Web: www.gradyemc.com	Cairo	GA	39828	229-377-4182	377-7176
Greystone Power Corp PO Box 897 Web: www.greystonepower.com	Douglasville	GA	30133	770-942-6576	489-0940
Habersham Electric Membership Corp PO Box 25 *Fax Area Code: 800 ■ TF: 800-640-6812 ■ Web: www.habershamemc.com	Clarkesville	GA	30523	706-754-2114	640-6813*
Hart Electric Membership Corp PO Box 250 *Fax Area Code: 800 ■ TF: 800-241-4109 ■ Web: www.hartemc.com	Hartwell	GA	30643	706-376-4714	486-3277*
Irwin Electric Membership Corp 915 W 4th St TF: 800-237-3745 ■ Web: www.irwinemc.com	Ocilla	GA	31774	229-468-7415	468-7009
Jackson Electric Membership Corp PO Box 38 TF: 800-462-3691 ■ Web: www.jacksonemc.com	Jefferson	GA	30549	706-367-5281	367-6102
Jefferson Energy Co-op 3077 Hwy 17 PO Box 457 TF: 800-342-0322 ■ Web: www.jeffersonenergy.com	North Wrens	GA	30833	706-547-2167	547-5075
Lamar Electric Membership Corp 1367 Hwy 341 S PO Box 40 TF: 877-358-1383 ■ Web: www.lamaremc.com	Barnesville	GA	30204	770-358-1383	358-6078
Little Ocmulgee Electric Membership Corp PO Box 150 Web: www.littleocmulgeeemc.com	Alamo	GA	30411	912-568-7171	568-7174
Middle Georgia Electric Membership Corp PO Box 190 TF: 800-342-0144 ■ Web: www.mgemc.com	Vienna	GA	31092	229-268-2671	268-7215
Mitchell Electric Membership Corp PO Box 409 TF: 800-479-6034 ■ Web: www.mitchellemc.com	Camilla	GA	31730	229-336-5221	336-7088
North Georgia Electric Membership Corp 1850 Cleveland Hwy TF: 800-282-4022 ■ Web: www.ngemc.com	Dalton	GA	30722	706-259-9441	259-9625
Ocmulgee Electric Membership Corp 5722 Eastman St TF: 800-342-5509 ■ Web: www.ocmulgeeemc.com	Eastman	GA	31023	478-374-7001	374-0759
Oconee Electric Membership Corp 3453 Hwy 80 W TF: 800-522-2930 ■ Web: www.oconeeemc.com	Dudley	GA	31022	478-676-3191	676-4200
Okefenoke Rural Electric Membership Corp 174 E Cleveland St TF: 800-262-5131 ■ Web: www.oremc.com	Nahunta	GA	31553	912-462-5131	462-6100
Pataula Electric Membership Corp 925 Barkley St PO Box 289 TF: 888-631-9757 ■ Web: www.pataulaemc.com	Cuthbert	GA	31740	229-732-3171	732-5191
Planters Electric Membership Corp 1740 Hwy 25 N TF: 800-324-4722 ■ Web: www.plantersemc.com	Millen	GA	30442	478-982-4722	982-4798
Rayle Electric Membership Corp 616 Lexington Ave Web: www.rayleemc.com	Washington	GA	30673	706-678-2116	678-5381
Satilla Rural Electric Membership Corp 101 W 17th St PO Box 906 TF: 888-738-6926 ■ Web: www.satillaemc.com	Alma	GA	31510	912-632-7222	632-8572
Sawnee Electric Membership Corp 543 Atlantic Hwy TF: 800-635-9131 ■ Web: www.sawnee.com	Cumming	GA	30028	770-887-2363	886-8119
Slash Pine Electric Membership Corp PO Box 356	Homerville	GA	31634	912-487-5201	487-2948
Snapping Shoals Electric Membership Corp 14750 Brown Bridge Rd Web: www.ssemc.com	Covington	GA	30016	770-786-3484	385-2720
Sumter Electric Membership Corp PO Box 1048 TF: 800-342-6978 ■ Web: www.sumteremc.com	Americus	GA	31709	229-924-8041	924-4982
Three Notch Electric Membership Corp PO Box 367 TF: 800-239-5377	Donalsonville	GA	39845	229-524-5377	524-8046
Tri-County Electric Membership Corp PO Box 487 TF: 800-342-3812 ■ Web: www.tri-countyemc.com	Gray	GA	31032	478-986-3134	986-4733
Tri-State Electric Membership Corp PO Box 68	McCaysville	GA	30555	706-492-3251	492-7617
Upson County Electric Membership Corp PO Box 31 Web: www.upsonemc.com	Thomaston	GA	30286	706-647-5475	647-8545
Walton Electric Membership Corp PO Box 260 Web: www.waltonemc.com	Monroe	GA	30655	770-267-2505	267-1223
Washington Electric Membership Corp PO Box 598 TF: 800-552-2577 ■ Web: www.washingtonemc.com	Sandersville	GA	31082	478-552-2577	552-5552

Idaho

				Phone	Fax
Clearwater Power Co 4230 Hatwai Rd PO Box 997 TF: 888-743-1501 ■ Web: www.clearwaterpower.com	Lewiston	ID	83501	208-743-1501	746-3902
Fall River Rural Electric Co-op Inc 1150 N 3400 East TF: 800-632-5726 ■ Web: www.frrec.com	Ashton	ID	83420	208-652-7431	652-7825
Idaho County Light & Power Co-op PO Box 300 TF: 877-212-0424 ■ Web: www.iclp.coop	Grangeville	ID	83530	208-983-1610	983-1432
Kootenai Electric Co-op Inc PO Box 278 Web: www.kec.com	Hayden	ID	83835	208-765-1200	772-5858
Lost River Electric Co-op Inc PO Box 420 Web: www.lrecoop.com	Mackay	ID	83251	208-588-3311	588-3038
Northern Lights Inc 421 Cherry St PO Box 269 TF: 800-326-9594 ■ Web: www.norlight.org	Sagle	ID	83860	208-263-5141	263-7412
Raft River Rural Electric Co-op Inc 155 N Main St PO Box 617 TF: 800-342-7732	Malta	ID	83342	208-645-2211	645-2300
Riverside Electric Co PO Box 12	Rupert	ID	83350	208-436-3855	431-3137
Salmon River Electric Co-op Inc 1130 Main St PO Box 384 TF: 877-806-2283 ■ Web: www.srec.org	Challis	ID	83226	208-879-2283	879-2596
South Side Electric Lines Inc PO Box 69	Declo	ID	83323	208-654-2313	
United Electric Co-op 1330 21st St Web: www.unitedelectric.org	Heyburn	ID	83336	208-679-2222	679-3333

Illinois

				Phone	Fax
Adams Electric Co-op 700 Eastwood St PO Box 247 TF: 800-232-4797 ■ Web: www.adamselectriccoop.com	Camp Point	IL	62320	217-593-7701	593-7120
Clinton County Electric Co-op Inc 475 N Main St TF: 800-526-7282 ■ Web: www.cceci.com	Breese	IL	62230	618-526-7282	526-4561
Coles-Moultrie Electric Co-op 104 DeWitt Ave E PO Box 709 TF: 888-661-2632 ■ Web: www.cmec.coop	Mattoon	IL	61938	217-235-0341	234-8342
Corn Belt Energy Corp 1 Energy Way PO Box 816 TF: 800-879-0339 ■ Web: www.cornbeltenergy.com	Bloomington	IL	61702	309-662-5330	663-4516
Eastern Illini Electric Co-op 330 W Ottawa PO Box 96 TF: 800-824-5102 ■ Web: www.eiec.org	Paxton	IL	60957	217-379-2131	379-2936
Egyptian Electric Co-op Assn PO Box 38 TF: 800-606-1505 ■ Web: www.egyptianelectric.coop	Steeleville	IL	62288	618-965-3434	965-3111
EnerStar Power Corp 11597 Illinois Hwy 1 TF: 800-635-4145 ■ Web: www.enerstar.com	Paris	IL	61944	217-463-4145	465-5801
Farmers Mutual Electric Co 1004 S Chicago St	Geneseo	IL	61254	309-944-4669	944-1173
Illinois Rural Electric Co-op 2 S Main St Web: www.e-co-op.com	Winchester	IL	62694	217-742-3128	742-3831
Jo-Carroll Energy PO Box 390 TF: 800-858-5522 ■ Web: www.jocarroll.com	Elizabeth	IL	61028	815-858-2207	858-3731
McDonough Power Co-op PO Box 352	Macomb	IL	61455	309-833-2101	833-2104
Menard Electric Co-op PO Box 200 TF: 800-872-1203 ■ Web: www.menard.com	Petersburg	IL	62675	217-632-7746	632-2578
MJM Electric Co-op Inc 264 N East St PO Box 80 TF: 800-648-4729 ■ Web: www.mjmelectric.coop	Carlinville	IL	62626	217-854-3137	854-3918
Norris Electric Co-op PO Box 6000 TF: 877-783-8765 ■ Web: www.norriselectric.com	Newton	IL	62448	618-783-8765	783-3673
Rural Electric Convenience Co-op Co 3973 W SR 104 PO Box 19 TF: 800-245-7322 ■ Web: www.recc.coop	Auburn	IL	62615	217-438-6197	438-3212
Shelby Electric Co-op Rt 128 N 6th St PO Box 560 TF: 800-677-2612 ■ Web: www.shelbyelectric.com	Shelbyville	IL	62565	217-774-3986	774-3330
SouthEastern Illinois Electric Co-op 585 Hwy 142 S PO Box 371 TF: 800-833-2611 ■ Web: www.seiec.com	Eldorado	IL	62930	618-273-2611	273-3886
Southern Illinois Electric Co-op 7420 US Hwy 51 S TF: 800-762-1400 ■ Web: www.siec.coop/	Dongola	IL	62926	618-827-3555	827-3585
Southwestern Electric Co-op Inc PO Box 549 TF: 800-637-8667 ■ Web: www.sweci.com	Greenville	IL	62246	618-664-1025	664-4179
Spoon River Electric Co-op Inc PO Box 340 TF: 877-404-2572 ■ Web: www.srecoop.com	Canton	IL	61520	309-647-2700	647-7354
Tri-County Electric Co-op Inc 3906 W Broadway PO Box 309 TF: 800-244-5151 ■ Web: www.tricountycoop.com	Mount Vernon	IL	62864	618-244-5151	244-1496
Wayne-White Counties Electric Co-op PO Drawer E TF: 888-871-7695 ■ Web: www.wwcec.com	Fairfield	IL	62837	618-842-2196	842-4497
Western Illinois Electrical Co-op PO Box 338 Web: www.wiec.net	Carthage	IL	62321	217-357-3125	357-3127

Indiana

				Phone	Fax
Bartholomew County Rural Electric Membership Corp 801 2nd St TF: 800-927-5672 ■ Web: www.bcremc.com	Columbus	IN	47201	812-372-2546	372-2112
Boone County Rural Electric Membership Corp 1207 Indianapolis Ave TF: 800-897-7362 ■ Web: www.bremc.com	Lebanon	IN	46052	765-482-2390	482-7869
Carroll County Rural Electric Membership Corp 119 W Franklin St PO Box 298 TF: 800-506-7362 ■ Web: www.remconline.net	Delphi	IN	46923	765-564-2057	564-4461
Central Indiana Power Corp 2243 Main St TF: 800-382-5544 ■ Web: www.cipower.com	Greenfield	IN	46140	317-477-2200	477-2213
Clark County Rural Electric Membership Corp 7810 SR 60 PO Box L TF: 800-462-6988 ■ Web: www.theremc.com	Sellersburg	IN	47172	812-246-3316	246-3947
Daviess-Martin County Rural Electric Membership Corp 12628 E 75 N PO Box 430 TF: 800-762-7362 ■ Web: www.dmremc.com	Loogootee	IN	47553	812-295-4200	
Decatur County Rural Electric Membership Corp 1430 W Main St PO Box 46 TF: 800-844-7362 ■ Web: www.dcremc.com	Greensburg	IN	47240	812-663-3391	663-8572
Dubois Rural Electric Co-op Inc PO Box 610 Web: www.duboisrec.com	Jasper	IN	47547	812-482-5454	482-7015
Fulton County Rural Electric Membership Corp PO Box 230 Web: www.fultoncountyremc.com	Rochester	IN	46975	574-223-3156	223-4353
Harrison County Rural Electric Membership Corp PO Box 517 Web: www.theremc.com	Corydon	IN	47112	812-738-4115	738-2378
Hendricks Power Co-op PO Box 309 TF: 800-876-5473 ■ Web: www.hendrickspower.com	Danville	IN	46122	317-745-5473	745-6865
Jackson County Rural Electric Membership Corp PO Box K TF: 800-200-4450 ■ Web: www.jacksonremc.com	Brownstown	IN	47220	812-358-4458	358-5719
Jasper County Rural Electric Membership Corp PO Box 129 TF: 888-866-7362 ■ Web: www.jasperremc.com	Rensselaer	IN	47978	219-866-4601	866-2199
Jay County Rural Electric Membership Corp PO Box 904 TF: 800-835-7362 ■ Web: www.jayremc.com	Portland	IN	47371	260-726-7121	726-6240
Johnson County Rural Electric Membership Corp PO Box 309 Web: www.jcremc.com	Franklin	IN	46131	317-736-6174	736-8185
Kankakee Valley Rural Electric Membership Corp 114 S Main St TF: 800-552-2622 ■ Web: www.kvremc.com	Wanatah	IN	46390	219-733-2511	733-2991
Kosciusko County Rural Electric Membership Corp 370 S 250 East TF: 800-790-7362 ■ Web: www.kosciuskoremc.com	Warsaw	IN	46582	574-267-6331	267-7273
LaGrange County Rural Electric Membership Corp PO Box 147 TF: 877-463-7165 ■ Web: www.lagrangeremc.com	LaGrange	IN	46761	260-463-7165	463-4329
Marshall County Rural Electric Membership Corp PO Box 250 Web: www.marshallcoremc.com	Plymouth	IN	46563	574-936-3161	935-4162
Miami-Cass County Rural Electric Membership Corp PO Box 168 TF: 800-844-6668 ■ Web: www.miami-cassremc.com	Peru	IN	46970	765-473-6668	473-8770
Newton County Rural Electric Membership Corp PO Box 125	Kentland	IN	47951	219-474-6224	474-6290
Noble Rural Electric Membership Corp PO Box 137 TF: 800-933-7362 ■ Web: www.nobleremc.com	Albion	IN	46701	260-636-2113	636-3319
Northeastern Rural Electric Membership Corp 4901 E Park 30 Dr Web: www.nremc.com	Columbia City	IN	46725	260-244-6111	625-3407
Orange County Rural Electric Membership Corp PO Box 208 TF: 888-337-5900 ■ Web: www.myremc.coop	Orleans	IN	47452	812-865-2229	865-2061
Parke County Rural Electric Membership Corp 119 W High St TF: 800-537-3913 ■ Web: www.parkecountyremc.com	Rockville	IN	47872	765-569-3133	569-3360
Rush Shelby Energy Inc 1504 S Harrison St TF: 800-427-0497 ■ Web: www.rse.coop	Shelbyville	IN	46176	317-398-6621	398-2898
South Central Indiana Rural Electric Membership Corp 300 Morton Ave PO Box 3100 TF: 800-264-7362 ■ Web: www.sciremc.com	Martinsville	IN	46151	765-342-3344	342-1335
Southeastern Indiana Rural Electric Membership Corp 712 Buckeye St TF: 800-737-4111 ■ Web: www.seiremc.com	Osgood	IN	47037	812-689-4111	689-6987
Southern Indiana Rural Electric Co-op Inc 1776 10th St PO Box 219 TF: 800-323-2316 ■ Web: www.sirec.com	Tell City	IN	47586	812-547-2316	547-6853
Steuben County Rural Electric Membership Corp PO Box 359 TF: 888-233-9088 ■ Web: www.remcsteuben.com	Angola	IN	46703	260-665-3563	665-7495

Indiana (Cont'd)

	City	State	ZIP	Phone	Fax
Tipmont Rural Electric Membership Corp PO Box 20 *TF:* 800-726-3953 ■ *Web:* www.tipmont.org	Linden	IN	47955	765-339-7211	339-4865
UDWI Rural Electric Membership Corp PO Box 427 *TF:* 800-489-7362 ■ *Web:* www.hepn.com/udwi/index.htm	Bloomfield	IN	47424	812-384-4446	384-3127
United Rural Electric Membership Corp PO Box 605 *TF:* 800-542-6339 ■ *Web:* www.unitedremc.com	Markle	IN	46770	260-758-3155	758-3157
Wabash County Rural Electric Membership Corp 350 Wedcor Ave *TF:* 800-563-2146	Wabash	IN	46992	260-563-2146	563-1523
Warren County Rural Electric Membership Corp 15 Midway St *TF:* 800-872-7319	Williamsport	IN	47993	765-762-6114	762-6117
White County Rural Electric Membership Corp PO Box 599 *TF:* 800-844-7161 ■ *Web:* www.whitecountyremc.com	Monticello	IN	47960	574-583-7161	583-4156
Whitewater Valley Rural Electric Membership Corp PO Box 349 *TF:* 800-529-5557 ■ *Web:* www.wvremc.com	Liberty	IN	47353	765-458-5171	458-5938
WIN Energy Rural Electric Membership Corp PO Box 577 *TF:* 800-882-5140 ■ *Web:* www.winenergyremc.com	Vincennes	IN	47591	812-882-5140	886-0306

Iowa

	City	State	ZIP	Phone	Fax
Access Energy Co-op 907 E Washington St *TF:* 866-242-4232 ■ *Web:* www.accessenergycoop.com	Mount Pleasant	IA	52641	319-385-1577	385-6873
Allamakee-Clayton Electric Co-op Inc 228 W Greene St *Web:* www.acrec.com	Postville	IA	52162	563-864-7611	864-7820
Butler County Rural Electric Co-op 521 N Main St *TF:* 888-267-2726 ■ *Web:* www.butlerrec.com	Allison	IA	50602	319-267-2726	267-2566
Calhoun County Electric Co-op Assn 1015 Tonawanda st *Web:* www.calhouncountyrec.coop	Rockwell City	IA	50579	712-297-7112	297-7211
Chariton Valley Electric Co-op 2090 Hwy 5 PO Box 486 *Web:* www.cvrec.com	Albia	IA	52531	641-932-7126	932-2534
Clarke Electric Co-op Inc 1103 N Main St *TF:* 800-362-2154 ■ *Web:* www.cecnet.net	Osceola	IA	50213	641-342-2173	342-6292
Consumers Energy 2075 Marshalltown Blvd PO Box 1058 *TF:* 800-696-6552 ■ *Web:* www.consumersenergy.net	Marshalltown	IA	50158	641-752-1593	752-5738
East-Central Iowa Rural Electric Co-op PO Box 248 *TF:* 877-850-4343 ■ *Web:* www.ecirec.com	Urbana	IA	52345	319-443-4343	443-4359
Eastern Iowa Light & Power Co-op 600 E 5th St Po Box 3003 *TF:* 800-728-1242 ■ *Web:* www.easterniowa.com	Wilton	IA	52778	563-732-2211	732-2219
Farmers Electric Co-op Inc 1959 Yoder Ave SW *TF:* 877-426-6540 ■ *Web:* www.feckalona.com	Kalona	IA	52247	319-683-2510	683-2506
Farmers Rural Electric Co-op Inc 102 SE 6th St *TF:* 800-397-4821 ■ *Web:* www.farmersrec.com	Greenfield	IA	50849	641-743-6146	343-7187
Franklin Rural Electric Co-op PO Box 437 *TF:* 800-750-3557 ■ *Web:* www.franklinrec.com	Hampton	IA	50441	641-456-2557	456-5183
Glidden Rural Electric Co-op PO Box 486 *TF:* 800-253-6211 ■ *Web:* www.gliddenrec.com	Glidden	IA	51443	712-659-3649	659-3716
Grundy County Rural Electric Co-op 102 E 'G' Ave *TF:* 800-390-7605 ■ *Web:* www.grundycountyrecia.org	Grundy Center	IA	50638	319-824-5251	824-3118
Guthrie County Rural Electric Co-op Assn PO Box 7 *TF:* 888-747-2206	Guthrie Center	IA	50115	641-747-2206	747-3701
Harrison County Rural Electric Co-op PO Box 2 *Web:* www.hcrec.coop	Woodbine	IA	51579	712-647-2727	647-2242
Hawkeye REC PO Box 90 *TF:* 800-658-2243 ■ *Web:* www.hawkeyerec.com	Cresco	IA	52136	563-547-3801	547-4033
Heartland Power Co-op 216 Jackson St PO Box 65 *TF:* 888-584-9732 ■ *Web:* www.heartlandpower.com	Thompson	IA	50478	641-584-2251	584-2253
Humboldt County Rural Electric Co-op 1210 13th St N *TF:* 800-994-3532 ■ *Web:* www.humboldtrec.com	Humboldt	IA	50548	515-332-1616	332-3007
Iowa Lakes Electric Co-op 702 S 1st St *TF:* 800-225-4532 ■ *Web:* www.ilec.coop	Estherville	IA	51334	712-362-7870	362-2819
Linn County Rural Electric Co-op PO Box 69 *Web:* www.linncountyrec.com	Marion	IA	52302	319-377-1587	377-5875
Lyon Rural Electric Co-op PO Box 629 *TF:* 800-658-3976 ■ *Web:* www.lyonrec.coop	Rock Rapids	IA	51246	712-472-2506	472-3925
Maquoketa Valley Rural Electric Co-op PO Box 370 *TF:* 800-927-6068 ■ *Web:* www.mvec.com	Anamosa	IA	52205	319-462-3542	462-3217
Midland Power Co-op 1005 E Lincolnway *Web:* www.midlandpower.com	Jefferson	IA	50129	515-386-4111	386-2385
Nishnabotna Valley Rural Electric Co-op PO Box 714 *TF:* 800-234-5122 ■ *Web:* www.nvrec.com	Harlan	IA	51537	712-755-2166	755-2351
North West Rural Electric Co-op 1505 Albany Pl SE *TF:* 800-383-0476 ■ *Web:* www.nwrec.com	Orange City	IA	51041	712-707-4935	707-4934
Osceola Electric Co-op Inc 204 8th St *TF:* 888-754-2519	Sibley	IA	51249	712-754-2519	754-2510
Pella Co-op Electric Assn 2615 Washington St *TF:* 800-619-1040 ■ *Web:* www.pella-cea.org	Pella	IA	50219	641-628-1040	628-4856
Prairie Energy Co-op 600 W 3rd St *Web:* www.prairieenergy.com	Garner	IA	50438	641-923-2654	923-3434
Sac County Rural Electric Co-op 601 E Main St PO Box 397 *TF:* 866-722-6732 ■ *Web:* www.sacrec.com	Sac City	IA	50583	712-662-4275	662-4538
Southern Iowa Electric Co-op Inc 800 E Franklin St *TF:* 800-607-2027 ■ *Web:* southerniowarec.coop	Bloomfield	IA	52537	641-664-2277	664-3502
Southwest Iowa Rural Electric Cooperative 626 Davis Ave *TF:* 888-591-1261 ■ *Web:* www.swiarec.coop	Corning	IA	50841	641-322-3165	322-5274
TIP Rural Electric Co-op PO Box 534 *TF:* 800-934-7976 ■ *Web:* www.tiprec.com	Brooklyn	IA	52211	641-522-9221	522-9271
Western Iowa Power Co-op PO Box 428 *TF:* 800-253-5189 ■ *Web:* www.wipco.com	Denison	IA	51442	712-263-2943	263-8655
Woodbury County Rural Electric Co-op Assn 1495 Humboldt Ave *TF:* 800-469-3125 ■ *Web:* showcase.netins.net/web/wdbyrec	Moville	IA	51039	712-873-3125	873-5377

Kansas

	City	State	ZIP	Phone	Fax
Ark Valley Electric Co-op Assn 10 E 10th St PO Box 1246 *TF:* 888-297-9212 ■ *Web:* www.arkvalley.com	South Hutchinson	KS	67504	620-662-6661	665-0148
Bluestem Electric Co-op Inc 614 E Hwy 24 PO Box 5 *TF:* 800-558-1580 ■ *Web:* www.bluestemelectric.com	Wamego	KS	66547	785-456-2212	456-2003
Brown-Atchison Electric Co-op Assn Inc 1712 Central Ave *Web:* www.baelectric.com	Horton	KS	66439	785-486-2117	486-3910
Butler Rural Electric Co-op Assn Inc 216 S Vine St PO Box 1242 *TF:* 800-464-0060 ■ *Web:* www.butler.coop	El Dorado	KS	67042	316-321-9600	321-9980
Caney Valley Electric Co-op Assn 401 Lawrence St *TF:* 800-310-8911 ■ *Web:* www.caneyvalley.com	Cedar Vale	KS	67024	620-758-2262	758-2926
CMS Electric Co-op Inc PO Box 790 *TF:* 800-794-2353 ■ *Web:* www.cmselectric.com	Meade	KS	67864	620-873-2184	873-5303
Doniphan Electric Co-op Assn Inc PO Box 699 *TF:* 800-699-0810 ■ *Web:* www.donrec.org	Troy	KS	66087	785-985-3523	985-2298
DS & O Rural Electric Co-op Assn 129 W Main St PO Box 286 *TF:* 800-376-3533 ■ *Web:* www.dsoelectric.com	Solomon	KS	67480	785-655-2011	655-2805
Flint Hills Rural Electric Co-op Assn Inc PO Box B *Web:* www.flinthillsrec.com	Council Grove	KS	66846	620-767-5144	767-6311
Heartland Rural Electric Co-op PO Box 40 *TF:* 888-835-9585 ■ *Web:* www.heartland-rec.com	Girard	KS	66743	620-724-8251	724-8253
Kaw Valley Electric Co-op Inc 1100 SW Auburn Rd *TF:* 800-794-2011 ■ *Web:* www.kawvalleyelectric.coop	Topeka	KS	66615	785-478-3444	478-1088
Lane-Scott Electric Co-op Inc PO Box 758 *Web:* www.lane-scott.com	Dighton	KS	67839	620-397-2321	397-5997
Leavenworth-Jefferson Electric Co-op Inc PO Box 70 *TF:* 888-796-6111 ■ *Web:* www.ljec.coop	McLouth	KS	66054	913-796-6111	796-6164
Lyon-Coffey Electric Co-op Inc PO Box 229 *TF:* 800-748-7395 ■ *Web:* www.lyon-coffey.com	Burlington	KS	66839	620-364-2116	364-5122
Midwest Energy Inc PO Box 898 *TF:* 800-222-3121 ■ *Web:* www.mwenergy.com	Hays	KS	67601	785-625-3437	625-1494
Nemaha-Marshall Electric Co-op PO Box O *TF:* 866-736-2347	Axtell	KS	66403	785-736-2345	736-2348
Pioneer Electric Co-op Inc 1850 W Oklahoma St PO Box 368 *TF:* 800-794-9302 ■ *Web:* www.pioneerelectric.cc	Ulysses	KS	67880	620-356-1211	356-1669
Prairie Land Electric Co-op Inc 1101 W Hwy 36 *TF:* 800-577-3323 ■ *Web:* www.prairielandelectric.com	Norton	KS	67654	785-877-3323	877-3572
Radiant Electric Co-op Inc 100 N 15th St *TF:* 800-821-0956	Fredonia	KS	66736	620-378-2161	378-3164
Rolling Hills Electric Co 122 W Main St *TF:* 877-906-5903	Mankato	KS	66956	785-378-3151	378-3219
Sedgwick County Electric Co-op 1355 S 383rd St W PO Box 220 *TF:* 866-542-4732 ■ *Web:* www.sedgwickcountyelectric.coop	Cheney	KS	67025	316-542-3131	542-3943
Sumner-Cowley Electric Co-op Inc PO Box 220 *TF:* 888-326-3356 ■ *Web:* www.sucocoop.com	Wellington	KS	67152	620-326-3356	326-6579
Twin Valley Electric Co-op PO Box 385 *TF:* 866-784-5500	Altamont	KS	67330	620-784-5500	784-2464
Victory Electric Co-op Assn Inc PO Box 1335 *TF:* 800-279-7915 ■ *Web:* www.victoryelectric.net	Dodge City	KS	67801	620-227-2139	227-8819
Western Co-op Electric Assn Inc 635 S 13th St *Web:* www.westerncoop.com	WaKeeney	KS	67672	785-743-5561	743-2717
Wheatland Electric Co-op Inc PO Box 230 *TF:* 800-762-0436 ■ *Web:* www.weci.net	Scott City	KS	67871	620-872-5885	872-7170

Kentucky

	City	State	ZIP	Phone	Fax
Big Sandy Rural Electric Co-op Corp 504 11th St	Paintsville	KY	41240	606-789-4095	789-5454
Blue Grass Energy Co-op Corp PO Box 990 *TF:* 888-546-4243 ■ *Web:* www.bgenergy.com	Nicholasville	KY	40340	859-885-4191	885-2854
Clark Energy Co-op Inc 2647 Iron Works Rd PO Box 748 *TF:* 800-992-3269 ■ *Web:* www.clarkenergy.com	Winchester	KY	40392	859-744-4251	744-4218
Cumberland Valley Electric Inc Cumberland Gap Pkwy PO Box 440 *TF:* 800-513-2677	Gray	KY	40734	606-528-2677	528-8458
Farmers Rural Electric Co-op Corp PO Box 1298 *TF:* 800-253-2191	Glasgow	KY	42141	270-651-2191	651-7332
Fleming Mason Energy Co-op PO Box 328 *TF:* 800-464-3144 ■ *Web:* www.fmenergy.com	Flemingsburg	KY	41041	606-845-2661	845-1008
Grayson Rural Electric Co-op Corp 109 Bagby Pk *Web:* www.graysonrecc.com	Grayson	KY	41143	606-474-5136	474-5862
Hickman-Fulton Counties Rural Electric Co-op Corp PO Box 190	Hickman	KY	42050	270-236-2521	236-3028
Inter-County Energy Co-op PO Box 87 *TF:* 888-266-7322 ■ *Web:* www.intercountyenergy.net	Danville	KY	40423	859-236-4561	236-3627
Jackson Energy Co-op PO Box 307 *TF:* 800-262-7480 ■ *Web:* www.jacksonenergy.com	McKee	KY	40447	606-364-1000	364-1007
Jackson Purchase Energy Corp 2900 Irvin Cobb Dr *TF:* 800-633-4044 ■ *Web:* www.jpenergy.com	Paducah	KY	42002	270-442-7321	442-5337
Kenergy Corp PO Box 18 *Web:* www.kenergycorp.com	Henderson	KY	42419	270-826-3991	826-3999
Licking Valley Rural Electric Co-op Corp PO Box 605	West Liberty	KY	41472	606-743-3179	743-2415
Meade County Rural Electric Co-op Corp PO Box 489 *Web:* www.mcrecc.coop	Brandenburg	KY	40108	270-422-2162	422-4705
Nolin Rural Electric Co-op Corp 411 Ring Rd *Web:* www.nolinrecc.com	Elizabethtown	KY	42701	270-765-6153	735-1053
Owen Electric Co-op Inc 510 S Main St PO Box 400 *TF:* 800-372-7612 ■ *Web:* www.owenelectric.com	Owenton	KY	40359	502-484-3471	484-2661
Pennyrile Rural Electric Co-op Corp PO Box 2900 *TF Cust Svc:* 800-297-4710 ■ *Web:* www.precc.com	Hopkinsville	KY	42241	270-886-2555	886-5933
Salt River Electric Co-op Corp 111 W Brashear Ave *TF:* 800-221-7465 ■ *Web:* www.srelectric.com	Bardstown	KY	40004	502-348-3931	348-1993
Shelby Energy Co-op Inc 620 Old Finchville Rd *TF:* 800-292-6585 ■ *Web:* www.shelbyenergy.com	Shelbyville	KY	40065	502-633-4420	633-2387
South Kentucky Rural Electrical Co-op 925 N Main St PO Box 910 *TF:* 800-264-5112 ■ *Web:* www.skrecc.com	Somerset	KY	42502	606-678-4121	679-8279
Taylor County Rural Electric Corp PO Box 100	Campbellsville	KY	42719	270-465-4101	789-3625
Warren Rural Electric Co-op Corp PO Box 1118 *Web:* www.wrecc.com	Bowling Green	KY	42102	270-842-6541	781-3299
West Kentucky Rural Electric Co-op Corp PO Box 589 *TF:* 877-495-7322 ■ *Web:* www.wkrecc.com	Mayfield	KY	42066	270-247-1321	247-8496

Louisiana

	City	State	ZIP	Phone	Fax
Beauregard Electric Co-op Inc 1010 E 1st St *TF:* 800-367-0275 ■ *Web:* www.beci.org	DeRidder	LA	70634	337-463-6221	463-2809
Claiborne Electric Co-op Inc 12525 Hwy 9 PO Box 719 *TF:* 800-929-3504 ■ *Web:* www.claiborneelectric.org	Homer	LA	71040	318-927-3504	927-6636
Concordia Electric Co-op Inc 1865 Hwy 84 W *TF:* 800-617-6282	Jonesville	LA	71343	318-339-7969	339-7462
DEMCO (Dixie Electric Membership Corp) PO Box 15659 *TF:* 800-262-0221 ■ *Web:* www.demco.org	Baton Rouge	LA	70895	225-261-1221	261-1383
Dixie Electric Membership Corp (DEMCO) PO Box 15659 *TF:* 800-262-0221 ■ *Web:* www.demco.org	Baton Rouge	LA	70895	225-261-1221	261-1383
Jefferson Davis Electric Co-op 906 N Lake Arthur Ave *TF:* 800-256-5332	Jennings	LA	70546	337-824-4330	824-8936
Northeast Louisiana Power Co-op Inc 1411 Landis St	Winnsboro	LA	71295	318-435-4523	435-3887
Pointe Coupee Electric Membership Corp 2506 False River Dr PO Box 160 *TF:* 800-738-7232 ■ *Web:* www.pcemc.org	New Roads	LA	70760	225-638-3751	638-8124
Southwest Louisiana Electric Membership Corp 3420 Hwy 167 N *TF:* 888-275-3626 ■ *Web:* www.slemco.com	Lafayette	LA	70509	337-896-5384	896-2533

Phone Fax

Valley Electric Membership Corp
1725 Texas St PO Box 659 .... Natchitoches LA 71458 318-352-3601 352-8570
TF: 800-733-8430 ■ *Web:* www.valleyelectric.coop

Washington-Saint Tammany Electric Co-op
950 Pearl St PO Box N .... Franklinton LA 70438 985-839-3562 839-4315
Web: www.wste.coop

Maine

Phone Fax

Eastern Maine Electric Co-op Inc PO Box 425 .... Calais ME 04619 207-454-7555 454-8376
TF: 800-696-7444 ■ *Web:* www.emec.com

Fox Islands Electric Co-op PO Box 527 .... Vinalhaven ME 04863 207-863-4636 863-4526
Web: www.foxislands.net

Maryland

Phone Fax

Choptank Electric Co-op Inc
24820 Meeting House Rd PO Box 430 .... Denton MD 21629 410-479-0380 479-3516
TF: 877-892-0001 ■ *Web:* www.choptankelectric.com

Southern Maryland Electric Co-op PO Box 1937 .... Hughesville MD 20637 301-274-3111 274-0086
TF: 888-440-3311 ■ *Web:* www.smeco.com

Michigan

Phone Fax

Alger Delta Co-op Electric Assn 426 N 9th St .... Gladstone MI 49837 906-428-4141 428-3840
TF: 800-562-0950 ■ *Web:* www.algerdelta.com

Cherryland Electric Co-op 5930 US Hwy 31 S .... Grawn MI 49637 231-486-9200 943-8204
TF: 800-442-8616 ■ *Web:* www.cecelec.com

Cloverland Electric Co-op 2916 W Hwy M-28 .... Dafter MI 49724 906-635-6800 635-6815
TF: 800-562-4953 ■ *Web:* www.cloverland.com

Great Lakes Energy Co-op 1323 Boyne Ave .... Boyne City MI 49712 888-485-2537 582-0003*
**Fax Area Code:* 231 ■ **Fax:* Cust Svc ■ *Web:* www.gtlakes.com

HomeWorks Tri-County Electric Co-op
7973 E Grand River Ave PO Box 350 .... Portland MI 48875 517-647-7554 647-4856
TF: 800-848-9333 ■ *Web:* www.homeworks.org

Midwest Energy Co-op PO Box 127 .... Cassopolis MI 49031 269-445-1000 445-3792
TF: 800-492-5989 ■ *Web:* www.teammidwest.com

Ontonagon County Rural Electric Assn 500 James K Paul St .... Ontonagon MI 49953 906-884-4151 884-6247
TF: 800-562-7128

Presque Isle Electric & Gas Co-op PO Box 308 .... Onaway MI 49765 989-733-8515 733-2247
TF: 800-423-6634 ■ *Web:* www.pieg.com

Thumb Electric Co-op Inc 2231 Main St .... Ubly MI 48475 989-658-8571 658-2571
Web: www.tecmi.com

Minnesota

Phone Fax

Agralite Electric Co-op 320 E Hwy 12 .... Benson MN 56215 320-843-4150 843-3738
TF: 800-950-8375 ■ *Web:* www.agralite.coop

Arrowhead Electric Co-op Inc 5401 W Hwy 61 .... Lutsen MN 55612 218-663-7239 663-7850
TF: 800-864-3744 ■ *Web:* www.aecimn.com

Beltrami Electric Co-op Inc 4111 Technology Dr NW .... Bemidji MN 56601 218-444-2540 444-3676
TF: 800-955-6083 ■ *Web:* www.beltramielectric.com

BENCO Electric Co-op 20946 549 Ave PO Box 8 .... Mankato MN 56002 507-387-7963 387-1269
TF: 888-792-3626 ■ *Web:* www.benco.org

Brown County Rural Electric Assn PO Box 529 .... Sleepy Eye MN 56085 507-794-3331 794-4282
TF: 800-658-2368 ■ *Web:* www.brownrea.com

Clearwater-Polk Electric Co-op 315 N Main Ave PO Box O .... Bagley MN 56621 218-694-6241 694-6245
TF: 888-694-3833 ■ *Web:* www.clearwater-polk.com

Connexus Energy Co-op 14601 Ramsey Blvd .... Ramsey MN 55303 763-323-2600 323-2603
TF: 800-642-1672 ■ *Web:* www.connexusenergy.com

Crow Wing Co-op Power & Light Co PO Box 507 .... Brainerd MN 56401 218-829-2827 825-2209
TF: 800-648-9401 ■ *Web:* www.cwpower.com

Dakota Electric Assn 4300 220th St W .... Farmington MN 55024 651-463-6212 463-6256
TF: 800-874-3409 ■ *Web:* www.dakotaelectric.com

East Central Energy PO Box 39 .... Braham MN 55006 800-254-7944 396-4114*
**Fax Area Code:* 320 ■ *Web:* www.eastcentralenergy.com

Federated Rural Electric Assn PO Box 69 .... Jackson MN 56143 507-847-3520 728-8366
TF: 800-321-3520 ■ *Web:* www.federatedrea.com

Freeborn-Mower Co-op Services PO Box 611 .... Albert Lea MN 56007 507-373-6421 377-7145
Web: www.fmcs.coop

Goodhue County Co-op Electric Assn PO Box 99 .... Zumbrota MN 55992 507-732-5117 732-5110
TF: 800-927-6864 ■ *Web:* www.gccea.com

Itasca-Mantrap Co-op Electrical Assn PO Box 192 .... Park Rapids MN 56470 218-732-3377 732-5890
Web: www.itasca-mantrap.com

Kandiyohi Power Co-op 1311 Hwy 71 NE .... Willmar MN 56201 320-235-4155 235-5236
TF: 800-551-4951 ■ *Web:* www.kpcoop.com

Lake Country Power 2810 Elida Dr .... Grand Rapids MN 55744 800-421-9959 326-8136*
**Fax Area Code:* 218 ■ *Web:* www.lakecountrypower.com

Lake Region Co-op Electrical Assn
1401 S Broadway PO Box 643 .... Pelican Rapids MN 56572 218-863-1171 863-1172
TF: 800-552-7658 ■ *Web:* www.lrec.coop

Lyon-Lincoln Electric Co-op Inc PO Box 639 .... Tyler MN 56178 507-247-5505 247-5508
TF: 800-927-6276 ■ *Web:* www.lyon-lincolnet.com

McLeod Co-op Power Assn 1231 Ford Ave N .... Glencoe MN 55336 320-864-3148 864-4850
TF: 800-494-6272 ■ *Web:* www.mcleodcoop.com

Meeker Co-op Light & Power Assn PO Box 522 .... Litchfield MN 55355 320-693-3231 693-2980
TF: 800-232-6257 ■ *Web:* www.meekercoop.com

Mille Lacs Electric Co-op PO Box 230 .... Aitkin MN 56431 218-927-2191 927-6822
TF: 800-450-2191 ■ *Web:* www.mlecmn.net

Minnesota Valley Co-op Light & Power Assn PO Box 248 .... Montevideo MN 56265 320-269-2163 269-2302
TF: 800-247-5051 ■ *Web:* www.mnvalleyrec.com

Minnesota Valley Electric Co-op
125 Minnesota Valley Electric Dr PO Box 77024 .... Jordan MN 55352 952-492-2313 492-8281
TF: 800-282-6832 ■ *Web:* www.mvec.net

Nobles Co-op Electric PO Box 788 .... Worthington MN 56187 507-372-7331 372-5148
TF: 800-776-0517 ■ *Web:* www.noblesce.com

North Itasca Electric Co-op Inc 301 Main Ave .... Bigfork MN 56628 218-743-3131 743-3644
TF: 800-762-4048 ■ *Web:* www.northitascaelectric.com

North Star Electric Co-op Inc 441 State Hwy 172 NW .... Baudette MN 56623 218-634-2202 634-2203
TF: 888-634-2202 ■ *Web:* www.northstarelectric.coop

People's Co-op Services 3935 Hwy 14 PO Box 339 .... Rochester MN 55903 507-288-4004 288-9438
TF: 800-214-2694 ■ *Web:* www.peoplesrec.com

PKM Electric Co-op Inc 406 N Minnesota St .... Warren MN 56762 218-745-4711 745-4713
TF: 800-552-7366 ■ *Web:* www.pkmcoop.com

Red Lake Electric Co-op Inc
412 International Dr SW PO Box 43 .... Red Lake Falls MN 56750 218-253-2168 253-2630
TF: 800-245-6068

Phone Fax

Red River Valley Co-op Power Assn 109 2nd Ave E .... Halstad MN 56548 218-456-2139 456-2102
Web: www.rrvcoop.com

Redwood Electric Co-op 60 Pine St PO Box 15 .... Clements MN 56224 507-692-2214 692-2211
TF: 888-251-5100

Renville-Sibley Co-op Power Assn 103 Oak St .... Danube MN 56230 320-826-2593 826-2679
TF: 800-826-2593 ■ *Web:* www.renville-sibley.coop

Roseau Electric Co-op Inc 903 3rd St NE .... Roseau MN 56751 218-463-1543 463-3713
TF: 888-847-8840 ■ *Web:* www.roseauelectric.coop

South Central Electric Assn 71176 Tiell Dr PO Box 150 .... Saint James MN 56081 507-375-3164 375-3166
TF: 888-805-7232 ■ *Web:* www.southcentralelectric.com

Stearns Co-op Electric Assn 900 E Kraft Dr .... Melrose MN 56352 320-256-4241 256-3618
TF: 800-962-0655 ■ *Web:* www.stearnselectric.org

Steele-Waseca Co-op Electric PO Box 485 .... Owatonna MN 55060 507-451-7340 446-4242
TF: 800-526-3514 ■ *Web:* www.swce.com

Todd-Wadena Electric Co-op PO Box 431 .... Wadena MN 56482 218-631-3120 631-4188
TF: 800-321-8932 ■ *Web:* www.toddwadena.com

Traverse Electric Co-op Inc PO Box 66 .... Wheaton MN 56296 320-563-8616 563-4863
TF: 800-927-5443 ■ *Web:* www.traverseelectric.com

Tri-County Electric Co-op PO Box 626 .... Rushford MN 55971 507-864-7783 864-2871
TF: 800-432-2285 ■ *Web:* www.tec.coop

Wild Rice Electric Co-op Inc 502 N Main PO Box 438 .... Mahnomen MN 56557 218-935-2517 935-2519
TF: 800-244-5709 ■ *Web:* www.wildriceelectric.com

Wright-Hennepin Co-op Electric Assn PO Box 330 .... Rockford MN 55373 763-477-3000 477-3054
TF: 800-943-2667 ■ *Web:* www.whe.org

Mississippi

Phone Fax

Alcorn County Electric Power Assn 1909 S Tate St .... Corinth MS 38834 662-287-4402 287-4088

Central Electric Power Assn 104 E Main St .... Carthage MS 39051 601-267-5671 267-6032
Web: www.centralepa.com

Coahoma Electric Power Assn 340 Hopson St .... Lyon MS 38645 662-624-8321 624-8327

Coast Electric Power Assn 302 Hwy 90 .... Bay Saint Louis MS 39521 228-467-6535 467-7066
TF Cust Svc: 800-624-3348 ■ *Web:* www.coastepa.com

Delta Electric Power Assn PO Box 935 .... Greenwood MS 30935 662-453-6352 453-6359

Dixie Electric Power Assn PO Box 88 .... Laurel MS 39441 601-425-2535 425-2535

East Mississippi Electric Power Assn PO Box 5517 .... Meridian MS 39302 601-483-7361 693-0464
Web: www.emepa.com

Four County Electric Power Assn PO Box 351 .... Columbus MS 39703 662-327-8900 327-8790
Web: www.4county.org

Magnolia Electric Power Assn PO Box 747 .... McComb MS 39649 601-684-4011 684-5535

Monroe County Electric Power Assn PO Box 300 .... Amory MS 38821 662-256-2962 257-9909

Natchez Trace Electric Power PO Box 609 .... Houston MS 38851 662-456-3037 456-2086
Web: www.ntepa.com

North East Mississippi Electric Power Assn 10 County Rd 2050 .... Oxford MS 38655 662-234-6331 234-0046
TF: 877-234-6331

Northcentral Mississippi Electric Power Assn
225 Hwy 309 S PO Box 405 .... Byhalia MS 38611 662-838-2151 838-4751

Pearl River Valley Electric Power Assn
1422 Hwy 13 N PO Box 1217 .... Columbia MS 39429 601-736-2666 736-9702
TF: 800-320-0312 ■ *Web:* www.prvepa.com

Pontotoc Electric Power Assn 12 S Main St .... Pontotoc MS 38863 662-489-3211 489-5156

Prentiss County Electric Power Assn 302 W Church St .... Booneville MS 38829 662-728-4433 728-4059

Singing River Electric Power Assn Inc
11187 Old Hwy 63 PO Box 767 .... Lucedale MS 39452 601-947-4211 947-6548
Web: www.singingriver.com

Southern Pine Electric Power Assn
110 Risher St PO Box 60 .... Taylorsville MS 39168 601-785-6511 785-4980
TF: 800-231-5240 ■ *Web:* www.spepa.com

Southwest Mississippi Electric Power Assn 18671 Hwy 61 .... Lorman MS 39096 601-437-3611 437-8736
TF: 800-287-8564 ■ *Web:* www.southwestepa.com

Tallahatchie Valley Electric Power Assn PO Box 513 .... Batesville MS 38606 662-563-4742 563-8615
Web: www.tvepa.com

Tishomingo County Electric Power Assn PO Box 560 .... Iuka MS 38852 662-423-3646 423-1763

Tombigbee Electric Power Assn Co-op PO Box 1789 .... Tupelo MS 38802 662-842-7635 842-0369

Twin County Electric Power Assn PO Box 158 .... Hollandale MS 38748 662-827-2262 827-2832

Yazoo Valley Electric Power Assn PO Box 8 .... Yazoo City MS 39194 662-746-4251 751-1060

Missouri

Phone Fax

Atchison-Holt Electric Co-op 18585 Industrial Rd .... Rock Port MO 64482 660-744-5344 744-5880
TF: 888-744-5366

Barry Electric Co-op 4015 Main St PO Box 307 .... Cassville MO 65625 417-847-2131 847-5524
TF: 866-847-2333 ■ *Web:* www.barryelectric.com

Barton County Electric Co-op 91 W Hwy 160 .... Lamar MO 64759 417-682-5636 682-5276
TF: 800-286-5636 ■ *Web:* www.bartonelectric.com

Black River Electric Co-op 2600 Hwy 67 PO Box 31 .... Fredericktown MO 63645 573-783-3381 783-7343
TF: 800-392-4711 ■ *Web:* www.blackriverelectric.com

Boone Electric Co-op 1413 Rangeline St .... Columbia MO 65205 573-449-4181 441-7272
TF: 800-225-8143 ■ *Web:* www.booneelectric.com

Callaway Electric Co-op 503 Truman Rd .... Fulton MO 65251 573-642-3326 642-3328
TF: 888-642-4840 ■ *Web:* www.callawayelectric.com

Central Missouri Electric Co-op Inc 22702 Hwy 65 PO Box 939 .... Sedalia MO 65302 660-826-2900 826-7180
Web: www.cmecinc.com

Citizens Electric Corp 150 Merchant St PO Box 311 .... Sainte Genevieve MO 63670 573-883-5339 883-3381
TF: 877-876-3511 ■ *Web:* www.citizenselectriccorp.com

Co-Mo Electric Co-op Inc 29868 Hwy 5 .... Tipton MO 65081 660-433-5521 433-5631
TF: 800-781-0157 ■ *Web:* www.co-moelectric.com

Consolidated Electric Co-op Hwy 54 E PO Box 540 .... Mexico MO 65265 573-581-3630 581-0990
TF: 800-621-0091 ■ *Web:* www.consolidatedelectric.com

Crawford Electric Co-op Inc 10301 N Service Rd PO Box 10 .... Bourbon MO 65441 573-732-4415 732-5409
TF: 800-677-2667 ■ *Web:* www.crawfordelec.com

Cuivre River Electric Co-op 1112 E Cherry St .... Troy MO 63379 636-528-8261 528-7696
TF: 800-392-3709 ■ *Web:* www.cuivre.com

Farmers' Electric Co-op Inc PO Box 680 .... Chillicothe MO 64601 660-646-4281 646-3569
TF: 800-279-0496 ■ *Web:* www.fec-co.com

Gascosage Electric Co-op PO Drawer G .... Dixon MO 65459 573-759-7146 759-6020
Web: www.gascosage.com

Grundy Electric Co-op Inc 4100 Oklahoma Ave .... Trenton MO 64683 660-359-3941 359-6030
TF: 800-279-2249 ■ *Web:* www.grundyec.com

Howard Electric Co-op Inc PO Box 391 .... Fayette MO 65248 660-248-3311 248-3543
Web: www.howardelectric.com

Howell-Oregon Electric Co-op Inc PO Box 649 .... West Plains MO 65775 417-256-2131 256-4571
TF: 888-463-7693 ■ *Web:* www.hoecoop.org

Intercounty Electric Co-op Assn 102 Maple Ave .... Licking MO 65542 573-674-2211 674-2888
Web: www.intercoelec.com

Laclede Electric Co-op PO Box M .... Lebanon MO 65536 417-532-3164 532-8321
TF: 800-299-3164 ■ *Web:* www.lacledeelectric.com

Lewis County Rural Electric Co-op Assn PO Box 68 .... Lewistown MO 63452 573-215-4000 215-4004
TF: 888-454-4485 ■ *Web:* www.lewiscountyrec.org

Macon Electric Co-op PO Box 157 .... Macon MO 63552 660-385-3157 385-3334
TF: 800-553-6901 ■ *Web:* www.maconelectric.com

New-Mac Electric Co-op Inc PO Box 310 .... Neosho MO 64850 417-451-1515 451-9042
Web: www.newmac.com

Missouri (Cont'd)

				Phone	Fax
North Central Missouri Electric Co-op Inc 1098 Hwy E PO Box 220	Milan	MO	63556	660-265-4404	265-4311
TF: 800-279-2264 ■ *Web:* www.northcentralelectric.com					
Osage Valley Electric Co-op Assn 1321 N Orange St	Butler	MO	64730	660-679-3131	679-3142
TF: 800-889-6832 ■ *Web:* www.osagevalley.com					
Ozark Border Electric Co-op 3281 S Westwood Blvd PO Box 400	Poplar Bluff	MO	63902	573-785-4631	785-1853
TF: 800-392-0567 ■ *Web:* www.ozarkborder.org					
Ozark Electric Co-op N Hwy 39 PO Box 420	Mount Vernon	MO	65712	417-466-2144	466-7239
TF: 800-947-6393 ■ *Web:* www.ozarkelectric.com					
Pemiscot-Dunklin Electric Co-op PO Box 657	Hayti	MO	63851	573-757-6641	757-6656
TF: 800-558-6641 ■ *Web:* www.pemdunk.com					
Platte-Clay Electric Co-op Inc 1000 W Hwy 92 PO Box 100	Kearney	MO	64060	816-628-3121	628-3141
TF: 800-431-2131 ■ *Web:* www.pcec.coop					
Ralls County Electric Co-op 17594 Hwy 19 PO Box 157	New London	MO	63459	573-985-8711	985-3658
TF: 877-985-8711					
Sac Osage Electric Co-op Inc 4815 E Hwy 54 PO Box 111	El Dorado Springs	MO	64744	417-876-2721	876-5368
TF: 800-876-2701 ■ *Web:* www.sacosage.com					
Se-Ma-No Electric Co-op 601 N Hwy 60	Mansfield	MO	65704	417-924-3243	924-8215
Semo Electric Co-op 505 S Main St PO Box 520	Sikeston	MO	63801	573-471-5821	471-1404
TF: 800-813-5230					
Three Rivers Electric Co-op 1324 E Main St PO Box 918	Linn	MO	65051	573-897-2251	897-3511
Web: www.threeriverselectric.com					
Tri-County Electric Co-op Assn PO Box 159	Lancaster	MO	63548	660-457-3733	457-3736
TF: 888-457-3734					
United Electric Co-op Inc 401 N Hwy 71 PO Box 319	Savannah	MO	64485	816-324-3155	324-3157
TF: 800-748-1488 ■ *Web:* www.ueci.org					
Webster Electric Co-op PO Box 87	Marshfield	MO	65706	417-859-2216	859-4579
TF: 800-643-4305 ■ *Web:* www.websterec.com					
West Central Electric Co-op Inc PO Box 452	Higginsville	MO	64037	660-584-2131	584-6286
Web: www.westcentralelectric.com					
White River Valley Electric Co-op Inc PO Box 969	Branson	MO	65615	417-335-9335	335-9250
TF: 800-879-4056 ■ *Web:* www.whiteriver.org					

Montana

				Phone	Fax
Beartooth Electric Co-op Inc 1306 N Broadway St PO Box 1110	Red Lodge	MT	59068	406-446-2310	446-3934
TF: 800-472-9821					
Big Flat Electric Co-op Inc 333 S 7th St E	Malta	MT	59538	406-654-2040	654-2292
TF: 800-242-2040 ■ *Web:* www.bigflatelectric.com					
Big Horn County Electric Co-op Inc 303 S Mitchell St	Hardin	MT	59034	406-665-2830	665-2644
Fergus Electric Co-op Inc 84423 US Hwy 87	Lewistown	MT	59457	406-538-3465	538-7391
Web: www.ferguselectric.coop					
Flathead Electric Co-op Inc 2510 Hwy 2 E	Kalispell	MT	59901	406-752-4483	752-4283
TF: 800-735-8489 ■ *Web:* www.flatheadelectric.com					
Glacier Electric Co-op Inc PO Box 2090	Cut Bank	MT	59427	406-873-5566	873-2071
TF: 800-347-6795 ■ *Web:* www.glacierelectric.com					
Goldenwest Electric Co-op Inc PO Box 177	Wibaux	MT	59353	406-796-2423	796-2445
Hill County Electric Co-op Inc PO Box 2330	Havre	MT	59501	406-394-7802	394-7801
TF: 877-394-7804 ■ *Web:* www.hcelectric.com					
Lincoln Electric Co-op Inc PO Box 628	Eureka	MT	59917	406-889-3301	889-3874
TF: 800-442-2994 ■ *Web:* www.lincolnelectric.org					
Lower Yellowstone Rural Electric Assn Inc PO Box 1047	Sidney	MT	59270	406-488-1602	488-6524
Web: www.lyrec.com					
Marias River Electric Co-op Inc PO Box 729	Shelby	MT	59474	406-434-5575	434-2531
Web: www.mariasriverec.com					
McCone Electric Co-op Inc PO Box 368	Circle	MT	59215	406-485-3430	485-3397
TF: 800-684-3605 ■ *Web:* www.mcconeelectric.coop					
Mid-Yellowstone Electric Co-op PO Box 386	Hysham	MT	59038	406-342-5521	342-5511
Missoula Electric Co-op Inc 1700 W Broadway	Missoula	MT	59808	406-541-4433	541-6318
TF: 800-352-5200 ■ *Web:* www.missoulaelectric.com					
Northern Electric Co-op Inc 75 Main St	Opheim	MT	59250	406-762-3411	762-3352
Park Electric Co-op Inc 5706 US Hwy 89 S PO Box 1119	Livingston	MT	59047	406-222-3100	222-3418
TF: 888-298-0657 ■ *Web:* www.parkelectric.coop					
Ravalli County Electric Co-op Inc 1051 NE Eastside Hwy PO Box 190	Corvallis	MT	59828	406-961-3001	961-3230
Web: www.ravallielectric.com					
Sheridan Electric Co-op Inc PO Box 227	Medicine Lake	MT	59247	406-789-2231	789-2234
Southeast Electric Co-op Inc 110 S Main St	Ekalaka	MT	59324	406-775-8762	775-8763
TF: 888-485-8762 ■ *Web:* www.midrivers.com/~seco/					
Sun River Electric Co-op Inc PO Box 309	Fairfield	MT	59436	406-467-2526	467-3108
TF: 800-452-7516 ■ *Web:* www.sunriverec.com					
Tongue River Electric Co-op Inc PO Box 138	Ashland	MT	59003	406-784-2341	784-2279
Valley Electric Co-op Inc PO Box 951	Glasgow	MT	59230	406-228-9351	367-9306
Vigilante Electric Co-op Inc PO Box 1049	Dillon	MT	59725	406-683-2327	683-4328
Web: www.vec.coop					
Yellowstone Valley Electric Co-op PO Box 249	Huntley	MT	59037	406-348-3411	348-3414
TF: 800-736-5323 ■ *Web:* www.yvec.com					

Nebraska

				Phone	Fax
Burt County Public Power District 613 N 13th St PO Box 209	Tekamah	NE	68061	402-374-2631	374-1605
TF: 888-835-1620 ■ *Web:* www.burtcoppd.com					
Butler County Rural Public Power District 1331 N 4th St	David City	NE	68632	402-367-3081	367-6114
TF: 800-230-0569 ■ *Web:* www.butlerppd.com					
Cedar-Knox Public Power District 56272 W Hwy 84	Hartington	NE	68739	402-254-6291	254-6991
Web: www.cedarknoxppd.com					
Chimney Rock Public Power District 805 W 8th St PO Box 608	Bayard	NE	69334	308-586-1824	586-2511
TF: 877-773-6300 ■ *Web:* www.crppd.com					
Cornhusker Public Power District NW Hwy 81 PO Box 9	Columbus	NE	68602	402-564-2821	564-9907
Web: www.cornhusker-power.com					
Cuming County Public Power District 500 S Main St	West Point	NE	68788	402-372-2463	372-5832
TF: 877-572-2463 ■ *Web:* www.ccppd.com					
Custer Public Power District 625 E South 'E' St PO Box 10	Broken Bow	NE	68822	308-872-2451	
TF: 888-749-2453 ■ *Web:* www.custerpower.com					
Dawson Public Power District PO Box 777	Lexington	NE	68850	308-324-2386	324-2907
TF: 800-752-8305 ■ *Web:* www.dawsonpower.com					
Elkhorn Rural Public Power District PO Box 310	Battle Creek	NE	68715	402-675-2185	675-6275
TF: 800-675-2185 ■ *Web:* www.erppd.com					
Howard Greeley Rural Public Power District PO Box 105	Saint Paul	NE	68873	308-754-4457	754-4230
TF: 800-280-4962					
KBR Rural Public Power District PO Box 187	Ainsworth	NE	69210	402-387-1120	387-1033
TF: 800-672-0009					
Loup River Public Power District PO Box 988	Columbus	NE	68602	402-564-3171	564-0970
TF: 888-564-3172 ■ *Web:* www.loup.com					
Loup Valleys Rural Public Power District 606 'S' St	Ord	NE	68862	308-728-3633	728-7726
TF: 888-880-3633					
McCook Public Power District PO Box 1147	McCook	NE	69001	308-345-2500	345-4772
TF: 800-658-4285					
Midwest Electric Co-op Corp PO Box 970	Grant	NE	69140	308-352-4356	352-4957
TF: 800-451-3691 ■ *Web:* www.midwestecc.com					
Niobrara Valley Electric Membership Corp PO Box 60	O'Neill	NE	68763	402-336-2803	336-4858
Web: www.nvemc.org					
Norris Public Power District PO Box 399	Beatrice	NE	68310	402-223-4038	228-2895
TF: 800-858-4707 ■ *Web:* www.norrisppd.com					
North Central Public Power District 1409 Main St	Creighton	NE	68729	402-358-5112	358-5129
TF: 800-578-1060 ■ *Web:* www.ncppd.com					
Northeast Nebraska Public Power District 303 Logan St PO Box 350	Wayne	NE	68787	402-375-1360	375-1233
TF: 800-750-9277					
Northwest Rural Public Power District PO Box 249	Hay Springs	NE	69347	308-638-4445	638-4448
TF: 800-847-0492 ■ *Web:* www.nrppd.com					
Perennial Public Power District 2122 S Lincoln Ave	York	NE	68467	402-362-3355	362-3623
TF: 800-289-0288 ■ *Web:* www.perennialpower.com					
Polk County Rural Public Power District 120 W 4th St PO Box 465	Stromsburg	NE	68666	402-764-4381	764-4382
TF: 888-242-5265 ■ *Web:* www.pcrppd.com					
Roosevelt Public Power District PO Box 97	Mitchell	NE	69357	308-635-2424	635-0632
Seward County Rural Public Power District 1363 Progressive Rd PO Box 69	Seward	NE	68434	402-643-2951	646-4695
South Central Public Power District 275 S Main St PO Box 406	Nelson	NE	68961	402-225-2351	225-2353
TF: 800-557-5254 ■ *Web:* www.southcentralppd.com					
Southern Public Power District PO Box 1687	Grand Island	NE	68802	308-384-2350	384-5018
TF: 800-652-2013 ■ *Web:* www.southernpd.com					
Southwest Public Power District 221 N Main St PO Box 289	Palisade	NE	69040	308-285-3295	285-3811
TF: 800-379-7977 ■ *Web:* www.swppd.com					
Stanton County Public Power District PO Box 319	Stanton	NE	68779	402-439-2228	439-7000
TF: 877-439-2300					
Twin Valleys Public Power District PO Box 160	Cambridge	NE	69022	308-697-3315	697-4877
TF: 800-658-4266 ■ *Web:* www.twinvalleysppd.com					
Wheat Belt Public Power District PO Box 177	Sidney	NE	69162	308-254-5871	254-2384
TF: 800-261-7114 ■ *Web:* www.wheatbelt.com					

Nevada

				Phone	Fax
Mount Wheeler Power Inc PO Box 15000	Ely	NV	89315	775-289-8981	289-8987
TF: 800-977-6937 ■ *Web:* www.mwpower.net					
Overton Power District # 5 615 N Moapa Valley Blvd PO Box 395	Overton	NV	89040	702-397-2512	397-2799
TF: 800-393-2512 ■ *Web:* www.opd5.com					
Valley Electric Assn PO Box 237	Pahrump	NV	89041	775-727-5312	727-6320
TF: 800-742-3330 ■ *Web:* www.valleyelectric.org					
Wells Rural Electric Co PO Box 365	Wells	NV	89835	775-752-3328	752-3407
Web: www.wellsrec.com					

New Hampshire

				Phone	Fax
New Hampshire Electric Co-op 579 Tenney Mountain Hwy	Plymouth	NH	03264	603-536-1800	536-8682
TF: 800-698-2007 ■ *Web:* www.nhec.com					

New Jersey

				Phone	Fax
Sussex Rural Electric Co-op PO Box 346	Sussex	NJ	07461	973-875-5101	875-4114
TF: 877-504-6463 ■ *Web:* www.sussexrec.com					

New Mexico

				Phone	Fax
Central New Mexico Electric Co-op Inc Hwy 55 PO Box 157	Mountainair	NM	87036	505-847-2521	847-2900
TF: 800-339-2521 ■ *Web:* www.cnmec.org					
Central Valley Electric Co-op Inc 1505 N 13th St PO Box 230	Artesia	NM	88211	505-746-3571	746-4219
Web: www.cvecoop.org					
Columbus Electric Co-op Inc 900 N Gold St	Deming	NM	88031	505-546-8838	546-3128
TF: 800-950-2667 ■ *Web:* www.columbusco-op.org					
Continental Divide Electric Co-op 200 E High St	Grants	NM	87020	505-285-6656	287-2234
Web: www.cdec.coop					
Farmers Electric Co-op Inc PO Box 550	Clovis	NM	88102	505-769-2116	769-2118
Web: www.farmerselectric.org					
Jemez Mountains Electric Co-op PO Box 128	Espanola	NM	87532	505-753-2105	753-6958
TF: 888-755-2105 ■ *Web:* www.jemezcoop.org					
Kit Carson Electric Co-op Inc PO Box 587	Taos	NM	87571	505-758-2258	758-4890
TF: 800-688-6780 ■ *Web:* www.kitcarson.com					
Lea County Electric Co-op Inc PO Drawer 1447	Lovington	NM	88260	505-396-3631	396-3634
TF: 800-510-5232 ■ *Web:* www.leacountyelectric.coop					
Mora-San Miguel Electric Co-op PO Box 240	Mora	NM	87732	505-387-2205	387-5975
Northern Rio Arriba Electric Co-op 1135 Camino Escondido Rd	Chama	NM	87520	505-756-2181	756-2200
Web: www.noraelectric.org					
Otero County Electric Co-op Inc 202 Burro Ave PO Box 227	Cloudcroft	NM	88317	505-682-2521	682-3109
TF: 800-548-4660 ■ *Web:* www.ocec-inc.com					
Roosevelt County Electric Co-op Inc 121 N Main St PO Box 389	Portales	NM	88130	505-356-4491	359-1651
Web: www.rcec.org					
Sierra Electric Co-op 610 Hwy 195 PO Box 290	Elephant Butte	NM	87935	505-744-5231	744-5819
Web: www.sierraelectric.org					
Socorro Electric Co-op Inc 215 E Manazannez St PO Box H	Socorro	NM	87801	505-835-0560	835-4449
TF: 800-351-7575 ■ *Web:* www.socorroelectric.com					
Southwestern Electric Co-op Inc PO Box 369	Clayton	NM	88415	505-374-2451	374-2030
Springer Electric Co-op Inc PO Box 698	Springer	NM	87747	505-483-2421	483-2692
TF: 800-288-1353 ■ *Web:* www.springercoop.com					

New York

				Phone	Fax
1st Rochdale Co-op Group Ltd 465 Grand St 2nd Fl	New York	NY	10002	212-673-3900	673-3902
TF: 877-624-3253 ■ *Web:* www.1strochdalenyc.net					
Delaware County Electric Co-op 39 Elm St PO Box 471	Delhi	NY	13753	607-746-2341	746-7548
Web: www.dce.coop					
Oneida-Madison Electric Co-op Inc 15630 Rt 20 PO Box 27	Bouckville	NY	13310	315-893-1851	893-1857
Web: www.oneida-madison.coop					
Otsego Electric Co-op Inc 3192 County Hwy 11	Hartwick	NY	13348	607-293-6622	293-6624
Web: www.otsegoec.coop					

Name / Address	City	State	Zip	Phone	Fax
Steuben Rural Electric Co-op Inc 9 Wilson Ave *TF:* 800-843-3414 ■ *Web:* www.steubenrec.com	Bath	NY	14810	607-776-4161	776-2293

North Carolina

Name / Address	City	State	Zip	Phone	Fax
Albemarle Electric Membership Corp 159 Creek Dr *TF:* 800-215-9915 ■ *Web:* www.albemarle-emc.com	Hertford	NC	27944	252-426-5735	426-8270
Blue Ridge Electric Membership Corp 1216 Blowing Rock Blvd NE *TF:* 800-451-5474	Lenoir	NC	28645	828-758-2383	758-2699
Brunswick Electric Membership Corp 795 Ocean Hwy W PO Box 226 *TF:* 800-842-5871 ■ *Web:* www.bemc.org	Supply	NC	28459	910-754-4391	755-4299
Cape Hatteras Electric Co-op 47109 Light Plant Rd PO Box 9 *TF:* 800-454-5616 ■ *Web:* www.chec.coop	Buxton	NC	27920	252-995-5616	995-4088
Carteret-Craven Electric Co-op 1300 Hwy 24 W PO Box 1490 *TF:* 800-682-2217 ■ *Web:* www.ccemc.com	Newport	NC	28570	252-247-3107	247-0235
Central Electric Membership Corp 128 Wilson Rd *TF:* 800-446-7752 ■ *Web:* www.centralelectriconline.com	Sanford	NC	27331	919-774-4900	774-1860
Cogentrix Energy Inc 9405 Arrowpoint Blvd *Web:* www.cogentrix.com	Charlotte	NC	28273	704-525-3800	529-5313
Edgecombe-Martin County Electric Membership Corp PO Box 188 *TF:* 800-445-6486	Tarboro	NC	27886	252-823-2171	823-4535
EnergyUnited Electric Membership Corp PO Box 1831 *TF:* 800-522-3793 ■ *Web:* www.energyunited.com	Statesville	NC	28687	704-873-5241	878-0161
Four County Electric Membership Corp PO Box 2000 *Web:* www.fourcty.org	Burgaw	NC	28425	910-259-2171	259-1860
French Broad Electric Membership Corp PO Box 9 *Web:* www.frenchbroademc.com	Marshall	NC	28753	828-649-2051	649-2989
Halifax Electric Membership Corp PO Box 667 *Web:* www.halifaxemc.com	Enfield	NC	27823	252-445-5111	445-2398
Harkers Island Electric Membership Corp PO Box 190	Harkers Island	NC	28531	252-728-2593	728-1253
Haywood Electric Membership Corp 1560 Asheville Rd *TF:* 800-951-6088 ■ *Web:* www.haywoodemc.com	Waynesville	NC	28786	828-452-2281	456-8803
Jones-Onslow Electric Membership Corp 259 Western Blvd *TF:* 800-682-1515 ■ *Web:* www.joemc.com	Jacksonville	NC	28546	910-353-1940	353-8000
Lumbee River Electric Membership Corp PO Box 830 *TF:* 800-683-5571 ■ *Web:* www.lumbeeriver.com	Red Springs	NC	28377	910-843-4131	843-5035
Pee Dee Electric Membership Corp 575 US Hwy 52 S *TF:* 800-992-1626 ■ *Web:* www.peedeeworld.net	Wadesboro	NC	28170	704-694-2114	694-9636
Piedmont Electric Membership Corp 2500 Hwy 86 S PO Drawer 1179 *Web:* www.pemc.org	Hillsborough	NC	27278	919-732-2123	644-1030
Pitt & Greene Electric Membership Corp 3989 W Wilson St *TF:* 800-622-1362	Farmville	NC	27828	252-753-3128	753-3136
Randolph Electric Membership Corp 879 McDowell Rd PO Box 40 *TF:* 800-672-8212 ■ *Web:* www.randolphemc.com	Asheboro	NC	27204	336-625-5177	626-1551
Roanoke Electric Co-op 401 N Main St *TF:* 800-433-2236 ■ *Web:* www.ezsdk.com	Rich Square	NC	27869	252-539-2236	539-3021
Rutherford Electric Membership Corp 186 Hudlow Rd PO Box 1569 *TF:* 800-521-0920 ■ *Web:* www.remc.com	Forest City	NC	28043	828-245-1621	248-2319
South River Electric Membership Corp 17494 US 421 S PO Box 931 *TF:* 800-338-5530 ■ *Web:* www.sremc.com	Dunn	NC	28335	910-892-8071	891-7189
Surry-Yadkin Electric Membership Corp PO Box 305 *TF:* 800-682-5903 ■ *Web:* www.syemc.com	Dobson	NC	27017	336-386-8241	386-9744
Tideland Electric Membership Corp PO Box 159 *TF:* 800-637-1079 ■ *Web:* www.tidelandemc.com	Pantego	NC	27860	252-943-3046	943-3510
Tri-County Electric Membership Corp PO Box 130	Dudley	NC	28333	919-735-2611	734-6277
Union Power Co-op PO Box 5014 *TF:* 800-922-6840 ■ *Web:* www.union-power.com	Monroe	NC	28111	704-289-3145	296-0408
Wake Electric Membership Corp 414 E Wait Ave *TF:* 800-474-6300 ■ *Web:* www.wemc.com	Wake Forest	NC	27587	919-863-6300	863-6379

North Dakota

Name / Address	City	State	Zip	Phone	Fax
Basin Electric Power Co-op 1717 E Interstate Ave *Web:* www.basinelectric.com	Bismarck	ND	58501	701-223-0441	224-5336
Burke-Divide Electric Co-op Inc Hwy 5 W *Web:* www.bdec.coop	Columbus	ND	58727	701-939-6671	939-6666
Capital Electric Co-op Inc PO Box 730 *Web:* www.capitalelec.com	Bismarck	ND	58502	701-223-1513	223-1557
Cass County Electric Co-op Inc 491 Elm St *TF:* 800-248-3292 ■ *Web:* www.kwh.com	Kindred	ND	58051	701-356-4400	356-4500
Cavalier Rural Electric Co-op Inc 1111 9th Ave	Langdon	ND	58249	701-256-5511	256-5513
Dakota Valley Electric Co-op 7296 Hwy 281 *TF:* 800-342-4671 ■ *Web:* www.dakotavalley.com	Edgeley	ND	58433	701-493-2281	493-2454
KEM Electric Co-op Inc 107 S Broadway *TF:* 800-472-2673 ■ *Web:* www.kemelectric.com	Linton	ND	58552	701-254-4666	254-4975
McKenzie Electric Co-op Inc 908 4th Ave NE *Web:* www.mckenzieelectric.com	Watford City	ND	58854	701-444-9288	444-3002
McLean Electric Co-op Inc PO Box 399 *TF:* 800-263-4922 ■ *Web:* www.mcleanelectric.com	Garrison	ND	58540	701-463-2291	337-5303
Mor-Gran-Sou Electric Co-op Inc PO Box 297 *TF:* 800-750-8212 ■ *Web:* www.morgransou.com	Flasher	ND	58535	701-597-3301	597-3915
Mountrail-Williams Electric Co-op PO Box 1346 *TF:* 800-279-2667 ■ *Web:* www.mwec.com	Williston	ND	58802	701-577-3765	577-3777
Nodak Electric Co-op Inc PO Box 13000 *TF:* 800-732-4373 ■ *Web:* www.nodakelectric.com	Grand Forks	ND	58208	701-746-4461	795-6701
North Central Electric Co-op Inc 501 11th St W *Web:* www.nceci.com	Bottineau	ND	58318	701-228-2202	228-2592
Northern Plains Electric Co-op 1515 W Main St *TF:* 800-882-2500 ■ *Web:* www.nplains.com	Carrington	ND	58421	701-652-3156	652-1848
Oliver-Mercer Electric Co-op Inc 800 Highway Dr *TF:* 800-748-5533 ■ *Web:* www.olivermercer.com	Hazen	ND	58545	701-748-2293	748-6500
Slope Electric Co-op Inc 116 E 12th St *TF:* 800-559-4191 ■ *Web:* www.slopeelectric.coop	New England	ND	58647	701-579-4191	579-4193
Verendrye Electric Co-op Inc 615 Hwy 52 W *TF:* 800-472-2141 ■ *Web:* www.verendrye.com	Velva	ND	58790	701-338-2855	624-0353
West Plains Electric Co-op Inc PO Box 1038 *TF:* 800-627-8470 ■ *Web:* www.wpec.net	Dickinson	ND	58602	701-483-5111	483-6057

Ohio

Name / Address	City	State	Zip	Phone	Fax
Adams Rural Electric Co-op Inc 4800 SR 125 *TF:* 800-283-1846 ■ *Web:* www.adamsrec.com	West Union	OH	45693	937-544-2305	544-3877
Buckeye Rural Electric Co-op Inc 4848 SR 325 S *TF:* 800-231-2732 ■ *Web:* www.buckeyerec.com	Patriot	OH	45658	740-379-2025	379-2048
Butler Rural Electric Co-op Inc 3888 Still-Beckett Rd *TF:* 800-255-2732 ■ *Web:* www.brecnet.com	Oxford	OH	45056	513-867-4400	867-4422
Carroll Electric Co-op Inc 350 Canton Rd NW *TF:* 800-232-7697 ■ *Web:* www.carrollelectriccoop.com	Carrollton	OH	44615	330-627-2116	627-7050
Consolidated Electric Co-op Inc 5255 SR 95 *TF:* 800-421-5863 ■ *Web:* www.conelec.com	Mount Gilead	OH	43338	419-947-3055	947-3082
Darke Rural Electric Co-op Inc 1120 Fort Jefferson Rd *TF:* 800-776-5612	Greenville	OH	45331	937-548-4114	548-0446
Firelands Electric Co-op Inc 1 Energy Pl PO Box 32 *TF:* 800-533-8658 ■ *Web:* www.firelandsec.com	New London	OH	44851	419-929-1571	929-8550
Frontier Power Co PO Box 280 *TF:* 800-624-8050 ■ *Web:* www.frontier-power.com	Coshocton	OH	43812	740-622-6755	622-0711
Guernsey-Muskingum Electric Co-op 17 S Liberty St *Web:* www.gmenergy.com	New Concord	OH	43762	740-826-7661	826-7171
Hancock-Wood Electric Co-op Inc PO Box 190 *TF:* 800-445-4840 ■ *Web:* www.hwelectric.com	North Baltimore	OH	45872	419-257-3241	257-3024
Holmes-Wayne Electric Co-op Inc PO Box 112 *TF:* 877-520-1055 ■ *Web:* www.hwecoop.com	Millersburg	OH	44654	330-674-1055	674-1869
Licking Rural Electrification Inc PO Box 4970 *TF:* 800-255-6815	Newark	OH	43058	740-892-2791	892-2429
Logan County Co-op Power & Light Assn Inc 1587 CR 32 N *Web:* www.loganrec.com	Bellefontaine	OH	43311	937-592-4781	592-5746
Lorain-Medina Rural Electric Co-op Inc PO Box 158 *TF:* 800-222-5673 ■ *Web:* www.lmre.org	Wellington	OH	44090	440-647-2133	647-4870
Mid Ohio Energy Co-op Inc PO Box 224 *TF:* 888-382-6732 ■ *Web:* www.midohioenergy.com	Kenton	OH	43326	419-673-7289	673-8388
Midwest Electric Inc PO Box 10 *TF:* 800-962-3830 ■ *Web:* www.midwestrec.com	Saint Marys	OH	45885	419-394-4110	394-8333
North Central Electric Co-op Inc PO Box 475 *TF:* 800-426-3072 ■ *Web:* www.ncelec.org	Attica	OH	44807	419-426-3072	426-1245
North Western Electric Co-op Inc 04125 SR 576 *TF:* 800-647-6932 ■ *Web:* www.nwec.com	Bryan	OH	43506	419-636-5051	636-0194
Paulding-Putman Electric Co-op 910 N Williams St *TF:* 800-686-2357 ■ *Web:* www.ppec.coop	Paulding	OH	45879	419-399-5015	399-3026
Pioneer Rural Electric Co-op Inc 344 W US Rt 36 PO Box 604 *TF:* 800-762-0997 ■ *Web:* www.pioneerec.com	Piqua	OH	45356	937-773-2523	773-7549
South Central Power Co Inc 2780 Coon Path Rd *TF:* 800-282-5064 ■ *Web:* www.southcentralpower.com	Lancaster	OH	43130	740-653-4422	681-4488
Tri-County Rural Electric Co-op Inc PO Box 100	Malinta	OH	43535	419-256-7900	256-6581
Union Rural Electric Co-op Inc 15461 US 36E *TF:* 800-642-1826 ■ *Web:* www.ure.com	Marysville	OH	43040	937-642-1826	644-4239
Washington Electric Co-op Inc PO Box 664 *TF:* 877-594-9324 ■ *Web:* www.weci.org	Marietta	OH	45750	740-373-2141	373-2941

Oklahoma

Name / Address	City	State	Zip	Phone	Fax
Alfalfa Electric Co-op Inc 121 E Main St *TF:* 888-736-3837 ■ *Web:* www.alfalfaelectric.com	Cherokee	OK	73728	580-596-3333	596-2464
Caddo Electric Co-op PO Box 70 *Web:* www.caddoelectric.com	Binger	OK	73009	405-656-2322	656-2327
Canadian Valley Electric Co-op PO Box 751 *Web:* www.canadianvalley.org	Seminole	OK	74868	405-382-3680	382-8808
Central Rural Electric Co-op 3304 S Boomer Rd PO Box 1809 *TF:* 800-375-2884 ■ *Web:* www.centralrec.org	Stillwater	OK	74076	405-372-2884	372-8559
Choctaw Electric Co-op Inc Hwy 93 N PO Box 758 *TF:* 800-780-6486 ■ *Web:* www.choctawelectric.com	Hugo	OK	74743	580-326-6486	326-2492
Cimarron Electric Co-op Hwy 81 N PO Box 299 *TF:* 800-375-4121 ■ *Web:* www.cimarronelectric.com	Kingfisher	OK	73750	405-375-4121	375-4209
Cookson Hills Electric Co-op Inc 1002 E Main St *TF:* 800-328-2368 ■ *Web:* www.cooksonhills.com	Stigler	OK	74462	918-967-4614	967-1200
Cotton Electric Co-op Inc 226 N Broadway *TF:* 800-522-3520 ■ *Web:* www.cottonelectric.com	Walters	OK	73572	580-875-3351	875-3101
East Central Oklahoma Electric Co-op Inc PO Box 1178 *TF:* 800-783-9317 ■ *Web:* www.ecoec.com	Okmulgee	OK	74447	918-756-0833	756-6347
Harmon Electric Assn Inc PO Box 393 *TF:* 800-643-7769 ■ *Web:* www.harmonelectric.com	Hollis	OK	73550	580-688-3342	688-2981
Indian Electric Co-op Inc PO Box 49 *TF:* 800-482-2750 ■ *Web:* www.iecok.com	Cleveland	OK	74020	918-358-2514	358-2518
Kay Electric Co-op PO Box 607 *TF:* 800-535-1079 ■ *Web:* www.kayelectric.com	Blackwell	OK	74631	580-363-1260	363-2308
Kiamichi Electric Co-op Inc PO Box 340 *TF:* 800-888-2731 ■ *Web:* www.kiamichielectric.org	Wilburton	OK	74578	918-465-2338	465-2405
Kiwash Electric Co-op Inc PO Box 100 *TF:* 888-832-3362 ■ *Web:* www.kiwash.coop	Cordell	OK	73632	580-832-3361	832-5174
Lake Region Electric Co-op Inc PO Box 127 *Web:* www.lrecok.coop	Hulbert	OK	74441	918-772-2526	772-2528
Northeast Oklahoma Electric Co-op Inc 443857 E Hwy 60 PO Box 948 *TF:* 800-256-6405 ■ *Web:* www.neelectric.com	Vinita	OK	74301	918-256-6405	256-9380
Northfork Electric Co-op 311 E Madden St PO Box 400 *Web:* www.nfecoop.com	Sayre	OK	73662	580-928-3366	928-3105
Northwestern Electric Co-op Inc 2925 William Ave *TF:* 800-375-7423 ■ *Web:* www.nwecok.coop	Woodward	OK	73802	580-256-7425	254-2858
Oklahoma Electric Co-op 242 24th Ave NW *Web:* www.okcoop.org	Norman	OK	73069	405-321-2024	217-6900
People's Electric Co-op 1130 W Main St *TF:* 877-455-3031 ■ *Web:* www.peoplesec.com	Ada	OK	74821	580-332-3031	436-0229
Red River Valley Rural Electric Assn 1003 Memorial Dr PO Box 220 *TF:* 800-749-3364 ■ *Web:* www.rrvrea.com	Marietta	OK	73448	580-276-3364	276-3828
Rural Electric Co-op Inc PO Box 609 *TF:* 800-259-3504 ■ *Web:* www.rural-electric.com	Lindsay	OK	73052	405-756-3104	756-8957
Southeastern Electric Co-op Inc 1514 E Hwy 70 *Web:* www.se-coop.com	Durant	OK	74702	580-924-2170	924-6402
Southwest Rural Electric Assn 700 N Broadway *TF:* 800-256-7973 ■ *Web:* www.swre.com	Tipton	OK	73570	580-667-5281	667-5284
Tri-County Electric Co-op Inc 302 E Glaydas St PO Box 880 *TF:* 800-522-3315 ■ *Web:* www.tri-countyelectric.coop	Hooker	OK	73945	580-652-2418	652-3151
Verdigris Valley Electric Co-op PO Box 219 *TF:* 800-870-5948 ■ *Web:* www.vvec.com	Collinsville	OK	74021	918-371-2584	371-9873

Oregon

Name / Address	City	State	Zip	Phone	Fax
Blachly-Lane Electric Co-op PO Box 70 *TF:* 800-446-8418 ■ *Web:* www.blachlylane.coop	Junction City	OR	97448	541-688-8711	688-8958
Central Electric Co-op Inc 2098 Hwy 97 N *Web:* www.cec-co.com	Redmond	OR	97756	541-548-2144	548-0366
Columbia Basin Electric Co-op 171 Linden Way PO Box 398 *Web:* www.rapidserve.net/cbec/	Heppner	OR	97836	541-676-9146	676-5159

Oregon (Cont'd)

	City	State	Zip	Phone	Fax
Columbia Power Co-op Assn 311 Wilson St PO Box 97	Monument	OR	97864	541-934-2311	934-2312
Consumers Power Inc 6990 W Hills Rd PO Box 1180 *TF:* 800-872-9036 ■ *Web:* www.cpi.coop	Philomath	OR	97370	541-929-3124	929-8673
Coos-Curry Electric Co-op Inc 43050 Hwy 101 *Web:* www.cooscurryelectric.com	Port Orford	OR	97465	541-332-3931	332-3501
Douglas Electric Co-op Inc PO Box 1327 *TF:* 800-233-2733 ■ *Web:* www.douglaselectric.com	Roseburg	OR	97470	541-673-6616	672-0863
Harney Electric Co-op Inc 1326 Hines Blvd *Web:* www.harneyelectric.org	Burns	OR	97720	541-573-2061	
Lane Electric Co-op PO Box 21410 *Web:* www.laneelectric.com	Eugene	OR	97402	541-484-1151	484-7316
Midstate Electric Co-op Inc PO Box 127 *TF:* 800-722-7219 ■ *Web:* www.midstateelectric.coop	La Pine	OR	97739	541-536-2126	536-1423
Northern Wasco County People's Utility District 2345 River Rd	The Dalles	OR	97058	541-296-2226	298-3320
Oregon Trail Electric Consumers Cooperative 4005 23rd St PO Box 226 *Web:* www.otec.coop	Baker City	OR	97814	541-523-3616	524-2865
Salem Electric PO Box 5588 *Web:* www.salemelectric.com	Salem	OR	97304	503-362-3601	371-2956
Tillamook People's Utility District PO Box 433 *TF:* 800-422-2535 ■ *Web:* www.tpud.org	Tillamook	OR	97141	503-842-2535	842-4161
Umatilla Electric Co-op Assn PO Box 1148 *Web:* www.ueinet.com	Hermiston	OR	97838	541-567-6414	567-8142
Wasco Electric Co-op Inc PO Box 1700 *Web:* www.wascoelectric.com	The Dalles	OR	97058	541-296-2740	296-7781
West Oregon Electric Co-op Inc PO Box 69 *TF:* 800-777-1276 ■ *Web:* www.westoregon.com	Vernonia	OR	97064	503-429-3021	429-8440

Pennsylvania

	City	State	Zip	Phone	Fax
Adams Electric Co-op Inc 1338 Biglerville Rd *TF:* 888-232-6732 ■ *Web:* www.adamsec.com	Gettysburg	PA	17325	717-334-9211	334-3980
Bedford Rural Electric Co-op Inc 8846 Lincoln Hwy *TF:* 800-808-2732 ■ *Web:* www.bedfordrec.com	Bedford	PA	15522	814-623-5101	623-7983
Claverack Rural Electric Co-op Inc RR 2 Box 17 *TF:* 800-326-9799 ■ *Web:* www.claverack.com	Wysox	PA	18854	570-265-2167	265-6019
New Enterprise Rural Electric Co-op Inc PO Box 75 *TF:* 800-270-3177 ■ *Web:* www.newenterpriserec.com	New Enterprise	PA	16664	814-766-3221	766-3319
Northwestern Rural Electric Co-op Assn Inc PO Box 207 **Fax Area Code:* 814 ■ *Web:* www.northwesternrec.com	Cambridge Springs	PA	16403	800-472-7910	734-5205*
REA Energy Co-op Inc 75 Airport Rd *TF:* 800-211-5667 ■ *Web:* www.reaenergy.com	Indiana	PA	15701	724-349-4800	349-7151
Somerset Rural Electric Co-op 223 Industrial Pk Rd PO Box 270 *TF:* 800-443-4255 ■ *Web:* www.somersetrec.com	Somerset	PA	15501	814-445-4106	445-5526
Sullivan County Rural Electric Co-op Inc PO Box 65 *TF:* 800-570-5081 ■ *Web:* www.screc.com	Forksville	PA	18616	570-924-3381	924-3383
Tri-County Rural Electric Co-op Inc PO Box 526 *TF:* 800-343-2559 ■ *Web:* www.tri-countyrec.com	Mansfield	PA	16933	570-662-2175	662-2142
United Electric Co-op Inc PO Box 688 *TF:* 888-581-8969 ■ *Web:* www.unitedpa.com	Du Bois	PA	15801	814-371-8570	371-9278
Valley Rural Electric Co-op Inc 11375 Standing Stone Rd PO Box 477 *TF:* 800-432-0680 ■ *Web:* www.valleyrec.com	Huntingdon	PA	16652	814-643-2650	643-1678
Warren Electric Co-op Inc 320 E Main St *TF:* 800-364-8640 ■ *Web:* www.warrenec.coop	Youngsville	PA	16371	814-563-7548	563-7012

South Carolina

	City	State	Zip	Phone	Fax
Aiken Electric Co-op Inc 2790 Wagener Rd *TF:* 800-922-1262 ■ *Web:* www.aikenelectric.net	Aiken	SC	29802	803-649-6245	641-8310
Berkeley Electric Co-op Inc 414 Hwy 52 N *Web:* www.becsc.com	Moncks Corner	SC	29461	843-761-8200	572-1280
Black River Electric Co-op Inc 1121 N Pike Rd W *Web:* www.blackriver.net	Sumter	SC	29153	803-469-8060	469-8320
Blue Ridge Electric Co-op Inc 734 W Main St *TF:* 800-240-3400 ■ *Web:* www.blueridgenet.com	Pickens	SC	29671	864-878-6326	878-6328
Broad River Electric Co-op Inc 811 Hamrick St *TF:* 866-687-2667 ■ *Web:* www.broadriverelectric.com	Gaffney	SC	29342	864-489-5737	487-7808
Coastal Electric Co-op Inc 2269 Jefferies Hwy *TF:* 877-538-5700 ■ *Web:* www.coastal.coop	Walterboro	SC	29488	843-538-5700	538-5081
Edisto Electric Co-op Inc PO Box 547 *TF:* 800-433-3292 ■ *Web:* www.edistoelectric.com	Bamberg	SC	29003	803-245-5141	245-0188
Fairfield Electric Co-op Inc PO Box 150 *Web:* www.fairelec.com	Winnsboro	SC	29180	803-635-4621	635-9614
Horry Electric Co-op Inc PO Box 119 *Web:* www.horryelectric.com	Conway	SC	29528	843-369-2211	369-6040
Laurens Electric Co-op Inc PO Box 700 *TF:* 800-942-3141 ■ *Web:* www.laurenselectric.com	Laurens	SC	29360	864-682-3141	683-5178
Little River Electric Co-op Inc PO Box 220 *TF:* 800-459-2141 ■ *Web:* www.littleriverelectric.com	Abbeville	SC	29620	864-366-2141	366-4524
Lynches River Electric Co-op Inc PO Box 308 *TF:* 800-922-3486 ■ *Web:* www.lynchesriver.com	Pageland	SC	29728	843-672-6111	672-6118
Marlboro Electric Co-op Inc PO Box 1057 *TF:* 800-922-9174 ■ *Web:* www.mecsc.net	Bennettsville	SC	29512	843-479-3855	479-8990
Mid-Carolina Electric Co-op Inc PO Box 669 *TF Cust Svc:* 888-813-8000 ■ *Web:* www.mcecoop.com	Lexington	SC	29071	803-749-6555	749-6466
Newberry Electric Co-op Inc PO Box 477 *TF:* 800-479-8838 ■ *Web:* www.nec.coop	Newberry	SC	29108	803-276-1121	276-4121
Palmetto Electric Co-op Inc 4063 Grays Hwy PO Box 820 *TF:* 800-922-5551 ■ *Web:* www.palelec.com	Ridgeland	SC	29936	843-726-5551	726-5632
Pee Dee Electric Co-op Inc PO Box 491 *Web:* www.peedeeelectric.com	Darlington	SC	29540	843-665-4070	669-7931
Santee Electric Co-op Inc 424 Sumter Hwy *TF:* 800-922-1604 ■ *Web:* www.santee.org	Kingstree	SC	29556	843-355-6187	355-0609
Tri-County Electric Co-op Inc PO Box 217 *TF:* 877-874-1215	Saint Matthews	SC	29135	803-874-1215	874-3888
York Electric Co-op Inc PO Box 150 *TF:* 800-582-8810 ■ *Web:* www.yorkelectric.net	York	SC	29745	803-684-4247	684-6306

South Dakota

	City	State	Zip	Phone	Fax
Black Hills Electric Co-op Inc 25191 Cooperative Way *TF:* 800-742-0085 ■ *Web:* www.bhec.com	Custer	SD	57730	605-673-4461	673-3147
Bon Homme Yankton Electric Assn 134 S Lidice St *Web:* www.byelectric.com	Tabor	SD	57063	605-463-2507	463-2419
Butte Electric Co-op Inc 109 S Dartmouth Ave *TF:* 800-928-8839 ■ *Web:* www.butteelectric.com	Newell	SD	57760	605-456-2494	456-2496
Cam-Wal Electric Co-op Inc 404 W Scranton St *Web:* www.cam-walnet.com	Selby	SD	57472	605-649-7676	649-7031
Central Electric Co-op 1420 N Main St PO Box 846 *TF:* 800-477-2892 ■ *Web:* www.centralec.com	Mitchell	SD	57301	605-996-7516	996-0869
Charles Mix Electric Assn Inc 440 Lake St *TF:* 800-208-8587 ■ *Web:* www.charles-mix.com	Lake Andes	SD	57356	605-487-7321	487-7868
Cherry-Todd Electric Co-op Inc Hwy 18 PO Box 169 *TF:* 800-856-4417	Mission	SD	57555	605-856-4416	856-4268
Clay-Union Electric Corp 1410 E Cherry St PO Box 317 *TF:* 800-696-2832 ■ *Web:* www.clayunionelectric.coop	Vermillion	SD	57069	605-624-2673	624-5526
Codington-Clark Electric Co-op 3 8th Ave *TF:* 800-463-8938	Watertown	SD	57201	605-886-5848	886-5934
Dakota Energy Co-op Inc 40294 US Hwy 14 PO Box 830 *TF:* 800-353-8591	Huron	SD	57350	605-352-8591	352-8578
Douglas Electric Co-op Inc PO Box 370	Armour	SD	57313	605-724-2323	724-2972
FEM Electric Assn Inc PO Box 468 *Web:* www.femelectric.coop	Ipswich	SD	57451	605-426-6891	426-6791
Grand Electric Co-op Inc 801 Coleman Ave PO Box 39 *TF:* 800-592-1803 ■ *Web:* www.grandelectric.coop	Bison	SD	57620	605-244-5211	244-7288
H-D Electric Co-op Inc PO Box 1007	Clear Lake	SD	57226	605-874-2171	874-8173
Kingsbury Electric Co-op Inc PO Box 126	De Smet	SD	57231	605-854-3522	854-3465
Lacreek Electric Assn Inc PO Box 220 *TF:* 800-655-9324	Martin	SD	57551	605-685-6581	685-6957
Lake Region Electric Assn Inc PO Box 341 *TF:* 800-657-5869 ■ *Web:* www.lakeregion.coop	Webster	SD	57274	605-345-3379	345-4442
McCook Electric Co-op Inc PO Box 250 *TF:* 800-942-3113	Salem	SD	57058	605-425-2661	425-2927
Moreau-Grand Electric Co-op Inc 405 9th St *TF:* 800-952-3158 ■ *Web:* www.mge.coop	Timber Lake	SD	57656	605-865-3511	865-3340
Northern Electric Co-op Inc 39456 133nd St. *TF:* 800-529-0310 ■ *Web:* www.northernelectric.coop	Bath	SD	57427	605-225-0310	225-1684
Oahe Electric Co-op Inc 102 S Cranford St PO Box 216 *TF:* 800-640-6243 ■ *Web:* www.oaheelectric.com	Blunt	SD	57522	605-962-6243	962-6306
Rosebud Electric Co-op Inc 512 Rosebud Ave PO Box 439 *Web:* www.rosebudelectric.com	Gregory	SD	57533	605-835-9624	835-9649
Sioux Valley-Southwestern Electric Co-op Inc 47092 SD Hwy 34 PO Box 216 *TF:* 800-234-1960 ■ *Web:* www.siouxvalleyenergy.com	Colman	SD	57017	605-534-3535	256-1693
Southeastern Electric Co-op Inc 501 S Broadway Ave *TF:* 800-333-2859	Marion	SD	57043	605-648-3619	648-3778
Union County Electric Co-op Inc PO Box 459	Elk Point	SD	57025	605-356-3395	356-3397
West Central Electric Co-op Inc 204 Main St *Web:* www.wcenet.com	Murdo	SD	57559	605-669-2472	669-2358
West River Electric Assn Inc PO Box 412 **Fax Area Code:* 605 ■ *Web:* www.westriver.com	Wall	SD	57790	888-279-2135	342-9587*
Whetstone Valley Electric Co-op Inc PO Box 512 *TF:* 800-568-6631 ■ *Web:* www.whetstoneelectric.com	Milbank	SD	57252	605-432-5331	432-5951

Tennessee

	City	State	Zip	Phone	Fax
Appalachian Electric Co-op 1109 Hill Dr *Web:* www.appalachianelectric.coop	New Market	TN	37820	865-475-2032	475-0888
Caney Fork Electric Co-op Inc 920 Smithville Hwy PO Box 272 *TF:* 888-505-3030 ■ *Web:* www.caneyforkec.com	McMinnville	TN	37110	931-473-3116	473-4939
Chickasaw Electric Co-op 17970 Hwy 64 PO Box 459 *TF:* 866-465-3591	Somerville	TN	38068	901-465-3591	465-5392
Cumberland Electric Membership Corp 1940 Madison St. *Web:* cemc.org	Clarksville	TN	37043	931-645-2481	542-9445
Duck River Electric Membership Corp PO Box 89 *Web:* www.dremc.com	Shelbyville	TN	37162	931-684-4621	685-0013
Fayetteville Electric System 408 W College St *TF:* 800-379-2534 ■ *Web:* www.fayelectric.com	Fayetteville	TN	37334	931-433-1522	433-0646
Forked Deer Electric Co-op Inc PO Box 67	Halls	TN	38040	731-836-7508	836-5070
Fort Loudoun Electric Co-op PO Box 1030 *Web:* www.flec.org	Vonroe	TN	37885	423-442-2487	442-6689
Gibson Electric Membership Corp PO Box 47 *Web:* www.gibsonemc.com	Trenton	TN	38382	731-855-4740	855-3944
Holston Electric Co-op Inc PO Box 190 *Web:* www.holstonelectric.com	Rogersville	TN	37857	423-272-8821	272-6051
La Follette Utilities Board 302 N Tennessee Ave PO Box 1411 *TF:* 800-352-1340 ■ *Web:* www.lub.org	La Follette	TN	37766	423-562-3316	566-0580
Meriwether Lewis Electric Co-op PO Box 240 *Web:* www.mlec.com	Centerville	TN	37033	931-729-3558	729-2267
Middle Tennessee Electric Membership Corp 555 New Salem Rd *Web:* www.mtemc.com	Murfreesboro	TN	37129	615-890-9762	895-3594
Mountain Electric Co-op Inc PO Box 180 *TF:* 888-721-9111 ■ *Web:* www.mountainelectric.com	Mountain City	TN	37683	423-727-1800	727-1822
Pickwick Electric Co-op 530 Mulberry Ave *TF:* 800-372-8258 ■ *Web:* www.pickwick-electric.com	Selmer	TN	38375	731-645-3411	645-7167
Plateau Electric Co-op 16200 Scott Hwy PO Box 4669 *Web:* www.plateauelectric.com	Oneida	TN	37841	423-569-8591	569-5726
Powell Valley Electric Co-op 325 Straight Creek Rd PO Box 1528 *Web:* www.pve.coop	New Tazewell	TN	37824	423-626-5204	626-0711
Sequachee Valley Electric Co-op 512 Cedar Ave PO Box 31 *TF:* 800-923-2203 ■ *Web:* www.svalleyec.com	South Pittsburg	TN	37380	423-837-8605	837-9836
Southwest Tennessee Electric Membership Corp PO Box 989 *TF:* 800-772-0472 ■ *Web:* www.stemc.com	Brownsville	TN	38012	731-772-1322	772-1037
Tennessee Valley Electric Co-op 590 Florence Rd *TF:* 866-925-4916 ■ *Web:* www.tennesseevalleyec.com	Savannah	TN	38372	731-925-4916	925-4919
Tri-County Electric Membership Corp PO Box 40 *TF:* 800-369-2111 ■ *Web:* www.tcemc.org	Lafayette	TN	37083	615-666-2111	688-2141
Upper Cumberland Electric Membership Corp 138 Gordonsville Hwy *TF:* 800-261-2940 ■ *Web:* www.ucemc.com	South Carthage	TN	37030	615-735-2940	735-2603
Volunteer Energy Co-op PO Box 277 *Web:* www.vec.org	Decatur	TN	37322	423-334-5721	334-7003

Texas

	City	State	Zip	Phone	Fax
Bailey County Electric Co-op Inc 305 East Ave B PO Drawer 1013 *TF:* 800-869-7049 ■ *Web:* www.bcecoop.com	Muleshoe	TX	79347	806-272-4504	272-4509

				Phone	Fax
Bandera Electric Co-op Inc 3172 State Hwy 16 N. *TF:* 866-226-3372 ■ *Web:* www.bandera-ec.com	Bandera	TX	78003	830-796-3741	460-3030
Bartlett Electric Co-op Inc PO Box 200 *Web:* www.bartlettec.coop	Bartlett	TX	76511	254-527-3551	527-3221
Belfalls Electric Co-op Inc PO Box 598 *Web:* www.belfalls.com	Rosebud	TX	76570	254-583-7955	583-7954
Big Country Electric Co-op 1010 W South 1st St *TF:* 888-662-2232 ■ *Web:* www.bigcountry.net	Roby	TX	79543	325-776-2244	776-2246
Bluebonnet Electric Co-op Inc 426 E Austin St. *TF:* 800-842-7708 ■ *Web:* www.bluebonnet.com	Giddings	TX	78942	979-542-3151	542-1187
Bowie-Cass Electric Co-op Inc 117 North St. *TF:* 800-794-2919 ■ *Web:* www.bcec.com	Douglassville	TX	75560	903-846-2311	846-2406
Central Texas Electric Co-op Inc 386 Friendship Ln. *TF:* 800-900-2832 ■ *Web:* www.centexec.com	Fredericksburg	TX	78624	830-997-2126	997-9034
Coleman County Electric Co-op Inc 3300 N Hwy 84. *TF:* 800-560-2128 ■ *Web:* www.colemancountyelectcoop.org	Coleman	TX	76834	325-625-2128	625-4600
Comanche Electric Co-op Assn PO Box 729 *TF:* 800-915-2533 ■ *Web:* ceca.coop	Comanche	TX	76442	325-356-2533	356-3038
Concho Valley Electric Co-op Inc 2530 Pulliam St. *Web:* www.cvec.coop	San Angelo	TX	76905	325-655-6957	655-6950
Cooke County Electric Co-op Assn 11799 W US Hwy 82 PO Box 530. *TF:* 800-962-0296 ■ *Web:* www.cceca.com	Muenster	TX	76252	940-759-2211	759-4122
CoServ Electric 7701 S Stemmons Fwy *TF:* 800-274-4014 ■ *Web:* www.coserv.com	Corinth	TX	76210	940-321-4640	270-6640
Deaf Smith Electric Co-op Inc PO Box 753 *TF:* 800-687-8189 ■ *Web:* www.dsec.org	Hereford	TX	79045	806-364-1166	364-5481
Deep East Texas Electric Co-op Inc PO Box 736 *TF:* 800-392-5986 ■ *Web:* www.deepeast.com	San Augustine	TX	75972	936-275-2314	275-2135
DeWitt Electric Co-op Inc PO Box 118 *Web:* www.dewittec.org	Gonzales	TX	78629	361-275-2334	275-5662
Fannin County Electric Co-op Inc PO Drawer 250 *TF:* 800-695-9020 ■ *Web:* www.fanninelectric.com	Bonham	TX	75418	903-583-2117	583-7384
Fayette Electric Co-op Inc PO Box 490 *TF:* 800-874-8290 ■ *Web:* www.fayette.coop	La Grange	TX	78945	979-968-3181	968-6752
Fort Belknap Electric Co-op Inc PO Box 486 *Web:* www.fortbelknapec.com	Olney	TX	76374	940-564-2343	564-3247
Grayson-Collin Electric Co-op Inc PO Box 548 *TF:* 800-967-5235 ■ *Web:* www.gcec.net	Van Alstyne	TX	75495	903-482-7100	482-5906
Greenbelt Electric Co-op Inc PO Box 948 *TF:* 800-527-3082	Wellington	TX	79095	806-447-2536	447-2434
Guadalupe Valley Electric Co-op Inc PO Box 118 *TF:* 800-223-4832 ■ *Web:* www.gvec.org	Gonzales	TX	78629	830-857-1200	857-1205
Hamilton County Electric Co-op Assn PO Box 753 *TF:* 800-595-3401	Hamilton	TX	76531	254-386-3123	386-8757
Hilco Electric Co-op Inc PO Box 127 *TF:* 800-338-6425 ■ *Web:* www.hilco.org	Itasca	TX	76055	254-687-2331	687-2428
Houston County Electric Co-op Inc PO Box 52 *TF:* 800-657-2445	Crockett	TX	75835	936-544-5641	544-4628
J-A-C Electric Co-op Inc PO Box 278 *Web:* www.jacelectric.com	Bluegrove	TX	76352	940-895-3311	895-3321
Jackson Electric Co-op Inc PO Box 1189 *Web:* www.jecec.com	Edna	TX	77957	361-782-7193	782-3252
Jasper-Newton Electric Co-op Inc 812 S Margaret Ave *TF:* 800-231-9340 ■ *Web:* www.jnec.com	Kirbyville	TX	75956	409-423-2241	423-3648
Karnes Electric Co-op Inc PO Box 7 *TF:* 888-807-3952 ■ *Web:* www.karnesec.org	Karnes City	TX	78118	830-780-3952	780-2347
Lamar County Electric Co-op Assn 1485 N Main St *TF:* 800-782-9010 ■ *Web:* www.lamarelectric.com	Paris	TX	75460	903-784-4303	784-7084
Lamb County Electric Co-op Inc 2415 S Phelps Ave. *Web:* www.lcec.coop	Littlefield	TX	79339	806-385-5191	385-5197
Lighthouse Electric Co-op Inc PO Box 600 *TF:* 800-657-7192 ■ *Web:* www.lighthouse.coop	Floydada	TX	79235	806-983-2814	983-2804
Lyntegar Electric Co-op Inc PO Box 970	Tahoka	TX	79373	806-561-4588	561-4724
Magic Valley Electric Co-op Inc PO Box 267 *Fax Area Code: 956 ■ *TF:* 800-880-6832 ■ *Web:* www.magval.com	Mercedes	TX	78570	866-225-5683	565-4182*
McLennan County Electric Co-op Inc PO Box 357 *TF:* 800-840-2957 ■ *Web:* www.mclennanelectric.com	McGregor	TX	76657	254-840-2871	840-4250
Medina Electric Co-op Inc PO Box 370 *TF:* 800-381-3334 ■ *Web:* www.medinaec.org	Hondo	TX	78861	830-741-4384	426-2796
Mid-South Electric Co-op Assn PO Box 970 *TF:* 888-525-6677 ■ *Web:* www.midsouthsynergy.com	Navasota	TX	77868	936-825-5100	825-5166
Navarro County Electric Co-op Inc PO Drawer 616 *TF:* 800-771-9095	Corsicana	TX	75151	903-874-7411	874-8422
Navasota Valley Electric Co-op PO Box 848 *Web:* www.navasotavalley.com	Franklin	TX	77856	979-828-3232	828-5563
North Plains Electric Co-op Inc 14585 Hwy 83 N. *TF:* 800-272-5482 ■ *Web:* www.npec.org	Perryton	TX	79070	806-435-5482	435-7225
Nueces Electric Co-op 709 E Main St *TF:* 800-632-9288 ■ *Web:* www.nueceselectriccoop.com	Robstown	TX	78380	361-387-2581	387-4139
Panola-Harrison Electric Co-op Inc 410 E Houston St *TF:* 800-972-1093	Marshall	TX	75670	903-935-7936	935-3361
Pedernales Electric Co-op Inc 300 Haley Rd PO Box 1 *Fax: Cust Svc ■ *TF:* 888-554-4732 ■ *Web:* www.lcra.org/pec	Johnson City	TX	78636	830-868-7155	868-4767*
Rio Grande Electric Co-op Inc Hwy 90 & State Hwy 131 PO Box 1509 *TF:* 800-749-1509 ■ *Web:* www.rgec.com	Brackettville	TX	78832	830-563-2444	563-2006
Rita Blanca Electric Co-op Inc PO Box 1947 *TF:* 800-299-4506	Dalhart	TX	79022	806-249-4506	249-5620
Rusk County Electric Co-op Inc 3162 State Hwy 43 E *Web:* www.rcelectric.org	Henderson	TX	75653	903-657-4571	657-5377
Sam Houston Electric Co-op Inc 150 E Church St PO Box 1121 *TF:* 800-458-0381 ■ *Web:* www.samhouston.net	Livingston	TX	77351	936-327-5711	328-1244
San Bernard Electric Co-op Inc 309 W Main St *TF:* 800-364-3171 ■ *Web:* www.sbec.org	Bellville	TX	77418	979-865-3171	865-9706
San Patricio Electric Co-op Inc 402 E Sinton St. *TF:* 888-740-2220 ■ *Web:* www.sanpatricioelectric.org	Sinton	TX	78387	361-364-2220	364-3467
South Plains Electric Co-op Inc 4727 S Loop 289 Suite 200 *TF:* 800-658-2655 ■ *Web:* www.spec-lbk.org	Lubbock	TX	79408	806-775-7732	775-7796
Southwest Texas Electric Co-op Inc 101 E Gillis St *TF:* 800-643-3980 ■ *Web:* www.swtec.com	Eldorado	TX	76936	325-853-2544	853-3141
Swisher Electric Co-op Inc 401 SW 2nd St PO Box 67 *TF:* 800-530-4344 ■ *Web:* www.swisherelectric.org	Tulia	TX	79088	806-995-3567	995-2249
Taylor Electric Co-op Inc PO Box 250 *TF:* 800-992-0086 ■ *Web:* www.taylorelectric.com	Merkel	TX	79536	325-928-4715	928-5216
Texas Electric Co-ops Inc 2550 S IH-35 *Web:* www.texas-ec.org	Austin	TX	78704	512-454-0311	
Tri-County Electric Co-op Inc 600 Northwest Pkwy *TF:* 800-367-8232 ■ *Web:* www.tcectexas.com	Azle	TX	76020	817-444-3201	444-3542
Trinity Valley Electric Co-op Inc PO Box 888 *TF:* 800-766-9576 ■ *Web:* www.tvec.net	Kaufman	TX	75142	972-932-2214	932-6466
United Co-op Services PO Box 16 *Web:* www.united-cs.com	Cleburne	TX	76033	817-556-4000	556-4068
Upshur Rural Electric Co-op Corp PO Box 70 *Web:* www.urecc.com	Gilmer	TX	75644	903-843-2536	843-2736
Victoria Electric Co-op Inc PO Box 2178 *Web:* www.vicec.org	Victoria	TX	77902	361-573-2428	573-5753
Wharton County Electric Co-op Inc PO Box 31 *TF:* 800-460-6271 ■ *Web:* www.wcecnet.net	El Campo	TX	77437	979-543-6271	543-6259
Wise Electric Co-op Inc PO Box 269 *TF:* 888-627-9326 ■ *Web:* www.wiseec.com	Decatur	TX	76234	940-627-2167	627-6540
Wood County Electric Co-op Inc PO Box 1827 *TF:* 800-762-2203 ■ *Web:* www.wcec.org	Quitman	TX	75783	903-763-2203	763-5693

Utah

				Phone	Fax
Dixie-Escalante Rural Electric Assn 71 E Hwy 56	Beryl	UT	84714	435-439-5311	439-5352
Flowell Electric Assn Inc 495 N 3200 West	Fillmore	UT	84631	435-743-6214	743-5722
GarKane Energy Inc PO Box 465 *TF:* 800-747-5403 ■ *Web:* www.garkaneenergy.com	Loa	UT	84747	435-836-2795	836-2497
Moon Lake Electric Assn Inc 188 W 200 North *Web:* mleainc.com/index.html	Roosevelt	UT	84066	435-722-2448	722-3752

Vermont

				Phone	Fax
Hardwick Electric Dept 123 N Main St PO Box 516	Hardwick	VT	05843	802-472-5201	472-6769
Vermont Electric Co-op Inc 42 Wescom Rd *TF:* 800-832-2667 ■ *Web:* www.vtcoop.com	Johnson	VT	05656	802-635-2331	635-7645
Washington Electric Co-op Inc PO Box 8 *TF:* 800-932-5245 ■ *Web:* www.washingtonelectric.coop	East Montpelier	VT	05651	802-223-5245	223-6780

Virginia

				Phone	Fax
A & N Electric Co-op 21275 Cooperative Way *Web:* www.anecop.com	Tasley	VA	23441	757-787-9750	787-9780
BARC Electric Co-op 100 High St PO Box 264 *TF:* 800-846-2272 ■ *Web:* www.barcelectric.com	Millboro	VA	24460	540-997-9124	997-9011
Central Virginia Electric Co-op 800 Cooperative Way PO Box 247 *TF:* 800-367-2832 ■ *Web:* www.forcvec.com	Lovingston	VA	22949	434-263-8336	263-8339
Community Electric Co-op 52 W Windsor Blvd *Web:* www.comelec.coop	Windsor	VA	23487	757-242-6181	242-3923
Craig-Botetourt Electric Co-op PO Box 265 *TF:* 800-760-2232	New Castle	VA	24127	540-864-5121	864-5461
Mecklenburg Electric Co-op PO Box 2451 *TF:* 800-989-4161 ■ *Web:* www.meckelec.org	Chase City	VA	23924	434-372-6100	372-6102
Northern Neck Electric Co-op Inc 85 Saint Johns St PO Box 288 *TF:* 800-243-2860 ■ *Web:* www.nnec.com	Warsaw	VA	22572	804-333-3621	333-5581
Northern Virginia Electric Co-op PO Box 2710 *TF:* 888-335-0500 ■ *Web:* www.novec.com	Manassas	VA	22110	703-335-0500	392-1546
Prince George Electric Co-op 7103 General Mahone Hwy PO Box 168 *Web:* www.pgec.coop	Waverly	VA	23890	804-834-2424	834-3544
Rappahannock Electric Co-op 247 Industrial Ct *Fax: Cust Svc ■ *TF:* 800-552-3904 ■ *Web:* www.rappelec.com	Fredericksburg	VA	22408	540-898-8500	891-5988*
Shenandoah Valley Electric Co-op PO Box 236 *TF:* 800-234-7832 ■ *Web:* www.shenvalleyelectric.com	Mount Crawford	VA	22841	540-434-2200	434-2227
Southside Electric Co-op Inc 2000 W Virgina Ave *TF:* 800-552-2118 ■ *Web:* www.sec.coop	Crewe	VA	23930	434-645-7721	645-1147

Washington

				Phone	Fax
Benton Rural Electric Assn 402 7th St *TF:* 800-221-6987 ■ *Web:* www.bentonrea.org	Prosser	WA	99350	509-786-2913	786-2231
Big Bend Electric Co-op Inc PO Box 348 *Web:* www.bbec.org	Ritzville	WA	99169	509-659-1700	659-1404
Columbia Rural Electric Assn Inc 115 E Main St *TF:* 800-642-1231 ■ *Web:* www.columbiarea.com	Dayton	WA	99328	509-382-2578	382-2736
Elmhurst Mutual Power & Light Co 120 132nd St S. *Web:* www.elmhurstmutual.org	Tacoma	WA	98444	253-531-4646	531-8969
Inland Power & Light Co Inc PO Box 4429 *TF:* 800-747-7151 ■ *Web:* www.inlandpower.com	Spokane	WA	99220	509-747-7151	747-7987
Nespelem Valley Electric Co-op Inc PO Box 31 *Web:* www.nvec.org	Nespelem	WA	99155	509-634-4571	634-8138
OHOP Mutual Light Co 34014 Mountain Hwy E	Eatonville	WA	98328	253-847-4364	847-2877
Okanogan County Electric Co-op PO Box 69	Winthrop	WA	98862	509-996-2228	996-2241
Orcas Power & Light Co-op 183 Mt Baker Rd *Web:* www.opalco.com	Eastsound	WA	98245	360-376-3500	376-3505
Parkland Light & Water Co 12918 Park Ave S PO Box 44426 *Web:* www.plw.coop	Tacoma	WA	98444	253-531-5666	531-2684
Peninsula Light Co PO Box 78 *TF:* 888-809-8021 ■ *Web:* www.penlight.org	Gig Harbor	WA	98335	253-857-5950	857-3100
Public Utility District #1 of Ferry County 686 S Clark Ave PO Box 1039 *Web:* www.fcpud.com	Republic	WA	99166	509-775-3325	775-3326
Public Utility District #1 of Kittitas County 1400 Vantage Hwy	Ellensburg	WA	98926	509-925-3164	933-7190
Tanner Electric Co PO Box 1426 *TF:* 800-472-0208	North Bend	WA	98045	425-888-0623	888-5688

West Virginia

				Phone	Fax
Harrison Rural Electrification Assn Inc Rt 6 Box 502 *TF:* 800-540-4732 ■ *Web:* www.harrisonrea.com	Clarksburg	WV	26301	304-624-6365	624-6366

Wisconsin

				Phone	Fax
Adams-Columbia Electric Co-op 401 E Lake St. *TF:* 800-831-8629	Friendship	WI	53934	608-339-3346	339-7756
Barron Electric Co-op 1434 State Hwy 25 W PO Box 40 *TF:* 800-322-1008 ■ *Web:* www.barronelectric.com	Barron	WI	54812	715-537-3171	537-5146
Bayfield Electric Co-op Inc 68325 Lee St PO Box 68 *Web:* www.bayfieldelectric.com	Iron River	WI	54847	715-372-4287	372-4318
Chippewa Valley Electric Co-op 317 S 8th St. *TF:* 800-300-6800 ■ *Web:* www.cvecoop.com	Cornell	WI	54732	715-239-6800	239-6160

Wisconsin (Cont'd)

	City	State	Zip	Phone	Fax
Clark Electric Co-op 124 N Main St PO Box 190 *TF:* 800-272-6188 ■ *Web:* www.cecoop.com	Greenwood	WI	54437	715-267-6188	267-7355
Dunn Energy Co-op PO Box 220 *TF:* 800-924-0630 ■ *Web:* www.dunnenergy.com	Menomonie	WI	54751	715-232-6240	232-6244
Eau Claire Electric Co-op PO Box 368 *TF:* 800-927-5090 ■ *Web:* www.ecec.com	Fall Creek	WI	54742	715-832-1603	832-2055
Jackson Electric Co-op PO Box 546 *TF:* 800-370-4607 ■ *Web:* www.jackelec.com	Black River Falls	WI	54615	715-284-5385	284-7143
Jump River Electric Co-op PO Box 99 *Web:* www.jrec.com	Ladysmith	WI	54848	715-532-5524	532-3065
Oakdale Electric Co-op 489 N Oakwood St PO Box 128 *TF:* 800-241-2468 ■ *Web:* www.oakdalerec.com	Oakdale	WI	54649	608-372-4131	372-5173
Oconto Electric Co-op 7478 Rea Rd PO Box 168 *TF:* 800-472-8410 ■ *Web:* www.ocontoelectric.com	Oconto Falls	WI	54154	920-846-2816	846-4327
Pierce-Pepin Electric Co-op 7725 US Hwy 10 *TF:* 800-924-2133 ■ *Web:* www.pp-rec.com	Ellsworth	WI	54011	715-273-4355	273-4476
Polk-Burnett Electric Co-op 1001 SR 35 *TF:* 800-421-0283 ■ *Web:* www.polk-burnett.org	Centuria	WI	54824	715-646-2191	646-2404
Price Electric Co-op Inc 508 N Lake Ave *TF:* 800-884-0881 ■ *Web:* www.price-electric.com	Phillips	WI	54555	715-339-2155	339-2921
Richland Electric Co-op 1027 N Jefferson St *Web:* www.richec.com	Richland Center	WI	53581	608-647-3173	647-4265
Riverland Energy Co-op 625 W Main St PO Box 277 *TF:* 800-411-9115 ■ *Web:* www.riverlandenergy.com	Arcadia	WI	54612	608-323-3381	323-3014
Rock County Electric Co-op Assn 2815 Kennedy Rd PO Box 1758 *TF:* 888-236-0665 ■ *Web:* www.rceca.com	Janesville	WI	53547	608-752-4550	752-6620
Saint Croix Electric Co-op 1925 Ridgeway St *TF:* 800-924-3407 ■ *Web:* www.scecnet.net	Hammond	WI	54015	715-796-7000	796-7070
Scenic Rivers Energy Co-op 231 N Sheridan St *TF:* 800-236-2141 ■ *Web:* www.scenicriversenergy.com	Lancaster	WI	53813	608-723-2121	723-2688
Taylor Electric Co-op N1831 State Hwy 13 *Web:* www.taylorelectric.org	Medford	WI	54451	715-678-2411	678-2555
Vernon Electric Co-op 110 N Main St *TF:* 800-447-5051 ■ *Web:* www.vernonelectric.org	Westby	WI	54667	608-634-3121	634-7452
Washington Island Electric Co-op Inc 1157 Main Rd	Washington Island	WI	54246	920-847-2541	847-3021

Wyoming

	City	State	Zip	Phone	Fax
Big Horn Rural Electric Co-op 208 S 5th St PO Box 270 *TF:* 800-564-2419	Basin	WY	82410	307-568-2419	568-2402
Bridger Valley Electric Assn Inc 40014 Business Loop 1-80 PO Box 399 *TF:* 800-276-3481 ■ *Web:* bvea.net	Mountain View	WY	82939	307-786-2800	786-4362
Carbon Power & Light Inc 110 E Spring St *TF:* 800-359-0249 ■ *Web:* www.carbonpower.com	Saratoga	WY	82331	307-326-5206	326-5934
Garland Light & Power Co 755 Hwy 14A	Powell	WY	82435	307-754-2881	754-5320
High Plains Power Inc PO Box 713 *TF:* 800-445-0613 ■ *Web:* www.highplainspower.org	Riverton	WY	82501	307-856-9426	856-4207
High West Energy Inc PO Box 519 *TF:* 888-834-1657 ■ *Web:* www.highwestenergy.com	Pine Bluffs	WY	82082	307-245-3261	245-9292
Lower Valley Energy PO Box 188 *TF:* 800-882-5875 ■ *Web:* www.lvenergy.com	Afton	WY	83110	307-885-3175	885-5787
Niobrara Electric Assn Inc PO Box 697 *TF:* 800-322-0544 ■ *Web:* www.tristategt.org/nb	Lusk	WY	82225	307-334-3221	334-2620
Powder River Energy Corp 221 Main St *TF:* 800-442-3630 ■ *Web:* www.precorp.org	Sundance	WY	82729	307-283-3531	283-3536
Wheatland Rural Electric Assn 2154 South Rd PO Box 1209 *TF:* 800-344-3351 ■ *Web:* www.wheatlandrea.com	Wheatland	WY	82201	307-322-2125	322-5340
Wyrulec Co PO Box 359 *TF:* 800-628-5266	Lingle	WY	82223	307-837-2225	837-2115

249 ELECTRICAL & ELECTRONIC EQUIPMENT & PARTS - WHOL

	City	State	Zip	Phone	Fax
ACF Components & Fasteners Inc 31012 Huntwood Ave *TF Cust Svc:* 800-227-2901 ■ *Web:* www.acfcom.com	Hayward	CA	94544	510-487-2100	471-7018
ACI Electronics Inc 125 Michael Dr Suite 105 *TF:* 800-645-4955 ■ *Web:* www.aci-elec.com	Syosset	NY	11791	516-730-8182	921-5023
ADDvantage Technologies Group Inc 1221 E Houston *AMEX: AEY* ■ *Web:* www.addvantagetech.com	Broken Arrow	OK	74012	918-251-9121	251-0792
Advanced MP Technology 1010 Calle Sombra *TF:* 800-492-3113 ■ *Web:* www.advancedmp.com	San Clemente	CA	92673	949-492-3113	492-6480
AE Petsche Co Inc 2112 W Division St *TF:* 800-777-9280 ■ *Web:* www.aepetsche.com	Arlington	TX	76012	817-461-9473	277-2887
Airtechnics Inc 3851 N Webb Rd *TF:* 800-544-4070 ■ *Web:* www.airtechnics.com	Wichita	KS	67226	316-315-1200	315-1298
All American Semiconductor Inc 16115 NW 52nd Ave *NASDAQ: SEMI* ■ **Fax:* Hum Res ■ *TF:* 800-762-2095 ■ *Web:* www.allamerican.com	Miami	FL	33014	305-621-8282	621-3121*
Allied Electronics Inc 7410 Pebble Dr *Web:* www.alliedelec.com	Fort Worth	TX	76118	817-595-3500	595-6404
Alltel Communications Products Inc 13560 Morris Rd *TF:* 800-501-1754 ■ *Web:* www.alltelcpi.com	Alpharetta	GA	30004	678-351-4000	351-8400
America II Corp Inc 2600 118th Ave N *TF:* 800-767-2637 ■ *Web:* www.americaii.com	Saint Petersburg	FL	33716	727-573-0900	572-9696
America II Electronics Inc 2600 118th Ave N *TF:* 800-767-2637 ■ *Web:* www.americaii.com	Saint Petersburg	FL	33716	727-573-0900	572-9696
American Electric Supply Inc 1872 W Pomona Rd *TF:* 800-877-8346 ■ *Web:* www.amelect.com	Corona	CA	92880	951-734-7910	737-9906
American Technology Corp 15378 Ave of Science Suite 100 *NASDAQ: ATCO* ■ *Web:* www.atcsd.com	San Diego	CA	92128	858-676-1112	676-1120
Anixter International Inc 2301 Patriot Blvd *NYSE: AXE* ■ *TF:* 800-264-9837 ■ *Web:* www.anixter.com	Glenview	IL	60025	224-521-8000	323-8166
Argo International Corp 140 Franklin St *TF:* 877-274-6468 ■ *Web:* www.argointl.com	New York	NY	10013	212-431-1700	226-9072
Arrow Electronics Inc 60 Marcus Dr *NYSE: ARW* ■ *TF Sales:* 800-777-2776 ■ *Web:* www.arrow.com	Melville	NY	11747	631-847-2000	847-2222
Astrex Inc 205 Express St *TF:* 800-633-6360 ■ *Web:* www.astrex.net	Plainview	NY	11803	516-433-1700	433-1796
Avnet Inc 2211 S 47th St *NYSE: AVT* ■ *TF:* 888-822-8638 ■ *Web:* www.avnet.com	Phoenix	AZ	85034	480-643-2000	
Avnet Memec 2211 S 47th St **Fax Area Code:* 858 ■ *TF:* 800-408-8353 ■ *Web:* www.em.avnet.com	Phoenix	AZ	85034	800-332-8638	314-8850*
Barnett Inc 801 W Bay St **Fax:* Mktg ■ *TF:* 800-288-2000 ■ *Web:* www.e-barnett.com	Jacksonville	FL	32204	904-384-6530	388-2723*
Beacon Electric Supply 9630 Chesapeake Dr *Web:* www.beaconelectric.com	San Diego	CA	92123	858-279-9770	279-9908
Bearcom Inc 4009 Distribution Dr Suite 200 *TF Sales:* 800-527-1670 ■ *Web:* www.bearcom.com	Garland	TX	75041	214-340-8876	
Becker Electric Supply Inc 1341 E 4th St *TF:* 800-762-9515 ■ *Web:* www.beckerelectric.com	Dayton	OH	45402	937-226-1341	226-1790
Bell Microproducts Inc 1941 Ringwood Ave *NASDAQ: BELM* ■ *TF:* 800-800-1513 ■ *Web:* www.bellmicro.com	San Jose	CA	95131	408-451-9400	451-1600
Benfield Electric Supply Co Inc 25 Lafayette Ave *Web:* www.benfieldelectric.com	North White Plains	NY	10603	914-948-6660	993-0558
Beyond Components 5 Carl Thompson Rd *Web:* www.beyondcomponents.com	Westford	MA	01886	978-392-9191	392-1199
Billows Electric Supply Co PO Box 828404 *Web:* www.billows.com	Philadelphia	PA	19182	215-332-9700	338-8320
Bisco Industries Inc 1500 N Lakeview Ave *TF:* 800-323-1232 ■ *Web:* www.biscoind.com	Anaheim	CA	92807	714-693-3670	693-9470
Blackburn Don & Co Inc 13335 Farmington Rd *TF:* 800-448-0528 ■ *Web:* www.donblackburn.com	Livonia	MI	48150	734-261-9100	261-7173
Boggis-Johnson Electric Co 2900 N 112th St PO Box 26068 *TF:* 800-333-7650 ■ *Web:* www.boggisjohnson.com	Milwaukee	WI	53226	414-475-6900	475-6607
Border States Electric Supply 105 25th St N *TF:* 800-676-5833 ■ *Web:* www.bseweb.com	Fargo	ND	58102	701-293-5834	237-9488
Braid Electric Co Inc 299 Cowan St *TF:* 800-342-1115 ■ *Web:* www.braidelectric.com	Nashville	TN	37213	615-242-6511	242-9684
Brightpoint Inc 501 Airtech Pkwy *NASDAQ: CELL* ■ *TF:* 800-952-2355 ■ *Web:* www.brightpoint.com	Plainfield	IN	46168	317-707-2355	707-2329
Brightstar Corp 2010 NW 84th Ave *TF:* 800-381-8402 ■ *Web:* www.brightstarcorp.com	Miami	FL	33122	305-477-8676	477-9072
Broken Arrow Electric Supply Inc 2350 W Vancouver *TF:* 877-999-2237 ■ *Web:* www.baes.com	Broken Arrow	OK	74012	918-258-3581	251-3799
Buckles-Smith 801 Savaker Ave *TF:* 800-833-7362 ■ *Web:* www.buckles-smith.com	San Jose	CA	95126	408-280-7777	280-0729
Butler Supply Inc 965 Horan Dr *Web:* www.butlersupply.com	Fenton	MO	63026	636-349-9000	349-7877
Cabletel Communications Corp 55 Valleywood Dr *TF:* 800-268-3231 ■ *Web:* www.cabletelgroup.com	Markham	ON	L3R5L9	905-475-1030	475-9571
Cain Electrical Supply Corp 204 Johnson St PO Box 2158 *TF:* 800-749-8421 ■ *Web:* www.cainelectrical.com	Big Spring	TX	79721	432-263-8421	267-6879
California Eastern Laboratories Inc 4590 Patrick Henry Dr *Web:* www.cel.com	Santa Clara	CA	95054	408-988-3500	988-0279
Capital Electric Supply Co 7310 W Roosevelt Suite 2 *Web:* www.capitalelectricsupplyco.com	Phoenix	AZ	85043	623-936-6789	936-6262
Cardello Electric Supply Co 701 N Point Dr *TF:* 800-333-0454 ■ *Web:* www.cardello.com	Pittsburgh	PA	15233	412-322-8031	322-9121
Carlton Bates Co 3600 W 69th St *TF:* 800-482-9313 ■ *Web:* www.carlton-bates.com	Little Rock	AR	72209	501-562-9100	562-4931
Cell-Tel Government Systems Inc 8226-B Phillips Hwy Suite 290 *TF:* 800-737-7545 ■ *Web:* www.cell-tel.com	Jacksonville	FL	32256	904-363-1111	363-0032
CellStar Corp 601 S Royal Ln *NASDAQ: CLST* ■ **Fax:* Hum Res ■ *TF:* 800-723-9070 ■ *Web:* www.cellstar.com	Coppell	TX	75019	972-462-2700	462-3520*
Cellular & Wireless Wholesale Corp 8240 NW 30th Terr *TF:* 888-918-4299	Miami	FL	33122	305-436-8999	436-8819
Central Wholesale Electrical Distributors Inc 6611 Preston Ave Suite E *TF:* 800-834-8122 ■ *Web:* www.cwed.com	Livermore	CA	94551	925-245-9310	245-9292
Century Fasteners Corp 50-20 Ireland St *TF:* 800-221-0769 ■ *Web:* www.centuryfasteners.com	Elmhurst	NY	11373	718-446-5000	426-8119
City Lighting Products Co 4307 W Papin St *TF:* 800-888-2572 ■ *Web:* www.citylighting.com	Saint Louis	MO	63109	314-534-1090	534-1314
Clifford of Vermont 1453 VT Route 107 **Fax:* Cust Svc ■ *TF:* 800-451-4381 ■ *Web:* www.cliffordvt.com	Royalton	VT	05068	802-234-9921	234-5006*
CLS Inc 270 Locust St *TF:* 800-842-8078 ■ *Web:* www.cls.com	Hartford	CT	06114	860-549-1230	527-3012
Codale Electric Supply Inc 3150 S 900 West *TF:* 800-300-6634 ■ *Web:* www.codale.com	Salt Lake City	UT	84119	801-975-7300	977-8833
Coghlin Electric/Electronics PO Box 5100 *TF:* 800-343-1201 ■ *Web:* www.ceewesco.com	Westborough	MA	01581	508-870-5000	870-5150
Communications Supply Corp 200 E Lies Rd *TF:* 800-468-2121 ■ *Web:* www.gocsc.com	Carol Stream	IL	60188	630-221-6400	221-6420
Comtel Corp 39830 Grand River Ave Suite B1-A *Web:* www.comtel.com	Novi	MI	48375	248-888-4730	888-4743
Consolidated Electrical Distributors Inc 31356 Via Colinas Suite 107 *Web:* www.ced-aec.com	Westlake Village	CA	91362	818-991-9000	991-6858
Cooper Electric Supply Co 70 Apple St *Web:* www.cooper-electric.com	Tinton Falls	NJ	07724	732-747-2233	576-8770
Corporate Telephone 56 Roland St *TF:* 800-274-1211 ■ *Web:* www.corporatetelephone.com	Boston	MA	02129	617-625-1200	625-1201
Crescent Electric Supply Co 7750 Dunleith Dr *Web:* www.cesco.com	East Dubuque	IL	61025	815-747-3145	747-7720
Cross Automation Inc 2001 Oak Pkwy PO Box 1026 *TF:* 800-866-4568 ■ *Web:* www.cross-automation.com	Belmont	NC	28012	704-523-2222	523-6500
Crum Electric Supply Co 1165 English Ave *TF:* 800-726-2239 ■ *Web:* www.crum.com	Casper	WY	82601	307-266-1278	577-1312
Dakota Supply Group 2601 3rd Ave N *TF:* 800-437-4702 ■ *Web:* www.dakotasupplygroup.com	Fargo	ND	58102	701-237-9440	237-6504
Dalis HL Inc 35-35 24th St *TF:* 800-453-2547 ■ *Web:* www.hldalis.com	Long Island City	NY	11106	718-361-1100	392-7654
Dee Electronics Inc 2500 16th Ave SW *TF:* 800-747-3331 ■ *Web:* www.dee-inc.com	Cedar Rapids	IA	52404	319-365-7551	365-8506
Dependable Component Supply Corp 1003 E Newport Ctr Dr *TF:* 800-336-7100 ■ *Web:* www.dependonus.com	Deerfield Beach	FL	33442	954-283-5800	283-5801
Desco Inc 1205 Lincolnton Rd *TF:* 800-222-2140 ■ *Web:* www.descoinc.com	Salisbury	NC	28145	704-633-6331	637-6966
DH Supply Co 6915 NE Expy *Web:* www.dhsupply.com	Doraville	GA	30340	770-409-0500	409-0403
Digi-Key Corp 701 Brooks Ave S *TF:* 800-344-4539 ■ *Web:* www.digikey.com	Thief River Falls	MN	56701	218-681-6674	681-3380
Diversified Supply Inc 210 N Holland Pk Ave *Web:* www.diversifiedsupply.com	Chattanooga	TN	37406	423-698-1551	698-1554
Dominion Electric Supply Co Inc 5053 Lee Hwy *TF:* 800-525-5006 ■ *Web:* www.dominionelectric.com	Arlington	VA	22207	703-536-4400	241-9047
Don Blackburn & Co Inc 13335 Farmington Rd *TF:* 800-448-0528 ■ *Web:* www.donblackburn.com	Livonia	MI	48150	734-261-9100	261-7173
Dow Electronics Inc 8603 Adamo Dr *TF:* 800-627-2900 ■ *Web:* www.dowelectronics.com	Tampa	FL	33619	813-626-5195	628-4990
E Sam Jones Distributor Inc 4898 S Atlanta Rd *TF:* 800-624-9849 ■ *Web:* www.esamjones.com	Smyrna	GA	30080	404-351-3250	351-4140
Eagle Electric Supply Co Inc 135 Will Dr *TF:* 800-462-5010 ■ *Web:* www.eagleweb.com	Canton	MA	02021	781-302-2000	302-2176
Eck Supply Co 1405 W Main St *Web:* www.ecksupply.com	Richmond	VA	23220	804-359-5781	358-1353
Edson Electric Supply Inc 2902 S 44th St *Web:* www.edsonelectric.com	Phoenix	AZ	85040	602-426-1377	426-1388
EIS Inc 2018 Powers Ferry Rd Suite 500 *Web:* www.eis-inc.com	Atlanta	GA	30339	678-255-3600	255-3725

Company	City	State	Zip	Phone	Fax
EIS Inc 13200 10th Ave N Suite E *TF:* 800-328-4662	Plymouth	MN	55441	763-513-7300	513-7351
Electric Fixture & Supply Co 1006 N 20th St *TF:* 800-642-9312 ■ *Web:* www.electricfixture.com	Omaha	NE	68102	402-342-3050	342-6874
Electric Supply & Equipment Co 1812 E Wendover Ave *TF:* 800-632-0268 ■ *Web:* www.ese-co.com	Greensboro	NC	27405	336-272-4123	274-4632
Electric Supply of Tampa Inc 4407 N Manhattan Ave *TF:* 800-678-1894 ■ *Web:* www.electricsupplyinc.com	Tampa	FL	33614	813-872-1894	874-1680
Electrical Wholesale Supply Co of Utah 158 E 4500 South *Web:* www.ewsutah.com	Salt Lake City	UT	84107	801-268-2555	268-3406
Electro Brand Inc 1127 S Mannheim Rd Suite 305 **Fax Area Code:* 708 ■ *TF:* 800-982-3954 ■ *Web:* www.electrobrand.com	Westchester	IL	60154	773-261-5000	338-4441*
Electro-Matic Products Inc 23409 Industrial Park Ct *TF:* 888-879-1088 ■ *Web:* www.electro-matic.com	Farmington Hills	MI	48335	248-478-1182	478-1472
Electro Sonic Inc 1100 Gordon Baker Rd *Web:* www.e-sonic.com	Willowdale	ON	M2H3B3	416-494-1666	496-3030
Elliott Electric Supply Co 2526 N Stallings Dr PO Box 630610 *TF:* 877-777-0242 ■ *Web:* www.elliottelectric.com	Nacogdoches	TX	75963	936-569-1184	569-1836
Englewood Electrical Supply 716 Belvedere Dr *TF:* 800-589-8886	Kokomo	IN	46901	765-452-4087	454-5138
Eoff Electric Co Inc 2950 22nd St SE *TF:* 877-371-3633	Salem	OR	97302	503-371-3633	585-2286
Equity Utility Service Co Inc 1060-D Triad Ct *TF:* 800-282-9695 ■ *Web:* action97.w1.com	Marietta	GA	30062	770-422-1005	427-8455
Eric Electronics 2220 Lundy Ave *TF:* 800-406-3742 ■ *Web:* www.ericnet.com	San Jose	CA	95131	408-432-1111	433-0570
ESCO LLC 2575 E Bayshore Rd **Fax Area Code:* 800 ■ *TF:* 800-622-3726 ■ *Web:* www.escollc.com	Palo Alto	CA	94303	650-856-9900	856-2006*
Essco Wholesale Electric Inc 175 E Corporate Pl *TF:* 888-812-3698 ■ *Web:* www.esscous.com	Chandler	AZ	85225	480-497-8000	497-9100
Essex Brownell Inc 84 Executive Ave *TF:* 800-228-8026	Edison	NJ	08817	732-287-3355	287-6819
Facility Solutions Group 4401 Westgate Blvd Suite 310 **Fax Area Code:* 512 ■ *TF:* 800-854-6465 ■ *Web:* www.fsgconnect.com	Austin	TX	78704	800-854-6465	440-0399*
Farmstead Telephone Group Inc 22 Prestige Park Cir *AMEX:* FTG ■ *TF:* 800-243-0234 ■ *Web:* www.farmstead.com	East Hartford	CT	06108	860-282-0010	610-6001
FD Lawrence Electric Co Inc 3450 Beekman St *TF Cust Svc:* 800-582-4490 ■ *Web:* www.fdlawrence.com	Cincinnati	OH	45223	513-542-1100	542-2422
Feldman Brothers Electrical Supply Co 26 Maryland Ave *Web:* www.feldmanbros.com	Paterson	NJ	07503	973-742-7329	742-2220
Fiber Instruments Sales Inc 161 Clear Rd *TF Sales:* 800-500-0347 ■ *Web:* www.fiberinstrumentsales.com	Oriskany	NY	13424	315-736-2206	736-2285
Fidelitone Inc 1260 Karl Ct *TF Cust Svc:* 800-342-2112 ■ *Web:* www.fidelitone.com	Wauconda	IL	60084	847-487-3300	487-2681
Fitzpatrick Electric Supply Co 1699 Wierengo Dr *TF:* 800-968-6621 ■ *Web:* www.fitzpatrick.com	Muskegon	MI	49442	231-723-6621	773-5523
Friedman Electric Supply 1321 Wyoming Ave *TF:* 800-545-5517 ■ *Web:* www.friedmanelectric.com	Exeter	PA	18643	570-654-3371	655-6194
Fromm Electric Supply Corp 2101 Centre Ave PO Box 15147 *TF:* 800-360-4441 ■ *Web:* www.frommelectric.com	Reading	PA	19612	610-374-4441	374-8756
FSG Lighting 4401 Westgate Blvd Suite 310 *TF:* 800-854-6465 ■ *Web:* www.fsgconnect.com/c	Austin	TX	78745	512-440-7985	440-0399
Future Electronics 237 Hymus Blvd *TF:* 800-388-8731 ■ *Web:* www.futureelectronics.com	Pointe-Claire	QC	H9R5C7	514-694-7710	695-3707
GE Supply 2 Corporate Dr PO Box 861 *Web:* www.gesupply.com	Shelton	CT	06484	203-944-3100	944-3348
Grainger WW Inc 100 Grainger Pkwy *NYSE:* GWW ■ *TF:* 888-361-8649 ■ *Web:* www.grainger.com	Lake Forest	IL	60045	847-535-1000	
Graybar Electric Co Inc 34 N Meramec Ave *TF:* 800-472-9227 ■ *Web:* www.graybar.com	Saint Louis	MO	63105	314-573-9200	573-9216
H Poll Electric Co 8 N Saint Clair St *TF:* 800-548-0196 ■ *Web:* www.hpoll.com	Toledo	OH	43697	419-255-1660	255-2915
Hagemeyer North America 12117 Insurance Way **Fax:* Cust Svc ■ *TF:* 800-638-3552 ■ *Web:* www.hagemeyer.com	Hagerstown	MD	21740	301-733-1212	790-2423*
Hammond Electronics Inc 1230 W Central Blvd *TF Sales:* 800-929-3672 ■ *Web:* www.hammondelec.com	Orlando	FL	32805	407-849-6060	872-0826
Hardware Specialty Co Inc 4875 36th St *TF:* 800-800-9269 ■ *Web:* www.hardwarespecialty.com	Long Island City	NY	11101	718-361-9393	706-0238
Harris Electric Supply Co Inc 656 Wedgewood Ave *TF:* 800-342-1479 ■ *Web:* www.harriselectricsupply.com	Nashville	TN	37203	615-255-4161	242-5683
Hartford Electric Supply Co (HESCO) 571 New Park Ave PO Box 331010 *TF:* 800-969-5444 ■ *Web:* www.hesconet.com	West Hartford	CT	06133	860-236-6363	236-0233
Heilind Electronics Inc 58 Jonspin Rd *TF:* 800-400-7041 ■ *Web:* www.heilind.com	Wilmington	MA	01887	978-657-4870	658-0278
HESCO (Hartford Electric Supply Co) 571 New Park Ave PO Box 331010 *TF:* 800-969-5444 ■ *Web:* www.hesconet.com	West Hartford	CT	06133	860-236-6363	236-0233
Hite Co PO Box 1754 *Web:* www.hiteco.com	Altoona	PA	16603	814-944-6121	944-3052
HL Dalis Inc 35-35 24th St *TF:* 800-453-2547 ■ *Web:* www.hldalis.com	Long Island City	NY	11106	718-361-1100	392-7654
Horizon Solutions Corp 4 Access Rd *TF:* 800-345-4621 ■ *Web:* www.hs-e.com	Albany	NY	12205	518-452-6904	452-6911
Houston Wire & Cable Co 10201 N Loop E *TF:* 800-468-9473 ■ *Web:* www.houwire.com	Houston	TX	77029	713-609-2100	609-2101
Hutton Communications Inc 2520 Marsh Ln **Fax Area Code:* 877 ■ *TF:* 800-435-9313 ■ *Web:* www.huttononline.com	Carrollton	TX	75006	972-417-0250	762-8274*
IBS Electronics Inc 3506 Lake Center Dr Unit D *TF:* 800-527-2888 ■ *Web:* www.ibselectronics.com	Santa Ana	CA	92704	714-751-6633	751-8159
ICS Telecom Inc 125 Highpower Rd *TF:* 800-836-8677 ■ *Web:* www.icstelecom.com	Rochester	NY	14623	585-427-7000	427-0863
IMS Inc 340 Progress Dr *TF:* 800-666-1626 ■ *Web:* www.imswire.com	Manchester	CT	06040	860-649-4415	649-0806
Independent Electric Supply Inc 1370 Bayport Ave *Web:* www.iesupply.com	San Carlos	CA	94070	650-594-9440	594-0484
Industrial Electric Wire & Cable Inc 5001 S Towne Dr *TF:* 800-344-2323 ■ *Web:* www.iewc.com	New Berlin	WI	53151	262-782-2323	957-1237
InfoSonics Corp 5880 Pacific Center Blvd *AMEX:* IFO ■ *TF:* 800-519-1599 ■ *Web:* www.infosonics.com	San Diego	CA	92121	858-373-1600	373-1505
Insulectro 20362 Windrow Dr *Web:* www.insulectro.com	Lake Forest	CA	92630	949-587-3200	454-0066
Integrated Electronics Corp 420 E 58th Ave *TF:* 800-876-8686	Denver	CO	80216	303-292-5537	296-1528
Interstate Electrical Supply Inc 2300 2nd Ave *TF:* 800-903-4409 ■ *Web:* www.interstate-electrical.com	Columbus	GA	31901	706-324-1000	576-5821
Irby Stuart C Co 815 S State St PO Box 1819 *TF:* 800-844-1811 ■ *Web:* www.irby.com	Jackson	MS	39215	601-969-1811	960-7277
Jaco Electronics Inc 145 Oser Ave *NASDAQ:* JACO ■ *TF:* 800-966-5226 ■ *Web:* www.jacoelectronics.com	Hauppauge	NY	11788	631-273-5500	273-5506
Jasco Products Inc 311 NW 122nd St *TF:* 800-654-8483 ■ *Web:* www.jascoproducts.com	Oklahoma City	OK	73114	405-752-0710	752-1537
JH Larson Co 10200 51st Ave N *TF:* 800-292-7970 ■ *Web:* www.jhlarson.com	Plymouth	MN	55442	763-545-1717	545-1144
K & M Electric Supply Inc 7641 Central Industrial Dr *Web:* www.kmelectric.com	Riviera Beach	FL	33404	561-842-4911	842-3834
Kendall Electric Inc 131 Grand Trunk Ave *TF:* 800-632-5422 ■ *Web:* www.kendallelectric.com	Battle Creek	MI	49015	269-963-5585	963-5606
Kendall Industrial Supplies Inc 4560 W Dickman Rd *TF:* 800-632-9606 ■ *Web:* www.kendallindustrial.com	Battle Creek	MI	49015	269-965-2211	965-3164
Kimball Electronics Inc 2233 S 300 East *Web:* www.kimballinc.com	Salt Lake City	UT	84115	801-466-0569	466-8636
King Wire Inc 2500 Commonwealth Ave *TF:* 800-453-5464 ■ *Web:* www.kingwire.com	North Chicago	IL	60064	847-688-1100	688-0244
Kirby Risk Corp 1815 Sagamore Pkwy N **Fax:* Sales ■ *Web:* www.kirbyrisk.com	Lafayette	IN	47904	765-448-4567	448-1342*
Larson JH Co 10200 51st Ave N *TF:* 800-292-7970 ■ *Web:* www.jhlarson.com	Plymouth	MN	55442	763-545-1717	545-1144
Lawrence FD Electric Co Inc 3450 Beekman St *TF Cust Svc:* 800-582-4490 ■ *Web:* www.fdlawrence.com	Cincinnati	OH	45223	513-542-1100	542-2422
Leff H Electric Co Inc 1163 E 40th St *TF:* 800-686-5333 ■ *Web:* www.leffelectric.com	Cleveland	OH	44114	216-432-3000	432-0051
Loeb Electric Co 915 Williams Ave *TF:* 800-837-2852 ■ *Web:* www.loebelectric.com	Columbus	OH	43212	614-294-6351	294-8142
Lowe Electric Inc PO Box 4767 *Web:* www.loweelectric.com	Macon	GA	31208	478-743-8661	742-3374
Loyd's Electric Supply Inc 838 Stonetree Dr PO Box 1169 *TF:* 800-492-4030 ■ *Web:* www.loydselectric.com	Branson	MO	65616	417-334-2171	334-6635
Madison Electric Co 31855 Van Dyke Ave *Web:* www.madisonelectric.com	Warren	MI	48093	586-825-0200	825-0225
Major Electric Supply Inc 123 High St *TF:* 800-444-1660 ■ *Web:* www.majorelectricsupply.com	Pawtucket	RI	02860	401-724-7100	727-7563
Maltby Electric Supply Co Inc 336 7th St *TF:* 800-339-0668 ■ *Web:* www.maltbyelec.com	San Francisco	CA	94103	415-863-5000	863-5011
Marcone Appliance Parts Inc 2300 Clark Ave **Fax:* Cust Svc ■ *TF:* 800-325-7588 ■ *Web:* www.marcone.com	Saint Louis	MO	63103	314-231-7141	231-5481*
Mars Electric Co 38868 Mentor Ave *TF:* 800-288-6277 ■ *Web:* www.mars-electric.com	Willoughby	OH	44094	440-946-2250	946-3214
Marsh Electronics Inc 1563 S 101st St *TF Cust Svc:* 800-558-1238 ■ *Web:* www.marshelectronics.com	Milwaukee	WI	53214	414-475-6000	771-2847
Master Distributors Inc 1220 Olympic Blvd *TF:* 800-421-8153 ■ *Web:* www.masterdistributors.com	Santa Monica	CA	90404	310-452-1229	399-8600
Maurice Electrical Supply Co 500 Penn St NE *Web:* www.mauriceelectric.com	Washington	DC	20002	202-675-9400	547-1956
Mayer Electric Supply Co 3405 4th Ave S *TF:* 800-444-8524 ■ *Web:* www.mayerelectric.com	Birmingham	AL	35222	205-583-3500	252-0315
McNaughton-McKay Electric Co Inc 1357 E Lincoln Ave *TF:* 800-527-5033 ■ *Web:* www.mc-mc.com	Madison Heights	MI	48071	248-399-7500	399-6828
Mercedes Electric Supply Inc 8550 NW South River Dr *TF:* 800-636-5550 ■ *Web:* www.mercedeselectric.com	Miami	FL	33166	305-887-5550	887-8761
Metron Technology 3100 Powers Ave Bldg 2 *Web:* www.metrontech.com	Santa Clara	CA	95052	408-719-4600	719-0452
Mid-Island Electrical Supply 59 Mall Dr *TF:* 877-324-2636 ■ *Web:* www.mid-island.com	Commack	NY	11725	631-864-4242	864-6644
Minnesota Electric Supply Co 1209 E Hwy 12 *TF:* 800-992-8830 ■ *Web:* www.mnelectric.com	Willmar	MN	56201	320-235-2255	214-4242
Mouser Electronics Corp 1000 N Main St *TF:* 800-346-6873 ■ *Web:* www.mouser.com	Mansfield	TX	76063	817-804-3888	804-3899
Nedco Electronics 594 American Way **Fax Area Code:* 800 ■ *TF:* 800-605-2323 ■ *Web:* www.nedcoelectronics.com	Payson	UT	84651	801-465-1790	605-3836*
Nedco Supply Inc 4200 W Spring Mountain Rd *Web:* www.nedco.com	Las Vegas	NV	89102	702-367-0400	362-8365
Nelson Electric Supply Co Inc 926 State St *TF:* 800-994-5666 ■ *Web:* www.nelson-electric.com	Racine	WI	53404	262-637-7661	637-2465
Newark In One 4801 N Ravenswood Ave **Fax Area Code:* 888 ■ **Fax:* Sales ■ *Web:* www.newark.com	Chicago	IL	60640	800-463-9275	551-4801*
NF Smith & Assoc LP 5306 Hollister Rd *TF:* 800-468-7866 ■ *Web:* www.smithweb.com	Houston	TX	77040	713-430-3000	430-3099
Northern Video Systems Inc 3625 Cincinnati Ave *TF:* 800-366-4472 ■ *Web:* www.northernvideo.com	Rocklin	CA	95765	916-543-4000	543-4020
Northwest Controls 1936 Spruce St *TF:* 800-888-6932 ■ *Web:* www.northwestcontrols.com	Defiance	OH	43512	419-782-9479	782-2206
Norvell Electronics Inc PO Box 701027 *TF:* 800-477-0021 ■ *Web:* www.norvell.com	Dallas	TX	75370	972-858-3713	490-7245
Nu Horizons Electronics Corp 70 Maxess Rd *NASDAQ:* NUHC ■ *TF:* 888-747-6846 ■ *Web:* www.nuhorizons.com	Melville	NY	11747	631-396-5000	396-5050
Nu-Lite Electrical Wholesalers 850 Edwards Ave *TF:* 800-250-1003 ■ *Web:* www.nulite.com	Harahan	LA	70123	504-733-3300	736-1617
Omni Cable Corp 2 Hagerty Blvd *TF:* 800-292-6664 ■ *Web:* www.omnicable.com	West Chester	PA	19382	610-701-0100	701-9870
OneSource Distributors Inc 3951 Oceanic Dr *TF:* 800-521-5092 ■ *Web:* www.1sourcedist.com	Oceanside	CA	92056	760-966-4500	966-4599
Paige Electric Corp 1160 Springfield Rd *TF:* 800-327-2443 ■ *Web:* www.paigeelectric.com	Union	NJ	07083	908-687-7810	687-2722
Peerless Electronics Inc 700 Hicksville Rd *TF:* 800-285-2121 ■ *Web:* www.peerlesselectronics.com	Bethpage	NY	11714	516-594-3500	593-2179
PEI-Genesis 2180 Hornig Rd *TF:* 800-523-0727 ■ *Web:* www.pei-genesis.com	Philadelphia	PA	19116	215-673-0400	552-8022
Petsche AE Co Inc 2112 W Division St *TF:* 800-777-9280 ■ *Web:* www.aepetsche.com	Arlington	TX	76012	817-461-9473	277-2887
Pill Ralph Electrical Supply Co 307 Dorchester Ave *TF:* 800-879-7455 ■ *Web:* www.ralphpill.com	Boston	MA	02127	617-269-8200	269-7582
Platt Electric Supply 10605 SW Allen Blvd *TF:* 800-257-5288 ■ *Web:* www.platt.com	Beaverton	OR	97005	503-641-6121	277-7494
PNS Inc 581 Dado St *TF:* 800-537-4767 ■ *Web:* www.pnsonline.com	San Jose	CA	95131	408-944-0500	944-0517
Powell Electronics Inc 200 Commodore Dr *TF:* 800-235-7880 ■ *Web:* www.powell.com	Swedesboro	NJ	68085	856-241-8000	241-8630
Power & Telephone Supply Co Inc 2673 Yale Ave *TF Cust Svc:* 800-238-7514 ■ *Web:* www.ptsupply.com	Memphis	TN	38112	901-324-6116	320-3082
Priority Wire & Cable Inc 8200 E Roosevelt Rd *TF:* 800-945-5542 ■ *Web:* www.prioritywire.com	North Little Rock	AR	72206	501-372-5444	372-3988
Professional Electric Products Co 33210 Lakeland Blvd *TF:* 800-872-7000 ■ *Web:* www.pepconet.com	Eastlake	OH	44095	440-946-3790	942-5883
Projections Unlimited Inc 14831 Myford Rd *TF:* 800-551-4405 ■ *Web:* www.gopui.com	Tustin	CA	92780	714-544-2700	544-8711
QED Inc 1661 W 3rd Ave *TF:* 800-700-5011 ■ *Web:* www.qedelectric.com	Denver	CO	80223	303-825-5011	893-5019
Ralph Pill Electrical Supply Co 307 Dorchester Ave *TF:* 800-879-7455 ■ *Web:* www.ralphpill.com	Boston	MA	02127	617-269-8200	269-7582
Rawson & Co Inc PO Box 924288 **Fax:* Sales ■ *TF:* 800-779-1414 ■ *Web:* www.rawson.net	Houston	TX	77292	713-684-1400	684-1409*
Red Peacock International Inc 1945 Gardena Ave *Web:* www.redpeacock.com	Glendale	CA	91204	818-265-7722	265-7750
Regency Lighting Co 16665 Arminta St *TF:* 800-284-2024 ■ *Web:* www.regencylighting.com	Van Nuys	CA	91406	818-901-0255	901-0118
Reily Electric Supply Inc 3011 Lausat St **Fax:* Sales ■ *TF:* 800-662-1906 ■ *Web:* www.wescodist.com/reilysite/index.asp	Metairie	LA	70001	504-835-8888	837-7320*
Rexel Canada Inc 5600 Keaton Crescent *Web:* www.rexel.ca	Mississauga	ON	L5R3G3	905-712-4004	712-4024

Company	City	State	ZIP	Phone	Fax
Rexel Electrical Supply Co 815A Central Ave *Web:* www.rexelusa.com	Linthicum	MD	21090	410-636-1051	354-7527
Rexel Inc 6606 LBJ Fwy Suite 200 **Fax:* Sales ■ *Web:* www.rexelusa.com	Dallas	TX	75240	972-387-3600	934-2056*
Rexel Ryall Electrical Supplies 2627 W 6th Ave **Fax:* Sales ■ *TF:* 800-759-2728 ■ *Web:* www.rexelusa.com	Denver	CO	80204	303-629-7721	825-7608*
Reynolds Co 2861 Merrell Rd *TF:* 800-851-0304 ■ *Web:* www.reynco.com	Dallas	TX	75229	214-630-9000	438-4617
RF Monolithics Inc 4441 Sigma Rd *NASDAQ: RFMI* ■ *TF:* 800-704-6079 ■ *Web:* www.rfm.com	Dallas	TX	75244	972-233-2903	387-8148
Richardson Electronics Ltd 40 W 267 Keslinger Rd PO Box 393 *NASDAQ: RELL* ■ *TF Sales:* 800-348-5580 ■ *Web:* www.rell.com	LaFox	IL	60147	630-208-2200	208-2550
Richmar Electronics Corp 1307 Butterfield Rd Suite 418 *Web:* www.richmarcorp.com	Downers Grove	IL	60515	630-968-0118	968-0197
Rochester Electronics Inc 16 Malcolm Hoyt Dr *Web:* www.rocelec.com	Newburyport	MA	01950	978-462-9332	462-9512
Rockingham Electrical Supply Co Inc 437 Shattuck Way *TF:* 800-727-2310 ■ *Web:* www.rockinghamelectric.com	Newington	NH	03801	603-436-2310	436-9665
Roden Electrical Supply Co 3317 S 5th Ave *Web:* www.rodenelectric.com	Birmingham	AL	35222	205-254-3192	254-0095
Roden Electrical Supply Co 170 Mabry Hood Rd *TF:* 800-532-8742 ■ *Web:* www.rodenelectric.com	Knoxville	TN	37922	865-546-8755	546-6076
Rohm Electronics USA LLC 10145 Pacific Heights Blvd Suite 1000 *TF:* 800-955-7646 ■ *Web:* www.rohmelectronics.com	San Diego	CA	92121	858-625-3600	625-3640
RS Electronics Inc 34443 Schoolcraft Rd *TF:* 800-366-7750 ■ *Web:* www.rselectronics.com	Livonia	MI	48150	734-525-1155	525-1184
Rumsey Electric Co 15 Colwell Ln *TF:* 800-462-2402 ■ *Web:* www.rumsey.com	Conshohocken	PA	19428	610-832-9000	941-8181
Sager Electronics Inc 19 Lorena Dr **Fax Area Code:* 508 ■ *TF:* 800-541-9371 ■ *Web:* www.sager.com	Middleboro	MA	02346	800-541-9371	923-6797*
Schaedler Yesco Distribution Inc 951 S 13th St *TF:* 800-998-1621 ■ *Web:* www.sydist.com	Harrisburg	PA	17104	717-233-1621	233-1626
Schuster Electronics Inc 11320 Grooms Rd *TF:* 800-877-6875 ■ *Web:* www.schusterusa.com	Cincinnati	OH	45242	513-489-1400	489-8686
Scott Electric 1000 S Main St PO Box S **Fax Area Code:* 800 ■ *TF:* 800-442-8045 ■ *Web:* www.scottelectricco.com	Greensburg	PA	15601	724-834-4321	426-9598*
SED International Inc 4916 N Royal Atlanta Dr *TF Sales:* 800-444-8962 ■ *Web:* www.sedonline.com	Tucker	GA	30084	770-491-8962	938-2814
Sennheiser Electronics Corp 1 Enterprise Dr *TF:* 877-736-6434 ■ *Web:* www.sennheiserusa.com	Old Lyme	CT	06371	860-434-9190	434-1759
Service Electric Supply Inc 15424 Oakwood Dr *Web:* www.servelectric.com	Romulus	MI	48174	734-229-9100	229-9101
Shepherd Electric Supply 7401 Pulaski Hwy *TF Sales:* 800-253-1777 ■ *Web:* www.shepherdelec.com	Baltimore	MD	21237	410-866-6000	866-6001
Singing Machine Co Inc 6601 Lyons Rd Bldg A-7 *AMEX: SMD* ■ *Web:* www.singingmachine.com	Coconut Creek	FL	33073	954-596-1000	596-2000
Smith NF & Assoc LP 5306 Hollister Rd *TF:* 800-468-7866 ■ *Web:* www.smithweb.com	Houston	TX	77040	713-430-3000	430-3099
Sommer Electric Corp 818 3rd St NE *TF:* 800-766-6373 ■ *Web:* www.sommerelectric.com	Canton	OH	44704	330-455-9454	455-6561
Sonepar USA 510 Walnut St Suite 400 *Web:* www.sonepar-usa.com	Philadelphia	PA	19106	215-399-5900	
South Dade Electrical Supply 13100 SW 87th Ave *Web:* www.south-dade.com	Miami	FL	33176	305-238-7131	251-5254
Springfield Electric Supply Co 700 N 9th St *TF:* 800-757-2101 ■ *Web:* www.springfieldelectric.com	Springfield	IL	62708	217-788-2100	788-2133
Sprint North Supply Co Inc 600 New Century Pkwy **Fax Area Code:* 800 ■ **Fax:* Sales ■ *TF:* 800-755-3004 ■ *Web:* www.sprintnorthsupply.com	New Century	KS	66031	913-791-7000	755-9023*
Standard Electric Co 2650 Trautner Dr PO Box 5289 *TF:* 800-322-0215 ■ *Web:* www.standardelectricco.com	Saginaw	MI	48603	989-497-2100	497-2101
Stanion Wholesale Electric Co 812 S Main St PO Box F *TF:* 800-880-2008 ■ *Web:* www.stanion.com	Pratt	KS	67124	620-672-5678	672-6220
State Electric Supply Co Inc 2010 2nd Ave *TF Cust Svc:* 800-624-3417 ■ *Web:* www.stateelectric.com	Huntington	WV	25703	304-523-7491	525-8917
Steiner Electric Co Inc 1250 Touhy Ave *TF:* 800-783-4637 ■ *Web:* www.stnr.com	Elk Grove Village	IL	60007	847-228-0400	228-1352
Steven Engineering Inc 230 Ryan Way **Fax Area Code:* 888 ■ *TF:* 800-258-9200 ■ *Web:* stevenengineering.com	South San Francisco	CA	94080	650-588-9200	258-9200*
Stokes Electric Co Inc 1701 McCalla Ave *TF:* 800-999-0351 ■ *Web:* www.stokeselec.com	Knoxville	TN	37915	865-525-0351	971-4149
Stoneway Electric Supply Co 402 N Perry St *TF:* 800-841-1408 ■ *Web:* www.stoneway.com	Spokane	WA	99202	509-535-2933	534-4512
Stuart C Irby Co 815 S State St PO Box 1819 *TF:* 800-844-1811 ■ *Web:* www.irby.com	Jackson	MS	39215	601-969-1811	960-7277
Summit Electric Supply Co 2900 Stanford NE *TF:* 800-824-4400 ■ *Web:* www.summit.com	Albuquerque	NM	87107	505-884-4400	346-1616
Surface Mount Distribution Inc 1 Oldfield Rd *TF:* 800-229-7634 ■ *Web:* www.smdinc.com	Irvine	CA	92618	949-470-7700	470-7777
Taitron Components Inc 28040 W Harrison Pkwy *NASDAQ: TAIT* ■ *TF:* 800-247-2232 ■ *Web:* www.taitroncomponents.com	Valencia	CA	91355	661-257-6060	257-6415
Tecot Electric Supply Co 55 Lukens Dr *TF:* 800-344-9905 ■ *Web:* rumsey.com	New Castle	DE	19720	302-421-3900	429-6268
Teleco Inc 430 Woodruff Rd Suite 300 *TF:* 800-800-6159 ■ *Web:* www.teleco.com	Greenville	SC	29607	864-297-4400	297-9983
Telmar Technology 6410 Via Real *TF:* 800-761-1206 ■ *Web:* www.telmarnt.com	Carpinteria	CA	93013	805-681-3322	681-3325
Terry-Durin Co 409 7th Ave SE *TF:* 800-332-8114 ■ *Web:* www.terrydurin.com	Cedar Rapids	IA	52401	319-364-4106	364-2562
TESSCO Technologies Inc 11126 McCormick Rd *NASDAQ: TESS* ■ *TF:* 800-472-7373 ■ *Web:* www.tessco.com	Hunt Valley	MD	21031	410-229-1000	527-0005
Thalner Electronics Laboratory Inc 7235 Jackson Rd *TF:* 800-686-7235 ■ *Web:* www.thalner.com	Ann Arbor	MI	48103	734-761-4506	761-9776
Tri-State Utility Products Inc 1030 Atlanta Industrial Dr *TF:* 800-282-7985 ■ *Web:* www.tristateutility.com	Marietta	GA	30066	770-427-3119	427-3945
TTI Inc 2441 Northeast Pkwy **Fax:* Hum Res ■ *TF Sales:* 800-845-5119 ■ *Web:* www.ttiinc.com	Fort Worth	TX	76106	817-740-9000	740-1622*
Turtle & Hughes Inc 1900 Lower Rd *Web:* www.turtle.com	Linden	NJ	07036	732-574-3600	574-3723
United Utility Supply Co-op Inc 4515 Bishop Ln *TF:* 800-357-5232 ■ *Web:* www.uus.org	Louisville	KY	40218	502-459-4011	815-6378
Van Meter Industrial Inc 240 33rd Ave SW *TF:* 800-332-8468 ■ *Web:* www.vanmeterindustrial.com	Cedar Rapids	IA	52404	319-366-5301	366-4709
Viking Electric Supply Inc 451 Industrial Blvd W *TF:* 800-435-3345 ■ *Web:* www.vikingelectric.com	Minneapolis	MN	55413	612-627-1300	627-1313
Voss Lighting 1601 Cushman Dr *TF:* 800-828-8677 ■ *Web:* www.vosslighting.com	Lincoln	NE	68512	402-328-2281	421-2282
Wabash Electric Supply Inc 1400 S Wabash St *TF:* 800-552-7777 ■ *Web:* www.wabashelectric.com	Wabash	IN	46992	260-563-4146	563-4140
Walker Component Group 420 E 58th Ave *TF:* 800-876-8686 ■ *Web:* www.walkercomponent.com	Denver	CO	80216	303-292-5537	296-1528
Walters Wholesale Electric Co 2825 Temple Ave *Web:* www.walterswholesale.com	Signal Hill	CA	90755	562-988-3100	988-3150
Warshauer Electric Supply Co 800 Shrewsbury Ave **Fax:* Sales ■ *Web:* www.warshauerelectric.com	Tinton Falls	NJ	07724	732-741-6400	741-3866*
Werner Electric Supply Co 2341 Industrial Dr *TF:* 800-236-5026 ■ *Web:* www.wernerelectric.com	Neenah	WI	54956	920-729-4500	729-4484
Wes-Garde Components Group Inc 190 Elliott St *TF:* 800-275-7089 ■ *Web:* www.wesgarde.com	Hartford	CT	06114	860-525-6907	527-6047
WESCO Distribution Inc 225 W Station Sq Dr Suite 700 *Web:* www.wescodist.com	Pittsburgh	PA	15219	412-454-2200	454-2505
Western Extralite Co 1470 Liberty St *TF:* 800-279-8833 ■ *Web:* www.westernextralite.com	Kansas City	MO	64102	816-421-8404	421-6211
Whitehill Lighting & Supplies Inc 1524 N Atherton St *TF:* 800-326-9940	State College	PA	16803	814-238-2449	238-1615
Whitlock Group 3900 Gaskins Rd *TF:* 800-726-9843 ■ *Web:* www.whitlock.com	Richmond	VA	23233	804-273-9100	273-9380
Wholesale Electric Supply Co LP 4040 Guls Fwy PO Box 230197 *TF:* 800-486-8563 ■ *Web:* www.wholesaleelectric.com	Houston	TX	77223	713-748-6100	749-8415
Wholesale Electric Supply Inc 1400 Waterall St *TF:* 800-869-8672 ■ *Web:* www.netwes.com	Texarkana	TX	75501	903-794-3404	792-2720
Williams Supply Inc 210 7th St *TF:* 800-533-6969 ■ *Web:* www.williams-supply.com	Roanoke	VA	24016	540-343-9333	342-3254
Winlectric Inc 3110 Kettering Blvd *Web:* www.winholesale.com	Dayton	OH	45439	937-294-6876	293-9591
Wolff Bros Supply Inc 6078 Wolff Rd *TF:* 800-879-6533 ■ *Web:* www.wolffbros.com	Medina	OH	44256	330-725-3451	725-5326
Womack Electric Supply Co 518 Newton St *Web:* www.womackelectric.com	Danville	VA	24541	434-793-5134	792-8256
World Electric Supply 11010 N 30th St Suite 106	Doral	FL	33172	305-436-1500	718-3820
WW Grainger Inc 100 Grainger Pkwy *NYSE: GWW* ■ *TF:* 888-361-8649 ■ *Web:* www.grainger.com	Lake Forest	IL	60045	847-535-1000	
XP ForeSight Co 990 Benicia Ave *TF:* 800-276-9378 ■ *Web:* www.fse-power.com	Sunnyvale	CA	94085	408-732-7777	522-8227
Zack Electronics Inc 1070 Hamilton Rd *TF:* 800-466-0449 ■ *Web:* www.zackelectronics.com	Duarte	CA	91010	626-303-0655	303-8694

250 ELECTRICAL EQUIPMENT FOR INTERNAL COMBUSTION ENGINES

SEE ALSO Automotive Parts & Supplies - Mfr p. 1360; Motors (Electric) & Generators p. 1983

Company	City	State	ZIP	Phone	Fax
Altronic Inc 712 Trumbull Ave *Web:* www.altronicinc.com	Girard	OH	44420	330-545-9768	545-9005
American Electronic Components 1101 Lafayette St *TF:* 888-847-6552 ■ *Web:* www.aecsensors.com	Elkhart	IN	46516	574-295-6330	293-8013
American Industrial Mfg Services Inc 41673 Corning Pl	Murrieta	CA	92562	951-698-3379	698-1379
Andover Inc PO Box 4848 *Web:* www.andovercoils.com	Lafayette	IN	47903	765-447-1157	447-1150
Autotronic Controls Corp DBA MSD Ignition 1490 Henry Brennan Dr *Web:* www.msdignition.com	El Paso	TX	79936	915-857-5200	857-3344
CE Niehoff & Co 2021 Lee St *TF Tech Supp:* 800-643-4633 ■ *Web:* www.ceniehoff.com	Evanston	IL	60202	847-866-6030	492-1242
CPX Inc 1400 E Buckeye St *Web:* www.cpxinc.com	North Vernon	IN	47265	812-346-8567	346-6616
Craft-Co Enterprises Inc 3269 Hwy 80 *Web:* www.craftco.net	Morton	MS	39117	601-732-6404	732-2481
Edge Products 1080 S Depot Dr *TF:* 888-360-3343 ■ *Web:* www.edgeproducts.com	Ogden	UT	84404	801-476-3343	476-3348
Electricfil Corp 11880 Belden Ct	Livonia	MI	48150	734-425-2774	425-3669
EMB Corp 1203 Hawkins Dr *Web:* www.embcorp.com	Elizabethtown	KY	42701	270-737-1996	737-1909
ETCO Inc Automotive Products Div 3004 62nd Ave E *Web:* www.etco.com/automotive_e.html	Bradenton	FL	34203	941-756-8426	758-7195
FAI Inc 1460 E 12th St *Web:* www.faiwiring.com	Mishawaka	IN	46544	574-259-3728	255-1079
Fargo Assembly of Pennsylvania Inc 800 W Washington St PO Box 550 *Web:* www.fargopa.com	Norristown	PA	19404	610-272-6850	272-6858
Fermag Inc 417 Union Pacific Blvd	Laredo	TX	78045	956-717-4130	717-4131
Fisher Electric Technology 2801 72nd St N *TF:* 800-789-2347 ■ *Web:* www.fisherelectric.com	Saint Petersburg	FL	33710	727-345-9122	345-2904
Goodall Mfg Co 7558 Washington Ave S *TF:* 800-328-7730 ■ *Web:* www.goodallmfg.com	Eden Prairie	MN	55344	952-941-6666	941-2617
Hitachi Automotive Products (USA) Inc 955 Warwick Rd *Web:* www.hap.com	Harrodsburg	KY	40330	859-734-9451	734-5309
Hood Cable Co PO Box 1253 *Web:* www.hoodcable.com	Prentiss	MS	39474	601-792-0375	792-4309
Ignition Systems & Controls LP 6300 W US Hwy 80 *Web:* www.ignition-systems.com	Midland	TX	79706	432-697-6472	697-0563
Interstate Industries Inc PO Box 1285	Kosciusko	MS	39090	662-289-3877	289-7439
Kelly Aerospace 1400 E South Blvd *Web:* www.kellyaerospace.com	Montgomery	AL	36116	334-286-8551	227-8596
KEM Mfg Co 18-35 River Rd *TF:* 800-289-5362 ■ *Web:* www.kemparts.com	Fair Lawn	NJ	07410	201-796-8000	796-3277
KenSa LLC 36199 Mound Rd *Web:* www.kensallc.com	Sterling Heights	MI	48310	586-983-4270	983-3531
Kongsberg Automotive 90 28th St *Web:* www.kongsbergautomotive.com	Grand-Mere	QC	G9T5Z8	819-533-3201	533-3901
M & G Electronics Corp 889 Seahawk Cir *Web:* www.mgelectronic.com	Virginia Beach	VA	23452	757-468-6000	
Mitsubishi Electric Automotive America Inc 4773 Bethany Rd *Web:* www.meaa-mea.com	Mason	OH	45040	513-398-2220	398-1121
Monona Wire Corp 301 W Spruce St	Monona	IA	52159	563-539-2011	539-4594
Motor Appliance Corp 555 Spirit of St Louis Blvd *TF:* 800-622-3406 ■ *Web:* www.macmc.com	Chesterfield	MO	63005	636-532-3406	532-4609
Motorcar Parts & Accessories 2929 California St *Web:* www.motorcarparts.com	Torrance	CA	90503	310-212-7910	212-7581
MSD Ignition 1490 Henry Brennan Dr *Web:* www.msdignition.com	El Paso	TX	79936	915-857-5200	857-3344
N/C Electronics Inc 42820 Port Orford Loop Rd	Port Orford	OR	97465	541-332-7004	
Niehoff CE & Co 2021 Lee St *TF Tech Supp:* 800-643-4633 ■ *Web:* www.ceniehoff.com	Evanston	IL	60202	847-866-6030	492-1242
Phelon RE Co Inc 895 University Pkwy *Web:* www.phelon.com	Aiken	SC	29801	803-649-1381	648-7309
Precision Parts & Remanufacturing Co 4411 SW 19th St *TF:* 800-654-3846 ■ *Web:* www.pprok.com	Oklahoma City	OK	73108	405-681-2592	681-2596
Prestolite Electric Inc 2311 Green Rd Suite B *TF Cust Svc:* 800-354-0560 ■ *Web:* www.prestolite.com	Ann Arbor	MI	48105	734-913-6600	913-6631
Prestolite Wire Corp 200 Galleria Officentre Suite 212 *TF:* 800-498-3132 ■ *Web:* www.prestolitewire.com	Southfield	MI	48034	248-355-4422	386-4462
Prettl Electric Corp 1721 White Horse Rd *Web:* www.prettlus.com	Greenville	SC	29605	864-220-1010	220-1020
RE Phelon Co Inc 895 University Pkwy *Web:* www.phelon.com	Aiken	SC	29801	803-649-1381	648-7309
Remy International Inc 2902 Enterprise Dr **Fax Area Code:* 888 ■ **Fax:* Cust Svc ■ *TF:* 800-372-5131 ■ *Web:* www.remyinc.com	Anderson	IN	46013	765-778-6499	372-3077*
Standard Motor Products Inc 37-18 Northern Blvd *NYSE: SMP* ■ *Web:* www.smpcorp.com	Long Island City	NY	11101	718-392-0200	729-4549

	City	State	ZIP	Phone	Fax
Sure Power Industries Inc 10189 SW Avery St	Tualatin	OR	97062	503-692-5360	692-9091
TF Tech Supp: 800-845-6269 ■ *Web:* www.surepower.com					
Syncro Corp PO Box 890	Arab	AL	35016	256-931-7800	931-7920
Web: www.syncrocorp.com					
Techma USA Inc PO Box 340	Gretna	VA	24557	434-656-3311	656-3211
Web: www.techma-usa.com					
Thales Avionics Ltd 3920 Park Ave	Edison	NJ	08820	732-494-1010	494-1421
TF: 800-573-9826 ■ *Web:* www.thales-avionics.com					
Transpo Electronics Inc 2150 Brengle Ave	Orlando	FL	32808	407-298-4563	298-4519
TF: 800-327-7792 ■ *Web:* www.transpo-usa.com					
Unison Industries Inc 7575 Baymeadows Way	Jacksonville	FL	32256	904-739-4000	739-4006
Web: www.unisonindustries.com					
Unit Parts Co Inc PO Box 6068	Edmond	OK	73083	405-677-3361	672-9979
Van Bergen & Greener Inc 1818 Madison St	Maywood	IL	60153	708-343-4700	343-9425
TF: 800-621-3889 ■ *Web:* www.starterdrives.com					
World Wide Automotive Inc 300 W Brooke Rd	Winchester	VA	22603	540-667-0106	662-7001

251 ELECTRICAL SIGNALS MEASURING & TESTING INSTRUMENTS

	City	State	ZIP	Phone	Fax
3M Telecommunications Div 6801 River Pl Blvd	Austin	TX	78726	651-733-1110	733-9973
Web: www.3m.com/market/telecom/index.jhtml					
Actron Mfg Co 15825 Industrial Pkwy	Cleveland	OH	44135	216-898-9200	898-1636
TF: 800-228-7667 ■ *Web:* www.actron.com					
Advanced Measurement Technology 801 S Illinois Ave	Oak Ridge	TN	37831	865-482-4411	483-0396
TF: 800-251-9750 ■ *Web:* www.ametek-online.com					
Advanced Test Products Inc 13515 Ballantyne Corporate Pl	Charlotte	NC	28277	704-752-4400	752-7488
TF: 800-533-6127 ■ *Web:* www.spx.com					
Advantest America Inc 3201 Scott Blvd	Santa Clara	CA	95054	408-988-7700	987-0680
NYSE: ATE ■ *Web:* www.advantest.com/aai.htm					
Aeroflex 400 New Century Pkwy	New Century	KS	66031	913-764-2452	782-5104*
**Fax:* Cust Svc ■ *TF:* 800-316-4981 ■ *Web:* www.aeroflex.com					
Aetrium Inc 2350 Helen St	North Saint Paul	MN	55109	651-770-2000	770-7975
NASDAQ: ATRM ■ *TF:* 800-274-3500 ■ *Web:* www.aetrium.com					
Agilent Technologies Inc 5301 Stevens Creek Blvd	Santa Clara	CA	95051	877-424-4536	345-8474*
NYSE: A ■ **Fax Area Code:* 408 ■ *TF:* 877-424-4536 ■ *Web:* www.agilent.com					
Allied Motion Technologies Inc 23 Inverness Way E Suite 150	Englewood	CO	80112	303-799-8520	799-8521
NASDAQ: AMOT ■ *Web:* www.alliedmotion.com					
AMETEK Inc Dixson Div 287 27 Rd	Grand Junction	CO	81503	970-244-1241	245-6267
TF: 888-302-0639 ■ *Web:* www.ametekdixson.com					
Analog Devices Inc 1 Technology Way PO Box 9106	Norwood	MA	02062	781-329-4700	461-3113
NYSE: ADI ■ *TF:* 800-262-5643 ■ *Web:* www.analog.com					
Anritsu Co 490 Jarvis Dr	Morgan Hill	CA	95037	408-778-2000	776-1744
TF: 800-267-4878 ■ *Web:* www.us.anritsu.com/					
Associated Equipment Corp 5043 Farlan Ave	Saint Louis	MO	63115	314-385-5178	385-3254
TF: 800-949-1472 ■ *Web:* www.associatedequip.com					
Avtron Mfg Inc 7900 E Pleasant Valley Rd	Independence	OH	44131	216-573-7600	642-6037
TF: 800-922-9751 ■ *Web:* www.avtron.com					
B & K Corp 5675 Dixie Hwy	Saginaw	MI	48601	989-777-2111	777-5620
TF: 800-977-3775 ■ *Web:* www.bkcorp.us					
Beede Electrical Instrument Co 88 Village St	Penacook	NH	03303	603-753-6362	753-6201
Web: www.beede.com					
BEI Technologies Inc Precision Systems & Space Div 1100 Murphy Dr	Maumelle	AR	72113	501-851-4000	851-5476
Web: www.beissd.com					
BI Technologies Corp 4200 Bonita Pl	Fullerton	CA	92835	714-447-2300	447-2745
Web: www.bitechnologies.com					
Bird Electronic Corp 30303 Aurora Rd	Solon	OH	44139	440-248-1200	248-5426
TF: 866-695-4569 ■ *Web:* www.bird-electronic.com					
Bruel & Kjaer Instruments Inc 2815-A Colonnades Ct	Norcross	GA	30071	770-209-6907	448-3246
TF: 800-241-9188 ■ *Web:* www.bkhome.com					
Cascade Microtech Inc 2430 NW 206th Ave	Beaverton	OR	97006	503-601-1000	601-1010
NASDAQ: CSCD ■ *TF:* 800-854-8400 ■ *Web:* www.cmicro.com					
Chatsworth Data Corp 20710 Lassen St	Chatsworth	CA	91311	818-341-9200	341-3002
TF: 800-423-5217 ■ *Web:* www.chatsworthdata.com					
Cohu Inc 12367 Crosthwaite Cir	Poway	CA	92064	858-848-8100	848-8185
NASDAQ: COHU ■ *Web:* www.cohu.com					
Communications Mfg Co 2239Colby Ave	Los Angeles	CA	90064	310-828-3200	481-0965
TF: 800-462-5532 ■ *Web:* www.gotocmc.com					
Credence Systems Corp 1421 California Cir	Milpitas	CA	95035	408-635-4300	635-4985
NASDAQ: CMOS ■ *TF:* 800 328 7016 ■ *Web:* www.credence.com					
Curtis Instruments Inc 200 Kisco Ave	Mount Kisco	NY	10549	914-666-2971	666-2188
Web: www.curtisinst.com					
CXR Larus Corp 894 Faulstich Ct	San Jose	CA	95112	408-573-2700	573-2708
TF: 800-999-9946 ■ *Web:* www.cxrlarus.com					
CyberOptics Corp 5900 Golden Hills Dr	Golden Valley	MN	55416	763-542-5000	542-5100
NASDAQ: CYBE ■ *TF Cust Svc:* 800-746-6315 ■ *Web:* www.cyberoptics.com					
Data Control Systems 213 Perry Pkwy	Gaithersburg	MD	20877	301-590-3300	590-3325
TF: 800-296-3333 ■ *Web:* www.compudyne.com/ies/dcs/					
Delta Design Inc 12367 Crosthwaite Cir	Poway	CA	92064	858-848-8000	848-8180*
**Fax:* Sales ■ *TF:* 800-776-0697 ■ *Web:* www.deltad.com					
Desco Industries Inc 3651 Walnut Ave	Chino	CA	91710	909-627-8178	627-7449
Web: www.desco.com					
DIT-MCO International Corp 5612 Brighton Terr	Kansas City	MO	64130	816-444-9700	444-6843
TF: 800-821-2168 ■ *Web:* www.ditmco.com					
Dixson Div AMETEK Inc 287 27 Rd	Grand Junction	CO	81503	970-244-1241	245-6267
TF: 888-302-0639 ■ *Web:* www.ametekdixson.com					
Dranetz-BMI 1000 New Durham Rd	Edison	NJ	08818	732-287-3680	287-9014
TF: 800-372-6832 ■ *Web:* www.dranetz-bmi.com					
DRS Test & Energy Management Inc 110 Wynn Dr	Huntsville	AL	35805	256-895-2000	895-2064
Web: www.drs-tem.com					
EADS North American Defense Test & Services Inc 4 Goodyear	Irvine	CA	92618	949-859-8999	859-7139*
**Fax:* Sales ■ *TF Cust Svc:* 800-722-2528 ■ *Web:* www.eads-nadefense.com					
EDAC Technologies Corp 1806 New Britain Ave	Farmington	CT	06032	860-678-8140	674-2718
Web: www.edactechnologies.com					
Electro-Metrics Corp 231 Enterprise Rd	Johnstown	NY	12095	518-762-2600	762-2812
Web: www.electro-metrics.com					
Electrodynamics Inc 1200 Hicks Rd	Rolling Meadows	IL	60008	847-259-0740	255-3827
Web: www.l-3com.com/edi					
Everett Charles Technologies Inc (ECT) 700 E Harrison Ave	Pomona	CA	91767	909-625-5551	624-9746
Web: www.ectinfo.com					
Everett Charles Technologies Inc Test Equipment Div 700 E Harrison Ave	Pomona	CA	91767	909-625-5551	624-9746
Web: www.ectinfo.com					
EXFO Electro-Optical Engineering Inc 400 Godin Ave	Vanier	QC	G1M2K2	418-683-0211	683-2170
NASDAQ: EXFO ■ *TF:* 800-663-3936 ■ *Web:* www.exfo.com					
Fluke Biomedical 6920 Seaway Blvd	Everett	WA	98203	425-446-6945	446-5716
TF: 800-443-5853 ■ *Web:* www.flukebiomedical.com					
Fluke Corp 6920 Seaway Blvd	Everett	WA	98203	425-446-6100	446-5116
TF: 800-753-5853 ■ *Web:* www.fluke.com					
Frequency Electronics Inc 55 Charles Lindbergh Blvd	Uniondale	NY	11553	516-794-4500	794-4340
AMEX: FEI ■ *Web:* www.freqelec.com					
Giga-Tronics Inc 4650 Norris Canyon Rd	San Ramon	CA	94583	925-328-4650	328-4700
NASDAQ: GIGA ■ *TF:* 800-726-4442 ■ *Web:* www.gigatronics.com					
Gleason M & M Precision Systems Corp 300 Progress Rd	Dayton	OH	45449	937-859-8273	859-4452
Web: www.gleason.com					
Hickok Inc 10514 Dupont Ave	Cleveland	OH	44108	216-541-8060	761-9879
TF: 800-342-5080 ■ *Web:* www.hickok-inc.com					
Hipotronics Inc 1650 Rt 22	Brewster	NY	10509	845-279-8091	279-2467
TF: 800-727-4476 ■ *Web:* www.hipotronics.com					
Hughes Corp Weschler Instruments Div 16900 Foltz Pkwy	Cleveland	OH	44149	440-238-2550	238-0660
TF: 800-557-0064 ■ *Web:* www.weschler.com					
ILX Lightwave Corp 31950 E Frontage Rd PO Box 6310	Bozeman	MT	59771	406-586-1244	586-9405
TF: 800-459-9459 ■ *Web:* www.ilxlightwave.com					
IMPulse NC Inc 100 IMPulse Way	Mount Olive	NC	28365	919-658-2200	658-2268
Web: www.impulsenc.com					
ISEC Inc 33 Inverness Dr E	Englewood	CO	80112	303-790-1444	799-8652
Web: www.iseinc.com					
Itron Inc 2111 N Molter Rd	Liberty Lake	WA	99019	509-924-9900	891-3355
NASDAQ: ITRI ■ *TF:* 800-635-5461 ■ *Web:* www.itron.com					
Ixia 26601 W Agoura Rd	Calabasas	CA	91302	818-871-1800	871-1805
NASDAQ: XXIA ■ *TF:* 877-367-4942 ■ *Web:* www.ixiacom.com					
JDS Uniphase Corp DBA JDSU 430 N McCarthy Blvd	Milpitas	CA	95035	408-546-5000	546-4300
NASDAQ: JDSU ■ *TF:* 800-543-1550 ■ *Web:* www.jdsu.com					
JDSU 430 N McCarthy Blvd	Milpitas	CA	95035	408-546-5000	546-4300
NASDAQ: JDSU ■ *TF:* 800-543-1550 ■ *Web:* www.jdsu.com					
Jewell Instruments LLC 850 Perimeter Rd	Manchester	NH	03103	603-669-6400	669-5962
TF: 800-638-3771 ■ *Web:* www.triplett.com					
Keithley Instruments Inc 28775 Aurora Rd	Cleveland	OH	44139	440-248-0400	248-6168
NYSE: KEI ■ *TF:* 800-552-1115 ■ *Web:* www.keithley.com					
KLA-Tencor Corp 160 Rio Robles	San Jose	CA	95134	408-875-3000	875-3030
NASDAQ: KLAC ■ *Web:* www.kla-tencor.com					
Knopp Inc 1307 66th St	Emeryville	CA	94608	510-653-1661	653-2202
TF: 800-227-1848 ■ *Web:* www.knoppinc.com					
LDS Test & Measurement LLC 8551 Research Way MS 140	Middleton	WI	53562	608-821-6600	821-6691*
**Fax:* Sales ■ *TF Sales:* 800-468-5365 ■ *Web:* www.lds-group.com					
LeCroy Corp 700 Chestnut Ridge Rd	Chestnut Ridge	NY	10977	845-425-2000	425-8967
NASDAQ: LCRY ■ *TF:* 800-553-2769 ■ *Web:* www.lecroy.com					
LTS Corp 7250 Woodmont Ave Suite 340	Bethesda	MD	20814	301-652-2121	951-9624
Web: www.ltscorporation.com					
LTX Corp 825 University Ave	Norwood	MA	02062	781-461-1000	461-0993
NASDAQ: LTXX ■ *TF:* 800-451-2400 ■ *Web:* www.ltx.com					
Mantas Inc 13650 Dulles Technology Dr	Herndon	VA	20171	703-673-0500	673-0510
TF: 866-462-6827 ■ *Web:* www.mantas.com					
Megger 4271 Bronze Way	Dallas	TX	75237	214-333-3201	331-7399
TF: 800-723-2861 ■ *Web:* www.megger.com/					
Micro Networks Corp 324 Clark St	Worcester	MA	01606	508-852-5400	853-8456
TF: 800-544-0052 ■ *Web:* www.mnc.com					
Micromanipulator Co Inc 1555 Forrest Way	Carson City	NV	89706	775-882-7377	882-7694
TF Cust Svc: 800-654-5659 ■ *Web:* www.micromanipulator.com					
Monroe Electronics Inc 100 Housel Ave	Lyndonville	NY	14098	585-765-2254	765-9330
TF: 800-821-6001 ■ *Web:* www.monroe-electronics.com					
Nartron Corp 5000 N US 131	Reed City	MI	49677	231-832-5513	832-3876
Web: www.nartron.com					
National Instruments Corp 11500 N Mopac Expy	Austin	TX	78759	512-794-0100	683-8411
NASDAQ: NATI ■ *TF Cust Svc:* 800-433-3488 ■ *Web:* www.ni.com					
NetTest North America Inc 6 Rhoads Dr	Utica	NY	13502	315-266-5000	798-4038
TF: 800-443-6154 ■ *Web:* www.nettest.com					
Newport Electronics Inc 2229 S Yale St	Santa Ana	CA	92704	714-540-4914	546-3022
TF Cust Svc: 800-639-7678 ■ *Web:* www.newportinc.com					
NH Research Inc 16601 Hale Ave	Irvine	CA	92606	949-474-3900	474-7062
Web: www.nhresearch.com					
PerkinElmer Inc 45 William St	Wellesley	MA	02481	781-237-5100	237-9386
NYSE: PKI ■ *Web:* www.perkinelmer.com					
PerkinElmer Instruments Inc 710 Bridgeport Ave	Shelton	CT	06484	203-925-4600	925-4654
TF: 800-762-4000 ■ *Web:* las.perkinelmer.com					
Phenix Technologies Inc 75 Speicher Dr	Accident	MD	21520	301-746-8118	895-5570
Web: www.phenixtech.com					
Photon Dynamics Inc 5970 Optical Ct	San Jose	CA	95138	408-226-9900	226-9910
NASDAQ: PHTN ■ *Web:* www.photondynamics.com					
Prime Technology LLC 344-352 Twin Lakes Rd PO Box 185	North Branford	CT	06471	203-481-5721	481-8937
Web: www.primetechnology.com					
Quest Technologies Inc 1060 Corporate Center Dr	Oconomowoc	WI	53066	262-567-9101	567-4047
TF: 800-245-0779 ■ *Web:* www.quest-technologies.com					
Radiodetection Corp 154 Portland Rd	Bridgton	ME	04009	207-647-3185	647-9496
TF: 800-524-1739 ■ *Web:* www.radiodetection.com					
Reliability Inc 15720 Park Row	Houston	TX	77084	281-492-0550	492-0615
Web: www.relinc.com					
Rodale Electronics Inc 20 Oser Ave	Hauppauge	NY	11788	631-231-0044	231-1345
Web: www.rodaleelectronics.com					
Schlumberger Ltd 5599 San Felipe	Houston	TX	77056	713-513-2000	350-8114*
NYSE: SLB ■ **Fax Area Code:* 212 ■ *Web:* www.slb.com					
Schneider Electric 2195 Keating Cross Rd	Saanichton	BC	V8M2A5	250-652-7100	652-0411
TF: 866-466-7627 ■ *Web:* www.schneider-electric.com					
Sencore Inc 3200 Sencore Dr	Sioux Falls	SD	57107	605-339-0100	335-6379
TF Cust Svc: 800-736-2673 ■ *Web:* www.sencore.com					
Simpson Electric Co 520 Simpson Ave	Lac Du Flambeau	WI	54538	715-588-3311	588-1248
Web: www.simpsonelectric.com					
Snap-on Diagnostics 420 Barclay Blvd	Lincolnshire	IL	60069	847-478-0700	478-7311
TF: 800-967-8030 ■ *Web:* www.snapondiagnostics.com					
Spirent Communications 15200 Omega Dr	Rockville	MD	20850	301-590-3600	590-3599
TF: 800-385-0110 ■ *Web:* www.spirentcom.com					
SPX Corp Service Solutions Div 8001 Angling Rd	Portage	MI	49024	269-329-7600	329-7645
Web: www.spx.com/Business_Segments					
TEGAM Inc 10 Tegam Way	Geneva	OH	44041	440-466-6100	466-6110
TF: 800-666-1010 ■ *Web:* www.tegam.com					
Tektronix Inc 14200 SW Karl Braun Dr PO Box 500	Beaverton	OR	97077	503-627-7111	627-3247*
NYSE: TEK ■ **Fax:* Sales ■ *TF:* 800-833-9200 ■ *Web:* www.tektronix.com					
Tempo Research Corp 1390 Aspen Way	Vista	CA	92083	760-598-8900	598-5634
TF: 800-642-2155 ■ *Web:* www.tempo.textron.com					
Teradyne Inc 600 Riverpark Dr	North Reading	MA	01864	978-370-2700	
NYSE: TER ■ *Web:* www.teradyne.com					
Teradyne Inc Assembly Test Div 600 Riverpark Dr	North Reading	MA	01864	978-370-2700	
Teradyne Inc Broadband Test Div 1405 Lake Cook Rd	Deerfield	IL	60015	847-940-9000	940-0344
Web: www.teradyne.com/prods/btd					
Teradyne Inc Industrial/Consumer Div 600 Riverpark Dr	North Reading	MA	01864	978-370-2700	
Teradyne Inc Semiconductor Test Div 30701 Agoura Rd	Agoura Hills	CA	91301	818-991-2900	735-5611*
**Fax:* Hum Res ■ *Web:* www.teradyne.com/prods/prodserv.html					
Texmate Inc 995 Park Center Dr	Vista	CA	92081	760-598-9899	598-9828
TF: 800-839-6283 ■ *Web:* www.texmate.com					
Trek Inc 11601 Maple Ridge Rd	Medina	NY	14103	585-798-3140	798-3106*
**Fax:* Sales ■ *TF:* 800-367-8735 ■ *Web:* www.trekinc.com					
Trilithic Inc 9710 Park Davis Dr	Indianapolis	IN	46235	317-895-3600	423-7604
TF: 800-344-2412 ■ *Web:* www.trilithic.com					
Trio-Tech International 14731 Califa St	Van Nuys	CA	91411	818-787-7000	787-9130
AMEX: TRT ■ *Web:* www.triotech.com					
Tyco Electronics Corp Corcom Div 62 S Butterfield Rd	Mundelein	IL	60060	847-680-7400	680-8169
Web: www.corcom.com					
United Industrial Corp 124 Industry Ln	Hunt Valley	MD	21030	410-628-3000	683-6498
NYSE: UIC ■ *TF:* 800-655-3964 ■ *Web:* www.unitedindustrial.com					

Company	City	State	Zip	Phone	Fax
Wems Electronics Inc 4650 W Rosecrans Ave	Hawthorne	CA	90250	310-644-0251	644-5334
Web: www.wems.com					
Weschler Instruments Div Hughes Corp 16900 Foltz Pkwy	Cleveland	OH	44149	440-238-2550	238-0660
TF: 800-557-0064 ■ *Web:* www.weschler.com					
Wireless Telecom Group Inc 25 Eastmans Rd	Parsippany	NJ	07054	973-386-9696	386-9191
AMEX: WTT ■ *Web:* www.noisecom.com					
Yokogawa Corp of America 2 Dart Rd	Newnan	GA	30265	770-253-7000	254-0928
TF: 800-888-6400 ■ *Web:* www.yokogawa.com/us					
Zetec Inc 8226 Bracken Pl SE Suite 100	Snoqualmie	WA	98065	425-974-2739	974-2621
TF: 800-643-1771 ■ *Web:* www.zetec.com					

252 ELECTRICAL SUPPLIES - PORCELAIN

Company	City	State	Zip	Phone	Fax
American Superconductor Corp 2 Technology Dr	Westborough	MA	01581	508-836-4200	836-4248
NASDAQ: AMSC ■ *Web:* www.amsuper.com					
American Technical Ceramics Corp 1 Norden Ln	Huntington Station	NY	11746	631-622-4700	622-4748
AMEX: AMK ■ *Web:* www.atceramics.com					
Bolt Technical Ceramics 12621 Hwy 105 W Suite 301	Conroe	TX	77304	936-539-2552	539-2548
Ceradyne Inc 3169 Redhill Ave	Costa Mesa	CA	92626	714-549-0421	549-5787*
NASDAQ: CRDN ■ **Fax:* Sales ■ *TF:* 800-839-2189 ■ *Web:* www.ceradyne.com					
CeramTec North America 1 Technology Pl	Laurens	SC	29360	864-682-3215	682-1121
TF: 800-845-9761 ■ *Web:* www.ceramtec.com					
CeramTec North America Corp 1 Technology Pl	Laurens	SC	29360	864-682-3215	682-1140
TF: 800-845-9761 ■ *Web:* www.ceramtec.com					
CoorsTek Inc 16000 Table Mountain Pkwy	Golden	CO	80403	303-278-4000	277-4574
TF: 800-821-6110 ■ *Web:* www.coorstek.com					
Custom Technical Ceramics Inc 8041 N I-70 Unit 6	Arvada	CO	80002	303-431-7798	431-6168
Web: www.customtechceramics.com					
Du-Co Ceramics Co Inc 155 S Rebecca St PO Box 568	Saxonburg	PA	16056	724-352-1511	352-1266
Web: www.ceramics.com/duco					
EDO Electro-Ceramic Products 2645 S 300 West	Salt Lake City	UT	84115	801-486-7481	484-3301
Web: www.edoceramic.com					
Fair-Rite Products Corp 1 Commerical Row PO Box J	Wallkill	NY	12589	845-895-2055	895-2629
TF: 888-324-7748 ■ *Web:* www.fair-rite.com					
Ferronics Inc 45 O'Connor Rd	Fairport	NY	14450	585-388-1020	388-0036
Web: www.ferronics.com					
International Ceramic Engineering 235 Brooks St	Worcester	MA	01606	508-853-4700	852-4101
TF: 800-779-3321 ■ *Web:* www.intlceramics.com					
Kane Magnetics International 700 Elk Ave	Kane	PA	16735	814-837-7000	837-9615
Web: www.kanemagnetics.com					
Kyocera Industrial Ceramics Corp 5713 E Fourth Plain Rd	Vancouver	WA	98661	360-696-8950	696-9804
TF: 800-826-0527 ■ *Web:* americas.kyocera.com/KICC					
Lapp Insulator Co 130 Gilbert St	Le Roy	NY	14482	585-768-6221	768-6219*
**Fax:* Cust Svc ■ *Web:* www.lappinsulator.com					
LTD Ceramics Inc 7411 Central Ave	Newark	CA	94560	510-789-2222	789-2231
Web: www.ltdceramics.com					
Maryland Ceramic & Steatite Co Inc PO Box 527	Bel Air	MD	21014	410-838-4114	457-4333
Web: www.marylandceramic.com					
Morgan Advanced Ceramics Inc 225 Theodore Rice Blvd	New Bedford	MA	02745	508-995-1725	995-6954
Web: www.morganadvancedceramics.com					
Morgan Advanced Ceramics Inc Alberox Div					
225 Theodore Rice Blvd	New Bedford	MA	02745	508-995-1725	995-6954
Web: www.alberox.com					
Morgan Advanced Ceramics Inc GBC Materials Div					
580 Monastery Dr	Latrobe	PA	15650	724-537-7791	537-4910
NTK Technical Ceramics 6 Whatney	Irvine	CA	92618	949-855-8278	855-8395
Web: www.ntktech.com					
PPC Insulators USA 225 N Patterson St	Carey	OH	43316	419-396-7621	396-7128
Web: www.ppcinsulators.com					
Precision Engineered Ceramics 812 Tradesman Pk Loop PO Box 938	Hutto	TX	78634	512-759-2994	846-2903
Web: www.peceramics.com					
Saint-Gobain Advanced Ceramics Latrobe 4702 Rt 982	Latrobe	PA	15650	724-539-6000	539-6070
TF: 800-438-7237 ■ *Web:* www.wrt.saint-gobain.com					
Saxonburg Ceramics Inc 100 N Isabella St PO Box 688	Saxonburg	PA	16056	724-352-1561	352-3580
TF: 800-245-1270 ■ *Web:* www.saxonburgceramics.com					
Steward Inc 1200 E 36th St	Chattanooga	TN	37407	423-867-4100	867-4102
TF Cust Svc: 800-634-2673 ■ *Web:* www.steward.com					
Superior Technical Ceramics Corp 600 Industrial Pk Rd	Saint Albans	VT	05478	802-527-7726	527-1181
Web: www.superiortechceramics.com					
TDK Ferrites Corp 5900 N Harrison St	Shawnee	OK	74804	405-275-2100	878-0574
Trans-Tech Inc 5520 Adamstown Rd	Adamstown	MD	21710	301-695-9400	695-7065
Web: www.trans-techinc.com					
Vesuvius McDanel Co 510 9th Ave	Beaver Falls	PA	15010	724-843-8300	843-5644
Web: www.ceramics.com/vesuvius					
Victor Insulators Inc 280 Maple Ave	Victor	NY	14564	585-924-2127	924-7906
Web: www.victorinsulators.com					
Wesgo Ceramics 2425 Whipple Rd	Hayward	CA	94544	510-491-1100	491-1175
Web: www.wesgo.com					
Wisconsin Porcelain Co PO Box 89	Sun Prairie	WI	53590	608-837-5155	837-0808

253 ELECTROMEDICAL & ELECTROTHERAPEUTIC EQUIPMENT

SEE ALSO Medical Instruments & Apparatus - Mfr p. 1953

Company	City	State	Zip	Phone	Fax
ABIOMED Inc 22 Cherry Hill Dr	Danvers	MA	01923	978-777-5410	777-8411
NASDAQ: ABMD ■ *TF:* 800-422-8666 ■ *Web:* www.abiomed.com					
Advanced Neuromodulation Systems Inc 6901 Preston Rd	Plano	TX	75024	972-309-8000	309-8150
TF: 800-727-7846 ■ *Web:* www.ans-medical.com					
Affymetrix Inc 3420 Central Expy	Santa Clara	CA	95051	408-731-5503	731-5380
NASDAQ: AFFX ■ *TF Tech Supp:* 888-362-2447 ■ *Web:* www.affymetrix.com					
Alere Medical Inc 595 Double Eagle Ct Suite 1000	Reno	NV	89521	775-829-8885	829-8637
Web: www.alere.com					
Analogic Corp 8 Centennial Dr	Peabody	MA	01960	978-977-3000	977-6810*
NASDAQ: ALOG ■ **Fax:* Hum Res ■ *Web:* www.analogic.com					
Angeion Corp 350 Oak Grove Pkwy	Saint Paul	MN	55127	651-484-4874	484-8941
NASDAQ: ANGN ■ *Web:* www.angeion.com					
Arrhythmia Research Technology Inc 25 Sawyer Passway	Fitchburg	MA	01420	978-345-0181	342-0168
AMEX: HRT ■ *Web:* www.arthrt.com					
ArthroCare Corp 680 Vaqueros Ave	Sunnyvale	CA	94085	408-736-0224	736-0226
NASDAQ: ARTC ■ *TF:* 800-348-8929 ■ *Web:* www.arthrocare.com					
Aspect Medical Systems Inc 1 Upland Rd	Norwood	MA	02062	617-559-7000	559-7400
NASDAQ: ASPM ■ *TF:* 888-247-4633 ■ *Web:* www.aspectms.com					
Astro-Med Inc 600 E Greenwich Ave	West Warwick	RI	02893	401-828-4000	822-2430
NASDAQ: ALOT ■ *TF:* 877-757-7978 ■ *Web:* www.astro-med.com					
Bio-logic Systems Corp 1 Bio-logic Plaza	Mundelein	IL	60060	847-949-5200	949-8615
TF Cust Svc: 800-323-8326 ■ *Web:* www.blsc.com					
Boston Scientific Corp 4100 Hamline Ave N	Saint Paul	MN	55112	651-582-4000	582-4166
TF: 800-405-9611 ■ *Web:* www.guidant.com					
Bovie Aaron Medical 7100 30th Ave N	Saint Petersburg	FL	33710	727-384-2323	347-9144
TF: 800-537-2790 ■ *Web:* www.aaronmed.com					
Bovie Medical Corp 734 Walt Whitman Rd Suite 207	Melville	NY	11747	631-421-5452	421-5821
AMEX: BVX ■ *TF:* 800-888-4999 ■ *Web:* www.boviemedical.com					
BSD Medical Corp 2188 W 2200 South	Salt Lake City	UT	84119	801-972-5555	972-5930
AMEX: BSM ■ *Web:* www.bsdmc.com					
Cardiac Science Corp 3303 Monte Villa Pkwy	Bothell	WA	98021	425-402-2000	402-2001
TF: 800-426-0337 ■ *Web:* www.quinton.com					
CardioDynamics International Corp					
6175 Nancy Ridge Dr Suite 300	San Diego	CA	92121	858-535-0202	623-0408
NASDAQ: CDIC ■ *TF:* 800-778-4825 ■ *Web:* www.cardiodynamics.com					
CAS Medical Systems Inc 44 E Industrial Rd	Branford	CT	06405	203-488-6056	488-9438
NASDAQ: CASM ■ *TF:* 800-227-4414 ■ *Web:* www.casmed.com					
Compumedics USA Ltd 7850 Paseo del Norte Suite 101	El Paso	TX	79912	915-845-5600	845-0355
TF: 877-717-3975 ■ *Web:* www.compumedics.com					
Computerized Thermal Imaging Inc (CTI) 1719 W 2800 South	Ogden	UT	84401	801-776-4700	459-6063
Web: www.cti-net.com					
CONMED Corp 525 French Rd	Utica	NY	13502	315-797-8375	438-3051*
NASDAQ: CNMD ■ **Fax Area Code:* 800 ■ **Fax:* Cust Svc ■ *TF:* 800-448-6506 ■ *Web:* www.conmed.com					
Cook Vascular Inc 1186 Montgomery Ln	Vandergrift	PA	15690	724-845-8621	845-2848
TF: 800-245-4715 ■ *Web:* www.cookvascular.com					
Covidien 5920 Longbow Dr	Boulder	CO	80301	303-530-2300	530-6285
TF: 800-255-8522 ■ *Web:* www.covidien.com					
Criticare Systems Inc 20925 Crossroads Cir Suite 100	Waukesha	WI	53186	262-798-8282	798-8290
AMEX: CMD ■ *TF:* 800-458-4615 ■ *Web:* www.csiusa.com					
Datascope Corp 14 Philips Pkwy	Montvale	NJ	07645	201-391-8100	307-5400
NASDAQ: DSCP ■ *TF:* 800-288-2121 ■ *Web:* www.datascope.com					
Draeger Medical Inc 3135 Quarry Rd	Telford	PA	18969	215-723-9824	721-9561*
**Fax:* Sales ■ *TF:* 800-437-2437 ■ *Web:* www.draegermedical.com					
Draeger Medical Infant Care Inc 3135 Quarry Rd	Telford	PA	18969	800-437-2437	675-1859*
**Fax Area Code:* 215 ■ *Web:* www.draeger-medical.com					
Dynatronics Corp 7030 Park Centre Dr	Salt Lake City	UT	84121	801-568-7000	221-1919*
NASDAQ: DYNT ■ **Fax Area Code:* 800 ■ *TF:* 800-874-6251 ■ *Web:* www.dynatronics.com					
EBI Medical Systems LP 100 Interpace Pkwy	Parsippany	NJ	07054	973-299-9300	524-0457*
**Fax Area Code:* 800 ■ *TF:* 800-526-2579 ■ *Web:* www.ebimedical.com					
Encision Inc 6797 Winchester Cir	Boulder	CO	80301	303-444-2600	444-2693
AMEX: ECI ■ *TF:* 800-998-0986 ■ *Web:* www.encision.com					
EP MedSystems Inc 575 Rt 73 N	West Berlin	NJ	08091	856-753-8533	753-8544
NASDAQ: EPMD ■ *TF:* 800-537-6285 ■ *Web:* www.epmedsystems.com					
Fisher & Paykel Healthcare Inc 15365 Barranca Pkwy	Irvine	CA	92618	949-453-4000	453-4001
TF: 800-446-3908 ■ *Web:* www.fphcare.co.nz					
Gambro Renal Products 10810 W Collins Ave	Lakewood	CO	80215	303-232-6800	231-4032*
**Fax:* Mktg ■ *TF:* 800-525-2623 ■ *Web:* www.usa-gambro.com					
GE Healthcare 3000 Grandview N	Waukesha	WI	53188	262-544-3011	548-2443*
**Fax:* Cust Svc ■ *TF:* 800-558-5102 ■ *Web:* www.gehealthcare.com					
GE Healthcare Information Technologies 8200 W Tower Ave	Milwaukee	WI	53223	414-355-5000	
TF: 800-558-5102					
HealthTronics Inc 1301 S Capital of Texas Hwy Suite B-200	Austin	TX	78746	512-328-2892	328-8510
NASDAQ: HTRN ■ *TF:* 888-252-6575 ■ *Web:* www.primemedical.com					
Inovio Biomedical Corp 11494 Sorrento Valley Rd	San Diego	CA	92121	858-597-6006	597-0451
AMEX: INO ■ *TF:* 877-446-6846 ■ *Web:* www.inovio.com					
IVY Biomedical Systems Inc 11 Business Park Dr	Branford	CT	06405	203-481-4183	481-8734
TF: 800-247-4614 ■ *Web:* www.ivybiomedical.com					
Masimo Corp 40 Parker	Irvine	CA	92618	949-297-7000	297-7001
TF: 800-326-4890 ■ *Web:* www.masimo.com					
Medical Graphics Corp 350 Oak Grove Pkwy	Saint Paul	MN	55127	651-484-4874	484-8941
TF: 800-333-4137 ■ *Web:* www.medgraph.com					
Medtronic of Canada Ltd 6733 Kitimat Rd	Mississauga	ON	L5N1W3	905-826-6020	826-6620
TF: 800-268-5346 ■ *Web:* www.medtronic.com					
Medtronic Emergency Response Systems					
11811 Willows Rd NE	Redmond	WA	98052	425-867-4000	881-2405*
**Fax:* Acctg ■ *TF:* 800-442-1142 ■ *Web:* www.medtronic-ers.com					
Medtronic Inc 710 Medtronic Pkwy NE	Minneapolis	MN	55432	763-514-4000	514-4879
NYSE: MDT ■ *TF Cust Svc:* 800-328-2518 ■ *Web:* www.medtronic.com					
Medtronic Perfusion Systems 7611 Northland Dr	Brooklyn Park	MN	55428	763-391-9000	391-9100
TF: 800-328-3320 ■ *Web:* www.medtronic.com					
Medtronic Powered Surgical Solutions 4620 N Beach St	Fort Worth	TX	76137	817-788-6400	788-6401*
**Fax:* Orders ■ *TF:* 800-433-7639 ■ *Web:* www.medtronic.com/neuro/midasrex					
Mennen Medical Corp 101 Witmer Rd Suite 100	Horsham	PA	19044	215-259-1020	675-6212
TF: 800-223-2201 ■ *Web:* www.mennenmedical.com					
Meridian Medical Technologies Inc					
6350 Stevens Forest Rd Suite 301	Columbia	MD	21046	443-259-7800	259-7801
TF: 800-638-8093 ■ *Web:* www.meridianmeds.com					
MicroMed Technology Inc 8965 Interchange Dr	Houston	TX	77054	713-838-9210	838-9214
Web: www.micromedtech.com					
Mortara Instrument Inc 7865 N 86th St	Milwaukee	WI	53224	414-354-1600	354-4760
TF: 800-231-7437 ■ *Web:* www.mortara.com					
Natus Medical Inc 1501 Industrial Rd	San Carlos	CA	94070	650-802-0400	802-0401
NASDAQ: BABY ■ *TF:* 800-255-3901 ■ *Web:* www.natusmed.com					
NeuroMetrix 62 4th Ave	Waltham	MA	02451	781-890-9989	890-1556
NASDAQ: NURO ■ *TF:* 888-786-7287 ■ *Web:* www.neurometrix.com					
Oscor Inc 3816 DeSoto Blvd	Palm Harbor	FL	34683	727-937-2511	934-9835
TF: 800-726-7267 ■ *Web:* www.oscor.com					
OSI Systems Inc 12525 Chadron Ave	Hawthorne	CA	90250	310-978-0516	644-1727
NASDAQ: OSIS ■ *Web:* www.osi-systems.com					
Paradigm Medical Industries Inc 2355 S 1070 West	Salt Lake City	UT	84119	801-977-8970	977-8973
TF: 800-742-0671 ■ *Web:* www.paradigm-medical.com					
QMed Inc 25 Christopher Way	Eatontown	NJ	07724	732-544-5544	544-5404
NASDAQ: QMED ■ *Web:* www.qmedinc.com					
Respironics Inc 1010 Murry Ridge Ln	Murrysville	PA	15668	724-387-5200	387-5245
NASDAQ: RESP ■ *TF:* 800-345-6443 ■ *Web:* www.respironics.com					
Respironics Novametrix Medical Systems Inc 5 Technology Dr	Wallingford	CT	06492	203-265-7701	284-0753
TF: 800-243-3444 ■ *Web:* www.novametrix.com					
Saint Jude Medical Inc Cardiac Rhythm Management Div					
15900 Valley View Ct	Sylmar	CA	91342	818-362-6822	364-5814
Web: www.sjm.com					
Saint Jude Medical Inc Heart Valve Div 1 Lillehei Plaza	Saint Paul	MN	55117	651-483-2000	482-8318
TF: 800-328-9634 ■ *Web:* www.sjm.com					
SensorMedics Corp 22745 Savi Ranch Pkwy	Yorba Linda	CA	92887	714-283-2228	283-8439*
**Fax:* Mktg ■ *TF:* 800-231-2466 ■ *Web:* www.sensormedics.com					
Siemens Medical Solutions Inc 51 Valley Stream Pkwy	Malvern	PA	19355	610-448-6300	219-3124
TF: 866-872-9745 ■ *Web:* www.medical.siemens.com					
Smiths Medical PM Inc N7 W22025 Johnson Rd	Waukesha	WI	53186	262-542-3100	542-0718
TF Cust Svc: 800-558-2345 ■ *Web:* www.smiths-medical.com					
Spacelabs Health Care 5150 220th Ave SE	Issaquah	WA	98029	425-657-7200	
TF: 800-287-7108 ■ *Web:* www.spacelabs.com					
Thoratec Corp 6035 Stoneridge Dr	Pleasanton	CA	94588	925-847-8600	847-8574
NASDAQ: THOR ■ *TF:* 800-528-2577 ■ *Web:* www.thoratec.com					
Vasomedical Inc 180 Linden Ave	Westbury	NY	11590	516-997-4600	997-2299
NASDAQ: VASO ■ *TF:* 800-455-3327 ■ *Web:* www.vasomedical.com					
Viasys Respiratory Care 1100 Bird Center Dr	Palm Springs	CA	92262	760-778-7200	778-7274*
**Fax:* Cust Svc ■ *Web:* www.viasyshealthcare.com					

Phone Fax

Welch Allyn Medical Products 4341 State Street Rd ...... Skaneateles Falls NY 13153 315-685-4100 685-3361
TF: 800-535-6663 ■ *Web:* www.welchallyn.com/medical

Welch Allyn Monitoring Inc 8500 SW Creekside Pl.............. Beaverton OR 97008 503-530-7500 526-4200*
**Fax:* Cust Svc ■ *TF Cust Svc:* 800-289-2500 ■ *Web:* www.monitoring.welchallyn.com

World Heart Inc 7799 Pardee Ln .... Oakland CA 94621 510-563-5000 563-5005
NASDAQ: WHRT ■ *Web:* www.worldheart.com

Zareba Systems Inc 13705 26th Ave N Suite 102 .... Minneapolis MN 55441 763-551-1125 509-7450
NASDAQ: ZRBA ■ *Web:* www.wtrs.com

ZOLL Medical Corp 269 Mill Rd .... Chelmsford MA 01824 978-421-9655 421-0025
NASDAQ: ZOLL ■ *TF:* 800-348-9011 ■ *Web:* www.zoll.com

254 ELECTRONIC BILL PRESENTMENT & PAYMENT SERVICES

SEE ALSO Application Service Providers (ASPs) p. 1281

Phone Fax

CheckFree Corp 4411 E Jones Bridge Rd..................... Norcross GA 30092 678-375-3000
NASDAQ: CKFR ■ *TF Cust Svc:* 800-305-3716 ■ *Web:* www.checkfree.com

Ecount.com 555 N Lane Suite 5040...................... Conshohocken PA 19428 610-941-4600 941-4660
Web: corp.ecount.com

Harbor Payments Inc 1900 Emery St NW 2nd Fl.................. Atlanta GA 30318 404-267-5000 267-5200
Web: www.harborpayments.com

Heartland Payment Systems Inc 90 Nassau St 2nd Fl............ Princeton NJ 08542 609-683-3831 683-3815
NYSE: HPY ■ *TF:* 888-798-3131 ■ *Web:* www.heartlandpaymentsystems.com

Internet Billing Co Ltd (iBill) 2200 SW 10th St............ Deerfield Beach FL 33442 954-363-4400 363-4401
TF: 888-237-1764 ■ *Web:* www.ibill.com

Kanbay International Inc 6400 Shafer Ct Suite 100 .... Rosemont IL 60018 847-384-6100 384-0500
NASDAQ: KBAY ■ *Web:* www.kanbay.com

LML Payment Systems Inc 1140 W Pender St Suite 1680........ Vancouver BC V6E4G1 604-689-4440 689-4413
NASDAQ: LMLP ■ *Web:* www.lmlpayment.com

Metavante Corp 4900 W Brown Deer Rd .... Brown Deer WI 53223 414-357-2290 357-9606
TF: 800-236-3282 ■ *Web:* www.metavante.com

PayPal Inc PO Box 45950.................................. Omaha NE 68145 402-935-2050 537-5734
Web: www.paypal.com

Paytrust Inc 4900 W Brown Deer Rd........................ Milwaukee WI 53223 800-729-8787
Web: www.paytrust.com

Princeton eCom Corp 650 College Rd E 2nd Fl .... Princeton NJ 08540 609-606-3000 606-3294
TF: 866-606-3000 ■ *Web:* www.princetonecom.com

TPi Billing Solutions PO Box 472330.............................. Tulsa OK 74147 918-664-0144 665-6677
TF: 800-332-0023 ■ *Web:* www.tpibillingsolutions.com

TROY Group Inc 2331 S Pullman St .... Santa Ana CA 92705 949-250-3280 250-8972
TF: 800-633-2266 ■ *Web:* www.troygroup.com

255 ELECTRONIC COMMUNICATIONS NETWORKS (ECNS)

SEE ALSO Securities & Commodities Exchanges p. 2309; Securities Brokers & Dealers p. 2307

ECNs are computerized trade-matching systems that unite best bid and offer prices and provide anonymity to investors.

Phone Fax

Archipelago Holdings LLC 100 S Wacker Dr Suite 1800 .... Chicago IL 60606 312-960-1696 960-1369
TF: 888-514-7284 ■ *Web:* www.tradearca.com

Bloomberg Tradebook LLC 731 Lexington Ave.................. New York NY 10022 212-893-5555
Web: tradebook.bloomberg.com

Instinet Group Inc 3 Times Sq .... New York NY 10036 212-310-9500
TF: 800-225-5008 ■ *Web:* www.instinet.com

Javelin Technologies 100 Wall St 26th Fl .... New York NY 10005 212-525-3000 809-1013
Web: www.javtech.com

MILCOM Systems Corp 532 Viking Dr...................... Virginia Beach VA 23452 757-463-2800 463-3052
TF: 800-967-0966 ■ *Web:* www.milcomsystems.com

NexTrade 301 S Missouri Ave.............................. Clearwater FL 33756 727-446-6660 441-8880
Web: nextrade1.com

NYFIX Inc 100 Wall St 26th Fl............................. New York NY 10005 212-809-3542 809-1013
Web: www.nyfix.com

Pink Sheets LLC 304 Hudson St 2nd Fl .... New York NY 10013 212-896-4400 868-3848
Web: www.pinksheets.com

SYS Technologies Inc 5050 Murphy Canyon Rd Suite 200....... San Diego CA 92123 858-715-5500 715-5510
AMEX: SYS ■ *Web:* www.systechnologies.com

256 ELECTRONIC COMPONENTS & ACCESSORIES - MFR

SEE ALSO Printed Circuit Boards p. 2138; Semiconductors & Related Devices p. 2312

Phone Fax

3M Electrical Products Div 6801 River Place Blvd 3M Austin Center..... Austin TX 78726 512-984-1800 245-0329*
**Fax Area Code:* 800 ■ *TF:* 800-245-3573 ■ *Web:* www.3m.com/elpd

3M Electro & Communications Div 3M Center .... Saint Paul MN 55144 651-733-1110 737-7117
TF: 800-364-3577

3M Electronic Handling & Protection Div 6801 River Place Blvd...... Austin TX 78726 800-328-1368 858-9136
Web: www.3m.com/ehpd

3M Interconnect Solutions Div 6801 River Place Blvd .... Austin TX 78726 512-984-1800 984-3417
TF: 800-225-5373 ■ *Web:* www.3m.com/us/electronics_mfg/interconnects

3M Transportation Div 3M Center......................... Saint Paul MN 55144 651-733-1110
TF: 888-364-3577

Aavid Thermal Technologies Inc 1 Eagle Sq Suite 509............ Concord NH 03301 603-224-1117 224-6673
Web: www.aavid.com

Aavid Thermalloy LLC 80 Commercial St .... Concord NH 03301 603-224-9988 223-1738
Web: www.aavidthermalloy.com

Actown-Electrocoil Inc 2414 Highview St .... Spring Grove IL 60081 815-675-6641 675-2050
TF: 800-531-6366 ■ *Web:* www.actown.com

AEM Inc 11525 Sorrento Valley Rd.......................... San Diego CA 92121 858-481-0210 481-1123
TF: 888-323-6462 ■ *Web:* www.aem-usa.com

Aeroflex Inc 35 S Service Rd .... Plainview NY 11803 516-694-6700 694-6771
NASDAQ: ARXX ■ *TF:* 800-843-1553 ■ *Web:* www.aeroflex.com

Aeroflex/Weinschel Inc 5305 Spectrum Dr .... Frederick MD 21703 301-846-9222 846-9116
TF Cust Svc: 800-638-2048 ■ *Web:* www.weinschel.com

Aerovox Inc 167 John Vertente Blvd...................... New Bedford MA 02745 508-994-9661 999-1000
TF: 800-343-3348 ■ *Web:* www.aerovox.com

Phone Fax

AESP Inc 16295 NW 13th Ave.................................. Miami FL 33169 305-944-7710 949-4483
TF: 800-446-2377 ■ *Web:* www.aesp.com

Alliance Fiber Optic Products Inc 275 Gibraltar Dr............. Sunnyvale CA 94089 408-736-6900 736-2466
NASDAQ: AFOP ■ *Web:* www.afop.com

Alpha Technologies Inc 3767 Alpha Way...................... Bellingham WA 98226 360-647-2360 671-4936*
**Fax:* Sales ■ *TF:* 800-322-5742 ■ *Web:* www.alpha.com

American Power Conversion Corp (APC) 132 Fairgrounds Rd ... West Kingston RI 02892 401-789-5735 789-3710
NASDAQ: APCC ■ *TF Cust Svc:* 800-788-2208 ■ *Web:* www.apcc.com

American Shizuki Corp 301 W 'O' St .... Ogallala NE 69153 308-284-3611 284-8324
Web: www.ascapacitor.com

AMETEK Automation & Process Technologies 1080 N Crooks Rd .... Clawson MI 48017 248-435-0700 435-8120
TF: 800-635-0289 ■ *Web:* www.ametekapt.com

Ametek HDR Power Systems Inc 3563 Interchange Rd........... Columbus OH 43204 614-308-5500 308-5506
TF: 888-797-2685 ■ *Web:* www.hdrpower.com

AMETEK Prestolite Power & Switch 2220 Corporate Dr.............. Troy OH 45373 937-440-0800 654-4024*
**Fax Area Code:* 800 ■ *TF:* 800-367-2002 ■ *Web:* www.powerandswitchproducts.com

AMETEK Solidstate Controls 875 Dearborn Dr.................. Columbus OH 43085 614-846-7500 885-3990
TF: 800-635-7300 ■ *Web:* www.solidstatecontrolsinc.com

Amphenol Aerospace 40-60 Delaware Ave .... Sidney NY 13838 607-563-5011 563-5157
TF: 800-678-0141 ■ *Web:* www.amphenol-aerospace.com

Amphenol Interconnect Products Corp 20 Valley St .... Endicott NY 13760 607-754-4444 786-4234*
**Fax:* Hum Res ■ *TF:* 888-275-2473 ■ *Web:* www.amphenol-aipc.com

Amphenol PCD 72 Cherry Hill Dr................................ Beverly MA 01915 978-624-3400 972-1513*
**Fax:* Sales ■ *Web:* www.amphenolpcd.com

Amphenol RF 4 Old Newtown Rd .... Danbury CT 06810 203-743-9272 796-2071
TF: 800-627-7100 ■ *Web:* www.amphenolrf.com

Amphenol Sine Systems 44724 Morley Dr .... Clinton Township MI 48036 586-465-3131
Web: www.sineco.com

Amphenol Spectra-Strip 720 Sherman Ave .... Hamden CT 06514 203-281-3200 281-5872
TF: 800-846-6400 ■ *Web:* www.spectra-strip.amphenol.com

Amphenol-Tuchel Electronics 6900 Haggerty Rd Suite 200 .... Canton MI 48187 734-451-6400 451-7197
TF: 800-380-8052 ■ *Web:* www.amphenol-tuchel.com

AmRad Engineering Inc 32 Hargrove Grade.................. Palm Coast FL 32137 386-445-6000 445-6871
TF: 800-445-6033 ■ *Web:* www.amradcapacitors.com

Anaren Microwave Inc 6635 Kirkville Rd .... East Syracuse NY 13057 315-432-8909 432-9121
NASDAQ: ANEN ■ *TF:* 800-544-2414 ■ *Web:* www.anaren.com

Antec Inc 47900 Fremont Blvd .... Fremont CA 94538 510-770-1200 770-1288
TF Cust Svc: 888-542-6832 ■ *Web:* www.antec-inc.com

APC (American Power Conversion Corp) 132 Fairgrounds Rd ... West Kingston RI 02892 401-789-5735 789-3710
NASDAQ: APCC ■ *TF Cust Svc:* 800-788-2208 ■ *Web:* www.apcc.com

API Delevan 270 Quaker Rd .... East Aurora NY 14052 716-652-3600 652-4814
Web: www.delevan.com

Aries Electronics Inc 62-A Trenton Ave PO Box 130........... Frenchtown NJ 08825 908-996-6841 996-3891
Web: www.arieselec.com

Astec America Inc 5810 Van Allen Way......................... Carlsbad CA 92008 760-930-4600 930-0698
TF: 888-412-7832 ■ *Web:* www.astecpower.com

Avanex Corp 40919 Encyclopedia Cir .... Fremont CA 94538 510-897-4188 897-4189
NASDAQ: AVNX ■ *Web:* www.avanex.com

AVG Automation 4140 Utica St............................. Battendorf IA 52722 630-462-5906 359-9094*
**Fax Area Code:* 563 ■ *TF:* 800-711-5109 ■ *Web:* www.avg.net/avgautomation

Avionic Instruments Inc 1414 Randolph Ave .... Avenel NJ 07001 732-388-3500 382-4996
Web: www.avionicinstruments.com

Avnet Electronics Marketing 2211 S 47th St .... Phoenix AZ 85034 480-643-2000
TF: 888-822-8638 ■ *Web:* www.em.avnet.com

AVX Corp 801 17th Ave S .... Myrtle Beach SC 29577 843-448-9411 444-0424
NYSE: AVX ■ *Web:* www.avxcorp.com

Ballard Power Systems Inc 9000 Glenlyon Pkwy.................. Burnaby BC V5J5J8 604-454-0900 412-4700
NASDAQ: BLDP ■ *Web:* www.ballard.com

Banner Engineering Corp 9714 10th Ave N .... Minneapolis MN 55441 763-544-3164 544-3213
TF: 888-373-6767 ■ *Web:* www.bannerengineering.com

Beacon Power Corp 234 Ballardvale St..................... Wilmington MA 01887 978-694-9121 694-9127
NASDAQ: BCON ■ *TF:* 888-938-9112 ■ *Web:* www.beaconpower.com

BEI Technologies Inc Duncan Electronics Div 170 Technology Dr..... Irvine CA 92618 949-341-9500 453-2700
Web: www.beiduncan.com

BEI Technologies Inc Industrial Encoder Div 7230 Hollister Ave ...... Goleta CA 93117 805-968-0782 968-3154
TF Sales: 800-350-2727 ■ *Web:* www.beiied.com

Belkin Corp 501 W Walnut St.............................. Compton CA 90220 310-898-1100 898-1100
TF: 800-223-5546 ■ *Web:* world.belkin.com

Bergquist Co 18930 W 78th St........................... Chanhassen MN 55317 952-835-2322 835-4156
TF: 800-347-4572 ■ *Web:* www.bergquistcompany.com

BH Electronics Inc 12219 Wood Lake Dr.................... Burnsville MN 55337 952-894-9590 894-9380
Web: www.bhelectronics.com

Bookham Inc 2584 Junction Ave........................... San Jose CA 95134 408-919-1500 919-6083
NASDAQ: BKHM ■ *TF:* 866-683-7287 ■ *Web:* www.bookham.com

C & D Technologies Inc 1400 Union Meeting Rd PO Box 3053 ..... Blue Bell PA 19422 215-619-2700 619-7840
NYSE: CHP ■ *TF:* 800-543-8630 ■ *Web:* www.cdtechno.com

C&D Technologies 11 Cabot Blvd.......................... Mansfield MA 02048 508-339-3000 339-6356
TF: 800-233-2765 ■ *Web:* www.cd4power.com

Celestica Inc 12 Concorde Pl 5th Fl .... Toronto ON M3C3R8 416-448-5800 448-4810
NYSE: CLS ■ *TF:* 888-899-9998 ■ *Web:* www.celestica.com

CeramTec North America 1 Technology Pl...................... Laurens SC 29360 864-682-3215 682-1121
TF: 800-845-9761 ■ *Web:* www.ceramtec.com

CeramTec North America Corp 1 Technology Pl .... Laurens SC 29360 864-682-3215 682-1140
TF: 800-845-9761 ■ *Web:* www.ceramtec.com

Circuit Assembly Corp 18 Thomas St............................ Irvine CA 92618 949-855-7887 855-4298
Web: www.circuitassembly.com

Cirrus Logic Inc 5980 N Shannon Rd........................... Tucson AZ 85741 520-690-8600 888-3329
TF: 800-421-1865 ■ *Web:* www.apexmicrotech.com

Coilcraft Inc 1102 Silver Lake Rd................................. Cary IL 60013 847-639-2361 639-1469
TF: 800-323-5045 ■ *Web:* www.coilcraft.com

Coils Inc 11716 Algonquin Rd PO Box 247 .... Huntley IL 60142 847-669-5115 669-5150
Web: www.coilsinc.com

Comdel Inc 11 Kondelin Rd............................. Gloucester MA 01930 978-282-0620 282-4980
TF: 800-468-3144 ■ *Web:* www.comdel.com

Communications & Power Industries DBA CPI Inc
811 Hansen Way PO Box 50750 .... Palo Alto CA 94303 650-846-2900 846-3276*
**Fax:* PR ■ *TF:* 800-231-4818 ■ *Web:* www.cpii.com

Communications & Power Industries Inc EIMAC Div DBA CPI Inc EIMAC Div 301 Industrial Rd............... San Carlos CA 94070 650-592-1221 592-9988
TF: 800-423-4622 ■ *Web:* www.cpii.com/eimac

Cooper Industries 600 Travis St Suite 5800.................... Houston TX 77002 713-209-8400 209-8995
NYSE: CBE ■ *Web:* www.cooperindustries.com

Corning Gilbert Inc 5310 W Camelback Rd .... Glendale AZ 85301 623-245-1050 934-5160
TF Cust Svc: 800-528-0199 ■ *Web:* www.corning.com/corninggilbert

Cornucopia Tool & Plastics Inc
448 Sherwood Rd PO Box 1915 .... Paso Robles CA 93447 805-369-0030 369-0033
TF: 800-235-4144 ■ *Web:* www.cornucopiaplastics.com

CPI Inc 811 Hansen Way PO Box 50750 .... Palo Alto CA 94303 650-846-2900 846-3276*
**Fax:* PR ■ *TF:* 800-231-4818 ■ *Web:* www.cpii.com

				Phone	Fax
Crystek Crystals Corp 12730 Commonwealth Dr Unit 6	Fort Myers	FL	33913	239-561-3311	561-1025
TF: 800-237-3061 ■ *Web:* www.crystek.com					
CTS Corp 905 West Blvd N	Elkhart	IN	46514	574-293-7511	293-6146
NYSE: CTS ■ *Web:* www.ctscorp.com					
Cyberex 5900 Eastport Blvd	Richmond	VA	23231	804-236-3300	236-4047
TF: 800-238-5000 ■ *Web:* www.cyberex.com					
Data Device Corp 105 Wilbur Pl	Bohemia	NY	11716	631-567-5600	567-6015
TF Cust Svc: 800-332-5757 ■ *Web:* www.ddc-web.com					
Dekko Technologies LLC 8645 E Backwater Rd PO Box 337	North Webster	IN	46555	574-834-2818	834-2794
Web: www.dekkotech.com					
Delta Electronics Mfg Corp 416 Cabot St	Beverly	MA	01915	978-927-1060	922-6430
Web: www.deltarf.com					
Delta Products Corp 4405 Cushing Pkwy	Fremont	CA	94538	510-668-5100	668-0696
Web: www.deltaww.com					
Diamond Antenna & Microwave Corp 59 Porter Rd	Littleton	MA	01460	978-486-0039	486-0079
Web: www.diamondantenna.com					
Dielectric Laboratories Inc 2777 Rt 20 E	Cazenovia	NY	13035	315-655-8710	655-8179
TF: 800-656-9499 ■ *Web:* www.dilabs.com					
Digital Power Corp 41920 Christy St	Fremont	CA	94538	510-657-2635	657-6634
AMEX: DPW ■ *Web:* www.digipwr.com					
Distributed Energy Systems Corp 10 Technology Dr	Wallingford	CT	06492	203-678-2000	949-8016
NASDAQ: DESC ■ *Web:* www.distributed-energy.com					
Dow-Key Microwave Corp 4822 McGrath St	Ventura	CA	93003	805-650-0260	650-1734
TF: 800-266-3695 ■ *Web:* www.dowkey.com					
DRS Laurel Technologies 246 Airport Rd	Johnstown	PA	15904	814-534-8900	534-8815
Web: www.drs.com					
Ducommun Technologies Inc 23301 Wilmington Ave	Carson	CA	90745	310-513-7200	513-7298
TF: 800-421-5032 ■ *Web:* www.ductech.com					
Duncan Electronics Div BEI Technologies Inc 170 Technology Dr	Irvine	CA	92618	949-341-9500	453-2700
Web: www.beiduncan.com					
Eby Co 4300 H St	Philadelphia	PA	19124	215-537-4700	537-4780
TF: 800-329-3430 ■ *Web:* www.ebycompany.com					
Elcon Products International Co 307 Constitution Dr	Menlo Park	CA	94025	650-361-3222	361-3223
TF: 800-227-8816 ■ *Web:* www.elconproducts.com					
ELDEC Corp 16700 13th Ave W	Lynnwood	WA	98037	425-743-1313	743-8234
TF: 800-464-0261 ■ *Web:* www.eldec.com					
Electro-Mechanical Corp 1 Goodson St	Bristol	VA	24201	276-466-8200	466-6931
Web: www.electro-mechanical.com					
Electroswitch Corp 180 King Ave	Weymouth	MA	02188	781-335-5200	335-4253
Web: www.electroswitch.com					
Elgar Electronics Corp 9250 Brown Deer Rd	San Diego	CA	92121	858-450-0085	458-0267*
**Fax:* Sales ■ *TF:* 800-733-5427 ■ *Web:* www.elgar.com					
Ellanef Mfg Corp 97-11 50th Ave	Corona	NY	11368	718-699-4000	592-0722
Web: www.ellanef.com					
Emerson Network Power Connectivity Solutions					
300 Lakeside Dr Suite 308-N	Bannockburn	IL	60015	847-739-0300	739-0301
Web: emersonnetworkpower.com					
Energy Conversion Devices Inc 2956 Waterview Dr	Rochester Hills	MI	48309	248-293-0440	844-1214
NASDAQ: ENER ■ *Web:* www.ovonic.com					
EPCOS Inc 186 Wood Ave S	Iselin	NJ	08830	732-906-4300	906-4395
NYSE: EPC ■ *TF:* 800-689-3717 ■ *Web:* www.usa.epcos.com					
eSilicon Corp 501 Macara Ave	Sunnyvale	CA	94085	408-616-4600	991-9567
Web: www.esilicon.com					
Espey Mfg & Electronics Corp 233 Ballston Ave	Saratoga Springs	NY	12866	518-584-4100	245-4425
AMEX: ESP ■ *Web:* www.espey.com					
Evolve Manufacturing Technologies 960 Linda Vista Ave	Mountain View	CA	94043	650-968-9292	968-9299
Web: portfolio.aplus.net/evolvemfg/company.htm					
Fawn Industries Inc 1920 Greenspring Dr Suite 140	Timonium	MD	21093	410-308-9200	308-9201
Web: www.fawn-ind.com					
Filnor Inc 227 N Freedom Ave PO Box 2328	Alliance	OH	44601	330-821-7667	829-3175
Web: www.filnor.com					
Flash Electronics Inc 4050 Starboard Dr	Fremont	CA	94538	510-440-2840	440-2844
Web: www.flashelec.com					
Flextronics International Ltd 2090 Fortune Dr	San Jose	CA	95131	408-428-1300	576-7988
NASDAQ: FLEX ■ *Web:* www.flextronics.com					
Framatome Connectors USA Inc (FCI) 47 E Industrial Pk Dr	Manchester	NH	03109	603-647-5000	647-5202*
**Fax:* Cust Svc ■ *TF:* 800-346-4175 ■ *Web:* www.fciconnect.com					
FuelCell Energy Inc 3 Great Pasture Rd	Danbury	CT	06810	203-825-6000	825-6100
NASDAQ: FCEL ■ *Web:* www.fuelcellenergy.com					
Fujitsu Components America Inc 250 E Caribbean Dr	Sunnyvale	CA	94089	408-745-4900	745-4970
Web: www.fujitsu.com/us					
G & H Technology Inc 750 W Ventura Blvd	Camarillo	CA	93010	805-484-0543	987-5062
Web: www.ghtech.com					
GE Aviation Electrical Power Systems 2855 W McNab Rd	Pompano Beach	FL	33069	954-984-7000	984-2479*
**Fax:* Sales ■ *TF:* 800-952-6909 ■ *Web:* www.geaviation.com					
Glasseal Div HCC Industries Inc 485 Oberlin Ave S	Lakewood	NJ	08701	732-370-9100	370-7107
Web: www.glasseal.com/home.htm					
Gore WL & Assoc Inc 551 Papermill Rd	Newark	DE	19711	302-738-4880	738-7710
Web: www.gore.com					
Greatbatch Inc 9645 Wehrle Dr	Clarence	NY	14031	716-759-5600	759-5654
NYSE: GB ■ *Web:* www.greatbatch.com					
GW Lisk Co Inc 2 South St	Clifton Springs	NY	14432	315-462-2611	462-7661
Web: www.gwlisk.com					
Harco Laboratories Inc 186 Cedar St	Branford	CT	06405	203-483-3700	483-0391
Web: www.harcolabs.com					
HCC Industries Inc 4232 Temple City Blvd	Rosemead	CA	91770	626-443-8933	575-2437
Web: www.hccindustries.com					
HCC Industries Inc Glasseal Div 485 Oberlin Ave S	Lakewood	NJ	08701	732-370-9100	370-7107
Web: www.glasseal.com/home.htm					
HCC Industries Inc Hermetic Seal Corp Div					
4232 Temple City Blvd	Rosemead	CA	91770	626-443-8931	443-6610
Web: www.hermeticseal.com/home.htm					
HCC Industries Inc Sealtron Div 9705 Reading Rd	Cincinnati	OH	45215	513-733-8400	733-0131
Web: www.sealtron.com/home.shtml					
Heraeus Shin-Etsu America Inc 4600 NW Pacific Rim Blvd	Camas	WA	98607	360-834-4004	834-3115
Heraeus Tenevo 100 Heraeus Blvd	Buford	GA	30518	770-945-2275	945-4741
TF: 800-848-4527 ■ *Web:* www.heraeusamersil.com					
Herley-CTI Inc 9 Whippany Rd	Whippany	NJ	07981	973-884-2580	887-6245
Web: www.herley.com					
Herley Industries Inc 101 N Point Blvd	Lancaster	PA	17603	717-735-8117	735-8123
NASDAQ: HRLY ■ *Web:* www.herley.com					
Herley New England 10 Sonar Dr	Woburn	MA	01801	781-729-9450	729-9547
Web: www.herleymdi.com					
Hermetic Seal Corp Div HCC Industries Inc					
4232 Temple City Blvd	Rosemead	CA	91770	626-443-8931	443-6610
Web: www.hermeticseal.com/home.htm					
HiRel Systems 11100 Wayzata Blvd Suite 501	Minnetonka	MN	55305	952-544-1344	544-1345
Web: www.hirelsystems.com					
Hirose Electric (USA) Inc 2688 Westhills Ct	Simi Valley	CA	93065	805-522-7958	522-3217
Web: www.hirose.com					
Hitachi Canada Ltd 2495 Meadowpine Blvd	Mississauga	ON	L5N6C3	905-821-4545	821-9435
TF: 800-906-4482 ■ *Web:* www.hitachi.ca					
Hitachi Electronic Devices (USA) Inc 575 Mauldin Rd	Greenville	SC	29607	864-299-2600	299-2700
Web: www.hedus.com					
Hitachi High Technologies America Inc					
10 N Martingale Rd Suite 500	Schaumburg	IL	60173	847-273-4141	273-4407
Web: www.hii-hitachi.com					
Honeywell Electronic Materials 1349 Moffett Park Dr	Sunnyvale	CA	94089	408-962-2000	980-1430
Web: www.honeywell.com/sites/sm/em					
Hubbell Power Systems Inc 210 N Allen St	Centralia	MO	65240	573-682-5521	682-8714
TF: 800-482-2355 ■ *Web:* www.hubbellpowersystems.com					
Hutchinson Technology Inc 40 W Highland Park Dr	Hutchinson	MN	55350	320-587-3797	587-1810
NASDAQ: HTCH ■ *Web:* www.htch.com					
Hydrogenics Corp 5985 McLaughlin Rd	Mississauga	ON	L5R1B8	905-361-3660	361-3626
NASDAQ: HYGS ■ *Web:* www.hydrogenics.com					
Illinois Capacitor Inc 3757 W Touhy Ave	Lincolnwood	IL	60712	847-675-1760	673-2850
TF: 800-323-5420 ■ *Web:* www.illcap.com					
Imaging & Sensing Technology Corp 100 IST Center	Horseheads	NY	14845	607-562-4300	562-4499
Web: www.istcorp.com					
Interconnect Devices Inc 5101 Richland Ave	Kansas City	KS	66106	913-342-4355	342-7043
Web: www.idinet.com					
International Components Corp					
4 Westbrook Corporate Ctr Suite 900	Westchester	IL	60154	708-836-3800	836-3801
TF: 800-210-1431 ■ *Web:* www.iccus.com					
International Resistive Co Inc (IRC) 736 Greenway Rd	Boone	NC	28607	828-264-8861	264-8865
TF: 800-472-6467 ■ *Web:* www.irctt.com					
Interpoint Corp PO Box 97005	Redmond	WA	98073	425-882-3100	882-1990
TF: 800-822-8782 ■ *Web:* www.interpoint.com					
inTEST Corp 7 Esterbrook Ln	Cherry Hill	NJ	08003	856-424-6886	751-1222
NASDAQ: INTT ■ *TF:* 800-501-6886 ■ *Web:* www.intest.com					
IRC (International Resistive Co Inc) 736 Greenway Rd	Boone	NC	28607	828-264-8861	264-8865
TF: 800-472-6467 ■ *Web:* www.irctt.com					
ITT Defense 1650 Tysons Blvd Suite 1700	McLean	VA	22102	703-790-6300	790-6360
Web: defense.itt.com					
ITT Industries Electronic Components 666 E Dyer Rd	Santa Ana	CA	92705	714-557-4700	628-2142
TF: 800-845-7000 ■ *Web:* www.itt.com					
ITT Industries Inc 4 W Red Oak Ln	White Plains	NY	10604	914-641-2000	696-2950
NYSE: ITT ■ *Web:* www.itt.com					
ITT Power Solutions 11 Interstate Dr	West Springfield	MA	01089	413-263-6200	737-0608
TF: 800-442-4334 ■ *Web:* www.ittpowersolutions.com					
ITW Paktron 1205 McConville Rd PO Box 4539	Lynchburg	VA	24502	434-239-6941	239-4730
TF: 888-227-7845 ■ *Web:* www.paktron.com					
JAE Electronics Inc 142 Technology Dr Suite 100	Irvine	CA	92618	949-753-2600	753-2699
TF: 800-523-7278 ■ *Web:* www.jae.com					
Jewell Instruments LLC 850 Perimeter Rd	Manchester	NH	03103	603-669-6400	669-5962
TF: 800-227-5955 ■ *Web:* www.jewellinstruments.com					
Johanson Mfg Corp 301 Rockaway Valley Rd	Boonton	NJ	07005	973-334-2676	334-2954*
**Fax:* Sales ■ *Web:* www.johansonmfg.com					
K & L Microwave Inc 2250 Northwood Dr	Salisbury	MD	21801	410-749-2424	749-1598
Web: www.klmicrowave.com					
Kaiser Systems Inc 126 Sohier Rd	Beverly	MA	01915	978-922-9300	922-8374
Web: www.kaisersys.com					
Kay Pentax 2 Bridgewater Ln	Lincoln Park	NJ	07035	973-628-6200	628-6363
TF: 800-289-5297 ■ *Web:* www.kaypentax.com					
KEMET Corp PO Box 5928	Greenville	SC	29606	864-963-6300	963-6322
NYSE: KEM ■ *Web:* www.kemet.com					
Kennedy MS Corp 4707 Dey Rd	Liverpool	NY	13088	315-701-6751	701-6752
Web: www.mskennedy.com					
Kepco Inc 131-38 Sanford Ave	Flushing	NY	11355	718-461-7000	767-1102
Web: www.kepcopower.com					
Knowles Electronics Inc 1151 Maplewood Dr	Itasca	IL	60143	630-250-5100	250-0575
Web: www.knowlesinc.com					
L-3 Communications Corp Display Systems Div					
1355 Bluegrass Lakes Pkwy	Alpharetta	GA	30004	770-752-7000	752-5525
Web: www-displays.tw.l-3com.com					
L-3 Communications Narda Microwave West 107 Woodmere Rd	Folson	CA	95630	916-351-4500	351-4550
Web: www.nardamicrowave.com					
La Marche Mfg Co 106 Bradrock Dr	Des Plaines	IL	60018	847-299-1188	299-3061
Web: www.lamarchemfg.com					
LaBarge Inc 9900 Clayton Rd	Saint Louis	MO	63124	314-997-0800	812-9437
AMEX: LB ■ *Web:* www.labarge.com					
Lambda America Inc 145 Marcus Blvd	Hauppauge	NY	11788	631-567-3000	967-3022
TF: 800-526-2325 ■ *Web:* www.lambdapower.com					
Lambda Americas 405 Essex Rd	Neptune	NJ	07753	732-922-9300	922-9334
Web: www.lambda-emi.com					
Larco 1902 13th St SE	Brainerd	MN	56401	218-829-9797	829-0139
TF Cust Svc: 800-523-6996 ■ *Web:* www.larcomfg.com					
Lexel Imaging Systems Inc 1500 Bull Lea Rd Suite 150	Lexington	KY	40511	859-243-5500	243-5555
Web: www.lexelimaging.com					
Linear LLC 1950 Camino Vida Roble Suite 150	Carlsbad	CA	92008	760-438-7000	931-1340
TF Cust Svc: 800-421-1587 ■ *Web:* www.linearcorp.com					
Lisk GW Co Inc 2 South St	Clifton Springs	NY	14432	315-462-2611	462-7661
Web: www.gwlisk.com					
Lumex Inc 290 E Helen Rd	Palatine	IL	60067	847-359-2790	359-8904
TF: 800-278-5666 ■ *Web:* www.lumex.com					
M-FLEX 1301 N Dynamics St	Anaheim	CA	92806	714-996-1248	996-3834
NASDAQ: MFLX ■ *Web:* www.mflex.com					
MagneTek Inc N49 W13650 Campbell Dr	Menomonee Falls	WI	53051	262-783-3500	298-3503*
NYSE: MAG ■ **Fax Area Code:* 800 ■ *TF:* 800-288-8178 ■ *Web:* www.magnetek.com					
Maida Development Co 20 Libby St	Hampton	VA	23663	757-723-0785	722-1194
Web: www.maida.com					
Marlow Industries Inc 10451 Vista Park Rd	Dallas	TX	75238	214-340-4900	341-5212
Web: www.marlow.com					
Maxwell Technologies Inc 9244 Balboa Ave	San Diego	CA	92123	858-503-3300	503-3301
NASDAQ: MXWL ■ *Web:* www.maxwell.com					
McDonald Technologies International Inc 1920 Diplomat Dr	Farmers Branch	TX	75234	972-243-6767	241-2643
TF: 800-678-7046 ■ *Web:* www.mcdonald-tech.com					
Meggitt Safety Systems Inc 1915 Voyager Ave	Simi Valley	CA	93063	805-584-4100	578-3400
Web: www.meggitt.com					
Melcor 1040 Spruce St	Trenton	NJ	08648	609-393-4178	393-9461
Web: www.melcor.com					
Merrimac Industries Inc 41 Fairfield Pl	West Caldwell	NJ	07006	973-575-1300	575-0531*
AMEX: MRM ■ **Fax:* Sales ■ *TF:* 800-575-1301 ■ *Web:* www.merrimacind.com					
Methode Electronics Inc 7401 W Wilson Ave	Chicago	IL	60706	708-867-6777	867-6999
NASDAQ: METH ■ *TF:* 877-316-7700 ■ *Web:* www.methode.com					
MGE UPS Systems 1660 Scenic Ave	Costa Mesa	CA	92626	714-557-1636	435-1445
TF: 800-523-0142 ■ *Web:* www.mgeups.com					
Micro Plastics Inc 801 E Mission Rd	San Marcos	CA	92069	760-744-0125	744-6081
TF: 888-774-3100 ■ *Web:* www.micro-plastics.com					
Midian Electronics Inc 2302 E 22nd St	Tucson	AZ	85713	520-884-7981	884-0422
TF Orders: 800-643-4267 ■ *Web:* www.midelec.com					
Miteq Inc 100 Davids Dr	Hauppauge	NY	11788	631-436-7400	436-7430
Web: www.miteq.com					
Mitsubishi Electric & Electronics USA Inc Elevator & Escalator					
Div 5665 Plaza Dr	Cypress	CA	90630	714-220-4822	220-4812
Web: www.mitsubishi-elevator.com					
Molex Inc 2222 Wellington Ct	Lisle	IL	60532	630-969-4550	969-1352
NASDAQ: MOLX ■ *TF Cust Svc:* 800-786-6539 ■ *Web:* www.molex.com					
Molex Inc Industrial Div 4 Aviation Dr	Gilford	NH	03249	603-524-5101	524-1627
Web: www.molex.com					
Morey Corp 100 Morey Dr	Woodridge	IL	60517	630-754-2300	754-2001
Web: www.moreycorp.com					
Motorola Inc 1301 E Algonquin Rd	Schaumburg	IL	60196	847-576-5000	538-3617*
NYSE: MOT ■ **Fax:* Hum Res ■ *TF:* 800-331-6456 ■ *Web:* www.motorola.com					

				Phone	Fax
MPD Inc 316 E 9th St *TF:* 866-225-5673 ■ *Web:* www.mpdinc.com	Owensboro	KY	42303	270-685-6200	685-6494
MS Kennedy Corp 4707 Dey Rd *Web:* www.mskennedy.com	Liverpool	NY	13088	315-701-6751	701-6752
MtronPTI 100 Douglas Ave *TF:* 800-762-8800 ■ *Web:* www.mtronpti.com	Yankton	SD	57078	605-665-9321	665-1709
Multi-Fineline Electronix Inc DBA M-FLEX 1301 N Dynamics St *NASDAQ: MFLX* ■ *Web:* www.mflex.com	Anaheim	CA	92806	714-996-1248	996-3834
Murata Electronics North America Inc 2200 Lake Park Dr *TF:* 800-241-6574 ■ *Web:* www.murata.com	Smyrna	GA	30080	770-436-1300	436-3030
Namco Controls Corp 201 W Meeting St **Fax Area Code:* 800 ■ *TF:* 800-626-8324 ■ *Web:* www.ncdjsolutions.com/namco	Lancaster	SC	29720	803-286-8491	678-6263*
Narda Microwave West 107 Woodmere Rd *Web:* www.nardamicrowave.com	Folson	CA	95630	916-351-4500	351-4550
Netcom Inc 599 Wheeling Rd *Web:* www.netcominc.com	Wheeling	IL	60090	847-537-6300	537-2700
Newport Corp 1791 Deere Ave *NASDAQ: NEWP* ■ **Fax:* Sales ■ *TF Sales:* 800-222-6440 ■ *Web:* www.newport.com	Irvine	CA	92606	949-863-3144	253-1680*
NMB Technologies Corp 9730 Independence Ave *Web:* www.nmbtech.com	Chatsworth	CA	91311	818-341-3355	341-8207
Nortech Systems Inc 1120 Wayzata Blvd E Suite 201 *NASDAQ: NSYS* ■ *TF:* 800-808-8281 ■ *Web:* www.nortechsys.com	Wayzata	MN	55391	952-345-2240	449-0442
Northern Technologies Corp 23123 E Mission Ave *TF:* 800-727-9119 ■ *Web:* www.northerntech.com	Liberty Lake	WA	99019	509-927-0401	927-0435
Novacap Inc 25136 Anza Dr *Web:* www.novacap.com	Valencia	CA	91355	661-295-5920	295-5928
NWL Transformers Inc 312 Rising Sun Rd *TF:* 800-742-5695 ■ *Web:* www.nwl.com	Bordentown	NJ	08505	609-298-7300	298-1982
Oeco LLC 4607 SE International Way *Web:* www.oeco.com	Milwaukie	OR	97222	503-659-7932	653-6310
OEM Worldwide Inc 2920 Kelly Ave PO Box 430 *TF:* 800-258-7989 ■ *Web:* www.oemworldwide.com	Watertown	SD	57201	605-886-2519	886-5123
Ohmite Mfg Co 1600 Golf Rd Suite 850 *TF:* 866-964-6483 ■ *Web:* www.ohmite.com	Rolling Meadows	IL	60008	847-258-0300	574-7501
OK International 12151 Monarch St *Web:* www.okinternational.com	Garden Grove	CA	92841	714-799-9910	799-9533
ONEAC Corp 27944 N Bradley Rd *TF:* 800-327-8801 ■ *Web:* www.oneac.com	Libertyville	IL	60048	847-816-6000	680-5124
Oppenheimer Precision Products 173 Gibraltar Rd *Web:* www.oppiprecision.com	Horsham	PA	19044	215-674-9100	675-5139
Optex America Inc 13661 Benson Ave Bldg C *TF:* 800-966-7839 ■ *Web:* www.optexamerica.com	Chino	CA	91710	909-993-5770	628-5560
Oren Elliott Products Inc 128 W Vine St *Web:* www.orenelliottproducts.com	Edgerton	OH	43517	419-298-2306	298-3545
OSI Systems Inc 12525 Chadron Ave *NASDAQ: OSIS* ■ *Web:* www.osi-systems.com	Hawthorne	CA	90250	310-978-0516	644-1727
OSRAM Sylvania Inc 100 Endicott St *Web:* www.sylvania.com	Danvers	MA	01923	978-777-1900	750-2152
Para Systems Inc 1455 LeMay Dr *TF:* 800-238-7272 ■ *Web:* www.minuteman-ups.com	Carrollton	TX	75007	972-446-7363	446-9011
PECO II Inc 1376 SR 598 *NASDAQ: PIII* ■ *TF:* 800-999-7326 ■ *Web:* www.peco2.com	Galion	OH	44833	419-468-7600	468-3688
PerkinElmer Inc 45 William St *NYSE: PKI* ■ *Web:* www.perkinelmer.com	Wellesley	MA	02481	781-237-5100	237-9386
Piller Inc 45 Turner Rd *TF:* 800-597-6937 ■ *Web:* www.piller.com	Middletown	NY	10941	845-695-5300	692-0295
Plastronics Socket Co Inc 2601 Texas Dr *TF Cust Svc:* 800-582-5822 ■ *Web:* www.locknest.com	Irving	TX	75062	972-258-1906	258-6771
Plug Power Inc 968 Albany-Shaker Rd *NASDAQ: PLUG* ■ *Web:* www.plugpower.com	Latham	NY	12110	518-782-7700	782-9060
Polyflon Co 1 Willard Rd *Web:* www.polyflon.com	Norwalk	CT	06851	203-840-7555	840-7565
Positronic Industries Inc 423 N Campbell Ave PO Box 8247 *TF:* 800-641-4054 ■ *Web:* www.connectpositronic.com	Springfield	MO	65801	417-866-2322	866-0210
Post Glover LifeLink Inc 167 Gap Way *TF:* 800-287-4123 ■ *Web:* www.postgloverhalsey.com	Erlanger	KY	41018	859-283-5900	372-6272
Post Glover Resistors Inc 4750 Olympic Blvd Bldg B *TF Cust Svc:* 800-537-6144 ■ *Web:* www.postglover.com	Erlanger	KY	41018	859-283-0778	283-2978
Power-One Inc 740 Calle Plano *NASDAQ: PWER* ■ *TF:* 800-678-9445 ■ *Web:* www.power-one.com	Camarillo	CA	93012	805-987-8741	987-5212
PowerLight Corp 2954 San Pablo Ave *TF:* 877-787-6527 ■ *Web:* www.powerlight.com	Berkeley	CA	94702	510-540-0550	540-0552
Powerware Corp 8609 Six Forks Rd *TF:* 800-554-3448 ■ *Web:* www.powerware.com	Raleigh	NC	27615	919-872-3020	878-2333
Precision Devices Inc 8840 N Greenview Dr *TF:* 800-274-9825 ■ *Web:* www.pdixtal.com	Middleton	WI	53562	608-831-4445	831-3343
Precision Interconnect Corp 10025 SW Freeman Ct *Web:* www.precisionint.com	Wilsonville	OR	97070	503-685-9300	685-9305
Progressive Dynamics Inc 507 Industrial Rd *Web:* www.progressivedyn.com	Marshall	MI	49068	269-781-4241	781-7802
Pulse Engineering Inc 12220 World Trade Dr *Web:* www.pulseeng.com	San Diego	CA	92128	858-674-8100	674-8262
Q P Semiconductor 2945 Oakmead Village Ct *Web:* www.qpsemi.com	Santa Clara	CA	95051	408-737-0992	736-8708
QC Onics Ventures LP 1410 Wohlert St PO Box 329 *Web:* www.qconics.com	Angola	IN	46703	260-665-9493	665-8744
QualiTau Inc 915 Walsh Ave *Web:* www.qualitau.com	Santa Clara	CA	95050	408-522-9200	522-8110
Quartzdyne Inc 1020 W Atherton Dr *TF:* 888-353-7956 ■ *Web:* www.quartzdyne.com	Salt Lake City	UT	84123	801-266-6958	266-7985
Raritan Computer Inc 400 Cottontail Ln *TF:* 800-724-8090 ■ *Web:* www.raritan.com	Somerset	NJ	08873	732-764-8886	764-8887
record-usa 4324 Phil Hargett Ct *TF Sales:* 800-438-1937 ■ *Web:* www.record-usa.com	Monroe	NC	28220	704-289-9212	289-2024
RF Industries 7610 Miramar Rd Bldg 6000 *NASDAQ: RFIL* ■ *TF:* 800-233-1728 ■ *Web:* www.rfindustries.com	San Diego	CA	92126	858-549-6340	549-6345
Sage Laboratories Inc 8 Executive Dr *Web:* www.sagelabs.com	Hudson	NH	03051	603-459-1600	459-1606
Samtec Inc 520 Parkeast Blvd *TF:* 800-726-8329 ■ *Web:* www.samtec.com	New Albany	IN	47150	812-944-6733	948-5047
SatCon Technology Corp 27 Dry Dock Ave *NASDAQ: SATC* ■ *TF:* 888-728-2760 ■ *Web:* www.satcon.com	Boston	MA	02210	617-897-2400	897-2401
Sawtek Inc 1818 S Hwy 441 *Web:* www.sawtek.com	Apopka	FL	32703	407-886-8860	886-7061
Schott Corp 1401 Air Wing Rd *Web:* www.schottcorp.com	San Diego	CA	92154	507-223-5572	223-5055
Schumacher Electric Corp 801 Business Center Dr *TF:* 800-621-5485 ■ *Web:* www.batterychargers.com	Mount Prospect	IL	60056	847-385-1600	298-1698
Sealtron Div HCC Industries Inc 9705 Reading Rd *Web:* www.sealtron.com/home.shtml	Cincinnati	OH	45215	513-733-8400	733-0131
Seiko Instruments USA Inc 12301 Technology Blvd *TF:* 800-358-0880 ■ *Web:* www.seikoinstruments.com	Austin	TX	78727	512-349-3800	349-3000
Seiko Instruments USA Inc Electronic Components Div 2990 Lomita Blvd *Web:* www.siielectroniccomponents.com	Torrance	CA	90505	310-517-7771	517-7709
Semicon Assoc 695 Laco Dr *Web:* www.semiconassociates.com	Lexington	KY	40510	859-255-3664	255-6829
Semiconductor Circuits Inc 49 Range Rd *Web:* www.dcdc.com	Windham	NH	03087	603-893-2330	893-6280
SEMX Corp 1 Labriola Ct *Web:* www.semx.com	Armonk	NY	10504	914-273-5500	273-5860
Sharp Microelectronics of the Americas 5700 NW Pacific Rim Blvd *Web:* www.sharpsma.com	Camas	WA	98607	360-834-2500	834-8903
Shelly Assoc Inc 17171 Murphy Ave *TF:* 888-669-9850 ■ *Web:* www.shellyinc.com	Irvine	CA	92614	949-417-8070	417-8075
Shogyo International Corp 6851 Jericho Tpke *Web:* www.shogyo.com	Syosset	NY	11791	516-921-9111	921-3777
Siemens Intelligent Transportation Systems 8004 Cameron Rd *TF:* 800-388-6882 ■ *Web:* www.itssiemens.com	Austin	TX	78754	512-837-8310	837-0196
Sigma Electronics Inc 1027 Commercial Ave *TF:* 866-569-2681 ■ *Web:* www.sigmaelectronics.com	East Petersburg	PA	17520	717-569-2681	569-4056
Signal Transformer Co Inc 500 Bayview Ave *TF:* 866-239-5777 ■ *Web:* www.signaltransformer.com	Inwood	NY	11096	516-239-5777	239-7208
Simclar Inc 2230 W 77th St *NASDAQ: SIMC* ■ *Web:* www.simclar.com	Hialeah	FL	33016	305-556-9210	827-5209
Simplex Inc 5300 Rising Moon Rd *TF:* 800-637-8603 ■ *Web:* www.simplexdirect.com	Springfield	IL	62711	217-483-1600	483-1616
SL Power Electronics Inc 6050 King Dr Bldg A **Fax Area Code:* 858 ■ *Web:* www.slpower.com	Ventura	CA	93003	805-486-4565	712-2040*
SMK Electronics Corp USA 1055 Tierra Del Rey *Web:* www.smk.co.jp	Chula Vista	CA	91910	619-216-6400	216-6498
SMTC Corp 635 Hood Rd *NASDAQ: SMTX* ■ *Web:* www.smtc.com	Markham	ON	L3R4N6	905-479-1810	479-1877
SNC Mfg Co Inc 101 W Waukau Ave *TF:* 800-558-3325 ■ *Web:* www.sncmfg.com	Oshkosh	WI	54902	920-231-7370	231-1090
Spang & Co 110 Delta Dr *Web:* www.spang.com	Pittsburgh	PA	15238	412-963-9363	696-0333
Sparton Corp 2400 E Ganson St *NYSE: SPA* ■ *TF:* 800-248-9579 ■ *Web:* www.sparton.com	Jackson	MI	49202	517-787-8600	787-8046
Spectrum Control Inc 8031 Avonia Rd *NASDAQ: SPEC* ■ *Web:* www.spectrumcontrol.com	Fairview	PA	16415	814-835-1650	474-4301
Spellman High Voltage Corp 1 Commerce Park *Web:* www.bertan.com	Valhalla	NY	10595	914-686-3600	686-5424
Spellman High Voltage Electronics Corp 475 Wireless Blvd **Fax:* Sales ■ *Web:* www.spellmanhv.com	Hauppauge	NY	11788	631-435-1600	435-1620*
Stacoswitch Inc 1139 Baker St *Web:* www.stacoswitch.com	Costa Mesa	CA	92626	714-549-3041	549-0930
Standex Electronics 4538 Camberwell Rd *Web:* www.standexelectronics.com	Cincinnati	OH	45209	513-871-3777	871-3779
STATS ChipPAC Test Services Inc 1768 McCandless Dr *Web:* www.statschippac.com	Milpitas	CA	95035	408-586-0600	586-0601
Stellar Microelectronics Inc 28575 Livingston Ave *Web:* www.stellarmicro.com	Valencia	CA	91355	661-775-3500	775-3522
Stevens Water Monitoring Systems 12067 NE Glenn Widing Dr Suite 106 *TF:* 800-452-5272 ■ *Web:* www.stevenswater.com	Portland	OR	97220	503-469-8000	469-8100
Stewart Connector Systems Inc 11118 Susquehanna Trail S *Web:* www.stewartconnector.com	Glen Rock	PA	17327	717-235-7512	235-7954
Stratos International Inc 7444 W Wilson Ave *NASDAQ: STLW* ■ *TF:* 800-323-6858 ■ *Web:* www.stratoslightwave.com	Harwood Heights	IL	60706	708-867-9600	867-0996
Suntron Corp 2401 W Grandview Rd Suite 1 *NASDAQ: SUNN* ■ *TF:* 888-520-3382 ■ *Web:* www.suntroncorp.com	Phoenix	AZ	85023	602-789-6600	789-6600
Superconductor Technologies Inc 460 Ward Dr *NASDAQ: SCON* ■ *Web:* www.suptech.com	Santa Barbara	CA	93111	805-683-7646	967-0342
Switchcraft Inc 5555 N Elston Ave *Web:* www.switchcraft.com	Chicago	IL	60630	773-792-2700	792-2129
Synergetix 310 S 51st St *Web:* www.synerget.com	Kansas City	KS	66106	913-342-0404	342-6623
Sypris Electronics LLC 10901 N McKinley Dr *Web:* www.grtk.com/electronics/	Tampa	FL	33612	813-972-6000	972-6168
Sypris Solutions Inc 101 Bullitt Ln Suite 450 *NASDAQ: SYPR* ■ *Web:* www.sypris.com	Louisville	KY	40222	502-329-2000	329-2050
Taiyo Yuden (USA) Inc 1930 N Thoreau Dr Suite 190 *TF:* 800-348-2496 ■ *Web:* www.t-yuden.com	Schaumburg	IL	60173	847-925-0888	925-0899
TDI-Transistor Devices Inc 85 Horsehill Rd *Web:* www.tdipower.com	Cedar Knolls	NJ	07927	973-267-1900	267-2047
TDK Corp of America 1221 Business Center Dr *Web:* www.component.tdk.com	Mount Prospect	IL	60056	847-803-6100	390-4370
Techneglas Inc 711 Southwood Ave *Web:* www.techneglas.com	Columbus	OH	43207	614-445-4700	445-1900
Technical Services for Electronics Inc 108 5th Ave NW *Web:* www.tseinc.net	Arlington	MN	55307	507-964-2237	964-2465
Technitrol Inc 1210 Northbrook Dr Suite 470 *NYSE: TNL* ■ *Web:* www.technitrol.com	Trevose	PA	19053	215-355-2900	355-7397
Teledyne Electronic Safety Products 8920 Quartz Ave *Web:* www.teledynesafetyproducts.com	Northridge	CA	91324	818-718-6640	998-3312
Teledyne Electronics & Communications 12964 Panama St *Web:* www.tet.com	Los Angeles	CA	90066	310-822-8229	574-2092
Teledyne Technologies Inc 12333 W Olympic Blvd *NYSE: TDY* ■ *Web:* www.teledynetechnologies.com	Los Angeles	CA	90064	310-893-1600	893-1613
Telonic Berkeley Inc 2825 Laguna Canyon Rd *TF:* 800-854-2436 ■ *Web:* www.telonicberkeley.com	Laguna Beach	CA	92651	949-494-9401	497-7331
Tempo Research Corp 1390 Aspen Way *TF:* 800-642-2155 ■ *Web:* www.tempo.textron.com	Vista	CA	92083	760-598-8900	598-5634
Toshiba America Inc 1251 Ave of the Americas Suite 4100 *TF:* 800-457-7777 ■ *Web:* www.toshiba.com	New York	NY	10020	212-596-0600	593-3875
Total Technologies Ltd 9 Studebaker *TF:* 800-669-4885 ■ *Web:* www.total-technologies.com	Irvine	CA	92618	949-465-0200	465-0212
TRAK Microwave Corp 4726 Eisenhower Blvd *TF:* 888-283-8444 ■ *Web:* www.trak.com	Tampa	FL	33634	813-884-1411	901-7490
Tri-Star Electronics International Inc 2201 Rosecrans Ave *Web:* www.tri-starelectronics.com	El Segundo	CA	90245	310-536-0444	536-9322
Triana Industries Inc 511 6th St *Web:* www.tiiconnects.com	Madison	AL	35756	256-772-9304	258-0411
Trompeter Electronics Inc 5550 E McDowell Rd *TF:* 800-778-4401 ■ *Web:* www.trompeter.com	Mesa	AZ	85215	480-985-9000	985-0334
Tyco Electronics Corp 1050 Westlakes Dr *NYSE: TEL* ■ *Web:* www.tycoelectronics.com	Berwyn	PA	19312	610-893-9800	
UTC Power 195 Governors Hwy *TF:* 866-383-5235 ■ *Web:* www.utcfuelcells.com	South Windsor	CT	06074	860-727-2200	727-2319
Valberg LLC 14792 172nd Dr SE *TF:* 800-487-2206 ■ *Web:* www.valbergllc.com	Monroe	WA	98272	360-794-9885	794-3314
Valpey Fisher Corp 75 South St *AMEX: VPF* ■ *TF:* 800-982-5737 ■ *Web:* www.valpeyfisher.com	Hopkinton	MA	01748	508-435-6831	435-5289
Vectron International 167 Lowell Rd **Fax:* Cust Svc ■ *TF:* 888-328-7661 ■ *Web:* www.vectron.com	Hudson	NH	03051	603-598-0070	598-0075*
VI Cinox Corp 4914 Gray Rd *Web:* www.cinox.com	Cincinnati	OH	45232	513-542-5555	542-5146
Viasystems Group Inc 101 S Hanley Rd Suite 400 *Web:* www.viasystems.com	Saint Louis	MO	63105	314-727-2087	746-2233
Viatran Corp 300 Industrial Dr *TF:* 800-688-0030 ■ *Web:* www.viatran.com	Grand Island	NY	14073	716-773-1700	773-2488

				Phone	Fax
Vicor Corp 25 Frontage Rd	Andover	MA	01810	978-470-2900	475-6715*
NASDAQ: VICR ■ **Fax:* Sales ■ *TF:* 800-869-5300 ■ *Web:* www.vicr.com					
Viking Technologies Group Ltd 80 E Montauk Hwy	Lindenhurst	NY	11757	631-957-7200	957-7203
TF: 800-280-1311 ■ *Web:* www.cardwellcondenser.com					
Vishay Intertechnology Inc 63 Lancaster Ave	Malvern	PA	19355	610-644-1300	296-0657
NYSE: VSH ■ *Web:* www.vishay.com					
Wakefield Thermal Solutions Inc 33 Bridge St	Pelham	NH	03076	603-635-2800	635-1900
TF: 800-325-1426 ■ *Web:* www.wakefield.com					
Western Electronics LLC 1550 S Tech Ln	Meridian	ID	83642	208-377-1557	955-9752
TF: 888-857-5775 ■ *Web:* www.westernelectronics.com					
Wilmore Electronics Co Inc					
607 Hwy 70-A East PO Box 1329	Hillsborough	NC	27278	919-732-9351	732-9359
Web: www.wilmoreelectronics.com					
Wireless Xcessories Group Inc					
1840 County Line Rd Suite 301	Huntingdon Valley	PA	19006	215-322-4600	233-0220*
AMEX: XWG ■ **Fax Area Code:* 888 ■ *TF:* 800-233-0013 ■					
Web: www.wirelessgroup.com					
WL Gore & Assoc Inc 551 Papermill Rd	Newark	DE	19711	302-738-4880	738-7710
Web: www.gore.com					
Xantrex Technology Inc 8999 Nelson Way	Burnaby	BC	V5A4B5	604-422-8595	420-1591
TF: 800-670-0707 ■ *Web:* www.xantrex.com					
Yazaki North America Inc 6801 Haggerty Rd	Canton	MI	48187	734-983-1000	
Web: www.yazaki-na.com					
Ziptronix Inc 800 Perimeter Park Dr Suite B	Morrisville	NC	27560	919-459-2400	459-2401
Web: www.ziptronix.com					

257 ELECTRONIC ENCLOSURES

				Phone	Fax
A & J Mfg Co 14831 Franklin Ave	Tustin	CA	92780	714-544-9570	544-4215
Web: www.aj-racks.com					
AMCO Engineering Co 3801 N Rose St	Schiller Park	IL	60176	847-671-6670	671-9469
Web: www.amcoengineering.com					
American Access Technologies Inc					
6670 Spring Lake Rd	Keystone Heights	FL	32656	352-473-6673	473-6572
NASDAQ: AATK ■ *TF:* 800-285-2070 ■ *Web:* www.aatk.com					
APW Electronic Solutions 14100 Danielson St	Poway	CA	92064	858-679-4550	679-4555
TF: 800-854-7086 ■ *Web:* www.apw.com					
APW Ltd N 22 W 23685 Ridgeview Pkwy W	Waukesha	WI	53188	262-523-7600	523-7588
TF: 800-599-5556 ■ *Web:* www.apw.com					
Buckeye ShapeForm 555 Marion Rd	Columbus	OH	43207	614-445-8433	445-8224
TF: 800-728-0776 ■ *Web:* www.buckeyeshapeform.com					
Bud Industries Inc 4605 E 355th St	Willoughby	OH	44094	440-946-3200	951-4015
Web: www.budind.com					
Cabtron Systems Inc 200 Anets Dr	Northbrook	IL	60062	847-498-6090	272-1943
Web: www.cabtron.com					
Commercial Sheet Metal Co 465 Turnpike St	Canton	MA	02021	781-828-7900	828-3565
Web: www.commercialsheetmetal.net					
Crenlo LLC 1600 4th Ave NW	Rochester	MN	55901	507-289-3371	287-3405*
**Fax:* Sales ■ *Web:* www.crenlo.com					
Dawson Metal Co Inc 825 Allen St	Jamestown	NY	14701	716-664-3815	664-3485
TF: 877-732-9766 ■ *Web:* www.dawsonmetal.com					
Electrol Specialties Co 441 Clark St PO Box 7	South Beloit	IL	61080	815-389-2291	389-2294
Web: www.esc4cip.com					
Emcor Enclosures 1600 4th Ave NW	Rochester	MN	55901	507-289-3371	287-3405*
**Fax:* Sales ■ *Web:* www.emcorenclosures.com					
Equipto Electronics Corp 351 Woodlawn Ave	Aurora	IL	60506	630-897-4691	897-5314
TF: 800-204-7225 ■ *Web:* www.equiptoelec.com					
General Kinetics Inc 110 Funray Dr	Johnston	PA	15905	814-255-6891	255-4106
Web: www.gki.com					
Gerome Mfg Co Inc PO Box 1089	Uniontown	PA	15401	724-438-8544	437-5608
Web: www.geromemfg.com					
Global MetalForm LP 733 Davis St	Scranton	PA	18505	570-346-3871	346-1612
TF: 800-233-4818 ■ *Web:* www.globalmetalform.com					
I-Bus Corp 3350 Scott Blvd Bldg 54	Santa Clara	CA	95054	408-450-7880	450-7881
TF: 877-777-4287 ■ *Web:* www.ibus.com					
JMR Electronics Inc 20400 Plummer St	Chatsworth	CA	91311	818-993-4801	727-2248*
**Fax:* Hum Res ■ *Web:* www.jmr.com					
National Mfg Co Inc 12 River Rd	Chatham	NJ	07928	973-635-8846	635-7810
Web: www.natlmfg.com					
Omega Tool 308 S Mountain View Ave	San Bernardino	CA	92408	909-888-0440	889-8740
Optima Electronic Packaging Systems					
2166 Mountain Industrial Blvd	Tucker	GA	30084	770-496-4000	496-4041*
**Fax:* Sales ■ *Web:* www.optimaeps.com					
Pentair Inc 5500 Wayzata Blvd Suite 800	Golden Valley	MN	55416	763-545-1730	656-5400
NYSE: PNR ■ *TF:* 800-328-9626 ■ *Web:* www.pentair.com					
Stahlin Enclosures 500 W Maple St	Belding	MI	48809	616-794-0700	794-3378
Web: www.stahlin.com					
TRI MAP International Inc 111 Val Dervin Pkwy	Stockton	CA	95206	209-234-0100	234-5990
TF: 888-687-4627 ■ *Web:* www.trimapintl.com					
Trio Metal Products Co Inc 1411 Clarkview Rd	Baltimore	MD	21209	410-828-5456	828-5467
Web: www.triometal.com					
Universal Enclosure Systems 1146 S Cedar Ridge Dr	Duncanville	TX	75137	972-298-0531	298-0614
Web: www.universalenclosures.com					
Zendex Corp 6780 Sierra Ct Suite A	Dublin	CA	94568	925-828-3000	828-1574
Web: www.zendex.com					
Zero Mfg Inc 500 W 200 North	North Salt Lake	UT	84054	801-298-5900	292-9450
TF: 800-545-1030 ■ *Web:* www.zerocases.com					

258 ELECTRONIC TRANSACTION PROCESSING

				Phone	Fax
Alliance Data Systems Corp 17655 Waterview Pkwy	Dallas	TX	75252	972-348-5100	348-5335*
NYSE: ADS ■ **Fax:* Hum Res ■ *Web:* www.alliancedatasystems.com					
Automated License Systems Inc					
3055 Lebanon Pike Bldg 2 Suite 2301	Nashville	TN	37214	615-263-4257	263-4271
Web: www.als-xtn.com					
BA Merchant Services LLC 1231 Durrett Ln	Louisville	KY	40213	502-315-2000	315-5739
TF: 800-949-7379 ■ *Web:* www.npc.net					
Ceridian Corp 3311 E Old Shakopee Rd	Minneapolis	MN	55425	952-853-8100	
NYSE: CEN ■ *TF:* 800-767-4969 ■ *Web:* www.ceridian.com					
Chase Paymentech Inc 14221 Dallas Pkwy Bldg 2	Dallas	TX	75254	214-849-2000	849-2015*
**Fax:* Hum Res ■ *TF:* 800-280-7061 ■ *Web:* www.chasepaymentech.com					
CheckFree 4411 E Jones Bridge Rd	Norcross	GA	30092	678-375-3000	697-9561*
**Fax Area Code:* 877 ■ *TF:* 800-309-7668 ■ *Web:* www.checkfree.com					
Covera Card Solutions 19 British American Blvd	Latham	NY	12110	518-437-8100	437-8500
TF: 866-526-8372 ■ *Web:* www.coverasolutions.com					
ECHO (Electronic Clearing House Inc) 730 Paseo Camarillo	Camarillo	CA	93010	800-262-3246	
NASDAQ: ECHO ■ *Web:* www.echo-inc.com					
Electracash 2501 Cherry Ave Suite 360	Signal Hill	CA	90755	562-498-5877	424-6481
TF Cust Svc: 800-444-6952 ■ *Web:* www.electracash.com					
Euronet Worldwide Inc 4601 College Blvd Suite 300	Leawood	KS	66211	913-327-4200	327-1921
NASDAQ: EEFT ■ *Web:* www.euronetworldwide.com					
Fidelity National Information Services Inc					
601 Riverside Ave	Jacksonville	FL	32204	904-854-5000	854-4124
NYSE: FIS ■ *TF:* 800-874-7359 ■ *Web:* www.fidelityinfoservices.com					
First Data Corp 6200 S Quebec St	Greenwood Village	CO	80111	303-488-8000	488-8705
NYSE: FDC ■ *TF:* 800-735-3362 ■ *Web:* www.firstdatacorp.com					
Global Payments Inc 10 Glenlake Pkwy North Tower	Atlanta	GA	30328	770-829-8000	
NYSE: GPN ■ *TF:* 800-560-2960 ■ *Web:* www.globalpaymentsinc.com					
Lynk Systems Inc 600 Morgan Falls Rd Suite 260	Atlanta	GA	30350	770-396-1616	551-9359*
**Fax:* Hum Res ■ *TF:* 800-200-5965 ■ *Web:* www.lynksystems.com					
National Bankcard Systems 2600 Via Fortuna Suite 240	Austin	TX	78749	512-494-9200	344-2979
TF: 800-823-6835 ■ *Web:* www.enbs.com					
NOVA Information Systems 1 Concourse Pkwy Suite 300	Atlanta	GA	30328	770-396-1456	
TF: 800-725-1243 ■ *Web:* www.novainfo.com					
Online Data Corp 2 Westbrook Corporate Ctr Suite 200	Westchester	IL	60154	708-562-2777	562-2729
Web: www.onlinedatacorp.com					
PayNet Merchant Services Inc					
950 S Old Woodward Suite 220	Birmingham	MI	48009	248-723-5760	723-5761
TF: 888-855-8644 ■ *Web:* www.visa-master.com					
Pershing LLC 95 Christopher Columbus Dr	Jersey City	NJ	07302	201-413-2000	413-3103*
**Fax:* Hum Res ■ *TF:* 800-443-4342 ■ *Web:* www.pershing.com					
Total System Services Inc 1600 1st Ave	Columbus	GA	31901	706-649-2310	649-4499
NYSE: TSS ■ *TF:* 800-241-0912 ■ *Web:* www.tsys.com					
Vital Processing Services LLC 8320 S Hardy Dr	Tempe	AZ	85284	480-333-7600	333-7553
Web: www.vitalps.com					

259 ELEVATORS, ESCALATORS, MOVING WALKWAYS

				Phone	Fax
CemcoLift Inc 2801 Township Line Rd	Hatfield	PA	19440	215-799-2900	703-0343
TF Sales: 800-962-3626 ■ *Web:* www.cemcolift.com					
Elevator Equipment Corp 4035 Goodwin Ave	Los Angeles	CA	90039	323-245-0147	245-9771
TF: 888-577-3326 ■ *Web:* www.elevatorequipment.com					
Fujitec America Inc 401 Fujitec Dr	Lebanon	OH	45036	513-932-8000	
Web: www.fujitecamerica.com					
Hollister-Whitney Elevator Corp 2603 N 24th St	Quincy	IL	62305	217-222-0466	222-0493
Web: www.hollisterwhitney.com					
Inclinator Co of America 2200 Paxton St	Harrisburg	PA	17105	717-234-8065	234-0941
TF: 800-343-9007 ■ *Web:* www.inclinator.com					
KONE Inc 1 Kone Ct	Moline	IL	61265	309-764-6771	743-5474
TF: 800-334-9556 ■ *Web:* www.us.kone.com					
Matot Inc 2501 Van Buren St	Bellwood	IL	60104	708-547-1888	547-1608
TF: 800-369-1070 ■ *Web:* www.matot.com					
Mitsubishi Electric & Electronics USA Inc Elevator & Escalator					
Div 5665 Plaza Dr	Cypress	CA	90630	714-220-4822	220-4812
Web: www.mitsubishi-elevator.com					
Oliver & Williams Elevator Co 3039 Roswell St	Los Angeles	CA	90065	323-478-2100	478-2130
Otis Elevator Co 10 Farm Springs Rd	Farmington	CT	06032	860-676-6000	676-6970
Web: www.otis.com					
Schindler Elevator Corp 20 Whippany Rd	Morristown	NJ	07960	973-397-6500	397-6485*
**Fax:* Mail Rm ■ *TF:* 800-225-3123 ■ *Web:* www.us.schindler.com					
Schumacher Elevator Co 1 Schumacher Way PO Box 393	Denver	IA	50622	319-984-5676	984-6316
Web: www.schumacherelevator.com					
Sematic USA DBA Tyler Elevator Products Inc					
6161 Halle Dr	Valley View	OH	44125	216-524-0100	524-9710
Web: www.tylerelevator.com					
ThyssenKrupp Access Inc 4001 E 138th St	Grandview	MO	64030	816-763-3100	763-4467
TF: 800-669-9047 ■ *Web:* www.tkaccess.com					
ThyssenKrupp Elevator 3965 Mendenhall Suite 110	Memphis	TN	38115	800-330-9730	365-5501*
**Fax Area Code:* 910 ■ *TF:* 877-230-0303 ■ *Web:* www.thyssenkruppelevator.com					

260 EMBASSIES & CONSULATES - FOREIGN, IN THE US

SEE ALSO Travel & Tourism Information - Foreign Travel p. 2384

Foreign embassies in the U.S. generally include consular services among their functions. These embassy-based consulates are listed here only if their address differs from the embassy's.

				Phone	Fax
Afghanistan					
Consulate General 360 Lexington Ave 11th Fl	New York	NY	10017	212-972-2276	972-9046
Embassy 2341 Wyoming Ave NW	Washington	DC	20008	202-483-6410	483-6488
Web: www.embassyofafghanistan.org					
Albania Embassy 2100 'S' St NW	Washington	DC	20008	202-223-4942	628-7342
Algeria					
Embassy 2118 Kalorama Rd NW	Washington	DC	20008	202-265-2800	667-2174
Web: www.algeria-us.org					
Embassy - Consular Section 2137 Wyoming Ave NW	Washington	DC	20008	202-265-2800	265-1978
Web: www.algeria-us.org					
Andorra Embassy 2 United Nations Plaza 27th Fl	New York	NY	10017	212-750-8064	750-6630
Web: www.andorra.ad					
Angola Embassy 2108 16th St NW	Washington	DC	20009	202-785-1156	822-9049
Web: www.angola.org					
Antigua & Barbuda					
Consulate General 25 SE 2nd Ave Suite 300	Miami	FL	33131	305-381-6762	381-7908
Embassy 3216 New Mexico Ave NW	Washington	DC	20016	202-362-5122	362-5225
Argentina					
Consulate General 5055 Wilshire Blvd Suite 210	Los Angeles	CA	90036	323-954-9155	934-9076
Consulate General 800 Brickell Ave PH 1	Miami	FL	33131	305-373-7794	373-1598
Consulate General 245 Peachtree Center Ave Suite 2101	Atlanta	GA	30303	404-880-0805	880-0806
Consulate General 205 N Michigan Ave Suite 4208	Chicago	IL	60601	312-819-2620	819-2612
Consulate General 12 W 56th St	New York	NY	10019	212-603-0400	541-7746
Web: www.congenargentinany.com					
Consulate General 3050 Post Oak Blvd Suite 1625	Houston	TX	77056	713-871-8935	871-0639
Embassy 1600 New Hampshire Ave NW	Washington	DC	20009	202-238-6400	332-3171
Web: www.embassyofargentina.us					
Armenia					
Consulate General 50 N La Cienega Blvd Suite 210	Beverly Hills	CA	90211	310-657-6102	657-7419
Embassy 2225 R St NW	Washington	DC	20008	202-319-1976	319-2982
Web: www.armeniaemb.org					

Entry	City	State	ZIP	Phone	Fax
Australia					
Consulate General					
2049 Century Park E Century Plaza Towers 19th Fl	Los Angeles	CA	90067	310-229-4800	277-3462
Web: www.austemb.org/losangeles.html					
Consulate General 1000 Bishop St PH	Honolulu	HI	96813	808-524-5050	531-5142
Web: www.austemb.org/honolulu.html					
Consulate General 123 N Wacker Dr Suite 1330	Chicago	IL	60606	312-419-1480	419-1499
Web: www.austemb.org/chicago.html					
Consulate General 150 E 42nd St 34th Fl	New York	NY	10017	212-351-6500	351-6501
Web: www.australianyc.org					
Embassy 1601 Massachusetts Ave NW	Washington	DC	20036	202-797-3000	797-3168
Web: www.austemb.org					
Austria					
Consulate General 11859 Wilshire Blvd Suite 501	Los Angeles	CA	90025	310-444-9310	477-9897
Web: www.austria.org/austriaintheus.shtml#5					
Consulate General 400 N Michigan Ave Suite 707	Chicago	IL	60611	312-222-1515	222-4113
Web: www.aussenministerium.at					
Consulate General 31 E 69th St	New York	NY	10021	212-737-6400	772-8926
Web: www.austria-ny.org					
Embassy 3524 International Ct NW	Washington	DC	20008	202-895-6700	895-6750
Web: www.austria.org					
Azerbaijan Embassy 2741 34th St NW	Washington	DC	20008	202-337-3500	337-5911
Web: www.azembassy.com					
Bahamas					
Consulate General 25 SE 2nd Ave	Miami	FL	33131	305-373-6295	373-6312
Consulate General 231 E 46th St	New York	NY	10017	212-421-6420	688-5926
Embassy 2220 Massachusetts Ave NW	Washington	DC	20008	202-319-2660	319-2668
Bahrain					
Consulate General 866 2nd Ave 14th Fl	New York	NY	10017	212-223-6200	223-6206
Web: www.un.int/bahrain/consulate.html					
Embassy 3502 International Dr NW	Washington	DC	20008	202-342-1111	362-2192
Web: www.bahrainembassy.org					
Bangladesh					
Consulate General 4201 Wilshire Blvd Suite 605	Los Angeles	CA	90010	323-932-0100	932-9703
Web: www.bangladeshconsulatela.com					
Consulate General 211 E 43rd St Suite 502	New York	NY	10017	212-599-6767	682-9211
Embassy 3510 International Dr NW	Washington	DC	20008	202-244-0183	244-2771
Web: www.bangladoot.org					
Barbados					
Consulate General 150 Alhambra Cir Suite 1000	Coral Gables	FL	33134	305-442-1994	567-2844
Consulate General 800 2nd Ave 2nd Fl	New York	NY	10017	212-867-8435	986-1030
Embassy 2144 Wyoming Ave NW	Washington	DC	20008	202-939-9200	332-7467
Vice Consulate 3440 Wilshire Blvd Suite 1207	Los Angeles	CA	90010	213-380-2198	384-2763
Belarus					
Consulate General 708 3rd Ave 21st Fl	New York	NY	10017	212-682-5392	682-5491
Embassy 1619 New Hampshire Ave NW	Washington	DC	20009	202-986-1606	986-1805
Web: www.belarusembassy.org					
Belgium					
Consulate General 6100 Wilshire Blvd Suite 1200	Los Angeles	CA	90048	323-857-1244	936-2564
Consulate General 230 Peachtree St NW Suite 2710	Atlanta	GA	30303	404-659-2150	659-8474
Consulate General 1065 Avenue of the Americas 22nd Fl	New York	NY	10018	212-586-5110	582-9657
Web: www.diplomatie.be/newyork/					
Consulate General 1065 Ave of the Americas 22nd Fl	New York	NY	10018	212-586-5110	582-9657
Embassy 3330 Garfield St NW	Washington	DC	20008	202-333-6900	333-3079
Web: www.diplobel.us					
Belize					
Consulate General					
4801 Wilshire Blvd Suite 250 Park Mile Plaza	Los Angeles	CA	90018	323-634-9900	634-9903
Embassy 2535 Massachusetts Ave NW	Washington	DC	20008	202-332-9636	332-6888
Web: www.embassyofbelize.org					
Benin Embassy 2124 Kalorama Rd NW	Washington	DC	20008	202-232-6656	265-1996
Web: www.beninembassy.us					
Bolivia					
Consulate General 3701 Wilshire Blvd Suite 1065	Los Angeles	CA	90010	213-388-0475	384-6272
Consulate General 211 E 43rd St Suite 702	New York	NY	10017	212-687-0530	687-0532
Web: www.boliviaweb.com/embassies.htm					
Embassy 3014 Massachusetts Ave NW	Washington	DC	20008	202-483-4410	328-3712
Web: www.boliviaweb.com/embassies.htm					
Bosnia & Herzegovina					
Consulate General 2109 E St NW	Washington	DC	20037	202-337-6478	337-2909
Web: www.bhembassy.org					
Embassy 2109 'E' St NW	Washington	DC	20037	202-337-1500	337-1502
Web: www.bhembassy.org					
Botswana Embassy 1531 New Hampshire Ave NW	Washington	DC	20036	202-244-4990	244-4164
Web: www.botswanaembassy.org					
Brazil					
Consulate General 8484 Wilshire Blvd Suite 711	Beverly Hills	CA	90211	323-651-2664	651-1274
Web: www.brazilian-consulate.org					
Consulate General 300 Montgomery St Suite 900	San Francisco	CA	94104	415-981-8170	981-3628
Web: www.brazilsf.org					
Consulate General 80 SW 8th St Suite 2600	Miami	FL	33130	305-285-6200	285-6259
Web: www.brazilmiami.org					
Consulate General 401 N Michigan Ave Suite 3050	Chicago	IL	60611	312-464-0244	464-0299
Consulate General 20 Park Plaza Suite 810	Boston	MA	02116	617-542-4000	542-4318
Web: www.consulatebrazil.org					
Consulate General 1185 6th Ave	New York	NY	10036	917-777-7777	827-0225*
*Fax Area Code: 212 ■ *Web:* www.brazilny.org					
Consulate General 1233 West Loop S Suite 1150	Houston	TX	77027	713-961-3063	961-3070
Web: www.brazilhouston.org					
Embassy 3006 Massachusetts Ave NW	Washington	DC	20008	202-238-2700	238-2827
TF: 800-727-2945 ■ *Web:* www.brasilemb.org					
Embassy - Consular Section 3009 Whitehaven St NW	Washington	DC	20008	202-238-2828	238-2818
Web: www.brasilemb.org					
Brunei Darussalam Embassy 3520 International Ct NW	Washington	DC	20008	202-237-1838	885-0560
Web: www.bruneiembassy.org					
Bulgaria					
Consulate General 121 E 62nd St	New York	NY	10021	212-935-4646	319-5955
Web: www.consulbulgaria-ny.org					
Embassy 1621 22nd St NW	Washington	DC	20008	202-387-0174	234-7973
Web: www.bulgaria-embassy.org					
Burkina Faso Embassy 2340 Massachusetts Ave NW	Washington	DC	20008	202-332-5577	667-1882
Web: www.burkinaembassy-usa.org					
Burundi Embassy 2233 Wisconsin Ave NW Suite 212	Washington	DC	20007	202-342-2574	342-2578
Web: www.burundiembassy-usa.org					
Cambodia Embassy 4530 16th St NW	Washington	DC	20011	202-726-7742	726-8381
Web: www.embassyofcambodia.org					
Cameroon Embassy 2349 Massachusetts Ave NW	Washington	DC	20008	202-265-8790	387-3826
Canada					
Consulate 200 S Biscayne Blvd Suite 1600	Miami	FL	33131	305-579-1600	374-6774
Web: geo.international.gc.ca/can-am/miami/					
Consulate General 550 S Hope St 9th Fl	Los Angeles	CA	90071	213-346-2700	620-8827
Web: www.dfait-maeci.gc.ca/los_angeles/					
Consulate General					
1175 Peachtree St NE 100 Colony Sq Suite 1700	Atlanta	GA	30361	404-532-2000	532-2050
Web: www.dfait-maeci.gc.ca/atlanta/					
Consulate General 180 N Stetson Ave Suite 2400	Chicago	IL	60601	312-616-1860	616-1877
Web: www.dfait-maeci.gc.ca/chicago					
Consulate General 3 Copley Pl Suite 400	Boston	MA	02116	617-262-3760	262-3415
Web: www.dfait-maeci.gc.ca/boston					
Consulate General 600 Renaissance Ctr Suite 1100	Detroit	MI	48243	313-567-2340	567-2164
Web: www.dfait-maeci.gc.ca/detroit					
Consulate General 701 4th Ave S Suite 900	Minneapolis	MN	55415	612-332-7486	332-4061
Web: www.dfait-maeci.gc.ca/minneapolis					
Consulate General 3000 HSBC Ctr	Buffalo	NY	14203	716-858-9500	852-2477
Web: www.dfait-maeci.gc.ca/buffalo/					
Consulate General					
1251 Ave of the Americas Concourse Level	New York	NY	10020	212-596-1628	596-1790
Web: geo.international.gc.ca/can-am/new_york/					
Consulate General 750 N Saint Paul St Suite 1700	Dallas	TX	75201	214-922-9806	922-9815
Web: www.dfait-maeci.gc.ca/dallas					
Consulate General 1501 4th Ave Suite 600	Seattle	WA	98101	206-443-1777	443-9662
Web: www.dfait-maeci.gc.ca/seattle/					
Embassy 501 Pennsylvania Ave NW	Washington	DC	20001	202-682-1740	682-7726
Web: www.canadianembassy.org					
Cape Verde					
Consulate General 607 Boylston St 4th Fl	Boston	MA	02116	617-353-0014	859-9798
Embassy 3415 Massachusetts Ave NW	Washington	DC	20007	202-965-6820	965-1207
Central African Republic Embassy 1618 22nd St NW	Washington	DC	20008	202-483-7800	332-9893
Chad Embassy 2002 R St NW	Washington	DC	20009	202-462-4009	265-1937
Web: www.chadembassy.org					
Chile					
Consulate General 6100 Wilshire Blvd Suite 1240	Los Angeles	CA	90048	323-933-3697	933-3842
Consulate General 870 Market St Suite 1058	San Francisco	CA	94102	415-982-7662	982-2384
Web: www.consuladochilesfo.com					
Consulate General 800 Brickell Ave Suite 1230	Miami	FL	33131	305-373-8623	379-6613
Consulate General 875 N Michigan Ave Suite 3352	Chicago	IL	60611	312-654-8780	654-8948
Consulate General 866 UN Plaza Suite 601	New York	NY	10017	212-980-3366	888-5288
Web: www.chileny.com					
Consulate General					
6th & Chestnut St Public Ledger Bldg Suite 1030	Philadelphia	PA	19106	215-829-9520	829-0594
Consulate General 1300 Post Oak Blvd Suite 1130	Houston	TX	77056	713-621-5853	621-8672
Embassy 1732 Massachusetts Ave NW	Washington	DC	20036	202-785-1746	887-5579
Web: www.chile-usa.org					
China People's Republic of					
Consulate General 443 Shatto Pl	Los Angeles	CA	90020	213-807-8088	807-8019
Web: www.chinaconsulatela.org					
Consulate General 1450 Laguna St	San Francisco	CA	94115	415-674-2900	563-0494
Web: www.chinaconsulatesf.org					
Consulate General 1 E Erie St	Chicago	IL	60611	312-803-0095	803-0110
Web: www.chinaconsulatechicago.org					
Consulate General 520 12th Ave	New York	NY	10036	212-244-9392	
Web: www.nyconsulate.prchina.org					
Consulate General 3417 Montrose Blvd	Houston	TX	77006	713-520-1462	524-7656
Web: www.chinahouston.org					
Embassy 2300 Connecticut Ave NW	Washington	DC	20008	202-328-2500	588-0032
Web: www.china-embassy.org					
Colombia					
Consulate 5901-C Peachtree Dunwoody Rd Suite 375	Atlanta	GA	30328	770-668-0512	668-0763
Consulate 535 Boylston St 3rd Fl	Boston	MA	02116	617-536-6222	536-9372
Consulate General 8383 Wilshire Blvd Suite 420	Beverly Hills	CA	90211	323-653-9863	653-2964
Consulate General 595 Market St Suite 2130	San Francisco	CA	94105	415-495-7195	777-3731
Consulate General 280 Aragon Ave	Coral Gables	FL	33134	305-448-5558	441-9537
Consulate General 500 N Michigan Ave Suite 2040	Chicago	IL	60611	312-923-1196	923-1197
Consulate General 10 E 46th St	New York	NY	10017	212-370-0004	972-1725
Consulate General 5851 San Felipe Suite 300	Houston	TX	77057	713-527-8919	529-3395
Web: www.colhouston.org					
Embassy 2118 Leroy Pl NW	Washington	DC	20008	202-387-8338	232-8643
Web: www.colombiaemb.org					
Embassy - Consular Section 1101 17th St NW Suite 1007	Washington	DC	20036	202-332-7573	332-7180
Web: www.colombiaemb.org					
Comoros Embassy 866 United Nations Plaza Suite 418	New York	NY	10017	212-750-1637	750-1657
Congo Democratic Republic of Embassy 1726 M St NW	Washington	DC	20036	202-234-7690	234-2609
Congo Republic of Embassy 4891 Colorado Ave NW	Washington	DC	20011	202-726-0825	726-1860
Costa Rica					
Consulate 3000 Wilcrest Dr Suite 112	Houston	TX	77042	713-266-0484	266-1527
Web: www.costarica-embassy.org/consular/consulates/default.htm					
Consulate General 1605 W Olympic Blvd Suite 400	Los Angeles	CA	90015	213-380-7915	380-5639
Web: www.costarica-embassy.org/consular/consulates					
Consulate General 2112 'S' St NW	Washington	DC	20008	202-328-6628	265-4795
Web: www.costarica-embassy.org/consular/consulates/default.htm					
Consulate General 1101 Brickell Ave Suite 401 North Tower	Miami	FL	33131	305-871-7485	871-0860
Web: www.costarica-embassy.org/consular/consulates/default.htm					
Consulate General 1870 The Exchange Suite 100	Atlanta	GA	30339	770-951-7025	951-7073
Web: www.costarica-embassy.org/consular/consulates/default.htm					
Consulate General 203 N Wabash Ave Suite 702	Chicago	IL	60601	312-263-2772	263-5807
Web: www.costarica-embassy.org/consular/consulates/default.htm					
Consulate General					
225 W 34th St Suite 1203 Penn Plaza Blvd	New York	NY	10122	212-509-3066	509-3068
Web: www.costarica-embassy.org/consular/consulates/default.htm					
Consulate General 3000 Wilcrest Dr Suite 112	Houston	TX	77042	713-266-0484	266-1527
Web: www.costarica-embassy.org/consular/consulates					
Embassy 2114 'S' St NW	Washington	DC	20008	202-234-2945	265-4795
Web: www.costarica-embassy.org					
Cote d'Ivoire Embassy 2424 Massachusetts Ave	Washington	DC	20008	202-797-0300	462-9444
Web: www.embaci.com					
Croatia					
Consulate General 11766 Wilshire Blvd Suite 1250	Los Angeles	CA	90025	310-477-1009	477-1866
Web: www.croatiaemb.org					
Consulate General 737 N Michigan Ave Suite 1030	Chicago	IL	60611	312-482-9902	482-9987
Web: www.croatiaemb.org					
Consulate General 369 Lexington Ave 11th Fl	New York	NY	10017	212-599-3066	599-3106
Web: www.croatiaemb.org					
Embassy 2343 Massachusetts Ave NW	Washington	DC	20008	202-588-5899	588-8936
Web: www.croatiaemb.org					
Cuba Interests Section					
Embassy of Switzerland 2630 16th St NW	Washington	DC	20009	202-797-8518	797-8521
Web: www.geocities.com/cubainte					
Cyprus					
Consulate General 13 E 40th St	New York	NY	10016	212-686-6016	686-3660
Embassy 2211 R St NW	Washington	DC	20008	202-462-5772	483-6710
Web: www.cyprusembassy.net					
Czech Republic					
Consulate General 10990 Wilshire Blvd Suite 1100	Los Angeles	CA	90024	310-473-0889	473-9813
Web: www.mzv.cz/losangeles					
Consulate General 1109-1111 Madison Ave	New York	NY	10028	646-981-4040	717-5064*
*Fax Area Code: 212 ■ *Web:* www.mfa.cz/newyork					
Embassy 3900 Spring of Freedom St NW	Washington	DC	20008	202-274-9100	966-8540
Web: www.mzv.cz/washington					
Denmark					
Consulate General 211 E Ontario St Suite 1800	Chicago	IL	60611	312-787-8780	787-8744
Web: www.consulatedk.org					
Consulate General					
1 Dag Hammarskjold Plaza 18th Fl 885 2nd Ave	New York	NY	10017	212-223-4545	754-1904
Web: www.denmark.org					

Phone | Fax

Embassy 3200 Whitehaven St NW ... Washington DC 20008 202-234-4300 328-1470
Web: www.ambwashington.um.dk/en
Djibouti Embassy 1156 15th St NW Suite 515 ... Washington DC 20005 202-331-0270 331-0302
Dominica
Consulate General 800 2nd Ave Suite 400-H ... New York NY 10017 212-599-8478 808-4975
Embassy 3216 New Mexico Ave NW ... Washington DC 20016 202-364-6781 364-6791
Dominican Republic
Consulate General 1516 Oak St Suite 321 ... Alameda CA 94501 510-864-7777 504-6617*
*Fax Area Code: 818 ■ *Web:* www.domrep.org
Consulate General 1715 22nd St NW ... Washington DC 20008 202-332-6280 387-2459
Web: www.domrep.org
Consulate General 1038 Brickell Ave ... Miami FL 33131 305-358-3220 358-2318
Web: consuladodominicanomiami.org
Consulate General
8700 Bryanmawr St Suite 818 Presidents Plaza
O'Hare Center ... Chicago IL 60631 773-714-4924
Web: www.domrep.org
Consulate General 20 Park Plaza Statler Bldg Suite 601 ... Boston MA 02116 617-482-2101 482-8133
Web: www.domrep.org
Consulate General 1501 Broadway Suite 410 ... New York NY 10036 212-768-2480 768-2677
Web: www.domrep.org
Embassy 1715 22nd St NW ... Washington DC 20008 202-332-6280 265-8057
Web: www.domrep.org
East Timor Embassy
4201 Massachusetts Ave NW Suite 504 ... Washington DC 20008 202-966-3202 966-3205
Ecuador
Consulate General 8484 Wilshire Blvd Suite 540 ... Beverly Hills CA 90211 323-658-6020 658-1198
Consulate General 235 Montgomery St Suite 944 ... San Francisco CA 94104 415-982-1819 982-1833
Consulate General 1101 Brickell Ave Suite M102 ... Miami FL 33131 305-539-8214 539-8313
Consulate General 30 S Michigan Ave Suite 204 ... Chicago IL 60603 312-338-1002 338-1004
Web: www.ecuador.org/consulates.htm
Consulate General 400 Market St 4th Fl ... Newark NJ 07105 973-344-6900 344-0008
Web: www.consuladoecuadornj.com
Consulate General 800 2nd Ave Suite 600 ... New York NY 10017 212-808-0170 808-0188
Web: www.consulecuadornewyork.com
Consulate General 4200 Westheimer Rd Suite 218 ... Houston TX 77027 713-572-8731 572-8732
Embassy 2535 15th St NW ... Washington DC 20009 202-234-7200 234-3429
Web: www.ecuador.org
Egypt
Consulate General 3001 Pacific Ave ... San Francisco CA 94115 415-346-9700 346-9480
Web: www.egy2000.com
Consulate General 500 N Michigan Ave Suite 1900 ... Chicago IL 60611 312-828-9162 828-9167
Web: www.eg2002.net
Consulate General 1110 2nd Ave Suite 201 ... New York NY 10022 212-759-7120 308-7643
Web: www.egyptnyc.net
Consulate General 1990 Post Oak Blvd Suite 2180 ... Houston TX 77056 713-961-4915 961-3868
Embassy 3521 International Ct NW ... Washington DC 20008 202-895-5400 244-4319
Web: www.egyptembassy.us
El Salvador
Consulate General 3450 Wilshire Blvd Suite 250 ... Los Angeles CA 90010 213-383-8580 383-8599
Web: www.elsalvador.org/home.nsf/consularinfo
Consulate General 507 Polk St Suite 280 ... San Francisco CA 94102 415-771-8524 771-8522
Web: www.elsalvador.org/home.nsf/consularinfo
Consulate General 2600 Douglas Rd Suite 104 ... Coral Gables FL 33134 305-774-0840 774-0850
Consulate General 104 S Michigan Ave Suite 816 ... Chicago IL 60603 312-332-1393 332-4446
Web: www.elsalvador.org/home.nsf/consularinfo
Consulate General 46 Park Ave ... New York NY 10016 212-889-3608 679-2835
Web: www.elsalvador.org/home.nsf/consularinfo
Consulate General 1555 W Mockingbird Ln Suite 216 ... Dallas TX 75235 214-637-0732 637-1106
Web: www.elsalvador.org/home.nsf/consularinfo
Consulate General 1702 Hillendahl Blvd ... Houston TX 77055 713-270-6239 270-9683
Web: www.elsalvador.org/home.nsf/consularinfo
Embassy 1400 16th St NW Suite 100 ... Washington DC 20036 202-595-7500 232-3763
Web: www.elsalvador.org
Equatorial Guinea Embassy 2020 16th St NW ... Washington DC 20009 202-518-5700 518-5252
Eritrea Embassy 1708 New Hampshire Ave NW ... Washington DC 20009 202-319-1991 319-1304
Estonia
Consulate General 600 3rd Ave 26th Fl ... New York NY 10016 212-883-0636 883-0648
Web: www.nyc.estemb.org
Embassy 2131 Massachusetts Ave NW ... Washington DC 20008 202-588-0101 588-0108
Web: www.estemb.org
Ethiopia Embassy 3506 International Dr NW ... Washington DC 20008 202-364-1200 587-0195
Web: www.ethiopianembassy.org
Fiji Embassy 2233 Wisconsin Ave NW Suite 240 ... Washington DC 20007 202-337-8320 337-1996
Web: www.fijiembassy.org
Finland
Consulate General 1801 Century Pk E Suite 2100 ... Los Angeles CA 90067 310-203-9903 203-9186
Web: www.finland.org/en/
Consulate General 866 UN Plaza Suite 250 ... New York NY 10017 212-750-4400 750-4418
Web: www.finland.org/en/
Embassy 3301 Massachusetts Ave NW ... Washington DC 20008 202-298-5800 298-6030
Web: www.finland.org
France
Consulate General 10990 Wilshire Blvd Suite 300 ... Los Angeles CA 90024 310-235-3200 312-0704
Web: www.consulfrance-losangeles.org
Consulate General 540 Bush St ... San Francisco CA 94108 415-397-4330 433-8357
Web: www.consulfrance-sanfrancisco.org
Consulate General 1395 Brickell Ave Suite 1050 ... Miami FL 33131 305-403-4185 403-4187
Web: www.consulfrance-miami.org
Consulate General 3475 Piedmont Rd NE Suite 1840 ... Atlanta GA 30305 404-495-1660 495-1661
Web: www.consulfrance-atlanta.org
Consulate General 205 N Michigan Ave Suite 3700 ... Chicago IL 60601 312-327-5200 327-5201
Web: www.consulfrance-chicago.org
Consulate General 1340 Poydras St Suite 1710 ... New Orleans LA 70112 504-569-2870 569-2871
Web: www.consulfrance-nouvelleorleans.org
Consulate General 31 Saint James Ave Suite 750 ... Boston MA 02116 617-832-4400
Web: www.consulfrance-boston.org
Consulate General 934 5th Ave ... New York NY 10021 212-606-3680 606-3614
Web: www.consulfrance-newyork.org
Consulate General 777 Post Oak Blvd Suite 600 ... Houston TX 77056 713-572-2799 572-2911
Web: www.consulfrance-houston.org
Embassy 4101 Reservoir Rd NW ... Washington DC 20007 202-944-6000 944-6175
Web: www.ambafrance-us.org
Gabon
Consulate 18 E 41st St 9th Fl ... New York NY 10017 212-686-9720 689-5769
Embassy 2034 20th St NW ... Washington DC 20009 202-797-1000 332-0668
Gambia Embassy 1156 15th St NW Suite 905 ... Washington DC 20005 202-785-1399 785-1430
Web: www.gambiaembassy.us
Georgia Embassy 1101 15th St NW Suite 602 ... Washington DC 20005 202-387-2390 393-4537
Web: www.georgiaemb.org
Germany
Consulate General 6222 Wilshire Blvd Suite 500 ... Los Angeles CA 90048 323-930-2703 930-2805
Consulate General 1960 Jackson St ... San Francisco CA 94109 415-775-1061 775-0187
Web: www.germany.info
Consulate General 100 N Biscayne Blvd Suite 2200 ... Miami FL 33132 305-358-0290 358-0307
Consulate General 285 Peachtree Center Ave NE Suite 901 ... Atlanta GA 30303 404-659-4760 659-1280
Consulate General 676 N Michigan Ave Suite 3200 ... Chicago IL 60611 312-202-0480 202-0466
Web: germany.info\chicago
Consulate General 3 Copley Pl Suite 500 ... Boston MA 02116 617-536-4414 536-8573
Consulate General 871 UN Plaza ... New York NY 10017 212-610-9700 610-9702
Consulate General 1330 Post Oak Blvd Suite 1850 ... Houston TX 77056 713-627-7770 627-0506
Web: www.germanconsulatehouston.org
Embassy 4645 Reservoir Rd NW ... Washington DC 20007 202-298-4000 298-4249
Web: www.germany-info.org
Ghana
Consulate General 19 E 47th St ... New York NY 10017 212-832-1300 751-6743
Embassy 3512 International Dr NW ... Washington DC 20008 202-686-4520 686-4527
Web: www.ghanaembassy.org
Greece
Consulate 3340 Peachtree Rd NE Tower Place 100 Suite 1670 ... Atlanta GA 30326 404-261-3313 262-2798
Consulate 520 Post Oak Blvd Suite 450 ... Houston TX 77027 713-840-7522 840-0614
Web: www.greekembassy.org/consular/houston
Consulate General 12424 Wilshire Blvd Suite 800 ... Los Angeles CA 90025 310-826-5555 826-8670
Web: www.greekembassy.org/consular/los_angeles
Consulate General 2441 Gough St ... San Francisco CA 94123 415-775-2102 776-6815
Web: www.greekembassy.org/consular/san_francisco
Consulate General 650 N Saint Clair St ... Chicago IL 60611 312-335-3915 335-3958
Web: www.greekembassy.org/consular/chicago
Consulate General 86 Beacon St ... Boston MA 02108 617-523-0100 523-0511
Web: www.greekembassy.org/consular/boston
Consulate General 69 E 79th St ... New York NY 10021 212-988-5500 734-8492
Web: www.greekembassy.org/consular/newyork
Embassy 2219 Massachusetts Ave NW ... Washington DC 20008 202-939-1300 939-1324
Web: www.greekembassy.org
Embassy - Consular Section 2217 Massachusetts Ave NW ... Washington DC 20008 202-939-1306 234-2803
Grenada
Consulate General 800 2nd Ave Suite 400-K ... New York NY 10017 212-599-0301 599-1540
Web: www.grenadaconsulate.org
Embassy 1701 New Hampshire Ave NW ... Washington DC 20009 202-265-2561 265-2468
Guatemala
Consulate General 1625 W Olympic Blvd Suite 1000 ... Los Angeles CA 90015 213-365-9251 365-9245
Consulate General 870 Market St Suite 667 ... San Francisco CA 94102 415-788-5651 788-5653
Consulate General 1101 Brickell Ave Suite 1003-S ... Miami FL 33131 305-679-9945 679-9983
Consulate General 203 N Wabash Ave Suite 910 ... Chicago IL 60601 312-332-1587 332-4256
Consulate General 57 Park Ave ... New York NY 10016 212-686-3837 447-6947
Consulate General 3013 Fountain View Dr Suite 210 ... Houston TX 77057 713-953-9531 953-9383
Embassy 2220 R St NW ... Washington DC 20008 202-745-4952 745-1908
Web: www.guatemala-embassy.org
Guinea Embassy 2112 Leroy Pl NW ... Washington DC 20008 202-986-4300 986-4800
Guyana
Consulate General 370 7th Ave Suite 402 ... New York NY 10001 212-947-5110 947-5163
Web: www.guyana.org/govt/govt_offices.html
Embassy 2490 Tracy Pl NW ... Washington DC 20008 202-265-6900 232-1297
Web: georgetown.usembassy.gov
Haiti
Consulate General 259 SW 13th St ... Miami FL 33130 305-859-2003 854-7441
Web: www.haiti.org/misyon.htm
Consulate General 220 S State St Suite 2110 ... Chicago IL 60604 312-922-4004 922-7122
Web: www.haitianconsulate.org
Consulate General 545 Boylston St Rm 201 ... Boston MA 02116 617-266-3660 778-6898
Web: www.haiti.org/misyon.htm
Consulate General 271 Madison Ave 5th Fl ... New York NY 10016 212-697-9767 681-6991
Web: www.haitianconsulate-nyc.org
Embassy 2311 Massachusetts Ave NW ... Washington DC 20008 202-332-4090 745-7215
Web: www.haiti.org
Holy See Apostolic Nunciature
3339 Massachusetts Ave NW ... Washington DC 20008 202-333-7121 337-4036
Web: www.vatican.va
Honduras
Consulate 1014 M St NW 2nd Fl ... Washington DC 20001 202-737-2972 737-2907
Web: www.hondurasemb.org/visas.htm
Consulate General 4040 E McDowell Rd Suite 305 ... Phoenix AZ 85008 602-273-0173 273-0547
Consulate General 3550 Wilshire Blvd Suite 410 ... Los Angeles CA 90010 213-383-9244 383-9309
Web: www.consuladodehonduras.com
Consulate General 870 Market St Suite 449 ... San Francisco CA 94102 415-392-0076 392-6726
Consulate General 7171 Coral Way Suite 309 ... Miami FL 33155 305-269-9399 269-9445
Consulate General 600 Houze Way Suite 3A ... Roswell GA 30076 770-645-8881 645-8808
Consulate General 4506 W Fullerton Ave ... Chicago IL 60639 773-342-8281 342-8293
Consulate General
World Trade Center 2 Canal St Suite 2340 ... New Orleans LA 70130 504-522-3118 523-0544
Consulate General 35 W 35th St 6th Fl ... New York NY 10001 212-714-9451 714-9453
Consulate General 6700 W Loop S Suite 360 ... Houston TX 77401 713-667-4693 667-4284
Embassy 3007 Tilden St NW Suite 4M ... Washington DC 20008 202-966-7702 966-9751
Web: www.hondurasemb.org
Hungary
Consulate General 11766 Wilshire Blvd Suite 410 ... Los Angeles CA 90025 310-473-9344 479-5119
Consulate General 223 E 52nd St ... New York NY 10022 212-752-0661 755-5986
Embassy 3910 Shoemaker St NW ... Washington DC 20008 202-362-6730 966-8135
Web: www.huembwas.org
Iceland
Consulate General 800 3rd Ave 36th Fl ... New York NY 10022 212-593-2700 282-9369*
*Fax Area Code: 646 ■ *Web:* www.iceland.org/us/nyc/
Embassy 1156 15th St NW Suite 1200 ... Washington DC 20005 202-265-6653 265-6656
Web: www.iceland.org/us
India
Consulate 2536 Massachusetts Ave NW ... Washington DC 20008 202-939-9806
Web: www.indianembassy.org/consular
Consulate General 540 Arguello Blvd ... San Francisco CA 94118 415-668-0662 668-9764
Web: www.cgisf.org
Consulate General 455 N Cityfront Plaza Dr Suite 850 ... Chicago IL 60611 312-595-0405 595-0417
Web: www.indianconsulate.com
Consulate General 3 E 64th St ... New York NY 10021 212-774-0600 861-3788
Web: www.indiacgny.org
Consulate General 1990 Post Oak Blvd Suite 600 ... Houston TX 77056 713-626-2148 626-2450
Web: www.cgihouston.org
Embassy 2107 Massachusetts Ave NW ... Washington DC 20008 202-939-7000 265-4351
Web: www.indianembassy.org
Indonesia
Consulate General 3457 Wilshire Blvd ... Los Angeles CA 90010 213-383-5126 487-3971
Consulate General 1111 Columbus Ave ... San Francisco CA 94133 415-474-9571 441-4320
Consulate General 211 W Wacker Dr 8th Fl ... Chicago IL 60606 312-920-1880 920-1881
Web: www.indonesiachicago.org
Consulate General 5 E 68th St ... New York NY 10021 212-879-0600 570-6206
Web: www.indony.org
Consulate General 10900 Richmond Ave ... Houston TX 77042 713-785-1691 780-9644
Embassy 2020 Massachusetts Ave NW ... Washington DC 20036 202-775-5200 775-5365
Web: www.embassyofindonesia.org
Iran Islamic Republic of Interests Section
Embassy of Pakistan 2209 Wisconsin Ave NW ... Washington DC 20007 202-965-4990 965-1073
Web: www.daftar.org

Phone | Fax

Ireland
Consulate General 100 Pine St 33rd Fl .... San Francisco CA 94111 415-392-4214 392-0885
Web: www.irelandemb.org/contact.html
Consulate General 400 N Michigan Ave Suite 911 .... Chicago IL 60611 312-337-1868 337-1954
Web: www.irelandemb.org/chicago.html
Consulate General 535 Boylston St .... Boston MA 02116 617-267-9330 267-6375
Web: www.irelandemb.org/contact.html
Consulate General 345 Park Ave 17th Fl .... New York NY 10154 212-319-2555 980-9475
Web: www.irelandemb.org/contact.html
Embassy 2234 Massachusetts Ave NW .... Washington DC 20008 202-462-3939 232-5993
Web: www.irelandemb.org

Israel
Consulate 230 S 15th St Suite 8 .... Philadelphia PA 19102 215-546-5556 545-3986
Consulate General 6380 Wilshire Blvd Suite 1700 .... Los Angeles CA 90048 323-852-5500 852-5555
Web: www.israelemb.org/la
Consulate General 456 Montgomery St Suite 2100 .... San Francisco CA 94104 415-844-7500 844-7555
Web: israelemb.org/sanfran
Consulate General 100 N Biscayne Blvd Suite 1800 .... Miami FL 33132 305-925-9400 925-9451
Web: www.israelemb.org/miami
Consulate General 1100 Spring St NW Suite 440 .... Atlanta GA 30309 404-487-6500 487-6555
Web: www.israelemb.org/atlanta
Consulate General 111 E Wacker Dr Suite 1308 .... Chicago IL 60601 312-297-4800 297-4855
Web: www.embassyofisrael.org/chicago
Consulate General 24 Greenway Plaza Suite 1500 .... Houston TX 77046 713-627-3780 627-0149
Web: www.israelemb.org/tx
Consulate General in New York 800 2nd Ave .... New York NY 10017 212-499-5300 499-5455
Web: www.israelfm.org
Embassy 3514 International Dr NW .... Washington DC 20008 202-364-5500 364-5429
Web: www.israelemb.org

Italy
Consulate 535 Griswold St Buhl Bldg Suite 1840 .... Detroit MI 48226 313-963-8560 963-8180
Web: www.italconsdetroit.org
Consulate General 12400 Wilshire Blvd Suite 300 .... Los Angeles CA 90025 310-820-0622 820-0727
Web: sedi.esteri.it/losangeles/
Consulate General 2590 Webster St .... San Francisco CA 94115 415-931-4924 931-7205
Web: www.italcons-sf.org
Consulate General 4000 Ponce de Leon Blvd Suite 590 ...... Coral Gables FL 33146 305-374-6322 374-7945
Web: www.consmiami.esteri.it/Consolato_Miami
Consulate General 500 N Michigan Ave Suite 1850 .... Chicago IL 60611 312-439-8600 467-1335
Web: www.consnewyork.esteri.it/Consolato_NewYork
Consulate General 600 Atlantic Ave 17th Fl. .... Boston MA 02210 617-722-9201 722-9407
Consulate General 690 Park Ave .... New York NY 10021 212-737-9100 249-4945
Web: www.italconsulnyc.org
Consulate General
150 S Independence Mall West Public Ledger Bldg
Suite 1026 .... Philadelphia PA 19106 215-592-7329 592-9808
Web: www.italconphila.org
Consulate General 1300 Post Oak Blvd Suite 660 .... Houston TX 77056 713-850-7520 850-9113
Web: www.italconshouston.org
Embassy 3000 Whitehaven St NW .... Washington DC 20008 202-612-4400 518-2154
Web: www.italyemb.org
Vice Consulate 1 Gateway Center Suite 100 .... Newark NJ 07102 973-643-1448 643-3043
Web: www.consnewark.esteri.it/Consolato_Newark

Ivory Coast Embassy 2424 Massachusetts Ave .... Washington DC 20008 202-797-0300 462-9444
Web: www.embaci.com

Jamaica
Consulate General 25 SE 2nd Ave Suite 842 .... Miami FL 33131 305-374-8431 577-4970
Embassy 1520 New Hampshire Ave NW .... Washington DC 20036 202-452-0660 452-0081
Web: www.jamaicaembassy.org

Japan
Consulate General 3601 C St Suite 1300 .... Anchorage AK 99503 907-562-8424 562-8434
Web: www.anchorage.us.emb-japan.go.jp
Consulate General 350 S Grand Ave Suite 1700 .... Los Angeles CA 90071 213-617-6700 617-6727
Web: www.la.us.emb-japan.go.jp
Consulate General 50 Fremont St Suite 2300 .... San Francisco CA 94105 415-777-3533 974-3660
Web: www.cgjsf.org
Consulate General 1225 17th St Suite 3000 .... Denver CO 80202 303-534-1151 534-3393
Web: www.denver.us.emb-japan.go.jp
Consulate General
80 SW 8th St Brickell Bay View Ctr Suite 3200 .... Miami FL 33130 305-530-9090 530-0950
Web: www.miami.us.emb-japan.go.jp
Consulate General 1 Alliance Ctr 3500 Lenox Rd Suite 1600 .... Atlanta GA 30326 404-240-4300 240-4311
Web: www.japanatlanta.org
Consulate General 1742 Nuuanu Ave .... Honolulu HI 96817 808-543-3111 543-3170
Web: www.honolulu.us.emb-japan.go.jp
Consulate General 737 N Michigan Ave Suite 1100 .... Chicago IL 60611 312-280-0400 280-9568
Web: www.chicago.us.emb-japan.go.jp
Consulate General 639 Loyola Ave Suite 2050 .... New Orleans LA 70113 504-529-2101 568-9847
Web: www.neworleans.us.emb-japan.go.jp
Consulate General
600 Atlantic Ave Federal Reserve Plaza 14th Fl. .... Boston MA 02210 617-973-9772 542-1329
Web: www.boston.us.emb-japan.go.jp
Consulate General 400 Renaissance Ctr Suite 1600 .... Detroit MI 48243 313-567-0120 567-0274
Web: www.detroit.us.emb-japan.go.jp
Consulate General 299 Park Ave 18th Fl .... New York NY 10171 212-371-8222 319-6357
Web: www.cgj.org
Consulate General
Wells Fargo Ctr 1300 SW 5th Ave Suite 2700 .... Portland OR 97201 503-221-1811 224-8936
Web: www.portland.us.emb-japan.go.jp
Consulate General
900 Fannin St Suite 3000 2 Houston Center .... Houston TX 77010 713-652-2977 651-7822
Web: www.houston.us.emb-japan.go.jp
Consulate General 601 Union St Suite 500 .... Seattle WA 98101 206-682-9107 624-9097
Web: www.seattle.us.emb-japan.go.jp
Embassy 2520 Massachusetts Ave NW .... Washington DC 20008 202-238-6700 328-2187
Web: www.embjapan.org

Jordan Embassy 3504 International Dr NW .... Washington DC 20008 202-966-2664 966-3110
Web: www.jordanembassyus.org

Kazakhstan
Consulate 866 UN Plaza Suite 586A .... New York NY 10017 212-888-3024 888-3025
Web: www.kazconsulny.org
Embassy 1401 16th St NW .... Washington DC 20036 202-232-5488 232-5845
Web: www.kazakhembus.com

Kenya Embassy 2249 R St NW .... Washington DC 20008 202-387-6101 462-3829
Web: www.kenyaembassy.com

Korea Republic of
Consulate General 3243 Wilshire Blvd .... Los Angeles CA 90010 213-385-9300 385-1849
Web: www.koreanconsulatela.org
Consulate General 3500 Clay St. .... San Francisco CA 94118 415-921-2251 921-5946
Web: www.koreanconsulatesf.org
Consulate General 2320 Massachusetts Ave NW .... Washington DC 20008 202-939-5661 342-1597
Consulate General
229 Peachtree St International Tower Suite 500 .... Atlanta GA 30303 404-522-1611 521-3169
Consulate General 2756 Pali Hwy .... Honolulu HI 96817 808-595-6109 595-3046
Consulate General
455 N City Front Plaza Dr NBC Tower Suite 2700 .... Chicago IL 60611 312-822-9485 822-9849
Consulate General 1 Gateway Ctr 2nd Fl .... Newton MA 02458 617-641-2830 641-2831
Web: www.kcgboston.org
Consulate General 335 E 45th St 4th Fl .... New York NY 10017 646-674-6000 674-6023
Web: www.koreanconsulate.org
Consulate General 1990 Post Oak Blvd Suite 1250 .... Houston TX 77056 713-961-0186 961-3340
Web: www.koreahouston.org/e
Consulate General 2033 6th Ave Suite 1125 .... Seattle WA 98121 206-441-1011 441-7912
Web: www.mofat.go.kr
Embassy 2450 Massachusetts Ave NW .... Washington DC 20008 202-939-5600 797-0595
Web: www.koreaembassyusa.org

Kuwait Embassy 2940 Tilden St NW .... Washington DC 20008 202-966-0702 966-0517
Kyrgyzstan Embassy 2360 Massachusetts Ave NW .... Washington DC 20008 202-449-9822 386-7550
Web: www.kyrgyzstan.org

Lao People's Democratic Republic Embassy
2222 'S' St NW .... Washington DC 20008 202-332-6416 332-4923
Web: www.laoembassy.com

Latvia Embassy 2306 Massachusetts Ave NW .... Washington DC 20008 202-328-2840 328-2860
Web: www.latvia-usa.org

Lebanon
Consulate General 660 S Figueroa St Suite 1050 .... Los Angeles CA 90017 213-243-0999
Consulate General 3031 W Grand Blvd Suite 560 .... Detroit MI 48202 313-758-0753 758-0756
Consulate General 9 E 76th St .... New York NY 10021 212-744-7905 794-1510
Web: www.lebconsny.org
Embassy 2560 28th St NW .... Washington DC 20008 202-939-6300 939-6324
Web: www.lebanonembassyus.org

Lesotho Embassy 2511 Massachusetts Ave NW .... Washington DC 20008 202-797-5533 234-6815
Web: www.lesothoemb-usa.gov.ls

Liberia
Consulate General 820 2nd Ave Suite 1300 .... New York NY 10017 212-687-1025 599-3189
Web: www.liberiaconsulate.com
Embassy 5201 16th St NW .... Washington DC 20011 202-723-0437 723-0436
Web: www.embassyofliberia.org

Liechtenstein Embassy 888 17th St NW Suite 1250 .... Washington DC 20006 202-331-0590 331-3221
Web: www.liechtenstein.li

Lithuania
Consulate General 211 E Ontario St Suite 1500 .... Chicago IL 60611 312-397-0382 397-0385
Web: www.ltembassyus.org
Consulate General 420 5th Ave 3rd Fl .... New York NY 10018 212-354-7840 354-7911
Web: www.ltembassyus.org
Embassy 4590 MacArthur Blvd NW Suite 200 .... Washington DC 20009 202-234-5860 328-0466
Web: www.ltembassyus.org

Luxembourg
Consulate General 1 Sansome St Suite 830 .... San Francisco CA 94104 415-788-0816 788-0985
Web: www.luxembourgsf.org
Consulate General 17 Beekman Pl .... New York NY 10022 212-888-6664 888-6116
Web: www.luxembourgnewyork.com
Embassy 2200 Massachusetts Ave NW .... Washington DC 20008 202-265-4171 328-8270
Web: www.luxembourg-usa.org

Macedonia
Consulate General 2000 Town Center Suite 1130 .... Southfield MI 48075 248-354-5537 354-5538
Embassy 2129 Wyoming Ave .... Washington DC 20008 202-667-0501 667-2131

Madagascar Embassy 2374 Massachusetts Ave NW .... Washington DC 20008 202-265-5525 265-3034
Malawi Embassy 1156 15th St NW Suite 320 .... Washington DC 20005 202-721-0270 721-0288

Malaysia
Consulate General 550 S Hope St Suite 400 .... Los Angeles CA 90071 213-892-1238 892-9031
Consulate General 313 E 43rd St .... New York NY 10017 212-490-2722 490-2049
Embassy 3516 International Ct NW .... Washington DC 20008 202-572-9700 572-9882

Mali Embassy 2130 R St NW .... Washington DC 20008 202-332-2249 332-6603
Web: www.maliembassy.us

Malta
Consulate 249 E 35th St .... New York NY 10016 212-725-2345 779-7097
Web: www.gov.mt
Embassy 2017 Connecticut Ave NW .... Washington DC 20008 202-462-3611 387-5470

Marshall Islands
Consulate General 1888 Lusitana St Suite 301 .... Honolulu HI 96813 808-545-7767 545-7211
Web: www.rmiembassyus.org
Embassy 2433 Massachusetts Ave NW .... Washington DC 20008 202-234-5414 232-3236
Web: www.rmiembassyus.org

Mauritania Embassy 2129 Leroy Pl NW .... Washington DC 20008 202-232-5700 319-2623
Web: www.ambarim-dc.org

Mauritius Embassy 4301 Connecticut Ave NW Suite 441 .... Washington DC 20008 202-244-1491 966-0983
Web: www.maurinet.com/embasydc.html

Mexico
Consulate 1201 F Ave .... Douglas AZ 85607 520-364-3107 364-1379
Consulate 571 N Grand Ave .... Nogales AZ 85621 520-287-2521 287-3175
Consulate 408 Heber Ave .... Calexico CA 92231 760-357-3863 357-6284
Consulate 2409 Merced St .... Fresno CA 93721 559-233-9770 233-6156
Consulate 293 N 'D' St .... San Bernardino CA 92401 909-889-9836 889-8285
Consulate 100 W Washington St .... Orlando FL 32801 407-422-0514 422-9633
Consulate 20 Park Plaza Suite 506 .... Boston MA 02116 617-426-4942 695-1957
TF: 800-601-1289 ■ *Web:* www.sre.gob.mx/boston
Consulate 645 Griswold Ave 8th Fl .... Detroit MI 48226 313-964-4515 964-4522
Web: www.sre.gob.mx/detroit
Consulate 1610 4th St NW .... Albuquerque NM 87102 505-247-2147 842-9490
Web: www.users.qwest.net/~consulmexalb
Consulate 1234 SW Morrison St .... Portland OR 97205 503-229-0790 274-1540
Web: www.sre.gob.mx/portland
Consulate
111 S Independence Mall E Bourse Bldg Suite 310 .... Philadelphia PA 19106 215-922-4262 923-7281
Consulate 301 Mexico Blvd .... Brownsville TX 78520 956-542-4431 542-7267
Web: www.sre.gob.mx/brownsville
Consulate 2398 Spur 239 PO Box 1275 .... Del Rio TX 78840 830-775-2352 774-6497
Consulate 2252 E Garrison St .... Eagle Pass TX 78852 830-773-9255 773-9397
Consulate 60 S Broadway St .... McAllen TX 78501 956-686-0244 686-4901
Consulate 2132 3rd Ave .... Seattle WA 98121 206-448-6819 448-4771
Web: www.sre.gob.mx/seattle
Consulate General 1990 W Camelback Rd Suite 110 .... Phoenix AZ 85015 602-242-7398 242-2957
Web: www.sre.gob.mx/phoenix
Consulate General 2401 W 6th St .... Los Angeles CA 90057 213-351-6800
Web: www.sre.gob.mx/losangeles
Consulate General 3151 W 5th St .... Oxnard CA 93030 805-984-8738 984-8747
Web: www.consulmexoxnard.com
Consulate General 1010 8th St .... Sacramento CA 95814 916-441-2987 441-3176
Web: www.mexico.us/consulate.htm
Consulate General 1549 India St .... San Diego CA 92101 619-231-8414
Web: www.sre.gob.mx/sandiego
Consulate General 532 Folsom St .... San Francisco CA 94105 415-392-5554 495-3971
Consulate General 540 N 1st St .... San Jose CA 95112 408-294-3414 294-4506
Web: www.consulmexsj.com
Consulate General 5350 Leesdale Dr .... Denver CO 80246 303-331-1110 331-1872
Web: www.consulmex-denver.com
Consulate General 5975 SW 72nd St Suite 101 .... Miami FL 33143 786-268-4900 268-4875
Web: www.sre.gob.mx/miami
Consulate General 2600 Apple Valley Rd .... Atlanta GA 30319 404-266-2233 266-2302
Web: www.consulmexatlanta.org
Consulate General 204 S Ashland Ave .... Chicago IL 60607 312-855-1380
Web: www.consulmexchicago.com

	City	State	ZIP	Phone	Fax
Consulate General 27 E 39th St	New York	NY	10016	212-217-6400	217-6493
Web: www.consulmexny.org					
Consulate General 800 Brazos St Suite 330	Austin	TX	78701	512-478-2866	478-8008
Web: www.sre.gob.mx/austin					
Consulate General 8855 N Stemmons Fwy	Dallas	TX	75247	214-252-9250	
Web: www.consulmexdallas.com					
Consulate General 910 E San Antonio St	El Paso	TX	79901	915-533-3644	532-7163
Web: www.sre.gob.mx/elpaso					
Consulate General 4506 Carolinas St	Houston	TX	77004	713-271-6800	271-3201
Web: www.sre.gob.mx/houston					
Consulate General 1612 Farragut St	Laredo	TX	78040	956-723-0990	723-1741
Web: www.sre.gob.mx/laredo					
Consulate General 127 Navarro St	San Antonio	TX	78205	210-227-9145	227-9817
Web: www.consulmexsat.org					
Embassy 1911 Pennsylvania Ave NW	Washington	DC	20006	202-728-1600	728-1766
Web: portal.sre.gob.mx/usa					
Micronesia Federated States of					
Consulate 3049 Ualena St suite 910	Honolulu	HI	96819	808-836-4775	836-6896
Embassy 1725 'N' St NW	Washington	DC	20036	202-223-4383	223-4391
Moldova Embassy 2101 'S' St NW	Washington	DC	20008	202-667-1130	667-1204
Web: www.embassyrm.org					
Mongolia Embassy 2833 M St NW	Washington	DC	20007	202-333-7117	298-9227
Web: www.mongolianembassy.us					
Morocco					
Consulate 10 E 40th St 23rd Fl	New York	NY	10016	212-213-9644	725-4198
Web: www.moroccanconsulate.com					
Consulate General 10 E 40th St 24th Fl	New York	NY	10016	212-758-2625	779-7441
Web: www.moroccanconsulate.com					
Embassy 1601 21st St NW	Washington	DC	20009	202-462-7980	462-7643
Mozambique Embassy 1990 M St NW Suite 570	Washington	DC	20036	202-293-7146	835-0245
Web: www.embamoc-usa.org					
Myanmar Embassy 2300 'S' St NW	Washington	DC	20008	202-332-3344	332-4351
Web: www.mewashingtondc.com					
Namibia Embassy 1605 New Hampshire Ave NW	Washington	DC	20009	202-986-0540	986-0443
Nepal					
Consulate General 820 2nd Ave Suite 17B	New York	NY	10017	212-370-3988	953-2038
Embassy 2131 Leroy Pl NW	Washington	DC	20008	202-667-4550	667-5534
Web: www.nepalembassyusa.org					
Netherlands					
Consulate General 11766 Wilshire Blvd Suite 1150	Los Angeles	CA	90025	310-268-1598	312-0989
Web: www.ncla.org					
Consulate General 701 Brickell Ave 5th Fl	Miami	FL	33131	786-866-0480	866-0497
Web: www.cgmiami.org					
Consulate General 303 E Wacker Dr Suite 2600	Chicago	IL	60601	312-856-0110	856-9218
TF: 877-388-2443 ■ *Web:* www.cgchicago.org					
Consulate General 1 Rockefeller Plaza 11th Fl	New York	NY	10020	212-246-1429	333-3603
Web: www.cgny.org					
Consulate General 2200 Post Oak Blvd Suite 610	Houston	TX	77056	713-622-8000	622-3581
Web: www.nlconsulatehouston.org					
Embassy 4200 Linnean Ave NW	Washington	DC	20008	202-244-5300	362-3430
Web: www.netherlands-embassy.org					
New Zealand					
Consulate General 2425 Olympic Blvd Suite 600-E	Santa Monica	CA	90404	310-566-6555	566-6556
Web: www.nzcgla.com					
Consulate General 222 E 41st St Suite 2510	New York	NY	10017	212-832-4038	832-7602
Embassy 37 Observatory Cir NW	Washington	DC	20008	202-328-4800	667-5227
Web: www.nzembassy.com					
Nicaragua					
Consulate 3550 Wilshire Blvd Suite 200	Los Angeles	CA	90010	213-252-1170	252-1177
Consulate General 870 Market St Suite 518	San Francisco	CA	94102	415-765-6825	765-6826
Consulate General 8532 SW 8th St Suite 270	Miami	FL	33144	305-265-1415	265-1780
Consulate General 820 2nd Ave Suite 802	New York	NY	10017	212-986-6562	983-2646
Consulate General 8989 Westheimer St Suite 103	Houston	TX	77063	713-789-2762	789-3164
Embassy 1627 New Hampshire Ave NW	Washington	DC	20009	202-939-6570	939-6542
Niger Embassy 2204 R St NW	Washington	DC	20008	202-483-4224	483-3169
Web: www.nigerembassyusa.org					
Nigeria					
Consulate General 828 2nd Ave	New York	NY	10017	212-850-2200	687-1476
Web: www.nigeriahouse.com					
Embassy 3519 International Ct NW	Washington	DC	20008	202-986-8400	362-6981
Web: www.nigeriaembassyusa.org					
Norway					
Consulate General 20 California St 6th Fl	San Francisco	CA	94111	415-986-0766	986-3318
Web: www.norway.org/embassy					
Consulate General 821 Marquette Ave Suite 800	Minneapolis	MN	55402	612-332-3338	332-1386
Web: www.norway.org/embassy					
Consulate General 825 3rd Ave 38th Fl	New York	NY	10022	212-421-7333	754-0583
Web: www.norway.org/embassy					
Consulate General 2777 Allen Pkwy Suite 1185	Houston	TX	77019	713-521-2900	521-9648
Web: www.norway.org/embassy					
Embassy 2720 34th St NW	Washington	DC	20008	202-333-6000	337-0870
Web: www.norway.org/embassy					
Oman Embassy 2535 Belmont Rd NW	Washington	DC	20008	202-387-1980	745-4933
Pakistan					
Consulate General 10850 Wilshire Blvd Suite 1250	Los Angeles	CA	90024	310-441-5114	441-9256
Consulate General 12 E 65th St	New York	NY	10021	212-879-5800	517-6987
Embassy 3517 International Ct NW	Washington	DC	20008	202-243-6500	686-1534
Web: www.embassyofpakistanusa.org					
Palau Embassy 1700 Pennsylvania Ave NW Suite 400	Washington	DC	20006	202-349-8598	349-8597
Web: www.palauembassy.com					
Panama					
Consulate General 5775 Blue Lagoon Dr Suite 200	Mimai	FL	33126	305-447-3700	447-4142
Consulate General 2424 World Trade Ctr 2 Canal St	New Orleans	LA	70130	504-525-3458	524-8960
Web: www.consulateofpanama.com					
Consulate General 1212 Ave of the Americas 6th Fl	New York	NY	10036	212-840-2450	840-2469
Consulate General 124 Chestnut St	Philadelphia	PA	19106	215-574-2994	625-4876
Consulate General 24 Greenway Plaza Suite 1307	Houston	TX	77046	713-622-4451	622-4468
Web: www.conpahouston.com					
Embassy 2862 McGill Terr NW	Washington	DC	20008	202-483-1407	483-8413
Web: www.embassyofpanama.org					
Papua New Guinea Embassy					
1779 Massachusetts Ave NW Suite 805	Washington	DC	20036	202-745-3680	745-3679
Web: www.pngembassy.org					
Paraguay					
Consulate General 25 SE 2nd Ave Suite 705	Miami	FL	33131	305-374-9090	374-5522
Consulate General 211 E 43rd St Suite 1400	New York	NY	10017	212-682-9441	682-9443
Embassy 2400 Massachusetts Ave NW	Washington	DC	20008	202-483-6960	234-4508
Peru					
Consulate General 3450 Wilshire Blvd Suite 800	Los Angeles	CA	90010	213-252-5910	252-8130
Web: www.consuladoperu.com/LosAngeles/index10.htm					
Consulate General 870 Market St Suite 1067	San Francisco	CA	94102	415-362-7136	362-2836
Consulate General 1001 S Monaco Pkwy Suite 210	Denver	CO	80224	303-355-8555	355-8555
Web: www.consuladoperu.com					
Consulate General 444 Brickell Ave Suite M135	Miami	FL	33131	305-374-1305	381-6027
Web: www.consulado-peru.com					
Consulate General 180 N Michigan Ave Suite 1830	Chicago	IL	60601	312-782-1599	704-6969
Consulate General 20 Park Plaza Suite 511	Boston	MA	02116	617-338-2227	338-2742
Consulate General 100 Hamilton Plaza Suite 1221	Paterson	NJ	07505	973-278-3324	278-0254
Consulate General 241 E 49th St	New York	NY	10017	646-735-3828	735-3866
Consulate General 5177 Richmond Ave Suite 695	Houston	TX	77056	713-355-9517	355-9377
Web: www.consuladoperu.com					
Embassy 1700 Massachusetts Ave NW	Washington	DC	20036	202-833-9860	659-8124
Web: www.embassyofperu.us					
Philippines					
Consulate General 3600 Wilshire Blvd Suite 500	Los Angeles	CA	90010	213-639-0980	639-0990
Web: www.pcgenla.org					
Consulate General 447 Sutter St 6th Fl	San Francisco	CA	94108	415-433-6666	421-2641
Web: www.philippineconsulate-sf.org					
Consulate General 2433 Pali Hwy	Honolulu	HI	96817	808-595-6316	595-2581
Consulate General 30 N Michigan Ave Suite 2100	Chicago	IL	60602	312-332-6458	332-3657
Web: www.chicagopcg.com					
Consulate General 556 5th Ave	New York	NY	10036	212-764-1330	382-1146
Web: www.pcgny.net					
Embassy 1600 Massachusetts Ave NW	Washington	DC	20036	202-467-9300	328-9417
Web: www.philippineembassy-usa.org					
Poland					
Consulate General 12400 Wilshire Blvd Suite 555	Los Angeles	CA	90025	310-442-8500	442-8515
Web: www.polishconsulatela.com					
Consulate General 820 N Orleans St Suite 335	Chicago	IL	60610	312-337-8166	337-7841
Web: www.polishconsulatechicago.org					
Consulate General 233 Madison Ave	New York	NY	10016	212-561-8160	237-2105*
**Fax Area Code:* 646 ■ *Web:* www.polandconsulateny.com					
Embassy 2224 Wyoming Ave NW	Washington	DC	20008	202-234-3800	328-2152
Web: www.polandembassy.org					
Portugal					
Consulate 2012 Massachusetts Ave NW	Washington	DC	20036	202-332-3007	387-2768
Consulate 628 Pleasant St Rm 204	New Bedford	MA	02740	508-997-6151	992-1068
Consulate 56 Pine St 6th Fl	Providence	RI	02903	401-272-2003	273-6247
Consulate General 3298 Washington St	San Francisco	CA	94115	415-346-3400	346-1440
Consulate General 699 Boylston St 7th Fl	Boston	MA	02116	617-536-8740	536-2503
Consulate General Legal Ctr 1 Riverfront Plaza	Newark	NJ	07102	973-643-4200	643-3900
Consulate General 590 5th Ave 3rd FL	New York	NY	10036	212-221-3165	221-3462
Embassy 2012 Massachusetts Ave NW	Washington	DC	20036	202-328-8610	462-3726
Qatar					
Consulate General 1990 Post Oak Blvd Suite 810	Houston	TX	77056	713-355-8221	355-8184
Embassy 2555 M St NW	Washington	DC	20037	202-274-1600	237-0061
Web: www.qatarembassy.net					
Romania					
Consulate General 11766 Wilshire Blvd Suite 560	Los Angeles	CA	90025	310-444-0043	445-0043
Web: www.consulateromania.org					
Consulate General 200 E 38th St 3rd Fl	New York	NY	10016	212-682-9120	972-8463
Web: www.romconsny.org					
Embassy 1607 23rd St NW	Washington	DC	20008	202-332-4846	232-4748
Web: www.roembus.org					
Russian Federation					
Consulate General 2790 Green St	San Francisco	CA	94123	415-928-6878	929-0306
Web: www.consulrussia.org					
Consulate General 9 E 91st St	New York	NY	10128	212-348-0926	831-9162
Consulate General 2001 6th Ave Westin Bldg Suite 2323	Seattle	WA	98121	206-728-1910	728-1871
Web: www.netconsul.org					
Embassy 2650 Wisconsin Ave NW	Washington	DC	20007	202-298-5700	298-5735
Web: www.russianembassy.org					
Rwanda Embassy 1714 New Hampshire Ave NW	Washington	DC	20009	202-232-2882	232-4544
Saint Kitts & Nevis Embassy 3216 New Mexico Ave NW	Washington	DC	20016	202-686-2636	686-5740
Web: www.stkittsnevis.org					
Saint Lucia					
Consulate General 800 2nd Ave 9th Fl	New York	NY	10017	212-697-9360	697-4993
Web: www.un.int/stlucia/consulate.htm					
Embassy 3216 New Mexico Ave NW	Washington	DC	20016	202-364-6792	364-6723
Saint Vincent & the Grenadines					
Consulate General 801 2nd Ave 21st Fl	New York	NY	10017	212-687-4490	949-5946
Embassy 3216 New Mexico Ave NW	Washington	DC	20016	202-364-6730	364-6736
Web: www.embsvg.com					
Samoa Embassy 800 2nd Ave Suite 400-J	New York	NY	10017	212-599-6196	599-0797
Saudi Arabia					
Consulate General 2045 Sawtelle Blvd	Los Angeles	CA	90025	310-479-6000	479-2752
Consulate General 866 2nd Ave 5th Fl	New York	NY	10017	212-752-2740	688-2719
Consulate General 5718 Westheimer Rd Suite 1500	Houston	TX	77057	713-785-5577	785-1163
Embassy 601 New Hampshire Ave NW	Washington	DC	20037	202-342-3800	944-5983
Web: www.saudiembassy.net					
Senegal Embassy 2112 Wyoming Ave NW	Washington	DC	20008	202-234-0540	332-6315
Web: www.senegalembassy-us.org					
Serbia & Montenegro					
Consulate General 201 E Ohio St Suite 200	Chicago	IL	60611	312-670-6707	670-6787
Web: www.scgchicago.org					
Embassy 2134 Kalorama Rd NW	Washington	DC	20008	202-332-0333	332-3933
Web: www.yuembusa.org					
Seychelles Embassy 800 2nd Ave Suite 400C	New York	NY	10017	212-972-1785	972-1786
Sierra Leone Embassy 1701 19th St NW	Washington	DC	20009	202-939-9261	483-1793
Web: www.embassyofsierraleone.org					
Singapore					
Consulate 231 E 51st St	New York	NY	10022	212-223-3331	826-5028
Web: www.mfa.gov.sg/newyork-consul					
Consulate General 595 Market St Suite 2450	San Francisco	CA	94105	415-543-4775	543-4788
Web: www.mfa.gov.sg/sanfrancisco					
Embassy 3501 International Pl NW	Washington	DC	20008	202-537-3100	537-0876
Web: www.mfa.gov.sg/washington					
Slovakia Embassy 3523 International Ct NW	Washington	DC	20008	202-237-1054	237-6438
Web: www.slovakembassy-us.org					
Slovenia					
Consulate 55 Public Sq Suite 945	Cleveland	OH	44113	216-589-9220	589-9210
Consulate General 600 3rd Ave 21st Fl	New York	NY	10016	212-370-3006	370-3581
Web: www.embassy.org/slovenia/offices.htm					
Embassy 1525 New Hampshire Ave NW	Washington	DC	20036	202-667-5363	667-4563
Solomon Islands Embassy 800 2nd Ave Suite 400L	New York	NY	10017	212-599-6192	661-8925
South Africa					
Consulate General 6300 Wilshire Blvd Suite 600	Los Angeles	CA	90048	323-651-0902	651-5969
Web: link2southafrica.com					
Consulate General 200 S Michigan Ave Suite 600	Chicago	IL	60604	312-939-7929	939-2588
Consulate General 333 E 38th St 9th Fl	New York	NY	10016	212-213-4880	213-0102
Web: www.southafrica-newyork.net					
Embassy 3051 Massachusetts Ave NW	Washington	DC	20008	202-232-4400	265-1607
Web: www.saembassy.org					
Spain					
Consulate General 5055 Wilshire Blvd Suite 860	Los Angeles	CA	90036	323-938-0158	938-2502
Consulate General 1405 Sutter St	San Francisco	CA	94109	415-922-2995	931-9706
Consulate General 2655 Le Jeune Rd Suite 203	Miami	FL	33134	305-446-5511	446-0585
Web: www.conspainmiami.org					
Consulate General 180 N Michigan Ave Suite 1500	Chicago	IL	60601	312-782-4588	782-1635
Web: www.consulate-spain-chicago.com					
Consulate General 2102 World Trade Ctr 2 Canal St	New Orleans	LA	70130	504-525-4951	525-4955
Consulate General 31 St James Ave Suite 905	Boston	MA	02116	617-536-2506	536-8512
Web: www.spainconsul-ny.org/boston.html					

Phone | Fax

Consulate General 150 E 58th St 30th Fl. .... New York NY 10155 212-355-4080 644-3751
Web: www.spainconsul-ny.org
Consulate General 1800 Bering Dr Suite 660 .... Houston TX 77057 713-783-6200 783-6166
Embassy 2375 Pennsylvania Ave NW .... Washington DC 20037 202-452-0100 833-5670
Web: www.spainemb.org

Sri Lanka
Consulate 630 3rd Ave 20th Fl .... New York NY 10017 212-986-7040 986-1838
Web: un.cti.depaul.edu/public/Sri_Lanka/0/
Consulate General 3250 Wilshire Blvd Suite 1405 .... Los Angeles CA 90010 213-387-0210 387-0216
Web: www.srilankaconsulatela.com
Embassy 2148 Wyoming Ave NW .... Washington DC 20008 202-483-4025 232-7181
Web: www.slembassyusa.org

Sudan Embassy 2210 Massachusetts Ave NW .... Washington DC 20008 202-338-8565 667-2406
Web: www.sudanembassy.org

Suriname
Consulate General 6303 Blue Lagoon Dr Suite 325 .... Miami FL 33126 305-265-4655 265-4599
Web: www.scgmia.com
Embassy 4301 Connecticut Ave NW Suite 460 .... Washington DC 20008 202-244-7488 244-5878
Web: www.surinameembassy.org

Swaziland Embassy 1712 New Hampshire Ave NW .... Washington DC 20009 202-234-5002 234-8254

Sweden
Consulate General 10940 Wilshire Blvd Suite 700 .... Los Angeles CA 90024 310-445-4008 473-2229
Web: www.swedenabroad.se/pages/start____7596.asp
Consulate General 120 Montgomery St Suite 2175 .... San Francisco CA 94104 415-788-2631 788-6841
Web: www.swedenabroad.com/pages/start____8372.asp
Consulate General
1 Dag Hammarskjold Plaza 885 2nd Ave 45th Fl .... New York NY 10017 212-583-2550 755-2732
Web: www.swedeninfo.com
Embassy 2900 K St NW .... Washington DC 20007 202-467-2600 467-2699
Web: www.swedenabroad.com/pages/start____6989.asp

Switzerland
Consulate General 11766 Wilshire Blvd Suite 1400 .... Los Angeles CA 90025 310-575-1145 575-1982
Web: www.eda.admin.ch/washington_emb
Consulate General 456 Montgomery St Suite 1500 .... San Francisco CA 94104 415-788-2272 788-1402
Web: www.eda.admin.ch/washington_emb
Consulate General
1349 W Peachtree St Suite 1000 2 Mid-Town Plaza .... Atlanta GA 30309 404-870-2000 870-2011
Web: www.eda.admin.ch/washington_emb
Consulate General 737 N Michigan Ave Suite 2301 .... Chicago IL 60611 312-915-0061 915-0388
Web: www.eda.admin.ch/washington_emb
Consulate General 633 3rd Ave 30th Fl .... New York NY 10017 212-599-5700 599-4266
Web: www.eda.admin.ch/washington_emb
Embassy 2900 Cathedral Ave NW .... Washington DC 20008 202-745-7900 387-2564
Web: www.swissemb.org

Syrian Arab Republic Embassy 2215 Wyoming Ave NW .... Washington DC 20008 202-232-6313 234-9548
Web: www.syrianembassy.us

Tajikistan Embassy 1005 New Hampshire Ave .... Washington DC 20037 202-223-6090 223-6091
Web: www.tjus.org

Tanzania United Republic of Embassy 2139 R St NW .... Washington DC 20008 202-939-6125 797-7408
Web: www.tanzaniaembassy-us.org

Thailand
Consulate General 611 N Larchmont Blvd 2nd Fl .... Los Angeles CA 90004 323-962-9574 962-2128
Web: www.thai-la.net
Consulate General 700 N Rush St .... Chicago IL 60611 312-664-3129 664-3230
Web: www.thaichicago.net
Consulate General 351 E 52nd St .... New York NY 10022 212-754-1770 754-1907
Web: www.thaiconsulnewyork.com
Embassy 1024 Wisconsin Ave NW Suite 401 .... Washington DC 20007 202-944-3600 944-3611
Web: www.thaiembdc.org

Timor-Leste Embassy
4201 Massachusetts Ave NW Suite 504 .... Washington DC 20008 202-966-3202 966-3205

Togo Embassy 2208 Massachusetts Ave NW .... Washington DC 20008 202-234-4212 232-3190

Tonga
Consulate General 360 Post St Suite 604 .... San Francisco CA 94108 415-781-0365 781-3964
Embassy 250 E 51st St .... New York NY 10022 917-369-1025 369-1024

Trinidad & Tobago
Consulate General 1000 Brickell Ave Suite 800 .... Miami FL 33131 305-374-2199 374-3199
Consulate General 475 5th Ave 4th Fl .... New York NY 10017 212-682-7272 986-2146
Embassy 1708 Massachusetts Ave NW .... Washington DC 20036 202-467-6490 785-3130

Tunisia Embassy 1515 Massachusetts Ave NW .... Washington DC 20005 202-862-1850 862-1858

Turkey
Consulate General 6300 Wilshire Blvd Suite 2010 .... Los Angeles CA 90048 323-655-8832
Web: www.turkiye.net/lacg
Consulate General 360 N Michigan Ave Suite 1405 .... Chicago IL 60601 312-263-0644 263-1449
Web: www.turkishembassy.org
Consulate General 821 UN Plaza 5th Fl .... New York NY 10017 212-949-0160 983-1293
Consulate General 1990 Post Oak Blvd Suite 1300 .... Houston TX 77056 713-622-5849 623-6639
TF: 888-566-7656
Embassy 2525 Massachusetts Ave NW .... Washington DC 20008 202-612-6700 319-1639
Web: www.turkishembassy.org

Turkmenistan Embassy 2207 Massachusetts Ave NW .... Washington DC 20008 202-588-1500 588-0697
Web: www.turkmenistanembassy.org

Uganda Embassy 5911 16th St NW .... Washington DC 20011 202-726-7100 726-1727
Web: www.ugandaembassy.com

Ukraine
Consulate General 10 E Huron St .... Chicago IL 60611 312-642-4388 642-4385
Web: www.ukrchicago.com
Embassy 3350 M St NW .... Washington DC 20007 202-333-0606 333-0817
TF: 800-779-8347 ■ *Web:* www.ukremb.com

United Arab Emirates Embassy 3522 International Ct NW .... Washington DC 20008 202-243-2400 243-2432
Web: www.uae-embassy.org

United Kingdom of Great Britain & Northern Ireland
Consulate World Trade Ctr 1675 Broadway Suite 1030 .... Denver CO 80202 303-592-5200 592-5209
Web: www.britainusa.com/denver
Consulate 1001 Brickell Bay Dr Suite 2800 .... Miami FL 33131 305-374-1522 374-8196
Web: www.britainusa.com/miami
Consulate 900 4th Ave Suite 3001 .... Seattle WA 98164 206-622-9255 622-4728
Web: www.britainusa.com/seattle
Consulate General 11766 Wilshire Blvd Suite 1200 .... Los Angeles CA 90025 310-481-0031 481-2960
Web: www.britainusa.com/la
Consulate General 1 Sansome St Suite 850 .... San Francisco CA 94104 415-617-1300 434-2018
Web: www.britainusa.com/sf
Consulate General
Georgia Pacific Ctr 133 Peachtree St NE Suite 3400 .... Atlanta GA 30303 404-954-7700 954-7702
Web: www.britainusa.com/atlanta
Consulate General 400 N Michigan Ave Suite 1300 .... Chicago IL 60611 312-970-3800 970-3854
Web: www.britainusa.com/chicago
Consulate General 1 Memorial Dr Suite 1500 .... Cambridge MA 02142 617-245-4500 621-0220
Web: www.britainusa.com/boston
Consulate General 845 3rd Ave .... New York NY 10022 212-745-0200 754-3062
Web: www.britainusa.com/ny
Consulate General 1000 Louisiana St Suite 1900 .... Houston TX 77002 713-659-6270 659-7094
Web: www.britainusa.com/houston
Embassy 3100 Massachusetts Ave NW .... Washington DC 20008 202-588-6500 588-7870
Web: www.britainusa.com/embassy
Vice Consulate 200 S Orange Ave Sun Trust Ctr Suite 2110 .... Orlando FL 32801 407-581-1540 254-3333
Web: www.britainusa.com/orlando

Uruguay
Consulate General 429 Santa Monica Blvd Suite 400 .... Santa Monica CA 90401 310-394-5777 394-5140
Consulate General 1077 Ponce De Leon Blvd .... Coral Gables FL 33134 305-443-9764 443-7802
Consulate General 420 Madison Ave 6th Fl .... New York NY 10017 212-753-8581 753-1603
Web: www.conuruyork.org
Embassy 1913 'I' St NW .... Washington DC 20006 202-331-1313 331-8142
Web: www.uruwashi.org

Uzbekistan
Consulate General 801 2nd Ave 20th Fl .... New York NY 10017 212-754-7403
Web: www.uzbekconsulny.org
Embassy 1746 Massachusetts Ave NW .... Washington DC 20036 202-887-5300 293-6804
Web: www.uzbekistan.org

Vatican City 3339 Massachusetts Ave NW .... Washington DC 20008 202-333-7121 337-4036
Web: www.vatican.va

Venezuela
Consulate General 311 California St Suite 620 .... San Francisco CA 94104 415-955-1982 955-1970
Consulate General 1101 Brickell Ave Suite 901 .... Miami FL 33131 305-577-4214 372-5167
Consulate General 20 N Wacker Dr Suite 1925 .... Chicago IL 60606 312-236-9655 580-1010
Consulate General
World Trade Ctr 2 Canal St Suite 2300 .... New Orleans LA 70130 504-522-3284 522-7092
Web: www.neworleans.embavenez-us.org
Consulate General 545 Boylston St 3rd Fl .... Boston MA 02116 617-266-9368 266-2350
Consulate General 7 E 51st St .... New York NY 10022 212-826-1660 644-7471
Web: consulado-ny.gov.ve
Consulate General 2925 Briarpark Dr Suite 900 .... Houston TX 77042 713-974-0028 974-1413
Web: www.consulvenhou.org
Embassy 1099 30th St NW .... Washington DC 20007 202-342-2214 342-6820
Web: www.embavenez-us.org

Vietnam
Consulate General 1700 California St Suite 430 .... San Francisco CA 94109 415-922-1707 922-1848
Web: www.vietnamconsulate-sf.org
Embassy 1233 20th St NW Suite 400 .... Washington DC 20036 202-861-0737 861-0917
Web: www.vietnamembassy.us

Yemen Embassy 2319 Wyoming Ave NW .... Washington DC 20008 202-965-4760 337-2017
Web: www.yemenembassy.org

Zambia Embassy 2419 Massachusetts Ave NW .... Washington DC 20008 202-265-9717 332-0826
Web: www.zambiaembassy.org

Zimbabwe Embassy 1608 New Hampshire Ave NW .... Washington DC 20009 202-332-7100 483-9326
Web: www.zimbabwe-embassy.us

261 EMBROIDERY & OTHER DECORATIVE STITCHING

Phone | Fax

Branded Emblem Co Inc 7920 Foster St .... Overland Park KS 66204 913-648-7920 648-7444
TF: 800-747-7920 ■ *Web:* www.brandedemblem.com
Carolace Embroidery Co Inc 65 Railroad Ave Unit 3 .... Ridgefield NJ 07657 201-945-2151 943-1990
Web: www.carolace.com
CR Daniels Inc 3451 Ellicott Ctr Dr .... Ellicott City MD 21043 410-461-2100 461-2987
TF: 800-933-2638 ■ *Web:* www.crdaniels.com
EmbroidMe Inc 2121 Vista Pkwy .... West Palm Beach FL 33411 561-640-7367 640-6062
TF: 877-877-0234 ■ *Web:* www.embroidme.com
Fabri-Quilt Inc 901 E 14th Ave PO Box 12479 .... North Kansas City MO 64116 816-421-2000 471-2853
TF: 800-279-0622 ■ *Web:* www.fabri-quilt.com
Jubilee Embroidery Co Inc PO Box 215 .... Lugoff SC 29078 803-438-2934 438-3733
Kasbar National Industries Inc 370 Reed Rd Suite 200 .... Broomall PA 19008 610-544-7117 544-9799
Web: www.kasbarnational.com
Lion Brothers Co Inc 10246 Reisterstown Rd .... Owings Mills MD 21117 410-363-1000 363-0181
TF Cust Svc: 800-365-6543 ■ *Web:* www.lionbrothers.com
Luv n' care Ltd PO Box 6050 .... Monroe LA 71211 318-388-4916 323-1899
TF: 800-588-6227 ■ *Web:* www.luvncare.com
Moritz Embroidery Works Inc PO Box 187 .... Mount Pocono PA 18344 570-839-9600 839-9430
TF: 800-533-4183 ■ *Web:* www.qdtmoritz.com/moritz/mewhome.asp
National Emblem Inc 17036 S Avalon Blvd .... Carson CA 90746 310-515-5055 515-5966
TF: 800-877-6185 ■ *Web:* www.nationalemblem.com
Penn Emblem Co 10909 Dutton Rd .... Philadelphia PA 19154 215-632-7800 632-6166
TF: 800-793-7366 ■ *Web:* www.pennemblem.com
Rockville Fabrics Corp Active Quilting Div 20 S River St .... Plains PA 18705 570-823-3127 829-3306
Saint Louis Embroidery 1759 Scherer Pkwy .... Saint Charles MO 63303 636-724-2200 946-3296
TF: 800-423-0450
Schweizer Emblem Co 1022 Busse Hwy .... Park Ridge IL 60068 847-292-1022 292-1028
TF Cust Svc: 800-942-5215 ■ *Web:* www.schweizer-emblem.com
Standard Swiss Embroidery Co
5900 S Eastern Ave Suite 166 .... Commerce CA 90040 323-582-8057 582-8097
TF: 800-443-8357
Superior Pleating & Stitching 3671 E Olympic Blvd .... Los Angeles CA 90023 323-261-3964 261-0122
Voyager Emblems Inc 3707 Lockport Rd .... Sanborn NY 14132 716-731-4121 731-2014
TF: 800-268-2204 ■ *Web:* www.voyager-emblems.com

262 EMPLOYMENT OFFICES - GOVERNMENT

Phone | Fax

Employment & Training Administration
200 Constitution Ave NW Rm S2307 .... Washington DC 20210 202-693-2700 693-2725
Web: www.doleta.gov
Veterans' Employment & Training Service
200 Constitution Ave NW Rm S1325 .... Washington DC 20210 202-693-4700 693-4754
Web: www.dol.gov/vets
Alabama Workforce Development Office
401 Adams Ave Suite 590 PO Box 5690 .... Montgomery AL 36103 334-353-1490 353-2005
Web: www.owd.alabama.gov
Alaska Employment Security Div PO Box 25509 .... Juneau AK 99802 907-465-2712 465-4537
Web: www.labor.state.ak.us/esd/home.htm
Arizona Employment Administration
1789 W Jefferson St Site 920Z .... Phoenix AZ 85007 602-542-3957 542-2491
Web: www.de.state.az.us/wia
Arkansas Workforce Services Dept PO Box 2981 .... North Little Rock AR 72203 501-682-2121 682-2273
Web: www.arkansas.gov/esd
California Employment Development Dept
800 Capitol Mall MIC 83 .... Sacramento CA 95814 916-654-8210 657-5294
Web: www.edd.ca.gov
Colorado Labor & Employment Dept 633 17th St Suite 201 .... Denver CO 80203 303-318-8000
TF: 800-390-7936 ■ *Web:* www.coworkforce.com
Connecticut Labor Dept 200 Folly Brook Blvd .... Wethersfield CT 06109 860-263-6000 263-6699
Web: www.ctdol.state.ct.us
Delaware Employment & Training Div 4425 N Market St .... Wilmington DE 19802 302-761-8085 761-6634
Web: www.vcnet.net
District of Columbia Employment Services Dept
609 H St NE .... Washington DC 20002 202-698-6044 546-8467
TF: 877-319-7346 ■ *Web:* does.ci.washington.dc.us

	City	State	Zip	Phone	Fax
Florida Workforce Florida Inc 1974 Commonwealth Ln *Web:* www.workforceflorida.com	Tallahassee	FL	32303	850-921-1119	921-1101
Georgia Employment Services Div 148 Andrew Young International Blvd NE *Web:* www.dol.state.ga.us	Atlanta	GA	30303	404-232-3515	
Hawaii Workforce Development Div 830 Punchbowl St Suite 329 *Web:* hawaii.gov/labor/wdd	Honolulu	HI	96813	808-586-8877	586-8822
Idaho Labor Dept 317 W Main St *Web:* cl.idaho.gov/portal	Boise	ID	83735	208-332-3570	334-6300
Illinois Employment Security Dept 33 S State St 9th Fl *Web:* www.ides.state.il.us	Chicago	IL	60603	312-793-5700	793-9834
Indiana Workforce Development Dept 10 N Senate Ave *Web:* www.in.gov/dwd	Indianapolis	IN	46204	317-232-7670	233-4793
Iowa Workforce Development 1000 E Grand Ave *Web:* www.iowaworkforce.org	Des Moines	IA	50319	515-281-5387	281-4698
Job Corps 200 Constitution Ave NW *Web:* jobcorps.dol.gov	Washington	DC	20210	202-693-3000	693-2767
Kansas Labor Dept 401 SW Topeka Blvd *Web:* www.dol.ks.gov	Topeka	KS	66603	785-296-5000	296-1926
Kentucky Workforce Investment Dept 500 Mero St 3rd Fl *Web:* workforce.ky.gov	Frankfort	KY	40601	502-564-6606	564-7967
Louisiana Labor Dept 1001 N 23rd St *TF:* 877-529-6757 ■ *Web:* www.laworks.net	Baton Rouge	LA	70802	225-342-3111	
Maine Employment Services Bureau 45 Commerce Dr *Web:* www.mainecareercenter.com	Augusta	ME	04330	207-623-7981	287-5933
Maryland Workforce Development Div 1100 N Eutaw St Rm 616 *Web:* www.dllr.state.md.us/employment	Baltimore	MD	21201	410-767-2400	767-2986
Massachusetts Workforce Development Dept 1 Ashburton Pl Rm 2112 *Web:* www.mass.gov/dlwd	Boston	MA	02108	617-626-7122	727-1090
Michigan Career Education & Workforce Programs 201 N Washington Sq 3rd Fl *TF:* 888-253-6855 ■ *Web:* www.michigan.gov/mdcd	Lansing	MI	48913	517-241-4000	373-0314
Minnesota Public Safety Dept 444 Cedar St Town Square Bldg *Web:* www.dps.state.mn.us/	Saint Paul	MN	55101	651-201-7000	
Mississippi Employment Security Commission 1235 Echelon Pkwy *Web:* www.mdes.ms.gov	Jackson	MS	39213	601-321-6000	321-6004
Missouri Employment Security Div 421 E Dunklin St *Web:* www.dolir.mo.gov/es/ui-tax/main.htm	Jefferson City	MO	65102	573-751-3215	751-4945
Montana Workforce Services Div PO Box 1728 *Web:* wsd.dli.mt.gov	Helena	MT	59624	406-444-4100	447-3037
Nebraska Workforce Development - Dept of Labor PO Box 94600 *Web:* www.dol.state.ne.us	Lincoln	NE	68509	402-471-9000	471-2318
Nevada Employment Training & Rehabilitation Dept 500 E 3rd St Rm 200 *Web:* detr.state.nv.us	Carson City	NV	89713	775-684-3911	684-3908
New Hampshire Employment Security Dept 32 S Main St *Web:* www.nhes.state.nh.us	Concord	NH	03301	603-224-3311	228-4145
New Jersey Workforce New Jersey PO Box 055 *Web:* www.wnjpin.net	Trenton	NJ	08625	609-292-2000	777-0483
New Mexico Governor's Office of Workforce Training & Development 1596 Pacheco St Suite 201 *Web:* www.dol.state.nm.us	Santa Fe	NM	87505	505-827-6827	827-6812
New York (State) Labor Dept WA Harriman Campus Bldg 12 *Web:* www.labor.state.ny.us	Albany	NY	12240	518-457-9000	457-6908
North Carolina Employment Security Commission PO Box 25903 *Web:* www.ncesc.com	Raleigh	NC	27611	919-733-3098	733-1129
North Dakota Job Service PO Box 5507 *TF:* 866-873-6042 ■ *Web:* www.jobsnd.com	Bismarck	ND	58506	701-328-2825	328-4000
Ohio Workforce Developement Office PO Box 1618 *Web:* www.ohioworkforce.org	Columbus	OH	43216	614-644-0677	728-8366
Oklahoma Employment Security Commission 2401 N Lincoln Blvd Suite 504 *Web:* www.oesc.state.ok.us	Oklahoma City	OK	73105	405-557-0200	557-5355
Oregon Employment Dept 875 Union St NE *Web:* egov.oregon.gov/EMPLOY	Salem	OR	97311	503-947-1394	947-1472
Pennsylvania Workforce Investment Board 901 N 7th St Suite 103 *Web:* www.paworkforce.state.pa.us	Harrisburg	PA	17120	717-705-8818	783-4660
Rhode Island Labor & Training Dept 1511 Pontiac Ave *Web:* www.dlt.state.ri.us	Cranston	RI	02920	401-462-8000	462-8872
South Carolina Employment Security Commission 1550 Gadsden St *Web:* www.sces.org	Columbia	SC	29201	803-737-2400	737-2642
South Dakota Career Center Div 116 W Missouri Ave *Web:* www.sdjobs.org	Pierre	SD	57501	605-773-3101	773-6680
Tennessee Labor & Workforce Development Dept 710 James Robertson Pkwy 8th Fl *Web:* www.state.tn.us/labor-wfd	Nashville	TN	37243	615-741-6642	741-5078
Texas Workforce Commission 101 E 15th St *Web:* www.twc.state.tx.us	Austin	TX	78778	512-463-2222	936-3504
USAJOBS Office of Personnel Management 1900 'E' St NW *Web:* www.usajobs.opm.gov	Washington	DC	20415	202-606-1800	
Utah Workforce Services Dept 140 E 300 South *Web:* jobs.utah.gov	Salt Lake City	UT	84111	801-526-9675	526-9211
Vermont Labor Dept 5 Green Mountain Dr *Web:* labor.vermont.gov	Montpelier	VT	05601	802-828-4000	828-4022
Virginia Employment Commission 703 E Main St *Web:* www.vec.virginia.gov	Richmond	VA	23219	804-786-1485	225-3923
Washington Employment Security Dept PO Box 9046 *Web:* www.wa.gov/esd	Olympia	WA	98507	360-902-9360	902-9287
West Virginia Workforce 112 California Ave *Web:* www.wvbep.org/bep/default.htm	Charleston	WV	25305	304-558-2630	558-2992
Wisconsin Workforce Development Dept 201 E Washington Ave *Web:* www.dwd.state.wi.us	Madison	WI	53702	608-267-9613	266-1784
Wyoming Employment Dept 1510 E Pershing Blvd *Web:* wydoe.state.wy.us	Cheyenne	WY	82002	307-777-7672	777-5805

263 EMPLOYMENT SERVICES - ONLINE

	City	State	Zip	Phone	Fax
4Jobs.com 1060 1st Ave Suite 100 *Web:* www.4jobs.com	King of Prussia	PA	19406	610-642-6999	642-6681
agriCAREERS Inc Hwy 92 W PO Box 140 *TF:* 888-224-5621 ■ *Web:* www.agricareersinc.com	Massena	IA	50853	712-779-3300	779-3366
Arbita 12 S 6th St Suite 730 **Fax Area Code:* 763 ■ *Web:* www.recruitusa.com	Minneapolis	MN	55402	612-278-0000	253-9392*
Avjobs Inc PO Box 260830 **Fax Area Code:* 888 ■ *Web:* www.avjobs.com	Littleton	CO	80163	303-683-2322	624-8691*
BestJobsUSA.com 550 Heritage Dr Suite 200 *Web:* www.bestjobsusa.com	Jupiter	FL	33458	561-686-6800	686-8043
Beyond.com Inc 1060 1st Ave Suite 100 *Web:* www.beyond.com	King of Prussia	PA	19406	610-642-6999	642-6681
BostonWorks.com c/o Boston Globe PO Box 55819 *TF:* 888-566-4562 ■ *Web:* bostonworks.boston.com	Boston	MA	02205	617-929-2000	929-3186
BrassRing Inc 343 Winter St *TF:* 888-265-6969 ■ *Web:* www.brassring.com	Waltham	MA	02451	781-530-5000	530-5500
CareerBuilder.com 200 N LaSalle St Suite 1100 **Fax Area Code:* 877 ■ *TF:* 800-638-4212 ■ *Web:* www.careerbuilder.com	Chicago	IL	60601	773-527-3600	349-4467*
CareerExposure 805 SW Broadway Suite 2250 *Web:* www.careerexposure.com	Portland	OR	97205	503-221-7779	221-7880
CareerMag.com 101 Gibraltar Rd Suite 100 *Web:* www.careermag.com	Horsham	PA	19044	215-675-1800	
CareerPark 101 N Point Blvd *TF:* 800-396-3306 ■ *Web:* www.careerpark.com	Lancaster	PA	17601	717-581-1966	
CareerShop Inc 12200 W Colonial Dr Suite 201 *TF:* 800-639-2060 ■ *Web:* www.careershop.com	Winter Garden	FL	34787	407-877-5992	877-5932
CareerWomen.com 805 SW Broadway Suite 2250 *Web:* www.careerwomen.com	Portland	OR	97205	503-221-7779	221-7780
Chronicle of Higher Education Career Network 1255 23rd St NW Suite 700 *Web:* chronicle.com/jobs	Washington	DC	20037	202-466-1000	452-1033
CollegeGrad.com Inc 576 N Washington Ave *Web:* www.collegegrad.com	Cedarburg	WI	53012	262-375-6700	375-6721
ComputerJobs.com Inc 280 Interstate North Pkwy SE Suite 300 *TF:* 800-850-0045 ■ *Web:* www.computerjobs.com	Atlanta	GA	30339	770-850-0045	850-0369
Cool Works PO Box 272 511 Hwy 89 *Web:* www.coolworks.com	Gardiner	MT	59030	406-848-2380	848-2320
CyberEdit Inc 2000 Lenox Dr 3rd Fl *TF:* 888-438-2633 ■ *Web:* www.cyberedit.com	Lawrenceville	NJ	08648	609-896-5401	896-4565
Dice Inc 3 Park Ave 33rd Fl *Web:* www.dice.com	New York	NY	10016	212-725-6550	725-6559
DiversitySearch 805 SW Broadway Suite 2250 *Web:* www.diversitysearch.com	Portland	OR	97205	503-221-7779	221-7780
EmplawyerNet 2331 Westwood Blvd Suite 331 *Web:* www.emplawyernet.com	Los Angeles	CA	90025	800-270-2688	
Employer Central c/o College Central Network Inc 245 8th Ave Suite 892 *TF:* 800-442-3614 ■ *Web:* www.employercentral.com	New York	NY	10001	212-967-0230	714-1688
EmploymentGuide.com 5301 Robin Hood Rd *TF:* 877-876-4039 ■ *Web:* www.employmentguide.com	Norfolk	VA	23513	757-446-2900	
Environmental Career Opportunities c/o Brubach Corp 700 Graves St **Fax Area Code:* 434 ■ *Web:* www.ecojobs.com	Charlottesville	VA	22902	800-315-9777	985-2331*
Environmental Careers Organization (ECO) 30 Windsor St 6th Fl *Web:* www.eco.org	Boston	MA	02108	617-426-4375	423-0998
ExecUNet Inc 295 Westport Ave *TF:* 800-637-3126 ■ *Web:* www.execunet.com	Norwalk	CT	06851	203-750-1030	840-8320
FedWorld Federal Job Search (NTIS) National Technical Information Service 5285 Port Royal Rd *Web:* www.fedworld.gov/jobs/jobsearch.html	Springfield	VA	22161	703-605-6000	
FindLaw 610 Opperman Dr **Fax Area Code:* 800 ■ *Web:* www.findlaw.com	Eagan	MN	55123	651-687-7000	392-6206*
Guru.com 5001 Baum Blvd Suite 760 *Web:* www.guru.com	Pittsburgh	PA	15213	412-687-1316	687-4466
HealthCareSource Inc 8 Winchester Pl Suite 201 *Web:* www.healthcaresource.com	Winchester	MA	01890	800-869-5200	829-6600
ihispano.com 4265 N Knox Ave Suite 300 *Web:* www.ihispano.com	Chicago	IL	60641	888-252-1220	
IMDiversity Inc 140 Carondelet St *Web:* www.imdiversity.com	New Orleans	LA	70130	504-523-0154	598-3894
InformationWeek Career Development InformationWeek Magazine 600 Community Dr *Web:* infoweek.techengine.com	Manhasset	NY	11030	516-562-5000	562-5036
International Foundation of Employee Benefit Plans Job Posting Service 18700 W Bluemound Rd PO Box 69 *Web:* www.ifebp.org/jobs	Brookfield	WI	53045	262-786-6700	786-8670
JobBank USA Inc 1417 Sadler Rd Box 331 **Fax Area Code:* 253 ■ *Web:* www.jobbankusa.com	Fernandina Beach	FL	32034	678-318-1775	295-8010*
JobWeb c/o National Assn of Colleges & Employers 62 Highland Ave *TF:* 800-544-5272 ■ *Web:* www.jobweb.org	Bethlehem	PA	18017	610-868-1421	868-0208
Lawjobs.com 10 United Nations Plaza 3rd Fl **Fax Area Code:* 415 ■ *Web:* www.lawjobs.com	San Francisco	CA	94102	800-628-1160	352-5287*
MarketingJobs.com Inc 15275 Collier Blvd Suite 201 *Web:* www.marketingjobs.com	Naples	FL	34119	877-348-5627	
MBA Careers 805 SW Broadway Suite 2250 *Web:* www.mbacareers.com	Portland	OR	97205	503-221-7779	221-7780
Monster Jobs 5 Clock Tower Pl Suite 500 *TF:* 800-666-7837 ■ *Web:* www.monster.com	Maynard	MA	01754	978-461-8000	461-8100
MonsterTRAK 11845 W Olympic Blvd Suite 500 *TF:* 800-999-8725 ■ *Web:* www.monstertrak.monster.com	Los Angeles	CA	90064	310-474-3377	475-7912
National Diversity Newspaper Job Bank c/o Morris Communications PO Box 936 *Web:* newsjobs.com	Augusta	GA	30903	800-622-6358	828-3830
NationJob Inc 601 SW 9th St Suites J & K *TF:* 800-292-7731 ■ *Web:* www.nationjob.com	Des Moines	IA	50309	515-280-3672	283-1223
Net-Temps Inc 55 Middlesex St Suite 220 *TF:* 800-307-0062 ■ *Web:* www.net-temps.com	North Chelmsford	MA	01863	978-251-7272	251-7250
Nonprofit Career Network PO Box 241 *TF:* 888-844-4870 ■ *Web:* www.nonprofitcareer.com	Haddam	CT	06438	860-345-3255	345-3299
NowHiring.com 130 S 1st St 3rd Fl *TF:* 800-669-4474 ■ *Web:* www.nowhiring.com	Ann Arbor	MI	48104	734-213-9500	213-9011
PowerOne Media Inc 99 Troy Rd *TF:* 800-676-9376 ■ *Web:* www.poweronemedia.com	East Greenbush	NY	12061	518-687-6000	687-6060
ProcureStaff Ltd 560 Lexington Ave 10th Fl *Web:* www.procurestaff.com	New York	NY	10022	212-901-2828	704-2477
Project Connect EPCS On-Line Services University of Wisconsin School of Education B150 Education Bldg 1000 Bascom Mall *Web:* careers.education.wisc.edu/projectconnect	Madison	WI	53706	608-262-1755	262-9074
Recruiters OnLine Network Inc (RON) 947 Essex Ln *Web:* www.recruitersonline.com	Medina	OH	44256	888-364-4667	237-8686
RON (Recruiters OnLine Network Inc) 947 Essex Ln *Web:* www.recruitersonline.com	Medina	OH	44256	888-364-4667	237-8686
Student Central c/o College Central Network Inc 245 8th Ave Suite 892 *Web:* www.studentcentral.com	New York	NY	10011	212-967-0230	714-1688
TechCareers c/o CMP Media LLC 600 Community Dr *Web:* www.techcareers.com	Manhasset	NY	11030	516-562-5000	562-7123
TrueCareers Inc 8420 W Bryn Mawr Ave *Web:* www.truecareers.com	Chicago	IL	60631	866-438-1485	

				Phone	Fax
TVJobs.com c/o Broadcast Employment Services PO Box 4116 *TF:* 800-374-0119 ■ *Web:* www.tvjobs.com	Oceanside	CA	92052	760-754-8177	754-2115
USAJOBS Office of Personnel Management 1900 'E' St NW *Web:* www.usajobs.opm.gov	Washington	DC	20415	202-606-1800	
Vault Inc 150 W 22nd St 5th Fl *Web:* www.vault.com	New York	NY	10011	212-366-4212	366-6117
WetFeet Inc 609 Mission St Suite 400 *TF:* 800-926-4562 ■ *Web:* www.wetfeet.com	San Francisco	CA	94105	415-284-7900	284-7910
Yahoo! HotJobs 45 W 18th St 6th Fl *Web:* hotjobs.yahoo.com	New York	NY	10011	646-351-5300	351-5301

264 ENGINEERING & DESIGN

SEE ALSO Surveying, Mapping, Related Services p. 2336

				Phone	Fax
3D/International Inc 1900 West Loop S Suite 400 *Web:* www.3di.com	Houston	TX	77027	713-871-7000	871-7171
A Epstein & Sons International Inc 600 W Fulton St 9th Fl *Web:* www.epstein-isi.com	Chicago	IL	60661	312-454-9100	559-1217
ABM Engineering Services Co 5300 S Eastern Ave Suite 100 *Web:* www.abm.com	Los Angeles	CA	90040	323-234-2001	724-9561
ADD Inc 210 Broadway *Web:* www.addinc.com	Cambridge	MA	02139	617-234-3100	661-7118
Advanced Engineering & Research Assoc Inc (AERA) 2800 Shirlington Rd 12th Fl *Web:* www.aera.com	Arlington	VA	22206	703-824-5000	824-5003
Advantis Technologies 1400 Bluegrass Lakes Pkwy *TF:* 888-452-7678 ■ *Web:* www.poolspacare.com	Alpharetta	GA	30004	770-521-5999	521-5959
AECOM Technology Corp 555 S Flower St 37th Fl *Web:* www.aecom.com	Los Angeles	CA	90071	213-593-8000	593-8730
AEI (Affiliated Engineers Inc) 5802 Research Pk Blvd *Web:* www.aeieng.com	Madison	WI	53719	608-238-2616	238-2614
AEP Pro Serv 1 Riverside Plaza *TF:* 800-777-1131 ■ *Web:* www.aep.com	Columbus	OH	43215	614-716-1000	716-1823
AEPCO Inc 15800 Crabbs Branch Way Suite 300 *Web:* www.aepco.com	Rockville	MD	20855	301-670-6770	670-9884
AERA (Advanced Engineering & Research Assoc Inc) 2800 Shirlington Rd 12th Fl *Web:* www.aera.com	Arlington	VA	22206	703-824-5000	824-5003
Affiliated Engineers Inc (AEI) 5802 Research Pk Blvd *Web:* www.aeieng.com	Madison	WI	53719	608-238-2616	238-2614
AGUIRRE Corp 12700 Park Central Dr 15th Fl *Web:* www.aguirre.com	Dallas	TX	75251	972-788-1508	788-1583
AI Signal Research Inc 3411 Triana Blvd SW *Web:* www.aisignal.com	Huntsville	AL	35805	256-551-0008	551-0099
AirPol Inc 199 Pomeroy Rd Suite 103 *Web:* www.airpol.com	Parsippany	NJ	07054	973-599-4400	428-6048
Aker Kvaerner 3600 Briarpark Dr *TF:* 800-859-8691 ■ *Web:* www.akerkvaerner.com/Internet/default.htm	Houston	TX	77042	713-988-2002	772-4673
AKRF Inc 117 E 29th St 5th Fl *TF:* 800-899-2573 ■ *Web:* www.akrf.com	New York	NY	10016	212-696-0670	779-9721
Albert-Garaudy & Assoc 3500 N Causeway Blvd Suite 600 *Web:* www.aga-engineers.com	Metairie	LA	70002	504-846-6400	838-8955
Albert Kahn Assoc Inc 7430 2nd Ave Albert Kahn Bldg *Web:* www.albertkahn.com	Detroit	MI	48202	313-202-7000	202-7001
Alfred Benesch & Co 205 N Michigan Ave Suite 2400 *TF:* 877-222-9995 ■ *Web:* www.benesch.com	Chicago	IL	60601	312-565-0450	565-2497
Alion Science & Technology 1750 Tysons Blvd Suite 1300 *TF:* 877-771-6252 ■ *Web:* www.alionscience.com	McLean	VA	22102	703-918-4480	933-6774
Allen & Hoshall Inc 1661 International Dr Suite 100 *TF:* 888-819-5005 ■ *Web:* www.allenhoshall.com	Memphis	TN	38120	901-820-0820	683-1001
Ambitech Engineering Corp 1333 Butterfield Rd Suite 200 *Web:* www.ambitech.com	Downers Grove	IL	60515	630-963-5800	963-8099
AMEC Earth & Environmental 221 18th St SE *Web:* www.amec.com/earthandenvironmental	Calgary	AB	T2E6J5	403-248-4331	248-2188
AMEC Inc 2020 Winston Park Dr Suite 700 *Web:* www.amec.com	Oakview	ON	L6H6X7	905-829-5400	829-5401
American Consulting Engineers PLC 400 E Vine St Suite 300 *Web:* www.ace-plc.com	Lexington	KY	40507	859-233-2100	254-9664
American Consulting Inc 7260 Shadeland Station *Web:* www.amercons.com	Indianapolis	IN	46256	317-547-5580	543-0270
Ammann & Whitney Inc 96 Morton St *Web:* www.ammann-whitney.com	New York	NY	10014	212-627-1190	929-5356
AMSEC LLC 2829 Guardian Ln *Web:* www.amsec.com	Virginia Beach	VA	23452	757-463-6666	463-9110
Anshen+Allen Architects 901 Market St *Web:* www.anshen.com	San Francisco	CA	94103	415-882-9500	882-9523
Apex Environmental Inc 15850 Crabbs Branch Way Suite 200 *Web:* www.apexenv.com	Rockville	MD	20855	301-417-0200	975-0169
Arcadis 630 Plaza Dr Suite 200 *Web:* www.arcadis-us.com	Highlands Ranch	CO	80129	720-344-3500	344-3535
Architects Collaborative International 124 Mt Auburn St Suite 200-N	Cambridge	MA	02138	617-576-5706	547-1431
Ardaman & Assoc Inc 8008 S Orange Ave *TF:* 800-432-3143 ■ *Web:* www.ardaman.com	Orlando	FL	32809	407-855-3860	859-8121
Arkel International Inc PO Box 4621 *Web:* www.arkel.com	Baton Rouge	LA	70821	225-343-0525	336-1849
Arquitectonica International Corp 801 Brickell Ave Suite 1100 *Web:* www.arquitectonica.com	Miami	FL	33131	305-372-1812	372-1175
Arthur Dyson & Assoc 754 P St Suite C *Web:* www.arthurdyson.com	Fresno	CA	93721	559-486-3582	486-3584
ASCG Inc 300 W 31st Ave *Web:* www.ascg.com	Anchorage	AK	99503	907-339-6500	339-5327
Astorino 227 Fort Pitt Blvd *TF:* 800-518-0464 ■ *Web:* www.ldastorino.com	Pittsburgh	PA	15222	412-765-1700	765-1711
Atkins Benham Inc 9400 N Broadway *Web:* www.benham.com	Oklahoma City	OK	73114	405-478-5353	478-5660
Atwell-Hicks Inc 500 Avis Dr *Web:* www.atwell-hicks.com	Ann Arbor	MI	48108	734-994-4000	994-1590
Austin Co 6095 Parkland Blvd *Web:* www.theaustin.com	Cleveland	OH	44124	440-544-2600	544-2661
AVCA Corp 1684 Woodland Dr	Maumee	OH	43537	419-893-2222	893-6115
Ayres Associates Inc 3433 Oakwood Hills Pkwy *Web:* www.ayresassociates.com	Eau Claire	WI	54701	715-834-3161	831-7500
Baker Michael Corp 100 Airsite Dr Airsite Business Pk *AMEX:* BKR ■ *TF:* 800-553-1153 ■ *Web:* www.mbakercorp.com	Moon Township	PA	15108	412-269-6300	375-3977
Ballinger 833 Chestnut St Suite 1400 *Web:* www.ballinger-ae.com	Philadelphia	PA	19107	215-446-0900	446-0901
Bard Rao + Athanas Consulting Engineers Inc 311 Arsenal St The Arsenal on the Charles *Web:* www.brplusa.com	Watertown	MA	02472	617-254-0016	924-9339
Barge Waggoner Sumner & Cannon 211 Commerce St Suite 600 *Web:* www.bargewaggoner.com	Nashville	TN	37201	615-254-1500	255-6572
Barletta Engineering Corp 10 Whipple Ave	Roslindale	MA	02131	617-524-4700	524-1201
Barr Engineering Co 4700 W 77th St *TF:* 800-632-2277 ■ *Web:* www.barr.com	Minneapolis	MN	55435	952-832-2600	832-2601
Bartlett & West Engineers Inc 1200 SW Executive Dr *TF:* 888-200-6464 ■ *Web:* www.bartwest.com/Default.htm	Topeka	KS	66615	785-272-2252	272-5694
Barton JF Contracting Co PO Box 73525 *TF:* 800-222-1472	Houston	TX	77273	281-443-3800	443-0649
Barton Malow Design 26500 American Dr Suite 451 *Web:* www.bartonmalowdesign.com	Southfield	MI	48034	248-351-4500	436-5001
Baxter & Woodman Inc 8678 Ridgefield Rd *Web:* www.baxwood.com	Crystal Lake	IL	60012	815-459-1260	455-0450
BBG-BBGM 515 Madison Ave 4th Fl *Web:* www.bbg-bbgm.com	New York	NY	10022	212-888-7663	935-3868
BCM Engineers 920 Germantown Pike Suite 200 *TF:* 800-221-1226	Plymouth Meeting	PA	19462	610-313-3100	313-3151
BE & K Inc PO Box 2332 *Web:* www.bek.com	Birmingham	AL	35201	205-969-3600	972-6300
Bechtel Corp 50 Beale St *Web:* www.bechtel.com	San Francisco	CA	94105	415-768-1234	768-9038
Bechtel North America 3000 Post Oak Blvd *Web:* www.bechtel.com	Houston	TX	77056	713-235-2000	960-9031
Belcan Engineering Group Inc 10200 Anderson Way *TF:* 800-423-5226 ■ *Web:* www.belcan.com	Cincinnati	OH	45242	513-891-0972	
Belt Collins 2153 N King St Suite 200 *Web:* www.beltcollins.com	Honolulu	HI	96819	808-521-5361	538-7819
Benatec Assoc Inc 200 Airport Rd *Web:* www.benatec.com	New Cumberland	PA	17070	717-901-7055	901-7059
Benesch Alfred & Co 205 N Michigan Ave Suite 2400 *TF:* 877-222-9995 ■ *Web:* www.benesch.com	Chicago	IL	60601	312-565-0450	565-2497
Berger Louis Group Inc 100 Halsted St *TF:* 800-323-4098 ■ *Web:* www.louisberger.com	East Orange	NJ	07018	973-678-1960	672-4284
Berger/ABAM Engineers Inc 33301 9th Ave S Suite 300 *Web:* www.abam.com	Federal Way	WA	98003	206-431-2300	431-2250
Bergmann Assoc Inc 28 E Main St 200 First Federal Plaza *TF:* 800-724-1168 ■ *Web:* www.bergmannpc.com	Rochester	NY	14614	585-232-5135	325-8493
Bermello Ajamil & Partners 2601 S Bayshore Dr *Web:* www.bamiami.com	Miami	FL	33133	305-859-2050	859-9638
Bernard Johnson Young Inc 1375 Piccard Dr Bldg 3 Suite 170 *Web:* www.bjy.com	Rockville	MD	20850	301-208-2600	208-2601
Berryman & Henigar 11590 W Bernardo Ct Suite 100 *TF:* 800-964-4274 ■ *Web:* www.bhiinc.com	San Diego	CA	92127	858-451-6100	451-2846
Beyer Blinder Belle Architects & Planners LLC 41 E 11th St 2nd Fl *Web:* www.beyerblinderbelle.com	New York	NY	10003	212-777-7800	475-7424
Bibb & Assoc Inc 8455 Lenexa Dr *Web:* www.bibb.com	Lenexa	KS	66214	913-928-7000	928-7500
Bionetics Corp 11833 Cannon Blvd Suite 100 *TF:* 800-868-0330 ■ *Web:* www.bionetics.com	Newport News	VA	23606	757-873-0900	873-6998
BKF Engineers 255 Shoreline Drq Suite 200 *Web:* www.bkf.com	Redwood City	CA	94065	650-482-6300	482-6399
BL Cos 355 Research Pkwy *TF:* 800-301-3077 ■ *Web:* www.blcompanies.com	Meriden	CT	06450	203-630-1406	630-2615
Blasland Bouck & Lee Engineers 6723 Towpath Rd *Web:* www.bbl-inc.com	Syracuse	NY	13214	315-446-9120	449-0017
BLM Architects 2520 Renaissance Blvd Suite 110 *Web:* www.blm-architects.com	King of Prussia	PA	19406	610-270-0599	270-0995
BMH Eagleton Inc 3900 Essex Ln Suite 300	Houston	TX	77027	713-871-8787	871-1914
Bolton & Menk Inc 1960 Premier Dr *Web:* www.bolton-menk.com	Mankato	MN	56001	507-625-4171	625-4177
Boswell Engineering 330 Phillips Ave *Web:* www.boswellengineering.com	South Hackensack	NJ	07606	201-641-0770	641-1831
Bourton Group LLC 11350 N Meridian St Suite 360 *Web:* www.bourtongroup.com	Carmel	IN	46032	317-818-8148	818-2434
Bowyer-Singleton & Assoc Inc 520 S Magnolia Ave *Web:* www.bsaorl.com	Orlando	FL	32801	407-843-5120	649-8664
Boyle Engineering Corp 1501 Quail St *Web:* www.boyleengineering.com	Newport Beach	CA	92660	949-476-3300	721-7142
BP Barber & Assoc Inc PO Box 1116 *Web:* www.bpbarber.com	Columbia	SC	29202	803-254-4400	771-6676
Braun Intertec Corp 11001 Hampshire Ave S *TF:* 800-279-6100 ■ *Web:* www.braunintertec.com	Bloomington	MN	55438	952-995-2000	995-2020
Bresslergroup 2400 Market St Suite 1 *Web:* www.bresslergroup.com	Philadelphia	PA	19103	215-561-5100	561-5101
Bricmont Inc 500 Technology Dr Southpointe Industrial Pk *TF:* 888-274-2462 ■ *Web:* www.bricmont.com	Canonsburg	PA	15317	724-746-2300	746-9420
Brinjac Engineering Inc PO Box 1290 *TF:* 877-274-6526 ■ *Web:* www.brinjac.com	Harrisburg	PA	17108	717-233-4502	233-0833
Brock Solutions Inc 86 Ardelt Ave *TF:* 877-702-7625 ■ *Web:* www.brocksolutions.com	Kitchener	ON	N2C2C9	519-571-1522	571-1721
Brown & Caldwell Consulting Engineers 201 N Civic Dr Suite 115 *Web:* www.brownandcaldwell.com	Walnut Creek	CA	94596	925-937-9010	937-9026
Brown Dayton T Inc 1175 Church St *TF:* 800-232-6300 ■ *Web:* www.daytontbrown.com	Bohemia	NY	11716	631-589-6300	589-4046
Brown & Gay Engineers Inc 11490 Westheimer Rd Suite 700 *Web:* www.browngay.com	Houston	TX	77077	281-558-8700	558-9701
Bryan A Stirrat & Assoc 1360 Valley Vista Dr *Web:* www.bas.com	Diamond Bar	CA	91765	909-860-7777	860-8017
BSA Life Structures 9365 Counselors Row *Web:* www.bsalifestructures.com	Indianapolis	IN	46240	317-819-7878	819-7288
BSK & Assoc 567 W Shaw Ave Suite B *Web:* www.bskinc.com	Fresno	CA	93704	559-497-2880	497-2864
BSW International Inc 1 W 3rd St Suite 800 *TF:* 800-749-8771 ■ *Web:* www.bswintl.com	Tulsa	OK	74103	918-582-8771	587-3594
Buchart Horn Inc/Basco Assoc PO Box 15040 *TF:* 800-274-2224 ■ *Web:* www.bh-ba.com	York	PA	17405	717-852-1400	852-1401
Bucher Willis & Ratliff Corp 609 W North St *TF:* 800-942-9807 ■ *Web:* www.bwrcorp.com	Salina	KS	67401	785-827-3603	827-3029
Burgess & Niple Inc 5085 Reed Rd *TF:* 800-282-1761 ■ *Web:* www.burgessniple.com	Columbus	OH	43220	614-459-2050	451-1385
Burk-Kleinpeter Inc (BKI) 4176 Canal St *Web:* www.bkiusa.com	New Orleans	LA	70119	504-486-5901	483-6298
Burns & McDonnell Engineering Architects & Consultants Inc 9400 Ward Pkwy *Web:* www.burnsmcd.com	Kansas City	MO	64114	816-333-9400	333-3690
Burns & Roe Enterprises Inc 800 Kinderkamack Rd *Web:* www.roe.com	Oradell	NJ	07649	201-986-4800	
Burt Hill Kosar Rittelmann Assoc 101 E Diamond St *Web:* www.burthill.com	Butler	PA	16001	724-285-4761	285-6815
Byers Engineering Co 6285 Barfield Rd 4th Fl *Web:* www.byers.com	Atlanta	GA	30328	404-843-1000	843-2116

Company	City	State	ZIP	Phone	Fax
C & S Cos 499 Col Eileen Collins Blvd *TF:* 877-277-6583 ■ *Web:* www.cscos.com	Syracuse	NY	13212	315-455-2000	455-9667
Callison Architecture Inc 1420 5th Ave Suite 2400 *Web:* www.callison.com	Seattle	WA	98101	206-623-4646	623-4625
Calmaquip Engineering Corp 7240 NW 12th St *Web:* www.calmaquip.com	Miami	FL	33126	305-592-4510	593-9618
Camp Dresser & McKee Inc 50 Hampshire St 1 Cambridge Pl *TF:* 800-343-7004 ■ *Web:* www.cdm.com	Cambridge	MA	02139	617-452-6000	452-8000
Cannon Design 2170 Whitehaven Rd *Web:* www.cannondesign.com	Grand Island	NY	14072	716-773-6800	773-5909
Carollo Engineers 3033 N 44th St Suite 101 *TF:* 800-523-5822 ■ *Web:* www.carollo.com	Phoenix	AZ	85018	602-263-9500	265-1422
Carter & Burgess Inc PO Box 901058 *TF:* 800-624-7959 ■ *Web:* www.c-b.com	Fort Worth	TX	76101	817-735-6000	735-6148
CAS Inc PO Box 11190 *TF:* 800-729-8686 ■ *Web:* www.cas-inc.com	Huntsville	AL	35814	256-922-4200	922-4243
CDI Engineering Group 1717 Arch St 35th Fl	Philadelphia	PA	19103	215-569-2200	636-1177
CDI Marine Co 9550 Regency Square Blvd Suite 400 *Web:* www.cdi-gs.com	Jacksonville	FL	32225	904-805-0700	805-0701
CEI Engineering Assoc Inc 3317 SW 'I' St *TF:* 800-433-4173 ■ *Web:* www.ceieng.com	Bentonville	AR	72712	479-273-9472	273-0844
CH Guernsey & Co 5555 N Grand Blvd *TF:* 800-845-2061 ■ *Web:* www.chguernsey.com	Oklahoma City	OK	73112	405-416-8100	416-8111
Chas H Sells Inc 555 Pleasantville Rd South Bldg *Web:* www.chashsells.com	Briarcliff Manor	NY	10510	914-747-1120	747-1956
Chastain-Skillman Inc PO Box 5710 *Web:* www.chastainskillman.com	Lakeland	FL	33807	863-646-1402	647-3806
Chemstress Consultant Co 39 S Main St *Web:* www.chemstress.com	Akron	OH	44308	330-535-5591	535-1431
Chemtex International Inc 1979 Eastwood Rd *TF:* 877-243-6839 ■ *Web:* www.chemtex.com	Wilmington	NC	28403	910-509-4400	509-4567
Chevron Energy Solutions 345 California St 18th Fl *Web:* www.chevronenergy.com	San Francisco	CA	94104	415-733-4500	733-4950
Chiang Patel & Yerby 1820 Regal Row Suite 200 *Web:* www.cpyi.com	Dallas	TX	75235	214-638-0500	638-3723
Civil & Environmental Consultants Inc 333 Baldwin Rd *TF:* 800-365-2324 ■ *Web:* www.cecinc.com	Pittsburgh	PA	15205	412-429-2324	429-2114
Clough Harbour & Assoc 3 Winners Circle *TF:* 800-836-0817 ■ *Web:* www.cloughharbour.com	Albany	NY	12205	518-453-4500	458-1735
Cochran Stephenson & Donkervoet Inc 323 W Camden St Suite 700 *Web:* www.csdarch.com	Baltimore	MD	21201	410-539-2080	752-5263
Coler & Colantonio Inc 101 Accord Pk Dr *Web:* www.col-col.com	Norwell	MA	02061	781-982-5400	982-5490
Columbia Research Corp 1201 'M' St SE Suite 010 *Web:* www.columbiaresearch.com	Washington	DC	20003	202-546-1435	546-0865
Comsearch 19700 Janelia Farm Blvd *Web:* www.comsearch.com	Ashburn	VA	20147	703-726-5500	726-5600
Concast America Inc 100 Sandusky St *Web:* www.concast-standard.com	Pittsburgh	PA	15212	412-237-8950	237-8951
Concepts NREC 217 Billings Farm Rd *Web:* www.nrec.com	White River Junction	VT	05001	802-296-2321	296-2325
Conestoga-Rovers & Assoc 2055 Niagara Falls Blvd Suite 3 *Web:* www.craworld.com	Niagara Falls	NY	14304	716-297-6150	297-2265
Consoer Townsend Envirodyne Engineers Inc 303 E Wacker Dr Suite 600 *Web:* www.cte-eng.com	Chicago	IL	60601	312-938-0300	938-1109
Continental Glass & Plastic Inc 841 W Cermak Rd *TF:* 888-676-5277 ■ *Web:* www.cgppkg.com	Chicago	IL	60608	312-666-2050	666-2088
Converse Consultants 222 E Huntington Dr Suite 211 *Web:* www.converseconsultants.com	Monrovia	CA	91016	626-930-1200	930-1212
Cooper Carry Inc 3520 Piedmont Rd NE Suite 200 *Web:* www.coopercarry.com	Atlanta	GA	30305	404-237-2000	237-0276
Corgan Assoc Inc 501 Elm St Suite 500 *Web:* www.corgan.com	Dallas	TX	75202	214-748-2000	653-8281
Corrpro Cos Inc 1055 W Smith Rd *TF:* 800-726-5082 ■ *Web:* www.corrpro.com	Medina	OH	44256	330-723-5082	722-7654
CPH Engineers PO Box 2808 *TF:* 800-609-0688 ■ *Web:* www.cphengineers.com	Sanford	FL	32772	407-322-6841	330-0639
CRA Engineering Group Inc 9181 Interline Ave Suite 220	Baton Rouge	LA	70809	225-927-4249	925-2897
Crawford Murphy & Tilly Inc 2750 W Washington St *Web:* www.cmtengr.com	Springfield	IL	62702	217-787-8050	787-8054
CSA Group Inc 8790 Governor's Hill Dr Suite 111 *Web:* www.csagroup.com	Cincinnati	OH	45249	513-677-4440	677-4443
CT Consultants Inc 35000 Kaiser Ct *Web:* www.ctconsultants.com	Willoughby	OH	44094	440-951-9000	951-7487
CTA Architects Engineers 13 N 23rd St *Web:* www.ctagroup.com	Billings	MT	59101	406-248-7455	248-3779
CTL/Thompson Inc 1971 W 12th Ave *Web:* www.ctlt.com	Denver	CO	80204	303-825-0777	825-4252
Cube Corp 45665 Willow Pond Plaza *Web:* www.cubecorp.com	Sterling	VA	20164	703-481-9101	481-9193
CUH2A Inc 1000 Lenox Dr *TF:* 877-992-8422 ■ *Web:* www.cuh2a.com	Lawrenceville	NJ	08648	609-844-1212	791-7700
Daly Leo A 8600 Indian Hills Dr *Web:* www.leoadaly.com	Omaha	NE	68114	402-391-8111	391-8564
David Evans & Assoc Inc 2100 SW River Pkwy *TF:* 800-721-1916 ■ *Web:* www.deainc.com	Portland	OR	97201	503-223-6663	223-2701
Davis & Floyd Inc PO Drawer 428 *Web:* www.davisfloyd.com	Greenwood	SC	29648	864-229-5211	229-7844
Dayton T Brown Inc 1175 Church St *TF:* 800-232-6300 ■ *Web:* www.daytontbrown.com	Bohemia	NY	11716	631-589-6300	589-4046
Degenkolb Engineers 225 Bush St Suite 1000 *Web:* www.degenkolb.com	San Francisco	CA	94104	415-392-6952	981-3157
Delon Hampton & Assoc Chartered 800 K St NW Suite 720 *Web:* www.delonhampton.com	Washington	DC	20001	202-898-1999	371-2073
DeStefano & Partners Ltd 445 E Illinois Ave Suite 250 *Web:* www.destefanoandpartners.com	Chicago	IL	60611	312-836-4321	836-4322
Dewberry & Davis 8401 Arlington Blvd *Web:* www.dewberry.com	Fairfax	VA	22031	703-849-0100	849-0118
Diversified Technology Consultants Inc 556 Washington Ave *Web:* www.teamdtc.com	North Haven	CT	06473	203-239-4200	234-7376
DLR Group Inc 400 Essex Ct *Web:* www.dlrgroup.com/home.htm#	Omaha	NE	68114	402-393-4100	393-8747
DLZ Corp 6121 Huntley Rd *TF:* 800-336-5352 ■ *Web:* www.dlzcorp.com	Columbus	OH	43229	614-888-0040	848-6712
DMJM & Harris 605 3rd Ave 31st Fl *TF:* 800-729-3656 ■ *Web:* www.dmjmharris.com	New York	NY	10158	212-973-2900	953-0399
DMJMH+N 999 Town & Country Rd *Web:* www.dmjmhn.aecom.com	Orange	CA	92868	714-567-2400	543-0955
DOWL Engineers 4040 B St *Web:* www.dowl.com	Anchorage	AK	99503	907-562-2000	563-3953
DRS Technical Services Segment 8300 Boone Blvd Suite 555 *Web:* www.drs.com	Vienna	VA	22182	703-761-7616	761-6713
Dufresne-Henry Inc 54 Rt 106 *Web:* www.dufresne-henry.com	North Springfield	VT	05150	802-886-2261	886-2260
Durrant Group Inc 700 Locust St Suite 942 *Web:* www.durrant.com	Dubuque	IA	52004	563-583-9131	557-9078
Dvirka & Bartilucci Consulting Engineers 330 Crossways Pk Dr *TF:* 888-364-9890 ■ *Web:* www.dvirkaandbartilucci.com	Woodbury	NY	11797	516-364-9890	364-9045
Dyer Riddle Mills & Precourt Inc 1505 E Colonial Dr *TF:* 800-375-3767 ■ *Web:* www.drmp.com	Orlando	FL	32803	407-896-0594	896-4836
Dynamac Corp 2275 Research Blvd Suite 300 *Web:* www.dynamac.com	Rockville	MD	20850	301-417-9800	417-6132
EA Engineering Science & Technology Inc 11019 McCormick Rd *TF:* 800-777-9750 ■ *Web:* www.eaest.com	Hunt Valley	MD	21031	410-584-7000	771-1625
EADS Group 1126 8th Ave *TF:* 800-626-0904 ■ *Web:* www.eadsgroup.com	Altoona	PA	16602	814-944-5035	944-4862
ECS Ltd 14026 Thunderbolt Pl Suite 100 *Web:* www.ecslimited.com	Chantilly	VA	20151	703-471-8400	834-5527
EDO Technical Services Operations 254 E Ave K-4 *Web:* www.edotso.com	Lancaster	CA	93535	661-723-7368	948-7003
Edwards & Kelcey Inc 299 Madison Ave *Web:* www.ekcorp.com	Morristown	NJ	07962	973-267-0555	267-3555
EI Assoc 8 Ridgedale Ave *Web:* www.eiassociates.com	Cedar Knolls	NJ	07927	973-775-7777	775-7770
Einhorn Yaffee Prescott 412 Broadway *Web:* www.eypae.com	Albany	NY	12207	518-431-3300	431-3333
Elkus/Manfredi Architects 300 A St *Web:* www.elkus-manfredi.com	Boston	MA	02210	617-426-1300	426-7502
Ellerbe Becket Co 800 LaSalle Ave *TF:* 800-344-6396 ■ *Web:* www.ellerbebecket.com	Minneapolis	MN	55402	612-376-2000	376-2271
EMA Services Inc 1970 Oakcrest Ave Suite 100 *Web:* www.ema-inc.com	Saint Paul	MN	55113	651-639-5600	639-5730
EMCON/OWT Inc 1 International Blvd Suite 700 *Web:* www.emconinc.com	Mahwah	NJ	07495	201-512-5700	512-5786
EN Engineering 7135 James Ave *Web:* www.enengineering.com	Woodridge	IL	60517	630-353-4000	353-7777
Enercon Services Inc 5100 E Skelly Dr Suite 450 *TF:* 800-735-7693 ■ *Web:* www.enercon.com	Tulsa	OK	74135	918-665-7693	665-7232
ENSCO Inc 5400 Port Royal Rd **Fax:* Hum Res ■ *TF:* 800-367-2682 ■ *Web:* www.ensco.com	Springfield	VA	22151	703-321-9000	321-4605*
ENSR International 2 Technology Pk Dr *TF:* 800-722-2440 ■ *Web:* www.ensr.aecom.com	Westford	MA	01886	978-589-3000	589-3100
ENTRANCO Inc 10900 NE 8th St Suite 300 *TF:* 800-454-5601 ■ *Web:* www.entranco.com	Bellevue	WA	98004	425-454-5600	454-0220
Epstein A & Sons International Inc 600 W Fulton St 9th Fl *Web:* www.epstein-isi.com	Chicago	IL	60661	312-454-9100	559-1217
Erdman Marshall & Assoc 5117 University Ave *TF:* 800-550-5117 ■ *Web:* www.erdman.com	Madison	WI	53705	608-238-0211	238-5604
ERM Group Inc 350 Eagle View Blvd *TF:* 800-662-1124 ■ *Web:* www.erm.com	Exton	PA	19341	610-524-3500	524-7335
ERM Southwest Inc 15810 Park Ten Place Suite 300	Houston	TX	77084	281-600-1000	600-1001
Essex Corp 6708 Alexander Bell Dr *NASDAQ:* KEYW ■ *TF:* 800-533-7739 ■ *Web:* www.essexcorp.com	Columbia	MD	21046	301-939-7000	953-7880
Evans David & Assoc Inc 2100 SW River Pkwy *TF:* 800-721-1916 ■ *Web:* www.deainc.com	Portland	OR	97201	503-223-6663	223-2701
Evans Mechwart Hambleton & Tilton Inc 5500 New Albany Rd *Web:* www.emht.com	Columbus	OH	43054	614-775-4500	775-4800
Ewing Cole 100 N 6th St *Web:* www.ewingcole.com	Philadelphia	PA	19106	215-923-2020	574-9163
Facility Group Inc 2233 Lake Pk Dr Suite 100 *TF:* 800-525-2463 ■ *Web:* www.facilitygroup.com	Smyrna	GA	30080	770-437-2700	437-7554
Fanning/Howey Assoc Inc 1200 Irmscher Blvd *TF:* 888-499-2292 ■ *Web:* www.fhai.com	Celina	OH	45822	419-586-2292	586-3393
Fata Hunter Co Inc 1040 Iowa Ave Suite 100 *TF:* 800-248-6837 ■ *Web:* www.fatahunter.com	Riverside	CA	92507	951-328-0200	328-9193
Fay Spofford & Thorndike LLC 5 Burlington Woods *TF:* 800-835-8666 ■ *Web:* www.fstinc.com	Burlington	MA	01803	781-221-1000	229-1115
Fentress Bradburn Architects Ltd 421 Broadway *Web:* www.fentressbradburn.com	Denver	CO	80203	303-722-5000	722-5080
Fishbeck Thompson Carr & Huber Inc 1515 Arboretum Dr SE *Web:* www.ftch.com	Grand Rapids	MI	49546	616-575-3824	464-3993
Flack & Kurtz Consulting Engineers Inc 475 5th Ave 9th Fl *Web:* www.flackandkurtz.com	New York	NY	10017	212-532-9600	689-7489
Flad & Assoc 644 Science Dr *Web:* www.flad.com	Madison	WI	53711	608-238-2661	238-6727
Fletcher-Thompson Inc 3 Corporate Dr *Web:* fletcherthompson.cosential.com	Shelton	CT	06484	203-225-6500	225-6800
Fluor Daniel Inc 1 Fluor Daniel Dr *Web:* www.fluor.com	Aliso Viejo	CA	92698	949-349-2000	349-2585
Ford Bacon & Davis 12021 Lakeland Pk Blvd *Web:* www.fbd.com	Baton Rouge	LA	70809	225-297-3201	297-3325
Foster Wheeler Development Corp 12 Peach Tree Hill Rd	Livingston	NJ	07039	973-535-2300	535-2242
Foster Wheeler Ltd 53 Frontage Rd Perryville Corporate Park *NASDAQ:* FWLT ■ **Fax:* Hum Res ■ *Web:* www.fwc.com	Clinton	NJ	08809	908-730-4000	730-5315*
Foster Wheeler USA Corp Perryville Corporate Pk *Web:* www.fwc.com	Clinton	NJ	08809	908-730-4000	730-5315
Foth & Van Dyke & Assoc Inc PO Box 19012 *TF:* 800-236-8690 ■ *Web:* www.foth.com	Green Bay	WI	54307	920-497-2500	497-8516
Framatome ANP Inc 3315 Old Forest Rd *Web:* www.framatech.com	Lynchburg	VA	24501	434-832-3000	832-2997
Freese & Nichols Inc 4055 International Plaza Suite 200 *Web:* www.freese.com	Fort Worth	TX	76109	817-735-7300	735-7491
Fru-Con Engineering Inc 15933 Clayton Rd *Web:* www.frucon.com	Ballwin	MO	63011	636-391-6700	391-4513
FSB Texas 6850 Manhattan Blvd Suite 200 *Web:* www.fsb-tx.com	Fort Worth	TX	73120	817-727-8348	451-4925
Fugro Consultants LP 6100 Hillcroft Ave *Web:* www.fugrosouth.com	Houston	TX	77081	713-369-5400	369-5518
Fuss & O'Neill Consulting Engineers Inc 146 Hartford Rd *Web:* www.fando.com	Manchester	CT	06040	860-646-2469	533-5143
GAI Consultants Inc 385 E Waterfront Dr *TF:* 800-437-2150 ■ *Web:* www.gaiconsultants.com	Homestead	PA	15120	412-476-2000	476-2020
Galaxy Scientific Corp 3120 Fire Rd *Web:* www.galaxyscientific.com	Egg Harbor Township	NJ	08234	609-645-0900	645-3316
Gannett Fleming Inc PO Box 67100 *TF:* 800-233-1055 ■ *Web:* www.gannettfleming.com	Harrisburg	PA	17106	717-763-7211	763-8150
Garver Engineers 1010 Battery St PO Box 50 *TF:* 800-264-3633 ■ *Web:* www.garverengineers.com	Little Rock	AR	72203	501-376-3633	372-8042
GDS Engineers Inc 9009 W Loop South Suite 800 *Web:* www.gdseng.com	Houston	TX	77096	713-667-9162	667-9241
GEI Consultants Inc 1021 Main St *TF:* 800-678-1503 ■ *Web:* www.geiconsultants.com	Winchester	MA	01890	781-721-4000	721-4073
Gensler 2 Harrison St Suite 400 *Web:* www.gensler.com	San Francisco	CA	94105	415-433-3700	836-4599

				Phone	Fax
GeoEngineers Inc 8410 154th Ave NE	Redmond	WA	98052	425-861-6000	861-6050
TF: 800-533-2158 ■ *Web:* www.geoengineers.com					
Geomatrix Consultants Inc 2101 Webster St 12th Fl	Oakland	CA	94612	510-663-4100	663-4141
TF: 800-999-6879 ■ *Web:* www.geomatrix.com					
George Butler Assoc Inc 9801 Renner Blvd	Lenexa	KS	66219	913-492-0400	577-8200
TF: 800-932-2468 ■ *Web:* www.gbutler.com					
George G Sharp Inc 100 Church St 14th Fl	New York	NY	10007	212-732-2800	732-2809
Web: www.georgesharp.com					
GeoSyntec Consultants Inc					
5901 Broken Sound Pkwy NW Suite 300	Boca Raton	FL	33487	561-995-0900	995-0925
TF: 800-765-4436 ■ *Web:* www.geosyntec.com					
Ghafari Assoc Inc 17101 Michigan Ave	Dearborn	MI	48126	313-441-3000	436-8624*
**Fax:* Hum Res ■ *Web:* www.ghafari.com					
Gibbs & Cox Inc 2711 Jefferson Davis Hwy Suite 1000	Arlington	VA	22202	703-416-3600	416-3679
Web: www.gibbscox.com					
Global Design Alliance Inc 3355 W Alabama St Suite 250	Houston	TX	77098	713-622-0101	622-6434
Web: www.globalda.com					
Global Marine Systems (Federal) Inc 1800 Eller Dr	Fort Lauderdale	FL	33316	954-530-8088	766-8853
Web: www.globalmarinesystems.com					
Golder Assoc Inc 3730 Chamblee Tucker Rd	Atlanta	GA	30341	770-496-1893	934-9476
Web: www.golder.com					
Gonzalez Design Group 29401 Stevenson Hwy	Madison Heights	MI	48071	248-548-6010	548-3160
Web: www.gonzalez-group.com					
Gould Evans International 4041 Mill St	Kansas City	MO	64111	816-931-6655	931-9640
Web: www.geaf.com					
GPD Group 520 S Main St Suite 2531	Akron	OH	44311	330-572-2100	572-2101
Web: www.gpdco.com					
Graef Anhalt Schloemer & Assoc Inc					
125 S 84th St Suite 401	Milwaukee	WI	53214	414-259-1500	259-0037
Web: www.gasai.com					
Grant Geophysical Inc PO Box 219950	Houston	TX	77218	281-398-9503	398-9996
TF: 800-390-5530 ■ *Web:* www.grantgeo.com					
Greeley & Hansen 100 S Wacker Dr Suite 1400	Chicago	IL	60606	312-558-9000	558-1006
TF: 800-837-9779 ■ *Web:* www.greeley-hansen.com					
Greenberg Farrow 1755 The Exchange	Atlanta	GA	30339	770-303-1033	303-2333
Web: www.greenbergfarrow.com					
Greenhorne & O'Mara Inc 6110 Frost Pl	Laurel	MD	20707	301-982-2800	220-2483
TF: 866-322-8905 ■ *Web:* www.g-and-o.com					
Greenman-Pedersen Inc 325 W Main St	Babylon	NY	11702	631-587-5060	587-5029
TF: 800-347-9221 ■ *Web:* www.gpinet.com					
Gresham Smith & Partners					
511 Union St 1400 Nashville City Ctr	Nashville	TN	37219	615-770-8100	770-8411
TF: 800-867-3384 ■ *Web:* www.gspnet.com					
Gruzen Samton LLC 320 W 13th St 9th Fl	New York	NY	10014	212-477-0900	477-1257
Web: www.gruzensamton.com					
GRW Engineers Inc 801 Corporate Dr	Lexington	KY	40503	859-223-3999	223-8917
TF: 800-432-9537 ■ *Web:* www.grwinc.com					
Gulf Interstate Engineering Co					
16010 Barkers Point Ln Suite 600	Houston	TX	77079	713-850-3400	850-3579
Web: www.gie.com					
H2M Group 575 Broad Hollow Rd	Melville	NY	11747	631-756-8000	694-4122
Web: www.h2m.com					
HAKS Engineers PC 161 Maiden Ln 5th Fl	New York	NY	10038	212-747-1997	747-1947
Web: www.haks.net					
Halcrow Yolles 207 Queens Quay W Suite 550 PO Box 132	Toronto	ON	M5J1A7	416-363-8123	363-0341
TF: 800-572-1759 ■ *Web:* www.halcrow.com/halcrowyolles/					
Haley & Aldrich Inc 465 Medford St Suite 2200	Boston	MA	02129	617-886-7400	886-7600
Web: www.haleyaldrich.com					
Halff Assoc Inc 8616 NW Plaza Dr	Dallas	TX	75225	214-346-6200	739-0095
TF: 800-425-3387 ■ *Web:* www.halff.com					
Hammel Green & Abrahamson Inc 701 Washington Ave N	Minneapolis	MN	55401	612-758-4000	758-4199
TF: 888-442-8255 ■ *Web:* www.hga.com					
Han-Padron Assoc LLP 22 Cortlandt St 33rd Fl	New York	NY	10007	212-608-3990	566-5059
Web: www.han-padron.com					
Hanson Engineers Inc 1525 S 6th St	Springfield	IL	62703	217-788-2450	788-2503
TF: 800-788-2450 ■ *Web:* www.hansonengineers.com					
Hardesty & Hanover LLP 1501 Broadway Suite 310	New York	NY	10036	212-944-1150	391-0297
Web: www.hardesty-hanover.com					
Harris Group Inc 200 W Thomas St Suite 200	Seattle	WA	98119	206-494-9400	494-9500
TF: 800-488-7410 ■ *Web:* www.harrisgroup.com					
Hart Crowser Inc 1910 Fairview Ave E	Seattle	WA	98102	206-324-9530	328-5581
TF: 800-925-9530 ■ *Web:* www.hartcrowser.com					
Hart Engineering Corp 800 P Scenic View Dr	Cumberland	RI	02864	401-658-4600	658-4609
TF: 800-492-4278					
Hatch Mott Macdonald Group 27 Bleeker St	Millburn	NJ	07041	973-379-3400	376-1072
Web: www.hatchmott.com					
Hayes Seay Mattern & Mattern Inc PO Box 13446	Roanoke	VA	24034	540-857-3100	857-3180
TF: 800-366-4766 ■ *Web:* www.hsmm.com					
Hazen & Sawyer PC 498 7th Ave 11th Fl	New York	NY	10018	212-777-8400	614-9049
TF: 800-858-9876 ■ *Web:* www.hazenandsawyer.com					
HC Nutting Co 611 Lunken Pk Dr	Cincinnati	OH	45226	513-321-5816	321-0294
Web: www.hcnutting.com					
HDR Engineering Inc 8404 Indian Hills Dr	Omaha	NE	68114	402-399-1000	548-5015*
**Fax:* Hum Res ■ *TF:* 800-366-4411 ■ *Web:* www.hdrinc.com					
Healy SA Co 1910 S Highland Ave Suite 300	Lombard	IL	60148	630-678-3110	678-3130
TF: 888-724-3259 ■ *Web:* www.sahealy.com					
Heery International Inc 999 Peachtree St NE Suite 300	Atlanta	GA	30309	404-881-9880	875-1283
Web: www.heery.com					
Hellmuth Obata & Kassabaum Inc					
211 N Broadway Suite 700	Saint Louis	MO	63102	314-421-2000	421-6073
Web: www.hok.com					
Herbert Rowland & Grubic Inc 369 E Park Dr	Harrisburg	PA	17111	717-564-1121	564-1158
Web: www.hrg-inc.com					
Hernandez Engineering Inc 17625 El Camino Real Suite 300	Houston	TX	77058	281-280-5159	480-7525
Web: www.hernandez-eng.com					
HF Lenz Co 1407 Scalp Ave	Johnstown	PA	15904	814-269-9300	269-9301
Web: www.hflenz.com					
High Technology Solutions Inc 4810 Eastgate Mall	San Diego	CA	92124	858-495-0508	495-0511
TF: 800-411-8483 ■ *Web:* www.htshq.com					
Hill International Inc 303 Lippincott Ctr	Marlton	NJ	08053	856-810-6200	810-0404
Web: www.hillintl.com					
Hillier Architecture Group 500 Alexander Pk	Princeton	NJ	08543	609-452-8888	452-8332
Web: www.hillier.com					
HKM Engineering PO Box 3588	Butte	MT	59702	406-723-8213	723-8328
Web: www.hkminc.com					
HKS Inc 1919 McKinney Ave	Dallas	TX	75201	214-969-5599	969-3397
Web: www.hksinc.com					
HLM Design Inc 121 W Trade St Suite 2950	Charlotte	NC	28202	704-358-0779	358-0229
Web: www.hlmdesign.com					
HLW International 115 5th Ave 5th Fl	New York	NY	10003	212-353-4600	353-4666
TF: 888-353-4601 ■ *Web:* www.hlw.com					
HMB Professional Engineers Inc 3 HMB Cir	Frankfort	KY	40601	502-695-9800	695-9810
Web: www.hmbconsultants.com					
HMC Archtiect 3270 Inland Empire Blvd	Ontario	CA	91764	909-989-9979	483-1400
TF: 800-350-9979 ■ *Web:* www.hmcgroup.com					
HNTB Corp 715 Kirk Dr	Kansas City	MO	64105	816-472-1201	472-4060
Web: www.hntb.com					

				Phone	Fax
Howard R Green Co 8710 Earhart Ln SW	Cedar Rapids	IA	52404	319-841-4000	841-4012
TF: 800-728-7805 ■ *Web:* www.hrgreen.com					
Howe-Baker Engineers Inc PO Box 956	Tyler	TX	75710	903-597-0311	595-7751
HPD Systems 23562 W Main St	Plainfield	IL	60544	815-609-2000	609-0490
TF: 800-927-0319 ■ *Web:* www.hpdsystems.com					
HSB Group Inc 1 State St PO Box 5024	Hartford	CT	06102	860-722-1866	722-5106
TF: 800-472-1866 ■ *Web:* www.hsb.com					
Hubbell Roth & Clark Inc 555 Hulet Dr PO Box 824	Bloomfield Hills	MI	48303	248-454-6300	338-2592
Web: www.hrc-engr.com					
Huitt-Zollars Inc 3131 McKinney Ave Suite 600	Dallas	TX	75204	214-871-3311	871-0757
Web: www.huitt-zollars.com					
Hunsaker & Assoc Irvine Inc 3 Hughes	Irvine	CA	92618	949-583-1010	583-0759
Web: www.hunsaker.com					
Hussey Gay Bell & DeYoung Inc					
329 Commercial Dr Suite 200	Savannah	GA	31406	912-354-4626	354-6754
Web: www.hgbd.com					
HW Lochner Inc 20 N Wacker Dr Suite 1200	Chicago	IL	60606	312-372-7346	372-8208
TF: 800-327-7346 ■ *Web:* www.hwlochner.com					
HWS Consulting Group Inc 825 J St	Lincoln	NE	68508	402-479-2200	479-2276
Web: www.hws-con.com					
ICF Consulting 9300 Lee Hwy	Fairfax	VA	22031	703-934-3000	934-3740
Web: www.icfconsulting.com					
IDEO 100 Forest Ave	Palo Alto	CA	94301	650-688-3400	289-3707
Web: www.ideo.com					
Inco Inc PO Box 2705	Rocky Mount	NC	27802	252-446-1174	977-3039
Inland Waters Pollution Control Inc 2021 S Schaefer Hwy	Detroit	MI	48217	313-841-5800	841-5270
TF: 800-992-9118 ■ *Web:* www.inlandwaters.com					
Intrinsix Corp 33 Lyman St	Westborough	MA	01581	508-836-4100	836-4222
TF: 800-783-0330 ■ *Web:* www.intrinsix.com					
Ionics Resources Conservation Co					
3006 Northup Way Suite 200	Bellevue	WA	98004	425-828-2400	828-0526
Jacobs Engineering Group Inc					
1111 S Arroyo Pkwy PO Box 7084	Pasadena	CA	91105	626-578-3500	578-6914*
NYSE: JEC ■ **Fax:* Hum Res ■ *Web:* www.jacobs.com					
Jacobs Facilities 1527 Cole Blvd	Golden	CO	80401	303-462-7000	462-7001
Web: www.jacobs.com					
Jeter Cook & Jepson Architects Inc 450 Church St	Hartford	CT	06103	860-247-9226	524-8067
Web: www.jcj.com					
JF Barton Contracting Co PO Box 73525	Houston	TX	77273	281-443-3800	443-0649
TF: 800-222-1472					
John A Martin & Assoc Inc 1212 S Flower St	Los Angeles	CA	90015	213-483-6490	483-3084
Web: www.johnmartin.com					
Johnson Fain 1201 N Broadway	Los Angeles	CA	90012	323-224-6000	224-6030
Web: www.jfpartners.com					
Johnson Mirmiran & Thompson 72 Loveton Cir	Sparks	MD	21152	410-329-3100	472-2200
TF: 800-472-2310 ■ *Web:* www.jmt-engineering.com					
Jones Edmunds & Assoc Inc 730 NE Waldo Rd	Gainesville	FL	32641	352-377-5821	377-3166
Web: www.jonesedmunds.com					
Jones & Stokes Assoc Inc 2600 V St	Sacramento	CA	95818	916-737-3000	737-3030
Web: www.jonesandstokes.com					
Jordan Jones & Goulding Inc 6801 Governors Lake Pkwy	Norcross	GA	30071	770-455-8555	455-7391
TF: 800-545-2373 ■ *Web:* www.jjg.com					
Joseph R Loring & Assoc 21 Pennsylvania Plaza 14th Fl	New York	NY	10001	212-563-7400	563-7382
Web: www.loringengineers.com					
Kadrmas Lee & Jackson Inc 677 27th Ave E PO Box 290	Dickinson	ND	58602	701-483-1284	483-2795
Web: www.kljeng.com					
Kahn Albert Assoc Inc 7430 2nd Ave Albert Kahn Bldg	Detroit	MI	48202	313-202-7000	202-7001
Web: www.albertkahn.com					
Kajima USA Inc 1251 Ave of the Americas 9th Fl	New York	NY	10020	212-355-4571	355-4576
Web: www.kajimausa.com					
Kaplan McLaughlin Diaz 222 Vallejo St 4th Fl	San Francisco	CA	94111	415-398-5191	394-7158
Web: www.kmd-arch.com					
KBR Inc 4100 Clinton Dr	Houston	TX	77020	713-753-3011	753-5353
TF: 800-231-8166 ■ *Web:* www.halliburton.com/kbr/index.jsp					
KCI Technologies Inc 10 N Park Dr	Hunt Valley	MD	21030	410-316-7800	316-7817
TF: 800-572-7496 ■ *Web:* www.kci.com/tech					
Keith Cos Inc 19 Technology Dr	Irvine	CA	92618	949-923-6000	923-6117
TF: 800-735-3484 ■ *Web:* www.keithco.com					
Keith & Schnars PA 6500 N Andrews Ave	Fort Lauderdale	FL	33309	954-776-1616	771-7690
Web: www.keithandschnars.com					
Kennedy/Jenks Consultants 622 Folsom St	San Francisco	CA	94107	415-243-2150	896-0999
Web: www.kennedyjenks.com					
Kimball L Robert & Assoc Inc 615 W Highland Ave	Ebensburg	PA	15931	814-472-7700	472-7712
Web: www.lrkimball.com					
Kinney AM Inc 150 E 4th St	Cincinnati	OH	45202	513-421-2265	421-2264
TF: 800-265-3682 ■ *Web:* www.amkinney.com					
Kirkham Michael Inc 12700 W Dodge Rd PO Box 542030	Omaha	NE	68154	402-393-5630	255-3850
Web: www.kirkham.com					
Kirksey 6909 Portwest Dr	Houston	TX	77024	713-850-9600	850-7308
Web: www.kirksey.com					
Kisinger Campo & Assoc Corp 2203 N Lois Ave Suite 1200	Tampa	FL	33607	813-871-5331	871-5135
Web: www.kcaeng.com					
KJWW Engineering Consultants PC 623 26th Ave	Rock Island	IL	61201	309-788-0673	786-5967
Web: www.kjww.com					
KKE Architects Inc 300 1st Ave N	Minneapolis	MN	55401	612-339-4200	342-9267
TF: 888-408-8569 ■ *Web:* www.kke.com					
Kleinfelder Inc 5015 Shoreham Pl	San Diego	CA	92122	858-320-2000	320-2001
Web: www.kleinfelder.com					
Kling 2301 Chestnut St	Philadelphia	PA	19103	215-569-2900	569-5963
TF: 800-888-2054 ■ *Web:* www.kling.us					
Kohn Pedersen Fox Assoc PC 111 W 57th St	New York	NY	10019	212-977-6500	956-2526
Web: www.kpf.com					
Koltanbar Engineering Co PO Box 3456	Troy	MI	48007	248-362-2400	362-2316
Web: www.koltanbar.com					
KPFF Consulting Engineers Inc 1601 5th Ave Suite 1600	Seattle	WA	98101	206-622-5822	622-8130
Web: www.kpff.com					
Krazan & Assoc Inc 215 W Dakota Ave	Clovis	CA	93612	559-348-2200	348-2201
Web: www.krazan.com					
L Robert Kimball & Assoc Inc 615 W Highland Ave	Ebensburg	PA	15931	814-472-7700	472-7712
Web: www.lrkimball.com					
Langan Engineering & Environmental Services Inc					
River Drive Center 1	Elmwood Park	NJ	07407	201-794-6900	794-7501
TF: 800-352-6426 ■ *Web:* www.langan.com					
Langdon Wilson Architecture Planning Interiors					
1055 Wilshire Blvd Suite 1500	Los Angeles	CA	90017	213-250-1186	482-4654
Web: www.langdonwilson.com					
Lawler Matusky & Skelly Engineers LLP 1 Blue Hill Plaza	Pearl River	NY	10965	845-735-8300	735-7466
Web: www.lmseng.com					
LBA Group Inc 3400 Tupper Dr	Greenville	NC	27834	252-757-0279	752-9155
TF: 800-522-4464 ■ *Web:* www.lbagroup.com					
Lee Burkhart Liu Inc 13335 Maxella Ave	Marina del Rey	CA	90292	310-829-2249	829-1736
Web: www.lblarch.com					
Lee Monte R & Co 100 NW 63rd St Suite 100	Oklahoma City	OK	73116	405-842-2405	848-8018
Web: www.mrleng.com					
Legat Architects Inc 24 N Chapel St Legat Ctr	Waukegan	IL	60085	847-263-3535	249-0436
Web: www.legat.com					

	City	State	ZIP	Phone	Fax
Leighton Group Inc 17781 Cowan St	Irvine	CA	92614	949-250-1421	250-1114
Web: www.leightongroup.com					
LeMessurier Consultants 675 Massachusetts Ave	Cambridge	MA	02139	617-868-1200	661-7520
Web: www.lemessurier.com					
Leo A Daly 8600 Indian Hills Dr	Omaha	NE	68114	402-391-8111	391-8564
Web: www.leoadaly.com					
LFR Inc 194 Forbes Rd Suite 100	Braintree	MA	02184	781-356-7300	356-2211
Web: www.lfr.com					
Lichtenstein Consulting Engineers 45 Eisenhower Dr	Paramus	NJ	07652	201-368-0400	368-7740
Web: www.lichtensteinengineers.com					
Lin TY International 2 Harrison St Suite 500	San Francisco	CA	94111	415-291-3700	433-0807
Web: www.tylin.com					
Lionakis Beaumont Design Group Inc 1919 19th St	Sacramento	CA	95814	916-558-1900	558-1919
Web: www.lbdg.com					
LiRo Group 6 Aerial Way	Syosset	NY	11791	516-938-5476	938-5491
Web: www.liro.com					
LJB Inc 3100 Research Blvd PO Box 20246	Dayton	OH	45420	937-259-5000	259-5100
TF: 866-552-3536 ■ *Web:* www.ljbinc.com					
LMN Architects 801 2nd Ave Suite 501	Seattle	WA	98104	206-682-3460	343-9388
TF: 800-966-3087 ■ *Web:* www.lmnarchitects.com					
Lockwood Andrews & Newnam Inc 2925 Briar Pk Dr	Houston	TX	77042	713-266-6900	266-2089
Web: www.lan-inc.com					
Lockwood Greene Engineers Inc PO Box 491	Spartanburg	SC	29304	864-578-2000	599-6400
Web: www.lg.com					
Lockwood Kessler & Bartlett Inc 1 Aerial Way	Syosset	NY	11791	516-938-0600	931-6344
Web: www.lkbinc.com					
Lohan Caprile Goettsch Architects 224 S Michigan Ave 17th Fl	Chicago	IL	60604	312-356-0600	356-0601
Web: www.lohan.com					
Loiederman Soltesz Assoc 1390 Piccard Dr Suite 100	Rockville	MD	20850	301-948-2750	948-6321
Web: www.lsassociates.net					
Looney Ricks Kiss Architects 175 Toyota Plaza Suite 600	Memphis	TN	38103	901-521-1440	525-2760
Web: www.lrk.com					
Louis Berger Group Inc 100 Halsted St	East Orange	NJ	07018	973-678-1960	672-4284
TF: 800-323-4098 ■ *Web:* www.louisberger.com					
LPA Group Inc 700 Huger St	Columbia	SC	29201	803-254-2211	779-8749
Web: www.lpagroup.com					
LPA Inc 5161 California Ave Suite 100	Irvine	CA	92612	949-261-1001	260-1190
Web: www.lpairvine.com					
LS3P Assoc Ltd 205 1/2 King St	Charleston	SC	29401	843-577-4444	722-4789
Web: www.ls3p.com					
LZA Assoc 641 Ave of the Americas 7th & 8th Fls	New York	NY	10011	917-661-7800	661-7801
Web: www.lzaassociates.com					
M-E Engineers Inc 10055 W 43rd Ave	Wheat Ridge	CO	80033	303-421-6655	421-0331
Web: www.me-engineers.com					
M & W Zander US Operations Inc 549 W Randolph St 1st Fl	Chicago	IL	60661	312-577-3200	577-3525
Web: www.mw-zander.com					
MacKay & Somps 5142 Franklin Dr Suite C	Pleasanton	CA	94588	925-416-1790	
Web: www.msce.com					
Magnusson Klemencic Assoc Inc 1301 5th Ave Suite 3200	Seattle	WA	98101	206-292-1200	292-1201
Web: www.mka.com					
Maguire Group Inc 33 Commercial St Suite 1	Foxboro	MA	02035	508-543-1700	543-5157
Web: www.maguiregroup.com					
Malcolm Pirnie Inc 104 Corporate Park Dr	White Plains	NY	10602	914-694-2100	694-9286
TF: 800-759-5020 ■ *Web:* www.pirnie.com					
Malouf Engineering International Inc					
17950 Preston Rd Suite 720	Dallas	TX	75252	972-783-2578	783-2583
Web: www.maloufengineering.com					
MAR Inc 1803 Research Blvd Suite 204	Rockville	MD	20850	301-231-0100	453-9871*
**Fax Area Code: 240* ■ *Web:* www.marinc.com					
MARISA Industries Inc 2965 LaPere Rd	Auburn Hills	MI	48326	248-475-9600	475-9908
Web: www.marisaind.com					
Mark Thomas & Co Inc 1960 Zanker Rd	San Jose	CA	95112	408-453-5373	453-5390
Web: www.markthomas.com					
Marshall Miller & Assoc					
Rt 720 Bluefield Industrial Pk PO Box 848	Bluefield	VA	24605	276-322-5467	322-3102
Web: www.mma1.com					
Martin John A & Assoc Inc 1212 S Flower St	Los Angeles	CA	90015	213-483-6490	483-3084
Web: www.johnmartin.com					
Maser Consulting PA					
331 Newman Springs Rd 1 River Centre Bldg 2	Red Bank	NJ	07701	732-383-1950	383-1984
Web: www.maserconsulting.com					
Mason & Hanger Group Inc 300 W Vine St Suite 1300	Lexington	KY	40507	859-252-9980	389-8870
TF: 800-586-2766 ■ *Web:* www.mhgrp.com					
MBH Architects 1115 Atlantic Ave	Alameda	CA	94501	510-865-8663	865-1611
TF: 888-689-8880 ■ *Web:* www.mbharch.com					
McClier Corp 401 E Illinois St Suite 625	Chicago	IL	60611	312-373-7700	373-7710
Web: www.mcclier.com					
McCormick Taylor & Assoc Inc 2 Commerce Sq 10th Fl	Philadelphia	PA	19103	215-592-4200	592-0682
Web: www.mccormicktaylor.com					
McDonough Assoc Inc 130 E Randolph St Suite 1000	Chicago	IL	60601	312-946-8600	946-7199
Web: www.maiengr.com					
MCG Architecture 1055 E Colorado Blvd Suite 400	Pasadena	CA	91106	626-793-9119	796-9295
Web: www.mcgarchitecture.com					
McKim & Creed PA 243 N Front St	Wilmington	NC	28401	910-343-1048	251-8282
Web: www.mckimcreed.com					
McLaughlin Research Corp 132 Johnnycake Hill Rd	Middletown	RI	02842	401-849-4010	847-9716
TF: 800-556-7154 ■ *Web:* www.mrcds.com					
McMahon Group 1445 McMahon Dr	Neenah	WI	54956	920-751-4200	751-4284
Web: www.mcmgrp.com					
Mead & Hunt Inc 6501 Watts Rd	Madison	WI	53719	608-273-6380	273-6391
Web: www.meadhunt.com					
Merrick & Co 2450 S Peoria St	Aurora	CO	80014	303-751-0741	751-2581
TF: 800-544-1714 ■ *Web:* www.merrick.com					
Metcalf & Eddy Inc 701 Edgewater Dr	Wakefield	MA	01880	781-246-5200	245-6293
Web: www.m-e.aecom.com					
Michael Baker Corp 100 Airsite Dr Airsite Business Pk	Moon Township	PA	15108	412-269-6300	375-3977
AMEX: BKR ■ *TF:* 800-553-1153 ■ *Web:* www.mbakercorp.com					
Middough Assoc Inc 1901 E 13th St	Cleveland	OH	44114	216-771-2060	367-6024*
**Fax: Hum Res* ■ *Web:* www.middough.com					
Midrex Technologies 2725 Water Ridge Pkwy Suite 100	Charlotte	NC	28217	704-373-1600	373-1611
Web: www.midrex.com					
MILCOM Systems Corp 532 Viking Dr	Virginia Beach	VA	23452	757-463-2800	463-3052
TF: 800-967-0966 ■ *Web:* www.milcomsystems.com					
Miller Architects & Builders Inc PO Box 1228	Saint Cloud	MN	56302	320-251-4109	251-4693
TF: 800-772-1758 ■ *Web:* www.millerab.com					
Miller & Lents Ltd 1100 Louisiana St 27th Fl	Houston	TX	77002	713-651-9455	654-9914
Web: www.millerandlents.com					
Modern Engineering Inc 633 South Blvd Suite 200	Rochester Hills	MI	48307	248-606-6100	606-0281
TF: 800-875-6423 ■ *Web:* www.modernengineering.com					
Modjeski & Masters Inc PO Box 2345	Harrisburg	PA	17105	717-790-9565	790-9564
Web: www.modjeski.com					
Moffatt & Nichol Engineers 320 Golden Shore Suite 300	Long Beach	CA	90802	562-590-6500	590-6512
Web: www.moffattnichol.com					
Monte R Lee & Co 100 NW 63rd St Suite 100	Oklahoma City	OK	73116	405-842-2405	848-8018
Web: www.mrleng.com					
Moody Nolan Inc 300 Spruce St Suite 300	Columbus	OH	43215	614-461-4664	280-8881
TF: 877-530-4984 ■ *Web:* www.moodynolan.com					
Moreland & Altobelli Assoc Inc					
2211 Beaver Ruin Rd Suite 190	Norcross	GA	30071	770-263-5945	263-0166
TF: 800-899-4689 ■ *Web:* www.moreland-altobelli.com					
Morris Architects 1001 Fannin St Suite 300	Houston	TX	77002	713-622-1180	622-7021
Web: www.morrisarchitects.com					
Morrison-Maierle Inc PO Box 6147	Helena	MT	59604	406-442-3050	442-8962
Web: www.m-m.net					
MS Consultants Inc 333 E Federal St	Youngstown	OH	44503	330-744-5321	744-5256
Web: www.msconsultants.com					
MSX International Inc 1950 Concept Dr	Warren	MI	48091	248-829-6300	
Web: www.msxi.com					
MTC Technologies Inc 4032 Linden Ave	Dayton	OH	45432	937-252-9199	258-3863
NASDAQ: MTCT ■ *Web:* www.mtctechnologies.com					
Mueser Rutledge Consulting Engineers 14 Penn Plaza 2nd Fl	New York	NY	10122	917-339-9300	339-9400
Web: www.mrce.com					
MulvanneyG2 Architecture 1110 112th Ave NE Suite 500	Bellevue	WA	98004	425-463-2000	463-2002
Web: www.mulvannyg2.com					
Mustang Engineering LP 16001 Park Ten Pl	Houston	TX	77084	713-215-8000	215-8506
Web: www.mustangeng.com					
MWH 301 North Lake Ave Suite 600	Pasadena	CA	91101	626-796-9141	568-6101
Web: www.mwhglobal.com					
Nadel Architects 1990 S Bundy Dr 4th Fl	Los Angeles	CA	90025	310-826-2100	826-0182
Web: www.nadelarc.com					
NBBJ 223 Yale Ave N	Seattle	WA	98109	206-223-5555	621-2300
Web: www.nbbj.com					
Neel-Schaffer Inc 666 North St Suite 201	Jackson	MS	39202	601-948-3071	948-3178
Web: www.neel-schaffer.com					
Neff Engineering Co 7114 Innovation Blvd	Fort Wayne	IN	46818	260-489-6007	489-6204
Web: www.neffengineering.com					
Nelson Waldemar S & Co Inc 1200 St Charles Ave	New Orleans	LA	70130	504-523-5281	523-4587
Web: www.wsnelson.com					
Newcomb & Boyd 303 Peachtree Ctr Ave NE Suite 525	Atlanta	GA	30303	404-730-8400	730-8401
Web: www.newcomb-boyd.com					
Niles Bolton Assoc Inc					
3060 Peachtree Rd NW Suite 600 1 Buckhead Plaza	Atlanta	GA	30305	404-365-7600	365-7610
Web: www.nilesbolton.com					
Ninyo & Moore 5710 Ruffin Rd	San Diego	CA	92123	858-576-1000	576-9600
TF: 800-427-0401 ■ *Web:* www.ninyoandmoore.com					
Nolte Assoc Inc 1750 Creekside Oaks Dr Suite 200	Sacramento	CA	95833	916-641-9100	641-9222
TF: 800-216-6583 ■ *Web:* www.nolte.com					
Northwestern Engineering Co PO Box 2624	Rapid City	SD	57709	605-394-3310	341-2558
Web: www.nwemanagement.com					
Nova Group Inc 7411 Napa-Vallejo Hwy	Napa	CA	94558	707-257-3200	257-2774
Web: www.novagrp.com					
NTD Stichler 2025 Financial Way Suite 106	Glendora	CA	91741	626-963-1401	963-5771
Web: www.ntdstichler.com					
O'Brien & Gere Engineers Inc 5000 Brittonfield Pkwy	East Syracuse	NY	13057	315-437-6100	463-7554
Web: www.obg.com					
Odell Assoc Inc 800 W Hill St 3rd Fl	Charlotte	NC	28208	704-414-1000	414-1111
Web: www.odell.com					
Olsson Assoc 1111 Lincoln Mall	Lincoln	NE	68508	402-474-6311	474-5160
Web: www.oaconsulting.com					
O'Neal Inc 10 Falcon Crest Dr	Greenville	SC	29607	864-298-2000	298-2200
Web: www.onealinc.com					
Operational Technologies Corp					
4100 NW Loop 410 Suite 230	San Antonio	TX	78229	210-731-0000	731-0008
TF: 800-677-8072 ■ *Web:* www.otcorp.com					
Orbital Engineering Inc 1344 5th Ave	Pittsburgh	PA	15219	412-261-9100	261-5351
Web: www.orbitalengr.com					
Orchard Hiltz & McCliment Inc 34000 Plymouth Rd	Livonia	MI	48150	734-522-6711	522-6427
Web: www.ohm-eng.com					
Ortloff Engineers Ltd 415 W Wall Ave Suite 2000	Midland	TX	79701	432-685-0277	685-0258
Web: www.ortloff.com					
Otak Inc 17355 SW Boones Ferry Rd	Lake Oswego	OR	97035	503-635-3618	635-5395
Web: www.otak.com					
Outokumpu Livernois Engineering Co 25315 Kean St	Dearborn	MI	48124	313-278-0200	278-5992
TF: 800-900-0200					
Overlook Systems Technologies Inc					
1950 Old Gallows Rd Suite 400	Vienna	VA	22182	703-893-1411	356-9029
Web: www.overlooksys.com					
Owen Group Inc 20 Morgan	Irvine	CA	92618	949-860-4800	860-4810
TF: 800-600-6936 ■ *Web:* www.owengroup.com					
Pace Resources Inc 40 S Richland Ave	York	PA	17404	717-852-1300	852-1301
TF: 800-274-2224					
Pacific Architects & Engineers Inc					
888 S Figueroa St Suite 1700	Los Angeles	CA	90017	213-481-2311	481-7189
Web: www.paegroup.com					
Pacifica Services Inc 106 S Mentor Ave Suite 200	Pasadena	CA	91106	626-405-0131	405-0059
Web: www.pacificaservices.com					
PageSoutherlandPage 1100 Louisiana St Suite 1	Houston	TX	77002	713-871-8484	871-8440
Web: www.pspaec.com					
Pape-Dawson Engineers Inc 555 E Ramsey	San Antonio	TX	78216	210-375-9000	375-9010
Web: www.pape-dawson.com					
Paragon Engineering Services Inc 10777 Clay Rd	Houston	TX	77041	713-570-1000	570-8910
TF: 800-324-7272 ■ *Web:* www.paraengr.com					
Parametrix Inc 1231 Fryar Ave	Sumner	WA	98390	253-863-5128	863-0946
Web: www.parametrix.com					
Parkhill Smith & Cooper Inc 4222 85th St	Lubbock	TX	79423	806-473-2200	473-3500
Web: www.team-psc.com					
Parsons 100 Summer St Suite 800	Boston	MA	02110	617-457-7900	457-7979
Web: www.parsons.com					
Parsons Brinckerhoff Inc 1 Penn Plaza 2nd Fl	New York	NY	10119	212-465-5000	465-5096
Web: www.pbworld.com					
Parsons Corp 100 W Walnut St	Pasadena	CA	91124	626-440-2000	440-2630
TF: 800-883-7300 ■ *Web:* www.parsons.com					
Parsons Energy & Chemicals Group Inc 5 Greenway Plaza	Houston	TX	77046	713-407-5000	407-5089
Parsons Harland Bartholomew & Assoc Inc					
400 Woods Mill Rd S Suite 330	Chesterfield	MO	63017	314-434-2900	576-2702
Web: www.parsons.com					
Parsons Infrastructure & Technology 100 W Walnut St	Pasadena	CA	91124	626-440-4000	440-6200
TF: 800-883-7300 ■ *Web:* www.parsons.com					
Parsons PFI 150 Federal St	Boston	MA	02110	617-946-9400	
TF: 800-555-0532 ■ *Web:* www.pfi.com					
Parsons Transportation Group 1133 15th St NW Suite 800	Washington	DC	20005	202-775-3300	775-3422
Patrick Engineering Inc 4970 Varsity Dr	Lisle	IL	60532	630-795-7200	724-1681
Web: www.patrickengineering.com					
Patton Harris Rust & Assoc PC 14532 Lee Rd	Chantilly	VA	20151	703-449-6700	449-6713
TF: 800-550-7472 ■ *Web:* www.phra.com					
Paulus Sokolowski & Sartor LLC 67A Mountain Blvd Ext	Warren	NJ	07059	732-560-9700	
Web: www.psands.com					
Payette Assoc Inc 285 Summer St	Boston	MA	02210	617-895-1000	895-1002
Web: www.payette.com					
PB-KBB Inc 11757 Katy Fwy Suite 600	Houston	TX	77079	281-496-5590	589-5865
Web: www.pbworld.com					
Pei Cobb Freed & Partners Architects LLP 88 Pine St	New York	NY	10005	212-751-3122	872-5443
Web: www.pcfandp.com					

				Phone	Fax
Pennoni Assoc Inc 3001 Market St.	Philadelphia	PA	19104	215-222-3000	222-3588
Web: www.pennoni.com					
Perkins Eastman Architects 115 5th Ave.	New York	NY	10003	212-353-7200	353-7676
Web: www.perkinseastman.com					
Perkins & Will 330 N Wabash Ave Suite 3600	Chicago	IL	60611	312-755-0770	755-0775
TF: 800-837-9455 ■ *Web:* www.perkinswill.com					
Perkowitz + Ruth Architects 111 W Ocean Blvd 21st Fl	Long Beach	CA	90802	562-628-8000	628-8001
Web: www.prarchitects.com					
Petrocon Engineering Inc PO Box 20397	Beaumont	TX	77720	409-840-2100	840-2200
TF: 800-256-5710 ■ *Web:* www.petrocon.com					
Phillips Swager Assoc 401 SW Water St Suite 701	Peoria	IL	61602	309-282-8000	282-8001
Web: www.psa-ae.com					
Pierce Goodwin Alexander & Linville					
5555 San Felipe St Suite 1000	Houston	TX	77056	713-622-1444	968-9333
Web: www.pgal.com					
Pittsburgh Design Services Inc PO Box 469	Carnegie	PA	15106	412-276-3000	276-1216
Poggemeyer Design Group Inc 1168 N Main St.	Bowling Green	OH	43402	419-352-7537	353-0187
Web: www.poggemeyer.com					
Polshek Partnership LLP 320 W 13 St.	New York	NY	10014	212-807-7171	807-5917
TF: 800-939-7790 ■ *Web:* www.polshek.com					
Post Buckley Schuh & Jernigan 2001 NW 107th Ave	Miami	FL	33172	305-592-7275	599-3809*
**Fax:* Mktg ■ *TF:* 800-597-7275 ■ *Web:* www.pbsj.com					
Power Engineering Corp PO Box 766	Wilkes-Barre	PA	18703	570-823-8822	823-8143
TF: 800-626-0903 ■ *Web:* www.powerengineeringcorp.com					
Power Engineers Inc PO Box 1066	Hailey	ID	83333	208-788-3456	788-2082
TF: 800-331-3902 ■ *Web:* www.powereng.com					
PPM Consultants Inc 2508 Ticheli Rd	Monroe	LA	71202	318-323-7270	323-6593
TF: 800-761-8675 ■ *Web:* www.ppmco.com					
Preston Partnership LLC 1000 Abernathy Rd NE Suite 600	Atlanta	GA	30328	770-396-7248	396-2945
Web: www.theprestonpartnership.com					
Product Development Technologies Inc 600 Heathrow Dr	Lincolnshire	IL	60069	847-821-3000	821-3030
TF: 800-747-6600 ■ *Web:* www.pdt.com					
Professional Engineering Consultants PA 303 S Topeka St	Wichita	KS	67202	316-262-2691	262-3003
Web: www.pec1.com					
Professional Service Industries Inc					
1901 S Meyers Rd Suite 400	Oakbrook Terrace	IL	60181	630-691-1490	691-1587
TF: 800-426-2897 ■ *Web:* www.psiusa.com					
ProjectDesign Consultants 701 B St Suite 800	San Diego	CA	92101	619-235-6471	234-0349
Web: www.projectdesign.com					
Psomas & Assoc 11444 W Olympic Blvd Suite 750	West Los Angeles	CA	90064	310-954-3700	954-3777
Web: www.psomas.com					
Qk4 815 W Market St Suite 300	Louisville	KY	40202	502-585-2222	581-0406
TF: 800-928-2222 ■ *Web:* www.qk4.com					
Quality Control Design Inc					
50495 Corporate Dr Suite 112	Shelby Township	MI	48315	586-726-6237	726-6325
Raymond Professional Group 550 W Van Buren St Suite 400	Chicago	IL	60607	312-935-3200	935-3201
Web: www.raymondgroup.com					
RBA Group Inc 1 Evergreen Pl PO Box 1927	Morristown	NJ	07962	973-898-0300	984-5421
Web: www.rbagroup.com					
RBF Consulting 14725 Alton Pkwy	Irvine	CA	92618	949-472-3505	472-8373
TF: 800-479-3808 ■ *Web:* www.rbf.com					
RD Zande & Assoc Inc 11500 Northlake Dr Suite 150	Cincinnati	OH	45249	513-769-5009	769-5030
TF: 800-340-2743 ■ *Web:* www.zande.com					
Reimelt Corp 13330 Byrd Dr.	Odessa	FL	33556	813-920-7434	920-3864
Web: www.reimelt.com					
Remington & Vernick Engineers Inc 232 Kings Hwy E	Haddonfield	NJ	08033	856-795-9595	795-1882
Web: www.rve.com					
Rentenbach Engineering Co 2400 Sutherland Ave	Knoxville	TN	37919	865-546-2440	546-3414
TF: 800-621-4941 ■ *Web:* www.rentenbach.com					
Research Management Consultants Inc					
816 Camarillo Springs Rd Suite J	Camarillo	CA	93012	805-987-5538	987-2868
Web: www.rmci.com					
Resource Consultants Inc 2650 Park Tower Dr Suite 800	Vienna	VA	22180	571-226-5000	573-8215*
**Fax Area Code:* 703 ■ *Web:* www.resourceconsultants.com					
Rettew Assoc Inc 3020 Columbia Ave	Lancaster	PA	17603	717-394-3721	394-1063
TF: 800-738-8395 ■ *Web:* www.rettew.com					
Reynolds Smith & Hills Inc 10748 Deerwood Park Blvd S	Jacksonville	FL	32256	904-256-2500	256-2501
TF: 800-741-2014 ■ *Web:* www.rsandh.com					
RG Vanderweil Engineers Inc 274 Summer St.	Boston	MA	02210	617-423-7423	423-7401
TF: 800-726-2840 ■ *Web:* www.vanderweil.com					
RM Towill Corp 420 Waiakamilo Rd Suite 411	Honolulu	HI	96817	808-842-1133	842-1937
Web: www.rmtowill.com					
RMT Inc 744 Heartland Trail	Madison	WI	53717	608-831-4444	831-3334
TF: 800 283 3443 ■ *Web:* www.rmtinc.com					
RNL Design 1515 Arapahoe St Tower 3 Suite 700	Denver	CO	80202	303-295-1717	292-0845
Web: www.rnldesign.com					
Roberts & Schaefer Co 222 S Riverside Plaza Suite 1800	Chicago	IL	60606	312-236-7292	726-2872
Web: www.r-s.com					
Ross & Baruzzini 6 S Old Orchard Ave	Webster Groves	MO	63119	314-918-8383	918-1766
Web: www.rossbar.com					
Rosser International 524 W Peachtree St NW	Atlanta	GA	30308	404-876-3800	888-6863*
**Fax:* Hum Res ■ *Web:* www.rosser.com					
Rothenbuhler Engineering 524 Rhodes Rd PO Box 708	Sedro Woolley	WA	98284	360-856-0836	856-2183
Web: www.rothenbuhlereng.com					
RSP Architects 1220 Marshall St NE	Minneapolis	MN	55413	612-677-7100	677-7499
Web: www.rsparch.com					
RTKL Assoc Inc 901 S Bond St.	Baltimore	MD	21231	410-537-6000	276-2136
TF: 800-345-7855 ■ *Web:* www.rtkl.com					
Rummel Klepper & Kahl LLP 81 Mosher St	Baltimore	MD	21217	410-728-2900	728-0282
TF: 800-787-3755 ■ *Web:* www.rkkengineers.com					
S & B Engineers & Constructors Ltd 7825 Park Place Blvd	Houston	TX	77087	713-645-4141	643-8029
Web: www.sbec.com					
S E A Consultants Inc 485 Massachusetts Ave	Cambridge	MA	02139	617-497-7800	498-4630
Web: www.seacon.com					
S Systems Corp 5777 W Century Blvd Suite 520	Los Angeles	CA	90045	310-215-0248	642-3738
Web: www.s-sc.com					
SA Healy Co 1910 S Highland Ave Suite 300	Lombard	IL	60148	630-678-3110	678-3130
TF: 888-724-3259 ■ *Web:* www.sahealy.com					
SAI Consulting Engineers Inc 1400 Penn Ave Suite 101	Pittsburgh	PA	15222	412-392-8750	392-8785
Web: www.saiengr.com					
Sandwell Inc 2300 Lake Pk Dr Suite 150	Smyrna	GA	30080	770-433-9336	433-9518
Web: www.sandwell.com					
Sargent & Lundy LLC 55 E Monroe St	Chicago	IL	60603	312-269-2000	269-3454
Web: www.sargentlundy.com					
Sasaki Assoc Inc 64 Pleasant St	Watertown	MA	02472	617-926-3300	924-2748
Web: www.sasaki.com					
Scale Models Unlimited 400 S Front St Suite 300	Memphis	TN	38103	901-577-5155	577-5157
Web: www.smu.com					
Schafer Corp 321 Billerica Rd	Chelmsford	MA	01824	978-256-2070	256-1404*
**Fax:* Hum Res ■ *Web:* www.schafercorp.com					
SchenkelShultz Architects 111 E Wayne St Suite 555	Fort Wayne	IN	46802	260-424-9080	424-1222
Web: www.schenkelshultz.com					
Schnabel Engineering Inc 1054 Technology Park Dr.	Glen Allen	VA	23059	804-264-3222	264-3244
Web: www.schnabel-eng.com					
Schneider Corp 8901 Otis Ave	Indianapolis	IN	46216	317-826-7100	826-7200
TF: 800-898-0332 ■ *Web:* www.theschneidercorp.com					

				Phone	Fax
Schoor DePalma Inc PO Box 900	Manalapan	NJ	07726	732-577-9000	577-9888
Web: www.schoordepalma.com					
Scientech Inc 200 S Woodruff Ave.	Idaho Falls	ID	83401	208-529-1000	524-9282
TF: 800-247-8818 ■ *Web:* www.scientech.com					
SCS Engineers 3711 Long Beach Blvd 9th Fl	Long Beach	CA	90807	562-426-9544	427-0805
TF: 800-326-9544 ■ *Web:* www.scsengineers.com					
SE Technologies Inc 98 Vanadium Rd Bldg D 2nd Fl	Bridgeville	PA	15017	412-221-1100	257-6103
TF: 800-685-0354 ■ *Web:* www.vanadium.com/companies/se.html					
Sear-Brown Group 85 Metro Park	Rochester	NY	14623	585-272-1814	427-9124
TF: 800-724-4131 ■ *Web:* www.searbrown.com					
Sebesta Blomberg & Assoc Inc 2381 Rosegate	Roseville	MN	55113	651-634-0775	634-7400
TF: 877-706-6858 ■ *Web:* www.sebesta.com					
SECOR International Inc 12034 134th Ct NE Suite 102	Redmond	WA	98052	425-372-1600	372-1688
Web: www.secor.com					
SENTEL Corp 2800 Eisenhower Ave Suite 300	Alexandria	VA	22314	703-739-0084	739-6028
Web: www.sentel.com					
SFA Inc 2200 Defense Hwy Suite 405	Crofton	MD	21114	301-858-1230	858-1233
TF: 800-787-2732 ■ *Web:* www.sfa.com					
Shannon & Wilson Inc PO Box 300303	Seattle	WA	98103	206-632-8020	633-6777
TF: 800-633-6800 ■ *Web:* www.shannonwilson.com					
Sharp George C Inc 100 Church St 14th Fl	New York	NY	10007	212-732-2800	732-2809
Web: www.georgesharp.com					
Shaw Stone & Webster Inc 100 Technology Center Dr	Stoughton	MA	02072	617-589-5111	589-2156
Sheladia Assoc Inc 15825 Shady Grove Rd Suite 100	Rockville	MD	20850	301-590-3939	948-7174
Web: www.sheladia.com					
Shepley Bulfinch Richardson & Abbott Inc 2 Seaport Ln	Boston	MA	02210	617-423-1700	451-2420
Web: www.sbra.com					
Shive-Hattery Inc PO Box 1803	Cedar Rapids	IA	52406	319-364-0227	364-4251
TF: 800-798-0227 ■ *Web:* www.shive-hattery.com					
Short-Elliott-Hendrickson Inc 3535 Vadnais Ctr Dr	Saint Paul	MN	55110	651-490-2000	490-2150
TF: 800-325-2055 ■ *Web:* www.sehinc.com					
SHW Group Inc 4000 McEwen Rd N	Dallas	TX	75244	972-701-0700	701-0799
Web: www.shwgroup.com					
Simpson Gumpertz & Heger Inc 41 Seyon St Bldg 1 Suite 500	Waltham	MA	02453	781-907-9000	907-9009
Web: www.sgh.com					
SJB Group Inc PO Box 1751	Baton Rouge	LA	70821	225-769-3400	769-3596
Web: www.sjbgroup.com					
Skelly & Loy Inc 2601 N Front St.	Harrisburg	PA	17110	717-232-0593	232-1799
TF: 800-892-5653 ■ *Web:* www.skellyloy.com					
Skidmore Owings & Merrill 224 S Michigan Ave Suite 1000	Chicago	IL	60604	312-554-9090	360-4545
Web: www.som.com					
S/L/A/M Collaborative 80 Glastonbury Blvd	Glastonbury	CT	06033	860-657-8077	657-3141
Web: www.slamcoll.com					
Smallwood Reynolds Stewart Stewart & Assoc Inc					
3565 Piedmont Rd Bldg 1 Suite 303	Atlanta	GA	30305	404-233-5453	264-0929
Web: www.srssa.com					
Smith Wilbur Assoc Inc PO Box 92	Columbia	SC	29202	803-758-4500	758-4610
Web: www.wilbursmith.com					
SmithGroup Inc 500 Griswold St Suite 1700	Detroit	MI	48226	313-983-3600	983-3636
Web: www.smithgroup.com					
SMMA (Symmes Maini & McKee Assoc)					
1000 Massachusetts Ave	Cambridge	MA	02138	617-547-5400	354-5758
Web: www.smma.com					
SMS Demag Inc 100 Sandusky St.	Pittsburgh	PA	15212	412-231-1200	231-3995
SNC Lavalin Group Inc 455 boul Rene Levesque O	Montreal	QC	H2Z1Z3	514-393-1000	866-0795
TSX: SNC ■ *Web:* www.snc-lavalin.com					
Sofec Inc 14741 Yorktown Plaza	Houston	TX	77070	713-510-6600	510-6601
TF: 800-462-6003					
Sonalysts Inc 215 Parkway N	Waterford	CT	06385	860-442-4355	447-8883
TF: 800-526-8091 ■ *Web:* www.sonalysts.com					
Southern Co Services Inc 42 Inverness Center Pkwy	Birmingham	AL	35242	205-992-6011	
SPACECO Inc 9575 W Higgins Rd Suite 700	Rosemont	IL	60018	847-696-4060	696-4065
TF: 888-772-2326 ■ *Web:* www.spacecoinc.com					
SPEC Services Inc 17101 Bushard St	Fountain Valley	CA	92708	714-963-8077	963-0364
Web: www.specservices.com					
Spillis Candela DMJM					
800 Douglas Entrance North Tower 2nd Fl	Coral Gables	FL	33134	305-444-4691	447-3580
TF: 800-999-4727 ■ *Web:* www.scpmiami.com					
SRF Consulting Group Inc 1 Carlson Pkwy N Suite 150	Minneapolis	MN	55447	763-475-0010	475-2429
Web: www.srfconsulting.com					
SSOE Inc 1001 Madison Ave	Toledo	OH	43624	419-255-3830	255-6101
Web: www.ssoe.com					
Stanley Consultants Inc 225 Iowa Ave.	Muscatine	IA	52761	563-264-6600	264-6658
Web: www.stanleygroup.com					
Stantec Inc 10160-112 St.	Edmonton	AB	T5K2L6	780-917-7000	917-7330
NYSE: SXC ■ *Web:* www.stantec.com					
Stellar Engineering Inc 5505 E 13-Mile Rd	Warren	MI	48092	586-978-8444	978-2315
Web: www.stellar-eng.com					
Strand Assoc Inc 910 W Wingra Dr	Madison	WI	53715	608-251-4843	251-8655
Web: www.strand.com					
Stratasys Inc 14950 Martin Dr	Eden Prairie	MN	55344	952-937-3000	
NASDAQ: SSYS ■ *Web:* www.stratasys.com					
STS Consultants Ltd 750 Corporate Woods Pkwy	Vernon Hills	IL	60061	847-279-2500	279-2510
TF: 800-859-7871 ■ *Web:* www.stsconsultants.com					
Stubbins Assoc 1030 Massachusetts Ave	Cambridge	MA	02138	617-491-6450	491-7104
Web: www.tsa-arch.com					
Studios Architecture 99 Green St.	San Francisco	CA	94111	415-398-7575	398-3829
Web: www.studiosarch.com					
STV Group Inc 205 W Welsh Dr	Douglassville	PA	19518	610-385-8200	385-8505
Web: www.stvinc.com					
STV Inc 225 Park Ave S 5th Fl	New York	NY	10003	212-777-4400	777-8463
Web: www.stvinc.com					
Sullivan International Group Inc					
409 Camino Del Rio S Suite 100	San Diego	CA	92108	619-260-1432	260-1421
TF: 888-744-1432 ■ *Web:* www.onesullivan.com					
Swanke Hayden Connell Ltd 295 Lafayette St	New York	NY	10012	212-226-9696	219-0059
Web: www.shca.com					
Symmes Maini & McKee Assoc (SMMA)					
1000 Massachusetts Ave	Cambridge	MA	02138	617-547-5400	354-5758
Web: www.smma.com					
Syska & Hennessy Group 11 W 42nd St	New York	NY	10036	212-921-2300	556-3333
TF: 800-328-1600 ■ *Web:* www.syska.com					
Systems & Electronics Inc 201 Evans Ln	Saint Louis	MO	63121	314-553-4600	553-4215*
**Fax:* Hum Res ■ *Web:* www.seistl.com					
T Moriarty & Son Inc 63 Creamer St	Brooklyn	NY	11231	718-858-4800	624-4059
Tait & Assoc Inc 701 N Parkcenter Dr	Santa Ana	CA	92705	714-560-8200	560-8244
Web: www.tait.com					
Tampa Bay Engineering Group Inc					
380 Park Pl Blvd Suite 300	Clearwater	FL	33759	727-531-3505	539-1294
TF: 800-861-8314 ■ *Web:* www.tbegroup.com					
Taylor Wiseman & Taylor 124 Gaither Dr Suite 150	Mount Laurel	NJ	08054	856-235-7200	722-9250
Web: www.taylorwiseman.com					
TECO Solutions 702 N Franklin St.	Tampa	FL	33602	813-228-1111	228-1527
Web: www.tecosolutions.com					
Teledyne Brown Engineering PO Box 070007	Huntsville	AL	35807	256-726-1000	726-3570*
**Fax:* Hum Res ■ *TF:* 800-933-2091 ■ *Web:* www.tbe.com					

Company	City	State	Zip	Phone	Fax
Terracon 16000 College Blvd *Web:* www.terracon.com	Lenexa	KS	66219	913-599-6886	599-0574
Testwell Laboratories Inc 47 Hudson St *TF:* 800-444-9013 ■ *Web:* www.testwelllabs.com	Ossining	NY	10562	914-762-9000	762-9638
Tetra Tech EC Inc 1000 The American Rd *TF:* 800-580-3765 ■ *Web:* www.tteci.com	Morris Plains	NJ	07950	973-630-8000	630-8165
Tetra Tech Inc 3475 E Foothill Blvd *NASDAQ: TTEK* ■ *Web:* www.tetratech.com	Pasadena	CA	91107	626-351-4664	351-5291
Tetra Tech MPS 710 Avis Dr *Web:* www.ttmps.com	Ann Arbor	MI	48108	734-665-6000	665-2570
Tetra Tech/KCM 1420 5th Ave Suite 600 *TF:* 800-443-5540 ■ *Web:* www.ttkcm.com	Seattle	WA	98101	206-883-9300	883-9301
Thomas Design & Engineering Service Co Inc 2029 S Elms Rd	Swartz Creek	MI	48473	810-733-6080	733-2995
Thompson Ventulett Stainback & Assoc Inc 1230 Peachtree St NE 2700 Promenade 2 *Web:* www.tvsa.com	Atlanta	GA	30309	404-888-6600	888-6700
Thornton-Tomasetti Group Inc 2000 L St NW Suite 840 *Web:* www.thettgroup.com	Washington	DC	20036	202-822-8222	822-8330
Tighe & Bond Inc 53 Southampton Rd *Web:* www.tighebond.com	Westfield	MA	01085	413-562-1600	562-5317
Timmons Group Inc 1001 Boulders Pkwy Suite 300 *Web:* www.timmons.com	Richmond	VA	23225	804-794-3500	794-7639
TLC Engineering for Architecture 1717 S Orange Ave Suite 300 *TF:* 800-835-9926 ■ *Web:* www.tlc-engineers.com	Orlando	FL	32806	407-841-9050	835-9926
TMAD Inc 320 N Halstead St Suite 200 *Web:* www.tmadengineers.com	Pasadena	CA	91107	626-351-8881	351-5319
TMP Architecture 1191 W Square Lake Rd Box 289 *Web:* www.tmp-architecture.com	Bloomfield Hills	MI	48302	248-338-4561	338-0223
Toledo Engineering Co Inc 3400 Executive Pkwy PO Box 2927 *Web:* www.teco.com	Toledo	OH	43606	419-537-9711	537-1369
Tolz King Duvall Anderson & Assoc Inc 444 Cedar St Suite 1500 *TF:* 800-247-1714 ■ *Web:* www.tkda.com	Saint Paul	MN	55101	651-292-4400	292-0083
Towill RM Corp 420 Waiakamilo Rd Suite 411 *Web:* www.rmtowill.com	Honolulu	HI	96817	808-842-1133	842-1937
Trandes Corp 4601 Presidents Dr Suite 360 *TF:* 800-878-0201 ■ *Web:* www.trandes.com	Lanham	MD	20706	301-459-0200	459-1069
TransCore Holdings Inc 8158 Adams Dr Bldg 200 *TF:* 800-233-2172 ■ *Web:* www.transcore.com	Hummelstown	PA	17036	717-561-2400	561-5939
TranSystems Corp 2400 Pershing Rd Suite 400 *Web:* www.transystems.com	Kansas City	MO	64108	816-329-8700	329-8703
TRC Worldwide Engineering Inc 217 Ward Cir *Web:* www.trcworldwide.com	Brentwood	TN	37027	615-661-7979	661-0644
TRO/The Richie Organization 80 Bridge St *Web:* www.troarch.com	Newton	MA	02458	617-969-9400	527-6753
Tsoi/Kobus & Assoc Inc 1 Brattle Sq PO Box 9114 *Web:* www.tka-architects.com	Cambridge	MA	02238	617-475-4000	475-4445
Turner Collie & Braden Inc PO Box 130089 *Web:* www.tcb.aecom.com	Houston	TX	77219	713-780-4100	780-0838
TY Lin International 2 Harrison St Suite 500 *Web:* www.tylin.com	San Francisco	CA	94111	415-291-3700	433-0807
UEC Technologies LLC 600 Grant St Rm 1614 *TF:* 800-245-4450 ■ *Web:* www.ussteel.com/corp/facilities/divisions/uec.htm	Pittsburgh	PA	15219	412-433-6527	433-6100
UFE Inc PO Box 7 *Web:* www.ufeinc.com	Stillwater	MN	55082	651-351-4100	351-4101
Ulteig Engineers Inc 3350 38th Ave S PO Box 9615 *TF:* 888-557-9090 ■ *Web:* www.ulteig.com	Fargo	ND	58104	701-237-3211	237-3191
Unidyne Corp 3835 E Princess Anne Rd	Norfolk	VA	23502	757-855-8037	853-3046
Unified Industries Inc 6551 Loisdale Ct Suite 400 *Web:* www.uii.com	Springfield	VA	22150	703-922-9800	971-5892
Universal Ensco Inc 4848 Loop Central Dr *TF:* 800-966-1811 ■ *Web:* www.uei-houston.com	Houston	TX	77081	713-977-7770	977-1047
Unwin Scheben Korynta Huettl Inc 2515 A St *TF:* 888-706-8754 ■ *Web:* www.uskh.com	Anchorage	AK	99503	907-276-4245	258-4653
Urbahn Architects 49 W 37th St 6th Fl *Web:* www.urbahn.com	New York	NY	10018	212-239-0220	563-5621
Urban Engineers Inc 530 Walnut St 14th Fl *Web:* www.urbanengineers.com	Philadelphia	PA	19106	215-922-8080	922-8082
Urbitran Group 71 W 23rd St 11th Fl *Web:* www.urbitran.com	New York	NY	10010	212-366-6200	366-6214
URS Corp 600 Montgomery St 25th Fl *NYSE: URS* ■ *Web:* www.urscorp.com	San Francisco	CA	94111	415-774-2700	398-1905
US Laboratories Inc 7895 Convoy Ct Suite 18 *TF:* 800-487-0355 ■ *Web:* www.uslaboratories.com	San Diego	CA	92111	858-715-5800	715-5810
Utility Engineering Corp Park Central Bldg 1515 Arapahoe St Tower 1 Suite 800 *Web:* www.ue-corp.com	Denver	CO	80202	303-928-4400	928-4368
Van Dijk Westlake Reed Leskosky 925 Euclid Ave Suite 1900 *Web:* www.vwrl.com	Cleveland	OH	44115	216-522-1350	522-1357
Vanadium Group Corp 134 Three Degree Rd *TF:* 800-685-0354 ■ *Web:* www.vanadium.com	Pittsburgh	PA	15237	412-367-6060	630-8430
Vanasse Hangen Brustlin Inc 101 Walnut St *Web:* www.vhb.com	Watertown	MA	02472	617-924-1770	924-2286
Vanderweil RG Engineers Inc 274 Summer St *TF:* 800-726-2840 ■ *Web:* www.vanderweil.com	Boston	MA	02210	617-423-7423	423-7401
Versar Inc 6850 Versar Ctr *AMEX: VSR* ■ *TF Cust Svc:* 800-283-7727 ■ *Web:* www.versar.com	Springfield	VA	22151	703-750-3000	642-6825
Vitetta 4747 S Broad St Philadelphia Naval Business Ctr *Web:* www.vitetta.com	Philadelphia	PA	19112	215-218-4747	218-4740
VOA Assoc Inc 224 S Michigan Ave Suite 1400 *Web:* www.voa.com	Chicago	IL	60604	312-554-1400	554-1412
Volkert & Assoc Inc 3809 Moffett Rd *TF:* 800-340-1070 ■ *Web:* www.volkert.com	Mobile	AL	36618	251-342-1070	342-7962
Vollmer Assoc 50 W 23rd St 8th Fl *TF:* 800-564-3434 ■ *Web:* www.vollmer.com	New York	NY	10010	212-366-5600	366-5629
Volt Telecom Group Inc 6400 Regency Pkwy Suite 650 *TF:* 800-521-8658 ■ *Web:* www.volt-telecom.com	Norcross	GA	30071	770-441-1331	662-5684
VSE Corp 2550 Huntington Ave *NASDAQ: VSEC* ■ *TF:* 800-455-4873 ■ *Web:* www.vsecorp.com	Alexandria	VA	22303	703-960-4600	329-4623
W & H Pacific 3350 Monte Villa Pkwy *Web:* www.whpacific.com	Bothell	WA	98021	425-951-4800	951-4808
Wade-Trim Group Inc 25251 Northline Rd *TF:* 800-482-2864 ■ *Web:* www.wadetrim.com	Taylor	MI	48180	734-947-9700	947-9726
Waldemar S Nelson & Co Inc 1200 St Charles Ave *Web:* www.wsnelson.com	New Orleans	LA	70130	504-523-5281	523-4587
Walker Parking Consultants/Restoration Engineers Inc 2121 Hudson Ave *Web:* www.walkerparking.com	Kalamazoo	MI	49008	269-381-6080	343-5811
Wallace Roberts & Todd LLC 1700 Market St 28th Fl *TF:* 800-978-4450 ■ *Web:* www.wrtdesign.com	Philadelphia	PA	19103	215-732-5215	732-2551
Walt Disney Imagineering 1401 Flower St PO Box 25020	Glendale	CA	91221	818-544-6500	544-7995
Walter P Moore 3131 Eastside St 2nd Fl *Web:* www.walterpmoore.com	Houston	TX	77098	713-630-7300	630-7396
Ware Malcomb 10 Edelman *Web:* www.waremalcomb.com	Irvine	CA	92618	949-660-9128	863-1581
Washington Corp PO Box 16630 *TF:* 800-832-7329 ■ *Web:* www.washcorp.com	Missoula	MT	59808	406-523-1300	523-1399
Washington Group International Inc PO Box 73 *NASDAQ: WGII* ■ **Fax:* Mktg ■ *Web:* www.wgint.com	Boise	ID	83729	208-386-5000	386-5658*
Watkins Hamilton Ross Architects Inc 1111 Louisiana St Suite 2600 *Web:* www.whrarchitects.com	Houston	TX	77002	713-665-5665	665-6213
WD Partners 1201 Dublin Rd *Web:* www.wdpartners.com	Columbus	OH	43215	614-221-0840	221-2484
Weidlinger Assoc 375 Hudson St 12th Fl *Web:* www.wai.com	New York	NY	10014	212-367-3000	367-3030
Westinghouse Electric Co PO Box 355 *Web:* www.westinghouse.com	Pittsburgh	PA	15230	412-374-4111	
Weston & Sampson Engineers Inc 5 Centennial Dr *TF:* 800-726-7766 ■ *Web:* www.wseinc.com	Peabody	MA	01960	978-532-1900	977-0100
Weston Solutions Inc 1400 Weston Way PO Box 2653 **Fax:* Hum Res ■ *TF:* 800-793-7866 ■ *Web:* www.westonsolutions.com	West Chester	PA	19380	610-692-3030	701-3795*
Whitman Requardt & Assoc 801 S Caroline St *TF:* 800-787-7100 ■ *Web:* www.wrallp.com	Baltimore	MD	21231	410-235-3450	243-5716
Whitney Bailey Cox & Magnani LLC 849 Fairmount Ave Suite 100 *Web:* www.wbcm.com	Baltimore	MD	21286	410-512-4500	324-4100
Wight & Co 2500 N Frontage Rd *Web:* www.wightco.com	Darien	IL	60561	630-969-7000	969-7979
Wilbur Smith Assoc Inc PO Box 92 *Web:* www.wilbursmith.com	Columbia	SC	29202	803-758-4500	758-4610
Willbros Engineers Inc 2087 E 71st St *TF:* 800-434-8970 ■ *Web:* www.willbros.com	Tulsa	OK	74136	918-496-0400	491-9436
Willdan 2401 E Katella Ave Suite 200 *TF:* 800-424-9144 ■ *Web:* www.willdan.com	Anaheim	CA	92806	714-940-6300	978-8299
Wilson & Co Inc 1700 E Iron Ave *Web:* www.wilsonco.com	Salina	KS	67401	785-827-0433	827-5949
WilsonMiller Inc 3200 Bailey Ln Suite 200 *TF:* 800-649-4336 ■ *Web:* www.wilsonmiller.com	Naples	FL	34105	239-649-4040	643-5716
Wimberly Allison Tong & Goo 700 Bishop St Suite 1800 *Web:* www.watg.com	Honolulu	HI	96813	808-521-8888	521-3888
Wink Inc 8641 United Plaza Blvd Suite 204 *Web:* www.winkinc.com	Baton Rouge	LA	70809	225-932-6000	932-9035
Winzler & Kelly Consulting Engineers 633 3rd St *Web:* www.w-and-k.com	Eureka	CA	95501	707-443-8326	444-8330
Wiss Janney Elstner Assoc Inc 330 Pfingsten Rd *TF:* 800-345-3199 ■ *Web:* www.wje.com	Northbrook	IL	60062	847-272-7400	291-9599
Wolfberg Alvarez & Partners 1500 San Remo Ave Suite 300 *Web:* www.wolfbergalvarez.com	Coral Gables	FL	33146	305-666-5474	666-4994
Woodard & Curran 41 Hutchins Dr *TF:* 800-426-4262 ■ *Web:* www.woodardcurran.com	Portland	ME	04102	207-774-2112	271-7952
Woolpert Inc 409 E Monument Ave *Web:* www.woolpert.com	Dayton	OH	45402	937-461-5660	461-0743
Zimmer Gunsul Frasca Partnership 320 SW Oak St Suite 500 *Web:* www.zgf.com	Portland	OR	97204	503-224-3860	224-2482

265 ENGINES & TURBINES

SEE ALSO Aircraft Engines & Engine Parts p. 1271; Automotive Parts & Supplies - Mfr p. 1360; Motors (Electric) & Generators p. 1983

Company	City	State	Zip	Phone	Fax
Alaska Diesel Electric Inc 4420 14th Ave NW *TF:* 800-762-0165 ■ *Web:* www.northern-lights.com	Seattle	WA	98107	206-789-3880	782-5455
Alturdyne Inc 660 Steele St *Web:* www.alturdyne.com	El Cajon	CA	92020	619-440-5531	442-0481
Arrow Engine Co 2301 E Independence St *TF:* 800-331-3662 ■ *Web:* www.arrowengines.com	Tulsa	OK	74110	918-583-5711	592-1481
Bombardier Recreational Products 565 de la Montagne *Web:* www.brp.com	Valcourt	QC	J0E2L0	450-532-2211	
Briggs & Stratton Corp PO Box 702 *NYSE: BGG* ■ *TF:* 800-444-7774 ■ *Web:* www.briggsandstratton.com	Milwaukee	WI	53201	414-259-5333	
Brunswick Corp 1 N Field Ct *NYSE: BC* ■ *Web:* www.brunswick.com	Lake Forest	IL	60045	847-735-4700	735-4765
Brunswick Corp Mercury Marine Div W 6250 Pioneer Rd *Web:* www.mercurymarine.com	Fond du Lac	WI	54935	920-929-5000	929-5781
Capstone Turbine Corp 21211 Nordhoff St *NASDAQ: CPST* ■ *Web:* www.microturbine.com	Chatsworth	CA	91311	818-734-5300	734-5320
Cascade Engine Center LLC 9800 40th Ave S *TF:* 800-238-3850 ■ *Web:* www.cascadediesel.com	Seattle	WA	98118	206-764-3850	764-3832
Caterpillar Inc 100 NE Adams St *NYSE: CAT* ■ **Fax:* PR ■ *Web:* www.cat.com	Peoria	IL	61629	309-675-1000	675-4332*
Caterpillar Remanufacturing Franklin 751 International Dr *TF Cust Svc:* 800-837-7697 ■ *Web:* www.franklinpower.com	Franklin	IN	46131	317-738-2117	738-4614
Chromium Corp 14911 Quorum Dr Suite 600 *Web:* www.chromcorp.com	Dallas	TX	75254	972-851-0460	851-0461
Clayton Industries 17477 Hurley St *TF:* 800-423-4585 ■ *Web:* www.claytonindustries.com	City of Industry	CA	91744	626-435-1200	435-0180
Concentric Inc 800 Hollywood Ave *Web:* www.concentricinc.com	Itasca	IL	60143	630-773-3355	773-1119
Cummins Inc 1000 5th St PO Box 3005 *NYSE: CMI* ■ *TF:* 800-343-7357 ■ *Web:* www.cummins.com	Columbus	IN	47201	812-377-5000	377-3334
DaimlerChrysler Corp 1000 Chrysler Dr *NYSE: DCX* ■ **Fax:* Cust Svc ■ *TF:* 800-992-1997 ■ *Web:* www.daimlerchrysler.com	Auburn Hills	MI	48326	248-576-5741	512-8084*
Deere & Co John Deere Power Systems Div 3801 W Ridgeway Ave *Web:* www.deere.com/en_US/rg	Waterloo	IA	50701	319-292-5643	292-5364
Delaware Mfg Industries Corp 3775 Commerce Ct *TF:* 800-248-3642 ■ *Web:* www.dmic.com	Wheatfield	NY	14120	716-743-4360	743-4370
Detroit Diesel Corp 13400 Outer Dr W *Web:* www.detroitdiesel.com	Detroit	MI	48239	313-592-5000	592-7580
Dresser Inc Waukesha Engine Div 1101 W St Paul Ave *Web:* waukeshaengine.dresser.com	Waukesha	WI	53188	262-547-3311	549-2795
Dresser-Rand Co Control Systems Div 1202 W Sam Houston Pkwy N *Web:* www.dresser-rand.com/controls	Houston	TX	77043	713-467-2221	365-2661
Dresser-Rand Co Steam Products Div 37 Coats St PO Box 592 *TF:* 800-828-2818 ■ *Web:* www.dresser-rand.com/steam	Wellsville	NY	14895	585-596-3100	593-5815
Dresser-Rand Steam Turbines 1106 Washington St PO Box 967 *Web:* www.dresser-rand.com	Burlington	IA	52601	319-753-5431	752-1616
Dresser-Rand Steam Turbines 299 Lincoln St *Web:* www.dresser-rand.com	Worcester	MA	01605	508-595-1700	595-1786
Electro Steam Generator Corp 50 Indel Ave *TF:* 800-634-8177 ■ *Web:* www.electrosteam.com	Rancocas	NJ	08073	609-288-9071	288-9078

Company	City	State	ZIP	Phone	Fax
Elliott Turbomachinery Co 901 N 4th St *TF:* 800-635-2208 ■ *Web:* www.elliott-turbo.com	Jeannette	PA	15644	724-527-2811	600-8442
EnPro Industries Inc 5605 Carnegie Blvd Suite 500 *NYSE: NPO* ■ *TF:* 866-663-6776 ■ *Web:* www.enproindustries.com	Charlotte	NC	28209	704-731-1500	731-1511
EnPro Industries Inc Fairbanks Morse Engine 701 White Ave *Fax: Mktg ■ *TF:* 800-356-6955 ■ *Web:* www.fairbanksmorse.com	Beloit	WI	53511	608-364-4411	364-8302*
Fairbanks Morse Engine EnPro Industries Inc 701 White Ave *Fax: Mktg ■ *TF:* 800-356-6955 ■ *Web:* www.fairbanksmorse.com	Beloit	WI	53511	608-364-4411	364-8302*
GE Aviation 1 Neumann Way *Web:* www.geaviation.com	Cincinnati	OH	45215	513-243-2000	
GE Energy 4200 Wildwood Pkwy *Fax Area Code: 800 ■ *TF:* 800-368-1316 ■ *Web:* www.gepower.com	Atlanta	GA	30339	770-859-6000	368-1317*
Globe Turbocharger Specialties Inc 201 Edison Way *Web:* www.globeturbocharger.com	Reno	NV	89502	775-856-7337	856-7338
Gopher Motor Rebuilding Inc 6530 James Ave N *TF:* 800-328-3994 ■ *Web:* www.gopherengines.com	Minneapolis	MN	55430	763-746-3440	746-3449
H & H Mfg Co Inc 2 Horne Dr	Folcroft	PA	19032	610-532-8100	461-4620
Hatch & Kirk Inc 5111 Leary Ave NW *TF:* 800-426-2818 ■ *Web:* www.hatchkirk.com	Seattle	WA	98107	206-783-2766	782-6482
HDM Hydraulics LLC 125 Fire Tower Dr *Web:* www.hdmco.com	Tonawanda	NY	14150	716-694-8004	694-4164
Hercules Engine Components Co 2770 S Erie St *TF:* 800-345-0662 ■ *Web:* www.herculesenginecompany.com	Massillon	OH	44646	330-830-2498	830-4081
Ingersoll-Rand Co 155 Chestnut Ridge Rd *NYSE: IR* ■ *Web:* www.irco.com	Montvale	NJ	07645	201-573-0123	573-3172
International Truck & Engine Corp 4201 Winfield Rd *Web:* www.navistar.com	Warrenville	IL	60555	630-753-5000	753-6888
JASPER Engines & Transmissions 815 Wernsing Rd PO Box 650 *TF:* 800-827-7455 ■ *Web:* www.jasperengines.com	Jasper	IN	47547	812-482-1041	634-1820
John Deere Power Systems Div Deere & Co 3801 W Ridgeway Ave *Web:* www.deere.com/en_US/rg	Waterloo	IA	50701	319-292-5643	292-5364
KMS Ventures Inc 1301 W 25th St Suite 300	Austin	TX	78705	512-474-6312	474-6389
Kohler Engines 444 Highland Dr *Fax: Sales ■ *TF:* 800-544-2444 ■ *Web:* www.kohlerengines.com	Kohler	WI	53044	920-457-4441	459-1570*
LM Glasfiber ND Inc 1580 S 48th St *Web:* www.lmglasfiber.com	Grand Forks	ND	58201	701-780-9910	780-9920
Marine Power Holding LLC 17506 Marine Power Industrial Park *Web:* www.marinepowerusa.com	Ponchatoula	LA	70454	985-386-2081	386-4010
Mercury Marine Div Brunswick Corp W 6250 Pioneer Rd *Web:* www.mercurymarine.com	Fond du Lac	WI	54935	920-929-5000	929-5781
Mercury Marine Ltd 2395 Meadowpine Blvd *Web:* www.mercurymarine.com	Mississauga	ON	L5N7W6	905-567-6372	567-7970
NREC Power Systems 5222 Hwy 311 *TF:* 800-851-6732 ■ *Web:* www.nrecps.com	Houma	LA	70360	985-872-5480	872-0611
Penske Corp Rt 10 Green Hills PO Box 563 *Fax: Acctg ■ *TF:* 800-222-0277 ■ *Web:* www.penske.com	Reading	PA	19603	610-775-6000	775-5064*
Pratt & Whitney Canada Inc 1000 Marie-Victorin Blvd *TF:* 800-268-8000 ■ *Web:* www.pwc.ca	Longueuil	QC	J4G1A1	450-677-9411	647-2888
Pratt & Whitney Power Systems Inc 80 Lamberton Rd *TF:* 800-525-8199	Windsor	CT	06095	860-565-5776	565-4619
Renk Corp 304 Tucapau Rd	Duncan	SC	29334	864-433-0069	433-0636
Rolls-Royce Energy System Inc 105 N Sandusky St *Web:* www.rolls-royce.com/energy	Mount Vernon	OH	43050	740-393-8888	393-8336
Salem Preferred Partners LLC 236 Rowan St *Web:* www.spplc.com	Salem	VA	24153	540-389-3922	389-3926
Sierra International Inc 1 Sierra Pl *TF:* 800-468-3976 ■ *Web:* www.sierramarine.com	Litchfield	IL	62056	217-324-9400	324-4396
Solar Turbines Inc 2200 Pacific Hwy *Fax: Sales ■ *Web:* mysolar.cat.com	San Diego	CA	92101	619-544-5000	544-2849*
Springfield ReManufacturing Corp 650 N Broadview Pl *TF:* 800-772-7733 ■ *Web:* www.srcreman.com	Springfield	MO	65802	417-862-3501	864-0625
SRC Holdings Corp 3140 E Division St	Springfield	MO	65802	417-862-4510	863-9778
Technetics Corp 1700 E International Speedway Blvd *Web:* www.techneticsfl.com	DeLand	FL	32724	386-736-7373	738-4533
TKA Atlas Inc 901 S US Rt 23	Fostoria	OH	44830	419-435-8531	436-5442
Unisom Engine Components 333 S 3rd St	Terre Haute	IN	47807	812-234-1591	231-7200
Voith Siemens Hydro Power 760 E Berlin Rd *Web:* www.voith.com	York	PA	17408	717-792-7000	792-7263
Volvo Penta of the Americas 1300 Volvo Penta Dr *Web:* www.volvopenta.com	Chesapeake	VA	23320	757-436-2800	436-5150
Walker Power Systems 1301 E Jackson St *Fax: Sales ■ *Web:* www.walkerpower.com	Phoenix	AZ	85034	602-257-8505	258-8684*
Wartsila North America Inc 16330 Air Center Blvd *TF:* 800-676-9945 ■ *Web:* www.wartsila.com/usa	Houston	TX	77032	281-233-6200	233-6250
Waukesha Engine Div Dresser Inc 1101 W St Paul Ave *Web:* waukeshaengine.dresser.com	Waukesha	WI	53188	262-547-3311	549-2795
Westerbeke Corp 150 John Hancock Rd Miles Standish Industrial Park *Web:* www.westerbeke.com	Taunton	MA	02780	508-823-7677	884-9688
Western Diesel Services Inc DBA CK Power 1100 Research Blvd *TF:* 800-495-8620 ■ *Web:* www.ckpower.com	Saint Louis	MO	63132	314-868-8620	868-9314
Woodward 5001 N 2nd St *NASDAQ: WGOV* ■ *TF:* 888-273-8839 ■ *Web:* www.woodward.com	Loves Park	IL	61111	815-877-7441	639-6033

266 ENVELOPES

Company	City	State	ZIP	Phone	Fax
ADM Corp 100 Lincoln Blvd *TF:* 800-327-0718 ■ *Web:* www.packinglist.com	Middlesex	NJ	08846	732-469-0900	469-0785
Alvah Bushnell Co 519 E Chelten Ave *TF:* 800-255-7434 ■ *Web:* www.bushnellco.com	Philadelphia	PA	19144	215-842-9520	843-7725
Ambassador Envelope Co 6705 Keaton Corp Pkwy *TF:* 800-325-4510 ■ *Web:* www.ambenv.com	O'Fallon	MO	63368	636-477-1300	477-7648
American Pad & Paper Co LLC 3101 E George Bush Hwy Suite 200 *Web:* www.ampad.com	Richardson	TX	75082	800-426-1368	558-0436
AmericanChurch Inc PO Box 3120 *TF:* 800-431-4134 ■ *Web:* www.apgroup.com	Youngstown	OH	44513	330-758-4545	758-3361
Ames Safety Envelope Co 12 Tyler St *TF:* 800-225-1138 ■ *Web:* www.amespage.com	Somerville	MA	02143	617-776-1142	623-7347
Atlantic Envelope Co 1325 Highlands Ridge Rd *TF:* 800-780-2326 ■ *Web:* www.atlanticenvelope.com	Smyrna	GA	30082	770-779-0111	779-0112
B & W Press Inc 401 E Main St *Web:* www.bwpress.com	Georgetown	MA	01833	978-352-6100	352-5955
Barkley Farling Corp 5370 Hwy 42 *Fax Area Code: 800 ■ *TF:* 800-522-0297	Hattiesburg	MS	39404	601-545-2200	423-7589*
Berlin & Jones Co LLC A Commercial Envelope Co 510 Commercial Ave	Carlstadt	NJ	07072	201-933-5900	933-4242
Bowers Envelope Co 5331 N Tacoma Ave *Web:* www.bowersenvelope.com	Indianapolis	IN	46220	317-253-4321	254-2239
Brenner Paper Products Co Inc 66-31 Otto Rd *TF:* 800-221-6980	Glendale	NY	11385	718-456-7817	497-0433
Cenveo Inc 1 Canterberry Green *NYSE: CVO* ■ *Web:* www.cenveo.com	Stamford	CT	06901	203-595-3000	595-3070
Colfax Envelope Corp 951 Commerce Ct *Web:* www.colfaxenv.com	Buffalo Grove	IL	60089	847-215-1122	215-1145
Colortree Inc of Virginia 8000 Villa Park Dr *TF:* 800-222-2962 ■ *Web:* www.colortreeva.com	Richmond	VA	23228	804-358-4245	358-0488
Curtis 1000 Inc 1725 Breckinridge Pkwy Suite 500 *Fax Area Code: 800 ■ *Fax: Mktg ■ *TF:* 800-683-8162 ■ *Web:* www.curtis1000.com	Duluth	GA	30096	678-380-9095	594-0518*
Envelope Printery Inc 24340 Northline Rd *Web:* www.envelopeprintery.com	Taylor	MI	48180	734-946-8505	946-7560
Federal Envelope Co 608 Country Club Dr *Web:* www.federalenvelope.com	Bensenville	IL	60106	630-595-2000	595-1212
Gaw-O'Hara Envelope Co 500 N Sacramento Blvd *TF:* 888-385-8439 ■ *Web:* www.gawoharaenvelope.com	Chicago	IL	60612	773-638-1200	638-1208
Heinrich Envelope Corp 925 Zane Ave N *TF:* 800-346-7957 ■ *Web:* www.heinrichenvelope.com	Minneapolis	MN	55422	763-544-3571	544-6287
Love Envelopes Inc 10733 E Ute St *TF:* 800-532-9747 ■ *Web:* www.loveenvelopes.com	Tulsa	OK	74116	918-836-3535	832-9978
Mackay Envelope Corp 2100 Elm St SE *TF:* 800-622-5299 ■ *Web:* www.mackayenvelope.com	Minneapolis	MN	55414	612-331-9311	331-8229
MeadWestvaco Corp Envelope Div 2001 Roosevelt Ave *TF:* 800-628-9265 ■ *Web:* www.meadwestvaco.com/cop.nsf	Springfield	MA	01104	413-736-7211	787-9625
Mercury Envelope Co Inc 100 Merrick Rd Suite 204E	Rockville Centre	NY	11570	516-678-6744	678-6764
Motion Envelope Inc 1455 Terre Colony Ct	Dallas	TX	75212	214-634-2131	634-2132
National Envelope Corp 29-10 Hunters Pt Ave *TF:* 800-877-9551 ■ *Web:* www.nationalenvelope.com	Long Island City	NY	11101	718-786-0300	361-3127
Oles Envelope Corp 532 E 25th St *TF:* 800-822-6537 ■ *Web:* www.olesenvelope.com	Baltimore	MD	21218	410-243-1520	243-1541
Papercone Corp 3200 Fern Valley Rd *TF:* 800-626-5308 ■ *Web:* www.papercone.com	Louisville	KY	40213	502-961-9493	961-9346
Poly-Pak Industries Inc 125 Spagnoli Rd *TF:* 800-969-1995 ■ *Web:* www.poly-pak.com	Melville	NY	11747	631-293-6767	454-6366
Quality Park 2520 Como Ave *TF:* 800-328-2990 ■ *Web:* www.qualitypark.com	Saint Paul	MN	55108	651-645-0251	659-3680
Rays Envelope Corp 7521 Pulaski Hwy	Baltimore	MD	21237	410-866-3550	866-6010
Response Envelope Inc 1340 S Baker Ave *TF:* 800-890-5959 ■ *Web:* www.response-envelope.com	Ontario	CA	91761	909-923-5855	923-3639
Roodhouse Envelope Co 414 S State St PO Box A	Roodhouse	IL	62082	217-589-4321	589-4425
Royal Envelope Co 4114 S Peoria St	Chicago	IL	60609	773-376-1212	376-0011
Sealed Air Corp 200 Riverfront Blvd *NYSE: SEE* ■ *Web:* www.sealedaircorp.com	Elmwood Park	NJ	07407	201-791-7600	
Stora Enso North America Corp 2 Landmark Sq 3rd Fl *NYSE: SEO* ■ *TF:* 888-807-8672 ■ *Web:* www.storaenso.com/na	Stamford	CT	06901	203-356-2300	356-2340
Tension Envelope Corp 819 E 19th St *TF:* 800-388-5122 ■ *Web:* www.tension.com	Kansas City	MO	64108	816-471-3800	283-1498
Top Flight Inc 1300 Central Ave *TF:* 800-777-3740 ■ *Web:* www.topflightpaper.com	Chattanooga	TN	37408	423-266-8171	266-6857
Tri-State Envelope Corp 20th & Market Sts 1 Orgler Pl *TF:* 800-233-3102 ■ *Web:* www.tristateenvelope.com	Ashland	PA	17921	570-875-0433	875-0125
Western States Envelope & Label Co 4480 N 132nd St *TF:* 800-558-0514 ■ *Web:* www.wsec.com	Butler	WI	53007	262-781-5540	781-5791
Wisco Envelope Co PO Box 880 *TF:* 800-777-9677 ■ *Web:* www.wiscoenv.com	Tullahoma	TN	37388	931-455-4584	454-0760
Wolf Envelope Co 725 S Adams Rd Suite 275 *TF:* 800-466-9653 ■ *Web:* www.wolfenvelope.com	Birmingham	MI	48009	248-258-5700	646-0350
Worcester Envelope Co 22 Millbury St PO Box 406 *Fax: Sales ■ *TF:* 800-343-1398 ■ *Web:* www.worcesterenvelope.com	Auburn	MA	01501	508-832-5394	832-3796*

267 EQUIPMENT RENTAL & LEASING

SEE ALSO Credit & Financing - Commercial p. 1580; Credit & Financing - Consumer p. 1581; Fleet Leasing & Management p. 1640

267-1 Computer Equipment Leasing

Company	City	State	ZIP	Phone	Fax
All Service Computer Rental 600 Sylvan Ave *TF:* 800-927-6555 ■ *Web:* www.ascr.com	Englewood Cliffs	NJ	07632	201-568-6555	568-4448
Applied Financial Inc 6975 Union Park Ctr Suite 200 *Web:* www.applied-financial.com	Midvale	UT	84047	801-566-9201	566-9306
Computer Sales International Inc (CSI) 9990 Old Olive St Rd *TF:* 800-955-0960 ■ *Web:* www.csileasing.com	Saint Louis	MO	63141	314-997-7010	997-7844
CRA Inc 11011 N 23rd Ave	Phoenix	AZ	85029	602-944-1548	628-7508
CSI (Computer Sales International Inc) 9990 Old Olive St Rd *TF:* 800-955-0960 ■ *Web:* www.csileasing.com	Saint Louis	MO	63141	314-997-7010	997-7844
Data Sales Co Inc 3450 W Burnsville Pkwy *TF:* 800-328-2730 ■ *Web:* www.datasales.com	Burnsville	MN	55337	952-890-8838	895-3369
Econocom USA Inc 6750 Poplar Ave Suite 202 *Web:* www.econocomusa.com	Memphis	TN	38138	901-685-0021	685-1105
El Camino Resources International Inc 6233 Variel Ave *Web:* www.elcamino.com	Woodland Hills	CA	91367	818-226-6600	226-6643
Electro Rent Corp 6060 Sepulveda Blvd *NASDAQ: ELRC* ■ *TF Sales:* 800-688-1111 ■ *Web:* www.electrorent.com	Van Nuys	CA	91411	818-787-2100	786-1827
Forsythe MacArthur Assoc Inc 7770 Frontage Rd *TF:* 800-843-4488 ■ *Web:* www.forsythe.com	Skokie	IL	60077	847-675-8000	675-2130
Halifax Corp 5250 Cherokee Ave *AMEX: HX* ■ *TF Cust Svc:* 800-425-2850 ■ *Web:* www.hxcorp.com	Alexandria	VA	22312	703-750-2202	658-2426
Hitachi Credit America Ltd 800 Connecticut Ave *TF:* 800-810-0952 ■ *Web:* www.hitachicreditamerica.com	Norwalk	CT	06854	203-956-3000	
JP Morgan Leasing Inc 1 Chase Sq *Web:* www.chaseleasing.com	Rochester	NY	14643	585-258-6475	258-6468
LaSalle Systems Leasing Inc 6111 N River Rd *Web:* www.elasalle.com	Rosemont	IL	60018	847-823-9600	823-1646
LEAF Financial Corp 1845 Walnut St Suite 1000	Philadelphia	PA	19103	215-574-1636	569-0675
Leasing Technologies International Inc 221 Danbury Rd *Web:* www.ltionthenet.com	Wilton	CT	06897	203-563-1100	563-1112
Meridian Technology Leasing Services 570 Lake Cook Rd Suite 300 *TF Cust Svc:* 800-426-3090 ■ *Web:* www.meridianleasing.com	Deerfield	IL	60015	847-940-1200	319-2209
Newport Leasing Inc 4750 Von Karman Ave *TF Cust Svc:* 800-678-9426 ■ *Web:* www.newportleasing.com	Newport Beach	CA	92660	949-476-8476	476-9200
Relational Technology Services 7720 Rivers Edge Dr Suite 200 *TF:* 866-999-4787 ■ *Web:* relationaltechnology.com	Columbus	OH	43235	614-431-4433	431-4434
Rent-A-PC Inc 265 Oser Ave *TF:* 877-736-8272 ■ *Web:* www.rentapc.com	Hauppauge	NY	11788	631-273-8888	273-8889
Rush Computer Rentals 29 North Plains Hwy PO Box 811 *TF:* 800-526-7368 ■ *Web:* www.rushcomputer.com	Wallingford	CT	06492	203-284-8277	284-8883

Computer Equipment Leasing (Cont'd)

Phone | Fax

Stamford Computer Group Inc 74 W Park Pl .... Stamford CT 06901 203-324-9495 324-3195
Web: www.scgcomputer.com
Summit Funding Group Inc 11500 Northlake Dr Suite 300 .... Cincinnati OH 45249 513-489-1222 489-1490
Web: www.summit-funding.com
Vicom Computer Services Inc 60 Carolyn Blvd .... Farmingdale NY 11735 631-694-3900 694-2640
Web: www.vicomnet.com

267-2 Home & Office Equipment Rental (General)

Phone | Fax

Aaron Rents Inc 309 E Paces Ferry Rd NE .... Atlanta GA 30305 404-231-0011 402-3567*
NYSE: RNT ■ **Fax Area Code:* 678 ■ **Fax:* Mktg ■ *TF:* 800-551-6015 ■
Web: www.aaronrents.com
Bestway Inc 12400 Coit Rd Suite 950 .... Dallas TX 75251 214-630-6655 630-8404
TF: 800-520-1107 ■ *Web:* www.bestwayrto.com
Brook Furniture Rental Inc 100 Field Dr Suite 220 .... Lake Forest IL 60045 847-810-4000 283-0478*
**Fax:* Cust Svc ■ *TF:* 800-933-7368 ■ *Web:* www.bfr.com
Celtic Leasing Corp 4 Park Plaza Suite 300 .... Irvine CA 92614 949-263-3880 263-1331
Web: www.celticleasing.com
Citicapital 1255 Wrights Ln .... West Chester PA 19380 610-719-4500 682-0600*
**Fax Area Code:* 888 ■ *TF:* 800-736-9033
CORT Business Services Corp 11250 Waples Mill Rd Suite 500 ...... Fairfax VA 22030 703-968-8500 968-8501
TF: 800-962-2678 ■ *Web:* www.cort1.com
CORT Furniture Rental 11250 Waples Mill Rd Suite 500 .... Fairfax VA 22030 703-968-8500 968-8503
TF: 800-962-2678 ■ *Web:* www.cort.net
General Furniture Leasing Co 4209-B Northeast Expy .... Doraville GA 30340 504-736-3606
GFC Leasing Co 2675 Research Park Dr .... Madison WI 53711 608-274-7877 271-9703
TF: 800-333-5905
Grand Rental Station 203 Jandus Rd .... Cary IL 60013 847-462-5440 516-9921
TF: 800-833-3004 ■ *Web:* www.grandrental.com
HSS RentX 1001 E Sunrise Blvd .... Fort Lauderdale FL 33304 954-766-2588 766-9889
TF: 877-711-7368 ■ *Web:* www.hssrentX.com
Initial Tropical Plant Services 3750 W Deerfield Rd .... Riverwoods IL 60015 847-634-4250 634-6820
TF: 800-345-0551 ■ *Web:* www.initialplants.com
Lease One Systems 7305 Manchester Rd Suite C-1 .... Saint Louis MO 63143 314-645-1300 645-2663
TF: 888-645-1300 ■ *Web:* www.lease-one.com
M & C Leasing Co Inc 1050 Union Rd Suite 102 .... West Seneca NY 14224 716-873-6800 873-1002
TF: 800-416-9080
Marlin Business Services Inc DBA Marlin Leasing Corp
124 Gaither Dr Suite 170 .... Mount Laurel NJ 08054 856-727-9526 479-9099*
NASDAQ: MRLN ■ **Fax Area Code:* 888 ■ *TF:* 888-479-9123 ■
Web: www.marlinleasing.com
Marlin Leasing Corp 124 Gaither Dr Suite 170 .... Mount Laurel NJ 08054 856-727-9526 479-9099*
NASDAQ: MRLN ■ **Fax Area Code:* 888 ■ *TF:* 888-479-9123 ■
Web: www.marlinleasing.com
Projection Presentation Technology
5803 Rolling Rd Suite 207 .... Springfield VA 22152 703-912-1334 912-1350
Web: www.projection.com
Rent-A-Center Inc 5700 Tennyson Pkwy .... Plano TX 75024 972-801-1100 943-0112*
NASDAQ: RCII ■ **Fax:* Cust Svc ■ *TF:* 800-275-2696 ■ *Web:* www.rentacenter.com
Rentway Inc 1 Rentway Pl .... Erie PA 16505 814-455-5378 461-5400
NYSE: RWY ■ *TF:* 800-736-8929 ■ *Web:* www.rentway.com
Rug Doctor LP 4701 Old Shepard Pl .... Plano TX 75093 972-673-1400 673-1401
TF: 800-234-6286 ■ *Web:* www.rugdoctor.com
Somerset Capital Group Ltd 1087 Broad St Suite 301 .... Bridgeport CT 06604 203-394-6182 394-6192
Web: www.somersetcapital.com
Taylor Rental 203 Jandus Rd .... Cary IL 60013 847-462-5440 516-9921
TF: 800-833-3004 ■ *Web:* www.taylorrental.com
Television Rental Co Inc 5502 Broadway .... Woodside NY 11377 718-458-2211 672-7223
TF: 888-875-8872 ■ *Web:* www.tvrc.com
Tri-Rentals Inc 3103 E Broadway Suite 400 .... Phoenix AZ 85040 602-232-9900 232-6001
TF: 800-678-3854 ■ *Web:* www.trirentals.com

267-3 Industrial & Heavy Equipment Rental

Phone | Fax

Able Builders Equipment Inc 7475 NW 63rd St .... Miami FL 33166 305-592-5940 592-2783
TF: 800-864-5387 ■ *Web:* www.ablebuildersequipment.com
Aero Rental Inc 3808 E Golf Links Rd .... Tucson AZ 85713 520-748-8776 748-7361
Web: www.aerorentalinc.com
Aggreko 4607 W Admiral Doyle Dr .... New Iberia LA 70560 337-367-7884 367-0870
TF: 800-323-6086 ■ *Web:* www.aggreko.com
AH Harris & Son Inc 367 Alumni Rd .... Newington CT 06111 860-665-9494 665-9444
TF: 800-382-6555 ■ *Web:* www.ahharris.com
Allied Steel Construction Co Inc
2211 NW 1st Terr PO Box 1111 .... Oklahoma City OK 73101 405-232-7531 236-3705
TF: 800-522-4658 ■ *Web:* www.alliedsteelerectors.com
American Classic Sanitation LLC 242 E Live Oak Ave .... Irwindale CA 91706 626-462-9110 254-0149
TF: 877-340-0004 ■ *Web:* www.americanclassicsanitation.com
American Equipment Co 2106 Anderson Rd .... Greenville SC 29611 864-295-7800 295-7956
Web: www.americanequipment.com
American Midwest Equipment Co
W 1361 Elmwood Ave PO Box 343 .... Ixonia WI 53036 920-261-8404 261-8428
Web: www.amequipmentco.com
APi Supply Inc 624 Arthur St NE .... Minneapolis MN 55413 612-379-8000 379-8038
Web: www.apisupplyinc.com
Atlas Lift Truck Rentals & Sales Inc 5050 N River Rd .... Schiller Park IL 60176 847-678-3450 678-1750
Web: www.atlaslift.com
Barnhart Crane & Rigging Inc 3022 Rower Hill Rd .... Powhatan VA 23139 804-598-8970 598-8971
Web: www.barnhartcrane.com
Bechtel Corp 50 Beale St .... San Francisco CA 94105 415-768-1234 768-9038
Web: www.bechtel.com
Beco Equipment Co 5555 Dahlia St .... Commerce City CO 80022 303-288-2613
Web: www.becoequipment.com
Blanchard Machinery Inc 14301 NE 19th Ave .... North Miami FL 33181 305-949-2581 949-9813
TF: 800-330-4242 ■ *Web:* blanchardmachinery.com
Bowles Stanley W Corp
2000 Virginia-Carolina Dr PO Box 4706 .... Martinsville VA 24115 276-632-3446 632-7624
Web: www.bowlesproperties.com
Brockman Forklift Inc 15800 Tireman Ave .... Detroit MI 48228 313-584-4550 584-2423
TF: 800-228-1957
Broussard Brothers Inc 25817 Louisiana Hwy 333 .... Abbeville LA 70510 337-893-5303 893-7148
TF: 800-299-5303 ■ *Web:* www.broussardbrothers.com
Burke Cyril J Inc 36000 Mound Rd .... Sterling Heights MI 48310 586-939-4400 939-3112
TF: 800-482-4952
Central Leasing USA Inc 7300 Turfway Rd Suite 510 .... Florence KY 41042 859-594-4380 594-4219
Chesapeake Industrial Leasing Co Inc 9512 Harford Rd .... Baltimore MD 21234 410-661-5000 661-5053
TF: 800-782-1022 ■ *Web:* www.cilc.com
Cloverdale Equipment Co 13133 Cloverdale St .... Oak Park MI 48237 248-399-6600 399-7730
TF: 800-822-7999 ■ *Web:* www.cloverdale-equip.com

Phone | Fax

Cyril J Burke Inc 36000 Mound Rd .... Sterling Heights MI 48310 586-939-4400 939-3112
TF: 800-482-4952
D & D Equipment Rental Inc
9016 Norwalk Blvd PO Box 2369 .... Santa Fe Springs CA 90670 562-595-4555 595-1265
TF: 866-446-1100 ■ *Web:* www.ddrental.com
Equipment Corp of America 1000 Station St PO Box 306 .... Coraopolis PA 15108 412-331-2000 264-1158
TF: 800-745-3872 ■ *Web:* www.ecanet.com
Essex Crane Rental Corp 1110 Lake Cook Rd Suite 220 .... Buffalo Grove IL 60089 847-215-6500 215-6535
Web: www.essexcrane.com
Force Construction Co Inc 990 N National Rd .... Columbus IN 47201 812-372-8441 372-5424
Web: www.forceco.com
G & C Equipment Corp 1875 W Redondo Beach Blvd Suite 102 ..... Gardena CA 90247 310-515-6715 515-5046
Web: www.gandccorp.com
Gammaloy Holdings LP 2001 Kirby Dr Suite 715 .... Houston TX 77019 713-522-9540 522-9559
Grand Rental Station 203 Jandus Rd .... Cary IL 60013 847-462-5440 516-9921
TF: 800-833-3004 ■ *Web:* www.grandrental.com
H & E Equipment Services Inc 11100 Mead Rd Suite 200 ...... Baton Rouge LA 70816 225-298-5200 298-5377
NASDAQ: HEES ■ *TF:* 877-700-7368 ■ *Web:* www.he-equipment.com
HB Rentals LC 5813 Hwy 90 E .... Broussard LA 70518 337-839-1641 839-1628
TF: 800-262-6790 ■ *Web:* www.hbrental.com
Hertz Big 4 Rents Inc 5500 Commerce Blvd .... Rohnert Park CA 94928 707-586-4444 586-4417
TF: 888-777-2700
Hertz Equipment Rental Corp 225 Brae Blvd .... Park Ridge NJ 07656 201-307-2000 307-2651
TF: 800-654-3131 ■ *Web:* www.hertzequip.com
Horizon Fleet Services Inc 341 NW 122nd St .... Oklahoma City OK 73114 405-755-9703 755-6829
TF: 800-357-2444 ■ *Web:* www.horizonfleet.com
Klochko Equipment Rental Co Inc 2782 Corbin Ave .... Melvindale MI 48122 313-386-7220 386-2530
TF: 800-783-7368 ■ *Web:* www.klochko.com
Kohler Rental Power Div of Kohler Co 4509 S Taylor Dr .... Sheboygan WI 53081 920-459-1634 459-1846
TF: 888-769-3794 ■ *Web:* www.kohlerrentalpower.com
Kreitz Morris & Sons Inc 220 N Park Rd .... Wyomissing PA 19610 610-376-7187 375-8747
Web: www.morriskreitz.com
Marco Crane & Rigging Co 221 S 35th Ave .... Phoenix AZ 85009 602-272-2671 352-0413
TF: 800-668-2671 ■ *Web:* www.marcocrane.com
Maxim Crane Works 1225 Washington Tpke .... Bridgeville PA 15017 412-504-0200 504-0132
TF: 866-629-4648 ■ *Web:* www.maximcrane.com
Medico Industries Inc 1500 Hwy 315 .... Wilkes-Barre PA 18711 570-825-7711 824-1169
TF: 800-633-0027 ■ *Web:* www.medico-ind.com
Mitcham Industries Inc 8141 Hwy 71 S PO Box 1175 .... Huntsville TX 77342 936-291-2277 295-0382
NASDAQ: MIND ■ *Web:* www.mitchamindustries.com
Modern Equipment Sales & Rental Co 24 Brookside Dr .... Wilmington DE 19804 302-658-5257 658-0135
TF: 800-227-2525 ■ *Web:* www.moderngroup.com
Morris Kreitz & Sons Inc 220 N Park Rd .... Wyomissing PA 19610 610-376-7187 375-8747
Web: www.morriskreitz.com
Morrow Equipment Co LLC 3218 Pringle Rd SE .... Salem OR 97302 503-585-5721 363-1172
TF: 800-505-7766 ■ *Web:* www.morrowequipment.com
Mustang Rental Services Inc 15907 I-10 E .... Channelview TX 77530 281-452-7368 457-0501
Web: www.mustangcat.com
National Construction Rentals Inc 15319 Chatsworth St ...... Mission Hills CA 91345 818-221-6000 221-6099
TF: 800-874-6285 ■ *Web:* www.rentnational.com
National Equipment Services Inc
8770 West Brynmawr Ave 4th Fl .... Chicago IL 60631 773-695-3999 714-0538
TF: 800-637-7368 ■ *Web:* www.n-e-s.com
NationsRent Inc 450 E Las Olas Blvd Suite 1400 .... Fort Lauderdale FL 33301 954-760-6550 760-6565
TF: 800-667-9328 ■ *Web:* www.nationsrent.com
Neff Corp 3750 NW 87th Ave Suite 400 .... Miami FL 33178 305-513-3350 513-4156
TF: 888-709-6333 ■ *Web:* www.neffrental.com
Quantum Analytics 363 Vintage Park Dr .... Foster City CA 94404 650-312-0900 312-0313
TF: 800-992-4199 ■ *Web:* www.lqa.com
Rental Service Corp 6929 E Greenway Pkwy Suite 200 .... Scottsdale AZ 85254 480-905-3300 905-3400
TF: 888-736-8772 ■ *Web:* www.rentalservice.com
Republic Leasing Corp 701 Xenia Ave S Suite 220 .... Golden Valley MN 55416 763-542-9900 545-3348
Rush Enterprises Inc 555 IH 35 S Suite 500 .... New Braunfels TX 78130 830-626-5200 626-5310
NASDAQ: RUSHA ■ *TF:* 800-973-7874 ■ *Web:* www.rushenterprises.com
Safway Services Inc N 19 W 24200 Riverwood Dr .... Waukesha WI 53188 262-523-6500 523-9880
TF: 800-558-4772 ■ *Web:* www.safway.com
Specialty Rental Tools & Supply Inc 1131 E FM 517 .... Alvin TX 77511 281-331-1800 331-1801
TF: 800-253-1985 ■ *Web:* www.stsrental.com
Stanley W Bowles Corp
2000 Virginia-Carolina Dr PO Box 4706 .... Martinsville VA 24115 276-632-3446 632-7624
Web: www.bowlesproperties.com
Star Rentals Inc 1919 4th Ave S .... Seattle WA 98134 206-622-7880 587-3280
TF: 800-825-7880 ■ *Web:* www.starrentals.com
Sterling Crane 2440 76th Ave .... Edmonton AB T6P1J5 780-440-4434 440-1954
Web: www.sterlingcrane.ca
Sunbelt Rentals Inc 1337 Hundred Oaks Dr .... Charlotte NC 28217 704-348-2676 602-7538
TF Mktg: 866-786-2358 ■ *Web:* www.sunbeltrentals.com
T & T Truck & Crane Service Inc 1375 N Olive St .... Ventura CA 93001 805-488-4475 648-5218
TF: 800-655-3348 ■ *Web:* www.truckandcrane.com
Taylor Rental 203 Jandus Rd .... Cary IL 60013 847-462-5440 516-9921
TF: 800-833-3004 ■ *Web:* www.taylorrental.com
Telogy Inc 3200 Whipple Rd .... Union City CA 94587 510-675-9500 675-1600
TF: 800-835-6494 ■ *Web:* www.tecentral.com
Tetra Corporate Services LLC
6925 Union Park Center Suite 520 .... Midvale UT 84047 801-566-2600 561-7844
Web: www.tetracsi.com
Timco Services Inc 1724 E Milton Rd .... Lafayette LA 70508 337-233-8664 856-8158
TF: 800-749-2054
Traffic Control Service Inc 1881 Betmor Ln .... Anaheim CA 92805 714-937-0422 937-1070
TF: 800-222-8274 ■ *Web:* www.tcsi.biz
United Crane Rentals Inc 111 N Michigan Ave .... Kenilworth NJ 07033 908-245-6260 245-1708
TF: 800-356-6260
United Rentals Inc 5 Greenwich Office Park .... Greenwich CT 06830 203-622-3131 622-6080
NYSE: URI ■ *TF:* 800-877-3687 ■ *Web:* www.ur.com
Utility Equipment Leasing Corp N4 W22610 Bluemound Rd ...... Waukesha WI 53186 262-547-1600 547-8407
TF: 800-558-0999 ■ *Web:* www.uelc.com
Volvo Rents 1 Volvo Dr .... Asheville NC 28803 866-387-3687 650-2504*
**Fax Area Code:* 828 ■ *Web:* www.volvorents.com
Waco Scaffolding & Equipment Co
4545 Spring Rd PO Box 318028 .... Cleveland OH 44131 216-749-8900 741-8486
TF: 800-901-2282 ■ *Web:* www.wacoscaf.com
Western Oilfields Supply Co 3404 State Rd .... Bakersfield CA 93308 661-399-9124 393-6897*
**Fax:* Acctg ■ *TF:* 800-350-7246 ■ *Web:* www.rainforrent.com

267-4 Medical Equipment Rental

Phone | Fax

American Shared Hospital Services
4 Embarcadero Ctr Suite 3700 .... San Francisco CA 94111 415-788-5300 788-5660
AMEX: AMS ■ *TF:* 800-735-0641 ■ *Web:* www.ashs.com
Apple Medical Inc 314 Franklin Ave .... Berlin MD 21811 410-641-3130 641-1630
First Lease Inc 185 Commerce Dr Unit 102 .... Fort Washington PA 19034 215-283-9727 283-9870
TF: 800-544-7607 ■ *Web:* www.firstleaseonline.com
Freedom Medical Inc 219 Welsh Pool Rd .... Exton PA 19341 610-903-0200 903-0180
TF: 800-784-8849 ■ *Web:* www.freedommedical.com

				Phone	Fax
King's Medical Co 1894 Georgetown Rd	Hudson	OH	44236	330-653-3968	656-0600
Web: www.kingsmedical.com					
M & C Leasing Co Inc 1050 Union Rd Suite 102	West Seneca	NY	14224	716-873-6800	873-1002
TF: 800-416-9080					
Modern Medical Modalities Corp PO Box 957	Union	NJ	07083	908-687-8840	687-8842
Universal Hospital Services Inc 7700 France Ave S Suite 275	Edina	MN	55435	952-893-3200	893-0704
TF: 800-847-7368 ■ *Web:* www.uhs.com					

267-5 Transport Equipment Rental

				Phone	Fax
Andersons Inc Rail Group 480 W Dussel Dr	Maumee	OH	43537	419-893-5050	891-2749
TF: 866-234-0505 ■ *Web:* www.ande-rail.com					
Chicago Freight Car Leasing Co 6250 N River Rd Suite 7000	Rosemont	IL	60018	847-318-8000	318-8045
Web: www.crdx.com					
Cronos Containers Inc 1 Front St Suite 925	San Francisco	CA	94111	800-821-7035	677-9396*
**Fax Area Code:* 415 ■ *Web:* www.cronos.com					
Cronos Containers Inc 517 Rt 1 S Suite 1000	Iselin	NJ	08830	732-602-0808	602-7722
TF: 800-221-4126 ■ *Web:* www.cronos.com					
Eurotainer Inc 5810 Wilson Rd Suite 200	Humble	TX	77396	832-300-5001	300-5050
Web: www.eurotainer.com					
EXSIF Worldwide Inc 100 Manhattanville Rd	Purchase	NY	10577	914-697-2600	697-2697
Web: www.exsifww.com					
Flexi-Van Leasing Inc 251 Monroe Ave	Kenilworth	NJ	07033	908-276-8000	276-7666
Web: www.flexi-van.com					
GATX Rail Canada 1801 Magill College Ave Suite 1475	Montreal	QC	H3A2N4	514-931-7343	931-5534
TF: 800-806-2489 ■ *Web:* www.cgtx.com					
GATX Rail Corp 500 W Monroe St	Chicago	IL	60661	312-621-6200	621-6272*
**Fax:* Sales ■ *Web:* www.gatx.com/rail					
GE Rail Car Services 161 N Clark St 7th Fl	Chicago	IL	60601	312-853-5000	853-5605
TF: 888-272-5793 ■ *Web:* www.ge.com/capital/rail					
GLNX Corp 10077 Grogan's Mill Rd Suite 450	The Woodlands	TX	77380	281-363-0185	363-7060
Web: www.glnx.com					
Greenbrier Co 1 Centerpointe Dr Suite 200	Lake Oswego	OR	97035	503-684-7000	684-7553
NYSE: GBX ■ *TF:* 800-343-7188 ■ *Web:* www.gbrx.com					
Highway Technologies Inc 915 Hager Rd Suite 350	Oak Brook	IL	60523	630-368-0920	368-8423
Web: www.highwaytech.net					
Interpool Inc 211 College Rd E	Princeton	NJ	08540	609-452-8900	452-8211
NYSE: IPX ■ *TF:* 800-388-7485 ■ *Web:* www.interpool.com					
Procor Ltd 2001 Speers Rd	Oakville	ON	L6J5E1	905-827-4111	827-0913
Web: www.procor.com					
Railserve Inc 1691 Phoenix Blvd Suite 110	Atlanta	GA	30349	770-996-6838	996-6830
TF: 800-345-7245 ■ *Web:* www.railserveinc.com					
Relco Locomotives Inc 113 Industrial Dr	Minooka	IL	60447	815-467-3030	467-3039
TF: 800-435-6091 ■ *Web:* www.relcolocomotives.com					
Southern Illinois Railcar Co 503 Buckeye Dr PO Box 510	Troy	IL	62294	618-667-2700	667-4175
Web: www.sircrail.com					
TAL International Group Inc 100 Manhattanville Rd	Purchase	NY	10577	914-251-9000	697-2549
NYSE: TAL ■ *Web:* www.talinternational.com					
TTX Co 101 N Wacker Dr	Chicago	IL	60606	312-853-3223	984-3790
TF: 800-621-5854 ■ *Web:* www.ttx.com					
Union Tank Car Co 175 W Jackson Blvd Suite 2100	Chicago	IL	60604	312-431-3111	347-5020
TF: 800-635-3770 ■ *Web:* www.utlx.com					
XTRA Corp 1801 Park 270 Dr Suite 400	Saint Louis	MO	63146	314-579-9300	542-0783
TF: 800-325-1453 ■ *Web:* www.xtracorp.com					

268 ETHICS COMMISSIONS

				Phone	Fax
Federal Election Commission 999 'E' St NW	Washington	DC	20463	202-694-1100	
TF: 800-424-9530 ■ *Web:* www.fec.gov					
US House of Representatives Standards of Official Conduct Committee HT-2 Capitol Bldg	Washington	DC	20515	202-225-7103	225-7392
Web: www.house.gov/ethics					
US Office of Government Ethics 1201 New York Ave NW Suite 500	Washington	DC	20005	202-482-9300	482-9237
Web: www.usoge.gov					
US Senate Select Committee on Ethics 220 Hart Bldg	Washington	DC	20510	202-224-2981	224-7416
Web: ethics.senate.gov					
Alabama Ethics Commission 100 N Union St Suite 104	Montgomery	AL	36104	334-242-2997	242-0248
Web: www.ethics.alalinc.net					
Alaska Legislative Ethics Committee PO Box 101468	Anchorage	AK	99510	907-269-0150	269-0152
Web: www.ethics.legis.state.ak.us					
Arkansas Ethics Commission 910 W 2nd St Suite 100	Little Rock	AR	72201	501-324-9600	324-9606
TF: 800-422-7773 ■ *Web:* www.arkansasethics.com					
California Fair Political Practices Commission 428 J St Suite 620	Sacramento	CA	95814	916-322-5660	322-0886
TF: 866-275-3772 ■ *Web:* www.fppc.ca.gov					
Connecticut Ethics Commission 20 Trinity St Suite 2	Hartford	CT	06106	860-566-4472	566-3806
Web: www.ethics.state.ct.us					
Delaware Public Integrity Commission 410 Federal St Suite 3	Dover	DE	19901	302-739-2399	739-2398
Web: www.state.de.us/pic					
District of Columbia Elections & Ethics Board 441 4th St NW Suite 250N	Washington	DC	20001	202-727-2525	347-2648
TF: 866-328-6837 ■ *Web:* www.dcboee.org					
Florida Ethics Commission 3600 Maclay Blvd S Suite 201	Tallahassee	FL	32312	850-488-7864	488-3077
Web: www.ethics.state.fl.us					
Georgia State Ethics Commission 205 Jesse Hill Jr Dr SE Suite 478 E Tower	Atlanta	GA	30334	404-463-1980	463-1988
Web: www.ethics.state.ga.us					
Hawaii State Ethics Commission PO Box 616	Honolulu	HI	96809	808-587-0460	587-0470
Web: www.state.hi.us/ethics					
Indiana State Ethics Commission 402 W Washington St Rm W-198	Indianapolis	IN	46204	317-232-3850	232-0707
Web: www.in.gov/ethics					
Iowa Ethics & Campaign Disclosure Board 510 E 12th St Suite 1-A	Des Moines	IA	50319	515-281-4028	281-3701
Web: www.state.ia.us/government/ecdb					
Kansas Governmental Ethics Commission 109 W 9th St Suite 504	Topeka	KS	66612	785-296-4219	296-2548
Web: www.accesskansas.org/ethics					
Kentucky					
Executive Branch Ethics Commission 403 Wapping St Suite 340 Bush Bldg	Frankfort	KY	40601	502-564-7954	564-2686
Web: ethics.ky.gov					
Legislative Ethics Commission 22 Mill Creek Pk	Frankfort	KY	40601	502-573-2863	573-2929
Web: klec.ky.gov					
Louisiana Ethics Board 2415 Quail Dr 3rd Fl	Baton Rouge	LA	70808	225-763-8777	763-8780
TF: 800-842-6630 ■ *Web:* www.ethics.state.la.us					
Maine Governmental Ethics & Election Practices Commission 135 State House Stn	Augusta	ME	04333	207-287-4179	287-6775
Web: www.state.me.us/ethics					
Maryland Ethics Commission 9 State Cir Suite 200	Annapolis	MD	21401	410-974-2068	974-2418
TF: 877-669-6085 ■ *Web:* ethics.gov.state.md.us/					
Massachusetts State Ethics Commission 1 Ashburton Pl Rm 619	Boston	MA	02108	617-727-0060	723-5851
Web: www.mass.gov/ethics					
Minnesota Campaign Finance & Public Disclosure Board 658 Cedar St Suite 190	Saint Paul	MN	55155	651-296-5148	296-1722
TF: 800-657-3889 ■ *Web:* www.cfboard.state.mn.us					
Mississippi Ethics Commission PO Box 22746	Jackson	MS	39225	601-359-1285	354-6253
Web: www.ethics.state.ms.us					
Montana Political Practices Commissioner's Office 1205 8th Ave	Helena	MT	59620	406-444-2942	444-1643
Web: www.state.mt.us/cpp					
Nebraska Accountability & Disclosure Commission PO Box 95086	Lincoln	NE	68509	402-471-2522	471-6599
Web: nadc.nol.org					
Nevada Ethics Commission 3476 Executive Pointe Way Suite 10	Carson City	NV	89706	775-687-5469	687-1279
Web: ethics.nv.gov					
New Jersey Ethical Standards Commission 28 W State St Rm 1407 PO Box 082	Trenton	NJ	08625	609-292-1892	633-9252
Web: www.state.nj.us/lps/ethics					
New Mexico Ethics Administration 325 Don Gaspar St Suite 300	Santa Fe	NM	87503	505-827-3600	827-4954
TF: 800-477-3632 ■ *Web:* www.sos.state.nm.us/ethics.htm					
New York (State) State Ethics Commission 39 Columbia St 4th Fl	Albany	NY	12207	518-432-8207	432-8255
Web: www.dos.state.ny.us/ethc/ethics.html					
North Carolina Ethics Board 116 W Jones St	Raleigh	NC	27603	919-733-2780	733-2785
Web: www.doa.state.nc.us/ethics					
Ohio Ethics Commission 8 E Long St 10th Fl	Columbus	OH	43215	614-466-7090	466-8368
Web: www.ethics.ohio.gov					
Oklahoma Ethics Commission 2300 N Lincoln Blvd Rm B5	Oklahoma City	OK	73105	405-521-3451	521-4905
Web: www.ethics.state.ok.us					
Oregon Government Standards & Practices Commission 100 High St SE Suite 220	Salem	OR	97301	503-378-5105	373-1456
Web: www.gspc.state.or.us					
Pennsylvania Ethics Commission PO Box 11470	Harrisburg	PA	17108	717-783-1610	787-0806
Web: www.ethics.state.pa.us					
Rhode Island Ethics Commission 40 Fountain St	Providence	RI	02903	401-222-3790	222-3382
Web: www.ethics.ri.gov					
South Carolina Ethics Commission 5000 Thurmond Mall Suite 250	Columbia	SC	29201	803-253-4192	253-7539
Web: www.state.sc.us/ethics					
Texas Ethics Commission 201 E 14th St 10th Fl	Austin	TX	78701	512-463-5800	463-5777
TF: 800-325-8506 ■ *Web:* www.ethics.state.tx.us					
Washington Public Disclosure Commission PO Box 40908	Olympia	WA	98504	360-753-1111	753-1112
Web: www.pdc.wa.gov					
West Virginia Ethics Commission 210 Brooks St Suite 300	Charleston	WV	25301	304-558-0664	558-2169
Web: www.wvethicscommission.org					
Wisconsin Ethics Board 44 E Mifflin St Suite 601	Madison	WI	53703	608-266-8123	264-9319
Web: ethics.state.wi.us					

269 EXECUTIVE RECRUITING FIRMS

				Phone	Fax
Aaron Consulting Inc PO Box 4757	Saint Louis	MO	63108	314-367-2627	367-2919
Web: www.aaronlaw.com					
AT Kearney Executive Search 222 W Adams St	Chicago	IL	60606	312-648-0111	223-6369
Web: www.atkearney.com					
Barton Assoc Inc 4314 Yoakum Blvd	Houston	TX	77006	713-961-9111	993-9399
Web: www.bartona.com					
Battalia Winston International 555 Madison Ave 19th Fl	New York	NY	10022	212-308-8080	308-1309
Web: www.battaliawinston.com					
Bialecki Inc 780 3rd Ave Suite 4203	New York	NY	10017	212-755-1090	755-1130
Web: www.bialecki.com					
Bishop Partners Ltd 708 3rd Ave Suite 2200	New York	NY	10017	212-986-3419	986-3350
Web: www.bishoppartners.com					
Boardroom Consultants 530 5th Ave Suite 2100	New York	NY	10036	212-328-0440	328-0441
Web: www.boardroomconsultants.com					
Boyden Global Executive Search 50 Broadway	Hawthorne	NY	10532	914-747-0093	747-0108
Web: www.boyden.com					
Boyden World Corp DBA Boyden Global Executive Search 50 Broadway	Hawthorne	NY	10532	914-747-0093	747-0108
Web: www.boyden.com					
Canny Bowen Inc 280 Park Ave West Tower 30th Fl	New York	NY	10017	212-949-6611	949-5191
Web: www.cannybowen.com					
Chadick Ellig Inc 300 Park Ave 25th Fl	New York	NY	10022	212-688-8671	308-4510
Web: www.chadickellig.com					
Chicago Legal Search Ltd 180 N LaSalle St Suite 3325	Chicago	IL	60601	312-251-2580	251-0223
Web: www.chicagolegalsearch.com					
Choi & Burns LLC 152 W 57th St 32nd Fl	New York	NY	10019	212-755-7051	355-2610
Web: www.choiburns.com					
Christian & Timbers 25825 Science Pk Dr Suite 100	Cleveland	OH	44122	216-464-8710	464-6160
TF: 800-380-9444 ■ *Web:* www.ctnet.com					
Cole Warren & Long Inc 2 Penn Ctr Plaza Suite 312	Philadelphia	PA	19102	215-563-0701	563-2907
TF: 800-394-8517 ■ *Web:* www.cwl-inc.com					
Compass Group Ltd 401 S Old Woodward Ave Suite 460	Birmingham	MI	48009	248-540-9110	647-8288
Web: www.compassgroup.com					
Dahl Morrow International 11260 Roger Bacon St Suite 204	Reston	VA	20190	703-787-8117	787-8114
Web: www.dahl-morrowintl.com					
Daniel & Yeager 6767 Old Madison Pike Suite 690	Huntsville	AL	35806	256-551-1070	551-1075
TF: 800-955-1919 ■ *Web:* www.daniel-yeager.com					
Davis Joseph A Consultants Inc 104 E 40th St Suite 203	New York	NY	10016	212-682-4006	661-0846
DHR International 10 S Riverside Plaza Suite 2220	Chicago	IL	60606	312-782-1581	782-2096
TF: 800-782-2210 ■ *Web:* www.dhrinternational.com					
Dieckmann & Assoc 233 N Michigan Ave Suite 2333	Chicago	IL	60601	312-819-5900	819-5924
Web: www.dieckmann-associates.com					
Diversified Search Cos 2005 Market St Suite 3300	Philadelphia	PA	19103	215-732-6666	568-8399
TF: 800-423-3932 ■ *Web:* www.divsearch.com					
DP Parker & Assoc Inc 1 Hollis St Suite 103	Wellesley	MA	02482	781-237-1220	237-4702
Web: www.dpparker.com					
Early Cochran & Olson LLC 1 E Wacker Dr Suite 2510	Chicago	IL	60601	312-595-4200	595-4209
Web: www.ecollc.com					
Eastman & Beaudine Inc 7201 Bishop Rd Suite 220	Plano	TX	75024	972-312-1012	312-1020
Web: www.eastman-beaudine.com					
Egon Zehnder International Inc 1 N Wacker Dr Suite 2300	Chicago	IL	60606	312-260-8800	782-2846
TF: 800-800-5567 ■ *Web:* www.egonzehnder.com					
Exec Solutions 5655 Lindero Canyon Rd Suite 521	Westlake Village	CA	91362	818-575-8080	575-8099
Fergus Partnership Consulting Inc 1325 6th Ave Suite 2302	New York	NY	10019	212-767-1775	315-0351
Web: ferguslex.com					

Phone *Fax*

Fischer Howard Assoc International
1800 Kennedy Blvd Suite 700 .... Philadelphia PA 19103 215-568-8363 568-4815
Web: www.hfischer.com
Gilbert Tweed Assoc Inc 415 Madison Ave 20th Fl .... New York NY 10017 212-758-3000 832-1040
TF: 800-456-3932 ■ *Web:* www.gilberttweed.com
Glaser Lawrence Assoc Inc 505 S Lenola Rd Suite 202 .... Moorestown NJ 08057 856-778-9500 778-4390
Web: www.lgasearch.com
Halbrecht Lieberman Assoc Inc 32 Surf Rd .... Westport CT 06880 203-222-4890 222-4895
Web: www.hlassoc.com
HC Smith Ltd 20600 Chagrin Blvd Tower East Suite 101 ..... Shaker Heights OH 44122 216-752-9966 752-9970
TF: 800-442-7583 ■ *Web:* www.hcsmith.com
HealthCare Recruiters International
5220 Spring Valley Rd Suite 40 .... Dallas TX 75254 972-702-0444 702-0432
Web: www.hcrintl.com
Heath/Norton Assoc 301 Crocus Ct Suite L-7 .... Dayton NJ 08810 732-329-4663
Heidrick & Struggles International Inc
233 S Wacker Dr Suite 4200 .... Chicago IL 60606 312-496-1000 496-1297
NASDAQ: HSII ■ *Web:* www.heidrick.com
Herbert Mines Assoc Inc 375 Park Ave Suite 801 .... New York NY 10152 212-355-0909 223-2186
Web: www.herbertmines.com
Higdon Partners LLC 230 Park Ave Suite 951 .... New York NY 10169 212-986-4662 986-5002
Web: www.higdonbarrett.com
Horton International LLC 433 S Main St .... West Hartford CT 06110 860-521-0101 521-0140
Web: www.horton-intl.com
Howard Fischer Assoc International
1800 Kennedy Blvd Suite 700 .... Philadelphia PA 19103 215-568-8363 568-4815
Web: www.hfischer.com
Howard-Sloan Search Inc 1140 Ave of the Americas .... New York NY 10036 212-704-0444 869-7999
TF: 800-221-1326 ■ *Web:* www.howardsloan.com
Hughes & Sloan Inc
1360 Peachtree St NE 1 Midtown Plaza Suite 1010 .... Atlanta GA 30309 404-873-3421 873-3861
Web: www.hughesandsloan.com
Hunt Howe Partners LLC 1 Dag Hammarskjold Plaza 26th Fl .... New York NY 10017 212-758-2800 758-7710
Web: www.hunthowe.com
IMC Group of Cos 120 White Plains Rd Suite 405 .... Tarrytown NY 10591 914-468-7050 468-7051
Web: www.the-imc.com
Isaacson Miller 334 Boylston St Suite 500 .... Boston MA 02116 617-262-6500 262-6509
TF: 888-472-2276 ■ *Web:* www.imsearch.com
Joseph A Davis Consultants Inc 104 E 40th St Suite 203 .... New York NY 10016 212-682-4006 661-0846
Kearney AT Executive Search 222 W Adams St .... Chicago IL 60606 312-648-0111 223-6369
Web: www.atkearney.com
Kenzer Corp 450 7th Ave Suite 2604 .... New York NY 10123 212-308-4300 308-1842
Web: www.kenzer.com
Kincannon & Reed 2106-C Gallows Rd .... Vienna VA 22182 703-761-4046 790-1533
Web: www.krsearch.com
Klein Landau & Romm 1725 K St NW .... Washington DC 20006 202-728-0100 728-0112
TF: 866-807-1931 ■ *Web:* www.klrsearch.com
Korn/Ferry International 200 Park Ave 37th Fl .... New York NY 10166 212-687-1834 986-5684
NYSE: KFY ■ *Web:* www.kornferry.com
Kovensky & Co 1250 Connecticut Ave NW Suite 200 .... Washington DC 20036 202-261-3555 832-1838*
**Fax Area Code: 413* ■ *Web:* www.kovenskyandcompany.com
Lawrence Glaser Assoc Inc 505 S Lenola Rd Suite 202 .... Moorestown NJ 08057 856-778-9500 778-4390
Web: www.lgasearch.com
Major Lindsey & Africa 938 B St .... San Rafael CA 94901 415-485-5111 485-5110
TF: 877-482-1010 ■ *Web:* www.mlaglobal.com
Management Recruiters International Worldwide Inc
1717 Arch St 36th Fl .... Philadelphia PA 19103 215-636-1200 751-1759
TF: 800-875-4000 ■ *Web:* www.mrinetwork.com
Medical Directions Inc 410 Saw Mill River Rd Suite 1005 .... Ardsley NY 10502 914-478-8500 478-8545
TF: 800-647-0573 ■ *Web:* www.medical-directions.com
Mestel & Co Inc 575 Madison Ave Suite 3000 .... New York NY 10022 646-356-0500 356-0545
Web: www.mestel.com
Mines Herbert Assoc Inc 375 Park Ave Suite 801 .... New York NY 10152 212-355-0909 223-2186
Web: www.herbertmines.com
Monster Worldwide Inc 622 3rd Ave 39th Fl .... New York NY 10017 212-351-7000 658-0541*
NASDAQ: MNST ■ **Fax Area Code: 646* ■ *TF:* 888-225-5867 ■
Web: www.monsterworldwide.com
MSI International Inc 650 Park Ave Suite 100 .... King of Prussia PA 19406 610-265-2000 265-2213
TF: 800-927-0919 ■ *Web:* www.msimsi.com
Nordeman Grimm 65 E 55th St 33rd Fl .... New York NY 10022 212-935-1000 980-1443
Web: www.nordemangrimm.com
Parker DP & Assoc Inc 1 Hollis St Suite 103 .... Wellesley MA 02482 781-237-1220 237-4702
Web: www.dpparker.com
Physicians Search 5581 E Stetson Ct .... Anaheim CA 92807 714-685-1047 685-1143
TF: 800-748-6320 ■ *Web:* www.physicianssearch.com
Pittleman & Assoc 336 E 43rd St .... New York NY 10017 212-370-9600 370-9608
Web: www.pittlemanassociates.com
Ray & Berndtson 405 Lexington Ave 26th Fl .... New York NY 10174 212-907-6501 907-6502
Web: www.rayberndtson.com
Reynolds Russell Assoc Inc 200 Park Ave 23rd Fl .... New York NY 10166 212-351-2000 370-0896
TF: 888-772-6200 ■ *Web:* www.russreyn.com
Rice Cohen International 301 Oxford Valley Rd Suite 1506A .... Yardley PA 19067 215-321-4100
Rusher Loscavio & LoPresto 100 Spear St Suite 935 .... San Francisco CA 94105 415-765-6600 546-2201
Web: www.rll.com
Russell Reynolds Assoc Inc 200 Park Ave 23rd Fl .... New York NY 10166 212-351-2000 370-0896
TF: 888-772-6200 ■ *Web:* www.russreyn.com
Sanford Rose Assoc 3737 Embassy Pkwy Suite 200 .... Akron OH 44333 330-670-9797 670-9798
TF: 800-731-7724 ■ *Web:* www.sanfordrose.com
Skott/Edwards Consultants 7 Royal Dr .... Cherry Quay NJ 08723 732-920-1883 477-1541
Web: www.skottedwards.com
Smith HC Ltd 20600 Chagrin Blvd Tower East Suite 101 ..... Shaker Heights OH 44122 216-752-9966 752-9970
TF: 800-442-7583 ■ *Web:* www.hcsmith.com
Spectra International 3200 N Hayden Rd Suite 210 .... Scottsdale AZ 85251 480-481-0411 893-8483*
**Fax Area Code: 800* ■ *TF:* 800-595-5617 ■ *Web:* www.spectra-az.com
Spencer Reed Group Inc 6900 College Blvd Suite 1 .... Overland Park KS 66211 913-663-4400 663-4410
TF: 800-477-5035 ■ *Web:* www.spencerreed.com
SpencerStuart 401 N Michigan Ave Suite 3400 .... Chicago IL 60611 312-822-0080 822-0116
Web: www.spencerstuart.com
Stanton Chase International 100 E Pratt St Suite 2530 .... Baltimore MD 21202 410-528-8400 528-8409
Web: www.stantonchase.com
Swan Legal Search 11500 Olympic Blvd Suite 370 .... Los Angeles CA 90064 310-445-5010 445-0621
TF: 888-860-1154 ■ *Web:* www.swanlegal.com
Tyler & Co 375 North Ridge Rd Suite 400 .... Atlanta GA 30350 770-396-3939 396-6693
Web: www.tylerandco.com
Viscusi Group Inc 200 Lexington Ave Suite 413 .... New York NY 10016 212-979-5700 979-5717
Web: www.viscusigroup.com
Whitney Group 850 3rd Ave 11th Fl .... New York NY 10022 212-508-3500 508-3589
Web: www.whitneygroup.com
Winston Personnel Service Inc 122 E 42nd St .... New York NY 10168 212-557-8181 682-1056
TF: 800-494-6786
Witt/Kieffer Ford Hadelman & Lloyd
2015 Spring Rd Suite 510 .... Oak Brook IL 60523 630-990-1370 990-1382
Web: www.wittkieffer.com
Wyatt & Jaffe 4999 France Ave S Suite 260 .... Minneapolis MN 55410 612-285-2858 285-2786
Web: www.wyattjaffe.com
Zehnder Egon International Inc 1 N Wacker Dr Suite 2300 .... Chicago IL 60606 312-260-8800 782-2846
TF: 800-800-5567 ■ *Web:* www.egonzehnder.com

270 EXERCISE & FITNESS EQUIPMENT

SEE ALSO Sporting Goods p. 2323

Phone *Fax*

Aerobics Inc 34 Fairfield Pl .... West Caldwell NJ 07006 973-276-9700 276-9001
Web: www.pacemaster.com
All Pro Exercise Products Inc PO Box 8268 .... Longboat Key FL 34228 941-387-9432 387-7901
TF: 800-735-9287 ■ *Web:* www.allproweights.com
Battle Creek Equipment Co 307 W Jackson St .... Battle Creek MI 49017 269-962-6181 962-8058
TF Cust Svc: 800-253-0854
Body Masters Sports Industries Inc 700 E Texas Ave PO Box 259 .... Rayne LA 70578 337-334-9611 334-4827
TF: 800-325-8964 ■ *Web:* www.body-masters.com
Body-Solid Inc 1900 S Des Plaines Ave .... Forest Park IL 60130 708-427-3500 427-3556
TF: 800-833-1227 ■ *Web:* www.bodysolid.com
Cybex International Inc 10 Trotter Dr .... Medway MA 02053 508-533-4300 533-5500
AMEX: CYB ■ *TF:* 888-462-9239 ■ *Web:* www.ecybex.com
Fitness Quest Inc 1400 Raff Rd SW .... Canton OH 44750 330-478-0755 478-2159
TF: 800-321-9236 ■ *Web:* www.fitnessquest.com
Heart-Rate Inc 3190 Airport Loop Dr Bldg E .... Costa Mesa CA 92626 714-850-9716 755-4973
TF: 800-237-2271 ■ *Web:* www.heartrateinc.com
Heartline Fitness Products Inc 19209 Orbit Dr .... Gaithersburg MD 20879 301-921-0661 330-5479
TF: 800-262-3348 ■ *Web:* www.heartlinefitness.com
Hoggan Health Industries Inc 8020 S 1300 West .... West Jordan UT 84088 801-572-6500 572-6514
TF: 800-678-7888 ■ *Web:* www.hogganhealth.com
Hoist Fitness Systems Inc 9990 Empire St Suite 130 .... San Diego CA 92126 858-578-7676 578-9558
TF: 800-548-5438 ■ *Web:* www.hoistfitness.com
HYDRO-FIT Inc 160 Madison St .... Eugene OR 97402 541-484-4361 484-1443
TF Cust Svc: 800-346-7295 ■ *Web:* www.hydrofit.com
ICON Health & Fitness Inc 1500 S 1000 West .... Logan UT 84321 435-750-5000 750-3632*
**Fax: Cust Svc* ■ *TF:* 800-999-3756 ■ *Web:* www.iconfitness.com
IronMaster LLC 21828 87th Ave SE Suite E .... Woodinville WA 98072 425-408-9040 483-2868
TF: 800-533-3339 ■ *Web:* www.ironmaster.com
Life Fitness 5100 N River Rd .... Schiller Park IL 60176 847-288-3300 288-3703
TF: 800-735-3867 ■ *Web:* www.lifefitness.com
Nautilus Inc 1400 NE 136th Ave .... Vancouver WA 98684 360-694-7722 694-7755
NYSE: NLS ■ *Web:* www.nautilusgroup.com
New York Barbells 160 Home St .... Elmira NY 14904 607-733-8038 733-1010
TF: 800-446-1833 ■ *Web:* www.newyorkbarbells.com
Paramount Fitness Corp 6450 E Bandini Blvd .... Los Angeles CA 90040 323-721-2121 724-2000
TF: 800-721-2121 ■ *Web:* www.paramountfitness.com
Precor Inc 20031 142nd Ave NE .... Woodinville WA 98072 425-486-9292 486-3856
TF: 800-786-8404 ■ *Web:* www.precor.com
Pro Star Sports Inc 1133 Winchester Ave .... Kansas City MO 64126 816-241-9737 241-2459
TF: 800-821-8482 ■ *Web:* www.prostarsports.com
Soloflex Inc 570 NE 53rd Ave .... Hillsboro OR 97124 503-640-8891 648-0864
TF: 800-547-8802 ■ *Web:* www.soloflex.com
Spirit Manufacturing Inc 2601 Commerce Dr .... Jonesboro AR 72402 870-935-1107 935-7611
TF: 800-258-4555 ■ *Web:* www.spiritfitness.com
Star Trac by Unisen Inc 14410 Myford Rd .... Irvine CA 92606 714-669-1660 838-6286
TF: 800-228-6635 ■ *Web:* www.startrac.com
Task Industries Inc 1325 E Franklin Ave .... Pomona CA 91766 909-629-1600 629-4967
TF: 800-961-9377 ■ *Web:* www.tuffstuff.net
True Fitness Technology Inc 865 Hoff Rd .... O'Fallon MO 63366 636-272-7100 272-7148
TF: 800-426-6570 ■ *Web:* www.truefitness.com
Vectra Fitness Inc 7901 S 190th St .... Kent WA 98032 425-291-9550 291-9650
Web: www.vectrafitness.com
Vision Fitness 500 South CP Ave .... Lake Mills WI 53551 920-648-4090 648-3373
TF: 800-335-4348 ■ *Web:* www.visionfitness.com
Woodway USA W229 N591 Foster Ct .... Waukesha WI 53186 262-548-6235 548-6239
TF: 800-966-3929 ■ *Web:* www.woodway.com
York Barbell Co Inc 3300 Board Rd .... York PA 17402 717-767-6481 764-0044
TF Cust Svc: 800-358-9675 ■ *Web:* www.yorkbarbell.com

271 EXPLOSIVES

Phone *Fax*

Accurate Energetics Systems LLC 5891 Hwy 230 W .... McEwen TN 37101 931-729-4207 729-4214
Web: www.aesys.biz
Action Mfg Co 100 E Erie Ave .... Philadelphia PA 19134 215-739-6400 423-7749
Web: www.action-mfg.com
Alliant Powder Rt 114 PO Box 6 .... Radford VA 24143 540-639-8503 639-8496
TF: 800-276-9337 ■ *Web:* www.alliantpowder.com
American Azide Corp 10622 W 6400 North .... Cedar City UT 84720 435-865-5000 865-5005
Apache Nitrogen Products Inc
1436 S Apache Powder Rd PO Box 700 .... Benson AZ 85602 520-720-2217 720-4158
Web: www.apachenitro.com
Austin Powder Co 25800 Science Park Dr Suite 300 .... Cleveland OH 44122 216-464-2400 591-1568
TF: 800-321-0752 ■ *Web:* www.austinpowder.com
Buckley Powder Co 42 Inverness Dr E .... Englewood CO 80112 303-790-7007 790-7033
TF: 800-333-2266 ■ *Web:* www.buckleypowder.com
Can-Blast Inc 755 Wallace Rd Unit 3 .... North Bay ON P1B8K4 705-474-3431 476-7643
Web: www.can-blast.com
Cartridge Actuated Devices Inc 51 Dwight Pl .... Fairfield NJ 07004 973-575-1312 575-6039
Web: www.mcselph.com/cad.html
Dyno Nobel Inc 2650 Decker Lake Blvd Suite 300 .... Salt Lake City UT 84119 801-364-4800 328-6452
TF: 800-473-2626 ■ *Web:* www.dynonobel.com
El Dorado Chemical Co 4500 Northwest Ave .... El Dorado AR 71730 870-863-1400 863-1426
Web: www.eldoradochemical.com
Ensign-Bickford Industries Inc 100 Grist Mill Rd .... Simsbury CT 06070 860-843-2000 843-1510
TF: 800-828-9814 ■ *Web:* www.ensign-bickfordind.com
GOEX Inc
Hwy 80 East Gate 4 Bldg 803 Camp Minden National Guard .... Minden LA 71055 318-382-9300 382-9303
Web: www.goexpowder.com
Hodgdon Powder Co Inc 6231 Robinson St .... Shawnee Mission KS 66202 913-362-9455 362-1307
Web: www.hodgdon.com
Keystone Fireworks & Specialty Sales Co Inc High St Ext .... Dunbar PA 15431 724-277-4294 277-0587
Mil-Spec Industries Corp 10 Mineola Ave .... Roslyn Heights NY 11577 516-625-5787 625-0988
Web: www.milspecindustries.com
Orica USA Inc 33101 E Quincy Ave .... Watkins CO 80137 303-268-5000 268-5250
Web: www.oricaexplosives.com
Pyrotechnic Specialties Inc 1661 Juniper Creek Rd .... Byron GA 31008 478-956-5400 956-5108
Web: www.pyrotechonline.com
Rozzi Inc 11605 N Lebanon Rd .... Loveland OH 45140 513-683-0620 683-2043
Web: www.rozzifireworks.com
Schaefer Pyrotechnics Inc DBA Schaefer Fireworks
376 Hartman Bridge Rd .... Ronks PA 17572 717-687-0647 687-8982
TF: 877-598-2264 ■ *Web:* www.schaeferfireworks.com
Senex Explosives Inc 710 Millers Run Rd .... Cuddy PA 15031 412-221-3218 221-6032
Sierra Chemical Co 2302 Larkin Cir .... Sparks NV 89431 775-358-0888 358-7799
TF: 800-777-8965

	City	State	Zip	Phone	Fax
Special Devices Inc 14370 White Sage Rd	Moorpark	CA	93021	805-553-1201	553-1201
TF: 888-782-0082 ■ *Web:* www.specialdevices.com					
Stresau Laboratory Inc N8265 Medley Rd	Spooner	WI	54801	715-635-2777	635-7979
Web: www.stresau.com					
Technical Ordnance Inc 9200 Nike Rd	Saint Bonifacius	MN	55375	952-446-1526	446-1990
Web: www.tekord.com					
Teledyne Reynolds Inc 5005 McConnell Ave	Los Angeles	CA	90066	310-823-5491	822-8046
Web: www.teledynereynolds.com					
Zambelli Internationale Fireworks Mfg					
20 S Mercer St 2nd Fl	New Castle	PA	16101	724-658-6611	658-8318
TF: 800-245-0397 ■ *Web:* www.zambellifireworks.com					

272 EYE BANKS

SEE ALSO Organ & Tissue Banks p. 2041; Transplant Centers - Blood Stem Cell p. 2378

Eye banks listed here are members of the Eye Bank Association of America (EBAA), an accrediting body for eye banks. The EBAA medical standards for member eye banks are endorsed by the American Academy of Ophthalmology.

	City	State	Zip	Phone	Fax
Alabama Eye Bank 500 Robert Jemison Rd	Birmingham	AL	35209	205-942-2120	942-2184
TF: 800-423-7811 ■ *Web:* www.alabamaeyebank.org					
Alcon Research Ltd 6201 South Fwy	Fort Worth	TX	76134	817-551-6929	777-2799*
**Fax Area Code: 800 ■ *TF:* 800-451-3937 ■ *Web:* www.alcon.com					
Arkansas Lions Eye Bank & Laboratory					
4301 W Markham St Slot 523-1	Little Rock	AR	72205	501-686-8388	603-1463
Web: www.uams.edu/jei/lions					
Banque D'Yeux de Quebec 5415 blvd l'Assomption	Montreal	QC	H1T2M4	514-252-3886	252-3821
Baton Rouge Regional Eye Bank 7777 Hennessy Blvd Suite 207	Baton Rouge	LA	70808	225-766-8996	765-4366
Web: www.eyebankbr.org					
Center for Organ Recovery & Education (CORE)					
204 Sigma Dr RIDC Park	Pittsburgh	PA	15238	412-366-6777	963-3596
TF: 800-366-6777 ■ *Web:* www.core.org					
Central Florida Tissue & Eye Bank Inc 8663 Commodity Cir	Orlando	FL	32819	407-226-3888	
TF: 800-753-9109 ■ *Web:* www.tissuebank.org					
Central New York Eye & Tissue Bank 475 Irving Ave Suite 100	Syracuse	NY	13210	315-476-0199	471-6060
TF: 800-393-7487 ■ *Web:* www.cnyeyebank.org					
Central Ohio Lions Eye Bank 262 Neil Ave Suite 1400	Columbus	OH	43215	614-293-8114	545-2067
TF: 800-301-4960 ■ *Web:* www.lionseyebank.net					
Cincinnati Eye Bank for Sight Restoration Inc					
4015 Executive Park Dr Suite 330	Cincinnati	OH	45241	513-861-3716	483-3984
Web: www.cintieb.org					
Cleveland Eye Bank 11100 Euclid Ave Wearn Bldg Room 615	Cleveland	OH	44106	216-844-3937	983-0069
TF: 800-251-9270					
Connecticut Eye Bank & Visual Research Foundation Inc					
100 Grand St	New Britain	CT	06052	860-224-5550	224-5720
TF: 800-355-5520 ■ *Web:* www.cteyebank.org					
CORE (Center for Organ Recovery & Education)					
204 Sigma Dr RIDC Park	Pittsburgh	PA	15238	412-366-6777	963-3596
TF: 800-366-6777 ■ *Web:* www.core.org					
Doheny Eye & Tissue Transplant Bank					
1127 Wilshire Blvd Suite 602	Los Angeles	CA	90017	213-482-9355	482-9343
Web: www.dettb.org					
Donor Network of Arizona 201 W Coolidge St	Phoenix	AZ	85013	602-222-2200	222-2202
TF: 800-447-9477 ■ *Web:* www.dnaz.org					
East Tennessee Lions Eye Bank 1924 Alcoa Hwy # U-26	Knoxville	TN	37920	865-544-9625	523-4869
Web: www.discoveret.org/eyebank					
EBAA (Eye Bank Assn of America) 1015 18th St NW Suite 1010	Washington	DC	20036	202-775-4999	429-6036
Web: www.restoresight.org					
Eye Bank Assn of America (EBAA) 1015 18th St NW Suite 1010	Washington	DC	20036	202-775-4999	429-6036
Web: www.restoresight.org					
Eye Bank of British Columbia					
2550 Willow St Eye Care Centre 3rd Fl	Vancouver	BC	V5Z3N9	604-875-4567	875-5316
Web: www.eyebankofbc.ca					
Eye Bank of Canada Ontario Div 1 Spadina Crescent Rm 114	Toronto	ON	M5S2J5	416-978-7355	978-1522
TF: 877-363-8456 ■ *Web:* eyebank.med.utoronto.ca					
Eye Bank for Sight Restoration Inc 120 Wall St 3rd Fl	New York	NY	10005	212-742-9000	269-3139
TF: 866-287-3937 ■ *Web:* www.eyedonation.org					
Great Plains Lions Eye Bank					
Texas Tech University Health Sciences Center 3601 4th St Suite BAB104-HSC	Lubbock	TX	79408	806-743-2242	743-1431
Web: www.ttuhsc.edu/eye					
Hawaii Lions Eye Bank & Makana Foundation					
614 South St Suite 101	Honolulu	HI	96813	808-536-7416	528-5032
Web: www.eyebank.org					
Heartland Lions Eye Bank					
10100 NW Ambassador Dr Suite 200-E	Kansas City	MO	64153	816-454-5454	454-5446
TF: 800-816-9264 ■ *Web:* www.mlerf.org					
Heartland Lions Eye Bank 4482 Woodson Rd Suite 7	Saint Louis	MO	63134	314-428-4373	428-3751
TF: 800-331-2636 ■ *Web:* www.mlerf.org					
Heartland Lions Eye Bank 3854 South Ave	Springfield	MO	65807	417-882-1532	882-8206
TF: 800-331-2636 ■ *Web:* www.mlerf.org					
Idaho Lions Eye Bank 1055 N Curtis Rd	Boise	ID	83706	208-367-2400	367-6843
TF: 800-546-6889 ■ *Web:* www.idaholions.org/pages/lionseye1.htm					
Indiana Lions Eye & Tissue Transplant Bank Indiana University Medical Center 702 Rotary Cir Rm 115	Indianapolis	IN	46202	317-274-8527	274-2180
TF: 800-232-4384 ■ *Web:* www.indianalions.org					
International Cornea Project 9444 Balboa Ave Suite 100	San Diego	CA	92123	858-694-0444	565-7368
TF: 888-393-2265 ■ *Web:* www.internationalcorneaproject.org					
International Sight Restoration Inc 3808 Gunn Hwy Suite B	Tampa	FL	33618	813-264-6003	264-6007
Web: www.internationalsight.com					
Iowa Lions Eye Bank 2346 Mormon Trek Blvd Suite 1500	Iowa City	IA	52246	319-356-2871	384-9781
TF: 866-435-7733 ■ *Web:* webeye.ophth.uiowa.edu/eyebank					
Laboratories at Bonfils 717 Yosemite St 2nd Fl	Denver	CO	80230	303-365-9000	343-6666
TF: 800-321-6088 ■ *Web:* www.labsatbonfils.com					
LifePoint Inc 4200 Faber Pl Dr	Charleston	SC	29405	843-763-7755	763-6393
TF: 800-462-0755 ■ *Web:* www.sceyebank.org					
LifePoint Inc 110-B Medical Cir	West Columbia	SC	29169	803-796-2195	794-1831
TF: 800-462-0755 ■ *Web:* www.sceyebank.org					
LifeShare of the Carolinas 86 Victoria Rd Bldg B	Asheville	NC	28801	828-258-9703	258-3219
TF: 800-932-4483 ■ *Web:* www.lifesharecarolinas.org					
LifeShare of the Carolinas 5000 D Airport Center Pkwy	Charlotte	NC	28208	704-697-3303	512-3056
TF: 800-932-4483 ■ *Web:* www.lifesharecarolinas.org					
Lions Eye Bank Alberta Society 7007 14th St SW	Calgary	AB	T2V1P9	403-943-3406	943-3244
Web: www.act4sight.com					
Lions Eye Bank of Lexington 3290 Blazer Pkwy Suite 201	Lexington	KY	40509	859-323-6740	323-5927
Web: www.mc.uky.edu/eyebank					
Lions Eye Bank for Long Island North Shore University Hospital 350 Community Dr	Manhasset	NY	11030	516-465-8430	465-8434
Web: www.lebli.org					
Lions Eye Bank of Manitoba & Northwest Ontario Inc					
691 Wolseley Ave Rm 105	Winnipeg	MB	R3C1A2	204-788-8507	783-6823
TF: 800-552-6820 ■ *Web:* www.lionseyebank.mb.ca					
Lions Eye Bank of Nebraska Inc University of Nebraska Medical Center 985541 Nebraska Medical Center	Omaha	NE	68198	402-559-4039	559-7705
TF: 877-633-1800 ■ *Web:* www.nebraskalionsfoundation.org/eyebank.html					
Lions Eye Bank of New Jersey 841 Mountain Ave	Springfield	NJ	07081	973-921-1222	921-1221
TF: 800-653-9379 ■ *Web:* www.lebnj.org					
Lions Eye Bank of North Dakota 301 N 4th St	Bismarck	ND	58501	701-250-9390	250-0805
TF: 800-372-3751					
Lions Eye Bank of Northwest Pennsylvania Inc 5105 Richmond St	Erie	PA	16509	814-866-3545	864-1875
Lions Eye Bank of Oregon 1010 NW 22nd Ave Suite N144	Portland	OR	97210	503-413-7523	413-6716
TF: 800-843-7793 ■ *Web:* www.orlions.org					
Lions Eye Bank of Puerto Rico PO Box 363311	San Juan	PR	00936	787-273-0597	273-0974
Web: www.prlionseyebank-org.com					
Lions Eye Bank of Saskatchewan Inc					
Regina Pasqua Hospital 4104 Dewdney Ave	Regina	SK	S4T1A5	306-655-8002	569-4122
Saskatoon City Hospital 701 Queen St Eye Care Ctr 4th Fl.	Saskatoon	SK	S7K0M7	306-655-1002	655-8846
Lions Eye Bank of Texas at Baylor College of Medicine Dept of Opthalmology 6565 Fannin St NC-205	Houston	TX	77030	713-798-5500	798-4645
Web: www.bayloreye.org/eyebank					
Lions Eye Bank of West Central Ohio					
1945 Southtown Blvd Suite E	Dayton	OH	45439	937-396-1000	396-1880
Lions Eye Bank of Wisconsin 2302 International Ln Suite 200	Madison	WI	53704	608-233-2354	233-2895
TF: 877-233-2354 ■ *Web:* www.eyebankwis.com					
Lions Eye Institute for Transplant & Research Inc					
5523 W Cypress St Suite 100	Tampa	FL	33607	813-289-1200	289-1800
TF: 800-277-2020 ■ *Web:* www.lionseyeinstitute.org					
Lions Medical Eye Bank & Research Center of Eastern Virginia Inc 600 Gresham Dr	Norfolk	VA	23507	757-388-2748	388-3744
TF: 800-453-6059 ■ *Web:* www.lionseyebank.org					
Lone Star Lions Eye Bank 102 E Wheeler St PO Box 347	Manor	TX	78653	512-457-0638	457-0658
TF: 800-977-3937 ■ *Web:* www.lsleb.org					
Medical Eye Bank of Florida 2177 E Michigan St Suite 2	Orlando	FL	32806	407-422-2020	425-7262
TF: 800-277-2020 ■ *Web:* www.medicaleyebank-florida.org					
Medical Eye Bank of Maryland 815 Park Ave	Baltimore	MD	21201	410-752-2020	783-6183
TF: 800-756-4824					
Medical Eye Bank of West Virginia 3 Courtney Dr	Charleston	WV	25304	304-926-9200	926-6779
Mid-America Transplant Services					
1139 Olivette Executive Pkwy	Saint Louis	MO	63132	314-991-1661	993-5179
TF: 888-376-4854 ■ *Web:* www.mts-stl.org					
Mid-Continent Eye Bank 625 N Carriage Pkwy Suite 190	Wichita	KS	67208	316-260-8220	260-8225
TF: 800-366-6791 ■ *Web:* www.mid-continent.org					
Midwest Eye Banks 4889 Venture Dr	Ann Arbor	MI	48108	734-780-2100	780-2111
TF: 800-247-7250 ■ *Web:* www.midwesteyebanks.org					
Minnesota Lions Eye Bank					
516 Delaware St SE Suite 9-318 MMC 493	Minneapolis	MN	55455	612-625-5159	626-1192
TF: 866-887-4448 ■ *Web:* www.mnlionseyebank.org					
Mississippi Lions Eye Bank 431 Katherine Dr	Flowood	MS	39232	601-420-5739	420-5743
TF: 800-213-0403					
Musculoskeletal Transplant Foundation 125 May St Suite 300	Edison	NJ	08837	732-661-0202	
Web: www.mtf.org					
National Disease Research Interchange (NDRI)					
1628 John F Kennedy Blvd 8 Penn Center 8th Fl	Philadelphia	PA	19103	215-557-7361	557-7154
TF: 800-222-6374 ■ *Web:* www.ndriresource.org					
NDRI (National Disease Research Interchange)					
1628 John F Kennedy Blvd 8 Penn Center 8th Fl	Philadelphia	PA	19103	215-557-7361	557-7154
TF: 800-222-6374 ■ *Web:* www.ndriresource.org					
Nevada Donor Network Inc 2085 E Sahara Ave	Las Vegas	NV	89104	702-796-9600	796-4225
Web: www.nvdonor.org					
New Brunswick Eye Bank Saint Joseph's Hospital					
130 Bayard Dr	Saint John	NB	E2L3L6	506-632-5541	632-5573
New England Eye & Tissue Transplant Bank					
1 Gateway Pl Suite 309	Newton	MA	02458	617-964-1809	965-1891
TF: 800-462-2566					
New Mexico Lions Eye Bank 2501 Yale Blvd SE Suite 100	Albuquerque	NM	87106	505-266-3937	266-5560
TF: 888-616-3937					
North Carolina Eye Bank Inc					
3900 Westpoint Blvd Suite F	Winston-Salem	NC	27103	336-765-0932	765-8803
TF: 800-552-9956 ■ *Web:* www.nceyebank.org					
Northeast Pennsylvania Lions Eye Bank Inc Lehigh Valley Hospital 17th & Chew Sts PO Box 7017	Allentown	PA	18105	610-969-2155	969-4254
TF: 800-637-2393 ■ *Web:* www.paeyebank.org					
Northern California Transplant Bank					
7700 Edgewater Dr Suite 526	Oakland	CA	94621	510-957-9595	957-9594
Northwest Lions Eye Bank 901 Boren Ave Suite 810	Seattle	WA	98104	206-682-8500	682-8504
TF: 800-847-5786 ■ *Web:* www.nleb.org					
Northwest Louisiana Lions Eye Bank 721 Boulevard St	Shreveport	LA	71104	318-222-7999	222-8779
TF: 800-960-0124					
Oklahoma Lions Eye Bank 3840 N Lincoln Blvd	Oklahoma City	OK	73105	405-557-1393	557-0086
Web: www.lionnet-oklahoma.org/eyebank.htm					
Old Dominion Eye Bank 9200 Arboretum Pkwy Suite 104	Richmond	VA	23236	804-560-7540	560-4752
Web: www.odef.org					
Regional Tissue Bank QEII Health Sciences Centre					
5788 University Ave Rm 431 McKenzie Bldg Ctr	Halifax	NS	B3H1V7	902-473-4171	473-2170
TF: 800-314-6515 ■ *Web:* www.cdha.nshealth.ca/tissuebank/tissueBank.html					
Rochester Eye & Human Parts Bank DBA Rochester/Finger Lakes Eye & Tissue Bank 524 White Spruce Blvd	Rochester	NY	14623	585-272-7890	272-7897
TF: 800-568-4321 ■ *Web:* www.rehpb.org					
Rochester/Finger Lakes Eye & Tissue Bank					
524 White Spruce Blvd	Rochester	NY	14623	585-272-7890	272-7897
TF: 800-568-4321 ■ *Web:* www.rehpb.org					
Rocky Mountain Lions Eye Bank					
1675 N Ursula Ave Rm El-2049	Aurora	CO	80045	720-848-3937	848-3938
TF: 800-444-7479 ■ *Web:* www.corneas.org					
San Antonio Eye Bank 8122 Datapoint Dr Suite 325	San Antonio	TX	78229	210-614-1209	614-1422
Web: www.tbionline.org					
San Diego Eye Bank 9444 Balboa Ave Suite 100	San Diego	CA	92123	858-694-0444	565-7368
TF: 800-393-2265 ■ *Web:* www.sdeb.org					
Sierra Eye & Tissue Donor Services					
1760 Creekside Oak Dr Suite 160	Sacramento	CA	95833	916-456-1450	569-0300
TF: 800-762-8819 ■ *Web:* www.dcids.org/sierra.htm					
Sight Society of Northeastern New York Inc Lions Eye Bank at Albany 6 Executive Park Dr	Albany	NY	12203	518-489-7606	489-7607
TF: 888-615-3937 ■ *Web:* www.lionseyebankalbany.com					
South Dakota Lions Eye Bank 1321 W 22nd St	Sioux Falls	SD	57105	605-373-1008	373-1261
TF: 800-245-7846 ■ *Web:* www.sdleb.org					
Southeast Texas Lions Eye Bank Inc					
700 University Blvd Suite 302	Galveston	TX	77550	409-747-5816	747-5817
TF: 866-902-3937 ■ *Web:* www.utmb.edu/stleb					
Southern Eye Bank 4621 W Napoleon Ave Suite 209	Metairie	LA	70001	504-891-3937	891-2401
Web: www.southerneyebank.com					
Tennessee District 12-O Lions Eye Bank					
979 E 3rd St Suite A250	Chattanooga	TN	37403	423-778-4000	778-4050

	City	State	ZIP	Phone	Fax
Tennessee Donor Services 1714 Hayes St *TF:* 800-216-0319 ■ *Web:* www.dcids.org	Nashville	TN	37203	615-234-5200	320-1655
Tissue Banks International 815 Park Ave *TF:* 800-756-4824 ■ *Web:* www.tbionline.org	Baltimore	MD	21201	410-752-2020	783-6183
Transplant Services Center University of Texas 5323 Harry Hines Blvd MC 9074 *TF:* 800-433-6667	Dallas	TX	75390	214-648-2609	648-2086
University of California San Francisco Tissue Bank 3924 Williams Rd Suite 201 *TF:* 800-553-5536	San Jose	CA	95117	408-345-3515	345-3520
University of Louisville Lions Eye Bank 301 E Muhammad Ali Blvd *Web:* www.ulleb.org	Louisville	KY	40202	502-852-5457	852-5471
Upstate New York Transplant Services Inc 110 Broadway *TF:* 800-227-4771 ■ *Web:* www.unyts.org	Buffalo	NY	14203	716-853-6667	853-6674
Utah Lions Eye Bank John A Moran Eye Center 65 N Medical Dr *Web:* www.utaheyebank.org	Salt Lake City	UT	84132	801-581-2039	585-5703
Vision Share 108 Acorn Hill Ln *TF:* 888-657-4448 ■ *Web:* www.visionshare.org	Apex	NC	27502	919-303-2584	303-2586
Washington Eye Bank 815 Park Ave *TF:* 800-756-4824	Baltimore	MD	21201	410-752-2020	783-6183
Western Texas Lions Eye Bank Alliance 102 N Magdalen St Suite 280 *TF:* 866-226-7632 ■ *Web:* www.wtleba.org	San Angelo	TX	76902	325-653-8666	655-2847

273 FABRIC STORES

SEE ALSO Patterns - Sewing p. 2089

	City	State	ZIP	Phone	Fax
Calico Corners 203 Gale Ln *TF Cust Svc:* 800-213-6366 ■ *Web:* www.calicocorners.com	Kennett Square	PA	19348	610-444-9700	444-1221
Everfast Inc DBA Calico Corners 203 Gale Ln *TF Cust Svc:* 800-213-6366 ■ *Web:* www.calicocorners.com	Kennett Square	PA	19348	610-444-9700	444-1221
Fabric & Home Bonanza Inc 249-26 Horace Harding Expy *Web:* www.fabricandhomebonanza.com	Douglaston	NY	11362	718-631-4326	631-4355
Fabric Place Inc 136 Howard St *TF:* 800-556-3700 ■ *Web:* www.fabricplace.com	Framingham	MA	01702	508-872-4888	872-2547
Fishman's Fabrics Inc 1101 S Des Plaines St *Web:* www.fishmansfabrics.com	Chicago	IL	60607	312-922-7250	922-7402
Hancock Fabrics Inc 1 Fashion Way *NYSE: HKF* ■ *Web:* www.hancockfabrics.com	Baldwyn	MS	38824	662-365-6000	365-6100
Jo-Ann Fabrics & Crafts 5555 Darrow Rd *TF:* 888-739-4120 ■ *Web:* www.jo-ann.com	Hudson	OH	44236	330-656-2600	463-6660
Jo-Ann Stores Inc 5555 Darrow Rd *NYSE: JAS* ■ *TF:* 800-739-4120 ■ *Web:* www.joann.com	Hudson	OH	44236	330-656-2600	463-6660
Mary Maxim Inc 2001 Holland Ave PO Box 5019 *TF:* 800-962-9504 ■ *Web:* www.marymaxim.com	Port Huron	MI	48061	810-987-2000	987-5056
Rag Shops Inc 111 Wagaraw Rd **Fax:* Orders ■ *Web:* www.ragshop.com	Hawthorne	NJ	07506	973-423-1303	427-6568*
Vogue Fabrics 718 Main St *Web:* www.voguefabricsstore.com	Evanston	IL	60202	847-864-9600	475-8958

274 FACILITIES MANAGEMENT SERVICES

SEE ALSO Correctional & Detention Management (Privatized) p. 1572

	City	State	ZIP	Phone	Fax
American Park 'n Swap 40 Fountain Plaza *TF:* 800-828-7240 ■ *Web:* www.americanparknswap.com	Buffalo	NY	14202	716-858-5185	858-5882
American Pool Enterprises Inc 11408 Cronridge Dr Suite G *Web:* www.americanpool.com	Owings Mills	MD	21117	443-471-1190	471-1189
Applied Geo Technologies Inc Moses Cook Rd Bldg 9100 *Web:* www.msaap.com	Stennis Space Center	MS	39529	228-689-8000	689-8800
ARAMARK Food & Support Services 1101 Market St *TF:* 800-999-8989	Philadelphia	PA	19107	215-238-3000	238-3333
ARAMARK Harrison Lodging 580 White Plains Rd *TF:* 800-422-6338 ■ *Web:* www.aramarkharrisonlodging.com	Tarrytown	NY	10591	914-631-8100	631-8362
ARAMARK Uniform & Career Apparel 1101 Market St *TF:* 800-999-8989 ■ *Web:* www.aramark-uniform.com	Philadelphia	PA	19107	215-238-3000	238-3333
Arctic Slope World Services 2 N Cascade Ave Suite 510 *Web:* www.arcticworld.com	Colorado Springs	CO	80903	719-473-8904	473-8907
Bechtel Bettis Inc 50 Beale St	San Francisco	CA	94105	415-768-1234	
CA One Services 40 Fountain Plaza *TF:* 800-828-7240	Buffalo	NY	14202	716-858-5000	858-5882
Conference Center Concepts LLC 205 N Michigan Ave	Chicago	IL	60601	312-938-2003	861-0324
Creative Dining Services 1 Royal Park Dr Suite 3 *Web:* www.creativedining.com	Zeeland	MI	49464	616-748-1700	748-1900
Delaware North Cos Gaming & Entertainment 40 Fountain Plaza *TF:* 800-828-7240 ■ *Web:* www.delawarenorth.com	Buffalo	NY	14202	716-858-5000	858-5926
Delaware North Cos Parks & Resorts 40 Fountain Plaza *TF:* 800-828-7240	Buffalo	NY	14202	716-858-5000	858-5882
Diversco Integrated Services Inc 105 Diversco Dr *TF:* 800-277-3420 ■ *Web:* www.diversco.com	Spartanburg	SC	29307	864-579-3420	579-9578
Elite Show Services Inc 2878 Camino Del Rio S Suite 260 *Web:* www.eliteshowservices.com	San Diego	CA	92108	619-574-1589	574-1588
FLIK International Corp Conference Center Management 3 International Dr 2nd Fl	Rye Brook	NY	10573	914-935-5300	935-5617
Johnson Controls Inc 7400 Birchmount Rd	Markham	ON	L3R4V5	905-475-7610	474-5436
Johnson Controls Inc 5757 N Green Bay Ave *NYSE: JCI* ■ *TF:* 800-972-8040 ■ *Web:* www.johnsoncontrols.com	Milwaukee	WI	53209	414-524-1200	524-3232
L & M Technologies Inc 4209 Balloon Park Rd NE *Web:* www.lmtechnologies.com	Albuquerque	NM	87109	505-343-0200	343-0300
Marenzana Group Inc 295 Main St S PO Box 845 *Web:* www.marenzana.com	Woodbury	CT	06798	203-263-3888	263-3815
Olympia Entertainment Inc 600 Civic Center Dr *Web:* www.olympiaentertainment.com	Detroit	MI	48226	313-396-7444	396-7993
OMNIPLEX World Services Corp 14840 Conference Center Dr **Fax:* Cust Svc ■ *TF:* 800-356-3406 ■ *Web:* www.omniplex.com	Chantilly	VA	20151	703-652-3100	652-3106*
Raytheon Technical Services Co LLC 12160 Sunrise Valley Dr *Web:* www.raytheon.com/businesses/rts	Reston	VA	20191	703-295-2502	295-2529
Serco Group Inc 2650 Park Tower Dr Suite 800 **Fax Area Code:* 703 ■ *Web:* www.serco.com	Vienna	VA	22180	571-226-5000	573-8215*
SKE Support Services Inc 14900 Landmark Blvd Suite 400 *Web:* www.firstvehicleservices.com/Newsletter/FSS.htm	Dallas	TX	75254	972-991-0800	233-2469
SMG 701 Market St 4th Fl *Web:* www.smgworld.com	Philadelphia	PA	19106	215-592-4100	592-6699
Sodexho Conferencing 9801 Washington Blvd Suite 1014 **Fax Area Code:* 301 ■ *Web:* www.sodexhoconferencing.com	Gaithersburg	MD	20878	800-763-3946	987-4068*
Sodexho Inc 9801 Washingtonian Blvd *TF:* 800-763-3946 ■ *Web:* www.sodexhousa.com	Gaithersburg	MD	20878	301-987-4000	987-4438
Sportservice Corp 40 Fountain Plaza **Fax:* Acctg ■ *TF:* 800-828-7240	Buffalo	NY	14202	716-858-5000	858-5882*
UNICCO Service Co 275 Grove St Suite 3-200 *TF:* 800-283-9222 ■ *Web:* www.unicco.com	Auburndale	MA	02466	617-527-5222	969-2210
United Space Alliance 1150 Gemini Ave *TF:* 800-329-4036 ■ *Web:* www.unitedspacealliance.com	Houston	TX	77058	281-212-6200	212-6636
VMS Inc 203 E Cary St Suite 200 *TF:* 888-547-4404 ■ *Web:* www.vmsom.com	Richmond	VA	23219	804-261-8000	264-1808
Xanterra Parks & Resorts 6312 S Fiddlers Green Cir Suite 600-N *Web:* www.xanterra.com	Greenwood Village	CO	80111	303-600-3400	600-3600

275 FACTORS

Factors are companies that buy accounts receivable (invoices) from other businesses at a discount.

	City	State	ZIP	Phone	Fax
1st AAA Factors Inc 321 N Mall Dr **Fax Area Code:* 775	Saint George	UT	84790	888-216-1235	587-2801*
Accord Financial Corp 77 Bloor St W *TSX: ACD* ■ *TF:* 800-967-0015 ■ *Web:* www.accordfinancial.com	Toronto	ON	M5S1M2	416-961-0007	961-9443
Accord Financial Inc 25 Woods Lake Rd Suite 102 *TF:* 800-231-2757 ■ *Web:* www.accordfinancialus.com	Greenville	SC	29607	864-271-4384	242-0863
Account Funding Inc 16055 Ventura Blvd Suite 924 *TF:* 800-666-3928 ■ *Web:* www.accountfunding.com	Encino	CA	91436	818-995-7272	995-3631
Accounts Receivable Funding Corp 317 Peoples St Suite 600 **Fax Area Code:* 877 ■ *TF:* 800-992-1717 ■ *Web:* www.arfc.com	Corpus Christi	TX	78401	361-884-7196	884-1292*
Action Capital Corp 230 Peachtree St Suite 910 *TF:* 800-525-7767 ■ *Web:* www.actioncapital.com	Atlanta	GA	30343	404-524-3181	577-4880
Advantage Funding Corp 1000 Parkwood Cir Suite 300 *TF:* 800-241-2274 ■ *Web:* www.advantagefunding.com	Atlanta	GA	30339	770-955-2274	955-0643
AmeriFactors 215 Celebration Pl Suite 150 *TF:* 800-884-3863 ■ *Web:* www.amerifactors.com	Celebration	FL	34747	407-566-1150	566-1250
Applied Capital Inc 3700 Rio Grande Blvd NW Suite 4 *Web:* www.appliedcapital.net	Albuquerque	NM	87107	505-342-1840	342-2246
Asta Funding Inc 210 Sylvan Ave *NASDAQ: ASFI* ■ *Web:* www.astafunding.com	Englewood Cliffs	NJ	07632	201-567-5648	569-4595
Bibby Financial Services 101 N Westlake Blvd Suite 204 *TF:* 866-446-2888 ■ *Web:* www.bibbyusa.com	Westlake Village	CA	91362	805-446-6111	370-0235
Bridgeport Capital Services Inc 5541 N University Dr Suite 101 *Web:* www.bridgeportcapital.com	Coral Springs	FL	33067	954-382-4336	345-5949
Capital Factors Inc 120 E Palmetto Pk Rd 5th Fl *Web:* www.capitalfactors.com	Boca Raton	FL	33432	561-368-5011	347-6265
Capital-Plus Inc 7620 Olentangy River Rd *Web:* www.capplus.com	Columbus	OH	43235	614-848-7620	841-3856
Crestmark Bank 5480 Corporate Dr Suite 350 *TF:* 888-999-6088 ■ *Web:* www.crestmark.com	Troy	MI	48098	248-641-5100	641-5101
Diversified Funding Services Inc PO Box 873 *TF:* 888-603-0055 ■ *Web:* www.divfunding.com	Jonesboro	GA	30237	770-603-0055	603-9823
DSA Factors 3126 N Lincoln Ave PO Box 577520 *Web:* www.dsafactors.com	Chicago	IL	60657	773-248-9000	248-9005
Goodman Factors 3010 LBJ Freeway Suite 140 *TF:* 877-446-6362 ■ *Web:* www.goodmanfactors.com	Dallas	TX	75234	972-241-3297	243-6285
Hamilton Group 100 Elwood Davis Rd *TF:* 800-351-3066 ■ *Web:* www.hamiltongroup.net	North Syracuse	NY	13212	315-413-0086	413-0087
Interface Financial Group 2182 Dupont Dr Suite 221 **Fax Area Code:* 866 ■ *TF:* 800-387-0860 ■ *Web:* www.interfacefinancial.com	Irvine	CA	92612	949-477-0665	475-8688*
JD Factors 500 Silver Spur Rd Suite 306 *TF:* 866-585-2274 ■ *Web:* www.jdfactors.com	Redondo Beach	CA	90275	310-544-5141	544-5142
LSQ Funding Group LC 1403 W Colonial Dr Suite B *TF:* 800-474-7606 ■ *Web:* www.lsqgroup.com	Orlando	FL	32804	407-206-0022	206-0025
Magnolia Financial Inc 187 W Broad St *Web:* www.magfinancial.com	Spartanburg	SC	29306	864-573-9900	573-9912
Mazon Assoc Inc 600 W Airport Fwy *TF:* 800-442-2740 ■ *Web:* www.mazon.com	Irving	TX	75062	972-554-6967	554-0951
Merchant Factors Corp 1430 Broadway 18th Fl *TF:* 800-929-3293 ■ *Web:* www.merchantfactors.com	New York	NY	10018	212-840-7575	869-1752
Montcap Financial Corp 3500 de Maisonneuve Blvd W Suite 1510 *TF:* 800-231-2977 ■ *Web:* www.montcap.com	Montreal	QC	H3Z3C1	514-932-8223	932-0076
Performance Funding 4105 N 20th St Suite 205 *Web:* www.performancefunding.com	Phoenix	AZ	85016	602-912-0200	912-0480
Porter Capital Corp 2112 1st Ave N *TF:* 800-737-7344 ■ *Web:* www.portercap.net	Birmingham	AL	35203	205-322-5442	322-7719
Prestige Capital Corp 2 Executive Dr400 Kelby St *Web:* www.pcc-cash.com	Fort Lee	NJ	07024	201-944-4455	944-9477
Quantum Corporate Funding Ltd 1140 Ave of the Americas 16th Fl *TF:* 800-352-2535 ■ *Web:* www.quantumfunding.com	New York	NY	10036	212-768-1200	944-8216
Riviera Finance 220 Ave I **Fax Area Code:* 651 ■ *TF:* 800-421-1327 ■ *Web:* www.rivierafinance.com	Redondo Beach	CA	90277	800-872-7484	454-8122*
Rockland Credit Finance LLC 6 Park Center Ct Suite 212 *TF:* 866-725-5263 ■ *Web:* www.rocklandcredit.com	Owings Mills	MD	21117	410-902-0393	902-0893
Rosenthal & Rosenthal Inc 1370 Broadway *TF:* 800-999-4800 ■ *Web:* www.rosenthalinc.com	New York	NY	10018	212-356-1400	356-0942
RTS Financial Service 8601 Monrovia *TF:* 800-860-7926 ■ *Web:* www.rtsfinancial.com	Lenexa	KS	66215	913-492-6351	492-1998
Seven Oaks Capital 5745 Essen Ln Suite 102 *TF:* 800-511-4588 ■ *Web:* www.sevenoakscapital.com	Baton Rouge	LA	70810	225-757-1919	757-1916
TCE Capital Corp 505 Consumers Rd Suite 707 *TF:* 800-465-0400 ■ *Web:* www.tcecapital.com	Toronto	ON	M2J4V8	416-497-7400	497-3139
Transport Clearing East Inc 210 E Woodlawn Rd Bldg 6 *Web:* www.tceast.com	Charlotte	NC	28217	704-527-1820	527-1851
United California Discount Corp 2035 S Myrtle Ave *TF:* 800-228-7151 ■ *Web:* www.ucdc.com	Monrovia	CA	91017	626-303-3551	303-5652
United Capital Funding Corp 146 2nd St N Suite 200 *Web:* www.ucfunding.com	Saint Petersburg	FL	33701	727-894-8232	898-4205
Working Capital Co 985 Moraga Rd Suite 210 PO Box 7007 *TF:* 800-899-3836 ■ *Web:* www.working-capital.com	Lafayette	CA	94549	925-283-4433	283-7755

276 FARM MACHINERY & EQUIPMENT - MFR

SEE ALSO Lawn & Garden Equipment p. 1888

Company	City	State	ZIP	Phone	Fax
ADM Alliance Nutrition Inc 1000 N 30th St *TF:* 800-292-3333 ■ *Web:* www.admani.com	Quincy	IL	62301	217-222-7100	222-4069
AGCO Corp 4205 River Green Pkwy *NYSE: AG* ■ *Web:* www.agcocorp.com	Duluth	GA	30096	770-813-9200	813-6140
Agile Mfg Inc 720 Industrial Park Rd *TF:* 800-704-7356 ■ *Web:* www.agilemfg.net	Anderson	MO	64831	417-845-6065	845-6069
Alamo Group Inc 1502 E Walnut St *NYSE: ALG* ■ *TF Cust Svc:* 800-356-6286 ■ *Web:* www.alamo-group.com	Seguin	TX	78155	830-379-1480	372-9679
Alliance Product Group 18107 US 224 W *TF:* 800-322-6301 ■ *Web:* www.allianceag.com	Kalida	OH	45853	419-532-3312	532-2021
Allied Systems Co 21433 SW Oregon St *TF:* 800-285-7000 ■ *Web:* www.alliedsystems.com	Sherwood	OR	97140	503-625-2560	625-7269
Amadas Industries Inc 1100 Holland Rd *Web:* www.amadas.com	Suffolk	VA	23434	757-539-0231	934-3264
Amarillo Wind Machine Co 20513 Ave 256 *TF:* 800-311-4498 ■ *Web:* www.amarillowind.com	Exeter	CA	93221	559-592-4256	592-4194
Amerequip Corp 1015 Calumet Ave *Web:* www.amerequip.com	Kiel	WI	53042	920-894-7063	894-3799
American Equipment Corp 47219 W Schweigers Cir *TF:* 800-624-0138	Sioux Falls	SD	57107	605-543-5606	543-5610
Art's-Way Mfg Co Inc 5556 Hwy 9 *NASDAQ: ARTW* ■ *Web:* www.artsway-mfg.com/	Armstrong	IA	50514	712-864-3131	864-3154
Automatic Equipment Mfg Co 1 Mill Rd Industrial Park *TF:* 800-228-9289 ■ *Web:* www.aemfg.com	Pender	NE	68047	402-385-3051	385-3360
B & H Mfg Inc 141 County Rd 34 E *TF:* 800-240-3288 ■ *Web:* www.bhmfg.com	Jackson	MN	56143	507-847-2802	847-4655
Behlen Mfg Co 4025 E 23rd St *TF:* 800-553-5520 ■ *Web:* www.behlenmfg.com	Columbus	NE	68601	402-564-3111	563-7405
Berg Equipment Co 2700 W Veterans Pkwy *TF:* 800-494-1738 ■ *Web:* www.bergsandmark.com	Marshfield	WI	54449	715-384-2151	387-6777
Big Dutchman Inc 3900 John F Donnelly Dr *Web:* www.bigdutchmanusa.com	Holland	MI	49424	616-392-5981	392-6188
Bou-Matic 1919 Stoughton Rd *Web:* www.bou-matic.com	Madison	WI	53716	608-222-3484	222-9314
Bowie Industries Inc 1004 E Wise St *TF:* 800-433-0934 ■ *Web:* www.bowieindustries.com	Bowie	TX	76230	940-872-1106	872-4792
Brillion Iron Works Inc 200 Park Ave PO Box 127 *TF:* 800-409-9749 ■ *Web:* www.brillionfarmeq.com	Brillion	WI	54110	920-756-2121	756-3550
Brock Grain Conditioning Group 1750 W SR-28 *TF:* 800-541-7900 ■ *Web:* www.graindryers.com	Frankfort	IN	46041	765-654-8517	654-8510
Brown Mfg Corp 6001 E Hwy 27 *TF:* 800-633-8909 ■ *Web:* www.brownmfgcorp.com	Ozark	AL	36360	334-795-6603	795-3029
Broyhill Co 1 N Market Sq *TF:* 800-228-1003 ■ *Web:* www.broyhill.com	Dakota City	NE	68731	402-987-3412	987-3601
Buhler Versatile Inc 1260 Clarence Ave *TF:* 866-291-7775 ■ *Web:* www.buhler.com	Winnipeg	MB	R3C4E8	204-284-6100	477-2325
Bush Hog LLC 2501 Griffin Ave PO Box 1039 *TF:* 800-363-6096 ■ *Web:* www.bushhog.com	Selma	AL	36702	334-872-6261	874-2701
Bushnell Illinois Tank Co 650 W Davis St *Web:* www.schuldbushnell.com	Bushnell	IL	61422	309-772-3106	772-2045
Cal-Coast Dairy Systems Inc 424 S Tegner Rd *TF Cust Svc:* 800-732-6826 ■ *Web:* www.calcoastinc.com	Turlock	CA	95380	209-634-9026	634-3458
Carter Day International Inc 500 73rd Ave NE *Web:* www.carterday.com	Minneapolis	MN	55432	763-571-1000	571-3012
Case IH 700 State St *Web:* www.caseih.com	Racine	WI	53404	262-636-6011	636-7006
Chick Master Incubator Co 945 Lafayette Rd *TF:* 800-727-8726 ■ *Web:* www.chickmaster.com	Medina	OH	44256	330-722-5591	723-0233
Conrad-American Inc 609 Main St *TF:* 800-553-1791 ■ *Web:* www.conradamer.com	Houghton	IA	52631	319-469-4111	469-4402
Continental Eagle Corp 201 Gin Shop Hill Rd *TF:* 866-266-3245 ■ *Web:* www.coneagle.com	Prattville	AL	36067	334-365-8811	361-7627
Covington Planter Co 410 Hodges Ave *Web:* www.covingtonplanter.com	Albany	GA	31701	229-888-2032	888-0448
CrustBuster/Speed King Inc 2300 E Trail *Web:* www.crustbuster.com	Dodge City	KS	67801	620-227-7106	227-7130
CTB Inc 611 N Higbee St PO Box 2000 *Web:* www.ctbinc.com	Milford	IN	46542	574-658-4101	658-3471
Custom Products of Litchfield Inc 1715 S Sibley Ave *TF:* 800-222-5463 ■ *Web:* www.800cabline.com	Litchfield	MN	55355	320-693-3221	693-7252
Cyclone Mfg Co Inc 151 N Washington St PO Box 67 *TF:* 800-972-6130	Urbana	IN	46990	260-774-3311	774-3416
Daco Inc 609 Airport Rd *Web:* www.dacoinc.com	North Aurora	IL	60542	630-897-8797	897-4076
Danuser Machine Co 500 E 3rd St *Web:* www.danuser.com	Fulton	MO	65251	573-642-2246	642-2240
David Mfg Co 1004 E Illinois St *TF:* 877-362-8033 ■ *Web:* www.dmc-davidmanufacturing.com	Assumption	IL	62510	217-226-4421	226-4445
Deere & Co John Deere Agriculture Div 1 John Deere Pl *TF:* 866-993-3373 ■ *Web:* www.deere.com/servlet/AgHomePageServlet	Moline	IL	61265	309-765-8000	765-5209
Dempster Industries Inc 711 S 6th St *TF:* 800-777-0212 ■ *Web:* www.dempsterinc.com	Beatrice	NE	68310	402-223-4026	228-4389
DuraTech Industries International Inc 3780 Hwy 281 SE *TF:* 800-243-4601 ■ *Web:* www.dura-ind.com	Jamestown	ND	58402	701-252-4601	252-0502
Edstrom Industries Inc 819 Bakke Ave *TF:* 800-558-5913 ■ *Web:* www.edstrom.com	Waterford	WI	53185	262-534-5181	534-5184
Empire Plow Co Inc 3140 E 65th St *Web:* www.mckayempire.com	Cleveland	OH	44127	216-641-2290	441-4709
EVH Mfg LLC 4895 Red Bluff Rd *TF:* 888-990-2555 ■ *Web:* www.evhmfg.com	Loris	SC	29569	843-756-4051	756-4436
EZ Trail Inc Hwy 133 E Box 168 *TF:* 800-677-2802 ■ *Web:* www.e-ztrail.com	Arthur	IL	61911	217-543-3471	543-3473
Farmtrac 111 Fairview St *TF:* 877-639-5194 ■ *Web:* www.farmtrac.com	Tarboro	NC	27886	252-823-4151	823-4576
Feterl Mfg Co 411 Center Ave W *TF:* 800-367-8660 ■ *Web:* www.feterl.com	Salem	SD	57058	605-425-2206	425-2183
Finn Corp 9281 Le Saint Dr *TF:* 800-543-7166 ■ *Web:* www.finncorp.com	Fairfield	OH	45014	513-874-2818	874-2914
Flint Cliffs Mfg Co 1600 Bluff Rd *TF:* 800-445-1867 ■ *Web:* squrl.8k.com	Burlington	IA	52601	319-752-2781	752-5538
Forsbergs Inc 1210 Pennington Ave *TF Cust Svc:* 800-654-1927 ■ *Web:* www.forsbergs.com	Thief River Falls	MN	56701	218-681-1927	681-2037
Gandy Co 528 Gandrud Rd *TF:* 800-443-2476 ■ *Web:* www.gandy.net	Owatonna	MN	55060	507-451-5430	451-2857
Gehl Co 143 Water St *NASDAQ: GEHL* ■ *Web:* www.gehl.com	West Bend	WI	53095	262-334-9461	338-7517
GMP Metal Products Inc 3883 Delor St *TF:* 800-325-9808 ■ *Web:* www.gmpmetal.com	Saint Louis	MO	63116	314-481-0300	481-1379
Gregory Mfg Co Inc 506 Oak Dr *TF:* 800-233-4734 ■ *Web:* www.gregorymfg.com	Lewiston	NC	27849	252-348-2531	348-2400
GSI Group Inc 1004 E Illinois St PO Box 20 *Web:* www.grainsystems.com	Assumption	IL	62510	217-226-5400	226-4445
Hagie Mfg Co 721 Central Ave W *TF:* 800-247-4885 ■ *Web:* www.hagie.com	Clarion	IA	50525	515-532-2861	532-3553
Hanson Silo Co 11587 County Rd 8 SE *TF:* 800-450-4171 ■ *Web:* www.hansonsilo.com	Lake Lillian	MN	56253	320-664-4171	664-4140
Hastings Equity Grain Bin Mfg Co 1900 Summit Ave *Web:* www.hastingstanks.com	Hastings	NE	68901	402-462-2189	462-2900
HCC Inc 1501 1st Ave *Web:* www.hccincorporated.com	Mendota	IL	61342	815-539-9371	539-7331
HD Hudson Mfg Co 500 N Michigan Ave Suite 2300 *TF:* 800-523-9284 ■ *Web:* www.hdhudson.com	Chicago	IL	60611	312-644-2830	644-7989
Henderson Mfg Inc 1085 S 3rd St *TF:* 800-359-4970 ■ *Web:* www.henderson-mfg.com	Manchester	IA	52057	563-927-2828	927-2521
Herschel-Adams Inc 1301 N 14th St **Fax Area Code:* 800 ■ *TF Cust Svc:* 800-247-2167 ■ *Web:* www.herschel-adams.com	Indianola	IA	50125	515-961-7481	524-7481*
Hiniker Co 58766 240th St **Fax:* Sales ■ *TF:* 800-433-5620 ■ *Web:* www.hiniker.com	Mankato	MN	56002	507-625-6621	625-5883*
Honiron Corp 400 S Canal St *Web:* www.honiron.com	Jeanerette	LA	70544	337-276-6314	276-3614
Howse Implement Co Inc 2013 Hwy 184 E *Web:* www.howseimplement.com	Laurel	MS	39443	601-428-0841	649-6759
Hudson HD Mfg Co 500 N Michigan Ave Suite 2300 *TF:* 800-523-9284 ■ *Web:* www.hdhudson.com	Chicago	IL	60611	312-644-2830	644-7989
Hutchinson/Mayrath/TerraTrack Industries 514 W Crawford St *TF:* 800-523-6993 ■ *Web:* www.hutchinson-mayrath.com	Clay Center	KS	67432	785-632-3133	632-5964
Irridelco International Corp 440 Sylvan Ave *Web:* www.irridelco.com	Englewood Cliffs	NJ	07632	201-569-3030	569-9237
John Deere Agriculture Div Deere & Co 1 John Deere Pl *TF:* 866-993-3373 ■ *Web:* www.deere.com/servlet/AgHomePageServlet	Moline	IL	61265	309-765-8000	765-5209
Johnson Farm Machinery Co Inc 38574 Kentucky Ave *Web:* www.jfmco.com	Woodland	CA	95695	530-662-1788	666-5585
K & M Mfg Co 308 NW 2nd St *TF:* 800-328-1752 ■ *Web:* www.kandmmanufacturing.com	Renville	MN	56284	320-329-3301	329-3709
Kelly Ryan Equipment Co 900 Kelly Ryan Dr *TF:* 800-640-6967 ■ *Web:* www.kryan.com	Blair	NE	68008	402-426-2151	426-2186
Kinze Mfg Inc 2172 M Ave *Web:* www.kinzemfg.com	Williamsburg	IA	52361	319-668-1300	668-3069
Kirby Mfg Inc 484 S Hwy 59 *Web:* www.kirbymfg.com	Merced	CA	95340	209-723-0778	723-3941
Krause Corp 305 S Monroe St *TF:* 800-957-2873 ■ *Web:* www.krauseco.com	Hutchinson	KS	67501	620-663-6161	663-6943
Kroy Industries Inc 701 S 17th St *TF:* 800-228-2883 ■ *Web:* www.kroyind.com	Henderson	NE	68371	402-723-5374	723-5378
Kubota Tractor Corp 3401 Del Amo Blvd *TF:* 800-582-6821 ■ *Web:* www.kubota.com	Torrance	CA	90503	310-370-3370	370-2370
Kuhn Knight Inc 1501 W 7th Ave *Web:* www.kuhnknight.com	Brodhead	WI	53520	608-897-2131	897-2561
Lely USA Inc 1610 Vermeer Rd E PO Box 437 *TF:* 888-245-4684 ■ *Web:* www.lely.com	Pella	IA	50219	641-621-7905	621-7881
Lewis/Mola Mfg LLC 183 Elle Dr *Web:* www.lewismola.com	Bennettsville	SC	29512	843-479-6231	479-7739
Lindsay Corp 214 E 2nd St *NYSE: LNN* ■ *TF:* 800-829-5300 ■ *Web:* lindsaymanufacturing.com	Lindsay	NE	68644	402-428-2131	428-7289
Loftness Specialized Farm Equipment Inc 650 S Main St *TF:* 800-828-7624 ■ *Web:* www.loftness.com	Hector	MN	55342	320-848-6266	848-6269
Lummus Carver Gump Corp 1 Lummus Dr *TF:* 800-458-6687 ■ *Web:* www.carver-inc.com	Savannah	GA	31407	912-748-5000	447-9250
Lund Precision Products Inc 791 Piper St *Web:* www.lundonline.com	Collierville	TN	38017	901-853-4761	853-5499
LZ Truck Equipment Co Inc 1881 Rice St *TF:* 800-247-1082 ■ *Web:* www.lztruckequipment.com	Roseville	MN	55113	651-488-2571	488-9857
Mathews Co 500 Industrial Ave *TF:* 800-323-7045 ■ *Web:* www.mathewscompany.com	Crystal Lake	IL	60012	815-459-2210	459-5889
Mertz Mfg LLC 1701 N Waverly St *TF:* 800-654-6433 ■ *Web:* www.mertzok.com	Ponca City	OK	74601	580-762-5646	767-8411
Miller Saint Nazianz Inc 511 E Main St *TF:* 800-247-5557 ■ *Web:* www.millerstn.com	Saint Nazianz	WI	54232	920-773-2121	773-1200
Modern Group Ltd 1655 Louisiana St *TF Cust Svc:* 800-231-8198 ■ *Web:* www.modernusa.com	Beaumont	TX	77701	409-833-2665	833-1766
Montgomery Industries International Inc 2017 Thelma St *Web:* www.montgomeryindustries.com	Jacksonville	FL	32206	904-355-4055	355-0401
Moorfeed Corp 1336 W Wiley Ave *TF:* 888-545-7171 ■ *Web:* www.moorfeed.com	Bluffton	IN	46714	260-353-1042	824-0129
Moridge Mfg Inc 105 Old US Hwy 81	Moundridge	KS	67107	620-345-6301	345-2301
New Holland Construction North America 245 E North Ave *TF:* 888-290-7377	Carol Stream	IL	60188	630-260-4000	462-7514
Orchard-Rite Ltd Inc PO Box 9308 *TF:* 800-676-4460 ■ *Web:* www.orchard-rite.com	Yakima	WA	98909	509-457-9196	457-9186
Orthman Mfg Inc 75765 Rd 435 PO Box B *TF:* 800-658-3270 ■ *Web:* www.orthman.com	Lexington	NE	68850	308-324-4654	324-5001
Osborne Industries Inc 120 N Industrial Ave *TF:* 800-255-0316 ■ *Web:* www.osborne-ind.com	Osborne	KS	67473	785-346-2192	346-2194
P & H Mfg Co 604 S Lodge St PO Box 349 *TF Sales:* 800-879-2123 ■ *Web:* www.phmfg.com	Shelbyville	IL	62565	217-774-2123	774-5341
Peerless Mfg Co US Hwy 82 E *TF:* 800-225-4617 ■ *Web:* www.peerlessmfg.cc	Shellman	GA	39886	229-679-5353	679-5542
Performance Feeders Inc 251 Dunbar *Web:* www.performancefeeders.com	Oldsmar	FL	34677	813-855-2685	855-4296
Precision Tank & Equipment Co Inc 3503 Conover Rd *TF:* 800-258-4197 ■ *Web:* www.precisiontank.com	Virginia	IL	62691	217-452-7228	452-3956
Rainbow Mfg Co 101 Rainbow Dr *TF Cust Svc:* 800-841-0323 ■ *Web:* www.rainbowirrigation.com	Fitzgerald	GA	31750	229-423-4341	423-4645
Rayne Land Planes Inc 200 Southeastern Ave *Web:* www.rayneplane.biz	Rayne	LA	70578	337-334-2101	334-7338
Reinke Mfg Co Inc 5325 Reinke Rd *Web:* www.reinke.com	Deshler	NE	68340	402-365-7251	365-4370
Reynolds International Equipment LP 5000 N 29th St *TF:* 800-441-8161 ■ *Web:* www.reynoldsinternational.com	McAllen	TX	78504	956-687-7500	630-5263
Ryan Kelly Equipment Co 900 Kelly Ryan Dr *TF:* 800-640-6967 ■ *Web:* www.kryan.com	Blair	NE	68008	402-426-2151	426-2186
Schuette Mfg & Steel Sales Inc 5028 Hwy 42 *Web:* www.knowlesmfgco.com	Manitowoc	WI	54220	920-758-2491	758-2599
Shivvers Inc 614 W English St *TF:* 800-245-9093 ■ *Web:* www.shivvers.com	Corydon	IA	50060	641-872-1005	872-1593
Simonsen Industries Inc 500 Hwy 31 E *TF:* 800-831-4860 ■ *Web:* www.simonsen-industries.com	Quimby	IA	51049	712-445-2211	445-2626
Sioux Steel Co 196 1/2 E 6th St *TF:* 800-557-4689 ■ *Web:* www.siouxsteel.com	Sioux Falls	SD	57104	605-336-1750	965-4252
Sprayrite Mfg Co Inc 4584 Hwy 49 PO Box 3289	West Helena	AR	72390	870-572-6737	572-6730
Spudnik Equipment Co 584 W 100 North Rd *Web:* www.spudnik.com	Blackfoot	ID	83221	208-785-0480	785-1497
Stock Equipment Co 16490 Chillicothe Rd *TF:* 800-268-3347 ■ *Web:* www.stock.com	Chagrin Falls	OH	44023	440-543-6000	543-5944

Company	City	State	ZIP	Phone	Fax
Sudenga Industries Inc 2002 Kingbird Ave TF: 888-783-3642 ■ *Web:* www.sudenga.com	George	IA	51237	712-475-3301	475-3320
Sukup Mfg Co 1555 255th St *Web:* www.sukupmfg.com	Sheffield	IA	50475	641-892-4222	892-4629
Summers Mfg Co Inc 338 Railway Ave TF: 800-732-4347 ■ *Web:* www.summersmfg.com	Maddock	ND	58348	701-438-2855	438-2680
Taylor Pittsburgh Manufacturing 7 Rocky Mount Rd TF: 800-456-7929 ■ *Web:* www.taylorpittsburgh.com	Athens	TN	37303	423-745-3110	744-9662
Toro Co Irrigation Div 5825 Jasmine St TF: 800-664-4740 ■ *Web:* www.toro.com	Riverside	CA	92502	951-688-9221	
Unverferth Mfg Co Inc 18107 US 224 W TF: 800-322-6301 ■ *Web:* www.unverferth.com	Kalida	OH	45853	419-532-3121	532-2468
Valco Inc 210 E Main St TF: 800-531-1064 ■ *Web:* www.valcompanies.com	Coldwater	OH	45828	419-678-8731	678-2200
Valmont Industries Inc 1 Valmont Plaza NYSE: VMI ■ TF: 800-825-6668 ■ *Web:* www.valmont.com	Omaha	NE	68154	402-963-1000	963-1100
Vermeer Mfg Co 1210 Vermeer Rd E *Fax: Mktg ■ *Web:* www.vermeer.com	Pella	IA	50219	641-628-3141	621-7734*
Wiese Industries Inc 1501 5th St PO Box 39 TF: 800-568-4391 ■ *Web:* www.wiesecorp.com	Perry	IA	50220	515-465-9854	465-9858
Woods Equipment Co 2606 S Illinois Rt 2 *Fax: Sales ■ TF: 800-319-6637 ■ *Web:* www.woodsonline.com	Oregon	IL	61061	815-732-2141	732-7580*
Woods Equipment Co 1000 W Cherokee St	Sioux Falls	SD	57104	605-336-3860	336-6750
Wylie & Son Mfg Co 101 N Main St TF Sales: 800-722-4001 ■ *Web:* www.wyliesprayers.com	Petersburg	TX	79250	806-667-3566	667-3392
Yetter Mfg Co Inc 109 S McDonough St TF: 800-447-5777 ■ *Web:* www.yetterco.com	Colchester	IL	62326	309-776-4111	776-3222

277 FARM MACHINERY & EQUIPMENT - WHOL

Company	City	State	ZIP	Phone	Fax
A & L Distributing Co 7933 SW Cirrus Dr TF: 800-234-9556	Beaverton	OR	97008	503-684-9384	684-5574
Ag-Land Implement Inc Hwy 63 N PO Box 31 *Web:* www.aglandimplement.com	New Hampton	IA	50659	641-394-4226	394-3936
Ag West Supply 9055 Rickreall Rd PO Box 47 TF: 800-842-2224 ■ *Web:* www.agwestsupply.com	Rickreall	OR	97371	503-363-2332	363-5662
Arends Brothers Inc Rt 54 N *Web:* www.arendsbros.com	Melvin	IL	60952	217-388-7717	388-2882
Arends & Sons Inc 715 S Sangamon Ave TF: 800-637-6052 ■ *Web:* www.arends-sons.com	Gibson City	IL	60936	217-784-4241	784-8749
B & G Equipment Inc 301 E 8th St TF: 800-382-9024 ■ *Web:* www.bgequipment.com	Greeley	CO	80631	970-352-2288	352-9179
Baker Implement Co 421 E Main St *Web:* www.bakerimplement.com	Portageville	MO	63873	573-379-5455	379-5313
Barnett Implement Co Inc 4220 Old Hwy 99 S TF: 800-453-9274 ■ *Web:* www.barnettimplement.com	Mount Vernon	WA	98273	360-424-7995	424-0403
BE Implement Co PO Box 752 TF: 800-725-5435 ■ *Web:* www.beimplement.com	Brownfield	TX	79316	806-637-3594	637-8992
Beatty Implement Co 1351 W Jackson St	Auburn	IL	62615	217-438-6111	438-6815
Belarus Tractor International Inc 7842 N Faulkner Rd *Fax: Sales ■ TF: 800-356-2336 ■ *Web:* www.belarus.com	Milwaukee	WI	53224	414-355-2000	355-6903*
Bell Equipment Inc PO Box 230 TF: 800-753-3373 ■ *Web:* www.jddealer.deere.com/bell/	Grangeville	ID	83530	208-983-1730	983-1903
Berchtold Equipment Co Inc 330 E 19th St *Web:* www.berchtold.com	Bakersfield	CA	93305	661-323-7817	325-4059
Blanchard Compact Equipment 1410 Ashville Hwy TF: 800-397-9075 ■ *Web:* www.blanchardmachinery.com	Spartanburg	SC	29303	864-582-1245	582-7121
Boston Tractor Co Inc PO Box 8	Dixie	GA	31629	229-263-4133	263-9178
Browning Equipment Inc 800 E Main St *Web:* www.browningequipment.com	Purcellville	VA	20132	540-338-7123	338-5835
Carco International Inc 2721 Midland Blvd TF: 800-824-3215	Fort Smith	AR	72904	479-441-3270	441-3273
Cash Hardware Co Inc 406 W Main St TF: 800-835-8311	Coulee City	WA	99115	509-632-5547	632-8720
Coleman Equipment Inc PO Box 456 *Web:* www.colemanequip.com	Bonner Springs	KS	66012	913-422-3040	422-3044
Deer Trail Implement Inc 1411 S 81 Hwy Bypass PO Box 1326 TF: 800-364-4020 ■ *Web:* www.jddealer.deere.com/deertrail/	McPherson	KS	67460	620-241-3553	241-3572
Deere John Ltd 295 Hunter Rd PO Box 1000 *Web:* www.deere.com	Grimsby	ON	L3M4H5	905-945-9281	945-0341
Delta Implement Co Inc 3180 Hwy 82 E	Greenville	MS	38704	662-332-2683	332-2911
Delta Ridge Implement Inc 1150 US Hwy 425 *Web:* www.jddealer.deere.com/deltaridge/	Rayville	LA	71269	318-728-6423	728-6426
Dexter Implement Co 20919 State Hwy 114 PO Box 217 *Web:* www.dexterimplement.com	Dexter	MO	63841	573-624-7467	624-3308
EJ Smith Group PO Box 7247 *Web:* www.ejsmithgroup.com	Charlotte	NC	28241	704-583-0422	583-0429
Empire Southwest Co 1725 S Country Club Dr TF: 800-367-4731 ■ *Web:* empire.cat.com	Mesa	AZ	85210	480-633-4000	633-4489
Ernie Williams Ltd 2613 Hwy 18 E *Web:* www.erniewilliamsltd.com	Algona	IA	50511	515-295-3561	295-3419
Farm Equipment Co Inc Hwy 165 *Web:* www.farmequipmentco.com	Portland	AR	71663	870-737-2211	737-4298
Farm Implement & Supply Co Inc 520 W Mill St TF: 888-589-6029 ■ *Web:* www.farmimp.com	Plainville	KS	67663	785-434-4824	434-7390
Farmers Supply Sales Inc 1409 'E' Ave TF: 877-656-2291	Kalona	IA	52247	319-656-2291	656-3873
Ferriday Farm Equipment Co Inc 503 Lake Dr Hwy 568 TF: 800-256-4576 ■ *Web:* www.ferridayfarm.com	Ferriday	LA	71334	318-757-4576	757-2607
Fields Equipment Co Inc 3203 Havendale Blvd *Web:* www.fieldsequip.com	Winter Haven	FL	33881	863-967-0602	967-8648
Finning International Inc 666 Burrard St Suite 1000 Park Place TSX: FTT ■ TF: 888-346-6464 ■ *Web:* www.finning.ca	Vancouver	AB	V6C2X8	604-691-6444	691-6440
Forks Equipment 5101 Gateway Dr TF: 888-456-0240 ■ *Web:* www.forksequipment.com	Grand Forks	ND	58203	701-746-4436	780-9550
French Implement Co Inc 497 S Hwy 105 TF: 800-325-8622 ■ *Web:* www.frenchimplement.com	Charleston	MO	63834	573-649-3021	649-5389
Fruit Growers Supply Co Inc 14130 Riverside Dr *Web:* www.fruitgrowers.com	Sherman Oaks	CA	91423	818-986-6480	783-1941
Gardner Inc 3641 Interchange Rd TF: 800-848-8946 ■ *Web:* www.gardnerinc.com	Columbus	OH	43204	614-456-4000	456-4001
Garton Tractor Inc 2400 N Golden State Blvd TF: 800-286-0490 ■ *Web:* www.garton-tractor.com	Turlock	CA	95380	209-632-3931	632-8006
Gebo Distributing Co Inc 3109 Olton Blvd PO Box 850	Plainview	TX	79073	806-293-4212	293-3992
Gem Equipment Inc 2670 Kimberley Rd E TF: 800-227-1007 ■ *Web:* jddealer.deere.com/gem	Twin Falls	ID	83301	208-733-7272	733-7290
German-Bliss Equipment Co Inc 624 W Spring St TF: 800-728-4734 ■ *Web:* www.germanbliss.com	Princeville	IL	61559	309-385-4316	385-2540
Giles & Ransome Inc Ransome Engine Power Div 2975 Galloway Rd TF: 800-753-4228 ■ *Web:* ransome.cat.com	Bensalem	PA	19020	215-639-4300	245-2779
Golden Spike Equipment Co 1352 W Main St PO Box 70 TF: 800-821-4474 ■ *Web:* www.gspike.com	Tremonton	UT	84337	435-257-5346	257-5719
Greenline Equipment 6068 S Redwood Rd TF: 888-201-5500 ■ *Web:* www.greenlineequipment.com	Salt Lake City	UT	84123	801-966-4231	966-4313
Grossenburg Implement Inc 31341 US Hwy 18 TF: 800-658-3440 ■ *Web:* www.grossenburg.com	Winner	SD	57580	605-842-2040	842-3485
Growers Equipment Co 8674 NW 58th St TF: 800-592-7890 ■ *Web:* www.growersford.com	Miami	FL	33166	305-592-7891	592-7892
Halferty HH & Sons Inc PO Box 298	Smithville	MO	64089	816-532-0221	532-0242
Hamilton Equipment Inc 567 S Reading Rd PO Box 478 *Web:* www.haminc.com	Ephrata	PA	17522	717-733-7951	733-1783
Hanley Co Inc 641 W Main St TF: 800-279-1422 ■ *Web:* www.hanleycompany.com	Sun Prairie	WI	53590	608-837-5111	837-0818
Harcourt Equipment 313 Hwy 169 & 175 E TF: 800-445-5646 ■ *Web:* www.harcourtequipment.com	Harcourt	IA	50544	515-354-5331	354-5328
Harry J Whelchel Co PO Box 5022	Chattanooga	TN	37406	423-698-4415	629-7395
Hayward Distributing Co 4061 Perimeter Dr TF: 800-282-1585	Columbus	OH	43228	614-272-5953	272-5959
HB Duvall Inc 901 E Patrick St TF: 800-423-4032 ■ *Web:* www.hbduvall.com	Frederick	MD	21701	301-662-1125	695-0265
HC Clark Implement Co 4411 E Hwy 12 TF: 800-532-6747	Aberdeen	SD	57401	605-225-8170	225-4671
Heartland Farm & Lawn 1880 Hwy 13 TF: 877-532-6766 ■ *Web:* www.heartlandfarmandlawn.com	Higginsville	MO	64037	660-584-7434	584-7412
Heath's Inc 600 W Bridge St TF: 800-443-2847 ■ *Web:* www.heaths.com	Monticello	IL	61856	217-762-2534	762-8032
Hector Turf & Garden Inc 1301 NW 3rd St TF: 877-343-2867 ■ *Web:* www.hectorturf.com	Deerfield Beach	FL	33442	954-429-3200	360-7657
HH Halferty & Sons Inc PO Box 298	Smithville	MO	64089	816-532-0221	532-0242
Hillsboro Equipment Inc E18898 State Hwy 33 E PO Box 583 TF: 800-521-5133 ■ *Web:* www.hillsboroequipment.com	Hillsboro	WI	54634	608-489-2275	489-2717
Hobbs Implement Co Inc PO Box 807 TF: 800-682-6457	Edenton	NC	27932	252-482-7411	482-7682
Hollingsworth Inc 1775 SW 30th St TF: 800-541-1612 ■ *Web:* www.jddealer.deere.com/hollings	Ontario	OR	97914	541-889-7254	889-8364
Holt Co of Texas 3302 South WW White Rd TF: 800-275-4658 ■ *Web:* www.holttexas.com	San Antonio	TX	78222	210-648-1111	648-0079
Hoober Inc 3452 Old Philadelphia Pike PO Box 518 TF: 800-732-0017 ■ *Web:* www.hoober.com	Intercourse	PA	17534	717-768-8231	768-3005
Horizon Equipment 402 6th St TF: 800-458-4431	Manning	IA	51455	712-653-2574	
Hoxie Implement Co 933 Oak Ave *Web:* www.hoxieimplement.com	Hoxie	KS	67740	785-675-3201	675-3438
Hultgren Implements Inc 5698 State Hwy 175 TF: 800-827-1650	Ida Grove	IA	51445	712-364-3105	364-2197
Hurst Farm Supply Inc 105 Ave D TF: 800-535-8903 ■ *Web:* www.hurstfs.com	Abernathy	TX	79311	806-298-2541	298-2936
Implement Sales Co LLC 1574 Stone Ridge Dr TF: 800-955-9592 ■ *Web:* www.implementsalesga.com	Stone Mountain	GA	30083	770-908-9439	908-8123
Jacobi Sales Inc 425 Main St NE TF: 800-489-3617 ■ *Web:* www.jacobisales.com	Palmyra	IN	47164	812-364-6141	364-6157
James River Equipment 11047 Leadbetter Rd TF: 800-969-6001 ■ *Web:* www.jrenet.com	Ashland	VA	23005	804-798-6001	752-7111
JD Equipment Inc 1660 US 42 NE TF: 800-659-5646 ■ *Web:* www.jdequipment.com	London	OH	43140	614-879-6620	879-5767
JJ Nichting Co Inc 1342 Pilot Grove Rd	Pilot Grove	IA	52648	319-469-4461	469-4703
JM Equipment Co Inc 819 S 9th St *Web:* www.jmequipment.com	Modesto	CA	95351	209-522-3271	522-5980
John Day Co 6263 Abbott Dr TF: 800-767-2273 ■ *Web:* www.johnday.com	Omaha	NE	68110	402-455-8000	457-3812
John Deere Ltd 295 Hunter Rd PO Box 1000 *Web:* www.deere.com	Grimsby	ON	L3M4H5	905-945-9281	945-0341
John Fayhee & Sons Inc 100 Ohio St PO box 109 TF: 800-637-2614	Prairie City	IL	61470	309-775-3317	775-4547
Johnson Implement Co Inc 1904 Hwy 82 W TF: 800-898-0160 ■ *Web:* www.johnsonimplement.net	Greenwood	MS	38930	662-453-6525	453-6544
JS Woodhouse Co Inc 1314 Union St *Web:* www.jswoodhouse.com	West Springfield	MA	01090	413-736-5462	732-3786
Kelly Sauder Rupiper Equipment LLC 805 E Howard St Box 77 *Web:* www.ksrequipment.com	Pontiac	IL	61764	815-842-1149	842-1085
L & L Implement Co Inc 704 E 8th Ave TF: 800-848-5482	Yuma	CO	80759	970-848-5482	848-5143
Laethem Farm Service Co 275 Columbia St	Caro	MI	48723	989-673-6172	693-6789
Landell-Thelen Inc 323 E Hwy 30 TF: 800-694-5674 ■ *Web:* www.landell-thelen.com	Shelton	NE	68876	308-647-6811	647-9100
Landmark Equipment Inc 1351 S Loop 12 *Web:* www.landmarkeq.com	Irving	TX	75060	972-579-9999	579-7871
Lansdowne-Moody Co LP 8445 East Fwy *Web:* www.lansdowne-moody.com	Houston	TX	77029	713-672-8366	672-8173
Larchmont Engineering & Irrigation Co 11 Larchmont Ln TF: 877-862-2550 ■ *Web:* www.larchmont-eng.com	Lexington	MA	02420	781-862-2550	862-0173
Lefeld Implement Inc 5228 SR-118 TF: 888-678-2375 ■ *Web:* www.lefeldimp.com	Coldwater	OH	45828	419-678-2375	678-8705
Leoti Greentech Inc PO Drawer L TF: 800-783-2621	Leoti	KS	67861	620-375-2621	375-4562
Liechty Farm Equipment Inc PO Box 67 TF: 800-272-5898 ■ *Web:* www.liechtyfarmequipment.com	Archbold	OH	43502	419-445-1565	445-1779
Linder Equipment Co 311 E Kern St *Web:* www.linderequipment.com	Tulare	CA	93274	559-685-5000	685-0452
Maine Potato Growers Inc 56 Parsons St PO Box 271 TF: 800-649-3358 ■ *Web:* www.mpgco-op.com	Presque Isle	ME	04769	207-764-3131	764-8450
McCranie Implement Co PO Box 628 TF: 800-245-9046 ■ *Web:* www.mccranietractor.com	Hawkinsville	GA	31036	478-892-9046	783-0778
McCranie Motors & Tractors Inc PO Box 770 TF: 800-841-4050 ■ *Web:* www.mccranietractor.com	Unadilla	GA	31091	478-627-3291	627-9283
MDMA Equipment N6387 US Hwy 25 *Web:* www.mdmaequipment.com	Durand	WI	54736	715-672-8444	
Mid-State Equipment Inc W 1115 Bristol Rd *Web:* www.midstateequipment.com	Columbus	WI	53925	920-623-4020	623-4376
Miller Machinery & Supply Co 127 NE 27th St TF: 800-273-3030	Miami	FL	33137	305-573-1300	576-9535
Monroe Tractor & Implement Co Inc 1001 Lehigh Station Rd *Web:* www.monroetractor.com	Henrietta	NY	14467	585-334-3867	334-0001
Northwood Equipment Inc Hwy 105 E	Northwood	IA	50459	641-324-1154	324-2132
Odessa Trading Co 9 W 1st Ave PO Box 277 TF: 800-726-2661 ■ *Web:* www.odessatrading.com	Odessa	WA	99159	509-982-2661	982-2540
Ohio Machinery Co 3993 E Royalton Rd TF: 800-837-6200 ■ *Web:* www.ohiomachinery.com	Broadview Heights	OH	44147	440-526-6200	526-9513
Olsen Implement Inc 2025 US Hwy 14 W TF: 800-627-5469 ■ *Web:* www.olsenimplement.com	Huron	SD	57350	605-352-7100	352-7071
Peterson Tractor Co 955 Marina Blvd TF: 888-738-3776 ■ *Web:* petersontractor.cat.com	San Leandro	CA	94577	510-357-6200	352-5952
Phillips Tractor 27225 Hwy 47	Gaston	OR	97119	503-662-3929	
Piggott Tractor & Equipment 197 E Pfeiffer St	Piggott	AR	72454	870-598-2221	598-2223
Polk County Farmers Co-op DBA Ag West Supply 9055 Rickreall Rd PO Box 47 TF: 800-842-2224 ■ *Web:* www.agwestsupply.com	Rickreall	OR	97371	503-363-2332	363-5662

Company	City	State	Zip	Phone	Fax
Price Brothers Equipment Co 619 S Washington St *Web:* www.pricebroseq.com	Wichita	KS	67211	316-265-9577	265-1062
R & W Supply Inc 2210 Hall Ave *TF:* 800-477-1191 ■ *Web:* www.rwsupply.com	Littlefield	TX	79339	806-385-4447	385-4449
Ransome Engine Power Div Giles & Ransome Inc 2975 Galloway Rd *TF:* 800-753-4228 ■ *Web:* ransome.cat.com	Bensalem	PA	19020	215-639-4300	245-2779
RDO Equipment Co 700 7th St S *Web:* www.rdoequipment.com	Fargo	ND	58103	701-239-8730	271-6328
Reliable Tractor Inc PO Box 808 *TF:* 800-255-4401 ■ *Web:* www.reliabletractor.com	Tifton	GA	31793	229-382-4400	386-8964
Revels Tractor Co Inc 2217 N Main St *TF:* 800-849-5469 ■ *Web:* www.revelstractor.com	Fuquay-Varina	NC	27526	919-552-5697	552-9321
RN Johnson Inc PO Box 448 *Web:* www.rnjohnsoninc.com	Walpole	NH	03608	603-756-3321	756-3452
Rockingham New Holland Inc 600 W Market St *TF:* 800-360-5313	Harrisonburg	VA	22802	540-434-6791	434-6780
Roeder Implement Inc 2550 Rockdale Rd *TF:* 800-557-1184 ■ *Web:* www.roederimplement.com	Dubuque	IA	52003	563-557-1184	583-1821
Rose Brothers Inc 302 Main St	Lingle	WY	82223	307-837-2292	837-2922
Schilling Brothers Inc 705 N Rt 49 *Web:* www.schillingbros.com	Casey	IL	62420	217-932-5941	932-2616
Schilling Brothers Inc 5400 US Hwy 45 *Web:* www.schillingbros.com	Mattoon	IL	61938	217-234-6478	235-3991
Schmidt Machine Co 7013 State Hwy 199 N *Web:* www.schmidtmachine.com	Upper Sandusky	OH	43351	419-294-3814	294-2607
Scott Truck & Tractor Co of Monroe Inc 1000 ML King Dr *Web:* www.scottcompanies.com	Monroe	LA	71203	318-387-4160	388-9297
Seedburo Equipment Co 1022 W Jackson Blvd *TF:* 800-284-5779 ■ *Web:* www.seedburo.com	Chicago	IL	60607	312-738-3700	738-3544
SEMA Equipment Inc 11555 Hwy 60 Blvd *TF:* 800-569-1377 ■ *Web:* www.semaequip.com	Wanamingo	MN	55983	507-824-2256	824-2668
Sloan Implement Co 120 N Business 51 *TF:* 800-745-4020 ■ *Web:* www.sloans.com	Assumption	IL	62510	217-226-4411	226-3351
Smith EJ Group PO Box 7247 *Web:* www.ejsmithgroup.com	Charlotte	NC	28241	704-583-0422	583-0429
Spartan Distributors Inc 487 W Division St *TF:* 800-822-2216	Sparta	MI	49345	616-887-7301	887-6288
Studer Super Service Inc PO Box 617 *Web:* www.studers.com	Monroe	WI	53566	608-328-8331	
Stull Enterprises Inc PO Box 887 *Web:* www.stullenterprises.com	Concordville	PA	19331	610-459-8406	459-8032
Teeter Irrigation Inc 2295 S Old Hwy 83 *TF:* 800-834-7481 ■ *Web:* www.teeterirrigation.com	Garden City	KS	67846	620-276-8257	276-2652
Texas Timberjack Inc 6004 S US Hwy 59 *Web:* www.texastimberjack.com	Lufkin	TX	75901	936-634-3365	634-9636
Titan Machinery Inc 7955 179th Ave SE *Web:* www.titanmachinery.com	Wahpeton	ND	58075	701-642-8424	642-9514
Tom Hassenfritz Equipment Co 1300 W Washington St *TF:* 800-634-4885 ■ *Web:* www.the-co.com	Mount Pleasant	IA	52641	319-385-3114	385-3731
Torgerson's LLC 4180 US Hwy 2 W PO Box 1111 *TF:* 800-800-3113 ■ *Web:* www.torgerson.biz	Havre	MT	59501	406-265-5887	265-4062
Torrence's Farm Implement Inc 190 E Hwy 86 PO Box C *Web:* www.torrencesfarmimplements.com	Heber	CA	92249	760-352-5355	352-8707
Tractor Supply Co 200 Powell Pl *NASDAQ: TSCO* ■ *TF:* 877-872-7721 ■ *Web:* www.mytscstore.com	Brentwood	TN	37027	615-366-4600	366-4686
Turf Professionals Equipment Co 9108 Bond St *TF:* 800-299-3245 ■ *Web:* www.turfproequipment.com	Overland Park	KS	66214	913-599-1449	599-0667
Unruh-Foster Inc 501 E Texcoco St *TF:* 800-279-7283 ■ *Web:* www.unruhfoster.com	Montezuma	KS	67867	620-846-2215	846-2371
Vincent Implements Inc 8258 Hwy 45 E South *TF:* 800-624-8754	Martin	TN	38237	731-587-3824	587-3827
Wade Inc 1505 Hwy 82 W *Web:* www.wadeincorporated.com	Greenwood	MS	38930	662-453-6312	455-3287
West Central Co-op 406 1st St PO Box 68 *TF:* 800-522-1946 ■ *Web:* www.west-central.com	Ralston	IA	51459	712-667-3200	667-3215
Western Implement Co Inc 2919 North Ave *Web:* www.westernimplement.com	Grand Junction	CO	81504	970-242-7960	242-5241
WG Leffelman & Sons Inc 340 N Metcalf Ave *TF:* 800-957-2513 ■ *Web:* www.wgleffelman.com	Amboy	IL	61310	815-857-2513	857-3105
White's Inc 4614 Navigation Blvd *TF:* 800-231-9559 ■ *Web:* www.whitesinc.com	Houston	TX	77011	713-928-2632	928-5374
Witmer's Inc 39821 Salem Unity Rd *TF:* 888-427-6025 ■ *Web:* www.witmersinc.com	Salem	OH	44460	330-427-2147	427-2611
Wolverine Tractor & Equipment Co 25900 W Eight-Mile Rd *TF:* 800-686-7482 ■ *Web:* www.wolverinetractor.com	Southfield	MI	48033	248-356-5200	356-2029
Wyandot Tractor & Implement Co PO Box 147 *TF:* 800-472-9554	Upper Sandusky	OH	43351	419-294-2349	294-5200
Wyatt-Quarles Seed Co 730 US Hwy 70 W *TF:* 800-662-7591 ■ *Web:* www.wqseeds.com	Garner	NC	27529	919-772-4243	772-4278

278 FARM PRODUCT RAW MATERIALS

Company	City	State	Zip	Phone	Fax
ADM-Benson Quinn 301 S 4th Ave Suite 1075	Minneapolis	MN	55415	612-340-5900	335-2959
ADM-Collingwood Grain Inc 1600 N Lorraine Suite 200	Hutchinson	KS	67501	620-669-5830	
ADM Grain Co 4666 E Faries Pkwy	Decatur	IL	62526	217-424-5200	424-4650
ADM Rice Inc 4666 Faries Pkwy	Decatur	IL	62526	217-424-5200	424-5580
ADM/Farmland 4666 E Faries Pkwy	Decatur	IL	62526	217-424-5200	424-5580
ADM/GROWMARK River System Inc 4666 E Faries Pkwy **Fax:* Hum Res ■ *TF:* 800-637-5843	Decatur	IL	62526	217-424-5900	424-4383*
Ag One Co-op Inc 141 W 500 North PO Box 2009 *Web:* www.agonecoop.com	Anderson	IN	46018	765-643-6639	643-4396
Ag Valley Co-op 103 S Commercial St *TF:* 800-233-4551 ■ *Web:* www.agvalley.com	Maywood	NE	69038	308-362-4244	362-4479
AGP Grain Co-op 390 E 5th St	Garner	IA	50438	641-923-2695	923-2444
Agri Co-op 310 Logan St *TF:* 800-658-4089 ■ *Web:* www.agrico-op.com	Holdrege	NE	68949	308-995-8626	995-5779
Allenberg Cotton Co 7255 Goodlett Farms Pkwy *Web:* www.allenberg.com	Cordova	TN	38016	901-383-5000	383-5010
Alliance Grain Co 1306 W 8th St *TF:* 800-222-2451 ■ *Web:* www.alliance-grain.com	Gibson City	IL	60936	217-784-4284	784-8949
Apache Farmers Co-op 201 W Floyd St *Web:* www.apachecoop.com	Apache	OK	73006	580-588-3351	588-9277
Auglaize Farmers Co-op Inc 601 S Logan St *Web:* www.auglaizeprovico.com	Wapakoneta	OH	45895	419-739-4600	738-2880
Aurora Co-op Elevator Co 605 12th St PO Box 209 *TF:* 800-642-6795 ■ *Web:* www.auroracoop.com	Aurora	NE	68818	402-694-2106	694-2060
Birdsong Peanuts 612 Madison Ave PO Box 1400	Suffolk	VA	23434	757-539-3456	539-7360
Bunge Ltd 50 Main St 6th Fl *NYSE: BG* ■ *Web:* www.bunge.com	White Plains	NY	10606	914-684-2800	684-3499
C & F Foods Inc 15620 E Valley Blvd *Web:* www.cnf-foods.com	City of Industry	CA	91744	626-723-1000	723-1212
Cargill Inc 15407 McGinty Rd **Fax:* Cust Svc ■ *TF:* 800-227-4455 ■ *Web:* www.cargill.com	Wayzata	MN	55391	952-742-7575	742-7209*
Cargill Ltd 240300 Graham Ave PO Box 5900 *Web:* www.cargill.com	Winnipeg	MB	R3C4C5	204-947-0141	947-6444
CBG Enterprises Inc PO Box 249 *Web:* www.cgb.com	Mandeville	LA	70470	985-867-3500	867-3506
Central Connecticut Co-op Farmers Assn 10 Apel Pl Box 8500 *TF:* 800-640-4523 ■ *Web:* www.cccfeeds.com	Manchester	CT	06040	860-649-4523	643-5305
Central Iowa Co-op 1st & Lyon St PO Box 190 *TF:* 800-728-0017 ■ *Web:* www.centraliowacoop.com	Jewell	IA	50130	515-827-5431	827-5904
Co-Alliance LLP 103 Lincoln St PO Box 560 *TF:* 800-525-0272 ■ *Web:* www.co-alliance.com	Danville	IN	46122	317-745-4491	718-1850
ConAgra Grain Cos 11 ConAgra Dr Suite 5024 *Web:* www.conagrafoods.com	Omaha	NE	68102	402-595-5637	943-5777
Cooperative Elevator Co 7211 E Michigan Ave PO Box 619 *TF:* 800-968-0601 ■ *Web:* www.coopelev.com	Pigeon	MI	48755	989-453-4500	453-3942
Cooperative Federee de Quebec 9001 boul de l'Acadie Bureau 200 *Web:* www.coopfed.qc.ca	Montreal	QC	H4N3H7	514-384-6450	384-7176
Dalhart Consumers Fuel Assn Inc Hwy 87 N PO Box 610 *TF:* 800-249-5695 ■ *Web:* www.dalhartconsumers.com	Dalhart	TX	79022	806-249-5695	249-5897
Davis NF Drier & Elevator Inc 9421 N Dos Palos Ave	Firebaugh	CA	93622	559-659-3035	659-2275
De Bruce Grain 300 Osage St PO Box 329 *TF:* 877-274-2676	Creston	IA	50801	641-782-6411	782-0160
DeBruce Grain Inc 4100 N Mulberry Dr Suite 300 *TF:* 800-821-5210 ■ *Web:* www.debruce.com	Kansas City	MO	64116	816-421-8182	584-2350
Dunavant Enterprises Inc 3797 New Getwell Rd **Fax:* Hum Res ■ *Web:* www.dunavant.com	Memphis	TN	38118	901-369-1500	369-1608*
Effingham Equity Inc 201 W Roadway Ave *TF:* 800-223-1337 ■ *Web:* www.effinghamequity.com	Effingham	IL	62401	217-342-4101	347-7601
Farmers Co-op Co 105 4th Ave SW PO Box 47	Dayton	IA	50530	515-547-2813	547-2282
Farmers Co-op Co 105 Garfield Ave *TF:* 800-642-6815 ■ *Web:* www.fccoop.com	Farnhamville	IA	50538	515-544-3213	544-3252
Farmers Co-op Co 1209 North St PO Box 80	Yale	IA	50277	641-439-2243	439-2309
Farmers Cooperative Elevator Co 208 W Depot *TF:* 800-642-6439 ■ *Web:* www.farmersco-operative.com	Dorchester	NE	68343	402-946-2211	946-2062
Federated Co-operatives Ltd 401 22nd St E *Web:* www.fcl.ca	Saskatoon	SK	S7K0H2	306-244-3311	244-3403
Frick Services Inc 3154 Depot St *TF:* 800-552-1754	Wawaka	IN	46794	260-761-3311	761-3112
Frontier Co-op Co 211 S Lincoln St *TF:* 800-869-0379 ■ *Web:* www.frontiercooperative.com	Brainard	NE	68626	402-545-2811	545-2821
Grand Prairie Co-op Inc 1 S Calhoun St *TF:* 800-252-4724 ■ *Web:* www.grandprairiecoop.com	Tolono	IL	61880	217-485-6630	485-5143
Growers Co-op Inc 2500 S 13th St *TF:* 800-283-8123 ■ *Web:* www.growerscoop.com	Terre Haute	IN	47802	812-235-8123	232-3857
Heart of Iowa Co-op 229 E Ash St *TF:* 800-662-4642 ■ *Web:* www.hoic.com	Roland	IA	50236	515-388-4341	388-4589
Heartland Co-op 2829 Westown Pkwy Suite 350 *TF:* 800-513-3938 ■ *Web:* www.heartlandcoop.com	West Des Moines	IA	50266	515-225-1334	225-8511
Interstate Commodities Inc 7 Madison St *TF:* 800-833-3636 ■ *Web:* www.interstate-commodities.com	Troy	NY	12181	518-272-7212	272-7299
Italgrani Elevator Co 7900 Van Buren St	Saint Louis	MO	63111	314-638-1447	752-7621
JaGee Corp 2918 Wingate St	Fort Worth	TX	76107	817-335-5881	335-1905
James Richardson International (JRI) 1 Lombard Pl Suite 2700 *Web:* www.jri.ca	Winnipeg	MB	R3B0X8	204-934-5961	947-2647
John I Haas Inc 5185 MacArthur Blvd NW Suite 300 *Web:* www.johnihaas.com	Washington	DC	20016	202-777-4800	777-4895
Kelley Bean Co Inc 2407 Circle Dr *Web:* www.kelleybean.com	Scottsbluff	NE	69361	308-635-6438	635-7345
Louis Dreyfus Group 20 Westport Rd *Web:* www.louisdreyfus.com	Wilton	CT	06897	203-761-2000	761-2375
MaxYield Cooperative 313 3rd Ave NE PO Box 49 *TF:* 800-383-0003 ■ *Web:* www.maxyieldcooperative.com	West Bend	IA	50597	515-887-7211	887-7291
Mid-Iowa Co-op 201 S Main St PO Box 160 *TF:* 800-458-9753	Conrad	IA	50621	641-366-2040	366-2855
Mont Eagle Mills Inc 804 W Main St	Oblong	IL	62449	618-592-4211	592-4214
NEW Cooperative Inc 2626 1st Ave S *TF:* 800-362-2233 ■ *Web:* www.newcoop.com	Fort Dodge	IA	50501	515-955-2040	955-5565
NF Davis Drier & Elevator Inc 9421 N Dos Palos Ave	Firebaugh	CA	93622	559-659-3035	659-2275
Northwest Grain 315 Broadway Ave N *Web:* www.northwestgrain.com	Saint Hilaire	MN	56754	218-964-5252	964-5818
Northwest Grain Growers Inc 850 N 4th Ave *TF:* 800-994-4290 ■ *Web:* www.nwgrgr.com	Walla Walla	WA	99362	509-525-6510	529-6050
Parrish & Heimbecker Ltd 201 Cottage Ave Suite 1400 *Web:* www.parheim.mb.ca	Winnipeg	MB	R3B3KG	204-956-2030	943-8233
Pendleton Grain Growers Inc 1000 SW Dorian St PO Box 1248 *TF:* 800-422-7611 ■ *Web:* www.pggcountry.com	Pendleton	OR	97801	541-276-7611	276-4839
Plains Cotton Co-op Assn 3301 E 50th St PO Box 2827 *TF:* 800-333-8011 ■ *Web:* www.pcca.com	Lubbock	TX	79408	806-763-8011	762-7400
Pro-Pet LLC 1400 McKinley Rd *TF:* 800-245-4125 ■ *Web:* www.joypetfood.com	Saint Marys	OH	45885	419-394-3374	394-8024
Richardson James International 1 Lombard Pl Suite 2700 *Web:* www.jri.ca	Winnipeg	MB	R3B0X8	204-934-5961	947-2647
Scoular Co 2027 Dodge St *TF:* 800-488-3500 ■ *Web:* www.scoular.com	Omaha	NE	68102	402-342-3500	342-5568
South Dakota Wheat Growers Assn 110 6th Ave SE *TF:* 888-429-4902 ■ *Web:* www.sdwg.com	Aberdeen	SD	57401	605-225-5500	225-0859
Southwestern Irrigated Cotton Growers Assn 3500 Doniphan Dr PO Box 1709 *Web:* www.swigcotton.com	El Paso	TX	79949	915-581-5441	581-4138
Staplcotn Co-op Assn Inc 214 W Market St *TF:* 800-293-6231 ■ *Web:* www.staplcotn.com	Greenwood	MS	38930	662-453-6231	453-6274
Stratton Equity Co-op Co Inc 98 Colorado Ave PO Box 25 *TF:* 800-752-2068	Stratton	CO	80836	719-348-5347	348-5506
SWIG Cotton 3500 Doniphan Dr PO Box 1709 *Web:* www.swigcotton.com	El Paso	TX	79949	915-581-5441	581-4138
United Farmers Co-op 340 Oak St PO Box 310 *TF:* 800-742-7813 ■ *Web:* www.ufcoop.com	Shelby	NE	68662	402-527-5511	527-5515
Viterra Inc 2625 Victoria Ave *TF:* 866-569-4411 ■ *Web:* www.viterra.ca	Regina	SK	S4T7T9	306-569-4411	569-4708
Watertown Co-op Elevator Assn 810 Burlington Northern Dr *TF:* 888-882-3039 ■ *Web:* www.watertowncoop.com	Watertown	SD	57201	605-886-3039	886-0601
Watonwan Farm Service 233 W Ciro St *TF:* 800-657-3282 ■ *Web:* www.wfsag.com	Truman	MN	56088	507-776-2831	776-2871
Weil Brothers Cotton Inc 444 Park Blvd PO Box 20100 *Web:* www.cotton.net	Montgomery	AL	36120	334-244-1800	271-4238
Western Iowa Co-op 3330 Moville St PO Box 106 *TF:* 800-488-3201 ■ *Web:* www.westerniowacoop.com	Hornick	IA	51026	712-874-3211	874-3230
Wheeler Brothers Grain Co Inc 501 W Russworm Dr PO Box 29	Watonga	OK	73772	580-623-7223	623-2686

279 FARM SUPPLIES

Company	City	State	Zip	Phone	Fax
Agland Inc 260 Factory Rd *Web:* www.aglandinc.com	Eaton	CO	80615	970-454-3391	454-2144
AgVantage FS Inc 1600 8th St SW *Web:* www.agvantagefs.com	Waverly	IA	50677	319-483-4900	483-4992
Auglaize Farmers Co-op Inc 601 S Logan St *Web:* www.auglaizeprovico.com	Wapakoneta	OH	45895	419-739-4600	738-2880
Battle Creek Farmers Co-op 400 W Front St Box 10 *TF:* 800-233-6679 ■ *Web:* www.bccoop.com	Battle Creek	NE	68715	402-675-2055	675-1645
Bleyhl Farm Service Inc 940 E Wine Country Rd *TF:* 800-862-6806 ■ *Web:* www.bleyhl.com	Grandview	WA	98930	509-882-2248	882-4208
Bradley Caldwell Inc 200 Kiwanis Blvd **Fax:* Cust Svc ■ *TF:* 800-257-9100 ■ *Web:* www.bradleycaldwell.com	Hazleton	PA	18202	570-455-7511	455-0385*
Cal/West Seeds 41970 E Main St PO Box 1428 *TF:* 800-327-3337 ■ *Web:* www.calwestseeds.com	Woodland	CA	95776	530-666-3331	666-5317
Carroll Service Co 505 W Illinois Rt 64	Lanark	IL	61046	815-493-2181	493-6173
CFC Farm & Home Center 15172 Brandy Rd PO Box 2002 *TF:* 800-284-2667 ■ *Web:* www.culpeperag.org/farms.asp	Culpeper	VA	22701	540-825-2200	825-2210
Chem Nut Inc 800 Business Park Dr *Web:* www.chemnut.com	Leesburg	GA	31763	229-883-7050	439-0842
CHS Inc 5500 Cenex Dr *NASDAQ: CHSCP* ■ *TF:* 800-232-3639 ■ *Web:* www.chsinc.com	Inver Grove Heights	MN	55077	651-355-6000	355-6432
Co-op Feed Dealers Inc 380 Broome Corporate Pkwy PO Box 670 *TF Cust Svc:* 800-333-0895 ■ *Web:* www.co-opfeed.com	Conklin	NY	13748	607-651-9078	651-9363
Countryside Co-op 514 E Main St *TF:* 800-236-7585 ■ *Web:* www.countrysidecoop.com	Durand	WI	54736	715-672-8947	672-5131
CropKing.com Inc 5050 Greenwich Rd *TF:* 800-321-5656 ■ *Web:* www.cropking.com	Seville	OH	44273	330-769-2002	335-1689
Dorchester Farmers Co-op 208 W Depot *TF:* 800-642-6439 ■ *Web:* www.dorchesterco-op.com	Dorchester	NE	68343	402-946-2211	946-2062
Evergreen FS Inc 402 N Hershey Rd *TF:* 877-963-2392 ■ *Web:* www.evergreen-fs.com	Bloomington	IL	61704	309-663-2392	663-0494
Farm Service Co 4040 S Expressway *TF:* 800-705-7666 ■ *Web:* www.farmservicecompany.com	Council Bluffs	IA	51502	712-323-7167	323-9667
Farm Service Co 2308 Pine St *TF:* 800-452-4372 ■ *Web:* www.fscoop.com	Harlan	IA	51537	712-755-3185	755-7098
Farmers Co-op Assn 105 Jackson St *TF:* 800-864-3847 ■ *Web:* www.fcajackson.com	Jackson	MN	56143	507-847-4160	847-2521
Farmers Co-op Oil Co 6th & Logan *TF:* 800-898-6292	Newman Grove	NE	68758	402-447-6292	447-2429
Farmers Co-op Supply & Shipping Assn 570 Commerce St *TF:* 800-657-5189	West Salem	WI	54669	608-786-1100	786-1606
Farmers Supply Co-op 714 Hwy 82 W	Greenwood	MS	38930	662-453-3612	453-5509
Farmway Co-op Inc 204 E Court St *TF:* 800-748-7038 ■ *Web:* www.farmwaycoop.com	Beloit	KS	67420	785-738-2241	
Federation Co-op 108 N Water St *TF:* 800-944-1784 ■ *Web:* www.fedcoop.com	Black River Falls	WI	54615	715-284-5354	284-9672
Florida Favorite Fertilizer Inc 1607 Olive St *TF:* 800-822-4474	Lakeland	FL	33815	863-688-2442	682-6652
Frenchman Valley Farmers Co-op Exchange 143 Broadway St *TF:* 800-538-2667 ■ *Web:* www.fvcoop.com	Imperial	NE	69033	308-882-3200	882-3242
Gold Star FS Inc 101 N East St *TF:* 800-443-8497 ■ *Web:* www.goldstarfs.com	Cambridge	IL	61238	309-937-3369	937-5465
GROWMARK Inc 1701 Towanda Ave *Web:* www.growmark.com	Bloomington	IL	61701	309-557-6000	829-8532
Helena Chemical Co 225 Schilling Blvd Suite 300 *Web:* www.helenachemical.com	Collierville	TN	38017	901-761-0050	683-2960
Hydro Agri North America Inc 100 N Tampa St Suite 3200 *TF:* 800-944-9376 ■ *Web:* www.hydro.com	Tampa	FL	33602	813-222-5700	875-5735
Illini FS Inc 1509 E University Ave *Web:* www.illinifs.com	Urbana	IL	61802	217-384-8300	384-6317
Intermountain Farmers Assn 1147 W 2100 South *TF:* 800-748-4432 ■ *Web:* www.ifa-coop.com	Salt Lake City	UT	84119	801-972-2122	972-2186
Jasper County Farm Bureau Co-op Assn 2530 N McKinley *TF:* 800-828-7516	Rensselaer	IN	47978	219-866-7131	866-7490
JS West & Cos 501 9th St PO Box 1041 *TF Cust Svc:* 800-675-9378 ■ *Web:* www.jswest.com	Modesto	CA	95353	209-577-3221	523-9828
Kugler Co 209 W 3rd St *TF:* 800-445-9116 ■ *Web:* www.kuglercompany.com	McCook	NE	69001	308-345-2280	345-7756
La Salle Farmers Grain Co 317 4th St NE *TF:* 800-245-5857 ■ *Web:* www.lasallefarmers.com	Madelia	MN	56062	507-642-3276	642-3299
Land O'Lakes Inc Western Feed Div 2407 Warren Ave *TF:* 800-328-6616	Twin Falls	ID	83301	208-459-3689	454-0012
LaPorte County Co-op Inc 512 State St	La Porte	IN	46350	219-362-2156	326-1058
Loveland Industries Inc 14520 WCR #64 *TF:* 800-356-8920	Greeley	CO	80631	970-356-8920	356-8926
Luckey Farmers Inc 1200 W Main St *Web:* www.luckeyfarmers.com	Woodville	OH	43469	419-849-2711	849-2720
Martrex Inc 14525 Hwy 7 *TF:* 800-328-3627 ■ *Web:* www.martrexinc.com	Minnetonka	MN	55345	952-933-5000	933-1889
McFarlane Mfg Co Inc 1259 Water St *TF:* 800-627-8569 ■ *Web:* www.mcfarlanesonline.com	Sauk City	WI	53583	608-643-3321	643-2309
Meadowland Farmers Co-op 101 1st Ave E *TF:* 800-527-5824	Lamberton	MN	56152	507-752-7352	752-7106
Meherrin Agricultural & Chemical Co Inc 413 Main St PO Box 200 *TF:* 800-775-0333	Severn	NC	27877	252-585-1744	585-1718
MFA Inc 201 Ray Young Dr *Web:* www.mfaincorporated.com	Columbia	MO	65201	573-874-5111	876-5430
Midland Co-op 101 S Main St *TF:* 800-404-2420 ■ *Web:* www.midlandcoop.com	Axtell	NE	68924	308-743-2424	743-2428
Miles Farm Supplies LLC 1401 B Spring Bank Dr *TF:* 800-666-4537 ■ *Web:* www.milesnmore.com	Owensboro	KY	42303	270-926-2420	683-7565
NC Plus Hybrids 3820 N 56th St *TF:* 800-279-7999 ■ *Web:* www.nc-plus.com	Lincoln	NE	68504	402-467-2517	467-4217
New Alliance FS 110 North E St *TF:* 800-672-2589 ■ *Web:* home.newalliancefs.com	Oskaloosa	IA	52577	641-672-2589	673-9735
NEW Cooperative Inc 2626 1st Ave S *TF:* 800-362-2233 ■ *Web:* www.newcoop.com	Fort Dodge	IA	50501	515-955-2040	955-5565
Northwestern Supply Co Inc 525 Progress Rd *TF:* 800-397-6972	Waite Park	MN	56387	320-251-0812	251-6210
Nyssa Co-op Supply 18 N 2nd St	Nyssa	OR	97913	541-372-2254	372-2453
Orange Belt Supply Co 25244 Rd 204 *Web:* www.orangebelt.net	Lindsay	CA	93247	559-562-2574	562-6043
Orscheln Farm & Home Supply 101 W Coates St *TF:* 800-662-2580 ■ *Web:* www.orscheln.com	Moberly	MO	65270	660-263-4335	269-3500
Osborne Distributing Co 3908 Wilbarger St	Vernon	TX	76384	940-552-7711	553-4056
Panhandle Co-op Assn 401 S Beltline Hwy W *TF Cust Svc:* 800-732-4546 ■ *Web:* www.panhandlecoop.com	Scottsbluff	NE	69361	308-632-5301	632-5375
Perham Co-op Creamery Assn 459 3rd Ave SE *Web:* www.perhamcoop.com	Perham	MN	56573	218-346-6240	346-6241
Pro Cooperative 303 S Railroad St *Web:* www.procooperative.com	Gilmore City	IA	50541	515-373-6174	373-6500
Rolling Hills Farm Service Inc 421 N 10th St *TF:* 800-352-3276 ■ *Web:* home.rollinghillsfs.com	Winterset	IA	50273	515-462-2644	462-3410
Rosen's Inc 1120 Lake Ave *TF:* 800-798-2000	Fairmont	MN	56031	507-238-4201	238-9966
South Central Co-op 40 W Park Dr *TF:* 800-690-6534	Gibbon	MN	55335	507-834-6534	834-6140
Southern FS Inc 1900 E Main St PO Box 728 *TF:* 800-492-7684 ■ *Web:* www.southernfs.com	Marion	IL	62959	618-993-2833	997-2526
Southern States Co-op Inc 6606 W Broad St *TF:* 800-826-2762 ■ *Web:* www.southernstates-coop.com	Richmond	VA	23230	804-281-1000	281-1141
Southern States Frederick Co-op Inc 500 E South St *Web:* www.southernstates.com	Frederick	MD	21701	301-663-6164	663-8173
Stanislaus Farm Supply Co 624 E Service Rd *TF:* 800-323-0725 ■ *Web:* www.stanislausfarmsupply.com	Modesto	CA	95358	209-538-7070	541-3191
Tennessee Farmers Co-op 180 Old Nashville Hwy *TF:* 800-366-2667 ■ *Web:* www.ourcoop.com	La Vergne	TN	37086	615-793-8011	793-8343
Terra Industries Inc 600 4th St Terra Center *NYSE: TRA* ■ **Fax:* Mktg ■ *Web:* www.terraindustries.com	Sioux City	IA	51101	712-277-1340	293-4601*
Transammonia Inc 320 Park Ave *Web:* www.transammonia.com	New York	NY	10022	212-223-3200	759-1410
TriOak Foods Inc 103 W Railroad St *Web:* www.trioak.com	Oakville	IA	52646	319-766-4411	766-4602
United Suppliers Inc 30473 260th St *TF:* 800-782-5123 ■ *Web:* www.uniteds.com	Eldora	IA	50627	641-858-2341	858-5493
Universal Cooperatives Inc 1300 Corporate Center Curve *TF:* 800-375-1121 ■ *Web:* www.ucoop.com	Eagan	MN	55121	651-239-1000	239-1203
Wabash Valley Service Co Inc 909 N Court St *TF:* 888-869-8127 ■ *Web:* home.wabashvalleyfs.com	Grayville	IL	62844	618-375-2311	375-5351
Watonwan Farm Service 208 S Main St *TF:* 800-830-0447	Delavan	MN	56023	507-854-3204	854-3290
West Agro Inc 11100 N Congress Ave *Web:* www.westagro.com	Kansas City	MO	64153	816-891-1600	891-1606
Western Farm Service Inc 3705 W Beechwood Ave Suite 101 *Web:* www.westernfarmservice.com	Fresno	CA	93711	559-436-2800	436-2890
Western Reserve Farm Co-op Inc 16003 E High St *Web:* www.wrfc.org	Middlefield	OH	44062	440-632-0271	632-5698
Westland Co-op 2112 Indianapolis Rd *TF:* 800-878-0952 ■ *Web:* www.westlandcoop.com	Crawfordsville	IN	47933	765-362-6700	362-7010
Wheaton-Dumont Farmer Co-op 1115 Broadway *TF:* 800-258-7444 ■ *Web:* www.wdcoop.com	Wheaton	MN	56296	320-563-8152	563-4392
Wilbur-Ellis Co 345 California St 27th Fl *Web:* www.wilburellis.com	San Francisco	CA	94104	415-772-4000	772-4011
Wilco Farmers 200 Industrial Way *TF:* 800-382-5339 ■ *Web:* www.wilco.coop	Mount Angel	OR	97362	503-845-6122	845-9310

280 FASHION DESIGN HOUSES

SEE ALSO Clothing & Accessories - Mfr p. 1449

Company	City	State	Zip	Phone	Fax
Anna Sui Corp 250 W 39th St 15th Fl *Web:* www.annasui.com	New York	NY	10018	212-768-1951	768-8825
Anne Klein & Co 1411 Broadway 15th Fl **Fax Area Code:* 917 ■ *Web:* www.anneklein.com	New York	NY	10018	212-536-9000	777-9354*
Armani Exchange 568 Broadway *TF:* 800-717-2929 ■ *Web:* www.armaniexchange.com	New York	NY	10012	212-431-6000	431-4669
Arnold Scaasi Inc 16 E 52nd St 3rd Fl	New York	NY	10022	212-755-5105	826-8332
Badgley Mischka 550 7th Ave 22nd Fl *Web:* www.badgleymischka.com	New York	NY	10018	212-921-1585	921-4171
BCBG Max Azria 2761 Fruitland Ave *TF:* 888-636-2224 ■ *Web:* www.bcbg.com	Vernon	CA	90058	323-589-2224	277-5454
Betsey Johnson Inc 498 7th Ave 21st Fl *Web:* www.betseyjohnson.com	New York	NY	10018	212-244-0843	244-0855
Bill Blass Ltd 550 7th Ave 12th Fl *Web:* www.billblass.com	New York	NY	10018	212-221-6660	398-5545
Calvin Klein Inc 205 W 39th St 3rd Fl *Web:* www.pvh.com	New York	NY	10018	212-719-2600	730-4818
Carolina Herrera Ltd 501 7th Ave 17th Fl *Web:* www.carolinaherrera.com	New York	NY	10018	212-944-5757	944-7996
Christian Dior 712 5th Ave 37th Fl *TF:* 800-929-3467 ■ *Web:* www.dior.com	New York	NY	10019	212-582-0500	582-1063
Cynthia Rowley 376 Bleecker St *Web:* www.cynthiarowley.com	New York	NY	10014	212-242-0847	242-4136
Dana Buchman 1441 Broadway 2nd Fl *TF:* 800-522-3262	New York	NY	10018	212-626-3000	626-1812
Diane Von Furstenberg 389 W 12th St *Web:* www.dvf.com	New York	NY	10014	212-753-1111	929-3971
Dolce & Gabbana 660 Madison Ave 10th Fl *Web:* www.dolcegabbana.it	New York	NY	10021	212-750-0055	750-5750
Donna Karan International Inc 550 7th Ave 15th Fl *TF:* 800-231-0884 ■ *Web:* www.donnakaran.com	New York	NY	10018	212-789-1500	789-1821
Ellen Tracy Inc 575 7th Ave 10th Fl *Web:* www.ellentracy.com	New York	NY	10018	212-944-6999	944-2446
Escada USA Inc 10 Mulholland Dr *Web:* www.escada.com	Hasbrouck Heights	NJ	07604	201-462-6000	462-6440
Giorgio Armani 114 5th Ave 17th Fl *Web:* www.giorgioarmani.com	New York	NY	10011	212-366-9720	366-9668
Halston 641 Lexington Ave 13th Fl *Web:* www.halston.com	New York	NY	10022	212-282-1200	
Hugo Boss Fashions Inc 601 W 26th St Suite 845 *TF:* 800-484-6207 ■ *Web:* www.hugo.com	New York	NY	10001	212-940-0600	940-0616
Jessica McClintock Inc 1400 16th St *TF:* 800-333-5301 ■ *Web:* www.jessicamcclintock.com	San Francisco	CA	94103	415-553-8200	553-8329
Jhane Barnes Inc 119 W 40th St 20th Fl *TF:* 888-465-4263 ■ *Web:* www.jhanebarnes.com	New York	NY	10018	212-575-2448	575-2506
Jill Stuart Inc 550 7th Ave 24th Fl *Web:* www.jillstuart.com	New York	NY	10018	212-921-2600	921-2850
Kamali Norma 11 W 56th St *Web:* www.normakamalicollection.com	New York	NY	10019	212-957-9797	956-1060
Liz Claiborne Inc 1441 Broadway 22nd Fl *NYSE: LIZ* ■ *Web:* www.lizclaiborneinc.com	New York	NY	10018	212-354-4900	626-1800
Manolo Blahnik Manolo Blahnik Press Office 31 W 54th St	New York	NY	10019	212-582-1583	582-5778
Marc Bouwer 27 W 20th St Suite 1201 *Web:* www.marcbouwer.com	New York	NY	10011	212-242-7510	242-2687
Marc Jacobs International 72 Spring St 8th Fl *Web:* www.marcjacobs.com	New York	NY	10012	212-343-0222	343-2960
Max Mara USA Inc 530 7th Ave 21st Fl	New York	NY	10018	212-536-6200	302-1134
Michael Kors 11 W 42nd St 21st Fl *Web:* www.michaelkors.com	New York	NY	10036	212-201-8100	
Miller Nicole 525 7th Ave 20th Fl *Web:* www.nicolemiller.com	New York	NY	10018	212-719-9200	391-4327
Nicole Miller 525 7th Ave 20th Fl *Web:* www.nicolemiller.com	New York	NY	10018	212-719-9200	391-4327

Phone Fax

Norma Kamali 11 W 56th St New York NY 10019 212-957-9797 956-1060
Web: www.normakamalicollection.com

Oscar De La Renta Ltd 550 7th Ave 8th Fl New York NY 10018 212-354-6777 768-9110
Web: www.oscardelarenta.com

Prada 610 W 52nd St New York NY 10019 212-307-9300
Web: www.prada.com

Ralph Lauren 650 Madison Ave New York NY 10022 212-318-7000 888-5780
TF: 800-377-7656 ■ *Web:* www.polo.com

Todd Oldham 120 Wooster St 3rd Fl New York NY 10012 212-226-4668 226-4873
Web: www.toddoldhamstudio.com

Tommy Hilfiger USA Inc 25 W 39th St New York NY 10018 212-840-8888
TF: 800-888-8802 ■ *Web:* www.tommy.com

Tyler Trafficante Inc 525 Mission St South Pasadena CA 91030 626-799-9961 799-9963

Vera Wang 225 W 39th St 9th Fl New York NY 10018 212-575-6400 354-2548*
**Fax:* PR ■ *TF:* 800-839-8372 ■ *Web:* www.verawang.com

Vivienne Tam 550 7th Ave 20th Fl New York NY 10018 212-840-6470 869-4043
Web: www.viviennetam.com

Yves Saint Laurent 3 E 57th St New York NY 10022 212-223-7463 223-8709
Web: www.ysl.com

281 FASTENERS & FASTENING SYSTEMS

SEE ALSO Hardware - Mfr p. 1770; Precision Machined Products p. 2133

Phone Fax

Air Industries Corp 12570 Knott St Garden Grove CA 92841 714-892-5571 892-7904
Web: www.air-industries.com

Alcoa Fastening Systems DBA Huck Fasteners
3724 E Columbia St Tucson AZ 85714 520-519-7400 519-7577*
**Fax:* Hum Res ■ *TF:* 800-326-1799 ■ *Web:* www.huck.com

Allfast Fastening Systems Inc 15200 Don Julian Rd City of Industry CA 91745 626-968-9388 968-9393
Web: www.allfastinc.com

Atlas Bolt & Screw Co 1628 Troy Rd Ashland OH 44805 419-289-6171 289-2564
TF: 800-321-6977 ■ *Web:* www.atlasfasteners.com

Avibank Mfg Inc 11500 Sherman Way North Hollywood CA 91605 818-392-2100 255-1762
Web: www.avibank.com

B & G Mfg Co Inc 3067 Unionville Pike Hatfield PA 19440 215-822-1925 822-1006*
**Fax:* Sales ■ *TF:* 800-366-3067 ■ *Web:* www.bgmfg.com

Brighton-Best Socket Screw Mfg Inc 1665 Heraeus Blvd Buford GA 30518 678-288-1000 288-1015
Web: www.brightonbest.com

Bristol Industries 630 E Lambert Rd Brea CA 92821 714-990-4121 529-6726*
**Fax:* Sales ■ *Web:* www.bristol-ind.com

Captive Fastener Corp 19 Thornton Rd Oakland NJ 07436 201-337-6800 337-1012
Web: www.captive-fastener.com

Chicago Rivet & Machine Co 901 Frontenac Rd Naperville IL 60563 630-357-8500 983-9314
AMEX: CVR ■ *Web:* www.chicagorivet.com

Cold Heading Co 21777 Hoover Rd Warren MI 48089 586-497-7000 497-7007
Web: www.coldheading.com

Decker Mfg Corp 703 N Clark St Albion MI 49224 517-629-3955 629-3535
Web: www.deckernut.com

Detroit Heading LLC 6421 Lynch Rd Detroit MI 48234 313-267-2240 267-2061
Web: www.detroitheading.com

Elgin Fastener Group PO Box 416 Versailles IN 47042 812-689-8959 689-6635
Web: www.elginfasteners.com

Entegra Fastener Corp 321 E Foster Ave Wood Dale IL 60191 630-595-6250 595-0336
Web: www.entegrafastener.com

Ford Fasteners Inc 110 S Newman St Hackensack NJ 07601 201-487-3151 487-1919
TF: 800-272-3673 ■ *Web:* www.fordfasteners.com

Gesipa Fasteners USA Inc 3150 Brunswick Pike Suite 310 Lawrenceville NJ 08648 609-883-8300 883-8301
TF: 800-257-9404 ■ *Web:* www.gesipausa.com

Hohmann & Barnard Inc 30 Rasons Ct Hauppauge NY 11788 631-234-0600 234-0683
TF: 800-323-7170 ■ *Web:* www.h-b.com

Huck Fasteners 3724 E Columbia St Tucson AZ 85714 520-519-7400 519-7577*
**Fax:* Hum Res ■ *TF:* 800-326-1799 ■ *Web:* www.huck.com

ITW Brands 955 National Pkwy Suite 95500 Schaumburg IL 60173 847-944-2260 619-8344
TF: 800-982-7178 ■ *Web:* www.itwbrands.com

ITW Buildex 1349 W Bryn Mawr Itasca IL 60143 630-595-3500 595-3549
TF: 800-284-5339 ■ *Web:* www.itwbuildex.com

Lake Erie Screw Corp 13001 Athens Ave Cleveland OH 44107 216-521-1800 228-9393
Web: www.lescrew.com

Metform LLC 2551 Wacker Rd Savanna IL 61074 815-273-2201 273-7837
Web: www.mfmvs.com

Monogram Aerospace Fasteners 3423 S Garfield Ave Los Angeles CA 90040 323-722-4760 721-1851
Web: www.monogramaerospace.com

National Rivet & Mfg Co 21 E Jefferson St Waupun WI 53963 920-324-5511 324-3388
TF: 888-324-5511 ■ *Web:* www.natriv.com

Ohio Nut & Bolt Co 33 Lou Groza Blvd Berea OH 44017 440-243-0200 243-4006
TF: 800-362-0291 ■ *Web:* www.on-b.com

Pan American Screw Inc 630 Reese Dr SW Conover NC 28613 828-466-0060 466-0070
TF: 800-951-2222 ■ *Web:* www.panamericanscrew.com

PennEngineering & Mfg Corp 5190 Old Easton Rd Danboro PA 18916 215-766-8853 766-3680
TF: 800-237-4736 ■ *Web:* www.penn-eng.com

Robertson Inc 97 Bronte St N Milton ON L9T2N8 905-878-2866 878-2867
TF: 800-268-5090 ■ *Web:* www.robertsonscrew.com

Scovill Fasteners Inc 1802 Scovill Dr Clarkesville GA 30523 706-754-1000 754-4000*
**Fax:* Cust Svc ■ *TF Cust Svc:* 800-756-4734 ■ *Web:* www.scovill.com

SPS Technologies Inc 301 Highland Ave Jenkintown PA 19046 215-572-3000 572-3193
Web: www.spstech.com

Stafast Products Inc 505 Lake Shore Blvd Painesville OH 44077 440-357-5546 357-7137
TF: 800-782-3278 ■ *Web:* www.stafast.com

Textron Fastening Systems 840 W Long Lake Rd Suite 450 Troy MI 48098 248-879-8660 813-6372
Web: www.textronfasteningsystems.com

TriMas Corp 39400 Woodward Ave Suite 130 Bloomfield Hills MI 48304 248-631-5450 631-5455
Web: www.trimascorp.com

282 FENCES - MFR

SEE ALSO Recycled Plastics Products p. 2208

Phone Fax

Acorn Wire & Iron Works Inc 4940 S Kilbourn Ave Chicago IL 60632 773-585-0600 585-2403
TF: 800-552-2676 ■ *Web:* www.acornwire.com

Dare Products Inc 157 Betterly Rd PO Box 157 Battle Creek MI 49016 269-965-2307 965-3261
TF: 800-922-3273 ■ *Web:* www.dareproducts.com

Fi-Shock Inc 5360 N National Dr Knoxville TN 37914 865-524-7380 673-4770
TF: 800-251-9288 ■ *Web:* www.fishock.com

Kalinich Fence Co Inc 12223 Prospect Rd Strongsville OH 44149 440-238-6127 238-2178
Web: www.kalinichfenceco.com

Master Halco Inc 4000 W Metropolitan Dr Suite 400 Orange CA 92868 714-385-0091 385-0107
TF: 800-883-8384 ■ *Web:* www.fenceonline.com

Merchants Metals Inc 3838 N Sam Houston Pkwy E Suite 600 Houston TX 77032 281-372-3800 372-3801
TF: 866-888-5611 ■ *Web:* www.merchantsmetals.com

Moultrie Mfg Co 1403 Georgia Hwy 133 S PO Box 2948 Moultrie GA 31776 229-985-1312 890-7245
TF: 800-841-8674 ■ *Web:* www.moultriemanufacturing.com

Superior Aluminum Products Inc 555 E Main St PO Box 430 Russia OH 45363 937-526-4065 526-3904
Web: www.superioraluminum.com

Tru-Link Fence Co 5440 W Touhy Ave Skokie IL 60077 847-568-9300 568-9600
TF: 888-568-9300 ■ *Web:* www.tru-link.com

283 FERTILIZERS & PESTICIDES

SEE ALSO Farm Supplies p. 1634

Phone Fax

Agricultural Commodities Inc 2224 Oxford Rd New Oxford PA 17350 717-624-8249 624-3216
TF: 800-359-8899

Agriliance 5500 Cenex Dr Inver Grove Heights MN 55077 651-451-5151 451-5568
TF: 800-535-4635 ■ *Web:* www.agriliance.com

Agrium Inc 13131 Lake Fraser Dr SE Calgary AB T2J7E8 403-225-7000 225-7609*
NYSE: AGU ■ **Fax:* PR ■ *TF:* 877-247-4861 ■ *Web:* www.agrium.com

Airgas Specialty Products 6340 Sugarloaf Pkwy Suite 300 Duluth GA 30097 770-717-2210 717-2222
TF: 800-226-4572 ■ *Web:* www.airgasspecialtyproducts.com

Alabama Farmers Co-op Inc 121 Somerville Rd NE Decatur AL 35601 256-353-6843 350-1770
TF: 800-737-6843 ■ *Web:* www.alafarm.com

Alco Industries Inc 820 Adams Ave Suite 130 Norristown PA 19403 610-666-0930 666-0752
Web: www.alcoind.com

Amvac Chemical Corp 4100 E Washington Blvd Los Angeles CA 90023 323-264-3910 268-1028
TF: 888-468-2726 ■ *Web:* www.amvac-chemical.com

Andersons Inc Plant Nutrient Group 8086 E CR 900 S Galveston IN 46932 574-626-2522 626-3174
TF: 800-552-3769 ■ *Web:* www.andersonsinc.com/ag/pnd/index.html

Andersons Inc Processing Group 480 W Dussel Dr Maumee OH 43537 419-893-5050 891-2914
TF: 800-537-3370

Apache Nitrogen Products Inc
1436 S Apache Powder Rd PO Box 700 Benson AZ 85602 520-720-2217 720-4158
Web: www.apachenitro.com

Arkema Inc 2000 Market St Philadelphia PA 19103 215-419-7000 419-7591
TF: 800-533-5552

Associated Tagline Inc 1504 Hwy 183 PO Box 1330 Salinas CA 93902 831-422-6452 758-8133

Atlantic FEC Fertilizer & Chemical Co 18375 SW 260 St Homestead FL 33031 305-247-8800 247-3328
TF: 800-432-3413 ■ *Web:* www.atlanticfec.com

Baker HJ & Bros Inc 228 Saugatuck Ave Westport CT 06880 203-682-9200 227-8351
Web: www.bakerbro.com

BASF Corp 100 Campus Dr Florham Park NJ 07932 973-245-6000 895-8002
NYSE: BF ■ *TF:* 800-526-1072 ■ *Web:* www.basf.com

Bay Zinc Co 301 W Charron Rd PO Box 167 Moxee WA 98936 509-248-4911 248-4916
Web: www.bayzinc.com

Bayer CropScience 2 TW Alexander Dr Research Triangle Park NC 27709 919-549-2000
Web: www.bayercropscienceus.com

Brandt Consolidated Inc 211 W Rt 125 PO Box 350 Pleasant Plains IL 62677 217-626-1123 626-1927
Web: www.brandtconsolidated.com

Cargill Inc North America 15407 McGinty Rd Wayzata MN 55391 952-742-7575
TF: 800-227-4455

Certis USA LLC 9145 Guilford Rd Suite 175 Columbia MD 21046 301-604-7340 604-7015
TF: 800-847-5620 ■ *Web:* www.certisusa.com

CF Industries Inc 4 Parkway N Deerfield IL 60015 847-405-2400 405-2711
Web: www.cfindustries.com

CFC Farm & Home Center 15172 Brandy Rd PO Box 2002 Culpeper VA 22701 540-825-2200 825-2210
TF: 800-284-2667 ■ *Web:* www.culpeperag.org/farms.asp

Clinton Nursery Products Inc 114 W Main St Clinton CT 06413 860-669-8611 669-4527
TF: 800-289-7645

Coastal Agrobusiness Inc 3702 Evans St PO Box 856 Greenville NC 27835 252-756-1126 756-3282
Web: www.coastalagro.com

Coffeyville Resources LLC 10 E Cambridge Circle Dr Kansas City KS 66103 913-982-0500 981-0001
Web: www.coffeyvillegroup.com

ConAgra International Fertilizer Co
5 Skidaway Village Walk Suite 201 Savannah GA 31411 912-598-8392 598-8692

Crop Production Services Inc PO Box 1467 Galesburg IL 61402 309-342-4100 342-4187
Web: www.cropproductionservices.com

Dow AgroSciences LLC 9330 Zionsville Rd Indianapolis IN 46268 317-337-3000 905-7326*
**Fax Area Code:* 800 ■ *TF:* 800-258-1470 ■ *Web:* www.dowagro.com

Drexel Chemical Co 1700 Channel Ave PO Box 13327 Memphis TN 38113 901-774-4370 774-4666
Web: www.drexchem.com

DuPont Agriculture & Nutrition
1007 Market St DuPont Bldg Wilmington DE 19898 302-774-1000 999-4399
TF: 800-441-7515

DuPont Crop Protection 1007 Market St DuPont Bldg Wilmington DE 19898 302-774-1000 999-4399
TF: 800-441-7515 ■ *Web:* cropprotection.dupont.com

EDEN Bioscience Corp 11816 N Creek Pkwy N Bothell WA 98011 425-806-7300 806-7400
NASDAQ: EDEN ■ *TF:* 888-522-5976 ■ *Web:* www.edenbio.com

Enforcer Products Inc PO Box 1060 Cartersville GA 30120 770-386-0801 386-1659
TF: 800-241-5656 ■ *Web:* www.enforcer.com

FMC Corp 1735 Market St Philadelphia PA 19103 215-299-6000 299-5998
NYSE: FMC ■ *Web:* www.fmc.com

FMC Corp Agricultural Products Group 1735 Market St Philadelphia PA 19103 215-299-6000 299-5998
Web: cropsolutions.fmc.com

Frit Industries Inc 1792 Jodie Parker Rd Ozark AL 36360 334-774-2515 774-9306
TF: 800-633-7685 ■ *Web:* www.fritinc.com

Good Earth Inc 5960 Broadway Lancaster NY 14086 716-684-8111 684-3722
Web: www.goodearth.org

Green Light Co 10511 Wetmore Rd San Antonio TX 78216 210-494-3481 494-5224
TF: 800-777-5702 ■ *Web:* www.greenlightco.com

Growers Fertilizer Corp 312 N Buena Vista Dr PO Box 1407 Lake Alfred FL 33850 863-956-1101 956-2629
TF: 800-343-1101

Helena Chemical Co 225 Schilling Blvd Suite 300 Collierville TN 38017 901-761-0050 683-2960
Web: www.helenachemical.com

Hintzsche Fertilizer Inc
2 S 181 County Line Rd PO Box 367 Maple Park IL 60151 630-557-2406 557-2557
TF: 800-446-3378 ■ *Web:* www.hintzsche.com

HJ Baker & Bros Inc 228 Saugatuck Ave Westport CT 06880 203-682-9200 227-8351
Web: www.bakerbro.com

Johnson SC & Son Inc 1525 Howe St Racine WI 53403 262-260-2000 260-2632
TF: 800-494-4855 ■ *Web:* www.scjohnson.com

JR Simplot Co 999 Main St Boise ID 83702 208-336-2110 389-7515
TF: 800-635-5008 ■ *Web:* www.simplot.com

JR Simplot Co AgriBusiness Group 999 Main St PO Box 70013 Boise ID 83707 208-672-2700 672-2760
TF: 800-635-9444 ■ *Web:* www.simplot.com/agricultural

Kellogg Supply Inc 350 W Sepulveda Blvd Carson CA 90745 310-830-2200 835-6174
TF Cust Svc: 800-232-2322 ■ *Web:* www.kellogggarden.com

Kirby Agri Inc 500 Running Pump Rd PO Box 6277 Lancaster PA 17607 717-299-2541 293-9306
TF: 800-745-7524 ■ *Web:* www.kirbyagri.com

	City	State	ZIP	Phone	Fax
Koch Nitrogen Co 4111 E 37th St N	Wichita	KS	67220	316-828-5500	828-4084
Web: www.kochind.com					
Kova Fertilizer Inc 1330 N Anderson St	Greensburg	IN	47240	812-663-5081	663-5370
TF: 800-346-1569					
Lebanon Seaboard Corp 1600 E Cumberland St	Lebanon	PA	17042	717-273-1685	273-9466
TF: 800-233-0628 ■ *Web:* www.lebsea.com					
LESCO Inc 1301 E 9th St Suite 1300	Cleveland	OH	44114	216-706-9250	706-5240*
NASDAQ: LSCO ■ **Fax:* Cust Svc ■ *TF:* 800-321-5325 ■ *Web:* www.lesco.com					
Living Earth Technology Co 5625 Crawford Rd	Houston	TX	77041	713-466-7360	466-7969
TF: 800-665-3826 ■ *Web:* www.livingearth.net					
MFA Inc 201 Ray Young Dr	Columbia	MO	65201	573-874-5111	876-5430
Web: www.mfaincorporated.com					
Miller Chemical & Fertilizer Corp 120 Radio Rd	Hanover	PA	17331	717-632-8921	632-4581
TF: 800-233-2040 ■ *Web:* www.millerchemical.com					
Mississippi Phosphate Corp 601 Industrial Rd PO Box 848	Pascagoula	MS	39568	228-762-3210	762-4173
Monsanto Co 800 N Lindbergh Blvd	Saint Louis	MO	63167	314-694-1000	694-8506
NYSE: MON ■ *Web:* www.monsanto.com					
Mosaic Co 3033 Campus Dr Suite E-490	Plymouth	MN	55441	763-577-2700	559-2860
NYSE: MOS ■ *TF:* 800-918-8270 ■ *Web:* www.mosaicco.com					
Na-Churs/Alpine Solutions 421 Leader St	Marion	OH	43302	740-382-5701	383-2615
TF: 800-622-4877 ■ *Web:* www.nachurs.com					
Nufarm Americas 150 Harvester Dr Suite 200	Burr Ridge	IL	60527	630-455-2000	455-2001
TF: 800-345-3330 ■ *Web:* www.ag.us.nufarm.com					
Pace International LLC 1201 3rd Ave Suite 5450	Seattle	WA	98101	800-722-2476	624-6593*
**Fax Area Code:* 206 ■ *TF:* 800-247-8711 ■ *Web:* www.paceint.com					
PBI/Gordon Corp 1217 W 12th St PO Box 014090	Kansas City	MO	64101	816-421-4070	474-0462
TF: 800-821-7925 ■ *Web:* www.pbigordon.com					
Pioneer Hi-Bred International Inc					
400 Locust St Capital Sq Suite 800	Des Moines	IA	50309	515-248-4800	
TF: 800-247-6803 ■ *Web:* www.pioneer.com					
Platte Chemical Co 419 18th St PO Box 1286	Greeley	CO	80632	970-353-9831	353-9590
Potash Corp 1101 Skokie Blvd	Northbrook	IL	60062	847-849-4200	849-4695
TF: 800-645-2183 ■ *Web:* www.potashcorp.com					
Potash Corp of Saskatchewan Inc 122 1st Ave S Suite 500	Saskatoon	SK	S7K7G3	306-933-8500	933-8844
NYSE: POT ■ *TF:* 800-667-3930 ■ *Web:* www.potashcorp.com					
Prentiss Inc 21 Vernon St CB 2000	Floral Park	NY	11001	516-326-1919	326-2312
TF: 800-645-1911 ■ *Web:* www.prentiss.com					
Pro-Serve Inc 400 E Brook Rd PO Box 161059	Memphis	TN	38109	901-332-7052	346-7157
TF: 877-776-7375 ■ *Web:* www.pro-serveinc.com					
Rohm & Haas Co 100 Independence Mall W	Philadelphia	PA	19106	215-592-3000	592-3377*
NYSE: ROH ■ **Fax:* Hum Res ■ *Web:* www.rohmhaas.com					
Safeguard Chemical Corp 411 Wales Ave	Bronx	NY	10454	718-585-3170	585-3657
TF: 800-536-3170 ■ *Web:* www.safeguardchemical.com					
Sara Lee Household & Body Care 707 Eagleview Blvd	Exton	PA	19341	610-321-1220	321-1440
TF: 800-879-5494 ■ *Web:* www.saralee.com					
SC Johnson & Son Inc 1525 Howe St	Racine	WI	53403	262-260-2000	260-2632
TF: 800-494-4855 ■ *Web:* www.scjohnson.com					
Scotts Miracle-Gro Co 14111 Scottslawn Rd	Marysville	OH	43041	937-644-0011	644-7600
NYSE: SMG ■ *TF Cust Svc:* 800-543-8873 ■ *Web:* www.scotts.com					
Scotts Miracle Gro Products Inc 14111 Scottslawn Rd	Marysville	OH	43041	937-644-0011	644-7600
TF: 800-543-8873 ■ *Web:* www.miracle-gro.com					
Share Corp 7821 N Faulkner Rd	Milwaukee	WI	53224	414-355-4000	355-0516
TF: 800-776-7192 ■ *Web:* www.sharecorp.com					
Simplot JR Co 999 Main St	Boise	ID	83702	208-336-2110	389-7515
TF: 800-635-5008 ■ *Web:* www.simplot.com					
Simplot JR Co AgriBusiness Group 999 Main St PO Box 70013	Boise	ID	83707	208-672-2700	672-2760
TF: 800-635-9444 ■ *Web:* www.simplot.com/agricultural					
Southern States Chemical Co 1600 E President St	Savannah	GA	31404	912-232-1101	232-1103
TF: 888-337-8922 ■ *Web:* www.sschemical.com					
Spectrum Brands 601 Rayovac Dr	Madison	WI	53711	314-427-4886	677-4770*
**Fax Area Code:* 888 ■ *TF:* 800-341-0020 ■ *Web:* www.spectrumbrands.com					
Standard Tar Products Co Inc 2456 W Cornell St	Milwaukee	WI	53209	414-873-7650	873-7737
TF: 800-825-7650 ■ *Web:* www.standardtar.com					
Stoller Enterprises Inc					
4001 W Sam Houston Pkwy N Suite 100	Houston	TX	77043	713-461-1493	461-4467
TF: 800-539-5283 ■ *Web:* www.keylate.com					
Summit Chemical Co 235 S Kresson St	Baltimore	MD	21224	410-522-0661	522-0833
TF: 800-227-8664 ■ *Web:* www.summitchemical.com					
Sunniland Corp 1721 Hwy 1735	Sanford	FL	32773	407-322-2421	324-5784
TF: 800-432-1130 ■ *Web:* www.sunniland.com					
Syngenta Corp 2200 Concord Pike	Wilmington	DE	19803	302-425-2000	425-2001
TF: 800-759-4500 ■ *Web:* www.syngenta.com					
Syngenta Crop Protection Inc 410 Swing Rd	Greensboro	NC	27409	336-632-6000	632-7650*
**Fax:* Sales ■ *TF:* 800-334-9481 ■ *Web:* www.syngenta.com					
Terra Industries Inc 600 4th St Terra Center	Sioux City	IA	51101	712-277-1340	293-4601*
NYSE: TRA ■ **Fax:* Mktg ■ *Web:* www.terraindustries.com					
Terra Nitrogen Co LP 600 4th St Terra Centre	Sioux City	IA	51101	712-277-1340	277-7364
Web: www.terranitrogen.com					
Town & Country Co-op Inc 686 E Main ST	Smithville	OH	44677	330-669-2711	669-3431
Trans-Resources Inc 200 W 57th St	New York	NY	10019	212-515-4100	515-4111
Web: www.trans-resources.com					
UAP Holding Corp 7251 W 4th St PO Box 1286	Greeley	CO	80632	970-356-4400	506-2462
NASDAQ: UAPH ■ *Web:* www.uap.com					
Valley Fertilizer & Chemical Co Inc					
201 Valley Rd PO Box 816	Mount Jackson	VA	22842	540-477-3121	477-3123
TF: 800-571-3121					
Van Diest Supply Co 1434 220th St PO Box 610	Webster City	IA	50595	515-832-2366	832-2955
TF: 800-779-2424 ■ *Web:* www.vdsc.com					
Whitmire Micro-Gen Research Laboratories Inc					
3568 Tree Court Industrial Blvd	Saint Louis	MO	63122	636-225-5371	225-3739
TF: 800-777-8570 ■ *Web:* www.wmmg.com					
Wolfkill Feed & Fertilizer Corp 217 E Stretch St PO Box 578	Monroe	WA	98272	360-794-7065	704-3561
TF: 800-525-4539					
Woodstream Corp 69 N Locust St	Lititz	PA	17543	717-626-2125	626-1912
TF: 800-800-1819 ■ *Web:* www.woodstreamcorp.com					
Y-Tex Corp 1825 Big Horn Ave	Cody	WY	82414	307-587-5515	527-6433
TF: 800-443-6401 ■ *Web:* www.y-tex.com					

284 FESTIVALS - BOOK

	City	State	ZIP	Phone	Fax
Alabama Bound 2100 Park Pl	Birmingham	AL	35203	205-226-3610	226-3743
Web: www.alabamabound.org					
Amelia Book Island Festival PO Box 824	Amelia Island	FL	32035	904-491-8176	
Web: www.bookisland.org					
Arizona Book Festival					
Arizona Humanities Council 1242 N Central Ave	Phoenix	AZ	85004	602-257-0335	257-0392
Web: www.azbookfestival.org					
Baltimore Book Festival					
Baltimore Office of Promotion 7 E Redwood St Suite 500	Baltimore	MD	21202	410-752-8632	385-0361
Web: www.bop.org					
Banff Mountain Book Festival					
The Banff Center Box 1020 Station 38	Banff	AB	T1L1H5	403-762-6675	762-6277
Web: www.banffcentre.ca/mountainculture/festivals					
Boston Globe Book Festival PO Box 2378 Public Affairs Dept	Boston	MA	02107	617-929-2649	929-2606
Web: bostonglobe.com/community/programs/books.stm					
Buckeye Book Fair 205 W Liberty St	Wooster	OH	44691	330-262-3244	
Web: www.buckeyebookfair.com					
Great Salt Lake Book Festival					
Utah Humanities Council 202 W 300 North	Salt Lake City	UT	84103	801-359-9670	531-7869
Web: www.utahhumanities.org					
Kentucky Book Fair PO Box 537	Frankfort	KY	40602	502-564-8300	564-5773
Web: www.kybookfair.com					
Latino Book & Family Festival 2777 Jefferson St Suite 200	Carlsbad	CA	92008	760-434-4484	434-7476
Web: www.latinobookfestival.com					
Lee County Reading Festival 2050 Central Ave	Fort Myers	FL	33901	239-479-4636	
Web: www.lee-county.com/library/ReadingFestivalHome.htm					
Los Angeles Times Festival of Books					
Los Angeles Times 202 W 1st St	Los Angeles	CA	90012	213-237-5000	237-2335
TF: 800-528-4637 ■ *Web:* www.latimes.com/extras/festivalofbooks					
Miami Book Fair International					
Miami-Dade Community College Wolfson Campus 300 NE 2nd Ave Suite 3704	Miami	FL	33132	305-237-3258	237-3978
Web: www.mdcc.edu/bookfair					
Montana Festival of the Book					
University of Montana Center for the Book 311 Brantly Hall	Missoula	MT	59812	406-243-6022	243-4836
Web: www.bookfest-mt.org					
Much Ado About Books					
Jacksonville Public Library Foundation PO Box 40103	Jacksonville	FL	32203	904-630-1703	
Web: www.muchadoaboutbooks.com/home.cfm					
National Book Festival					
Library of Congress 101 Independence Ave SE	Washington	DC	20540	888-714-4696	707-9199*
**Fax Area Code:* 202 ■ *Web:* www.loc.gov/bookfest					
New York Center for Independent Publishing					
Small Press Center 20 W 44th St	New York	NY	10036	212-764-7021	840-2046
Web: www.nycip.org/					
New York is Book Country C2 Media 423 W 55th St	New York	NY	10019	646-557-6300	557-6400
Web: www.nyisbookcountry.com					
Northern Arizona Book Festival PO Box 1871	Flagstaff	AZ	86002	928-380-8682	
Web: www.nazbookfestival.org					
NOVELLO Festival of Reading					
Public Library of Charlotte & Mecklenburg County 310 N Tryon St	Charlotte	NC	28202	704-336-2725	336-2002
Web: www.novellofestival.net					
Printers Row Book Fair Chicago Tribune 435 N Michigan Ave	Chicago	IL	60611	312-527-8280	
Web: www.chicagotribune.com/extras/printersrow					
South Carolina Book Festival PO Box 5287	Columbia	SC	29250	803-771-2477	771-2487
Web: www.schumanities.org/bookfestival.htm					
Southern Festival of Books					
Humanities Tennessee 306 Gay St Suite 306	Nashville	TN	37201	615-770-0006	321-4586
Web: tn-humanities.org/sfbmain.htm					
Southern Kentucky Book Fest					
Western Kentucky University Libraries & Museum Cravens Library Room 106	Bowling Green	KY	42101	270-745-5016	745-6422
Web: www.sokybookfest.org					
Texas Book Festival 610 Brazos St Suite 200	Austin	TX	78701	512-477-4055	322-0722
Web: www.texasbookfestival.org					
Times Festival of Reading					
490 1st Ave S 4th Fl St Petersburg Times Promotion Dept	Saint Petersburg	FL	33701	727-445-4142	892-2992
TF: 800-333-7505 ■ *Web:* www.festivalofreading.com					
Vancouver International Writers & Readers Festival					
1398 Cartwright St	Vancouver	BC	V6H3R8	604-681-6330	681-8400
Web: www.writersfest.bc.ca/2004festival/index.htm					
Vegas Valley Book Festival					
Nevada Humanities Committee 4505 Maryland Pkwy	Las Vegas	NV	89154	702-895-1878	895-1877
TF: 800-382-5023 ■ *Web:* www.nevadahumanities.org/bookfest.htm					
Virginia Festival of the Book					
Virginia Foundation for the Humanities 145 Ednam Dr	Charlottesville	VA	22903	434-924-3296	296-4714
Web: www.vabook.org					

285 FESTIVALS - FILM

	City	State	ZIP	Phone	Fax
AFI Fest American Film Institute 2021 N Western Ave	Los Angeles	CA	90027	323-856-7600	467-4578
Web: www.afifest.com					
American Black Film Festival 584 Broadway PO Box 688	New York	NY	10012	212-966-2411	966-2497
Web: www.abff.com					
Anchorage Film Festival 1410 Rudakof Cir	Anchorage	AK	99508	907-338-3690	338-3857
Web: www.anchoragefilmfestival.com					
Ann Arbor Film Festival PO Box 8232	Ann Arbor	MI	48107	734-995-5356	995-5396
Web: www.aafilmfest.org					
Arpa International Film Festival 2919 Maxwell St	Los Angeles	CA	90027	323-663-1882	663-1882
Web: www.affma.org					
Asian American International Film Festival					
133 W 19th St Suite 300	New York	NY	10011	212-989-1422	727-3584
Web: www.asiancinevision.org					
Atlanta Film Festival 535 Means St NW Suite C	Atlanta	GA	30318	404-352-4225	352-0173
Web: www.atlantafilmfestival.com					
Austin Film Festival 1604 Nueces St	Austin	TX	78701	512-478-4795	478-6205
TF: 800-310-3378 ■ *Web:* www.austinfilmfestival.com					
Beverly Hills Film Festival					
9663 Santa Monica Blvd Suite 777	Beverly Hills	CA	90210	310-779-1206	
Web: www.beverlyhillsfilmfestival.com					
Boston Film Festival 9B Hamilton Pl	Boston	MA	02108	617-523-8388	
Web: www.bostonfilmfestival.org					
Brooklyn International Film Festival 180 S 4th St Suite 2S	Brooklyn	NY	11211	718-486-8181	599-5039
Web: www.brooklynfilmfestival.org					
Chicago Indiefest Film Festival PO Box 148849	Chicago	IL	60614	773-665-7600	665-7660
Web: www.indiefestchicago.com					
Chicago International Film Festival					
Cinema Chicago 30 E Adams St Suite 800	Chicago	IL	60603	312-683-0121	683-0122
Web: www.chicagofilmfestival.com					
Cleveland International Film Festival 2510 Market Ave	Cleveland	OH	44133	216-623-3456	623-0103
Web: www.clevelandfilm.org					
DC Independent Film Festival 2950 Van Ness St NW	Washington	DC	20008	202-537-9493	686-8867
Web: www.dciff.org					
Denver International Film Festival					
Denver Film Society 1725 Blake St	Denver	CO	80202	303-595-3456	595-0956
Web: www.denverfilm.org					
Film Fest New Haven PO Box 9644	New Haven	CT	06536	203-776-6789	776-4260
Web: www.filmfest.org					

	City	State	Zip	Phone	Fax
Fort Lauderdale International Film Festival 503 SE 6th St *Web:* www.fliff.com	Fort Lauderdale	FL	33301	954-760-9898	760-9099
Full Frame Documentary Film Festival 324 Blackwell St Suite 500 Washington Bldg Bay 5 *Web:* www.fullframefest.org	Durham	NC	27701	919-687-4100	687-4200
Green Mountain Film Festival 26 Main St *Web:* savoytheater.com/gmff	Montpelier	VT	05602	802-229-0598	229-2662
Heartland Film Festival 200 S Meridian St Suite 220 *Web:* www.heartlandfilmfestival.com	Indianapolis	IN	46225	317-464-9405	464-9409
High Falls Film Festival 45 East Ave Suite 400 *Web:* www.highfallsfilmfestival.com	Rochester	NY	14604	585-279-8330	232-4822
Hot Springs Documentary Film Festival 819 Central Ave *Web:* www.docufilminst.org	Hot Springs	AR	71901	501-321-4747	321-0211
Long Beach International Film Festival 2005 Palo Verde Suite 309 *Web:* www.longbeachfilmfestival.com	Long Beach	CA	90815	562-938-9687	938-9687
Los Angeles Film Festival Film Independent 9911 W. Pico Blvd. *TF:* 866-345-6337 ■ *Web:* www.lafilmfest.com	Beverly Hills	CA	90211	310-432-1240	
Los Angeles International Film Festival American Film Institute 2021 N Western Ave *Web:* www.afifest.com	Los Angeles	CA	90027	323-856-7600	467-4578
Los Angeles International Short Film Festival 1610 Argyle Ave Suite 113 *Web:* lashortsfest.com	Hollywood	CA	90028	323-461-4400	
Malibu International Film Festival PO Box 4166 *Web:* www.malibufilmfestival.org	Venice	CA	90294	310-452-6688	
Maryland Film Festival 107 E Read St *Web:* www.mdfilmfest.com	Baltimore	MD	21202	410-752-8083	752-8273
Miami International Film Festival Miami Dade College 25 NE 2nd St Bldg 5 Rm 5501 *Web:* www.miamifilmfestival.com	Miami	FL	33132	305-237-3456	237-7344
Mill Valley Film Festival 38 Miller Ave Suite 6 *Web:* www.mvff.com	Mill Valley	CA	94941	415-383-5256	383-8606
Minneapolis/St Paul International Film Festival Minnesota Film Arts 309 Oak St SE *Web:* www.mnfilmarts.org	Minneapolis	MN	55414	612-331-7563	378-7750
Montreal World Film Festival 1432 rue de Bleury *Web:* www.ffm-montreal.org	Montreal	QC	H3A2J1	514-848-3883	848-3886
Nashville Film Festival 161 Rains Ave *Web:* www.nashvillefilmfestival.org	Nashville	TN	37203	615-742-2500	742-1004
New Hampshire Film Expo 155 Fleet St *Web:* www.nhfilmexpo.com	Portsmouth	NH	03801	603-647-6439	
New Orleans Film Festival 843 Carondelet St Upper Suite 1 *Web:* www.neworleansfilmfest.com	New Orleans	LA	70130	504-309-6633	309-0923
New York Film Festival 70 Lincoln Center Plaza *Web:* www.filmlinc.com	New York	NY	10023	212-875-5638	875-5636
Newport International Film Festival PO Box 146 *Web:* www.newportfilmfestival.com	Newport	RI	02840	401-846-9100	846-6665
Olympia Film Festival 416 Washington St SE Suite 208 *Web:* www.olyfilm.org	Olympia	WA	98501	360-754-3675	943-9100
Outfest-Los Angeles Gay & Lesbian Film Festival *Web:* www.outfest.org	Los Angeles	CA		213-480-7088	
Philadelphia Film Festival 234 Market St 4th Fl *Fax Area Code: 215 ■ *Web:* www.phillyfests.com	Philadelphia	PA	19106	267-765-9700	733-0668*
Phoenix Film Festival 2345 E Thomas Rd Suite 100 *Web:* www.phoenixfilmfestival.com	Phoenix	AZ	85016	602-955-6444	955-0966
Portland International Film Festival Northwest Film Center 1219 SW Park Ave *Web:* www.nwfilm.org	Portland	OR	97205	503-221-1156	294-0874
Riverrun International Film Festival 870 W 4th St *Web:* www.riverrunfilm.com	Winston-Salem	NC	27101	336-724-1502	724-1112
Rochester International Film Festival PO Box 17746 *Web:* www.rochesterfilmfest.org	Rochester	NY	14617	585-234-7411	
Saint Louis International Film Festival 3547 Olive St *Web:* www.cinemastlouis.org	Saint Louis	MO	63103	314-289-4150	289-4159
San Diego Film Festival 7974 Mission Bonita Dr *Web:* www.sdff.org	San Diego	CA	92120	619-582-2368	286-8324
San Francisco International Asian American Film Festival 145 9th St Suite 350 *Web:* www.naatanet.org/festival	San Francisco	CA	94103	415-863-0814	863-7428
San Francisco International Film Festival 39 Mesa St Suite 110 The Presidio *Web:* www.sfiff.org	San Francisco	CA	94129	415-561-5000	561-5099
San Jose Film Festival - CineQuest PO Box 720040 *Web:* www.cinequest.org	San Jose	CA	95172	408-995-5033	995-5713
Santa Barbara International Film Festival 1528 Chapala St Suite 203 *Web:* www.sbfilmfestival.org	Santa Barbara	CA	93101	805-963-0023	962-2524
Sarasota Film Festival 332 Cocoanut Ave *Web:* www.sarasotafilmfestival.com	Sarasota	FL	34236	941-364-9514	364-8411
Savannah Film Festival PO Box 3146 *Web:* www.scad.edu/filmfest	Savannah	GA	31402	912-525-5051	525-5052
Seattle International Film Festival 400 9th Ave N *Web:* www.seattlefilm.com	Seattle	WA	98109	206-464-5830	264-7919
Sidewalk Moving Picture Festival 2312 1st Ave N *Web:* www.sidewalkfest.com	Birmingham	AL	35203	205-324-0888	324-2488
Sonoma Valley Film Festival 569 1st St W *Web:* www.sonomafilmfest.org	Sonoma	CA	95476	707-933-2600	933-2612
South by Southwest Film Festival PO Box 4999 *Web:* www.sxsw.com	Austin	TX	78765	512-467-7979	451-0754
Sundance Film Festival PO Box 3630 *Web:* www.sundance.org	Salt Lake City	UT	84110	801-328-3456	575-5175
Tambay Film & Video Festival 16002 Saddle Creek Dr *Web:* www.tambayfilmfest.com	Tampa	FL	33694	813-964-9781	
Telluride Film Festival 800 Jones St *Web:* www.telluridefilmfestival.com	Berkeley	CA	94710	510-665-9494	665-9589
Telluride Indiefest PO Box 860 *Web:* tellurideindiefest.com	Telluride	CO	81435	970-708-1529	728-8128
Three Rivers Film Festival 477 Melwood Ave *Web:* 3rff.com	Pittsburgh	PA	15213	412-681-5449	681-5503
Toronto International Film Festival 2 Carlton St Suite 1600 *Web:* www.e.bell.ca/filmfest	Toronto	ON	M5B1J3	416-967-7371	967-9477
Utah Short Film & Video Festival Utah Film & Video Ctr 20 SW Temple *Web:* www.ufvc.org	Salt Lake City	UT	84101	801-534-1158	
Vermont International Film Festival 1 Main St Suite 307 *Web:* www.vtiff.org	Burlington	VT	05401	802-660-2600	860-9555
Worldfest Houston International Film Festival PO Box 56566 *TF:* 866-965-9955 ■ *Web:* www.worldfest.org	Houston	TX	77256	713-965-9955	965-9960

286 FIRE PROTECTION SYSTEMS

SEE ALSO Personal Protective Equipment & Clothing p. 2105; Safety Equipment - Mfr p. 2302; Security Products & Services p. 2309

	City	State	Zip	Phone	Fax
Autronics Corp 12701 Schabarum Ave *Web:* www.autronics.com	Irwindale	CA	91706	626-851-3100	960-8500
BRK Brands Inc 3901 Liberty Street Rd *TF:* 800-323-9005 ■ *Web:* www.firstalert.com	Aurora	IL	60504	630-851-7330	851-9015
Chemetron Fire Systems 4801 Southwick Dr 3rd Fl *TF Cust Svc:* 800-878-5631 ■ *Web:* www.chemetron.com	Matteson	IL	60443	708-748-1503	748-2847
Cooper Wheelock 273 Branchport Ave *TF Cust Svc:* 800-631-2148 ■ *Web:* www.wheelockinc.com	Long Branch	NJ	07740	732-222-6880	222-8707
Detector Electronics Corp 6901 W 110th St *TF:* 800-765-3473 ■ *Web:* www.detronics.com	Minneapolis	MN	55438	952-941-5665	829-8750
Faraday LLC 805 S Maumee St *TF:* 800-465-7115 ■ *Web:* www.faradayfirealarms.com	Tecumseh	MI	49286	517-423-2111	423-2320
Fenwal Safety Systems 4200 Airport Dr NW *Web:* www.fenwalsafety.com	Wilson	NC	27896	252-237-7004	246-7181
Fike Corp 704 SW 10th St *TF:* 877-342-3453 ■ *Web:* www.fike.com	Blue Springs	MO	64015	816-229-3405	228-9277
Fire-Lite Alarms 1 Fire-Lite Pl *TF:* 800-289-3473 ■ *Web:* www.firelite.com	Northford	CT	06472	203-484-7161	484-7118
Firecom Inc 39-27 59th St *TF:* 800-347-3266 ■ *Web:* www.firecominc.com	Woodside	NY	11377	718-899-6100	899-1932
First Alert Inc 3901 Liberty Street Rd *TF:* 800-323-9005 ■ *Web:* www.firstalert.com	Aurora	IL	60504	630-851-7330	851-7538
Gamewell Co 12 Clintonville Rd *TF:* 800-606-1983 ■ *Web:* www.gamewell.com	Northford	CT	06472	203-484-7161	
General Monitors Inc 26776 Simpatica Cir *TF:* 866-686-0741 ■ *Web:* www.generalmonitors.com	Lake Forest	CA	92630	949-581-4464	581-1151
Harrington Signal Co 2519 4th Ave *TF:* 800-577-5758 ■ *Web:* www.harringtonsignal.com	Moline	IL	61265	309-762-0731	762-8215
Honeywell Fire Solutions DBA Fire-Lite Alarms 1 Fire-Lite Pl. *TF:* 800-289-3473 ■ *Web:* www.firelite.com	Northford	CT	06472	203-484-7161	484-7118
Kidde Aerospace 4200 Airport Dr NW *Fax: Hum Res ■ *Web:* www.kiddeaerospace.com	Wilson	NC	27896	252-237-7004	246-7184*
Meggitt Safety Systems Inc 1915 Voyager Ave *Web:* www.meggitt.com	Simi Valley	CA	93063	805-584-4100	578-3400
Potter Electric Signal Co Inc 2081 Craig Rd *TF:* 800-325-3936 ■ *Web:* www.pottersignal.com	Saint Louis	MO	63146	314-878-4321	878-7264
Siemens Building Technologies Inc Fire Safety Div 8 Fernwood Rd *TF:* 800-222-0108 ■ *Web:* www.sbt.siemens.com/fis	Florham Park	NJ	07932	973-593-2600	
Silent Knight 7550 Meridian Cir Suite 100 *TF:* 800-328-0103 ■ *Web:* www.silentknight.com	Maple Grove	MN	55369	763-493-6400	493-6475
SimplexGrinnell Ltd 50 Technology Dr *Fax: Hum Res ■ *TF:* 800-746-7539 ■ *Web:* www.simplexgrinnell.com	Westminster	MA	01441	978-731-2500	731-7867*
Viking Corp 210 N Industrial Pk Dr *TF:* 800-968-9501 ■ *Web:* www.vikingcorp.com	Hastings	MI	49058	269-945-9501	945-9599

287 FIREARMS & AMMUNITION (NON-MILITARY)

SEE ALSO Sporting Goods p. 2323; Weapons & Ordnance (Military) p. 2413

	City	State	Zip	Phone	Fax
American Derringer Corp 127 N Lacy Dr *Web:* www.amderringer.com	Waco	TX	76705	254-799-9111	799-7935
Beeman Precision Airguns 5454 Argosy Dr *TF:* 800-227-2744 ■ *Web:* www.beeman.com	Huntington Beach	CA	92649	714-890-4800	890-4808
Beretta USA Corp 17601 Beretta Dr *TF:* 800-636-3420 ■ *Web:* www.beretta.com	Accokeek	MD	20607	301-283-2191	283-0435
Colt's Mfg Co LLC PO Box 1868 *TF:* 800-962-2658 ■ *Web:* www.coltsmfg.com	Hartford	CT	06144	860-236-6311	244-1442
Connecticut Valley Arms 5988 Peachtree Corners E *Web:* www.cva.com	Norcross	GA	30071	770-449-4687	242-8546
Crosman Corp Rts 5 & 20 *TF:* 800-724-7486 ■ *Web:* www.crosman.com	East Bloomfield	NY	14443	585-657-6161	657-5405
Defense Technology/Federal Laboratories 1855 S Loop PO Box 248 *TF:* 877-248-3835 ■ *Web:* www.defense-technology.com	Caspar	WY	82601	307-235-2136	473-2713
Eldorado Cartridge Corp 12801 US Hwy 95 S *Web:* www.pmcammo.com	Boulder City	NV	89005	702-294-0025	294-0121
Federal Cartridge Co 900 Ehlen Dr *Fax: Hum Res ■ *TF:* 800-322-2342 ■ *Web:* www.federalcartridge.com	Anoka	MN	55303	763-323-2300	323-2506*
Freedom Arms Inc 314 Hwy 239 *TF:* 800-833-4432 ■ *Web:* www.freedomarms.com	Freedom	WY	83120	307-883-2468	883-2005
Galion LLC 515 N East St *Web:* www.galionllc.com	Galion	OH	44833	419-468-5214	468-1661
Glock Inc 6000 Highlands Pkwy *Web:* www.glock.com	Smyrna	GA	30082	770-432-1202	433-8719
Green Mountain Rifle Barrel Co PO Box 2670 *Web:* www.gmriflebarrel.com	Conway	NH	03818	603-447-1095	447-1099
Gun Parts Corp 226 Williams Ln *Fax Area Code: 877 ■ *Web:* www.gunpartscorp.com	West Hurley	NY	12491	845-679-4867	486-7278*
H & R 1871 60 Industrial Rowe *TF:* 866-776-9292 ■ *Web:* www.hr1871.com	Gardner	MA	01440	978-632-9393	632-2300
Heckler & Koch Inc 7661 Commerce Ln *Web:* www.hecklerkoch-usa.com	Trussville	AL	35173	205-655-8299	655-7078
Heritage Mfg Inc 4600 NW 135th St *Web:* www.heritagemfg.com	Opa Locka	FL	33054	305-685-5966	687-6721
Hornady Mfg Co 3625 Old Potash Hwy *TF Cust Svc:* 800-338-3220 ■ *Web:* www.hornady.com	Grand Island	NE	68803	308-382-1390	382-5761
Knight Rifles 21852 Hwy J46 *Web:* www.knightrifles.com	Centerville	IA	52544	641-856-2626	856-2628
Lyman Products Corp 475 Smith St *TF:* 800-225-9626 ■ *Web:* www.lymanproducts.com	Middletown	CT	06457	860-632-2020	632-1699
Marksman Products Inc 5482 Argosy Dr *Fax Area Code: 800 ■ *Fax: Cust Svc ■ *TF:* 800-822-8005 ■ *Web:* www.marksman.com	Huntington Beach	CA	92649	714-898-7535	822-8542*
Marlin Firearms Co 100 Kenna Dr *TF Cust Svc:* 800-544-8892 ■ *Web:* www.marlinfirearms.com	North Haven	CT	06473	203-239-5621	234-7991
MDS Caswell 2540 2nd St NE	Minneapolis	MN	55418	612-379-2000	379-2367
Meggitt Defense Systems Caswell (MDSC) 2540 2nd St NE	Minneapolis	MN	55418	612-379-2000	379-2367
Mossberg OF & Sons Inc 7 Grasso Ave *Fax: Mktg ■ *TF:* 800-989-4867 ■ *Web:* www.mossberg.com	North Haven	CT	06473	203-230-5300	230-5420*
OF Mossberg & Sons Inc 7 Grasso Ave *Fax: Mktg ■ *TF:* 800-989-4867 ■ *Web:* www.mossberg.com	North Haven	CT	06473	203-230-5300	230-5420*
Olin Corp Metals & Ammunition Segment 427 N Shamrock St	East Alton	IL	62024	618-258-2000	258-3084

Company	City	State	Zip	Phone	Fax
Olin Corp Winchester Div 427 N Shamrock St *TF:* 800-356-2666 ■ *Web:* www.winchester.com	East Alton	IL	62024	618-258-2000	258-3084
Remington Arms Co Inc 870 Remington Dr PO Box 700 *TF:* 800-243-9700 ■ *Web:* www.remington.com	Madison	NC	27025	336-548-8700	548-7801
Savage Arms Inc 100 Springdale Rd *TF:* 800-370-0712 ■ *Web:* www.savagearms.com	Westfield	MA	01085	413-568-7001	562-7764
SIGARMS Inc 18 Industrial Dr *TF Orders:* 800-325-3693 ■ *Web:* www.sigarms.com	Exeter	NH	03833	603-772-2302	772-9082
Smith & Wesson Corp 2100 Roosevelt Ave *TF Cust Svc:* 800-331-0852 ■ *Web:* www.smith-wesson.com	Springfield	MA	01104	413-781-8300	747-3317
Smith & Wesson Holding Corp 2100 Roosevelt Ave *AMEX:* SWB ■ *TF:* 800-331-0852 ■ *Web:* www.smith-wesson.com	Springfield	MA	01104	413-781-8300	747-3317
Springfield Armory 420 W Main St *TF:* 800-680-6866 ■ *Web:* www.springfield-armory.com	Geneseo	IL	61254	309-944-5631	944-3676
Sturm Ruger & Co Inc 1 Lacey Pl *NYSE:* RGR ■ *Web:* www.ruger-firearms.com	Southport	CT	06890	203-259-7843	254-2195
Taurus International Mfg Inc 16175 NW 49th Ave *Web:* www.taurususa.com	Miami	FL	33014	305-624-1115	623-7506
Thompson Center Arms Co Inc PO Box 5002 *Web:* www.tcarms.com	Rochester	NH	03866	603-332-2333	332-5133
Weatherby Inc 1065 Commerce Way *TF:* 800-334-4423 ■ *Web:* www.weatherby.com	Paso Robles	CA	93446	805-227-2600	237-0427
Williams Gun Sight Co 7389 Lapeer Rd *TF:* 800-530-9028 ■ *Web:* www.williamsgunsight.com	Davison	MI	48423	810-653-2131	658-2140
Winchester Div Olin Corp 427 N Shamrock St *TF:* 800-356-2666 ■ *Web:* www.winchester.com	East Alton	IL	62024	618-258-2000	258-3084

288 FISHING - COMMERCIAL

Company	City	State	Zip	Phone	Fax
All Alaskan Seafood Ventures PO Box 601	Edmonds	WA	98020	206-285-8200	285-2313
American Seafoods Holdings LLC 2025 1st Ave Suite 900 *AMEX:* SEA ■ *TF:* 800-275-2019 ■ *Web:* www.americanseafoods.com	Seattle	WA	98121	206-448-0300	448-4867
Arctic Storm Inc 400 N 34th St Suite 306 *TF:* 800-929-0908	Seattle	WA	98103	206-547-6557	547-3165
Blue North Fisheries 2930 Westlake Ave N Suite 300 *TF:* 877-878-3263	Seattle	WA	98109	206-352-9252	352-9380
Bon Secour Fisheries Inc 17449 County Rd 49 S PO Box 60 *TF:* 800-633-6854 ■ *Web:* www.bonsecourfisheries.com	Bon Secour	AL	36511	251-949-7411	949-6478
Canadian Fishing Co Foot of Gore Ave *TF:* 888-526-2929 ■ *Web:* www.canfisco.com	Vancouver	BC	V6A2Y7	604-681-0211	681-3277
Canfisco Foot of Gore Ave *TF:* 888-526-2929 ■ *Web:* www.canfisco.com	Vancouver	BC	V6A2Y7	604-681-0211	681-3277
JH Miles & Co Inc 902 S Hampton Ave	Norfolk	VA	23510	757-622-9264	622-9261
Little Bay Lobster Co 18 Old Dover Rd *Web:* www.littlebaylobster.com	Newington	NH	03801	603-431-3170	431-3496
Lund's Fisheries Inc 997 Ocean Dr *Web:* www.lundsfish.com	Cape May	NJ	08204	609-884-7600	884-0664
Miles JH & Co Inc 902 S Hampton Ave	Norfolk	VA	23510	757-622-9264	622-9261
North Pacific Corp 5612 Lake Washington Blvd Suite 102 *Web:* www.npc-usa.com	Kirkland	WA	98033	425-822-1001	822-1004
Nova Fisheries 2532 Yale Ave E *TF:* 888-458-6682 ■ *Web:* www.novafish.com	Seattle	WA	98102	206-781-2000	781-9011
Ocean Beauty Seafoods Inc 1100 W Ewing St *TF:* 800-877-0185 ■ *Web:* www.oceanbeauty.com	Seattle	WA	98119	206-285-6800	285-9190
Point Judith Fishermen's Co 75 State St	Narragansett	RI	02882	401-782-1500	782-1599
Raffield Fisheries Inc 1624 Grouper Ave *Web:* www.raffieldfisheries.com	Port Saint Joe	FL	32456	850-229-8229	229-8782
Sahlman Seafoods Inc 1601 Sahlman Dr *Web:* www.sahlmanseafood.com	Tampa	FL	33605	813-248-5726	247-5787
Trident Seafood Corp 5303 Shilshole Ave NW *TF:* 800-426-5490 ■ *Web:* www.tridentseafoods.com	Seattle	WA	98107	206-783-3818	782-7195
Wanchese Fish Co 2000 Northgate Commerce Pkwy *Web:* www.wanchese.com	Suffolk	VA	23435	757-673-4500	673-4550

289 FIXTURES - OFFICE & STORE

SEE ALSO Furniture - Mfr - Commercial & Industrial Furniture p. 1681

Company	City	State	Zip	Phone	Fax
Abco Wire & Metal Products 4061 E Castro Valley Blvd Suite 474 *Web:* www.abcowire.com	Castro Valley	CA	94552	510-782-6121	782-7310
Able Steel Equipment Co Inc 50-02 23rd St *Web:* ablesteelequipment.com	Long Island City	NY	11101	718-361-9240	937-5742
ADAPTO Storage Products 225 Main St **Fax Area Code:* 888 ■ *Web:* www.adapto.com	Tatamy	PA	18085	800-923-2786	859-2121*
Advanced Equipment Corp 2401 W Commonwealth Ave *Web:* www.advancedequipment.com	Fullerton	CA	92833	714-635-5350	525-6083
AGI Schutz Merchandising Co 376 Pine St Ext *TF:* 800-662-2150 ■ *Web:* www.agischutz.com	Forest City	NC	28043	828-245-9871	248-4990
Amco Corp 11230 Harland Dr **Fax Area Code:* 800 ■ *TF:* 800-621-4023	Covington	GA	30014	770-787-9830	577-2210*
American Sanitary Partition Corp 300 Enterprise St PO Box 99 *Web:* www.am-sanitary-partition.com	Ocoee	FL	34761	407-656-0611	656-8189
Ampco Products Inc 11400 NW 36th Ave *Web:* www.ampco.com	Miami	FL	33167	305-821-5700	557-0764
Amstore Corp 540 Danforth St *TF:* 800-933-6681 ■ *Web:* www.amstore.com	Coopersville	MI	49404	616-837-3700	837-3705
Angola Wire Products Inc 803 Wohlert St *TF:* 800-800-7225 ■ *Web:* www.angolawire.com	Angola	IN	46703	260-665-9447	665-6182
Architectural Bronze Aluminum Corp 655 Deerfield Rd Suite 100 *TF:* 800-339-6581 ■ *Web:* www.architecturalbronze.com	Deerfield	IL	60015	847-266-7300	266-7301
Aspects Inc 9441 Opal Ave	Mentone	CA	92359	909-794-7722	794-6996
Bassett Russ Co 8189 Byron Rd *TF:* 800-350-2445 ■ *Web:* www.russbassett.com	Whittier	CA	90606	562-945-2445	698-8972
Bel-Mar Wire Products Inc 2343 N Damen Ave *Web:* www.belmarwire.net	Chicago	IL	60647	773-342-3800	342-0038
Benner-Nawman Inc 3450 Sabin Brown Rd *TF:* 800-992-3833 ■ *Web:* www.benner-nawman.com	Wickenburg	AZ	85390	928-684-2813	684-7041
Bennett Mfg Co Inc 13315 Railroad St *TF:* 800-345-2142 ■ *Web:* www.bennettmfg.com	Alden	NY	14004	716-937-9161	937-3137
Best-Rite Mfg 2885 Lorraine Ave PO Box D **Fax Area Code:* 866 ■ *TF:* 866-866-6935 ■ *Web:* www.bestrite.com	Temple	TX	76503	254-778-4727	888-7483*
Bob-Leon Plastics Inc 5151 Franklin Blvd *Web:* www.bob-leon.com	Sacramento	CA	95820	916-452-4063	452-3759
Boden Store Fixtures Inc 5335 NE 109th Ave *TF:* 800-733-1923 ■ *Web:* www.boden.com	Portland	OR	97220	503-252-4728	252-4932
Boos John & Co 315 S 1st St PO Box 609 *Web:* www.johnboos.com	Effingham	IL	62401	217-347-7701	347-7705
Borroughs Corp 3002 N Burdick St *TF:* 800-748-0227 ■ *Web:* www.borroughs.com	Kalamazoo	MI	49004	269-342-0161	342-4161
Boston Retail Products 400 Riverside Ave *TF:* 800-225-1633 ■ *Web:* www.bostonretail.com	Medford	MA	02155	781-395-7417	395-0155
Brewster Panel Inc 435 12th St SW PO Box 669 *TF:* 800-243-8198	Vernon	AL	35592	205-695-6841	695-6465
Buckley Co PO Box 337	Cohasset	MA	02025	781-871-0700	447-3876
Cal-Partitions Inc 23814 President Ave *Web:* www.calpartitions.com	Harbor City	CA	90710	310-539-1911	539-5816
Cano Corp 225 Industrial Rd *TF:* 800-237-1358 ■ *Web:* www.canocorp.com	Fitchburg	MA	01420	978-342-0953	342-5082
Carolina Cabinet Co PO Box 157 *Web:* www.carolinacabinet.net	Black Creek	NC	27813	252-291-5181	291-8039
Center Fixture Operations 1010 Logansport St	Center	TX	75935	936-598-5645	598-4641
Churchill Cabinet Co 4616 W 19th St	Cicero	IL	60804	708-780-0070	780-9762
ClosetMaid Corp PO Box 4400 *TF Cust Svc:* 800-874-0008 ■ *Web:* www.closetmaid.com	Ocala	FL	34478	352-401-6000	867-8583
Columbia Showcase & Cabinet Co 11034 Sherman Way *Web:* www.columbiashowcase.com	Sun Valley	CA	91352	818-765-9710	255-0750
Consolidated Storage Cos DBA EQUIPTO 225 Main St **Fax Area Code:* 888 ■ *TF Cust Svc:* 800-323-0801 ■ *Web:* www.equipto.com	Tatamy	PA	18085	610-253-2775	859-2121*
Cres-Cor 5925 Heisley Rd *TF:* 877-273-7267 ■ *Web:* www.crescor.com	Mentor	OH	44060	440-350-1100	350-7267
Crown Metal Mfg Co 765 S SR 83 *Web:* www.crownmetal.com	Elmhurst	IL	60126	630-279-9800	279-9807
Custom Fold Doors Inc 110 W Ash Ave **Fax Area Code:* 818 ■ *TF:* 800-913-3573 ■ *Web:* www.customfold.net	Burbank	CA	91502	323-849-3225	846-0744*
DAC Products 100 Century Point Dr *TF:* 800-431-1982 ■ *Web:* www.dacproducts.com	East Bend	NC	27018	336-699-2900	699-2231
Dann Dee Display Fixtures Inc 7555 N Caldwell Ave *TF:* 800-888-8515 ■ *Web:* www.danndee.com	Niles	IL	60714	847-588-1600	588-1620
Darling LA Co 1401 Hwy 49B *TF:* 800-643-3499 ■ *Web:* www.ladarling.com	Paragould	AR	72450	870-239-9564	239-6427
Datum Filing Systems Inc 89 Church Rd *TF:* 800-828-8018 ■ *Web:* www.datumfiling.com	Emigsville	PA	17318	717-764-6350	764-6656
DeBourgh Mfg Co 27505 Otero Ave PO Box 981 *TF:* 800-328-8829 ■ *Web:* www.all-american-lockers.com	La Junta	CO	81050	719-384-8161	384-7713
Design Fabricators Inc 12777 Claude Ct *Web:* www.designfab.com	Thornton	CO	80241	303-661-9800	661-9814
Design Workshops 486 Lesser St *Web:* www.design-workshops.com	Oakland	CA	94601	510-434-0727	434-0409
Dixie Store Fixtures & Sales Co Inc 2425 1st Ave N *TF:* 800-323-4943 ■ *Web:* www.dixiestorefixtures.com	Birmingham	AL	35203	205-322-2442	322-2445
Durham Mfg Co Inc 201 Main St PO Box 230 *TF:* 800-243-3774 ■ *Web:* www.durhammfg.com	Durham	CT	06422	860-349-3427	
Econoco Corp 300 Karin Ln **Fax Area Code:* 800 ■ *TF:* 800-645-7032 ■ *Web:* www.econoco.com	Hicksville	NY	11801	516-935-7700	505-8300*
Edsal Mfg Co Inc 4400 S Packers Ave *Web:* www.edsal.com	Chicago	IL	60609	773-254-0600	
Edwards Products Inc 11385 Sebring Dr *TF:* 800-543-1835 ■ *Web:* www.edwardsproducts.com	Cincinnati	OH	45240	513-851-3000	851-9300
Egli WJ Co Inc PO Box 2605 *Web:* www.wjegli.com	Alliance	OH	44601	330-823-3666	823-0011
Electrorack Inc 1443 S Sunkist St *TF:* 800-433-6745 ■ *Web:* www.electrorack.com	Anaheim	CA	92806	714-776-5420	776-9683
Environments Inc 5700 Baker Rd *Web:* www.environmentsinc.com	Minnetonka	MN	55345	952-933-9981	933-6048
EQUIPTO 225 Main St **Fax Area Code:* 888 ■ *TF Cust Svc:* 800-323-0801 ■ *Web:* www.equipto.com	Tatamy	PA	18085	610-253-2775	859-2121*
Eugene Welding Co 2420 Wills St *TF:* 800-959-0857 ■ *Web:* www.ewco.net	Marysville	MI	48040	810-364-7421	364-4347
Ex-Cell Metal Products Inc 11240 Melrose St *TF:* 800-392-3557 ■ *Web:* www.ex-cell.com	Franklin Park	IL	60131	847-451-0451	451-0458
Eyelematic Mfg Co Inc 1 Seemar Rd *Web:* www.eyelematic.com	Watertown	CT	06795	860-274-6791	274-8464
Farmington Displays Inc 21 Hyde Rd *Web:* www.fdi-group.com	Farmington	CT	06032	860-677-2497	677-1418
Ferrante Mfg Co 6626 Gratiot Ave *Web:* www.ferrantemfg.com	Detroit	MI	48207	313-571-1111	571-0325
Fetzers' Inc 6223 W Double Eagle Cir *Web:* www.fetzersinc.com	Salt Lake City	UT	84118	801-484-6103	484-6122
Fixtures International Inc 501 Yale St PO Box 7774 *TF:* 800-444-1253 ■ *Web:* www.fixturesintl.com	Houston	TX	77007	713-869-3228	869-0970
Fleetwood Fixtures 3001 St Lawrence Ave *Web:* www.fleetwoodfixtures.com	Reading	PA	19606	610-779-7700	779-4829
Frazier Industrial Co 91 Fairview Ave *Web:* www.frazier.com	Long Valley	NJ	07853	908-876-3001	876-3615
General Partitions Mfg Corp 1702 Peninsula Dr PO Box 8370 *Web:* www.genpartitions.com	Erie	PA	16505	814-833-1154	838-3473
Giannelli Cabinets 19443 Londelius St	Northridge	CA	91324	818-882-9787	
Giffin Interior & Fixture Inc 500 Scotti Dr	Bridgeville	PA	15017	412-221-1166	221-3745
Goebel Fixture Co 528 Dale St *TF:* 800-727-4646 ■ *Web:* www.gf.com	Hutchinson	MN	55350	320-587-2112	587-2378
Guilford Corp 901 9th St S	Rockford	IL	61104	815-962-5362	
Hale TJ Co W 139 N 9499 Hwy 145 PO Box 250 *TF:* 800-236-4253 ■ *Web:* www.tjhale.com	Menomonee Falls	WI	53051	262-255-5555	255-5678
Hamilton Fixture 3550 Symmes Rd *TF:* 800-889-2165 ■ *Web:* www.hamiltonfixture.com	Hamilton	OH	45015	513-874-2016	870-8741
Hamilton Sorter Co Inc 3158 Production Dr **Fax Area Code:* 800 ■ *TF:* 800-503-9966 ■ *Web:* www.hamiltonsorter.com	Fairfield	OH	45014	513-870-4400	503-9968*
Harbor Industries Inc 14130 172nd Ave *TF:* 800-968-6993 ■ *Web:* www.harbor-ind.com	Grand Haven	MI	49417	616-842-5330	842-1385
HC Osvold Co 2828 University Ave SE *Web:* www.osvold.com	Minneapolis	MN	55414	612-331-1581	331-5540
Hirsh Industries MEG Div 502 S Green St PO Box 240 *TF Cust Svc:* 800-645-3315 ■ *Web:* www.megfixtures.com	Cambridge City	IN	47327	765-478-3141	478-4439
HMC Industries Inc 21020 63rd Ave N **Fax Area Code:* 206 ■ *Web:* www.hmcindinc.com	Lynnwood	WA	98036	425-778-3144	624-4434*
Holcomb & Hoke Mfg Co Inc 1545 Van Buren St *Web:* www.foldoor.com	Indianapolis	IN	46203	317-784-2444	781-9164
Hoosier Co 5421 W 86th St PO Box 681064 *TF:* 800-521-4184 ■ *Web:* www.hoosierco.com	Indianapolis	IN	46268	317-872-8125	872-7183
Hufcor Inc 2101 Kennedy Rd *TF:* 800-356-6968 ■ *Web:* www.hufcor.com	Janesville	WI	53545	608-756-1241	756-1246
Hurco Design & Mfg 200 W 33rd St *TF:* 877-859-6840 ■ *Web:* www.hurcoind.com	Ogden	UT	84401	801-394-9471	394-8218
IDX Baltimore 1710 Midway Rd *TF:* 800-638-9667 ■ *Web:* www.idxcorporation.com	Odenton	MD	21113	410-551-3600	551-9076
IDX Seattle 1301 N Levee Rd *Web:* www.idxcorporation.com	Puyallup	WA	98371	253-445-9000	445-8754
Imperial Counters Inc 725 Spiral Blvd *Web:* www.imperialcounters.com	Hastings	MN	55033	651-437-3903	438-3855
Inland Showcase & Fixture Co Inc 1473 N Thesta St	Fresno	CA	93703	559-237-4158	237-7238

Phone Fax

InterMetro Industries Corp 651 N Washington St .... Wilkes-Barre PA 18705 570-825-2741 824-7520*
*Fax: Hum Res ■ TF Cust Svc: 800-992-1776 ■ Web: www.metro.com
International Visual Corp (IVC) 4765 Des Grandes Prairies.........Montreal QC H1R1A5 514-643-0570 643-4867
TF: 866-643-0570 ■ Web: www.ivcweb.com
IVC (International Visual Corp) 4765 Des Grandes Prairies.........Montreal QC H1R1A5 514-643-0570 643-4867
TF: 866-643-0570 ■ Web: www.ivcweb.com
Jarke Corp - Div of Leggett & Platt Inc
750 Pinecrest Dr .... Prospect Heights IL 60070 847-541-6500 541-0858
TF: 800-722-5255 ■ Web: www.jarke.com
Jesco-Wipco Industries Inc 950 Anderson Rd PO Box 388 .... Litchfield MI 49252 517-542-2903 542-2501
TF: 800-455-0019 ■ Web: www.jesco-wipco.com
JL Industries Inc 4450 W 78th Street Cir.................. Bloomington MN 55435 952-835-6850 835-2218
TF: 800-554-6077 ■ Web: www.jlindustries.com
John Boos & Co 315 S 1st St PO Box 609 ....Effingham IL 62401 217-347-7701 347-7705
Web: www.johnboos.com
JR Jones Fixture Co 3216 Winnetka Ave N ....Minneapolis MN 55427 763-544-4239 544-3106
Kardex Systems Inc 114 Westview Ave PO Box 171 .... Marietta OH 45750 740-374-9300 374-9953*
*Fax: Mktg ■ TF: 800-234-3654 ■ Web: www.kardex.com
Karges Furniture Co Inc 1501 W Maryland St..................Evansville IN 47710 812-425-2291 425-4016
TF: 800-252-7437 ■ Web: www.karges.com
Kawneer Co Inc 555 Guthridge Ct .... Norcross GA 30092 770-449-5555 734-1560
Web: www.kawneer.com
Kay Co Inc The 509 W Barner St.......................... Frankfort IN 46041 765-659-3388 659-2956
Kent Corp 4446 Pinson Valley Pkwy.........................Birmingham AL 35215 205-853-3420 856-3622
TF: 800-252-5368 ■ Web: www.kentcorp.com
Killion Industries Inc 1380 Poinsettia Ave........................Vista CA 92083 760-727-5102 727-5108
TF: 800-421-5352 ■ Web: www.killionindustries.com
Knickerbocker Partition Corp 193 Hanse Ave PO Box 3035........ Freeport NY 11520 516-546-0550 546-0549
Web: www.knickerbockerpartition.com
Kwik-Wall Co 1010 E Edwards St...........................Springfield IL 62703 217-522-5553 522-1170
TF: 800-280-5945 ■ Web: www.kwik-wall.com
LA Darling Co 1401 Hwy 49B ....Paragould AR 72450 870-239-9564 239-6427
TF: 800-643-3499 ■ Web: www.ladarling.com
Lista International Corp 106 Lowland St......................Holliston MA 01746 508-429-1350 429-0711
TF Cust Svc: 800-722-3020 ■ Web: www.listaintl.com
Lodi Metal Tech 37555 Sycamore St...........................Newark CA 94560 510-795-1602 794-6156*
*Fax: Sales
Lozier Corp 6336 John J Pershing Dr..........................Omaha NE 68110 402-457-8000 457-8478*
*Fax: Cust Svc ■ TF: 800-228-9882 ■ Web: www.lozier.com
Lundia Div MII Inc 600 Capitol Way.........................Jacksonville IL 62650 217-243-8585 479-8191
TF: 800-726-9663 ■ Web: www.lundiausa.com
Lyon Work Space Products 420 N Main St .... Montgomery IL 60538 630-892-8941 892-8966
TF: 800-433-8488 ■ Web: www.lyonworkspace.com
Madix Store Fixtures 500 Airport Rd ....Terrell TX 75160 972-563-5744 563-0792
TF Cust Svc: 800-776-2349 ■ Web: www.madixinc.com
Markley Enterprises Inc 800 Lillian Ave.......................Elkhart IN 46516 574-295-4195 522-2230
Marlton Technologies Inc 2828 Charter Rd Suite 101..........Philadelphia PA 19154 215-676-6900 664-6900*
*Fax Area Code: 610 ■ Web: www.marltontechnologies.com
MEG Div Hirsh Industries 502 S Green St PO Box 240...... Cambridge City IN 47327 765-478-3141 478-4439
TF Cust Svc: 800-645-3315 ■ Web: www.megfixtures.com
Metpar Corp 95 State St..Westbury NY 11590 516-333-2600 333-2618
TF: 888-638-7271 ■ Web: www.metpar.com
MII Inc Lundia Div 600 Capitol Way.........................Jacksonville IL 62650 217-243-8585 479-8191
TF: 800-726-9663 ■ Web: www.lundiausa.com
MII Inc Myers Div 2100 W 5th St Rd..........................Lincoln IL 62656 217-735-1241 735-6645
Web: www.mii-inc.com
Miller/Zell Inc 4715 Frederick Dr SW.........................Atlanta GA 30336 404-691-7400 699-2189
Web: www.millerzell.com
Millrock Div Modular Brand Group LLC 405 West St ......West Bridgewater MA 02379 508-584-0084 687-7700*
*Fax Area Code: 617 ■ TF: 800-645-7625 ■ Web: www.millrock.com
Modern Metals Industries Inc PO Box 888 .... El Segundo CA 90245 310-516-0851 516-0464
TF: 800-437-6633
Modern Woodcrafts LLC
PO Box 464 Farmington Industrial Park ....Farmington CT 06034 860-677-7371 676-8381
Web: www.modernwoodcrafts.com
Modernfold Inc 215 W New Rd ....Greenfield IN 46140 317-468-6700 468-6760
TF: 800-869-9685 ■ Web: www.modernfold.com
Modular Brand Group LLC Millrock Div 405 West St ......West Bridgewater MA 02379 508-584-0084 687-7700*
*Fax Area Code: 617 ■ TF: 800-645-7625 ■ Web: www.millrock.com
Modular Systems Inc 169 W Park St PO Box 399...............Fruitport MI 49415 231-865-3167 865-6101
TF: 877-847-5989 ■ Web: www.mod-eez.com
Monarch Industries Inc 99 Main St ....Warren RI 02885 401-247-5200 247-5601*
*Fax: Sales ■ TF: 800-669-9663 ■ Web: www.monarchinc.com
National Partitions & Interiors Inc 10300 Goldenfern Ln......... Knoxville TN 37931 800-999-7266 362-5688*
*Fax Area Code: 305 ■ TF: 866-528-4616 ■ Web: www.n-p.com
Northway Industries Inc 434 Paxtonville Rd PO Box 277 ....Middleburg PA 17842 570-837-1564 837-1575
Web: www.northwayind.com
Northwestern Inc 15054 Oxnard St.........................Van Nuys CA 91411 818-786-1581 786-5063
Oak & More Ltd 4949 SE 25th Ave.............................Portland OR 97202 503-245-4522 245-4503
Osvold HC Co 2828 University Ave SE .... Minneapolis MN 55414 612-331-1581 331-5540
Web: www.osvold.com
Pacific Fixture Co Inc 9725 Variel Ave ....Chatsworth CA 91311 818-727-1545 727-1582
TF: 800-272-2349 ■ Web: www.pacificfixture.com
Packard Industries Inc 1515 US 31 N...........................Niles MI 49120 269-684-2550 684-2422
TF Orders: 800-253-0866 ■ Web: www.packardindustries.com
Pan-Osten Co 6944 Louisville Rd .... Bowling Green KY 42101 270-783-3900 783-3911*
TF: 800-472-6678
Panelfold Inc 10700 NW 36th Ave ....Miami FL 33167 305-688-3501 688-0185
Web: www.panelfold.com
Penloyd LLC 2900 E Apache St.............................. Tulsa OK 74110 918-836-3794 836-3835*
*Fax: Sales ■ TF: 800-233-3794 ■ Web: www.penloyd.com
Pentwater Wire Products Inc 474 Carol St PO Box 947..........Pentwater MI 49449 231-869-6911 869-4020
TF: 877-869-6911 ■ Web: www.pentwaterwire.com
Peterson Mfg Co 24133 W 143rd St .... Plainfield IL 60544 815-436-9201 436-2863
TF: 800-547-8995 ■ Web: www.peterson-mfg.com
Plasticrest Products Inc 4519 W Harrison St .... Chicago IL 60624 773-826-2163 826-4227
TF: 800-828-2163
Premier Metal Products Co 55 Walnut St Suite 201 .... Norwood NJ 07648 201-750-4900 750-4937
Web: www.pmpwest.com
Principle Fixture & Millwork 105 Prospect Way PO Box 698....... Osceola WI 54020 715-294-1400 294-1456
Web: www.pfmi.com
Production Aids Inc 2930 Anthony Ln N .... Minneapolis MN 55418 612-638-1330 638-1341
Rapid Rack Industries Inc 14421 Bonelli St............... City of Industry CA 91746 626-333-7225 333-5265
TF: 800-736-7225 ■ Web: www.rapidrack.com
RC Smith Co 14200 Southcross Dr W.........................Burnsville MN 55306 952-854-0711 854-8160
TF: 800-747-7648 ■ Web: www.rcsmith.com
Reeve Store Equipment Co 9131 Bermudez St PO Box 276 ..... Pico Rivera CA 90660 562-949-2535 949-3862
TF: 800-927-3383 ■ Web: www.reeveco.com
Republic Storage Systems LLC 1038 Belden Ave NE...............Canton OH 44705 330-438-5800 454-7772
TF Sales: 800-477-1255 ■ Web: www.republicstorage.com
Ridg-U-Rak Inc 120 S Lake St PO Box 150 .... North East PA 16428 814-725-8751 725-5659
TF: 866-479-7225 ■ Web: www.ridgurak.com
Russ Bassett Co 8189 Byron Rd.............................. Whittier CA 90606 562-945-2445 698-8972
TF: 800-350-2445 ■ Web: www.russbassett.com
Sandusky Cabinets Inc 16125 Widmere Rd PO Box 517............. Arvin CA 93203 661-854-5551 854-2003
TF: 800-336-0674 ■ Web: www.sanduskycabinets.com

Phone Fax

Schulte Corp 12115 Ellington Ct...............................Cincinnati OH 45249 513-489-9300 277-3701
TF: 800-669-3225 ■ Web: www.schultestorage.com
Semasys Inc 702 Ashland St.................................Houston TX 77007 713-869-8331 869-5077
TF Cust Svc: 800-231-1425 ■ Web: www.semasys.com
Showbest Fixture Corp 4112 Sarellen Rd...................... Richmond VA 23231 804-222-5535 222-7220
Web: www.showbest.com
Smith RC Co 14200 Southcross Dr W.........................Burnsville MN 55306 952-854-0711 854-8160
TF: 800-747-7648 ■ Web: www.rcsmith.com
Source Interlink Cos Inc 27500 Riverview Ctr Blvd..........Bonita Springs FL 34134 239-949-4450 949-7633
NASDAQ: SORC ■ TF: 866-276-5584 ■ Web: www.sourceinterlink.com
Southern Imperial Inc 1400 Eddy Ave .... Rockford IL 61103 815-877-7041
TF Cust Svc: 800-747-4665 ■ Web: www.southernimperial.com
Southern Metal Industries Inc
8767 Alabama Hwy PO Box 219 .... Ringgold GA 30736 706-935-4486 935-6854
TF: 800-241-5246 ■ Web: www.southernmetal.com
SpaceGuard Products Inc 711 S Commerce Dr.................. Seymour IN 47274 812-523-3044 428-5758*
*Fax Area Code: 800 ■ TF: 800-841-0680 ■ Web: www.spaceguardproducts.com
Spacesaver Corp 1450 Janesville Ave......................Fort Atkinson WI 53538 920-563-6362 563-2702
TF: 800-492-3434 ■ Web: www.spacesaver.com
Sparks Custom Retail LLC 2828 Charter Rd.................Philadelphia PA 19154 215-602-8100 676-8020
Web: www.sparksretail.com
Spectrum Industries Inc 1600 Johnson St................Chippewa Falls WI 54729 715-723-6750 335-0473*
*Fax Area Code: 800 ■ *Fax: Sales ■ TF: 800-235-1262 ■
Web: www.spectrumfurniture.com
Stanley Vidmar Storage Technologies 11 Grammes Rd..........Allentown PA 18103 610-797-6600 523-9934*
*Fax Area Code: 800 ■ TF: 800-523-9462 ■ Web: www.stanleyvidmar.com
Stanly Fixtures Co Inc 11635 NC 138 Hwy PO Box 616.......... Norwood NC 28128 704-474-3184 474-3011
TF: 800-476-3184
Stevens Industries Inc 704 W Main St..................... Teutopolis IL 62467 217-857-6411 540-3101
Web: www.stevensind.com
Stevens Wire Products Inc 351 NW 'F' St PO Box 1146......... Richmond IN 47375 765-966-5534 962-3586
Web: www.stevenswire.com
Store Kraft Mfg Co 500 Irving St............................ Beatrice NE 68310 402-223-2348 223-1268
Web: www.storekraft.com
Streater Inc 411 S 1st Ave .... Albert Lea MN 56007 507-373-0611 373-7630
TF: 800-527-4197 ■ Web: www.streater.com
Structural Concepts Corp 888 Porter Rd .... Muskegon MI 49441 231-798-8888 798-4960
TF: 800-433-9489 ■ Web: www.structuralconcepts.com
Syndicate Systems 402 N Main St..........................Middlebury IN 46540 574-825-9561 825-7194
Systems Mfg Corp 1037 Powers Rd.............................Conklin NY 13748 607-775-1100 775-5080
TF Cust Svc: 800-762-7587 ■ Web: www.smcplus.com
Tarrant Interiors 5000 South Fwy..........................Fort Worth TX 76115 817-922-5000 922-5015
Tesko Welding & Mfg Co 7350 W Montrose Ave ....Norridge IL 60706 708-452-0045 452-0112
TF: 800-621-4514
Timely Inc 10241 Norris Ave.................................Pacoima CA 91331 818-896-3094 899-2677
TF: 800-247-6242 ■ Web: www.timelyframes.com
TJ Hale Co W 139 N 9499 Hwy 145 PO Box 250 ....Menomonee Falls WI 53051 262-255-5555 255-5678
TF: 800-236-4253 ■ Web: www.tjhale.com
Transwall Office Systems Inc 1220 Wilson Dr ....West Chester PA 19380 610-429-1400 429-1411
TF: 800-441-9255 ■ Web: www.transwall.com
Trendway Corp 13467 Quincy St PO Box 9016 ....Holland MI 49422 616-399-3900 399-2231
TF: 800-968-5344 ■ Web: www.trendway.com
Tri Palm International 265 N Hamilton Rd.....................Columbus OH 43213 614-861-1350 322-4557*
*Fax: Cust Svc ■ TF: 800-950-3226 ■ Web: www.tripalmint.com
Trion Industries Inc 297 Laird St .... Wilkes-Barre PA 18702 570-824-1000 824-0802
TF: 800-444-4665 ■ Web: www.triononline.com
Unarco Material Handling Inc 701 16th Ave E .... Springfield TN 37172 615-384-3531 382-2777
TF: 800-862-7261 ■ Web: www.unarcorack.com
United Steel & Wire Co 4909 Wayne Rd .... Battle Creek MI 49015 269-962-5571 962-5577
TF: 800-227-7887 ■ Web: www.unitedsteelandwire.com
Universal Display & Fixtures Co 726 E Hwy 121............... Lewisville TX 75057 972-221-5022 221-6624
TF: 800-235-0701 ■ Web: www.udfc.com
Viking Metal Cabinet Co Inc 5321 W 65th St.................... Chicago IL 60638 708-594-1111 594-1028
TF: 800-776-7767 ■ Web: www.vikingmetal.com
Vira Mfg Inc 1 Buckingham Ave........................... Perth Amboy NJ 08861 732-442-8472 442-8464
TF: 800-305-8472 ■ Web: www.viranet.com
Volunteer Fabricators Inc 985 Hwy 11 W PO Box 398........ Bean Station TN 37708 865-993-2417 993-5246*
*Fax: Cust Svc
Weis/Robart Partitions Inc 3737 S Venoy Rd .... Wayne MI 48184 734-467-8711 467-8710
Web: www.weisrobart.com
Westco Inc 4010 S Orchard St Suite 108.......................New York NY 10001 212-685-5050 213-1382
Western Pacific Storage Systems Inc 300 E Arrow Hwy ....San Dimas CA 91773 909-451-0303 451-0311
TF: 800-732-9777 ■ Web: www.wpss.com
White Systems Inc 30 Boright Ave.............................Kenilworth NJ 07033 908-272-6700 272-5920
TF: 800-275-1442 ■ Web: www.whitesystems.com
WJ Egli Co Inc PO Box 2605 .... Alliance OH 44601 330-823-3666 823-0011
Web: www.wjegli.com
W/M Display Group 1040-50 W 40th St .... Chicago IL 60609 773-254-3700 254-3188
TF: 800-443-2000 ■ Web: www.wmdisplay.com
Woodworkers of Denver Inc 1475 S Acoma St .... Denver CO 80223 303-777-7656 744-8550
Web: www.woodworkersofdenver.com

290 FLAGS, BANNERS, PENNANTS

Phone Fax

Annin & Co 105 Eisenhower Pkwy .... Roseland NJ 07068 973-228-9400 228-4095
TF: 800-526-1390 ■ Web: www.annin.com
Collegiate Pacific Inc 532 Luck Ave ....Roanoke VA 24016 540-981-0281 981-0337
AMEX: BOO ■ TF: 800-336-5996 ■ Web: www.collegiatepacific.com
Eder Flag Mfg Co Inc 1000 W Rawson Ave.................. Oak Creek WI 53154 414-764-3522 764-1039
TF: 800-558-6044 ■ Web: www.ederflag.com
Metro Flag 47 Bassett Hwy..Dover NJ 07802 973-366-1776 366-0956
TF: 800-666-3524
National Banner Co 11938 Harry Hines Blvd ....Dallas TX 75234 972-241-2131 241-6282
TF: 800-527-0860
Olympus Flag & Banner 9000 W Heather Ave .... Milwaukee WI 53224 414-355-2010 355-1931
TF: 800-558-9620 ■ Web: www.olympus-flag.com
Valley Forge Flag Co Inc 1700 Conrad Weiser Pkwy ....Womelsdorf PA 19567 610-589-5888 589-4971
TF Cust Svc: 800-743-5247 ■ Web: www.valleyforgeflag.com

291 FLASH MEMORY DEVICES

Phone Fax

Advanced Micro Devices Inc (AMD) 1 AMD Pl PO Box 3453 ..... Sunnyvale CA 94088 408-749-4000 749-4291
NYSE: AMD ■ TF: 800-538-8450 ■ Web: www.amd.com
EDGE Tech Corp 327 E 14th St.....................................Ada OK 74820 580-332-6581 310-6518
Web: www.edgetechcorp.com
Kingston Technology Co 17600 Newhope St............. Fountain Valley CA 92708 714-435-2600 435-2699
TF: 800-835-6575 ■ Web: www.kingston.com

	City	State	Zip	Phone	Fax
Lexar Media Inc 47300 Bayside Pkwy *NASDAQ: LEXR* ■ *Web:* www.lexarmedia.com	Fremont	CA	94538	510-413-1200	440-3499
M-Systems Flash Disk Pioneers Ltd 8371 Central Ave Suite A *NASDAQ: FLSH* ■ *Web:* www.m-sys.com	Newark	CA	94560	408-470-4440	470-4470
Micron Quantum Devices Inc 2125 Onel Dr	San Jose	CA	95131	408-588-1300	822-0201
Micron Technology Inc 8000 S Federal Way *NYSE: MU* ■ *Web:* www.micron.com	Boise	ID	83707	208-368-4000	368-4617
PNY Technologies Inc 299 Webro Rd **Fax:* Sales ■ *TF:* 800-769-7079 ■ *Web:* www.pny.com	Parsippany	NJ	07054	973-515-9700	560-5590*
Samsung Semiconductors Inc 3655 N 1st St *TF:* 800-726-7864 ■ *Web:* www.usa.samsungsemi.com	San Jose	CA	95134	408-544-4000	544-4980
SanDisk Corp 140 Caspian Ct *NASDAQ: SNDK* ■ *Web:* www.sandisk.com	Sunnyvale	CA	94089	408-542-0500	542-0503
Sharp Microelectronics of the Americas 5700 NW Pacific Rim Blvd *Web:* www.sharpsma.com	Camas	WA	98607	360-834-2500	834-8903
Silicon Storage Technology Inc 1171 Sonora Ct *NASDAQ: SSTI* ■ *Web:* www.sst.com	Sunnyvale	CA	94086	408-735-9110	735-9036
SimpleTech Inc 3001 Daimler St *NASDAQ: STEC* ■ *TF:* 800-367-7330 ■ *Web:* www.simpletech.com	Santa Ana	CA	92705	949-476-1180	476-1209
Sony Electronics Inc 1 Sony Dr **Fax:* Hum Res ■ *TF Cust Svc:* 800-222-7669 ■ *Web:* www.sony.com	Park Ridge	NJ	07656	201-930-1000	358-4058*
Spansion Inc 915 DeGuigne Dr *NASDAQ: SPSN* ■ *TF:* 866-772-6746 ■ *Web:* www.spansion.com	Sunnyvale	CA	94088	408-962-2500	

292 FLEET LEASING & MANAGEMENT

	City	State	Zip	Phone	Fax
Automotive Resources International 9000 Midlantic Dr *Web:* www.arifleet.com	Mount Laurel	NJ	08054	856-778-1500	778-6200
Avis Budget Group Inc 6 Sylvan Way *NYSE: CAR* ■ *Web:* www.avisbudgetgroup.com	Parsippany	NJ	07054	973-496-3500	
Bank of America Leasing Corp 2059 Northlake Pkwy 4th Fl	Tucker	GA	30084	770-270-8400	270-8404
Donlen Corp 2315 Sanders Rd *TF:* 800-323-1483 ■ *Web:* www.donlen.com	Northbrook	IL	60062	847-714-1400	714-1500
Emkay Inc 805 W Thorndale Ave *TF:* 800-621-2001 ■ *Web:* www.emkaynet.com	Itasca	IL	60143	630-250-7400	250-7422
Enterprise Fleet Services 5105 Johnson Rd *TF:* 800-325-8007 ■ *Web:* www.enterprise.com/fleets	Coconut Creek	FL	33073	954-354-5400	
Executive Car Leasing Inc 7807 Santa Monica Blvd *TF:* 800-994-2277 ■ *Web:* www.executivecarleasing.com	Los Angeles	CA	90046	323-654-5000	848-9015
Ford Leasing Development Co 550 Town Center Dr Suite 200	Dearborn	MI	48126	313-322-4200	390-0779
Frank Consolidated Enterprises Inc 666 Garland Pl	Des Plaines	IL	60016	847-699-7000	699-0681
GE Capital Fleet Services 3 Capital Dr **Fax:* Hum Res ■ *TF:* 800-469-0044 ■ *Web:* www.gefleet.com/fleet/	Eden Prairie	MN	55344	952-828-1000	828-1040*
GE Equipment Services 120 Long Ridge Rd *Web:* www.geem.com	Stamford	CT	06927	203-357-4000	
Lease Plan USA 1165 Sanctuary Pkwy **Fax Area Code:* 678 ■ *TF:* 800-457-8721 ■ *Web:* www.leaseplan.com	Alpharetta	GA	30004	770-933-9090	202-8700*
Leasing Assoc Inc PO Box 243 *TF:* 800-449-4807 ■ *Web:* www.theleasingcompany.com	Houston	TX	77001	713-522-9771	528-1259
Lily Transportation Corp 145 Rosemary St *Web:* www.lily.com	Needham	MA	02494	781-449-8811	449-7128
Motorlease Corp 1506 New Britain Ave *TF:* 800-243-0182 ■ *Web:* www.motorleasecorp.com	Farmington	CT	06032	860-677-9711	674-8677
PHH Arval 940 Ridgebrook Rd *TF:* 800-665-9744 ■ *Web:* www.phh.com	Sparks	MD	21152	410-771-1900	771-3362
RUAN Transportation Management Systems 666 Grand Ave Suite 3100 *TF:* 800-678-3210 ■ *Web:* www.ruan.com	Des Moines	IA	50309	515-245-2500	
Transervice Lease Corp 5 Dakota Dr Suite 209 *TF:* 800-645-8018 ■ *Web:* www.transervice.com	Lake Success	NY	11042	516-488-3400	488-3574
Trinity Railcar Leasing & Management Services 2525 Stemmons Fwy	Dallas	TX	75207	214-631-4420	589-8271
Wheels Inc 666 Garland Pl **Fax:* Mail Rm ■ *Web:* www.wheels.com	Des Plaines	IL	60016	847-699-7000	699-4047*

FLOOR COVERINGS - MFR

SEE Carpets & Rugs p. 1408; Flooring - Resilient p. 1640; Tile - Ceramic (Wall & Floor) p. 2367

293 FLOOR COVERINGS STORES

	City	State	Zip	Phone	Fax
Augusta Flooring Inc 202 Bobby Jones Expy *Web:* www.gcocarpet.com	Augusta	GA	30907	706-650-0400	650-2167
Budget Floor Store 3636 W Reno	Oklahoma City	OK	73157	405-947-5575	942-5783
Carpet City Inc 2811 E 15th St	Tulsa	OK	74104	918-744-0088	744-0092
Carpet Exchange 1251 1st Ave S *Web:* www.greatfloors.com	Seattle	WA	98134	206-624-7800	622-8407
Carpet King Inc 1815 W River Rd *Web:* www.carpet-king.com	Minneapolis	MN	55411	612-287-1700	588-2401
Carpet Network Inc 109 Gaither Dr Suite 302 *TF:* 800-428-1067 ■ *Web:* www.carpetnetwork.com	Mount Laurel	NJ	08054	856-273-9393	273-0160
Carpet World Inc 2837 NW 36th St	Oklahoma City	OK	73112	405-947-5555	949-5559
Carpetile Plano Inc 8-10 W Main St	Plano	IL	60545	630-552-3400	552-3044
Century Tile Supply Co 747 E Roosevelt Rd *Web:* www.century-tile.com	Lombard	IL	60148	630-495-2300	495-8645
Clark-Dunbar Carpets 3232 Empire Dr *TF:* 800-256-1467	Alexandria	LA	71301	318-445-0262	473-9246
Clark & Mitchell Inc 7820 Bluffton Rd *TF:* 800-319-2366 ■ *Web:* www.clarkandmitchell.com	Fort Wayne	IN	46809	260-747-7431	747-3464
Coyle Carpet One Inc 250 W Beltline Hwy *TF:* 800-842-6953 ■ *Web:* www.coylecarpet.com	Madison	WI	53713	608-257-0291	258-7248
Dawn Co 101-A W Sumner St *Web:* www.carpetcave.com	Bakersfield	CA	93301	661-324-9893	
Dent & Ding Appliance Co 3423 N Main St *Web:* www.dentandding.com	Joplin	MO	64801	417-781-5516	781-5537
Drexel Interior Inc 19355 W Bluemound Rd *Web:* www.drexelinteriors.com	Brookfield	WI	53045	262-786-2250	786-9787
Ducks Carpet & Flooring 1133 Hwy 45 Bypass *TF:* 800-372-1000	Jackson	TN	38301	731-664-2871	668-2929
Einstein-Moomjy Inc 10 New Maple Ave *Web:* www.einsteinmoomjy.com	Pine Brook	NJ	07058	973-575-0895	575-4306
Everett Carpet Co 318 Ashman St	Midland	MI	48640	989-835-7191	835-7621
Finer Floor Covering Inc 1098 S 6th St *Web:* www.finerfloors.com	San Jose	CA	95112	408-297-0420	
Floor Coverings International 200 Technology Ct Suite 1200 *TF Sales:* 800-955-4324 ■ *Web:* floorcoveringsinternational.com	Smyrna	GA	30082	770-874-7600	874-7605
Floorcraft 7842 159th Pl NE *Web:* www.floorcraft.org	Redmond	WA	98052	425-885-4161	881-5617
Flooring Sales Group DBA Carpet Exchange 1251 1st Ave S *Web:* www.greatfloors.com	Seattle	WA	98134	206-624-7800	622-8407
Harry L Murphy Inc 42 Bonaventura Dr *TF:* 800-439-6777	San Jose	CA	95134	408-955-1100	955-1111
Lumber Liquidators Inc 1455 VFW Pkwy *TF:* 877-645-5347 ■ *Web:* www.lumberliquidators.com	West Roxbury	MA	02132	617-327-1222	327-2039
Miller's Carpet One 15615 Hwy 99 *Web:* carpetone.com	Lynnwood	WA	98037	425-743-3213	742-4141
MMM Carpets Unlimited Inc 3100 Molinaro St *TF:* 800-355-4666 ■ *Web:* www.mmmcarpets.com	Santa Clara	CA	95054	408-988-4661	988-5181
Nationwide Floorcover & Window Coverings 111 E Kilbourn Ave Suite 2400 *TF:* 800-366-8088 ■ *Web:* www.floorsandwindows.com	Milwaukee	WI	53202	414-765-9900	765-1300
O'Krent Floor Covering Co 2075 N Loop 1604 E *TF:* 800-369-7387 ■ *Web:* www.okrentfloors.com	San Antonio	TX	78232	210-227-7387	227-7390
Pace Stone Inc 663 Washington St *TF:* 800-789-0236 ■ *Web:* www.pacestone.com	Eden	NC	27288	336-623-2158	623-3347
Saint Paul Linoleum & Carpet Co 2956 Center Ct *Web:* www.stpaullinocpt.com	Eagan	MN	55121	651-686-7770	686-6660
Super Tiles 3290 NW 79th Ave	Miami	FL	33122	305-593-6000	593-0249

294 FLOORING - RESILIENT

SEE ALSO Recycled Plastics Products p. 2208

	City	State	Zip	Phone	Fax
American Biltrite Inc 57 River St *AMEX: ABL* ■ *Web:* ambilt.com	Wellesley Hills	MA	02481	781-237-6655	237-6880
American Floor Products Co Inc 7977 Cessna Ave *TF:* 800-342-0424 ■ *Web:* www.afco-usa.com	Gaithersburg	MD	20879	301-987-0490	987-0422
Amtico International Inc 6480 Roswell Rd *TF:* 800-268-4260 ■ *Web:* www.amtico.com	Atlanta	GA	30328	404-267-1900	267-1901
Armstrong World Industries Inc 2500 Columbia Ave **Fax:* Hum Res ■ *TF Cust Svc:* 800-233-3823 ■ *Web:* www.armstrong.com/armstrong_home.jsp	Lancaster	PA	17603	717-397-0611	396-6133*
Columbia Forest Products Inc 222 SW Columbia St Suite 1575 *TF:* 800-547-4261 ■ *Web:* www.columbiaforestproducts.com	Portland	OR	97201	503-224-5300	224-5294
Congoleum Corp 3500 Quakerridge Rd PO Box 3127 *AMEX: CGM* ■ *TF:* 800-274-3266 ■ *Web:* congoleum.com	Mercerville	NJ	08619	609-584-3000	584-3305
Dodge-Regupol Inc 715 Fountain Ave *TF:* 800-322-1923 ■ *Web:* www.regupol.com	Lancaster	PA	17601	717-295-3400	295-3414
DuPont Flooring Systems 3445 Millennium Ct *TF:* 800-572-7823	Columbus	OH	43219	614-476-1043	473-8543
Expanko Cork Co Inc 3135 Lower Valley Rd *TF Cust Svc:* 800-345-6202 ■ *Web:* www.expanko.com	Parkesburg	PA	19365	610-593-3000	593-3027
Forbo Industries Inc PO Box 667 **Fax:* Cust Svc ■ *TF Cust Svc:* 800-842-7839 ■ *Web:* www.forbo-industries.com	Hazleton	PA	18201	570-459-0771	450-0258*
Formica Corp 10155 Reading Rd *TF:* 800-367-6422 ■ *Web:* www.formica.com	Cincinnati	OH	45241	513-786-3400	
Hambro Forest Products Inc 445 Elk Valley Rd PO Box 129 *TF:* 800-442-6276 ■ *Web:* www.hambro.biz	Crescent City	CA	95531	707-464-6131	464-9375
Mannington Commercial 345 Marine Dr PO Box 12281 *TF:* 800-241-2262 ■ *Web:* www.mannington.com	Calhoun	GA	30703	706-629-7301	629-2365
Mannington Mills Inc 75 Mannington Mills Rd *TF Cust Svc:* 800-356-6787 ■ *Web:* www.mannington.com	Salem	NJ	08079	856-935-3000	339-6099
Natco Products Corp 155 Brookside Ave	West Warwick	RI	02893	401-828-0300	823-7670
Pergo Inc 3128 Highwoods Blvd Suite 100 *TF:* 800-222-1827 ■ *Web:* www.pergo.com	Raleigh	NC	27604	919-773-6000	773-6004
RCA Rubber Co 1833 E Market St *TF:* 800-321-2340 ■ *Web:* www.rcarubber.com	Akron	OH	44305	330-784-1291	784-2899
Roppe Corp 1602 N Union St *TF:* 800-537-9527 ■ *Web:* www.roppe.com	Fostoria	OH	44830	419-435-8546	435-1056
SRI Sports Inc 809 Kenner St *TF:* 800-723-8873 ■ *Web:* www.srisports.com	Dalton	GA	30721	706-272-4200	278-4898
Stonhard Inc 1 Park Ave *TF Cust Svc:* 800-854-0310 ■ *Web:* www.stonhard.com	Maple Shade	NJ	08052	856-779-7500	321-7510
Superior Mfg Group 7171 W 65th St *TF:* 800-621-2802 ■ *Web:* www.notrax.com	Chicago	IL	60638	708-458-4600	458-4723
Tarkett Inc 1139 Lehigh Ave *TF:* 800-367-8275 ■ *Web:* www.tarkettna.com	Whitehall	PA	18052	610-266-5500	266-5609
Tarkett Inc 1001 Yamaska St E *TF:* 800-363-9276 ■ *Web:* www.tarkettna.com	Farnham	QC	J2N1J7	450-293-3173	293-6644
Wilsonart International Inc 2400 Wilson Pl *TF Cust Svc:* 800-433-3222 ■ *Web:* www.wilsonart.com	Temple	TX	76504	254-207-7000	207-2384

295 FLORISTS

SEE ALSO Flowers-by-Wire Services p. 1641; Garden Centers p. 1687

	City	State	Zip	Phone	Fax
1-800-Flowers.com Inc 1 Old Country Rd *NASDAQ: FLWS* ■ *TF:* 800-356-9377 ■ *Web:* ww2.1800flowers.com	Carle Place	NY	11514	516-237-6000	237-6124
Alan Preuss Florists 17680-E W Bluemound Rd *TF:* 800-839-8400 ■ *Web:* www.alanpreussflorists.com	Brookfield	WI	53045	262-786-7900	796-8944
Amlings Flowerland 7101 S Adams St *TF:* 888-265-4647 ■ *Web:* www.amlings.com	Willowbrook	IL	60527	630-850-5070	654-0512
Anthony's Florist & Gifts Inc 701 E Hallandale Beach Blvd *TF:* 800-989-8765 ■ *Web:* www.anthonysflorist.com	Hallandale	FL	33009	954-457-8520	457-8669
Arrow Florist & Park Avenue Greenhouses Inc 757 Park Ave *TF:* 800-556-7097	Cranston	RI	02910	401-785-1900	785-4120
Bachman's Inc 6010 Lyndale Ave S *TF:* 888-222-4626 ■ *Web:* www.florists.ftd.com/bachmans	Minneapolis	MN	55419	612-861-7600	861-7730
Boesen the Florist 3422 Beaver Ave *TF:* 800-274-4761 ■ *Web:* www.boesen.com	Des Moines	IA	50310	515-274-4761	274-6369
Cactus Flower Florists 7077 E Bell Rd Suite 100 **Fax:* Sales ■ *TF:* 800-922-2887 ■ *Web:* www.cactusflower.com	Scottsdale	AZ	85254	480-483-9200	483-9200*
Calyx & Corolla Inc DBA Calyx Flowers 3975 Zoth St Suite 6 **Fax Area Code:* 772 ■ *TF:* 888-882-2599 ■ *Web:* www.calyxandcorolla.com	Vero Beach	FL	32960	800-882-2599	299-1208*

				Phone	Fax
Carter's & La Rue's Flower Shop 2600 N MacArthur Blvd *TF:* 800-874-1462 ■ *Web:* www.cartersflowers.com	Oklahoma City	OK	73127	405-943-3314	948-1079
Connell's Flowers 2408 E Main St *TF:* 800-790-8980 ■ *Web:* www.connellsflowers.com	Bexley	OH	43209	614-237-8653	235-8239
Conroy's Inc 2550 N Hollywood Way Suite 206 *TF:* 800-266-7697 ■ *Web:* 1-800conroys.com	Burbank	CA	91505	818-843-8280	843-6362
Country Lane Flower Shops Inc 729 S Michigan Ave **Fax:* Sales ■ *TF:* 800-764-7673 ■ *Web:* www.countrylaneflowers.com	Howell	MI	48843	517-546-1111	546-5168*
DeLoache Flowers 2927 Millwood Ave *TF:* 800-922-2707	Columbia	SC	29205	803-256-1681	256-5002
Don Wan Florist Ltd 5644 W 63rd St *TF:* 800-336-6926 ■ *Web:* www.chicagoflowers-florist.com	Chicago	IL	60638	773-585-2225	585-9572
Dr Delphinium Designs & Events 5806 W Lovers Lane & Tollway *TF:* 800-783-8790 ■ *Web:* www.drdelphinium.com	Dallas	TX	75225	214-522-9911	525-1240
Eastern Floral & Gift Shop 2836 Broadmoor Ave SE *TF:* 800-494-2202 ■ *Web:* www.easternfloral.com	Grand Rapids	MI	49512	616-949-2200	949-9009
Felly's Flowers Inc PO Box 6620 *TF:* 800-993-7673 ■ *Web:* www.fellys.net	Madison	WI	53716	608-223-3285	
Field of Flowers Inc 5101 S University Dr *TF:* 800-963-7374 ■ *Web:* www.fieldofflowers.com	Davie	FL	33328	954-680-2406	680-2116
Florist 800 Network 973 Vale Terrace Blvd Suite 102 **Fax Area Code:* 800 ■ *TF:* 800-688-1299 ■ *Web:* www.800send.com	Vista	CA	92084	760-732-1260	947-8552*
Flower Patch Inc 4645 S Riverside Dr *TF:* 888-865-6858 ■ *Web:* www.flowerpatch.com	Murray	UT	84123	801-268-6566	266-6746
Flower Pot Florists 2314 N Broadway St *TF:* 800-824-7792 ■ *Web:* www.knoxvilleflowerpot.com	Knoxville	TN	37917	865-523-5121	524-8654
Flower World 1530 S Delaware St *TF:* 800-257-7880 ■ *Web:* www.floworld.com	Paulsboro	NJ	08066	856-429-5800	661-8049
FlowerClub PO Box 60910 *TF:* 800-800-7363 ■ *Web:* www.flowerclub.com	Los Angeles	CA	90060	405-440-6001	
Flowers from Holland Ltd 835A Franklin Ct **Fax Area Code:* 678 ■ **Fax:* Sales ■ *TF:* 800-647-8182 ■ *Web:* www.flowersfromholland.com	Marietta	GA	30067	800-647-8182	385-7128*
Foster City Flowers & Gifts 1185 Chess Dr Suite G *TF:* 800-970-7673 ■ *Web:* www.fostercity-flowers.com	Foster City	CA	94404	650-573-6607	573-5968
FTD Inc 3113 Woodcreek Dr *TF:* 800-736-3383 ■ *Web:* www.ftd.com	Downers Grove	IL	60515	630-719-7800	724-6019
Grower Direct Fresh Cut Flowers Inc 4220 98th St Suite 118 *Web:* www.growerdirect.com	Edmonton	AB	T6E6A1	780-436-7774	436-3336
Higdon Florist 201 E 32nd St *TF:* 800-641-4726 ■ *Web:* www.higdonflorist.com	Joplin	MO	64804	417-624-7171	624-7244
Howard Brothers Florists 7101 Southwestern Ave *TF:* 800-648-0524 ■ *Web:* www.howardbrothersflorist.com	Oklahoma City	OK	73139	405-632-4747	632-1672
John Wolf Florist 6228 Waters Ave *TF:* 800-944-6435 ■ *Web:* www.ftdfloristsonline.com/johnwolfflorist	Savannah	GA	31406	912-352-9843	353-8843
Johnston the Florist Inc 14179 Lincoln Way *TF:* 800-232-4795 ■ *Web:* www.johnstontheflorist.com	North Huntingdon	PA	15642	412-751-2821	751-2961
Joyce Florist 2729 S Hampton Rd *TF:* 800-527-1520 ■ *Web:* www.joyceflorist.com	Dallas	TX	75224	214-942-1776	331-6272
Ken's Flower Shop 140 W South Boundary St *TF:* 800-253-0100 ■ *Web:* www.florists.ftd.com/kensflowershops	Perrysburg	OH	43551	419-874-1333	874-3441
Kuhn Flowers Inc 3802 Beach Blvd *TF:* 800-458-5846 ■ *Web:* www.florists.ftd.com/kuhn	Jacksonville	FL	32207	904-398-8601	348-7379
Lehrer's Flowers Inc 3191 W 38th Ave *TF:* 800-537-1308 ■ *Web:* www.thinkflowers.com	Denver	CO	80211	303-455-1234	433-0028
Lester's Florist Inc 2100 Bull St *TF:* 800-841-1103 ■ *Web:* www.lestersflorist.com	Savannah	GA	31401	912-233-6066	233-3654
Locker's Florist 1640 S 83rd St *TF:* 877-276-7673 ■ *Web:* www.lockersflorist.com	West Allis	WI	53214	414-276-7673	
Maple Lee Flowers Inc 615 High St *TF:* 800-414-0000	Worthington	OH	43085	614-885-5350	885-4194
Martina's Flowers & Gifts 3830 Washington Rd West Town Market Sq *TF:* 800-927-1204 ■ *Web:* www.martinas.com	Martinez	GA	30907	706-863-7172	860-7590
Metropolitan Plant & Flower Exchange 2125 Fletcher Ave *TF:* 800-942-1050 ■ *Web:* www.florists.ftd.com/metro	Fort Lee	NJ	07024	201-944-1050	944-7970
Nanz & Kraft Florists Inc 141 Breckenridge Ln *TF:* 800-897-6551 ■ *Web:* www.nanzandkraft.com	Louisville	KY	40207	502-897-6551	897-2082
National Floral Supply Inc PO Box 190 *Web:* www.flowersonbase.com	Bryantown	MD	20617	301-932-7600	932-7906
Norton's Flowers & Gifts 2900 Washtenaw Ave **Fax:* Sales ■ *TF Sales:* 800-682-8667 ■ *Web:* www.nortonsflowers.com	Ypsilanti	MI	48197	734-434-2700	434-1140*
Phillip's Flower Shops Inc 524 N Cass Ave *TF:* 800-350-7257 ■ *Web:* www.800florals.com	Westmont	IL	60559	630-719-5200	719-2292
Phoenix Flower Shops 5733 E Thomas Rd Suite 4 **Fax Area Code:* 480 ■ *TF:* 800-995-7673 ■ *Web:* www.phoenixflowershops.com	Scottsdale	AZ	85251	602-840-1200	970-0344*
Preuss Alan Florists 17680-E W Bluemound Rd *TF:* 800-839-8400 ■ *Web:* www.alanpreussflorists.com	Brookfield	WI	53045	262-786-7900	796-8944
Proflowers.com 5005 Wateridge Vista Dr 2nd Fl *TF:* 800-776-3569 ■ *Web:* www.proflowers.com	San Diego	CA	92121	858-454-9850	638-4725
Provide Commerce Inc 5005 Wateridge Vista Dr *TF Cust Svc:* 800-776-3569 ■ *Web:* www.prvd.com	San Diego	CA	92121	858-638-4900	638-4724
Royer's Flower Shops 810 S 12th St *TF:* 888-276-9377 ■ *Web:* www.royers.com	Lebanon	PA	17042	717-273-2683	306-5353
Russell Florist Inc 5001 Gravois Ave *TF:* 800-351-9003 ■ *Web:* www.florists.ftd.com/russellfloriststlouis	Saint Louis	MO	63116	314-351-4676	351-6842
Schroeder's Flowerland Inc 1530 S Webster Ave *TF:* 800-236-4769 ■ *Web:* www.florists.ftd.com/schroeder	Green Bay	WI	54301	920-436-6363	433-9685
Stephenson's Flower Shops 810 S 12th St *TF:* 800-735-6937 ■ *Web:* www.florists.ftd.com/stephensons	Lebanon	PA	17042	717-761-5990	975-0481
Strange's Florist Inc 3313 Mechanicsville Pike *TF:* 800-421-4070 ■ *Web:* www.netfloral.com	Richmond	VA	23223	804-321-2200	329-5576
Thrifty Flowers Inc 24001 Telegraph Rd *Web:* www.thriftyflorist.net	Southfield	MI	48034	248-386-8900	386-4195
Veldkamp's Flowers 9501 W Colfax Ave *TF:* 800-247-3730 ■ *Web:* www.veldkamps.com	Lakewood	CO	80215	303-232-2673	234-5686
Villere's Florist 1107 Veterans Blvd *TF:* 800-845-5373 ■ *Web:* www.florists.ftd.com/villeresflorist	Metairie	LA	70005	504-833-3716	830-4513
Winston Brothers Inc 160 Southampton St *TF:* 800-457-4901 ■ *Web:* www.winstonflowers.com	Boston	MA	02118	617-541-1100	541-1126
Wolf John Florist 6228 Waters Ave *TF:* 800-944-6435 ■ *Web:* www.ftdfloristsonline.com/johnwolfflorist	Savannah	GA	31406	912-352-9843	353-8843

296 FLOWERS & NURSERY STOCK - WHOL

SEE ALSO Horticultural Products Growers p. 1789

				Phone	Fax
Agriflora Corp 9475 NW 13th St *TF:* 800-851-2098 ■ *Web:* www.agriflora.com	Miami	FL	33172	305-477-0291	593-7042
Ardinger HT & Son Co 1990 Lake Point Dr **Fax:* Acctg ■ *TF:* 800-683-0498	Lewisville	TX	75057	214-631-9830	819-1523*
Atwoods Distributing Inc 500 S Garland Rd *Web:* www.atwoods.com	Enid	OK	73703	580-233-3702	234-4332
Ball Horticultural Co 622 Town Rd *TF:* 800-879-2255 ■ *Web:* www.ballhort.com	West Chicago	IL	60185	630-231-3600	231-3605
Bill Doran Co Inc 619 W Jefferson St *TF:* 800-822-8815 ■ *Web:* www.billdoran.com	Rockford	IL	61103	815-965-6042	968-3223
Carlstedt Oscar G Co 577 College St *TF:* 800-654-5739	Jacksonville	FL	32204	904-354-8474	354-2829
Celebrity Inc 4520 Old Troup Hwy Suite C **Fax Area Code:* 800 ■ *TF:* 800-527-8446 ■ *Web:* www.celebrity-inc.com	Tyler	TX	75707	903-561-3981	850-4329*
Central Garden & Pet Co 1340 Treat Blvd Suite 600 *NASDAQ: CENT* ■ *Web:* www.centralgardenandpet.com	Walnut Creek	CA	94597	925-948-4000	287-0601
Claymore C Sieck Wholesale Florist 311 E Chase St *TF:* 800-624-7134 ■ *Web:* www.sieck.com	Baltimore	MD	21202	410-685-4660	685-1547
Cleveland Plant & Flower Co 12920 Corporate Dr *TF:* 800-688-8012 ■ *Web:* www.cpfco.com	Parma	OH	44130	216-898-3500	898-1075
Cut Flower Wholesale Inc 2122 Faulkner Rd *TF:* 888-997-8367 ■ *Web:* www.cutflower.com	Atlanta	GA	30324	404-320-1619	634-7922
Delaware Valley Wholesale Florist 520 Mantua Blvd N *TF:* 800-676-1212 ■ *Web:* www.dvwf.com	Sewell	NJ	08080	856-468-7000	464-2750
Denver Wholesale Florists Co 4800 Dahlia St *Web:* www.dwfwholesale.com	Denver	CO	80216	303-399-0970	376-3123
Distinctive Designs International Inc 120 Sibley Dr *TF:* 800-243-4787 ■ *Web:* www.distinctivedesigns.com	Russellville	AL	35654	256-332-7390	332-7890
Esprit Miami 3043 NW 107th Ave *TF:* 800-327-2320 ■ *Web:* www.espritmiami.com	Miami	FL	33172	305-591-2244	591-2603
Florist Distributing Inc 2403 Bell Ave *TF:* 800-373-3741 ■ *Web:* www.fdionline.net	Des Moines	IA	50321	515-243-5228	282-9241
Glacier Mountain Floral Suppliers 115 E Pacific Ave *Web:* www.glaciermtn.net	Spokane	WA	99202	509-624-0121	747-8509
Greenleaf Wholesale Florists Inc 13239 Weld County Rd 4 *TF:* 800-659-8000 ■ *Web:* www.greenleafwholesale.com	Brighton	CO	80601	303-659-8000	659-4022
Hill Floral Products Inc 2117 Peacock Rd *TF:* 800-526-4733	Richmond	IN	47374	765-973-6660	962-2920
Houff Roy Co 6200 S Oak Park Ave *TF:* 800-366-1769 ■ *Web:* www.royhouff.com	Chicago	IL	60638	773-586-8118	586-8785
HT Ardinger & Son Co 1990 Lake Point Dr **Fax:* Acctg ■ *TF:* 800-683-0498	Lewisville	TX	75057	214-631-9830	819-1523*
John Deere Landscapes 5610 McGinnis Ferry Rd *Web:* www.johndeerelandscapes.com	Alpharetta	GA	30005	770-442-8881	442-3214
Karthauser & Sons Inc W 147 N 11100 Fond du Lac Ave *TF:* 800-338-8620 ■ *Web:* www.karthauser.net	Germantown	WI	53022	262-255-7815	255-6920
L & L Nursery Supply Co Inc 5350 G St *TF:* 800-624-2517 ■ *Web:* www.llnurserysupply.com	Chino	CA	91710	909-591-0461	591-3280
Lee Wholesale Floral Inc 917 N 8th St *TF:* 800-677-2626	Abilene	TX	79601	325-673-7381	673-7398
Manatee Cortez Floral Co 1320 33rd St W *TF:* 800-752-9845 ■ *Web:* www.manateefloral.com	Palmetto	FL	34221	941-722-3279	729-5151
Norben Import Corp 99 S Newman St *TF:* 800-526-4652 ■ *Web:* www.norben.com	Hackensack	NJ	07601	201-487-0855	487-0787
Oscar G Carlstedt Co 577 College St *TF:* 800-654-5739	Jacksonville	FL	32204	904-354-8474	354-2829
Pennock Co 3601 Island Ave *TF:* 888-736-6625 ■ *Web:* www.pennock.com	Philadelphia	PA	19153	215-844-6600	492-7901
Pittsburgh Cut Flower Co 1901 Liberty Ave *TF:* 800-837-2837 ■ *Web:* www.pittsburghcutflower.com	Pittsburgh	PA	15222	412-355-7000	391-0649
Platz Flowers & Supply Inc 8501 Frontage Rd *TF:* 888-752-8048 ■ *Web:* www.platzwholesale.com	Morton Grove	IL	60053	847-966-3100	556-6471
Reliance Trading Corp of America 2222 W 138th St **Fax Area Code:* 800 ■ *TF:* 800-782-7673	Blue Island	IL	60406	708-597-2300	579-8174*
Rexius Forest By-Products Inc 1275 Bailey Hill Rd *TF:* 800-473-9487 ■ *Web:* www.rexius.com	Eugene	OR	97402	541-342-1835	343-4802
Roman J Claprood Co 242 N Grant Ave *TF:* 800-966-7695	Columbus	OH	43215	614-221-5515	
Roy Houff Co 6200 S Oak Park Ave *TF:* 800-366-1769 ■ *Web:* www.royhouff.com	Chicago	IL	60638	773-586-8118	586-8785
Shemin Nurseries 1081 King St *Web:* www.sheminnurseries.com	Greenwich	CT	06831	203-531-6700	531-7393
Southern Importers Inc 3859 Battleground Ave Suite 300 *TF Cust Svc:* 800-334-9658 ■ *Web:* www.southernimporters.com	Greensboro	NC	27410	336-292-4521	852-6397
Spokane Flower Growers Inc DBA Glacier Mountain Floral Suppliers 115 E Pacific Ave *Web:* www.glaciermtn.net	Spokane	WA	99202	509-624-0121	747-8509
Tapscott's 1403 E 18th St *TF:* 800-626-1922 ■ *Web:* www.tapfloral.com	Owensboro	KY	42303	270-684-2308	683-3702
Tennessee Florist Supply Inc 2713 John Deere Dr *TF:* 800-951-7451	Knoxville	TN	37917	865-524-7451	637-8155
Teters Floral Products Inc 1425 S Lillian Ave *TF:* 800-999-5996 ■ *Web:* www.teters.com	Bolivar	MO	65613	417-326-7654	326-8061
Teufel Nursery Inc 12345 NW Barnes Rd *TF:* 800-483-8335 ■ *Web:* www.teufel.com	Portland	OR	97229	503-646-1111	646-1112
Van Bloem Gardens 8079 Van Zyverden Rd PO Box 500 **Fax Area Code:* 646 ■ *TF:* 800-332-2852 ■ *Web:* www.vanbloem.com	Meridian	MS	39302	601-679-1050	839-2605*
Van Well Nursery 2821 Grant Rd *TF:* 800-572-1553 ■ *Web:* www.vanwell.net	East Wenatchee	WA	98802	509-886-8189	886-0294
Van Zyverden Inc 8079 Van Zyverden Rd *TF:* 800-332-2852 ■ *Web:* www.vanzyverdenusa.com	Meridian	MS	39305	601-679-8274	679-8039
Western Organics Inc 420 E Southern Ave *TF:* 800-352-3245 ■ *Web:* www.westernorganics.com	Tempe	AZ	85202	602-269-5756	269-7621
Worthington Farms Inc 3661 Ballards Crossroads Rd *Web:* www.worthingtonfarms.com	Greenville	NC	27834	252-756-3827	756-9442
Zieger & Sons Inc 6215 Ardleigh St *TF:* 800-752-2003 ■ *Web:* www.zieger.com	Philadelphia	PA	19138	215-438-7060	438-8729

297 FLOWERS-BY-WIRE SERVICES

				Phone	Fax
FTD Group Inc 3113 Woodcreek Dr *NYSE: FTD* ■ *TF:* 800-788-9000 ■ *Web:* www.ftd.com	Downers Grove	IL	60515	630-719-7800	719-6183
FTD Inc 3113 Woodcreek Dr *TF:* 800-736-3383 ■ *Web:* www.ftd.com	Downers Grove	IL	60515	630-719-7800	724-6019
Teleflora Inc 11444 W Olympic Blvd 4th Fl **Fax:* Hum Res ■ *TF:* 800-321-2654 ■ *Web:* www.teleflora.com	Los Angeles	CA	90064	310-231-9199	966-3612*

298 FOIL & LEAF - METAL

				Phone	Fax
Chemetal 39 O'Neil St *TF:* 800-807-7341 ■ *Web:* www.chmetal.com	Easthampton	MA	01027	413-529-0718	529-9898

				Phone	Fax
Crown Roll Leaf Inc 91 Illinois Ave *TF:* 800-631-3831 ■ *Web:* www.crownrollleaf.com	Paterson	NJ	07503	973-742-4000	742-0219
DEXMET Corp 14 Commercial St *Web:* www.dexmet.com	Branford	CT	06405	203-481-4277	488-6902
Gould Electronics Inc 2929 W Chandler Blvd *Web:* www.gould.com	Chandler	AZ	85224	480-899-0343	963-2119
M Swift & Sons Inc 10 Love Ln *TF:* 800-628-0380 ■ *Web:* www.mswiftandsons.com	Hartford	CT	06112	860-522-1181	249-5934
Oak-Mitsui Inc 80 1st St *Web:* www.oakmitsui.com	Hoosick Falls	NY	12090	518-686-4961	686-8080
October Co Inc PO Box 71 *TF:* 800-628-9346	Easthampton	MA	01027	413-527-9380	527-0091
Swift M & Sons Inc 10 Love Ln *TF:* 800-628-0380 ■ *Web:* www.mswiftandsons.com	Hartford	CT	06112	860-522-1181	249-5934

299 FOOD PRODUCTS - MFR

SEE ALSO Agricultural Products p. 1262; Bakeries p. 1367; Beverages - Mfr p. 1376; Ice - Manufactured p. 1851; Livestock & Poultry Feeds - Prepared p. 1917; Meat Packing Plants p. 1952; Pet Products p. 2106; Poultry Processing p. 2132; Salt p. 2303

299-1 Bakery Products - Fresh

				Phone	Fax
Alessi Bakeries Inc 2909 W Cypress St *Web:* www.alessibakeries.com	Tampa	FL	33609	813-879-4544	872-9103
Alfred Nickles Bakery Inc 26 N Main St *TF:* 800-635-1110 ■ *Web:* www.nicklesbakery.com	Navarre	OH	44662	330-879-5635	879-5896
Alpha Baking Co Inc 4545 W Lyndale Ave *Web:* www.alphabaking.com	Chicago	IL	60639	773-489-5400	489-2711
Amoroso's Baking Co 845 S 55th St *TF:* 800-377-6557 ■ *Web:* www.amorosobaking.com/	Philadelphia	PA	19143	215-471-4740	472-5299
Arnie's Inc 722 Leonard St NW *TF:* 800-343-4361	Grand Rapids	MI	49504	616-458-1107	458-3085
Bama Pie Ltd 2745 E 11th St *TF:* 800-756-2262	Tulsa	OK	74104	918-592-0778	732-2811
Bays Corp PO Box 1455 *Web:* www.bays.com	Chicago	IL	60690	312-346-5757	226-3435
Better Baked Foods Inc 56 Smedley St *Web:* www.betterbaked.com	North East	PA	16428	814-725-8778	725-8785
Bimbo Bakeries USA 7301 South Fwy *Web:* www.bimbobakeriesusa.com	Fort Worth	TX	76134	817-293-6230	615-3091
Brownie Products Co 423 Industry Ave	Gardner	IL	60424	815-237-2163	237-2644
Brown's Bakery Inc 505 Downs St	Defiance	OH	43512	419-784-3330	784-5346
Butter Krust Baking Co Inc 249 N 11th St *TF:* 800-332-8521 ■ *Web:* www.holsum.com	Sunbury	PA	17801	570-286-5845	286-0780
Byrnes & Kiefer Co 131 Kline Ave *TF:* 877-444-2240 ■ *Web:* www.bkcompany.com	Callery	PA	16024	724-538-5200	538-9292
Carolina Foods Inc 1807 S Tryon St *TF:* 800-234-0441	Charlotte	NC	28203	704-333-9812	940-0040
Cassones Bakery Inc 202 S Regent St	Port Chester	NY	10573	914-939-1568	939-3811
Chattanooga Bakery Inc 900 Manufacture Rd *TF:* 800-251-3404 ■ *Web:* www.moonpie.com	Chattanooga	TN	37401	423-267-3351	266-2169
Cloverhill Bakery Inc 2035 N Narragansett Ave *TF:* 800-745-9822 ■ *Web:* www.cloverhill.com	Chicago	IL	60639	773-745-9800	745-1647
Colchester Bakery 96 Lebanon Ave *Web:* www.colchesterbakery.com	Colchester	CT	06415	860-537-2415	
Colombo Baking Co 580 Julie Ann Way *TF:* 888-661-7687 ■ *Web:* www.sourdoughbread.com	Oakland	CA	94621	510-729-6232	
Country Hearth Breads 3355 W Memorial Blvd *TF:* 800-283-8093	Lakeland	FL	33815	863-682-1155	686-9252
Country Oven Bakery Inc 2840 Pioneer Dr	Bowling Green	KY	42101	270-782-3200	782-7170
Dakota Brands International 2121 13th St NE *TF:* 800-844-5073 ■ *Web:* www.dakotabrands.com	Jamestown	ND	58401	701-252-5073	251-1047
Derst Baking Co 1311 W 52nd St *TF:* 800-778-8486 ■ *Web:* www.derst.com	Savannah	GA	31405	912-233-2235	234-3611
Dinkel's Bakery 3329 N Lincoln Ave *TF:* 800-822-8817 ■ *Web:* www.dinkels.com	Chicago	IL	60657	773-281-7300	281-6169
Dolly Madison Cakes 12 E Armour Blvd	Kansas City	MO	64111	816-502-4000	502-4126
Drake Bakeries Inc 75 Demarest Dr	Wayne	NJ	07470	973-696-5010	696-2485
Ellison Bakery 4108 W Ferguson Rd *Web:* www.ebakery.com	Fort Wayne	IN	46809	260-747-6136	747-1954
Fantini Baking Co Inc 375 Washington St *TF:* 800-223-9037	Haverhill	MA	01832	978-373-1273	373-6250
Federal Bakers USA 5015 Lee Hwy Suite 101	Arlington	VA	22207	703-469-1500	312-6051
Flowers Foods Inc 1919 Flowers Cir *NYSE: FLO* ■ **Fax: Mktg* ■ *Web:* www.flowersfoods.com	Thomasville	GA	31757	229-226-9110	226-1318*
Franklin Baking Co 500 W Grantham St	Goldsboro	NC	27530	919-735-0344	735-6629
Franz Bakery 340 NE 11th Ave *TF:* 800-935-5679 ■ *Web:* www.usbakery.com	Portland	OR	97232	503-232-2191	234-7036
Franz Family Bakeries Gai's Div 2006 S Weller St *Web:* www.franzbakery.com	Seattle	WA	98144	206-322-0931	726-7555
Franz Family Bakeries William's Div 2000 Nugget Way **Fax Area Code: 503*	Eugene	OR	97403	541-485-8211	546-7140*
Fresh Start Bakeries 145 S State College Blvd Suite 200 *Web:* www.freshstartbakeries.com	Brea	CA	92821	714-256-8900	256-8916
Gai's Div Franz Family Bakeries 2006 S Weller St *Web:* www.franzbakery.com	Seattle	WA	98144	206-322-0931	726-7555
George Weston Bakeries Inc 55 Paradise Ln **Fax: Sales* ■ *TF:* 800-842-9595 ■ *Web:* www.gwbakeries.com	Bay Shore	NY	11706	631-273-6000	951-5582*
H & S Bakery Inc 601 S Caroline St *TF:* 800-959-7655 ■ *Web:* www.hsbakery.com	Baltimore	MD	21231	410-276-7254	558-3096
Heinemann's Bakeries Inc 6355 Belmont Ave Suite 140 *Web:* www.heinemanns.com	Belmont	MI	49306	616-885-9094	885-9031
Heiners Bakery Inc 1300 Adams Ave *TF:* 800-776-8411	Huntington	WV	25704	304-523-8411	525-9268
Hostess Cake Bakery 12 E Armour Blvd	Kansas City	MO	64111	816-502-4000	502-4126
Jenny Lee Bakery Inc 620 Island Ave *Web:* www.jennyleebakery.com	McKees Rocks	PA	15136	412-331-8900	331-8903
Klosterman Baking Co Inc 4760 Paddock Rd *TF:* 877-301-1004 ■ *Web:* www.klostermanbakery.com	Cincinnati	OH	45229	513-242-1004	242-8257
Leidenheimer Baking Co 1501 Simon Bolivar Ave *TF:* 800-259-9099 ■ *Web:* www.leidenheimer.com	New Orleans	LA	70113	504-525-1575	525-1596
Lepage Bakeries Inc 1 Country Kitchen Plaza PO Box 1900 *Web:* www.lepagebakeries.com	Auburn	ME	04211	207-783-9161	783-3300
Lewis Bakeries Inc 500 N Fulton Ave *TF:* 800-365-2812	Evansville	IN	47710	812-425-4642	425-7609
Little Dutch Boy Bakery Inc 12349 S 970 East *TF:* 800-382-2594	Draper	UT	84020	801-571-3800	571-3802
Mama Kayer's Baltimore Bakery Inc 1140 Kingwood Ave *TF:* 800-627-7850	Norfolk	VA	23502	757-855-4731	
Martin's Famous Pastry Shoppe Inc 1000 Potato Roll Ln *TF Cust Svc:* 800-548-1200 ■ *Web:* www.mfps.com	Chambersburg	PA	17201	717-263-9580	263-4452
Mary Ann's Baking Co 8371 Carbide Ct	Sacramento	CA	95828	916-681-7444	681-7470
Mary of Puddin Hill Inc 201 E I-30 *TF Orders:* 800-545-8889 ■ *Web:* www.puddinhill.com	Greenville	TX	75403	903-455-2651	455-4522
Maurice Lenell Cooky Co 4474 N Harlem Ave *TF:* 800-323-1760	Norridge	IL	60706	708-456-6500	456-6552
McKee Foods Corp PO Box 750 **Fax: Hum Res* ■ *TF Cust Svc:* 800-522-4499 ■ *Web:* www.mckeefoods.com	Collegedale	TN	37315	423-238-7111	238-7174*
Merita Bakeries 12 E Armour Blvd	Kansas City	MO	64111	816-502-4000	502-4126
Morabito Baking Co Inc 757 Kohn St *TF:* 800-525-7747 ■ *Web:* www.morabito.com	Norristown	PA	19401	610-275-5419	275-0358
Mrs Baird's Bakeries Inc 7301 South Fwy *TF:* 800-366-7921 ■ *Web:* www.mrsbairds.com	Fort Worth	TX	76134	817-293-6230	615-3091
Nickles Alfred Bakery Inc 26 N Main St *TF:* 800-635-1110 ■ *Web:* www.nicklesbakery.com	Navarre	OH	44662	330-879-5635	879-5896
Old London Foods 1776 Eastchester Rd *TF:* 888-266-4445 ■ *Web:* www.oldlondonmelba.com	Bronx	NY	10461	718-409-1776	430-0301
Orlando Baking Co Inc 7777 Grand Ave *TF:* 800-362-5504 ■ *Web:* www.orlandobaking.com	Cleveland	OH	44104	216-361-1872	391-3469
Ottenberg's Bakery Inc 655 Taylor St NE *TF:* 800-334-7264	Washington	DC	20017	202-529-5800	529-3121
Palagonia Bakery 508 Junius St	Brooklyn	NY	11212	718-272-5400	272-5427
Pan-O-Gold Baking Co 444 E Saint Germain St *TF:* 800-444-7005	Saint Cloud	MN	56304	320-251-9361	252-0249
Parco Foods LLC 2200 W 138th St *TF:* 888-371-9200 ■ *Web:* www.parcofoods.com	Blue Island	IL	60406	708-371-9200	239-4156
Pechters Baking 840 Jersey St *TF:* 800-525-5779	Harrison	NJ	07029	973-483-3374	481-2319
Pepperidge Farm Inc 595 Westport Ave *TF PR:* 888-737-7374 ■ *Web:* www.pepperidgefarm.com	Norwalk	CT	06851	203-846-7000	846-7369
Philadelphia Baking Co 2550 Grant Ave *TF:* 800-775-5623	Philadelphia	PA	19114	215-464-4242	464-5701
Piantedosi Baking Co Inc 240 Commercial St *TF:* 800-339-0080 ■ *Web:* www.piantedosi.com	Malden	MA	02148	781-321-3400	324-5647
Quality Bakery Products Inc 888 E Las Olas Blvd Suite 700 **Fax Area Code: 305*	Fort Lauderdale	FL	33301	954-779-3663	779-7678*
Quinzani's Bakery 380 Harrison Ave *TF:* 800-999-1062 ■ *Web:* www.quinzanisbakery.com	Boston	MA	02118	617-426-2114	451-8075
Ralcorp Frozen Bakery Products 999 Oakmont Plaza Dr Suite 610 *Web:* www.ralcorpfrozen.com	Westmont	IL	60559	630-455-5200	455-5202
Richmond Baking Co PO Box 698 *Web:* www.richmondbaking.com	Richmond	IN	47374	765-962-8535	962-2253
Roskam Baking Co PO Box 202 *TF:* 877-684-2879	Grand Rapids	MI	49501	616-574-5757	574-1117
Saputo Inc 6869 boul Metropolitain *TSX: SAP* ■ *Web:* www.saputo.com	Saint-Leonard	QC	H1P1X8	514-328-6662	328-3310
Sara Lee Food & Beverage 3500 Lacey Rd *TF:* 866-727-2533 ■ *Web:* www.saraleefoods.com	Downers Grove	IL	60515	630-598-7892	598-8221
Schafers Bakery Inc 5085 W Grand River Ave	Lansing	MI	48906	517-886-3842	886-4276
Schmidt Baking Co Inc 7801 Fitch Ln *TF:* 800-456-2253 ■ *Web:* www.schmidtbaking.com	Baltimore	MD	21236	410-668-8200	882-2051
Schwebel Baking Co PO Box 6018 *TF:* 800-860-2867 ■ *Web:* www.schwebels.com	Youngstown	OH	44501	330-783-2860	782-1774
Snyder's Bakery Inc 31 N 4th Ave	Yakima	WA	98902	509-453-8223	249-4102
Sokol & Co 5315 Dansher Rd *TF Cust Svc:* 800-328-7656 ■ *Web:* www.solofoods.com	Countryside	IL	60525	708-482-8250	482-9750
Southern Bakeries LLC 2700 E 3rd St *TF:* 800-643-1542 ■ *Web:* www.southernbakeries.com	Hope	AR	71802	870-777-9031	777-2406
Specialty Bakers Inc 450 S State Rd *TF:* 800-233-0778 ■ *Web:* www.sbiladyfingers.com	Marysville	PA	17053	717-957-2131	957-0156
Stroehmann Bakeries Inc 255 Business Center Dr *TF:* 800-355-1260	Horsham	PA	19044	215-672-8010	672-6988
Svenhard's Swedish Bakery Inc 335 Adeline St *TF:* 800-333-7836 ■ *Web:* www.svenhards.com	Oakland	CA	94607	510-834-5035	839-6797
Sweetheart Bakery 5150 Midland Rd	Billings	MT	59101	406-248-4800	248-1499
Table Talk Pies Inc 120 Washington St *Web:* www.tabletalkpie.com	Worcester	MA	01610	508-798-8811	798-0848
Tasty Baking Co 2801 W Hunting Park Ave *NASDAQ: TSTY* ■ *TF:* 800-338-8677 ■ *Web:* www.tastykake.com	Philadelphia	PA	19129	215-221-8500	223-3288
TJ Cinnamons 1155 Perimeter Center W *TF:* 800-487-2729	Atlanta	GA	30338	678-514-4100	
Turano Baking Co 6501 W Roosevelt Rd *TF:* 800-458-5662 ■ *Web:* www.turanobakery.com	Berwyn	IL	60402	708-788-9220	788-3075
US Bakery DBA Franz Bakery 340 NE 11th Ave *TF:* 800-935-5679 ■ *Web:* www.usbakery.com	Portland	OR	97232	503-232-2191	234-7036
Weston George Bakeries Inc 55 Paradise Ln **Fax: Sales* ■ *TF:* 800-842-9595 ■ *Web:* www.gwbakeries.com	Bay Shore	NY	11706	631-273-6000	951-5582*
Wolferman's Inc 14350 Santa Fe Trail Dr *TF Cust Svc:* 800-919-1888 ■ *Web:* www.wolfermans.com	Lenexa	KS	66215	913-888-4499	492-5195
Wonder Bread Bakeries 12 E Armour Blvd *Web:* www.wonderbread.com	Kansas City	MO	64111	816-502-4000	502-4126

299-2 Bakery Products - Frozen

				Phone	Fax
Athens Pastries & Frozen Foods Inc 13600 Snow Rd *TF:* 800-837-5683 ■ *Web:* www.athens.com	Cleveland	OH	44142	216-676-8500	676-0609
Bako Products 1425 Del Paso Blvd *Web:* www.bakoproducts.com	Sacramento	CA	95815	916-929-6868	922-9091
Best Brands Corp 111 Cheshire Ln Suite 100 *TF:* 800-328-2068 ■ *Web:* www.bestbrandscorp.com	Minnetonka	MN	55305	952-404-7500	404-7501
Bridgford Foods Corp 1308 N Patt St *NASDAQ: BRID* ■ *TF:* 800-854-3255 ■ *Web:* www.bridgford.com	Anaheim	CA	92801	714-526-5533	526-4360
Brooks Food Group Inc 940 Orange St *TF:* 800-873-4934 ■ *Web:* www.brooksfoodgroup.com	Bedford	VA	24523	540-586-8284	586-1072
Chef Solutions Inc 1000 Universal Dr *TF:* 800-877-1157 ■ *Web:* www.chefsolutions.com	North Haven	CT	06473	203-234-0115	234-7620
Cookietree Bakeries PO Box 57888 *TF:* 800-998-0111 ■ *Web:* www.cookietree.com	Salt Lake City	UT	84157	801-268-2253	265-2727
Country Home Bakers Inc 3 Enterprise Dr Suite 404 *TF Cust Svc:* 800-243-0008 ■ *Web:* www.countryhomebakers.com	Shelton	CT	06484	203-225-2333	929-2177
Country Oven Bakery Inc 2840 Pioneer Dr	Bowling Green	KY	42101	270-782-3200	782-7170
Eli's Cheesecake Co 6701 W Forest Preserve Dr *TF:* 800-999-8300 ■ *Web:* www.elicheesecake.com	Chicago	IL	60634	773-736-3417	205-3801
Evans Frozen Baked Goods Inc PO Box 284 *TF Cust Svc:* 800-222-5641 ■ *Web:* www.evansbakery.com	Cozad	NE	69130	308-784-2409	784-2459
Gregory's Foods Inc 2514 Northland Dr **Fax Area Code: 651* ■ *TF:* 800-347-8700 ■ *Web:* www.gregorysfoods.com	Mendota Heights	MN	55120	800-231-4734	454-2254*
Guttenplans Frozen Dough 100 Hwy 36 *TF:* 888-422-4357 ■ *Web:* www.guttenplan.com	Middletown	NJ	07748	732-495-9480	495-2415

	City	State	Zip	Phone	Fax
James Skinner Baking Co 4657 G St *TF:* 800-358-7428 ■ *Web:* www.skinnerbaking.com	Omaha	NE	68117	402-734-1672	734-0516
Main Street Gourmet Inc 170 Muffin Ln *TF:* 800-678-6246 ■ *Web:* www.mainstreetgourmet.com	Cuyahoga Falls	OH	44223	330-929-0000	920-8329
Maple Leaf Bakery Inc 220 S Orange Ave *Web:* www.mapleleaf.com	Livingston	NJ	07039	973-597-1991	597-1183
Maplehurst Inc 50 Maplehurst Dr *TF:* 800-428-3200 ■ *Web:* www.maplehurstbakeries.com	Brownsburg	IN	46112	317-858-9000	858-9009
New York Frozen Foods Inc 25900 Fargo Ave	Bedford Heights	OH	44146	216-292-5655	292-5978
Orange Bakery Inc 17751 Cowan Ave *TF:* 800-576-6836	Irvine	CA	92614	949-863-1377	863-1932
Pierre Foods Inc 9990 Princeton Rd *Web:* www.pierrefoods.com	Cincinnati	OH	45246	513-874-8741	874-1756
Rhino Foods Inc 79 Industrial Pkwy *TF:* 800-639-3350 ■ *Web:* www.rhinofoods.com	Burlington	VT	05401	802-862-0252	865-4145
Sara Lee Food & Beverage 3500 Lacey Rd *TF:* 866-727-2533 ■ *Web:* www.saraleefoods.com	Downers Grove	IL	60515	630-598-7892	598-8221
Schroeder's Cosmopolitan Bakery Inc PO Box 183 *TF:* 800-850-7763	Buffalo	NY	14213	716-885-4894	885-0369
Vie de France Yamazaki Inc 2070 Chain Bridge Rd Suite 500 *TF:* 800-446-4404 ■ *Web:* www.vdfy.com	Vienna	VA	22182	703-442-9205	821-2695

299-3 Butter (Creamery)

	City	State	Zip	Phone	Fax
Agri-Mark Inc PO Box 5800 *Web:* www.agrimark.net	Lawrence	MA	01842	978-689-4442	794-8304
AMPI 315 N Broadway *TF:* 800-533-3580 ■ *Web:* www.ampi.com	New Ulm	MN	56073	507-354-8295	359-8668
Cabot Creamery 1 Home Farm Way *TF:* 888-792-2268 ■ *Web:* cabotcheese.com	Montpelier	VT	05602	802-229-9361	
California Dairies Inc 11709 E Artesia Blvd *TF:* 800-821-5588 ■ *Web:* www.californiadairies.com	Artesia	CA	90701	562-865-1291	860-8633
Challenge Dairy Products Inc 11875 Dublin Blvd Suite B230 *TF:* 800-733-2374 ■ *Web:* www.challengedairy.com	Dublin	CA	94568	925-828-6160	551-7591
Crystal Cream & Butter Co 1013 D St *TF:* 800-272-7326 ■ *Web:* www.crystal-milk.com	Sacramento	CA	95814	916-444-7200	448-0284
Farmers Co-op Creamery Inc 700 N Hwy 99 W	McMinnville	OR	97128	503-472-2157	472-3821
Grassland Dairy Products Co Inc N 8790 Fairgrounds Ave PO Box 160 *TF:* 800-428-8837 ■ *Web:* www.grassland.com	Greenwood	WI	54437	715-267-6182	267-6044
Land O'Lakes Inc 4001 Lexington Ave N **Fax:* Hum Res ■ *TF:* 800-328-9680 ■ *Web:* www.landolakesinc.com	Arden Hills	MN	55126	651-481-2222	481-2488*
Madison Dairy Produce Co 1002 E Washington Ave	Madison	WI	53703	608-256-5561	256-0985
Milkco Inc 220 Deaverview Rd *TF:* 800-842-8021	Asheville	NC	28806	828-254-9560	252-9560
O-AT-KA Milk Products Co-op Inc PO Box 718 *TF:* 800-828-8152 ■ *Web:* www.oatkamilk.com	Batavia	NY	14021	585-343-0536	343-4473
Plainview Milk Products Co-Op 130 2nd St SW *TF:* 800-356-5606	Plainview	MN	55964	507-534-3872	534-3992
Ramey Farmers Co-op Creamery 5139 345th Ave *TF:* 888-219-1768	Foley	MN	56329	320-355-2313	355-2320
Schreiber Foods Inc 425 Pine St *TF:* 800-344-0333 ■ *Web:* www.schreiberfoods.com	Green Bay	WI	54301	920-437-7601	455-2700
Sommermaid Creamery Inc PO Box 350 *Web:* www.sommermaid.com	Doylestown	PA	18901	215-345-6160	345-4945
WestFarm Foods 635 Elliott Ave W *TF:* 800-333-6455 ■ *Web:* www.westfarm.com	Seattle	WA	98119	206-284-7220	281-3456

299-4 Cereals (Breakfast)

	City	State	Zip	Phone	Fax
Arrowhead Mills Inc 110 S Lawton St PO Box 2059 *TF:* 800-858-4308	Hereford	TX	79045	806-364-0730	364-8242
Barbara's Bakery Inc 3900 Cypress Dr *Web:* www.barbarasbakery.com	Petaluma	CA	94954	707-765-2273	765-2927
Beech-Nut Nutrition Corp 100 S 4th St Suite 1010 *TF:* 800-233-2468 ■ *Web:* www.beechnut.com	Saint Louis	MO	63102	314-436-7667	436-7679
Big G Cereals 1 General Mills Blvd PO Box 9452 *TF:* 800-328-1144 ■ *Web:* www.generalmills.com	Minneapolis	MN	55440	763-764-7600	764-3232
Blue Planet Foods Inc PO Box 2178 *TF:* 877-396-3145 ■ *Web:* www.blueplanetfoods.net	Collegedale	TN	37315	423-396-3145	396-3470
Bob's Red Mill Natural Foods Inc 5209 SE International Way *TF:* 800-553-2258 ■ *Web:* www.bobsredmill.com	Milwaukie	OR	97222	503-654-3215	653-1339
Breadshop Inc 16100 Foothill Blvd **Fax Area Code:* 626	Irwindale	CA	91706	800-334-3204	969-0939*
ConAgra Store Brands 21340 Hayes Ave	Lakeville	MN	55044	952-469-4971	469-5550
General Mills Inc 1 General Mills Blvd *NYSE:* GIS ■ *TF:* 800-328-1144 ■ *Web:* www.generalmills.com	Minneapolis	MN	55426	763-764-7600	764-8330
General Mills Inc International Foods Div 1 General Mills Blvd *TF:* 800-328-1144 ■ *Web:* www.generalmills.com	Minneapolis	MN	55426	763-764-7600	764-3232
Gilster-Mary Lee Corp 1037 State St *TF:* 800-851-5371	Chester	IL	62233	618-826-2361	826-2973
Grain Millers of Iowa Inc 606 Hwy 218 N	Saint Ansgar	IA	50472	641-713-4801	713-4839
Healthy Times Inc 13200 Kirkham Way Bldg 104	Poway	CA	92064	858-513-1550	513-1533
Homestead Mills 221 N River St PO Box 1115 *TF:* 800-652-5233 ■ *Web:* www.homesteadmills.com	Cook	MN	55723	218-666-5233	666-5236
Honeyville Grain Inc 11600 Dayton Dr *TF:* 888-810-3212 ■ *Web:* www.honeyvillegrain.com	Rancho Cucamonga	CA	91730	909-980-9500	980-6503
Kashi Co 4250 Executive Sq Suite 600 PO Box 8557 *Web:* www.kashi.com	La Jolla	CA	92038	858-274-8870	274-8894
Kellogg Co 1 Kellogg Sq *NYSE:* K ■ *TF Cust Svc:* 800-962-1413 ■ *Web:* www.kelloggs.com	Battle Creek	MI	49016	269-961-2000	961-2871
Kellogg USA Inc PO Box 3599	Battle Creek	MI	49016	269-961-2000	961-2871
Little Crow Foods PO Box 1038 *TF:* 800-288-2769 ■ *Web:* www.littlecrowfoods.com	Warsaw	IN	46581	574-267-7141	267-2370
Lundberg Family Farms 5370 Church St PO Box 369 *Web:* www.lundberg.com	Richvale	CA	95974	530-882-4551	882-4500
Malt-O-Meal Inc 80 S 8th St Suite 2700 *TF:* 800-328-4452 ■ *Web:* www.malt-o-meal.com	Minneapolis	MN	55402	612-338-8551	359-5424
Nature's Hand Inc 1800 E Cliff Rd Suite 7	Burnsville	MN	55337	952-890-6033	890-6040
New England Natural Bakers 74 Fairview St E *Web:* www.nenb.com	Greenfield	MA	01301	413-772-2239	772-2936
Organic Milling Co 505 W Allen Ave *TF:* 800-638-8686	San Dimas	CA	91773	909-599-0961	599-5180
Pacific Grain Products International Inc PO Box 2060 *TF Cust Svc:* 800-747-0161 ■ *Web:* www.pacgrain.com	Woodland	CA	95776	530-662-5056	662-6074
Quaker Foods North America 555 W Monroe St *TF:* 800-555-6287 ■ *Web:* www.quakeroats.com	Chicago	IL	60661	312-821-1000	
Ralston Foods PO Box 618 *Web:* www.ralstonfoods.com	Saint Louis	MO	63188	314-877-7000	877-7771
US Mills Inc 200 Reservoir St Suite 200 *TF:* 800-422-1125 ■ *Web:* www.usmillsinc.com	Needham	MA	02494	781-444-0440	444-3411

	City	State	Zip	Phone	Fax
Weetabix Co Inc 20 Cameron St *TF:* 800-343-0590	Clinton	MA	01510	978-368-0991	365-7268
Wildtime Foods 1201 Pearl St *TF:* 800-356-4458 ■ *Web:* www.grizzliesbrand.com	Eugene	OR	97441	541-747-1654	747-5067

299-5 Cheeses - Natural, Processed, Imitation

	City	State	Zip	Phone	Fax
Agri-Mark Inc PO Box 5800 *Web:* www.agrimark.net	Lawrence	MA	01842	978-689-4442	794-8304
McCadam Cheese 39 McCadam Ln **Fax Area Code:* 802 ■ *TF:* 800-639-4031 ■ *Web:* www.mccadam.com	Chateaugay	NY	12920	518-497-6644	371-1210*
Alpine Lace Brands Inc PO Box 64101 *Web:* www.alpinelace.com	Saint Paul	MN	55164	651-481-2222	481-2022
Alto Dairy Co-op N 3545 County Trunk EE *Web:* www.altodairy.com	Waupun	WI	53963	920-346-2215	346-2377
AMPI 315 N Broadway *TF:* 800-533-3580 ■ *Web:* www.ampi.com	New Ulm	MN	56073	507-354-8295	359-8668
Bel/Kaukauna USA 1500 E North Ave *TF:* 800-558-3500 ■ *Web:* www.kaukaunacheese.com	Little Chute	WI	54140	920-788-3524	788-9725
Berner Foods Inc 2034 E Factory Rd *TF:* 800-819-8199 ■ *Web:* www.bernerfoods.com	Dakota	IL	61018	815-563-4222	563-4017
Boar's Head Provisions Co Inc 1819 Main St Suite 800 *Web:* www.boarshead.com	Sarasota	FL	34236	941-955-0994	906-8213
Bongards' Creameries 13200 County Rd 51 *Web:* bongardscheese.com	Norwood	MN	55368	952-466-5521	466-5556
Bongrain Cheese USA 400 S Custer Ave **Fax:* Mktg ■ *TF:* 800-253-6637	New Holland	PA	17557	717-355-8500	355-8546*
Brewster Dairy Inc PO Box 98 *TF:* 800-874-8874 ■ *Web:* www.brewstercheese.com	Brewster	OH	44613	330-767-3492	767-3386
Burnett Dairy Co-op 11631 SR 70 *Web:* www.burnettdairy.com	Grantsburg	WI	54840	715-689-2468	689-2135
Cabot Creamery 1 Home Farm Way *TF:* 888-792-2268 ■ *Web:* cabotcheese.com	Montpelier	VT	05602	802-229-9361	
Cacique Inc 14923 Procter Ave **Fax:* Sales ■ *TF:* 800-521-6987 ■ *Web:* www.caciqueusa.com	La Puente	CA	91746	626-961-3399	961-4676*
Calabro Cheese Corp 580 Coe Ave *TF:* 800-969-1311 ■ *Web:* www.calabrocheese.com	East Haven	CT	06512	203-469-1311	469-6929
California Dairies Inc 11709 E Artesia Blvd *TF:* 800-821-5588 ■ *Web:* www.californiadairies.com	Artesia	CA	90701	562-865-1291	860-8633
Churny Co Inc 1 Kraft Ct	Glenview	IL	60025	847-646-5500	646-5590
Colonna Brothers Inc 4102 Bergen Tpke	North Bergen	NJ	07047	201-864-1115	864-0144
ConAgra Foods Retail Products Co Dairy Foods Group 215 W Diehl Rd **Fax Area Code:* 800 ■ *TF:* 800-444-7360 ■ *Web:* www.conagrafoods.com	Naperville	IL	60563	630-857-5200	444-7072*
ConAgra Foods Retail Products Co Deli Foods Group 215 W Field Rd *TF:* 800-325-7424	Naperville	IL	60563	630-857-1000	512-1124
Crowley Foods Inc 95 Court St *TF:* 800-637-0019 ■ *Web:* www.crowleyfoods.com	Binghamton	NY	13901	607-779-3289	779-3439
Dairy Farmers of America Inc 10220 N Ambassador Dr Northpointe Tower *TF:* 888-332-6455 ■ *Web:* www.dfamilk.com	Kansas City	MO	64153	816-801-6455	801-6592
Ellsworth Co-op Creamery Inc PO Box 610	Ellsworth	WI	54011	715-273-4311	273-5318
Elm City Cheese Co Inc 2240 State St	Hamden	CT	06517	203-865-5768	865-8303
Empire Cheese Inc 4520 Haskell Rd	Cuba	NY	14727	585-968-1552	968-2660
F & A Cheese Corp PO Box 19127 *TF:* 800-634-4109	Irvine	CA	92623	949-221-8255	221-8256
F & A Dairy Products Inc PO Box 278	Dresser	WI	54009	715-755-3485	755-3480
Farmdale Creamery Inc 1049 W Baseline St	San Bernardino	CA	92411	909-889-3002	888-2541
First District Assn 101 S Swift Ave *Web:* www.firstdistrict.com	Litchfield	MN	55355	320-693-3236	693-6243
Fleur de Lait BC USA 400 S Custer Ave *TF:* 800-322-2743	New Holland	PA	17557	717-355-8500	355-8546
Friendship Dairies Inc 1 Jericho Plaza *Web:* www.friendshipdairies.com	Jericho	NY	11753	516-719-4000	719-3880
Galaxy Nutritional Foods Inc 2441 Viscount Row *AMEX:* GXY ■ *TF Cust Svc:* 800-808-2325 ■ *Web:* www.galaxyfoods.com	Orlando	FL	32809	407-855-5500	855-7485
Golden Cheese Co of California 1138 W Rincon St **Fax:* Hum Res ■ *TF Cust Svc:* 800-842-0264	Corona	CA	92880	951-493-4700	493-4749*
Gossner Foods Inc 1051 N 1000 West *TF:* 800-944-0454 ■ *Web:* www.gossner.com	Logan	UT	84321	435-752-9365	752-3147
Grande Cheese Co Dairy Rd **Fax:* Hum Res ■ *Web:* www.grandecig.com	Brownsville	WI	53006	920-583-3122	269-1435*
Great Lakes Cheese Co Inc 17825 Great Lakes Pkwy *TF:* 800-677-7181 ■ *Web:* www.greatlakescheese.com	Hiram	OH	44234	440-834-2500	834-1002
Heluva Good Cheese Inc 6551 Pratt Rd PO Box 410 *TF:* 800-323-2188 ■ *Web:* www.heluvagood.com	Sodus	NY	14551	315-483-6971	483-9927
Hilmar Cheese Co Inc PO Box 910 *TF:* 888-300-4465 ■ *Web:* www.hilmarcheese.com	Hilmar	CA	95324	209-667-6076	634-1408
Holmes Cheese Co 9444 SR-39	Millersburg	OH	44654	330-674-6451	674-6673
Ideal Dairy 10 Executive Ave *TF:* 800-332-4791	Edison	NJ	08817	732-442-6337	287-1326
Jerome Cheese Co 47 W 100 S	Jerome	ID	83338	208-324-8806	324-8892
Kolb-Lena Cheese Co 3990 N Sunnyside Rd	Lena	IL	61048	815-369-4577	369-4914
Kraft Canada Inc 95 Moatfield Dr **Fax:* PR ■ *Web:* www.kraftcanada.com	Don Mills	ON	M3B3L6	416-441-5000	441-5328*
Kraft Foods Inc 3 Lakes Drive *NYSE:* KFT ■ *Web:* www.kraft.com	Northfield	IL	60093	847-646-2000	646-6005
Kraft Foods North America Inc 3 Lakes Dr *Web:* www.kraft.com	Northfield	IL	60093	847-646-2000	646-2922
Lactoprot USA Inc PO Box 7 *TF Cust Svc:* 800-236-3300	Blue Mounds	WI	53517	608-437-5598	437-8850
Land O'Lakes Inc 4001 Lexington Ave N **Fax:* Hum Res ■ *TF:* 800-328-9680 ■ *Web:* www.landolakesinc.com	Arden Hills	MN	55126	651-481-2222	481-2488*
Le Sueur Cheese Co Inc 719 N Main St *TF:* 800-247-0871	Le Sueur	MN	56058	507-665-3353	665-2820
Leprino Foods Co 1830 W 38th Ave *TF:* 800-537-7466 ■ *Web:* www.leprinofoods.com	Denver	CO	80211	303-480-2600	480-2682
Lucille Farms Inc 150 River Rd *TF:* 800-654-6844 ■ *Web:* www.lucille-farms.com	Montville	NJ	07045	973-334-6030	402-6361
Mancuso Cheese Co 612 Mills Rd	Joliet	IL	60433	815-722-2475	722-1302
Marathon Cheese Corp PO Box 185	Marathon	WI	54448	715-443-2211	443-2211
Miceli Dairy Products Co 2721 E 90th St *TF:* 800-551-7196 ■ *Web:* www.miceli-dairy.com	Cleveland	OH	44104	216-791-6222	231-2504
Milkco Inc 220 Deaverview Rd *TF:* 800-842-8021	Asheville	NC	28806	828-254-9560	252-9560
Minerva Cheese Factory Inc PO Box 60 *Web:* www.minervacheese.com	Minerva	OH	44657	330-868-4196	868-7947
Nelson Ricks Creamery Co 1755 S Fremont Dr	Salt Lake City	UT	84104	801-364-3607	364-3600
Pace Dairy Foods Co 2700 Valleyhigh Dr NW *TF:* 800-533-1687	Rochester	MN	55901	507-288-6315	288-6856
rondele Specialty Foods 8100 Hwy 'K' S *Web:* www.rondele.com	Merrill	WI	54452	715-675-3326	536-3028
Saputo Inc 6869 boul Metropolitain *TSX:* SAP ■ *Web:* www.saputo.com	Saint-Leonard	QC	H1P1X8	514-328-6662	328-3310

Cheeses - Natural, Processed, Imitation (Cont'd)

Company	City	State	ZIP	Phone	Fax
Sargento Foods Inc 1 Persnickety Pl *TF:* 800-558-5802 ■ *Web:* www.sargentocheese.com	Plymouth	WI	53073	920-893-8484	893-8399
Sartori Food Corp 107 Pleasant View Rd *TF Cust Svc:* 800-558-5888 ■ *Web:* www.sartorifoods.com	Plymouth	WI	53073	920-893-6061	892-2732
Schreiber Foods Inc 425 Pine St *TF:* 800-344-0333 ■ *Web:* www.schreiberfoods.com	Green Bay	WI	54301	920-437-7601	455-2700
Sorrento Lactalis Inc 2376 S Park Ave *TF:* 800-828-7031 ■ *Web:* www.sorrentocheese.com	Buffalo	NY	14220	716-823-6262	823-6454
Sun-Re Cheese Corp 178 Lenker Ave	Sunbury	PA	17801	570-286-1511	286-5123
Swiss Valley Farms Co 21100 Holden Dr *TF:* 800-747-6113 ■ *Web:* www.swissvalley.com	Davenport	IA	52806	563-391-3341	391-7479
Tillamook County Creamery Assn Inc 4185 Hwy 101 N *Web:* www.tillamookcheese.com	Tillamook	OR	97141	503-842-4481	842-6039
Valley Queen Cheese Factory Inc 200 E Railway Ave *Web:* www.vqcheese.com	Milbank	SD	57252	605-432-4563	432-9383
Wapsie Valley Creamery Inc 300 10th St NE	Independence	IA	50644	319-334-7193	334-4914
Westby Co-op Creamery 401 S Main St *TF:* 800-492-9282 ■ *Web:* www.westbycreamery.com	Westby	WI	54667	608-634-3181	634-3194
WestFarm Foods 635 Elliott Ave W *TF:* 800-333-6455 ■ *Web:* www.westfarm.com	Seattle	WA	98119	206-284-7220	281-3456
Wisconsin Cheeseman Inc 301 Broadway Dr *TF Orders:* 800-698-1721 ■ *Web:* www.wisconsincheeseman.com	Sun Prairie	WI	53590	608-837-5166	837-5493

299-6 Chewing Gum

Company	City	State	ZIP	Phone	Fax
Concord Confections Ltd 345 Courtland Ave *TF:* 800-793-5548 ■ *Web:* www.concordconfectionsinc.com	Concord	ON	L4K5A6	905-660-8989	660-8979
Dreyfus LA Co 3775 Park Ave	Edison	NJ	08820	732-549-1600	549-1685
Ford Gum & Machine Co Inc 18 Newton Ave *TF:* 800-225-5535 ■ *Web:* www.fordgum.com	Akron	NY	14001	716-542-4561	542-4610
Lotte USA Inc 5243 Wayne Rd	Battle Creek	MI	49015	269-963-6664	963-6695
Topps Co Inc 1 Whitehall St *NASDAQ: TOPP* ■ *Web:* www.topps.com	New York	NY	10004	212-376-0300	376-0573
Wm Wrigley Jr Co 410 N Michigan Ave *NYSE: WWY* ■ *TF:* 888-824-9681 ■ *Web:* www.wrigley.com	Chicago	IL	60611	312-644-2121	644-0353

299-7 Coffee - Roasted (Ground, Instant, Freeze-Dried)

Company	City	State	ZIP	Phone	Fax
Allegro Coffee Co 12799 Claude Ct *TF Cust Svc:* 800-530-3993 ■ *Web:* www.allegro-coffee.com	Thornton	CO	80241	303-444-4844	920-5468
American Coffee Co Inc 800 Magazine St *TF:* 800-554-7234 ■ *Web:* www.frenchmarketcoffee.com	New Orleans	LA	70130	504-581-7234	581-7518
Andresen Ryan Coffee Co 2206 Winter St *TF:* 800-293-2726	Superior	WI	54880	715-392-4771	392-4776
Araban Coffee Co Inc 2 Keith Way *TF:* 800-225-2474	Hingham	MA	02043	781-740-4441	740-4005
Autocrat Coffee Inc PO Box 285 *TF:* 800-288-6272 ■ *Web:* www.autocrat.com	Lincoln	RI	02865	401-333-3300	333-3719
Bargreen Coffee Co 2821 Rucker Ave *Web:* www.bargreencoffee.com	Everett	WA	98201	425-252-3161	259-4673
Boyd Coffee Co 19730 NE Sandy Blvd *TF Cust Svc:* 800-545-4077 ■ *Web:* www.boyds.com	Portland	OR	97230	503-666-4545	669-2223
Cadillac Coffee Co 1801 Michael St *TF:* 800-438-6900 ■ *Web:* www.cadillaccoffee.com	Madison Heights	MI	48071	248-545-2266	584-4184
Caravali Coffees Inc 717 Del Paso Rd *TF:* 800-647-5282	Sacramento	CA	95834	916-565-5500	565-5519
Coffee Holding Co Inc 4401 1st Ave *AMEX: JVA* ■ *TF:* 800-458-2233 ■ *Web:* www.coffeeholding.com	Brooklyn	NY	11232	718-832-0800	832-0892
Community Coffee Co PO Box 791 *TF:* 800-688-0990 ■ *Web:* www.communitycoffee.com	Baton Rouge	LA	70821	225-291-3900	368-4510
DeCoty Coffee Co Inc 1920 Austin St *TF:* 800-588-8001 ■ *Web:* www.decotycoffee.com	San Angelo	TX	76903	325-655-5607	655-6837
deLima Paul Co Inc PO Box 4813 *TF:* 800-962-8864 ■ *Web:* www.delimacoffee.com	Syracuse	NY	13221	315-457-3722	457-3730
Don Francisco Coffee Traders Inc PO Box 58271 **Fax Area Code: 800* ■ *TF:* 800-697-5282 ■ *Web:* www.don-francisco.com	Los Angeles	CA	90058	323-581-0671	697-9947*
Excellent Coffee Co Inc 259 East Ave	Pawtucket	RI	02860	401-724-6393	724-0560
F Gavina & Sons Inc 2700 Fruitland Ave *TF:* 800-428-4627 ■ *Web:* www.gavina.com	Vernon	CA	90058	323-582-0671	581-1127
Farmer Brothers Co 20333 S Normandie Ave *NASDAQ: FARM* ■ *TF:* 800-735-3226	Torrance	CA	90502	310-787-5200	320-2436
Folger Coffee Co 1 Procter & Gamble Plaza *Web:* www.folgers.com	Cincinnati	OH	45202	513-983-1100	562-4500
Frontier Natural Products Co-op 3021 78th St PO Box 299 *TF:* 800-669-3275 ■ *Web:* www.frontiercoop.com	Norway	IA	52318	319-227-7996	227-7966
Great Atlantic & Pacific Tea Co Inc 2 Paragon Dr *NYSE: GAP* ■ *Web:* www.aptea.com	Montvale	NJ	07645	201-573-9700	571-8820
Green Mountain Coffee Roasters Inc 33 Coffee Ln *NASDAQ: GMCR* ■ **Fax: Sales* ■ *TF Cust Svc:* 800-432-4627 ■ *Web:* www.greenmountaincoffee.com	Waterbury	VT	05676	802-244-5621	244-6565*
Hawaiian Isles Kona Coffee Co 2839 Mokumoa St *TF Orders:* 800-749-9103 ■ *Web:* www.hawaiianisles.com	Honolulu	HI	96819	808-833-2244	833-6328
JFG Coffee Co 3434 Mynatt Ave *TF:* 800-627-1988	Knoxville	TN	37919	865-546-2120	524-8725
Kauai Coffee Co Inc 1 Numila Rd *TF:* 800-545-8605 ■ *Web:* www.kauaicoffee.com	Kaleheo	HI	96741	808-335-5497	335-3149
McCullagh SJ Inc 245 Swan St *TF:* 800-753-3473 ■ *Web:* www.mccullaghcoffee.com	Buffalo	NY	14204	716-856-3473	856-3486
Melitta Canada Inc 1 Greensboro Dr Suite 202 *TF:* 800-565-4882 ■ *Web:* www.melitta.ca	Rexdale	ON	M9W1C8	416-243-8979	243-1808
Nestle USA Inc 800 N Brand Blvd **Fax: Sales* ■ *Web:* www.nestle.com	Glendale	CA	91203	818-549-6000	549-6952*
New England Coffee Co 100 Charles St *TF:* 800-225-3537 ■ *Web:* www.necoffeeco.com	Malden	MA	02148	781-324-8094	388-2838
Old Mansion Foods Inc 1558 W Washington St PO Box 2026 *TF:* 800-476-1877 ■ *Web:* www.oldmansionfoods.com	Petersburg	VA	23803	804-862-9889	861-8816
Paul deLima Co Inc PO Box 4813 *TF:* 800-962-8864 ■ *Web:* www.delimacoffee.com	Syracuse	NY	13221	315-457-3722	457-3730
Procter & Gamble Mfg Co 1 Procter & Gamble Plaza *Web:* www.pg.com	Cincinnati	OH	45202	513-983-1100	
Red Diamond Inc 1701 Vanderbilt Rd PO Box 2168 *TF:* 800-292-4651 ■ *Web:* www.reddiamond.com	Birmingham	AL	35201	205-254-3138	254-6062
Reily William B & Co Inc 640 Magazine St *TF:* 800-535-1961	New Orleans	LA	70130	504-524-6131	539-5427
Rowland Coffee Roasters Inc 5605 NW 82nd Ave *TF:* 800-990-9039	Miami	FL	33166	305-594-9039	594-7603
Royal Cup Inc 160 Cleage Dr *TF:* 800-366-5836 ■ *Web:* www.royalcupcoffee.com	Birmingham	AL	35217	205-849-5836	271-6071
S & D Coffee Inc 300 Concord Pkwy PO Box 1628 *TF Cust Svc:* 800-933-2210 ■ *Web:* www.sndcoffee.com	Concord	NC	28026	704-782-3121	721-5792
Sara Lee Food & Beverage 3500 Lacey Rd *TF:* 866-727-2533 ■ *Web:* www.saraleefoods.com	Downers Grove	IL	60515	630-598-7892	598-8221
SJ McCullagh Inc 245 Swan St *TF:* 800-753-3473 ■ *Web:* www.mccullaghcoffee.com	Buffalo	NY	14204	716-856-3473	856-3486
Stewarts Private Blend Food Inc 4110 W Wrightwood Ave *TF:* 800-654-2862 ■ *Web:* www.stewarts.com	Chicago	IL	60639	773-489-2500	489-2148
Tetley USA Inc 100 Commerce Dr Suite 210 PO Box 856 *Web:* www.tetleyusa.com	Shelton	CT	06484	203-929-9200	929-9263
Texas Coffee Co Inc 3291 ML King Pkwy S PO Box 31 *TF:* 800-259-3400 ■ *Web:* www.texjoy.com	Beaumont	TX	77704	409-835-3434	835-4248
Torke Coffee Roasting Co Inc 3455 Paine Ave PO Box 694 *TF:* 800-242-7671	Sheboygan	WI	53081	920-458-4114	458-0488
Van Rooy Coffee Co 4569 Spring Rd *TF:* 877-826-7669 ■ *Web:* www.vanrooycoffee.com	Cleveland	OH	44131	216-749-7069	749-7039
White Cloud Coffee Co 199 E 52nd St *TF:* 800-627-0309 ■ *Web:* www.whitecloudcoffee.com	Boise	ID	83714	208-322-1166	322-6226
White Coffee Corp 1835 38th St *TF:* 800-221-0140 ■ *Web:* www.whitecoffee.com	Long Island City	NY	11105	718-204-7900	956-8504
William B Reily & Co Inc 640 Magazine St *TF:* 800-535-1961	New Orleans	LA	70130	504-524-6131	539-5427

299-8 Confectionery Products

Company	City	State	ZIP	Phone	Fax
Adams & Brooks Inc 1915 S Hoover St PO Box 7303 *TF Orders:* 800-999-9808 ■ *Web:* www.adams-brooks.com	Los Angeles	CA	90007	213-749-3226	746-7614
ADM Cocoa Div 4666 E Faries Pkwy *TF:* 800-558-9958	Decatur	IL	62526	217-424-5200	424-4296
American Licorice Co 3701 W 128th Pl *TF:* 800-220-2399 ■ *Web:* www.redvines.com	Alsip	IL	60803	708-371-1414	371-0231
Andes Candies Inc 1400 E Wisconsin St	Delavan	WI	53115	262-728-9121	728-6794
Anthony-Thomas Candy Co 1777 Arlingate Ct *TF:* 877-226-3921 ■ *Web:* www.anthony-thomas.com	Columbus	OH	43228	614-274-8405	274-0019
Asher's Chocolates 80 Wambold Rd *TF:* 800-223-4420 ■ *Web:* www.ashers.com	Souderton	PA	18964	215-721-3000	721-3265
Atkinson Candy Co 1608 W Frank Ave *TF:* 800-231-1203 ■ *Web:* www.atkinsoncandy.com	Lufkin	TX	75904	936-639-2333	639-2337
Banner Candy Mfg Corp 700 Liberty Ave *TF:* 800-221-0934	Brooklyn	NY	11208	718-647-4747	647-7192
Barry Callebaut USA LLC 400 Industrial Pk Rd *TF:* 800-556-8845 ■ *Web:* www.barry-callebaut.com	Saint Albans	VT	05478	802-524-9711	524-5148
Beecher Katharine Candies 1250 Slate Hill Rd *TF:* 800-708-3641 ■ *Web:* www.padutchcandies.com	Camp Hill	PA	17011	717-761-5440	761-2206
Ben Myerson Candy Co Inc 928 Towne Ave *TF:* 800-421-8448 ■ *Web:* www.sunkistcandy.com	Los Angeles	CA	90021	213-623-6266	688-7571
Best Sweet Inc 288 Mazeppa Rd **Fax: Mktg* ■ *TF:* 888-211-5530 ■ *Web:* www.bestsweet.com	Mooresville	NC	28115	704-664-4300	664-9640*
Blommer Chocolate Co 600 W Kinzie St *TF:* 800-621-1606 ■ *Web:* www.blommer.com	Chicago	IL	60610	312-226-7700	226-4141
Boyer Candy Inc 821 17th St *Web:* www.boyercandies.com	Altoona	PA	16602	814-944-9401	943-2354
Brach's Confections Inc 19111 N Dallas Pkwy Suite 200 *TF:* 800-999-0204 ■ *Web:* www.brachs.com	Dallas	TX	75287	972-930-3600	
Brown & Haley 1940 E 11th St *TF:* 800-426-8400 ■ *Web:* www.brown-haley.com	Tacoma	WA	98421	253-620-3000	272-6742
Cambridge Brands Inc 810 Main St	Cambridge	MA	02139	617-491-2500	547-2381
Cargill Foods 15407 McGinty Rd *TF:* 800-227-4455 ■ *Web:* www.cargillfoods.com	Wayzata	MN	55391	952-742-7575	
Cargill Inc North America 15407 McGinty Rd *TF:* 800-227-4455	Wayzata	MN	55391	952-742-7575	
Ce De Candy Inc 1091 Lousons Rd *TF:* 800-631-7968	Union	NJ	07083	908-964-0660	964-0911
Charms Co 7401 S Cicero Ave *TF:* 800-877-7655	Chicago	IL	60629	773-838-3400	838-3564
Cherrydale Farms Inc 1035 Mill Rd *TF:* 800-333-4525 ■ *Web:* www.cherrydale.com	Allentown	PA	18106	610-366-1606	391-9345
Chocolate House Inc 4121 S 35th St *Web:* www.fudgiebear.com	Milwaukee	WI	53221	414-281-7800	423-2484
Chocolates a la Carte Inc 28455 Livingston Ave **Fax: Sales* ■ *TF Cust Svc:* 800-818-2462 ■ *Web:* www.chocolatesalacarte.com	Valencia	CA	91355	661-257-3700	257-4999*
Classic Caramel Co 231 W College Ave *Web:* www.classiccaramel.com	York	PA	17403	717-843-0921	854-9743
ConAgra Foods Retail Products Co Grocery Foods Group 3353 Michelson Dr	Irvine	CA	92612	949-437-1000	437-3342
ConAgra Specialty Snacks 8064 Chivvis Dr	Saint Louis	MO	63123	314-832-2602	832-3015
Concord Confections Ltd 345 Courtland Ave *TF:* 800-793-5548 ■ *Web:* www.concordconfectionsinc.com	Concord	ON	L4K5A6	905-660-8989	660-8979
Dahlgren & Co Inc 1220 Sunflower St *TF:* 800-346-6050 ■ *Web:* www.sunflowerseed.com	Crookston	MN	56716	218-281-2985	281-6218
Decko Products Inc 2105 Superior St *TF:* 800-537-6143 ■ *Web:* www.decko.com	Sandusky	OH	44870	419-626-5757	626-3135
Eaton Farm Confectioners Inc 30 Burbank Rd *TF:* 800-343-9300 ■ *Web:* www.eatonfarmcandies.com	Sutton	MA	01590	508-865-5235	865-7087
Elmer Candy Corp 401 N 5th St *TF:* 800-843-9537 ■ *Web:* www.elmercandy.com	Ponchatoula	LA	70454	985-386-6166	386-6245
Esther Price Candies Inc 1709 Wayne Ave *TF:* 800-782-0326 ■ *Web:* www.estherprice.com	Dayton	OH	45410	937-253-2121	253-3294
Farley's & Sathers Candy Co Inc 1 Sather Plaza *TF:* 800-533-0330 ■ *Web:* www.farleysandsathers.com	Round Lake	MN	56167	507-945-8181	945-8343
FB Washburn Candy Corp 137 Perkins Ave *Web:* www.fbwashburncandy.com	Brockton	MA	02302	508-588-0820	588-2205
Ferrara Bakery & Cafe Inc 195 Grand St 3rd Fl *TF:* 800-871-6068 ■ *Web:* www.ferraracafe.com	New York	NY	10013	212-226-6150	226-0667
Ferrara Pan Candy Co 7301 W Harrison St *TF:* 800-323-1768 ■ *Web:* www.ferrarapan.com	Forest Park	IL	60130	708-366-0500	366-5921
Ferrero USA Inc 600 Cottontail Ln *TF:* 800-337-7376 ■ *Web:* www.tictacpoints.com	Somerset	NJ	08873	732-764-9300	764-2700
Fowler's Chocolate Co 100 River Rock Dr *TF:* 800-824-2263 ■ *Web:* www.fowlerschocolate.com	Buffalo	NY	14207	716-877-9983	877-9959
Frankford Candy & Chocolate Co Inc 9300 Ashton Rd *Web:* www.frankfordcandy.com	Philadelphia	PA	11914	215-735-5200	735-0721
Ganong Brothers Ltd 1 Chocolate Dr *Web:* www.ganong.com	Saint Stephen	NB	E3L2X5	506-465-5600	465-5610
Gayle's Chocolates 417 S Washington Ave *Web:* www.gayleschocolates.com	Royal Oak	MI	48067	248-398-0001	399-5106
Gertrude Hawk Chocolates Inc 9 Keystone Park *TF:* 800-822-2032 ■ *Web:* www.gertrudehawkchocolates.com	Dunmore	PA	18512	570-342-7556	342-0261
Ghirardelli Chocolate Co 1111 139th Ave *TF:* 800-877-9338 ■ *Web:* www.ghirardelli.com	San Leandro	CA	94578	510-483-6970	297-2649
Godiva Chocolatier Inc 355 Lexington Ave 16th Fl *TF:* 800-732-7333 ■ *Web:* www.godiva.com	New York	NY	10017	212-984-5900	984-5901
Goetze's Candy Co Inc 3900 E Monument St *TF Orders:* 800-295-8058 ■ *Web:* www.goetzecandy.com	Baltimore	MD	21205	410-342-2010	522-7681

	City	State	ZIP	Phone	Fax
Golden Stream Quality Foods 11899 Exit 5 Pkwy	Fishers	IN	46038	317-845-5534	577-3588
TF: 800-837-2855 ■ *Web:* www.goldenstream.com					
Guittard Chocolate Co 10 Guittard Rd	Burlingame	CA	94010	650-697-4427	692-2761
TF: 800-468-2462 ■ *Web:* www.guittard.com					
Harry London Candies Inc 5353 Lauby Road	North Canton	OH	44720	330-494-0833	499-6902
TF Cust Svc: 800-321-0444 ■ *Web:* www.londoncandies.com					
Hawk Gertrude Chocolates Inc 9 Keystone Park	Dunmore	PA	18512	570-342-7556	342-0261
TF: 800-822-2032 ■ *Web:* www.gertrudehawkchocolates.com					
HB Reese Candy Co 925 Reese Ave	Hershey	PA	17033	717-534-4106	
TF Cust Svc: 800-468-1714					
Hershey Co 100 Crystal A Dr.	Hershey	PA	17033	717-534-4200	534-6760
NYSE: HSY ■ *TF Cust Svc:* 800-468-1714 ■ *Web:* www.thehersheycompany.com					
Hillside Candy Co 35 Hillside Ave	Hillside	NJ	07205	973-926-2300	926-4440
TF: 800-524-1304 ■ *Web:* www.hillsidecandy.com					
James Candy Co 1519 Boardwalk	Atlantic City	NJ	08401	609-344-1519	344-0246
TF: 800-441-1404 ■ *Web:* www.jamescandy.com					
James P Linette Inc DBA Linette Quality Chocolates PO Box 212	Womelsdorf	PA	19567	610-589-4526	589-2706
Jelly Belly Candy Co 1 Jelly Belly Ln	Fairfield	CA	94533	707-428-2800	428-0819*
**Fax:* Cust Svc ■ *TF:* 800-323-9380 ■ *Web:* www.jellybelly.com					
Joyva Corp 53 Varick Ave	Brooklyn	NY	11237	718-497-0170	366-8504
Web: www.joyva.com					
Judson-Atkinson Candies 4266 Dividend St PO Box 200669	San Antonio	TX	78220	210-359-8380	359-8392
Web: www.judsonatkinsoncandies.com					
Just Born Inc 1300 Stefko Blvd	Bethlehem	PA	18017	610-867-7568	867-7870
TF: 800-445-5787 ■ *Web:* www.justborn.com					
Kalva Corp 3940 Porett Dr	Gurnee	IL	60031	847-336-1200	336-0712
TF: 800-525-8220 ■ *Web:* www.kalvacorp.com					
Katharine Beecher Candies 1250 Slate Hill Rd	Camp Hill	PA	17011	717-761-5440	761-2206
TF: 800-708-3641 ■ *Web:* www.padutchcandies.com					
Koeze Co 2555 Burlingame Ave SW	Grand Rapids	MI	49509	616-724-2601	530-1819
TF: 888-253-6887 ■ *Web:* www.koeze.com					
Kopper's Chocolate 39 Clarkson St	New York	NY	10014	212-243-0220	
TF: 800-325-0026 ■ *Web:* www.kopperschocolate.com					
Lammes Candies Since 1885 Inc 200 B Parker Dr Suite 500	Austin	TX	78728	512-310-1885	310-2280
TF: 800-252-1885 ■ *Web:* www.lammes.com					
Lincoln Snacks Co 5020 S 19th St	Lincoln	NE	68512	402-421-5500	421-5519
Web: www.lincolnsnacks.com					
Lindt & Sprungli USA 1 Fine Chocolate Pl	Stratham	NH	03885	603-778-8100	778-3102
TF: 877-695-4638 ■ *Web:* www.lindtusa.com					
Linette James P Inc DBA Linette Quality Chocolates PO Box 212	Womelsdorf	PA	19567	610-589-4526	589-2706
Linette Quality Chocolates PO Box 212	Womelsdorf	PA	19567	610-589-4526	589-2706
London Harry Candies Inc 5353 Lauby Road	North Canton	OH	44720	330-494-0833	499-6902
TF Cust Svc: 800-321-0444 ■ *Web:* www.londoncandies.com					
Lucks Co 3003 S Pine St	Tacoma	WA	98409	253-383-4815	674-7250*
**Fax Area Code:* 206 ■ *TF:* 800-426-9778 ■ *Web:* www.lucks.com					
Madelaine Chocolate Novelties Inc 9603 Beach Channel Dr	Rockaway Beach	NY	11693	718-945-1500	318-4607
TF: 800-322-1505 ■ *Web:* madelainechocolate.com					
Malleys Chocolates 13400 Brookpark Rd	Cleveland	OH	44135	216-362-8700	362-7240
TF: 800-835-5684 ■ *Web:* secure.malleys.com					
Mars Snack Food 800 High St	Hackettstown	NJ	07840	908-852-1000	850-2734
TF: 800-432-1093 ■ *Web:* www.mars.com					
Marshmallow Cone Co 5141 Fischer Pl	Cincinnati	OH	45217	513-641-2345	641-2557
TF: 800-641-8551 ■ *Web:* www.marshmallowcone.com					
Masterson Co Inc 4023 W National Ave	Milwaukee	WI	53215	414-647-1132	647-1170
TF: 800-558-0990 ■ *Web:* www.mastersoncompany.com					
Maxfield Candy Co 1050 S 200 West	Salt Lake City	UT	84101	801-355-5321	355-5546
TF: 800-288-8002 ■ *Web:* www.maxfieldcandy.com					
Melster Candies Inc 500 E Madison St	Cambridge	WI	53523	608-423-3221	423-3195
TF: 800-535-4401					
Morley Candy Makers Inc 23770 Hall Rd	Clinton Township	MI	48036	586-468-4300	468-9407
TF: 800-682-2760 ■ *Web:* www.morleycandy.com					
Munson's Candy Kitchen Inc DBA Munson's Chocolates 174 Hop River Rd	Bolton	CT	06043	860-649-4332	649-7209
TF: 888-686-7667 ■ *Web:* www.munsonschocolates.com					
Myerson Ben Candy Co Inc 928 Towne Ave	Los Angeles	CA	90021	213-623-6266	688-7571
TF: 800-421-8448 ■ *Web:* www.sunkistcandy.com					
NECCO (New England Confectionery Co) 135 American Legion Hwy	Revere	MA	02151	781-485-4500	485-4509
TF: 800-225-5508 ■ *Web:* www.necco.com					
Nestle Canada Inc 25 Sheppard Ave W	Toronto	ON	M2N0З0	416-512-9000	218-2654
Web: www.nestle.ca					
Nestle USA Inc 800 N Brand Blvd	Glendale	CA	91203	818-549-6000	549-6952*
**Fax:* Sales ■ *Web:* www.nestle.com					
New England Confectionery Co (NECCO) 135 American Legion Hwy	Revere	MA	02151	781-485-4500	485-4509
TF: 800-225-5508 ■ *Web:* www.necco.com					
Orville Redenbacher/Swiss Miss Foods Co PO Box 3768	Omaha	NE	68103	949-255-4100	
TF: 800-243-0303					
Palmer Candy Co 311 Bluff St	Sioux City	IA	51103	712-258-5543	258-3224
TF: 800-831-0828 ■ *Web:* www.palmercandy.com					
Palmer RM Co 77 S 2nd Ave	West Reading	PA	19611	610-372-8971	378-5208
Web: www.rmpalmer.com					
Paradise Inc 1200 W MLK Blvd PO Drawer Y	Plant City	FL	33564	813-752-1155	754-3168
TF: 800-330-8952 ■ *Web:* www.paradisefruitco.com					
Pearson's Candy Co 2140 W 7th St	Saint Paul	MN	55116	651-698-0356	696-2222
TF Cust Svc: 800-328-6507 ■ *Web:* www.pearsoncandy.com					
Peerless Confection Co 1250 W Schubert Ave	Chicago	IL	60614	773-281-6100	281-5812
Web: www.peerlesscandy.com					
Pennsylvania Dutch Candies 1250 Slate Hill Rd	Camp Hill	PA	17011	717-761-5440	761-2206
TF: 800-233-7082 ■ *Web:* www.padutchcandies.com					
Peter Paul 889 New Haven Rd	Naugatuck	CT	06770	203-729-0221	
Pez Candy Inc 35 Prindle Hill Rd	Orange	CT	06477	203-795-0531	799-1679
TF: 800-243-6087 ■ *Web:* www.pez.com					
Price Esther Candies Inc 1709 Wayne Ave	Dayton	OH	45410	937-253-2121	253-3294
TF: 800-782-0326 ■ *Web:* www.estherprice.com					
Quigley Mfg Inc DBA Simon Candy Co 31 N Spruce St	Elizabethtown	PA	17022	717-367-2441	367-4055
TF: 800-367-2441 ■ *Web:* www.simoncandy.com					
Reese HB Candy Co 925 Reese Ave	Hershey	PA	17033	717-534-4106	
TF Cust Svc: 800-468-1714					
RM Palmer Co 77 S 2nd Ave	West Reading	PA	19611	610-372-8971	378-5208
Web: www.rmpalmer.com					
Russell Stover Candies Inc 4900 Oak St	Kansas City	MO	64112	816-842-9240	
TF: 800-477-8683 ■ *Web:* www.russellstover.com					
Santa Cruz Nutritionals 2200 Delaware Ave	Santa Cruz	CA	95060	831-457-3200	460-0610*
**Fax:* Sales ■ *Web:* www.scnutr.com					
Scott's of Wisconsin 301 Broadway Dr	Sun Prairie	WI	53590	608-837-8020	837-0763
See's Candies Inc 210 El Camino Real	South San Francisco	CA	94080	650-761-2490	875-6825
TF Cust Svc: 800-951-7337 ■ *Web:* www.sees.com					
Sherwood Brands Inc 1803 Research Blvd Suite 201	Rockville	MD	20850	301-309-6161	309-6162*
**Fax:* Cust Svc ■ *Web:* www.sherwoodbrands.com					
Simon Candy Co 31 N Spruce St	Elizabethtown	PA	17022	717-367-2441	367-4055
TF: 800-367-2441 ■ *Web:* www.simoncandy.com					
Sorbee International Ltd 9990 Global Rd	Philadelphia	PA	19115	215-677-5200	677-7736
TF: 800-654-3997 ■ *Web:* www.sorbee.com					
Spangler Candy Co 400 N Portland St PO Box 71	Bryan	OH	43506	419-636-4221	636-3695
TF Sales: 800-653-8638 ■ *Web:* www.spanglercandy.com					
Standard Candy Co Inc 715 Massman Dr	Nashville	TN	37210	615-889-6360	889-7775
TF: 800-226-4340 ■ *Web:* www.googoo.com					
Storck USA LP 325 N LaSalle St Suite 400	Chicago	IL	60610	312-467-5700	467-9722
TF: 800-621-7772 ■ *Web:* www.storck.com					
Supreme Chocolatier LLC 1150 South Ave	Staten Island	NY	10314	718-761-9600	761-5279
Web: www.supremechocolatier.com/					
Sweet Candy Co Inc 3780 W Directors Row	Salt Lake City	UT	84104	801-886-1444	886-1404
TF: 800-669-8669 ■ *Web:* www.sweetcandy.com					
Tootsie Roll Industries Inc 7401 S Cicero Ave	Chicago	IL	60629	773-838-3400	838-3534
NYSE: TR ■ *TF:* 800-877-7655 ■ *Web:* www.tootsie.com					
Warner Candy Co Inc 1099 Pratt Blvd	Elk Grove Village	IL	60007	847-928-7200	928-2115
Web: www.warnercandy.com					
Washburn FB Candy Corp 137 Perkins Ave	Brockton	MA	02302	508-588-0820	588-2205
Web: www.fbwashburncandy.com					
Wolfgang Candy Co 50 E 4th Ave	York	PA	17404	717-843-5536	845-2881
TF: 800-248-4273 ■ *Web:* www.wolfgangcandy.com					
World's Finest Chocolate Inc 4801 S Lawndale Ave	Chicago	IL	60632	773-847-4600	847-4006
TF: 800-366-2462 ■ *Web:* www.wfchocolate.com					
Y & S Candies 400 Running Pump Rd	Lancaster	PA	17603	717-299-1261	394-9109
Zachary Confections Inc 2130 W SR-28	Frankfort	IN	46041	765-659-4751	659-1491
TF Cust Svc: 800-445-4222 ■ *Web:* www.zacharyconfections.com					

299-9 Cookies & Crackers

	City	State	ZIP	Phone	Fax
Archway & Mother's Cookie Co 67 W Michigan Ave Suite 608	Battle Creek	MI	49017	269-962-6205	962-8149
TF: 800-444-6205					
B Manischewitz Co LLC 1 Manischewitz Plaza	Jersey City	NJ	07302	201-333-3700	333-1809
Web: www.manischewitz.com					
Bakery Resources -Ms Desserts 2275 Rolling Run Dr	Baltimore	MD	21244	410-281-2000	944-5427
TF Cust Svc: 800-876-7117					
Benzel's Pretzel Bakery Inc 5200 6th Ave	Altoona	PA	16602	814-942-5062	942-4133
TF: 800-344-4438 ■ *Web:* www.benzels.com					
Bremner Biscuit Co 4600 Joliet St	Denver	CO	80239	303-371-8180	371-8185
TF: 800-722-1871 ■ *Web:* www.bremnerbiscuitco.com					
Bremner Inc 800 Market St PO Box 618	Saint Louis	MO	63101	314-877-7000	877-7667
TF Cust Svc: 800-445-8338 ■ *Web:* www.bremnerbiscuit.com					
California Pretzel Co 7607 W Goshen Ave	Visalia	CA	93291	559-651-0600	651-0604
Web: www.calpretzel.com					
Chatham Village Foods Div T Marzetti Co 15 Kendrick Rd	Wareham	MA	02571	508-291-2304	291-0133
TF: 800-771-3888 ■ *Web:* www.marzetti.com					
Christie Cookie Co 1205 3rd Ave N	Nashville	TN	37208	615-242-3817	242-5572
TF: 800-458-2447 ■ *Web:* www.christiecookies.com					
Consolidated Biscuit Co 312 Rader Rd	McComb	OH	45858	419-293-2911	293-3366
Crackin Good Bakers Inc 701 N Forrest St	Valdosta	GA	31601	229-242-7850	671-7040
TF: 800-323-7850					
DF Stauffer Biscuit Co PO Box 1426 Belmont & 6th Ave	York	PA	17405	717-843-9016	843-0592
TF: 800-673-2473 ■ *Web:* www.stauffers.net					
Ellison Bakery 4108 W Ferguson Rd	Fort Wayne	IN	46809	260-747-6136	747-1954
Web: www.ebakery.com					
Ferrara Bakery & Cafe Inc 195 Grand St 3rd Fl	New York	NY	10013	212-226-6150	226-0667
TF: 800-871-6068 ■ *Web:* www.ferraracafe.com					
George Weston Bakeries Inc 55 Paradise Ln	Bay Shore	NY	11706	631-273-6000	951-5582*
**Fax:* Sales ■ *TF:* 800-842-9595 ■ *Web:* www.gwbakeries.com					
Holland American Wafer Co 3300 Roger B Chaffee Blvd SE	Grand Rapids	MI	49548	616-243-0191	243-0342
TF: 800-253-8350					
Interbake Foods LLC 2821 Emerywood Pkwy Suite 210	Richmond	VA	23294	804-755-7107	
Web: www.interbakefoods.com					
J & J Snack Foods Corp 6000 Central Hwy	Pennsauken	NJ	08109	856-665-9533	665-6718
NASDAQ: JJSF ■ *TF:* 800-486-9533 ■ *Web:* www.jjsnack.com					
Joy Cone Co 3435 Lamor Rd	Hermitage	PA	16148	724-962-5747	962-7103
TF: 800-242-2663 ■ *Web:* www.joycone.com					
Joyce Food Products Inc 80 Ave K	Newark	NJ	07105	973-491-9696	589-6145*
**Fax:* Sales					
Keebler Foods Co 1 Kellogg Sq PO Box 3599	Battle Creek	MI	49016	269-961-2000	530-8773*
**Fax Area Code:* 630 ■ *Web:* www.keebler.com					
Keystone Pretzels 124 W Airport Rd Flyway Business Pk	Lititz	PA	17543	717-560-1882	560-2241
TF: 888-572-4500 ■ *Web:* www.keystonepretzels.com					
Kraft Foods Inc 3 Lakes Drive	Northfield	IL	60093	847-646-2000	646-6005
NYSE: KFT ■ *Web:* www.kraft.com					
Kraft Foods North America Inc 3 Lakes Dr	Northfield	IL	60093	847-646-2000	646-2922
Web: www.kraft.com					
Lance Inc 8600 South Blvd	Charlotte	NC	28273	704-554-1421	554-5562
NASDAQ: LNCE ■ *TF:* 888-722-1163 ■ *Web:* www.lance.com					
Little Dutch Boy Bakery Inc 12349 S 970 East	Draper	UT	84020	801-571-3800	571-3802
TF: 800-382-2594					
Manischewitz B Co LLC 1 Manischewitz Plaza	Jersey City	NJ	07302	201-333-3700	333-1809
Web: www.manischewitz.com					
Mrs Alison's Cookie Co Inc 1600 Pk 370 Pl Suite 2	Hazelwood	MO	63042	314-298-2595	875-3291*
**Fax Area Code:* 800 ■ *TF:* 800-878-6772					
Norse Dairy Systems PO Box 1869	Columbus	OH	43216	614-294-4931	
TF: 800-338-7465 ■ *Web:* www.norse.com					
Pretzels Inc 123 Harvest Rd PO Box 503	Bluffton	IN	46714	260-824-4838	824-0895
TF: 800-456-4838 ■ *Web:* www.pretzels-inc.com					
Richmond Baking Co PO Box 698	Richmond	IN	47374	765-962-8535	962-2253
Web: www.richmondbaking.com					
Rudolph Foods Co Inc 6575 Bellefontaine Rd	Lima	OH	45804	419-648-3611	648-4087
TF: 800-241-7675 ■ *Web:* www.rudolphfoods.com					
Schulze & Burch Biscuit Co 1133 W 35th St	Chicago	IL	60609	773-927-6622	376-4528
Shur-Good Biscuit Co Inc 2950 Robertson Ave 4th Fl	Cincinnati	OH	45209	513-458-6200	458-6212
Silver Lake Cookie Co Inc 141 Freeman Ave	Islip	NY	11751	631-581-4000	581-4510
TF: 800-645-9048 ■ *Web:* www.silverlakecookie.com					
Snyder's of Hanover 1250 York St PO Box 6917	Hanover	PA	17331	717-632-4477	632-7207
TF: 800-233-7125 ■ *Web:* www.snydersofhanover.com					
Stauffer DF Biscuit Co PO Box 1426 Belmont & 6th Ave	York	PA	17405	717-843-9016	843-0592
TF: 800-673-2473 ■ *Web:* www.stauffers.net					
Stella D'oro Biscuit Co Inc 184 W 237th St	Bronx	NY	10463	718-549-3700	884-6494
Web: www.kraftfoods.com/stelladoro/					
Sturgis Tom Pretzels Inc 2267 Lancaster Pike	Reading	PA	19607	610-775-0335	796-1418*
**Fax:* Sales ■ *TF:* 800-817-3834 ■ *Web:* www.tomsturgispretzels.com					
Sweet Street Desserts PO Box 15127	Reading	PA	19612	610-921-8113	921-8195
TF Orders: 800-793-3897 ■ *Web:* www.sweetstreet.com					
T Marzetti Co Chatham Village Foods Div 15 Kendrick Rd	Wareham	MA	02571	508-291-2304	291-0133
TF: 800-771-3888 ■ *Web:* www.marzetti.com					
Tom Sturgis Pretzels Inc 2267 Lancaster Pike	Reading	PA	19607	610-775-0335	796-1418*
**Fax:* Sales ■ *TF:* 800-817-3834 ■ *Web:* www.tomsturgispretzels.com					
Venus Wafers Inc 70 Research Rd	Hingham	MA	02043	781-740-1002	749-7195
TF: 800-545-4538 ■ *Web:* www.venuswafers.com					
Vista Bakery Inc 3000 Mt Pleasant St PO Box 888	Burlington	IA	52601	319-754-6551	752-0063
TF: 800-553-2343 ■ *Web:* www.vistabakery.com					

Cookies & Crackers (Cont'd)

Company	City	State	Zip	Phone	Fax
Wege Pretzel Co 116 N Blettner Ave *Fax Area Code: 717 ■ Web: www.wege.com	Hanover	PA	17331	800-233-1933	632-4190*
Weston George Bakeries Inc 55 Paradise Ln *Fax: Sales ■ TF: 800-842-9595 ■ Web: www.gwbakeries.com	Bay Shore	NY	11706	631-273-6000	951-5582*
Willmar Cookie & Nut Co Inc 1118 E Hwy 12	Willmar	MN	56201	320-235-0600	235-0659

299-10 Dairy Products - Dry, Condensed, Evaporated

Company	City	State	Zip	Phone	Fax
Abbott Laboratories Ross Products Div 625 Cleveland Ave *Fax: PR ■ TF PR: 800-227-5767 ■ Web: www.rosslabs.com	Columbus	OH	43215	614-624-7677	624-7616*
American Casein Co 109 Elbow Ln TF: 800-699-6455 ■ Web: www.americancasein.com	Burlington	NJ	08016	609-387-3130	387-7204
AMPI 315 N Broadway TF: 800-533-3580 ■ Web: www.ampi.com	New Ulm	MN	56073	507-354-8295	359-8668
California Dairies Inc 11709 E Artesia Blvd TF: 800-821-5588 ■ Web: www.californiadairies.com	Artesia	CA	90701	562-865-1291	860-8633
Dairy Farmers of America Inc 10220 N Ambassador Dr Northpointe Tower TF: 888-332-6455 ■ Web: www.dfamilk.com	Kansas City	MO	64153	816-801-6455	801-6592
Davisco International Inc PO Box 69 TF: 800-323-4503 ■ Web: www.daviscofoods.com	Le Sueur	MN	56058	507-665-8811	665-3701
Diehl Inc 24 N Clinton St Web: www.diehlinc.com	Defiance	OH	43512	419-782-5010	784-5924
Dietrichs Milk Products Inc 100 McKinley Ave TF: 800-526-6455	Reading	PA	19605	610-929-5736	921-9330
DMV USA 1285 Rudy St TF Cust Svc: 877-300-7676	Onalaska	WI	54650	608-779-7676	779-7666
Erie Foods International Inc 401 7th Ave TF: 800-447-1887 ■ Web: www.eriefoods.com	Erie	IL	61250	309-659-2233	659-7270
Farmers Co-op Creamery Inc 700 N Hwy 99 W	McMinnville	OR	97128	503-472-2157	472-3821
Foremost Farms USA E10889A Penny Ln TF: 800-362-9196 ■ Web: www.foremostfarms.com	Baraboo	WI	53913	608-356-8316	355-6701
Galloway Co Inc 601 S Commercial St Web: www.gallowaycompany.com	Neenah	WI	54956	920-722-7741	722-1927
Gehl's Guernsey Farms Inc N116 W15970 Main St TF: 800-521-2873 ■ Web: www.gehls.com	Germantown	WI	53022	262-251-8570	251-8744
Humboldt Creamery Assn 572 Hwy 1 TF: 800-248-8879 ■ Web: www.humboldtcreamery.com	Fortuna	CA	95540	707-725-6182	725-6186
Instantwhip Foods Inc 2200 Cardigan Ave *Fax: Sales ■ TF Cust Svc: 800-544-9447 ■ Web: www.instantwhip.com	Columbus	OH	43215	614-488-2536	488-0307*
Jackson-Mitchell Inc PO Box 934 TF: 800-343-1185 ■ Web: www.meyenberg.com	Turlock	CA	95381	209-667-2019	668-4753
Land O'Lakes Inc 4001 Lexington Ave N *Fax: Hum Res ■ TF: 800-328-9680 ■ Web: www.landolakesinc.com	Arden Hills	MN	55126	651-481-2222	481-2488*
Maple Island Inc 2497 7th Ave E Suite 105 TF: 800-369-1022 ■ Web: www.maple-island.com	North Saint Paul	MN	55109	651-773-1000	773-2155
Mead Johnson Canada 333 Preston St Suite 600 Web: www.meadjohnson.ca	Ottawa	ON	K1S5N4	613-567-3536	239-3996
Mead Johnson Nutritionals 2400 W Lloyd Expy Web: www.meadjohnson.com	Evansville	IN	47721	812-429-5000	429-7538
Milnot Co 100 S 4th St Suite 1010 TF Sales: 800-877-6455 ■ Web: www.milnot.com	Saint Louis	MO	63102	314-436-7667	436-7679
Morningstar Foods 2515 McKinney Ave Suite 1200	Dallas	TX	75201	214-303-3400	303-3499
Nestle USA Inc 800 N Brand Blvd *Fax: Sales ■ Web: www.nestle.com	Glendale	CA	91203	818-549-6000	549-6952*
O-AT-KA Milk Products Co-op Inc PO Box 718 TF: 800-828-8152 ■ Web: www.oatkamilk.com	Batavia	NY	14021	585-343-0536	343-4473
Ohio Processors Inc PO Box 594	London	OH	43140	740-852-9243	852-5445
Penn Maid Foods Inc 10975 Dutton Rd TF: 800-220-7063 ■ Web: www.pennmaid.com	Philadelphia	PA	19154	215-824-2800	824-2820
Rich Products Corp 1 Robert Rich Way TF: 800-828-2021 ■ Web: www.richs.com	Buffalo	NY	14213	716-878-8000	
Ross Products Div Abbott Laboratories 625 Cleveland Ave *Fax: PR ■ TF PR: 800-227-5767 ■ Web: www.rosslabs.com	Columbus	OH	43215	614-624-7677	624-7616*
Saputo Cheese USA 325 Tompkins St TF: 800-345-9714 ■ Web: www.saputo.com	Fond du Lac	WI	54935	920-922-0600	922-4702
Sinton Dairy Foods Co LLC 3801 N Sinton Rd TF: 800-388-4970 ■ Web: www.sintondairy.com	Colorado Springs	CO	80907	719-633-3821	633-4376
WestFarm Foods 635 Elliott Ave W TF: 800-333-6455 ■ Web: www.westfarm.com	Seattle	WA	98119	206-284-7220	281-3456

299-11 Diet & Health Foods

Company	City	State	Zip	Phone	Fax
Alle Processing Corp 56-20 59th St Web: www.moncuisine.com	Maspeth	NY	11378	718-894-2000	326-4642
AMS Health Sciences Inc 711 NE 39th AMEX: AMM ■ TF: 800-426-4267 ■ Web: www.amsonline.com	Oklahoma City	OK	73105	405-842-0131	843-4935
Balance Bar Co 800 W Chester Ave PO Box 1031 *Fax Area Code: 914 ■ TF: 800-678-4246 ■ Web: www.balancebar.com	Rye Brook	NY	10573	800-678-4246	335-8412*
Cascadian Farm Inc 719 Metcalf St TF: 800-624-4123 ■ Web: www.cascadianfarm.com	Sedro Woolley	WA	98284	360-855-0100	855-0444
ConAgra Foods Retail Products Co Grocery Foods Group 3353 Michelson Dr	Irvine	CA	92612	949-437-1000	437-3342
Continental Culture Specialists Inc 1358 E Colorado St Web: www.continentalyogurt.com	Glendale	CA	91205	818-240-7400	243-3601
Eden Foods Inc 701 Tecumseh Rd TF Cust Svc: 800-248-0320 ■ Web: www.edenfoods.com	Clinton	MI	49236	517-456-7424	456-6075
Enjoy Life Foods LLC 1601 N Natchez Ave TF: 888-503-6569 ■ Web: www.enjoylifefoods.com	Chicago	IL	60707	773-889-5070	
French Meadow Bakery Inc 2610 Lyndale Ave S TF: 877-669-3278 ■ Web: www.frenchmeadow.com	Minneapolis	MN	55408	612-870-4740	870-0907
Golden Temple Inc 2545 Prairie Rd TF: 800-285-6457 ■ Web: www.goldentemple.com	Eugene	OR	97402	541-461-2160	461-2191
Great American Health Foods 4075 40th Ave SW *Fax Area Code: 800 ■ TF: 800-437-2733	Fargo	ND	58108	701-356-2760	450-5047*
Grow Co Inc 55 Railroad Ave	Richfield	NJ	07657	201-941-8777	
Health Hut 1512 1st Ave NE	Cedar Rapids	IA	52402	319-362-7345	369-0440
Herbalife International Inc 1800 Century Park E *Fax: Hum Res ■ TF: 866-866-4744 ■ Web: www.herbalife.com	Los Angeles	CA	90067	310-410-9600	557-3941*
Lehman Sugarfree Confections Inc 4512 Farragut Rd TF: 800-438-3327 ■ Web: www.sugarfree-edas.com	Brooklyn	NY	11203	718-469-3057	469-3060
Medifast Inc 11445 Cronhill Dr AMEX: MED ■ TF: 866-463-3432 ■ Web: www.medifastdiet.com	Owings Mills	MD	21117	410-581-8042	581-8070
Nutrition 21 Inc 4 Manhattanville Rd NASDAQ: NXXI ■ TF: 800-699-3533 ■ Web: www.nutrition21.com	Purchase	NY	10577	914-701-4500	696-0860
Optimal Nutrients Inc 1163 Chess Dr Unit F TF: 800-966-8874 ■ Web: www.optimalnutrients.com	Foster City	CA	94404	650-525-0112	349-1686
PowerBar Inc 2150 Shattuck Ave *Fax Area Code: 866 ■ TF: 800-850-8030 ■ Web: www.powerbar.com	Berkeley	CA	94704	510-843-1330	574-6420*
RC Fine Foods PO Box 236 TF: 800-526-3953 ■ Web: www.rcfinefoods.com	Belle Mead	NJ	08502	908-359-5500	359-6957
Seasons' Enterprises Ltd 1790 W Cortland Ct Suite B PO Box 965 TF: 800-789-0211 ■ Web: www.seasonssnacks.com	Addison	IL	60101	630-628-0211	628-0385
Sigco Sun Products Inc PO Box 331 TF: 800-654-4145 ■ Web: www.sigcosun.com	Breckenridge	MN	56520	218-643-8467	643-4555
Slim-Fast Foods Co 800 Sylvan Ave TF: 877-375-4632 ■ Web: www.slim-fast.com	Englewood Cliffs	NJ	07632	201-567-8000	871-5550
Tahitian Noni International 333 W Riverpark Dr TF: 800-445-2969 ■ Web: www.tahitiannoni.com	Provo	UT	84604	801-431-6000	234-1007
Vitaminerals Inc 1815 Flower St Web: www.vitamineralsinc.com	Glendale	CA	91201	818-500-8718	240-2785
Vitarich Foods Inc 4365 Arnold Ave TF: 800-817-9999 ■ Web: www.vitarichlabs.com	Naples	FL	34104	239-430-2266	430-4930
Weight Watchers Gourmet Food Co 357 6th Ave Heinz 57 Ctr TF: 800-762-0228	Pittsburgh	PA	15222	412-237-5757	237-5291
Worldwide Sport Nutrition 851 Broken Sound Pkwy NW Suite 133 *Fax Area Code: 866 ■ TF: 800-854-5019 ■ Web: www.sportnutrition.com	Boca Raton	FL	33487	561-241-9400	857-6152*
XELR8 Inc DBA XELR8 Holdings Inc 480 S Holly St AMEX: PRH ■ TF: 888-935-7808 ■ Web: www.xelr8.com	Denver	CO	80246	303-316-8577	316-8078

299-12 Fats & Oils - Animal or Marine

Company	City	State	Zip	Phone	Fax
American Proteins Inc 4705 Leland Dr TF: 800-346-7476 ■ Web: www.americanproteins.com	Cumming	GA	30041	770-886-2250	886-2296
Anamax Corp PO Box 10067 Web: www.anamax.com	Green Bay	WI	54307	920-494-5233	494-9141
Baker Commodities Inc 4020 Bandini Blvd TF: 800-427-0696	Los Angeles	CA	90023	323-268-2801	268-5166
Beaufort Fisheries Inc PO Box 240	Beaufort	NC	28516	252-728-3144	728-7992
Carolina By-Products 1309 Industrial Dr TF: 800-476-8675	Fayetteville	NC	28301	910-483-0473	213-1140
Central Bi-Products 590 W Park Rd PO Box 319	Redwood Falls	MN	56283	507-637-2938	637-5409
Coast Packing Co 3275 E Vernon Ave	Los Angeles	CA	90058	323-277-7700	277-7712
Darling International Inc 251 O'Connor Ridge Blvd Suite 300 AMEX: DAR ■ TF: 800-800-4841 ■ Web: www.darlingii.com	Irving	TX	75038	972-717-0300	717-1588
GA Wintzer & Son Co 5 N Blackhoof St PO Box 406 TF: 800-331-1801	Wapakoneta	OH	45895	419-738-3771	
Griffin Industries 4221 Alexandria Pike TF: 800-743-7413 ■ Web: www.griffinind.com	Cold Spring	KY	41076	859-781-2010	572-2575
Griffin Industries Inc 4413 Tanner Church Rd TF: 800-536-3935	Ellenwood	GA	30294	404-363-1320	363-1335
HRR Enterprises 2129 W Pershing Rd	Chicago	IL	60609	773-376-7735	376-7739
Inland Products Inc PO Box 2228	Columbus	OH	43216	614-444-1127	443-5127
Jacob Stern & Sons Inc 1464 E Valley Rd TF: 800-223-7054 ■ Web: www.jacobstern.com	Santa Barbara	CA	93108	805-565-1411	565-1415
Kaluzny Brothers Inc 2324 Mound Rd	Joliet	IL	60436	815-744-1453	729-5078
Modesto Tallow Co 925 Crows Landing Rd	Modesto	CA	95351	209-522-7224	575-0278
National By-Products Inc 907 Walnut St Suite 400 TF: 888-773-5430 ■ Web: www.nationalby-products.com	Des Moines	IA	50309	515-288-2166	288-1007
Neatsfoot Oil Refineries Corp E Ontario & Bath St	Philadelphia	PA	19134	215-739-1291	425-3370
Omega Protein Inc 835-B Pride Dr NYSE: OME ■ Web: www.buyomegaprotein.com	Hammond	LA	70401	985-345-5553	419-2797
San Luis Tallow Co Inc PO Box 3835 TF: 800-281-8660	San Luis Obispo	CA	93403	805-543-8660	
Werner G Smith Inc 1730 Train Ave	Cleveland	OH	44113	216-861-3676	861-3680
Zapata Corp 100 Meridian Ctr Suite 350 NYSE: ZAP ■ Web: www.zapatacorp.com	Rochester	NY	14618	585-242-2000	242-8677

299-13 Fish & Seafood - Canned

Company	City	State	Zip	Phone	Fax
Alyeska Seafoods Inc PO Box 31359	Seattle	WA	98103	206-547-2100	547-1808
Annette Island Packing Co PO Box 10 Web: www.metlakatlaseafood.com	Metlakatla	AK	99926	907-886-4661	886-4660
Appert's Foodservice 900 S Hwy 10 TF: 800-225-3883 ■ Web: www.apperts.com	Saint Cloud	MN	56304	320-251-3200	259-0747
Beaver Street Fisheries Inc 1741 W Beaver St TF: 800-874-6426 ■ Web: www.beaverfish.com	Jacksonville	FL	32209	904-354-8533	
Bumble Bee Seafoods Inc PO Box 85362 TF: 800-800-8572 ■ Web: www.bumblebee.com	San Diego	CA	92186	858-715-4000	560-6045
Cape May Foods Inc 35 Indian Trail Rd TF: 800-922-1141	Burleigh	NJ	08210	609-465-4551	465-3927
Chicken of the Sea International Inc 9330 Scranton Rd Suite 500 TF: 800-456-1511 ■ Web: www.chickenofthesea.com	San Diego	CA	92121	858-558-9662	597-4574
Cossack Caviar Inc PO Box 267 Web: www.cossackcaviar.com	LaConner	WA	98257	360-466-0176	466-1029
DLM Foods LLC 1075 Progress St	Pittsburgh	PA	15212	412-237-5757	
Doxsee Sea Clam Co Inc PO Box 120	Point Lookout	NY	11569	516-432-0529	432-3140
Fishking Alabama Inc PO Box 1068 TF: 800-445-0729	Bayou La Batre	AL	36509	251-824-2118	824-7181
Florida Smoked Fish Div SeaSpecialties Inc 1111 NW 159th Dr TF: 800-654-6682 ■ Web: www.seaspecialties.com	Miami	FL	33169	305-625-5112	625-5528
Hegg & Hegg Elwha Fish Co 801 Marine Dr TF: 800-435-3474 ■ Web: www.elwhafish.com	Port Angeles	WA	98363	360-457-3344	457-1205
High Liner Foods Inc PO Box 839 Web: www.highlinerfoods.com	Portsmouth	NH	03802	603-431-6865	430-9205
Icicle Seafoods Inc 4019 21st Ave W Web: www.icicleseafoods.com	Seattle	WA	98199	206-282-0988	282-7222
Inlet Fish Producers Inc PO Box 114 2000 Columbia St TF: 800-478-9275 ■ Web: www.inletsalmon.com	Kenai	AK	99611	907-283-9275	283-4097
LASCCO (Los Angeles Smoking & Curing Co) PO Box 53236	Los Angeles	CA	90053	213-622-0724	624-2369
Los Angeles Smoking & Curing Co (LASCCO) PO Box 53236	Los Angeles	CA	90053	213-622-0724	624-2369
Nelson Crab Inc PO Box 520 TF: 800-262-0069 ■ Web: www.nelsoncrabonline.com	Tokeland	WA	98590	360-267-2911	267-2921
Noon Hour Food Products Inc 215 N Des Plaines TF Cust Svc: 800-621-6636	Chicago	IL	60661	312-382-1177	382-9420
Overwaitea Food Group 19855 92A Ave TF: 800-242-9229 ■ Web: www.owfg.com	Langley	BC	V1M3B6	604-888-1213	
Pacific Choice Seafoods Co 1 Commercial St	Eureka	CA	95501	707-442-2981	442-2985
Pacific Seafood Co PO Box 97 TF: 800-388-1101 ■ Web: www.pacseafood.com	Clackamas	OR	97015	503-657-1101	
Peter Pan Seafoods Inc 2200 6th Ave Suite 1000 Web: www.ppsf.com	Seattle	WA	98121	206-728-6000	441-9090
Petersburg Fisheries PO Box 1147 Web: www.hookedonfish.com/locations/ptg	Petersburg	AK	99833	907-772-4294	772-4472
Rich-SeaPak Corp PO Box 20670 TF: 800-654-9731 ■ Web: www.seapak.com	Saint Simons Island	GA	31522	912-638-5000	634-3104

Phone Fax
RJ Peacock Canning Co PO Box 189 ... Lubec ME 04652 207-733-5556 733-0936
Robinson Canning Co Inc 129 E Oakridge Pk ... Metairie LA 70005 504-835-1177
Sea Garden Seafoods Inc PO Box 181 ... Meridian GA 31319 912-832-4437 832-6834
Sea Safari Ltd PO Box 369 ... Belhaven NC 27810 252-943-3091 943-3083
Web: www.seasafari.com
SeaSpecialties Inc Florida Smoked Fish Div 1111 NW 159th Dr ... Miami FL 33169 305-625-5112 625-5528
TF: 800-654-6682 ■ *Web:* www.seaspecialties.com
Silver Lining Seafoods Co PO Box 6092 ... Ketchikan AK 99901 907-225-9865 225-3891
Web: www.silverliningseafoods.com
Snow's/Doxsee Inc 994 Ocean Dr ... Cape May NJ 08204 609-884-0440 898-2409
TF: 800-459-0396 ■ *Web:* www.snows.com
Stinson Seafood Co PO Box 69 ... Prospect Harbor ME 04669 207-963-7331 963-4169
Vita Food Products Inc 2222 W Lake St ... Chicago IL 60612 312-738-4500 738-3215
AMEX: VSF ■ *TF:* 800-989-8482 ■ *Web:* www.vitafoodproducts.com
Wards Cove Packing Co PO Box 5030 ... Seattle WA 98105 206-323-3200 323-9165

299-14 Fish & Seafood - Fresh or Frozen

Phone Fax
All Alaskan Seafood Ventures PO Box 601 ... Edmonds WA 98020 206-285-8200 285-2313
American Seafoods International 40 Herman Melville Blvd ... New Bedford MA 02740 508-997-0031 997-5820
TF: 800-343-8046
America's Catch Inc PO Box 584 ... Itta Bena MS 38941 662-254-7207 254-9776
TF: 800-242-0041 ■ *Web:* www.catfish.com
Bama Sea Products 756 28th St S ... Saint Petersburg FL 33712 727-327-3474 322-0580
TF: 800-833-3474 ■ *Web:* www.bamasea.com
Blount Seafood Corp 630 Currant Rd ... Fall River MA 02720 774-888-1300 888-1399
TF: 800-274-2526 ■ *Web:* www.blountseafood.com
Bon Secour Fisheries Inc
17449 County Rd 49 S PO Box 60 ... Bon Secour AL 36511 251-949-7411 949-6478
TF: 800-633-6854 ■ *Web:* www.bonsecourfisheries.com
Chesapeake Fish Co Inc 535 Harbor Ln ... San Diego CA 92101 619-238-0526 238-5592
Web: www.chesapeakefish.com
ConAgra Seafood Cos PO Box 2819 ... Tampa FL 33601 813-241-1500 247-2019
TF: 800-732-3663
ConFish Inc PO Box 271 ... Isola MS 38754 662-962-3101 962-0114
TF: 800-228-3474 ■ *Web:* www.confish.com
Delta Pride Catfish Inc 1301 Industrial Pkwy ... Indianola MS 38751 662-887-5401 887-9083
TF: 800-421-1045 ■ *Web:* www.deltapride.com
Eastern Shore Seafood PO Box 38 ... Mappsville VA 23407 757-824-5651 824-4135
TF Sales: 800-446-8550
Fishermen's Pride Processors DBA Neptune Foods
4510 S Alameda St ... Los Angeles CA 90058 323-232-8300 232-8833
Web: www.neptunefoods.com
Fishking Processors Inc PO Box 21385 ... Market Station CA 90021 213-746-1307 746-5089*
**Fax:* Hum Res ■ *Web:* www.mrsfridays.com
Frog Island Seafood PO Box 2107 ... Elizabeth City NC 27906 252-453-2879 453-4527
Gorton's Inc 128 Rogers St ... Gloucester MA 01930 978-283-3000 281-8295
TF: 800-225-0572 ■ *Web:* www.gortons.com
Graham & Rollins Inc 19 Rudd Ln ... Hampton VA 23669 757-723-3831 722-3762
Gulf City Seafood Inc PO Box 1346 ... Pascagoula MS 39568 228-762-3271 762-3962
TF: 800-666-3300
Iceland Seafood Corp 190 Enterprise Dr ... Newport News VA 23603 757-820-4000 888-6250
Icelandic USA Inc 190 Enterprise Dr ... Newport News VA 23603 757-820-4000 888-6250
Web: www.icelandic.com
Icicle Seafoods Inc 4019 21st Ave W ... Seattle WA 98199 206-282-0988 282-7222
Web: www.icicleseafoods.com
Indian Ridge Shrimp Co 120 Dr Hugh St Martin Rd ... Chauvin LA 70344 985-594-3361 594-9641
King & Prince Seafood Corp 1 King & Prince Blvd ... Brunswick GA 31520 912-265-5155 264-4812
TF: 800-841-0205 ■ *Web:* www.kpseafood.com
Kitchens Seafood 1001 E Baker St ... Plant City FL 33563 813-750-1888 750-1889
TF: 800-327-0132
Martin Brothers Seafood Co Inc PO Box 219 ... Westwego LA 70094 504-341-2251
Matlaw's Food Products Inc 135 Front Ave ... West Haven CT 06516 203-934-5233 933-8506
TF Cust Svc: 800-934-8266
Metompkin Bay Oyster Co PO Box 671 ... Crisfield MD 21817 410-968-0660 968-0670
Web: www.metompkinseafood.com
Morey's Seafood International LLC PO Box 248 ... Motley MN 56466 218-352-6345 352-6523
Web: www.moreys.com
Nanticoke Foods LLC PO Box 70 ... Nanticoke MD 21840 410-873-2811 873-2982
Neptune Foods 4510 S Alameda St ... Los Angeles CA 90058 323-232-8300 232-8833
Web: www.neptunefoods.com
NorQuest Seafoods Inc 5245 Shilshole Ave NW ... Seattle WA 98107 206-281-7022 285-8159
Web: www.norquest.com
Ocean Beauty Seafoods Inc 1100 W Ewing St ... Seattle WA 98119 206-285-6800 285-9190
TF: 800-877-0185 ■ *Web:* www.oceanbeauty.com
Oceantrawl Inc 2223 Alaskan Way Suite 220 ... Seattle WA 98121 206-448-9200 448-5057
Overwaitea Food Group 19855 92A Ave ... Langley BC V1M3B6 604-888-1213
TF: 800-242-9229 ■ *Web:* www.owfg.com
Pacific Coast Seafood Co PO Box 70 ... Warrenton OR 97146 503-861-2201 861-3302*
**Fax:* Acctg
Perona Farms Food Specialties 350 Andover Sparta Rd ... Andover NJ 07821 973-729-7878 729-4424
TF: 800-750-6190 ■ *Web:* www.peronafarms.com
Pinnacle Foods Corp 6 Executive Campus Suite 100 ... Cherry Hill NJ 08002 856-969-7100
TF: 800-486-8816 ■ *Web:* www.pinnaclefoodscorp.com
Riverside Foods Inc 2520 Wilson St ... Two Rivers WI 54241 920-793-4511 794-7332
Sau-Sea Foods Inc 303 S Broadway Suite 224 ... Tarrytown NY 10591 914-631-1717 631-0865
TF: 800-677-0346
Sea Harvest Packing Co PO Box 818 ... Brunswick GA 31521 912-264-3212 264-2749
TF: 800-627-4300 ■ *Web:* www.seaharvest.com
Sea Watch International Ltd 8978 Glebe Pk Dr ... Easton MD 21601 410-822-7500 822-1266
TF: 800-732-2526 ■ *Web:* www.seaclam.com
Seafood Producers Co-op 2875 Roeder Ave ... Bellingham WA 98225 360-733-0120 733-0513
Web: www.spcsales.com
Shemper Seafood Packing Co 367 Bayview Ave ... Biloxi MS 39530 228-435-2703 432-2104
Simmons Farm Raised Catfish Inc 2628 Erickson Rd ... Yazoo City MS 39194 662-746-5687 746-8625
Web: www.simmonscatfish.com
Singleton Seafood Co 5024 Uceta Rd ... Tampa FL 33619 813-241-1500 247-2019
TF: 800-732-3663
Smith Luther & Son Inc PO Box 67 ... Atlantic NC 28511 252-225-3341 225-6391
Stoller Fisheries Inc PO Box B ... Spirit Lake IA 51360 712-336-1750 336-4681
TF: 800-831-5174 ■ *Web:* www.stollerfisheries.com
Tampa Bay Fisheries Inc 3060 Gallagher Rd ... Dover FL 33527 813-752-8883 752-3168
TF: 800-234-2561 ■ *Web:* www.tampabayfisheries.com
Tampa Maid Foods Inc 1600 Kathleen Rd ... Lakeland FL 33805 863-687-4411 683-8713
TF: 800-237-7637 ■ *Web:* www.tampamaid.com
Texas Pack Inc PO Box 1643 ... Port Isabel TX 78578 956-943-5461 943-6630
Thomas Seafood of Carteret Inc 421 Merrimon Rd ... Beaufort NC 28516 252-728-2391 728-6792
Three Star Smoked Fish Co 1300 Factory Pl ... Los Angeles CA 90013 213-624-2101 624-2369
Tichon Seafood Corp 7 Conway St ... New Bedford MA 02740 508-999-5607 990-8271
Trident Seafood Corp 5303 Shilshole Ave NW ... Seattle WA 98107 206-783-3818 782-7195
TF: 800-426-5490 ■ *Web:* www.tridentseafoods.com
UniSea Inc 15400 NE 90th St PO Box 97019 ... Redmond WA 98073 425-881-8181 861-5249
TF: 800-535-8509 ■ *Web:* www.unisea.com
Viking Seafoods Inc 50 Crystal St ... Malden MA 02148 781-324-1050 397-0527
TF: 800-225-3920 ■ *Web:* www.vikingseafoods.com

Phone Fax
Wanchese Fish Co 2000 Northgate Commerce Pkwy ... Suffolk VA 23435 757-673-4500 673-4550
Web: www.wanchese.com
Washington Crab Producers Inc PO Box 1488 ... Westport WA 98595 360-268-9161 268-9410

299-15 Flavoring Extracts & Syrups

Phone Fax
Aroma Tech Inc 130 Industrial Pkwy ... Somerville NJ 08876 908-707-0707 707-1704
TF: 800-542-7662 ■ *Web:* www.aromatec.com
BFI Innovations 420-C Airport Rd ... Elgin IL 60123 847-214-4860 214-4880
TF: 800-323-7009
Brady Enterprises Inc 167 Moore Rd ... East Weymouth MA 02189 781-337-5000 337-9338
TF: 800-225-5126 ■ *Web:* www.brady-ent.com
Cadbury Schweppes Americas Beverages 5301 Legacy Dr ... Plano TX 75024 972-673-7000 673-7980
Web: www.cadburyschweppes.com/EN
Cleveland Syrup Corp 5000 Track Rd PO Box 91959 ... Cleveland OH 44101 216-883-1845 883-6204
David Michael & Co Inc 10801 Decatur Rd ... Philadelphia PA 19154 215-632-3100 637-3920
TF: 800-523-3806 ■ *Web:* www.dmflavors.com
DD Williamson & Co Inc 100 S Spring St ... Louisville KY 40206 502-895-2438
Web: www.caramel.com
Edlong Corp 225 Scott St ... Elk Grove Village IL 60007 847-439-9230 439-0053
TF: 888-698-2783 ■ *Web:* www.edlong.com
Elan Chemical Co 268 Doremus Ave ... Newark NJ 07105 973-344-8014 344-1948
Web: www.elan-chemical.com
Emerald Kalama Chemical LLC 1296 3rd St NW ... Kalama WA 98625 360-673-2550 673-3564
Web: www.emeraldmaterials.com
Ensign-Bickford Industries Inc 100 Grist Mill Rd ... Simsbury CT 06070 860-843-2000 843-1510
TF: 800-828-9814 ■ *Web:* www.ensign-bickfordind.com
Firmenich Inc PO Box 5880 ... Princeton NJ 08543 609-452-1000 452-0564
TF: 800-257-9591 ■ *Web:* www.firmenich.com
Food Producers International
10505 Wayzata Blvd Suite 400 ... Minnetonka MN 55305 952-544-2763
TF: 800-443-1336
Frutarom Corp 9500 Railroad Ave ... North Bergen NJ 07047 201-861-9500 861-9267*
**Fax:* Cust Svc ■ *TF:* 800-526-7147 ■ *Web:* www.frutarom.com
Givaudan Flavors Corp 1199 Edison Dr ... Cincinnati OH 45216 513-948-8000 948-2157*
**Fax:* Cust Svc ■ *TF:* 800-892-1199 ■ *Web:* www.givaudan.com
I Rice & Co Inc 11500 Roosevelt Blvd Bldg D ... Philadelphia PA 19116 215-673-7423 673-2616
TF: 800-232-6022 ■ *Web:* www.iriceco.com
International Flavors & Fragrances Inc 521 W 57th St ... New York NY 10019 212-765-5500 708-7132
NYSE: IFF ■ *Web:* www.iff.com
Jel Sert Co Rt 59 & Conde St PO Box 261 ... West Chicago IL 60186 630-231-7590 231-3993
TF: 800-323-2592 ■ *Web:* www.jelsert.com
Jordan Industries Inc Flavor & Fragrance Group
1751 Lake Cook Rd ArborLake Ctr Suite 550 ... Deerfield IL 60015 847-945-5591 945-3645
Kalsec Inc 300 Turwill Ln PO Box 50511 ... Kalamazoo MI 49005 269-349-9711 382-3060
TF: 800-323-9320 ■ *Web:* www.kalsec.com
Kerry North America 1 Millington Rd ... Beloit WI 53511 608-363-1200
TF: 800-334-4788 ■ *Web:* www.kerryingredients.com
Lemix Inc 400 W Nassau St Suite C ... East Canton OH 44730 330-488-3072 488-3076
Limpert Brothers Inc 202 Northwest Blvd PO Box 1480 ... Vineland NJ 08362 856-691-1353 794-8968
TF: 800-691-1353 ■ *Web:* www.limpertbrothers.com
Lyons Magnus Inc 3158 E Hamilton Ave ... Fresno CA 93702 559-268-5966 233-8249
TF: 800-344-7130 ■ *Web:* www.lyonsmagnus.com
M & F Worldwide Corp 35 E 62nd St ... New York NY 10021 212-572-8600 572-8400
NYSE: MFW ■ *Web:* www.mandfworldwide.com
Mafco Worldwide Corp 3rd St & Jefferson Ave ... Camden NJ 08104 856-964-8840 964-6029
Mastertaste 6133 N River Rd Suite 670 ... Rosemont IL 60018 847-823-9300 823-9301
Web: www.mastertaste.com
McCormick & Co Inc Food Service Div 226 Schilling Cir ... Hunt Valley MD 21031 410-771-7500 771-1111
TF: 800-327-6838 ■ *Web:* www.mccormick.com/foodservice
McCormick & Co Inc McCormick Flavor Div
226 Schilling Cir ... Hunt Valley MD 21031 410-771-7500 771-1111
TF: 800-327-6838 ■ *Web:* www.mccormick.com
McCormick & Co Inc US Consumer Products Div
211 Schilling Cir ... Hunt Valley MD 21031 410-527-6000 771-1111
TF: 800-292-5300 ■ *Web:* www.mccormick.com
Mother Murphy's Labs Inc 2826 S Elm St PO Box 16846 ... Greensboro NC 27416 336-273-1737 273-2615
TF: 800-849-1277 ■ *Web:* www.mothermurphys.com
Nielsen-Massey Vanillas Inc 1550 Shields Dr ... Waukegan IL 60085 847-578-1550 578-1570
TF: 800-525-7873 ■ *Web:* www.nielsenmassey.com
Northwestern Flavors Inc 120 N Aurora St ... West Chicago IL 60185 630-231-6111 876-5042
Nuvex Ingredients Inc 1640 W 1st St PO Box 158 ... Blue Earth MN 56013 507-526-4362 526-2838
Web: www.nuvexingredients.com
Ottens Flavors 7800 Holstein Ave ... Philadelphia PA 19153 215-365-7800 365-7801
TF: 800-523-0767 ■ *Web:* www.ottensflavors.com
Phillips Syrup Corp 28025 Ranney Pkwy ... Westlake OH 44145 440-835-8001 835-1148
Web: www.phillipssyrup.com
Quest International Flavors & Fragrances Inc
10 Painters Mill Rd ... Owings Mills MD 21117 410-363-2550 363-7514
TF: 800-743-1399 ■ *Web:* www.quest.nl
Robertet Flavors Inc 10 Colonial Dr ... Piscataway NJ 08854 732-981-8300 981-1717
Sea Breeze Inc 441 Rt 202 ... Towaco NJ 07082 973-334-7777 334-2617
TF: 800-732-2733 ■ *Web:* www.seabreezesyrups.com
Seco & Golden 100 Dairies of Florida Inc 1600 Essex Ave ... DeLand FL 32724 386-734-3906 738-1378
Web: www.golden100.com
Sensient Technologies Corp 777 E Wisconsin Ave 11th Fl ... Milwaukee WI 53202 414-271-6755 347-4783
NYSE: SXT ■ *TF:* 800-558-9892 ■ *Web:* www.sensient-tech.com
Sethness Products Co 3422 W Touhy Ave ... Lincolnwood IL 60712 847-329-2080 329-2090
TF: 888-772-1880 ■ *Web:* www.sethness.com
Symrise Inc 300 North St ... Teterboro NJ 07608 201-288-3200 288-0843
TF: 800-422-1559 ■ *Web:* www.symrise.com
Tatz William Industries Inc 11 Railroad Pl ... Belleville NJ 07109 973-751-0720 751-0166
United Specialty Food Ingredients Cos 125 Wall St ... Glendale Heights IL 60139 630-671-4300
V & E Kohnstamm Inc 882 3rd Ave ... Brooklyn NY 11232 718-788-6320 768-3978
TF: 800-847-4500
Virginia Dare Extract Co Inc 882 3rd Ave ... Brooklyn NY 11232 718-788-1776 768-3978
TF: 800-847-4500 ■ *Web:* www.virginiadare.com
Western Syrup Co 13766 Milroy Pl ... Santa Fe Springs CA 90670 562-921-4485 921-5170
TF: 800-229-6686
Wild Flavors Inc 1261 Pacific Ave ... Erlanger KY 41018 859-342-3600 342-3736*
**Fax:* Sales ■ *TF:* 888-945-3352 ■ *Web:* www.wildflavors.com
William Tatz Industries Inc 11 Railroad Pl ... Belleville NJ 07109 973-751-0720 751-0166
Williamson DD & Co Inc 100 S Spring St ... Louisville KY 40206 502-895-2438
Web: www.caramel.com
Zink & Triest Co Inc 150 Domorah Dr ... Montgomeryville PA 18936 215-469-1950 469-1951
TF: 800-537-5070

299-16 Flour Mixes & Doughs

Phone Fax
Abitec Corp Inc PO Box 569 ... Columbus OH 43216 614-429-6464 299-8279
TF Sales: 800-555-1255 ■ *Web:* www.abiteccorp.com
Attala Co PO Box 697 ... Kosciusko MS 39090 662-289-3121

Flour Mixes & Doughs (Cont'd)

	City	State	Zip	Phone	Fax
BakeMark Ingredients (East) Inc					
1933 N Meacham Rd Suite 530	Schaumburg	IL	60173	847-925-2100	925-2101
Web: www.bakemark.com					
BakeMark Ingredients (West) Inc 7351 Crider Ave	Pico Rivera	CA	90660	562-949-1054	
Web: www.bakemark.com					
Bake'n Joy Foods Inc 351 Willow St S	North Andover	MA	01845	978-683-1414	683-1713
TF: 800-666-4937 ■ Web: www.bakenjoy.com					
Best Brands Corp 111 Cheshire Ln Suite 100	Minnetonka	MN	55305	952-404-7500	404-7501
TF: 800-328-2068 ■ Web: www.bestbrandscorp.com					
Betty Crocker 1 General Mills Blvd	Minneapolis	MN	55426	763-764-7600	764-3232*
*Fax: PR ■ Web: www.bettycrocker.com					
Caravan Products Co Inc 100 Adams Dr	Totowa	NJ	07512	973-256-8886	256-8395
TF: 800-526-5261 ■ Web: www.caravanproducts.com					
Cereal Food Processors Inc					
2001 Shawnee Mission Pkwy	Mission Woods	KS	66205	913-890-6300	890-6382
TF: 800-743-5687 ■ Web: www.cerealfood.com					
Champion Foods LLC 23900 Bell Rd	New Boston	MI	48164	734-753-3663	753-5366
Web: www.championfoods.com					
Continental Mills Inc PO Box 88176	Seattle	WA	98138	253-872-8400	872-7954
TF: 800-457-7744 ■ Web: www.continentalmills.com					
Dawn Food Products Inc 2021 Micor Dr	Jackson	MI	49203	517-789-4400	789-4465
TF: 800-248-1144 ■ Web: www.dawnfoods.com					
General Mills Inc International Foods Div					
1 General Mills Blvd	Minneapolis	MN	55426	763-764-7600	764-3232
TF: 800-328-1144 ■ Web: www.generalmills.com					
Gilster-Mary Lee Corp 1037 State St	Chester	IL	62233	618-826-2361	826-2973
TF: 800-851-5371					
HC Brill Co Inc 1912 Montreal Rd	Tucker	GA	30084	770-938-3823	939-2934
Web: www.hcbrill.com					
Langlois Co 10810 San Sevaine Way	Mira Loma	CA	91752	951-360-3900	360-3465
TF: 800-962-5993					
Modern Products Inc PO Box 248	Thiensville	WI	53092	262-242-2400	242-2751
Pinnacle Foods Corp 6 Executive Campus Suite 100	Cherry Hill	NJ	08002	856-969-7100	
TF: 800-486-8816 ■ Web: www.pinnaclefoodscorp.com					
Puratos Corp 1941 Old Cuthbert Rd	Cherry Hill	NJ	08034	856-428-4300	428-2939
TF: 800-654-0036 ■ Web: www.puratos.com					
Rhodes International Inc PO Box 25487	Salt Lake City	UT	84125	801-972-0122	972-0286
TF: 800-876-7333 ■ Web: www.rhodesbread.com					
Roman Meal Co 2101 S Tacoma Way	Tacoma	WA	98409	253-475-0964	475-1906
TF: 800-426-3600 ■ Web: www.romanmeal.com					
Southern Maid Donut Flour Co 3615 Cavalier Dr	Garland	TX	75042	972-272-6425	276-3549
TF: 800-936-6887 ■ Web: www.southernmaiddonuts.com					
Subco Foods Inc 4350 S Taylor Dr	Sheboygan	WI	53081	920-457-7761	457-3899
TF: 800-473-0757 ■ Web: www.subcofoods.com					

299-17 Food Emulsifiers

	City	State	Zip	Phone	Fax
ADM Arkady Products 100 Paniplus Rd	Olathe	KS	66061	913-782-8800	782-1792*
*Fax: Cust Svc ■ TF: 800-255-6637 ■ Web: food.admworld.com					
ADM Oil Refinery 1940 E Hull Ave	Des Moines	IA	50316	515-263-2112	263-2110
TF: 800-637-5843					
ADM Specialty Food Ingredients Div 4666 E Faries Pkwy	Decatur	IL	62526	217-424-5200	424-4702
Web: www.admworld.com					
American Casein Co 109 Elbow Ln	Burlington	NJ	08016	609-387-3130	387-7204
TF: 800-699-6455 ■ Web: www.americancasein.com					
American Ingredients Co 3947 Broadway	Kansas City	MO	64111	816-561-9050	561-9909
TF: 800-669-4092 ■ Web: www.americaningredients.com					
American Lecithin Co Inc 115 Hurley Rd Unit 2B	Oxford	CT	06478	203-262-7100	262-7101
TF: 800-364-4416 ■ Web: www.americanlecithin.com					
Bunge Ltd 50 Main St 6th Fl	White Plains	NY	10606	914-684-2800	684-3499
NYSE: BG ■ Web: www.bunge.com					
Crest Foods Co Inc PO Box 371	Ashton	IL	61006	815-453-7411	453-7744
Web: www.crestfoods.com					
Frutarom Corp 9500 Railroad Ave	North Bergen	NJ	07047	201-861-9500	861-9267*
*Fax: Cust Svc ■ TF: 800-526-7147 ■ Web: www.frutarom.com					
Honeymead Products Co PO Box 3247	Mankato	MN	56002	507-625-7911	345-2254
TF: 800-328-3445					
Lonza Inc 90 Boroline Rd	Allendale	NJ	07401	201-316-9200	785-9989*
*Fax: Cust Svc ■ TF Cust Svc: 800-631-3647 ■ Web: www.lonzagroup.com					

299-18 Fruits & Vegetables - Dried or Dehydrated

	City	State	Zip	Phone	Fax
Basic American Foods 2999 Oak Rd Suite 100	Walnut Creek	CA	94597	925-472-4000	472-4360*
*Fax: Mktg ■ TF: 800-227-4050 ■ Web: www.baf.com					
Bernard Food Industries Inc 1125 Hartrey Ave	Evanston	IL	60204	847-869-5222	962-1546*
*Fax Area Code: 800 ■ TF: 800-323-3663 ■ Web: www.bernardfoods.com					
Betty Crocker 1 General Mills Blvd	Minneapolis	MN	55426	763-764-7600	764-3232*
*Fax: PR ■ Web: www.bettycrocker.com					
ConAgra Store Brands 21340 Hayes Ave	Lakeville	MN	55044	952-469-4971	469-5550
Concord Foods Inc 10 Minuteman Way	Brockton	MA	02301	508-580-1700	584-9425
Web: www.concordfoods.com					
Crystals International Inc 600 W ML King Jr Blvd	Plant City	FL	33563	813-754-2691	757-6448
TF: 800-237-7620 ■ Web: www.crystals-inc.com					
Custom Culinary 2021 West Dr	Oakbrook	IL	60532	630-928-4880	928-4899
TF Cust Svc: 800-621-8827 ■ Web: www.customculinary.com					
Dean Distributors Inc 1350 Bayshore Hwy Suite 400	Burlingame	CA	94010	650-340-1738	928-2090*
*Fax Area Code: 800 ■ TF: 800-792-0816 ■ Web: www.deandistributors.com					
Del Monte Foods Co					
The Landmark @ 1 Market PO Box 193575	San Francisco	CA	94105	415-247-3000	247-3565
NYSE: DLM ■ TF Cust Svc: 800-543-3090 ■ Web: www.delmonte.com					
Fantastic Foods Inc 580 Gateway Dr	Napa	CA	94558	707-254-3700	254-0742
Web: www.fantasticfoods.com					
Garry Packing Inc PO Box 249	Del Rey	CA	93616	559-888-2126	888-2848
TF: 800-248-2126 ■ Web: www.garryscountrystore.com					
Graceland Fruit Inc 1123 Main St	Frankfort	MI	49635	231-352-7181	352-4711
TF: 800-352-7181 ■ Web: www.gracelandfruit.com					
Halben Food Mfg Co Inc 4553 Gustine Ave	Saint Louis	MO	63116	314-832-1906	832-4668
Idaho Fresh-Pak Inc DBA Idahoan Foods					
529 N 3500 East PO Box 130	Lewisville	ID	83431	208-754-4686	754-0094
TF: 800-635-6100 ■ Web: www.idahoan.com					
Idaho-Pacific Corp PO Box 478	Ririe	ID	83443	208-538-6971	538-5082
TF Sales: 800-238-5503 ■ Web: www.idahopacific.com					
Idaho Supreme Potatoes Inc 614 E 800 North PO Box 246	Firth	ID	83236	208-346-6841	346-4104
Lamanuzzi & Pantaleo Inc 11767 Rd 27 1/2	Madera	CA	93637	559-432-3844	299-5902
Larsen Farms 2650 N 2375 E	Hamer	ID	83425	208-662-5501	662-5568
Web: www.larsenfarms.com					
Lipton Co 800 Sylvan Ave	Englewood Cliffs	NJ	07632	201-567-8000	871-8198*
*Fax: Hum Res ■ Web: www.lipton.com					
Meridian Foods PO Box 155	Eaton	IN	47338	765-396-3344	396-3430
MicroSoy Corp 300 E MicroSoy Dr	Jefferson	IA	50129	515-386-2100	386-3287
Web: www.microsoyflakes.com					
National Raisin Co PO Box 219	Fowler	CA	93625	559-834-5981	834-1055
TF: 800-874-3726 ■ Web: www.nationalraisin.com					
Nonpareil Corp 40 N 400 W	Blackfoot	ID	83221	208-785-5880	785-3656
TF: 800-522-2223 ■ Web: www.nonparl.com					
Northwest Pea & Bean Co Inc 6109 E Desmet Ave	Spokane	WA	99212	509-534-3821	534-4350
Oregon Freeze Dry Inc PO Box 1048	Albany	OR	97321	541-926-6001	967-6527
TF: 800-547-4060 ■ Web: www.ofd.com					
Quest International Fruit & Vegetable Products PO Box 157	Silverton	OR	97381	503-873-3600	873-7807
Sensient Dehydrated Flavors PO Box 1524	Turlock	CA	95381	209-667-2777	634-6235
Small Planet Foods Inc 719 Metcalf St	Sedro Woolley	WA	98284	360-855-0100	855-0444
TF: 800-624-4123 ■ Web: www.smallplanetfoods.com					
Stapleton-Spence Packing Co 1530 The Alameda Suite 320	San Jose	CA	95126	408-297-8815	297-0611
TF: 800-297-8815 ■ Web: www.stapleton-spence.com					
Sun-Maid Growers of California 13525 S Bethel Ave	Kingsburg	CA	93631	559-896-8000	897-2362
TF Sales: 800-272-4746 ■ Web: www.sun-maid.com					
Sunsweet Growers Inc 901 N Walton Ave	Yuba City	CA	95993	530-674-5010	751-5238
TF: 800-417-2253 ■ Web: www.sunsweet.com					
Tree Top Inc 220 E 2nd Ave	Selah	WA	98942	509-697-7251	697-0421
TF: 800-237-0515 ■ Web: www.treetop.com					
Tule River Co-op Dryer Inc 16548 Rd 168 PO Box 4477	Woodville	CA	93258	559-784-3396	686-8061
Unilever Bestfoods North America 800 Sylvan Ave	Englewood Cliffs	NJ	07632	201-894-4000	
Web: www.bestfoods.com					
Victor Packing Inc 11687 Rd 27 1/2	Madera	CA	93637	559-673-5908	673-4225
Web: www.victorpacking.com					
Winnemucca Farms Inc 1 Potato Pl	Winnemucca	NV	89445	775-623-2900	623-3310
Zoria Farms Inc 3487 McKee Rd Suite 54	San Jose	CA	95127	408-258-2900	258-0117
Web: www.zoria.com					

299-19 Fruits & Vegetables - Pickled

	City	State	Zip	Phone	Fax
B & G Foods Inc 4 Gatehall Dr Suite 110	Parsippany	NJ	07054	973-401-6500	630-6553
AMEX: BGF ■ Web: www.bgfoods.com					
Baumer Foods Inc 2424 Edenborn Ave Suite 510	Metairie	LA	70001	504-482-5761	483-2425
TF Sales: 800-222-0694 ■ Web: www.baumerfoods.com					
Bay Valley Foods 857 School Pl	Green Bay	WI	54303	920-497-7131	497-4604
TF: 800-558-4700 ■ Web: www.bayvalleyfoods.com					
Bay View Food Products Inc 2606 N Huron Rd	Pinconning	MI	48650	989-879-3555	879-2659
Web: www.bayviewfoods.com					
Beaverton Foods Inc PO Box 687	Beaverton	OR	97075	503-646-8138	644-9204
TF: 800-223-8076 ■ Web: www.beavertonfoods.com					
Cain's Foods Inc 114 E Main St PO Box 347	Ayer	MA	01432	978-772-0300	772-9254
TF: 800-225-0601 ■ Web: www.cainsfoods.com					
Cajun Chef Products Inc PO Box 248	Saint Martinville	LA	70582	337-394-7112	394-7115
Claussen Pickle Co 1300 Claussen Dr	Woodstock	IL	60098	815-338-7000	338-9244
TF: 800-435-2817					
Clorox Co 1221 Broadway	Oakland	CA	94612	510-271-7000	832-1463
NYSE: CLX ■ TF Cust Svc: 800-292-2808 ■ Web: www.thecloroxcompany.com					
ConAgra Foods Retail Products Co Grocery Foods Group					
3353 Michelson Dr	Irvine	CA	92612	949-437-1000	437-3342
Conway Import Co Inc 11051 West Addison St	Franklin Park	IL	60131	847-455-5600	455-5630
TF: 800-323-8801					
Daltons Best Maid Products Inc 1400 S Riverside Dr	Fort Worth	TX	76104	817-335-5494	534-7117
TF: 800-447-3581 ■ Web: www.bestmaidproducts.com					
Eastern Foods Inc 1000 Naturally Fresh Blvd	Atlanta	GA	30349	404-765-9000	765-9016*
*Fax: Hum Res ■ TF: 800-765-1950 ■ Web: www.naturallyfresh.com					
Gedney MA Co 2100 Stoughton Ave	Chaska	MN	55318	952-448-2612	448-1790
Web: www.gedneypickle.com					
Gold Pure Food Products Inc 1 Brooklyn Rd	Hempstead	NY	11550	516-483-5600	483-5798
TF: 800-422-4681 ■ Web: www.goldshorseradish.com					
Great Lakes Kraut Co 400 Clark St	Bear Creek	WI	54922	715-752-4105	752-3432
Web: www.krispkraut.com					
Green Garden Food Products Inc 5851 S 194th St	Kent	WA	98032	253-395-4460	395-0408
Web: www.ggfoods.com					
Henri's Food Products Co Inc 8622 N 87th St	Milwaukee	WI	53224	414-365-5720	354-3958
TF Cust Svc: 800-338-8831					
Hudson Cos 101 Hudson St	Troy	AL	36079	334-566-6274	670-0116
HV Food Products Co PO Box 24305	Oakland	CA	94623	510-271-7000	832-1463
Web: www.hiddenvalley.com					
JG Van Holten & Son Inc 703 W Madison St PO Box 66	Waterloo	WI	53594	920-478-2144	478-2316
Web: www.vanholtenpickles.com					
Kaplan & Zubrin Inc PO Box 1006	Camden	NJ	08101	856-964-1083	964-0510
Ken's Foods Inc 1 D'Angelo Dr	Marlborough	MA	01752	508-485-7540	485-6882
TF: 800-633-5800 ■ Web: www.kensfoods.com					
Kikkoman Foods Inc N 1365 6th Corners Rd PO Box 69	Walworth	WI	53184	262-275-6181	275-9452
Web: www.kikkoman.com					
Kruger Foods Inc 18362 E Hwy 4	Stockton	CA	95215	209-941-8518	941-0345
Web: www.krugerfoods.com					
KT's Kitchens Inc 1065 E Walnut St	Carson	CA	90746	310-764-0850	764-0855
Langlois Co 10810 San Sevaine Way	Mira Loma	CA	91752	951-360-3900	360-3465
TF: 800-962-5993					
Lawry's Foods Inc 222 E Huntington Dr	Monrovia	CA	91016	800-952-9797	
Web: www.lawrys.com					
Lee Kum Kee Inc 14841 don Julian Rd	City of Industry	CA	91746	626-709-1888	709-1899
TF Orders: 800-654-5082 ■ Web: home.lkk.com					
Litehouse Inc 1109 N Ella Ave	Sandpoint	ID	83864	208-263-7569	263-7821
TF: 800-669-3169 ■ Web: www.litehousefoods.com					
MA Gedney Co 2100 Stoughton Ave	Chaska	MN	55318	952-448-2612	448-1790
Web: www.gedneypickle.com					
Marzetti T Co 1105 Schrock Rd Suite 300	Columbus	OH	43229	614-846-2232	848-8330
Web: www.marzetti.com					
Maurice's Gourmet Barbeque PO Box 6847	West Columbia	SC	29171	803-791-5887	791-8707
TF: 800-628-7423 ■ Web: www.mauricesbbq.com					
McCormick & Co Inc McCormick Flavor Div					
226 Schilling Cir	Hunt Valley	MD	21031	410-771-7500	771-1111
TF: 800-327-6838 ■ Web: www.mccormick.com					
McIlhenny Co Hwy 329	Avery Island	LA	70513	337-365-8173	365-9613
TF Orders: 800-634-9599 ■ Web: www.tabasco.com					
Moody Dunbar Inc 2000 Waters Edge Dr Suite 21	Johnson City	TN	37604	423-952-0100	952-0289
TF: 800-251-8202					
Morehouse Foods Inc 760 Epperson Dr	City of Industry	CA	91748	626-854-1655	854-1656
TF: 888-297-9800 ■ Web: www.morehousefoods.com					
Mount Olive Pickle Co PO Box 609	Mount Olive	NC	28365	919-658-2535	658-6296
TF: 800-672-5041 ■ Web: www.mtolivepickles.com					
Mullins Food Products Inc 2200 S 25th Ave	Broadview	IL	60155	708-344-3224	344-0153
Web: www.mullinsfood.com					
Musco Olive Products Inc 17950 Via Nicolo	Tracy	CA	95377	209-836-4600	836-0518
TF: 800-523-9828					
Newman's Own Inc 246 Post Rd E	Westport	CT	06880	203-222-0136	
Web: www.newmansown.com					
NORPAC Foods Inc 930 W Washington St	Stayton	OR	97383	503-769-2101	769-1273
TF Sales: 800-733-9311 ■ Web: www.norpac.com					
Old Dutch Mustard Co 98 Cutter Mill Rd	Great Neck	NY	11021	516-466-0522	466-0762

				Phone	Fax
Olds Products Co 10700 88th Ave	Pleasant Prairie	WI	53158	262-947-3500	947-3517
TF: 800-233-8064					
Pacific Choice Brands Inc 4667 E Date Ave	Fresno	CA	93725	559-237-5583	237-2078
Web: www.pacificchoicebrands.com					
Pfiffer Foods Div T Marzetti Co 683 Lake St	Wilson	NY	14172	716-751-9371	751-6218
Piknik Products Co Inc 3806 Day St	Montgomery	AL	36108	334-265-1567	265-9490
TF Cust Svc: 800-300-8557 ■ *Web:* www.piknikproducts.com					
Plochman Inc 1333 Boudreau Rd	Manteno	IL	60950	815-468-3434	468-8755
Web: www.plochman.com					
Portion Pac Inc 7325 Snider Rd	Mason	OH	45040	513-398-0400	459-5309
TF: 800-232-4829 ■ *Web:* www.portionpac.com					
Ralph Sechler & Son Inc 5686 State Rd 1	Saint Joe	IN	46785	260-337-5461	337-5771
TF: 800-332-5461 ■ *Web:* www.sechlerspickles.com					
Reckitt Benckiser Inc 399 Interpace Pkwy PO Box 225	Parsippany	NJ	07054	973-404-2600	404-5700
TF Cust Svc: 800-333-3899 ■ *Web:* www.reckitt.com					
Reily William B & Co Inc 640 Magazine St	New Orleans	LA	70130	504-524-6131	539-5427
TF: 800-535-1961					
Richelieu Group Inc 25 Braintree Hill Office Pk Suite 405	Braintree	MA	02184	781-848-1110	848-1112
Web: www.richelieufoods.com					
Sechler Ralph & Son Inc 5686 State Rd 1	Saint Joe	IN	46785	260-337-5461	337-5771
TF: 800-332-5461 ■ *Web:* www.sechlerspickles.com					
Spectrum Organic Products Inc 5341 Old Redwood Hwy	Petaluma	CA	94954	707-778-8900	765-8470
TF: 800-995-2705 ■ *Web:* www.spectrumnaturals.com					
Spring Glen Fresh Foods Inc 314 Spring Glen Dr PO Box 518	Ephrata	PA	17522	717-733-2201	738-4335
TF: 800-641-2853 ■ *Web:* www.springglen.com					
Swanson Pickle Co Inc 11561 Heights Ravenna Rd	Ravenna	MI	49451	231-853-2289	853-6281
T Marzetti Co 1105 Schrock Rd Suite 300	Columbus	OH	43229	614-846-2232	848-8330
Web: www.marzetti.com					
T Marzetti Co Pfiffer Foods Div 683 Lake St	Wilson	NY	14172	716-751-9371	751-6218
Thor-Shackel Horseradish Co 16 W 224th Shore Ct	Burr Ridge	IL	60527	630-986-1333	986-0125
TF: 800-951-9696					
TODDS Enterprises Inc 610 S 56th Ave	Phoenix	AZ	85043	602-484-9584	484-9585
TF: 800-242-7687 ■ *Web:* www.toddsfoods.com					
Tulkoff Products Co Inc 1101 S Conkling St	Baltimore	MD	21224	410-327-6585	327-7033
TF: 800-638-7343 ■ *Web:* www.tulkoff.com					
Van Holten JG & Son Inc 703 W Madison St PO Box 66	Waterloo	WI	53594	920-478-2144	478-2316
Web: www.vanholtenpickles.com					
Van Law Food Products Inc PO Box 2388	Fullerton	CA	92837	714-870-9091	870-5609
Victoria Packing Corp 443 E 100th St	Brooklyn	NY	11236	718-927-3000	649-7069
Web: www.victoriapacking.com					
Walden Farms 1209 W St Georges Ave	Linden	NJ	07036	908-925-9494	925-9537
TF: 800-229-1706 ■ *Web:* www.waldenfarms.com					
William B Reily & Co Inc 640 Magazine St	New Orleans	LA	70130	504-524-6131	539-5427
TF: 800-535-1961					
Yamasa Corp USA 3500 Fairview Industrial Dr SE	Salem	OR	97302	503-363-8550	363-8710
Web: www.yamasausa.com					

299-20 Fruits, Vegetables, Juices - Canned or Preserved

				Phone	Fax
All Juice Food & Beverage Corp 352 Jett St	Hendersonville	NC	28792	828-685-8821	685-8495
TF: 800-232-8717					
Allen Canning Co 305 E Main St	Siloam Springs	AR	72761	479-524-6431	524-3291
TF: 800-234-2553 ■ *Web:* www.allencanning.com					
AM Braswell Jr Food Co Inc 226 N Zetterower Ave	Statesboro	GA	30458	912-764-6191	489-1572
TF: 800-673-9388 ■ *Web:* www.braswells.com					
American Spoon Foods Inc 1668 Clarion Ave	Petoskey	MI	49770	231-347-9030	347-2512
TF: 800-222-5886 ■ *Web:* www.spoon.com					
Apple & Eve Inc 2 Seaview Blvd	Port Washington	NY	11050	516-621-1122	625-9474
TF: 800-969-8018 ■ *Web:* www.appleandeve.com					
Ardmore Farms Inc 1915 N Woodland Blvd	DeLand	FL	32720	386-734-4634	736-8894
TF: 800-365-8423 ■ *Web:* www.juice4u.com					
Authentic Specialty Foods Inc 4340 Eucalyptus Ave	Chino	CA	91710	909-631-2000	636-2100
TF: 888-236-2272 ■ *Web:* www.asf-inc.com					
B & G Foods Inc 4 Gatehall Dr Suite 110	Parsippany	NJ	07054	973-401-6500	630-6553
AMEX: BGF ■ *Web:* www.bgfoods.com					
Baumer Foods Inc 2424 Edenborn Ave Suite 510	Metairie	LA	70001	504-482-5761	483-2425
TF Sales: 800-222-0694 ■ *Web:* www.baumerfoods.com					
Beckman & Gast Co Inc					
282 W Kremer-Hoying Rd PO Box 307	Saint Henry	OH	45883	419-678-4195	
Web: www.beckmangast.com					
Bell-Carter Foods Inc 3742 Mount Diablo Blvd	Lafayette	CA	94549	925-284-5933	284-2377
TF: 000 252 0557					
Birds Eye Foods Inc 90 Linden Oaks	Rochester	NY	14625	585-383-1850	385-2857
TF: 800-999-5044 ■ *Web:* www.birdseyefoods.com					
Bonduelle Inc 8615 Saint-Laurent Blvd Suite 200	Montreal	QC	H2P2M9	514-384-4281	384-7992
Web: www.bonduelle.ca					
Braswell AM Jr Food Co 226 N Zetterower Ave	Statesboro	GA	30458	912-764-6191	489-1572
TF: 800-673-9388 ■ *Web:* www.braswells.com					
Brooklyn Bottling Co 143 South Rd PO Box 808	Milton	NY	12547	845-795-2171	795-2589
Bruce Foods Corp PO Drawer 1030	New Iberia	LA	70562	337-365-8101	364-3742
TF: 800-299-9082 ■ *Web:* www.brucefoods.com					
Burnette Foods Inc 701 US 31 PO Box 128	Elk Rapids	MI	49629	231-264-8116	264-9597
Web: www.burnettefoods.com					
Bush Brothers & Co 1016 E Weisgarber Rd	Knoxville	TN	37909	865-588-7685	584-8157
Web: www.bushbeans.com					
California Fruit & Tomato Kitchen					
2906 Santa Fe St PO Box 827	Riverbank	CA	95367	209-869-9300	869-9060
Web: www.calfruittom.com					
Campbell Soup Co 1 Campbell Pl	Camden	NJ	08103	856-342-4800	342-3878
NYSE: CPB ■ *TF:* 800-772-8467					
Cargill Foods 15407 McGinty Rd	Wayzata	MN	55391	952-742-7575	
TF: 800-227-4455 ■ *Web:* www.cargillfoods.com					
Cargill Inc North America 15407 McGinty Rd	Wayzata	MN	55391	952-742-7575	
TF: 800-227-4455					
Carriage House Cos Inc 196 Newton St	Fredonia	NY	14063	716-673-1000	673-8443*
*Fax: Sales ■ *TF:* 800-828-8915 ■ *Web:* www.carriagehousecos.com					
Cascadian Farm Inc 719 Metcalf St	Sedro Woolley	WA	98284	360-855-0100	855-0444
TF: 800-624-4123 ■ *Web:* www.cascadianfarm.com					
Centennial Specialty Foods Corp					
10700 E Geddes Ave Suite 170	Centennial	CO	80112	303-292-4018	292-4364
Web: www.centennialspecialtyfoods.com					
Cherry Growers Inc 6331 US 31 S PO Box 90	Grawn	MI	49637	231-276-9241	276-7075
Web: www.cherrygrowers.net					
Cincinnati Preserving Co Inc 3015 E Kemper Rd	Sharonville	OH	45241	513-771-2000	771-8381
TF: 800-222-9966					
Clement Pappas & Co Inc 1010 N Parsonage Rd	Seabrook	NJ	08302	856-455-1000	455-8746
TF: 800-257-7019 ■ *Web:* www.clementpappas.com					
Cliffstar Corp 1 Cliffstar Ave	Dunkirk	NY	14048	716-366-6100	366-6161
TF: 800-777-2389 ■ *Web:* www.cliffstar.com					
ConAgra Foods Retail Products Co Grocery Foods Group					
3353 Michelson Dr	Irvine	CA	92612	949-437-1000	437-3342
ConAgra Hunt-Wesson Foodservice Co 3353 Michelson Dr	Irvine	CA	92612	949-437-1000	
TF: 800-633-0112 ■ *Web:* www.conagrafoodservice.com					
Country Pure Foods Inc 681 W Waterloo Rd	Akron	OH	44314	330-753-2293	745-7838
Web: www.countrypurefoods.com					
Daily Juice Products 1 Daily Way	Verona	PA	15147	412-828-9020	828-8876
TF: 800-245-2929					
Del Monte Foods Co					
The Landmark @ 1 Market PO Box 193575	San Francisco	CA	94105	415-247-3000	247-3565
NYSE: DLM ■ *TF Cust Svc:* 800-543-3090 ■ *Web:* www.delmonte.com					
Del Monte Fresh Produce Co 241 Sevilla Ave	Coral Gables	FL	33134	305-520-8400	520-8455
Web: www.freshdelmonte.com					
Diana Fruit Co Inc 651 Mathew St	Santa Clara	CA	95050	408-727-9631	727-9890
Web: www.dianafruit.com					
Dole Packaged Foods Co 1 Dole Dr	Westlake Village	CA	91362	818-874-4000	874-4893
Don Pepino Sales Co 123 Railroad Ave	Williamstown	NJ	08094	856-629-7429	629-6340
Web: www.donpepino.com					
ED Smith & Sons Ltd 944 Hwy 8	Winona	ON	L8E5S3	905-643-1211	643-3328
TF: 800-263-9246 ■ *Web:* www.edsmith.com					
Escalon Premier Brands 1905 McHenry Ave	Escalon	CA	95320	209-838-7341	838-6785
TF: 800-343-9556 ■ *Web:* www.escalon.net					
Faribault Foods Inc 222 S 9th St Suite 3380	Minneapolis	MN	55402	612-333-6461	342-2908
Web: www.faribaultfoods.com					
Fremont Co 802 N Front St	Fremont	OH	43420	419-334-8995	334-8120
Friel's Inc 100 Friel Pl	Queenstown	MD	21658	410-827-8811	827-9472
TF: 800-739-2676					
Furmano Foods Inc 770 Cannery Rd PO Box 500	Northumberland	PA	17857	570-473-3516	473-7367
TF: 877-877-6032 ■ *Web:* www.furmanos.com					
Garner TW Food Co 4045 Indiana Ave PO Box 4239	Winston-Salem	NC	27115	336-661-1550	661-1901
Web: www.texaspete.com					
Giorgio Foods Inc 1161 Park Rd	Blandon	PA	19510	610-926-2139	926-7012
TF: 800-220-2139 ■ *Web:* www.giorgiofoods.com					
Gray & Co 2331 23rd Ave	Forest Grove	OR	97116	503-357-3141	357-8837
TF: 800-333-8876 ■ *Web:* www.cherryman.com					
Growers Co-op Grape Juice Co Inc					
112 N Portage St PO Box 399	Westfield	NY	14787	716-326-3161	326-6566
Web: www.concordgrapejuice.com					
Hanover Foods Corp 1550 York St PO Box 334	Hanover	PA	17331	717-632-6000	632-6681
TF: 800-888-4646 ■ *Web:* www.hanoverfoods.com					
Hawaiian Sun Products Inc 259 Sand Island Access Rd	Honolulu	HI	96819	808-845-3211	842-0532
Web: www.hawaiiansunproducts.com					
Heinz North America 357 6th Ave Heinz 57 Center	Pittsburgh	PA	15222	412-237-5757	237-5377
Hi-Country Foods Corp 1 Railroad Ave PO Box 338	Selah	WA	98942	509-697-7292	697-3498
Hirzel Canning Co Inc 411 Lemoyne Rd	Northwood	OH	43619	419-693-0531	693-4859
TF: 800-837-1631 ■ *Web:* www.hirzel.com					
HJ Heinz Co 600 Grant St	Pittsburgh	PA	15219	412-456-5700	456-6128
NYSE: HNZ ■ *TF:* 800-255-5750 ■ *Web:* www.heinz.com					
Home Juice Co 2000 N 15th Ave	Melrose Park	IL	60160	708-345-3350	345-3361
HR Nicholson Co 1332 Londontown Blvd	Saint James	MD	21781	410-764-2323	764-9125
TF Cust Svc: 800-638-3514 ■ *Web:* www.hrnicholson.com					
Independent Food Processors					
303 E 'D' St Suite 5 PO Box 1588	Yakima	WA	98907	509-457-6487	457-7983
Indian Summer Co-op 3958 W Chauvez Rd	Ludington	MI	49431	231-845-6248	843-9453*
*Fax: Sales					
Ingomar Packing Co 9950 S Ingomar Grade PO Box 1448	Los Banos	CA	93635	209-826-9494	854-6292
Web: www.ingomarpacking.com					
International Juice Concentrates Inc 625 W Anaheim St	Long Beach	CA	90813	562-599-5831	599-5107
Web: intljuice.com					
Jasper Wyman & Son PO Box 100	Milbridge	ME	04658	207-546-2311	546-2074
TF: 800-341-1758 ■ *Web:* www.wymans.com					
JM Smucker Co 1 Strawberry Ln	Orrville	OH	44667	330-682-3000	684-6410
NYSE: SJM ■ *TF:* 800-553-0952 ■ *Web:* www.smucker.com					
JM Smucker Pennsylvania Inc 300 Keck Ave	New Bethlehem	PA	16242	814-275-1323	275-1340
Johanna Foods Inc 20 Johanna Farm Rd	Flemington	NJ	08822	908-788-2200	788-2200
TF: 800-727-6700 ■ *Web:* www.johannafoods.com					
Juice Bowl Products Inc 2090 Bartow Rd	Lakeland	FL	33802	863-665-5515	667-7137
Knouse Foods Co-op Inc 800 Peach Glen-Idaville Rd	Peach Glen	PA	17375	717-677-8181	677-7069
TF: 800-827-7537 ■ *Web:* www.knouse.com					
Lakeside Foods Inc PO Box 1327	Manitowoc	WI	54221	920-684-3356	686-4033
Web: www.lakesidefoods.com					
Langers Juice Co Inc 16195 Stephens St	City of Industry	CA	91745	626-336-1666	961-2021
Web: www.langers.com					
Lawrence Foods Inc 2200 Lunt Ave	Elk Grove Village	IL	60007	847-437-2400	437-2567
TF: 800-323-7848 ■ *Web:* www.lawrencefoods.com					
Leelanau Fruit Co 2900 SW Bayshore Dr	Suttons Bay	MI	49682	231-271-3514	271-4367
TF: 800-431-0718 ■ *Web:* www.leelanaufruit.com					
LiDestri Foods Inc 815 Whitney Rd W	Fairport	NY	14450	585-377-7700	377-8150
TF: 800-397-5222					
Litehouse Chadalee Farms Inc 1400 Foreman Rd	Lowell	MI	49331	616-897-5911	897-6720
Louis Dreyfus Group 20 Westport Rd	Wilton	CT	06897	203-761-2000	761-2375
Web: www.louisdreyfus.com					
Louis Maull Co 219 N Market St	Saint Louis	MO	63102	314-241-8410	
Web: www.maull.com					
Luigino's Inc 525 S Lake Ave	Duluth	MN	55802	218-723-5555	723-8356
TF: 800-521-1281 ■ *Web:* www.michelinas.com					
Lyons Magnus Inc 3158 E Hamilton Ave	Fresno	CA	93702	559-268-5966	233-8249
TF: 800-344-7130 ■ *Web:* www.lyonsmagnus.com					
Maui Land & Pineapple Co Ltd 120 Kane St PO Box 187	Kahului	HI	96733	808-877-3351	871-0953
AMEX: MLP ■ *Web:* www.mauiland.com					
Maull Louis Co 219 N Market St	Saint Louis	MO	63102	314-241-8410	
Web: www.maull.com					
Mayer Brothers Apple Products Inc 3300 Transit Rd	West Seneca	NY	14224	716-668-1787	668-2437
Web: mayerbrothers.com					
Minute Maid Co 2000 St James Pl	Houston	TX	77056	713-888-5000	888-5959
TF: 800-888-6488 ■ *Web:* www.minutemaid.com					
Monticello Canning Co Inc 711 Sparta Dr	Crossville	TN	38555	931-484-3696	484-3696
Moody Dunbar Inc 2000 Waters Edge Dr Suite 21	Johnson City	TN	37604	423-952-0100	952-0289
TF: 800-251-8202					
Morgan Foods Inc 90 W Morgan St	Austin	IN	47102	812-794-1170	794-1211
TF: 888-430-1780 ■ *Web:* www.morganfoods.com					
Morning Star Packing Co 13448 Volta Rd	Los Banos	CA	93635	209-826-8000	826-8266
Web: www.morningstarco.com					
Mott's Inc 900 King St	Rye Brook	NY	10573	914-612-4000	612-4100
TF: 800-426-4891 ■ *Web:* www.motts.com					
Mrs Clark's Foods LLC 740 SE Dalby Dr	Ankeny	IA	50021	515-964-8100	964-8397
TF: 866-971-6500 ■ *Web:* www.mrsclarks.com					
Muir Glen Organic Tomato Products 719 Metcalf St	Sedro Woolley	WA	98284	360-855-0100	
TF: 800-832-6345 ■ *Web:* www.muirglen.com					
Mullins Food Products Inc 2200 S 25th Ave	Broadview	IL	60155	708-344-3224	344-0153
Web: www.mullinsfood.com					
Mushroom Canning Co 902 Woods Rd	Cambridge	MD	21613	410-221-8970	221-8952
Web: www.mushroomcanning.com					
Naked Juice Co 935 W 8th St	Azusa	CA	91702	626-852-2500	852-2560
TF: 800-800-0689 ■ *Web:* www.nakedjuice.com					
National Fruit Product Co Inc					
701 Fairmont Ave PO Box 2040	Winchester	VA	22604	540-662-3401	665-4670*
*Fax: Sales ■ *TF:* 800-551-5167 ■ *Web:* www.whitehousefoods.com					
New Era Canning Co 4856 1st St	New Era	MI	49446	231-861-2151	861-4068
Web: www.neweracanning.com					
Nicholson HR Co 1332 Londontown Blvd	Saint James	MD	21781	410-764-2323	764-9125
TF Cust Svc: 800-638-3514 ■ *Web:* www.hrnicholson.com					

Fruits, Vegetables, Juices - Canned or Preserved (Cont'd)

Company	City	State	Zip	Phone	Fax
NORPAC Foods Inc 930 W Washington St *TF Sales:* 800-733-9311 ■ *Web:* www.norpac.com	Stayton	OR	97383	503-769-2101	769-1273
Northwest Packing Co 1701 W 16th St PO Box 30 *TF:* 800-543-4356	Vancouver	WA	98666	360-696-4356	696-0050
Ocean Spray Cranberries Inc 1 Ocean Spray Dr *TF:* 800-662-3263 ■ *Web:* www.oceanspray.com	Lakeville-Middleboro	MA	02349	508-946-1000	946-7704
Odwalla Inc 120 Stone Pine Rd *TF:* 800-639-2552 ■ *Web:* www.odwalla.com	Half Moon Bay	CA	94019	650-726-1888	560-9009
Pacific Coast Producers 631 N Cluff Ave *Web:* www.pcoastp.com	Lodi	CA	95240	209-367-8800	367-1084
Packers Canning Co Inc 72100 M 40 S PO Box 907	Lawton	MI	49065	269-624-4681	624-6009
Pastorelli Food Products Inc 162 N Sangamon St *TF:* 800-767-2829 ■ *Web:* www.pastorelli.com	Chicago	IL	60607	312-666-2041	666-2415
PepsiCo Beverages North America 700 Anderson Hill Rd *Web:* www.pepsi.com	Purchase	NY	10577	914-253-2000	253-2070
President Global Corp 6965 Aragon Cir	Buena Park	CA	90620	714-994-2990	523-3142
Pro-Fac Co-op Inc 590 Willow Brook Office Park *NASDAQ: PFACP* ■ *TF:* 877-894-2869 ■ *Web:* www.profaccoop.com	Fairport	NY	14450	585-218-4210	218-4241
Ray Brothers & Noble Canning Co Inc 3720 E 150 South PO Box 314 *Web:* www.noblecanning.com	Hobbs	IN	46047	765-675-7451	675-7400
Red Gold Inc 120 E Oak St *Web:* www.redgold.com	Orestes	IN	46063	765-754-7527	754-3230
Rohtstein Corp 70 Olympia Ave *TF:* 800-225-1661	Woburn	MA	01888	781-935-8400	932-3917
Seneca Foods Corp 3736 S Main St *NASDAQ: SENEA* ■ *Web:* www.senecafoods.com	Marion	NY	14505	315-926-8100	926-8300
Simply Orange Juice Co 2659 Orange Ave *Web:* www.simplyorangejuice.com	Apopka	FL	32703	800-871-2653	
Smith ED & Sons Ltd 944 Hwy 8 *TF:* 800-263-9246 ■ *Web:* www.edsmith.com	Winona	ON	L8E5S3	905-643-1211	643-3328
Smucker JM Co 1 Strawberry Ln *NYSE: SJM* ■ *TF:* 800-553-0952 ■ *Web:* www.smucker.com	Orrville	OH	44667	330-682-3000	684-6410
Smucker JM Pennsylvania Inc 300 Keck Ave	New Bethlehem	PA	16242	814-275-1323	275-1340
Southern Gardens Citrus 1820 Country Rd 833	Clewiston	FL	33440	863-983-3030	983-3060
Stanislaus Food Products Co 1202 D St *TF:* 800-327-7201 ■ *Web:* www.stanislausfoodproducts.com	Modesto	CA	95354	209-522-7201	521-4014
Stapleton-Spence Packing Co 1530 The Alameda Suite 320 *TF:* 800-297-8815 ■ *Web:* www.stapleton-spence.com	San Jose	CA	95126	408-297-8815	297-0611
Sun Orchard Inc 1198 W Fairmont Dr *TF:* 800-505-8423 ■ *Web:* www.sunorchard.com	Tempe	AZ	85282	480-966-1770	921-1426
Talk O'Texas Brands Inc 1610 Roosevelt St *TF:* 800-749-6572 ■ *Web:* www.talkotexas.com	San Angelo	TX	76905	325-655-6077	655-7967
Texas Citrus Exchange 702 E Expy 83 *Web:* www.texascitrusexchange.com	Mission	TX	78572	956-585-8321	585-1655
Tip Top Canning Co 505 S 2nd St PO Box 126 *TF:* 800-352-2635	Tipp City	OH	45371	937-667-3713	667-3802
Tree Top Inc 220 E 2nd Ave *TF:* 800-237-0515 ■ *Web:* www.treetop.com	Selah	WA	98942	509-697-7251	697-0421
Truitt Brothers Inc 1105 Front St NE **Fax:* Sales ■ *TF:* 800-547-8712 ■ *Web:* www.truittbros.com	Salem	OR	97301	503-362-3674	588-2868*
TW Garner Food Co 4045 Indiana Ave PO Box 4239 *Web:* www.texaspete.com	Winston-Salem	NC	27115	336-661-1550	661-1901
UniMark Group Inc 1425 Greenway Dr Suite 160	Irving	TX	75038	972-518-1155	518-1405
Valley Processing Inc 108 E Blaine Ave PO Box 246	Sunnyside	WA	98944	509-837-8084	837-3481
Vegetable Juices Inc 7400 S Narragansett Ave *TF:* 888-776-9752 ■ *Web:* www.vegetablejuices.com	Bedford Park	IL	60638	708-924-9500	924-9510
Vita-Pakt Citrus Products 707 N Barranca Ave *Web:* vita-pakt.com	Covina	CA	91723	626-332-1101	915-4107
Vitality Food Service Inc 400 N Tampa St Suite 1700 *TF:* 888-863-6726 ■ *Web:* www.vitalityfoodservice.com	Tampa	FL	33602	813-301-4600	301-4650
Welch's Inc 3 Concord Farms 575 Virginia Rd *Web:* www.welchs.com	Concord	MA	01742	978-371-1000	
Whitlock Packaging Corp 1701 S Lee St *TF:* 800-833-9382 ■ *Web:* www.whitlockpkg.com	Fort Gibson	OK	74434	918-478-4300	478-7362
Wyman Jasper & Son PO Box 100 *TF:* 800-341-1758 ■ *Web:* www.wymans.com	Milbridge	ME	04658	207-546-2311	546-2074
Zeigler Beverage Co 1513 N Broad St *TF Sales:* 800-854-6123 ■ *Web:* www.zeiglers.com	Lansdale	PA	19446	215-855-5161	855-4548

299-21 Fruits, Vegetables, Juices - Frozen

Company	City	State	Zip	Phone	Fax
Allen GM & Son Inc Rt 15 PO Box 454	Blue Hill	ME	04614	207-469-7060	469-2308
American Fruit Processors 10725 Sutter Ave **Fax:* Sales ■ *Web:* www.americanfruit.com	Pacoima	CA	91331	818-899-9574	899-6042*
Ardmore Farms Inc 1915 N Woodland Blvd *TF:* 800-365-8423 ■ *Web:* www.juice4u.com	DeLand	FL	32720	386-734-4634	736-8894
Berry Jack M Inc PO Box 459	La Belle	FL	33975	863-675-2769	675-6851
Birds Eye Foods Inc 90 Linden Oaks *TF:* 800-999-5044 ■ *Web:* www.birdseyefoods.com	Rochester	NY	14625	585-383-1850	385-2857
Bonduelle Inc 8615 Saint-Laurent Blvd Suite 200 *Web:* www.bonduelle.ca	Montreal	QC	H2P2M9	514-384-4281	384-7992
Brooks Food Group Inc 940 Orange St *TF:* 800-873-4934 ■ *Web:* www.brooksfoodgroup.com	Bedford	VA	24523	540-586-8284	586-1072
Cargill Citro-Pure LP PO Box 2000 **Fax:* Cust Svc	Frostproof	FL	33843	863-635-2211	635-8040*
Cascadian Farm Inc 719 Metcalf St *TF:* 800-624-4123 ■ *Web:* www.cascadianfarm.com	Sedro Woolley	WA	98284	360-855-0100	855-0444
Cherry Central Co-op Inc 1771 N US Hwy 31 S PO Box 988 *TF:* 800-678-1860 ■ *Web:* www.cherrycentral.com	Traverse City	MI	49685	231-946-1860	941-4167
Cherry Growers Inc 6331 US 31 S PO Box 90 *Web:* www.cherrygrowers.net	Grawn	MI	49637	231-276-9241	276-7075
Cherryfield Foods Inc PO Box 128	Cherryfield	ME	04622	207-546-7573	546-2713
Coloma Frozen Foods Inc 4145 Coloma Rd *TF:* 800-462-7608 ■ *Web:* www.colomafrozen.com	Coloma	MI	49038	269-849-0500	849-0886
ConAgra Foods Retail Products Co Frozen Foods Group 5 ConAgra Dr *Web:* www.conagrafoods.com	Omaha	NE	68102	402-595-6000	
Del Mar Food Products Corp 1720 W Beach Rd	Watsonville	CA	95076	831-722-3516	722-7690
Dole Food Co Inc 1 Dole Dr **Fax:* Hum Res ■ *TF:* 800-232-8888 ■ *Web:* www.dole.com	Westlake Village	CA	91362	818-879-6600	874-4893*
Frozsun Inc 701 W Kimberly Ave Suite 210 *Web:* www.frozsun.com	Placentia	CA	92870	714-630-2170	630-0920
General Mills Green Giant 915 E Pleasant St **Fax:* Cust Svc ■ *Web:* www.greengiant.com	Belvidere	IL	61008	815-547-5311	547-5896*
Giorgio Foods Inc 1161 Park Rd *TF:* 800-220-2139 ■ *Web:* www.giorgiofoods.com	Blandon	PA	19510	610-926-2139	926-7012
GM Allen & Son Inc Rt 15 PO Box 454	Blue Hill	ME	04614	207-469-7060	469-2308
Graceland Fruit Inc 1123 Main St *TF:* 800-352-7181 ■ *Web:* www.gracelandfruit.com	Frankfort	MI	49635	231-352-7181	352-4711
Hi-Country Foods Corp 1 Railroad Ave PO Box 338	Selah	WA	98942	509-697-7292	697-3498
HJ Heinz Co 600 Grant St *NYSE: HNZ* ■ *TF:* 800-255-5750 ■ *Web:* www.heinz.com	Pittsburgh	PA	15219	412-456-5700	456-6128
Holly Hill Fruit Products Co Inc 315 US Hwy 17-92 N	Davenport	FL	33837	863-422-1131	422-1136
Jack M Berry Inc PO Box 459	La Belle	FL	33975	863-675-2769	675-6851
Jewel Apple & Summer Prize Co PO Box 27	Yakima	WA	98907	509-248-7200	
JR Simplot Co 999 Main St *TF:* 800-635-5008 ■ *Web:* www.simplot.com	Boise	ID	83702	208-336-2110	389-7515
JR Simplot Co Food Group 6360 S Federal Way *TF:* 800-635-0408 ■ *Web:* www.simplot.com	Boise	ID	83716	208-384-8000	384-8015
Lakeside Foods Inc PO Box 1327 *Web:* www.lakesidefoods.com	Manitowoc	WI	54221	920-684-3356	686-4033
Lamb Weston Inc 8701 W Gage Blvd *Web:* www.lambweston.com	Kennewick	WA	99336	509-735-4651	736-0399
Leelanau Fruit Co 2900 SW Bayshore Dr *TF:* 800-431-0718 ■ *Web:* www.leelanaufruit.com	Suttons Bay	MI	49682	231-271-3514	271-4367
Lewis Dreyfus Citrus Inc PO Box 770399 *TF:* 800-549-4272 ■ *Web:* www.ldcitrusfl.com	Winter Garden	FL	34777	407-656-1000	656-1229
Louis Dreyfus Group 20 Westport Rd *Web:* www.louisdreyfus.com	Wilton	CT	06897	203-761-2000	761-2375
Maine Wild Blueberry Co PO Box 128	Cherryfield	ME	04622	207-255-8364	255-8341
McCain Foods Ltd 107 Main St *Web:* www.mccain.com	Florenceville	NB	E7L1B2	506-392-5541	392-8156
McCain Foods USA Inc 2275 Cabot Dr *TF:* 800-938-7799 ■ *Web:* www.mccainusa.com	Lisle	IL	60532	630-955-0400	857-4560
McCain Snack Foods 555 N Hickory Farm Ln PO Box 2518 *TF:* 800-767-7377 ■ *Web:* www.mccainusa.com	Appleton	WI	54913	920-997-2828	997-7604
Milne Fruit Products Inc PO Box 111 *Web:* www.milnefruit.com	Prosser	WA	99350	509-786-2611	786-4915
Minute Maid Co 2000 St James Pl *TF:* 800-888-6488 ■ *Web:* www.minutemaid.com	Houston	TX	77056	713-888-5000	888-5959
Mr Dell Foods Inc 300 W Major St *Web:* www.mrdells.com	Kearney	MO	64060	816-628-4644	628-4633
Mrs Clark's Foods LLC 740 SE Dalby Dr *TF:* 866-971-6500 ■ *Web:* www.mrsclarks.com	Ankeny	IA	50021	515-964-8100	964-8397
National Frozen Foods Corp 1600 Fairview Ave E 2nd Fl *Web:* www.nationalfrozenfoods.com	Seattle	WA	98102	206-322-8900	322-4458
NORPAC Foods Inc 930 W Washington St *TF Sales:* 800-733-9311 ■ *Web:* www.norpac.com	Stayton	OR	97383	503-769-2101	769-1273
Ocean Spray Cranberries Inc 1 Ocean Spray Dr *TF:* 800-662-3263 ■ *Web:* www.oceanspray.com	Lakeville-Middleboro	MA	02349	508-946-1000	946-7704
Ochoa Egg & Unlimited Foods Inc PO Box 747	Warden	WA	98857	509-349-2210	349-2375
Patterson Frozen Foods Inc PO Box 114 *TF:* 800-821-1007 ■ *Web:* www.pattersonfrozenfoods.com	Patterson	CA	95363	209-892-2611	892-5209
PepsiCo Beverages North America 700 Anderson Hill Rd *Web:* www.pepsi.com	Purchase	NY	10577	914-253-2000	253-2070
Peterson Farms Inc 3104 W Baseline Rd *Web:* www.petersonfarmsinc.com	Shelby	MI	49455	231-861-6333	861-6550
Pro-Fac Co-op Inc 590 Willow Brook Office Park *NASDAQ: PFACP* ■ *TF:* 877-894-2869 ■ *Web:* www.profaccoop.com	Fairport	NY	14450	585-218-4210	218-4241
Seabrook Brothers & Sons Inc 85 Finley Rd *Web:* www.seabrookfarms.com	Seabrook	NJ	08302	856-455-8080	455-9282
Seneca Foods Corp 3736 S Main St *NASDAQ: SENEA* ■ *Web:* www.senecafoods.com	Marion	NY	14505	315-926-8100	926-8300
Sill Farms Market Inc 50241 Red Arrow Hwy	Lawrence	MI	49064	269-674-3755	674-3756
Simplot JR Co 999 Main St *TF:* 800-635-5008 ■ *Web:* www.simplot.com	Boise	ID	83702	208-336-2110	389-7515
Simplot JR Co Food Group 6360 S Federal Way *TF:* 800-635-0408 ■ *Web:* www.simplot.com	Boise	ID	83716	208-384-8000	384-8015
Smucker Quality Beverages Inc PO Box 369 *Web:* www.knudsenjuices.com	Chico	CA	95927	530-899-5000	891-6397
Sun Orchard of Florida Inc PO Box 2008 *TF:* 877-875-8423 ■ *Web:* www.sunorchard.com	Haines City	FL	33844	863-422-5062	422-5176
Townsend Farms Inc 23303 NE Sandy Blvd	Fairview	OR	97024	503-666-1780	618-8257
Tree Top Inc 220 E 2nd Ave *TF:* 800-237-0515 ■ *Web:* www.treetop.com	Selah	WA	98942	509-697-7251	697-0421
Twin City Foods Inc 10120 269th Pl NW	Stanwood	WA	98292	360-629-2111	629-3533
UniMark Group Inc 1425 Greenway Dr Suite 160	Irving	TX	75038	972-518-1155	518-1405
United Foods Inc 10 Pictsweet Dr **Fax Area Code:* 800 ■ *TF:* 800-367-7412 ■ *Web:* www.pictsweet.com	Bells	TN	38006	731-422-7600	561-8810*
Valley Foods Inc PO Box C	Lindsay	CA	93247	559-562-5169	562-5691
Value Frozen Foods Inc RR 1 PO Box 130	Edcouch	TX	78538	956-262-4723	262-1038
Ventura Coastal Corp 2325 Vista del Mar Dr	Ventura	CA	93002	805-653-7000	648-4915
Vita-Pakt Citrus Products 707 N Barranca Ave *Web:* vita-pakt.com	Covina	CA	91723	626-332-1101	915-4107
Wawona Frozen Foods Inc 100 W Alluvial Ave *TF:* 800-669-2966 ■ *Web:* www.wawona.com	Clovis	CA	93611	559-299-2901	299-1921
Welch's Inc 3 Concord Farms 575 Virginia Rd *Web:* www.welchs.com	Concord	MA	01742	978-371-1000	
World Citrus West Inc 130 W Santa Fe Ave *Web:* www.floridasnatural.com	Fullerton	CA	92832	714-870-6171	871-4100

299-22 Gelatin

Company	City	State	Zip	Phone	Fax
ConAgra Hunt-Wesson Foodservice Co 3353 Michelson Dr *TF:* 800-633-0112 ■ *Web:* www.conagrafoodservice.com	Irvine	CA	92612	949-437-1000	
Gelita USA Inc PO Box 927 *TF:* 888-443-5482 ■ *Web:* www.gelita.com	Sioux City	IA	51102	712-943-5516	943-3372
Kraft Food Ingredients Corp 8000 Horizon Ctr Blvd *TF:* 800-458-8324	Memphis	TN	38133	901-381-6500	381-6524
Langlois Co 10810 San Sevaine Way *TF:* 800-962-5993	Mira Loma	CA	91752	951-360-3900	360-3465
Milligan & Higgins PO Box 506 *Web:* www.milligan1868.com	Johnstown	NY	12095	518-762-4638	762-7039
Nitta Gelatin Inc 201 W Passaic St *TF:* 800-278-7680 ■ *Web:* www.nitta-gelatin.com	Rochelle Park	NJ	07662	201-368-0071	368-0282
PB Leiner 366 N Broadway Suite 307 *Web:* www.gelatin.com	Jericho	NY	11753	516-822-4040	822-4044
Precision Foods Inc 11457 Olde Cabin Rd *TF:* 800-442-5242 ■ *Web:* www.precisionfoods.com	Saint Louis	MO	63141	314-567-7400	567-7421
Subco Foods Inc 4350 S Taylor Dr *TF:* 800-473-0757 ■ *Web:* www.subcofoods.com	Sheboygan	WI	53081	920-457-7761	457-3899
Swagger Foods Corp 900 Corporate Woods Pkwy *Web:* www.swaggerfoods.com	Vernon Hills	IL	60061	847-913-1200	913-1263
Vyse Gelatin Co 5010 N Rose St *TF:* 800-533-2152 ■ *Web:* www.vyse.com	Schiller Park	IL	60176	847-678-4780	678-0329

299-23 Grain Mill Products

Company	City	State	Zip	Phone	Fax
ACH Food Cos Inc 7171 Goodlett Farms Pkwy *TF:* 800-691-1106 ■ *Web:* www.achfood.com	Cordova	TN	38016	901-381-3000	381-2968
ADM Corn Processing Div 4666 E Faries Pkwy	Decatur	IL	62526	217-424-5200	424-5978

Phone Fax

ADM Milling Co 8000 W 110th St Suite 300 Overland Park KS 66210 913-491-9400 491-0035
TF: 800-422-1688
ADM Specialty Feed Ingredients Div 4666 E Faries Pkwy. Decatur IL 62526 217-424-5200 424-5978
Ag Processing Inc 12700 W Dodge Rd PO Box 2047 Omaha NE 68103 402-496-7809 498-5548
TF: 800-247-1345 ■ *Web*: www.agp.com
Allen Brothers Milling Co PO Box 1437 Columbia SC 29202 803-779-2460 252-0014
American Rice Inc 10700 North Fwy Suite 800 Houston TX 77037 281-272-8800 272-9707
Web: www.amrice.com
Anderson Custom Processing Inc 121 Lindbergh Dr S Little Falls MN 56345 320-632-2338 632-9194
Arrowhead Mills Inc 110 S Lawton St PO Box 2059 Hereford TX 79045 806-364-0730 364-8242
TF: 800-858-4308
Azteca Milling Co 501 W Chapin St Edinburg TX 78539 956-383-4911 383-8346
TF: 800-262-7322
Bartlett & Co 4800 Main St Suite 600 Kansas City MO 64112 816-753-6300 753-0063
TF: 800-888-6300 ■ *Web*: www.bartlettandco.com
Bay State Milling Co 100 Congress St Quincy MA 02169 617-328-4400 479-8910
TF: 800-553-5687 ■ *Web*: www.bsm.com
Beaumont Rice Mills Inc 1800 Pecos St Beaumont TX 77701 409-832-2521 832-6927
Birkett Mills 163 Main St Penn Yan NY 14527 315-536-3311 536-6740
Web: www.thebirkettmills.com
Blendex Co Inc 11208 Electron Dr Louisville KY 40299 502-267-1003 267-1024
TF: 800-626-6354 ■ *Web*: www.blendex.com
Bunge Milling 321 E North St Danville IL 61832 217-442-1800 443-9829
California Food Processors Inc 1861 E 55th St Los Angeles CA 90058 323-585-0131 587-2658
Cargill 616 S Jefferson St Paris IL 61944 217-465-5331 463-1644
Cargill Foods 15407 McGinty Rd Wayzata MN 55391 952-742-7575
TF: 800-227-4455 ■ *Web*: www.cargillfoods.com
Cargill Inc North America 15407 McGinty Rd Wayzata MN 55391 952-742-7575
TF: 800-227-4455
Cereal Food Processors Inc
2001 Shawnee Mission Pkwy Mission Woods KS 66205 913-890-6300 890-6382
TF: 800-743-5687 ■ *Web*: www.cerealfood.com
Cereal Foods Inc 416 N Main St McPherson KS 67460 620-241-2410 241-7167
TF: 800-835-2067
Chelsea Milling Co 201 W North St PO Box 460 Chelsea MI 48118 734-475-1361 475-4630
Web: www.jiffymix.com
ConAgra Food Ingredients Co 11 ConAgra Dr Omaha NE 68102 402-595-7300 595-7497*
*Fax: Hum Res
ConAgra Food Ingredients Co Grain Processing Group
9 ConAgra Dr Omaha NE 68102 402-595-7368 978-5553
Web: www.conagramilling.com
Cormier Rice Milling Co Inc 501 W 3rd St PO Box 152 De Witt AR 72042 870-946-3561 946-3029
Corn Products International Inc
5 Westbrook Corporate Center Westchester IL 60154 708-551-2600 551-2700
NYSE: CPO ■ *Web*: www.cornproducts.com
Farmers Rice Co-op PO Box 15223 Sacramento CA 95851 916-923-5100 920-3321
TF: 800-326-2799 ■ *Web*: www.farmersrice.com
Farmers Rice Milling Co 3211 Hwy 397 S Lake Charles LA 70615 337-433-5205 433-1735
Web: www.frmco.com
Florida Crystals Corp 1 N Clematis St Suite 200 West Palm Beach FL 33401 561-655-6303 659-3206
Web: www.floridacrystals.com
Foxtail Foods 6075 Poplar Ave Suite 800 Memphis TN 38119 901-766-6400 537-7141
TF Cust Svc: 800-487-2253 ■ *Web*: www.foxtailfoods.com
General Mills Inc 1 General Mills Blvd Minneapolis MN 55426 763-764-7600 764-8330
NYSE: GIS ■ *TF*: 800-328-1144 ■ *Web*: www.generalmills.com
Gold Medal 1 General Mills Blvd Minneapolis MN 55426 763-764-7600 764-3232*
*Fax: PR
Grain Processing Corp 1600 Oregon St Muscatine IA 52761 563-264-4211 264-4216
Web: www.grainprocessing.com
Henry & Henry Inc 3765 Walden Ave Lancaster NY 14086 716-685-4000 685-0160
TF: 800-828-7130 ■ *Web*: www.henryandhenry.com
HFM FoodService 716 UMI St Honolulu HI 96819 808-843-3200 843-3211
Web: www.hfmfoodservice.com
Hopkinsville Milling Co 2001 S Walnut St Hopkinsville KY 42240 270-886-1231 886-6407
Horizon Milling LLC 15407 McGinty Rd W Wayzata MN 55391 952-742-2361 742-7934
TF: 888-423-0138 ■ *Web*: www.horizonmilling.com
House-Autry Mills Inc 7000 US Hwy 301 S Four Oaks NC 27524 919-963-6200 963-6458
TF: 800-849-0802 ■ *Web*: www.house-autry.com
HR Wentzel Sons Inc 5521 Waggoners Gap Rd PO Box 125 Landisburg PA 17040 717-789-3306
Indian Harvest Specialtifoods Inc 1012 Paul Bunyan Dr SE Bemidji MN 56601 218-751-8500 751-8519
TF Orders: 800-346-7032 ■ *Web*: www.indianharvest.com
JR Short Milling Co 1580 Grinnell Rd Chicago IL 60601 815-937-2633 937-8806
TF: 800-544-8734 ■ *Web*: www.shortmill.com
King Milling Co 115 S Broadway St Lowell MI 49331 616-897-9264 897-4350
Web: www.kingmilling.com
Knappen Milling Co 110 S Water St Augusta MI 49012 269-731-4141 731-5441
TF: 800-562-7736 ■ *Web*: www.knappen.com
Lacey Milling Co 217 W 5th St Hanford CA 93230 559-584-6634 584-9165
Mallet & Co Inc 51 Arch St Ext Carnegie PA 15106 412-276-9000 276-9002
TF: 800-245-2757 ■ *Web*: www.malletoil.com
Manildra Milling Corp
4210 Shawnee Mission Pkwy Suite 312A Shawnee Mission KS 66205 913-362-0777 362-0052
Mars Snack Food 800 High St Hackettstown NJ 07840 908-852-1000 850-2734
TF: 800-432-1093 ■ *Web*: www.mars.com
Mennel Milling Co 128 W Crocker St Fostoria OH 44830 419-435-8151 436-5150
TF: 800-688-8151 ■ *Web*: www.mennel.com
MGP Ingredients Inc 1300 Main St Atchison KS 66002 913-367-1480 367-0192
NASDAQ: MGPI ■ *TF*: 800-255-0302 ■ *Web*: www.midwestgrain.com
Midstate Mills Inc 324 E 'A' St Newton NC 28658 828-464-1611 465-5139
TF: 800-222-1032 ■ *Web*: www.midstatemills.com
Minn-Dak Growers Ltd PO Box 13276 Grand Forks ND 58208 701-746-7453 780-9050
Web: www.minndak.com
Minnesota Corn Processors Inc 400 W Erie Rd Marshall MN 56258 507-537-2676 537-2642
TF: 800-328-4150
Minnesota Grain Pearling Co
1380 Corporate Ctr Curve Suite 101 Eagan MN 55121 651-681-1460 681-7975
Monahan Thomas Co Inc 202 N Oak St Arcola IL 61910 217-268-4955 268-3113
TF: 800-637-7739 ■ *Web*: www.thomasmonahan.com
Morrison Milling Co 319 E Prairie St Denton TX 76201 940-387-6111 566-5992
TF: 800-866-5487
North Dakota Mill 1823 Mill Rd Grand Forks ND 58208 701-795-7000 795-7251
TF: 800-538-7721 ■ *Web*: www.ndmill.com
Pacific Grain Products International Inc PO Box 2060 Woodland CA 95776 530-662-5056 662-6074
TF Cust Svc: 800-747-0161 ■ *Web*: www.pacgrain.com
Pacific International Rice Mills Inc PO Box 652 Woodland CA 95776 530-666-1691 668-8515
TF: 800-747-4764 ■ *Web*: www.pirmi.com
Producers Rice Mill Inc 518 E Harrison St Stuttgart AR 72160 870-673-4444 673-8131
Web: www.producersrice.com
Riceland Foods Inc 2120 S Park Ave Stuttgart AR 72160 870-673-5500 673-3366
TF: 800-264-1283 ■ *Web*: www.riceland.com
Riviana Foods Inc PO Box 2636 Houston TX 77252 713-529-3251 529-1661
Web: www.riviana.com
Rocky Mountain Milling LLC 400 Platte St Platteville CO 80651 970-785-2794 785-0575
TF: 888-785-7636 ■ *Web*: www.bsm.com/rockymountainmilling
Roman Meal Milling Co Inc 4014 15th Ave NW Fargo ND 58102 701-282-9656 282-9743
Roquette America Inc 1417 Exchange St Keokuk IA 52632 319-524-5757 526-2345
TF: 800-553-7030
Seaboard Flour Corp 822 Boylston St Suite 301 Chestnut Hill MA 02467 617-739-4480 739-4487
Shawnee Milling Co Inc 201 S Broadway PO Box 1567 Shawnee OK 74802 405-273-7000 273-7333
TF: 800-654-2600 ■ *Web*: www.shawneemilling.com
Short JR Milling Co 1580 Grinnell Rd Chicago IL 60601 815-937-2633 937-8806
TF: 800-544-8734 ■ *Web*: www.shortmill.com
Siemer Milling Co 111 W Main St PO Box 670 Teutopolis IL 62467 217-857-3131 857-3092
TF: 800-826-1065 ■ *Web*: www.siemermilling.com
Stafford County Flour Mills Co 108 Church St PO Box 7 Hudson KS 67545 620-458-4121 458-5121
TF: 800-530-5640 ■ *Web*: www.flour.com
SunOpta Inc 2838 Bovaird Dr W Brampton ON L7A0H2 905-455-1990 455-2529
NASDAQ: STKL ■ *Web*: www.sunopta.com
Supreme Rice Mill Inc PO Box 490 Crowley LA 70527 337-783-5222 783-3204
Web: www.supremerice.com
Thomas Monahan Co Inc 202 N Oak St Arcola IL 61910 217-268-4955 268-3113
TF: 800-637-7739 ■ *Web*: www.thomasmonahan.com
Wentzel HR Sons Inc 5521 Waggoners Gap Rd PO Box 125 Landisburg PA 17040 717-789-3306
White Lily Foods Co 218 E Depot Ave Knoxville TN 37917 865-546-5511 521-7725
TF: 800-264-5459 ■ *Web*: www.whitelily.com
Wilkins-Rogers Inc 27 Frederick Rd Ellicott City MD 21043 410-465-5800 750-0163
TF Cust Svc: 800-735-3585

299-24 Honey

Phone Fax

Adee Honey Farm PO Box 368 Bruce SD 57220 605-627-5621 627-5622
Web: www.adeehoneyfarms.com
Artesian Honey Producers PO Box 6 Artesian SD 57314 605-527-2423
Burleson TW & Son Inc 301 Peters St Waxahachie TX 75165 972-937-4810 937-8711
Web: www.burlesons-honey.com
Dutch Gold Honey Inc 2220 Dutch Gold Dr Lancaster PA 17601 717-393-1716 393-8687
Web: www.dutchgoldhoney.com
Fisher Honey Co 1 Belle Ave Bldg 21 Lewistown PA 17044 717-242-4373 242-3978
Web: www.fisherhoney.com
Glorybee Foods Inc PO Box 2744 Eugene OR 97402 541-689-0913 689-9692
TF: 800-456-7923 ■ *Web*: www.glorybee.com
Golden Heritage Foods LLC 120 Santa Fe St Hillsboro KS 67063 620-947-3173 947-3640
TF: 800-947-3640 ■ *Web*: www.ghfllc.com
Honey Acres 1557 Hwy 67 N Ashippun WI 53003 920-474-4411 474-4018
TF: 800-558-7745 ■ *Web*: www.honeyacres.com
Honeytree Inc PO Box 310 Onsted MI 49265 517-467-2482 467-2056
TF: 800-968-1889
Hoyt's Honey Farm 11711 I-10 E Baytown TX 77520 281-576-5383 576-2191
Mel-O Foods Inc 515 Cannon Industrial Blvd Cannon Falls MN 55009 507-263-8599 263-8611
Web: www.mel-o.com
Mel-O Honey Inc 515 Cannon Industrial Blvd Cannon Falls MN 55009 507-263-8599 263-8611
Web: www.mel-o.com
Miller's Honey Co Inc PO Box 65807 Salt Lake City UT 84165 801-486-8479 486-8494
Web: www.millerhoney.com
Pure Sweet Honey Farm Inc 514 Commerce Pkwy Verona WI 53593 608-845-9601
Silverbow Honey Co Inc 1120 E Wheeler Rd Moses Lake WA 98837 509-765-6616 765-6549
Web: www.silverbowhoney.com
Sioux Honey Assn Co-op PO Box 388 Sioux City IA 51102 712-258-0638 258-1332
TF: 888-270-6956 ■ *Web*: www.suebee.com/
TW Burleson & Son Inc 301 Peters St Waxahachie TX 75165 972-937-4810 937-8711
Web: www.burlesons-honey.com
Wixson Honey Inc 4937 Lakemont-Himrod Rd Dundee NY 14837 607-243-7301 243-7143

299-25 Ice Cream & Frozen Desserts

Phone Fax

Anderson Erickson Dairy Co 2420 E University Ave Des Moines IA 50317 515-265-2521 263-6301*
TF: 800-234-7257 ■ *Web*: www.aedairy.com
Atlanta Dairies Inc 777 Memorial Dr SE Atlanta GA 30316 404-688-2671 523-0385
Baldwin Richardson Foods Co Inc
20201 S La Grange Rd Suite 200 Frankfort IL 60423 815-464-9994 464-9995
TF Cust Svc: 800-762-6458 ■ *Web*: www.brfoods.com
Barber Dairies Inc 36 Barber Ct Birmingham AL 35209 205-942-2351 943-0297
Web: www.barbersdairy.com
Ben & Jerry's Homemade Inc 30 Community Dr South Burlington VT 05403 802-846-1500 846-1556
Web: www.benjerry.com
Berkeley Farms Inc 25500 Clawiter Rd Hayward CA 94545 510-265-8600 265-8754*
*Fax: Sales ■ *Web*: www.berkeleyfarms.com
Blue Bell Creameries Inc 1101 Blue Bell Rd Brenham TX 77833 979-836-7977 830-7398
Web: www.bluebell.com
Braum WH Inc 3000 NE 63rd St Oklahoma City OK 73121 405-478-1656 475-2460
Web: www.braums.com
Brigham's Inc 30 Mill St Arlington MA 02476 781-648-9000 646-0507
TF: 800-274-4426 ■ *Web*: www.brighams.com
Broughton Foods Co 1701 Green St Marietta OH 45750 740-373-4121 373-2861
TF: 800-283-2479
Cedar Crest Specialties Inc 7269 Hwy 60 PO Box 260 Cedarburg WI 53012 262-377-7252 377-5554
TF: 800-877-8341 ■ *Web*: www.cedarcresticecream.com
Central Dairy & Ice Cream Co 610 Madison St Jefferson City MO 65101 573-635-6148 634-3028
TF: 800-422-2148
Coleman Dairy Inc 6901 I-30 Little Rock AR 72209 501-565-1551 568-1710
TF: 800-365-1551 ■ *Web*: www.colemandairy.com
CoolBrands International Inc 8300 Woodbine Ave 5th Fl Markham ON L3R9Y7 905-479-8762 479-5235
TSX: COB ■ *Web*: www.coolbrandsinc.com
Country Fresh Inc 355 Mart St SW Grand Rapids MI 49548 616-243-0173 243-5926
TF: 800-748-0480 ■ *Web*: www.enjoycountryfresh.com
Creamland Dairies Inc 010 Indian School Rd NW Albuquerque NM 87102 505-247-0721 246-9696
TF: 800-334-3865 ■ *Web*: www.creamland.com
Crossroad Farms Dairy 400 S Shortridge Rd Indianapolis IN 46219 317-229-7600 229-7676
TF: 800-334-7502
Dairy Fresh Corp 915 Tuscaloosa St Greensboro AL 36744 334-624-3041
Dreyer's Grand Ice Cream Holdings Inc 5929 College Ave Oakland CA 94618 510-317-1415 450-4621
TF: 800-888-3442 ■ *Web*: www.dreyersinc.com
Driggs Farm of Indiana Inc 400 S Chamber Dr Decatur IN 46733 260-724-2136 724-4109
Web: www.driggsfarms.net
Edy's Grand Ice Cream 5929 College Ave Oakland CA 94618 510-652-8187 450-4621
TF: 800-888-3442
Elgin Dairy Foods Inc 3707 W Harrison St Chicago IL 60624 773-722-7100 722-3230
TF: 800-786-9900 ■ *Web*: www.elgindairy.com
Farr Better Foods 286 21st St Ogden UT 84401 801-393-8629 399-0516
Web: www.farrsicecream.com
Flav-O-Rich 1105 N William St Goldsboro NC 27530 919-734-0728 735-6344
TF: 877-321-1158
Friendly Ice Cream Corp 1855 Boston Rd Wilbraham MA 01095 413-543-2400 543-3966
AMEX: FRN ■ *Web*: www.friendlys.com
Galliker Dairy Co Inc 143 Donald Ln Johnstown PA 15904 814-266-8702 266-4619
TF: 800-477-6455 ■ *Web*: www.gallikers.com
Gandy's Dairies Inc PO Box 992 San Angelo TX 76902 325-655-6965 655-5266
TF: 800-200-3326 ■ *Web*: www.gandysdairy.com
Good Humor-Breyers Ice Cream PO Box 19007 Green Bay WI 54307 920-499-5151 497-6523
Web: www.icecreamusa.com

Ice Cream & Frozen Desserts (Cont'd)

				Phone	Fax
Heisler's Cloverleaf Dairy 743 Catawissa Rd	Tamaqua	PA	18252	570-668-3399	668-3041
Web: www.heislersdairy.com					
Hershey Creamery Co 301 S Cameron St	Harrisburg	PA	17101	717-238-8134	233-7195
TF: 888-240-1905 ■ Web: www.hersheyicecream.com					
Hiland Dairy Co 1133 E Kearney St PO Box 2270	Springfield	MO	65801	417-862-9311	837-1106
TF: 800-641-4022 ■ Web: www.hilanddairy.com					
Holland Dairies Inc 304 Main St	Holland	IN	47541	812-536-2310	536-4320
TF: 800-634-2509					
Hood HP LLC 90 Everett Ave	Chelsea	MA	02150	617-887-3000	887-8484
TF Cust Svc: 800-662-4468 ■ Web: www.hphood.com					
HP Hood LLC 90 Everett Ave	Chelsea	MA	02150	617-887-3000	887-8484
TF Cust Svc: 800-662-4468 ■ Web: www.hphood.com					
Ice Cream Specialties 8419 Hanley Industrial Dr	Saint Louis	MO	63144	314-962-2550	962-1990
TF: 800-662-7550					
Integrated Brands 4175 Veterans Memorial Hwy	Ronkonkoma	NY	11779	631-737-9700	737-9792
TF: 800-423-2763					
J & J Snack Foods Corp 6000 Central Hwy	Pennsauken	NJ	08109	856-665-9533	665-6718
NASDAQ: JJSF ■ TF: 800-486-9533 ■ Web: www.jjsnack.com					
Jackson Ice Cream Co Inc 2600 E 4th Ave	Hutchinson	KS	67501	620-663-1244	663-1952
Kemps Food Inc 150 Roosevelt Ave	York	PA	17401	717-767-4016	767-5902
TF: 800-233-2007					
Kemps LLC 1270 Energy Ln	Saint Paul	MN	55108	651-379-6500	379-6806
TF: 800-322-9566 ■ Web: www.kemps.com					
Klinke Brothers Ice Cream Co 2450 Scaper Cove	Memphis	TN	38114	901-743-8250	743-8254
Kohler Mix Specialties Inc 4041 Hwy 61	White Bear Lake	MN	55110	651-426-1633	426-7876
Land O'Sun Dairies LLC 2900 Bristol Hwy	Johnson City	TN	37601	423-283-5700	283-5716
TF: 800-683-0765					
Louis Trauth Dairy Inc 16 E 11th St	Newport	KY	41071	859-431-7553	431-0349
TF: 800-544-6455 ■ Web: www.trauthdairy.com					
Luvel Dairy Products Inc 926 Hwy 35 Bypass S	Kosciusko	MS	39090	662-289-2511	289-2572
Maola Milk & Ice Cream Co 305 Ave C	New Bern	NC	28563	252-638-1131	638-2268
TF: 800-476-1021 ■ Web: www.maolamilk.com					
Melody Farms/Stroh's Ice Cream Co 1000 Maple St	Detroit	MI	48207	313-568-5100	568-1029
TF: 800-968-7980 ■ Web: www.melodyfarms.com					
Mid States Dairy Co 6040 N Lindbergh Blvd	Saint Louis	MO	63042	314-731-1150	731-1198
TF: 800-473-1150					
Milkco Inc 220 Deaverview Rd	Asheville	NC	28806	828-254-9560	252-9560
TF: 800-842-8021					
Newport Creamery Inc 35 Stockanosset Rd	Cranston	RI	02920	401-946-4000	946-4392
Web: www.newportcreamery.com					
Perry's Ice Cream Co Inc 1 Ice Cream Plaza	Akron	NY	14001	716-542-5492	542-2544
TF: 800-873-7797 ■ Web: www.perrysicecream.com					
Richman Ice Cream Co 91 18th Ave	Paterson	NJ	07513	973-684-8935	684-8935
TF: 800-883-3332					
Schwan Food Co 115 W College Dr	Marshall	MN	56258	507-532-3274	
TF: 800-533-5290 ■ Web: www.theschwanfoodcompany.com					
Smith Dairy Wayne Div 1590 NW 11th St	Richmond	IN	47375	765-935-7521	962-5269
TF: 800-875-9296					
Stonyfield Farm Inc 10 Burton Dr	Londonderry	NH	03053	603-437-4040	437-7594
TF: 800-776-2697 ■ Web: www.stonyfield.com					
Sugar Creek Foods Inc 301 N El Paso St	Russellville	AR	72810	479-968-1005	968-5651
TF: 800-445-2715					
Tofutti Brands Inc 50 Jackson Dr	Cranford	NJ	07016	908-272-2400	272-9492
AMEX: TOF ■ Web: www.tofutti.com					
Trauth Louis Dairy Inc 16 E 11th St	Newport	KY	41071	859-431-7553	431-0349
TF: 800-544-6455 ■ Web: www.trauthdairy.com					
Turkey Hill Dairy Inc 2601 River Rd	Conestoga	PA	17516	717-872-5461	872-4130
TF: 800-688-7539 ■ Web: www.turkeyhill.com					
Umpqua Dairy Products 333 SE Sykes Ave	Roseburg	OR	97470	541-672-2638	673-0256
Web: www.umpquadairy.com					
United Dairy Farmers 3955 Montgomery Rd	Cincinnati	OH	45212	513-396-8700	396-8736
TF: 800-654-2809 ■ Web: www.udf.com					
Upstate Farms Co-op 25 Anderson Rd	Buffalo	NY	14225	716-892-3156	892-3157
TF: 800-724-6455 ■ Web: www.upstatefarmscoop.com					
Velda Farms LLC 402 S Kentucky Ave Suite 500	Lakeland	FL	33801	863-686-4441	644-6113*
*Fax Area Code: 888 ■ TF Cust Svc: 800-795-4649 ■ Web: www.veldafarms.com					
Wayne Div Smith Dairy 1590 NW 11th St	Richmond	IN	47375	765-935-7521	962-5269
TF: 800-875-9296					
Wells' Dairy Inc 1 Blue Bunny Dr	Le Mars	IA	51031	712-546-4000	546-1782
TF: 800-942-3800 ■ Web: www.wellsdairy.com					
WestFarm Foods 635 Elliott Ave W	Seattle	WA	98119	206-284-7220	281-3456
TF: 800-333-6455 ■ Web: www.westfarm.com					
WH Braum Inc 3000 NE 63rd St	Oklahoma City	OK	73121	405-478-1656	475-2460
Web: www.braums.com					
Yarnell Ice Cream Co 205 S Spring St	Searcy	AR	72143	501-268-2414	279-0846
TF: 800-666-2414 ■ Web: www.yarnells.com					
YoCream International Inc 5858 NE 87th Ave	Portland	OR	97220	503-256-3754	256-3976
TF: 800-962-7326 ■ Web: www.yocream.com					

299-26 Meat Products - Prepared

				Phone	Fax
A to Z Kosher Meat Products Co Inc DBA Empire National Kosher 123 Grand St	Brooklyn	NY	11211	718-384-7400	384-7403
Web: www.empirenational.com					
Alderfer Inc 382 Main St PO Box 2	Harleysville	PA	19438	215-256-8818	256-6120
TF Sales: 877-253-6328 ■ Web: www.alderfermeats.com					
American Foods Group Inc PO Box 8547	Green Bay	WI	54308	920-437-6330	436-6510
TF: 800-345-0293 ■ Web: www.americanfoodsgroup.com					
Ball Park Brands 3500 Lacey Rd	Downers Grove	IL	60515	630-598-7892	598-8221
TF Cust Svc: 866-727-2533 ■ Web: www.ballparkfranks.com					
Ballard's Farm Sausage Inc 2131 Right Fork Wilson Creek Rd PO Box 699	Wayne	WV	25570	304-272-5147	272-5336
TF: 800-346-7675 ■ Web: www.ballardsfarm.com					
Bar-S Foods Co 3838 N Central Ave Suite 1900	Phoenix	AZ	85012	602-264-7272	285-5252
Web: www.bar-s.com					
Beef Products Inc 891 Two Rivers Dr	Dakota Dunes	SD	57049	605-217-8000	217-8001
Web: www.beefproducts.com					
Berks Packing Co Inc 307-323 Bingaman St PO box 5919	Reading	PA	19610	610-376-7291	378-1210
TF: 800-882-3757 ■ Web: www.berksfoods.com					
Best Kosher Foods Corp 3500 Lacey Rd	Downers Grove	IL	60515	630-598-7892	598-8221
TF: 866-727-2533 ■ Web: www.bests-kosher.com					
Best Provision Co Inc 144 Avon Ave	Newark	NJ	07108	973-242-5000	648-0041
TF: 800-631-4466					
Bison Products Co Inc 81 Dingens St	Buffalo	NY	14206	716-826-2700	826-0603
TF: 800-248-2705					
Blue Grass Quality Meats 2645 Commerce Dr	Crescent Springs	KY	41017	859-331-7100	331-4273
TF: 888-236-4455					
Boar's Head Provisions Co Inc 1819 Main St Suite 800	Sarasota	FL	34236	941-955-0994	906-8213
Web: www.boarshead.com					
Boyle's Famous Corned Beef Co 1638 St Louis Ave	Kansas City	MO	64101	816-221-6283	221-3888
TF: 800-821-3626					
Bridgford Foods Corp 1308 N Patt St	Anaheim	CA	92801	714-526-5533	526-4360
NASDAQ: BRID ■ TF: 800-854-3255 ■ Web: www.bridgford.com					
Bryan Foods Inc 100 Church Hill Rd	West Point	MS	39773	662-494-3741	495-4439*
*Fax: Hum Res ■ Web: www.bryanfoods.com					
Buddig Carl & Co 950 W 175th St	Homewood	IL	60430	708-798-0900	798-3178
TF: 800-621-0868 ■ Web: www.buddig.com					
Burger's Ozark Country Cured Hams Inc 32819 Hwy 87 S	California	MO	65018	573-796-3134	796-3137
TF: 800-203-4424 ■ Web: www.smokehouse.com					
Carando Inc 20 Carando Dr	Springfield	MA	01104	413-781-5620	737-7314
TF: 800-628-9524 ■ Web: www.carando.com					
Cargill Foods 15407 McGinty Rd	Wayzata	MN	55391	952-742-7575	
TF: 800-227-4455 ■ Web: www.cargillfoods.com					
Cargill Inc North America 15407 McGinty Rd	Wayzata	MN	55391	952-742-7575	
TF: 800-227-4455					
Cargill Value Added Meats 200 S Ember Ln	Milwaukee	WI	53233	414-645-6500	647-6009
TF: 800-558-2000 ■ Web: www.cargill.com/about/organization/value_added_meats.htm					
Caribbean Products Ltd 3624 Falls Rd	Baltimore	MD	21211	410-235-7700	235-1513
Carl Buddig & Co 950 W 175th St	Homewood	IL	60430	708-798-0900	798-3178
TF: 800-621-0868 ■ Web: www.buddig.com					
Carlton Food Products Inc 880 Hwy 46 E PO Box 311385	New Braunfels	TX	78131	830-625-7583	629-7814
TF: 800-628-9849					
Carmelita Chorizo 2901 W Floral Dr	Monterey Park	CA	91754	323-262-6751	262-3503
TF: 800-924-6749 ■ Web: www.carmelitachorizo.com					
Carolina Pride 1 Packer Ave	Greenwood	SC	29646	864-229-5611	229-5386
Web: www.carolinaprideonline.com					
Carriage House Foods DBA Grand Choice Foods 1131 Dayton Ave	Ames	IA	50010	515-232-2273	232-3003
TF: 800-250-3860					
Casing Assoc Inc 1120 Close Ave	Bronx	NY	10472	718-842-7151	617-6894
TF: 800-223-8318					
Cattaneo Brothers Inc 769 Caudill St	San Luis Obispo	CA	93401	805-543-7188	543-4698
TF: 800-243-8537 ■ Web: www.cattaneobros.com					
Cher-Make Sausage Co 2915 Calumet Ave	Manitowoc	WI	54220	920-683-5980	682-2588
TF: 800-242-7679 ■ Web: www.cher-make.com					
Chicago Meat Authority Inc 1120 W 47th Pl	Chicago	IL	60609	773-254-3811	254-5851
TF: 800-383-3811 ■ Web: www.chicagomeat.com					
Chicopee Provision Co Inc 19 Sitarz St	Chicopee	MA	01014	413-594-4765	594-2584
TF: 800-924-6328 ■ Web: www.bluesealkielbasa.com					
Citterio USA Corp 2008 SR 940	Freeland	PA	18224	570-636-3171	636-1267
TF: 800-435-8888 ■ Web: www.citterio.com					
Clifty Farm Country Ham Co Inc 1500 Hwy 641 S PO Box 1146	Paris	TN	38242	731-642-9740	642-7129
TF: 800-486-4267 ■ Web: www.cliftyfarm.com					
Cloverdale Foods Co Inc 3015 34th St NW PO Box 667	Mandan	ND	58554	701-663-9511	663-0690
TF: 800-669-9511 ■ Web: www.cloverdalefoods.com					
Coleman Natural Foods 1767 Denver West Blvd Suite 200	Golden	CO	80401	303-468-2500	
TF: 800-442-8666 ■ Web: www.colemannatural.com					
ConAgra/Hebrew National 2 Jericho Plaza Suite 304	Jericho	NY	11753	516-949-7500	933-4620
TF: 800-275-5454 ■ Web: www.hebrewnational.com					
Conti Packing Co Inc 2299 Brighton Henritta Town Line Rd PO box 23025	Rochester	NY	14692	585-424-2500	424-2504
Continental-Capri Inc 250 Jackson St	Englewood	NJ	07631	201-568-7100	568-7180
Cook's Ham Inc 200 S 2nd St	Lincoln	NE	68508	402-475-6700	
Web: www.cooksham.com					
Counts Sausage Co Inc 220 Church St PO Box 390	Prosperity	SC	29127	803-364-2392	364-1570
TF: 800-868-0041					
Cudahy Patrick Inc 1 Sweet Apple-Wood Ln	Cudahy	WI	53110	414-744-2000	744-4213
TF: 800-486-6900 ■ Web: www.patrickcudahy.com					
Daniel Weaver Co 1415 Weavertown Rd PO Box 525	Lebanon	PA	17042	717-274-6100	274-6103
TF: 800-932-8377					
Dearborn Sausage Co Inc 2450 Wyoming Ave	Dearborn	MI	48120	313-842-2375	842-2640
Web: www.dearbornsausage.com					
Dewied International Inc 5010 E IH-10	San Antonio	TX	78219	210-661-6161	662-6112
TF: 800-992-5600 ■ Web: www.dewied.com					
Dial Corp 15501 N Dial Blvd	Scottsdale	AZ	85260	480-754-3425	
TF Cust Svc: 800-258-3425 ■ Web: www.dialcorp.com					
Dietz & Watson Inc 5701 Tacony St	Philadelphia	PA	19135	215-831-9000	831-1044
TF: 800-333-1974 ■ Web: www.dietzandwatson.com					
Dold Foods Inc 2929 N Ohio St	Wichita	KS	67204	316-838-9101	838-9053
Ed Miniat Inc 1055 W 175th St Suite 201	Homewood	IL	60430	708-957-3800	957-7413
TF: 800-621-8793 ■ Web: www.miniat.com					
Empire National Kosher 123 Grand St	Brooklyn	NY	11211	718-384-7400	384-7403
Web: www.empirenational.com					
Fabbri Sausage Mfg Co 166 N Aberdeen St	Chicago	IL	60607	312-829-6363	
Web: www.fabbrisausage.com					
Fairbank Farms 1 Fairbank Rd	Ashville	NY	14710	716-782-2000	782-2900
Family Brands International LLC 1001 Elm Hill Rd PO Box 429	Lenoir City	TN	37771	865-986-8005	986-7171
TF: 800-356-4455 ■ Web: www.fbico.com					
Fargo Packing & Sausage Co 307 E Main Ave	West Fargo	ND	58078	701-282-3211	282-0325
Farm Boy Meats 2751 N Kentucky Ave PO Box 996	Evansville	IN	47706	812-425-5231	428-8432
TF: 800-852-3976 ■ Web: www.farmboyfoodservice.com					
Farmland Foods Inc 7501 NW Tiffany Springs Pkey	Kansas City	MO	64153	816-801-4300	801-1959
TF: 888-327-6526 ■ Web: www.farmlandfoods.com					
FB Purnell Sausage Co Inc 6931 Shelbyville Rd PO Box 366	Simpsonville	KY	40067	502-722-5626	722-5586
TF: 800-262-6584 ■ Web: www.itsgooo-od.com					
Fisher Meats Inc 85 Front St N	Issaquah	WA	98027	425-392-3131	392-0168
Frank Wardynski & Sons Inc 336 Peckham St	Buffalo	NY	14206	716-854-6083	854-4887
Web: www.wardynski.com					
Fred Usinger Inc 1030 N Old World 3rd St	Milwaukee	WI	53203	414-276-9100	291-5277
TF: 800-558-9997 ■ Web: www.usinger.com					
Freedom Sausage Inc 4155 E 1650th Rd	Earlville	IL	60518	815-792-8276	792-8283
Freirich Julian Food Products Inc 815 W Kerr St	Salisbury	NC	28144	704-636-2621	636-4650
TF: 800-554-4788 ■ Web: www.freirich.com					
Gallo Salami 2411 Baumann Ave	San Lorenzo	CA	94580	510-276-1300	278-2177
TF: 800-321-1097					
Gold Star Sausage Co Inc 2800 Walnut St PO Box 4245	Denver	CO	80204	303-295-6400	294-0495
TF: 800-258-7229					
Golden State Foods 18301 Von Karman Ave Suite 1100	Irvine	CA	92612	949-252-2000	252-2080
Web: www.goldenstatefoods.com					
Grand Choice Foods 1131 Dayton Ave	Ames	IA	50010	515-232-2273	232-3003
TF: 800-250-3860					
Great Lakes Packing Co 1535 W 43rd St	Chicago	IL	60609	773-927-6660	927-8587
Green Bay Dressed Beef Inc 544 Acme St PO Box 8547	Green Bay	WI	54308	920-437-4311	436-6510
TF: 800-345-0293					
Green Tree Packing Co 65 Central Ave	Passaic	NJ	07055	973-473-1305	473-7975
TF: 800-221-5754					
Greenwood Packing Plant DBA Carolina Pride 1 Packer Ave	Greenwood	SC	29646	864-229-5611	229-5386
Web: www.carolinaprideonline.com					
Grote & Weigel Inc 76 Granby St	Bloomfield	CT	06002	860-242-8528	242-4162
TF: 800-973-6370 ■ Web: www.groteandweigel.com					
Gwaltney of Smithfield Ltd 601 N Church St	Smithfield	VA	23430	757-357-3131	
TF: 800-888-7521 ■ Web: www.gwaltneyfoods.com					
H & H Meat Products Inc DBA H & H Foods 2009 E Expy 83 PO Box 358	Mercedes	TX	78570	956-565-6363	565-4108
TF: 800-365-4632 ■ Web: www.hhfoods.com					

				Phone	Fax
Habbersett Scrapple Inc 701 Ashland Ave Suite A-4	Folcroft	PA	19032	610-532-9973	586-2396
Web: www.habbersettscrapple.com					
Hahn Brothers Inc 440 Hahn Rd PO Box 395	Westminster	MD	21158	410-848-4200	848-1247
TF: 800-227-7675					
Hansel 'n Gretel Brand Inc 79-36 Cooper Ave	Glendale	NY	11385	718-326-0041	326-2069
TF: 800-635-3354					
Hatfield Quality Meats Inc 2700 Funks Rd PO Box 902	Hatfield	PA	19440	215-368-2500	
TF: 800-523-5291 ■ *Web:* www.hatfieldqualitymeats.com					
Hazle Park Packing Co 260 Washington Ave Hazle Park	West Hazleton	PA	18202	570-455-7571	455-6030
Hebrew National 2 Jericho Plaza Suite 304	Jericho	NY	11753	516-949-7500	933-4620
TF: 800-275-5454 ■ *Web:* www.hebrewnational.com					
Henry's Hickory House Inc 249 Copeland St	Jacksonville	FL	32204	904-354-6839	354-6028
Hi Grade Meats Inc 2160 S West Temple St	Salt Lake City	UT	84115	801-487-5818	487-4343
Hillshire Farm & Kahn's 3241 Spring Grove Ave	Cincinnati	OH	45225	513-541-4000	853-1592
TF: 800-543-4465 ■ *Web:* www.hillshirefarm.com					
Hormel Foods Corp 1 Hormel Pl	Austin	MN	55912	507-437-5611	437-5489*
NYSE: HRL ■ **Fax:* Sales ■ *TF:* 800-523-4635 ■ *Web:* www.hormel.com					
Hormel Foods International Corp 1 Hormel Pl	Austin	MN	55912	507-437-5478	437-5113
TF: 800-523-4635 ■ *Web:* www.hormel.com					
Hummel Brothers Inc 180 Sargent Dr	New Haven	CT	06511	203-787-4113	498-1755
TF: 800-828-8978					
Ito Cariani Foods Div Itoham America Inc 3190 Corporate Pl	Hayward	CA	94545	510-887-0882	
Web: www.itocariani.com					
JC Potter Sausage Co 1914 Hwy 70 E	Durant	OK	74701	580-924-2414	924-2415
TF: 800-321-8549 ■ *Web:* www.jcpotter.com					
John Hofmeister & Son Inc 2386 S Blue Island Ave	Chicago	IL	60608	773-847-0700	847-6624
Web: www.hofhaus.com					
John Morrell & Co 805 E Kemper Rd	Cincinnati	OH	45246	513-346-3540	346-7552*
**Fax:* Cust Svc ■ *TF:* 800-445-2013 ■ *Web:* www.johnmorrell.com					
Johnsonville Sausage LLC					
W4202 County Hwy J PO Box 906	Sheboygan Falls	WI	53085	920-467-2641	467-2818
TF: 888-733-2728 ■ *Web:* www.johnsonville.com					
Jones Dairy Farm 800 Jones Ave PO Box 808	Fort Atkinson	WI	53538	920-563-2431	563-6801
TF: 800-635-6637 ■ *Web:* www.jonesdairyfarm.com					
Joseph McSweeney & Sons Inc					
1618 Ownby Ln PO Box 26409	Richmond	VA	23260	804-359-6024	358-2852
TF: 800-552-6927					
Karl Ehmer Inc 63-35 Fresh Pond Rd	Ridgewood	NY	11385	718-456-8100	456-2270
TF: 800-487-5275 ■ *Web:* www.karlehmer.com					
Kayem Foods Inc 75 Arlington St	Chelsea	MA	02150	617-889-1600	889-5931
TF: 800-426-6100 ■ *Web:* www.kayem.com					
Kessler's Inc 1201 Hummel Ave	Lemoyne	PA	17043	717-763-7162	763-4982
TF: 800-382-1328 ■ *Web:* www.kesslerfoods.com					
Keystone Foods LLC					
300 Bar Harbor Dr Suite 600 5 Tower Bridge	West Conshohocken	PA	19428	610-667-6700	667-1460
Web: www.keystonefoods.com					
Klement Sausage Co Inc 207 E Lincoln Ave	Milwaukee	WI	53207	414-744-2330	744-2438
TF: 800-553-6368 ■ *Web:* www.klements.com					
Koegel Meats Inc 3400 W Bristol Rd	Flint	MI	48507	810-238-3685	238-2467
Web: www.koegelmeats.com					
Kowalski Sausage Co Inc 2270 Holbrook Ave	Hamtramck	MI	48212	313-873-8200	873-4220
TF: 800-482-2400					
Kraft Foods Inc Oscar Mayer Foods Div 910 Mayer Ave	Madison	WI	53704	608-241-3311	
Web: www.kraftfoods.com/om					
Kunzler & Co Inc 652 Manor St	Lancaster	PA	17603	717-299-6301	390-2170
TF: 888-586-9537 ■ *Web:* www.kunzler.com					
Land O'Frost Inc 16850 Chicago Ave	Lansing	IL	60438	708-474-7100	474-9329
TF: 800-323-3308 ■ *Web:* www.landofrost.com					
Levonian Brothers Inc 27 River St PO Box 629	Troy	NY	12180	518-274-3610	274-0098
TF Cust Svc: 800-538-6642					
Lopez Foods Inc 9500 NW 4th St	Oklahoma City	OK	73127	405-789-7500	499-0114
Web: www.lopezfoods.com					
Lykes Meat Group 4611 Lykes Rd	Plant City	FL	33566	813-752-1102	759-4201
Maid-Rite Steak Co Inc 105 Keystone Industrial Park	Dunmore	PA	18512	570-343-4748	969-2878
TF: 800-233-4259 ■ *Web:* www.maidritesteak.com					
Makowski's Real Sausage Co 2710 S Poplar Ave	Chicago	IL	60608	312-842-5330	842-5414
Maple Leaf Consumer Foods 321 Cortland Ave E	Kitchener	ON	N2G3X8	519-741-5000	749-7400
TF: 800-567-3212 ■ *Web:* www.mapleleaf.ca					
Maple Leaf Foods Inc 30 Saint Clair Ave W Suite 1500	Toronto	ON	M4V3A2	416-926-2000	926-2018
TSX: MFI ■ *Web:* www.mapleleaf.ca					
Marathon Enterprises Inc 9 Smith St	Englewood	NJ	07631	201-935-3330	935-5693
TF: 800-722-7388					
Martin Rosol Inc 45 Grove St	New Britain	CT	06053	860-223-2707	229-6690
Web: www.martinrosols.com					
McSweeney Joseph & Sons Inc					
1618 Ownby Ln PO Box 26409	Richmond	VA	23260	804-359-6024	358-2852
TF: 800-552-6927					
Meadow Farms Sausage Co 6215 S Western Ave	Los Angeles	CA	90047	323-752-2300	752-5640
Milan Salami Co Inc 1155 67th St	Oakland	CA	94608	510-654-7055	654-7257
Miller Packing Co 1122 Industrial Way PO Box 1390	Lodi	CA	95241	209-339-2310	334-0848
TF: 800-624-2328 ■ *Web:* www.millerhotdogs.com					
Miniat Ed Inc 1055 W 175th St Suite 201	Homewood	IL	60430	708-957-3800	957-7413
TF: 800-621-8793 ■ *Web:* www.miniat.com					
Mongolia Casing Corp 4706 Grand Ave	Maspeth	NY	11378	718-628-4500	628-5800
TF: 800-221-4887					
Morrell John & Co 805 E Kemper Rd	Cincinnati	OH	45246	513-346-3540	346-7552*
**Fax:* Cust Svc ■ *TF:* 800-445-2013 ■ *Web:* www.johnmorrell.com					
Murry's Inc 8300 Pennsylvania Ave	Upper Marlboro	MD	20772	301-420-6400	967-4816
TF: 800-638-0215 ■ *Web:* www.murrys.com					
Natural Casing Co 410 E Railroad St	Peshtigo	WI	54157	715-582-3736	582-3931
Neto Sausage Co Inc 3499 Alameda St PO Box 578	Santa Clara	CA	95052	408-296-0818	296-0538
TF: 888-482-6386 ■ *Web:* www.netosausage.com					
North Side Foods Corp 2200 Rivers Edge Dr	Arnold	PA	15068	724-335-5800	335-2249
Oberto Sausage Co 7060 S 238th St	Kent	WA	98032	253-437-6100	437-6153
TF: 877-234-7902 ■ *Web:* www.oberto.com					
Odom's Tennessee Pride Sausage Inc 1201 Neelys Bend Rd	Madison	TN	37115	615-868-1360	860-4703
TF: 800-327-6269 ■ *Web:* www.tnpride.com					
Old Wisconsin Sausage Co 5030 Claybird Rd	Sheboygan	WI	53083	920-458-4304	458-2716
TF: 800-558-7840					
Oscar Mayer Foods Div Kraft Foods Inc 910 Mayer Ave	Madison	WI	53704	608-241-3311	
Web: www.kraftfoods.com/om					
OSI Industries LLC 1225 Corporate Blvd	Aurora	IL	60504	630-851-6600	851-8223
Web: www.osigroup.com					
Owens Country Sausage Inc 1403 E Lookout Dr	Richardson	TX	75082	972-235-7181	235-2135
TF: 800-966-9367 ■ *Web:* www.owensinc.com					
Palama Meat Co Inc 2029 Lauwiliwili St	Kapolei	HI	96707	808-682-8305	834-8895
Palmyra Bologna Co Inc DBA Seltzer's Smokehouse Meats					
230 N College St PO Box 111	Palmyra	PA	17078	717-838-6336	838-5345
TF: 800-282-6336 ■ *Web:* www.seltzerslebanonbologna.com					
Park 100 Foods Inc 326 E Adams St	Tipton	IN	46072	765-675-3480	675-3474
Web: www.park100foods.com					
Peer Foods Group Inc 1200 W 35th St Suite 5E	Chicago	IL	60609	773-927-1440	927-9859
TF: 800-365-5644 ■ *Web:* www.peerfoods.com					
Phillips Brothers Country Ham Inc 1523 S Fayetteville St	Asheboro	NC	27205	336-625-4321	625-4322
Web: phillipsbrotherscountryhams.com					
Pierre Foods Inc 9990 Princeton Rd	Cincinnati	OH	45246	513-874-8741	874-1756
Web: www.pierrefoods.com					
Pine Ridge Farms 1800 Maury St	Des Moines	IA	50317	515-266-4100	266-9889
Web: www.pineridgefarmspork.com					
Plumrose USA Inc 7 Lexington Ave	East Brunswick	NJ	08816	732-257-6600	257-6644
TF: 800-526-4909 ■ *Web:* www.plumroseusa.com					
Potter JC Sausage Co 1914 Hwy 70 E	Durant	OK	74701	580-924-2414	924-2415
TF: 800-321-8549 ■ *Web:* www.jcpotter.com					
Premio Foods Inc 50 Utter Ave	Hawthorne	NJ	07506	973-427-1106	427-1140
TF: 800-864-7622 ■ *Web:* www.premiofoods.com					
Purnell FB Sausage Co Inc					
6931 Shelbyville Rd PO Box 366	Simpsonville	KY	40067	502-722-5626	722-5586
TF: 800-262-6584 ■ *Web:* www.itsgooo-od.com					
Reser's Fine Foods Inc 15570 SW Jenkins Rd PO Box 8	Beaverton	OR	97075	503-643-6431	
TF: 800-333-6431 ■ *Web:* www.resers.com					
Rosol Martin Inc 45 Grove St	New Britain	CT	06053	860-223-2707	229-6690
Web: www.martinrosols.com					
Russer Foods Inc 665 Perry St	Buffalo	NY	14210	716-826-6400	822-4628
TF: 800-826-6400					
Saags Products Inc 1799 Factor Ave	San Leandro	CA	94577	510-352-8000	352-4100
TF: 800-352-7224 ■ *Web:* www.saags.com					
Sabrett Food Products Corp 9 Smith St	Englewood	NJ	07631	201-935-3330	935-5693
TF: 800-722-7388 ■ *Web:* www.sabrett.com					
Sara Lee Food & Beverage 3500 Lacey Rd	Downers Grove	IL	60515	630-598-7892	598-8221
TF: 866-727-2533 ■ *Web:* www.saraleefoods.com					
Schaller & Weber Inc 22-35 46th St	Astoria	NY	11105	718-721-5480	956-9157
TF Orders: 800-847-4115 ■ *Web:* www.schallerweber.com					
Seltzer's Smokehouse Meats 230 N College St PO Box 111	Palmyra	PA	17078	717-838-6336	838-5345
TF: 800-282-6336 ■ *Web:* www.seltzerslebanonbologna.com					
Silver Star Meats Inc 1720 Middletown Rd PO Box 393	McKees Rocks	PA	15136	412-771-5539	
TF: 800-548-1321 ■ *Web:* www.silverstarmeats.com					
Simeus Foods International Inc 812 S 5th Ave	Mansfield	TX	76063	817-473-1562	473-2017
TF: 888-772-3663 ■ *Web:* www.simeusfoods.com					
Smith Packing Co Inc 105-125 Washington St	Utica	NY	13503	315-732-5125	732-5129
Web: www.smithpacking.com					
Smithfield Foods Inc 200 Commerce St	Smithfield	VA	23430	757-365-3000	365-3017*
NYSE: SFD ■ **Fax:* Cust Svc ■ *TF:* 800-276-6158 ■ *Web:* www.smithfieldfoods.com					
Smithfield Ham & Products Co Inc 311 Court St Suite 201	Portsmouth	VA	23705	800-628-2242	673-7006*
**Fax Area Code:* 757 ■ *TF:* 800-628-2242 ■ *Web:* www.smithfield-companies.com					
Sparrer Sausage Co Inc 4320 W Ogden Ave	Chicago	IL	60623	773-762-3334	521-9368
TF: 800-666-3287 ■ *Web:* www.sparrers.com					
Specialty Foods Group Inc 603 Pilot House Dr 4th Fl	Newport News	VA	23606	757-952-1200	952-1201
Web: www.sfgtrust.com					
Standard Casing Co Inc 165 Chubb Ave	Lyndhurst	NJ	07071	201-434-6300	434-1508
TF: 800-847-4141					
Stevison Ham Co 125 Stevison Ham Rd	Portland	TN	37148	615-325-4161	325-5914
TF: 800-844-4267					
Stock Yards Packing Co Inc 340 N Oakley Blvd	Chicago	IL	60612	312-733-6050	733-0738
TF: 800-621-3687 ■ *Web:* www.stockyards.com					
Storer Meats Co Inc 3007 Clinton Ave	Cleveland	OH	44113	216-621-7538	361-0622
TF: 800-355-7537					
Suzanna's Kitchen Inc 4025 Buford Hwy	Duluth	GA	30096	770-476-9900	476-8899
TF: 800-241-2455 ■ *Web:* www.suzannaskitchen.com					
Swift & Co 1770 Promontory Cir	Greeley	CO	80634	970-506-8000	506-8719
TF: 800-727-5366 ■ *Web:* www.swiftbrands.com					
Taylor Provisions 63 Perrine Ave PO Box 5108	Trenton	NJ	08638	609-392-1113	392-1354
Teepak LLC 1011 Warrenville Rd Suite 255	Lisle	IL	60532	630-493-9080	719-3805
TF: 800-544-9861 ■ *Web:* www.teepak.com					
Tyson Prepared Foods Inc 5701 McNutt Rd	Santa Teresa	NM	88008	505-589-0100	589-1903*
**Fax:* Acctg ■ *TF:* 800-351-8184 ■ *Web:* www.tyson.com					
Usinger Fred Inc 1030 N Old World 3rd St	Milwaukee	WI	53203	414-276-9100	291-5277
TF: 800-558-9997 ■ *Web:* www.usinger.com					
Vienna Sausage Mfg Co 2501 N Damen Ave	Chicago	IL	60647	773-278-7800	278-4759
TF: 800-621-8183 ■ *Web:* www.viennabeef.com					
Vincent Giordano Corp 2600 Washington Ave	Philadelphia	PA	19146	215-467-6629	467-6339
Web: www.vgiordano.com					
Vollwerth & Co 200 Hancock St PO Box 239	Hancock	MI	49930	906-482-1550	482-0842
TF: 800-562-7620 ■ *Web:* www.vollwerth.com					
Wardynski Frank & Sons Inc 336 Peckham St	Buffalo	NY	14206	716-854-6083	854-4887
Web: www.wardynski.com					
Weaver Daniel Co 1415 Weavertown Rd PO Box 525	Lebanon	PA	17042	717-274-6100	274-6103
TF: 800-932-8377					
Wimmer's Meat Products Inc 126 W Grant St PO Box 286	West Point	NE	68788	402-372-2437	372-5659
TF Sales: 800-358-0761 ■ *Web:* www.wimmersmeats.com					
Wolfson Casing Corp 700 S Fulton Ave	Mount Vernon	NY	10550	914-668-9000	668-6900
TF: 800-221-8042 ■ *Web:* www.wolfsoncasing.com					
Wright Brand Foods Inc 700 Wheeler St	Vernon	TX	76385	940-553-1811	553-3747
TF: 800-772-0844 ■ *Web:* www.wrightbrand.com					
Zartic Inc 438 Lavender Dr	Rome	GA	30165	706-234-3000	291-6068
TF Cust Svc: 800-241-0516 ■ *Web:* www.zartic.com					
Zweigles Inc 651 Plymouth Ave N	Rochester	NY	14608	585-546-1740	546-8721
Web: www.zweigles.com					

299-27 Milk & Cream Products

				Phone	Fax
Agri-Mark Inc PO Box 5800	Lawrence	MA	01842	978-689-4442	794-8304
Web: www.agrimark.net					
Agropur Co-op Agro-alimentaire 510 rue Principale	Granby	QC	J2G7G2	450-375-1991	375-2099
TF: 800-363-6190					
Allen Milk Div T Marzetti Co 1709 Frank Rd	Columbus	OH	43223	614-279-8673	279-5674
Alta Dena Dairy 17637 E Valley Blvd	City of Industry	CA	91744	626-964-6401	965-1960
TF Orders: 800-533-2479 ■ *Web:* www.altadenadairy.com					
AMPI 315 N Broadway	New Ulm	MN	56073	507-354-8295	359-8668
TF: 800-533-3580 ■ *Web:* www.ampi.com					
Anderson Dairy Inc 801 Searles Ave	Las Vegas	NV	89101	702-642-7507	642-3480
Web: www.andersondairy.com					
Anderson Erickson Dairy Co 2420 E University Ave	Des Moines	IA	50317	515-265-2521	263-6301
TF: 800-234-7257 ■ *Web:* www.aedairy.com					
Atlanta Dairies Inc 777 Memorial Dr SE	Atlanta	GA	30316	404-688-2671	523-0385
Barber Dairies Inc 36 Barber Ct	Birmingham	AL	35209	205-942-2351	943-0297
Web: www.barbersdairy.com					
Barber Pure Milk Co 19 Green Briar Rd	Anniston	AL	36201	256-240-9141	240-9672
TF: 800-264-4157					
Bartlett Dairy Inc 150-03 150th St	Jamaica	NY	11433	718-658-2299	725-2527
Web: www.bartlettny.com					
Berkeley Farms Inc 25500 Clawiter Rd	Hayward	CA	94545	510-265-8600	265-8754*
**Fax:* Sales ■ *Web:* www.berkeleyfarms.com					
Broughton Foods Co 1701 Green St	Marietta	OH	45750	740-373-4121	373-2861
TF: 800-283-2479					
California Dairies Inc 11709 E Artesia Blvd	Artesia	CA	90701	562-865-1291	860-8633
TF: 800-821-5588 ■ *Web:* www.californiadairies.com					
Century Foods International 400 Century Ct PO Box 257	Sparta	WI	54656	608-269-1900	269-1910
Web: www.centuryfoods.com					
CF Burger Creamery Co 8101 Greenfield Rd	Detroit	MI	48228	313-584-4040	584-9870
TF: 800-229-2322					
Clover Farms Dairy PO Box 14627	Reading	PA	19612	610-921-9111	
TF Cust Svc: 800-323-0123 ■ *Web:* www.farmersdairy.com					

Milk & Cream Products (Cont'd)

				Phone	Fax
Cloverland Green Spring Dairy Inc 2701 Loch Raven Rd	Baltimore	MD	21218	410-235-4477	889-3690
TF Orders: 800-876-6455 ■ *Web:* www.cloverlanddairy.com					
Coleman Dairy Inc 6901 I-30	Little Rock	AR	72209	501-565-1551	568-1710
TF: 800-365-1551 ■ *Web:* www.colemandairy.com					
Country Fresh Inc 355 Mart St SW	Grand Rapids	MI	49548	616-243-0173	243-5926
TF: 800-748-0480 ■ *Web:* www.enjoycountryfresh.com					
Crossroad Farms Dairy 400 S Shortridge Rd	Indianapolis	IN	46219	317-229-7600	229-7676
TF: 800-334-7502					
Dairy Fresh Corp 915 Tuscaloosa St	Greensboro	AL	36744	334-624-3041	
Dairymen's Milk Co 3068 W 106th St	Cleveland	OH	44111	216-671-2300	944-0232*
**Fax Area Code:* 800 ■ *TF:* 800-944-2301					
Dannon Co 100 Hillside Ave	White Plains	NY	10603	914-872-8400	872-1573*
**Fax:* Hum Res ■ *Web:* www.dannon.com					
Dean Foods Co 2515 McKinney Ave Suite 1200 Box 30	Dallas	TX	75201	214-303-3400	303-3499
NYSE: DF ■ *Web:* www.deanfoods.com					
Fairmont Products Inc 15 Kishacoquillas St	Belleville	PA	17004	717-935-2121	935-5473
TF: 800-525-9338					
Farmers Select LLC 7321 N Loop Rd	El Paso	TX	79915	915-772-2736	772-0907
Farmland Dairies LLC 520 Main Ave	Wallington	NJ	07057	973-777-2500	777-7648*
**Fax:* Sales ■ *TF:* 800-275-4645 ■ *Web:* www.farmlanddairies.com					
Flav-O-Rich 1105 N William St	Goldsboro	NC	27530	919-734-0728	735-6344
TF: 877-321-1158					
Galliker Dairy Co Inc 143 Donald Ln	Johnstown	PA	15904	814-266-8702	266-4619
TF: 800-477-6455 ■ *Web:* www.gallikers.com					
Garelick Farms Inc					
124 Grove St Franklin Oaks Office Park Suite 100	Franklin	MA	02038	508-528-9000	553-5475*
**Fax:* Sales ■ *TF:* 800-343-4982					
Gillette Dairy of the Black Hills Inc PO Box 2553	Rapid City	SD	57709	605-348-1500	348-6934
TF: 800-933-3247					
Guida-Seibert Dairy Co 433 Park St	New Britain	CT	06051	860-224-2404	225-0035
TF: 800-832-8929 ■ *Web:* www.supercow.com					
Gustafson's Dairy Inc 4169 County Rd 15-A	Green Cove Springs	FL	32043	904-284-3750	284-5570
TF: 800-342-1092 ■ *Web:* www.gustafsonsdairy.com					
H Meyer Dairy Co 415 John St	Cincinnati	OH	45215	513-948-8811	948-8837*
**Fax:* Sales ■ *TF:* 800-347-6455 ■ *Web:* meyerdairy.com					
Harrisburg Dairies Inc 2001 Herr St	Harrisburg	PA	17105	717-233-8701	231-4584
TF: 800-692-7429 ■ *Web:* www.harrisburgdairies.com					
Heritage Foods LLC 4002 Westminster Ave	Santa Ana	CA	92703	714-775-5000	239-6027*
**Fax Area Code:* 800 ■ *TF Orders:* 800-321-5960					
Hiland Dairy Co 1133 E Kearney St PO Box 2270	Springfield	MO	65801	417-862-9311	837-1106
TF: 800-641-4022 ■ *Web:* www.hilanddairy.com					
Hood HP LLC 90 Everett Ave	Chelsea	MA	02150	617-887-3000	887-8484
TF Cust Svc: 800-662-4468 ■ *Web:* www.hphood.com					
HP Hood LLC 90 Everett Ave	Chelsea	MA	02150	617-887-3000	887-8484
TF Cust Svc: 800-662-4468 ■ *Web:* www.hphood.com					
Johanna Foods Inc 20 Johanna Farm Rd	Flemington	NJ	08822	908-788-2200	788-2200
TF: 800-727-6700 ■ *Web:* www.johannafoods.com					
Kemps LLC 1270 Energy Ln	Saint Paul	MN	55108	651-379-6500	379-6806
TF: 800-322-9566 ■ *Web:* www.kemps.com					
Kinney Dairy Inc 1215 N Johnson St	Bay City	MI	48708	989-893-9741	
Land O'Lakes Inc 4001 Lexington Ave N	Arden Hills	MN	55126	651-481-2222	481-2488*
**Fax:* Hum Res ■ *TF:* 800-328-9680 ■ *Web:* www.landolakesinc.com					
Land O'Lakes Inc Dairyman's Div 400 S 'M' St	Tulare	CA	93274	559-687-8287	685-6911*
**Fax:* Sales					
Lee TG Foods Inc 315 N Bumby Ave	Orlando	FL	32803	407-894-4941	896-4757
Lehigh Valley Dairies Inc 880 Allentown Rd	Lansdale	PA	19446	215-855-8205	855-9834
TF: 800-937-3233 ■ *Web:* www.lehighmilk.com					
Lifeway Foods Inc 6431 W Oakton St	Morton Grove	IL	60053	847-967-1010	967-6558
NASDAQ: LWAY ■ *Web:* www.lifeway.net					
Luvel Dairy Products Inc 926 Hwy 35 Bypass S	Kosciusko	MS	39090	662-289-2511	289-2572
Maola Milk & Ice Cream Co 305 Ave C	New Bern	NC	28563	252-638-1131	638-2268
TF: 800-476-1021 ■ *Web:* www.maolamilk.com					
Maple Hill Farms Inc 12 Burr Rd PO Box 767	Bloomfield	CT	06002	860-242-9689	243-2490
TF: 800-243-0067					
Marcus Dairy Inc 3 Sugar Hollow Rd	Danbury	CT	06810	203-748-5611	791-2759
TF: 800-243-2511 ■ *Web:* www.marcusdairy.com					
Mayfield Dairy Farms Inc PO Box 310	Athens	TN	37371	423-745-2151	745-6385
TF: 800-362-9546 ■ *Web:* www.mayfielddairy.com					
McArthur Dairy Inc 500 Sawgrass Corporate Pkwy	Sunrise	FL	33325	954-846-1234	846-0429
TF: 877-803-6565 ■ *Web:* www.mcarthurdairy.com					
Meadow Brook Dairy 2365 Buffalo Rd	Erie	PA	16510	814-899-3191	899-9426
TF: 800-458-2304 ■ *Web:* www.meadowbrookdairy.com					
Meyer H Dairy Co 415 John St	Cincinnati	OH	45215	513-948-8811	948-8837*
**Fax:* Sales ■ *TF:* 800-347-6455 ■ *Web:* meyerdairy.com					
Michigan Milk Producers Assn 41310 Bridge St	Novi	MI	48375	248-474-6672	474-0924
Web: www.mimilk.com					
Mid States Dairy Co 6040 N Lindbergh Blvd	Saint Louis	MO	63042	314-731-1150	731-1198
TF: 800-473-1150					
Milkco Inc 220 Deaverview Rd	Asheville	NC	28806	828-254-9560	252-9560
TF: 800-842-8021					
Oakhurst Dairy 364 Forest Ave	Portland	ME	04101	207-772-7468	874-0714
TF: 800-482-0718 ■ *Web:* www.oakhurstdairy.com					
Oberlin Farms Dairy Inc DBA Dairymen's Milk Co					
3068 W 106th St	Cleveland	OH	44111	216-671-2300	944-0232*
**Fax Area Code:* 800 ■ *TF:* 800-944-2301					
Parmalat Canada Ltd 405 The West Mall 10th Fl	Toronto	ON	M9C5J1	416-626-1973	620-3123
Web: www.parmalat.ca					
Penn Maid Foods Inc 10975 Dutton Rd	Philadelphia	PA	19154	215-824-2800	824-2820
TF: 800-220-7063 ■ *Web:* www.pennmaid.com					
Prairie Farms Dairy Inc 1100 N Broadway St	Carlinville	IL	62626	217-854-2547	854-6426
TF: 800-654-2547 ■ *Web:* www.prairiefarms.com					
Pride of Main Street Dairy 214 Main St S	Sauk Centre	MN	56378	320-351-8300	351-8500
Producers Dairy Foods Inc 250 E Belmont Ave	Fresno	CA	93701	559-264-6583	264-2218*
**Fax:* Orders ■ *TF:* 800-244-6024 ■ *Web:* www.producersdairy.com					
Purity Dairies Inc 360 Murfreesboro Rd	Nashville	TN	37210	615-244-1900	242-8547
TF: 800-947-6455 ■ *Web:* www.puritydairies.com					
Readington Farms Inc 12 Mill Rd	Whitehouse Station	NJ	08889	908-534-2121	534-5235
TF: 800-426-1707					
Roberts Dairy 3805 S Emanuel Cleaver II Blvd	Kansas City	MO	64128	816-921-7370	921-3437
TF: 800-279-1692 ■ *Web:* www.robertsdairy.com					
Royal Crest Dairy Inc 350 S Pearl St	Denver	CO	80209	303-777-2227	744-9173
Web: www.royalcrestdairy.com					
Rutter Dairy Inc 2100 N George St	York	PA	17404	717-848-9827	845-8751
Web: www.rutters.com					
Saputo Inc 6869 boul Metropolitain	Saint-Leonard	QC	H1P1X8	514-328-6662	328-3310
TSX: SAP ■ *Web:* www.saputo.com					
Schneider Valley Farms Dairy 1860 E 3rd St	Williamsport	PA	17701	570-326-2021	326-2736
TF: 800-332-8563					
Schneider's Dairy Inc 726 Frank St	Pittsburgh	PA	15227	412-881-3525	881-7722
Schroeder Milk Co Inc 2080 Rice St	Maplewood	MN	55113	651-487-1471	487-1476
TF: 800-354-6775 ■ *Web:* www.schroedermilk.com					
Shamrock Foods Co Inc 2540 N 29th Ave	Phoenix	AZ	85009	602-233-6400	477-6469
TF: 800-388-3247 ■ *Web:* www.shamrockfoods.com					
Shenandoah's Pride Dairy Inc					
168 Dinkel Ave PO Box 120	Mount Crawford	VA	22841	540-442-6000	442-6111
TF: 888-840-6001					
Smith Dairy 1381 Dairy Ln	Orrville	OH	44667	330-683-8710	683-1079
TF: 800-776-7076 ■ *Web:* www.smithdairy.com					
Smith Dairy Wayne Div 1590 NW 11th St	Richmond	IN	47375	765-935-7521	962-5269
TF: 800-875-9296					
Southeast Milk Inc 1950 SE Hwy 484	Belleview	FL	34420	352-245-2437	307-5528
TF: 800-598-7866 ■ *Web:* www.southeastmilk.org					
Southern Belle Dairy Co Inc 607 E Bourne Ave PO Box 1020	Somerset	KY	42502	606-679-1131	441-8931*
**Fax Area Code:* 800 ■ *TF:* 800-468-4798 ■ *Web:* www.southernbelledairy.com					
Steuben Foods Inc 155-04 Liberty Ave	Jamaica	NY	11433	718-291-3333	291-0560
Stonyfield Farm Inc 10 Burton Dr	Londonderry	NH	03053	603-437-4040	437-7594
TF: 800-776-2697 ■ *Web:* www.stonyfield.com					
Superior Dairy Inc 4719 Navarre Rd SW	Canton	OH	44706	330-477-4515	477-5908
TF: 800-683-2479					
T Marzetti Co Allen Milk Div 1709 Frank Rd	Columbus	OH	43223	614-279-8673	279-5674
TG Lee Foods Inc 315 N Bumby Ave	Orlando	FL	32803	407-894-4941	896-4757
Tuscan Dairy Farms Inc 750 Union Ave	Union	NJ	07083	908-686-1500	686-1193
TF: 800-672-1137					
UC Milk Co Inc 234 N Scott St	Madisonville	KY	42431	270-821-7221	821-7292
TF: 800-462-2354					
Umpqua Dairy Products 333 SE Sykes Ave	Roseburg	OR	97470	541-672-2638	673-0256
Web: www.umpquadairy.com					
United Dairy Farmers 3955 Montgomery Rd	Cincinnati	OH	45212	513-396-8700	396-8736
TF: 800-654-2809 ■ *Web:* www.udfinc.com					
United Dairy Inc 300 N 5th St	Martins Ferry	OH	43935	740-633-1451	633-6759
TF: 800-252-1542 ■ *Web:* www.uniteddairy.com					
Upstate Farms Co-op 25 Anderson Rd	Buffalo	NY	14225	716-892-3156	892-3157
TF: 800-724-6455 ■ *Web:* www.upstatefarmscoop.com					
Velda Farms LLC 402 S Kentucky Ave Suite 500	Lakeland	FL	33801	863-686-4441	644-6113*
**Fax Area Code:* 888 ■ *TF Cust Svc:* 800-795-4649 ■ *Web:* www.veldafarms.com					
Verifine Dairy Products Co Inc 1606 Erie Ave	Sheboygan	WI	53081	920-457-7733	457-5372
TF: 800-236-6455					
Wayne Div Smith Dairy 1590 NW 11th St	Richmond	IN	47375	765-935-7521	962-5269
TF: 800-875-9296					
Wengert's Dairy Inc 2401 Walnut St	Lebanon	PA	17042	717-273-2658	273-2794
WestFarm Foods 635 Elliott Ave W	Seattle	WA	98119	206-284-7220	281-3456
TF: 800-333-6455 ■ *Web:* www.westfarm.com					
WhiteWave Foods Co 12002 Airport Way	Broomfield	CO	80021	303-635-4000	
Web: www.whitewave.com					
Whittier Farms Inc 237 W Main St	Shrewsbury	MA	01545	508-842-2881	845-6522
Web: www.whittierfarms.com					
Wilcox Farms Inc 40400 Harts Lake Valley Rd	Roy	WA	98580	360-458-7774	458-6950
TF: 800-568-6456 ■ *Web:* www.wilcoxfarms.com					
Worcester Creameries Corp 2 Railroad Ave	Worcester	NY	12197	607-397-8791	397-8539
Yoplait USA Inc 1 General Mills Blvd PO Box 1113	Minneapolis	MN	55440	763-764-7600	541-5114
TF: 800-967-5248 ■ *Web:* www.yoplaitusa.com					

299-28 Nuts - Edible

				Phone	Fax
AL Bazzini Co Inc 200 Food Center Dr	Bronx	NY	10474	718-842-8644	842-8582
TF Cust Svc: 800-228-0172					
Azar Nut Co 1800 Northwestern Dr	El Paso	TX	79912	915-877-4079	877-1198
TF: 800-351-8178					
Bazzini AL Co Inc 200 Food Center Dr	Bronx	NY	10474	718-842-8644	842-8582
TF Cust Svc: 800-228-0172					
Beer Nuts Inc 103 N Robinson St	Bloomington	IL	61701	309-827-8580	827-0914
TF: 800-233-7688 ■ *Web:* www.beernuts.com					
Blue Diamond Growers 1802 C St	Sacramento	CA	95814	916-442-0771	446-8620
TF: 888-285-1351 ■ *Web:* www.bluediamond.com					
ConAgra Specialty Snacks 8064 Chivvis Dr	Saint Louis	MO	63123	314-832-2602	832-3015
Dahlgren & Co Inc 1220 Sunflower St	Crookston	MN	56716	218-281-2985	281-6218
TF: 800-346-6050 ■ *Web:* www.sunflowerseed.com					
Diamond of California 1050 S Diamond St	Stockton	CA	95205	209-467-6000	461-7309
NASDAQ: DMND ■ *Web:* www.diamondnuts.com					
Diamond Foods Inc DBA Diamond of California					
1050 S Diamond St	Stockton	CA	95205	209-467-6000	461-7309
NASDAQ: DMND ■ *Web:* www.diamondnuts.com					
Diamond Walnut Growers Inc PO Box 1727	Stockton	CA	95201	209-467-6000	467-6257
Web: www.diamondnuts.com					
Fisher Nut Co 2299 Busse Rd	Elk Grove Village	IL	60007	847-593-2300	593-9826
TF: 800-323-1288					
Flavor House Products PO Box 8084	Dothan	AL	36304	334-983-5643	983-4796
TF: 800-233-5979					
Georgia Nut Co 1742 Glenview Rd	Glenview	IL	60025	847-724-8405	724-8408
Web: www.georgianut.com					
Hines Nut Co Inc 990 S Saint Paul St	Dallas	TX	75201	214-939-0253	761-0720
TF: 800-580-0580 ■ *Web:* www.hinesnut.com					
John B Sanfilippo & Son Inc 2299 Busse Rd	Elk Grove Village	IL	60007	847-593-2300	593-3085
NASDAQ: JBSS ■ *TF:* 800-323-6887 ■ *Web:* www.jbssinc.com					
Kar Nut Products Co Inc 1200 E 14 Mile Rd	Madison Heights	MI	48071	248-588-1903	588-1902
TF: 800-527-6887 ■ *Web:* www.karsnuts.net/shop					
King Nut Co 31900 Solon Rd	Solon	OH	44139	440-248-8484	248-0153
TF: 800-860-5464 ■ *Web:* www.kingnut.com					
Koeze Co 2555 Burlingame Ave SW	Grand Rapids	MI	49509	616-724-2601	530-1819
TF: 888-253-6887 ■ *Web:* www.koeze.com					
Koinonia Partners Inc 1324 Georgia Hwy 49 S	Americus	GA	31719	229-924-0391	924-6504
TF: 877-738-1741 ■ *Web:* www.koinoniapartners.org/cartpages					
Leavitt Corp 100 Santilli Hwy	Everett	MA	02149	617-389-2600	387-9085
Web: www.teddie.com					
Mauna Loa Macadamia Nut Corp HC01 Box 3	Hilo	HI	96720	808-982-6562	966-8410*
**Fax:* Cust Svc ■ *TF Cust Svc:* 800-832-9993 ■ *Web:* www.maunaloa.com					
Nutcracker Brands Inc PO Box 420	Billerica	MA	01821	978-663-5400	667-8596
TF: 800-638-6887 ■ *Web:* www.nutcrackerbrands.com					
Old Dominion Peanut Corp 208 W 24th St	Norfolk	VA	23517	757-622-1633	624-9415
TF: 800-368-6887					
Pippin Snack Pecan Co PO Box 3330	Albany	GA	31706	229-432-9316	438-0464
Priester Pecan Co Inc PO Box 381	Fort Deposit	AL	36032	334-227-4301	227-4294
TF: 800-277-3226 ■ *Web:* www.priesters.com					
Sanfilippo John B & Son Inc 2299 Busse Rd	Elk Grove Village	IL	60007	847-593-2300	593-3085
NASDAQ: JBSS ■ *TF:* 800-323-6887 ■ *Web:* www.jbssinc.com					
Severn Peanut Co Inc PO Box 710	Severn	NC	27877	252-585-0838	585-1718
South Georgia Pecan Co 309 S Lee St	Valdosta	GA	31601	229-244-1321	247-6361
TF: 800-627-6630 ■ *Web:* www.georgiapecan.com					
Superior Nut Co Inc 225 Monsignor O'Brien Hwy	Cambridge	MA	02141	617-876-3808	876-8225
Web: www.superiornut.com					
Trophy Nut Co Inc 320 N 2nd St	Tipp City	OH	45371	937-667-8478	667-4656
TF: 800-729-6887 ■ *Web:* www.trophynut.com					
Warner Candy Co Inc 1099 Pratt Blvd	Elk Grove Village	IL	60007	847-928-7200	928-2115
Web: www.warnercandy.com					
Willmar Cookie & Nut Co Inc 1118 E Hwy 12	Willmar	MN	56201	320-235-0600	235-0659
Wricley Nut Products Co 480 Pattison Ave	Philadelphia	PA	19148	215-467-1106	467-4127
TF: 800-523-1303					

Phone Fax

Young Pecan Shelling Co PO Box 5779 ... Florence SC 29502 843-664-2330 664-2344
TF Sales: 800-829-6864 ■ *Web:* www.youngpecan.com
Zenobia Co LLC/House of Pistachio Nuts 5774 Mosholv Ave ... Bronx NY 10471 718-796-7700 548-2313
Web: www.nutsonthenet.com

299-29 Oil Mills - Cottonseed, Soybean, Other Vegetable Oils

Phone Fax

Abitec Corp Inc PO Box 569 ... Columbus OH 43216 614-429-6464 299-8279
TF Sales: 800-555-1255 ■ *Web:* www.abiteccorp.com
ADM North American Oilseed Processing Div
4666 E Faries Pkwy ... Decatur IL 62526 217-424-5200
ADM Oil Refinery 1940 E Hull Ave ... Des Moines IA 50316 515-263-2112 263-2110
TF: 800-637-5843
ADM Quincy 1900 Gardner Expy ... Quincy IL 62301 217-224-1800
Ag Processing Inc 12700 W Dodge Rd PO Box 2047 ... Omaha NE 68103 402-496-7809 498-5548
TF: 800-247-1345 ■ *Web:* www.agp.com
American Lecithin Co Inc 115 Hurley Rd Unit 2B ... Oxford CT 06478 203-262-7100 262-7101
TF: 800-364-4416 ■ *Web:* www.americanlecithin.com
Bunge Ltd 50 Main St 6th Fl ... White Plains NY 10606 914-684-2800 684-3499
NYSE: BG ■ *Web:* www.bunge.com
Cargill Foods 15407 McGinty Rd ... Wayzata MN 55391 952-742-7575
TF: 800-227-4455 ■ *Web:* www.cargillfoods.com
Cargill Inc 15407 McGinty Rd ... Wayzata MN 55391 952-742-7575 742-7209*
**Fax:* Cust Svc ■ *TF:* 800-227-4455 ■ *Web:* www.cargill.com
Cargill Inc North America 15407 McGinty Rd ... Wayzata MN 55391 952-742-7575
TF: 800-227-4455
ConAgra Foods Retail Products Co Grocery Foods Group
3353 Michelson Dr ... Irvine CA 92612 949-437-1000 437-3342
Delta Oil Mill PO Box 29 ... Jonestown MS 38639 662-358-4481 358-4629
Web: www.deltaoilmill.com
Hartsville Oil Mill PO Box 1057 ... Darlington SC 29540 843-393-1501 395-2690
Honeymead Products Co PO Box 3247 ... Mankato MN 56002 507-625-7911 345-2254
TF: 800-328-3445
HUMKO Oil Products 7171 Goodlett Farms Pkwy ... Cordova TN 38016 901-381-3000 381-3136
TF: 800-344-8656
Kraft Food Ingredients Corp 8000 Horizon Ctr Blvd ... Memphis TN 38133 901-381-6500 381-6524
TF: 800-458-8324
New Southern of Rocky Mount Inc PO Box 109 ... Rocky Mount NC 27802 252-977-1000 977-1079
Owensboro Grain Co 719 E 2nd St ... Owensboro KY 42303 270-926-2032 686-6509
TF: 800-874-0305 ■ *Web:* www.owensborograin.com
Planters Cotton Oil Mill Inc 2901 Planters Dr ... Pine Bluff AR 71601 870-534-3631 534-1421
Web: www.plantersoil.com
Producers Co-op Oil Mill 6 SE 4th St ... Oklahoma City OK 73129 405-232-7555 236-4887
Web: www.producerscoop.net
Pyco Industries Inc PO Box 841 ... Lubbock TX 79041 806-747-3434 744-3221
Web: www.pycoindustries.com
Sessions Co Inc 801 N Main PO Box 1310 ... Enterprise AL 36331 334-393-0200 393-0240
Web: www.peanutsouth.com
Southern Cotton Oil Co PO Box 1470 ... Decatur IL 62525 217-424-5526 424-4131
TF: 800-637-5824
Valley Co-op Oil Mill PO Box 533609 ... Harlingen TX 78553 956-425-4545 425-4264
TF: 800-775-3382
WA Cleary Products 1049 Rt 27 ... Somerset NJ 08873 732-247-8000 247-6977
TF: 800-238-7813 ■ *Web:* www.wacklearyproducts.com
Wesson/Peter Pan Foods Co 3353 Michelson Dr ... Irvine CA 92612 949-437-1000 437-3347

299-30 Oils - Edible (Margarine, Shortening, Table Oils, etc)

Phone Fax

ACH Food Cos Inc 7171 Goodlet Farms Pkwy ... Cordova TN 38016 901-381-3000 381-2968
TF: 800-691-1106 ■ *Web:* www.achfood.com
Bertolli USA Inc 920 Sylvan Ave ... Englewood Cliffs NJ 07632 800-908-9789
Web: www.bertolli.com
ConAgra Hunt-Wesson Foodservice Co 3353 Michelson Dr ... Irvine CA 92612 949-437-1000
TF: 800-633-0112 ■ *Web:* www.conagrafoodservice.com
Creative Foods LLC 710 N Pearl St ... Osceola AR 72370 870-563-2601 563-2223
TF: 800-643-0006
Delizia Brand Olive Oil Co 1991 Dennison St ... Oakland CA 94606 510-535-6833 532-2837
TF: 800-370-5554 ■ *Web:* www.evoliveoil.com
Golden Foods/Golden Brands LLC 2520 7th Street Rd ... Louisville KY 40208 502-636-3712 636-3904
TF: 800-622-3055 ■ *Web:* www.gfgb.com
Kraft Canada Inc 95 Moatfield Dr ... Don Mills ON M3B3L6 416-441-5000 441-5328*
**Fax:* PR ■ *Web:* www.kraftcanada.com
Kraft Foods North America Inc 3 Lakes Dr ... Northfield IL 60093 847-646-2000 646-2922
Web: www.kraft.com
Par-Way Tryson Co 107 Bolte Ln ... Saint Clair MO 63077 636-629-4545 629-1330
TF: 800-844-4554 ■ *Web:* www.parwaytryson.com
Star Fine Foods 4652 E Date Ave ... Fresno CA 93725 559-498-2900 498-2920
TF: 800-694-4872 ■ *Web:* www.starfinefoods.com
Unilever Bestfoods North America 800 Sylvan Ave ... Englewood Cliffs NJ 07632 201-894-4000
Web: www.bestfoods.com
Ventura Foods LLC 40 Point Dr ... Brea CA 92821 714-257-3700 257-4009
TF: 800-421-6257 ■ *Web:* www.venturafoods.com
Veronica Foods Co DBA Delizia Brand Olive Oil Co
1991 Dennison St ... Oakland CA 94606 510-535-6833 532-2837
TF: 800-370-5554 ■ *Web:* www.evoliveoil.com

299-31 Pasta

Phone Fax

A Zerega's Sons Inc 20-01 Broadway ... Fair Lawn NJ 07410 201-797-1400 797-0148
Web: www.zerega.com
American Italian Pasta Co 4100 N Mulberry Dr Suite 200 ... Kansas City MO 64116 816-584-5000 584-5100
NYSE: PLB ■ *Web:* www.aipc.com
Borden Foods Corp 180 E Broad St ... Columbus OH 43215 614-225-4000
D Merlino & Sons 1001 83rd Ave ... Oakland CA 94621 510-568-2151 568-2220
Everfresh Food Corp 501 Huron Blvd SE ... Minneapolis MN 55414 612-331-6393 331-1172
TF: 800-428-9999
Foulds Inc 520 E Church St ... Libertyville IL 60048 847-362-3062 362-6658
German Village Products 715 W Linfoot St ... Wauseon OH 43567 419-335-1515 337-0514
Gilster-Mary Lee Corp 1037 State St ... Chester IL 62233 618-826-2361 826-2973
TF: 800-851-5371
Golden Grain 555 W Monroe St ... Chicago IL 60661 312-222-7111
Inn Maid Products PO Box 27 ... Millersburg OH 44654 330-674-2993 674-3293
Joyce Food Products Inc 80 Ave K ... Newark NJ 07105 973-491-9696 589-6145*
**Fax:* Sales
Larinascente Macaroni Co 41 James St ... South Hackensack NJ 07606 201-342-2500 342-4351
Marzetti Frozen Pasta 803 8th St SW ... Altoona IA 50009 515-967-4254 967-4147
TF: 800-247-4194 ■ *Web:* www.marzetti.com
Merlino D & Sons 1001 83rd Ave ... Oakland CA 94621 510-568-2151 568-2220
Monterey Pasta Co 1528 Moffett St ... Salinas CA 93905 831-753-6262 753-6255
NASDAQ: PSTA ■ *TF:* 800-588-7782 ■ *Web:* www.montereypasta.com
Nanka Seimen Co 3030 Leonis Blvd ... Vernon CA 90058 323-585-9967
New World Pasta Co 85 Shannon Rd ... Harrisburg PA 17112 717-526-2200 526-2469*
**Fax:* Sales ■ *TF Sales:* 800-227-2782 ■ *Web:* www.newworldpasta.com
Nissin Foods USA Co Inc 2001 W Rosecrans Ave ... Gardena CA 90249 310-327-8478 515-3751*
**Fax:* Sales ■ *Web:* www.nissinfoods.com
Noodles By Leonardo Inc 1702 Schwan Ave PO Box 860 ... Devils Lake ND 58301 701-662-8300 662-2216
OB Macaroni Co PO Box 53 ... Fort Worth TX 76101 817-335-4629 335-4726
TF Orders: 800-553-4336 ■ *Web:* www.obpasta.com
Original Italian Pasta Products Co Inc 6 ConAgra Dr ... Omaha NE 68102 402-595-6935 595-6964
TF: 800-563-9786
Pasta USA Inc E 3405 Bismark Ct PO Box 7399 ... Spokane WA 99207 509-489-7219 489-2848
TF: 800-456-2084 ■ *Web:* www.pastausa.com
Peking Noodle Co Inc 1514 N San Fernando Rd ... Los Angeles CA 90065 323-223-2023 223-3211
Web: www.pekingnoodle.com
Philadelphia Macaroni Co 760 S 11th St ... Philadelphia PA 19147 215-923-3141 925-9904
Web: www.conteluna.com
Provena Foods Inc 5010 Eucalyptus Ave ... Chino CA 91710 909-627-1082 627-7315
AMEX: PZA
Unilever Bestfoods North America 800 Sylvan Ave ... Englewood Cliffs NJ 07632 201-894-4000
Web: www.bestfoods.com

299-32 Peanut Butter

Phone Fax

Algood Food Co 7401 Trade Port Dr ... Louisville KY 40258 502-637-3631 637-1502
Web: www.algoodfood.com
Baumer Foods Inc 2424 Edenborn Ave Suite 510 ... Metairie LA 70001 504-482-5761 483-2425
TF Sales: 800-222-0694 ■ *Web:* www.baumerfoods.com
Carriage House Cos Inc 196 Newton St ... Fredonia NY 14063 716-673-1000 673-8443*
**Fax:* Sales ■ *TF:* 800-828-8915 ■ *Web:* www.carriagehousecos.com
ConAgra Foods Retail Products Co Grocery Foods Group
3353 Michelson Dr ... Irvine CA 92612 949-437-1000 437-3342
ConAgra Hunt-Wesson Foodservice Co 3353 Michelson Dr ... Irvine CA 92612 949-437-1000
TF: 800-633-0112 ■ *Web:* www.conagrafoodservice.com
Edwards-Freeman Inc 441 E Hector St ... Conshohocken PA 19428 610-828-7441 832-0126
TF: 877-448-6887 ■ *Web:* www.edwardsfreeman.com
Fisher Nut Co 2299 Busse Rd ... Elk Grove Village IL 60007 847-593-2300 593-9826
TF: 800-323-1288
HB Reese Candy Co 925 Reese Ave ... Hershey PA 17033 717-534-4106
TF Cust Svc: 800-468-1714
Jimbo's Jumbos Inc 185 Peanut Dr PO Box 465 ... Edenton NC 27932 252-482-2193 482-7857
TF: 800-334-4771 ■ *Web:* www.originalnuthouse.com
JM Smucker Co 1 Strawberry Ln ... Orrville OH 44667 330-682-3000 684-6410
NYSE: SJM ■ *TF:* 800-553-0952 ■ *Web:* www.smucker.com
John B Sanfilippo & Son Inc 2299 Busse Rd ... Elk Grove Village IL 60007 847-593-2300 593-3085
NASDAQ: JBSS ■ *TF:* 800-323-6887 ■ *Web:* www.jbssinc.com
Koeze Co 2555 Burlingame Ave SW ... Grand Rapids MI 49509 616-724-2601 530-1819
TF: 888-253-6887 ■ *Web:* www.koeze.com
Leavitt Corp 100 Santilli Hwy ... Everett MA 02149 617-389-2600 387-9085
Web: www.teddie.com
Producers Peanut Co Inc 337 Moore Ave ... Suffolk VA 23434 757-539-7496 934-7730
TF: 800-847-5491 ■ *Web:* www.producerspeanut.com
Sanfilippo John B & Son Inc 2299 Busse Rd ... Elk Grove Village IL 60007 847-593-2300 593-3085
NASDAQ: JBSS ■ *TF:* 800-323-6887 ■ *Web:* www.jbssinc.com
Sessions Co Inc 801 N Main PO Box 1310 ... Enterprise AL 36331 334-393-0200 393-0240
Web: www.peanutsouth.com
Smucker JM Co 1 Strawberry Ln ... Orrville OH 44667 330-682-3000 684-6410
NYSE: SJM ■ *TF:* 800-553-0952 ■ *Web:* www.smucker.com
Wesson/Peter Pan Foods Co 3353 Michelson Dr ... Irvine CA 92612 949-437-1000 437-3347
William B Reily & Co Inc 640 Magazine St ... New Orleans LA 70130 504-524-6131 539-5427
TF: 800-535-1961

299-33 Salads - Prepared

Phone Fax

A Camacho Inc 2502 Walden Woods Dr ... Plant City FL 33566 813-305-4534 305-4545*
**Fax:* Cust Svc ■ *TF:* 800-881-4534 ■ *Web:* www.acamacho.com
Chef Solutions Inc 1000 Universal Dr ... North Haven CT 06473 203-234-0115 234-7620
TF: 800-877-1157 ■ *Web:* www.chefsolutions.com
Danner Salads 725 W Giles Ln ... Peoria IL 61614 309-691-0289 691-5267
D'Arrigo Brothers Co of California Inc PO Box 850 ... Salinas CA 93902 831-424-3955 424-3136
Web: www.andyboy.com
Dole Fresh Vegetables Co PO Box 1759 ... Salinas CA 93902 831-754-5244 757-0973
TF Sales: 800-333-5454 ■ *Web:* www.dole.com
Earth Island 9201 Owensmouth Ave ... Chatsworth CA 91311 818-725-2820 725-2812
Herold's Salads Inc 17512 Miles Ave ... Cleveland OH 44128 216-991-7500 991-9565
TF: 800-427-2523 ■ *Web:* www.heroldssalads.com
Home Made Brand Foods Inc 2 Opportunity Way ... Newburyport MA 01950 978-462-3663 462-7117
Web: www.hmbf.com
Kayem Foods Inc 75 Arlington St ... Chelsea MA 02150 617-889-1600 889-5931
TF: 800-426-6100 ■ *Web:* www.kayem.com
Naked Juice Co 935 W 8th St ... Azusa CA 91702 626-852-2500 852-2560
TF: 800-800-0689 ■ *Web:* www.nakedjuice.com
Reser's Fine Foods Inc 15570 SW Jenkins Rd PO Box 8 ... Beaverton OR 97075 503-643-6431
TF: 800-333-6431 ■ *Web:* www.resers.com
Sandridge Food Corp 133 Commerce Dr ... Medina OH 44256 330-725-2348 722-3998
TF: 800-280-7951 ■ *Web:* www.sandridge.com
Star Food Products Inc PO Box 1479 ... Burlington NC 27216 336-227-4079 227-2109
TF: 800-672-5310
Suter Co Inc 258 May St ... Sycamore IL 60178 815-895-9186 895-4814
TF: 800-435-6942 ■ *Web:* www.suterco.com
Sweet Earth Natural Foods 207 16th St ... Pacific Grove CA 93950 831-375-8673 375-3441

299-34 Sandwiches - Prepared

Phone Fax

Bridgford Foods Corp 1308 N Patt St ... Anaheim CA 92801 714-526-5533 526-4360
NASDAQ: BRID ■ *TF:* 800-854-3255 ■ *Web:* www.bridgford.com
Camino Real Foods Inc 2638 E Vernon Ave ... Vernon CA 90058 323-585-6599 585-5420
TF: 800-421-6201 ■ *Web:* www.crfoods.com
Cloverdale Foods Co Inc 3015 34th St NW PO Box 667 ... Mandan ND 58554 701-663-9511 663-0690
TF: 800-669-9511 ■ *Web:* www.cloverdalefoods.com
Downs Food Group 400 Armstrong Blvd N ... Saint James MN 56081 507-375-3111 375-3048
TF: 800-533-0452
Fishers Bakery & Sandwich Co 1519 Brookside Dr ... Raleigh NC 27604 919-832-6494 832-4865
TF: 800-849-8093
Hormel Foods Corp 1 Hormel Pl ... Austin MN 55912 507-437-5611 437-5489*
NYSE: HRL ■ **Fax:* Sales ■ *TF:* 800-523-4635 ■ *Web:* www.hormel.com
Konop Cos 1725 Industrial Dr ... Green Bay WI 54302 920-468-8517 468-1190
TF: 800-770-0477 ■ *Web:* www.konopcompanies.com
Landshire Inc 9200 W Main St ... Belleville IL 62223 618-398-8122 398-7627
TF: 800-468-3354 ■ *Web:* www.landshire.com
Southern Belle Sandwich Co 1969 N Lobdell Blvd ... Baton Rouge LA 70806 225-927-4670 928-5661

Sandwiches - Prepared (Cont'd)

Company	City	State	ZIP	Phone	Fax
Sunburst Foods Inc 1002 Sunburst Dr TF: 800-849-3196 ■ Web: www.sunburstfoods.net	Goldsboro	NC	27534	919-778-2151	778-9203
Sweet Earth Natural Foods 207 16th St	Pacific Grove	CA	93950	831-375-8673	375-3441

299-35 Snack Foods

Company	City	State	ZIP	Phone	Fax
American Pop Corn Co 1 Fun Pl PO Box 178 Web: www.jollytime.com	Sioux City	IA	51102	712-239-1232	239-1268
Bachman Co 1 Park Plaza TF: 800-523-8253 ■ Web: www.bachmanco.com	Wyomissing	PA	19610	610-320-7800	320-7897
Barrel O' Fun Snack Foods Co 800 4th St NW TF: 800-346-4910 ■ Web: www.barrelofunsnacks.com	Perham	MN	56573	218-346-7000	346-7003
Better Made Snack Foods Inc 10148 Gratiot Ave *Fax Area Code: 989 ■ Web: www.bettermadesnackfoods.com	Detroit	MI	48213	313-925-4774	684-6390*
Bickel's Snack Foods 1120 Zinns Quarry Rd *Fax: Cust Svc ■ TF: 800-233-1933 ■ Web: www.bickelssnacks.com	York	PA	17404	717-843-0738	843-4569*
Cape Cod Potato Chip Co 100 Breed's Hill Rd TF: 888-881-2447 ■ Web: www.capecodchips.com	Hyannis	MA	02601	508-775-3358	775-2808
Chester Inc 555 Eastport Center Dr Web: www.chesters.com	Valparaiso	IN	46383	219-462-1131	462-2652
CJ Vitner & Co 4202 W 45th St TF: 800-397-7629	Chicago	IL	60632	773-523-7900	523-9143
ConAgra Foods Retail Products Co Grocery Foods Group 3353 Michelson Dr	Irvine	CA	92612	949-437-1000	437-3342
Evans Food Products Co 4118 S Halsted St TF: 866-254-7400 ■ Web: www.evansfood.com	Chicago	IL	60609	773-254-7400	254-7791
F & F Foods Inc 3501 W 48th Pl TF: 800-621-0225 ■ Web: www.fffoods.com	Chicago	IL	60632	773-927-3737	927-3906
Frito-Lay North America 7701 Legacy Dr TF: 866-374-8677 ■ Web: www.fritolay.com	Plano	TX	75024	972-334-7000	334-2019
General Mills Inc 1 General Mills Blvd NYSE: GIS ■ TF: 800-328-1144 ■ Web: www.generalmills.com	Minneapolis	MN	55426	763-764-7600	764-8330
General Mills Inc International Foods Div 1 General Mills Blvd TF: 800-328-1144 ■ Web: www.generalmills.com	Minneapolis	MN	55426	763-764-7600	764-3232
Golden Flake Snack Foods Inc 1 Golden Flake Dr TF: 800-239-2447 ■ Web: www.goldenflake.com	Birmingham	AL	35205	205-323-6161	458-7121
Herr Foods Inc 20 Herr Dr PO Box 300 TF: 800-344-3777 ■ Web: www.herrs.com	Nottingham	PA	19362	610-932-9330	932-8007
Husman Snack Foods Co 1845 Airport Exchange Blvd Bldg B Suite 100 TF: 800-487-6267 ■ Web: www.birdseyefoods.com/husmans	Erlanger	KY	41018	859-282-7490	282-7491
Ira Middleswarth & Sons Inc 250 Furnace Rd	Middleburg	PA	17842	570-837-1431	837-1731
Jays Foods Inc 825 E 99th St TF: 800-621-6152 ■ Web: www.jaysfoods.com	Chicago	IL	60628	773-731-8400	933-2100
Keystone Food Products Inc 3767 Hecktown Rd TF: 800-523-9426	Easton	PA	18045	610-258-0888	250-0721
Lance Inc 8600 South Blvd NASDAQ: LNCE ■ TF: 888-722-1163 ■ Web: www.lance.com	Charlotte	NC	28273	704-554-1421	554-5562
Martin's Famous Pastry Shoppe Inc 1000 Potato Roll Ln TF Cust Svc: 800-548-1200 ■ Web: www.mfps.com	Chambersburg	PA	17201	717-263-9580	263-4452
Martin's Potato Chips Inc 5847 Lincoln Hwy W TF: 800-272-4477 ■ Web: www.martinschips.com	Thomasville	PA	17364	717-792-3565	792-4906
Mike-Sell's Potato Chip Co 333 Leo St TF: 800-257-4742 ■ Web: www.mike-sells.com	Dayton	OH	45404	937-228-9400	461-5707
Mission Foods 2110 Santa Fe Dr TF: 800-821-3187 ■ Web: www.missionfoods.com	Pueblo	CO	81006	719-543-4350	545-3681
Old Dutch Foods Inc 2375 Terminal Rd TF: 800-989-2447 ■ Web: www.olddutchfoods.com	Roseville	MN	55113	651-633-8810	633-8894
Orville Redenbacher/Swiss Miss Foods Co PO Box 3768 TF: 800-243-0303	Omaha	NE	68103	949-255-4100	
Ozuna Food Products Corp 510 Martin Ave	Santa Clara	CA	95050	408-727-5481	727-2009
Procter & Gamble Mfg Co 1 Procter & Gamble Plaza Web: www.pg.com	Cincinnati	OH	45202	513-983-1100	
Snacks Unlimited 1 General Mills Blvd TF: 800-438-9473 ■ Web: www.generalmills.com	Minneapolis	MN	55426	763-764-7600	
Snyder of Berlin 1313 Stadium Dr TF: 800-374-7949 ■ Web: www.birdseyefoods.com/snyder	Berlin	PA	15530	814-267-4641	267-5648
Tim's Cascade Snacks 1150 Industry Dr N TF: 800-533-8467 ■ Web: www.timschips.com	Algona	WA	98001	253-833-0255	939-9411
Troyer Potato Products Inc 810 Rt 97S TF: 800-458-0485 ■ Web: www.troyerfarms.com	Waterford	PA	16441	814-796-2611	796-6757
Utz Quality Foods Co 900 High St TF: 800-367-7629 ■ Web: www.utzsnacks.com	Hanover	PA	17331	717-637-6644	633-5102
Wachusett Potato Chip Co 759 Water St TF: 800-551-5539	Fitchburg	MA	01420	978-342-6038	345-4894
Weaver Potato Chip Co 1600 Center Park Rd Web: www.affinitysnacks.com	Lincoln	NE	68512	402-423-6625	423-0492
Wise Foods Inc 245 Townpark Dr Suite 450 TF: 800-438-9473 ■ Web: www.wisesnacks.com	Kennesaw	GA	30144	770-426-5821	426-0971
Wyandot Inc 135 Wyandot Ave *Fax: Cust Svc ■ TF: 800-992-6368 ■ Web: www.wyandotsnacks.com	Marion	OH	43302	740-383-4031	382-0115*

299-36 Specialty Foods

Company	City	State	ZIP	Phone	Fax
AFP Advanced Food Products LLC 402 S Custer Ave Web: www.afpllc.com	New Holland	PA	17557	717-355-8667	355-8848
Alphin Brothers Inc 2302 US 301 S TF: 800-672-4502 ■ Web: www.alphinbrothers.com	Dunn	NC	28334	910-892-8751	892-2709
Amigos Canning Co 600 Carswell TF: 800-580-3477 ■ Web: www.amigosfoods.com	San Antonio	TX	78226	210-798-5360	798-5365
Amy's Kitchen Inc 2227 Capricorn Way Suite 201 Web: www.amyskitchen.com	Santa Rosa	CA	95407	707-578-7188	578-7995
Appetizers And Inc 2555 N Elston Ave Web: www.appetizersandinc.com	Chicago	IL	60647	773-227-0400	227-0448
Arden International Kitchens Inc 21150 Hamburg Ave TF: 800-368-7337	Lakeville	MN	55044	952-469-2000	985-5822
Armanino Foods of Distinction Inc 30588 San Antonio St TF: 800-255-5855 ■ Web: www.armaninofoods.com	Hayward	CA	94544	510-441-9300	441-0101
Ateeco Inc DBA Mrs T's Pierogies 600 E Center St PO Box 606 TF: 800-233-3170 ■ Web: www.pierogy.com	Shenandoah	PA	17976	570-462-2745	462-1392
Avanti Foods Co 109 Depot St Web: www.avantifoods.com	Walnut	IL	61376	815-379-2155	
Beckman & Gast Co Inc 282 W Kremer-Hoying Rd PO Box 307 Web: www.beckmangast.com	Saint Henry	OH	45883	419-678-4195	
Beech-Nut Nutrition Corp 100 S 4th St Suite 1010 TF: 800-233-2468 ■ Web: www.beechnut.com	Saint Louis	MO	63102	314-436-7667	436-7679
Bernardi's Italian Foods Co Inc 301 W 3rd St PO Box 767	Toluca	IL	61369	815-452-2361	452-2822
Boca Foods Co 1 Kraft Ct *Fax Area Code: 570 ■ TF: 877-966-8769 ■ Web: www.bocafoods.com	Glenview	WI	60025	847-646-2000	301-5275*
Border Foods Inc 4065 J St SE Web: www.borderfoodsinc.com	Deming	NM	88030	505-546-8863	546-8676
Bruce Foods Corp PO Drawer 1030 TF: 800-299-9082 ■ Web: www.brucefoods.com	New Iberia	LA	70562	337-365-8101	364-3742
Buddy's Kitchen Inc 12105 Nicollet Ave Web: www.buddyskitchen.com	Burnsville	MN	55337	952-894-2540	895-1664
Bush Brothers & Co 1016 E Weisgarber Rd Web: www.bushbeans.com	Knoxville	TN	37909	865-588-7685	584-8157
California Fruit & Tomato Kitchen 2906 Santa Fe St PO Box 827 Web: www.calfruittom.com	Riverbank	CA	95367	209-869-9300	869-9060
Camino Real Foods Inc 2638 E Vernon Ave TF: 800-421-6201 ■ Web: www.crfoods.com	Vernon	CA	90058	323-585-6599	585-5420
Campbell Soup Co 1 Campbell Pl NYSE: CPB ■ TF: 800-772-8467	Camden	NJ	08103	856-342-4800	342-3878
Castleberry's Food Co 1621 15th St PO Box 1010 TF: 800-241-3520 ■ Web: www.castleberrys.com	Augusta	GA	30903	706-733-7765	736-5061
Champion Foods LLC 23900 Bell Rd Web: www.championfoods.com	New Boston	MI	48164	734-753-3663	753-5366
Chungs Gourmet Foods 3907 Dennis St TF: 800-824-8647 ■ Web: www.chungsfoods.com	Houston	TX	77004	713-741-2118	741-2330
ConAgra Foods Culinary Products 1805 Santa Fe Ave PO Box 4188 TF: 800-388-5505 ■ Web: www.conagrafoods.com	Compton	CA	90221	310-223-1499	223-1698
ConAgra Foods Retail Products Co Frozen Foods Group 5 ConAgra Dr Web: www.conagrafoods.com	Omaha	NE	68102	402-595-6000	
ConAgra Foods Retail Products Co Grocery Foods Group 3353 Michelson Dr	Irvine	CA	92612	949-437-1000	437-3342
Continental Mills Inc PO Box 88176 TF: 800-457-7744 ■ Web: www.continentalmills.com	Seattle	WA	98138	253-872-8400	872-7954
Cromers Inc 1055 Berea Rd PO box 163 TF: 800-322-7688 ■ Web: www.cromers.com	Columbia	SC	29202	803-779-1147	779-4743
Cuisine Solutions Inc 85 S Bragg St Suite 600 AMEX: FZN ■ TF: 888-285-4679 ■ Web: www.cuisinesolutions.com	Alexandria	VA	22312	703-270-2900	750-1158
D & D Foods Inc 9425 N 48th St TF: 800-272-5234	Omaha	NE	68152	402-571-4113	571-8245
Del Monte Foods Co The Landmark @ 1 Market PO Box 193575 NYSE: DLM ■ TF Cust Svc: 800-543-3090 ■ Web: www.delmonte.com	San Francisco	CA	94105	415-247-3000	247-3565
Deli Express 16101 W 78th St TF: 866-787-8862 ■ Web: www.deliexpress.com	Eden Prairie	MN	55344	952-937-9440	937-0186
Don Miguel Mexican Foods Inc 1501 W Orangewood Ave Web: www.donmiguel.com	Orange	CA	92868	714-634-8441	978-3743
Durrset Amigos Ltd DBA Amigos Canning Co 600 Carswell TF: 800-580-3477 ■ Web: www.amigosfoods.com	San Antonio	TX	78226	210-798-5360	798-5365
Ebro Foods Inc 1330 W 43rd St Web: www.ebrofoods.com	Chicago	IL	60609	773-696-0150	696-0151
Eden Foods Inc 701 Tecumseh Rd TF Cust Svc: 800-248-0320 ■ Web: www.edenfoods.com	Clinton	MI	49236	517-456-7424	456-6075
Edwards-Freeman Inc 441 E Hector St TF: 877-448-6887 ■ Web: www.edwardsfreeman.com	Conshohocken	PA	19428	610-828-7441	832-0126
El Encanto Inc 2001 4th St SW PO Box 293 TF: 800-888-7336 ■ Web: www.buenofoods.com	Albuquerque	NM	87103	505-243-2722	242-1680
Ener-G Foods Inc 5960 1st Ave S PO Box 84487 TF: 800-331-5222 ■ Web: www.ener-g.com	Seattle	WA	98124	206-767-6660	764-3398
Fairmont Foods of Minnesota 905 E 4th St Web: www.fairmontfoods.com	Fairmont	MN	56031	507-238-9001	238-9560
Fiesta Canning Co Inc 3117 N 16th St TF: 877-524-4537	Phoenix	AZ	85016	602-212-2424	274-7233
Frozen Specialties Inc 720 Barre Rd	Archbold	OH	43502	419-445-9015	445-9465
Gardenburger Inc 15615 Alton Pkwy Suite 350 TF: 800-636-0109 ■ Web: www.gardenburger.com	Irvine	CA	92618	949-255-2000	255-2010
Gerber Products Co 445 State St TF: 800-443-7237 ■ Web: www.gerber.com	Fremont	MI	49413	231-928-2000	928-2723
Goya Foods Inc 100 Seaview Dr Web: www.goya.com	Secaucus	NJ	07096	201-348-4900	348-6609
Grandma Brown's Beans Inc 5837 Scenic Ave	Mexico	NY	13114	315-963-7221	963-4072
Hain Celestial Group Inc 58 S Service Rd Suite 250 NASDAQ: HAIN ■ Web: www.hain-celestial.com	Melville	NY	01747	631-730-2200	730-2550
Hanover Foods Corp 1550 York St PO Box 334 TF: 800-888-4646 ■ Web: www.hanoverfoods.com	Hanover	PA	17331	717-632-6000	632-6681
Heinz North America 357 6th Ave Heinz 57 Center	Pittsburgh	PA	15222	412-237-5757	237-5377
HJ Heinz Co 600 Grant St NYSE: HNZ ■ TF: 800-255-5750 ■ Web: www.heinz.com	Pittsburgh	PA	15219	412-456-5700	456-6128
Home Market Foods Inc 140 Morgan Dr TF: 800-367-8325 ■ Web: www.homemarketfoods.com	Norwood	MA	02062	781-948-1500	702-6171
Home Run Inn Frozen Foods Corp 1300 International Pkwy Web: www.homeruninn.com	Woodridge	IL	60517	630-783-9696	783-0069
Homestead Pasta Co 315 S Maple Ave Bldg 106 TF: 800-334-3397 ■ Web: www.homesteadpasta.com	South San Francisco	CA	94080	650-615-0750	615-0764
Hormel Foods Corp 1 Hormel Pl NYSE: HRL ■ *Fax: Sales ■ TF: 800-523-4635 ■ Web: www.hormel.com	Austin	MN	55912	507-437-5611	437-5489*
JC World Foods Inc 310 Johnson Ave	Brooklyn	NY	11206	718-386-1130	386-1715
JM Smucker Co 1 Strawberry Ln NYSE: SJM ■ TF: 800-553-0952 ■ Web: www.smucker.com	Orrville	OH	44667	330-682-3000	684-6410
Juanita's Foods Inc 645 N Eubank St PO Box 847 Web: www.juanitasfoods.com	Wilmington	CA	90748	310-834-5339	835-6516
Kedem Food Products/Royal Wine Corp 63 Le Fante Ln TF: 800-382-8299 ■ Web: www.kedem.com	Bayonne	NJ	07002	718-384-2400	384-5329
Kraft Pizza Co 940 S Whelen Ave TF: 800-624-5186 ■ Web: www.kraft.com	Medford	WI	54451	715-748-5550	748-7330
La Choy Foodservice 3353 Michelson Dr TF: 800-663-0112 ■ Web: www.conagrafoodservice.com	Irvine	CA	92612	949-255-4100	
La Reina Inc 316 N Ford Blvd TF: 800-367-7522 ■ Web: www.lareinainc.com	Los Angeles	CA	90022	323-268-2791	265-4295
Lamb Weston Inc 8701 W Gage Blvd Web: www.lambweston.com	Kennewick	WA	99336	509-735-4651	736-0399
Leon's Texas Cuisine Co 2100 Redbud Blvd TF: 800-527-1243 ■ Web: www.texascuisine.com	McKinney	TX	75069	972-529-5050	529-2244
Little Lady Foods Inc 2323 Pratt Blvd TF: 800-439-1440 ■ Web: www.littleladyfoods.com	Elk Grove Village	IL	60007	847-806-1440	806-0026
Logan International Ltd 2 Marina Dr PO Box 1000 Web: www.loganinternational.com	Boardman	OR	97818	541-481-2081	481-3388
Luigino's Inc 525 S Lake Ave TF: 800-521-1281 ■ Web: www.michelinas.com	Duluth	MN	55802	218-723-5555	723-8356
Mancini Packing Co 3500 Mancini Pl PO Box 157 TF: 800-741-1778 ■ Web: www.mancinipacking.com	Zolfo Springs	FL	33890	863-735-2000	735-1172
Marzetti Frozen Pasta 803 8th St SW TF: 800-247-4194 ■ Web: www.marzetti.com	Altoona	IA	50009	515-967-4254	967-4147
McCain Foods Ltd 107 Main St Web: www.mccain.com	Florenceville	NB	E7L1B2	506-392-5541	392-8156
McCain Foods USA Inc 2275 Cabot Dr TF: 800-938-7799 ■ Web: www.mccainusa.com	Lisle	IL	60532	630-955-0400	857-4560

Phone Fax

McCain Snack Foods 555 N Hickory Farm Ln PO Box 2518........Appleton WI 54913 920-997-2828 997-7604
TF: 800-767-7377 ■ Web: www.mccainusa.com
Michael Angelo's Gourmet Foods Inc 200 Michael Angelo Way.......Austin TX 78728 512-218-3500 218-3600
TF: 800-526-4918 ■ Web: www.michaelangelos.com
Morgan Foods Inc 90 W Morgan St.............................Austin IN 47102 812-794-1170 794-1211
TF: 888-430-1780 ■ Web: www.morganfoods.com
Mott's Inc 900 King St.............................Rye Brook NY 10573 914-612-4000 612-4100
TF: 800-426-4891 ■ Web: www.motts.com
Mrs T's Pierogies 600 E Center St PO Box 606..............Shenandoah PA 17976 570-462-2745 462-1392
TF: 800-233-3170 ■ Web: www.pierogy.com
Nardone Bros Baking Co Inc 420 New Commerce Blvd........ Wilkes-Barre PA 18706 570-823-0141 823-2581
TF: 800-822-5320 ■ Web: www.nardonebros.com
National Coney Island Chili Co Inc 6700 E Davidson St............Detroit MI 48212 313-365-5611 365-3150
Neiman Brothers Co Inc 3322 W Newport Ave ....Chicago IL 60618 773-463-3000 463-3181
Web: www.neimanbrothers.com
Ole Mexican Foods Inc 6585 Crescent Dr.....................Norcross GA 30071 770-582-9200 447-8580
TF: 800-878-6307 ■ Web: www.olemexicanfoods.com
On-Cor Frozen Foods LLC 627 Landwehr Rd...................Northbrook IL 60062 847-205-1040 205-1070
Web: www.on-cor.com
Orville Redenbacher/Swiss Miss Foods Co PO Box 3768...........Omaha NE 68103 949-255-4100
TF: 800-243-0303
Overhill Farms Inc 2727 E Vernon Ave.........................Vernon CA 90058 323-582-9977 582-6122
AMEX: OFI ■ Web: www.overhillfarms.com
Panhandle Foods Inc 1980 Smith Township SR ....Burgettstown PA 15021 724-947-2216 947-4940
Park 100 Foods Inc 326 E Adams St.........................Tipton IN 46072 765-675-3480 675-3474
Web: www.park100foods.com
Pastorelli Food Products Inc 162 N Sangamon St ....Chicago IL 60607 312-666-2041 666-2415
TF: 800-767-2829 ■ Web: www.pastorelli.com
Pinnacle Foods Corp 6 Executive Campus Suite 100............Cherry Hill NJ 08002 856-969-7100
TF: 800-486-8816 ■ Web: www.pinnaclefoodscorp.com
Preferred Meal Systems Inc 5240 Saint Charles Rd ....Berkeley IL 60163 708-318-2500 493-2690
TF Cust Svc: 800-886-6325
Proferas Inc 1136 Moosic St ....Scranton PA 18505 570-342-4181 342-4853
TF: 800-360-7763 ■ Web: www.proferaspizza.com
Progresso Quality Foods Co 500 W Elmer Rd....................Vineland NJ 08360 856-691-1565
TF: 800-200-9377 ■ Web: www.bettycrocker.com/products/prod_progresso.asp
Quaker Foods North America 555 W Monroe St ....Chicago IL 60661 312-821-1000
TF: 800-555-6287 ■ Web: www.quakeroats.com
Randall Food Products Inc 8050 Hosbrook Rd..................Cincinnati OH 45236 513-793-6525 793-6442
Web: www.randallbeans.com
Readi-Bake Inc 361 Benigno Blvd.............................Bellmawr NJ 08031 856-931-7052 931-7423
TF: 800-852-2253 ■ Web: www.readi-bake.com
Request Foods Inc PO Box 2577 ....Holland MI 49422 616-786-0900 786-9180
TF Sales: 800-748-0378 ■ Web: www.requestfoods.com
Reynaldo's Mexican Food Co Inc 11929 Woodruff Ave............ Downey CA 90241 562-803-3188 803-3196
TF: 800-686-4911 ■ Web: www.rmfood.com
Rich Products Corp 1 Robert Rich Way ....Buffalo NY 14213 716-878-8000
TF: 800-828-2021 ■ Web: www.richs.com
Rokeach Food Corp 80 Ave K.................................Newark NJ 07105 973-589-4900 589-5298
Web: www.rokeach.com
Rosarita Food Service 3353 Michelson Dr.......................Irvine CA 92612 949-255-4100
Web: www.conagrafoods.com
Ruiz Foods Inc 501 S Alta Ave ....Dinuba CA 93618 559-591-5510 591-1968
TF: 800-477-6474 ■ Web: www.ruizfoods.com
Sanderson Farms Inc Foods Div 4418 Mangum Dr...............Flowood MS 39232 601-939-9790 932-2037
TF: 800-844-8291
Schwan Food Co 115 W College Dr ....Marshall MN 56258 507-532-3274
TF: 800-533-5290 ■ Web: www.theschwanfoodcompany.com
Small Planet Foods Inc 719 Metcalf St ....Sedro Woolley WA 98284 360-855-0100 855-0444
TF: 800-624-4123 ■ Web: www.smallplanetfoods.com
Smucker JM Co 1 Strawberry Ln ....Orrville OH 44667 330-682-3000 684-6410
NYSE: SJM ■ TF: 800-553-0952 ■ Web: www.smucker.com
State Fair Foods 3900 Meacham Blvd .... Haltom City TX 76117 817-427-7700 427-7777
TF: 800-641-6412
Stockpot Inc 22505 SR 9 ....Woodinville WA 98072 425-415-2000 415-2004
TF: 800-468-1611 ■ Web: www.stockpot.com
Suter Co Inc 258 May St....................................Sycamore IL 60178 815-895-9186 895-4814
TF: 800-435-6942 ■ Web: www.suterco.com
Symons Frozen Foods Inc 619 Goodrich Rd.....................Centralia WA 98531 360-736-1321 736-6328
Web: www.symonsfrozenfoods.com
Tastefully Simple Inc
1920 Turning Leaf Ln SW PO Box 3006 .... Alexandria MN 56308 320-763-0695 763-2458
TF: 866-448-6446 ■ Web: www.tastefullysimple.com
TODDS Enterprises Inc 610 S 56th Ave ....Phoenix AZ 85043 602-484-9584 484-9585
TF: 800-242-7087 ■ Web: www.toddsfoods.com
Unilever Bestfoods North America 800 Sylvan Ave........ Englewood Cliffs NJ 07632 201-894-4000
Web: www.bestfoods.com
Unilever Food Solutions 2200 Cabot Dr..........................Lisle IL 60532 630-955-5508 955-5231*
*Fax: Cust Svc ■ TF: 800-786-6988 ■ Web: www.unileverusa.com
Vanee Foods Co Inc 5418 McDermott Dr........................Berkeley IL 60163 708-449-7300 449-2558
TF Cust Svc: 800-654-6647 ■ Web: www.vaneefoods.com
Windsor Foods 3355 W Alabama St Suite 730....................Houston TX 77098 713-843-5200 960-9709
TF: 800-437-6936 ■ Web: www.windsorfoods.com
Winter Gardens Quality Foods Inc 304 Commerce St.......... New Oxford PA 17350 717-624-4911 624-7729
TF: 800-242-7637 ■ Web: www.wintergardens.com
Wornick Co 10825 Kenwood Rd..............................Cincinnati OH 45242 513-794-9800 794-0107
TF: 800-860-4555 ■ Web: www.wornick.com

299-37 Spices, Seasonings, Herbs

Phone Fax

Abco Laboratories Inc 2450 S Watney Way.....................Fairfield CA 94533 707-432-2200 432-2240
TF: 800-678-2226 ■ Web: www.abcolabs.com
Alberto-Culver Consumer Products Worldwide
2525 Armitage Ave.......................................Melrose Park IL 60160 708-450-3000
TF: 800-333-0005 ■ Web: www.alberto.com
All American Seasonings 10600 E 54th Ave ....Denver CO 80239 303-623-2320 623-1920
Web: www.allamericanseasonings.com
Basic American Foods 2999 Oak Rd Suite 100..............Walnut Creek CA 94597 925-472-4000 472-4360*
*Fax: Mktg ■ TF: 800-227-4050 ■ Web: www.baf.com
Benson's Gourmet Seasonings PO Box 638........................Azusa CA 91702 626-969-4443 969-2912
TF: 800-325-5619 ■ Web: www.bensonsgourmetseasonings.com
Blendex Co Inc 11208 Electron Dr ....Louisville KY 40299 502-267-1003 267-1024
TF: 800-626-6354 ■ Web: www.blendex.com
Cargill Foods 15407 McGinty Rd ....Wayzata MN 55391 952-742-7575
TF: 800-227-4455 ■ Web: www.cargillfoods.com
ConAgra Food Ingredients Co SpiceTec-USF Group
195 Alexandra Way ....Carol Stream IL 60188 630-682-5600 462-9953
TF: 800-872-9236 ■ Web: www.conagrafoods.com
Custom Culinary 2021 West Dr.................................Oakbrook IL 60532 630-928-4880 928-4899
TF Cust Svc: 800-621-8827 ■ Web: www.customculinary.com
El Guapo Spice Inc 6200 E Slauson Ave ....Commerce CA 90040 323-890-8900 890-0910
TF: 800-995-8906
Frontier Natural Products Co-op 3021 78th St PO Box 299.........Norway IA 52318 319-227-7996 227-7966
TF: 800-669-3275 ■ Web: www.frontiercoop.com

Phone Fax

Fuchs North America 9740 Reisterstown Rd .... Owings Mills MD 21117 410-363-1700 363-6619
TF: 800-365-3229 ■ Web: www.fuchsnorthamerica.com
Griffith Laboratories USA 1 Griffith Center.........................Alsip IL 60803 708-371-0900 597-3294
TF Cust Svc: 800-346-9494 ■ Web: www.griffithlabs.com
Johnny's Fine Foods Inc 319 E 25th St .... Tacoma WA 98421 253-383-4597 572-8742
TF Orders: 800-962-1462 ■ Web: www.johnnys-inc.com
Lawry's Foods Inc 222 E Huntington Dr....................... Monrovia CA 91016 800-952-9797
Web: www.lawrys.com
Lipton Co 800 Sylvan Ave .... Englewood Cliffs NJ 07632 201-567-8000 871-8198*
*Fax: Hum Res ■ Web: www.lipton.com
Lucile's Famous Creole Seasonings 2124 14th St .... Boulder CO 80302 303-442-4743 939-9848
Web: www.luciles.com
McCormick & Co Inc 18 Loveton Cir .... Sparks MD 21152 410-771-7301 771-7462
NYSE: MKC ■ TF: 800-632-5847 ■ Web: www.mccormick.com
McCormick & Co Inc Food Service Div 226 Schilling Cir .... Hunt Valley MD 21031 410-771-7500 771-1111
TF: 800-327-6838 ■ Web: www.mccormick.com/foodservice
McCormick & Co Inc McCormick Flavor Div
226 Schilling Cir....................................... Hunt Valley MD 21031 410-771-7500 771-1111
TF: 800-327-6838 ■ Web: www.mccormick.com
McCormick & Co Inc US Consumer Products Div
211 Schilling Cir....................................... Hunt Valley MD 21031 410-527-6000 771-1111
TF: 800-292-5300 ■ Web: www.mccormick.com
McCormick Ingredients 10901 Gilroy Rd .... Hunt Valley MD 21031 410-771-5025 527-6005
TF: 800-632-5847 ■ Web: www.mccormick.com
Newly Weds Foods Inc 4140 W Fullerton Ave .... Chicago IL 60639 773-489-7000 292-7612
TF Cust Svc: 800-621-7521 ■ Web: www.newlywedsfoods.com
Old Mansion Foods Inc
1558 W Washington St PO Box 2026............................Petersburg VA 23803 804-862-9889 861-8816
TF: 800-476-1877 ■ Web: www.oldmansionfoods.com
Precision Foods Inc 11457 Olde Cabin Rd.....................Saint Louis MO 63141 314-567-7400 567-7421
TF: 800-442-5242 ■ Web: www.precisionfoods.com
Presco Food Seasonings Inc 26 Minneakoning Rd ....Flemington NJ 08822 908-782-4919 782-6993
TF: 800-526-1713
REX Fine Foods 1690 S Causeway Blvd .... Metairie LA 70001 504-831-9295 831-9962
TF: 800-344-8314 ■ Web: www.rexfoods.com
Spice Hunter Inc 184 Suburban Rd .... San Luis Obispo CA 93403 805-544-4466 544-3824*
*Fax: Cust Svc ■ TF: 800-444-3061 ■ Web: www.spicehunter.com
Spice World Inc 8101 Presidents Dr.............................. Orlando FL 32809 407-851-9432 857-7171
TF: 800-433-4979 ■ Web: www.spiceworldinc.com
Tampico Spice Co Inc 5941 S Central Ave......................Los Angeles CA 90001 323-235-3154 232-8686
Web: www.tampicospice.com
Unilever Bestfoods North America 800 Sylvan Ave........ Englewood Cliffs NJ 07632 201-894-4000
Web: www.bestfoods.com
United Specialty Food Ingredients Cos 125 Wall St....... Glendale Heights IL 60139 630-671-4300
World Spice Inc 223-235 Highland Pkwy ....Roselle NJ 07203 908-245-0600 245-0696
TF: 800-234-1060 ■ Web: www.wsispice.com
Zatarain's Inc 82 1st St .... Gretna LA 70053 504-367-2950 362-2004
Web: www.zatarain.com

299-38 Sugar & Sweeteners

Phone Fax

ADM Specialty Food Ingredients Div 4666 E Faries Pkwy.......... Decatur IL 62526 217-424-5200 424-4702
Web: www.admworld.com
Alma Plantation Ltd 4612 Alma Rd.............................Lakeland LA 70752 225-627-6666 627-5138
Amalgamated Sugar Co LLC 3184 Elder St........................... Boise ID 83705 208-383-6500 383-6684
American Crystal Sugar Co 101 N 3rd St.........................Moorhead MN 56560 218-236-4400 236-4702
Web: www.crystalsugar.com
American Sugar Refining Co DBA Domino Sugar 1 Federal St ...... Yonkers NY 10702 914-963-2400 963-1030
Atlantic Sugar Assn PO Box 1570 ....Belle Glade FL 33430 561-996-6541 996-8021
C & H Sugar Co Inc 830 Loring Ave .... Crockett CA 94525 510-787-2121 787-1791
TF: 800-888-0118 ■ Web: www.chsugar.com
Cajun Sugar Co-op Inc 2711 Northside Rd.......................New Iberia LA 70563 337-365-3401 365-7820
Cora-Texas Mfg Co Inc 32505 Texas Rd PO Box 280..........White Castle LA 70788 225-545-3679 545-8360
Web: www.coratexas.com
Cumberland Packing Corp 2 Cumberland St ....Brooklyn NY 11205 718-858-4200 260-9017
TF: 800-221-1763 ■ Web: www.sweetnlow.com
Domino Sugar 1 Federal St .... Yonkers NY 10702 914-963-2400 963-1030
Florida Crystals Corp 1 N Clematis St Suite 200......... West Palm Beach FL 33401 561-655-6303 659-3206
Web: www.floridacrystals.com
Hawaiian Commercial & Sugar Co PO Box 266...................Puunono HI 06781 808 877 0081 871 7663
Web: www.hcsugar.com
Imperial Sugar Co 8016 Hwy 90 A .... Sugar Land TX 77478 281-491-9181 490-9530
NASDAQ: IPSU ■ TF: 800-727-8427 ■ Web: www.imperialsugar.com
Lafourche Sugars Corp 141 Leighton Quarters Rd .... Thibodaux LA 70301 985-447-3210 447-8728
Lantic Sugar Ltd 4026 Notre-Dame St NE .... Montreal QC H1W2K3 514-527-8686 527-8406
Web: www.lantic.ca
Louisiana Sugar Co-op Inc 6092 Resweber Hwy ....Saint Martinville LA 70582 337-394-3255 394-3787
Web: www.lasuca.com
Lula Westfield LLC 451 Hwy 1005 PO Box 10...............Paincourtville LA 70391 985-369-6450 369-6139
MA Patout & Son Ltd 3512 J Patout Burns Rd .... Jeanerette LA 70544 337-276-4592 276-4247
Web: www.mapatout.com
McNeil Nutritionals 601 Office Center Dr............... Fort Washington PA 19034 215-273-7000 273-4074
Merisant Worldwide Inc 10 S Riverside Plaza Suite 850........... Chicago IL 60606 312-840-6000 840-5400
Web: www.merisant.com
Michigan Sugar Co Inc 2600 S Euclid Ave........................ Bay City MI 48706 989-686-0161 671-3695
Web: www.michigansugar.com
Minn-Dak Farmers Co-op 7525 Red River Rd ....Wahpeton ND 58075 701-642-8411 642-6814
Web: www.mdfarmerscoop.com
Mueka Kea Agribusiness Co Inc PO Box 15 .... Papaikou HI 96781 808-964-8405 964-8426
NutraSweet Co 200 World Trade Center Merchandise Mart.......... Chicago IL 60654 312-873-5000 873-5055*
*Fax: Cust Svc ■ TF Cust Svc: 800-323-5321 ■ Web: www.nutrasweet.com
Okeelanta Corp 21250 US Hwy 27 PO Box 86.................. South Bay FL 33493 561-996-9072 992-5815
Osceola Farms Co 32298 US 98 PO Box 679 .... Pahokee FL 33476 561-924-7156 924-3246
Rio Grande Valley Sugar Growers PO Box 459 .... Santa Rosa TX 78593 956-636-1411 636-1046
Web: www.rgvsugar.com
Rogers Sugar Ltd 4026 Notre-Dame St E..........................Montreal QC H1W2K3 514-527-8686 527-8406
Web: www.rogerssugar.com
Saint Mary Sugar Co-op Inc 20056 Hwy 182 PO Box 269 .... Jeanerette LA 70544 337-276-6761 276-4297
South Louisiana Sugars Cooperative
5354 Saint James Co-op St PO Box 67 ....Saint James LA 70086 225-265-4056 265-4060
Web: www.slscoop.com
Southern Minnesota Beet Sugar Cooperative
83550 CR 21 PO Box 500.. Renville MN 56284 320-329-8305 329-3252
Web: www.smbsc.com
Stadt Corp 2 Cumberland St ....Brooklyn NY 11205 718-858-4200 260-9017
TF: 800-221-1763
Sterling Sugars Inc 611 Irish Bend Rd........................... Franklin LA 70538 337-828-0620 828-1757
Sugar Cane Growers Co-op of Florida PO Box 666.............Belle Glade FL 33430 561-996-5556 996-4747
Web: www.scgc.org
US Sugar Corp 111 Ponce de Leon Ave ....Clewiston FL 33440 863-983-8121 902-2889*
*Fax: Hum Res ■ Web: www.ussugar.com
Western Sugar Cooperative 7555 E Hampden Ave Suite 600 .... Denver CO 80231 303-830-3939 830-3941
TF: 800-523-7497 ■ Web: www.westernsugar.com

299-39 Syrup - Maple

				Phone	Fax
Carriage House Cos Inc 196 Newton St	Fredonia	NY	14063	716-673-1000	673-8443*
*Fax: Sales ■ TF: 800-828-8915 ■ Web: www.carriagehousecos.com					
Food Producers International					
10505 Wayzata Blvd Suite 400	Minnetonka	MN	55305	952-544-2763	
TF: 800-443-1336					
Foxtail Foods 6075 Poplar Ave Suite 800	Memphis	TN	38119	901-766-6400	537-7141
TF Cust Svc: 800-487-2253 ■ Web: www.foxtailfoods.com					
Golden Eagle Syrup Co Inc PO Box 690	Fayette	AL	35555	205-932-5294	932-5296
Web: www.goldeneaglesyrup.com					
H Fox & Co Inc 416 Thatford Ave	Brooklyn	NY	11212	718-385-4600	345-4283
Web: www.foxs-syrups.com					
HJ Heinz Co of Canada Ltd 90 Shepherd Ave E Suite 400	North York	ON	M2N7K5	416-226-5757	226-5064
Kalva Corp 3940 Porett Dr	Gurnee	IL	60031	847-336-1200	336-0712
TF: 800-525-8220 ■ Web: www.kalvacorp.com					
Maple Grove Farms of Vermont Inc 1052 Portland St	Saint Johnsbury	VT	05819	802-748-5141	748-9647
TF: 800-525-2540 ■ Web: www.maplegrove.com					
Maple Hollow/Waterloo USA W 1887 Robinson Dr	Merrill	WI	54452	715-536-7251	536-1295
Phillips Syrup Corp 28025 Ranney Pkwy	Westlake	OH	44145	440-835-8001	835-1148
Web: www.phillipssyrup.com					
Pinnacle Foods Corp 6 Executive Campus Suite 100	Cherry Hill	NJ	08002	856-969-7100	
TF: 800-486-8816 ■ Web: www.pinnaclefoodscorp.com					
Richards Maple Products Inc 545 Water St	Chardon	OH	44024	440-286-4160	286-7203
TF: 800-352-4052 ■ Web: www.richardsmapleproducts.com					
Sea Breeze Inc 441 Rt 202	Towaco	NJ	07082	973-334-7777	334-2617
TF: 800-732-2733 ■ Web: www.seabreezesyrups.com					
Spring Tree Maple Products 28 Vernon St Suite 412	Brattleboro	VT	05301	802-254-8784	254-8648
Web: www.springtree.com					

299-40 Tea

				Phone	Fax
Celestial Seasonings Inc 4600 Sleepytime Dr	Boulder	CO	80301	303-581-1202	581-1520*
*Fax: Cust Svc ■ TF: 800-525-0347 ■ Web: www.celestialseasonings.com					
Eastern Tea Corp 1 Engelhard Dr	Monroe Township	NJ	08831	609-860-1100	860-1105
TF: 800-221-0865 ■ Web: www.easterntea.com					
Fee Brothers Inc 453 Portland Ave	Rochester	NY	14605	585-544-9530	
TF: 800-961-3337 ■ Web: www.feebrothers.com					
Four C Foods Corp 580 Fountain Ave	Brooklyn	NY	11208	718-272-4242	272-2899
Web: www.4c.com					
JFG Coffee Co 3434 Mynatt Ave	Knoxville	TN	37919	865-546-2120	524-8725
TF: 800-627-1988					
Lipton Co 800 Sylvan Ave	Englewood Cliffs	NJ	07632	201-567-8000	871-8198*
*Fax: Hum Res ■ Web: www.lipton.com					
Old Mansion Foods Inc					
1558 W Washington St PO Box 2026	Petersburg	VA	23803	804-862-9889	861-8816
TF: 800-476-1877 ■ Web: www.oldmansionfoods.com					
Oregon Chai Inc 20925 Watertown Rd	Waukesha	WI	53186	262-317-3900	317-3993
TF: 888-874-2424 ■ Web: www.oregonchai.com					
Redco Foods Inc 1 Hansen Island	Little Falls	NY	13365	315-823-1300	823-2069
TF: 800-556-6674 ■ Web: www.redrosetea.com					
S & D Coffee Inc 300 Concord Pkwy PO Box 1628	Concord	NC	28026	704-782-3121	721-5792
TF Cust Svc: 800-933-2210 ■ Web: www.sndcoffee.com					
Sara Lee Food & Beverage 3500 Lacey Rd	Downers Grove	IL	60515	630-598-7892	598-8221
TF: 866-727-2533 ■ Web: www.saraleefoods.com					
SJ McCullagh Inc 245 Swan St	Buffalo	NY	14204	716-856-3473	856-3486
TF: 800-753-3473 ■ Web: www.mccullaghcoffee.com					
Stash Tea Co Inc PO Box 910	Portland	OR	97207	503-684-4482	624-4424*
*Fax: Orders ■ TF: 800-547-1514 ■ Web: www.stashtea.com					
Tetley USA Inc 100 Commerce Dr Suite 210 PO Box 856	Shelton	CT	06484	203-929-9200	929-9263
Web: www.tetleyusa.com					
Texas Coffee Co Inc 3291 ML King Pkwy S PO Box 31	Beaumont	TX	77704	409-835-3434	835-4248
TF: 800-259-3400 ■ Web: www.texjoy.com					
Unilever Bestfoods North America 800 Sylvan Ave	Englewood Cliffs	NJ	07632	201-894-4000	
Web: www.bestfoods.com					
Van Rooy Coffee Co 4569 Spring Rd	Cleveland	OH	44131	216-749-7069	749-7039
TF: 877-826-7669 ■ Web: www.vanrooycoffee.com					
White Coffee Corp 1835 38th St	Long Island City	NY	11105	718-204-7900	956-8504
TF: 800-221-0140 ■ Web: www.whitecoffee.com					

299-41 Vinegar & Cider

				Phone	Fax
A Camacho Inc 2502 Walden Woods Dr	Plant City	FL	33566	813-305-4534	305-4545*
*Fax: Cust Svc ■ TF: 800-881-4534 ■ Web: www.acamacho.com					
Agrusa Inc 117 Ft Lee Rd	Leonia	NJ	07605	201-592-5950	585-7244
Assouline & Ting Inc 2050 Richmond St	Philadelphia	PA	19125	215-627-3000	627-3517
TF: 800-521-4491 ■ Web: www.icaviar.com					
Bertolli USA Inc 920 Sylvan Ave	Englewood Cliffs	NJ	07632	800-908-9789	
Web: www.bertolli.com					
Boyajian Inc 144 Will Dr	Canton	MA	02021	781-828-9966	828-9922
TF: 800-965-0665 ■ Web: www.boyajianinc.com					
Consumers Vinegar & Spice Co Inc 4723 S Washtenaw Ave	Chicago	IL	60632	773-376-4100	376-6224
Creole Fermentation Industries Inc 7331 Den Frederick Rd	Abbeville	LA	70510	337-898-9377	898-9376
Daltons Best Maid Products Inc 1400 S Riverside Dr	Fort Worth	TX	76104	817-335-5494	534-7117
TF: 800-447-3581 ■ Web: www.bestmaidproducts.com					
Gedney MA Co 2100 Stoughton Ave	Chaska	MN	55318	952-448-2612	448-1790
Web: www.gedneypickle.com					
Gold Pure Food Products Inc 1 Brooklyn Rd	Hempstead	NY	11550	516-483-5600	483-5798
TF: 800-422-4681 ■ Web: www.goldshorseradish.com					
Heintz & Weber Co Inc 150 Reading Ave	Buffalo	NY	14220	716-852-7171	852-7173
Web: www.webersmustard.com					
Heinz North America 357 6th Ave Heinz 57 Center	Pittsburgh	PA	15222	412-237-5757	237-5377
Inter-State Cider & Vinegar Co Inc 101 N Warwick Ave	Baltimore	MD	21223	410-947-1529	947-7585
Ken's Foods Inc 1 D'Angelo Dr	Marlborough	MA	01752	508-485-7540	485-6882
TF: 800-633-5800 ■ Web: www.kensfoods.com					
Knouse Foods Co-op Inc 800 Peach Glen-Idaville Rd	Peach Glen	PA	17375	717-677-8181	677-7069
TF: 800-827-7537 ■ Web: www.knouse.com					
MA Gedney Co 2100 Stoughton Ave	Chaska	MN	55318	952-448-2612	448-1790
Web: www.gedneypickle.com					
Mizkan Americas Inc 1661 Feehanville Dr Suite 300	Mount Prospect	IL	60056	847-590-0059	590-0405
TF: 800-323-4358 ■ Web: www.mizkan.com					
National Fruit Product Co Inc					
701 Fairmont Ave PO Box 2040	Winchester	VA	22604	540-662-3401	665-4670*
*Fax: Sales ■ TF: 800-551-5167 ■ Web: www.whitehousefoods.com					
National Vinegar Co 8460 Watson Rd	Saint Louis	MO	63119	314-842-2822	842-7298
Pastorelli Food Products Inc 162 N Sangamon St	Chicago	IL	60607	312-666-2041	666-2415
TF: 800-767-2829 ■ Web: www.pastorelli.com					
REX Fine Foods 1690 S Causeway Blvd	Metairie	LA	70001	504-831-9295	831-9962
TF: 800-344-8314 ■ Web: www.rexfoods.com					
Rex Wine Vinegar Co 828-30 Raymond Blvd	Newark	NJ	07105	973-589-6911	589-5788
Silver Palate 300 Knickerbocker Rd PO Box 512	Cresskill	NJ	07626	201-568-0110	568-8844
TF: 800-872-5283 ■ Web: www.silverpalate.com					

299-42 Yeast

				Phone	Fax
Abco Laboratories Inc 2450 S Watney Way	Fairfield	CA	94533	707-432-2200	432-2240
TF: 800-678-2226 ■ Web: www.abcolabs.com					
ADM Arkady Products 100 Paniplus Rd	Olathe	KS	66061	913-782-8800	782-1792*
*Fax: Cust Svc ■ TF: 800-255-6637 ■ Web: food.admworld.com					
Bakon Yeast Inc PO Box 651	Rhinelander	WI	54501	715-362-6533	362-6530
Brolite Products Inc 1900 S Park Ave	Streamwood	IL	60107	630-830-0340	830-0356
TF: 888-276-5483 ■ Web: www.bakewithbrolite.com					
DSM Food Specialties Inc 45 Waterview Blvd	Parsippany	NJ	07054	800-662-4478	257-8265*
*Fax Area Code: 973 ■ TF: 800-662-4478 ■ Web: www.dsm.com/dfs					
Lake States Yeast 515 W Davenport St	Rhinelander	WI	54501	715-369-4356	369-4141
Web: www.wplakestates.com					
Lesaffre Yeast Corp 433 E Michigan St	Milwaukee	WI	53202	414-615-4055	615-4003
TF: 877-677-7000 ■ Web: www.lesaffreyeastcorp.com					
Minn-Dak Yeast Co Inc 18175 Red River Rd W	Wahpeton	ND	58075	701-642-3300	642-1908
TF: 800-348-0991					
Sensient Flavors Inc 5600 W Raymond St	Indianapolis	IN	46241	317-243-3521	240-1524*
*Fax: Sales ■ TF: 800-445-0073 ■ Web: www.sensient-tech.com					

300 FOOD PRODUCTS - WHOL

SEE ALSO Beverages - Whol p. 1377

300-1 Baked Goods - Whol

				Phone	Fax
Country Home Bakers Inc 3 Enterprise Dr Suite 404	Shelton	CT	06484	203-225-2333	929-2177
TF Cust Svc: 800-243-0008 ■ Web: www.countryhomebakers.com					
Fresh Start Bakeries 145 S State College Blvd Suite 200	Brea	CA	92821	714-256-8900	256-8916
Web: www.freshstartbakeries.com					
Horizon Food Group 7066 Las Positas Rd Suite G	Livermore	CA	94551	925-373-7700	373-8271
TF: 800-229-2552 ■ Web: www.horizonfoodgroup.com					
Interstate Bakeries Corp 12 E Armour Blvd	Kansas City	MO	64111	816-502-4000	502-4126
Web: www.interstatebakeriescorp.com					
Stroehmann Bakeries Inc 255 Business Center Dr	Horsham	PA	19044	215-672-8010	672-6988
TF: 800-355-1260					
Tri-State Baking Co 6800 S Washington St	Amarillo	TX	79120	806-373-6696	345-7893
Turano Baking Co 6501 W Roosevelt Rd	Berwyn	IL	60402	708-788-9220	788-3075
TF: 800-458-5662 ■ Web: www.turanobakery.com					

300-2 Coffee & Tea - Whol

				Phone	Fax
Barrie House Coffee Co Inc 945 Nepperhan Ave	Yonkers	NY	10703	914-423-8400	423-8499
Web: www.barriehouse.com					
Becharas Brothers Coffee Co Inc 14501 Hamilton Ave	Highland Park	MI	48203	313-869-4700	869-7940
TF: 800-944-9675					
Capricorn Coffees Inc 353 10th St	San Francisco	CA	94103	415-621-8500	621-9875
TF: 800-541-0758 ■ Web: www.capricorncoffees.com					
Coex Coffee International Inc					
2121 Ponce de Leon Blvd Suite 930	Coral Gables	FL	33134	305-444-0568	444-4541
TF: 800-426-0343 ■ Web: www.coexgroup.com					
Coffee Bean International 2181 NW Nicolai St	Portland	OR	97210	503-227-4490	225-9604
TF: 800-877-0474 ■ Web: www.coffeebeanintl.com					
Coffee Masters Inc 7606 Industrial Ct	Spring Grove	IL	60081	815-675-0088	675-3166
TF: 800-334-6485 ■ Web: www.coffeemasters.com					
Don Francisco Coffee Traders Inc PO Box 58271	Los Angeles	CA	90058	323-581-0671	697-9947*
*Fax Area Code: 800 ■ TF: 800-697-5282 ■ Web: www.don-francisco.com					
Paramount Coffee Co 130 N Larch Ave	Lansing	MI	48912	517-372-5500	372-2870
TF: 800-968-1222 ■ Web: www.paramountcoffee.com					
Procter & Gamble Distributing Co 1 Procter & Gamble Plaza	Cincinnati	OH	45202	513-983-1100	983-1100
Red Diamond Inc 1701 Vanderbilt Rd PO Box 2168	Birmingham	AL	35201	205-254-3138	254-6062
TF: 800-292-4651 ■ Web: www.reddiamond.com					
Royal Cup Inc 160 Cleage Dr	Birmingham	AL	35217	205-849-5836	271-6071
TF: 800-366-5836 ■ Web: www.royalcupcoffee.com					
Texas Coffee Co Inc 3291 ML King Pkwy S PO Box 31	Beaumont	TX	77704	409-835-3434	835-4248
TF: 800-259-3400 ■ Web: www.texjoy.com					

300-3 Confectionery & Snack Foods - Whol

				Phone	Fax
AMCON Distributing Co 7405 Irvington Rd	Omaha	NE	68122	402-331-3727	331-4834
AMEX: DIT ■ TF: 800-369-6200 ■ Web: www.amcon.com					
Annabelle Candy Co Inc 27211 Industrial Blvd	Hayward	CA	94545	510-783-2900	785-7675
Web: www.annabelle-candy.com					
Anpesil Distribution Services 333 Swedesboro Ave	Gibbstown	NJ	08027	856-687-0000	687-0017
Web: www.anpesil.com					
AW Marshall Co PO Box 16127	Salt Lake City	UT	84116	801-328-4713	328-9600
TF: 800-273-4713					
Barentsen Candy Co 147 5th St	Benton Harbor	MI	49022	269-927-3171	925-4570
Brown & Haley 1940 E 11th St	Tacoma	WA	98421	253-620-3000	272-6742
TF: 800-426-8400 ■ Web: www.brown-haley.com					
Burklund Distributors Inc 2500 N Main St Suite 3	East Peoria	IL	61611	309-694-1900	694-6788
TF: 800-322-2876 ■ Web: www.burklund.com					
Candy Direct 745 Design Ct Suite 602	Chula Vista	CA	91911	619-216-0116	374-2930
Web: www.candydirect.com					
Chocolate House Inc 4121 S 35th St	Milwaukee	WI	53221	414-281-7800	423-2484
Web: www.fudgiebear.com					
Diamond Bakery Co 756 Moowaa St	Honolulu	HI	96817	808-847-3551	847-7482
Web: www.diamondbakery.com					
Eby-Brown Co 280 W Shuman Blvd Suite 280	Naperville	IL	60563	630-778-2800	778-2831
TF: 800-553-8249 ■ Web: www.eby-brown.com					
Foreign Candy Co Inc 1 Foreign Candy Dr	Hull	IA	51239	712-439-1496	439-1434
TF: 800-767-4575 ■ Web: www.foreigncandy.com					
Frito-Lay North America 7701 Legacy Dr	Plano	TX	75024	972-334-7000	334-2019
TF: 866-374-8677 ■ Web: www.fritolay.com					
Gold Harbor Commodities Inc 9750 3rd Ave NE	Seattle	WA	98115	206-527-3494	522-7321
Hammons Products Co 105 Hammons Dr PO Box 140	Stockton	MO	65785	417-276-5181	276-5187
TF: 888-429-6887 ■ Web: www.hammonsproducts.com					
Harold Levinson Assoc (HLA) 21 Banfi Plaza	Farmingdale	NY	11735	631-962-2400	962-9000
TF: 800-325-2512 ■ Web: www.hlacigars.com					
Hershey International					
2700 S Commerce Pkwy Weston Corporate Ctr 4th Fl	Weston	FL	33331	954-385-2600	385-2625
Web: www.hersheys.com					
Hines Nut Co Inc 990 S Saint Paul St	Dallas	TX	75201	214-939-0253	761-0720
TF: 800-580-0580 ■ Web: www.hinesnut.com					

Phone Fax

HLA (Harold Levinson Assoc) 21 Banfi Plaza .... Farmingdale NY 11735 631-962-2400 962-9000
TF: 800-325-2512 ■ *Web:* www.hlacigars.com
J Polep Distribution Services Inc 705 Meadow St .... Chicopee MA 01013 413-592-4141 592-5870
TF: 800-447-6537 ■ *Web:* www.jpolep.com
J Sosnick & Sons Inc 258 Littlefield Ave .... South San Francisco CA 94080 650-952-2226 952-2439
TF: 800-443-6737 ■ *Web:* www.sosnick.com
Keilson-Dayton Co 107 Commerce Park Dr .... Dayton OH 45404 937-236-1070 236-2124
TF: 800-759-3174
Kennedy Wholesale Inc 16014 Adelante St .... Irwindale CA 91706 818-241-9977 241-3046
TF: 877-292-2639 ■ *Web:* www.kennedywholesale.com
Marshall AW Co PO Box 16127 .... Salt Lake City UT 84116 801-328-4713 328-9600
TF: 800-273-4713
McDonald Candy Co 2350 W Broadway St..................... Eugene OR 97402 541-345-8421 345-7146
TF: 877-722-5503
Mound City Industries Inc 1315 Cherokee St. .... Saint Louis MO 63118 314-773-5200 773-7453
TF: 800-727-1548 ■ *Web:* www.moundcityind.com
New Britain Candy Co 24 Maple St .... Wethersfield CT 06129 860-257-7058 257-7495
TF: 800-382-0515 ■ *Web:* www.newbritaincandy.com
Old Dutch Foods Inc 2375 Terminal Rd .... Roseville MN 55113 651-633-8810 633-8894
TF: 800-989-2447 ■ *Web:* www.olddutchfoods.com
Pennsylvania Dutch Candies 1250 Slate Hill Rd .... Camp Hill PA 17011 717-761-5440 761-2206
TF: 800-233-7082 ■ *Web:* www.padutchcandies.com
Perugina Brands of America 800 N Brand Blvd 8th Fl .... Glendale CA 91203 818-551-3530 543-7811
TF: 800-544-1672
Polep J Distribution Services Inc 705 Meadow St .... Chicopee MA 01013 413-592-4141 592-5870
TF: 800-447-6537 ■ *Web:* www.jpolep.com
Procter & Gamble Distributing Co 1 Procter & Gamble Plaza...... Cincinnati OH 45202 513-983-1100 983-1100
Scott's of Wisconsin 301 Broadway Dr .... Sun Prairie WI 53590 608-837-8020 837-0763
Sosnick J & Sons Inc 258 Littlefield Ave .... South San Francisco CA 94080 650-952-2226 952-2439
TF: 800-443-6737 ■ *Web:* www.sosnick.com
Superior Nut Co Inc 225 Monsignor O'Brien Hwy .... Cambridge MA 02141 617-876-3808 876-8225
Web: www.superiornut.com
Taste of Nature Inc 400 S Beverly Dr Suite 214 .... Beverly Hills CA 90212 310-396-4433 396-4432
TF Cust Svc: 800-898-2783 ■ *Web:* www.candyasap.com
Trophy Nut Co Inc 320 N 2nd St .... Tipp City OH 45371 937-667-8478 667-4656
TF: 800-729-6887 ■ *Web:* www.trophynut.com
Tzetzo Brothers Inc 1100 Military Rd.......................... Buffalo NY 14217 716-877-0800 877-0385
TF: 800-248-2881
Zenobia Co LLC/House of Pistachio Nuts 5774 Mosholv Ave .... Bronx NY 10471 718-796-7700 548-2313
Web: www.nutsonthenet.com

300-4 Dairy Products - Whol

Phone Fax

Abbott's Premium Ice Cream Inc PO Box 411................... Conway NH 03818 603-356-2344 356-3957
Ambriola Co Inc 2 Burma Rd .... Jersey City NJ 07305 201-434-6289 434-5505
TF: 800-962-8224 ■ *Web:* www.ambriola.com
AMPI 315 N Broadway.. New Ulm MN 56073 507-354-8295 359-8668
TF: 800-533-3580 ■ *Web:* www.ampi.com
Broughton Foods Co 1701 Green St............................ Marietta OH 45750 740-373-4121 373-2861
TF: 800-283-2479
Clofine Dairy Products Inc 1407 New Rd .... Linwood NJ 08221 609-653-1000 653-0127
TF: 800-441-1001 ■ *Web:* www.clofinedairy.com
Country Classic Dairies Inc DBA Darigold Farms of Montana
PO Box 968 .... Bozeman MT 59771 406-586-5426 586-5110
TF: 800-321-4563 ■ *Web:* www.darigold-mt.com
Country Fresh Inc 355 Mart St SW .... Grand Rapids MI 49548 616-243-0173 243-5926
TF: 800-748-0480 ■ *Web:* www.enjoycountryfresh.com
Cream-O-Land Dairy Inc 529 Cedar Ln Box 146.................. Florence NJ 08518 609-499-3601 499-3896
TF: 800-220-6455 ■ *Web:* www.creamoland.com
Crystal Farms Refrigerated Distribution Co
6465 Wayzata Blvd Suite 200 .... Minneapolis MN 55426 952-544-8101 544-8069
TF: 877-279-7825 ■ *Web:* www.crystalfarms.com
Dairylea Co-op Inc 5001 Brittonfield Pkwy................. East Syracuse NY 13057 315-433-0100 433-2345
TF: 800-654-8838 ■ *Web:* www.dairylea.com
Darigold Farms of Montana PO Box 968 .... Bozeman MT 59771 406-586-5426 586-5110
TF: 800-321-4563 ■ *Web:* www.darigold-mt.com
DMV USA 1285 Rudy St....................................... Onalaska WI 54650 608-779-7676 779-7666
TF Cust Svc: 877-300-7676
Erie Foods International Inc 401 7th Ave .... Erie IL 61250 309-659-2233 659-7270
TF: 800-447-1887 ■ *Web:* www.eriefoods.com
Fleur de Lait BC USA 400 S Custer Ave.................... New Holland PA 17557 717-355-8500 355-8546
TF: 800-322-2743
Fonterra USA 100 Corporate Center Dr Suite 101 .... Camp Hill PA 17011 717-920-4000 920-4089
TF: 800-358-9096 ■ *Web:* www.fonterra.com
Foremost Farms USA E10889A Penny Ln......................... Baraboo WI 53913 608-356-8316 355-6701
TF: 800-362-9196 ■ *Web:* www.foremostfarms.com
Graf Creamery Co PO Box 49 .... Zachow WI 54182 715-758-2137 758-8020
Hautly Cheese Co Inc 5130 Northrup Ave .... Saint Louis MO 63110 314-772-9339 772-0243
TF: 800-729-9339 ■ *Web:* www.hautlycheese.com
Ideal Dairy 10 Executive Ave.................................. Edison NJ 08817 732-442-6337 287-1326
TF: 800-332-4791
Jack & Jill Ice Cream Co 101 Commerce Dr.................. Moorestown NJ 08057 856-813-2300
TF: 800-220-2300 ■ *Web:* www.jackjillicecream.com
Kraft Foods International Inc 3 Lakes Dr .... Northfield IL 60093 847-646-2000 335-9395*
**Fax Area Code:* 914 ■ *TF:* 800-323-0768 ■ *Web:* www.kraft.com
Lowville Producers Dairy Co-op 7396 Utica Blvd................. Lowville NY 13367 315-376-3921 376-3442
Web: www.gotgoodcheese.com
Maryland & Virginia Milk Producers Co-op Assn Inc
1985 Isaac Newton Sq W .... Reston VA 20190 703-742-6800 742-7459
TF: 800-552-1976 ■ *Web:* www.mdvamilk.com
Masters Gallery Foods Inc 328 County Hwy PP .... Plymouth WI 53073 920-893-8431 893-6075
TF: 800-236-8431 ■ *Web:* www.mastersgalleryfoods.com
Matanuska Maid Dairy 814 W Northern Lights Blvd .... Anchorage AK 99503 907-561-5223 563-7492
TF: 800-478-5223 ■ *Web:* www.matmaid.com
Pevely Dairy Co 1001 S Grand Blvd .... Saint Louis MO 63104 314-771-4400 771-6695
TF: 800-727-4407
Plains Dairy Products 300 N Taylor St........................ Amarillo TX 79107 806-374-0385 374-0396
TF: 800-365-5608 ■ *Web:* www.plainsdairy.com
Prairie Farms Dairy Inc 1100 N Broadway St .... Carlinville IL 62626 217-854-2547 854-6426
TF: 800-654-2547 ■ *Web:* www.prairiefarms.com
Purity Dairies Inc 360 Murfreesboro Rd....................... Nashville TN 37210 615-244-1900 242-8547
TF: 800-947-6455 ■ *Web:* www.puritydairies.com
Queensboro Farm Products Inc 156-02 Liberty Ave .... Jamaica NY 11433 718-658-5000 658-0408
TF: 800-696-8970
Reilly Dairy & Food Co PO Box 130197............................ Tampa FL 33681 813-839-8458 839-0394
Web: www.reillydairy.com
Reiter Dairy Inc 1415 W Waterloo Rd .... Akron OH 44314 330-745-1123 745-4363
TF: 800-362-0825 ■ *Web:* www.reiterdairy.com
Roberts Dairy Co PO Box 3825.................................. Omaha NE 68103 402-344-4321 346-0277
TF: 800-779-4321 ■ *Web:* www.robertsdairy.com
Rockview Dairies Inc PO Box 668 .... Downey CA 90241 562-927-5511 928-9866
TF: 800-423-2479 ■ *Web:* www.rockviewfarms.com
Schenkel's Dairy 1019 Flax Mill Rd .... Huntington IN 46750 260-356-4225 359-5045
TF: 800-552-2791
Schneider's Dairy Inc 726 Frank St .... Pittsburgh PA 15227 412-881-3525 881-7722

Phone Fax

Simco Sales Service of Pennsylvania Inc DBA Jack & Jill Ice Cream Co 101 Commerce Dr............................ Moorestown NJ 08057 856-813-2300
TF: 800-220-2300 ■ *Web:* www.jackjillicecream.com
Sunshine Dairy Foods Inc 801 NE 21st Ave...................... Portland OR 97232 503-234-7526 233-9441
TF: 800-544-0554 ■ *Web:* www.sunshinedairyfoods.com
Sure Winner Foods Inc PO Box 430................................. Saco ME 04072 207-282-1258 286-1410
TF: 800-640-6447 ■ *Web:* www.swfoods.com
Tillamook County Creamery Assn Inc 4185 Hwy 101 N .... Tillamook OR 97141 503-842-4481 842-6039
Web: www.tillamookcheese.com
Tuscan Dairy Farms Inc 750 Union Ave............................ Union NJ 07083 908-686-1500 686-1193
TF: 800-672-1137
Umpqua Dairy Products 333 SE Sykes Ave .... Roseburg OR 97470 541-672-2638 673-0256
Web: www.umpquadairy.com
United Dairymen of Arizona Inc PO Box 26877................... Tempe AZ 85285 480-966-7211 829-7491
Velda Farms LLC 402 S Kentucky Ave Suite 500.................. Lakeland FL 33801 863-686-4441 644-6113*
**Fax Area Code:* 888 ■ *TF Cust Svc:* 800-795-4649 ■ *Web:* www.veldafarms.com
Wapsie Valley Creamery Inc 300 10th St NE................ Independence IA 50644 319-334-7193 334-4914

300-5 Fish & Seafood - Whol

Phone Fax

Amory LD & Co Inc 101 S King St .... Hampton VA 23669 757-722-1915 723-1184
Barnett Paul Seafoods Inc PO Box 630446............................ Ojus FL 33163 305-652-4800 652-3236
Beaver Street Fisheries Inc 1741 W Beaver St .... Jacksonville FL 32209 904-354-8533
TF: 800-874-6426 ■ *Web:* www.beaverfish.com
Becker Food Co Inc 4160 N Port Washington Rd .... Milwaukee WI 53212 414-964-5353 964-4523
Blount Seafood Corp 630 Currant Rd........................... Fall River MA 02720 774-888-1300 888-1399
TF: 800-274-2526 ■ *Web:* www.blountseafood.com
Bon Secour Fisheries Inc
17449 County Rd 49 S PO Box 60 .... Bon Secour AL 36511 251-949-7411 949-6478
TF: 800-633-6854 ■ *Web:* www.bonsecourfisheries.com
California Shellfish Co PO Box 2028 .... San Francisco CA 94126 415-923-7400 923-7422
ConAgra Foods Foodservice Co 1 ConAgra Dr..................... Omaha NE 68102 402-595-4000
Web: www.conagrafoodservice.com
Empress International Ltd 5 Dakota Dr Suite 303 .... Lake Success NY 11042 516-740-4100 621-8318
TF Sales: 800-645-6244
Fishery Products International 18 Electronics Ave .... Danvers MA 01923 978-777-2660 777-6849
TF: 800-374-4770 ■ *Web:* www.fpil.com
Fjord Seafoods DBA Windward Seafoods
8550 NW 17 St Suite 105 .... Miami FL 33126 305-591-8550 670-8883
TF: 800-780-3474 ■ *Web:* www.windwardseafoods.com
Gorton Slade Co Inc 225 Southampton St .... Boston MA 02118 617-442-5800 442-9090
TF: 800-225-1573 ■ *Web:* www.sladegorton.com
Handy John T Co Inc PO Box 309 .... Crisfield MD 21817 410-968-1772 968-1771
TF: 800-426-3977 ■ *Web:* fis.com/handycrab
Inland Seafood Corp 1222 Menlo Dr .... Atlanta GA 30318 404-350-5850 350-5871
TF: 800-883-3474 ■ *Web:* www.choicemall.com/inlandseafood
Interamerican Trading & Products Corp PO Box 402427 ...... Miami Beach FL 33140 305-885-9666 885-0402
TF: 800-999-7123
Intersea Fisheries Ltd
777 Terrace Ave Heights Plaza .... Hasbrouck Heights NJ 07604 201-692-9000 692-9460
Web: www.intersea-fish.com
Ipswich Shellfish Co Inc 8 Hayward St .... Ipswich MA 01938 978-356-4371 356-9235
TF: 800-477-9424 ■ *Web:* www.ipswichshellfish.com
John Keeler & Co Inc 3000 NW 109th Ave .... Miami FL 33172 305-836-6858 836-6859
TF: 888-663-2722 ■ *Web:* www.onecrab.com
John T Handy Co Inc PO Box 309 .... Crisfield MD 21817 410-968-1772 968-1771
TF: 800-426-3977 ■ *Web:* fis.com/handycrab
Keeler John & Co Inc 3000 NW 109th Ave .... Miami FL 33172 305-836-6858 836-6859
TF: 888-663-2722 ■ *Web:* www.onecrab.com
LD Amory & Co Inc 101 S King St .... Hampton VA 23669 757-722-1915 723-1184
M Slavin & Sons Ltd 31 Belmont Ave.............................. Brooklyn NY 11212 718-485-1823 485-6769
Web: www.mslavin.com
Maine Lobster Direct 48 Union Wharf .... Portland ME 04101 207-772-9056 772-0169
TF: 800-556-2783 ■ *Web:* www.mainelobsterdirect.com
Mazzetta Co 1990 St Johns Ave............................. Highland Park IL 60035 847-433-1150 433-8973
Web: www.mazzetta.com
Metropolitan Poultry & Seafood Co 1920 Stanford Ct .... Landover MD 20785 301-772-0060 772-1013
TF: 800-522-0060 ■ *Web:* www.metropoultry.com
Michael's Finer Meats & Seafoods 3775 Zane Trace Dr.......... Columbus OH 43228 614-527-4900 527-4520
TF: 800-282-0518 ■ *Web:* www.michaelsmeats.com
Morey's Seafood International LLC PO Box 248 .... Motley MN 56466 218-352-6345 352-6523
Web: www.moreys.com
Morley Sales Co Inc 809 W Madison St............................ Chicago IL 60607 312-829-1125 829-3680
TF: 800-828-0424 ■ *Web:* www.morleysales.com
Ore-Cal Corp 634 S Crocker St.............................. Los Angeles CA 90021 213-680-9540 623-3063
TF: 800-827-7474 ■ *Web:* www.ore-cal.com
Paul Barnett Seafoods Inc PO Box 630446............................ Ojus FL 33163 305-652-4800 652-3236
Premier Pacific Seafoods Inc 111 W Harrison St................... Seattle WA 98119 206-286-8584 286-8810
Quirch Foods Co 7600 NW 82nd Pl .... Miami FL 33166 305-691-3535 593-0272
TF: 800-458-5252 ■ *Web:* www.quirchfoods.com
Red Chamber Co 1912 E Vernon Ave .... Vernon CA 90058 323-234-9000 231-8888
Web: www.redchamber.com
Robert Wholey & Co Inc 1501 Penn Ave .... Pittsburgh PA 15222 412-261-3693 261-4834
TF: 800-248-0568 ■ *Web:* www.wholey.com
SeaSpecialties Inc 1111 NW 159th Dr............................. Miami FL 33169 305-625-5112 625-5528
TF: 800-654-6682 ■ *Web:* www.seaspecialties.com
Slade Gorton Co Inc 225 Southampton St .... Boston MA 02118 617-442-5800 442-9090
TF: 800-225-1573 ■ *Web:* www.sladegorton.com
Slavin M & Sons Ltd 31 Belmont Ave.............................. Brooklyn NY 11212 718-485-1823 485-6769
Web: www.mslavin.com
Southern Foods Inc 3500 Old Battleground Rd .... Greensboro NC 27410 336-545-3800 545-3822
TF: 800-441-3663 ■ *Web:* www.southernfoods.com
Stavis Seafoods Inc 212 Northern Ave Suite 305 .... Boston MA 02210 617-482-6349 482-1340
TF: 800-390-5103 ■ *Web:* www.stavis.com
Sunnyvale Seafood Corp 1651 Pomona Ave........................ San Jose CA 95110 408-289-9198 289-9100
TF: 800-726-2326 ■ *Web:* www.sunnyvaleseafood.com
Suram Trading Corp 2655 Le Jeune Rd Suite 1006........... Coral Gables FL 33134 305-448-7165 445-7185
Tichon Seafood Corp 7 Conway St............................ New Bedford MA 02740 508-999-5607 990-8271
Tropic Fish & Vegetable Center Inc 1020 Auahi St .... Honolulu HI 96814 808-591-2936 591-2934
Troyer Foods Inc PO Box 608.................................... Goshen IN 46527 574-533-0302 533-3851
TF: 800-876-9377 ■ *Web:* www.troyers.com
Wholey Robert & Co Inc 1501 Penn Ave .... Pittsburgh PA 15222 412-261-3693 261-4834
TF: 800-248-0568 ■ *Web:* www.wholey.com
Windward Seafoods 8550 NW 17 St Suite 105 .... Miami FL 33126 305-591-8550 670-8883
TF: 800-780-3474 ■ *Web:* www.windwardseafoods.com

300-6 Frozen Foods (Packaged) - Whol

Phone Fax

Advantage Sales & Marketing 19100 Von Karman Ave Suite 600 ..... Irvine CA 92612 949-797-2900 797-9112
Web: www.asmnet.com
Cirelli Foods Inc 30 Commerce Blvd .... Middleboro MA 02346 508-947-8778 947-8004
TF: 800-242-0939 ■ *Web:* www.cirelli.com

Frozen Foods (Packaged) - Whol (Cont'd)

	City	State	Zip	Phone	Fax
ConAgra Foods Foodservice Co 1 ConAgra Dr.	Omaha	NE	68102	402-595-4000	
Web: www.conagrafoodservice.com					
Dot Foods Inc 1 Dot Way PO Box 192	Mount Sterling	IL	62353	217-773-4411	773-3321
TF: 800-366-3687 ■ Web: www.dotfoods.com					
Happy & Healthy Products Inc 1600 S Dixie Hwy Suite 200	Boca Raton	FL	33432	561-367-0739	368-5267
TF: 800-378-4854 ■ Web: www.fruitfull.com					
HJ Heinz Co of Canada Ltd 90 Shepherd Ave E Suite 400	North York	ON	M2N7K5	416-226-5757	226-5064
Mrs Smith's Foodservice Group 2855 Rolling Pin Ln	Suwanee	GA	30024	678-482-3000	482-3451
Web: www.mrssmithsfs.com					
Muir Enterprises Inc 3575 W 900 South	Salt Lake City	UT	84104	801-363-7695	355-0221*
*Fax: Sales ■ TF: 877-268-2002 ■ Web: www.coppercanyonfarms.com					
Paris Foods Corp 1632 Carman St	Camden	NJ	08105	856-964-0915	964-9719
Web: www.parisfoods.com					
Superior Foods Inc 275 Westgate Dr	Watsonville	CA	95076	831-728-3691	722-0926
TF: 888-373-7871 ■ Web: www.superiorfd.com					
Wilcox Frozen Foods Inc 2200 Oakdale Ave.	San Francisco	CA	94124	415-282-4116	282-3044
TF: 800-827-7858					

300-7 Fruits & Vegetables - Fresh - Whol

	City	State	Zip	Phone	Fax
Adams Brothers Produce Co					
302 Fenley Ave W PO Box 2682	Birmingham	AL	35202	205-323-7161	251-4867
TF: 800-292-6532					
Albert's Organics Inc 3268 E Vernon Ave	Vernon	CA	90058	323-587-6367	587-6567
TF: 800-899-4595 ■ Web: www.albertsorganics.com					
Amerifresh 17767 N Perimeter Dr Suite B-103	Scottsdale	AZ	85255	480-933-4900	927-4909
TF: 800-568-3235 ■ Web: www.amerifresh.com					
Anthony Marano Co Inc 3000 S Ashland Ave.	Chicago	IL	60608	312-829-5055	321-7800*
*Fax Area Code: 773 ■ Web: www.anthonymarano.com					
Banacol Marketing Corp 2655 Le Jeune Rd Suite 1015	Coral Gables	FL	33134	305-441-9036	446-4291
TF: 800-824-6585 ■ Web: www.banacol.com					
Belair Produce Co Inc 7226 Parkway Dr	Hanover	MD	21076	410-782-8000	782-8009
TF: 888-782-8008 ■ Web: belairproduce.com					
Bell-Carter Foods Inc 3742 Mount Diablo Blvd	Lafayette	CA	94549	925-284-5933	284-2377
TF: 800-252-3557					
Bix Produce Co 1415 L'Orient St	Saint Paul	MN	55117	651-487-8000	489-1310
TF: 800-642-9514 ■ Web: www.bixproduce.com					
Calavo Growers Inc 1141-A Cummings Rd	Santa Paula	CA	93060	805-525-1245	921-3287
NASDAQ: CVGW ■ TF: 800-422-5286 ■ Web: www.calavo.com					
Caro Foods Inc 2324 Bayou Blue Rd	Houma	LA	70364	985-872-1483	876-0825
TF: 800-395-2276 ■ Web: www.carofoods.com					
Castellini Co 2 Plum St PO Box 721610	Newport	KY	41066	859-442-4600	442-4666
TF: 800-233-8560 ■ Web: castellinico.com					
Cleveland Growers Marketing Co 12200 Corporate Dr	Parma	OH	44130	216-898-3900	898-3901
Web: clevegrowers.com					
CM Holtzinger Fruit Co 1312 N 6th Ave PO Box 169	Yakima	WA	98902	509-457-5115	248-1514
Web: holtzingerfruit.com					
Community Suffolk Inc 304 2nd St.	Everett	MA	02149	617-389-5200	389-6680
TF: 800-225-4470					
Consumers Produce Co 1 21st St.	Pittsburgh	PA	15222	412-281-0722	281-6541
TF: 800-245-0698 ■ Web: www.consumersproduce.com					
Costa Fruit & Produce 18 Bunker Hill Industrial Park	Charlestown	MA	02129	617-241-8007	241-8718
TF: 800-343-0836 ■ Web: www.freshideas.com					
Crosset Co Inc 10295 Toebben Dr	Independence	KY	41051	859-283-5830	817-7634
TF: 800-347-4902					
Custom Apple 2701 Euclid Ct	Wenatchee	WA	98801	509-662-8131	663-3484
D'Arrigo Brothers Co of Massachusetts Inc					
105 New England Produce Center	Chelsea	MA	02150	617-884-0316	884-1304
TF: 800-327-7446					
D'Arrigo Brothers Co of New York Inc 315 NYC Terminal Market	Bronx	NY	10474	718-991-5900	960-0544
TF: 800-223-8080					
Del Monte Fresh Produce Co 241 Sevilla Ave	Coral Gables	FL	33134	305-520-8400	520-8455
Web: www.freshdelmonte.com					
DiMare Brothers/New England Farms Packing Co					
84 New England Produce Ctr.	Chelsea	MA	02150	617-889-3800	889-2067
Web: www.dimareinc.com					
DiMare Fresh Inc 1049 Ave H East	Arlington	TX	76011	817-385-3000	385-3015
TF: 800-322-2184 ■ Web: www.dimarefresh.com					
DNE World Fruit Sales 1900 Old Dixie Hwy	Fort Pierce	FL	34946	772-465-1110	465-1181
TF: 800-327-6676 ■ Web: www.dneworld.com					
Dole Distribution Center 802 Mapunapuna St	Honolulu	HI	96819	808-861-8015	861-8020
TF: 800-697-9100 ■ Web: www.dolefruithawaii.com					
East Coast Fruit Co Inc 3335 Edgewood Ave N.	Jacksonville	FL	32254	904-355-7591	791-8331
TF: 800-541-4602 ■ Web: www.eastcoastfruit.com					
Federal Fruit & Produce Co 1890 E 58th Ave	Denver	CO	80216	303-292-1303	292-3103
TF: 800-621-7166 ■ Web: www.fedfruit.com					
FreshPoint Inc 1390 Enclave Pkwy	Houston	TX	77077	281-899-4242	899-4295
Web: www.freshpoint.com					
Frieda's Inc 4465 Corporate Center Dr.	Los Alamitos	CA	90720	714-826-6100	816-0273*
*Fax: Sales ■ TF: 800-421-9477 ■ Web: www.friedas.com					
General Produce Co 1330 N 'B' St	Sacramento	CA	95814	916-441-6431	441-2483
TF: 800-366-4985 ■ Web: www.generalproduce.com					
Giumarra Brothers Fruit Co Inc					
1601 E Olympic Blvd Bldg 400 Suite 408	Los Angeles	CA	90021	213-627-2900	628-4878
Web: www.giumarra.com					
Gold Harbor Commodities Inc 9750 3rd Ave NE	Seattle	WA	98115	206-527-3494	522-7321
Graves Menu Maker Foods Inc 913 Big Horn Dr.	Jefferson City	MO	65109	573-893-3000	893-2172
TF: 800-557-6623 ■ Web: www.menumakerfoods.com.futuresite.register.com					
HC Schmeiding Produce Co					
2330 N Thompson St PO Box 369	Springdale	AR	72764	479-751-4517	751-6831
TF: 800-643-3607					
Hearn Kirkwood 7251 Standard Dr	Hanover	MD	21076	410-712-6000	712-0020
TF: 888-866-2905 ■ Web: www.hearnkirkwood.com					
Heeren Bros Inc 1060 Hall St SW	Grand Rapids	MI	49503	616-452-2101	243-7070
TF: 800-253-4620 ■ Web: www.heerenbros.com					
Hollar & Greene Produce Co Inc 230 Cabbage Rd PO Box 3500	Boone	NC	28607	828-264-2177	264-4413
TF: 800-222-1077 ■ Web: www.hollarandgreene.com					
Indianapolis Fruit Co Inc 4501 Massachusetts Ave	Indianapolis	IN	46218	317-546-2425	543-0521
TF: 800-377-2425 ■ Web: www.indyfruit.com					
Lamanuzzi & Pantaleo Inc 11767 Rd 27 1/2	Madera	CA	93637	559-432-3844	299-5902
Lee Ray-Tarantino Co Inc					
155 Terminal Ct PO Box 2408	South San Francisco	CA	94083	650-761-2854	873-0364
TF: 800-321-1035					
Maine Potato Growers Inc 56 Parsons St PO Box 271	Presque Isle	ME	04769	207-764-3131	764-8450
TF: 800-649-3358 ■ Web: www.mpgco-op.com					
Melissa's/World Variety Produce Inc 5325 S Soto St	Vernon	CA	90058	323-588-0151	588-1768
TF: 800-468-7111 ■ Web: www.melissas.com					
Mission Produce Inc 2500 Vineyard Ave Suite 300 PO Box 5267	Oxnard	CA	93031	805-981-3650	981-3660
Web: www.missionpro.com					
Moore Food Distributors Co 9910 Page Ave	Saint Louis	MO	63132	314-426-1300	426-6690
TF: 800-467-7878 ■ Web: moorefooddist.com					
Muir Enterprises Inc 3575 W 900 South	Salt Lake City	UT	84104	801-363-7695	355-0221*
*Fax: Sales ■ TF: 877-268-2002 ■ Web: www.coppercanyonfarms.com					
Natural Selection Foods 1721 San Juan Hwy	San Juan Bautista	CA	95045	831-623-7880	623-4988
TF: 888-624-1004 ■ Web: www.nsfoods.com					
Oneonta Trading Corp 1 Oneonta Way	Wenatchee	WA	98801	509-663-2631	663-6333
TF: 800-688-2191 ■ Web: www.oneonta.com					
Organic Valley Family of Farms 1 Organic Way	LaFarge	WI	54639	608-625-2602	625-2600
TF: 888-444-6455 ■ Web: www.organicvalley.coop					
Pandol Brothers Inc 401 Rd 192	Delano	CA	93215	661-725-3755	725-4741
Web: www.pandol.com					
Paramount Export Co 175 Filbert St Suite 201	Oakland	CA	94607	510-839-0150	839-1002
TF: 800-869-0150 ■ Web: www.paramountexport.net					
Peak of the Market 1200 King Edward St	Winnipeg	MB	R3H0R5	204-633-7325	694-7325
TF: 888-289-7325 ■ Web: www.peakmarket.com					
Peirone Produce Co 524 Spokane Falls Blvd	Spokane	WA	99202	509-838-3515	838-3916
TF: 800-552-5837 ■ Web: www.peirone.com					
Sandridge Food Corp 133 Commerce Dr	Medina	OH	44256	330-725-2348	722-3998
TF: 800-280-7951 ■ Web: www.sandridge.com					
Schmieding HC Produce Co					
2330 N Thompson St PO Box 369	Springdale	AR	72764	479-751-4517	751-6831
TF: 800-643-3607					
Simonian Fruit Co 511 N 7th St	Fowler	CA	93625	559-834-5307	834-2363
Web: www.simonianfruit.com					
Snokist Growers Co-op 10 W Mead Ave PO Box 1587	Yakima	WA	98907	509-453-5631	453-9359
TF: 800-258-0470 ■ Web: www.snokist.com					
Sunkist Growers Inc 14130 Riverside Dr	Sherman Oaks	CA	91423	818-986-4800	379-7511*
*Fax: PR ■ TF: 800-383-7141 ■ Web: www.sunkist.com					
Superior Foods Inc 275 Westgate Dr	Watsonville	CA	95076	831-728-3691	722-0926
TF: 888-373-7871 ■ Web: www.superiorfd.com					
Tony Vitrano Co Maryland Wholesale Produce Market Bldg B	Jessup	MD	20794	410-799-7444	799-2464
Tropic Fish & Vegetable Center Inc 1020 Auahi St	Honolulu	HI	96814	808-591-2936	591-2934
United Foods Inc 10 Pictsweet Dr	Bells	TN	38006	731-422-7600	561-8810*
*Fax Area Code: 800 ■ TF: 800-367-7412 ■ Web: www.pictsweet.com					
William H Kopke Jr Inc 3000 Marcus Ave Suite 3E4	Lake Success	NY	11042	516-328-6800	328-6874

300-8 Groceries - General Line

	City	State	Zip	Phone	Fax
Abbott Sysco Food Service 2400 Harrison Rd	Columbus	OH	43204	614-272-0658	272-8409*
*Fax: Sales ■ TF: 800-686-3663 ■ Web: www.abbottfoods.com					
Abraham S & Sons Inc 4001 Three-Mile Rd NW	Walker	MI	49501	616-453-6358	453-9309
TF: 877-477-5455 ■ Web: www.sasinc.com					
Advantage Sales & Marketing 19100 Von Karman Ave Suite 600	Irvine	CA	92612	949-797-2900	797-9112
Web: www.asmnet.com					
Affiliated Foods Inc 1401 Farmers Ave	Amarillo	TX	79118	806-372-3851	374-1721*
*Fax: Sales ■ TF: 800-234-3661 ■ Web: www.afiama.com					
Affiliated Foods Midwest 1301 Omaha Ave.	Norfolk	NE	68701	402-371-0555	371-1884
Web: www.afmidwest.com					
Affiliated Foods Southwest Inc 12103 I-30	Little Rock	AR	72209	501-455-3590	455-6549*
*Fax: Mktg ■ Web: www.affiliatedfoods.com					
AJC International 5188 Roswell Rd NW	Atlanta	GA	30342	404-252-6750	252-9340
TF: 800-252-3663 ■ Web: www.ajcfood.com					
Albert Guarnieri Co 1133 E Market St	Warren	OH	44483	330-394-5636	394-4982
TF: 800-686-2639 ■ Web: www.albertguarnieri.com					
Allen Foods Inc 8543 Page Ave	Saint Louis	MO	63114	314-426-4100	426-0391
TF: 800-888-4855 ■ Web: www.allenfoods.com					
AMCON Distributing Co 7405 Irvington Rd.	Omaha	NE	68122	402-331-3727	331-4834
AMEX: DIT ■ TF: 800-369-6200 ■ Web: www.amcon.com					
American Seaway Foods Inc 5300 Richmond Rd	Bedford Heights	OH	44146	216-292-7000	968-1618*
*Fax Area Code: 412					
Amster-Kirtz Co 2830 Cleveland Ave NW	Canton	OH	44709	330-493-1800	493-8207
TF: 800-257-9338					
Anderson-DuBose Co 6575 Davis Industrial Pkwy	Solon	OH	44139	440-248-8800	248-6208
TF: 800-248-1080					
Associated Food Stores Inc 1850 W 2100 South	Salt Lake City	UT	84119	801-973-4400	978-8551
TF Cust Svc: 888-574-9000 ■ Web: www.afstores.com					
Associated Grocers of Florida Inc 1141 SW 12th Ave	Pompano Beach	FL	33069	954-876-3000	876-3039
Web: www.agfla.com					
Associated Grocers Inc 8600 Anselmo Ln	Baton Rouge	LA	70810	225-769-2020	763-6194
TF: 800-637-2021 ■ Web: www.agbr.com					
Associated Grocers Inc 3301 S Norfolk St	Seattle	WA	98118	206-762-2100	767-8785
TF: 800-562-9729 ■ Web: www.agsea.com					
Associated Grocers of Maine Inc 47 AG Dr	Gardiner	ME	04345	207-582-6500	582-3461
TF: 800-852-6550 ■ Web: www.agofme.com					
Associated Grocers of New England Inc 11 Cooperative Way	Pembroke	NH	03275	603-223-6710	223-5672
TF: 800-242-2248 ■ Web: www.agne.com					
Associated Grocers of the South 3600 Vanderbilt Rd	Birmingham	AL	35217	205-841-6781	808-4920
TF: 800-695-6051 ■ Web: www.agsouth.com					
Associated Wholesale Grocers Inc 5000 Kansas Ave	Kansas City	KS	66106	913-288-1000	288-1587
Web: www.awginc.com					
Associated Wholesalers Inc PO Box 67	Robesonia	PA	19551	610-693-3161	693-3171*
*Fax: Orders ■ TF: 800-927-7771 ■ Web: www.awiweb.com					
Atalanta Corp 1 Atalanta Plaza	Elizabeth	NJ	07206	908-351-8000	351-1693
Web: www.atalanta1.com					
Banta Foods Inc 1620 N Packer Rd	Springfield	MO	65803	417-862-6644	865-7223
TF: 800-492-2682 ■ Web: www.bantafoods.com					
Ben E Keith Co 7650 Will Rogers Blvd	Fort Worth	TX	76140	817-759-6000	759-6238
TF: 877-317-6100 ■ Web: www.benekeith.com					
Bozzuto's Inc 275 School House Rd	Cheshire	CT	06410	203-272-3511	250-2880*
*Fax: Sales ■ Web: www.bozzutos.com					
Brenham Wholesale Grocery Co 602 W 1st St	Brenham	TX	77833	979-836-7925	830-0346
TF: 800-324-3232 ■ Web: www.bwgroc.com					
C & S Wholesale Grocers Inc 47 Old Ferry Rd PO Box 821	Brattleboro	VT	05302	802-257-4371	257-6613*
*Fax: Hum Res ■ Web: www.cswg.com					
Cash-Wa Distributing Co 401 W 4th St	Kearney	NE	68845	308-237-3151	234-6018
TF: 800-652-0010 ■ Web: www.cashwa.com					
CB Ragland Co 2720 Eugenia Ave.	Nashville	TN	37211	615-259-4622	254-2130*
*Fax: Hum Res ■ TF: 800-234-4455 ■ Web: www.cbragland.com					
CD Hartnett Co 302 N Main St	Weatherford	TX	76086	817-594-3813	594-9714
TF: 877-594-3813 ■ Web: www.cd-hartnett.com					
Central Grocers Co-op Inc 11100 Belmont Ave	Franklin Park	IL	60131	847-451-0660	288-8710
Web: www.central-grocers.com					
Certified Grocers Midwest Inc 1 Certified Dr.	Hodgkins	IL	60525	708-579-2100	579-9786
Web: www.certisaver.com					
Coastal Pacific Food Distributors Inc 1015 Performance Dr	Stockton	CA	95206	209-983-2454	983-8009
Web: www.cpfd.com					
ConAgra Grocery Products Co 3353 Michelson Dr	Irvine	CA	92612	949-437-1000	437-3310
Web: www.conagrafoods.com					
Core-Mark International Inc					
395 Oyster Point Blvd Suite 415	South San Francisco	CA	94080	650-589-9445	952-4284
TF: 800-622-1713 ■ Web: www.coremark.com					
Dearborn Wholesale Grocers Inc 2801 S Western Ave	Chicago	IL	60608	773-254-4300	847-3838
TF: 800-999-3663 ■ Web: www.dearbornwholesale.com					
Di Giorgio Corp 380 Middlesex Ave.	Carteret	NJ	07008	732-541-5555	541-3602
Web: www.whiterose.com					

Phone | Fax

Di Giorgio Corp White Rose Food Div 380 Middlesex Ave. Carteret NJ 07008 732-541-5555 541-3730
Web: www.whiterose.com
DiCarlo Distributors Inc 1630 N Ocean Ave Holtsville NY 11742 631-758-6000 758-6096
TF: 800-342-2756 ■ *Web:* www.dicarlofood.com
Dutch Valley Bulk Food Distributors Inc
7615 Lancaster Ave Myerstown PA 17067 717-933-4191 933-5466
TF: 800-733-4191 ■ *Web:* www.dutchvalleyfoods.com
Farner-Bocken Co 1751 US Hwy 30 E Carroll IA 51401 712-792-3503 792-7352
TF: 800-274-8692 ■ *Web:* www.farner-bocken.com
Feesers Inc 5561 Grayson Rd Harrisburg PA 17111 717-564-4636 558-7450
TF: 800-326-2828 ■ *Web:* www.feesers.com
Food Services of America Inc 4025 Delridge Way SW Suite 400 Seattle WA 98106 206-933-5000 933-5283
TF: 800-372-3663 ■ *Web:* www.fsafood.com
Glazier Foods Co 11303 Antoine Dr Houston TX 77066 832-375-6300 375-6114
TF: 800-989-6411 ■ *Web:* www.glazierfoods.com
Gordon Food Service 333 50th St SW Grand Rapids MI 49548 616-530-7000 717-7600
TF: 800-968-7500 ■ *Web:* www.gfs.com
Henry Lee Div 3301 NW 125th St Miami FL 33167 305-685-5851 459-8731
TF: 800-274-4533 ■ *Web:* www.gfs-henrylee.com
Grocers Supply Co Inc 3131 E Holcombe Blvd Houston TX 77021 713-747-5000 746-5611*
**Fax:* Acctg ■ *TF:* 800-352-8003 ■ *Web:* www.grocerssupply.com
Grocery Supply Co 130 Hillcrest Dr Sulphur Springs TX 75482 903-885-7621 439-3249
TF: 800-231-1938 ■ *Web:* www.grocerysupply.com
Guarnieri Albert Co 1133 E Market St Warren OH 44483 330-394-5636 394-4982
TF: 800-686-2639 ■ *Web:* www.albertguarnieri.com
Hackney HT Inc 1200 Burris Rd Newton NC 28658 828-464-1010 466-3464
TF: 800-876-4641 ■ *Web:* www.hthackney.com
Hannaford Bros Co 145 Pleasant Hill Rd Scarborough ME 04074 207-883-2911
TF: 800-341-6393 ■ *Web:* www.hannaford.com
Hartnett CD Co 302 N Main St Weatherford TX 76086 817-594-3813 594-9714
TF: 877-594-3813 ■ *Web:* www.cd-hartnett.com
HT Hackney Inc 1200 Burris Rd Newton NC 28658 828-464-1010 466-3464
TF: 800-876-4641 ■ *Web:* www.hthackney.com
IJ Co 4720 Singleton Station Rd Louisville TN 37777 865-970-7800 970-5495*
**Fax:* Cust Svc ■ *TF:* 800-251-9516 ■ *Web:* www.ijcompany.com
Imperial Trading Co Inc 701 Edwards Ave PO Box 23508 Elmwood LA 70123 504-733-1400 736-4156
TF Cust Svc: 800-743-1761 ■ *Web:* www.imperialtrading.com
Institution Food House Inc 543 12th Street Dr NW Hickory NC 28603 828-323-4500 725-4500
TF: 800-800-0434 ■ *Web:* www.institutionfoodhouse.com
Institutional Distributors Inc PO Box 520 East Bernstadt KY 40729 606-843-2100 843-2108
TF: 800-442-7885 ■ *Web:* www.idifoods.com
International Multifoods Corp 111 Cheshire Ln Suite 100 Minnetonka MN 55305 952-404-7500 404-7670
TF: 800-866-3300 ■ *Web:* www.multifoods.com
Jetro Cash & Carry Enterprises Inc 15-24 132nd St College Point NY 11356 718-762-8700 463-8598
Web: www.jetro.com
JM Swank Co 395 Herky St North Liberty IA 52317 319-626-3683 626-3666
TF: 800-593-6375 ■ *Web:* www.jmswank.com/index2.html
Jordano's Inc 550 S Patterson Ave Santa Barbara CA 93111 805-964-0611 964-3821
TF: 800-325-2278 ■ *Web:* www.jordanos.com
JT Davenport & Sons Inc PO Box 1105 Sanford NC 27331 919-774-9444 774-4282
TF Cust Svc: 800-868-7550 ■ *Web:* www.jtdavenport.com
Kehe Food Distributors Inc 900 N Schmidt Rd Romeoville IL 60446 815-886-0700 886-1111
TF: 800-995-5343
Keith Ben E Co 7650 Will Rogers Blvd Fort Worth TX 76140 817-759-6000 759-6238
TF: 877-317-6100 ■ *Web:* www.benekeith.com
Key Food Stores Co-op Inc 1200 South Ave Staten Island NY 10314 718-370-4200 370-4232*
**Fax:* Mktg ■ *Web:* www.keyfoods.com
Klein Wholesale Distributors 100 W End Rd Wilkes-Barre PA 18703 570-823-2447 823-9670
TF: 800-824-6965 ■ *Web:* www.kleinwd.com
Kraft Foods International Inc 3 Lakes Dr Northfield IL 60093 847-646-2000 335-9395*
**Fax Area Code:* 914 ■ *TF:* 800-323-0768 ■ *Web:* www.kraft.com
Krasdale Foods Inc 400 Food Ctr Dr Bronx NY 10474 914-694-6400 697-5225
Web: www.krasdalefoods.com
Labatt Food Service 4500 Industry Park Dr San Antonio TX 78218 210-661-4216 661-0973
TF: 800-324-8732 ■ *Web:* www.labattfood.com
Laurel Grocery Co Inc PO Box 4100 London KY 40743 606-878-6601 864-5693
TF: 800-467-6601 ■ *Web:* www.laurelgrocery.com
Loblaw Cos Ltd 22 St Clair Ave E Toronto ON M4T2S7 416-922-8500 922-4395
TF: 877-525-4762 ■ *Web:* www.loblaw.com
Long Wholesale Distributors Inc 5173 Pioneer Dr PO Box 70 Meridian MS 39301 601-482-3144 482-3109
TF: 800-748-3847 ■ *Web:* www.longdistribution.com
Luke Soules Acosta 1920 Westridge Dr Irving TX 75038 972-518-1442 751-0983
TF: 800-486-0928
Maines Paper & Food Service Co 101 Broome Corporate Pkwy Conklin NY 13748 607-772-1936 723-3245*
**Fax:* Cust Svc ■ *TF:* 800-366-3669 ■ *Web:* www.maines.net
MBM Corp PO Box 800 Rocky Mount NC 27801 252-985-7200 985-7241*
**Fax:* Cust Svc
MBM Corp Proficient Food Co Div
9408 Richmond Pl Rancho Cucamonga CA 91730 909-484-6100 484-6127
McLane Co Inc 4747 McLane Pkwy Temple TX 76504 254-771-7500 771-7244
TF: 800-299-1401 ■ *Web:* www.mclaneco.com
McLane Foodservice Inc 2085 Midway Rd Carrollton TX 75006 972-364-2000 364-2088
TF: 888-792-9300 ■ *Web:* www.mclaneco.com
Mendez & Co PO Box 363348 San Juan PR 00936 787-793-8888 783-9498
Merchants Co 1100 Edwards St Hattiesburg MS 39401 601-583-4351 582-5333
TF: 800-844-3663 ■ *Web:* www.themerchantscompany.com
Merchants Distributors Inc 5001 Alex Lee Blvd Hickory NC 28601 828-323-4100 323-4527
TF: 800-800-2634 ■ *Web:* www.merchantsdistributors.com
Metro Inc 11011 Maurice-Duplessis Blvd Montreal QC H1C1V6 514-643-1055 643-1215
TF: 800-361-4681 ■ *Web:* www.metro.ca
Mid-Mountain Foods Inc 26331 Hillman Hwy PO Box 129 Abingdon VA 24212 276-623-5000 623-5404
Millbrook Distribution Services 88 Huntoon Memorial Hwy Leicester MA 01524 508-892-8171 892-4827
TF: 800-225-7398 ■ *Web:* www.millbrookds.com
Nash Finch Co 7600 France Ave S Edina MN 55435 952-832-0534 844-1231*
NASDAQ: NAFC ■ **Fax:* Mktg ■ *Web:* www.nashfinch.com
Nobel/Sysco Food Services Inc 5000 Beeler St Denver CO 80238 303-585-2000
TF: 800-366-6696 ■ *Web:* www.nobelsysco.com
Olean Wholesale Grocery Co-op Inc 1587 Haskell Rd Olean NY 14760 716-372-2020 372-2039
TF: 866-774-9751 ■ *Web:* www.oleanwholesale.com
Oppenheimer Cos Inc 877 W Main St Suite 700 Boise ID 83702 208-343-4883 343-4490
TF: 800-727-9939 ■ *Web:* www.oppcos.com
Pegler-Sysco Food Services Co 1700 Center Park Rd Lincoln NE 68512 402-423-1031 421-5291
TF: 800-366-1031
Penn Traffic Co 1200 State Fair Blvd Syracuse NY 13209 315-453-7284 461-2387*
**Fax:* Acctg ■ *TF:* 800-275-9005 ■ *Web:* www.penntraffic.com
Performance Food Group Co 12500 W Creek Pkwy Richmond VA 23238 804-484-7700 484-7701
NASDAQ: PFGC ■ *Web:* www.pfgc.com
Perishable Distributors of Iowa Ltd 2741 SE PDI Pl Ankeny IA 50021 515-965-6300 965-1105
Web: www.contactpdi.com
PFG/AFI Foodservice 1 Center Dr Elizabeth NJ 07207 908-629-1800 629-0500
TF: 800-275-0155 ■ *Web:* www.metrofresh.com
Piggly Wiggly Alabama Distributing Co Inc
2400 JT Wooten Dr Bessemer AL 35020 205-481-2300 481-2383
Web: www.pwadc.com
Piggly Wiggly Carolina Co Inc PO Box 118047 Charleston SC 29423 843-554-9880 745-2730
TF: 800-243-9880 ■ *Web:* www.thepig.net

Phone | Fax

Pocahontas Foods USA Inc PO Box 9729 Richmond VA 23228 804-262-8614 261-4394
Web: www.pocahontasfoods.com
Proficient Food Co Div MBM Corp
9408 Richmond Pl Rancho Cucamonga CA 91730 909-484-6100 484-6127
Purity Wholesale Grocers Inc
5400 Broken Sound Blvd NW Suite 100 Boca Raton FL 33487 561-994-9360 994-9629
TF: 800-323-6838 ■ *Web:* www.pwg-inc.com
Quality-PFG 4901 Asher Ave Little Rock AR 72204 501-568-3141 565-8821
TF: 800-568-3141 ■ *Web:* www.qfi.com
Ragland CB Co 2720 Eugenia Ave Nashville TN 37211 615-259-4622 254-2130*
**Fax:* Hum Res ■ *TF:* 800-234-4455 ■ *Web:* www.cbragland.com
Reinhart FoodService Inc 1500 Saint James St La Crosse WI 54603 608-782-2660 784-1674
TF: 800-827-4010 ■ *Web:* www.reinhartfoodservice.com
Roundy's Inc 875 E Wisconsin Ave Milwaukee WI 53202 414-231-5000 231-7939
Web: www.roundys.com
S Abraham & Sons Inc 4001 Three-Mile Rd NW Walker MI 49501 616-453-6358 453-9309
TF: 877-477-5455 ■ *Web:* www.sasinc.com
Shamrock Foods Co Inc 2540 N 29th Ave Phoenix AZ 85009 602-233-6400 477-6469
TF: 800-388-3247 ■ *Web:* www.shamrockfoods.com
Soules Luke Acosta 1920 Westridge Dr Irving TX 75038 972-518-1442 751-0983
TF: 800-486-0928
Southco Distributing Co 2201 S John St Goldsboro NC 27530 919-735-8012 735-0097
TF: 800-969-3172 ■ *Web:* www.southcodistributing.com
Spartan Stores Inc 850 76th St SW PO Box 8700 Grand Rapids MI 49518 616-878-2000
NASDAQ: SPTN ■ *TF:* 800-343-4422 ■ *Web:* www.spartanstores.com
Super Store Industries 16888 McKinley Ave PO Box 549 Lathrop CA 95330 209-858-2010 858-5674
SUPERVALU Inc 11840 Valley View Rd Eden Prairie MN 55344 952-828-4000 828-8998
NYSE: SVU ■ *TF Cust Svc:* 888-256-2800 ■ *Web:* www.supervalu.com
SUPERVALU International 495 E 19th St Tacoma WA 98421 253-593-3198 593-7828
TF: 877-787-8254 ■ *Web:* www.supervaluinternational.com
Swank JM Co 395 Herky St North Liberty IA 52317 319-626-3683 626-3666
TF: 800-593-6375 ■ *Web:* www.jmswank.com/index2.html
SYGMA Network Inc 2000 Westbelt Dr Columbus OH 43228 614-771-3801 771-3830
TF: 800-347-7344 ■ *Web:* www.sygmanetwork.com
SYSCO Corp 1390 Enclave Pkwy Houston TX 77077 281-584-1390 584-2721*
NYSE: SYY ■ **Fax:* PR ■ *Web:* www.sysco.com
Sysco Food Services of Metro New York LLC
20 Theodore Conrad Dr Jersey City NJ 07305 201-433-2000 433-1338
Web: www.syscometrony.com
Sysco Foodservice 21 Four Seasons Dr Etobicoke ON M9B6J8 416-234-2668 234-2650
Web: www.sysco.ca
Thomas & Howard Wholesale Grocers Inc 209 Flintlake Rd Columbia SC 29223 803-788-5520 699-9097
Web: www.tohoco.com
Thoms Proestler Co 8001 TPC Rd Rock Island IL 61204 309-787-1234 787-1254
TF: 800-747-1234 ■ *Web:* www.tpcinfo.com
Topco Assoc LLC 7711 Gross Pt Rd Skokie IL 60077 847-676-3030 676-4949
TF: 888-423-0139 ■ *Web:* www.topco.com
Tree of Life Inc 405 Golfway W Dr Saint Augustine FL 32095 904-824-1846 447-8917*
**Fax Area Code:* 800 ■ **Fax:* Cust Svc ■ *TF Cust Svc:* 800-260-2424 ■
Web: www.treeoflife.com
Tripifoods Inc 1427 William St Buffalo NY 14240 716-853-7400 852-7400
TF: 800-851-7400 ■ *Web:* www.tripifoods.com
Unified Western Grocers Inc 6433 S E Lake Rd Portland OR 97222 503-833-1000 833-1008
TF: 800-777-3305 ■ *Web:* www.uwgrocers.com
UniPro Foodservice Inc 2500 Cumberland Pkwy Suite 600 Atlanta GA 30339 770-952-0871 952-0872
TF: 800-366-7723 ■ *Web:* www.uniprofoodservice.com
United Natural Foods Inc 260 Lake Rd Dayville CT 06241 860-779-2800 779-2811
NASDAQ: UNFI ■ *TF:* 800-877-8898 ■ *Web:* www.unfi.com
United Wholesale Grocery Co 25700 W Eight Mile Rd Southfield MI 48033 248-356-7300 356-7301
US Foodservice Inc 9755 Patuxent Woods Dr Columbia MD 21046 410-312-7100 312-7591*
**Fax:* Hum Res ■ *TF:* 800-236-0805 ■ *Web:* www.usfoodservice.com
Vistar/VSA Corp 12650 E Arapahoe Rd Bldg D Centennial CO 80112 303-662-7100 662-7570
TF: 800-880-9900 ■ *Web:* www.vistarvsa.com
Wakefern Food Corp 600 York St Elizabeth NJ 07207 908-527-3300 527-3397
TF: 800-746-7748 ■ *Web:* www.shoprite.com
Western Family Foods Inc 6700 SW Sandburg St Tigard OR 97223 503-639-6300 684-3469
Web: www.westernfamily.com
White Rose Food Div Di Giorgio Corp 380 Middlesex Ave Carteret NJ 07008 732-541-5555 541-3730
Web: www.whiterose.com
Winkler Inc PO Box 68 Dale IN 47523 812-937-4421 937-2044
TF: 800-621-3843 ■ *Web:* www.winklerinc.com
Wood-Fruitticher Grocery Co Inc 2900 Alton Rd Birmingham AL 35210 205-836-9663 836-9681
TF: 800-489-4500 ■ *Web:* www.woodfruitticher.com

300-9 Meats & Meat Products - Whol

Phone | Fax

Agar Supply Co Inc 225 John Hancock Rd Taunton MA 02780 508-821-2060 880-5113*
**Fax Area Code:* 617 ■ **Fax:* Sales ■ *TF:* 800-669-6040 ■ *Web:* www.agarsupply.com
Aurora Packing Co Inc 125 S Grant St North Aurora IL 60542 630-897-0551 897-0647
Auth Brothers Inc 1905 Clarkson Way Landover MD 20785 301-322-8400 322-3185
TF: 800-424-2610 ■ *Web:* www.authbros.com
Becker Food Co Inc 4160 N Port Washington Rd Milwaukee WI 53212 414-964-5353 964-4523
Bruss Co 3548 N Kostner Ave Chicago IL 60641 773-282-2900 282-6966
TF: 800-621-3882
Casing Assoc Inc 1120 Close Ave Bronx NY 10472 718-842-7151 617-6894
TF: 800-223-8318
Colorado Boxed Beef Co PO Box 899 Winter Haven FL 33882 863-967-0636 965-2222
TF: 800-955-0636 ■ *Web:* www.coloradoboxedbeef.com
ConAgra Foods Foodservice Co 1 ConAgra Dr Omaha NE 68102 402-595-4000
Web: www.conagrafoodservice.com
Cusack Wholesale Meat Inc PO Box 25111 Oklahoma City OK 73125 405-232-2114 232-2127
TF: 800-241-6328 ■ *Web:* www.cusackmeats.com
Cypress Food Distributors Inc
3111 N University Dr Suite 612 Coral Springs FL 33065 954-344-2900 344-3607
Day-Lee Foods Inc 13055 E Molette St Santa Fe Springs CA 90670 562-802-6800 926-0646
Web: www.day-lee.com
Deen Wholesale Meats 813 E Northside Dr Fort Worth TX 76102 817-335-2257 338-9256
TF: 800-333-3953 ■ *Web:* www.deenmeat.com
Durham Meat Co 2026 Martin Ave Santa Clara CA 95050 800-444-5687 748-1267*
**Fax Area Code:* 408 ■ *TF:* 800-233-8742
Earp Distribution Co 6550 Kansas Ave Kansas City KS 66111 913-287-3311 287-3297
TF: 800-866-3277 ■ *Web:* www.earpdistribution.com
Empire Beef Co Inc 171 Weidner Rd Rochester NY 14624 585-235-7350 235-1573
TF: 800-462-6804 ■ *Web:* www.empirebeef.com
Freedman Food Service of San Antonio DBA Texas Meat Purveyor 4241 Director Dr San Antonio TX 78219 210-337-1011 333-9410
TF: 800-552-3234 ■ *Web:* www.freedmanfoods.com
Green Tree Packing Co 65 Central Ave Passaic NJ 07055 973-473-1305 473-7975
TF: 800-221-5754
Harker's Distribution Inc 801 6th St SW Le Mars IA 51031 712-546-8171 546-3109*
**Fax:* Sales ■ *TF:* 800-798-9800 ■ *Web:* www.harkers.com
Holten Meat Inc 1682 Sauget Business Blvd Sauget IL 62206 618-337-8400 337-3292
TF: 800-851-4684 ■ *Web:* www.holtenmeat.com
Interstate Meat Service Inc 2309 Myers Rd Albert Lea MN 56007 507-377-2228 377-9305
Web: www.interstatemeats.com

Meats & Meat Products - Whol (Cont'd)

	City	State	Zip	Phone	Fax
Keystone Foods LLC 300 Bar Harbor Dr Suite 600 5 Tower Bridge *Web:* www.keystonefoods.com	West Conshohocken	PA	19428	610-667-6700	667-1460
Leidy's Inc 266 W Cherry Ln PO Box 64257 *TF:* 800-222-2319 ■ *Web:* www.leidys.com	Souderton	PA	18964	215-723-4606	721-2003
Manda Fine Meats 2445 Sorrel Ave *TF:* 800-343-2642 ■ *Web:* www.mandafinemeats.com	Baton Rouge	LA	70802	225-344-7636	344-7647
Maryland Quality Meats Inc 701 W Hamburg St *TF:* 800-368-2579 ■ *Web:* www.mqm.biz	Baltimore	MD	21230	410-539-7055	685-6720
Michael's Finer Meats & Seafoods 3775 Zane Trace Dr *TF:* 800-282-0518 ■ *Web:* www.michaelsmeats.com	Columbus	OH	43228	614-527-4900	527-4520
Midamar Corp PO Box 218 *TF:* 800-362-3711 ■ *Web:* www.midamar.com	Cedar Rapids	IA	52406	319-362-3711	362-4111
Middendorf Meat Co Inc 3737 N Broadway *TF:* 800-949-6328 ■ *Web:* www.middendorfmeat.com	Saint Louis	MO	63147	314-241-4800	241-5386
Nationwide Foods/Brookfield Farms 700 E 107th St *TF:* 800-243-1014	Chicago	IL	60628	773-787-4900	264-1270
Northwestern Meat Inc 2100 NW 23rd St *Web:* www.numeat.com	Miami	FL	33142	305-633-8112	633-6907
Peyton Meats Inc 3 Butterfield Trail Suite 101 *TF:* 800-351-1024	El Paso	TX	79906	915-751-6632	771-9687
Porky Products Corp 400 Port Carteret Dr *TF:* 800-952-0265 ■ *Web:* www.porkyproducts.com	Carteret	NJ	07008	732-541-0200	969-6043
Quality Meats & Seafoods 700 Center St *TF:* 800-959-4250 ■ *Web:* www.qualitymeats.com	West Fargo	ND	58078	701-282-0202	282-0583
Quirch Foods Co 7600 NW 82nd Pl *TF:* 800-458-5252 ■ *Web:* www.quirchfoods.com	Miami	FL	33166	305-691-3535	593-0272
Randall Foods Inc 2905 E 50th St **Fax:* Hum Res ■ *TF:* 800-372-6581	Vernon	CA	90058	323-587-2383	586-1587*
Sampco Inc 651 W Washington Blvd Suite 300 *TF:* 800-767-0689	Chicago	IL	60661	312-346-1506	346-8302
Scavuzzo's Inc 2840 Gwinnot St *TF:* 800-800-4707	Kansas City	MO	64120	816-231-1517	231-1590
Schisa Brothers Inc PO Box 3350 *TF:* 800-676-3287 ■ *Web:* www.schisabros.com	Syracuse	NY	13220	315-463-0213	463-0248
Sherwood Food Distributors 18615 Sherwood Ave *Web:* www.sherwoodfoods.com	Detroit	MI	48234	313-366-3100	366-8825
Southern Foods Inc 3500 Old Battleground Rd *TF:* 800-441-3663 ■ *Web:* www.southernfoods.com	Greensboro	NC	27410	336-545-3800	545-3822
Stadler's Country Hams Inc PO Box 397 *TF:* 800-262-1795	Elon	NC	27244	336-584-1396	584-9483
Texas Meat Purveyor 4241 Director Dr *TF:* 800-552-3234 ■ *Web:* www.freedmanfoods.com	San Antonio	TX	78219	210-337-1011	333-9410
Thumann Inc 670 Dell Rd *Web:* www.thumanns.com	Carlstadt	NJ	07072	201-935-3636	935-2226
Troyer Foods Inc PO Box 608 *TF:* 800-876-9377 ■ *Web:* www.troyers.com	Goshen	IN	46527	574-533-0302	533-3851
Wolfson Casing Corp 700 S Fulton Ave *TF:* 800-221-8042 ■ *Web:* www.wolfsoncasing.com	Mount Vernon	NY	10550	914-668-9000	668-6900

300-10 Poultry, Eggs, Poultry Products - Whol

	City	State	Zip	Phone	Fax
Acme Farms Inc PO Box 3065 *TF:* 800-542-8309	Seattle	WA	98114	206-323-4300	323-3900
Agar Supply Co Inc 225 John Hancock Rd **Fax Area Code:* 617 ■ **Fax:* Sales ■ *TF:* 800-669-6040 ■ *Web:* www.agarsupply.com	Taunton	MA	02780	508-821-2060	880-5113*
Consolidated Poultry & Egg Co PO Box 11958	Memphis	TN	38111	901-322-6466	324-7283
Crystal Farms Refrigerated Distribution Co 6465 Wayzata Blvd Suite 200 *TF:* 877-279-7825 ■ *Web:* www.crystalfarms.com	Minneapolis	MN	55426	952-544-8101	544-8069
Durbin Marshall Food Corp 2830 Commerce Blvd *TF:* 800-768-2456 ■ *Web:* www.marshalldurbin.com	Irondale	AL	35210	205-956-3505	380-3251
Dutt & Wagner of Virginia Inc PO Box 518 *TF:* 800-688-2116	Abingdon	VA	24212	276-628-2116	628-4619
El Jay Poultry Corp 1010 Haddonfield-Berlin Rd Suite 402	Voorhees	NJ	08043	856-435-0900	435-3019
Harker's Distribution Inc 801 6th St SW **Fax:* Sales ■ *TF:* 800-798-9800 ■ *Web:* www.harkers.com	Le Mars	IA	51031	712-546-8171	546-3109*
Hemmelgarn & Sons Inc 3763 Philothea Rd	Coldwater	OH	45828	419-678-2351	678-4922
House of Raeford Farms Inc PO Box 100 *TF:* 800-888-7539 ■ *Web:* www.houseofraeford.com	Raeford	NC	28376	910-875-5161	875-8300
Lincoln Poultry & Egg Co 2005 'M' St *TF:* 800-477-4433 ■ *Web:* www.lincolnpoultry.com	Lincoln	NE	68510	402-477-3757	477-1800
Marshall Durbin Food Corp 2830 Commerce Blvd *TF:* 800-768-2456 ■ *Web:* www.marshalldurbin.com	Irondale	AL	35210	205-956-3505	380-3251
Metropolitan Poultry & Seafood Co 1920 Stanford Ct *TF:* 800-522-0060 ■ *Web:* www.metropoultry.com	Landover	MD	20785	301-772-0060	772-1013
Norbest Inc 6875 S 900 East *TF:* 800-453-5327 ■ *Web:* www.norbest.com	Midvale	UT	84047	801-566-5656	255-2309
Nulaid Foods Inc 200 W 5th St *TF:* 800-788-8871 ■ *Web:* www.nulaid.com	Ripon	CA	95366	209-599-2121	599-5220
Park Farms Inc 1925 30th St NE *TF:* 800-683-6511 ■ *Web:* www.parkfarms.com	Canton	OH	44705	330-455-0241	455-5820
Petaluma Poultry Processors PO Box 7368 *TF:* 800-556-6789 ■ *Web:* www.petalumapoultry.com	Petaluma	CA	94955	707-763-1904	763-3924
Quirch Foods Co 7600 NW 82nd Pl *TF:* 800-458-5252 ■ *Web:* www.quirchfoods.com	Miami	FL	33166	305-691-3535	593-0272
Randall Foods Inc 2905 E 50th St **Fax:* Hum Res ■ *TF:* 800-372-6581	Vernon	CA	90058	323-587-2383	586-1587*
RW Sauder Inc 570 Furnace Hills Pike *Web:* www.saudereggs.com	Lititz	PA	17543	717-626-2074	626-0493
Sauder RW Inc 570 Furnace Hills Pike *Web:* www.saudereggs.com	Lititz	PA	17543	717-626-2074	626-0493
Troyer Foods Inc PO Box 608 *TF:* 800-876-9377 ■ *Web:* www.troyers.com	Goshen	IN	46527	574-533-0302	533-3851
Valley Fresh Inc 680 D St PO Box 339 *TF:* 800-526-3189 ■ *Web:* www.valleyfreshkitchen.com	Turlock	CA	95381	209-668-3695	668-0770
Zacky Farms 13200 Crossroads Pkwy N Suite 250 *TF:* 800-888-0235 ■ *Web:* www.zacky.com	City of Industry	CA	91746	562-641-2020	641-2040

300-11 Specialty Foods - Whol

	City	State	Zip	Phone	Fax
Camerican International Inc 45 Eisenhower Dr **Fax:* Hum Res	Paramus	NJ	07652	201-587-0101	587-2043*
ConAgra Foods Foodservice Co 1 ConAgra Dr *Web:* www.conagrafoodservice.com	Omaha	NE	68102	402-595-4000	
Condal Distributors 531 Dupont St *Web:* www.condalfoods.com	Bronx	NY	10474	718-589-1100	589-9200
Connell Rice & Sugar Co Inc 1 Connell Dr *Web:* www.connellco.com/CRISU.htm	Berkeley Heights	NJ	07922	908-673-3700	673-3800
Conway Import Co Inc 11051 West Addison St *TF:* 800-323-8801	Franklin Park	IL	60131	847-455-5600	455-5630
Diaz Wholesale & Mfg Co Inc 5501 Fulton Industrial Blvd *TF:* 800-394-4639 ■ *Web:* www.diazfoods.com	Atlanta	GA	30336	404-344-5421	344-3003
Distribution Plus Inc (DPI) 825 Green Bay Rd Suite 200 *Web:* www.distribution-plus.com	Wilmette	IL	60091	847-256-8289	256-8299
Essex Grain Products 9 Lee Blvd *TF:* 800-441-1017 ■ *Web:* www.essexgrain.com	Frazer	PA	19355	610-647-3800	647-4990
Golombeck Morris J Inc 960 Franklin Ave *Web:* www.golombeck.com	Brooklyn	NY	11225	718-284-3505	693-1941
Gourmet Award Foods 7225 W Marcia Rd *TF:* 800-726-7205 ■ *Web:* www.gourmetaward.com	Milwaukee	WI	53223	414-365-7000	365-7016
Grande Foods 671 N Poplar St	Orange	CA	92868	714-978-0061	978-0436
Gregory's Foods Inc 2514 Northland Dr **Fax Area Code:* 651 ■ *TF:* 800-347-8700 ■ *Web:* www.gregorysfoods.com	Mendota Heights	MN	55120	800-231-4734	454-2254*
Hain Celestial Group Inc 58 S Service Rd Suite 250 *NASDAQ: HAIN* ■ *Web:* www.hain-celestial.com	Melville	NY	01747	631-730-2200	730-2550
I & K Distributors Inc 1600 Gressel Dr *TF:* 800-472-9920 ■ *Web:* www.ikdist.com	Delphos	OH	45833	419-695-5015	695-7585
Indiana Sugars Inc 911 Virginia St *TF:* 800-333-9666 ■ *Web:* www.sugars.com	Gary	IN	46402	219-886-9151	886-5124
J Sosnick & Sons Inc 258 Littlefield Ave *TF:* 800-443-6737 ■ *Web:* www.sosnick.com	South San Francisco	CA	94080	650-952-2226	952-2439
JF Braun & Sons Inc 265 Post Ave Suite 360 PO Box 1806 *TF:* 800-997-7177 ■ *Web:* www.jfbny.com	Westbury	NY	11590	516-997-2200	997-2478
JFC International Inc 540 Forbes Blvd *TF:* 800-633-1004 ■ *Web:* www.jfc.com	South San Francisco	CA	94080	650-873-8400	952-3272
John E Koerner & Co Inc PO Box 10218 *TF:* 800-333-1913 ■ *Web:* www.koerner-co.com	New Orleans	LA	70181	504-734-1100	734-0630
King Milling Co 115 S Broadway St *Web:* www.kingmilling.com	Lowell	MI	49331	616-897-9264	897-4350
Koerner John E & Co Inc PO Box 10218 *TF:* 800-333-1913 ■ *Web:* www.koerner-co.com	New Orleans	LA	70181	504-734-1100	734-0630
Kraft Foods International Inc 3 Lakes Dr **Fax Area Code:* 914 ■ *TF:* 800-323-0768 ■ *Web:* www.kraft.com	Northfield	IL	60093	847-646-2000	335-9395*
Liberty Richter Inc 300 Broadacres Dr *Web:* www.libertyrichter.com	Bloomfield	NJ	07003	973-338-0300	338-0382
Lomar Distributing 2500 Dixon St *TF:* 800-369-3663	Des Moines	IA	50316	515-244-3105	244-0515
Losurdo Foods Inc 20 Owens Rd *TF:* 888-567-8736 ■ *Web:* www.losurdofoods.com	Hackensack	NJ	07601	201-343-6680	343-8078
Mitsui Foods Inc 35 Maple St *TF:* 800-777-2322 ■ *Web:* www.mitsui-foods.com	Norwood	NJ	07648	201-750-0500	750-0150
Morris J Golombeck Inc 960 Franklin Ave *Web:* www.golombeck.com	Brooklyn	NY	11225	718-284-3505	693-1941
Mutual Trading Co Ltd 431 Crocker St *Web:* www.lamtc.com	Los Angeles	CA	90013	213-626-9458	626-5130
Neiman Brothers Co Inc 3322 W Newport Ave *Web:* www.neimanbrothers.com	Chicago	IL	60618	773-463-3000	463-3181
Otis McAllister Inc 353 Sacramento St Suite 300 *Web:* www.otismac.com	San Francisco	CA	94111	415-421-6010	421-6016
Producers Rice Mill Inc 518 E Harrison St *Web:* www.producersrice.com	Stuttgart	AR	72160	870-673-4444	673-8131
Riceland Foods Inc 2120 S Park Ave *TF:* 800-264-1283 ■ *Web:* www.riceland.com	Stuttgart	AR	72160	870-673-5500	673-3366
Roma Food Enterprises Inc 1 Roma Blvd *TF:* 800-526-7662 ■ *Web:* www.romafood.com	Piscataway	NJ	08854	732-463-7662	356-4852
Shonfeld's USA Inc 3100 S Susan St *TF:* 877-447-8933 ■ *Web:* www.shonfelds.com	Santa Ana	CA	92704	714-429-1922	429-7971
Sosnick J & Sons Inc 258 Littlefield Ave *TF:* 800-443-6737 ■ *Web:* www.sosnick.com	South San Francisco	CA	94080	650-952-2226	952-2439
Sturm Foods Inc PO Box 287 *TF:* 800-347-8876 ■ *Web:* www.sturmfoods.com	Manawa	WI	54949	920-596-2511	596-3040
Sugar Foods Corp 950 3rd Ave 21st Fl *TF:* 800-666-3285 ■ *Web:* www.sugarfoods.com	New York	NY	10022	212-753-6900	753-6988
Sunsweet Growers Inc 901 N Walton Ave *TF:* 800-417-2253 ■ *Web:* www.sunsweet.com	Yuba City	CA	95993	530-674-5010	751-5238
Syrian Bakery & Grocery Inc 5400 W 35th St *Web:* www.ziyad.com	Cicero	IL	60804	708-222-8330	222-1442
United Sugars Corp 7401 Metro Blvd Suite 350 *Web:* www.unitedsugars.com	Edina	MN	55439	952-896-0131	
Westway Trading Corp 365 Canal St Suite 2900 *Web:* www.westwaytrading.com	New Orleans	LA	70130	504-525-9741	522-1638

301 FOOD PRODUCTS MACHINERY

SEE ALSO Food Service Equipment & Supplies p. 1664

	City	State	Zip	Phone	Fax
Acme Pizza & Bakery Equipment Inc 7039 E Slauson Ave *TF:* 800-428-2263 ■ *Web:* www.acmepbe.com	Commerce	CA	90040	323-722-7900	726-4700
Adamatic Corp 607 Industrial Way W *TF:* 800-526-2807 ■ *Web:* www.adamatic.com	Eatontown	NJ	07724	732-544-8400	544-0735
Alto-Shaam Inc W 164 N 9221 Water St PO Box 450 *TF:* 800-329-8744 ■ *Web:* www.alto-shaam.com	Menomonee Falls	WI	53052	262-251-3800	251-7067
American Permanent Ware Inc 729 3rd Ave *TF:* 800-527-2100 ■ *Web:* www.apwwyott.com	Dallas	TX	75226	214-421-7366	565-0976
Anderson International Corp 6200 Harvard Ave *TF:* 800-336-4730 ■ *Web:* www.andersonintl.net	Cleveland	OH	44105	216-641-1112	641-0709
Anetsberger Brothers Inc 180 N Anets Dr *TF:* 800-837-2638 ■ *Web:* www.anetsberger.com	Northbrook	IL	60062	847-272-0770	272-1095
APV Canada Inc 3280 Langstaff Rd *TF:* 800-263-3958	Concord	ON	L4K4Z8	905-760-1852	760-1865
Ashton Food Machinery Co Inc 1128 Peachtree Ln	Mountainside	NJ	07092	908-317-5433	289-1060
Atlas Metal Industries 1135 NW 159th Dr *TF Cust Svc:* 800-762-7565 ■ *Web:* www.atlasfoodserv.com	Miami	FL	33169	305-625-2451	623-0475
Atlas Pacific Engineering Co 1 Atlas Ave *TF:* 800-227-0682 ■ *Web:* www.atlaspacific.com	Pueblo	CO	81001	719-948-3040	948-3058
Baader-Johnson 2955 Fairfax Trafficway *TF:* 800-288-3434 ■ *Web:* www.baader-johnson.com	Kansas City	KS	66115	913-621-3366	621-1729
Baker Perkins Inc 3223 Kraft Ave SE *Web:* www.bakerperkinsgroup.com	Grand Rapids	MI	49512	616-784-3111	784-0973
Beehive Machinery Inc 9100 S 500 West PO Box 5002 *TF:* 800-621-8438	Sandy	UT	84091	801-561-4211	562-5857
Belshaw Brothers Inc 1750 22nd Ave S *TF:* 800-578-2547 ■ *Web:* www.belshaw.com	Seattle	WA	98144	206-322-5474	322-5425
Bepex International LLC 333 Taft St NE *Web:* www.bepex.com	Minneapolis	MN	55413	612-331-4370	627-1444
Biro Mfg Co Inc 1114 W Main St *Web:* www.birosaw.com	Marblehead	OH	43440	419-798-4451	798-9106
Blakeslee Inc 1844 S Laramie Ave *TF:* 888-656-0660 ■ *Web:* www.blakesleeinc.com	Cicero	IL	60804	708-656-0660	656-0017

Company	City	State	ZIP	Phone	Fax
Brewmatic Co 20333 S Normandie Ave	Torrance	CA	90509	310-787-5444	787-5412
TF: 800-421-6860 ■ *Web:* www.brewmatic.com					
Brown International Corp 681 Arron Grand Cir	Covina	CA	91722	626-966-8361	332-7921
TF: 800-423-1843 ■ *Web:* www.brown-intl.com					
C Cretors & Co 3243 N California Ave	Chicago	IL	60618	773-588-1690	588-7141
TF: 800-228-1885 ■ *Web:* www.cretors.com					
Carlisle Cos Inc 13925 Ballantyne Corporate Pl Suite 400	Charlotte	NC	28277	704-501-1100	501-1190
NYSE: CSL ■ *Web:* www.carlisle.com					
Carpigiani USA 3760 Industrial Dr PO Box 4069	Winston-Salem	NC	27115	336-661-9893	661-9895
TF: 800-648-4389 ■ *Web:* www.carpigiani-usa.com					
Carrier Commercial Refrigeration Inc 9300 Harris Corners Pkwy Suite 200	Charlotte	NC	28269	704-494-2600	494-2558
Web: www.ccr.carrier.com					
Carter Lewis M Mfg Co Hwy 84 W	Donalsonville	GA	39845	229-524-2197	524-2531
Web: www.lmcarter.com					
Casa Herrerra Inc 2655 N Pine St	Pomona	CA	91767	909-392-3930	392-0231
TF: 800-624-3916 ■ *Web:* www.casaherrera.com					
CE Rogers Co 1895 Frontage Rd	Mora	MN	55051	320-679-2172	679-2180
TF: 800-279-8081 ■ *Web:* www.cerogers.com					
Chester-Jensen Co Inc PO Box 908	Chester	PA	19016	610-876-6276	876-0485
TF: 800-685-3750 ■ *Web:* www.chester-jensen.com					
Cleveland Range Co 1333 E 179th St	Cleveland	OH	44110	216-481-4900	481-3782
TF: 800-338-2204 ■ *Web:* www.clevelandrange.com					
Colborne Corp 28495 N Ballard Dr	Lake Forest	IL	60045	847-371-0101	371-0199
TF: 800-279-1879 ■ *Web:* www.colborne.com					
CPM Wolverine Proctor LLC 251 Gibraltar Rd	Horsham	PA	19044	215-443-5200	443-5206*
**Fax:* Sales ■ *Web:* www.cpmroskamp.com/wolverine					
Cretors C & Co 3243 N California Ave	Chicago	IL	60618	773-588-1690	588-7141
TF: 800-228-1885 ■ *Web:* www.cretors.com					
Curtis Wilbur Co Inc 6913 Acco St	Montebello	CA	90640	323-837-2300	837-2406
TF: 800-421-6150 ■ *Web:* www.wilburcurtis.com					
Delfield Co 980 S Isabella Rd	Mount Pleasant	MI	48858	989-773-7981	773-3210
TF: 800-733-8821 ■ *Web:* www.delfield.com					
Duke Mfg Co 2305 N Broadway	Saint Louis	MO	63102	314-231-1130	231-5074
TF: 800-735-3853 ■ *Web:* www.dukemfg.com					
Dupps Co 548 N Cherry St	Germantown	OH	45327	937-855-6555	855-6554
Web: www.dupps.com					
Edlund Co Inc 159 Industrial Pkwy	Burlington	VT	05401	802-862-9661	862-4822
TF: 800-772-2126 ■ *Web:* www.edlundco.com					
Evergreen Packaging Equipment 2400 6th St SW	Cedar Rapids	IA	52406	319-399-3200	399-3543
Web: www.evergreenpackaging.com					
Exact Equipment Corp 920 Town Center Dr	Langhorne	PA	19047	215-295-2000	295-2080
Web: www.exactequipment.com					
Fedco Systems Co Super Grain Div 500 Vandenmark Rd PO Box 769	Sidney	OH	45365	937-492-4158	492-3688
TF: 800-999-3327 ■ *Web:* www.fedcosystems.com					
Fish Oven & Equipment Corp 120 W Kemp Ave	Wauconda	IL	60084	847-526-8686	526-7447
TF: 877-526-8720 ■ *Web:* www.fishoven.com					
Fitzpatrick Co 832 Industrial Dr	Elmhurst	IL	60126	630-530-3333	530-0832
Web: www.fitzmill.com					
FMC Technologies Inc FoodTech Unit 200 E Randolph Dr	Chicago	IL	60601	312-861-6000	861-6011
Web: www.fmctechnologies.com/FoodTech					
Food Warming Equipment Co Inc 7900 SR 31	Crystal Lake	IL	60014	815-459-7500	459-7989
TF Sales: 800-222-4393 ■ *Web:* www.fweco.com					
Fulton Iron & Mfg LLC 3844 Walsh St	Saint Louis	MO	63116	314-752-2400	353-2987
Web: www.fultoniron.net					
Garland Commercial Industries 185 E South St	Freeland	PA	18224	570-636-1000	624-0218*
**Fax Area Code:* 800 ■ *TF:* 800-424-2411 ■ *Web:* www.garland-group.com					
Globe Food Equipment Co 2153 Dryden Rd	Dayton	OH	45439	937-299-5493	299-4147
TF: 800-347-5423 ■ *Web:* www.globeslicers.com					
Gold Medal Products Co 10700 Medallion Dr	Cincinnati	OH	45241	513-769-7676	769-8500
TF Cust Svc: 800-543-0862 ■ *Web:* www.gmpopcorn.com					
Great Western Mfg Co Inc 2017 S 4th St PO Box 149	Leavenworth	KS	66048	913-682-2291	682-1431
TF: 800-682-3121 ■ *Web:* www.gwmfg.com					
Grindmaster Crathco Systems Inc PO Box 35020	Louisville	KY	40232	502-425-4776	425-4664
TF: 800-695-4500 ■ *Web:* www.grindmaster.com					
GS Blodgett Corp 44 Lakeside Ave	Burlington	VT	05401	802-658-6600	864-0183
TF: 800-331-5842 ■ *Web:* www.blodgett.com					
Hayes & Stolz Industrial Mfg Co Ltd 3521 Hemphill St PO Box 11217	Fort Worth	TX	76110	817-926-3391	926-4133
TF: 800-725-7272 ■ *Web:* www.hayes-stolz.com					
Healdsburg Machine Co 452 Healdsburg Ave	Healdsburg	CA	95448	707-433-3348	433-3340
Heat & Control Inc 21121 Cabot Blvd	Hayward	CA	94545	510-259-0500	259-0600
TF: 800-227-5980 ■ *Web:* www.heatandcontrol.com					
Henny Penny Corp 1219 US 35 W	Eaton	OH	45320	937-456-4171	417-8402*
**Fax Area Code:* 800 ■ *TF:* 800-417-8417 ■ *Web:* www.hennypenny.com					
Hobart Corp 701 S Ridge Ave	Troy	OH	45374	937-332-3000	332-2852
TF Cust Svc: 800-333-7447 ■ *Web:* www.hobartcorp.com					
Hollymatic Corp 600 E Plainfield Rd	Countryside	IL	60525	708-579-3700	579-1057
Web: www.hollymatic.com					
Horix Mfg Co 1384 Island Ave	McKees Rocks	PA	15136	412-771-1111	331-8599
Web: www.horixmfg.com					
Howes S Co Inc 25 Howard St	Silver Creek	NY	14136	716-934-2611	934-2081
TF: 888-255-2611 ■ *Web:* www.showes.com					
Idaho Steel Products Co 255 Anderson St	Idaho Falls	ID	83401	208-522-1275	522-6041
Web: www.idahosteel.com					
Insinger Machine Co 6245 State Rd	Philadelphia	PA	19135	215-624-4800	624-6966
TF: 800-344-4802 ■ *Web:* www.insingermachine.com					
Invensys APV 105 Crosspoint Pkwy	Getzville	NY	14068	716-692-3000	
Web: www.apv.com					
ITW Food Equipment Group 701 S Ridge Ave	Troy	OH	45374	937-332-3000	332-2852
TF Cust Svc: 800-333-7447					
Jarvis Products Corp 33 Anderson Rd	Middletown	CT	06457	860-347-7271	347-6978
Web: www.jarvisproducts.com					
Kasco Corp 1569 Tower Grove Ave	Saint Louis	MO	63110	314-771-1550	771-5162
TF: 800-325-8940 ■ *Web:* www.kasco.com					
Key Technology Inc 150 Avery St	Walla Walla	WA	99362	509-529-2161	522-3378
NASDAQ: KTEC ■ *Web:* www.keyww.com					
Kuhl Corp 39 Kuhl Rd	Flemington	NJ	08822	908-782-5696	782-2751
Web: www.kuhlcorp.com					
Kwik Lok Corp 2712 S 16th Ave PO Box 9548	Yakima	WA	98909	509-248-4770	457-6531
TF: 800-688-5945 ■ *Web:* www.kwiklok.com					
Lewis M Carter Mfg Co Hwy 84 W	Donalsonville	GA	39845	229-524-2197	524-2531
Web: www.lmcarter.com					
Load King Mfg Co 1357 W Beaver St PO Box 40606	Jacksonville	FL	32203	904-354-8882	353-1984
TF: 800-531-4975 ■ *Web:* www.loadking.com					
Lucks Co 3003 S Pine St	Tacoma	WA	98409	253-383-4815	674-7250*
**Fax Area Code:* 206 ■ *TF:* 800-426-9778 ■ *Web:* www.lucks.com					
Luker Inc 514 National Ave	Augusta	GA	30901	706-724-0244	724-1050
TF: 800-982-9534 ■ *Web:* www.lukerinc.com					
Luthi Machinery Co Inc 1 Atlas Ave	Pueblo	CO	81001	719-948-1110	948-3058
TF: 800-227-0682 ■ *Web:* www.luthi.com					
M-E-C Co 1400 W Main St	Neodesha	KS	66757	620-325-2673	325-2678
Web: www.m-e-c.com					
Manitowoc Beverage Equipment 2100 Future Dr	Sellersburg	IN	47172	812-246-7000	246-9922
TF: 800-367-4233 ■ *Web:* www.manitowocbeverage.com					
Manitowoc Co Inc 2400 S 44th St	Manitowoc	WI	54220	920-684-4410	652-9778
NYSE: MTW ■ *Web:* www.manitowoc.com					
Market Forge Industries Inc 35 Garvey St	Everett	MA	02149	617-387-4100	227-2659*
**Fax Area Code:* 800 ■ *TF:* 888-259-7076 ■ *Web:* www.mfii.com					
Merco-Savory Inc 1111 N Hadley Rd	Fort Wayne	IN	46804	260-459-8200	436-0735
TF Cust Svc: 800-547-2513 ■ *Web:* www.mercosavory.com					
Meyer Machine Co Inc 3528 Fredericksburg Rd PO Box 5460	San Antonio	TX	78201	210-736-1811	736-9452
Web: www.meyer-industries.com					
Microfluidics International Corp 30 Ossipee Rd PO Box 9101	Newton	MA	02464	617-969-5452	965-1213
TF: 800-370-5452 ■ *Web:* www.microfluidicscorp.com					
Middleby Corp 1400 Toastmaster Dr	Elgin	IL	60120	847-741-3300	741-0015
NASDAQ: MIDD ■ *Web:* www.middleby.com					
Myers Engineering Inc 8376 Salt Lake Ave	Bell	CA	90201	323-560-4723	771-7789
Web: www.myersmixer.com					
National Drying Machinery Co 4850 Street Rd Suite 150	Trevose	PA	19053	215-464-6070	464-4096
Web: www.nationaldrying.com					
Nitta Casings Inc 141 Southside Ave PO Box 858	Somerville	NJ	08876	908-218-4400	725-2835
TF Cust Svc: 800-526-3970 ■ *Web:* www.nittacasings.com					
Oliver Products Co 445 6th St NW	Grand Rapids	MI	49504	616-456-7711	456-5820
TF: 800-253-3893 ■ *Web:* www.oliverproducts.com					
Peerless Machinery Corp 500 S Vandenmark Rd PO Box 769	Sidney	OH	45365	937-492-4158	492-3688
TF: 800-999-3327 ■ *Web:* www.thepeerlessgroup.us					
Peters Machinery Inc 500 S Vandemark Rd	Sidney	OH	45365	937-492-4158	492-3688
TF: 800-999-3327 ■ *Web:* www.petersmachinery.com					
Piper Products Inc 300 S 84th Ave	Wausau	WI	54401	715-842-2724	842-3125
TF: 800-558-5880 ■ *Web:* www.pdgi.com					
Pitco Frialator Inc PO Box 501	Concord	NH	03302	603-225-6684	225-8472
TF: 800-258-3708 ■ *Web:* www.blodgett.com/pitco_hm.shtml					
Planet Products Corp 4200 Malsbary Rd	Cincinnati	OH	45242	513-984-5544	984-5580
Web: www.planet-products.com					
Prince Castle Inc 355 E Kehoe Blvd	Carol Stream	IL	60188	630-462-8800	462-1460
TF: 800-722-7853 ■ *Web:* www.princecastle.com					
Resina West Inc 27455 Bostik Ct	Temecula	CA	92590	951-296-6585	296-5018
Web: www.resina.com					
RMF Steel Products Co 4417 E 119th St	Grandview	MO	64030	816-765-4101	765-0067
Web: www.rmfsteel.com					
Rogers CE Co 1895 Frontage Rd	Mora	MN	55051	320-679-2172	679-2180
TF: 800-279-8081 ■ *Web:* www.cerogers.com					
Ross Industries Inc 5321 Midland Rd	Midland	VA	22728	540-439-3271	439-2740
TF: 800-336-6010 ■ *Web:* www.rossindinc.com					
S Howes Co Inc 25 Howard St	Silver Creek	NY	14136	716-934-2611	934-2081
TF: 888-255-2611 ■ *Web:* www.showes.com					
SaniServ Inc 451 E County Line Rd	Mooresville	IN	46158	317-831-7030	831-7036
TF: 800-733-8073 ■ *Web:* www.saniserv.com					
Schebler Co 5665 Senno Rd PO Box 1008	Bettendorf	IA	52722	563-359-0110	359-8430
Web: www.schebler.com					
Schlueter Co 320 N Main St PO Box 548	Janesville	WI	53547	608-755-5455	755-5440
TF: 800-359-1700					
Server Products Inc 3601 Pleasant Hill Rd PO Box 98	Richfield	WI	53076	262-628-5600	628-5110
TF: 800-558-8722 ■ *Web:* www.server-products.com					
Simmons Engineering Co 91 Simmons Industrial Pl PO Box 546	Dallas	GA	30132	770-445-6085	443-9058
Sonic Corp 1 Research Dr	Stratford	CT	06615	203-375-0063	378-4079
Web: www.sonicmixing.com					
Southbend Co Inc 1100 Old Honeycutt Rd	Fuquay-Varina	NC	27526	919-552-9161	552-9798
TF: 800-348-2558 ■ *Web:* www.southbendnc.com					
Stoelting Inc 502 Hwy 67	Kiel	WI	53042	920-894-2293	894-7029
TF: 800-558-5807 ■ *Web:* www.stoelting.com					
Stolle Machinery Co LLC 6949 S Potomac St	Centennial	CO	80112	303-708-9044	708-9045
TF: 800-228-4593 ■ *Web:* www.stollemachinery.com					
Stork Gamco Inc 1024 Airport Pkwy PO Box 1258	Gainesville	GA	30503	770-532-7041	532-9867
TF: 800-347-8675 ■ *Web:* www.stork-gamco.com					
Taylor 750 N Blackhawk Blvd	Rockton	IL	61072	815-624-8333	624-8000
TF: 800-624-8333 ■ *Web:* www.taylor-company.com					
Tomlinson Industries 13700 Broadway Ave	Garfield Heights	OH	44125	216-587-3400	526-9634*
**Fax Area Code:* 800 ■ *TF:* 800-945-4589 ■ *Web:* www.tomlinsonind.com					
Town Food Service Equipment Co 72 Beadel St	Brooklyn	NY	11222	718-388-5650	388-5860
TF: 800-221-5032 ■ *Web:* www.townfood.com					
Townsend Engineering Co 2425 Hubbell Ave PO Box 1433	Des Moines	IA	50305	515-265-8181	263-3344
TF: 800-247-8609 ■ *Web:* www.townsendeng.com					
Ultrafryer Systems 302 Spencer Ln	San Antonio	TX	78201	210-731-5000	731-5099
TF: 800-545-9189 ■ *Web:* www.ultrafryer.com					
Union Standard Equipment Co 801 E 141st St	Bronx	NY	10454	718-585-0200	993-2650
TF: 800-237-8873 ■ *Web:* unionmachinery.com					
United Bakery Equipment Co Inc 15815 W 110th St	Lenexa	KS	66219	913-541-8700	541-0789
Web: www.ubeusa.com					
Univex Corp 3 Old Rockingham Rd	Salem	NH	03079	603-893-6191	893-1249
TF: 800-258-6358 ■ *Web:* www.univexcorp.com					
Urschel Laboratories Inc 2503 Calumet Ave	Valparaiso	IN	46383	219-464-4811	462-3879
Web: www.urschel.com					
Van Doren Sales Inc 10 NE Cascade Ave	East Wenatchee	WA	98802	509-886-1837	886-2837
Web: www.vandorensales.com					
Vendome Copper & Brass Works Inc 729 Franklin St	Louisville	KY	40202	502-587-1930	589-0639
Web: www.vendomecopper.com					
Volckening Inc 6700 3rd Ave	Brooklyn	NY	11220	718-836-4000	748-2811
TF: 800-221-0876 ■ *Web:* www.volckening.com					
Vulcan-Hart Corp 2006 Northwestern Pkwy	Louisville	KY	40203	502-778-2791	772-7831
TF Cust Svc: 800-814-2028 ■ *Web:* www.vulcanhart.com					
Walker Stainless Equipment Co LLC 625 State St	New Lisbon	WI	53950	608-562-3151	562-3142
TF: 800-356-5734 ■ *Web:* www.walkerstainless.com					
Weiler & Co Inc 1116 E Main St	Whitewater	WI	53190	262-473-5254	473-5867
TF Sales: 800-558-9507 ■ *Web:* www.weilerinc.com					
Wells Bloomfield Industries 2 Erik Cir PO Box 280	Verdi	NV	89439	775-345-0444	356-5142*
**Fax Area Code:* 800 ■ **Fax:* Cust Svc ■ *TF:* 800-777-0450 ■ *Web:* www.wellsbloomfield.com					
Wenger Mfg Inc 714 Main St	Sabetha	KS	66534	785-284-2133	284-3771
TF: 800-833-0174 ■ *Web:* www.wenger.com					
Wilbur Curtis Co Inc 6913 Acco St	Montebello	CA	90640	323-837-2300	837-2406
TF: 800-421-6150 ■ *Web:* www.wilburcurtis.com					
Winston Industries LLC 2345 Carton Dr	Louisville	KY	40299	502-495-5400	495-5458
TF: 800-234-5286 ■ *Web:* www.winstonind.com					
Wisco Industries Inc 736 Janesville St	Oregon	WI	53575	608-835-3106	835-7399
TF: 800-999-4726 ■ *Web:* www.wiscoind.com					
Witte Co Inc 507 Rt 31 S PO Box 47	Washington	NJ	07882	908-689-6500	537-6806
TF: 866-265-4071 ■ *Web:* www.witte.com					
Wolf Range Co 2006 Northwestern Pkwy	Louisville	KY	40203	502-778-2791	775-4053
TF: 888-435-9653 ■ *Web:* www.wolfrange.com					

302 FOOD SERVICE

SEE ALSO Restaurant Companies p. 2229

				Phone	Fax
Aircraft Service International Group 201 S Orange Ave Suite 1100 *TF*: 800-557-2744 ■ *Web*: www.asig.com	Orlando	FL	32801	407-648-7373	206-5391
All Seasons Services Inc 5 Campanelli Cir 2nd Fl *TF*: 888-558-2557 ■ *Web*: www.allseasonsservices.com	Canton	MA	02021	781-828-2345	828-0427
ARAMARK Food & Support Services 1101 Market St *TF*: 800-999-8989	Philadelphia	PA	19107	215-238-3000	238-3333
ARAMARK Uniform & Career Apparel 1101 Market St *TF*: 800-999-8989 ■ *Web*: www.aramark-uniform.com	Philadelphia	PA	19107	215-238-3000	238-3333
Atlas Food Systems & Services Inc 205 Woods Lake Rd *TF*: 800-476-1123 ■ *Web*: www.atlasfoods.com	Greenville	SC	29607	864-232-1885	232-1671
Blue Line Foodservice Distribution 24120 Haggerty Rd *TF*: 866-310-1187 ■ *Web*: www.bluelinedist.com	Farmington Hills	MI	48335	248-478-6200	442-4570
Bon Appetit Management Co 100 Hamilton Ave Suite 300 *Web*: www.bamco.com	Palo Alto	CA	94301	650-798-8000	798-8090
Canteen Correctional Services 38 Pond St Suite 308 *TF*: 800-357-0012	Franklin	MA	02030	508-520-4334	520-7666
Canteen Vending Services 2400 Yorkmont Rd *TF*: 800-357-0012 ■ *Web*: www.canteen-usa.com	Charlotte	NC	28217	704-329-4000	424-5086
Cara Operations Ltd 6303 Airport Rd *TF*: 800-860-4082 ■ *Web*: www.cara.com	Mississauga	ON	L4V1R8	905-405-6500	405-6777
Centerplate 201 E Broad St *AMEX*: CVP ■ **Fax*: Sales ■ *TF*: 800-698-6992 ■ *Web*: www.centerplate.com	Spartanburg	SC	29306	864-598-8600	598-8695*
CL Swanson Corp 4501 Femrite Dr *Web*: www.swansons.net	Madison	WI	53716	608-221-7640	221-7648
Coburn Catering Co PO Box 122447	Fort Worth	TX	76121	817-732-5251	
COI Foodservice 2629 Eugenia Ave *TF*: 877-503-5212 ■ *Web*: www.coifoodservice.com	Nashville	TN	37211	615-231-4300	231-4334
Compass Group North American Div 2400 Yorkmont Rd **Fax*: Hum Res ■ *TF*: 800-357-0012 ■ *Web*: www.cgnad.com	Charlotte	NC	28217	704-329-4000	424-5086*
Culinaire International 2100 Ross Ave Suite 3100 *TF*: 866-324-9093 ■ *Web*: www.culinaireintl.com	Dallas	TX	75201	214-754-1880	754-1881
Custom Food Group 2627 Midway Ave *TF*: 800-256-8828 ■ *Web*: www.customfoodgroup.com	Shreveport	LA	71108	318-632-8000	632-8088
Edsung Foodservice Equipment Co PO Box 17100	Honolulu	HI	96817	808-845-3931	842-4702
Excelsior Grand 2380 Hylan Blvd *Web*: www.excelsiorgrand.com	Staten Island	NY	10306	718-987-4800	987-4803
Filterfresh Coffee Service Inc 378 University Ave *TF*: 800-461-8734 ■ *Web*: www.filterfresh.com	Westwood	MA	02090	781-461-8734	461-8732
Five Star Food Service Inc 1019 14th St *TF*: 800-327-0043 ■ *Web*: www.fivestar-food.com	Columbus	GA	31901	706-327-0303	324-1038
Flying Food Group 212 N Sangamon St Suite 1-A *Web*: www.flyingfood.com	Chicago	IL	60607	312-243-2122	243-5088
Forever/NPC Resorts LLC 7501 McCormick Blvd *TF*: 800-455-3509	Scottsdale	AZ	85258	480-998-8888	998-8887
Gate Gourmet 11710 Plaza America Dr Suite 800 **Fax*: Sales ■ *Web*: www.gategourmet.com	Reston	VA	20190	703-964-2300	964-2399*
General Mills Inc Foodservice Div 1 General Mills Blvd *Web*: www.generalmills.com	Minneapolis	MN	55426	763-764-7600	
Gourmet Services Inc 82 Piedmont Ave	Atlanta	GA	30303	404-876-5700	876-2240
Guckenheimer Enterprises Inc 3 Lagoon Dr Suite 325 *TF*: 800-466-5303 ■ *Web*: www.guckenheimer.com	Redwood Shores	CA	94065	650-592-3800	592-0406
Guest Services Inc 3055 Prosperity Ave *TF*: 800-345-7534 ■ *Web*: www.guestservices.com	Fairfax	VA	22031	703-849-9300	641-4690
HDS Services Inc 39395 W 12-Mile Rd Suite 101 *Web*: www.hdsservices.com	Farmington Hills	MI	48331	248-324-9500	324-1825
HMSHost Corp 6600 Rockledge Dr **Fax*: PR ■ *Web*: www.hmshost.com	Bethesda	MD	20817	240-694-4100	694-4626*
Host America Corporate Dining 1 Leonardo Dr *Web*: www.hostamericacorp.com	North Haven	CT	06473	203-239-4678	234-1503
Hot Stuff Foods LLC 2930 W Maple St *Web*: www.hotstufffoods.com	Sioux Falls	SD	57107	605-330-7531	336-0141
Institution Food House Inc 543 12th Street Dr NW *TF*: 800-800-0434 ■ *Web*: www.institutionfoodhouse.com	Hickory	NC	28603	828-323-4500	725-4500
Institutional Distributors Inc PO Box 520 *TF*: 800-442-7885 ■ *Web*: www.idifoods.com	East Bernstadt	KY	40729	606-843-2100	843-2108
Institutional Wholesale Co 535 Dry Valley Rd **Fax*: Cust Svc ■ *TF*: 800-239-9588	Cookeville	TN	38503	931-537-4000	537-4017*
International In-Flight Catering Co Ltd 310 Rogers Blvd	Honolulu	HI	96819	808-836-2431	836-5815
Lackmann Culinary Services 303 Crossways Park Dr *Web*: www.lackmann.com	Woodbury	NY	11797	516-364-2300	364-9788
Martin's Inc 6821 Dogwood Rd	Baltimore	MD	21244	410-265-1300	265-1328
Mobil-Teria Catering Co Inc 5035 Raytown Rd	Kansas City	MO	64133	816-356-8600	
Morrison Management Specialists Inc 5801 Peachtree Dunwoody Rd *TF*: 800-622-1035 ■ *Web*: www.iammorrison.com	Atlanta	GA	30342	404-845-3330	845-3333
Open Kitchen Inc 1161 W 21st St *TF*: 800-339-5334 ■ *Web*: www.openkitchens.com	Chicago	IL	60608	312-666-5334	666-9242
Regal Food Service Inc 3515 Eastex Fwy	Houston	TX	77026	713-222-8231	222-2549
Restaurant Assoc Inc 120 W 45th St 16th Fl *Web*: www.restaurantassociates.com	New York	NY	10036	212-789-8100	302-8032
Sanese Services Inc 6465 Busch Blvd *TF*: 800-589-3410 ■ *Web*: www.sanese.com	Columbus	OH	43229	614-436-1234	436-1592
SeamlessWeb Professional Solutions Inc 232 Madison Ave Suite 1409 *Web*: www.seamlessweb.com	New York	NY	10016	212-944-7755	
Shamrock Food Service 3055 Prosperity Ave *TF*: 800-345-7534	Fairfax	VA	22031	703-849-9300	641-4690
Signature Services Corp 2705 Hawes Ave PO Box 35885 *TF*: 800-929-5519 ■ *Web*: www.signatureservices.com	Dallas	TX	75235	214-353-2661	353-4843
Sodexho Inc 9801 Washingtonian Blvd *TF*: 800-763-3946 ■ *Web*: www.sodexhousa.com	Gaithersburg	MD	20878	301-987-4000	987-4438
Sportservice Corp 40 Fountain Plaza **Fax*: Acctg ■ *TF*: 800-828-7240	Buffalo	NY	14202	716-858-5000	858-5882*
Summit Food Service Distributors Inc 580 Industrial Rd *TF*: 800-265-9267 ■ *Web*: www.summitfoods.com	London	ON	N5V1V1	519-453-3410	453-5148
Swanson CL Corp 4501 Femrite Dr *Web*: www.swansons.net	Madison	WI	53716	608-221-7640	221-7648
Taher Inc 5570 Smetana Dr *Web*: www.taher.com	Minnetonka	MN	55343	952-945-0505	945-0444
Universal Sodexho 5749 Susitna Dr *TF*: 800-535-1946 ■ *Web*: www.sodexhousa.com	Harahan	LA	70123	504-733-5761	731-1679
Valley Inc 4400 Mangum Dr *TF*: 800-748-9985 ■ *Web*: www.valleyservicesi.com	Flowood	MS	39232	601-664-3100	664-3399
V/Gladieux Enterprises Inc 3400 Executive Pkwy	Toledo	OH	43606	419-473-3009	473-2335
Volume Services America Holdings Inc DBA Centerplate 201 E Broad St *AMEX*: CVP ■ **Fax*: Sales ■ *TF*: 800-698-6992 ■ *Web*: www.centerplate.com	Spartanburg	SC	29306	864-598-8600	598-8695*
Williams Food Service 227 S 30th St *Web*: www.williamsfood.com	Louisville	KY	40212	502-778-1641	213-5675
Zaugs Inc 4100 W Wisconsin Ave	Appleton	WI	54913	920-734-9881	734-4322

303 FOOD SERVICE EQUIPMENT & SUPPLIES

SEE ALSO Food Products Machinery p. 1662

				Phone	Fax
Adams-Burch Inc 1901 Stanford Ct *TF Cust Svc*: 800-347-8093 ■ *Web*: www.adams-burch.com	Landover	MD	20785	301-341-1600	341-5114
Advance Tabco 200 Heartland Blvd *TF*: 800-645-3166 ■ *Web*: www.advancetabco.com	Edgewood	NY	11717	631-242-4800	242-6900
Anderson-DuBose Co 6575 Davis Industrial Pkwy *TF*: 800-248-1080	Solon	OH	44139	440-248-8800	248-6208
Arranaga Robert & Co Inc 216 S Alameda St *TF*: 800-639-0059	Los Angeles	CA	90012	213-622-1261	473-9800
Atlanta Fixture & Sales Co 3185 Northeast Expy *TF*: 800-282-1977 ■ *Web*: www.atlantafixture.com	Atlanta	GA	30341	770-455-8844	986-9202
Blue Line Foodservice Distribution 24120 Haggerty Rd *TF*: 866-310-1187 ■ *Web*: www.bluelinedist.com	Farmington Hills	MI	48335	248-478-6200	442-4570
Boelter Cos Inc 11100 W Silver Spring Rd *TF*: 800-392-3278 ■ *Web*: www.boelter.com	Milwaukee	WI	53225	414-461-3400	461-5058
Bolton & Hay Inc 2701 Delaware Ave *TF*: 800-362-1861 ■ *Web*: www.boltonhay.com	Des Moines	IA	50317	515-265-2554	265-6090
Browne & Co 100 Esna Park Dr *TF*: 877-327-6963 ■ *Web*: www.browneco.com	Markham	ON	L3R1E3	905-475-6104	475-5843
Browne-Halco Inc 2840 Morris Ave *TF*: 888-289-1005 ■ *Web*: www.halco.com	Union	NJ	07083	908-964-9200	964-6677
Buffalo Hotel Supply Co Inc 375 Commerce Dr PO Box 646 *TF*: 800-333-1678 ■ *Web*: www.ebhsonline.com	Amherst	NY	14226	716-691-8080	691-3255
Cambro Mfg Co 5801 Skylab Rd **Fax*: Cust Svc ■ *TF*: 800-833-3003 ■ *Web*: www.cambro.com	Huntington Beach	CA	92647	714-848-1555	842-3430*
Carlisle FoodService Products Inc 4711 E Hefner Rd *TF*: 800-654-8210 ■ *Web*: www.carlislefsp.com	Oklahoma City	OK	73131	405-475-5600	475-5607
Cecilware Corp 43-05 20th Ave *TF*: 800-935-2211 ■ *Web*: www.cecilware.com	Astoria	NY	11105	718-932-1414	932-7860
Chudnow Mfg Co Inc 3055 New St PO Box 10 *Web*: www.chudnowmfg.com	Oceanside	NY	11572	516-593-4222	593-4156
Clark Foodservice Inc 950 Arthur Ave *Web*: www.clarkfoodservice.com	Elk Grove Village	IL	60007	847-956-1730	956-0199
Curtis Restaurant Supply & Equipment Co 6577 E 40th St *TF*: 800-766-2878 ■ *Web*: www.curtisequipment.com	Tulsa	OK	74145	918-622-7390	665-0990
Don Edward & Co 2500 S Harlem Ave *TF Cust Svc*: 800-777-4366 ■ *Web*: www.don.com	North Riverside	IL	60546	708-883-8000	883-8676
Eagle Group 100 Industrial Blvd *TF*: 800-441-8440 ■ *Web*: www.eaglegrp.com	Clayton	DE	19938	302-653-3000	653-2065
Economy Hotel & Restaurant Supply 5059 Edgewater Dr	Orlando	FL	32810	407-294-0300	294-8565
Edsung Foodservice Equipment Co PO Box 17100	Honolulu	HI	96817	808-845-3931	842-4702
Edward Don & Co 2500 S Harlem Ave *TF Cust Svc*: 800-777-4366 ■ *Web*: www.don.com	North Riverside	IL	60546	708-883-8000	883-8676
Enodis Corp 2227 Welbilt Blvd *Web*: www.enodis.com	New Port Richey	FL	34655	727-375-7010	375-0894
Fountain Products Inc 220 Persimmon Dr	Saint Charles	IL	60174	630-443-1113	443-1344
Gardner & Benoit Inc PO Box 7246 *TF*: 800-467-6676	Charlotte	NC	28241	704-504-1151	504-5529
Genpak Carthage 505 E Cotton St **Fax Area Code*: 800 ■ *TF*: 800-340-4005 ■ *Web*: www.genpak.com	Carthage	TX	75633	903-693-7151	932-5222*
Gordon Food Service 333 50th St SW *TF*: 800-968-7500 ■ *Web*: www.gfs.com	Grand Rapids	MI	49548	616-530-7000	717-7600
Henry Lee Div 3301 NW 125th St *TF*: 800-274-4533 ■ *Web*: www.gfs-henrylee.com	Miami	FL	33167	305-685-5851	459-8731
Groen 1055 Mendell Davis Dr *TF*: 800-676-9040 ■ *Web*: www.groen.com	Jackson	MS	39272	601-372-3903	373-9587
HB Hunter Co 1512 Brown Ave PO Box 1599 *TF*: 800-446-8314 ■ *Web*: www.hbhunter.com	Norfolk	VA	23501	757-664-5200	664-2372
Hunter HB Co 1512 Brown Ave PO Box 1599 *TF*: 800-446-8314 ■ *Web*: www.hbhunter.com	Norfolk	VA	23501	757-664-5200	664-2372
Intedge Mfg 1875 Chumley Rd *Web*: www.intedge.com	Woodruff	SC	29388	864-969-9601	969-9604
InterMetro Industries Corp 651 N Washington St **Fax*: Hum Res ■ *TF Cust Svc*: 800-992-1776 ■ *Web*: www.metro.com	Wilkes-Barre	PA	18705	570-825-2741	824-7520*
Kittredge Equipment Co Inc 2155 Columbus Ave *TF*: 800-423-7082 ■ *Web*: www.kittredgeequipment.com	Springfield	MA	01104	413-788-6101	781-3352
Lancaster Colony Commercial Products Inc 3902 Indianola Ave *TF*: 800-292-7260 ■ *Web*: www.lccpinc.com	Columbus	OH	43214	614-263-2850	263-2857
Maines Equipment & Supply Co 101 Broome Corporate Pkwy *TF*: 800-306-3669 ■ *Web*: www.maines.net	Conklin	NY	13748	607-772-0055	772-0550
Maines Paper & Food Service Co 101 Broome Corporate Pkwy **Fax*: Cust Svc ■ *TF*: 800-366-3669 ■ *Web*: www.maines.net	Conklin	NY	13748	607-772-1936	723-3245*
McLane Foodservice Inc 2085 Midway Rd *TF*: 888-792-9300 ■ *Web*: www.mclaneco.com	Carrollton	TX	75006	972-364-2000	364-2088
N Wasserstrom & Sons Inc 2300 Lockbourne Rd *TF*: 800-444-4697 ■ *Web*: www.wasserstrom.com	Columbus	OH	43207	614-228-5550	737-8501
PBI Market Equipment Inc 2667 Gundry Ave *TF*: 800-421-3753 ■ *Web*: www.pbimarketing.com	Signal Hill	CA	90755	562-595-4785	426-2262
Perkins Equipment Div 7 Perimeter Rd *TF*: 800-258-3040 ■ *Web*: www.perkins1.com	Manchester	NH	03103	603-669-3400	641-6140
QualServ Corp 1222 Ozark Rd *TF*: 800-477-1414 ■ *Web*: www.qualservcorp.com	North Kansas City	MO	64116	816-221-7300	221-4979
RAPIDS Wholesale Equipment Co 6201 S Gateway Dr *TF*: 800-472-7431 ■ *Web*: www.rapidswholesale.com	Marion	IA	52302	319-447-1670	447-1680
Regal Ware Inc 1675 Reigle Dr *Web*: www.regalware.com	Kewaskum	WI	53040	262-626-2121	626-8565
Reinhart Food Service 7735 Westside Industrial Dr *TF*: 888-781-5464 ■ *Web*: www.rfsdelivers.com	Jacksonville	FL	32219	904-781-9888	786-7035
Restaurant & Stores Equipment Co 230 W 700 South *TF*: 800-877-0087	Salt Lake City	UT	84101	801-364-1981	355-2029
Robert Arranaga & Co Inc 216 S Alameda St *TF*: 800-639-0059	Los Angeles	CA	90012	213-622-1261	473-9800
Service Ideas Inc 2354 Ventura Dr *TF*: 800-328-4493 ■ *Web*: www.serviceideas.com	Woodbury	MN	55125	651-730-8800	730-8880
Singer Equipment Co Inc 150 S Twin Valley Rd *TF*: 800-422-8126 ■ *Web*: www.singerequipment.com	Elverson	PA	19520	610-286-8000	286-8050
Sofco a Div of Bunzl 3366 Walden Ave **Fax*: Sales ■ *TF Cust Svc*: 800-724-2571 ■ *Web*: www.bunzldistribution.com	Depew	NY	14043	716-685-6001	685-6020*
Sofco a Div of Bunzl 702 Potential Pkwy *TF Orders*: 800-836-7632 ■ *Web*: www.bunzldistribution.com	Scotia	NY	12302	518-374-7810	374-8437
Southern Foods Inc 3500 Old Battleground Rd *TF*: 800-441-3663 ■ *Web*: www.southernfoods.com	Greensboro	NC	27410	336-545-3800	545-3822
Standex International Corp Food Service Equipment Group 908 Hwy 15 N *TF*: 800-647-1284 ■ *Web*: www.standex.com/bus/1busfood.htm	New Albany	MS	38652	662-534-9061	534-8180

Phone Fax

Strategic Equipment & Supply Corp 5980 Golden Hills Dr ..... Golden Valley MN 55416 763-231-3900 231-3901
TF: 800-328-5133 ■ *Web:* www.strategicequipment.com
Sunlow Master Marketing 1071 Howell Mill Rd NW ..... Atlanta GA 30318 404-872-8135 872-0471
TF: 800-678-6569
Superior Products Catalog Co 510 W County Rd D ..... Saint Paul MN 55112 651-636-1110 636-3671
TF Sales: 800-328-9800 ■ *Web:* www.superprod.com
SYSCO Corp 1390 Enclave Pkwy ..... Houston TX 77077 281-584-1390 584-2721*
NYSE: SYY ■ **Fax: PR* ■ *Web:* www.sysco.com
Sysco Foodservice 21 Four Seasons Dr ..... Etobicoke ON M9B6J8 416-234-2668 234-2650
Web: www.sysco.ca
Traex Co 101 Traex Plaza ..... Dane WI 53529 608-849-2500 849-2580
Web: www.traex.com/
TriMark USA Inc 505 Collins St ..... South Attleboro MA 02703 508-399-2400 761-3600
TF: 800-755-5580 ■ *Web:* www.trimarkusa.com
Unified Foodservice Purchasing Co-op LLC
950 Breckenridge Ln ..... Louisville KY 40207 502-896-5900 893-4150
TF: 800-444-4144 ■ *Web:* www.ufpc.com
UniPro Foodservice Inc 2500 Cumberland Pkwy Suite 600 ..... Atlanta GA 30339 770-952-0871 952-0872
TF: 800-366-7723 ■ *Web:* www.uniprofoodservice.com
United Restaurant Equipment Co Inc 297 Central St ..... Lowell MA 01852 978-453-7223 453-2765
Web: www.unitedrestaurant.com
Vollrath Co LLC 1236 N 18th St PO Box 611 ..... Sheboygan WI 53082 920-457-4851 459-6570
TF: 800-624-2051 ■ *Web:* www.vollrathco.com
Wasserstrom Co 477 S Front St ..... Columbus OH 43215 614-228-6525 228-8776
TF: 800-999-9277 ■ *Web:* www.wasserstrom.com
Wasserstrom N & Sons Inc 2300 Lockbourne Rd ..... Columbus OH 43207 614-228-5550 737-8501
TF: 800-444-4697 ■ *Web:* www.wasserstrom.com
Western Pioneer Sales Co 406 E Colorado St ..... Glendale CA 91205 818-244-1466 245-7285*
**Fax Area Code:* 323

304 FOOTWEAR

Phone Fax

ACI International 844 Moraga Dr ..... Los Angeles CA 90049 310-889-3400 889-3500
Web: www.aciint.com
Acor Orthopaedic Inc 18530 S Miles Pkwy ..... Cleveland OH 44128 216-662-4500 662-4547
TF: 800-237-2267 ■ *Web:* www.acor.com
Acton Enterprises Inc 253 America Pl ..... Jeffersonville IN 47130 812-288-7659 288-7747
Web: www.actonenterprises.com
Acushnet Co 333 Bridge St ..... Fairhaven MA 02719 508-979-2000 979-3900*
**Fax:* Hum Res ■ *TF:* 800-225-8500 ■ *Web:* www.acushnet.com
adidas America 5055 N Greeley Ave ..... Portland OR 97217 971-234-2300 234-2450
TF: 888-234-3270 ■ *Web:* www.adidas.com
Aerosoles Inc 201 Meadow Rd ..... Edison NJ 08817 732-985-6900 985-1332
TF: 800-798-9478 ■ *Web:* www.aerosoles.com
Aldo Shoes 2300 Emile Belanger ..... Saint-Laurent QC H4R3J4 514-747-2536 747-7993
TF: 888-818-2536 ■ *Web:* www.aldoshoes.com
Allen-Edmonds Shoe Corp 201 E Seven Hills Rd ..... Port Washington WI 53074 262-235-6000 235-6265
TF Cust Svc: 800-235-2348 ■ *Web:* www.allenedmonds.com
American Shoe Shank Co Inc 53 E Main St ..... Avon MA 02322 508-584-8273 559-6407
American Sporting Goods Corp 101 Enterprise Suite 100 ..... Aliso Viejo CA 92656 949-267-2800
TF: 800-848-8698
Asics America Corp 16275 Laguna Canyon Rd ..... Irvine CA 92618 949-453-8888 453-0292
TF: 800-333-8404 ■ *Web:* www.asicsamerica.com
Athlete's Foot Group Inc 5840 El Camino Real Suite 106 ..... Norcross GA 30093 770-514-4500 514-4903
TF: 800-524-6444 ■ *Web:* www.theathletesfoot.com
ATP Mfg LLC 761 Great Rd ..... North Smithfield RI 02896 401-765-8600 766-5327
TF: 800-315-5246 ■ *Web:* www.atp-usa.com
BA Mason 1251 1st Ave ..... Chippewa Falls WI 54774 715-723-1871 446-2329*
**Fax Area Code:* 800 ■ *TF:* 800-893-8508 ■ *Web:* www.bamason.com
Badorf Shoe Co Inc 1633 Rothsville Rd PO Box 367 ..... Lititz PA 17543 717-626-8521 627-4952
TF: 800-325-1545 ■ *Web:* www.badorfshoe.com
Bakers Footwear Group Inc 2815 Scott Ave ..... Saint Louis MO 63103 314-621-0699 621-1018
NASDAQ: BKRS ■ *Web:* www.bakersshoes.com
Barbour Welting Co Div Barbour Corp 1001 N Montello St ..... Brockton MA 02301 508-583-8200 583-4113
TF: 800-955-9649 ■ *Web:* www.barbourcorp.com
Bass GH & Co Inc 1001 Frontier Rd Suite 100 ..... Bridgewater NJ 08807 908-685-0050
TF Cust Svc: 800-950-2277 ■ *Web:* www.pvh.com
Bates Shoe Co 9341 Courtland Dr NE ..... Rockford MI 49351 616-866-5500 866-5658
Web: www.wolverineworldwide.com
Beacon Shoe Co Inc 213 Lions Estates Dr ..... Jonesburg MO 63351 636-488-5444 488-3103
TF: 800-325-7463
BFG 117 Kendrick St Suite 300 ..... Needham MA 02494 617-303-3200
Web: www.brownshoe.com
Birkenstock Footprint Sandals Inc 8171 Redwood Blvd ..... Novato CA 94945 415-892-4200 937-2475*
**Fax Area Code:* 888 ■ **Fax:* Cust Svc ■ *TF:* 800-487-9255 ■
Web: www.birkenstockusa.com
Bottega Veneta Inc 699 5th Ave ..... New York NY 10022 212-371-5511 371-4361
TF: 877-362-1715 ■ *Web:* www.bottegaveneta.com
Brooks Sports Inc 19910 North Creek Pkwy Suite 200 ..... Bothell WA 98011 425-488-3131 483-8181
TF: 800-227-6657 ■ *Web:* www.brookssports.com
Brown HH Shoe Co Inc 124 W Putnam Ave ..... Greenwich CT 06830 203-661-2424 661-1818
TF: 888-444-2769 ■ *Web:* www.hhbrown.com
Brown Shoe Co Inc 8300 Maryland Ave ..... Saint Louis MO 63105 314-854-4000 854-4274
NYSE: BWS ■ *TF Cust Svc:* 800-766-6465 ■ *Web:* www.brownshoe.com
Bryer International 408 Rudolph Ave ..... Nashville TN 37206 888-262-7717 258-3338*
**Fax Area Code:* 615 ■ *TF:* 800-628-2668 ■ *Web:* www.texasbootco.com
Capezio/Ballet Makers Inc 1 Campus Rd ..... Totowa NJ 07512 973-595-9000 595-9120
TF: 800-595-9002 ■ *Web:* www.capeziodance.com
Cardinal Shoe Corp 468 Canal St ..... Lawrence MA 01840 978-686-9706 686-9707
Carolina Shoe Co 250 N 8th St ..... Lebanon PA 17046 717-272-5724 272-5769
TF: 800-438-7026 ■ *Web:* www.hhbrown.com/carolina/carolina_about.asp
Cavender's 2025 SW Loop 323 ..... Tyler TX 75701 903-561-4992 561-4849
Web: www.cavenders.com
Cels Enterprises Inc 3485 S La Cienega Blvd ..... Los Angeles CA 90016 310-838-2103 838-8732
Web: www.chineselaundry.com
Charles David of California 5731 Buckingham Pkwy ..... Culver City CA 90230 310-348-5050 348-5041
Web: www.charlesdavid.com
Cherokee Inc 6835 Valjean Ave ..... Van Nuys CA 91406 818-908-9868 908-9191
NASDAQ: CHKE ■ *Web:* www.cherokeegroup.com
Chinese Laundry Shoes 3485 S La Cienega Blvd ..... Los Angeles CA 90016 310-838-2103 838-8732
Web: www.chineselaundry.com
Clark Cos NA 156 Oak St ..... Newton Upper Falls MA 02464 617-964-1222 243-4213
TF Cust Svc: 800-425-2757 ■ *Web:* www.clarksusa.com
Cole-Haan 1 Cole Haan Dr ..... Yarmouth ME 04096 207-846-2500 846-1491
TF: 800-488-2000 ■ *Web:* www.colehaan.com
Cole Kenneth Productions Inc 603 W 50th St ..... New York NY 10019 212-265-1500 583-3811*
NYSE: KCP ■ **Fax Area Code:* 201 ■ **Fax:* Cust Svc ■ *TF:* 800-536-2653 ■
Web: www.kennethcole.com
Conaway-Winter Inc 718 E Park St ..... Willow Springs MO 65793 417-469-3125 469-1259
TF: 800-331-9476
Connors Footwear 20 Whitcher St ..... Lisbon NH 03585 603-838-6694 838-2278
Web: www.whitemt.com

Phone Fax

Consolidated Shoe Co Inc 22290 Timberlake Rd ..... Lynchburg VA 24502 434-239-0391 582-5631*
**Fax:* Sales ■ *TF:* 800-368-7463 ■ *Web:* www.nicoleshoes.com
Converse Inc 1 High St ..... North Andover MA 01845 978-983-3300 983-3521*
**Fax:* Mktg ■ *TF Cust Svc:* 800-428-2667 ■ *Web:* www.converse.com
Cowtown Boot Co 11401 Gateway Blvd W ..... El Paso TX 79936 915-593-2565 593-9441
TF: 800-580-2698
Crocs Inc 6273 Monarch Park Pl ..... Niwot CO 80503 303-468-4260 468-4266
NASDAQ: CROX ■ *Web:* www.crocs.com
D Myers & Sons Inc 4311 Erdman Ave ..... Baltimore MD 21213 410-522-7500 522-7575
TF: 800-367-7463 ■ *Web:* www.dmyers.com
Dan Post Boot Co 1751 Alpine Dr ..... Clarksville TN 37040 931-645-4466 645-6557
TF: 800-340-2668 ■ *Web:* www.danpostboots.com
Danner Shoe Mfg Co 17634 NE Airport ..... Portland OR 97230 503-251-1100 251-1119
TF Cust Svc: 800-345-0430 ■ *Web:* www.danner.com
Deckers Outdoor Corp 495-A S Fairview Ave ..... Goleta CA 93117 805-967-7611 967-9722
NASDAQ: DECK ■ *TF:* 800-858-5342 ■ *Web:* www.deckers.com
Drew Shoe Corp 252 Quarry Rd ..... Lancaster OH 43130 740-653-4271 654-4979
TF: 800-837-3739 ■ *Web:* www.drewshoe.com
DSW Inc 4150 E 5th Ave ..... Columbus OH 43219 614-237-7100 238-4209
NYSE: DSW ■ *TF Cust Svc:* 800-477-8595 ■ *Web:* www.dswshoe.com
E Shoe Sale Inc 60 Enterprise Ave N ..... Secaucus NJ 07094 201-319-0853 319-0853
TF: 877-474-6372 ■ *Web:* www.eshoesale.com
Eastland Shoe Mfg Corp 4 Meeting House Rd ..... Freeport ME 04032 207-865-6314 865-9261
Web: www.eastlandshoe.com
Easy Spirit Shoes 1129 Westchester Ave ..... White Plains NY 10604 914-640-6400 640-3575*
**Fax:* Hum Res ■ *TF:* 800-284-9955 ■ *Web:* www.easyspirit.com
EJ Footwear Corp 120 Plaza Dr Suite B ..... Vestal NY 13850 607-584-5000 584-5098
TF: 800-223-5029
ES Originals Inc 450 W 33rd St 9th Fl ..... New York NY 10001 212-736-8124 736-8366
TF: 800-677-6577 ■ *Web:* www.esoriginals.com
Eurostar Inc 13425 S Figueroa St ..... Los Angeles CA 90061 310-354-1387 767-2169
TF Cust Svc: 800-276-2002
Falcon Shoe Mfg Co 2 Cedar St ..... Lewiston ME 04240 207-784-9186 782-9522
Famous Footwear 7010 Mineral Point Rd ..... Madison WI 53717 608-829-3668 827-3353
TF Cust Svc: 800-888-7198 ■ *Web:* www.famousfootwear.com
Fancy Feet Inc 26650 Harding St ..... Oak Park MI 48237 248-398-8460 398-5650
TF: 800-858-8460 ■ *Web:* www.shoebedoo.com
Fendi NA Inc 720 5th Ave 5th Fl ..... New York NY 10019 212-920-8100 767-0545
TF: 800-336-3469 ■ *Web:* www.fendi.com
Fila USA Inc 1 Fila Way ..... Sparks MD 21152 410-773-3000 773-4973
TF: 800-787-3452 ■ *Web:* www.fila.com
Finish Line Inc 3308 N Mitthoeffer Rd ..... Indianapolis IN 46235 317-899-1022 899-0237
NASDAQ: FINL ■ *TF:* 800-370-6061 ■ *Web:* www.finishline.com
Florsheim Group Inc 333 W Estabrook Blvd ..... Glendale WI 53212 414-908-1600 908-1601
Web: www.florsheim.com
Foot Locker Inc 112 W 34th St ..... New York NY 10120 212-720-3700 720-4460
NYSE: FL ■ *TF:* 800-991-6682 ■ *Web:* www.footlocker-inc.com
Foot-So-Port Shoe Corp 405 E Forest St PO Box 247 ..... Oconomowoc WI 53066 262-567-4416 567-5323
TF: 800-679-7463 ■ *Web:* www.footsoport.com
Foot Solutions Inc 2359 Windy Hill Rd Suite 400 ..... Marietta GA 30067 770-955-0099 953-6270
TF: 866-338-2597 ■ *Web:* www.footsolutions.com
Footaction USA 112 W 34th St ..... New York NY 10120 212-720-3700 720-3831
TF: 800-863-8932 ■ *Web:* www.footaction.com
Footstar Inc 933 MacArthur Blvd ..... Mahwah NJ 07430 201-934-2000 934-0398
TF: 800-777-1330 ■ *Web:* www.footstar.com
Gateway Shoe Co 910 Kehro Mill Rd Suite 112 ..... Ballwin MO 63011 636-256-7050 527-3797
TF: 800-539-6063 ■ *Web:* www.gatewayshoes.com
Gator Industries Inc 1000 SE 8th St ..... Hialeah FL 33010 305-888-5000 885-6536
Genesco Inc 1415 Murfreesboro Rd ..... Nashville TN 37217 615-367-7000
NYSE: GCO ■ *Web:* www.genesco.com
Georgia Boot Inc 235 Noah Dr ..... Franklin TN 37068 615-794-1556 790-4229
TF: 800-251-3388 ■ *Web:* www.georgiaboot.com
GH Bass & Co Inc 1001 Frontier Rd Suite 100 ..... Bridgewater NJ 08807 908-685-0050
TF Cust Svc: 800-950-2277 ■ *Web:* www.pvh.com
Global Brand Marketing Inc 6500 Hollister Ave ..... Santa Barbara CA 93117 805-562-5600 562-5620
Web: www.gbmi.net
Gucci Group Inc 50 Hartz Way ..... Secaucus NJ 07094 201-867-8800 617-2398*
**Fax:* Hum Res ■ *Web:* www.guccigroup.com
HH Brown Shoe Co Inc 124 W Putnam Ave ..... Greenwich CT 06830 203-661-2424 661-1818
TF: 888-444-2769 ■ *Web:* www.hhbrown.com
Hi-Tec Sports USA Inc 4801 Stoddard Rd ..... Modesto CA 95356 209-545-1111 545-2543
TF: 800-521-1698 ■ *Web:* www.hi-tecsports.com
Hush Puppies Co 9341 Courtland Dr NE ..... Rockford MI 49351 616-866-5500 852-9258*
**Fax Area Code:* 800 ■ **Fax:* Acctg ■ *TF:* 800-626-8696 ■
Web: www.hushpuppiesshoes.com
Ilani Shoes Ltd 1350 Broadway ..... New York NY 10018 212-947-5830 947-2319
IMA International Marketing Inc 10821 Lakeview Ave ..... Lenexa KS 66219 913-599-5995 599-2288
TF: 800-321-1098 ■ *Web:* www.imalimited.com
Impo International Inc PO Box 639 ..... Santa Maria CA 93456 805-922-7753 925-0450
TF: 800-367-4676
Inter-Pacific Corp 2257 Colby Ave ..... Los Angeles CA 90064 310-473-7591 479-8701
Iron Age Corp 200 Friberg Pkwy Suite 2000 ..... Westborough MA 01581 508-768-4100 836-2227
TF Cust Svc: 800-223-8912 ■ *Web:* www.ironageshoes.com
Jack Schwartz Shoes Inc 155 6th Ave 9th Fl ..... New York NY 10013 212-691-4700 691-5350
Jimlar Corp 160 Great Neck Rd ..... Great Neck NY 11021 516-829-1717 829-2970
TF: 800-883-3453 ■ *Web:* www.fryeboots.com
John Reyer Shoe Store Reyers City Ctr 40 S Water Ave ..... Sharon PA 16146 724-981-2200 983-8269
TF Cust Svc: 800-245-1550 ■ *Web:* www.reyers.com
Johnston & Murphy Inc 1415 Murfreesboro Rd ..... Nashville TN 37217 615-367-8101 367-7139
TF: 800-424-2854 ■ *Web:* www.johnstonmurphy.com
Justin Boot Co Inc 610 W Daggett St ..... Fort Worth TX 76104 817-332-4385 348-2809*
**Fax:* Cust Svc ■ *TF Cust Svc:* 866-240-8853 ■ *Web:* www.justinboots.com
K-Swiss Inc 31248 Oak Crest Dr ..... Westlake Village CA 91361 818-706-5100 706-5390
NASDAQ: KSWS ■ *TF:* 800-938-8000 ■ *Web:* www.kswiss.com
Kaepa USA Inc 9050 Autobahn Dr Suite 500 ..... Dallas TX 75237 972-296-7300 296-7319
TF: 800-880-9200 ■ *Web:* www.kaepa.com
Keds Corp 191 Spring St ..... Lexington MA 02421 617-824-6000 824-6868
TF: 800-428-6575 ■ *Web:* www.keds.com
Kenneth Cole Productions Inc 603 W 50th St ..... New York NY 10019 212-265-1500 583-3811*
NYSE: KCP ■ **Fax Area Code:* 201 ■ **Fax:* Cust Svc ■ *TF:* 800-536-2653 ■
Web: www.kennethcole.com
LA Gear Inc 844 Moraga Dr ..... Los Angeles CA 90049 310-889-3410 889-3500
TF: 800-252-4327 ■ *Web:* www.lagear.com
La Sportiva North America Inc 3850 Frontier Ave Suite 100 ..... Boulder CO 80301 303-443-8710 442-7541
Web: www.sportiva.com
LaCrosse Footwear Inc 17634 NE Airport ..... Portland OR 97230 503-766-1010 766-1015
NASDAQ: BOOT ■ *TF Cust Svc:* 800-323-2668 ■ *Web:* www.lacrosse-outdoors.com
Lady Foot Locker 112 W 34th St ..... New York NY 10120 212-720-3700 628-6302*
**Fax Area Code:* 800 ■ *TF:* 800-877-5239 ■ *Web:* www.ladyfootlocker.com
Lake Catherine Footwear 190 Elmwood Dr ..... Hot Springs AR 71901 501-262-6000 262-6165
TF: 800-826-8676
Lama Tony Boot Co Inc 1137 Tony Lama St ..... El Paso TX 79915 915-778-8311 771-6107
TF: 800-866-9526 ■ *Web:* www.tonylama.com
Lamey-Wellehan Inc 940 Turner St ..... Auburn ME 04210 207-784-6595 784-9650
TF: 800-370-6900 ■ *Web:* www.lwshoes.com
Lehigh Safety Shoe Co 120 Plaza Dr Suite B ..... Vestal NY 13850 607-584-5000 584-5134
TF: 800-223-5029 ■ *Web:* www.lehighsafetyshoes.com

				Phone	Fax
Lucchese Boot Co Inc 40 Walter Jones Blvd *Fax Area Code: 888 ■ *Fax: Cust Svc ■ TF: 800-637-6888 ■ Web: www.lucchese.com	El Paso	TX	79906	915-778-8585	238-0468*
Lugz Inc 155 6th Ave 9th Fl TF: 800-648-8602 ■ Web: www.lugz.com	New York	NY	10013	212-691-4700	691-5350
Lyn-Flex West Inc 405 Red Oak Rd PO Box 570 Web: www.lynflex.com	Owensville	MO	65066	573-437-4125	437-2350
Madden Steven Ltd 52-16 Barnett Ave NASDAQ: SHOO ■ TF: 800-747-6233 ■ Web: www.stevemadden.com	Long Island City	NY	11104	718-446-1800	446-5599
Marty's Shoes Inc 60 Enterprise Ave N TF Cust Svc: 800-262-7897 ■ Web: www.martyshoes.com	Secaucus	NJ	07094	201-319-0500	319-1446
McRae Footwear Hwy 109 N	Mount Gilead	NC	27306	910-439-6149	439-9596
Meldisco Inc 933 MacArthur Blvd TF: 800-777-1330 ■ Web: www.meldisco.com	Mahwah	NJ	07430	201-934-2000	934-0398
Meramec Group Inc 338 Ramsey St Web: www.meramec.com	Sullivan	MO	63080	573-468-3101	860-3101
Mercury International 19 Alice Agnew Dr Box 222	North Attleboro	MA	02761	508-699-9000	699-9099
Merrell Footwear 9341 Courtland Dr NE *Fax Area Code: 800 ■ TF Cust Svc: 888-637-7001 ■ Web: www.merrellboot.com	Rockford	MI	49351	616-866-5500	637-7001*
Minor PW & Son Inc 3 Tread Easy Ave PO Box 678 TF: 800-524-1084 ■ Web: www.pwminor.com	Batavia	NY	14020	585-343-1500	343-1514
Mizuno USA 4925 Avalon Ridge Pkwy TF: 800-333-7888 ■ Web: www.mizunousa.com	Norcross	GA	30071	770-441-5553	448-3234
Montello Heel Mfg Inc 13 Emerson Ave TF: 800-245-4335	Brockton	MA	02305	508-586-0603	559-9270
Munro & Co 190 Elmwood Dr TF: 800-826-8676 ■ Web: www.munroshoe.com	Hot Springs	AR	71901	501-262-6000	262-6084
New Balance Athletic Shoe Inc 20 Guest St Brighton Landing TF: 800-343-4648 ■ Web: www.newbalance.com	Boston	MA	02135	617-783-4000	783-7050
Nike Inc 1 Bowerman Dr NYSE: NKE ■ TF Cust Svc: 800-344-6453 ■ Web: www.nike.com	Beaverton	OR	97005	503-671-6453	671-6300
Nina Footwear Co Inc 730 5th Ave 8th Fl TF: 800-233-6462 ■ Web: www.ninashoes.com	New York	NY	10019	212-399-2323	246-6837
Nine West Group Inc 1129 Westchester Ave Nine West Plaza TF: 800-260-2227 ■ Web: www.ninewest.com	White Plains	NY	10604	914-640-6400	640-3599
Nocona Boot Co 610 W Daggett St *Fax: Cust Svc ■ TF: 866-240-8854 ■ Web: www.nocona.com	Fort Worth	TX	76104	817-332-4385	877-0365*
Nunn-Bush Shoe Co Inc 333 W Estabrook Blvd	Milwaukee	WI	53201	414-908-1600	908-1605
ONGUARD Industries 1850 Clark Rd TF: 800-365-2282 ■ Web: www.onguardindustries.com	Havre de Grace	MD	21078	410-272-2000	272-3346
Otomix Inc 3691 Lenawee Ave TF: 800-701-7867 ■ Web: www.otomix.com	Los Angeles	CA	90016	310-815-4700	815-4720
Payless ShoeSource Inc 3231 SE 6th Ave NYSE: PSS ■ *Fax: Mail Rm ■ TF: 800-426-1141 ■ Web: www.payless.com	Topeka	KS	66607	785-233-5171	295-6233*
Pentland USA Inc 3333 New Hyde Pk Rd Suite 200 Web: www.pentland.com	New Hyde Park	NY	11042	516-365-1333	365-2333
Phoenix Footwear Group Inc 5759 Fleet St Suite 220 AMEX: PXG ■ TF: 800-341-1550 ■ Web: www.phoenixfootwear.com	Carlsbad	CA	92008	760-602-9688	602-0152
Pierre Shoes Inc 10-G Roessler Rd Suite 524	Woburn	MA	01801	781-933-6900	935-7023
Propet USA Inc 25612 74th Ave S TF: 800-877-6738 ■ Web: www.propetusa.com	Kent	WA	98032	253-854-7600	854-7607
Puma North America Inc 5 Lyberty Way TF: 800-662-7862 ■ Web: www.puma.com	Westford	MA	01886	978-698-1000	698-1150
PW Minor & Son Inc 3 Tread Easy Ave PO Box 678 TF: 800-524-1084 ■ Web: www.pwminor.com	Batavia	NY	14020	585-343-1500	343-1514
Quabaug Corp 18 School St TF: 800-325-5022 ■ Web: www.vibram.com	North Brookfield	MA	01535	508-867-7731	867-4600
Rack Room Shoes 8310 Technology Dr Web: www.rackroomshoes.com	Charlotte	NC	28262	704-547-9200	547-8159
Red Wing Shoe Co Inc 314 Main St TF Cust Svc: 800-733-9464 ■ Web: www.redwingshoes.com	Red Wing	MN	55066	651-388-8211	388-7415
Reebok International Ltd 1895 JW Foster Blvd *Fax: Cust Svc ■ TF: 800-843-4444 ■ Web: www.reebok.com	Canton	MA	02021	781-401-5000	401-4516*
Reef Brazil 9660 Chesapeake Dr TF: 800-423-6855 ■ Web: www.reefbrazil.com	San Diego	CA	92123	858-514-3600	514-3620
RG Barry Corp 13405 Yarmouth Dr NW AMEX: DFZ ■ TF: 800-848-7560 ■ Web: www.rgbarry.com	Pickerington	OH	43147	614-864-6400	866-9787
Riddell Footwear 2047 Westport Ctr Dr TF: 888-698-0717 ■ Web: www.riddellfootwear.com	Saint Louis	MO	63146	314-432-7171	692-2133
Rockport Co Inc 1895 JW Foster Blvd *Fax: Cust Svc ■ TF: 800-762-5767 ■ Web: www.rockport.com	Canton	MA	02021	781-401-5000	401-5230*
Rocky Shoes & Boots Inc 39 E Canal St NASDAQ: RCKY ■ TF: 800-421-5151 ■ Web: www.rockyboots.com	Nelsonville	OH	45764	740-753-1951	753-4024
Romika USA LLC 3405 Del Webb Ave NE Web: www.romikausa.com	Salem	OR	97301	503-485-1848	588-3013
Ryka Inc 101 Enterprise Suite 100 TF: 800-848-8698 ■ Web: www.ryka.com	Aliso Viejo	CA	92656	949-267-2800	862-4890
Salomon North America 5055 N Greeley Ave TF: 877-272-5666 ■ Web: www.salomonsports.com	Portland	OR	97217	971-234-2300	234-2450
SAS Shoemakers 1717 SAS Dr TF: 877-782-7463 ■ Web: www.sasshoes.com	San Antonio	TX	78224	210-924-6561	921-7896
Saucony Inc 191 Spring St TF: 800-365-4933 ■ Web: www.saucony.com	Lexington	MA	02421	617-824-6000	
Schottenstein Stores Corp 1800 Moler Rd *Fax: Cust Svc ■ TF: 800-743-4577	Columbus	OH	43207	614-221-9200	449-4880*
Schwartz & Benjamin Inc 20 W 57th St 4th Fl	New York	NY	10019	212-541-9092	974-0609
Schwartz Jack Shoes Inc 155 6th Ave 9th Fl	New York	NY	10013	212-691-4700	691-5350
Sebago Inc 9341 Courtland Dr *Fax Area Code: 800 ■ TF: 800-253-2184 ■ Web: www.sebago.com	Rockford	MI	49351	616-863-4815	862-6230*
SG Footwear Inc 20 E Broadway Web: www.sgfootwear.com	Hackensack	NJ	07601	201-342-1200	342-4405
Sherman Shoes 116 N Old Woodward Ave Web: www.shopshermans.com	Birmingham	MI	48009	248-646-8431	646-5018
Shoe Carnival Inc 8233 Baumgart Rd NASDAQ: SCVL ■ TF Cust Svc: 800-430-7463 ■ Web: www.shoecarnival.com	Evansville	IN	47725	812-867-6471	867-3625
Shoe Pavillion Inc 1380 Fitzgerald Dr NASDAQ: SHOE ■ TF: 800-736-5523 ■ Web: www.shoepavillion.com	Pinole	CA	94564	510-222-4405	222-4506
Shoe Show of Rocky Mountain Inc 2201 Trinity Church Rd TF Cust Svc: 888-557-4637 ■ Web: www.shoeshow.com	Concord	NC	28027	704-782-4143	782-3411
Shoes.com Inc 6755 Hollywood Blvd 4th Fl *Fax Area Code: 310 ■ TF: 888-233-6743 ■ Web: www.shoes.com	Los Angeles	CA	90028	888-233-6743	566-7933*
Shtofman Co 1905 W Gentry Pkwy	Tyler	TX	75702	903-592-0861	592-8380
Skechers USA Inc 228 Manhattan Beach Blvd Suite 200 NYSE: SKX ■ TF Cust Svc: 800-243-0443 ■ Web: www.skechers.com	Manhattan Beach	CA	90266	310-318-3100	318-5019
South Cone Inc DBA Reef Brazil 9660 Chesapeake Dr TF: 800-423-6855 ■ Web: www.reefbrazil.com	San Diego	CA	92123	858-514-3600	514-3620
Spalding 150 Brookdale Dr TF Cust Svc: 800-772-5346 ■ Web: www.spalding.com	Springfield	MA	01104	413-735-1400	735-1570
Spenco Medical Corp 6301 Imperial Dr TF: 800-877-3626 ■ Web: www.spenco.com	Waco	TX	76712	254-772-6000	772-6536
Sperry Top-Sider Inc 191 Spring St TF Cust Svc: 800-666-5689 ■ Web: www.sperrytopsider.com	Lexington	MA	02421	617-824-6000	824-6666
Sporto Corp 65 Sprague St TF Cust Svc: 888-277-6786 ■ Web: www.sporto.net	Boston	MA	02136	617-364-3001	364-3118
Stanbee Co Inc 70 Broad St Web: www.stanbee.com	Carlstadt	NJ	07072	201-933-9666	933-7985
Steven Madden Ltd 52-16 Barnett Ave NASDAQ: SHOO ■ TF: 800-747-6233 ■ Web: www.stevemadden.com	Long Island City	NY	11104	718-446-1800	446-5599
Stride Rite Corp 191 Spring St NYSE: SRR ■ *Fax Area Code: 800 ■ TF Cust Svc: 800-666-5689 ■ Web: www.striderite.com	Lexington	MA	02421	617-824-6000	428-2767*
Super Shoe Stores Inc 601 Dual Hwy TF: 888-392-2204 ■ Web: www.supershoe.com	Hagerstown	MD	21740	301-766-7513	393-3923
Teva Sport Sandals 515 N Beaver St TF Orders: 800-367-8382 ■ Web: www.teva.com	Flagstaff	AZ	86001	928-779-5938	779-6004
Timberland Co 200 Domain Dr NYSE: TBL ■ TF: 800-258-0855 ■ Web: www.timberland.com	Stratham	NH	03885	603-772-9500	773-1640
Tony Lama Boot Co Inc 1137 Tony Lama St TF: 800-866-9526 ■ Web: www.tonylama.com	El Paso	TX	79915	915-778-8311	771-6107
Topline Corp 13150 SE 32nd St Web: www.toplinecorp.com	Bellevue	WA	98005	425-643-3003	643-3846
Trimfoot Co LLC 115 Trimfoot Terr TF: 800-325-6116 ■ Web: www.trimfootco.com	Farmington	MO	63640	573-756-6616	756-8482
TT Group Inc 702 Carnation Dr TF: 800-445-0886 ■ Web: www.tt-group.com	Aurora	MO	65605	417-678-2181	678-6901
Unisa America Inc 10814 NW 33rd St Suite 100 Web: www.unisashoes.com	Miami	FL	33172	305-591-9397	594-2154
United Retail Group Inc 365 W Passaic St NASDAQ: URGI ■ TF: 877-708-8740 ■ Web: www.unitedretail.com	Rochelle Park	NJ	07662	201-845-0880	909-2114
Vans Inc 15700 Shoemaker Ave TF: 800-826-7800 ■ Web: www.vans.com	Santa Fe Springs	CA	90670	562-565-8267	565-8407
Walking Co 2473 Towns Gate Rd Suite 200 Web: www.walkingco.com	West Lake Village	CA	91361	805-496-3005	496-3240
Weinbrenner Shoe Co Inc 108 S Polk St TF Cust Svc: 800-826-0002 ■ Web: www.weinbrennerusa.com	Merrill	WI	54452	715-536-5521	536-1172
Wellco Enterprises Inc 150 Westwood Cir AMEX: WLC ■ TF: 800-840-3155 ■ Web: www.wellco.com	Waynesville	NC	28786	828-456-3545	456-3547
Wesco 52828 NW Shoe Factory Ln PO Box 607 TF: 800-326-2711 ■ Web: www.westcoastshoe.com	Scappoose	OR	97056	503-543-7114	543-7110
West Coast Shoe Co 52828 NW Shoe Factory Ln PO Box 607 TF: 800-326-2711 ■ Web: www.westcoastshoe.com	Scappoose	OR	97056	503-543-7114	543-7110
Weyco Group Inc 333 W Estabrook Blvd NASDAQ: WEYS ■ Web: www.weycogroup.com	Glendale	WI	53212	414-908-1600	908-1601
Willits Footwear Worldwide Inc 208 N River Rd TF: 800-544-3633	Halifax	PA	17032	717-896-3411	896-3470
Wolff Shoe Co 910 Kehrs Mill Rd	Fenton	MO	63026	636-343-7770	326-4922
Wolverine World Wide Inc 9341 Courtland Dr NYSE: WWW ■ *Fax Area Code: 800 ■ TF: 800-365-5505 ■ Web: www.wolverineworldwide.com	Rockford	MI	49351	616-866-5500	862-6230*
Wolverine Worldwide Inc 9341 Courtland Dr *Fax Area Code: 800 ■ TF: 800-253-2184 ■ Web: www.wolverineworldwide.com	Rockford	MI	49351	616-866-5500	325-8164*

305 FORESTRY SERVICES

SEE ALSO Timber Tracts p. 2367

				Phone	Fax
Cascade Timber Consulting Inc 3210 Hwy 20	Sweet Home	OR	97386	541-367-2111	367-2117
Columbia River Log Scaling & Grading Bureau 260 Oakway Ctr Web: www.crls.com	Eugene	OR	97401	541-342-6007	485-3086
Environmental Consultants Inc 301 Lakeside Dr Web: www.eci-consulting.com	Southampton	PA	18966	215-322-4040	322-9404
Georgia Timberlands Inc 3250 Waterville Rd	Macon	GA	31206	478-788-4660	781-0246
International Air Response Inc 22000 S Old Price Rd Web: www.internationalairresponse.com	Chandler	AZ	85248	520-796-5188	796-1064
International Forest Products Ltd (Interfor) 1055 Sunsmuir St Suite 3500 Web: www.interfor.com	Vancouver	BC	V7X1H7	604-689-6800	688-0313
Lower Dixie Timber Co 2285 Bashi Rd PO Box 248 TF: 800-824-9525	Thomasville	AL	36784	334-636-1500	636-1861
Resource Management Service LLC 31 Inverness Center Pkwy Suite 360 TF: 800-995-9516 ■ Web: www.resourcemgt.com	Birmingham	AL	35242	205-991-9516	991-2807
Sealaska Corp 1 Sealaska Plaza Suite 400 Web: www.sealaska.com	Juneau	AK	99801	907-586-1512	586-8191
Sustainable Forestry 1201 W Lothrop Ave PO Box 1391	Savannah	GA	31402	912-238-6220	238-6111
UAP Timberland LLC 140 Arkansas St TF: 800-752-7009 ■ Web: www.uaptimberland.com	Monticello	AR	71655	870-367-8561	367-1804
Western Forest Products Inc 435 Trunk Rd 3rd Fl TSX: WEF ■ Web: www.westernforest.com	Duncan	BC	V9L2P9	250-748-3711	748-6630

306 FOUNDATIONS - COMMUNITY

SEE ALSO Associations & Organizations - General - Charitable & Humanitarian Organizations p. 1294

				Phone	Fax
Arizona Community Foundation 2201 E Camelback Rd Suite 202 TF: 800-222-8221 ■ Web: www.azfoundation.org	Phoenix	AZ	85016	602-381-1400	381-1575
Boston Foundation 75 Arlington St 10th Fl Web: www.tbf.org	Boston	MA	02116	617-338-1700	338-1604
California Community Foundation 445 S Figueroa St Suite 3400 Web: www.calfund.org	Los Angeles	CA	90071	213-413-4130	383-2046
California Endowment 21650 Oxnard St Suite 1200 TF: 800-449-4149 ■ Web: www.calendow.org	Woodland Hills	CA	91367	818-703-3311	703-4193
California Wellness Foundation 6320 Canoga Ave Suite 1700 Web: www.tcwf.org	Woodland Hills	CA	91367	818-593-6600	593-6614
Chicago Community Trust & Affiliates 111 E Wacker Dr Suite 1400 Web: www.cct.org	Chicago	IL	60601	312-616-8000	616-7955
Cleveland Foundation 1422 Euclid Ave Suite 1300 TF: 800-869-3810 ■ Web: www.clevelandfoundation.org	Cleveland	OH	44115	216-861-3810	861-1729
Colorado Trust 1600 Sherman St TF: 888-847-9140 ■ Web: www.coloradotrust.org	Denver	CO	80203	303-837-1200	839-9034
Columbus Foundation 1234 E Broad St Web: www.columbusfoundation.org	Columbus	OH	43205	614-251-4000	251-4009
Communities Foundation of Texas Inc 5500 Caruth Haven Ln Web: www.cftexas.org	Dallas	TX	75225	214-750-4222	750-4210

	City	State	ZIP	Phone	Fax
Community Foundation for Greater Atlanta Inc					
50 Hurt Plaza Suite 449	Atlanta	GA	30303	404-688-5525	688-3060
Web: www.atlcf.org					
Community Foundation of Greater Memphis 1900 Union Ave	Memphis	TN	38104	901-728-4600	722-0010
Web: www.cfgm.org					
Community Foundation for Greater New Haven					
70 Audubon St	New Haven	CT	06510	203-777-2386	787-6584
Web: www.cfgnh.org					
Community Foundation for the National Capital Region					
1201 15th St NW Suite 420	Washington	DC	20005	202-955-5890	955-8084
Web: www.cfncr.org					
Community Foundation Serving Richmond & Central Virginia					
7325 Beaufont Springs Dr Suite 210	Richmond	VA	23225	804-330-7400	330-5992
Web: www.tcfrichmond.org					
Community Foundation Silicon Valley					
60 S Market St Suite 1000	San Jose	CA	95113	408-278-2200	278-0280
Web: www.cfsv.org					
Dayton Foundation 2300 Kettering Tower	Dayton	OH	45423	937-222-0410	222-0636
TF: 877-222-0410 ■ *Web:* www.daytonfoundation.org					
El Pomar Foundation 10 Lake Cir	Colorado Springs	CO	80906	719-633-7733	577-5702
TF: 800-554-7711 ■ *Web:* www.elpomar.org					
Foundation for the Carolinas 217 S Tryon St	Charlotte	NC	28202	704-973-4500	973-4599
TF: 800-973-7244 ■ *Web:* www.fftc.org					
Greater Cincinnati Foundation 200 W 4th St	Cincinnati	OH	45202	513-241-2880	852-6886
Web: www.greatercincinnatifdn.org					
Greater Kansas City Community Foundation & Affiliated Trusts 1055 Broadway Suite 130	Kansas City	MO	64105	816-842-0944	842-8079
Web: www.gkccf.org					
Greater Milwaukee Foundation 1020 N Broadway Suite 112	Milwaukee	WI	53202	414-272-5805	272-6235
Web: www.greatermilwaukeefoundation.org					
Hartford Foundation for Public Giving 85 Gillett St	Hartford	CT	06105	860-548-1888	524-8346
Web: www.hfpg.org					
Hawaii Community Foundation 1164 Bishop St Suite 800	Honolulu	HI	96813	808-537-6333	521-6286
TF: 888-731-3863 ■ *Web:* www.hawaiicommunityfoundation.org					
Houston Endowment Inc 600 Travis St Suite 6400	Houston	TX	77002	713-238-8100	238-8101
Web: www.houstonendowment.org					
Marin Community Foundation 5 Hamilton Landing Suite 200	Novato	CA	94949	415-464-2500	464-2555
TF: 800-270-0295 ■ *Web:* www.marincf.org					
Minneapolis Foundation 80 8th St 800 IDS Ctr	Minneapolis	MN	55402	612-672-3878	672-3846
Web: www.mplsfoundation.org					
New York Community Trust 909 3rd Ave 22nd Fl	New York	NY	10022	212-686-0010	532-8528
Web: www.nycommunitytrust.org					
Northwest Area Foundation 60 Plato Blvd E Suite 400	Saint Paul	MN	55107	651-224-9635	225-7701
TF: 888-904-9821 ■ *Web:* www.nwaf.org					
Oklahoma City Community Foundation					
1300 N Broadway Dr	Oklahoma City	OK	73103	405-235-5603	235-5612
Web: www.occf.org					
Omaha Community Foundation 302 S 36th St Suite 100	Omaha	NE	68131	402-342-3458	342-3582
Web: www.omahacf.org					
Oregon Community Foundation 1221 SW Yamhill St Suite 100	Portland	OR	97205	503-227-6846	274-7771
Web: www.ocf1.org					
Peninsula Community Foundation					
1700 S El Camino Real Suite 300	San Mateo	CA	94402	650-358-9369	358-9817
Web: www.pcf.org					
Pittsburgh Foundation 1 PPG Pl 30th Fl	Pittsburgh	PA	15222	412-391-5122	391-7259
Web: www.pittsburghfoundation.org					
Rhode Island Foundation 1 Union Stn	Providence	RI	02903	401-274-4564	331-8085
Web: www.rifoundation.org					
Saint Paul Foundation 55 E 5th St Suite 600	Saint Paul	MN	55101	651-224-5463	224-8123
TF: 800-875-6167 ■ *Web:* saintpaulfoundation.org					
San Diego Foundation 1420 Kettner Blvd Suite 500	San Diego	CA	92101	619-235-2300	239-1710
Web: www.sdfoundation.org					
San Francisco Foundation 225 Bush St Suite 500	San Francisco	CA	94104	415-733-8500	477-2785
Web: www.sff.org					
Seattle Foundation 1200 5th Ave Suite 1300	Seattle	WA	98101	206-622-2294	622-7673
Web: www.seattlefoundation.org					

307 FOUNDATIONS - CORPORATE

SEE ALSO Associations & Organizations - General - Charitable & Humanitarian Organizations p. 1294

	City	State	ZIP	Phone	Fax
3M Foundation Inc 3M Center Bldg 225-1S-23	Saint Paul	MN	55144	651-733-0144	737-3061
Abbott Laboratories Fund					
100 Abbott Park Rd Dept 379 Bldg 6D	Abbott Park	IL	60064	847-935-0853	935-5051
Web: abbott.com/citizenship/fund/fund.shtml					
Aetna Foundation Inc 151 Farmington Ave	Hartford	CT	06156	860-273-6382	273-4764
Web: www.aetna.com/foundation					
Alabama Power Foundation Inc 600 N 18th St	Birmingham	AL	35291	205-257-2508	257-1860
Web: www.southerncompany.com/alpower					
Alcoa Foundation 201 Isabella St	Pittsburgh	PA	15212	412-553-2348	553-4498
Web: www.alcoa.com/foundation					
Allstate Foundation 2775 Sanders Rd Suite F4	Northbrook	IL	60062	847-402-5502	326-7517
Web: www.allstate.com/foundation					
Anheuser-Busch Foundation 1 Busch Pl	Saint Louis	MO	63118	314-577-2453	577-3251
Archer Daniels Midland Foundation 4666 E Faries Pkwy	Decatur	IL	62526	217-424-5200	424-5581
TF: 800-637-5843					
Bank of America Charitable Foundation 100 N Tryon St	Charlotte	NC	28202	800-218-9946	622-3469*
**Fax Area Code:* 415 ■ *TF:* 888-488-9802 ■ *Web:* www.bankofamerica.com/foundation					
Baxter International Foundation 1 Baxter Pkwy	Deerfield	IL	60015	847-948-4605	948-4559
Web: www.baxter.com/investors/citizenship/foundatio					
Boeing-McDonnell Foundation PO Box 516 MC S100-1510	Saint Louis	MO	63166	314-234-0456	232-7654
Bristol-Myers Squibb Foundation Inc 345 Park Ave	New York	NY	10154	212-546-4000	546-9574
Web: www.bms.com/sr/philanthropy					
Burroughs Wellcome Fund					
21 TW Alexander Dr PO Box 13901	Research Triangle Park	NC	27709	919-991-5100	941-5160
Web: www.bwfund.org					
Cargill Foundation 15407 McGinty Rd W MS PA-50	Wayzata	MN	55391	952-742-2546	742-7224
TF: 800-227-4455 ■ *Web:* www.cargill.com/commun/found.htm					
Caterpillar Foundation 100 NE Adams St	Peoria	IL	61629	309-675-4464	675-4332
Web: www.cat.com/foundation					
CIGNA Foundation 1601 Chestnut St	Philadelphia	PA	19192	215-761-6054	761-5715
Web: www.cigna.com/general/about/community/contributions.html					
Cisco Systems Foundation 170 W Tasman Dr	San Jose	CA	95134	408-527-3040	
TF: 800-553-6387 ■ *Web:* www.cisco.com/go/foundation					
Citigroup Foundation 850 3rd Ave 13th Fl	New York	NY	10022	212-559-9163	793-5944
Web: www.citigroup.com/citigroup/citizen					
Coca-Cola Foundation Inc PO Box 1734	Atlanta	GA	30301	404-676-2568	676-8804
Web: www2.coca-cola.com/citizenship/foundation_coke.html					
DaimlerChrysler Corp Fund 1000 Chrysler Dr	Auburn Hills	MI	48326	248-512-2502	512-2503
Web: www.fund.daimlerchrysler.com					
Dell Foundation 1 Dell Way	Round Rock	TX	78682	512-338-4400	283-6161
TF: 800-854-6245					
Dominion Resources Foundation					
625 Liberty Ave Dominion Tower 21st Fl	Pittsburgh	PA	15222	412-690-1430	690-7608
Web: www.dom.com/about/community/index.jsp					
Dow Chemical Co Foundation 2030 Dow Ctr	Midland	MI	48674	989-636-1000	636-4460
TF: 800-331-6451 ■ *Web:* www.dow.com/about/corp/social/social.htm					
Eastman Kodak Charitable Trust 343 State St	Rochester	NY	14650	585-724-2434	724-1376
Eli Lilly & Co Foundation Lilly Corporate Ctr	Indianapolis	IN	46285	317-276-2000	277-6719
TF: 800-545-5979 ■ *Web:* www.lilly.com/products/access/foundation.html					
Emerson Charitable Trust 8000 W Florissant Ave	Saint Louis	MO	63136	314-553-3621	
ExxonMobil Foundation Inc 5959 Las Colinas Blvd	Irving	TX	75039	972-444-1000	444-1405
Fidelity Foundation 82 Devonshire St Suite S-2	Boston	MA	02109	617-563-6806	476-9130
Web: www.fidelityfoundation.org					
Ford Motor Co Fund 1 American Rd Suite 211	Dearborn	MI	48126	313-845-8711	337-6680
Freddie Mac Foundation 8250 Jones Branch Dr	McLean	VA	22102	703-918-8888	918-8895
TF: 800-373-3343 ■ *Web:* www.freddiemacfoundation.org					
GE Foundation 3135 Easton Tpke	Fairfield	CT	06828	203-373-3216	373-3029
Web: www.ge.com/foundation					
General Mills Foundation 1 General Mills Blvd	Minneapolis	MN	55426	763-764-2211	764-4114
Web: www.generalmills.com/foundation					
General Motors Foundation Inc					
3044 W Grand Blvd 11-134 GM Bldg	Detroit	MI	48202	313-665-0824	
Web: www.gm.com/company/gmability					
Georgia Power Foundation Inc					
241 Ralph McGill Blvd NE Bin 10131	Atlanta	GA	30308	404-506-6784	506-1485
Web: www.southerncompany.com/gapower/charitable					
GlaxoSmithKline Foundation 5 Moore Dr	Research Triangle Park	NC	27709	919-483-2140	315-3015
TF: 888-825-5249 ■ *Web:* www.gsk.com/community					
Hallmark Corp Foundation 2501 McGee St	Kansas City	MO	64108	816-274-8516	274-8547
Hasbro Children's Foundation 1027 Newport Ave	Pawtucket	RI	02862	401-431-8697	
Web: www.hasbro.org/hcf					
HCA Foundation 1 Park Plaza	Nashville	TN	37203	615-344-2343	344-5722
Web: www.hcacaring.org					
Hess Foundation Inc 1185 Ave of the Americas	New York	NY	10036	212-997-8500	536-8390
HJ Heinz Co Foundation 600 Grant St 60th Fl	Pittsburgh	PA	15219	412-456-5773	442-3227
Web: www.heinz.com/jsp/foundation.jsp					
Honeywell International Foundation 101 Columbia Rd	Morristown	NJ	07962	973-455-2000	455-4807
Humana Foundation Inc 500 W Main St Humana Bldg	Louisville	KY	40202	502-580-3613	580-1256
Web: www.humanafoundation.org					
IBM International Foundation 1 New Orchard Rd	Armonk	NY	10504	914-499-5242	499-7684
Web: www.ibm.com/ibm/ibmgives					
Intel Foundation 5200 NE Elam Young Pkwy MS AG6-601	Hillsboro	OR	97124	503-696-8080	
Johnson & Johnson Family of Cos Contribution Fund					
1 Johnson & Johnson Plaza	New Brunswick	NJ	08933	732-524-3255	524-3300
Kimberly-Clark Foundation 351 Phelps Dr	Irving	TX	75038	972-281-1477	281-1490
Web: www.kimberly-clark.com/aboutus/kc_foundation.asp					
Koch Foundation Inc 4421 NW 39th Ave Suite 1	Gainesville	FL	32606	352-373-7491	
Web: www.kochenterprises.com/corporate/foundation.htm					
Levi Strauss Foundation 1155 Battery St	San Francisco	CA	94111	415-501-6000	501-6575
Web: www.levistrauss.com/responsibility/foundation					
Lucent Technologies Foundation					
600 Mountain Ave Rm 3A-312	Murray Hill	NJ	07974	908-508-8080	508-2576
Web: www.lucent.com/news/foundation					
Lutheran Community Foundation 625 4th Ave S Suite 200	Minneapolis	MN	55415	612-340-4110	340-4109
TF: 800-365-4172 ■ *Web:* www.thelcf.org					
Mead Corp Foundation Courthouse Plaza NE	Dayton	OH	45463	937-495-6323	495-4103
TF: 800-345-6323					
Mellon Financial Corp Fund 1 Mellon Ctr Rm 1830	Pittsburgh	PA	15258	412-234-2732	234-0831
Web: www.mellon.com/aboutmellon/communityinvolvement					
Merck Co Foundation 1 Merck Dr PO Box 100	Whitehouse Station	NJ	08889	908-423-2042	
MetLife Foundation					
2701 Queens Plaza N MetLife Plaza	Long Island City	NY	11101	212-578-6272	578-0617
Web: www.metlife.org					
Motorola Foundation 1303 E Algonquin Rd	Schaumburg	IL	60196	847-576-7895	538-4055
Web: www.motorola.com/MotorolaFoundation					
New York Life Foundation 51 Madison Ave Suite 1600	New York	NY	10010	212-576-7341	
Web: www.newyorklife.com/foundation					
New York Times Co Foundation Inc 229 W 43rd St	New York	NY	10036	212-556-1091	556-4450
Web: www.nytco.com/company/foundation					
Northwestern Mutual Foundation 720 E Wisconsin Ave	Milwaukee	WI	53202	414-665-2200	665-2199
PepsiCo Foundation Inc 700 Anderson Hill Rd	Purchase	NY	10577	914-253-2000	253-3553
Pfizer Foundation Inc 235 E 42nd St	New York	NY	10017	212-733-2323	573-2883
TF: 800-733-4717 ■ *Web:* www.pfizer.com/pfizer/subsites/philanthropy/index.jsp					
Playboy Foundation 680 N Lake Shore Dr	Chicago	IL	60611	312-751-8000	751-2818
Web: www.playboyenterprises.com/foundation					
Principal Financial Group Foundation Inc 711 High St	Des Moines	IA	50392	515-247-7227	246-5475
TF: 800-986-3343 ■ *Web:* www.principal.com/about/giving					
Procter & Gamble Fund PO Box 599	Cincinnati	OH	45201	513-983-1100	
Prudential Foundation 751 Broad St 15th Fl	Newark	NJ	07102	973-802-4791	802-3345
Revlon Foundation Inc 237 Park Ave	New York	NY	10017	212-527-6974	527-5710
Sara Lee Foundation 3 First National Plaza	Chicago	IL	60602	312-558-8448	419-3192
TF: 800-727-2533 ■ *Web:* www.saraleefoundation.org					
SBC Foundation 130 E Travis St Suite 350	San Antonio	TX	78205	800-591-9663	351-2599*
**Fax Area Code:* 210 ■ *TF:* 800-591-9663 ■ *Web:* www.sbc.com/foundation					
Scripps Howard Foundation 312 Walnut St PO Box 5380	Cincinnati	OH	45201	513-977-3035	977-3800
TF: 800-888-3000 ■ *Web:* foundation.scripps.com/foundation					
Shell Oil Co Foundation PO Box 2099	Houston	TX	77252	713-241-4512	241-0633
Siemens Foundation 170 Wood Ave S	Iselin	NJ	08830	732-603-5886	603-5890
TF: 877-822-5233 ■ *Web:* www.siemens-foundation.org					
State Farm Cos Foundation 1 State Farm Plaza Suite B-4	Bloomington	IL	61710	309-766-2161	766-2314
Steelcase Foundation PO Box 1967	Grand Rapids	MI	49501	616-246-4695	475-2200
Target Foundation 1000 Nicollete Mall TPS 3080	Minneapolis	MN	55403	612-696-6098	696-5088
TF: 800-440-0680 ■					
Web: www.targetcorp.com/targetcorp_group/community/foundation.jhtml					
Tenet Healthcare Foundation 13737 Noel Rd Suite 100	Dallas	TX	75240	469-893-6502	
Web: www.tenethealth.com/tenethealth/TenetFoundatio					
Union Pacific Foundation 1400 Douglas St MS 1560	Omaha	NE	68179	402-544-5600	
Web: www.up.com/found					
UPS Foundation 55 Glenlake Pkwy NE	Atlanta	GA	30328	404-828-6451	828-7435
Web: www.community.ups.com/philanthropy/main.html					
US Bancorp Foundation 800 Nicollet Mall	Minneapolis	MN	55402	612-303-0737	303-0787
Verizon Foundation 1255 Corporate Dr	Irving	TX	75038	800-360-7955	840-6988*
**Fax Area Code:* 212 ■ *Web:* foundation.verizon.com					
Wachovia Foundation 301 S College St	Charlotte	NC	28288	704-374-4085	374-2484
Web: www.wachovia.com/wachoviafoundation					
Wal-Mart Foundation 702 SW 8th St	Bentonville	AR	72716	800-530-9925	273-6850*
**Fax Area Code:* 479 ■ *Web:* www.walmartfoundation.org					
Wells Fargo Foundation 431 S Palm Canyon Dr Suite 202	Palm Springs	CA	92262	760-864-1047	322-6695
Web: www.wellsfargo.com					
Whirlpool Foundation 2000 North M-63	Benton Harbor	MI	49022	269-923-5584	925-0154
TF: 800-446-2574 ■ *Web:* www.whirlpoolcorp.com					
Xerox Foundation 45 Glover Ave PO Box 4504	Norwalk	CT	06856	203-968-3000	

308 FOUNDATIONS - PRIVATE

SEE ALSO Associations & Organizations - General - Charitable & Humanitarian Organizations p. 1294

Phone / Fax

Adolph Coors Foundation 4100 E Mississippi Ave Suite 1850 ... Denver CO 80246 303-388-1636 388-1684
Web: www.acoorsfdn.org
Ahmanson Foundation 9215 Wilshire Blvd ... Beverly Hills CA 90210 310-278-0770
Albertson JA & Kathryn Foundation PO Box 70002 ... Boise ID 83707 208-424-2600 424-2626
Web: www.jkaf.org
Alfred P Sloan Foundation 630 5th Ave Suite 2550 ... New York NY 10111 212-649-1649 757-5117
Web: www.sloan.org
Allen Paul G Family Foundation 505 5th Ave S Suite 900 ... Seattle WA 98104 206-342-2000 342-3000
Web: www.pgafamilyfoundation.org
Amon G Carter Foundation PO Box 1036 ... Fort Worth TX 76101 817-332-2783 332-2787
Web: www.agcf.org
Andrew W Mellon Foundation 140 E 62nd St ... New York NY 10021 212-838-8400 888-4172
Web: www.mellon.org
Annenberg Foundation 150 N Radnor-Chester Rd Suite 200 ... Radnor PA 19087 610-341-9066 964-8688
Web: www.annenbergfoundation.org
Annie E Casey Foundation 701 Saint Paul St ... Baltimore MD 21202 410-547-6600 547-6624
TF: 800-222-1099 ■ *Web:* www.aecf.org
Archibald Bush Foundation 332 Minnesota St Suite E-900 ... Saint Paul MN 55101 651-227-0891 297-6485
Web: www.bushfoundation.org
Arthur S DeMoss Foundation
777 S Flagler Dr Suite 1600-W ... West Palm Beach FL 33401 561-804-9000 804-9025
Arthur Vining Davis Foundations 225 Water St Suite 1510 ... Jacksonville FL 32202 904-359-0670 359-0675
Web: www.avdfdn.org
Ave Maria Foundation 1 Ave Maria Dr PO Box 373 ... Ann Arbor MI 48106 734-930-3150 930-4453
Web: www.avemariafoundation.org
Barr Foundation 136 NE Olive Way ... Boca Raton FL 33432 561-394-6514 391-7601
Web: www.oandp.com/barr
Benton Foundation 1625 K St NW 11th Fl ... Washington DC 20006 202-638-5770 638-5771
Web: www.benton.org
Bill & Melinda Gates Foundation PO Box 23350 ... Seattle WA 98102 206-709-3100 709-3180
TF: 888-452-6352 ■ *Web:* www.gatesfoundation.org
Bradley Lynde & Harry Foundation Inc 1241 N Franklin Pl ... Milwaukee WI 53202 414-291-9915 291-9991
Web: www.bradleyfdn.org
Brown Foundation Inc PO Box 130646 ... Houston TX 77219 713-523-6867 523-2917
Web: www.brownfoundation.org
Cafritz Morris & Gwendolyn Foundation
1825 K St NW 14th Fl ... Washington DC 20006 202-223-3100 296-7567
Web: www.cafritzfoundation.org
Campbell J Bulow Foundation 50 Hurt Plaza Suite 850 ... Atlanta GA 30303 404-658-9066 659-4802
Web: www.jbcf.org
Carnegie Corp of New York 437 Madison Ave 26th Fl ... New York NY 10022 212-371-3200 754-4073
Web: www.carnegie.org
Carter Amon G Foundation PO Box 1036 ... Fort Worth TX 76101 817-332-2783 332-2787
Web: www.agcf.org
Carver Roy J Charitable Trust 202 Iowa Ave ... Muscatine IA 52761 563-263-4010 263-1547
Web: www.carvertrust.org
Casey Annie E Foundation 701 Saint Paul St ... Baltimore MD 21202 410-547-6600 547-6624
TF: 800-222-1099 ■ *Web:* www.aecf.org
Champlin Foundations 300 Centerville Rd Suite 300S ... Warwick RI 02886 401-736-0370 736-7248
Web: fdncenter.org/grantmaker/champlin
Charles Hayden Foundation 140 Broadway 51st Fl ... New York NY 10005 212-785-3677 785-3689
Web: fdncenter.org/grantmaker/hayden
Charles & Helen Schwab Foundation
1650 S Amphlett Blvd Suite 300 ... San Mateo CA 94402 650-655-2412 655-2411
Web: www.schwabfoundation.org
Charles Stewart Mott Foundation 503 S Saginaw St Suite 1200 ... Flint MI 48502 810-238-5651 766-1753
Web: www.mott.org
Chatlos Foundation PO Box 915048 ... Longwood FL 32791 407-862-5077 862-0708
Web: www.chatlos.org
Clark Edna McConnell Foundation 415 Madison Ave 10th Fl ... New York NY 10017 212-551-9100 421-9325
Web: www.emcf.org
Colonial Williamsburg Foundation PO Box 1776 ... Williamsburg VA 23187 757-229-1000 220-7259*
**Fax:* Hum Res ■ *TF:* 800-447-8679 ■ *Web:* www.history.org
Commonwealth Fund 1 E 75th St ... New York NY 10021 212-606-3800 606-3500
Web: www.cmwf.org
Conrad N Hilton Foundation 100 W Liberty St Suite 840 ... Reno NV 89501 775-323-4221 323-4150
Web: www.hiltonfoundation.org
Coors Adolph Foundation 4100 E Mississippi Ave Suite 1850 ... Denver CO 80246 303-388-1636 388-1684
Web: www.acoorsfdn.org
Corporation for Public Broadcasting (CPB) 401 9th St NW ... Washington DC 20004 202-879-9600 879-9700
TF: 800-272-2190 ■ *Web:* www.cpb.org
Dave Thomas Foundation for Adoption 4150 Tuller Rd Suite 204 ... Dublin OH 43017 614-764-8454 766-3871
TF: 800-275-3832 ■ *Web:* www.davethomasfoundationforadoption.org
David & Lucile Packard Foundation 300 2nd St ... Los Altos CA 94022 650-948-7658 948-5793
Web: www.packard.org
Davis Arthur Vining Foundations 225 Water St Suite 1510 ... Jacksonville FL 32202 904-359-0670 359-0675
Web: www.avdfdn.org
DeMoss Arthur S Foundation
777 S Flagler Dr Suite 1600-W ... West Palm Beach FL 33401 561-804-9000 804-9025
Dodge Geraldine R Foundation
163 Madison Ave PO Box 1239 ... Morristown NJ 07962 973-540-8442 540-1211
Web: www.grdodge.org
Donald W Reynolds Foundation 1701 Village Ctr Cir ... Las Vegas NV 89134 702-804-6000 804-6099
Web: www.dwreynolds.org
Doris Duke Charitable Foundation 650 5th Ave 19th Fl ... New York NY 10019 212-974-7000 974-7590
Web: fdncenter.org/grantmaker/dorisduke
Dow Herbert H & Grace A Foundation 1018 W Main St ... Midland MI 48640 989-631-3699 631-0675
TF: 800-362-4849 ■ *Web:* www.hhdowfoundation.org
Duke Doris Charitable Foundation 650 5th Ave 19th Fl ... New York NY 10019 212-974-7000 974-7590
Web: fdncenter.org/grantmaker/dorisduke
Duke Endowment 100 N Tryon St Suite 3500 ... Charlotte NC 28202 704-376-0291 376-9336
Web: www.dukeendowment.org
E L Wiegand Foundation 165 W Liberty St Suite 200 Wiegand Ctr ... Reno NV 89501 775-333-0310 333-0314
Eccles Foundation 79 S Main St 12th Fl ... Salt Lake City UT 84111 801-246-5355 350-3510
Web: www.gsecclesfoundation.org
Edna McConnell Clark Foundation 415 Madison Ave 10th Fl ... New York NY 10017 212-551-9100 421-9325
Web: www.emcf.org
Educational Foundation of America 35 Church Ln ... Westport CT 06880 203-226-6498 227-0424
Web: www.efaw.org
Ellison Medical Foundation 4710 Bethesda Ave Suite 204 ... Bethesda MD 20814 301-657-1830 657-1828
Web: www.ellisonfoundation.org
Evelyn & Walter Haas Jr Fund
1 Market St Suite 400 Landmark Bldg ... San Francisco CA 94105 415-856-1400 856-1500
Web: www.haasjr.org
Ewing Marion Kauffman Foundation 4801 Rockhill Rd ... Kansas City MO 64110 816-932-1000 932-1100
TF: 800-489-4900 ■ *Web:* web.kauffman.org
Ford Family Foundation 1600 NW Stewart Pkwy ... Roseburg OR 97470 541-957-5574 957-5720
Web: www.tfff.org

Phone / Fax

Ford Foundation 320 E 43rd St ... New York NY 10017 212-573-5000 351-3677
Web: www.fordfound.org
Gates Bill & Melinda Foundation PO Box 23350 ... Seattle WA 98102 206-709-3100 709-3180
TF: 888-452-6352 ■ *Web:* www.gatesfoundation.org
Gates Family Foundation 3575 Cherry Creek North Dr Suite 100 ... Denver CO 80209 303-722-1881 316-3038
Web: www.gatesfamilyfoundation.org
George S & Dolores Dore Eccles Foundation
79 S Main St 12th Fl ... Salt Lake City UT 84111 801-246-5355 350-3510
Web: www.gsecclesfoundation.org
Geraldine R Dodge Foundation
163 Madison Ave PO Box 1239 ... Morristown NJ 07962 973-540-8442 540-1211
Web: www.grdodge.org
Getty J Paul Trust 1200 Getty Center Dr Suite 403 ... Los Angeles CA 90049 310-440-7340 440-7722
Web: www.getty.edu
Goizueta Foundation 4401 Northside Pkwy Suite 520 ... Atlanta GA 30327 404-239-0390 239-0018
Web: www.goizuetafoundation.org
Goldsmith Horace W Foundation 375 Park Ave Rm 1602 ... New York NY 10152 212-319-8700 319-2881
Guggenheim John Simon Memorial Foundation
90 Park Ave 33rd Fl ... New York NY 10016 212-687-4470 697-3248
Web: www.gf.org
Haas Evelyn & Walter Jr Fund
1 Market St Suite 400 Landmark Bldg ... San Francisco CA 94105 415-856-1400 856-1500
Web: www.haasjr.org
Haas Walter & Elise Fund 1 Lombard St Suite 305 ... San Francisco CA 94111 415-398-4474
Web: www.haassr.org
Hall Family Foundation
2501 McGee St PO Box 419580 MD 323 ... Kansas City MO 64141 816-274-8516 274-8547
Web: www.hallfamilyfoundation.org
Hearst William Randolph Foundation 300 W 57th St 26th Fl ... New York NY 10019 212-586-5404 586-1917
Web: hearstfdn.org
Heinz Vira I Endowment 625 Liberty Ave 30 Dominion Tower ... Pittsburgh PA 15222 412-281-5777 281-5788
Web: www.heinz.org
Henry J Kaiser Family Foundation 2400 Sand Hill Rd ... Menlo Park CA 94025 650-854-9400 854-4800
Web: www.kff.org
Henry Luce Foundation Inc 111 W 50th St Suite 4601 ... New York NY 10020 212-489-7700 581-9541
Web: www.hluce.org
Herbert H & Grace A Dow Foundation 1018 W Main St ... Midland MI 48640 989-631-3699 631-0675
TF: 800-362-4849 ■ *Web:* www.hhdowfoundation.org
Hewlett William & Flora Foundation 2121 Sand Hill Rd ... Menlo Park CA 94025 650-234-4500 234-4501
Web: www.hewlett.org
Hilton Conrad N Foundation 100 W Liberty St Suite 840 ... Reno NV 89501 775-323-4221 323-4150
Web: www.hiltonfoundation.org
Horace W Goldsmith Foundation 375 Park Ave Rm 1602 ... New York NY 10152 212-319-8700 319-2881
Hudson-Webber Foundation 333 W Fort St Suite 1310 ... Detroit MI 48226 313-963-7777 963-2818
Web: www.hudson-webber.org
Irvine James Foundation 575 Market St Suite 3400 ... San Francisco CA 94105 415-777-2244 777-0869
Web: www.irvine.org
J Bulow Campbell Foundation 50 Hurt Plaza Suite 850 ... Atlanta GA 30303 404-658-9066 659-4802
Web: www.jbcf.org
J Paul Getty Trust 1200 Getty Center Dr Suite 403 ... Los Angeles CA 90049 310-440-7340 440-7722
Web: www.getty.edu
JA & Kathryn Albertson Foundation PO Box 70002 ... Boise ID 83707 208-424-2600 424-2626
Web: www.jkaf.org
James Irvine Foundation 575 Market St Suite 3400 ... San Francisco CA 94105 415-777-2244 777-0869
Web: www.irvine.org
JE & LE Mabee Foundation Inc 401 S Boston Ave 30th Fl ... Tulsa OK 74103 918-584-4286 585-5540
Web: www.mabeefoundation.com
John D & Catherine T MacArthur Foundation
140 S Dearborn St Suite 1200 ... Chicago IL 60603 312-726-8000 920-6284*
**Fax:* Hum Res ■ *TF:* 800-662-8004 ■ *Web:* www.macfound.org
John S & James L Knight Foundation
200 S Biscayne Blvd Suite 3300 ... Miami FL 33131 305-908-2600 908-2698
TF: 800-711-2004 ■ *Web:* www.knightfdn.org
John Simon Guggenheim Memorial Foundation
90 Park Ave 33rd Fl ... New York NY 10016 212-687-4470 697-3248
Web: www.gf.org
John Templeton Foundation
300 Conshohocken State Rd Suite 500 ... West Conshohocken PA 19428 610-941-2828 825-1730
Web: www.templeton.org
Johnson Magic Foundation Inc
9100 Wilshire Blvd Suite 700-E ... Beverly Hills CA 90212 310-246-4400 246-1106
TF: 888-624-4205 ■ *Web:* www.magicjohnson.org
Johnson Robert Wood Foundation PO Box 2316 ... Princeton NJ 08543 609-452-8701 627-6701
Web: www.rwjf.org
Joyce Foundation 70 W Madison St Suite 2750 ... Chicago IL 60602 312-782-2464 782-4160
Web: www.joycefdn.org
Kaiser Henry J Family Foundation 2400 Sand Hill Rd ... Menlo Park CA 94025 650-854-9400 854-4800
Web: www.kff.org
Kate B Reynolds Charitable Trust 128 Reynolda Village ... Winston-Salem NC 27106 336-723-1456 723-7765
Web: www.kbr.org
Keck WM Foundation 550 S Hope St Suite 2500 ... Los Angeles CA 90071 213-680-3833
Web: www.wmkeck.org
Kellogg WK Foundation 1 Michigan Ave E ... Battle Creek MI 49017 269-968-1611 968-0413
Web: www.wkkf.org
Kiewit Peter Foundation 8805 Indian Hills Dr Suite 225 ... Omaha NE 68114 402-344-7890 344-8099
Kiwanis International Foundation 3636 Woodview Trace ... Indianapolis IN 46268 317-875-8755 471-8323
TF: 800-549-2647 ■ *Web:* kif.kiwanis.org
Knight John S & James L Foundation
200 S Biscayne Blvd Suite 3300 ... Miami FL 33131 305-908-2600 908-2698
TF: 800-711-2004 ■ *Web:* www.knightfdn.org
Koret Foundation 33 New Montgomery St Suite 1090 ... San Francisco CA 94105 415-882-7740 882-7775
Web: www.koretfoundation.org
Lilly Endowment Inc 2801 N Meridian St ... Indianapolis IN 46208 317-924-5471 926-4431
Web: www.lillyendowment.org
Lois Pope LIFE Foundation 6274 Linton Blvd Suite 103 ... Delray Beach FL 33484 561-865-0955 865-0938
Web: www.life-edu.org
Longwood Foundation Inc 100 W 10th St Suite 1109 ... Wilmington DE 19801 302-654-2477 654-2323
Luce Henry Foundation Inc 111 W 50th St Suite 4601 ... New York NY 10020 212-489-7700 581-9541
Web: www.hluce.org
Lumina Foundation for Education
30 S Meridian St Suite 700 ... Indianapolis IN 46204 317-951-5342 951-5063
TF: 800-834-5756 ■ *Web:* www.luminafoundation.org
Lynde & Harry Bradley Foundation Inc 1241 N Franklin Pl ... Milwaukee WI 53202 414-291-9915 291-9991
Web: www.bradleyfdn.org
Lyndhurst Foundation 517 E 5th St ... Chattanooga TN 37403 423-756-0767 756-0770
Web: www.lyndhurstfoundation.org
Mabee JE & LE Foundation Inc 401 S Boston Ave 30th Fl ... Tulsa OK 74103 918-584-4286 585-5540
Web: www.mabeefoundation.com
MacArthur John D & Catherine T Foundation
140 S Dearborn St Suite 1200 ... Chicago IL 60603 312-726-8000 920-6284*
**Fax:* Hum Res ■ *TF:* 800-662-8004 ■ *Web:* www.macfound.org
Magic Johnson Foundation Inc
9100 Wilshire Blvd Suite 700-E ... Beverly Hills CA 90212 310-246-4400 246-1106
TF: 888-624-4205 ■ *Web:* www.magicjohnson.org
McCormick Robert R Tribune Foundation
435 N Michigan Ave Suite 770 ... Chicago IL 60611 312-222-3512 222-3523
Web: www.mccormicktribune.org

				Phone	Fax
McCune Foundation 6 PPG Pl Suite 750 *Web:* www.mccune.org	Pittsburgh	PA	15222	412-644-8779	644-8059
McKnight Foundation 710 2nd St S Suite 400 *Web:* www.mcknight.org	Minneapolis	MN	55401	612-333-4220	332-3833
Meadows Foundation Inc 3003 Swiss Ave *TF:* 800-826-9431 ■ *Web:* www.mfi.org	Dallas	TX	75204	214-826-9431	827-7042
Mellon Andrew W Foundation 140 E 62nd St *Web:* www.mellon.org	New York	NY	10021	212-838-8400	888-4172
Mellon Richard King Foundation 500 Grant St Suite 4106 *Web:* fdncenter.org/grantmaker/rkmellon	Pittsburgh	PA	15219	412-392-2800	392-2837
Meyer Memorial Trust 425 NW 10th Ave Suite 400 *Web:* www.mmt.org	Portland	OR	97209	503-228-5512	228-5840
Michael J Fox Foundation for Parkinson's Research PO Box 4777 Grand Central Stn *Web:* www.michaeljfox.org	New York	NY	10163	800-708-7644	
Milken Family Foundation 1250 4th St *Web:* www.mff.org	Santa Monica	CA	90401	310-570-4800	570-4801
MJ Murdock Charitable Trust 703 Broadway St Suite 710 *Web:* www.murdock-trust.org	Vancouver	WA	98660	360-694-8415	694-1819
Moody Foundation 2302 Post Office St Suite 704 *TF:* 866-742-1133 ■ *Web:* www.moodyf.org	Galveston	TX	77550	409-763-5333	763-5564
Morris & Gwendolyn Cafritz Foundation 1825 K St NW 14th Fl *Web:* www.cafritzfoundation.org	Washington	DC	20006	202-223-3100	296-7567
Mott Charles Stewart Foundation 503 S Saginaw St Suite 1200 *Web:* www.mott.org	Flint	MI	48502	810-238-5651	766-1753
National Foundation for Cancer Research (NFCR) 4600 East West Hwy Suite 525 *TF:* 800-321-2873 ■ *Web:* www.nfcr.org	Bethesda	MD	20814	301-654-1250	654-5824
Nellie Mae Education Foundation 1250 Hancock St Suite 205N *TF:* 877-635-5436 ■ *Web:* www.nmefdn.org	Quincy	MA	02169	781-348-4200	348-4299
NFCR (National Foundation for Cancer Research) 4600 East West Hwy Suite 525 *TF:* 800-321-2873 ■ *Web:* www.nfcr.org	Bethesda	MD	20814	301-654-1250	654-5824
Open Society Institute 400 W 59th St *Web:* www.soros.org	New York	NY	10019	212-548-0600	548-4679
Packard David & Lucile Foundation 300 2nd St *Web:* www.packard.org	Los Altos	CA	94022	650-948-7658	948-5793
Packard Humanities Institute 300 2nd St *Web:* www.packhum.org	Los Altos	CA	94022	650-948-0150	948-4135
Paul G Allen Family Foundation 505 5th Ave S Suite 900 *Web:* www.pgafamilyfoundation.org	Seattle	WA	98104	206-342-2000	342-3000
Penn William Foundation 100 N 18th St 2 Logan Sq 11th Fl *Web:* www.wpennfdn.org	Philadelphia	PA	19103	215-988-1830	988-1823
Peter Kiewit Foundation 8805 Indian Hills Dr Suite 225	Omaha	NE	68114	402-344-7890	344-8099
Pew Charitable Trusts 2005 Market St 1 Commerce Sq Suite 1700 *TF:* 800-634-4850 ■ *Web:* www.pewtrusts.org	Philadelphia	PA	19103	215-575-9050	575-4939
Pope Lois LIFE Foundation 6274 Linton Blvd Suite 103 *Web:* www.life-edu.org	Delray Beach	FL	33484	561-865-0955	865-0938
Pritzker Foundation 71 S Wacker Dr Suite 47	Chicago	IL	60606	312-750-8400	750-8545
Public Welfare Foundation 1200 U St NW *TF:* 800-275-7934 ■ *Web:* www.publicwelfare.org	Washington	DC	20009	202-965-1800	265-8852
Research Corp 4703 E Camp Lowell Dr Suite 201 *Web:* www.rescorp.org	Tucson	AZ	85712	520-571-1111	571-1119
Retirement Research Foundation 8765 W Higgins Rd Suite 430 *Web:* www.rrf.org	Chicago	IL	60631	773-714-8080	714-8089
Reynolds Donald W Foundation 1701 Village Ctr Cir *Web:* www.dwreynolds.org	Las Vegas	NV	89134	702-804-6000	804-6099
Reynolds Kate B Charitable Trust 128 Reynolda Village *Web:* www.kbr.org	Winston-Salem	NC	27106	336-723-1456	723-7765
Richard King Mellon Foundation 500 Grant St Suite 4106 *Web:* fdncenter.org/grantmaker/rkmellon	Pittsburgh	PA	15219	412-392-2800	392-2837
Richardson Smith Foundation Inc 60 Jesup Rd *Web:* www.srf.org	Westport	CT	06880	203-222-6222	222-6282
Robert A Welch Foundation 5555 San Felipe St Suite 1900 *Web:* www.welch1.org	Houston	TX	77056	713-961-9884	961-5168
Robert R McCormick Tribune Foundation 435 N Michigan Ave Suite 770 *Web:* www.mccormicktribune.org	Chicago	IL	60611	312-222-3512	222-3523
Robert W Woodruff Foundation Inc 50 Hurt Plaza Suite 1200 *Web:* www.woodruff.org	Atlanta	GA	30303	404-522-6755	522-7026
Robert Wood Johnson Foundation PO Box 2316 *Web:* www.rwjf.org	Princeton	NJ	08543	609-452-8701	627-6701
Rockefeller Brothers Fund 437 Madison Ave 37th Fl *Web:* www.rbf.org	New York	NY	10022	212-812-4200	812-4299
Rockefeller Foundation 420 5th Ave **Fax:* Mail Rm ■ *TF:* 800-645-1133 ■ *Web:* www.rockfound.org	New York	NY	10018	212-869-8500	764-3468*
Rosie's For All Kids Foundation Inc PO Box 1001 *Web:* www.forallkids.org	New York	NY	10105	212-703-7388	703-7381
Roy J Carver Charitable Trust 202 Iowa Ave *Web:* www.carvertrust.org	Muscatine	IA	52761	563-263-4010	263-1547
Schwab Charles & Helen Foundation 1650 S Amphlett Blvd Suite 300 *Web:* www.schwabfoundation.org	San Mateo	CA	94402	650-655-2412	655-2411
Skillman Foundation 100 Falon Centre Dr Suite 100 *Web:* www.skillman.org	Detroit	MI	48207	313-393-1185	393-1187
Sloan Alfred P Foundation 630 5th Ave Suite 2550 *Web:* www.sloan.org	New York	NY	10111	212-649-1649	757-5117
Smith Richardson Foundation Inc 60 Jesup Rd *Web:* www.srf.org	Westport	CT	06880	203-222-6222	222-6282
Spencer Foundation 625 N Michigan Ave Suite 1600 *Web:* www.spencer.org	Chicago	IL	60611	312-337-7000	337-0282
Starr Foundation 399 Park Ave 17th Fl *Web:* fdncenter.org/grantmaker/starr	New York	NY	10022	212-909-3600	750-3536
Sunshine Lady Foundation Inc 4900 Randall Pkwy Suite H *TF:* 866-255-7742 ■ *Web:* www.sunshineladyfdn.org	Wilmington	NC	28403	910-397-7742	397-0023
Surdna Foundation Inc 330 Madison Ave 30th Fl *Web:* www.surdna.org	New York	NY	10017	212-557-0010	557-0003
Terra Foundation for American Art 664 N Michigan Ave *Web:* www.terraamericanart.org	Chicago	IL	60611	312-664-3939	664-2052
Thomas Jefferson Foundation PO Box 316 *Web:* www.monticello.org	Charlottesville	VA	22902	434-984-9808	977-7757
Turner Foundation Inc 133 Luckie St 2nd Fl *Web:* www.turnerfoundation.org	Atlanta	GA	30303	404-681-9900	681-0172
Valley Wayne & Gladys Foundation 1939 Harrison St Suite 510	Oakland	CA	94612	510-466-6060	466-6067
Van Andel Institute 333 Bostwick Ave NE *Web:* www.vai.org	Grand Rapids	MI	49503	616-234-5000	234-5001
Vira I Heinz Endowment 625 Liberty Ave 30 Dominion Tower *Web:* www.heinz.org	Pittsburgh	PA	15222	412-281-5777	281-5788
Wallace Foundation 510 Penn Plaza 7th Fl *Web:* www.wallacefoundation.org	New York	NY	10001	212-251-9700	679-6990
Walter & Elise Haas Fund 1 Lombard St Suite 305 *Web:* www.haassr.org	San Francisco	CA	94111	415-398-4474	
Walton Family Foundation Inc PO Box 2030 *Web:* www.wffhome.com	Bentonville	AR	72712	479-464-1570	464-1580
Warren William K Foundation 6585 S Yale Ave Suite 900	Tulsa	OK	74136	918-492-8100	481-7935
Wayne & Gladys Valley Foundation 1939 Harrison St Suite 510	Oakland	CA	94612	510-466-6060	466-6067
Weingart Foundation 1055 W 7th St Suite 3050 *Web:* www.weingartfnd.org	Los Angeles	CA	90017	213-688-7799	688-1515
Welch Robert A Foundation 5555 San Felipe St Suite 1900 *Web:* www.welch1.org	Houston	TX	77056	713-961-9884	961-5168
Whitehall Foundation Inc 380 South County Rd PO Box 3423 *Web:* www.whitehall.org	Palm Beach	FL	33480	561-655-4474	659-4978
Wiegand EL Foundation 165 W Liberty St Suite 200 Wiegand Ctr	Reno	NV	89501	775-333-0310	333-0314
William & Flora Hewlett Foundation 2121 Sand Hill Rd *Web:* www.hewlett.org	Menlo Park	CA	94025	650-234-4500	234-4501
William K Warren Foundation 6585 S Yale Ave Suite 900	Tulsa	OK	74136	918-492-8100	481-7935
William Penn Foundation 100 N 18th St 2 Logan Sq 11th Fl *Web:* www.wpennfdn.org	Philadelphia	PA	19103	215-988-1830	988-1823
William Randolph Hearst Foundation 300 W 57th St 26th Fl *Web:* hearstfdn.org	New York	NY	10019	212-586-5404	586-1917
WK Kellogg Foundation 1 Michigan Ave E *Web:* www.wkkf.org	Battle Creek	MI	49017	269-968-1611	968-0413
WM Keck Foundation 550 S Hope St Suite 2500 *Web:* www.wmkeck.org	Los Angeles	CA	90071	213-680-3833	
Woodruff Robert W Foundation Inc 50 Hurt Plaza Suite 1200 *Web:* www.woodruff.org	Atlanta	GA	30303	404-522-6755	522-7026

309 FOUNDRIES - INVESTMENT

				Phone	Fax
Aero Metals Inc 1201 E Lincoln Way *Web:* www.aerometals.com	La Porte	IN	46350	219-326-1976	326-1972
Bescast Inc 4600 E 355th St *Web:* www.bescast.com	Willoughby	OH	44094	440-946-5300	946-8437
Bimac Corp 3034 Dryden Rd *Web:* www.bimac.com	Dayton	OH	45439	937-299-7333	299-7367
Consolidated Casting Corp 1501 S I-45 *Web:* www.consolicast.com	Hutchins	TX	75141	972-225-7305	225-2970
Dolphin Inc 740 S 59th Ave *Web:* www.dolphincasting.com	Phoenix	AZ	85043	602-272-6747	233-9570
Doncasters Medical Technologies Inc 13963 Fir St PO Box 1990 *Web:* www.doncasters.com	Oregon City	OR	97045	503-656-9653	656-1788
Engineered Precision Casting Co Inc 952 Palmer Ave *Web:* www.epcast.com	Middletown	NJ	07748	732-671-2424	671-8615
Fansteel Intercast Inc 3600 Formosa Ave Suite 13	McAllen	TX	78503	956-688-6406	688-6106
FS Precision Tech Co LLC 3025 E Victoria St *Web:* www.fs-precision.com	Rancho Dominguez	CA	90221	310-638-0595	631-2884
Hitchiner Mfg Co Inc 117 Old Wilton Rd PO Box 2001 *Web:* www.hitchiner.com	Milford	NH	03055	603-673-1100	673-7960
Northern Precision Casting Co 300 Interchange N PO Box 580 *TF:* 800-934-4903 ■ *Web:* www.northernprecision.com	Lake Geneva	WI	53147	262-248-4461	248-1796
PCC Structurals Inc 4600 SE Harney Dr *Web:* www.pcc-structurals.com	Portland	OR	97206	503-777-3881	652-3593
Pennsylvania Precision Cast Parts Inc 521 N 3rd Ave PO Box 1429 *Web:* www.ppcpinc.com	Lebanon	PA	17042	717-273-3338	273-2662
Post Precision Castings Inc 21 Walnut St *Web:* www.postprecision.com	Strausstown	PA	19559	610-488-1011	488-6928
Precision Castparts Corp 4650 SW Macadam Ave Suite 440 *NYSE:* PCP ■ *Web:* www.precast.com	Portland	OR	97239	503-417-4800	417-4817
Precision Metalsmiths Inc 1081 E 200th St *Web:* www.precisionmetalsmiths.com	Cleveland	OH	44117	216-481-8900	481-8903
Precision Technology Inc 551 Old Swede Rd *Web:* www.prectech.com	Douglassville	PA	19518	610-385-6091	385-6959
Remet Corp 210 Commons Rd *TF:* 800-445-2424 ■ *Web:* www.remet.com	Utica	NY	13502	315-797-8700	797-4477
Southern Tool Inc 508 Hamric Dr W PO Box 7610	Oxford	AL	36203	256-831-2811	835-8116
Stainless Foundry & Engineering Inc 5110 N 35th St *Web:* www.stainlessfoundry.com	Milwaukee	WI	53209	414-462-7400	462-7303
Waltek Inc 14310 Sunfish Lake Blvd NW *TF:* 800-937-9496 ■ *Web:* www.waltekinc.com	Ramsey	MN	55303	763-427-3181	427-3216
Wyman-Gordon Co 244 Worcester St *TF:* 800-343-6070 ■ *Web:* www.wyman-gordon.com	North Grafton	MA	01536	508-839-4441	839-7500

310 FOUNDRIES - IRON & STEEL

SEE ALSO Foundries - Nonferrous (Castings) p. 1670

				Phone	Fax
Aarrowcast Inc 2900 E Richmond St *Web:* www.aarrowcast.com	Shawano	WI	54166	715-526-3600	526-9758
Alabama Ductile Castings Co 210 Ann Ave	Brewton	AL	36426	251-867-5481	867-0525
Allegheny Technologies Inc 6 PPG Pl Suite 1000 *NYSE:* ATI ■ **Fax:* Hum Res ■ *TF Sales:* 800-258-3586 ■ *Web:* www.alleghenytechnologies.com	Pittsburgh	PA	15222	412-394-2800	395-2804*
Alloy Engineering & Casting Co 1700 W Washington St *Web:* www.aecco.com	Champaign	IL	61821	217-398-3200	398-3208
American Cast Iron Pipe Co (ACIPCO) 2916 16th St N *TF:* 800-442-2347 ■ *Web:* www.acipco.com	Birmingham	AL	35207	205-325-7701	307-2747
American Drill Bushing Co 7141 Paramount Blvd *TF:* 800-423-4425 ■ *Web:* www.americandrillbushing.com	Pico Rivera	CA	90660	323-725-1515	725-8740
AMSTED Industries Inc 180 N Stetson St Suite 1800 **Fax:* Hum Res ■ *Web:* www.amsted.com	Chicago	IL	60601	312-645-1700	819-8504*
ASF-Keystone Inc 1700 Walnut St *Web:* www.asf-usa.com	Granite City	IL	62040	618-452-2111	452-7115
Atchison Steel Casting & Machine 400 S 4th St *Web:* www.atchisoncasting.com/sub_atchison.asp	Atchison	KS	66002	913-367-2121	367-2130
Atlantic States Cast Iron Pipe Co 183 Sitgreaves St *TF:* 800-859-1161 ■ *Web:* www.atlanticstates.com	Phillipsburg	NJ	08865	908-454-1161	454-1026
Atlas Castings & Technology 3021 S Wilkeson St *Web:* www.atlasfoundry.com	Tacoma	WA	98409	253-475-4600	473-8710
Atlas Foundry Co Inc PO Box 688 *Web:* www.atlasfdry.com	Marion	IN	46952	765-662-2525	662-2902

	City	State	ZIP	Phone	Fax
Badger Foundry Co 1058 E Mark St	Winona	MN	55987	507-452-5760	452-6469
Web: www.badgerfoundry.com					
Baker Mfg Co 133 Enterprise St	Evansville	WI	53536	608-882-5100	882-6776
Web: www.bakermfg.com					
Bay Cast Inc PO Box 126	Bay City	MI	48707	989-892-0511	892-0599
Web: www.baycastinc.com					
Benton Foundry Inc 5297 SR 487	Benton	PA	17814	570-925-6711	925-6929
Web: www.bentonfoundry.com					
Bentonville Casting Co PO Box 1109	Bentonville	AR	72712	479-273-7723	273-0770
Blackhawk Foundry & Machine Co 323 S Clark St	Davenport	IA	52802	563-323-3621	323-2105
Bremen Castings Inc 500 N Baltimore St	Bremen	IN	46506	574-546-2411	546-5016
TF: 800-837-2411 ■ *Web:* www.bremencastings.com					
Buck Co Inc 897 Lancaster Pike	Quarryville	PA	17566	717-284-4114	284-3737
Web: www.buckcompany.com					
Burnham Foundry LLC 2345 Licking Rd	Zanesville	OH	43701	740-452-9371	450-8081
Web: www.burnhamfoundry.com					
Campbell Foundry Co 800 Bergen St	Harrison	NJ	07029	973-483-5480	483-1843
TF: 800-843-4766 ■ *Web:* www.campbellfoundry.com					
Canada Alloy Casting Co 529 Manitou Dr	Kitchener	ON	N2C1S2	519-895-1161	895-1169
Web: www.cac.ca					
Cast-Fab Technologies Inc 3040 Forrer St	Cincinnati	OH	45209	513-758-1000	758-1002
Web: www.cast-fab.com					
Castalloy Inc 1701 Industrial Ln	Waukesha	WI	53189	262-547-0070	547-2215
TF: 800-211-0900 ■ *Web:* www.castalloycpg.com					
Casting Service 300 Philadelphia St	La Porte	IN	46350	219-362-1000	362-0119
Web: www.castingservice.com					
Citation Corp 2700 Corporate Dr Suite 100	Birmingham	AL	35242	205-871-5731	870-8211
Web: www.citation.net					
Clow Water Systems Co 2266 S 6th St	Coshocton	OH	43812	740-622-6651	622-8551
Web: www.clowwatersystems.com					
Columbia Steel Casting Co Inc PO Box 83095	Portland	OR	97283	503-286-0685	286-1743
TF: 800-547-9471 ■ *Web:* www.columbiasteel.com					
Columbus Foundries Inc 1600 Northside Industrial Blvd	Columbus	GA	31904	706-323-5221	596-2224
Columbus Steel Castings Co 2211 Parsons Ave	Columbus	OH	43207	614-444-2121	445-2125
Web: www.columbussteel.com					
Dalton Corp PO Box 230	Warsaw	IN	46581	574-267-8111	371-5299
Web: www.daltonfoundries.com					
Delta Centrifugal Corp 3402 Center St PO Box 1043	Temple	TX	76503	254-773-9055	773-8988
TF Sales: 800-433-3100 ■ *Web:* www.deltacentrifugal.com					
Didion & Sons Foundry Co 4894 N Service Rd	Saint Peters	MO	63376	636-928-1130	447-8640
Web: www.didionfoundry.com					
Donsco Inc PO Box 2001	Wrightsville	PA	17368	717-252-1561	252-4530
Web: www.donsco.com					
Dotson Co Inc 200 W Rock St	Mankato	MN	56001	507-345-5018	345-1270
Web: www.dotson.com					
Duraloy Technologies Inc 120 Bridge St	Scottdale	PA	15683	724-887-5100	887-5224*
**Fax:* Sales ■ *TF:* 800-823-5101 ■ *Web:* www.duraloy.com					
Eagle Foundry Co Inc PO Box 250	Eagle Creek	OR	97022	503-637-3048	637-3091
Web: www.eaglefoundryco.com					
East Jordan Iron Works Inc 301 Spring St	East Jordan	MI	49727	231-536-2261	536-4458
TF: 800-874-4100 ■ *Web:* www.ejiw.com					
Elyria Foundry Co 120 Filbert St	Elyria	OH	44036	440-322-4657	323-1101
Web: www.elyriafoundry.com					
Eureka Foundry Co 1601 Carter St	Chattanooga	TN	37402	423-267-3328	756-2607
Web: www.eurekafoundryco.com					
Farrar Corp 142 W Burns St	Norwich	KS	67118	620-478-2212	478-2200
Web: www.farrarusa.com					
Frazier & Frazier Industries Inc 817 S 1st St	Coolidge	TX	76635	254-786-2293	786-2284
Web: ffcastings.com					
Gartland Foundry Co Inc PO Box 1564	Terre Haute	IN	47808	812-232-0226	232-7569
TF: 800-237-0226 ■ *Web:* www.gartlandfoundry.com					
Goldens' Foundry & Machine Co 600 12th St	Columbus	GA	31901	706-323-0471	596-2850
TF: 800-328-8379 ■ *Web:* www.gfmco.com					
Great Lakes Castings Corp 800 N Washington Ave	Ludington	MI	49431	231-843-2501	845-1534
Web: www.glccadv.com					
Grede Foundries Inc 9898 W Bluemound Rd	Milwaukee	WI	53226	414-257-3600	256-9399*
**Fax:* Sales ■ *Web:* www.grede.com					
Grede Vassar Foundries 700 E Huron Ave	Vassar	MI	48768	989-823-8411	823-7400
Gregg Industries Inc 10460 Hickson St	El Monte	CA	91731	626-575-7664	401-0971
Web: www.greggind.com					
Harrison Steel Castings Co Inc 900 S Mound St	Attica	IN	47918	765-762-2481	762-2487
Web: www.hscast.com					
Hensley Industries Inc 2108 Joe Field Rd PO Box 29779	Dallas	TX	75229	972-241-2321	241-0915*
**Fax:* Cust Svc ■ *TF:* 888-406-6262 ■ *Web:* www.hensleyind.com					
Hunt Rodney Co Inc 46 Mill St	Orange	MA	01364	978-544-2511	544-7204
TF: 800-448-8860 ■ *Web:* www.rodneyhunt.com					
Huron Casting Inc 7050 Hartley St PO Box 679	Pigeon	MI	48755	989-453-3933	453-3319
Web: www.huroncasting.com					
Intermet Corp 700 Tower Dr 4th Fl	Troy	MI	48098	248-952-2500	952-2501
Web: www.intermet.com					
Interstate Castings Co 3823 Massachusetts Ave	Indianapolis	IN	46218	317-546-2427	546-4004
Web: www.interstatecastings.com					
Jencast 1004 W 14th	Coffeyville	KS	67337	620-251-7802	251-3622
TF: 800-796-6630 ■ *Web:* www.jencast.com					
Johnson Brass & Machine Foundry Inc 270 N Mill St	Saukville	WI	53080	262-377-9440	284-7066
Web: www.johnsonbrass.com					
Johnstown Specialty Castings Inc 545 Central Ave	Johnstown	PA	15902	814-535-9000	536-0868*
**Fax:* Sales					
KP Iron Foundry Inc 4731 E Vine Ave	Fresno	CA	93725	559-233-2591	233-8094
TF: 800-655-2590					
Lodge Mfg Co 204 E 5th St	South Pittsburg	TN	37380	423-837-7181	837-8279
Web: www.lodgemfg.com					
Lufkin Industries Inc 601 S Raguet St	Lufkin	TX	75902	936-634-2211	637-5474
NASDAQ: LUFK ■ *Web:* www.lufkin.com					
Mabry Castings 6531 Industrial Rd	Beaumont	TX	77705	409-842-2223	842-2894
Web: www.iron-casting.com					
Maddox Foundry & Machine Works Inc 13370 SW 170th St	Archer	FL	32618	352-495-2121	495-3962
TF: 800-347-0789 ■ *Web:* www.maddoxfoundry.com					
Maynard Steel Casting Co 2856 S 27th St	Milwaukee	WI	53215	414-645-0440	645-7378
Web: www.maynardsteel.com					
McWane Cast Iron Pipe Co 1201 Vanderbilt Rd	Birmingham	AL	35234	205-322-3521	324-7250*
**Fax:* Sales					
McWane Inc 2900 Hwy 280 Suite 300	Birmingham	AL	35223	205-414-3100	414-3170
Web: www.mcwane.com					
ME Global 3901 University Ave NE	Minneapolis	MN	55421	763-788-1651	788-2874
TF: 800-328-3858 ■ *Web:* www.meglobal.com					
Milwaukee Malleable & Grey Iron Works PO Box 2039	Milwaukee	WI	53201	414-645-0200	645-2892
Minnotte Corp Minnotte Sq	Pittsburgh	PA	15220	412-922-2963	922-1244
TF: 800-809-7068 ■ *Web:* www.minnotte.com					
Motor Castings Co 1323 S 65th St	Milwaukee	WI	53214	414-476-1434	476-2845
Web: www.motorcastings.com					
Neenah Foundry Co 2121 Brooks Ave	Neenah	WI	54956	920-725-7000	729-3661
TF: 800-558-5075 ■ *Web:* www.nfco.com					
Northern Iron & Machine 867 Forest St	Saint Paul	MN	55106	651-778-3300	778-1321
Web: www.northernim.com					
Omaha Steel Castings Co 4601 Farnam St	Omaha	NE	68106	402-558-6000	558-0327
Web: www.omahasteel.com					
Osco Industries Inc PO Box 1388	Portsmouth	OH	45662	740-354-3183	353-1504
Web: www.oscoind.com					
Pacific States Cast Iron Pipe Co 2550 S Industrial Pkwy PO Box 1219	Provo	UT	84606	801-373-6910	377-0338*
**Fax:* Sales ■ *Web:* www.pscipco.com					
Pacific Steel Casting Co Inc 1333 2nd St	Berkeley	CA	94710	510-525-9200	524-4673
Web: www.pacificsteel.com					
Paxton-Mitchell Co 2614 Martha St	Omaha	NE	68105	402-345-6767	345-6772
Web: www.paxton-mitchell.com					
Prospect Foundry Inc 1225 Winter St NE	Minneapolis	MN	55413	612-331-9282	331-4122
Web: www.prospectfoundry.com					
Quaker City Castings Inc 310 Euclid St	Salem	OH	44460	330-332-1566	332-1159
Web: www.qccast.com					
Quality Castings Co 1200 N Main St	Orrville	OH	44667	330-682-6010	683-3153
Web: www.qcfoundry.com					
Robinson Foundry Inc 505 Robinson Ct	Alexander City	AL	35010	256-329-8481	329-0503
Web: www.robinsonfoundry.com					
Rodney Hunt Co Inc 46 Mill St	Orange	MA	01364	978-544-2511	544-7204
TF: 800-448-8860 ■ *Web:* www.rodneyhunt.com					
Sawbrook Steel Castings Co 425 Shepherd Ave	Cincinnati	OH	45215	513-554-1700	554-0092
Web: www.sawbrooksteel.com					
Signa Corp Hwy 22 W	Alexander City	AL	35010	256-234-2514	234-4956
TF: 800-824-4513					
Sioux City Foundry Co 801 Division St	Sioux City	IA	51102	712-252-4181	252-4197
TF: 800-831-0874 ■ *Web:* www.siouxcityfoundry.com					
Sivyer Steel Corp 225 S 33rd St	Bettendorf	IA	52722	563-355-1811	355-3946
TF: 800-474-8937 ■ *Web:* www.sivyersteel.com					
Smith Foundry Co 1855 E 28th St	Minneapolis	MN	55407	612-729-9395	725-2519
Web: www.smithfoundry.com					
Southern Tool Inc 508 Hamric Dr W PO Box 7610	Oxford	AL	36203	256-831-2811	835-8116
Spokane Steel Foundry Co 3808 N Sullivan Rd Bldg 1	Spokane	WA	99216	509-924-0440	924-9448
TF: 800-541-3601 ■ *Web:* www.spokaneindustries.com/steelfoundry					
Standard Alloys & Mfg PO Box 969	Port Arthur	TX	77640	409-983-3201	983-7837
TF: 800-231-8240 ■ *Web:* www.standardalloys.com					
T & B Foundry Co 2469 E 71st St	Cleveland	OH	44104	216-391-4200	391-4206
Talladega Castings & Machine Co Inc 228 N Court St	Talladega	AL	35160	256-362-5550	362-1321
TF: 800-766-6708 ■ *Web:* www.tmsco.com					
Talladega Machinery & Supply Co Inc 301 N Johnson Ave PO Box 736	Talladega	AL	35161	256-362-4124	761-2565
TF Cust Svc: 800-289-8672 ■ *Web:* www.tmsco.com					
Taylor & Fenn Co 22 Deerfield Rd	Windsor	CT	06095	860-249-7531	525-2961
Web: www.taylorfenn.com					
ThyssenKrupp Budd Co 3155 W Big Beaver Rd PO Box 2601	Troy	MI	48007	248-643-3500	643-3593
Web: www.buddcompany.com					
Thyssenkrupp Waupaca Inc 1955 Brunner Dr	Waupaca	WI	54981	715-258-6611	258-9268
Web: www.waupacafoundry.com					
Tyler Pipe Co 11910 CR 492	Tyler	TX	75706	903-882-5511	882-2522
TF: 800-527-8478 ■ *Web:* www.tylerpipe.com					
Unicast Co 241 N Washington St	Boyertown	PA	19512	610-367-0155	367-2787
Web: www.unicastco.com					
Union Electric Steel Corp 726 Bell Ave	Carnegie	PA	15106	412-429-7655	276-1711
Web: www.uniones.com					
Urick Foundry Co 1501 Cherry St	Erie	PA	16502	814-454-2461	454-1397
Web: www.urickfoundry.com					
US Pipe & Foundry Co 3300 1st Ave N	Birmingham	AL	35222	205-254-7000	254-7149
Web: www.uspipe.com					
Wabtec Foundry 40 Mason St	Wallaceburg	ON	N8A4M1	519-627-3314	627-1768
Walker Machine & Foundry Corp PO Box 4587	Roanoke	VA	24015	540-344-6265	342-2278
Web: www.walkerfoundry.com					
Waukesha Foundry Co Inc 1300 Lincoln Ave	Waukesha	WI	53186	262-542-0741	549-8440*
**Fax:* Sales ■ *TF:* 800-727-0741 ■ *Web:* www.waukeshafoundry.com					
Wells Mfg Co 2100 W Lake Shore Dr	Woodstock	IL	60098	815-338-3900	338-3950
TF: 800-227-6455 ■ *Web:* www.wellsmanufacturing.com					
Willman Industries Inc 338 S Main St	Cedar Grove	WI	53013	920-668-8526	668-8998
Web: www.willmanind.com					
Wollaston Alloys Inc 205 Wood Rd	Braintree	MA	02184	781-848-3333	848-3993
Web: www.wollastonalloys.com					
Zurn Cast Metals Operation 1301 Raspberry St	Erie	PA	16502	814-455-0921	456-2754
TF: 877-875-1404 ■ *Web:* www.zurn.com					

311 FOUNDRIES - NONFERROUS (CASTINGS)

SEE ALSO Foundries - Iron & Steel p. 1669

	City	State	ZIP	Phone	Fax
Ace Precision Castings LLC 610 S 12th Ave PO Box 657	Marshalltown	IA	50158	641-753-5566	753-0150
Web: www.aceprecisioncastings.com					
Advance Die Casting Co 3760 N Holton St	Milwaukee	WI	53212	414-964-0284	963-6088
Ahresty Wilmington Corp 2627 S South St	Wilmington	OH	45177	937-382-6112	382-5871
Web: www.ahresty.com					
Akron Foundry Co 2728 Wingate Ave	Akron	OH	44314	330-745-3101	745-7999
Web: www.akronfoundry.com					
Alloy Die Casting Co 6550 Caballero Blvd	Buena Park	CA	90620	714-521-9800	521-5510*
**Fax:* Sales ■ *Web:* www.alloydie.com					
Arrow Acme Inc PO Box 218	Webster City	IA	50595	515-832-3120	832-3145
Arrow Pattern & Foundry Co 9725 Industrial Dr	Bridgeview	IL	60455	708-598-0300	598-0310
Web: www.arrowpattern.com					
Atchison Steel Casting & Machine 400 S 4th St	Atchison	KS	66002	913-367-2121	367-2130
Web: www.atchisoncasting.com/sub_atchison.asp					
Aurora Metals Divison LLC 1995 Greenfield Ave	Montgomery	IL	60538	630-844-4900	844-6839
Web: www.aurorametals.com					
Bardane Mfg PO Box 70	Jermyn	PA	18433	570-876-4844	876-1938
Web: www.bardane.com					
Basic Aluminum Castings Co 1325 E 168th St	Cleveland	OH	44110	216-481-5606	481-7031
Web: www.basicaluminum.com					
Blaser Die Casting Co 5700 3rd Ave S	Seattle	WA	98108	206-767-7800	767-7055
Web: www.blaser-die.com					
Blue Ridge Pressure Casting Inc PO Box 208	Lehighton	PA	18235	610-377-2510	377-5066
Bodine Aluminum Inc 2100 Walton Rd	Saint Louis	MO	63114	314-423-8200	423-0318
Web: www.bodinealuminum.com					
Brillcast Inc 3400 Wentworth Dr SW	Grand Rapids	MI	49519	616-534-4977	534-0880
Web: www.brillcast.com					
Buck Co Inc 897 Lancaster Pike	Quarryville	PA	17566	717-284-4114	284-3737
Web: www.buckcompany.com					
Buddy Bar Casting Corp 10801 S Sessler St	South Gate	CA	90280	562-861-9664	861-9323
Bunting Bearings Corp 1001 Holland Park Blvd	Holland	OH	43528	419-866-7000	866-0653
TF: 888-228-9899 ■ *Web:* www.buntingbearings.com					
C & H Die Casting Inc PO Box 1170	Temple	TX	76503	254-938-2541	938-7117
TF: 800-433-3148 ■ *Web:* www.chdiecasting.com					

Company	City	State	Zip	Phone	Fax
Cambridge Tool & Mfg Co Inc 67 Faulkner St *TF:* 888-333-9798 ■ *Web:* www.cambridgetool.com	North Billerica	MA	01862	978-667-8400	667-4104
Cast-Rite Corp 515 E Airline Way *Web:* www.cast-rite.com	Gardena	CA	90248	310-532-2080	532-0605
Cast Technologies Inc 1100 SW Washington St	Peoria	IL	61602	309-676-2157	676-2167
Chicago White Metal Casting Inc 649 N Rt 83 *Web:* www.cwmdiecast.com	Bensenville	IL	60106	630-595-4424	595-4474
Citation Corp 2700 Corporate Dr Suite 100 *Web:* www.citation.net	Birmingham	AL	35242	205-871-5731	870-8211
Consolidated Foundries Inc 8333 Wilcox Ave *Web:* www.cfi-pac.com	Cudahy	CA	90201	323-773-2363	562-3174
Consolidated Metco Inc 13940 N Rivergate Blvd **Fax:* Sales ■ *TF Sales:* 800-547-9473 ■ *Web:* www.conmet.com	Portland	OR	97203	503-286-5741	240-5488*
Deco Products Co 506 Sanford St *TF:* 800-327-9751 ■ *Web:* www.decoprod.com	Decorah	IA	52101	563-382-4264	382-9845
Del Mar Die Casting Co 12901 S Western Ave **Fax Area Code:* 310 ■ *TF:* 800-624-7468 ■ *Web:* www.delmardiecasting.com	Gardena	CA	90249	323-321-0600	327-1951*
Delta Centrifugal Corp 3402 Center St PO Box 1043 *TF Sales:* 800-433-3100 ■ *Web:* www.deltacentrifugal.com	Temple	TX	76503	254-773-9055	773-8988
Denison Industries 22 Fielder Dr *Web:* www.denisonindustries.com	Denison	TX	75020	903-786-4444	786-6570
Dynacast Inc 7810 Ballantyne Commons Pkwy Suite 200 *TF:* 800-811-7839 ■ *Web:* www.dynacast.com	Charlotte	NC	28277	704-927-2790	927-2791
Eck Industries Inc 1602 N 8th St PO Box 967 *Web:* www.eckindustries.com	Manitowoc	WI	54221	920-682-4618	682-9298
Electric Materials Co 50 S Washington St *TF:* 800-356-2211 ■ *Web:* www.elecmat.com	North East	PA	16428	814-725-9621	725-3620
Empire Die Casting Co Inc 635 Highland Rd E *Web:* www.empiredie.com	Macedonia	OH	44056	330-467-0750	908-3052
Falcon Foundry Co 96 6th St *TF:* 800-253-8624 ■ *Web:* www.falconfoundry.com	Lowellville	OH	44436	330-536-6221	536-6371
Fall River Group 670 S Main St	Fall River	WI	53932	920-484-3311	484-2233
Fansteel Inc 570 Lake Cook Rd Suite 200 *Web:* www.fansteel.com	Deerfield	IL	60015	847-689-4900	689-0307
Fansteel/Wellman Dynamics Corp 1746 Commerce Rd	Creston	IA	50801	641-782-8521	782-7672
Foundry Systems International 5159 S Prospect St *Web:* www.fsigroup.com	Ravenna	OH	44266	330-296-9053	296-1921
Gamco Products Co 1105 5th St PO Box 318	Henderson	KY	42419	270-826-9573	826-8982
General Die Casters Inc 2150 Highland Rd *TF:* 800-332-2278 ■ *Web:* www.generaldie.com	Twinsburg	OH	44087	330-657-2300	657-2192
Gibbs Die Casting Corp 369 Community Dr *Web:* www.gibbsdc.com	Henderson	KY	42420	270-827-1801	827-7840
H-J Enterprises Inc 3010 High Ridge Blvd *Web:* www.h-jenterprises.com	High Ridge	MO	63049	636-677-3421	376-1915
Halex Co 23901 Aurora Rd *TF:* 800-749-3261 ■ *Web:* www.halexco.com	Bedford Heights	OH	44146	440-439-1616	439-1792
Harmony Castings LLC 251 Perry Hwy *Web:* www.harmonycastings.com	Harmony	PA	16037	724-452-5811	452-0118
Heick Die Casting Corp 6550 W Diversey Ave *Web:* www.heick.com	Chicago	IL	60707	773-637-1100	637-1101
Hoffmann Die Cast Corp 229 Kerth St *Web:* www.hoffmanndc.com	Saint Joseph	MI	49085	269-983-1102	983-2928
Howmet Castings 1 Misco Dr *Web:* www.alcoa.com/howmet	Whitehall	MI	49461	231-894-5686	894-7607
ICG Castings Inc 101 Poplar St *Web:* www.icgcastings.com	Dowagiac	MI	49047	269-782-2108	783-3104
Imperial Die Casting Co 2249 Old Liberty Rd *Web:* www.rcmindustries.com/imperial.html	Liberty	SC	29657	864-859-0202	855-1597
Intermet Corp 700 Tower Dr 4th Fl *Web:* www.intermet.com	Troy	MI	48098	248-952-2500	952-2501
Johnson Brass & Machine Foundry Inc 270 N Mill St *Web:* www.johnsonbrass.com	Saukville	WI	53080	262-377-9440	284-7066
Ken-Dec Inc 1145 S Dixie Hwy PO Box 129	Horse Cave	KY	42749	270-786-2111	786-3133
Kennedy Die Castings Inc 15 Coppage Dr *Web:* www.kennedydc.com	Worcester	MA	01603	508-791-5594	791-6338
Kitchen-Quip Inc PO Box 548 *Web:* www.kqcasting.com	Waterloo	IN	46793	260-837-8311	837-7919
Lansco Die Casting Inc 711 S Stimson Ave *Web:* www.lanscodiecasting.com	City of Industry	CA	91745	626-961-3441	369-7129
Lee Brass Co 1800 Golden Springs Dr *TF:* 800-876-1811 ■ *Web:* www.leebrass.com	Anniston	AL	36207	256-831-2501	831-8380
Littlestown Foundry Inc 150 Charles St PO Box 69 *TF:* 800-471-0844 ■ *Web:* www.littlestownfoundry.com	Littlestown	PA	17340	717-359-4141	359-5010
Madison-Kipp Corp 201 Waubesa St **Fax:* Mktg ■ *Web:* www.madison-kipp.com	Madison	WI	53704	608-244-3511	242-5284*
Madison Precision Products Inc 94 E 400 North *Web:* www.madisonprecision.com	Madison	IN	47250	812-273-4702	273-2451
Magnolia Metal Corp 6161 Abbott Dr *TF:* 800-228-4043 ■ *Web:* www.magnoliabronze.com	Omaha	NE	68119	402-455-8760	455-8762
Martin Brass Foundry Inc 2341 Jefferson St **Fax Area Code:* 310 ■ *Web:* www.martinbrass.com	Torrance	CA	90501	323-775-3803	320-4971*
Matthews International Corp 2 Northshore Ctr Suite 200 *NASDAQ: MATW* ■ *TF:* 800-223-4964 ■ *Web:* www.matthewsinternational.com	Pittsburgh	PA	15212	412-442-8200	442-8291
Matthews International Corp Bronze Div 1315 W Liberty Ave *TF:* 888-838-8890 ■ *Web:* www.matthewsbronze.com	Pittsburgh	PA	15226	412-571-5500	571-5514
Minnotte Corp Minnotte Sq *TF:* 800-809-7068 ■ *Web:* www.minnotte.com	Pittsburgh	PA	15220	412-922-2963	922-1244
New Products Corp 448 North Shore Dr	Benton Harbor	MI	49022	269-925-2161	925-5184
NGK Metals Corp 917 US Hwy 11 S **Fax Area Code:* 877 ■ *TF Sales:* 800-523-8268 ■ *Web:* www.ngkmetals.com	Sweetwater	TN	37874	423-337-5500	645-2328*
Ohio Aluminum Industries Inc 4840 Warner Rd *Web:* www.fsigroup.com/ohioalum.htm	Garfield Heights	OH	44125	216-641-8865	641-8847
Ohio Decorative Products Inc 220 S Elizabeth St *Web:* www.ohiodec.com	Spencerville	OH	45887	419-647-4191	647-4202
Pace Industries Inc PO Box 1198 *Web:* www.legalumimum.com/harrison	Harrison	AR	72601	870-741-8255	741-4998
Pacific Die Casting Corp 6155 S Eastern Ave *Web:* www.pacdiecast.com	Commerce	CA	90040	323-725-1332	728-1115
Park-Ohio Holdings Corp 23000 Euclid Ave *NASDAQ: PKOH* ■ *Web:* www.pkoh.com	Cleveland	OH	44117	216-692-7200	692-7174
PHB Inc 7900 W Ridge Rd *Web:* www.phbcorp.com	Fairview	PA	16415	814-474-5511	474-2063
Piad Precision Casting Corp 161 Devereux Dr *TF:* 800-441-9858 ■ *Web:* www.piad.com	Greensburg	PA	15601	724-838-5500	838-5520
Premier Die Casting Co 1177 Rahway Ave *TF:* 800-394-3006 ■ *Web:* www.diecasting.com	Avenel	NJ	07001	732-634-3000	634-0590
Premier Tool & Die Cast Corp 9886 N Tudor Rd *TF:* 800-417-8717 ■ *Web:* www.premierdiecast.com	Berrien Springs	MI	49103	269-471-7715	471-3855
Presto Casting Co 5401 Luke Ave	Glendale	AZ	85301	623-939-9441	934-7062
Progress Casting Group Inc 2600 Niagara Ln N *TF:* 800-866-3025 ■ *Web:* www.progresscasting.com	Plymouth	MN	55447	763-557-1000	557-0320
Quad City Die Casting Co 3800 River Dr *Web:* www.quadcitydiecasting.com	Moline	IL	61265	309-762-7346	762-3134
Ravenna Aluminum Foundries 5159 S Prospect St *Web:* www.fsigroup.com/ravenna.htm	Ravenna	OH	44266	330-296-9053	296-1921
Reliable Castings Corp 3530 Spring Grove Ave *Web:* www.reliablecastings.com	Cincinnati	OH	45223	513-541-2627	541-5696
Ridco Casting Co 6 Beverage Hill Ave *Web:* www.ridco.com	Pawtucket	RI	02860	401-724-0400	724-6320
Robinson Foundry Inc 505 Robinson Ct *Web:* www.robinsonfoundry.com	Alexander City	AL	35010	256-329-8481	329-0503
Ross Aluminum Foundries 815 N Oak Ave *Web:* www.rossal.com	Sidney	OH	45365	937-492-4134	498-1883
Saint Clair Die Casting LLC 225 St Clair Industrial Park Dr *TF:* 800-367-7232 ■ *Web:* www.stclairdiecasting.com	Saint Clair	MO	63077	636-629-2550	629-0594
Southern Centrifugal Inc 4180 S Creek Rd *TF:* 800-722-7277 ■ *Web:* www.metaltekint.com/Southern	Chattanooga	TN	37406	423-622-4131	622-2227
Southern Tool Inc 508 Hamric Dr W PO Box 7610	Oxford	AL	36203	256-831-2811	835-8116
Stroh Die Casting Co Inc 11123 W Burleigh St *TF Cust Svc:* 800-843-2871 ■ *Web:* www.stroh.com	Milwaukee	WI	53222	414-771-7100	771-1329
Talladega Castings & Machine Co Inc 228 N Court St *TF:* 800-766-6708 ■ *Web:* www.tmsco.com	Talladega	AL	35160	256-362-5550	362-1321
Techni-Cast Corp 11220 Garfield Ave **Fax:* Sales ■ *TF:* 800-923-4585 ■ *Web:* www.techni-cast.com	South Gate	CA	90280	562-923-4585	861-4259*
Texas Die Casting Inc 600 S Loop 485 *Web:* www.texasdiecasting.com	Gladewater	TX	75647	903-845-2224	845-6155
ThyssenKrupp Stahl Co 11 E Pacific PO Box 6 *TF:* 888-395-1042 ■ *Web:* www.stahlspecialty.com	Kingsville	MO	64061	816-597-3322	597-3485
Top Die Casting Co 13910 Dearborn Ave *Web:* www.topdie.com	South Beloit	IL	61080	815-389-2599	389-3057
Travis Pattern & Foundry Inc 1413 E Hawthorne Rd *Web:* www.pduinc.com	Spokane	WA	99218	509-466-3545	467-6465
Twin City Die Castings Co 1070 33rd Ave SE *Web:* www.tcdcinc.com	Minneapolis	MN	55414	651-645-3611	644-5280
Virginia Metalcrafters Inc 1010 E Main St *Web:* www.virginiametalcrafters.com	Waynesboro	VA	22980	540-949-9400	949-9446
Walker Die Casting Inc 1125 Higgs Rd PO Box 1189	Lewisburg	TN	37091	931-359-6206	359-9703
Ward Aluminum Casting Co 642 Growth Ave *TF:* 866-427-8700 ■ *Web:* www.wardcorp.com	Fort Wayne	IN	46808	260-426-8700	420-1919
Watry Industries Inc 3312 Lakeshore Dr *Web:* www.watry.com	Sheboygan	WI	53081	920-457-4886	457-5241
Wisconsin Aluminum Foundry Co Inc 838 S 16th St *Web:* www.wafco.com	Manitowoc	WI	54220	920-682-8286	682-7285
Wollaston Alloys Inc 205 Wood Rd *Web:* www.wollastonalloys.com	Braintree	MA	02184	781-848-3333	848-3993
Wolverine Bronze Co 28178 Hayes Rd **Fax:* Sales ■ *Web:* www.wolverinebronze.com	Roseville	MI	48066	586-776-8180	776-4510*
Yoder Die Casting Corp 727 Kiser St *Web:* www.yoderdiecasting.com	Dayton	OH	45404	937-222-6734	222-6805
Yoder Industries Inc 2520 Needmore Rd *Web:* www.yoderindustries.com	Dayton	OH	45414	937-278-5769	278-6321

312 FRAMES & MOULDINGS

Company	City	State	Zip	Phone	Fax
Alexander Moulding Mill Co Hwy 281 S	Hamilton	TX	76531	254-386-3187	386-3675
Alexandria Moulding 20352 Powerdam Rd *TF:* 866-377-2539 ■ *Web:* www.alexmo.com	Alexandria	ON	K0C1A0	613-525-2784	525-4677
Art-O-Rama Inc 560 S 3rd Ave *TF:* 800-421-2438	Mount Vernon	NY	10550	914-662-2961	662-2966
Best Moulding Corp 100 Alameda Rd NW *Web:* www.bestmoulding.com	Albuquerque	NM	87114	505-898-6770	898-1301
Contact Lumber Co 9200 SE Sunnybrook Blvd Suite 200 *TF:* 800-547-1038 ■ *Web:* www.contactlumber.com	Clackamas	OR	97015	503-228-7361	221-1340
Dallas Wood Craft Inc 2829 Sea Harbor Rd	Dallas	TX	75212	214-631-2782	905-1029
Groovfold Inc 1050 W State St *TF:* 800-367-1133 ■ *Web:* www.groovfold.com	Newcomerstown	OH	43832	740-498-8363	498-8782
Homeshield Colonial Craft 2270 Woodale Dr *TF:* 800-727-5187 ■ *Web:* www.home-shield.com	Mounds View	MN	55112	763-231-4000	783-7218
Kendall-Hartcraft 1480 Independence Ave PO Box 270465 *TF:* 800-558-7834 ■ *Web:* www.kendallhartcraft.com	Hartford	WI	53027	262-673-3440	673-3052
Kendall-Hartcraft Inc 334 Dan Tibbs Rd **Fax Area Code:* 888 ■ *TF:* 800-421-7435 ■ *Web:* www.kendallhartcraft.com	Huntsville	AL	35806	256-859-5533	545-0398*
Larson-Juhl 3900 Steve Reynolds Blvd **Fax:* Hum Res ■ *TF:* 800-438-5031 ■ *Web:* www.larsonjuhl.com	Norcross	GA	30093	770-279-5200	279-5297*
Lasercraft Inc 1 Thorndale Dr Suite 268	San Rafael	CA	94903	415-472-8388	472-8389
Monarch Industries Inc 99 Main St **Fax:* Sales ■ *TF:* 800-669-9663 ■ *Web:* www.monarchinc.com	Warren	RI	02885	401-247-5200	247-5601*
Muench Woodwork Co Inc 2701 Jackson Ave *Web:* www.muenchwoodwork.com	South Chicago Heights	IL	60411	708-754-2108	754-5562
Nordic Interior Inc 56-01 Maspeth Ave *TF:* 800-464-0066	Maspeth	NY	11378	718-456-7000	456-9340
North American Enclosures Inc 65 Jetson Ln *TF:* 800-645-9209 ■ *Web:* www.naeframes.com	Central Islip	NY	11722	631-234-9500	234-9504
PB & H Moulding Corp 124 Pickard Dr E *TF:* 800-746-9724 ■ *Web:* www.pbhmoulding.com	Syracuse	NY	13211	315-455-5602	455-8748
Peterson Picture Frame Co Inc 2720 W Belmont Ave *Web:* www.peterson-picture.com	Chicago	IL	60618	773-463-8888	463-4603
Pinnacle Frames & Accents Inc 2606 Hwy 67 S PO Box 507 **Fax:* Sales ■ *TF:* 800-231-9974	Pocahontas	AR	72455	870-892-5227	892-3959*
Royal Mouldings Ltd 135 Bearcreek Rd **Fax:* Sales ■ *TF:* 800-368-3117 ■ *Web:* www.royalmouldings.com	Marion	VA	24354	276-783-8161	782-3292*
Sunset Moulding Co Inc 2231 Paseo Ave *Web:* www.sunsetmoulding.com	Live Oak	CA	95953	530-695-1801	695-2560
Tara Picture Frames 7615 Siempre Viva Rd *TF:* 800-241-8129 ■ *Web:* www.tarapf.com	San Diego	CA	92154	619-671-1018	671-1019
Tewa Moulding LLC 100 Daniel Rd NW *TF:* 800-821-3769	Albuquerque	NM	87107	505-898-0420	898-9636
Thunderbird Forest Products 8180 Industrial Pkwy *TF:* 800-824-5104	Sacramento	CA	95824	916-381-4200	381-0803
Uniek Inc 805 Uniek Dr *TF:* 800-248-6435 ■ *Web:* www.uniekinc.com	Waunakee	WI	53597	608-849-9999	849-9799
Williamson Co PO Box 409 **Fax Area Code:* 800 ■ *TF Orders:* 800-851-2467 ■ *Web:* www.williamsonco.com	Fairfield	IL	62837	618-842-4555	468-4762*
Woodgrain Distribution 80 S Shelby St **Fax:* Sales ■ *TF:* 800-756-0199 ■ *Web:* www.woodgraindistribution.com	Montevallo	AL	35115	205-665-2546	665-3432*

FRAMES & MOULDINGS - METAL

SEE Doors & Windows - Metal p. 1590

313 FRANCHISES

SEE ALSO Auto Supply Stores p. 1357; Automotive Services p. 1363; Bakeries p. 1367; Beauty Salons p. 1374; Business Service Centers p. 1403; Candles p. 1405; Car Rental Agencies p. 1406; Children's Learning Centers p. 1445; Cleaning Services p. 1447; Construction - Special Trade Contractors - Remodeling, Refinishing, Resurfacing Contractors p. 1546; Convenience Stores p. 1559; Health Food Stores p. 1774; Home Inspection Services p. 1788; Hotels & Hotel Companies p. 1832; Ice Cream & Dairy Stores p. 1851; Laundry & Drycleaning Services p. 1887; Optical Goods Stores p. 2040; Pest Control Services p. 2106; Printing Companies - Commercial Printers p. 1503; Real Estate Agents & Brokers p. 1397; Restaurant Companies p. 2229; Staffing Services p. 2331; Travel Agency Networks p. 2383; Weight Loss Centers & Services p. 2415

Please see the category on Hotel & Resort Operation & Management for listings of hotel franchises.

Phone *Fax*

1-800-DryClean LLC 3948 Ranchero Dr ... Ann Arbor MI 48108 866-822-6115 822-6888*
Fax Area Code: 734 ■ *TF:* 800-379-2532 ■ *Web:* www.1-800-dryclean.com

1-800-Got-Junk? 1523 W 3rd Ave 3rd Floor ... Vancouver BC V6J1J8 800-468-5865 751-0634*
Fax Area Code: 801 ■ *Web:* www.1800gotjunk.com

1-800-Water Damage 1167 Mercer St ... Seattle WA 98109 206-381-3047 381-3052
TF: 800-940-9745 ■ *Web:* www.1800waterdamage.com

7-Eleven Inc 2711 N Haskell Ave PO Box 711 ... Dallas TX 75221 214-828-7011 828-7848
TF: 800-255-0711 ■ *Web:* www.7-eleven.com

A & W Restaurants Inc 1441 Gardiner Ln ... Louisville KY 40213 502-874-8300 874-3183
Web: www.awrestaurants.com

AAMCO Transmissions Inc 1 Presidential Blvd ... Bala Cynwyd PA 19004 610-668-2900 664-1226
TF Cust Svc: 800-523-0401 ■ *Web:* www.aamcotransmissions.com

Aaron Rents Inc 309 E Paces Ferry Rd NE ... Atlanta GA 30305 404-231-0011 402-3567*
NYSE: RNT ■ **Fax Area Code:* 678 ■ **Fax:* Mktg ■ *TF:* 800-551-6015 ■
Web: www.aaronrents.com

ABC Seamless 3001 Fiechtner Dr ... Fargo ND 58103 701-293-5952 293-3107
TF: 800-732-6577 ■ *Web:* www.abcseamless.com

Abrakadoodle Inc 1800 Robert Fulton Dr ... Reston VA 22191 703-860-6570 860-6574
Web: www.abrakadoodle.com

ACE Cash Express Inc 1231 Greenway Dr Suite 800 ... Irving TX 75038 972-550-5000 550-5150
NASDAQ: AACE ■ *TF Sales:* 800-713-3338 ■ *Web:* www.acecashexpress.com

ActionCOACH 5670 Wynn Rd Suite C ... Las Vegas NV 89118 702-795-3188 795-3183
TF: 888-483-2828 ■ *Web:* www.actioncoach.com

Affiliated Car Rental LC 96 Freneau Ave Suite 2 ... Matawan NJ 07747 732-583-8500 290-8305
TF: 800-367-5159 ■ *Web:* www.sensiblecarrental.com

Affordable Car Rental System Inc 105 Hwy 36 ... Eatontown NJ 07724 732-380-0888 380-0404
TF: 800-631-2290 ■ *Web:* www.sensiblecarrental.com

AIM Mail Centers 15550-D Rockfield Blvd ... Irvine CA 92618 949-837-4151 837-4537
TF: 800-669-4246 ■ *Web:* www.aimmailcenters.com

Aire-Master of America Inc 1821 N Highway CC PO Box 2310 ... Nixa MO 65714 417-725-2691 725-5737
TF: 800-525-0957 ■ *Web:* www.airemaster.com

Aire Serv Heating & Air Conditioning Inc 1020 N University Parks Dr ... Waco TX 76707 800-583-2662 745-5098*
**Fax Area Code:* 254 ■ *Web:* www.aireserv.com

All About Honeymoons 7887 E Belleview ... Englewood CO 80110 720-259-4546 753-1796*
**Fax Area Code:* 303 ■ *TF:* 888-845-4488 ■ *Web:* www.aahfranchise.com

All Tune & Lube Brakes & More Inc 8334 Veteran's Hwy ... Millersville MD 21108 410-987-1011 987-9080
TF: 800-935-8863 ■ *Web:* www.alltuneandlube.com

All Tune and Lube International Inc ATL International Inc
8334 Veterans Hwy ... Millersville MD 21108 410-987-1011 987-9080
TF: 800-935-8863 ■ *Web:* www.alltuneandlube.com

Allegra Network LLC 21680 Haggerty Rd ... Northville MI 48167 248-596-8600 596-8601
TF: 800-726-9050 ■ *Web:* www.allegranetwork.com

AlphaGraphics Inc 268 S State St Suite 300 ... Salt Lake City UT 84111 801-595-7270 595-7271
TF: 800-955-6246 ■ *Web:* www.alphagraphics.com

Alternative Board 1640 Grant St Suite 200 ... Denver CO 80203 303-839-1200 839-0012
TF: 800-727-0126 ■ *Web:* www.tabboards.com

American Leak Detection 888 Research Dr Suite 100 ... Palm Springs CA 92262 760-320-9991 320-1288
TF: 800-755-6697 ■ *Web:* www.americanleakdetection.com

American Poolplayers Assn (APA)
1000 Lake St Louis Blvd Suite 325 ... Lake Saint Louis MO 63367 636-625-8611 625-2975
TF: 800-372-2536 ■ *Web:* www.poolplayers.com

AmeriSpec Inc 889 Ridge Lake Blvd ... Memphis TN 38120 901-820-8500 820-8520
TF: 800-426-2270 ■ *Web:* www.amerispec.com

Anago Franchising Inc 3111 N University Dr Suite 625 ... Coral Springs FL 33065 954-752-3111 752-1200
TF: 800-213-5857 ■ *Web:* www.anagousa.com

Anytime Fitness Inc 330 E Marie Ave ... West Saint Paul MN 55118 651-554-0144 554-0311
TF: 800-704-5004 ■ *Web:* www.anytimefitness.com

Applebee's International Inc 4551 W 107th St ... Overland Park KS 66207 913-967-4000 341-1694
NASDAQ: APPB ■ *Web:* www.applebees.com

Arby's Restaurant Group Inc 1155 Perimeter Center W ... Atlanta GA 30338 678-514-4100
TF: 800-487-2729 ■ *Web:* www.arbys.com

Archadeck 2112 W Laburnum Ave Suite 100 ... Richmond VA 23227 804-353-6999 353-2364
TF: 800-722-4668 ■ *Web:* www.archadeck.com

Assist-2-Sell Inc 1610 Meadow Wood Ln ... Reno NV 89502 775-688-6060 688-6069
TF: 800-528-7816 ■ *Web:* www.assist2sell.com

Auntie Anne's Inc 160-A Rt 41 ... Gap PA 17527 717-442-4766 442-4139
Web: www.auntieannes.com

Avalar Network Inc PO Box 82010 ... Las Vegas NV 89180 702-895-8988 895-8998
TF: 877-895-8988 ■ *Web:* www.avalar.biz

Back Yard Burgers Inc 1657 Shelby Oaks Dr N Suite 105 ... Memphis TN 38134 901-367-0888 367-0999
NASDAQ: BYBI ■ *TF:* 800-292-6939 ■ *Web:* www.backyardburgers.com

Bad Ass Coffee Co of Hawaii Inc 155 W Malvern Ave ... Salt Lake City UT 84115 801-463-1966 463-2606
TF: 888-422-3277 ■ *Web:* www.badasscoffee.com

Bark Busters Home Training 250 Lehow Ave Suite B ... Englewood CO 80110 303-471-4935 283-2819*
**Fax Area Code:* 720 ■ *Web:* www.barkbusters.com

Barnie's Coffee & Tea Co Inc 2126 Landstreet Rd Suite 300 ... Orlando FL 32809 407-854-6600 854-6601
TF: 800-854-1416 ■ *Web:* www.barniescoffee.com

Baskin-Robbins Inc 130 Royall St ... Canton MA 02021 781-737-3000
TF: 800-859-5339 ■ *Web:* www.baskinrobbins.com

Batteries Plus LLC 925 Walnut Ridge Dr ... Hartland WI 53029 262-369-0690 912-3100
TF: 800-274-9155 ■ *Web:* www.batteriesplus.com

Beef O'Bradys Inc 5510 W LaSalle St Suite 200 ... Tampa FL 33607 813-226-2333 226-0030
TF: 800-728-8878 ■ *Web:* www.beefobradys.com

Bellacino's Corp 10096 Shaver Rd ... Portage MI 49024 269-329-0782 329-0930
TF: 877-379-0700 ■ *Web:* www.bellacinos.com

Ben Franklin Stores Promotions Unlimited Corp 087601 ... Racine WI 53408 262-681-7000
Web: www.benfranklinstores.com

Ben & Jerry's Homemade Inc 30 Community Dr ... South Burlington VT 05403 802-846-1500 846-1556
Web: www.benjerry.com

Benjamin Franklin Plumbing
50 Central Ave Suite 920 Plaza Five Points ... Sarasota FL 34236 941-366-9692 951-0942
TF: 800-695-3579 ■ *Web:* www.benfranklinplumbing.com

Phone *Fax*

Bennigan's 6500 International Pkwy Suite 1000 ... Plano TX 75093 972-588-5000 588-5280*
**Fax:* Cust Svc ■ *TF:* 800-727-8355 ■ *Web:* www.bennigans.com

Bevinco Bar Systems Ltd 510-505 Consumers Rd ... Toronto ON M2J4V8 416-490-6266 490-6899
TF: 888-238-4626 ■ *Web:* www.bevinco.com

Big Apple Bagels 500 Lake Cook Rd Suite 475 ... Deerfield IL 60015 847-948-7520 405-8140
TF: 800-251-6101 ■ *Web:* www.babcorp.com

Big Boy Restaurants International LLC 4199 Marcy St ... Warren MI 48091 586-759-6000 755-8531*
**Fax:* Cust Svc ■ *TF:* 800-837-3003 ■ *Web:* www.bigboy.com

Big O Tires Inc 12650 E Briarwood Ave Suite 2D ... Englewood CO 80112 303-728-5500 728-5700
TF: 800-321-2446 ■ *Web:* www.bigotires.com

Blockbuster Inc 1201 Elm St Suite 2100 ... Dallas TX 75270 214-854-3000 683-8165*
NYSE: BBI ■ **Fax Area Code:* 972 ■ *Web:* www.blockbuster.com

Bojangles' Restaurants Inc 9432 Southern Pine Blvd ... Charlotte NC 28273 704-527-2675 523-6676
TF: 800-366-9921 ■ *Web:* www.bojangles.com

Bonus Building Care Inc 14331 Proton Rd ... Dallas TX 75244 972-789-9400 789-9399
TF: 800-931-1102 ■ *Web:* www.bonusbuildingcare.com

Boston Pizza International Inc 5500 Parkwood Way ... Richmond BC V6V2M4 604-270-1108 270-4168
Web: www.bostonpizza.com

Boston Pizza Restaurants LP 1501 LBJ Fwy Suite 450 ... Dallas TX 75234 972-484-9022 484-7630
Web: www.bostonsgourmet.com

Breadeaux Pizza Inc 2300 Frederick St ... Saint Joseph MO 64506 816-364-1088 364-3739
TF: 800-835-6534 ■ *Web:* www.breadeauxpizza.com

BrickKicker Inc 849 N Ellsworth St ... Naperville IL 60563 630-420-9900 420-2270
TF: 800-821-1820 ■ *Web:* www.brickkicker.com

Brooke Corp 10950 Grandview Dr Suite 600 ... Overland Park KS 66210 913-661-0123 451-3183
NASDAQ: BXXX ■ *TF:* 800-642-1872 ■ *Web:* www.brookecorp.com

Bruegger's Enterprises 159 Bank St ... Burlington VT 05401 802-660-4020 652-9293
Web: www.brueggers.com

Bruster's Ice Cream Inc 730 Mulberry St ... Bridgewater PA 15009 724-774-4250 774-0666
Web: www.brusters.com

Budget Blinds Inc 1927 N Glassell St ... Orange CA 92865 714-637-2100 637-1400
TF: 800-800-9250 ■ *Web:* www.budgetblinds.com

Buffalo Wild Wings Inc 1600 Utica Ave S Suite 700 ... Minneapolis MN 55416 952-593-9943 593-9787
NASDAQ: BWLD ■ *TF:* 800-499-9586 ■ *Web:* www.buffalowildwings.com

BuildingStars Inc 11489 Page Service Dr ... Saint Louis MO 63146 314-991-3356 991-3198
Web: www.buildingstars.com

Burger King Corp 5505 Blue Lagoon Dr ... Miami FL 33126 305-378-7011 378-7262
Web: www.bk.com

Burger King Restaurants of Canada Inc 401 The West Mall 7th Fl ... Etobicoke ON M9C5J4 416-626-6464 626-6684*
**Fax:* Mktg ■ *TF:* 888-252-8280

Camille's Sidewalk Cafe 8801 S Yale Suite 400 ... Tulsa OK 74137 800-230-7004 497-1916*
**Fax Area Code:* 918 ■ *Web:* www.camillescafe.com

Candy Bouquet International Inc 423 E 3rd St ... Little Rock AR 72201 501-375-9990 375-9998
TF: 877-226-3901 ■ *Web:* www.candybouquet.com

Captain D's LLC 1717 Elm Hill Pike Suite A-1 ... Nashville TN 37210 615-391-5461 231-2309
TF: 800-314-4819 ■ *Web:* www.captainds.com

Car-X Assoc Corp 1375 E Woodfield Rd Suite 500 ... Schaumburg IL 60173 847-273-8920 619-3310
TF: 800-359-2359 ■ *Web:* www.carx.com

CardSmart Retail Corp 430 Pine St ... Central Falls RI 02863 877-227-3762 726-2384*
**Fax Area Code:* 401 ■ *Web:* www.cardsmart.com

Carl's Jr Restaurants 6307 Carpinteria Ave Suite A ... Carpinteria CA 93013 714-774-5796 778-7183
TF Cust Svc: 877-799-7827 ■ *Web:* www.carlsjr.com

Carlson Wagonlit Travel Inc 701 Carlson Pkwy ... Minnetonka MN 55305 763-212-5000 212-5458
TF: 800-335-8747 ■ *Web:* www.carlsonwagonlit.com

Cartex Ltd 42816 Mound Rd ... Sterling Heights MI 48314 586-739-4330 739-4331
TF: 800-421-7328 ■ *Web:* www.fabrion.net

Cartridge World 6460 Hollis St ... Emeryville CA 94608 510-594-9900 594-9991
Web: www.cartridgeworldusa.com

Carvel Franchising 200 Glenridge Point Pkwy Suite 200 ... Atlanta GA 30342 404-255-3250 255-4978
TF: 800-227-8353 ■ *Web:* www.carvel.com

Century 21 Real Estate Corp 1 Campus Dr ... Parsippany NJ 07054 973-428-9700 496-5966*
**Fax:* Hum Res ■ *TF:* 800-992-8023 ■ *Web:* www.century21.com

CertaPro Painters Ltd 150 Green Tree Rd Suite 1003 ... Oaks PA 19456 610-983-9411 650-9997
TF: 800-462-3782 ■ *Web:* www.certapro.com

Certified Restoration DryCleaning Network LLC 2060 Coolidge Hwy ... Berkley MI 48072 800-963-2736 246-7868*
**Fax Area Code:* 248 ■ *Web:* www.restorationdrycleaning.com

Charley's Grilled Subs 2500 Farmers Dr Suite 140 ... Columbus OH 43235 614-923-4700 923-4701
TF: 800-437-8325 ■ *Web:* www.charleys.com

Checkers Drive-In Restaurants Inc 4300 W Cypress St Suite 600 ... Tampa FL 33607 813-283-7000 283-7001
NASDAQ: CHKR ■ *TF:* 800-800-8072 ■ *Web:* www.checkers.com

Cheeburger Cheeburger Restaurants Inc
15951 McGregor Blvd Suite 2A ... Fort Myers FL 33908 239-437-1611 437-1512
TF: 800-487-6211 ■ *Web:* www.cheeburger.com

Chem-Dry 1530 N 1000 West ... Logan UT 84321 435-755-0099 755-0021
TF: 800-243-6379 ■ *Web:* www.chemdry.com

Chester's International LLC 3500 Colonnade Pkwy Suite 325 ... Birmingham AL 32543 800-288-1555 298-0332*
**Fax Area Code:* 205 ■ *Web:* www.chestersinternational.com

CHIP - The Child ID Program Inc 705 Lakefield Rd Bldg G ... Westlake Village CA 91361 805-557-0577 557-0587
TF: 866-999-2447 ■ *Web:* www.4childid.com

Christmas Decor Inc 206 23rd St ... Lubbock TX 79404 800-687-9551 722-9627*
**Fax Area Code:* 806 ■ *Web:* www.christmasdecor.net

Church's Chicken Inc 980 Hammond Dr NE Suite 1100 ... Atlanta GA 30328 770-350-3800 512-3920
Web: www.churchs.com

CiCi Enterprises LP 1080 W Bethel Rd ... Coppell TX 75019 972-745-4200 745-4204
Web: www.cicispizza.com

Cinnabon Inc 200 Glenridge Point Pkwy Suite 200 ... Atlanta GA 30342 404-255-3250 255-4978
Web: www.cinnabon.com

Cleaning Authority 6994 Columbia Gateway Dr Suite 100 ... Columbia MD 21046 410-740-1900 685-6243*
**Fax Area Code:* 866 ■ *TF:* 800-783-6243 ■ *Web:* www.thecleaningauthority.com

CleanNet USA 9861 Brokenland Pkwy Suite 208 ... Columbia MD 21046 410-720-6444 720-5307
TF: 800-735-8838 ■ *Web:* www.cleannetusa.com

Closet Factory 12800 S Broadway ... Los Angeles CA 90061 310-516-7000 516-8065
TF: 800-318-8800 ■ *Web:* www.closetfactory.com

Club Z! Inc 15310 Amberly Dr Suite 185 ... Tampa FL 33647 813-931-5516 932-2485
TF: 800-434-2582 ■ *Web:* www.clubztutoring.com

Coffee Beanery Ltd 3429 Pierson Pl ... Flushing MI 48433 810-733-1020 733-1536
TF: 800-728-2326 ■ *Web:* www.coffeebeanery.com

Coffee News USA PO Box 84444 ... Bangor ME 04402 207-941-0860 941-1050
Web: www.coffeenewsusa.com

Cold Stone Creamery Inc 9311 E Via De Ventura ... Scottsdale AZ 85258 480-362-4800 362-4812
TF Cust Svc: 866-464-9467 ■ *Web:* www.coldstonecreamery.com

Coldwell Banker Real Estate Corp 1 Campus Dr ... Parsippany NJ 07054 973-496-2653 496-7217
Web: www.coldwellbanker.com

Color-Glo International 7111 Ohms Ln ... Minneapolis MN 55439 952-835-1338 835-1395
TF: 800-328-6347 ■ *Web:* www.colorglo.com

Color Me Mine Enterprises Inc 5140 Lankershim Blvd ... North Hollywood CA 91601 818-505-2100 509-9778
TF: 888-265-6764 ■ *Web:* www.colormemine.com

Colors on Parade 642 Century Cir ... Conway SC 29526 843-347-8818 347-0349
TF: 800-929-3363 ■ *Web:* www.colorsonparade.com

Comet Cleaners 406 W Division St ... Arlington TX 76011 817-461-3555 861-4779
Web: www.cometcleaners.com

ComForcare Senior Services Inc
2510 Telegraph Rd Suite 100 ... Bloomfield Hills MI 48302 248-745-9700 745-9763
TF: 800-886-4044 ■ *Web:* www.comforcare.com

	City	State	Zip	Phone	Fax
Comfort Keepers Franchising Inc 6640 Poe Ave Suite 200	Dayton	OH	45414	937-264-1933	264-3103
TF: 800-387-2415 ■ *Web:* www.comfortkeepers.com					
Complete Music Inc 7877 L St	Omaha	NE	68127	402-339-0001	339-1285
TF: 800-843-3866 ■ *Web:* www.cmusic.com					
Computer Renaissance 500 S Florida Ave Suite 400	Lakeland	FL	33801	863-669-1155	665-6324*
**Fax Area Code:* 800 ■ *Web:* www.compren.com					
Computer Troubleshooters USA 755 Commerce Dr Suite 412	Decatur	GA	30030	404-477-1300	234-6162*
**Fax Area Code:* 770 ■ *TF:* 877-704-1702 ■ *Web:* www.comptroub.com/us					
Computertots/Computer Explorers 12715 Telge Rd	Cypress	TX	77429	281-256-4100	373-4450
TF: 800-531-5053 ■ *Web:* www.computertots.com					
Contours Express Inc 156 Imperial Way	Nicholasville	KY	40356	859-885-6441	241-2234
TF: 877-227-2282 ■ *Web:* www.contoursexpress.com					
Cookies By Design Inc 1865 Summit Ave Suite 605	Plano	TX	75074	972-398-9536	398-9542
TF: 800-945-2665 ■ *Web:* www.cookiesbydesign.com					
Cost Cutters Family Hair Salon Div Regis Corp					
7201 Metro Blvd	Minneapolis	MN	55439	952-947-7777	947-7801
TF: 888-888-7778 ■ *Web:* www.costcutters.com					
Cottman Transmission Systems LLC					
201 Gibraltar Rd Suite 150	Horsham	PA	19044	215-643-5885	643-2519
TF: 800-394-6116 ■ *Web:* www.cottman.com					
Coverall Cleaning Concepts 5201 Congress Ave Suite 275	Boca Raton	FL	33487	561-922-2500	922-2423
TF: 800-537-3371 ■ *Web:* www.coverall.com					
CP Franchising LLC DBA Cruise Planners					
3300 University Dr Suite 602	Coral Springs	FL	33065	954-344-8060	344-4479
TF: 800-683-0206 ■ *Web:* www.cruiseplanners.com					
Craters & Freighters 331 Corporate Cir Suite J	Golden	CO	80401	800-736-3335	399-9964*
**Fax Area Code:* 303 ■ *Web:* www.cratersandfreighters.com					
Creative Colors International Inc 19015 S Jodi Rd Suite E	Mokena	IL	60448	708-478-1437	478-1636
TF: 800-933-2656 ■ *Web:* www.creativecolorsintl.com					
Crest Foods Inc DBA Nestle Toll House Cafe by Chip					
101 W Renner Rd Suite 240	Richardson	TX	75802	214-495-9533	853-5347
Web: www.nestlecafe.com					
Crestcom International Ltd					
6900 E Belleview Ave Suite 300	Greenwood Village	CO	80111	303-267-8200	267-8207
TF: 888-273-7826 ■ *Web:* www.crestcom.com					
Critter Control Inc 9435 Cherry Bend Rd	Traverse City	MI	49684	231-947-2400	947-9440
TF: 800-451-6544 ■ *Web:* www.crittercontrol.com					
Crown Trophy 9 Skyline Dr	Hawthorne	NY	10532	800-583-8228	347-0211*
**Fax Area Code:* 914 ■ *Web:* www.crowntrophy.com					
Cruise Holidays International Inc 701 Carlson Pkwy	Minnetonka	MN	55305	800-866-7245	212-5266*
**Fax Area Code:* 763 ■ *Web:* www.cruiseholidays.com					
Cruise Planners 3300 University Dr Suite 602	Coral Springs	FL	33065	954-344-8060	344-4479
TF: 800-683-0206 ■ *Web:* www.cruiseplanners.com					
CruiseOne Inc 1415 NW 62nd St Suite 205	Fort Lauderdale	FL	33309	954-958-3700	958-3703
TF: 800-832-3592 ■ *Web:* www.cruiseone.com					
Culver Franchising System Inc 540 Water St	Prairie du Sac	WI	53578	608-643-7980	643-7982
Web: www.culvers.com					
Curves International Inc 100 Ritchie Rd	Waco	TX	76712	254-399-9285	399-9731
TF: 800-848-1096 ■ *Web:* www.curves.com					
Cuts Fitness For Men 1120 Raritan Rd	Clark	NJ	07066	732-381-9300	574-1130
Web: www.cutsfitness.com					
Dairy Queen 7505 Metro Blvd	Minneapolis	MN	55439	952-830-0200	830-0480
TF: 800-679-6556 ■ *Web:* www.dairyqueen.com					
D'Angelo Sandwich Shops 600 Providence Hwy	Dedham	MA	02026	781-461-1200	461-1896
TF: 800-727-2446 ■ *Web:* www.dangelos.com					
Deck The Walls Inc 101 S Hanley Rd Suite 1280	Saint Louis	MO	63105	314-719-8200	
TF: 866-719-8200 ■ *Web:* www.deckthewalls.com					
Decor & You Inc 900 Main St South Bldg 2	Southbury	CT	06488	203-264-3500	264-5095
TF: 800-477-3326 ■ *Web:* www.decorandyou.com					
Decorating Den Systems Inc DBA Interiors By Decorating Den					
8659 Commerce Dr	Easton	MD	21601	410-822-9001	
TF: 800-332-3367 ■ *Web:* www.decoratingden.com					
Denny's Inc 203 E Main St	Spartanburg	SC	29319	864-597-8000	597-8780*
**Fax:* Mktg ■ *Web:* www.dennys.com					
Dingo Inc DBA Bark Busters Home Training					
250 Lehow Ave Suite B	Englewood	CO	80110	303-471-4935	283-2819*
**Fax Area Code:* 720 ■ *Web:* www.barkbusters.com					
DirectBuy Inc 8450 Broadway	Merrillville	IN	46410	219-755-6211	755-6208
TF: 800-827-6400 ■ *Web:* www.directbuy.com					
Domino's Pizza Inc 30 Frank Lloyd Wright Dr	Ann Arbor	MI	48106	734-930-3030	930-3580*
NYSE: DPZ ■ **Fax:* Mail Rm ■ *TF:* 888-366-4667 ■ *Web:* www.dominos.com					
Dr Vinyl & Assoc Ltd 201 NW Victoria Dr	Lee's Summit	MO	64086	816-525-6060	525-6333
TF: 800 531 6600 ■ *Web:* www.drvinyl.com					
DreamMaker Bath & Kitchen by Worldwide					
1020 N University Parks Dr	Waco	TX	76707	254-745-2477	745-2588
TF: 800-583-9099 ■ *Web:* www.dreammaker-remodel.com					
Dry Cleaning Station 8301 Golden Valley Rd Suite 240	Minneapolis	MN	55427	763-541-0832	542-2246
TF: 800-655-8134 ■ *Web:* www.drycleaningstation.com					
Dryclean USA Inc 290 NE 68th St	Miami	FL	33138	305-758-0066	751-8390
AMEX: DCU ■ *TF:* 800-746-4583 ■ *Web:* www.drycleanusa.com					
Dunkin' Donuts 130 Royall St	Canton	MA	02021	781-737-3000	737-4000
TF Cust Svc: 800-859-5339 ■ *Web:* www.dunkindonuts.com					
Duraclean International Inc 220 Campus Dr	Arlington Heights	IL	60004	847-704-7100	704-7101
TF Cust Svc: 800-251-7070 ■ *Web:* www.duraclean.com					
E.nopi Daekyo USA Inc 701 E Palisades Ave Suite 201	Englewood Cliffs	NJ	07632	201-894-1212	894-8686
TF: 888-835-1212 ■ *Web:* www.enopi.com					
East of Chicago Pizza Co 512 E Tiffin St	Willard	OH	44890	419-935-3033	935-3278
Web: www.eastofchicago.com					
Edible Arrangements LLC 1952 Whitney Ave	Hamden	CT	06517	203-907-0066	230-0792
TF: 800-236-7101 ■ *Web:* www.ediblearrangements.com					
Educate Inc 1001 Fleet St	Baltimore	MD	21202	410-843-8000	843-8717
NASDAQ: EEEE ■ *TF:* 888-338-2283 ■ *Web:* www.educate-inc.com					
El Pollo Loco 3333 Michelson Dr Suite 550	Irvine	CA	92612	949-399-2000	399-2175
Web: www.elpolloloco.com					
EmbroidMe Inc 2121 Vista Pkwy	West Palm Beach	FL	33411	561-640-7367	640-6062
TF: 877-877-0234 ■ *Web:* www.embroidme.com					
Emerging Vision Inc 100 Quentin Roosevelt Blvd Suite 508	Garden City	NY	11530	516-390-2100	390-2110
TF: 800-332-6302					
ERA Franchise Systems Inc 1 Campus Dr	Parsippany	NJ	07054	973-428-9700	261-6275*
**Fax Area Code:* 800 ■ *TF:* 800-869-1260 ■ *Web:* www.era.com					
Expetic Technology Service 12 2nd Ave SW	Aberdeen	SD	57401	605-225-4122	225-5176
TF: 888-297-2292 ■ *Web:* www.expetec.biz					
Express Oil Change 1880 S Park Dr	Hoover	AL	35244	205-945-1771	940-6025
TF: 888-945-1771 ■ *Web:* www.expressoil.com					
Express Personnel Services 8516 NW Expressway	Oklahoma City	OK	73162	405-840-5000	717-5665
TF: 800-222-4057 ■ *Web:* www.expresspersonnel.com					
Express Tax Franchise Corp 3030 Hartley Rd Suite 320	Jacksonville	FL	32257	904-262-0031	262-2864
TF: 888-417-4461 ■ *Web:* www.expresstaxservice.com					
Extreme Pita 2187 Dunwin Dr	Mississauga	ON	L5L1X2	905-820-7887	820-8448
TF: 888-729-7482 ■ *Web:* www.extremepita.com					
Famous Dave's of America Inc					
12701 Whitewater Dr Suite 200	Minnetonka	MN	55343	952-294-1300	294-0242
NASDAQ: DAVE ■ *TF:* 800-210-4040 ■ *Web:* www.famousdaves.com					
Fantastic Sams Inc 50 Dunham Rd 3rd Fl	Beverly	MA	01915	978-232-5600	232-5601
Web: www.fantasticsams.com					
Fast-Fix Jewelry & Watch Repairs					
1300 NW 17th Ave Suite 170	Delray Beach	FL	33445	561-330-6060	330-6062
TF: 800-359-0407 ■ *Web:* www.fastfix.com					
Fastframe USA Inc 1200 Lawrence Dr Suite 300	Newbury Park	CA	91320	805-498-4463	498-8983
TF: 888-863-7263 ■ *Web:* www.fastframe.com					
FasTracKids International Ltd					
6900 E Belleview Ave Suite 100	Greenwood Village	CO	80111	303-224-0200	224-0222
TF: 888-576-6888 ■ *Web:* www.fastrackids.com					
FASTSIGNS International Inc 2542 Highlander Way	Carrollton	TX	75006	972-447-0777	248-8201
TF: 800-827-7446 ■ *Web:* www.fastsigns.com					
Figaro's Italian Pizza Inc 1500 Liberty St SE Suite 160	Salem	OR	97302	503-371-9318	363-5364
TF: 888-344-2767 ■ *Web:* figaros.com					
Filta Group Inc 5401 S Kirkman Rd Suite 740	Orlando	FL	32819	407-996-5550	996-5551
TF: 866-513-4582 ■ *Web:* www.filtafry.com					
Firehouse Subs 3410 Kori Rd	Jacksonville	FL	32257	904-886-8300	886-2111
TF: 800-388-3473 ■ *Web:* www.firehousesubs.com					
Firehouse Restaurant Group Inc DBA Firehouse Subs					
3410 Kori Rd	Jacksonville	FL	32257	904-886-8300	886-2111
TF: 800-388-3473 ■ *Web:* www.firehousesubs.com					
Fish Window Cleaning Services Inc 200 Enchanted Pkwy	Saint Louis	MO	63021	636-530-7334	530-7856
TF: 877-707-3474 ■ *Web:* www.fishwindowcleaning.com					
Floor Coverings International 200 Technology Ct Suite 1200	Smyrna	GA	30082	770-874-7600	874-7605
TF Sales: 800-955-4324 ■ *Web:* floorcoveringsinternational.com					
Flowerama of America Inc 3165 W Airline Hwy	Waterloo	IA	50703	319-291-6004	291-8676
TF: 800-728-6004 ■ *Web:* www.flowerama.com					
Foot Solutions Inc 2359 Windy Hill Rd Suite 400	Marietta	GA	30067	770-955-0099	953-6270
TF: 866-338-2597 ■ *Web:* www.footsolutions.com					
Fox's Pizza Den Inc 3243 Old Frankstown Rd	Pittsburgh	PA	15239	724-733-7888	325-5479
TF: 800-899-3697 ■ *Web:* www.foxspizza.com					
Framing & Art Centre 1800 Appleby Line Rd	Burlington	ON	L7L6A1	800-563-7263	565-5755
Web: www.framingartcentre.com					
Franchise Concepts Inc 101 S Hanley Rd Suite 1280	Saint Louis	MO	63105	314-719-8200	719-8290
TF: 866-719-8200 ■ *Web:* www.franchiseconceptsinc.com					
Friendly Computers 3440 W Cheyenne Suite 100	North Las Vegas	NV	89032	702-458-2780	869-2780
TF: 800-656-3115 ■ *Web:* www.friendlycomputers.com					
Friendly Ice Cream Corp 1855 Boston Rd	Wilbraham	MA	01095	413-543-2400	543-3966
AMEX: FRN ■ *Web:* www.friendlys.com					
Frullati Cafe & Bakery 7730 E Greenway Rd Suite 104	Scottsdale	AZ	85260	480-443-0200	443-1972
TF: 800-438-2590 ■ *Web:* www.frullati.com					
Fuddruckers Inc 5700 MopaC Expy S Bldg C Suite 300	Austin	TX	78749	512-275-0400	275-0670
Web: www.fuddruckers.com					
Furniture Medic 3839 Forrest Hill Irene Rd	Memphis	TN	38125	901-597-8600	597-8630
TF: 800-877-9933 ■ *Web:* www.furnituremedic.com					
Gateway Newstands 9555 Yonge St Suite 400	Richmond Hill	ON	L4C9M5	905-737-7755	737-7757
TF: 800-942-5351 ■ *Web:* www.gatewaynewstands.com					
Geeks On Call America Inc 814 Kempsville Rd Suite 106	Norfolk	VA	23502	757-466-3448	466-3457
TF: 800-905-4335 ■ *Web:* www.geeksoncall.com					
Glass Doctor 1020 N University Parks Dr	Waco	TX	76707	254-745-2480	745-5073
TF: 800-280-9959 ■ *Web:* www.glassdoctor.com					
GNC Corp 300 6th Ave	Pittsburgh	PA	15222	412-288-4600	338-8905*
**Fax:* Cust Svc ■ *TF Cust Svc:* 888-462-2548 ■ *Web:* www.gnc.com					
Goddard Systems Inc 1016 W Ninth Ave	King of Prussia	PA	19406	610-265-8510	265-6931
TF: 800-463-3273 ■ *Web:* www.goddardschool.com					
Golden Chick 11488 Luna Rd Suite 100B	Dallas	TX	75234	972-831-0911	831-0401
Web: www.goldenchick.com					
Golden Corral Corp 5151 Glenwood Ave	Raleigh	NC	27612	919-781-9310	881-4485
TF: 800-284-5673 ■ *Web:* www.goldencorral.net					
Golden Krust Carribean Bakery & Grill 3958 Park Ave	Bronx	NY	10457	718-655-7878	583-1883
Web: www.goldenkrustbakery.com					
Gold's Gym International Inc					
125 E John Carpenter Fwy Suite 1300	Irving	TX	75062	214-574-4653	
TF: 800-457-5375 ■ *Web:* www.goldsgym.com					
Golf Etc of America Inc 2201 Commercial Ln	Granbury	TX	76048	817-279-7888	579-1793
TF: 800-806-8633 ■ *Web:* www.golfetc.com					
Golf USA 3705 W Memorial Rd Suite 801	Oklahoma City	OK	73134	405-751-0015	755-0065
TF: 800-488-1107 ■ *Web:* www.golfusainc.com					
Gotcha Covered 1611 N Stemmons Fwy Suite 318	Carrollton	TX	75006	972-466-2544	446-6774
Web: www.gotchacoveredblinds.com					
Grand Rental Station 203 Jandus Rd	Cary	IL	60013	847-462-5440	516-9921
TF: 800-833-3004 ■ *Web:* www.grandrental.com					
Granite Transformations 2700 Biscayne Blvd	Miami	FL	33137	786-497-3007	438-1578*
**Fax Area Code:* 305 ■ *TF:* 866-685-5300 ■ *Web:* www.granitetransformations.com					
Grease Monkey International Inc					
7100 E Belleview Ave Suite 305	Greenwood Village	CO	80111	303-308-1660	308-5908
TF: 800-822-7706 ■ *Web:* www.greasemonkey.net					
Great American Cookie Co Inc 4685 Frederick Dr SW	Atlanta	GA	30336	404-696-1700	699-0887
TF: 800-332-4856 ■ *Web:* www.greatamericancookies.com					
Great Clips Inc 7700 France Ave S Suite 425	Minneapolis	MN	55435	952-893-9088	844-3444
TF: 800-999-5959 ■ *Web:* www.greatclips.com					
Great Frame Up The 101 S Hanley Rd Suite 1280	Saint Louis	MO	63105	314-719-8200	
TF: 866-719-8200 ■ *Web:* www.greatframeup.com					
Great Harvest Bread Co 28 S Montana St	Dillon	MT	59725	406-683-6842	683-5537
TF: 800-442-0424 ■ *Web:* www.greatharvest.com					
Great Steak & Potato Co 188 N Brookwood Ave Suite 100	Hamilton	OH	45013	513-896-9695	896-3750
Web: www.thegreatsteak.com					
Great Wraps! Inc 4 Executive Pk E Suite 315	Atlanta	GA	30329	404-248-9900	248-0180
TF: 888-489-7277 ■ *Web:* www.greatwraps.com					
Griswold Special Care Inc 717 Bethlehem Pike Suite 300	Erdenheim	PA	19038	215-402-0200	402-0202
TF: 888-777-7630 ■ *Web:* www.griswoldspecialcare.com					
Growth Coach 10700 Montgomery Rd Suite 300	Cincinnati	OH	45242	513-563-8339	563-2691
TF: 888-292-7992 ■ *Web:* www.thegrowthcoach.com					
Gymboree Corp 500 Howard St	San Francisco	CA	94105	415-278-7000	278-7100
NASDAQ: GYMB ■ *TF:* 800-222-7758 ■ *Web:* www.gymboree.com					
Gymboree Corp Play & Music Program 500 Howard St	San Francisco	CA	94105	415-278-7000	278-7100
TF: 800-520-7529 ■ *Web:* www.gymboree.com					
Handyman Connection Inc 9403 Kenwood Rd Suite D-207	Cincinnati	OH	45242	513-771-1122	771-2030
TF: 800-466-5530 ■ *Web:* www.handymanconnection.com					
Handyman Matters Inc 12567 W Cedar Dr Suite 250	Lakewood	CO	80228	303-984-0177	984-0133
TF: 866-808-8401 ■ *Web:* www.handymanmatters.com					
Happy & Healthy Products Inc 1600 S Dixie Hwy Suite 200	Boca Raton	FL	33432	561-367-0739	368-5267
TF: 800-378-4854 ■ *Web:* www.fruitfull.com					
Hardee's Food Systems Inc 505 N 7th St Suite 2000	Saint Louis	MO	63101	314-259-6200	259-6300*
**Fax:* Cust Svc ■ *TF Cust Svc:* 877-799-7827 ■ *Web:* www.hardees.com					
Harvey's 6303 Airport Rd	Mississauga	ON	L4V1R8	905-405-6500	405-6650
TF: 877-439-1125 ■ *Web:* www.harveys.ca					
Hayes Handpiece Franchises Inc					
5375 Avenida Encinas Suite C	Carlsbad	CA	92008	760-602-0521	602-0505
TF: 800-228-0521 ■ *Web:* www.hayeshandpiece.com					
Heavenly Ham Franchising Co 5445 Triangle Pkwy Suite 400	Norcross	GA	30092	770-752-1999	752-4653
TF: 800-989-0509 ■ *Web:* www.heavenlyham.com					
Heaven's Best Carpet & Upholstery Cleaning PO Box 607	Rexburg	ID	83440	208-359-1106	359-1236
TF: 800-359-2095 ■ *Web:* www.heavensbest.com					
Help-U-Sell Real Estate 900 W Castleton Rd Suite 230	Castle Rock	CO	80109	303-814-1400	814-3400
TF: 800-366-1177 ■ *Web:* www.helpusell.com					
Hobbytown USA 6301 S 58th St	Lincoln	NE	68516	402-434-5385	
TF: 800-869-0424 ■ *Web:* www.hobbytown.com					

Company	City	State	Zip	Phone	Fax
Hollywood Tans 1120 Rt 73 S CSC Plaza Suite 400	Mount Laurel	NJ	08054	856-914-9090	914-9099
Web: www.hollywoodtans.com					
Home Helpers Inc 10700 Montgomery Rd	Cincinnati	OH	45242	513-563-8339	563-2691
TF: 800-216-4196 ■ *Web:* www.homehelpers.cc					
Home Instead Inc 13330 California St Suite 200	Omaha	NE	68154	402-498-4466	498-5757
TF: 888-484-5759 ■ *Web:* www.homeinstead.com					
Homes & Land Magazine Affiliates LLC 1830 E Park Ave	Tallahassee	FL	32301	850-574-2111	575-9567
TF: 800-726-6683 ■ *Web:* www.homesandland.com					
HomeTeam Inspection Service Inc 575 Chamber Dr	Milford	OH	45150	513-831-1300	831-6010
TF: 800-598-5297 ■ *Web:* www.hometeaminspection.com					
HomeVestors of America Inc 10670 N Central Expwy Suite 700	Dallas	TX	75231	972-761-0046	761-9022
Web: www.homevestors.com					
Homewatch CareGivers 2865 S Colorado Blvd	Denver	CO	80222	303-758-7290	758-1724
TF: 800-777-9770 ■ *Web:* www.homewatchcaregivers.com					
Honeybaked Ham Co 5445 Triangle Pkwy Suite 400	Norcross	GA	30092	678-966-3100	966-3134
TF: 800-367-2426 ■ *Web:* www.honeybakedonline.com					
Hot Stuff Foods LLC 2930 W Maple St	Sioux Falls	SD	57107	605-330-7531	336-0141
Web: www.hotstufffoods.com					
Houlihan's Restaurant Group Inc					
8700 State Line Rd Suite 100	Leawood	KS	66206	913-901-2500	901-2651
Web: www.houlihans.com					
House Doctors 575 Chamber Dr	Milford	OH	45150	513-831-0100	831-6010
TF: 800-319-3359 ■ *Web:* www.housedoctors.com					
HouseMaster 421 W Union Ave	Bound Brook	NJ	08805	732-469-6565	469-7405
TF: 800-526-3939 ■ *Web:* www.housemaster.com					
Huddle House Inc 2969 E Ponce de Leon Ave	Decatur	GA	30030	404-377-5700	377-4142
TF: 800-418-9555 ■ *Web:* www.huddlehouse.com					
Hungry Howie's Pizza & Subs Inc					
30300 Stephenson Hwy Suite 200	Madison Heights	MI	48071	248-414-3300	414-3301
TF: 800-624-8122 ■ *Web:* www.hungryhowies.com					
Huntington Learning Centers Inc 23 Jefferson Ave	Westwood	NJ	07675	201-261-8600	
TF: 800-226-5327 ■ *Web:* www.huntingtonlearning.com					
Ident-A-Kid Services of America					
2810 Scherer Dr Suite 100	Saint Petersburg	FL	33716	727-577-4646	576-8258
Web: www.ident-a-kid.com					
IHOP Corp 450 N Brand Blvd 7th Fl	Glendale	CA	91203	818-240-6055	543-4178
NYSE: IHP ■ *TF:* 800-241-4467 ■ *Web:* www.ihop.com					
Instant Imprints 9808 Waples St	San Diego	CA	92121	858-642-4848	453-6513
TF: 800-542-3437 ■ *Web:* www.instantimprints.com					
Interface Financial Group 2182 Dupont Dr Suite 221	Irvine	CA	92612	949-477-0665	475-8688*
**Fax Area Code:* 866 ■ *TF:* 800-387-0860 ■ *Web:* www.interfacefinancial.com					
Interim HealthCare Inc 1601 Sawgrass Corporate Pkwy	Sunrise	FL	33323	954-858-6000	858-2820
TF: 800-338-7786 ■ *Web:* www.interimhealthcare.com					
Interiors By Decorating Den 8659 Commerce Dr	Easton	MD	21601	410-822-9001	
TF: 800-332-3367 ■ *Web:* www.decoratingden.com					
Island Ink-Jet Systems Inc 244 4th St	Courtenay	BC	V9N1G6	250-897-0067	897-0021
TF: 877-446-5538 ■ *Web:* www.islandinkjet.com					
iSold It 129 N Hill Ave Suite 202	Pasadena	CA	91106	626-584-0440	584-6540
Web: www.i-soldit.com					
It's A Grind Inc 6272 E Pacific Coast Hwy Suite E	Long Beach	CA	90803	562-594-5600	594-4100
TF: 866-424-5282 ■ *Web:* www.itsagrind.com					
It's Just Lunch! Inc 101 W Grand Ave Suite 502	Chicago	IL	60610	312-644-9999	644-9474
Web: www.itsjustlunch.com					
Jack in the Box 9330 Balboa Ave	San Diego	CA	92123	858-571-2121	571-2101
TF: 800-500-5225 ■ *Web:* www.jackinthebox.com					
Jackson Hewitt Inc 7 Sylvan Way	Parsippany	NJ	07054	973-496-1040	229-8935*
NYSE: JTX ■ **Fax Area Code:* 605 ■ *TF:* 800-234-1040 ■ *Web:* www.jacksonhewitt.com					
Jan-Pro International Inc 11605 Haynes Bridge Rd Suite 425	Alpharetta	GA	30004	678-336-1780	336-1781
TF: 800-668-1001 ■ *Web:* www.jan-pro.com					
Jani-King International Inc 16885 Dallas Pkwy	Addison	TX	75001	972-991-0900	526-4546*
**Fax Area Code:* 800 ■ *TF:* 800-552-5264 ■ *Web:* www.janiking.com					
Jazzercise Inc 2460 Impala Dr	Carlsbad	CA	92010	760-476-1750	602-7180
TF Cust Svc: 800-348-4748 ■ *Web:* www.jazzercise.com					
Jenny Craig International Inc 5770 Fleet St	Carlsbad	CA	92008	760-696-4000	696-4506
TF: 800-443-2331 ■ *Web:* www.jennycraig.com					
Jet's America Inc 37177 Mound Rd	Sterling Heights	MI	48130	586-268-5870	268-6762
TF: 888-446-5870 ■ *Web:* www.jetspizza.com					
Jiffy Lube International Inc 700 Milam St	Houston	TX	77002	713-546-4000	
TF: 800-327-9532 ■ *Web:* www.jiffylube.com					
Jimmy John's Franchise Inc 2212 Fox Dr	Champaign	IL	61820	217-356-9900	359-2956
TF: 800-546-6904 ■ *Web:* www.jimmyjohns.com					
Johnny Rockets Group Inc					
25550 Commerce Centre Dr Suite 200	Lake Forest	CA	92630	949-643-6100	643-6200
TF: 888-236-9100 ■ *Web:* www.johnnyrockets.com					
Juice It Up! Franchise Corp 17915 Sky Park Cir Suite J	Irvine	CA	92614	949-475-0146	475-0137
Web: www.juiceitup.com					
Kampgrounds of America Inc (KOA) PO Box 30558	Billings	MT	59114	406-248-7444	248-7414
Web: www.koakampgrounds.com					
Karmelkorn Shoppes Inc 7505 Metro Blvd	Minneapolis	MN	55439	952-830-0200	830-0270
Web: www.karmelkorn.com					
Keller Williams Realty Inc 807 Las Cimas Pkwy Suite 200	Austin	TX	78746	512-327-3070	328-1433
Web: www.kw.com					
KFC Corp 1441 Gardiner Ln	Louisville	KY	40213	502-874-8300	874-2759
TF: 800-544-5774 ■ *Web:* www.kfc.com					
Kid to Kid 452 E 500 South	Salt Lake City	UT	84111	801-359-0071	359-3207
TF: 888-543-2543 ■ *Web:* www.kidtokid.com					
Kiddie Academy International Inc 108 Wheel Rd Suite 200	Bel Air	MD	21015	410-515-0788	569-2729
TF: 800-554-3343 ■ *Web:* www.kiddieacademy.com					
Kinderdance International Inc 1333 Gateway Dr Suite 1033	Melbourne	FL	32901	321-984-4448	984-4490
TF: 800-554-2334 ■ *Web:* www.kinderdance.com					
Kitchen Solvers Inc 401 Jay St	La Crosse	WI	54601	608-791-5516	784-2917
TF: 800-845-6779 ■ *Web:* www.kitchensolvers.com					
Kitchen Tune-Up Inc 813 Circle Dr	Aberdeen	SD	57401	605-225-4049	225-1371
TF: 800-333-6385 ■ *Web:* www.kitchentuneup.com					
Krystal Co 1 Union Sq	Chattanooga	TN	37402	423-757-1550	757-5644
TF: 800-458-5841 ■ *Web:* www.krystalco.com					
Kumon North America Inc					
300 Frank W Burr Blvd Glenpointe Ctr E 5th Fl	Teaneck	NJ	07666	201-928-0444	928-0044
TF: 877-586-6673 ■ *Web:* www.kumon.com					
L & L Hawaiian Barbecue 931 University Ave Suite 202	Honolulu	HI	96826	808-951-9888	951-0888
Web: www.hawaiianbarbecue.com					
L & L Franchise Inc DBA L & L Hawaiian Barbecue					
931 University Ave Suite 202	Honolulu	HI	96826	808-951-9888	951-0888
Web: www.hawaiianbarbecue.com					
L & W Investigations Inc 23332 Mill Creek Dr Suite 130	Laguna Hills	CA	92653	949-305-7383	305-8928
Web: www.lwfranchise.com					
LA Weight Loss Centers 747 Dresher Rd Suite 100	Horsham	PA	19044	215-346-4400	
TF: 877-524-3571 ■ *Web:* www.laweightloss.com					
Labor Finders International Inc 11426 N Jog Rd	Palm Beach Gardens	FL	33418	561-627-6507	627-6556
Web: www.laborfinders.com					
Lady of America Franchise Corp					
500 E Broward Blvd Suite 1650	Fort Lauderdale	FL	33394	954-527-5373	527-5436
TF: 800-833-5239 ■ *Web:* www.ladyofamerica.com					
Lawn Doctor Inc 142 SR 34	Holmdel	NJ	07733	732-946-0029	946-9089
TF: 800-631-5660 ■ *Web:* www.lawndoctor.com					
Leadership Management Inc 4567 Lake Shore Dr	Waco	TX	76710	254-776-2060	772-9588
TF: 800-568-1241 ■ *Web:* www.lmi-bus.com					
Learning Express Inc 29 Buena Vista St	Devens	MA	01434	978-889-1000	889-1010
TF: 800-924-2296 ■ *Web:* www.learningexpress.com					
LEDO Pizza System Inc 2001 Tidewater Colony Dr Suite 203	Annapolis	MD	21401	410-721-6887	266-6888
Web: www.ledopizza.com					
Lee Myles Assoc Corp 650 From Rd 4th Fl South Lobby	Paramus	NJ	07652	201-262-0555	262-5177
TF: 800-533-6953 ■ *Web:* www.leemyles.com					
Liberty Tax Service Inc 1716 Corporate Landing Pkwy	Virginia Beach	VA	23454	757-493-8855	493-0169
TF: 800-790-3863 ■ *Web:* www.libertytax.com					
Lil' Angels LLC 4041 Hatcher Cir	Memphis	TN	38118	901-682-4470	682-2018
TF: 800-358-9101 ■ *Web:* www.angelsus.com					
Line-X Corp 2400 S Garnsey St	Santa Ana	CA	92707	714-850-1662	850-8759
TF: 800-831-3232 ■ *Web:* www.goline-x.com					
Little Caesars Inc 2211 Woodward Ave	Detroit	MI	48201	313-983-6000	983-6166*
**Fax:* Cust Svc ■ *TF:* 800-722-3727 ■ *Web:* www.littlecaesars.com					
Little Gym International Inc 8970 E Raintree Dr Suite 200	Scottsdale	AZ	85260	480-948-2878	948-2765
TF: 888-228-2878 ■ *Web:* www.thelittlegym.com					
Long John Silver's Restaurants Inc 1441 Gardiner Ln	Louisville	KY	40213	502-874-8300	874-8306
Web: www.ljsilvers.com					
M & M Meat Shops Ltd PO Box 2488 Station C	Kitchener	ON	N2H6M3	519-895-1075	895-0762
Web: www.mmmeatshops.com					
MAACO LLC 381 Brooks Rd	King of Prussia	PA	19406	610-265-6606	337-6113
TF: 800-523-1180 ■ *Web:* www.maaco.com					
Mad Science Group 8360 Bougainville St Suite 201	Montreal	QC	H4P2G1	514-344-4181	344-6695
TF: 800-586-5231 ■ *Web:* www.madscience.org					
MaggieMoo's International LLC					
10025 Governor Warfield Pkwy Suite 301	Columbia	MD	21044	800-949-8114	740-1500*
**Fax Area Code:* 410 ■ *Web:* www.maggiemoos.com					
Magnetsigns Advertising Inc 4225 38th St	Camrose	AB	T4V3Z3	780-672-8720	672-8716
TF: 800-219-8977 ■ *Web:* www.magnetsigns.com					
Maid Brigade USA/Minimaid Canada					
4 Concourse Pkwy Suite 200	Atlanta	GA	30328	770-551-9630	391-9092
TF: 800-722-6243 ■ *Web:* www.maidbrigade.com					
Maid to Perfection Corp 1101 Opal Ct 2nd Fl	Hagerstown	MD	21740	301-790-7900	790-3949
TF: 800-648-6243 ■ *Web:* www.maidtoperfectioncorp.com					
MaidPro Corp 180 Canal St	Boston	MA	02114	617-742-8787	720-0700
TF: 888-624-3776 ■ *Web:* www.maidpro.com					
Maids Home Services 4820 Dodge St	Omaha	NE	68132	402-558-5555	558-4112
TF: 800-843-6243 ■ *Web:* www.maids.com					
Maids International DBA Maids Home Services 4820 Dodge St	Omaha	NE	68132	402-558-5555	558-4112
TF: 800-843-6243 ■ *Web:* www.maids.com					
Mail Boxes Etc 6060 Cornerstone Ct W	San Diego	CA	92121	858-455-8800	546-7493
TF: 800-789-4623 ■ *Web:* www.mbe.com					
Manchu Wok 85 Citizen Ct Unit 9	Markham	ON	L6G1A8	905-946-7200	946-7201
TF: 800-361-8864 ■ *Web:* www.manchuwok.com					
Manhattan Bagel Co Inc 100 Horizon Ctr Blvd	Hamilton	NJ	08691	609-631-7000	631-7068
TF: 800-308-2457 ■ *Web:* www.manhattanbagel.com					
Marble Slab Creamery Inc 3100 S Gessner Suite 305	Houston	TX	77063	713-780-3601	780-0264
Web: www.marbleslab.com					
Marco's Franchising LLC 5252 Monroe St	Toledo	OH	43623	419-885-7000	885-5215
TF: 800-262-7267 ■ *Web:* www.marcos.com					
MARS International Inc 2001 E Division St Suite 101	Arlington	TX	76011	817-226-6277	230-2859*
**Fax Area Code:* 800 ■ *Web:* www.marsinternational.com					
Martinizing Dry Cleaning 422 Wards Corner Rd	Loveland	OH	45140	513-351-6211	731-0818
TF: 800-827-0207 ■ *Web:* www.martinizing.com					
Matco Tools 4403 Allen Rd	Stow	OH	44224	330-929-4949	926-5320
TF: 800-368-6651 ■ *Web:* www.matcotools.com					
Mathnasium LLC 5120 W Goldleaf Cir Suite 130	Los Angeles	CA	90056	877-531-6284	943-2111*
**Fax Area Code:* 310 ■ *Web:* www.mathnasium.com					
Maui Wowi Inc 5445 DTC Pkwy Suite 1050	Greenwood Village	CO	80111	303-781-7800	781-2438
Web: www.mauiwowi.com					
McAlister's Corp 731 S Pear Orchard Rd Suite 51	Ridgeland	MS	39157	601-952-1100	957-0964
TF: 888-855-3354 ■ *Web:* www.mcalistersdeli.com					
McDonald's Corp 1 McDonald's Plaza	Oak Brook	IL	60523	630-623-3000	623-5500
NYSE: MCD ■ *TF:* 800-234-6227 ■ *Web:* www.mcdonalds.com					
Medicap Pharmacies Inc					
4350 Westown Pkwy Suite 400	West Des Moines	IA	50266	515-224-8400	224-8415
TF Cust Svc: 800-445-2244 ■ *Web:* www.medicaprx.com					
Medicine Shoppe International Inc 1100 N Lindbergh Blvd	Saint Louis	MO	63132	314-993-6000	872-5500
TF Cust Svc: 800-325-1397 ■ *Web:* www.medshoppe.com					
Meineke Car Care Centers 128 S Tryon St Suite 900	Charlotte	NC	28202	704-377-8855	377-1490
TF: 800-275-5200 ■ *Web:* www.meineke.com					
Melting Pot Restaurants Inc 8810 Twin Lakes Blvd	Tampa	FL	33614	813-881-0055	889-9361
TF: 800-783-0867 ■ *Web:* www.meltingpot.com					
Merle Norman Cosmetics Inc 9130 Bellanca Ave	Los Angeles	CA	90045	310-641-3000	641-7144
TF: 800-421-2060 ■ *Web:* www.merlenorman.com					
Merlin 200,000 Mile Shops 1 N River Lane Suite 206	Geneva	IL	60134	630-208-9900	208-8601
TF: 800-637-5467 ■ *Web:* www.merlins.com					
Merry Maids 3839 Forrest Hill-Irene Rd	Memphis	TN	38125	901-597-8100	597-8140
TF: 800-798-8000 ■ *Web:* www.merrymaids.com					
Midas International Corp 1300 Arlington Heights Rd	Itasca	IL	60143	630-438-3000	438-3700
TF: 800-621-0144 ■ *Web:* www.midas.com					
Minuteman Press International Inc 61 Executive Blvd	Farmingdale	NY	11735	631-249-1370	249-5618
TF: 800-645-3006 ■ *Web:* minutemanpress.com					
Miracle Method US Corp					
4239 N Nevada Ave Suite 115	Colorado Springs	CO	80907	719-594-9091	594-9282
TF: 800-444-8827 ■ *Web:* www.miraclemethodusa.com					
Moe's Southwest Grill LLC 2915 Peachtree Rd	Atlanta	GA	30305	404-351-3500	442-8320
Web: www.moes.com					
Molly Maid Inc 3948 Ranchero Dr	Ann Arbor	MI	48108	734-822-6800	822-6888
TF: 800-665-5962 ■ *Web:* www.mollymaid.com					
Money Mailer LLC 12131 Western Ave	Garden Grove	CA	92841	714-889-3800	889-4618
TF: 800-234-2771 ■ *Web:* www.moneymailer.com					
Mr Appliance Corp 1010 N University Parks Dr	Waco	TX	76707	800-290-1422	745-5073*
**Fax Area Code:* 254 ■ *Web:* www.mrappliance.com					
Mr Electric Corp 1010 N University Parks Dr	Waco	TX	76707	800-253-9151	745-5068*
**Fax Area Code:* 254 ■ *Web:* www.mrelectric.com					
Mr Handyman International LLC 3948 Ranchero Dr	Ann Arbor	MI	48108	800-289-4600	822-6888*
**Fax Area Code:* 734 ■ *TF Cust Svc:* 877-674-2639 ■ *Web:* www.mrhandyman.com					
Mr Hero Restaurants 7010 Engle Rd Suite 100	Middleburg Heights	OH	44130	440-625-3080	625-3081
TF: 888-860-5082 ■ *Web:* www.mrhero.com					
Mr Payroll Check Cashing 1600 W 7th St	Fort Worth	TX	76102	817-335-1100	570-1738
TF: 800-322-3250 ■ *Web:* www.cashamerica.com					
Mr Rooter Corp 1010 N University Pk Dr	Waco	TX	76707	254-745-2444	745-2501
TF: 800-583-8003 ■ *Web:* www.mrrooter.com					
Mr Sub 4576 Yonge St Suite 600	Toronto	ON	M2N6P1	416-225-5545	225-5536
TF: 800-668-7827 ■ *Web:* www.mrsub.ca					
Mrs Fields Original Cookies Inc					
2855 E Cottonwood Pkwy Suite 400	Salt Lake City	UT	84121	801-736-5600	736-5970
TF: 800-348-6311 ■ *Web:* www.mrsfields.com					
MTY Food Group Inc 3465 Thimens Blvd	Sainte-Laurent	QC	H4R1V5	514-336-8885	336-9222
Web: www.mtygroup.com					
My Favorite Muffin 500 Lake Cook Rd Suite 475	Deerfield	IL	60015	847-948-7520	405-8140
TF: 800-251-6101 ■ *Web:* www.babcorp.com					
My Gym Enterprises Inc 15300 Ventura Blvd Suite 414	Sherman Oaks	CA	91403	800-469-4967	907-0735*
**Fax Area Code:* 818 ■ *TF:* 800-426-4573 ■ *Web:* www.my-gym.com					
N-Hance 1530 N 1000 West	Logan	UT	84321	435-755-0099	755-0021
Web: www.nhancefranchise.com					

Company	City	State	ZIP	Phone	Fax
Nathan's Famous Inc 1400 Old Country Rd Suite 400 *NASDAQ: NATH* ■ *TF:* 800-628-4267 ■ *Web:* www.nathansfamous.com	Westbury	NY	11590	516-338-8500	338-7220
National Property Inspections Inc (NPI) 9375 Burt St Suite 201 **Fax Area Code:* 800 ■ *TF:* 800-333-9807 ■ *Web:* www.npiweb.com	Omaha	NE	68114	402-333-9807	933-2508*
Nationwide Floorcover & Window Coverings 111 E Kilbourn Ave Suite 2400 *TF:* 800-366-8088 ■ *Web:* www.floorsandwindows.com	Milwaukee	WI	53202	414-765-9900	765-1300
NaturaLawn of America Inc 1 E Church St *TF:* 800-989-5444 ■ *Web:* www.nl-amer.com	Frederick	MD	21701	301-694-5440	846-0320
Navis Pack & Ship Centers 5675 DTC Blvd Suite 280 *TF:* 800-525-6309 ■ *Web:* www.gonavis.com	Greenwood Village	CO	80111	303-741-6626	741-6653
Nestle Toll House Cafe by Chip 101 W Renner Rd Suite 240 *Web:* www.nestlecafe.com	Richardson	TX	75802	214-495-9533	853-5347
Norwalk Furniture Corp 100 Furniture Pkwy *TF Orders:* 800-837-2565 ■ *Web:* www.norwalkfurniture.com	Norwalk	OH	44857	419-744-3200	668-6223
NOVUS Auto Glass Eagle Creek Commerce Ctr 12800 Hwy 13 S Suite 500 *TF:* 800-328-1137 ■ *Web:* www.novusglass.com	Minneapolis	MN	55378	952-944-8000	944-2542
Nutrilawn Inc 185 The West Mall Suite 115 *TF:* 800-396-6096 ■ *Web:* www.nutri-lawn.com	Toronto	ON	M9C5K8	416-620-7100	620-7771
OctoClean Franchising Systems 5225 Canyon Crest Dr Suite 71-339 *Web:* www.octoclean.com	Riverside	CA	92507	951-683-5859	779-0270
Once Upon A Child 4200 Dahlberg Dr Suite 100 *TF:* 800-433-2540 ■ *Web:* www.ouac.com	Minneapolis	MN	55422	763-520-8500	520-8510
One Hour Air Conditioning & Heating 2 N Tamiami Trail Suite 806 *TF:* 800-746-0458 ■ *Web:* www.onehourair.com	Sarasota	FL	34236	941-552-5100	552-5130
OpenWorks 4742 N 24th St Suite 300 *TF:* 800-777-6736 ■ *Web:* www.openworksweb.com	Phoenix	AZ	85016	602-224-0440	468-3788
Orange Julius of America 7505 Metro Blvd PO Box 39286 **Fax:* Mktg ■ *TF:* 800-679-6556 ■ *Web:* www.orangejulius.com	Minneapolis	MN	55439	952-830-0200	830-0480*
Outdoor Connection Inc 424 Neosho *Web:* www.outdoor-connection.com	Burlington	KS	66839	620-364-5500	364-5563
Oxford Learning Centers Inc 97B S Livingston Ave *TF:* 888-559-2212 ■ *Web:* www.oxfordlearning.com	Livingston	NJ	07039	973-597-4300	
Padgett Business Services 160 Hawthorne Park *TF:* 800-723-4388 ■ *Web:* www.smallbizpros.com	Athens	GA	30606	706-548-1040	543-8537
Pak Mail Centers of America Inc 7173 S Havana St Suite 600 *TF:* 800-778-6665 ■ *Web:* pakmail.com	Englewood	CO	80112	303-957-1000	790-9445
Palm Beach Tan Inc 13800 Senlac Dr Suite 200 *Web:* www.palmbeachtan.com	Farmers Branch	TX	75234	972-406-2400	406-2515
Papa John's International Inc 2002 Papa John's Blvd *NASDAQ: PZZA* ■ **Fax:* Cust Svc ■ *TF:* 877-547-7272 ■ *Web:* www.papajohns.com	Louisville	KY	40299	502-261-7272	261-4331*
Papa Murphy's International Inc 8000 NE Parkway Dr Suite 350 *Web:* www.papamurphys.com	Vancouver	WA	98662	360-260-7272	260-0500
Parcel Plus Inc 12715 Telge Rd *TF:* 800-662-5553 ■ *Web:* www.parcelplus.com	Cypress	TX	77429	281-256-4100	373-4450
Party America 980 Atlantic Ave Suite 103 *Web:* www.partyamerica.com	Alameda	CA	94501	510-747-1800	747-1810
Party City Corp 400 Commons Way *TF:* 800-883-2100 ■ *Web:* www.partycity.com	Rockaway	NJ	07866	973-983-0888	983-1313
Party Land Inc 5215 Militia Hill Rd **Fax Area Code:* 610 ■ *TF:* 800-778-9563 ■ *Web:* www.partyland.com	Plymouth Meeting	PA	19462	484-342-6213	941-6301*
Paul Davis Restoration Inc 1 Independent Dr Suite 2300 *TF:* 800-722-1818 ■ *Web:* www.pdrestoration.com	Jacksonville	FL	32202	904-737-2779	737-4204
Payless Car Rental System Inc 2350-N 34th St N *TF:* 800-729-5255 ■ *Web:* www.paylesscarrental.com	Saint Petersburg	FL	33713	727-321-6352	322-6540
Pearle Vision Inc 4000 Luxottica Pl **Fax Area Code:* 330 ■ *TF:* 800-282-3931 ■ *Web:* www.pearlevision.com	Mason	OH	45040	877-486-6486	486-3596*
Penn Station Inc 8276 Beechmont Ave *Web:* www.penn-station.com	Cincinnati	OH	45255	513-474-5957	474-7116
Perkins Restaurant & Bakery 6075 Poplar Ave Suite 800 *TF:* 800-877-7375 ■ *Web:* www.perkinsrestaurants.com	Memphis	TN	38119	901-766-6400	766-6482
Perma-Glaze Inc 1638 Research Loop Rd Suite 160 *TF:* 800-332-7397 ■ *Web:* www.permaglaze.com	Tucson	AZ	85710	520-722-9718	296-4393
Pet Supplies "Plus" Inc 22710 Haggerty Rd Suite 100 *TF:* 866-477-7747 ■ *Web:* www.petsuppliesplus.com	Farmington Hills	MI	48335	248-374-1900	374-7900
Pet Valu Canada Inc 121 McPherson St *TSX: PVC* ■ *TF:* 800-738-8258 ■ *Web:* www.petvalu.com	Markham	ON	L3R3L3	905-946-1200	305-6166
Petland Inc 250 Riverside St *TF:* 800-221-5935 ■ *Web:* www.petland.com	Chillicothe	OH	45601	740-775-2464	775-2574
Philly Connection 120 Interstate N Pkwy E Suite 112 *TF:* 800-886-8826 ■ *Web:* www.phillyconnection.com	Atlanta	GA	30339	770-952-6152	952-3168
Philly Franchising Co DBA Philly Connection 120 Interstate N Pkwy E Suite 112 *TF:* 800-886-8826 ■ *Web:* www.phillyconnection.com	Atlanta	GA	30339	770-952-6152	952-3168
Physicians Weight Loss Centers of America Inc 395 Springside Dr *TF:* 800-205-7887 ■ *Web:* www.pwlc.com	Akron	OH	44333	330-666-7952	666-2197
Pillar to Post Inc 13902 N Dale Mabry Hwy Suite 300 *TF:* 800-294-5591 ■ *Web:* www.pillartopost.com	Tampa	FL	33618	813-962-4461	963-5301
Pinch A Penny Inc PO Box 6025 *TF:* 800-509-5571 ■ *Web:* www.pinchapenny.com	Clearwater	FL	33758	727-531-8913	536-8066
PIP Printing & Document Services Inc 26722 Plaza Dr Suite 200 *Web:* www.pip.com	Mission Viejo	CA	92691	949-282-3800	282-3899
Pizza Factory Inc 49430 Rd 426 *TF:* 800-654-4840 ■ *Web:* www.pizzafactoryinc.com	Oakhurst	CA	93644	559-683-3377	683-6879
Pizza Hut Inc 14841 N Dallas Pkwy **Fax:* Cust Svc ■ *TF:* 800-948-8488 ■ *Web:* www.pizzahut.com	Dallas	TX	75254	972-338-7700	338-6869*
Pizza Inn Inc 3551 Plano Pkwy *NASDAQ: PZZI* ■ *TF:* 800-880-9955 ■ *Web:* www.pizzainn.com	The Colony	TX	75056	469-384-5000	384-5054
Pizza Pizza Ltd 580 Jarvis St *TF:* 800-265-9762 ■ *Web:* www.pizzapizza.ca	Toronto	ON	M4Y2H9	416-967-1010	967-0891
Pizza Ranch Inc 1121 Main St *TF:* 800-321-3401 ■ *Web:* www.pizzaranch.com	Hull	IA	51239	712-439-1150	439-1125
Plato's Closet 4200 Dahlberg Dr Suite 100 *Web:* www.platoscloset.com	Minneapolis	MN	55422	763-520-8500	520-8410
Play It Again Sports 4200 Dahlberg Dr Suite 100 *TF:* 800-433-2540 ■ *Web:* www.playitagainsports.com	Minneapolis	MN	55422	763-520-8500	520-8470
Ponderosa Steakhouses 6500 International Pkwy Suite 1000 **Fax:* Cust Svc ■ *TF:* 800-727-8355 ■ *Web:* www.ponderosasteakhouses.com	Plano	TX	75093	972-588-5000	588-5973*
Popeyes Chicken & Biscuits 5555 Glenridge Connector NE Suite 300 *TF:* 866-232-4403 ■ *Web:* www.popeyes.com	Atlanta	GA	30342	404-459-4450	459-4533
Port of Subs Inc 5365 Mae Anne Ave Suite A-29 *TF:* 800-245-0245 ■ *Web:* www.portofsubs.com	Reno	NV	89523	775-747-0555	747-1510
Postal Connections of America 1081 Camino del Rio S Suite 109 *TF:* 800-767-8257 ■ *Web:* www.postalconnections.com	San Diego	CA	92108	619-294-7550	294-4550
PostalAnnex+ Inc 7580 Metropolitan Dr Suite 200 *TF:* 800-456-1525 ■ *Web:* www.postalannex.com	San Diego	CA	92108	619-563-4800	563-9850
PostNet International Franchise Corp 1819 Wazee St *TF:* 800-841-7171 ■ *Web:* www.postnet.com	Denver	CO	80202	303-771-7100	771-7133
Powerhouse Gym International 24385 Halsted Rd Suite 2000 *Web:* www.powerhousegym.com	Farmington Hills	MI	48335	248-476-2888	476-4732
Precision Auto Care Inc 748 Miller Dr SE *TF:* 800-438-8863 ■ *Web:* www.precisionac.com	Leesburg	VA	20175	703-777-9095	771-7108
PremierGarage Systems LLC 1616 W Williams Dr *TF:* 866-483-4272 ■ *Web:* www.premiergarage.com	Phoenix	AZ	85027	480-483-3030	483-7895
Pressed4Time Inc 8 Clock Tower Pl Suite 110 *TF:* 800-423-8711 ■ *Web:* www.pressed4time.com	Maynard	MA	01754	978-823-8300	823-8301
Primrose School Franchising Co 3660 Cedarcrest Rd *TF:* 800-745-0677 ■ *Web:* www.primroseschools.com	Acworth	GA	30101	770-529-4100	529-1551
Priority Management Systems Inc 13251 Delf Pl Suite 420 *TF:* 800-665-5448 ■ *Web:* www.prioritymanagement.com	Richmond	BC	V6V2A2	604-214-7772	214-7773
Pro Golf Inc 37735 Enterprise Ct Suite 600 *Web:* www.progolfamerica.com	Farmington Hills	MI	48331	248-994-0553	489-9334
Pro Image Franchise LC 233 N 1250 West Suite 200 *TF:* 888-477-6326 ■ *Web:* www.proimage.net	Centerville	UT	84014	801-296-9999	296-1319
Professional Carpet Systems Inc (PCS) 4211 Atlantic Ave *TF:* 800-925-5055 ■ *Web:* www.procarpetsys.com	Raleigh	NC	27604	919-875-8871	875-9855
ProForma 8800 E Pleasant Valley Rd *TF:* 800-825-1525 ■ *Web:* www.proforma.com	Independence	OH	44131	216-520-8400	520-8444
Property Damage Appraisers Inc PO Box 9230 **Fax Area Code:* 800 ■ *TF:* 800-749-7324 ■ *Web:* www.pdahomeoffice.com	Fort Worth	TX	76147	817-731-5555	725-5553*
Prudential Real Estate Affiliates Inc 3333 Michelson Dr Suite 1000 **Fax:* Mktg ■ *TF:* 800-999-1120 ■ *Web:* www.prudential.com/realestate	Irvine	CA	92612	949-794-7900	794-7036*
Pump It Up 1249 Quarry Ln Suite 150 *TF:* 866-325-9663 ■ *Web:* www.pumpitupparty.com	Pleasanton	CA	94566	925-397-1300	600-0279
Qdoba Mexican Grill 4865 Ward Rd Suite 500 *TF:* 877-261-4783 ■ *Web:* www.qdoba.com	Wheat Ridge	CO	80033	720-898-2300	898-2396
Qdoba Restaurant Corp DBA Qdoba Mexican Grill 4865 Ward Rd Suite 500 *TF:* 877-261-4783 ■ *Web:* www.qdoba.com	Wheat Ridge	CO	80033	720-898-2300	898-2396
Quik Internet 3151 Airway Ave Suite M-3 *Web:* www.quik.com	Costa Mesa	CA	92626	714-429-1040	429-1038
QuikDrop International 3151 Airway Ave Suite M3 *Web:* www.quikdropfranchise.com	Costa Mesa	CA	92626	714-429-1040	429-1038
Quiznos Corp 1475 Lawrence St Suite 400 *Web:* www.quiznos.com	Denver	CO	80202	720-359-3300	359-3399
RadioShack 300 Radioshack Cir *TF:* 800-843-7422 ■ *Web:* www.radioshack.com	Fort Worth	TX	76102	817-415-3011	415-3240
Rainbow International 1010 N University Park Dr *TF:* 800-583-9100 ■ *Web:* www.rainbowintl.com	Waco	TX	76707	254-745-2444	745-2592
Rally's Hamburgers Inc 4300 W Cypress St Suite 600 *TF:* 800-800-8072 ■ *Web:* www.rallyshamburgers.com	Tampa	FL	33607	813-283-7000	283-7001
Re-Bath LLC 1055 S Country Club Dr *TF:* 800-426-4573 ■ *Web:* www.re-bath.com	Mesa	AZ	85210	480-844-1575	833-7199
Real Living Inc 77 E Nationwide Blvd *TF:* 800-848-7400 ■ *Web:* www.realliving.com	Columbus	OH	43215	614-459-7400	457-6807
Realty Executives International Inc 2398 E Camelback Rd Suite 900 *TF:* 800-252-3366 ■ *Web:* www.realtyexecutives.com	Phoenix	AZ	85016	602-957-0747	224-5542
Red Robin Gourmet Burgers Inc 6312 S Fiddlers Green Cir Suite 200-N *NASDAQ: RRGB* ■ *Web:* www.redrobin.com	Greenwood Village	CO	80111	303-846-6000	846-6013
Regis Corp Cost Cutters Family Hair Salon Div 7201 Metro Blvd *TF:* 888-888-7778 ■ *Web:* www.costcutters.com	Minneapolis	MN	55439	952-947-7777	947-7801
Regis Corp Pro-Cuts Div 7201 Metro Blvd *TF:* 888-888-7778 ■ *Web:* www.pro-cuts.com	Minneapolis	MN	55439	952-947-7777	
Regis Corp Supercuts Div 7201 Metro Blvd *TF:* 888-888-7778 ■ *Web:* www.supercuts.com	Minneapolis	MN	55439	952-947-7777	947-7801
Relax The Back Corp 6 Center Point Dr Suite 350 **Fax Area Code:* 714 ■ *Web:* www.relaxtheback.com	La Palma	CA	90623	800-222-5728	523-2419*
RE/MAX International Inc 8390 E Crescent Pkwy Suite 500 *TF Cust Svc:* 800-525-7452 ■ *Web:* www.remax.com	Greenwood Village	CO	80111	303-770-5531	796-3599
Remedy Temp Inc 101 Enterprise Suite 100 *NASDAQ: REMX* ■ *TF:* 800-828-3726 ■ *Web:* www.remedystaff.com	Aliso Viejo	CA	92656	949-425-7600	425-7980
Rescuecom Corp 2560 Burnet Ave **Fax Area Code:* 315 ■ *Web:* www.rescuecom.com	Syracuse	NY	13206	800-737-2837	433-5228*
Results Travel 701 Carlson Pkwy *TF:* 800-523-2200 ■ *Web:* www.resultstravel.com	Minnetonka	MN	55305	763-212-5000	212-2302
Right at Home Inc 11949 Q St Suite 100 *TF:* 877-697-7537 ■ *Web:* www.rightathome.net	Omaha	NE	68137	402-697-7537	697-0289
Rita's Water Ice Franchise Co LLC 1210 Northbrook Dr *TF:* 800-677-7482 ■ *Web:* www.ritasice.com	Trevose	PA	19053	215-876-9300	
Rocky Mountain Chocolate Factory Inc 265 Turner Dr *NASDAQ: RMCF* ■ *TF Cust Svc:* 888-525-2462 ■ *Web:* www.rmcf.com	Durango	CO	81303	970-259-0554	259-5895
Rooter-Man 268 Rangeway Rd *TF:* 800-700-8062 ■ *Web:* www.rooterman.com	North Billerica	MA	01862	978-667-1144	663-0061
RSVP Publications 6730 W Linebaugh Ave Suite 201 *TF:* 800-360-7787 ■ *Web:* www.rsvppublications.com	Tampa	FL	33625	813-960-7787	549-3306
Ruby Tuesday Inc 150 W Church Ave *NYSE: RI* ■ **Fax:* Mktg ■ *TF:* 800-325-0755 ■ *Web:* www.ruby-tuesday.com	Maryville	TN	37801	865-379-5700	379-6826*
Saladworks Inc Eight Tower Bridge 161 Washington St Suite 225 *Web:* www.saladworks.com	Conshohocken	PA	19428	610-825-3080	825-3280
Sandler Sales Institute 10411 Stevenson Rd *TF:* 800-638-5686 ■ *Web:* www.sandler.com	Stevenson	MD	21153	410-653-1993	358-7858
Scotts Lawn Service 14111 Scottslawn Rd *TF:* 888-872-6887 ■ *Web:* www.scottslawnservice.com	Marysville	OH	43040	937-644-0011	578-5444
Screenmobile 72-050A Corporate Way *Web:* www.screenmobile.com	Thousand Palms	CA	92276	760-343-3500	343-7543
Sea Tow Services International Inc 1560 Youngs Ave PO Box 1178 *TF:* 800-473-2869 ■ *Web:* www.seatow.com	Southold	NY	11971	631-765-3660	765-5208
Second Cup Ltd 6303 Airport Rd *TF:* 800-338-2610 ■ *Web:* www.secondcup.com	Mississauga	ON	L4V1R8	905-405-6700	405-6479
Sensible Car Rental 105 Hwy 36 *TF:* 800-631-2290 ■ *Web:* www.sensiblecarrental.com	Eatontown	NJ	07724	732-380-0888	380-0404
ServiceMaster Clean 3839 Forrest Hill Irene Rd *TF:* 800-633-5703 ■ *Web:* www.servicemasterclean.com	Memphis	TN	38125	901-597-7500	597-7600
Servpro Industries Inc 801 Industrial Blvd *TF:* 800-826-9586 ■ *Web:* www.servpro.com	Gallatin	TN	37066	615-451-0600	451-4861
Shefield Group 2265 W Railway St *Web:* www.shefieldgourmet.com	Abbotsford	BC	V2S2E3	604-859-1014	859-1711
Shoney's Restaurants Inc 1717 Elm Hill Pike Suite B1 *TF:* 877-474-6639 ■ *Web:* www.shoneys.com	Nashville	TN	37210	615-391-5395	231-2498
Sign-A-Rama 2121 Vista Pkwy *TF:* 800-776-8105 ■ *Web:* www.sign-a-rama.com	West Palm Beach	FL	33411	561-640-5570	640-5580
Signs Now 6976 Professional Pkwy E *TF:* 800-356-3373 ■ *Web:* www.signsnow.com	Sarasota	FL	34240	941-373-1958	388-9507
Signs by Tomorrow USA Inc 8681 Robert Fulton Dr *TF:* 800-765-7446 ■ *Web:* www.signsbytomorrow.com	Columbia	MD	21046	410-312-3600	312-3520

				Phone	Fax
Sir Speedy Inc 26722 Plaza Dr / *TF:* 800-854-8297 ■ *Web:* www.sirspeedy.com	Mission Viejo	CA	92691	949-348-5000	348-5010
Smitty's Canada Ltd 600-501 18th Ave SW / *Web:* www.smittys.ca	Calgary	AB	T2S0C7	403-229-3838	229-3899
Smoothie King Franchises Inc 2400 Veterans Blvd Suite 110 / *TF:* 800-577-4200 ■ *Web:* www.smoothieking.com	Kenner	LA	70062	504-467-4006	469-1274
Snap-on Inc 2801 80th St / *NYSE: SNA* ■ *Web:* www.snapon.com	Kenosha	WI	53143	262-656-5200	656-5577
Sonic Drive-in Restaurants 300 Johnny Bench Dr / *TF:* 800-569-6656 ■ *Web:* www.sonicdrivein.com	Oklahoma City	OK	73104	405-225-5000	225-5963
Sonny's Franchise Co DBA Sonny's Real Pit Bar-B-Q 2605 Maitland Ctr Pkwy Suite C / *Web:* www.sonnysbbq.com	Maitland	FL	32751	407-660-8888	660-9050
Sonny's Real Pit Bar-B-Q 2605 Maitland Ctr Pkwy Suite C / *Web:* www.sonnysbbq.com	Maitland	FL	32751	407-660-8888	660-9050
Sparkle International Inc 26851 Richmond Rd / *TF:* 800-321-0770 ■ *Web:* www.sparklewash.com	Cleveland	OH	44146	216-464-4212	464-8869
Spherion Corp 2050 Spectrum Blvd / *NYSE: SFN* ■ **Fax:* Hum Res ■ *TF:* 866-435-7456 ■ *Web:* www.spherion.com	Fort Lauderdale	FL	33309	954-308-7600	308-7666*
Sport Clips Inc 110 Briarwood Dr / *TF:* 800-872-4247 ■ *Web:* www.sportclips.com	Georgetown	TX	78628	512-869-1201	869-0366
Spring-Green Lawn Care Corp 11909 Spaulding School Dr / *TF:* 800-435-4051 ■ *Web:* www.spring-green.com	Plainfield	IL	60544	815-436-8777	436-9056
Stained Glass Overlay Inc 1827 N Case St / *TF:* 800-944-4746 ■ *Web:* www.stainedglassoverlay.com	Orange	CA	92865	714-974-6124	974-6529
Stanley Steemer International Inc 5500 Stanley Steemer Pkwy / *TF:* 800-848-7496 ■ *Web:* www.stanleysteemer.com	Dublin	OH	43016	614-764-2007	764-1506
Steak Escape 222 Neilston St / *Web:* www.steakescape.com	Columbus	OH	43215	614-224-0300	224-6460
Steak n Shake Co 36 S Pennsylvania St Suite 500 / *NYSE: SNS* ■ *TF:* 800-437-2406 ■ *Web:* www.steaknshake.com	Indianapolis	IN	46204	317-633-4100	633-4105
Sterling Optical 100 Quentin Roosevelt Blvd / *TF:* 800-332-6302 ■ *Web:* www.sterlingoptical.com	Garden City	NY	11530	516-390-2100	390-2110
Stork News of America Inc 1305 Hope Mills Rd Suite A / *TF:* 800-633-6395 ■ *Web:* www.storknews.com	Fayetteville	NC	28304	910-426-1357	426-2473
Stretch-N-Grow International Inc PO Box 7599 / *TF:* 800-348-0166 ■ *Web:* www.stretch-n-grow.com	Seminole	FL	33775	727-596-7614	596-7633
StrollerFit Inc 100 E-Business Way Suite 290 / *TF:* 866-222-9348 ■ *Web:* www.strollerfit.com	Cincinnati	OH	45241	513-489-2920	489-2964
Subway Restaurants 325 Bic Dr / *TF:* 800-888-4848 ■ *Web:* www.subway.com	Milford	CT	06460	203-877-4281	783-7614
Successories Inc 2520 Diehl Rd / *TF:* 800-621-1423 ■ *Web:* www.successories.com	Aurora	IL	60504	630-820-7200	820-3003
Sunbelt Business Advisors Network LLC 7100 E Pleasant Valley Rd Suite 260 / **Fax Area Code:* 216 ■ *Web:* www.sunbeltnetwork.com	Independence	OH	44131	800-771-7866	674-0650*
Super Wash Inc 707 W Lincolnway / *Web:* www.superwash.com	Morrison	IL	61270	815-772-2111	772-7160
SuperCoups 350 Revolutionary Dr / *TF:* 800-626-2620 ■ *Web:* www.supercoups.com	East Taunton	MA	02718	508-977-2000	977-0644
Supercuts Div Regis Corp 7201 Metro Blvd / *TF:* 888-888-7778 ■ *Web:* www.supercuts.com	Minneapolis	MN	55439	952-947-7777	947-7801
SuperGlass Windshield Repair Inc 6101 Chancellor Dr Suite 200 / *TF:* 866-557-7497 ■ *Web:* www.sgwr.com	Orlando	FL	32809	407-240-1920	240-3266
SuperShuttle International Inc 14500 N Northsight Blvd Suite 329 / *Web:* www.supershuttle.com	Scottsdale	AZ	85260	480-609-3000	607-9317
Surf City Squeeze 7730 E Greenway Rd Suite 104 / *Web:* www.surfcitysqueeze.com	Scottsdale	AZ	85260	480-443-0200	443-1972
Swensen's Ice Cream Co 4175 Veterans Memorial Hwy / *TF:* 800-423-2763	Ronkonkoma	NY	11779	631-737-9898	737-9792
Swisher Hygiene Co 6849 Fairview Rd / **Fax Area Code:* 800 ■ *TF:* 800-444-4138 ■ *Web:* www.swisheronline.com	Charlotte	NC	28210	704-364-7707	444-4565*
Sylvan Learning Centers 1001 Fleet St / *TF:* 800-627-4267 ■ *Web:* educate-inc.com	Baltimore	MD	21202	410-843-8000	880-8717
System4 10060 Brecksville Rd / *Web:* www.system4usa.com	Brecksville	OH	44141	440-746-0440	746-9544
Taco Bell Corp 17901 Von Karman Ave / *Web:* www.tacobell.com	Irvine	CA	92614	949-863-4500	863-2214
Taco Maker Inc 4605 Harrison Blvd PO Box 84415 / *TF:* 800-207-5804 ■ *Web:* www.tacomaker.com	Ogden	UT	84403	801-476-9780	476-9788
Taco Time International Inc 7730 E Greenway Rd Suite 104 / *TF:* 800-547-8907 ■ *Web:* www.tacotime.com	Scottsdale	AZ	85260	480-443-0200	443-1972
Taylor Rental 203 Jandus Rd / *TF:* 800-833-3004 ■ *Web:* www.taylorrental.com	Cary	IL	60013	847-462-5440	516-9921
TCBY Enterprises Inc 2855 E Cottonwood Pkwy Suite 400 / *TF:* 888-900-8229 ■ *Web:* www.tcby.com	Salt Lake City	UT	84121	801-736-5600	736-5970
Terminix International Co LP 860 Ridge Lake Blvd / **Fax:* Mktg ■ *TF:* 800-654-7848 ■ *Web:* www.terminix.com	Memphis	TN	38120	901-766-1333	766-1491*
TGI Friday's Worldwide Inc 4201 Marsh Ln / **Fax:* Mktg ■ *TF:* 800-374-3297 ■ *Web:* www.tgifridays.com	Carrollton	TX	75007	972-662-5400	662-5739*
Tim Hortons Inc 874 Sinclair Rd / *NYSE: THI* ■ *TF:* 888-601-1616 ■ *Web:* www.timhortons.com	Oakville	ON	L6K2Y1	905-845-6511	845-0265
Tony Roma's Inc 9304 Forest Ln Suite 200 / *TF:* 800-286-7662 ■ *Web:* www.tonyromas.com	Dallas	TX	75243	214-343-7800	343-2680
Treats International Franchise Corp 1550-A Laperriere Ave Suite 201 / *TF:* 800-461-4003 ■ *Web:* www.treats.com	Ottawa	ON	K1Z7T2	613-563-4073	563-1982
Tropical Smoothie Cafe 4100 Legendary Dr Suite 250 / *Web:* www.tropicalsmoothie.com	Destin	FL	32541	850-269-9850	269-9845
Truly Nolen of America Inc 3636 E Speedway Blvd / *TF:* 800-528-3442 ■ *Web:* www.trulynolen.com	Tucson	AZ	85716	520-327-3447	322-4011
Tuffy Assoc Corp 1414 Baronial Plaza Dr / *TF:* 800-228-8339 ■ *Web:* www.tuffy.com	Toledo	OH	43615	419-865-6900	865-7343
Tutor Time Child Care/Learning Centers 21333 Haggerty Rd Suite 300 / *TF:* 800-275-1235 ■ *Web:* www.tutortime.com	Novi	MI	48375	248-697-9000	697-9001
Tutoring Club Inc 14870 Hwy 4 Suite B / *TF:* 888-674-6425 ■ *Web:* www.tutoringclub.com	Discovery Bay	CA	94514	925-513-7784	513-8443
Two Men & A Truck International Inc 3400 Belle Chase Way / *TF:* 800-345-1070 ■ *Web:* www.twomen.com	Lansing	MI	48911	517-394-7210	394-7432
UBuildIt Corp 12006 98th Ave NE Suite 200 / *TF:* 800-992-4357 ■ *Web:* www.ubuildit.com	Kirkland	WA	98034	425-821-6200	821-6876
United Financial Services Group 400 Market St Suite 1030 / *TF:* 800-826-0787 ■ *Web:* www.unitedfsg.com	Philadelphia	PA	19106	215-238-0300	238-9056
United Shipping Solutions 6985 Union Park Center Suite 565 / *TF:* 866-744-7486 ■ *Web:* www.usshipit.com	Midvale	UT	84047	801-352-0012	352-0339
Uno Chicago Grill 100 Charles Park Rd / *TF:* 866-600-8667 ■ *Web:* www.unos.com	Boston	MA	02132	617-323-9200	469-3949
UPS Store The 6060 Cornerstone Ct W / *Web:* theupsstore.com	San Diego	CA	92121	858-455-8800	546-7492
US Lawns 4407 Vineland Rd Suite D-15 / **Fax Area Code:* 407 ■ *Web:* www.uslawns.com	Orlando	FL	32811	800-875-2967	246-1623*
V2K Window Fashions Inc 1127 Auraria Pkwy Suite 204 / **Fax Area Code:* 303 ■ *Web:* www.v2k.com	Denver	CO	80204	800-200-0835	202-5201*
Valpak Direct Marketing Systems Inc 8605 Largo Lakes Dr / *TF:* 800-237-6266 ■ *Web:* www.valpak.com	Largo	FL	33773	727-393-1270	393-8060
Vanguard Cleaning Systems Inc 655 Mariners Island Blvd Suite 303 / *TF:* 800-564-6422 ■ *Web:* www.vanguardcleaning.com	San Mateo	CA	94404	650-594-1500	591-1545
Village Inn 400 W 48th Ave / **Fax:* Cust Svc ■ *TF:* 800-800-3644 ■ *Web:* www.vicorpinc.com	Denver	CO	80216	303-296-2121	672-2676*
Visiting Angels 28 W Eagle Rd Suite 204 / *TF:* 800-365-4189 ■ *Web:* www.livingassistance.com	Havertown	PA	19083	610-924-0630	924-9690
Volvo Rents 1 Volvo Dr / **Fax Area Code:* 828 ■ *Web:* www.volvorents.com	Asheville	NC	28803	866-387-3687	650-2504*
We The People USA Inc 1436 Lancaster Ave Suite 300 / **Fax Area Code:* 610 ■ *Web:* www.wethepeopleusa.com	Berwyn	PA	19312	866-429-2790	296-2038*
Weed Man 2399 Royal Windsor / *Web:* www.weedmanusa.com	Mississauga	ON	L5J1K9	905-823-8550	823-4594
Weichert Realtors 225 Littleton Rd / *TF:* 800-872-7653 ■ *Web:* www.weichert.com	Morris Plains	NJ	07950	973-359-8377	292-1428
Wendy's International Inc 1 Dave Thomas Blvd / *NYSE: WEN* ■ *Web:* www.wendys.com	Dublin	OH	43017	614-764-3100	764-3459
Westaff Inc 298 N Wiget Ln / *NASDAQ: WSTF* ■ *TF:* 800-872-8367 ■ *Web:* www.westaff.com	Walnut Creek	CA	94598	925-930-5300	256-1515
Western Sizzlin Corp 1338 Plantation Rd / *TF:* 800-247-8325 ■ *Web:* www.western-sizzlin.com	Roanoke	VA	24012	540-345-3195	345-0831
Wetzel's Pretzels LLC 35 Hugus Alley Suite 300 / *Web:* www.wetzels.com	Pasadena	CA	91103	626-432-6900	432-6904
White Hen Pantry Inc 700 E Butterfield Rd Suite 300 / *TF:* 800-726-8791 ■ *Web:* www.whitehen.com	Lombard	IL	60148	630-366-3100	366-3447
Wienerschnitzel 4450 Von Karman Ave Suite 220 / *Web:* www.wienerschnitzel.com	Newport Beach	CA	92660	949-752-5800	
Wild Birds Unlimited Inc 11711 N College Ave Suite 146 / *TF:* 800-326-4928 ■ *Web:* www.wbu.com	Carmel	IN	46032	317-571-7100	571-7110
WIN Home Inspections 6500 6th Ave NW / *TF:* 800-967-8127 ■ *Web:* www.wini.com	Seattle	WA	98117	206-728-8100	
Window Gang 405 Arendell St / *TF:* 877-946-4264 ■ *Web:* www.windowgang.com	Morehead City	NC	28557	252-726-1463	726-2837
WineStyles Inc 5100 W Copans Rd Suite 310 / *TF:* 866-424-9463 ■ *Web:* winestyles.net	Margate	FL	33063	954-984-0070	984-0074
Wing Zone Franchise Corp 900 Circle 75 Pkwy Suite 930 / *TF:* 877-946-4966 ■ *Web:* www.wingzone.com	Atlanta	GA	30339	404-875-5045	875-6631
Wingstop Restaurants Inc 1101 E Arapaho Rd Suite 150 / *Web:* www.wingstop.com	Richardson	TX	75081	972-686-6500	686-6502
Wireless Toyz Ltd 23399 Commerce Dr Suite B-1 / *TF:* 866-237-2624 ■ *Web:* www.wirelesstoyz.com	Farmington Hills	MI	48335	248-426-8200	671-0346
Wireless Zone 34 Industrial Park Pl / *TF:* 800-411-2355 ■ *Web:* www.wirelesszone.com	Middletown	CT	06457	860-632-9494	632-9343
Women's Health Boutique Franchise System Inc 12715 Telge Rd / *TF:* 888-280-2053 ■ *Web:* www.w-h-b.com	Cypress	TX	77429	281-256-4100	373-4450
Woodcraft Supply LLC 1177 Rosemar Rd PO Box 1686 / *TF Cust Svc:* 800-535-4482 ■ *Web:* www.woodcraft.com	Parkersburg	WV	26105	304-422-5412	428-8271
World Gym International 226 E Palm Ave / *TF:* 800-544-7441 ■ *Web:* www.worldgym.com	Burbank	CA	91502	818-955-8905	
World Inspection Network International Inc 6500 6th Ave NW / *TF:* 800-967-8127 ■ *Web:* www.wini.com	Seattle	WA	98117	206-728-8100	
Worldwide Express 2828 Routh St Suite 400 / *TF:* 800-758-7447 ■ *Web:* www.wwex.com	Dallas	TX	75201	214-720-2400	720-2446
WSI Internet 5580 Explorer Dr Suite 600 / *TF:* 888-678-7588 ■ *Web:* www.wsicorporate.com	Mississauga	ON	L4W4Y1	905-678-7588	678-7242
Yogen Früz 8300 Woodbine Ave 5th Fl / *Web:* www.yogenfruz.com	Markham	ON	L3R9Y7	905-479-8762	479-5235
Young Rembrandts 23 N Union St / *Web:* www.youngrembrandts.com	Elgin	IL	60123	847-742-6966	742-7197
Ziebart International Corp 1290 E Maple Rd / **Fax:* Orders ■ *TF:* 800-877-1312 ■ *Web:* www.ziebart.com	Troy	MI	48083	248-588-4100	588-2513*

314 FREIGHT FORWARDERS

SEE ALSO Logistics Services (Transportation & Warehousing) p. 1918

				Phone	Fax
Adcom Worldwide Inc PO Box 390048 / *TF:* 800-829-7991 ■ *Web:* www.adcomworldwide.com	Edina	MN	55439	952-829-7990	829-9124
Air Cargo International & Domestic 180 Admiral Cochrane Dr Suite 305 / *TF:* 800-747-6505 ■ *Web:* www.aircargoinc.com	Annapolis	MD	21401	410-280-5578	268-3154
Airways Freight Corp 3849 W Wedington Dr / *TF:* 800-643-3525 ■ *Web:* www.airwaysfreight.com	Fayetteville	AR	72704	479-442-6301	442-6522
Alba Wheels Up International Inc 525 Washington Blvd Suite 2402 / *Web:* www.albawheelsup.com	Jersey City	NJ	07310	201-435-7050	435-5650
ALG Admiral Inc 745 Dillon Dr / *TF:* 800-323-0289 ■ *Web:* www.admiralusa.com	Wood Dale	IL	60191	630-766-3900	350-7616
Allstates WorldCargo Inc 4 Lakeside Dr S / *TF:* 800-575-5575 ■ *Web:* www.allstatesair.com	Forked River	NJ	08731	609-693-5950	693-6667
Argents Express Group 7025 Metroplex Dr / *TF:* 800-229-2231 ■ *Web:* www.argents.com	Romulus	MI	48174	734-326-9499	326-1172
Central Global Express PO Box 698 / *TF:* 800-982-3924 ■ *Web:* www.centralglobalexpress.com	Taylor	MI	48180	734-955-2555	955-2829
Continental Traffic Service Inc (CTSI) 5100 Poplar Ave Clark Tower Bldg Suite 1750 / *Web:* www.continental-traffic.com	Memphis	TN	38137	901-766-1500	766-1520
CTSI (Continental Traffic Service Inc) 5100 Poplar Ave Clark Tower Bldg Suite 1750 / *Web:* www.continental-traffic.com	Memphis	TN	38137	901-766-1500	766-1520
Dynamic Ocean Services International Inc 1201 Hahlo St / *Web:* www.dynamicosi.com	Houston	TX	77020	713-672-0515	672-0786
FESCO Agencies NA Inc 1000 2nd Ave Suite 1310 / *TF:* 800-275-3372 ■ *Web:* www.fesco-na.com	Seattle	WA	98104	206-583-0860	583-0889
Graulich International Inc 6411 NW 35th Ave / *TF:* 800-836-2709 ■ *Web:* www.graulichinternational.com	Miami	FL	33147	305-836-1700	836-1763
Guaranteed Air Freight & Forwarding Inc 4555 McDonnell Blvd / *TF:* 800-445-0738 ■ *Web:* www.gaffinc.com	Saint Louis	MO	63134	314-427-7709	427-5392
Hassett Air Express 877 S Rt 83 / *TF:* 800-323-9422 ■ *Web:* www.hassettair.com	Elmhurst	IL	60126	630-530-6515	530-9859
Lynden Inc 18000 International Blvd Suite 800 / *TF:* 800-426-3201 ■ *Web:* www.lynden.com	Seattle	WA	98188	206-241-8778	243-8415
Maher MG & Co 1 Canal Pl Suite 1600 / *Web:* www.mgmaher.com	New Orleans	LA	70130	504-581-3320	529-2611
MG Maher & Co 1 Canal Pl Suite 1600 / *Web:* www.mgmaher.com	New Orleans	LA	70130	504-581-3320	529-2611
Nippon Express USA Inc 590 Madison Ave Suite 2401 / *Web:* www.nipponexpressusa.com	New York	NY	10022	212-758-6100	758-2595

	City	State	Zip	Phone	Fax
Pacific CMA Inc 153-04 Rockaway Blvd *AMEX: PAM* ■ *Web:* www.pacificcma.com	Jamaica	NY	11434	212-247-0049	247-0245
Phoenix International Freight Services Ltd 712 N Central Ave *TF:* 800-959-9590 ■ *Web:* www.phoenixintl.com	Wood Dale	IL	60191	630-766-9444	766-6395
Ram International Inc 4664 World Pkwy Cir *TF:* 800-884-4726 ■ *Web:* www.ram-intl.com	Saint Louis	MO	63134	314-427-3000	427-5068
Senderex Cargo Inc 10425 S La Cienega Blvd *TF:* 800-421-5846 ■ *Web:* www.senderex.com	Los Angeles	CA	90045	310-342-2900	642-0427
Sho-Air International 5401 Argosy Ave *TF:* 800-227-9111 ■ *Web:* www.shoair.com	Huntington Beach	CA	92649	949-476-9111	476-9991
Target Logistic Services Inc 1400 Glenn Curtiss St *TF:* 800-283-8888 ■ *Web:* www.targetlogistics.com	Carson	CA	90746	310-900-1974	223-2610
Tricor America Inc 717 Airport Blvd *TF:* 800-669-7631 ■ *Web:* www.tricor.com	South San Francisco	CA	94080	650-877-3650	583-3197
Velocity Express 1 Morningside Dr N Bldg B Suite 300 **Fax Area Code:* 201 ■ *TF:* 800-899-7296 ■ *Web:* www.velocityexp.com	Westport	CT	06880	888-839-7669	489-6974*
WR Zanes & Co of Louisiana Inc 223 Tchoupitoulas St *Web:* www.wrzanes.com	New Orleans	LA	70130	504-524-1301	524-1309
Zanes WR & Co of Louisiana Inc 223 Tchoupitoulas St *Web:* www.wrzanes.com	New Orleans	LA	70130	504-524-1301	524-1309

315 FREIGHT TRANSPORT - DEEP SEA (DOMESTIC PORTS)

	City	State	Zip	Phone	Fax
Alaska Marine Lines Inc 5615 W Marginal Way SW *TF:* 800-950-4265 ■ *Web:* www.aml.lynden.com	Seattle	WA	98106	206-763-4244	764-5782
Coastal Transportation Inc 4025 13th Ave W *TF:* 800-544-2580 ■ *Web:* www.coastaltrans.com	Seattle	WA	98119	206-282-9979	283-9121
Crowley Maritime Corp 555 12th St Suite 2130 *TF:* 800-276-9539 ■ *Web:* www.crowley.com	Oakland	CA	94607	510-251-7500	251-7510
ENSCO Offshore Co 620 Moulin Rd *TF:* 800-322-8217 ■ *Web:* www.enscous.com	Broussard	LA	70518	337-837-8500	837-8540
Express Marine Inc PO Box 329 *Web:* www.expressmarine.com	Pennsauken	NJ	08110	856-541-4600	541-0338
Hapag-Lloyd America Inc 401 E Jackson St *TF:* 800-276-4600 ■ *Web:* www.hapag-lloyd.com/en	Tampa	FL	33631	813-276-4600	276-4873
Horizon Lines Inc 4064 Colony Rd Suite 200 *NYSE: HRZ* ■ *TF Cust Svc:* 877-678-7447 ■ *Web:* www.horizonlines.com	Charlotte	NC	28211	704-973-7000	973-7075
Inchcape Shipping Services Inc 118 N Royal St Suite 400 *Web:* www.iss-shipping.com	Mobile	AL	36602	251-461-2700	461-5067
International Shipholding Corp 650 Poydras St Suite 1700 *NYSE: ISH* ■ **Fax:* Hum Res ■ *Web:* www.intship.com	New Orleans	LA	70130	504-529-5461	593-2571*
K Line America Inc 8730 Stony Point Pkwy Suite 400 *TF:* 800-609-3221 ■ *Web:* www.k-line.com	Richmond	VA	23235	804-560-3600	560-3463
Keystone Shipping Co 1 Bala Plaza Suite 600	Bala Cynwyd	PA	19004	610-617-6800	617-6899
Marine Transport Corp 9487 Regency Sq Blvd *Web:* www.crowley.com/petroleum-chemical-transportation	Jacksonville	FL	32225	904-727-2200	727-2501
Maritrans Inc 2 Harbor Pl 302 Knights Run Ave Suite 1200 *NYSE: TUG* ■ *Web:* www.maritrans.com	Tampa	FL	33602	813-209-0600	221-3189
Matson Navigation Co 555 12th St *TF Cust Svc:* 800-462-8766 ■ *Web:* www.matson.com	Oakland	CA	94607	510-628-4000	628-7380
Mormac Marine Group Inc 1 Landmark Sq Suite 710	Stamford	CT	06901	203-977-8900	977-8933
Northland Services Inc 6700 W Marginal Way SW Suite 600 *TF:* 800-426-3113 ■ *Web:* www.northlandservicesinc.com	Seattle	WA	98106	206-763-3000	767-5579
NYK Line North America Inc 300 Lighting Way 5th Fl *Web:* www.nykline.com	Secaucus	NJ	07094	201-330-3000	617-1367
Overseas Shipholding Group Inc 666 3rd Ave *NYSE: OSG* ■ *TF:* 800-223-1722 ■ *Web:* www.osg.com	New York	NY	10017	212-953-4100	578-1832
Penn-Attransco Corp 10 E Baltimore St Suite 1102	Baltimore	MD	21202	410-347-7000	347-7001
SC Loveland Co Inc PO Box 368 *TF:* 800-523-2687	Pennsville	NJ	08070	856-935-8100	935-7417
Sea Star Line LLC 100 Bell Tel Way Suite 300 *TF:* 877-775-7447 ■ *Web:* www.seastarline.com	Jacksonville	FL	32216	904-855-1260	724-3011
Seaboard Marine Ltd 8001 NW 79th Ave *TF:* 800-753-0681 ■ *Web:* www.seaboardmarine.com	Miami	FL	33166	305-863-4444	863-4400
TECO Ocean Shipping 1300 E 8th Ave Suite S-300 *TF:* 800-835-4161 ■ *Web:* www.tecooceanshipping.com	Tampa	FL	33605	813-209-4200	242-4849
TECO Transport 702 N Franklin St *TF:* 800-835-4161 ■ *Web:* www.tecotransport.com	Tampa	FL	33602	813-228-1111	273-0248
Totem Ocean Trailer Express Inc (TOTE) 32001 32nd Ave S Suite 200 *TF:* 800-426-0074 ■ *Web:* www.totemocean.com	Federal Way	WA	98001	253-449-8100	449-8225
Trailer Bridge Inc 10405 New Berlin Rd E *NASDAQ: TRBR* ■ *TF:* 800-554-1589 ■ *Web:* www.trailerbridge.com	Jacksonville	FL	32226	904-751-7100	751-7444
US Shipping Partners LP 399 Thornall St 8th Fl *NYSE: USS* ■ *Web:* www.usshipllc.com	Edison	NJ	08837	732-635-1500	635-1918
Waterman Steamship Corp 1 Whitehall St 20th Fl *TF:* 888-972-5274 ■ *Web:* www.waterman-steamship.com	New York	NY	10004	212-747-8550	747-8588
Western Pioneer Inc 4601 Shilshole Ave NW *TF:* 800-426-6783 ■ *Web:* www.westernpioneer.com	Seattle	WA	98107	206-789-1930	781-2486
Young Brothers Ltd PO Box 3288 *TF:* 800-572-2743 ■ *Web:* www.htbyb.com	Honolulu	HI	96801	808-543-9311	543-9458

316 FREIGHT TRANSPORT - DEEP SEA (FOREIGN PORTS)

	City	State	Zip	Phone	Fax
Alcoa Steamship Co Inc 201 Isabella St	Pittsburgh	PA	15212	412-553-4545	553-1060
American Overseas Marine Corp 100 Newport Ave Ext	Quincy	MA	02171	617-786-8300	472-4925
American President Lines Ltd 1111 Broadway *TF:* 800-999-7733 ■ *Web:* www.apl.com	Oakland	CA	94607	510-272-8000	272-2818
Antillean Marine Shipping Corp 3038 NW North River Dr *Web:* www.antillean.com	Miami	FL	33142	305-633-6361	894-3880
APL Ltd 1111 Broadway *TF:* 800-999-7733 ■ *Web:* www.apl.com	Oakland	CA	94607	510-272-8000	272-2818
Atlantic Container Line 194 Wood Ave S Suite 500 **Fax:* Hum Res ■ *TF:* 800-225-1235 ■ *Web:* www.aclcargo.com	Iselin	NJ	08830	732-452-5400	452-5492*
Brennan International Transport Inc 2665 E Del Amo Blvd *TF:* 866-427-3662 ■ *Web:* www.brennanusa.com	Rancho Dominguez	CA	90221	310-637-7000	637-9550
Direct Container Line Inc 857 E 230th St *TF:* 888-325-4325 ■ *Web:* www.dclusa.com	Carson	CA	90745	310-518-1773	830-5316
Energy Transportation Group 654 Madison Ave *Web:* www.etgglobal.com	New York	NY	10021	212-813-9360	813-9390
Fednav Ltd 1000 rue de la Gauchetière O Bureau 3500 *TF:* 800-678-4842 ■ *Web:* www.fednav.com	Montreal	QC	H3B4W5	514-878-6500	878-6642
General Maritime Corp 299 Park Ave 2nd Fl *NYSE: GMR* ■ *Web:* www.generalmaritimecorp.com	New York	NY	10171	212-763-5600	763-5603
Hamburg Sud North America Inc 465 South St *TF:* 800-901-7447 ■ *Web:* www.hamburgsud.com	Morristown	NJ	07960	973-775-5300	775-5310
Hapag-Lloyd America Inc 401 E Jackson St *TF:* 800-276-4600 ■ *Web:* www.hapag-lloyd.com/en	Tampa	FL	33631	813-276-4600	276-4873
Höegh Autoliners Inc 500 N Broadway Jericho Atrium Bldg Suite 233 *Web:* www.hoegh.com/autoliners	Jericho	NY	11753	516-935-1600	935-2604
Inchcape Shipping Services Inc 118 N Royal St Suite 400 *Web:* www.iss-shipping.com	Mobile	AL	36602	251-461-2700	461-5067
International Shipholding Corp 650 Poydras St Suite 1700 *NYSE: ISH* ■ **Fax:* Hum Res ■ *Web:* www.intship.com	New Orleans	LA	70130	504-529-5461	593-2571*
K Line America Inc 8730 Stony Point Pkwy Suite 400 *TF:* 800-609-3221 ■ *Web:* www.k-line.com	Richmond	VA	23235	804-560-3600	560-3463
Liberty Maritime Corp 1979 Marcus Ave Suite 200	Lake Success	NY	11042	516-488-8800	488-8806
Maersk Inc 2 Giralda Farms PO Box 880 *TF:* 800-321-8807 ■ *Web:* www.maersksealand.com	Madison	NJ	07940	973-514-5000	514-5410
Marine Transport Corp 9487 Regency Sq Blvd *Web:* www.crowley.com/petroleum-chemical-transportation	Jacksonville	FL	32225	904-727-2200	727-2501
Mitsui OSK Lines (America) Inc 160 Fieldcrest Ave PO Box 7804	Edison	NJ	08818	732-512-5200	512-5300
OMI Corp 1 Station Pl Metro Center *NYSE: OMM* ■ **Fax:* Hum Res ■ *TF:* 800-344-9711 ■ *Web:* www.omicorp.net	Stamford	CT	06902	203-602-6700	602-6701*
Orient Overseas Container Line Inc 17777 Center Court Dr N Suite 500 *TF:* 800-822-6625 ■ *Web:* www.oocl.com	Cerritos	CA	90703	562-499-2600	499-4401
Overseas Shipholding Group Inc 666 3rd Ave *NYSE: OSG* ■ *TF:* 800-223-1722 ■ *Web:* www.osg.com	New York	NY	10017	212-953-4100	578-1832
Pasha Group Inc 5725 Paradise Dr Suite 1000 *Web:* www.pashagroup.com	Corte Madera	CA	94925	415-927-6400	924-5672
Red River Shipping Corp 6110 Executive Blvd Suite 620	Rockville	MD	20852	301-230-0854	770-6131
Seaboard Marine Ltd 8001 NW 79th Ave *TF:* 800-753-0681 ■ *Web:* www.seaboardmarine.com	Miami	FL	33166	305-863-4444	863-4400
SEACOR Marine Inc 5005 Railroad Ave *Web:* www.seacormarine.com	Morgan City	LA	70380	985-385-3475	385-1130
Stolt-Nielsen Transportation Group 800 Connecticut Ave *NASDAQ: SNSA* ■ *Web:* www.stoltnielsen.com	Norwalk	CT	06854	203-299-3600	299-0067
Sunmar Inc 500 108th Ave NE Suite 1710 *TF:* 800-443-4127 ■ *Web:* www.sunmar.com	Bellevue	WA	98004	425-577-1870	577-1880
Sunmar Shipping Inc 500 108th Ave NE Suite 1710 *TF:* 800-443-4127 ■ *Web:* www.sunmar.com/ssi	Bellevue	WA	98004	425-577-1870	577-1880
TECO Ocean Shipping 1300 E 8th Ave Suite S-300 *TF:* 800-835-4161 ■ *Web:* www.tecooceanshipping.com	Tampa	FL	33605	813-209-4200	242-4849
Tidewater Inc 601 Poydras St Suite 1900 *NYSE: TDW* ■ *TF:* 800-678-8433 ■ *Web:* www.tdw.com	New Orleans	LA	70130	504-568-1010	566-4580
Tropical Shipping 4 E Port Rd *TF:* 800-367-6200 ■ *Web:* www.tropical.com	Riviera Beach	FL	33404	561-881-3900	840-2840
Wallenius Wilhelmsen Lines Americas 188 Broadway **Fax:* Hum Res ■ *Web:* www.wlna.com	Woodcliff Lake	NJ	07677	201-505-5100	307-9576*
Waterman Steamship Corp 1 Whitehall St 20th Fl *TF:* 888-972-5274 ■ *Web:* www.waterman-steamship.com	New York	NY	10004	212-747-8550	747-8588
Westwood Shipping Lines 840 S 333rd St PO Box 9777 *TF:* 800-200-9751 ■ *Web:* www.weyerhaeuser.com/ourbusinesses/transportation/westwood/	Federal Way	WA	98063	253-924-4399	924-5956

317 FREIGHT TRANSPORT - INLAND WATERWAYS

	City	State	Zip	Phone	Fax
American Commercial Barge Lines Co 1701 E Market St *TF:* 800-457-6377 ■ *Web:* www.acbl.net	Jeffersonville	IN	47130	812-288-0100	288-1664
American Commercial Lines Inc 1701 E Market St *NASDAQ: ACLI* ■ *TF:* 800-457-6377 ■ *Web:* www.aclines.com	Jeffersonville	IN	47130	812-288-0100	288-0413
American River Transportation Co 4666 E Faries Pkwy *TF:* 800-637-5824	Decatur	IL	62526	217-424-5200	451-4270
American Steamship Co 500 Essjay Rd Centerpointe Corporate Pk *Web:* www.americansteamship.com	Williamsville	NY	14221	716-635-0222	635-0220
Andrie Inc 561 E Western Ave *Web:* www.andrie.com	Muskegon	MI	49442	231-728-2226	726-6747
Bluegrass Marine Inc 2308 S 4th St *TF:* 800-456-9404 ■ *Web:* www.marquettetrans.com	Paducah	KY	42001	270-443-9404	441-7544
Boston Towing & Transportation Co LP 36 New St *TF:* 800-836-8847	East Boston	MA	02128	617-567-9100	567-2583
Bouchard Transportation Co Inc 58 S Service Rd Suite 150 *Web:* www.bouchardtransport.com	Melville	NY	11747	631-390-4900	390-4905
Canal Barge Co Inc 835 Union St Suite 300 *Web:* www.canalbarge.com	New Orleans	LA	70112	504-581-2424	584-1505
Cargill Cargo Carriers 15407 McGinty Rd *Web:* www.cargill.com	Wayzata	MN	55391	952-742-7575	742-6289
Celtic Marine Corp 3888 S Sherwood Forest Blvd Celtic Centre Bldg 1 *Web:* www.celticmarine.com	Baton Rouge	LA	70816	225-752-2490	752-2582
Crounse Corp 2626 Broadway *Web:* www.crounse.com	Paducah	KY	42001	270-444-9611	444-9615
Crowley Maritime Corp 555 12th St Suite 2130 *TF:* 800-276-9539 ■ *Web:* www.crowley.com	Oakland	CA	94607	510-251-7500	251-7510
Fednav Ltd 1000 rue de la Gauchetière O Bureau 3500 *TF:* 800-678-4842 ■ *Web:* www.fednav.com	Montreal	QC	H3B4W5	514-878-6500	878-6642
Hannah Marine Corp 13155 Grant Rd *TF:* 800-257-5458 ■ *Web:* www.hannahmarine.com	Lemont	IL	60439	630-257-5458	257-9049
Ingram Barge Co 4400 Harding Rd 1 Belle Meade Pl *TF:* 800-876-2047 ■ *Web:* www.ingrambarge.com	Nashville	TN	37205	615-298-8200	298-8379
K-Sea Transportation Partners LP 3245 Richmond Terr *NYSE: KSP* ■ *Web:* www.k-sea.com	Staten Island	NY	10303	718-720-7207	448-3083
Kirby Corp 55 Waugh Dr Suite 1000 *NYSE: KEX* ■ *TF:* 800-324-2441 ■ *Web:* www.kmtc.com	Houston	TX	77007	713-435-1000	435-1011
L & M Botruc Rental Inc 18692 W Main St *TF:* 800-256-1186 ■ *Web:* www.botruc.com	Galliano	LA	70354	985-475-5733	475-5669
M-G Transport Service Inc 7000 Midland Blvd *TF:* 800-543-2644	Amelia	OH	45102	513-943-7300	947-4026
Marquette Transportation Co Inc 2308 S 4th St *TF:* 800-456-9404 ■ *Web:* www.marquettetrans.com	Paducah	KY	42001	270-443-9404	441-7544
Midwest Energy Resources Co W Winter St & Ajax Rd *Web:* www.midwestenergy.com	Superior	WI	54880	715-392-9807	392-9137
Patton-Tully Transportation LLC 1242 N 2nd St *Web:* www.patton-tully.com	Memphis	TN	38107	901-576-1400	576-1486
Port Amherst Industries 2 Port Amherst Dr	Charleston	WV	25306	304-926-1100	926-1136
Seafreight Agencies Inc 2800 NW 105th Ave *Web:* www.seafreightagencies.com	Miami	FL	33172	305-592-6060	471-9555
Shaver Transportation Co Inc 4900 NW Front Ave *TF:* 888-228-8850	Portland	OR	97210	503-228-8850	274-7098
TECO Transport 702 N Franklin St *TF:* 800-835-4161 ■ *Web:* www.tecotransport.com	Tampa	FL	33602	813-228-1111	273-0248
Tidewater Barge Lines Inc 6305 NW Old Lower River Rd *TF:* 800-562-4345 ■ *Web:* www.tidewater.com	Vancouver	WA	98660	360-693-1491	694-8981
Transerve Marine Inc 500 E Indian River Rd	Norfolk	VA	23523	757-545-7301	545-5692
Warrior & Gulf Navigation Co 50 Viaduct RD PO Box 11397 *TF:* 800-452-6100 ■ *Web:* www.tstarinc.com/wgn	Chickasaw	AL	36671	251-452-6000	452-6014

Phone Fax

Western Kentucky Navigation Inc 631 S 2nd St................Paducah KY 42003 270-415-9956 415-9950
TF: 800-811-8133 ■ *Web:* www.wkynav.com

318 FRUIT GROWERS

SEE ALSO Agricultural Services - Crop Preparation Services p. 1265; Beverages - Mfr - Wines - Mfr p. 1376

318-1 Berry Growers

Phone Fax

AD Makepeace Co Inc 158 Tihonet Rd........................Wareham MA 02571 508-295-1000 291-7453
Web: www.admakepeace.com
Adkin Blue Ribbon Packing Co Inc 70333 Baseline Rd........South Haven MI 49090 269-637-5740 637-3274
Atlantic Blueberry Co 7201 Weymouth Rd ....Hammonton NJ 08037 609-561-8600 561-5033
Web: www.atlanticblueberry.com
Brady Farms Inc 14786 Winans St..........................West Olive MI 49460 616-842-3916 842-8357
California Giant Inc 75 Sakata Ln ....Watsonville CA 95076 831-728-1773 728-0613
Web: www.calgiant.com
Cherryfield Foods Inc PO Box 128..........................Cherryfield ME 04622 207-546-7573 546-2713
Coastal Berry Co LLC 480 W Beach St PO Box 1570 ....Watsonville CA 95077 831-724-1366 722-1407
Columbia Empire Farms Inc PO Box 1..........................Dundee OR 97115 503-538-2156 538-4393
Web: www.columbiaempirefarms.com
Cranberry Growers Service Inc 2417 Cranberry Hwy.............Wareham MA 02571 508-295-2222 291-0144
Cutler Cranberry Co N11569 County Rd H.................Camp Douglas WI 54618 608-427-3268
Driscoll Strawberry Assoc Inc 345 Westridge Dr..............Watsonville CA 95077 831-763-5100 761-1090
TF: 800-871-3333 ■ *Web:* www.driscollsberries.com
Fujii Farms 2511 S Troutdale Rd ....Troutdale OR 97060 503-665-6659 661-2799
Habelman Bros Co Inc PO Box 150 ....Tomah WI 54660 608-372-2444 372-2566
Jasper Wyman & Son PO Box 100 ....Milbridge ME 04658 207-546-2311 546-2074
TF: 800-341-1758 ■ *Web:* www.wymans.com
Maine Wild Blueberry Co PO Box 128.........................Cherryfield ME 04622 207-255-8364 255-8341
Merrill Blueberry Farms Inc 63 Thorsen Rd PO Box 149 ....Ellsworth ME 04605 207-667-2541 667-4052
TF: 800-711-6551 ■ *Web:* www.merrillwildblueberries.com
Michigan Blueberry Growers Assn DBA MBG Marketing
04726 CR 215 PO Box 322...............................Grand Junction MI 49056 269-434-6791 434-6997
TF: 866-269-1511 ■ *Web:* www.blueberries.com
Naturipe Berry Growers 1020 Merrill St 2nd Fl ....Salinas CA 93901 831-722-2430 728-9398
Web: www.naturipe.com
Northland Cranberries Inc
2321 W Grand Ave PO Box 8020 ....Wisconsin Rapids WI 54495 715-424-4444 422-6800
Web: www.northlandcran.com
Reenders Blueberries Farms 14079 168th Ave ....Grand Haven MI 49417 616-842-5238 842-0890
Reiter Affiliated Cos 1767 San Juan Rd ....Aromas CA 95004 831-726-3256 726-3219
Sandy Farms 34500 SE Hwy 211 ....Boring OR 97009 503-668-4525 668-8813
Web: www.sandyfarms.com
Sunrise Growers 701 W Kimberly St Suite 210 ....Placentia CA 92870 714-630-2050 630-0215
Web: sunrisegrowers.com
Variety Farms Inc 548 Pleasant Mills Rd....................Hammonton NJ 08037 609-561-0612 561-1051

318-2 Citrus Growers

Phone Fax

A Duda & Sons Inc PO Box 620257 ....Oviedo FL 32762 407-365-2111 365-2010
Web: www.duda.com
Alico Inc PO Box 338 ....La Belle FL 33975 863-675-2966 675-6928
NASDAQ: ALCO ■ *Web:* www.alicoinc.com
Barron Collier Co 1320 N 15th St..........................Immokalee FL 34142 239-658-6060 657-2337
Web: www.barroncollier.com
Ben Hill Griffin Inc 700 S SR 17 PO Box 127 ....Frostproof FL 33843 863-635-2251 635-7333
Berry Jack M Inc PO Box 459 ....La Belle FL 33975 863-675-2769 675-6851
Blood's Hammock Groves 4600 Linton Blvd.................Delray Beach FL 33445 561-498-3400 451-3011*
**Fax Area Code: 888* ■ **Fax: Orders* ■ *TF:* 800-255-5188 ■ *Web:* www.bloodsgroves.com
Blue Banner Co Inc 2601 3rd St PO Box 226 ....Riverside CA 92502 951-686-2422 686-6440
TF: 800-426-2422
Bob Paul Inc 2020 Dundee Rd PO Box 898................Winter Haven FL 33882 863-293-9906 297-5156
Bowen Brothers Fruit Co Inc 305 Ave 'E' SW ....Winter Haven FL 33880 863-299-1183 293-1889
Callery-Judge Grove 4001 Seminole-Pratt Whitney Rd ....Loxahatchee FL 33470 561-793-1676 790-5466
TF: 800-967-2643 ■ *Web:* www.cjgrove.com
Consolidated Citrus LP 4210 Metro Pkwy Suite 250............Fort Myers FL 33916 239-275-4060 275-4973
Corona College Heights Orange & Lemon Assn
8000 Lincoln Ave..Riverside CA 92504 951-688-1811 689-5115
Web: www.cchcitrus.com
Duda A & Sons Inc PO Box 620257 ....Oviedo FL 32762 407-365-2111 365-2010
Web: www.duda.com
Edinburg Citrus Assn 401 W Chapin Rd.......................Edinburg TX 78539 956-383-2743 383-2435
Egan Bernard & Co DBA DNE World Fruit Sales
1900 Old Dixie Hwy...Fort Pierce FL 34946 772-465-1110 465-1181
TF: 800-327-6676 ■ *Web:* www.dneworld.com
Evans Properties Inc 660 Beachland Blvd Suite 301 ....Vero Beach FL 32963 772-234-2410 234-3690
G & S Packing Co Inc 16600 S Hwy C 25.......................Weirsdale FL 32195 352-821-2251 821-5000
Web: www.gspacking.com
Gracewood Fruit Co 1626 90th Ave ....Vero Beach FL 32966 772-567-1151 567-2719
TF: 800-678-8911 ■ *Web:* www.egracewoodgroves.com
Graves Brothers Co 5135 87th St...............................Wabasso FL 32970 772-589-4356 589-5901
TF Sales: 877-999-8499 ■ *Web:* www.graves-bros.com
Heller Brothers Packing Corp 288 9th St...................Winter Garden FL 34787 407-656-2124 656-1751
TF: 800-823-2124 ■ *Web:* www.hellerbros.com
Highland Exchange Service Co-op 5916 SR 540 E PO Box K.......Waverly FL 33877 863-439-3661 439-5383
TF: 800-237-3989 ■ *Web:* www.hesco-fl.com
Jack M Berry Inc PO Box 459 ....La Belle FL 33975 863-675-2769 675-6851
JW Yonce & Sons Farms Inc 37 Yonce Pond Rd PO Box 175 .....Johnston SC 29832 803-275-3244 275-3852
Lake Wales Citrus Growers Assn 111 N 1st St PO Box 1739........Dundee FL 33838 863-439-5710 439-1535
Leroy E Smith's Sons Inc 4776 Old Dixie Hwy................Vero Beach FL 32967 772-567-3421 567-8428*
**Fax: Orders*
Limoneira Co 1141 Cummings Rd ....Santa Paula CA 93060 805-525-5541 525-8211
TF: 800-350-5541 ■ *Web:* www.limoneira.com
Nelson & Co Inc 110 E Broadway PO Box 620789 ....Oviedo FL 32762 407-365-6631 366-0145
Orange Cove-Sanger Citrus Assn 180 South Ave............Orange Cove CA 93646 559-626-4453 626-7357
TF: 800-533-8871
Paramount Citrus Assn 1901 S Lexington St.....................Delano CA 93215 661-720-2400 720-2403
Web: www.paramountcitrus.com
Roper Growers Co-op 120 S Dillard St....................Winter Garden FL 34787 407-656-3233 656-4999
TF: 800-872-5032
Saticoy Lemon Assn 7560 E Bristol Rd ....Ventura CA 93003 805-654-6500 654-6587
Web: www.saticoylemon.com
Seald-Sweet Growers Inc 1991 74th Ave......................Vero Beach FL 32966 772-569-2244 562-9038
TF Sales: 800-336-2926 ■ *Web:* www.sealdsweet.com
Silver Springs Citrus Inc 25411 N Mare Ave.............Howey in the Hills FL 34737 352-324-2101 324-3422
TF: 800-940-2277 ■ *Web:* www.silverspringscitrus.com

Phone Fax

South Valley Citrus Assn PO Box 10055 ....Terra Bella CA 93270 559-535-4422 535-4206
Southern Gardens Citrus 1820 Country Rd 833.................Clewiston FL 33440 863-983-3030 983-3060
Sunkist Growers Inc 14130 Riverside Dr ....Sherman Oaks CA 91423 818-986-4800 379-7511*
**Fax: PR* ■ *TF:* 800-383-7141 ■ *Web:* www.sunkist.com
Villa Park Orchards Assn 960 3rd St PO Box 307...............Fillmore CA 93016 805-524-0411 524-5912

318-3 Deciduous Tree Fruit Growers

Phone Fax

All State Apple Exchange PO Box 246............................Milton NY 12547 845-795-2121 795-2618
Appletree Orchards Inc 12025 Four-Mile Rd NE ....Lowell MI 49331 616-897-9216 897-8066
TF: 800-922-0635
Associated Fruit Co 3721 Colver Rd ....Phoenix OR 97535 541-535-1787 535-6936
Auvil Fruit Co 21902 SR 97 ....Orondo WA 98843 509-784-1033 784-1712
Web: www.auvilfruit.com
Barbee Orchards 131 Bella Terra Rd..............................Zillah WA 98953 509-865-4591 865-3220
Bertuccio Farms 2410 Airline Hwy ....Hollister CA 95023 831-636-0821 637-9393
Web: www.bertuccios.com
Big Six Farms 5575 Zenith Mill Rd ....Fort Valley GA 31030 478-825-7504 825-1194
Web: www.bigsixfarm.com
Blue Bird Inc 10135 Mill Rd ....Peshastin WA 98847 509-548-1700 548-0288
Blue Mountain Growers Inc
231 E Broadway PO Box 156.........................Milton-Freewater OR 97862 541-938-4401 938-5304
Blue Star Growers Inc 100 SE Blue Star Way ....Cashmere WA 98815 509-782-2922 782-3646
Borton & Sons Inc 2550 Borton Rd ....Yakima WA 98903 509-966-3905 966-3994
Web: www.bortonfruit.com
Brandt EW & Sons Inc PO Box B ....Parker WA 98939 509-877-3193 877-2544
Web: www.ewbrandt.com
Broetje Orchards 1111 Fishhook Park Rd.......................Prescott WA 99348 509-749-2217 749-2354
California Prune Packing 2200 Encinal Rd ....Live Oak CA 95953 530-671-4200 695-3654
Capital Agricultural Property Services Inc
801 Warrenville Rd Suite 150 ....Lisle IL 60532 630-434-9150 434-9343
TF: 800-243-2060 ■ *Web:* www.capitalag.com
Chappell Farms Inc 166 Boiling Springs Rd.....................Barnwell SC 29812 803-584-2565 584-3676
Web: www.chappellfarms.com
Chelan Fruit Co 8 Howser Rd...................................Chelan WA 98816 509-682-2591 682-2656
Cherry Central Co-op Inc
1771 N US Hwy 31 S PO Box 988 ....Traverse City MI 49685 231-946-1860 941-4167
TF: 800-678-1860 ■ *Web:* www.cherrycentral.com
Cowiche Growers Inc 251 Cowiche City Rd ....Cowiche WA 98923 509-678-4168 678-4160
Web: www.cowichegrowers.com
Danna & Danna Inc 625 Cooper St.............................Yuba City CA 95992 530-673-5131 673-5131
Evans Farms Hwy 96 E & 50 Evans Rd PO Box 913 ....Fort Valley GA 31030 478-825-2095 825-3670
Evans Fruit Farm 200 Cowiche City Rd ....Cowiche WA 98923 509-678-4127
TF: 800-255-7513
EW Brandt & Sons Inc PO Box B ....Parker WA 98939 509-877-3193 877-2544
Web: www.ewbrandt.com
Fagundes Agribusiness 8700 Fargo Ave.........................Hanford CA 93230 559-582-4080 582-0683
Web: www.oldworldcheese.com
Farmland Management Services 138 Regis St Suite A.............Turlock CA 95382 209-669-0742 669-0811
Fowler Brothers Inc 10273 Lummisville Rd......................Wolcott NY 14590 315-594-8068 594-8060
Fowler Packing Co Inc 8570 S Cedar Ave ....Fresno CA 93725 559-834-5911 834-5272
Gerawan Farming 15749 E Ventura St ....Sanger CA 93657 559-787-8780 787-8798
Gerbbers Farms 908 Hwy 97....................................Brewster WA 98812 509-689-3424 689-2997
TF: 800-967-3634
Henggeler Packing Co Inc 6730 Elmore Rd PO Box 313 ....Fruitland ID 83619 208-452-4212 452-5416
Highland Fruit Growers Inc 8304 Wide Hollow Rd ....Yakima WA 98908 509-966-3990 966-3992
Holmes Lewis F & Son 1137 Hwy 191............................Johnston SC 29832 803-275-4779 275-4115
Hudson Valley Farms Inc 381 Vineyard Ave.....................Highland NY 12528 845-691-2181 691-2613
TF: 800-336-2252
Ito Packing Co Inc PO Box 707 ....Reedley CA 93654 559-638-2531 638-2282
Web: www.itopack.com
Jack Frost/Marley Orchards Corp 2820 River Rd PO Box 1552 ......Yakima WA 98907 509-248-5231 248-7358
JW Yonce & Sons Farms Inc 37 Yonce Pond Rd PO Box 175 .....Johnston SC 29832 803-275-3244 275-3852
Lane Packing Inc 50 Ln Rd PO Box 1087 ....Fort Valley GA 31030 478-825-3592 825-7995
TF: 800-277-3224 ■ *Web:* www.lanepacking.com
Marchese Family Properties 270 E Main St ....Los Gatos CA 95030 408-395-8375 395-9675
McDougal & Sons 3887 Pioneer Way.............................Monitor WA 98836 509-662-2136 782-4491
Mount Konocti Growers Inc 2550 Big Valley Rd PO Box 365 ...Kelseyville CA 95451 707-279-4213 279-2251
National Fruit Product Co Inc
701 Fairmont Ave PO Box 2040 ....Winchester VA 22604 540-662-3401 665-4670*
**Fax: Sales* ■ *TF:* 800-551-5167 ■ *Web:* www.whitehousefoods.com
Naumes Inc 2 Barnett Rd ....Medford OR 97501 541-772-6268 772-2135
Web: www.naumes.com
Northwestern Fruit & Produce Co 3581 Maple Way Rd ....Yakima WA 98908 509-966-4830 965-5945
Orchard View Farms Inc 4055 Skyline Rd ....The Dalles OR 97058 541-298-4496 298-1808
Web: www.orchardviewfarms.com
Oregon Cherry Growers Inc PO Box 7357 ....Salem OR 97303 541-296-5487 296-2509
Web: www.orcherry.com
P-R Farms Inc 2917 E Shepherd Ave ....Clovis CA 93619 559-299-0201 299-7292
Web: www.prfarms.com
Premiere Partners 2407 S Neil St PO Box 3009 ....Champaign IL 61826 217-352-6000 352-9048
Rice Fruit Co 2760 Carlisle Rd PO Box 66.....................Gardners PA 17324 717-677-8131 677-9842
TF: 800-627-3359 ■ *Web:* www.ricefruit.com
Royal Valley Fruit Growers Assn
10881 S Englehart Ave PO Box 152 ....Reedley CA 93654 559-638-2540 638-8540
Southern Orchard Supply Co DBA Lane Packing Inc
50 Ln Rd PO Box 1087 ....Fort Valley GA 31030 478-825-3592 825-7995
TF: 800-277-3224 ■ *Web:* www.lanepacking.com
Stadelman Fruit Inc PO Box 445 ....Zillah WA 98953 509-829-5145 829-5164
Stemilt Growers Inc PO Box 2779 ....Wenatchee WA 98807 509-663-1451 665-4376
Web: www.stemilt.com
Sun Valley Packing Co 7381 Ave 432 PO Box 351 ....Reedley CA 93654 559-591-1515 591-1616
Sun World International Inc 16350 Driver Rd ....Bakersfield CA 93308 661-392-5000 392-4678
Web: www.sun-world.com
Symms Fruit Ranch Inc 14068 Sunny Slope Rd....................Caldwell ID 83607 208-459-4821 459-6932
Taylor Orchards Hwy 96 W PO Box 975.........................Reynolds GA 31076 478-847-4186 847-4464
Web: www.taylororchards.com
Thiara Brothers Orchards 1205 Kibby Rd.........................Merced CA 95340 209-383-6126 383-1012
Titan Farms 5 RW Du Bose Rd.............................Ridge Spring SC 29129 803-685-5381 685-5885
TF: 888-848-2672 ■ *Web:* www.titanfarms.com
Twin Hill Ranch 1689 Pleasant Hill Rd......................Sebastopol CA 95472 707-823-2815 823-6268
Web: www.twinhillranch.com
Valley View Packing Co Inc PO Box 5699.......................San Jose CA 95150 408-289-8300 289-8897
Web: www.valleyviewpacking.com
Woodmont Orchards Inc 15 Pillsbury Rd ....Londonderry NH 03053 603-432-3311 432-7931

318-4 Fruit Growers (Misc)

Phone Fax

Barkley Co PO Box 2706..Yuma AZ 85366 928-343-2918 343-2940
Web: www.barkleyag.com
Brooks Tropicals Inc 18400 SW 256th St PO Box 900160.......Homestead FL 33090 305-247-3544 246-5827*
**Fax: Sales* ■ *TF:* 800-327-4833 ■ *Web:* www.brookstropicals.com

Phone Fax

Calavo Growers Inc 1141-A Cummings Rd .... Santa Paula CA 93060 805-525-1245 921-3287
NASDAQ: CVGW ■ TF: 800-422-5286 ■ Web: www.calavo.com
Chiquita Brands International Inc 250 E 5th St ....Cincinnati OH 45202 513-784-8000 784-8030
NYSE: CQB ■ Web: www.chiquita.com
Del Monte Fresh Produce Co 241 Sevilla Ave .... Coral Gables FL 33134 305-520-8400 520-8455
Web: www.freshdelmonte.com
Dole Food Co Inc 1 Dole Dr ....Westlake Village CA 91362 818-879-6600 874-4893*
*Fax: Hum Res ■ TF: 800-232-8888 ■ Web: www.dole.com
Elmore & Stahl Inc 4012 E Goodwin Rd .... Mission TX 78572 956-585-4540 585-5825
Jewel Date Co 48440 Prairie Dr ....Palm Desert CA 92260 760-399-4474 399-4476
Web: www.jeweldate.com
Martori Farms 7332 E Butherus Dr......................... Scottsdale AZ 85260 480-998-1444 483-6723
TF: 800-627-8674 ■ Web: www.martorifarms.com
Maui Land & Pineapple Co Ltd 120 Kane St PO Box 187...........Kahului HI 96733 808-877-3351 871-0953
AMEX: MLP ■ Web: www.mauiland.com
Mission Produce Inc 2500 Vineyard Ave Suite 300 PO Box 5267..... Oxnard CA 93031 805-981-3650 981-3660
Web: www.missionpro.com
Mount Dora Farms 1500 Port Blvd..............................Miami FL 33132 305-530-4700 375-0971
Web: www.mountdorafarms.com
Pecos Cantaloupe Co Inc 2101 Bickley Ave......................Pecos TX 79772 432-447-2123 447-6871*
*Fax: Orders
Valley Fig Growers 2028 S 3rd St .... Fresno CA 93702 559-237-3893 237-3898
Web: www.valleyfig.com
Virginia Fork Produce Inc PO Box 148 .... Edenton NC 27932 252-482-2165 482-3515
TF: 800-334-7716
West Pak Avocado Inc 42322 Avenida Alvarado ....Temecula CA 92590 951-296-5757 296-5745
TF: 800-266-4414 ■ Web: www.westpak.com

318-5 Grape Vineyards

Phone Fax

Agro Farming Corp 3800 Herring Rd .... Arvin CA 93203 661-854-2203 854-2203
Baker Farming Co 45499 W Panoche Rd.....................Firebaugh CA 93622 559-659-3942 659-7114
Beringer Blass Wine Estates 610 Airpark Rd PO Box 4500 ....Napa CA 94558 707-259-4500 259-4542
Web: www.beringer.com
Del Rey Packing 5287 S Del Rey Ave .... Del Rey CA 93616 559-888-2031 888-2715
Delicato Vineyards 12001 S Hwy 99 ....Manteca CA 95336 209-824-3600 824-3400
TF: 888-599-4637 ■ Web: www.delicato.com
E & J Gallo Winery 600 Yosemite Blvd.......................Modesto CA 95354 209-341-3111 341-3307
TF: 800-322-2389 ■ Web: www.gallo.com
Gallo E & J Winery 600 Yosemite Blvd.......................Modesto CA 95354 209-341-3111 341-3307
TF: 800-322-2389 ■ Web: www.gallo.com
Giumarra Vineyards Corp 11220 Edison Hwy.................... Edison CA 93220 661-395-7000 366-7134
J & L Farms PO Box 906...................................... Gonzales CA 93926 831-675-2302
John J Kovacevich & Sons PO Box 488............................ Arvin CA 93203 661-854-8430 854-8430*
*Fax: Orders
John Kautz Farms 5490 Bear Creek Rd .... Lodi CA 95240 209-334-4786 339-1689
Lion Raisins 9500 S De Wols Ave PO Box 1350 ....Selma CA 93662 559-834-6677 834-6622
Web: www.lionraisins.com
National Grape Co-op Assn Inc 2 S Portage St .... Westfield NY 14787 716-326-5200 326-5494
Web: www.nationalgrape.com
National Raisin Co PO Box 219 .... Fowler CA 93625 559-834-5981 834-1055
TF: 800-874-3726 ■ Web: www.nationalraisin.com
Pacific Agri Lands Inc 5206 Hammett Rd ....Modesto CA 95358 209-545-1623
Pandol & Sons 401 Rd 192......................................Delano CA 93215 661-725-3755 725-4741
Web: www.pandol.com
Royal Madera Vineyards 7770 Rd 33...........................Madera CA 93638 559-673-2291 661-1427
Scheid Vineyards Inc 305 Hilltown Rd..........................Salinas CA 93908 831-455-9990 455-9998
NASDAQ: SVIN ■ TF: 888-772-4343 ■ Web: www.scheidvineyards.com
Spring Mountain Vineyards 2805 Spring Mountain Rd ....Saint Helena CA 94574 707-967-4188 963-2753
TF: 877-769-4637 ■ Web: www.springmtn.com
Ste Michelle Wine Estates 14111 NE 145th St............... Woodinville WA 98072 425-488-1133 415-3657
TF: 800-267-6793 ■ Web: www.ste-michelle.com
Sun Valley Packing Co 7381 Ave 432 PO Box 351 .... Reedley CA 93654 559-591-1515 591-1616
Sun World International Inc 16350 Driver Rd ....Bakersfield CA 93308 661-392-5000 392-4678
Web: www.sun-world.com
Symms Fruit Ranch Inc 14068 Sunny Slope Rd.................Caldwell ID 83607 208-459-4821 459-6932
Tejon Ranch Co PO Box 1000......................................Lebec CA 93243 661-248-3000 248-3100
NYSE: TRC ■ Web: www.tejonranch.com
Trinchero Family Estates
100 Saint Helena Hwy S PO Box 248 ....Saint Helena CA 94574 707-963-3104 963-2381*
*Fax: Mktg ■ Web: www.tfewines.com
Valley Farm Management Inc 11131 John Fox Rd .... Hughson CA 95326 209-883-0401 883-0402
Vino Farms Inc 1377 E Lodi Ave .... Lodi CA 95240 209-334-6975 369-8765
Windsor Vineyards 9600 Bell Rd PO Box 368 ....Windsor CA 95492 707-836-5000 836-5924
TF: 800-289-9463 ■ Web: www.windsorwines.com

319 FUEL DEALERS

Phone Fax

Able Energy Inc 198 Green Pond Rd PO Box 630..............Rockaway NJ 07866 973-625-1012 586-9866
NASDAQ: ABLE ■ TF: 800-564-1012 ■ Web: www.ableenergy.com
AC & T Co Inc 11535 Hopewell Rd.......................... Hagerstown MD 21740 301-582-2700 582-2719
TF: 800-458-3835 ■ Web: www.acandt.com
All Star Gas Corp 119 W Commercial St ....Lebanon MO 65536 417-532-3103 532-8529
Web: www.allstargas.com
Alvin Hollis & Co Inc 1 Hollis St ....South Weymouth MA 02190 781-335-2100 335-6134
TF: 800-649-5090 ■ Web: www.alvinhollis.com
AmeriGas Inc 460 N Gulph Rd .... King of Prussia PA 19406 610-337-7000 768-7647
Web: www.amerigas.com
AmeriGas Partners LP 460 N Gulph Rd .... King of Prussia PA 19406 610-337-1000 768-7647
NYSE: APU ■ Web: www.amerigas.com
Automotive Service Inc 910 Mountain Home Rd PO Box 2157...... Reading PA 19608 610-678-3421 678-3515
TF: 800-383-3421
Besche Oil Co Inc 3045 Old Washington Rd .... Waldorf MD 20601 301-645-7061 645-8727
Web: www.bescheoil.com
Blossman Gas Inc 801 Washington Ave PO Box 1110.......Ocean Springs MS 39566 228-875-2261 875-9307
TF: 800-234-1110 ■ Web: www.blossmangas.com
Brinker's/Swartley Oil Co PO Box 816 .... Doylestown PA 18901 215-348-2670 348-8398
Butane Power & Equipment Co 507 N Beverly St PO Box 2628...... Casper WY 82602 307-234-8985 265-7330
TF: 800-734-3404
Carolane Propane Gas Inc 339 S Main St......................Lexington NC 27292 336-249-8981 248-5711
TF: 800-838-1982
Carroll Independent Fuel Co 2700 Loch Raven Rd .... Baltimore MD 21218 410-235-1066 235-3842
TF: 800-834-8590 ■ Web: www.carrollfuel.com
Cenex 5500 Cenex Dr ....Inver Grove Heights MN 55077 651-355-6000
TF: 800-232-3639 ■ Web: www.cenex.com
Consumer Oil & Supply Co 100 Railroad St.....................Braymer MO 64624 660-645-2215 645-2426
Cutter DJ & Co Inc 88 Freeport St ....Dorchester MA 02122 617-825-1300 825-0203
Davis Melvin L Oil Co Inc 11042 Blue Star Hwy PO Box C..... Stony Creek VA 23882 434-246-2600 246-5308
Diamond/Delchester 841 Lincoln Ave.......................West Chester PA 19381 610-692-3366 692-8953
TF: 888-835-3535

Phone Fax

District Petroleum Products Inc 1814 River Rd Suite 100..........Huron OH 44839 419-433-8373 433-9646
DJ Cutter & Co Inc 88 Freeport St ....Dorchester MA 02122 617-825-1300 825-0203
Empire State Fuel Co 1640 McDonald Ave.......................Brooklyn NY 11230 718-627-5100 627-5166
Web: www.oilheatusa.com
Energy Transfer Equity LP 2828 Woodside St.....................Dallas TX 75204 214-981-0700 981-0703
NYSE: ETE ■ Web: www.energytransfer.com
Energy Transfer Partners LP 2838 Woodside St ....Dallas TX 75204 214-981-0700 981-0703
NYSE: ETP ■ Web: www.energytransfer.com
Farm & Home Oil Co 3115 State Rd PO Box 389..................Telford PA 18969 215-257-0131 257-2088
TF: 800-473-1562 ■ Web: www.fhoil.com
FC Haab Co Inc 1700 Schuylkill Ave........................ Philadelphia PA 19103 215-563-0800 563-9448
TF: 800-486-5663 ■ Web: www.fchaab.com
Ferrellgas Partners LP 1 Liberty Plaza........................... Liberty MO 64068 816-792-1600 792-7985
NYSE: FGP ■ TF: 800-816-3048 ■ Web: www.ferrellgas.com
Fred M Schildwachter & Sons Inc 1400 Ferris Pl ....Bronx NY 10461 718-828-2500 828-3661
TF: 800-642-3646 ■ Web: www.schildwachteroil.com
Gas Inc 77 Jefferson Pkwy .... Newnan GA 30263 770-502-8800 502-8833
Web: www.gasincorporated.com
Glassmere Fuel Service Inc 1967 Saxonburg Blvd ....Tarentum PA 15084 724-224-0880 265-3588
TF: 800-235-9054 ■ Web: www.glassmerefuel.com
Griffith Energy Services Inc 2510 Schuster Dr ....Cheverly MD 20781 301-322-5100 772-8183*
*Fax: Cust Svc ■ TF: 800-633-4328 ■ Web: www.griffithoil.com
Herring Gas Co Inc 33 Main St E .... Meadville MS 39653 601-384-5833 384-2205
TF: 800-543-9049
Hollis Alvin & Co Inc 1 Hollis St ....South Weymouth MA 02190 781-335-2100 335-6134
TF: 800-649-5090 ■ Web: www.alvinhollis.com
Hometown Inc 1518 E North Ave .... Milwaukee WI 53202 414-276-9311 276-6061
Huntley Oil & Gas Co Inc 137 Hwy 74 PO Box 369............Wadesboro NC 28170 704-694-2144 694-2145
Inergy LP 2 Brush Creek Blvd Suite 200......................Kansas City MO 64112 816-842-8181 842-1904
NASDAQ: NRGY ■ TF: 877-446-3749 ■ Web: www.inergypropane.com
Jenkins Gas & Oil Co Inc 221 Main St.....................Pollocksville NC 28573 252-224-4551 224-1443
Web: www.jenkinsgas.com
JS West & Cos 501 9th St PO Box 1041 ....Modesto CA 95353 209-577-3221 523-9828
TF Cust Svc: 800-675-9378 ■ Web: www.jswest.com
King Service Inc PO Box 838 .... Troy NY 12180 518-274-4200 274-0582
Kingston Oil Supply Corp 15 N Broadway PO Box 760 .... Port Ewen NY 12466 845-331-0770 331-3760
TF: 800-755-6726 ■ Web: www.kingstonoil.com
Kocolene Marketing LLC 1725 E Tipton St .... Seymour IN 47274 812-522-2224 522-6264
TF: 800-457-9886
Lansing Ice & Fuel Co 911 Center St.......................... Lansing MI 48906 517-372-3850 485-9482
Lawes Coal Co Inc Sycamore Ave PO Box 258 ....Shrewsbury NJ 07702 732-741-6300 741-8527
Lincoln Land Oil Co 2026 Republic St ....Springfield IL 62702 217-523-5050 523-5001
TF: 800-238-4912 ■ Web: www.lincolnlandoil.com
Local Oil Co Inc 2015 7th Ave N PO Box 517 ....Anoka MN 55303 763-421-4923 421-0304
Martin LP Gas Inc 2606 N Longview St .... Kilgore TX 75662 903-984-0781 986-3519
TF: 800-441-8569 ■ Web: www.martinlpgas.com
Meenan Oil Co Inc 520 Broadhollow Rd Suite 200-W...............Melville NY 11747 516-495-1100 495-1101
Melvin L Davis Oil Co Inc 11042 Blue Star Hwy PO Box C...... Stony Creek VA 23882 434-246-2600 246-5308
Metro Energy Group 1011 Hudson Ave...........................Ridgefield NJ 07657 201-941-3470 941-6854
TF: 800-866-4680 ■ Web: www.metrocomfort.com
Midwest Bottle Gas Co 3600 State Trunk Hwy 157..............La Crosse WI 54602 608-781-1010 781-3094
TF: 800-522-1055
Mirabito Fuel Group 44 Grand St................................ Sidney NY 13838 607-561-2700 563-1460
TF: 800-934-9480 ■ Web: www.mirabitofuel.com
Mitchell Supreme Fuel Co 532 Freeman St ....Orange NJ 07050 973-678-1800 672-0148
TF: 800-832-7090 ■ Web: www.mitchellsupreme.com
Mutual Liquid Gas & Equipment Co Inc 17117 S Broadway St...... Gardena CA 90248 323-321-3771 515-2633*
*Fax Area Code: 310 ■ Web: www.mutualpropane.com
New London Energy 410 Bank St .... New London CT 06320 860-271-2020 271-2050
TF: 800-944-8803
Oliver Oil Co Inc PO Box 248 ....Chambersburg PA 17201 717-264-5165 264-1733
TF: 800-634-8729
Peoples Community Oil Co-op 427 Main St................... Darlington WI 53530 608-776-4437 776-3156
Peterson William R Oil Co 276 Main St Suite 1 PO box 31 .... Portland CT 06480 860-342-3560 342-2543
TF: 800-622-6971
Petro Heat & Power Corp 28 Southfield Ave .... Stamford CT 06902 203-323-2121 359-4072
TF: 800-645-4328 ■ Web: www.petro.com
Petroleum Marketers Inc 3000 Ogden Rd ....Roanoke VA 24014 540-772-4900 772-6900
Web: www.petroleummarketers.com
Planters Oil Inc 217 S Main St................................Fitzgerald GA 31750 229-423-2096 423-4836
Polsinello Fuels Inc 41 Riverside Ave ....Rensselaer NY 12144 518-463-0084 463-4086
TF: 800-334-5823 ■ Web: www.polsinello.com
Prairie Pride Cooperative 1100 E Main St....................... Marshall MN 56258 507-532-9686 532-1394
TF: 888-532-9686 ■ Web: www.prairiepridecoop.com
Pro-Gas Sales & Service Co 1535 S Walker Rd................. Muskegon MI 49442 231-773-3261 773-3463
Range Co-op Inc 102 S Hoover Rd............................... Virginia MN 55792 218-741-7393 741-7396
TF: 800-862-8628
Rawls SW Inc 100 Bowers Rd.................................... Franklin VA 23851 757-562-3115 562-1227
Web: www.swrawls.com
Reynolds Industries Inc 33 Mt Auburn St .... Watertown MA 02472 617-484-1443 923-9019
Robison Oil Corp 500 Executive Blvd .... Elmsford NY 10523 914-345-5700 345-5792
Web: www.robisonoil.com
Rose Fuel & Materials Inc 918 Oliver Plow Ct .... South Bend IN 46601 574-234-2133 232-2645
Web: www.rosebrick.com
Schierl Oil Co Inc PO Box 308 ....Stevens Point WI 54481 715-345-5060 345-5075
Web: www.tsctoday.com/schierloil.html
Schildwachter Fred M & Sons Inc 1400 Ferris Pl ....Bronx NY 10461 718-828-2500 828-3661
TF: 800-642-3646 ■ Web: www.schildwachteroil.com
Sharp Energy Inc 648 Ocean Hwy.........................Pocomoke City MD 21851 410-957-0422 957-0716
Web: www.sharpenergy.com
Shipley Energy 550 E King St.................................... York PA 17405 717-848-4100 854-5496
TF: 800-839-1849 ■ Web: www.shipleyenergy.com
SJ Fuel Co Inc 601 Union St...................................Brooklyn NY 11215 718-855-6060 625-5696
Web: www.sjfuelco.com
Southeast Fuels Inc 604 Green Valley Rd Suite 207 .... Greensboro NC 27408 336-854-1106 547-8720
Web: www.southeastfuels.com
Spencer Oil Co Inc 16410 Common Rd .... Roseville MI 48066 586-775-5022 775-3111
TF: 800-445-7562 ■ Web: www.spenceroil.com
Star Gas Partners LP 2187 Atlantic St .... Stamford CT 06902 203-328-7300 328-7406*
NYSE: SGU ■ *Fax: Hum Res ■ TF: 800-966-9827 ■ Web: www.star-gas.com
Streicher Mobile Fueling Inc
200 W Cypress Creek Rd Suite 400 .... Fort Lauderdale FL 33309 954-308-4200 308-4222
NASDAQ: FUEL ■ TF: 800-383-5734 ■ Web: www.mobilefueling.com
Suburban Gas Inc 2800 Dartmouth Ave ....Bessemer AL 35020 205-424-4464 424-0667
Suburban Propane Partners LP 240 Rt 10 W....................Whippany NJ 07981 973-887-5300 515-5970*
NYSE: SPH ■ *Fax: Mktg ■ TF: 800-526-0620 ■ Web: www.suburbanpropane.com
Susser Holdings LLC 4433 Baldwin Blvd..................... Corpus Christi TX 78408 361-693-3600 884-2494
TF: 800-569-3585 ■ Web: www.susser.com
SW Rawls Inc 100 Bowers Rd.................................... Franklin VA 23851 757-562-3115 562-1227
Web: www.swrawls.com
Webber Energy Fuels 700 Main St.............................. Bangor ME 04401 207-942-5501 941-9597
TF: 800-932-2371 ■ Web: www.wenergy.com
Western Natural Gas Co 2960 Strickland St................ Jacksonville FL 32254 904-387-3511 387-6034
Web: www.westernnaturalgas.com
WH Riley & Son Inc 35 Chestnut St .... North Attleboro MA 02761 508-695-9391 699-7712
Web: www.whriley.com

Phone Fax

William R Peterson Oil Co 276 Main St Suite 1 PO box 31 .... Portland CT 06480 860-342-3560 342-2543
TF: 800-622-6971

Wilson of Wallingford Inc 221 Rogers Ln PO box 185 .... Wallingford PA 19086 610-566-7600 566-7608
Web: www.wilsonoil.com

Woodruff Energy 73 Water St .... Bridgeton NJ 08302 856-455-1111 455-4085
TF: 800-557-1121 ■ *Web:* www.woodruffenergy.com

320 FUND-RAISING SERVICES

Phone Fax

Adams Hussey & Assoc 1400 'I' St NW Suite 650 .... Washington DC 20005 202-682-2500 682-5100
Web: www.ahadirect.com

Alford Group Inc 1603 Orrington Ave 2nd Fl .... Evanston IL 60201 847-425-9800 425-4114
TF: 800-291-8913 ■ *Web:* www.alford.com

Barton Cotton Inc 1405 Parker Rd .... Baltimore MD 21227 410-247-4800 247-3681
TF: 800-638-4652 ■ *Web:* www.bartoncotton.com

Bentz Whaley Flessner 7251 Ohms Ln .... Minneapolis MN 55439 952-921-0111 921-0109
TF: 800-921-0111 ■ *Web:* www.bwf.com

Brakeley Briscoe Inc 51 Locust Ave Suite 204 .... New Canaan CT 06804 203-972-0282 972-0263
TF: 800-486-5171 ■ *Web:* www.brakeleybriscoe.com

Cargill Assoc Inc 4701 Altamesa Blvd .... Fort Worth TX 76133 817-292-9374 292-6205
TF: 800-433-2233 ■ *Web:* www.cargillassociates.com

Carlton & Co 101 Federal St Suite 1900 .... Boston MA 02110 617-342-7257 738-8962*
**Fax Area Code: 252* ■ *TF:* 800-622-0194

Community Counselling Service 461 5th Ave 3rd Fl .... New York NY 10017 212-695-1175 967-6451
TF: 800-223-6733 ■ *Web:* www.ccsfundraising.com

Cull Martin & Assoc Inc 59 Court St 4th Fl .... Binghamton NY 13901 607-722-3884 722-4264
Web: www.cullmartin.com

Dragul Group 312 Walnut St Suite 1600 .... Cincinnati OH 45202 513-762-7828 721-4628

Gift Planning Assoc 223 Clipper St .... San Francisco CA 94114 415-970-2380
Web: www.giftplanner1.com

Gonser Gerber Tinker Stuhr LLP 400 E Diehl Rd Suite 380 .... Naperville IL 60563 630-505-1433 505-7710
TF: 800-446-4487 ■ *Web:* www.ggts.com

Goodale Assoc 52 E 66th St .... New York NY 10021 212-472-0300 472-0311
Web: www.tkgoodale.com

Grenzebach Glier & Assoc Inc 401 N Michigan Ave Suite 2800 .... Chicago IL 60611 312-372-4040 372-7911
Web: www.grenzebachglier.com

Hodge Cramer & Assoc Inc 5400 Frantz Rd Suite 120 .... Dublin OH 43016 614-761-3005 761-9920
TF: 800-978-9212 ■ *Web:* www.hodgecramer.com

Institutional Advancement Programs Inc
65 Main St Suite 208 .... Tuckahoe NY 10707 914-779-4092 961-3114

Jackson & Assoc Inc 30294 Inverness Ln .... Evergreen CO 80439 303-670-1100 670-1127
TF: 800-824-8447 ■ *Web:* www.jacksonandassoc.com

John B Cummings Co Inc 3333 Lee Pkwy Suite 600 .... Dallas TX 75219 214-526-1772 665-9590
Web: www.cummingsco.com

John Brown Ltd Inc 46 Grove St PO Box 296 .... Peterborough NH 03458 603-924-3834 924-7998
Web: www.johnbrownlimited.com

Ketchum Inc 5151 Belt Line Rd Suite 900 .... Dallas TX 75254 214-866-7600 866-7750
TF: 800-242-2161 ■ *Web:* www.ketchum.viscern.com

Kintera Inc 9605 Scranton Rd Suite 240 .... San Diego CA 92121 858-795-3000 795-3010
NASDAQ: KNTA ■ *Web:* www.kintera.com

KMA Direct Communications 7160 Dallas Pkwy Suite 400 .... Plano TX 75024 972-244-1900 244-1901
TF: 800-562-4161 ■ *Web:* www.kma.com

Lipman Hearne Inc 200 S Michigan Ave Suite 1600 .... Chicago IL 60604 312-356-8000 356-4005
Web: www.lipmanhearne.com

LW Robbins Assoc 201 Summer St .... Holliston MA 01746 508-893-0210 893-0212
TF: 800-229-5972 ■ *Web:* www.lwra.com

MacIntyre Assoc Inc 106 W State St .... Kennett Square PA 19348 610-925-5925
TF: 888-575-0903 ■ *Web:* www.macintyreassociates.com

McGrath & Co 113 N Cass Ave .... Westmont IL 60559 630-852-9900 852-4567
Web: www.mcgrathco.com

Netzel Assoc Inc 9696 Culver Blvd Suite 105 .... Culver City CA 90232 310-836-7624 836-9357
Web: www.netzelinc.com

PEP Direct Inc 19 Stoney Brook Dr .... Wilton NH 03086 603-654-6141 654-2159
TF: 877-782-3782 ■ *Web:* www.pep-direct.com

Phillips & Assoc PO Box 241040 .... Los Angeles CA 90024 310-247-0963 247-0966
Web: www.phillipsontheweb.com

Robbins LW Assoc 201 Summer St .... Holliston MA 01746 508-893-0210 893-0212
TF: 800-229-5972 ■ *Web:* www.lwra.com

Ruotolo Assoc Inc 29 Broadway Suite 210 .... Cresskill NJ 07626 201-568-3898 568-8783
TF: 800-786-8656 ■ *Web:* www.ruotoloassoc.com

Sanky Perlowin Assoc Inc 589 8th Ave 10th Fl .... New York NY 10018 212-868-4300 868-4310
Web: www.sankyperlowin.com

Skystone Ryan 635 W 7th St Suite 107 .... Cincinnati OH 45203 513-241-6778 241-0551
TF: 800-883-0801 ■ *Web:* www.skystoneryan.com

Stanford Group 211 W 56th St Suite 3-M .... New York NY 10019 212-333-5514 581-4202

Ter Molen Watkins & Brandt LLC 500 N Dearborn St Suite 726 .... Chicago IL 60610 312-222-0560 222-0565
Web: www.twbfundraising.com

Van Groesbeck & Co 2211 Dickens Rd Suite 300 .... Richmond VA 23230 804-285-3175 285-2059
Web: www.vangroesbeck.com

Whitney Jones Inc 119 Brookstown Ave Suite 302 .... Winston-Salem NC 27101 336-722-2371
Web: www.whitneyjonesinc.com

321 FURNACES & OVENS - INDUSTRIAL PROCESS

Phone Fax

AFC Holcroft LLC 49630 Pontiac Trail .... Wixom MI 48393 248-624-8191 624-3710
Web: www.afc-holcroft.com

AGF Burner Inc 1955 Swarthmore Ave Unit 2 .... Lakewood NJ 08701 732-730-8090 730-8060
Web: www.agfburner.com

Ajax Electric Co 60 Tomlinson Rd .... Huntingdon Valley PA 19006 215-947-8500 947-6757
Web: www.ajaxelectric.com

Ajax Tocco Magnethermic Corp 1745 Overland Ave NE .... Warren OH 44483 330-372-8511 372-8644
TF: 800-321-0153 ■ *Web:* www.ajaxtocco.com

Alpha 1 Induction Service Center Inc
1525 Old Alum Creek Dr .... Columbus OH 43209 614-253-8900 253-8981
TF: 800-991-2599 ■ *Web:* www.alpha1induction.com

AVS Inc 60 Fitchburg Rd .... Ayer MA 01432 978-772-0710 772-6462
TF: 800-272-0710 ■ *Web:* www.avsinc.com

Belco Industries Inc 115 E Main St .... Belding MI 48809 616-794-0410 794-3424
Web: www.belcoind.com

BH Thermal Corp 1055 Gibbard Ave .... Columbus OH 43201 614-294-3376 294-3807
TF: 800-848-7673 ■ *Web:* www.bhthermal.com

Bloom Engineering Co Inc 5460 Horning Rd .... Pittsburgh PA 15236 412-653-3500 653-2253
TF: 800-451-5491 ■ *Web:* www.bloomeng.com

Callidus Technologies Inc 7130 S Lewis St Suite 335 .... Tulsa OK 74136 918-496-7599 496-7587
Web: www.callidus.com

CCI Thermal Technologies Inc 5918 Roper Rd .... Edmonton AB T6B3E1 780-466-3178 468-5904
TF: 800-661-8529 ■ *Web:* www.ccithermal.com

Phone Fax

CI Hayes 33 Freeway Dr .... Cranston RI 02920 401-467-5200 467-2108
Web: www.cihayes.com

Cincinnati Industrial Machinery An Armor Metal Group Co
4600 N Mason-Montgomery Rd .... Mason OH 45040 513-923-5600 923-5694*
**Fax: Sales* ■ *TF:* 800-677-0076 ■ *Web:* www.armormetal.com

CMI EFCO Inc 435 W Wilson St .... Salem OH 44460 330-332-4661 332-1853
Web: www.cmiefco.com

Consarc Corp 100 Indel Ave .... Rancocas NJ 08073 609-267-8000 267-1366*
**Fax: Sales* ■ *Web:* www.consarc.com

Consutech Systems LLC PO Box 15119 .... Richmond VA 23227 804-746-4120 730-9056
Web: www.consutech.com

Core Furnace Systems 100 Corporate Center Dr .... Coraopolis PA 15108 412-262-2240 262-3064
TF: 800-355-4826 ■ *Web:* www.corefurnace.com

Delta Manufacturing/Acra PO Box 9889 .... Tulsa OK 74157 918-224-6755 224-6866
Web: www.acraelectric.com

Despatch Industries Inc 8860 207th St W .... Lakeville MN 55044 952-469-5424 469-4513
Web: www.despatch.com

Detroit Radiant Product Co 21400 Hoover Rd .... Warren MI 48089 586-756-0950 756-2626
TF: 800-222-1100 ■ *Web:* www.reverberray.com

Detroit Stoker Co 1510 E 1st St .... Monroe MI 48161 734-241-9500 241-0216
TF: 800-786-5374 ■ *Web:* www.detroitstoker.com

Eclipse Inc 1665 Elmwood Rd .... Rockford IL 61103 815-877-3031 877-3336*
**Fax: Cust Svc* ■ *TF:* 800-676-3254 ■ *Web:* www.eclipsenet.com

Eisenmann Corp 150 E Dartmoor Dr .... Crystal Lake IL 60014 815-455-4100 455-1018
Web: www.eisenmann.com

Electric Heating Equipment Co 1240 Oronoque Rd .... Milford CT 06460 203-882-0199 882-8937
TF: 800-958-9998

Fast Heat Inc 776 Oaklawn Ave .... Elmhurst IL 60126 630-833-5400 833-2040
TF: 800-982-4328 ■ *Web:* www.fastheat.com

Fostoria Industries Inc 1200 N Main St .... Fostoria OH 44830 419-435-9201 435-0842
TF: 800-495-4525 ■ *Web:* www.fostoriaindustries.com

Gas-Fired Products Inc PO Box 36485 .... Charlotte NC 28236 704-372-3485 332-5843
TF: 800-830-3983 ■ *Web:* www.gasfiredproducts.com

GC Broach Co 7667 E 46th Pl .... Tulsa OK 74145 918-664-7420 627-4083
Web: www.broach.com

Glenn Electric Heater Corp 2111 E 30th St .... Erie PA 16510 814-898-4000 898-1719
Web: www.glennelectricheater.com

Glenro Inc 39 McBride Ave .... Paterson NJ 07501 973-279-5900 279-9103
TF: 800-922-0106 ■ *Web:* www.glenro.com

Glo-Quartz Electric Heater Co Inc 7084 Maple St .... Mentor OH 44060 440-255-9701 255-7852
TF Sales: 800-321-3574 ■ *Web:* www.gloquartz.com

Global Finishing Solutions LLC 1625 W Crosby Rd Suite 124 .... Carrollton TX 75006 800-848-8738 633-1108
Web: globalfinishing.com

Harper International Corp W Drullard Ave .... Lancaster NY 14086 716-684-7400 684-7405
Web: www.harperintl.com

Hauck Mfg Co PO Box 90 .... Lebanon PA 17042 717-272-3051 273-9882
Web: www.hauckburner.com

Hayes CI 33 Freeway Dr .... Cranston RI 02920 401-467-5200 467-2108
Web: www.cihayes.com

Heatrex Inc PO Box 515 .... Meadville PA 16335 814-724-1800 333-6580
TF: 800-394-6589 ■ *Web:* www.heatrex.com

Henry F Teichmann Inc 3009 Washington Rd .... McMurray PA 15317 724-941-9550 941-3479
Web: www.hft.com

Hotwatt Inc 128 Maple St .... Danvers MA 01923 978-777-0070 774-2409*
**Fax: Sales* ■ *Web:* www.hotwatt.com

Huppert KH Co Inc 16850 S State St .... South Holland IL 60473 708-339-2020 339-2225
Web: www.huppert.com

Inductoheat Inc 32251 N Avis Dr .... Madison Heights MI 48071 248-585-9393 589-1062
TF: 800-642-8903 ■ *Web:* www.inductoheat.com

Inductotherm Corp 10 Indel Ave .... Rancocas NJ 08073 609-267-9000 267-3537
TF: 800-257-9527 ■ *Web:* www.inductotherm.com

Inductotherm Industries Inc 10 Indel Ave .... Rancocas NJ 08073 609-267-9000 267-3537
TF: 800-257-9527 ■ *Web:* www.inductothermgroup.com

Industrial Combustion Inc 351 21st St .... Monroe WI 53566 608-325-3141 325-4379
Web: www.ind-comb.com

Industrial Engineering & Equipment Co
425 Hanley Industrial Ct .... Saint Louis MO 63144 314-644-4300 644-5332
Web: www.indeeco.com

Industrial Heater Corp 30 Knotter Dr .... Cheshire CT 06410 203-250-0500 250-0599
TF: 800-822-4426 ■ *Web:* www.industrialheater.com

Industronics Service Co 489 Sullivan Ave PO Box 649 .... South Windsor CT 06074 860-289-1551 289-3526
TF: 800-878-1551 ■ *Web:* www.industronics.com

International Thermal Systems LLC 4697 W Greenfield Ave .... Milwaukee WI 53214 414-672-7700 672-8800
TF: 877-683-6797 ■ *Web:* www.itsllcusa.com

IntriCon Corp 1260 Red Fox Rd .... Arden Hills MI 55112 651-636-9770 636-9503
AMEX: IIN ■ *TF:* 800-523-6500 ■ *Web:* www.intricon.com

Ipsen International Inc PO Box 6266 .... Rockford IL 61125 815-332-4941 332-4549
TF: 800-727-7625 ■ *Web:* www.ipsen-international.com

John Zink Co LLC PO Box 21220 .... Tulsa OK 74121 918-234-1800 234-2700
TF: 800-421-9242 ■ *Web:* www.johnzink.com

Johnson Gas Appliance Co 520 E Ave NW .... Cedar Rapids IA 52405 319-365-5267 365-6282
TF: 800-553-5422 ■ *Web:* www.mendotahearth.com

Johnson ST Co PO Box 8627 .... Emeryville CA 94662 510-652-6000 652-4302
Web: www.stjohnson.com

JT Thorpe & Son Inc 1060 Hensley St .... Richmond CA 94801 510-233-2500 233-2901
TF: 800-577-1755 ■ *Web:* www.jtthorpe.com

KH Huppert Co Inc 16850 S State St .... South Holland IL 60473 708-339-2020 339-2225
Web: www.huppert.com

Koch Chemical Technology Group LLC 4111 E 37th St N .... Wichita KS 67220 316-828-5500 828-4704
Web: www.kochchemtech.com

Lanly Co 26201 Tungsten Rd .... Cleveland OH 44132 216-731-1115 731-7900
Web: www.lanly.com

Larose RF Systems Inc 150 Dover Rd .... Millis MA 02054 508-376-0850 376-9944
Web: www.radiofrequency.com

Lepel Corp 200-G Executive Dr .... Edgewood NY 11717 631-586-3300 586-3232
TF: 800-548-8520 ■ *Web:* www.inductionheating.com

Mestek Inc 260 N Elm St .... Westfield MA 01085 413-568-9571 562-7630
NYSE: MCC ■ *Web:* www.mestek.com

Novatec Inc 222 E Thomas Ave .... Baltimore MD 21225 410-789-4811 789-4638
TF: 800-237-8379 ■ *Web:* www.novatec.com

Nutec Bickley USA PO Box 369 .... Bensalem PA 19020 215-638-4500
Web: www.nutecbickley.com

Paragon Industries Inc 2011 South Town E Blvd .... Mesquite TX 75149 972-288-7557 222-0646
TF: 800-876-4328 ■ *Web:* www.paragonweb.com

Phoenix Solutions Co 3324 Winpark Dr .... Crystal MN 55427 763-544-2721 546-5617
Web: www.phoenixsolutionsco.com

Pillar Induction Co 21905 Gateway Rd .... Brookfield WI 53045 262-317-5300 317-5353
TF: 800-558-7733 ■ *Web:* www.pillar.com

Procedyne Corp 11 Industrial Dr .... New Brunswick NJ 08901 732-249-8347 249-7220
Web: www.procedyne.com

Process Combustion Corp 5460 Horning Rd .... Pittsburgh PA 15236 412-655-0955 650-5569
Web: www.pcc-sterling.com

Pyronics Inc 17700 Miles Rd .... Cleveland OH 44128 216-662-8800 663-8954
Web: www.pyronics.com

Radiant Technology Corp 1335 S Acacia Ave .... Fullerton CA 92831 714-991-0200 991-0600
Web: www.radianttech.com

Phone | Fax

Radio Frequency Co Inc 150 Dover Rd PO Box 158 ... Millis MA 02054 508-376-9555 376-9944
Web: www.radiofrequency.com
Radyne Corp 211 W Boden St ... Milwaukee WI 53207 414-481-8360 481-8303
TF: 800-236-8360 ■ *Web:* www.radyne.com
Rapid Engineering Inc 1100 7-Mile Rd NW ... Comstock Park MI 49321 616-784-0500 784-1910
TF: 800-536-3461 ■ *Web:* www.rapidengineering.com
Ray Burner/RD Miners Co 401 Parr Blvd ... Richmond CA 94801 510-236-4972 236-4083
TF: 800-729-2876 ■ *Web:* www.rayburner.com
Red-Ray Mfg Co Inc 10-22 County Line Rd ... Branchburg NJ 08876 908-722-0040 722-2535
Web: www.red-ray.com
SECO/Warwick Corp 180 Mercer St ... Meadville PA 16335 814-724-1400 724-1407
TF: 800-458-6071 ■ *Web:* www.secowarwick.com
SPX Corp Lindberg Div 3827 Riverside Rd ... Riverside MI 49084 269-849-2700 849-3021
TF: 800-759-4782 ■ *Web:* www.heat-treat.com
ST Johnson Co PO Box 8627 ... Emeryville CA 94662 510-652-6000 652-4302
Web: www.stjohnson.com
Steelman Industries Inc 2800 Hwy 135 N ... Kilgore TX 75662 903-984-3061 984-1384
TF: 800-287-6633 ■ *Web:* www.steelman.com
StrikoDynarad 501 E Roosevelt Ave ... Zeeland MI 49464 616-772-3705 772-5271
Web: www.strikodynarad.com
Surface Combustion Inc 1700 Indian Wood Cir ... Maumee OH 43537 419-891-7150 891-7151
TF: 800-537-8980 ■ *Web:* www.surfacecombustion.com
Swindell Dressler International Co PO Box 15541 ... Pittsburgh PA 15244 412-788-7100 788-7110
Web: www.swindelldressler.com
T-M Vacuum Products Inc 630 S Warrington Ave ... Cinnaminson NJ 08077 856-829-2000 829-0990
Web: www.tmvacuum.com
Tempco Electric Heater Corp 607 N Central Ave ... Wood Dale IL 60191 630-350-2252 350-0232
TF: 800-323-6859 ■ *Web:* www.tempco.com
Thermal Circuits Inc 1 Technology Way ... Salem MA 01970 978-745-1162 741-3420
TF: 800-808-4328 ■ *Web:* www.thermalcircuits.com
Thermal Engineering Corp 2741 The Boulevard ... Columbia SC 29209 803-783-0750 783-0756
TF: 800-331-0097 ■ *Web:* www.tecinfrared.com
Thermal Equipment Corp 1301 W 228th St ... Torrance CA 90501 310-328-6600 320-2692
Web: www.thermalequipment.com
Thermex Thermatron Inc 400 Oser Ave Suite 1800 ... Hauppauge NY 11788 631-231-7800 231-5399
Web: www.thermex-thermatron.com
Todd Combustion Group 2 Armstrong Rd 3rd Fl ... Shelton CT 06484 203-925-0380 925-0384
TF: 800-225-0085
Trent Inc 201 Leverington Ave ... Philadelphia PA 19127 215-482-5000 482-9389
TF: 800-544-8736 ■ *Web:* www.trentheat.com
Truheat Inc 700 Grand St ... Allegan MI 49010 269-673-2145 673-7219
TF: 800-879-6199 ■ *Web:* www.truheat.com
United Industrial Corp 124 Industry Ln ... Hunt Valley MD 21030 410-628-3000 683-6498
NYSE: UIC ■ *TF:* 800-655-3964 ■ *Web:* www.unitedindustrial.com
Watlow Electric Mfg Co 12001 Lackland Rd ... Saint Louis MO 63146 314-878-4600 878-6814
TF: 800-492-8569 ■ *Web:* www.watlow.com
Webster Engineering & Mfg Co LLC 619 Industrial Rd ... Winfield KS 67156 620-221-7464 221-9447
Web: www.webster-engineering.com
Wisconsin Oven Corp 2675 Main St ... East Troy WI 53120 262-642-3938 363-4018
Web: www.wisoven.com
Zink John Co LLC PO Box 21220 ... Tulsa OK 74121 918-234-1800 234-2700
TF: 800-421-9242 ■ *Web:* www.johnzink.com

322 FURNITURE - MFR

SEE ALSO Baby Products p. 1366; Cabinets - Wood p. 1403; Fixtures - Office & Store p. 1638; Mattresses & Adjustable Beds p. 1950; Recycled Plastics Products p. 2208

322-1 Commercial & Industrial Furniture

Phone | Fax

Abco Office Furniture 4121 Rushton St ... Florence AL 35630 256-767-4100 760-1247
TF: 800-336-0070 ■ *Web:* www.abcofurniture.com
Adelphia Steel Equipment Co 7372 State Rd ... Philadelphia PA 19136 215-333-6300 331-6090
TF: 800-865-8211 ■ *Web:* www.adelphiafurniture.com
Allied Plastics Co Inc 2001 Walnut St ... Jacksonville FL 32206 904-359-0386 353-4746
TF Cust Svc: 800-999-0386 ■ *Web:* www.alliedplasticsco.com
Allsteel Inc 2210 2nd Ave ... Muscatine IA 52761 563-262-4800 272-4887
TF Cust Svc: 800-553-8230 ■ *Web:* www.allsteeloffice.com
American of Martinsville 128 E Church St ... Martinsville VA 24112 276-632-2061 638-8810
Web: www.americanofmartinsville.com
Anthro Corp 10450 SW Manhasset Dr ... Tualatin OR 97062 503-691-2556 691-2409
TF: 800-325-3841 ■ *Web:* www.anthro.com
Bernhardt Furniture Co Inc 1839 Morganton Blvd SW ... Lenoir NC 28645 828-758-9811 759-6634
TF: 800-523-8824 ■ *Web:* www.bernhardt.com
Bestar Inc 4220 Villeneuve St ... Lac-Megantic QC G6B2C3 819-583-1017 583-5370
TSX: BES ■ *TF:* 888-823-7827 ■ *Web:* www.bestar.ca
Bevco Precision Mfg Co 2246A Bluemound Rd ... Waukesha WI 53186 262-798-9200 798-9201
TF: 800-864-2991 ■ *Web:* www.bevco.com
BGD Cos Inc 275 Market St Suite 192 ... Minneapolis MN 55405 612-338-6804 338-4942
TF: 800-699-3537 ■ *Web:* www.bgdmidwest.com
Biofit Engineered Products 15500 Biofit Way ... Bowling Greene OH 43402 419-823-1089 823-1342
TF: 800-597-0246 ■ *Web:* www.biofit.com
BK Barrit Corp 4011 G St ... Philadelphia PA 19124 267-345-1200 739-1709*
**Fax Area Code:* 215 ■ *TF:* 888-256-2020 ■ *Web:* www.bkbarrit.com
Boling Furniture Co 311 NE Church Rd PO Box 1059 ... Mount Olive NC 28365 919-635-2400 635-4845
TF: 888-779-6546 ■ *Web:* www.bolingfurniture.com
Borroughs Corp 3002 N Burdick St ... Kalamazoo MI 49004 269-342-0161 342-4161
TF: 800-748-0227 ■ *Web:* www.borroughs.com
Brayton International Inc 250 Swathmoore Ave ... High Point NC 27263 336-434-4151 434-8247
TF: 800-627-6770 ■ *Web:* www.brayton.com
Bright Chair Co 51 Railroad Ave PO Box 269 ... Middletown NY 10940 845-343-2196 343-4958
TF: 888-524-5997 ■ *Web:* www.brightchair.com
CabotWrenn 405 Rink Dam Rd ... Hickory NC 28601 828-495-4607 495-1294
Web: www.cabotwrenn.com
Carolina Business Furniture LLC 535 Archdale Blvd ... Archdale NC 27263 336-431-9400 431-9511
TF: 800-763-0212 ■ *Web:* www.carolinabusinessfurniture.com
Carson's Inc 4299 Cheyenne Dr PO Box 14186 ... Archdale NC 27263 336-431-1101 431-0677
Web: www.carsonsofhp.com
CF Group 10650 Gateway Blvd ... Saint Louis MO 63132 314-991-9200 991-9227
Web: www.commercialfurnituregroup.com
Chairmasters Inc 200 E 146th St ... Bronx NY 10451 718-292-0600 292-0613
Web: www.chairmasters.com
Chromcraft Revington Inc 1330 Win Hentschel Blvd ... West Lafayette IN 47906 765-807-2640 807-2660
AMEX: CRC
Commercial Furniture Group 10650 Gateway Blvd ... Saint Louis MO 63132 314-991-9200 991-9227
Web: www.commercialfurnituregroup.com
Cramer Inc 1222 Quebec St ... North Kansas City MO 64116 816-471-4433 471-7188
TF: 800-366-6700 ■ *Web:* www.cramerinc.com

Phone | Fax

CTB Corp 26327 Fallbrook Ave ... Wyoming MN 55092 651-462-3550 462-8806
Web: www.ctbcorp.com
Danver 1 Grand St ... Wallingford CT 06492 203-269-2300 265-6190
Web: www.danver.com
Dar-Ran Furniture Industries 2402 Shore St ... High Point NC 27263 336-861-2400 861-6485
TF: 800-334-7891 ■ *Web:* www.darran.com
Dauphin North America 300 Myrtle Ave ... Boonton NJ 07005 973-263-1100 263-3551
TF Cust Svc: 800-631-1186 ■ *Web:* www.dauphin.com
Davis Furniture Industries Inc 2401 S College Dr ... High Point NC 27261 336-889-2009 889-0031
TF: 877-463-2847 ■ *Web:* www.davis-furniture.com
Delco Assoc Inc Delco Office Systems Div
55 Old Field Point Rd PO Box 423 ... Greenwich CT 06830 203-661-5101 661-9829
TF: 800-243-8528 ■ *Web:* www.mailingstuff.com/delco
Delco Office Systems Div Delco Assoc Inc
55 Old Field Point Rd PO Box 423 ... Greenwich CT 06830 203-661-5101 661-9829
TF: 800-243-8528 ■ *Web:* www.mailingstuff.com/delco
Design Options 5202 Eagle Trail Dr ... Tampa FL 33634 813-885-4950 885-2994
TF Cust Svc: 877-800-3560 ■ *Web:* www.designoptions.com
DMI Furniture Inc 9780 Ormsby Station Rd Suite 2000 ... Louisville KY 40223 502-426-4351 755-2878*
**Fax Area Code:* 800 ■ *TF:* 888-372-1927 ■ *Web:* www.dmifurniture.com
Easi File Mfg Corp 6 Wrigley St ... Irvine CA 92618 949-855-4121 380-0561*
**Fax:* Sales ■ *TF:* 800-800-5563 ■ *Web:* www.easifileusa.com
EBSCO Industries Inc Luxor Div 2245 Delany Rd ... Waukegan IL 60087 847-244-1800 327-1698*
**Fax Area Code:* 800 ■ *TF:* 800-323-4656 ■ *Web:* www.luxorfurn.com
Emeco Industries Inc 805 W Elm Ave PO Box 179 ... Hanover PA 17331 717-637-5951 633-6018
TF: 800-366-5951 ■ *Web:* www.emeco.net
Engineered Data Products Inc 1250 W 124th Ave ... Denver CO 80234 303-465-2800 465-4936
TF: 800-432-1337 ■ *Web:* www.edp-usa.com
Ergotron Inc 1181 Trapp Rd ... Eagan MN 55121 651-681-7600 681-7710
TF Sales: 800-888-8458 ■ *Web:* www.ergotron.com
Executive Office Concepts Inc 1715 S Anderson Ave ... Compton CA 90220 310-537-1657 603-9100
TF: 800-421-5927 ■ *Web:* www.eoccorp.com
Fairfield Chair Co 1331 Harper Ave SW ... Lenoir NC 28645 828-758-5571 758-0211
Web: www.fairfieldchair.com
Fillip Metal Cabinet Co 701 N Albany Ave ... Chicago IL 60612 773-826-7373 826-6420
TF: 800-535-0733 ■ *Web:* www.fillipmetal.com
First Office 1204 E 6th St PO Box 100 ... Huntingburg IN 47542 812-683-4848 683-7155*
**Fax:* Cust Svc ■ *TF:* 800-521-5381 ■ *Web:* www.firstoffice.com
Fixtures Furniture Inc 1642 Crystal Ave ... Kansas City MO 64126 816-241-4500 245-5884
TF Cust Svc: 800-821-3500 ■ *Web:* www.fixturesfurniture.com
Flex-Y-Plan Industries Inc 6960 W Ridge Rd ... Fairview PA 16415 814-474-1565 474-2129
TF Cust Svc: 800-458-0552 ■ *Web:* www.fyp.com
Flexible-Montisa 323 Acorn St ... Plainwell MI 49080 269-685-6831 685-9195
TF Cust Svc: 800-875-6836 ■ *Web:* www.flexiblefurniture.com
Flexsteel Industries Inc 3400 Jackson St ... Dubuque IA 52001 563-556-7730 556-8345*
NASDAQ: FLXS ■ **Fax:* Cust Svc ■ *Web:* www.flexsteel.com
Foldcraft Co 615 Centennial Dr ... Kenyon MN 55946 507-789-5111 544-0480*
**Fax Area Code:* 800 ■ *TF:* 800-759-6653 ■ *Web:* www.plymold.com
Franke Foodservice Systems 305 Tech Park Dr ... La Vergne TN 37086 615-287-8200 287-8250
TF: 888-437-2653 ■ *Web:* www.frankefs.com
Furniture Values International LLC 2929 NW Grand Ave ... Phoenix AZ 85017 602-233-0224 269-6810
TF: 888-484-5874
Geiger International Inc 6095 Fulton Industrial Blvd SW ... Atlanta GA 30336 404-344-1100 836-7519
TF: 800-444-8812 ■ *Web:* www.hmgeiger.com
GF Office Furniture Ltd 525 Steam Plant Rd ... Gallatin TN 37066 615-452-9120 230-1533
TF Cust Svc: 800-321-4005 ■ *Web:* www.gfoffice.com
Global Industries Inc 17 W Stow Rd ... Marlton NJ 08053 856-596-3390 596-5684
TF: 800-220-1900 ■ *Web:* www.globaltotaloffice.com
Groupe Lacasse LLC 147 St-Pierre St ... Sainte-Pie QC J0H1W0 450-772-2495 248-1865*
**Fax Area Code:* 888 ■ **Fax:* Cust Svc ■ *TF:* 888-522-2773 ■
Web: www.groupelacasse.com
Gunlocke Co LLC 1 Gunlocke Dr ... Wayland NY 14572 585-728-5111 728-8334*
**Fax:* Hum Res ■ *TF Cust Svc:* 800-828-6300 ■ *Web:* www.gunlocke.com
H Wilson Co 555 W Taft Dr ... South Holland IL 60473 708-339-5111 245-8224*
**Fax Area Code:* 800 ■ *TF:* 800-245-7224 ■ *Web:* www.hwilson.com
Harden Furniture Inc 8550 Mill Pond Way ... McConnellsville NY 13401 315-245-1000 245-2884
Web: www.harden.com
Harter 11451 Harter Dr ... Middlebury IN 46540 574-825-5871 825-3258
TF: 800-543-5449 ■ *Web:* www.harter.com
Hausmann Industries Inc 130 Union St ... Northvale NJ 07647 201-767-0255 767-1369
TF: 888-428-7626 ■ *Web:* www.hausmann.com
Haworth Inc 1 Haworth Center ... Holland MI 49423 616-393-3000 393-1570
TF: 800-765-4100 ■ *Web:* www.haworth.com
Herman Miller Inc 855 E Main Ave ... Zeeland MI 49464 616-654-3000 654-5385
NASDAQ: MLHR ■ *TF:* 888-443-4357 ■ *Web:* www.hermanmiller.com
High Point Furniture Industries Inc
1104 Bedford St PO Box 2063 ... High Point NC 27261 336-431-7101 434-1964
TF: 800-447-3462 ■ *Web:* www.hpfi.com
Hirsh Industries Inc 11229 Aurora Ave ... Urbandale IA 50322 515-299-3200 299-3374
TF: 800-383-7414 ■ *Web:* www.hirshindustries.com
HON Co 200 Oak St ... Muscatine IA 52761 563-264-7400 264-7206
TF: 800-553-8230 ■ *Web:* www.hon.com
Huot Mfg Co 550 Wheeler St N ... Saint Paul MN 55104 651-646-1869 646-0457
TF: 800-832-3838 ■ *Web:* www.huot.com
IAC Industries 895 Beacon St ... Brea CA 92821 714-990-8997 990-0557
TF: 800-229-1422 ■ *Web:* www.iacindustries.com
Indiana Furniture 1224 Mill St ... Jasper IN 47546 812-482-5727 482-9035
TF: 800-422-5727 ■ *Web:* www.indianafurniture.com
Institutional & Office Services Inc 4 Cara Ct ... Randolph NJ 07869 973-895-9002 895-9003
TF: 800-223-1210
Interior Crafts Inc 2513 W Cullerton Ave ... Chicago IL 60608 773-376-8160 376-9578
Intrex LLC 40 Park St ... Brooklyn NY 11206 718-455-5042 919-5202
TF: 877-946-8739 ■ *Web:* www.intrexfurniture.com
Invincible Office Furniture Co 842 S 26th St PO Box 1117 ... Manitowoc WI 54220 920-682-4601 683-2970
TF: 800-558-4417 ■ *Web:* www.invinciblefurniture.com
Inwood Office Environments 1108 E 15th St ... Jasper IN 47546 812-482-6121 482-9732
TF: 800-786-6121 ■ *Web:* www.inwood.net
izzydesign 17237 Van Wagoner Rd ... Spring Lake MI 49456 616-847-7000 847-6540
Web: www.izzydesign.com
izzydesign 1 Industrial Park ... Belton TX 76513 254-939-3517 939-1630
TF Cust Svc: 800-345-6034 ■ *Web:* www.izzydesign.com
Jami Inc 7300 W 110th St Suite 210 ... Overland Park KS 66210 913-663-3459 663-1556
TF: 800-707-7288 ■ *Web:* www.jamiinc.com
Jasper Desk Co 415 E 6th St ... Jasper IN 47546 812-482-4132 482-9552
TF Cust Svc: 800-365-7994 ■ *Web:* www.jasperdesk.com
Jasper Seating Co Inc 225 Clay St ... Jasper IN 47546 812-482-3204 482-1548
TF: 800-622-5661 ■ *Web:* www.jasperseating.com
Jebco Inc 405 Mayfield Rd ... Warrenton GA 30828 706-465-3378 465-2481
Web: www.jebcomfg.com
Jofco International 402 E 13th St ... Jasper IN 47546 812-482-5154 634-2392
TF: 800-235-6326 ■ *Web:* www.jofco.com
JSJ Corp 700 Robbins Rd ... Grand Haven MI 49417 616-842-6350 847-3112
Web: www.jsjcorp.com
KI 1330 Bellevue St ... Green Bay WI 54302 920-468-8100 468-0280
TF: 877-231-8555 ■ *Web:* www.ki-inc.com
Kimball Hospitality 1180 E 16th St ... Jasper IN 47549 812-482-1600 634-4324
TF: 800-634-9510 ■ *Web:* www.kimballhospitality.com

Commercial & Industrial Furniture (Cont'd)

	City	State	ZIP	Phone	Fax
Kimball Office Furniture Co 1600 Royal St TF: 800-482-1818 ■ Web: www.kimballoffice.com	Jasper	IN	47549	812-482-1600	482-8300
Knoll Inc 1235 Water St NYSE: KNL ■ TF Cust Svc: 800-343-5665 ■ Web: www.knoll.com	East Greenville	PA	18041	215-679-7991	679-1755
Lakeside Mfg Inc 4900 W Electric Ave TF: 800-558-8565 ■ Web: www.elakeside.com	West Milwaukee	WI	53219	414-902-6400	902-6446
LB Furniture Industries LLC 99 S 3rd St TF: 800-403-0833 ■ Web: www.lbempire.com	Hudson	NY	12534	518-828-1501	828-3219
Lincoln Office 77 Commerce Dr TF: 800-374-1555 ■ Web: www.lincolnoffice.com	Morton	IL	61550	309-263-7777	692-1018
Loewenstein Inc 4200 Tudor Ln TF: 877-396-5356 ■ Web: www.loewensteininc.com	Greensboro	NC	27410	336-740-3100	855-4934
Luxor Div EBSCO Industries Inc 2245 Delany Rd *Fax Area Code: 800 ■ TF: 800-323-4656 ■ Web: www.luxorfurn.com	Waukegan	IL	60087	847-244-1800	327-1698*
Magna Design Inc 5804 204th St SW TF: 800-233-2304 ■ Web: www.magnadesign.com	Lynnwood	WA	98046	425-776-2181	778-5466
Martin Furniture 7757 St Andrews Ave TF: 800-268-5669 ■ Web: www.martinfurniture.com	San Diego	CA	92154	619-671-5100	671-5199
Marvel Group Inc 3843 W 43rd St *Fax Area Code: 800 ■ *Fax: Cust Svc ■ TF Cust Svc: 800-621-8846 ■ Web: www.marvelgroup.com	Chicago	IL	60632	773-523-4804	237-0358*
Maxon Furniture Inc 660 SW 39th St Suite 150 TF Cust Svc: 800-289-1274 ■ Web: www.maxonfurniture.com	Renton	WA	98057	253-872-0396	872-7572
Mayline Group 619 N Commerce St TF: 800-822-8037 ■ Web: www.mayline.com	Sheboygan	WI	53081	920-457-5537	457-7388
McDowell-Craig Office Furniture 13146 Firestone Blvd TF: 877-921-2100 ■ Web: www.mcdowellcraig.com	Norwalk	CA	90650	562-921-4441	921-9648
Metacom Office & Computer Furniture 501 'O' Ave	Anacortes	WA	98221	360-293-0122	293-2724
Metro 7220 Edgewater Dr Web: www.metrofurniture.com	Oakland	CA	94621	510-567-5200	562-2915
Midwest Commercial Interiors 987 S West Temple TF: 800-351-4553 ■ Web: www.midwestoffice.com	Salt Lake City	UT	84101	801-359-7681	355-2713
Miller Herman Inc 855 E Main Ave NASDAQ: MLHR ■ TF: 888-443-4357 ■ Web: www.hermanmiller.com	Zeeland	MI	49464	616-654-3000	654-5385
MLP Seating Corp 2125 Lively Blvd TF: 800-723-3030 ■ Web: www.mlpseating.com	Elk Grove Village	IL	60007	847-956-1700	956-1776
MTS Seating Inc 7100 Industrial Dr *Fax Area Code: 800 ■ Web: www.mtsseating.com	Temperance	MI	48182	734-847-3875	329-0687*
National Business Services 1601 Magoffin Ave TF Sales: 800-777-7807 ■ Web: www.nbsinc.com	El Paso	TX	79901	915-544-1271	544-0325
National Office Furniture 1205 Kimball Blvd TF: 800-482-1717 ■ Web: www.nationalonline.com	Jasper	IN	47549	812-482-1717	482-8800
NER Data Products Inc 307 S Delsea Dr *Fax Area Code: 800 ■ TF: 800-257-5235 ■ Web: www.nerdata.com	Glassboro	NJ	08028	856-881-5524	637-2217*
Neutral Posture Inc 3904 N Texas Ave TF: 800-446-3746 ■ Web: www.igoergo.com	Bryan	TX	77803	979-778-0502	778-0408
Nova Solutions Inc 421 W Industrial Ave *Fax Area Code: 800 ■ TF: 800-730-6682 ■ Web: www.novadesk.com	Effingham	IL	62401	217-342-7070	940-6682*
Office Chairs Inc 14815 Radburn Ave TF: 866-624-4968 ■ Web: www.officechairsinc.com	Santa Fe Springs	CA	90670	562-802-0464	926-5561
Omni International Inc 435 12th St SW PO Box 1409 TF: 800-844-6664 ■ Web: www.omniinternational.com	Vernon	AL	35592	205-695-9173	695-6465
Omni Remanufacturing 2700 NE Winter St Suite 200 TF: 888-627-1633 ■ Web: www.omniremanufacturing.com	Minneapolis	MN	55413	612-362-2300	362-2301
Open Plan Systems Inc 14140 N Washington Hwy PO Box 1810 TF: 800-849-7239 ■ Web: www.openplan.com	Ashland	VA	23005	804-228-5600	228-5656
Orna Metal Inc 1200 Stafford St PO Box 608 Web: www.ornametal.com	Washington	MO	63090	636-239-7867	239-0789
Paoli Inc 201 E Martin St TF: 800-457-7415 ■ Web: www.paoli.com	Orleans	IN	47452	812-723-2791	865-1516
Paramount Mfg Corp 353 Middlesex Ave	Wilmington	MA	01887	978-657-4300	658-5215
Penco Products Inc 99 Brower Ave TF: 800-562-1000 ■ Web: www.pencoproducts.com	Oaks	PA	19456	610-666-0500	666-7561
Plymold Seating 615 Centennial Dr *Fax Area Code: 800 ■ TF: 800-759-6653 ■ Web: www.plymold.com	Kenyon	MN	55946	507-789-5111	544-0480*
Pucel Enterprises Inc 1440 E 36th St TF: 800-336-4986 ■ Web: www.pucel-grizzly.com	Cleveland	OH	44114	216-881-4604	881-6731
Reconditioned Systems Inc 2636 S Wilson St Suite 105 TF: 800-280-5000 ■ Web: www.resy.net	Tempe	AZ	85282	480-968-1772	894-1907
Robertson Furniture Co Inc 720 Elberton St PO Box 847 TF: 800-241-0713 ■ Web: www.robertson-furniture.com	Toccoa	GA	30577	706-886-1494	886-8998
RomWeber Co 4 S Park Ave PO Box 191 Web: www.romweber.com	Batesville	IN	47006	812-934-3485	934-5042
Rush Industries Inc 118 N Wrenn St Web: www.rushfurniture.com	High Point	NC	27260	336-886-7700	886-2227
Safco Products Co 9300 W Research Center Rd TF: 800-328-3020 ■ Web: www.safcoproducts.com	New Hope	MN	55428	763-536-6700	536-6784
Sedgewick Industries 667 W Ward Ave TF: 888-882-8565 ■ Web: www.sedgewick.com	High Point	NC	27260	336-885-9300	885-9174
Shafer Commercial Seating Inc 4101 E 48th Ave Web: www.shafer.com	Denver	CO	80216	303-322-7792	393-1836
Shure Mfg Corp 1901 W Main St TF: 800-227-4873 ■ Web: www.shureusa.com	Washington	MO	63090	636-390-7100	390-7171
Signore Inc 55-57 Jefferson St TF: 800-828-2808 ■ Web: www.signore.com	Ellicottville	NY	14731	716-699-2361	699-8025
Sligh Furniture Co 217 E 24th St Suite 102 TF: 866-277-0258 ■ Web: www.sligh.com	Holland	MI	49423	616-392-7101	392-9495
Southwood Furniture Corp 2860 Nathan St Web: www.southwoodfurn.com	Hickory	NC	28602	828-465-1776	465-0858
Spectrum Industries Inc 1600 Johnson St *Fax Area Code: 800 ■ *Fax: Sales ■ TF: 800-235-1262 ■ Web: www.spectrumfurniture.com	Chippewa Falls	WI	54729	715-723-6750	335-0473*
Statton Furniture Mfg Co Inc 504 E 1st St Web: www.statton.com	Hagerstown	MD	21740	301-739-0360	739-8421
Steelcase Inc 801 44th St SE PO Box 1967 NYSE: SCS ■ *Fax: Mail Rm ■ TF: 888-783-3522 ■ Web: www.steelcase.com	Grand Rapids	MI	49501	616-247-2710	247-2256*
Stevens Industries Inc 704 W Main St Web: www.stevensind.com	Teutopolis	IL	62467	217-857-6411	540-3101
Studios Q Furniture 3060 Main Ave SE TF: 800-356-5732 ■ Web: www.studioqfurniture.com	Hickory	NC	28602	828-322-1794	322-8462
Stylex Inc Tungsten Rd PO Box 5038 TF: 800-257-5742 ■ Web: www.stylexseating.com	Delanco	NJ	08075	856-461-5600	461-5574
TAB Products Co 605 4th St TF: 888-822-9777 ■ Web: www.tab.com	Mayville	WI	53050	920-387-3131	387-1805
Taylor Cos 1 Taylor Pkwy TF: 888-758-2956 ■ Web: www.thetaylorcompanies.com	Bedford	OH	44146	440-232-0700	439-6720
Techline USA LLC 500 S Division St TF: 800-356-8400 ■ Web: www.techlineusa.com	Waunakee	WI	53597	608-849-4181	850-2379
Teknion Corp 1150 Flint Rd Web: www.teknion.com	Toronto	ON	M3J2J5	416-661-3370	661-2647
Tennsco Corp 201 Tennsco Dr PO Box 1888 *Fax Area Code: 800 ■ TF Cust Svc: 800-251-8184 ■ Web: www.tennsco.com	Dickson	TN	37056	615-446-8000	722-0134*
Trendway Corp 13467 Quincy St PO Box 9016 TF: 800-968-5344 ■ Web: www.trendway.com	Holland	MI	49422	616-399-3900	399-2231
Tuohy Furniture Corp 42 St Albans Pl TF Cust Svc: 800-533-1696 ■ Web: www.tuohyfurniture.com	Chatfield	MN	55923	507-867-4280	867-3374
Turnbull Enterprises Inc 3100 Viona Ave Web: www.turnbullenterprises.com	Baltimore	MD	21230	410-789-1700	789-1706
Ulrich Planfiling Equipment Corp 2120 4th Ave PO Box 135 TF: 800-346-2875 ■ Web: www.ulrichcorp.com	Lakewood	NY	14750	716-763-1815	763-1818
United Chair Co 147 St-Pierre St *Fax Area Code: 888 ■ TF: 888-522-2773 ■ Web: www.unitedchair.com	Sainte-Pie	QC	J0H1W0	450-772-2495	248-1865*
Van San Corp 16735 E Johnson Dr TF: 800-423-1829 ■ Web: www.vansan.com	City of Industry	CA	91745	626-961-7211	369-9510
Vecta 1800 S Great Southwest Pkwy Web: www.vecta.com	Grand Prairie	TX	75051	972-641-2860	603-4896
Viking Acoustical Corp 21480 Heath Ave TF: 800-328-8385 ■ Web: www.vikingusa.com	Lakeville	MN	55044	952-469-3405	469-4503
Vitro Seating Products Inc 201 Madison St TF Cust Svc: 800-325-7093 ■ Web: www.vitroseating.com	Saint Louis	MO	63102	314-241-2265	241-8723
West Coast Industries Inc 10 Jackson St TF: 800-243-3150 ■ Web: www.westcoastindustries.com	San Francisco	CA	94111	415-621-6656	552-5368
Whitehall Furniture 201 E Martin St *Fax Area Code: 800 ■ TF: 800-467-3585 ■ Web: www.wfi.com	Orleans	IN	47452	812-865-3898	888-5817*
Wilson H Co 555 W Taft Dr *Fax Area Code: 800 ■ TF: 800-245-7224 ■ Web: www.hwilson.com	South Holland	IL	60473	708-339-5111	245-8224*
Woodland Products Co Inc 1480 E Grand Ave	Pomona	CA	91766	909-622-3456	622-2042
Workdeck Furniture 4990 W Greenbrooke SE Web: www.workdeckfurniture.com	Kentwood	MI	49512	616-698-2664	698-2665
Workplace Systems Inc 562 Mammoth Rd TF: 800-258-9700 ■ Web: www.workplacesystemsinc.com	Londonderry	NH	03053	603-622-3727	622-0174
Workspaces Inc 14311 SE 77th Ct TF: 800-466-4123 ■ Web: www.workspaces.com	Newcastle	WA	98059	425-226-4398	226-9468
Wright Line LLC 160 Gold Star Blvd *Fax: Hum Res ■ TF: 800-225-7348 ■ Web: www.wrightline.com	Worcester	MA	01606	508-852-4300	365-6161*
Zoom Seating 1644 Crystal Ave *Fax Area Code: 866 ■ TF: 866-839-9666 ■ Web: www.zoomseating.com	Kansas City	MO	64126	816-245-5930	839-9777*

322-2 Household Furniture

	City	State	ZIP	Phone	Fax
Aaron Rents Inc MacTavish Furniture Industries Div 23400 Hwy 319N Web: www.aaronrents.com	Coolidge	GA	31738	229-346-3505	346-3261
Acacia Home & Garden Inc 101 McLin Creek Rd N PO Box 426 Web: www.acaciahomeandgarden.com	Conover	NC	28613	828-465-1700	465-4205
Advantage Furniture Hwy 145 S PO Box 369 Web: www.advantagefurniture.com	Nettleton	MS	38858	662-895-3800	963-0574
Alan White Co 1122 E Antigo St	Stamps	AR	71860	870-533-4471	533-8858
American Drew 4620 Grandover Pkwy TF: 800-933-0243 ■ Web: www.americandrew.com	Greensboro	NC	27417	336-294-5233	315-4391
Ameriwood Industries Inc 410 E South 1st St TF: 800-454-0283 ■ Web: www.ameriwood.com	Wright City	MO	63390	636-745-3351	745-1007
Ashley Furniture Industries Inc 1 Ashley Way TF: 800-477-2222 ■ Web: www.ashleyfurniture.com	Arcadia	WI	54612	608-323-3377	323-6008
Aston Garrett International 911 Canada Ct Bldg A Web: www.astongarrettintl.com	City of Industry	CA	91748	626-912-1454	810-0354
Astro-Lounger/Davis Furniture 119 Industrial Pk Dr TF: 800-700-6945	Houlka	MS	38850	662-568-3385	568-3384
Aubrey Mfg Inc 6709 S Main St	Union	IL	60180	815-923-2101	923-4687
Baby's Dream Furniture Inc 411 Industrial Blvd PO Box 579 TF: 800-835-2742 ■ Web: www.babysdream.com	Buena Vista	GA	31803	229-649-4404	649-2007
Baker Furniture 1661 Monroe Ave NW *Fax: Acctg ■ TF: 800-592-2537 ■ Web: www.kohlerinteriors.com	Grand Rapids	MI	49505	616-361-7321	361-7067*
Barcalounger Corp 1450 Atlantic Ave Web: www.barcalounger.com	Rocky Mount	NC	27801	252-977-6395	977-2864
Bassett Furniture Industries Inc 3525 Fairystone Park Hwy NASDAQ: BSET ■ Web: www.bassettfurniture.com	Bassett	VA	24055	276-629-6000	629-6346
Bauhaus USA Inc 1 Bauhaus Dr Web: www.bauhaususa.com	Saltillo	MS	38866	662-869-2664	869-5910
Bellini 495 Central Ave Web: www.bellini.com	Scarsdale	NY	10583	914-472-7336	
Berg Furniture Inc 120 E Gloucester Pike Web: www.bergfurniture.com	Barrington	NJ	08007	856-310-0511	310-0512
Berkline BenchCraft LLC 1 Berkline Dr Web: www.berkline.com	Morristown	TN	37814	423-585-1500	585-1760
Best Home Furnishings Inc 1 Best Dr Web: www.bestchairs.com	Ferdinand	IN	47532	812-367-1761	367-2345
Bielecky Brothers Inc 50-22 72nd St Web: bieleckybrothers.com	Woodside	NY	11377	718-424-4764	898-4737
Bradington-Young 920 E 1st St Web: www.bradington-young.com	Cherryville	NC	28021	704-435-5881	435-4276
Brooks Furniture Mfg Inc 110 Maples Ln TF: 800-427-6657	Tazewell	TN	37879	423-626-1111	626-8346
Brookwood Furniture Co Inc 263 Brookwood Dr *Fax Area Code: 800	Pontotoc	MS	38863	662-489-1100	680-8649*
Broyhill Furniture Industries Inc 1 Broyhill Pk *Fax: Sales ■ TF Cust Svc: 800-327-6944 ■ Web: www.broyhillfurn.com	Lenoir	NC	28633	828-758-3111	758-3538*
Brueton Industries Inc 145-68 228th St TF Cust Svc: 800-221-6783 ■ Web: www.brueton.com	Springfield Gardens	NY	11413	718-527-3000	712-6783
Bush Industries Inc 1 Mason Dr TF: 800-228-2874 ■ Web: www.bushfurniture.com	Jamestown	NY	14701	716-665-2000	665-2074
Bushline Inc 707 Industrial Park Dr TF: 800-627-1682 ■ Web: www.bushline.com	New Tazewell	TN	37825	423-626-5246	626-7237
Canadel Furniture Inc 700 Canadel Ave Web: www.canadel.com	Louiseville	QC	J5V2L6	819-228-8471	228-8389
Canalli Furniture 183 Grand St Web: www.canallifurniture.com	Paterson	NJ	07501	973-247-7222	278-9118
Capri Industries Inc 1401 Burkemont Ave PO box 8040	Morganton	NC	28680	828-437-4243	438-9318
Capris Furniture Industries Inc 1401 NW 27th Ave *Fax Area Code: 800 ■ Web: www.caprisfurniture.com	Ocala	FL	34475	352-629-8889	226-0765*
Carson Marge Inc 9056 Garvey Ave Web: www.margecarson.com	Rosemead	CA	91770	626-571-1111	571-0924
Carson's Inc 4299 Cheyenne Dr PO Box 14186 Web: www.carsonsofhp.com	Archdale	NC	27263	336-431-1101	431-0677
Century Furniture LLC 401 11th St NW Web: www.centuryfurniture.com	Hickory	NC	28601	828-328-1851	328-2176
Charles Inc 518 N 10th St TF: 800-831-5878 ■ Web: www.charlesfurniture.com	Council Bluffs	IA	51503	712-328-2603	328-8270
Charles Schneider Furniture 518 N 10th St TF: 800-831-5878 ■ Web: charlesfurniture.com/cschneider	Council Bluffs	IA	51503	712-328-1587	328-8270
Child Craft Industries Inc 1010 Keller Dr Web: www.childcraftindustries.com	New Salisbury	IN	47161	812-206-2200	206-2250
Chromcraft Revington Inc 1330 Win Hentschel Blvd AMEX: CRC	West Lafayette	IN	47906	765-807-2640	807-2660

Phone Fax

Classic Leather Inc 203 Simpson St .... Conover NC 28613 828-328-2046 324-6212
Web: www.classic-leather.com

Clayton Marcus Co Inc 166 Teague Town Rd .... Hickory NC 28601 828-495-2200 495-2260
Web: www.claytonmarcus.com

Cochrane Furniture Co 190 Cochrane Rd.......... Lincolnton NC 28092 704-732-1151 752-6109*
**Fax Area Code:* 800 ■ *Web:* www.cochrane-furniture.com

Community Products LLC DBA Community Playthings
359 Gibson Hill Rd.......... Chester NY 10918 845-572-3410 336-5948*
**Fax Area Code:* 800 ■ **Fax:* Cust Svc ■ *TF:* 800-777-4244 ■
Web: www.communityplaythings.com

Conover Chair Co Inc 210 4th St SW.......... Conover NC 28613 828-464-0251 465-4535
Web: www.conoverchair.com

Councill Cos LLC 267 Councill Access Rd .... Denton NC 27239 336-859-2155 859-5284
Web: www.councill.com

Craftmaster Furniture Corp 221 Craftmaster Rd .... Hiddenite NC 28636 828-632-9786 632-0301

Crawford Furniture Mfg Corp 1021 Allen St Ext .... Jamestown NY 14701 716-661-9100 483-2634
TF: 800-325-7368 ■ *Web:* www.crawfordfurniture.com

Cresent Mfg Co 350 Maple St.......... Gallatin TN 37066 615-452-1671 451-0332
Web: www.cresent.com

DeFehr Furniture Ltd 125 Furniture Pk.......... Winnipeg MB R2G1B9 204-988-5630 663-4458
Web: www.defehr.com

DMI Furniture Inc 9780 Ormsby Station Rd Suite 2000 .... Louisville KY 40223 502-426-4351 755-2878*
**Fax Area Code:* 800 ■ *TF:* 888-372-1927 ■ *Web:* www.dmifurniture.com

Dorel Industries Inc 1255 Greene Ave Suite 300.......... Montreal QC H3Z2A4 514-934-3034 934-9379
NASDAQ: DIIB ■ *Web:* www.dorel.com

Douglas Furniture of California LLC
4000 Redondo Beach Ave .... Redondo Beach CA 90278 310-643-7200 536-0626
Web: www.douglasfurniture.com

Drexel Heritage Furnishings Inc 1925 Eastchester Dr.......... High Point NC 27265 336-888-4800 888-4815
TF: 866-450-3434 ■ *Web:* www.drexelheritage.com

Durham Furniture Inc 450 Lambton St W .... Durham ON N0G1R0 519-369-2345 369-6515
Web: www.durhamfurniture.com

Dutailier Group Inc 299 rue Chaput .... Sainte-Pie QC J0H1W0 450-772-2403 772-5055
TF: 800-363-9817 ■ *Web:* www.dutailier.com

Eagle Industries LLC 610 Hope St .... Bowling Green KY 42101 270-843-3363 843-3609
Web: www.eagle-ind.com

El Ran Furniture Ltd 2751 Transcanada Hwy.......... Pointe-Claire QC H9R1B4 514-630-5656 630-9150
TF: 800-361-6546 ■ *Web:* www.elran.com

Elegant Bebe 1430 W Pine Lake.......... Montgomery TX 77316 281-584-0190 416-7923*
**Fax Area Code:* 713 ■ *TF:* 888-886-8307 ■ *Web:* www.elegantbebe.com

Elliott's Designs Inc 2473 E Rancho Del Amo Pl.......... Rancho Dominguez CA 90220 310-631-4931 631-4531
TF: 800-435-5468 ■ *Web:* www.elliottsdesigns.com

Ello Furniture Mfg Co 1350 Preston St .... Rockford IL 61102 815-964-8601 964-9985
Web: www.ellofurniture.com

Entourage LA 100 Wilshire Blvd Suite 800.......... Santa Monica CA 90401 310-656-0499 656-0269
Web: www.entouragela.com

Ethan Allen Interiors Inc Ethan Allen Dr .... Danbury CT 06811 203-743-8000 743-8298
NYSE: ETH ■ *Web:* www.ethanallen.com

Evenflo Co Inc 1801 Commerce Dr.......... Piqua OH 45356 937-415-3300 415-3112*
**Fax:* Hum Res ■ *TF:* 800-233-5921 ■ *Web:* www.evenflo.com

Fairfield Chair Co 1331 Harper Ave SW.......... Lenoir NC 28645 828-758-5571 758-0211
Web: www.fairfieldchair.com

Ficks Reed Co 6245 Creek Rd .... Cincinnati OH 45242 513-985-0606 985-9293
Web: www.ficksreed.com

Flexsteel Industries Inc 3400 Jackson St .... Dubuque IA 52001 563-556-7730 556-8345*
NASDAQ: FLXS ■ **Fax:* Cust Svc ■ *Web:* www.flexsteel.com

Founders Furniture Rt 460 E .... Appomattox VA 24522 434-352-7181 352-8726*
**Fax:* Cust Svc ■ *TF:* 800-548-7704 ■ *Web:* www.foundersfurniture.com

Fraenkel Co Inc 10600 S Choctaw Dr PO Box 15385 .... Baton Rouge LA 70895 225-275-8111 272-7319
TF: 800-847-2580 ■ *Web:* www.fraenkel.com

Franklin Corp 600 Franklin Dr.......... Houston MS 38851 662-456-4286 456-3156
Web: www.franklincorp.com

Fredman Brothers Furniture Co Inc 908 SW Washington St.......... Peoria IL 61602 309-674-2011 674-0407
TF: 800-248-5228

Furniture Brands International Inc
101 S Hanley Rd Suite 1900.......... Saint Louis MO 63105 314-863-1100 863-5306
NYSE: FBN ■ *TF:* 866-873-3667 ■ *Web:* www.furniturebrands.com

Furniture Values International LLC 2929 NW Grand Ave .... Phoenix AZ 85017 602-233-0224 269-6810
TF: 888-484-5874

Gold Mitchell & Bob Williams Co 135 One Comfortable Pl.......... Taylorsville NC 28681 828-632-9200 635-0613
TF: 800-789-5401 ■ *Web:* www.mgandbw.com

GuildCraft of California 18626 S Reyes Ave .... Rancho Dominguez CA 90221 310-223-4200 639-1859
TF: 800-283-6716 ■ *Web:* www.guildcraft.com

Hammary Furniture Co 2464 Norwood St SW .... Lenoir NC 28645 828-728-3231 443-2920*
**Fax Area Code:* 800 ■ *TF:* 800-362-3387 ■ *Web:* www.hammary.com

Hancock & Moore Inc 166 Hancock & Moore Ln .... Hickory NC 28601 828-495-8235 495-3021
Web: www.hancockandmoore.com

Harden Furniture Inc 8550 Mill Pond Way.......... McConnellsville NY 13401 315-245-1000 245-2884
Web: www.harden.com

Hekman Furniture Co 1400 Buchanan Ave SW .... Grand Rapids MI 49507 616-452-1411 452-1000
TF: 800-253-9249 ■ *Web:* www.hekman.com

Henkel Harris Co Inc 2983 S Pleasant Valley Rd.......... Winchester VA 22601 540-667-4900 667-8261
Web: www.henkelharris.com

Henredon Furniture Industries Inc 400 Henredon Rd .... Morganton NC 28655 828-437-5261 437-5264
TF: 800-444-3682 ■ *Web:* www.henredon.com

Hickory Chair Co 37 9th St Pl SE.......... Hickory NC 28602 828-328-1801 328-8954
TF: 800-349-4579 ■ *Web:* www.hickorychair.com

Hickory Hill Furniture Corp 501 Hoyle St SW .... Valdese NC 28690 828-874-2124 874-3622
TF: 800-737-4432 ■ *Web:* www.hickoryhillfurniture.com

Hickory White Co 856 7th Ave SE .... Hickory NC 28602 828-322-8624 322-3942
Web: www.hickorywhite.com

Hooker Furniture Corp 440 E Commonwealth Blvd .... Martinsville VA 24112 276-632-0459 388-2289*
NASDAQ: HOFT ■ **Fax Area Code:* 800 ■ **Fax:* Cust Svc ■ *TF Cust Svc:* 888-462-6877 ■ *Web:* www.hookerfurniture.com

Hughes Furniture Industries Inc 952 Stout St.......... Randleman NC 27317 336-498-8700 498-8750
Web: www.hughesfurniture.com

Interactive Health Inc 3030 Walnut Ave .... Long Beach CA 90807 562-426-8700 426-9690
TF: 800-742-5493 ■ *Web:* www.interhealth.com

Interior Crafts Inc 2513 W Cullerton Ave.......... Chicago IL 60608 773-376-8160 376-9578

J-Art Iron Co 9435 W Jefferson Blvd .... Culver City CA 90232 310-202-1126 202-1642
Web: www.jartiron.com

Jack-Post Corp 800 E 3rd St .... Buchanan MI 49107 269-695-7000 695-7603
TF Cust Svc: 800-800-4950

Jackson Furniture Industries Inc 1910 King Edward Ave .... Cleveland TN 37311 423-476-8544 961-7343
Web: www.catnapper.com

Jensen Industries Inc 1946 E 46th St .... Los Angeles CA 90058 323-235-6800 235-6878
TF: 800-325-8351 ■ *Web:* www.jensen-ind.com

Johnston Tombigbee Furniture Mfg Co 1402 Waterworks Rd.......... Columbus MS 39701 662-328-1685 327-1814
TF: 800-654-3876 ■ *Web:* www.jtbfurniture.com

Kessler Industries 8600 Gateway Blvd S .... El Paso TX 79906 915-591-8161 598-7353
Web: www.kesslerind.com

Khoury Inc 1600 W Breitung Ave .... Kingsford MI 49802 906-774-6333 779-7178
TF Cust Svc: 800-553-5446 ■ *Web:* www.khouryfurniture.com

KidsChairs Inc 1364 London Bridge Rd Suite 101.......... Virginia Beach VA 23453 757-301-7464 301-7551
Web: www.kidschairs.com

Kimball Home Furniture 1600 Royal St .... Jasper IN 47549 812-482-1600 482-8012*
**Fax:* Cust Svc ■ *TF:* 800-482-1616 ■ *Web:* www.kimball.com

Kincaid Furniture Co Inc 240 Pleasant Hill Rd.......... Hudson NC 28638 828-728-3261 728-0223
TF: 800-438-8207 ■ *Web:* www.kincaidfurniture.com

Kindel Furniture Co 100 Garden St SE.......... Grand Rapids MI 49507 616-243-3676 243-6248
Web: www.kindelfurniture.com

King Hickory Furniture Co 1820 Main Ave SE .... Hickory NC 28601 828-322-6025 328-2159
Web: www.kinghickory.com

Klaussner Furniture Industries Inc 405 Lewallen Rd.......... Asheboro NC 27205 336-625-6174 626-0905
TF Cust Svc: 800-828-9534 ■ *Web:* www.klaussner.com

La-Z-Boy Inc 1284 N Telegraph Rd .... Monroe MI 48162 734-242-1444 457-2005*
NYSE: LZB ■ **Fax:* Sales ■ *Web:* www.lazboy.com

Lamont Ltd 1530 N Bluff Rd .... Burlington IA 52601 319-753-5131 753-0946
TF: 800-553-5621 ■ *Web:* www.lamontlimited.com

Lane Furniture Industries Inc 5380 Hwy 145 .... Tupelo MS 38801 662-566-7211 566-3474
Web: www.lanefurniture.com

Lea Industries Inc 4620 Grandover Pkwy.......... Greensboro NC 27417 336-294-5233 315-4391
TF: 888-299-5619 ■ *Web:* www.leaindustries.com

Leathercraft Inc 102 Section House Rd .... Conover NC 28613 828-322-3305 322-7812
TF: 800-627-1561 ■ *Web:* www.leathercraft-furniture.com

Lexington Home Brands 1300 National Hwy.......... Thomasville NC 27360 336-474-5300 474-5506
TF: 800-539-4636 ■ *Web:* www.lexington.com

Little Tikes Co 2180 Barlow Rd .... Hudson OH 44236 330-650-3000 650-3877
TF Cust Svc: 800-321-0183 ■ *Web:* www.littletikes.com

Mactavish Furniture Industries Div Aaron Rents Inc
23400 Hwy 319N.......... Coolidge GA 31738 229-346-3505 346-3261
Web: www.aaronrents.com

Mantua Mfg Co 7900 Northfield Rd .... Walton Hills OH 44146 440-232-8865 232-5622
TF Orders: 800-333-8333 ■ *Web:* www.bedframes.com

Marge Carson Inc 9056 Garvey Ave .... Rosemead CA 91770 626-571-1111 571-0924
Web: www.margecarson.com

McGuire Furniture Co 1201 Bryant St .... San Francisco CA 94103 415-626-1414 864-8593
TF: 800-662-4847 ■ *Web:* www.mcguirefurniture.com

Michael Thomas Furniture Inc 100 E Newberry St .... Liberty NC 27298 336-622-3075 622-4112
Web: www.michaelthomasfurniture.com

Million Dollar Baby 841 Washington Blvd .... Montebello CA 90640 323-728-8988 722-8866
Web: www.milliondollarbaby.com

Minson Corp 1 Minson Way .... Montebello CA 90640 323-513-1041 513-1047
TF: 800-251-6537 ■ *Web:* www.minson.com

Mitchell Gold & Bob Williams Co 135 One Comfortable Pl.......... Taylorsville NC 28681 828-632-9200 635-0613
TF: 800-789-5401 ■ *Web:* www.mgandbw.com

Moore Sam Furniture Industries 1556 Dawn Dr .... Bedford VA 24523 540-586-8253 586-8497
Web: www.sammoore.com

Nichols & Stone Co 232 Sherman St .... Gardner MA 01440 978-632-2770 632-2623
Web: www.nichols-stone.com

Norwalk Furniture Corp 100 Furniture Pkwy .... Norwalk OH 44857 419-744-3200 668-6223
TF Orders: 800-837-2565 ■ *Web:* www.norwalkfurniture.com

Orleans Furniture Inc 1481 N Main St.......... Columbia MS 39429 601-736-9002 731-2823
Web: www.orleansfurniture.com

O'Sullivan Furniture 1900 Gulf St.......... Lamar MO 64759 417-682-3322 673-3767*
**Fax Area Code:* 800 ■ *TF Cust Svc:* 800-327-9782 ■ *Web:* www.osullivan.com

Pearson Co 1420 Progress Ave.......... High Point NC 27260 336-882-8135 885-5508
Web: www.pearsoncompany.com

Pennsylvania House Co 166 Teague Town Rd .... Hickory NC 28601 828-495-2200 456-2788*
**Fax Area Code:* 800 ■ *TF:* 800-782-9663 ■ *Web:* www.pennsylvaniahouse.com

PeopLoungers Inc 389 Hwy 6 E .... Nettleton MS 38858 662-963-7301 963-2504
Web: www.peoploungers.net

Perdue Woodworks Inc 2415 Creek Dr.......... Rapid City SD 57703 605-341-2101 341-1565
Web: www.perduesinc.com

Peters-Revington Corp 1100 N Washington St .... Delphi IN 46923 765-564-2586 564-3722
Web: www.peters-revington-furniture.com

Progressive Furniture Inc 502 Middle St PO Box 308.......... Archbold OH 43502 419-446-4500 446-4550
Web: www.progressivefurniture.com

Pulaski Furniture Corp 1 Pulaski Sq.......... Pulaski VA 24301 540-980-7330 994-5468
Web: www.pulaskifurniture.com

Realistic Furniture Industries 405 Lewallen Rd.......... Asheboro NC 27205 336-625-6174 626-0905
TF: 800-828-9534

Richardson Brothers Co 904 Monroe St.......... Sheboygan Falls WI 53085 920-467-4631 467-3850*
**Fax:* Cust Svc ■ *TF:* 800-558-7709 ■ *Web:* www.richardsonbrothers.com

Riverside Furniture Corp 1400 S 6th St.......... Fort Smith AR 72902 479-785-8100 785-8149
Web: www.riverside-furniture.com

Robern Inc 701 N Wilson Ave.......... Bristol PA 19007 215-826-9800 826-9633
TF: 800-877-2376 ■ *Web:* www.robern.com

Rochelle Furniture PO Box 649 .... Ludington MI 49431 800-223-6047 843-9276*
**Fax Area Code:* 231 ■ *Web:* www.rochellefurniture.com

RomWeber Co 4 S Park Ave PO Box 191.......... Batesville IN 47006 812-934-3485 934-5042
Web: www.romweber.com

Rowe Fine Furniture Inc 8300 Greensboro Dr Suite 425.......... McLean VA 22102 703-847-8670 847-8686
TF: 800-334-7693 ■ *Web:* www.rowefurniture.com

RT Mfg 1186 N Industrial Park Dr.......... Orem UT 84057 801-226-2648 226-2707
TF: 877-826-6800 ■ *Web:* www.rumbletuff.com

Rush Industries Inc 118 N Wrenn St .... High Point NC 27260 336-886-7700 886-2227
Web: www.rushfurniture.com

Sam Moore Furniture Industries 1556 Dawn Dr .... Bedford VA 24523 540-586-8253 586-8497
Web: www.sammoore.com

Sandberg Furniture Mfg Co Inc 5685 Alcoa Ave .... Los Angeles CA 90058 323-582-0711 589-5507
Web: www.sandbergfurniture.com

Sauder Woodworking Co 502 Middle St PO Box 156.......... Archbold OH 43502 419-446-2711 446-3692
TF Cust Svc: 800-523-3987 ■ *Web:* www.sauder.com

Schnadig Corp 1111 E Touhy Ave Suite 500 .... Des Plaines IL 60018 847-803-6000 803-6050
TF: 800-468-8730 ■ *Web:* www.schnadig.com

Schneider Charles Furniture 518 N 10th St.......... Council Bluffs IA 51503 712-328-1587 328-8270
TF: 800-831-5878 ■ *Web:* charlesfurniture.com/cschneider

Shermag Inc 2171 King St W .... Sherbrooke QC J1J2G1 819-566-1515 566-7323
TF Sales: 800-363-2635 ■ *Web:* www.shermag.com

Sherrill Furniture Co 2405 Highland Ave NE .... Hickory NC 28601 828-322-2640 324-8207
Web: www.sherrillfurniture.com

Sico North America Inc 7525 Cahill Rd .... Minneapolis MN 55439 952-941-1700 941-6737
TF: 800-328-6138 ■ *Web:* www.sicoinc.com

Sligh Furniture Co 217 E 24th St Suite 102.......... Holland MI 49423 616-392-7101 392-9495
TF: 866-277-0258 ■ *Web:* www.sligh.com

Southwood Furniture Corp 2860 Nathan St .... Hickory NC 28602 828-465-1776 465-0858
Web: www.southwoodfurn.com

Standard Furniture Mfg Co Inc 801 Hwy 31 S .... Bay Minette AL 36507 251-937-6741 520-7667*
**Fax Area Code:* 800 ■ **Fax:* Cust Svc ■ *TF:* 800-827-7866 ■
Web: www.standard-furniture.com

Stanley Furniture Co Inc 1641 Fairystone Pk Hwy.......... Stanleytown VA 24168 276-627-2000 629-4334
NASDAQ: STLY ■ *Web:* www.stanleyfurniture.com

Statton Furniture Mfg Co Inc 504 E 1st St .... Hagerstown MD 21740 301-739-0360 739-8421
Web: www.statton.com

Storkcraft Baby 11511 Number Five Rd.......... Richmond BC V7A4E8 604-274-5121 274-9727
TF: 877-274-0277 ■ *Web:* www.storkcraft.com

Style Line Furniture Inc 116 Godfrey Rd.......... Verona MS 38879 662-566-1113 566-7657

Swaim Inc 1801 S College Dr.......... High Point NC 27260 336-885-6131 885-6227
Web: www.swaim-inc.com

Techline USA LLC 500 S Division St.......... Waunakee WI 53597 608-849-4181 850-2379
TF: 800-356-8400 ■ *Web:* www.techlineusa.com

Household Furniture (Cont'd)

Phone | Fax

Thomasville Furniture Industries Inc
401 E Main St PO Box 339 .... Thomasville NC 27361 336-472-4000 472-4085
Web: www.thomasville.com

Vanguard Furniture Co Inc 109 Simpson St .... Conover NC 28613 828-328-5631 328-9816
TF: 800-968-1702 ■ *Web:* www.vanguardfurniture.com

Vaughan Furniture Co Inc 816 Glendale Rd .... Galax VA 24333 276-236-6111 238-3238
Web: www.vaughanfurniture.com

Vermont Tubbs 1 Tubbs Ave .... Brandon VT 05733 802-247-3414 247-6395
TF: 800-327-7026 ■ *Web:* www.vermonttubbs.com

Webb Furniture Enterprises Inc PO Box 1277 .... Galax VA 24333 276-236-2984 236-2899
Web: www.webbfurn.com

White Alan Co 1122 E Antigo St .... Stamps AR 71860 870-533-4471 533-8858

Whitecraft Inc 1855 Griffin Rd Suite C212 .... Dania Beach FL 33004 954-921-0775 921-7363
Web: www.whitecraft.net

Whittier Wood Products 3787 W 1st Ave .... Eugene OR 97402 541-687-0213 687-2060*
**Fax:* Cust Svc ■ *TF:* 800-653-3336 ■ *Web:* www.whittierwood.com

Woodland Furniture LLC 4475 S 15th West .... Idaho Falls ID 83402 208-523-9006 523-9194
Web: www.woodlandfurniture.com

Zenith Products Corp 400 Lukens Dr .... New Castle DE 19720 302-326-8200 326-8400*
**Fax:* Cust Svc ■ *TF:* 800-892-3986 ■ *Web:* www.zenith-interiors.com

322-3 Institutional & Other Public Buildings Furniture

Phone | Fax

Adden Furniture Inc 26 Jackson St .... Lowell MA 01852 978-454-7848 453-1449
TF: 800-625-3876 ■ *Web:* www.addenfurniture.com

American Desk Mfg Co Inc PO Box 608 .... Temple TX 76503 254-778-1811 773-7370
TF: 800-433-3142 ■ *Web:* www.amdesk.com

American of Martinsville 128 E Church St .... Martinsville VA 24112 276-632-2061 638-8810
Web: www.americanofmartinsville.com

American Seating Co 401 American Seating Ctr .... Grand Rapids MI 49504 616-732-6600 732-6401
TF Cust Svc: 800-748-0268 ■ *Web:* www.americanseating.com

Artco-Bell Corp PO Box 608 .... Temple TX 76503 254-778-1811 771-0827
TF: 800-950-5850 ■ *Web:* www.artcobell.com

Bay Concepts Inc PO Box 7229 .... Oakland CA 94601 510-534-4511 534-4515
TF: 888-534-4511 ■ *Web:* www.bayconcepts.com

Brandrud Furniture Co Inc 1502 20th St NW .... Auburn WA 98001 253-838-6500 333-6302
Web: www.brandrud.com

Brayton International Inc 250 Swathmoore Ave .... High Point NC 27263 336-434-4151 434-8247
TF: 800-627-6770 ■ *Web:* www.brayton.com

Bretford Mfg Inc 11000 Seymour Ave .... Franklin Park IL 60131 847-678-2545 343-1779*
**Fax Area Code:* 800 ■ *TF:* 800-521-9614 ■ *Web:* www.bretford.com

Brodart Co 500 Arch St .... Williamsport PA 17701 570-326-2461 326-6769
TF: 800-233-8467 ■ *Web:* www.brodart.com

Buckstaff Co PO Box 2506 .... Oshkosh WI 54903 920-235-5890 235-2018
TF: 800-755-5890 ■ *Web:* www.buckstaff.com

Collegedale Casework LLC PO Box 810 .... Collegedale TN 37315 423-238-4131 238-4130
Web: www.collegedale.com

Columbia Mfg Inc PO Box 1230 .... Westfield MA 01086 413-562-3664 568-5345
Web: www.columbiamfginc.com

EBSCO Industries Inc Luxor Div 2245 Delany Rd .... Waukegan IL 60087 847-244-1800 327-1698*
**Fax Area Code:* 800 ■ *TF:* 800-323-4656 ■ *Web:* www.luxorfurn.com

Enochs Medical Furniture Inc PO Box 50559 .... Indianapolis IN 46250 317-580-2940 580-2944
TF Cust Svc: 800-428-2305 ■ *Web:* www.enochsmed.com

Fetzers' Inc 6223 W Double Eagle Cir .... Salt Lake City UT 84118 801-484-6103 484-6122
Web: www.fetzersinc.com

Fleetwood Group Inc 11832 James St .... Holland MI 49424 616-396-1142 396-8022
TF: 800-257-6390 ■ *Web:* www.fleetwoodgroup.com

Fordham Equipment Co 3308 Edson Ave .... Bronx NY 10469 718-379-7300 379-7312
TF: 800-249-5922 ■ *Web:* www.fordhamequip.com

Furniture by Thurston 12250 Charles Dr .... Grass Valley CA 95945 530-272-4331 272-4962
Web: www.furniturebythurston.com

Gaylord Brothers PO Box 4901 .... Syracuse NY 13221 315-457-5070 457-8387*
**Fax:* Cust Svc ■ *TF Cust Svc:* 800-634-6304 ■ *Web:* www.gaylord.com

Gunlocke Co LLC 1 Gunlocke Dr .... Wayland NY 14572 585-728-5111 728-8334*
**Fax:* Hum Res ■ *TF Cust Svc:* 800-828-6300 ■ *Web:* www.gunlocke.com

Hard Mfg Co Inc 230 Grider St .... Buffalo NY 14215 716-893-1800 896-2579
TF: 800-873-4273 ■ *Web:* www.hardmfg.com

Herman Miller for Health Care 855 E Main Ave PO Box 302 .... Zeeland MI 49464 616-654-3000
TF: 888-443-4357 ■ *Web:* www.hermanmiller.com/healthcare

Hill-Rom Services Inc 1069 SR 46 E .... Batesville IN 47006 812-934-7777 931-3592*
**Fax:* Hum Res ■ *Web:* www.hill-rom.com

Hussey Seating Co 38 Dyer St Ext .... North Berwick ME 03906 207-676-2271 676-2222*
**Fax:* Sales ■ *TF:* 800-341-0401 ■ *Web:* www.husseyseating.com

Imperial Woodworks Inc 7201 Mars Dr PO Box 7835 .... Waco TX 76714 254-741-0606 741-0736
TF: 800-234-6624 ■ *Web:* www.imperialww.com

Interkal Inc 5981 E Cork St .... Kalamazoo MI 49048 269-349-1521 349-6530
Web: www.interkal.com

Inwood Office Environments 1108 E 15th St .... Jasper IN 47546 812-482-6121 482-9732
TF: 800-786-6121 ■ *Web:* www.inwood.net

Irwin Seating Co Inc PO Box 2429 .... Grand Rapids MI 49501 616-784-2621 574-7411*
**Fax:* Sales ■ *TF:* 800-759-7328 ■ *Web:* www.irwinseating.com

Jasper Seating Co Inc 225 Clay St .... Jasper IN 47546 812-482-3204 482-1548
TF: 800-622-5661 ■ *Web:* www.jasperseating.com

KI 1330 Bellevue St .... Green Bay WI 54302 920-468-8100 468-0280
TF: 877-231-8555 ■ *Web:* www.ki-inc.com

Kimball Hospitality 1180 E 16th St .... Jasper IN 47549 812-482-1600 634-4324
TF: 800-634-9510 ■ *Web:* www.kimballhospitality.com

KLN Steel Products Co PO Box 34690 .... San Antonio TX 78265 210-227-4747 227-4047
TF: 800-624-9101 ■ *Web:* www.kln.com

LB Furniture Industries LLC 99 S 3rd St .... Hudson NY 12534 518-828-1501 828-3219
TF: 800-403-0833 ■ *Web:* www.lbempire.com

List Industries Inc 401 Jim Moran Blvd .... Deerfield Beach FL 33442 954-429-9155 428-3843
TF: 800-776-1342 ■ *Web:* www.listindustries.com

Luxor Div EBSCO Industries Inc 2245 Delany Rd .... Waukegan IL 60087 847-244-1800 327-1698*
**Fax Area Code:* 800 ■ *TF:* 800-323-4656 ■ *Web:* www.luxorfurn.com

Mastercraft Specialties Inc 800 Maple St .... Red Lion PA 17356 717-244-8508 244-9483
Web: www.mastercraftspecialties.com

Meco Corp 1500 Industrial Rd .... Greeneville TN 37745 423-639-1171 639-2570
TF: 800-251-7558 ■ *Web:* www.meco.net

Midwest Folding Products Inc 1414 S Western Ave .... Chicago IL 60608 312-666-3366 666-2606
TF: 800-621-4716 ■ *Web:* www.midwestfolding.com

Miller Herman for Health Care 855 E Main Ave PO Box 302 .... Zeeland MI 49464 616-654-3000
TF: 888-443-4357 ■ *Web:* www.hermanmiller.com/healthcare

Mitchell Furniture Systems Inc 1700 W St Paul Ave .... Milwaukee WI 53201 414-342-3111 342-4239
TF: 800-290-5960 ■ *Web:* www.mitchell-tables.com

MITY Enterprises Inc 1301 W 400 North .... Orem UT 84057 801-224-0589 224-6191
NASDAQ: MITY ■ *TF:* 800-327-1692 ■ *Web:* www.mitylite.com

MLP Seating Corp 2125 Lively Blvd .... Elk Grove Village IL 60007 847-956-1700 956-1776
TF: 800-723-3030 ■ *Web:* www.mlpseating.com

Monroe Table Co 316 N Walnut St .... Colfax IA 50054 515-674-3511 674-3513
TF: 800-247-2488 ■ *Web:* www.monroetables.com

Phone | Fax

Nemschoff Chairs Inc 909 N 8th St .... Sheboygan WI 53081 920-457-7726 457-7537
TF Cust Svc: 800-203-8916 ■ *Web:* www.nemschoff.com

New Holland Church Furniture 313 Prospect St .... New Holland PA 17557 717-354-4521 354-2481
TF: 800-648-9663 ■ *Web:* www.newhollandwood.com

Omni International Inc 435 12th St SW PO Box 1409 .... Vernon AL 35592 205-695-9173 695-6465
TF: 800-844-6664 ■ *Web:* www.omniinternational.com

Parisi Royal Inc 305 Pheasant Run .... Newtown PA 18940 215-968-6677 968-3580
Web: www.parisi-royal.com

Reliance Medical Products Inc 3535 Kings Mills Rd .... Mason OH 45040 513-398-3937 398-0256
TF: 800-735-0357 ■ *Web:* www.reliance-medical.com

Royal Seating Ltd 1110 Industrial Blvd .... Cameron TX 76520 254-605-5500 605-5516
TF Cust Svc: 800-460-4916 ■ *Web:* www.royalseating.com

Scholarcraft Inc PO Box 170748 .... Birmingham AL 35217 205-841-1922 841-1992
TF Cust Svc: 888-765-5200 ■ *Web:* www.scholarcraft.com

Shelby Williams Industries Inc 150 Shelby Williams Dr .... Morristown TN 37813 423-586-7000 586-2260
TF: 800-732-8464 ■ *Web:* www.shelbywilliams.com

Sico North America Inc 7525 Cahill Rd .... Minneapolis MN 55439 952-941-1700 941-6737
TF: 800-328-6138 ■ *Web:* www.sicoinc.com

Spectrum Industries Inc 1600 Johnson St .... Chippewa Falls WI 54729 715-723-6750 335-0473*
**Fax Area Code:* 800 ■ **Fax:* Sales ■ *TF:* 800-235-1262 ■
Web: www.spectrumfurniture.com

Sturdisteel Co 131 Ava Dr .... Hewitt TX 76643 254-666-5155 666-4472
TF: 800-433-3116 ■ *Web:* www.sturdisteel.com

Sunrise Medical Continuing Care Group 5001 Joerns Dr .... Stevens Point WI 54481 715-341-3600 341-3962
TF: 800-972-7581

Sunrise Medical Inc 2382 Faraday Ave Suite 200 .... Carlsbad CA 92008 760-930-1500 930-1585
TF: 800-278-6747 ■ *Web:* www.sunrisemedical.com

Texwood Furniture Corp 1203 Industrial Blvd .... Cameron TX 76520 254-605-5500 605-5552
TF: 888-878-0000 ■ *Web:* www.texwood.com

TMI Systems Design Corp 50 S 3rd Ave West .... Dickinson ND 58601 701-456-6716 456-6700
TF: 800-456-6716 ■ *Web:* www.tmisystems.com

Trinity Furniture Mfg 2885 Lorraine Ave .... Temple TX 76501 254-778-4727 773-0500
TF: 800-256-7397 ■ *Web:* www.pews.com

United Metal Fabricators Inc 1316 Eisenhower Blvd .... Johnstown PA 15904 814-266-8726 266-1870
TF Sales: 800-638-5322 ■ *Web:* www.umf-exam.com

Valley City Mfg Co Ltd 64 Hatt St .... Dundas ON L9H2G3 905-628-2255 628-4470
TF: 800-828-7628 ■ *Web:* www.valleycity.com

Virco Mfg Corp 2027 Harpers Way .... Torrance CA 90501 310-533-0474 258-7367*
AMEX: VIR ■ **Fax Area Code:* 800 ■ *TF Cust Svc:* 800-448-4726 ■
Web: www.virco-mfg.com

Wieland 13737 Main St PO Box 1000 .... Grabill IN 46741 260-627-3686 627-6496
TF: 800-777-5055 ■ *Web:* www.wielandhealthcare.com

Winco Inc 5516 SW 1st Ln .... Ocala FL 34474 352-854-2929 854-9544
TF: 800-237-3377 ■ *Web:* www.wincomfg.com

Worden Co Inc 199 E 17th St .... Holland MI 49423 616-392-1848 392-2542
TF: 800-748-0561 ■ *Web:* www.wordencompany.com

322-4 Outdoor Furniture

Phone | Fax

All-Luminum Products Inc 10981 Decatur Rd .... Philadelphia PA 19154 215-632-2800 824-1172
Web: www.all-luminum.com

Basta Sole 5 Marconi .... Irvine CA 92618 949-951-2010 972-5714*
**Fax Area Code:* 800 ■ **Fax:* Cust Svc ■ *TF Cust Svc:* 800-654-7000

Belson Outdoors Inc 111 N River Rd .... North Aurora IL 60542 630-897-8489 897-0573
TF: 800-323-5664 ■ *Web:* www.belson.com

Bemis Mfg Co PO Box 901 .... Sheboygan Falls WI 53085 920-467-4621 467-8573
TF: 800-558-7651 ■ *Web:* www.bemismfg.com

Brown Jordan Co 9860 Gidley St .... El Monte CA 91731 626-443-8971 575-0126
TF: 800-743-4252 ■ *Web:* www.brownjordan.com

Brown Jordan International Inc 1801 N Andrews Ave .... Pompano Beach FL 33069 954-960-1117 960-1849
Web: www.brownjordan.com

CFI Mfg Inc DBA Carter Grandle 2150 Whitfield Ave .... Sarasota FL 34243 941-751-1000 755-0977
Web: www.cartergrandle.com

Cox Industries Inc 860 Cannon Bridge Rd PO Box 1124 .... Orangeburg SC 29116 803-534-7467 534-1410
TF: 800-476-4401 ■ *Web:* www.coxwood.com

DuMor Inc PO Box 142 .... Mifflintown PA 17059 717-436-2106 436-9839
TF: 800-598-4018 ■ *Web:* www.dumor.com

Gardenside Ltd 999 Andersen Dr Suite 140 .... San Rafael CA 94901 415-455-4500 455-4505
TF: 888-999-8325 ■ *Web:* www.gardenside.com

Hatteras Hammocks Inc PO Box 1602 .... Greenville NC 27835 252-758-0641 758-0375
TF: 800-643-3522 ■ *Web:* www.hatterashammocks.com

Hill Co 8615 Germantown Ave .... Philadelphia PA 19118 215-247-7600 247-7603
Web: www.hill-company.com

Homecrest Industries Inc PO Box 350 .... Wadena MN 56482 218-631-1000 631-2609
TF: 888-346-4852 ■ *Web:* www.homecrest.com

Kay Park Recreation Corp 1301 Pine St .... Janesville IA 50647 319-987-2313 987-2900*
**Fax:* Cust Svc ■ *TF Cust Svc:* 800-553-2476 ■ *Web:* www.kaypark.com

Kessler Industries 8600 Gateway Blvd S .... El Paso TX 79906 915-591-8161 598-7353
Web: www.kesslerind.com

Kingsley-Bate Ltd 7200 Gateway Ct .... Manassas VA 20109 703-361-7000 361-7001
Web: www.kingsleybate.com

Lloyd/Flanders Industries Inc 3010 10th St .... Menominee MI 49858 906-863-4491 863-6700
TF: 800-526-9894 ■ *Web:* www.lloydflanders.com

Mallin Casual Furniture 1 Minson Way .... Montebello CA 90640 323-513-1041 513-1047
TF: 800-251-6537 ■ *Web:* www.mallinfurniture.com

Meadowcraft Inc 4700 Pinson Valley Pkwy .... Birmingham AL 35215 205-853-2220 854-4054
Web: www.meadowcraft.com

Minson Corp 1 Minson Way .... Montebello CA 90640 323-513-1041 513-1047
TF: 800-251-6537 ■ *Web:* www.minson.com

Moultrie Mfg Co 1403 Georgia Hwy 133 S PO Box 2948 .... Moultrie GA 31776 229-985-1312 890-7245
TF: 800-841-8674 ■ *Web:* www.moultriemanufacturing.com

OW Lee Co Inc 1822 E Francis St .... Ontario CA 91761 909-947-3771 947-6614
TF: 800-776-9533 ■ *Web:* www.owlee.com

Plantation Patterns Inc 4700 Pinson Valley Pkwy .... Birmingham AL 35215 205-853-2220 854-4054
Web: www.plantationpatterns.com

RJ Thomas Mfg Co Inc PO Box 946 .... Cherokee IA 51012 712-225-5115 225-5796
TF: 800-725-5115 ■ *Web:* www.pilotrock.com

Syroco Inc 7528 State Fair Blvd .... Baldwinsville NY 13027 315-635-9911 635-5388
TF: 800-853-9272 ■ *Web:* www.syroco.com

Telescope Casual Furniture Inc 82 Church St .... Granville NY 12832 518-642-1100 642-2536
Web: www.telescopecasual.com

Texacraft Inc 603 SE 14th St .... Ocala FL 34471 352-351-5777 368-3762
TF: 800-231-9790 ■ *Web:* www.texacraft.com

Tropitone Furniture Co Inc 5 Marconi .... Irvine CA 92618 949-951-2010 972-5714*
**Fax Area Code:* 800 ■ **Fax:* Cust Svc ■ *TF Cust Svc:* 800-654-7000 ■
Web: www.tropitone.com

Twin Oaks Hammocks 138 Twin Oaks Rd .... Louisa VA 23093 540-894-5125 894-4112
TF: 800-688-8946 ■ *Web:* www.twinoakstore.com

Wabash Valley Mfg Inc 505 E Main St .... Silver Lake IN 46982 260-352-2102 352-2160
TF: 800-253-8619 ■ *Web:* www.wabashvalley.com

Walpole Woodworkers Inc 767 East St PO Box 151 .... Walpole MA 02081 508-668-2800 668-7301
TF: 800-343-6948 ■ *Web:* www.walpolewoodworkers.com

Winston Furniture PO Box 868 .... Haleyville AL 35565 205-486-9211 486-9349
Web: www.winstonfurniture.com

Phone Fax

Woodard LLC 168 N Clinton Suite 300 Chicago IL 60661 312-423-5600 423-5561
Web: www.woodard-furniture.com

323 FURNITURE - WHOL

Phone Fax

A Pomerantz & Co 701 Market St Suite 7000 Philadelphia PA 19106 215-408-2100 408-2110
TF: 800-344-9135 ■ *Web:* www.pomerantz.com
Adirondack Chair Co Inc 31-01 Vernon Blvd Long Island City NY 11106 718-932-4003 204-4537
TF: 800-477-1330 ■ *Web:* www.adirondackchair.com
Adirondack Direct 31-01 Vernon Blvd Long Island City NY 11101 718-204-4500 204-4537
TF: 800-221-2444 ■ *Web:* www.adirondackdirect.com
AFD Contract Furniture Inc 88 West End Ave New York NY 10023 212-721-7100 721-7175
Web: www.afd-inc.com
Angel Line 88 Industrial Park Rd Pennsville NJ 08070 856-678-6300 678-6328
Web: www.angelline.com
ATD-American Co 135 Greenwood Ave Wyncote PA 19095 215-576-1380 523-2300*
**Fax Area Code:* 800 ■ *Web:* www.atd.com
Barclay Dean Interiors 11100 NE 8th St Suite 900 Bellevue WA 98004 425-451-8940 454-1705
Web: www.barclaydean.com
BCinteriors DBA Bottom Line Design LLC 1930 Central Ave Boulder CO 80301 303-443-3666 443-0406
Web: www.bcinteriors.com
BKM Enterprises Inc 300 E River Dr East Hartford CT 06108 860-528-9981 528-1843
TF: 800-786-4350 ■ *Web:* www.bkm.com
Bodine Inc 2141 14th Ave S Birmingham AL 35205 205-933-9100 933-8607
Web: www.bodineinc.com
Booker-Price Co 1318 McHenry St Louisville KY 40217 502-637-2531 637-1535
TF: 800-928-1080
Brown & Saenger PO Box 84040 Sioux Falls SD 57118 605-336-1960 332-0963
TF Sales: 800-952-3509 ■ *Web:* www.brown-saenger.com
Business Furniture Corp 6102 Victory Way Indianapolis IN 46278 317-216-1600 216-1602
TF: 800-774-5544 ■ *Web:* www.bfcindy.com
Business Furniture Inc 10 Lanidex Ctr W Parsippany NJ 07054 973-503-0730 503-1565
Web: www.bfionline.com
California Business Furnishings 4450 N Brawley St Suite 125 Fresno CA 93722 559-276-0511 276-0963
Web: www.deskschairsandmore.com
California Office Furniture Inc 1724 10th St Sacramento CA 95814 916-442-6959 442-3480
TF: 877-442-6959 ■ *Web:* www.caloffice.com
Capitol Motion Picture Supply Corp 630 9th Ave Suite 301 New York NY 10036 212-757-4510 265-5648
Carithers Wallace Courtenay Co 4343 Northeast Expy Atlanta GA 30340 770-493-8200 491-6374
TF: 800-292-8220 ■ *Web:* www.c-w-c.com
Carroll Seating Co Inc 2105 Lunt Ave Elk Grove Village IL 60007 847-434-0909 434-0910
TF: 800-972-3779 ■ *Web:* www.carrollseating.com
Champion Industries Inc 2450-90 1st Ave Huntington WV 25703 304-528-2791 528-2746*
NASDAQ: CHMP ■ **Fax:* Cust Svc ■ *TF:* 800-624-3431 ■
Web: www.champion-industries.com
COECO Office Systems Co
2521 N Church St PO Box 2088 Rocky Mount NC 27804 252-977-1121 985-1566
TF: 800-682-6844 ■ *Web:* www.coeco.com
Corporate Environments 1636 Northeast Expwy Atlanta GA 30329 404-679-8999 679-8950
Web: www.corporateenvironments.com
Dancker Sellew & Douglas 100 Broadway 5th Fl New York NY 10005 212-267-2200 619-6799
TF: 800-326-2537 ■ *Web:* www.dancker.com
Decorize Inc 1938 E Phelps St Springfield MO 65802 417-879-3326 879-3330
AMEX: DCZ ■ *TF:* 877-669-3326 ■ *Web:* www.decorize.com
Douron Inc 30 New Plant Ct Owings Mills MD 21117 410-363-2600 363-1659
TF: 888-833-8350 ■ *Web:* www.douron.com
Empire Office Inc 125 Maiden Ln New York NY 10038 212-607-5500 607-5650
TF: 877-533-6747 ■ *Web:* www.empireoffice.com
Enriching Spaces 1360 Kemper Meadow Dr Cincinnati OH 45240 513-851-0933 742-6415
Web: www.enrichingspaces.com
Finn Distributing Co Inc 430 S Commerce St Wichita KS 67202 316-265-1624
Flowers School Equipment Inc 10286 Staples Mill Rd Glen Allen VA 23060 804-672-8033 672-8455
Forrer Business Interiors Inc 555 W Estabrook Blvd Glendale WI 53212 414-906-3200 906-3299
Furniture Consultants Inc 641 Ave of the Americas 2nd Fl New York NY 10011 212-229-4500 807-0036
Web: www.e-fci.com
General Office Environment Inc 18 Railroad Ave Rochelle Park NJ 07662 201-845-0010 845-0034
Web: www.goeinc.com
General Office Products Co 4521 Hwy 7 Minneapolis MN 55416 952-925-7500 925-7531
Web: www.gopco.com
Glover Equipment Solco Group LLC
221 Cockeysville Rd PO Box 405 Cockeysville MD 21030 410-771-8000 771-8010
TF: 800-966-9016 ■ *Web:* www.gloverequipment.com
Haldeman-Homme Inc 430 Industrial Blvd NE Minneapolis MN 55413 612-331-4880 378-2236
TF: 800-795-0696 ■ *Web:* www.haldemanhomme.com
Hart Furniture Co Inc 12 Harold Hart Rd Siler City NC 27344 919-742-4141 663-2925
Web: www.hartfurnitureco.com
Henricksen & Co 1101 W River Pkwy Suite 100 Minneapolis MN 55415 612-455-2200 877-3300
Web: www.henricksen.com
Highsmith Inc W 5527 SR 106 PO Box 800 Fort Atkinson WI 53538 920-563-9571 563-7395
TF: 800-558-3899 ■ *Web:* www.highsmith.com
Holland House Furniture 9420 E 33rd St Indianapolis IN 46235 317-895-4300 895-4310
TF: 800-634-4666
Hunters Inc 120 Mokauea St Honolulu HI 96819 808-841-8002 847-7301
Huntington Wholesale Furniture Co Inc PO Box 1300 Huntington WV 25715 304-523-9415 523-9419
TF Orders: 800-788-3858
Intereum 845 Berkshire Ln N Plymouth MN 55441 763-417-3300 417-3309
Web: www.intereum.com
Interior Services Inc DBA Enriching Spaces
1360 Kemper Meadow Dr Cincinnati OH 45240 513-851-0933 742-6415
Web: www.enrichingspaces.com
Interiors Inc 1325 N Dutton Ave Santa Rosa CA 95401 707-544-4770 544-0722
J L Business Interiors Inc 515 Schoenhaar Dr PO Box 303 West Bend WI 53095 262-338-2221 338-2269
TF: 866-338-5524 ■ *Web:* www.jlbusinessinteriors.com
Johnson & Assoc Business Interiors Inc
833 W Jackson Blvd 4th Fl Chicago IL 60607 312-649-0074 649-0342
Web: www.johnsonassoc.net
Jules Seltzer Assoc 8833 Beverly Blvd Los Angeles CA 90048 310-274-7243 274-5626
Web: www.julesseltzer.com
KBM Workspace 320 S 1st St San Jose CA 95113 408-351-7100 938-0699
Web: www.kbmworkspace.com
Kimbrell Furniture Distributors PO Box 11117 Charlotte NC 28220 704-523-3424 522-1137
Web: www.kimbrells.com
Kyle RH Furniture Co 1352 Hansford St Charleston WV 25301 304-346-0671 346-0674
TF: 800-624-9170 ■ *Web:* www.kylefurniture.com
Lake County Office Equipment Inc DBA Office Plus of Lake County PO Box 8758 Waukegan IL 60079 847-662-5393 662-8761
TF: 800-468-8104 ■ *Web:* www.getofficeplus.com
Lee Co Inc 27 S 12th St PO Box 567 Terre Haute IN 47808 812-235-8155 235-3587
Web: www.leecompanyinc.com
Lenoir Empire Furniture 1625 Cherokee Rd Johnson City TN 37604 423-929-7283 929-7040
Web: www.lenoirempirefurniture.com
Loth Inc 3574 E Kemper Rd Cincinnati OH 45241 513-554-4900 554-8700
Web: www.lothmbi.com

Phone Fax

MG West 1787 Tribute Rd Suite A Sacramento CA 95815 916-641-3000 641-3008
Web: www.mgwest.com
MISSCO Contract Sales 2510 Lakeland Terr Suite 100 Jackson MS 39216 601-987-8600 987-3038
TF: 800-647-5333 ■ *Web:* www.missco.com
National Business Furniture Inc 735 N Water St Suite 440 Milwaukee WI 53202 414-276-8511 276-8371
TF Sales: 800-558-1010 ■ *Web:* www.nationalbusinessfurniture.com
Nova International Inc 3401 K St NW Suite 201 Washington DC 20007 202-338-4009 338-4138
TF: 800-257-6682 ■ *Web:* www.novainternational.com
OEC Bsuiness Interiors 900 N Church Rd Elmhurst IL 60126 630-589-5500 589-5637
Web: www.oecbusinessinteriors.com
Office Concepts 965 W Chicago Ave Chicago IL 60622 312-942-1100 942-9840
Web: www.officeconcepts.com
Office Environments Inc PO Box 411248 Charlotte NC 28241 704-714-7200 714-7400
Web: www.office-environments.com
Office Plus of Lake County PO Box 8758 Waukegan IL 60079 847-662-5393 662-8761
TF: 800-468-8104 ■ *Web:* www.getofficeplus.com
Ohio Desk Co 1122 Prospect Ave E Cleveland OH 44115 216-623-0600 623-0611
TF: 800-326-0601 ■ *Web:* www.ohiodesk.com
OneWorkplace 475 Brannan St San Francisco CA 94107 415-357-2200 357-2201
Web: www.oneworkplace.com
Pacific Design Center 8687 Melrose Ave West Hollywood CA 90069 310-657-0800 652-8576
Web: www.pacificdesigncenter.com
Peabody Office Furniture Corp 234 Congress St Boston MA 02110 617-542-1902 542-1609
Web: www.peabodyoffice.com
Pivot Interiors 2740 Zanker Rd Suite 100 San Jose CA 95134 408-432-5600 432-5601
Web: www.pivotinteriors.com
Pomerantz A & Co 701 Market St Suite 7000 Philadelphia PA 19106 215-408-2100 408-2110
TF: 800-344-9135 ■ *Web:* www.pomerantz.com
R & M Office Furniture Inc 9615 Oates Dr Sacramento CA 95827 916-362-1756 362-1086
TF: 800-660-1756 ■ *Web:* www.randmoffice.com
Red Willow Office Interiors
558 Castle Pines Pkwy Unit D4-314 Castle Rock CO 80108 303-373-9950 371-3710
Web: www.redwillowoffice.com
RH Kyle Furniture Co 1352 Hansford St Charleston WV 25301 304-346-0671 346-0674
TF: 800-624-9170 ■ *Web:* www.kylefurniture.com
Ruff T W & Co Inc 2400 Corporate Exchange Dr Suite 300 Columbus OH 43231 614-487-4000 487-8281
TF: 800-828-0234 ■ *Web:* www.thomasruff.com
Sarreid Ltd 3905 Airport Dr NW Wilson NC 27896 252-291-1414 237-1592
Web: www.sarreid.com
Seltzer Jules Assoc 8833 Beverly Blvd Los Angeles CA 90048 310-274-7243 274-5626
Web: www.julesseltzer.com
Servco Pacific Inc 900 4th St Mall Suite 600 Honolulu HI 96813 808-521-6511 523-3937
Web: www.servco.com
Southern Office Furniture Distributors Inc
719 N Regional Rd Greensboro NC 27409 336-668-4192 668-2076
TF: 800-933-6369 ■ *Web:* www.southernofficefurniture.com
Storage Equipment Co Inc 1258 Titan Dr Dallas TX 75247 214-630-9221 637-6340
TF: 800-443-1791 ■ *Web:* www.storageequip.com
T W Ruff & Co Inc 2400 Corporate Exchange Dr Suite 300 Columbus OH 43231 614-487-4000 487-8281
TF: 800-828-0234 ■ *Web:* www.thomasruff.com
Tangram Interiors Inc 9200 Sorensen Ave Santa Fe Springs CA 90670 562-365-5000 365-5399
TF: 800-700-1377 ■ *Web:* www.tangraminteriors.com
Valiant Products Corp 2727 5th Ave W Denver CO 80204 303-892-1234 892-5535
TF Cust Svc: 800-347-2727 ■ *Web:* www.valiantproducts.com
Waldner's Business Environment 125 Rt 110 Farmingdale NY 11735 631-694-1522 694-3503
TF: 800-473-9253 ■ *Web:* www.waldners.com
Walsh Brothers Inc 1636 N Central Ave PO Box 1711 Phoenix AZ 85001 602-252-6971 252-8222
TF: 800-527-3437 ■ *Web:* www.walshbros.com
Wasserstrom Co 477 S Front St Columbus OH 43215 614-228-6525 228-8776
TF: 800-999-9277 ■ *Web:* www.wasserstrom.com
WB Wood Co 890 Mountain Ave New Providence NJ 07974 908-771-9000 665-6500
Web: www.wbwood.com
Western Office Interiors 500 Citadel Dr Suite 250 Los Angeles CA 90040 323-271-1800 271-1801
Web: www.westernoffice.com
Wilson Office Interiors 1540 Champion Dr Carrollton TX 75006 972-488-4100 488-8815
Web: www.wilsonoi.com
Workplace Integrators 30800 Telegraph Rd Suite 4800 Bingham Farms MI 48025 248-430-2345 430-2346
TF: 800-429-9172 ■ *Web:* www.wp-int.com
Workscapes Inc 1040 Arlington St Orlando FL 32805 407-599-6770 599-6780
Web: www.workscapes.com

324 FURNITURE STORES

SEE ALSO Department Stores p. 1586

Phone Fax

American Furniture Warehouse Co 8501 Grant St Thornton CO 80229 303-289-3311 288-1726
TF: 800-992-7997 ■ *Web:* www.4americanfurniture.com
American Home Furnishings 3535 Menaul Blvd NE Albuquerque NM 87107 505-883-2211 883-2119
TF: 800-876-4454 ■ *Web:* www.americanhome.com
Art Van Furniture Co 6500 E14-Mile Rd Warren MI 48092 586-939-0800 979-9064*
**Fax:* Mktg ■ *TF:* 877-511-8364 ■ *Web:* www.artvan.com
Atlantic Corporate Interiors Inc
4600 Powder Mill Rd Suite 300 Beltsville MD 20705 301-931-3600 931-3601
Web: www.aciinc.com
Babies 'R' Us 545 Rt 17 S Paramus NJ 07652 201-251-3191 251-2469
Web: www.babiesrus.com
Badcock WS Corp 200 N Phosphate Blvd Mulberry FL 33860 863-425-4921 425-7513*
**Fax:* Hum Res ■ *TF:* 800-223-2625 ■ *Web:* www.badcock.com
Badcock's Economy Furniture Store Inc
3931 RCA Blvd Suite 3122 Palm Beach Gardens FL 33410 561-694-8588 694-8113
Web: www.badcock.com
Baer's Furniture 1589 NW 12th Ave Pompano Beach FL 33069 954-946-8001 946-8006
TF: 800-543-2092 ■ *Web:* www.baersfurniture.com
Barn Furniture Mart Inc 62221/2 N Sepulveda Blvd Van Nuys CA 91411 818-780-4070 780-4749
TF: 888-302-2276 ■ *Web:* www.barnfurniture.com
Bedroom Store Inc 2440 Adie Rd Saint Louis MO 63043 314-569-3669 569-0352
Web: www.thebedroomstore.com
Big Sandy Furniture Co Inc 8375 Gallia Pike Franklin Furnace OH 45629 740-574-2113 574-1078
Web: www.bigsandysuperstore.com
Big Sur Waterbeds Inc 13333 E 37th Ave Denver CO 80239 303-371-8560 371-9420
Bombay Co Inc 550 Bailey Ave Fort Worth TX 76107 817-347-8200 332-7066
NYSE: BBA ■ *TF:* 800-829-7789 ■ *Web:* www.bombaycompany.com
Cabot House Inc 10 Industrial Way Amesbury MA 01913 978-834-9280 388-0792
Web: cabothouse.com
Carls Furniture 6650 N Federal Hwy Boca Raton FL 33487 561-226-1111 226-1497
Web: www.carls.com
Carol House Furniture Co 2332 Millpark Dr Maryland Heights MO 63043 314-427-4200 427-8176
Web: www.carolhouse.com
Carter's Furniture Co 410 N Vine St Urbana IL 61802 217-367-4066 367-4094
City Furniture Inc 6701 N Hiatus Rd Tamarac FL 33321 954-597-2200 718-3328
TF: 866-208-2489 ■ *Web:* www.city-furniture.com

				Phone	Fax
Coulter's Furniture 1324 Windsor Ave *TF:* 888-238-4778 ■ *Web:* www.coulters.com	Windsor	ON	N8X3L9	519-253-7422	253-3744
CS Wo & Sons Ltd 702 S Beretenia St *Web:* www.cswo.com	Honolulu	HI	96813	808-545-5966	543-5366
Darvin Furniture 15400 S La Grange Rd *TF:* 800-232-7846 ■ *Web:* www.darvin.com	Orland Park	IL	60462	708-460-4100	460-9132
Dearden's Furniture Co 700 S Main St *Web:* www.deardens.com	Los Angeles	CA	90014	213-627-9601	624-0775
Desks Inc Business Furniture 1385 S Santa Fe Dr *Web:* www.dibf.net	Denver	CO	80223	303-777-7778	698-7139
Domain Home 51 Morgan Dr *TF:* 877-436-6246 ■ *Web:* www.domain-home.com	Norwood	MA	02062	781-769-9130	769-3580
Dufresne Furniture Ltd 230 Panet Rd **Fax:* Claims ■ *Web:* www.dufresne.ca	Winnipeg	MB	R2J0S3	204-989-9907	237-4923*
Ed Marling Stores Inc 2950 SW McClure Rd *Web:* www.marlings.com	Topeka	KS	66614	785-273-6970	271-2910
El Dorado Furniture Corp 4200 NW 167th St *TF:* 800-236-6256 ■ *Web:* www.eldoradofurniture.com	Miami Gardens	FL	33054	305-624-9700	430-9698
Elder-Beerman Stores Corp 332 W Wisconsin Ave *Web:* www.elderbeerman.com	Milwaukee	WI	53203	414-347-1152	
Ethan Allen Interiors Inc Ethan Allen Dr *NYSE: ETH* ■ *Web:* www.ethanallen.com	Danbury	CT	06811	203-743-8000	743-8298
Expressions Custom Furniture PO Box 608 *Web:* www.expressions-furniture.com	Hickory	NC	28603	828-328-1851	267-8749
Farmers Furniture 1851 Telfair St *TF:* 800-456-0424 ■ *Web:* www.farmersfurniture.com	Dublin	GA	31021	478-275-3150	275-6276
Finger Furniture Co Inc 1601 Gillingham Ln *Web:* www.fingerfurniture.com	Sugar Land	TX	77478	713-221-4441	221-4601
Franklin Interiors Inc 2740 Smallman St Suite 600 *TF:* 800-371-5001 ■ *Web:* www.franklininteriors.com	Pittsburgh	PA	15222	412-261-2525	255-4089
Fredman Brothers Furniture Co Inc 908 SW Washington St *TF:* 800-248-5228	Peoria	IL	61602	309-674-2011	674-0407
Furnitureland South Inc 5635 Riverdale Dr **Fax:* Cust Svc ■ *TF:* 866-553-4200 ■ *Web:* www.furniturelandsouth.com	Jamestown	NC	27282	336-841-4328	822-3082*
Gabberts Inc 3501 Galleria *Web:* www.gabberts.com	Minneapolis	MN	55435	952-927-1500	927-1555
Gallery Furniture Inc 6006 I-45 N Fwy *TF:* 800-518-0008 ■ *Web:* www.galleryfurniture.com	Houston	TX	77076	713-694-5570	696-4524
Goldberg Furniture 506 S Main St	North Syracuse	NY	13212	315-458-0855	458-4229
Goodmans Inc 1400 E Indian School Rd *Web:* www.goodmansinc.com	Phoenix	AZ	85014	602-263-1110	263-0624
Gordon's Furniture Stores 214 N Center St *Web:* www.gordonsfurn.com	Statesville	NC	28687	704-768-8000	768-8001
Gorman's Gallery Inc 29145 Telegraph Rd *Web:* www.gormans.com	Southfield	MI	48034	248-353-9880	353-6855
Grand Furniture Discount Store 836 E Little Creek Rd *Web:* www.grandfurniture.com	Norfolk	VA	23518	757-588-1331	583-9075
Grand Home Furnishings 4235 Electric Rd SW Suite 100 *Web:* www.grandhomefurnishings.com	Roanoke	VA	24018	540-776-7000	776-5528
Granite Furniture Co PO Box 526199	Salt Lake City	UT	84152	801-486-3333	485-1561
Hansen's Furniture Co 916 W Division St *Web:* www.hansensfurniture.com	Mount Vernon	WA	98273	360-424-7188	
Hart Furniture Co Inc 12 Harold Hart Rd *Web:* www.hartfurnitureco.com	Siler City	NC	27344	919-742-4141	663-2925
Haverty Furniture Cos Inc 780 Johnson Ferry Rd NE Suite 800 *NYSE: HVT* ■ *TF:* 800-241-4599 ■ *Web:* www.havertys.com	Atlanta	GA	30342	404-443-2900	443-4180
Haynes Furniture Co Inc 5324 Virginia Beach Blvd *Web:* www.haynesfurniture.com	Virginia Beach	VA	23462	757-497-9681	552-1545
Hurwitz-Mintz Furniture Co 1751 Airline Dr *TF:* 800-597-9555 ■ *Web:* www.hurwitzmintz.com	Metairie	LA	70001	504-378-1000	523-7273
IKEA 420 Alan Wood Rd *TF:* 800-434-4532 ■ *Web:* www.ikea.com	Conshohocken	PA	19428	610-834-0180	834-0872
Jennifer Convertibles Inc 419 Crossways Park Dr *AMEX: JEN* ■ *TF:* 800-595-1422 ■ *Web:* www.jenniferfurniture.com	Woodbury	NY	11797	516-496-1900	390-8638
Jerome's Furniture Warehouse 16960 Mesamint St *TF:* 888-537-6637 ■ *Web:* www.jeromes.com	San Diego	CA	92127	858-753-1500	753-0826
Jordan's Furniture Co 100 Stockwell Dr *Web:* www.jordans.com	Avon	MA	02322	508-580-4600	580-3440
K Town Corp 136 Oak Ave *Web:* www.k-townfurniture.com	Kannapolis	NC	28081	704-932-3111	938-7079
Kacey Fine Furniture 900 S Santa Fe Dr Dock 4 Unit 25 *TF:* 800-574-1979 ■ *Web:* www.kacey.com	Denver	CO	80223	303-778-6400	778-0530
Kalin Enterprises Inc 5252 S Tamiami Trail	Sarasota	FL	34231	941-924-1271	923-0045
Kane Furniture Corp 5700 70th Ave N *Web:* www.kanesfurniture.com	Pinellas Park	FL	33781	727-545-9555	541-6960
Kelly's Furniture 20 Bruckner Blvd	Bronx	NY	10454	718-665-8344	993-6590
Kimbrell's 4524-C South Blvd *Web:* www.kimbrells.com	Charlotte	NC	28209	704-523-3424	522-1137
Lack's Stores Inc PO Box 2088 *TF:* 800-242-1123 ■ *Web:* www.lacks.com	Victoria	TX	77902	361-578-3571	576-9814
Lack's Valley Stores Ltd 1300 San Patricia St	Pharr	TX	78577	956-702-3361	782-5740
Levin Furniture Co 301 Fritzhenry Rd *Web:* www.levinfurniture.com	Smithton	PA	15479	724-872-2050	872-2060
LFD Inc 725 E Esperanza Ave	McAllen	TX	78501	956-686-2271	686-3548
Loth Inc 3574 E Kemper Rd *Web:* www.lothmbi.com	Cincinnati	OH	45241	513-554-4900	554-8700
Low's Furniture 906 Main St *Web:* www.lows.com	Fortuna	CA	95540	707-725-3331	725-1268
Market Square 305 W High St	High Point	NC	27260	336-821-1500	821-1575
Marling Ed Stores Inc 2950 SW McClure Rd *Web:* www.marlings.com	Topeka	KS	66614	785-273-6970	271-2910
Marlo Furniture Co Inc 725 Rockville Pike *Web:* www.marlofurniture.com	Rockville	MD	20852	301-738-9595	838-2970
Marshall Field & Co 111 N State St *Web:* www.fields.com	Chicago	IL	60602	312-781-1000	
Mathis Brothers Furniture Inc 3434 W Reno Ave *TF:* 800-329-3434 ■ *Web:* www.mathisbrothers.com	Oklahoma City	OK	73107	405-943-3434	949-1366
McGregor Co PO Box 517 *Web:* www.mcgregorsfurniture.com	Marshalltown	IA	50158	641-753-3381	753-0175
Mecklenburg Furniture Shop 520 Providence Rd	Charlotte	NC	28207	704-376-8401	347-0499
Miskelly Furniture 101 Airport Rd *Web:* www.miskellyfurniture.com	Jackson	MS	39208	601-939-6288	933-5975
Mott Haven Furniture Co Inc DBA Kelly's Furniture 20 Bruckner Blvd	Bronx	NY	10454	718-665-8344	993-6590
Nebraska Furniture Mart Inc 700 S 72nd St *TF:* 800-359-1200 ■ *Web:* www.nfm.com	Omaha	NE	68114	402-397-6100	392-3386
Norwalk Furniture Corp 100 Furniture Pkwy *TF Orders:* 800-837-2565 ■ *Web:* www.norwalkfurniture.com	Norwalk	OH	44857	419-744-3200	668-6223
Olinde's Furniture 9536 Airline Hwy *Web:* www.olindes.com	Baton Rouge	LA	70815	225-926-3380	924-2063
Olum's of Binghamton Inc 3701 Vestal Pkwy E *TF Cust Svc:* 800-964-5690 ■ *Web:* www.olums.com	Vestal	NY	13850	607-729-5775	729-6166
Parker Furniture 10375 SW Beaverton-Hillsdale Hwy *TF:* 800-877-9491 ■ *Web:* www.parker-furniture.com	Beaverton	OR	97005	503-644-0155	644-0170
Peerless Mattress & Furniture Co G-3437 Miller Rd *TF:* 800-253-0937 ■ *Web:* www.peerlessfurn.com	Flint	MI	48507	810-230-7440	230-0143
Pier 1 Kids 100 Pier 1 Pl *Web:* www.pier1kids.com	Fort Worth	TX	76102	817-252-8000	252-8174
Plunkett Furniture Co Inc 222 W Roosevelt Rd *Web:* www.plunkettfurniture.com	Lombard	IL	60148	630-629-6100	629-9775
Porters of Racine 301 6th St *TF:* 800-558-3245 ■ *Web:* www.portersofracine.com	Racine	WI	53403	262-633-6363	633-5011
Raymour & Flanigan Furniture PO Box 220 **Fax:* Mktg ■ *Web:* www.raymourflanigan.com	Liverpool	NY	13088	315-453-2500	453-2551*
RC Willey & Son Inc 2301 S 300 West *TF:* 800-444-3876 ■ *Web:* www.rcwilley.com	Salt Lake City	UT	84115	801-461-3900	461-3990
RH Kuhn Co DBA Roomful Express 2250 Roswell Dr *TF:* 888-696-7378 ■ *Web:* www.roomfulexpress.com	Pittsburgh	PA	15205	412-784-1250	799-0439
Robb & Stucky Furniture Inc 13170 S Cleveland Ave *Web:* www.robbstucky.com	Fort Myers	FL	33907	239-936-8541	437-5940
Roomful Express 2250 Roswell Dr *TF:* 888-696-7378 ■ *Web:* www.roomfulexpress.com	Pittsburgh	PA	15205	412-784-1250	799-0439
Rooms To Go Inc 11540 US Hwy 92 E *TF Cust Svc:* 800-766-6786 ■ *Web:* www.roomstogo.com	Seffner	FL	33584	813-623-5400	620-1717
Rothman Furniture Stores Inc 2101 E Terra Ln **Fax Area Code:* 636 ■ *Web:* www.rothmanfurniture.com	O'Fallon	MO	63366	314-291-1199	978-7057*
Rotmans Furniture & Carpet 725 Southbridge St *TF:* 800-768-6267 ■ *Web:* www.rotmans.com	Worcester	MA	01610	508-755-5276	752-4258
Routzahn's 1931 N Market St *Web:* www.routzahns.com	Frederick	MD	21701	301-662-2141	662-7215
Royal Discount Furniture Co Inc 122 S Main St *Web:* www.royalfurniture.com	Memphis	TN	38103	901-527-6407	527-8166
Royals Inc 324 SW 16th St	Belle Glade	FL	33430	561-996-6581	996-1369
Scan International Inc 1800-I Rockville Pike *TF:* 800-386-0989 ■ *Web:* www.scanfurniture.com	Rockville	MD	20852	301-984-2960	984-0755
Schewel Furniture Co Inc 1031 Main St *Web:* www.schewels.com	Lynchburg	VA	24504	434-522-0200	522-0207
Schottenstein Stores Corp 1800 Moler Rd **Fax:* Cust Svc ■ *TF:* 800-743-4577	Columbus	OH	43207	614-221-9200	449-4880*
Scott Rice Office Works 14720 W 105th St *Web:* www.scottrice.com	Lenexa	KS	66215	913-888-7600	227-7793
Sedlak Interiors Inc 34300 Solon Rd *TF:* 800-260-2949 ■ *Web:* www.sedlakinteriors.com	Solon	OH	44139	440-248-2424	349-8724
See Ltd 8806 Beverly Blvd *Web:* www.seeltd.com	Los Angeles	CA	90048	310-385-1919	385-1999
Selden's Home Furnishings & Interior Design 1802 62nd Ave E *TF:* 800-870-7880 ■ *Web:* www.seldens.com	Tacoma	WA	98424	253-922-5700	922-2924
Seven Seas Rattan Co 2138 Sepulveda Blvd *Web:* www.sevenseasrattan.com	Los Angeles	CA	90025	310-477-5995	
Shops at Carolina Furniture 5425 Richmond Rd *Web:* www.carolina-furniture.com	Williamsburg	VA	23188	757-565-3000	565-4476
Sit 'n Sleep 3853 Overland Ave *Web:* www.sitnsleep.com	Culver City	CA	90232	310-842-6850	842-6844
Sleepy's Inc 175 Central Ave S *TF:* 800-753-3797 ■ *Web:* www.sleepys.com	Bethpage	NY	11714	516-844-8800	844-8887
Smith's Furniture 8055 National Tpke *Web:* www.smithsfurniture.net	Louisville	KY	40214	502-368-9917	368-5369
Smulekoff's Fine Home Furnishings PO Box 74090 *TF:* 888-384-6995 ■ *Web:* www.smulekoffs.com	Cedar Rapids	IA	52407	319-362-2181	362-2180
Star Furniture Co Inc 16666 Barker Springs Rd *TF:* 800-364-6661 ■ *Web:* www.starfurniture.com	Houston	TX	77084	281-492-6661	579-5900
Steinhafels W 231 N 1013 County Hwy F *TF:* 866-351-4600 ■ *Web:* www.steinhafels.com	Waukesha	WI	53189	262-436-4600	436-4602
Sterling Furniture Co 2051 S 1100 East	Salt Lake City	UT	84106	801-467-1579	
Stevens Furniture 1258 Hickory Blvd SW *Web:* www.stevensfurniture.com	Lenoir	NC	28645	828-728-5511	728-5518
Town & Country Furniture 6545 Airline Hwy *TF:* 800-375-6660 ■ *Web:* www.tcfurniture.com	Baton Rouge	LA	70805	225-355-6666	355-7459
USA Baby 793 Springer Dr *TF:* 800-323-4108 ■ *Web:* www.usababy.com	Lombard	IL	60148	630-652-0600	652-9080
Value City Furniture 1800 Moler Rd **Fax:* Cust Svc ■ *TF:* 800-743-4577 ■ *Web:* www.vcf.com	Columbus	OH	43207	614-221-9200	449-4880*
Walsh Brothers Inc 1636 N Central Ave PO Box 1711 *TF:* 800-527-3437 ■ *Web:* www.walshbros.com	Phoenix	AZ	85001	602-252-6971	252-8222
Warehouse Home Furnishings Distributors Inc DBA Farmers Furniture 1851 Telfair St *TF:* 800-456-0424 ■ *Web:* www.farmersfurniture.com	Dublin	GA	31021	478-275-3150	275-6276
Weirs Furniture Village 3219 Knox St *TF:* 888-889-3477 ■ *Web:* www.weirsfurniture.com	Dallas	TX	75205	214-528-0321	521-4302
Wenger Furniture & Appliance Co 4552 Whittier Blvd *Web:* www.wengerfurniture.com	Los Angeles	CA	90022	323-261-1136	261-0968
Western Contract Furnishers 11455 Folsom Blvd *Web:* www.westerncontract.com	Rancho Cordova	CA	95742	916-638-3338	638-2698
Wickes Furniture Co 250 S Gary Ave *TF:* 888-942-5372 ■ *Web:* www.wickesfurniture.com	Carol Stream	IL	60188	847-541-0100	279-7511
Wieser & Cawley Inc 1301 Colegate Dr *TF:* 800-339-0094	Marietta	OH	45750	740-373-1676	373-9336
Willey RC & Son Inc 2301 S 300 West *TF:* 800-444-3876 ■ *Web:* www.rcwilley.com	Salt Lake City	UT	84115	801-461-3900	461-3990
Wo CS & Sons Ltd 702 S Beretenia St *Web:* www.cswo.com	Honolulu	HI	96813	808-545-5966	543-5366
Wolf Furniture Inc 1620 N Tuckahoe St *Web:* www.wolffurniture.com	Bellwood	PA	16617	814-742-4380	742-4389
Wood You Distributors Inc 3333 N Canal St PO Box 12469 *Web:* www.woodyou.com	Jacksonville	FL	32209	904-354-0300	354-6983
WS Badcock Corp 200 N Phosphate Blvd **Fax:* Hum Res ■ *TF:* 800-223-2625 ■ *Web:* www.badcock.com	Mulberry	FL	33860	863-425-4921	425-7513*

325 GAMES & GAMING

SEE ALSO Casino Companies p. 1409; Casinos p. 1409; Lotteries, Games, Sweepstakes p. 1922; Toys, Games, Hobbies p. 2375

				Phone	Fax
Alaska Bingo Supply 3707 Woodland Dr Suite 3 *TF:* 800-478-7003 ■ *Web:* www.alaskabingosupply.com	Anchorage	AK	99517	907-243-7003	248-0895
Alliance Gaming Corp 6601 S Bermuda Rd *NYSE: AGI* ■ **Fax:* Hum Res ■ *TF:* 877-462-2559 ■ *Web:* www.ally.com	Las Vegas	NV	89119	702-896-7700	896-7838*
American Gaming & Electronics 9500 W 55th St *TF:* 800-336-6630 ■ *Web:* www.age-gaming.com	McCook	IL	60525	708-290-2100	290-2200
American Wagering Inc 675 Grier Dr *Web:* www.americanwagering.com	Las Vegas	NV	89119	702-735-0101	735-0142
Amtote International Inc 11200 Pepper Rd **Fax:* Acctg ■ *TF:* 800-345-1566 ■ *Web:* www.amtote.com	Hunt Valley	MD	21031	410-771-8700	785-5279*
Arachnid Inc 6212 Material Ave *TF:* 800-435-8319 ■ *Web:* www.bullshooter.com	Loves Park	IL	61111	815-654-0212	654-0447
Aristocrat Technologies 7230 Amigo St *TF:* 800-748-4156 ■ *Web:* www.aristocrat.com.au	Las Vegas	NV	89119	702-270-1000	270-1469

Phone Fax

Bally Gaming & Systems 6601 S Bermuda Rd. Las Vegas NV 89119 702-896-7700 896-7823*
*Fax: Sales ■ TF: 877-462-2559 ■ Web: www.ballygaming.com

Bally-Sierra Design Group 300 Sierra Manor Dr Reno NV 89511 775-850-1500 850-1501
TF: 888-404-8838 ■ Web: www.sierradesign.com

Douglas Press Inc 2810 Madison St. Bellwood IL 60104 708-547-8400 547-0296
TF: 800-323-0705 ■ Web: www.douglaspress.com

eLottery Inc 46 Southfield Ave 3 Stamford Landing Suite 370 Stamford CT 06902 203-388-1800 388-1809
Web: www.elottery.com

Florida Gaming Corp 3500 NW 37th Ave Miami FL 33142 305-633-6400 633-4386
Web: www.fla-gaming.com

FortuNet Inc 2950 S Highland Dr Suite C. Las Vegas NV 89109 702-796-9090 796-9069
NASDAQ: FNET ■ Web: www.fortunet.com

GameTech International Inc 900 Sandhill Rd Reno NV 89521 775-850-6000 850-6090
NASDAQ: GMTC ■ TF: 800-487-8510 ■ Web: www.gametech-inc.com

Gaming & Entertainment Group Inc 4501 Hayvenhurst Ave Encino CA 91436 818-400-5930 723-2141*
*Fax Area Code: 413 ■ Web: www.gaming-group.com

Gaming Partners International Corp 1700 Industrial Rd Las Vegas NV 89102 702-384-2425 384-1965
NASDAQ: GPIC ■ TF: 800-728-5766 ■ Web: www.gpigaming.com

GTECH Holdings Corp 55 Technology Way West Greenwich RI 02817 401-392-1000 392-1234
NYSE: GTK ■ Web: www.gtech.com

IGT Inc 1085 Palms Airport Dr Las Vegas NV 89119 702-263-7588 263-7595
TF: 888-254-7568 ■ Web: www.acresgaming.com

Interactive Systems Worldwide Inc 2 Andrews Dr West Paterson NJ 07424 973-256-8181 256-8211
NASDAQ: ISWI ■ Web: www.sportxction.com

International Game Technology 9295 Prototype Dr. Reno NV 89521 775-448-7777 448-1600*
NYSE: IGT ■ *Fax: Hum Res ■ TF: 800-688-7890 ■ Web: www.igt.com

International Lottery & Totalizator Systems Inc
2131 Faraday Ave. Carlsbad CA 92008 760-931-4000 931-1789
Web: www.ilts.com

Konami Gaming Inc 585 Trade Center Dr Las Vegas NV 89119 702-616-1400 367-0001
TF: 866-544-7568 ■ Web: www.konamigaming.com

Littlefield Corp 2501 North Lamar Blvd Austin TX 78705 512-476-5141 476-5680
Web: www.littlefield.com

Mondial International Corp 101 Secor Ln PO Box 889 Pelham Manor NY 10803 914-738-7411 738-7521
Web: www.mondialgroup.com

Multimedia Games Inc 206 Wild Basin Rd S Bldg B 4th Fl Austin TX 78746 512-371-7100 334-7695
NASDAQ: MGAM ■ Web: www.multimediagames.com

Poker Chips Online LLC 342 Warren Ave Portland ME 04103 506-575-8827 575-1081
TF: 888-797-2200 ■ Web: www.pokerchips.com

PokerTek Inc 1020 Crews Rd Suite J Matthews NC 28106 704-849-0860
NASDAQ: PTEK ■ Web: pokertek.com

Progressive Gaming International Corp 920 Pilot Rd Las Vegas NV 89119 702-896-3890 896-2461
NASDAQ: PGIC ■ TF: 800-336-8449 ■ Web: www.mikohn.com

Scientific Games Corp 750 Lexington Ave 25th Fl. New York NY 10022 212-754-2233 754-2372
NASDAQ: SGMS ■ TF: 800-367-9345 ■ Web: www.scigames.com

Shuffle Master Inc 10901 Valley View Rd Eden Prairie MN 55344 952-943-1951 914-0764
NASDAQ: SHFL ■ Web: www.shufflemaster.com

Sigma Game Inc 7160 S Amigo St Las Vegas NV 89119 702-260-3100 260-0677
Web: www.sigmagame.com

Skee-Ball Inc 121 Liberty Ln Chalfont PA 18914 215-997-8900 997-8982
Web: www.skeeball.com

Smart Industries Corp 1626 Delaware Ave Des Moines IA 50317 515-265-9900 265-3148
TF: 800-553-2442 ■ Web: www.smartind.com

United Tote Co 11505 Susquehanna Trail. Glen Rock PA 17327 717-227-4350 227-4351
TF: 800-238-8683 ■ Web: www.unitedtote.com

Valley-Dynamo 2525 Handley Ederville Rd Richland Hills TX 76118 817-299-3070 299-3170
TF: 800-248-2837 ■ Web: www.valley-dynamo.com

VendingData Corp 6830 Spencer St Las Vegas NV 89119 702-733-7195 733-7197
AMEX: VNX ■ Web: www.vendingdata.com

Video King Gaming Systems 2717 N 118 Cir Suite 210 Omaha NE 68164 402-951-2970 951-2990
TF: 800-635-9912 ■ Web: www.bingoking.com

VirtGame Corp 6969 Corte Santa Fe Suite A. San Diego CA 92121 858-373-5001 373-5007
Web: www.virtgame.com

Vision Gaming & Technology Inc 2055 Boggs Rd NW Duluth GA 30096 770-923-9900 923-0097
Web: www.vision-gaming.com

Western Regional Off-Track Betting Corp 700 Ellicott St Batavia NY 14020 585-343-1423 343-6873
TF: 800-724-2000 ■ Web: www.westernotb.com

WMS Gaming Inc 3401 N California Ave Chicago IL 60618 773-961-1000 961-1060*
*Fax: Hum Res ■ TF: 800-932-3021 ■ Web: www.wmsgaming.com

WMS Industries Inc 800 S Northpoint Blvd Waukegan IL 60085 847-785-3000 785-3058
NYSE: WMS ■ Web: www.wmsgaming.com

326 GARDEN CENTERS

SEE ALSO Horticultural Products Growers p. 1789; Seed Companies p. 2311

Phone Fax

Armstrong Garden Centers Inc 2200 E Rt 66 Suite 200 Glendora CA 91740 626-914-1091 335-0257
TF: 800-229-1707 ■ Web: www.armstronggarden.com

Behnke Nurseries Co 11300 Baltimore Ave Beltsville MD 20705 301-937-1100 937-8034
Web: www.behnkes.com

Breck's LLC PO Box 65 Guilford IN 47022 812-537-3149 537-9653*
*Fax: Orders ■ Web: www.brecks.com

Cal Herbold Nursery 9403 E Ave. Hesperia CA 92340 760-244-6125

Calloway's Nursery Inc 4200 Airport Fwy Suite 200 Fort Worth TX 76117 817-222-1122 302-0031
Web: www.calloways.com

Capital Nursery Co 4700 Freeport Blvd. Sacramento CA 95822 916-455-2601 455-2141
Web: www.capitalnursery.com

Cornelius Nurseries Inc 2233 S Voss Rd. Houston TX 77057 713-782-7611 780-2878
Web: www.corneliusnurseries.com

DA Hoerr & Sons Inc 8020 N Shadetree Dr Peoria IL 61615 309-691-4561 691-1834
Web: www.hoerrnursery.com

Earl May Seed & Nursery 208 N Elm St. Shenandoah IA 51603 712-246-1020 246-2210
TF: 800-843-9608 ■ Web: www.earlmay.com

Farmers Market Garden Center Inc 4110 N Elston Ave. Chicago IL 60618 773-539-1200 539-1482
Web: www.gardenchicago.com

Flowerland 765 28th St SW Wyoming MI 49509 616-532-7404 531-7858
Web: www.myflowerland.com

Flowerwood Garden Center 7625 US Hwy 14 Crystal Lake IL 60012 815-459-6200 459-3711
TF: 800-852-3114 ■ Web: www.flowerwoodinc.com

Fruit Basket Gardens Inc DBA Flowerland 765 28th St SW Wyoming MI 49509 616-532-7404 531-7858
Web: www.myflowerland.com

Gardener's Supply Co 128 Intervale Rd Burlington VT 05401 802-660-3500 660-3501
TF: 800-863-1700 ■ Web: www.gardeners.com

Green Thumb International Inc 21812 Sherman Way Canoga Park CA 91303 818-340-6400 340-8598
Web: www.supergarden.com

Greenbrier Farms Inc 225 Sign Pine Rd. Chesapeake VA 23322 757-421-2141 421-2159
TF: 800-821-2141 ■ Web: www.greenbrierfarms.info

Home Depot Inc 2455 Paces Ferry Rd NW Atlanta GA 30339 770-433-8211 384-2356
NYSE: HD ■ TF Cust Svc: 800-553-3199 ■ Web: www.homedepot.com

Home & Garden Showplace 8600 W Bryn Mawr Chicago IL 60631 773-695-5000 695-7049
TF: 888-474-9752 ■ Web: www.gardenplace.com

Phone Fax

Jackson & Perkins 2500 S Pacific Hwy PO Box 1028 Medford OR 97501 541-776-2000 864-2194
TF Cust Svc: 800-872-7673 ■ Web: www.jacksonandperkins.com

Johnson's Garden Centers 2707 W 13th St Wichita KS 67203 316-942-1443 942-1494
TF: 888-542-8463 ■ Web: www.johnsonsgarden.com

Jung JW Seed Co 335 S High St Randolph WI 53956 920-326-3121 692-5864*
*Fax Area Code: 800 ■ TF: 800-297-3123 ■ Web: www.jungseed.com

JW Jung Seed Co 335 S High St Randolph WI 53956 920-326-3121 692-5864*
*Fax Area Code: 800 ■ TF: 800-297-3123 ■ Web: www.jungseed.com

Lakeland Equipment Inc 4751 County Rd 5 PO Box 265 Hall NY 14463 585-526-6325 526-6073
Web: www.jddealer.deere.com/lakelandequipment

Langeveld Bulb Co Inc 725 Vassar Ave Lakewood NJ 08701 732-367-2000 942-3801
TF: 800-526-0467 ■ Web: www.langeveld.com

Lowe's Cos Inc 1000 Lowe's Blvd Mooresville NC 28117 704-758-1000 658-4766*
NYSE: LOW ■ *Fax Area Code: 336 ■ TF: 800-445-6937 ■ Web: www.lowes.com

M & R Nurseries Inc 1601 W Beauregard Ave San Angelo TX 76901 325-653-3341 653-3342

Mahoney's Garden Center 242 Cambridge St Winchester MA 01890 781-729-5900 721-1277
Web: www.mahoneysgarden.com

Master Nursery Garden Centers Inc 2151 Salvio St Suite 255 Concord CA 94520 925-288-3060 288-3061
TF: 800-576-5102 ■ Web: www.masternursery.com

McKay Nursery Co Inc 750 S Monroe St Waterloo WI 53594 920-478-2121 478-3615
TF: 800-236-4242 ■ Web: www.mckaynursery.com

Merrygro Farms Inc 34135 Cardinal Ln Eustis FL 32736 888-301-7673 589-8138*
*Fax Area Code: 352 ■ TF: 888-637-7947 ■ Web: www.merrygro.com

Michigan Bulb Co PO Box 4180 Lawrenceburg IN 47025 812-539-2494 354-1499*
*Fax Area Code: 513 ■ Web: michiganbulb.com

Milaeger's Inc 4838 Douglas Ave Racine WI 53402 262-639-2040 639-1855
TF: 800-669-1229 ■ Web: www.milaegers.com

North Haven Gardens Inc 7700 Northaven Rd Dallas TX 75230 214-363-6715 987-1511
TF: 800-347-2342 ■ Web: www.nhg.com

Panhandle Co-op Assn 401 S Beltline Hwy W Scottsbluff NE 69361 308-632-5301 632-5375
TF Cust Svc: 800-732-4546 ■ Web: www.panhandlecoop.com

Pike Nurseries Holding LLC 4020 Steve Reynolds Blvd Norcross GA 30093 770-921-1022 638-6940
Web: www.pikenursery.com

Plant Delights Nursery Inc 9241 Sauls Rd. Raleigh NC 27603 919-772-4794 662-0370
Web: www.plantdel.com

Plants of the Southwest 3095 Agua Fria St. Santa Fe NM 87507 505-438-8888 438-8800
TF: 800-788-7333 ■ Web: www.plantsofthesouthwest.com

Pursley Inc 9115 58th Dr E Suite A Bradenton FL 34202 941-753-7851 758-9583
TF: 800-683-7584

Rain or Shine LandscapeUSA 13126 NE Airport Way Portland OR 97230 503-255-1981 255-9201
TF: 800-248-1981 ■ Web: www.landscapeusa.com

San Gabriel Nursery & Florist 632 S San Gabriel Blvd San Gabriel CA 91776 626-286-3782 286-0047
Web: www.sgnursery.com

Shanti Bithi Nursery Inc 3047 High Ridge Rd Stamford CT 06903 203-329-0768 329-8872
Web: www.webcom.com/shanti

Siebenthaler Co 3001 Catalpa Dr Dayton OH 45405 937-274-1154 274-9448
Web: www.siebenthaler.com

Sloat Garden Center Inc 420 Coloma St Sausalito CA 94965 415-332-0657 332-1009
Web: www.sloatgardens.com

Smith & Hawken Inc 4 Hamilton Landing Suite 100 Novato CA 94949 415-506-3700 506-3900
Web: www.smith-hawken.com

Star Nursery Inc 125 Cassia Way Henderson NV 89014 702-568-7000 568-7028
TF: 866-584-7827 ■ Web: www.starnursery.com

Stein Garden & Gift Centers Inc 5400 S 27th St. Milwaukee WI 53221 414-761-5400 761-5420
Web: www.steingg.com

Summerwinds Nursery 17826 N Tatum Blvd. Phoenix AZ 85032 602-867-1822
Web: www.summerwindsnursery.com

Target Stores 1000 Nicollet Mall Minneapolis MN 55403 612-304-6073 307-8870
TF: 800-440-0680 ■ Web: www.target.com

TLC Forest & Greenhouse Inc 105 W Memorial Rd. Oklahoma City OK 73114 405-751-0630 751-1300
TF: 800-366-4852 ■ Web: www.tlcgarden.com

Treelands Inc 1000 Huntington Tpke Bridgeport CT 06610 203-372-3511 371-6023

Twombly Nursery 163 Barn Hill Rd Monroe CT 06468 203-261-2133 261-9230
Web: www.twomblynursery.com

Van Bourgondien & Sons Inc 245 Rt 109 Babylon NY 11702 631-669-3500 669-1228
TF: 800-622-9997 ■ Web: www.dutchbulbs.com

Village Nurseries 1589 N Main St Orange CA 92867 714-279-3100 279-3199
TF: 800-542-0209 ■ Web: www.villagenurseries.com

Wal-Mart Stores Inc 702 SW 8th St. Bentonville AR 72716 479-273-4000 273-4053*
NYSE: WMT ■ *Fax: PR ■ TF Cust Svc: 800-925-6278 ■ Web: www.walmartstores.com

Waterloo Gardens Inc 200 N Whitford Rd Exton PA 19341 610-363-0800 363-6416
Web: www.waterloogardens.com

White Flower Farm Inc 30 Irene St Torrington CT 06790 860-496-9624 496-1418
TF Cust Svc: 800-411-6159 ■ Web: www.whiteflowerfarm.com

Zamzows Inc 1201 N Franklin Blvd Nampa ID 83687 208-465-3630 465-3468
Web: www.zamzows.com

327 GAS STATIONS

SEE ALSO Convenience Stores p. 1559

Phone Fax

AMBEST Inc 5250 Virginia Way Suite 250 Brentwood TN 37027 615-371-5187 371-5186
TF: 800-910-7220 ■ Web: www.am-best.com

AT Williams Oil Co 5446 University Pkwy Winston-Salem NC 27105 336-767-6280 767-6283
TF: 800-642-0945 ■ Web: www.wilcousa.com

BP Plc 28100 Torch Pkwy. Warrenville IL 60555 630-420-5111 298-0738*
NYSE: BP ■ *Fax Area Code: 281 ■ TF: 866-427-6947 ■ Web: www.bp.com

Burns Brothers Inc 4800 SW Meadows Rd Suite 475 Lake Oswego OR 97035 503-697-0666 697-0541

Busler Enterprises Inc 2601 St Joseph Ave. Evansville IN 47720 812-424-7511 429-0669
TF Whse: 800-457-3232

Canadian Tire Corp Ltd PO Box 770 Stn K Toronto ON M4P2V8 416-480-3000 544-7715
TSX: CTR ■ TF: 800-387-8803 ■ Web: www2.canadiantire.ca

Chevron Corp 6001 Bollinger Canyon Rd San Ramon CA 94583 925-842-1000 420-0335*
NYSE: CVX ■ *Fax Area Code: 866 ■ TF Cust Svc: 800-243-8766 ■
Web: www.chevron.com

CITGO Petroleum Corp 1293 Eldridge Pkwy Houston TX 77077 832-486-4000
Web: www.spsecurities.com

Colonial Group Inc 101 N Lathrop Ave. Savannah GA 31415 912-236-1331 235-2938

Commercial Truck Terminal Inc 35647 Hwy 27 Haines City FL 33844 863-422-1148 422-6060
Web: www.commercialtrktrm.com

Cone Oil Co Inc 6185 Cockrill Bend Cir Nashville TN 37209 615-350-6141 350-6137

Crystal Flash Petroleum Corp 5221 Ivy Tech Dr Indianapolis IN 46268 317-879-2849 879-2855
TF: 800-886-3835 ■ Web: www.crystal-flash.com

Detroiter Travel Center 21055 West Rd. Woodhaven MI 48183 734-675-0222 692-4015
Web: www.detroiter.net

Dixie Oil Co Inc PO Box 1007 Tifton GA 31793 229-382-2700 387-6905

Dunlap Oil Co Inc 759 S Haskell Ave Willcox AZ 85643 520-384-2240 384-5159

Englefield Oil Co 447 James Pkwy. Heath OH 43056 740-928-8215 928-3844
TF: 800-282-1675 ■ Web: www.englefieldoil.com

Erickson Oil Products Inc 1231 Industrial St. Hudson WI 54016 715-386-8241 386-2022
TF: 800-521-0104 ■ Web: www.freedomvalu.com

Company	City	State	Zip	Phone	Fax
Exxon Mobil Corp 5959 Las Colinas Blvd *NYSE: XOM* ■ *TF:* 800-252-1800 ■ *Web:* www.exxon.mobil.com/corporate/	Irving	TX	75039	972-444-1000	444-1198
Fisca Oil Co 4830 Rainbow Blvd	Shawnee Mission	KS	66205	913-236-7000	236-7128
FL Roberts & Co Inc PO Box 1964 *TF:* 800-628-4004 ■ *Web:* www.flroberts.com	Springfield	MA	01102	413-781-7444	781-4328
Flying J Inc 1104 Country Hill Dr *TF:* 800-842-6428 ■ *Web:* www.flyingj.com	Ogden	UT	84403	801-624-1000	395-8005
Forward Corp 219 N Front St *TF:* 800-664-4501 ■ *Web:* www.forwardcorp.com	Standish	MI	48658	989-846-4501	846-4412
Fowler MM Inc 4220 Neal Rd *TF:* 800-313-6635	Durham	NC	27705	919-309-2925	309-9924
Freedom Oil Co 814 W Chestnut St *TF:* 800-397-6147 ■ *Web:* www.freedomoil.com	Bloomington	IL	61701	309-828-7750	829-3813
Gaseteria Oil Corp 364 Maspeth Ave	Brooklyn	NY	11211	718-782-4200	782-5175
Gate Petroleum Co 9540 San Jose Blvd *Web:* www.gatepetro.com	Jacksonville	FL	32257	904-737-7220	732-7660
Getty Realty Corp 125 Jericho Tpke Suite 103 *NYSE: GTY* ■ *TF:* 866-399-4335 ■ *Web:* www.gettyrealty.com	Jericho	NY	11753	516-478-5400	478-5490
Gibbs Oil Co LP 90 Everett Ave PO Box 9151 *TF:* 800-352-3558 ■ *Web:* www.gibbsoil.com	Chelsea	MA	02150	617-889-9000	884-6075
Griffin Rip Truck Travel Center Inc PO Box 10128 *TF:* 800-333-9330 ■ *Web:* www.ripgriffin.com	Lubbock	TX	79408	806-795-8785	795-6574
Harper Oil Co 2319 W Jefferson	Springfield	IL	62702	217-698-4088	698-7088
Hawkeye Oil Co Inc PO Box 1506	Cedar Rapids	IA	52406	319-364-7146	364-7148
Herdrich Petroleum 210 E US 52	Rushville	IN	46173	765-932-3224	932-4622
Imperial Oil Resources Ltd 237 4th Ave SW PO Box 2480 Stn M	Calgary	AB	T2P3M9	403-237-3737	237-2072
Iowa 80 Group Inc PO Box 630 *TF:* 800-336-9889 ■ *Web:* www.iowa80group.com	Walcott	IA	52773	563-284-6965	284-6475
J & H Oil Co PO Box 9464 *TF:* 800-442-9110 ■ *Web:* www.jhoil.com	Wyoming	MI	49509	616-534-2181	534-1663
Jubitz Corp 33 NE Middlefield Rd *TF:* 800-399-5480 ■ *Web:* www.jubitz.com	Portland	OR	97211	503-283-1111	240-5834
Kent Oil Inc PO Box 908001 *TF:* 800-375-5368 ■ *Web:* www.kentoil.com	Midland	TX	79708	432-699-5822	697-8911
Keystops LLC PO Box 2809 *TF:* 800-346-6456	Franklin	KY	42135	270-586-8283	586-3112
Lassus Brothers Oil Inc 1800 Magnavox Way *TF:* 800-686-2836 ■ *Web:* www.lassus.com	Fort Wayne	IN	46804	260-436-1415	436-0340
MAPCO Express Inc 7102 Commerce Way *Web:* www.mapcoexpress.com	Brentwood	TN	37027	615-771-6701	771-8098
Midstream Fuel Service LLC 3 Riverway Suite 400 *TF:* 800-368-5990	Houston	TX	77056	713-350-6800	350-6801
MM Fowler Inc 4220 Neal Rd *TF:* 800-313-6635	Durham	NC	27705	919-309-2925	309-9924
NELLA Oil Co 2360 Lindbergh St *TF:* 800-995-0401 ■ *Web:* www.nellaoil.com	Auburn	CA	95602	530-885-0401	885-5851
O'Connell Oil Assoc Inc PO Box 1387 *TF:* 800-464-4894 ■ *Web:* www.baygo.com/oconnell	Pittsfield	MA	01202	413-499-4800	499-6072
Petro Stopping Centers 6080 Surety Dr *TF:* 800-331-8809 ■ *Web:* www.petrotruckstops.com	El Paso	TX	79905	915-779-4711	774-7373
Pilot Travel Centers LLC PO Box 10146 **Fax:* Cust Svc ■ *TF:* 800-562-6210 ■ *Web:* www.pilotcorp.com	Knoxville	TN	37939	865-588-7487	450-2800*
Platolene 500 Inc PO Box 3088	Terre Haute	IN	47803	812-877-1556	877-2510
Premium Oil Co 2005 S 300 West	Salt Lake City	UT	84115	801-487-4721	
RaceTrac Petroleum Inc 3225 Cumberland Blvd Suite 100 *TF:* 888-636-5589 ■ *Web:* www.racetrac.com	Atlanta	GA	30339	770-431-7600	563-8129
Rip Griffin Truck Travel Center Inc PO Box 10128 *TF:* 800-333-9330 ■ *Web:* www.ripgriffin.com	Lubbock	TX	79408	806-795-8785	795-6574
Roberts FL & Co Inc PO Box 1964 *TF:* 800-628-4004 ■ *Web:* www.flroberts.com	Springfield	MA	01102	413-781-7444	781-4328
Russell Petroleum Corp 3378 Tankview Ct	Montgomery	AL	36108	334-834-3750	834-3755
Sapp Brothers Truck Stops Inc 9915 S 148th St *Web:* www.sappbrostruckstops.com	Omaha	NE	68138	402-895-7038	895-1957
Schmitt Sales Inc 2101 St Rita's Ln *TF:* 800-873-8080 ■ *Web:* www.schmittsales.com	Buffalo	NY	14221	716-639-1500	639-1511
Service Oil Inc 1718 E Main Ave *TF:* 800-726-0133 ■ *Web:* www.stamart.com	West Fargo	ND	58078	701-277-1050	277-1723
Shell Oil Co 910 Louisanna St *TF:* 888-467-4355 ■ *Web:* www.shellus.com	Houston	TX	77002	713-241-6161	241-4044
Sinclair Oil Corp 550 E South Temple *TF:* 800-552-8695 ■ *Web:* www.sinclairoil.com	Salt Lake City	UT	84102	801-524-2700	524-2720
Speedway SuperAmerica LLC 500 Speedway Dr *TF Cust Svc:* 800-643-1948 ■ *Web:* www.speedway.com	Enon	OH	45323	937-864-3000	
Spencer Cos Inc 120 Woodson St NW *TF:* 800-633-2910 ■ *Web:* www.spencercos.com	Huntsville	AL	35801	256-533-1150	535-2910
Swifty Gas PO Box 1002 *TF:* 800-742-8497	Seymour	IN	47274	812-522-1640	522-8554
Swifty Oil Co Inc DBA Swifty Gas PO Box 1002 *TF:* 800-742-8497	Seymour	IN	47274	812-522-1640	522-8554
Thornton Oil Corp DBA Thorntons Inc 10101 Linn Station Rd Suite 200 *TF:* 800-928-8022 ■ *Web:* www.thorntonsinc.com	Louisville	KY	40223	502-425-8022	327-9026
Thorntons Inc 10101 Linn Station Rd Suite 200 *TF:* 800-928-8022 ■ *Web:* www.thorntonsinc.com	Louisville	KY	40223	502-425-8022	327-9026
TravelCenters of America 24601 Center Ridge Rd Suite 200 **Fax:* Mktg ■ *TF:* 800-872-7024 ■ *Web:* www.tatravelcenters.com	Westlake	OH	44145	440-808-9100	808-3209*
Tri Star Marketing Inc 2211 W Bradley Ave *Web:* www.superpantry.com	Champaign	IL	61821	217-367-8386	367-3920
Triple A Oil 12342 Inwood Rd *TF:* 800-657-9595	Dallas	TX	75244	972-503-3333	503-0007
Tucson Truck Terminal Inc 5451 E Benson Hwy	Tucson	AZ	85706	520-574-0050	574-9606
Ultramar Ltd 2200 ave McGill College *TF Cust Svc:* 800-363-6949 ■ *Web:* www.ultramar.ca	Montreal	QC	H3A3L3	514-499-6111	499-6320
Urbieta Enterprises Inc 9701 NW 89th Ave *Web:* www.urbietaoil.com	Medley	FL	33178	305-884-0008	883-1927
USA Petroleum Corp 905 Rancho Conejo Blvd	Newbury Park	CA	91320	805-214-9200	214-0919
W & H Co-op Oil Co 407 13th St N *TF:* 800-392-3816	Humboldt	IA	50548	515-332-2782	332-1559
Wallace Enterprises Inc 5370 Oakdale Rd	Smyrna	GA	30082	404-799-9400	799-0322
Wesco Inc 1460 Whitehall Rd *TF:* 800-968-0200 ■ *Web:* www.gowesco.com	Muskegon	MI	49445	231-719-4300	719-4301
Williams AT Oil Co 5446 University Pkwy *TF:* 800-642-0945 ■ *Web:* www.wilcousa.com	Winston-Salem	NC	27105	336-767-6280	767-6283

328 GAS TRANSMISSION - NATURAL GAS

Companies that transmit or store natural gas but do not distribute it.

Company	City	State	Zip	Phone	Fax
ANR Pipeline Co PO Box 2511 *Web:* www.anrpl.com	Houston	TX	77011	800-827-5267	
ANR Storage Inc 27725 Stansbury Blvd Suite 200 *TF:* 800-998-3847	Farmington Hills	MI	48334	248-994-4100	994-4301
Atlas Pipeline Partners LP 3500 Massillon Rd Suite 100 *NYSE: APL* ■ *Web:* www.resourceamerica.com/atlaspp.html	Uniontown	OH	44685	330-896-8510	896-8518
Belden & Blake Corp 5200 Stoneham Rd *TF:* 800-837-4344	North Canton	OH	44720	330-497-5471	497-5463
Boardwalk Pipeline Partners LP 3800 Frederica St *NYSE: BWP* ■ *TF:* 877-686-3620	Owensboro	KY	42301	270-926-8686	688-5872
British Gas Services Inc 5444 Westheimer Rd Suite 1775	Houston	TX	77056	713-622-7100	622-7244
Cheniere Energy Inc 717 Texas Ave Suite 3100 *AMEX: LNG* ■ *TF:* 888-948-2036 ■ *Web:* www.cheniere.com	Houston	TX	77002	713-659-1361	659-5459
CMS Gas Transmission & Storage Co 1 Energy Plaza *Web:* www.cmsenergy.com	Jackson	MI	49201	517-788-0550	
CMS Panhandle Eastern Pipe Line Co 5444 Westheimer Rd *TF:* 800-275-7375 ■ *Web:* www.panhandleenergy.com	Houston	TX	77056	713-627-4272	989-1178
CMS Trunkline Gas Co 5444 Westheimer Rd *TF:* 800-275-7375 ■ *Web:* www.panhandleenergy.com	Houston	TX	77056	713-627-4272	989-1178
CNX Gas Corp 4000 Brownsville Rd *NYSE: CXG* ■ *Web:* www.cnxgas.com	South Park	PA	15129	412-854-6719	
Colorado Interstate Gas Co PO Box 1087 *Web:* www.cigco.com	Colorado Springs	CO	80944	719-473-2300	520-4318
Columbia Gas Transmission Corp 1700 MacCorkle Ave SE *TF:* 800-832-3242 ■ *Web:* www.columbiagastrans.com/tco.html	Charleston	WV	25314	304-357-2000	357-2424
Columbia Gulf Transmission Co 2603 Augusta Dr Suite 300 *TF:* 888-880-4853 ■ *Web:* www.columbiagastrans.com/cgt.html	Houston	TX	77057	713-267-4100	267-4110
ConocoPhillips Alaska Inc PO Box 100360 *TF:* 800-622-5501 ■ *Web:* www.conocophillipsalaska.com	Anchorage	AK	99510	907-276-1215	263-4731
Copano Energy LLC 2727 Allen Pkwy Suite 1200 *NASDAQ: CPNO* ■ *TF:* 800-621-9556 ■ *Web:* www.copanoenergy.com	Houston	TX	77019	713-621-9547	
Crossroads Pipeline Co 12801 Fair Lakes Pkwy *TF:* 888-499-3450 ■ *Web:* www.crossroadspipeline.com	Fairfax	VA	22033	703-227-3200	227-3378
Crosstex Energy LP 2501 Cedar Springs Rd Suite 600 *NASDAQ: XTEX* ■ *Web:* www.crosstexenergy.com	Dallas	TX	75201	214-953-9500	953-9501
DCP Midstream Partners LP 370 17th St Suite 2775 *NYSE: DPM*	Denver	CO	80202	303-633-2900	605-2225
Dominion Transmission PO Box 2450 **Fax:* Mktg ■ *TF:* 800-624-3101	Clarksburg	WV	26302	304-623-8000	627-3321*
Duke Energy Algonquin Gas 1284 Soldiers Field Rd	Brighton	MA	02135	617-254-4050	
Duke Energy Gas Transmission 5400 Westheimer Ct	Houston	TX	77056	713-627-5400	627-4145
Duke Energy Trading & Marketing 5400 Westheimer Ct *TF:* 800-873-3853 ■ *Web:* www.duke-energy.com	Houston	TX	77056	713-260-1800	627-4145
El Paso Corp 1001 Louisiana St *NYSE: EP* ■ *TF:* 800-351-0004 ■ *Web:* www.elpaso.com	Houston	TX	77002	713-420-2600	420-4417
El Paso Natural Gas Co PO Box 1087 **Fax:* Mktg ■ *Web:* www.epenergy.com	Colorado Springs	CO	80944	719-473-2300	520-4878*
Enbridge Midcoast Energy Inc 1100 Louisiana St Suite 3300 *TF:* 888-650-8900	Houston	TX	77002	713-650-8900	650-3232
Enogex Inc 515 Central Park Dr Suite 600 *TF:* 800-736-8492 ■ *Web:* www.oge.com/enogex	Oklahoma City	OK	73105	405-525-7788	557-7904
Enterprise GP Holdings LP 2727 N Loop W Suite 101 *NYSE: EPE* ■ *Web:* www.enterprisegp.com	Houston	TX	77008	713-426-4500	
Enterprise Products Partners LP 2727 N Loop West PO Box 4324 *NYSE: EPD* ■ *Web:* www.eprod.com	Houston	TX	77210	713-880-6500	880-6573
Equitrans LP 200 Allegheny Center Mall *TF:* 800-654-6335 ■ *Web:* www.eqt.com/equitrans	Pittsburgh	PA	15212	412-231-4888	395-3290
Fort Chicago Energy Partners LP 222 3rd Ave SW Suite 440 *Web:* www.fortchicago.com	Calgary	AB	T2P0B4	403-296-0140	213-3648
Granite State Gas Transmission Co 325 West Rd	Portsmouth	NH	03801	603-436-0310	427-6839
Great Lakes Gas Transmission Co 5250 Corporate Dr *Web:* www.greatlakesgas.com	Troy	MI	48098	248-205-7400	205-7571
Gulf South Pipeline Co LP 20 E Greenway Plaza Suite 900 *TF:* 866-820-6000 ■ *Web:* www.gulfsouthpl.com	Houston	TX	77046	713-544-6000	
GulfTerra Energy Partners LP 1001 Louisiana St **Fax:* Hum Res ■ *TF:* 800-594-2018 ■ *Web:* www.gulfterra.com	Houston	TX	77002	713-420-2131	420-6969*
Hiland Partners LP 205 W Maple Ave Suite 1100 *NASDAQ: HLND* ■ *Web:* www.hilandpartners.com	Enid	OK	73701	580-242-6040	548-5188
Iroquois Gas Transmission System LP 1 Corporate Dr Suite 600 *Web:* www.iroquois.com	Shelton	CT	06484	203-925-7200	929-9501
Kentucky West Virginia Gas Co LLC 748 N Lake Dr *TF:* 800-654-9754	Prestonsburg	KY	41653	606-886-2311	886-7246
Kern River Gas Transmission Co 2755 E Cottonwood Pkwy Suite 300 *TF:* 800-420-7500	Salt Lake City	UT	84158	801-937-6000	
Kinder Morgan Energy Partners LP 500 Dallas St Suite 1000 *NYSE: KMP* ■ **Fax:* Hum Res ■ *TF:* 888-844-5657 ■ *Web:* www.kindermorgan.com	Houston	TX	77002	713-369-9000	369-9411*
Kinder Morgan Management LLC 500 Dallas St 1 Allen Ctr Suite 1000 *NYSE: KMR* ■ *TF:* 800-324-2900 ■ *Web:* www.kindermorgan.com	Houston	TX	77002	713-369-9000	369-9100
Kinder Morgan Texas Pipeline LP 500 Dallas St Suite 1000 *TF:* 800-324-2900 ■ *Web:* www.kindermorgan.com	Houston	TX	77002	713-369-9000	369-9100
Louisiana Intrastate Gas Corp LLC 1201 Louisiana	Houston	TX	77002	832-668-1000	668-1122
Mid Louisiana Gas Co 1100 Louisiana St Suite 2950 *TF:* 888-650-8900	Houston	TX	77002	713-650-8900	650-3232
Mississippi River Transmission Inc 1600 S Brentwood Blvd Suite 590 *TF Cust Svc:* 800-325-4005	Saint Louis	MO	63144	314-991-9900	991-2317
Mojave Pipeline Operating Co 5401 E Brundage Ln	Bakersfield	CA	93307	661-363-4000	363-4050
Natural Gas Pipeline Co of America 747 E 22nd St	Lombard	IL	60148	630-691-3000	691-3829
Natural Gas Transmission Services (NGTS) 8150 N Central Expy Suite 801	Dallas	TX	75206	214-365-0600	365-9670
Northern Border Partners LP 13710 FNB Pkwy *NYSE: NBP* ■ *Web:* www.northernborderpartners.com	Omaha	NE	68154	402-492-7300	398-7214
Northern Border Pipeline Co 13710 FND Pkwy *Web:* www.nbpl.nborder.com	Omaha	NE	68154	402-492-7300	492-7481
Northern Natural Gas Co 1111 S 103rd St	Omaha	NE	68124	402-398-7200	398-7214
Northern Plains Natural Gas Co 13710 FND Pkwy	Omaha	NE	68154	402-492-7300	492-7481
Paiute Pipeline Co PO Box 94197 *Web:* www.paiutepipeline.com	Las Vegas	NV	89193	702-876-7178	873-3820
Penn Octane Corp 77-530 Enfield Ln Bldg D *NASDAQ: POCC* ■ *TF:* 877-419-6265 ■ *Web:* www.pennoctane.com	Palm Desert	CA	92211	760-772-9080	772-8588
PG & E Gas Transmission-Northwest 1400 SW 5th Ave Suite 900	Portland	OR	97201	503-833-4000	833-4906
PG Energy Co 1 PEI Ctr *TF Cust Svc:* 800-432-8017 ■ *Web:* www.pgenergy.com	Wilkes-Barre	PA	18711	570-829-8600	829-8743
PRB Gas Transportation Inc 1401 17th St Suite 650 *AMEX: PRB* ■ *Web:* www.prbtrans.com	Denver	CO	80202	303-308-1330	308-1590
Questar Gas Management Co PO Box 45601 *TF:* 800-323-5517	Salt Lake City	UT	84145	801-324-2400	324-3880
Questar Pipeline Co PO Box 45360 **Fax:* Cust Svc ■ *Web:* www.questarpipeline.com	Salt Lake City	UT	84145	801-324-2400	324-2684*
Regency Energy Partners LP 1700 Pacific Suite 2900 *NASDAQ: RGNC* ■ *Web:* www.regencyenergy.com	Dallas	TX	75201	214-750-1771	750-1749
Rio Vista Energy Partners LP 820 Gessner Rd Suite 1285 *NASDAQ: RVEP*	Houston	TX	77024	713-467-8235	467-8258
SemGroup LP 6120 S Yale Ave Suite 700 *Web:* www.semgrouplp.com	Tulsa	OK	74136	918-388-8100	388-8290

Phone | Fax

South Carolina Pipeline Corp PO Box 102407 . . . Columbia SC 29224 803-699-3111 217-2104

Southern Natural Gas Co PO Box 2563 . . . Birmingham AL 35202 205-325-7410 325-7578
Web: www.epenergy.com

Tengasco Inc 10215 Technology Dr Suite 301 . . . Knoxville TN 37902 865-675-1554 675-1621
AMEX: TGC ■ *Web:* www.tengasco.com

Tennessee Gas Pipeline Co 1001 Louisiana St . . . Houston TX 77002 713-420-2131 420-6969*
**Fax:* Hum Res ■ *Web:* www.epenergy.com

TEPPCO Partners LP 2929 Allen Pkwy . . . Houston TX 77019 713-759-3636 759-3783
NYSE: TPP ■ *TF:* 800-877-3636 ■ *Web:* www.teppco.com

Texas Eastern Transmission Corp 4227 Decker Dr . . . Baytown TX 77020 713-759-3636 627-4145

Trailblazer Pipeline Co PO Box 27 . . . Heartwell NE 68945 308-563-3221 563-2270

TransCanada Energy USA Inc 4211 S 143rd Cir . . . Omaha NE 68137 402-505-8800 505-4500

TransCanada Pipelines Ltd 450 1st St SW . . . Calgary AB T2P5H1 403-920-2000 920-2200
NYSE: TRP ■ *TF:* 800-661-3805 ■ *Web:* www.transcanada.com

Transwestern Pipeline Co 5444 Westheimer Rd . . . Houston TX 77056 713-989-7000 646-2551
Web: www.tw.enron.com

TXU Lone Star Pipeline 301 S Harwood St . . . Dallas TX 75201 214-875-4887 875-5134
Web: www.txu.com/us/ourbus/pipeline

Viking Gas Transmission Co 3140 Neil Armstrong Blvd Suite 208 . . . Eagan MN 55121 651-994-0332 994-0334
Web: www.viking-gas.com

WBI Holdings Inc PO Box 5601 . . . Bismarck ND 58506 701-530-1500 530-1599
TF: 800-238-8350 ■ *Web:* www.wbip.com

Williams Gas Pipeline 2800 Post Oak Blvd . . . Houston TX 77056 713-215-2000 215-4620*
**Fax:* Cust Svc

Williams Gas Pipelines Transco PO Box 1396 . . . Houston TX 77251 713-215-2000 215-4608*
**Fax:* Cust Svc ■ *TF:* 888-215-8475

Williams Gas Pipelines West PO Box 58900 . . . Salt Lake City UT 84158 801-583-8800 584-6483

Williams Partners LP 1 Williams Ctr . . . Tulsa OK 74172 918-573-2000 573-8805
NYSE: WPZ ■ *TF:* 800-945-5426 ■ *Web:* www.williamslp.com

Williston Basin Interstate Pipeline Co 1250 W Century Ave . . . Bismarck ND 58503 701-530-1600 530-1699
TF: 800-238-8350 ■ *Web:* www.wbip.com

329 GASKETS, PACKING, SEALING DEVICES

SEE ALSO Automotive Parts & Supplies - Mfr p. 1360

Phone | Fax

Accratronics Seals Corp 2211 Kenmere Ave . . . Burbank CA 91504 818-843-1500 841-2117
Web: www.accratronics.com

Accro Gasket Inc 17365 Daimler St . . . Irvine CA 92614 949-261-5846 261-5840
Web: www.accrogasket.com

Akron Gasket & Packing Enterprises Inc 1244 Home Ave . . . Akron OH 44310 330-633-3742 888-2088*
**Fax Area Code:* 800 ■ *TF:* 800-289-7318 ■ *Web:* www.akrongasket.com

American Casting & Mfg Corp 51 Commercial St . . . Plainview NY 11803 516-349-7010 349-8389
TF: 800-342-0333 ■ *Web:* www.americancasting.com

American Gasket & Rubber Co 119 E Commerce Dr . . . Schaumburg IL 60173 847-882-8333 882-9333

American Packing & Gasket Co 6039 Armour Dr . . . Houston TX 77020 713-675-5271 675-2730
TF: 800-888-5223 ■ *Web:* www.apandg.com

APM Hexseal Corp 44 Honeck St . . . Englewood NJ 07631 201-569-5700 569-4106
Web: www.apmhexseal.com

Apple Rubber Products Inc 310 Erie St . . . Lancaster NY 14086 716-684-6560 684-8302
TF Cust Svc: 800-828-7745 ■ *Web:* www.applerubber.com

Artus Corp 201 S Dean St . . . Englewood NJ 07631 201-568-1000 568-8865
Web: www.artuscorp.com

Atlantic Gasket Corp 3908 Frankford Ave . . . Philadelphia PA 19124 215-533-6400 533-4130
TF: 800-229-8881 ■ *Web:* www.atlanticgasket.com

Auburn Mfg Co 29 Stack St . . . Middletown CT 06457 860-346-6677 346-1334
TF: 800-427-5387 ■ *Web:* www.auburn-mfg.com

Avica Inc 1785 Voyager Ave . . . Simi Valley CA 93063 805-584-4150 584-4155
Web: www.avicausa.com

AW Chesterton Co 225 Fallon Rd . . . Stoneham MA 02180 781-438-7000 481-2500
Web: www.chesterton.com

Bal Seal Engineering Co Inc 19650 Pauling . . . Foothill Ranch CA 92610 949-460-2100 460-2300
TF: 800-366-1006 ■ *Web:* www.balseal.com

Bar's Products 720 W Rose St . . . Holly MI 48442 248-634-8278 634-1505
TF: 800-521-7475 ■ *Web:* www.barsproducts.com

Beaverite Corp 9394 Bridge St128 Main St . . . Beaver Falls NY 13305 315-346-6011 346-1575
TF Cust Svc: 800-424-6337 ■ *Web:* www.beaverite.com

Bentley Mfg Co Inc 15123 Colorado Ave . . . Paramount CA 90723 562-634-4051 634-4309
TF: 800-424-2425 ■ *Web:* www.gasketsonline.com

Brooks EJ Co 8 Microlab Rd . . . Livingston NJ 07039 973-597-2900 597-2919
TF: 800-458-7325 ■ *Web:* www.ejbrooks.com

Burly Seal Products Co 1865 W 'D' Ave . . . Tooele UT 84074 800-877-7325 877-6979
TF: 800-877-7325 ■ *Web:* www.burlyseal.com

California Gasket & Rubber Corp 1601 W 134th St . . . Gardena CA 90249 310-323-4250 329-9721
TF: 800-635-7084 ■ *Web:* www.calgasket.com

Calpico Inc 1387 San Mateo Ave . . . South San Francisco CA 94080 650-588-2241 872-7325*
**Fax Area Code:* 800 ■ *TF:* 800-998-9115 ■ *Web:* www.calpicoinc.com

Carbon Technology Inc 659 S County Trail . . . Exeter RI 02822 401-295-8877 295-7035
TF: 800-222-7266

CE Conover & Co Inc 4106 Blanche Rd . . . Bensalem PA 19020 215-639-6666 639-1799
TF: 800-266-6837

Centurion Products PerkinElmer Fluid Sciences Inc
15 Pioneer Ave . . . Warwick RI 02888 401-781-4700 781-0930
Web: www.perkinelmer.com

CGR Products Inc 4655 US 29 N . . . Greensboro NC 27405 336-621-4568 375-5324
Web: www.cgrproducts.com

Chambers Gasket & Mfg Co 4701 W Rice St . . . Chicago IL 60651 773-626-8800 626-1430
Web: www.chambersgasket.com

Chesterton AW Co Inc 225 Fallon Rd . . . Stoneham MA 02180 781-438-7000 481-2500
Web: www.chesterton.com

Chicago-Allis Mfg Corp 113 N Green St . . . Chicago IL 60607 312-666-5050 666-4930
Web: www.chicagoallis.com

Chicago Gasket Co 1285 W North Ave . . . Chicago IL 60622 773-486-3060 486-3784
TF: 800-833-5666 ■ *Web:* www.chicagogasket.com

Chicago Rawhide Industries 900 N State St . . . Elgin IL 60123 847-742-7840 742-7845
TF Cust Svc: 800-882-0008 ■ *Web:* www2.chicago-rawhide.com

Chicago-Wilcox Mfg Co 16928 State St . . . South Holland IL 60473 708-339-5000 339-9876
TF: 800-323-5282 ■ *Web:* www.chicagowilcox.com

Cincinnati Gasket Packing & Mfg Inc 40 Illinois Ave . . . Cincinnati OH 45215 513-761-3458 761-2994
Web: www.cincinnatigasket.com

Conover CE & Co Inc 4106 Blanche Rd . . . Bensalem PA 19020 215-639-6666 639-1799
TF: 800-266-6837

Cooper Mfg Co 410 S 1st Ave . . . Marshalltown IA 50158 641-752-6736 752-7476

Crane John Canada 423 Green Rd N . . . Stoney Creek ON L8E3A1 905-662-6191 662-1564
TF: 800-263-6860 ■ *Web:* www.johncrane.com

Crane John Inc 6400 W Oakton St . . . Morton Grove IL 60053 847-967-2400 967-3513
TF: 800-732-5464 ■ *Web:* www.johncrane.com

DAR Industrial Products Inc 128 Front St . . . West Conshohocken PA 19428 610-825-4900 825-4901
Web: www.darindustrial.com

Delta Rubber Co 39 Wauregan Rd PO Box 300 . . . Danielson CT 06239 860-779-0300 774-0402
Web: www.nnbr.com

Phone | Fax

Eagle Burgmann Industries LP 10035 Brookriver Dr . . . Houston TX 77040 713-939-9515 939-9091
TF: 800-303-7735 ■ *Web:* www.burgmann-bsa.com

EJ Brooks Co 8 Microlab Rd . . . Livingston NJ 07039 973-597-2900 597-2919
TF: 800-458-7325 ■ *Web:* www.ejbrooks.com

EnPro Industries Inc 5605 Carnegie Blvd Suite 500 . . . Charlotte NC 28209 704-731-1500 731-1511
NYSE: NPO ■ *TF:* 866-663-6776 ■ *Web:* www.enproindustries.com

Excelsior Inc 720 Chestnut St . . . Rockford IL 61105 815-987-2900 962-5466
TF: 800-435-4671 ■ *Web:* www.excelsiorinc.com

Flow Dry Technology Ltd 379 Albert Rd . . . Brookville OH 45309 937-833-2161 833-3208
TF: 800-533-0077 ■ *Web:* www.stanhope.com

Flowserve Corp 5215 N O'Connor Blvd Suite 2300 . . . Irving TX 75039 972-443-6500 443-6800
NYSE: FLS ■ *Web:* www.flowserve.com

Forest City Technologies Inc 299 Clay St . . . Wellington OH 44090 440-647-2115 647-2644
Web: www.forestcitytech.com

France Compressor Products 4410 Greenbriar Dr . . . Stafford TX 77477 281-207-4600 207-4611
TF: 800-675-6646 ■ *Web:* www.francecomp.com

Freudenberg-NOK General Partnership 47690 E Anchor Ct . . . Plymouth MI 48170 734-451-0020 451-0125
TF: 800-533-5656 ■ *Web:* www.freudenberg-nok.com

Garlock Sealing Technologies 1666 Division St . . . Palmyra NY 14522 315-597-4811 597-3290*
**Fax:* Cust Svc ■ *TF:* 800-448-6688 ■ *Web:* www.garlock.net

Gasket Engineering Co Inc
4500 E 75th Terr PO Box 320288 . . . Kansas City MO 64132 816-363-8333 363-3558
Web: www.gasketeng.com

Gasket Mfg Co 18001 S Main St . . . Gardena CA 90248 310-217-5600 217-5608
TF: 800-442-7538 ■ *Web:* www.gasketmfg.com

Gaskets Inc 301 W Hwy 16 PO Box 398 . . . Rio WI 53960 920-992-3137 992-3124
TF: 800-558-1833 ■ *Web:* www.gasketsinc.com

Greene Tweed & Co 2075 Detwiler Rd . . . Kulpsville PA 19443 215-256-9521 256-0189
Web: www.gtweed.com

Gunite Supply & Equipment Co 1726 S Magnolia Ave . . . Monrovia CA 91016 626-359-9361 359-7985
TF: 888-393-8635 ■ *Web:* www.mesa-intl.com/gunitesupply.htm

Hahn Elastomer Corp 14601 Keel St . . . Plymouth MI 48170 734-455-3300 455-0546
Web: www.hahnelastomer.com

Higbee Inc 6741 Thompson Rd N . . . Syracuse NY 13221 315-432-8021 432-0227
TF: 800-255-4800 ■ *Web:* www.higbee-inc.com

Holm Industries Inc 745 S Gardner St . . . Scottsburg IN 47170 812-752-2526 752-3563

Hoosier Gasket Corp 3333 Massachusetts Ave . . . Indianapolis IN 46218 317-545-2000 545-5500
TF: 800-442-7705 ■ *Web:* www.hoosiergasket.com

Hydro Components Research & Development Corp
901 Phoenix Lake Ave . . . Streamwood IL 60107 630-289-1500 289-5434
Web: www.hcrd.com

IGS (Industrial Gasket & Shim Co Inc)
200 Country Club Rd . . . Meadow Lands PA 15347 724-222-5800 222-5898
TF: 800-229-1447 ■ *Web:* www.igscorp.com

Ilene Industries Inc 301 Stanley Blvd . . . Shelbyville TN 37160 931-684-8731 684-8735
TF: 800-251-1602 ■ *Web:* www.ileneindustries.com

Indian Springs Mfg Co Inc
2095 W Genesse Rd PO Box 469 . . . Baldwinsville NY 13027 315-635-6101 635-7473
Web: www.indiansprings.com

Industrial Custom Products Inc 2801 37th Ave NE . . . Minneapolis MN 55421 612-781-2255 781-1144
TF: 800-654-0886 ■ *Web:* www.industrialcustom.com

Industrial Gasket Inc 720 S Sara Rd . . . Mustang OK 73064 405-376-9393 376-3933
TF: 800-654-8433 ■ *Web:* www.igok.com

Industrial Gasket & Shim Co Inc (IGS)
200 Country Club Rd . . . Meadow Lands PA 15347 724-222-5800 222-5898
TF: 800-229-1447 ■ *Web:* www.igscorp.com

Intek Plastic Inc 800 E 10th St . . . Hastings MN 55033 651-437-7700 437-3805
TF Cust Svc: 800-451-4544 ■ *Web:* www.intekplastics.com

Interface Solutions Inc 216 Wohlsen Way . . . Lancaster PA 17603 717-207-6000 207-6080
TF: 800-942-7538 ■ *Web:* www.sealinfo.com

International Seal Co Inc 2041 E Wilshire Ave . . . Santa Ana CA 92705 714-834-0602 834-0590

ITT Conoflow 5154 Hwy 78 PO Box 768 . . . Saint George SC 29477 843-563-9281 563-2131*
**Fax:* Cust Svc ■ *Web:* www.ittconoflow.com

ITW Southland 5700 Ward Ave . . . Virginia Beach VA 23455 757-543-5701 318-9165
TF: 800-804-4744 ■ *Web:* www.itwsouthland.com

JM Clipper Corp 403 Industrial Dr PO Drawer 632340 . . . Nacogdoches TX 75964 936-560-8900 560-8998
TF: 800-233-3900 ■ *Web:* www.jmclipper.com

John Crane Canada Inc 423 Green Rd N . . . Stoney Creek ON L8E3A1 905-662-6191 662-1564
TF: 800-263-6860 ■ *Web:* www.johncrane.com

John Crane Inc 6400 W Oakton St . . . Morton Grove IL 60053 847-967-2400 967-3513
TF: 800-732-5464 ■ *Web:* www.johncrane.com

Kaydon Ring & Seal Inc 1600 Wicomico St . . . Baltimore MD 21230 410-547-7700 576-9059
Web: www.kaydon.com/ringseal/default.htm

Lamons Gasket Co 7300 Airport Blvd . . . Houston TX 77061 713-222-0284 547-9502
TF: 800-231-6906 ■ *Web:* www.lamonsgasket.com

Manufactured Rubber Products Co 4501 Tacony St . . . Philadelphia PA 19124 215-533-3600 533-3912

Marsh Industries Inc 49680 Leona Dr . . . Chesterfield MI 48051 586-949-9300 949-1290
Web: www.marshindustries.com

Melrath Gasket Inc 2901 W Hunting Park Ave . . . Philadelphia PA 19129 215-223-6000 229-6235
TF: 800-635-7284 ■ *Web:* www.melrath.com

Mesa Rubber Co 1726 S Magnolia Ave . . . Monrovia CA 91016 626-359-9361 359-7985
TF: 888-393-8635 ■ *Web:* www.mesa-intl.com

MG Industries Inc 1427 W 16th St . . . Long Beach CA 90813 562-436-9095 436-6844

Mr Gasket Inc 10601 Memphis Ave Bldg 12-A . . . Cleveland OH 44144 216-688-8300 688-8301
Web: www.mrgasket.com

Netherland Rubber Co 2931 Exon Ave . . . Cincinnati OH 45241 513-733-0883 733-1096
TF: 800-582-1877 ■ *Web:* www.netherlandrubber.com

Newco Automotive Inc 101 Ellen Dr . . . Orion Township MI 48359 248-333-2320 239-3900
Web: www.newcoautomotive.com

Nott-Atwater Co 1309 N Bradley Rd . . . Spokane WA 99212 509-922-4522 922-9820
TF: 800-288-7278 ■ *Web:* www.nottatwater.com

Ohio Gasket & Shim Co Inc 976 Evans Ave . . . Akron OH 44305 330-630-2030 630-2075
TF: 800-321-2438 ■ *Web:* www.ohiogasket.com

Omega Shielding Products Inc 1384 Pompton Ave . . . Cedar Grove NJ 07009 973-890-7455 890-9714
TF: 800-828-5784 ■ *Web:* www.omegashielding.com

Pacific States Felt & Mfg Co Inc 23850 Clawiter Rd . . . Hayward CA 94545 510-783-0277 783-4725
TF: 800-566-8866 ■ *Web:* www.pacificstatesfelt.com

Parco Inc 1801 S Archibald Ave . . . Ontario CA 91761 909-947-2200 923-0288
Web: www.parcoinc.com

Parker EPS Redmond Plastics Ops 3967 Buffalo St . . . Marion NY 14505 315-926-4211 926-4498
Web: www.acadiapolymers.com

Parker Hannifin Corp Composite Sealing Systems Div
7664 Panasonic Way . . . San Diego CA 92154 619-661-7000 671-3202
TF: 800-272-7537 ■ *Web:* www.parker.com/sg/parkerseals/css.asp

Parker Hannifin Corp TechSeal Div 3025 W Croft Cir . . . Spartanburg SC 29302 864-573-7332 583-4299
Web: www.parker.com/sg/parkerseals

Pemko Mfg Co Inc 4226 Transport St . . . Ventura CA 93003 805-642-2600 642-4109
TF: 800-283-9988 ■ *Web:* www.pemko.com

Performance Polymer Technologies Co
8801 Washington Blvd Suite 109 . . . Roseville CA 95678 916-677-1414 677-1474
Web: www.pptech.com

PerkinElmer Fluid Sciences Inc Centurion Products
15 Pioneer Ave . . . Warwick RI 02888 401-781-4700 781-0930
Web: www.perkinelmer.com

Plastomer Corp 37819 Schoolcraft Rd . . . Livonia MI 48150 734-464-0700 464-4792
Web: www.plastomer.com

Phone Fax

PPC Mechanical Seals 2769 Mission Dr .... Baton Rouge LA 70805 225-356-4333 355-2126
TF: 800-731-7325 ■ Web: www.ppcmechanicalseals.com

Precision Gasket Co 5625 W 78th St....................... Minneapolis MN 55439 952-942-6711 942-6712
Web: www.precisiongasket.com

Presray Corp 159 Charles Coleman Blvd........................ Pawling NY 12564 845-855-1220 855-1137
Web: www.presray.com

Press-Seal Gasket Corp 2424 W State Blvd.................. Fort Wayne IN 46808 260-436-0521 436-1908
TF: 800-348-7325 ■ Web: www.press-seal.com

Presscut Industries Inc 1540 Selene Dr Suite 100 ....Carrollton TX 75006 972-389-0615 245-2488
TF: 800-442-4924 ■ Web: www.presscut.com

Punch Products Mfg Co 500 S Kolmar Ave........................ Chicago IL 60624 773-533-2800 533-2801

Pureflex Inc 4617 E Paris Ave SE............................Kentwood MI 49512 616-554-1100 554-3633
Web: www.pureflex.com

Redmond Plastics Div JM Clipper Corp 3967 Buffalo St............ Marion NY 14505 315-926-4211 926-4498
Web: www.acadiapolymers.com

Rhopac Fabricators Inc 450 Enterprise Pkwy .... Lake Zurich IL 60047 847-540-7400 540-6690
Web: www.rhopac.com

Rotor Clip Co Inc 187 Davidson Ave.......................... Somerset NJ 08873 732-469-7333 469-7898
TF Cust Svc: 800-631-5857 ■ Web: www.rotorclip.com

Rubbercraft Corp of California 15627 S Broadway .... Gardena CA 90248 310-328-5402 618-1832
TF: 800-782-2379 ■ Web: www.rubbercraft.com

Santa Fe Rubber Products Inc 12306 E Washington Blvd.......... Whittier CA 90606 562-693-2776 693-4936
Web: www.santaferubber.com

Schlegel Systems Inc 1555 Jefferson Rd.......................Rochester NY 14623 585-427-7200 427-7216
TF: 800-828-6237 ■ Web: www.schlegel.com

Seal Methods Inc 11915 Shoemaker Ave................ Santa Fe Springs CA 90670 562-944-0291 946-9439
TF: 800-423-4777 ■ Web: www.sealmethodsinc.com

Sealing Devices Inc 4400 Walden Ave.........................Lancaster NY 14086 716-684-7600 684-0760
TF Cust Svc: 800-727-3257 ■ Web: www.sealingdevices.com

Sealing Equipment Products Co Inc 123 Airpark Industrial Rd..... Alabaster AL 35007 205-403-7500 403-7592
TF Cust Svc: 800-633-4770 ■ Web: www.sepcousa.com

Serra Mfg Corp 3039 E Las Hermanas St.............. Rancho Dominguez CA 90221 310-537-4560 537-1153
Web: www.serramfg.com

Southern California Oil Tool Co 8220 Atlantic Ave PO Box 30.......Cudahy CA 90201 323-560-1794 560-6946

Southern Rubber Co Inc 2209 Patterson St.................. Greensboro NC 27407 336-299-2456 294-4970
Web: www.southernrubber.com

Specification Rubber Products Inc 1568 1st St N .... Alabaster AL 35007 205-663-2521 663-1875
TF: 800-633-3415 ■ Web: www.specrubber.com

Standard Washer & Mat Inc 299 Progress Dr................ Manchester CT 06040 860-643-5125 647-7964
Web: www.standardwasher.com

Standco Industries Inc 2701 Clinton Dr........................Houston TX 77020 713-224-6311 229-9312
TF: 800-231-6018 ■ Web: www.standco.net

Stanley Harrison Corp 3020 Empire Ave........................ Burbank CA 91504 818-842-2131 842-6042
Web: www.stanleyaviation.com

Stein Seal Co Inc 1500 Industrial Blvd........................Kulpsville PA 19443 215-256-0201 256-4818
Web: www.steinseal.com

Stillman Seal 6020 Avenida Encinas...........................Carlsbad CA 92009 760-438-1011 438-7536
Web: www.stillmanseal.com

Stillman Seal Div Hutchinson Seal Corp 6020 Avenida Encinas .....Carlsbad CA 92009 760-438-1011 438-7536
Web: www.stillmanseal.com

Sur-Seal Gasket & Packing Inc 6156 Wesselman Rd ....Cincinnati OH 45248 513-574-8500 574-2220
TF: 800-345-8966 ■ Web: www.sur-seal.com

T & E Industries Inc 215 Watchung Ave..........................Orange NJ 07050 973-672-5454 672-0180
TF Sales: 800-245-7080 ■ Web: www.teindustries.com

TechSeal Div Parker Hannifin Corp 3025 W Croft Cir..........Spartanburg SC 29302 864-573-7332 583-4299
Web: www.parker.com/sg/parkerseals

Trelleborg Sealing Solutions 2531 Bremer Rd................ Fort Wayne IN 46803 260-749-2709
Web: www.trelleborg.com

Trostel Ltd 901 Maxwell St.............................. Lake Geneva WI 53147 262-248-4481 249-8100
Web: www.trostel.com

TRUARC Co LLC 125 Bronico Way.......................... Phillipsburg NJ 08865 800-526-7055 859-6529*
*Fax Area Code: 908 ■ TF: 800-228-4460 ■ Web: www.truarc.com

Tyden Brammall Inc 409 Hoosier Dr........................... Angola IN 46703 260-665-3176 665-8309
TF: 800-348-4777 ■ Web: www.tydenbrammall.com

United Gasket Corp 1633 S 55th Ave............................Cicero IL 60804 708-656-3700 656-6292
Web: www.unitedgasket.com

UTEX Industries Inc 10810 Old Katy Rd........................Houston TX 77043 713-467-1000 467-3609
TF: 800-359-9230 ■ Web: www.utexind.com

Vellumoid Inc 54 Rockdale St............................. Worcester MA 01606 508-853-2500 852-0741
TF: 800-609-5558 ■ Web: www.vellumoid.com

Wolverine Gasket Co 2638 Princess St .... Inkster MI 48141 313-562-6400 562-8248

330 GIFT SHOPS

SEE ALSO Card Shops p. 1407; Duty-Free Shops p. 1594; Home Furnishings Stores p. 1786

Phone Fax

Afromart Gift Enterprises 20 La Rue St......................... Riverside CA 92508 951-686-0078
TF: 877-215-0284 ■ Web: www.afromart.net

Arribas Brothers Inc 1500 Live Oak Ln .... Lake Buena vista FL 32830 407-828-4840 828-8019
TF: 888-828-4840 ■ Web: www.arribasbrothers.com

Ashford.com 14001 NW 4th St...............................Sunrise FL 33325 954-453-2874 835-2236
TF: 888-342-6663 ■ Web: www.ashford.com

Barbeques Galore 10 Orchard Rd Suite 200................. Lake Forest CA 92630 949-597-2400 597-2434
TF: 800-752-3085 ■ Web: www.bbqgalore.com

Berry's Gifts & Collectibles Inc 2571 E Lincoln Hwy ....New Lenox IL 60451 815-485-6724 485-0707

Brookstone Inc 1 Innovation Way........................... Merrimack NH 03054 603-880-9500 577-8003
TF Cust Svc: 866-806-4887 ■ Web: www.brookstone.com

Candleman Corp 15025 Glazier Ave Suite 400 ....Apple Valley MN 55124 800-328-3453 997-6224*
*Fax Area Code: 952 ■ TF: 800-328-3453 ■ Web: www.candleman.com

Christmas Tree Shops 261 White's Path................ South Yarmouth MA 02664 508-394-1206 394-7153
Web: www.christmastreeshops.com

CM Paula Co 6049 Hi-Tek Ct .... Mason OH 45040 513-336-3100 336-3119
TF: 800-543-4464 ■ Web: www.cmpaula.com

Crown House of Gifts 2910 Huron Pkwy .... Ann Arbor MI 48105 734-761-4359 761-1457
TF: 800-521-3088

Disney Consumer Products 500 S Buena Vista St................ Burbank CA 91521 818-560-1000 560-1930*
*Fax: Cust Svc ■ TF PR: 800-723-4763

Disney Store Inc 101 N Brand Blvd Suite 400...................Glendale CA 91203 818-265-3435 543-1604*
*Fax: Hum Res ■ Web: disney.store.go.com

EBSCO Industries Inc Military Service Co Div
PO Box 1943 .... Birmingham AL 35201 205-991-6600 408-4826
TF: 800-255-3722 ■ Web: www.militaryservicecompany.com

Friendly Gift Shop Inc 4 Branmar Plaza..................... Wilmington DE 19810 302-475-6560 475-4605

GiftCertificates.com 11510 Blondo St Suite 103................... Omaha NE 68164 800-522-8207 445-0075*
*Fax Area Code: 402 ■ TF: 800-773-7368 ■ Web: www.giftcertificates.com

GoCollect Inc 65 Broadway 7th Fl..........................New York NY 10006 212-430-6520
Web: www.gocollect.com

Hazelwood Enterprises Inc 402 N 32nd St...................... Phoenix AZ 85008 602-275-7709 275-4658
TF: 800-680-4667 ■ Web: www.hazelwoods.com

Phone Fax

Historical Research Center International Inc
2019 Corporate Dr.................................Boynton Beach FL 33426 561-732-5263 740-0497
TF: 800-940-7991 ■ Web: www.names.com

Hummel Gift Shop 1656 E Garfield Rd ....New Springfield OH 44443 330-549-3728 549-0879
TF: 800-354-5438 ■ Web: www.hummelgiftshop.com

Illuminations 1736 Corporate Cir .... Petaluma CA 94954 707-769-2700 769-8700
TF: 800-226-3537 ■ Web: www.illuminations.com

Kirlins Inc 532 Maine St....................................... Quincy IL 62305 217-224-8953 224-9400
Web: www.kirlins.com

Limited Edition 2170 Sunrise Hwy ....Merrick NY 11566 516-623-4400 867-3701
TF Orders: 800-645-2864 ■ Web: www.thelimitededition.com

Military Service Co Div EBSCO Industries Inc
PO Box 1943 .... Birmingham AL 35201 205-991-6600 408-4826
TF: 800-255-3722 ■ Web: www.militaryservicecompany.com

Mole Hollow Candles Ltd 3 Deerfield Ave .... Shelburne Falls MA 01370 413-625-6337 625-9669
TF Cust Svc: 800-445-6653 ■ Web: www.molehollowcandles.com

Napa Valley Candle Factory & Gift Shop 3037 California Blvd.........Napa CA 94558 707-255-0902 255-0902
Web: members.napanet.net/candlman

Only in San Francisco Pier 39 Space B-11................. San Francisco CA 94133 415-397-0143 956-8124
Web: www.onlyinsanfrancisco.net

Oregon Connection 1125 S 1st St ....Coos Bay OR 97420 541-267-7804 267-6497
TF: 800-255-5318 ■ Web: www.oregonconnection.com

Pacific Trade International Inc 5515 Security Ln Suite 1100...... Rockville MD 20852 301-816-4200 816-4220

Paradies Shops 5950 Fulton Industrial Blvd SW .... Atlanta GA 30336 404-344-7905 349-3226
Web: www.theparadiesshops.com

Paula CM Co 6049 Hi-Tek Ct .... Mason OH 45040 513-336-3100 336-3119
TF: 800-543-4464 ■ Web: www.cmpaula.com

Plaza Gift Center 111 Japanese Village Plaza Mall.............Los Angeles CA 90012 213-680-3288 680-1980

Razorback Gift Shops Inc 579 W Vanburen St............. Eureka Springs AR 72632 479-253-8294 253-9232

RedEnvelope Inc 149 New Montgomery St .... San Francisco CA 94105 415-371-9100 371-1134
NASDAQ: REDE ■ TF: 877-733-3683 ■ Web: www.redenvelope.com

Remembering You Inc PO Box 275 ....Glenelg MD 21737 410-489-9500 489-5423

San Francisco Music Box Co 6411 Burleson Rd ....Austin TN 78744 800-227-2190 369-6192*
*Fax Area Code: 512 ■ TF: 800-227-2190 ■ Web: www.sfmusicbox.com

Sanrio Inc 570 Eccles Ave........................ South San Francisco CA 94080 650-952-2880 872-2730
TF: 800-325-8316 ■ Web: www.sanrio.com

Soap Plant 4633 Hollywood Blvd ....Los Angeles CA 90027 323-663-0122 663-0243
Web: www.soapplant.com

Spencer Gifts Inc 6826 Black Horse Pike........... Egg Harbor Township NJ 08234 609-645-3300 645-5797
TF: 800-762-0419 ■ Web: www.spencergifts.com

Symphony Store 220 S Michigan Ave .... Chicago IL 60604 312-294-3345 294-3329
Web: www.cso.org

Things Remembered Inc 5500 Avion Park Dr............ Highland Heights OH 44143 440-473-2000 473-2018
TF: 800-874-2653 ■ Web: www.thingsremembered.com

Tipton & Hurst Inc 1801 N Grant St......................... Little Rock AR 72207 501-666-3333 666-4205
TF: 800-633-3036 ■ Web: www.tiptonhurst.com

Tuesday Morning Corp 6250 LBJ Fwy ....Dallas TX 75240 972-387-3562 991-5403
NASDAQ: TUES ■ TF: 800-457-0099 ■ Web: www.tuesdaymorning.com

Virginia's Gift Shop 8039 Beach Blvd...................... Buena Park CA 90620 714-220-5323

WeddingChannel.com 700 S Flower Suite 600...............Los Angeles CA 90017 888-750-1550 599-4180*
*Fax Area Code: 213 ■ Web: www.weddingchannel.com

Wendell August Forge Inc 620 Madison Ave................. Grove City PA 16127 724-458-8360 458-5952
TF: 800-923-4438 ■ Web: www.wendellaugust.com

Yankee Candle Co Inc 16 Yankee Candle Way............ South Deerfield MA 01373 413-665-8306 665-4815
NYSE: YCC ■ TF: 800-839-6038 ■ Web: www.yankeecandle.com

331 GIFTS & NOVELTIES - WHOL

Phone Fax

ABC Distributing Inc PO Box 610130.......................North Miami FL 33261 305-944-6200 944-1918
Web: www.abcdistributing.com

Accoutrements PO Box 30811 .... Seattle WA 98113 425-349-3838 349-5188
TF: 800-886-2221 ■ Web: www.accoutrements.com

Aerial Photography Services Inc 2511 S Tryon St .... Charlotte NC 28203 704-333-5143 333-5148
Web: www.aps-1.com

Angel Sales Inc 4147 N Ravenswood Ave .... Chicago IL 60613 773-883-8858 883-8889
Web: angelsales.com

BalloonZone 1 American Rd .... Cleveland OH 44144 216-252-7300 252-6778
TF Sales: 800-321-3040 ■ Web: www.agballoonzone.com

Blair Cedar & Novelty Works Inc 680 W Hwy 54 ....Camdenton MO 65020 573-346-2235 346-5534
TF: 800-325-3943 ■ Web: www.blaircedar.com

Boyds Collection Ltd 350 South St.................... McSherrystown PA 17344 717-633-9898 633-5511
TF: 800-377-3050 ■ Web: www.boydsstuff.com

Enesco Group Inc 225 Windsor Dr................................ Itasca IL 60143 630-875-5300 875-5350
NYSE: ENC ■ TF Cust Svc: 800-632-7968 ■ Web: www.enesco.com

Fridgedoor.com 21 Dixwell Ave.................................. Quincy MA 02169 617-770-7913 801-8026
TF: 800-955-3741 ■ Web: www.fridgedoor.com

Giftco Inc 700 Woodlands Pkwy...........................Vernon Hills IL 60061 847-478-8400 777-3232*
*Fax Area Code: 800 ■ *Fax: Cust Svc ■ TF: 800-443-8261

Hayes Specialties Corp 1761 E Genesee ....Saginaw MI 48601 989-755-6541 755-2341
TF: 800-248-3603 ■ Web: www.ehayes.com

Healthy Planet Products Inc 43 Moraga Way Suite 205............ Orinda CA 94563 925-253-9595 362-5999*
*Fax Area Code: 800 ■ TF: 800-424-4422 ■ Web: www.healthyplanet.com

Hornung's Golf Products Inc 815 Morris St..................Fond du Lac WI 54935 920-922-2640 922-4986
TF: 800-323-3569 ■ Web: www.hornungs.com

JR Industries Inc 2 Central Ave Suite 1 ....Tarrytown NY 10591 914-524-8602 524-8606

Lenox Group Inc 6436 City W Pkwy 1 Village Pl ....Eden Prairie MN 55344 952-944-5600 943-4500
NYSE: LNX ■ TF: 800-348-3749 ■ Web: www.department56.com

Northwestern Products Inc 721 Industrial Park Rd .... Ashland WI 54806 715-685-9500 685-9545
TF: 800-328-7317 ■ Web: www.nwproductsinc.com

Sanrio Inc 570 Eccles Ave........................ South San Francisco CA 94080 650-952-2880 872-2730
TF: 800-325-8316 ■ Web: www.sanrio.com

Star Sales Co Inc 1803 N Central St .... Knoxville TN 37917 865-524-0771 524-4889
TF: 800-347-9494

Unique Industries Inc 4750 League Island Blvd............... Philadelphia PA 19112 215-336-4300 888-1490*
*Fax Area Code: 800 ■ TF: 800-888-1705 ■ Web: www.favors.com

Variety Distributors Inc 7th & Spring Sts PO Box 728 .... Harlan IA 51537 712-755-2184 755-5041
TF: 800-274-1095 ■ Web: www.varietydistributors.com

Western Slope Sales Service Inc 720 Alfred Noble Dr ....Hercules CA 94547 510-724-9080 724-9084
TF: 888-777-2770

WinCraft Inc 1124 W 5th St..................................Winona MN 55987 507-454-5510 454-6403
TF: 800-533-8006 ■ Web: www.wincraft.com

Zims Inc 4370 S 300 West ....Salt Lake City UT 84107 801-268-2505 268-9859
TF Orders: 800-453-6420 ■ Web: www.zimscrafts.com

332 GLASS - FLAT, PLATE, TEMPERED

Phone Fax

ACI Distribution 965 Ridge Lake Blvd Suite 300 .... Memphis TN 38120 901-767-7111 683-9351
TF: 800-238-6057 ■ Web: www.acidistribution.com

				Phone	Fax
AFG Industries IncAGC Flat Galss North America Inc 11175 Cicero Dr.	Alpharetta	GA	30022	404-446-4200	446-4221
TF: 800-251-0441 ■ Web: www.na.agc-flatglass.com					
Anthony International 12391 Montera Ave.	Sylmar	CA	91342	818-365-9451	361-9611
TF: 800-772-0900 ■ Web: www.anthonydoors.com					
Apogee Enterprises Inc 7900 Xerxes Ave S Suite 1800	Minneapolis	MN	55431	952-835-1874	835-3196
NASDAQ: APOG ■ Web: www.apog.com					
Asahi Glass America Inc 2201 Water Ridge Pkwy Suite 400	Charlotte	NC	28217	704-357-3631	357-6328
Basco Shower Enclosures 7201 Snider Rd	Mason	OH	45040	513-573-1900	573-1919
TF: 800-543-1938 ■ Web: www.bascoshowerdoor.com					
Binswanger Glass 965 Ridge Lake Blvd Suite 300	Memphis	TN	38120	901-767-7111	683-9351
TF: 800-238-6057 ■ Web: www.binswangerglass.com					
Binswanger Mirror PO Box 1400	Grenada	MS	38901	662-226-5551	226-9787
TF: 800-221-8408 ■ Web: www.binswangermirror.com					
Cameron Glass Inc 3550 W Tacoma St	Broken Arrow	OK	74012	918-254-6000	252-4665
TF: 800-331-3666 ■ Web: www.camglass.com					
Cardinal Glass Co 1087 Research Pkwy	Rockford	IL	61109	815-394-1400	397-1750
TF: 800-728-3468					
Century Glass Inc 4620 Andrews St	North Las Vegas	NV	89031	702-385-9309	385-1296
TF: 800-654-7027					
Corning Display Technologies 1 Riverfront Plaza	Corning	NY	14831	607-974-5439	974-7097
Web: www.corning.com/displaytechnologies					
D & W Inc 941 Oak St.	Elkhart	IN	46514	574-264-9674	264-9859
TF: 800-255-0829 ■ Web: www.dwincorp.com					
Delbar Products Inc 601 W Spruce St	Perkasie	PA	18944	215-257-6892	453-0122
Gemtron Corp 615 Hwy 68	Sweetwater	TN	37874	423-337-3522	337-7979
Web: www.gemtron.com					
Gentex Corp 600 N Centennial St	Zeeland	MI	49464	616-772-1800	772-7348
NASDAQ: GNTX ■ TF: 800-444-4689 ■ Web: www.gentex.com					
Globe Amerada Glass Co 2001 Greenleaf Ave	Elk Grove Village	IL	60007	847-364-2900	364-2909
TF: 800-323-8776 ■ Web: www.globeamerada.com					
Golden Gate Glass & Mirror Co Inc 2011 Folsom St.	San Francisco	CA	94110	415-522-0220	
Gray Glass Co 217-44 98th Ave	Queens Village	NY	11429	718-217-2943	217-0280
TF: 800-523-3320 ■ Web: grayglass.net					
Guardian Industries Corp 2300 Harmon Rd	Auburn Hills	MI	48326	248-340-1800	340-9988
TF: 800-327-5888 ■ Web: www.guardian.com					
Hehr International Inc 3333 Casitas Ave	Los Angeles	CA	90039	323-663-1261	666-9458
Web: www.hehrintl.com					
Kokomo Opalescent Glass Co 1310 S Market St	Kokomo	IN	46902	765-457-8136	459-5177
Web: www.kog.com					
Magna Donnelly 49 W 3rd St	Holland	MI	49423	616-786-7000	786-6233
Web: www.magnadon.com					
Maran-Wurzell Glass & Mirror Co 1683 Mount Vernon Ave	Pomona	CA	91768	909-623-1665	623-1695
Naturalite 750 Airport Rd	Terrell	TX	75160	972-551-6400	551-6420
TF: 800-527-4018 ■ Web: www.naturalite.com/Naturalite					
Northwestern Industries Inc 2500 W Jameson St	Seattle	WA	98199	206-285-3140	285-3603
TF: 800-426-2771 ■ Web: www.nwiglass.com					
ODL Inc 215 E Roosevelt Ave	Zeeland	MI	49464	616-772-9111	772-9110*
*Fax: Cust Svc ■ TF: 800-288-1800 ■ Web: www.odl.com					
Oregon Glass Co 10450 SW Ridder Rd	Wilsonville	OR	97070	503-682-3846	682-0252
TF: 800-547-0217 ■ Web: www.oregonglass.com					
Paul Wissmach Glass Co Inc PO Box 228	Paden City	WV	26159	304-337-2253	337-8800
Web: www.wissmachglass.com					
Pilkington Holdings Inc 811 Madison Ave PO Box 0799	Toledo	OH	43697	419-247-3731	247-3821
Web: www.pilkington.com					
PPG Industries Inc 1 PPG Pl.	Pittsburgh	PA	15272	412-434-3131	434-2011*
NYSE: PPG ■ *Fax: Hum Res ■ Web: www.ppg.com					
Rainbow Art Glass Inc 1761 Rt 34 S	Wall	NJ	07727	732-681-6003	681-4984
TF: 800-526-2356 ■ Web: www.rainbowartglass.com					
Rambusch Decorating Co 160 Cornelison Ave	Jersey City	NJ	07304	201-333-2525	433-3355
Web: www.rambusch.com					
Saint-Gobain Corp 750 E Swedesford Rd	Valley Forge	PA	19482	610-341-7000	341-7797
TF: 800-274-8530 ■ Web: www.saint-gobain.com/us					
SCHOTT North America Inc 555 Taxter Rd	Elmsford	NY	10523	914-831-2200	831-2201
Web: www.us.schott.com					
Shower Rite Inc 7519 S Greenwood Ave	Chicago	IL	60619	773-483-5400	483-5409
TF: 800-925-9131					
Spectrum Glass Co PO Box 646	Woodinville	WA	98072	425-483-6699	483-9007
TF: 800-426-3120 ■ Web: www.spectrumglass.com					
Stanley Home Decor 480 Myrtle St	New Britain	CT	06053	860-225-5111	827-3895
TF: 800-782-6539					
Super Sky Products Inc 10301 N Enterprise Dr	Mequon	WI	53092	262-242-2000	242-7409
TF: 800-558-0467 ■ Web: www.supersky.com					
Thermoseal Glass Corp 400 Water St	Gloucester	NJ	08130	856-456-3109	456-0989
TF: 800-456-7788 ■ Web: www.thermoseal.com					
Torstenson Glass Co 3233 N Sheffield Ave	Chicago	IL	60657	773-525-0435	525-0009
Web: www.tglass.com					
Tru-Vue Glass & Artboard Co 9400 W 55th St	McCook	IL	60525	708-485-5080	485-5980
TF Cust Svc: 800-621-8339 ■ Web: www.tru-vue.com					
Viracon Inc 800 Park Dr	Owatonna	MN	55060	507-451-9555	444-3555
TF: 800-533-2080 ■ Web: www.viracon.com					
Virginia Mirror Co Inc PO Box 5431	Martinsville	VA	24115	276-632-9816	632-2488
TF: 800-826-4776					
VVP America Inc 965 Ridge Lake Blvd Suite 300	Memphis	TN	38120	901-767-7111	683-9351
TF: 800-238-6057 ■ Web: www.vvpamerica.com					
Wasco Products Inc 22 Pioneer Ave PO Box 351	Sanford	ME	04073	207-324-8060	490-1218
TF: 800-388-0293 ■ Web: www.wascoproducts.com					
Water Bonnet Mfg Inc PO Box 180427	Casselberry	FL	32718	407-831-2122	831-5069

333 GLASS FIBERS

				Phone	Fax
Corning Inc 1 Riverfront Plaza	Corning	NY	14831	607-974-9000	974-8688*
NYSE: GLW ■ *Fax: Hum Res ■ Web: www.corning.com					
Corning Optical Fiber PO Box 7429	Endicott	NY	13760	607-786-8125	539-3632*
*Fax Area Code: 800 ■ TF: 800-525-2524 ■ Web: www.corning.com/opticalfiber					
Evanite Fiber Corp PO Box E	Corvallis	OR	97339	541-753-1211	753-0388
TF Cust Svc: 800-441-5567 ■ Web: www.evanite.com					
Fiber Glass Industries Inc 69 Edson St	Amsterdam	NY	12010	518-842-4000	842-4408
TF: 800-842-4413 ■ Web: www.fiberglassindustries.com					
Fiberoptics Technology Inc 1 Quassett Rd	Pomfret	CT	06258	860-928-0443	928-7664
TF: 800-433-5248 ■ Web: www.fiberoptix.com					
Incom Inc PO Box G	Southbridge	MA	01550	508-765-9151	765-0041
Web: www.incomusa.com					

334 GLASS JARS & BOTTLES

				Phone	Fax
Anchor Glass Container Corp 4343 Anchor Plaza Pkwy.	Tampa	FL	33634	813-882-0000	886-3456*
*Fax: Mail Rm ■ TF: 800-326-2467					
Arkansas Glass Container Corp PO Box 1717	Jonesboro	AR	72403	870-932-4564	268-6217
Web: www.agcc.com					
Glenshaw Glass Co Inc 1101 William Flynn Hwy	Glenshaw	PA	15116	412-486-9100	486-9252
TF: 800-326-2467					
Gujarat Glass International Inc 401 Rt 73 N Bldg 10 Suite 202 Lake Center Executive Park	Marlton	NJ	08053	856-293-6400	293-6401
Web: www.theglassgroup.com					
Jarden Corp 555 Theodore Fremd Ave Suite B-302	Rye	NY	10580	914-967-9400	
NYSE: JAH ■ Web: www.jardencorp.com					
Leone Industries Co 443 Southeast Ave	Bridgeton	NJ	08302	856-455-2000	455-3491
Web: www.leoneglass.com					
New High Glass Inc 12713 SW 125th Ave	Miami	FL	33186	305-232-0840	251-4622
TF: 800-452-7787 ■ Web: www.newhigh.com					
Owens-Brockway Glass Containers 1 SeaGate	Toledo	OH	43666	419-247-5000	247-5098*
*Fax: Sales					
Owens-Illinois Inc 1 SeaGate	Toledo	OH	43666	419-247-5000	247-7107
NYSE: OI ■ Web: www.o-i.com					
Saint-Gobain Containers Inc 1509 S Macedonia Ave	Muncie	IN	47302	765-741-7000	741-7012
TF: 800-428-8642 ■ Web: www.sgcontainers.com					

335 GLASS PRODUCTS - INDUSTRIAL (CUSTOM)

				Phone	Fax
Abrisa USPG PO Box 3258	Ventura	CA	93006	805-525-4902	525-8604
TF: 800-350-5000 ■ Web: www.abrisa.com					
ACCU-GLASS Div Becton Dickinson & Co 10765 Trenton Ave.	Saint Louis	MO	63132	314-423-0300	423-0413
TF: 800-325-4796 ■ Web: www.bd.com/accu-glass					
Becton Dickinson & Co ACCU-GLASS Div 10765 Trenton Ave.	Saint Louis	MO	63132	314-423-0300	423-0413
TF: 800-325-4796 ■ Web: www.bd.com/accu-glass					
Elan Technology 169 Elan Ct PO Box 779	Midway	GA	31320	912-880-3526	880-3000
Web: www.elantechnology.com					
Flex-O-Lite Inc 801 Corporate Ctr Dr Suite 300	Saint Charles	MO	63304	636-300-2700	300-2820
TF: 800-325-9525 ■ Web: www.flexolite.com					
Fredericks Co Inc 2400 Philmont Ave PO Box 67	Huntingdon Valley	PA	19006	215-947-2500	947-7464
Web: www.frederickscom.com					
Garner Glass Co 177 S Indian Hill Blvd	Claremont	CA	91711	909-624-5071	625-0173
Web: www.garnerglass.com					
Lancaster Glass Corp 240 W Main St.	Lancaster	OH	43130	740-653-0311	653-9501
TF: 800-264-6826 ■ Web: www.lancasterglasscorp.com					
Lenoir Mirror Co Inc PO Box 1650	Lenoir	NC	28645	828-728-3271	728-5010
TF: 800-438-8204 ■ Web: www.lenoirmirror.com					
Morgan Advanced Ceramics Inc GBC Materials Div 580 Monastery Dr	Latrobe	PA	15650	724-537-7791	537-4910
Naugatuck Glass Co PO Box 71	Naugatuck	CT	06770	203-729-5227	729-8781*
*Fax: Sales ■ TF: 800-533-3513 ■ Web: www.naugatuckglass.com					
Photo Sciences Inc 2542 W 237th St	Torrance	CA	90505	310-539-9040	784-3642
Web: www.photo-sciences.com					
Precision Electronic Glass Inc 1013 Hendee Rd	Vineland	NJ	08360	856-691-2234	691-3090
TF: 800-982-4734 ■ Web: www.pegglass.com					
Richland Glass Co Inc 1640 Southwest Blvd	Vineland	NJ	08360	800-959-0312	691-4525*
*Fax Area Code: 856 ■ Web: www.richlandglass.com					
Schott Corp 3 Odell Plaza	Yonkers	NY	10701	914-968-8900	968-4422
TF: 800-633-4505					
Swift Glass Co Inc 131 W 22nd St.	Elmira Heights	NY	14903	607-733-7166	732-5829
TF: 800-537-9438 ■ Web: www.swiftglass.com					

336 GLASSWARE - LABORATORY & SCIENTIFIC

				Phone	Fax
Ace Glass Inc 1430 Northwest Blvd PO Box 688	Vineland	NJ	08360	856-692-3333	543-6752*
*Fax Area Code: 800 ■ TF: 800-223-4524 ■ Web: www.aceglass.com					
Bellco Glass Inc 340 Edrudo Rd.	Vineland	NJ	08360	856-691-1075	691-3247
TF: 800-257-7043 ■ Web: www.bellcoglass.com					
Corning Inc 1 Riverfront Plaza	Corning	NY	14831	607-974-9000	974-8688*
NYSE: GLW ■ *Fax: Hum Res ■ Web: www.corning.com					
Eden Labs 1601 W 5th St Suite 240	Columbus	OH	43212	614-374-2455	469-0148*
*Fax Area Code: 801 ■ Web: www.edenlabs.org					
Erie Scientific Co 20 Post Rd.	Portsmouth	NH	03801	603-431-8410	431-8996
TF: 800-258-0834 ■ Web: www.eriesci.com					
Gujarat Glass International Coded Products 5176 Harding Hwy	Mays Landing	NJ	08330	609-625-2291	625-7173
TF: 800-442-7533 ■ Web: www.gujaratglassinternational.com					
Quadrex Corp PO Box 3881	Woodbridge	CT	06525	203-393-3112	393-0391
TF Sales: 800-275-7033 ■ Web: www.quadrexcorp.com					
SCHOTT North America Inc 555 Taxter Rd	Elmsford	NY	10523	914-831-2200	831-2201
Web: www.us.schott.com					
Super Glass Corp 1020 E 48th St	Brooklyn	NY	11203	718-469-9300	469-5480
TF: 800-237-2211					
Wale Apparatus Co Inc PO Box D	Hellertown	PA	18055	610-838-7047	838-7440
TF: 800-444-9253 ■ Web: www.waleapparatus.com					

337 GLASSWARE & POTTERY - HOUSEHOLD

SEE ALSO Table & Kitchen Supplies - China & Earthenware p. 2337

				Phone	Fax
Anchor Hocking Co 519 Pierce Ave	Lancaster	OH	43130	740-681-6478	681-6040
Web: www.anchorhocking.com					
Berney-Karp Inc 3350 E 26th St.	Los Angeles	CA	90023	323-260-7122	260-7245
TF: 800-237-6395 ■ Web: www.ceramic-source.com					
Blenko Glass Co Inc Fairground Rd	Milton	WV	25541	304-743-9081	743-0547
TF: 877-425-3656 ■ Web: www.blenkoglass.com					
Boehm Edward Marshall Inc 25 Princess Diana Ln.	Trenton	NJ	08638	609-392-2207	392-1437
TF: 800-257-9410					
Carolina Mirror Co 600 Elkin Hwy	North Wilkesboro	NC	28659	336-838-2151	838-9734
TF: 800-334-7245 ■ Web: www.carolinamirror.com					
CDP Corp 1399 Executive Dr W.	Richardson	TX	75081	972-234-8565	231-9239
TF: 800-527-4356 ■ Web: www.cdpintl.com					
Ceramo Co Inc 681 Kasten Dr.	Jackson	MO	63755	573-243-3138	243-3130
TF: 800-325-8303 ■ Web: www.ceramousa.com					
Creative Bath Products 250 Creative Dr.	Central Islip	NY	11722	631-582-8000	582-2020
Web: www.creativebath.com					

Phone | Fax

Crystal Clear Industries 2 Bergen Tpke Ridgefield Park NJ 07660 201-440-4200 440-1758
TF Orders: 800-841-4014 ■ *Web:* www.crystalclear.com
Culver Industries Inc
1000 Industrial Blvd Hopewell Industrial Park Aliquippa PA 15001 724-857-5770 857-5707
TF: 800-862-0070 ■ *Web:* www.culverind.com
Dacra Glass Inc 1144 S State Rd 3 S Hartford City IN 47348 765-348-2190 348-2191
TF: 800-359-3189 ■ *Web:* www.dacraglass.com
Dansk International Designs Ltd 1414 Radcliff St Bristol PA NJ 19007 267-525-7800 844-1576*
**Fax Area Code:* 609 ■ *TF Cust Svc:* 800-293-2675 ■ *Web:* www.dansk.com
Edward Marshall Boehm Inc 25 Princess Diana Ln Trenton NJ 08638 609-392-2207 392-1437
TF: 800-257-9410
Enesco Corp 225 Windsor Dr Itasca IL 60143 630-875-5300 875-5350
TF: 800-436-3726 ■ *Web:* www.enesco.com
Fenton Art Glass Co 700 Elizabeth St Williamstown WV 26187 304-375-6122 375-6459
TF Cust Svc: 800-933-6766 ■ *Web:* www.fentonartglass.com
Fitz & Floyd Corp Inc 501 Corporate Dr Lewisville TX 75057 972-874-3480 353-7718
TF: 800-243-2058 ■ *Web:* www.fitzandfloyd.com
Friedman Brothers Decorative Arts Inc 9015 NW 105th Way Medley FL 33178 305-887-3170 885-5331
TF: 800-327-1065 ■ *Web:* www.homeportfolio.com
Gainey Ceramics Inc 1200 Arrow Hwy La Verne CA 91750 909-593-3533 596-9337
TF Cust Svc: 800-451-8155 ■ *Web:* www.gaineyceramics.com
Gardner Glass Products Inc 600 Elkin Hwy North Wilkesboro NC 28659 336-651-9300 667-0185
TF: 800-334-7267 ■ *Web:* www.gardnerglass.com
Haeger Industries Inc 7 Maiden Ln Dundee IL 60118 847-426-3441 426-0017
TF: 800-288-2529 ■ *Web:* www.haegerpotteries.com
Haeger Potteries of Macomb 411 W Calhoun St Macomb IL 61455 309-833-2171 833-3860
Web: www.haegerpotteries.com
Haggerty Enterprises Inc 321 W Lake St Suite G Elmhurst IL 60126 630-315-3300 315-3392
TF: 800-352-5282 ■ *Web:* www.lavaworld.com
Hollohaza USA 920 E Colorado Blvd Suite 542 Pasadena CA 91106 626-666-1431 568-3275
Web: www.hollohaza.com
Indiana Glass Co Div Lancaster Colony Corp 717 W 'E' St Dunkirk IN 47336 765-768-6789 768-1272
Web: www.indianaglass.com
Lancaster Colony Corp Indiana Glass Co Div 717 W 'E' St Dunkirk IN 47336 765-768-6789 768-1272
Web: www.indianaglass.com
LE Smith Glass Co 1900 Liberty St Mount Pleasant PA 15666 724-547-3544 547-2077
TF: 800-537-6484 ■ *Web:* www.lesmithglass.com
Lenox Inc 100 Lenox Dr Lawrenceville NJ 08648 609-896-2800 895-0139
TF Cust Svc: 800-635-3669 ■ *Web:* www.lenox.com
LH Selman Ltd 123 Locust St Santa Cruz CA 95060 831-427-1177 427-0111
TF: 800-538-0766 ■ *Web:* www.paperweight.com
Libbey Inc 300 Madison Ave PO Box 10060 Toledo OH 43699 419-325-2100 325-2369
NYSE: LBY ■ *TF:* 888-794-8469 ■ *Web:* www.libbey.com
Marshall Pottery 4901 Elysian Fields Rd Marshall TX 75670 903-927-5400 938-8222
TF: 888-768-8721 ■ *Web:* www.marshallpottery.com
Martin's Herend Imports Inc 21440 Pacific Blvd Sterling VA 20167 703-450-1601 450-1605
TF: 800-643-7363 ■ *Web:* www.herendusa.com
Media Arts Group Inc 900 Lightpost Way Morgan Hill CA 95037 408-201-5000
TF: 800-366-3733 ■ *Web:* www.mediaarts.com
Mikasa Inc 100 Plaza Dr Secaucus NJ 07094 201-867-9210 867-0580
TF Cust Svc: 800-833-4681 ■ *Web:* www.mikasa.com
Noritake Co Inc 15-22 Fair Lawn Ave Fair Lawn NJ 07410 201-475-5200 796-2269
TF: 888-296-3423 ■ *Web:* www.noritake.com
Oneida Ltd 163-181 Kenwood Ave Oneida NY 13421 315-361-3000 361-3475
TF: 800-877-6667 ■ *Web:* www.oneida.com
Papel Giftware 373 S Monte Vista Dr Suite C Palm Springs CA 92262 760-327-2211 327-8211
Web: www.papeldesigns.com
Pfaltzgraff Co 140 E Market St York PA 17401 717-848-5500 771-1433*
**Fax:* Cust Svc ■ *TF:* 800-999-2811 ■ *Web:* www.pfaltzgraff.com
Rauch Industries Inc 2408 Forbes Rd Gastonia NC 28056 704-867-5333 864-2081
Royal Doulton USA Inc 200 Cottontail Ln Somerset NJ 08873 732-356-7880 764-4974
TF: 800-682-4462 ■ *Web:* www.royaldoulton.com
Steuben Glass 1 Steuben Way Corning NY 14830 607-974-8584 974-8850
TF: 800-424-4240 ■ *Web:* steuben.com
Stroupe Mirror Co PO Box 728 Thomasville NC 27360 336-475-2181 475-4833
Swarovski Consumer Goods Ltd 1 Kenney Dr Cranston RI 02920 401-463-6400 463-5257
TF: 800-289-4900 ■ *Web:* www.swarovski.com
United Design Corp PO Box 1200 Noble OK 73068 405-872-3468 360-4442
TF: 800-527-4883 ■ *Web:* www.united-design.com
Waterford Wedgwood USA Inc 1330 Campus Pkwy Wall NJ 07719 732-938-5800 938-6915
Web: www.wwusa.com
Willitts Designs International 1129 Industrial Ave Petaluma CA 94952 707-778-7211 769-0304
TF: 800-358-9184 ■ *Web:* www.willitts.com
World Kitchen Inc 11911 Freedom Dr Suite 600 Reston VA 20190 703-456-4700 456-2020
TF Cust Svc: 800-999-3436 ■ *Web:* www.worldkitchen.com

338 GLOBAL DISTRIBUTION SYSTEMS (GDSS)

A global distribution system (GDS) is a computer reservations system that includes reservations databases of air travel suppliers in many countries. GDSs typically are owned jointly by airlines operating in different countries.

Phone | Fax

Amadeus North America LLC 9250 NW 36 St Miami FL 33178 305-499-6000 499-6889
TF: 888-262-3387 ■ *Web:* www.us.amadeus.com
Galileo International Inc 7 Sylvan Way Parsippany NJ 07054 973-496-6000
Web: www.galileo.com
Pegasus Solutions Inc 8350 N Central Expy Suite 1900 Dallas TX 75206 214-234-4000 234-4040
NASDAQ: PEGS ■ *TF:* 800-528-2422 ■ *Web:* www.pegs.com
Sabre Inc 3150 Sabre Dr Southlake TX 76092 682-605-1000
NYSE: TSG ■ *Web:* www.sabre.com
Travelport 7 Sylvan Way Parsippany NJ 07054 973-428-9700
Web: www.travelport.com
WorldRes Inc 999 Baker Way Suite 290 San Mateo CA 94404 650-372-1700 372-1701
Web: www.worldres.com
Worldspan LP 300 Galleria Pkwy NW Atlanta GA 30339 770-563-7400 563-7004
Web: www.worldspan.com
Worldspan Technologies Inc 300 Galleria Pkwy NW Atlanta GA 30339 770-563-7400 563-7004
Web: www.worldspan.com

339 GOURMET SPECIALTY SHOPS

Phone | Fax

Dean & DeLuca Inc 560 Broadway New York NY 10012 212-226-6800 781-4050*
**Fax Area Code:* 800 ■ *TF:* 800-999-0306 ■ *Web:* www.deandeluca.com
Eatzi's Market & Bakery LLC 2508 Highlander Way Suite 220 Carrollton TX 75006 972-248-5200 248-5249
Web: www.eatzis.com
EthnicGrocer.com Inc 1090 Industrial Dr Suite 5 Bensenville IL 60106 630-860-1733
Web: www.ethnicgrocer.com
Graber Olive House Inc 315 E 4th St Ontario CA 91764 909-983-1761 984-2180
TF: 800-996-5483 ■ *Web:* www.graberolives.com
Harry & David Holdings Inc 2500 S Pacific Hwy Medford OR 97501 541-776-2121 233-2300*
**Fax Area Code:* 877 ■ *TF Cust Svc:* 800-345-5655 ■ *Web:* www.harryanddavid.com
Heavenly Ham Franchising Co 5445 Triangle Pkwy Suite 400 Norcross GA 30092 770-752-1999 752-4653
TF: 800-989-0509 ■ *Web:* www.heavenlyham.com
Hickory Farms Inc 1505 Holland Rd Maumee OH 43537 419-893-7611 893-0164
TF: 800-288-7327 ■ *Web:* www.hickoryfarms.com
Honeybaked Ham Co 5445 Triangle Pkwy Suite 400 Norcross GA 30092 678-966-3100 966-3134
TF: 800-367-2426 ■ *Web:* www.honeybakedonline.com
Jerky Hut International PO Box 308 Hubbard OR 97032 503-981-7191 981-7692
TF: 800-223-5759 ■ *Web:* www.4mymeat.com
Logan Farms Honey Glazed Hams 10560 Westheimer Rd Houston TX 77042 713-781-3773 977-0532
TF: 800-833-4267 ■ *Web:* www.loganfarmsinc.com
M & M Meat Shops Ltd PO Box 2488 Station C Kitchener ON N2H6M3 519-895-1075 895-0762
Web: www.mmmeatshops.com
Omaha Steaks International Inc 10909 John Galt Blvd Omaha NE 68137 402-597-8370 597-8125*
**Fax:* Hum Res ■ *TF:* 800-960-8400 ■ *Web:* www.omahasteaks.com
Stew Leonard's 100 Westport Ave Norwalk CT 06851 203-847-9088 750-6178*
**Fax:* Hum Res ■ *TF:* 800-729-7839 ■ *Web:* www.stew-leonards.com
Your Northwest 31461 NE Bell Rd Sherwood OR 97140 503-554-9060 537-9693
TF: 888-252-0699 ■ *Web:* www.yournw.com
Zabar's & Co Inc 2245 Broadway New York NY 10024 212-787-2000 580-4477
TF: 800-697-6301 ■ *Web:* www.zabars.com

340 GOVERNMENT - CITY

Phone | Fax

Abilene 555 Walnut St Abilene TX 79601 325-676-6200 676-6229
Web: www.abilenetx.com
Akron 166 S High St Suite 200 Akron OH 44308 330-375-2345 375-2468
Web: www.ci.akron.oh.us
Albany 24 Eagle St Suite 102 Albany NY 12207 518-434-5100 434-5013
Web: www.albanyny.org
Albuquerque PO Box 1293 Albuquerque NM 87103 505-768-3000 768-3019
Web: www.cabq.gov
Alexandria 301 King St Alexandria VA 22314 703-838-4000 838-6433
Web: alexandriava.gov
Allentown 435 Hamilton St Allentown PA 18101 610-437-7539 437-7554
Web: www.allentownpa.org
Amarillo 509 E 7th Ave Amarillo TX 79101 806-378-3000 378-9394
Web: www.ci.amarillo.tx.us
Anaheim 200 S Anaheim Blvd Anaheim CA 92805 714-765-5162 765-5164
Web: www.anaheim.net
Anchorage PO Box 196650 Anchorage AK 99519 907-343-4431 343-4499
Web: www.muni.org
Ann Arbor 100 N 5th Ave Ann Arbor MI 48104 734-994-2700 332-5966
Web: www.a2gov.org/
Annapolis 160 Duke of Gloucester St Annapolis MD 21401 410-263-7997 216-9284
Web: www.ci.annapolis.md.us
Arlington (TX) 101 W Abram St Arlington TX 76010 817-275-3271 459-6120
Web: www.ci.arlington.tx.us
Asheville 70 Court Plaza PO Box 7148 Asheville NC 28802 828-259-5600 259-5499
Web: www.ashevillenc.gov/
Atlanta 55 Trinity Ave SW Atlanta GA 30303 404-330-6000 266-1949
Web: www.atlantaga.gov
Atlantic City 1301 Bacharach Blvd Atlantic City NJ 08401 609-347-5300 347-6408
Web: www.cityofatlanticcity.org
Augusta (GA) 530 Greene St Augusta GA 30911 706-821-1820 821-1838
Web: www.augustaga.gov
Augusta (ME) 16 Cony St Augusta ME 04330 207-626-2310 626-2304
Web: www.ci.augusta.me.us
Aurora 15151 E Alameda Pkwy Aurora CO 80012 303-739-7015 739-7594
Web: www.ci.aurora.co.us
Austin PO Box 1088 Austin TX 78767 512-974-2000 974-2337
Web: www.cityofaustin.org
Bakersfield 1501 Truxtun Ave Bakersfield CA 93301 661-326-3751 324-1850
Web: www.bakersfieldcity.us
Baltimore 100 N Holliday St Baltimore MD 21202 410-396-3100 576-9425
Web: www.baltimorecity.gov
Bangor 73 Harlow St Bangor ME 04401 207-945-4400 945-4449
Web: www.bangormaine.gov
Bar Harbor 93 Cottage St Bar Harbor ME 04609 207-288-4098 288-4461
Web: www.ci.bar-harbor.me.us
Baton Rouge PO Box 1471 Baton Rouge LA 70821 225-389-3100 389-5203
Web: www.brgov.com
Billings PO Box 1178 Billings MT 59103 406-657-8210 657-8390
Web: ci.billings.mt.us
Biloxi PO Box 429 Biloxi MS 39533 228-435-6254 435-6129
Web: www.biloxi.ms.us
Birmingham 710 N 20th St Birmingham AL 35203 205-254-2000 254-2115
Web: www.informationbirmingham.com
Bismarck 500 E Front St Bismarck ND 58501 701-355-1300 222-6470
Web: www.bismarck.org
Bloomington 401 N Morton St Bloomington IN 47404 812-339-2261 349-3570
Web: www.bloomington.in.gov
Boise PO Box 500 Boise ID 83701 208-384-4422 384-4420
Web: www.cityofboise.org
Boston 1 City Hall Plaza Boston MA 02201 617-635-4601 248-1937
Web: www.cityofboston.gov
Boulder PO Box 791 Boulder CO 80306 303-441-3388 441-4478
Web: www.ci.boulder.co.us
Branson 110 W Maddux St Suite 205 Branson MO 65616 417-334-3345 335-4354
Web: www.cityofbranson.org
Bridgeport 999 Broad St Bridgeport CT 06604 203-576-7201 576-3913
Web: www.ci.bridgeport.ct.us
Brownsville 1001 E Elizabeth St Brownsville TX 78520 956-548-6000 546-4021
Web: www.cob.us
Buffalo 65 Niagara Sq Buffalo NY 14202 716-851-4200 851-4360
Web: www.ci.buffalo.ny.us
Burlington 149 Church St Burlington VT 05401 802-865-7000 865-7014
Web: www.ci.burlington.vt.us
Calgary PO Box 2100 Stn M Calgary AB T2P2M5 403-268-2489 538-6111
Web: www.calgary.ca
Carson City 201 N Carson St Carson City NV 89701 775-887-2100 882-8408
Web: www.carson-city.nv.us
Casper 200 N David St Casper WY 82601 307-235-8400 235-7575
Web: www.cityofcasperwy.com
Cedar Rapids 50 2nd Ave Bridge Cedar Rapids IA 52401 319-286-5060 286-5130
Web: www.cedar-rapids.org
Champaign 102 N Neil St Champaign IL 61820 217-403-8700 403-8980
Web: www.ci.champaign.il.us

	City	State	Zip	Phone	Fax
Charleston (SC) 50 Broad St	Charleston	SC	29401	843-577-6970	720-3959
Web: www.charlestoncity.info/					
Charleston (WV) 501 Virginia St E	Charleston	WV	25301	304-348-8000	348-8157
Web: www.cityofcharleston.org					
Charlotte					
Charlotte-Mecklenburg Government Center 600 E 4th St	Charlotte	NC	28202	704-336-2241	336-6644
Web: www.ci.charlotte.nc.us					
Chattanooga 101 E 11th St Suite 100	Chattanooga	TN	37402	423-757-5152	757-0005
Web: www.chattanooga.gov					
Chesapeake 306 Cedar Rd 6th Fl	Chesapeake	VA	23322	757-382-6345	421-3176
Web: www.chesapeake.va.us					
Cheyenne 2101 O'Neil Ave	Cheyenne	WY	82001	307-637-6200	637-6454
Web: www.cheyennecity.org					
Chicago 121 N La Salle St	Chicago	IL	60602	312-744-4000	744-2324
Web: egov.cityofchicago.org					
Chula Vista 276 4th Ave	Chula Vista	CA	91910	619-691-5044	476-5379
Web: www.ci.chula-vista.ca.us					
Cincinnati 801 Plum St	Cincinnati	OH	45202	513-352-3000	352-5020
Web: www.cincinnati-oh.gov					
Cleveland 601 Lakeside Ave	Cleveland	OH	44114	216-664-2000	664-3837
Web: www.cleveland-oh.gov					
Colorado Springs 107 N Nevada Ave Suite 205	Colorado Springs	CO	80903	719-385-5900	385-5488
Web: www.springsgov.com					
Columbia (MO) 701 E Broadway 5th Fl	Columbia	MO	65201	573-874-7214	442-8828
Web: www.ci.columbia.mo.us					
Columbus (GA) 100 10th St	Columbus	GA	31901	706-653-4000	653-4970
Web: www.columbusga.com					
Columbus (OH) 90 W Broad St	Columbus	OH	43215	614-645-8100	645-5818
Web: ci.columbus.oh.us					
Concord 41 Green St	Concord	NH	03301	603-225-8500	225-8592
Web: www.ci.concord.nh.us					
Corpus Christi PO Box 9277	Corpus Christi	TX	78469	361-880-3000	880-3113
Web: www.cctexas.com					
Dallas 1500 Marilla St	Dallas	TX	75201	214-670-3011	670-3946
Web: www.dallascityhall.com					
Dayton 101 W 3rd St	Dayton	OH	45402	937-333-3333	333-4297
Web: www.ci.dayton.oh.us					
Daytona Beach 301 S Ridgewood Ave Rm 210	Daytona Beach	FL	32114	386-671-8022	671-8035
Web: www.ci.daytona-beach.fl.us					
Denver 201 W Colfax Ave Rm 101	Denver	CO	80202	720-865-8400	865-8580
Web: www.denvergov.org					
Des Moines 400 Robert D Ray Dr 2nd Fl	Des Moines	IA	50309	515-283-4209	237-1645
Web: www.dmgov.org					
Detroit 2 Woodward Ave Suite 200	Detroit	MI	48226	313-224-3270	224-1466
Web: www.ci.detroit.mi.us					
Dover 15 E Loockerman St	Dover	DE	19901	302-736-7008	736-7177
Web: www.cityofdover.com					
Dubuque 50 W 13th St	Dubuque	IA	52001	563-589-4100	589-0890
Web: www.cityofdubuque.org					
Duluth 411 W 1st St	Duluth	MN	55802	218-730-5500	730-5923
Web: www.ci.duluth.mn.us					
Durham 101 City Hall Plaza	Durham	NC	27701	919-560-4100	560-4835
Web: www.durhamnc.gov					
Edmonton 1 Sir Winston Churchill Sq	Edmonton	AB	T5J2R7	780-496-8200	496-8210
Web: www.edmonton.ca					
El Paso 2 Civic Center Plaza	El Paso	TX	79901	915-541-4000	541-4501
Web: www.elpasotexas.gov					
Erie 626 State St	Erie	PA	16501	814-870-1234	870-1296
Web: www.ci.erie.pa.us					
Eugene 777 Pearl St Rm 105	Eugene	OR	97401	541-682-5010	682-5414
Web: www.eugene-or.gov					
Evansville 1 NW ML King Jr Blvd	Evansville	IN	47708	812-436-4992	436-4999
Web: www.evansvillegov.net					
Fairbanks 800 Cushman St	Fairbanks	AK	99701	907-459-6771	459-6710*
**Fax:* City Clerk ■ *Web:* www.ci.fairbanks.ak.us					
Fargo 200 N 3rd St	Fargo	ND	58102	701-241-1310	476-4136
Web: www.cityoffargo.com					
Flagstaff 211 W Aspen Ave	Flagstaff	AZ	86001	928-774-5281	779-7696
Web: www.flagstaff.az.gov					
Flint 1101 S Saginaw St Rm 101	Flint	MI	48502	810-766-7346	766-7218
Web: www.cityofflint.com					
Fort Collins 300 W LaPorte Ave	Fort Collins	CO	80521	970-221-6505	224-6107
Web: www.fcgov.com					
Fort Lauderdale 100 N Andrews Ave	Fort Lauderdale	FL	33301	954-828-5000	828-5017
Web: www.fortlauderdale.gov					
Fort Smith 623 Garrison Ave	Fort Smith	AR	72901	479-784-2208	784-2256
Web: www.fsark.com					
Fort Wayne 1 Main St	Fort Wayne	IN	46802	260-427-1221	427-1371
Web: www.cityoffortwayne.org					
Fort Worth 1000 Throckmorton St	Fort Worth	TX	76102	817-392-8900	392-6187
Web: www.fortworthgov.org					
Frankfort PO Box 697	Frankfort	KY	40602	502-875-8500	875-8502
Web: frankfort.ky.gov/					
Fremont PO Box 5006	Fremont	CA	94537	510-284-4000	284-4001
Web: www.fremont.gov					
Fresno 2600 Fresno St Rm 2064	Fresno	CA	93721	559-621-7770	621-7776
Web: www.fresno.gov					
Garden Grove 11222 Acacia Pkwy	Garden Grove	CA	92840	714-741-5100	741-5044
Web: www.ci.garden-grove.ca.us					
Garland 200 N 5th St	Garland	TX	75040	972-205-2000	205-2504
Web: www.ci.garland.tx.us					
Gettysburg 59 E High St	Gettysburg	PA	17325	717-334-1160	334-7258
Web: www.gettysburg-pa.gov/					
Glendale (AZ) 5850 W Glendale Ave	Glendale	AZ	85301	623-930-2000	915-2690
Web: www.glendaleaz.com/					
Glendale (CA) 613 E Broadway Rm 110	Glendale	CA	91206	818-548-2090	241-5386
Web: www.ci.glendale.ca.us					
Grand Forks 255 N 4th St	Grand Forks	ND	58203	701-746-2626	787-3740
Web: www.grandforksgov.com					
Grand Rapids 300 Monroe Ave NW	Grand Rapids	MI	49503	616-456-3010	456-4607
Web: www.ci.grand-rapids.mi.us					
Great Falls 2 Park Dr S	Great Falls	MT	59403	406-771-1180	727-0005
Web: www.ci.great-falls.mt.us					
Green Bay 100 N Jefferson St Rm 106	Green Bay	WI	54301	920-448-3010	448-3016
Web: www.ci.green-bay.wi.us					
Greensboro PO Box 3136	Greensboro	NC	27402	336-373-2000	373-2117
Web: www.greensboro-nc.gov					
Greenville 206 S Main St	Greenville	SC	29601	864-232-2273	467-5725
TF: 800-849-4339 ■ *Web:* www.greatergreenville.com					
Gulfport 2309 15th St	Gulfport	MS	39501	228-868-5700	868-5800
Web: www.ci.gulfport.ms.us					
Halifax PO Box 1749	Halifax	NS	B3J3A5	902-490-4210	490-4208
Web: www.halifax.ca					
Harrisburg 10 N 2nd St	Harrisburg	PA	17101	717-255-3060	255-3081
Web: www.harrisburgpa.gov					
Hartford 550 Main St	Hartford	CT	06103	860-522-4888	
Web: www.hartford.gov					

	City	State	Zip	Phone	Fax
Hattiesburg 200 Forest St	Hattiesburg	MS	39401	601-545-4550	545-4529
Web: www.hattiesburgms.com					
Helena 316 N Park Ave	Helena	MT	59623	406-447-8410	447-8434
Web: www.ci.helena.mt.us					
Hialeah 501 Palm Ave Suite 310	Hialeah	FL	33010	305-883-5820	883-5814
Web: www.ci.hialeah.fl.us					
Hilton Head Island 1 Town Center Ct	Hilton Head Island	SC	29928	843-341-4600	842-7728
Web: www.ci.hilton-head-island.sc.us					
Honolulu 530 S King St	Honolulu	HI	96813	808-523-4385	527-6888
Web: www.co.honolulu.hi.us					
Hot Springs PO Box 700	Hot Springs	AR	71902	501-321-6800	321-6809
Web: www.ci.hot-springs.ar.us					
Houston 901 Bagby St	Houston	TX	77002	713-247-1000	247-2355
Web: www.houstontx.gov/					
Huntington Beach 2000 Main St	Huntington Beach	CA	92648	714-536-5511	374-1557
Web: www.ci.huntington-beach.ca.us					
Huntsville PO Box 308	Huntsville	AL	35804	256-427-5000	427-5257
Web: www.hsvcity.com/					
Independence 111 E Maple Ave	Independence	MO	64050	816-325-7000	325-7012
Web: www.ci.independence.mo.us					
Indianapolis 200 E Washington St Suite 2501	Indianapolis	IN	46204	317-327-3601	327-3980
Web: www.indygov.org					
Irving 825 W Irving Blvd	Irving	TX	75060	972-721-2600	721-2420
Web: www.ci.irving.tx.us					
Jackson (MS) 219 S President St	Jackson	MS	39205	601-960-1084	960-2193
Web: www.city.jackson.ms.us					
Jackson (WY) 150 E Pearl Ave	Jackson	WY	83001	307-733-3932	739-0919
Web: www.ci.jackson.wy.us					
Jacksonville 117 W Duval St Suite 400	Jacksonville	FL	32202	904-630-1776	630-2391
Web: www.coj.net					
Jefferson City 320 E McCarty St	Jefferson City	MO	65101	573-634-6304	634-6329
Web: www.jeffcitymo.org					
Jersey City 280 Grove St	Jersey City	NJ	07302	201-547-5000	547-5461
Web: www.cityofjerseycity.com					
Johnson City 601 E Main St	Johnson City	TN	37601	423-434-6000	434-6295
Web: www.johnsoncitytn.com					
Juneau 155 S Seward St	Juneau	AK	99801	907-586-5278	586-2536
Web: www.juneau.org					
Kansas City (KS) 701 N 7th St Municipal Office Bldg.	Kansas City	KS	66101	913-573-5000	573-5210
Web: www.wycokck.org					
Kansas City (MO) 414 E 12th St 25th Fl	Kansas City	MO	64106	816-513-3360	513-3353
Web: www.kcmo.org					
Key West 525 Angela St	Key West	FL	33040	305-809-3834	809-3833
Web: www.keywestcity.com					
Knoxville 400 Main St Rm 691	Knoxville	TN	37902	865-215-2000	215-2085
Web: www.ci.knoxville.tn.us					
Lafayette PO Box 4017C	Lafayette	LA	70502	337-291-8200	291-8399
Web: www.lafayettegov.org					
Lansing 124 W Michigan Ave 9th Fl	Lansing	MI	48933	517-483-4131	377-0068
Web: cityoflansingmi.com					
Las Cruces 200 N Church St	Las Cruces	NM	88001	505-541-2000	541-2117
Web: www.las-cruces.org					
Las Vegas 400 Stewart Ave 1st Fl	Las Vegas	NV	89101	702-229-6011	382-4803
Web: www.lasvegasnevada.gov					
Lincoln 555 S 10th St	Lincoln	NE	68508	402-441-7511	441-7120
Web: www.lincoln.ne.gov					
Little Rock 500 W Markham St	Little Rock	AR	72201	501-371-4500	371-4498
Web: www.littlerock.org					
Long Beach 333 W Ocean Blvd	Long Beach	CA	90802	562-570-6101	570-6789
Web: www.longbeach.gov					
Los Angeles 200 N Spring St Rm 360	Los Angeles	CA	90012	213-978-1022	978-1027
Web: www.lacity.org					
Louisville 601 W Jefferson St	Louisville	KY	40202	502-574-1100	574-4420
Web: louisvilleky.gov/					
Lubbock 1625 13th St	Lubbock	TX	79401	806-775-3000	775-3002
Web: www.ci.lubbock.tx.us					
Macon 700 Poplar St	Macon	GA	31201	478-751-7170	751-7931
Web: www.macon.ga.us					
Madison 210 ML King Jr Blvd Rm 403	Madison	WI	53703	608-266-4611	267-8671
Web: www.cityofmadison.com					
Manchester 1 City Hall Plaza	Manchester	NH	03101	603-624-6455	624-6481
Web: www.manchesternh.gov					
Memphis 125 N Main St	Memphis	TN	38103	901-576-6500	576-6200
Web: www.cityofmemphis.org					
Mesa 55 N Center St	Mesa	AZ	85201	480-644-2011	644-2821
Web: www.cityofmesa.org					
Miami 3500 Pan American Dr	Miami	FL	33133	305-250-5400	250-5410
Web: www.ci.miami.fl.us					
Milwaukee 200 E Wells St	Milwaukee	WI	53202	414-286-2150	286-3456
Minneapolis 350 S 5th St	Minneapolis	MN	55415	612-673-3000	673-3812
Web: www.ci.minneapolis.mn.us					
Mobile PO Box 1827	Mobile	AL	36633	251-208-7411	208-7576
Web: www.cityofmobile.org					
Modesto PO Box 642	Modesto	CA	95353	209-577-5200	571-5152
Web: www.modestogov.com					
Monterey 580 Pacific St	Monterey	CA	93940	831-646-3935	646-3702
Web: www.monterey.org					
Montgomery PO Box 1111	Montgomery	AL	36101	334-241-4400	241-2266
Web: www.montgomeryal.gov/					
Montpelier 39 Main St	Montpelier	VT	05602	802-223-9502	223-9519
Web: montpelier-vt.org					
Montreal 275 Notre-Dame St E	Montreal	QC	H2Y1C6	514-872-6395	872-2896
Web: www.ville.montreal.qc.ca					
Morgantown 389 Spruce St	Morgantown	WV	26505	304-284-7439	284-7525
Web: www.morgantown.com					
Myrtle Beach 937 Broadway St	Myrtle Beach	SC	29577	843-918-1000	918-1028
Web: www.cityofmyrtlebeach.com					
Naples 735 8th St S	Naples	FL	34102	239-213-1015	213-1025
Web: www.naplesgov.com					
Nashville & Davidson County 225 Polk Ave	Nashville	TN	37203	615-862-6000	862-6040
Web: www.nashville.gov					
New Haven 165 Church St	New Haven	CT	06510	203-946-8200	946-7683
Web: www.cityofnewhaven.com					
New Orleans 1300 Perdido St	New Orleans	LA	70112	504-658-4000	658-4938
Web: www.cityofno.com					
New York Broadway & Murray Sts	New York	NY	10007	212-788-3000	788-2460
Web: www.nyc.gov					
Newark 920 Broad St	Newark	NJ	07102	973-733-8004	733-5352
Web: www.ci.newark.nj.us					
Newport 43 Broadway	Newport	RI	02840	401-846-9600	845-2510
Web: www.cityofnewport.com					
Newport News 2400 Washington Ave	Newport News	VA	23607	757-926-8411	926-8599
Web: www.ci.newport-news.va.us					
Norfolk 810 Union St	Norfolk	VA	23510	757-664-4000	664-4226
Web: www.norfolk.gov					
Oakland 1 Frank H Ogawa Plaza 3rd Fl	Oakland	CA	94612	510-238-3301	238-3301
Web: www.oaklandnet.com					

	City	State	Zip	Phone	Fax
Ocean City 301 Baltimore Ave TF: 800-626-2326 ■ Web: www.town.ocean-city.md.us	Ocean City	MD	21842	410-289-8931	289-7385
Ogden 2549 Washington Blvd Web: www.ogdencity.com	Ogden	UT	84401	801-629-8150	629-8154
Oklahoma City 200 N Walker Ave Web: www.okc.gov	Oklahoma City	OK	73102	405-297-2578	297-3124
Olympia PO Box 1967 Web: www.ci.olympia.wa.us	Olympia	WA	98507	360-753-8447	709-2791
Omaha 1819 Farnam St Suite LC1 Web: www.ci.omaha.ne.us	Omaha	NE	68183	402-444-5550	444-5263
Orlando 400 S Orange Ave Web: www.cityoforlando.net	Orlando	FL	32801	407-246-2221	246-2842
Ottawa 110 Laurier Ave W Web: city.ottawa.on.ca	Ottawa	ON	K1P1J1	613-580-2400	580-2495
Oxnard 305 W 3rd St Web: www.ci.oxnard.ca.us	Oxnard	CA	93030	805-385-7803	385-7806
Palm Springs 3200 E Tahquitz Canyon Way Web: www.ci.palm-springs.ca.us	Palm Springs	CA	92262	760-323-8299	322-8332
Paterson 155 Market St Web: www.patcity.com	Paterson	NJ	07506	973-321-1500	321-1311
Pensacola 180 Governmental Center Web: www.ci.pensacola.fl.us	Pensacola	FL	32521	850-435-1626	436-5208
Peoria 419 Fulton St Suite 401 Web: www.ci.peoria.il.us	Peoria	IL	61602	309-494-8565	494-8574
Philadelphia Broad & Market Sts Web: www.phila.gov	Philadelphia	PA	19107	215-686-1776	686-2180
Phoenix 200 W Washington St 11th Fl Web: www.phoenix.gov	Phoenix	AZ	85003	602-262-7111	495-5583
Pierre 222 E Dakota Ave Web: ci.pierre.sd.us	Pierre	SD	57501	605-773-7407	773-7406
Pittsburgh 414 Grant St City-County Bldg Web: www.city.pittsburgh.pa.us	Pittsburgh	PA	15219	412-255-2100	255-2821
Plano 1520 Ave K Web: www.plano.gov/	Plano	TX	75074	972-941-7000	423-9587
Pocatello 911 N 7th Ave Web: www.pocatello.us	Pocatello	ID	83201	208-234-6163	234-6297
Portland (ME) 389 Congress St Web: www.portlandmaine.gov	Portland	ME	04101	207-874-8610	874-8612
Portland (OR) 1221 SW 4th Ave Web: www.portlandonline.com/	Portland	OR	97204	503-823-4000	823-3588
Providence 25 Dorrance St Web: www.providenceri.com	Providence	RI	02903	401-421-7740	421-6492
Provo 351 W Center St Web: www.provo.org	Provo	UT	84601	801-852-6100	852-6107
Quebec 2 des Jardins St Rm 216 Web: www.ville.quebec.qc.ca	Quebec	QC	G1R4S9	418-641-6010	641-6318
Raleigh PO Box 590 Web: www.raleigh-nc.org	Raleigh	NC	27602	919-890-3100	890-3058
Rapid City 300 6th St Web: www.rcgov.org	Rapid City	SD	57701	605-394-4110	394-6793
Rehoboth Beach 229 Rehoboth Ave Web: www.cityofrehoboth.com	Rehoboth Beach	DE	19971	302-227-6181	227-4643
Reno PO Box 1900 Web: www.cityofreno.com	Reno	NV	89505	775-334-2030	334-2432
Richmond 900 E Broad St Rm 201 Web: www.richmondgov.com	Richmond	VA	23219	804-646-7977	646-7978
Riverside 3900 Main St Web: www.riversideca.gov	Riverside	CA	92522	951-826-5312	826-5470
Roanoke 215 Church Ave SW Web: www.roanokegov.com	Roanoke	VA	24011	540-853-2000	853-1145
Rochester (MN) 201 4th St SE Web: www.ci.rochester.mn.us	Rochester	MN	55904	507-285-8082	287-7979
Rochester (NY) 30 Church St Web: www.ci.rochester.ny.us	Rochester	NY	14614	585-428-7045	428-6059
Rockford 425 E State St Web: www.ci.rockford.il.us	Rockford	IL	61104	815-987-5590	967-6952
Sacramento 915 'I' St Web: www.cityofsacramento.org	Sacramento	CA	95814	916-808-7200	808-7672
Saint Augustine 75 King St Web: www.staugustinegovernment.com	Saint Augustine	FL	32084	904-825-1007	823-4311
Saint Louis 1200 Market St Web: stlouis.missouri.org	Saint Louis	MO	63103	314-622-3201	622-4061
Saint Paul 15 W Kellogg Blvd 390 City Hall Web: www.stpaul.gov	Saint Paul	MN	55101	651-266-8500	266-8513
Saint Petersburg 175 5th St N Web: www.stpete.org	Saint Petersburg	FL	33701	727-893-7448	892-5102
Salem 555 Liberty St SE Rm 220 Web: www.cityofsalem.net	Salem	OR	97301	503-588-6255	588-6354
Salt Lake City 451 S State St Web: www.slcgov.com	Salt Lake City	UT	84111	801-535-7704	535-6331
San Antonio PO Box 839966 Web: www.sanantonio.gov	San Antonio	TX	78283	210-207-7040	207-7027
San Bernardino 300 N 'D' St Web: www.ci.san-bernardino.ca.us	San Bernardino	CA	92418	909-384-5002	384-5158
San Diego 202 C St Web: www.sandiego.gov	San Diego	CA	92101	619-533-4000	533-4045
San Francisco 1 Dr Carleton B Goodlett Pl Rm 200 Web: www.sfgov.org	San Francisco	CA	94102	415-554-6141	554-6141
San Jose 200 Santa Clara St Web: www.sanjoseca.gov	San Jose	CA	95113	408-535-3500	292-6731
Santa Ana 20 Civic Center Plaza Web: www.ci.santa-ana.ca.us	Santa Ana	CA	92701	714-647-6900	647-6954
Santa Fe 200 Lincoln Ave Web: www.santafenm.gov	Santa Fe	NM	87501	505-955-6520	955-6910
Savannah PO Box 1027 Web: www.ci.savannah.ga.us	Savannah	GA	31402	912-651-6441	651-4260
Scottsdale 3939 Civic Center Dr Web: www.scottsdaleaz.gov	Scottsdale	AZ	85251	480-312-2600	312-2738
Scranton 340 N Washington Ave Web: www.scrantonpa.gov/	Scranton	PA	18503	570-348-4113	348-4207
Seattle 600 4th Ave Web: seattle.gov	Seattle	WA	98104	206-386-1234	684-5360
Shreveport PO Box 31109 Web: www.ci.shreveport.la.us	Shreveport	LA	71130	318-673-2489	673-5099
Sioux Falls 224 W 9th St Web: www.siouxfalls.org	Sioux Falls	SD	57104	605-367-8000	367-7801
South Bend 227 W Jefferson Blvd 455 County-City Bldg Web: www.ci.south-bend.in.us	South Bend	IN	46601	574-235-9221	235-9173
Spokane 808 W Spokane Falls Blvd Web: www.spokanecity.org	Spokane	WA	99201	509-625-6350	625-6217
Springfield (IL) 800 E Monroe St Rm 300 Web: www.springfield.il.us	Springfield	IL	62701	217-789-2306	789-2109
Springfield (MA) 36 Court St Web: www.springfieldcityhall.com/COS/	Springfield	MA	01103	413-787-6000	
Springfield (MO) 840 Boonville Ave Web: www.springfieldmo.gov/home	Springfield	MO	65802	417-864-1000	864-1649
Stamford 888 Washington Blvd 10th Fl Web: www.cityofstamford.org	Stamford	CT	06904	203-977-4150	977-5845
Stockton 425 N El Dorado St 2nd Fl Web: www.stocktongov.com	Stockton	CA	95202	209-937-8212	937-7149
Syracuse 233 E Washington St Web: www.syracuse.ny.us	Syracuse	NY	13202	315-448-8216	448-8489
Tacoma 747 Market St Web: www.cityoftacoma.org	Tacoma	WA	98402	253-591-5000	591-5300
Tallahassee 300 S Adams St Web: www.talgov.com	Tallahassee	FL	32301	850-891-0010	891-8542
Tampa 306 E Jackson St Web: www.tampagov.net	Tampa	FL	33602	813-274-8251	274-7050
Tempe 31 E 5th St Web: www.tempe.gov	Tempe	AZ	85281	480-350-8221	350-8930
Toledo 670 Jackson Ave 1 Government Center Web: www.ci.toledo.oh.us	Toledo	OH	43604	419-245-1001	245-1370
Topeka 215 SE 7th St Web: www.topeka.org	Topeka	KS	66603	785-368-3754	368-3966
Toronto 100 Queen St W Web: www.toronto.ca	Toronto	ON	M5H2N2	416-392-8016	392-2980
Trenton 319 E State St Web: www.ci.trenton.nj.us	Trenton	NJ	08608	609-989-3185	989-3190
Tucson 255 W Alameda St Web: www.ci.tucson.az.us	Tucson	AZ	85701	520-791-4204	791-5198
Tulsa 200 Civic Center Web: www.cityoftulsa.org	Tulsa	OK	74103	918-596-2100	596-9010
Tupelo 71 E Troy St Web: www.ci.tupelo.ms.us	Tupelo	MS	38804	662-841-6513	840-2075
Tuscaloosa 2201 University Blvd Web: www.ci.tuscaloosa.al.us	Tuscaloosa	AL	35401	205-349-2010	349-0147
Vancouver (BC) 453 W 12th Ave Web: www.city.vancouver.bc.ca	Vancouver	BC	V5Y1V4	604-873-7011	873-7419
Vancouver (WA) 210 E 13th St Web: www.ci.vancouver.wa.us	Vancouver	WA	98660	360-696-8121	696-8049
Virginia Beach 2401 Courthouse Dr Municipal Center Bldg 1 Web: www.vbgov.com	Virginia Beach	VA	23456	757-385-8151	
Washington 1350 Pennsylvania Ave NW Web: www.dc.gov	Washington	DC	20004	202-727-1000	727-0505
West Palm Beach 200 2nd St Web: www.cityofwpb.com	West Palm Beach	FL	33401	561-659-8000	822-1424
Wheeling 1500 Chapline St Web: www.cityofwheelingwv.org	Wheeling	WV	26003	304-234-3694	234-6419
Wichita 455 N Main St 1st Fl Web: www.wichita.gov	Wichita	KS	67202	316-268-4331	268-4567
Williamsburg 401 Lafayette St Web: www.ci.williamsburg.va.us	Williamsburg	VA	23185	757-220-6100	220-6107
Wilmington 800 French St Web: www.ci.wilmington.de.us	Wilmington	DE	19801	302-576-2489	571-4607
Winnipeg 510 Main St Main Fl Web: www.winnipeg.ca	Winnipeg	MB	R3B1B9	204-986-2171	947-3452
Winston-Salem 101 N Main St Suite 170 Web: www.cityofws.org	Winston-Salem	NC	27101	336-727-2123	748-3060
Worcester 455 Main St Web: www.ci.worcester.ma.us	Worcester	MA	01608	508-799-1000	799-1208
Yonkers 40 S Broadway Web: www.cityofyonkers.com	Yonkers	NY	10701	914-377-6000	377-6029
Youngstown 26 S Phelps St Web: www.cityofyoungstownoh.org	Youngstown	OH	44503	330-742-8710	742-8707

341 GOVERNMENT - COUNTY

Alabama

	City	State	Zip	Phone	Fax
Autauga County 134 N Court St Rm 106 Web: www.autaugaco.org/	Prattville	AL	36067	334-361-3701	361-3724
Baldwin County 312 Court House Sq Suite 12 Web: www.co.baldwin.al.us	Bay Minette	AL	36507	251-937-9561	580-2500
Barbour County PO Box 398	Clayton	AL	36016	334-775-3203	775-1102
Bibb County PO Box 185 Web: www.bibbcountyalabama.com/	Centreville	AL	35042	205-926-3103	926-3132
Blount County 220 2nd Ave E Rm 106 Web: www.co.blount.al.us/	Oneonta	AL	35121	205-625-4160	625-5961
Bullock County PO Box 472 Web: www.unionspringsalabama.com/	Union Springs	AL	36089	334-738-3883	738-3839
Butler County PO Box 756	Greenville	AL	36037	334-382-3612	382-3506
Calhoun County 1702 Noble St Suite 103 Web: www.calhounchamber.com	Anniston	AL	36201	256-241-2800	231-1744
Chambers County 2 Lafayette St Courthouse Web: www.chamberscounty.com	Lafayette	AL	36862	334-864-4348	
Cherokee County 260 Cedar Bluff Rd Suite 103 Web: www.cherokee-chamber.org	Centre	AL	35960	256-927-3668	927-3669
Chilton County PO Box 1948	Clanton	AL	35046	205-755-1551	280-7204
Choctaw County 117 S Mulberry St Suite 9	Butler	AL	36904	205-459-2417	459-4248
Clarke County PO Box 548	Grove Hill	AL	36451	251-275-3507	275-8517
Clay County PO Box 187	Ashland	AL	36251	256-354-7888	354-3208
Cleburne County 120 Vickery St Rm 202	Heflin	AL	36264	256-463-2651	463-2257
Coffee County 230-M Court Ave	Elba	AL	36323	334-897-2954	
Colbert County 201 N Main St Web: www.colbertcounty.org	Tuscumbia	AL	35674	256-386-8500	386-8510
Conecuh County 409 Bellville St	Evergreen	AL	36401	251-578-2066	578-7013
Coosa County PO Box 10	Rockford	AL	35136	256-377-2420	377-2524
Covington County 1 Court Sq County Courthouse	Andalusia	AL	36420	334-428-2540	428-2575
Crenshaw County PO Box 227	Luverne	AL	36049	334-335-6568	335-3616
Cullman County 500 2nd Ave SW Rm 202 Web: www.co.cullman.al.us	Cullman	AL	35055	256-739-3530	739-3525
Dale County 202 Hwy 123 S Suite C	Ozark	AL	36360	334-774-6025	774-1841
Dallas County PO Box 987	Selma	AL	36702	334-874-2560	874-2587
DeKalb County 111 Grand Ave SW Suite 200 Web: www.dekalbcountyal.us	Fort Payne	AL	35967	256-845-8500	845-8502
Elmore County PO Box 310 Web: elmoreco.org	Wetumpka	AL	36092	334-567-1124	567-5957
Escambia County PO Box 856 Web: www.co.escambia.al.us	Brewton	AL	36427	251-867-0305	867-0365
Etowah County 800 Forrest Ave Web: www.etowahcounty.org	Gadsden	AL	35901	256-549-5300	549-5400
Fayette County 103 1st Ave NW Courthouse Annex Suite 2	Fayette	AL	35555	205-932-4510	932-2902
Franklin County PO Box 1028 Web: www.franklincountychamber.org	Russellville	AL	35653	256-332-8851	332-8855
Geneva County PO Box 86	Geneva	AL	36340	334-684-5620	684-5605

Name / Address	City	State	ZIP	Phone	Fax
Greene County PO Box 307	Eutaw	AL	35462	205-372-3598	372-1510
Web: greenecountyalabama.com					
Hale County PO Box 396	Greensboro	AL	36744	334-624-4257	624-1715
Web: www.halecoal.org					
Henry County 101 Court Sq Suite J	Abbeville	AL	36310	334-585-2753	585-5006
Houston County PO Drawer 6406	Dothan	AL	36302	334-677-4741	794-6633
Web: www.houstoncounty.org					
Jackson County 102 E Laurel St Suite 47 Courthouse	Scottsboro	AL	35768	256-574-9280	574-9321
Jefferson County 716 Richard Arrington Jr Blvd N Suite 210	Birmingham	AL	35203	205-325-5555	325-4860
Web: www.jeffcointouch.com					
Lamar County PO Box 338	Vernon	AL	35592	205-695-7333	695-8522
Lauderdale County PO Box 1059	Florence	AL	35631	256-760-5750	760-5703
Web: lauderdalecountyonline.com					
Lawrence County PO Box 307	Moulton	AL	35650	256-974-0663	974-2403
Web: www.naiap.com					
Lee County PO Box 666	Opelika	AL	36803	334-745-9767	742-9478
Limestone County 310 W Washington St	Athens	AL	35611	256-233-6400	233-6403
Web: www.co.limestone.al.us					
Lowndes County PO Box 65	Hayneville	AL	36040	334-548-2331	548-5101
Macon County 101 E Northside St Courthouse	Tuskegee	AL	36083	334-727-5120	724-2621
Madison County 100 Northside Sq	Huntsville	AL	35801	256-532-3492	532-6994
Web: www.co.madison.al.us					
Marengo County PO Box 480715	Linden	AL	36748	334-295-2200	295-2254
Marion County PO Box 1595	Hamilton	AL	35570	205-921-7451	952-9851
Web: www.sonet.net/marioncounty/					
Marshall County 424 Blount Ave	Guntersville	AL	35976	256-571-7701	571-7703
Web: www.marshallco.org					
Mobile County 205 Government St	Mobile	AL	36644	251-574-5077	
Web: www.mobilecounty.org					
Monroe County PO Box 8	Monroeville	AL	36461	251-743-4107	575-7934
Web: www.monroecountyal.com					
Montgomery County PO Box 1667	Montgomery	AL	36102	334-832-1210	832-2533
Web: www.mc-ala.org					
Morgan County PO Box 668	Decatur	AL	35602	256-351-4730	351-4738
Web: www.co.morgan.al.us					
Perry County PO Box 505	Marion	AL	36756	334-683-6106	
Pickens County PO Box 460	Carrollton	AL	35447	205-367-2020	367-2025
Pike County PO Box 1147	Troy	AL	36081	334-566-6374	566-0142
Randolph County PO Box 328	Wedowee	AL	36278	256-357-4551	357-9012
Russell County 501 14th St	Phenix City	AL	36867	334-298-0516	297-6250
Saint Clair County 165 5th Ave Suite 100	Ashville	AL	35953	205-594-2100	594-2110
Web: www.stclairco.com					
Shelby County PO Box 1810	Columbiana	AL	35051	205-669-3760	669-3786
Web: www.shelbycountyalabama.com					
Sumter County PO Box 936	Livingston	AL	35470	205-652-2291	
Talladega County PO Box 6170	Talladega	AL	35161	256-362-1357	761-2147
Web: www.talladegacounty.com					
Tallapoosa County 125 N Broadnax St Rm 131	Dadeville	AL	36853	256-825-4268	825-1009
Tuscaloosa County 714 Greensboro Ave	Tuscaloosa	AL	35401	205-349-3870	
Web: www.tuscco.com/					
Walker County PO Box 1447	Jasper	AL	35502	205-384-7230	384-7003
Web: www.walkercounty.com					
Washington County PO Box 146	Chatom	AL	36518	251-847-2208	847-3677
Web: www.washingtoncountyalgov.com					
Wilcox County PO Box 608	Camden	AL	36726	334-682-4126	682-4025
Winston County PO Box 309	Double Springs	AL	35553	205-489-5533	489-5140

Alaska

Name / Address	City	State	ZIP	Phone	Fax
Aleutians East Borough PO Box 349	Sand Point	AK	99661	907-383-2699	383-3496
TF: 888-383-2699 ■ *Web:* www.aleutianseast.org					
Anchorage Municipality PO Box 196650	Anchorage	AK	99519	907-343-4311	343-4313
Web: www.muni.org/homepage/index.cfm					
Bristol Bay Borough PO Box 189	Naknek	AK	99633	907-246-4224	246-6633
Web: www.theborough.com					
Denali Borough PO Box 480	Healy	AK	99743	907-683-1330	683-1340
Web: www.denaliborough.govoffice.com					
Fairbanks North Star Borough 809 Pioneer Rd	Fairbanks	AK	99701	907-459-1000	459-1224
Web: www.co.fairbanks.ak.us					
Haines Borough PO Box 1209	Haines	AK	99827	907-766-2711	766-2716
Web: www.haines.ak.us					
Juneau City & Borough 155 S Seward St	Juneau	AK	99801	907-586-5278	586-5385
Web: www.juneau.org					
Kenai Peninsula Borough 144 N Binkley St	Soldotna	AK	99669	907-262-4441	262-8615
Web: www.borough.kenai.ak.us					
Ketchikan Gateway Borough 344 Front St	Ketchikan	AK	99901	907-228-6605	247-8439
Web: www.borough.ketchikan.ak.us					
Kodiak Island Borough 710 Mill Bay Rd	Kodiak	AK	99615	907-486-9311	486-9391
Web: www.kib.co.kodiak.ak.us					
Lake & Peninsula Borough PO Box 495	King Salmon	AK	99613	907-246-3421	246-6602
Matanuska-Susitna Borough 350 E Dahlia Ave	Palmer	AK	99645	907-745-4801	745-9845
Web: www.co.mat-su.ak.us					
North Slope Borough PO Box 69	Barrow	AK	99723	907-852-2611	852-0229
Web: www.co.north-slope.ak.us					
Northwest Arctic Borough PO Box 1110	Kotzebue	AK	99752	907-442-2500	442-2930
Web: www.nwabor.org					
Sitka City & Borough 100 Lincoln St	Sitka	AK	99835	907-747-3294	747-7403
Web: www.cityofsitka.com					
Yakutat City & Borough PO Box 160	Yakutat	AK	99689	907-784-3323	784-3281
Web: www.yakutat.net					

Arizona

Name / Address	City	State	ZIP	Phone	Fax
Apache County PO Box 365	Saint Johns	AZ	85936	928-337-4364	337-2771
Web: www.co.apache.az.us					
Cochise County 1415 W Melody Ln	Bisbee	AZ	85603	520-432-9200	432-5016
Web: www.co.cochise.az.us					
Coconino County 219 E Cherry Ave	Flagstaff	AZ	86001	928-774-5011	779-6785
TF: 800-559-9289 ■ *Web:* www.coconino.az.gov					
Gila County 1400 E Ash St	Globe	AZ	85501	928-425-3231	425-0319
TF: 800-304-4452 ■ *Web:* www.co.gila.az.us					
Graham County 800 W Main	Safford	AZ	85546	928-428-3250	428-5951
Web: www.graham.az.gov					
Greenlee County PO Box 908	Clifton	AZ	85533	928-865-2072	865-4417
Web: www.co.greenlee.az.us					
La Paz County 1108 Joshua Ave	Parker	AZ	85344	928-669-6115	669-9709
Web: www.co.la-paz.az.us					
Maricopa County 301 W Jefferson St 10th Fl	Phoenix	AZ	85003	602-506-3415	506-6402
Web: www.maricopa.gov					
Mohave County PO Box 7000	Kingman	AZ	86402	928-753-0729	753-5103
Web: www.co.mohave.az.us					
Navajo County PO Box 668	Holbrook	AZ	86025	928-524-4188	524-4261
Web: www.co.navajo.az.us					
Pima County 130 W Congress St 10th Fl	Tucson	AZ	85701	520-740-8661	740-8171
Web: www.co.pima.az.us					
Pinal County 31 N Pinal St	Florence	AZ	85232	520-866-6000	866-6512
Web: www.co.pinal.az.us					
Santa Cruz County 2150 N Congress Dr	Nogales	AZ	85621	520-761-7800	761-7700
Web: www.co.santa-cruz.az.us					
Yavapai County 1015 Fair St Rm 310	Prescott	AZ	86305	928-771-3200	771-3257
Web: www.co.yavapai.az.us					
Yuma County 198 S Main St	Yuma	AZ	85364	928-329-2104	329-2001
Web: www.co.yuma.az.us					

Arkansas

Name / Address	City	State	ZIP	Phone	Fax
Arkansas County PO Box 719	Stuttgart	AR	72160	870-673-7311	
Ashley County 205 E Jefferson St Box 5	Hamburg	AR	71646	870-853-2020	853-2082
Baxter County 1 E 7th St Room 103	Mountain Home	AR	72653	870-425-3475	424-5105
Web: www.baxtercounty.org					
Benton County 215 E Central St Suite 217	Bentonville	AR	72712	479-271-1013	271-1019
Web: www.co.benton.ar.us					
Boone County 100 N Main St Suite 201	Harrison	AR	72601	870-741-8428	741-9724
Bradley County 101 E Cedar St	Warren	AR	71671	870-226-3853	226-8401
Calhoun County PO Box 1175	Hampton	AR	71744	870-798-2517	798-2428
Carroll County 210 W Church St	Berryville	AR	72616	870-423-2022	423-7400
Chicot County 108 Main St County Courthouse	Lake Village	AR	71653	870-265-8000	265-8018
Clark County 401 Clay St	Arkadelphia	AR	71923	870-246-4491	246-6505
Web: www.clarkcountyarkansas.com					
Clay County PO Box 306	Piggott	AR	72454	870-598-2813	598-2813
Cleburne County 301 W Main St	Heber Springs	AR	72543	501-362-4620	362-4622
Cleveland County PO Box 368	Rison	AR	71665	870-325-6521	325-6144
Columbia County 1 Court Sq Suite 1	Magnolia	AR	71753	870-235-3774	235-3773
Conway County 117 S Moose St	Morrilton	AR	72110	501-354-9621	354-9610
Craighead County PO Box 1167	Jonesboro	AR	72403	870-933-4520	933-4514
Web: www.craigheadcounty.org					
Crawford County 300 Main St County Courthouse Rm 7	Van Buren	AR	72956	479-474-1312	471-3236
Crittenden County 100 Court St County Courthouse	Marion	AR	72364	870-739-4434	739-3072
Cross County 705 E Union St Rm 8	Wynne	AR	72396	870-238-5735	238-5739
Dallas County 206 W 3rd St	Fordyce	AR	71742	870-352-2307	352-7179
Desha County PO Box 188	Arkansas City	AR	71630	870-877-2426	877-2531
Drew County 210 S Main St	Monticello	AR	71655	870-460-6250	460-6246
Faulkner County 801 Locust St	Conway	AR	72034	501-450-4909	450-4938
Franklin County 211 W Commercial St	Ozark	AR	72949	479-667-3607	667-4247
Fulton County PO Box 219	Salem	AR	72576	870-895-3310	895-3383
Garland County 501 Ouachita Ave	Hot Springs	AR	71901	501-622-3610	624-0665
Web: www.garlandcounty.org					
Grant County 101 W Center St County Courthouse Rm 106	Sheridan	AR	72150	870-942-2631	942-3564
Greene County PO Box 62	Paragould	AR	72451	870-239-6311	239-3550
Web: www.greenecounty.org					
Hempstead County PO Box 1420	Hope	AR	71802	870-777-2241	777-7829
Hot Spring County 210 Locust St	Malvern	AR	72104	501-332-2291	332-2221
Howard County 421 N Main St Rm 10	Nashville	AR	71852	870-845-7502	845-7505
Independence County 192 E Main St	Batesville	AR	72501	870-793-8828	793-8831
Izard County PO Box 95	Melbourne	AR	72556	870-368-4316	368-4748
Jackson County 208 Main St County Courthouse	Newport	AR	72112	870-523-7420	523-7404
Jefferson County PO Box 6317	Pine Bluff	AR	71611	870-541-5322	541-5324
Web: www.jeffersoncountyark.com					
Johnson County 215 Main St	Clarksville	AR	72830	479-754-3967	754-2286
Lafayette County 1 Courthouse Sq	Lewisville	AR	71845	870-921-4858	921-4505
Lawrence County PO Box 526	Walnut Ridge	AR	72476	870-886-1111	886-1122
Lee County 15 E Chestnut St	Marianna	AR	72360	870-295-7715	295-7766
Lincoln County 300 S Drew St	Star City	AR	71667	870-628-5114	628-5794
Little River County 351 N 2nd St	Ashdown	AR	71822	870-898-7208	898-7207
Logan County 366 N Broadway Ave	Booneville	AR	72927	479-675-2951	675-2952
Lonoke County 301 N Center St	Lonoke	AR	72086	501-676-2368	676-3038
Madison County 201 Main St	Huntsville	AR	72740	479-738-2747	738-2735
Marion County PO Box 545	Yellville	AR	72687	870-449-6231	449-4979
Miller County 400 Laurel St Rm 105	Texarkana	AR	71854	870-774-1501	773-4090
Mississippi County 200 W Walnut St Rm 103	Blytheville	AR	72315	870-762-2411	838-7784
Web: mcagov.missconet.com					
Monroe County 123 Madison St	Clarendon	AR	72029	870-747-3632	747-5961
Montgomery County PO Box 717	Mount Ida	AR	71957	870-867-3114	867-4354
Nevada County PO Box 621	Prescott	AR	71857	870-887-2710	887-5795
Newton County PO Box 410	Jasper	AR	72641	870-446-5125	446-5775
Ouachita County PO Box 644	Camden	AR	71711	870-837-2210	837-2218
Perry County 310 W Main St Suite 105	Perryville	AR	72126	501-889-5126	889-5759
Phillips County 620 Cherry St Suite 202 County Courthouse	Helena	AR	72342	870-338-5505	338-5509
Pike County PO Box 219	Murfreesboro	AR	71958	870-285-2231	285-3281
Poinsett County County Courthouse 401 Market St	Harrisburg	AR	72432	870-578-5333	
Polk County 507 Church Ave	Mena	AR	71953	479-394-8123	394-8115
Pope County 102 W Main St County Courthouse Suite 6	Russellville	AR	72801	479-968-6064	967-2291
Prairie County PO Box 1011	Des Arc	AR	72040	870-256-4434	
Pulaski County 401 W Markham St Suite 100	Little Rock	AR	72201	501-340-8500	340-8340
Web: www.co.pulaski.ar.us					
Randolph County 107 W Broadway	Pocahontas	AR	72455	870-892-5264	892-2269
Saint Francis County PO Box 1653	Forrest City	AR	72336	870-261-1725	630-1210
Saline County 215 N Main St Suite 9	Benton	AR	72015	501-303-5630	776-2412
Web: www.salinecounty.org					
Scott County 190 W 1st St Box 10	Waldron	AR	72958	479-637-2642	637-0124
Searcy County PO Box 998	Marshall	AR	72650	870-448-3807	448-5005
Sebastian County 35 S 6th St Rm 102	Fort Smith	AR	72901	479-782-5065	784-1567
Web: www.sebastiancountyonline.com					
Sevier County County Courthouse 115 N 3rd St Rm 102	De Queen	AR	71832	870-642-2852	642-3896
Sharp County PO Box 307	Ash Flat	AR	72513	870-994-7361	994-7712
Web: www.sharpcounty.org					
Stone County 107 W Main St Suite C	Mountain View	AR	72560	870-269-3351	269-3176
Union County 101 N Washington Rm 102 County Courthouse	El Dorado	AR	71730	870-864-1910	864-1927
Van Buren County 451 Main St Suite 2	Clinton	AR	72031	501-745-4140	745-7400
Washington County 280 N College Ave Suite 300	Fayetteville	AR	72701	479-444-1711	444-1894
Web: www.co.washington.ar.us					
White County 300 N Spruce St	Searcy	AR	72143	501-279-6200	279-6233
Web: www.whitecountyar.org					
Woodruff County Woodruff County Courthouse 500 N 3rd St	Augusta	AR	72006	870-347-2871	347-2608
Yell County PO Box 219	Danville	AR	72833	479-495-4850	

California

Name / Address	City	State	ZIP	Phone	Fax
Alameda County 1221 Oak St Suite 555	Oakland	CA	94612	510-272-6984	272-3784
Web: www.acgov.org					
Alpine County 99 Waters St	Markleeville	CA	96120	530-694-2281	694-2491
Web: www.alpinecountyca.com					
Amador County 810 Court St	Jackson	CA	95642	209-223-6470	257-0619
Web: www.co.amador.ca.us					

California (Cont'd)

	City	State	Zip	Phone	Fax
Butte County 25 County Center Dr	Oroville	CA	95965	530-538-7691	538-7975
Web: www.buttecounty.net					
Calaveras County 891 Mountain Ranch Rd	San Andreas	CA	95249	209-754-6370	754-6733
Web: www.co.calaveras.ca.us					
Colusa County 546 Jay St	Colusa	CA	95932	530-458-0500	458-0512
Web: www.colusacountyclerk.com					
Contra Costa County 651 Pine St 3rd Fl	Martinez	CA	94553	925-335-1080	335-1098
Web: www.co.contra-costa.ca.us					
Del Norte County 981 H St Suite 200	Crescent City	CA	95531	707-464-7204	464-1165
Web: www.co.del-norte.ca.us					
El Dorado County 360 Fair Ln Bldg B	Placerville	CA	95667	530-621-5490	621-2147
Web: co.el-dorado.ca.us					
Fresno County 2281 Tulare St Rm 304 Hall of Records	Fresno	CA	93721	559-488-1710	488-1830
Web: www.co.fresno.ca.us					
Glenn County 526 W Sycamore St	Willows	CA	95988	530-934-6400	934-6419
Web: www.countyofglenn.net					
Humboldt County 825 5th St	Eureka	CA	95501	707-445-7256	
Web: www.co.humboldt.ca.us					
Imperial County 940 W Main St Rm 202	El Centro	CA	92243	760-482-4427	482-4271
Web: www.co.imperial.ca.us					
Inyo County PO Drawer N	Independence	CA	93526	760-878-0292	878-2241
Web: www.countyofinyo.org					
Kern County 1115 Truxtun Ave 5th Fl	Bakersfield	CA	93301	661-868-3198	868-3190
Web: www.co.kern.ca.us					
Kings County 1400 W Lacey Blvd	Hanford	CA	93230	559-582-3211	582-6639
Web: www.co.kings.ca.us					
Lake County 255 N Forbes St	Lakeport	CA	95453	707-263-2371	263-2207
Web: www.co.lake.ca.us					
Lassen County 220 S Lassen St Suite 5	Susanville	CA	96130	530-251-8217	257-3480
Web: www.co.lassen.ca.us					
Los Angeles County 500 W Temple St	Los Angeles	CA	90012	213-974-1311	680-1122
Web: lacounty.info					
Madera County 209 W Yosemite Ave	Madera	CA	93637	559-675-7721	675-7870
Web: www.madera-county.com					
Marin County 3501 Civic Center Dr	San Rafael	CA	94903	415-499-6407	
Web: www.marin.org					
Mariposa County PO Box 28	Mariposa	CA	95338	209-966-2005	742-6860
Web: www.mariposacounty.org					
Mendocino County 501 Low Gap Rd Rm 1020	Ukiah	CA	95482	707-463-4376	463-4257
Web: www.co.mendocino.ca.us					
Merced County 2222 M St	Merced	CA	95340	209-385-7637	385-7375
Web: www.co.merced.ca.us					
Modoc County 204 S Court St Rm 204	Alturas	CA	96101	530-233-6200	233-2434
Web: www.modoccounty.us					
Mono County PO Box 237	Bridgeport	CA	93517	760-932-5530	932-5531
Web: www.monocounty.ca.gov					
Monterey County 168 W Alisal St	Salinas	CA	93901	831-755-5115	757-5792
Web: www.co.monterey.ca.us					
Napa County 1195 3rd St Rm 310	Napa	CA	94559	707-253-4421	253-4176
Web: www.co.napa.ca.us					
Nevada County 201 Church St Suite 5	Nevada City	CA	95959	530-265-1293	
Web: www.co.nevada.ca.us					
Orange County 12 Civic Center Plaza	Santa Ana	CA	92702	714-834-2500	834-2675
Web: www.oc.ca.gov					
Placer County 2954 Richardson Dr	Auburn	CA	95603	530-886-5600	886-5687
Web: www.placer.ca.gov					
Plumas County 520 Main St Rm 104	Quincy	CA	95971	530-283-6305	283-6415
Web: www.countyofplumas.com					
Riverside County 4080 Lemon St 4th Fl	Riverside	CA	92501	951-955-1100	955-1105
Web: www.co.riverside.ca.us					
Sacramento County 700 H St Rm 7650	Sacramento	CA	95814	916-874-5833	874-5885
Web: www.saccounty.net					
San Benito County 440 5th St Rm 206	Hollister	CA	95023	831-636-4029	636-2939
Web: www.san-benito.ca.us					
San Bernardino County 222 W Hospitality Ln	San Bernardino	CA	92415	909-387-8306	376-8940
Web: www.co.san-bernardino.ca.us					
San Diego County PO Box 121750	San Diego	CA	92112	619-237-0502	557-4155
Web: www.co.san-diego.ca.us					
San Francisco City & County 1 Dr Carlton B Goodlett Pl City Hall Rm 168	San Francisco	CA	94102	415-554-4950	554-4951
Web: www.sfgov.org					
San Joaquin County 222 E Weber Ave Rm 707	Stockton	CA	95202	209-468-3211	468-2875
Web: www.sjgov.org					
San Luis Obispo County 1155 Monterey St Rm D-120	San Luis Obispo	CA	93408	805-781-5245	781-1111
Web: www.slocounty.org					
San Mateo County 555 County Ctr	Redwood City	CA	94063	650-363-4712	363-4843
Web: www.co.sanmateo.ca.us					
Santa Barbara County PO Box 159	Santa Barbara	CA	93102	805-568-2550	568-3247
Web: www.countyofsb.org					
Santa Clara County 70 W Hedding St 11th Fl East Wing	San Jose	CA	95110	408-299-5105	293-5649
Web: claraweb.co.santa-clara.ca.us					
Santa Cruz County 701 Ocean St Rm 230	Santa Cruz	CA	95060	831-454-2800	
Web: www.co.santa-cruz.ca.us					
Shasta County 1643 Market St	Redding	CA	96099	530-225-5378	225-5454
Web: www.co.shasta.ca.us					
Sierra County 110 Courthouse Sq Rm 11	Downieville	CA	95936	530-289-3295	289-2830
Web: www.sierracounty.ws/					
Siskiyou County 201 4th St	Yreka	CA	96097	530-842-8005	842-8013
Web: www.co.siskiyou.ca.us					
Solano County 675 Texas St Suite 1900	Fairfield	CA	94533	707-784-7485	784-6311
Web: www.co.solano.ca.us					
Sonoma County 575 Administration Dr Suite 104A	Santa Rosa	CA	95403	707-565-2431	565-3778
Web: www.sonoma-county.org					
Stanislaus County PO Box 1670	Modesto	CA	95353	209-525-5251	525-5239
Web: www.co.stanislaus.ca.us					
Sutter County 433 2nd St	Yuba City	CA	95991	530-822-7120	822-7214
Web: www.co.sutter.ca.us					
Tehama County 633 Washington St Rm 11	Red Bluff	CA	96080	530-527-3350	527-1745
Web: www.co.tehama.ca.us					
Trinity County 101 Court St	Weaverville	CA	96093	530-623-1222	623-8398
Web: www.trinitycounty.org					
Tulare County 2800 W Burrel Ave	Visalia	CA	93291	559-733-6271	733-6898
Web: www.co.tulare.ca.us					
Tuolumne County 2 S Green St	Sonora	CA	95370	209-533-5511	533-5510
Web: www.tuolumnecounty.ca.gov					
Ventura County 800 S Victoria Ave	Ventura	CA	93009	805-654-2267	662-6543
Web: www.countyofventura.org					
Yolo County 625 Court St Suite 202	Woodland	CA	95695	530-666-8150	668-4029
Web: www.yolocounty.org					
Yuba County 915 8th St Suite 115	Marysville	CA	95901	530-749-7575	749-7312
Web: www.co.yuba.ca.us					

Colorado

	City	State	Zip	Phone	Fax
Adams County 450 S 4th Ave	Brighton	CO	80601	303-659-2120	654-6011
Web: www.co.adams.co.us					
Alamosa County PO Box 178	Alamosa	CO	81101	719-589-4848	589-1900
Web: www.ccionline.org/counties/alamosa.html					
Arapahoe County 5334 S Prince St	Littleton	CO	80166	303-795-4200	794-4625
Web: www.co.arapahoe.co.us					
Archuleta County PO Box 2589	Pagosa Springs	CO	81147	970-264-5633	264-6423
Web: www.archuletacounty.org					
Baca County 741 Main St	Springfield	CO	81073	719-523-4372	523-4881
Web: www.springfieldcolorado.com/countygov.html					
Bent County PO Box 350	Las Animas	CO	81054	719-456-1600	456-0375
Web: www.bentcounty.org					
Boulder County 1425 Pearl St 1st Fl	Boulder	CO	80301	303-413-7770	413-7775
Web: www.co.boulder.co.us					
Broomfield City & County 1 DesCombes Dr	Broomfield	CO	80020	303-469-3301	438-6296
Web: www.ci.broomfield.co.us					
Chaffee County PO Box 699	Salida	CO	81201	719-539-4004	539-8588
Web: www.chaffeecounty.org					
Cheyenne County PO Box 567	Cheyenne Wells	CO	80810	719-767-5685	767-5540
Clear Creek County PO Box 2000	Georgetown	CO	80444	303-679-2312	679-2440
Web: www.co.clear-creek.co.us					
Conejos County PO Box 157	Conejos	CO	81129	719-376-5565	376-5661
Costilla County PO Box 301	San Luis	CO	81152	719-672-3681	672-4493
Web: www.costilla-county.com					
Crowley County 631 Main St Suite 102	Ordway	CO	81063	719-267-4643	267-4608
Web: crowleycounty.net					
Custer County 205 S 6th St	Westcliffe	CO	81252	719-783-2441	783-2885
Web: www.custercountygov.com					
Delta County 501 Palmer St Suite 211	Delta	CO	81416	970-874-2150	874-2161
Web: www.deltacounty.com					
Denver City & County 201 W Colfax Ave 1st Fl	Denver	CO	80202	720-865-8400	
Web: www.denvergov.org					
Dolores County PO Box 608	Dove Creek	CO	81324	970-677-2383	677-2815
Web: www.dolorescounty.org					
Douglas County 100 3rd St	Castle Rock	CO	80104	303-660-7401	688-1293
Web: www.douglas.co.us					
Eagle County PO Box 850	Eagle	CO	81631	970-328-8612	328-8716
Web: www.eaglecounty.us					
El Paso County 200 S Cascade Ave	Colorado Springs	CO	80903	719-520-6200	520-6212
Web: www.elpasoco.com					
Elbert County PO Box 597	Kiowa	CO	80117	303-621-3132	621-3166
Web: www.elbertcolorado.com					
Fremont County 136 Justice Ctr Rd Rm 103	Canon City	CO	81212	719-269-0100	269-0134
Web: www.fremontco.com					
Garfield County 109 8th St Suite 200	Glenwood Springs	CO	81601	970-945-2377	947-1078
Web: www.garfield-county.com					
Gilpin County 203 Eureka St	Central City	CO	80427	303-582-5321	582-3086
Web: www.co.gilpin.co.us					
Grand County 308 Byers Ave PO Box 120	Hot Sulphur Springs	CO	80451	970-725-3347	725-0100
Web: co.grand.co.us					
Gunnison County 221 N Wisconsin St Suite C	Gunnison	CO	81230	970-641-1516	641-7956
Web: www.co.gunnison.co.us					
Hinsdale County PO Box 277	Lake City	CO	81235	970-944-2225	944-2630
Web: www.hinsdalecountycolorado.us					
Huerfano County 401 Main St Suite 201	Walsenburg	CO	81089	719-738-2370	738-3996
Web: www.huerfanococc.com					
Jackson County 404 4th St	Walden	CO	80480	970-723-4660	723-4706
Jefferson County 100 Jefferson County Pkwy	Golden	CO	80419	303-271-8106	271-8197
Web: www.jeffco.us					
Kiowa County PO Box 37	Eads	CO	81036	719-438-5421	438-5327
Web: www.kiowacountycolo.com					
Kit Carson County PO Box 249	Burlington	CO	80807	719-346-8638	346-7242
Web: www.kitcarsoncounty.org					
La Plata County 1060 E 2nd Ave Suite 134	Durango	CO	81301	970-382-6280	382-6285
Web: www.co.laplata.co.us					
Lake County PO Box 917	Leadville	CO	80461	719-486-1410	486-3972
Larimer County PO Box 1280	Fort Collins	CO	80522	970-498-7860	498-7906
Web: www.larimer.org					
Las Animas County PO Box 115	Trinidad	CO	81082	719-846-3314	845-2573
Web: www.trinidadco.com/Main/CityCounty.asp					
Lincoln County PO Box 67	Hugo	CO	80821	719-743-2444	743-2524
Web: www.lincolncountyco.us.					
Logan County 315 Main St	Sterling	CO	80751	970-522-0888	522-4018
Web: www.loganco.gov					
Mesa County PO Box 20000-5007	Grand Junction	CO	81502	970-244-1800	256-1588
Web: www.co.mesa.co.us					
Mineral County PO Box 70	Creede	CO	81130	719-658-2440	658-2931
Web: www.creede.com					
Moffat County 221 W Victory Way	Craig	CO	81625	970-824-9104	824-4975
Web: www.co.moffat.co.us					
Montezuma County 109 W Main St Rm 302	Cortez	CO	81321	970-565-8317	565-3420
Web: www.co.montezuma.co.us					
Montrose County 161 S Townsend	Montrose	CO	81401	970-249-3362	249-7761
Web: www.co.montrose.co.us					
Morgan County PO Box 1399	Fort Morgan	CO	80701	970-542-3521	542-3520
Web: www.co.morgan.co.us					
Otero County PO Box 511	La Junta	CO	81050	719-383-3020	383-3026
Ouray County PO Box C	Ouray	CO	81427	970-325-4961	325-0452
Web: www.co.ouray.co.us					
Park County PO Box 220	Fairplay	CO	80440	719-836-4227	836-4348
Web: www.co.park.co.us					
Phillips County 221 S Interocean Ave	Holyoke	CO	80734	970-854-3131	854-4745
Web: www.phillipscountyco.org					
Pitkin County 530 E Main St Suite 101	Aspen	CO	81611	970-920-5180	920-5196
Web: county.aspenpitkin.com					
Prowers County 301 S Main St Suite 210	Lamar	CO	81052	719-336-8011	336-5306
Web: www.prowerscounty.net					
Pueblo County 215 W 10th St	Pueblo	CO	81003	719-583-6000	583-4894
Web: www.co.pueblo.co.us					
Rio Blanco County PO box 1067	Meeker	CO	81641	970-878-5068	878-3587
Web: www.co.rio-blanco.co.us					
Rio Grande County 965 6th St PO Box 160	Del Norte	CO	81132	719-657-3334	657-2621
Web: www.riograndecounty.org					
Routt County 136 6th St	Steamboat Springs	CO	80477	970-879-0108	879-3992
Web: www.co.routt.co.us					
Saguache County 501 4th St PO Box 176	Saguache	CO	81149	719-655-2512	655-2730
Web: saguache.org					
San Juan County PO Box 466	Silverton	CO	81433	970-387-5671	387-5671
San Miguel County PO Box 548	Telluride	CO	81435	970-728-3954	728-4808
Web: www.sanmiguelcounty.org					
Sedgwick County PO Box 50	Julesburg	CO	80737	970-474-3346	474-0954
Summit County PO Box 1538	Breckenridge	CO	80424	970-453-2561	453-3540
Web: www.co.summit.co.us					
Teller County PO Box 959	Cripple Creek	CO	80813	719-689-2988	686-7900
Web: www.co.teller.co.us					

	City	State	ZIP	Phone	Fax
Washington County 150 Ash Ave	Akron	CO	80720	970-345-2701	345-2702
Weld County PO Box 758	Greeley	CO	80632	970-336-7204	352-0242
Web: www.co.weld.co.us					
Yuma County 310 Ash St Suite F	Wray	CO	80758	970-332-5809	332-5919
Web: www.yumacounty.net					

Connecticut

	City	State	ZIP	Phone	Fax
Fairfield County 1061 Main St	Bridgeport	CT	06604	203-579-6527	382-8406
Hartford County 550 Main St	Hartford	CT	06103	860-522-4888	
Web: www.hartford.gov					
Litchfield County 15 West St	Litchfield	CT	06759	860-567-0885	567-4779
Web: www.litchfieldcty.com					
Middlesex County 1 Court St	Middletown	CT	06457	860-343-6400	343-6423
New Haven County 165 Church St	New Haven	CT	06510	203-946-8200	946-7683
Web: www.cityofnewhaven.com					
New London County 70 Huntington St	New London	CT	06320	860-443-5363	442-7703
Tolland County 69 Brooklyn St	Rockville	CT	06066	860-896-4920	
Windham County PO Box 191	Putnam	CT	06260	860-928-7749	928-7076

Delaware

	City	State	ZIP	Phone	Fax
Kent County 555 Bay Rd	Dover	DE	19901	302-744-2305	736-2279
Web: www.co.kent.de.us					
New Castle County 87 Reads Way New Castle Corporate Commons	New Castle	DE	19720	302-395-5101	395-5268
Web: www.co.new-castle.de.us					
Sussex County PO Box 589	Georgetown	DE	19947	302-855-7743	855-7749
Web: www.sussexcountyde.gov/					

Florida

	City	State	ZIP	Phone	Fax
Alachua County 12 SE 1st St	Gainesville	FL	32601	352-374-5210	338-7303
Web: www.co.alachua.fl.us					
Baker County 339 E Macclenny Ave	Macclenny	FL	32063	904-259-8113	259-4176
Web: bakercountyfl.org					
Bay County 300 E 4th St	Panama City	FL	32401	850-763-9061	747-5188
Web: www.co.bay.fl.us					
Bradford County PO Drawer B	Starke	FL	32091	904-964-6280	964-4454
Web: www.bradford-co-fla.org					
Brevard County 400 South St County Courthouse	Titusville	FL	32780	321-264-6942	633-2115
Web: www.brevardcounty.us					
Broward County 115 S Andrews Ave Rm 421	Fort Lauderdale	FL	33301	954-357-7000	357-7295
Web: www.co.broward.fl.us					
Calhoun County 20859 Central Ave E Rm 130	Blountstown	FL	32424	850-674-4545	674-5553
Web: www.calhounco.org/index.htm					
Charlotte County 18500 Murdoch Cir	Port Charlotte	FL	33948	941-743-1200	743-1530
Web: www.co.charlotte.fl.us					
Citrus County 110 N Apopka Ave	Inverness	FL	34450	352-341-6400	341-6491
Web: www.clerk.citrus.fl.us					
Clay County 825 N Orange Ave	Green Cove Springs	FL	32043	904-269-6302	
Web: www.claycountygov.com					
Collier County 3301 Tamiami Trail E	Naples	FL	34112	239-774-8383	774-4010
Web: www.colliergov.net/					
Columbia County PO Box 2069	Lake City	FL	32056	386-755-4100	758-1337
Web: www.columbiacountyfla.com					
DeSoto County 201 E Oak St	Arcadia	FL	34266	863-993-4800	993-4809
Web: www.co.desoto.fl.us					
Dixie County PO Box 1206	Cross City	FL	32628	352-498-1200	498-1201
Web: www.dixiecounty.org					
Duval County 117 W Duval St	Jacksonville	FL	32202	904-630-1178	630-2906
Web: www.coj.net					
Escambia County PO Box 1591	Pensacola	FL	32591	850-595-4900	595-4908
Web: www.co.escambia.fl.us					
Flagler County 1200 E Moody Blvd Suite 1	Bunnell	FL	32110	386-437-7480	437-7399
Web: www.flaglercounty.org					
Franklin County 33 Market St Suite 203	Apalachicola	FL	32320	850-653-8861	653-2261
Web: www.franklincountyflorida.com					
Gadsden County PO Box 1649	Quincy	FL	32353	850-875-8601	875-8612
Web: www.gadsdengov.net					
Gilchrist County PO Box 37	Trenton	FL	32693	352-463-3170	463-3166
Web: www.co.gilchrist.fl.us					
Glades County 500 Ave J Suite 102	Moore Haven	FL	33471	863-946-6010	946-0560
Web: www.gladescofl.us					
Gulf County 1000 Cecil Costin Sr Blvd	Port Saint Joe	FL	32456	850-229-6113	229-6174
Web: www.gulfcountygovernment.com					
Hamilton County 207 NE 1st St Rm 106	Jasper	FL	32052	386-792-1288	792-3524
Web: www.hamiltoncountyflorida.com					
Hardee County 412 W Orange St Rm A-203	Wauchula	FL	33873	863-773-6952	773-0958
Web: www.hardeecounty.net					
Hendry County PO Box 1760	La Belle	FL	33975	863-675-5217	675-5238
Web: www.hendryfla.net					
Hernando County 20 N Main St Rm 460	Brooksville	FL	34601	352-754-4000	754-4477
Web: www.co.hernando.fl.us					
Highlands County 430 S Commerce Ave	Sebring	FL	33870	863-402-6500	402-6507
Web: www.hcbcc.net					
Hillsborough County 800 E Twigg St	Tampa	FL	33602	813-276-8100	276-2437
Web: www.hillsboroughcounty.org					
Holmes County PO Box 397	Bonifay	FL	32425	850-547-1100	547-6630
Web: www.holmescountyonline.com					
Indian River County 1840 25th St	Vero Beach	FL	32960	772-567-8000	978-1822
Web: indian-river.fl.us					
Jackson County PO Box 510	Marianna	FL	32447	850-482-9552	482-7849
Web: www.jacksoncounty-fl.com					
Jefferson County County Courthouse Rm 10	Monticello	FL	32344	850-342-0218	342-0222
Web: www.co.jefferson.fl.us					
Lafayette County PO Box 88	Mayo	FL	32066	386-294-1600	294-4231
Lake County PO Box 7800	Tavares	FL	32778	352-742-4102	742-4110
Web: www.lakegovernment.com					
Lee County PO Box 398	Fort Myers	FL	33902	239-533-2259	485-2143
Web: www.lee-county.com					
Leon County 301 S Monroe St Suite 108	Tallahassee	FL	32301	850-487-2220	488-6293
Web: www.co.leon.fl.us					
Levy County PO Box 610	Bronson	FL	32621	352-486-5100	486-5166
Web: www.naturecoast.org					
Liberty County PO Box 399	Bristol	FL	32321	850-643-5404	643-2866
Web: www.libertycountyflorida.com					
Madison County PO Box 237	Madison	FL	32341	850-973-1500	973-2059
Web: www.madisonfl.org					
Manatee County PO Box 25400	Bradenton	FL	34206	941-749-1800	741-4083
Web: www.co.manatee.fl.us					
Marion County 601 SE 25th Ave	Ocala	FL	34471	352-620-3307	620-3392
Web: www.marioncountyfl.org					
Martin County PO Box 9016	Stuart	FL	34995	772-288-5576	288-5548
Web: www.martin.fl.us					
Miami-Dade County 111 NW 1st St Suite 220	Miami	FL	33128	305-375-5124	375-5569
Web: miamidade.gov					
Monroe County 1100 SimontonSt	Key West	FL	33040	305-294-4641	
Web: monroecofl.virtualtownhall.net/					
Nassau County PO Box 456	Fernandina Beach	FL	32035	904-548-4600	321-5723
Web: www.nassauclerk.org					
Okaloosa County 101 E James Lee Blvd	Crestview	FL	32536	850-689-5000	689-5818
Web: www.co.okaloosa.fl.us					
Okeechobee County 304 NW 2nd St	Okeechobee	FL	34972	863-763-6441	763-9529
Web: www.co.okeechobee.fl.us					
Orange County 201 S Rosalind Ave	Orlando	FL	32801	407-836-7350	836-5879
Web: www.orangecountyfl.net					
Osceola County 2 Courthouse Sq	Kissimmee	FL	34741	407-343-3500	343-3699
Web: www.osceola.org					
Palm Beach County 301 N Olive Ave	West Palm Beach	FL	33407	561-355-2001	355-3990
Web: www.co.palm-beach.fl.us					
Pasco County 7530 Little Rd	New Port Richey	FL	34654	727-847-8190	
Web: www.pascocountyfl.net					
Pinellas County 315 Court St Rm 601	Clearwater	FL	33756	727-464-3485	464-4384
Web: www.pinellascounty.org					
Polk County PO Box 9005 Drawer BC01	Bartow	FL	33831	863-534-6000	534-7655
Web: www.polk-county.net					
Putnam County PO Box 758	Palatka	FL	32178	386-329-0361	329-0888
Web: www.co.putnam.fl.us					
Saint Johns County 4010 Lewis Speedway	Saint Augustine	FL	32084	904-819-3600	819-3661
Web: www.co.st-johns.fl.us					
Saint Lucie County PO Box 700	Fort Pierce	FL	34954	772-462-6900	
Web: www.stlucieco.gov					
Santa Rosa County 68655 Caroline St	Milton	FL	32570	850-983-1974	983-1986
Web: www.co.santa-rosa.fl.us					
Sarasota County PO Box 3079	Sarasota	FL	34230	941-861-7400	
Web: www.co.sarasota.fl.us					
Seminole County 1101 E 1st St	Sanford	FL	32771	407-665-7945	665-7939*
*Fax: Hum Res ■ *Web:* www.seminolecountyfl.gov					
Sumter County 209 N Florida St	Bushnell	FL	33513	352-793-0200	793-0207
Web: www.bocc.co.sumter.fl.us					
Suwannee County 200 S Ohio Ave	Live Oak	FL	32064	386-364-3498	362-0548
Web: www.suwanneechamber.com					
Taylor County PO Box 620	Perry	FL	32348	850-838-3506	838-3549
Web: taco.perryfl.com					
Union County 55 W Main St Rm 103	Lake Butler	FL	32054	386-496-3711	496-1718
Web: www.unioncofl.com					
Volusia County 123 W Indiana Ave	DeLand	FL	32720	386-736-5920	822-5707
Web: volusia.org					
Wakulla County 3056 Crawfordville Hwy	Crawfordville	FL	32327	850-926-0905	926-0938
Web: www.clerk.wakulla.fl.us					
Walton County PO Box 1260	De Funiak Springs	FL	32435	850-892-8115	892-7551
Web: www.co.walton.fl.us					
Washington County PO Box 647	Chipley	FL	32428	850-638-6285	638-6297
Web: www.washingtonfl.com					

Georgia

	City	State	ZIP	Phone	Fax
Appling County 60 Tippins St Suite 201	Baxley	GA	31513	912-367-8100	367-8161
Web: www.baxley.org/site/					
Athens-Clarke County PO Box 1868	Athens	GA	30603	706-613-3031	613-3033
Web: www.athensclarkecounty.com					
Atkinson County PO Box 518	Pearson	GA	31642	912-422-3391	422-3429
Augusta-Richmond County 530 Greene St	Augusta	GA	30911	706-821-2400	821-2819
Web: www.augustaga.gov					
Bacon County PO Box 356	Alma	GA	31510	912-632-5214	632-2757
Baker County PO Box 10	Newton	GA	39870	229-734-3004	734-7770
Baldwin County 121 N Wilkinson St Suite 314	Milledgeville	GA	31061	478-445-4791	445-6320
Web: www.baldwincountyga.com					
Banks County 144 Yonah Homer Rd PO Box 337	Homer	GA	30547	706-677-6240	677-6294
Web: www.bankscountyga.org					
Barrow County 233 E Broad St	Winder	GA	30680	770-307-3005	307-3141
Web: www.barrowga.org					
Bartow County 135 W Cherokee Ave Suite 251	Cartersville	GA	30120	770-387-5030	387-5023
Web: www.bartowga.org					
Ben Hill County 402A E Pine St	Fitzgerald	GA	31750	229-426-5112	426-5106
Web: www.benhillcounty.com					
Berrien County 201 N Davis St	Nashville	GA	31639	229-686-5421	686-2785
Bibb County 601 Mulberry St	Macon	GA	31201	478-621-6400	621-6329
Web: www.co.bibb.ga.us					
Bleckley County 306 SE 2nd St	Cochran	GA	31014	478-934-3200	934-0822
Web: www.bleckley.org					
Brantley County PO Box 398	Nahunta	GA	31553	912-462-6285	462-5538
Web: www.brantleycounty.org					
Brooks County PO Box 272	Quitman	GA	31643	229-263-5561	263-9345
Web: www.brooks-county.org					
Bryan County 116 Lanier St PO Box 430	Pembroke	GA	31321	912-653-3819	653-4691
Web: www.bryancountyga.org					
Bulloch County PO Box 347	Statesboro	GA	30459	912-764-6245	764-8634
Web: www.bullochcounty.net					
Burke County PO Box 89	Waynesboro	GA	30830	706-554-2324	554-0350
Web: www.burkecounty-ga.gov					
Butts County 25 3rd St Suite 4	Jackson	GA	30233	770-775-8200	775-8211
Web: www.buttscounty.org					
Calhoun County PO Box 226	Morgan	GA	39866	229-849-4835	849-2100
Camden County PO Box 99	Woodbine	GA	31569	912-576-5649	576-5647
Web: www.co.camden.ga.us					
Candler County 705 N Lewis St	Metter	GA	30439	912-685-2835	685-4823
Carroll County PO Box 338	Carrollton	GA	30112	770-830-5800	830-5992
Web: www.carrollcountyga.com					
Catoosa County 875 Lafayette St	Ringgold	GA	30736	706-935-4231	
Web: www.catoosa.com					
Charlton County 100 S 3rd St	Folkston	GA	31537	912-496-2549	496-1156
Chatham County 124 Bull St	Savannah	GA	31401	912-652-7869	652-7874
Web: www.chathamcounty.org					
Chattooga County PO Box 211	Summerville	GA	30747	706-857-0701	857-0742
Cherokee County 90 North St Suite 310	Canton	GA	30114	678-493-6000	493-6013
Web: www.cherokeega.com/ie.cfm					
Clay County PO Box 519	Fort Gaines	GA	39851	229-768-3238	768-3672
Web: www.claycountyga.org					
Clayton County 112 Smith St	Jonesboro	GA	30236	770-477-3211	477-3217
Web: www.co.clayton.ga.us					
Clinch County PO Box 433	Homerville	GA	31634	912-487-5854	487-3083

Georgia (Cont'd)

	City	State	ZIP	Phone	Fax
Cobb County 100 Cherokee St Suite 300	Marietta	GA	30090	770-528-3300	528-2606
Web: www.cobbcounty.org					
Coffee County 101 S Peterson Ave	Douglas	GA	31533	912-384-4799	384-0291
Colquitt County PO Box 517	Moultrie	GA	31776	229-890-1805	
Columbia County PO Box 498	Evans	GA	30809	706-868-3379	868-3348
Web: www.columbiacountyga.gov					
Columbus-Muscogee County PO Box 1340	Columbus	GA	31902	706-653-4013	653-4016
Web: www.columbusga.com					
Cook County 1200 Hutchinson Ave	Adel	GA	31620	229-896-6888	896-7629
Coweta County 22 E Broad St	Newnan	GA	30263	770-254-2601	254-2606
Web: www.coweta.ga.us					
Crawford County 1011 Hwy 341 N	Roberta	GA	31078	478-836-3782	836-5818
Crisp County 210 S 7th St	Cordele	GA	31015	229-276-2672	276-2675
Web: www.crispcounty.com					
Cusseta-Chattahoochee County PO Box 299	Cusseta	GA	31805	706-989-3602	989-2005
Web: chattahoocheecounty.georgia.gov					
Dade County PO Box 417	Trenton	GA	30752	706-657-4778	657-8284
Web: www.dadega.com					
Dawson County 76 Howard Ave E Suite 120	Dawsonville	GA	30534	706-344-3501	344-3504
Web: www.dawsoncounty.org					
Decatur County PO Box 726	Bainbridge	GA	39818	229-248-3030	246-2062
DeKalb County 556 N McDonough St	Decatur	GA	30030	404-371-2000	371-2002
Web: www.co.dekalb.ga.us					
Dodge County 5016 Courthouse Cir Suite 102	Eastman	GA	31023	478-374-4361	374-8121
Dooly County PO Box 322	Vienna	GA	31092	229-268-4228	268-4230
Web: www.doolychamber.com					
Dougherty County PO Box 1827	Albany	GA	31702	229-431-2121	438-3967
Web: www.dougherty.ga.us					
Douglas County 8700 Hospital Dr	Douglasville	GA	30134	770-920-7266	920-7357
Web: www.co.douglas.ga.us					
Early County PO Box 849	Blakely	GA	39823	229-723-3033	723-4411
Echols County PO Box 190	Statenville	GA	31648	229-559-6538	559-6158
Effingham County 601 N Laurel St	Springfield	GA	31329	912-754-2153	754-4157
Web: www.effinghamcounty.org					
Elbert County PO Box 619	Elberton	GA	30635	706-283-2005	213-7286
Web: www.elbertga.com					
Emanuel County 101 N Main St	Swainsboro	GA	30401	478-237-3881	237-2593
Evans County 3 Freeman St	Claxton	GA	30417	912-739-1141	739-0111
Web: www.claxtonevanschamber.com					
Fannin County 400 W Main St Suite 100	Blue Ridge	GA	30513	706-632-2203	632-2507
Web: www.fannincountyga.org					
Fayette County 140 Stonewall Ave W	Fayetteville	GA	30214	770-460-5730	460-9412
Web: www.fayettecountyga.gov					
Floyd County 12 E 4th Ave Suite 209	Rome	GA	30162	706-291-5110	291-5248
Web: www.floydcountyga.org					
Forsyth County 100 Courthouse Sq Suite 010	Cumming	GA	30040	770-781-2120	886-2858
Web: www.co.forsyth.ga.us					
Franklin County 9492 Lavonia Rd PO Box 70	Carnesville	GA	30521	706-384-2514	
Web: www.franklin-county.com					
Fulton County 141 Pryor St SW Suite 10061	Atlanta	GA	30303	404-730-8320	893-6511
Web: www.co.fulton.ga.us					
Gilmer County 1 West Side Sq	Ellijay	GA	30540	706-635-4361	635-4359
Web: www.gilmerchamber.com					
Glascock County PO Box 231	Gibson	GA	30810	706-598-2084	598-2577
Glynn County 1803 Gloucester St Rm 114	Brunswick	GA	31520	912-554-7400	267-5691
Web: www.glynncounty.com					
Gordon County 201 N Wall St	Calhoun	GA	30701	706-629-3795	629-9516
Web: www.gordoncounty.org					
Grady County 250 N Broad St	Cairo	GA	39828	229-377-1512	377-1039
Web: www.gradycountyga.gov					
Greene County 113 N Main St 3rd Fl Suite 306	Greensboro	GA	30642	706-453-7716	453-9555
Web: www.greenecountyga.gov					
Gwinnett County 75 Langley Dr Gwinnett Justice & Administration Ctr	Lawrenceville	GA	30045	770-822-7000	822-7097
Web: www.co.gwinnett.ga.us					
Habersham County 555 Monroe St Unit 20	Clarkesville	GA	30523	706-754-6270	754-1014
Web: www.co.habersham.ga.us					
Hall County PO Box 1275	Gainesville	GA	30503	770-531-7025	531-7070
Web: www.hallcounty.org					
Hancock County 601 Broad St Courthouse Sq	Sparta	GA	31087	706-444-5746	444-6221
Haralson County PO Box 489	Buchanan	GA	30113	770-646-2002	646-2035
Web: www.haralsoncountyga.org					
Harris County PO Box 528	Hamilton	GA	31811	706-628-4944	628-7039
Web: www.harriscountychamber.org					
Hart County 800 Chandler St	Hartwell	GA	30643	706-376-2024	376-9477
Web: www.hartcountyga.org					
Heard County PO Box 40	Franklin	GA	30217	706-675-3821	675-2493
Henry County 140 Henry Pkwy	McDonough	GA	30253	770-954-2400	954-2418
Web: www.co.henry.ga.us					
Houston County 201 Perry Pkwy County Courthouse	Perry	GA	31069	478-542-2115	923-5697
Web: www.houstoncountyga.com					
Irwin County 207 S Irwin Ave Suite 2	Ocilla	GA	31774	229-468-9441	468-9672
Web: www.irwincounty.net					
Jackson County 67 Athens St	Jefferson	GA	30549	706-367-6312	367-9083
Web: www.jacksoncountygov.com					
Jasper County 126 W Greene St Suite 18	Monticello	GA	31064	706-468-4900	468-4942
Jeff Davis County PO Box 609	Hazlehurst	GA	31539	912-375-6611	375-0378
Jefferson County 217 E Broad St	Louisville	GA	30434	478-625-3332	625-4007
Web: www.jeffersoncounty.org					
Jenkins County 611 Winthrop Ave	Millen	GA	30442	478-982-2563	982-4750
Johnson County PO Box 321	Wrightsville	GA	31096	478-864-3484	864-1343
Jones County PO Box 1359	Gray	GA	31032	478-986-6405	986-9682
Web: www.jonescounty.org					
Lamar County 326 Thomaston St	Barnesville	GA	30204	770-358-5146	358-5149
Web: www.barnesville.org					
Lanier County 100 W Main St	Lakeland	GA	31635	229-482-2088	482-8187
Laurens County 117 E Jackson St	Dublin	GA	31040	478-272-4755	272-3895
Web: www.co.laurens.ga.us					
Lee County 104 Leslie Hwy PO Box 889	Leesburg	GA	31763	229-759-6000	759-6050
Web: www.lee.ga.us					
Liberty County PO Box 829	Hinesville	GA	31310	912-876-2164	369-0204
Web: www.libertycounty.org					
Lincoln County PO Box 340	Lincolnton	GA	30817	706-359-4444	359-4729
Web: www.lincolncountyga.com					
Long County 49 E McDonald St	Ludowici	GA	31316	912-545-2143	545-2150
Lowndes County 325 W Savannah Ave	Valdosta	GA	31601	229-671-2400	245-5222
Web: www.lowndescounty.com					
Lumpkin County 99 Courthouse Hill Suite A	Dahlonega	GA	30533	706-864-3742	864-4760
Web: www.lumpkincounty.gov					
Macon County 121 S Sumter St	Oglethorpe	GA	31068	478-472-7021	472-5643
Web: www.maconcountyga.org					
Madison County PO Box 147	Danielsville	GA	30633	706-795-5664	795-2997
Web: www.madisonco.us					
Marion County PO Box 481	Buena Vista	GA	31803	229-649-2603	649-3702
McDuffie County PO Box 158	Thomson	GA	30824	706-595-2134	595-9150
Web: www.dca.state.ga.us/snapshots					
McIntosh County PO Box 584	Darien	GA	31305	912-437-6671	437-6416
Web: www.mcintoshcounty.com					
Meriwether County PO Box 428	Greenville	GA	30222	706-672-1314	672-1886
Miller County 179 S Cuthbert St	Colquitt	GA	39837	229-758-4104	758-2229
Mitchell County 26 N Court St PO Box 187	Camilla	GA	31730	229-336-2000	336-2003
Web: www.mitchellcountyga.net					
Monroe County 38 W Main St	Forsyth	GA	31029	478-994-7000	994-7294
Web: www.monroecountygeorgia.com					
Montgomery County PO Box 295	Mount Vernon	GA	30445	912-583-2363	583-2026
Morgan County 355 Hancock St	Madison	GA	30650	706-342-0725	343-6450
Web: www.morganga.org					
Murray County PO Box 1129	Chatsworth	GA	30705	706-695-2413	695-8721
Newton County 1124 Clark St	Covington	GA	30014	770-784-2000	784-2007
Web: www.co.newton.ga.us					
Oconee County PO Box 145	Watkinsville	GA	30677	706-769-5120	769-0705
Web: www.oconeecounty.net					
Oglethorpe County PO Box 261	Lexington	GA	30648	706-743-5270	743-8371
Paulding County 166 Confederate Ave	Dallas	GA	30132	770-505-1352	505-1353
Web: www.paulding.gov					
Peach County 205 W Church St	Fort Valley	GA	31030	478-825-2535	825-2678
Web: www.peachcounty.net					
Pickens County PO Box 130	Jasper	GA	30143	706-253-8766	
Web: www.georgiamarble-mountain.org					
Pierce County PO Box 679	Blackshear	GA	31516	912-449-2022	449-2024
Pike County PO Box 377	Zebulon	GA	30295	770-567-3406	567-2006
Web: www.co.pike.ga.us					
Polk County PO Box 948	Cedartown	GA	30125	770-749-2114	749-2148
Web: www.polkcountygeorgia.us					
Pulaski County 105 Lumpkin St	Hawkinsville	GA	31036	478-783-4154	783-9209
Putnam County 108 S Madison Ave Suite 300	Eatonton	GA	31024	706-485-5826	485-5578
Web: www.putnamcountyga.us					
Quitman County PO Box 307	Georgetown	GA	39854	229-334-2578	334-3991
Rabun County 25 Courthouse Sq Suite 201	Clayton	GA	30525	706-782-5271	782-7588
Web: www.gamountains.com					
Randolph County PO Box 221	Cuthbert	GA	39840	229-732-6440	732-5364
Rockdale County 922 Court St	Conyers	GA	30012	770-929-4021	
Web: www.rockdalecounty.org					
Schley County PO Box 352	Ellaville	GA	31806	229-937-2609	937-5880
Screven County PO Box 159	Sylvania	GA	30467	912-564-7535	564-2562
Seminole County 200 S Knox Ave	Donalsonville	GA	39845	229-524-2878	524-8984
Spalding County PO Box 1046	Griffin	GA	30224	770-467-4309	
Web: www.spaldingcounty.com					
Stephens County PO Box 386	Toccoa	GA	30577	706-886-9491	886-2185
Web: www.stephenscounty-ga.gov					
Stewart County PO Box 157	Lumpkin	GA	31815	229-838-6769	838-9856
Web: www.stewartcountyga.gov					
Sumter County 605 Spring St PO Box 295	Americus	GA	31709	229-928-4500	928-4503
Web: sumtercountyga.us					
Talbot County PO Box 325	Talbotton	GA	31827	706-665-3239	665-8637
Web: www.talbotgeorgia.com					
Taliaferro County PO Box 182	Crawfordville	GA	30631	706-456-2123	456-2749
Tattnall County PO Box 25	Reidsville	GA	30453	912-557-4335	557-6088
Web: www.tattnall.com					
Taylor County 109 Ivy St	Butler	GA	31006	478-862-3336	862-2871
Telfair County 713 Telfair Ave	McRae	GA	31055	229-868-5688	868-7950
Terrell County PO Box 525	Dawson	GA	39842	229-995-4476	995-4320
Thomas County 110 N Crawford St PO Box 920	Thomasville	GA	31799	229-225-4100	226-3430
Web: www.thomascountyboc.org					
Tift County 225 N Tift Ave PO Box 354	Tifton	GA	31793	229-386-7810	386-7813
Web: www.tiftcounty.org					
Toombs County 100 Courthouse Sq	Lyons	GA	30436	912-526-3311	526-1004
Towns County 48 River St Suite B	Hiawassee	GA	30546	706-896-2276	896-4628
Web: www.mountaintopga.com					
Treutlen County PO Box 79	Soperton	GA	30457	912-529-3664	529-6062
Troup County PO Box 866	LaGrange	GA	30241	706-883-1740	883-1724
Web: www.troupcountyga.org					
Turner County PO Box 106	Ashburn	GA	31714	229-567-2011	567-0450
Web: www.turnerchamber.com					
Twiggs County 425 N Railroad St	Jeffersonville	GA	31044	478-945-3629	945-3988
Web: www.twiggscounty.us					
Union County 114 Courthouse St Box 1	Blairsville	GA	30512	706-439-6000	439-6004
Web: www.unioncounty.gov					
Upson County 106 E Lee St Suite 110	Thomaston	GA	30286	706-647-7012	647-7030
Walker County PO Box 445	La Fayette	GA	30728	706-638-1437	638-1453
Web: www.co.walker.ga.us					
Walton County 303 S Hammond Dr Suite 330	Monroe	GA	30655	770-267-1301	267-1400
Web: www.waltoncountyga.org					
Ware County 800 Church St	Waycross	GA	31501	912-287-4300	287-4301
Web: www.warecounty.com					
Warren County 521 Main St PO Box 46	Warrenton	GA	30828	706-465-2171	465-1300
Web: www.warrencountyga.com					
Washington County 119 Jones St	Sandersville	GA	31082	478-552-2325	552-7424
Web: www.washingtoncounty-ga.com					
Wayne County PO Box 270	Jesup	GA	31598	912-427-5900	427-5906
Web: www.co.wayne.ga.us					
Webster County PO Box 29	Preston	GA	31824	229-828-5775	828-2105
Wheeler County PO Box 181	Alamo	GA	30411	912-568-7135	568-1909
White County 59 S Main St Suite A	Cleveland	GA	30528	706-865-2235	865-1324
Web: www.whitecounty.net					
Whitfield County PO Box 868	Dalton	GA	30722	706-275-7450	275-7456
Web: www.whitfieldcountyga.com					
Wilcox County 103 N Broad St	Abbeville	GA	31001	229-467-2737	467-2000
Wilkes County 23 E Court St Rm 222	Washington	GA	30673	706-678-2511	678-3033
Web: www.washingtonwilkes.org					
Wilkinson County 100 Bacon St	Irwinton	GA	31042	478-946-2236	946-3767
Worth County 201 N Main St Rm 30	Sylvester	GA	31791	229-776-8200	776-8232
Web: www.worthcounty.com					

Hawaii

	City	State	ZIP	Phone	Fax
Hawaii County 25 Aupuni St Rm 209	Hilo	HI	96720	808-961-8255	961-8912
Web: www.hawaii-county.com					
Honolulu City & County 530 S King St Rm 100	Honolulu	HI	96813	808-768-3810	768-3835
Web: www.co.honolulu.hi.us					
Kauai County 4396 Rice St Rm 206	Lihue	HI	96766	808-241-6371	241-6349
Web: www.kauai.gov					
Maui County 200 S High St	Wailuku	HI	96793	808-270-7748	270-7171
Web: www.co.maui.hi.us					

Idaho

County / Address	City	State	ZIP	Phone	Fax
Ada County 200 W Front St Suite 3255	Boise	ID	83702	208-287-7000	287-7009
Web: www.adaweb.net					
Adams County PO Box 48	Council	ID	83612	208-253-4561	253-4880
Web: www.co.adams.id.us					
Bannock County PO Box 4016	Pocatello	ID	83205	208-236-7211	236-7363
Web: www.co.bannock.id.us					
Bear Lake County 7 E Center St PO Box 190	Paris	ID	83261	208-945-2212	945-2780
Web: www.bearlakecounty.info					
Benewah County 701 College Ave	Saint Maries	ID	83861	208-245-3212	245-3046
Bingham County 501 N Maple St Suite 205	Blackfoot	ID	83221	208-782-3163	785-4131
Web: www.co.bingham.id.us					
Blaine County 206 1st Ave S Suite 200	Hailey	ID	83333	208-788-5505	788-5501
Web: www.co.blaine.id.us					
Boise County 420 Main St PO Box 1300	Idaho City	ID	83631	208-392-4431	392-4473
Web: www.co.boise.id.us					
Bonner County 215 S 1st Ave	Sandpoint	ID	83864	208-265-1432	265-1447
Web: www.co.bonner.id.us					
Bonneville County 900 Environmental Way	Idaho Falls	ID	83402	208-529-1354	529-1379
Web: www.co.bonneville.id.us					
Boundary County PO Box 419	Bonners Ferry	ID	83805	208-267-5504	267-7814
Web: www.boundarycountyid.org					
Butte County 248 W Grand Ave PO Box 737	Arco	ID	83213	208-527-3021	527-3295
Camas County PO Box 430	Fairfield	ID	83327	208-764-2242	764-2349
Canyon County 1115 Albany St	Caldwell	ID	83605	208-454-7574	454-7525
Web: www.canyoncounty.org					
Caribou County PO Box 775	Soda Springs	ID	83276	208-547-4324	547-4759
Cassia County 1459 Overland Ave	Burley	ID	83318	208-878-7302	878-9109
Web: www.cassiacounty.org					
Clark County 320 W Main St PO Box 205	Dubois	ID	83423	208-374-5402	374-5609
Clearwater County PO Box 586	Orofino	ID	83544	208-476-3615	476-3127
Web: www.clearwatercounty.org					
Custer County 801 Main St	Challis	ID	83226	208-879-2360	879-5246
Web: www.co.custer.id.us					
Elmore County 150 S 4th East St Suite 5	Mountain Home	ID	83647	208-587-2129	587-2134
Web: www.elmorecounty.org					
Franklin County 39 W Oneida St	Preston	ID	83263	208-852-1090	852-1094
Fremont County 151 W 1st North St	Saint Anthony	ID	83445	208-624-7332	624-7335
Web: www.co.fremont.id.us					
Gem County 415 E Main St	Emmett	ID	83617	208-365-4561	365-7795
Web: www.co.gem.id.us					
Gooding County 624 Main St	Gooding	ID	83330	208-934-4841	934-5085
Web: goodingidaho.net					
Idaho County 320 W Main St Rm 5	Grangeville	ID	83530	208-983-2751	983-1458
Web: www.idahocounty.org					
Jefferson County 210 Courthouse Way Suite 100	Rigby	ID	83442	208-745-7756	745-9397
Web: www.co.jefferson.id.us					
Jerome County 300 N Lincoln Ave Rm 301	Jerome	ID	83338	208-644-2704	644-2709
Web: www.co.jerome.id.us					
Kootenai County PO Box 9000	Coeur d'Alene	ID	83816	208-446-1000	446-1188
Web: www.co.kootenai.id.us					
Latah County 522 S Adams St PO Box 8068	Moscow	ID	83843	208-882-8580	883-7203
Web: www.latah.id.us					
Lemhi County 206 Courthouse Dr	Salmon	ID	83467	208-756-2815	756-8424
Web: www.lemhicountyidaho.org					
Lewis County 510 Oak St Rm 1	Nezperce	ID	83543	208-937-2251	937-9233
Web: www.lewiscountyid.org					
Lincoln County 111 W 'B' St Suite C	Shoshone	ID	83352	208-886-7641	886-2798
Madison County PO Box 389	Rexburg	ID	83440	208-356-3662	356-8396
Web: www.co.madison.id.us					
Minidoka County 715 G St PO Box 368	Rupert	ID	83350	208-436-7111	436-0737
Web: www.minidoka.id.us					
Nez Perce County 1230 Main St PO Box 896	Lewiston	ID	83501	208-799-3020	799-3070
Web: www.co.nezperce.id.us					
Oneida County 10 Court St	Malad City	ID	83252	208-766-4116	766-2990
Web: www.co.oneida.id.us					
Owyhee County PO Box 128	Murphy	ID	83650	208-495-2421	495-1173
Web: owyheecounty.net					
Payette County 1130 3rd Ave N Rm 104	Payette	ID	83661	208-642-6000	642-6011
Web: www.payettecounty.org					
Power County 543 Bannock Ave	American Falls	ID	83211	208-226-7611	226-7612
Web: www.co.power.id.us					
Shoshone County 700 Bank St	Wallace	ID	83873	208-752-3331	753-2711
Teton County 89 N Main St Suite 1	Driggs	ID	83422	208-354-2905	354-8776
Twin Falls County PO Box 126	Twin Falls	ID	83303	208-736-4004	736-4182
Web: www.twinfallscounty.org					
Valley County PO Box 1350	Cascade	ID	83611	208-382-4297	382-7107
Washington County PO Box 670	Weiser	ID	83672	208-414-2092	414-3925
Web: www.co.washington.id.us					

Illinois

County / Address	City	State	ZIP	Phone	Fax
Adams County 507 Vermont St	Quincy	IL	62301	217-277-2150	277-2155
Web: www.co.adams.il.us					
Alexander County 2000 Washington Ave	Cairo	IL	62914	618-734-7000	734-7002
Bond County 203 W College Ave	Greenville	IL	62246	618-664-0449	664-9414
Boone County 601 N Main St Suite 201	Belvidere	IL	61008	815-547-4770	547-3579
Web: www.boonecountyil.org					
Brown County 200 Court St Rm 4	Mount Sterling	IL	62353	217-773-3421	773-2233
Bureau County 700 S Main St	Princeton	IL	61356	815-875-2014	879-4803
Web: www.bureaucounty-il.com					
Calhoun County 102 County Rd PO Box 187	Hardin	IL	62047	618-576-2351	576-2895
Carroll County PO Box 152	Mount Carroll	IL	61053	815-244-0221	244-3709
Web: www.gocarrollcounty.com					
Cass County 100 E Springfield St	Virginia	IL	62691	217-452-7217	452-7219
Champaign County 1776 E Washington St	Urbana	IL	61802	217-384-3776	384-3896
Web: www.co.champaign.il.us					
Christian County 101 S Main St PO Box 647	Taylorville	IL	62568	217-824-4969	824-5105
Clark County 501 Archer Ave County Courthouse	Marshall	IL	62441	217-826-8311	826-2519
Web: www.clarkcountyil.org					
Clay County PO Box 160	Louisville	IL	62858	618-665-3626	665-3607
Clinton County PO Box 308	Carlyle	IL	62231	618-594-2464	594-0195
Web: www.clintonco.org					
Coles County 651 Jackson Ave Rm 122	Charleston	IL	61920	217-348-0501	348-7337
Web: www.co.coles.il.us					
Cook County 118 N Clark St Rm 820	Chicago	IL	60602	312-603-4660	603-4479
Web: www.co.cook.il.us					
Crawford County PO Box 616	Robinson	IL	62454	618-546-1212	546-0140
Web: www.crawfordcountycentral.com					
Cumberland County 140 Courthouse Sq PO Box 146	Toledo	IL	62468	217-849-2631	849-2968
DeKalb County 110 E Sycamore St	Sycamore	IL	60178	815-895-7149	895-7148
Web: www.dekalbcounty.org					
DeWitt County 201 W Washington St PO Box 439	Clinton	IL	61727	217-935-2119	935-4596
Web: www.dewittcountyill.com					
Douglas County 401 S Center St PO Box 465	Tuscola	IL	61953	217-253-2411	253-2233
DuPage County 421 N County Farm Rd	Wheaton	IL	60187	630-407-5500	407-5501
Web: www.dupageco.org					
Edgar County 115 W Court St Rm J County Courthouse	Paris	IL	61944	217-466-7433	466-7430
Web: www.edgarcounty-il.gov					
Edwards County 50 E Main St	Albion	IL	62806	618-445-2115	445-4941
Effingham County 101 N 4th St PO Box 628	Effingham	IL	62401	217-342-6535	342-3577
Web: www.co.effingham.il.us					
Fayette County PO Box 401	Vandalia	IL	62471	618-283-5000	283-5004
Ford County 200 W State St Rm 101	Paxton	IL	60957	217-379-2721	379-3258
Web: fordiroq.prairienet.org/ford.htm					
Franklin County PO Box 607	Benton	IL	62812	618-438-3221	435-3405
Fulton County 100 N Main St	Lewistown	IL	61542	309-547-3041	547-3326
Web: www.outfitters.com/illinois/fulton/					
Gallatin County PO Box 550	Shawneetown	IL	62984	618-269-3025	269-3343
Greene County 519 N Main St	Carrollton	IL	62016	217-942-5443	942-9323
Web: www.greene-county.com					
Grundy County PO Box 675	Morris	IL	60450	815-941-3222	942-2222
Web: www.grundyco.org					
Hamilton County 100 S Jackson St County Courthouse	McLeansboro	IL	62859	618-643-2721	
Hancock County PO Box 39	Carthage	IL	62321	217-357-3911	
Hardin County PO Box 187	Elizabethtown	IL	62931	618-287-2251	287-2661
Web: www.hardincountyil.org					
Henderson County PO Box 308	Oquawka	IL	61469	309-867-2911	867-2033
Web: www.outfitters.com/illinois/henderson/					
Henry County 307 W Center St	Cambridge	IL	61238	309-937-3575	
Web: www.co.henry.il.us					
Iroquois County 1001 E Grant St	Watseka	IL	60970	815-432-6960	432-3894
Web: fordiroq.prairienet.org/iroquois.htm					
Jackson County 1001 Walnut St County Courthouse	Murphysboro	IL	62966	618-687-7360	687-7359
Web: www.co.jackson.il.us					
Jasper County 204 W Washington St Suite 2	Newton	IL	62448	618-783-3124	783-4137
Jefferson County 100 S 10th St County Courthouse	Mount Vernon	IL	62864	618-244-8000	244-8111
Jersey County 200 N Lafayette St Suite 1	Jerseyville	IL	62052	618-498-5571	498-7721
Web: www.jerseycounty.org					
Jo Daviess County 330 N Bench St	Galena	IL	61036	815-777-0161	777-3688
Web: www.jodaviess.org					
Johnson County PO Box 96	Vienna	IL	62995	618-658-3611	658-2908
Kane County 719 Rt 31	Geneva	IL	60134	630-232-5950	232-5866
Web: www.co.kane.il.us					
Kankakee County 189 E Court St	Kankakee	IL	60901	815-937-2990	939-8831
Web: www.co.kankakee.il.us					
Kendall County 111 W Fox St	Yorkville	IL	60560	630-553-4104	553-4119
Web: www.co.kendall.il.us					
Knox County 200 S Cherry St	Galesburg	IL	61401	309-345-3860	345-0098
Web: www.knoxcountyil.com					
Lake County 18 N County St	Waukegan	IL	60085	847-377-2000	
Web: www.co.lake.il.us					
LaSalle County 707 E Etna Rd	Ottawa	IL	61350	815-434-8205	434-8319
Web: www.lasallecounty.org					
Lawrence County 1100 State St County Courthouse	Lawrenceville	IL	62439	618-943-2346	943-5205
Web: www.lawrencecountyillinois.com					
Lee County 112 E 2nd St	Dixon	IL	61021	815-288-3309	288-6492
Web: www.leecountyillinois.com					
Livingston County 112 W Madison St	Pontiac	IL	61764	815-844-2006	842-1844
Web: www.livingstoncounty-il.org					
Logan County 601 Broadway St Rm 20	Lincoln	IL	62656	217-732-4148	732-6064
Web: www.co.logan.il.us					
Macon County 141 S Main St Rm 104	Decatur	IL	62523	217-424-1305	423-0922
Macoupin County PO Box 107	Carlinville	IL	62626	217-854-3214	854-7347
Web: www.macoupincountyonline.net					
Madison County 157 N Main St Suite 109	Edwardsville	IL	62025	618-692-6290	692-8903
Web: www.co.madison.il.us					
Marion County PO Box 637	Salem	IL	62881	618-548-3400	548-2226
Marshall County PO Box 328	Lacon	IL	61540	309-246-6325	246-3667
Web: www.co.marshall.il.us					
Mason County PO Box 77	Havana	IL	62644	309-543-6661	543-2085
Web: www.masoncountyil.org					
Massac County PO Box 429	Metropolis	IL	62960	618-524-5213	524-8514
McDonough County 1 Courthouse Sq	Macomb	IL	61455	309-833-2474	836-3368
Web: www.outfitters.com/illinois/mcdonough/					
McHenry County 2200 N Seminary Ave	Woodstock	IL	60098	815-334-4000	334-8727
Web: www.co.mchenry.il.us					
McLean County 115 E Washington St Rm 102	Bloomington	IL	61701	309-888-5190	888-5932
Web: www.co.mclean.il.us					
Menard County PO Box 465	Petersburg	IL	62675	217-632-2415	632-4301
Web: www.menardil.com					
Mercer County PO Box 66	Aledo	IL	61231	309-582-7021	582-7022
Monroe County 100 S Main St	Waterloo	IL	62298	618-939-8681	939-8639
Montgomery County 1 Courthouse Sq PO Box 595	Hillsboro	IL	62049	217-532-9530	532-9581
Web: www.montgomeryco.com					
Morgan County PO Box 1387	Jacksonville	IL	62651	217-243-8581	243-8368
Web: www.morgancounty-il.com					
Moultrie County County Courthouse 10 S Main St Suite 6	Sullivan	IL	61951	217-728-4389	728-8178
Ogle County PO Box 357	Oregon	IL	61061	815-732-3201	732-6273
Web: www.oglecounty.org					
Peoria County 324 Main St Rm 101	Peoria	IL	61602	309-672-6059	672-6063
Web: www.co.peoria.il.us					
Perry County PO Box 438	Pinckneyville	IL	62274	618-357-5116	357-3194
Web: www.perrycountyil.org					
Piatt County PO Box 558	Monticello	IL	61856	217-762-9487	762-7563
Web: www.piattcounty.org					
Pike County 100 E Washington St Courthouse	Pittsfield	IL	62363	217-285-6812	285-5820
Web: www.pikeil.org					
Pope County PO Box 216	Golconda	IL	62938	618-683-4466	683-4466
Pulaski County PO Box 118	Mound City	IL	62963	618-748-9360	748-9305
Putnam County PO Box 236	Hennepin	IL	61327	815-925-7129	925-7549
Randolph County 1 Taylor St	Chester	IL	62233	618-826-2510	826-3750
Richland County 103 W Main St	Olney	IL	62450	618-392-3111	393-4005
Rock Island County 1504 3rd Ave	Rock Island	IL	61201	309-786-4451	
Web: www.co.rock-island.il.us					
Saint Clair County 10 Public Sq	Belleville	IL	62220	618-277-6600	277-8783
Web: co.st-clair.il.us					
Saline County 10 E Poplar St	Harrisburg	IL	62946	618-253-8197	252-3073
Sangamon County 200 S 9th St	Springfield	IL	62701	217-753-6706	535-3233
Web: www.co.sangamon.il.us					
Schuyler County PO Box 200	Rushville	IL	62681	217-322-4734	322-6164
Scott County County Courthouse 35 E Market St	Winchester	IL	62694	217-742-3178	742-5853
Shelby County PO Box 230	Shelbyville	IL	62565	217-774-4421	774-5291
Stark County PO Box 97	Toulon	IL	61483	309-286-5911	286-4039
Web: www.outfitters.com/illinois/stark/					
Stephenson County 15 N Galena Ave Suite 1	Freeport	IL	61032	815-235-8289	235-8378
Web: www.co.stephenson.il.us					
Tazewell County 11 S 4th St	Pekin	IL	61554	309-477-2264	477-2244
Web: www.tazewell.com					
Union County 309 W Market St Rm 100	Jonesboro	IL	62952	618-833-5711	833-8712
Web: www.shawneeheartland.com					

Illinois (Cont'd)

				Phone	Fax
Vermilion County 6 N Vermilion St Courthouse Annex	Danville	IL	61832	217-554-1900	554-1914
Web: www.co.vermilion.il.us					
Wabash County PO Box 277	Mount Carmel	IL	62863	618-262-4561	
Warren County 100 W Broadway	Monmouth	IL	61462	309-734-8592	734-7406
Web: www.outfitters.com/illinois/warren/					
Washington County 101 E Saint Louis St County Courthouse	Nashville	IL	62263	618-327-8314	327-3582
Wayne County PO Box 187	Fairfield	IL	62837	618-842-5182	842-6427
White County PO Box 339	Carmi	IL	62821	618-382-7211	382-2322
Web: www.whitecounty-il.gov					
Whiteside County 200 E Knox St	Morrison	IL	61270	815-772-5100	772-7673
Web: www.whiteside.org					
Will County 302 N Chicago St	Joliet	IL	60432	815-740-4615	740-4699
Web: www.willcountyillinois.com					
Williamson County 200 W Jefferson St	Marion	IL	62959	618-997-1301	993-2071
Winnebago County 404 Elm St	Rockford	IL	61101	815-987-3050	969-0259
Web: www.co.winnebago.il.us					
Woodford County 115 N Main St Rm 202	Eureka	IL	61530	309-467-2822	467-7391

Indiana

				Phone	Fax
Adams County PO Box 189	Decatur	IN	46733	260-724-5300	724-5313
Web: www.co.adams.in.us					
Allen County 715 S Calhoun St County Courthouse Rm 201	Fort Wayne	IN	46802	260-449-7245	449-7929
Web: www.co.allen.in.us					
Bartholomew County PO Box 924	Columbus	IN	47202	812-379-1600	379-1675
Web: www.bartholomewco.com					
Benton County 706 E 5th St Suite 37	Fowler	IN	47944	765-884-0930	884-0322
Web: www.bentoncounty.org					
Blackford County 110 W Washington St	Hartford City	IN	47348	765-348-1620	348-7222*
**Fax:* Acctg ■ *Web:* www.supertiles.com					
Boone County Courthouse Sq Rm 212	Lebanon	IN	46052	765-482-3510	485-0150
Brown County PO Box 85	Nashville	IN	47448	812-988-5510	988-5562
Web: www.browncounty.org					
Carroll County 101 W Main St	Delphi	IN	46923	765-564-4485	564-1835
Web: www.carrollnet.org					
Cass County 200 Court Pk	Logansport	IN	46947	574-753-7740	722-1556
Clark County 501 E Court Ave Rm 137	Jeffersonville	IN	47130	812-285-6244	285-6372
Web: www.co.clark.in.us					
Clay County 609 E National Ave Rm 213	Brazil	IN	47834	812-448-9024	446-9602
Web: www.claycountyin.org					
Clinton County 265 Courthouse Sq	Frankfort	IN	46041	765-659-6335	
Crawford County PO Box 375	English	IN	47118	812-338-2565	338-2507
Daviess County PO Box 739	Washington	IN	47501	812-254-8664	254-8698
Web: www.daviesscounty.org					
Dearborn County 215 W High St	Lawrenceburg	IN	47025	812-537-8877	532-2021
Web: www.dearborncounty.org					
Decatur County 150 Courthouse Sq Suite 244	Greensburg	IN	47240	812-663-8223	662-6627
Web: www.decaturcounty.in.gov					
DeKalb County PO Box 230	Auburn	IN	46706	260-925-0912	925-5126
Web: www.dekalbnet.org					
Delaware County 100 W Main St	Muncie	IN	47305	765-747-7730	747-7899
Web: www.co.delaware.in.us					
Dubois County 1 Courthouse Sq	Jasper	IN	47546	812-481-7035	481-7044
Web: www.duboiscounty.org					
Elkhart County 117 N 2nd St Rm 101	Goshen	IN	46526	574-535-6409	
Web: www.elkhartcountygov.org					
Fayette County PO Box 607	Connersville	IN	47331	765-825-1813	827-4902
Web: www.co.fayette.in.us					
Floyd County PO Box 1056	New Albany	IN	47151	812-948-5415	948-4711
Web: www.warrickcounty.gov					
Fountain County PO Box 183	Covington	IN	47932	765-793-2192	793-5002
Web: www.co.fountain.in.us					
Franklin County 459 Main St	Brookville	IN	47012	765-647-5111	647-3224
Fulton County 815 Main St	Rochester	IN	46975	574-223-2911	223-8304
Web: www.fultoncounty-in.org					
Gibson County PO Box 630	Princeton	IN	47670	812-386-8401	385-5025
Grant County 101 E 4th St	Marion	IN	46952	765-668-8121	668-6541
Web: www.grantcounty.net					
Greene County PO Box 229	Bloomfield	IN	47424	812-384-8532	384-8458
Web: www.in-map.net/counties/GREENE/					
Hamilton County 1 Hamilton County Sq Suite 106	Noblesville	IN	46060	317-776-9629	776-9664
Web: www.co.hamilton.in.us					
Hancock County 9 E Main St Rm 201	Greenfield	IN	46140	317-462-1109	
Web: www.hancockcoingov.org					
Harrison County 300 N Capitol Ave	Corydon	IN	47112	812-738-8241	738-0531
Web: www.harrisonchamber.org					
Hendricks County PO Box 599	Danville	IN	46122	317-745-9231	745-9306
Web: www.co.hendricks.in.us					
Henry County PO Box B	New Castle	IN	47362	765-529-6401	521-7046
Howard County PO Box 9004	Kokomo	IN	46904	765-456-2204	456-2267
Web: co.howard.in.us					
Huntington County 201 N Jefferson St County Courthouse Rm 103	Huntington	IN	46750	260-358-4822	358-4823
Web: www.huntington.in.us					
Jackson County PO Box 318	Brownstown	IN	47220	812-358-6116	358-6187
Jasper County Courthouse 115 W Washington St Suite 204	Rensselaer	IN	47978	219-866-4926	866-9450
Web: www.jaspercountyin.com					
Jay County 120 N Court St 2nd Fl	Portland	IN	47371	260-726-6920	726-6922
Web: www.co.jay.in.us					
Jefferson County 300 E Main St Courthouse Rm 203	Madison	IN	47250	812-265-8922	265-8950
Web: www.madisonindiana.org/govern.html					
Jennings County PO Box 385	Vernon	IN	47282	812-352-3070	352-3076
Web: www.jenningsco.org					
Johnson County 5 E Jefferson St PO Box 368	Franklin	IN	46131	317-736-3708	736-3749
Web: www.co.johnson.in.us					
Knox County 101 N 7th St	Vincennes	IN	47591	812-885-2521	895-4929
Kosciusko County 121 N Lake St	Warsaw	IN	46580	574-372-2334	372-2338
Web: www.kcgov.com					
La Porte County 813 Lincolnway	La Porte	IN	46350	216-326-6808	326-5615
Web: www.alco.org					
LaGrange County 105 N Detroit St	LaGrange	IN	46761	260-499-6368	463-2187
Web: www.lagrangecounty.com					
Lake County 2293 N Main St	Crown Point	IN	46307	219-755-3440	755-3447
Web: www.lakecountyin.org					
Lawrence County 916 15th St Rm 31	Bedford	IN	47421	812-275-7543	277-2024
Web: bedfordonline.com/government/lawrence/					
Madison County 16 E 9th St	Anderson	IN	46016	765-641-9419	648-1375
Web: www.madisoncty.com					
Marion County 200 E Washington St City County Bldg Rm W122	Indianapolis	IN	46204	317-327-4740	327-3893
Web: www.indygov.org/county					
Marshall County 112 W Jefferson St	Plymouth	IN	46563	574-935-8510	936-4863
Web: www.co.marshall.in.us					
Martin County PO Box 120	Shoals	IN	47581	812-247-3651	247-2791
Miami County PO Box 184	Peru	IN	46970	765-472-3901	472-1778
Monroe County 301 N College Ave Rm 201	Bloomington	IN	47404	812-349-2600	349-2610
Web: www.co.monroe.in.us					
Montgomery County PO Box 768	Crawfordsville	IN	47933	765-364-6430	364-6355
Web: www.mcedonline.com					
Morgan County PO Box 1556	Martinsville	IN	46151	765-342-1025	342-1111
Newton County PO Box 49	Kentland	IN	47951	219-474-6081	474-5749
Noble County 101 N Orange St	Albion	IN	46701	260-636-2736	636-4000
Web: www.nobleco.org					
Ohio County 413 Main St PO Box 185	Rising Sun	IN	47040	812-438-2610	438-1215
Orange County 1 Court St	Paoli	IN	47454	812-723-2649	723-0239
Web: www.co.orange.in.us					
Owen County 60 S Main St County Courthouse	Spencer	IN	47460	812-829-5000	829-5004
Web: www.owencounty.org					
Parke County 116 W High St Rm 204	Rockville	IN	47872	765-569-5132	569-4222
Web: www.parkecounty.com					
Perry County County Courthouse 2219 Payne St	Tell City	IN	47586	812-547-3741	547-9782
Web: www.perrycountyin.org					
Pike County 801 Main St PO Box 125	Petersburg	IN	47567	812-354-6025	354-6369
Web: www.pikecountyin.org					
Porter County 155 Indiana Ave	Valparaiso	IN	46383	219-465-3445	465-3592
Web: www.co.porter.in.us					
Posey County 126 E 3rd St Rm 220	Mount Vernon	IN	47620	812-838-1300	838-1344
Web: www.poseycounty.org					
Pulaski County 112 E Main St Rm 230	Winamac	IN	46996	574-946-3313	946-4953
Putnam County 1 Courthouse Sq Rm 20	Greencastle	IN	46135	765-653-5513	653-5992*
**Fax:* Acctg ■ *Web:* www.putnamcountyin.org					
Randolph County County Courthouse 100 S Main St PO Box 230	Winchester	IN	47394	765-584-7207	584-2958
Web: www.randolphcounty.us					
Ripley County PO Box 177	Versailles	IN	47042	812-689-6115	689-6000
Web: www.ripleycounty.com					
Rush County 101 E 2nd St County Courthouse	Rushville	IN	46173	765-932-2077	938-1163*
**Fax:* Acctg ■ *Web:* www.rushcounty.in.gov					
Saint Joseph County 101 S Main St	South Bend	IN	46601	574-235-9635	235-9838
Web: www.stjosephcountyindiana.com					
Scott County 1 E McClain Ave Suite 120	Scottsburg	IN	47170	812-752-4769	752-5459
Web: www.greatscottindiana.org					
Shelby County 25 W Polk St	Shelbyville	IN	46176	317-392-6330	392-6393
Web: www.shelbychamber.net					
Spencer County PO Box 12	Rockport	IN	47635	812-649-6027	649-6030
Web: www.spencerco.org					
Starke County 53 E Washington St County Courthouse	Knox	IN	46534	574-772-9128	772-9169
Steuben County 55 S Public Sq	Angola	IN	46703	260-668-1000	668-3702
Web: www.co.steuben.in.us					
Sullivan County PO Box 370	Sullivan	IN	47882	812-268-4657	268-7027
Web: www.sctb.net					
Switzerland County 212 W Main St County Courthouse	Vevay	IN	47043	812-427-3302	427-3179
Tippecanoe County 20 N 3rd St	Lafayette	IN	47901	765-423-9215	423-9196
Web: www.county.tippecanoe.in.us					
Tipton County 101 E Jefferson St	Tipton	IN	46072	765-675-2794	675-3194*
**Fax:* Acctg ■ *Web:* www.tiptoncounty.org					
Union County 26 W Union St	Liberty	IN	47353	765-458-6121	458-5263
Vanderburgh County 1 NW ML King Jr Blvd	Evansville	IN	47708	812-435-5241	435-5963
Web: www.vanderburghgov.org					
Vermillion County PO Box 10	Newport	IN	47966	765-492-3500	492-5001
Vigo County PO Box 8449	Terre Haute	IN	47808	812-462-3211	232-2921
Web: www.vigocountyin.com					
Wabash County 69 W Hill St	Wabash	IN	46992	260-563-0661	569-1352
Web: www.wabashcountycvb.com					
Warren County 125 N Monroe St Suite 11	Williamsport	IN	47993	765-762-3510	762-7251
Web: www.warrenco.net					
Warrick County 107 W Locust St Suite 301	Boonville	IN	47601	812-897-6120	897-6189
Web: www.warrickcounty.gov					
Washington County 99 Public Sq Suite 102	Salem	IN	47167	812-883-5748	883-8108
Web: www.washingtoncountyindiana.com					
Wayne County 401 E Main St	Richmond	IN	47374	765-973-9237	973-9321
Web: www.co.wayne.in.us					
Wells County 102 W Market St Rm 205	Bluffton	IN	46714	260-824-6470	824-6475
Web: www.wellscounty.org					
White County 110 N Main St	Monticello	IN	47960	574-583-7032	583-1532
Whitley County 101 W Van Buren St	Columbia City	IN	46725	260-248-3102	248-3137

Iowa

				Phone	Fax
Adair County 400 Public Sq	Greenfield	IA	50849	641-743-2546	743-2565
Adams County PO Box 484	Corning	IA	50841	641-322-4711	322-4523
Web: www.co.adams.ia.us					
Allamakee County 110 Allamakee St	Waukon	IA	52172	563-568-3318	568-6353
Web: www.allamakeecounty.com					
Appanoose County PO Box 400	Centerville	IA	52544	641-856-6101	856-2282
Web: www.appanoosecounty.net					
Audubon County 318 Leroy St No 6	Audubon	IA	50025	712-563-4275	563-4276
Web: www.auduboncounty.org					
Benton County PO Box 719	Vinton	IA	52349	319-472-2766	
Web: www.cobentoniaus.com					
Black Hawk County 316 E 5th St	Waterloo	IA	50703	319-833-3012	833-3170
Web: www.co.black-hawk.ia.us					
Boone County 201 State St	Boone	IA	50036	515-433-0500	432-8102
Web: www.co.boone.ia.us					
Bremer County 415 E Bremer Ave	Waverly	IA	50677	319-352-0130	352-0602
Web: www.co.bremer.ia.us					
Buchanan County PO Box 259	Independence	IA	50644	319-334-2196	334-7455
Web: www.buchanancounty.com					
Buena Vista County PO Box 1186	Storm Lake	IA	50588	712-749-2546	749-2700
Web: www.co.buena-vista.ia.us					
Butler County 428 6th St	Allison	IA	50602	319-267-2487	267-2488
Web: www.butlercoiowa.org					
Calhoun County 416 4th St Suite 5	Rockwell City	IA	50579	712-297-8122	297-5082
Web: www.calhouncountyiowa.com					
Carroll County 114 E 6th St	Carroll	IA	51401	712-792-4923	792-9423
Web: www.co.carroll.ia.us					
Cass County 5 W 7th St	Atlantic	IA	50022	712-243-4570	243-6660
Web: www.casscountyiowa.org					
Cedar County 400 Cedar St	Tipton	IA	52772	563-886-2101	886-3594
Web: www.iowacity.com/cedarco/#cedar					
Cerro Gordo County 220 N Washington Ave	Mason City	IA	50401	641-421-3022	421-3072
Web: www.co.cerro-gordo.ia.us					
Cherokee County 520 W Main St PO Box F	Cherokee	IA	51012	712-225-6744	225-6749
Web: www.cherokeeia.com					
Chickasaw County PO Box 311	New Hampton	IA	50659	641-394-2100	394-5541*
**Fax:* Acctg ■ *Web:* www.chickasawcoia.org					

	City	State	ZIP	Phone	Fax
Clarke County 100 S Main St Courthouse *Web:* www.clarkecountyia.org	Osceola	IA	50213	641-342-6096	342-2463
Clay County 215 W 4th St *Web:* www.co.clay.ia.us	Spencer	IA	51301	712-262-4335	262-6042
Clayton County 111 High St NE *Web:* www.claytoncountyiowa.net	Elkader	IA	52043	563-245-2204	245-1175
Clinton County 1900 N 3rd St *Web:* www.clintoncountyiowa.com	Clinton	IA	52733	563-243-6210	243-5869
Crawford County 1202 Broadway *Web:* www.crawfordcounty.org	Denison	IA	51442	712-263-2242	263-5753
Dallas County 801 Court St *Web:* www.co.dallas.ia.us	Adel	IA	50003	515-993-5814	993-4752
Davis County 100 Courthouse Sq *Web:* www.daviscounty.org	Bloomfield	IA	52537	641-664-2011	664-2041
Decatur County 207 N Main St	Leon	IA	50144	641-446-4382	446-7159
Delaware County 301 E Main St *Web:* www.delawarecountyia.com	Manchester	IA	52057	563-927-4942	927-3074
Des Moines County PO Box 158 *Web:* www.co.des-moines.ia.us	Burlington	IA	52601	319-753-8272	753-8253
Dickinson County 1802 Hill Ave *Web:* www.co.dickinson.ia.us	Spirit Lake	IA	51360	712-336-3356	336-2677
Dubuque County 720 Central Ave *Web:* www.dubuquecounty.org	Dubuque	IA	52001	563-589-4418	
Emmet County 609 1st Ave N *Web:* www.emmetcountyia.com	Estherville	IA	51334	712-362-4261	362-7454
Fayette County 114 N Vine St	West Union	IA	52175	563-422-5694	422-3137
Floyd County 101 S Main St *Web:* www.floydcoia.org	Charles City	IA	50616	641-228-7777	228-7772
Franklin County 12 1st Ave NW PO Box 28	Hampton	IA	50441	641-456-5626	456-5628
Fremont County PO Box 549 *Web:* www.co.fremont.ia.us	Sidney	IA	51652	712-374-2232	374-3330
Greene County 114 N Chestnut St *Web:* www.jeffersoniowa.com	Jefferson	IA	50129	515-386-2516	386-2321
Grundy County 706 G Ave *Web:* www.grundycounty.org	Grundy Center	IA	50638	319-824-5229	824-3447
Guthrie County 200 N 5th St	Guthrie Center	IA	50115	641-747-3415	747-2420
Hamilton County 2300 Superior St *Web:* www.hamiltoncounty.org	Webster City	IA	50595	515-832-9510	832-9514
Hancock County PO Box 70 *Web:* www.hancockcountyia.org	Garner	IA	50438	641-923-2532	923-3521
Hardin County 1215 Edgington Ave County Courthouse *Web:* hardincountyonline.com	Eldora	IA	50627	641-939-8109	939-8245
Harrison County 111 N 2nd Ave *Web:* www.harrisoncountyia.org	Logan	IA	51546	712-644-2665	644-2615
Henry County PO Box 176 *Web:* www.co.henry.ia.us	Mount Pleasant	IA	52641	319-385-2632	385-4144
Howard County 137 N Elm St County Courthouse *Web:* www.crescoia.com/howardcounty/index.html	Cresco	IA	52136	563-547-2661	547-3605
Humboldt County 203 Main St *Web:* www.ci.humboldt.ia.us	Dakota City	IA	50529	515-332-1571	332-1738
Ida County 401 Moorehead St	Ida Grove	IA	51445	712-364-2626	364-3929
Iowa County PO Box 266 *Web:* www.co.iowa.ia.us	Marengo	IA	52301	319-642-3914	
Jackson County 201 W Platt St *Web:* www.jacksoncountyiowa.com	Maquoketa	IA	52060	563-652-3144	652-6975
Jasper County PO Box 944 *Web:* www.co.jasper.ia.us	Newton	IA	50208	641-792-7016	792-1053
Jefferson County 51 E Briggs Ave *Web:* www.jeffersoniowa.com	Fairfield	IA	52556	641-472-2840	
Johnson County 913 S Dubuque St Suite 201 *Web:* www.jacksoncountyiowa.com	Iowa City	IA	52240	319-356-6000	356-6036
Jones County PO Box 19 *Web:* www.co.jones.ia.us	Anamosa	IA	52205	319-462-4341	462-5827
Keokuk County 101 S Main St Courthouse *Web:* www.keokukcountyia.com	Sigourney	IA	52591	641-622-2210	622-2171
Kossuth County 114 W State St *Web:* www.co.kossuth.ia.us	Algona	IA	50511	515-295-2718	295-3071
Lee County PO Box 488 *Web:* www.leecounty.org	Fort Madison	IA	52627	319-372-6557	372-8200
Linn County 930 1st St SW *Web:* www.linncounty.org	Cedar Rapids	IA	52404	319-892-5005	892-5009
Louisa County 117 S Main St *Web:* www.louisacountyiowa.org	Wapello	IA	52653	319-523-4541	523-4542
Lucas County 916 Braden St	Chariton	IA	50049	641-774-4421	774-8669
Lyon County 206 S 2nd Ave *Web:* www.lyoncountyiowa.com	Rock Rapids	IA	51246	712-472-2623	472-2422
Madison County 112 N 1st St *Web:* www.madisoncounty.com	Winterset	IA	50273	515-462-4451	462-9825
Mahaska County 106 S 1st St Mahaska Courthouse *Web:* www.mahaskacounty.org	Oskaloosa	IA	52577	641-673-7786	672-1256
Marion County PO Box 497 *Web:* www.redrockarea.com	Knoxville	IA	50138	641-828-2207	828-7580
Marshall County 1 E Main St 3rd Fl *Web:* www.co.marshall.ia.us	Marshalltown	IA	50158	641-754-6355	754-6349
Mills County 418 Sharp St County Courthouse *Web:* www.millscoia.us	Glenwood	IA	51534	712-527-4880	527-4936
Mitchell County 508 State St	Osage	IA	50461	641-732-3726	732-3728
Monona County 610 Iowa Ave	Onawa	IA	51040	712-423-2491	423-2744
Monroe County 10 Benton Ave E	Albia	IA	52531	641-932-5212	932-3245
Montgomery County PO Box 469	Red Oak	IA	51566	712-623-4986	623-4987
Muscatine County 401 E 3rd St *Web:* www.co.muscatine.ia.us	Muscatine	IA	52761	563-263-5821	263-7248
O'Brien County PO Box 340 *Web:* www.obriencounty.com	Primghar	IA	51245	712-957-3045	957-3046
Osceola County 300 7th St *Web:* www.osceolacountyia.com	Sibley	IA	51249	712-754-2241	754-3743
Page County PO Box 263	Clarinda	IA	51632	712-542-3214	542-5460
Palo Alto County PO Box 387	Emmetsburg	IA	50536	712-852-3603	852-2274
Plymouth County 215 4th Ave SE *Fax: Acctg ■ *Web:* www.co.plymouth.ia.us	Le Mars	IA	51031	712-546-6100	546-5784*
Pocahontas County 99 Court Sq County Courthouse	Pocahontas	IA	50574	712-335-4208	335-5045
Polk County 111 Court Ave *Web:* www.polkcountyiowa.gov	Des Moines	IA	50309	515-286-3000	323-5250
Pottawattamie County PO Box 476 *Web:* www.pottcounty.com	Council Bluffs	IA	51502	712-328-5604	
Poweshiek County PO Box 218	Montezuma	IA	50171	641-623-5644	623-5320
Ringgold County 109 W Madison St *Web:* www.ringgoldcounty.us	Mount Ayr	IA	50854	641-464-3234	464-2478
Sac County PO Box 368 *Web:* www.saccounty.org	Sac City	IA	50583	712-662-7791	662-7978
Scott County 416 W 4th St *Web:* www.co.scott.ia.us	Davenport	IA	52801	563-326-8647	326-8298
Shelby County PO Box 431 *Web:* www.shco.org	Harlan	IA	51537	712-755-5543	755-2667
Sioux County PO Box 47 *Web:* www.siouxcounty.org	Orange City	IA	51041	712-737-2286	737-8908

	City	State	ZIP	Phone	Fax
Story County 1315 South B Ave *Web:* www.storycounty.com	Nevada	IA	50201	515-382-7410	
Tama County PO Box 306 *Web:* www.tamacounty.org	Toledo	IA	52342	641-484-3721	484-6403
Taylor County 405 Jefferson St County Courthouse	Bedford	IA	50833	712-523-2095	523-2936
Union County 300 N Pine St *Web:* www.unioncountyiowa.org	Creston	IA	50801	641-782-7315	782-8241
Van Buren County PO Box 475 *Web:* www.800-tourvbc.com	Keosauqua	IA	52565	319-293-3129	293-6404
Wapello County 101 W 4th St *Web:* www.wapellocounty.org	Ottumwa	IA	52501	641-683-0060	683-0064
Warren County 115 N Howard St *Web:* www.co.warren.ia.us	Indianola	IA	50125	515-961-1033	961-1071
Washington County PO Box 391 *Web:* co.washington.ia.us	Washington	IA	52353	319-653-7741	653-7787
Wayne County PO Box 424 *Web:* www.waynecountyiowa.com	Corydon	IA	50060	641-872-2264	872-2431
Webster County 701 Central Ave *Web:* www.webstercountyia.org	Fort Dodge	IA	50501	515-574-3719	574-3714
Winnebago County 126 S Clark St	Forest City	IA	50436	641-585-3412	
Winneshiek County 201 W Main St	Decorah	IA	52101	563-382-2469	382-0603
Woodbury County 620 Douglas St *Web:* www.woodbury-ia.com	Sioux City	IA	51101	712-279-6611	279-6021
Worth County 1000 Central Ave *Web:* www.worthcounty.org	Northwood	IA	50459	641-324-2840	324-2360
Wright County 115 N Main St *Web:* www.wrightcounty.org	Clarion	IA	50525	515-532-2771	532-2669

Kansas

	City	State	ZIP	Phone	Fax
Allen County 1 N Washington St *Web:* www.allencounty.org	Iola	KS	66749	620-365-1407	365-1441
Anderson County 100 E 4th Ave	Garnett	KS	66032	785-448-6841	448-5621
Atchison County 423 N 5th St *Web:* www.atchisoncountyks.org	Atchison	KS	66002	913-367-1653	367-0227
Barber County 120 E Washington Ave *Web:* www.barbercounty.net	Medicine Lodge	KS	67104	620-886-3961	886-5425
Barton County 1400 Main St Suite 202 *Web:* www.bartoncounty.org	Great Bend	KS	67530	620-793-1835	793-1990
Bourbon County 210 S National Ave *Web:* www.bourboncountyks.org	Fort Scott	KS	66701	620-223-3800	223-5832
Brown County 601 Oregon St *Web:* www.brown.kansasgov.com	Hiawatha	KS	66434	785-742-2581	742-7705
Butler County 205 W Central Ave *Web:* www.bucoks.com	El Dorado	KS	67042	316-322-4239	321-1011
Chase County PO Box 529 *Web:* www.chasecountyks.org	Cottonwood Falls	KS	66845	620-273-6423	273-6617
Chautauqua County 215 N Chautauqua St	Sedan	KS	67361	620-725-5800	725-5801
Cherokee County PO Box 14	Columbus	KS	66725	620-429-2042	429-1042
Cheyenne County PO Box 985 *Web:* www.cheyennecounty.org	Saint Francis	KS	67756	785-332-8800	332-8825
Clark County 913 Highland St	Ashland	KS	67831	620-635-2813	635-2393
Clay County PO Box 98 *Web:* www.claycountyks.org	Clay Center	KS	67432	785-632-2552	632-5856
Cloud County 811 Washington St *Web:* www.cloudcountyks.org	Concordia	KS	66901	785-243-8110	243-8123
Coffey County 110 S 6th St *Web:* www.coffeycountyks.org	Burlington	KS	66839	620-364-2191	364-8975
Comanche County PO Box 776 *Web:* www.comanchecounty.com	Coldwater	KS	67029	620-582-2361	582-2426
Cowley County 311 E 9th Ave *Web:* www.cowleycounty.org	Winfield	KS	67156	620-221-5400	221-5498
Crawford County PO Box 249 *Web:* www.crawfordcountykansas.org	Girard	KS	66743	620-724-6115	724-6007
Decatur County PO Box 28 *Web:* www.oberlinkansas.org	Oberlin	KS	67749	785-475-8102	475-8130
Dickinson County PO Box 248 *Web:* www.dkcoks.com	Abilene	KS	67410	785-263-3774	263-2045
Doniphan County PO Box 278	Troy	KS	66087	785-985-3513	985-3723
Douglas County 111 E 11 St *Web:* www.douglas-county.com	Lawrence	KS	66044	785-832-5132	832-5174
Edwards County 312 Massachusetts Ave *Web:* www.edwardscounty.org	Kinsley	KS	67547	620-659-3000	659-2583
Elk County 127 N Pine *Web:* www.elk.kansasgov.com	Howard	KS	67349	620-374-2490	374-2771
Ellis County PO Box 720 *Web:* www.ellisco.org	Hays	KS	67601	785-628-9410	628-9413
Ellsworth County 210 N Kansas St *Web:* www.ellsworthcounty.org	Ellsworth	KS	67439	785-472-4161	472-3818
Finney County 311 N 9th St PO Box M *Web:* www.finneycounty.org	Garden City	KS	67846	620-272-3542	272-3599
Ford County 100 Gunsmoke St *Web:* www.fordcounty.net	Dodge City	KS	67801	620-227-4500	227-4699
Franklin County 315 S Main St *Web:* www.co.franklin.ks.us	Ottawa	KS	66067	785-229-3410	229-3419
Geary County PO Box 927 *Web:* www.geary.kansasgov.com	Junction City	KS	66441	785-238-3912	238-5419
Gove County 520 Washington St	Gove	KS	67736	785-938-2300	938-4486
Graham County 410 N Pomeroy St	Hill City	KS	67642	785-421-3453	421-6374
Grant County 108 S Glenn St *Web:* www.grantcoks.org	Ulysses	KS	67880	620-356-1335	356-3081
Gray County PO Box 487	Cimarron	KS	67835	620-855-3618	855-3107
Greeley County PO Box 277 *Web:* www.greeleycountygovernment.org	Tribune	KS	67879	620-376-4256	376-2294
Greenwood County 311 N Main St	Eureka	KS	67045	620-583-8121	583-8124
Hamilton County PO Box 1167	Syracuse	KS	67878	620-384-5629	384-5853
Harper County 201 N Jennings Ave *Web:* www.harpercounty.org	Anthony	KS	67003	620-842-5555	842-3455
Harvey County PO Box 687 *Web:* www.harveycounty.com	Newton	KS	67114	316-284-6840	284-6856
Haskell County PO Box 518 *Web:* www.haskellcounty.org	Sublette	KS	67877	620-675-2263	675-2681
Hodgeman County PO Box 247	Jetmore	KS	67854	620-357-6421	357-6161
Jackson County 400 New York Ave 2nd Fl *Web:* www.jackson.kansasgov.com	Holton	KS	66436	785-364-2891	364-4204
Jefferson County PO Box 321 *Web:* www.jfcountyks.com	Oskaloosa	KS	66066	785-863-2272	863-3135
Jewell County 307 N Commercial St	Mankato	KS	66956	785-378-4020	378-4075
Johnson County 111 S Cherry St Suite 1200 *Web:* www.jocoks.com	Olathe	KS	66061	913-715-0775	715-0800
Kearny County PO Box 86 *Web:* www.kearnycountykansas.com	Lakin	KS	67860	620-355-6422	355-7382
Kingman County 130 N Spruce St	Kingman	KS	67068	620-532-2521	532-2037
Kiowa County 211 E Florida Ave	Greensburg	KS	67054	620-723-3366	723-3234

Kansas (Cont'd)

				Phone	Fax
Labette County PO Box 387	Oswego	KS	67356	620-795-2138	795-2928
Web: www.labettecounty.com					
Lane County PO Box 788	Dighton	KS	67839	620-397-5356	397-5419
Leavenworth County 300 Walnut St Suite 106	Leavenworth	KS	66048	913-684-0421	684-0406
Web: www.leavenworthcounty.org					
Lincoln County 216 E Lincoln Ave	Lincoln	KS	67455	785-524-4757	524-5008
Linn County PO Box 350	Mound City	KS	66056	913-795-2660	795-2004
Web: www.linncountyks.com					
Logan County 710 W 2nd St	Oakley	KS	67748	785-672-4244	672-3341
Lyon County 430 Commercial St	Emporia	KS	66801	620-341-3243	341-3415
Web: www.lyoncounty.org					
Marion County 200 S 3rd Courthouse Sq	Marion	KS	66861	620-382-2185	382-3420
Web: www.marioncoks.net					
Marshall County 1201 Broadway	Marysville	KS	66508	785-562-5361	562-5262
Web: www.marshall.kansasgov.com					
McPherson County 117 N Maple	McPherson	KS	67460	620-241-3656	241-1168
Web: www.mcphersoncountyks.us					
Meade County PO Box 278	Meade	KS	67864	620-873-8700	873-8713
Miami County 201 S Pearl St Suite 102	Paola	KS	66071	913-294-3976	294-9544
Web: www.miamicountyks.org					
Mitchell County PO Box 190	Beloit	KS	67420	785-738-3652	738-5524
Web: www.mcks.org					
Montgomery County PO Box 446	Independence	KS	67301	620-330-1200	330-1202
Web: www.mgcountyks.org					
Morris County 501 W Main St	Council Grove	KS	66846	620-767-5518	767-6861
Morton County PO Box 1116	Elkhart	KS	67950	620-697-2157	697-2159
Web: www.mtcoks.com					
Nemaha County PO Box 186	Seneca	KS	66538	785-336-3570	336-3373
Neosho County PO Box 138	Erie	KS	66733	620-244-3811	244-3810
Ness County 202 W Sycamore St	Ness City	KS	67560	785-798-2401	798-3829
Norton County PO Box 70	Norton	KS	67654	785-877-5720	877-5722
Osage County PO Box 226	Lyndon	KS	66451	785-828-4812	828-4749
Web: www.osage.kansasgov.com					
Osborne County PO Box 160	Osborne	KS	67473	785-346-2431	346-5252
Web: www.osbornecounty.org					
Ottawa County 307 N Concord St Suite 130	Minneapolis	KS	67467	785-392-2279	392-2011
Web: www.ottawacounty.org					
Pawnee County 715 Broadway	Larned	KS	67550	620-285-3721	285-3802
Web: www.pawneecountykansas.com					
Phillips County 301 State St	Phillipsburg	KS	67661	785-543-6825	543-6827
Web: www.phillipscounty.org					
Pottawatomie County PO Box 187	Westmoreland	KS	66549	785-457-3314	457-3507
Web: www.pottcounty.org					
Pratt County PO Box 885	Pratt	KS	67124	620-672-4115	672-9541
Web: www.prattcounty.org					
Rawlins County 607 Main St	Atwood	KS	67730	785-626-3351	626-9019
Web: www.rawlinscounty.info					
Reno County 206 W 1st St	Hutchinson	KS	67501	620-694-2934	694-2534
Web: www.rngov.reno.ks.us					
Republic County 1815 M St	Belleville	KS	66935	785-527-7231	527-2668
Web: www.nckcn.com/repco					
Rice County 101 W Commercial St	Lyons	KS	67554	620-257-2232	257-3039
Web: www.ricecounty.us					
Riley County 110 Courthouse Plaza	Manhattan	KS	66502	785-537-6300	537-6394
Web: www.co.riley.ks.us					
Rooks County 115 N Walnut St	Stockton	KS	67669	785-425-6391	425-6015
Web: www.rookscounty.net					
Rush County PO Box 220	La Crosse	KS	67548	785-222-2731	222-3559
Web: www.rushcounty.org					
Russell County PO Box 113	Russell	KS	67665	785-483-4641	483-5725
Web: www.russellcounty.org					
Saline County PO Box 5040	Salina	KS	67402	785-309-5820	309-5826
Web: www.co.saline.ks.us					
Scott County 303 Court St	Scott City	KS	67871	620-872-2420	872-7145
Web: www.scott.kansasgov.com					
Sedgwick County 525 N Main St Rm 211	Wichita	KS	67203	316-660-9222	383-7961
Web: www.sedgwick.ks.us					
Seward County 415 N Washington Ave Suite 109	Liberal	KS	67901	620-626-3200	626-3211
Web: www.seward.kansasgov.com					
Shawnee County 200 SE 7th St	Topeka	KS	66603	785-233-8200	291-4912
Web: www.co.shawnee.ks.us					
Sheridan County PO Box 899	Hoxie	KS	67740	785-675-3361	675-3487
Sherman County 813 Broadway Rm 102	Goodland	KS	67735	785-899-4800	899-4844
Web: www.sherman.kansasgov.com					
Smith County 218 S Grant St	Smith Center	KS	66967	785-282-5110	282-5114
Stafford County 209 N Broadway St	Saint John	KS	67576	620-549-3509	549-3481
Web: www.staffordcounty.org					
Stanton County PO Box 190	Johnson	KS	67855	620-492-2140	492-2688
Stevens County 200 E 6th St	Hugoton	KS	67951	620-544-2541	544-4094
Web: www.stevenscoks.org					
Sumner County 501 N Washington Ave	Wellington	KS	67152	620-326-3395	326-2116
Web: co.sumner.ks.us					
Thomas County 300 N Court Ave	Colby	KS	67701	785-460-4500	460-4512
Trego County 216 N Main St	WaKeeney	KS	67672	785-743-5773	743-5594
Unified Government of Wyandotte County/Kansas City 701 N 7th St	Kansas City	KS	66101	913-573-5260	321-0237
Web: www.wycokck.org					
Wabaunsee County 215 Kansas Ave PO box 278	Alma	KS	66401	785-765-3414	765-3704
Web: www.wabaunsee.kansasgov.com					
Wallace County PO Box 70	Sharon Springs	KS	67758	785-852-4282	852-4783
Washington County 214 C St	Washington	KS	66968	785-325-2974	325-2303
Wichita County PO Box 968	Leoti	KS	67861	620-375-2731	375-4350
Wilson County 615 Madison St	Fredonia	KS	66736	620-378-2186	378-3841
Web: www.wilson.kansasgov.com					
Woodson County 105 W Rutledge St	Yates Center	KS	66783	620-625-2179	625-8670
Web: www.woodsoncounty.net					

Kentucky

				Phone	Fax
Adair County 424 Public Sq	Columbia	KY	42728	270-384-2801	384-4805
Web: columbia-adaircounty.com					
Allen County 201 W Main St Rm 6	Scottsville	KY	42164	270-237-3706	237-9206
Web: www.allencountykentucky.com					
Anderson County 151 S Main St	Lawrenceburg	KY	40342	502-839-3041	839-3043
Ballard County PO Box 145	Wickliffe	KY	42087	270-335-5168	335-3081
Web: www.ballardconet.com					
Barren County 117 N Public Sq Suite 1A	Glasgow	KY	42141	270-651-3783	651-1083
Web: www.barrencounty.com					
Bath County PO Box 609	Owingsville	KY	40360	606-674-2613	674-9526
Bell County PO Box 157	Pineville	KY	40977	606-337-6143	337-5415
Boone County 2950 E Washington St	Burlington	KY	41005	859-334-3642	334-2193
Web: www.boonecountyky.org					
Bourbon County 301 Main St Suite 106	Paris	KY	40361	859-987-2142	987-5660
Web: www.parisky.com					
Boyd County PO Box 523	Catlettsburg	KY	41129	606-739-5116	739-6357
Boyle County 321 W Main St Rm 123	Danville	KY	40422	859-238-1110	238-1114
Web: www.danville-ky.com					
Bracken County PO Box 147	Brooksville	KY	41004	606-735-2952	735-2867
Breathitt County 1137 Main St	Jackson	KY	41339	606-666-3810	666-3807
Web: www.breathittcounty.com					
Breckinridge County PO Box 538	Hardinsburg	KY	40143	270-756-2246	756-1569
Web: www.breckinridgecounty.net					
Bullitt County 149 N Walnut St	Shepherdsville	KY	40165	502-543-2513	543-9121
Web: www.bullittcounty.org					
Butler County PO Box 449	Morgantown	KY	42261	270-526-5676	526-2658
Caldwell County 100 E Market St Rm 23	Princeton	KY	42445	270-365-6754	365-7447
Calloway County 101 S 5th St 2nd Fl	Murray	KY	42071	270-753-3923	759-9611
Campbell County 340 York St	Newport	KY	41071	859-292-3845	292-0615
Web: www.campbellcountyky.org					
Carlisle County PO Box 176	Bardwell	KY	42023	270-628-3233	628-0191
Carroll County 440 Main St Courthouse	Carrollton	KY	41008	502-732-7005	732-7007
Web: www.carrollcountyky.com					
Carter County 300 W Main St Rm 232	Grayson	KY	41143	606-474-5188	474-6883
Casey County PO Box 306	Liberty	KY	42539	606-787-6154	787-6154
Christian County 511 S Main St	Hopkinsville	KY	42240	270-887-4105	885-5925
Web: www.christiancounty.org					
Clark County 34 S Main St Rm 103	Winchester	KY	40391	859-745-0200	737-5678
Clay County 316 Main St Suite 108	Manchester	KY	40962	606-598-3663	598-4047
Clinton County County Courthouse 100 S Croff St	Albany	KY	42602	606-387-5943	387-5258
Crittenden County 107 S Main St	Marion	KY	42064	270-965-4200	965-4572
Cumberland County 601 Courthouse Sq Rm 6	Burkesville	KY	42717	270-864-3726	864-5884
Daviess County PO Box 609	Owensboro	KY	42302	270-685-8434	686-7111
Web: www.daviessky.org					
Edmonson County PO Box 830	Brownsville	KY	42210	270-597-2624	597-9714
Elliott County PO Box 788	Sandy Hook	KY	41171	606-738-5238	738-6962
Estill County PO Box 59	Irvine	KY	40336	606-723-5156	723-5108
Web: www.estill.net					
Fleming County 201 Court Sq	Flemingsburg	KY	41041	606-845-7571	845-1312
Web: www.flemingcountyky.org					
Floyd County PO Box 1089	Prestonsburg	KY	41653	606-886-3816	886-8089
Web: www.floydcountykentucky.com					
Franklin County 315 W Main St	Frankfort	KY	40602	502-875-8702	875-8718
Fulton County PO Box 126	Hickman	KY	42050	270-236-2727	236-2522
Gallatin County PO Box 1309	Warsaw	KY	41095	859-567-5411	567-5444
Web: www.gallatincountyky.com					
Garrard County 15 Public Sq County Courthouse	Lancaster	KY	40444	859-792-3071	792-6751
Grant County 107 N Main St	Williamstown	KY	41097	859-824-3321	824-3367
Web: www.grantco.org					
Graves County County Courthouse 101 E South St Suite 2	Mayfield	KY	42066	270-247-1676	247-1274
Grayson County 10 Public Sq	Leitchfield	KY	42754	270-259-3201	259-9264
Web: www.graysoncountychamber.com					
Green County 203 W Court St	Greensburg	KY	42743	270-932-5386	932-6241
Greenup County PO Box 686	Greenup	KY	41144	606-473-7394	473-5354
Hancock County PO Box 146	Hawesville	KY	42348	270-927-6117	927-8639
Web: www.hancockcounty-ky.com					
Hardin County PO Box 1030	Elizabethtown	KY	42702	270-765-2171	769-2682
Web: www.hcky.org					
Harlan County PO Box 670	Harlan	KY	40831	606-573-3636	573-0064
Harrison County 313 Oddville Ave	Cynthiana	KY	41031	859-234-7130	234-8049
Hart County PO Box 277	Munfordville	KY	42765	270-524-2751	524-0458
Web: www.hartcounty.com					
Henderson County 20 N Main St	Henderson	KY	42420	270-826-3906	826-9677
Web: www.hendersonky.com					
Henry County 27 S Property Rd	New Castle	KY	40050	502-845-5705	845-5708
Web: www.henryweb.com					
Hickman County 110 E Clay St County Courthouse	Clinton	KY	42031	270-653-2131	653-4248
Hopkins County 10 S Main St	Madisonville	KY	42431	270-821-7361	825-5009
Web: www.hopkinscounty.net					
Jackson County PO Box 339	McKee	KY	40447	606-287-7800	287-4505
Web: www.eastky.net/jacksonco/					
Jessamine County 101 N Main St	Nicholasville	KY	40356	859-885-4161	885-5837
Web: www.jessamineco.com					
Johnson County 230 Court St	Paintsville	KY	41240	606-789-2557	789-2559
Kenton County 303 Court St	Covington	KY	41011	859-392-1600	392-1639
Web: www.kentoncounty.org					
Knott County PO Box 446	Hindman	KY	41822	606-785-5651	785-0996
Knox County PO Box 173	Barbourville	KY	40906	606-546-8915	546-6196
LaRue County 209 W High St	Hodgenville	KY	42748	270-358-3544	358-4528
Web: www.laruecounty.org					
Laurel County 101 S Main St Rm 203	London	KY	40741	606-864-5158	864-7369
Lawrence County 122 S Main Cross St	Louisa	KY	41230	606-638-4102	638-0638
Lee County PO Box 551	Beattyville	KY	41311	606-464-4115	464-4102
Leslie County PO Box 619	Hyden	KY	41749	606-672-3200	672-7373
Web: www.lesliecounty.net					
Letcher County 156 Main St Suite 102	Whitesburg	KY	41858	606-633-2432	632-9282
Web: www.letchercountykentucky.net					
Lewis County 514 2nd St	Vanceburg	KY	41179	606-796-2722	796-0822
Lexington-Fayette County 162 E Main St	Lexington	KY	40507	859-253-3344	231-9619
Web: www.lfucg.com					
Lincoln County 102 E Main St County Courthouse	Stanford	KY	40484	606-365-4570	365-4572
Web: www.lincolnky.com					
Livingston County 335 Court St	Smithland	KY	42081	270-928-2162	928-2162
Web: www.livingstonco.ky.gov					
Logan County 229 W 3rd St PO Box 358	Russellville	KY	42276	270-726-6061	726-4355
Web: www.loganchamber.com					
Louisville-Jefferson County 527 W Jefferson St	Louisville	KY	40202	502-574-5700	574-5784
Web: www.louisvilleky.gov					
Lyon County PO Box 310	Eddyville	KY	42038	270-388-2331	388-0634
Web: www.lyoncounty.com					
Madison County 101 W Main St	Richmond	KY	40475	859-624-4703	623-3071
Magoffin County PO Box 430	Salyersville	KY	41465	606-349-2313	349-2109
Marion County 120 W Main St Suite 3	Lebanon	KY	40033	270-692-2651	692-9811
Web: www.lebanonky.org					
Marshall County 1101 Main St	Benton	KY	42025	270-527-4740	527-4738
Web: www.marshallcounty.net					
Martin County PO Box 460	Inez	KY	41224	606-298-2810	298-0143
Mason County 27 W 3rd St PO Box 234	Maysville	KY	41056	606-564-3341	564-8979
Web: www.masoncounty-ky.com					
McCracken County PO Box 609	Paducah	KY	42002	270-444-4700	444-4704
Web: www.co.mccracken.ky.us					
McCreary County PO Box 699	Whitley City	KY	42653	606-376-2411	376-3898
Web: www.mccrearycounty.com					
McLean County PO Box 57	Calhoun	KY	42327	270-273-3082	273-5084
Meade County PO Box 614	Brandenburg	KY	40108	270-422-2152	422-2158
Web: www.meadecountyclerk.ky.gov					
Menifee County PO Box 123	Frenchburg	KY	40322	606-768-3512	768-6738
Mercer County PO Box 426	Harrodsburg	KY	40330	859-734-6310	734-6309
Web: www.merceronline.com/mercer.htm					
Metcalfe County PO Box 25	Edmonton	KY	42129	270-432-4821	432-5176

	City	State	ZIP	Phone	Fax
Monroe County 200 N Main St Suite D	Tompkinsville	KY	42167	270-487-5471	487-5976
Montgomery County PO Box 414	Mount Sterling	KY	40353	859-498-8700	498-8729
Morgan County PO Box 26	West Liberty	KY	41472	606-743-3949	743-2111
Muhlenberg County PO Box 525	Greenville	KY	42345	270-338-1441	338-1774
Nelson County 113 E Steven Foster St	Bardstown	KY	40004	502-348-1820	348-1822
Nicholas County PO Box 227	Carlisle	KY	40311	859-289-3730	289-3705
Web: www.carlisle-nicholascounty.org					
Ohio County PO Box 85	Hartford	KY	42347	270-298-4423	298-4425
Oldham County 100 W Jefferson St	LaGrange	KY	40031	502-222-9311	222-3208
Web: www.oldhamcounty.net					
Owen County 100 N Thomas St	Owenton	KY	40359	502-484-3405	484-1004
Web: www.owenton.net					
Owsley County PO Box 500	Booneville	KY	41314	606-593-5735	593-5737
Web: www.owsleycountykentucky.org					
Pendleton County 233 Main St	Falmouth	KY	41040	859-654-4321	654-5047
Web: www.pendletoncountyky.org					
Perry County PO Box 150	Hazard	KY	41702	606-436-4614	439-0557
Pike County PO Box 631	Pikeville	KY	41502	606-432-6240	432-6222
Powell County PO Box 548	Stanton	KY	40380	606-663-6444	663-6406
Pulaski County PO Box 724	Somerset	KY	42502	606-679-2042	678-0073
Web: www.pulaskicountygovt.com					
Robertson County PO Box 75	Mount Olivet	KY	41064	606-724-5212	724-5022
Web: www.robertsoncountyky.com					
Rockcastle County 205 E Main St Box 6	Mount Vernon	KY	40456	606-256-2831	256-4302
Web: www.rockcastlecountyky.com					
Rowan County 627 E Main St 2nd Fl	Morehead	KY	40351	606-784-5212	784-2923
Russell County 410 Monument Sq Rm 103	Jamestown	KY	42629	270-343-2125	343-4700
Web: www.russellcountyky.com					
Scott County 101 E Main St	Georgetown	KY	40324	502-863-7850	863-7852
Web: www.scottky.com					
Shelby County 501 Main St	Shelbyville	KY	40065	502-633-1220	633-7623
Web: www.shelbyvilleky.com					
Simpson County PO Box 268	Franklin	KY	42135	270-586-8161	586-6464
Web: www.simpsoncountyclerk.ky.gov					
Spencer County 2 W Main St	Taylorsville	KY	40071	502-477-3215	477-3216
Web: www.spencercountyky.gov					
Taylor County 203 N Court St Suite 5	Campbellsville	KY	42718	270-465-6677	789-1144
Todd County PO Box 307	Elkton	KY	42220	270-265-2363	265-2588
Trigg County PO Box 1310	Cadiz	KY	42211	270-522-6661	522-6662
Trimble County 30 Hwy 42 E	Bedford	KY	40006	502-255-7174	255-7045
Web: www.trimblecounty.com					
Union County PO Box 119	Morganfield	KY	42437	270-389-1334	389-9135
Web: www.ucky.org/v2/					
Warren County 429 E 10th St Courthouse	Bowling Green	KY	42102	270-842-9416	842-9416
Web: www.warrencounty.state.ky.us					
Washington County PO Box 446	Springfield	KY	40069	859-336-5425	336-5408
Wayne County PO Box 565	Monticello	KY	42633	606-348-6661	348-8303
Web: www.monticellokychamber.com					
Webster County PO Box 155	Dixon	KY	42409	270-639-5042	639-7009
Web: www.webstercountyky.com					
Whitley County PO Box 8	Williamsburg	KY	40769	606-549-6002	549-2790
Wolfe County PO Box 400	Campton	KY	41301	606-668-3515	668-3492
Woodford County 103 S Main St County Courthouse	Versailles	KY	40383	859-873-3421	873-0196
Web: www.woodfordchamber-ky.com					

Louisiana

	City	State	ZIP	Phone	Fax
Acadia Parish N Parkson Court Cir 3rd Fl	Crowley	LA	70526	337-788-8800	788-2421
Web: www.acadiaparishpolicejury.org					
Allen Parish PO Drawer G	Oberlin	LA	70655	337-639-4396	639-4326
Web: www.allenparish.com					
Ascension Parish PO Box 1659	Gonzales	LA	70707	225-621-5709	621-5704
Web: www.ascensionparish.net					
Assumption Parish PO Box 249	Napoleonville	LA	70390	985-369-6653	369-2032
Web: www.assumptionla.com/ala/					
Avoyelles Parish 312 N Main St Courthouse Bldg Suite D	Marksville	LA	71351	318-253-9208	253-4614
Beauregard Parish PO Box 100	DeRidder	LA	70634	337-463-8595	462-3916
Bienville Parish 100 Courthouse Dr Rm 100	Arcadia	LA	71001	318-263-2123	263-7426
Web: www.bienvilleparish.org					
Bossier Parish 204 Burt Blvd 2nd Fl	Benton	LA	71006	318-965-2336	965-2713
Web: www.mybossier.com					
Caddo Parish 505 Travis St 8th Fl	Shreveport	LA	71101	318-226-6900	429-7630
Web: www.caddo.org					
Calcasieu Parish PO Box 1030	Lake Charles	LA	70602	337-437-3550	437-3350
Web: www.cppj.net					
Caldwell Parish PO Box 1737	Columbia	LA	71418	318-649-2681	649-5930
Cameron Parish PO Box 549	Cameron	LA	70631	337-775-5316	775-7172
Web: www.cameronparish.net					
Catahoula Parish PO Box 654	Harrisonburg	LA	71340	318-744-5497	744-5488
Claiborne Parish 512 E Main St PO Box 330	Homer	LA	71040	318-927-9601	927-2345
Web: www.claiborneone.org					
Concordia Parish PO Box 790	Vidalia	LA	71373	318-336-4204	336-8777
DeSoto Parish PO Box 1206	Mansfield	LA	71052	318-872-3110	872-4202
East Baton Rouge Parish 1755 Florida St	Baton Rouge	LA	70802	225-389-3129	389-3118
Web: www.brgov.com					
East Carroll Parish 400 1st St	Lake Providence	LA	71254	318-559-2399	559-0037
Web: www.eastcarroll.net/home.htm					
East Feliciana Parish PO Box 599	Clinton	LA	70722	225-683-5145	683-3556
Web: www.felicianatourism.org					
Evangeline Parish PO Drawer 347	Ville Platte	LA	70586	337-363-5671	363-5780
Web: www.evangelinetourism.com					
Franklin Parish PO Box 1564	Winnsboro	LA	71295	318-435-5133	435-5134
Grant Parish PO Box 263	Colfax	LA	71417	318-627-3246	627-3201
Iberia Parish PO Box 12010	New Iberia	LA	70562	337-365-7282	365-0737
Web: www.iberiaparishgovernment.com					
Iberville Parish PO Box 423	Plaquemine	LA	70765	225-687-5160	687-5260
Web: www.ibervilleparish.com					
Jackson Parish PO Box 730	Jonesboro	LA	71251	318-259-2424	395-0386
Web: www.jacksonparishpolicejury.org					
Jefferson Davis Parish PO Box 799	Jennings	LA	70546	337-824-8340	
Web: www.jeffdavis.org					
Jefferson Parish 200 Durbigny St	Gretna	LA	70053	504-364-2600	
Web: www.jeffparish.net					
Lafayette Consolidated Government PO Box 2009	Lafayette	LA	70502	337-233-0150	291-6392
Web: www.lafayettegov.org					
Lafourche Parish PO Box 5548	Thibodaux	LA	70302	985-446-8427	446-8459
Web: www.lapage.com/parishes/lafou.htm					
LaSalle Parish PO Box 1288	Jena	LA	71342	318-992-2101	992-2103
Lincoln Parish 100 W Texas Ave	Ruston	LA	71270	318-251-5150	251-5149
Web: www.lincolnparish.org					
Livingston Parish PO Box 427	Livingston	LA	70754	225-686-2266	686-7079
Web: www.lapage.com/parishes/livin.htm					
Madison Parish PO Box 1710	Tallulah	LA	71282	318-574-0655	574-3961
Morehouse Parish PO Box 1543	Bastrop	LA	71221	318-281-3343	281-3775
Natchitoches Parish PO Box 799	Natchitoches	LA	71458	318-352-2714	357-2208
Web: nppj.org					
Orleans Parish 1300 Perdido St Rm 9-E-06	New Orleans	LA	70112	504-658-4000	658-8647
Web: www.neworleans.com					
Ouachita Parish PO Box 1862	Monroe	LA	71210	318-327-1444	327-1462
Plaquemines Parish 301 Main St	Belle Chasse	LA	70037	504-392-4969	297-5195
Web: www.plaqueminesparish.com					
Pointe Coupee Parish PO Box 86	New Roads	LA	70760	225-638-9596	638-9590
Rapides Parish PO Box 952	Alexandria	LA	71309	318-473-8153	473-4667
Web: www.rppj.com					
Red River Parish PO Box 485	Coushatta	LA	71019	318-932-6741	932-3126
Richland Parish 708 Julia St	Rayville	LA	71269	318-728-2061	728-7004
Sabine Parish 400 S Capitol St	Many	LA	71449	318-256-6223	256-9037
Web: www.sabineparish.com					
Saint Bernard Parish 8201 W Judge Perez Dr	Chalmette	LA	70043	504-277-6371	278-4329
Web: www.st-bernard.la.us					
Saint Charles Parish 15045 River Rd	Hahnville	LA	70057	985-783-5000	783-2067
Web: www.st-charles.la.us					
Saint Helena Parish PO Box 308	Greensburg	LA	70441	225-222-4514	222-3443
TF: 866-345-6185					
Saint James Parish PO Box 106	Convent	LA	70723	225-562-2270	562-2279
Web: www.stjamesla.com					
Saint John the Baptist Parish 1801 W Airline Hwy	LaPlace	LA	70068	985-652-9569	652-4131
Web: www.sjbparish.com					
Saint Landry Parish 118 S Court St Suite 109	Opelousas	LA	70571	337-942-5606	948-7265
Web: www.stlandry.org					
Saint Martin Parish PO Box 308	Saint Martinville	LA	70582	337-394-2210	394-7772
Web: stmartinparish-la.org					
Saint Mary Parish PO Box 1231	Franklin	LA	70538	337-828-4100	828-2509
Web: www.parish.st-mary.la.us					
Saint Tammany Parish 701 N Columbia St	Covington	LA	70433	985-809-8700	
Web: www.stpgov.org					
Tangipahoa Parish PO Box 215	Amite	LA	70422	985-748-3211	748-7576
Web: www.tangipahoa.org					
Tensas Parish PO Box 78	Saint Joseph	LA	71366	318-766-3921	766-3926
Terrebonne Parish PO Box 1569	Houma	LA	70361	985-872-0466	868-5143
Web: www.terrebonneparish.com					
Union Parish 100 E Bayou St Suite 105	Farmerville	LA	71241	318-368-3055	368-3861
Vermilion Parish County Courthouse 100 N State St Suite 101	Abbeville	LA	70510	337-898-1992	898-9803
Web: www.vermilion.org					
Vernon Parish 215 S 4th St	Leesville	LA	71446	337-238-1384	238-9902
Washington Parish 909 Pearl St	Franklinton	LA	70438	985-839-7825	839-7828
Webster Parish PO Box 370	Minden	LA	71058	318-371-0366	371-0226
Web: www.wppj.org					
West Baton Rouge Parish PO Box 757	Port Allen	LA	70767	225-383-4755	387-0218
Web: www.wbrcouncil.org					
West Carroll Parish PO Box 1078	Oak Grove	LA	71263	318-428-3281	428-9896
West Feliciana Parish PO Box 1921	Saint Francisville	LA	70775	225-635-3864	635-3705
Web: www.westfelicianaparish.org					
Winn Parish PO Box 951	Winnfield	LA	71483	318-628-5824	628-7336

Maine

	City	State	ZIP	Phone	Fax
Androscoggin County 2 Turner St Unit 2	Auburn	ME	04210	207-784-8390	782-5367
Web: www.androscoggincounty.com					
Aroostook County 144 Sweden St	Caribou	ME	04736	207-498-8125	
Web: www.aroostook.me.us					
Cumberland County 142 Federal St Rm 102	Portland	ME	04101	207-871-8380	871-8292
Web: www.cumberlandcounty.org					
Franklin County 140 Main St	Farmington	ME	04938	207-778-6614	778-5899
Web: www.franklincountymaine.com					
Hancock County 50 State St Suite 7	Ellsworth	ME	04605	207-667-9542	667-1412
Web: www.co.hancock.me.us					
Kennebec County 125 State St	Augusta	ME	04330	207-622-0971	623-4083
Web: www.kennebeccounty.org					
Knox County 62 Union St	Rockland	ME	04841	207-594-0420	594-0443
Web: knoxcounty.midcoast.com					
Lincoln County PO Box 249	Wiscasset	ME	04578	207-882-6311	882-4320
Web: www.co.lincoln.me.us					
Oxford County PO Box 179	South Paris	ME	04281	207-743-6359	743-1545
Web: www.oxfordcounty.org					
Penobscot County 97 Hammond St	Bangor	ME	04401	207-942-0535	945-6027
Piscataquis County 159 E Main St	Dover-Foxcroft	ME	04426	207-564-2161	564-3022
Web: www.pcedc.org					
Sagadahoc County 752 High St	Bath	ME	04530	207-443-8200	443-8213
Web: www.sagcounty.com					
Somerset County County Courthouse 41 Court St	Skowhegan	ME	04976	207-474-9861	474-7405
Web: www.somersetcountymaine.org					
Waldo County PO Box D	Belfast	ME	04915	207-338-1710	338-6360
Web: www.waldocountyme.gov					
Washington County PO Box 297	Machias	ME	04654	207-255-3127	255-3313
Web: www.washingtoncountymaine.com					
York County 45 Kennebunk Rd PO Box 399	Alfred	ME	04002	207-324-1571	324-9494
Web: www.yorkcountyme.gov					

Maryland

	City	State	ZIP	Phone	Fax
Allegany County 701 Kelly Rd	Cumberland	MD	21502	301-777-5911	777-5819
Web: www.allconet.org					
Anne Arundel County 44 Calvert St	Annapolis	MD	21401	410-222-7000	
Web: www.co.anne-arundel.md.us					
Baltimore County 401 Bosley Ave	Towson	MD	21204	410-887-2697	887-3062
Web: www.co.ba.md.us					
Baltimore (Independent City) 100 N Holliday St	Baltimore	MD	21202	410-396-3100	396-9568
Web: www.ci.baltimore.md.us					
Calvert County 175 Main St	Prince Frederick	MD	20678	410-535-1600	535-9572
Web: www.co.cal.md.us					
Caroline County 109 Market St	Denton	MD	21629	410-479-0660	479-4060
Web: www.carolinemd.org					
Carroll County 225 N Center St Rm 300	Westminster	MD	21157	410-386-2400	386-2485
Web: www.ccgov.carr.org					
Cecil County 129 E Main St Rm 108	Elkton	MD	21921	410-996-5375	392-6032
Web: www.ccgov.org					
Charles County PO Box 2150	La Plata	MD	20646	301-645-0600	645-0560
Web: www.charlescounty.org					
Dorchester County 501 Court Ln	Cambridge	MD	21613	410-228-1700	228-9641
Web: www.commissioners.net					
Frederick County 12 E Church St	Frederick	MD	21701	301-694-1100	694-1849
Web: www.co.frederick.md.us					
Garrett County 203 S 4th St Rm 207	Oakland	MD	21550	301-334-8970	334-5000
Web: www.garrettcounty.org					
Harford County 220 S Main St	Bel Air	MD	21014	410-838-6000	638-1387
Web: www.co.ha.md.us					

Maryland (Cont'd)

	City	State	ZIP	Phone	Fax
Howard County 3430 Courthouse Dr *Web:* www.co.ho.md.us	Ellicott City	MD	21043	410-313-2011	313-3051
Kent County 400 High St *Web:* www.kentcounty.com	Chestertown	MD	21620	410-778-7435	778-7482
Montgomery County 101 Monroe St *Web:* www.montgomerycountymd.gov	Rockville	MD	20850	240-777-2500	777-2517
Prince George's County 14741 Governor Oden Bowie Dr *Web:* www.goprincegeorgescounty.com	Upper Marlboro	MD	20772	301-952-3600	952-4862
Queen Anne's County 107 N Liberty St *Web:* www.qac.org	Centreville	MD	21617	410-758-4098	758-1170
Saint Mary's County PO Box 676 *Web:* www.co.saint-marys.md.us	Leonardtown	MD	20650	301-475-4567	475-4470
Somerset County 11916 Somerset Ave Rm 111 *Web:* www.visitsomerset.com	Princess Anne	MD	21853	410-651-0320	651-0366
Talbot County 11 N Washington St County Courthouse *Web:* www.co.talbot.md.us	Easton	MD	21601	410-770-8010	770-8007
Washington County 100 W Washington St *Web:* www.washco-md.net/	Hagerstown	MD	21740	240-313-2200	313-2201
Wicomico County 125 N Division St *Web:* www.wicomicocounty.org	Salisbury	MD	21803	410-548-4801	548-4803
Worcester County 1 W Market St Rm 1103 *Web:* www.co.worcester.md.us	Snow Hill	MD	21863	410-632-1194	632-3131

Massachusetts

	City	State	ZIP	Phone	Fax
Barnstable County 3195 Main St *Web:* www.tsic.com	Barnstable	MA	02630	508-362-2511	362-4136
Berkshire County 76 East St	Pittsfield	MA	01201	413-499-1940	499-7990
Bristol County 9 Court St	Taunton	MA	02780	508-824-9681	821-3101
Dukes County PO Box 190 *Web:* www.dukescounty.org	Edgartown	MA	02539	508-696-3840	696-3841
Essex County 36 Federal St County Administration Bldg 1st Fl	Salem	MA	01970	978-741-0200	
Franklin County 425 Main St PO Box 1573 *Web:* www.co.franklin.ma.us	Greenfield	MA	01302	413-774-5535	774-4770
Hampden County 50 State St	Springfield	MA	01102	413-748-8600	
Hampshire County 99 Main St Rm 205	Northampton	MA	01060	413-584-0557	584-1465
Middlesex County 40 Thorndike St	Cambridge	MA	02141	617-494-4300	494-9129
Nantucket County 16 Broad St	Nantucket	MA	02554	508-228-7216	325-5313
Norfolk County 614 High St *Web:* www.norfolkcounty.org	Dedham	MA	02026	781-461-6105	326-6480
Plymouth County Court St *Web:* www.seeplymouth.com	Plymouth	MA	02360	508-747-6911	830-0676
Suffolk County 3 Pemberton Sq Government Center	Boston	MA	02108	617-725-8787	
Worcester County 2 Main St County Courthouse	Worcester	MA	01608	508-798-7717	798-7746

Michigan

	City	State	ZIP	Phone	Fax
Alcona County PO Box 308	Harrisville	MI	48740	989-724-5374	724-5838
Alger County PO Box 538	Munising	MI	49862	906-387-2076	387-2156
Allegan County 113 Chestnut St *Web:* www.allegancounty.org	Allegan	MI	49010	269-673-0450	673-0298
Alpena County 720 W Chisholm St *Web:* www.alpenacounty.org	Alpena	MI	49707	989-356-0930	354-9648
Antrim County PO Box 520 *Web:* www.antrimcounty.org	Bellaire	MI	49615	231-533-6353	533-6935
Arenac County PO Box 747 *Web:* www.arenaccountygov.com	Standish	MI	48658	989-846-4626	
Baraga County 16 N 3rd St	L'Anse	MI	49946	906-524-6183	524-6186
Barry County 220 W State St *Web:* www.barrycounty.org	Hastings	MI	49058	269-948-4810	945-0209
Bay County 515 Center Ave Suite 101 *Web:* www.co.bay.mi.us	Bay City	MI	48708	989-895-4280	895-4284
Benzie County 448 Court Pl *Web:* www.benzieco.net	Beulah	MI	49617	231-882-9671	882-5941
Berrien County 811 Port St *Web:* www.berriencounty.org	Saint Joseph	MI	49085	269-983-7111	982-8642
Branch County 31 Division St *Web:* www.co.branch.mi.us	Coldwater	MI	49036	517-279-4301	278-4130
Calhoun County 315 W Green St *Web:* www.calhouncountymi.org	Marshall	MI	49068	269-781-0730	781-0721
Cass County PO Box 132 *Web:* casscountymi.org	Cassopolis	MI	49031	269-445-3701	445-5018
Charlevoix County 203 Antrim St *Web:* www.charlevoixcounty.org	Charlevoix	MI	49720	231-547-7200	547-7217
Cheboygan County PO Box 70 *Web:* www.cheboygancounty.net	Cheboygan	MI	49721	231-627-8808	627-8453
Chippewa County 319 Court St *Web:* users.lighthouse.net/chippewa/	Sault Sainte Marie	MI	49783	906-635-6300	635-6851
Clare County 225 W Main St *Web:* clarecountyinternet.com	Harrison	MI	48625	989-539-7131	539-6616
Clinton County PO Box 69 *Web:* www.clinton-county.org	Saint Johns	MI	48879	989-224-5140	224-5102
Crawford County 200 W Michigan Ave *Web:* www.crawfordco.org	Grayling	MI	49738	989-344-3206	344-3223
Delta County 310 Ludington St *Web:* www.deltami.org	Escanaba	MI	49829	906-789-5105	789-5196
Dickinson County PO Box 609 *Web:* www.dickinsoncountymi.org	Iron Mountain	MI	49801	906-774-0988	774-4660
Eaton County 1045 Independence Blvd *Web:* www.co.eaton.mi.us	Charlotte	MI	48813	517-543-7500	541-0666
Emmet County 200 Division St *Web:* www.co.emmet.mi.us	Petoskey	MI	49770	231-348-1744	348-0602
Genesee County 900 S Saginaw St Rm 202 *Web:* www.co.genesee.mi.us	Flint	MI	48502	810-257-3282	257-3464
Gladwin County 401 W Cedar Ave *Web:* www.gladwinco.com	Gladwin	MI	48624	989-426-7351	426-6917
Gogebic County 200 N Moore St *Web:* www.gogebic.org	Bessemer	MI	49911	906-663-4518	663-4660
Grand Traverse County 400 Boardman Ave *Web:* www.grandtraverse.org	Traverse City	MI	49684	231-922-4760	922-4658
Gratiot County County Courthouse 214 E Center St PO Box 437 *Web:* www.gratiotcounty.org	Ithaca	MI	48847	989-875-5215	875-5284
Hillsdale County 29 N Howell St *Web:* www.co.hillsdale.mi.us	Hillsdale	MI	49242	517-437-3391	437-3392
Houghton County 401 E Houghton Ave *Web:* www.houghtoncounty.net	Houghton	MI	49931	906-482-1150	483-0364
Huron County 250 E Huron Ave Rm 305 *Web:* www.huroncounty.com	Bad Axe	MI	48413	989-269-8242	269-6152
Ingham County 315 S Jefferson St *Web:* www.ingham.org	Mason	MI	48854	517-676-7204	676-7254
Ionia County 100 Main St *Web:* www.ioniacounty.org	Ionia	MI	48846	616-527-5322	527-8201
Iosco County PO Box 778 *Web:* iosco.m33access.com	Tawas City	MI	48764	989-362-4212	984-1002
Iron County 2 S 6th St *Web:* www.iron.org	Crystal Falls	MI	49920	906-875-3221	875-6775
Isabella County 200 N Main St *Web:* www.isabellacounty.org	Mount Pleasant	MI	48858	989-772-0911	773-7431
Jackson County 312 S Jackson St 1st Fl *Web:* www.co.jackson.mi.us	Jackson	MI	49201	517-788-4265	788-4601
Kalamazoo County 201 W Kalamazoo Ave *Web:* www.kalcounty.com	Kalamazoo	MI	49007	269-383-8840	384-8143
Kalkaska County PO Box 10 *Web:* www.kalkaskami.com	Kalkaska	MI	49646	231-258-3300	258-3337
Kent County 300 Monroe Ave NW *Web:* www.accesskent.com	Grand Rapids	MI	49503	616-632-7640	632-7645
Keweenaw County 5095 Forest St *Web:* www.keweenaw.org	Eagle River	MI	49950	906-337-2229	337-2795
Lake County 800 10th St Suite 200 *Web:* www.lakecountymichigan.com	Baldwin	MI	49304	231-745-2725	745-8632
Lapeer County 255 Clay St *Web:* www.county.lapeer.org	Lapeer	MI	48446	810-667-0356	667-0362
Leelanau County 8527 E Government Center Dr Suite 103 *Web:* www.leelanaucounty.com	Suttons Bay	MI	49682	231-256-9824	256-8295
Lenawee County 425 N Main St *Web:* www.lenawee.mi.us	Adrian	MI	49221	517-264-4606	264-4790
Livingston County 200 E Grand River Ave *Web:* www.co.livingston.mi.us	Howell	MI	48843	517-546-0500	546-4354
Luce County 407 W Harrie St	Newberry	MI	49868	906-293-5521	293-0050
Mackinac County 100 S Marley St *Web:* www.mackinaccounty.net	Saint Ignace	MI	49781	906-643-7300	643-7302
Macomb County 40 N Main St 1st Fl *Web:* macombcountymi.gov	Mount Clemens	MI	48043	586-469-5120	
Manistee County 415 3rd St *Web:* www.manisteecounty.net	Manistee	MI	49660	231-398-5000	723-1795
Marquette County 234 W Baraga Ave *Web:* www.co.marquette.mi.us	Marquette	MI	49855	906-225-8330	228-1572
Mason County 304 E Ludington Ave *Web:* www.masoncounty.net	Ludington	MI	49431	231-843-8202	843-1972
Mecosta County 400 Elm St *Web:* www.co.mecosta.mi.us	Big Rapids	MI	49307	231-796-2505	592-0121
Menominee County 839 10th Ave *Web:* www.menomineecounty.com	Menominee	MI	49858	906-863-9968	863-8839
Midland County 220 W Ellsworth St *Web:* www.co.midland.mi.us	Midland	MI	48640	989-832-6739	832-6680
Missaukee County 111 S Canal PO Box 800 *Web:* www.missaukee.org	Lake City	MI	49651	231-839-4967	839-3684
Monroe County 106 E 1st St *Web:* www.co.monroe.mi.us	Monroe	MI	48161	734-240-7020	240-7045
Montcalm County PO Box 368	Stanton	MI	48888	989-831-7339	831-7474
Montmorency County PO Box 789	Atlanta	MI	49709	989-785-8013	785-8014
Muskegon County 990 Terrace St *Web:* www.co.muskegon.mi.us	Muskegon	MI	49442	231-724-6221	724-6262
Newaygo County 1087 Newell St *Web:* www.countyofnewaygo.com	White Cloud	MI	49349	231-689-7200	689-7205
Oakland County 1200 N Telegraph Rd *Web:* www.co.oakland.mi.us	Pontiac	MI	48341	248-858-0582	452-9221
Oceana County 100 State St Suite 1 *Web:* www.oceana.mi.us	Hart	MI	49420	231-873-4328	873-1391
Ogemaw County 806 W Houghton Ave	West Branch	MI	48661	989-345-0215	345-7223
Ontonagon County 725 Greenland Rd *Web:* www.ontonagonmi.com	Ontonagon	MI	49953	906-884-4255	884-2916
Osceola County 301 W Upton Ave *Web:* www.osceola-county.org	Reed City	MI	49677	231-832-3261	832-6149
Oscoda County PO Box 399	Mio	MI	48647	989-826-1109	826-1136
Otsego County 225 W Main St *Web:* www.otsegocountymi.gov	Gaylord	MI	49735	989-732-6484	732-1562
Ottawa County 414 Washington St *Web:* www.co.ottawa.mi.us	Grand Haven	MI	49417	616-846-8312	846-8138
Presque Isle County PO Box 110	Rogers City	MI	49779	989-734-3288	734-7635
Roscommon County 500 Lake St *Web:* www.roscommoncounty.net	Roscommon	MI	48653	989-275-5923	275-8640
Saginaw County 111 S Michigan Ave *Web:* www.saginawcounty.com	Saginaw	MI	48602	989-790-5251	790-5254
Saint Clair County 201 McMorran Blvd *Web:* www.stclaircounty.org	Port Huron	MI	48060	810-985-2200	985-4796
Saint Joseph County PO Box 189 *Web:* www.stjosephcountymi.org	Centreville	MI	49032	269-467-5602	467-5628
Sanilac County 60 W Sanilac Ave Rm 203 *Web:* www.sanilaccounty.net	Sandusky	MI	48471	810-648-3212	648-5466
Schoolcraft County 300 Walnut St Rm 164	Manistique	MI	49854	906-341-3618	341-5680
Shiawassee County 208 N Shiawassee St *Web:* www.co.shiawassee.mi.us	Corunna	MI	48817	989-743-2242	743-2241
Tuscola County 440 N State St *Web:* www.tuscolacounty.org	Caro	MI	48723	989-672-3780	672-4266
Van Buren County 212 E Paw Paw St Suite 101 *Web:* www.vbco.org	Paw Paw	MI	49079	269-657-8218	657-8298
Washtenaw County PO Box 8645 *Web:* www.ewashtenaw.org	Ann Arbor	MI	48107	734-222-6850	222-6715
Wayne County 211 Coleman A Young Municipal Center *Web:* www.co.wayne.mi.us	Detroit	MI	48226	313-224-6262	224-5364
Wexford County 437 E Division St *Web:* www.wexfordcounty.org	Cadillac	MI	49601	231-779-9453	779-9745

Minnesota

	City	State	ZIP	Phone	Fax
Aitkin County 209 2nd St NW *Web:* www.co.aitkin.mn.us	Aitkin	MN	56431	218-927-7350	927-4535
Anoka County 325 E Main St *Web:* www.co.anoka.mn.us	Anoka	MN	55303	763-422-7350	422-6919
Becker County 915 Lake Ave **Fax:* Acctg ■ *Web:* www.co.becker.mn.us	Detroit Lakes	MN	56501	218-846-7301	846-7257*
Beltrami County 619 Beltrami Ave NW Courthouse *Web:* www.co.beltrami.mn.us	Bemidji	MN	56601	218-333-4120	333-4209
Benton County 615 Hwy 23 PO Box 189 *Web:* www.co.benton.mn.us	Foley	MN	56329	320-968-5205	968-5353
Big Stone County 20 SE 2nd St *Web:* www.bigstonecounty.org	Ortonville	MN	56278	320-839-2537	839-2537
Blue Earth County 204 S 5th St *Web:* www.co.blue-earth.mn.us	Mankato	MN	56002	507-389-8100	389-8437
Brown County 14 S State St PO Box 248 *Web:* www.co.brown.mn.us	New Ulm	MN	56073	507-233-6600	359-1430

	City	State	ZIP	Phone	Fax
Carlton County PO Box 130	Carlton	MN	55718	218-384-9166	384-9182
Web: www.co.carlton.mn.us					
Carver County 606 E 4th St	Chaska	MN	55318	952-361-1500	361-1491
Web: www.co.carver.mn.us					
Cass County 303 Minnesota Ave W PO Box 3000	Walker	MN	56484	218-547-3300	547-2440
Web: www.co.cass.mn.us					
Chippewa County 629 N 11th St	Montevideo	MN	56265	320-269-7447	269-7412*
**Fax:* Acctg ■ *Web:* www.co.chippewa.mn.us					
Chisago County 313 N Main St Rm 174	Center City	MN	55012	651-213-1300	213-0359
Web: www.co.chisago.mn.us					
Clay County PO Box 280	Moorhead	MN	56560	218-299-5002	299-5195
Web: www.co.clay.mn.us					
Clearwater County 213 Main Ave N	Bagley	MN	56621	218-694-6520	694-6244*
**Fax:* Acctg ■ *Web:* www.co.clearwater.mn.us					
Cook County 411 W 2nd St	Grand Marais	MN	55604	218-387-3000	387-3007
Web: www.co.cook.mn.us					
Cottonwood County 900 3rd Ave	Windom	MN	56101	507-831-1905	831-4553
Web: www.co.cottonwood.mn.us					
Crow Wing County 326 Laurel St	Brainerd	MN	56401	218-824-1000	824-1046
Web: www.co.crow-wing.mn.us					
Dakota County 1560 Hwy 55	Hastings	MN	55033	651-438-8100	438-4405
Web: www.co.dakota.mn.us					
Dodge County 22 6th St E	Mantorville	MN	55955	507-635-6239	635-6265
Web: www.co.dodge.mn.us					
Douglas County 305 8th Ave W	Alexandria	MN	56308	320-762-3877	762-2389
Web: www.co.douglas.mn.us					
Faribault County 415 N Main St	Blue Earth	MN	56013	507-526-6277	526-3054
Web: www.co.faribault.mn.us					
Fillmore County 101 Fillmore St	Preston	MN	55965	507-765-3356	765-4571
Web: www.co.fillmore.mn.us					
Freeborn County 411 S Broadway	Albert Lea	MN	56007	507-377-5116	377-5109
Web: www.co.freeborn.mn.us					
Goodhue County 454 W 6th St	Red Wing	MN	55066	651-267-4800	267-4986
Web: www.co.goodhue.mn.us					
Grant County PO Box 1007 County Courthouse	Elbow Lake	MN	56531	218-685-4825	685-5349
Web: www.co.grant.mn.us					
Hennepin County 300 S 6th St	Minneapolis	MN	55487	612-348-3000	
Web: www.co.hennepin.mn.us					
Houston County 304 S Marshall St	Caledonia	MN	55921	507-725-5806	725-5550
Web: www.geocities.com/houstoncountymn/HC.html					
Hubbard County 301 Court Ave County Courthouse	Park Rapids	MN	56470	218-732-2300	732-3645*
**Fax:* Acctg ■ *Web:* www.co.hubbard.mn.us					
Isanti County 555 18th Ave SW	Cambridge	MN	55008	763-689-3859	689-8226
Web: www.co.isanti.mn.us					
Itasca County 123 NE 4th St	Grand Rapids	MN	55744	218-327-2847	327-2848
Web: www.co.itasca.mn.us					
Jackson County PO Box 226	Jackson	MN	56143	507-847-2763	847-4718
Web: www.co.jackson.mn.us					
Kanabec County 18 N Vine St	Mora	MN	55051	320-679-6466	679-6431
Web: www.kanabeccounty.org					
Kandiyohi County PO Box 936	Willmar	MN	56201	320-231-6202	231-6263
Web: www.co.kandiyohi.mn.us					
Kittson County 410 5th St S Suite 214	Hallock	MN	56728	218-843-2655	843-2656
Web: www.visitnwminnesota.com/Kittson.htm					
Koochiching County 715 4th St	International Falls	MN	56649	218-283-1152	283-1151
Web: www.co.koochiching.mn.us					
Lac qui Parle County 600 6th St	Madison	MN	56256	320-598-7444	598-3125
Web: www.ci.madison.mn.us/					
Lake County 601 3rd Ave	Two Harbors	MN	55616	218-834-8300	834-8360
Web: www.co.lake.mn.us					
Lake of the Woods County 206 8th Ave SE	Baudette	MN	56623	218-634-2836	634-2509
Web: www.co.lake-of-the-woods.mn.us					
Le Sueur County 88 South Pk	Le Center	MN	56057	507-357-2251	357-6433
Web: www.co.le-sueur.mn.us					
Lincoln County 319 N Rebecca St	Ivanhoe	MN	56142	507-694-1529	694-1198*
**Fax:* Acctg ■ *Web:* www.co.lincoln.mn.us					
Lyon County 607 W Main St	Marshall	MN	56258	507-537-6728	537-6091*
**Fax:* Acctg ■ *Web:* www.lyonco.org					
Mahnomen County PO Box 379	Mahnomen	MN	56557	218-935-5669	935-5946*
**Fax:* Acctg					
Marshall County 208 E Colvin Ave	Warren	MN	56762	218-745-4851	745-5089
Web: www.visitnwminnesota.com/Marshall.htm					
Martin County 201 Lake Ave Suite 201	Fairmont	MN	56031	507-238-3211	238-3259*
**Fax:* Acctg ■ *Web:* www.co.martin.mn.us					
McLeod County 830 11th St E Suite 106	Glencoe	MN	55336	320-864-1281	864-5905
Web: www.co.mcleod.mn.us					
Meeker County 325 N Sibley Ave	Litchfield	MN	55355	320-693-5230	693-5254
Web: www.co.meeker.mn.us					
Mille Lacs County 635 2nd St SE	Milaca	MN	56353	320-983-8313	983-8384
Web: www.co.mille-lacs.mn.us					
Morrison County 213 SE 1st Ave	Little Falls	MN	56345	320-632-0293	632-0294
Web: www.co.morrison.mn.us					
Mower County 201 1st St NE	Austin	MN	55912	507-437-9535	437-9471
Web: www.co.mower.mn.us					
Murray County 2500 28th St	Slayton	MN	56172	507-836-6148	836-8904
Web: www.murray-countymn.com					
Nicollet County 501 S Minnesota Ave	Saint Peter	MN	56082	507-931-6800	931-9220
Web: www.co.nicollet.mn.us					
Nobles County 1530 Airport Rd	Worthington	MN	56187	507-372-8263	372-4994
Web: www.co.nobles.mn.us					
Norman County 16 3rd Ave E PO Box 146	Ada	MN	56510	218-784-5473	784-4531
Web: www.co.norman.mn.us					
Olmsted County 151 4th St SE	Rochester	MN	55904	507-285-8115	287-2693
Web: www.olmstedcounty.com					
Otter Tail County 520 Fir Ave W	Fergus Falls	MN	56537	218-998-8000	998-8438
Web: www.co.ottertail.mn.us					
Pennington County County Courthouse 101 Main Ave N	Thief River Falls	MN	56701	218-683-7000	683-7026
Web: www.visitnwminnesota.com/Pennington.htm					
Pine County 315 Main St S Suite 9	Pine City	MN	55063	320-629-5634	629-5762
Web: www.pinecounty.org					
Pipestone County 416 S Hiawatha Ave	Pipestone	MN	56164	507-825-6740	825-6741*
**Fax:* Acctg ■ *Web:* www.mncounties.org/pipestone/					
Polk County 816 Marion Ave Suite 210	Crookston	MN	56716	218-281-2332	281-2204
Web: www.co.polk.mn.us					
Pope County 130 E Minnesota Ave	Glenwood	MN	56334	320-634-5705	634-3087*
**Fax:* Acctg ■ *Web:* www.mncounties.org/pope/					
Ramsey County 15 W Kellogg Blvd Rm 250	Saint Paul	MN	55102	651-266-8000	266-8039
Web: www.co.ramsey.mn.us					
Red Lake County PO Box 367	Red Lake Falls	MN	56750	218-253-2598	253-4894
Web: www.prairieagcomm.com/redlakecounty/index.cfm					
Redwood County					
PO Box 130 3rd & Jefferson Courthouse Sq	Redwood Falls	MN	56283	507-637-4013	637-4072*
**Fax:* Acctg ■ *Web:* www.mncounties2.org/redwood/					
Renville County 500 E DePue Ave 3rd Fl	Olivia	MN	56277	320-523-3680	523-3689
Web: www.co.renville.mn.us					
Rice County 320 NW 3rd St	Faribault	MN	55021	507-332-6101	332-5999
Web: www.co.rice.mn.us					
Rock County 204 E Brown St	Luverne	MN	56156	507-283-5020	283-5017
Web: www.co.rock.mn.us					
Roseau County 606 5th Ave SW Rm 20	Roseau	MN	56751	218-463-2541	463-1889
Web: www.visitnwminnesota.com/Roseau.htm					
Saint Louis County 100 North 5th Ave W Rm 214	Duluth	MN	55802	218-726-2380	725-5060*
**Fax:* Acctg ■ *Web:* www.co.st-louis.mn.us					
Scott County 200 4th Ave W	Shakopee	MN	55379	952-445-7750	496-8257
Web: www.co.scott.mn.us					
Sherburne County 13880 Hwy 10	Elk River	MN	55330	763-241-2800	241-2816
Web: www.co.sherburne.mn.us					
Sibley County 400 Court St	Gaylord	MN	55334	507-237-4051	237-4062
Web: www.co.sibley.mn.us					
Stearns County 705 Courthouse Sq Rm 121	Saint Cloud	MN	56303	320-656-3601	656-6393
Web: www.co.stearns.mn.us					
Steele County 111 E Main St	Owatonna	MN	55060	507-444-7700	444-7491
Web: www.co.steele.mn.us					
Stevens County PO Box 530	Morris	MN	56267	320-589-7287	589-7288
Web: www.co.stevens.mn.us					
Swift County PO Box 110	Benson	MN	56215	320-843-2744	843-4124
Web: www.swiftcounty.com					
Todd County 221 1st Ave S Suite 200	Long Prairie	MN	56347	320-732-4469	732-4001*
**Fax:* Acctg ■ *Web:* www.co.todd.mn.us					
Traverse County PO Box 428	Wheaton	MN	56296	320-563-4242	563-4424*
**Fax:* Acctg					
Wabasha County 625 Jefferson Ave	Wabasha	MN	55981	651-565-2648	565-2774*
**Fax:* Acctg ■ *Web:* www.co.wabasha.mn.us					
Wadena County 415 S Jefferson St	Wadena	MN	56482	218-631-7634	631-7635
Web: www.co.wadena.mn.us					
Waseca County 307 N State St	Waseca	MN	56093	507-835-0610	835-0633*
**Fax:* Acctg ■ *Web:* www.co.waseca.mn.us					
Washington County 14949 62nd St N	Stillwater	MN	55082	651-430-6001	430-6017
Web: www.co.washington.mn.us					
Watonwan County 710 7th Ave S	Saint James	MN	56081	507-375-1236	375-5010
Web: www.extension.umn.edu/county/watonwan/					
Wilkin County PO Box 219	Breckenridge	MN	56520	218-643-7172	643-7167
Web: www.co.wilkin.mn.us					
Winona County 177 Main St	Winona	MN	55987	507-457-6350	454-9365
Web: www.co.winona.mn.us/					
Wright County 10 2nd St NW Rm 201	Buffalo	MN	55313	763-682-7539	682-7300
Web: www.co.wright.mn.us					
Yellow Medicine County 415 9th Ave	Granite Falls	MN	56241	320-564-3325	564-4435
Web: www.yellowmedicine.govoffice.com					

Mississippi

	City	State	ZIP	Phone	Fax
Adams County PO Box 1006	Natchez	MS	39121	601-446-6684	445-7913
Alcorn County 305 S Fulton Dr	Corinth	MS	38834	662-286-7700	286-7773
Amite County PO Box 680	Liberty	MS	39645	601-657-8022	657-8288
Attala County 230 W Washington St	Kosciusko	MS	39090	662-289-2921	289-7662
Benton County PO Box 218	Ashland	MS	38603	662-224-6300	224-6303
Bolivar County 200 Court St PO Box 698	Cleveland	MS	38732	662-846-5877	846-5880
Web: www.co.bolivar.ms.us					
Calhoun County PO Box 8	Pittsboro	MS	38951	662-412-3117	412-3128
Carroll County PO Box 60	Carrollton	MS	38917	662-237-9274	237-9642
Chickasaw County County Courthouse 1 Pinson Sq	Houston	MS	38851	662-456-2513	456-5295
Choctaw County PO Box 250	Ackerman	MS	39735	662-285-6329	285-3444
Claiborne County 410 Market St	Port Gibson	MS	39150	601-437-5841	437-4543
Clarke County PO Box 689	Quitman	MS	39355	601-776-2126	776-2756
Clay County PO Box 815	West Point	MS	39773	662-494-3124	492-4059
Coahoma County PO Box 98	Clarksdale	MS	38614	662-624-3000	624-3040
Copiah County PO Box 507	Hazlehurst	MS	39083	601-894-3021	894-4081
Web: www.copiahcounty.org					
Covington County PO Box 1679	Collins	MS	39428	601-765-4242	765-5016
DeSoto County 365 Losher St	Hernando	MS	38632	662-429-1460	429-4116
Web: www.desotoms.com					
Forrest County 700 N Main St	Hattiesburg	MS	39401	601-582-3213	545-6065
Web: www.co.forrest.ms.us					
Franklin County PO Box 297	Meadville	MS	39653	601-384-2330	384-5864
Web: www.franklincountyms.com					
George County 355 Cox St Suite A	Lucedale	MS	39452	601-947-4801	947-1300
Greene County PO Box 610	Leakesville	MS	39451	601-394-2377	394-4445
Grenada County PO Drawer 1208	Grenada	MS	38902	662-226-1821	227-2860
Hancock County 3068 Longfellow Dr	Bay Saint Louis	MS	39520	228-467-5404	467-3159
Web: www.hancockcountyms.org					
Harrison County PO Drawer CC	Gulfport	MS	39502	228-865-4036	868-1480
Web: www.co.harrison.ms.us					
Hinds County 316 S President St	Jackson	MS	39205	601-968-6501	968-6794
Web: www.co.hinds.ms.us					
Holmes County PO Box 239	Lexington	MS	39095	662-834-2508	834-3020
Humphreys County 102 Castleman St PO Box 547	Belzoni	MS	39038	662-247-1740	247-0101
Issaquena County PO Box 27	Mayersville	MS	39113	662-873-2761	873-2061
Itawamba County PO Box 776	Fulton	MS	38843	662-862-3421	862-3421
Web: www.itawamba.com					
Jackson County PO Box 998	Pascagoula	MS	39568	228-769-3089	769-3348
Web: www.co.jackson.ms.us					
Jasper County PO Box 1047	Bay Springs	MS	39422	601-764-3368	764-3999
Jefferson County PO Box 145	Fayette	MS	39069	601-786-3021	786-6009
Jefferson Davis County PO Box 1137	Prentiss	MS	39474	601-792-4204	792-2894
Jones County PO Box 1468	Laurel	MS	39441	601-428-0527	428-3610
Web: www.edajones.com					
Kemper County PO Box 188	De Kalb	MS	39328	601-743-2460	743-2789
Lafayette County PO Box 1240	Oxford	MS	38655	662-234-7563	234-5038
Web: www.oxfordms.com					
Lamar County PO Box 247	Purvis	MS	39475	601-794-8504	794-3903
Web: www.lamarcounty.com					
Lauderdale County PO Box 1587	Meridian	MS	39302	601-482-9714	486-4943
Web: www.lauderdalecounty.org					
Lawrence County PO Box 821	Monticello	MS	39654	601-587-7162	587-0767
Web: www.lawrencecounty.org					
Leake County PO Box 72	Carthage	MS	39051	601-267-7372	267-6137
Web: www.leakems.com					
Lee County PO Box 7127	Tupelo	MS	38802	662-841-9100	680-6091
Web: www.leecoms.com					
Leflore County 306 W Market St	Greenwood	MS	38930	662-453-1435	455-1278
Lincoln County PO Box 555	Brookhaven	MS	39602	601-835-3479	835-3423
Web: www.co.lincoln.ms.us					
Lowndes County 505 2nd Ave N	Columbus	MS	39701	662-329-5888	329-5881
Madison County PO Box 404	Canton	MS	39046	601-859-1177	859-5875
Web: www.madison-co.com					
Marion County 250 Broad St Suite 2	Columbia	MS	39429	601-736-2691	444-0206
Marshall County PO Box 219	Holly Springs	MS	38635	662-252-4431	252-0004
Monroe County PO Box 578	Aberdeen	MS	39730	662-369-8143	369-7928
Web: www.gomonroe.org					
Montgomery County PO Box 71	Winona	MS	38967	662-283-2333	283-2233

Mississippi (Cont'd)

County / Address	City	State	Zip	Phone	Fax
Neshoba County 401 Beacon St Suite 107	Philadelphia	MS	39350	601-656-3581	656-5915
Web: www.neshoba.org					
Newton County PO Box 447	Decatur	MS	39327	601-635-2368	635-3210
Noxubee County PO Box 147	Macon	MS	39341	662-726-4243	726-2272
Web: www.noxubeecounty.org					
Oktibbeha County 101 E Main St	Starkville	MS	39759	662-323-5834	338-1064
Web: www.gtpdd.com/counties/oktibbeha/					
Panola County 151 Public Sq	Batesville	MS	38606	662-563-6205	563-6277
Pearl River County PO Box 431	Poplarville	MS	39470	601-403-2300	795-3093
Web: www.pearlrivercounty.net					
Perry County PO Box 198	New Augusta	MS	39462	601-964-8398	964-8746
Pike County PO Box 309	Magnolia	MS	39652	601-783-3363	783-5982
Web: www.co.pike.ms.us					
Pontotoc County PO Box 209	Pontotoc	MS	38863	662-489-3900	489-3940
Prentiss County PO Box 477	Booneville	MS	38829	662-728-8151	728-2007
Quitman County 230 Chestnut St County Courthouse	Marks	MS	38646	662-326-2661	326-8004
Rankin County PO Box 1599	Brandon	MS	39043	601-825-1466	825-1465
Web: www.rankincounty.org					
Scott County PO Box 630	Forest	MS	39074	601-469-1922	469-5180
Sharkey County PO Box 218	Rolling Fork	MS	39159	662-873-2755	873-6045
Simpson County PO Box 367	Mendenhall	MS	39114	601-847-2626	847-7004
Smith County PO Box 517	Raleigh	MS	39153	601-782-4751	782-4007
Stone County PO Drawer 7	Wiggins	MS	39577	601-928-5266	928-6464
Web: www.stonecounty.com					
Sunflower County PO Box 988	Indianola	MS	38751	662-887-4703	887-7054
Tallahatchie County PO Box 350	Charleston	MS	38921	662-647-5551	647-8490
Tate County PO Box 309	Senatobia	MS	38668	662-562-5661	560-6205
Tippah County 101 Spring St	Ripley	MS	38663	662-837-7374	837-7148
Web: www.tippahcounty.ripley.ms					
Tishomingo County 1008 Battleground Dr	Iuka	MS	38852	662-423-7010	423-7005
Web: www.tunicacounty.com					
Tunica County PO Box 217	Tunica	MS	38676	662-363-2451	357-5934
Web: www.tunicacounty.com					
Union County PO Box 847	New Albany	MS	38652	662-534-1900	534-1907
Web: www.ucda-newalbany.com					
Walthall County PO Box 351	Tylertown	MS	39667	601-876-4947	876-6026
Web: www.walthallcountychamber.org					
Warren County PO Box 351	Vicksburg	MS	39181	601-636-4415	630-8016
Web: www.co.warren.ms.us					
Washington County PO Box 309	Greenville	MS	38702	662-332-1595	334-2725
Web: www.thedelta.org					
Wayne County 609 Azalea Dr County Courthouse	Waynesboro	MS	39367	601-735-2873	735-6224
Web: www.wayneco.com					
Webster County PO Box 398	Walthall	MS	39771	662-258-4131	258-6657
Web: www.webstercountyms.com/county/					
Wilkinson County PO Box 516	Woodville	MS	39669	601-888-4381	888-6776
Winston County PO Box 69	Louisville	MS	39339	662-773-3631	773-8814
Web: www.winstoncounty.com					
Yalobusha County PO Box 664	Water Valley	MS	38965	662-473-5024	473-3622
Yazoo County 211 E Broadway	Yazoo City	MS	39194	662-746-2661	746-3893
Web: www.yazoo.org					

Missouri

County / Address	City	State	Zip	Phone	Fax
Adair County 106 W Washington St County Courthouse	Kirksville	MO	63501	660-665-3350	785-3233
Andrew County PO Box 206	Savannah	MO	64485	816-324-3624	324-6154
Atchison County PO Box 280	Rock Port	MO	64482	660-744-2707	744-5705
Audrain County 101 N Jefferson St Rm 101	Mexico	MO	65265	573-473-5820	581-2380
Web: www.audraincounty.org					
Barry County 700 Main St Suite 2	Cassville	MO	65625	417-847-2561	847-5311
Barton County 1004 Gulf St	Lamar	MO	64759	417-682-3529	682-4100
Web: www.bartoncounty.com					
Bates County 1 N Delaware St	Butler	MO	64730	660-679-3371	679-9922
Web: www.batescounty.net					
Benton County PO Box 1238	Warsaw	MO	65355	660-438-7326	438-3275
Bollinger County PO Box 110	Marble Hill	MO	63764	573-238-1900	238-4511
Boone County 801 E Walnut St	Columbia	MO	65201	573-886-4295	886-4300
Web: www.co.boone.mo.us					
Buchanan County 411 Jules St	Saint Joseph	MO	64501	816-271-1411	271-1535
Web: www.co.buchanan.mo.us					
Butler County 100 N Main St Courthouse Rm 202	Poplar Bluff	MO	63901	573-686-8050	686-8066
Caldwell County PO Box 67	Kingston	MO	64650	816-586-2571	586-3600
Callaway County 10 E 5th St	Fulton	MO	65251	573-642-0730	642-7181
Web: callaway.county.missouri.org					
Camden County 1 Court Cir Suite 2	Camdenton	MO	65020	573-346-4440	346-5181
Web: www.camdenmo.org					
Cape Girardeau County 1 Barton Sq	Jackson	MO	63755	573-243-3547	204-2418
Web: www.showme.net/CapeCounty/					
Carroll County 8 S Main St Suite 6	Carrollton	MO	64633	660-542-0615	542-0621
Carter County 105 Main St	Van Buren	MO	63965	573-323-4527	323-4527
Cass County 2501 W Wall St	Harrisonville	MO	64701	816-380-8100	380-8101
Web: www.casscounty.com					
Cedar County 113 South St PO Box 126	Stockton	MO	65785	417-276-6700	276-3461
Chariton County 306 S Cherry St	Keytesville	MO	65261	660-288-3273	288-3403
Christian County 100 W Church St Rm 206	Ozark	MO	65721	417-581-6360	581-8331
Web: www.christiancountymo.gov					
Clark County 111 E Court St	Kahoka	MO	63445	660-727-3283	727-1051
Clay County 1 Courthouse Sq	Liberty	MO	64068	816-792-7733	792-7777
Web: www.claycogov.com					
Clinton County PO Box 245	Plattsburg	MO	64477	816-539-3713	539-3072
Cole County 311 E High St	Jefferson City	MO	65101	573-634-9100	634-8031
Web: www.colecounty.org					
Cooper County 200 Main St	Boonville	MO	65233	660-882-2114	882-5645
Crawford County 302 Main St	Steelville	MO	65565	573-775-2376	775-3066
Dade County 300 W Water St	Greenfield	MO	65661	417-637-2724	637-1006
Dallas County 102 S Cedar St	Buffalo	MO	65622	417-345-2632	345-5321
Daviess County 102 N Main St	Gallatin	MO	64640	660-663-2641	663-3376
DeKalb County PO Box 248	Maysville	MO	64469	816-449-5402	449-2440
Dent County 400 N Main St	Salem	MO	65560	573-729-4144	729-6106
Web: www.salemmissouri.com/government.html					
Douglas County 283 SE 2nd Ave	Ava	MO	65608	417-683-4714	683-1017
Dunklin County Courthouse Sq PO Box 188	Kennett	MO	63857	573-888-1374	888-2832
Franklin County 300 E Main St Rm 201	Union	MO	63084	636-583-6355	583-7320
Web: www.franklinmo.org					
Gasconade County 119 E 1st St Rm 2	Hermann	MO	65041	573-486-5427	486-8893
Web: www.gscnd.com					
Gentry County 200 W Clay St	Albany	MO	64402	660-726-3618	726-4102
Greene County 940 N Boonville Ave	Springfield	MO	65802	417-868-4055	868-4170
Web: www.greenecountymo.org					
Grundy County 700 Main St	Trenton	MO	64683	660-359-6305	359-6786
Harrison County PO Box 525	Bethany	MO	64424	660-425-6424	425-3772
Henry County 100 W Franklin St	Clinton	MO	64735	660-885-7204	890-2693
Hickory County PO Box 3	Hermitage	MO	65668	417-745-6450	745-6057
Holt County PO Box 437	Oregon	MO	64473	660-446-3303	446-3353
Howard County 1 Courthouse Sq	Fayette	MO	65248	660-248-2284	248-1075
Howell County 1 Courthouse	West Plains	MO	65775	417-256-2591	256-2512
Web: www.howellcounty.net					
Iron County 25 S Main St	Ironton	MO	63650	573-546-2912	546-6499
Web: www.ironcounty.org					
Jackson County 415 E 12th St	Kansas City	MO	64106	816-881-3000	881-3133
Web: www.co.jackson.mo.us					
Jasper County 302 S Main St Rm 102	Carthage	MO	64836	417-358-0416	358-0415
Web: www.jaspercounty.org					
Jefferson County PO Box 100	Hillsboro	MO	63050	636-797-5478	797-5360
Web: www.jeffcomo.org					
Johnson County 300 N Holden St County Courthouse	Warrensburg	MO	64093	660-747-6161	747-9332
Web: www.jaspercounty.org					
Knox County 107 N 4th St	Edina	MO	63537	660-397-2184	397-3331
Laclede County 200 N Adams Ave	Lebanon	MO	65536	417-532-5471	588-9288
Web: www.lacledecountymissouri.org					
Lafayette County 1001 Main St	Lexington	MO	64067	660-259-4315	259-6109
Web: www.historiclexington.com/LafayetteOfficials.html					
Lawrence County 1 Courthouse Sq Suite 101	Mount Vernon	MO	65712	417-466-2638	466-4348
Lewis County 100 Lafayette St	Monticello	MO	63457	573-767-5205	767-8245
Lincoln County 201 Main St	Troy	MO	63379	636-528-6300	528-5528
Web: www.lcmo.us					
Linn County 108 N High St	Linneus	MO	64653	660-895-5417	895-5527
Livingston County 700 Webster St	Chillicothe	MO	64601	660-646-2293	646-6139
Macon County PO Box 96	Macon	MO	63552	660-385-2913	385-7203
Web: www.maconcounty.org					
Madison County 1 Courthouse Sq	Fredericktown	MO	63645	573-783-2176	783-5351
Maries County 211 4th St	Vienna	MO	65582	573-422-3388	422-3269
Marion County 100 S Main St	Palmyra	MO	63461	573-769-2549	769-4312
McDonald County 602 Main St	Pineville	MO	64856	417-223-4717	223-7519
Mercer County 802 Main St County Courthouse	Princeton	MO	64673	660-748-3425	748-3180
Miller County PO Box 12	Tuscumbia	MO	65082	573-369-1900	369-2910
Mississippi County 200 n Main St	Charleston	MO	63834	573-683-2146	683-6071
Web: www.misscomo.net					
Moniteau County 200 E Main St	California	MO	65018	573-796-4661	796-3082
Monroe County 300 N Main St Rm 204	Paris	MO	65275	660-327-5106	327-1019
Montgomery County 211 E 3rd St	Montgomery City	MO	63361	573-564-3357	564-8088
Web: www.montgomerycountymo.org					
Morgan County 100 E Newton St	Versailles	MO	65084	573-378-5436	378-5991
New Madrid County 450 Main St	New Madrid	MO	63869	573-748-2524	748-9269
Newton County 101 S Wood St	Neosho	MO	64850	417-451-8220	451-7434
Nodaway County PO Box 218	Maryville	MO	64468	660-582-2251	582-5282
Oregon County PO Box 324	Alton	MO	65606	417-778-7475	778-7488
Osage County 106 E Main St	Linn	MO	65051	573-897-2139	897-4741
Web: www.osagecountymo.com					
Ozark County PO Box 416	Gainesville	MO	65655	417-679-3516	679-3209
Pemiscot County 610 Ward Ave	Caruthersville	MO	63830	573-333-4203	333-0440
Perry County 321 N Main St Suite 2	Perryville	MO	63775	573-547-4242	547-7367
Web: www.perryvillemo.com/county/					
Pettis County 415 S Ohio St	Sedalia	MO	65301	660-826-5395	829-0717
Phelps County 200 N Main St	Rolla	MO	65401	573-364-1891	458-6119
Web: www.phelpscounty.org					
Pike County 115 W Main St	Bowling Green	MO	63334	573-324-2412	324-5154
Web: www.pikecountytourism.com					
Platte County 415 3rd St	Platte City	MO	64079	816-858-2232	858-3363
Web: www.co.platte.mo.us					
Polk County 102 E Broadway	Bolivar	MO	65613	417-326-4031	326-3525
Web: www.polkcountymo.org					
Pulaski County 301 Historic 66 E Suite 101	Waynesville	MO	65583	573-774-4701	774-5601
Web: www.visitpulaskicounty.org					
Putnam County Rm 204 County Courthouse	Unionville	MO	63565	660-947-2674	947-4214
Ralls County 311 S Main St	New London	MO	63459	573-985-7111	985-6100
Randolph County 110 S Main St	Huntsville	MO	65259	660-277-4717	277-3246
Web: www.randolphcountymo.com					
Ray County 100 W Main St County Courthouse	Richmond	MO	64085	816-776-4502	776-4512
Reynolds County Hwy 21 & Courthouse Sq PO Box 10	Centerville	MO	63633	573-648-2494	648-2449
Ripley County County Courthouse 100 Courthouse Sq	Doniphan	MO	63935	573-996-3215	996-9774
Web: www.ripleycountymissouri.org/ripley.asp					
Saint Charles County 201 N 2nd St	Saint Charles	MO	63301	636-949-7550	949-7552
Web: www.saintcharlescounty.org					
Saint Clair County 655 2nd St	Osceola	MO	64776	417-646-2315	646-8080
Saint Francois County 1 N Washington St Rm 206	Farmington	MO	63640	573-756-5411	431-6967
Saint Louis County 41 S Central Ave	Clayton	MO	63105	314-615-5432	615-7890
Web: www.stlouisco.com					
Saint Louis (Independent City) 1200 Market St	Saint Louis	MO	63103	314-622-3201	622-4061
Web: stlouis.missouri.org					
Sainte Genevieve County 55 S 3rd St	Sainte Genevieve	MO	63670	573-883-5589	883-5312
Saline County 101 E Arrow St County Courthouse	Marshall	MO	65340	660-886-3331	886-2644
Schuyler County PO Box 187	Lancaster	MO	63548	660-457-3842	457-3016
Scotland County					
County Courthouse 117 S Market St Suite 100	Memphis	MO	63555	660-465-7027	465-7785
Web: www.scotlandcounty.net					
Scott County 131 S Winchester St	Benton	MO	63736	573-545-3549	545-3540
Shannon County 111 N Main St	Eminence	MO	65466	573-226-3414	226-5321
Shelby County 100 E Main St	Shelbyville	MO	63469	573-633-2181	633-1004
Stoddard County 316 S Prairie St	Bloomfield	MO	63825	573-568-3339	568-2194
Stone County 108 4th St	Galena	MO	65656	417-357-6127	357-6861
Web: www.stoneco-mo.us					
Sullivan County 109 N Main St	Milan	MO	63556	660-265-3786	265-3724
Taney County 266-A Main St	Forsyth	MO	65653	417-546-7200	546-2519
Web: www.co.taney.mo.us					
Texas County 210 N Grand Ave	Houston	MO	65483	417-967-2112	967-3837
Vernon County 100 W Cherry St	Nevada	MO	64772	417-448-2500	667-6035
Web: www.vernoncountymo.org					
Warren County 104 W Main St	Warrenton	MO	63383	636-456-3331	456-1801
Web: www.co.warren.mo.us					
Washington County 102 N Missouri St	Potosi	MO	63664	573-438-4901	438-4038
Wayne County 109 Walnut St County Courthouse	Greenville	MO	63944	573-224-3011	224-5609
Webster County					
101 S Crittenden St County Courthouse Rm 12	Marshfield	MO	65706	417-468-2223	468-5307
Worth County PO Box 450	Grant City	MO	64456	660-564-2219	564-2432
Wright County 125 Court Sq	Hartville	MO	65667	417-741-6661	741-6142
Web: www.wrightcountymo.com					

Montana

County / Address	City	State	Zip	Phone	Fax
Anaconda-Deer Lodge County 800 Main St	Anaconda	MT	59711	406-563-4060	563-4001
Web: www.anacondamt.org					
Beaverhead County 2 S Pacific St	Dillon	MT	59725	406-683-5245	683-3769
Web: www.beaverhead.com					
Big Horn County 121 W 3rd St	Hardin	MT	59034	406-665-9735	665-9738
Blaine County 400 Ohio St	Chinook	MT	59523	406-357-3250	357-2199

				Phone	Fax
Broadwater County 515 Broadway	Townsend	MT	59644	406-266-3443	266-3674
Butte-Silver Bow County 155 W Granite St	Butte	MT	59703	406-497-6200	497-6328
Web: www.co.silverbow.mt.us					
Carbon County 17 W 11th St	Red Lodge	MT	59068	406-446-1220	446-2640
Web: www.co.carbon.mt.us/gp/					
Carter County 214 Park St	Ekalaka	MT	59324	406-775-8749	775-8750
Web: www.cartercountymt.com					
Cascade County 121 4th St N Suite 1B-1	Great Falls	MT	59401	406-454-6800	454-6703
Web: www.co.cascade.mt.us					
Chouteau County 1308 Franklin St	Fort Benton	MT	59442	406-622-5151	622-3012
Web: www.co.chouteau.mt.us					
Custer County 1010 Main St	Miles City	MT	59301	406-874-3343	874-3452
Web: www.co.chouteau.mt.us					
Daniels County 213 Main St	Scobey	MT	59263	406-487-5561	487-5583
Web: www.scobey.org					
Dawson County 207 W Bell St	Glendive	MT	59330	406-377-3058	377-1717
Web: www.dawsoncountymontana.org					
Fallon County 10 W Fallon St	Baker	MT	59313	406-778-7114	778-2815
Fergus County 712 W Main St	Lewistown	MT	59457	406-538-5119	538-9023
Web: www.co.fergus.mt.us					
Flathead County 800 S Main St	Kalispell	MT	59901	406-758-5503	758-5861
Web: www.co.flathead.mt.us					
Gallatin County 311 W Main St Rm 203	Bozeman	MT	59715	406-582-3050	582-3068
Web: www.co.gallatin.mt.us					
Garfield County 352 Leavitt St	Jordan	MT	59337	406-557-6254	557-2567
Web: www.garfieldcounty.com					
Glacier County 512 E Main St	Cut Bank	MT	59427	406-873-5063	873-2125
Web: www.glaciercountymt.org					
Golden Valley County 107 Kemp St	Ryegate	MT	59074	406-568-2231	568-2598
Web: www.co.golden-valley.mt.us					
Granite County 220 N Sansome St PO Box 925	Philipsburg	MT	59858	406-859-3771	859-3817
Web: www.co.granite.mt.us					
Hill County 315 4th St	Havre	MT	59501	406-265-5481	265-3693
Web: co.hill.mt.us					
Jefferson County PO Box H	Boulder	MT	59632	406-225-4020	225-4149
Web: www.co.jefferson.mt.us					
Judith Basin County 11 3rd St NW	Stanford	MT	59479	406-566-2277	566-2211
Lake County 106 4th Ave E	Polson	MT	59860	406-883-7208	883-7283
Web: www.lakecounty-mt.org					
Lewis & Clark County 316 N Park Ave	Helena	MT	59623	406-447-8200	447-8370
Web: www.co.lewis-clark.mt.us					
Liberty County 111 1st St E	Chester	MT	59522	406-759-5365	759-5395
Web: www.co.lewis-clark.mt.us					
Lincoln County 512 California Ave	Libby	MT	59923	406-293-7781	293-8577
Web: www.lincolncountymt.us/					
Madison County 100 Wallace St	Virginia City	MT	59755	406-843-4230	843-5207
McCone County 1004 C Ave	Circle	MT	59215	406-485-3505	485-2689
Web: circle-montana.com					
Meagher County 15 W Main St	White Sulphur Springs	MT	59645	406-547-3612	547-3388
Mineral County 300 River St	Superior	MT	59872	406-822-3520	822-3579
Web: www.co.mineral.mt.us					
Missoula County 200 W Broadway St	Missoula	MT	59802	406-523-4780	258-4899
Web: www.co.missoula.mt.us					
Musselshell County 506 Main St	Roundup	MT	59072	406-323-1104	323-3303
Park County 414 E Callender St	Livingston	MT	59047	406-222-4110	
Web: www.parkcounty.org					
Petroleum County 201 E Main St	Winnett	MT	59087	406-429-5311	429-6328
Phillips County 314 S 2nd Ave W PO Box 360	Malta	MT	59538	406-654-2423	654-2429
Pondera County 20 4th Ave SW	Conrad	MT	59425	406-271-4000	271-4070
Web: www.ponderacountymontana.org					
Powder River County PO Box 270	Broadus	MT	59317	406-436-2657	436-2151
Powell County 409 Missouri Ave	Deer Lodge	MT	59722	406-846-3680	846-2784
Web: www.powellcountymontana.com					
Prairie County 217 W Park St	Terry	MT	59349	406-635-5575	635-5576
Ravalli County 215 S 4th St Suite C	Hamilton	MT	59840	406-375-6212	375-6326
Web: www.co.ravalli.mt.us					
Richland County 201 W Main St	Sidney	MT	59270	406-433-1708	482-3731
Web: www.richland.org					
Roosevelt County 400 2nd Ave S	Wolf Point	MT	59201	406-653-6250	653-6289
Rosebud County 1200 Main St	Forsyth	MT	59327	406-346-2251	356-7551
Sanders County 111 Main St	Thompson Falls	MT	59873	406-827-6942	827-4388
Web: www.co.sanders.mt.us					
Sheridan County 100 W Laurel Ave	Plentywood	MT	59254	406-765-2310	765-2609
Web: www.co.sheridan.mt.us					
Stillwater County 400 3rd Ave N	Columbus	MT	59019	406-322-8000	322-8007
Web: www.co.stillwater.mt.us					
Sweet Grass County 200 W 1st Ave	Big Timber	MT	59011	406-932-5152	932-5177
Web: www.co.sweetgrass.mt.us					
Teton County 1 S Main St	Choteau	MT	59422	406-466-2151	466-2138
Web: www.tetoncomt.org					
Toole County 226 1st St S	Shelby	MT	59474	406-424-8310	424-8301
Treasure County PO Box 392	Hysham	MT	59038	406-342-5547	342-5445
Valley County 501 Court Sq Box 2	Glasgow	MT	59230	406-228-6220	228-9027
Wheatland County 201 A Ave NW	Harlowton	MT	59036	406-632-4891	632-4880
Wibaux County 200 S Wibaux St	Wibaux	MT	59353	406-796-2484	
Yellowstone County 217 N 27th St Rm 401	Billings	MT	59101	406-256-2785	256-2736
Web: www.co.yellowstone.mt.us					

Nebraska

				Phone	Fax
Adams County PO Box 2067	Hastings	NE	68902	402-461-7104	461-7185
Web: www.adamscounty.org					
Antelope County 501 Main St	Neligh	NE	68756	402-887-4410	887-4719
Web: www.co.antelope.ne.us					
Arthur County PO Box 126	Arthur	NE	69121	308-764-2203	764-2216
Banner County 204 State St PO Box 67	Harrisburg	NE	69345	308-436-5265	436-4180
Web: www.co.banner.ne.us					
Blaine County Lincoln Ave Bldg 1	Brewster	NE	68821	308-547-2222	547-2228
Web: www.blainecounty.ne.gov					
Boone County 222 S 4th St	Albion	NE	68620	402-395-2055	
Web: www.co.boone.ne.us					
Box Butte County PO Box 678	Alliance	NE	69301	308-762-6565	762-2867
Web: www.co.box-butte.ne.us					
Boyd County PO Box 26	Butte	NE	68722	402-775-2391	775-2146
Brown County 148 W 4th St	Ainsworth	NE	69210	402-387-2705	387-0918
Web: www.co.brown.ne.us					
Buffalo County PO Box 1270	Kearney	NE	68848	308-236-1226	233-3649
Web: www.buffalogov.org					
Burt County PO Box 87	Tekamah	NE	68061	402-374-2955	374-2956
Web: www.burtcounty.ne.gov					
Butler County PO Box 289	David City	NE	68632	402-367-7430	367-3329
Web: www.co.butler.ne.us					
Cass County 346 Main St	Plattsmouth	NE	68048	402-296-9300	296-9332
Web: www.cassne.org					
Cedar County 101 S Broadway	Hartington	NE	68739	402-254-7411	254-7410
Web: www.co.cedar.ne.us					
Chase County PO Box 1299	Imperial	NE	69033	308-882-5266	882-7552
Web: www.co.chase.ne.us					
Cherry County PO Box 120	Valentine	NE	69201	402-376-2771	376-3095
Web: www.co.cherry.ne.us					
Cheyenne County PO Box 217	Sidney	NE	69162	308-254-2141	254-5049*
*Fax: Hum Res ■ *Web:* www.co.cheyenne.ne.us					
Clay County 111 W Fairfield St PO Box 67	Clay Center	NE	68933	402-762-3463	762-3506
Web: www.claycounty.ne.gov					
Colfax County 411 E 11th St	Schuyler	NE	68661	402-352-8504	352-8515
Web: www.colfaxcounty.ne.gov					
Cuming County 200 S Lincoln St PO Box 290	West Point	NE	68788	402-372-6002	372-6013
Web: www.co.cuming.ne.us					
Custer County 431 S 10th St	Broken Bow	NE	68822	308-872-5701	872-2811
Web: www.co.custer.ne.us					
Dakota County 1601 Broadway	Dakota City	NE	68731	402-987-2126	494-9228
Web: www.dakotacountyne.org					
Dawes County 451 Main St	Chadron	NE	69337	308-432-0100	432-5179
Web: www.co.dawes.ne.us					
Dawson County PO Box 370	Lexington	NE	68850	308-324-2127	324-6106
Web: www.dawsoncountyne.net					
Deuel County PO Box 327	Chappell	NE	69129	308-874-3308	874-3472
Web: www.co.deuel.ne.us					
Dixon County PO Box 395	Ponca	NE	68770	402-755-2881	755-2632
Web: www.co.dixon.ne.us					
Dodge County 435 N Park Ave Rm 102	Fremont	NE	68025	402-727-2767	727-2764
Web: www.dodgecounty.ne.gov					
Douglas County 1819 Farnam St	Omaha	NE	68183	402-444-6762	444-6456
Web: www.co.douglas.ne.us					
Dundy County PO Box 506	Benkelman	NE	69021	308-423-2058	
Web: www.co.dundy.ne.us					
Fillmore County PO Box 307	Geneva	NE	68361	402-759-4931	759-4307
Web: www.fillmorecounty.org					
Franklin County PO Box 146	Franklin	NE	68939	308-425-6202	425-6093
Frontier County PO Box 40	Stockville	NE	69042	308-367-8641	367-8730
Web: www.co.frontier.ne.us					
Furnas County PO Box 387	Beaver City	NE	68926	308-268-4145	268-3205
Gage County PO Box 429	Beatrice	NE	68310	402-223-1300	223-1371
Web: www.co.gage.ne.us					
Garden County PO Box 486	Oshkosh	NE	69154	308-772-3924	772-0124
Web: www.co.garden.ne.us					
Garfield County PO Box 218	Burwell	NE	68823	308-346-4161	
Web: www.garfieldcounty.ne.gov					
Gosper County 507 Smith Ave PO Box 136	Elwood	NE	68937	308-785-2611	785-2300
Web: www.co.gosper.ne.us					
Grant County 105 E Harrison St PO Box 139	Hyannis	NE	69350	308-458-2488	458-2780
Greeley County PO Box 287	Greeley	NE	68842	308-428-3625	428-3022
Hall County 121 S Pine St	Grand Island	NE	68801	308-385-5080	385-5184
Web: www.hcgi.org					
Hamilton County 1111 13th St Suite 1	Aurora	NE	68818	402-694-3443	694-2397
Web: www.co.hamilton.ne.us					
Harlan County PO Box 698	Alma	NE	68920	308-928-2173	928-2079
Hayes County PO Box 370	Hayes Center	NE	69032	308-286-3413	286-3208
Web: www.geocities.com/hayes_county/					
Hitchcock County PO Box 248	Trenton	NE	69044	308-334-5646	334-5398
Web: www.co.hitchcock.ne.us					
Holt County PO Box 329	O'Neill	NE	68763	402-336-1762	336-1762
Web: www.co.holt.ne.us					
Hooker County PO Box 184	Mullen	NE	69152	308-546-2244	546-2490
Web: www.co.hooker.ne.us					
Howard County PO Box 25	Saint Paul	NE	68873	308-754-4343	754-4125
Web: www.howardcounty.ne.gov					
Jefferson County 411 4th St	Fairbury	NE	68352	402-729-2323	729-2016
Web: www.co.jefferson.ne.us					
Johnson County PO Box 416	Tecumseh	NE	68450	402-335-6300	335-6311
Web: www.co.johnson.ne.us					
Kearney County PO Box 339	Minden	NE	68959	308-832-2723	832-2729
Web: www.kearneycounty.ne.gov					
Keith County PO Box 149	Ogallala	NE	69153	308-284-4726	284-6277
Web: www.co.keith.ne.us					
Keya Paha County PO Box 349	Springview	NE	68778	402-497-3791	497-3799
Web: www.co.keya-paha.ne.us					
Kimball County 114 E 3rd St	Kimball	NE	69145	308-235-2241	235-3654
Web: www.co.kimball.ne.us					
Knox County PO Box 166	Center	NE	68724	402-288-5604	288-5605
Web: www.co.knox.ne.us					
Lancaster County 555 S 10th St Rm 108	Lincoln	NE	68508	402-441-7481	441-8728
Web: www.lancaster.ne.gov					
Lincoln County 301 N Jeffers St	North Platte	NE	69101	308-534-4350	535-3527
Web: www.co.lincoln.ne.us					
Logan County 317 Main St PO Box 8	Stapleton	NE	69163	308-636-2311	
Web: www.co.logan.ne.us					
Loup County 408 4th St	Taylor	NE	68879	308-942-3135	942-3103
Web: www.co.loup.ne.us					
Madison County PO Box 290	Madison	NE	68748	402-454-3311	454-6682
Web: www.co.madison.ne.us					
McPherson County PO Box 122	Tryon	NE	69167	308-587-2363	
Merrick County PO Box 27	Central City	NE	68826	308-946-2881	946-2332
Morrill County PO Box 610	Bridgeport	NE	69336	308-262-0860	262-1469
Web: www.co.morrill.ne.us					
Nance County 209 Esther St PO Box 338	Fullerton	NE	68638	308-536-2331	536-2742
Web: www.co.nance.ne.us					
Nemaha County 1824 'N' St	Auburn	NE	68305	402-274-4285	274-4389
Web: www.visitnemahacounty.org					
Nuckolls County PO Box 366	Nelson	NE	68961	402-225-4361	225-4301
Web: www.nuckollscounty.ne.gov					
Otoe County 1021 Central Ave Rm 103	Nebraska City	NE	68410	402-873-9500	873-9506
Web: www.co.otoe.ne.us					
Pawnee County 625 6th St	Pawnee City	NE	68420	402-852-2962	852-2963
Web: www.co.pawnee.ne.us					
Perkins County PO Box 156	Grant	NE	69140	308-352-4643	352-2455
Web: www.co.perkins.ne.us					
Phelps County PO Box 404	Holdrege	NE	68949	308-995-4469	995-4368
Web: www.phelpsgov.org					
Pierce County 111 W Court St Rm 1	Pierce	NE	68767	402-329-4225	329-6439
Web: www.co.pierce.ne.us					
Platte County 2610 14th St	Columbus	NE	68601	402-563-4904	564-4164
Web: www.plattecounty.net					
Polk County PO Box 276	Osceola	NE	68651	402-747-5431	747-2656
Web: www.polkcounty.ne.gov					
Red Willow County 502 Norris Ave	McCook	NE	69001	308-345-1552	345-4460
Web: www.co.red-willow.ne.us					
Richardson County 1700 Stone St	Falls City	NE	68355	402-245-2911	245-2946
Web: www.co.richardson.ne.us					
Rock County 400 State St	Bassett	NE	68714	402-684-3933	684-2741
Web: www.co.rock.ne.us					

Nebraska (Cont'd)

Phone | Fax

Saline County 215 S Court ST ... Wilber NE 68465 402-821-2374 821-3381
Web: www.co.saline.ne.us
Sarpy County 1210 Golden Gate Dr Suite 1118 ... Papillion NE 68046 402-593-2105 593-4360
Web: www.co.sarpy.ne.us
Saunders County PO Box 61 ... Wahoo NE 68066 402-443-8101 443-5010
Web: www.co.saunders.ne.us
Scotts Bluff County 1825 10th St ... Gering NE 69341 308-436-6600 436-3178
Web: www.scottsbluffcounty.org
Seward County PO Box 190 ... Seward NE 68434 402-643-2883 643-9243
Web: connectseward.org/cgov/
Sheridan County 301 E 2nd St PO Box 39 ... Rushville NE 69360 308-327-5650 327-5624
Sherman County PO Box 456 ... Loup City NE 68853 308-745-1513 745-1820
Web: www.co.sherman.ne.us
Sioux County PO Box 158 ... Harrison NE 69346 308-668-2443 668-2443
Web: www.co.sioux.ne.us
Stanton County PO Box 347 ... Stanton NE 68779 402-439-2222 439-2200
Web: www.co.stanton.ne.us
Thayer County PO Box 208 ... Hebron NE 68370 402-768-6126 768-2129
Web: www.thayercounty.ne.gov
Thomas County PO Box 226 ... Thedford NE 69166 308-645-2261 645-2623
Thurston County PO Box G ... Pender NE 68047 402-385-2343 385-3544
Valley County 125 S 15th St ... Ord NE 68862 308-728-3700 728-7725
Web: www.co.valley.ne.us
Washington County PO Box 466 ... Blair NE 68008 402-426-6822 426-6825
Wayne County PO Box 248 ... Wayne NE 68787 402-375-2288 375-4137
Web: county.waynene.org
Webster County PO Box 250 ... Red Cloud NE 68970 402-746-2716 746-2710
Web: www.co.webster.ne.us
Wheeler County PO Box 127 ... Bartlett NE 68622 308-654-3235 654-3470
York County 510 Lincoln Ave ... York NE 68467 402-362-7759 362-7558
Web: www.yorkcounty.ne.gov

Nevada

Phone | Fax

Carson City (Independent City) 201 N Carson St ... Carson City NV 89701 775-887-2100 887-2286
Web: www.carson-city.nv.us
Churchill County 155 N Taylor St Suite 153 ... Fallon NV 89406 775-423-5136 423-0717
Web: www.churchillcounty.org
Clark County 200 S Lewis Ave 3rd Fl ... Las Vegas NV 89101 702-671-0500 474-2434
Web: www.co.clark.nv.us
Douglas County PO Box 218 ... Minden NV 89423 775-782-9020 782-9016
Web: www.co.douglas.nv.us
Elko County 569 Court St ... Elko NV 89801 775-738-5398 753-8535
Web: www.elkocountynv.net
Esmeralda County PO Box 547 ... Goldfield NV 89013 775-485-6367 485-6376
Web: www.governet.net/NV/CO/ESM/home.cfm
Eureka County PO Box 677 ... Eureka NV 89316 775-237-5262 237-6015
Web: www.co.eureka.nv.us
Humboldt County 50 W 5th St County Courthouse Rm 205 ... Winnemucca NV 89445 775-623-6300 623-6302
Web: www.hcnv.us
Lander County 315 S Humboldt St ... Battle Mountain NV 89820 775-635-5738 635-5761
Web: www.landercounty.org
Lincoln County PO Box 90 ... Pioche NV 89043 775-962-5390 962-5180
Web: www.co.lincoln.nv.us
Lyon County 27 S Main St ... Yerington NV 89447 775-463-6503 463-6533
Web: www.lyon-county.org
Mineral County PO Box 1450 ... Hawthorne NV 89415 775-945-2446 945-0706
Nye County PO Box 1031 ... Tonopah NV 89049 775-482-8127 482-8133
Web: www.co.nye.nv.us
Pershing County PO Box 820 ... Lovelock NV 89419 775-273-2208 273-3015
Web: www.pershingcounty.net
Storey County Drawer D ... Virginia City NV 89440 775-847-0968 847-0949
Washoe County PO Box 30083 ... Reno NV 89520 775-328-3260 328-3582
Web: www.co.washoe.nv.us
White Pine County 801 Clark St Suite 4 ... Ely NV 89301 775-289-2341 289-2544
Web: www.co.white-pine.nv.us

New Hampshire

Phone | Fax

Belknap County 34 County Dr ... Laconia NH 03246 603-527-5400 527-5409
Web: www.belknapcounty.org
Carroll County PO Box 152 ... Ossipee NH 03864 603-539-2428 539-4287
Cheshire County 12 Court St ... Keene NH 03431 603-352-6902
Web: www.co.cheshire.nh.us
Coos County 55 School St Suite 301 ... Lancaster NH 03584 603-788-4900
Grafton County 3855 Dartmouth College Hwy Box 1 ... North Haverhill NH 03774 603-787-6941 787-2345
Web: www.graftoncountynh.us
Hillsborough County 329 Mast Rd ... Golfstown NH 03045 603-627-5600 627-5603
Web: www.hillsboroughcountynh.org
Merrimack County 4 Court St Suite 2 ... Concord NH 03301 603-228-0331 224-2665
Web: www.ci.concord.nh.us
Rockingham County PO Box 1258 ... Kingston NH 03848 603-642-5256
Web: www.co.rockingham.nh.us
Strafford County 259 County Farm Rd ... Dover NH 03820 603-742-1458 743-4407
Web: www.co.strafford.nh.us
Sullivan County 14 Main St ... Newport NH 03773 603-863-2560 863-9314
Web: www.sullivancountynh.gov

New Jersey

Phone | Fax

Atlantic County 5901 E Main St ... Mays Landing NJ 08330 609-641-7867 625-4738
Web: www.aclink.org
Bergen County 1 Bergen County Plaza Rm 580 ... Hackensack NJ 07601 201-336-7300 336-7304
Web: www.co.bergen.nj.us
Burlington County 49 Rancocas Rd ... Mount Holly NJ 08060 609-265-5122 265-0696
Web: www.co.burlington.nj.us
Camden County 520 Market St Rm 102 ... Camden NJ 08102 856-225-5300 225-5316
Web: www.co.camden.nj.us
Cape May County 7 N Main St PO Box 5000 ... Cape May Court House NJ 08210 609-465-1010 465-8625
Web: www.capemaycountygov.net
Cumberland County 60 W Broad St ... Bridgeton NJ 08302 856-451-8000 455-1410
Web: www.co.cumberland.nj.us
Essex County 465 ML King Jr Blvd Rm 247 ... Newark NJ 07102 973-621-4921
Web: www.co.essex.nj.us
Gloucester County 1 N Broad St Rm 101 ... Woodbury NJ 08096 856-853-3237 853-3327
Web: www.co.gloucester.nj.us

Phone | Fax

Hudson County 583 Newark Ave Brennan Courthouse ... Jersey City NJ 07306 201-795-6112 795-2581
Web: www.hudsoncountynj.org
Hunterdon County 71 Main St ... Flemington NJ 08822 908-788-1221 782-4068
Web: www.co.hunterdon.nj.us
Mercer County PO Box 8068 ... Trenton NJ 08650 609-989-6470 989-1111
Web: nj.gov/counties/mercer/
Middlesex County 75 Bayard St ... New Brunswick NJ 08903 732-745-3828 745-3642
Web: co.middlesex.nj.us
Monmouth County Market Yard ... Freehold NJ 07728 732-431-7324 409-7566
Web: www.co.monmouth.nj.us
Morris County PO Box 315 ... Morristown NJ 07963 973-285-6120 285-5231
Web: www.co.morris.nj.us
Ocean County 118 Washington St ... Toms River NJ 08753 732-929-2018 349-4334
Web: www.co.ocean.nj.us
Passaic County 401 Grand St ... Paterson NJ 07505 973-225-3632 754-1920
Web: www.passaiccountynj.org
Salem County PO Box 18 ... Salem NJ 08079 856-935-7510 935-8882
Web: www.salemco.org
Somerset County 20 Grove St ... Somerville NJ 08876 908-231-7006 253-8853
Web: www.co.somerset.nj.us
Sussex County 4 Park Pl ... Newton NJ 07860 973-579-0900 383-7493
Web: www.sussex.nj.us
Union County 2 Broad St Rm 115 ... Elizabeth NJ 07207 908-527-4999 558-2589
Web: www.unioncountynj.org
Warren County 413 2nd St ... Belvidere NJ 07823 908-475-6211 475-6208
Web: www.co.warren.nj.us

New Mexico

Phone | Fax

Bernalillo County 1 Civic Plaza NW 10th Fl ... Albuquerque NM 87102 505-768-4240 768-4329
Web: www.bernco.gov
Catron County 100 Main St ... Reserve NM 87830 505-533-6423 533-6433
Web: www.mylocalgov.com/catroncountynm/Index.asp
Chaves County PO Box 580 ... Roswell NM 88202 505-624-6614 624-6523
Web: www.co.chaves.nm.us
Cibola County 515 W High Ave ... Grants NM 87020 505-287-9431 285-2562
Web: www.grants.org
Colfax County 230 N 3rd St ... Raton NM 87740 505-445-5551 445-4031
Curry County 700 N Main St Suite 7 ... Clovis NM 88101 505-763-5591 763-4232
Web: www.currycounty.org
De Baca County 548 E Ave C ... Fort Sumner NM 88119 505-355-2601 355-2441
Dona Ana County 845 N Mortel Blvd ... Las Cruces NM 88007 505-647-7200 647-7302
Web: www.co.dona-ana.nm.us
Eddy County 101 W Greene St Suite 225 ... Carlsbad NM 88220 505-887-9511 887-1039
Web: www.carlsbadnm.com/ecourt
Grant County PO Box 898 ... Silver City NM 88062 575-574-0000 574-0073
Web: www.grantcountynm.com
Guadalupe County 420 Parker Ave Suite 1 ... Santa Rosa NM 88435 505-472-3791 472-4791
Harding County 35 Pine St ... Mosquero NM 87733 505-673-2301 673-2922
Web: www.hardingcounty.org
Hidalgo County 300 Shakespeare St ... Lordsburg NM 88045 505-542-9213 542-3193
Lea County 100 N Main St Suite 11 ... Lovington NM 88260 505-396-8521 396-5684
Web: www.leacounty.net
Lincoln County 300 Central Ave PO Box 338 ... Carrizozo NM 88301 505-648-2394 648-2576
TF: 800-687-2705 ■ *Web:* www.lincolncountynm.net
Los Alamos County 2300 Trinity Dr Rm 230 ... Los Alamos NM 87544 505-662-8080 662-8079
Web: www.lac-nm.us
Luna County 110 N Gold St ... Deming NM 88031 505-546-0491 544-4187
Web: www.lunacountynm.com
McKinley County 207 W Hill Ave ... Gallup NM 87301 505-863-6866 863-1419
Web: www.co.mckinley.nm.us
Mora County 518 Mile Marker 29 PO Box 360 ... Mora NM 87732 505-387-2448 387-9023
Otero County 1000 New York Ave Rm 101 ... Alamogordo NM 88310 505-437-7427 443-2904
Web: www.co.otero.nm.us
Quay County 300 S 3rd St ... Tucumcari NM 88401 505-461-2112 461-6208
Web: www.tucumcarinm.com
Rio Arriba County PO Box 127 ... Tierra Amarilla NM 87575 505-588-7255 588-7418
Roosevelt County County Courthouse 109 W 1st St ... Portales NM 88130 505-356-8562 356-3560
Web: www.rooseveltcounty.com
San Juan County 100 S Oliver Dr ... Aztec NM 87410 505-334-9471 334-3635
Web: www.co.san-juan.nm.us
San Miguel County
County Courthouse 500 W National St Suite 100 ... Las Vegas NM 87701 505-425-9333 425-7019
Web: www.smcounty.net
Sandoval County 711 Camino del Pueblo ... Bernalillo NM 87004 505-867-7572 771-8610
Web: www.sandovalcounty.com
Santa Fe County 102 Grant Ave ... Santa Fe NM 87504 505-986-6200 995-2740
TF: 800-894-7028 ■ *Web:* www.co.santa-fe.nm.us
Sierra County 100 N Date St ... Truth or Consequences NM 87901 505-894-6215 894-9548
Web: www.truthorconsequencesnm.net
Socorro County 210 Park St ... Socorro NM 87801 505-835-0589 835-4629
Web: www.socorro-nm.com
Taos County 105 Albright St Suite A ... Taos NM 87571 505-737-6300 751-8637
Web: www.taoscounty.org
Torrance County 205 9th & Allen St PO Box 767 ... Estancia NM 87016 505-384-2221 384-4080
Web: www.torrancecountynm.org
Union County 200 Court St ... Clayton NM 88415 505-374-9491 374-9442
Web: www.claytonnewmexico.org
Valencia County 444 Luna Ave ... Los Lunas NM 87031 505-866-2073 866-2023
Web: www.co.valencia.nm.us

New York

Phone | Fax

Albany County 112 State St Rm 200 ... Albany NY 12207 518-447-7040 447-5589
Web: www.albanycounty.com
Allegany County 7 Court St County Courthouse ... Belmont NY 14813 585-268-9270 268-9659
Web: www.alleganyco.com
Bronx County 851 Grand Concourse Suite 301 ... Bronx NY 10451 718-590-3500 590-3537
Web: www.nyc.gov
Broome County PO Box 2062 ... Binghamton NY 13902 607-778-2451 778-2243
Web: www.gobroomecounty.com
Cattaraugus County 303 Court St ... Little Valley NY 14755 716-938-9111 938-6009
Web: www.co.cattaraugus.ny.us
Cayuga County 160 Genesee St ... Auburn NY 13021 315-253-1271 253-1673
Web: www.co.cayuga.ny.us
Chautauqua County 3 N Erie St Gerace Office Bldg ... Mayville NY 14757 716-753-4211 753-4756
Web: www.chautco.com
Chemung County PO Box 588 ... Elmira NY 14902 607-737-2920 737-2897
Web: www.chemungcounty.com
Chenango County 5 Court St ... Norwich NY 13815 607-337-1450 337-1455
Web: www.co.chenango.ny.us
Clinton County 137 Margaret St Suite 208 ... Plattsburgh NY 12901 518-565-4600 565-4616
Web: www.co.clinton.ny.us

	City	State	ZIP	Phone	Fax
Columbia County 560 Warren St.	Hudson	NY	12534	518-828-3339	
Web: www.govt.co.columbia.ny.us					
Cortland County 46 Greenbush St Suite 101	Cortland	NY	13045	607-753-5021	753-5378
Web: www.cortland-co.org					
Delaware County PO Box 426	Delhi	NY	13753	607-746-2123	746-6924
Web: www.co.delaware.ny.us					
Dutchess County 22 Market St	Poughkeepsie	NY	12601	845-486-2120	
Web: www.co.dutchess.ny.us					
Erie County 92 Franklin St.	Buffalo	NY	14202	716-858-8785	858-6550
Web: www.erie.gov					
Essex County 7559 Court St	Elizabethtown	NY	12932	518-873-3600	873-3548
Web: www.co.essex.ny.us					
Franklin County 355 W Main St PO Box 70	Malone	NY	12953	518-481-1681	483-9143
Web: www.adirondacklakes.org					
Fulton County 223 W Main St.	Johnstown	NY	12095	518-736-5555	762-3839
Web: www.fultoncountyny.org					
Genesee County 7 Main St	Batavia	NY	14020	585-344-2550	344-8582
Web: www.co.genesee.ny.us					
Greene County 411 Main St	Catskill	NY	12414	518-943-2050	719-3284
Web: www.greene-ny.com					
Hamilton County PO Box 204 Rt 8	Lake Pleasant	NY	12108	518-548-7111	548-9740
Web: hamiltoncounty.com					
Herkimer County 109 Mary St Suite 1111	Herkimer	NY	13350	315-867-1129	866-4396
Web: www.herkimercounty.org					
Jefferson County 175 Arsenal St	Watertown	NY	13601	315-785-3081	785-5145
Web: www.co.jefferson.ny.us					
Kings County 360 Adams St	Brooklyn	NY	11201	718-643-7037	643-8187
Web: www.nyc.gov					
Lewis County PO Box 232	Lowville	NY	13367	315-376-5333	376-3768
Web: lewiscountyny.org					
Livingston County 6 Court St Rm 201	Geneseo	NY	14454	585-243-7010	
Web: www.co.livingston.state.ny.us					
Madison County PO Box 668	Wampsville	NY	13163	315-366-2261	366-2615
Web: www.madisoncounty.org					
Monroe County 39 W Main St Rm 101	Rochester	NY	14614	585-428-5151	753-1650
Web: www.monroecounty.gov					
Montgomery County PO Box 1500	Fonda	NY	12068	518-853-3834	853-8220
Web: www.co.montgomery.ny.us					
Nassau County 240 Old Country Rd	Mineola	NY	11501	516-571-2664	742-4099
Web: www.nassaucountyny.gov					
New York County 60 Centre St	New York	NY	10007	646-386-5955	374-5790*
*Fax Area Code: 212 ■ *Web:* www.nyc.gov					
Niagara County PO Box 461	Lockport	NY	14095	716-439-7022	439-7066
Web: www.niagaracounty.com					
Oneida County 800 Park Ave.	Utica	NY	13501	315-798-5776	798-6440
Web: www.oneidacounty.org					
Onondaga County 401 Montgomery St Rm 200	Syracuse	NY	13202	315-435-2226	435-3455
Web: www.ongov.net					
Ontario County 20 Ontario St	Canandaigua	NY	14424	585-396-4200	393-2951
Web: www.co.ontario.ny.us					
Orange County 255 Main St	Goshen	NY	10924	845-291-2700	291-2724
Web: www.co.orange.ny.us					
Orleans County 3 S Main St	Albion	NY	14411	585-589-5334	589-0181
Web: www.orleansny.com					
Oswego County 46 E Bridge St	Oswego	NY	13126	315-349-8385	349-8383
Web: www.co.oswego.ny.us/					
Otsego County PO Box 710	Cooperstown	NY	13326	607-547-4275	547-7544
Web: www.otsegocounty.com					
Putnam County 40 Gleneida Ave	Carmel	NY	10512	845-225-3641	228-0231
Web: www.putnamcountyny.com					
Queens County 120-55 Queens Blvd	Kew Gardens	NY	11424	718-286-3000	
Web: www.nyc.gov					
Rensselaer County 1600 7th Ave	Troy	NY	12180	518-270-2900	270-2961
Web: www.rensco.com					
Richmond County 130 Stuyvesant Pl	Staten Island	NY	10301	718-390-5393	390-5269
Web: www.nyc.gov					
Rockland County 11 New Hempstead Rd	New City	NY	10956	845-638-5100	638-5675
Web: www.co.rockland.ny.us					
Saint Lawrence County 48 Court St	Canton	NY	13617	315-379-2237	379-2302
Web: www.co.st-lawrence.ny.us					
Saratoga County 40 McMaster St	Ballston Spa	NY	12020	518-885-5381	884-4726
Web: www.co.saratoga.ny.us					
Schenectady County 620 State St.	Schenectady	NY	12305	518-388-4222	388-4224
Web: www.schenectadycounty.com					
Schoharie County 284 Main St	Schoharie	NY	12157	518-295-8347	295-8482
Web: www.schohariecounty-ny.gov					
Schuyler County 105 9th St	Watkins Glen	NY	14891	607-535-8133	535-8130
Web: www.schuylercounty.us					
Seneca County 1 DiPronio Dr	Waterloo	NY	13165	315-539-1770	539-3789
Web: www.co.seneca.ny.us					
Steuben County 3 E Pulteny Sq	Bath	NY	14810	607-776-9631	664-2158
Web: www.steubencony.org					
Suffolk County 310 Center Dr	Riverhead	NY	11901	631-852-2000	852-2004
Web: www.co.suffolk.ny.us					
Sullivan County 100 North St	Monticello	NY	12701	845-794-3000	794-6928
Web: www.co.sullivan.ny.us					
Tioga County PO Box 307	Owego	NY	13827	607-687-8660	687-8686
Web: www.tiogacountyny.com					
Tompkins County 320 N Tioga St	Ithaca	NY	14850	607-274-5431	274-5445
Web: www.co.tompkins.ny.us					
Ulster County PO Box 1800	Kingston	NY	12402	845-340-3288	340-3299
Web: www.co.ulster.ny.us					
Warren County 1340 State Rt 9	Lake George	NY	12845	518-761-6429	761-6551
Web: www.co.warren.ny.us					
Washington County 383 Broadway Bldg A	Fort Edward	NY	12828	518-746-2170	746-2177
Web: www.co.washington.ny.us					
Wayne County 26 Church St	Lyons	NY	14489	315-946-5400	946-5407
Web: www.co.wayne.ny.us					
Westchester County 110 Dr ML King Jr Blvd 3rd Fl	White Plains	NY	10601	914-995-3080	
Web: www.westchestergov.com/firstvisit.htm					
Wyoming County 143 N Main St.	Warsaw	NY	14569	585-786-8810	786-3703
Web: www.wyomingco.net					
Yates County 417 Liberty St	Penn Yan	NY	14527	315-536-5120	536-5545
Web: www.yatescounty.org					

North Carolina

	City	State	ZIP	Phone	Fax
Alamance County 124 W Elm St.	Graham	NC	27253	336-228-1312	570-6788
Web: www.alamance-nc.com					
Alexander County 621 Liledoun Rd.	Taylorsville	NC	28681	828-632-9332	632-0059
Web: www.co.alexander.nc.us					
Alleghany County PO Box 61	Sparta	NC	28675	336-372-8949	372-4899
Web: www.alleghanycounty-nc.gov					
Anson County 114 N Green St Courthouse Rm 30	Wadesboro	NC	28170	704-694-2796	694-7015
Web: www.co.anson.nc.us					
Ashe County 150 Government Cir Suite 3100	Jefferson	NC	28640	336-246-5641	246-4276
Web: www.ashechamber.com					
Avery County PO Box 115	Newland	NC	28657	828-733-2900	733-8410
Web: www.averycounty.com					
Beaufort County 121 W 3rd St	Washington	NC	27889	252-946-0079	946-7722
Web: www.co.beaufort.nc.us					
Bertie County 106 Dundee St PO Box 530	Windsor	NC	27983	252-794-5300	794-5327
Web: www.co.bertie.nc.us					
Bladen County 166 E Broad St Rm 105	Elizabethtown	NC	28337	910-862-6700	862-6767
Web: www.bladeninfo.org					
Brunswick County PO Box 249	Bolivia	NC	28422	910-253-2000	253-2022
Web: www.brunsco.net					
Buncombe County 205 College St Suite 300	Asheville	NC	28801	828-250-4100	250-6077
Web: www.buncombecounty.org					
Burke County PO Box 219	Morganton	NC	28680	828-439-4340	438-2782
Web: www.co.burke.nc.us					
Cabarrus County 65 Church St SE	Concord	NC	28025	704-920-2100	920-2820
Web: www.cabarruscounty.us					
Caldwell County PO Box 2200	Lenoir	NC	28645	828-757-1300	757-1295
Web: www.co.caldwell.nc.us					
Camden County PO Box 190	Camden	NC	27921	252-335-4691	333-1603
Web: www.camdencountync.gov					
Carteret County Courthouse Sq	Beaufort	NC	28516	252-728-8450	728-2092
Web: www.co.carteret.nc.us					
Caswell County PO Box 790	Yanceyville	NC	27379	336-694-4171	694-7338
Web: www.caswellcountync.gov					
Catawba County PO Box 389	Newton	NC	28658	828-465-8201	465-8392
Web: www.co.catawba.nc.us					
Chatham County PO Box 369	Pittsboro	NC	27312	919-542-3240	542-1402
Web: www.co.chatham.nc.us					
Cherokee County 75 Peachtree St.	Murphy	NC	28906	828-837-5527	837-9684
Web: www.cherokeecounty-nc.org					
Chowan County 115 E King St PO Box 1030	Edenton	NC	27932	252-482-8431	482-0126
Web: www.chowancounty-nc.gov					
Clay County PO Box 506	Hayesville	NC	28904	828-389-8334	389-3329
Web: www.main.nc.us/clay/					
Cleveland County PO Box 1210	Shelby	NC	28151	704-484-4800	484-4930
Web: www.clevelandcounty.com					
Columbus County PO Box 1587	Whiteville	NC	28472	910-641-3000	641-3027
Web: www.columbusco.org					
Craven County 406 Craven St	New Bern	NC	28560	252-636-6600	637-0526
Web: www.co.craven.nc.us					
Cumberland County PO Box 1829	Fayetteville	NC	28302	910-678-7700	678-7717
Web: www.co.cumberland.nc.us					
Currituck County 153 Courthouse Rd PO Box 39	Currituck	NC	27929	252-232-2075	232-3551
Web: www.co.currituck.nc.us					
Dare County PO Box 1000	Manteo	NC	27954	252-475-5800	473-1817
Web: www.co.dare.nc.us					
Davidson County PO Box 1067	Lexington	NC	27293	336-242-2200	248-8440
Web: www.co.davidson.nc.us/dcinfo.htm					
Davie County 123 S Main St	Mocksville	NC	27028	336-751-5513	751-7408
Web: www.co.davie.nc.us					
Duplin County PO Box 189	Kenansville	NC	28349	910-296-1686	296-2310
Web: www.duplincounty.org					
Durham County 200 E Main St	Durham	NC	27701	919-560-0000	560-0020
Web: www.co.durham.nc.us					
Edgecombe County PO Box 10	Tarboro	NC	27886	252-641-7833	641-0456
Web: www.edgecombecountync.gov					
Forsyth County PO Box 20099	Winston-Salem	NC	27120	336-761-2250	761-2018
Web: www.co.forsyth.nc.us					
Franklin County 113 Market St	Louisburg	NC	27549	919-496-5994	496-2683
Web: www.co.franklin.nc.us					
Gaston County PO Box 1578	Gastonia	NC	28053	704-866-3100	866-3147
Web: www.co.gaston.nc.us					
Gates County PO Box 148	Gatesville	NC	27938	252-357-1240	357-0073
Web: www.albemarle-nc.com/gates/					
Graham County 12 N Main St	Robbinsville	NC	28771	828-479-7973	479-6417
Web: main.nc.us/graham/					
Granville County PO Box 906	Oxford	NC	27565	919-693-4761	690-1766
Web: www.granvillecounty.org					
Greene County PO Box 675	Snow Hill	NC	28580	252-747-3505	747-2700
Web: www.co.greene.nc.us					
Guilford County PO Box 3427	Greensboro	NC	27402	336-641-3383	641-6833
Web: www.co.guilford.nc.us					
Halifax County PO Box 38	Halifax	NC	27839	252-583-1131	583-9921
Web: www.halifaxnc.com					
Harnett County PO Box 759	Lillington	NC	27546	910-893-7555	814-2662
Web: www.harnett.org					
Haywood County 215 N Main St	Waynesville	NC	28786	828-452-6625	452-6715
Web: www.gov.co.haywood.nc.us					
Henderson County 100 N King St	Hendersonville	NC	28792	828-697-4808	692-9855
Web: www.hendersoncountync.org					
Hertford County PO Box 86	Winton	NC	27986	252-358-7845	358-0793
Web: www.co.hertford.nc.us					
Hoke County PO Box 210	Raeford	NC	28376	910-875-8751	875-9222
TF: 800-597-8751 ■ *Web:* www.hoke-raeford.com					
Hyde County PO Box 188	Swanquarter	NC	27885	252-926-4178	926-3701
Web: www.hydecounty.org					
Iredell County 200 S Center St PO Box 788	Statesville	NC	28687	704-878-3000	878-5355
Web: www.co.iredell.nc.us					
Jackson County 401 Grindstaff Cove Rd	Sylva	NC	28779	828-586-4055	586-7528
Web: www.jacksonnc.org					
Johnston County PO Box 297	Smithfield	NC	27577	919-934-3191	934-5857
Web: www.co.johnston.nc.us					
Jones County PO Box 280	Trenton	NC	28585	252-448-7351	448-1607
Web: www.co.jones.nc.us					
Lee County PO Box 4209	Sanford	NC	27331	919-708-4400	775-3483
Web: www.leecountync.com					
Lenoir County PO Box 3289	Kinston	NC	28502	252-559-6450	559-6454
Web: www.co.lenoir.nc.us					
Lincoln County 115 W Main St	Lincolnton	NC	28092	704-736-8471	736-8718
Web: www.co.lincoln.nc.us					
Macon County 5 W Main St	Franklin	NC	28734	828-349-2025	349-2400
Web: www.maconnc.org					
Madison County PO Box 579	Marshall	NC	28753	828-649-2531	649-2829
Web: www.main.nc.us/madison/					
Martin County PO Box 807	Williamston	NC	27892	252-792-2515	792-6668
Web: www.martincountyncgov.com					
McDowell County 60 E Court St	Marion	NC	28752	828-652-7121	659-3484
Web: www.mcdowellgov.com					
Mecklenburg County 600 E 4th St 11th Fl Charlotte-Mecklenburg Government Center	Charlotte	NC	28202	704-336-2472	336-5887
Web: www.co.mecklenburg.nc.us					
Mitchell County PO Box 409	Bakersville	NC	28705	828-688-2434	688-4443
Web: www.mitchellcounty.org					

North Carolina (Cont'd)

	City	State	Zip	Phone	Fax
Montgomery County PO Box 527 *Web:* www.montgomery-county.com	Troy	NC	27371	910-576-4211	576-5020
Moore County PO Box 905 *Web:* www.co.moore.nc.us	Carthage	NC	28327	910-947-6363	947-1874
Nash County 120 W Washington St Suite 3072 *Web:* www.co.nash.nc.us	Nashville	NC	27856	252-459-9800	459-9817
New Hanover County 320 Chestnut St Rm 502 *Web:* www.co.new-hanover.nc.us	Wilmington	NC	28401	910-341-7184	341-4027
Northampton County PO Box 808 *Web:* www.northamptonnc.com	Jackson	NC	27845	252-534-2501	534-1166
Onslow County 118 Old Bridge St *Web:* www.co.onslow.nc.us	Jacksonville	NC	28540	910-347-4717	455-7878
Orange County 106 E Margaret Ln *Web:* www.co.orange.nc.us	Hillsborough	NC	27278	919-732-8181	644-3043
Pamlico County PO Box 776 *Web:* www.co.pamlico.nc.us	Bayboro	NC	28515	252-745-3133	745-5514
Pasquotank County PO Box 39 *Web:* www.co.pasquotank.nc.us	Elizabeth City	NC	27907	252-335-0865	335-0866
Pender County PO Box 5 *Web:* www.pender-county.com	Burgaw	NC	28425	910-259-1200	259-1402
Perquimans County PO Box 45 *Web:* www.co.perquimans.nc.us	Hertford	NC	27944	252-426-8484	426-4034
Person County 304 S Morgan St Rm 212 *Web:* www.personcounty.net	Roxboro	NC	27573	336-597-1720	599-1609
Pitt County 1717 W 5th St *Web:* www.pittcountync.gov	Greenville	NC	27834	252-902-2951	830-6311
Polk County 40 Courthouse Sq *Web:* www.co.polk.nc.us	Columbus	NC	28722	828-894-3301	894-2263
Randolph County PO Box 4728 *Web:* www.co.randolph.nc.us	Asheboro	NC	27204	336-318-6300	318-6853
Richmond County 125 S Hancock St *Web:* www.co.richmond.nc.us	Rockingham	NC	28379	910-997-8211	997-8208
Robeson County 701 N Elm St *Web:* www.co.robeson.nc.us	Lumberton	NC	28358	910-671-3022	671-3010
Rockingham County PO Box 206 *Web:* www.co.rockingham.nc.us	Wentworth	NC	27375	336-342-8101	342-8105
Rowan County 130 W Innes St *Web:* www.co.rowan.nc.us	Salisbury	NC	28144	704-636-0361	638-3092
Rutherford County 289 N Main St *Web:* www.rutherfordgov.org	Rutherfordton	NC	28139	828-287-6060	287-6262
Sampson County 435 Rowan Rd *Web:* www.sampsonnc.com	Clinton	NC	28328	910-592-6308	592-1945
Scotland County PO Box 489 *Web:* www.scotlandcounty.org	Laurinburg	NC	28353	910-277-2406	277-2411
Stanly County 201 S 2nd St *Web:* www.co.stanly.nc.us	Albemarle	NC	28001	704-986-3600	983-3133
Stokes County PO Box 250 *Web:* www.co.stokes.nc.us	Danbury	NC	27016	336-593-9173	593-5459
Surry County 202 Kapp St *Web:* www.co.surry.nc.us	Dobson	NC	27017	336-386-3700	386-9879
Swain County PO Box 1397 *Web:* www.swaincounty.org	Bryson City	NC	28713	828-488-2288	488-9360
Transylvania County 28 E Main St *Web:* www.transylvaniacounty.org	Brevard	NC	28712	828-884-3100	884-3119
Tyrrell County 108 S Water St PO Box 449 **Fax:* Acctg ■ *Web:* albemarle-nc.com/columbia/	Columbia	NC	27925	252-796-1371	796-1188*
Union County 500 N Main St Rm 921 *Web:* www.co.union.nc.us	Monroe	NC	28112	704-283-3672	282-0121
Vance County 122 Young St Suite F *Web:* www.vancecounty.org	Henderson	NC	27536	252-738-2110	
Wake County PO Box 550 *Web:* www.wakegov.com	Raleigh	NC	27602	919-856-6160	856-6168
Warren County PO Box 709 *Web:* www.warrencountync.org	Warrenton	NC	27589	252-257-3261	257-5529
Washington County PO Box 1007 *Web:* www.washingtoncountygov.com	Plymouth	NC	27962	252-793-5823	793-1183
Watauga County 842 W King St Courthouse *Web:* www.wataugacounty.org	Boone	NC	28607	828-265-8000	264-3230
Wayne County PO Box 227 *Web:* www.waynegov.com	Goldsboro	NC	27533	919-731-1435	731-1446
Wilkes County 110 North St *Web:* www.wilkescounty.net	Wilkesboro	NC	28697	336-651-7345	651-7546
Wilson County PO Box 1728 *Web:* www.wilson-co.com	Wilson	NC	27894	252-399-2810	237-4341
Yadkin County PO Box 146 *Web:* www.yadkincounty.gov	Yadkinville	NC	27055	336-679-4200	679-6005
Yancey County 110 Town Square Rm 11 *Web:* www.main.nc.us/yancey/	Burnsville	NC	28714	828-682-3971	682-4301

North Dakota

	City	State	Zip	Phone	Fax
Adams County 602 Adams Ave PO Box 469 *Web:* www.hettingernd.com	Hettinger	ND	58639	701-567-2460	567-2910
Barnes County 230 4th St NW Rm 202 *Web:* www.co.barnes.nd.us	Valley City	ND	58072	701-845-8500	845-8548
Benson County PO Box 213	Minnewaukan	ND	58351	701-473-5345	473-5571
Billings County PO Box 138	Medora	ND	58645	701-623-4491	623-4896
Bottineau County 314 W 5th St *Web:* www.bottineau.com	Bottineau	ND	58318	701-228-3983	228-2336
Bowman County PO Box 379 *Web:* www.bowmannd.com	Bowman	ND	58623	701-523-3450	523-5443
Burke County PO Box 219 *Web:* www.burkecountynd.com	Bowbells	ND	58721	701-377-2718	377-2020
Burleigh County PO Box 1055 *Web:* www.co.burleigh.nd.us	Bismarck	ND	58502	701-222-6761	221-3756
Cass County PO Box 2806 *Web:* www.casscountynd.gov/	Fargo	ND	58108	701-241-5601	241-5728
Cavalier County 901 3rd St Suite 15 *Web:* www.ccjda.org	Langdon	ND	58249	701-256-2229	256-2566
Dickey County PO Box 215	Ellendale	ND	58436	701-349-3249	349-4639
Divide County PO Box 68	Crosby	ND	58730	701-965-6831	965-6943
Dunn County PO Box 105	Manning	ND	58642	701-573-4448	573-4323
Eddy County 524 Central Ave	New Rockford	ND	58356	701-947-2434	947-2067
Emmons County PO Box 129	Linton	ND	58552	701-254-4807	254-4012
Foster County PO Box 257 *Web:* www.fostercounty.com	Carrington	ND	58421	701-652-1001	652-2173
Golden Valley County 150 1st Ave SE PO Box 9 *Web:* www.beachnd.com	Beach	ND	58621	701-872-3713	
Grand Forks County 124 S 4th St *Web:* www.grandforkscountygov.com	Grand Forks	ND	58201	701-787-2715	787-2716
Grant County 102 2nd Ave	Carson	ND	58529	701-622-3615	622-3717
Griggs County PO Box 326 *Web:* www.cooperstownnd.com	Cooperstown	ND	58425	701-797-2772	797-3587
Hettinger County PO Box 668 *Web:* www.hettingercounty.org	Mott	ND	58646	701-824-2645	824-2717
Kidder County 120 E Broadway Kidder County Courthouse	Steele	ND	58482	701-475-2632	475-2202
LaMoure County PO Box 128 *Web:* lamoco.drtel.net	La Moure	ND	58458	701-883-5301	883-4240
Logan County 301 Broadway St *Web:* www.napoleonnd.com	Napoleon	ND	58561	701-754-2751	754-2270
McHenry County PO Box 117	Towner	ND	58788	701-537-5729	537-5969
McIntosh County PO Box 179	Ashley	ND	58413	701-288-3450	288-3671
McKenzie County PO Box 524 *Web:* www.4eyes.net	Watford City	ND	58854	701-444-3452	444-3916
McLean County PO Box 1108 *Web:* www.visitmcleancounty.com	Washburn	ND	58577	701-462-8541	462-8212
Mercer County PO Box 39 *Web:* www.mercercountynd.com	Stanton	ND	58571	701-745-3262	745-3710
Morton County 210 2nd Ave NW *Web:* www.co.morton.nd.us	Mandan	ND	58554	701-667-3300	667-3453
Mountrail County PO Box 69	Stanley	ND	58784	701-628-2915	628-3975
Nelson County 210 B Ave W Suite 203	Lakota	ND	58344	701-247-2462	247-2412
Oliver County PO Box 125	Center	ND	58530	701-794-8777	794-3476
Pembina County 301 Dakota St W Suite 6 *Web:* pembinacountynd.gov	Cavalier	ND	58220	701-265-4275	265-4876
Pierce County 240 SE 2nd St PO Box 258	Rugby	ND	58368	701-776-6161	776-5707
Ramsey County 524 4th Ave Rm 4 *Web:* www.co.ramsey.nd.us	Devils Lake	ND	58301	701-662-7006	662-7063
Ransom County PO Box 626	Lisbon	ND	58054	701-683-5823	683-5826
Renville County 205 Main St E *Web:* www.renvillecounty.org	Mohall	ND	58761	701-756-6398	756-6398
Richland County 418 2nd Ave N *Web:* www.mylocalgov.com/richlandcountynd/	Wahpeton	ND	58075	701-671-1524	671-1512
Rolette County 102 2nd Ave PO Box 460 *Web:* www.rolettecounty.com	Rolla	ND	58367	701-477-3816	477-8594
Sargent County PO Box 176 *Web:* mylocalgov.com/SargentCountyND/	Forman	ND	58032	701-724-6241	724-6244
Sheridan County PO Box 409 *Web:* mylocalgov.com/SheridanCountyND/	McClusky	ND	58463	701-363-2207	363-2953
Sioux County PO Box L **Fax:* Acctg	Fort Yates	ND	58538	701-854-3481	854-3854*
Slope County PO Box JJ	Amidon	ND	58620	701-879-6275	879-6278
Stark County PO Box 130 **Fax:* Acctg	Dickinson	ND	58602	701-456-7630	456-7634*
Steele County PO Box 296	Finley	ND	58230	701-524-2152	524-1325
Stutsman County 511 2nd Ave SE *Web:* www.co.stutsman.nd.us	Jamestown	ND	58401	701-252-9035	251-6325
Towner County PO Box 517 *Web:* www.mylocalgov.com/townercountynd/	Cando	ND	58324	701-968-4340	968-4344
Traill County 114 W Caledonia Ave *Web:* mylocalgov.com/traillcountynd	Hillsboro	ND	58045	701-636-4454	636-4457
Walsh County 600 Cooper Ave *Web:* mylocalgov.com/WalshCountyND/	Grafton	ND	58237	701-352-2851	352-3340
Ward County PO Box 5005 *Web:* www.co.ward.nd.us	Minot	ND	58702	701-857-6600	857-6623
Wells County PO Box 155 *Web:* mylocalgov.com/wellscountynd/	Fessenden	ND	58438	701-547-3122	547-3840
Williams County PO Box 2047 *Web:* www.williamsnd.com	Williston	ND	58802	701-577-4540	577-4535

Ohio

	City	State	Zip	Phone	Fax
Adams County 110 W Main St Rm 25 County Courthouse *Web:* www.adamscountytravel.org	West Union	OH	45693	937-544-2011	544-8911
Allen County 301 N Main St *Web:* www.allencountyohio.com	Lima	OH	45801	419-228-3700	222-8427
Ashland County 142 W 2nd St *Web:* www.ashlandcounty.org	Ashland	OH	44805	419-289-0000	282-4240
Ashtabula County 25 W Jefferson St *Web:* www.co.ashtabula.oh.us	Jefferson	OH	44047	440-576-3637	576-2819
Athens County PO Box 290 *Web:* www.athenscountygovernment.com	Athens	OH	45701	740-592-3242	592-3282
Auglaize County 201 Willipie St Suite 211 *Web:* www.auglaizecounty.org	Wapakoneta	OH	45895	419-738-4219	738-7953
Belmont County 101 W Main St Courthouse	Saint Clairsville	OH	43950	740-695-2121	695-5305
Brown County 800 Mount Orab Pike Suite 101 *Web:* www.county.brown.oh.us	Georgetown	OH	45121	937-378-3956	378-6324
Butler County 315 High St *Web:* www.butlercountyohio.org	Hamilton	OH	45011	513-887-3278	887-3966
Carroll County 119 S Lisbon St Suite 201 *Web:* www.carrollcountyohio.net	Carrollton	OH	44615	330-627-4869	627-6656
Champaign County 1512 S US Hwy 68 *Web:* www.co.champaign.oh.us	Urbana	OH	43078	937-484-1611	484-1609
Clark County 101 N Limestone St *Web:* www.co.clark.oh.us	Springfield	OH	45502	937-328-2458	328-2436
Clermont County 101 E Main St *Web:* www.co.clermont.oh.us	Batavia	OH	45103	513-732-7300	732-7826
Clinton County 46 S South St *Web:* www.co.clinton.oh.us	Wilmington	OH	45177	937-382-2103	383-2884
Columbiana County 105 S Market St *Web:* www.columbianacounty.org	Lisbon	OH	44432	330-424-7777	424-3960
Coshocton County 349 1/2 Main St *Web:* www.co.coshocton.oh.us	Coshocton	OH	43812	740-622-1753	622-4917
Crawford County 112 E Mansfield St *Web:* www.crawford-co.org	Bucyrus	OH	44820	419-562-5876	562-3491
Cuyahoga County 1219 Ontario St *Web:* www.cuyahogacounty.us	Cleveland	OH	44113	216-443-7010	443-5091
Darke County 504 S Broadway St *Web:* www.co.darke.oh.us	Greenville	OH	45331	937-547-7370	547-7367
Defiance County 500 Court St Suite A *Web:* www.defiance-county.com/	Defiance	OH	43512	419-782-4761	782-8449
Delaware County 101 N Sandusky St *Web:* www.co.delaware.oh.us	Delaware	OH	43015	740-833-2100	833-2099
Erie County 323 Columbus Ave *Web:* www.erie-county-ohio.net	Sandusky	OH	44870	419-627-7705	624-6873
Fairfield County 210 E Main St *Web:* www.co.fairfield.oh.us	Lancaster	OH	43130	740-687-7190	687-6048
Fayette County 133 S Main St Suite 401 *Web:* www.fayette-co-oh.com	Washington Court House	OH	43160	740-335-0720	333-3530
Franklin County 369 S High St 3rd Fl *Web:* www.co.franklin.oh.us	Columbus	OH	43215	614-462-3650	462-4325
Fulton County 152 S Fulton St Suite 270 *Web:* www.fultoncountyoh.com	Wauseon	OH	43567	419-337-9255	337-9285
Gallia County 18 Locust St *Web:* www.galliacounty.org	Gallipolis	OH	45631	740-446-4374	446-4804

				Phone	Fax
Geauga County 470 Center St Bldg 4	Chardon	OH	44024	440-285-2222	286-9177
Web: www.co.geauga.oh.us					
Greene County 35 Green St.	Xenia	OH	45385	937-562-5006	562-5331
Web: www.co.greene.oh.us					
Guernsey County 627 Wheeling Ave Suite 53	Cambridge	OH	43725	740-432-9200	432-9359
Web: www.guernseycounty.org					
Hamilton County 138 E Court St Rm 603	Cincinnati	OH	45202	513-946-4400	946-4444
Web: www.hamilton-co.org					
Hancock County 300 S Main St	Findlay	OH	45840	419-424-7037	424-7801
Web: www.co.hancock.oh.us					
Hardin County 1 Courthouse Sq Suite 100	Kenton	OH	43326	419-674-2205	674-2272
Web: www.co.hardin.oh.us					
Harrison County 100 W Market St	Cadiz	OH	43907	740-942-8861	942-8860
Web: www.harrisoncountyohio.org					
Henry County 1853 Oakwood Ave	Napoleon	OH	43545	419-592-4876	
Web: www.henrycountyohio.com					
Highland County 114 Governor Foraker Pl	Hillsboro	OH	45133	937-393-1911	393-5850
Web: www.highland-co.com					
Hocking County 1 E Main St	Logan	OH	43138	740-385-5195	385-1105
Web: www.co.hocking.oh.us					
Holmes County 2 Court St	Millersburg	OH	44654	330-674-0286	674-0566
Web: www.holmescounty.com/gov					
Huron County County Courthouse 2 E Main St 2nd Fl	Norwalk	OH	44857	419-668-5113	663-4048
Web: www.hccommissioners.com					
Jackson County 275 Portsmouth St	Jackson	OH	45640	740-286-3301	286-4061
Jefferson County 301 Market St Courthouse	Steubenville	OH	43952	740-283-8500	283-8599
Web: www.jeffersoncountyoh.com					
Knox County 117 E High St Suite 161	Mount Vernon	OH	43050	740-393-6703	393-6705
Web: www.knoxcountyohio.org					
Lake County 25 N Park Pl	Painesville	OH	44077	440-350-2500	
Web: www.lakecountyohio.org					
Lawrence County PO Box 208	Ironton	OH	45638	740-533-4355	533-4383
Web: www.lawrencecountyohio.org					
Licking County 20 S 2nd St	Newark	OH	43055	740-670-5110	670-5119
Web: www.lcounty.com					
Logan County 117 E Columbus St	Bellefontaine	OH	43311	937-599-7283	599-7268
Web: www.co.logan.oh.us					
Lorain County 225 Court St	Elyria	OH	44035	440-329-5536	329-5404
Web: www.loraincounty.us					
Lucas County 1 Government Center Suite 800	Toledo	OH	43604	419-213-4500	213-4532
Web: www.co.lucas.oh.us					
Madison County PO Box 618	London	OH	43140	740-852-2972	845-1660
Web: www.co.madison.oh.us					
Mahoning County 120 Market St	Youngstown	OH	44503	330-740-2104	740-2105
Web: www.mahoningcountyoh.gov					
Marion County 100 N Main St	Marion	OH	43302	740-223-4270	223-4279
Web: www.co.marion.oh.us					
Medina County 93 Public Sq	Medina	OH	44256	330-725-9722	
Web: www.co.medina.oh.us					
Meigs County PO Box 151	Pomeroy	OH	45769	740-992-5290	992-4429
Web: www.meigscountyohio.com					
Mercer County 220 W Livingston St Rm A201	Celina	OH	45822	419-586-3178	586-1699
Web: www.mercercountyohio.org					
Miami County 201 W Main St	Troy	OH	45373	937-440-5900	
Web: www.co.miami.oh.us					
Monroe County 101 N Main St Rm 35	Woodsfield	OH	43793	740-472-5181	472-2526
Web: www.monroecountyohio.net					
Montgomery County 41 N Perry St	Dayton	OH	45422	937-496-7591	496-7627
Web: www.co.montgomery.oh.us/					
Morgan County 19 E Main St	McConnelsville	OH	43756	740-962-4752	962-4522
Web: www.morgancounty.org					
Morrow County 48 E High St	Mount Gilead	OH	43338	419-947-4085	947-1860
Web: www.co.morrow.oh.us					
Muskingum County 401 Main St	Zanesville	OH	43701	740-455-7104	
Web: www.muskingumcounty.org					
Noble County County Courthouse Rm 210	Caldwell	OH	43724	740-732-2969	732-5702
Web: www.noblecountyohio.com					
Ottawa County 315 Madison St	Port Clinton	OH	43452	419-734-6710	734-6898
Web: www.co.ottawa.oh.us					
Paulding County					
County Courthouse 115 N Williams St Rm 104	Paulding	OH	45879	419-399-8210	399-8248
Perry County 121 W Brown St PO Box 248	New Lexington	OH	43764	740-342-2045	342-5505
Web: www.perrycountyohiocofc.com					
Pickaway County 139 W Franklin St	Circleville	OH	43113	740-474-6093	474-8988
Web: www.pickaway.org					
Pike County 100 E 2nd St	Waverly	OH	45690	740-947-2715	947-1729
Web: www.piketravel.com					
Portage County 449 S Meridian St	Ravenna	OH	44266	330-297-3600	297-3610
Web: www.co.portage.oh.us					
Preble County 101 E Main St	Eaton	OH	45320	937-456-8143	456-8114
Web: www.prebco.org					
Putnam County 245 E Main St Suite 101	Ottawa	OH	45875	419-523-3656	523-9213
Web: www.putnamcountyohio.com					
Richland County 50 Park Ave E	Mansfield	OH	44902	419-774-5549	774-5547
Web: www.richlandcountyohio.org					
Ross County 2 N Paint St Suite B	Chillicothe	OH	45601	740-702-3010	702-3018
Web: www.co.ross.oh.us					
Sandusky County 622 Croghan St	Fremont	OH	43420	419-334-6100	334-6104
Web: www.sandusky-county.org					
Scioto County 602 7th St Rm 205	Portsmouth	OH	45662	740-355-8218	354-2057
Web: www.sciotocountyohio.com					
Seneca County 81 Jefferson St	Tiffin	OH	44883	419-447-4550	447-0556
Web: www.senecacounty.com					
Shelby County 129 E Court St Suite 100	Sidney	OH	45365	937-498-7226	498-1293
Web: www.co.shelby.oh.us					
Stark County 225 4th St NE	Canton	OH	44702	330-451-7432	451-7190
Web: www.co.stark.oh.us					
Summit County 175 S Main St	Akron	OH	44308	330-643-2500	643-2507
Web: www.co.summit.oh.us					
Trumbull County 160 High St NW 5th Fl Administration Bldg	Warren	OH	44481	330-675-2451	675-2462
Web: www.co.trumbull.oh.us					
Tuscarawas County 125 E High Ave Rm 230	New Philadelphia	OH	44663	330-365-3243	343-4682
Web: www.co.tuscarawas.oh.us					
Union County 233 W 6th St	Marysville	OH	43040	937-645-3012	645-3002
Web: www.co.union.oh.us					
Van Wert County 114 E Main St	Van Wert	OH	45891	419-238-6159	238-4528
Web: vanwertcounty.org					
Vinton County 100 E Main St County Courthouse	McArthur	OH	45651	740-596-4571	596-4571
Web: www.vintoncounty.com					
Warren County 550 Justice Dr	Lebanon	OH	45036	513-695-1370	695-2990
Web: www.co.warren.oh.us					
Washington County 205 Putnam St	Marietta	OH	45750	740-373-6623	373-2085
Web: www.co.washington.oh.us					
Wayne County 428 W Liberty St	Wooster	OH	44691	330-287-5400	287-5407
Web: www.wayneohio.org					
Williams County 1 Courthouse Sq	Bryan	OH	43506	419-636-2059	636-0643
Web: www.co.williams.oh.us					
Wood County 1 Courthouse Sq PO Box 829	Bowling Green	OH	43402	419-354-9280	354-9241
Web: www.co.wood.oh.us					
Wyandot County					
109 S Sandusky Ave County Courthouse	Upper Sandusky	OH	43351	419-294-1432	294-6414
Web: www.co.wyandot.oh.us					

Oklahoma

				Phone	Fax
Adair County PO Box 169	Stilwell	OK	74960	918-696-7198	696-2603
Alfalfa County 300 S Grand Ave	Cherokee	OK	73728	580-596-3158	
Atoka County 200 E Court St	Atoka	OK	74525	580-889-2643	889-2608
Web: www.atokacity.org					
Beaver County PO Box 338	Beaver	OK	73932	580-625-3151	625-3430
Beckham County PO Box 67	Sayre	OK	73662	580-928-2457	928-2467
Blaine County 212 N Weigle	Watonga	OK	73772	580-623-5890	
Web: www.watonga.com					
Bryan County PO Box 1789	Durant	OK	74702	580-924-2202	924-2289
Caddo County SW 2nd & Oklahoma PO Box 68	Anadarko	OK	73005	405-247-6609	247-6510
Canadian County 201 N Choctaw St	El Reno	OK	73036	405-262-1070	422-2411
Web: www.canadiancounty.org					
Carter County PO Box 1236	Ardmore	OK	73402	580-223-8162	221-5508
Web: www.brightok.net/cartercounty/					
Cherokee County 213 W Delaware St Rm 200	Tahlequah	OK	74464	918-456-3171	458-6508
Choctaw County 300 E Duke St	Hugo	OK	74743	580-326-3778	326-6787
Cimarron County Courthouse Sq PO Box 145	Boise City	OK	73933	580-544-2251	544-2251
Web: www.ccccok.org					
Cleveland County 641 E Robinson St Rm 300	Norman	OK	73071	405-366-0240	366-0229
Coal County 4 N Main St	Coalgate	OK	74538	580-927-3122	927-4003
Comanche County 315 SW 5th St Suite 304	Lawton	OK	73501	580-355-5214	
Web: www.comanchecounty.us					
Cotton County 301 N Broadway	Walters	OK	73572	580-875-3026	875-3756
Craig County PO Box 397	Vinita	OK	74301	918-256-2507	256-3617
Creek County 317 E Lee St Rm 100	Sapulpa	OK	74066	918-224-4084	
Custer County Broadway & B St	Arapaho	OK	73620	580-323-1221	
Delaware County PO Box 309	Jay	OK	74346	918-253-4520	253-8352
Dewey County Broadway & Ruble PO Box 368	Taloga	OK	73667	580-328-5361	
Ellis County PO Box 197	Arnett	OK	73832	580-885-7301	885-7258
Garfield County 114 W Broadway	Enid	OK	73701	580-237-0225	249-5951
Garvin County 201 W Grant St	Pauls Valley	OK	73075	405-238-2772	238-6283
Grady County 326 Choctaw St	Chickasha	OK	73018	405-224-7388	222-4506
Web: www.gradycountyok.com					
Grant County 112 E Guthrie St PO Box 167	Medford	OK	73759	580-395-2274	395-2086
Greer County PO Box 207	Mangum	OK	73554	580-782-3664	782-3803
Web: www.greercounty-ok.com					
Harmon County 114 W Hollis St	Hollis	OK	73550	580-688-3658	688-9784
Harper County PO Box 369	Buffalo	OK	73834	580-735-2130	735-6034
Haskell County 202 E Main St	Stigler	OK	74462	918-967-2885	967-2885
Hughes County 200 N Broadway St Suite 7	Holdenville	OK	74848	405-379-2746	379-6739
Jackson County PO Box 515	Altus	OK	73522	580-482-4070	482-4472
Web: www.intplsrv.net/jacksoncounty/					
Jefferson County 220 N Main St Rm 103	Waurika	OK	73573	580-228-2029	228-3608
Johnston County 403 W Main St	Tishomingo	OK	73460	580-371-3058	371-2174
Kay County 201 S Main St	Newkirk	OK	74647	580-362-2537	362-3300
Web: www.courthouse.kay.ok.us/home.html					
Kingfisher County 101 S Main St Rm 3	Kingfisher	OK	73750	405-375-3887	375-6033
Web: www.kingfisherco.com					
Kiowa County PO Box 73	Hobart	OK	73651	580-726-5286	726-6033
Latimer County 109 N Central St	Wilburton	OK	74578	918-465-2021	465-3736
LeFlore County PO Box 218	Poteau	OK	74953	918-647-5738	647-8930
Lincoln County 811 Manuel St Suite 5	Chandler	OK	74834	405-258-1264	258-0439
Logan County 301 E Harrison Ave Suite 102	Guthrie	OK	73044	405-282-0266	282-0267
Love County 405 W Main St Suite 203	Marietta	OK	73448	580-276-3059	
Major County 500 E Broadway	Fairview	OK	73737	580-227-4732	227-2736
Marshall County 1 County Courthouse Rm 106	Madill	OK	73446	580-795-3165	795-3165
Mayes County 1 Court Pl Suite 120	Pryor	OK	74361	918-825-2426	825-3803
McClain County 121 N 2nd St Suite 303	Purcell	OK	73080	405-527-3360	
McCurtain County 108 N Central St	Idabel	OK	74745	580-286-2370	286-1040
McIntosh County PO Box 110	Eufaula	OK	74432	918-689-2741	689-3385
Murray County PO Box 240	Sulphur	OK	73086	580-622-3777	622-6209
Muskogee County PO Box 1008	Muskogee	OK	74402	918-682-7781	682-8803
Noble County 300 Courthouse Dr Rm 11	Perry	OK	73077	580-336-2141	336-2481
Nowata County 229 N Maple St	Nowata	OK	74048	918-273-0175	273-1936
Okfuskee County PO Box 26	Okemah	OK	74859	918-623-0939	623-0635
Oklahoma County 320 Robert S Kerr Ave	Oklahoma City	OK	73102	405-270-0082	
Web: www.oklahomacounty.org					
Okmulgee County PO Box 904	Okmulgee	OK	74447	918-756-0788	758-1261
Osage County PO Box 87	Pawhuska	OK	74056	918-287-3136	287-4979
Ottawa County 102 E Central Ave Suite 203	Miami	OK	74354	918-542-3332	542-8260
Pawnee County 500 Harrison St Rm 203	Pawnee	OK	74058	918-762-3741	762-3714
Web: www.cityofpawnee.com/cofc/					
Payne County 315 W 6th St Suite 202	Stillwater	OK	74074	405-747-8310	747-8304
Web: www.paynecounty.org					
Pittsburg County 115 E Carl Albert Pkwy Suite 1A	McAlester	OK	74501	918-423-6865	423-7304
Pontotoc County 100 W 13th St	Ada	OK	74820	580-332-1425	
Pottawatomie County 325 N Broadway	Shawnee	OK	74801	405-273-8222	275-6898
Pushmataha County 304 SW 'B' St	Antlers	OK	74523	580-298-2512	298-5299
Roger Mills County PO Box 708	Cheyenne	OK	73628	580-497-3365	497-3199
Rogers County 219 S Missouri St	Claremore	OK	74017	918-341-2518	341-4529
Web: www.rogerscounty.org					
Seminole County PO Box 1180	Wewoka	OK	74884	405-257-2501	257-6422
Sequoyah County 120 E Chickasaw Ave	Sallisaw	OK	74955	918-775-4516	775-1218
Stephens County 101 S 11th St	Duncan	OK	73533	580-255-4193	255-1771
Texas County 319 N Main St	Guymon	OK	73942	580-338-3233	338-4311
Web: www.txcountyok.com					
Tillman County 201 N Main St	Frederick	OK	73542	580-335-3421	335-3795
Tulsa County 500 S Denver Ave Suite 120	Tulsa	OK	74103	918-596-5801	596-5819
Web: www.tulsacounty.org					
Wagoner County PO Box 156	Wagoner	OK	74477	918-485-6171	485-7709
Washington County 400 S Johnstone Ave Rm 100	Bartlesville	OK	74003	918-337-2840	337-2894
Web: www.co.washington.ok.us					
Washita County PO Box 380	Cordell	OK	73632	580-832-2284	832-3526
Woods County 407 Government St	Alva	OK	73717	580-327-2126	327-1219
Woodward County 1600 Main St Suite 9	Woodward	OK	73801	580-256-8097	254-6840

Oregon

				Phone	Fax
Baker County 1995 3rd St Suite 150	Baker City	OR	97814	541-523-8207	523-8240
Web: www.bakercounty.org					
Benton County 408 SW Monroe Ave Suite 111	Corvallis	OR	97339	541-766-6800	766-6893
Web: www.co.benton.or.us					
Clackamas County 2051 Kaen Rd	Oregon City	OR	97045	503-655-8551	650-5688
Web: www.co.clackamas.or.us					

Oregon (Cont'd)

	City	State	ZIP	Phone	Fax
Clatsop County 820 Exchange St 2nd Fl *Web:* www.co.clatsop.or.us	Astoria	OR	97103	503-325-8511	325-9307
Columbia County County Courthouse 230 Strand St *Web:* www.co.columbia.or.us	Saint Helens	OR	97051	503-397-3796	397-7266
Coos County 250 N Baxter St *Web:* www.co.coos.or.us	Coquille	OR	97423	541-396-3121	396-4861
Crook County 300 NE 3rd St Rm 23 *Web:* www.co.crook.or.us	Prineville	OR	97754	541-447-6553	416-2145
Curry County 29821 Ellensburg Ave *Web:* www.co.curry.or.us	Gold Beach	OR	97444	541-247-3295	247-6440
Deschutes County 1300 NW Wall St Suite 200 *Web:* www.co.deschutes.or.us	Bend	OR	97701	541-388-6570	385-3202
Douglas County 1036 SE Douglas St *Web:* www.co.douglas.or.us	Roseburg	OR	97470	541-440-4323	440-4408
Gilliam County 221 S Oregon St	Condon	OR	97823	541-384-2311	384-2166
Grant County 201 S Humbolt St Suite 290 *Web:* www.grantcounty.cc	Canyon City	OR	97820	541-575-1675	575-2248
Harney County 450 N Buena Vista Ave *Web:* www.co.harney.or.us	Burns	OR	97720	541-573-6641	573-8370
Hood River County 601 State St *Web:* www.co.hood-river.or.us	Hood River	OR	97031	541-386-3970	386-9392
Jackson County 10 S Oakdale Ave Rm 214 Courthouse *Web:* www.co.jackson.or.us	Medford	OR	97501	541-774-6035	774-6455
Jefferson County 66 SE 'D' St Suite C	Madras	OR	97741	541-475-4451	325-5018
Josephine County 500 NW 6th St *Web:* www.co.josephine.or.us	Grants Pass	OR	97526	541-474-5240	474-5246
Klamath County 305 Main St *Web:* www.co.klamath.or.us	Klamath Falls	OR	97601	541-883-5134	883-5165
Lake County 513 Center St *Web:* www.lakecountyor.org	Lakeview	OR	97630	541-947-6006	947-6015
Lane County 125 E 8th Ave *Web:* www.co.lane.or.us	Eugene	OR	97401	541-682-4203	682-4616
Lincoln County 225 W Olive St Rm 201 *Web:* www.co.lincoln.or.us	Newport	OR	97365	541-265-4121	265-4114
Linn County 300 4th Ave SW *Web:* www.co.linn.or.us	Albany	OR	97321	541-967-3831	926-5109
Malheur County 251 B St W *Web:* www.malheurco.org	Vale	OR	97918	541-473-5151	473-5523
Marion County 100 High St NE Rm 1331 *Web:* www.co.marion.or.us	Salem	OR	97301	503-588-5225	373-4408
Morrow County 100 Court St *Web:* morrowcountyoregon.com	Heppner	OR	97836	541-676-9061	676-9876
Multnomah County 1021 SW 4th Ave *Web:* www.co.multnomah.or.us	Portland	OR	97204	503-988-3957	988-5773
Polk County 850 Main St *Web:* www.co.polk.or.us	Dallas	OR	97338	503-623-9217	623-0717
Sherman County 500 Court St *Web:* www.sherman-county.com	Moro	OR	97039	541-565-3606	565-3312
Tillamook County 201 Laurel Ave *Web:* www.co.tillamook.or.us	Tillamook	OR	97141	503-842-3403	842-1384
Umatilla County 216 SE 4th St *Web:* www.co.umatilla.or.us	Pendleton	OR	97801	541-278-6236	278-6345
Union County 1106 K Ave *Web:* www.union-county.org	La Grande	OR	97850	541-963-1001	963-1079
Wallowa County 101 S River St Rm 100 *Web:* www.co.wallowa.or.us	Enterprise	OR	97828	541-426-4543	426-5901
Wasco County 511 Washington St *Web:* www.co.wasco.or.us	The Dalles	OR	97058	541-506-2500	298-3607
Washington County 155 N 1st Ave Rm 340 *Web:* www.co.washington.or.us	Hillsboro	OR	97124	503-846-8747	846-8636
Wheeler County 701 Adams St *Web:* www.wheelercounty-oregon.com	Fossil	OR	97830	541-763-2400	763-2026
Yamhill County 535 NE 5th St *Web:* www.co.yamhill.or.us	McMinnville	OR	97128	503-434-7518	434-7520

Pennsylvania

	City	State	ZIP	Phone	Fax
Adams County 111-117 Baltimore St *Web:* www.adamscounty.us	Gettysburg	PA	17325	717-334-6781	334-2091
Allegheny County 436 Grant St County Courthouse Rm 119 *Web:* www.county.allegheny.pa.us/	Pittsburgh	PA	15219	412-350-5300	350-3581
Armstrong County 450 E Market St Courthouse Complex *Web:* www.armstrongcounty.com	Kittanning	PA	16201	724-543-2500	548-3285
Beaver County 810 3rd St Courthouse *Web:* www.co.beaver.pa.us	Beaver	PA	15009	724-728-3934	728-0725
Bedford County 211 S Juliana St *Web:* bedford.sapdc.org	Bedford	PA	15522	814-623-4807	623-0991
Berks County 633 Court St 4th Fl *Web:* www.co.berks.pa.us	Reading	PA	19601	610-478-6550	478-6570
Blair County 423 Allegheny St Suite 142	Hollidaysburg	PA	16648	814-693-3030	693-3033
Bradford County 301 Main St Courthouse *Web:* www.bradfordcountypa.org	Towanda	PA	18848	570-265-1727	265-1729
Bucks County 55 E Court St *Web:* www.buckscounty.org	Doylestown	PA	18901	215-348-6000	348-6571
Butler County 290 S Main St PO Box 1208 *Web:* www.co.butler.pa.us	Butler	PA	16003	724-284-5233	284-5244
Cambria County 200 S Center St *Web:* www.co.cambria.pa.us	Ebensburg	PA	15931	814-472-6176	472-6940
Cameron County 20 E 5th St *Web:* www.cameroncountypa.com	Emporium	PA	15834	814-486-2315	486-3176
Carbon County 2 Hazard Sq *Web:* www.carboncounty.com	Jim Thorpe	PA	18229	570-325-3611	325-3622
Centre County 420 Holmes St Willowbank Office Bldg *Web:* www.co.centre.pa.us	Bellefonte	PA	16823	814-355-6700	355-6980
Chester County 2 N High St Suite 512 PO Box 2748 *Web:* dsf.chesco.org	West Chester	PA	19380	610-344-6100	344-5995
Clarion County 421 Main St Courthouse *Web:* www.co.clarion.pa.us	Clarion	PA	16214	814-226-1119	227-2501
Clearfield County 230 E Market St *Web:* www.clearfieldco.org	Clearfield	PA	16830	814-765-2641	765-2640
Clinton County 232 E Main St 3rd Fl *Web:* www.clintoncountypa.com	Lock Haven	PA	17745	570-893-4000	893-4041
Columbia County 35 W Main St *Web:* www.columbiapa.org	Bloomsburg	PA	17815	570-389-5600	784-0257
Crawford County 903 Diamond Pk *Web:* www.co.crawford.pa.us	Meadville	PA	16335	814-333-7400	337-0457
Cumberland County 1 Courthouse Sq *Web:* www.ccpa.net/cumberland/	Carlisle	PA	17013	717-240-6150	240-6448
Dauphin County 2 S 2nd St *TF:* 800-328-0058 ■ *Web:* www.dauphincounty.org	Harrisburg	PA	17101	717-780-6300	255-2684
Delaware County 201 W Front St Government Center Bldg *Web:* www.co.delaware.pa.us	Media	PA	19063	610-891-4000	891-0647
Elk County PO Box 448 *Web:* www.co.elk.pa.us	Ridgway	PA	15853	814-776-1161	776-5379
Erie County 140 W 6th St Rm 116 *Web:* www.eriecountygov.org	Erie	PA	16501	814-451-6303	451-6350
Fayette County 61 E Main St *Web:* www.fayettepa.org	Uniontown	PA	15401	724-430-1201	430-1265
Forest County 526 Elm St Suite 3 *Web:* www.co.forest.pa.us	Tionesta	PA	16353	814-755-3537	755-8837
Franklin County 14 N Main St *Web:* www.co.franklin.pa.us	Chambersburg	PA	17201	717-261-3810	267-3438
Fulton County 116 W Market St Suite 203 *Web:* fulton.sapdc.org	McConnellsburg	PA	17233	717-485-3691	485-9411
Greene County 93 E High St *Web:* www.co.greene.pa.us	Waynesburg	PA	15370	724-852-5210	852-5327
Huntingdon County 223 Penn St County Courthouse *Web:* www.huntingdoncounty.net	Huntingdon	PA	16652	814-643-3091	643-8152
Indiana County 825 Philadelphia St Courthouse *Web:* www.indianacounty.org	Indiana	PA	15701	724-465-3805	465-3953
Jefferson County 155 Main St Jefferson Pl *Web:* www.jeffersoncountypa.com	Brookville	PA	15825	814-849-1653	849-4084
Juniata County PO Box 68 *Web:* www.co.juniata.pa.us	Mifflintown	PA	17059	717-436-7715	436-7734
Lackawanna County 436 Spruce St *Web:* www.lackawannacounty.org	Scranton	PA	18503	570-963-6723	963-6387
Lancaster County 50 N Duke St *Web:* www.co.lancaster.pa.us	Lancaster	PA	17602	717-299-8000	293-7208
Lawrence County County Courthouse 430 Court St *Web:* www.co.lawrence.pa.us	New Castle	PA	16101	724-658-2541	652-9646
Lebanon County 400 S 8th St *Web:* dsf.pacounties.org/lebanon/	Lebanon	PA	17042	717-274-2801	274-8094
Lehigh County 455 W Hamilton St Rm 132 *Web:* www.lehighcounty.org	Allentown	PA	18101	610-782-3148	770-3840
Luzerne County 200 N River St *Web:* www.luzernecounty.org	Wilkes-Barre	PA	18711	570-825-1500	825-9343
Lycoming County 48 W 3rd St *Web:* www.lyco.org	Williamsport	PA	17701	570-327-2256	327-2505
McKean County PO Box 1507 *Web:* www.mckeancountypa.org	Smethport	PA	16749	814-887-5571	887-2242
Mercer County Mercer County Courthouse Rm 103 *Web:* www.merlink.org/mcjac/governmt.htm	Mercer	PA	16137	724-662-3800	662-1530
Mifflin County 20 N Wayne St *Web:* www.co.mifflin.pa.us	Lewistown	PA	17044	717-248-6733	248-3695
Monroe County County Courthouse Sq *Web:* www.co.monroe.pa.us	Stroudsburg	PA	18360	570-420-3400	420-3458
Montgomery County PO Box 311 *Web:* www.montcopa.org	Norristown	PA	19404	610-278-3346	278-5188
Montour County 29 Mill St *Web:* www.montourco.org	Danville	PA	17821	570-271-3012	271-3071
Northampton County 669 Washington St *Web:* www.northamptoncounty.org	Easton	PA	18042	610-559-6700	559-6702
Northumberland County 201 Market St Rt 7 *Web:* www.northumberlandco.org	Sunbury	PA	17801	570-988-4151	
Perry County 25 W Main St PO Box 37 *Web:* www.perryco.org	New Bloomfield	PA	17068	717-582-2131	582-5162
Philadelphia County City Hall Broad & Market Sts *Web:* www.phila.gov	Philadelphia	PA	19107	215-686-1776	567-7380
Pike County 506 Broad St *Web:* www.pikepa.org	Milford	PA	18337	570-296-7613	296-6055
Potter County 1 E 2nd St Rm 22 *Web:* www.pottercountypa.net	Coudersport	PA	16915	814-274-8290	274-8284
Schuylkill County 401 N 2nd St *Web:* www.co.schuylkill.pa.us	Pottsville	PA	17901	570-628-1200	628-1210
Snyder County 9 W Market St *Web:* www.snydercounty.org	Middleburg	PA	17842	570-837-4207	837-4282
Somerset County 300 N Center Ave *Web:* www.co.somerset.pa.us	Somerset	PA	15501	814-445-1400	445-1447
Sullivan County PO Box 157 Main & Muncy Sts *Web:* www.sullivancounty-pa.us	Laporte	PA	18626	570-946-5201	946-4421
Susquehanna County 11 Maple St *Web:* www.susquehanna.pa.us	Montrose	PA	18801	570-278-4600	278-9268
Tioga County 118 Main St *Web:* www.visittiogapa.com	Wellsboro	PA	16901	570-723-8191	
Union County 103 S 2nd St *Web:* www.unionco.org	Lewisburg	PA	17837	570-524-8600	524-8635
Venango County Courthouse Annex 1174 Elk St *Web:* www.co.venango.pa.us	Franklin	PA	16323	814-432-9510	432-3149
Warren County 204 4th Ave *Web:* www.warren-county.net	Warren	PA	16365	814-728-3400	728-3479
Washington County 1 S Main St Suite 1005 *Web:* www.co.washington.pa.us	Washington	PA	15301	724-228-6787	
Wayne County 925 Court St *Web:* www.co.wayne.pa.us	Honesdale	PA	18431	570-253-5970	253-5432
Westmoreland County 2 N Main St Courthouse Sq Suite 101 *Web:* www.co.westmoreland.pa.us	Greensburg	PA	15601	724-830-3100	830-3029
Wyoming County 1 Courthouse Sq *Web:* www.pacounties.org/wyoming	Tunkhannock	PA	18657	570-836-3200	836-7244
York County 45 N George St *Web:* www.york-county.org	York	PA	17401	717-771-9612	771-9096

Rhode Island

	City	State	ZIP	Phone	Fax
Bristol County 10 Court St	Bristol	RI	02809	401-253-7000	253-3080
Kent County 222 Quaker Ln Suite 6	Warwick	RI	02886	401-822-1311	
Newport County 45 Washington Sq	Newport	RI	02840	401-841-8330	846-1673
Providence County 1 Dorrance Plaza	Providence	RI	02903	401-458-5400	
Washington County 4800 Tower Hill Rd	Wakefield	RI	02879	401-782-4121	782-4190

South Carolina

	City	State	ZIP	Phone	Fax
Abbeville County Courthouse PO Box 99 *Web:* www.sccounties.org/counties/Abbeville.htm	Abbeville	SC	29620	864-366-5312	366-4595
Aiken County 828 Richland Ave W *Web:* www.aikencounty.net	Aiken	SC	29801	803-642-2012	642-2124
Allendale County PO Box 190 *Web:* www.allendalecounty.com	Allendale	SC	29810	803-584-3438	584-7042
Anderson County 100 S Main St *Web:* www.andersoncountysc.org	Anderson	SC	29624	864-260-4000	260-4106
Bamberg County PO Box 150 *Web:* bambergsc.com	Bamberg	SC	29003	803-245-3025	245-3088
Barnwell County PO Box 723 *Web:* www.barnwellcountysc.com	Barnwell	SC	29812	803-541-1020	541-1025

	City	State	Zip	Phone	Fax
Beaufort County 102 Ribaut Rd	Beaufort	SC	29902	843-470-5218	470-5248
Web: www.co.beaufort.sc.us					
Berkeley County PO Box 219	Moncks Corner	SC	29461	843-719-4403	719-4511
Web: www.co.berkeley.sc.us					
Calhoun County 102 Courthouse Dr Suite 108 Courthouse Annex	Saint Matthews	SC	29135	803-874-2435	874-1242
Charleston County 4045 Bridge View	Charleston	SC	29405	843-958-4030	958-4035
Web: www.charlestoncounty.org					
Cherokee County 210 N Limestone St	Gaffney	SC	29340	864-487-2562	487-2594
Web: www.cherokeecounty-sc.org					
Chester County PO Box 580	Chester	SC	29706	803-385-2605	581-7975
Web: www.chesterchamber.com					
Chesterfield County PO Box 529	Chesterfield	SC	29709	843-623-2574	623-6944
Web: www.chesterfield.k12.sc.us					
Clarendon County 3 W Key St	Manning	SC	29102	803-435-8424	435-8258
Web: www.clarendoncounty.com					
Colleton County PO Box 157	Walterboro	SC	29488	843-549-1725	549-7215
Web: www.colletoncounty.org					
Darlington County PO Box 1177	Darlington	SC	29540	843-398-4330	393-6871
Web: www.darcosc.com					
Dillon County PO Box 449	Dillon	SC	29536	843-774-1400	774-1443
Web: www.dilloncounty.org					
Dorchester County 101 Ridge St	Saint George	SC	29477	843-563-0121	563-0178
Web: www.dorchestercounty.net					
Edgefield County 129 Courthouse Sq Suite 205	Edgefield	SC	29824	803-637-4080	637-4007
Web: www.edgefieldcounty.sc.gov					
Fairfield County PO Drawer 60	Winnsboro	SC	29180	803-635-1415	635-5969
Web: www.fairfieldchamber.org					
Florence County 180 N Irby	Florence	SC	29501	843-665-3031	665-3097
Web: www.florenceco.org					
Georgetown County PO Drawer 421270	Georgetown	SC	29442	843-545-3063	545-3292
Web: www.georgetowncountysc.org					
Greenville County 305 E North St	Greenville	SC	29601	864-467-8551	467-8540
Web: www.greenvillecounty.org					
Greenwood County 600 Monument St Box P-103	Greenwood	SC	29646	864-942-8500	942-8566
Web: www.co.greenwood.sc.us					
Hampton County 201 Jackson Ave W	Hampton	SC	29924	803-943-7561	943-7502
Web: www.hamptoncountysc.org					
Horry County PO Box 677	Conway	SC	29528	843-915-5080	915-6081
Web: www.horrycounty.org					
Jasper County PO Box 248	Ridgeland	SC	29936	843-726-7710	726-7782
Web: www.jaspersc.org					
Kershaw County 1121 Broad St Rm 202	Camden	SC	29020	803-425-1500	425-6044
Web: www.kershawcountysc.org					
Lancaster County PO Box 1809	Lancaster	SC	29721	803-285-1581	416-9388
Web: www.lancastercountysc.net					
Laurens County PO Box 287	Laurens	SC	29360	864-984-3538	984-3726
Web: www.laurenscountysc.org					
Lee County PO Box 387	Bishopville	SC	29010	803-484-5341	484-1632
Lexington County 205 E Main St County Courthouse	Lexington	SC	29072	803-785-8212	785-8314
Web: www.co.lexington.sc.us					
Marion County PO Box 183	Marion	SC	29571	843-423-3904	423-8306
Web: www.co.marion.sc.us					
Marlboro County PO Box 419	Bennettsville	SC	29512	843-479-5600	479-5639
Web: www.marlborocounty.sc.gov					
McCormick County 133 S Mine St Rm 102	McCormick	SC	29835	864-465-2195	465-0071
Web: www.mccormickcountysc.com					
Newberry County 1226 College St PO Drawer 10	Newberry	SC	29108	803-321-2110	321-2111
Web: www.newberrycounty.net					
Oconee County 415 S Pine St	Walhalla	SC	29691	864-638-4242	638-4241
Web: www.oconeesc.com					
Orangeburg County PO Drawer 9000	Orangeburg	SC	29116	803-533-6243	534-3848
Web: www.orangeburgcounty.org					
Pickens County PO Box 215	Pickens	SC	29671	864-898-5866	898-5863
Web: www.co.pickens.sc.us					
Richland County 2020 Hampton St	Columbia	SC	29204	803-576-2050	576-2137
Web: www.richlandonline.com					
Saluda County 100 E Church St Suite 6	Saluda	SC	29138	864-445-3303	445-3772
Web: www.saludacounty.sc.gov					
Spartanburg County 180 Magnolia St	Spartanburg	SC	29306	864-596-2591	596-2239
Web: www.spartanburgcounty.org					
Sumter County 141 N Main St	Sumter	SC	29150	803-436-2227	436-2223
Web: www.sumtercountysc.org					
Union County PO Box 703	Union	SC	29379	864-429-1630	429-1715
Web: www.countyofunion.com					
Williamsburg County 147 W Main St	Kingstree	SC	29556	843-355-9321	355-2106
Web: www.williamsburgsc.com					
York County 2 S Congress St PO Box 649	York	SC	29745	803-684-8507	684-8575
Web: www.yorkcountygov.com					

South Dakota

	City	State	Zip	Phone	Fax
Aurora County PO Box 366	Plankinton	SD	57368	605-942-7165	942-7170
Beadle County PO Box 1358	Huron	SD	57350	605-353-7165	353-0118
Web: www.beadlecounty.org					
Bennett County PO Box 281	Martin	SD	57551	605-685-6969	685-1075
Bon Homme County 300 W 18th Ave	Tyndall	SD	57066	605-589-4215	589-4245
Brookings County 314 6th Ave	Brookings	SD	57006	605-692-6284	696-8211
Web: www.brookingscountysd.gov					
Brown County 25 Market St Suite 1	Aberdeen	SD	57401	605-626-7110	626-4010
Web: www.brown.sd.us					
Brule County 300 S Courtland St Suite 111	Chamberlain	SD	57325	605-734-4580	734-4582
Web: bruleco.tripod.com					
Buffalo County PO Box 148	Gann Valley	SD	57341	605-293-3234	293-3240
Butte County PO Box 250	Belle Fourche	SD	57717	605-892-2516	892-2836
Campbell County PO Box 146	Mound City	SD	57646	605-955-3536	955-5303
Charles Mix County PO Box 490	Lake Andes	SD	57356	605-487-7131	487-7221*
**Fax:* Acctg					
Clark County 200 N Commercial St	Clark	SD	57225	605-532-5921	532-5931
Clay County 211 W Main St Suite 200	Vermillion	SD	57069	605-677-7120	677-7104
Web: www.claycountysd.org					
Codington County PO Box 1054	Watertown	SD	57201	605-882-5095	882-5384
Web: www.codington.org					
Corson County PO Box 175	McIntosh	SD	57641	605-273-4201	273-4597
Custer County RR 1 Box 101	Custer	SD	57730	605-673-8100	
Web: www.custercountysd.com					
Davison County 200 E 4th Ave	Mitchell	SD	57301	605-995-8105	995-8112
Web: www.davisoncounty.org					
Day County 711 W 1st St	Webster	SD	57274	605-345-3771	345-3818
Deuel County PO Box 308	Clear Lake	SD	57226	605-874-2120	874-2916
Web: www.deuelcountysd.com					
Dewey County PO Box 277	Timber Lake	SD	57656	605-865-3672	865-3691
Douglas County PO Box 36	Armour	SD	57313	605-724-2585	724-2508
Edmunds County PO Box 384	Ipswich	SD	57451	605-426-6671	426-6323
Fall River County 906 N River St	Hot Springs	SD	57747	605-745-5132	745-6835
Faulk County PO Box 309	Faulkton	SD	57438	605-598-6224	
Grant County 210 E 5th Ave	Milbank	SD	57252	605-432-6711	432-9004*
**Fax:* Acctg					
Gregory County PO Box 430	Burke	SD	57523	605-775-2665	775-2965
Haakon County PO Box 698	Philip	SD	57567	605-859-2800	
Hamlin County PO Box 256	Hayti	SD	57243	605-783-3751	783-2157
Hand County 415 W 1st Ave	Miller	SD	57362	605-853-3337	853-3779
Hanson County PO Box 127	Alexandria	SD	57311	605-239-4446	239-9446
Harding County 410 Ramsland St PO Box 534	Buffalo	SD	57720	605-375-3351	375-3432
Hughes County PO Box 1238	Pierre	SD	57501	605-773-3713	
Web: www.hughescounty.org/					
Hutchinson County 140 Euclid St Rm 36	Olivet	SD	57052	605-387-4215	387-4208
Hyde County PO Box 306	Highmore	SD	57345	605-852-2512	852-2767
Jackson County PO Box 128	Kadoka	SD	57543	605-837-2121	837-2120
Jerauld County PO Box 435	Wessington Springs	SD	57382	605-539-1202	539-1203
Jones County PO Box 448	Murdo	SD	57559	605-669-2361	669-2641
Kingsbury County PO Box 176	De Smet	SD	57231	605-854-3811	854-9080
Lake County 200 E Center St	Madison	SD	57042	605-256-5644	256-5012
Lawrence County 90 Sherman St	Deadwood	SD	57732	605-578-1941	578-1065*
**Fax:* Acctg ■ *Web:* www.lawrence.sd.us					
Lincoln County 100 E 5th St	Canton	SD	57013	605-764-2581	764-5932*
**Fax:* Acctg					
Lyman County PO Box 38	Kennebec	SD	57544	605-869-2247	869-2203*
**Fax:* Acctg					
Marshall County PO Box 130	Britton	SD	57430	605-448-5213	448-5213
McCook County PO Box 504	Salem	SD	57058	605-425-2781	425-3144
McPherson County PO Box 248	Leola	SD	57456	605-439-3361	439-3394
Meade County PO Box 939	Sturgis	SD	57785	605-347-4411	347-3526
Web: www.meadecounty.org					
Mellette County PO Box 257	White River	SD	57579	605-259-3230	259-3030
Miner County PO Box 265	Howard	SD	57349	605-772-4612	772-4412
Web: www.howardsd.com					
Minnehaha County 415 N Dakota Ave	Sioux Falls	SD	57104	605-367-4206	367-8314
Web: www.minnehahacounty.org					
Moody County 101 E Pipestone Ave	Flandreau	SD	57028	605-997-3181	997-3861
Pennington County 315 Saint Joseph St	Rapid City	SD	57701	605-394-2171	394-6833
Web: www.co.pennington.sd.us					
Perkins County PO Box 426	Bison	SD	57620	605-244-5626	244-7110
Potter County 201 S Exene St PO Box 67	Gettysburg	SD	57442	605-765-9472	765-9670
Roberts County 411 2nd Ave E	Sisseton	SD	57262	605-698-7336	698-4277*
**Fax:* Acctg					
Sanborn County PO Box 56	Woonsocket	SD	57385	605-796-4515	796-4502
Shannon County 906 N River St	Hot Springs	SD	57747	605-745-5131	745-5688
Spink County 210 E 7th Ave	Redfield	SD	57469	605-472-1825	472-2410
Stanley County PO Box 595	Fort Pierre	SD	57532	605-223-7780	223-7791
Sully County PO Box 188	Onida	SD	57564	605-258-2535	258-2270
Todd County 200 E 3rd St	Winner	SD	57580	605-842-3727	842-1116
Tripp County 200 E 3rd St	Winner	SD	57580	605-842-2266	842-2267
Turner County PO Box 446	Parker	SD	57053	605-297-3115	297-2115
Union County 209 E Main St Suite 230	Elk Point	SD	57025	605-356-2132	356-3687
Walworth County PO Box 199	Selby	SD	57472	605-649-7878	649-7867*
**Fax:* Acctg					
Yankton County 410 Walnut St	Yankton	SD	57078	605-668-3080	668-5411
Web: www.co.yankton.sd.us					
Ziebach County PO Box 68	Dupree	SD	57623	605-365-5157	365-5204*
**Fax:* Acctg					

Tennessee

	City	State	Zip	Phone	Fax
Anderson County 100 N Main St Rm 111	Clinton	TN	37716	865-457-5400	259-0116
Web: www.andersoncountychamber.org					
Bedford County 104 Northside Sq	Shelbyville	TN	37160	931-684-1921	685-9590
Web: www.shelbyvilletn.com					
Benton County 1 E Court Sq Rm 102	Camden	TN	38320	731-584-6011	584-4640
Bledsoe County 104 N Frazier St	Pikeville	TN	37367	423-447-6855	447-7265
Blount County 341 Court St	Maryville	TN	37804	865-273-5700	273-5705
Web: www.blounttn.org					
Bradley County 155 N Ocoee St	Cleveland	TN	37311	423-728-7226	478-8845
Web: www.bradleyco.net					
Campbell County 195 Kentucky St Suite 2	Jacksboro	TN	37757	423-562-4985	566-3852
Web: co.campbell.tn.us					
Cannon County 1 County Courthouse Public Sq	Woodbury	TN	37190	615-563-4278	563-1289
Carroll County 625 High St Suite 103	Huntingdon	TN	38344	731-986-1961	986-1978
Web: www.carrollcounty-tn-chamber.com					
Carter County 801 E Elk Ave Courthouse Bldg	Elizabethton	TN	37643	423-542-1814	547-1502
Web: www.tourelizabethton.com					
Cheatham County 100 Public Sq Suite 105	Ashland City	TN	37015	615-792-4316	792-2001
Web: www.cheathamcounty.net					
Chester County PO Box 205	Henderson	TN	38340	731-989-2233	989-9602
Claiborne County 1740 Main St	Tazewell	TN	37879	423-626-3284	626-3604
Web: www.claibornecounty.com					
Clay County PO Box 387	Celina	TN	38551	931-243-2161	243-2436
Web: www.dalehollowlake.org/county.htm					
Cocke County 360 E Main St Room 146 Courthouse Annex	Newport	TN	37821	423-623-8791	623-8792
Web: www.cockecounty.com					
Coffee County 1327 McArthur Dr Suite 1	Manchester	TN	37355	931-723-5106	723-8248
Web: www.coffeecountytn.org					
Crockett County 1 S Bells St Suite 3	Alamo	TN	38001	731-696-5460	696-4101
Cumberland County 2 N Main St Suite 206	Crossville	TN	38555	931-484-6442	484-6440
Web: www.crossville-chamber.com					
Davidson County 205 Metro Courthouse	Nashville	TN	37201	615-862-6770	862-6774
Web: www.nashville.gov					
Decatur County PO Box 488	Decaturville	TN	38329	731-852-2131	852-2130
Web: www.decaturcountytn.org					
DeKalb County 1 Public Sq Rm 205	Smithville	TN	37166	615-597-5177	597-1404
Web: www.smithvilletn.com					
Dickson County PO Box 267	Charlotte	TN	37036	615-789-7003	789-6075
Web: www.dicksoncounty.net					
Dyer County PO Box 1360	Dyersburg	TN	38025	731-286-7814	288-7719
Web: www.co.dyer.tn.us					
Fayette County PO Box 218	Somerville	TN	38068	901-465-5213	465-5293
Web: www.fayettecountychamber.com					
Fentress County PO Box 823	Jamestown	TN	38556	931-879-8014	879-8438
Web: www.jamestowntn.org					
Franklin County 1 S Jefferson St	Winchester	TN	37398	931-967-2541	962-3394
Web: www.franklincountychamber.com					
Gibson County 1 Court Sq Suite 100	Trenton	TN	38382	731-855-7642	855-7643
Web: www.gibsoncountytn.com					
Giles County 1 Public Sq	Pulaski	TN	38478	931-363-1509	424-4795
Web: www.gilescounty-tn.us					
Grainger County Hwy 11 W PO Box 126 Courthouse Sq	Rutledge	TN	37861	865-828-3513	828-4284
Web: www.graingertn.com					
Greene County 204 N Cutler St Suite 200	Greeneville	TN	37745	423-798-1708	798-1822
Web: www.greenecountypartnership.com					
Grundy County PO Box 177	Altamont	TN	37301	931-692-3718	692-3721

Tennessee (Cont'd)

	City	State	Zip	Phone	Fax
Hamblen County 511 W 2nd North St	Morristown	TN	37814	423-586-1993	318-2508
Web: www.hamblencountygovernment.us					
Hamilton County 625 Georgia Ave Rm 201	Chattanooga	TN	37402	423-209-6500	209-6501
Web: www.hamiltontn.gov					
Hancock County 418 Harrison St Suite 96	Sneedville	TN	37869	423-733-2519	733-4509
Hardeman County 100 N Main St	Bolivar	TN	38008	731-658-3541	658-3482
Web: www.hardemancotn.org					
Hardin County 465 Main St Courthouse	Savannah	TN	38372	731-925-3921	926-4313
Web: www.tourhardincounty.org					
Hawkins County 110 E Main St	Rogersville	TN	37857	423-272-7002	272-5801
Web: www.hawkinscounty.org					
Haywood County 1 N Washington St	Brownsville	TN	38012	731-772-1432	772-3864
Henderson County 17 Monroe Ave Suite 2	Lexington	TN	38351	731-968-2856	968-6644
Henry County 101 W Washington St Suite 100 PO Box 24	Paris	TN	38242	731-642-2412	644-0947
Web: www.henryco.com					
Hickman County 101 S Public Sq	Centerville	TN	37033	931-729-2621	729-9951
Web: www.hickmanco.com					
Houston County PO Box 388	Erin	TN	37061	931-289-4165	289-2603
Humphreys County Courthouse Annex Rm 1	Waverly	TN	37185	931-296-7795	296-5011
Jackson County PO Box 617	Gainesboro	TN	38562	931-268-9888	268-9060
Web: www.jacksonco.com					
Jefferson County 214 W Main St	Dandridge	TN	37725	865-397-2935	397-3839
Web: www.jefferson-tn-chamber.org					
Johnson County 222 Main St	Mountain City	TN	37683	423-727-9633	727-7047
Web: www.johnsoncountytn.org					
Knox County City-County Bldg 400 Main St Suite 603	Knoxville	TN	37902	865-215-2534	215-2038
Web: www.knoxcounty.org					
Lake County 116 S Court St	Tiptonville	TN	38079	731-253-7582	253-6815
Lauderdale County 100 Court Sq	Ripley	TN	38063	731-635-2561	635-9682
Lawrence County 240 W Gaines St	Lawrenceburg	TN	38464	931-762-7700	766-2291
Web: www.co.lawrence.tn.us					
Lewis County 110 N Park St Rm 108	Hohenwald	TN	38462	931-796-3378	796-6010
Web: www.lewisedc.org					
Lincoln County 112 Main St S	Fayetteville	TN	37334	931-433-2454	433-9304
Web: www.vallnet.com/lincolncounty					
Loudon County 101 Mulberry St Suite 200	Loudon	TN	37774	865-458-2726	458-9891
Web: www.loudoncounty.org					
Macon County County Courthouse Rm 104	Lafayette	TN	37083	615-666-2333	666-2202
Web: www.maconcountytn.com					
Madison County 100 E Main St Rm 105	Jackson	TN	38301	731-423-6022	424-4903
Web: www.co.madison.tn.us					
Marion County 24 Courthouse Sq	Jasper	TN	37347	423-942-2515	942-0815
Web: www.marioncountychamber.com					
Marshall County 1107 Courthouse Annex	Lewisburg	TN	37091	931-359-1072	359-0559
Web: www.marshallcountytn.com					
Maury County 10 Public Sq	Columbia	TN	38401	931-381-3690	381-1016
Web: www.mauryalliance.com					
McMinn County 5 S Hill St Suite A	Athens	TN	37303	423-745-4440	744-1657
Web: www.mcminnco.org					
McNairy County County Courthouse Rm 102	Selmer	TN	38375	731-645-3511	646-1414
Web: www.mcnairy.com					
Meigs County PO Box 218	Decatur	TN	37322	423-334-5747	
Web: www.meigscountytnchamber.org					
Monroe County 103 College St	Madisonville	TN	37354	423-442-2220	442-9542
Web: www.monroegovernment.org					
Montgomery County PO Box 687	Clarksville	TN	37041	931-648-5711	553-5160
Web: www.montgomerycountytn.org					
Moore County PO Box 206	Lynchburg	TN	37352	931-759-7346	759-6394
Web: www.lynchburgtenn.com					
Morgan County 415 Kingston St	Wartburg	TN	37887	423-346-3480	346-4161
Obion County 2 Bill Burnett Cir	Union City	TN	38261	731-885-3831	885-0287
Web: www.obioncountytennessee.com					
Overton County					
317 University St Courthouse Annex Suite 22	Livingston	TN	38570	931-823-2631	823-7036
Perry County PO Box 16	Linden	TN	37096	931-589-2216	589-2215
Web: www.perrycountytennessee.com					
Pickett County 1 Courthouse Sq Suite 201	Byrdstown	TN	38549	931-864-3879	864-7885
Web: www.dalehollow.com/government.htm					
Polk County 6239 Hwy 411	Benton	TN	37307	423-338-4524	338-8611
Web: www.ocoeetn.org					
Putnam County 29 N Washington Ave	Cookeville	TN	38501	931-526-7106	372-8201
Web: www.putnamcountytn.gov					
Rhea County 375 Church St Suite 101	Dayton	TN	37321	423-775-7808	775-7898
Web: www.rheacountyetc.com					
Roane County 200 E Race St	Kingston	TN	37763	865-376-5556	717-4121
Web: www.roanealliance.org					
Robertson County 511 S Brown St	Springfield	TN	37172	615-384-5895	384-2218
Web: www.robertsoncountytn.org					
Rutherford County 319 N Maple St	Murfreesboro	TN	37130	615-898-7799	898-7830
Web: www.rutherfordcounty.org					
Scott County 283 Court St	Huntsville	TN	37756	423-663-2588	663-3969
Web: www.scottcounty.com					
Sequatchie County 307 Cherry St E Rm 6	Dunlap	TN	37327	423-949-2522	949-6316
Web: www.sequatchie.com					
Sevier County 125 Court Ave Suite 202 E	Sevierville	TN	37862	865-453-5502	453-6830
Web: www.seviercountytn.org					
Shelby County 160 N Main St Suite 450	Memphis	TN	38103	901-545-4301	545-4283
Web: www.co.shelby.tn.us					
Smith County 122 Turner High Cir	Carthage	TN	37030	615-735-9833	735-8252
Web: www.smithcountychamber.org					
Stewart County PO Box 67	Dover	TN	37058	931-232-7616	232-4934
Web: www.stewartcountygovernment.com					
Sullivan County 3258 Hwy 126	Blountville	TN	37617	423-323-6428	279-2725
Web: www.sullivancounty.org					
Sumner County 355 N Belvedere Dr	Gallatin	TN	37066	615-452-4063	452-9371
Web: www.sumnertn.org					
Tipton County PO Box 528	Covington	TN	38019	901-476-0207	476-0227
Web: tiptonco.com					
Trousdale County 200 E Main St Rm 2	Hartsville	TN	37074	615-374-2906	374-1100
Unicoi County 100 Main St	Erwin	TN	37650	423-743-9391	743-8007
Web: www.unicoicounty.org					
Union County 901 Main St Suite 119	Maynardville	TN	37807	865-992-8043	992-4992
Web: www.unioncountytn.org					
Van Buren County PO Box 827	Spencer	TN	38585	931-946-2121	946-7572
Warren County 201 Locust St Suite 2P	McMinnville	TN	37110	931-473-2623	473-8622
Web: www.warrentn.com					
Washington County 100 E Main St	Jonesborough	TN	37659	423-753-1621	753-4716
Web: www.washingtoncountytn.com/					
Wayne County PO Box 848	Waynesboro	TN	38485	931-722-3653	722-5994
Web: www.waynecountytn.org					
Weakley County PO Box 587	Dresden	TN	38225	731-364-2285	364-5236
Web: www.weakleycountytn.gov					
White County County Courthouse Rm 205	Sparta	TN	38583	931-836-3203	836-3204
Web: www.sparta-chamber.net					
Williamson County 1320 W Main St PO Box 624	Franklin	TN	37065	615-790-5712	790-5610
Web: www.williamson-tn.org					
Wilson County PO Box 950	Lebanon	TN	37088	615-444-0314	443-2615
Web: www.wilsoncountytn.com					

Texas

	City	State	Zip	Phone	Fax
Anderson County 500 N Church St	Palestine	TX	75801	903-723-7432	723-4625
Web: www.co.anderson.tx.us					
Andrews County 215 NW 1st St Annex Bldg	Andrews	TX	79714	432-524-1426	
Web: www.co.andrews.tx.us					
Angelina County PO Box 908	Lufkin	TX	75902	936-634-8339	634-8460
Web: www.angelinacounty.net					
Aransas County 301 N Live Oak St	Rockport	TX	78382	361-790-0122	790-0119
Web: www.aransascounty.org					
Archer County PO Box 815	Archer City	TX	76351	940-574-4615	574-2432
Web: www.co.archer.tx.us					
Armstrong County PO Box 309	Claude	TX	79019	806-226-2081	226-5301
Web: www.co.armstrong.tx.us					
Atascosa County 1 Courthouse Circle Dr Suite 102	Jourdanton	TX	78026	830-767-2511	769-1021
Web: www.co.atascosa.tx.us					
Austin County 1 E Main St	Bellville	TX	77418	979-865-5911	865-8786
Web: www.austincounty.com					
Bailey County 300 S 1st St	Muleshoe	TX	79347	806-272-3044	272-3538
Web: www.co.bailey.tx.us					
Bandera County 500 Main St PO Box 823	Bandera	TX	78003	830-796-3332	796-8323
Web: www.banderacounty.org					
Bastrop County 804 Pecan St	Bastrop	TX	78602	512-332-7244	332-7249
Web: www.bastropcounty.com					
Baylor County PO Box 689	Seymour	TX	76380	940-889-3322	
Bee County 105 W Corpus Christi St Rm 103	Beeville	TX	78102	361-362-3245	362-3247
Web: www.co.bee.tx.us					
Bell County PO Box 480	Belton	TX	76513	254-933-5160	933-5176
Web: www.bellcountytx.com					
Bexar County 100 Dolorosa St	San Antonio	TX	78205	210-335-2011	335-2252
Web: www.bexar.org					
Blanco County 101 E Pecan Dr Po Box 65	Johnson City	TX	78636	830-868-7357	868-7788
Web: www.co.blanco.tx.us					
Borden County Po Box 156	Gail	TX	79738	806-756-4391	756-4405
Web: www.co.borden.tx.us					
Bosque County PO Box 617	Meridian	TX	76665	254-435-2201	435-2152
Web: users.htcomp.net/bosque					
Bowie County 710 James Bowie Dr	New Boston	TX	75570	903-628-2571	628-6729
Web: www.co.bowie.tx.us					
Brazoria County 111 E Locust St Suite 200	Angleton	TX	77515	979-849-5711	864-1358
Web: www.brazoria-county.com					
Brazos County 300 E 26th St Suite 120	Bryan	TX	77803	979-361-4135	361-4125
Web: www.co.brazos.tx.us					
Brewster County 201 W Ave E	Alpine	TX	79830	432-837-3366	837-6217
Web: www.co.brewster.tx.us					
Briscoe County PO Box 555	Silverton	TX	79257	806-823-2134	823-2359
Web: www.co.briscoe.tx.us					
Brooks County PO Box 427	Falfurrias	TX	78355	361-325-5604	325-4944
Brown County 200 S Broadway	Brownwood	TX	76801	325-643-2594	
Burleson County 100 W Buck St Suite 203	Caldwell	TX	77836	979-567-2329	567-2376
Web: www.co.burleson.tx.us					
Burnet County 220 S Pierce St	Burnet	TX	78611	512-756-5420	756-5410
Web: www.burnetcountytexas.org					
Caldwell County 110 S Main St	Lockhart	TX	78644	512-398-1824	398-1816
Web: www.co.caldwell.tx.us					
Calhoun County 211 S Ann St	Port Lavaca	TX	77979	361-553-4411	553-4420
Web: www.tisd.net/~calhoun/					
Callahan County 100 W 4th St	Baird	TX	79504	325-854-1155	854-1227
Web: www.co.callahan.tx.us					
Cameron County 964 E Harrison St	Brownsville	TX	78520	956-544-0815	544-0813
Web: www.co.cameron.tx.us					
Camp County 126 Church St	Pittsburg	TX	75686	903-856-2731	856-2309
Web: www.co.camp.tx.us					
Carson County PO Box 487	Panhandle	TX	79068	806-537-3873	537-3623
Web: www.co.carson.tx.us					
Cass County PO Box 449	Linden	TX	75563	903-756-5071	756-8057
Web: www.co.cass.tx.us					
Castro County 100 E Bedford St	Dimmitt	TX	79027	806-647-3338	647-5438
Web: www.co.castro.tx.us					
Chambers County 404 Washington Ave	Anahuac	TX	77514	409-267-8309	267-8315
Web: www.co.chambers.tx.us					
Cherokee County PO Box 420	Rusk	TX	75785	903-683-2350	683-5931
Web: www.co.cherokee.tx.us					
Childress County Courthouse Box 4	Childress	TX	79201	940-937-6143	937-3479
Web: www.co.childress.tx.us					
Clay County PO Box 548	Henrietta	TX	76365	940-538-4631	538-5597
Web: www.co.clay.tx.us					
Cochran County County Courthouse Rm 102	Morton	TX	79346	806-266-5450	266-9027
Web: www.co.cochran.tx.us					
Coke County PO Box 150	Robert Lee	TX	76945	325-453-2631	453-2650
Coleman County PO Box 591	Coleman	TX	76834	325-625-2889	
Web: www.co.coleman.tx.us					
Collin County 200 S McDonald St Suite 120	McKinney	TX	75069	972-548-4134	547-5731
Web: www.co.collin.tx.us					
Collingsworth County					
800 West Ave County Courthouse Box 10	Wellington	TX	79095	806-447-2408	447-2409
Web: www.co.collingsworth.tx.us					
Colorado County PO Box 68	Columbus	TX	78934	979-732-2155	732-8852
Web: www.co.colorado.tx.us					
Comal County 150 N Seguin St	New Braunfels	TX	78130	830-620-5513	620-3410
Web: www.co.comal.tx.us					
Comanche County County Courthouse 101 W Central Ave	Comanche	TX	76442	325-356-2655	356-5764
Concho County PO Box 98	Paint Rock	TX	76866	325-732-4322	732-2040
Web: www.co.concho.tx.us					
Cooke County 100 S Dixon St	Gainesville	TX	76240	940-668-5420	668-5440
Web: www.co.cooke.tx.us					
Coryell County 620 E Main St PO Box 237	Gatesville	TX	76528	254-865-5911	865-8631
Web: www.co.coryell.tx.us					
Cottle County PO Box 717	Paducah	TX	79248	806-492-3823	492-2625
Web: www.co.cottle.tx.us					
Crane County 201 W 6th St	Crane	TX	79731	432-558-3581	558-1185
Web: www.co.crane.tx.us					
Crockett County PO Box C	Ozona	TX	76943	325-392-2022	392-3742
Web: www.co.crockett.tx.us					
Crosby County 201 W Aspen St Suite 102	Crosbyton	TX	79322	806-675-2334	
Web: www.co.crosby.tx.us					
Culberson County 300 La Caverna St	Van Horn	TX	79855	432-283-2058	283-9234
Web: www.co.culberson.tx.us					
Dallam County PO Box 1352	Dalhart	TX	79022	806-244-4751	244-3751
Web: www.dallam.org/county/					

Phone Fax

Dallas County 411 Elm St ... Dallas TX 75202 214-653-7361 653-7057
Web: www.dallascounty.org
Dawson County PO Box 1268 ... Lamesa TX 79331 806-872-3778 872-2473
Web: www.co.dawson.tx.us
Deaf Smith County 235 E 3rd St Rm 203 ... Hereford TX 79045 806-363-7077 363-7023
Web: www.co.deaf-smith.tx.us
Delta County 90 Texas Hwy 24 S ... Cooper TX 75432 903-395-4118 395-4455
Denton County 1450 E McKinney ... Denton TX 76209 940-349-2012 349-2019
Web: www.co.denton.tx.us
DeWitt County 307 N Gonzales St ... Cuero TX 77954 361-275-3724 275-8994
Web: www.co.dewitt.tx.us
Dickens County PO Box 120 ... Dickens TX 79229 806-623-5531 623-5319
Dimmit County 103 N 5th St ... Carrizo Springs TX 78834 830-876-2323 876-5036
Web: www.dimmitcountytx.com
Donley County PO Box U ... Clarendon TX 79226 806-874-3436 874-3351
Web: www.donleytx.com
Duval County PO Box 248 ... San Diego TX 78384 361-279-6274
Eastland County PO Box 110 ... Eastland TX 76448 254-629-1583 629-8125
Web: county.eastlandcountytexas.com
Ector County 300 N Grant Ave Rm 111 ... Odessa TX 79761 432-498-4130 498-4177
Web: www.co.ector.tx.us
Edwards County PO Box 184 ... Rocksprings TX 78880 830-683-2235 683-5376
El Paso County 500 E San Antonio Ave ... El Paso TX 79901 915-546-2000 546-2012
Web: www.co.el-paso.tx.us
Ellis County 1201 N Hwy 77 Suite B ... Waxahachie TX 75165 972-825-5071 923-5010
Web: www.co.ellis.tx.us
Erath County 100 W Washington St County Courthouse ... Stephenville TX 76401 254-965-1482 965-5732
Web: www.co.erath.tx.us
Falls County PO Box 458 ... Marlin TX 76661 254-883-1408 883-1406
Fannin County
101 Sam Rayburn Dr County Courthouse Suite 102 ... Bonham TX 75418 903-583-7486 583-7811
Web: www.co.fannin.tx.us
Fayette County PO Box 59 ... La Grange TX 78945 979-968-3251 968-8531
Web: www.co.fayette.tx.us
Fisher County PO Box 368 ... Roby TX 79543 325-776-2401 776-3274
Web: www.co.fisher.tx.us
Floyd County 100 Main St Courthouse Rm 101 ... Floydada TX 79235 806-983-4900 983-4909
Foard County PO Box 539 ... Crowell TX 79227 940-684-1365 684-1947
Fort Bend County 301 Jackson St Suite 101 ... Richmond TX 77469 281-341-8685 341-8669
Web: www.co.fort-bend.tx.us
Franklin County PO Box 68 ... Mount Vernon TX 75457 903-537-4252
Web: www.co.franklin.tx.us
Freestone County PO Box 1010 ... Fairfield TX 75840 903-389-2635 389-6533
Frio County 500 E San Antonio St Rm 6 ... Pearsall TX 78061 830-334-2214 334-0021
Web: www.co.frio.tx.us
Gaines County 101 S Main St Rm 107 ... Seminole TX 79360 432-758-4003 758-1442
Web: www.gainescountyonline.us
Galveston County 722 Moody St ... Galveston TX 77550 409-766-2200 770-5133
Web: www.co.galveston.tx.us
Garza County PO Box 366 ... Post TX 79356 806-495-4430 495-4431
Web: www.garzacounty.net
Gillespie County 101 W Main St Unit 13 ... Fredericksburg TX 78624 830-997-6515 997-9958
Web: www.gillespiecounty.org
Glasscock County 117 E Currie St ... Garden City TX 79739 432-354-2371
Web: www.co.glasscock.tx.us
Goliad County 127 N Courthouse Sq ... Goliad TX 77963 361-645-3294 645-3858
Web: www.goliadcogovt.org
Gonzales County 1709 Sarah Dewitt Dr ... Gonzales TX 78629 830-672-2801 672-2636
Web: www.co.gonzales.tx.us
Gray County PO Box 1902 ... Pampa TX 79066 806-669-8004 669-8054
Web: www.co.gray.tx.us
Grayson County 100 W Houston St ... Sherman TX 75090 903-813-4207 868-9691
Web: www.co.grayson.tx.us
Gregg County PO Box 3049 ... Longview TX 75606 903-236-8430 237-2574
Web: www.co.gregg.tx.us
Grimes County PO Box 209 ... Anderson TX 77830 936-873-2662 873-2056
Web: www.co.grimes.tx.us
Guadalupe County PO Box 990 ... Seguin TX 78156 830-303-4188 401-0300
Web: www.co.guadalupe.tx.us
Hale County 500 Broadway St Suite 140 ... Plainview TX 79072 806-291-5261 291-9810
Web: www.texasonline.net/halecounty/
Hall County 512 Main St County Courthouse ... Memphis TX 79245 806-259-2627 259-5078
Web: www.co.hall.tx.us
Hamilton County County Courthouse ... Hamilton TX 76531 254-386-3518 386-8727
Web: www.co.hamilton.tx.us
Hansford County 15 NW Court ... Spearman TX 79081 806-659-4110 659-4168
Web: www.co.hansford.tx.us
Hardeman County PO Box 30 ... Quanah TX 79252 940-663-2901
Hardin County 300 Monroe St Suite B-110 ... Kountze TX 77625 409-246-5185
Web: www.co.hardin.tx.us
Harris County 201 Caroline St 4th Fl ... Houston TX 77002 713-755-5000
Web: www.co.harris.tx.us
Harrison County PO Box 1365 ... Marshall TX 75671 903-935-8403
Web: www.co.harrison.tx.us
Hartley County PO Box Q ... Channing TX 79018 806-235-3582 235-2316
Web: www.co.hartley.tx.us
Haskell County PO Box 725 ... Haskell TX 79521 940-864-2451 864-6164
Web: www.co.haskell.tx.us
Hays County 110 E Martin Luther King St ... San Marcos TX 78666 512-393-7738 393-7735
Web: www.co.hays.tx.us
Hemphill County PO Box 867 ... Canadian TX 79014 806-323-6212
Henderson County Courthouse Sq Rm 107 ... Athens TX 75751 903-675-6140 675-6105
Web: www.co.henderson.tx.us/
Hidalgo County PO Box 58 ... Edinburg TX 78540 956-318-2100 318-2105
Web: www.co.hidalgo.tx.us
Hill County PO Box 398 ... Hillsboro TX 76645 254-582-4030 582-4003
Web: www.co.hill.tx.us
Hockley County 802 Houston St Suite 213 ... Levelland TX 79336 806-894-4404
Web: www.co.hockley.tx.us
Hood County PO Box 339 ... Granbury TX 76048 817-579-3222 579-3227
Web: www.co.hood.tx.us
Hopkins County PO Box 288 ... Sulphur Springs TX 75483 903-438-4074 438-4110
Web: www.hopkinscountytx.org
Houston County PO Box 370 ... Crockett TX 75835 936-544-3256 544-1954
Web: www.co.houston.tx.us
Howard County 300 Main St ... Big Spring TX 79720 432-264-2213 264-2215
Web: www.co.howard.tx.us
Hudspeth County PO Box 58 ... Sierra Blanca TX 79851 915-369-2301 369-2407
Hunt County PO Box 1316 ... Greenville TX 75403 903-408-4130 408-4287
Web: www.huntcounty.net
Hutchinson County PO Box 1186 ... Stinnett TX 79083 806-878-4002
Web: www.co.hutchinson.tx.us
Irion County PO Box 736 ... Mertzon TX 76941 325-835-2421 835-2008
Web: www.co.irion.tx.us
Jack County 100 Main St ... Jacksboro TX 76458 940-567-2111 567-6641
Jackson County 115 W Main St Rm 101 ... Edna TX 77957 361-782-3563
Web: www.co.jackson.tx.us

Jasper County P121 N Austin St Rm 103 ... Jasper TX 75951 409-384-2632 384-7198
Web: www.co.jasper.tx.us
Jeff Davis County 100 Woodward Ave ... Fort Davis TX 79734 432-426-3251 426-3760
Web: www.co.jeff-davis.tx.us
Jefferson County 114 Pearl St ... Beaumont TX 77701 409-835-8475 839-2394
Web: www.co.jefferson.tx.us
Jim Hogg County PO Box 878 ... Hebbronville TX 78361 361-527-4031 527-5843
Web: www.co.jim-hogg.tx.us
Jim Wells County PO Box 1459 ... Alice TX 78333 361-668-5702
Web: www.co.jim-wells.tx.us
Johnson County PO Box 662 ... Cleburne TX 76033 817-556-6323 556-6327
Web: www.johnsoncountytx.org
Jones County PO Box 552 ... Anson TX 79501 325-823-3762 823-4223
Web: www.co.jones.tx.us
Karnes County 101 N Panna Maria Ave Suite 9 ... Karnes City TX 78118 830-780-3938 780-4576
Web: www.co.karnes.tx.us
Kaufman County 100 W Mulberry St ... Kaufman TX 75142 972-932-4331 932-8018
Web: www.kaufmancounty.net
Kendall County 201 E San Antonio St ... Boerne TX 78006 830-249-9343 249-1763
Web: www.co.kendall.tx.us
Kenedy County PO Box 227 ... Sarita TX 78385 361-294-5220 294-5218
Kent County PO Box 9 ... Jayton TX 79528 806-237-3881 237-2632
Web: www.co.kent.tx.us
Kerr County 700 Main St Rm 122 ... Kerrville TX 78028 830-792-2255 792-2274
Web: www.kerrcounty.org
Kimble County 501 Main St Courthouse ... Junction TX 76849 325-446-3353 446-2986
Web: www.co.kimble.tx.us
King County PO Box 135 ... Guthrie TX 79236 806-596-4412 596-4664
Kinney County PO Box 9 ... Brackettville TX 78832 830-563-2521 563-2644
Web: www.co.kinney.tx.us
Kleberg County PO Box 1327 ... Kingsville TX 78364 361-595-8548 593-1355
Web: www.co.kleberg.tx.us
Knox County PO Box 196 ... Benjamin TX 79505 940-459-2441 459-2005
Web: www.knoxcountytexas.com
La Salle County PO Box 340 ... Cotulla TX 78014 830-879-3033 879-2933
Web: www.lasallecountytx.org
Lamar County 119 N Main St Rm 109 ... Paris TX 75460 903-737-2420 782-1000
Web: 66.165.115.117
Lamb County 100 6th St Rm 103 ... Littlefield TX 79339 806-385-4222 385-6485
Lampasas County 409 Pecan St ... Lampasas TX 76550 512-556-8271
Web: www.co.lampasas.tx.us
Lavaca County 109 N La Grange St ... Hallettsville TX 77964 361-798-3612 798-1610
Web: www.co.lavaca.tx.us
Lee County PO Box 419 ... Giddings TX 78942 979-542-3684 542-2623
Web: www.co.lee.tx.us
Leon County PO Box 98 ... Centerville TX 75833 903-536-2352
Web: www.co.leon.tx.us
Liberty County 1923 Sam Houston St ... Liberty TX 77575 936-336-4600 336-4640
Web: www.co.liberty.tx.us
Limestone County PO Box 350 ... Groesbeck TX 76642 254-729-5504 729-2951
Web: www.co.limestone.tx.us
Lipscomb County 1 Courthouse Sq PO Box 70 ... Lipscomb TX 79056 806-862-3091 862-3004
Web: www.co.lipscomb.tx.us
Live Oak County PO Box 280 ... George West TX 78022 361-449-2733
Web: www.co.live-oak.tx.us
Llano County PO Box 40 ... Llano TX 78643 325-247-4455 247-2406
Web: www.co.llano.tx.us
Loving County 100 Bell St PO Box 194 ... Mentone TX 79754 432-377-2441 377-2701
Web: www.co.loving.tx.us
Lubbock County 904 Broadway St Rm 207 ... Lubbock TX 79401 806-775-1043
Web: www.co.lubbock.tx.us
Lynn County PO Box 937 ... Tahoka TX 79373 806-561-4750 561-4988
Web: www.co.lynn.tx.us
Madison County 101 W Main St Rm 102 ... Madisonville TX 77864 936-348-2638 348-5858
Web: www.co.madison.tx.us
Marion County PO Box 763 ... Jefferson TX 75657 903-665-3971 665-8732
Web: www.co.marion.tx.us
Martin County 301 N Saint Peter St ... Stanton TX 79782 432-756-3412 607-2212
Mason County PO Box 702 ... Mason TX 76856 325-347-5253 347-6868
Web: www.co.mason.tx.us
Matagorda County 1700 7th St Rm 202 ... Bay City TX 77414 979-244-7680 244-7688
Web: www.co.matagorda.tx.us
Maverick County PO Box 4050 ... Eagle Pass TX 78853 830-773-2829 752-4479
Web: www.maverickcounty.org
McCulloch County 199 County Courthouse Sq ... Brady TX 76825 325-597-0733 597-1731
Web: www.co.mcculloch.tx.us
McLennan County PO Box 1727 ... Waco TX 76703 254-757-5078 757-5146
Web: www.co.mclennan.tx.us
McMullen County PO Box 235 ... Tilden TX 78072 361-274-3215 274-3858
Medina County 1100 16th St Rm 109 ... Hondo TX 78861 830-741-6001 741-6015
Menard County PO Box 1038 ... Menard TX 76859 325-396-4682 396-2047
Midland County 200 W Wall Suite 105 ... Midland TX 79701 432-688-4401 688-4925
Web: www.co.midland.tx.us
Milam County 107 W Main St ... Cameron TX 76520 254-697-7049 697-7055
Web: www.co.milam.tx.us
Mills County PO Box 646 ... Goldthwaite TX 76844 325-648-2711 648-3251
Web: www.co.mills.tx.us
Mitchell County 349 Oak St Rm 103 ... Colorado City TX 79512 325-728-3481 728-5322
Montague County PO Box 77 ... Montague TX 76251 940-894-2461 894-3110
Web: www.co.montague.tx.us
Montgomery County PO Box 959 ... Conroe TX 77305 936-539-7885 760-6990
Web: www.co.montgomery.tx.us
Moore County 715 S Dumas Ave Rm 105 ... Dumas TX 79029 806-935-6164 935-9004
Web: www.co.moore.tx.us
Morris County 500 Broadnax St ... Daingerfield TX 75638 903-645-3911 645-5729
Web: www.co.morris.tx.us
Motley County PO Box 660 ... Matador TX 79244 806-347-2621 347-2220
Web: www.co.motley.tx.us
Nacogdoches County 101 W Main St Rm 205 ... Nacogdoches TX 75961 936-560-7733 559-5926
Web: www.co.nacogdoche
Navarro County PO Box 423 ... Corsicana TX 75151 903-654-3036 654-3097
Web: www.co.navarro.tx.us
Newton County 110 Court St ... Newton TX 75966 409-379-5341 379-9049
Web: www.co.newton.tx.us
Nolan County 100 E 3rd St Suite 108 ... Sweetwater TX 79556 325-235-2462 236-9416
Web: www.co.nolan.tx.us
Nueces County 901 Leopard St Suite 201 ... Corpus Christi TX 78401 361-888-0580 888-0329
Web: www.co.nueces.tx.us
Ochiltree County 511 S Main St ... Perryton TX 79070 806-435-8039 435-2081
Web: www.co.ochiltree.tx.us
Oldham County PO Box 360 ... Vega TX 79092 806-267-2667 267-2671
Web: www.co.oldham.tx.us
Orange County 801 Division St ... Orange TX 77631 409-883-7740 882-7012
Web: www.co.orange.tx.us
Palo Pinto County PO Box 219 ... Palo Pinto TX 76484 940-659-1277
Web: www.co.palo-pinto.tx.us

Texas (Cont'd)

	City	State	Zip	Phone	Fax
Panola County 110 Sycamore St Rm 201 *Web:* www.carthagetexas.com	Carthage	TX	75633	903-693-0302	693-2726
Parker County PO Box 819 *Web:* www.co.parker.tx.us	Weatherford	TX	76086	817-594-7461	594-9540
Parmer County PO Box 356 *Web:* www.co.parmer.tx.us	Farwell	TX	79325	806-481-3691	
Pecos County 103 W Callaghan St *Web:* www.co.pecos.tx.us	Fort Stockton	TX	79735	432-336-7555	336-7557
Polk County PO Drawer 2119 *Web:* www.co.polk.tx.us	Livingston	TX	77351	936-327-6804	327-6874
Potter County PO Box 9638 *Web:* www.co.potter.tx.us	Amarillo	TX	79105	806-379-2275	379-2296
Presidio County 320 N Highland Ave *Web:* www.co.presidio.tx.us	Marfa	TX	79843	432-729-4812	729-4313
Rains County PO Box 187 *Web:* www.co.rains.tx.us	Emory	TX	75440	903-474-9999	474-9390
Randall County PO Box 660 *Web:* www.randallcounty.org	Canyon	TX	79015	806-468-5505	468-5509
Reagan County PO Box 100	Big Lake	TX	76932	325-884-2442	884-1503
Real County PO Box 750 *Web:* www.co.real.tx.us	Leakey	TX	78873	830-232-5202	232-6888
Red River County 200 N Walnut St *Web:* www.co.red-river.tx.us	Clarksville	TX	75426	903-427-2401	427-5510
Reeves County 100 E 4th St	Pecos	TX	79772	432-445-5467	445-3997
Refugio County 808 Commerce St PO Box 704 *Web:* www.co.refugio.tx.us	Refugio	TX	78377	361-526-2233	526-1325
Roberts County PO Box 477 *Web:* www.co.roberts.tx.us	Miami	TX	79059	806-868-2341	868-3381
Robertson County PO Box 1029 *Web:* www.co.robertson.tx.us	Franklin	TX	77856	979-828-4130	828-1260
Rockwall County 1101 Ridge Rd Suite 101 *Web:* www.rockwallcountytexas.com	Rockwall	TX	75087	972-882-0220	882-0229
Runnels County PO Box 189 *Web:* www.co.runnels.tx.us	Ballinger	TX	76821	325-365-2720	365-3408
Rusk County 115 N Main St Suite 206 *Web:* www.co.rusk.tx.us	Henderson	TX	75652	903-657-0330	
Sabine County PO Box 580 *Web:* www.sabinecountytexas.com	Hemphill	TX	75948	409-787-3786	787-2044
San Augustine County Courthouse Rm 106 *Web:* www.co.san-augustine.tx.us	San Augustine	TX	75972	936-275-2452	275-9579
San Jacinto County 1 State Hwy 150 Rm 2 *Web:* www.co.san-jacinto.tx.us	Coldspring	TX	77331	936-653-2324	653-8312
San Patricio County PO Box 578 *Web:* www.co.san-patricio.tx.us	Sinton	TX	78387	361-364-6290	364-6112
San Saba County 500 E Wallace St County Courthouse *Web:* www.sansabacounty.org	San Saba	TX	76877	325-372-3614	
Schleicher County PO Drawer 580 *Web:* www.co.schleicher.tx.us	Eldorado	TX	76936	325-853-2833	853-2768
Scurry County 1806 25th St Suite 300 *Web:* www.co.scurry.tx.us	Snyder	TX	79549	325-573-5332	573-7396
Shackelford County PO Box 247 *Web:* www.co.shackelford.tx.us	Albany	TX	76430	325-762-2232	762-2830
Shelby County PO Box 1987 *Web:* www.co.shelby.tx.us	Center	TX	75935	936-598-6361	598-3701
Sherman County PO Box 270 *Web:* www.co.sherman.tx.us	Stratford	TX	79084	806-366-2371	396-5670
Smith County PO Box 1018 *Web:* www.smith-county.com	Tyler	TX	75710	903-535-0630	535-0684
Somervell County PO Box 1098 *Web:* www.glenrose.org	Glen Rose	TX	76043	254-897-4427	897-3233
Starr County County Courthouse Rm 201	Rio Grande City	TX	78582	956-487-2954	487-6227
Stephens County 200 W Walker St *Web:* www.co.stephens.tx.us	Breckenridge	TX	76424	254-559-3700	559-9645
Sterling County PO Box 55 *Web:* www.co.sterling.tx.us	Sterling City	TX	76951	325-378-5191	378-2266
Stonewall County PO Drawer P	Aspermont	TX	79502	940-989-2272	989-2715
Sutton County 300 E Oak St Suite 3 *Web:* www.co.sutton.tx.us	Sonora	TX	76950	325-387-3815	387-6028
Swisher County County Courthouse 119 S Maxwell St *Web:* www.co.swisher.tx.us	Tulia	TX	79088	806-995-3294	995-4121
Tarrant County 100 W Weatherford St *Web:* www.tarrantcounty.com	Fort Worth	TX	76196	817-884-1195	884-3295
Taylor County 300 Oak St *Web:* www.taylorcountytexas.org	Abilene	TX	79602	325-674-1202	674-1279
Terrell County 108 Hackberry St *Web:* www.co.terrell.tx.us	Sanderson	TX	79848	432-345-2391	345-2274
Terry County 500 W Main St Rm 105 *Web:* www.co.terry.tx.us	Brownfield	TX	79316	806-637-8551	637-4874
Throckmorton County PO Box 309 *Web:* www.co.throckmorton.tx.us	Throckmorton	TX	76483	940-849-2501	849-3220
Titus County 100 W 1st Suite 204 *Web:* www.co.titus.tx.us	Mount Pleasant	TX	75455	903-577-6796	572-5078
Tom Green County 124 W Beauregard Ave *Web:* www.co.tom-green.tx.us/county/index.html	San Angelo	TX	76903	325-659-6553	659-3251
Travis County PO Box 1748 *Web:* www.co.travis.tx.us	Austin	TX	78767	512-854-9343	854-9542
Trinity County PO Box 456 *Web:* www.co.trinity.tx.us	Groveton	TX	75845	936-642-1208	642-3004
Tyler County 100 Bluff St Rm 110 *Web:* www.co.tyler.tx.us	Woodville	TX	75979	409-283-2281	283-6305
Upshur County PO Box 730 *Web:* www.countyofupshur.com	Gilmer	TX	75644	903-843-4015	843-5492
Upton County 205 E 10th St *Web:* www.co.upton.tx.us	Rankin	TX	79778	432-693-2861	693-2129
Uvalde County PO Box 284 *Web:* www.uvaldecounty.com	Uvalde	TX	78802	830-278-6614	278-8692
Val Verde County PO Box 1267	Del Rio	TX	78841	830-774-7564	774-7608
Van Zandt County 121 E Dallas St Rm 202 *Web:* www.vanzandtcounty.org	Canton	TX	75103	903-567-6503	567-6722
Victoria County PO Box 1968 *Web:* www.victoriacountytx.org	Victoria	TX	77902	361-575-1478	575-6276
Walker County PO Box 1207 *Web:* www.co.walker.tx.us	Huntsville	TX	77342	936-436-4933	436-4930
Waller County 836 Austin St *Web:* www.wallercounty.org	Hempstead	TX	77445	979-826-3357	826-8317
Ward County County Courthouse 400 S Allen St Suite 101 *Web:* www.co.ward.tx.us	Monahans	TX	79756	432-943-3294	943-6054
Washington County 100 E Main St Suite 102 *Web:* www.co.washington.tx.us	Brenham	TX	77833	979-277-6200	277-6278
Webb County 1000 Houston County Courthouse *Web:* www.webbcounty.com	Laredo	TX	78040	956-721-2500	726-6906
Wharton County PO Box 69 *Web:* www.co.wharton.tx.us	Wharton	TX	77488	979-532-2381	532-8426
Wheeler County PO Box 465 *Web:* www.co.wheeler.tx.us	Wheeler	TX	79096	806-826-5544	826-3282
Wichita County PO Box 1679 *Web:* www.co.wichita.tx.us	Wichita Falls	TX	76307	940-766-8144	716-8554
Wilbarger County 1700 Wilbarger St County Courthouse Rm 15 *Web:* www.co.wilbarger.tx.us	Vernon	TX	76384	940-552-5486	
Willacy County 540 W Hidalgo St 1st Fl	Raymondville	TX	78580	956-689-2710	689-0937
Williamson County 405 ML King St *Web:* www.co.williamson.tx.us	Georgetown	TX	78626	512-930-4300	943-1616
Wilson County PO Box 27	Floresville	TX	78114	830-393-7308	393-7334
Winkler County 100 E Winkler ST *Web:* www.co.wichita.tx.us	Kermit	TX	79745	432-586-3401	
Wise County PO Box 359 *Web:* www.co.wise.tx.us	Decatur	TX	76234	940-627-3351	627-2138
Wood County PO Box 1796 *Web:* www.co.wood.tx.us	Quitman	TX	75783	903-763-2711	763-2902
Yoakum County PO Box 309 *Web:* www.co.yoakum.tx.us	Plains	TX	79355	806-456-2721	456-2258
Young County 516 4th St Rm 104	Graham	TX	76450	940-549-8432	521-0305
Zapata County PO Box 789 *Web:* www.zapatausa.com	Zapata	TX	78076	956-765-9915	765-9933
Zavala County 200 E Uvalde St County Courthouse *Web:* www.co.zavala.tx.us	Crystal City	TX	78839	830-374-2331	374-5955

Utah

	City	State	Zip	Phone	Fax
Beaver County 105 E Center St *Web:* www.beaver.state.ut.us	Beaver	UT	84713	435-438-6463	438-6462
Box Elder County 01 S Main St *Web:* www.boxeldercounty.org	Brigham City	UT	84302	435-734-3300	723-7562
Cache County 179 N Main St Suite 102 *Web:* www.cachecounty.org	Logan	UT	84321	435-716-7150	752-3597
Carbon County 120 E Main St *Web:* www.co.carbon.ut.us	Price	UT	84501	435-636-3200	636-3210
Daggett County 95 N & 100 W PO Box 219 *Web:* www.dsdf.org/county	Manila	UT	84046	435-784-3154	784-3335
Davis County PO Box 618 *Web:* www.co.davis.ut.us	Farmington	UT	84025	801-451-3324	451-3421
Duchesne County 734 N Center St *Web:* www.duchesnegov.net	Duchesne	UT	84021	435-738-1101	738-5522
Emery County 95 E Main *Web:* www.co.emery.ut.us	Castle Dale	UT	84513	435-381-5106	381-5183
Garfield County 55 S Main St *TF:* 800-636-8826 ■ *Web:* www.utahreach.org/garfield/	Panguitch	UT	84759	435-676-8826	676-8239
Grand County 125 E Center St *Web:* www.grandcountyutah.net	Moab	UT	84532	435-259-1321	259-2959
Iron County 68 S 100 East *Web:* www.ironcounty.net	Parowan	UT	84761	435-477-3375	477-8847
Juab County 160 N Main St *Web:* www.co.juab.ut.us	Nephi	UT	84648	435-623-3410	623-5936
Kane County 76 N Main St *Web:* www.kaneutah.com	Kanab	UT	84741	435-644-2458	644-2052
Millard County 765 S Hwy 99 Suite 6 *Web:* www.millardcounty.com	Fillmore	UT	84631	435-743-6223	743-6923
Morgan County PO Box 886 *Web:* www.morgan-county.net	Morgan	UT	84050	801-845-4011	829-6176
Piute County 550 N Main St *Web:* www.millardcounty.com	Junction	UT	84740	435-577-2840	577-2433
Rich County 20 S Main St *Web:* utahreach.org/rich/	Randolph	UT	84064	435-793-2415	793-2410
Salt Lake County 2001 S State St Suite S2200 *Web:* www.co.slc.ut.us	Salt Lake City	UT	84190	801-468-3000	468-3440
San Juan County 117 S Main St *Web:* www.sanjuancounty.org	Monticello	UT	84535	435-587-3223	587-2425
Sanpete County 160 N Main St *Web:* utahreach.org/sanpete/govt/index.htm	Manti	UT	84642	435-835-2131	835-2135
Sevier County 250 N Main St *Web:* www.sevierutah.net	Richfield	UT	84701	435-896-9262	896-8888
Summit County 60 N Main St *Web:* www.co.summit.ut.us	Coalville	UT	84017	435-336-3203	336-3030
Tooele County 47 S Main St *Web:* www.co.tooele.ut.us	Tooele	UT	84074	435-843-3140	882-7317
Uintah County 147 E Main St *TF:* 800-966-4680 ■ *Web:* www.co.uintah.ut.us	Vernal	UT	84078	435-781-0770	781-6701
Utah County 100 E Center St Suite 2300 *Web:* www.co.utah.ut.us	Provo	UT	84606	801-851-8136	851-8146
Wasatch County 25 N Main St *Web:* www.co.wasatch.ut.us	Heber City	UT	84032	435-654-3211	654-9924
Washington County 197 E Tabernacle St *Web:* www.washco.state.ut.us	Saint George	UT	84770	435-634-5700	634-5753
Wayne County 18 S Main St *Web:* www.waynecnty.com	Loa	UT	84747	435-836-2765	836-2479
Weber County 2380 Washington Blvd Suite 350 *Web:* www.co.weber.ut.us	Ogden	UT	84401	801-399-8454	399-8314

Vermont

	City	State	Zip	Phone	Fax
Addison County 7 Mahady Ct *Web:* www.addisoncountychamber.com	Middlebury	VT	05753	802-388-7741	388-4621
Bennington County PO Box 4157 *Web:* www.bennington.com	Bennington	VT	05201	802-447-2700	447-2703
Caledonia County 1126 Main St	Saint Johnsbury	VT	05819	802-748-6600	748-6603
Chittenden County PO Box 187 *Web:* www.ccrpcvt.org/	Burlington	VT	05402	802-863-3467	
Essex County PO Box 75	Guildhall	VT	05905	802-676-3910	676-3463
Franklin County PO Box 808 *Web:* www.stalbanschamber.com	Saint Albans	VT	05478	802-524-3863	
Grand Isle County 9 Hyde Rd PO Box 49	Grand Isle	VT	05458	802-372-8830	372-8815
Lamoille County PO Box 490 *Web:* www.lamoilleeconomy.org	Hyde Park	VT	05655	802-888-2207	
Orange County 5 Court St	Chelsea	VT	05038	802-685-4610	685-3246
Orleans County 247 Main St	Newport	VT	05855	802-334-3344	334-3385
Rutland County 83 Center St Suite 3 *Web:* www.rutlandvermont.com	Rutland	VT	05701	802-775-4394	775-2291
Washington County 65 State St	Montpelier	VT	05602	802-828-2091	
Windham County PO Box 207	Newfane	VT	05345	802-365-7979	365-4360
Windsor County PO Box 458	Woodstock	VT	05091	802-457-2121	457-3446

Virginia

	City	State	Zip	Phone	Fax
Accomack County PO Box 388 *Web:* www.co.accomack.va.us	Accomac	VA	23301	757-787-5700	787-2468

	City	State	ZIP	Phone	Fax
Albemarle County 401 McIntire Rd *Web:* www.albemarle.org	Charlottesville	VA	22902	434-296-5841	296-5800
Alexandria (Independent City) 301 King St Suite 2300 *Web:* ci.alexandria.va.us	Alexandria	VA	22314	703-838-4500	838-6433
Alleghany County 9212 Winterberry Ave Suite C *Web:* www.co.alleghany.va.us	Covington	VA	24426	540-863-6600	863-6606
Amelia County PO Box A *Web:* www.ameliacova.us	Amelia Court House	VA	23002	804-561-3039	561-6039
Amherst County 153 Washington St *Web:* www.countyofamherst.com	Amherst	VA	24521	434-946-9400	946-9370
Appomattox County 297 Court St *Web:* www.appomattox.com	Appomattox	VA	24522	434-352-5275	352-2781
Arlington County 2100 Clarendon Blvd Suite 300 *Web:* www.co.arlington.va.us	Arlington	VA	22201	703-228-3130	228-7430
Augusta County 18 Government Center Ln *Web:* www.co.augusta.va.us	Verona	VA	24482	540-245-5600	245-5621
Bath County PO Box 309 *Web:* www.bathcountyva.org	Warm Springs	VA	24484	540-839-7221	839-7222
Bedford County 122 E Main St Suite 202 *Web:* www.co.bedford.va.us	Bedford	VA	24523	540-586-7601	586-0406
Bedford (Independent City) 215 E Main St *Web:* www.ci.bedford.va.us	Bedford	VA	24523	540-587-6001	586-7134
Bland County PO Box 295 *Web:* www.bland.org	Bland	VA	24315	276-688-4562	688-2438
Botetourt County 1 W Main St 1st Fl *Web:* www.co.botetourt.va.us	Fincastle	VA	24090	540-473-8220	
Bristol (Independent City) 497 Cumberland St Rm 210 *Web:* www.bristolva.org	Bristol	VA	24201	276-645-7321	821-6097
Brunswick County 216 N Main St *Web:* www.tourbrunswick.org	Lawrenceville	VA	23868	434-848-2215	848-4307
Buchanan County PO Box 950	Grundy	VA	24614	276-935-6500	935-4479
Buckingham County PO Box 252	Buckingham	VA	23921	434-969-4242	969-1638
Buena Vista (Independent City) 2039 Sycamore Ave *Web:* www.buenavistavirginia.org	Buena Vista	VA	24416	540-261-8611	261-8727
Campbell County 732 Village Hwy *Web:* www.co.campbell.va.us	Rustburg	VA	24588	434-332-9517	332-9518
Caroline County PO Box 447 *Web:* www.co.caroline.va.us	Bowling Green	VA	22427	804-633-5380	633-4970
Carroll County 605-1 Pine St PO Box 218 *Web:* www.chillsnet.org	Hillsville	VA	24343	276-730-3070	730-3071
Charles City County PO Box 128	Charles City	VA	23030	804-829-9201	829-5819
Charlotte County 125 David Bruce Ave *Web:* www.co.charlotte.va.us	Charlotte Court House	VA	23923	434-542-5147	542-4336
Charlottesville (Independent City) 605 E Main St *Web:* www.charlottesville.org	Charlottesville	VA	22902	434-970-3101	970-3890
Chesapeake (Independent City) 306 Cedar Rd *Web:* www.chesapeake.va.us	Chesapeake	VA	23322	757-382-6151	382-6678
Chesterfield County PO Box 70 *Web:* www.co.chesterfield.va.us	Chesterfield	VA	23832	804-748-1201	751-4993
Clarke County 102 N Church St *Web:* www.co.clarke.va.us	Berryville	VA	22611	540-955-5100	955-4002
Colonial Heights (Independent City) PO Box 3401 *Web:* www.colonial-heights.com	Colonial Heights	VA	23834	804-520-9265	520-9207
Covington (Independent City) 333 W Locust St *Web:* www.covington.va.us	Covington	VA	24426	540-965-6300	965-6303
Craig County 303 Main St *Web:* www.co.craig.va.us	New Castle	VA	24127	540-864-6141	864-7471
Culpeper County 302 N Main St *Web:* www.culpepercounty.gov	Culpeper	VA	22701	540-727-3427	727-3460
Cumberland County 1 Courthouse Cir *Web:* www.cumberlandcounty.virginia.gov	Cumberland	VA	23040	804-492-4280	492-3342
Danville (Independent City) 401 Patton St *Web:* www.ci.danville.va.us	Danville	VA	24544	434-799-5168	799-6502
Dickenson County PO Box 190 *Web:* www.dickensonctyva.com	Clintwood	VA	24228	276-926-1616	926-6465
Dinwiddie County PO Drawer 70 *Web:* www.dinwiddieva.us	Dinwiddie	VA	23841	804-469-4500	469-4503
Emporia (Independent City) 201 S Main St *Web:* www.ci.emporia.va.us	Emporia	VA	23847	434-634-3332	634-0003
Essex County PO Box 445 *Web:* www.essex-virginia.org	Tappahannock	VA	22560	804-443-3541	445-1216
Fairfax County 12000 Government Ctr Pkwy *Web:* www.co.fairfax.va.us	Fairfax	VA	22035	703-324-2531	324-3956
Fairfax (Independent City) 10455 Armstrong St *Web:* www.co.fairfax.va.us	Fairfax	VA	22030	703-385-7936	385-7811
Falls Church (Independent City) 300 Park Ave *Web:* www.ci.falls-church.va.us	Falls Church	VA	22046	703-248-5001	248-5146
Fauquier County 10 Hotel St *Web:* www.fauquiercounty.gov	Warrenton	VA	20186	540-347-8680	349-2331
Floyd County 120 W Oxford St *Web:* www.fin.org	Floyd	VA	24091	540-745-9300	745-9305
Fluvanna County 132 Main St *Web:* www.co.fluvanna.va.us	Palmyra	VA	22963	434-591-1910	591-1911
Franklin County 40 E Court St *Web:* www.franklincountyva.org	Rocky Mount	VA	24151	540-483-3030	483-3035
Franklin (Independent City) 120 Pretlow St *Web:* www.ci.franklin.va.us	Franklin	VA	23851	757-562-8559	562-8561
Frederick County 107 N Kent St *Web:* www.co.frederick.va.us	Winchester	VA	22601	540-665-5600	667-0370
Fredericksburg (Independent City) 715 Princess Ann St *Web:* fredericksburgchamber.org	Fredericksburg	VA	22401	540-372-1010	372-1201
Galax (Independent City) 111 E Grayson St *Web:* www.ingalax.net	Galax	VA	24333	276-236-5773	236-2889
Giles County 501 Wenonah Ave *Web:* www.gilescounty.org	Pearisburg	VA	24134	540-921-1722	921-3825
Gloucester County PO Box 329 *Web:* www.co.gloucester.va.us	Gloucester	VA	23061	804-693-4042	693-6004
Goochland County 1800 Sandy Hook Rd *Web:* www.co.goochland.va.us	Goochland	VA	23063	804-556-5800	556-4617
Grayson County 129 Davis St PO Box 130 *Web:* www.ls.net/~grayson/index.html	Independence	VA	24348	276-773-2231	773-3338
Greene County 22 Court St *Web:* www.gcva.us	Stanardsville	VA	22973	434-985-5208	985-6723
Greensville County 337 S Main St *Web:* www.greensvillecountyva.gov	Emporia	VA	23847	434-348-4215	348-4020
Halifax County 134 S Main St *Web:* www.halifax.com/county	Halifax	VA	24558	434-476-3300	476-3384
Hampton (Independent City) 22 Lincoln St *Web:* www.hampton.va.us	Hampton	VA	23669	757-727-8311	
Hanover County 7516 County Complex Rd PO Box 470 *Web:* www.co.hanover.va.us	Hanover	VA	23069	804-365-6000	365-6234
Harrisonburg (Independent City) 345 S Main St *Web:* www.ci.harrisonburg.va.us	Harrisonburg	VA	22801	540-432-7701	432-7778
Henrico County PO Box 27032 *Web:* www.co.henrico.va.us	Richmond	VA	23273	804-501-4202	501-5214
Henry County PO Box 7 *Web:* www.martinsville.com	Collinsville	VA	24078	276-634-4601	634-4781

	City	State	ZIP	Phone	Fax
Highland County Main St PO Box 190 *Web:* www.highlandcova.org	Monterey	VA	24465	540-468-2447	468-3447
Hopewell (Independent City) 300 N Main St *Web:* www.ci.hopewell.va.us	Hopewell	VA	23860	804-541-2243	541-2248
Isle of Wight County PO Box 80 *Web:* www.co.isle-of-wight.va.us	Isle of Wight	VA	23397	757-365-6204	357-9171
James City County PO Box 8784 *Web:* www.james-city.va.us	Williamsburg	VA	23187	757-253-6728	253-6833
King George County 9483 Kings Hwy Suite 3 *Web:* www.king-george.va.us	King George	VA	22485	540-775-3322	775-5466
King & Queen County PO Box 177 *Web:* www.kingandqueenco.net	King & Queen Court House	VA	23085	804-785-5975	785-5999
King William County PO Box 215 *Web:* www.co.king-william.va.us	King William	VA	23086	804-769-4927	769-4964
Lancaster County PO Box 99 *Web:* www.lancova.com	Lancaster	VA	22503	804-462-5611	
Lee County PO Box 367 *Web:* www.leecountyvachamber.org	Jonesville	VA	24263	276-346-7714	346-7712
Lexington (Independent City) 300 E Washington St *Web:* www.ci.lexington.va.us	Lexington	VA	24450	540-463-7133	463-5310
Loudoun County 1 Harrison St SE PO Box 7000 *Web:* www.co.loudoun.va.us	Leesburg	VA	20177	703-777-0200	777-0325
Louisa County 1 Woolfolk Ave *Web:* www.louisacounty.com	Louisa	VA	23093	540-967-0401	967-3411
Lunenburg County 11435 Courthouse Rd *Web:* www.lunenburgva.org	Lunenburg	VA	23952	434-696-2230	696-3931
Lynchburg (Independent City) 900 Church St *Web:* www.ci.lynchburg.va.us	Lynchburg	VA	24504	434-847-1443	847-1536
Madison County 1 Main St *Web:* www.madison-va.com	Madison	VA	22727	540-948-6888	948-3759
Manassas (Independent City) PO Box 560 *Web:* www.manassascity.org	Manassas	VA	20108	703-257-8200	335-0042
Manassas Park (Independent City) 1 Park Center Ct *Web:* www.cityofmanassaspark.us	Manassas Park	VA	20111	703-335-8800	335-0053
Martinsville (Independent City) PO Box 1112 *Web:* www.ci.martinsville.va.us	Martinsville	VA	24114	276-656-5180	403-5280
Mathews County PO Box 463 *Web:* www.co.mathews.va.us	Mathews	VA	23109	804-725-2550	725-7456
Mecklenburg County 393 Washington St *Web:* www.mecklenburgva.com	Boydton	VA	23917	434-738-6191	738-6861
Middlesex County PO Box 158 *Web:* www.co.middlesex.va.us	Saluda	VA	23149	804-758-5317	758-8637
Montgomery County 755 Roanoke St *Web:* www.montva.com	Christiansburg	VA	24073	540-382-6954	382-6943
Nelson County 84 Courthouse Sq *Web:* www.nelsoncounty.com	Lovingston	VA	22949	434-263-7000	263-7004
New Kent County PO Box 98 *Web:* www.newkent.com	New Kent	VA	23124	804-966-9520	966-9528
Newport News (Independent City) 2400 Washington Ave *Web:* www.newport-news.va.us	Newport News	VA	23607	757-926-8411	926-3503
Norfolk (Independent City) 810 Union St Rm 1101 *Web:* www.norfolk.gov	Norfolk	VA	23510	757-664-4242	664-4239
Northampton County PO Box 36 *Web:* www.co.northampton.va.us	Eastville	VA	23347	757-678-0465	678-5410
Northumberland County PO Box 217 *Web:* www.co.northumberland.va.us	Heathsville	VA	22473	804-580-3700	580-2261
Norton (Independent City) PO Box 618 *Web:* www.nortonva.org	Norton	VA	24273	276-679-1160	679-3510
Nottoway County 325 W Court House Rd	Nottoway	VA	23955	434-645-9043	645-2201
Orange County 112 W Main St Suite 202 PO Box 111 *Fax Area Code: 276 ■ *Web:* www.orangecova.com	Orange	VA	22960	540-672-3313	672-1679*
Page County 117 S Court St *Web:* www.co.page.va.us	Luray	VA	22835	540-743-4142	743-4533
Patrick County PO Box 148 *Web:* www.co.patrick.va.us	Stuart	VA	24171	276-694-7213	694-6943
Petersburg (Independent City) City Hall 135 N Union St *Web:* www.petersburg-va.org	Petersburg	VA	23803	804-733-2301	732-9212
Pittsylvania County 11 Bank St 2nd Fl *Web:* www.pittgov.org	Chatham	VA	24531	434-432-7879	432-7915
Poquoson (Independent City) 500 City Hall Ave *Web:* www.ci.poquoson.va.us	Poquoson	VA	23662	757-868-3000	868-3101
Portsmouth (Independent City) PO Box 820 *Web:* www.portsmouth.va.us	Portsmouth	VA	23705	757-393-8746	393-5378
Powhatan County PO Box 37 *Web:* www.powhatanva.com	Powhatan	VA	23139	804-598-5660	598-5608
Prince Edward County 111 South St *Web:* www.co.prince-edward.va.us	Farmville	VA	23901	434-392-5145	
Prince George County 6602 Courts Dr PO Box 68 *Web:* www.princegeorgeva.org	Prince George	VA	23875	804-733-2600	732-3604
Prince William County 1 County Complex Ct *Web:* www.pwcgov.org	Prince William	VA	22192	703-792-6600	792-7484
Pulaski County 143 3rd St NW Suite 1 *Web:* www.pulaskicounty.org	Pulaski	VA	24301	540-980-7705	980-7717
Radford (Independent City) 619 2nd St *Web:* www.radford.va.us	Radford	VA	24141	540-731-3603	731-3699
Rappahannock County 290 Gay St PO Box 519 *Web:* www.rappahannockcountyva.gov	Washington	VA	22747	540-675-5330	675-3698
Richmond County 101 Court Cir *Web:* www.co.richmond.va.us	Warsaw	VA	22572	804-333-3781	333-5396
Richmond (Independent City) 900 E Broad St Rm 201 *Web:* www.ci.richmond.va.us	Richmond	VA	23219	804-780-7970	646-7987
Roanoke County 5204 Bernard Dr *Web:* www.co.roanoke.va.us	Roanoke	VA	24018	540-772-2006	772-2193
Roanoke (Independent City) 215 Church Ave SW *Web:* www.roanokeva.gov	Roanoke	VA	24011	540-853-2000	853-1138
Rockbridge County 150 S Main St *Web:* www.co.rockbridge.va.us	Lexington	VA	24450	540-463-4361	463-5981
Rockingham County Court Sq *Web:* www.co.rockingham.va.us	Harrisonburg	VA	22801	540-564-3000	564-3127
Russell County 121 E Main St PO Box 1208 *Web:* www.russellcountyva.org	Lebanon	VA	24266	276-889-8000	889-8011
Salem (Independent City) 114 N Broad St *Web:* www.ci.salem.va.us	Salem	VA	24153	540-375-3016	375-4048
Scott County 112 Water St Suite 1 *Web:* www.scottcountyva.com	Gate City	VA	24251	276-386-6521	386-9198
Shenandoah County 600 N Main St Suite 102 *Web:* www.co.shenandoah.va.us	Woodstock	VA	22664	540-459-6165	459-6168
Smyth County 109 W Main St Rm 144 *Web:* www.smythcounty.org	Marion	VA	24354	276-782-4044	782-4045
Southampton County PO Box 190 *Web:* www.southamptoncounty.org	Courtland	VA	23837	757-653-2200	653-2547
Spotsylvania County 1905 Courthouse Rd *Web:* www.spotsylvania.va.us	Spotsylvania	VA	22553	540-582-7010	582-9308
Stafford County 1300 Court House Rd *Web:* www.co.stafford.va.us	Stafford	VA	22554	540-658-8605	658-7643
Staunton (Independent City) 116 W Beverly St *Web:* www.staunton.va.us	Staunton	VA	24401	540-332-3800	332-3807

Virginia (Cont'd)

				Phone	Fax
Suffolk (Independent City) 441 Market St *Web:* www.suffolk.va.us	Suffolk	VA	23434	757-923-2085	923-2091
Surry County PO Box 65 *Web:* www.surrycounty.govoffice2.com	Surry	VA	23883	757-294-5271	294-5204
Sussex County 20233 Thornton Sq *Web:* sussexcounty.govoffice.com	Sussex	VA	23884	434-246-5511	246-6013
Tazewell County PO Box 968 *Web:* www.tazewellcounty.org	Tazewell	VA	24651	276-988-1222	988-7501
Virginia Beach (Independent City) 2401 Courthouse Dr Municipal Ctr Bldg 1 *Web:* www.vbgov.com	Virginia Beach	VA	23456	757-427-4242	427-5626
Warren County 220 N Commerce Ave Suite 100 *Web:* www.warrencountyva.net	Front Royal	VA	22630	540-636-4600	636-6066
Washington County 205 Academy Dr *Web:* www.washcova.com	Abingdon	VA	24210	276-676-6202	676-6201
Waynesboro (Independent City) 503 W Main St *Web:* www.waynesboro.va.us	Waynesboro	VA	22980	540-942-6600	942-6671
Westmoreland County PO Box 1000 *Web:* www.westmoreland-county.org	Montross	VA	22520	804-493-0130	493-0134
Williamsburg (Independent City) 401 Lafayette St *Web:* www.ci.williamsburg.va.us	Williamsburg	VA	23185	757-220-6100	220-6107
Winchester (Independent City) 5 N Kent St *Web:* www.ci.winchester.va.us	Winchester	VA	22601	540-667-5770	545-8711
Wise County PO Box 570 *Web:* www.wisecounty.org	Wise	VA	24293	276-328-2321	328-9780
Wythe County 340 S 6th St *Web:* www.wytheco.org	Wytheville	VA	24382	276-223-6020	223-6030
York County 300 Ballard St PO Box 316 *Web:* www.co.york.va.us	Yorktown	VA	23690	757-890-3450	890-3459

Washington

				Phone	Fax
Adams County 210 W Broadway *Web:* www.co.adams.wa.us	Ritzville	WA	99169	509-659-3257	659-0118
Asotin County 135 2nd St *Web:* www.co.asotin.wa.us	Asotin	WA	99402	509-243-2081	243-4978
Benton County 7122 W Okanogan Pl MS C *Web:* www.co.benton.wa.us	Kennewick	WA	99336	509-735-8388	
Chelan County 350 Orondo Ave *Web:* www.co.chelan.wa.us	Wenatchee	WA	98801	509-667-6380	667-6611
Clallam County 223 E 4th St Suite 2 *Web:* www.clallam.net	Port Angeles	WA	98362	360-452-7831	417-2493
Clark County 1200 Franklin St *Web:* www.co.clark.wa.us	Vancouver	WA	98660	360-397-2000	397-6099
Columbia County 341 E Main St *Web:* www.columbiaco.com	Dayton	WA	99328	509-382-4542	382-2490
Cowlitz County 312 SW 1st Ave *Web:* www.co.cowlitz.wa.us	Kelso	WA	98626	360-577-3016	577-2323
Douglas County 203 Ranier St *Web:* www.douglascountywa.net	Waterville	WA	98858	509-745-8537	745-9045
Ferry County 290 E Tessie Ave *Web:* www.ferry-county.com	Republic	WA	99166	509-775-5229	775-5230
Franklin County 1016 N 4th Ave *Web:* www.co.franklin.wa.us	Pasco	WA	99301	509-545-3535	545-3573
Garfield County 789 Main St *Web:* www.palouse.org/garfield.htm	Pomeroy	WA	99347	509-843-3731	843-1224
Grant County 35 C St NW *Web:* www.co.grant.wa.us	Ephrata	WA	98823	509-754-2011	754-6098
Grays Harbor County 102 W Broadway St Rm 203 *Web:* www.co.grays-harbor.wa.us	Montesano	WA	98563	360-249-3842	249-6381
Island County PO Box 5000 *Web:* www.islandcounty.net	Coupeville	WA	98239	360-679-7354	679-7381
Jefferson County PO Box 1220 *Web:* www.co.jefferson.wa.us	Port Townsend	WA	98368	360-385-9100	385-9382
King County 701 5th Ave Suite 3210 *TF:* 800-325-6165 ■ *Web:* www.metrokc.gov	Seattle	WA	98104	206-296-4040	296-0194
Kitsap County 614 Division St MS 4 *Web:* www.kitsapgov.com	Port Orchard	WA	98366	360-337-7146	337-4632
Kittitas County 205 W 5th Ave Rm 108 *Web:* www.co.kittitas.wa.us	Ellensburg	WA	98926	509-962-7508	962-7679
Klickitat County 205 S Columbus Ave Rm 204 MS CH3 *Web:* www.klickitatcounty.org	Goldendale	WA	98620	509-773-5744	773-4559
Lewis County 360 NW North St *Web:* fortress.wa.gov/lewisco/home	Chehalis	WA	98532	360-748-9121	748-1639
Lincoln County 450 Logan St *Web:* www.co.lincoln.wa.us	Davenport	WA	99122	509-725-1401	725-1150
Mason County PO Box 340 *Web:* www.co.mason.wa.us	Shelton	WA	98584	360-427-9670	
Okanogan County 149 N 3rd St *Web:* www.okanogancounty.org	Okanogan	WA	98840	509-422-7275	422-7277
Pacific County PO Box 67 *Web:* www.co.pacific.wa.us	South Bend	WA	98586	360-875-9300	875-9321
Pend Oreille County 229 S Garden Ave *Web:* www.co.pend-oreille.wa.us	Newport	WA	99156	509-447-2435	447-2734
Pierce County 930 Tacoma Ave S Rm 110 *Web:* www.co.pierce.wa.us	Tacoma	WA	98402	253-798-3495	798-3428
San Juan County 350 Court St Rm 7 *Web:* www.co.san-juan.wa.us	Friday Harbor	WA	98250	360-378-2163	378-3967
Skagit County 205 W Kincaid St Rm 103 *Web:* www.skagitcounty.net	Mount Vernon	WA	98273	360-336-9440	
Skamania County 240 Vancouver Ave *Web:* www.skamaniacounty.org	Stevenson	WA	98648	509-427-9430	427-7386
Snohomish County 3000 Rockefeller Ave MS 605 *Web:* www1.co.snohomish.wa.us	Everett	WA	98201	425-388-3466	388-3806
Spokane County 1116 W Broadway Ave *Web:* www.spokanecounty.org	Spokane	WA	99260	509-477-2265	477-2274
Stevens County 215 S Oak St *Web:* www.co.stevens.wa.us	Colville	WA	99114	509-684-3751	684-8310
Thurston County 2000 Lakeridge Dr SW Bldg 2 *Web:* www.co.thurston.wa.us	Olympia	WA	98502	360-786-5430	753-4033
Wahkiakum County PO Box 116 *Web:* www.co.wahkiakum.wa.us	Cathlamet	WA	98612	360-795-3558	795-8813
Walla Walla County 315 W Main St *Web:* www.co.walla-walla.wa.us	Walla Walla	WA	99362	509-527-3200	527-3235
Whatcom County 311 Grand Ave Rm 301 *Web:* www.co.whatcom.wa.us	Bellingham	WA	98225	360-676-6777	676-6693
Whitman County 400 N Main St *Web:* www.co.whitman.wa.us	Colfax	WA	99111	509-397-4622	397-6355
Yakima County 128 N 2nd St Rm 323 *Web:* www.co.yakima.wa.us	Yakima	WA	98901	509-574-1430	574-1473

West Virginia

				Phone	Fax
Barbour County 8 N Main St	Philippi	WV	26416	304-457-2232	457-2790
Berkeley County 100 W King St Rm 1 *Web:* www.berkeleycountycomm.org	Martinsburg	WV	25401	304-264-1925	267-1794
Boone County 200 State St *Web:* www.boonecountywv.org	Madison	WV	25130	304-369-3925	369-7329
Braxton County 300 Main St PO Box 486 *Web:* www.braxtonwv.org/CourtHouse.htm	Sutton	WV	26601	304-765-2833	765-2093
Brooke County 632 Main St	Wellsburg	WV	26070	304-737-3661	737-4023
Cabell County 750 5th Ave Rm 108 *Web:* www.cabellcounty.org	Huntington	WV	25701	304-526-8625	526-8632
Calhoun County PO Box 230	Grantsville	WV	26147	304-354-6725	354-6725
Clay County PO Box 190	Clay	WV	25043	304-587-4259	587-7329
Doddridge County 118 E Court St Rm 102	West Union	WV	26456	304-873-2631	873-1840
Fayette County 100 Court St *Web:* www.fayettecounty.com	Fayetteville	WV	25840	304-574-4348	574-4314
Gilmer County 10 Howard St	Glenville	WV	26351	304-462-7641	462-8855
Grant County 5 Highland Ave *Web:* www.grantcounty-wv.com	Petersburg	WV	26847	304-257-4422	257-9645
Greenbrier County PO Box 506 *Web:* www.greenbrierwv.com	Lewisburg	WV	24901	304-647-6602	647-6694
Hampshire County PO Box 806 *Web:* www.co.hampshire.wv.us	Romney	WV	26757	304-822-5112	822-4039
Hancock County PO Box 367	New Cumberland	WV	26047	304-564-3311	564-5941
Hardy County 204 Washington St Rm 111 *Web:* hardycountywv.com	Moorefield	WV	26836	304-530-0250	530-0251
Harrison County 301 W Main St County Courthouse *Web:* www.harrisoncountywv.com	Clarksburg	WV	26301	304-624-8611	624-8575
Jackson County PO Box 800	Ripley	WV	25271	304-372-2011	372-1107
Jefferson County PO Box 208 *Web:* www.jeffersoncountywv.org	Charles Town	WV	25414	304-728-3215	728-1957
Kanawha County 409 Virginia St E *Web:* www.kanawha.us	Charleston	WV	25301	304-357-0130	357-0585
Lewis County 110 Center Ave PO Box 87 *Web:* www.stonewallcountry.com	Weston	WV	26452	304-269-8215	269-8202
Lincoln County PO Box 497 *Web:* www.co.lincoln.wv.us	Hamlin	WV	25523	304-824-7990	824-2444
Logan County 300 Stratton St Rm 101 *Web:* www.logancountychamberofcommerce.com	Logan	WV	25601	304-792-8600	792-8621
Marion County PO Box 1267 *Web:* www.marioncountywv.com	Fairmont	WV	26555	304-367-5440	367-5448
Marshall County PO Box 459 *Web:* www.marshallcountytourism.com	Moundsville	WV	26041	304-845-1220	845-5891
Mason County 200 6th St	Point Pleasant	WV	25550	304-675-1110	675-4982
McDowell County 90 Wyoming St Suite 109	Welch	WV	24801	304-436-8544	436-8576
Mercer County 1501 Main St *Web:* www.mccvb.com	Princeton	WV	24740	304-487-8311	487-9842
Mineral County 150 Armstrong St *Web:* www.mineralcountywv.com	Keyser	WV	26726	304-788-3924	788-4109
Mingo County PO Box 1197	Williamson	WV	25661	304-235-0381	235-0365
Monongalia County 243 High St Rm 123 *Web:* www.co.monongalia.wv.us	Morgantown	WV	26505	304-291-7230	291-7233
Monroe County PO Box 350 *Web:* www.travelmonroe.com	Union	WV	24983	304-772-3096	772-4191
Morgan County 77 Fairfax St Suite 1A *Web:* www.morgancountyeda.com/gov	Berkeley Springs	WV	25411	304-258-8547	258-8545
Nicholas County 700 Main St Suite 2	Summersville	WV	26651	304-872-7848	872-9600
Ohio County 1500 Chapline St Rm 205	Wheeling	WV	26003	304-234-3656	234-3829
Pendleton County PO Box 1167 *Web:* www.pendletoncounty.net/pccom/	Franklin	WV	26807	304-358-2505	358-2473
Pleasants County 301 Court Ln Rm 101	Saint Marys	WV	26170	304-684-7542	684-7569
Pocahontas County 900C 10th Ave *Web:* www.pocahontascountywv.com	Marlinton	WV	24954	304-799-4549	799-6947
Preston County 101 W Main St Rm 201	Kingwood	WV	26537	304-329-0070	329-0198
Putnam County 3389 Winfield Rd *Web:* www.putnamcounty.org	Winfield	WV	25213	304-586-0202	586-0280
Raleigh County 215 Main St	Beckley	WV	25801	304-255-9126	255-9355
Randolph County PO Box 368	Elkins	WV	26241	304-636-0543	636-0544
Ritchie County 115 E Main St Rm 201	Harrisville	WV	26362	304-643-2164	643-2906
Roane County 200 Main St	Spencer	WV	25276	304-927-2860	927-2489
Summers County PO Box 97 *Web:* www.summerscvb.com	Hinton	WV	25951	304-466-7104	466-7146
Taylor County 214 W Main St	Grafton	WV	26354	304-265-1401	265-3016
Tucker County 215 1st St Suite 3 *Web:* www.canaanvalley.org	Parsons	WV	26287	304-478-2414	478-2217
Tyler County PO Box 66	Middlebourne	WV	26149	304-758-2102	758-2126
Upshur County 40 W Main St Rm 101 *Web:* www.buchamber.com	Buckhannon	WV	26201	304-472-1068	472-1029
Wayne County PO Box 248	Wayne	WV	25570	304-272-6369	272-5318
Webster County 2 Court Sq Rm G1 *Web:* www.websterwv.com	Webster Springs	WV	26288	304-847-2508	847-5780
Wetzel County PO Box 156	New Martinsville	WV	26155	304-455-8224	455-5256
Wirt County PO Box 53	Elizabeth	WV	26143	304-275-4271	275-3418
Wood County PO Box 1474 *Web:* www.woodcountywv.com	Parkersburg	WV	26102	304-424-1850	424-1864
Wyoming County PO Box 309	Pineville	WV	24874	304-732-8000	732-9659

Wisconsin

				Phone	Fax
Adams County PO Box 278 *Web:* www.adamscountywi.com	Friendship	WI	53934	608-339-4200	339-4514
Ashland County 201 W Main St Rm 202 *Web:* www.co.ashland.wi.us	Ashland	WI	54806	715-682-7000	682-7032
Barron County 330 E LaSalle Ave Rm 210 *Web:* www.co.barron.wi.us	Barron	WI	54812	715-537-6200	537-6277
Bayfield County PO Box 878 *Web:* www.bayfieldcounty.org	Washburn	WI	54891	715-373-6100	373-6153
Brown County 305 E Walnut Suite 120 *Web:* www.co.brown.wi.us	Green Bay	WI	54301	920-448-4016	448-4498
Buffalo County 407 S 2nd St *Web:* www.buffalocounty.com	Alma	WI	54610	608-685-6209	685-6213
Burnett County 7410 County Rd K Box 115 *Web:* www.burnettcounty.com/gov	Siren	WI	54872	715-349-2147	349-7659
Calumet County 206 Court St *Web:* www.co.calumet.wi.us	Chilton	WI	53014	920-849-2361	849-1469
Chippewa County 711 N Bridge St *Web:* www.co.chippewa.wi.us	Chippewa Falls	WI	54729	715-726-7980	726-7987
Clark County 517 Court St *Web:* www.co.clark.wi.us	Neillsville	WI	54456	715-743-5148	743-5154
Columbia County PO Box 177 *Web:* www.co.columbia.wi.us	Portage	WI	53901	608-742-9654	742-9602
Crawford County 220 N Beaumont Rd *Web:* www.wisconline.com/counties/crawford/	Prairie du Chien	WI	53821	608-326-0200	326-0213

Phone Fax

Dane County 210 ML King Jr Blvd Rm 112 Madison WI 53703 608-266-4121
Web: www.co.dane.wi.us
Dodge County 127 E Oak St Juneau WI 53039 920-386-3602 386-3928
Web: www.co.dodge.wi.us
Door County PO Box 670 Sturgeon Bay WI 54235 920-746-2200 746-2330
Web: www.co.door.wi.gov
Douglas County 1313 Belknap St Superior WI 54880 715-395-1341 395-1421
Web: www.douglascountywi.org
Dunn County 800 Wilson Ave Menomonie WI 54751 715-232-1677 232-2534
Web: dunncountywi.govoffice2.com
Eau Claire County 721 Oxford Ave Eau Claire WI 54703 715-839-4803 839-4854
Web: www.co.eau-claire.wi.us
Florence County PO Box 410 Florence WI 54121 715-528-3201 528-4762
Web: www.florencewisconsin.com
Fond du Lac County PO Box 1557 Fond du Lac WI 54936 920-929-3000 929-3293
Web: www.co.fond-du-lac.wi.us
Forest County 200 E Madison St Crandon WI 54520 715-478-2422 478-5175
Web: www.forestcountywi.com
Grant County 111 S Jefferson St Lancaster WI 53813 608-723-2675 723-4048
Web: grantcounty.org/govt/index.html
Green County 1016 16th Ave Monroe WI 53566 608-328-9430 328-2835
Web: greencounty.org
Green Lake County PO Box 3188 Green Lake WI 54941 920-294-4005 294-4009
Web: www.co.green-lake.wi.us
Iowa County 222 N Iowa St Suite 102 Dodgeville WI 53533 608-935-5445 935-3024
Web: www.iowacounty.org
Iron County 300 Taconite St Hurley WI 54534 715-561-3375 561-2928
Web: www.ironcountywi.com
Jackson County 307 Main St Black River Falls WI 54615 715-284-0208 284-0270
Web: www.co.jackson.wi.us
Jefferson County 320 S Main St Rm 109 Jefferson WI 53549 920-674-7140 674-7368
Web: www.co.jefferson.wi.us
Juneau County 220 E State St Mauston WI 53948 608-847-9300 847-9402
Web: www.juneaucounty.com
Kenosha County 1010 56th St Kenosha WI 53140 262-653-2552 653-2564
Web: www.co.kenosha.wi.us
Kewaunee County 613 Dodge St Kewaunee WI 54216 920-388-7144 388-3199
Web: www.kewauneeco.org
La Crosse County 400 N 4th St Rm 1210 La Crosse WI 54601 608-785-9581 785-9741
Web: www.co.la-crosse.wi.us
Lafayette County 626 Main St PO Box 40 Darlington WI 53530 608-776-4850 776-8893
Web: www.co.lafayette.wi.gov
Langlade County 800 Clermont St Antigo WI 54409 715-627-6200 627-6303
Web: www.co.langlade.wi.us
Lincoln County 1110 E Main St Merrill WI 54452 715-536-0312 536-6528
Web: www.co.lincoln.wi.us
Manitowoc County PO Box 2000 Manitowoc WI 54221 920-683-4030 683-2733
Web: www.co.manitowoc.wi.us
Marathon County 500 Forest St Wausau WI 54403 715-261-1500 261-1515
Web: www.co.marathon.wi.us
Marinette County 1926 Hall Ave Marinette WI 54143 715-732-7406 732-7532
Web: www.marinettecounty.com
Marquette County PO Box 186 Montello WI 53949 608-297-9136 297-7609
Web: www.co.marquette.wi.us
Menominee County PO Box 279 Keshena WI 54135 715-799-3311 799-1322
Web: www.wisconline.com/counties/menominee/
Milwaukee County 901 N 9th St Milwaukee WI 53233 414-278-4067 278-4075
Web: www.co.milwaukee.wi.us
Monroe County 202 S 'K' St Sparta WI 54656 608-269-8705 269-8747
Web: www.co.monroe.wi.us
Oconto County 301 Washington St Oconto WI 54153 920-834-6800 834-6867
Web: www.co.oconto.wi.us
Oneida County PO Box 400 Rhinelander WI 54501 715-369-6144 369-6230
Web: www.co.oneida.wi.gov
Outagamie County 410 S Walnut St Appleton WI 54911 920-832-5077 832-2200
Web: www.co.outagamie.wi.us
Ozaukee County PO Box 994 Port Washington WI 53074 262-284-8110 284-8100
Web: www.co.ozaukee.wi.us
Pepin County 740 7th Ave W Durand WI 54736 715-672-8857 672-8677
Web: www.co.pepin.wi.us
Pierce County 414 W Main St PO Box 119 Ellsworth WI 54011 715-273-6796 273-6861
Web: www.co.pierce.wi.us
Polk County 100 Polk County Plaza Suite 110 Balsam Lake WI 54810 715-485-9271 485-9104
Web: www.co.polk.wi.us
Portage County 1516 Church St Stevens Point WI 54481 715-346-1351 346-1486
Web: www.co.portage.wi.us
Price County 126 Cherry St Phillips WI 54555 715-339-3325 339-3089
Web: www.co.price.wi.us
Racine County 730 Wisconsin Ave Racine WI 53403 262-636-3121 636-3491
Web: www.racineco.com
Richland County 181 W Seminary St PO Box 310 Richland Center WI 53581 608-647-2197 647-6134
Web: www.co.richland.wi.us
Rock County 51 S Main St Janesville WI 53545 608-757-5660 757-5662
Web: www.co.rock.wi.us
Rusk County 311 Miner Ave E Ladysmith WI 54848 715-532-2100 532-2237
Web: www.ruskcounty.org
Saint Croix County 1101 Carmichael Rd Hudson WI 54016 715-386-4600 381-4400
Web: www.co.saint-croix.wi.us
Sauk County 505 Broadway Baraboo WI 53913 608-355-3286 355-3522
Web: www.co.sauk.wi.us
Sawyer County PO Box 836 Hayward WI 54843 715-634-4866 634-3666
Web: www.sawyercountygov.org
Shawano County 311 N Main St Shawano WI 54166 715-526-9150 524-5157
Web: www.co.shawano.wi.us
Sheboygan County 508 New York Ave Sheboygan WI 53081 920-459-3003 459-0304
Web: www.co.sheboygan.wi.us
Taylor County 224 S 2nd St Medford WI 54451 715-748-1460 748-1415
Web: www.co.taylor.wi.us
Trempealeau County 36245 Main St Whitehall WI 54773 715-538-2311 538-4210
Web: www.tremplocounty.com
Vernon County Courthouse Annex Rm 108 Viroqua WI 54665 608-637-5380 637-5556
Web: www.wisconline.com/counties/vernon/
Vilas County 330 Court St Eagle River WI 54521 715-479-3600 479-3605
Web: www.co.vilas.wi.us
Walworth County PO Box 1001 Elkhorn WI 53121 262-741-4241 741-4287
Web: www.co.walworth.wi.us
Washburn County PO Box 639 Shell Lake WI 54871 715-468-4600 468-4725
Web: www.co.washburn.wi.us
Washington County 432 E Washington St PO Box 1986 West Bend WI 53095 262-335-4305 306-2208
Web: www.co.washington.wi.us
Waukesha County 1320 Pewaukee Rd Rm 120 Waukesha WI 53188 262-548-7010 548-7722
Web: www.waukeshacounty.gov
Waupaca County 811 Harding St Waupaca WI 54981 715-258-6200 258-6212
Web: www.co.waupaca.wi.us
Waushara County 209 S Saint Marie St Wautoma WI 54982 920-787-0441 787-0481
Web: www.1waushara.com
Winnebago County PO Box 2808 Oshkosh WI 54903 920-236-4800 303-3025
Web: www.co.winnebago.wi.us
Wood County PO Box 8095 Wisconsin Rapids WI 54495 715-421-8460 421-8808
Web: www.co.wood.wi.us

Wyoming

Phone Fax

Albany County 525 Grand Ave County Courthouse Rm 202 Laramie WY 82070 307-721-2541 721-2544
Web: www.co.albany.wy.us
Big Horn County 420 W 'C' St Basin WY 82410 307-568-2357 568-9375
Web: www.bighorncountywy.gov
Campbell County PO Box 3010 Gillette WY 82717 307-682-7285 687-6455
Web: ccg.co.campbell.wy.us
Carbon County PO Box 6 Rawlins WY 82301 307-328-2668 328-2669
Web: www.wyomingcarboncounty.com
Converse County 107 N 5th St Suite 114 Douglas WY 82633 307-358-2244 358-5998
Web: www.conversecounty.org
Crook County 309 Cleveland St Sundance WY 82729 307-283-1323 283-3038
Web: www.newedc.net/crook/index.htm
Fremont County 450 N 2nd St Rm 220 Lander WY 82520 307-332-2405 332-1132
Web: www.fremontcounty.org
Goshen County 2125 E 'A' St PO Box 160 Torrington WY 82240 307-532-4051 532-7375
Web: goshencounty.org
Hot Springs County 415 Arapahoe St Thermopolis WY 82443 307-864-3515 864-3333
Web: www.hscounty.com
Johnson County 76 N Main St Buffalo WY 82834 307-684-7272 684-2708
Web: www.johnsoncountywyoming.org
Laramie County 309 W 20th St Cheyenne WY 82001 307-633-4264 633-4240
Web: webgate.co.laramie.wy.us
Lincoln County PO Box 670 Kemmerer WY 83101 307-877-9056 877-3101
Web: www.lcwy.org
Natrona County 200 N Center St Casper WY 82601 307-235-9200
Web: www.natronacounty-wy.gov
Niobrara County 424 S Elm St PO Box 420 Lusk WY 82225 307-334-2211 334-3013
Web: www.newedc.net/niobrara/index.htm
Park County 1002 Sheridan Ave Cody WY 82414 307-754-8600 527-8626
Web: www.parkcounty.us
Platte County PO Box 728 Wheatland WY 82201 307-322-3555 322-2245
Sheridan County 224 S Main St Suite B-2 Sheridan WY 82801 307-674-2500
Web: www.sheridancounty.com
Sublette County PO Box 250 Pinedale WY 82941 307-367-4372 367-6396
Web: www.visitsublettecounty.com
Sweetwater County PO Box 730 Green River WY 82935 307-872-6400 872-6337
Web: www.co.sweet.wy.us
Teton County PO Box 1727 Jackson WY 83001 307-733-4430 739-8681
Web: www.tetonwyo.org
Uinta County PO Box 810 Evanston WY 82931 307-783-0306 783-0376
Web: www.uintacounty.com
Washakie County PO Box 260 Worland WY 82401 307-347-3131 347-9366
Web: www.washakiecounty.net
Weston County 1 W Main St Newcastle WY 82701 307-746-4744 746-9505

342 GOVERNMENT - STATE

342-1 Alabama

Phone Fax

State Government Information AL 334-242-8000
Web: www.alabama.gov
Administrative Office of Alabama Courts 300 Dexter Ave Montgomery AL 36104 334-242-0300 242-2099
Web: www.judicial.state.al.us
Agriculture & Industries Dept
1445 Federal Dr PO Box 3336 Montgomery AL 36109 334-240-7171 240-7190
Web: www.agi.state.al.us
Archives & History Dept 624 Washington Ave Montgomery AL 30130 334-242-4435 240-3433
Web: www.archives.state.al.us
Arts Council 201 Monroe St Suite 110 Montgomery AL 36130 334-242-4076 240-3269
Web: www.arts.alabama.gov
Attorney General State House 11 S Union St Montgomery AL 36130 334-242-7300 242-7458
Web: www.ago.state.al.us
Banking Dept 401 Adams Ave Suite 680 Montgomery AL 36130 334-242-3452 242-3500
Web: www.bank.state.al.us
Bill Status-House State House 11 S Union St Montgomery AL 36130 334-242-7627 242-2489
Web: alisdb.legislature.state.al.us/acas
Bill Status-Senate State House 11 S Union St Rm 716 Montgomery AL 36130 334-242-7826 242-8819
TF: 800-499-3051 ■ *Web:* alisdb.legislature.state.al.us/acas
Child Support Enforcement Div 50 Ripley St Montgomery AL 36130 334-242-9300 242-0606
Children's Affairs Dept 201 Monroe St Suite 1670 Montgomery AL 36130 334-223-0502 240-3054
Web: www.dca.state.al.us
Student Assistance Office PO Box 302000 Montgomery AL 36130 334-242-1998 242-0268
Web: www.ache.state.al.us/StudentAsst/Programs.htm
Conservation & Natural Resources Dept
64 N Union St PO Box 301450 Montgomery AL 36130 334-242-3486 242-1880
TF: 800-262-3151 ■ *Web:* www.outdooralabama.com
Consumer Affairs Office 11 S Union St Montgomery AL 36130 334-242-7334 242-2433
Web: www.ago.state.al.us/consumer.cfm
Corrections Dept PO Box 301501 Montgomery AL 36130 334-353-3883 353-3891
Web: www.doc.state.al.us
Crime Victims Compensation Commission
100 N Union St Suite 736 Montgomery AL 36102 334-242-4007 353-1401
Web: www.acvcc.state.al.us
Economic & Community Affairs Dept PO Box 5690 Montgomery AL 36103 334-242-5100 242-5099
Web: www.adeca.state.al.us
Education Dept 50 N Ripley St PO Box 302101 Montgomery AL 36104 334-242-9700 242-9708
Web: www.alsde.edu
Emergency Management Agency
5898 County Rd 41 PO Drawer 2160 Clanton AL 35046 205-280-2200 280-2410
TF: 800-843-0699 ■ *Web:* www.ema.alabama.gov
Environmental Management Dept 1400 Coliseum Blvd Montgomery AL 36110 334-271-7700 271-7950
Web: www.adem.state.al.us
Ethics Commission 100 N Union St Suite 104 Montgomery AL 36104 334-242-2997 242-0248
Web: www.ethics.alalinc.net
Finance Dept 600 Dexter Ave Rm N-105 Montgomery AL 36130 334-242-7160 353-3300
Web: www.finance.state.al.us
Forensic Sciences Dept PO Box 3510 Montgomery AL 36131 334-844-4648 877-7531
Web: www.adfs.state.al.us
Governor State Capitol 600 Dexter Ave Suite N-104 Montgomery AL 36130 334-242-7100 353-0004
Web: www.governor.state.al.us

Alabama (Cont'd)

	City	State	ZIP	Phone	Fax
Higher Education Commission 100 N Union St PO Box 302000 *Web:* www.ache.state.al.us	Montgomery	AL	36130	334-242-1998	242-0268
Highway Patrol Div PO Box 1511 *Web:* www.dps.state.al.us/public/highwaypatrol	Montgomery	AL	36102	334-242-4393	242-4385
Historical Commission 468 S Perry St *Web:* www.preserveala.org	Montgomery	AL	36130	334-242-3184	240-3477
Homeland Security Dept PO Box 304115 *TF:* 800-361-4454 ■ *Web:* www.dhs.alabama.gov	Montgomery	AL	36130	334-956-7250	223-1120
Housing Finance Authority PO Box 230909 *Web:* www.ahfa.com	Montgomery	AL	36123	334-244-9200	244-9214
Human Resources Dept 50 Ripley St PO Box 304000 *Web:* www.dhr.state.al.us	Montgomery	AL	36130	334-242-1160	242-0198
Industrial Relations Dept 649 Monroe St *Web:* dir.alabama.gov	Montgomery	AL	36131	334-242-8005	242-3960
Information Services Div 64 N Union St Suite 200 *Web:* www.isd.state.al.us	Montgomery	AL	36130	334-242-3800	242-7002
Insurance Dept 201 Monroe St Suite 1700 *Web:* www.aldoi.org	Montgomery	AL	36104	334-269-3550	241-4192
Labor Dept PO Box 303500 *Web:* www.alalabor.state.al.us	Montgomery	AL	36130	334-242-3460	240-3417
Legislature 11 S Union St *Web:* www.legislature.state.al.us	Montgomery	AL	36130	334-242-7800	242-8819
Lieutenant Governor 11 S Union St Suite 725 *Web:* www.ltgov.state.al.us	Montgomery	AL	36130	334-242-7900	242-4661
Mental Health & Mental Retardation Dept 100 N Union St Suite 520 PO Box 301410 *Web:* www.mh.state.al.us	Montgomery	AL	36130	334-242-3417	242-0684
Military Dept 1730 Congressman William L Dickinson Dr *Web:* www.alguard.state.al.us	Montgomery	AL	36109	334-271-7400	271-7426
Motor Vehicle Div 50 N Ripley St 12th Fl *Web:* www.ador.state.al.us/motorvehicle/index.html	Montgomery	AL	36104	334-242-9000	242-8038
Pardons & Paroles Board 301 S Ripley St *Web:* www.pardons.state.al.us	Montgomery	AL	36104	334-242-8700	242-1809
Postsecondary Education Dept PO Box 302130 *Web:* www.acs.cc.al.us	Montgomery	AL	36130	334-242-2900	242-2888
Prepaid Affordable College Tuition (PACT) Program 100 N Union St Suite 660 *TF:* 800-252-7228 ■ *Web:* www.treasury.state.al.us	Montgomery	AL	36130	334-242-7514	242-7041
Public Health Dept PO Box 303017 *Web:* www.adph.org	Montgomery	AL	36130	334-206-5300	206-5534
Public Safety Dept PO Box 1511 *Web:* www.dps.state.al.us	Montgomery	AL	36102	334-242-4371	353-8477
Public Service Commission PO Box 304260 *TF:* 800-392-8050 ■ *Web:* www.psc.state.al.us	Montgomery	AL	36130	334-242-5218	242-0509
Rehabilitation Services Dept 2129 E South Blvd *TF:* 800-441-7607 ■ *Web:* www.rehab.state.al.us	Montgomery	AL	36116	334-281-8780	281-1973
Revenue Dept 50 N Ripley St Rm 4112 *Web:* www.ador.state.al.us	Montgomery	AL	36104	334-242-1170	242-0550
Secretary of State PO Box 5616 *Web:* www.sos.state.al.us	Montgomery	AL	36103	334-242-7200	242-4993
Securities Commission 770 Washington Ave Suite 570 *TF:* 800-222-1253 ■ *Web:* asc.state.al.us	Montgomery	AL	36130	334-242-2984	242-0240
Senior Services Dept 770 Washington Ave Suite 470 *TF:* 877-425-2243 ■ *Web:* www.adss.state.al.us	Montgomery	AL	36130	334-242-5743	242-5594
State Parks Div 64 N Union St *TF:* 800-252-7275 ■ *Web:* www.alapark.com	Montgomery	AL	36130	334-242-3334	353-8629
State Port Authority PO Box 1588 *Web:* www.asdd.com	Mobile	AL	36633	251-441-7200	441-7216
Supreme Court 300 Dexter Ave *Web:* www.judicial.state.al.us	Montgomery	AL	36104	334-242-4609	242-0588
Tourism & Travel Bureau 401 Adams Ave Suite 126 *TF:* 800-252-2262 ■ *Web:* www.touralabama.org	Montgomery	AL	36104	334-242-4169	242-4554
Transportation Dept 1409 Coliseum Blvd *Web:* www.dot.state.al.us	Montgomery	AL	36130	334-242-6356	353-6542
Treasury Dept 600 Dexter Ave Suite S-106 *Web:* www.treasury.state.al.us	Montgomery	AL	36130	334-242-7500	242-7592
Veterans Affairs Dept PO Box 1509 *Web:* www.va.state.al.us	Montgomery	AL	36102	334-242-5077	242-5102
Vital Records Center for Health Statistics PO Box 5625 *Web:* ph.state.al.us/chs/Index.htm	Montgomery	AL	36103	334-206-5418	262-9563
Weights & Measures Div PO Box 3336 *Web:* www.agi.state.al.us/weights_measures.htm	Montgomery	AL	36109	334-240-7133	240-7175
Wildlife & Freshwater Fisheries Div 64 N Union St *Web:* www.dcnr.state.al.us/about/awff	Montgomery	AL	36104	334-242-3465	242-3032
Workers' Compensation Div 649 Monroe St *Web:* dir.alabama.gov/wc	Montgomery	AL	36131	334-353-0990	353-8262
Workforce Development Office 401 Adams Ave Suite 590 PO Box 5690 *Web:* www.owd.alabama.gov	Montgomery	AL	36103	334-353-1490	353-2005

342-2 Alaska

	City	State	ZIP	Phone	Fax
State Government Information *Web:* www.state.ak.us		AK		907-465-2111	
Aging Commission PO Box 116093 *Web:* www.alaskaaging.org	Juneau	AK	99811	907-465-3250	465-1396
Agriculture Div 1800 Glenn Hwy Suite 12 *Web:* www.dnr.state.ak.us/ag	Palmer	AK	99645	907-761-3851	745-7112
Arts Council 411 W 4th Ave Suite 1E *Web:* www.eed.state.ak.us/AKSCA	Anchorage	AK	99501	907-269-6610	269-6601
Attorney General PO Box 110300 *Web:* www.law.state.ak.us	Juneau	AK	99811	907-465-3600	465-2075
Banking Securities & Corporations Div 150 3rd St Rm 217 *Web:* www.dced.state.ak.us/bsc	Juneau	AK	99801	907-465-2521	465-2549
Behavioral Health Div PO Box 110620 *Web:* www.hss.state.ak.us/dbh	Juneau	AK	99811	907-465-3370	465-2668
Bill Status State Capitol MS 3100 *Web:* www.legis.state.ak.us/basis	Juneau	AK	99801	907-465-4648	465-2864
Child Support Enforcement Div 550 W 7th Ave Suite 310 *Web:* www.csed.state.ak.us	Anchorage	AK	99501	907-269-6900	269-6650
Children's Services Office PO Box 110630 *Web:* www.hss.state.ak.us/ocs	Juneau	AK	99811	907-465-3191	465-3397
Commerce Community & Economic Development Dept 333 Willoughby Ave PO Box 11080 *Web:* www.commerce.state.ak.us	Juneau	AK	99811	907-465-2500	465-5442
Corrections Dept PO Box 112000 *Web:* www.correct.state.ak.us	Juneau	AK	99811	907-465-3342	465-3253
Court System 303 K St *Web:* www.state.ak.us/courts	Anchorage	AK	99501	907-264-0547	264-0585
Education & Early Development Dept 801 W 10th St Suite 200 *Web:* www.eed.state.ak.us	Juneau	AK	99801	907-465-2800	465-4156
Employment Security Div PO Box 25509 *Web:* www.labor.state.ak.us/esd/home.htm	Juneau	AK	99802	907-465-2712	465-4537
Enterprise Technology Services Div PO Box 110206 *Web:* www.state.ak.us/admin/info	Juneau	AK	99811	907-465-2220	465-3450
Environmental Conservation Dept 410 Willoughby Ave Suite 303 *Web:* www.state.ak.us/dec	Juneau	AK	99801	907-465-5066	465-5070
Fish & Game Dept 1255 W 8th St PO Box 25526 *Web:* www.adfg.state.ak.us	Juneau	AK	99802	907-465-4100	465-2332
Governor PO Box 110011 *Web:* www.gov.state.ak.us	Juneau	AK	99811	907-465-3500	465-3532
Health & Social Services Dept PO Box 110601 *Web:* www.hss.state.ak.us	Juneau	AK	99811	907-465-3030	465-3068
History & Archeology Office 550 W 7th Ave Suite 1310 *Web:* www.dnr.state.ak.us/parks/oha_web	Anchorage	AK	99501	907-269-8721	269-8908
Homeland Security & Emergency Services Div PO Box 5750 *Web:* www.ak-prepared.com	Fort Richardson	AK	99505	907-428-7000	428-7009
Housing Finance Corp PO Box 101020 *Web:* www.ahfc.state.ak.us	Anchorage	AK	99510	907-338-6100	338-7940
Insurance Div PO Box 110805 *Web:* www.commerce.state.ak.us/insurance	Juneau	AK	99811	907-465-2515	465-3422
Labor & Workforce Development Dept 111 W 8th St PO Box 21149 *Web:* www.labor.state.ak.us	Juneau	AK	99802	907-465-2700	465-2784
Legislative Ethics Committee PO Box 101468 *Web:* www.ethics.legis.state.ak.us	Anchorage	AK	99510	907-269-0150	269-0152
Lieutenant Governor PO Box 110015 *Web:* www.gov.state.ak.us/ltgov	Juneau	AK	99811	907-465-3520	465-5400
Measurement Standards Div 12050 Industry Way Bldg O Suite 6 *Web:* www.dot.state.ak.us/mscve	Anchorage	AK	99515	907-345-7750	345-6835
Military & Veterans Affairs Dept PO Box 5800 *Web:* www.ak-prepared.com/dmva	Fort Richardson	AK	99505	907-428-6003	428-6019
Motor Vehicles Div 3300 B Fairbanks St *Web:* www.state.ak.us/dmv	Anchorage	AK	99503	907-269-5559	269-6084
Natural Resources Dept 500 W 7th Ave Suite 1400 *Web:* www.dnr.state.ak.us	Anchorage	AK	99501	907-269-8431	269-8918
Occupational Licensing Div PO Box 110806 *Web:* www.dced.state.ak.us/occ	Juneau	AK	99811	907-465-2534	465-2974
Parks & Outdoor Recreation Div 550 W 7th Ave Suite 1380 *Web:* www.dnr.state.ak.us/parks	Anchorage	AK	99501	907-269-8700	269-8907
Parole Board PO Box 112000 *Web:* www.correct.state.ak.us/corrections/Parole	Juneau	AK	99811	907-465-3384	465-3110
Permanent Fund Dividend Div 333 Willoughby Ave 11th Fl *Web:* www.pfd.state.ak.us	Juneau	AK	99811	907-465-2326	465-3470
Personnel Div 333 Willoughby Ave PO Box 110201 *Web:* dop.state.ak.us	Juneau	AK	99811	907-465-4430	465-2576
Postsecondary Education Commission 3030 Vintage Blvd *TF Cust Svc:* 800-441-3293 ■ *Web:* alaskaadvantage.state.ak.us	Juneau	AK	99801	907-465-6740	465-5316
Public Assistance Div PO Box 110640 *Web:* www.hss.state.ak.us/dpa	Juneau	AK	99811	907-465-3347	465-5154
Real Estate Commission 550 W 7th Ave Suite 1500 *Web:* www.commerce.state.ak.us/occ/prec.htm	Anchorage	AK	99501	907-269-8197	269-8196
Regulatory Commission 550 W 8th Ave Suite 300 *Web:* www.state.ak.us/rca	Anchorage	AK	99501	907-276-6222	276-0160
Revenue Dept PO Box 110400 *Web:* www.revenue.state.ak.us	Juneau	AK	99811	907-465-2300	465-2389
State Legislature State Capitol *Web:* www.legis.state.ak.us	Juneau	AK	99801	907-465-4648	465-2864
State Libraries Archives & Museums Div PO Box 110571 *Web:* www.eed.state.ak.us/lam	Juneau	AK	99811	907-465-2910	465-2151
State Medical Examiner 4500 Boniface Pkwy *Web:* www.hss.state.ak.us/dph/sme	Anchorage	AK	99507	907-334-2200	334-2216
State Troopers Div 5700 E Tudor Rd *Web:* www.dps.state.ak.us/ast	Anchorage	AK	99507	907-269-5641	337-2059
Student Aid Office PO Box 110505 *TF:* 800-441-2962 ■ *Web:* alaskaadvantage.state.ak.us	Juneau	AK	99811	907-465-2962	465-5316
Supreme Court 303 K St	Anchorage	AK	99501	907-264-0612	264-0878
Tourism Development Office PO Box 11801 *Web:* www.commerce.state.ak.us/oed/toubus/home.cfm	Juneau	AK	99811	907-465-2012	465-3767
Transportation & Public Facilities Dept 3132 Channel Dr *Web:* www.dot.state.ak.us	Juneau	AK	99801	907-465-3900	586-8365
Violent Crimes Compensation Board PO Box 1102030 *Web:* www.state.ak.us/admin/vccb	Juneau	AK	99811	907-465-3040	465-2379
Vital Statistics Bureau 5441 Commercial Blvd *Web:* www.hss.state.ak.us/dph/bvs	Juneau	AK	99801	907-465-3391	465-3618
Vocational Rehabilitation Div 801 W 10th St Suite 200 *TF:* 800-478-2815 ■ *Web:* www.labor.state.ak.us/dvr	Juneau	AK	99801	907-465-2814	465-2856
Workers' Compensation Div PO Box 25512 *Web:* www.labor.state.ak.us/wc	Juneau	AK	99802	907-465-2790	465-2797

342-3 Arizona

	City	State	ZIP	Phone	Fax
State Government Information *Web:* www.az.gov		AZ		602-542-4900	
Administrative Office of the Courts 1501 W Washington St *Web:* www.supreme.state.az.us/nav2/aoc.htm	Phoenix	AZ	85007	602-542-9301	542-9484
Aging & Adult Administration 1789 W Jefferson St MS 001A *Web:* www.de.state.az.us/aaa	Phoenix	AZ	85007	602-542-6572	542-6575
Agriculture Dept 1688 W Adams St *Web:* www.azda.gov	Phoenix	AZ	85007	602-542-4373	542-5420
Arts Commission 417 W Roosevelt St *Web:* www.arizonaarts.org	Phoenix	AZ	85003	602-255-5882	256-0282
Attorney General 1275 W Washington St *TF:* 888-377-6108 ■ *Web:* www.azag.gov	Phoenix	AZ	85007	602-542-5025	542-4085
Banking Dept 2910 N 44th St Suite 310 *Web:* www.azbanking.com	Phoenix	AZ	85018	602-255-4421	381-1225
Bill Status-House Capitol Complex 1700 W Washington St *TF:* 800-352-8404 ■ *Web:* www.azleg.state.az.us/legtext/bills.htm	Phoenix	AZ	85007	602-542-4900	542-4009
Boxing Commission 1110 W Washington St Suite 260	Phoenix	AZ	85007	602-364-1721	364-1703
Child Support Enforcement Div PO Box 40458 *Fax: Cust Svc ■ *Web:* www.de.state.az.us/dcse	Phoenix	AZ	85067	602-274-7646	274-8250*
Children Youth & Families Div 1789 W Jefferson St *TF:* 877-543-7633 ■ *Web:* www.de.state.az.us/dcyf	Phoenix	AZ	85007	602-542-2277	542-3330
Commerce Dept 1700 W Washington St Suite 600 *Web:* www.azcommerce.com	Phoenix	AZ	85007	602-771-1100	771-1200
Consumer Protection & Antitrust Unit 1275 W Washington St *Web:* www.azag.gov/consumer	Phoenix	AZ	85007	602-542-5763	542-4579
Corporation Commission 1200 W Washington St *Web:* www.cc.state.az.us	Phoenix	AZ	85007	602-542-2237	542-4111
Corrections Dept 1601 W Jefferson St *Web:* www.adc.state.az.us	Phoenix	AZ	85007	602-542-5536	542-2859
Criminal Justice Commission 1110 W Washington St Suite 230 *Web:* acjc.state.az.us	Phoenix	AZ	85007	602-364-1146	364-1175

	City	State	ZIP	Phone	Fax
Economic Security Dept 1717 W Jefferson St	Phoenix	AZ	85007	602-542-4791	542-5339
Web: www.de.state.az.us					
Education Dept 1535 W Jefferson St	Phoenix	AZ	85007	602-542-4361	542-5440
Web: www.ade.state.az.us					
Emergency & Military Affairs Dept 5636 E McDowell Rd	Phoenix	AZ	85008	602-267-2700	267-2954
Web: www.azdema.gov					
Employement Administration 1789 W Jefferson St Site 920Z	Phoenix	AZ	85007	602-542-3957	542-2491
Web: www.de.state.az.us/wia					
Environmental Quality Dept 1110 W Washington St	Phoenix	AZ	85007	602-207-2300	207-2218
TF: 800-234-5677 ■ *Web:* www.azdeq.gov					
Executive Clemency Board 1645 W Jefferson St Rm 101	Phoenix	AZ	85007	602-542-5656	542-5680
Web: azboec.gov					
Game & Fish Dept 2222 W Greenway Rd	Phoenix	AZ	85023	602-942-3000	789-3924
Web: www.azgfd.com					
Government Information Technology Agency 100 N 15th Ave Suite 440	Phoenix	AZ	85007	602-364-4482	364-4799
Web: www.azgita.gov					
Governor 1700 W Washington St Executive Tower 9th Fl	Phoenix	AZ	85007	602-542-4331	542-7601
Web: www.governor.state.az.us					
Health Services Dept 150 N 18th Ave	Phoenix	AZ	85007	602-542-1000	542-1062
Web: www.azdhs.gov					
Highway Patrol Div PO Box 6638	Phoenix	AZ	85005	602-223-2000	223-2916
Web: www.dps.state.az.us					
Historic Preservation Office 1300 W Washington St	Phoenix	AZ	85007	602-542-4009	542-4180
Web: www.azstateparks.com					
Housing Dept 1700 W Washington St Suite 210	Phoenix	AZ	85007	602-771-1000	771-1002
Web: www.housingaz.com					
Industrial Commission 800 W Washington St	Phoenix	AZ	85007	602-542-4411	542-3373
Web: www.ica.state.az.us					
Insurance Dept 2910 N 44th St 2nd Fl	Phoenix	AZ	85018	602-912-8400	912-8452
Web: www.id.state.az.us					
Land Dept 1616 W Adams St	Phoenix	AZ	85007	602-542-4602	542-5223
Web: www.land.state.az.us					
Legislature Capitol Complex 1700 W Washington St	Phoenix	AZ	85007	602-542-4900	542-3429
TF: 800-352-8404 ■ *Web:* www.azleg.state.az.us					
Lottery 4740 E University Dr	Phoenix	AZ	85034	480-921-4400	921-5512
Web: www.arizonalottery.com					
Medical Board 9545 Doubletree Ranch Rd	Scottsdale	AZ	85258	480-551-2700	551-2704
Web: www.azmdboard.org					
Motor Vehicle Div 1801 W Jefferson St	Phoenix	AZ	85007	602-712-8152	712-6539
Web: www.dot.state.az.us/mvd					
Nursing Board 1651 E Morten Ave Suite 210	Phoenix	AZ	85020	602-331-8111	906-9365
Web: www.azboardofnursing.org					
Postsecondary Education Commission 2020 N Central Ave Suite 550	Phoenix	AZ	85004	602-258-2435	258-2483
Web: www.azhighered.org					
Racing Dept 1110 W Washington St Suite 260	Phoenix	AZ	85007	602-364-1700	364-1703
Web: www.azracing.gov					
Real Estate Dept 2910 N 44th St 1st Fl	Phoenix	AZ	85018	602-468-1414	468-0562
Web: www.re.state.az.us					
Rehabilitation Services Administration 1789 W Jefferson St 2nd Fl NW	Phoenix	AZ	85007	602-542-3332	542-3778
TF: 800-563-1221 ■ *Web:* www.azdes.gov/rsa					
Revenue Dept 1600 W Monroe St	Phoenix	AZ	85007	602-716-6090	542-4772
Web: www.azdor.gov					
Secretary of State 1700 W Washington St West Wing 7th Fl	Phoenix	AZ	85007	602-542-4285	542-1575
Web: www.azsos.gov					
Securities Div 1300 W Washington St 3rd Fl	Phoenix	AZ	85007	602-542-4242	594-7470
Web: www.ccsd.cc.state.az.us					
State Boards Office 1400 W Washington St Suite 230	Phoenix	AZ	85007	602-542-3095	542-3093
State Compensation Fund 3031 N 2nd St	Phoenix	AZ	85012	602-631-2000	631-2213
Web: www.scfaz.com					
State Parks 1300 W Washington St	Phoenix	AZ	85007	602-542-4174	542-4188
Web: www.azstateparks.com					
Supreme Court 1501 W Washington St	Phoenix	AZ	85007	602-542-9300	542-9480
Web: www.supreme.state.az.us					
Tourism Office 1110 W Washington St Suite 155	Phoenix	AZ	85007	602-364-3700	364-3701
TF: 888-520-3434 ■ *Web:* www.arizonaguide.com					
Transportation Dept 206 S 17th Ave	Phoenix	AZ	85007	602-712-7227	712-6941
Web: www.dot.state.az.us					
Treasurer 1700 W Washington St West Wing 1st Fl	Phoenix	AZ	85007	602-542-1463	542-7176
Web: www.aztreasury.state.az.us					
Veterans' Service Dept 3839 N 3rd St Suite 200	Phoenix	AZ	85012	602-255-3373	255-1038
Web: www.azdvs.gov					
Vital Records Office 1818 W Adams St	Phoenix	AZ	85007	602-364-1300	364-1257
Web: www.azdhs.gov/vitalrcd					
Weights & Measures Dept 4425 W Olive Ave Suite 134	Glendale	AZ	85302	602-255-5211	255-1950
Web: www.azdwm.gov					

342-4 Arkansas

	City	State	ZIP	Phone	Fax
State Government Information		AR		501-682-3000	
Web: www.arkansas.gov					
Administrative Office of the Courts 625 Marshall St	Little Rock	AR	72201	501-682-9400	682-9410
Web: courts.state.ar.us/courts/aoc.html					
Aging & Adult Services Div PO Box 1437 Slot 5530	Little Rock	AR	72203	501-682-2441	682-8155
Web: www.arkansas.gov/dhhs/aging					
Arts Council 323 Center St Suite 1400	Little Rock	AR	72201	501-324-9766	324-9207
Web: www.arkansasarts.com					
Athletic Commission 9110 Lew Dr	Little Rock	AR	72209	501-666-5544	666-5546
Attorney General 323 Center St Suite 200	Little Rock	AR	72201	501-682-2007	682-8084
TF Consumer Inf: 800-482-8982 ■ *Web:* www.ag.state.ar.us					
Bank Dept 400 Hardin Rd Suite 100	Little Rock	AR	72211	501-324-9019	324-9028
Web: www.state.ar.us/bank					
Bill Status-House State Capitol Rm 350	Little Rock	AR	72201	501-682-7771	
Web: www.arkleg.state.ar.us					
Bill Status-Senate State Capitol Rm 320	Little Rock	AR	72201	501-682-5951	
Web: www.arkleg.state.ar.us					
Child Support Enforcement Office PO Box 8133	Little Rock	AR	72203	501-682-6169	682-6002
Web: www.state.ar.us/dfa/childsupport					
Children & Family Services Div PO Box 1437 Slot 5560	Little Rock	AR	72203	501-682-8772	682-6968
Web: www.arkansas.gov/dhhs/chilnfam					
Consumer Protection Div 323 Center St Tower Bldg Suite 200	Little Rock	AR	72201	501-682-6150	682-8118
TF: 800-482-8982 ■ *Web:* www.ag.state.ar.us/consumer/home.htm					
Contractors Licensing Board 4100 Richards Rd	North Little Rock	AR	72117	501-372-4661	372-2247
Web: www.state.ar.us/clb					
Correction Dept PO Box 8707	Pine Bluff	AR	71611	870-267-6200	267-6258
Web: www.state.ar.us/doc					
Cosmetology Board 101 E Capitol Ave Suite 108	Little Rock	AR	72201	501-682-2168	682-5640
Web: www.accessarkansas.org/cos					
Crime Victims Reparations Board 323 Center St Suite 200	Little Rock	AR	72201	501-682-1323	682-5313
TF: 800-448-3014 ■ *Web:* www.ag.state.ar.us/outreach					
Development Finance Authority 423 Main St Suite 500	Little Rock	AR	72201	501-682-5900	682-5859
Web: www.accessarkansas.org/adfa					
Economic Development Dept 1 Capitol Mall Suite 4C-300	Little Rock	AR	72201	501-682-1121	682-7394
TF: 800-275-2672 ■ *Web:* www.1800arkansas.com					
Education Dept 4 Capitol Mall	Little Rock	AR	72201	501-682-4475	682-1079
Web: arkedu.state.ar.us					
Emergency Management Dept PO Box 758	Conway	AR	72033	501-730-9750	730-9754
Web: www.adem.state.ar.us					
Environmental Quality Dept 8001 National Dr	Little Rock	AR	72209	501-682-0744	682-0798
Web: www.adeq.state.ar.us					
Ethics Commission 910 W 2nd St Suite 100	Little Rock	AR	72201	501-324-9600	324-9606
TF: 800-422-7773 ■ *Web:* www.arkansasethics.com					
Finance & Administration Dept 1509 W 7th St	Little Rock	AR	72201	501-682-2242	682-1029
Web: www.state.ar.us/dfa					
Financial Aid Office 114 E Capitol St	Little Rock	AR	72201	501-371-2013	371-2001
TF: 800-547-8839 ■ *Web:* www.arkansashighered.com/financial.html					
Game & Fish Commission 2 Natural Resource Dr	Little Rock	AR	72205	501-223-6300	223-6444
TF: 800-364-4263 ■ *Web:* www.agfc.state.ar.us					
General Assembly State Capitol Bldg	Little Rock	AR	72201	501-682-6107	682-2917
Web: www.arkleg.state.ar.us					
Governor State Capitol Bldg	Little Rock	AR	72201	501-682-2345	682-1382
Web: www.arkansas.gov/governor					
Health Dept 4815 W Markham St	Little Rock	AR	72205	501-661-2000	671-1450
Web: www.healthyarkansas.com					
Heritage Dept 323 Center St Suite 1500	Little Rock	AR	72201	501-324-9150	324-9154
Web: www.arkansasheritage.com					
Higher Education Dept 114 E Capitol Ave	Little Rock	AR	72201	501-371-2000	371-2001
Web: www.arkansashighered.com					
Highway & Transportation Dept PO Box 2261	Little Rock	AR	72203	501-569-2000	569-2400
Web: www.arkansashighways.com					
Human Services Dept PO Box 1437	Little Rock	AR	72203	501-682-1001	682-6571
Web: www.arkansas.gov/dhhs					
Information Systems Dept PO Box 3155	Little Rock	AR	72203	501-682-3038	682-4310
Web: www.dis.state.ar.us					
Insurance Dept 1200 W 3rd St	Little Rock	AR	72201	501-371-2600	371-2618
TF: 800-282-9134 ■ *Web:* www.state.ar.us/insurance					
Labor Dept 10421 W Markham St	Little Rock	AR	72205	501-682-4500	682-4535
Web: www.ark.org/labor					
Lieutenant Governor State Capitol Bldg Rm 270	Little Rock	AR	72201	501-682-2144	682-2894
Web: www.state.ar.us/ltgov					
Motor Vehicle Office 1900 W 7th St Rm 2030	Little Rock	AR	72203	501-682-4630	682-1116
Web: www.state.ar.us/dfa/motorvehicle					
Parks & Tourism Dept 1 Capitol Mall	Little Rock	AR	72201	501-682-7777	682-1364
TF: 800-628-8725 ■ *Web:* www.arkansas.com					
Public Accountancy Board 101 E Capitol Ave Suite 430	Little Rock	AR	72201	501-682-1520	682-5538
Web: www.state.ar.us/asbpa					
Public Service Commission PO Box 400	Little Rock	AR	72203	501-682-2051	682-5731
Web: www.state.ar.us/psc					
Racing Commission 1515 W 7th St Rm 505	Little Rock	AR	72203	501-682-1467	682-5273
Web: www.state.ar.us/dfa/racing					
Real Estate Commission 612 S Summit St	Little Rock	AR	72201	501-683-8010	683-8020
Web: www.state.ar.us/arec					
Rehabilitation Services 1616 Brookwood Dr	Little Rock	AR	72202	501-296-1600	296-1655
TF: 800-330-0632 ■ *Web:* www.arsinfo.org					
Revenue Div PO Box 1272	Little Rock	AR	72203	501-682-7025	682-7900
Web: www.state.ar.us/arsec					
Secretary of State State Capitol Bldg Rm 256	Little Rock	AR	72201	501-682-1010	682-3510
Web: www.sosweb.state.ar.us					
Securities Dept 201 E Markham St Rm 300	Little Rock	AR	72201	501-324-9260	324-9268
TF: 800-981-4429 ■ *Web:* www.accessarkansas.org/arsec					
Soil & Water Conservation Commission 101 E Capitol Suite 350	Little Rock	AR	72201	501-682-1611	682-3991
Web: www.aswcc.arkansas.gov					
Standards Bureau 4608 W 61st St	Little Rock	AR	72209	501-570-1159	562-7605
Web: www.plantboard.org/bureau_about.html					
State Medical Board 2100 Riverfront Dr	Little Rock	AR	72202	501-296-1802	296-1805
Web: www.armedicalboard.org					
State Police 1 State Police Plaza Dr	Little Rock	AR	72209	501-618-8000	618-8222
Web: www.asp.state.ar.us					
Supreme Court 625 Marshall St 1st Fl N	Little Rock	AR	72201	501-682-6849	682-6877
Web: courts.state.ar.us/courts/sc.html					
Treasurer State Capitol Bldg Rm 220	Little Rock	AR	72201	501-682-5888	682-3842
Web: avcf.uark.edu:81/TREAWeb					
Veterans Affairs Dept 2200 Fort Roots Dr Bldg 65 Rm 119	North Little Rock	AR	72114	501-370-3820	370-3829
Web: www.nasdva.com/arkansas.html					
Vital Records Div 4815 W Markham St Slot 44	Little Rock	AR	72205	501-661-2174	663-2832
TF: 800-637-9314 ■ *Web:* www.healthyarkansas.com					
Worker's Compensation Commission PO Box 950	Little Rock	AR	72203	501-682-3930	682-2777
TF: 800-622-4472 ■ *Web:* www.awcc.state.ar.us					
Employment Security Dept PO Box 2981	North Little Rock	AR	72203	501-682-2121	682-2273
Web: www.arkansas.gov/esd					

342-5 California

	City	State	ZIP	Phone	Fax
State Government Information		CA		916-657-9900	
Web: www.ca.gov					
Administrative Office of the Courts 455 Golden Gate Ave 3rd Fl	San Francisco	CA	94102	415-865-4200	865-4205
Web: www.courtinfo.ca.gov					
Aging Dept 1300 National Dr Suite 200	Sacramento	CA	95834	916-419-7500	928-2268
Web: www.aging.ca.gov					
Arts Council 1300 'I' St Suite 930	Sacramento	CA	95814	916-322-6555	322-6575
TF: 800-201-6201 ■ *Web:* www.cac.ca.gov					
Athletic Commission 1424 Howe Ave Suite 33	Sacramento	CA	95825	916-263-2195	263-2197
Web: www.dca.ca.gov/csac					
Attorney General PO Box 944255	Sacramento	CA	95244	916-445-9555	324-5341
Web: caag.state.ca.us					
Bill Status-Assembly State Capitol Rm 3196	Sacramento	CA	95814	916-445-2323	
Web: www.leginfo.ca.gov/bilinfo.html					
Bill Status-Senate State Capitol Rm 3044	Sacramento	CA	95814	916-445-4251	445-4450
Web: www.leginfo.ca.gov/bilinfo.html					
Child Support Services Dept PO Box 269112	Sacramento	CA	95826	916-464-5000	464-5211
TF: 866-249-0773 ■ *Web:* www.childsup.ca.gov					
Community Services & Development Dept PO Box 1947	Sacramento	CA	95814	916-341-4200	341-4203
Web: www.csd.ca.gov					
Conservation Dept 801 K St MS 24-01	Sacramento	CA	95814	916-322-1080	445-0732
Web: www.consrv.ca.gov					
Consumer Affairs Dept 400 R St	Sacramento	CA	95814	916-445-1254	445-3755
Web: www.dca.ca.gov					
Corporations Dept 1515 K St Suite 200	Sacramento	CA	95814	916-445-7205	322-3205
Web: www.corp.ca.gov					
Corrections Dept PO Box 942883	Sacramento	CA	94283	916-445-7682	322-2877
Web: www.corr.ca.gov					
Economic Development Dept 801 K St Suite 1700	Sacramento	CA	95814	916-322-1394	322-2865
Web: commerce.ca.gov					

California (Cont'd)

	City	State	Zip	Phone	Fax
Education Dept 1430 'N' St Suite 5602 *Web:* www.cde.ca.gov	Sacramento	CA	95812	916-319-0800	319-0100
Emergency Services Office 3650 Schriever Ave *Web:* www.oes.ca.gov	Mather	CA	95655	916-845-8510	845-8910
Employment Development Dept 800 Capitol Mall MIC 83 *Web:* www.edd.ca.gov	Sacramento	CA	95814	916-654-8210	657-5294
Energy Commission 1516 9th St *Web:* www.energy.ca.gov	Sacramento	CA	95814	916-654-4287	654-4420
Environmental Protection Agency 1001 'I' St 25th Fl *Web:* www.calepa.ca.gov	Sacramento	CA	95814	916-445-3846	445-6401
Fair Political Practices Commission 428 J St Suite 620 *TF:* 866-275-3772 ■ *Web:* www.fppc.ca.gov	Sacramento	CA	95814	916-322-5660	322-0886
Finance Dept State Capitol Rm 1145 *Web:* www.dof.ca.gov	Sacramento	CA	95814	916-445-3878	324-7311
Financial Institutions Dept 111 Pine St Suite 1100 *TF Consumer Inf:* 800-622-0620 ■ *Web:* www.dfi.ca.gov	San Francisco	CA	94111	415-263-8500	989-5310
Fish & Game Dept 1416 9th St 12th Fl *Web:* www.dfg.ca.gov	Sacramento	CA	95814	916-654-7667	653-7387
Food & Agriculture Dept 1220 'N' St *Web:* www.cdfa.ca.gov	Sacramento	CA	95814	916-654-0433	654-0403
Governor State Capitol 1st Fl *Web:* www.governor.ca.gov	Sacramento	CA	95814	916-445-2841	445-4633
Health & Human Services Agency PO Box 942732 *Web:* www.dhs.ca.gov	Sacramento	CA	95814	916-440-7400	
Highway Patrol 2555 1st Ave *Web:* www.chp.ca.gov	Sacramento	CA	95818	916-657-7261	657-8639
Historic Preservation Office PO Box 942896 *Web:* ohp.parks.ca.gov	Sacramento	CA	94296	916-653-6624	653-9824
Horse Racing Board 1010 Hurley Way Rm 300 *Web:* www.chrb.ca.gov	Sacramento	CA	95825	916-263-6000	263-6042
Housing & Community Development Dept 1800 3rd St Suite 450 *Web:* www.hcd.ca.gov	Sacramento	CA	95814	916-445-4782	323-9242
Housing Finance Agency 1415 L St Suite 500 *Web:* www.calhfa.ca.gov	Sacramento	CA	95814	916-322-3991	322-1994
Industrial Relations Dept 455 Golden Gate Ave *Web:* www.dir.ca.gov	San Francisco	CA	94102	415-703-5050	703-5058
Insurance Dept 300 Capitol Mall Suite 1700 *Web:* www.insurance.ca.gov	Sacramento	CA	95814	916-492-3500	445-5280
Lieutenant Governor State Capitol Rm 1114 *Web:* www.ltg.ca.gov	Sacramento	CA	95814	916-445-8994	323-4998
Medical Board 1426 Howe Ave Suite 54 *Web:* www.medbd.ca.gov	Sacramento	CA	95825	916-263-2382	263-2944
Mental Health Dept 1600 9th St Rm 151 *Web:* www.dmh.ca.gov	Sacramento	CA	95814	916-654-3565	654-3198
Military Dept 9800 Goethe Rd PO Box 269101 *TF:* 800-321-2752	Sacramento	CA	95826	916-854-3000	854-3671
Motor Vehicles Dept PO Box 942869 MS E-254 *Web:* www.dmv.ca.gov	Sacramento	CA	95818	916-657-6437	657-5716
Parks & Recreation Dept PO Box 942896 *TF:* 800-777-0369 ■ *Web:* www.parks.ca.gov	Sacramento	CA	94296	916-653-6995	657-3903
Postsecondary Education Commission 1303 J St Suite 500 *Web:* www.cpec.ca.gov	Sacramento	CA	95814	916-445-7933	327-4417
Prison Terms Board 1515 K St Suite 600 *Web:* www.bpt.ca.gov	Sacramento	CA	95814	916-445-4072	445-5242
Public Utilities Commission 505 Van Ness Ave *TF:* 800-848-5580 ■ *Web:* www.cpuc.ca.gov	San Francisco	CA	94102	415-703-2782	703-1758
Real Estate Dept 2201 Broadway *Web:* www.dre.ca.gov	Sacramento	CA	95818	916-227-0782	227-0777
Rehabilitation Dept 2000 Evergreen St *Web:* www.rehab.ca.gov	Sacramento	CA	95815	916-263-8981	263-7474
Secretary of State 1500 11th St *Web:* www.ss.ca.gov	Sacramento	CA	95814	916-653-6814	653-4620
Social Services Dept 744 P St *Web:* www.dss.cahwnet.gov	Sacramento	CA	95814	916-445-6951	445-7311
State Legislature State Capitol *Web:* www.leginfo.ca.gov	Sacramento	CA	95814	916-322-4311	445-1830
State Lottery Commission 600 N 10th St *Web:* www.calottery.com	Sacramento	CA	95814	916-323-7095	323-7087
Student Aid Commission PO Box 419027 *TF:* 888-224-7268 ■ *Web:* www.csac.ca.gov	Rancho Cordova	CA	95741	916-526-8999	526-8002
Supreme Court 350 McAllister St *Web:* www.courtinfo.ca.gov/courts/supreme	San Francisco	CA	94102	415-865-7000	865-7183
Teacher Credentialing Commission 1900 Capitol Ave *TF:* 888-921-2682 ■ *Web:* www.ctc.ca.gov	Sacramento	CA	95814	916-445-7254	
Transportation Dept 1120 'N' St *Web:* www.dot.ca.gov	Sacramento	CA	95814	916-654-5266	654-6608
Travel & Tourism Commission PO Box 1499 *Web:* www.visitcalifornia.com	Sacramento	CA	95812	916-444-4429	322-3402
Treasurer PO Box 942809 *Web:* www.treasurer.ca.gov	Sacramento	CA	94209	916-653-2995	653-3125
Veterans Affairs Dept 1227 'O' St *TF:* 800-221-8998 ■ *Web:* www.cdva.ca.gov	Sacramento	CA	95814	916-653-2158	653-2456
Victim Compensation Program PO Box 3036 *TF:* 800-777-9229 ■ *Web:* www.boc.ca.gov	Sacramento	CA	95812	916-324-0400	
Vital Records & Statistics Office PO Box 997410 **Fax Area Code:* 800 ■ *Web:* www.dhs.ca.gov/chs/OVR	Sacramento	CA	95899	916-445-2684	858-5553*
Workers' Compensation Div PO Box 420603 *Web:* www.dir.ca.gov/dwc	San Francisco	CA	94142	415-703-4600	703-4664

342-6 Colorado

	City	State	Zip	Phone	Fax
State Government Information *Web:* www.colorado.gov		CO		303-866-5000	
Aging & Adult Services Div 1575 Sherman St 10th Fl	Denver	CO	80203	303-866-2800	866-2696
Agriculture Dept 700 Kipling St Suite 4000 *Web:* www.ag.state.co.us	Lakewood	CO	80215	303-239-4100	239-4125
Arts Council 1380 Lawrence St Suite 1200 *TF:* 800-291-2787 ■ *Web:* www.coloarts.state.co.us	Denver	CO	80204	303-866-2723	866-4266
Attorney General 1525 Sherman St 5th Fl *Web:* www.ago.state.co.us	Denver	CO	80203	303-866-3617	866-5691
Banking Div 1560 Broadway St Suite 975 *Web:* www.dora.state.co.us/banking	Denver	CO	80202	303-894-7575	894-7570
Bill Status 200 E Colfax Ave *Web:* www.leg.state.co.us	Denver	CO	80203	303-866-3055	866-4543
Child Support Enforcement Div 1575 Sherman St 5th Fl *Web:* www.childsupport.state.co.us	Denver	CO	80203	303-866-4300	866-4360
Children Youth & Families Office 1575 Sherman St *Web:* www.cdhs.state.co.us/cyf/CYF_Home.html	Denver	CO	80203	303-866-5700	866-2214
CollegeInvest 1801 Broadway Suite 1300 *TF:* 800-478-5651 ■ *Web:* www.prepaidtuition.org	Denver	CO	80202	303-295-1981	296-4811
Consumer Protection Div 1525 Sherman St 5th Fl *Web:* www.cdphe.state.co.us/cp	Denver	CO	80203	303-866-5189	866-5691
Corrections Dept 2862 S Circle Dr *Web:* www.doc.state.co.us	Colorado Springs	CO	80906	719-226-4701	226-4755
Economic Development Commission 1625 Broadway Suite 1700 *Web:* www.state.co.us/oed/edc	Denver	CO	80202	303-892-3840	892-3848
Education Dept 201 E Colfax Ave *Web:* www.cde.state.co.us	Denver	CO	80203	303-866-6600	830-0793
Educator Licensing Unit 201 E Colfax Ave *Web:* www.cde.state.co.us/index_license.htm	Denver	CO	80203	303-866-6628	866-6866
Emergency Management Office 9195 E Mineral Ave Suite 200 *Web:* www.dola.state.co.us	Centennial	CO	80112	720-852-6600	852-6750
General Assembly State Capitol 200 E Colfax Ave Rm 048 *Web:* www.leg.state.co.us	Denver	CO	80203	303-866-3521	
Governor 136 State Capitol Bldg *Web:* www.colorado.gov/governor	Denver	CO	80203	303-866-2471	866-2003
Higher Education Commission 1380 Lawrence St Suite 1200 *Web:* www.state.co.us/cche_dir/hecche.html	Denver	CO	80203	303-866-2723	866-4266
Historical Society 1300 Broadway *Web:* www.coloradohistory.org	Denver	CO	80203	303-866-3682	866-5739
Housing & Finance Authority 1981 Blake St *TF:* 800-877-2432 ■ *Web:* www.colohfa.org	Denver	CO	80202	303-297-2432	297-2615
Human Services Dept 1575 Sherman St *Web:* www.cdhs.state.co.us	Denver	CO	80203	303-866-5700	866-4214
Innovation & Technology Office 225 E 16th Ave Suite 260 *Web:* www.oit.state.co.us	Denver	CO	80203	303-866-6060	866-6454
Insurance Div 1560 Broadway Suite 850 *Web:* www.dora.state.co.us/insurance	Denver	CO	80202	303-894-7499	894-7455
Labor & Employment Dept 633 17th St Suite 201 *TF:* 800-390-7936 ■ *Web:* www.coworkforce.com	Denver	CO	80203	303-318-8000	
Lieutenant Governor 130 State Capitol Bldg	Denver	CO	80203	303-866-2087	866-5469
Lottery Div 212 W 3rd St Suite 210 *TF:* 800-999-2959 ■ *Web:* www.coloradolottery.com	Pueblo	CO	81003	719-546-2400	546-5208
Measurements Standards Section 3125 Wyandot St *Web:* www.ag.state.co.us/ics/ics.html	Denver	CO	80211	303-477-4220	477-4248
Medical Examiners Board 1560 Broadway Suite 1300 *Web:* www.dora.state.co.us/medical	Denver	CO	80202	303-894-7690	894-7692
Motor Vehicle Div 1881 Pierce St *Web:* www.mv.state.co.us/mv.html	Lakewood	CO	80214	303-205-5600	205-5975
Natural Resources Dept 1313 Sherman St Rm 718 *TF:* 800-536-5308 ■ *Web:* www.dnr.state.co.us	Denver	CO	80203	303-866-3311	866-2115
Parks & Outdoor Recreation Div 1313 Sherman St Rm 618 *TF Campground R:* 800-678-2267 ■ *Web:* parks.state.co.us	Denver	CO	80203	303-866-3437	866-3206
Parole Board 1600 W 24th St Bldg 54	Pueblo	CO	81003	719-583-5800	583-5805
Public Health & Environment Dept 4300 Cherry Creek Dr S *Web:* www.cdphe.state.co.us	Denver	CO	80246	303-692-2035	782-0095
Public Utilities Commission 1580 Logan St 2nd Fl *Web:* www.dora.state.co.us/puc	Denver	CO	80203	303-894-2000	894-2065
Real Estate Commission 1900 Grant St Suite 600 *Web:* www.dora.state.co.us/real-estate	Denver	CO	80203	303-894-2166	894-2683
Regulatory Agencies Dept 1560 Broadway Suite 1550 *TF:* 800-886-7675 ■ *Web:* www.dora.state.co.us	Denver	CO	80202	303-894-7855	894-7885
Revenue Dept 1375 Sherman St Rm 404 *Web:* www.revenue.state.co.us	Denver	CO	80261	303-866-3091	866-2400
Secretary of State 1700 Broadway 2nd Fl *Web:* www.sos.state.co.us	Denver	CO	80290	303-894-2200	894-4860
Securities Div 1580 Lincoln St Suite 420 *Web:* www.dora.state.co.us/securities	Denver	CO	80203	303-894-2320	861-2126
State Court Administrator 1301 Pennsylvania St Suite 300 *TF:* 800-888-0001 ■ *Web:* www.courts.state.co.us	Denver	CO	80203	303-837-3668	837-2340
State Patrol 700 Kipling St *Web:* www.csp.state.co.us	Denver	CO	80215	303-239-4500	239-4485
Supreme Court 2 E 14th Ave 4th Fl *Web:* www.courts.state.co.us/supct/supctindex.htm	Denver	CO	80203	303-837-3790	
Tourism Office 1625 Broadway Suite 1700 *TF:* 800-265-6723 ■ *Web:* www.colorado.com	Denver	CO	80202	303-892-3885	892-3848
Transportation Dept 4201 E Arkansas Ave *Web:* www.dot.state.co.us	Denver	CO	80222	303-757-9228	757-9153
Treasurer 140 State Capitol Bldg *Web:* www.treasurer.state.co.us	Denver	CO	80203	303-866-2441	866-2123
Veterans Affairs Div 789 Sherman St Suite 260	Denver	CO	80203	303-894-7474	894-7442
Victims Programs Office 700 Kipling St Suite 3000 *TF:* 888-282-1080 ■ *Web:* dcj.state.co.us/ovp	Denver	CO	80215	303-239-4442	239-4491
Vital Records Section 4300 Cherry Creek Dr S *Web:* www.cdphe.state.co.us/hs/certs.asp	Denver	CO	80246	303-692-2200	691-9307
Vocational Rehabilitation Div 2211 W Evans Ave Bldg B *Web:* www.cdhs.state.co.us/ods/dvr	Denver	CO	80223	303-866-4150	866-3419
Wildlife Div 6060 Broadway *Web:* wildlife.state.co.us	Denver	CO	80216	303-297-1192	294-0874
Workers Compensation Div 633 17th St Suite 400 *TF:* 888-390-7936 ■ *Web:* www.coworkforce.com/dwc	Denver	CO	80202	303-318-8700	318-8710

342-7 Connecticut

	City	State	Zip	Phone	Fax
State Government Information *Web:* www.ct.gov		CT		860-622-2200	
Accountancy Board 30 Trinity St	Hartford	CT	06106	860-509-6179	509-6247
Administrative Services Dept 165 Capitol Ave 4th Fl *Web:* www.das.state.ct.us	Hartford	CT	06106	860-713-5000	713-7459
Aging Commission 210 Capitol Ave Suite 508 *Web:* www.cga.ct.gov/coa	Hartford	CT	06106	860-240-5200	240-5204
Agriculture Dept 165 Capitol Ave *TF:* 800-861-9931 ■ *Web:* www.ct.gov/doag	Hartford	CT	06106	860-713-2500	713-2515
Attorney General 55 Elm St *Web:* www.cslib.org/attygenl	Hartford	CT	06106	860-808-5318	808-5387
Banking Dept 260 Constitution Plaza *TF:* 800-831-7225 ■ *Web:* www.state.ct.us/dob	Hartford	CT	06103	860-240-8299	240-8178
Bill Status Legislative Office Bldg	Hartford	CT	06106	860-240-0555	
Chief Medical Examiner 11 Shuttle Rd *TF:* 800-846-8820 ■ *Web:* www.state.ct.us/ocme	Farmington	CT	06032	860-679-3980	679-1257
Child Support Assistance 55 Elm St	Hartford	CT	06106	860-808-5150	808-5383
Children & Families Dept 505 Hudson St *TF:* 800-842-2288 ■ *Web:* www.state.ct.us/dcf	Hartford	CT	06106	860-566-2497	566-7947
Arts Commission 755 Main St 1 Financial Plaza *Web:* www.cultureandtourism.org	Hartford	CT	06103	860-256-2800	256-2811
Consumer Protection Dept 165 Capitol Ave *TF:* 800-842-2649 ■ *Web:* www.ct.gov/dcp	Hartford	CT	06106	860-713-6020	713-7239
Correction Dept 24 Wolcott Hill Rd *Web:* www.ct.gov/doc/	Wethersfield	CT	06109	860-692-7780	692-7783
Economic & Community Development Dept 505 Hudson St *Web:* www.ct.gov/ecd	Hartford	CT	06106	860-270-8000	270-8188
Education Dept 165 Capitol Ave *Web:* www.state.ct.us/sde	Hartford	CT	06106	860-713-6548	713-7005

Agency	City	State	ZIP	Phone	Fax
Environmental Protection Dept 79 Elm St *Web:* dep.state.ct.us	Hartford	CT	06106	860-424-3000	424-4051
Ethics Commission 20 Trinity St Suite 2 *Web:* www.ethics.state.ct.us	Hartford	CT	06106	860-566-4472	566-3806
General Assembly Legislative Office Bldg *Web:* www.cga.state.ct.us	Hartford	CT	06106	860-240-0100	240-0122
Governor 210 Capitol Ave *Web:* www.ct.gov/governorrell	Hartford	CT	06106	860-566-4840	524-7395
Higher Education Dept 61 Woodland St *TF:* 800-842-0229 ■ *Web:* www.ctdhe.org	Hartford	CT	06105	860-947-1800	947-1310
Historical Commission 59 S Prospect St	Hartford	CT	06106	860-566-3005	566-5078
Homeland Security Div 25 Sigourney St 6th Fl *Web:* www.ct.gov/hls	Hartford	CT	06106	860-256-0800	256-0815
Housing Finance Authority 999 West St *Web:* www.chfa.org	Rocky Hill	CT	06067	860-721-9501	571-4367
Information Technology Dept 101 E River Dr *Web:* www.ct.gov/doit	East Hartford	CT	06108	860-622-2400	610-0672
Insurance Dept PO Box 816 *Web:* www.ct.gov/cid	Hartford	CT	06142	860-297-3800	566-7410
Judicial Branch 231 Capitol Ave *Web:* www.jud.state.ct.us	Hartford	CT	06106	860-757-2100	757-2130
Labor Dept 200 Folly Brook Blvd *Web:* www.ctdol.state.ct.us	Wethersfield	CT	06109	860-263-6000	263-6699
Lieutenant Governor 210 Capitol Ave Rm 304 *Web:* www.ct.gov/ltgovksullivan	Hartford	CT	06106	860-524-7384	524-7304
Lottery Corp 270 John Downey Dr *Web:* www.ctlottery.org	New Britain	CT	06051	860-348-4000	348-4015
Motor Vehicles Dept 60 State St *Web:* www.ct.gov/dmv	Wethersfield	CT	06161	860-263-5700	524-4898
Parole Board 55 W Main St Suite 520 *Web:* www.ct.gov/doc	Waterbury	CT	06702	203-805-6605	805-6652
Public Health Dept 410 Capitol Ave *Web:* www.dph.state.ct.us	Hartford	CT	06134	860-509-8000	509-7111
Public Utility Control Dept 10 Franklin Sq *TF:* 800-382-4586 ■ *Web:* www.state.ct.us/dpuc	New Britain	CT	06051	860-827-2622	827-2613
Real Estate & Professional Trades Div 165 Capitol Ave Rm 110	Hartford	CT	06106	860-713-6135	713-7239
Regulatory Services Bureau 410 Capitol Ave PO Box 340308	Hartford	CT	06134	860-509-8045	509-7539
Rehabilitation Services Bureau 25 Sigourney St 11th Fl *TF:* 800-537-2549 ■ *Web:* www.brs.state.ct.us	Hartford	CT	06106	860-424-4844	424-4850
Revenue Services Dept 25 Sigourney St *Web:* www.ct.gov/drs	Hartford	CT	06106	860-297-5650	297-5714
Secretary of State 210 Capitol Ave Rm 104 *Web:* www.sots.state.ct.us	Hartford	CT	06106	860-509-6200	509-6209
Securities & Business Investments Div 260 Constitution Plaza *Web:* www.state.ct.us/dob/pages/secdiv.htm	Hartford	CT	06103	860-240-8230	240-8295
Certification & Professional Development Bureau PO Box 150471 *Web:* www.state.ct.us/sde/dtl	Hartford	CT	06115	860-713-6969	713-7017
State Parks Div 79 Elm St *TF:* 866-287-2757 ■ *Web:* www.dep.state.ct.us/stateparks	Hartford	CT	06106	860-424-3200	424-4070
State Police Div 1111 Country Club Rd *Web:* www.state.ct.us/dps/csp.htm	Middletown	CT	06457	860-685-8000	685-8354
Student Financial Aid Office 61 Woodland St *Web:* www.ctdhe.org/SFA	Hartford	CT	06105	860-947-1800	947-1310
Supreme Court 231 Capitol Ave *Web:* www.jud.state.ct.us/external/supapp	Hartford	CT	06106	860-757-2200	757-2217
Tourism Div 505 Hudson St *TF:* 888-288-4748 ■ *Web:* www.ctbound.org	Hartford	CT	06106	860-270-8080	270-8077
Transportation Dept 2800 Berlin Tpke *Web:* www.ct.gov/dot	Newington	CT	06111	860-594-2000	594-3008
Treasurer 55 Elm St *Web:* www.state.ct.us/ott	Hartford	CT	06106	860-702-3000	702-3043
Veterans Affairs Dept 287 West St *TF:* 800-447-0961 ■ *Web:* www.ct.gov/ctva	Rocky Hill	CT	06067	860-721-5891	721-5904
Victim Services Office 31 Cookes St *TF:* 800-822-8428 ■ *Web:* www.jud.state.ct.us/faq/crime.html	Plainville	CT	06062	860-747-3994	747-6428
Vital Records Unit PO Box 340308 *Web:* www.dph.state.ct.us/OPPE/hpvital.htm	Hartford	CT	06134	860-509-7897	509-7964
Weights & Measures Div 165 Capitol Ave Rm 165	Hartford	CT	06106	860-713-6300	566-7630
Workers' Compensation Commission 21 Oak St 4th Fl *TF:* 800-223-9675 ■ *Web:* wcc.state.ct.us	Hartford	CT	06106	860-493-1500	247-1361

342-8 Delaware

Agency	City	State	ZIP	Phone	Fax
State Government Information *Web:* www.delaware.gov		DE		302-739-4000	
Administrative Office of the Courts 500 N King St 11th Fl *Web:* courts.delaware.gov	Wilmington	DE	19801	302-255-0090	255-2217
Aging & Adults with Physical Disabilites Services Div 1901 N DuPont Hwy *Web:* www.dhss.delaware.gov	New Castle	DE	19720	302-255-9390	577-4445
Agriculture Dept 2320 S DuPont Hwy *TF:* 800-286-8685 ■ *Web:* www.state.de.us/deptagri	Dover	DE	19901	302-739-4811	697-6287
Arts Div 820 N French St 4th Fl *Web:* www.artsdel.org	Wilmington	DE	19801	302-577-8278	577-6561
Attorney General 820 N French St *Web:* www.state.de.us/attgen	Wilmington	DE	19801	302-577-8400	577-6630
Bank Commissioner 555 E Loockerman St Suite 210	Dover	DE	19901	302-739-4235	739-3609
Bill Status Legislative Hall PO Box 1401 *Web:* www.legis.state.de.us	Dover	DE	19903	302-739-4114	739-3895
Chief Medical Examiner 200 S Adam St *Web:* www.dhss.delaware.gov/dhss/ocme	Wilmington	DE	19801	302-577-3420	577-3416
Child Support Enforcement Div PO Box 904 *Web:* www.dhss.delaware.gov/dhss/dcse	New Castle	DE	19720	302-577-7171	577-4873
Consumer Protection Unit 820 N French St 5th Fl *Web:* www.state.de.us/attgen/	Wilmington	DE	19801	302-577-8600	577-6499
Correction Dept 245 McKee Rd **Fax:* Mail Rm ■ *Web:* www.state.de.us/correct	Dover	DE	19904	302-739-5601	739-8223*
Economic Development Office 99 Kings Hwy *Web:* www.state.de.us/dedo	Dover	DE	19901	302-739-4271	739-5749
Education Dept 401 Federal St Suite 2 *Web:* www.doe.state.de.us	Dover	DE	19901	302-739-4601	739-4654
Emergency Management Agency 165 Brick Store Landing Rd *TF:* 877-729-3362 ■ *Web:* www.state.de.us/dema	Smyrna	DE	19977	302-659-3362	659-6855
Employment & Training Div 4425 N Market St *Web:* www.vcnet.net	Wilmington	DE	19802	302-761-8085	761-6634
Finance Dept 820 N French St 8th Fl *Web:* www.state.de.us/finance	Wilmington	DE	19801	302-577-8979	577-8982
Fish & Wildlife Div 89 Kings Hwy *Web:* www.dnrec.state.de.us/fw	Dover	DE	19901	302-739-9910	739-6157
General Assembly Legislative Hall Box 1401 *Web:* www.legis.state.de.us	Dover	DE	19903	302-739-4114	739-3895
Governor 150 William Penn St 2nd Fl *Web:* www.state.de.us/governor	Dover	DE	19901	302-577-3210	739-2775
Harness Racing Commission 2320 S Dupont Hwy *Web:* www.state.de.us/deptagri/harness	Dover	DE	19901	302-698-4599	697-6287
Health & Social Services Dept 1901 N DuPont Hwy *Web:* www.dhss.delaware.gov/dhss	New Castle	DE	19720	302-355-9040	255-4429
Higher Education Commission 820 N French St 5th Fl *TF:* 800-292-7935 ■ *Web:* www.doe.state.de.us/high-ed	Wilmington	DE	19801	302-577-3240	577-6765
Historical & Cultural Affairs Div 21 The Green	Dover	DE	19901	302-739-5313	739-6711
Housing Authority 18 The Green *Web:* www2.state.de.us/dsha	Dover	DE	19901	302-739-4263	739-6122
Insurance Dept 841 Silver Lake Blvd *Web:* www.state.de.us/inscom	Dover	DE	19904	302-739-4251	739-5280
Labor Dept 4425 N Market St *Web:* www.delawareworks.com	Wilmington	DE	19802	302-761-8000	761-6621
Lieutenant Governor 150 William Penn St 3rd Fl *Web:* www.state.de.us/ltgov	Dover	DE	19901	302-744-4333	739-6965
Motor Vehicles Div PO Box 698 *Web:* www.dmv.de.gov	Dover	DE	19903	302-744-2500	739-3152
Natural Resources & Environmental Control Dept 89 Kings Hwy *Web:* www.dnrec.state.de.us	Dover	DE	19901	302-739-9902	739-6242
Parks & Recreation Div 89 Kings Hwy *TF Campground R:* 877-987-2757 ■ *Web:* www.destateparks.com	Dover	DE	19901	302-739-9200	739-3817
Parole Board 820 N French St 5th Fl *Web:* www.state.de.us/parole	Wilmington	DE	19801	302-577-5233	577-3501
Professional Regulation Div 861 Silver Lake Blvd Suite 203 *Web:* www.professionallicensing.state.de.us	Dover	DE	19904	302-739-4500	739-2711
Professional Standards Board 401 Federal St Suite 2 *Web:* www.doe.state.de.us/ProfStandardsBoard	Dover	DE	19901	302-739-2771	739-4483
Public Integrity Commission 410 Federal St Suite 3 *Web:* www.state.de.us/pic	Dover	DE	19901	302-739-2399	739-2398
Public Service Commission 861 Silver Lake Blvd Suite 100 *TF:* 800-282-8574 ■ *Web:* www.state.de.us/delpsc	Dover	DE	19904	302-739-4247	739-4849
Revenue Div 820 N French St 1st Fl *Web:* www.state.de.us/revenue	Wilmington	DE	19801	302-577-8200	577-8202
Secretary of State 401 Federal St Suite 3 *Web:* www.state.de.us/sos/sos.shtml	Dover	DE	19901	302-739-4111	739-3811
Securities Div 820 N French St 5th Fl *Web:* www.state.de.us/securities	Wilmington	DE	19801	302-577-8424	577-6987
Services for Children Youth & Their Families Dept 1825 Faulkland Rd *Web:* www.state.de.us/kids	Wilmington	DE	19805	302-633-2500	995-8290
Social Services Div 1901 N DuPont Hwy *Web:* www.state.de.us/dhss/dss/dsshome.html	New Castle	DE	19720	302-577-4400	577-4405
State Lottery 1575 McKee Rd Suite 102 *TF:* 800-338-6200 ■ *Web:* lottery.state.de.us	Dover	DE	19904	302-739-5291	739-6706
State Police Div PO Box 430 *Web:* www.state.de.us/dsp	Dover	DE	19903	302-739-5911	739-5966
Supreme Court 820 N French St *Web:* courts.delaware.gov	Wilmington	DE	19899	302-577-8425	577-3702
Technology & Information Dept 801 Silver Lake Blvd *Web:* www.state.de.us/dti	Dover	DE	19904	302-739-9500	739-6251
Thoroughbred Racing Commission 2320 S DuPont Hwy **Fax Area Code:* 512 ■ *Web:* www.state.de.us/deptagri/thoroughbred	Dover	DE	19901	302-698-4599	463-1376*
Tourism Office 99 Kings Hwy *TF:* 866-284-7483 ■ *Web:* www.visitdelaware.net	Dover	DE	19901	302-739-4271	739-5749
Transportation Dept 800 Bay Rd *TF:* 800-652-5600 ■ *Web:* www.deldot.net	Dover	DE	19903	302-760-2080	739-4329
Treasurer 540 S DuPont Hwy Suite 4 *Web:* www.state.de.us/treasure	Dover	DE	19903	302-744-1000	739-5635
Unemployment Insurance Div 4425 N Market St *Web:* www.delawareworks.com/Unemployment/welcome.shtml	Wilmington	DE	19802	302-761-8351	761-6637
Veterans Affairs Commission 802 Silverlake Blvd Suite 100 *Web:* www.state.de.us/veteran/	Dover	DE	19904	302-739-2792	739-2794
Violent Crimes Compensation Board 240 N James St Suite 203 *Web:* courts.delaware.gov/vccb	Newport	DE	19804	302-995-8383	995-8387
Vital Statistics Office PO Box 637 *TF:* 800-464-4357 ■ *Web:* www.dhss.delaware.gov/dhss/dph/ss/vitalstats.html	Dover	DE	19903	302-739-4721	736-1862
Vocational Rehabilitation Div 4425 N Market St *Web:* www.delawareworks.com/divisions/dvr/welcome.htm	Wilmington	DE	19809	302-761-8300	761-6633
Weights & Measures Office 2320 S DuPont Hwy *TF:* 800-282-8685 ■ *Web:* www.state.de.us/deptagri/weightsm	Dover	DE	19901	302-739-4811	697-6287

342-9 District of Columbia

Agency	City	State	ZIP	Phone	Fax
Government Information *Web:* www.dc.gov		DC		202-727-1000	
Aging Office 441 4th St NW Suite 900 S *Web:* dcoa.dc.gov	Washington	DC	20001	202-724-5622	724-4979
Banking & Financial Institutions Office PO Box 96378	Washington	DC	20090	202-727-8000	535-1197
Bill Status 1350 Pennsylvania Ave NW Suite 10 *Web:* www.dccouncil.washington.dc.us/lims/default.asp	Washington	DC	20004	202-724-8050	
Commission on the Arts & Humanities 2901 14th St NW 1st Fl *Web:* www.dcarts.dc.gov/dcarts/	Washington	DC	20010	202-724-5613	727-4135
Consumer & Regulatory Affairs Dept 941 N Capitol St NE *Web:* dcra.dc.gov/dcra/	Washington	DC	20002	202-442-4400	442-9445
Convention & Tourism Corp 901 7th Street NW 4th Fl *TF:* 800-422-8644 ■ *Web:* www.washington.org	Washington	DC	20001	202-789-7000	789-7037
Crime Victims Compensation Program 515 5th St NW Room 104 *Web:* www.dccourts.gov/dccourts/superior/cvcp.jsp	Washington	DC	20001	202-879-4216	879-4230
Department of Insurance & Securities Regulation 810 1st St NE Suite 701 *Web:* disr.washingtondc.gov	Washington	DC	20002	202-727-8000	
Economic Development 1350 Pennsylvania Ave NW Suite 317 *Web:* www.dcbiz.dc.gov	Washington	DC	20004	202-727-6365	727-6703
Elections & Ethics Board 441 4th St NW Suite 250N *TF:* 866-328-6837 ■ *Web:* www.dcboee.org	Washington	DC	20001	202-727-2525	347-2648
Employment Services Dept 609 H St NE *TF:* 877-319-7346 ■ *Web:* does.ci.washington.dc.us	Washington	DC	20002	202-698-6044	546-8467
Historic Preservation Div 801 N Capitol St NE	Washington	DC	20002	202-442-8800	
Emergency Preparedness Office 2720 Martin Luther King Jr Ave SE 8th Fl *Web:* dcema.dc.gov/dcema/	Washington	DC	20032	202-727-6161	
Housing Finance Agency 815 Florida Ave NW *Web:* www.dchfa.org	Washington	DC	20001	202-777-1600	
Human Services Dept 64 New York Ave NE 6th Fl *Web:* www.dhs.dc.gov	Washington	DC	20002	202-671-4200	
Lottery Board 2101 ML King Jr Ave SE *Web:* www.dclottery.com	Washington	DC	20020	202-645-8000	645-8077
Occupational & Professional Licensing Administration 941 N Capitol St NE	Washington	DC	20002	202-442-4320	442-4528
Paternity & Child Support Enforcement Office 441 4th St NW Suite 550	Washington	DC	20001	202-442-9900	

District of Columbia (Cont'd)

				Phone	Fax
Public Service Commission 1333 'H' St NW 2nd Fl W	Washington	DC	20005	202-626-5100	393-1389
Web: www.dcpsc.org					
Rehabilitation Services Administration 810 1st St NE 9th Fl	Washington	DC	20002	202-442-8400	
Securities Office 810 1st St NE 7th Fl	Washington	DC	20002	202-727-8000	535-1199
Web: www.disb.dc.gov					
Tuition Assistance Grant Program 441 4th St NW Rm 350N	Washington	DC	20001	202-727-2824	727-2834
TF: 877-485-6751 ■ *Web:* www.tuitiongrant.dc.gov					
Vital Records Branch 825 N Capitol St NE 1st Fl	Washington	DC	20002	202-671-5000	
Web: dchealth.dc.gov					
Weights & Measures Branch 1110 U St SE	Washington	DC	20020	202-698-2130	

342-10 Florida

				Phone	Fax
State Government Information		FL		850-488-1234	
Web: www.myflorida.com					
Agriculture & Consumer Services Dept State Capitol PL-10	Tallahassee	FL	32399	850-488-3022	488-7585
Web: www.doacs.state.fl.us					
Attorney General State Capitol PL-01	Tallahassee	FL	32399	850-487-1963	487-2564
Web: myfloridalegal.com					
Bill Status 111 W Madison St Rm 704	Tallahassee	FL	32399	850-488-4371	922-1534
TF: 800-342-1827 ■ *Web:* www.leg.state.fl.us					
Business & Professional Regulation Dept 1940 N Monroe St	Tallahassee	FL	32399	850-487-1395	488-1830
Web: www.myflorida.com/dbpr					
Chief Financial Officer 200 E Gaines St	Tallahassee	FL	32399	850-413-2850	
Web: www.fldfs.com					
Child Support Enforcement Program PO Box 8030	Tallahassee	FL	32314	800-622-5437	
Web: www.myflorida.com/dor/childsupport					
Children & Families Dept 1317 Winewood Blvd	Tallahassee	FL	32399	850-488-6294	487-4682
Web: www.state.fl.us/cf_web					
Citrus Dept 1115 E Memorial Blvd PO Box 148	Lakeland	FL	33802	863-499-2500	284-4300
Web: www.floridajuice.com					
Colleges & Universities Div 325 W Gaines St	Tallahassee	FL	32399	850-254-0466	245-9685
Web: www.fldcu.org					
Consumer Services Div 2005 Apalachee Pkwy	Tallahassee	FL	32399	850-922-2966	487-4177
TF: 800-435-7352 ■ *Web:* www.800helpfla.com					
Corrections Dept 2601 Blair Stone Rd	Tallahassee	FL	32399	850-488-5021	488-4534*
*Fax: Hum Res ■ *Web:* www.dc.state.fl.us					
Cultural Affairs Div 1001 DeSoto Park Dr	Tallahassee	FL	32301	850-254-6470	245-6497
Web: www.florida-arts.org					
Education Dept 325 W Gaines St	Tallahassee	FL	32399	850-245-0505	245-9667
Web: www.fdoe.org					
Elder Affairs Dept 4040 Esplanade Way	Tallahassee	FL	32399	850-414-2000	414-2004
Web: elderaffairs.state.fl.us					
Emergency Management Div 2555 Shumard Oak Blvd	Tallahassee	FL	32399	850-413-9900	488-7841
Web: www.floridadisaster.org					
Environmental Protection Dept 3900 Commonwealth Blvd MS 10	Tallahassee	FL	32399	850-245-2118	245-2128
Web: www.dep.state.fl.us					
Ethics Commission 3600 Maclay Blvd S Suite 201	Tallahassee	FL	32312	850-488-7864	488-3077
Web: www.ethics.state.fl.us					
Financial Regulation Office 200 E Gaines St	Tallahassee	FL	32399	850-410-9111	410-9448
Web: www.fldfs.com/OFR					
Financial Services Dept 200 E Gaines St	Tallahassee	FL	32399	850-413-3100	488-2349
TF: 800-342-2762 ■ *Web:* www.fldfs.com					
Fish & Wildlife Conservation Commission 620 S Meridian St	Tallahassee	FL	32399	850-488-4676	488-6988
Web: www.floridaconservation.org					
Governor State Capitol	Tallahassee	FL	32399	850-488-4441	487-0801
Web: www.myflorida.com					
Health Dept 4052 Bald Cypress Way Bin A00	Tallahassee	FL	32399	850-245-4443	487-3729
Web: www.doh.state.fl.us					
Highway Safety & Motor Vehicles Dept 2900 Apalachee Pkwy	Tallahassee	FL	32399	850-922-9000	922-6274
Web: www.hsmv.state.fl.us					
Historical Resources Div 500 S Bronough St Suite 305	Tallahassee	FL	32399	850-245-6300	245-6435
Web: dhr.dos.state.fl.us					
Housing Finance Corp 227 N Bronough St Suite 5000	Tallahassee	FL	32301	850-488-4197	488-9809
Web: www.floridahousing.org					
Insurance Regulation Office 200 E Gaines St	Tallahassee	FL	32399	850-413-3132	
TF: 800-342-2762 ■ *Web:* www.fldfs.com/companies					
Law Enforcement Dept PO Box 1489	Tallahassee	FL	32302	850-410-7000	410-7440
Web: www.fdle.state.fl.us					
Legislature State Capitol	Tallahassee	FL	32399	850-488-4371	922-0183
Web: www.leg.state.fl.us					
Lieutenant Governor State Capitol PL-05	Tallahassee	FL	32399	850-488-4711	921-6114
Lottery Dept 250 Marriott Dr	Tallahassee	FL	32301	850-487-7777	487-7796*
*Fax: Hum Res ■ *Web:* www.flalottery.com					
Medical Quality Assurance Div 4052 Bald Cypress Way	Tallahassee	FL	32399	850-488-0595	487-9622
Web: www.doh.state.fl.us/mqa					
Military Affairs Dept St Francis Barracks 82 Marine St	Saint Augustine	FL	32084	904-823-0364	823-0125
Web: www.dma.state.fl.us					
Parole Commission 2601 Blair Stone Rd Bldg C	Tallahassee	FL	32399	850-488-3417	414-1915
Web: fpc.state.fl.us					
Prepaid College Board PO Box 6567	Tallahassee	FL	32314	850-488-8514	309-1766*
*Fax: Cust Svc ■ *TF:* 800-552-4723 ■ *Web:* www.florida529plans.com					
Public Service Commission 2540 Shumard Oak Blvd	Tallahassee	FL	32399	850-413-6042	487-1716
Web: www.floridapsc.com					
Recreation & Parks Div 3900 Commonwealth Blvd MS 500	Tallahassee	FL	32399	850-245-2157	245-3041
TF Campground R: 800-326-3521 ■ *Web:* www.dep.state.fl.us/parks					
Revenue Dept 501 S Calhoun St Suite 104	Tallahassee	FL	32399	850-488-5050	488-0024
Web: myflorida.com/dor					
Secretary of State 500 S Bronough St	Tallahassee	FL	32399	850-245-6500	245-6125
Web: www.dos.state.fl.us					
State Boxing Commission 1940 N Monroe St	Tallahassee	FL	32399	850-488-8500	922-2249
Web: www.state.fl.us/dbpr/sbc					
State Courts Administrator Office 500 S Duval St	Tallahassee	FL	32399	850-922-5081	488-0156
Web: www.flcourts.org					
State Technology Office 4030 Esplanade Way	Tallahassee	FL	32399	850-410-4777	922-5162
Web: sto.myflorida.com					
Student Financial Assistance Office 1940 N Monroe St Suite 70	Tallahassee	FL	32303	850-410-5200	488-3612
TF: 888-827-2004 ■ *Web:* www.floridastudentfinancialaid.org					
Supreme Court 500 S Duval St	Tallahassee	FL	32399	850-488-0125	
Web: www.flcourts.org					
Tourism Commission 661 E Jefferson St Suite 300	Tallahassee	FL	32301	850-488-5607	224-2938
TF: 888-735-2872 ■ *Web:* www.visitflorida.com					
Transportation Dept 605 Suwannee St	Tallahassee	FL	32399	850-414-5200	414-5201
Web: www.dot.state.fl.us					
Veterans' Affairs Dept 11351 Ulmerton Rd Rm 311-K	Largo	FL	33778	727-518-3202	518-3216
Web: www.floridavets.org					
Victim Services & Criminal Justice Programs State Capitol PL-01	Tallahassee	FL	32399	850-414-3300	487-1595
Web: myfloridalegal.com/victims					
Vital Records Bureau PO Box 210	Jacksonville	FL	32231	904-359-6900	359-6993
Web: www.doh.state.fl.us/planning_eval/vital_statistics					
Vocational Rehabilitation Services Div 2002 Old St Augustine Rd Bldg A	Tallahassee	FL	32301	850-245-3399	
TF: 800-451-4327 ■ *Web:* www.rehabworks.org					
Workers' Compensation Div 200 E Gaines St	Tallahassee	FL	32399	850-413-1601	
Web: www.fldfs.com/wc					
Workforce Florida Inc 1974 Commonwealth Ln	Tallahassee	FL	32303	850-921-1119	921-1101
Web: www.workforceflorida.com					

342-11 Georgia

				Phone	Fax
State Government Information		GA		404-656-2000	
Web: www.georgia.gov					
Administrative Office of the Courts 244 Washington St SW Suite 300	Atlanta	GA	30334	404-656-5171	651-6449
Web: www.georgiacourts.org/aoc					
Aging Services Div 2 Peachtree St NW Suite 9-385	Atlanta	GA	30303	404-657-5255	657-5285
Web: aging.dhr.georgia.gov					
Agriculture Dept 19 ML King Jr Dr SW	Atlanta	GA	30334	404-656-3600	656-9380
Web: www.agr.state.ga.us					
Arts Council 260 14th St NW Suite 401	Atlanta	GA	30318	404-685-2787	685-2788
Web: www.gaarts.org					
Attorney General 40 Capitol Sq SW	Atlanta	GA	30334	404-656-3300	657-8733
Web: www.state.ga.us/ago					
Banking & Finance Dept 2990 Brandywine Rd Suite 200	Atlanta	GA	30341	770-986-1633	986-1654
Web: www.ganet.org/dbf					
Bill Status-House State Capitol Rm 309	Atlanta	GA	30334	404-656-5015	
Web: www.legis.state.ga.us					
Bill Status-Senate State Capitol Rm 353	Atlanta	GA	30334	404-656-5040	656-5043
Web: www.legis.state.ga.us					
Child Support Enforcement Office 2 Peachtree St NW	Atlanta	GA	30303	404-657-0634	
Web: ocse.dhr.georgia.gov					
Community Affairs Dept 60 Executive Park South NE	Atlanta	GA	30329	404-656-4940	679-0589
Web: www.dca.state.ga.us					
Consumer Affairs Office 2 ML King Jr Dr SE Suite 356	Atlanta	GA	30334	404-656-6800	651-9018
Web: consumer.georgia.gov					
Corrections Dept 2 ML King Jr Dr SE Suite 866	Atlanta	GA	30334	404-656-9770	651-8335
Web: www.dcor.state.ga.us					
Crime Victim Compensation Program 503 Oak Pl Suite 540	Atlanta	GA	30349	404-559-4949	559-4960
Defense Dept PO Box 17965	Atlanta	GA	30316	404-624-6001	624-6005
Web: www.dod.state.ga.us					
Economic Development Dept 285 Peachtree Center Ave NW Suites 1000 & 1100	Atlanta	GA	30303	404-962-4000	463-7299
Web: www.georgia.org					
Education Dept 205 Jesse Hill Jr Dr SE Suite 2066E	Atlanta	GA	30334	404-656-2800	651-8737
Web: www.gadoe.org					
Emergency Management Agency PO Box 18055	Atlanta	GA	30316	404-635-7000	635-7205
Web: www.gema.state.ga.us					
Employment Services Div 148 Andrew Young International Blvd NE	Atlanta	GA	30303	404-232-3515	
Web: www.dol.state.ga.us					
Environmental Protection Div 2 ML King Jr Dr SE Suite 1152E	Atlanta	GA	30334	404-657-5947	651-5778
TF: 888-373-5947 ■ *Web:* www.dnr.state.ga.us/dnr/environ					
Family & Children Services Div 2 Peachtree St NW Suite 19-400	Atlanta	GA	30303	404-651-9361	657-5105
Web: dfcs.dhr.georgia.gov					
General Assembly State Capitol	Atlanta	GA	30334	404-656-5000	651-8086
Web: www.legis.state.ga.us					
Governor State Capitol Rm 203	Atlanta	GA	30334	404-656-1776	657-7332
Web: www.gov.state.ga.us					
Historic Preservation Div 47 Trinity Ave SW Suite 141-H	Atlanta	GA	30303	404-656-2840	651-8739
Web: www.gashpo.org					
Housing Finance Div 60 Executive Park South NE	Atlanta	GA	30329	404-679-0607	679-4837
Web: www.dca.state.ga.us					
Human Resources Dept 2 Peachtree St NW Suite 29-250	Atlanta	GA	30303	404-656-5680	651-8669
Web: dhr.georgia.gov					
Information Technology Office 2 Peachtree St NW Suite 4-400	Atlanta	GA	30303	404-656-5440	
Web: oit.dhr.georgia.gov					
Insurance Commissioner 2 ML King Jr Dr SE 7th Fl	Atlanta	GA	30334	404-656-2056	656-4030
Web: www.gainsurance.org					
Labor Dept 148 Andrew Young International Blvd NE	Atlanta	GA	30303	404-232-7300	657-9996
Web: www.dol.state.ga.us					
Lieutenant Governor State Capitol Rm 240	Atlanta	GA	30334	404-656-5030	656-6739
Web: ltgov.georgia.gov					
Lottery Corp 250 Williams St NW Suite 3000	Atlanta	GA	30303	404-215-5000	215-8871
Web: www.galottery.com					
Medical Examiners Composite State Board 2 Peachtree St NW 36th Fl	Atlanta	GA	30303	404-656-3913	656-9723
Web: medicalboard.georgia.gov					
Mental Health Developmental Disabilities & Addictive Diseases Div 2 Peachtree St NW Suite 22-224	Atlanta	GA	30303	404-657-2252	657-1137
Web: mhddad.dhr.georgia.gov					
Motor Vehicle Safety Dept 2206 East View Pkwy	Conyers	GA	33013	678-413-8650	
Web: www.dmvs.ga.gov					
Natural Resources Dept 2 ML King Jr Dr SE Suite 1252E	Atlanta	GA	30334	404-656-3500	656-0770
Web: www.gadnr.org					
Pardons & Paroles Board 2 ML King Jr Dr SE East Tower Suite 458	Atlanta	GA	30334	404-656-5651	651-8502
Web: www.pap.state.ga.us					
Parks Recreation & Historic Sites Div 2 ML King Jr Dr SE Suite 1352E	Atlanta	GA	30334	404-656-2770	651-5871
TF: 800-862-7275 ■ *Web:* www.gastateparks.org					
Ports Authority PO Box 2406	Savannah	GA	31402	912-964-3811	964-3921
TF: 800-342-8012 ■ *Web:* www.gaports.com					
Professional Licensing Boards Div 237 Coliseum Dr	Macon	GA	31217	478-207-1300	207-1363
Web: www.sos.state.ga.us/plb					
Public Health Div 2 Peachtree St NW Suite 15-470	Atlanta	GA	30303	404-657-2700	657-2715
Web: health.state.ga.us					
Public Service Commission 244 Washington St SW Suite 126	Atlanta	GA	30334	404-656-4501	656-2341
Web: www.psc.state.ga.us					
Rehabilitation Services Div 140 Andrew Young International Blvd NE Suite 510	Atlanta	GA	30303	404-232-3910	
Web: www.vocrehabga.org					
Revenue Dept 1800 Century Center Blvd NE	Atlanta	GA	30345	404-417-4477	417-2101
Web: www.etax.dor.ga.gov					
Secretary of State State Capitol Rm 214	Atlanta	GA	30334	404-656-2881	656-0513
Web: www.sos.state.ga.us					
Securities & Business Regulation Div 2 ML King Jr Dr SE West Tower Suite 802	Atlanta	GA	30334	404-656-3920	657-8410
Web: www.sos.state.ga.us/securities					

	City	State	Zip	Phone	Fax
State Ethics Commission 205 Jesse Hill Jr Dr SE Suite 478 E Tower *Web:* www.ethics.state.ga.us	Atlanta	GA	30334	404-463-1980	463-1988
State Patrol PO Box 1456 *Web:* dps.georgia.gov	Atlanta	GA	30371	404-624-7000	624-7498
Student Finance Commission 2082 E Exchange Pl Suite 200 *TF:* 800-505-4732 ■ *Web:* www.gsfc.org	Tucker	GA	30084	770-724-9000	724-9004
Supreme Court 244 Washington St SW *Web:* www.gasupreme.us	Atlanta	GA	30334	404-656-3470	656-2253
Tourism Div 285 Peachtree Center Ave NE Suite 1000 *TF:* 800-847-4842 ■ *Web:* www.georgiaonmymind.org	Atlanta	GA	30303	404-656-2000	651-9063
Transportation Dept 2 Capitol Sq *Web:* www.dot.state.ga.us	Atlanta	GA	30334	404-656-5267	656-3507
Treasury & Fiscal Services Office 200 Piedmont Ave Suite 1202W *Web:* otfs.georgia.gov	Atlanta	GA	30334	404-656-2168	656-9048
University System Board of Regents 270 Washington St SW *Web:* www.usg.edu	Atlanta	GA	30334	404-656-2250	651-9301
Veterans Service Dept 2 ML King Jr Dr SE Suite 970E *Web:* sdvs.georgia.gov	Atlanta	GA	30303	404-656-2300	656-7006
Vital Records Office 2600 Skyland Dr NE *Web:* health.state.ga.us/programs/vitalrecords	Atlanta	GA	30319	404-679-4701	524-4278
Wildlife Resources Div 2070 US Hwy 278 SE **Fax Area Code: 706* ■ *Web:* georgiawildlife.dnr.state.ga.us	Social Circle	GA	30025	770-918-6400	557-3030*
Workers' Compensation Board 270 Peachtree St NW *Web:* sbwc.georgia.gov	Atlanta	GA	30303	404-656-2048	651-9467

342-12 Hawaii

	City	State	Zip	Phone	Fax
State Government Information *Web:* www.hawaii.gov		HI		808-586-2211	
Administrative Office of the Courts 417 S King St Rm 206 *Web:* www.courts.state.hi.us	Honolulu	HI	96812	808-539-4900	539-4855
Aging Office 250 S Hotel St Rm 406 *Web:* www4.hawaii.gov/eoa	Honolulu	HI	96813	808-586-0100	586-0185
Agriculture Dept 1428 S King St *Web:* www.hawaii.gov/hdoa	Honolulu	HI	96814	808-973-9600	973-9613
Attorney General 425 Queen St *Web:* www.state.hi.us/ag	Honolulu	HI	96813	808-586-1500	586-1239
Bill Status 415 S Beretania St Rm 401 *Web:* www.capitol.hawaii.gov	Honolulu	HI	96813	808-587-0478	587-0793
Budget & Finance Dept PO Box 150 *Web:* www.state.hi.us/budget	Honolulu	HI	96810	808-586-1518	586-1976
Business Economic Development & Tourism Dept PO Box 2359 *Web:* www.hawaii.gov/dbedt	Honolulu	HI	96804	808-586-2355	586-2377
Child Support Enforcement Agency 601 Kamokila Blvd Suite 251 *TF:* 888-317-9081 ■ *Web:* www.hawaii.gov/csea/csea.htm	Kapolei	HI	96707	808-692-7000	692-7060
Civil Defense Div 3949 Diamond Head Rd *Web:* www.scd.state.hi.us	Honolulu	HI	96816	808-733-4300	733-4287
Commerce & Consumer Affairs Dept PO Box 541 *Web:* www.state.hi.us/dcca	Honolulu	HI	96809	808-586-2830	586-2877
Consumer Protection Office 235 S Beretania St Rm 801 *Web:* www.hawaii.gov/dcca/ocp	Honolulu	HI	96813	808-586-2630	586-2640
Corrections Div 919 Ala Moana Blvd 4th Fl	Honolulu	HI	96814	808-587-1340	587-1282
Crime Victims Compensation Commission 1136 Union Mall Rm 600 *Web:* www.hawaii.gov/cvcc	Honolulu	HI	96813	808-587-1143	587-1146
Education Dept PO Box 2360 *Web:* doe.k12.hi.us	Honolulu	HI	96804	808-586-3230	586-3234
Financial Institutions Div PO Box 2054 *Web:* www.hawaii.gov/dcca/areas/dfi	Honolulu	HI	96805	808-586-2820	586-2818
Forestry & Wildlife Div 1151 Punchbowl St Rm 325 *Web:* www.dofaw.net	Honolulu	HI	96813	808-587-0166	587-0160
Governor 415 S Beretania St State Capitol *Web:* gov.state.hi.us	Honolulu	HI	96813	808-586-0034	586-0006
Health Dept 1250 Punchbowl St *Web:* www.state.hi.us/doh	Honolulu	HI	96813	808-586-4400	586-4444
Historic Preservation Div 601 Kamokila Blvd Rm 555 *Web:* www.hawaii.gov/dlnr/hpd/hpgreeting.htm	Kapolei	HI	96707	808-692-8015	692-8020
Housing & Community Development Corp 677 Queen St Suite 300 *Web:* www.hcdch.state.hi.us	Honolulu	HI	96813	808-587-0597	587-0588
Human Resources Development Dept 235 S Beretania St Rm 1400 *Web:* www.state.hi.us/hrd	Honolulu	HI	96813	808-587-1100	587-1106
Human Services Dept PO Box 339 *Web:* www.state.hi.us/dhs	Honolulu	HI	96809	808-586-4997	586-4890
Information & Communication Services Div 1151 Punchbowl St Rm B-10 *Web:* www.hawaii.gov/icsd	Honolulu	HI	96813	808-586-1920	586-1922
Insurance Div PO Box 3614 *Web:* www.hawaii.gov/dcca/areas/ins	Honolulu	HI	96811	808-586-2790	586-2806
Labor & Industrial Relations Dept 830 Punchbowl St *Web:* www.dlir.state.hi.us	Honolulu	HI	96813	808-586-8842	586-9099
Land & Natural Resources Dept 1151 Punchbowl St *Web:* www.hawaii.gov/dlnr	Honolulu	HI	96813	808-587-0400	587-0390
Legislature 415 S Beretania St *Web:* www.capitol.hawaii.gov	Honolulu	HI	96813	808-587-0666	587-0681
Lieutenant Governor 415 S Beretania St 5th Fl *Web:* www.hawaii.gov/ltgov	Honolulu	HI	96813	808-586-0255	586-0231
Measurement Standards Branch 1851 Auiki St *Web:* www.hawaiiag.org/hdoa/qad_ms.htm	Honolulu	HI	96819	808-832-0690	832-0683
Motor Vehicle Safety Office 601 Kamokila Blvd Rm 511	Kapolei	HI	96707	808-692-7650	692-7665
Paroling Authority 1177 Alakea St 1st Fl	Honolulu	HI	96813	808-587-1293	587-1314
Postsecondary Education Commission 2444 Dole St Bachman Hall Rm 209	Honolulu	HI	96822	808-956-8213	956-5156
Professional & Vocational Licensing Div PO Box 3469 *Web:* www.hawaii.gov/dcca/areas/pvl	Honolulu	HI	96801	808-586-3000	586-3031
Public Utilities Commission 465 S King St Rm 103 *Web:* www.state.hi.us/budget/puc/puc.htm	Honolulu	HI	96813	808-586-2020	586-2066
Securities Compliance Div 335 Merchant St Rm 203 *Web:* www.hawaii.gov/dcca/areas/sec	Honolulu	HI	96813	808-586-2744	586-2733
Sheriffs Div 1111 Alakea St 2nd Fl	Honolulu	HI	96813	808-538-5665	538-5661
Social Services Div 810 Richards St Suite 400 *Web:* www.state.hi.us/dhs	Honolulu	HI	96813	808-586-5701	586-5700
State Ethics Commission PO Box 616 *Web:* www.state.hi.us/ethics	Honolulu	HI	96809	808-587-0460	587-0470
State Foundation for Culture & the Arts 250 S Hotel St 2nd Fl *Web:* www.state.hi.us/sfca	Honolulu	HI	96813	808-586-0300	586-0308
State Parks Div PO Box 621 *Web:* www.state.hi.us/dlnr/dsp/dsp.html	Honolulu	HI	96809	808-587-0300	587-0311
Supreme Court 417 S King St *Web:* www.courts.state.hi.us	Honolulu	HI	96813	808-539-4919	539-4928
Taxation Dept PO Box 259 *TF:* 800-222-3229 ■ *Web:* www.state.hi.us/tax/tax.html	Honolulu	HI	96809	808-587-1510	587-1506
Teacher Standards Board 650 Iwilei Rd Suite 201 *Web:* www.htsb.org	Honolulu	HI	96817	808-586-2600	586-2606
Tourism Authority 1801 Kalakaua Ave *Web:* www.hawaii.gov/tourism	Honolulu	HI	96815	808-973-2255	973-2253
Transportation Dept 869 Punchbowl St *Web:* www.hawaii.gov/dot	Honolulu	HI	96813	808-587-2160	587-2313
Veterans Services Office 459 Patterson Rd E Wing Suite 1-A103 *Web:* www.dod.state.hi.us/ovs	Honolulu	HI	96819	808-433-0420	433-0385
Vital Records Section PO Box 3378 *Web:* www.state.hi.us/doh/records	Honolulu	HI	96801	808-586-4533	586-4606
Vocational Rehabilitation Div 601 Kamokila Blvd Rm 514	Kapolei	HI	96707	808-692-7715	692-7727
Workforce Development Div 830 Punchbowl St Suite 329 *Web:* hawaii.gov/labor/wdd	Honolulu	HI	96813	808-586-8877	586-8822

342-13 Idaho

	City	State	Zip	Phone	Fax
State Government Information *TF:* 877-443-3468 ■ *Web:* www.idaho.gov		ID		208-334-2411	
Accountancy Board PO Box 83720 *Web:* www.isba.idaho.gov	Boise	ID	83720	208-334-2490	334-2615
Administrative Director of the Courts 451 W State St *Web:* www.isc.idaho.gov	Boise	ID	83702	208-334-2246	947-7590
Aging Commission 3380 Americana Terr Suite 120 *Web:* www.idahoaging.com	Boise	ID	83706	208-334-3833	334-3033
Agriculture Dept PO Box 790 *Web:* www.agri.state.id.us	Boise	ID	83701	208-332-8500	334-2170
Arts Commission 2410 Old Penitentiary Rd *TF:* 800-278-3863 ■ *Web:* www.arts.idaho.gov	Boise	ID	83712	208-334-2119	334-2488
Attorney General PO Box 83720 *TF:* 800-432-3545 ■ *Web:* www2.state.id.us/ag	Boise	ID	83720	208-334-2400	334-2530
Bill Status PO Box 83720 *Web:* www3.state.id.us/legislat/legtrack.html	Boise	ID	83720	208-334-2475	334-2125
Board of Medicine 1755 Westgate Dr Suite 140 *TF:* 800-333-0073 ■ *Web:* www.bom.state.id.us	Boise	ID	83704	208-327-7000	327-7005
Certification & Professional Standards Bureau PO Box 83720 *Web:* www.sde.idaho.gov	Boise	ID	83720	208-332-6880	334-4664
Child Support Services Bureau PO Box 83720 *Web:* www.healthandwelfare.idaho.gov	Boise	ID	83720	208-334-2479	334-0666
Consumer Protection Unit PO Box 83720 *Web:* www2.state.id.us/ag/consumer	Boise	ID	83720	208-334-2424	334-4151
Correction Board 1299 N Orchard St Suite 110 *Web:* www.corr.state.id.us	Boise	ID	83706	208-658-2000	327-7404
Crime Victims Compensation Program PO Box 83720 *TF:* 800-950-2110 ■ *Web:* www.iic.idaho.gov/cv/crimevictims.htm	Boise	ID	83720	208-334-6080	332-7559
Economic Development Div PO Box 83720 *TF:* 800-842-5858 ■ *Web:* www.idoc.state.id.us	Boise	ID	83720	208-334-2470	334-2631
Education Dept 650 W State St PO Box 83720 *Web:* www.sde.state.id.us	Boise	ID	83720	208-332-6800	334-2228
Family & Community Services Div 450 W State St *Web:* www.healthandwelfare.idaho.gov	Boise	ID	83702	208-334-5700	332-7330
Finance Dept PO Box 83720 *Web:* finance.state.id.us	Boise	ID	83720	208-332-8000	332-8096
Fish & Game Dept PO Box 25 *Web:* fishandgame.idaho.gov	Boise	ID	83707	208-334-3700	334-2114
Governor State Capitol Bldg 2nd Fl *Web:* gov.idaho.gov	Boise	ID	83720	208-334-2100	334-3454
Health & Welfare Dept 450 W State St 10th Fl PO Box 83720 **Fax:* PR ■ *Web:* www.healthandwelfare.idaho.gov	Boise	ID	83720	208-334-5500	334-5926*
Historical Society 2205 Old Penitentiary Rd *TF:* 877-653-4367 ■ *Web:* www.idahohistory.net	Boise	ID	83712	208-334-2682	334-2774
Disaster Services Bureau 4040 W Guard St Bldg 600 *TF:* 800-344-0984 ■ *Web:* www.bhs.idaho.gov	Boise	ID	83705	208-422-3040	422-3044
Housing & Finance Assn 565 W Myrtle Ave *TF:* 800-526-7145 ■ *Web:* www.ihfa.org	Boise	ID	83702	208-331-4882	331-4804
Information Technology & Communication Services Div 650 W State St Rm 100 *Web:* adm.idaho.gov	Boise	ID	83702	208-332-1841	334-5315
Insurance Dept 700 W State St 3rd Fl PO Box 83720 *Web:* www.doi.state.id.us	Boise	ID	83720	208-334-4250	334-4398
Labor Dept 317 W Main St *Web:* cl.idaho.gov/portal	Boise	ID	83735	208-332-3570	334-6300
Lands Dept PO Box 83720 *Web:* www.idl.idaho.gov/index.htm	Boise	ID	83720	208-334-0200	334-2339
Legislature PO Box 83720 *TF:* 800-626-0471 ■ *Web:* www.legislature.idaho.gov	Boise	ID	83720	208-332-1000	334-5397
Lieutenant Governor PO Box 83720 *Web:* lgo.idaho.gov	Boise	ID	83720	208-334-2200	334-3259
State Lottery 1199 Shoreline Ln Suite 100 *TF:* 800-432-5688 ■ *Web:* www.idaholottery.com	Boise	ID	83702	208-334-2600	334-2610
Motor Vehicles Div PO Box 7129 *Web:* itd.idaho.gov	Boise	ID	83707	208-334-8606	334-8739
Occupational Licenses Bureau 1109 Main St Suite 220 *Web:* www.ibol.idaho.gov	Boise	ID	83702	208-334-3233	334-3945
Pardon & Parole Commission PO Box 83720 *Web:* www2.state.id.us/parole	Boise	ID	83720	208-334-2520	334-3501
Parks & Recreation Dept 5657 Warm Springs Ave *Web:* www.idahoparks.org	Boise	ID	83716	208-334-4199	334-3741
Public Utilities Commission PO Box 83720 *TF:* 800-432-0369 ■ *Web:* www.puc.state.id.us	Boise	ID	83720	208-334-0300	334-3762
Racing Commission PO Box 700 *Web:* www.isp.state.id.us/race	Meridian	ID	83680	208-884-7080	884-7098
Real Estate Commission PO Box 83720 *Web:* www.idahorealestatecommission.com	Boise	ID	83720	208-334-3285	334-2050
Scholarship Office PO Box 83720 *Web:* www.idahoboardofed.org/scholarships.asp	Boise	ID	83720	208-334-2270	334-2632
Secretary of State 700 W Jefferson St Rm 203 *Web:* www.idsos.state.id.us	Boise	ID	83720	208-334-2300	334-2282
Securities Bureau PO Box 83720 *Web:* finance.idaho.gov	Boise	ID	83720	208-332-8004	332-8099
State Police Div PO Box 700 *Web:* www.isp.state.id.us	Meridian	ID	83680	208-884-7000	884-7290
Supreme Court PO Box 83720 *Web:* www.isc.idaho.gov	Boise	ID	83720	208-334-2210	334-2616
Tax Commission PO Box 36 *TF:* 800-972-7660 ■ *Web:* tax.idaho.gov	Boise	ID	83722	208-334-7660	334-7844
Tourism Div 700 W State St PO Box 83720 *TF:* 800-842-5858 ■ *Web:* www.visitid.org	Boise	ID	83720	208-334-2470	334-2631
Transportation Dept PO Box 7129 *Web:* itd.idaho.gov	Boise	ID	83707	208-334-8000	334-3858

Idaho (Cont'd)

	City	State	ZIP	Phone	Fax
Treasurer PO Box 83720 *Web:* sto.idaho.gov	Boise	ID	83720	208-334-3200	332-2960
Veterans Services Div 320 Collins Rd *Web:* www.idvs.state.id.us	Boise	ID	83702	208-334-3513	334-2627
Vital Records & Health Statistics Bureau PO Box 83720 *Web:* www.healthandwelfare.idaho.gov/	Boise	ID	83720	208-334-5988	
Vocational Rehabilitation Div 650 W State St Rm 150 *Web:* www.vr.idaho.gov	Boise	ID	83720	208-334-3390	334-5305
Weights & Measures Bureau PO Box 790 *Web:* www.agri.state.id.us	Boise	ID	83701	208-332-8690	334-2378

342-14 Illinois

	City	State	ZIP	Phone	Fax
State Government Information *Web:* www.illinois.gov		IL		217-782-2000	
Administrative Office of the Illinois Courts 3101 Old Jacksonville Rd *Web:* www.state.il.us/court	Springfield	IL	62704	217-558-4490	785-3903
Aging Dept 421 E Capitol Ave Suite 100 *Web:* www.state.il.us/aging	Springfield	IL	62701	217-785-3356	785-4477
Agriculture Dept PO Box 19281 *Web:* www.agr.state.il.us	Springfield	IL	62794	217-782-2172	785-4505
Arts Council 100 W Randolph St Suite 10-500 *TF:* 800-237-6994 ■ *Web:* www.state.il.us/agency/iac	Chicago	IL	60601	312-814-4831	814-1471
Attorney General 500 S 2nd St *Web:* www.illinoisattorneygeneral.gov	Springfield	IL	62706	217-782-1090	782-7046
Banks & Real Estate Div 500 E Monroe St 3rd Fl *Web:* www.idfpr.com	Springfield	IL	62701	217-782-3000	558-4297
Bill Status 705 Stratton Bldg *Web:* www.ilga.gov/legislation	Springfield	IL	62706	217-782-3944	524-6059
Child Support Enforcement Div 509 S 6th St *Fax Area Code: 217 ■ *TF:* 800-447-4278 ■ *Web:* www.ilchildsupport.com	Springfield	IL	62701	800-447-4278	524-4608*
Children & Family Services Dept 406 E Monroe St *Web:* www.state.il.us/dcfs	Springfield	IL	62701	217-785-2509	524-0014
Commerce Commission 527 E Capitol Ave *Web:* www.state.il.us/icc	Springfield	IL	62701	217-782-7295	524-0673
Commerce & Economic Opportunity Dept 620 E Adams St *Web:* www.commerce.state.il.us	Springfield	IL	62701	217-782-7500	524-0864
Community College Board 401 E Capitol Ave *Web:* www.iccb.state.il.us	Springfield	IL	62701	217-785-0123	524-4981
Consumer Protection Div 100 W Randolph St 12th Fl *Web:* www.illinoisattorneygeneral.gov/consumers	Chicago	IL	60601	312-814-3000	814-2549
Corrections Dept 1301 Concordia Ct *Web:* www.idoc.state.il.us	Springfield	IL	62702	217-522-2666	522-0355
Crime Victims Services Div 100 W Randolf Rd 13th Fl *TF:* 800-228-3368 ■ *Web:* www.illinoisattorneygeneral.gov/victims	Chicago	IL	60601	312-814-2581	814-7105
Driver Services Office 2701 S Dirksen Pkwy *Web:* www.cyberdriveillinois.com/departments/drivers	Springfield	IL	62723	217-785-6212	
Emergency Management Agency 2200 S Dirksen Pkwy *Web:* www.state.il.us/iema	Springfield	IL	62703	217-782-7860	782-2589
Employment Security Dept 33 S State St 9th Fl *Web:* www.ides.state.il.us	Chicago	IL	60603	312-793-5700	793-9834
Environmental Protection Agency 1021 N Grand Ave E *Web:* www.epa.state.il.us	Springfield	IL	62794	217-782-2829	782-9039
General Assembly State House *Web:* www.ilga.gov	Springfield	IL	62706	217-782-2000	
Governor State Capitol Bldg Rm 207 *Web:* www.illinois.gov/gov	Springfield	IL	62706	217-782-6830	524-4049
Public Aid Dept 201 S Grand Ave E 3rd Fl *Web:* www.hfs.illinois.gov	Springfield	IL	62763	217-782-1200	524-7979
Higher Education Board 431 E Adams St 2nd Fl *Web:* www.ibhe.org	Springfield	IL	62701	217-782-2551	782-8548
Historic Preservation Agency 1 Old State Capitol Plaza *Web:* www.state.il.us/HPA	Springfield	IL	62701	217-785-7930	785-7937
Housing Development Authority 401 N Michigan Ave Suite 900 *Web:* www.ihda.org	Chicago	IL	60611	312-836-5200	832-2136
Human Services Dept 100 S Grand Ave E 3rd Fl *TF:* 800-843-6154 ■ *Web:* www.dhs.state.il.us	Springfield	IL	62762	217-557-1601	557-1651
Insurance Div 320 W Washington St 4th Fl *Web:* www.ins.state.il.us	Springfield	IL	62767	217-782-4515	782-5020
Labor Dept 160 N LaSalle St Suite C-1300 *Web:* www.state.il.us/agency/idol	Chicago	IL	60601	312-793-2800	793-5257
Lieutenant Governor State Capitol Bldg Rm 214 *Web:* www.state.il.us/ltgov	Springfield	IL	62706	217-782-7884	524-6262
Lottery Dept 101 W Jefferson St *TF:* 800-252-1775 ■ *Web:* www.illinoislottery.com	Springfield	IL	62702	217-524-5155	558-2468
Mental Health Div 100 W Randolf St Suite 3-400 *TF:* 800-252-2923 ■ *Web:* www.commerce.state.il.us/bus	Chicago	IL	60601	312-814-2811	814-6732
Military Affairs Dept 1301 N MacArthur Blvd *Web:* www.il.ngb.army.mil	Springfield	IL	62702	217-761-3569	761-3527
Natural Resources Dept 1 Natural Resources Way *Web:* dnr.state.il.us	Springfield	IL	62702	217-782-6302	782-0179
Professional Regulation Div 320 W Washington St 3rd Fl *Web:* www.ildpr.com	Springfield	IL	62786	217-785-0800	782-7645
Public Health Dept 535 W Jefferson St *Web:* www.idph.state.il.us	Springfield	IL	62761	217-782-4977	782-3987
Racing Board 100 W Randolph St Suite 11-100 *Web:* www.state.il.us/agency/irb	Chicago	IL	60601	312-814-2600	814-5062
Revenue Dept 101 W Jefferson St *TF:* 800-732-8866 ■ *Web:* www.revenue.state.il.us	Springfield	IL	62702	217-782-3336	782-4217
Secretary of State State Capitol Bldg Rm 213 *Web:* www.sos.state.il.us	Springfield	IL	62756	217-782-2201	785-0358
Securities Dept 300 W Jefferson St Suite 300-A *Web:* www.cyberdriveillinois.com/departments/securities	Springfield	IL	62702	217-782-2256	782-8876
State Board of Education 100 N 1st St *Web:* www.isbe.state.il.us	Springfield	IL	62777	217-782-4321	524-4928
State Police PO Box 19461 *Web:* www.isp.state.il.us	Springfield	IL	62794	217-782-7263	785-2821
Student Assistance Commission 1755 Lake Cook Rd *Fax: Cust Svc ■ *TF:* 800-899-4722 ■ *Web:* www.collegezone.com	Deerfield	IL	60015	847-948-8500	831-8549*
Supreme Court 200 E Capitol Ave *Web:* www.state.il.us/court	Springfield	IL	62701	217-782-2035	782-3520
Tourism Bureau 100 W Randolph St Suite 3-400 *TF:* 800-226-6632 ■ *Web:* www.enjoyillinois.com	Chicago	IL	60601	312-814-4732	814-6175
Transportation Dept 2300 S Dirksen Pkwy *Web:* www.dot.state.il.us	Springfield	IL	62764	217-782-7820	782-6828
Treasurer State Capitol Bldg Rm 219 *Web:* www.treasurer.il.gov	Springfield	IL	62706	217-782-2211	785-2777
Veterans Affairs Dept 833 S Spring St *TF:* 800-437-9824 ■ *Web:* www.state.il.us/agency/dva	Springfield	IL	62794	217-782-6641	524-0344
Vital Records Div 605 W Jefferson St *Web:* www.idph.state.il.us/vitalrecords	Springfield	IL	62702	217-782-6553	785-3209
Wildlife Resources Div 1 Natural Resources Way *Web:* www.dnr.state.il.us/orc/wildlifeResources	Springfield	IL	62702	217-782-6384	
Industrial Commission 100 W Randolph St 8th Fl *TF:* 866-352-3033 ■ *Web:* www.iwcc.il.gov	Chicago	IL	60601	312-814-6611	814-6523

342-15 Indiana

	City	State	ZIP	Phone	Fax
State Government Information *Web:* www.in.gov		IN		317-233-0800	
Agriculture Commission 101 W Ohio St Suite 1200 *Web:* www.in.gov/isda	Indianapolis	IN	46204	317-232-8770	232-1362
Arts Commission 150 W Market St Suite 618 *Web:* www.in.gov/arts	Indianapolis	IN	46204	317-232-1268	232-5595
Attorney General 302 W Washington St 5th Fl *Web:* www.in.gov/attorneygeneral	Indianapolis	IN	46204	317-232-6201	232-7979
Bill Status State House 200 W Washington St Suite 301 *Web:* www.in.gov/apps/lsa/session/billwatch	Indianapolis	IN	46204	317-232-9856	
Child Support Bureau 402 W Washington St Rm W360 *Web:* www.in.gov/dcs/support	Indianapolis	IN	46204	317-232-4877	233-4925
Community Development Div 1 N Capitol Ave Suite 600 *TF:* 800-824-2476 ■ *Web:* www.iedc.in.gov	Indianapolis	IN	46204	317-232-8911	233-3597
Consumer Protection Div 402 W Washington St 5th Fl *TF:* 800-382-5516 ■ *Web:* www.in.gov/attorneygeneral/consumer	Indianapolis	IN	46204	317-232-6330	233-4393
Correction Dept 302 W Washington St Rm E334 *Web:* www.in.gov/indcorrection	Indianapolis	IN	46204	317-232-5715	232-6798
Disability Aging & Rehabilitative Services Div 402 W Washington St Rm W451 *TF:* 800-545-7763 ■ *Web:* www.in.gov/fssa/servicedisabl	Indianapolis	IN	46207	317-232-1147	232-1240
Commerce Dept 1 N Capitol Ave Suite 700 *Web:* www.iedc.in.gov	Indianapolis	IN	46204	317-232-8800	232-4146
Education Dept State House 200 W Washington St Rm 229 *Web:* www.doe.state.in.us	Indianapolis	IN	46204	317-232-6610	232-9121
Environmental Management Dept 100 N Senate Ave Rm 1301 *TF:* 800-451-6027 ■ *Web:* www.in.gov/idem	Indianapolis	IN	46204	317-232-8611	233-6647
Family & Social Services Administration 402 W Washington St Rm W461 *TF:* 800-545-7763 ■ *Web:* www.in.gov/fssa	Indianapolis	IN	46207	317-233-4454	233-4693
Development Finance Authority 1 N Capitol Ave Suite 900 *Web:* www.in.gov/idfa	Indianapolis	IN	46204	317-233-4332	232-6786
Financial Institutions Dept 30 S Meridian St Suite 300 *Web:* www.in.gov/dfi	Indianapolis	IN	46204	317-232-3955	232-7655
Fish & Wildlife Div 402 W Washington St Rm W273 *Web:* www.in.gov/dnr/fishwild	Indianapolis	IN	46204	317-232-4080	232-8150
General Assembly State House 200 W Washington St *Web:* www.in.gov/legislative	Indianapolis	IN	46204	317-232-9600	232-2554
Governor State House 200 W Washington St Rm 206 *Web:* www.in.gov/gov	Indianapolis	IN	46204	317-232-4567	232-3443
Health Dept 2 N Meridian St *Web:* www.in.gov/isdh	Indianapolis	IN	46204	317-233-1325	233-7394
Higher Education Commission 101 W Ohio St Suite 550 *Web:* www.che.state.in.us	Indianapolis	IN	46204	317-464-4400	464-4410
Historical Bureau 140 N Senate Ave Rm 130 *Web:* www.in.gov/history	Indianapolis	IN	46204	317-232-2537	232-3728
State Emergency Management Agency 302 W Washington St Rm E208 *Web:* www.in.gov/dhs	Indianapolis	IN	46204	317-232-3980	232-3895
Horse Racing Commission 150 W Market St Suite 530 *Web:* www.in.gov/ihrc	Indianapolis	IN	46204	317-233-3119	233-4470
Housing Finance Authority 30 S Meridian St Suite 1000 *Web:* www.in.gov/ihfa	Indianapolis	IN	46204	317-232-7777	232-7778
Insurance Dept 311 W Washington St Suite 300 *TF Cust Svc:* 800-622-4461 ■ *Web:* www.in.gov/idoi	Indianapolis	IN	46204	317-232-2385	232-5251
Labor Dept 402 W Washington St Rm W195 *Web:* www.in.gov/labor	Indianapolis	IN	46204	317-232-2655	233-3790
Lieutenant Governor State House 200 W Washington St Rm 333 *Web:* www.in.gov/lgov	Indianapolis	IN	46204	317-232-4545	232-4788
Indiana Lottery 201 S Capitol Ave Suite 1100 *TF:* 800-955-6886 ■ *Web:* www.in.gov/hoosierlottery	Indianapolis	IN	46225	317-264-4800	264-4933
Motor Vehicles Bureau 100 N Senate Ave Rm N440 *Web:* www.in.gov/bmv	Indianapolis	IN	46204	317-233-6000	233-3135
Natural Resources Dept 402 W Washington St *Web:* www.in.gov/dnr	Indianapolis	IN	46204	317-232-4200	233-6811
Parole Services Div 302 W Washington St	Indianapolis	IN	46204	317-232-5726	232-5728
Port Commission 150 W Market St Suite 100 *TF:* 800-232-7678 ■ *Web:* www.portsofindiana.com	Indianapolis	IN	46204	317-232-9200	232-0137
Professional Licensing Agency 302 W Washington St Rm E034 *Web:* www.in.gov/pla	Indianapolis	IN	46204	317-232-2980	232-2312
Professional Standards Board 101 W Ohio St Suite 300 *Web:* www.doe.state.in.us/dps	Indianapolis	IN	46204	317-232-9010	232-9023
Revenue Dept 100 N Senate Ave Rm N128 *Web:* www.in.gov/dor	Indianapolis	IN	46204	317-232-2240	232-2103
Secretary of State State House 200 W Washington St Rm 201 *Web:* www.in.gov/sos	Indianapolis	IN	46204	317-232-6531	233-3283
Securities Div 302 W Washington St Rm E111 *Web:* www.in.gov/sos/securities	Indianapolis	IN	46204	317-232-6681	233-3675
State Court Administration Div 115 W Washington St Suite 1080 *Web:* www.in.gov/judiciary	Indianapolis	IN	46204	317-232-2542	233-6586
State Ethics Commission 402 W Washington St Rm W-198 *Web:* www.in.gov/ethics	Indianapolis	IN	46204	317-232-3850	232-0707
State Parks & Reservoirs Div 402 W Washington Rm W-298 *TF:* 800-622-4931 ■ *Web:* www.in.gov/dnr/parks	Indianapolis	IN	46204	317-232-4124	232-4132
State Police 100 N Senate Ave 3rd Fl *Web:* www.in.gov/isp	Indianapolis	IN	46204	317-232-8248	232-0652
Students Assistance Commission 150 W Market St Suite 500 *TF:* 888-528-4719 ■ *Web:* www.in.gov/ssaci	Indianapolis	IN	46204	317-232-2350	232-3260
Supreme Court State House 200 W Washington St Rm 315 *Web:* www.in.gov/judiciary/supreme	Indianapolis	IN	46204	317-232-2540	232-8372
Information Technology Div 100 N Senate Ave Suite N-551 *Web:* www.in.gov/iot	Indianapolis	IN	46204	317-232-3172	232-0748
Tourism Div 1 N Capitol Ave Suite 100 *TF:* 888-365-6946 ■ *Web:* www.in.gov/enjoyindiana	Indianapolis	IN	46204	317-232-8860	233-6887
Transportation Dept 100 N Senate Ave Rm N755 *Web:* www.in.gov/dot	Indianapolis	IN	46204	317-232-5533	232-0238
Treasurer State House 200 W Washington St Rm 242 *Web:* www.in.gov/tos	Indianapolis	IN	46204	317-232-6386	233-1780
Utility Regulatory Commission 302 W Washington St Rm E306 *Web:* www.in.gov/iurc	Indianapolis	IN	46204	317-232-2701	232-6758

				Phone	Fax
Veterans' Affairs Dept 302 W Washington St Rm E120 *Web:* www.in.gov/veteran	Indianapolis	IN	46204	317-232-3910	232-7721
Victims Services Div 1 N Capitol Ave Suite 1000 *TF:* 800-353-1484 ■ *Web:* www.in.gov/cji/victim	Indianapolis	IN	46204	317-232-1233	233-3912
Vital Records Office 6 West Washington St *Web:* www.in.gov/isdh/bdcertifs/bdcert.html	Indianapolis	IN	46204	317-233-2700	233-7210
Weights & Measures Div 2525 Shadeland Ave Unit D3 *Web:* www.in.gov/isdh/regsvcs/wtmsr/welcome.html	Indianapolis	IN	46219	317-356-7078	351-2877
Worker's Compensation Board 402 W Washington St Rm W196 *Web:* www.in.gov/workcomp	Indianapolis	IN	46204	317-232-3808	233-5493
Workforce Development Dept 10 N Senate Ave *Web:* www.in.gov/dwd	Indianapolis	IN	46204	317-232-7670	233-4793

342-16 Iowa

				Phone	Fax
State Government Information *Web:* www.iowa.gov		IA		515-281-5011	
Adult Children & Family Services Div 1305 E Walnut St 5th Fl *TF:* 800-972-2017 ■ *Web:* www.dhs.state.ia.us/ACFS/ACFS.asp	Des Moines	IA	50319	515-281-5521	281-4597
Agriculture & Land Stewardship Dept 502 E 9th St *Web:* www.agriculture.state.ia.us	Des Moines	IA	50319	515-281-5321	281-6236
Arts Council 600 E Locust *Web:* www.iowaartscouncil.org	Des Moines	IA	50319	515-281-6412	242-6498
Attorney General 1305 E Walnut St 2nd Fl *Web:* www.state.ia.us/government/ag	Des Moines	IA	50319	515-281-8373	281-4209
Banking Div 200 E Grand Ave Suite 300 *Web:* www.state.ia.us/government/com/bank/bank.htm	Des Moines	IA	50309	515-281-4014	281-4862
Bill Status State Capitol Bldg Rm 16 *Web:* www.legis.state.ia.us/Bills.html	Des Moines	IA	50319	515-281-5129	
Child Support Recovery Unit 1901 Bell Ave *TF:* 888-229-9223 ■ *Web:* childsupport.dhs.state.ia.us	Des Moines	IA	50309	515-242-5530	
College Student Aid Commission 200 10th St 4th Fl *TF:* 800-383-4222 ■ *Web:* www.iowacollegeaid.org	Des Moines	IA	50309	515-281-3501	725-3401
Commerce Dept 1918 SE Hulsizer Rd *Web:* www.state.ia.us/government/com	Ankeny	IA	50021	515-281-7400	281-5329
Community Development Div 200 E Grand Ave *Web:* www.state.ia.us/government/ided/crd	Des Moines	IA	50309	515-242-4780	242-4809
Conservation & Recreation Div 502 E 9th St *Web:* www.iowadnr.com	Des Moines	IA	50319	515-281-5529	281-6794
Consumer Protection Div 1305 E Walnut St 2nd Fl *Web:* www.iowaattorneygeneral.org	Des Moines	IA	50319	515-281-5926	281-6771
Corrections Dept 420 Watson Powell Jr Way *Web:* www.doc.state.ia.us	Des Moines	IA	50309	515-242-5702	281-7345
Crime Victim Assistance Div 321 E 12th St Rm 018 *TF:* 800-373-5044 ■ *Web:* www.state.ia.us/government/ag/CVAD	Des Moines	IA	50319	515-281-5044	281-8199
Economic Development Dept 200 E Grand Ave *Web:* www.state.ia.us/government/ided	Des Moines	IA	50309	515-242-4700	242-4722
Education Dept 400 E 14th St *Web:* www.state.ia.us/educate	Des Moines	IA	50319	515-281-3436	242-4722
Educational Examiners Board 400 E 14th St Grimes State Office Bldg *TF:* 800-778-7856 ■ *Web:* www.state.ia.us/boee	Des Moines	IA	50319	515-281-5849	281-7669
Elder Affairs Dept 200 10th St 3rd Fl *TF:* 800-532-3213 ■ *Web:* www.state.ia.us/elderaffairs	Des Moines	IA	50309	515-242-3333	242-3300
Emergency Management Div 1305 E Walnut St Level A *Web:* www.iowahomelandsecurity.org	Des Moines	IA	50319	515-281-3231	281-7539
Environmental Protection Div 502 E 9th St *Web:* www.iowadnr.com/epc	Des Moines	IA	50319	515-281-5918	281-8895
Ethics & Campaign Disclosure Board 510 E 12th St Suite 1-A *Web:* www.state.ia.us/government/ecdb	Des Moines	IA	50319	515-281-4028	281-3701
General Assembly State Capitol *Web:* www.legis.state.ia.us	Des Moines	IA	50319	515-281-5129	
Governor State Capitol Bldg *Web:* www.governor.state.ia.us	Des Moines	IA	50319	515-281-5211	281-6611
Human Services Dept 1305 E Walnut St *TF:* 800-972-2017 ■ *Web:* www.dhs.state.ia.us	Des Moines	IA	50319	515-281-2817	281-4457
Information Technology Dept 1305 E Walnut St Level B *Web:* www.state.ia.us/government/its	Des Moines	IA	50319	515-281-5503	281-6137
Insurance Div 330 Maple St *Web:* www.iid.state.ia.us	Des Moines	IA	50319	515-281-5705	281-3059
Lieutenant Governor State Capitol Bldg	Des Moines	IA	50319	515-281-5211	281-6611
Lottery 2323 Grand Ave **Fax:* Hum Res ■ *Web:* www.ialottery.com	Des Moines	IA	50312	515-281-7900	281-7882*
Medical Examiners Board 400 SW 8th St Suite C *Web:* www.docboard.org/ia/ia_home.htm	Des Moines	IA	50309	515-281-5171	242-5908
Motor Vehicle Div PO Box 9204 *TF:* 800-532-1121 ■ *Web:* www.dot.state.ia.us/mvd	Des Moines	IA	50306	515-244-9124	237-3152
Natural Resources Dept 502 E 9th St *Web:* www.iowadnr.com	Des Moines	IA	50319	515-281-5918	281-6794
Parks & Preserves Bureau 502 E 9th St *Web:* www.iowadnr.com	Des Moines	IA	50319	515-281-5918	281-6794
Parole Board 420 Watson Powell Jr Way *Web:* www.bop.state.ia.us	Des Moines	IA	50309	515-242-5747	242-5762
Professional Licensing & Regulation Div 200 E Grand Ave Suite 300 *Web:* www.state.ia.us/government/com/prof	Ankeny	IA	50309	515-281-4041	281-4862
Public Health Dept 321 E 12th St *Web:* idph.state.ia.us	Des Moines	IA	50319	515-281-5787	281-4958
Regents Board 11260 Aurora Ave *Web:* www2.state.ia.us/regents	Urbandale	IA	50322	515-281-3934	281-6420
Revenue & Finance Dept 1305 E Walnut St 4th Fl *Web:* www.state.ia.us/tax	Des Moines	IA	50319	515-281-3204	242-6040
Secretary of State 321 E 12th St 1st Fl *Web:* www.sos.state.ia.us	Des Moines	IA	50319	515-281-5204	242-5953
Securities Bureau 340 E Maple St *Web:* www.iid.state.ia.us/division/securities	Des Moines	IA	50319	515-281-4441	281-3059
State Court Administration State House 1111 E Court Ave *Web:* www.judicial.state.ia.us/courtadmin	Des Moines	IA	50319	515-281-5241	242-0014
State Historical Society 600 E Locust St *Web:* www.iowahistory.org	Des Moines	IA	50319	515-281-5111	242-6498
State Patrol Div 502 E 9th St *Web:* www.state.ia.us/government/dps/isp	Des Moines	IA	50319	515-281-5824	242-6305
Supreme Court 1111 E Court Ave *Web:* www.judicial.state.ia.us/supreme	Des Moines	IA	50319	515-281-5911	242-6164
Tourism Office 200 E Grand Ave *TF:* 888-472-6035 ■ *Web:* www.traveliowa.com	Des Moines	IA	50309	515-242-4705	242-4718
Transportation Dept 800 Lincoln Way *Web:* www.dot.state.ia.us	Ames	IA	50010	515-239-1101	239-1639
Treasurer 1007 E Grand Ave *Web:* www.treasurer.state.ia.us	Des Moines	IA	50319	515-281-5368	281-7562
Utilities Board 350 E Maple St *Web:* www.state.ia.us/government/com/util	Des Moines	IA	50319	515-281-5167	281-8821
Veterans Affairs Commission 7105 NW 70th Ave Camp Dodge Bldg A6A *TF:* 800-838-4692 ■ *Web:* www2.state.ia.us/icva	Johnston	IA	50131	515-242-5331	242-5659
Vital Records Office 321 E 12th St Lucas State Office Bldg 1st Fl *Web:* www.idph.state.ia.us/eh/health_statistics.asp#vital	Des Moines	IA	50319	515-281-4944	281-0479
Vocational Rehabilitation Services Div 510 E 12th St *Web:* www.dvrs.state.ia.us	Des Moines	IA	50319	515-281-4311	281-7645
Weights & Measures Bureau 2230 S Ankeny Blvd	Ankeny	IA	50021	515-725-1492	725-1459
Workforce Development 1000 E Grand Ave *Web:* www.iowaworkforce.org	Des Moines	IA	50319	515-281-5387	281-4698

342-17 Kansas

				Phone	Fax
State Government Information *Web:* www.kansas.gov		KS		785-296-0111	
Accountancy Board 900 SW Jackson St Suite 556 *Web:* www.ksboa.org	Topeka	KS	66612	785-296-2162	291-3501
Aging Dept 503 S Kansas Ave *Web:* www.agingkansas.org/kdoa	Topeka	KS	66603	785-296-4986	296-0256
Agriculture Dept 109 SW 9th St *Web:* www.accesskansas.org/kda	Topeka	KS	66612	785-296-3556	296-8389
Arts Commission 700 SW Jackson St Suite 1004 *Web:* arts.state.ks.us	Topeka	KS	66603	785-296-3335	296-4989
Attorney General 120 SW 10th Ave 2nd Fl *Web:* www.ksag.org	Topeka	KS	66612	785-296-2215	296-6296
Banking Commissioner 700 SW Jackson St Suite 300 *Web:* www.osbckansas.org	Topeka	KS	66603	785-296-2266	296-0168
Bill Status 300 SW 10th Ave State Capitol Bldg Rm 343N *Web:* www.kslegislature.org	Topeka	KS	66612	785-296-3296	296-6650
Certification & Teacher Education Div 120 SE 10th Ave *Web:* www.ksbe.state.ks.us/cert/cert.html	Topeka	KS	66612	785-296-8010	296-4318
Child Support Enforcement Program PO Box 497	Topeka	KS	66601	785-296-3237	296-5206
Commerce & Housing Dept 1000 SW Jackson St Suite 100 *Web:* kdoch.state.ks.us	Topeka	KS	66612	785-296-3481	296-5055
Conservation Commission 109 SW 9th St Suite 500 *Web:* www.accesskansas.org/kscc	Topeka	KS	66612	785-296-3600	296-6172
Consumer Protection Div 120 SW 10th Ave Rm 430 *TF:* 800-432-2310 ■ *Web:* www.accesskansas.org/ksag	Topeka	KS	66612	785-296-3751	291-3699
Corporation Commission 1500 SW Arrowhead Rd *Web:* www.kcc.state.ks.us	Topeka	KS	66604	785-271-3220	271-3354
Corrections Dept 900 SW Jackson St Suite 400 *Web:* docnet.dc.state.ks.us	Topeka	KS	66612	785-296-3317	296-0014
Cosmetology Board 714 SW Jackson St Suite 100 *Web:* www.accesskansas.org/kboc	Topeka	KS	66603	785-296-3155	296-3002
Crime Victims Compensation Board 120 SW 10th Ave 2nd Fl *Web:* www.accesskansas.org/ksag/Divisions/Cvcb/main.htm	Topeka	KS	66612	785-296-2359	296-0652
Education Dept 120 SE 10th Ave *Web:* www.ksbe.state.ks.us	Topeka	KS	66612	785-296-3201	296-7933
Emergency Management Div 2800 SW Topeka Blvd *Web:* www.accesskansas.org/kdem	Topeka	KS	66611	785-274-1409	274-1426
Governmental Ethics Commission 109 W 9th St Suite 504 *Web:* www.accesskansas.org/ethics	Topeka	KS	66612	785-296-4219	296-2548
Governor State Capitol Bldg 2nd Fl *Web:* www.ksgovernor.org	Topeka	KS	66612	785-296-3232	296-7973
Healing Arts Board 235 S Topeka Blvd *Web:* www.ksbha.org	Topeka	KS	66603	785-296-7413	296-0852
Health & Environment Dept 1000 SW Jackson St *Web:* www.kdhe.state.ks.us	Topeka	KS	66612	785-296-1500	296-6231
Highway Patrol 122 SW 7th St *Web:* www.kansashighwaypatrol.org	Topeka	KS	66603	785-296-6800	296-5956
Historical Society 6425 SW 6th Ave *Web:* www.kshs.org	Topeka	KS	66615	785-272-8681	272-8682
Housing Div 611 S Kansas Ave Suite 300 *Web:* kshousingcorp.org	Topeka	KS	66603	785-296-5865	296-8985
Information Systems & Communications Div 900 SW Jackson Rm 751S *Web:* da.state.ks.us/disc	Topeka	KS	66612	785-296-3343	296-1168
Insurance Dept 420 SW 9th St *TF:* 800-432-2484 ■ *Web:* www.ksinsurance.org	Topeka	KS	66612	785-296-3071	296-2283
Judicial Administrator 301 W 10th St Kansas Judicial Ctr *Web:* www.kscourts.org	Topeka	KS	66612	785-296-2256	296-7076
Kansas Inc 632 SW Van Buren St Suite 100 *Web:* www.kansasinc.org	Topeka	KS	66603	785-296-1460	296-1463
Human Resources Dept 401 SW Topeka Blvd *Web:* www.dol.ks.gov	Topeka	KS	66603	785-296-5000	296-1926
Legislature 300 SW 10th Ave State Capitol Bldg *Web:* www.kslegislature.org	Topeka	KS	66612	785-296-2391	296-1153
Lieutenant Governor 300 SW 10th Ave State Capitol Bldg Rm 222 *Web:* www.ksgovernor.org/lt_gov.html	Topeka	KS	66612	785-296-2213	296-5669
Lottery 128 N Kansas Ave *TF:* 800-544-9467 ■ *Web:* www.kslottery.com	Topeka	KS	66603	785-296-5700	296-5712
Motor Vehicles Div 915 SW Harrison St Rm 162 *Web:* www.ksrevenue.org/dmv.htm	Topeka	KS	66626	785-296-3601	291-3755
Parole Board 900 SW Jackson St 4th Fl	Topeka	KS	66612	785-296-3469	296-7949
Real Estate Commission 120 SE 6th Ave Suite 200 *Web:* www.accesskansas.org/krec	Topeka	KS	66603	785-296-3411	296-1771
Regents Board 1000 SW Jackson St Suite 520 *Web:* www.kansasregents.org	Topeka	KS	66612	785-296-3421	296-0983
Rehabilitation Services Div 3640 SW Topeka Blvd Suite 150 *Web:* www.srskansas.org/rehab	Topeka	KS	66611	785-267-5301	267-0263
Revenue Dept 915 SW Harrison St *Web:* www.ksrevenue.org	Topeka	KS	66612	785-296-3041	368-8392
Secretary of State 120 SW 10th Ave 1st Fl *Web:* www.kssos.org	Topeka	KS	66612	785-296-4564	296-4570
Securities Commission 618 S Kansas Ave 2nd Fl *Web:* www.securities.state.ks.us	Topeka	KS	66603	785-296-3307	296-6872
Social & Rehabilitation Services Dept 915 SW Harrison St 6th Fl *Web:* www.srskansas.org	Topeka	KS	66612	785-296-3959	296-2173
Student Financial Aid Div 1000 SW Jackson St Suite 520 *Web:* www.kansasregents.org/financial_aid	Topeka	KS	66612	785-296-3518	296-0983
Supreme Court 301 SW 10th Ave Rm 374 *Web:* www.kscourts.org/supct	Topeka	KS	66612	785-296-3229	296-1028
Technical Professions Board 900 SW Jackson St Suite 507 *Web:* www.accesskansas.org/ksbtp	Topeka	KS	66612	785-296-3053	
Transportation Dept 700 SW Harrison St *Web:* www.ink.org/public/kdot	Topeka	KS	66603	785-296-3566	296-1095
Travel & Tourism Development Div 1000 SW Jackson St Suite 100 *TF:* 800-252-6727 ■ *Web:* www.travelks.org	Topeka	KS	66612	785-296-5403	296-6988
Treasurer 900 SW Jackson St Suite 201 *Web:* www.treasurer.state.ks.us	Topeka	KS	66612	785-296-3171	296-7950

Kansas (Cont'd)

				Phone	Fax
Veterans Affairs Commission 700 SW Jackson St Suite 701 *Web:* www.kcva.org	Topeka	KS	66603	785-296-3976	296-1462
Vital Statistics Div 1000 SW Jackson St Suite 120 *Web:* www.kdhe.state.ks.us/vital	Topeka	KS	66612	785-296-1400	296-8075
Weights & Measures Div PO Box 19282 *Web:* www.accesskansas.org/kda/W&M/mainpage.htm	Topeka	KS	66619	785-862-2415	862-2460
Wildlife & Parks Dept 1020 S Kansas Ave Suite 200 *Web:* www.kdwp.state.ks.us	Topeka	KS	66612	785-296-2281	296-6953
Workers' Compensation Div 800 SW Jackson St Suite 600 *TF:* 800-332-0353 ■ *Web:* www.hr.state.ks.us/wc/html/wc.htm	Topeka	KS	66612	785-296-4000	296-0839

342-18 Kentucky

				Phone	Fax
State Government Information *Web:* www.kentucky.gov		KY		502-564-2500	
Accountancy Board 332 W Broadway Suite 310 *Web:* cpa.ky.gov	Louisville	KY	40202	502-595-3037	595-4500
Administrative Office of the Courts 100 Millcreek Pk *TF:* 800-928-2350 ■ *Web:* www.kycourts.net	Frankfort	KY	40601	502-573-2350	695-1759
Aging Services Office 275 E Main St 3rd Fl W *Web:* chs.state.ky.us/aging	Frankfort	KY	40621	502-564-6930	564-4595
Agriculture Dept Capitol Annex 702 Capitol Ave Suite 188 *Web:* www.kyagr.com	Frankfort	KY	40601	502-564-5126	564-5016
Arts Council 500 Mero St 21st Fl *TF:* 888-833-2787 ■ *Web:* www.kyarts.org	Frankfort	KY	40601	502-564-3757	564-2839
Athletic Commission 100 Airport Rd Suite 300 *Web:* ppr.ky.gov/kac	Frankfort	KY	40601	502-564-7760	564-3969
Attorney General State Capitol Bldg 700 Capitol Ave Rm 118 *Web:* www.law.state.ky.us	Frankfort	KY	40601	502-696-5300	564-2894
Bill Status State Capitol Bldg 700 Capitol Ave Rm 300 *Web:* www.lrc.state.ky.us/legislat/legislat.htm	Frankfort	KY	40601	502-564-8100	564-6543
Child Support Enforcement Commission 275 E Main St *TF:* 800-248-1163 ■ *Web:* chfs.ky.gov	Frankfort	KY	40621	502-564-2285	564-5988
Corrections Dept 275 E Main St Rm G-41 PO Box 2400 *Web:* www.corrections.ky.gov	Frankfort	KY	40602	502-564-4726	564-5037
Crime Victims Compensation Board 130 Brighton Park Blvd *TF:* 800-469-2120 ■ *Web:* cvcb.ppr.ky.gov	Frankfort	KY	40601	502-573-2290	573-4817
Economic Development Cabinet 500 Mero St 24th Fl *Web:* www.thinkkentucky.com	Frankfort	KY	40601	502-564-7670	564-3256
Education Dept 500 Mero St *Web:* www.education.ky.gov/KDE/	Frankfort	KY	40601	502-564-4770	564-5680
Education Professional Standards Board 100 Airport Dr 3rd Fl *TF:* 888-598-7667 ■ *Web:* www.kyepsb.net	Frankfort	KY	40601	502-564-4606	564-7080
Emergency Management Div 100 Minuteman Pkwy *Web:* kyem.ky.gov	Frankfort	KY	40601	502-607-1680	607-1614
Environmental Protection Dept 14 Reilly Rd *Web:* www.dep.ky.gov	Frankfort	KY	40601	502-564-2150	564-4245
Executive Branch Ethics Commission 403 Wapping St Suite 340 Bush Bldg *Web:* ethics.ky.gov	Frankfort	KY	40601	502-564-7954	564-2686
Finance & Administration Cabinet Capitol Annex 702 Capitol Ave Rm 383 *Web:* www.state.ky.us/agencies/finance	Frankfort	KY	40601	502-564-4240	564-6785
Financial Institutions Dept 1025 Capital Center Dr Suite 200 *TF:* 800-223-2579 ■ *Web:* www.dfi.state.ky.us	Frankfort	KY	40601	502-573-3390	573-8787
Fish & Wildlife Resources Dept 1 Game Farm Rd *TF:* 800-858-1549 ■ *Web:* www.kdfwr.state.ky.us	Frankfort	KY	40601	502-564-3400	564-6508
General Assembly State Capitol Bldg 700 Capitol Ave *TF:* 800-372-7181 ■ *Web:* www.lrc.state.ky.us	Frankfort	KY	40601	502-564-8100	564-6543
Governor State Capitol Bldg 700 Capitol Ave Rm 100 *Web:* governor.ky.gov	Frankfort	KY	40601	502-564-2611	564-2517
Governor's Office for Technology 101 Cold Harbor Dr *Web:* got.state.ky.us	Frankfort	KY	40601	502-564-7680	564-6856
Hairdressers & Cosmetologists Board 111 St James Ct Suite A	Frankfort	KY	40601	502-564-4262	564-0481
Families & Children Cabinet 275 E Main St 4th Fl W *Web:* chfs.ky.gov	Frankfort	KY	40621	502-564-7130	564-3866
Health Services Cabinet 275 E Main St 5th Fl W *Web:* chfs.ky.gov	Frankfort	KY	40621	502-564-7042	564-7091
Higher Education Assistance Authority PO Box 798 *TF:* 800-928-8926 ■ *Web:* www.kheaa.com	Frankfort	KY	40602	502-696-7200	696-7345
Historical Society 100 W Broadway *TF:* 877-444-7867 ■ *Web:* www.kyhistory.org	Frankfort	KY	40601	502-564-1792	564-4701
Horse Racing Authority 4063 Iron Works Pkwy Bldg B *Web:* krc.ppr.ky.gov	Lexington	KY	40602	859-246-2040	246-2039
Housing Corp 1231 Louisville Rd *TF:* 800-633-8896 ■ *Web:* www.kyhousing.org	Frankfort	KY	40601	502-564-7630	564-5708
Insurance Dept 215 W Main St *TF:* 800-595-6053 ■ *Web:* doi.ppr.ky.gov/kentucky	Frankfort	KY	40602	502-564-3630	564-6090
Labor Cabinet 1047 US Hwy 127 S Suite 4 *Web:* www.labor.ky.gov	Frankfort	KY	40601	502-564-3070	564-5387
Legislative Ethics Commission 22 Mill Creek Pk *Web:* klec.ky.gov	Frankfort	KY	40601	502-573-2863	573-2929
Lieutenant Governor State Capitol Bldg 700 Capitol Ave Rm 100 *Web:* ltgov.state.ky.us	Frankfort	KY	40601	502-564-2611	564-2849
Lottery Corp 1011 W Main St *TF:* 800-937-8946 ■ *Web:* www.kylottery.com	Louisville	KY	40202	502-560-1500	560-1532
Medical Licensure Board 310 Whittington Pkwy Suite 1B *Web:* www.kbml.org	Louisville	KY	40222	502-429-7150	429-7158
Natural Resources Dept 2 Hudson Hollow *Web:* www.naturalresources.ky.gov	Frankfort	KY	40601	502-564-6940	564-5848
Parks Dept 500 Mero St Suite 1100 *TF:* 800-255-7275 ■ *Web:* www.kystateparks.com	Frankfort	KY	40601	502-564-2172	564-6100
Parole Board PO Box 2400 *Web:* www.justice.ky.gov/parolebd	Frankfort	KY	40602	502-564-3620	564-8995
Postsecondary Education Council 1024 Capital Center Dr Suite 320 *Web:* cpe.ky.gov	Frankfort	KY	40601	502-573-1555	573-1535
Public Service Commission PO Box 615 *TF:* 800-772-4636 ■ *Web:* www.psc.state.ky.us	Frankfort	KY	40602	502-564-3940	564-3460
Real Estate Commission 10200 Linn Station Rd Suite 201 *TF:* 888-373-3300 ■ *Web:* www.krec.net	Louisville	KY	40223	502-429-7250	429-7246
Revenue Cabinet 200 Fair Oaks Ln *Web:* www.revenue.state.ky.us	Frankfort	KY	40620	502-564-4581	564-3685
Secretary of State State Capitol Bldg 700 Capitol Ave Rm 152 *Web:* sos.ky.gov	Frankfort	KY	40601	502-564-3490	564-5687
State Police Dept 919 Versailles Rd *Web:* www.kentuckystatepolice.org	Frankfort	KY	40601	502-695-6300	573-1479
Supreme Court State Capitol Bldg 700 Capitol Ave Rm 235 *Web:* www.kycourts.net/Supreme/SC_Main.shtm	Frankfort	KY	40601	502-564-5444	564-5491
Transportation Cabinet 200 Mero St *Web:* www.kytc.state.ky.us	Frankfort	KY	40622	502-564-4890	564-4809
Travel Dept 500 Mero St Suite 2200 *TF:* 800-225-8747 ■ *Web:* www.kentuckytourism.com	Frankfort	KY	40601	502-564-4930	564-5695
Treasury Capitol Annex 702 Capitol Ave Rm 183 *Web:* www.kytreasury.com	Frankfort	KY	40601	502-564-4722	564-6545
Vehicle Regulation Div 200 Mero St 3rd Fl *Web:* www.kytc.state.ky.us	Frankfort	KY	40622	502-564-7000	564-6403
Veterans Affairs Dept 1111 Louisville Rd *Web:* www.kdva.net	Frankfort	KY	40601	502-564-9203	564-9240
Vital Statistics Div 275 E Main St Suite 1EA *Web:* chfs.ky.gov	Frankfort	KY	40621	502-564-4212	227-0032
Vocational Rehabilitation Dept 209 Saint Clair St Rm 200 *TF:* 800-372-7172	Frankfort	KY	40601	502-564-4440	564-6745
Workers Claims Dept 657 Chamberlin Ave *TF:* 800-554-8601 ■ *Web:* dwc.state.ky.us	Frankfort	KY	40601	502-564-5550	564-5732
Workforce Development Cabinet 500 Mero St 3rd Fl *Web:* workforce.ky.gov	Frankfort	KY	40601	502-564-6606	564-7967
Consumer Protection Div 1024 Capital Center Dr Suite 200 *TF:* 888-432-9257 ■ *Web:* ag.ky.gov/cp/	Frankfort	KY	40601	502-696-5389	573-8317

342-19 Louisiana

				Phone	Fax
State Government Information *Web:* www.louisiana.gov		LA		225-342-6600	
Agriculture & Forestry Dept PO Box 631 *Web:* www.ldaf.state.la.us	Baton Rouge	LA	70821	225-922-1234	922-1253
Arts Div PO Box 44247 *Web:* www.crt.state.la.us/arts	Baton Rouge	LA	70804	225-342-8180	342-8173
Attorney General PO Box 94005 *Web:* www.ag.state.la.us	Baton Rouge	LA	70804	225-326-6705	326-6793
Bill Status State Capitol 900 N 3rd St 13th Fl *TF:* 800-256-3793 ■ *Web:* www.legis.state.la.us	Baton Rouge	LA	70804	225-342-2456	
Board of Regents PO Box 3677 *Web:* www.regents.state.la.us	Baton Rouge	LA	70821	225-342-4253	342-6926
Certified Public Accountants Board 601 Poydras St Suite 1770 *Web:* www.cpaboard.state.la.us	New Orleans	LA	70130	504-566-1244	566-1252
Child Support Enforcement Services PO Box 260222 *Web:* www.dss.state.la.us	Baton Rouge	LA	70826	225-342-4780	
Community Services Office PO Box 3318 *Web:* www.dss.state.la.us/departments/ocs/Index.html	Baton Rouge	LA	70821	225-342-2297	342-2268
Consumer Protection Office PO Box 94095 *Web:* www.ag.state.la.us/Consumers.aspx	Baton Rouge	LA	70804	225-342-7900	342-9637
Contractors Licensing Board PO Box 14419 *Web:* www.lslbc.state.la.us	Baton Rouge	LA	70898	225-765-2301	765-2431
Crime Victims Reparations Board 1885 Wooddale Blvd Rm 1230 *Web:* www.lcle.state.la.us/programs/cvr	Baton Rouge	LA	70806	225-925-4437	925-6649
Culture Recreation & Tourism Dept PO Box 94361 *Web:* www.crt.state.la.us	Baton Rouge	LA	70804	225-342-8115	342-3207
Economic Development Dept PO Box 94185 *TF:* 800-450-8115 ■ *Web:* www.lded.state.la.us	Baton Rouge	LA	70804	225-342-3000	342-9095
Education Dept PO Box 94064 **Fax Area Code: 225* ■ *Web:* www.doe.state.la.us	Baton Rouge	LA	70804	877-453-2721	342-0193*
Elderly Affairs Office 412 N 4th St 3rd Fl *Web:* goea.louisiana.gov	Baton Rouge	LA	70802	225-342-7100	342-7133
Environmental Quality Dept 602 N Fifth St *TF:* 866-896-5337 ■ *Web:* www.deq.state.la.us	Baton Rouge	LA	70802	225-219-5337	
Ethics Board 2415 Quail Dr 3rd Fl *TF:* 800-842-6630 ■ *Web:* www.ethics.state.la.us	Baton Rouge	LA	70808	225-763-8777	763-8780
Financial Institutions Office PO Box 94095 *Web:* www.ofi.state.la.us	Baton Rouge	LA	70804	225-925-4660	925-4548
Governor PO Box 94004 *TF:* 866-366-1121 ■ *Web:* www.gov.state.la.us	Baton Rouge	LA	70804	225-342-7015	342-7099
Health & Hospitals Dept PO Box 629 *Web:* www.dhh.state.la.us	Baton Rouge	LA	70821	225-342-9500	342-5568
Historic Preservation Div PO Box 44247 *Web:* www.crt.state.la.us/hp/	Baton Rouge	LA	70804	225-342-8160	342-8173
Emergency Preparedness Office 7667 Independence Blvd *Web:* www.loep.state.la.us	Baton Rouge	LA	70806	225-925-7500	925-7501
Housing Finance Agency 2415 Quail Dr *TF:* 888-454-2001 ■ *Web:* www.lhfa.state.la.us	Baton Rouge	LA	70808	225-763-8700	763-8710
Information Technology Office PO Box 94095 *Web:* www.doa.state.la.us/ois	Baton Rouge	LA	70804	225-342-0900	342-0902
Insurance Dept PO Box 94214 *TF:* 800-259-5300 ■ *Web:* www.ldi.state.la.us	Baton Rouge	LA	70804	225-342-5900	342-8622
Judicial Administrators Office 400 Royal St Suite 1190 *Web:* www.lasc.org/judicial_admin	New Orleans	LA	70130	504-310-2550	
Labor Dept 1001 N 23rd St *TF:* 877-529-6757 ■ *Web:* www.laworks.net	Baton Rouge	LA	70802	225-342-3111	
Legislature PO Box 94062 *TF:* 800-256-3793 ■ *Web:* www.legis.state.la.us	Baton Rouge	LA	70804	225-342-2456	
Lieutenant Governor 1051 N Third St *Web:* www.crt.state.la.us/ltgovernor/	Baton Rouge	LA	70802	225-342-7009	342-1949
Lottery Corp 555 Laurel St *Web:* www.louisianalottery.com	Baton Rouge	LA	70801	225-297-2000	297-2005
Medical Examiners Board 630 Camp St *Web:* www.lsbme.org	New Orleans	LA	70130	504-568-6820	
Motor Vehicles & Drivers License Office PO Box 64886 *TF:* 877-368-5463 ■ *Web:* omv.dps.state.la.us	Baton Rouge	LA	70896	225-925-6335	925-1838
Natural Resources Dept PO Box 94396 *Web:* www.dnr.state.la.us	Baton Rouge	LA	70804	225-342-4500	342-5861
Public Safety & Corrections Dept PO Box 94304 *Web:* www.doc.louisiana.gov	Baton Rouge	LA	70804	225-342-6741	342-3095
Public Service Commission PO Box 91154 *TF:* 800-256-2397 ■ *Web:* www.lpsc.org	Baton Rouge	LA	70821	225-342-4404	342-2831
Racing Commission 320 N Carrollton Ave Suite 2-B *Web:* horseracing.la.gov	New Orleans	LA	70119	504-483-4000	483-4898
Real Estate Commission PO Box 14785 *TF:* 800-821-4529 ■ *Web:* www.lrec.state.la.us	Baton Rouge	LA	70898	225-765-0191	765-0637
Rehabilitation Services 627 N 4th St *TF:* 800-737-2958	Baton Rouge	LA	70802	225-219-2225	
Revenue Dept PO Box 201 *Web:* www.rev.state.la.us	Baton Rouge	LA	70821	225-219-2700	
Secretary of State PO Box 94125 *Web:* www.sec.state.la.us	Baton Rouge	LA	70804	225-922-1000	922-0002
Securities Commission 8660 United Plaza Blvd 2nd Fl	Baton Rouge	LA	70809	225-925-4660	925-4548
Social Services Dept 627 N Fourth St *Web:* www.dss.state.la.us	Baton Rouge	LA	70802	225-342-0286	342-8636
State Parks Office PO Box 44426 *TF:* 888-677-1400 ■ *Web:* www.lastateparks.com	Baton Rouge	LA	70804	225-342-8111	342-8107
State Police PO Box 66614 *Web:* www.lsp.org	Baton Rouge	LA	70896	225-925-6006	925-3742

	City	State	Zip	Phone	Fax
Student Financial Assistance Office PO Box 91202	Baton Rouge	LA	70821	225-922-1011	922-1089
TF: 800-259-5626 ■ *Web:* www.osfa.state.la.us					
Supreme Court 400 Royal St	New Orleans	LA	70112	504-310-2300	
Web: www.lasc.org					
Teacher Standards Assessment & Certification Div PO Box 94064	Baton Rouge	LA	70804	225-342-3490	342-3499
Web: www.doe.state.la.us					
Tourism Office PO Box 94291	Baton Rouge	LA	70804	225-342-8100	342-8390
Web: www.louisianatravel.com					
Transportation & Development Dept PO Box 94245	Baton Rouge	LA	70804	225-379-1100	379-1856
TF: 877-452-3683 ■ *Web:* www.dotd.state.la.us					
Treasurer PO Box 44154	Baton Rouge	LA	70804	225-342-0010	342-0046
Web: www.treasury.state.la.us					
Veterans Affairs Dept PO Box 94095 Capital Stn	Baton Rouge	LA	70804	225-922-0500	922-0511
Web: www.ldva.org					
Vital Records Registry PO Box 60630	New Orleans	LA	70160	504-568-5152	
TF: 877-605-8562 ■ *Web:* www.oph.dhh.state.la.us					
Weights & Measures Div PO Box 91081	Baton Rouge	LA	70821	225-925-3780	923-4877
Web: www.ldaf.state.la.us/divisions/acs/weights-measures.asp					
Wildlife & Fisheries Dept PO Box 98000	Baton Rouge	LA	70898	225-765-2800	765-2892
Web: www.wlf.state.la.us					
Workers' Compensation Office PO Box 94040	Baton Rouge	LA	70804	225-342-7555	342-5665
Web: www.laworks.net/WorkersComp/OWC_WorkerMenu.asp					

342-20 Maine

	City	State	Zip	Phone	Fax
State Government Information		ME		207-624-9494	
Web: www.maine.gov					
Finance Authority of Maine (FAME) PO Box 949	Augusta	ME	04332	207-623-3263	623-0095
TF: 800-228-3734 ■ *Web:* www.famemaine.com					
Administrative Office of the Courts PO Box 4820	Portland	ME	04112	207-822-0792	
Web: www.courts.state.me.us					
Agriculture Dept 28 State House Stn	Augusta	ME	04333	207-287-3871	287-7548
Web: www.state.me.us/agriculture					
Arts Commission 25 State House Stn	Augusta	ME	04333	207-287-2724	287-2725
Web: www.mainearts.com					
Attorney General 6 State House Stn	Augusta	ME	04333	207-626-8800	
Web: www.state.me.us/ag					
Bill Status State House 100 State House Station	Augusta	ME	04333	207-287-1692	287-1580
Web: www.mainelegislature.org/legis/bills/					
Chief Medical Examiner 37 State House Stn	Augusta	ME	04333	207-624-7180	624-7178
Web: www.state.me.us/ag					
Child & Family Services Bureau 221 State St	Augusta	ME	04333	207-287-5060	287-5031
Web: www.maine.gov/dhhs/bcfs					
Conservation Dept 22 State House Stn	Augusta	ME	04333	207-287-2211	287-2400
Web: www.state.me.us/doc					
Consumer Protection Div 6 State House Stn	Augusta	ME	04333	207-626-8849	
TF: 800-436-2131 ■ *Web:* www.state.me.us/ag					
Corrections Dept 25 Tyson Drive 3rd Fl 111 State House Stn	Augusta	ME	04333	207-287-2711	287-4370
Web: www.state.me.us/corrections					
Economic & Community Development Dept 59 State House Stn	Augusta	ME	04333	207-624-9800	
TF: 800-541-5872 ■ *Web:* www.econdevmaine.com					
Education Dept 23 State House Stn	Augusta	ME	04333	207-624-6600	624-6700
Web: www.maine.gov/education/					
Elder & Adult Services Bureau 11 State House Stn 442 Civic Center Dr	Augusta	ME	04333	207-287-9200	287-9229
Web: www.maine.gov/dhhs/beas					
Emergency Management Agency 72 State House Stn	Augusta	ME	04333	207-624-4432	287-3189
TF: 800-452-8735 ■ *Web:* www.state.me.us/mema					
Employment Services Bureau 45 Commerce Dr	Augusta	ME	04330	207-623-7981	287-5933
Web: www.mainecareercenter.com					
Environmental Protection Dept 17 State House Stn	Augusta	ME	04333	207-287-7688	287-7814
TF: 800-452-1942 ■ *Web:* www.state.me.us/dep					
Financial Institutions Bureau 36 State House Stn	Augusta	ME	04333	207-624-8570	624-8590
Web: www.state.me.us/pfr/bkg/bkg_index.htm					
Governmental Ethics & Election Practices Commission 135 State House Stn	Augusta	ME	04333	207-287-4179	287-6775
Web: www.state.me.us/ethics					
Governor 1 State House Stn	Augusta	ME	04333	207-287-3531	287-1034
Web: www.maine.gov/governor					
Health Bureau 11 State House Stn	Augusta	ME	04333	207-287-8016	287-9058
Web: www.mainepublichealth.gov					
Historic Preservation Commission 65 State House Stn	Augusta	ME	04333	207-287-2132	287-2335
Web: www.state.me.us/mhpc					
Housing Authority 353 Water St	Augusta	ME	04330	207-626-4600	626-4678
Web: www.mainehousing.org					
Human Services Dept 11 State House Stn	Augusta	ME	04333	207-287-3707	287-3005
Web: www.state.me.us/dhs					
Information Services Bureau 145 State House Stn	Augusta	ME	04333	207-624-8800	287-4563
Web: www.state.me.us/bis					
Inland Fisheries & Wildlife Dept 41 State House Stn	Augusta	ME	04333	207-287-8000	287-6395
Web: www.state.me.us/ifw					
Insurance Bureau 34 State House Stn	Augusta	ME	04333	207-624-8475	624-8599
Web: www.maine.gov/pfr/insurance/					
Labor Dept PO Box 259	Augusta	ME	04332	207-623-7900	
Web: www.state.me.us/labor					
Legislature 115 State House Stn	Augusta	ME	04333	207-287-1615	287-1621
Web: janus.state.me.us/legis					
Licensing & Registration Office 35 State House Stn	Augusta	ME	04333	207-624-8500	624-8637
Web: www.state.me.us/pfr/olr					
Licensure in Medicine Board 137 State House Stn	Augusta	ME	04333	207-287-3601	287-6590
Web: www.docboard.org/me/me_home.htm					
Motor Vehicles Bureau 29 State House Stn	Augusta	ME	04333	207-624-9000	624-9013
Web: www.maine.gov/sos/bmv/					
Parks & Land Bureau 22 State House Stn	Augusta	ME	04333	207-287-3821	287-6170
TF Campground R: 800-332-1501 ■ *Web:* www.state.me.us/doc/parks					
Parole Board 111 State House Stn	Augusta	ME	04333	207-287-4381	287-4370
Public Utilities Commission 18 State House Stn	Augusta	ME	04333	207-287-3831	287-1039
Web: www.state.me.us/mpuc					
Quality Assurance & Regulations Div 28 State House Stn	Augusta	ME	04333	207-287-2161	287-5576
Web: www.state.me.us/agriculture/qar					
Rehabilitation Services Bureau 150 State House Stn	Augusta	ME	04333	800-698-4440	287-5292*
**Fax Area Code:* 207 ■ *TF:* 800-760-1573 ■ *Web:* www.maine.gov/rehab/					
Revenue Services 24 State House Stn	Augusta	ME	04333	207-287-2076	287-3618
Web: www.state.me.us/revenue					
Secretary of State 148 State House Stn	Augusta	ME	04333	207-626-8400	287-8598
Web: www.maine.gov/sos/					
Securities Div 121 State House Stn	Augusta	ME	04333	207-624-8551	624-8590
Web: www.maine.gov/pfr/securities/index.shtml					
State Lottery 8 State House Stn	Augusta	ME	04333	207-287-3721	287-6769
Web: www.mainelottery.com					
State Police 45 Commerce Dr	Augusta	ME	04333	207-624-7200	624-7088
Web: www.maine.gov/dps/msp/					
Support Enforcement & Recovery Div 11 State House Stn	Augusta	ME	04333	207-624-4100	287-5096
Web: www.state.me.us/dhhs/bfi/dser					
Supreme Court PO Box 368	Portland	ME	04112	207-822-4146	
Web: www.courts.state.me.us/mainecourts/supreme					
Teacher Certification & Placement Office 23 State House Stn	Augusta	ME	04333	207-624-6603	624-6851
Web: www.state.me.us/education/cert/cert.htm					
Tourism Office 59 State House Stn	Augusta	ME	04333	207-287-5711	287-8070
TF: 888-624-6345 ■ *Web:* www.visitmaine.com					
Transportation Dept 16 State House Stn	Augusta	ME	04333	207-624-3000	624-3001
Web: www.maine.gov/mdot					
Treasurer 39 State House Stn	Augusta	ME	04333	207-624-7477	287-2367
Web: www.state.me.us/treasurer					
University of Maine System Board of Trustees 16 Central St	Bangor	ME	04401	207-973-3211	973-3296
Web: www.maine.edu/bot3.html					
Veterans' Services Bureau 117 State House Stn	Augusta	ME	04333	207-626-4271	626-4509
Web: www.state.me.us/va/defense/hmpgmvs.htm					
Victims' Compensation Program State House Stn 6	Augusta	ME	04333	207-624-7882	624-7730
Web: www.maine.gov/ag/					
Vital Records Office 11 State House Stn	Augusta	ME	04333	207-287-3181	287-1093
Web: www.maine.gov/dhhs					
Workers' Compensation Board 27 State House Stn	Augusta	ME	04333	207-287-3751	287-7198
Web: www.state.me.us/wcb					

342-21 Maryland

	City	State	Zip	Phone	Fax
State Government Information		MD		410-974-3901	
Web: www.maryland.gov					
Administrative Office of the Courts 580 Taylor Ave	Annapolis	MD	21401	410-260-1400	974-2169
Web: www.courts.state.md.us					
Aging Dept 301 W Preston St Rm 1007	Baltimore	MD	21201	410-767-1100	333-7943
Web: www.mdoa.state.md.us					
Agriculture Dept 50 Harry S Truman Pkwy	Annapolis	MD	21401	410-841-5700	841-5914
Web: www.mda.state.md.us					
Assessments & Taxation Dept 301 W Preston St 8th Fl	Baltimore	MD	21201	410-767-1184	333-5873
Web: www.dat.state.md.us					
Attorney General 200 St Paul Pl 16th Fl	Baltimore	MD	21202	410-576-6300	576-7040
Web: www.oag.state.md.us					
Business & Economic Development Dept 217 E Redwood St	Baltimore	MD	21202	410-767-6300	333-6911
Web: www.choosemaryland.org					
Chief Medical Examiner 111 Penn St	Baltimore	MD	21201	410-333-3250	333-3063
Child Support Enforcement Administration 311 W Saratoga St	Baltimore	MD	21201	410-767-7674	333-8992
TF: 800-332-6347 ■ *Web:* www.dhr.state.md.us/csea					
Consumer Protection Div 200 St Paul Pl	Baltimore	MD	21202	410-528-8662	576-7040
Web: www.oag.state.md.us/Consumer					
Court of Appeals 361 Rowe Blvd 4th Fl	Annapolis	MD	21401	410-260-1500	
Web: www.courts.state.md.us/coappeals					
Criminal Injuries Compensation Board 6776 Reisterstown Rd Suite 206	Baltimore	MD	21215	410-585-3010	764-3815
TF: 888-679-9347 ■ *Web:* www2.dpscs.state.md.us					
Bill Status 90 State Cir	Annapolis	MD	21401	410-946-5400	946-5405
TF: 800-492-7122 ■ *Web:* mlis.state.md.us					
Education Dept 200 W Baltimore St	Baltimore	MD	21201	410-767-0100	333-2226
TF: 888-246-0016 ■ *Web:* www.marylandpublicschools.org/msde					
Emergency Management Agency 5401 Rue Saint Lo Dr	Reisterstown	MD	21136	410-517-3600	517-3610
TF: 877-636-2872 ■ *Web:* memaportal.mema.state.md.us					
Environment Dept 1800 Washington Blvd	Baltimore	MD	21230	410-537-3000	537-3888
TF: 800-633-6101 ■ *Web:* www.mde.state.md.us					
Ethics Commission 9 State Cir Suite 200	Annapolis	MD	21401	410-974-2068	974-2418
TF: 877-669-6085 ■ *Web:* ethics.gov.state.md.us/					
Financial Regulation Div 500 N Calvert St Rm 402	Baltimore	MD	21202	410-230-6097	333-0475
TF: 888-784-0136 ■ *Web:* www.dllr.state.md.us/finance					
Fisheries Service 580 Taylor Ave	Annapolis	MD	21401	410-260-8281	260-8279
Web: www.dnr.state.md.us/fisheries					
General Assembly 90 State Cir	Annapolis	MD	21401	410-841-3000	841-3850
Web: mlis.state.md.us					
Governor State House 100 State Cir	Annapolis	MD	21401	410-974-3901	974-3275
Web: www.gov.state.md.us					
Health & Mental Hygiene Dept 201 W Preston St 5th Fl	Baltimore	MD	21201	410-767-6500	767-6489
Web: dhmh.state.md.us					
Higher Education Commision 839 Bestgate Rd Suite 400	Annapolis	MD	21401	410-260-4500	260-3200
TF: 800-974-0203 ■ *Web:* www.mhec.state.md.us					
Historical & Cultural Programs Div 100 Community Pl 3rd Fl	Crownsville	MD	21032	410-514-7600	514-7678
Web: www.marylandhistoricaltrust.net					
Housing & Community Development Dept 100 Community Pl	Crownsville	MD	21032	410-514-7206	987-4070
TF: 800-756-0119 ■ *Web:* www.dhcd.state.md.us					
Information Technology Office 45 Calvert St	Annapolis	MD	21401	410-260-7259	
Web: www.dbm.state.md.us					
Insurance Administration 525 St Paul Pl	Baltimore	MD	21202	410-468-2000	468-2020
TF: 800-492-6116 ■ *Web:* www.mdinsurance.state.md.us					
Labor & Industry Div 1100 N Eutaw St Rm 606	Baltimore	MD	21201	410-767-2241	767-2986
Web: www.dllr.state.md.us/labor					
Lieutenant Governor 100 State Cir	Annapolis	MD	21401	410-974-2804	974-5882
TF: 800-811-8336 ■ *Web:* www.gov.state.md.us					
Motor Vehicle Administration 6601 Ritchie Hwy NE	Glen Burnie	MD	21062	410-768-7274	768-7506
Web: www.mva.state.md.us					
Natural Resources Dept 580 Taylor Ave	Annapolis	MD	21401	410-260-8021	260-8024
TF: 877-620-8367 ■ *Web:* www.dnr.state.md.us					
Occupational & Professional Licensing Div 500 N Calvert St 3rd Fl	Baltimore	MD	21202	410-230-6231	333-6314
Web: www.dllr.state.md.us/license/occprof					
Parole & Probation Div 6776 Reisterstown Rd Suite 305	Baltimore	MD	21215	410-585-3500	764-4091
TF: 877-227-8031 ■ *Web:* www2.dpscs.state.md.us					
Physician Quality Assurance Board 4201 Patterson Ave	Baltimore	MD	21215	410-764-4777	358-2252
Web: www.bpqa.state.md.us					
Public Safety & Correctional Services Dept 300 E Joppa Rd Suite 1000	Towson	MD	21286	410-339-5000	339-4240
TF: 877-379-8636 ■ *Web:* www.dpscs.state.md.us					
Public Service Commission 6 Saint Paul St 16th Fl	Baltimore	MD	21202	410-767-8000	333-6495
TF: 800-492-0474 ■ *Web:* www.psc.state.md.us/psc					
Racing Commission 500 N Calvert St Rm 201	Baltimore	MD	21202	410-230-6330	333-8308
Web: www.dllr.state.md.us/racing					
Rehabilitation Services Div 2301 Argonne Dr	Baltimore	MD	21218	410-554-9385	554-9412
TF: 888-554-0334 ■ *Web:* www.dors.state.md.us					
Secretary of State 16 Francis St Jeffery Bldg 1st Fl	Annapolis	MD	21401	410-974-5521	974-5190
Web: www.sos.state.md.us					
Securities Div 200 St Paul Pl 20th Fl	Baltimore	MD	21202	410-576-6360	576-6532
Web: www.oag.state.md.us/Securities					
Social Services Administration 311 W Saratoga St	Baltimore	MD	21201	410-767-7216	333-0127
Web: www.dhr.state.md.us/ssa					
State Archives 350 Rowe Blvd	Annapolis	MD	21401	410-260-6400	974-2525
Web: www.mdarchives.state.md.us					
State Arts Council 175 W Ostend St Suite E	Baltimore	MD	21230	410-767-6555	333-1062
Web: www.msac.org					

Maryland (Cont'd)

	City	State	Zip	Phone	Fax
State Athletic Commission 500 N Calvert St Rm 304	Baltimore	MD	21202	410-230-6223	333-6314
Web: www.dllr.state.md.us/license/occprof/athlet.html					
State Forest & Park Service 580 Taylor Ave Rm E-3	Annapolis	MD	21401	410-260-8186	260-8191
TF Campground R: 800-830-3970 ■ *Web:* www.dnr.state.md.us/publiclands					
Lottery Agency 1800 Washington Blvd Suite 330	Baltimore	MD	21230	410-230-8790	230-8728
Web: www.mdlottery.com					
State Police 1201 Reisterstown Rd	Pikesville	MD	21208	410-486-3101	653-4269
Web: www.mdsp.maryland.gov					
Student Financial Assistance Office 839 Bestgate Rd Suite 400	Annapolis	MD	21401	410-260-4565	260-3200
TF: 800-974-0203 ■ *Web:* www.mhec.state.md.us					
Teacher Certification & Accreditation Div 200 W Baltimore St	Baltimore	MD	21201	410-767-0412	
TF: 866-772-8922 ■ *Web:* certification.msde.state.md.us					
Tourism Development Office 217 E Redwood St 9th Fl	Baltimore	MD	21202	410-767-3400	333-6643
TF: 800-543-1036 ■ *Web:* www.mdisfun.org					
Transportation Dept 7201 Corporate Center Dr	Hanover	MD	21076	410-865-1000	865-1334
TF: 888-713-1414 ■ *Web:* www.mdot.state.md.us					
Treasurer 80 Calvert St Rm 109	Annapolis	MD	21401	410-260-7533	974-3530
TF: 800-974-0468 ■ *Web:* www.treasurer.state.md.us					
Veterans Affairs Dept 31 Hopkins Plaza Rm 1231	Baltimore	MD	21201	410-230-4444	230-4445
TF: 800-446-4926 ■ *Web:* www.mdva.state.md.us					
Vital Records Div 6550 Reisterstown Rd	Baltimore	MD	21215	410-764-3038	358-0738
TF: 800-832-3277 ■ *Web:* mdpublichealth.org/vsa					
Weights & Measures Section 50 Harry S Truman Pkwy Rm 410	Annapolis	MD	21401	410-841-5790	841-2765
Web: www.mda.state.md.us					
Workers' Compensation Commission 10 E Baltimore St	Baltimore	MD	21202	410-864-5100	564-5101
Web: www.wcc.state.md.us					
Employment & Training Div 1100 N Eutaw St Rm 616	Baltimore	MD	21201	410-767-2400	767-2986
Web: www.dllr.state.md.us/employment					

342-22 Massachusetts

	City	State	Zip	Phone	Fax
State Government Information		MA		866-888-2808	
Web: www.mass.gov					
Agricultural Resources Dept 251 Causeway St Suite 500	Boston	MA	02114	617-626-1700	626-1850
Web: www.mass.gov/agr					
Attorney General 1 Ashburton Pl Suite 2010	Boston	MA	02108	617-727-2200	727-6016
Web: www.ago.state.ma.us					
Banks Div 1 South Stn 3rd Fl	Boston	MA	02110	617-956-1500	956-1599
Web: www.mass.gov/dob					
Bill Status 1 Ashburton Pl Rm 1611	Boston	MA	02108	617-727-7030	742-4528
TF: 800-392-6090 ■ *Web:* www.mass.gov/legis/ltsform.htm					
Business Development Office 10 Park Plaza Rm 3720	Boston	MA	02116	617-973-8600	973-8797
Web: www.state.ma.us/mobd					
Child Support Enforcement Div 51 Sleeper St 3rd Fl	Boston	MA	02205	617-626-4170	626-3894
TF: 800-332-2733 ■ *Web:* www.cse.state.ma.us					
Correction Dept 50 Maple St	Milford	MA	01757	508-422-3300	422-3386
Web: www.mass.gov/doc					
Cultural Council 10 St James Ave 3rd Fl	Boston	MA	02116	617-727-3668	727-0044
Web: www.massculturalcouncil.org					
Education Dept 350 Main St	Malden	MA	02148	781-388-3300	388-3392
Web: www.doe.mass.edu					
Educational Financing Authority 125 Summer St Suite 300	Boston	MA	02110	617-261-9760	261-9765
TF: 800-449-6332 ■ *Web:* www.mefa.org					
Elder Affairs Office 1 Ashburton Pl 5th Fl	Boston	MA	02108	617-727-7750	727-9368
TF: 800-243-4636 ■ *Web:* www.state.ma.us/elder					
Emergency Management Agency 400 Worcester Rd	Framingham	MA	01702	508-820-2000	820-2030
Web: www.mass.gov/portal/					
Environmental Protection Dept 1 Winter St 2nd Fl	Boston	MA	02108	617-292-5856	574-6880
Web: www.mass.gov/eops					
Executive Office of Transportation 10 Park Plaza Rm 3170	Boston	MA	02116	617-973-7000	973-8031
Web: www.eot.state.ma.us					
Fish & Game Dept 251 Causeway St Suite 400	Boston	MA	02214	617-626-1500	626-1505
Web: www.mass.gov/dfwele/					
General Court State House	Boston	MA	02133	617-722-2000	267-8658
Web: www.mass.gov/legis					
Governor State House Executive Office Rm 360	Boston	MA	02133	617-725-4000	727-9725
Web: www.mass.gov/gov					
Higher Education Board 1 Ashburton Pl Rm 1401	Boston	MA	02108	617-994-6950	727-6397
Web: www.mass.edu					
Historical Commission 220 Morrissey Blvd	Boston	MA	02125	617-727-8470	727-5128
Web: www.sec.state.ma.us/mhc/mhcidx.htm					
Housing & Community Development Dept 100 Cambridge St	Boston	MA	02114	617-573-1100	573-1285
Web: www.mass.gov/dhcd					
Housing Finance Agency 1 Beacon St	Boston	MA	02108	617-854-1000	854-1029
Web: www.masshousing.com					
Information Technology Div 1 Ashburton Pl Rm 801	Boston	MA	02108	617-727-2040	727-2779
Web: www.mass.gov/itd					
Insurance Div 1 South Stn 5th Fl	Boston	MA	02110	617-521-7794	521-7770
Web: www.mass.gov/doi					
Lieutenant Governor State House Rm 360	Boston	MA	02133	617-727-4005	727-3666
Web: www.mass.gov/gov					
Medical Examiner 720 Albany St	Boston	MA	02118	617-267-6767	266-6763
Web: www.mass.gov./eops					
Mental Health Dept 25 Staniford St	Boston	MA	02214	617-626-8000	
Web: www.mass.gov/dmh					
Parole Board PO Box 647	Medfield	MA	02052	508-242-8001	242-8100
Web: www.mass.gov/parole					
Port Authority 1 Harborside Dr Suite 200S	East Boston	MA	02128	617-568-1000	568-1022
Web: www.massport.com					
Professional Licensure Div 239 Causeway St 5th Fl	Boston	MA	02114	617-727-3074	727-2197
Web: www.mass.gov/dpl					
Public Health Dept 250 Washington St	Boston	MA	02108	617-624-6000	624-5206
Web: www.mass.gov/dph					
Public Protection Bureau 100 Cambridge St	Boston	MA	02114	617-727-2200	727-5762
Registry of Motor Vehicles PO Box 199100	Roxbury	MA	02119	617-351-4500	351-9519
Web: www.mass.gov/rmv					
Rehabilitation Commission 27 Wormwood St Suite 600	Boston	MA	02210	617-204-3600	727-1539
Web: www.state.ma.us/mrc					
Revenue Dept 51 Sleeper St	Boston	MA	02205	617-626-2201	626-2299
Web: www.dor.state.ma.us					
Secretary of the Commonwealth State House Rm 337	Boston	MA	02133	617-727-9180	742-4722
Web: www.sec.state.ma.us					
Securities Div 1 Ashburton Pl 17th Fl	Boston	MA	02108	617-727-3548	248-0177
Web: www.sec.state.ma.us/sct					
Social Services Dept 24 Farnsworth St	Boston	MA	02210	617-748-2000	261-7435
Web: www.mass.gov/dss					
Standards Div 1 Ashburton Pl Rm 1115	Boston	MA	02108	617-727-3480	727-5705
Web: www.mass.gov/consumer					
State Boxing Commission 1 Ashburton Pl Rm 1301	Boston	MA	02108	617-727-3200	727-5732
Web: www.mass.gov/mbc					
State Ethics Commission 1 Ashburton Pl Rm 619	Boston	MA	02108	617-727-0060	723-5851
Web: www.mass.gov/ethics					
Lottery Commission 60 Columbian St	Braintree	MA	02184	781-849-5555	849-5546
Web: www.masslottery.com					
State Parks & Recreation Div 251 Causeway St Suite 600	Boston	MA	02214	617-626-4986	626-4999
Web: www.mass.gov/dcr/forparks.htm					
State Police Dept 470 Worcester Rd	Framingham	MA	01701	508-820-2300	820-9630
Web: www.state.ma.us/msp					
State Racing Commission 1 Ashurton Pl Rm 1313	Boston	MA	02108	617-727-2581	227-6062
Web: www.state.ma.us/src					
Supreme Judicial Court 1 Pemberton Sq Suite 2500	Boston	MA	02108	617-557-1000	723-3577
Web: www.mass.gov/courts					
Telecommunications & Energy Dept 1 South Stn 2nd Fl	Boston	MA	02202	617-305-3500	345-9101
Web: www.mass.gov/dte					
Transitional Assistance Dept 600 Washington St	Boston	MA	02111	617-348-8400	348-8575
Web: www.mass.gov/dta					
Travel & Tourism Office 10 Park Plaza Suite 4510	Boston	MA	02116	617-973-8500	973-8525
TF: 800-227-6277 ■ *Web:* www.mass-vacation.com					
Treasurer State House Rm 227	Boston	MA	02133	617-367-6900	248-0372
Web: www.mass.gov/treasury					
Veterans' Services Dept 600 Washington St Suite 1100	Boston	MA	02111	617-727-3578	727-5903
Web: www.state.ma.us/veterans					
Victim Compensation & Assistance Div 1 Ashburton Pl	Boston	MA	02108	617-727-2200	367-3906
Web: www.ago.state.ma.us					
Vital Records & Statistics Registry 150 Mt Vernon St 1st Fl	Dorchester	MA	02125	617-740-2600	423-2038
Web: www.mass.gov/dph/bhsre/rvr/rvr.htm					
Labor & Workforce Development Dept 1 Ashburton Pl Rm 2112	Boston	MA	02108	617-626-7122	727-1090
Web: www.mass.gov/dlwd					

342-23 Michigan

	City	State	Zip	Phone	Fax
State Government Information		MI		517-373-1837	
Web: www.michigan.gov					
Aging Services Office PO Box 30676	Lansing	MI	48909	517-373-8230	373-4092
Web: www.miseniors.net					
Agriculture Dept PO Box 30017	Lansing	MI	48909	517-373-1104	335-7071
TF: 800-292-3939 ■ *Web:* www.michigan.gov/mda					
Arts & Cultural Affairs Council 702 W Kalamazoo St PO Box 30705	Lansing	MI	48909	517-241-4011	241-3979
Web: www.michigan.gov/hal					
Attorney General PO Box 30212	Lansing	MI	48909	517-373-1110	373-3042
TF: 877-765-8388 ■ *Web:* www.michigan.gov/ag					
Bill Status PO Box 30036	Lansing	MI	48909	517-373-0630	
Web: www.legislature.mi.gov					
Career Development Office 201 N Washington Sq 3rd Fl	Lansing	MI	48913	517-241-4000	373-0314
TF: 888-253-6855 ■ *Web:* www.michigan.gov/mdcd					
Child Support Office 235 S Grand Ave Suite 1215	Lansing	MI	48933	866-661-0005	
Web: www.michigan.gov/dhs					
Civil Rights Dept Capitol Tower Bldg Suite 800	Lansing	MI	48933	517-335-3165	241-0546
Web: www.michigan.gov/mdcr					
Civil Service Dept Capitol Commons Center 400 S Pine St	Lansing	MI	48913	517-373-3030	373-7690
TF: 800-788-1766 ■ *Web:* www.michigan.gov/mdcs					
Community Health Dept Capitol View Bldg 201 Townsend St	Lansing	MI	48913	517-373-3740	
Web: www.michigan.gov/mdch					
Consumer Protection Div PO Box 30213	Lansing	MI	48909	517-373-1140	241-3771
Web: www.michigan.gov/ag					
Corrections Dept 206 E Michigan Ave Grandview Plaza PO Box 30003	Lansing	MI	48909	517-335-1426	373-6883
Web: www.michigan.gov/corrections					
Crime Victims Services Commission 320 S Walnut St 5th Fl	Lansing	MI	48913	517-373-7373	
Web: www.mivictims.org/services/cvsc/					
Driver & Vehicle Bureau 7064 Crowner Dr	Lansing	MI	48918	517-322-1460	322-5458
Web: www.michigan.gov/sos					
Mental Health & Substance Abuse Office 320 S Walnut St Lewis Cass Bldg 5th Fl	Lansing	MI	48913	517-373-4700	241-2199
Web: www.michigan.gov/mdch					
Economic Development Corp 300 N Washington Sq 3rd Fl	Lansing	MI	48913	517-373-9808	241-3683
TF: 888-522-0103 ■ *Web:* medc.michigan.org					
Education Board 608 W Allegan St PO Box 30008	Lansing	MI	48909	517-373-3324	
Web: www.michigan.gov/mde					
Education Trust PO Box 30198	Lansing	MI	48909	517-335-4767	373-6967
TF: 800-638-4543 ■ *Web:* www.michigan.gov/treasury					
Michigan eLibrary Information 702 W Kalamazoo St PO Box 30007	Lansing	MI	48909	517-373-4331	373-5700
Web: www.michigan.gov/hal/					
Emergency Management Div PO Box 30636	Lansing	MI	48909	517-336-6198	333-4987
Environmental Quality Dept PO Box 30473	Lansing	MI	48909	517-373-7917	
Web: www.michigan.gov/deq					
Financial Institutions & Insurance Services Office PO Box 30220	Lansing	MI	48909	517-373-0220	335-4978
TF: 877-999-6442 ■ *Web:* www.michigan.gov/ofis					
Consumer & Industry Services Dept 1500 Abbott Rd Suite 400	East Lansing	MI	48823	517-241-0040	241-0510
Web: www.michigan.gov/mgcb					
Governor PO Box 30013	Lansing	MI	48909	517-373-3400	335-6863
Web: www.michigan.gov/gov					
Human Services Dept PO Box 30037 235 S Grand Ave	Lansing	MI	48909	517-373-2035	335-6101
Web: www.michigan.gov/dhs					
Information Technology Dept George W Romney Bldg 8th Fl 111 S Capitol Ave	Lansing	MI	48913	517-335-4000	373-8213
Web: www.michigan.gov/dit					
Labor & Economic Growth Dept PO Box 30004	Lansing	MI	48909	517-373-1820	373-2129
Web: www.michigan.gov/dleg					
Legislature State Capitol	Lansing	MI	48909	517-373-0170	373-0171
Web: www.legislature.mi.gov					
Lieutenant Governor PO Box 30013	Lansing	MI	48909	517-373-6800	241-3956
Web: www.michigan.gov/ltgov					
Management & Budget Dept PO Box 30026	Lansing	MI	48909	517-373-1004	373-7268
Web: www.michigan.gov/dmb					
Military & Veterans Affairs Dept 3411 N ML King Blvd	Lansing	MI	48906	517-481-8000	
Web: www.michigan.gov/dmva					
Natural Resources Dept PO Box 30028	Lansing	MI	48909	517-241-3230	
Web: www.michigan.gov/dnr					
Parks & Recreation Bureau PO Box 30257	Lansing	MI	48909	517-373-9900	373-4625
TF Campground R: 800-447-2757 ■ *Web:* www.michigan.gov/dnr					
Public Service Commission PO Box 30221	Lansing	MI	48909	517-241-6180	241-6181
Web: www.michigan.gov/mpsc					
Racing Commissioners Office 525 W Allegan St PO Box 30773	Lansing	MI	48909	517-335-1420	241-3018
Web: www.michigan.gov/horseracing/					
Rehabilitation Services 201 N Washington Sq 4th Fl	Lansing	MI	48933	517-373-3390	335-7277
Web: www.michigan.gov/mdcd					
Secretary of State 430 W Allegan St 4th Fl	Lansing	MI	48918	517-373-2510	241-3442
Web: www.michigan.gov/sos					

				Phone	Fax
State Court Administrator 925 W Ottawa St *Web:* courts.michigan.gov/scao	Lansing	MI	48913	517-373-0130	373-7517
State Historic Preservation Office 702 W Kalamazoo St PO Box 30740 *Web:* www.michigan.gov/hal	Lansing	MI	48909	517-373-1630	
State Housing Development Authority PO Box 30044 *Web:* www.michigan.gov/mshda	Lansing	MI	48909	517-373-8370	335-4797
State Lottery Bureau 101 E Hillsdale St PO Box 30023 *Web:* www.michigan.gov/lottery	Lansing	MI	48909	517-335-5600	335-5644
State Police Dept 714 S Harrison Rd *Web:* www.michigan.gov/msp	East Lansing	MI	48823	517-332-2521	336-6255
Student Financial Services Bureau Austin Bldg 430 West Allegan *TF:* 800-642-5626 ■ *Web:* www.michigan.gov/mistudentaid	Lansing	MI	48922	517-373-4897	
Supreme Court PO Box 30052 *Web:* courts.michigan.gov/supremecourt	Lansing	MI	48909	517-373-0120	
Transportation Dept PO Box 30050 *Web:* www.michigan.gov/mdot	Lansing	MI	48909	517-373-2090	373-0167
Travel Michigan 300 N Washington Sq *TF:* 888-784-7328 ■ *Web:* travel.michigan.org	Lansing	MI	48913	517-373-0670	373-0059
Treasurer 430 W Allegan St *Web:* www.michigan.gov/treasury	Lansing	MI	48922	517-373-3200	373-4968
Commercial Services Bureau Cadillac Place 3024 W Grand Blvd *Web:* www.michigan.gov/uia	Detroit	MI	48202	313-456-2400	456-2424
Vital Records Div 201 Townsend St Capitol View Bldg 3rd Fl *Web:* www.michigan.gov/mdch	Lansing	MI	48913	517-335-8656	321-5884
Wildlife Div PO Box 30444 *Web:* www.michigan.gov/dnr	Lansing	MI	48909	517-373-1263	373-6705
Workers Compensation Agency PO Box 30016 *Web:* www.michigan.gov/wca	Lansing	MI	48909	517-322-1106	322-6689

342-24 Minnesota

				Phone	Fax
State Government Information *Web:* www.state.mn.us		MN		651-296-6013	
Aging Board 540 Cedar St *TF:* 800-657-3889 ■ *Web:* www.mnaging.org	Saint Paul	MN	55155	651-431-2500	431-7415
Agriculture Dept 625 Robert St N *TF:* 800-967-2474 ■ *Web:* www.mda.state.mn.us	Saint Paul	MN	55155	651-201-6000	
Arts Board 400 Sibley St Suite 200 *TF:* 800-866-2787 ■ *Web:* www.arts.state.mn.us	Saint Paul	MN	55101	651-215-1600	215-1602
Attorney General 1400 Bremer Tower 445 Minnesota St *TF:* 800-657-3787 ■ *Web:* www.ag.state.mn.us	Saint Paul	MN	55101	651-296-3353	297-4193
Bill Status-House 75 ML King Jr Blvd Rm 211 *Web:* www.leg.state.mn.us/leg/legis.asp	Saint Paul	MN	55155	651-296-6646	
Bill Status-Senate 75 ML King Jr Blvd Rm 231 *Web:* www.leg.state.mn.us/leg/legis.asp	Saint Paul	MN	55155	651-296-2887	
Campaign Finance & Public Disclosure Board 658 Cedar St Suite 190 *TF:* 800-657-3889 ■ *Web:* www.cfboard.state.mn.us	Saint Paul	MN	55155	651-296-5148	296-1722
Child Support Enforcement Div 444 Lafayette Rd *Web:* www.dhs.state.mn.us	Saint Paul	MN	55155	651-431-2000	431-7517
Children Families & Learning Dept 1500 Hwy 36 W *Web:* children.state.mn.us	Roseville	MN	55113	651-582-8200	582-8202
Children's Services Administration 444 Lafayette Rd *Web:* www.dhs.state.mn.us	Saint Paul	MN	55155	651-431-4660	297-5840
Commerce Dept 85 7th Pl E Suite 500 *Web:* www.commerce.state.mn.us	Saint Paul	MN	55101	651-296-4026	297-1959
Consumer Protection Office 445 Minnesota St Suite 1400 *TF:* 800-657-3787 ■ *Web:* www.ag.state.mn.us	Saint Paul	MN	55101	651-296-3353	
Corrections Dept 1450 Energy Park Dr Suite 200 *Web:* www.corr.state.mn.us	Saint Paul	MN	55108	651-361-7200	642-0223
Crime Victims Reparations Board 445 Minnesota St Suite 2300 *TF:* 888-622-8799	Saint Paul	MN	55101	651-201-7300	296-5787
Driver & Vehicle Services Div 445 Minnesota St Rm 196 *Web:* www.dps.state.mn.us/dvs	Saint Paul	MN	55101	651-296-4544	296-3141
Trade & Economic Development Dept 332 Minnesota St Suite E200 *TF:* 800-657-3858 ■ *Web:* www.deed.state.mn.us	Saint Paul	MN	55101	651-259-7114	
Technology Office 658 Cedar St	Saint Paul	MN	55155	651-296-8888	
Finance Dept 658 Cedar St Suite 400 *TF:* 800-627-3529 ■ *Web:* www.finance.state.mn.us	Saint Paul	MN	55155	651-201-8000	296-8685
Fisheries Div 500 Lafayette Rd *Web:* www.dnr.state.mn.us/fishwildlife/	Saint Paul	MN	55155	651-259-5180	297-7272
Governor 130 State Capitol 75 Rev Dr Martin Luther King Jr Blvd *TF:* 800-657-3717 ■ *Web:* www.governor.state.mn.us	Saint Paul	MN	55155	651-296-3391	296-2089
Health Dept PO Box 64975 *TF:* 888-345-0823 ■ *Web:* www.health.state.mn.us	Saint Paul	MN	55164	651-201-5000	
Historical Society 345 Kellogg Blvd W *TF:* 800-657-3773 ■ *Web:* www.mnhs.org	Saint Paul	MN	55102	651-259-3000	
Emergency Management Div 444 Cedar St Suite 223 *Web:* www.dps.state.mn.us/dhsem/hsemhome.asp	Saint Paul	MN	55101	651-201-7400	296-0459
Housing Finance Authority 400 Sibley St Suite 300 *TF:* 800-657-3769 ■ *Web:* www.mhfa.state.mn.us	Saint Paul	MN	55101	651-296-7608	296-8139
Human Services Dept 444 Lafayette Rd *Web:* www.dhs.state.mn.us	Saint Paul	MN	55155	651-431-2000	296-6244
Labor & Industry Dept 443 Lafayette Rd N *TF:* 800-342-5354 ■ *Web:* www.doli.state.mn.us	Saint Paul	MN	55155	651-284-5005	284-5727
Legislature 75 Constitution Ave State Capitol *TF:* 800-657-3550 ■ *Web:* www.leg.state.mn.us	Saint Paul	MN	55155	651-296-2146	
Licensing Div 85 7th Pl E Suite 600 *TF:* 800-657-3978	Saint Paul	MN	55101	651-296-6319	284-4107
Lieutenant Governor 130 State Capitol 75 Rev Dr Martin Luther King Jr Blvd *TF:* 800-657-3717 ■ *Web:* www.governor.state.mn.us	Saint Paul	MN	55155	651-296-3391	296-2089
Medical Practice Board 2829 University Ave SE Suite 500 *TF:* 800-657-3709 ■ *Web:* www.bmp.state.mn.us	Minneapolis	MN	55414	612-617-2130	617-2166
Natural Resources Dept 500 Lafayette Rd *TF:* 888-646-6367 ■ *Web:* www.dnr.state.mn.us	Saint Paul	MN	55155	651-296-6157	296-3618
Higher Education Services Office 1450 Energy Park Dr Suite 350 *TF:* 800-657-3866 ■ *Web:* www.ohe.state.mn.us	Saint Paul	MN	55108	651-642-0567	642-0675
Pardon Board 1450 Energy Park Dr Suite 200	Saint Paul	MN	55108	651-642-0284	643-2575
Parks & Recreation Div 500 Lafayette Rd *Web:* www.dnr.state.mn.us/parks_recreation	Saint Paul	MN	55155	651-259-5591	
Economic Security Dept 444 Cedar St Town Square Bldg *Web:* www.dps.state.mn.us/	Saint Paul	MN	55101	651-201-7000	
Public Utilities Commission 121 7th Pl E Suite 350 *TF:* 800-657-3782 ■ *Web:* www.puc.state.mn.us	Saint Paul	MN	55101	651-296-7124	297-7073
Rehabilitation Services Branch 332 Minnesota St Suite E200 *TF:* 800-328-9095 ■ *Web:* www.deed.state.mn.us/rehab	Saint Paul	MN	55101	651-296-5616	297-5159
Revenue Dept 6000 N Roberts St *Web:* www.taxes.state.mn.us	Saint Paul	MN	55146	651-296-3403	297-5309
Secretary of State 60 Empire Dr Suite 100 *Web:* www.sos.state.mn.us	Saint Paul	MN	55103	651-296-2803	215-0682
Securities Registration Div 85 7th Pl E	Saint Paul	MN	55101	651-296-4973	
State Court Administrator 25 Rev Dr Martin Luther King Jr Blvd Rm 135 *Web:* www.courts.state.mn.us	Saint Paul	MN	55155	651-296-2474	297-5636
State Lottery 2645 Long Lake Rd *Web:* www.mnlottery.com	Roseville	MN	55113	651-297-7456	
State Patrol Div 444 Cedar St Suite 130 *Web:* www.dps.state.mn.us/patrol	Saint Paul	MN	55101	651-201-7100	
Supreme Court 25 Rev Dr Martin Luther King Jr Blvd *Web:* www.courts.state.mn.us	Saint Paul	MN	55155	651-297-7650	
Teacher Licensing Office 1500 Hwy 36 W	Roseville	MN	55113	651-582-8691	582-8809
Tourism Office 121 7th Pl E Suite 100 *TF:* 888-868-7476 ■ *Web:* www.exploreminnesota.com	Saint Paul	MN	55101	651-296-5029	
Transportation Dept 395 John Ireland Blvd *TF:* 800-657-3774 ■ *Web:* www.dot.state.mn.us	Saint Paul	MN	55155	651-296-3000	
Veterans Affairs Dept 20 W 12th St 2nd Fl *Web:* www.mdva.state.mn.us	Saint Paul	MN	55155	651-296-2562	296-3954
Vital Statistics Section PO Box 64882 *Web:* www.health.state.mn.us/divs/chs/osr/	Saint Paul	MN	55164	651-201-5970	291-0101
Weights & Measures Div 14305 Southcross Dr Suite 150 **Fax Area Code:* 952	Burnsville	MN	55306	651-215-5821	435-4040*
Workers' Compensation Div 443 Lafayette Rd *TF:* 800-342-5354 ■ *Web:* www.doli.state.mn.us/workcomp.html	Saint Paul	MN	55155	651-284-5005	296-9634

342-25 Mississippi

				Phone	Fax
State Government Information *Web:* www.mississippi.gov		MS		601-359-1000	
Administrative Office of the Courts PO Box 117	Jackson	MS	39205	601-354-7406	354-7459
Aging & Adult Services Div 750 N State St *Web:* www.mdhs.state.ms.us/aas.html	Jackson	MS	39202	601-359-4929	359-4370
Archives & History Dept PO Box 571 *Web:* www.mdah.state.ms.us	Jackson	MS	39205	601-576-6850	576-6899
Arts Commission 501 N West St Suite 1101-A *Web:* www.arts.state.ms.us	Jackson	MS	39201	601-359-6030	359-6008
Attorney General PO Box 220 *Web:* www.ago.state.ms.us	Jackson	MS	39205	601-359-3680	359-3796
Banking & Consumer Finance Dept PO Box 23729 *TF:* 800-844-2499 ■ *Web:* www.dbcf.state.ms.us	Jackson	MS	39225	601-359-1031	359-3557
Bill Status PO Box 1018 *Web:* billstatus.ls.state.ms.us	Jackson	MS	39215	601-359-3719	
Child Support Enforcement Div PO Box 352 *TF:* 800-948-4010 ■ *Web:* www.mdhs.state.ms.us/cse.html	Jackson	MS	39205	601-359-4861	359-4415
Consumer Protection Div PO Box 1609 *TF:* 800-551-1830	Jackson	MS	39215	601-359-1111	359-1175
Contractors Board 215 Woodline Dr Suite B *TF:* 800-880-6161 ■ *Web:* www.msboc.state.ms.us	Jackson	MS	39232	601-354-6161	354-6715
Corrections Dept 723 N President St *Web:* www.mdoc.state.ms.us	Jackson	MS	39202	601-359-5600	359-5624
Crime Victim Compensation Program PO Box 220 *TF:* 800-829-6766 ■ *Web:* www.ago.state.ms.us/divisions/crime_victim	Jackson	MS	39205	601-359-6766	576-4445
Development Authority PO Box 849 *Web:* www.mississippi.org	Jackson	MS	39205	601-359-3449	359-2832
Education Dept PO Box 771 *Web:* www.mde.k12.ms.us	Jackson	MS	39205	601-359-3513	359-2566
Emergency Management Agency PO Box 4501 *TF:* 800-222-6362 ■ *Web:* www.msema.org	Jackson	MS	39296	601-933-6875	933-6800
Employment Security Commission 1235 Echelon Pkwy *Web:* www.mdes.ms.gov	Jackson	MS	39213	601-321-6000	321-6004
Enviromental Quality Dept PO Box 20305 *Web:* www.deq.state.ms.us	Jackson	MS	39289	601-961-5000	354-6965
Ethics Commission PO Box 22746 *Web:* www.ethics.state.ms.us	Jackson	MS	39225	601-359-1285	354-6253
Family & Children Services Div 750 N State St *Web:* www.mdhs.state.ms.us/fcs.html	Jackson	MS	39202	601-359-4500	359-4363
Finance & Administration Dept PO Box 267 *Web:* www.dfa.state.ms.us	Jackson	MS	39205	601-359-3402	359-2405
Governor PO Box 139 *Web:* www.governorbarbour.com	Jackson	MS	39205	601-359-3150	359-3741
Health Dept PO Box 1700 *Web:* www.msdh.state.ms.us	Jackson	MS	39215	601-576-7400	576-7948
Higher Learning Institutions Board of Trustees 3825 Ridgewood Rd Suite 915 *Web:* www.ihl.state.ms.us	Jackson	MS	39211	601-432-6611	432-6972
Highway Safety Patrol PO Box 958 *Web:* www.dps.state.ms.us	Jackson	MS	39205	601-987-1500	987-1498
Historic Preservation Div PO Box 571 *Web:* mdah.state.ms.us/hpres/	Jackson	MS	39205	601-576-6940	576-6955
Home Corp PO Box 23369 *Web:* www.mshomecorp.com	Jackson	MS	39225	601-718-4642	718-4643
Human Services Dept 750 N State St *Web:* www.mdhs.state.ms.us	Jackson	MS	39205	601-359-4500	359-4510
Information Technology Services Dept 301 N Lamar St Suite 508 *Web:* www.its.state.ms.us	Jackson	MS	39201	601-359-1395	354-6016
Insurance Dept PO Box 79 *Web:* www.doi.state.ms.us	Jackson	MS	39205	601-359-3569	359-2474
Legislature New Capitol Box 1018 *Web:* www.ls.state.ms.us	Jackson	MS	39215	601-359-3770	359-3935
Lieutenant Governor PO Box 1018 *Web:* www.ls.state.ms.us/ltgov	Jackson	MS	39215	601-359-3200	359-4054
Medical Licensure Board 1867 Crane Ridge Dr Suite 200-B *Web:* www.msbml.state.ms.us	Jackson	MS	39216	601-987-3079	987-4159
Motor Vehicle Commission PO Box 16873 *Web:* www.mmvc.state.ms.us	Jackson	MS	39236	601-987-3995	987-3997
Parks & Recreation Div PO Box 451 *TF:* 800-467-2757 ■ *Web:* www.mdwfp.com/parks.asp	Jackson	MS	39205	601-432-2266	432-2236
Parole Board 201 W Capitol St Suite 800 *Web:* www.mpb.state.ms.us	Jackson	MS	39201	601-354-7716	354-7725
Prepaid Affordable College Tuition Program (MPACT) 501 N West St PO Box 120 *TF:* 800-987-4450 ■ *Web:* www.collegesavingsmississippi.com	Jackson	MS	39205	601-359-5255	359-5234
Public Accountancy Board 5 Old River Pl Suite 104 *Web:* www.msbpa.state.ms.us	Jackson	MS	39202	601-354-7320	354-7290
Public Health Statistics Bureau 571 Stadium Dr PO Box 1700 *Web:* www.msdh.state.ms.us/phs	Jackson	MS	39215	601-576-7960	576-7505
Public Service Commission PO Box 1174 *Web:* www.psc.state.ms.us	Jackson	MS	39215	601-961-5434	961-5469
Real Estate Appraiser Licensing & Certification Commission PO Box 12685 *Web:* www.mrec.state.ms.us	Jackson	MS	39236	601-932-9191	932-2990
Rehabilitation Services Dept PO Box 1698 *TF:* 800-443-1000 ■ *Web:* www.mdrs.state.ms.us	Jackson	MS	39215	601-853-5100	853-5205

Mississippi (Cont'd)

Name / Address	City	State	Zip	Phone	Fax
Secretary of State PO Box 136 *Web:* www.sos.state.ms.us	Jackson	MS	39205	601-359-1350	359-1499
Securities Div PO Box 136 *Web:* www.sos.state.ms.us/regenf/securities/securities.asp	Jackson	MS	39201	601-359-1350	359-2663
State Medical Examiner 1700 E Woodrow Wilson Ave *Web:* www.dps.state.ms.us	Jackson	MS	39216	601-987-1600	987-1445
Student Financial Aid Office 3825 Ridgewood Rd *TF:* 800-327-2980 ■ *Web:* www.ihl.state.ms.us/financialaid	Jackson	MS	39211	601-432-6997	432-6527
Supreme Court PO Box 117 *Web:* www.mssc.state.ms.us	Jackson	MS	39205	601-359-3694	359-2407
Tax Commission PO Box 22828 *Web:* www.mstc.state.ms.us	Jackson	MS	39225	601-923-7000	923-7404
Teacher Licensure Office PO Box 771 *Web:* www.mde.k12.ms.us	Jackson	MS	39205	601-359-3483	359-2778
Tourism Development Div PO Box 849 *TF:* 866-733-6477 ■ *Web:* www.visitmississippi.org	Jackson	MS	39205	601-359-3297	359-5757
Transportation Dept PO Box 1850 *Web:* www.gomdot.com	Jackson	MS	39215	601-359-7002	359-7050
Treasury Dept PO Box 138 *Web:* www.treasury.state.ms.us	Jackson	MS	39205	601-359-3600	359-2001
Veterans Affairs Board PO Box 5947 *Web:* www.vab.state.ms.us	Pearl	MS	39288	601-576-4850	576-4868
Weights & Measures Div PO Box 1609	Jackson	MS	39215	601-359-1149	359-1175
Wildlife Fisheries & Parks Dept 1505 Eastover Dr *Web:* www.mdwfp.com	Jackson	MS	39211	601-432-2400	432-2024
Worker's Compensation Commission PO Box 5300 *Web:* www.mwcc.state.ms.us	Jackson	MS	39296	601-987-4200	987-4233

342-26 Missouri

Name / Address	City	State	Zip	Phone	Fax
State Government Information *Web:* www.missouri.gov		MO		573-751-2000	
Agriculture Dept PO Box 630 *Web:* www.mda.state.mo.us	Jefferson City	MO	65102	573-751-4211	751-1784
Arts Council 815 Olive St Suite 16 *Web:* www.missouriartscouncil.org	Saint Louis	MO	63101	314-340-6845	340-7215
Attorney General PO Box 899 *Web:* www.moago.org	Jefferson City	MO	65102	573-751-3321	751-0774
Bill Status 117A State Capitol *Web:* www.house.state.mo.us/jointsearch.asp	Jefferson City	MO	65101	573-751-4633	751-0130
Child Support Enforcement Div 221 W High St PO Box 1527 *TF:* 800-859-7999 ■ *Web:* dss.missouri.gov/cse	Jefferson City	MO	65102	573-751-4301	751-8450
Conservation Dept 2901 W Truman Blvd *Web:* www.mdc.mo.gov	Jefferson City	MO	65109	573-751-4115	751-4467
Consumer Protection Div PO Box 899 *Web:* www.moago.org/divisions/consumerprotection.htm	Jefferson City	MO	65102	573-751-6887	751-7948
Corrections Dept PO Box 236 *Web:* www.corrections.state.mo.us	Jefferson City	MO	65102	573-526-6500	751-4099
Crime Victims' Compensation Unit PO Box 3001 *Web:* www.dolir.state.mo.us/wc/cv_help.htm	Jefferson City	MO	65102	573-526-6006	526-4940
Economic Development Dept PO Box 1157 *Web:* www.ded.state.mo.us	Jefferson City	MO	65102	573-751-3946	751-7258
Elementary & Secondary Education Dept PO Box 480 *Web:* www.dese.state.mo.us	Jefferson City	MO	65102	573-751-4212	751-8613
Emergency Management Agency PO Box 116 *Web:* www.sema.state.mo.us	Jefferson City	MO	65102	573-526-9101	634-7966
Employment Security Div 421 E Dunklin St *Web:* www.dolir.mo.gov/es/ui-tax/main.htm	Jefferson City	MO	65102	573-751-3215	751-4945
Family Services Div PO Box 2320 *Web:* dss.missouri.gov/dfs	Jefferson City	MO	65102	573-751-3221	751-3203
Finance Div PO Box 716 *Web:* www.missouri-finance.org	Jefferson City	MO	65102	573-751-3242	751-9192
General Assembly State Capitol **Fax:* PR ■ *Web:* www.moga.state.mo.us	Jefferson City	MO	65101	573-751-3824	751-8640*
Governor PO Box 720 *Web:* www.gov.state.mo.us	Jefferson City	MO	65102	573-751-3222	751-1495
Healing Arts Board PO Box 4 *Web:* www.ded.state.mo.us	Jefferson City	MO	65102	573-751-0098	751-3166
Health & Senior Services Dept PO Box 570 *Web:* www.dhss.state.mo.us	Jefferson City	MO	65102	573-751-6400	751-6010
Higher Education Dept 3515 Amazonas Dr *TF:* 800-473-6757 ■ *Web:* www.dhe.mo.gov	Jefferson City	MO	65109	573-751-2361	751-6635
Historical Preservation Office 1101 Riverside Dr *Web:* www.dnr.mo.gov/shpo	Jefferson City	MO	65101	573-751-7858	522-6262
Homeland Security Office PO Box 809 *Web:* www.homelandsecurity.state.mo.us	Jefferson City	MO	65102	573-522-3007	751-7819
Housing Development Commission 3435 Broadway *Web:* www.mhdc.com	Kansas City	MO	64111	816-759-6600	759-6828
Insurance Dept 301 W High St Suite 530 *Web:* www.insurance.state.mo.us	Jefferson City	MO	65101	573-751-4126	751-1165
Labor & Industrial Relations Dept PO Box 504 *Web:* www.dolir.state.mo.us	Jefferson City	MO	65102	573-751-4091	526-4135
Lieutenant Governor State Capitol Rm 224 *Web:* www.ltgov.state.mo.us	Jefferson City	MO	65102	573-751-4727	751-9422
Lottery PO Box 1603 *Web:* www.molottery.state.mo.us	Jefferson City	MO	65102	573-751-4050	751-5188
Motor Vehicles & Drivers Licensing Div 301 W High St Rm 470 *Web:* dor.mo.gov/mvdl	Jefferson City	MO	65101	573-751-4450	526-4774
Natural Resources Dept PO Box 176 *Web:* www.dnr.state.mo.us	Jefferson City	MO	65102	573-751-3443	751-7627
Probation & Parole Board 1511 Christy Dr *Web:* www.corrections.state.mo.us/division/prob/prob.htm	Jefferson City	MO	65101	573-751-8488	751-8501
Professional Registration Div PO Box 1335 *Web:* www.ded.state.mo.us	Jefferson City	MO	65102	573-751-0293	751-4176
Public Service Commission PO Box 360 *Web:* www.psc.state.mo.us	Jefferson City	MO	65102	573-751-3234	751-1847
Real Estate Commission PO Box 1339 *Web:* www.ded.state.mo.us	Jefferson City	MO	65102	573-751-2628	751-2777
Revenue Dept PO Box 311 *Web:* www.dor.state.mo.us	Jefferson City	MO	65105	573-751-4450	751-7150
Secretary of State PO Box 778 *Web:* www.sos.state.mo.us	Jefferson City	MO	65102	573-751-4936	526-4903
Securities Div 600 W Main St 2nd Fl *Web:* www.sos.state.mo.us/securities	Jefferson City	MO	65101	573-751-4136	526-3124
Social Services Dept PO Box 1527 *Web:* www.dss.state.mo.us	Jefferson City	MO	65102	573-751-4815	751-3203
State Courts Administrator PO Box 104480 *Web:* www.osca.state.mo.us	Jefferson City	MO	65110	573-751-3585	751-5540
State Highway Patrol PO Box 568 *Web:* www.mshp.state.mo.us	Jefferson City	MO	65102	573-751-3313	751-9419
State Parks Div PO Box 176 *TF:* 800-334-6946 ■ *Web:* www.mostateparks.com	Jefferson City	MO	65102	573-751-2479	751-8656
Student Assistance Resource Services (MOSTARS) 3515 Amazonas Dr. *TF:* 800-473-6757 ■ *Web:* www.dhe.mo.gov	Jefferson City	MO	65109	573-751-2361	751-6635
Supreme Court PO Box 150 *Web:* www.osca.state.mo.us/sup/index.nsf	Jefferson City	MO	65102	573-751-4144	751-7514
Teacher Certification Office PO Box 480 *Web:* dese.mo.gov/divteachqual/teachcert	Jefferson City	MO	65102	573-751-0051	
Tourism Div PO Box 1055 *TF:* 800-877-1234 ■ *Web:* www.missouritourism.org	Jefferson City	MO	65102	573-526-5900	751-5160
Transportation Dept PO Box 270 *TF:* 888-275-6636 ■ *Web:* www.modot.state.mo.us	Jefferson City	MO	65102	573-751-2551	751-6555
Treasurer PO Box 210 *Web:* www.sto.state.mo.us	Jefferson City	MO	65102	573-751-2411	751-9443
Veterans Commission PO Drawer 147 *Web:* www.mvc.dps.mo.gov	Jefferson City	MO	65102	573-751-3779	751-6836
Vital Records Bureau PO Box 570 *Web:* www.dhss.state.mo.us	Jefferson City	MO	65102	573-751-6387	526-3846
Vocational & Adult Education Div 3024 Dupont Cir *Web:* dese.mo.gov/divcareered	Jefferson City	MO	65109	573-751-3251	751-1441
Weights & Measures Div PO Box 630 *Web:* www.mda.state.mo.us/Consumer/j.htm	Jefferson City	MO	65102	573-751-4278	751-0281
Workers' Compensation Div PO Box 58 *Web:* www.dolir.state.mo.us/wc	Jefferson City	MO	65102	573-751-4231	751-2012

342-27 Montana

Name / Address	City	State	Zip	Phone	Fax
State Government Information *Web:* www.mt.gov		MT		406-444-2511	
Agriculture Dept PO Box 59620-0201 *Web:* agr.state.mt.us	Helena	MT	59620	406-444-3144	444-5409
Arts Council PO Box 202201 *TF:* 800-282-3092 ■ *Web:* art.mt.gov/	Helena	MT	59620	406-444-6430	444-6548
Attorney General PO Box 201401 *Web:* doj.mt.gov/	Helena	MT	59620	406-444-2026	444-3549
Banking & Financial Institutions Div PO Box 200546 *TF:* 800-914-8423 ■ *Web:* banking.mt.gov	Helena	MT	59620	406-841-2920	841-2930
Business & Occupational Licensing Bureau PO Box 200513 *Web:* www.state.mt.us/dli/bsd	Helena	MT	59620	406-841-2300	841-2305
Child & Family Services Div 1400 Broadway PO Box 8005 *Web:* www.dphhs.state.mt.us	Helena	MT	59604	406-444-5900	444-5956
Child Support Enforcement Div PO Box 202943 *Web:* www.dphhs.state.mt.us	Helena	MT	59620	406-444-9767	444-9626
Commerce Dept PO Box 200501 *Web:* commerce.state.mt.us	Helena	MT	59620	406-841-2700	841-2701
Community Development Div 1424 9th Ave *Web:* www.commerce.state.mt.us/CDD/CDD_Home.html	Helena	MT	59620	406-444-3814	444-1872
Consumer Protection Office 2225 11th Ave PO Box 200501 *TF:* 800-481-6896 ■ *Web:* doj.mt.gov/consumer/	Helena	MT	59620	406-444-4500	444-9680
Corrections Dept PO Box 201301 *Web:* www.cor.state.mt.us	Helena	MT	59620	406-444-3930	444-4920
Court Administration 215 N Sanders St Rm 315 *Web:* www.montanacourts.org	Helena	MT	59620	406-444-2621	444-0834
Disability Services Div 111 N Sanders St *Web:* www.dphhs.mt.gov/dsd/	Helena	MT	59604	406-444-2590	444-3632
Disaster & Emergency Services Div PO Box 4789 *Web:* www.state.mt.us/dma/des	Helena	MT	59604	406-841-3911	841-3965
Environmental Quality Dept PO Box 200901 *Web:* www.deq.state.mt.us	Helena	MT	59620	406-444-2544	444-4386
Fish Wildlife & Parks Dept 1420 E 6th Ave *Web:* fwp.state.mt.us	Helena	MT	59620	406-444-2535	444-4952
Forensic Science Div 2679 Palmer St *Web:* doj.mt.gov/department/	Missoula	MT	59808	406-728-4970	549-1067
Governor PO Box 200801 *Web:* www.governor.mt.gov	Helena	MT	59620	406-444-3111	444-4151
Healthcare Licensing Bureau 301 S Park Ave Rm 430 *Web:* www.discoveringmontana.com/dli/bsd	Helena	MT	59620	406-841-2303	841-2305
Higher Education Board of Regents 46 N Last Change Gulch PO Box 203201 *Web:* www.montana.edu/wwwbor	Helena	MT	59620	406-444-6570	444-1469
Highway Patrol Div 2550 Prospect Ave *Web:* www.doj.state.mt.us/department	Helena	MT	59620	406-444-7000	444-4169
Historical Society 225 N Roberts St. *TF:* 800-243-9900 ■ *Web:* www.his.state.mt.us	Helena	MT	59601	406-444-2694	444-2696
Horse Racing Board PO Box 200512 *Web:* www.mt.gov/liv/HorseRacing/index.asp	Helena	MT	59620	406-444-4287	444-4305
Housing Div PO Box 200528 *Web:* www.housing.mt.gov	Helena	MT	59620	406-841-2840	841-2841
Information Technology Services Div PO Box 200113 *TF:* 800-628-4917 ■ *Web:* itsd.mt.gov/	Helena	MT	59620	406-444-2700	444-2701
Insurance Div 840 Flelena Ave *Web:* www.discoveringmontana.com/sao/insurance	Helena	MT	59601	406-444-2040	444-3497
Labor & Industry Dept PO Box 1728 *Web:* www.dli.mt.gov	Helena	MT	59624	406-444-3555	444-1419
Bill Status PO Box 201706 *Web:* leg.state.mt.us/css/bills	Helena	MT	59620	406-444-4800	444-3036
Lieutenant Governor State Capitol PO Box 200801 *Web:* governor.mt.gov	Helena	MT	59620	406-444-5551	444-4648
Lottery 2525 N Montana Ave. *Web:* www.montanalottery.com	Helena	MT	59601	406-444-5825	444-5830
Motor Vehicle Div PO Box 201430 *Web:* doj.mt.gov	Helena	MT	59620	406-444-1772	444-1631
Natural Resources & Conservation Dept 1625 11th Ave. *Web:* dnrc.mt.gov	Helena	MT	59620	406-444-2074	444-2684
Parks Div PO Box 200701 *Web:* www.fwp.state.mt.us/parks	Helena	MT	59620	406-444-3750	444-4952
Political Practices Commissioner's Office 1205 8th Ave *Web:* www.state.mt.us/cpp	Helena	MT	59620	406-444-2942	444-1643
Promotion Div (Travel Montana) PO Box 200533 *TF:* 800-847-4868 ■ *Web:* www.visitmt.com	Helena	MT	59620	406-841-2870	841-2871
Public Education Board 46 N Last Chance Gulch PO Box 200601 *Web:* www.bpe.state.mt.us	Helena	MT	59620	406-444-6576	444-0847
Public Health & Human Services Dept PO Box 4210 *Web:* www.dphhs.mt.gov	Helena	MT	59604	406-444-5622	444-1970
Public Instruction Office PO Box 202501 *TF:* 888-231-9393 ■ *Web:* www.opi.state.mt.us	Helena	MT	59620	406-444-3680	444-2893
Public Service Commission PO Box 202601 *Web:* www.psc.state.mt.us	Helena	MT	59620	406-444-6199	444-7618
Revenue Dept PO Box 5805 *Web:* discoveringmontana.com/revenue	Helena	MT	59604	406-444-6900	444-3696
Secretary of State PO BOx 202801 *Web:* www.sos.state.mt.us	Helena	MT	59620	406-444-2034	444-3976

				Phone	Fax
Securities Dept 840 Helena Ave	Helena	MT	59601	406-444-2040	444-5558
Web: sao.mt.gov/					
Senior & Long Term Care Div 111 N Sanders St Rm 210	Helena	MT	59604	406-444-4077	444-7743
Web: www.dphhs.state.mt.us/sltc					
State Auditor Office 840 Helena Ave	Helena	MT	59601	406-444-2040	444-3497
Web: sao.mt.gov/					
State Legislature State Capitol	Helena	MT	59620	406-444-4800	444-3036
Web: leg.state.mt.us					
Supreme Court 215 N Sanders St Rm 323	Helena	MT	59620	406-444-3858	444-5705
Web: www.lawlibrary.state.mt.us					
Transportation Dept 2701 Prospect Ave PO Box 201001	Helena	MT	59620	406-444-6200	444-7643
Web: www.mdt.mt.gov/					
Veterans' Affairs Board PO Box 5715	Helena	MT	59604	406-324-3740	324-3145
Web: dma.mt.gov/mvad/					
Victim Services Office PO Box 201410	Helena	MT	59620	406-444-3653	444-9680
Web: www.doj.state.mt.us/department					
Vital Records Bureau PO Box 4210	Helena	MT	59604	406-444-4228	444-1803
TF: 888-877-1946 ■ *Web:* www.dphhs.mt.gov					
Weights & Measures Bureau PO Box 200516	Helena	MT	59620	406-841-2240	841-2060
Web: www.state.mt.us/dli/bsd/wm					
Worker's Compensation Court PO Box 537	Helena	MT	59624	406-444-7794	444-7798
Web: www.wcc.dli.mt.gov					
Workforce Services Div PO Box 1728	Helena	MT	59624	406-444-4100	447-3037
Web: wsd.dli.mt.gov					

342-28 Nebraska

				Phone	Fax
State Government Information		NE		402-471-2311	
Web: www.nebraska.gov					
Accountability & Disclosure Commission PO Box 95086	Lincoln	NE	68509	402-471-2522	471-6599
Web: nadc.nol.org					
Aging Div PO Box 95026	Lincoln	NE	68509	402-471-2307	471-4619
Web: www.hhs.state.ne.us/ags/agsindex.htm					
Agriculture Dept 301 Centennial Mall S	Lincoln	NE	68509	402-471-2341	471-2759
Web: www.agr.state.ne.us					
Arts Council 1004 Farnam St	Omaha	NE	68131	402-595-2122	595-2334
TF: 800-341-4067 ■ *Web:* www.nebraskaartscouncil.org					
Attorney General PO Box 98920	Lincoln	NE	68509	402-471-2682	471-3297
Web: www.ago.state.ne.us					
Banking & Finance Dept PO Box 95006	Lincoln	NE	68509	402-471-2171	471-3062
Web: www.ndbf.org					
Bill Status 2018 State Capitol Bldg	Lincoln	NE	68509	402-471-2709	
Web: www.unicam.state.ne.us/					
Child Support Enforcement Div PO Box 94728	Lincoln	NE	68509	402-471-8715	471-7311
TF: 877-631-9973 ■ *Web:* www.hhs.state.ne.us/cse/cseindex.htm					
Children's Services Div PO Box 95026	Lincoln	NE	68509	402-471-9331	471-9034
Web: www.hhs.state.ne.us/chs/chsindex.htm					
Consumer Protection Div 2115 State Capitol Bldg	Lincoln	NE	68509	402-471-2682	471-0006
TF: 800-727-6432 ■ *Web:* www.ago.state.ne.us					
Coordinating Commission for Postsecondary Education 140 N 8th St Suite 300 PO Box 95005	Lincoln	NE	68509	402-471-2847	471-2886
Web: www.ccpe.state.ne.us					
Correctional Services Dept PO Box 94661	Lincoln	NE	68509	402-471-2654	479-5119
Web: www.corrections.state.ne.us					
Crime Victim Reparations Programs PO Box 94946	Lincoln	NE	68509	402-471-2828	471-2837
Economic Development Dept 301 Centennial Mall S PO Box 94666	Lincoln	NE	68509	402-471-3747	471-3778
TF: 800-426-6505 ■ *Web:* www.neded.org					
Education Dept PO Box 94987	Lincoln	NE	68509	402-471-5020	471-0117
Web: www.nde.state.ne.us					
Emergency Management Agency 1300 Military Rd	Lincoln	NE	68508	402-471-7421	471-7433
TF: 877-297-2368 ■ *Web:* www.nema.ne.gov					
Environmental Quality Dept 1200 'N' St Suite 400	Lincoln	NE	68508	402-471-2186	471-2909
TF: 877-253-2603 ■ *Web:* www.deq.state.ne.us					
Game & Parks Commission PO Box 30370	Lincoln	NE	68503	402-471-0641	471-5528
Web: www.ngpc.state.ne.us					
Governor PO Box 94848	Lincoln	NE	68509	402-471-2244	471-6031
Web: gov.nol.org					
Health & Human Services Dept PO Box 95044	Lincoln	NE	68509	402-471-3121	471-9449
TF: 800-430-3244 ■ *Web:* www.hhs.state.ne.us					
Health Regulations & Licensure Div PO Box 95026	Lincoln	NE	68509	402-471-2133	471-9449
Web: www.hhs.state.ne.us					
Historical Society 1500 R St	Lincoln	NE	68501	402-471-3270	471-3100
TF: 800-833-6747 ■ *Web:* www.nebraskahistory.org					
Insurance Dept 941 'O' St Suite 400	Lincoln	NE	68508	402-471-2201	471-4610
TF: 877-564-7323 ■ *Web:* www.doi.ne.gov					
Investment Finance Authority 1230 'O' St Suite 200	Lincoln	NE	68508	402-434-3900	434-3921
TF: 800-204-6432 ■ *Web:* www.nifa.org					
Lieutenant Governor PO Box 94863	Lincoln	NE	68509	402-471-2256	471-6031
Web: www.ltgov.ne.gov					
Lottery PO Box 98901	Lincoln	NE	68509	402-471-6100	471-6108
TF: 800-587-5200 ■ *Web:* www.nelottery.com					
Motor Vehicles Dept PO Box 94789	Lincoln	NE	68509	402-471-3900	471-9594
Web: www.dmv.state.ne.us					
Natural Resources Dept 301 Centennial Mall S 4th Fl	Lincoln	NE	68509	402-471-2363	471-2900
Web: www.dnr.state.ne.us					
Parks Div 2200 N 33rd St	Lincoln	NE	68503	402-471-0641	471-5528
Web: www.ngpc.state.ne.us/parks					
Parole Board PO Box 94754	Lincoln	NE	68509	402-471-2156	471-2453
Web: www.parole.state.ne.us					
Power Review Board PO Box 94713	Lincoln	NE	68509	402-471-2301	471-3715
Web: www.nprb.state.ne.us					
Public Accountancy Board PO Box 94725	Lincoln	NE	68509	402-471-3595	471-4484
Web: www.nbpa.ne.gov					
Public Service Commission 1200 'N' St Suite 300	Lincoln	NE	68508	402-471-3101	471-0254
Web: www.psc.state.ne.us					
Real Estate Commission PO Box 94667	Lincoln	NE	68509	402-471-2004	471-4492
Web: www.nrec.state.ne.us					
Revenue Dept PO Box 94818	Lincoln	NE	68509	402-471-5604	471-5608
Web: www.revenue.state.ne.us					
Secretary of State PO Box 94608	Lincoln	NE	68509	402-471-2554	471-3237
Web: www.sos.state.ne.us					
Securities Bureau PO Box 95006	Lincoln	NE	68509	402-471-3445	471-3062
Web: www.ndbf.org					
State Court Administrator PO Box 98910	Lincoln	NE	68509	402-471-3730	471-2197
Web: court.nol.org					
State Patrol PO Box 94907	Lincoln	NE	68509	402-471-4545	479-4002
Web: www.nsp.state.ne.us					
State Racing Commission 301 Centennial Mall S 6th Fl PO Box 95014	Lincoln	NE	68509	402-471-4155	471-2339
Web: www.horseracing.state.ne.us					
Supreme Court PO Box 98910	Lincoln	NE	68509	402-471-3731	471-3480
Web: court.nol.org					
Teacher Certification Office PO Box 94987	Lincoln	NE	68509	402-471-2496	471-9735
Web: www.nde.state.ne.us/tcert/tcert.html					
Travel & Tourism Div PO Box 98907	Lincoln	NE	68509	402-471-3796	471-3026
TF: 877-632-7275 ■ *Web:* www.visitnebraska.org					
Treasurer PO Box 94788	Lincoln	NE	68509	402-471-2455	471-4390
Web: www.treasurer.state.ne.us					
Unicameral Legislature PO Box 94604	Lincoln	NE	68509	402-471-2271	471-2126
Web: www.unicam.state.ne.us					
Veterans' Affairs Dept PO Box 95083	Lincoln	NE	68509	402-471-2458	471-2491
Web: www.vets.state.ne.us					
Vital Statistics Div PO Box 95065	Lincoln	NE	68509	402-471-2871	
Web: www.nebraska.gov					
Vocational Rehabilitation Services Div PO Box 94987	Lincoln	NE	68509	402-471-3644	471-0788
TF: 877-637-3422 ■ *Web:* www.vocrehab.state.ne.us					
Weights & Measures Div PO Box 94757	Lincoln	NE	68509	402-471-4292	471-2759
Web: www.agr.state.ne.us/division/wam/wam.htm					
Workers' Compensation Court PO Box 98908	Lincoln	NE	68509	402-471-6468	471-2700
TF: 800-599-5155 ■ *Web:* www.wcc.ne.gov					
Workforce Development - Dept of Labor PO Box 94600	Lincoln	NE	68509	402-471-9000	471-2318
Web: www.dol.state.ne.us					

342-29 Nevada

				Phone	Fax
State Government Information		NV		775-687-5000	
Web: www.nv.gov					
Accountancy Board 1325 Airmotive Way Suite 220	Reno	NV	89502	775-786-0231	786-0234
Web: www.nvaccountancy.com					
Administrative Office of the Courts 201 S Carson St Suite 250	Carson City	NV	89701	775-684-1700	684-1723
Web: www.nvsupremecourt.us/aoc/aoc.html					
Aging Services Div 1860 E Sahara Ave	Las Vegas	NV	89104	702-486-3545	486-3572
Web: aging.state.nv.us					
Agriculture Dept 350 Capitol Hill Ave	Reno	NV	89502	775-688-1180	688-1178
Web: agri.state.nv.us					
Arts Council 716 N Carson St Suite A	Carson City	NV	89701	775-687-6680	687-6688
Web: dmla.clan.lib.nv.us/docs/arts					
Attorney General 100 N Carson St	Carson City	NV	89701	775-684-1100	684-1108
Web: ag.state.nv.us					
Bill Status 401 S Carson St	Carson City	NV	89701	775-684-3360	
TF: 800-992-6761 ■ *Web:* www.leg.state.nv.us					
Business & Industry Dept 555 E Washington Ave Suite 4900	Las Vegas	NV	89101	702-486-2750	486-2758
Web: dbi.state.nv.us					
Child & Family Services Div 4126 Technology Way 3rd Fl	Carson City	NV	89706	775-684-4400	684-4455
Web: dcfs.state.nv.us					
Child Support Enforcement Office 1470 College Pkwy	Carson City	NV	89706	775-684-0500	684-0646
TF: 800-992-0900 ■ *Web:* dwss.nv.gov					
Conservation & Natural Resources Dept 901 S Stewart St Suite 5001	Carson City	NV	89701	775-684-2700	684-2715
Web: dcnr.nv.gov					
Consumer Affairs Div 1850 E Sahara Ave Suite 101	Las Vegas	NV	89104	702-486-7355	486-7371
Web: www.fyiconsumer.org					
Corrections Dept PO Box 7011	Carson City	NV	89702	775-887-3285	687-6715
Web: www.doc.nv.gov					
Cultural Affairs Dept 716 N Carson St Suite B	Carson City	NV	89701	775-687-8393	684-5446
Web: dmla.clan.lib.nv.us					
Economic Development Commission 108 E Proctor St	Carson City	NV	89701	775-687-4325	687-4450
TF: 800-336-1600 ■ *Web:* www.expand2nevada.com					
Education Dept 700 E 5th St	Carson City	NV	89701	775-687-9200	687-9101
Web: www.nde.state.nv.us					
Emergency Management Div 2478 Fairview Dr	Carson City	NV	89701	775-687-0300	687-0322
Web: dem.state.nv.us					
Employment Training & Rehabilitation Dept 500 E 3rd St Rm 200	Carson City	NV	89713	775-684-3911	684-3908
Web: detr.state.nv.us					
Environmental Protection Div 901 S Stewart St Suite 4001	Carson City	NV	89701	775-687-4670	687-5856
Web: ndep.nv.gov					
Ethics Commission 3476 Executive Pointe Way Suite 10	Carson City	NV	89706	775-687-5469	687-1279
Web: ethics.nv.gov					
Financial Institutions Div 2785 E Desert Inn Rd Suite 180	Las Vegas	NV	89121	775-486-4120	486-4563
Web: fid.state.nv.us					
Gaming Commission PO Box 8003	Carson City	NV	89702	775-684-7750	687-8221
Web: gaming.nv.gov					
Governor 101 N Carson St	Carson City	NV	89701	775-684-5670	684-5683
Web: gov.state.nv.us					
Health Div 4150 Technology Way Suite 300	Carson City	NV	89706	775-684-4200	684-4211
Web: health2k.state.nv.us					
Highway Patrol Div 555 Wright Way	Carson City	NV	89711	775-687-5300	684-4879
Web: ps.state.nv.us/NHP					
Historic Preservation Office 100 N Stewart St	Carson City	NV	89701	775-684-3440	684-3442
Web: dmla.clan.lib.nv.us/docs/shpo					
Housing Div 1535 Old Hot Springs Rd Suite 50	Carson City	NV	89706	775-687-2040	687-4040
Web: nvhousing.state.nv.us					
Human Resources Dept 4126 Technology Way Rm 100	Carson City	NV	89706	775-684-4000	684-4010
Web: hr.state.nv.us					
Information Technology Dept 400 W King St Suite 300	Carson City	NV	89703	775-684-5800	684-5846
Web: doit.nv.gov					
Insurance Div 788 Fairview Dr Suite 300	Carson City	NV	89701	775-687-4270	687-3937
Web: doi.state.nv.us					
Legislature 401 S Carson St	Carson City	NV	89701	775-684-6800	687-5962
Web: www.leg.state.nv.us					
Lieutenant Governor 101 N Carson St Suite 2	Carson City	NV	89701	775-684-7111	684-7110
Web: www.ltgov.nv.gov/					
Medical Examiners Board 1105 Terminal Way Suite 301	Reno	NV	89502	775-688-2559	688-2321
Web: medboard.nv.gov					
Motor Vehicles Dept 555 Wright Way	Carson City	NV	89711	775-684-4368	684-4770
TF: 877-368-7828 ■ *Web:* www.dmvnv.com					
Parole & Probation Div 1445 Old Hot Springs Rd Suite 104	Carson City	NV	89706	775-687-5040	684-2699
Web: dps.nv.gov/pandp/index.htm					
Postsecondary Education Commission 1820 E Sahara Ave Suite 111	Las Vegas	NV	89104	702-486-7330	486-7340
Web: www.cpe.state.nv.us					
Public Safety Dept 555 Wright Way	Carson City	NV	89711	775-684-4556	684-4809
Public Utilities Commission 1150 E William St	Carson City	NV	89701	775-684-6101	687-6110
Web: pucweb1.state.nv.us/pucn/					
Real Estate Div 2501 E Sahara Ave Suite 102	Las Vegas	NV	89104	702-486-4033	486-4275
Web: www.red.state.nv.us					
Rehabilitation Div 1370 S Curry St	Carson City	NV	89703	775-684-4040	684-4184
Web: www.nv.gov					
Secretary of State 101 N Carson St Suite 3	Carson City	NV	89701	775-684-5708	684-5725
TF: 800-450-8594 ■ *Web:* sos.state.nv.us					
Securities Div 555 E Washington Ave Suite 5200	Las Vegas	NV	89101	702-486-2440	486-2452
TF: 800-758-6440 ■ *Web:* sos.state.nv.us/securities					
State Athletic Commission 555 E Washington Ave Suite 3300	Las Vegas	NV	89101	702-486-2575	486-2577
Web: boxing.nv.gov					
State Parks Div 901 S Stewart St 5th Fl	Carson City	NV	89701	775-684-2770	684-2777
Web: parks.nv.gov					

Nevada (Cont'd)

	City	State	Zip	Phone	Fax
Supreme Court 201 S Carson St Suite 201 *Web:* www.nvsupremecourt.us	Carson City	NV	89701	775-684-1600	
University & Community College System 2601 Enterprise Rd *Web:* www.nevada.edu	Reno	NV	89512	775-784-4901	784-1127
Taxation Dept 1550 E College Pkwy Suite 115 *Web:* tax.state.nv.us	Carson City	NV	89706	775-684-2000	684-2020
Teacher Licensure Office 700 E 5th St *Web:* www.doe.nv.gov	Carson City	NV	89701	775-687-9115	687-9101
Tourism Commission 401 N Carson St *TF:* 800-237-0774 ■ *Web:* www.travelnevada.com	Carson City	NV	89701	775-687-4322	687-6159
Transportation Dept 1263 S Stewart St *Web:* www.nevadadot.com	Carson City	NV	89712	775-888-7000	888-7115
Treasurer 101 N Carson St Rm 4 *Web:* nevadatreasurer.gov	Carson City	NV	89701	775-684-5600	684-5623
Veterans Services Office 5460 Reno Corporate Dr *Web:* veterans.nv.gov	Reno	NV	89511	775-688-1653	688-1656
Vital Statistics Office 4150 Technology Way Suite 104 *Web:* health2k.state.nv.us/vital	Carson City	NV	89706	775-684-4242	684-4156
Weights & Measures Bureau 2150 Frazier Ave *Web:* agri.state.nv.us	Sparks	NV	89431	775-688-1166	688-2533
Welfare Div 1470 College Pkwy *Web:* welfare.state.nv.us	Carson City	NV	89706	775-684-0500	684-0646

342-30 New Hampshire

	City	State	Zip	Phone	Fax
State Government Information *Web:* www.nh.gov		NH		603-271-1110	
Elderly & Adult Services Div 129 Pleasant St *Web:* www.dhhs.nh.gov/DHHS/BEAS	Concord	NH	03301	603-271-4680	271-4643
Accountancy Board 78 Regional Dr Bldg 2 *Web:* www.nh.gov/accountancy	Concord	NH	03301	603-271-3286	271-8702
Administrative Office of the Courts 2 Charles Doe Dr *Web:* www.courts.state.nh.us	Concord	NH	03301	603-271-2521	513-5454
Agriculture Markets & Food Dept PO Box 2042 *Web:* agriculture.nh.gov	Concord	NH	03302	603-271-3551	271-1109
Arts Council 2 1/2 Beacon St 2nd Fl *Web:* www.nh.gov/nharts	Concord	NH	03301	603-271-2789	271-3584
Attorney General 33 Capitol St *Web:* www.nh.gov/nhdoj/	Concord	NH	03301	603-271-3658	271-2110
Banking Dept 64B Old Suncook Rd *Web:* www.nh.gov/banking	Concord	NH	03301	603-271-3561	271-1090
Bill Status 107 N Main St *Web:* gencourt.state.nh.us	Concord	NH	03301	603-271-3420	
Board of Medicine 2 Industrial Park Dr Suite 8 *Web:* www.nh.gov/medicine	Concord	NH	03301	603-271-1203	271-6702
Chief Medical Examiner 246 Pleasant St Suite 218	Concord	NH	03301	603-271-1235	271-6308
Child Support Services 129 Pleasant St *Web:* www.dhhs.state.nh.us/DHHS/DCSS	Concord	NH	03301	603-271-4754	271-4787
Children Youth & Families Div 129 Pleasant St 4th Fl *Web:* www.dhhs.state.nh.us/DHHS/DCYF	Concord	NH	03301	603-271-4451	271-4729
Consumer Protection Bureau 33 Capitol St *Web:* doj.nh.gov/consumer/	Concord	NH	03301	603-271-3641	271-2110
Corrections Dept PO Box 1806 *Web:* www.state.nh.us/nhdoc	Concord	NH	03302	603-271-5600	271-5643
Education Dept 101 Pleasant St *Web:* www.ed.state.nh.us	Concord	NH	03301	603-271-3494	271-1953
Emergency Management Office 33 Hazen Dr *Web:* www.nhoem.state.nh.us	Concord	NH	03305	603-271-2231	225-7341
Employment Security Dept 32 S Main St *Web:* www.nhes.state.nh.us	Concord	NH	03301	603-224-3311	228-4145
Environmental Services Dept 29 Hazen Dr *Web:* www.des.state.nh.us	Concord	NH	03301	603-271-3503	271-2867
Fish & Game Dept 11 Hazen Dr *Web:* www.wildlife.state.nh.us	Concord	NH	03301	603-271-3511	271-1438
General Court 1 Noble Dr *Web:* gencourt.state.nh.us	Concord	NH	03301	603-271-1110	271-2105
Governor State House 107 N Main St Rm 208 *Web:* www.nh.gov/governor	Concord	NH	03301	603-271-2121	271-7680
Health & Human Services Dept 129 Pleasant St *Web:* www.dhhs.state.nh.us	Concord	NH	03301	603-271-4685	271-4912
Historical Resources Div 19 Pillsbury St *Web:* www.nh.gov/nhdhr	Concord	NH	03301	603-271-3483	271-3433
Housing Finance Authority PO Box 5087 *TF:* 800-439-7247 ■ *Web:* www.nhhfa.org	Manchester	NH	03108	603-472-8623	472-8501
Insurance Dept 21 S Fruit St Suite 14 *Web:* www.nh.gov/insurance	Concord	NH	03301	603-271-2261	271-1406
Joint Board of Licensure & Certification 57 Regional Dr *Web:* www.state.nh.us/jtboard/home.htm	Concord	NH	03301	603-271-2219	271-6990
Labor Dept 95 Pleasant St *Web:* www.labor.state.nh.us	Concord	NH	03301	603-271-3171	271-6852
Sweepstakes Commission 14 Integra Dr *Web:* www.nhlottery.org	Concord	NH	03301	603-271-3391	271-6289
Motor Vehicles Div 23 Hazen Dr *Web:* www.nh.gov/dmv	Concord	NH	03305	603-271-2251	271-1061
Parks & Recreation Div PO Box 1856 *Web:* www.nhparks.state.nh.us	Concord	NH	03302	603-271-3556	271-3553
Parole Board PO Box 14	Concord	NH	03302	603-271-2569	271-6179
Postsecondary Education Commission 3 Barrell Ct Suite 300 *TF:* 800-735-2964 ■ *Web:* www.nh.gov/postsecondary	Concord	NH	03301	603-271-2555	271-2696
Public Utilities Commission 21 S Fruit St Suite 10 *Web:* www.puc.state.nh.us	Concord	NH	03301	603-271-2431	271-3878
Real Estate Commission 25 Capitol St Rm 434 *Web:* www.nh.gov/nhrec	Concord	NH	03301	603-271-2701	271-1039
Resources & Economic Development Dept PO Box 1856 *Web:* www.dred.state.nh.us	Concord	NH	03302	603-271-2412	271-2629
Revenue Administration Dept 45 Chenell Dr *Web:* www.nh.gov/revenue	Concord	NH	03301	603-271-2191	271-1756
Secretary of State 107 N Main St State House Rm 204 *Web:* www.sos.nh.gov	Concord	NH	03301	603-271-3242	271-6316
Securities Regulation Bureau State House Rm 204 *Web:* www.sos.nh.gov/securities	Concord	NH	03301	603-271-1463	271-7933
State Police Div 10 Hazen Dr *Web:* www.nh.gov/safety/nhsp	Concord	NH	03305	603-271-2575	271-2527
Supreme Court 1 Charles Doe Dr *Web:* www.courts.state.nh.us/supreme	Concord	NH	03301	603-271-2646	513-4575
Teacher Credentialing Bureau 101 Pleasant St *Web:* www.ed.state.nh.us	Concord	NH	03301	603-271-2408	271-1953
Transportation Dept PO Box 483 *Web:* www.nh.gov/dot	Concord	NH	03301	603-271-3734	271-3914
Travel & Tourism Development Office PO Box 1856 *TF:* 800-262-6660 ■ *Web:* www.visitnh.gov	Concord	NH	03302	603-271-2665	271-6870
Treasury Dept 25 Capitol St Rm 121 *Web:* www.nh.gov/treasury	Concord	NH	03301	603-271-2621	271-3922
Veterans Council 275 Chestnut St Rm 517 *Web:* www.nh.gov/nhveterans	Manchester	NH	03101	603-624-9230	624-9236
Victims' Assistance Commission 33 Capitol St *TF:* 800-300-4500 ■ *Web:* www.nh.gov/nhdoj	Concord	NH	03301	603-271-1284	223-6291
Vital Records Bureau 71 S Fruit St *Web:* www.sos.nh.gov/vitalrecords	Concord	NH	03301	603-271-4650	271-3447
Vocational Rehabilitation Office 21 Fruit St *Web:* www.ed.state.nh.us/VR	Concord	NH	03301	603-271-3471	271-7095
Weights & Measures Bureau PO Box 2042 *Web:* agriculture.nh.gov/about/weights_measures.htm	Concord	NH	03302	603-271-3700	271-1109
Worker's Compensation Div 95 Pleasant St *TF:* 800-272-4353 ■ *Web:* www.labor.state.nh.us	Concord	NH	03301	603-271-3176	271-6149

342-31 New Jersey

	City	State	Zip	Phone	Fax
State Government Information *Web:* www.newjersey.gov		NJ		609-292-2121	
Administrative Office of the Courts 25 Market St PO Box 037 *Web:* www.judiciary.state.nj.us	Trenton	NJ	08625	609-984-0275	984-6968
Aging & Community Services Div PO Box 807 *Web:* www.newjersey.gov/health/senior	Trenton	NJ	08625	609-943-3437	588-3317
Agriculture Dept PO Box 330 *Web:* www.state.nj.us/agriculture	Trenton	NJ	08625	609-292-3976	292-3978
Arts Council 225 W State St PO Box 306 *Web:* www.njartscouncil.org	Trenton	NJ	08625	609-292-6130	989-1440
Attorney General 25 Market St PO Box 080 *Web:* www.state.nj.us/lps/oag	Trenton	NJ	08625	609-292-4925	292-3508
Banking & Insurance Dept PO Box 325 *Web:* www.state.nj.us/dobi	Trenton	NJ	08625	609-292-5360	984-5273
Bill Status State House Annex PO Box 068 *TF:* 800-792-8630 ■ *Web:* www.njleg.state.nj.us	Trenton	NJ	08625	609-292-4840	777-2440
Child Support Office PO Box 716 *TF:* 800-621-5437 ■ *Web:* www.njchildsupport.org	Trenton	NJ	08625	609-588-2385	588-2354
Commerce Economic Growth & Tourism Commission 20 W State St PO Box 820 *Web:* www.state.nj.us/commerce	Trenton	NJ	08625	609-777-0885	777-4097
Community Affairs Dept 101 S Broad St PO Box 800 *Web:* www.nj.gov/dca	Trenton	NJ	08625	609-292-6055	984-6696
Consumer Affairs Div 124 Halsey St *Web:* www.state.nj.us/lps/ca	Newark	NJ	07102	973-504-6200	648-3538
Corrections Dept PO Box 863 *Web:* www.state.nj.us/corrections	Trenton	NJ	08625	609-292-4036	292-9083
Economic Development Authority PO Box 990 *Fax: PR ■ *Web:* www.njeda.com	Trenton	NJ	08625	609-292-1800	292-5722*
Education Dept PO Box 500 *Web:* www.state.nj.us/education	Trenton	NJ	08625	609-292-4450	777-4099
Emergency Management Office PO Box 7068 *Web:* www.njsp.org/ems/ems.html	West Trenton	NJ	08628	609-882-2000	538-0345
Environmental Protection Dept 401 E State St PO Box 402 *Web:* www.state.nj.us/dep	Trenton	NJ	08625	609-292-2885	292-1921
Ethical Standards Commission 28 W State St Rm 1407 PO Box 082 *Web:* www.state.nj.us/lps/ethics	Trenton	NJ	08625	609-292-1892	633-9252
Fish Game & Wildlife Div PO Box 400 *Web:* www.state.nj.us/dep/fgw	Trenton	NJ	08625	609-292-9410	984-1414
Governor 125 W State St Box 001 *Web:* www.state.nj.us/governor	Trenton	NJ	08625	609-292-6000	292-3454
Health & Senior Services Dept PO Box 360 *Web:* www.state.nj.us/health	Trenton	NJ	08625	609-292-7837	984-5474
Higher Education Commission 20 W State St PO Box 542 *Web:* www.state.nj.us/highereducation	Trenton	NJ	08625	609-292-4310	292-7225
Higher Education Student Assistance Authority 4 Quakerbridge Plaza PO Box 540 *TF:* 800-792-8670 ■ *Web:* www.hesaa.org	Trenton	NJ	08625	609-588-7944	588-7389
Historical Commission 225 W State St PO Box 305 *Web:* www.state.nj.us/state/history	Trenton	NJ	08625	609-292-6062	633-8168
Housing & Mortgage Finance Agency 637 S Clinton Ave PO Box 18550 *Web:* www.state.nj.us/dca/hmfa	Trenton	NJ	08650	609-278-7400	278-1754
Human Services Dept 240 W State St PO Box 700 *Web:* www.state.nj.us/humanservices	Trenton	NJ	08625	609-292-3717	292-3824
Information Technology Office PO Box 212 *Web:* www.nj.gov/it/oit	Trenton	NJ	08625	609-777-3861	633-8888
Labor & Workforce Development Dept PO Box 110 *Web:* www.state.nj.us/labor	Trenton	NJ	08625	609-292-2323	633-9271
Lottery Div PO Box 041 *Web:* www.njlottery.net	Trenton	NJ	08625	609-599-5800	599-5935
Mental Health Services Div PO Box 272 *TF:* 800-382-9717 ■ *Web:* www.state.nj.us/humanservices/dmhs	Trenton	NJ	08625	609-777-0700	777-0662
Military & Veterans' Affairs Dept 101 Eggert Crossing Rd *TF:* 800-624-0508 ■ *Web:* www.state.nj.us/military	Lawrenceville	NJ	08648	609-530-4600	530-7100
Motor Vehicles Commission 225 E State St PO Box 160 *TF:* 888-486-3339 ■ *Web:* www.state.nj.us/mvc	Trenton	NJ	08666	609-292-6500	777-4171
Parks & Forestry Div PO Box 404 *Web:* www.state.nj.us/dep/parksandforests	Trenton	NJ	08625	609-292-2733	984-0503
Parole Board PO Box 862 *Web:* www.state.nj.us/parole	Trenton	NJ	08625	609-292-4257	984-2188
Personnel Dept 44 S Clinton Ave PO Box 317 *Web:* www.state.nj.us/personnel	Trenton	NJ	08625	609-292-4144	984-1064
Public Utilities Board 2 Gateway Ctr *Web:* www.state.nj.us/bpu	Newark	NJ	07102	973-648-2013	648-4195
Racing Commission 140 E Front St *Web:* www.njpublicsafety.org/racing	Trenton	NJ	08625	609-292-0613	599-1785
Real Estate Commission 20 W State St PO Box 328 *Web:* www.state.nj.us/dobi/remnu.shtml	Trenton	NJ	08625	609-292-8300	292-0944
Secretary of State 125 W State St PO Box 300 *Web:* www.state.nj.us/state	Trenton	NJ	08625	609-984-1900	292-7665
Securities Bureau PO Box 47029 *Web:* www.state.nj.us/lps/ca/bos.htm	Newark	NJ	07101	973-504-3610	504-3639
State Athletic Control Board 140 E Front St *Web:* www.state.nj.us/lps/sacb	Trenton	NJ	08625	609-292-0317	292-3756
State Legislature State House Annex PO Box 068 *Web:* www.njleg.state.nj.us	Trenton	NJ	08625	609-292-4840	777-2440
State Medical Examiner 325 Norfolk St *Web:* www.state.nj.us/lps/dcj/sme.htm	Newark	NJ	07103	973-648-4500	648-4469
State Police PO Box 7068 *Web:* www.state.nj.us/lps/njsp	West Trenton	NJ	08628	609-882-2000	882-6920
Supreme Court PO Box 970 *Web:* www.judiciary.state.nj.us/supreme/index.htm	Trenton	NJ	08625	609-292-4837	396-9056
Transportation Dept 1035 Parkway Ave PO Box 600 *Web:* www.state.nj.us/transportation	Trenton	NJ	08625	609-530-2000	530-3294
Travel & Tourism Div PO Box 820 *TF:* 800-847-4865 ■ *Web:* www.state.nj.us/travel	Trenton	NJ	08625	609-777-0885	633-7418

				Phone	Fax
Treasurer State House PO Box 002	Trenton	NJ	08625	609-292-5031	292-6145
Web: www.state.nj.us/treasury					
Victims of Crime Compensation Board 50 Park Pl	Newark	NJ	07102	973-648-6219	648-7031
Web: www.state.nj.us/victims					
Vital Statistics Bureau PO Box 370	Trenton	NJ	08625	609-292-4087	392-4292
Web: www.state.nj.us/health/vital/vital.shtml					
Vocational Rehabilitation Services Div PO Box 398	Trenton	NJ	08625	609-292-7318	
Web: www.state.nj.us/labor/dvrs/vrsindex.html					
Weights & Measures Office 126 Rts 1 & 9 S	Avenel	NJ	07001	732-815-4840	382-5298
Web: www.state.nj.us/lps/ca/owm.htm					
Workers' Compensation Div PO Box 381	Trenton	NJ	08625	609-292-2414	984-2515
Web: www.state.nj.us/labor/wc/wcindex.html					
Workforce New Jersey PO Box 055	Trenton	NJ	08625	609-292-2000	777-0483
Web: www.wnjpin.net					

342-32 New Mexico

				Phone	Fax
State Government Information		NM		505-476-2200	
Web: www.state.nm.us					
Accountancy Board 1650 University Blvd NE Suite 400A	Albuquerque	NM	87102	505-841-9108	476-6511
Web: www.rld.state.nm.us/accountancy/index.html					
Administrative Office of the Courts 237 Don Gaspar St Rm 25	Santa Fe	NM	87501	505-827-4800	827-4824
Web: www.nmcourts.com					
Adult Parole Board 45 Penitentiary Rd	Santa Fe	NM	87508	505-827-8825	827-8933
Aging Agency 2550 Cerrillos Rd	Santa Fe	NM	87505	505-476-4799	476-4836
Web: www.nmaging.state.nm.us					
Agriculture Dept MSC 3189 PO Box 30005	Las Cruces	NM	88003	505-646-3007	646-1820
Web: nmdaweb.nmsu.edu					
Arts Div 407 Galisteo St Suite 270	Santa Fe	NM	87501	505-827-6490	827-6043
Web: www.nmoca.org/					
Attorney General PO Drawer 1508	Santa Fe	NM	87504	505-827-6000	827-5826
Web: www.nmag.gov					
Child Support Enforcement Div PO Box 25110	Santa Fe	NM	87504	505-476-7207	476-7045
Web: www.state.nm.us/hsd/csed.html					
Children Youth & Families Dept PO Drawer 5160	Santa Fe	NM	87502	505-827-7610	827-9978
TF: 800-610-7610 ■ *Web:* www.cyfd.org					
Consumer Protection Div PO Drawer 1508	Santa Fe	NM	87504	505-827-6060	827-6685
Web: www.ago.state.nm.us					
Corrections Dept PO Box 27116	Santa Fe	NM	87502	505-827-8709	827-8220
Web: www.state.nm.us/corrections					
Crime Victims Reparation Commission 8100 Mountain Rd NE Suite 106	Albuquerque	NM	87110	505-841-9432	841-9437
TF: 800-306-6262 ■ *Web:* www.state.nm.us/cvrc					
Cultural Affairs Office 407 Galisteo St	Santa Fe	NM	87501	505-827-6490	827-6043
Web: www.nmoca.org					
Labor Dept 401 Broadway NE PO Box 1928	Albuquerque	NM	87103	505-841-8409	841-8491
Web: www.dws.state.nm.us					
Economic Development Dept PO Box 20003	Santa Fe	NM	87504	505-827-0300	827-0328
TF: 800-374-3061 ■ *Web:* www.edd.state.nm.us					
Education Dept 300 Don Gaspar St	Santa Fe	NM	87501	505-827-5800	827-6696
Web: sde.state.nm.us					
Energy Minerals & Natural Resources Dept PO Box 6429	Santa Fe	NM	87505	505-476-3200	476-3220
Web: www.emnrd.state.nm.us					
Environment Dept 1190 St Francis Dr Suite 4050	Santa Fe	NM	87502	505-827-2855	827-2836
TF: 800-219-6157 ■ *Web:* www.nmenv.state.nm.us					
Ethics Administration 325 Don Gaspar St Suite 300	Santa Fe	NM	87503	505-827-3600	827-4954
TF: 800-477-3632 ■ *Web:* www.sos.state.nm.us/ethics.htm					
Finance & Administration Dept 407 Galisteo St Rm 180	Santa Fe	NM	87501	505-827-4985	827-4984
Web: www.state.nm.us/clients/dfa					
Financial Aid & Student Services Unit 1068 Cerrillos Rd	Santa Fe	NM	87505	505-476-6500	476-6511
TF: 800-279-9777 ■ *Web:* hed.state.nm.us					
Financial Institutions Div PO Box 25101	Santa Fe	NM	87504	505-476-4515	
Web: www.rld.state.nm.us/fid/					
Game & Fish Dept PO Box 25112	Santa Fe	NM	87504	505-476-8000	476-8116
Web: www.wildlife.state.nm.us					
Governor State Capitol Bldg 490 Santa Fe Trail Rm 400	Santa Fe	NM	87501	505-827-3000	476-2226
Web: www.governor.state.nm.us					
Job Training Div 1596 Pacheco St Suite 201	Santa Fe	NM	87505	505-827-6827	827-6812
Web: www.dol.state.nm.us					
Health Dept 1190 S St Francis Dr Suite N-4100	Santa Fe	NM	87505	505-827-2613	827-2530
Web: www.health.state.nm.us					
Higher Education Commission 1068 Cerrillos Rd	Santa Fe	NM	87505	505-476-1100	476-6511
TF: 800-279-9777 ■ *Web:* hed.state.nm.us					
Highway & Transportation Dept PO Box 1149	Santa Fe	NM	87504	505-827-5100	827-3214
TF: 877-887-7094 ■ *Web:* www.nmshtd.state.nm.us					
Historic Preservation Div 228 E Palace Ave Rm 320	Santa Fe	NM	87501	505-827-6320	827-6338
Web: www.nmoca.com/historicpreservation.html					
Human Services Dept PO Box 2348	Santa Fe	NM	87504	505-827-7750	827-6286
Web: www.state.nm.us/hsd					
Information Technology Management Office 715 Alta Vista	Santa Fe	NM	87505	505-827-2051	
Web: cio.state.nm.us					
Bill Status 490 Old Santa Fe Trail Rm 411	Santa Fe	NM	87501	505-986-4600	986-4680
Web: www.legis.state.nm.us					
Lieutenant Governor State Capitol Bldg Rm 417	Santa Fe	NM	87501	505-476-2250	476-2257
TF: 800-432-4406					
Lottery PO Box 93190	Albuquerque	NM	87199	505-342-7600	342-7511
Web: www.nmlottery.com					
Medical Examiners Board 2055 S Pacheco Bldg 400	Santa Fe	NM	87505	505-476-7220	476-7237
Web: www.nmmb.state.nm.us					
Medical Investigator UNM Health Science Center MSC11 6030	Albuquerque	NM	87131	505-272-6053	272-0727
Web: omi.unm.edu					
Mortgage Finance Authority 344 4th St SW	Albuquerque	NM	87102	505-843-6880	243-3289
TF: 800-444-6880 ■ *Web:* www.nmmfa.org					
Motor Vehicles Div PO Box 1028	Santa Fe	NM	87504	505-827-2296	827-2267
TF: 888-683-4636 ■ *Web:* www.state.nm.us/tax/mvd					
Professional (Educator) Licensure Unit 300 Don Gaspar St	Santa Fe	NM	87501	505-827-6581	827-4148
Web: www.ped.state.nm.us/div/ais/lic					
Public Regulation Commission PO Box 1269	Santa Fe	NM	87504	505-827-4500	827-4747
Web: www.nmprc.state.nm.us					
Public Safety Dept PO Box 1628	Santa Fe	NM	87504	505-827-9000	827-3434
Web: www.dps.nm.org					
Racing Commission 300 San Mateo NE Suite 110	Albuquerque	NM	87108	505-841-6400	841-6413
Web: nmrc.state.nm.us					
Regulation & Licensing Dept 2550 Cerrillos Rd	Santa Fe	NM	87505	505-476-4500	476-4511
Web: www.rld.state.nm.us					
Secretary of State 325 Don Gaspar Ave Suite 300	Santa Fe	NM	87503	505-827-3600	827-8081
TF: 800-477-3632 ■ *Web:* www.sos.state.nm.us					
Securities Div 2550 Cerrillos Rd	Santa Fe	NM	87505	505-476-4580	984-0617
Web: www.rld.state.nm.us/Securities					
Standards & Consumers Services Div MSC 3170 Box 30005	Las Cruces	NM	88003	505-646-1616	646-2361
TF: 800-371-7099 ■ *Web:* nmdaweb.nmsu.edu/DIVISIONS/scs.html					
State Legislature State Capitol Rm 411	Santa Fe	NM	87501	505-986-4600	986-4680
Web: legis.state.nm.us					
State Parks Div PO Box 1147	Santa Fe	NM	87504	505-476-3355	476-3361
TF: 888-667-2757 ■ *Web:* www.emnrd.state.nm.us/nmparks					
State Police Div PO Box 1628	Santa Fe	NM	87504	505-827-9002	827-3395
Web: www.nmsp.com					
Supreme Court PO Box 848	Santa Fe	NM	87504	505-827-4860	827-4837
Web: www.supremecourt.nm.org					
Taxation & Revenue Dept PO Box 630	Santa Fe	NM	87504	505-827-0700	827-0331
Web: www.state.nm.us/tax					
Tourism Dept 491 Old Santa Fe Trail	Santa Fe	NM	87503	505-827-7400	827-7402
TF: 800-545-2070 ■ *Web:* www.newmexico.org					
Treasurer PO Box 608	Santa Fe	NM	87504	505-995-1120	995-1195
Web: www.stonm.org					
Veterans' Service Commission PO Box 2324	Santa Fe	NM	87504	505-827-6300	827-6372
TF: 866-433-8387 ■ *Web:* www.state.nm.us/veterans					
Vital Records & Health Statistics Bureau 1105 S St Francis Dr	Santa Fe	NM	87505	505-827-0121	984-1048
Web: dohewbs2.health.state.nm.us/VitalRec					
Vocational Rehabilitation Div 435 St Michaels Dr Bldg D	Santa Fe	NM	87505	505-954-8500	954-8562
TF: 800-224-7005 ■ *Web:* www.dvrgetsjobs.com					
Workers' Compensation Administration PO Box 27198	Albuquerque	NM	87125	505-841-6000	841-6009
Web: www.state.nm.us/wca					

342-33 New York

				Phone	Fax
State Government Information		NY		518-474-2121	
Web: www.state.ny.us					
Aging Office 2 Empire State Plaza	Albany	NY	12223	518-474-7158	
Web: aging.state.ny.us					
Agriculture & Markets Dept 10A Airline Dr	Albany	NY	12235	518-457-3880	457-3087
TF: 800-554-4501 ■ *Web:* www.agmkt.state.ny.us					
Arts Council 175 Varick St 3rd Fl	New York	NY	10014	212-627-4455	620-5911
Web: www.nysca.org					
Athletic Commission 123 William St 20th Fl	New York	NY	10038	212-417-5700	417-4987
TF: 866-269-3769 ■ *Web:* www.dos.state.ny.us/athletic					
Attorney General State Capitol	Albany	NY	12224	518-474-7330	474-5481
Web: www.oag.state.ny.us					
Banking Dept 1 State St	New York	NY	10004	212-709-5470	709-3582*
**Fax:* Hum Res ■ *TF:* 877-226-5697 ■ *Web:* www.banking.state.ny.us					
Bill Status 55 Elk St	Albany	NY	12210	518-455-7545	455-7681
TF: 800-342-9860 ■ *Web:* www.assembly.state.ny.us					
Child Support Enforcement Div 40 N Pearl St	Albany	NY	12243	518-474-9081	
Web: newyorkchildsupport.com					
Children & Family Services Office 52 Washington St	Rensselaer	NY	12144	518-473-7793	486-7550
Web: www.ocfs.state.ny.us					
Consumer Protection Board 5 Empire State Plaza Suite 2101	Albany	NY	12223	518-474-3514	474-2474
TF: 800-697-1220 ■ *Web:* www.consumer.state.ny.us					
Correctional Services Dept 1220 Washington Ave Bldg 2	Albany	NY	12226	518-457-8126	457-7070
Web: www.docs.state.ny.us					
Court Administration Office 25 Beaver St	New York	NY	10004	212-428-2100	428-2188
Web: www.nycourts.gov					
Court of Appeals 20 Eagle St	Albany	NY	12207	518-455-7700	
Web: www.nycourts.gov/ctapps					
Crime Victims Board 845 Central Ave	Albany	NY	12206	518-457-8727	457-8658
Web: www.cvb.state.ny.us					
Education Dept 89 Washington Ave	Albany	NY	12234	518-474-3852	474-5631*
**Fax:* Hum Res ■ *Web:* www.nysed.gov					
Emergency Management Office 1220 Washington Ave Bldg 22 Suite 101	Albany	NY	12226	518-457-8900	457-8924
Web: www.nysemo.state.ny.us					
Empire State Development Corp 30 S Pearl St	Albany	NY	12245	518-292-5100	292-5812
TF: 800-782-8369 ■ *Web:* www.empire.state.ny.us					
Environmental Conservation Dept 625 Broadway 14th Fl	Albany	NY	12233	518-402-8540	402-9016
Web: www.dec.state.ny.us					
Fish Wildlife & Marine Resources Div 625 Broadway 5th Fl	Albany	NY	12233	518-402-8924	402-8925
Web: www.dec.state.ny.us/website/dfwmr					
Governor State Capitol Executive Chamber	Albany	NY	12224	518-474-8390	474-1513
Web: www.state.ny.us/governor					
Health Dept Empire State Plaza Corning II Tower	Albany	NY	12237	518-473-8600	473-7071
Web: www.health.state.ny.us					
Higher Education Office State Education Bldg 2nd Fl West Mezzanine	Albany	NY	12234	518-474-3862	486-2175
Web: www.highered.nysed.gov					
Higher Education Services Corp 99 Washington Ave	Albany	NY	12255	518-473-1574	473-3749
TF: 888-697-4372 ■ *Web:* www.hesc.com					
Historic Preservation Div PO Box 219	Waterford	NY	12188	518-237-8643	235-4248
Web: www.nysparks.com					
Housing Finance Agency 641 Lexington Ave	New York	NY	10022	212-688-4000	872-0789
Web: www.nyhomes.org/hfa/hfa.html					
Insurance Dept 1 Commerce Plaza	Albany	NY	12257	518-474-6600	473-6814
Web: www.ins.state.ny.us					
Investor Protection & Securities Bureau 120 Broadway 23rd Fl	New York	NY	10271	212-416-8200	416-8816
Web: www.oag.state.ny.us					
Labor Dept WA Harriman Campus Bldg 12	Albany	NY	12240	518-457-9000	457-6908
Web: www.labor.state.ny.us					
Lieutenant Governor State Capitol Executive Chamber Rm 246	Albany	NY	12224	518-474-4623	486-4170
Web: www.state.ny.us/governor/ltgov					
Lower Manhattan Development Corp 1 Liberty Plaza 20th Fl	New York	NY	10006	212-962-2300	962-2431
Web: www.renewnyc.com					
Mental Health Office 44 Holland Ave	Albany	NY	12239	518-474-4403	474-2149
Web: www.omh.state.ny.us					
Military & Naval Affairs Div 330 Old Niskayuna Rd	Latham	NY	12110	518-786-4500	786-4785
Web: www.dmna.state.ny.us					
Motor Vehicles Dept 6 Empire State Plaza	Albany	NY	12228	518-473-5595	474-9578
Web: www.nydmv.state.ny.us					
Office of the Professions 89 Washington Ave 2nd Fl	Albany	NY	12234	518-474-3817	474-1449
Web: www.op.nysed.gov					
Parks Recreation & Historic Preservation Office 1 Empire State Plaza	Albany	NY	12238	518-474-0456	486-2924
TF Campground R: 800-456-2267 ■ *Web:* www.nysparks.com					
Parole Div 97 Central Ave	Albany	NY	12206	518-473-9400	473-6037
Web: www.parole.state.ny.us					
Power Authority 30 S Pearl St 10th Fl	Albany	NY	12207	518-433-6700	433-6780
Web: www.nypa.gov					
Public Service Commission 3 Empire State Plaza	Albany	NY	12223	518-474-7080	473-2838
Web: www.dps.state.ny.us					
Racing & Wagering Board 1 Waterliet Ave Ext Suite 2	Albany	NY	12206	518-453-8460	453-8490
Web: www.racing.state.ny.us					
Secretary of State 41 State St	Albany	NY	12231	518-474-0050	474-4765
Web: www.dos.state.ny.us					
State Comptroller 110 State St 15th Fl	Albany	NY	12236	518-474-4404	473-3004
Web: www.osc.state.ny.us					
State Ethics Commission 39 Columbia St 4th Fl	Albany	NY	12207	518-432-8207	432-8255
Web: www.dos.state.ny.us/ethc/ethics.html					

New York (Cont'd)

Entry	City	State	ZIP	Phone	Fax
State Legislature Legislative Office Bldg *Web:* public.leginfo.state.ny.us	Albany	NY	12247	518-455-2800	456-3332
State Lottery PO Box 7500 **Fax:* PR ■ *Web:* www.nylottery.org	Schenectady	NY	12301	518-388-3300	388-3403*
State Police Div 1220 Washington Ave Bldg 22 *Web:* www.troopers.state.ny.us	Albany	NY	12226	518-457-6811	457-3207
Taxation & Finance Dept WA Harriman Campus Bldg 8 *TF:* 800-225-5829 ■ *Web:* www.tax.state.ny.us	Albany	NY	12227	518-457-2244	457-2486
Technology Office PO Box 2062 *Web:* www.oft.state.ny.us	Albany	NY	12220	518-473-9450	402-2976
Temporary & Disability Assistance Office 40 N Pearl St *Web:* www.otda.state.ny.us	Albany	NY	12243	518-474-9003	474-7870
Tourism Div PO Box 2603 *TF:* 800-225-5697 ■ *Web:* www.iloveny.com	Albany	NY	12220	518-474-4116	486-6416
Transportation Dept 50 Wolf Rd *Web:* www.dot.state.ny.us	Albany	NY	12232	518-457-4422	457-5583
Veterans' Affairs Div 5 Empire State Plaza Suite 2836 *Web:* veterans.state.ny.us	Albany	NY	12223	518-474-6784	473-0379
Vital Records Office PO Box 2602 *Web:* www.health.state.ny.us/vital_records	Albany	NY	12220	518-474-3077	474-9168
Vocational & Educational Services for Individuals with Disabilities 1 Commerce Plaza Rm 1606 *Web:* www.vesid.nysed.gov	Albany	NY	12234	518-474-2714	474-8802
Workers' Compensation Board 20 Park St *Web:* www.wcb.state.ny.us	Albany	NY	12207	518-474-6674	473-1415

342-34 North Carolina

Entry	City	State	ZIP	Phone	Fax
State Government Information *Web:* www.ncgov.com		NC		919-733-1110	
Administrative Office of the Courts PO Box 2448 *Web:* www.nccourts.org	Raleigh	NC	27602	919-733-7107	715-5779
Aging & Adult Service Div 693 Palmer Dr *Web:* www.dhhs.state.nc.us/aging	Raleigh	NC	27603	919-733-3983	733-0443
Agriculture Dept 2 W Edenton St 1001 MSC *Web:* www.agr.state.nc.us	Raleigh	NC	27699	919-733-7125	733-1141
Arts Council MSC 4632 Dept of Cultural Resources *Web:* www.ncarts.org	Raleigh	NC	27699	919-807-6500	807-6532
Attorney General MSC 9001 *Web:* www.ncdoj.com	Raleigh	NC	27699	919-716-6400	716-6750
Banking Commission 316 W Edenton St *Web:* www.nccob.org	Raleigh	NC	27603	919-733-3016	733-6918
Bill Status 16 W Jones St Rm 2226 *Web:* www.ncleg.net	Raleigh	NC	27601	919-733-7778	
Chief Medical Examiner Campus Box 7580 *Web:* www.ocme.med.unc.edu	Chapel Hill	NC	27599	919-966-2253	962-6263
Child Support Enforcement Section PO Box 20800 *Web:* www.dhhs.state.nc.us/dss/cse	Raleigh	NC	29619	919-255-3800	
Commerce Dept 301 N Wilmington St *Web:* www.nccommerce.com	Raleigh	NC	27699	919-733-4151	733-9299
Community College System 200 W Jones St *Web:* www.ncccs.cc.nc.us	Raleigh	NC	27603	919-807-7100	807-7164
Consumer Protection Section PO Box 629 *Web:* www.ncdoj.com/consumerprotection/cp_about.jsp	Raleigh	NC	27602	919-716-6000	716-6050
Corrections Dept 214 W Jones St 4201 MSC *Web:* www.doc.state.nc.us	Raleigh	NC	27699	919-716-3700	716-3794
Cultural Resources Dept 109 E Jones St *Web:* www.ncdcr.gov	Raleigh	NC	27601	919-807-7385	733-1620
Economic Development Board 301 N Wilmington St *Web:* www.ncedb.com	Raleigh	NC	27603	919-733-7978	
Emergency Management Div 116 W Jones St *Web:* www.ncem.org	Raleigh	NC	27611	919-715-8000	733-5406
Employment Security Commission PO Box 25903 *Web:* www.ncesc.com	Raleigh	NC	27611	919-733-3098	733-1129
Environment & Natural Resources Dept 1601 MSC *Web:* www.enr.state.nc.us	Raleigh	NC	27699	919-733-4984	715-3060
Ethics Board 116 W Jones St *Web:* www.doa.state.nc.us/ethics	Raleigh	NC	27603	919-733-2780	733-2785
General Assembly 16 W Jones St *Web:* www.ncleg.net	Raleigh	NC	27601	919-733-7928	715-2880
Governor 166 W Jones St 20301 MSC *Web:* www.governor.state.nc.us	Raleigh	NC	27699	919-733-5811	733-2120
Health & Human Services Dept 2001 MSC *Web:* www.dhhs.state.nc.us	Raleigh	NC	27699	919-733-4534	715-4645
Housing Finance Agency 3508 Bush St *Web:* www.nchfa.com	Raleigh	NC	27609	919-877-5700	877-5701
Information Technology Services Office PO Box 17209 *Web:* www.its.state.nc.us	Raleigh	NC	27619	919-981-5555	981-2548
Insurance Dept 1201 MSC *Web:* www.ncdoi.com	Raleigh	NC	27699	919-733-7349	733-0085
Labor Dept 4 W Edenton St *Web:* www.dol.state.nc.us	Raleigh	NC	27601	919-733-7166	733-6197
Lieutenant Governor 310 N Blount St 20401 MSC *Web:* www.ltgov.state.nc.us	Raleigh	NC	27699	919-733-7350	733-6595
Marine Fisheries Div PO Box 769 *TF:* 800-682-2632 ■ *Web:* www.ncfisheries.net	Morehead City	NC	28557	252-726-7021	
Mental Health Developmental Disabilities & Substance Abuse Services Div 3009 MSC *Web:* www.dhhs.state.nc.us/mhddsas	Raleigh	NC	27699	919-715-3197	733-4962
Motor Vehicles Div 1100 New Bern Ave *Web:* www.ncdot.org/DMV	Raleigh	NC	27697	919-861-3015	733-0126
Parks & Recreation Div 1615 MSC *Web:* ils.unc.edu/parkproject/ncparks.html	Raleigh	NC	27699	919-733-4181	715-3085
Parole Commission 4222 MSC *Web:* www.doc.state.nc.us/parole	Raleigh	NC	27699	919-716-3010	716-3987
Public Instruction Dept 301 N Wilmington St *Web:* www.ncpublicschools.org	Raleigh	NC	27601	919-807-3300	807-3445
Real Estate Commission 1313 Navajo Dr *Web:* www.ncrec.state.nc.us	Raleigh	NC	27609	919-875-3700	877-4221
Revenue Dept 501 N Wilmington St *Web:* www.dor.state.nc.us	Raleigh	NC	27604	919-733-7211	733-0023
Secretary of State PO Box 29622 *Web:* www.secstate.state.nc.us	Raleigh	NC	27699	919-807-2005	807-2010
Securities Div PO Box 29622 *Web:* www.secretary.state.nc.us/sec	Raleigh	NC	27626	919-733-3924	821-0818
Social Services Div 2401 MSC *Web:* www.dhhs.state.nc.us/dss	Raleigh	NC	27699	919-733-3055	733-9386
Standards Div 2 W Edenton St 1050 MSC *Web:* www.agr.state.nc.us/standard	Raleigh	NC	27699	919-733-3313	715-0524
State Education Assistance Authority PO Box 14103 *TF:* 800-700-1775 ■ *Web:* www.ncseaa.edu	Research Triangle Park	NC	27709	919-549-8614	549-8481
Highway Patrol Div 4702 MSC *Web:* www.nccrimecontrol.org	Raleigh	NC	27699	919-733-7952	733-1189
State Historic Preservation Office 4610 MSC *Web:* www.hpo.dcr.state.nc.us	Raleigh	NC	27699	919-733-4763	733-8653
State Personnel Office 1331 MSC *Web:* www.osp.state.nc.us	Raleigh	NC	27699	919-733-7108	715-9750
State Ports Authority 2202 Burnett Blvd PO Box 9002 *TF:* 800-334-0682 ■ *Web:* www.ncports.com	Wilmington	NC	28402	910-763-1621	343-6225
State Treasurer 325 N Salisbury St *Web:* www.nctreasurer.com	Raleigh	NC	27603	919-508-5176	508-5167
Supreme Court PO Box 2170 *Web:* www.nccourts.org	Raleigh	NC	27602	919-733-3723	733-0105
Tourism Div 301 N Wilmington St *TF:* 800-847-4862 ■ *Web:* www.visitnc.com	Raleigh	NC	27601	919-733-4171	733-8582
Transportation Dept 1 S Wilmington St *Web:* www.ncdot.org	Raleigh	NC	27611	919-733-2520	733-9150
Utilities Commission 4325 MSC *Web:* www.ncuc.commerce.state.nc.us	Raleigh	NC	27699	919-733-7328	733-7300
Veterans Affairs Div 1315 MSC *Web:* www.doa.state.nc.us/vets/va.htm	Raleigh	NC	27699	919-733-3851	733-2834
Victims Compensation Services Div 4703 MSC *Web:* www.nccrimecontrol.org/vjs	Raleigh	NC	27699	919-733-7974	715-4209
Vital Records Unit 1903 MSC *Web:* vitalrecords.dhhs.state.nc.us	Raleigh	NC	27699	919-733-3526	829-1359
Vocational Rehabilitation Services Div 2801 MSC *Web:* dvr.dhhs.state.nc.us	Raleigh	NC	27699	919-855-3500	733-7968

342-35 North Dakota

Entry	City	State	ZIP	Phone	Fax
State Government Information *Web:* www.nd.gov		ND		701-328-2000	
Accountancy Board 2701 S Columbia Rd *TF:* 800-532-5904 ■ *Web:* www.state.nd.us/ndsba	Grand Forks	ND	58201	701-775-7100	775-7430
Aging Services Div 600 E Boulevard Ave Dept 325	Bismarck	ND	58505	701-328-4601	328-4061
Agriculture Dept 600 E Boulevard Ave Dept 602 *TF:* 800-242-7535 ■ *Web:* www.agdepartment.com	Bismarck	ND	58505	701-328-2231	328-4567
Arts Council 1600 E Century Ave Suite 6 *Web:* www.state.nd.us/arts	Bismarck	ND	58503	701-328-7590	328-7595
Attorney General 600 E Boulevard Ave Dept 125 *Web:* www.ag.state.nd.us	Bismarck	ND	58505	701-328-2210	328-2226
Child Support Enforcement Div 1600 E Century Ave Suite 7 *TF:* 800-231-4255 ■ *Web:* www.nd.gov/dhs/services/childsupport/	Bismarck	ND	58501	701-328-3582	328-6575
Children & Family Services Div 600 E Boulevard Ave *Web:* www.nd.gov	Bismarck	ND	58505	701-328-2316	328-3538
Consumer Protection Div 600 E Boulevard Ave Dept 125 *Web:* www.ag.state.nd.us	Bismarck	ND	58505	701-328-3404	328-5568
Corrections & Rehabilitation Dept 3100 Railroad Ave *Web:* www.state.nd.us/docr	Bismarck	ND	58501	701-328-6390	328-6651
Court Administrator Office 600 E Boulevard Ave Dept 180 *Web:* www.ndcourts.com	Bismarck	ND	58505	701-328-4216	328-2092
Crime Victims Compensation Program PO Box 5521	Bismarck	ND	58506	701-328-6195	328-6186
Drivers License & Traffic Safety Div 608 E Boulevard Ave *Web:* www.dot.nd.gov/dl	Bismarck	ND	58505	701-328-2600	328-2435
Economic Development & Finance Div 1600 E Century Ave Suite 200-B *TF:* 866-432-5682 ■ *Web:* www.growingnd.com	Bismarck	ND	58503	701-328-5300	328-5320
Education Standards & Practices Board 2718 Gateway Ave Dept 303 *Web:* www.state.nd.us/espb	Bismarck	ND	58503	701-328-9641	328-9647
Emergency Management Div PO Box 5511 *Web:* www.nd.gov/des/	Bismarck	ND	58506	701-328-8100	328-8181
Financial Institutions Dept 2000 Schafer St Suite G *Web:* www.nd.gov/dfi/	Bismarck	ND	58501	701-328-9933	328-9955
Game & Fish Dept 100 N Bismarck Expy *Web:* gf.nd.gov/	Bismarck	ND	58501	701-328-6300	328-6352
Governor 600 E Boulevard Ave Dept 101 *Web:* governor.state.nd.us	Bismarck	ND	58505	701-328-2200	328-2205
Health Dept 600 E Boulevard Ave Dept 301 *Web:* www.health.state.nd.us	Bismarck	ND	58505	701-328-2372	328-4727
Highway Patrol 600 E Boulevard Ave Dept 504 *Web:* www.state.nd.us/ndhp	Bismarck	ND	58505	701-328-2455	328-1717
Historical Society 612 E Boulevard Ave *Web:* www.state.nd.us/hist	Bismarck	ND	58505	701-328-2666	328-3710
Housing Finance Agency PO Box 1535 *TF:* 800-292-8621 ■ *Web:* www.ndhfa.org	Bismarck	ND	58502	701-328-8080	328-8090
Human Services Dept 600 E Boulevard Ave Dept 325 *TF:* 800-472-2622 ■ *Web:* www.state.nd.us/humanservices	Bismarck	ND	58505	701-328-2310	328-2359
Indian Affairs Commission 600 E Boulevard Ave Rm 117 *Web:* www.health.state.nd.us/ndiac	Bismarck	ND	58505	701-328-2428	328-1537
Information Technology Dept 600 E Boulevard Ave Dept 112 *Web:* www.state.nd.us/itd	Bismarck	ND	58505	701-328-3190	328-3000
Insurance Dept 600 E Boulevard Ave Dept 401 *TF:* 800-247-0560 ■ *Web:* www.state.nd.us/ndins	Bismarck	ND	58505	701-328-2440	328-4880
Job Service PO Box 5507 *TF:* 866-873-6042 ■ *Web:* www.jobsnd.com	Bismarck	ND	58506	701-328-2825	328-4000
Labor Dept 600 E Boulevard Ave Dept 406 *Web:* www.nd.gov/labor/	Bismarck	ND	58505	701-328-2660	328-2031
Legislative Assembly State Capitol 600 E Boulevard Ave *Web:* www.legis.nd.gov/	Bismarck	ND	58505	701-328-2916	328-3615
Bill Status State Capitol Bldg 600 E Boulevard Ave *Web:* www.state.nd.us/lr	Bismarck	ND	58505	701-328-2916	328-3615
Lieutenant Governor 600 E Boulevard Ave Dept 101	Bismarck	ND	58505	701-328-2200	328-2205
Medical Examiners Board 418 E Broadway Suite 12 *Web:* www.ndbomex.com	Bismarck	ND	58501	701-328-6500	328-6505
Parks & Recreation Dept 1600 E Century Ave Suite 301-N *TF Campground R:* 800-807-4723 ■ *Web:* www.ndparks.com	Bismarck	ND	58503	701-328-5357	328-5363
Parole & Probation Div 3100 E Railroad Ave *Web:* www.nd.gov/docr/	Bismarck	ND	58501	701-328-6190	328-6651
Public Instruction Dept 600 E Boulevard Ave Dept 201 *Web:* www.dpi.state.nd.us	Bismarck	ND	58505	701-328-2260	328-2461
Public Service Commission 600 E Boulevard Ave Dept 408 *Web:* www.psc.state.nd.us	Bismarck	ND	58505	701-328-2400	328-2410
Racing Commission 500 N 9th St *Web:* www.ndracingcommission.com	Bismarck	ND	58501	701-328-4290	328-4300
Real Estate Commission 200 E Main Ave Suite 204 *Web:* www.realestatend.org	Bismarck	ND	58501	701-328-9749	328-9750
Secretary of State 600 E Boulevard Ave Dept 108 *TF:* 800-352-0867 ■ *Web:* www.nd.gov/sos/	Bismarck	ND	58505	701-328-2900	328-2992
Securities Dept 600 E Boulevard Ave Dept 414 *Web:* www.ndsecurities.com	Bismarck	ND	58505	701-328-2910	328-2946
Student Financial Assistance Program 600 E Boulevard Ave 10th Fl Dept 215 *Web:* www.ndus.nodak.edu	Bismarck	ND	58505	701-328-2960	328-2961
Supreme Court 600 E Boulevard Ave Dept 180 *Web:* www.ndcourts.com	Bismarck	ND	58505	701-328-2221	328-4480

				Phone	Fax
Tax Dept 600 E Boulevard Ave *Web:* www.nd.gov/tax/	Bismarck	ND	58505	701-328-2770	328-3700
Testing & Safety Div 600 E Boulevard Ave Dept 408 *Web:* www.psc.state.nd.us	Bismarck	ND	58505	701-328-2400	328-2410
Tourism Div 1600 Eentury Ave Suite 200S *TF:* 800-435-5663 ■ *Web:* www.ndtourism.com	Bismarck	ND	58502	701-328-2525	328-4878
Transportation Dept 608 E Boulevard Ave *Web:* www.state.nd.us/dot	Bismarck	ND	58505	701-328-2500	328-1420
Treasurer 600 E Boulevard Ave *Web:* www.nd.gov/ndtreas/	Bismarck	ND	58505	701-328-2643	328-3002
University System 600 E Boulevard Ave Dept 215 *Web:* www.ndus.edu	Bismarck	ND	58505	701-328-2960	328-2961
Veterans Affairs Dept 1411 32nd St S *TF:* 866-634-8387 ■ *Web:* www.nd.gov/veterans/	Fargo	ND	58106	701-239-7165	239-7166
Vital Records Div 600 E Boulevard Ave Dept 301 *Web:* www.vitalnd.com	Bismarck	ND	58505	701-328-2360	328-1850
Vocational Rehabilitation Div 1237 W Divide Ave Suite 1B *TF:* 800-755-2745	Bismarck	ND	58501	701-328-8950	328-8969
Workers Compensation 1600 E Century Ave Suite 1000 *TF:* 800-777-5033 ■ *Web:* www.workforcesafety.com	Bismarck	ND	58503	701-328-3800	328-3820

342-36 Ohio

				Phone	Fax
State Government Information *Web:* www.ohio.gov		OH		614-466-2000	
Adjutant General's Dept 2825 W Dublin-Granville Rd *Web:* www.ohionationalguard.com	Columbus	OH	43235	614-336-7000	336-7410
Administrative Director of the Supreme Court 35 S Front St *Web:* www.sconet.state.oh.us	Columbus	OH	43215	614-387-9000	387-9509
Adoption Services Section 225 E Main St 3rd Fl *Web:* jfs.ohio.gov/oapl	Columbus	OH	43215	614-466-9274	466-0164
Aging Dept 50 W Broad St 9th Fl *Web:* www.goldenbuckeye.com	Columbus	OH	43215	614-466-5500	466-5741
Agriculture Dept 8995 E Main St *TF:* 800-282-1955 ■ *Web:* www.ohioagriculture.gov	Reynoldsburg	OH	43068	614-728-6200	466-6124
Arts Council 727 E Main St *Web:* www.oac.state.oh.us	Columbus	OH	43205	614-466-2613	466-4494
Attorney General 30 E Broad St 17th Fl *Web:* www.ag.state.oh.us	Columbus	OH	43215	614-466-4320	466-5087
Child Support Office 30 E Broad St 32nd Fl *TF:* 800-686-1556 ■ *Web:* jfs.ohio.gov/OCS	Columbus	OH	43215	614-752-6561	752-9760
Commerce Dept 77 S High St 23rd Fl *Web:* www.com.state.oh.us	Columbus	OH	43215e	614-466-3636	644-8292
Consumer Protection Section 30 E Broad St 25th Fl *Web:* www.ag.state.oh.us/sections	Columbus	OH	43215	614-466-8831	466-8898
Crime Victim Services 150 E Gay St 25th Fl *TF:* 800-582-2877 ■ *Web:* www.ag.state.oh.us/sections	Columbus	OH	43215	614-466-5610	752-2732
Development Dept 77 S High St *TF:* 800-848-1300 ■ *Web:* www.odod.state.oh.us	Columbus	OH	43215	614-466-2480	644-5167
Education Dept 25 S Front St *TF:* 877-644-6338 ■ *Web:* www.ode.state.oh.us	Columbus	OH	43215	614-466-3641	466-0599
Emergency Management Agency 2855 W Dublin-Granville Rd *Web:* ema.ohio.gov	Columbus	OH	43235	614-889-7150	889-7183
Environmental Protection Agency 122 S Front St PO Box 1049 *Web:* www.epa.state.oh.us	Columbus	OH	43216	614-644-3020	644-3184
Ethics Commission 8 E Long St 10th Fl *Web:* www.ethics.ohio.gov	Columbus	OH	43215	614-466-7090	466-8368
Financial Institutions Div 77 S High St 21st Fl *Web:* www.com.state.oh.us/dfi	Columbus	OH	43266	614-728-8400	644-1631
General Assembly State House *Web:* www.legislature.state.oh.us	Columbus	OH	43215	614-466-8842	
Governor 77 S High St 30th Fl *Web:* governor.ohio.gov	Columbus	OH	43215	614-466-3555	466-9354
Governor's Office on Veterans Affairs 77 S High St 7th Fl *Web:* veteransaffairs.ohio.gov	Columbus	OH	43215	614-644-0898	
Health Dept 246 N High St *Web:* www.odh.ohio.gov	Columbus	OH	43215	614-466-3542	644-0085
Highway Patrol 1970 W Broad St PO Box 182074 *Web:* statepatrol.ohio.gov	Columbus	OH	43223	614-466-2660	644-9749
Historical Society 1982 Velma Ave *Web:* www.ohiohistory.org	Columbus	OH	43211	614-297-2300	297-2411
Housing Finance Agency 57 E Main St *Web:* www.ohiohome.org	Columbus	OH	43215	614-466-7970	644-5393
Information Technology Office 30 E Broad St 40th Fl *Web:* oit.ohio.gov	Columbus	OH	43215	614-644-6446	644-9152
Insurance Dept 2100 Stella Ct *TF:* 800-686-1526 ■ *Web:* www.ohioinsurance.gov	Columbus	OH	43215	614-644-2658	644-3743
Job & Family Services Dept 30 E Broad St 32nd Fl *Web:* jfs.ohio.gov	Columbus	OH	43215	614-466-6282	466-2815
Bill Status 77 S High St *TF:* 800-282-0253 ■ *Web:* www.legislature.state.oh.us	Columbus	OH	43215	614-466-8842	644-1721
Lieutenant Governor 77 S High St 30th Fl *Web:* ltgovernor.ohio.gov	Columbus	OH	43215	614-466-3396	644-0575
Lottery Commission 615 W Superior Ave *Web:* www.ohiolottery.com	Cleveland	OH	44113	216-787-3200	787-3313
Mental Health Dept 30 E Broad St 8th Fl *Web:* www.mh.state.oh.us	Columbus	OH	43215	614-466-2596	752-9453
Motor Vehicles Bureau 1970 W Broad St Box 16520 *Web:* bmv.ohio.gov	Columbus	OH	43216	614-752-7500	752-7972
Natural Resources Dept 2045 Morse Rd *Web:* www.ohiodnr.com	Columbus	OH	43229	614-265-6565	261-9601
Parks & Recreation Div 2045 Morse Rd Bldg C-3 *TF:* 800-282-7275 ■ *Web:* www.ohiodnr.com/parks	Columbus	OH	43229	614-265-6561	261-8407
Parole Board 1050 Freeway Dr N *Web:* www.drc.state.oh.us/web/parboard.htm	Columbus	OH	43229	614-752-1200	752-1251
Public Utilities Commission 180 E Broad St *Web:* www.puco.ohio.gov	Columbus	OH	43215	614-466-3016	644-9546
Racing Commission 77 S High St 18th Fl *Web:* www.racing.ohio.gov	Columbus	OH	43215	614-466-2757	466-1900
Regents Board 30 E Broad St 36th Fl *Web:* www.regents.state.oh.us	Columbus	OH	43266	614-466-6000	466-5866
Rehabilitation & Correction Dept 1050 Freeway Dr N *Web:* www.drc.state.oh.us	Columbus	OH	43229	614-752-1159	752-1086
Rehabilitation Services Commission 400 E Campus View Blvd *TF:* 800-282-4536 ■ *Web:* rsc.ohio.gov	Columbus	OH	43235	614-438-1200	438-1257
Secretary of State 180 E Broad St 16th Fl *Web:* www.sos.state.oh.us	Columbus	OH	43215	614-466-2655	644-0649
Securities Div 77 S High St 22nd Fl *Web:* www.securities.state.oh.us	Columbus	OH	43215	614-644-7381	466-3316
State Grants & Scholarships Office 30 E Broad St 36th Fl PO Box 182452 *TF:* 888-833-1133 ■ *Web:* regents.ohio.gov/sgs	Columbus	OH	43218	614-466-7420	752-5903
Supreme Court 65 S Front St *Web:* www.sconet.state.oh.us	Columbus	OH	43215	614-387-9530	387-9539
Taxation Dept 30 E Broad St 22nd Fl *Web:* tax.ohio.gov	Columbus	OH	43215	614-466-2166	466-6401
Transportation Dept 1980 W Broad St *Web:* www.dot.state.oh.us	Columbus	OH	43223	614-466-7170	644-8662
Travel & Tourism Div PO Box 1001 *TF:* 800-282-5393 ■ *Web:* www.discoverohio.com	Columbus	OH	43216	614-466-8844	466-6744
Treasurer 30 E Broad St 9th Fl *Web:* www.treasurer.state.oh.us	Columbus	OH	43215	614-466-2160	644-7313
Tuition Trust Authority 580 S High St Suite 208 *TF Cust Svc:* 800-233-6734 ■ *Web:* www.collegeadvantage.com	Columbus	OH	43215	614-752-9400	466-4486
Vital Statistics Unit 246 N High St PO Box 15098 *Web:* www2.odh.ohio.gov/VitStats/vsmain1.htm	Columbus	OH	43215	614-466-2531	
Weights & Measures Div 8995 E Main St *Web:* www.ohioagriculture.gov/weights	Reynoldsburg	OH	43068	614-728-6290	728-6424
Wildlife Div 2045 Morse Rd Bldg G *TF:* 800-945-3543 ■ *Web:* www.ohiodnr.com/wildlife	Columbus	OH	43229	614-265-6300	262-1143
Workers' Compensation Bureau 30 W Spring St *Fax Area Code: 877 ■ *TF:* 800-644-6292 ■ *Web:* www.ohiobwc.com	Columbus	OH	43215	614-644-6292	526-6446*
Workforce Services Bureau PO Box 1618 *Web:* www.ohioworkforce.org	Columbus	OH	43216	614-644-0677	728-8366
Youth Services Dept 51 N High St *Web:* www.dys.ohio.gov	Columbus	OH	43215	614-466-4314	728-9859

342-37 Oklahoma

				Phone	Fax
State Government Information *Web:* www.ok.gov		OK		405-521-2011	
Administrative Office of the Courts 1915 N Stiles Ave Suite 305	Oklahoma City	OK	73105	405-521-2450	521-6815
Aging Services Div 312 NE 28th St *Web:* www.okdhs.org/aging	Oklahoma City	OK	73105	405-521-2327	521-2086
Agriculture Food & Forestry Dept 2800 N Lincoln Blvd *Web:* www.oda.state.ok.us	Oklahoma City	OK	73105	405-521-3864	521-4912
Arts Council PO Box 52001-2001 *Web:* www.arts.state.ok.us	Oklahoma City	OK	73152	405-521-2931	521-6418
Attorney General 313 NE 21st St *Web:* www.oag.state.ok.us	Oklahoma City	OK	73105	405-521-3921	521-6246
Banking Dept 4545 N Lincoln Blvd Suite 164 *Web:* www.osbd.state.ok.us	Oklahoma City	OK	73105	405-521-2782	522-2993
Chief Medical Examiner 901 N Stonewall Ave *Web:* www.state.ok.us/~ocme	Oklahoma City	OK	73117	405-239-7141	239-2430
Child Support Enforcement Div PO Box 53552 *Web:* www.okdhs.org/childsupport	Oklahoma City	OK	73152	405-522-5871	522-2753
Children & Family Services Div PO Box 25352 *Web:* www.okdhs.org/dcfs	Oklahoma City	OK	73125	405-521-3777	521-4373
Commerce Dept 900 N Stiles Ave *TF:* 800-879-6552 ■ *Web:* www.okcommerce.gov	Oklahoma City	OK	73104	405-815-6552	815-5199
Conservation Commission 2800 N Lincoln Blvd Suite 160 *Web:* www.okcc.state.ok.us	Oklahoma City	OK	73105	405-521-2384	521-6686
Consumer Protection Div 4545 N Lincoln Blvd Rm 112 *Web:* www.oag.state.ok.us/oagweb.nsf/Consumer	Oklahoma City	OK	73105	405-521-4274	528-1867
Corporation Commission PO Box 52000 *Web:* www.occ.state.ok.us	Oklahoma City	OK	73152	405-521-2211	522-1623
Corrections Dept 3400 ML King Ave *Web:* www.doc.state.ok.us	Oklahoma City	OK	73111	405-425-2500	425-2886
Development Finance Authority 5900 N Classen Ct	Oklahoma City	OK	73118	405-842-1145	848-3314
Education Dept 2500 N Lincoln Blvd *Web:* www.sde.state.ok.us	Oklahoma City	OK	73105	405-521-3301	521-6205
Emergency Management Dept PO Box 53365 *Web:* www.ok.gov/oem	Oklahoma City	OK	73152	405-521-2481	521-4053
Employment Security Commission 2401 N Lincoln Blvd Suite 504 *Web:* www.oesc.state.ok.us	Oklahoma City	OK	73105	405-557-0200	557-5355
Environmental Quality Dept 707 N Robinson Ave PO Box 1677 *TF:* 800-869-1400 ■ *Web:* www.deq.state.ok.us	Oklahoma City	OK	73101	405-702-1000	702-7101
Ethics Commission 2300 N Lincoln Blvd Rm B5 *Web:* www.ethics.state.ok.us	Oklahoma City	OK	73105	405-521-3451	521-4905
Governor State Capitol Rm 212 *Web:* www.governor.state.ok.us	Oklahoma City	OK	73105	405-521-2342	521-3353
Health Dept 1000 NE 10th St *Web:* www.health.state.ok.us	Oklahoma City	OK	73117	405-271-4200	271-3431
Highway Patrol PO Box 11415 *Web:* www.dps.state.ok.us	Oklahoma City	OK	73136	405-425-2006	419-2029
Historical Society 2100 N Lincoln Blvd *Web:* www.ok-history.mus.ok.us	Oklahoma City	OK	73105	405-521-2491	521-2492
Housing Finance Agency 1140 NW 63rd St Suite 200 *TF:* 800-256-1489 ■ *Web:* www.ohfa.org	Oklahoma City	OK	73116	405-848-1144	840-1109
Human Services Dept PO Box 25352 *Web:* www.okdhs.org	Oklahoma City	OK	73125	405-521-3646	521-6458
Indian Affairs Commission 2500 N Lincoln Blvd Suite 282 *Web:* www.oiac.state.ok.us	Oklahoma City	OK	73105	405-521-3828	522-4447
Insurance Dept 2401 NW 23rd St Suite 28 PO Box 53408 *Web:* www.oid.state.ok.us	Oklahoma City	OK	73152	405-521-2828	521-6635
Labor Dept 4001 N Lincoln Blvd *Web:* www.okdol.state.ok.us	Oklahoma City	OK	73105	405-528-1500	528-5751
Bill Status 2300 N Lincoln Blvd Rm B30 *Web:* www.lsb.state.ok.us	Oklahoma City	OK	73105	405-521-4081	521-5507
Legislature 2300 N Lincoln Blvd *Web:* www.lsb.state.ok.us	Oklahoma City	OK	73105	405-524-0126	521-5507
Lieutenant Governor 2300 N Lincoln Blvd Suite 211 *Web:* www.ltgov.state.ok.us	Oklahoma City	OK	73105	405-521-2161	525-2702
Mental Health & Substance Abuse Services Dept 1200 NE 13th St PO Box 53277 *Web:* www.odmhsas.org	Oklahoma City	OK	73152	405-522-3908	522-3650
Military Dept 3501 Military Cir *Web:* www.omd.state.ok.us	Oklahoma City	OK	73111	405-228-5000	228-5524
Motor Vehicle Commission 4334 Northwest Expy Suite 183 *Web:* www.youroklahoma.com/omvc	Oklahoma City	OK	73116	405-607-8227	607-8909
Pardon & Parole Board 120 N Robinson Ave Suite 900W *Web:* www.ppb.state.ok.us	Oklahoma City	OK	73102	405-602-5863	602-6437
Parks Div PO Box 52002 *TF:* 800-654-8240 ■ *Web:* touroklahoma.com	Oklahoma City	OK	73152	405-230-8300	521-2428
Personnel Management Office 2101 N Lincoln Blvd Suite G-80 *Web:* www.opm.state.ok.us	Oklahoma City	OK	73105	405-521-2177	524-6942
Plant Industry & Consumer Services 2800 N Lincoln Blvd *Web:* www.oda.state.ok.us/pics-weighthome.htm	Oklahoma City	OK	73105	405-521-3864	522-4584

Oklahoma (Cont'd)

				Phone	Fax
Real Estate Commission 2401 NW 23rd St Suite 18 *Web:* www.orec.state.ok.us	Oklahoma City	OK	73107	405-521-3387	521-2189
Rehabilitative Services Dept 3535 NW 58th St Suite 500 *TF:* 800-845-8476 ■ *Web:* www.okrehab.org	Oklahoma City	OK	73112	405-951-3400	951-3529
Secretary of State 2300 N Lincoln Blvd Rm 101 *Web:* www.sos.state.ok.us	Oklahoma City	OK	73105	405-521-3912	521-3771
Securities Dept 120 N Robinson St Suite 860 *Web:* www.securities.state.ok.us	Oklahoma City	OK	73102	405-280-7700	280-7742
State Regents for Higher Education 655 Research Pkwy Suite 200 *Web:* www.okhighered.org	Oklahoma City	OK	73104	405-225-9100	225-9235
Supreme Court 2300 N Lincoln Blvd Rm 245 *Web:* www.oscn.net	Oklahoma City	OK	73105	405-521-2163	528-1607
Tax Commission 2501 N Lincoln Blvd *Web:* www.oktax.state.ok.us	Oklahoma City	OK	73194	405-521-3160	521-3826
Tourism & Recreation Dept 15 N Robinson St Suite 100 *TF:* 800-652-6552 ■ *Web:* tourism.state.ok.us	Oklahoma City	OK	73105	405-521-2406	521-3992
Transportation Dept 200 NE 21st St *Web:* www.okladot.state.ok.us	Oklahoma City	OK	73105	405-521-2631	522-1044
Treasurer 2300 N Lincoln Rd Rm 217 *Web:* www.treasurer.state.ok.us	Oklahoma City	OK	73105	405-521-3191	521-4994
Veterans Affairs Dept 2311 N Central Ave *Web:* www.odva.state.ok.us	Oklahoma City	OK	73105	405-521-3684	521-6533
Victim Services Unit 2300 N Lincoln Blvd Rm 112 *Web:* www.oag.state.ok.us/oagweb.nsf/VServices	Oklahoma City	OK	73105	405-521-3921	521-6246
Vital Records Div 1000 NE 10th St Rm 111 *Web:* www.health.state.ok.us/program/vital	Oklahoma City	OK	73117	405-271-4040	
Wildlife Conservation Dept PO Box 53465 *Web:* www.wildlifedepartment.com	Oklahoma City	OK	73152	405-521-4660	521-6505
Workers' Compensation Div 4001 N Lincoln Blvd *TF:* 888-269-5353 ■ *Web:* www.okdol.state.ok.us/workcomp	Oklahoma City	OK	73105	405-528-1500	528-5751

342-38 Oregon

				Phone	Fax
Accountancy Board 2600 State St Suite 110 *Web:* egov.oregon.gov/ODF	Salem	OR	97310	503-945-7200	945-7212
Agriculture Dept 635 Capitol St NE *Web:* egov.oregon.gov/ODA	Salem	OR	97301	503-986-4550	986-4750
Arts Commission 775 Summer St NE Suite 200 *Web:* www.oregonartscommission.org	Salem	OR	97301	503-986-0082	986-0260
Attorney General 1162 Court St NE Justice Bldg *Web:* www.doj.state.or.us	Salem	OR	97301	503-378-4400	378-4017
Child Support Div 494 State St Suite 300 *Web:* dcs.state.or.us	Salem	OR	97301	503-986-6166	986-6158
Children Adults & Families Div 500 Summer St NE *Web:* egov.oregon.gov/DHS/children	Salem	OR	97310	503-945-5600	373-7032
Community Colleges & Workforce Development Dept 255 Capitol St NE *Web:* www.workforce.state.or.us	Salem	OR	97310	503-378-8648	378-8434
Consumer & Business Services Dept 350 Winter St NE PO Box 14480 *Web:* egov.oregon.gov/DCBS	Salem	OR	97309	503-378-4100	378-6444
Corrections Dept 2575 Center St NE *Web:* egov.oregon.gov/DOC	Salem	OR	97301	503-945-0920	373-1173
Crime Victims Assistance Section 1162 Court St NE *Web:* www.doj.state.or.us/CrimeV/welcome1.htm	Salem	OR	97301	503-378-4400	378-5738
Driver & Motor Vehicle Services Div 1905 Lana Ave NE *Web:* www.oregon.gov/ODOT/DMV	Salem	OR	97314	503-945-5000	945-5254
Economic & Community Development Dept 775 Summer St NE Suite 200 *Web:* egov.oregon.gov/ECDD	Salem	OR	97301	503-986-0123	581-5115
Education Dept 255 Capitol St NE *Web:* www.ode.state.or.us	Salem	OR	97310	503-378-3600	373-5156
Emergency Management PO Box 14370 *Web:* egov.oregon.gov/OOHS/OEM	Salem	OR	97309	503-378-2911	373-7933
Employment Dept 875 Union St NE *Web:* egov.oregon.gov/EMPLOY	Salem	OR	97311	503-947-1394	947-1472
Energy Dept 625 Marion St NE *Web:* egov.oregon.gov/ENERGY	Salem	OR	97301	503-378-4040	373-7806
Environmental Quality Dept 811 SW 6th Ave *Web:* www.deq.state.or.us	Portland	OR	97204	503-229-5696	229-6124
Finance & Corporate Securities Div PO Box 14480 *Web:* www.cbs.state.or.us/external/dfcs	Salem	OR	97309	503-378-4140	947-7862
Financial Fraud/Consumer Protection Section 1162 Court St NE *Web:* www.doj.state.or.us/FinFraud/welcome3.htm	Salem	OR	97301	503-378-4400	373-7067
Fish & Wildlife Dept 3406 Cherry Ave NE *TF:* 800-720-6339 ■ *Web:* www.dfw.state.or.us	Salem	OR	97303	503-947-6000	947-6042
Government Standards & Practices Commission 100 High St SE Suite 220 *Web:* www.gspc.state.or.us	Salem	OR	97301	503-378-5105	373-1456
Governor 900 Court St NE *Web:* www.governor.state.or.us	Salem	OR	97301	503-378-3111	378-6827
Heritage Conservation Div 725 Summer St NE Suite C *Web:* egov.oregon.gov/OPRD/HCD	Salem	OR	97301	503-986-0671	986-0793
Homeland Security Office 3225 State St PO Box 14370 *Web:* egov.oregon.gov/OOHS	Salem	OR	97309	503-378-3056	
Housing & Community Services Dept 725 Summer St NE Suite B PO Box 14508 *Web:* egov.oregon.gov/OHCS	Salem	OR	97309	503-986-2000	986-2020
Human Services Dept 500 Summer St NE *Web:* egov.oregon.gov/DHS	Salem	OR	97310	503-945-5733	378-2897
Information Resources Management Div 1225 Ferry St SE *Web:* irmd.das.state.or.us	Salem	OR	97301	503-378-2135	373-5200
Insurance Div 350 Winter St NE Rm 440 *Web:* www.cbs.state.or.us/external/ins	Salem	OR	97301	503-947-7980	378-4351
Labor & Industries Bureau 800 NE Oregon St Suite 1045 *Web:* www.boli.state.or.us	Portland	OR	97232	503-731-4200	731-4103
Land Conservation & Development Dept 635 Capitol St NE Suite 150 *Web:* www.lcd.state.or.us	Salem	OR	97302	503-373-0050	378-5518
Legislative Assembly 900 Court St NE *Web:* www.leg.state.or.us	Salem	OR	97310	503-986-1180	373-1527
State Lottery 500 Airport Rd SE *Web:* www.oregonlottery.org	Salem	OR	97301	503-540-1000	540-1001
Measurement Standards Div 635 Capitol St NE *Web:* egov.oregon.gov/ODA/MSD	Salem	OR	97301	503-986-4670	986-4784
Medical Examiners Board 1500 SW 1st Ave Suite 620 *Web:* www.bme.state.or.us	Portland	OR	97201	503-229-5770	229-6543
Military Dept 1776 Militia Way SE PO Box 14350 *Web:* egov.oregon.gov/OMD	Salem	OR	97309	503-584-3980	584-3987
Parks & Recreation Dept 725 Summer St NE Suite C *TF:* 800-551-6949 ■ *Web:* egov.oregon.gov/OPRD	Salem	OR	97301	503-986-0667	986-0794
Parole & Post-Prison Supervision Board 2575 Center St NE Suite 100 *Web:* www.paroleboard.state.or.us	Salem	OR	97301	503-945-0900	373-7558
Public Health Div 800 NE Oregon St *Web:* egov.oregon.gov/DHS/ph	Salem	OR	97323	503-731-4000	731-4031
Public Utility Commission 550 Capitol St NE Suite 215 PO Box 2148 *Web:* www.puc.state.or.us	Salem	OR	97308	503-378-6611	378-5505
Bill Status 900 Court St NE Rm 49 *Web:* www.leg.state.or.us/bills_laws	Salem	OR	97310	503-986-1180	373-1527
Racing Commission 800 NE Oregon St Suite 310 *Web:* egov.oregon.gov/RACING	Portland	OR	97232	503-731-4052	731-4053
Revenue Dept 955 Center St NE *Web:* egov.oregon.gov/DOR	Salem	OR	97301	503-378-4988	945-8738
Secretary of State 900 Court St NE Rm 136 *Web:* www.sos.state.or.us	Salem	OR	97301	503-986-1500	986-1616
Seniors & People with Disabilities Div 500 Summer St NE 2nd Fl *TF:* 800-282-2096 ■ *Web:* egov.oregon.gov/DHS/spwpd	Salem	OR	97310	503-945-5811	378-7823
State Court Administrator Office 1163 State St *Web:* www.ojd.state.or.us/osca	Salem	OR	97301	503-986-5500	986-5503
State Police Dept 225 Capitol St Suite 400 *Web:* egov.oregon.gov/OSP	Salem	OR	97310	503-378-3720	378-8282
Student Assistance Commission 1500 Valley River Dr Suite 100 *TF:* 800-452-8807 ■ *Web:* www.osac.state.or.us	Eugene	OR	97401	541-687-7400	687-7419
Supreme Court 1163 State St *Web:* www.ojd.state.or.us/courts/supreme	Salem	OR	97301	503-986-5550	986-5560
Tourism Commission 670 Hawthorne Ave SE Suite 240 *TF:* 800-547-7842 ■ *Web:* www.traveloregon.com	Salem	OR	97301	503-378-8850	
Transportation Dept 355 Capitol St NE Suite 135 *TF:* 888-275-6368 ■ *Web:* egov.oregon.gov/ODOT	Salem	OR	97301	503-986-3200	986-3432
Treasurer 350 Winter St NE Suite 100 *Web:* www.ost.state.or.us	Salem	OR	97301	503-378-4000	373-7051
University System 506 SW Mill St Suite 530 PO Box 751 *Web:* www.ous.edu	Portland	OR	97207	503-725-5700	725-5709
Veterans' Affairs Dept 700 Summer St NE *Web:* www.odva.state.or.us	Salem	OR	97301	503-373-2000	373-2362
Vital Records Unit PO Box 14050 *Web:* www.dhs.state.or.us/publichealth/chs	Portland	OR	97293	503-731-4095	234-8417
Vocational Rehabilitation Services Office 500 Summer St NE *TF:* 800-452-2147 ■ *Web:* egov.oregon.gov/DHS/vr	Salem	OR	97310	503-945-5880	947-5025
Workers' Compensation Board 2601 SE 25th St Suite 150 *Web:* www.cbs.state.or.us/wcb	Salem	OR	97302	503-378-3308	373-1684

342-39 Pennsylvania

				Phone	Fax
State Government Information *Web:* www.state.pa.us		PA		717-787-2121	
Administrative Office of the Courts 1515 Market St Suite 1414 *Web:* www.courts.state.pa.us	Philadelphia	PA	19102	215-560-6300	560-6315
Aging Dept 555 Walnut St 5th Fl *Web:* www.aging.state.pa.us	Harrisburg	PA	17101	717-783-1550	783-6842
Agriculture Dept 2301 N Cameron St *Web:* www.agriculture.state.pa.us	Harrisburg	PA	17110	717-772-2853	772-2780
Arts Council 216 Finance Bldg *Web:* www.pacouncilonthearts.org	Harrisburg	PA	17120	717-787-6883	783-2538
Attorney General Strawberry Sq 16th Fl *Web:* www.attorneygeneral.gov	Harrisburg	PA	17120	717-787-3391	787-8242
Banking Dept 333 Market St 16th Fl *Web:* www.banking.state.pa.us	Harrisburg	PA	17101	717-214-8343	787-8773
Bill Status Main Capitol Bldg Rm 648 *Web:* www.legis.state.pa.us	Harrisburg	PA	17120	717-787-2342	
Child Support Enforcement Bureau PO Box 8018 *Web:* www.dpw.state.pa.us/Child/ChildSupport	Harrisburg	PA	17105	717-787-2600	787-9706
Children Youth & Families Office PO Box 2675 *Web:* www.dpw.state.pa.us/Child	Harrisburg	PA	17105	717-787-4756	787-0414
Community & Economic Development Dept 400 North St 4th Fl *Web:* www.newpa.com	Harrisburg	PA	17120	717-787-3003	787-6866
Conservation & Natural Resources Dept PO Box 8767 *Web:* www.dcnr.state.pa.us	Harrisburg	PA	17105	717-787-2869	705-2832
Consumer Advocate 555 Walnut St 5th Fl *Web:* www.oca.state.pa.us	Harrisburg	PA	17101	717-783-5048	783-7152
Corrections Dept PO Box 598 *Web:* www.cor.state.pa.us	Camp Hill	PA	17001	717-975-4859	787-0132
Driver & Vehicle Services Bureau 1101 S Front St *Web:* www.dmv.state.pa.us	Harrisburg	PA	17104	717-787-2977	705-1046
Education Dept 333 Market St *Web:* www.pde.state.pa.us	Harrisburg	PA	17126	717-783-6788	783-4517
Emergency Management Agency 2605 Interstate Dr *Web:* www.pema.state.pa.us	Harrisburg	PA	17110	717-651-2001	651-2021
Environmental Protection Dept PO Box 2063 *Web:* www.dep.state.pa.us	Harrisburg	PA	17105	717-783-2300	783-8926
Ethics Commission PO Box 11470 *Web:* www.ethics.state.pa.us	Harrisburg	PA	17108	717-783-1610	787-0806
Fish & Boat Commission PO Box 67000 *Web:* www.fish.state.pa.us	Harrisburg	PA	17106	717-705-7800	705-7802
Game Commission 2001 Elmerton Ave *Web:* www.pgc.state.pa.us	Harrisburg	PA	17110	717-787-4250	772-2411
General Assembly Capitol Bldg *Web:* www.legis.state.pa.us	Harrisburg	PA	17120	717-787-5920	772-2344
General Services Dept PO Box 1365 *Web:* www.dgs.state.pa.us	Harrisburg	PA	17125	717-787-2121	772-2026
Governor 225 Main Capitol Bldg *Web:* www.governor.state.pa.us	Harrisburg	PA	17120	717-787-2500	772-8284
Health Dept Health & Welfare Bldg Box 90 *Web:* www.dsf.health.state.pa.us	Harrisburg	PA	17108	717-787-6436	772-6959
Higher Education Assistance Agency 1200 N 7th St *TF:* 800-692-7392 ■ *Web:* www.pheaa.org	Harrisburg	PA	17102	717-720-2860	720-3644
Historical & Museum Commission PO Box 1026 *Web:* www.phmc.state.pa.us	Harrisburg	PA	17108	717-787-3362	783-9924
Homeland Security Office 2605 Interstate Dr *Web:* www.homelandsecurity.state.pa.us	Harrisburg	PA	17110	717-772-8052	
Housing Finance Agency PO Box 8029 *Web:* www.phfa.org	Harrisburg	PA	17105	717-780-3800	780-3905
Information Technology Office 209 Finance Bldg *Web:* www.oit.state.pa.us	Harrisburg	PA	17120	717-787-5440	787-4523
Insurance Dept 1326 Strawberry Sq *Web:* www.ins.state.pa.us	Harrisburg	PA	17120	717-787-7000	783-3898
Labor & Industry Dept 1700 Labor & Industry Bldg *Web:* www.dli.state.pa.us	Harrisburg	PA	17120	717-787-5279	787-8826

	City	State	Zip	Phone	Fax
Lieutenant Governor Capitol Bldg Suite 200 *Web:* www.governor.state.pa.us	Harrisburg	PA	17120	717-787-3300	783-0150
Civil Service Commission PO Box 2675 *Web:* www.dpw.state.pa.us/Family	Harrisburg	PA	17105	717-787-6443	
Military & Veterans Affairs Dept Fort Indiantown Gap *Web:* www.dmva.state.pa.us	Annville	PA	17003	717-861-8500	861-8211
Probation & Parole Board 1101 S Front St Suite 5100 *Web:* www.pbpp.state.pa.us	Harrisburg	PA	17104	717-787-5100	772-2157
Professional & Occupational Affairs Bureau PO Box 2649 *Web:* www.dos.state.pa.us/bpoa	Harrisburg	PA	17105	717-783-7192	783-0510
Public Utility Commission PO Box 3265 *Web:* www.puc.state.pa.us	Harrisburg	PA	17105	717-783-1740	787-6641
Public Welfare Dept PO Box 2675 *Web:* www.dpw.state.pa.us	Harrisburg	PA	17105	717-787-2600	772-2062
Revenue Dept Strawberry Sq 11th Fl *Web:* www.revenue.state.pa.us	Harrisburg	PA	17128	717-783-3680	787-3990
Secretary of the Commonweath 302 North Office Bldg *Web:* www.dos.state.pa.us	Harrisburg	PA	17120	717-787-6458	787-1734
Securities Commission 1010 N 7th St 2nd Fl *Web:* www.psc.state.pa.us	Harrisburg	PA	17102	717-787-8061	783-5122
State Athletic Commission 2601 N 3rd St *Web:* www.dos.state.pa.us/sac	Harrisburg	PA	17110	717-787-5720	783-0824
State Lottery 2850 Turnpike Industrial Dr *TF:* 800-692-7481 ■ *Web:* www.palottery.com	Middletown	PA	17057	717-986-4699	986-4767
State Parks Bureau PO Box 8551 *TF:* 888-727-2757 ■ *Web:* www.dcnr.state.pa.us/stateparks	Harrisburg	PA	17105	717-787-6640	787-8817
State Police 1800 Elmerton Ave *Web:* www.psp.state.pa.us	Harrisburg	PA	17110	717-783-5599	787-2948
State System of Higher Education 2986 N 2nd St *TF:* 800-457-7743 ■ *Web:* www.passhe.edu	Harrisburg	PA	17110	717-720-4000	720-4011
Supreme Court City Hall Suite 468 *Web:* www.courts.state.pa.us	Philadelphia	PA	19107	215-560-6370	
Transportation Dept 400 North St *TF:* 800-932-4600 ■ *Web:* www.dot.state.pa.us	Harrisburg	PA	17120	717-787-2838	787-1739
Treasury Dept 129 Finance Bldg *Web:* www.treasury.state.pa.us	Harrisburg	PA	17120	717-787-2465	783-9760
Tuition Account Plan (TAP 529) PO Box 55463 *Fax Area Code: 781 ■ *TF:* 800-440-4000 ■ *Web:* tap529.com	Boston	MA	02205	800-440-4000	707-8981*
Victims Compensation Assistance Program PO Box 1167 *Web:* www.pccd.state.pa.us	Harrisburg	PA	17101	717-783-5153	787-4306
Vital Records Div PO Box 1528 *Web:* www.health.state.pa.us/vitalrecords	New Castle	PA	16103	724-656-3100	652-8951
Vocational Rehabilitation Office 909 Green St *TF:* 800-442-6351	Harrisburg	PA	17120	717-787-5244	783-5221
Workers Compensation Bureau 1171 S Cameron St Rm 324	Harrisburg	PA	17104	717-783-5421	772-0342
Workforce Investment Board 901 N 7th St Suite 103 *Web:* www.paworkforce.state.pa.us	Harrisburg	PA	17120	717-705-8818	783-4660
Tourism Office 404 North St 4th Fl *TF:* 800-847-4872 ■ *Web:* www.visitpa.com	Harrisburg	PA	17120	717-720-1301	787-0687

342-40 Rhode Island

	City	State	Zip	Phone	Fax
State Government Information *Web:* www.ri.gov		RI		401-222-2000	
Adjustant General's Office 645 New London Ave *Web:* www.riguard.com	Cranston	RI	02920	401-275-4100	275-4338
Agriculture & Resource Marketing Div 235 Promenade St	Providence	RI	02908	401-222-2781	222-6047
Arts Council 1 Capitol Hill 3rd Fl *Web:* www.arts.ri.gov	Providence	RI	02908	401-222-3880	222-3018
Attorney General 150 S Main St *Web:* www.riag.state.ri.us	Providence	RI	02903	401-274-4400	222-1331
Banking Div 233 Richmond St *Web:* www.dbr.state.ri.us/banking.html	Providence	RI	02903	401-222-2405	222-5628
Bill Status State House Rm 1 *Web:* www.rilin.state.ri.us	Providence	RI	02903	401-222-3580	
Child Support Services 77 Dorrance St	Providence	RI	02903	401-222-2847	222-2887
Children Youth & Families Dept 101 Friendship St *Web:* www.dcyf.state.ri.us	Providence	RI	02903	401-528-3575	528-3590
Consumer Protection Unit 150 S Main St *Web:* www.riag.ri.gov/civil/consumer.php	Providence	RI	02903	401-274-4400	222-5110
Corrections Dept 40 Howard Ave *Web:* www.doc.state.ri.us	Cranston	RI	02920	401-462-1000	462-2630
Court Administrators Office 250 Benefit St *Web:* www.courts.state.ri.us	Providence	RI	02903	401-222-3263	222-5131
Crime Victim Compensation Program 40 Fountain St 1st Fl *Web:* www.treasury.state.ri.us/vcfund.htm	Providence	RI	02903	401-222-8590	222-4577
Economic Development Corp 1 W Exchange St *Web:* www.riedc.com	Providence	RI	02903	401-222-2601	222-2102
Elderly Affairs Dept 35 Howard Ave *Web:* www.dea.state.ri.us	Cranston	RI	02920	401-462-4000	462-0586
Elementary & Secondary Education Dept 255 Westminster St *Web:* www.ridoe.net	Providence	RI	02903	401-222-4600	222-6178
Emergency Management Agency 645 New London Ave *Web:* www.riema.ri.gov	Cranston	RI	02920	401-946-9996	944-1891
Environmental Management Dept 235 Promenade St Suite 450 *Web:* www.state.ri.us/dem	Providence	RI	02908	401-222-6800	222-6802
Ethics Commission 40 Fountain St *Web:* www.ethics.ri.gov	Providence	RI	02903	401-222-3790	222-3382
Fish & Wildlife Div 4808 Tower Hill Rd	Wakefield	RI	02879	401-778-9304	783-4460
General Assembly State House *Web:* www.rilin.state.ri.us	Providence	RI	02903	401-222-2466	222-6142
Governor State House *Web:* www.governor.state.ri.us	Providence	RI	02903	401-222-2080	273-5729
Health Dept 3 Capitol Hill *Web:* www.health.ri.gov	Providence	RI	02908	401-222-2231	222-6548
Higher Education Assistance Authority 560 Jefferson Blvd *TF:* 800-922-9855 ■ *Web:* www.riheaa.org	Warwick	RI	02886	401-736-1100	732-3541
Higher Education Office 301 Promenade St *Web:* www.ribghe.org	Providence	RI	02908	401-455-9300	455-9314
Historical Preservation & Heritage Commission 150 Benefit St *Web:* www.preservation.ri.gov	Providence	RI	02903	401-222-2678	222-2968
Housing & Mortgage Finance Corp 44 Washington St *Web:* www.rihousing.com	Providence	RI	02903	401-751-5566	
Human Services Dept 600 New London Ave *Web:* www.dhs.state.ri.us	Cranston	RI	02920	401-462-5300	462-1876
Insurance Div 233 Richmond St *Web:* www.dbr.state.ri.us/insurance.html	Providence	RI	02903	401-222-2223	222-5475
Labor & Training Dept 1511 Pontiac Ave *Web:* www.dlt.state.ri.us	Cranston	RI	02920	401-462-8000	462-8872
Library & Information Services Office 1 Capitol Hill *Web:* www.olis.state.ri.us	Providence	RI	02908	401-222-4444	222-2083
Lieutenant Governor 116 State House *Web:* www.ltgov.state.ri.us	Providence	RI	02903	401-222-2371	222-2012
Lottery 1425 Pontiac Ave *Web:* www.rilot.com	Cranston	RI	02920	401-463-6500	463-5008
Medical Examiner 48 Orms St	Providence	RI	02904	401-222-5500	222-5517
Mental Health Retardation & Hospitals Dept 14 Harrington Rd *Web:* www.mhrh.ri.gov	Cranston	RI	02920	401-262-1000	462-3204
Motor Vehicle Div 100 Main St *Web:* www.dmv.state.ri.us	Pawtucket	RI	02860	401-588-3020	
Parks & Recreation Div 2321 Hartford Ave *Web:* www.riparks.com	Johnston	RI	02919	401-222-2632	934-0610
Parole Board 1 Center Pl	Providence	RI	02903	401-222-3262	222-1418
Professional Regulation Div 1511 Pontiac Ave Howard Ctr Bldg 70 *Web:* www.dlt.ri.gov/profregs	Cranston	RI	02920	401-462-8580	
Public Utilities Commission 89 Jefferson Blvd *Web:* www.ripuc.org	Warwick	RI	02888	401-941-4500	941-1694
Racing & Athletics Div 233 Richmond St *Web:* www.dbr.state.ri.us/race-athletics.html	Providence	RI	02903	401-222-6541	222-6131
Rehabilitation Services Office 40 Fountain St *Web:* www.ors.state.ri.us	Providence	RI	02903	401-421-7005	222-3574
Secretary of State 217 State House *Web:* www.state.ri.us	Providence	RI	02903	401-222-2357	222-1356
Securities Div 233 Richmond St Suite 232 *Web:* www.dbr.state.ri.us/securities.html	Providence	RI	02903	401-222-3048	222-5629
State Police 311 Danielson Pike *Web:* www.risp.state.ri.us	North Scituate	RI	02857	401-444-1000	444-1105
Supreme Court 250 Benefit St *Web:* www.courts.state.ri.us	Providence	RI	02903	401-222-3272	222-3599
Taxation Div 1 Capitol Hill *Web:* www.tax.state.ri.us	Providence	RI	02908	401-222-3050	222-6006
Transportation Dept 2 Capitol Hill *Web:* www.dot.state.ri.us	Providence	RI	02903	401-222-2481	222-2086
Treasurer 102 State House *Web:* www.treasury.state.ri.us	Providence	RI	02903	401-222-2397	222-6140
Veterans' Affairs Div 600 New London Ave *Web:* www.dhs.state.ri.us/dhs/dvetaff.htm	Cranston	RI	02910	401-462-0350	
Vital Records Div 3 Capitol Hill Rm 101 *Web:* www.health.state.ri.us/chic/vital	Providence	RI	02908	401-222-2811	222-4393
Weights & Measures Office 1511 Pontiac Ave Bldg 70	Cranston	RI	02920	401-457-8555	
Worker's Compensation Unit 1511 Pontiac Ave Bldg 69 2nd Fl *Web:* www.dlt.ri.gov/wc/	Cranston	RI	02920	401-460-8100	462-8105
Tourism Div 1 W Exchange St *TF:* 800-556-2484 ■ *Web:* visitrhodeisland.com	Providence	RI	02903	401-222-2601	273-8270

342-41 South Carolina

	City	State	Zip	Phone	Fax
State Government Information *Web:* www.sc.gov		SC		803-896-0000	
Adoption Services Div PO Box 1520 *Web:* www.state.sc.us/dss/adoption	Columbia	SC	29202	803-898-7561	898-7641
Agriculture Dept 1200 Senate St PO Box 11280 *Web:* www.scda.state.sc.us	Columbia	SC	29211	803-734-2190	734-2192
Arts Commission 1800 Gervais St *Web:* www.state.sc.us/arts	Columbia	SC	29201	803-734-8696	734-8526
Attorney General PO Box 11549 *Web:* www.scattorneygeneral.org	Columbia	SC	29211	803-734-3970	734-3971
Bill Status PO Box 142 *Web:* www.scstatehouse.net	Columbia	SC	29201	803-212-6720	
Child Support Enforcement Office PO Box 1469 *TF:* 800-768-5858 ■ *Web:* www.state.sc.us/dss/csed	Columbia	SC	29202	803-898-9210	898-9126
Commerce Dept 1201 Main St Suite 1600 *Web:* www.sccommerce.com	Columbia	SC	29201	803-737-0400	737-0418
Higher Education Commission 1333 Main St Suite 200 *Web:* www.che400.state.sc.us	Columbia	SC	29201	803-737-2260	737-2297
Consumer Affairs Dept PO Box 5757 *TF:* 800-922-1594 ■ *Web:* www.scconsumer.gov	Columbia	SC	29250	803-734-4200	734-4286
Corrections Dept PO Box 21787 *Web:* www.doc.sc.gov	Columbia	SC	29221	803-896-8500	896-3972
Court Administration 1015 Sumter St 2nd Fl *Web:* www.judicial.state.sc.us	Columbia	SC	29201	803-734-1800	734-1821
Disabilities & Special Needs Dept 3440 Harden St Ext PO Box 4706 *TF:* 888-376-4636 ■ *Web:* www.state.sc.us/ddsn	Columbia	SC	29240	803-898-9600	898-9653
Education Dept 1429 Senate St *Web:* www.myscschools.com	Columbia	SC	29201	803-734-8500	734-8527
Education Lottery 1333 Main St 4th Fl *Web:* www.sceducationlottery.com	Columbia	SC	29201	803-737-2002	737-2005
Emergency Management Div 1100 Fish Hatchery Rd *Web:* www.scemd.org	West Columbia	SC	29172	803-737-8500	737-8570
Employment Security Commission 1550 Gadsden St *Web:* www.sces.org	Columbia	SC	29201	803-737-2400	737-2642
Ethics Commission 5000 Thurmond Mall Suite 250 *Web:* www.state.sc.us/ethics	Columbia	SC	29201	803-253-4192	253-7539
Financial Institutions Board PO Box 11778 *Web:* www.state.sc.us/treas	Columbia	SC	29211	803-734-2001	734-2013
Governor PO Box 12267 *Web:* www.scgovernor.com	Columbia	SC	29211	803-734-2100	734-5167
Health & Environmental Control Dept 2600 Bull St *Web:* www.scdhec.net	Columbia	SC	29201	803-898-3432	898-3323
Health & Human Services Dept PO Box 8206 *Web:* www.dhhs.state.sc.us	Columbia	SC	29202	803-898-2500	898-4515
Higher Education Tuition Grants Commission 101 Business Park Blvd Suite 2100 *Web:* www.sctuitiongrants.com	Columbia	SC	29203	803-896-1120	896-1126
Highway Patrol 5400 Broad River Rd *Web:* www.schp.org	Columbia	SC	29210	803-896-7920	896-7922
Historic Preservation Office 8301 Parklane Rd *Web:* www.state.sc.us/scdah/histrcpl.htm	Columbia	SC	29223	803-896-6100	896-6167
Insurance Dept 300 Arbor Lake Suite 1200 *Web:* www.doi.state.sc.us	Columbia	SC	29223	803-737-6160	737-6229
Jobs-Economic Development Authority 1441 Main St Suite 900 *Web:* businesscarolina.net	Columbia	SC	29201	803-461-3801	461-3826
Labor Licensing & Regulation Dept PO Box 11329 *Web:* www.llr.state.sc.us	Columbia	SC	29211	803-896-4300	896-4393
Law Enforcement Div 4400 Broad River Rd PO Box 21398 *Web:* www.sled.state.sc.us	Columbia	SC	29221	803-896-7001	896-7041
Legislature State House PO Box 142 *Web:* www.scstatehouse.net	Columbia	SC	29202	803-212-6200	212-6299
Lieutenant Governor PO Box 142 *Web:* www.state.sc.us/ltgov	Columbia	SC	29202	803-734-2080	734-2082
Medical Examiners Board PO Box 11289 *Web:* www.llr.state.sc.us/POL/Medical	Columbia	SC	29211	803-896-4500	896-4515

South Carolina (Cont'd)

				Phone	Fax
Mental Health Dept 2414 Bull St PO Box 485 *Web:* www.state.sc.us/dmh	Columbia	SC	29202	803-898-8581	898-8316
Motor Vehicles Div PO Box 1498 *TF:* 800-422-1368 ■ *Web:* www.scdps.org/dmv	Blythewood	SC	29016	803-896-5000	
Natural Resources Dept PO Box 167 *Web:* www.dnr.state.sc.us	Columbia	SC	29202	803-734-4007	734-4300
Parks Recreation & Tourism Dept 1205 Pendleton St *Web:* southcarolinaparks.com	Columbia	SC	29201	803-734-1650	734-0133
Probation Parole & Pardon Services Dept PO Box 50666 *Web:* www.dppps.sc.gov	Columbia	SC	29250	803-734-9220	734-9440
Professional & Occupational Licensing Boards PO Box 11329 *Web:* www.llr.state.sc.us/pol	Columbia	SC	29211	803-896-4300	896-4310
Public Service Commission PO Drawer 11649 *Web:* www.psc.state.sc.us	Columbia	SC	29211	803-896-5133	896-5246
Revenue Dept PO Box 125 *Web:* www.sctax.org	Columbia	SC	29214	803-898-5000	898-5888
Secretary of State PO Box 11350 *Web:* www.scsos.com	Columbia	SC	29211	803-734-2170	734-1661
Securities Div PO Box 11549 *TF:* 877-232-5378 ■ *Web:* www.scsecurities.com	Columbia	SC	29211	803-734-9916	734-0032
Senior Services Bureau 1801 Main St *Web:* www.dhhs.state.sc.us/InsideDHHS/Bureaus	Columbia	SC	29202	803-898-2850	898-4515
Social Services Dept PO Box 1520 *Web:* www.state.sc.us/dss	Columbia	SC	29202	803-898-7601	898-7277
State Housing Finance & Development Authority 300 Outlet Pointe Blvd Suite C *Web:* www.sha.state.sc.us	Columbia	SC	29210	803-896-9001	896-9012
State Ports Authority 176 Concord St *TF:* 800-845-7106 ■ *Web:* www.scspa.com	Charleston	SC	29401	843-723-8651	577-8626
Supreme Court PO Box 11330 *Web:* www.judicial.state.sc.us/supreme	Columbia	SC	29211	803-734-1080	734-1499
Transportation Dept 955 Park St *Web:* www.dot.state.sc.us	Columbia	SC	29201	803-737-1302	737-2038
Treasurer PO Box 11778 *Web:* www.state.sc.us/treas	Columbia	SC	29211	803-734-2101	734-2690
Veterans Affairs Div 1205 Pendleton St Rm 447 *Web:* www.govoepp.state.sc.us/vetaff.htm	Columbia	SC	29201	803-734-0200	734-0197
Victim Assistance Div 1205 Pendleton St Rm 401 *Web:* www.govoepp.state.sc.us/sova	Columbia	SC	29201	803-734-1900	734-1708
Vital Records Div 2600 Bull St *Web:* www.scdhec.gov/vr	Columbia	SC	29201	803-898-3630	898-3761
Vocational Rehabilitation Dept PO Box 15 *Web:* www.scvrd.net	West Columbia	SC	29171	803-896-6500	896-6529
Wildlife & Freshwater Fisheries Div PO Box 167 *Web:* www.dnr.state.sc.us/wild	Columbia	SC	29202	803-734-3889	734-6020
Workers' Compensation Commission PO Box 1715 *Web:* www.wcc.state.sc.us	Columbia	SC	29202	803-737-5700	737-5764

342-42 South Dakota

				Phone	Fax
State Government Information *Web:* www.state.sd.us		SD		605-773-3011	
Adult Services & Aging Office 700 Governors Dr *Web:* www.state.sd.us/social/asa	Pierre	SD	57501	605-773-3656	773-6834
Agriculture Dept 523 E Capitol Ave *Web:* www.state.sd.us/doa	Pierre	SD	57501	605-773-3375	773-5926
Arts Council 800 Governors Dr *Web:* www.artscouncil.sd.gov	Pierre	SD	57501	605-773-3131	773-6962
Attorney General 1302 E Hwy 14 *Web:* www.state.sd.us/attorney	Pierre	SD	57501	605-773-3215	773-4106
Banking Div 217 1/2 W Missouri Ave *Web:* www.state.sd.us/drr2/reg/bank	Pierre	SD	57501	605-773-3421	773-5367
Bill Status 500 E Capitol *Web:* legis.state.sd.us	Pierre	SD	57501	605-773-3251	
Career Center Div 116 W Missouri Ave *Web:* www.sdjobs.org	Pierre	SD	57501	605-773-3101	773-6680
Child Protection Services 700 Governors Dr *Web:* www.state.sd.us/social/CPS	Pierre	SD	57501	605-773-3227	773-6834
Child Support Div 700 Governors Dr *TF:* 800-286-9145 ■ *Web:* www.state.sd.us/social/DCS	Pierre	SD	57501	605-773-3641	773-7295
Consumer Protection Div 500 E Capitol Ave *Web:* www.state.sd.us/attorney	Pierre	SD	57501	605-773-4400	773-7163
Corrections Dept 500 E Capital Ave *Web:* www.state.sd.us/corrections/corrections.html	Pierre	SD	57501	605-773-3478	773-3194
Crime Victims' Compensation Program 700 Governors Dr *TF:* 800-696-9476 ■ *Web:* www.state.sd.us/social/cvc	Pierre	SD	57501	605-773-6317	773-6834
Economic Development Office 711 E Wells Ave *TF:* 800-872-6190 ■ *Web:* www.sdgreatprofits.com	Pierre	SD	57501	605-773-3301	773-3256
Education & Cultural Affairs Dept 700 Governors Dr *Web:* doe.sd.gov	Pierre	SD	57501	605-773-3134	773-6139
Emergency Management Office 118 W Capitol Ave *Web:* oem.sd.gov/home.htm	Pierre	SD	57501	605-773-3231	773-5380
Environment & Natural Resources Dept 523 E Capitol Ave *Web:* www.state.sd.us/denr	Pierre	SD	57501	605-773-3151	773-6035
Finance & Management Bureau 500 E Capitol Ave Rm A-216 *Web:* www.state.sd.us/bfm	Pierre	SD	57501	605-773-3411	773-4711
Game Fish & Parks Dept 523 E Capitol Ave *Web:* www.sdgfp.info	Pierre	SD	57501	605-773-3485	773-6245
Gaming Commission 221 W Capitol Ave Suite 101 *Web:* www.state.sd.us/drr2/reg/gaming	Pierre	SD	57501	605-773-6050	773-6053
Governor 500 E Capitol Ave *Web:* www.state.sd.us/governor	Pierre	SD	57501	605-773-3212	773-5844
Health Dept 600 E Capitol Ave *Web:* www.state.sd.us/doh	Pierre	SD	57501	605-773-3361	773-5683
Highway Patrol Div 118 W Capitol Ave *Web:* hp.state.sd.us	Pierre	SD	57501	605-773-3105	773-6046
Historical Society 900 Governors Dr *Web:* www.sdhistory.org	Pierre	SD	57501	605-773-3458	773-6041
Housing Development Authority PO Box 1237 *Web:* www.sdhda.org	Pierre	SD	57501	605-773-3181	773-5154
Human Services Dept 500 E Capitol Ave *Web:* www.state.sd.us/dhs	Pierre	SD	57501	605-373-5990	773-5483
Information & Telecommunications Bureau 700 Governors Dr *Web:* www.state.sd.us/bit	Pierre	SD	57501	605-773-5110	773-6040
Insurance Div 445 E Capitol Ave *Web:* www.state.sd.us/drr2/reg/insurance	Pierre	SD	57501	605-773-3563	773-5369
Labor Dept 700 Governors Dr *Web:* www.state.sd.us/dol	Pierre	SD	57501	605-773-3101	773-4211
Legislature Capitol Bldg 500 E Capitol Ave *Web:* legis.state.sd.us	Pierre	SD	57501	605-773-3251	773-4576
Lieutenant Governor 500 E Capitol Ave *Web:* www.state.sd.us/Lt.Gov	Pierre	SD	57501	605-773-3661	773-4711
Lottery PO Box 7107 *Web:* www.sdlottery.org	Pierre	SD	57501	605-773-5770	773-5786
Military & Veterans Affairs Dept 2823 W Main St *Web:* www.state.sd.us/military/military.html	Rapid City	SD	57702	605-737-6200	737-6677
Motor Vehicle Div 445 E Capital Ave *Web:* www.state.sd.us/drr2/motorvehicle	Pierre	SD	57501	605-773-3541	773-5129
Pardons & Parole Board PO Box 5911 *Web:* www.state.sd.us/corrections/parole.htm	Sioux Falls	SD	57117	605-367-5040	367-5025
Parks & Recreation Div 523 E Capitol Ave *TF Campground R:* 800-710-2267 ■ *Web:* www.sdgfp.info/Parks	Pierre	SD	57501	605-773-3391	773-6245
Personnel Bureau 500 E Capitol Ave *Web:* www.state.sd.us/jobs	Pierre	SD	57501	605-773-3148	773-4356
Public Utilities Commission 500 E Capitol Ave *Web:* www.state.sd.us/puc	Pierre	SD	57501	605-773-3201	773-3809
Real Estate Commission 221 W Capitol Ave Suite 101 *Web:* www.state.sd.us/sdrec	Pierre	SD	57501	605-773-3600	773-4356
Regents Board 306 E Capitol Ave Suite 200 *Web:* www.sdbor.edu	Pierre	SD	57501	605-773-3455	733-5320
Rehabilitation Services Div 500 E Capitol Ave *TF:* 800-265-9684 ■ *Web:* www.state.sd.us/dhs/drs	Pierre	SD	57501	605-773-3195	773-5483
Revenue & Regulation Dept 445 E Capitol Ave *Web:* www.state.sd.us/drr	Pierre	SD	57501	605-773-3311	773-5129
Secretary of State 500 E Capitol Ave Suite 204 *Web:* www.sdsos.gov	Pierre	SD	57501	605-773-3537	773-6580
Securities Div 445 E Capitol Ave *Web:* www.state.sd.us/drr2/reg/securities	Pierre	SD	57501	605-773-4823	773-5953
Social Services Dept 700 Governors Dr *Web:* www.state.sd.us/social	Pierre	SD	57501	605-773-3165	773-4855
State Court Administrator 500 E Capitol Ave *Web:* www.sdjudicial.com	Pierre	SD	57501	605-773-3474	773-5627
Supreme Court 500 E Capitol Ave *Web:* www.sdjudicial.com	Pierre	SD	57501	605-773-3511	773-6128
Transportation Dept 700 E Broadway Ave *Web:* www.sddot.com	Pierre	SD	57501	605-773-3265	773-3921
Treasurer 500 E Capitol Ave Suite 212 *Web:* www.sdtreasurer.com	Pierre	SD	57501	605-773-3378	773-3115
Tribal Government Relations Office 711 E Wells Ave *Web:* www.sdtribalrelations.com	Pierre	SD	57501	605-773-3415	773-6592
Vital Records 600 E Capitol Ave *TF:* 800-738-2301 ■ *Web:* www.state.sd.us/doh/VitalRec	Pierre	SD	57501	605-773-4961	773-5683
Weights & Measures Office 118 W Capitol Ave *Web:* www.state.sd.us/dps/wm	Pierre	SD	57501	605-773-3697	773-6631
Tourism Office 711 E Wells Ave *TF:* 800-952-3625 ■ *Web:* www.travelsd.com	Pierre	SD	57501	605-773-3301	773-3256

342-43 Tennessee

				Phone	Fax
State Government Information *Web:* www.tennessee.gov		TN		615-741-3011	
Administrative Office of the Courts 511 Union St Suite 600 *Web:* www.tsc.state.tn.us	Nashville	TN	37219	615-741-2687	741-6285
Aging & Disability Commission 500 Deaderick St 8th Fl *Web:* www.state.tn.us/comaging	Nashville	TN	37243	615-741-2056	741-3309
Agriculture Dept 440 Hogan Rd PO Box 40627 *Web:* www.state.tn.us/agriculture	Nashville	TN	37204	615-837-5100	837-5333
Arts Commission 401 Charlotte Ave *Web:* www.arts.state.tn.us	Nashville	TN	37243	615-741-1701	741-8559
Attorney General PO Box 20207 *Web:* www.attorneygeneral.state.tn.us	Nashville	TN	37202	615-741-3491	741-2009
Baccalaureate Education System Trust (BEST) PO Box 198786 *TF:* 888-486-2378 ■ *Web:* www.treasury.state.tn.us/best.htm	Nashville	TN	37219	615-532-8056	734-6467
Bill Status 320 6th Ave N 1st Fl *Web:* www.legislature.state.tn.us	Nashville	TN	37243	615-741-3511	
Boxing & Racing Board 500 James Robertson Pkwy 2nd Fl	Nashville	TN	37243	615-741-2384	741-5995
Child Support Services Div 400 Deaderick St 12th Fl *TF:* 800-838-6911 ■ *Web:* www.state.tn.us/humanserv/child_support.htm	Nashville	TN	37248	615-313-4880	532-2791
Children's Services Dept 436 6th Ave N 7th Fl *Web:* www.state.tn.us/youth	Nashville	TN	37243	615-741-9699	532-8079
Commerce & Insurance Dept 500 James Robertson Pkwy 5th Fl *Web:* www.state.tn.us/commerce	Nashville	TN	37423	615-741-6007	532-6934
Consumer Affairs Div 500 James Robertson Pkwy 5th Fl *Web:* www.state.tn.us/consumer	Nashville	TN	37243	615-741-4737	532-4994
Correction Dept 320 6th Ave N 4th Fl *Web:* www.state.tn.us/correction	Nashville	TN	37243	615-741-1000	741-4605
Criminal Injuries Compensation Program 710 James Robertson Pkwy 9th Fl *Web:* www.treasury.state.tn.us/injury.htm	Nashville	TN	37243	615-741-2734	532-4979
Economic & Community Development Dept 312 8th Ave N 11th Fl *Web:* www.tnecd.gov	Nashville	TN	37243	615-741-1888	741-7306
Education Dept 710 James Robertson Pkwy 6th Fl *Web:* www.state.tn.us/education	Nashville	TN	37243	615-741-2731	532-4791
Emergency Management Agency 3041 Sidco Dr *Web:* www.tnema.org	Nashville	TN	37204	615-741-0001	242-9635
Environment & Conservation Dept 401 Church St L & C Annex 1st Fl *Web:* www.state.tn.us/environment	Nashville	TN	37243	615-532-0109	532-0120
Finance & Administration Dept State Capitol 1st Fl *Web:* www.state.tn.us/finance	Nashville	TN	37243	615-741-2401	741-9872
Financial Institutions Dept 511 Union St 4th Fl *Web:* www.state.tn.us/financialinst	Nashville	TN	37219	615-741-2236	741-2883
General Assembly 320 6th Ave N *Web:* www.legislature.state.tn.us	Nashville	TN	37243	615-741-3511	532-6973
Governor State Capitol 1st Fl *Web:* www.tennessee.gov/governor	Nashville	TN	37243	615-741-2001	532-9711
Health Dept 425 5th Ave N 3rd Fl *Web:* www.state.tn.us/health	Nashville	TN	37247	615-741-3111	741-2491
Higher Education Commission 404 James Robertson Pkwy Suite 1900 *Web:* state.tn.us/thec	Nashville	TN	37243	615-741-3605	741-6230
Highway Patrol 1150 Foster Ave *Web:* www.state.tn.us/safety/thp.htm	Nashville	TN	37249	615-251-5175	532-1051
Historical Commission 2941 Lebanon Rd *Web:* www.state.tn.us/environment/hist	Nashville	TN	37214	615-532-1550	532-1549
Homeland Security Office 312 8th Ave N 25th Fl *Web:* www.tennessee.gov/homelandsecurity	Nashville	TN	37243	615-532-7825	253-5379
Housing Development Agency 404 James Robertson Pkwy Suite 1114 *Web:* www.state.tn.us/thda	Nashville	TN	37243	615-741-2400	741-9634
Human Services Dept 400 Deaderick St *Web:* www.state.tn.us/humanserv	Nashville	TN	37248	615-313-4700	741-4165

				Phone	Fax
Information Resources Office 312 8th Ave N 16th Fl *Web:* www.state.tn.us/finance/oir	Nashville	TN	37243	615-741-3700	532-0471
Insurance Div 500 James Robertson Pkwy 5th Fl *Web:* www.state.tn.us/commerce/insurance	Nashville	TN	37243	615-741-2176	532-2788
Labor & Workforce Development Dept 710 James Robertson Pkwy 8th Fl *Web:* www.state.tn.us/labor-wfd	Nashville	TN	37243	615-741-6642	741-5078
Lieutenant Governor 1 Legislative Plaza	Nashville	TN	37243	615-741-2368	741-9349
Lottery 200 Athens Way Suite 200 *Web:* www.tnlottery.com	Nashville	TN	37228	615-324-6500	
Mental Health & Developmental Disabilities Dept 425 5th Ave N 3rd Fl *TF:* 800-669-1851 ■ *Web:* www.state.tn.us/mental	Nashville	TN	37243	615-532-6500	532-6514
Military Dept 3041 Sidco Dr *Web:* www.tnmilitary.org	Nashville	TN	37204	615-313-3001	313-3129
Personnel Dept 505 Deaderick St *Web:* www.state.tn.us/personnel	Nashville	TN	37243	615-741-2958	532-0728
Probation & Parole Board 404 James Robertson Pkwy Suite 1300 *Web:* www2.tennessee.gov/bopp	Nashville	TN	37243	615-741-1673	532-8581
Real Estate Commission 500 James Robertson Pkwy Suite 180 *TF:* 800-342-4031 ■ *Web:* www.state.tn.us/commerce/boards/trec	Nashville	TN	37243	615-741-2273	741-0313
Regulatory Authority 460 James Robertson Pkwy *Web:* www.state.tn.us/tra	Nashville	TN	37243	615-741-2904	741-5015
Regulatory Boards Div 500 James Robertson Pkwy *Web:* www.state.tn.us/commerce/boards	Nashville	TN	37243	615-741-3449	741-6470
Rehabilitation Services Div 400 Deaderick St 11th Fl *Web:* www.state.tn.us/humanserv/rehabilitation.htm	Nashville	TN	37248	615-313-4700	741-4165
Revenue Dept 500 Deaderick St *Web:* www.state.tn.us/revenue	Nashville	TN	37242	615-741-2461	741-0682
Secretary of State State Capitol 1st Fl *Web:* www.state.tn.us/sos	Nashville	TN	37243	615-741-2819	532-9547
Securities Div 500 James Robertson Pkwy Suite 680 *Web:* www.state.tn.us/commerce/securities	Nashville	TN	37243	615-741-2947	532-8375
State Parks Div 401 Church St 7th Fl *TF:* 888-867-2757 ■ *Web:* www.state.tn.us/environment/parks	Nashville	TN	37243	615-532-0001	532-0732
Student Assistance Corp 404 James Robertson Pkwy Suite 1510 *TF:* 800-257-6526 ■ *Web:* state.tn.us/tsac	Nashville	TN	37243	615-741-1346	741-6101
Supreme Court 401 7th Ave N *Web:* www.tsc.state.tn.us	Nashville	TN	37219	615-253-1470	532-8757
Title & Registration Div 44 Vantage Way Suite 160 *Web:* www.state.tn.us/safety/titleandregistration	Nashville	TN	37243	615-741-3101	401-6782
Tourist Development Dept 312 8th Ave N 25th Fl *Web:* www.state.tn.us/tourdev	Nashville	TN	37243	615-741-2159	741-7225
Transportation Dept 505 Deaderick St Suite 700 *Web:* www.tdot.state.tn.us	Nashville	TN	37243	615-741-2848	741-2508
Treasury Dept State Capitol 1st Fl *Web:* www.treasury.state.tn.us	Nashville	TN	37243	615-741-2956	532-1591
Veterans Affairs Dept 215 8th Ave N *Web:* www.state.tn.us/veteran	Nashville	TN	37243	615-741-2931	741-4785
Vital Records Div 421 5th Ave N 1st Fl *Web:* www2.state.tn.us/health/vr	Nashville	TN	37247	615-741-1763	741-9860
Wildlife Resources Agency PO Box 40747 *Web:* www.state.tn.us/twra	Nashville	TN	37204	615-781-6500	741-4606
Workers Compensation Div 710 James Robertson Pkwy 2nd Fl *Web:* www.state.tn.us/labor-wfd/wcomp.html	Nashville	TN	37243	615-741-2395	532-1468

342-44 Texas

				Phone	Fax
State Government Information *Web:* www.texas.gov		TX		512-463-4630	
Aging & Disability Services Dept 701 W 51st St PO Box 149030 *Web:* www.dads.state.tx.us	Austin	TX	78714	512-438-3011	438-4747
Agriculture Dept PO Box 12847 *Web:* www.agr.state.tx.us	Austin	TX	78711	512-463-7476	463-1104
Arts Commission PO Box 13406 *Web:* www.arts.state.tx.us	Austin	TX	78711	512-463-5535	475-2699
Assistive & Rehabilitation Services Dept 4800 N Lamar Blvd 3rd Fl *TF:* 800-252-5204 ■ *Web:* www.dars.state.tx.us	Austin	TX	78756	512-377-0500	407-3251
Attorney General PO Box 12548 *Web:* www.oag.state.tx.us	Austin	TX	78711	512-463-2191	463-2063
Banking Dept 2601 N Lamar Blvd *Web:* www.banking.state.tx.us	Austin	TX	78705	512-475-1300	475-1313
Bill Status State Capitol 1100 Congress Ave Rm 2N-3 *TF:* 877-824-7038 ■ *Web:* www.capitol.state.tx.us	Austin	TX	78711	512-463-2182	475-4626
Child Support Div MC 040 PO Box 12017 *TF:* 800-252-8014 ■ *Web:* www.oag.state.tx.us/child/index.shtml	Austin	TX	78711	512-460-6000	834-9712
Comptroller of Public Accounts 111 E 17th St *TF:* 800-531-5441 ■ *Web:* www.cpa.state.tx.us	Austin	TX	78774	512-463-4600	475-0352
Consumer Protection Div PO Box 12548 *TF:* 800-621-0508 ■ *Web:* www.oag.state.tx.us/consumer/consumer.shtml	Austin	TX	78711	512-463-2185	473-8301
Court Administration Office 205 W 14th St *Web:* www.courts.state.tx.us	Austin	TX	78711	512-463-1625	463-1648
Crime Victims Compensation Div PO Box 12198 *TF:* 800-983-9933 ■ *Web:* www.oag.state.tx.us/victims/cvc.shtml	Austin	TX	78711	512-936-1200	320-8270
Criminal Justice Dept PO Box 13084 *Web:* www.tdcj.state.tx.us	Austin	TX	78711	512-475-3250	305-9398
Economic Development Dept 1700 N Congress Ave PO Box 12728 *Web:* www.tded.state.tx.us	Austin	TX	78711	512-936-0100	936-0440
Education Agency 1701 N Congress Ave *Web:* www.tea.state.tx.us	Austin	TX	78701	512-463-9734	463-9838
Emergency Management Div PO Box 4087 *Web:* www.demwmd.net	Austin	TX	78773	512-424-2138	424-2444
Environmental Quality Commission 12100 Park 35 Cir PO Box 13087 *Web:* www.tceq.state.tx.us	Austin	TX	78711	512-239-1000	239-5533
Ethics Commission 201 E 14th St 10th Fl *TF:* 800-325-8506 ■ *Web:* www.ethics.state.tx.us	Austin	TX	78701	512-463-5800	463-5777
Family & Protective Services Dept 701 W 51st St PO Box 149030 *Web:* www.dfps.state.tx.us	Austin	TX	78752	512-438-4800	438-3525
General Land Office 1700 N Congress Ave *Web:* www.glo.state.tx.us	Austin	TX	78701	512-463-5001	475-1558
Governor PO Box 12428 *Web:* www.governor.state.tx.us	Austin	TX	78711	512-463-2000	463-1849
Higher Education Coordinating Board PO Box 12788 *Web:* www.thecb.state.tx.us	Austin	TX	78711	512-427-6101	427-6169
Historical Commission PO Box 12276 *Web:* www.thc.state.tx.us	Austin	TX	78711	512-463-6100	463-8222
Housing & Community Affairs Dept 507 Sabine St PO Box 13941 *Web:* www.tdhca.state.tx.us	Austin	TX	78711	512-475-3800	472-8526
Information Resources Dept 300 W 15th St Suite 1300 *Web:* www.dir.state.tx.us	Austin	TX	78701	512-475-4700	475-4759
Insurance Dept 333 Guadalupe St PO Box 149104 *Web:* www.tdi.state.tx.us	Austin	TX	78714	512-463-6169	475-2005
Legislature State Capitol *Web:* www.capitol.state.tx.us	Austin	TX	78711	512-463-4630	463-0694
Licensing & Regulation Dept PO Box 12157 *Web:* www.license.state.tx.us	Austin	TX	78711	512-463-6599	475-2874
Lieutenant Governor PO Box 12068 *Web:* www.ltgov.state.tx.us	Austin	TX	78711	512-463-0001	936-6700
Lottery Commission PO Box 16630 *TF:* 800-375-6886 ■ *Web:* www.txlottery.org	Austin	TX	78761	512-344-5000	478-3682
Medical Examiners Board PO Box 2018 *Web:* www.tsbme.state.tx.us	Austin	TX	78768	512-305-7010	305-7008
Motor Vehicle Div 125 E 11th St *Web:* www.dot.state.tx.us/mvd	Austin	TX	78701	512-416-4800	416-4890
Pardons & Parole Board PO Box 13401 Suite 50 *Web:* www.tdcj.state.tx.us/bpp	Austin	TX	78701	512-936-6351	463-8120
Parks & Wildlife Dept 4200 Smith School Rd *TF:* 800-792-1112 ■ *Web:* www.tpwd.state.tx.us	Austin	TX	78744	512-389-4800	389-4814
Public Safety Dept 5805 N Lamar Blvd *Web:* www.txdps.state.tx.us	Austin	TX	78752	512-424-2000	424-5708
Public Utility Commission PO Box 13326 *TF:* 888-782-8477 ■ *Web:* www.puc.state.tx.us	Austin	TX	78711	512-936-7000	936-7003
Racing Commission 8505 Cross Park Dr Suite 110 *Web:* www.txrc.state.tx.us	Austin	TX	78754	512-833-6699	833-6907
Railroad Commission PO Box 12967 *Web:* www.rrc.state.tx.us	Austin	TX	78711	512-463-7288	463-7161
Real Estate Commission PO Box 12188 *Web:* www.trec.state.tx.us	Austin	TX	78711	512-465-3900	465-3910
Secretary of State PO Box 12697 *Web:* www.sos.state.tx.us	Austin	TX	78711	512-463-5770	475-2761
State Health Services Dept 1100 W 49th St *Web:* www.tdh.texas.gov	Austin	TX	78756	512-458-7111	458-7750
Securities Board PO Box 13167 *Web:* www.ssb.state.tx.us	Austin	TX	78711	512-305-8300	305-8310
Supreme Court 201 W 14th St PO Box 12248 *Web:* www.supreme.courts.state.tx.us	Austin	TX	78711	512-463-1312	463-1365
Tourism Div PO Box 12728 *TF:* 800-888-8839 ■ *Web:* www.traveltex.com	Austin	TX	78711	512-462-9191	936-0089
Transportation Dept 125 E 11th St *Web:* www.dot.state.tx.us	Austin	TX	78701	512-463-8585	463-9896
Veterans Commission PO Box 12277 *Web:* www.tvc.state.tx.us	Austin	TX	78711	512-463-5538	475-2395
Vital Statistics Bureau PO Box 12040 **Fax Area Code:* 512 ■ *Web:* www.tdh.state.tx.us/bvs	Austin	TX	78711	888-963-7111	458-7111*
Workers Compensation Commission 7551 Metro Center Dr *TF:* 800-372-7713 ■ *Web:* www.twcc.state.tx.us	Austin	TX	78744	512-804-4000	804-4001
Workforce Commission 101 E 15th St *Web:* www.twc.state.tx.us	Austin	TX	78778	512-463-2222	936-3504
Youth Commission 4900 N Lamar Blvd *Web:* www.tyc.state.tx.us	Austin	TX	78751	512-424-6130	424-6236

342-45 Utah

				Phone	Fax
State Government Information *Web:* www.utah.gov		UT		801-538-3000	
Administrative Office of the Courts 450 S State St *Web:* www.utcourts.gov	Salt Lake City	UT	84114	801-578-3800	578-3843
Aging & Adult Services Div 120 N 200 West Rm 325 *Web:* www.hsdaas.utah.gov	Salt Lake City	UT	84103	801-538-3910	538-4395
Agriculture & Food Dept PO Box 146500 *Web:* www.ag.utah.gov	Salt Lake City	UT	84114	801-538-7100	538-7126
Arts Council 617 E South Temple *Web:* arts.utah.gov	Salt Lake City	UT	84102	801-236-7555	236-7556
Attorney General PO Box 142320 *Web:* attorneygeneral.utah.gov	Salt Lake City	UT	84114	801-538-9600	538-1121
Bill Status 419 State Capitol *Web:* le.utah.gov/Documents/bills.htm	Salt Lake City	UT	84114	801-538-1588	538-1728
Child & Family Services Div 120 N 200 West Rm 225 *Web:* www.hsdcfs.utah.gov	Salt Lake City	UT	84103	801-538-4100	538-3993
Child Support Div 515 E 100 South 8th Fl *Web:* attorneygeneral.utah.gov/childsupport.html	Salt Lake City	UT	84114	801-536-8300	536-8315
Commerce Dept PO Box 146701 *Web:* www.commerce.utah.gov	Salt Lake City	UT	84114	801-530-6701	530-6446
Community & Economic Development Dept 324 S State St Suite 500 *Web:* dced.utah.gov	Salt Lake City	UT	84111	801-538-8700	538-8888
Consumer Protection Div 160 E 300 South *Web:* www.commerce.utah.gov/dcp	Salt Lake City	UT	84114	801-530-6601	530-6001
Corrections Dept 14717 S Minuteman Dr *Web:* www.corrections.utah.gov	Draper	UT	84020	801-265-5500	265-5726
Crime Victim Reparations Office 350 E 500 South Suite 200 *Web:* www.crimevictim.utah.gov	Salt Lake City	UT	84111	801-238-2360	533-4127
Education Office 250 E 500 South *Web:* www.usoe.k12.ut.us	Salt Lake City	UT	84111	801-538-7500	538-7521
Emergency Services & Homeland Security Div 1110 State Office Bldg *Web:* des.utah.gov	Salt Lake City	UT	84114	801-538-3400	538-3770
Environmental Quality Dept 168 N 1950 West *Web:* www.eq.state.ut.us	Salt Lake City	UT	84116	801-536-4400	536-0061
Financial Institutions Dept PO Box 146800 *Web:* www.dfi.utah.gov	Salt Lake City	UT	84114	801-538-8830	538-8894
Governor PO Box 142220 *Web:* www.utah.gov/governor	Salt Lake City	UT	84114	801-538-1000	538-1528
Health Dept 288 N 1460 West *Web:* health.utah.gov	Salt Lake City	UT	84116	801-538-6111	538-6306
Higher Education Assistance Authority 60 S 400 West *TF:* 877-336-7378 ■ *Web:* www.uheaa.org	Salt Lake City	UT	84101	801-321-7294	366-8431
Higher Education System 60 S 400 West *Web:* www.utahsbr.edu	Salt Lake City	UT	84101	801-321-7101	321-7199
Highway Patrol 4501 S 2700 West *Web:* highwaypatrol.utah.gov	Salt Lake City	UT	84119	801-965-4518	965-4716
Housing Corp 2479 Lake Park Blvd *Web:* www.utahhousingcorp.org	West Valley City	UT	84120	801-902-8200	
Human Resource Management Dept 2120 State Office Bldg *Web:* www.dhrm.utah.gov	Salt Lake City	UT	84114	801-538-3025	538-3403
Human Services Dept PO Box 45500 *Web:* www.dhs.utah.gov	Salt Lake City	UT	84145	801-538-4171	538-4016
Information Technology Services 6000 State Office Bldg *Web:* www.its.state.ut.us	Salt Lake City	UT	84114	801-538-3833	538-3622
Insurance Dept 3110 State Office Bldg *Web:* www.insurance.utah.gov	Salt Lake City	UT	84114	801-538-3800	538-3829

Utah (Cont'd)

				Phone	Fax
Labor Commission PO Box 146600 *Web:* www.labor.state.ut.us	Salt Lake City	UT	84114	801-530-6800	530-6390
Legislature State Capitol Complex West Bldg *Web:* le.utah.gov	Salt Lake City	UT	84114	801-538-1029	538-1908
Lieutenant Governor PO Box 142220 *Web:* www.utah.gov/ltgovernor	Salt Lake City	UT	84114	801-538-1000	538-1557
Medical Examiner 48 Medical Dr *Web:* health.utah.gov/ome	Salt Lake City	UT	84113	801-584-8410	584-8435
Motor Vehicle Div 210 N 1950 West *Web:* dmv.utah.gov	Salt Lake City	UT	84134	801-297-7780	297-3570
Natural Resources Dept 1594 W North Temple Suite 3710 *Web:* www.nr.utah.gov	Salt Lake City	UT	84116	801-538-7200	538-7315
Occupational & Professional Licensing Div PO Box 146741 *Web:* www.dopl.utah.gov	Salt Lake City	UT	84111	801-530-6628	530-6511
Pardons & Parole Board 448 E 6400 South Suite 300 *Web:* bop.utah.gov	Murray	UT	84107	801-261-6464	261-6481
Parks & Recreation Div PO Box 146001 *TF Campground R:* 800-322-3770 ■ *Web:* www.stateparks.utah.gov	Salt Lake City	UT	84114	801-538-7220	538-7378
Public Service Commission PO Box 45585 *Web:* www.psc.state.ut.us	Salt Lake City	UT	84145	801-530-6716	530-6796
Real Estate Div PO Box 146711 *Web:* www.commerce.utah.gov/dre	Salt Lake City	UT	84114	801-530-6747	530-6749
Rehabilitation Office 250 E 500 South *TF:* 800-473-7530 ■ *Web:* www.usor.utah.gov	Salt Lake City	UT	84111	801-538-7530	538-7522
Securities Div 160 E 300 South *Web:* www.securities.state.ut.us	Salt Lake City	UT	84114	801-530-6600	530-6980
Sports Commission 201 S Main St Suite 2002 *Web:* www.utahsportscommission.com	Salt Lake City	UT	84111	801-328-2372	328-2389
State History Div 300 S Rio Grande St *Web:* history.utah.gov	Salt Lake City	UT	84101	801-533-3500	533-3503
State Treasurer PO Box 142315 *Web:* www.treasurer.utah.gov	Salt Lake City	UT	84114	801-538-1042	538-1465
Supreme Court 450 S State St *Web:* www.utcourts.gov/courts/sup	Salt Lake City	UT	84114	801-238-7967	238-7980
Tax Commission 210 N 1950 West *Web:* www.tax.utah.gov	Salt Lake City	UT	84134	801-297-2200	297-3891
Transportation Dept 4501 S 2700 West *Web:* udot.utah.gov	Salt Lake City	UT	84119	801-965-4000	965-4338
Travel Development Div 300 N State St *TF:* 800-200-1160 ■ *Web:* travel.utah.gov	Salt Lake City	UT	84114	801-538-1900	538-1399
Veterans' Affairs Office 550 Foothills Blvd Suite 206 *Web:* www.ut.ngb.army.mil/veterans	Salt Lake City	UT	84108	801-326-2372	326-2369
Vital Records & Statistics Office PO Box 141012 *Web:* health.utah.gov/vitalrecords	Salt Lake City	UT	84114	801-538-6105	538-9467
Wildlife Resources Div 1594 W North Temple Suite 2110 *Web:* www.wildlife.utah.gov	Salt Lake City	UT	84116	801-538-4700	538-4709
Workers' Compensation Fund PO Box 57929	Murray	UT	84157	801-288-8000	288-8938
Workforce Services Dept 140 E 300 South *Web:* jobs.utah.gov	Salt Lake City	UT	84111	801-526-9675	526-9211

342-46 Vermont

				Phone	Fax
State Government Information *Web:* www.vermont.gov		VT		802-828-1110	
Aging & Disabilities Dept 103 S Main St *Web:* dail.vermont.gov/	Waterbury	VT	05671	802-241-2401	241-2325
Agriculture Food & Markets Dept 116 State St *Web:* www.vermontagriculture.com	Montpelier	VT	05620	802-828-2430	828-2361
Arts Council 136 State St *Web:* www.vermontartscouncil.org	Montpelier	VT	05633	802-828-3291	828-3363
Attorney General 109 State St *Web:* www.state.vt.us/atg	Montpelier	VT	05609	802-828-3171	828-2154
Banking Div 89 Main St *Web:* www.bishca.state.vt.us	Montpelier	VT	05620	802-828-3307	828-1477
Bill Status 115 State St State House *Web:* www.leg.state.vt.us	Montpelier	VT	05633	802-828-2231	828-2424
Chief Medical Examiner 111 Colchester Ave	Burlington	VT	05401	802-863-7320	863-7265
Child Support Office 103 S Main St *TF:* 800-786-3214 ■ *Web:* www.ocs.state.vt.us	Waterbury	VT	05671	802-241-2319	244-1483
Consumer Assistance Program 104 Morrill Hall UVM *Web:* www.atg.state.vt.us	Burlington	VT	05405	802-656-3183	656-1423
Insurance Div 89 Main St *Web:* www.bishca.state.vt.us	Montpelier	VT	05620	802-828-3301	
Corrections Dept 103 S Main St *Web:* www.doc.state.vt.us	Waterbury	VT	05671	802-241-2442	241-2565
Court Administrator 109 State St *Web:* www.vermontjudiciary.org	Montpelier	VT	05609	802-828-3278	828-3457
Crime Victim Services Center 58 S Main St *Web:* www.ccvs.state.vt.us	Waterbury	VT	05676	802-241-1250	241-4337
Prevention Assistance Transition & Health Access (PATH) Dept 103 S Main St *Web:* www.dpath.state.vt.us	Waterbury	VT	05671	802-241-2853	241-2830
Economic Development Dept National Life North Bldg 1 National Life Dr 6th Fl *Web:* www.thinkvermont.com	Montpelier	VT	05620	802-828-3080	828-3258
Education Dept 120 State St *Web:* www.state.vt.us/educ	Montpelier	VT	05620	802-828-3135	828-3140
Educator Licensing Div 120 State St *Web:* education.vermont.gov/	Montpelier	VT	05620	802-828-2445	828-5107
Emergency Management Office 103 S Main St *TF:* 800-347-0488 ■ *Web:* www.dps.state.vt.us/vem	Waterbury	VT	05671	802-244-8721	241-5556
Environmental Conservation Dept 103 S Main St *Web:* www.anr.state.vt.us/dec/dec.htm	Waterbury	VT	05671	802-241-3800	244-5141
Fish & Wildlife Dept 103 S Main St Bldg 10S *Web:* www.anr.state.vt.us/fw/fwhome	Waterbury	VT	05671	802-241-3700	241-3295
General Assembly 115 State St *Web:* www.leg.state.vt.us	Montpelier	VT	05633	802-828-2228	828-2424
Governor 109 State St 5th Fl *Web:* www.vermont.gov/governor	Montpelier	VT	05609	802-828-3333	828-3339
Health Dept 108 Cherry St *Web:* healthvermont.gov/	Burlington	VT	05402	802-863-7200	865-7754
Historic Preservation Div National Life Bldg 1 National Life Dr *TF:* 800-341-2211 ■ *Web:* www.historicvermont.org	Montpelier	VT	05620	802-828-3211	828-3206
Housing & Community Affairs Dept National Life Bldg 1 National Life Dr 6th Fl *TF:* 800-622-4553 ■ *Web:* www.dhca.state.vt.us	Montpelier	VT	05620	802-828-3211	828-2928
Employment & Training Administration Dept 5 Green Mountain Dr *Web:* labor.vermont.gov	Montpelier	VT	05601	802-828-4000	828-4022
Labor & Industry Dept 5 Green Mountain Dr PO Box 488 *Web:* www.state.vt.us/labind	Montpelier	VT	05601	802-828-2288	828-2195
Licensing & Professional Regulation Office National Life Bldg N 2nd Fl *Web:* vtprofessionals.org	Montpelier	VT	05620	802-828-2367	828-2368
Lieutenant Governor State House *Web:* ltgov.vermont.gov/	Montpelier	VT	05633	802-828-2226	828-3198
Lottery Commission 1311 US Route 302 Suite 100 *Web:* www.vtlottery.com	Barre	VT	05641	802-479-5686	479-4294
Medical Practice Board PO Box 70 *Web:* healthvermont.gov/	Burlington	VT	05402	802-657-4220	657-4227
Motor Vehicles Dept 120 State St *Web:* www.aot.state.vt.us/dmv/dmvhp.htm	Montpelier	VT	05603	802-828-2000	828-2098
Natural Resources Agency 103 S Main St *Web:* www.anr.state.vt.us	Waterbury	VT	05671	802-241-3600	244-1102
Parks Div 103 S Main St Bldg 10S *TF Campground R:* 888-409-7579 ■ *Web:* www.vtstateparks.com	Waterbury	VT	05671	802-241-3655	244-1481
Public Service Board 112 State St 4th Fl *Web:* www.state.vt.us/psb	Montpelier	VT	05620	802-828-2358	828-3351
Real Estate Commission 81 River St Drawer 9	Montpelier	VT	05609	802-828-3228	828-2368
Secretary of State 26 Terrace St Drawer 9 *Web:* www.sec.state.vt.us	Montpelier	VT	05609	802-828-2363	828-2496
Securities Div 89 Main St *Web:* www.bishca.state.vt.us	Montpelier	VT	05620	802-828-3420	828-2896
Social & Rehabilitation Services Dept 103 S Main St *Web:* www.dcf.state.vt.us/	Waterbury	VT	05671	802-241-2100	241-2407
State Police 103 S Main St *Web:* www.dps.state.vt.us/vtsp	Waterbury	VT	05671	802-244-7345	241-5551
Supreme Court 109 State St *Web:* www.vermontjudiciary.org	Montpelier	VT	05609	802-828-3278	828-3457
Taxes Dept 133 State St *Web:* www.state.vt.us/tax	Montpelier	VT	05609	802-828-2505	828-2701
Tourism & Marketing Dept 6 Baldwin St drawer 22 *TF:* 800-837-6668 ■ *Web:* www.vermontvacation.com	Montpelier	VT	05633	802-828-3237	828-3233
Transportation Agency 1 National Life Dr *Web:* www.aot.state.vt.us	Montpelier	VT	05633	802-828-2657	828-2024
Treasurer 109 State St 4th Fl *Web:* www.vermonttreasurer.gov/	Montpelier	VT	05609	802-828-2301	828-2772
Veterans Affairs Office 118 State St *Web:* www.va.state.vt.us	Montpelier	VT	05620	802-828-3379	828-5932
Vital Records Section PO Box 70 *Web:* healthvermont.gov/	Burlington	VT	05402	802-863-7275	651-1787
Vocational Rehabilitation Div 103 S Main St *TF:* 866-879-6757 ■ *Web:* vocrehab.vermont.gov	Waterbury	VT	05671	802-241-2186	241-3359
Workers' Compensation Div 50 Green Mountain Dr PO Box 488 *Web:* www.labor.vermont.gov/	Montpelier	VT	05601	802-828-2286	828-2195

342-47 Virginia

				Phone	Fax
State Government Information *Web:* www.virginia.gov		VA		804-786-0000	
Aging Dept 1600 Forest Ave Suite 100 *Web:* www.vda.virginia.gov	Richmond	VA	23229	804-662-9333	662-9354
Agriculture & Consumer Services Dept 1100 Bank St Suite 210 *Web:* www.vdacs.virginia.gov	Richmond	VA	23219	804-786-3501	371-2945
Arts Commission 223 Governor St 2nd Fl *Web:* www.arts.state.va.us	Richmond	VA	23219	804-225-3132	225-4327
Attorney General 900 E Main St *Web:* www.oag.state.va.us	Richmond	VA	23219	804-786-2071	786-1991
Bill Status PO Box 406 *Web:* legis.state.va.us	Richmond	VA	23218	804-698-1500	786-3215
Chief Medical Examiner 400 E Jackson St *Web:* www.vdh.virginia.gov/medexam	Richmond	VA	23219	804-786-3174	371-8595
Child Support Enforcement Div 730 E Broad St *TF:* 800-468-8894 ■ *Web:* www.dss.state.va.us/family/dcse.html	Richmond	VA	23219	804-692-1501	692-2553
College Savings Plan PO Box 607 *TF:* 888-567-0540 ■ *Web:* www.virginia529.com	Richmond	VA	23218	804-786-0719	786-2453
Commerce & Trade Office 202 N 9th St Suite 723 *Web:* www.commerce.virginia.gov	Richmond	VA	23219	804-786-7831	371-0250
Community College System 101 N 14th St 15th Fl *Web:* www.vccs.edu	Richmond	VA	23219	804-819-4901	819-4766
Conservation & Recreation Dept 203 Governor St Suite 302 *Web:* www.dcr.state.va.us	Richmond	VA	23219	804-786-6124	786-6141
Consumer Affairs Office PO Box 1163 *Web:* www.vdacs.virginia.gov/consumers	Richmond	VA	23218	804-786-2042	225-2666
Corrections Dept 6900 Atmore Dr *Web:* www.vadoc.state.va.us	Richmond	VA	23225	804-674-3000	674-3509
Criminal Injuries Compensation Fund 11513 Allecingie Pkwy *TF:* 800-522-4007 ■ *Web:* www.vwc.state.va.us	Richmond	VA	23235	804-378-3434	378-4390
Economic Development Partnership 901 E Byrd St *Web:* www.yesvirginia.org	Richmond	VA	23219	804-371-8100	371-8112
Education Dept PO Box 2120 *Web:* www.pen.k12.va.us	Richmond	VA	23218	804-225-2020	371-2099
Emergency Management Dept 10501 Trade Ct *Web:* www.vdem.state.va.us	Richmond	VA	23236	804-897-6500	897-6506
Employment Commission 703 E Main St *Web:* www.vec.virginia.gov	Richmond	VA	23219	804-786-1485	225-3923
Environmental Quality Dept PO Box 10009 *Web:* www.deq.state.va.us	Richmond	VA	23240	804-698-4000	698-4500
Financial Institutions Bureau 1300 E Main St Suite 800 PO Box 640 *Web:* www.scc.virginia.gov/division/banking	Richmond	VA	23218	804-371-9657	371-9416
Game & Inland Fisheries Dept 4010 W Broad St *Web:* www.dgif.state.va.us	Richmond	VA	23230	804-367-1000	367-0405
General Assembly General Assembly Bldg PO Box 396 *Web:* legis.state.va.us	Richmond	VA	23218	804-698-7410	698-7651
Governor Capitol Bldg 3rd Fl *Web:* www.governor.virginia.gov	Richmond	VA	23219	804-786-2211	371-6351
Health Dept PO Box 2448 *Web:* www.vdh.virginia.gov	Richmond	VA	23218	804-864-7001	864-7022
Health Professions Dept 6606 W Broad St 5th Fl *Web:* www.dhp.virginia.gov	Richmond	VA	23230	804-662-9900	662-9943
Historic Resources Dept 2801 Kensington Ave *Web:* www.dhr.state.va.us	Richmond	VA	23221	804-367-2323	367-2391
Housing Development Authority 601 S Belvidere St *TF:* 800-968-7837 ■ *Web:* www.vhda.com	Richmond	VA	23220	804-782-1986	783-6704
Human Resource Management Dept 101 N 14th St 12th Fl *Web:* www.dhrm.virginia.gov	Richmond	VA	23219	804-225-2131	371-7401
Information Technologies Agency 411 E Franklin St Suite 500 *Web:* www.vita.virginia.gov	Richmond	VA	23219	804-225-8482	
Insurance Bureau PO Box 1157 *Web:* www.scc.virginia.gov/division/boi	Richmond	VA	23218	804-371-9741	371-9873

	City	State	Zip	Phone	Fax
Labor & Industry Dept 13 S 13th St	Richmond	VA	23219	804-371-2327	371-6524
Web: www.doli.state.va.us					
Lieutenant Governor 900 E Main St 1st Fl West	Richmond	VA	23219	804-786-2078	786-7514
Web: www.ltgov.virginia.gov					
Lottery Dept 900 E Main St	Richmond	VA	23219	804-692-7777	692-7775
Web: www.valottery.com					
Mental Health Mental Retardation & Substance Abuse Services Dept 1220 Bank St	Richmond	VA	23219	804-786-3921	371-6638
Web: www.dmhmrsas.virginia.gov					
Motor Vehicles Dept PO Box 27412	Richmond	VA	23269	804-367-6600	367-6631
Web: www.dmv.state.va.us					
Parole Board 6900 Atmore Dr	Richmond	VA	23225	804-674-3081	674-3284
Port Authority 600 World Trade Ctr	Norfolk	VA	23510	757-683-8000	683-8500
Web: www.vaports.com					
Professional & Occupational Regulation Dept 3600 W Broad St	Richmond	VA	23230	804-367-8500	367-9537
Web: www.state.va.us/dpor					
Racing Commission 3600 W Broad St	Richmond	VA	23230	804-367-8590	367-2474
Web: www.vrc.virginia.gov					
Rehabilitative Services Dept 8004 Franklin Farms Dr	Richmond	VA	23229	804-662-7000	662-9532
TF: 800-552-5019 ■ *Web:* www.vadrs.org					
Secretary of the Commonwealth 830 E Main St 14th Fl	Richmond	VA	23219	804-786-2441	371-0017
Web: www.soc.state.va.us					
Securities Div PO Box 1197	Richmond	VA	23218	804-371-9051	371-9911
Web: www.scc.virginia.gov/division/srf					
Social Services Dept 7 N 8th St	Richmond	VA	23219	804-726-7000	
Web: www.dss.state.va.us					
State Corporation Commission 1300 E Main St PO Box 1197	Richmond	VA	23218	804-371-9967	371-9836
Web: www.scc.virginia.gov					
State Council of Higher Education 101 N 14th St 9th Fl	Richmond	VA	23219	804-225-2600	225-2604
Web: www.schev.edu					
State Court Administrator 100 N 9th St 3rd Fl	Richmond	VA	23219	804-786-6455	786-4542
Web: www.courts.state.va.us					
State Parks Div 203 Governor St Suite 213	Richmond	VA	23219	804-786-1712	786-9294
TF Resv: 800-933-7275 ■ *Web:* www.dcr.virginia.gov/parks					
State Police PO Box 27472	Richmond	VA	23261	804-674-2000	674-2267
Web: www.vsp.state.va.us					
Supreme Court 100 N 9th St	Richmond	VA	23219	804-786-2251	786-6249
Web: www.courts.state.va.us/scv					
Taxation Dept PO Box 1115	Richmond	VA	23218	804-367-8031	786-3536
Web: www.tax.virginia.gov					
Tourism Corp 901 E Byrd St	Richmond	VA	23219	804-786-2051	786-1919
TF: 800-847-4882 ■ *Web:* www.vatc.org					
Transportation Dept 1401 E Broad St Suite 311	Richmond	VA	23219	804-786-2701	786-2940
Web: virginiadot.org					
Treasury Dept PO Box 1879	Richmond	VA	23218	804-225-2142	225-3187
Web: www.trs.virginia.gov					
Veterans Services Dept 270 Franklin Rd SW Rm 503	Roanoke	VA	24011	540-857-7104	857-7573
Web: www.vdva.vipnet.org					
Vital Records Div PO Box 1000	Richmond	VA	23218	804-662-6200	644-2550
Web: www.vdh.virginia.gov/vitalrec					
Workers Compensation Commission 1000 DMV Dr	Richmond	VA	23220	804-367-8600	367-9740
Web: www.vwc.state.va.us					

342-48 Washington

	City	State	Zip	Phone	Fax
State Government Information		WA		360-753-5000	
Web: access.wa.gov					
Administrative Office of the Courts 1112 Quince St SE PO Box 41174	Olympia	WA	98504	360-753-3365	586-8869
Web: www.courts.wa.gov					
Aging & Disability Services Administration PO Box 45600	Olympia	WA	98504	360-725-2300	407-0369
Web: www.aasa.dshs.wa.gov					
Agriculture Dept PO Box 42560	Olympia	WA	98504	360-902-1800	902-2092
Web: www.agr.wa.gov					
Arts Commission 711 Capitol Way S Suite 600	Olympia	WA	98504	360-753-3860	586-5351
Web: www.arts.wa.gov					
Attorney General PO Box 40100	Olympia	WA	98504	360-753-6200	664-0228
Web: www.atg.wa.gov					
Bill Status PO Box 40600	Olympia	WA	98504	360-786-7573	
TF: 800-562-6000 ■ *Web:* www.leg.wa.gov					
Child Support Div PO Box 45860	Olympia	WA	98504	360-664-5440	586-3274
TF: 800-457-6202 ■ *Web:* www.dshs.wa.gov/dcs					
Children's Administration PO Box 45710	Olympia	WA	98504	360-902-7920	902-7903
Web: www1.dshs.wa.gov/ca					
Community Trade & Economic Development Dept PO Box 42525	Olympia	WA	98504	360-725-4000	586-8440
Web: www.cted.wa.gov					
Consumer Protection Div PO Box 40118	Olympia	WA	98504	360-753-6210	664-2585
Web: www.atg.wa.gov/consumer					
Corrections Dept PO Box 41100	Olympia	WA	98504	360-753-1573	664-4056
Web: www.doc.wa.gov					
Crime Victim Compensation Program PO Box 44520	Olympia	WA	98504	360-902-5355	902-5333
TF: 800-547-8367 ■ *Web:* www.lni.wa.gov/insurance/CrimeVictims					
Ecology Dept PO Box 47600	Olympia	WA	98504	360-407-6000	407-6989
Web: www.ecy.wa.gov					
Emergency Management Div Camp Murray Bldg 20 TA-20	Tacoma	WA	98430	253-512-7000	512-7200
Web: www.emd.wa.gov					
Employment Security Dept PO Box 9046	Olympia	WA	98507	360-902-9360	902-9287
Web: www.wa.gov/esd					
Financial Institutions Dept PO Box 41200	Olympia	WA	98504	360-902-8700	586-5068
Web: www.dfi.wa.gov					
Fish & Wildlife Dept 600 Capitol Way N	Olympia	WA	98501	360-902-2200	902-2156
Web: wdfw.wa.gov					
Governor 302 14th St SW PO Box 40002	Olympia	WA	98504	360-902-4111	753-4110
Web: www.governor.wa.gov					
Health Dept PO Box 47890	Olympia	WA	98504	360-236-4501	586-7424
TF: 800-525-0127 ■ *Web:* www.doh.wa.gov					
Higher Education Coordinating Board 917 Lakeridge Way PO Box 43430	Olympia	WA	98504	360-753-7800	753-7808
Web: www.hecb.wa.gov					
Historical Society 1911 Pacific Ave	Tacoma	WA	98402	253-272-3500	272-9518
TF: 888-238-4378 ■ *Web:* www.wshs.org					
Horse Racing Commission 6326 Martin Way Suite 209	Olympia	WA	98516	360-459-6462	459-6461
Web: www.whrc.wa.gov					
Housing Finance Commission 1000 2nd Ave Suite 2700	Seattle	WA	98104	206-464-7139	587-5113
TF: 800-767-4663 ■ *Web:* www.wshfc.org					
Indeterminate Sentence Review Board PO Box 40907	Olympia	WA	98504	360-493-9266	493-9287
Web: www.srb.wa.gov					
Information Services Dept PO Box 42445	Olympia	WA	98504	360-902-3470	664-0733
Web: www.dis.wa.gov					
Insurance Commissioner PO Box 40255	Olympia	WA	98504	360-725-7000	586-3535
Web: www.insurance.wa.gov					
Labor & Industries Dept PO Box 44000	Olympia	WA	98504	360-902-5800	902-4202
Web: www.lni.wa.gov					
Legislature State Capitol	Olympia	WA	98504	360-786-7550	786-7520
Web: www.leg.wa.gov					
Licensing Dept PO Box 9020	Olympia	WA	98504	360-902-3600	902-4042
Web: www.dol.wa.gov					
Lieutenant Governor PO Box 40400	Olympia	WA	98504	360-786-7700	786-7749
Web: www.ltgov.wa.gov					
Mental Health Div PO Box 45320	Olympia	WA	98504	360-902-8070	902-0809
TF: 888-713-6010 ■ *Web:* www1.dshs.wa.gov/mentalhealth					
Natural Resources Dept PO Box 47001	Olympia	WA	98504	360-902-1000	902-1775
Web: www.wa.gov/dnr					
Personnel Dept PO Box 47500	Olympia	WA	98504	360-664-1960	586-4694
Web: hr.dop.wa.gov					
Professional Educator Standards Board PO Box 47236	Olympia	WA	98504	360-725-6275	586-4548
Web: www.pesb.wa.gov					
Public Disclosure Commission PO Box 40908	Olympia	WA	98504	360-753-1111	753-1112
Web: www.pdc.wa.gov					
Public Instruction Dept PO Box 47200	Olympia	WA	98504	360-753-6000	753-6712
Web: www.k12.wa.us					
Revenue Dept PO Box 47454	Olympia	WA	98504	360-753-5574	586-5543
Web: dor.wa.gov					
Secretary of State PO Box 40220	Olympia	WA	98504	360-902-4151	586-5629
Web: www.secstate.wa.gov					
Securities Div PO Box 9033	Olympia	WA	98507	360-902-8760	902-0524
Web: www.dfi.wa.gov/sd					
Social & Health Services Dept PO Box 45010	Olympia	WA	98504	360-902-8400	902-7848
Web: www.wa.gov/dshs					
State Lottery PO Box 43000	Olympia	WA	98504	360-664-4720	664-2630
Web: www.walottery.com					
State Parks & Recreation Commission PO Box 42650	Olympia	WA	98504	360-902-8500	753-1594
TF Campground R: 888-226-7688 ■ *Web:* www.parks.wa.gov					
State Patrol PO Box 42600	Olympia	WA	98504	360-753-6540	753-2492
Web: www.wa.gov/wsp					
Supreme Court PO Box 40929	Olympia	WA	98504	360-357-2077	357-2102
Web: www.courts.wa.gov					
Tourism Div PO Box 42525	Olympia	WA	98504	360-725-4172	753-4470
Web: www.experiencewashington.com					
Transportation Dept PO Box 47300	Olympia	WA	98504	360-705-7000	705-6800
Web: www.wsdot.wa.gov					
Treasurer PO Box 40200	Olympia	WA	98504	360-902-9000	902-9044
Web: www.tre.wa.gov					
Utilities & Transportation Commission PO Box 47250	Olympia	WA	98504	360-664-1160	664-1150
Web: www.wutc.wa.gov					
Vehicle Services Div PO Box 9020	Olympia	WA	98507	360-902-3820	586-6703
Web: www.dol.wa.gov					
Veterans Affairs Dept PO Box 41150	Olympia	WA	98504	360-753-5586	725-2197
TF: 800-562-2308 ■ *Web:* www.dva.wa.gov					
Vital Records Div PO Box 9709	Olympia	WA	98507	360-236-4300	352-2586
Web: www.doh.wa.gov/EHSPHL/CHS/cert.htm					
Vocational Rehabilitation Div PO Box 45340	Olympia	WA	98504	360-438-8000	438-8007
TF: 800-637-5627 ■ *Web:* www1.dshs.wa.gov/dvr					

342-49 West Virginia

	City	State	Zip	Phone	Fax
State Government Information		WV		304-558-3456	
Web: www.wv.gov					
Accountancy Board 106 Capitol St Suite 100	Charleston	WV	25301	304-558-3557	558-1325
Web: www.wvboacc.org					
Administrative Office of the Courts 1900 Kanawha Blvd E Suite E-100	Charleston	WV	25305	304-558-0145	558-1212
Web: www.state.wv.us/wvsca/AO.htm					
Agriculture Dept 1900 Kanawha Blvd E Bldg 1 Rm E-28	Charleston	WV	25305	304-558-2201	558-2203
Web: www.wvagriculture.org					
Arts Commission 1900 Kanawha Blvd E Cultural Center	Charleston	WV	25305	304-558-0220	558-2779
Web: www.wvculture.org/arts					
Attorney General 1900 Kanawha Blvd E Bldg 1 Rm 26-E	Charleston	WV	25305	304-558-2021	558-0140
Web: www.wvago.gov					
Banking Div 1900 Kanawha Blvd E Bldg 3 Rm 311	Charleston	WV	25305	304-558-2294	558-0442
Web: www.wvdob.org					
Bill Status State Capitol Rm MB27	Charleston	WV	25305	304-347-4831	347-4901
TF: 877-565-3447 ■ *Web:* www.legis.state.wv.us					
Board of Medicine 101 Dee Dr Suite 103	Charleston	WV	25311	304-558-2921	558-2084
Web: www.wvdhhr.org/wvbom					
Public Health Bureau 350 Capitol St Rm 702	Charleston	WV	25301	304-558-2971	558-1035
Web: www.wvdhhr.org/bph					
Chief Medical Examiner 619 Virginia St W	Charleston	WV	25302	304-558-3920	558-7886
Web: www.wvdhhr.org/ocme					
Child Support Enforcement Bureau 350 Capitol St Rm 147	Charleston	WV	25301	304-558-3780	558-4092
TF: 800-249-3778 ■ *Web:* www.wvdhhr.org/bcse					
Children & Families Bureau 350 Capitol St Rm R-730	Charleston	WV	25301	304-558-0628	558-4194
TF: 800-642-8589 ■ *Web:* www.wvdhhr.org/bcf					
Commerce Bureau 80 MacCorkle Ave SW	South Charleston	WV	25303	304-558-2200	558-2956
TF: 800-225-5982 ■ *Web:* www.boc.state.wv.us					
Community Development Div 1900 Kanawha Blvd E Bldg 6 Rm 553	Charleston	WV	25305	304-558-4010	558-3248
TF: 800-982-3386 ■ *Web:* www.wvdo.org/community/index.html					
Consumer Protection Div 812 Quarrier St 1st Fl	Charleston	WV	25301	304-558-8986	558-0184
TF: 800-368-8808 ■ *Web:* www.state.wv.us/wvag					
Corrections Div 112 California Ave Bldg 4 Rm 300	Charleston	WV	25305	304-558-2036	558-5367
Web: www.wvdoc.com/wvdoc/					
Crime Victims Compensation Fund 1900 Kanawha Blvd E Rm W-334	Charleston	WV	25305	304-347-4850	347-4915
TF: 877-562-6878 ■ *Web:* www.legis.state.wv.us/ADA_legishp1a.html					
Tax & Revenue Dept State Capitol Bldg 1 Rm W-300	Charleston	WV	25305	304-558-0211	558-2324
Web: www.wvrevenue.gov					
Development Office 1900 Kanawah Blvd E Bldg 6 Rm 525B	Charleston	WV	25305	304-558-2234	558-1189
TF: 800-982-3386 ■ *Web:* www.wvdo.org					
Education Dept 1900 Kanawha Blvd E Bldg 6 Rm 358	Charleston	WV	25305	304-558-2681	558-0048
Web: wvde.state.wv.us					
Emergency Services Office 1900 Kanawha Blvd E Bldg 1 Rm EB-80	Charleston	WV	25305	304-558-5380	344-4538
Web: www.wvdhsem.gov					
Environmental Protection Dept 601 57th St	Charleston	WV	25304	304-926-0440	926-0446
Web: www.dep.state.wv.us					
Ethics Commission 210 Brooks St Suite 300	Charleston	WV	25301	304-558-0664	558-2169
Web: www.wvethicscommission.org					
Governor State Capitol Bldg 1900 Kanawha Blvd E	Charleston	WV	25305	304-558-2000	342-7025
Web: www.wvgov.org					
Higher Education Policy Commission 1018 Kanawha Blvd E Suite 700	Charleston	WV	25301	304-558-2101	558-5719
TF: 888-825-5707 ■ *Web:* www.hepc.wvnet.edu/students					
Historic Preservation Unit 1900 Kanawha Blvd E	Charleston	WV	25305	304-558-0220	558-2779
Web: www.wvculture.org/shpo					
Housing Development Fund 814 Virginia St E	Charleston	WV	25301	304-345-6475	340-9943
TF: 800-933-9843 ■ *Web:* www.wvhdf.com					

West Virginia (Cont'd)

				Phone	Fax
Insurance Commission PO Box 50540 TF: 888-879-9842 ■ Web: www.wvinsurance.gov	Charleston	WV	25305	304-558-3354	558-0412
Labor Div 1900 Kanawha Blvd E Bldg 6 Rm 749-B TF: 877-558-5134 ■ Web: www.state.wv.us/labor	Charleston	WV	25305	304-558-7890	558-3797
Lottery PO Box 2067 TF: 800-982-4946 ■ Web: www.wvlottery.com	Charleston	WV	25327	304-558-0500	558-0129
Motor Vehicles Div 1800 Kanawha Blvd E Bldg 3 Web: www.wvdot.com/6_motorists/dmv/6G_DMV.HTM	Charleston	WV	25317	304-558-3900	558-1987
Natural Resources Div 1900 Kanawha Blvd E Bldg 3 Rm 669 TF: 800-225-3982 ■ Web: www.dnr.state.wv.us	Charleston	WV	25305	304-558-2754	558-2768
Information Services & Communications Div 321-323 Capitol St Web: www.state.wv.us/ot/	Charleston	WV	25305	304-558-5472	
Parks & Recreation 1900 E Kanawha Blvd E Bldg 3 Rm 714 TF: 800-225-5982 ■ Web: www.wvstateparks.com	Charleston	WV	25305	304-558-2764	558-0077
Probation & Parole Board 112 California Ave Bldg 4 Rm 307	Charleston	WV	25305	304-558-6366	558-5678
Public Service Commission PO Box 812 Web: www.psc.state.wv.us	Charleston	WV	25323	304-340-0300	340-0325
Racing Commission 106 Dee Dr Web: www.wvf.state.wv.us/racing	Charleston	WV	25311	304-558-2150	558-6319
Real Estate Commission 300 Capitol St Suite 400 Web: www.wvrec.org	Charleston	WV	25301	304-558-3555	558-6442
Rehabilitation Services Div State Capitol PO Box 50890 TF: 800-642-8207 ■ Web: www.wvdrs.org	Charleston	WV	25305	304-766-4600	766-4905
Secretary of State 1900 Kanawha Blvd E Bldg 1 Suite 157K TF: 866-767-8683 ■ Web: www.wvsos.com	Charleston	WV	25305	304-558-6000	558-0900
Securities Div 1900 Kanawha Blvd E Bldg 1 Rm W-100 TF: 877-982-9148 ■ Web: www.wvsao.gov	Charleston	WV	25305	304-558-2257	558-4211
Senior Services Bureau 1900 Kanawha Blvd E Bldg 10 TF: 877-987-3646 ■ Web: www.state.wv.us/seniorservices	Charleston	WV	25305	304-558-3317	558-0004
State Legislature State Capitol Rm 212 Web: www.legis.state.wv.us	Charleston	WV	25305	304-347-4836	347-4919
State Police 725 Jefferson Rd Web: www.wvstatepolice.com	South Charleston	WV	25309	304-746-2100	746-2230
Supreme Court of Appeals 1900 Kanawha Blvd E Bldg 1 Rm E-317 Web: www.state.wv.us/wvsca	Charleston	WV	25305	304-558-2601	558-3815
Teacher Certification Office 1900 Kanawha Blvd E Bldg 6 Rm 252 TF: 800-982-2378 ■ Web: wvde.state.wv.us/certification	Charleston	WV	25305	304-558-7010	558-7843
Tourism Div 90 MacCorkle Ave SW TF: 800-225-5982 ■ Web: www.wvtourism.com	Charleston	WV	25303	304-558-2200	558-2956
Transportation Dept 1900 Kanawha Blvd E Bldg 5 Rm A-109 Web: www.wvdot.com	Charleston	WV	25305	304-558-0444	558-1004
Treasurer 1900 Kanawha Blvd E Bldg 1 Suite E-145 TF: 800-422-7498 ■ Web: www.wvtreasury.com	Charleston	WV	25305	304-558-5000	558-4097
Veterans Affairs Div 1321 Plaza East Suite 101 TF: 888-838-2332 ■ Web: www.state.wv.us/va	Charleston	WV	25301	304-558-3540	558-8197
Vital Statistics 350 Capitol St Rm 165 Web: www.wvdhhr.org/bph/oehp/hsc/vr/birtcert.htm	Charleston	WV	25301	304-558-2931	558-1051
Weights & Measures Div 570 W MacCorkle Ave	Saint Albans	WV	25177	304-722-0602	722-0605
Employment Programs Bureau 112 California Ave Web: www.wvbep.org/bep/default.htm	Charleston	WV	25305	304-558-2630	558-2992

342-50 Wisconsin

				Phone	Fax
State Government Information Web: www.wisconsin.gov		WI		608-266-2211	
Aging & Long Term Care Resources Bureau PO Box 7851 Web: www.dhfs.state.wi.us/aging	Madison	WI	53707	608-266-2536	267-3203
Agriculture Trade & Consumer Protection Dept PO Box 8911 Web: datcp.state.wi.us	Madison	WI	53708	608-224-5012	224-5045
Arts Board 101 E Wilson St 1st Fl Web: arts.state.wi.us	Madison	WI	53702	608-266-0190	267-0380
Attorney General PO Box 7857 Web: www.doj.state.wi.us	Madison	WI	53707	608-266-1221	267-2779
Bill Status 1 E Main St TF: 800-362-9472 ■ Web: www.legis.state.wi.us	Madison	WI	53708	608-266-9960	
Board of Regents 1220 Linden Dr 1860 Van Hise Hall Web: www.uwsa.edu/bor	Madison	WI	53706	608-262-2324	262-5739
Child Support Bureau PO Box 7935 Web: www.dwd.state.wi.us/bcs	Madison	WI	53707	608-266-9909	267-2824
Children & Family Services Div PO Box 8916 Web: www.dhfs.state.wi.us/aboutDHFS/DCFS/dcfs.htm	Madison	WI	53708	608-267-3905	266-6836
Commerce Dept PO Box 7970 Web: www.commerce.state.wi.us	Madison	WI	53707	608-266-1018	266-3447
Consumer Protection Office PO Box 7857 Web: www.doj.state.wi.us/columns	Madison	WI	53707	608-266-3861	267-2779
Corrections Dept PO Box 7925 Web: www.wi-doc.com	Madison	WI	53707	608-240-5000	240-3300
Crime Victims Services Office PO Box 7951 Web: www.doj.state.wi.us/cvs	Madison	WI	53707	608-264-9446	264-6368
Director of State Courts PO Box 1688 Web: www.courts.state.wi.us	Madison	WI	53701	608-266-6828	267-0980
Economic Development Div PO Box 7970	Madison	WI	53707	608-266-9467	264-6451
Education Investment Program PO Box 7871 TF: 888-338-3789 ■ Web: www.edvest.com	Madison	WI	53707	608-264-7899	266-2647
Emergency Management Div PO Box 7865 Web: emergencymanagement.wi.gov	Madison	WI	53707	608-242-3232	242-3247
Ethics Board 44 E Mifflin St Suite 601 Web: ethics.state.wi.us	Madison	WI	53703	608-266-8123	264-9319
Fisheries Management & Habitat Protection Bureau PO Box 7921 Web: www.dnr.state.wi.us/fish/	Madison	WI	53707	608-267-7498	266-2244
Governor State Capitol PO Box 7863 Web: www.wisgov.state.wi.us	Madison	WI	53707	608-266-1212	267-8983
Health & Family Services Dept PO Box 7850 Web: www.dhfs.state.wi.us	Madison	WI	53707	608-266-1865	266-7882
Health Professions Bureau PO Box 8935 Web: drl.wi.gov	Madison	WI	53708	608-266-2112	261-7083
Higher Educational Aids Board PO Box 7885 Web: heab.state.wi.us	Madison	WI	53707	608-267-2206	267-2808
Historical Society 816 State St Web: www.wisconsinhistory.org	Madison	WI	53706	608-264-6400	
Housing & Economic Development Authority PO Box 1728 TF: 800-334-6873 ■ Web: www.wheda.com	Madison	WI	53701	608-266-7884	267-1099
Insurance Commission PO Box 7873 TF: 800-236-8517 ■ Web: oci.wi.gov	Madison	WI	53707	608-266-3585	266-9935
Legislature State Capitol Web: www.legis.state.wi.us	Madison	WI	53702	608-266-2211	266-7038
Lieutenant Governor 19 E State Capitol Web: www.ltgov.state.wi.us	Madison	WI	53702	608-266-3516	267-3571
Lottery PO Box 8941 Web: www.wilottery.com	Madison	WI	53708	608-261-8800	264-6644
Motor Vehicles Div 4802 Sheboygan Ave Web: www.dot.wisconsin.gov/drivers	Madison	WI	53707	608-266-2233	261-0136
Natural Resources Dept 101 S Webster St PO Box 7921 Web: www.dnr.state.wi.us	Madison	WI	53707	608-266-2621	261-4380
Parks & Recreation Bureau PO Box 7921 Web: dnr.wi.gov/org/land/parks	Madison	WI	53707	608-266-2181	267-7474
Parole Commission PO Box 7960 Suite 201	Madison	WI	53707	608-240-7280	240-7299
Public Instruction Dept PO Box 7841 Web: www.dpi.state.wi.us	Madison	WI	53707	608-266-1771	267-1052
Public Service Commission PO Box 7854 Web: psc.wi.gov	Madison	WI	53707	608-267-7897	266-3957
Regulation & Licensing Dept PO Box 8935 Web: drl.wi.gov	Madison	WI	53708	608-266-2112	267-0644
Revenue Dept PO Box 8933 Web: www.dor.state.wi.us	Madison	WI	53708	608-266-6466	266-5718
Secretary of State PO Box 7848 Web: www.sos.state.wi.us	Madison	WI	53707	608-266-8888	266-3159
Securities Div PO Box 1768 Web: www.wdfi.org/fi/securities	Madison	WI	53701	608-266-3431	256-1259
State Patrol Div PO Box 7912 Web: www.dot.wisconsin.gov/statepatrol	Madison	WI	53707	608-266-3212	267-4495
Supreme Court PO Box 1688 Web: www.courts.state.wi.us/supreme	Madison	WI	53701	608-266-1880	267-0640
Teacher Education & Licensing Bureau PO Box 7841 Web: www.dpi.state.wi.us/dpi/dlsis/tel	Madison	WI	53707	608-266-1879	264-9558
Tourism Dept 201 W Washington Ave 2nd Fl TF: 800-432-8747 ■ Web: www.travelwisconsin.com	Madison	WI	53703	608-266-2161	266-3403
Transportation Dept PO Box 7910 Web: www.dot.state.wi.us	Madison	WI	53707	608-266-1113	266-9912
Treasurer PO Box 7871 Web: www.ost.state.wi.us	Madison	WI	53707	608-266-1714	266-2647
Veterans Affairs Dept PO Box 7843 TF: 800-947-8387 ■ Web: dva.state.wi.us	Madison	WI	53707	608-266-1311	267-0403
Vital Records Office PO Box 309 Web: www.dhfs.state.wi.us/vitalrecords	Madison	WI	53701	608-266-1373	255-2035
Vocational Rehabilitation Div PO Box 7852 TF: 800-442-3477 ■ Web: www.dwd.state.wi.us/dvr	Madison	WI	53707	608-261-0050	266-1133
Worker's Compensation Div PO Box 7901 Web: www.dwd.state.wi.us/wc	Madison	WI	53707	608-266-1340	267-0394
Workforce Development Dept 201 E Washington Ave Web: www.dwd.state.wi.us	Madison	WI	53702	608-267-9613	266-1784

342-51 Wyoming

				Phone	Fax
State Government Information Web: wyoming.gov		WY		307-777-7220	
Aging Div 6101 Yellowstone Rd N Rm 259B TF: 800-442-2766 ■ Web: wdhfs.state.wy.us/aging	Cheyenne	WY	82002	307-777-7986	777-5340
Agriculture Dept 2219 Carey Ave Web: wyagric.state.wy.us	Cheyenne	WY	82002	307-777-7321	777-6593
Arts Council 2320 Capitol Ave Web: wyoarts.state.wy.us/	Cheyenne	WY	82002	307-777-7742	777-5499
Attorney General 123 Capitol 200 W 24th St Web: attorneygeneral.state.wy.us	Cheyenne	WY	82002	307-777-7841	777-6869
Banking Div 122 W 25th St Herschler Bldg 3rd Fl E Web: audit.state.wy.us/banking	Cheyenne	WY	82202	307-777-7797	777-3555
Board of Medicine 211 W 19th St Colony Bldg 2nd Fl Web: wyomedboard.state.wy.us	Cheyenne	WY	82002	307-778-7053	778-2069
Business Council 214 W 15th St Web: www.wyomingbusiness.org	Cheyenne	WY	82002	307-777-2800	777-2838
Certified Public Accountants Board 2020 Carey Ave Suite 702 Web: cpaboard.state.wy.us	Cheyenne	WY	82002	307-777-7551	777-3796
Child Support Enforcement 2300 Capital Ave 3rd Fl Web: dfsweb.state.wy.us/cse_enforce.html	Cheyenne	WY	82002	307-777-6948	777-3693
Community College Commission 2020 Carey Ave 8th Fl Web: www.commission.wcc.edu	Cheyenne	WY	82002	307-777-7763	777-6567
Community Development Authority PO Box 634 Web: www.wyomingcda.com	Casper	WY	82602	307-265-0603	266-5414
Consumer Protection Unit 123 State Capitol Bldg Web: attorneygeneral.state.wy.us/consumer.htm	Cheyenne	WY	82002	307-777-7874	777-7956
Corrections Dept 700 W 21st St Web: doc.state.wy.us/corrections.asp	Cheyenne	WY	82002	307-777-7208	777-7479
Education Dept 2300 Capitol Ave 2nd Fl Web: www.k12.wy.us	Cheyenne	WY	82002	307-777-7675	777-6234
Employment Dept 1510 E Pershing Blvd Web: wydoe.state.wy.us	Cheyenne	WY	82002	307-777-7672	777-5805
Environmental Quality Dept 122 W 25th St Herschler Bldg Web: deq.state.wy.us	Cheyenne	WY	82002	307-777-7937	777-7682
Family Services Dept 2300 Capitol Ave 3rd Fl Web: dfsweb.state.wy.us	Cheyenne	WY	82002	307-777-7561	777-7747
Game & Fish Dept 5400 Bishop Blvd Web: gf.state.wy.us	Cheyenne	WY	82006	307-777-4600	777-4610
Governor State Capitol 200 W 24th St Rm 124 Web: wyoming.gov/governor	Cheyenne	WY	82202	307-777-7434	632-3909
Health Dept 2300 Capitol Ave Suite 401 Web: wdhfs.state.wy.us	Cheyenne	WY	82002	307-777-7656	777-7439
Highway Patrol 5300 Bishop Blvd Web: whp.state.wy.us	Cheyenne	WY	82009	307-777-4301	777-4288
Historic Preservation Office 2301 Central Ave 3rd Fl Web: wyoshpo.state.wy.us	Cheyenne	WY	82002	307-777-7697	777-6421
Emergency Management Agency 122 W 25th St Herschler Bldg 1st Fl Web: wyohomelandsecurity.state.wy.us	Cheyenne	WY	82002	307-777-4900	635-6017
Information Technology Div 2001 Capitol Ave Web: ai.state.wy.us/ITD	Cheyenne	WY	82002	307-777-5003	
Insurance Dept 106 E 6th Ave Web: insurance.state.wy.us	Cheyenne	WY	82002	307-777-7401	777-2446
Bill Status State Capitol Bldg Rm 213 TF: 800-342-9570 ■ Web: legisweb.state.wy.us	Cheyenne	WY	82002	307-777-7881	777-5466
Legislature State Capitol Bldg Web: legisweb.state.wy.us	Cheyenne	WY	82002	307-777-7881	777-5466
Motor Vehicles Services Div 5300 Bishop Blvd Web: dot.state.wy.us	Cheyenne	WY	82009	307-777-4714	777-4772
Probation & Parole Div 700 W 21st St Suite 200	Cheyenne	WY	82002	307-777-7208	777-5386
Professional Teaching Standards Board 1920 Thomes Ave Suite 400 Web: ptsb.state.wy.us	Cheyenne	WY	82002	307-777-7291	777-8718
Public Service Commission 2515 Warren Ave Suite 300 Web: psc.state.wy.us	Cheyenne	WY	82002	307-777-7427	777-5700
Real Estate Commission 2020 Carey Ave Suite 702 Web: realestate.state.wy.us	Cheyenne	WY	82002	307-777-7141	777-3796

	City	State	Zip	Phone	Fax
Revenue Dept 122 W 25th St 2nd Fl *Web:* revenue.state.wy.us	Cheyenne	WY	82002	307-777-5287	777-7722
Secretary of State 200 W 24th St *Web:* soswy.state.wy.us	Cheyenne	WY	82002	307-777-7378	777-6217
Securities Div 200 W 24th St Rm 109 *Web:* soswy.state.wy.us/securiti/securiti.htm	Cheyenne	WY	82002	307-777-7370	777-5339
State Parks & Historical Sites Div 122 W 25th St 1st Fl E *TF Campground R:* 877-996-7275 ■ *Web:* wyoparks.state.wy.us	Cheyenne	WY	82002	307-777-5598	777-6472
Supreme Court 2300 Capitol Ave *Web:* courts.state.wy.us	Cheyenne	WY	82002	307-777-7316	777-6129
Technical Services Div 2219 Carey Ave *Web:* wyagric.state.wy.us/techserv/tsindex.html	Cheyenne	WY	82202	307-777-6590	777-6593
Tourism Div 1520 Etchepare Cir *TF:* 800-225-5996 ■ *Web:* www.wyomingtourism.org	Cheyenne	WY	82007	307-777-7777	777-2877
Transportation Dept 5300 Bishop Blvd *Web:* www.dot.state.wy.us	Cheyenne	WY	82009	307-777-4375	777-4163
Treasurer 200 W 24th St *Web:* treasurer.state.wy.us	Cheyenne	WY	82002	307-777-7408	777-5411
Veterans' Affairs Commission 851 Werner Ct Suite 120 *TF:* 800-833-5987	Casper	WY	82601	307-265-7372	265-7392
Victims Services Div 122 W 25 St 1st Fl W *TF:* 888-996-8816 ■ *Web:* vssi.state.wy.us	Cheyenne	WY	82002	307-777-7200	777-6683
Vital Records Services Hathaway Bldg *Web:* wdhfs.state.wy.us/vital_records	Cheyenne	WY	82002	307-777-7591	
Vocational Rehabilitation Div 122 W 25th St Suite 1100 *Web:* www.wyomingworkforce.org	Cheyenne	WY	82002	307-777-7389	777-5939
Workers' Safety & Compensation Div 1510 E Pershing Blvd *Web:* wydoe.state.wy.us/wscd	Cheyenne	WY	82002	307-777-7159	777-6552
Workforce Services Dept 122 W 25th St 2nd Fl E *Web:* www.wyomingworkforce.org	Cheyenne	WY	82002	307-777-8650	777-7106

343 GOVERNMENT - US - EXECUTIVE BRANCH

SEE ALSO Cemeteries - National p. 1412; Coast Guard Installations p. 1457; Correctional Facilities - Federal p. 1572; Military Bases p. 1969; Parks - National - US p. 2050

	City	State	Zip	Phone	Fax
Office of the President 1600 Pennsylvania Ave NW *Web:* www.whitehouse.gov/president	Washington	DC	20500	202-456-1414	456-2461
Office of the Vice President Eisenhower Executive Office Bldg 1650 Pennsylvania Ave NW *Web:* www.whitehouse.gov/vicepresident	Washington	DC	20501	202-456-0373	
Council of Economic Advisers 1800 G St NW 8th Fl *Web:* www.whitehouse.gov/cea	Washington	DC	20502	202-395-5084	395-6958
Council on Environmental Quality 730 Jackson Pl NW *Web:* www.whitehouse.gov/ceq	Washington	DC	20503	202-395-5750	456-6546
Domestic Policy Council Executive Office of the President 1600 Pennsylvania Ave NW *Web:* www.whitehouse.gov/dpc	Washington	DC	20502	202-456-5594	456-5557
National Economic Council 1600 Pennsylvania Ave NW *Web:* www.whitehouse.gov/nec	Washington	DC	20500	202-456-2800	456-2223
National Security Council (NSC) Eisenhower Executive Office Bldg 1650 Pennsylvania Ave NW *Web:* www.whitehouse.gov/nsc	Washington	DC	20504	202-456-9491	456-9270
Office of Faith-Based & Community Initiatives 708 Jackson Pl NW *Web:* www.whitehouse.gov/government/fbci	Washington	DC	20502	202-456-6708	456-7019
Office of the First Lady 1600 Pennsylvania Ave NW 200 East Wing *Web:* www.whitehouse.gov/firstlady	Washington	DC	20500	202-456-7064	456-6771
Office of Management & Budget (OMB) 725 17th St NW *Web:* www.whitehouse.gov/omb	Washington	DC	20503	202-395-3080	395-3888
Office of National AIDS Policy 736 Jackson Pl NW *Web:* www.whitehouse.gov/onap/aids.html	Washington	DC	20503	202-456-7320	456-7315
Office of National Drug Control Policy PO Box 6000 **Fax Area Code:* 301 ■ *Web:* www.whitehousedrugpolicy.gov	Rockville	MD	20849	800-666-3332	519-5212*
Office of Science & Technology Policy 725 17th St NW Rm 5228 *Web:* www.ostp.gov	Washington	DC	20502	202-456-7116	456-6021
Office of the US Trade Representative 600 17th St NW *Web:* www.ustr.gov	Washington	DC	20508	202-395-7360	
President's Foreign Intelligence Advisory Board White House 1600 Pennsylvania Ave *Web:* www.whitehouse.gov/pfiab	Washington	DC	20500	202-456-1414	456-2461
USA Freedom Corps 1600 Pennsylvania Ave NW West Wing *Web:* www.usafreedomcorps.gov	Washington	DC	20500	877-872-2677	
White House Office 1600 Pennsylvania Ave NW *Web:* www.whitehouse.gov	Washington	DC	20500	202-456-1111	
White House Press Secretary 1600 Pennsylvania Ave NW West Wing 1st Fl	Washington	DC	20500	202-456-2673	456-0126

343-1 US Department of Agriculture

	City	State	Zip	Phone	Fax
Department of Agriculture (USDA) 1400 Independence Ave SW *Web:* www.usda.gov	Washington	DC	20250	202-720-3631	720-2166
Agricultural Marketing Service 1400 Independence Ave SW *Web:* www.ams.usda.gov	Washington	DC	20250	202-720-5115	720-8477
Agricultural Research Service (ARS) US Dept of Agriculture 1400 Independence Ave SW *Web:* www.ars.usda.gov	Washington	DC	20250	202-720-3656	720-5427
Animal & Plant Health Inspection Service (APHIS) 4700 River Rd *Web:* www.aphis.usda.gov	Riverdale	MD	20737	301-734-7799	734-5221
National Veterinary Services Laboratories 1800 Dayton Ave PO Box 844 *Web:* www.aphis.usda.gov/vs/nvsl	Ames	IA	50010	515-663-7200	663-7402
Center for Nutrition Policy & Promotion 3101 Park Center Dr *Web:* www.cnpp.usda.gov	Alexandria	VA	22302	703-305-7600	305-3300
Commodity Credit Corp 1400 Independence Ave SW *Web:* www.fsa.usda.gov/ccc	Washington	DC	20250	202-720-3111	720-9105
Cooperative State Research Education & Extension Service US Dept of Agriculture 1400 Independence Ave SW MS 2201 *Web:* www.csrees.usda.gov	Washington	DC	20250	202-720-7441	720-8987
Economic Research Service (ERS) US Dept of Agriculture 1800 M St NW *Web:* www.ers.usda.gov	Washington	DC	20036	202-694-5050	694-5757
Farm Service Agency 1400 Independence Ave SW MS 0506 *Web:* www.fsa.usda.gov	Washington	DC	20250	202-720-3865	
Food & Nutrition Service 3101 Park Center Dr *Web:* www.fns.usda.gov	Alexandria	VA	22302	703-305-2062	305-2908
Food Stamp Program 3101 Park Center Dr *TF:* 800-221-5689 ■ *Web:* www.fns.usda.gov/fsp	Alexandria	VA	22302	703-305-2022	305-2454
Food & Nutrition Service Regional Offices					
Mid-Atlantic Region 300 Corporate Blvd *Web:* www.fns.usda.gov/fns/	Robbinsville	NJ	08691	609-259-5025	259-5185
Midwest Region 77 W Jackson Blvd 20th Fl	Chicago	IL	60604	312-353-6664	
Mountain Plains Region 1244 Speer Blvd Rm 903	Denver	CO	80204	303-844-0300	844-2160
Northeast Region Federal Bldg 10 Causeway St Rm 501	Boston	MA	02222	617-565-6370	565-6473
Southeast Region 61 Forsyth St SW Suite 8T36	Atlanta	GA	30303	404-562-1801	562-1807
Southwest Region USDA 1100 Commerce St Rm 522	Dallas	TX	75242	214-290-9800	767-0271
Western Region 90 7th St Suite 10-100	San Francisco	CA	94103	415-705-1310	705-1353
Food Safety & Inspection Service 1400 Independence Ave SW Rm 331E *Web:* www.fsis.usda.gov	Washington	DC	20250	202-720-7025	205-0158
Foreign Agricultural Service 1400 Independence Ave SW *Web:* www.fas.usda.gov	Washington	DC	20250	202-720-3935	690-2159
Forest Service (USFS) 1400 Independence Ave SW *TF:* 800-832-1355 ■ *Web:* www.fs.fed.us	Washington	DC	20050	202-205-8333	
Forest Service Regional Offices					
Region 1 (Northern Region) PO Box 7669 *Web:* www.fs.fed.us/r1	Missoula	MT	59807	406-329-3511	329-3347
Region 2 (Rocky Mountain Region) 740 Simms St *Web:* www.fs.fed.us/r2	Golden	CO	80401	303-275-5350	275-5366
Region 3 (Southwestern Region) 333 Broadway Blvd SE *Web:* www.fs.fed.us/r3	Albuquerque	NM	87102	505-842-3292	
Region 4 (Intermountain Region) 324 25th St *Web:* www.fs.fed.us/r4	Ogden	UT	84401	801-625-5306	625-5127
Region 5 (Pacific Southwest Region) 1323 Club Dr *Web:* www.fs.fed.us/r5	Vallejo	CA	94592	707-562-8737	562-9130
Region 6 (Pacific Northwest Region) 333 SW 1st Ave PO Box 3623 *Web:* www.fs.fed.us/r6	Portland	OR	97208	503-808-2468	808-2469
Region 8 (Southern Region) 1720 Peachtree St Suite 760S *TF:* 877-372-7248 ■ *Web:* www.fs.fed.us/r8	Atlanta	GA	30309	404-347-4177	347-4821
Region 9 (Eastern Region) 626 E Wisconsin Ave *Web:* www.fs.fed.us/r9	Milwaukee	WI	53202	414-297-3600	297-3808
Region 10 (Alaska Region) Box 21628 *Web:* www.fs.fed.us/r10	Juneau	AK	99802	907-586-8806	586-7876
Grain Inspection Packers & Stockyards Administration 1400 Independence Ave SW MS-3601 *TF:* 800-998-3447 ■ *Web:* www.gipsa.usda.gov	Washington	DC	20250	202-720-0219	205-9237
National Agricultural Library Abraham Lincoln Bldg 10301 Baltimore Ave *Web:* www.nal.usda.gov	Beltsville	MD	20705	301-504-5755	504-6110
National Agricultural Statistics Service (NASS) 1400 Independence Ave SW *TF:* 800-727-9540 ■ *Web:* www.nass.usda.gov	Washington	DC	20250	202-720-2707	720-9013
National Veterinary Services Laboratories 1800 Dayton Ave PO Box 844 *Web:* www.aphis.usda.gov/vs/nvsl	Ames	IA	50010	515-663-7200	663-7402
Natural Resources Conservation Service 1400 Independence Ave SW Rm 5105A *Web:* www.nrcs.usda.gov	Washington	DC	20250	202-720-7246	720-7690
Risk Management Agency 1400 Independence Ave SW MS 0801 *Web:* www.rma.usda.gov	Washington	DC	20250	202-690-2803	690-2818
Rural Business-Cooperative Service 1400 Independence Ave SW *Web:* www.rurdev.usda.gov/rbs	Washington	DC	20250	202-690-4730	690-4737
Rural Development 1400 Independence Ave SW *Web:* www.rurdev.usda.gov	Washington	DC	20250	202-720-4581	720-2080
Rural Housing Service 1400 Independence Ave SW Rm 5014 *Web:* www.rurdev.usda.gov/rhs	Washington	DC	20250	202-690-1533	690-0500
Rural Utilities Service 1400 Independence Ave SW Rm 5135S *Web:* www.rurdev.usda.gov/rus	Washington	DC	20250	202-720-9540	720-1725
Secretary of Agriculture 1400 Independence Ave SW Rm 200A *Web:* www.usda.gov	Washington	DC	20250	202-720-3631	720-2166
USDA (Department of Agriculture) 1400 Independence Ave SW *Web:* www.usda.gov	Washington	DC	20250	202-720-3631	720-2166
USDA Graduate School 600 Maryland Ave SW **Fax Area Code:* 866 ■ *TF:* 888-744-4723 ■ *Web:* grad.usda.gov	Washington	DC	20024	202-314-3300	329-4723*
World Agricultural Outlook Board 1400 Independence Ave SW *Web:* www.usda.gov/oce/commodity	Washington	DC	20250	202-720-6030	720-4043

343-2 US Department of Commerce

	City	State	Zip	Phone	Fax
Department of Commerce Hoover Bldg 1401 Constitution Ave NW *Web:* www.commerce.gov	Washington	DC	20230	202-482-4883	482-5168
Bureau of the Census 4600 Silver Hill Rd *Web:* www.census.gov	Washington	DC	20233	301-763-2135	763-3761
Bureau of Economic Analysis (BEA) US Dept of Commerce 1441 L St NW *Web:* www.bea.gov	Washington	DC	20230	202-606-9900	606-5311
Bureau of Industry & Security Hoover Bldg 1401 Constitution Ave NW *Web:* www.bis.doc.gov	Washington	DC	20230	202-482-2000	
Economic Development Administration 1401 Constitution Ave NW *Web:* www.eda.gov	Washington	DC	20230	202-482-4687	482-5671
Economic Development Administration Regional Offices					
Atlanta 401 W Peachtree St NW Suite 1820 *Web:* www.eda.gov	Atlanta	GA	30308	404-730-3002	730-3025
Austin 504 Lavaca St Suite 1100 *Web:* www.eda.gov	Austin	TX	78701	512-381-8144	381-8177
Chicago 111 N Canal St Suite 855	Chicago	IL	60606	312-353-7706	353-8575
Denver Federal Bldg 1244 Speer Blvd Rm 670	Denver	CO	80204	303-844-4715	844-3968
Philadelphia Curtis Center 601 Walnut St Suite 140-S	Philadelphia	PA	19106	215-597-4603	597-1063
Seattle Federal Bldg 915 2nd Ave Rm 1890	Seattle	WA	98174	206-220-7660	220-7657

US Department of Commerce (Cont'd)

Phone Fax

Economics & Statistics Administration
1401 Constitution Ave NW ... Washington DC 20230 202-482-5710 482-3417
Web: www.esa.doc.gov
International Trade Administration
1401 Constitution Ave NW ... Washington DC 20230 202-482-3809 482-5819
Web: www.ita.doc.gov
Minority Business Development Agency (MBDA)
1401 Constitution Ave NW ... Washington DC 20230 202-482-5061 501-4698
Web: www.mbda.gov
Minority Business Development Agency Regional Offices
Atlanta Region 401 W Peachtree St NW Suite 1715 ... Atlanta GA 30308 404-730-3300 730-3313
Web: www.mbda.gov
Chicago Region 55 E Monroe St Suite 2810 ... Chicago IL 60603 312-353-0182 353-0191
TF: 888-324-1551 ■ *Web:* www.mbda.gov
Dallas Region 1100 Commerce St Rm 726 ... Dallas TX 75242 214-767-8001 767-0613
Web: www.mbda.gov
New York Region 26 Federal Plaza Suite 3720 ... New York NY 10278 212-264-3262 264-0725
Web: www.mbda.gov
San Francisco Region 221 Main St Suite 1280 ... San Francisco CA 94105 415-744-3001 744-3061
Web: www.mbda.gov
National Environmental Satellite Data & Information Service (NCDDC) National Coastal Data Development Center Bldg 1100 Suite 101 ... Stennis Space Center MS 39529 228-688-2936 688-2010
TF: 866-732-2382 ■ *Web:* www.ncddc.noaa.gov
National Environmental Satellite Data & Information Service (NESDIS) 1335 East-West Hwy SSMC1 8th Fl ... Silver Spring MD 20910 301-713-3578 713-1249
Web: www.nesdis.noaa.gov
National Climatic Data Center 151 Patton Ave Rm 120 ... Asheville NC 28801 828-271-4800 271-4876
Web: www.ncdc.noaa.gov
National Geophysical Data Center E/GC 325 Broadway ... Boulder CO 80305 303-497-6826 497-6513
Web: www.ngdc.noaa.gov
National Oceanographic Data Center
1315 East-West Hwy 4th Fl ... Silver Spring MD 20910 301-713-3270 713-3300
Web: www.nodc.noaa.gov
National Hurricane Center 11691 SW 17th St ... Miami FL 33165 305-229-4470 553-1901
Web: www.nhc.noaa.gov
National Institute of Standards & Technology (NIST)
100 Bureau Dr MS 2500 ... Gaithersburg MD 20899 301-975-6478 926-1630
Web: www.nist.gov
National Marine Fisheries Service (NMFS)
1315 East-West Hwy 9th Fl ... Silver Spring MD 20910 301-713-2379 713-2384
Web: www.nmfs.noaa.gov
National Marine Fisheries Service Regional Offices
Alaska Region PO Box 21668 ... Juneau AK 99802 907-586-7221 586-7249
Web: www.fakr.noaa.gov
Northeast Region 1 Blackburn Dr ... Gloucester MA 01930 978-281-9300 281-9333
Web: www.nero.noaa.gov
Northwest Region 7600 Sand Point Way NE ... Seattle WA 98115 206-526-6150 526-6426
Web: www.nwr.noaa.gov
Pacific Islands Region 1601 Kapiolani Blvd Suite 1110 ... Honolulu HI 96814 808-944-2200 973-2941
Web: swr.nmfs.noaa.gov/pir
Southeast Region 263 13th Ave S ... Saint Petersburg FL 33701 727-824-5301 824-5320
Web: sero.nmfs.noaa.gov
Southwest Region 501 W Ocean Blvd Suite 4200 ... Long Beach CA 90802 562-980-4000 980-4018
Web: swr.nmfs.noaa.gov
National Ocean Service 1305 East-West Hwy ... Silver Spring MD 20910 301-713-3074 713-4269
Web: www.nos.noaa.gov
National Oceanic & Atmospheric Administration (NOAA)
1401 Constitution Ave NW ... Washington DC 20910 202-482-6090 482-3154
Web: www.noaa.gov
National Sea Grant Program
1315 East-West Hwy SSMC-3 11th Fl ... Silver Spring MD 20910 301-734-1077 713-0799
Web: www.nsgo.seagrant.org
National Technical Information Service (NTIS)
5285 Port Royal Rd ... Springfield VA 22161 703-605-6000 605-6900
TF Orders: 800-553-6847 ■ *Web:* www.ntis.gov
National Telecommunications & Information Administration (NTIA) 1401 Constitution Ave NW Hoover Bldg ... Washington DC 20230 202-482-7002
Web: www.ntia.doc.gov
National Weather Service (NWS)
1325 East-West Hwy Metro Ctr 2 ... Silver Spring MD 20910 301-713-0689 713-0662
Web: www.weather.gov
National Hurricane Center 11691 SW 17th St ... Miami FL 33165 305-229-4470 553-1901
Web: www.nhc.noaa.gov
National Weather Service Regional Offices
Alaska Region 222 W 7th Ave # 23 Rm 517 ... Anchorage AK 99513 907-271-5088 271-3711
Web: www.arh.noaa.gov
Central Region 7220 NW 101st Terr ... Kansas City MO 64153 816-891-7734 891-8362
Web: www.crh.noaa.gov
Eastern Region 630 Johnson Ave ... Bohemia NY 11716 631-244-0101 244-0167
Web: www.erh.noaa.gov
Pacific Region 737 Bishop St Suite 2200 ... Honolulu HI 96813 808-532-6416 532-5569
Web: www.prh.noaa.gov/pr
Southern Region 819 Taylor St Rm 10A05C ... Fort Worth TX 76102 817-978-1000 978-4740
Web: www.srh.noaa.gov
Western Region 125 S State St ... Salt Lake City UT 84103 801-524-5122 524-5270
Web: www.wrh.noaa.gov
NESDIS (National Environmental Satellite Data & Information Service) 1335 East-West Hwy SSMC1 8th Fl ... Silver Spring MD 20910 301-713-3578 713-1249
Web: www.nesdis.noaa.gov
NOAA (National Oceanic & Atmospheric Administration)
1401 Constitution Ave NW ... Washington DC 20910 202-482-6090 482-3154
Web: www.noaa.gov
North American Industry Classification System (NAICS)
US Census Bureau 4600 Silver Hill Rd ... Washington DC 20233 301-763-4636 457-4436
TF: 888-756-2427 ■ *Web:* www.census.gov/epcd/www/naics.html
Secretary of Commerce
1401 Constitution Ave NW HCHB Rm 5858 ... Washington DC 20230 202-482-2112 482-2741
Web: www.commerce.gov
STAT-USA 14th St & Constitution Ave NW Rm 4885 ... Washington DC 20230 202-482-1986 482-2164
TF: 800-782-8872 ■ *Web:* www.stat-usa.gov
US Census Bureau 4600 Silver Hill Rd ... Washington DC 20233 301-763-2135 763-3761
Web: www.census.gov
US Census Bureau Regional Offices
Atlanta 101 Marietta St NW Suite 3200 ... Atlanta GA 30303 404-730-3832 730-3835
TF: 800-424-6974 ■ *Web:* www.census.gov/roatl/www
Boston 4 Copley Pl Suite 301 ... Boston MA 02117 617-424-4501 424-0547
TF: 800-562-5721 ■ *Web:* www.census.gov/robos/www
Charlotte 901 Center Park Dr Suite 106 ... Charlotte NC 28217 704-424-6400 424-6944
TF: 800-331-7360 ■ *Web:* www.census.gov/rocha/www
Chicago 1111 W 22nd St Suite 400 ... Oak Brook IL 60523 630-288-9200 288-9288
TF: 800-865-6384 ■ *Web:* www.census.gov/rochi/www
Dallas 8585 N Stemmons Fwy Suite 800-S ... Dallas TX 75247 214-253-4400 655-5362
TF: 800-835-9752 ■ *Web:* www.census.gov/rodal/www
Denver 6900 W Jefferson Ave Suite 100 ... Denver CO 80235 303-264-0202 969-6777
TF: 800-852-6159 ■ *Web:* www.census.gov/roden/www
Detroit 1395 Brewery Park Blvd Suite 100 ... Detroit MI 48207 313-259-1158 259-5045
TF: 800-432-1495 ■ *Web:* www.census.gov/rodet/www
Kansas City 1211 N 8th St ... Kansas City KS 66101 913-551-6728 551-6789
TF: 800-728-4748 ■ *Web:* www.census.gov/rokan/www
Los Angeles 15350 Sherman Way Suite 300 ... Van Nuys CA 91406 818-267-1700 904-6429
TF: 800-992-3530 ■ *Web:* www.census.gov/rolax/www
New York 395 Hudson St Suite 800 ... New York NY 10014 212-584-3400 478-4800
TF: 800-991-2520 ■ *Web:* www.census.gov/ronyc/www
Philadelphia 833 Chestnut St Suite 504 ... Philadelphia PA 19107 215-717-1800 717-0755
TF: 800-262-4236 ■ *Web:* www.census.gov/rophi/www
Seattle 601 Union St Suite 3800 ... Seattle WA 98101 206-381-6200 381-6310
TF: 800-233-3308 ■ *Web:* www.census.gov/rosea/www
US Patent & Trademark Office PO Box 1450 ... Alexandria VA 22313 571-272-1000 273-8300
TF: 800-786-9199 ■ *Web:* www.uspto.gov

343-3 US Department of Defense

Phone Fax

Department of Defense (DOD) The Pentagon ... Washington DC 20301 703-545-6700
Web: www.defenselink.mil
American Forces Information Service (AFIS)
601 N Fairfax St ... Alexandria VA 22314 703-428-1200 428-0903
Web: www.defenselink.mil/afis
Defense Advanced Research Projects Agency (DARPA)
3701 N Fairfax Dr ... Arlington VA 22203 703-696-2400 696-2209
Web: www.darpa.mil
Defense Commissary Agency 1300 E Ave ... Fort Lee VA 23801 804-734-8253
TF: 800-699-5063 ■ *Web:* www.commissaries.com
Defense Contract Audit Agency
8725 John J Kingman Rd Suite 2135 ... Fort Belvoir VA 22060 703-767-3265 767-3267
Web: www.dcaa.mil
Defense Contract Management Agency
6350 Walker Ln Suite 300 ... Alexandria VA 22310 703-428-1833
TF: 888-576-3262 ■ *Web:* www.dcma.mil
Defense Finance & Accounting Service 1851 Bell St Rm 920 ... Arlington VA 22240 703-607-2616 607-1384
Web: www.dod.mil/dfas
Defense Hotline for Fraud Waste & Abuse ... Washington DC 20301 703-604-8799 604-8567
TF: 800-424-9098 ■ *Web:* www.dodig.osd.mil/hotline
Defense Information Systems Agency PO Box 4502 ... Arlington VA 22204 703-607-6900 607-4081
Web: www.disa.mil
Defense Intelligence Agency (DIA) 7400 Defense Pentagon ... Washington DC 20301 703-695-0071
Web: www.dia.mil
Defense Logistics Agency
8725 John J Kingman Rd Rm 2545 ... Fort Belvoir VA 22060 703-767-6200 767-6287
Defense Office of Economic Adjustment
400 Army-Navy Dr Suite 200 ... Arlington VA 22202 703-604-6020 604-5843
Web: www.oea.gov
Defense Prisoner of War/Missing Personnel Office
2900 Defense Pentagon ... Washington DC 20301 703-699-1102 602-1890
Web: www.dtic.mil/dpmo
Defense Security Cooperation Agency
201 12th St S Suite 203 ... Arlington VA 22202 703-604-6604 602-5403
Web: www.dsca.osd.mil
Defense Security Service
Office of Communication 1340 Braddock Pl ... Alexandria VA 22314 703-325-9471 325-6545
Web: www.dss.mil
Defense Technical Information Center (DTIC)
8725 John J Kingman Rd Suite 0944 ... Fort Belvoir VA 22060 703-767-9100 767-9183
TF: 800-225-3842 ■ *Web:* www.dtic.mil
Defense Threat Reduction Agency
8725 John T Kingman Rd MS 6201 ... Fort Belvoir VA 22060 703-767-5870 767-4450
TF: 800-701-5096 ■ *Web:* www.dtra.mil
Joint Chiefs of Staff Chairman
9999 Joint Chiefs of Staff Pentagon ... Washington DC 20318 703-697-9121 697-6002
Web: www.dtic.mil/jcs
Missile Defense Agency 7100 Defense Pentagon ... Washington DC 20301 703-693-0891 693-1526
Web: www.mda.mil
National Defense University Fort McNair 300 5th Ave SW ... Washington DC 20319 202-685-4700
Web: www.ndu.edu
National Geospatial-Intelligence Agency
3838 Vogel Rd MS L-89 ... Arnold MO 63010 314-263-4210 263-4875
TF: 800-455-0899 ■ *Web:* www.nga.mil
National Security Agency (NSA) 9800 Savage Rd ... Fort Meade MD 20755 301-688-6524 688-6198
Web: www.nsa.gov
Secretary of Defense 1000 Defense Pentagon ... Washington DC 20301 703-692-7100 571-8951
Web: www.defenselink.mil/osd/topleaders.html
Uniformed Services University of the Health Sciences
4301 Jones Bridge Rd ... Bethesda MD 20814 301-295-1956 295-1960
TF Admissions: 800-772-1743 ■ *Web:* www.usuhs.mil

343-4 US Department of Defense - Department of the Air Force

Phone Fax

Department of the Air Force 1670 Air Force Pentagon ... Washington DC 20330 703-695-9664 693-9601
Web: www.af.mil
North American Aerospace Defense Command
250 Vandenberg St Suite B-016 ... Peterson AFB CO 80914 719-554-6889 554-3165
Web: www.norad.mil
Air Combat Command 205 Dodd Blvd ... Langley AFB VA 23665 757-764-3204 764-3589
Web: www.acc.af.mil
Air Education & Training Command 100 H St Suite 4 ... Randolph AFB TX 78150 210-652-6307 652-2027
Web: www.aetc.randolph.af.mil
Air Force Chief of Staff 1670 Air Force Pentagon ... Washington DC 20330 703-697-9225 693-9297
Web: www.af.mil/library/afchain.asp
Air Force Materiel Command 4375 Chidlaw Rd ... Wright-Patterson AFB OH 45433 937-257-6033
Web: www.afmc.af.mil
Air Force Reserve Command 155 Richard Ray Blvd ... Robins AFB GA 31098 478-327-1009 327-0082
Web: www.afrc.af.mil
Air Force Space Command 150 Vandenberg St ... Peterson AFB CO 80914 719-554-3731 554-6013
Web: www.afspc.af.mil
Air Force Special Operations Command
229 Cody Ave Suite 103 ... Hurlburt Field FL 32544 850-884-5515 884-7249
Web: www2.afsoc.af.mil
Air Mobility Command ... Scott AFB IL 62225 618-229-7843
Web: www.amc.af.mil
Air National Guard 1411 Jefferson Davis Hwy ... Arlington VA 22202 703-607-2388 607-3678
Web: www.ang.af.mil

343-5 US Department of Defense - Department of the Army

Phone Fax

Department of the Army 1500 Army Pentagon ... Washington DC 20310 703-697-4200
Web: www.army.mil

Phone Fax

Army Board for Correction of Military Records
1901 Jefferson Davis Hwy Crystal Mall Bldg 4 . . . . Arlington VA 22202 703-607-1621 602-0935
Web: arba.army.pentagon.mil/abcmr.htm
Army Discharge Review Board
1941 Jefferson Davis Hwy Crystal Mall Bldg 4 . . . . Arlington VA 22202 703-607-1607
Web: arba.army.pentagon.mil/adrb.htm
Chief of Staff of the US Army 200 Army Pentagon. . . . . Washington DC 20310 703-697-0900 614-5268
Web: www.army.mil/leaders/csa
Judge Advocate General's Corps 1777 N Kent St . . . . Rosslyn VA 22209 703-697-5151 588-0155
TF: 800-208-7178 ■ *Web:* www.jagcnet.army.mil
US Army Center of Military History
103 3rd Ave SW Fort McNair Bldg 35. . . . . Washington DC 20319 202-685-2194 685-2081
Web: www.history.army.mil
US Army Legal Services Agency 901 N Stuart St Suite 700. . . . . . Arlington VA 22203 703-588-6357 696-8403
Web: www.jagcnet.army.mil/usalsa
Army National Guard
Army National Guard Readiness Center 111 S George Mason Dr . . . . Arlington VA 22204 703-607-7000 607-7088
Web: www.arng.army.mil
US Army Corps of Engineers 441 G St NW . . . . Washington DC 20314 202-761-0010 761-1803
Web: www.usace.army.mil
US Army Corps of Engineers Regional Offices
Great Lakes & Ohio River Div 550 Main St. . . . . Cincinnati OH 45202 513-684-3010 684-3755
Web: www.lrd.usace.army.mil
Mississippi Valley Div 1400 Walnut St . . . . Vicksburg MS 39180 601-634-7783
Web: www.mvd.usace.army.mil
North Atlantic Div 302 General Lee Ave Fort Hamilton . . . . Brooklyn NY 11252 718-765-7018 765-7170
Web: www.nad.usace.army.mil
Northwestern Div PO Box 2870. . . . . Portland OR 97208 503-808-3700 808-3706
Web: www.nwd.usace.army.mil
Pacific Ocean Div Fort Shafter Bldg 525 . . . . Honolulu HI 96858 808-438-8319 438-2656
Web: www.pod.usace.army.mil
South Atlantic Div 60 Forsyth St SW Rm 9M15 . . . . Atlanta GA 30303 404-562-5011
Web: www.sad.usace.army.mil
South Pacific Div 1455 Market St . . . . San Francisco CA 94103 415-503-6514
Web: www.spd.usace.army.mil
Southwestern Div 1100 Commerce St. . . . . Dallas TX 75242 469-487-7007
Web: www.swd.usace.army.mil
US Army Criminal Investigation Command
Public Affairs Office 6010 6th St. . . . . Fort Belvoir VA 22060 703-806-0372
Web: www.cid.army.mil
US Army Forces Command 1777 Hardee Ave SW . . . . Fort McPherson GA 30330 404-464-7276 464-5628
Web: www.forscom.army.mil
US Army Intelligence & Security Command 8825 Beulah St. . . . . Fort Belvoir VA 22060 703-706-2002
Web: www.inscom.army.mil
US Army Materiel Command 9301 Chapek Rd. . . . . Fort Belvoir VA 22060 703-806-8010 806-8031
Web: www.amc.army.mil
US Army Medical Command
2050 Worth Rd Bldg 2792. . . . . Fort Sam Houston TX 78234 210-221-6213
Web: www.armymedicine.army.mil
US Army Military District of Washington
103 3rd Ave SW Bldg 39 Fort McNair. Washington DC 20319 202-685-2812 685-3481
Web: www.mdw.army.mil
US Army Reserve Command 1401 Deshler St SW . . . . Fort McPherson GA 30330 404-464-8500
Web: www.armyreserve.army.mil/ARWEB
US Army Space & Missile Defense Command PO Box 1500. . . . . . . Huntsville AL 35807 256-955-6338 955-6344
Web: www.smdc.army.mil
US Army Special Operations Command . . . . Fort Bragg NC 28310 910-432-6005
Web: www.soc.mil
US Army Training & Doctrine Command
66 Ingalls Rd Bldg 27 . . . . Fort Monroe VA 23651 757-788-3333 788-3358
Web: www-tradoc.army.mil
US Army War College 122 Forbes Ave . . . . Carlisle PA 17013 717-245-3131 245-4224
TF: 800-453-0992 ■ *Web:* www.carlisle.army.mil
Walter Reed Army Medical Center 6900 Georgia Ave NW . . . . . . Washington DC 20307 202-782-3501 782-2478
Web: www.wramc.amedd.army.mil

343-6 US Department of Defense - Department of the Navy

Phone Fax

Department of the Navy 1000 Navy Pentagon . . . . Washington DC 20350 703-695-8400
Web: www.navy.mil
Chief of Naval Operations 2000 Navy Pentagon . . . . Washington DC 20350 703-695-5664 693-9408
Web: www.navy.mil
Judge Advocate General's Corps
1332 Patterson Ave Suite 3000 Washington Navy Yard . . . . . Washington DC 20374 202-685-5190 685-8510
Web: www.jag.navy.mil
Medicine & Surgery Bureau 2300 'E' St NW. . . . . Washington DC 20372 202-762-3218
Web: navymedicine.med.navy.mil
Office of Naval Intelligence
National Maritime Intelligence Center 4251 Suitland Rd . . . . . Washington DC 20395 301-669-3001 669-3099
Web: www.nmic.navy.mil
Office of Naval Research
1 Liberty Center 875 N Randolph St Suite 1425. . . . . Arlington VA 22203 703-696-5031 696-5940
Web: www.onr.navy.mil
Military Sealift Command
914 Charles Morris Ct SE Washington Navy Yard. . . . . Washington DC 20398 202-685-5055 685-5067
TF: 888-732-5438 ■ *Web:* www.msc.navy.mil
Naval Air Systems Command
47123 Buse Rd Bldg 2272 Suite 075 . . . . Patuxent River MD 20670 301-757-1487 757-1525
Web: www.navair.navy.mil
Naval Education & Training Command 250 Dallas St . . . . Pensacola FL 32508 850-452-4858 452-4900
Web: www.cnet.navy.mil
Naval Facilities Engineering Command
1322 Patterson Ave SE Washington Navy Yard. . . . . Washington DC 20374 202-685-1423 685-1484
Web: www.navfac.navy.mil
Naval Network Warfare Command 2465 Guadalcanal Rd. . . . . Norfolk VA 23521 757-417-6706
Web: www.netwarcom.navy.mil
Naval Sea Systems Command
1333 Isaac Hull Ave SE Washington Navy Yard . . . . Washington DC 20376 202-781-3889
Web: www.navsea.navy.mil
Naval Special Warfare Command 2000 Trident Way . . . . Coronado CA 92155 619-522-2824 522-2831
Web: www.navsoc.navy.mil
Navy Personnel Command 5720 Integrity Dr . . . . Millington TN 38055 901-874-3165 874-3165
Web: www.npc.navy.mil
Space & Naval Warfare Systems Command
4301 Pacific Hwy . . . . San Diego CA 92110 619-524-7000 524-7010
Web: www.spawar.navy.mil
US Naval Observatory 3450 Massachusetts Ave NW . . . . Washington DC 20392 202-762-1438 762-1489*
**Fax:* PR ■ *Web:* www.usno.navy.mil

343-7 US Department of Defense - US Marine Corps

Phone Fax

US Marine Corps (USMC)
USMC Headquarters 3000 Marine Corps Pentagon. . . . . Washington DC 20350 703-614-2500 697-7246
Web: www.usmc.mil
Commandant The Pentagon. . . . . Washington DC 20350 703-614-2500 697-7246
Web: www.usmc.mil/cmc/33cmc.nsf/cmcmain
Public Affairs Div The Pentagon . . . . Washington DC 20350 703-614-8010 697-5362
Web: www.usmc.mil
Marine Corps Recruiting Command 3280 Russell Rd . . . . Quantico VA 22134 703-784-9400 784-9863
Web: www.marines.com
Marine Corps Systems Command 2200 Lester St . . . . Quantico VA 22134 703-432-1800 432-3535
Web: www.marcorsyscom.usmc.mil

343-8 US Department of Education

Phone Fax

Department of Education 400 Maryland Ave SW. . . . . Washington DC 20202 202-401-2000 401-0689
TF: 800-872-5327 ■ *Web:* www.ed.gov
Inspector General's Fraud & Abuse Hotline
400 Maryland Ave SW . . . . Washington DC 20202 800-647-8733 245-7047*
**Fax Area Code:* 202 ■ *Web:* www.ed.gov/about/offices/list/oig/hotline.html
Institute of Education Sciences
555 New Jersey Ave NW Rm 600. . . . . Washington DC 20208 202-219-1385 219-1402
Web: www.ed.gov/about/offices/list/ies
Office of Elementary & Secondary Education
400 Maryland Ave SW . . . . Washington DC 20202 202-401-0113 205-0303
Web: www.ed.gov/about/offices/list/oese
Office of English Language Acquisition 550 12th St SW . . . . . . Washington DC 20202 202-245-7100 245-7168
Web: www.ed.gov/about/offices/list/oela
Office of Innovation & Improvement
400 Maryland Ave SW . . . . Washington DC 20202 202-205-4500 401-4123
Web: www.ed.gov/about/offices/list/oii
Office of Postsecondary Education 1990 K St NW . . . . Washington DC 20006 202-502-7750 502-7677
Web: www.ed.gov/about/offices/list/ope
Office of Safe & Drug-Free Schools
400 Maryland Ave SW Rm 3E300. . . . . Washington DC 20202 202-260-3954 260-7767
Web: www.ed.gov/about/offices/list/osdfs
Office of Special Education & Rehabilitation Services
550 12th St SW . . . . Washington DC 20202 202-245-7468 245-7638
Web: www.ed.gov/about/offices/list/osers
Office of Vocational & Adult Education 550 12th St SW. . . . . . . Washington DC 20202 202-245-7700 245-7837
TF: 800-872-5327 ■ *Web:* www.ed.gov/about/offices/list/ovae
Department of Education Regional Offices
Region 1 33 Arch St Suite 1030 . . . . Boston MA 02110 617-289-0100 289-0151
Region 2 Financial Sq 32 Old Slip 25th Fl. . . . . New York NY 10005 646-428-3905 428-3904
Region 3 100 Penn Sq E Suite 505. . . . . Philadelphia PA 19107 215-656-6010 656-6020
Region 4 Federal Center 61 Forsyth St SW Suite 19T40 . . . . Atlanta GA 30303 404-562-6225 562-6520
Region 5 500 W Madison St Suite 1427. . . . . Chicago IL 60661 312-730-1700 730-1704
Region 6 1999 Bryan St Suite 1510. . . . . Dallas TX 75201 214-661-9500 661-9594
Region 7 8930 Ward Pkwy Suite 2002 . . . . Kansas City MO 64114 816-268-0405 823-1400
Region 8 Federal Bldg 1244 Speer Blvd Suite 310. . . . . Denver CO 80204 303-844-3544 844-2524
Region 9 50 Beale St Rm 9100. . . . . San Francisco CA 94105 415-486-5700
Region 10 Federal Bldg 915 2nd Ave Rm 3362 . . . . Seattle WA 98174 206-220-7800 220-7806
National Center for Education Statistics 1990 K St NW . . . . Washington DC 20006 202-502-7300 502-7466
Web: nces.ed.gov
National Institute for Literacy (NIFL)
1775 'I' St NW Suite 730. . . . . Washington DC 20006 202-233-2025 233-2050
TF: 800-228-8813 ■ *Web:* www.nifl.gov
National Library of Education 400 Maryland Ave SW . . . . Washington DC 20202 202-205-5015 260-7364
TF: 800-424-1616 ■ *Web:* ies.ed.gov/ncee/projects/nat_ed_library.asp
Office of Federal Student Aid
Union Center Plaza 830 1st St NE. . . . . Washington DC 20202 202-377-3000 275-5000
TF: 800-433-3243 ■ *Web:* www.ed.gov/about/offices/list/fsa
Federal Student Aid Information Center PO Box 84 . . . . Washington DC 20044 800-433-3243
Web: studentaid.ed.gov
Secretary of Education 400 Maryland Ave SW . . . . Washington DC 20202 202-401-3000 260-7867
TF: 800-872-5327 ■ *Web:* www.ed.gov/news/staff/bios/spellings.html

343-9 US Department of Energy

Phone Fax

Department of Energy (DOE) 1000 Independence Ave SW. . . . . . . Washington DC 20585 202-586-5575 586-5823
Web: www.energy.gov
Office of Civilian Radioactive Waste Management
1000 Independence Ave SW . . . . Washington DC 20585 202-586-6842 586-6638
TF: 800-225-6972 ■ *Web:* www.ocrwm.doe.gov
Office of Electricity Delivery & Energy Reliability
1000 Independence Ave SW . . . . Washington DC 20585 202-586-1411 586-1472
Web: www.electricity.doe.gov
Office of Energy Efficiency & Renewable Energy
1000 Independence Ave SW . . . . Washington DC 20585 202-586-5570 586-9260
TF: 877-337-3463 ■ *Web:* www.eere.energy.gov
Office of Environmental Management
1000 Independence Ave SW . . . . Washington DC 20585 202-586-7709 586-7757
Web: www.em.doe.gov
Office of Fossil Energy 1000 Independence Ave SW. . . . . Washington DC 20585 202-586-6660 586-7847
Web: www.fe.doe.gov
Office of Legacy Management
1000 Independence Ave SW Office of Stakeholder Relations LM-5. . . . . Washington DC 20585 202-586-7550 586-1540
Web: www.lm.doe.gov
Office of Nuclear Energy 1000 Independence Ave SW . . . . Washington DC 20585 202-586-6630 586-0544
Web: www.ne.doe.gov
Office of Science 1000 Independence Ave SW . . . . Washington DC 20585 202-586-5430 586-4120
Web: www.sc.doe.gov
Energy Information Administration
1000 Independence Ave SW . . . . Washington DC 20585 202-586-8800 586-0727
Web: www.eia.doe.gov
Federal Energy Regulatory Commission (FERC)
888 1st St NE. . . . . Washington DC 20426 202-502-8004 208-2106
TF: 866-208-3372 ■ *Web:* www.ferc.gov
Federal Energy Regulatory Commission Regional Offices
Atlanta 3125 Presidential Pkwy Suite 300. . . . . Atlanta GA 30340 770-452-3800 452-3810
Web: www.ferc.gov/contact-us/tel-num/regional.asp
Chicago Federal Bldg 230 S Dearborn St Rm 3130 . . . . Chicago IL 60604 312-596-4430 596-4460
Web: www.ferc.gov/contact-us/tel-num/regional.asp
New York 19 W 34th St Suite 400 . . . . New York NY 10001 212-273-5900 631-8124
Web: www.ferc.gov/contact-us/tel-num/regional.asp
Portland 805 SW Broadway Suite 550. . . . . Portland OR 97205 503-552-2700 552-2799
Web: www.ferc.gov/contact-us/tel-num/regional.asp
San Francisco 901 Market St Suite 350 . . . . San Francisco CA 94103 415-369-3300 369-3322
Web: www.ferc.gov/contact-us/tel-num/regional.asp

US Department of Energy (Cont'd)

Phone Fax

National Nuclear Security Administration
1000 Independence Ave SW ... Washington DC 20585 202-586-5555 586-4892
Web: www.nnsa.doe.gov
Power Marketing Administrations
Bonneville Power Administration 905 NE 11th Ave ... Portland OR 97232 503-230-3000
Web: www.bpa.gov
Southeastern Power Administration 1166 Athens Tech Rd ... Elberton GA 30635 706-213-3800 213-3884
Web: www.sepa.doe.gov
Southwestern Power Administration 1 W 3rd St ... Tulsa OK 74103 918-595-6600 595-6656
Web: www.swpa.gov
Western Area Power Administration PO Box 281213 ... Lakewood CO 80228 720-962-7000 962-7200
Web: www.wapa.gov
Secretary of Energy 1000 Independence Ave SW ... Washington DC 20585 202-586-6210 586-4403
Web: www.energy.gov/organization

343-10 US Department of Health & Human Services

Phone Fax

Department of Health & Human Services (HHS)
200 Independence Ave SW ... Washington DC 20201 202-619-0257
TF: 877-696-6775 ■ *Web:* www.dhhs.gov
Department of Health & Human Services Regional Offices
Region 1 JFK Federal Bldg Suite 2100 ... Boston MA 02203 617-565-1500 565-1491
Web: www.hhs.gov/region1
Region 2 26 Federal Plaza ... New York NY 10278 212-264-4600 264-3620
Web: www.hhs.gov/region2
Region 3 150 S Independence Mall W ... Philadelphia PA 19106 215-861-4633 861-4625
Web: www.hhs.gov/region3
Region 4 Federal Center 61 Forsyth St SW ... Atlanta GA 30303 404-562-7888 562-7899
Web: www.hhs.gov/region4
Region 5 233 N Michigan Ave Suite 1300 ... Chicago IL 60601 312-353-5160 353-4144
Web: www.hhs.gov/region5
Region 6 1301 Young St Suite 1124 ... Dallas TX 75202 214-767-3301 767-3617
Web: www.hhs.gov/region6
Region 7 601 E 12th St ... Kansas City MO 64106 816-426-2821 426-2178
Web: www.hhs.gov/region7
Region 8 Federal Bldg 1961 Stout St ... Denver CO 80294 303-844-3372 844-4545
Web: www.hhs.gov/region8
Region 9 50 United Nations Plaza Rm 431 ... San Francisco CA 94102 415-437-8500 437-8505
Web: www.hhs.gov/region9
Region 10 2201 6th Ave Rm 1036 ... Seattle WA 98121 206-615-2010 615-2087
Web: www.hhs.gov/region10
Administration on Aging (AoA) 1 Massachusetts Ave NW ... Washington DC 20201 202-619-0724 357-3555
Web: www.aoa.gov
Administration on Aging Regional Offices
Region I JFK Federal Bldg Rm 2075 ... Boston MA 02203 617-565-1158 565-4511
Web: www.aoa.gov/about/contact/contact.asp
Regions II & III 26 Federal Plaza Rm 38-102 ... New York NY 10278 212-264-2977 264-0114
Web: www.aoa.gov/about/contact/contact.asp
Region IV Atlanta Federal Ctr 61 Forsyth St SW Suite 5M69 ... Atlanta GA 30303 404-562-7600 562-7598
Web: www.aoa.gov/about/contact/contact.asp
Region V 233 N Michigan Ave Suite 790 ... Chicago IL 60601 312-353-3141 886-8533
Web: www.aoa.gov/about/contact/contact.asp
Region VI 1301 Young St Suite 736 ... Dallas TX 75201 214-767-2971 767-2951
Web: www.aoa.gov/about/contact/contact.asp
Region VII 601 E 12th St Suite 1731 ... Kansas City MO 64106 816-426-3511 426-3516
Web: www.aoa.gov/about/contact/contact.asp
Region VIII Federal Bldg 1961 Stout St Rm 358 ... Denver CO 80294 303-844-2951 844-2943
Web: www.aoa.gov/about/contact/contact.asp
Region IX 50 United Nations Plaza Rm 455 ... San Francisco CA 94102 415-437-8780 437-8782
Web: www.aoa.gov/about/contact/contact.asp
Region X Blanchard Plaza 2201 6th Ave Rm 1202 MS RX-33 ... Seattle WA 98121 206-615-2298 615-2305
Web: www.aoa.gov/about/contact/contact.asp
Administration for Children & Families (ACF) 901 D St SW ... Washington DC 20447 202-401-9215 401-5450
Web: www.acf.dhhs.gov
Administration for Children & Families Regional Offices
Atlanta 61 Forsyth St SW Suite 4M60 ... Atlanta GA 30303 404-562-2900 562-2981
Web: www.acf.hhs.gov/programs/region4
Boston JFK Federal Bldg Rm 2000 ... Boston MA 02203 617-565-1020 565-2493
Web: www.acf.hhs.gov/programs/region1
Chicago 233 N Michigan Ave Suite 400 ... Chicago IL 60601 312-353-4237 353-2204
Web: www.acf.hhs.gov/programs/region5
Dallas 1301 Young St Suite 914 ... Dallas TX 75202 214-767-9648 767-3743
Web: www.acf.hhs.gov/programs/region6
Denver Federal Office Bldg 1961 Stout St 9th Fl ... Denver CO 80294 303-844-3100 844-2313
Web: www.acf.hhs.gov/programs/region8
Kansas City Federal Office Bldg 601 E 12th St Rm 276 ... Kansas City MO 64106 816-426-3981 426-2888
Web: www.acf.hhs.gov/programs/region7
New York 26 Federal Plaza Rm 4114 ... New York NY 10278 212-264-2890 264-4881
Web: www.acf.hhs.gov/programs/region2
Philadelphia 150 S Independence Mall W Suite 864 ... Philadelphia PA 19106 215-861-4000 861-4070
Web: www.acf.hhs.gov/programs/region3
San Francisco 50 United Nations Plaza Rm 450 ... San Francisco CA 94102 415-437-8400 437-8444
Web: www.acf.hhs.gov/programs/region9
Seattle Blanchard Plaza 2201 6th Ave Rm 300 MS RX-70 ... Seattle WA 98121 206-615-2547 615-2574
Web: www.acf.hhs.gov/programs/region10
Agency for Healthcare Research & Quality 540 Gaither Rd ... Rockville MD 20850 301-427-1200 427-1201
TF: 800-358-9295 ■ *Web:* www.ahrq.gov
Agency for Toxic Substances & Disease Registry
1600 Clifton Rd NE Bldg 37 MS E-29 ... Atlanta GA 30333 404-498-0110 498-0093
TF: 888-422-8737 ■ *Web:* www.atsdr.cdc.gov
AIDSinfo PO Box 6303 ... Rockville MD 20849 301-519-0459 519-6616
TF: 800-448-0440 ■ *Web:* www.aidsinfo.nih.gov
Alzheimer's Disease Education & Referral Center
PO Box 8250 ... Silver Spring MD 20907 800-438-4380 495-3334*
*Fax Area Code: 301 ■ *Web:* www.nia.nih.gov/alzheimers
Cancer Information Service
National Cancer Institute 9000 Rockville Pike Bldg 31 ... Bethesda MD 20892 800-422-6237
Web: cis.nci.nih.gov
Centers for Disease Control & Prevention (CDC)
1600 Clifton Rd NE ... Atlanta GA 30333 404-639-7000 639-7111
Web: www.cdc.gov
National Center on Birth Defects & Developmental Disabilities
12 Executive Park Dr West NE ... Atlanta GA 30329 770-498-3800 498-3070
Web: www.cdc.gov/ncbddd
National Center for Chronic Disease Prevention & Health Promotion 2900 Woodcock Blvd ... Atlanta GA 30341 404-639-8000 639-8600
Web: www.cdc.gov/nccdphp
National Center for Environmental Health
4770 Buford Hwy Bldg 101 ... Chamblee GA 30341 770-498-0004 488-0083
TF: 888-232-6789 ■ *Web:* www.cdc.gov/nceh
National Center for Health Marketing 1600 Clifton Rd NE ... Atlanta GA 30333 404-498-1515
TF: 800-311-3435 ■ *Web:* www.cdc.gov/healthmarketing
National Center for Health Statistics 6525 Belcrest Rd ... Hyattsville MD 20782 301-458-4000
Web: www.cdc.gov/nchs
National Center for HIV/AIDS Viral Hepatitis STD & TB Prevention
1108 Corporate Sq Bldg 8 ... Atlanta GA 30329 404-639-8187 639-8609
Web: www.cdc.gov/nchstp/od/nchstp.html
National Center for Immunization & Respiratory Diseases
1600 Clifton Rd NE MS E-05 ... Atlanta GA 30333 800-832-4636
Web: www.cdc.gov/vaccines
National Center for Injury Prevention & Control
2858 Woodcock Blvd ... Atlanta GA 30333 770-488-4696 488-4422
Web: www.cdc.gov/ncipc
National Center for Preparedness Detection & Control of Infectious Diseases 1600 Clifton Rd NE MS C-14 ... Atlanta GA 30333 404-639-3534 639-2945
TF: 800-311-3435 ■ *Web:* www.cdc.gov/ncpdcid
National Center for Public Health Informatics
1600 Clifton Rd NE MS E-78 ... Atlanta GA 30333 404-498-2475 498-6570
Web: www.cdc.gov/ncphi
National Institute for Occupational Safety & Health
200 Independence Ave SW ... Washington DC 20201 202-401-6997
TF: 800-356-4674 ■ *Web:* www.cdc.gov/niosh
National Office of Public Health Genomics
4770 Buford Hwy MS K-89 ... Atlanta GA 30341 770-488-8510 488-8355
Web: www.cdc.gov/genomics
Centers for Disease Control & Prevention (CDC NPIN) National Prevention Information Network PO Box 6003 ... Rockville MD 20849 919-361-4892 282-7681*
*Fax Area Code: 888 ■ *TF:* 800-458-5231 ■ *Web:* www.cdcnpin.org
Centers for Disease Control & Prevention (CDC) Travelers' Health
1600 Clifton Rd NE ... Atlanta GA 30333 877-394-8747 232-3299*
*Fax Area Code: 888 ■ *Web:* wwwn.cdc.gov/travel
Centers for Disease Control & Prevention National Center for Zoonotic Vector-Borne & Enteric Diseases 1600 Clifton Rd MS D-76 ... Atlanta GA 30333 404-639-3311
Web: www.cdc.gov/nczved
Centers for Medicare & Medicaid Services (CMS)
7500 Security Blvd ... Baltimore MD 21244 410-786-1800 786-1810
Web: www.cms.hhs.gov
Medicare Hotline ... Baltimore MD 21207 800-633-4227
Web: www.medicare.gov
Centers for Medicare & Medicaid Services Regional Offices
Region I JFK Federal Bldg Rm 2325 ... Boston MA 02203 617-565-1188 565-1339
Web: www.cms.hhs.gov/RegionalOffices
Region II 26 Federal Plaza 38th Fl ... New York NY 10278 212-616-2205 264-6189
Web: www.cms.hhs.gov/RegionalOffices
Region III 150 S Independence Mall W Suite 216 ... Philadelphia PA 19106 215-861-4140 861-4240
Web: www.cms.hhs.gov/RegionalOffices
Region IV 61 Forsyth St SW Suite 4T20 ... Atlanta GA 30303 404-562-7500 562-7162
Web: www.cms.hhs.gov/RegionalOffices
Region V 233 N Michigan Ave Suite 600 ... Chicago IL 60601 312-886-6432 353-0252
Web: www.cms.hhs.gov/RegionalOffices
Region VI 1301 Young St Suite 714 ... Dallas TX 75202 214-767-6423 767-6400
Web: www.cms.hhs.gov/RegionalOffices
Region VII Federal Bldg 601 E 12th St Rm 235 ... Kansas City MO 64106 816-426-5233 426-3548
Web: www.cms.hhs.gov/RegionalOffices
Region VIII 1600 Broadway Suite 700 ... Denver CO 80202 303-844-2111 844-6374
Web: www.cms.hhs.gov/RegionalOffices
Region IX 75 Hawthorne St ... San Francisco CA 94105 415-744-3501 744-3517
Web: www.cms.hhs.gov/RegionalOffices
Region X 2201 6th Ave MS 40 ... Seattle WA 98121 206-615-2306 615-2027
Web: www.cms.hhs.gov/RegionalOffices
Child Welfare Information Gateway
1250 Maryland Ave SW 8th Fl ... Washington DC 20024 703-385-7565 385-3206
TF: 800-394-3366 ■ *Web:* www.childwelfare.gov
Fogarty International Center 31 Center Dr MSC 2220 ... Bethesda MD 20892 301-496-2075 594-1211
Web: www.fic.nih.gov
Food & Drug Administration (FDA) 5600 Fishers Ln ... Rockville MD 20857 301-827-2410 443-3100
TF: 888-463-6332 ■ *Web:* www.fda.gov
Center for Biologics Evaluation & Research
1401 Rockville Pike Suite 200N MS HFM-4 ... Rockville MD 20852 301-827-0372
Web: www.fda.gov/cber
Center for Devices & Radiological Health
9200 Corporate Blvd Suite 100G ... Rockville MD 20850 800-638-2041 443-8818*
*Fax Area Code: 301 ■ *Web:* www.fda.gov/cdrh
Center for Drug Evaluation & Research
5515 Security Ln Suite 5100 ... Rockville MD 20852 301-594-5400 594-6197
Web: www.fda.gov/cder
Center for Food Safety & Applied Nutrition
5100 Paint Branch Pkwy ... College Park MD 20740 301-436-1600
TF: 888-723-3366 ■ *Web:* www.cfsan.fda.gov
Center for Veterinary Medicine
7519 Standish Pl Metro Park N 4 ... Rockville MD 20855 240-276-9000
Web: www.fda.gov/cvm
FoodSafety.gov 5100 Paint Branch Pkwy ... College Park MD 20740 888-723-3366
Web: www.foodsafety.gov
MedWatch
Center for Drug Evaluation & Research 5515 Security Ln Suite 5100 ... Rockville MD 20852 888-463-6332
Web: www.fda.gov/medwatch
National Center for Toxicological Research 3900 NCTR Rd ... Jefferson AR 72079 870-543-7000 543-7576
TF: 800-638-3321 ■ *Web:* www.fda.gov/nctr
Food & Drug Administration Regional Offices
Central Region 900 US Custom House 200 Chestnut St ... Philadelphia PA 19106 215-597-4390
Northeast Region 158-15 Liberty Ave ... Jamaica NY 11433 718-662-5416 662-5434
Pacific Region Federal Bldg 1301 Clay St Suite 1180N ... Oakland CA 94612 510-637-3960 637-3976
Southeast Region 60 8th St NE ... Atlanta GA 30309 404-253-1171 253-1207
Southwest Region 4040 N Central Expwy Suite 900 ... Dallas TX 75204 214-253-4904 253-4965
Health Resources & Services Administration (HRSA)
5600 Fishers Ln ... Rockville MD 20857 301-443-2216
TF: 888-275-4772 ■ *Web:* www.hrsa.gov
Indian Health Service (IHS) 801 Thompson Ave Suite 400 ... Rockville MD 20852 301-443-1083 443-4794
Web: www.ihs.gov
National Child Care Information Center (NCCIC)
10530 Rosehaven St Suite 400 ... Fairfax VA 22030 800-616-2242 716-2242
Web: nccic.org
National Clearinghouse for Alcohol & Drug Information
PO Box 2345 ... Rockville MD 20847 301-468-2600
TF: 800-729-6686 ■ *Web:* ncadi.samhsa.gov
National Disaster Medical System
200 Independence Ave SW Rm 638-G ... Washington DC 20201 202-205-2882
Web: www.ndms.dhhs.gov
National Hansen's Disease Program (NHDP)
1770 Physicians Park Dr ... Baton Rouge LA 70816 800-642-2477
Web: www.hrsa.gov/hansens
National Health Information Center (NHIC) PO Box 1133 ... Washington DC 20013 301-565-4167 984-4256
TF: 800-336-4797 ■ *Web:* www.health.gov/nhic
National Institute for Occupational Safety & Health
200 Independence Ave SW ... Washington DC 20201 202-401-6997
TF: 800-356-4674 ■ *Web:* www.cdc.gov/niosh

Phone Fax

National Institutes of Health (NIH) 9000 Rockville Pike Bethesda MD 20892 301-496-4000
Web: www.nih.gov
Center for Scientific Review 6701 Rockledge Dr MSC 7768 Bethesda MD 20892 301-435-1115
Web: cms.csr.nih.gov
Clinical Center 10 Center Dr Bldg 10 Bethesda MD 20892 301-496-2563 402-2984
Web: www.cc.nih.gov
John E Fogarty International Center 31 Center Dr MSC 2220 Bethesda MD 20892 301-496-2075 594-1211
Web: www.fic.nih.gov
National Cancer Institute
Public Inquiries Office 6116 Executive Blvd Rm 3036A Bethesda MD 20892 301-435-3848 402-2594
TF: 800-422-6237 ■ Web: www.cancer.gov
National Cancer Institute - Cancer Information Service
National Cancer Institute 9000 Rockville Pike Bldg 31 Bethesda MD 20892 800-422-6237
Web: cis.nci.nih.gov
National Center for Complementary & Alternative Medicine
National Institutes of Health 31 Center Dr Bldg 31 Bethesda MD 20892 301-519-3153 464-3616*
*Fax Area Code: 866 ■ TF: 888-644-6226 ■ Web: nccam.nih.gov
National Center on Minority Health & Health Disparities
6707 Democracy Blvd Suite 800 MSC 5465 Bethesda MD 20892 301-402-1366 480-4049
Web: ncmhd.nih.gov
National Eye Institute 2020 Vision Pl Bethesda MD 20892 301-496-5248
Web: www.nei.nih.gov
National Heart Lung & Blood Institute
31 Center Dr Bldg 31 Rm 5A48 MSC 2486 Bethesda MD 20892 301-496-5166 402-0818
Web: www.nhlbi.nih.gov
National Human Genome Research Institute
31 Center Dr Bldg 31 Rm 4B09 Bethesda MD 20892 301-402-0911 402-2218
Web: www.genome.gov
National Institute on Aging
31 Center Dr Bldg 31 Rm 5C27 MSC 2292 Bethesda MD 20892 301-496-1752 496-1072
Web: www.nia.nih.gov
National Institute on Alcohol Abuse & Alcoholism
5635 Fishers Ln MSC 9304 Bethesda MD 20892 301-443-3885
Web: www.niaaa.nih.gov
National Institute of Allergy & Infectious Diseases
6610 Rockledge Dr MSC 6612 Bethesda MD 20892 301-496-5717 402-3573
Web: www.niaid.nih.gov
National Institute of Arthritis & Musculoskeletal & Skin Diseases 31 Center Dr MSC 2350 Bldg 31 Rm 4C02 Bethesda MD 20892 301-496-8190 480-2814
Web: www.niams.nih.gov
National Institute of Biomedical Imaging & Bioengineering
6707 Democracy Blvd Bethesda MD 20892 301-496-8859 480-0679
Web: www.nibib.nih.gov
National Institute of Child Health & Human Development
31 Center Dr Bldg 31 Rm 2A32 Bethesda MD 20892 301-496-5133 496-7101
TF: 800-370-2943 ■ Web: www.nichd.nih.gov
National Institute on Deafness & Other Communication Disorders 31 Center Dr MSC 2320 Bethesda MD 20892 301-496-7243 402-0018
Web: www.nidcd.nih.gov
National Institute of Dental & Craniofacial Research
31 Center Dr Bethesda MD 20892 301-496-3571
Web: www.nidcr.nih.gov
National Institute of Diabetes & Digestive & Kidney Diseases
31 Center Dr MSC 2560 Bethesda MD 20892 301-496-3583 496-4722
Web: www.niddk.nih.gov
National Institute on Drug Abuse
6001 Executive Blvd Rm 5274 Bethesda MD 20892 301-443-6480 443-8908
Web: www.nida.nih.gov
National Institute of Environmental Health Sciences PO Box 12233 Research Triangle Park NC 27709 919-541-3201 541-2260
Web: www.niehs.nih.gov
National Institute of General Medical Sciences
45 Center Dr MSC 6200 Bethesda MD 20892 301-496-7301
Web: www.nigms.nih.gov
National Institute of Mental Health
6001 Executive Blvd Rm 8184 MSC 9663 Bethesda MD 20892 301-443-4513 443-4279
TF: 866-615-6464 ■ Web: www.nimh.nih.gov
National Institute of Neurological Disorders & Stroke
PO Box 5801 Bethesda MD 20824 301-496-5751
TF: 800-352-9424 ■ Web: www.ninds.nih.gov
National Institute of Nursing Research
31 Center Dr Bldg 31 Rm 5B05 Bethesda MD 20892 301-496-8230
Web: www.nih.gov/ninr
National Library of Medicine
National Institutes of Health 8600 Rockville Pike Bldg 38 Bethesda MD 20894 301-594-5983 402-1384
TF: 888-346-3656 ■ Web: www.nlm.nih.gov
Office of Communications & Public Liason
9000 Rockville Pike Bldg 1 Bethesda MD 20892 301-496-4461 496-0017
Office of Dietary Supplements
6100 Executive Blvd Suite 3B01 Bethesda MD 20892 301-435-2920 480-1845
Web: ods.od.nih.gov
Office of Rare Diseases 6100 Executive Blvd Suite 3B01 Bethesda MD 20892 301-402-4336 480-9655
Web: rarediseases.info.nih.gov
National Library of Medicine
National Institutes of Health 8600 Rockville Pike Bldg 38 Bethesda MD 20894 301-594-5983 402-1384
TF: 888-346-3656 ■ Web: www.nlm.nih.gov
Lister Hill National Center for Biomedical Communications
8600 Rockville Pike Bldg 38A 7th Fl Bethesda MD 20894 301-496-4441 480-3035
Web: lhncbc.nlm.nih.gov
National Center for Biotechnology Information
8600 Rockville Pike Bldg 38A Bethesda MD 20894 301-496-2475 480-9241
Web: www.ncbi.nlm.nih.gov
National Mental Health Information Center PO Box 42557 Washington DC 20015 240-747-5484 747-5470
TF: 800-789-2647 ■ Web: mentalhealth.samhsa.gov
National Women's Health Information Center
8270 Willow Oaks Corporate Dr Fairfax VA 22031 800-994-9662
Web: www.womenshealth.gov
NIH Osteoporosis & Related Bone Diseases - National Resource Center 2 AMS Cir Bethesda MD 20892 202-223-0344 293-2356
TF: 800-624-2663 ■ Web: www.niams.nih.gov/bone
Office of Public Health & Science
200 Independence Ave SW Rm 716G Washington DC 20201 202-690-7694 690-6960
Web: www.hhs.gov/ophs
Office of Public Health & Science Regional Offices
Region I JFK Federal Bldg Rm 2100 Boston MA 02203 617-565-1505 565-1491
Web: www.hhs.gov/ophs/rha
Region II 26 Federal Plaza Suite 3835 New York NY 10278 212-264-2560
Web: www.hhs.gov/ophs/rha
Region III 150 S Independence Mall W Suite 436 Philadelphia PA 19106 215-861-4639
Web: www.hhs.gov/ophs/rha
Region IV 61 Forsyth St SW Suite 5B95 Atlanta GA 30303 404-562-7888 562-7899
Web: www.hhs.gov/ophs/rha
Region V 233 N Michigan Ave Suite 1300 Chicago IL 60601 312-353-1385 353-0718
Web: www.hhs.gov/ophs/rha
Region VI 1301 Young St Suite 1124 Dallas TX 75202 214-767-3879 767-3617
Web: www.hhs.gov/ophs/rha
Region VII Federal Bldg 601 E 12th St Kansas City MO 64106 816-426-3291 426-2178
Web: www.hhs.gov/ophs/rha
Region VIII Federal Bldg 1961 Stout St Denver CO 80294 303-844-6163 844-2019
Web: www.hhs.gov/ophs/rha
Region IX 50 United Nations Plaza Suite 327 San Francisco CA 94102 415-437-8096 437-8004
Web: www.hhs.gov/ophs/rha
Region X 2201 6th Ave MS RX-20 Seattle WA 98121 206-615-2469 615-2481
Web: www.hhs.gov/ophs/rha
President's Council on Physical Fitness & Sports
Dept W 200 Independence Ave SW Rm 738-H Washington DC 20201 202-690-9000 690-5211
Web: www.fitness.gov
Secretary of Health & Human Services
200 Independence Ave SW Rm 615-F Washington DC 20201 202-690-7000 690-7755
Web: www.hhs.gov/about
Substance Abuse & Mental Health Services Administration (SAMHSA) 1 Choke Cherry Rd Rockville MD 20857 240-276-2000 276-2010
Web: www.samhsa.gov
Center for Mental Health Services 1 Choke Cherry Ln Rockville MD 20857 240-276-1310 276-1320
Web: www.mentalhealth.samhsa.gov/cmhs
Center for Substance Abuse Prevention 1 Choke Cherry Rd Rockville MD 20850 240-276-2420 276-2760
TF: 800-729-6686 ■ Web: prevention.samhsa.gov
Center for Substance Abuse Treatment 1 Choke Cherry Rd Rockville MD 20857 240-276-2757 276-1670
Web: csat.samhsa.gov
US Surgeon General 5600 Fishers Ln Rm 18-67 Rockville MD 20857 301-443-4000 443-5890
Web: www.surgeongeneral.gov

343-11 US Department of Homeland Security

Phone Fax

Department of Homeland Security (DHS) Washington DC 20528 202-282-8000 282-8401
Web: www.dhs.gov
Ready Campaign Washington DC 20528 202-282-8000 282-8401
Web: www.ready.gov
Federal Air Marshal Service 601 S 12th St Arlington VA 22202 703-487-3400 487-3405
Web: www.tsa.gov
Federal Emergency Management Agency (FEMA)
500 C St SW Washington DC 20472 800-621-3362
Web: www.fema.gov
FEMA for Kids 500 C St SW Washington DC 20472 202-646-4600
Web: www.fema.gov/kids
National Flood Insurance Program 500 C St SW Washington DC 20472 888-379-9531 646-2818*
*Fax Area Code: 202 ■ Web: www.floodsmart.gov
US Fire Administration 16825 S Seton Ave Emmitsburg MD 21727 301-447-1000 447-1346
Web: www.usfa.dhs.gov
Federal Emergency Management Agency Regional Offices
Region 1 99 High St 6th Fl Boston MA 02110 877-336-2734
Web: www.fema.gov/about/regions
Region 2 26 Federal Plaza Suite 1311 New York NY 10278 212-680-3600 680-3681
Web: www.fema.gov/about/regions
Region 3 1 Independence Mall 615 Chestnut St 6th Fl Philadelphia PA 19106 215-931-5600 931-5621
TF: 800-621-3362 ■ Web: www.fema.gov/about/regions
Region 4 3003 Chamblee-Tucker Rd Atlanta GA 30341 770-220-5200 220-5230
Web: www.fema.gov/about/regions
Region 5 536 S Clark St 6th Fl Chicago IL 60605 312-408-5500 408-5234
TF: 877-336-2564 ■ Web: www.fema.gov/about/regions
Region 6 FRC 800 North Loop 288 Denton TX 76209 940-898-5399 898-5325
TF: 800-426-5460 ■ Web: www.fema.gov/about/regions
Region 7 9221 Ward Pkwy Suite 300 Kansas City MO 64114 816-283-7061 283-7582
Web: www.fema.gov/about/regions
Region 8 Denver Federal Center Bldg 710 Box 25267 Denver CO 80225 303-235-4900 235-4976
Web: www.fema.gov/about/regions
Region 9 1111 Broadway Suite 1200 Oakland CA 94607 510-627-7100 627-7112
Web: www.fema.gov/about/regions
Region 10 Federal Regional Ctr 130 228th St SW Bothell WA 98021 425-487-4600 487-4622
TF: 800-772-1252 ■ Web: www.fema.gov/about/regions
Federal Law Enforcement Training Center
1131 Chapel Crossing Rd Glynco GA 31524 912-267-2100
Web: www.fletc.gov
FEMA (Federal Emergency Management Agency)
500 C St SW Washington DC 20472 800-621-3362
Web: www.fema.gov
Immigration & Naturalization Service (now US Citizenship & Immigration Services) 20 Massachusetts Ave NW Washington DC 20529 202-272-1000 272-1134
TF: 800-375-5283 ■ Web: uscis.gov
Ready.gov Washington DC 20528 202-282-8000 282-8401
Web: www.ready.gov
Secretary of Homeland Security Naval Security Station Washington DC 20528 202-282-8000 282-8401
Web: www.dhs.gov/dhspublic
Transportation Security Administration (TSA) 601 S 12th St Arlington VA 22202 202-282-8000 227-1300
TF: 866-289-9673 ■ Web: www.tsa.gov
Federal Air Marshal Service 601 S 12th St Arlington VA 22202 703-487-3400 487-3405
Web: www.tsa.gov
US Citizenship & Immigration Services (USCIS)
20 Massachusetts Ave NW Washington DC 20529 202-272-1000 272-1134
TF: 800-375-5283 ■ Web: uscis.gov
US Citizenship & Immigration Services Regional Offices
Central Region 7701 N Stemmons Fwy Dallas TX 75247 214-905-5430 905-5435
Eastern Region 70 Kimball Ave South Burlington VT 05403 802-660-5000 660-5114
Western Region 24000 Avila Rd PO Box 30080 Laguna Niguel CA 92607 949-360-2995 360-3081
TF: 800-375-5283 ■ Web: www.uscis.gov
US Coast Guard (USCG) 2100 2nd St SW Washington DC 20593 202-372-4620 372-4986
Web: www.uscg.mil
Boating Safety Office 2100 2nd St SW Washington DC 20593 202-372-1051
Web: www.uscgboating.org
Law Enforcement Office 2100 2nd St SW Washington DC 20593 202-372-2183
Web: www.uscg.mil/hq/g-o/g-opl
National Maritime Center 100 Forbes Dr Martinsburg WV 25404 304-433-3400
TF: 888-427-5662 ■ Web: www.uscg.mil/stcw
National Pollution Funds Center
4200 Wilson Blvd Suite 1000 Arlington VA 22203 202-493-6700 493-6900
Web: www.uscg.mil/hq/npfc
Navigation Center 7323 Telegraph Rd Alexandria VA 22315 703-313-5900 313-5920
Web: www.navcen.uscg.gov
Search & Rescue Office 2100 2nd St SW Rm 3106 Washington DC 20593 202-372-2076
Web: www.uscg.mil/hq/g-o/g-opr/g-opr.htm
US Coast Guard Academy 15 Mohegan Ave New London CT 06320 860-444-8500
TF: 800-883-8724 ■ Web: www.cga.edu
US Computer Emergency Readiness Team (CERT)
US-CERT Information Request MS 8500 245 Murray Ln SW Bldg 410 Washington DC 20528 703-235-5110
Web: www.us-cert.gov
US Customs & Border Protection
1300 Pennsylvania Ave NW Washington DC 20229 703-526-4200
TF: 877-227-5511 ■ Web: www.customs.ustreas.gov
US Immigration & Customs Enforcement (ICE)
425 'I' St NW Washington DC 20536 202-514-1900
TF: 866-347-2423 ■ Web: www.ice.gov

US Department of Homeland Security (Cont'd)

Phone Fax

US Secret Service 245 Murray Dr Bldg 410 .... Washington DC 20223 202-406-5708
Web: www.secretservice.gov

343-12 US Department of Housing & Urban Development

Phone Fax

Department of Housing & Urban Development (HUD)
451 7th St SW .... Washington DC 20410 202-708-0685 619-8153
TF: 800-569-4287 ■ Web: www.hud.gov
Public Affairs Office 451 7th St SW MC W .... Washington DC 20410 202-708-0980 619-8153
Department of Housing & Urban Development Regional Offices
Great Plains Region 400 State Ave .... Kansas City KS 66101 913-551-5644 551-5469
Mid-Atlantic Region 100 Penn Sq E .... Philadelphia PA 19107 215-656-0500 656-3445
TF: 800-225-5342
Midwest Region Federal Bldg 77 W Jackson Blvd .... Chicago IL 60604 312-353-6236 886-2729
New England Region Federal Bldg 10 Causeway St .... Boston MA 02222 617-994-8200 565-6558
New York/New Jersey Region 26 Federal Plaza Rm 3541 .... New York NY 10278 212-264-8000 264-2780
Northwest/Alaska Region Federal Bldg 909 1st Ave Suite 200 .... Seattle WA 98104 206-220-5101 220-5108
TF: 877-741-3281
Pacific/Hawaii Region 600 Harrison St .... San Francisco CA 94107 415-489-6400 489-6419
TF: 800-347-3739
Rocky Mountain Region 1670 Broadway 25th Fl .... Denver CO 80202 303-672-5440 672-5004
Southeast/Caribbean Region
Five Points Plaza Bldg 40 Marietta St .... Atlanta GA 30303 404-331-5001 730-2392
Southwest Region 801 N Cherry St Unit 45 Suite 2500 .... Fort Worth TX 76102 817-978-5965 978-5569
Federal Housing Administration 451 7th St SW Suite 9100 .... Washington DC 20410 202-708-1112
TF: 800-767-7468 ■ Web: www.hud.gov/offices/hsg/fhahistory.cfm
Ginnie Mae 451 7th St SW Suite B-133 .... Washington DC 20410 202-708-1535 708-0490
Web: www.ginniemae.gov
Government National Mortgage Assn DBA Ginnie Mae
451 7th St SW Suite B-133 .... Washington DC 20410 202-708-1535 708-0490
Web: www.ginniemae.gov
HUD Office of Community Planning & Development
451 7th St SW MC-D .... Washington DC 20410 202-708-2690 708-3336
Web: www.hud.gov/offices/cpd
Affordable Housing Programs Office
451 7th St SW MS-DGH .... Washington DC 20410 202-708-2684 708-1744
Web: www.hud.gov/offices/cpd/affordablehousing/programs
Block Grant Assistance Office 451 7th St SW MS-DGB .... Washington DC 20410 202-708-3587
Web: www.hud.gov/offices/cpd/communitydevelopment
HIV/AIDS Housing Office 451 7th St SW Rm 7212 .... Washington DC 20410 202-708-1934 708-9313
Web: www.hud.gov/offices/cpd/aidshousing
Special Needs Assistance Programs Office
451 7th St SW MS-DESP .... Washington DC 20410 202-708-4300 708-0053
Web: www.hud.gov/offices/cpd/homeless
HUD Office of Fair Housing & Equal Opportunity
451 7th St SW MC E .... Washington DC 20410 202-708-4252 708-4483
TF: 800-669-9777 ■ Web: www.hud.gov/offices/fheo
Housing Discrimination Hotline .... Washington DC 20410 800-669-9777
Web: www.hud.gov/complaints/housediscrim.cfm
HUD Office of Healthy Homes & Lead Hazard Control
451 7th St SW MC-L .... Washington DC 20410 202-708-0310 755-1000
Web: www.hud.gov/offices/lead
HUD Office of Housing - Federal Housing Administration (FHA) 451 7th St SW Suite 9100 .... Washington DC 20410 202-708-1112
TF: 800-767-7468 ■ Web: www.hud.gov/offices/hsg/fhahistory.cfm
HUD Office of Policy Development & Research
451 7th St SW MC R .... Washington DC 20410 202-708-1600 619-8000
Web: www.huduser.org
HUD Office of Public & Indian Housing
451 7th St SW Rm 4100 .... Washington DC 20410 202-708-0950 619-8478
TF: 800-955-2232 ■ Web: www.hud.gov/offices/pih
Real Estate Assessment Center 550 12th St SW Suite 100 .... Washington DC 20410 888-245-4860
Web: www.hud.gov/offices/reac
Real Estate Assessment Center 550 12th St SW Suite 100 .... Washington DC 20410 888-245-4860
Web: www.hud.gov/offices/reac
Secretary of Housing & Urban Development
451 7th St SW .... Washington DC 20410 202-708-0417 619-8365
Web: www.hud.gov/about

343-13 US Department of the Interior

Phone Fax

Department of the Interior (DOI) 1849 C St NW .... Washington DC 20240 202-208-3100
Web: www.doi.gov
Nationalatlas.gov
US Geological Survey 508 National Ctr 12201 Sunrise Valley Dr .... Reston VA 20192 703-648-5953
TF: 888-275-8747 ■ Web: nationalatlas.gov
Bureau of Indian Affairs (BIA) 1849 C St NW MS 4141 .... Washington DC 20240 202-208-7163 208-5320
Web: www.doi.gov/bureau-indian-affairs.html
Bureau of Indian Affairs Regional Offices
Alaska Region 709 W 9th St 3rd Fl PO Box 25520 .... Juneau AK 99802 907-586-7177 586-7252
TF: 800-645-8397
Eastern Oklahoma Region PO Box 8002 .... Muskogee OK 74402 918-781-4600 781-4604
Eastern Region 545 Marriott Dr Suite 700 .... Nashville TN 37214 615-564-6700 564-6701
TF: 888-258-6118
Great Plains Region 115 4th Ave SE .... Aberdeen SD 57401 605-226-7343 226-7446
Midwest Region Federal Bldg 1 Federal Dr Rm 550 .... Minneapolis MN 55111 612-713-4400 713-4401
Navajo Region PO Box 1060 .... Gallup NM 87305 505-863-8314 863-8324
Northwest Region Federal Complex 911 NE 11th Ave .... Portland OR 97232 503-231-6702 231-2201
Pacific Region
Federal Bldg 2800 Cottage Way Suite W-2820 .... Sacramento CA 95825 916-978-6000 978-6099
Rocky Mountain Region Federal Courthouse 316 N 26th St .... Billings MT 59101 406-247-7943 247-7976
Southern Plains Region PO Box 368 .... Anadarko OK 73005 405-247-6673 247-5611
Southwest Region 1001 Indian School Rd NW .... Albuquerque NM 87104 505-563-3103 563-3101
Western Region 400 N 5th St 12th Fl 12 Arizona Center .... Phoenix AZ 85001 602-379-6600 379-4413
Bureau of Land Management (BLM) 1849 C St NW .... Washington DC 20240 202-208-3801 208-5242
Web: www.blm.gov
National Wild Horse & Burro Program PO Box 3270 .... Sparks NV 89432 775-475-2222
TF: 866-468-7826 ■ Web: www.blm.gov/wo/st/en/prog/wild_horse_and_burro.html
Bureau of Land Management Regional Offices
Alaska State Office 222 W 7th Ave Suite 13 .... Anchorage AK 99513 907-271-5960 271-3684
Web: www.blm.gov/ak/blmaso.html
Arizona State Office 1 N Central Ave Suite 800 .... Phoenix AZ 85004 602-417-9200 417-9556
Web: www.blm.gov/az
California State Office 2800 Cottage Way Suite W-1834 .... Sacramento CA 95825 916-978-4400 978-4416
Web: www.blm.gov/ca
Colorado State Office 2850 Youngfield St .... Lakewood CO 80215 303-239-3600 239-3933
Web: www.co.blm.gov
Eastern States Office 7450 Boston Blvd .... Springfield VA 22153 703-440-1600
Web: www.es.blm.gov
Idaho State Office 1387 S Vinnell Way .... Boise ID 83709 208-373-4000 373-3899
Web: www.id.blm.gov
Montana State Office 5001 Southgate Dr .... Billings MT 59101 406-896-5000
Web: www.mt.blm.gov
Nevada State Office 1340 Financial Blvd .... Reno NV 89502 775-861-6400 861-6606
Web: www.nv.blm.gov
New Mexico State Office 1474 Rodeo Rd .... Santa Fe NM 87505 505-438-7400 438-7435
Web: www.nm.blm.gov
Oregon/Washington State Office 333 SW 1st Ave .... Portland OR 97204 503-808-6001 808-6422
Web: www.blm.gov/or
Utah State Office PO Box 45155 .... Salt Lake City UT 84145 801-539-4001 539-4013
Web: www.ut.blm.gov
Wyoming State Office 5353 Yellowstone Rd PO Box 1828 .... Cheyenne WY 82003 307-775-6256 775-6129
Web: www.wy.blm.gov
Bureau of Reclamation 1849 C St NW .... Washington DC 20240 202-513-0501 513-0314
Web: www.usbr.gov
Bureau of Reclamation Regional Offices
Great Plains Region PO Box 36900 .... Billings MT 59107 406-247-7600 247-7604
Web: www.usbr.gov/gp
Lower Colorado Region PO Box 61470 .... Boulder City NV 89006 702-293-8411 293-8333
Web: www.usbr.gov/lc
Mid-Pacific Region Federal Bldg 2800 Cottage Way .... Sacramento CA 95825 916-978-5000 978-5005
Web: www.usbr.gov/mp
Pacific Northwest Region 1150 N Curtis Rd Suite 100 .... Boise ID 83706 208-378-5012 378-5019
Web: www.usbr.gov/pn
Upper Colorado Region 125 S State St Rm 6107 .... Salt Lake City UT 84138 801-524-3600 524-5499
Web: www.usbr.gov/uc
Minerals Management Service 1849 C St NW .... Washington DC 20240 202-208-3500 208-7242
Web: www.mms.gov
National Interagency Fire Center 3833 S Development Ave .... Boise ID 83705 208-387-5512 387-5797
Web: www.nifc.gov
National Park Service (NPS) 1849 C St NW Rm 1013 .... Washington DC 20240 202-208-6843 219-0910
Web: www.nps.gov
Conservation & Outdoor Recreation Programs
National Park Service 1849 C St NW Org Code 2220 .... Washington DC 20246 202-354-6900 371-5179
Web: www.nps.gov/ncrc
National Register of Historic Places
c/o National Park Service 1201 Eye St NW 8th Fl .... Washington DC 20005 202-354-2213
Web: www.cr.nps.gov/nr
National Park Service Regional Offices
Alaska Region 240 W 5th Ave Suite 114 .... Anchorage AK 99501 907-644-3510 644-3816
Intermountain Region 12795 W Alameda Pkwy .... Denver CO 80225 303-969-2500
Midwest Region 601 Riverfront Dr .... Omaha NE 68102 402-661-1524 661-1984
National Capital Region 1100 Ohio Dr SW .... Washington DC 20242 202-619-7000 619-7220
Web: www.nps.gov/ncro
Northeast Region US Custom House 200 Chestnut St .... Philadelphia PA 19106 215-597-7013 597-0815
Web: www.nps.gov/nero
Pacific West Region 1111 Jackson St Suite 700 .... Oakland CA 94607 510-817-1304 817-1485
Southeast Region 100 Alabama St SW 1924 Building .... Atlanta GA 30303 404-562-3100
National Register of Historic Places
c/o National Park Service 1201 Eye St NW 8th Fl .... Washington DC 20005 202-354-2213
Web: www.cr.nps.gov/nr
Office of Surface Mining Reclamation & Enforcement
1951 Constitution Ave NW SIB Rm 233 .... Washington DC 20240 202-208-4006 219-5106
Web: www.osmre.gov
Office of Surface Mining Reclamation & Enforcement Regional Offices
Appalachian Region 3 Parkway Center .... Pittsburgh PA 15220 412-937-2804
Web: www.arcc.osmre.gov
Mid-Continent Region 501 Belle St .... Alton IL 62002 618-463-6460 463-6470
Web: www.mcrcc.osmre.gov
Western Region 1999 Broadway Suite 3320 PO Box 46667 .... Denver CO 80201 303-293-5000
Web: www.wrcc.osmre.gov
Secretary of the Interior 1849 C St NW Rm 6156 .... Washington DC 20240 202-208-7351 208-5048
Web: www.doi.gov/welcome.html
US Board on Geographic Names
US Geological Survey 12201 Sunrise Valley Dr MS 523 .... Reston VA 20192 703-605-4575
Web: geonames.usgs.gov
US Fish & Wildlife Service (USFWS) 1849 C St NW .... Washington DC 20240 202-208-4717 208-6965
TF: 800-344-9453 ■ Web: www.fws.gov
US Fish & Wildlife Service Regional Offices
Alaska Region 1011 E Tudor Rd .... Anchorage AK 99503 907-786-3309 786-3495
Web: alaska.fws.gov
California & Nevada Region 2800 Cottage Way .... Sacramento CA 95825 916-414-6464 414-6486
Web: www.fws.gov/cno
Great Lakes/Big Rivers Region 1 Federal Dr .... Fort Snelling MN 55111 612-713-5360 713-5280
Web: www.fws.gov/midwest
Mountain-Prairie Region 134 Union Blvd .... Lakewood CO 80228 303-236-7905 236-8295
Web: mountain-prairie.fws.gov
Northeast Region 300 Westgate Center Dr .... Hadley MA 01035 413-253-8200 253-8308
Web: www.fws.gov/northeast
Pacific Region Eastside Federal Complex 911 NE 11th Ave .... Portland OR 97232 503-231-6828 872-2716
Web: www.fws.gov/pacific/
Southeast Region 1875 Century Blvd .... Atlanta GA 30345 404-679-4000 679-4006
Web: www.fws.gov/southeast
Southwest Region 500 Gold Ave SW .... Albuquerque NM 87102 505-248-6911 248-6910
Web: www.fws.gov/southwest
US Geological Survey (USGS) 12201 Sunrise Valley Dr .... Reston VA 20192 703-648-4000 648-4454
TF: 888-275-8747 ■ Web: www.usgs.gov
Ask USGS 12201 Sunrise Valley Dr .... Reston VA 20192 888-275-8747
Web: ask.usgs.gov

343-14 US Department of Justice

Phone Fax

Department of Justice (DOJ) 950 Pennsylvania Ave NW .... Washington DC 20530 202-514-2007 514-5331
Web: www.usdoj.gov
Department of Justice Antitrust Div Regional Offices
Atlanta Field Office Federal Bldg 75 Spring St SW Suite 1176 .... Atlanta GA 30303 404-331-7100 331-7110
Chicago Field Office 209 S LaSalle St Suite 600 .... Chicago IL 60604 312-353-7530 353-1046
Cleveland Field Office 55 Erieview Plaza Suite 700 .... Cleveland OH 44114 216-522-4070 522-8332
Dallas Field Office 1601 Elm St Suite 3900 .... Dallas TX 75201 214-880-9401 880-9423
New York Field Office 26 Federal Plaza Rm 3630 .... New York NY 10278 212-264-0391 264-0678
Philadelphia Field Office
170 S Independence Mall W Suite 650 W .... Philadelphia PA 19106 215-597-7405 597-8838
San Francisco Field Office
US Courthouse 450 Golden Gate Ave Rm 10-0101 .... San Francisco CA 94102 415-436-6660 436-6687
Department of Justice (DOJ)
Antitrust Div 950 Pennsylvania Ave NW .... Washington DC 20530 202-514-2401 616-2645
Web: www.usdoj.gov/atr
Civil Div 950 Pennsylvania Ave NW .... Washington DC 20530 202-514-3301 514-8071
Web: www.usdoj.gov/civil
Civil Rights Div 950 Pennsylvania Ave NW .... Washington DC 20530 202-514-4609 307-2572
Web: www.usdoj.gov/crt

	City	State	Zip	Phone	Fax
Community Relations Service 600 'E' St NW	Washington	DC	20530	202-305-2935	305-3009
Web: www.usdoj.gov/crs					
Criminal Div 601 D St NW	Washington	DC	20530	202-514-7200	514-9412
Web: www.usdoj.gov/criminal					
Environment & Natural Resources Div 950 Pennsylvania Ave NW	Washington	DC	20530	202-514-2701	514-0557
Web: www.usdoj.gov/enrd					
National Security Division 950 Pennsylvania Ave NW	Washington	DC	20530	202-514-1057	353-9836
Web: www.usdoj.gov/nsd					
Office of Information & Privacy 1425 New York Ave NW Suite 11050	Washington	DC	20530	202-514-3642	514-1009
Web: www.usdoj.gov/oip/oip.html					
Public Affairs Office 950 Pennsylvania Ave NW	Washington	DC	20530	202-616-2777	
Web: www.usdoj.gov/opa					
Tax Div 950 Pennsylvania Ave NW 4th Fl	Washington	DC	20530	202-514-2901	514-5479
Web: www.usdoj.gov/tax					
ATF (Bureau of Alcohol Tobacco Firearms & Explosives) 650 Massachusetts Ave NW	Washington	DC	20226	202-927-7777	927-7862
Web: www.atf.gov					
Attorney General 950 Pennsylvania Ave NW	Washington	DC	20530	202-514-2000	307-6777
Web: www.usdoj.gov/ag					
Bureau of Alcohol Tobacco Firearms & Explosives (ATF) 650 Massachusetts Ave NW	Washington	DC	20226	202-927-7777	927-7862
Web: www.atf.gov					
Bureau of Alcohol Tobacco Firearms & Explosives Regional Offices					
Atlanta Field Div 2600 Century Pkwy NE	Atlanta	GA	30345	404-417-2600	417-2601
Web: www.atf.gov/field/atlanta					
Baltimore Field Div 31 Hopkins Plaza 5th Fl	Baltimore	MD	21201	410-779-1700	779-1701
Web: www.atf.gov/field/baltimore					
Boston Field Div 10 Causeway St Suite 791	Boston	MA	02222	617-557-1200	577-1201
Web: www.atf.gov/field/boston					
Charlotte Field Div 6701 Carmel Rd Suite 200	Charlotte	NC	28226	704-716-1800	716-1801
Web: www.atf.gov/field/charlotte					
Chicago Field Div 525 W Van Buren St Suite 600	Chicago	IL	60607	312-846-7200	846-7201
Web: www.atf.gov/field/chicago					
Columbus Field Div 37 W Broad St Suite 200	Columbus	OH	43215	614-827-8400	827-8401
Web: www.atf.gov/field/columbus					
Dallas Field Div 1114 Commerce St Rm 303	Dallas	TX	75242	469-227-4300	227-4330
Web: www.atf.gov/field/dallas					
Denver Field Div Byron Rogers Federal Bldg 1961 Stout St Rm 674	Denver	CO	80294	303-844-7450	844-7535
Web: www.atf.gov/field/denver					
Detroit Field Div 1155 Brewery Park Blvd Suite 300	Detroit	MI	48207	313-259-8050	393-6054
Web: www.atf.gov/field/detroit					
Houston Field Div 15355 Vantage Pkwy W Suite 200	Houston	TX	77032	281-372-2900	372-2919
Web: www.atf.gov/field/houston					
Kansas City Field Div 2600 Grand Ave Suite 200	Kansas City	MO	64108	816-559-0700	559-0701
Web: www.atf.gov/field/kansascity					
Los Angeles Field Div 350 S Figueroa St Suite 800	Los Angeles	CA	90071	213-534-2450	534-2415
Web: www.atf.gov/field/losangeles					
Louisville Field Div 600 Dr ML King Jr Pl Suite 322	Louisville	KY	40202	502-753-3400	753-3401
Web: www.atf.gov/field/louisville					
Miami Field Div 5225 NW 87th Ave Suite 300	Miami	FL	33178	305-597-4800	597-4801
Web: www.atf.gov/field/miami					
Nashville Field Div 5300 Maryland Way Suite 200	Brentwood	TN	37027	615-565-1400	565-1401
Web: www.atf.gov/field/nashville					
New Orleans Field Div 428 E Boston 2nd Fl	Covington	LA	70433	985-246-7000	246-7038
Web: www.atf.gov/field/neworleans					
New York Field Div 241 37th St 3rd Fl	Brooklyn	NY	11232	718-650-4000	650-4001
Web: www.atf.gov/field/newyork					
Philadelphia Field Div Curtis Center 601 Walnut St Suite 1000E	Philadelphia	PA	19106	215-446-7800	446-7811
Web: www.atf.gov/field/philadelphia					
Phoenix Field Div 201 E Washington St Suite 940	Phoenix	AZ	85004	602-776-5400	776-5429
Web: www.atf.gov/field/phoenix					
Saint Paul Field Div 30 E 7th St Suite 1900	Saint Paul	MN	55101	651-726-0200	726-0201
Web: www.atf.gov/field/stpaul					
San Francisco Field Div 5601 Arnold Rd Suite 400	Dublin	CA	94568	925-479-7500	829-7612
Web: www.atf.gov/field/sanfrancisco					
Seattle Field Div 915 2nd Ave Rm 790	Seattle	WA	98174	206-389-5800	389-5829
Web: www.atf.gov/field/seattle					
Tampa Field Div 501 E Polk St Suite 700	Tampa	FL	33602	813-202-7300	202-7301
Web: www.atf.gov/field/tampa					
Washington (DC) Field Div 1401 H St NW Suite 900	Washington	DC	20226	202-648-8010	648-8001
Web: www.atf.gov/field/washington					
Bureau of Justice Assistance 810 7th St NW	Washington	DC	20531	202-616-6500	305-1367
Web: www.ojp.usdoj.gov/BJA					
Community Oriented Policing Services (COPS) 1100 Vermont Ave NW 10th Fl	Washington	DC	20530	202-616-2888	
TF: 800-421-6770 ■ *Web:* www.cops.usdoj.gov					
DEA (Drug Enforcement Administration) 700 Army-Navy Dr	Arlington	VA	22202	202-307-8000	
Web: www.dea.gov					
Drug Enforcement Administration (DEA) 700 Army-Navy Dr	Arlington	VA	22202	202-307-8000	
Web: www.dea.gov					
DEA Training Academy PO Box 1475	Quantico	VA	22134	703-632-5000	
Web: www.usdoj.gov/dea/programs/training.htm					
El Paso Intelligence Center 11339 Simms St	El Paso	TX	79908	915-760-2000	
Web: www.dea.gov/programs/epic.htm					
Drug Enforcement Administration Regional Offices					
Atlanta Div Federal Bldg 75 Spring St SW	Atlanta	GA	30303	404-893-7000	893-7110
Web: www.dea.gov/pubs/states/atlanta.html					
Boston Div 15 New Sudbury St Rm E400	Boston	MA	02203	617-557-2100	557-2135
Web: www.dea.gov/pubs/states/boston.html					
Chicago Div Federal Bldg 230 S Dearborn St	Chicago	IL	60604	312-353-7875	886-8439
Web: www.dea.gov/pubs/states/chicago.html					
Dallas Div 10160 Technology Blvd E	Dallas	TX	75220	214-366-6900	366-6914
Web: www.dea.gov/pubs/states/dallas.html					
Denver Div 115 Inverness Dr E	Englewood	CO	80112	303-705-7300	705-7414
Web: www.dea.gov/pubs/states/denver.html					
Detroit Div 431 Howard St	Detroit	MI	48226	313-234-4000	234-4141
Web: www.dea.gov/pubs/states/detroit.html					
El Paso Div 660 S Mesa Hills Suite 2000	El Paso	TX	79912	915-832-6000	832-6001
Web: www.dea.gov/pubs/states/elpaso.html					
Houston Div 1433 West Loop S Suite 600	Houston	TX	77027	713-693-3000	
Web: www.dea.gov/pubs/states/houston.html					
Los Angeles Div Federal Bldg 255 E Temple St 20th Fl	Los Angeles	CA	90012	213-621-6700	
Web: www.dea.gov/pubs/states/la.html					
Miami Div 8400 NW 53rd St	Miami	FL	33166	305-994-4870	994-4500
Web: www.dea.gov/pubs/states/miami.html					
New Jersey Div 80 Mulberry St	Newark	NJ	07102	973-273-5000	645-6297
Web: www.dea.gov/pubs/states/newark.html					
New Orleans Div 3838 N Causeway Blvd Suite 1800	Metairie	LA	70002	504-840-1100	
Web: www.dea.gov/pubs/states/neworleans.html					
New York Div 99 10th Ave	New York	NY	10011	212-337-3900	337-2799
Web: www.dea.gov/pubs/states/nyc.html					
Philadelphia Div Federal Bldg 600 Arch St Rm 10224	Philadelphia	PA	19106	215-861-3474	861-1979
Web: www.dea.gov/pubs/states/phila.html					

	City	State	Zip	Phone	Fax
Phoenix Div 3010 N 2nd St Suite 301	Phoenix	AZ	85012	602-664-5600	664-5616
Web: www.dea.gov/pubs/states/phoenix.html					
Saint Louis Div 317 S 16th St	Saint Louis	MO	63103	314-538-4600	538-4798
Web: www.dea.gov/pubs/states/stlouis.html					
San Diego Div 4560 Viewridge Ave	San Diego	CA	92123	858-616-4100	616-4084
Web: www.dea.gov/pubs/states/sandiego.html					
San Francisco Div 450 Golden Gate Ave	San Francisco	CA	94102	415-436-7900	436-7810
Web: www.dea.gov/pubs/states/sanfran.html					
Seattle Div 400 2nd Ave W	Seattle	WA	98119	206-553-5443	553-1576
Web: www.dea.gov/pubs/states/seattle.html					
Washington DC Div 800 K St NW Suite 500	Washington	DC	20001	202-305-8500	305-5760
Web: www.dea.gov/pubs/states/wdo.html					
Executive Office for Immigration Review 5107 Leesburg Pike	Falls Church	VA	22041	703-305-0289	605-0365
Web: www.usdoj.gov/eoir					
Executive Office for US Attorneys 950 Pennsylvania Ave NW	Washington	DC	20530	202-514-2121	616-2278
Web: www.usdoj.gov/usao/eousa					
Executive Office for US Trustees 20 Massachusetts Ave NW Suite 8000	Washington	DC	20530	202-307-1391	307-0672
Web: www.usdoj.gov/ust					
Federal Bureau of Investigation (FBI) 935 Pennsylvania Ave NW	Washington	DC	20535	202-324-3000	
Web: www.fbi.gov					
Criminal Justice Information Services 1000 Custer Hollow Rd	Clarksburg	WV	26306	304-625-2700	
Web: www.fbi.gov/hq/cjisd/cjis.htm					
FBI Academy	Quantico	VA	22135	703-632-1000	
Web: www.fbi.gov/hq/td/academy/academy.htm					
FBI Laboratory FBI Academy	Quantico	VA	22135	703-632-1000	
Web: www.fbi.gov/hq/lab/labhome.htm					
Federal Bureau of Prisons 320 1st St NW	Washington	DC	20534	202-307-3250	514-6620
Web: www.bop.gov					
Management & Specialty Training Center 791Chambers Rd	Aurora	CO	80011	303-340-7800	
Web: www.bop.gov/about/train					
National Institute of Corrections 320 1st St NW	Washington	DC	20534	202-307-3106	
TF: 800-995-6423 ■ *Web:* nicic.org					
National Institute of Corrections Information Center 1860 Industrial Cir Suite A	Longmont	CO	80501	303-682-0213	682-0558
TF: 800-877-1461 ■ *Web:* nicic.org					
Federal Bureau of Prisons Regional Offices					
Mid-Atlantic Region 302 Sentinel Dr Suite 200	Annapolis Junction	MD	20701	301-317-3100	
Web: www.bop.gov/about/ro/mxr					
North Central Region 400 State Ave Suite 800	Kansas City	KS	66101	913-621-3939	
Web: www.bop.gov/about/ro/ncr					
Northeast Region 2nd & Chestnut St 7th Fl	Philadelphia	PA	19106	215-521-7301	
Web: www.bop.gov/about/ro/ner					
South Central Region 4211 Cedar Springs Rd	Dallas	TX	75219	214-224-3389	
Web: www.bop.gov/about/ro/scr					
Southeast Region 3800 Camp Creek Pk SW Bldg 2000	Atlanta	GA	30331	678-686-1200	
Web: www.bop.gov/about/ro/ser					
Western Region 7950 Dublin Blvd 3rd Fl	Dublin	CA	94568	925-803-4700	
Web: www.bop.gov/about/ro/wxr					
Foreign Claims Settlement Commission of the US 600 'E' St NW	Washington	DC	20579	202-616-6975	616-6993
Web: www.usdoj.gov/fcsc					
Freedom of Information Act 1425 New York Ave NW Suite 11050	Washington	DC	20530	202-514-3642	514-1009
Web: www.usdoj.gov/oip/oip.html					
National Criminal Justice Reference Service PO Box 6000	Rockville	MD	20849	301-519-5500	519-5212
TF: 800-851-3420 ■ *Web:* www.ncjrs.org					
National Drug Intelligence Center 319 Washington St 5th Fl	Johnstown	PA	15901	814-532-4601	532-4690
Web: www.usdoj.gov/ndic					
National Institute of Corrections 320 1st St NW	Washington	DC	20534	202-307-3106	
TF: 800-995-6423 ■ *Web:* nicic.org					
National Institute of Justice 810 7th St NW	Washington	DC	20531	202-307-2942	307-6394
Web: www.ojp.usdoj.gov/nij					
Office of Justice Programs (OJP) 810 7th St NW	Washington	DC	20531	202-307-0703	
Web: www.ojp.usdoj.gov					
Bureau of Justice Assistance 810 7th St NW	Washington	DC	20531	202-616-6500	305-1367
Web: www.ojp.usdoj.gov/BJA					
Bureau of Justice Statistics 810 7th St NW	Washington	DC	20531	202-307-0765	307-5846
TF: 800-851-3420 ■ *Web:* www.ojp.usdoj.gov/bjs					
Community Capacity Development Office 810 7th St NW	Washington	DC	20531	202-616-1152	616-1159
Web: www.ojp.usdoj.gov/ccdo					
National Institute of Justice 810 7th St NW	Washington	DC	20531	202-307-2942	307-6394
Web: www.ojp.usdoj.gov/nij					
Office of Juvenile Justice & Delinquency Prevention 810 7th St NW	Washington	DC	20531	202-307-5911	307-2093
Web: ojjdp.ncjrs.org					
Office for Victims of Crime 810 7th St NW 8th Fl	Washington	DC	20531	202-307-5983	514-6383
Web: www.ojp.usdoj.gov/ovc					
Office of the Pardon Attorney 1425 New York Ave NW Suite 1100	Washington	DC	20530	202-616-6070	616-6069
Web: www.usdoj.gov/pardon					
Office of Special Counsel for Immigration-Related Unfair Employment Practices 950 Pennsylvania Ave NW	Washington	DC	20038	202-616-5594	616-5509
TF Hotline: 800-255-7688 ■ *Web:* www.usdoj.gov/crt/osc					
Office of Tribal Justice 950 Pennsylvania Ave NW Rm 2200C	Washington	DC	20530	202-514-8812	514-9078
Web: www.usdoj.gov/otj					
Office for Victims of Crime 810 7th St NW 8th Fl	Washington	DC	20531	202-307-5983	514-6383
Web: www.ojp.usdoj.gov/ovc					
Office on Violence Against Women 800 K St NW Suite 920	Washington	DC	20530	202-307-6026	307-3911
Web: www.ovw.usdoj.gov					
US Marshals Service 1735 Jefferson Davis Hwy	Arlington	VA	22202	202-307-9100	307-8729
TF: 800-336-0102 ■ *Web:* www.usmarshals.gov					
US National Central Bureau of INTERPOL (INTERPOL)	Washington	DC	20530	202-616-9000	616-8400
Web: www.usdoj.gov/usncb					
US Parole Commission 5550 Friendship Blvd Rm 420	Chevy Chase	MD	20815	301-492-5990	492-5543
Web: www.usdoj.gov/uspc					

343-15 US Department of Labor

	City	State	Zip	Phone	Fax
Department of Labor (DOL) 200 Constitution Ave NW	Washington	DC	20210	202-693-4650	693-4674
TF: 866-487-2365 ■ *Web:* www.dol.gov					
Department of Labor Regional Offices					
Region 1 - Boston JFK Federal Bldg Rm E-335	Boston	MA	02203	617-656-2282	565-2280
Region 2 - New York 201 Varick St Rm 605B	New York	NY	10014	212-337-2387	337-2386
Region 3 - Philadelphia 170 S Independence Mall W Suite 635E	Philadelphia	PA	19106	215-861-5027	861-5029
Region 4 - Atlanta Federal Center 61 Forsyth St SW Suite 6B75	Atlanta	GA	30303	404-562-2076	562-2081
Region 5 - Chicago Federal Bldg 230 S Dearborn St	Chicago	IL	60604	312-353-4591	353-8679
Region 6 - Dallas Federal Bldg 525 S Griffin St Suite 731	Dallas	TX	75202	214-676-6800	767-6809

US Department of Labor (Cont'd)

Phone Fax

Region 8 - Denver 1999 Broadway ... Denver CO 80201 303-844-1256 844-1257
Region 10 - Seattle 1111 3rd Ave Suite 920 ... Seattle WA 98101 206-553-0574 553-2086
Department of Labor (DOL)
GovBenefits.gov 200 Constitution Ave NW ... Washington DC 20210 800-333-4636
TF: 866-487-2365 ■ *Web:* www.govbenefits.gov
Job Corps 200 Constitution Ave NW ... Washington DC 20210 202-693-3000 693-2767
Web: jobcorps.dol.gov
Office of Administrative Law Judges
800 K St NW Suite 400 N ... Washington DC 20001 202-693-7300 693-7365
Web: www.oalj.dol.gov
Public Affairs Office 200 Constitution Ave NW Rm S2514 ... Washington DC 20210 202-693-4676 693-5057
TF: 866-487-2365
Bureau of International Labor Affairs
200 Constitution Ave NW Rm C4325 ... Washington DC 20210 202-693-4770 693-4780
Web: www.dol.gov/ilab
Bureau of Labor Statistics 2 Massachusetts Ave NE ... Washington DC 20212 202-691-5200 691-7890
Web: www.bls.gov
Consumer Price Index
2 Massachusetts Ave NE Suite 3130 ... Washington DC 20212 202-691-7000 691-6325
Web: www.bls.gov/cpi
Bureau of Labor Statistics Regional Offices
Mid-Atlantic Information Office
170 S Independence Mall W Suite 610 E ... Philadelphia PA 19106 215-597-3282 861-5720
Web: www.bls.gov/ro3
Midwest Information Office
Federal Bldg 230 S Dearborn St Rm 960 ... Chicago IL 60604 312-353-1880 353-1886
Web: www.bls.gov/ro5
Mountain-Plains Information Office
2300 Main St Suite 1190 ... Kansas City MO 64108 816-285-7000 285-7009
Web: www.bls.gov/ro7
New England Information Office JFK Federal Bldg Rm E-310 ... Boston MA 02203 617-565-2327 565-4182
Web: www.bls.gov/ro1
New York-New Jersey Information Office
201 Varick St Rm 808 ... New York NY 10014 212-264-3600 337-2532
Web: www.bls.gov/ro2
Southeast Information Office
Federal Center 61 Forsyth St SW Suite 7T50 ... Atlanta GA 30303 404-893-4222 893-4221
Web: www.bls.gov/ro4
Southwest Information Office
Federal Bldg 525 Griffin St Rm 221 ... Dallas TX 75202 214-767-6970 767-8881
Web: www.bls.gov/ro6
Western Information Office PO Box 193766 ... San Francisco CA 94119 415-625-2270 625-2351
Web: www.bls.gov/ro9
Employee Benefits Security Administration
200 Constitution Ave NW Rm S2524 ... Washington DC 20210 202-693-8300 219-5526
Web: www.dol.gov/ebsa
Employment Standards Administration
200 Constitution Ave NW Rm S2321 ... Washington DC 20210 202-693-0200 693-0218
TF: 866-487-2365 ■ *Web:* www.dol.gov/esa
Office of Labor-Management Standards
200 Constitution Ave NW Rm N5605 ... Washington DC 20210 202-693-0122
Web: www.dol.gov/esa/olms_org.htm
Office of Workers' Compensation Programs
200 Constitution Ave Rm S3524 ... Washington DC 20210 202-693-0031 693-1378
Web: www.dol.gov/esa/owcp_org.htm
Wage & Hour Div 200 Constitution Ave NW ... Washington DC 20210 202-693-0051 693-1406
Web: www.dol.gov/esa/whd
Employment & Training Administration
200 Constitution Ave NW Rm S2307 ... Washington DC 20210 202-693-2700 693-2725
Web: www.doleta.gov
Employment & Training Administration Regional Offices
Region I - Boston JFK Federal Bldg Rm E-350 ... Boston MA 02203 617-788-0170 788-0101
Web: www.doleta.gov/regions/reg01bos
Region II - Philadelphia
Curtis Center 170 S Independence Mall West
Suite 825E ... Philadelphia PA 19106 215-861-5200 861-5260
Web: www.doleta.gov/regions/reg02
Region III - Atlanta
Federal Center 61 Forsyth St SW Rm 6M12 ... Atlanta GA 30303 404-302-5300 302-5382
Web: www.doleta.gov/regions/reg03
Region IV - Dallas Federal Bldg 525 Griffin St Rm 317 ... Dallas TX 75202 972-850-4600 850-4605
Web: www.doleta.gov/regions/reg04
Region V - Chicago Federal Bldg 230 S Dearborn St 6th Fl ... Chicago IL 60604 312-596-5400
Web: www.doleta.gov/regions/reg05
Region VI - San Francisco 90 7th St Suite 17-300 ... San Francisco CA 94103 415-625-7900 625-7903
Web: www.doleta.gov/regions/reg06
Labor Racketeering & Fraud Investigations Office
200 Constitution Ave NW Rm S5014 ... Washington DC 20210 202-693-5229
Web: www.oig.dol.gov/olrfi.htm
Mine Safety & Health Administration (MSHA)
1100 Wilson Blvd ... Arlington VA 22209 202-693-9400 693-9401
TF: 800-746-1553 ■ *Web:* www.msha.gov
Coal Mine Safety & Health Office 1100 Wilson Blvd ... Arlington VA 22209 202-693-9500 693-9501
Web: www.msha.gov/programs/coal.htm
Metal & Non-Metal Mine Safety & Health Office
1100 Wilson Blvd ... Arlington VA 22209 202-693-9600 693-9601
Web: www.msha.gov/programs/metal.htm
National Mine Health & Safety Academy 1301 Airport Rd ... Beaver WV 25813 304-256-3100 256-3324
Web: www.msha.gov/programs/epd2.htm
National Mine Health & Safety Academy 1301 Airport Rd ... Beaver WV 25813 304-256-3100 256-3324
Web: www.msha.gov/programs/epd2.htm
Occupational Safety & Health Administration (OSHA)
200 Constitution Ave NW ... Washington DC 20210 202-693-1999 693-1659
TF: 800-321-6735 ■ *Web:* www.osha.gov
Occupational Safety & Health Administration Regional Offices
Region 1 JFK Federal Bldg Rm E-340 ... Boston MA 02203 617-565-9860 565-9827
TF: 800-321-6742 ■ *Web:* www.osha.gov/oshdir/r01.html
Region 2 201 Varick St Suite 670 ... New York NY 10014 212-337-2378 337-2371
TF: 800-321-6742 ■ *Web:* www.osha.gov/oshdir/r02.html
Region 3
Curtis Center 170 S Independence Mall W Suite 740W ... Philadelphia PA 19106 215-861-4900 861-4904
TF: 800-321-6742 ■ *Web:* www.osha.gov/oshdir/r03.html
Region 4 61 Forsyth St SW Rm 6T50 ... Atlanta GA 30303 404-562-2300 562-2295
Web: www.osha.gov/oshdir/r04.html
Region 5 Federal Bldg 230 S Dearborn St Rm 3244 ... Chicago IL 60604 312-353-2220 353-7774
Web: www.osha.gov/oshdir/r05.html
Region 6 Federal Bldg 525 Griffin St Rm 602 ... Dallas TX 75202 972-850-4145 850-4149
Web: www.osha.gov/oshdir/r06.html
Region 7 2300 Main St Suite 1010 ... Kansas City MO 64108 816-283-8745 283-0547
Web: www.osha.gov/oshdir/r07.html
Region 8 1999 Broadway Suite 1690 ... Denver CO 80202 720-264-6550 264-6585
Web: www.osha.gov/oshdir/r08.html
Region 9 90 7th St Suite 18100 ... San Francisco CA 94103 415-625-2547 625-2534
Web: www.osha.gov/oshdir/r09.html
Region 10 1111 3rd Ave Suite 715 ... Seattle WA 98101 206-553-5930 553-6499
TF: 800-321-6742 ■ *Web:* www.osha.gov/oshdir/r10.html
Office of Disability Employment Policy
200 Constitution Ave NW Suite S1303 ... Washington DC 20210 202-693-7880 693-7888
TF: 866-633-7365 ■ *Web:* www.dol.gov/odep
Secretary of Labor 200 Constitution Ave NW Rm S2018 ... Washington DC 20210 202-693-6000 693-6111
TF: 866-487-2365 ■ *Web:* www.dol.gov
Veterans' Employment & Training Service
200 Constitution Ave NW Rm S1325 ... Washington DC 20210 202-693-4700 693-4754
Web: www.dol.gov/vets
Women's Bureau 200 Constitution Ave NW Rm S3002 ... Washington DC 20210 202-693-6710 693-6746
TF: 800-827-5335 ■ *Web:* www.dol.gov/wb
Women's Bureau Regional Offices
Region 1 JFK Federal Bldg Rm 525-A ... Boston MA 02203 617-565-1988 565-1986
Web: www.dol.gov/wb
Region 2 201 Varick St Rm 602 ... New York NY 10014 212-337-2389 337-2394
TF: 800-827-5335 ■ *Web:* www.dol.gov/wb
Region 3 170 S Independence Mall W Suite 631E ... Philadelphia PA 19106 215-861-4860 861-4867
TF: 800-827-5335 ■ *Web:* www.dol.gov/wb
Region 4 Federal Center 61 Forsyth St SW Suite 7T95 ... Atlanta GA 30303 404-562-2336 562-2413
TF: 800-827-5335 ■ *Web:* www.dol.gov/wb
Region 5 Federal Bldg 230 S Dearborn St Rm 1022 ... Chicago IL 60604 312-353-6985 353-6986
TF: 800-827-5335 ■ *Web:* www.dol.gov/wb
Region 6 Federal Bldg 525 Griffin St Suite 735 ... Dallas TX 75202 972-850-4700 850-4704
TF: 800-827-5335 ■ *Web:* www.dol.gov/wb
Region 7 2300 Main St Suite 1050 ... Kansas City MO 64108 816-285-7233 285-7237
TF: 800-827-5335 ■ *Web:* www.dol.gov/wb
Region 8 1999 Broadway Suite 1620 PO Box 46550 ... Denver CO 80201 303-844-1286 844-1283
TF: 800-827-5335 ■ *Web:* www.dol.gov/wb
Region 9 90 7th St Suite 2650 ... San Francisco CA 94103 415-625-2638 625-2641
TF: 800-827-5335 ■ *Web:* www.dol.gov/wb
Region 10 1111 3rd Ave Rm 925 ... Seattle WA 98101 206-553-1534 553-5085
TF: 800-827-5335 ■ *Web:* www.dol.gov/wb

343-16 US Department of State

Phone Fax

Department of State 2201 C St NW ... Washington DC 20520 202-647-4000 647-3344
Web: www.state.gov
Bureau of Consular Affairs 2201 C St NW Rm 6811 ... Washington DC 20520 202-647-9576 647-9622
Web: travel.state.gov
Office of Children's Issues
2201 C St NW 4th Fl MS SA-29 ... Washington DC 20520 202-736-9130 736-9133
TF: 888-407-4747 ■ *Web:* travel.state.gov/family
Overseas Citizens Services 2201 C St NW 4th Fl SA-29 ... Washington DC 20520 202-647-5225
TF: 888-407-4747 ■ *Web:* travel.state.gov/travel/overseas.html
Passport Services 2100 Pennsylvania Ave NW ... Washington DC 20037 202-663-2463
TF: 877-487-2778 ■ *Web:* travel.state.gov/passport
Visa Services 2401 'E' St NW SA-1 ... Washington DC 20522 202-663-1225 663-3899
Web: travel.state.gov/visa
Bureau of Diplomatic Security
DS Public Affairs 2201 C St NW ... Washington DC 20522 571-345-2502
Web: www.state.gov/m/ds
Foreign Service Institute 4000 Arlington Blvd ... Arlington VA 22204 703-302-6703 302-7461
Web: www.state.gov/m/fsi
International Boundary Commission - US & Canada
1250 23rd St NW Suite 100 ... Washington DC 20037 202-736-9100
Web: www.internationalboundarycommission.org
International Boundary & Water Commission - US & Mexico
4171 N Mesa Suite C-100 ... El Paso TX 79902 915-832-4790 832-4190
TF: 800-262-8857 ■ *Web:* www.ibwc.state.gov
National Passport Information Center ... Washington DC 20520 877-487-2778
Web: travel.state.gov/passport
Passport Services 2100 Pennsylvania Ave NW ... Washington DC 20037 202-663-2463
TF: 877-487-2778 ■ *Web:* travel.state.gov/passport
Passport Services Regional Offices
Boston Agency
Tip O'Neill Federal Bldg 10 Causeway St Rm 247 ... Boston MA 02222 877-487-2778
Web: travel.state.gov/passport/ppt_bn.html
Chicago Agency
Kluczynski Federal Bldg 230 S Dearborn St Suite 1803 ... Chicago IL 60604 877-487-2778
Web: travel.state.gov/passport/ppt_cg.html
Colorado Agency 3151 S Vaughn Way Suite 600 ... Aurora CO 80014 877-487-2778
Connecticut Agency 50 Washington St ... Norwalk CT 06854 877-487-2778 299-3434*
**Fax Area Code:* 203 ■ *Web:* travel.state.gov/passport/ppt_ct.html
Honolulu Agency 300 Ala Moana Bld Suite 1-330 ... Honolulu HI 96850 877-487-2778
Web: travel.state.gov/passport/ppt_hh.html
Houston Agency Federal Bldg 1919 Smith St Suite 1100 ... Houston TX 77002 877-487-2778
Web: travel.state.gov/passport/ppt_hn.html
Los Angeles Agency 11000 Wilshire Blvd Suite 1000 ... Los Angeles CA 90024 877-487-2778
Web: travel.state.gov/passport/ppt_la.html
Miami Agency
Claude Pepper Federal Bldg 51 SW 1st Ave 3rd Fl ... Miami FL 33130 877-487-2778
Web: travel.state.gov/passport/ppt_mm.html
New Orleans Agency 365 Canal St Suite 1300 ... New Orleans LA 70130 877-487-2778
Web: travel.state.gov/passport/ppt_no.html
New York Agency 376 Hudson St 10th Fl ... New York NY 10014 877-487-2778
Web: travel.state.gov/passport/ppt_ny.html
Philadelphia Agency
US Custom House 200 Chesnut St Rm 103 ... Philadelphia PA 19106 877-487-2778
Web: travel.state.gov/passport/ppt_pa.html
San Francisco Agency 95 Hawthorne St 5th Fl ... San Francisco CA 94105 877-487-2778 538-2715*
**Fax Area Code:* 415 ■ *Web:* travel.state.gov/passport/ppt_sf.html
Seattle Agency Federal Bldg 915 2nd Ave Suite 992 ... Seattle WA 98174 877-487-2778
Web: travel.state.gov/passport/ppt_se.html
Washington (DC) Agency 1111 19th St NW Rm 300 ... Washington DC 20036 877-487-2778
Web: travel.state.gov/passport/ppt_wn.html
Secretary of State 2201 C St NW 7th Fl ... Washington DC 20520 202-647-9572 647-2283
Web: www.state.gov/secretary
Bureau of Intelligence & Research
2201 C St NW Rm 6531 ... Washington DC 20520 202-647-9177 736-4688
Web: www.state.gov/s/inr
Office of the Chief of Protocol 2201 C St NW Rm 1238 ... Washington DC 20520 202-647-2648 647-3980
Web: www.state.gov/s/cpr
Office of the Coordinator for Counterterrorism
2201 C St NW Rm 2509 ... Washington DC 20520 202-647-9892 647-9256
Web: www.state.gov/s/ct
Under Secretary for Arms Control & International Security
Bureau of International Security & Nonproliferation
2201 C St NW Rm 7531 ... Washington DC 20520 202-647-9610 647-4920
Web: www.state.gov/t/isn
Bureau of Political-Military Affairs
2201 C St NW Rm 6212 ... Washington DC 20520 202-647-9022 736-4779
Web: www.state.gov/t/pm
Bureau of Verification Compliance & Implementation
2201 C St NW Rm 5950 ... Washington DC 20520 202-647-5315 647-1321
Web: www.state.gov/t/vci

				Phone	Fax
Under Secretary for Democracy & Global Affairs					
Bureau of Democracy Human Rights & Labor					
2201 C St NW Rm 7802	Washington	DC	20520	202-647-2590	647-3209
Web: www.state.gov/g/drl					
Bureau of Oceans & International Environmental & Scientific Affairs 2201 C St NW Rm 7831	Washington	DC	20520	202-647-1554	647-0217
Web: www.state.gov/g/oes					
Bureau of Population Refugees & Migration 2201C St NW	Washington	DC	20520	202-647-7360	647-8162
Web: www.state.gov/g/prm					
Under Secretary for Economic Energy & Agricultural Affairs					
Bureau of Economic Energy & Business Affairs 2201 C St NW	Washington	DC	20520	202-647-7971	647-5713
Web: www.state.gov/e/eb					
Under Secretary for Political Affairs					
Bureau of African Affairs 2201 C St NW Rm 6234A	Washington	DC	20520	202-647-2530	647-6301
Web: www.state.gov/p/af					
Bureau of East Asian & Pacific Affairs					
2201 C St NW Rm 6205	Washington	DC	20520	202-647-9596	647-7350
Web: www.state.gov/p/eap					
Bureau of European & Eurasian Affairs					
2201 C St NW Rm 4515	Washington	DC	20520	202-647-9761	647-5116
Web: www.state.gov/p/eur					
Bureau of International Narcotics & Law Enforcement Affairs					
2201 C St NW Rm 7333	Washington	DC	20520	202-647-8464	736-4885
Web: www.state.gov/p/inl					
Bureau of International Organization Affairs					
2201 C St NW	Washington	DC	20520	202-647-9600	736-4116
Web: www.state.gov/p/io					
Bureau of Near Eastern Affairs 2201 C St NW Rm 6242	Washington	DC	20520	202-647-7209	736-4462
Web: www.state.gov/p/nea					
Bureau of South & Central Asian Affairs					
2201 C St NW Rm 6254	Washington	DC	20520	202-736-4325	736-4333
Web: www.state.gov/p/sca					
Bureau of Western Hemisphere Affairs					
2201 C St NW Rm 6262	Washington	DC	20520	202-647-5780	647-0834
Web: www.state.gov/p/wha					
Under Secretary for Public Diplomacy & Public Affairs					
Bureau of Educational & Cultural Affairs					
301 4th St SW Suite 800	Washington	DC	20547	202-203-5118	203-5115
Web: exchanges.state.gov					
Bureau of International Information Programs					
301 4th St SW	Washington	DC	20547	202-736-4405	
Web: www.state.gov/r/iip					
Bureau of Public Affairs 2201 C St NW Rm 2206	Washington	DC	20520	202-647-8411	647-3344
Web: www.state.gov/r/pa					
Visa Services 2401 'E' St NW SA-1	Washington	DC	20522	202-663-1225	663-3899
Web: travel.state.gov/visa					

343-17 US Department of Transportation

				Phone	Fax
Department of Transportation (DOT)					
1200 New Jersey Ave SE	Washington	DC	20590	202-366-4000	
Web: www.dot.gov					
Federal Aviation Administration (FAA)					
800 Independence Ave SW	Washington	DC	20591	866-835-5322	
Web: www.faa.gov					
Accident Investigation Office					
800 Independence Ave SW Rm 840	Washington	DC	20591	202-267-9612	267-5265
Web: www.faa.gov/about/office_org/headquarters_offices/avs					
Air Traffic Organization					
800 Independence Ave SW Rm 1002	Washington	DC	20591	202-267-3666	267-5456
Web: www.faa.gov/about/office_org/headquarters_offices/ato					
Aircraft Certification Service					
800 Independence Ave SW Suite 800 E	Washington	DC	20591	202-267-8235	267-5364
Web: www.faa.gov/about/office_org/headquarters_offices/avs/offices/air/					
Commercial Space Transportation Office					
800 Independence Ave SW Rm 331	Washington	DC	20591	202-267-7793	267-5450
Web: ast.faa.gov					
FAA Academy					
Mike Monroney Aeronautical Center 6500 S MacArthur Blvd	Oklahoma City	OK	73169	405-954-6900	954-3018
Web: www.academy.faa.gov					
Flight Standards Service					
800 Independence Ave SW Rm 821	Washington	DC	20591	202-267-8237	267-5230
Web: www.faa.gov/about/office_org/headquarters_offices/avs					
International Aviation Office 800 Independence Ave SW	Washington	DC	20591	202-385-8900	267-7198
Web: www.intl.faa.gov					
Mike Monroney Aeronautical Center					
6500 S MacArthur Blvd	Oklahoma City	OK	73125	405-954-3011	
Web: www.faa.gov/about/office_org					
Safety Hotline	Washington	DC	20591	800-255-1111	
William J Hughes Technical Center					
Atlantic City International Airport	Atlantic City	NJ	08405	609-485-4000	
Web: www.faa.gov/about/office_org/tc					
Federal Aviation Administration Regional Offices					
Alaskan Region 222 W 7th Ave	Anchorage	AK	99513	907-271-5296	
Web: www.alaska.faa.gov					
Central Region Federal Bldg 901 Locust St	Kansas City	MO	64106	816-329-3050	329-3055
Web: www.faa.gov/cen					
Eastern Region 1 Aviation Plaza 159-30 Rockaway Blvd	Jamaica	NY	11434	718-553-3000	
Web: aea.faa.gov					
Great Lakes Region 2300 E Devon Ave	Des Plaines	IL	60018	847-294-7294	294-8490
Web: www.agl.faa.gov					
New England Region 12 New England Executive Pk	Burlington	MA	01803	781-238-7020	238-7005
Web: www.faa.gov/region/ane					
Northwest Mountain Region 1601 Lind Ave SW	Renton	WA	98057	425-227-2001	227-1006
Web: www.nw.faa.gov					
Southern Region 1701 Columbia Ave	College Park	GA	30337	404-305-5000	305-5010
Web: www.faa.gov/aso					
Western Pacific Region 15000 Aviation Blvd	Lawndale	CA	90261	310-725-3550	725-6811
Web: www.awp.faa.gov					
Federal Highway Administration (FHWA) 400 7th St SW	Washington	DC	20590	202-366-0660	
Web: www.fhwa.dot.gov					
National Highway Institute 4600 N Fairfax Dr Suite 800	Arlington	VA	22203	703-235-0500	235-0593
TF: 877-558-6873 ■ *Web:* www.nhi.fhwa.dot.gov					
Federal Motor Carrier Safety Administration (FMCSA)					
1200 New Jersey Ave SE	Washington	DC	20590	800-832-5660	
Web: www.fmcsa.dot.gov					
Federal Railroad Administration 1200 New Jersey Ave Se	Washington	DC	20590	202-493-6000	
Web: www.fra.dot.gov					
Federal Railroad Administration Regional Offices					
Region 1 55 Broadway Suite 1077	Cambridge	MA	02142	617-494-2302	494-2967
Region 2 Baldwin Tower Suite 660 1510 Chester Pike	Crum Lynne	PA	19022	610-521-8200	521-8225
Region 3 61 Forsyth St SW Suite 16T20	Atlanta	GA	30303	404-562-3800	562-3830
TF: 800-724-5993					
Region 4 200 W Adams St Suite 310	Chicago	IL	60606	312-353-6203	886-9634
Region 5 4100 International Plaza Suite 450	Fort Worth	TX	76109	817-862-2200	862-2204
Region 6 901 Locust St Suite 464	Kansas City	MO	64106	816-329-3840	329-3867
TF: 800-724-5996					
Region 7 801 'I' St Suite 466	Sacramento	CA	95814	916-498-6540	498-6546
Web: www.fra.dot.gov					
Region 8 West Coast Bank Bldg 500 E Broadway Suite 240	Vancouver	WA	98660	360-696-7536	696-7548
TF: 800-724-5998 ■ *Web:* www.fra.dot.gov					
Federal Transit Administration 1200 New Jersey Ave SE	Washington	DC	20590	202-366-4043	366-9854
Web: www.fta.dot.gov					
Federal Transit Administration Regional Offices					
Region 1 55 Broadway Suite 920	Cambridge	MA	02142	617-494-2055	494-2865
Web: www.fta.dot.gov					
Region 2 1 Bowling Green Suite 429	New York	NY	10004	212-668-2170	668-2136
Web: www.fta.dot.gov					
Region 3 1760 Market St Suite 500	Philadelphia	PA	19103	215-656-7100	656-7260
Web: www.fta.dot.gov					
Region 4 230 Peachtree St NW Suite 800	Atlanta	GA	30303	404-865-5600	865-5605
Web: www.fta.dot.gov					
Region 5 200 W Adams St Suite 320	Chicago	IL	60606	312-353-2789	886-0351
Web: www.fta.dot.gov					
Region 6 819 Taylor St Rm 8A36	Fort Worth	TX	76102	817-978-0550	978-0575
Web: www.fta.dot.gov					
Region 7 901 Locust St Suite 404	Kansas City	MO	64106	816-329-3920	329-3921
Web: www.fta.dot.gov					
Region 8 12300 W Dakota Ave Suite 310	Lakewood	CO	80228	720-963-3300	963-3333
Web: www.fta.dot.gov					
Region 9 201 Mission St Suite 1650	San Francisco	CA	94105	415-744-3133	744-2726
Web: www.fta.dot.gov					
Region 10 Federal Bldg 915 2nd Ave Suite 3142	Seattle	WA	98174	206-220-7954	220-7959
Web: www.fta.dot.gov					
Maritime Administration Division of Gulf Operations					
500 Poydras St Suite 1223	New Orleans	LA	70130	504-589-2000	589-6559
Web: www.marad.dot.gov/Offices/MRG-3100.html					
Maritime Administration (MARAD) 1200 New Jersey Ave SE	Washington	DC	20590	202-366-5807	366-3791
TF Hotline: 800-996-2723 ■ *Web:* www.marad.dot.gov					
National Maritime Resource & Education Center					
1200 New Jersey Ave SE	Washington	DC	20590	202-366-1931	366-6988
Web: www.marad.dot.gov/NMREC					
US Merchant Marine Academy 300 Steamboat Rd	Kings Point	NY	11024	516-773-5387	773-5509
Web: www.usmma.edu					
Maritime Administration Regional Offices					
Great Lakes Region 1701 E Woodfield Rd Suite 203	Schaumburg	IL	60173	847-995-0122	995-0133
Web: www.marad.dot.gov/Offices/MRG-6100.html					
North Atlantic Region 1 Bowling Green Rm 418	New York	NY	10004	212-668-3330	668-3382
Web: www.marad.dot.gov/Offices/MRG-2100.html					
South Atlantic Region 7737 Hampton Blvd	Norfolk	VA	23505	757-441-6393	440-0812
Web: www.marad.dot.gov/Offices/MRG-7100.html					
Western Region 201 Mission St Suite 2200	San Francisco	CA	94105	415-744-3125	744-2576
Web: www.marad.dot.gov/Offices/MRG-4100.html					
National Highway Traffic Safety Administration (NHTSA)					
1200 New Jersey Ave SE	Washington	DC	20590	202-366-9550	366-6916
TF: 888-327-4236 ■ *Web:* www.nhtsa.dot.gov					
Defects Investigation Office 1200 New Jersey Ave SE	Washington	DC	20590	202-366-9550	366-1767
TF: 888-327-4236 ■ *Web:* www-odi.nhtsa.dot.gov					
National Center for Statistics & Analysis					
1200 New Jersey Ave SE	Washington	DC	20590	202-366-1503	366-3189
TF: 800-934-8517 ■ *Web:* www-nrd.nhtsa.dot.gov/departments/nrd-30/ncsa					
Vehicle Research & Test Center					
10820 SR 347 PO Box B37	East Liberty	OH	43319	937-666-4511	666-3590
TF: 800-262-8309 ■ *Web:* www.nhtsa.gov					
National Highway Traffic Safety Administration Regional Offices					
NHTSA Region 1 Volpe Center Kendall Sq MS 903	Cambridge	MA	02142	617-494-3427	494-3646
Web: www.nhtsa.dot.gov/nhtsa/whatis/regions/Region01					
NHTSA Region 2 222 Mamaroneck Ave Suite 204	White Plains	NY	10605	914-682-6162	682-6239
Web: www.nhtsa.dot.gov/nhtsa/whatis/regions/Region02					
NHTSA Region 3 10 S Howard St Suite 6700	Baltimore	MD	21201	410-962-0900	962-2770
Web: www.nhtsa.dot.gov/nhtsa/whatis/regions/Region03					
NHTSA Region 4					
Federal Center 61 Forsyth St SW Suite 17T30	Atlanta	GA	30303	404-562-3739	562-3763
Web: www.nhtsa.dot.gov/nhtsa/whatis/regions/Region04					
NHTSA Region 5 19900 Governors Dr Suite 201	Olympia Fields	IL	60461	708-503-8822	503-8991
TF: 888-327-4235 ■ *Web:* www.nhtsa.dot.gov/nhtsa/whatis/regions/Region05					
NHTSA Region 6 Federal Bldg 819 Taylor St Rm 8A38	Fort Worth	TX	76102	817-978-3653	978-8339
Web: www.nhtsa.dot.gov/nhtsa/whatis/regions/Region06					
NHTSA Region 7 901 Locust St Rm 466	Kansas City	MO	64106	816-329-3900	329-3910
Web: www.nhtsa.dot.gov/nhtsa/whatis/regions/Region07					
NHTSA Region 8 12300 W Dakota Ave Suite 140	Lakewood	CO	80228	720-963-3100	963-3124
Web: www.nhtsa.dot.gov/nhtsa/whatis/regions/Region08					
NHTSA Region 9 201 Mission St Suite 2230	San Francisco	CA	94105	415-744-3089	744-2532
Web: www.nhtsa.dot.gov/nhtsa/whatis/regions/Region09					
NHTSA Region 10 915 2nd Ave Suite 3140	Seattle	WA	98174	206-220-7640	220-7651
Web: www.nhtsa.dot.gov/nhtsa/whatis/regions/Region10					
National Maritime Resource & Education Center					
1200 New Jersey Ave SE	Washington	DC	20590	202-366-1931	366-6988
Web: www.marad.dot.gov/NMREC					
Pipeline & Hazardous Materials Safety Administration (PHMSA) 1200 New Jersey Ave SE East Bldg 2nd Fl	Washington	DC	20590	202-366-4433	366-3666
Web: www.phmsa.dot.gov					
Office of Hazardous Materials Safety					
1200 New Jersey Ave SE	Washington	DC	20590	202-366-0656	366-5713
TF: 800-467-4922 ■ *Web:* hazmat.dot.gov					
Office of Pipeline Safety					
1200 New Jersey Ave SE Suite E-22-2311	Washington	DC	20590	202-366-4595	493-2311
Web: ops.dot.gov					
Pipeline & Hazardous Materials Safety Administration Regional Offices					
Central Region (Pipeline) 901 Locust St Rm 462	Kansas City	MO	64106	816-329-3800	329-3831
Web: www.phmsa.dot.gov/about/region.html					
Eastern Region (Pipeline) 409 3rd St SW Suite 300	Washington	DC	20024	202-260-8500	260-8530
Web: www.phmsa.dot.gov/about/region.html					
Southern Region 233 Peachtree St NE Suite 602	Atlanta	GA	30303	404-832-1140	832-1168
Web: www.phmsa.dot.gov/about/region.html					
Southwest Region 8701 Gessner Rd Suite 1110	Houston	TX	77074	713-272-2820	272-2821
Web: www.phmsa.dot.gov/about/region.html					
Western Region (Pipeline) 12300 W Dakota Ave Suite 110	Lakewood	CO	80228	720-963-3160	963-3161
Web: www.phmsa.dot.gov/about/region.html					
Research & Innovative Technology Administration (RITA)					
400 7th St SW Suite 3103	Washington	DC	20590	202-366-7582	493-2381
Web: www.rita.dot.gov					
Bureau of Transportation Statistics					
1200 New Jersey Ave SE	Washington	DC	20590	202-366-1270	366-3640
TF: 800-853-1351 ■ *Web:* www.bts.gov					
Office of Research Development & Technology					
1200 New Jersey Ave SE	Washington	DC	20590	202-366-3492	
TF: 800-853-1351 ■ *Web:* www.rita.dot.gov/agencies_and_offices/research					

US Department of Transportation (Cont'd)

	City	State	Zip	Phone	Fax
Transportation Safety Institute					
6500 S MacArthur Blvd PO Box 25082	Oklahoma City	OK	73125	405-954-3153	954-3521
TF: 800-954-3521 ■ *Web:* www.tsi.dot.gov					
Volpe National Transportation Systems Center					
55 Broadway	Cambridge	MA	02142	617-494-2000	
Web: www.volpe.dot.gov					
Saint Lawrence Seaway Development Corp					
1200 New Jersey Ave SE Suite W-32-300	Washington	DC	20590	202-366-0091	366-7147
TF: 800-785-2779 ■ *Web:* www.seaway.dot.gov					
Secretary of Transportation					
1200 New Jersey Ave SE Suite W-96-300	Washington	DC	20590	202-366-1111	366-7202
Web: www.dot.gov/ost					
Surface Transportation Board 395 E St SW	Washington	DC	20423	202-245-0230	245-0461
Web: www.stb.dot.gov					

343-18 US Department of the Treasury

	City	State	Zip	Phone	Fax
Department of the Treasury 1500 Pennsylvania Ave NW	Washington	DC	20220	202-622-2000	622-6415
Web: www.ustreas.gov					
Treasurer of the US 1500 Pennsylvania Ave NW	Washington	DC	20220	202-622-0100	622-6464
Web: www.treas.gov/offices/treasurer					
Alcohol & Tobacco Tax & Trade Bureau (TTB)					
1310 G St NW 3rd Fl	Washington	DC	20220	202-927-5000	927-5611
Web: www.ttb.gov					
National Revenue Center 550 Main St Suite 8002	Cincinnati	OH	45202	513-684-3334	684-2159
TF: 877-882-3277 ■ *Web:* www.ttb.gov/nrc					
Bureau of Engraving & Printing 14th & C Sts SW	Washington	DC	20228	202-874-8888	874-3177
TF: 877-874-4114 ■ *Web:* www.moneyfactory.gov					
Bureau of the Public Debt 799 9th St NW	Washington	DC	20239	202-504-3500	504-3630
Web: www.publicdebt.treas.gov					
TreasuryDirect PO Box 7015	Parkersburg	WV	26106	304-480-7711	
TF: 800-722-2678 ■ *Web:* www.savingsbonds.gov					
Comptroller of the Currency 250 'E' St SW	Washington	DC	20219	202-874-5000	874-4950
TF Cust Svc: 800-613-6743 ■ *Web:* www.occ.treas.gov					
Financial Crimes Enforcement Network (FinCEN)					
2070 Chain Bridge Rd PO Box 39	Vienna	VA	22183	703-905-3591	905-3690
Web: www.fincen.gov					
Financial Management Service 401 14th St SW	Washington	DC	20227	202-874-6950	
Web: www.fms.treas.gov					
Internal Revenue Service (IRS) 1111 Constitution Ave NW	Washington	DC	20224	202-622-9511	622-5156
TF: 800-829-1040 ■ *Web:* www.irs.gov					
Appeals Office 1099 14th St NW	Washington	DC	20005	202-435-5600	994-1804
Web: www.irs.gov					
Large & Mid-Size Business Div					
1111 Constitution Ave NW	Washington	DC	20224	202-283-8710	283-8508
Web: www.irs.gov/businesses					
Small Business/Self-Employed Div					
1111 Constitution Ave NW	Washington	DC	20442	202-622-0600	622-5046
Web: www.irs.gov/businesses					
Tax Exempt & Government Entities Div					
1111 Constitution Ave NW	Washington	DC	20224	202-283-2500	283-9973
Web: www.irs.gov/charities					
Taxpayer Advocate Service 1111 Constitution Ave NW	Washington	DC	20224	202-622-6100	622-7854
TF: 877-777-4778 ■ *Web:* www.irs.gov/advocate					
Wage & Investment Div 401 W Peachtree St NW	Atlanta	GA	30308	404-338-7060	338-7054
National Revenue Center 550 Main St Suite 8002	Cincinnati	OH	45202	513-684-3334	684-2159
TF: 877-882-3277 ■ *Web:* www.ttb.gov/nrc					
Office of Thrift Supervision 1700 G St NW	Washington	DC	20552	202-906-6000	898-0230
Web: www.ots.treas.gov					
Secretary of the Treasury					
1500 Pennsylvania Ave NW Rm 3330	Washington	DC	20220	202-622-1100	622-0073
Web: www.treas.gov/organization/officials.html					
US Mint 801 9th St NW	Washington	DC	20220	202-354-7200	
TF Cust Svc: 800-872-6468 ■ *Web:* www.usmint.gov					
Denver 320 W Colfax Ave	Denver	CO	80204	303-405-4600	405-4604
Philadelphia 151 N Independence Mall East	Philadelphia	PA	19106	215-408-0367	408-2700
San Francisco 155 Hermann St	San Francisco	CA	94102	415-575-8000	575-7765
TF: 800-872-6468 ■ *Web:* www.usmint.gov					
US Bullion Depository PO Box 965	Fort Knox	KY	40121	502-942-1194	942-2153
West Point (NY) PO Box 37	West Point	NY	10996	845-446-6200	446-6258

343-19 US Department of Veterans Affairs

	City	State	Zip	Phone	Fax
Department of Veterans Affairs (VA) 810 Vermont Ave NW	Washington	DC	20420	202-461-7600	
TF Cust Svc: 800-827-1000 ■ *Web:* www.va.gov					
Public & Intergovernmental Affairs Office					
810 Vermont Ave NW	Washington	DC	20420	202-273-5750	273-7635
Web: www1.va.gov/opa					
National Cemetery Administration 810 Vermont Ave NW	Washington	DC	20420	202-273-5146	273-6709
Web: www.cem.va.gov					
Secretary of Veterans Affairs 810 Vermont Ave NW	Washington	DC	20420	202-273-4809	273-4877
Web: www1.va.gov/opa/bios					
Board of Veterans' Appeals 811 Vermont Ave NW	Washington	DC	20420	202-565-5001	565-5587
Web: www.va.gov/vbs/bva					
Center for Minority Veterans					
810 Vermont Ave NW Rm 436	Washington	DC	20420	202-273-6708	273-7092
Web: www1.va.gov/centerforminorityveterans					
Center for Veterans Enterprise 1722 I St NW Rm UM2	Washington	DC	20006	202-303-3260	254-0238
TF: 866-584-2344 ■ *Web:* www.vetbiz.gov					
Center for Women Veterans					
810 Vermont Ave NW Rm 438	Washington	DC	20420	202-273-6193	273-7092
Web: www1.va.gov/womenvet					
Veterans Benefits Administration 810 Vermont Ave NW	Washington	DC	20420	202-273-6763	275-3591
TF: 800-827-1000 ■ *Web:* www.vba.va.gov					
Veterans Canteen Service 1 Jefferson Barracks Rd Bldg 25	Saint Louis	MO	63125	314-845-1207	845-1201
Web: www.vacanteen.va.gov					
Veterans Health Administration 810 Vermont Ave NW	Washington	DC	20420	202-273-5400	
Web: www1.va.gov/health					
Gulf War Veterans Information 50 Irving St NW	Washington	DC	20422	202-745-8000	
TF: 800-749-8387 ■ *Web:* www1.va.gov/gulfwar					
National Center for Post-Traumatic Stress Disorder					
215 N Main St	White River Junction	VT	05009	802-296-5132	296-5135
Web: www.ncptsd.va.gov					
Office of Research & Development					
810 Vermont Ave NW MC 12	Washington	DC	20420	202-254-0185	254-0460
Web: www.research.va.gov					

343-20 US Independent Agencies Government Corporations & Quasi-Official Agencies

Included also among these listings are selected Federal Boards, Committees, and Commissions.

	City	State	Zip	Phone	Fax
Access Board 1331 F St NW Suite 1000	Washington	DC	20004	202-272-0080	272-0081
TF: 800-872-2253 ■ *Web:* www.access-board.gov					
Advisory Council on Historic Preservation					
1100 Pennsylvania Ave NW Rm 803	Washington	DC	20004	202-606-8503	606-8647
Web: www.achp.gov					
African Development Foundation 1400 'I' St NW 10th Fl	Washington	DC	20005	202-673-3916	673-3810
Web: www.adf.gov					
American Battle Monuments Commission					
Courthouse Plaza II Suite 500	Arlington	VA	22201	703-696-6900	696-6666
Web: www.abmc.gov					
AmeriCorps USA 1201 New York Ave NW	Washington	DC	20525	202-606-5000	
Web: www.americorps.org					
Amtrak 60 Massachusetts Ave NE	Washington	DC	20002	202-906-3000	
TF: 800-872-7245 ■ *Web:* www.amtrak.com					
Appalachian Regional Commission					
1666 Connecticut Ave NW Suite 700	Washington	DC	20009	202-884-7700	884-7691
Web: www.arc.gov					
Architectural & Transportation Barriers Compliance Board					
1331 F St NW Suite 1000	Washington	DC	20004	202-272-0080	272-0081
TF: 800-872-2253 ■ *Web:* www.access-board.gov					
Broadcasting Board of Governors					
330 Independence Ave SW	Washington	DC	20237	202-203-4545	203-4585
Web: www.bbg.gov					
International Broadcasting Bureau					
330 Independence Ave SW	Washington	DC	20237	202-203-4515	
Web: www.ibb.gov					
Office of Cuba Broadcasting 4201 NW 77th Ave	Miami	FL	33166	305-437-7012	437-7004
Web: www.martinoticias.com					
Voice of America 330 Independence Ave SW	Washington	DC	20237	202-203-4959	203-4960
Web: www.voanews.com					
Central Intelligence Agency (CIA) Office of Public Affairs	Washington	DC	20505	703-482-0623	482-1739
Web: www.cia.gov					
CIA (Central Intelligence Agency) Office of Public Affairs	Washington	DC	20505	703-482-0623	482-1739
Web: www.cia.gov					
Commission of Fine Arts 401 F St NW Suite 312	Washington	DC	20001	202-504-2200	504-2195
Web: www.cfa.gov					
Commission on Presidential Scholars					
Department of Education 400 Maryland Ave SW					
Rm 5E115	Washington	DC	20202	202-401-0961	260-7464
Web: www.ed.gov/programs/psp/commission.html					
Commission on Security & Cooperation in Europe					
234 Ford House Office Bldg 3rd & D Sts SW	Washington	DC	20515	202-225-1901	226-4199
Web: www.csce.gov					
Committee on Foreign Investments in the US					
Department of the Treasury Office of International					
Investment 1500 Pennsylvania Ave NW Rm 5221	Washington	DC	20220	202-622-9066	
Web: www.treas.gov/offices/international-affairs/exon-florio					
Committee for Purchase from People Who Are Blind or Severely					
Disabled 1421 Jefferson Davis Hwy Jefferson Plaza 2					
Suite 10800	Arlington	VA	22202	703-603-7740	603-0655
Web: www.abilityone.gov					
Commodity Futures Trading Commission (CFTC)					
3 Lafayette Center 1155 21 St NW	Washington	DC	20581	202-418-5000	418-5521
TF: 866-366-2382 ■ *Web:* www.cftc.gov					
Commodity Futures Trading Commission Regional Offices					
Central Region 525 W Monroe St	Chicago	IL	60661	312-596-0700	596-0713
Web: www.cftc.gov					
Eastern Region 140 Broadway 19th Fl	New York	NY	10005	646-746-9700	746-9938
Web: www.cftc.gov					
Southwestern Region 2 Emanuel Cleaver II Blvd Suite 300	Kansas City	MO	64112	816-960-7700	960-7750
Web: www.cftc.gov					
Consumer Product Safety Commission (CPSC)					
4330 East West Hwy	Bethesda	MD	20814	301-504-7923	504-0051
TF: 800-638-2772 ■ *Web:* www.cpsc.gov					
Coordinating Council on Juvenile Justice & Delinquency					
Prevention 810 7th St NW	Washington	DC	20531	202-307-5911	307-2093
Web: www.juvenilecouncil.gov					
Corporation for National & Community Service					
1201 New York Ave NW	Washington	DC	20525	202-606-5000	
Web: www.cns.gov					
AmeriCorps USA 1201 New York Ave NW	Washington	DC	20525	202-606-5000	
Web: www.americorps.org					
Learn & Serve America 1201 New York Ave NW	Washington	DC	20525	202-606-5000	
Web: www.learnandserve.org					
Senior Corps 1201 New York Ave NW	Washington	DC	20525	202-606-5000	
Web: www.seniorcorps.org					
Court Services & Offender Supervision Agency for the					
District of Columbia 633 Indiana Ave NW	Washington	DC	20004	202-220-5300	220-5350
Web: www.csosa.gov					
Defense Nuclear Facilities Safety Board					
625 Indiana Ave NW Suite 700	Washington	DC	20004	202-694-7000	
TF: 800-788-4016 ■ *Web:* www.dnfsb.gov					
Denali Commission 510 L St Suite 410	Anchorage	AK	99501	907-271-1414	271-1415
TF: 888-480-4321 ■ *Web:* www.denali.gov					
EEOC (Equal Employment Opportunity Commission)					
1801 L St NW	Washington	DC	20507	202-663-4191	
TF: 800-669-4000 ■ *Web:* www.eeoc.gov					
Environmental Protection Agency (EPA)					
1200 Pennsylvania Ave NW	Washington	DC	20460	202-564-4700	501-1450
TF: 888-372-8255 ■ *Web:* www.epa.gov					
US National Response Team 1200 Pennsylvania Ave NW	Washington	DC	20593	202-267-2675	267-1322
TF: 800-424-9346 ■ *Web:* www.nrt.org					
Environmental Protection Agency Regional Offices					
Region 1 1 Congress St Suite 1100	Boston	MA	02114	617-918-1111	918-0101
TF: 888-372-7341 ■ *Web:* www.epa.gov/region1					
Region 2 290 Broadway	New York	NY	10007	212-637-3000	
Web: www.epa.gov/region2					
Region 3 1650 Arch St	Philadelphia	PA	19103	215-814-5000	
TF: 800-438-2474 ■ *Web:* www.epa.gov/region3					
Region 4 Federal Ctr 61 Forsyth St SW	Atlanta	GA	30303	404-562-9900	562-8174
TF: 800-241-1754 ■ *Web:* www.epa.gov/region4					
Region 5 77 W Jackson Blvd	Chicago	IL	60604	312-353-2000	
Web: www.epa.gov/region5					
Region 6 1445 Ross Ave Suite 1200	Dallas	TX	75202	214-665-2200	665-2182
TF: 800-887-6063 ■ *Web:* www.epa.gov/region6					
Region 7 901 N 5th St	Kansas City	KS	66101	913-551-7003	
Web: www.epa.gov/region7					
Region 8 1595 Wynkoop St	Denver	CO	80202	303-312-6312	
TF: 800-227-8917 ■ *Web:* www.epa.gov/region8					

				Phone	Fax
Region 9 75 Hawthorne St	San Francisco	CA	94105	415-947-8000	947-3598
TF: 866-372-9378 ■ Web: www.epa.gov/region9					
Region 10 1200 6th Ave Suite 900	Seattle	WA	98101	206-553-1200	553-0059
TF: 800-424-4372 ■ Web: www.epa.gov/region10					
EPA (Environmental Protection Agency)					
1200 Pennsylvania Ave NW	Washington	DC	20460	202-564-4700	501-1450
TF: 888-372-8255 ■ Web: www.epa.gov					
Equal Employment Opportunity Commission (EEOC)					
1801 L St NW	Washington	DC	20507	202-663-4191	
TF: 800-669-4000 ■ Web: www.eeoc.gov					
Equal Employment Opportunity Commission Regional Offices					
Atlanta District 100 Alabama St SW Suite 4R30	Atlanta	GA	30303	404-562-6800	562-6909
TF: 800-669-4000 ■ Web: www.eeoc.gov/atlanta					
Birmingham District 1130 22nd St S Suite 2000	Birmingham	AL	35205	205-212-2100	212-2105
TF: 800-669-4000 ■ Web: www.eeoc.gov/birmingham					
Charlotte District 129 W Trade St Suite 400	Charlotte	NC	28202	704-344-6682	344-6734
TF: 800-669-4000 ■ Web: www.eeoc.gov/charlotte					
Chicago District 500 W Madison St Suite 2800	Chicago	IL	60661	312-353-2713	353-4041
Web: www.eeoc.gov/chicago					
Dallas District 207 S Houston St 3rd Fl	Dallas	TX	75202	214-253-2700	253-2720
TF: 800-669-4000 ■ Web: www.eeoc.gov/dallas					
Houston District Federal Bldg 1919 Smith St 6th Fl	Houston	TX	77002	713-209-3377	209-3381
TF: 800-669-4000 ■ Web: www.eeoc.gov/houston					
Indianapolis District 101 W Ohio St Suite 1900	Indianapolis	IN	46204	317-226-7212	226-7953
Web: www.eeoc.gov/indianapolis					
Los Angeles District 255 E Temple St 4th Fl	Los Angeles	CA	90012	213-894-1096	894-1118
TF: 800-669-4000 ■ Web: www.eeoc.gov/losangeles					
Memphis District 1407 Union Ave Suite 621	Memphis	TN	38104	901-544-0115	544-0111
TF: 800-669-4000 ■ Web: www.eeoc.gov/memphis					
Miami District 2 S Biscayne Blvd Suite 2700	Miami	FL	33131	305-808-1740	808-1834
Web: www.eeoc.gov/miami					
New York District 33 Whitehall St 5th Fl	New York	NY	10004	212-336-3620	336-3790
TF: 866-408-8075 ■ Web: www.eeoc.gov/newyork					
Philadelphia District 21 S 5th St Suite 400	Philadelphia	PA	19106	215-440-2600	440-2606
TF: 866-408-8075 ■ Web: www.eeoc.gov/philadelphia					
Phoenix District 3300 N Central Ave Suite 690	Phoenix	AZ	85012	602-640-5000	640-5071
Web: www.eeoc.gov/phoenix					
Saint Louis District 1222 Spruce St Suite 8.100	Saint Louis	MO	63103	314-539-7800	539-7894
TF: 800-669-4000 ■ Web: www.eeoc.gov/stlouis					
San Francisco District 350 The Embarcadero Suite 500	San Francisco	CA	94105	415-625-5600	625-5609
Web: www.eeoc.gov/sanfrancisco					
Export-Import Bank of the US 811 Vermont Ave NW	Washington	DC	20571	202-565-3946	
TF: 800-565-3946 ■ Web: www.exim.gov					
Farm Credit Administration 1501 Farm Credit Dr	McLean	VA	22102	703-883-4000	734-5784
Web: www.fca.gov					
Farm Credit Administration Regional Offices					
Bloomington (MN) Field Office					
2051 Killebrew Dr Suite 610	Bloomington	MN	55425	952-854-7151	854-4736
TF: 877-322-2566 ■ Web: www.fca.gov					
Dallas Field Office 511 E Carpenter Fwy Suite 650	Irving	TX	75062	972-869-0550	869-9531
Denver Field Office 3131 S Vaughn Way Suite 250	Aurora	CO	80014	303-696-9737	696-7114
Web: www.fca.gov					
McLean Field Office 1501 Farm Credit Dr	McLean	VA	22102	703-883-4497	883-2704
TF: 877-625-3261 ■ Web: www.fca.gov					
Sacramento Field Office 2180 Harvard St Suite 300	Sacramento	CA	95815	916-648-1118	649-0512
Web: www.fca.gov					
Federal Accounting Standards Advisory Board					
441 G St NW Suite 6814	Washington	DC	20548	202-512-7350	512-7366
Web: www.fasab.gov					
Federal Communications Commission (FCC)					
445 12th St SW	Washington	DC	20554	888-225-5322	418-0232*
*Fax Area Code: 202 ■ Web: www.fcc.gov					
Federal Deposit Insurance Corp (FDIC) 550 17th St NW	Washington	DC	20429	202-898-7192	
TF: 877-275-3342 ■ Web: www.fdic.gov					
Federal Deposit Insurance Corp Regional Offices					
Atlanta Area Office 10 10th St NE Suite 800	Atlanta	GA	30309	678-916-2200	
TF: 800-765-3342 ■ Web: www.fdic.gov					
Boston Area Office 15 Braintree Hill Office Pk Suite 300	Braintree	MA	02184	781-794-5500	794-5533
TF: 866-728-9953 ■ Web: www.fdic.gov					
Chicago Area Office 500 W Monroe St Suite 3300	Chicago	IL	60661	312-382-6000	282-7507
TF: 800-944-5343 ■ Web: www.fdic.gov					
Dallas Area Office 1601 Bryan St	Dallas	TX	75201	214-754-0098	
TF: 800-568-9161 ■ Web: www.fdic.gov					
Kansas City Area Office 2345 Grand Blvd Suite 1200	Kansas City	MO	64108	816-234-8000	234-8004
TF: 800-209-7459 ■ Web: www.fdic.gov					
Memphis Area Office 5100 Poplar Ave Suite 1900	Memphis	TN	38137	901-685-1603	821-5308
TF: 800-210-6354 ■ Web: www.fdic.gov					
New York Area Office 20 Exchange Pl 4th Fl	New York	NY	10005	917-320-2500	320-2903
TF: 800-334-9594					
San Francisco Area Office					
25 Jessie St at Ecker Sq Suite 2300	San Francisco	CA	94105	415-546-0160	
TF: 800-756-3558 ■ Web: www.fdic.gov					
Federal Election Commission 999 'E' St NW	Washington	DC	20463	202-694-1100	
TF: 800-424-9530 ■ Web: www.fec.gov					
Federal Financing Bank					
Department of the Treasury 1500 Pennsylvania Ave NW	Washington	DC	20220	202-622-2470	622-0707
Web: www.treas.gov/ffb					
Federal Housing Finance Board 1625 'I' St NW	Washington	DC	20006	202-408-2500	408-1435
Web: www.fhfb.gov					
Federal Labor Relations Authority 1400 K St NW	Washington	DC	20424	202-357-6029	482-6724
Web: www.flra.gov					
Federal Labor Relations Authority Regional Offices					
Atlanta Region 285 Peachtree Center Ave Suite 701	Atlanta	GA	30303	404-331-5300	331-5280
Web: www.flra.gov					
Boston Region Federal Bldg 10 Causeway St Suite 472	Boston	MA	02222	617-565-5100	565-6262
Web: www.flra.gov					
Chicago Region 55 W Monroe St Suite 1150	Chicago	IL	60603	312-886-3465	886-5977
Web: www.flra.gov					
Dallas Region 525 S Griffin St Suite 926 LB-107	Dallas	TX	75202	214-767-6266	767-0156
Web: www.flra.gov					
Denver Region 1244 Speer Blvd Suite 100	Denver	CO	80204	303-844-5224	844-2774
San Francisco Region 901 Market St Suite 220	San Francisco	CA	94103	415-356-5000	356-5017
Web: www.cftc.gov					
Washington (DC) Region 1400 K St NW 2nd Fl	Washington	DC	20424	202-357-6029	482-6724
Web: www.flra.gov					
Federal Laboratory Consortium for Technology Transfer					
950 N Kings Hwy Suite 208	Cherry Hill	NJ	08034	856-667-7727	667-8009
Web: www.federallabs.org					
Federal Maritime Commission 800 N Capitol St NW	Washington	DC	20573	202-523-5725	523-0014
Web: www.fmc.gov					
Federal Maritime Commission Regional Offices					
Los Angeles Area 839 S Beacon St Rm 1018	San Pedro	CA	90733	310-514-4905	514-3931
New Orleans Area 1515 Poydras St Rm 1723	New Orleans	LA	70112	504-589-6662	589-6663
Web: www.fmc.gov					
New York Area JFK International Airport Bldg 75 Rm 205B	Jamaica	NY	11430	718-553-2228	553-2229
Web: www.fca.gov					

				Phone	Fax
Seattle Area 7 S Nevada St Suite 100	Seattle	WA	98134	206-553-0221	553-0222
Web: www.fmc.gov					
South Florida Area PO Box 813609	Hollywood	FL	33081	954-963-5362	963-5630
Web: www.fmc.gov					
Federal Mediation & Conciliation Service 2100 K St NW	Washington	DC	20427	202-606-8100	606-4251
Web: www.fmcs.gov					
Federal Mediation & Conciliation Service Regional Offices					
Eastern Region 6161 Oak Tree Blvd Suite 120	Independence	OH	44131	216-520-4800	520-4819
Web: www.fmcs.gov					
Western Region 1300 Godward St Suite 3950	Minneapolis	MN	55413	612-331-6670	331-5272
Web: www.fmcs.gov					
Federal Mine Safety & Health Review Commission					
601 New Jersey Ave NW	Washington	DC	20001	202-434-9900	434-9944
Web: www.fmshrc.gov					
Federal Reserve System 20th St & Constitution Ave NW	Washington	DC	20551	202-452-3000	452-3819
Web: www.federalreserve.gov					
Federal Retirement Thrift Investment Board 1250 H St NW	Washington	DC	20005	202-942-1600	942-1675
Web: www.frtib.gov					
Federal Trade Commission (FTC) 600 Pennsylvania Ave NW	Washington	DC	20580	202-326-2222	326-2396
TF: 877-382-4357 ■ Web: www.ftc.gov					
National Do Not Call Registry	Washington	DC	20580	888-382-1222	
Web: www.ftc.gov/donotcall					
Federal Trade Commission Regional Offices					
East Central Region 1111 Superior Ave Suite 200	Cleveland	OH	44114	216-263-3455	263-3426
TF: 877-382-4357 ■ Web: www.ftc.gov/ro/eastcentral.htm					
Midwest Region 55 W Monroe St Suite 1825	Chicago	IL	60603	312-960-5634	960-5600
Web: www.ftc.gov/ro/midwest.htm					
Northeast Region 1 Bowling Green Suite 318	New York	NY	10004	212-607-2829	607-2822
Web: www.ftc.gov/ro/northeast.htm					
Northwest Region 915 2nd Ave Suite 2896	Seattle	WA	98174	206-220-6350	220-6366
Web: www.ftc.gov/ro/northwest.htm					
Southeast Region 225 Peachtree St NE Suite 1500	Atlanta	GA	30303	404-656-1390	656-1379
TF: 877-282-4357 ■ Web: www.ftc.gov/ro/southeast.htm					
Southwest Region 1999 Bryan St Suite 2150	Dallas	TX	75201	214-979-9350	953-3079
Web: www.ftc.gov/ro/southwest.htm					
Western Region 18077 Wilshire Blvd Suite 700	Los Angeles	CA	90024	310-824-4343	824-4380
TF: 877-382-4357 ■ Web: www.ftc.gov/ro/western.htm					
FTC (Federal Trade Commission) 600 Pennsylvania Ave NW	Washington	DC	20580	202-326-2222	326-2396
TF: 877-382-4357 ■ Web: www.ftc.gov					
General Services Administration (GSA) 1800 F St NW	Washington	DC	20405	202-501-0800	
Web: www.gsa.gov					
FCIC National Contact Center	Pueblo	CO	81009	800-333-4636	
Web: www.info.gov					
Federal Citizen Information Center	Pueblo	CO	81009	888-878-3256	
Web: www.pueblo.gsa.gov					
Regulatory Information Service Center					
1800 F St NW Rm 3039	Washington	DC	20405	202-482-7340	482-7360
Web: gsa.gov/risc					
USA.gov					
Office of Citizen Services & Communications 1800 F St NW Suite G-142	Washington	DC	20405	800-488-3111	
Web: www.usa.gov					
General Services Administration Regional Offices					
Region 1 - New England					
Thomas P O'Neill Federal Bldg 10 Causeway St Rm 1010	Boston	MA	02222	617-565-5860	
TF: 866-734-1727 ■ Web: www.gsa.gov					
Region 2 - Northeast & Caribbean 26 Federal Plaza	New York	NY	10278	212-264-2600	
Web: www.gsa.gov					
Region 3 - Mid-Atlantic Strawbridge Bldg 20 N 8th St	Philadelphia	PA	19107	215-446-5100	
TF: 800-333-4636 ■ Web: www.gsa.gov					
Region 4 - Southeast Sunbelt 77 Forsyth St Suite 600	Atlanta	GA	30303	404-331-3200	331-0931
Web: www.gsa.gov					
Region 5 - Great Lakes 230 S Dearborn St	Chicago	IL	60604	312-886-8900	886-8901
Web: www.gsa.gov					
Region 6 - Heartland 1500 E Bannister Rd	Kansas City	MO	64131	816-926-7201	926-7513
Web: www.gsa.gov					
Region 7 - Greater Southwest 819 Taylor St	Fort Worth	TX	76102	817-978-2321	978-4867
Web: www.gsa.gov					
Region 8 - Rocky Mountain Denver Federal Ctr Bldg 41	Denver	CO	80225	303-236-7329	
TF: 888-999-4777 ■ Web: www.gsa.gov					
Region 9 - Pacific Rim 450 Golden Gate Ave	San Francisco	CA	94102	415-522-3001	522-3005
Web: www.gsa.gov					
Region 10 - Northwest/Arctic 400 15th St SW	Auburn	WA	98001	253-931-7000	
Web: www.gsa.gov					
Region 11 - National Capital Region 301 7th St SW	Washington	DC	20407	202-708-9100	708-9966
Web: www.gsa.gov					
Harry S Truman Scholarship Foundation					
712 Jackson Pl NW	Washington	DC	20006	202-395-4831	395-6995
Web: www.truman.gov					
Indian Arts & Crafts Board					
Department of the Interior 1849 C St NW MS 2528-MIB	Washington	DC	20240	202-208-3773	208-5196
TF: 888-278-3253 ■ Web: www.iacb.doi.gov					
Institute of Museum & Library Services					
1800 M St NW 9th Fl	Washington	DC	20036	202-653-4657	653-4600
Web: www.imls.gov					
Inter-American Foundation (IAF) 901 N Stuart St 10th Fl	Arlington	VA	22203	703-306-4301	306-4365
Web: www.iaf.gov					
Interagency Council on Homelessness					
409 3rd St SW Suite 310	Washington	DC	20024	202-708-4663	708-1216
Web: www.ich.gov					
Japan-US Friendship Commission					
1201 15th St NW Suite 330	Washington	DC	20005	202-653-9800	653-9802
Web: www.jusfc.gov					
Joint Board for the Enrollment of Actuaries					
Internal Revenue Service SE:OPR 1111 Constitution Ave NW	Washington	DC	20224	202-622-8229	622-8300
Web: www.irs.gov/taxpros/actuaries					
Legal Services Corp 3333 K St NW 3rd Fl	Washington	DC	20007	202-295-1500	337-6797
Web: www.lsc.gov					
Marine Mammal Commission 4340 East West Hwy Rm 700	Bethesda	MD	20814	301-504-0087	504-0099
Web: www.mmc.gov					
Merit Systems Protection Board (MSPB) 1615 M St NW	Washington	DC	20419	202-653-7200	653-7130
TF: 800-209-8960 ■ Web: www.mspb.gov					
Merit Systems Protection Board Regional Offices					
Atlanta Region 401 W Peachtree St NW 10th Fl	Atlanta	GA	30308	404-730-2755	730-2767
TF: 800-209-8960 ■ Web: www.mspb.gov					
Central Region 230 S Dearborn St 31st Fl	Chicago	IL	60604	312-353-2923	886-4231
Web: www.mspb.gov					
Dallas Field Office 1100 Commerce St Rm 620	Dallas	TX	75242	214-767-0555	767-0102
Web: www.mspb.gov					
Denver Field Office 165 S Union Blvd Suite 318	Lakewood	CO	80228	303-969-5101	969-5109
New York Field Office 26 Federal Plaza Rm 3137-A	New York	NY	10278	212-264-9372	264-1417
Northeastern Region 1601 Market St Suite 1700	Philadelphia	PA	19103	215-597-9960	597-3456
Washington (DC) Region 1800 Diagonal Rd Suite 205	Alexandria	VA	22314	703-756-6250	756-7112
Web: www.mspb.gov/-					
Western Region 201 Mission St	San Francisco	CA	94105	415-904-6772	904-0580

US Independent Agencies Government Corporations & Quasi-Official Agencies (Cont'd)

Phone Fax

Migratory Bird Conservation Commission
4401 N Fairfax Dr MS ARLSQ-622 .... Arlington VA 22203 703-358-1716 358-2223
Web: www.fws.gov/realty/mbcc.html
Millenium Challenge Corp 875 15th St NW .... Washington DC 20005 202-521-3600
Web: www.mcc.gov
Morris K Udall Foundation 130 S Scott Ave .... Tucson AZ 85701 520-670-5529 670-5530
Web: www.udall.gov
National Aeronautics & Space Administration (NASA)
300 'E' St SW .... Washington DC 20546 202-358-0001 358-3469
Web: www.nasa.gov
National Archives & Records Administration (NARA)
8601 Adelphi Rd .... College Park MD 20740 866-272-6272 837-0483*
*Fax Area Code: 301 ■ *Web:* www.archives.gov
Archival Research Catalog 8601 Adelphi Rd .... College Park MD 20740 866-272-6272
Web: www.archives.gov/research/arc
Office of the Federal Register
800 N Capitol St NW Suite 700-K .... Washington DC 20002 202-741-6000 741-6012
Web: www.archives.gov/federal-register
Office of Presidential Libraries
8601 Adelphi Rd Suite 2200 .... College Park MD 20740 301-837-3250 837-3199
Web: www.archives.gov/presidential_libraries
National Archives & Records Administration Regional Offices
Central Plains Region 2312 E Bannister Rd .... Kansas City MO 64131 816-268-8000
Web: www.archives.gov/central-plains
Great Lakes Region 7358 S Pulaski Rd .... Chicago IL 60629 773-948-9001
Web: www.archives.gov/great-lakes
Mid Atlantic Region 900 Market St .... Philadelphia PA 19107 215-606-0100 606-0116
Web: www.archives.gov/midatlantic
Northeast Region 380 Trapelo Rd .... Waltham MA 02452 781-663-0130 663-0154
TF: 866-406-2379 ■ *Web:* www.archives.gov/northeast
Pacific Alaska Region 6125 Sand Point Way NE .... Seattle WA 98115 206-336-5115 336-5112
TF: 866-325-7208 ■ *Web:* www.archives.gov/pacific-alaska
Pacific Region 1000 Commodore Dr .... San Bruno CA 94066 650-238-3500 238-3507
Web: www.archives.gov/pacific
Rocky Mountain Region PO Box 25307 .... Denver CO 80225 303-407-5740 407-5709
Web: www.archives.gov/rocky-mountain
Southeast Region 5780 Jonesboro Rd .... Morrow GA 30260 770-968-2100 968-2547
Web: www.archives.gov/southeast
Southwest Region 501 W Felix St Bldg 1 PO Box 6216 .... Fort Worth TX 76115 817-831-5620 334-5621
Web: www.archives.gov/southwest
National Capital Planning Commission
401 9th St NW North Lobby Suite 500 .... Washington DC 20004 202-482-7200 482-7272
Web: www.ncpc.gov
National Commission on Libraries & Information Science
1800 M St NW Suite 350 North Tower .... Washington DC 20036 202-606-9200 606-9203
Web: www.nclis.gov
National Council on Disability (NCD)
1331 F St NW Suite 850 .... Washington DC 20004 202-272-2004 272-2022
Web: www.ncd.gov
National Credit Union Administration 1775 Duke St .... Alexandria VA 22314 703-518-6300 518-6319
TF Fraud Hotlin: 800-827-9650 ■ *Web:* www.ncua.gov
National Credit Union Administration Regional Offices
Region 1 9 Washington Sq Washington Ave Ext. .... Albany NY 12205 518-862-7400 862-7420
Web: www.ncua.gov
Region 2 1775 Duke St Suite 4206 .... Alexandria VA 22314 703-519-4600 519-4620
Web: www.ncua.gov
Region 3 7000 Central Pkwy Suite 1600 .... Atlanta GA 30328 678-443-3000 443-3020
Web: www.ncua.gov
Region 4 4807 Spicewood Springs Rd Suite 5200 .... Austin TX 78759 512-342-5600 342-5620
Web: www.ncua.gov
Region 5 1230 W Washington St Suite 301 .... Tempe AZ 85281 602-302-6000 302-6024
Web: www.ncua.gov
National Endowment for the Arts (NEA)
1100 Pennsylvania Ave NW .... Washington DC 20506 202-682-5400
Web: www.arts.gov
National Endowment for the Humanities (NEH)
1100 Pennsylvania Ave NW .... Washington DC 20506 202-606-8400
TF: 800-634-1121 ■ *Web:* www.neh.gov
National Indian Gaming Commission
1441 L St NW Suite 9100 .... Washington DC 20005 202-632-7003 632-7066
Web: www.nigc.gov
National Labor Relations Board (NLRB) 1099 14th St NW ...... Washington DC 20570 202-273-1991
TF: 866-667-6572 ■ *Web:* www.nlrb.gov
National Labor Relations Board Regional Offices
Region 1 Federal Bldg 10 Causeway St 6th Fl .... Boston MA 02222 617-565-6700 565-6725
TF: 866-667-6572 ■ *Web:* www.nlrb.gov
Region 2 26 Federal Plaza Rm 3614 .... New York NY 10278 212-264-0300 264-2450
Web: www.nlrb.gov
Region 3 Niagara Center Bldg 130 S Elmwood Ave Suite 630 ...... Buffalo NY 14202 716-551-4931 551-4972
TF: 866-667-6572 ■ *Web:* www.nlrb.gov
Region 4 615 Chestnut St 7th Fl .... Philadelphia PA 19106 215-597-7601 597-7658
Web: www.nlrb.gov
Region 5 103 S Gay St 8th Fl .... Baltimore MD 21202 410-962-2822 962-2198
Web: www.nlrb.gov
Region 6 112 Washington Pl .... Pittsburgh PA 15219 412-395-4400 395-5986
Web: www.nlrb.gov
Region 7 477 Michigan Ave Rm 300 .... Detroit MI 48226 313-226-3200 226-2090
Web: www.nlrb.gov
Region 8 1240 E 9th St Rm 1695 .... Cleveland OH 44199 216-522-3716 522-2418
TF: 866-667-6572 ■ *Web:* www.nlrb.gov
Region 9 1240 E 9th St Rm 1695 .... Cleveland OH 44199 216-522-3716 522-2418
TF: 866-667-6572 ■ *Web:* www.nlrb.gov
Region 10 233 Peachtree St NE Suite 1000 .... Atlanta GA 30303 404-331-2896 331-2858
Web: www.nlrb.gov
Region 11 4035 University Pkwy Suite 200 .... Winston-Salem NC 27106 336-631-5201 631-5210
TF: 866-667-6572 ■ *Web:* www.nlrb.gov
Region 12 201 E Kennedy Blvd Suite 530 .... Tampa FL 33602 813-228-2641 228-2874
Web: www.nlrb.gov
Region 13 209 S LaSalle St Suite 900 .... Chicago IL 60604 312-353-7570 886-1341
Web: www.nlrb.gov
Region 14 1222 Spruce St Rm 8.302 .... Saint Louis MO 63103 314-539-7770 539-7794
TF: 866-667-6572 ■ *Web:* www.nlrb.gov
Region 15 1515 Poydras St Rm 610 .... New Orleans LA 70112 504-589-6361 589-4069
Web: www.nlrb.gov
Region 16 Federal Bldg 819 Taylor St Rm 8A24 .... Fort Worth TX 76102 817-978-2921 978-2928
TF: 866-667-6572 ■ *Web:* www.nlrb.gov
Region 17 8600 Farley St Suite 100 .... Overland Park KS 66212 913-967-3000 967-3010
Web: www.nlrb.gov
Region 18 330 2nd Ave S Suite 790 .... Minneapolis MN 55401 612-348-1757 348-1785
TF: 866-667-6572 ■ *Web:* www.nlrb.gov
Region 19 Federal Bldg 915 2nd Ave Rm 2948 .... Seattle WA 98174 206-220-6300 220-6305
Web: www.nlrb.gov
Region 20 901 Market St Suite 400 .... San Francisco CA 94103 415-356-5130 356-5156
TF: 866-667-6572 ■ *Web:* www.nlrb.gov
Region 21 888 S Figueroa St 9th Fl .... Los Angeles CA 90017 213-894-5200 894-2778
Web: www.nlrb.gov
Region 22 20 Washington Pl 5th Fl .... Newark NJ 07102 973-645-2100 645-3852
Web: www.nlrb.gov
Region 24 525 FD Roosevelt Ave Suite 1002 .... San Juan PR 00918 787-766-5347 766-5478
Web: www.nlrb.gov
Region 25 Federal Bldg 575 N Pennsylvania St Rm 238 ...... Indianapolis IN 46204 317-226-7381 226-5103
TF: 866-667-6572 ■ *Web:* www.nlrb.gov
Region 26 80 Monroe Ave Suite 350 .... Memphis TN 38103 901-544-0018 544-0008
Web: www.nlrb.gov
Region 27 600 17th St 7th Fl North Tower .... Denver CO 80202 303-844-3551 844-6249
Web: www.nlrb.gov
Region 28 2600 N Central Ave Suite 1800 .... Phoenix AZ 85004 602-640-2160 640-2178
Web: www.nlrb.gov
Region 29
2 Metro Tech Center N Jay St & Myrtle Ave 5th Fl .... Brooklyn NY 11201 718-330-7713 330-7579
Web: www.nlrb.gov
Region 30 310 W Wisconsin Ave Suite 700 .... Milwaukee WI 53203 414-297-3861 297-3880
Web: www.nlrb.gov
Region 31 11150 W Olympic Blvd Suite 700 .... Los Angeles CA 90064 310-235-7352 235-7420
TF: 866-667-6572 ■ *Web:* www.nlrb.gov
Region 32 1301 Clay St Rm 300N .... Oakland CA 94612 510-637-3300 637-3315
Web: www.nlrb.gov
Region 34 280 Trumbull St 21st Fl .... Hartford CT 06103 860-240-3522 240-3564
Web: www.nlrb.gov
National Mediation Board 1301 K St NW Suite 250E .... Washington DC 20005 202-692-5050
Web: www.nmb.gov
National Railroad Passenger Corp DBA Amtrak
60 Massachusetts Ave NE .... Washington DC 20002 202-906-3000
TF: 800-872-7245 ■ *Web:* www.amtrak.com
National Science Foundation (NSF) 4201 Wilson Blvd .... Arlington VA 22230 703-292-5111 292-9232
Web: www.nsf.gov
National Transportation Safety Board (NTSB)
490 L'Enfant Plaza SW .... Washington DC 20594 202-314-6000 314-6293
Web: www.ntsb.gov
NLRB (National Labor Relations Board) 1099 14th St NW ...... Washington DC 20570 202-273-1991
TF: 866-667-6572 ■ *Web:* www.nlrb.gov
NRC (Nuclear Regulatory Commission) .... Washington DC 20555 301-415-8200
TF: 800-368-5642 ■ *Web:* www.nrc.gov
NTSB (National Transportation Safety Board)
490 L'Enfant Plaza SW .... Washington DC 20594 202-314-6000 314-6293
Web: www.ntsb.gov
Nuclear Regulatory Commission (NRC) .... Washington DC 20555 301-415-8200
TF: 800-368-5642 ■ *Web:* www.nrc.gov
Nuclear Regulatory Commission Regional Offices
Region 1 475 Allendale Rd .... King of Prussia PA 19426 610-337-5000
TF: 800-432-1156
Region 2 61 Forsyth St SW Suite 23T85 .... Atlanta GA 30303 404-562-4400 562-4900
TF: 800-577-8510 ■ *Web:* www.nrc.gov
Region 3 2443 Warrenville Rd Suite 210 .... Lisle IL 60532 630-829-9500 515-1078
TF: 800-522-3025 ■ *Web:* www.nrc.gov
Region 4
Texas Health Resources Tower 611 Ryan Plaza Suite 400 ..... Arlington TX 76011 817-860-8100 860-8210
TF: 800-952-9677
Nuclear Waste Technical Review Board (NWTRB)
2300 Clarendon Blvd Suite 1300 .... Arlington VA 22201 703-235-4473 235-4495
Web: www.nwtrb.gov
Occupational Safety & Health Review Commission
1120 20th St NW 9th Fl .... Washington DC 20036 202-606-5400 606-5050
Web: www.oshrc.gov
Occupational Safety & Health Review Commission Regional Offices
Atlanta Region 100 Alabama St SW Rm 2R90 .... Atlanta GA 30303 404-562-1640 562-1650
Web: www.oshrc.gov
Denver Region 1244 Speer Blvd Rm 250 .... Denver CO 80204 303-844-3409 844-3759
Office of Compliance 110 2nd St SE Rm LA 200 .... Washington DC 20540 202-724-9250 426-1913
Web: www.compliance.gov
Office of the National Counterintelligence Executive (NCIX)
CS5 Rm 300 .... Washington DC 20511 703-682-4500 682-4510
Web: www.ncix.gov
Office of Personnel Management (OPM) 1900 'E' St NW .... Washington DC 20415 202-606-1800
Web: www.opm.gov
Office of Special Counsel 1730 M St NW Suite 218 .... Washington DC 20036 202-254-3600 653-5151
TF: 800-872-9855 ■ *Web:* www.osc.gov
Office of Special Counsel Regional Offices
Dallas Field Office 525 Griffin St Rm 824 Box 103 .... Dallas TX 75202 214-747-1519 767-2764
TF: 800-872-9855 ■ *Web:* www.osc.gov
Midwest Field Office 477 Michigan Ave Suite 495 .... Detroit MI 48226 313-226-4496 226-5606
San Francisco Bay Area Field Office
Federal Bldg 1301 Clay St Suite 1220-N .... Oakland CA 94612 510-637-3460 637-3474
TF: 800-872-9855 ■ *Web:* www.osc.gov
Overseas Private Investment Corp (OPIC)
1100 New York Ave NW .... Washington DC 20527 202-336-8400 408-9859
Web: www.opic.gov
Peace Corps 1111 20th St NW .... Washington DC 20526 202-692-2100 692-2101
TF: 800-424-8580 ■ *Web:* www.peacecorps.gov
Peace Corps Regional Offices
Atlanta Regional Office 100 Alabama St Bldg 1924 Suite 2R70 ..... Atlanta GA 30303 404-562-3456 562-3455
TF: 800-424-8508 ■ *Web:* www.peacecorps.gov
Chicago Regional Office 55 W Monroe St Suite 450 .... Chicago IL 60603 312-353-4990 353-4192
TF: 800-424-8580 ■ *Web:* www.peacecorps.gov
Dallas Regional Office 110 Commerce St Suite 427 .... Dallas TX 75242 214-253-5400 253-5401
TF: 800-424-8580 ■ *Web:* www.peacecorps.gov
Denver Regional Office 1999 Broadway Suite 2205 .... Denver CO 80202 303-844-7020 844-7010
TF: 800-424-8580 ■ *Web:* www.peacecorps.gov
Los Angeles Regional Office
2361 Rosecrans Ave Suite 155 .... El Segundo CA 90245 310-356-1100 356-1125
TF: 800-424-8580 ■ *Web:* www.peacecorps.gov
Mid-Atlantic Regional Office 1525 Wilson Blvd Suite 100 .... Arlington VA 22209 202-692-1040 692-1041
TF: 800-424-8580 ■ *Web:* www.peacecorps.gov
Minneapolis Regional Office 330 2nd Ave S Suite 420 .... Minneapolis MN 55401 612-348-1480 348-1474
TF: 800-424-8580 ■ *Web:* www.peacecorps.gov
New England Regional Office
Federal Bldg 10 Causeway St Rm 559 .... Boston MA 02222 617-565-5555 565-5539
TF: 800-424-8580 ■ *Web:* www.peacecorps.gov
New York Regional Office 201 Varick St Suite 1025 .... New York NY 10014 212-352-5440 352-5441
TF: 800-424-8580 ■ *Web:* www.peacecorps.gov
Northwest Regional Office 1601 5th Ave Suite 605 .... Seattle WA 98101 206-553-5490 553-2343
TF: 800-424-8580 ■ *Web:* www.peacecorps.gov
San Francisco Regional Office 1301 Clay St Suite 620-N .... Oakland CA 94610 510-452-8444 452-8441
TF: 800-424-8580 ■ *Web:* www.peacecorps.gov
Pension Benefit Guaranty Corp 1200 K St NW .... Washington DC 20005 202-326-4000 326-4047
TF Cust Svc: 800-400-7242 ■ *Web:* www.pbgc.gov
Postal Regulatory Commission
901 New York Ave NW Suite 200 .... Washington DC 20268 202-789-6800 789-6886
Web: www.prc.gov
Presidio Trust PO Box 29052 34 Graham St .... San Francisco CA 94129 415-561-5300 561-5315
Web: www.presidio.gov

				Phone	Fax
Railroad Retirement Board 844 N Rush St	Chicago	IL	60611	312-751-4500	
TF: 800-808-0772 ■ Web: www.rrb.gov					
Regulatory Information Service Center					
1800 F St NW Rm 3039	Washington	DC	20405	202-482-7340	482-7360
Web: gsa.gov/risc					
SBA (Small Business Administration) 409 3rd St SW	Washington	DC	20416	202-205-6600	205-6802
TF: 800-827-5722 ■ Web: www.sba.gov					
Securities & Exchange Commission (SEC) 100 F St NE	Washington	DC	20549	202-942-8088	772-9295
TF: 800-732-0330 ■ Web: www.sec.gov					
Office of Investor Education & Advocacy 100 F St NE	Washington	DC	20549	202-942-8088	772-9295
Web: www.sec.gov/investor.shtml					
Securities & Exchange Commission Regional Offices					
Atlanta Regional Office 3475 Lenox Rd NE Suite 1000	Atlanta	GA	30326	404-842-7600	
Web: www.sec.gov					
Boston Regional Office 33 Arch St 23rd Fl	Boston	MA	02110	617-573-8900	
Chicago Regional Office 175 W Jackson Blvd Suite 900	Chicago	IL	60604	312-353-7390	353-7398
Web: www.sec.gov					
Denver Regional Office 1801 California St Suite 1500	Denver	CO	80202	303-844-1000	844-1010
Web: www.sec.gov					
Fort Worth Regional Office					
Burnett Plaza Suite 1900 801 Cherry St Unit 18	Fort Worth	TX	76102	817-978-3821	
Los Angeles Regional Office 5670 Wilshire Blvd 11th Fl	Los Angeles	CA	90036	323-965-3998	965-3815
Web: www.sec.gov					
Miami Regional Office 801 Brickell Ave Suite 1800	Miami	FL	33131	305-982-6300	
Web: www.sec.gov					
New York Regional Office					
3 World Financial Center Suite 400	New York	NY	10281	212-336-1100	
Web: www.sec.gov					
Philadelphia Regional Office					
Mellon Independence Ctr 701 Market St	Philadelphia	PA	19106	215-597-3100	
Salt Lake Regional Office					
15 W South Temple St Suite 1800	Salt Lake City	UT	84101	801-524-5796	
San Francisco Regional Office					
44 Montgomery St Suite 2600	San Francisco	CA	94104	415-705-2500	
Selective Service System 1515 Wilson Blvd	Arlington	VA	22209	703-605-4000	
Web: www.sss.gov					
Selective Service System Regional Offices					
Region 1 2500 Green Bay Rd Bldg 3400 Suite 276	North Chicago	IL	60064	847-688-4540	688-3433
Region 2 2400 Lake Park Dr Suite 270	Smyrna	GA	30080	770-319-6036	319-5631
Web: www.sss.gov					
Region 3 3401 Quebec St	Denver	CO	80207	720-941-1670	941-1685
Web: www.sss.gov					
Small Business Administration (SBA) 409 3rd St SW	Washington	DC	20416	202-205-6600	205-6802
TF: 800-827-5722 ■ Web: www.sba.gov					
National Women's Business Council					
409 3rd St SW Suite 210	Washington	DC	20024	202-205-3850	205-6825
Web: www.nwbc.gov					
Small Business Administration Regional Offices					
Region 1 10 Causeway St Suite 812	Boston	MA	02222	617-565-8415	565-8420
Web: www.sba.gov/region1					
Region 2 26 Federal Plaza Suite 3108	New York	NY	10278	212-264-1450	264-0038
Web: www.sba.gov/region2					
Region 3 900 Market St 5th Fl	Philadelphia	PA	19107	215-580-2807	580-2800
Web: www.sba.gov/region3					
Region 4 233 Peachtree St NE Suite 1800	Atlanta	GA	30303	404-331-4999	331-2354
Web: www.sba.gov/region4					
Region 5 Citicorp Center 500 W Madison St Suite 1240	Chicago	IL	60661	312-353-4626	353-3426
Web: www.sba.gov/region5					
Region 6 4300 Amon Carter Blvd Suite 108	Fort Worth	TX	76155	817-684-5581	684-5588
Web: www.sba.gov/region6					
Region 7 100 Walnut Suite 530	Kansas City	MO	64106	816-426-4840	426-4848
Web: www.sba.gov/region7					
Region 8 721 19th St Suite 400	Denver	CO	80202	303-844-0500	844-0506
Web: www.sba.gov/region8					
Region 9 330 N Brand Blvd Suite 1270	Glendale	CA	91203	818-552-3434	552-3440
Web: www.sba.gov/region9					
Region 10 2401 4th Ave Suite 400	Seattle	WA	98121	206-553-5676	553-4155
Web: www.sba.gov/region10					
Smithsonian Institution					
SI Bldg Rm 153 MRC 010 PO Box 37012	Washington	DC	20113	202-633-1000	
Web: www.si.edu					
Social Security Administration (SSA) 6401 Security Blvd	Baltimore	MD	21235	410-965-5738	966-1463
TF: 800-772-1213 ■ Web: www.ssa.gov					
Social Security Administration Regional Offices					
Region 1 JFK Federal Bldg Rm 1900	Boston	MA	02203	617-565-2870	565-2143
Web: www.ssa.gov/boston					
Region 2 26 Federal Plaza Rm 40-102	New York	NY	10278	212-264-3915	264-6847
TF: 800-772-1213 ■ Web: www.ssa.gov/ny					
Region 3 300 Spring Garden St PO Box 8788	Philadelphia	PA	19101	215-597-5157	597-2827
TF: 800-772-1213 ■ Web: www.ssa.gov/phila					
Region 4 61 Forsyth St SW Suite 23T30	Atlanta	GA	30303	404-562-5600	562-5608
Web: www.ssa.gov/atlanta					
Region 5 600 W Madison St PO Box 8280	Chicago	IL	60680	312-575-4000	575-4016
TF: 800-772-1213 ■ Web: www.ssa.gov/chicago					
Region 6 1301 Young St	Dallas	TX	75202	214-767-4212	767-8986
TF: 800-772-1213 ■ Web: www.ssa.gov/dallas					
Region 7 Federal Bldg 601 E 12th St Rm 436	Kansas City	MO	64106	816-936-5700	936-5972
Web: www.ssa.gov/kc					
Region 8 Federal Bldg 1961 Stout St	Denver	CO	80294	303-844-2388	844-6767
Web: www.ssa.gov/denver					
Region 9 PO Box 4201	Richmond	CA	94804	510-970-8430	970-8218
TF: 800-772-1213 ■ Web: www.ssa.gov/sf					
Region 10 701 5th Ave Suite 2900	Seattle	WA	98104	206-615-2100	615-2193
TF: 800-772-1213 ■ Web: www.ssa.gov/seattle					
Social Security Advisory Board					
400 Virginia Ave SW Suite 625	Washington	DC	20024	202-475-7700	475-7715
Web: www.ssab.gov					
State Justice Institute (SJI) 1650 King St Suite 600	Alexandria	VA	22314	703-684-6100	684-7618
Web: www.statejustice.org					
Susquehanna River Basin Commission 1721 N Front St	Harrisburg	PA	17102	717-238-0423	238-2436
Web: www.srbc.net					
Tennessee Valley Authority (TVA) 400 W Summit Hill Dr	Knoxville	TN	37902	865-632-2101	
Web: www.tva.gov					
US Agency for International Development (USAID)					
1300 Pennsylvania Ave NW	Washington	DC	20523	202-712-0000	216-3524
Web: www.usaid.gov					
US Arctic Research Commission 4350 N Fairfax Dr Suite 510	Arlington	VA	22203	703-525-0111	525-0114
Web: www.arctic.gov					
US Chemical Safety & Hazard Investigation Board					
2175 K St NW Suite 400	Washington	DC	20037	202-261-7600	261-7650
Web: www.chemsafety.gov					
US Commission on Civil Rights 624 9th St NW	Washington	DC	20425	202-376-7700	376-7672
Web: www.usccr.gov					
US Commission on Civil Rights Regional Offices					
Central Regional Office 400 State Ave Suite 908	Kansas City	KS	66101	913-551-1400	551-1413
Web: www.usccr.gov					
Eastern Regional Office 624 9th St NW Suite 700	Washington	DC	20425	202-376-7700	376-7672
Web: www.usccr.gov					
Midwestern Regional Office 55 W Monroe St Suite 410	Chicago	IL	60603	312-353-8311	353-8324
TF: 800-552-6843 ■ Web: www.usccr.gov					
Rocky Mountain Regional Office 1961 Stout St Suite 240	Denver	CO	80294	303-866-1040	866-1050
Web: www.usccr.gov					
Southern Regional Office 61 Forsyth St SW Suite 18T40	Atlanta	GA	30303	404-562-7000	562-7005
Western Regional Office					
300 N Los Angeles St Suite 2010	Los Angeles	CA	90012	213-894-3437	894-0508
Web: www.usccr.gov					
US Commission on International Religious Freedom (USCIRF)					
800 N Capitol St NW Suite 790	Washington	DC	20002	202-523-3240	523-5020
Web: www.uscirf.gov					
US Election Assistance Commission					
1225 New York Ave NW Suite 1100	Washington	DC	20005	202-566-3100	566-3127
TF: 866-747-1471 ■ Web: www.eac.gov					
US Helsinki Commission					
234 Ford House Office Bldg 3rd & D Sts SW	Washington	DC	20515	202-225-1901	226-4199
Web: www.csce.gov					
US Institute of Peace 1200 17th St NW	Washington	DC	20036	202-457-1700	429-6063
Web: www.usip.org					
US International Trade Commission 500 'E' St SW	Washington	DC	20436	202-205-2000	205-2316
Web: www.usitc.gov					
US Office of Government Ethics					
1201 New York Ave NW Suite 500	Washington	DC	20005	202-482-9300	482-9237
Web: www.usoge.gov					
US Postal Service (USPS) 475 L'Enfant Plaza West SW	Washington	DC	20260	202-268-2000	
TF Cust Svc: 800-275-8777 ■ Web: www.usps.com					
US Trade & Development Agency					
1000 Wilson Blvd Suite 1600	Arlington	VA	22209	703-875-4357	875-4009
Web: www.ustda.gov					
Vietnam Education Foundation (VEF)					
2111 Wilson Blvd Suite 700	Arlington	VA	22201	703-351-5053	351-1423
Web: www.vef.gov					
White House Commission on the National Moment of Remembrance 1750 New York Ave NW	Washington	DC	20006	202-783-4665	783-1168
Web: www.remember.gov					

344 GOVERNMENT - US - JUDICIAL BRANCH

				Phone	Fax
Administrative Office of the US Courts					
Federal Judiciary Bldg 1 Columbus Cir NE	Washington	DC	20544	202-502-2600	
Web: www.uscourts.gov					
Alien Terrorist Removal Court					
US Courthouse 333 Constitution Ave NW	Washington	DC	20001	202-354-3050	354-3067
Federal Judicial Center					
Thurgood Marshall Federal Judiciary Bldg 1 Columbus Cir NE	Washington	DC	20002	202-502-4000	502-4099
Web: www.fjc.gov					
Judicial Conference of the US					
Thurgood Marshall Federal Judiciary Bldg 1 Columbus Cir NE Rm 7-425 S	Washington	DC	20544	202-502-2400	502-1144
Web: www.uscourts.gov/judconf.html					
Judicial Panel on Multidistrict Litigation					
Thurgood Marshall Federal Judiciary Bldg 1 Columbus Cir NE Rm G-255 N Lobby	Washington	DC	20002	202-502-2800	502-2888
Web: www.jpml.uscourts.gov					
Supreme Court of the US					
US Supreme Court Bldg 1 1st St NE	Washington	DC	20543	202-479-3211	
Web: www.supremecourtus.gov					
US Court of Appeals for the Armed Forces 450 'E' St NW	Washington	DC	20442	202-761-1448	761-4672
Web: www.armfor.uscourts.gov					
US Court of Appeals for Veterans Claims					
625 Indiana Ave NW Suite 900	Washington	DC	20004	202-501-5970	501-5848
Web: www.vetapp.uscourts.gov					
US Court of Federal Claims 717 Madison Pl NW	Washington	DC	20005	202-357-6400	
Web: www.uscfc.uscourts.gov					
US Court of International Trade 1 Federal Plaza	New York	NY	10278	212-264-2800	264-1085
Web: www.cit.uscourts.gov					
US Sentencing Commission					
Thurgood Marshall Federal Judiciary Bldg 1 Columbus Cir NE South Lobby	Washington	DC	20002	202-502-4500	
Web: www.ussc.gov					
US Tax Court 400 2nd St NW	Washington	DC	20217	202-521-0700	
Web: www.ustaxcourt.gov					

344-1 US Appeals Courts

				Phone	Fax
US Court of Appeals					
Federal Circuit 717 Madison Pl NW	Washington	DC	20439	202-633-6550	633-9623
Web: www.fedcir.gov					
Circuit 1 US Courthouse 1 Courthouse Way Suite 2500	Boston	MA	02210	617-748-9057	
Web: www.ca1.uscourts.gov					
Circuit 2 US Courthouse 40 Foley Sq	New York	NY	10007	212-857-8500	
Web: www.ca2.uscourts.gov					
Circuit 3 US Courthouse 601 Market St	Philadelphia	PA	19106	215-597-2995	
Web: www.ca3.uscourts.gov					
Circuit 4 US Courthouse Annex 1100 E Main St	Richmond	VA	23219	804-916-2700	
Web: www.ca4.uscourts.gov					
Circuit 5 600 S Maestri Pl	New Orleans	LA	70130	504-310-7700	
Web: www.ca5.uscourts.gov					
Circuit 6 540 Potter Stewart US Courthouse 100 E 5th St	Cincinnati	OH	45202	513-564-7000	564-7090
Web: www.ca6.uscourts.gov					
Circuit 7 US Courthouse 219 S Dearborn St	Chicago	IL	60604	312-435-5850	
Web: www.ca7.uscourts.gov					
Circuit 8 US Courthouse 111 S 10th St	Saint Louis	MO	63102	314-244-2400	244-2780
Web: www.ca8.uscourts.gov					
Circuit 9 95 7th St PO Box 193939	San Francisco	CA	94103	415-355-8000	
Web: www.ca9.uscourts.gov					
Circuit 10 US Courthouse 1823 Stout St	Denver	CO	80257	303-844-3157	
Web: www.ca10.uscourts.gov					
Circuit 11 56 Forsyth St NW 1st Fl	Atlanta	GA	30303	404-335-6100	
Web: www.ca11.uscourts.gov					
District of Columbia Circuit					
US Courthouse 33 Constitution Ave NW Rm 5523	Washington	DC	20001	202-216-7000	
Web: www.cadc.uscourts.gov					

344-2 US Bankruptcy Courts

	City	State	Zip	Phone	Fax
US Bankruptcy Court					
Alabama Middle 1 Church St	Montgomery	AL	36104	334-954-3800	954-3819
Web: www.almb.uscourts.gov					
Alabama Northern 1800 5th Ave N Rm 120	Birmingham	AL	35203	205-714-4000	714-3913
Web: www.alnb.uscourts.gov					
Alabama Southern 201 Saint Louis St	Mobile	AL	36602	251-441-5391	441-6286
Web: www.alsb.uscourts.gov					
Alaska 605 W 4th Ave Suite 138	Anchorage	AK	99501	907-271-2655	271-2645
TF: 800-859-8059 ■ Web: www.akb.uscourts.gov					
Arizona 230 N 1st Ave Suite 101	Phoenix	AZ	85003	602-682-4000	
Web: www.azb.uscourts.gov					
Arkansas 300 W 2nd St	Little Rock	AR	72201	501-918-5500	918-5520
Web: www.arb.uscourts.gov					
California Central 255 E Temple St	Los Angeles	CA	90012	213-894-3118	
Web: www.cacb.uscourts.gov					
California Eastern 501 'I' St Suite 3-200	Sacramento	CA	95814	916-930-4400	
Web: www.caeb.uscourts.gov					
California Northern PO Box 7 PO Box 7341	San Francisco	CA	94120	415-268-2300	
Web: www.canb.uscourts.gov					
California Southern 325 W 'F' St	San Diego	CA	92101	619-557-5620	
Web: www.casb.uscourts.gov					
Colorado US Custom House 721 19th St	Denver	CO	80202	720-904-7300	
Web: www.cob.uscourts.gov					
Connecticut 450 Main St 7th Fl	Hartford	CT	06103	860-240-3675	240-3595
Web: www.ctb.uscourts.gov					
Delaware 824 N Market St 3rd Fl	Wilmington	DE	19801	302-252-2900	
Web: www.deb.uscourts.gov					
District of Columbia 333 Constitution Ave NW	Washington	DC	20001	202-565-2500	
Web: www.dcb.uscourts.gov					
Florida Middle 801 N Florida Ave Suite 727	Tampa	FL	33602	813-301-5162	
Web: www.flmb.uscourts.gov					
Florida Northern 110 E Park Ave Suite 100	Tallahassee	FL	32301	850-521-5001	
Web: www.flnb.uscourts.gov					
Florida Southern 51 SW 1st Ave	Miami	FL	33130	305-714-1800	
Web: www.flsb.uscourts.gov					
Georgia Middle 433 Cherry St PO Box 1957	Macon	GA	31202	478-752-3506	
Web: www.gamb.uscourts.gov					
Georgia Northern 75 Spring St SW	Atlanta	GA	30303	404-215-1000	
Web: www.ganb.uscourts.gov					
Georgia Southern PO Box 8347	Savannah	GA	31412	912-650-4100	
Web: www.gasb.uscourts.gov					
Hawaii 1132 Bishop St	Honolulu	HI	96813	808-522-8100	522-8120
Web: www.hib.uscourts.gov					
Idaho 550 W Fort St	Boise	ID	83724	208-334-1074	
Web: www.id.uscourts.gov					
Illinois Central 600 E Monroe St Rm 226	Springfield	IL	62701	217-492-4551	
Web: www.ilcb.uscourts.gov					
Illinois Northern 219 S Dearborn St Rm 713	Chicago	IL	60604	312-435-5694	408-7750
Web: www.ilnb.uscourts.gov					
Illinois Southern 750 Missouri Ave	East Saint Louis	IL	62201	618-482-9400	
Web: www.ilsb.uscourts.gov					
Indiana Northern 401 S Michigan St	South Bend	IN	46601	574-968-2100	
Web: www.innb.uscourts.gov					
Indiana Southern 46 E Ohio St	Indianapolis	IN	46204	317-229-3800	229-3801
Web: www.insb.uscourts.gov					
Iowa Northern PO Box 74890	Cedar Rapids	IA	52407	319-286-2200	286-2280
Web: www.ianb.uscourts.gov					
Iowa Southern 110 E Court Ave PO Box 9264	Des Moines	IA	50306	515-284-6230	284-6303
TF: 888-219-5534 ■ Web: www.iasb.uscourts.gov					
Kansas 401 N Market St Rm 167	Wichita	KS	67202	316-269-6486	269-6181
Web: www.ksb.uscourts.gov					
Kentucky Eastern 100 E Vine St Suite 200	Lexington	KY	40507	859-233-2608	
Web: www.kyeb.uscourts.gov					
Kentucky Western 601 W Broadway Suite 450	Louisville	KY	40202	502-627-5700	
Web: www.kywb.uscourts.gov					
Louisiana Eastern 500 Poydras St Suite B-601	New Orleans	LA	70130	504-589-7878	
Web: www.laeb.uscourts.gov					
Louisiana Middle 707 Florida St Suite 119	Baton Rouge	LA	70801	225-389-0211	
Web: www.lamb.uscourts.gov					
Louisiana Western 300 Fannin St Suite 2201	Shreveport	LA	71101	318-676-4267	
Web: www.lawb.uscourts.gov					
Maine 537 Congress St 2nd Fl	Portland	ME	04101	207-780-3482	780-3679
Web: www.meb.uscourts.gov					
Maryland 101 W Lombard St Suite 8308	Baltimore	MD	21201	410-962-2688	
Web: www.mdb.uscourts.gov					
Massachusetts Federal Bldg 10 Causeway St Rm 1101	Boston	MA	02222	617-565-8950	565-6650
Web: www.mab.uscourts.gov					
Michigan Eastern 211 W Fort St Suite 2100	Detroit	MI	48226	313-234-0065	
Web: www.mieb.uscourts.gov					
Michigan Western 1 Division Ave N Rm 200	Grand Rapids	MI	49503	616-456-2693	
Web: www.miwb.uscourts.gov					
Minnesota 300 S 4th St Rm 301	Minneapolis	MN	55415	612-664-5200	
TF: 800-959-9002 ■ Web: www.mnb.uscourts.gov					
Mississippi Northern					
Thad Cochran US Courthouse 703 Hwy 145 N	Aberdeen	MS	39730	662-369-2596	
Web: www.msnb.uscourts.gov					
Mississippi Southern PO Box 2448	Jackson	MS	39225	601-965-5301	
Web: www.mssb.uscourts.gov					
Missouri Eastern 111 S 10th St 4th Fl	Saint Louis	MO	63102	314-244-4500	244-4990
TF: 866-803-9517 ■ Web: www.moeb.uscourts.gov					
Missouri Western 400 E 9th St Rm1510	Kansas City	MO	64106	816-512-1800	
Web: www.mow.uscourts.gov					
Montana 400 NW Main St	Butte	MT	59701	406-782-3354	
Web: www.mtb.uscourts.gov					
Nebraska 111 S 18th Plaza Suite 1125	Omaha	NE	68102	402-661-7444	
Web: www.neb.uscourts.gov					
Nevada 300 Las Vegas Blvd S	Las Vegas	NV	89101	702-388-6257	
Web: www.nvb.uscourts.gov					
New Hampshire 1000 Elm St 10th Fl	Manchester	NH	03101	603-222-2600	222-2697
Web: www.nhb.uscourts.gov					
New Jersey PO Box 1352	Newark	NJ	07102	973-645-4764	
Web: www.njb.uscourts.gov					
New Mexico PO Box 546	Albuquerque	NM	87103	505-348-2500	348-2473
TF: 866-291-6805 ■ Web: www.nmcourt.fed.us					
New York Eastern 271 Cadman Plaza E	Brooklyn	NY	11201	347-394-1700	
Web: www.nyeb.uscourts.gov					
New York Northern 445 Broadway Suite 330	Albany	NY	12207	518-257-1661	257-1643
Web: www.nynb.uscourts.gov					
New York Southern US Custom House 1 Bowling Green	New York	NY	10004	212-668-2870	668-2878
Web: www.nysb.uscourts.gov					
New York Western 100 State St Rm 1220	Rochester	NY	14614	585-613-4200	
Web: www.nywb.uscourts.gov					
North Carolina Eastern 1760-A Parkwood Blvd	Wilson	NC	27893	252-237-0248	243-4870
Web: www.nceb.uscourts.gov					
North Carolina Middle					
101 S Edgeworth St 1st Fl PO Box 26100	Greensboro	NC	27420	336-358-4000	
Web: www.ncmb.uscourts.gov					
North Carolina Western 401 W Trade St PO Box 34189	Charlotte	NC	28234	704-350-7500	344-6403
TF: 800-884-9868 ■ Web: www.ncwb.uscourts.gov					
North Dakota 655 1st Ave N Suite 210	Fargo	ND	58102	701-297-7100	297-7166
Web: www.ndb.uscourts.gov					
Ohio Northern 201 Superior Ave	Cleveland	OH	44114	216-615-4300	
Web: www.ohnb.uscourts.gov					
Ohio Southern 120 W 3rd St	Dayton	OH	45402	937-225-2516	225-7574
Web: www.ohsb.uscourts.gov					
Oklahoma Eastern 111 W 4th St PO Box 1347	Okmulgee	OK	74447	918-758-0126	756-9248
Web: www.okeb.uscourts.gov					
Oklahoma Northern 224 S Boulder Ave Rm 105	Tulsa	OK	74103	918-699-4000	699-4045
Web: www.oknb.uscourts.gov					
Oklahoma Western 215 Dean A McGee Ave	Oklahoma City	OK	73102	405-609-5700	609-5752
Web: www.okwb.uscourts.gov					
Oregon 1001 SW 5th Ave Rm 700	Portland	OR	97204	503-326-1500	
Web: www.orb.uscourts.gov					
Pennsylvania Eastern 900 Market St Suite 400	Philadelphia	PA	19107	215-408-2800	
Web: www.paeb.uscourts.gov					
Pennsylvania Middle 197 S Main St	Wilkes-Barre	PA	18701	570-826-6450	826-6401
Web: www.pamb.uscourts.gov					
Pennsylvania Western 5414 US Steel Tower 600 Grant St	Pittsburgh	PA	15219	412-644-2700	
Web: www.pawb.uscourts.gov					
Puerto Rico 300 Calle Del Recinto Sur	San Juan	PR	00901	787-977-6000	977-6008
Web: www.prb.uscourts.gov					
Rhode Island Federal Center 380 Westminster Mall 6th Fl	Providence	RI	02903	401-626-3100	626-3150
Web: www.rib.uscourts.gov					
South Carolina 1100 Laurel St	Columbia	SC	29201	803-765-5436	
Web: www.scb.uscourts.gov					
South Dakota 400 S Phillips Ave Rm 104	Sioux Falls	SD	57104	605-357-2400	357-2401
Web: www.sdb.uscourts.gov					
Tennessee Eastern 800 Market St Suite 330	Knoxville	TN	37902	865-545-4279	
Web: www.tneb.uscourts.gov					
Tennessee Middle 701 Broadway Suite 160	Nashville	TN	37203	615-736-5584	736-2305
Web: www.tnmb.uscourts.gov					
Tennessee Western 200 Jefferson Ave Suite 413	Memphis	TN	38103	901-328-3500	
Web: www.tnwb.uscourts.gov					
Texas Eastern 110 N College Ave 9th Fl	Tyler	TX	75702	903-590-3200	
Web: www.txeb.uscourts.gov					
Texas Northern 1100 Commerce St Rm 1254	Dallas	TX	75242	214-753-2000	753-2038
TF: 800-442-6850 ■ Web: www.txnb.uscourts.gov					
Texas Southern PO Box 61010	Houston	TX	77208	713-250-5500	
Web: www.txs.uscourts.gov					
Texas Western 615 E Houston St	San Antonio	TX	78205	210-472-6720	
Web: www.txwb.uscourts.gov					
US Virgin Islands					
US Courthouse 5500 Veterans Dr Rm 310	Saint Thomas	VI	00802	340-774-8310	776-5615
Web: www.vid.uscourts.gov					
Utah 350 S Main St Rm 301	Salt Lake City	UT	84101	801-524-6687	524-4409
Web: www.utb.uscourts.gov					
Vermont PO Box 6648	Rutland	VT	05702	802-776-2000	776-2020
Web: www.vtb.uscourts.gov					
Virginia Eastern 1100 E Main St Rm 301	Richmond	VA	23219	804-916-2400	
Web: www.vaeb.uscourts.gov					
Virginia Western 210 Church Ave SW Rm 200	Roanoke	VA	24011	540-857-2391	857-2873
Web: www.vawb.uscourts.gov					
Washington Eastern 904 W Riverside Ave Suite 304	Spokane	WA	99201	509-353-2404	
TF: 800-519-2549 ■ Web: www.waeb.uscourts.gov					
Washington Western 700 Stewart St 6th Fl	Seattle	WA	98101	206-370-5200	
Web: www.wawb.uscourts.gov					
West Virginia Northern 1125 Chapline St 3rd Fl PO Box 70	Wheeling	WV	26003	304-233-1655	233-0185
Web: www.wvnb.uscourts.gov					
West Virginia Southern					
US Courthouse 300 Virginia St E Rm 3200	Charleston	WV	25301	304-347-3003	
Web: www.wvsb.uscourts.gov					
Wisconsin Eastern					
US Courthouse 517 E Wisconsin Ave Rm 126	Milwaukee	WI	53202	414-297-3291	
TF: 877-781-7277 ■ Web: www.wieb.uscourts.gov					
Wisconsin Western PO Box 548	Madison	WI	53701	608-264-5178	
Web: www.wiwb.uscourts.gov					
Wyoming 2120 Capitol Ave Suite 6004	Cheyenne	WY	82001	307-433-2200	433-2214
Web: www.wyb.uscourts.gov					

344-3 US District Courts

	City	State	Zip	Phone	Fax
US District Court Alabama Middle					
1 Church St PO Box 711	Montgomery	AL	36101	334-954-3600	954-3615
Web: www.almd.uscourts.gov					
US District Court Alabama Northern 1729 5th Ave N	Birmingham	AL	35203	205-278-1700	
Web: www.alnd.uscourts.gov					
US District Court Alabama Southern					
US Courthouse 113 Saint Joseph St	Mobile	AL	36602	251-690-2371	694-4297
Web: www.als.uscourts.gov					
US District Court Alaska 222 W 7th Ave	Anchorage	AK	99513	907-677-6100	
TF: 866-243-3814 ■ Web: www.akd.uscourts.gov					
US District Court Arizona 401 W Washington St Suite 130	Phoenix	AZ	85003	602-322-7200	322-7209
Web: www.azd.uscourts.gov					
US District Court Arkansas Eastern					
600 W Capitol Ave Suite A-149	Little Rock	AR	72201	501-604-5351	
Web: www.are.uscourts.gov					
US District Court Arkansas Western Federal Bldg 30 6th St	Fort Smith	AR	72901	479-783-6833	783-6308
Web: www.arwd.uscourts.gov					
US District Court California Central 312 N Spring St	Los Angeles	CA	90012	213-894-1565	
Web: www.cacd.uscourts.gov					
US District Court California Eastern 501 'I' St Suite 4-200	Sacramento	CA	95814	916-930-4000	
Web: www.caed.uscourts.gov					
US District Court California Northern					
450 Golden Gate Ave 16th Fl Rm 161111	San Francisco	CA	94102	415-522-2000	
Web: www.cand.uscourts.gov					
US District Court California Southern 880 Front St Rm 4290	San Diego	CA	92101	619-557-6348	702-9900
Web: www.casd.uscourts.gov					
US District Court Colorado 901 19th St 2nd Fl	Denver	CO	80294	303-844-3433	335-2040
Web: www.co.uscourts.gov					
US District Court Connecticut 141 Church St	New Haven	CT	06510	203-773-2140	773-2334
Web: www.ctd.uscourts.gov					
US District Court Delaware Federal Bldg 844 N King St	Wilmington	DE	19801	302-573-6170	
Web: www.ded.uscourts.gov					
US District Court District of Columbia					
US Courthouse 333 Constitution Ave NW	Washington	DC	20001	202-354-3000	
Web: www.dcd.uscourts.gov					
US District Court Florida Middle					
401 W Central Blvd Suite 1200	Orlando	FL	32801	407-835-4200	
Web: www.flmd.uscourts.gov					

Entry	City	State	ZIP	Phone	Fax
US District Court Florida Northern 111 N Adams St 3rd Fl *Web:* www.flnd.uscourts.gov	Tallahassee	FL	32301	850-521-3501	521-3656
US District Court Florida Southern 301 N Miami Ave *Web:* www.flsd.uscourts.gov	Miami	FL	33128	305-523-5100	
US District Court Georgia Middle 475 Mulberry St PO Box 128 *Web:* www.gamd.uscourts.gov	Macon	GA	31202	478-752-3497	752-3496
US District Court Georgia Northern 75 Spring St SW Rm 2211 *Web:* www.gand.uscourts.gov	Atlanta	GA	30303	404-215-1600	
US District Court Georgia Southern PO Box 8286 *Web:* www.gasd.uscourts.gov	Savannah	GA	31412	912-650-4020	
US District Court Guam 520 W Soledad Ave 4th Fl *Web:* www.gud.uscourts.gov	Hagatna	GU	96910	671-473-9100	
US District Court Hawaii 300 Ala Moana Blvd Rm C-338 *Web:* www.hid.uscourts.gov	Honolulu	HI	96850	808-541-1300	
US District Court Idaho 550 W Fort St *Web:* www.id.uscourts.gov	Boise	ID	83724	208-334-1361	
US District Court Illinois Central 600 E Monroe St *Web:* www.ilcd.uscourts.gov	Springfield	IL	62701	217-492-4020	492-4028
US District Court Illinois Northern 219 S Dearborn St 20th Fl *Web:* www.ilnd.uscourts.gov	Chicago	IL	60604	312-435-5670	
US District Court Illinois Southern PO Box 249 *Web:* www.ilsd.uscourts.gov	East Saint Louis	IL	62202	618-482-9371	482-9383
US District Court Indiana Northern 204 S Main St *Web:* www.innd.uscourts.gov	South Bend	IN	46601	574-246-8000	
US District Court Indiana Southern 46 E Ohio St *Web:* www.insd.uscourts.gov	Indianapolis	IN	46204	317-229-3700	229-3959
US District Court Iowa Northern 101 1st St SE *Web:* www.iand.uscourts.gov	Cedar Rapids	IA	52401	319-286-2300	286-2301
US District Court Iowa Southern PO Box 9344 *Web:* www.iasd.uscourts.gov	Des Moines	IA	50306	515-284-6421	284-6418
US District Court Kansas 500 State Ave *Web:* www.ksd.uscourts.gov	Kansas City	KS	66101	913-551-6719	551-6942
US District Court Kentucky Eastern 101 Barr St *Web:* www.kyed.uscourts.gov	Lexington	KY	40507	859-233-2503	
US District Court Kentucky Western 601 W Broadway Rm 106 *Web:* www.kywd.uscourts.gov	Louisville	KY	40202	502-625-3500	625-3880
US District Court Louisiana Eastern 500 Poydras St Rm C-151 *Web:* www.laed.uscourts.gov	New Orleans	LA	70130	504-589-7650	589-7697
US District Court Louisiana Middle 777 Florida St Suite 139 *Web:* www.lamd.uscourts.gov	Baton Rouge	LA	70801	225-389-3500	389-3501
US District Court Louisiana Western 300 Fannin St Suite 1167 *Web:* www.lawd.uscourts.gov	Shreveport	LA	71101	318-676-4273	676-3962
US District Court Maine 156 Federal St *Web:* www.med.uscourts.gov	Portland	ME	04101	207-780-3356	
US District Court Maryland 101 W Lombard St *Web:* www.mdd.uscourts.gov	Baltimore	MD	21201	410-962-2600	
US District Court Massachusetts 1 Courthouse Way Suite 2300 *Web:* www.mad.uscourts.gov	Boston	MA	02210	617-748-9152	
US District Court Michigan Eastern 231 W Lafayette Blvd *Web:* www.mied.uscourts.gov	Detroit	MI	48226	313-234-5005	
US District Court Michigan Western 110 Michigan St NW Rm 399 *Web:* www.miwd.uscourts.gov	Grand Rapids	MI	49503	616-456-2381	456-2058
US District Court Minnesota 300 S 4th St Suite 202 *Web:* www.mnd.uscourts.gov	Minneapolis	MN	55415	612-664-5000	664-5033
US District Court Mississippi Northern 911 Jackson Ave E Rm 369 *Web:* www.msnd.uscourts.gov	Oxford	MS	38655	662-234-1971	236-5210
US District Court Mississippi Southern PO Box 23552 *Web:* www.mssd.uscourts.gov	Jackson	MS	39225	601-965-4439	
US District Court Missouri Eastern 111 S 10th St Suite 3.300 *Web:* www.moed.uscourts.gov	Saint Louis	MO	63102	314-244-7900	244-7909
US District Court Missouri Western 400 E 9th St *Web:* www.mow.uscourts.gov	Kansas City	MO	64106	816-512-5000	
US District Court Montana PO Box 8537 *Web:* www.mtd.uscourts.gov	Missoula	MT	59807	406-542-7260	542-7272
US District Court Nebraska 111 S 18th Plaza Suite 1152 *TF:* 866-220-4381 ■ *Web:* www.ned.uscourts.gov	Omaha	NE	68102	402-661-7350	661-7387
US District Court Nevada 333 Las Vegas Blvd S 1st Fl *Web:* www.nvd.uscourts.gov	Las Vegas	NV	89101	702-464-5400	
US District Court New Hampshire 55 Pleasant St Rm 110 *Web:* www.nhd.uscourts.gov	Concord	NH	03301	603-225-1423	
US District Court New Jersey 50 Walnut St Rm 4015 *Web:* pacer.njd.uscourts.gov	Newark	NJ	07102	973-645-3730	
US District Court New Mexico 333 Lomas Blvd NW *Web:* www.nmcourt.fed.us	Albuquerque	NM	87102	505-348-2000	348-2028
US District Court New York Eastern 225 Cadman Plaza E *Web:* www.nyed.uscourts.gov	Brooklyn	NY	11201	718-613-2600	
US District Court New York Northern 100 S Clinton St PO Box 7367 *Web:* www.nynd.uscourts.gov	Syracuse	NY	13261	315-234-8500	
US District Court New York Southern 500 Pearl St *Web:* www.nysd.uscourts.gov	New York	NY	10007	212-805-0136	
US District Court New York Western 68 Court St *Web:* www.nywd.uscourts.gov	Buffalo	NY	14202	716-551-4211	551-4850
US District Court North Carolina Eastern PO Box 25670 *Web:* www.nced.uscourts.gov	Raleigh	NC	27611	919-645-1700	645-1750
US District Court North Carolina Middle 324 W Market St 4th Fl *Web:* www.ncmd.uscourts.gov	Greensboro	NC	27401	336-332-6000	332-6060
US District Court North Carolina Western 401 W Trade St *TF:* 866-851-1605 ■ *Web:* www.ncwd.uscourts.gov	Charlotte	NC	28202	704-350-7400	350-7421
US District Court North Dakota PO Box 1193 *Web:* www.ndd.uscourts.gov	Bismarck	ND	58502	701-530-2300	530-2312
US District Court Ohio Northern 801 W Superior Ave *Web:* www.ohnd.uscourts.gov	Cleveland	OH	44113	216-357-7000	357-7040
US District Court Ohio Southern 85 Marconi Blvd *Web:* www.ohsd.uscourts.gov	Columbus	OH	43215	614-719-3000	719-3005
US District Court Oklahoma Eastern PO Box 607 *Web:* www.oked.uscourts.gov	Muskogee	OK	74402	918-684-7920	684-7902
US District Court Oklahoma Northern 333 W 4th St *TF:* 866-213-1957 ■ *Web:* www.oknd.uscourts.gov	Tulsa	OK	74103	918-699-4700	
US District Court Oklahoma Western 200 NW 4th St Rm 1210 *Web:* www.okwd.uscourts.gov	Oklahoma City	OK	73102	405-609-5000	609-5099
US District Court Oregon 1000 SW 3rd Ave Suite 740 *Web:* www.ord.uscourts.gov	Portland	OR	97204	503-326-8008	
US District Court Pennsylvania Eastern 601 Market St *Web:* www.paed.uscourts.gov	Philadelphia	PA	19106	215-597-7704	597-6390
US District Court Pennsylvania Middle 235 N Washington Ave PO Box 1148 *Web:* www.pamd.uscourts.gov	Scranton	PA	18501	570-207-5600	207-5650
US District Court Pennsylvania Western 700 Grant St *Web:* www.pawd.uscourts.gov	Pittsburgh	PA	15219	412-208-7500	
US District Court Puerto Rico 150 Carlos Chardon Ave Rm 150 Federal Bldg *Web:* www.prd.uscourts.gov	San Juan	PR	00918	787-772-3000	766-5693
US District Court Rhode Island 1 Exchange Terr *Web:* www.rid.uscourts.gov	Providence	RI	02903	401-752-7200	752-7247
US District Court South Carolina 901 Richland St *Web:* www.scd.uscourts.gov	Columbia	SC	29201	803-765-5816	765-5960
US District Court South Dakota 400 S Phillips Ave Rm 128 *Web:* www.sdd.uscourts.gov	Sioux Falls	SD	57104	605-330-6600	
US District Court Tennessee Eastern 800 Market St Suite 130 *Web:* www.tned.uscourts.gov	Knoxville	TN	37902	865-545-4228	545-4247
US District Court Tennessee Middle 801 Broadway Rm 800 *Web:* www.tnmd.uscourts.gov	Nashville	TN	37203	615-736-5498	736-7488
US District Court Tennessee Western 167 N Main St Rm 242 *Web:* www.tnwd.uscourts.gov	Memphis	TN	38103	901-495-1200	495-1250
US District Court Texas Eastern 211 W Ferguson St *Web:* www.txed.uscourts.gov	Tyler	TX	75702	903-590-1000	
US District Court Texas Northern 1100 Commerce St Rm 1452 *Web:* www.txnd.uscourts.gov	Dallas	TX	75242	214-753-2200	753-2266
US District Court Texas Southern PO Box 61010 *Web:* www.txs.uscourts.gov	Houston	TX	77208	713-250-5500	
US District Court Texas Western 655 E Durango Blvd Rm G65 *TF:* 800-659-2497 ■ *Web:* www.txwd.uscourts.gov	San Antonio	TX	78206	210-472-6550	472-6513
US District Court US Virgin Islands 3013 Estate Golden Rock *Web:* www.vid.uscourts.gov	Saint Croix	VI	00820	340-773-1130	773-1563
US District Court Utah 350 S Main St Rm 150 *Web:* www.utd.uscourts.gov	Salt Lake City	UT	84101	801-524-6100	526-1175
US District Court Vermont 11 Elmwood Ave *Web:* www.vtd.uscourts.gov	Burlington	VT	05401	802-951-6301	
US District Court Virginia Eastern 401 Courthouse Sq 2nd Fl *Web:* www.vaed.uscourts.gov	Alexandria	VA	22314	703-299-2100	
US District Court Virginia Western PO Box 1234 *Web:* www.vawd.uscourts.gov	Roanoke	VA	24006	540-857-5100	857-5110
US District Court Washington Eastern 920 W Riverside Ave Suite 840 *Web:* www.waed.uscourts.gov	Spokane	WA	99201	509-458-3400	458-3420
US District Court Washington Western 700 Stewart St *Web:* www.wawd.uscourts.gov	Seattle	WA	98101	206-370-8400	
US District Court West Virginia Northern 300 3rd St *Web:* www.wvnd.uscourts.gov	Elkins	WV	26241	304-636-1445	636-5746
US District Court West Virginia Southern 300 Virginia St E Rm 2400 *Web:* www.wvsd.uscourts.gov	Charleston	WV	25301	304-347-3000	
US District Court Wisconsin Eastern 517 E Wisconsin Ave *Web:* www.wied.uscourts.gov	Milwaukee	WI	53202	414-297-3372	
US District Court Wisconsin Western 120 N Henry St *Web:* www.wiwd.uscourts.gov	Madison	WI	53703	608-264-5156	264-5925
US District Court Wyoming 2120 Capitol Ave 2nd Fl *Web:* www.wyd.uscourts.gov	Cheyenne	WY	82001	307-433-2120	433-2152

344-4 US Supreme Court

Entry	City	State	ZIP	Phone	Fax
Roberts John G Jr US Supreme Court Bldg 1 1st St NE *Web:* www.supremecourtus.gov	Washington	DC	20543	202-479-3000	
Alito Samuel A Jr US Supreme Court Bldg 1 1st St NE *Web:* www.supremecourtus.gov	Washington	DC	20543	202-479-3000	
Breyer Stephen G US Supreme Court Bldg 1 1st St NE *Web:* www.supremecourtus.gov	Washington	DC	20543	202-479-3000	
Ginsburg Ruth Bader US Supreme Court Bldg 1 1st St NE *Web:* www.supremecourtus.gov	Washington	DC	20543	202-479-3000	
Kennedy Anthony M US Supreme Court Bldg 1 1st St NE *Web:* www.supremecourtus.gov	Washington	DC	20543	202-479-3000	
Scalia Antonin US Supreme Court Bldg 1 1st St NE *Web:* www.supremecourtus.gov	Washington	DC	20543	202-479-3000	
Souter David H US Supreme Court Bldg 1 1st St NE *Web:* www.supremecourtus.gov	Washington	DC	20543	202-479-3000	
Stevens John Paul US Supreme Court Bldg 1 1st St NE *Web:* www.supremecourtus.gov	Washington	DC	20543	202-479-3000	
Thomas Clarence US Supreme Court Bldg 1 1st St NE *Web:* www.supremecourtus.gov	Washington	DC	20543	202-479-3000	

345 GOVERNMENT - US - LEGISLATIVE BRANCH

SEE ALSO Legislation Hotlines p. 1890

Entry	City	State	ZIP	Phone	Fax
Congressional Budget Office Ford House Office Bldg 4th Fl *Web:* www.cbo.gov	Washington	DC	20515	202-226-2602	
Government Accountability Office (GAO) 441 G St NW *Web:* www.gao.gov	Washington	DC	20548	202-512-4800	
Atlanta Office 2635 Century Pkwy Suite 700 *Web:* www.gao.gov	Atlanta	GA	30345	404-679-1900	679-1819
Boston Office 10 Causeway St Rm 575 *Web:* www.gao.gov	Boston	MA	02222	617-788-0500	788-0505
Chicago Office 200 W Adams St Suite 700 *Web:* www.gao.gov	Chicago	IL	60606	312-220-7600	220-7726
Dallas Office 1999 Bryan St Suite 2200 *Web:* www.gao.gov	Dallas	TX	75201	214-777-5600	777-5758
Dayton Office 2196 D St Area B Bldg 39 *Web:* www.gao.gov	Wright-Patterson AFB	OH	45433	937-258-7900	258-7118
Denver Office 1244 Speer Blvd Suite 800 *Web:* www.gao.gov	Denver	CO	80204	303-572-7306	572-7433
Huntsville Office 6767 Old Madison Pike Bldg 5 Suite 520 *Web:* www.gao.gov	Huntsville	AL	35806	256-922-7500	971-9240
Los Angeles Office 350 S Figueroa St Suite 1010 *Web:* www.gao.gov	Los Angeles	CA	90071	213-830-1000	830-1180
Norfolk Office 5029 Corporate Woods Dr Suite 300 *Web:* www.gao.gov	Virginia Beach	VA	23462	757-552-8100	552-8197
San Francisco Office 301 Howard St Suite 1200 *Web:* www.gao.gov	San Francisco	CA	94105	415-904-2000	904-2111
Seattle Office 701 5th Ave Suite 2700 *Web:* www.gao.gov	Seattle	WA	98104	206-287-4800	287-4872
Legislative Information (LEGIS)	Washington	DC	20215	202-225-1772	
Library of Congress 101 Independence Ave SE *Web:* www.loc.gov	Washington	DC	20540	202-707-5000	

				Phone	Fax
American Folklife Center 101 Independence Ave SE	Washington	DC	20540	202-707-5510	707-2076
Web: www.loc.gov/folklife					
Congressional Research Service 101 Independence Ave SE	Washington	DC	20540	202-707-5700	707-6745
Web: www.loc.gov/crsinfo					
Law Library of Congress 101 Independence Ave SE	Washington	DC	20540	202-707-5079	707-1820
Web: www.loc.gov/rr/law					
National Library Service for the Blind & Physically Handicapped 1291 Taylor St NW	Washington	DC	20011	202-707-5100	707-0712
TF: 888-657-7323 ■ *Web:* www.loc.gov/nls					
Online Catalog Library of Congress 101 Independence Ave SE	Washington	DC	20540	202-707-5000	707-5844
Web: catalog.loc.gov					
THOMAS: Legislative Information on the Internet 101 Independence Ave SE	Washington	DC	20540	202-707-5000	707-5844
Web: thomas.loc.gov					
US Copyright Office 101 Independence Ave SE	Washington	DC	20559	202-707-3000	
Web: www.copyright.gov					
US Government Printing Office (GPO) 732 N Capitol St NW Suite 700	Washington	DC	20401	202-512-1800	512-2104
TF: 866-512-1800 ■ *Web:* www.gpoaccess.gov					
Federal Register Online 800 N Capitol St NW	Washington	DC	20001	202-741-6000	741-6012
Web: www.gpoaccess.gov/fr					
Online Bookstore 732 N Capitol St NW	Washington	DC	20401	202-512-1800	512-2104
Web: bookstore.gpo.gov					
US House of Representatives	Washington	DC	20515	202-225-3121	
Web: www.house.gov					
US Senate	Washington	DC	20510	202-224-3121	
Web: www.senate.gov					

345-1 US Congressional Committees

				Phone	Fax
US Congress					
Joint Committee on Printing 305 Russell Senate Office Bldg	Washington	DC	20510	202-224-3205	224-1912
Web: www.house.gov/jcp					
Joint Committee on Taxation 1015 Longworth Bldg	Washington	DC	20515	202-225-3621	225-0832
Web: www.house.gov/jct					
Joint Economic Committee G-01 Dirksen Bldg	Washington	DC	20510	202-224-5171	224-0240
Web: jec.senate.gov					
US House of Representatives					
Agriculture Committee 1301 Longworth Bldg	Washington	DC	20515	202-225-2171	225-0917
Web: www.agriculture.house.gov					
Appropriations Committee H-218 Capitol Bldg	Washington	DC	20515	202-225-2771	
Web: appropriations.house.gov					
Armed Services Committee 2120 Rayburn Bldg	Washington	DC	20515	202-225-4151	225-9077
Web: www.house.gov/hasc					
Budget Committee Cannon House Office Bldg Suite B-71	Washington	DC	20515	202-226-7270	226-7174
Web: www.budget.house.gov					
Committee on Education & Labor 2181 Rayburn Bldg	Washington	DC	20515	202-225-4527	
Web: edlabor.house.gov					
Committee on Natural Resources 1324 Longworth Bldg	Washington	DC	20515	202-225-6065	225-1031
Web: resourcescommittee.house.gov					
Energy & Commerce Committee 2125 Rayburn Bldg	Washington	DC	20515	202-225-2927	225-2525
Web: energycommerce.house.gov					
Financial Services Committee 2129 Rayburn Bldg	Washington	DC	20515	202-225-4247	225-6952
Web: financialservices.house.gov					
Government Reform Committee 2157 Rayburn Bldg	Washington	DC	20515	202-225-5074	225-3974
Web: reform.house.gov					
Homeland Security Committee 117 Ford House Office Bldg	Washington	DC	20515	202-226-8417	226-3399
Web: www.hsc.house.gov					
House Administration Committee 1309 Longworth Bldg	Washington	DC	20515	202-225-2061	226-2774
Web: www.house.gov/cha					
House Committee on Foreign Affairs 2170 Rayburn Bldg	Washington	DC	20515	202-225-5021	225-2035
Web: www.internationalrelations.house.gov					
Judiciary Committee 2138 Rayburn Bldg	Washington	DC	20515	202-225-3951	225-7680
Web: judiciary.house.gov					
Permanent Select Committee on Intelligence H-405 Capitol Bldg	Washington	DC	20515	202-225-4121	226-5068
TF: 877-858-9040 ■ *Web:* intelligence.house.gov					
Rules Committee H-312 Capitol Bldg	Washington	DC	20515	202-225-9191	225-1061
Web: www.rules.house.gov					
Science Committee 2320 Rayburn Bldg	Washington	DC	20515	202-225-6371	225-0113
Web: www.house.gov/science					
Small Business Committee 2361 Rayburn Bldg	Washington	DC	20515	202-225-5821	225-3587
Web: wwwc.house.gov/smbiz					
Standards of Official Conduct Committee HT-2 Capitol Bldg	Washington	DC	20515	202-225-7103	225-7392
Web: www.house.gov/ethics					
Transportation & Infrastructure Committee 2165 Rayburn Bldg	Washington	DC	20515	202-225-9446	225-6782
Web: www.house.gov/transportation					
Veterans Affairs Committee 335 Cannon Bldg	Washington	DC	20515	202-225-3527	
Web: www.house.gov/va					
Ways & Means Committee 1102 Longworth Bldg	Washington	DC	20515	202-225-3625	225-2610
Web: waysandmeans.house.gov					
US Senate					
Agriculture Nutrition & Forestry Committee SR-328A Russell Bldg	Washington	DC	20510	202-224-2035	228-4576
Web: agriculture.senate.gov					
Appropriations Committee S-131 Capitol Bldg	Washington	DC	20510	202-224-7363	224-2100
Web: appropriations.senate.gov					
Armed Services Committee 228 Russell Bldg	Washington	DC	20510	202-224-3871	228-0036
Web: armed-services.senate.gov					
Banking Housing & Urban Affairs Committee 534 Dirksen Bldg	Washington	DC	20510	202-224-7391	224-5137
Web: banking.senate.gov					
Budget Committee 624 Dirksen Bldg	Washington	DC	20510	202-224-0642	224-4835
Web: www.senate.gov/~budget					
Commerce Science & Transportation Committee 508 Dirksen Bldg	Washington	DC	20510	202-224-5115	
Web: commerce.senate.gov					
Energy & Natural Resources Committee 304 Dirksen Bldg	Washington	DC	20510	202-224-4971	224-6163
Web: energy.senate.gov					
Environment & Public Works Committee 410 Dirksen Bldg	Washington	DC	20510	202-224-6176	224-1273
Web: epw.senate.gov					
Finance Committee 219 Dirksen Bldg	Washington	DC	20510	202-224-4515	228-0554
Web: finance.senate.gov					
Foreign Relations Committee 450 Dirksen Bldg	Washington	DC	20510	202-224-4651	228-3612
Web: foreign.senate.gov					
Health Education Labor & Pensions Committee 428 Dirksen Bldg	Washington	DC	20510	202-224-5375	228-4000
Web: help.senate.gov					
Homeland Security & Governmental Affairs Committee 340 Dirksen Bldg	Washington	DC	20510	202-224-4751	224-9603
Web: www.senate.gov/~gov_affairs					
Indian Affairs Committee 838 Hart Bldg	Washington	DC	20510	202-224-2251	
Web: indian.senate.gov					
Judiciary Committee SD-224 Dirksen Bldg	Washington	DC	20510	202-224-5225	224-9102
Web: judiciary.senate.gov					
Rules & Administration Committee 305 Russell Bldg	Washington	DC	20510	202-224-6352	228-2401
Web: rules.senate.gov					
Select Committee on Ethics 220 Hart Bldg	Washington	DC	20510	202-224-2981	224-7416
Web: ethics.senate.gov					
Select Committee on Intelligence 211 Hart Bldg	Washington	DC	20510	202-224-1700	224-1772
Web: intelligence.senate.gov					
Small Business & Entrepreneurship Committee 428A Russell Bldg	Washington	DC	20510	202-224-5175	224-5619
Web: sbc.senate.gov					
Special Committee on Aging SD-G31 Dirksen Bldg	Washington	DC	20510	202-224-5364	224-9926
Web: aging.senate.gov					
Veterans Affairs Committee 412 Russell Bldg	Washington	DC	20510	202-224-9126	224-9575
Web: veterans.senate.gov					

345-2 US Senators, Representatives, Delegates

The circled letter S denotes that a listing is for a senator.

Alabama

				Phone	Fax
Aderholt Robert (Rep R-AL) 1433 Longworth Bldg	Washington	DC	20515	202-225-4876	225-5587
Web: aderholt.house.gov					
Bachus Spencer (Rep R-AL) 2246 Rayburn House Bldg	Washington	DC	20515	202-225-4921	225-2082
Web: bachus.house.gov					
Bonner Jo (Rep R-AL) 422 Cannon House Office Bldg	Washington	DC	20515	202-225-4931	225-0562
TF: 800-288-8721 ■ *Web:* bonner.house.gov					
Cramer Bud (Rep D-AL) 2184 Rayburn Bldg	Washington	DC	20515	202-225-4801	225-4392
Web: cramer.house.gov					
Davis Artur (Rep D-AL) 208 Cannon Bldg	Washington	DC	20515	202-225-2665	226-9567
Web: www.house.gov/arturdavis					
Everett Terry (Rep R-AL) 2312 Rayburn Bldg	Washington	DC	20515	202-225-2901	225-8913
Web: wwwc.house.gov/everett					
Rogers Mike D (Rep R-AL) 324 Cannon Bldg	Washington	DC	20515	202-225-3261	226-8485
Web: www.house.gov/mike-rogers					
Ⓢ**Sessions Jeff (Sen R-AL)** 335 Russell Bldg	Washington	DC	20510	202-224-4124	224-3149
Web: sessions.senate.gov					
Ⓢ**Shelby Richard C (Sen R-AL)** 110 Hart Bldg	Washington	DC	20510	202-224-5744	224-3416
Web: shelby.senate.gov					

Alaska

				Phone	Fax
Ⓢ**Murkowski Lisa (Sen R-AK)** 709 Hart Bldg	Washington	DC	20510	202-224-6665	224-5301
Web: murkowski.senate.gov					
Ⓢ**Stevens Ted (Sen R-AK)** 522 Hart Bldg	Washington	DC	20510	202-224-3004	224-2354
Web: stevens.senate.gov					
Young Don (Rep R-AK) 2111 Rayburn Bldg	Washington	DC	20515	202-225-5765	225-0425
Web: donyoung.house.gov					

American Samoa

				Phone	Fax
Faleomavaega Eni FH (Del D-AS) 2422 Rayburn Bldg	Washington	DC	20515	202-225-8577	225-8757
Web: www.house.gov/faleomavaega					

Arizona

				Phone	Fax
Flake Jeff (Rep R-AZ) 240 Cannon Bldg	Washington	DC	20515	202-225-2635	226-4386
Web: www.house.gov/flake					
Franks Trent (Rep R-AZ) 1237 Longworth Bldg	Washington	DC	20525	202-225-4576	225-6328
Web: www.house.gov/franks					
Giffords Gabrielle (Rep D-AZ) 502 Cannon Bldg	Washington	DC	20515	202-225-2542	225-0378
Web: giffords.house.gov					
Grijalva Raul M (Rep D-AZ) 1440 Longworth Bldg	Washington	DC	20515	202-225-2435	225-1541
Web: www.house.gov/grijalva					
Ⓢ**Kyl Jon (Sen R-AZ)** 730 Hart Bldg	Washington	DC	20510	202-224-4521	224-2207
Web: kyl.senate.gov					
Ⓢ**McCain John (Sen R-AZ)** 241 Russell Bldg	Washington	DC	20510	202-224-2235	228-2862
Web: mccain.senate.gov					
Mitchell Harry E (Rep D-AZ) 2434 Rayburn Bldg	Washington	DC	20515	202-225-2190	225-3263
Web: mitchell.house.gov					
Pastor Ed (Rep D-AZ) 2465 Rayburn Bldg	Washington	DC	20515	202-225-4065	225-1655
Web: www.house.gov/pastor					
Renzi Rick (Rep R-AZ) 418 Cannon Bldg	Washington	DC	20515	202-225-2315	226-9739
TF: 866-537-2800 ■ *Web:* www.house.gov/renzi					
Shadegg John (Rep R-AZ) 306 Cannon Bldg	Washington	DC	20515	202-225-3361	225-3462
Web: johnshadegg.house.gov					

Arkansas

				Phone	Fax
Berry Marion (Rep D-AR) 2305 Rayburn Bldg	Washington	DC	20515	202-225-4076	225-5602
Web: www.house.gov/berry					
Boozman John (Rep R-AR) 1519 Longworth Bldg	Washington	DC	20515	202-225-4301	225-5713
Web: www.boozman.house.gov					
Ⓢ**Lincoln Blanche L (Sen D-AR)** 355 Dirksen Bldg	Washington	DC	20510	202-224-4843	228-1371
Web: lincoln.senate.gov					
Ⓢ**Pryor Mark (Sen D-AR)** 257 Dirksen Bldg	Washington	DC	20510	202-224-2353	228-0908
Web: pryor.senate.gov					
Ross Mike (Rep D-AR) 314 Cannon Bldg	Washington	DC	20515	202-225-3772	225-1314
Web: www.house.gov/ross					
Snyder Vic (Rep D-AR) 1330 Longworth Bldg	Washington	DC	20515	202-225-2506	225-5903
Web: www.house.gov/snyder					

California

				Phone	Fax
Baca Joe (Rep D-CA) 1527 Longworth Bldg	Washington	DC	20515	202-225-6161	225-8671
Web: www.house.gov/baca					

Name / Address	City	State	Zip	Phone	Fax
Becerra Xavier (Rep D-CA) 1119 Longworth Bldg *Web:* becerra.house.gov	Washington	DC	20515	202-225-6235	225-2202
Berman Howard L (Rep D-CA) 2221 Rayburn Bldg *Web:* www.house.gov/berman	Washington	DC	20515	202-225-4695	225-3196
Bilbray Brian (Rep R-CA) 227 Cannon Bldg *Web:* www.house.gov/bilbray	Washington	DC	20515	202-225-0508	225-2558
Bono Mary (Rep R-CA) 104 Cannon Bldg *Web:* www.house.gov/bono	Washington	DC	20515	202-225-5330	225-2961
Ⓢ**Boxer Barbara (Sen D-CA)** 112 Hart Bldg *Web:* boxer.senate.gov	Washington	DC	20510	202-224-3553	224-0454
Calvert Ken (Rep R-CA) 2201 Rayburn Bldg *Web:* calvert.house.gov	Washington	DC	20515	202-225-1986	225-2004
Campbell John (Rep R-CA) 1728 Longworth Bldg *Web:* campbell.house.gov	Washington	DC	20515	202-225-5611	225-9177
Capps Lois (Rep D-CA) 1110 Longworth Bldg *Web:* www.house.gov/capps	Washington	DC	20515	202-225-3601	225-5632
Cardoza Dennis (Rep D-CA) 435 Cannon Bldg *Web:* www.house.gov/cardoza	Washington	DC	20515	202-225-6131	225-0819
Costa Jim (Rep D-CA) 1314 Longworth House Office Bldg *Web:* www.house.gov/costa	Washington	DC	20515	202-225-3341	225-9308
Davis Susan A (Rep D-CA) 1526 Longworth Bldg *Web:* www.house.gov/susandavis	Washington	DC	20515	202-225-2040	225-2948
Doolittle John T (Rep R-CA) 2410 Rayburn Bldg *Web:* www.house.gov/doolittle	Washington	DC	20515	202-225-2511	225-5444
Dreier David (Rep R-CA) 233 Cannon Bldg *Web:* www.dreier.house.gov	Washington	DC	20515	202-225-2305	225-7018
Eshoo Anna G (Rep D-CA) 205 Cannon Bldg *Web:* eshoo.house.gov	Washington	DC	20515	202-225-8104	225-8890
Farr Sam (Rep D-CA) 1221 Longworth Bldg *Web:* www.farr.house.gov	Washington	DC	20515	202-225-2861	225-6791
Ⓢ**Feinstein Dianne (Sen D-CA)** 331 Hart Bldg *Web:* feinstein.senate.gov	Washington	DC	20510	202-224-3841	228-3954
Filner Bob (Rep D-CA) 2428 Rayburn Bldg *Web:* www.house.gov/filner	Washington	DC	20515	202-225-8045	225-9073
Gallegly Elton (Rep R-CA) 2309 Rayburn Bldg *Web:* www.house.gov/gallegly	Washington	DC	20515	202-225-5811	225-1100
Harman Jane (Rep D-CA) 2400 Rayburn Bldg *Web:* www.house.gov/harman	Washington	DC	20515	202-225-8220	226-7290
Herger Wally (Rep R-CA) 2268 Rayburn Bldg *Web:* www.house.gov/herger	Washington	DC	20515	202-225-3076	226-0852
Honda Michael M (Rep D-CA) 1713 Longworth Bldg *Web:* www.honda.house.gov	Washington	DC	20515	202-225-2631	225-2699
Hunter Duncan (Rep R-CA) 2265 Rayburn Bldg *Web:* www.house.gov/hunter	Washington	DC	20515	202-225-5672	225-0235
Issa Darrell E (Rep R-CA) 211 Cannon Bldg *Web:* www.issa.house.gov	Washington	DC	20515	202-225-3906	225-3303
Lee Barbara (Rep D-CA) 2444 Rayburn Bldg *Web:* www.house.gov/lee	Washington	DC	20515	202-225-2661	225-9817
Lewis Jerry (Rep R-CA) 2112 Rayburn Bldg *Web:* www.house.gov/jerrylewis	Washington	DC	20515	202-225-5861	225-6498
Lofgren Zoe (Rep D-CA) 102 Cannon Bldg *Web:* www.house.gov/lofgren	Washington	DC	20515	202-225-3072	225-3336
Lungren Daniel E (Rep R-CA) 2448 Rayburn Bldg *Web:* lungren.house.gov	Washington	DC	20515	202-225-5716	226-1298
Matsui Doris O (Rep D-CA) 222 Cannon Bldg *Web:* matsui.house.gov	Washington	DC	20515	202-225-7163	225-0566
McCarthy Kevin (Rep R-CA) 1523 Longworth Bldg *Web:* kevinmccarthy.house.gov	Washington	DC	20515	202-225-2915	225-2908
McKeon Buck (Rep D-CA) 2351 Rayburn Bldg *Web:* mckeon.house.gov	Washington	DC	20515	202-225-1956	226-0683
McNerney Jerry (Rep R-CA) 312 Cannon Bldg *Web:* mcnerney.house.gov	Washington	DC	20515	202-225-1947	225-4060
Miller Gary G (Rep R-CA) 2438 Rayburn Bldg *Web:* www.house.gov/garymiller	Washington	DC	20515	202-225-3201	226-6962
Miller George (Rep D-CA) 2205 Rayburn Bldg *Web:* georgemiller.house.gov	Washington	DC	20515	202-225-2095	225-5609
Napolitano Grace Flores (Rep D-CA) 1610 Longworth Bldg *Web:* www.napolitano.house.gov	Washington	DC	20515	202-225-5256	225-0027
Nunes Devin (Rep R-CA) 1013 Longworth Bldg *Web:* www.nunes.house.gov	Washington	DC	20515	202-225-2523	225-3404
Pelosi Nancy (Rep D-CA) 235 Cannon Bldg *Web:* www.house.gov/pelosi	Washington	DC	20515	202-225-4965	225-4188
Radanovich George (Rep R-CA) 2367 Rayburn Bldg *Web:* www.radanovich.house.gov	Washington	DC	20515	202-225-4540	225-3402
Rohrabacher Dana (Rep R-CA) 2300 Rayburn Bldg *Web:* rohrabacher.house.gov	Washington	DC	20515	202-225-2415	225-0145
Roybal-Allard Lucille (Rep D-CA) 2330 Rayburn Bldg *Web:* www.house.gov/roybal-allard	Washington	DC	20515	202-225-1766	226-0350
Royce Ed (Rep R-CA) 2185 Rayburn Bldg *Web:* www.royce.house.gov	Washington	DC	20515	202-225-4111	226-0335
Sanchez Linda T (Rep D-CA) 1222 Longworth Bldg *Web:* www.house.gov/lindasanchez	Washington	DC	20515	202-225-6676	226-1012
Sanchez Loretta (Rep D-CA) 1230 Longworth Bldg *Web:* www.lorettasanchez.house.gov	Washington	DC	20515	202-225-2965	225-5859
Schiff Adam B (Rep D-CA) 326 Cannon Bldg *Web:* schiff.house.gov	Washington	DC	20515	202-225-4176	225-5828
Sherman Brad (Rep D-CA) 2242 Rayburn Bldg *Web:* www.house.gov/sherman	Washington	DC	20515	202-225-5911	225-5879
Solis Hilda L (Rep D-CA) 1414 Longworth Bldg *Web:* solis.house.gov	Washington	DC	20515	202-225-5464	225-5467
Speier Jackie (Rep D-CA) 2413 Rayburn Bldg *Web:* speier.house.gov	Washington	DC	20515	202-225-3531	226-4183
Stark Pete (Rep D-CA) 239 Cannon Bldg *Web:* www.house.gov/stark	Washington	DC	20515	202-225-5065	226-3805
Tauscher Ellen (Rep D-CA) 2459 Rayburn Bldg *Web:* www.house.gov/tauscher	Washington	DC	20515	202-225-1880	225-5914
Thompson Mike (Rep D-CA) 231 Cannon Bldg *Web:* mikethompson.house.gov	Washington	DC	20515	202-225-3311	225-4335
Waters Maxine (Rep D-CA) 2344 Rayburn Bldg *Web:* www.house.gov/waters	Washington	DC	20515	202-225-2201	225-7854
Watson Diane E (Rep D-CA) 125 Cannon Bldg *Web:* www.house.gov/watson	Washington	DC	20515	202-225-7084	225-2422
Waxman Henry A (Rep D-CA) 2204 Rayburn Bldg *Web:* www.house.gov/waxman	Washington	DC	20515	202-225-3976	225-4099
Woolsey Lynn C (Rep D-CA) 2263 Rayburn Bldg *Web:* woolsey.house.gov	Washington	DC	20515	202-225-5161	225-5163

Colorado

Name / Address	City	State	Zip	Phone	Fax
Ⓢ**Allard Wayne (Sen R-CO)** 521 Dirksen Bldg *Web:* allard.senate.gov	Washington	DC	20510	202-224-5941	224-6471
DeGette Diana (Rep D-CO) 2421 Rayburn Bldg *Web:* www.house.gov/degette	Washington	DC	20515	202-225-4431	225-5657
Lamborn Doug (Rep R-CO) 437 Cannon Bldg *Web:* lamborn.house.gov	Washington	DC	20515	202-225-4422	226-2638
Musgrave Marilyn N (Rep R-CO) 1507 Longworth Bldg *Web:* musgrave.house.gov	Washington	DC	20515	202-225-4676	225-5870
Perlmutter Ed (Rep D-CO) 415 Cannon Bldg *Web:* perlmutter.house.gov	Washington	DC	20515	202-225-2645	225-5278
Salazar John T (Rep D-CO) 1531 Longworth Bldg *Web:* www.house.gov/salazar	Washington	DC	20515	202-225-4761	226-9669
Ⓢ**Salazar Ken (Sen D-CO)** 702 Hart Bldg *Web:* salazar.senate.gov	Washington	DC	20510	202-224-5852	228-5036
Tancredo Tom (Rep R-CO) 1131 Longworth Bldg *Web:* tancredo.house.gov	Washington	DC	20515	202-225-7882	226-4623
Udall Mark (Rep D-CO) 100 Cannon Bldg *Web:* markudall.house.gov	Washington	DC	20515	202-225-2161	226-7840

Connecticut

Name / Address	City	State	Zip	Phone	Fax
Courtney Joe (Rep D-CT) 215 Cannon Bldg *Web:* courtney.house.gov	Washington	DC	20515	202-225-2076	225-4977
DeLauro Rosa (Rep D-CT) 2262 Rayburn Bldg *Web:* www.house.gov/delauro	Washington	DC	20515	202-225-3661	225-4890
Ⓢ**Dodd Christopher J (Sen D-CT)** 448 Russell Bldg *Web:* dodd.senate.gov	Washington	DC	20510	202-224-2823	224-1083
Larson John B (Rep D-CT) 1005 Longworth Bldg *Web:* www.house.gov/larson	Washington	DC	20515	202-225-2265	225-1031
Ⓢ**Lieberman Joseph I (Sen D-CT)** 706 Hart Bldg *Web:* lieberman.senate.gov	Washington	DC	20510	202-224-4041	224-9750
Murphy Chris (Rep D-CT) 501 Cannon Bldg *Web:* chrismurphy.house.gov	Washington	DC	20515	202-225-4476	225-5933
Shays Christopher (Rep R-CT) 1126 Longworth Bldg *Web:* www.house.gov/shays	Washington	DC	20515	202-225-5541	225-9629

Delaware

Name / Address	City	State	Zip	Phone	Fax
Ⓢ**Biden Joseph R Jr (Sen D-DE)** 201 Russell Bldg *Web:* biden.senate.gov	Washington	DC	20510	202-224-5042	224-0139
Ⓢ**Carper Thomas (Sen D-DE)** 513 Hart Bldg *Web:* carper.senate.gov	Washington	DC	20510	202-224-2441	228-2190
Castle Michael N (Rep R-DE) 1233 Longworth Bldg *Web:* www.castle.house.gov	Washington	DC	20515	202-225-4165	225-2291

District of Columbia

Name / Address	City	State	Zip	Phone	Fax
Norton Eleanor Holmes (Del D-DC) 2136 Rayburn Bldg *Web:* www.norton.house.gov	Washington	DC	20515	202-225-8050	225-3002

Florida

Name / Address	City	State	Zip	Phone	Fax
Bilirakis Gus Michael (Rep R-FL) 1630 Longworth Bldg *Web:* www.house.gov/bilirakis	Washington	DC	20515	202-225-5755	225-4085
Boyd Allen (Rep D-FL) 1227 Longworth Bldg *Web:* www.house.gov/boyd	Washington	DC	20515	202-225-5235	225-5615
Brown Corrine (Rep D-FL) 2336 Rayburn Bldg *Web:* www.house.gov/corrinebrown	Washington	DC	20515	202-225-0123	225-2256
Brown-Waite Ginny (Rep D-FL) 414 Cannon Bldg *Web:* www.house.gov/brown-waite	Washington	DC	20515	202-225-1002	226-6559
Buchanan Vern (Rep R-FL) 1516 Longworth Bldg *Web:* buchanan.house.gov	Washington	DC	20515	202-225-5015	226-0828
Castor Kathy (Rep D-FL) 317 Cannon Bldg *Web:* castor.house.gov	Washington	DC	20515	202-225-3376	225-5652
Crenshaw Ander (Rep R-FL) 127 Cannon Bldg *Web:* crenshaw.house.gov	Washington	DC	20515	202-225-2501	225-2504
Diaz-Balart Lincoln (Rep R-FL) 2244 Rayburn Bldg *Web:* diaz-balart.house.gov	Washington	DC	20515	202-225-4211	225-8576
Diaz-Balart Mario (Rep R-FL) 328 Cannon Bldg *Web:* www.house.gov/mariodiaz-balart	Washington	DC	20515	202-225-2778	226-0346
Feeney Tom C (Rep R-FL) 323 Cannon Bldg *Web:* www.house.gov/feeney	Washington	DC	20515	202-225-2706	226-6299
Hastings Alcee L (Rep D-FL) 2353 Rayburn Bldg *Web:* alceehastings.house.gov	Washington	DC	20515	202-225-1313	225-1171
Keller Ric (Rep R-FL) 419 Cannon Bldg *Web:* keller.house.gov	Washington	DC	20515	202-225-2176	225-0999
Klein Ron (Rep D-FL) 313 Cannon Bldg *Web:* klein.house.gov	Washington	DC	20515	202-225-3026	225-8398
Mack Connie IV (Rep R-FL) 115 Cannon Bldg *Web:* mack.house.gov	Washington	DC	20515	202-225-2536	226-0439
Mahoney Tim (Rep D-FL) 1541 Longworth Bldg *Web:* www.mahoney.house.gov	Washington	DC	20515	202-225-5792	225-3132
Ⓢ**Martinez Mel R (Sen R-FL)** 356 Russell Bldg *Web:* martinez.senate.gov	Washington	DC	20510	202-224-3041	228-5172
Meek Kendrick (Rep D-FL) 1039 Longworth Bldg *Web:* kendrickmeek.house.gov	Washington	DC	20515	202-225-4506	226-0777
Mica John L (Rep R-FL) 2313 Rayburn Bldg *Web:* www.house.gov/mica	Washington	DC	20515	202-225-4035	226-0821
Miller Jeff (Rep R-FL) 1535 Longworth Bldg *Web:* jeffmiller.house.gov	Washington	DC	20515	202-225-4136	225-3414
Ⓢ**Nelson Bill (Sen D-FL)** 716 Hart Bldg *Web:* billnelson.senate.gov	Washington	DC	20510	202-224-5274	228-2183
Putnam Adam (Rep R-FL) 1725 Longworth Bldg *TF:* 866-534-3530 ■ *Web:* www.house.gov/putnam	Washington	DC	20515	202-225-1252	226-0585
Ros-Lehtinen Ileana (Rep R-FL) 2160 Rayburn Bldg *Web:* www.house.gov/ros-lehtinen	Washington	DC	20515	202-225-3931	225-5620
Stearns Cliff (Rep R-FL) 2370 Rayburn Bldg *Web:* www.house.gov/stearns	Washington	DC	20515	202-225-5744	225-3973
Wasserman Schultz Debbie (Rep D-FL) 118 Cannon Bldg *Web:* www.house.gov/schultz	Washington	DC	20515	202-225-7931	226-2052
Weldon Dave (Rep R-FL) 2347 Rayburn Bldg *Web:* weldon.house.gov	Washington	DC	20515	202-225-3671	225-3516
Wexler Robert (Rep D-FL) 2241 Rayburn Bldg *Web:* wexler.house.gov	Washington	DC	20515	202-225-3001	225-5974
Young CW Bill (Rep R-FL) 2407 Rayburn Bldg *Web:* www.house.gov/young	Washington	DC	20515	202-225-5961	225-9764

Georgia

Name / Address	City	State	Zip	Phone	Fax
Barrow John (Rep D-GA) 213 Cannon Bldg *Web:* barrow.house.gov	Washington	DC	20515	202-225-2823	225-3377
Bishop Sanford D Jr (Rep D-GA) 2429 Rayburn Bldg *Web:* www.house.gov/bishop	Washington	DC	20515	202-225-3631	225-2203

US Senators, Representatives, Delegates (Cont'd)

Georgia (Cont'd)

				Phone	Fax
Ⓢ**Chambliss Saxby (Sen R-GA)** 416 Russell Bldg *Web:* chambliss.senate.gov	Washington	DC	20510	202-224-3521	224-0103
Deal Nathan (Rep R-GA) 2133 Rayburn Bldg *Web:* www.house.gov/deal	Washington	DC	20515	202-225-5211	225-8272
Gingrey Phil (Rep R-GA) 119 Cannon Bldg *Web:* gingrey.house.gov	Washington	DC	20515	202-225-2931	225-2944
Ⓢ**Isakson Johnny (Sen R-GA)** 120 Russell Bldg *Web:* isakson.senate.gov	Washington	DC	20510	202-224-3643	228-0724
Johnson Henry C (Rep D-GA) 1133 Longworth Bldg *Web:* hankjohnson.house.gov	Washington	DC	20515	202-225-1605	226-0691
Kingston Jack (Rep R-GA) 2368 Rayburn Bldg *Web:* www.house.gov/kingston	Washington	DC	20515	202-225-5831	226-2269
Lewis John (Rep D-GA) 343 Cannon Bldg *Web:* johnlewis.house.gov	Washington	DC	20515	202-225-3801	225-0351
Linder John (Rep R-GA) 1026 Longworth Bldg *Web:* linder.house.gov	Washington	DC	20515	202-225-4272	225-4696
Marshall James C (Rep D-GA) 504 Cannon Bldg *Web:* www.house.gov/marshall	Washington	DC	20515	202-225-6531	225-3013
Price Tom (Rep R-GA) 424 Cannon Bldg *Web:* tomprice.house.gov	Washington	DC	20515	202-225-4501	225-0802
Scott David (Rep D-GA) 417 Cannon Bldg *Web:* davidscott.house.gov	Washington	DC	20515	202-225-2939	225-4628
Westmoreland Lynn (Rep R-GA) 1213 Longworth Bldg *Web:* www.house.gov/westmoreland	Washington	DC	20515	202-225-5901	225-2515

Guam

				Phone	Fax
Bordallo Madeleine Z (Del D-GU) 427 Cannon Bldg *Web:* www.house.gov/bordallo	Washington	DC	20515	202-225-1188	226-0341

Hawaii

				Phone	Fax
Abercrombie Neil (Rep D-HI) 1502 Longworth House Office Bldg *Web:* www.house.gov/abercrombie	Washington	DC	20515	202-225-2726	225-4580
Ⓢ**Akaka Daniel K (Sen D-HI)** 141 Hart Bldg *Web:* akaka.senate.gov	Washington	DC	20510	202-224-6361	224-2126
Hirono Mazie K (Rep D-HI) 1229 Longworth Bldg *Web:* hirono.house.gov	Washington	DC	20515	202-225-4906	225-4987
Ⓢ**Inouye Daniel K (Sen D-HI)** 722 Hart Bldg *Web:* inouye.senate.gov	Washington	DC	20510	202-224-3934	224-6747

Idaho

				Phone	Fax
Ⓢ**Craig Larry E (Sen R-ID)** 520 Hart Bldg *Web:* craig.senate.gov	Washington	DC	20510	202-224-2752	228-1067
Ⓢ**Crapo Mike (Sen R-ID)** 239 Dirksen Bldg *Web:* crapo.senate.gov	Washington	DC	20510	202-224-6142	228-1375
Sali William (Rep R-ID) 508 Cannon Bldg *Web:* sali.house.gov	Washington	DC	20515	202-225-6611	225-3029
Simpson Mike (Rep R-ID) 1339 Longworth Bldg *Web:* www.house.gov/simpson	Washington	DC	20515	202-225-5531	225-8216

Illinois

				Phone	Fax
Bean Melissa L (Rep D-IL) 318 Cannon Bldg *Web:* www.house.gov/bean	Washington	DC	20515	202-225-3711	225-7830
Biggert Judy (Rep R-IL) 1034 Longworth Bldg *Web:* judybiggert.house.gov	Washington	DC	20515	202-225-3515	225-9420
Costello Jerry F (Rep D-IL) 2408 Rayburn Bldg *Web:* www.house.gov/costello	Washington	DC	20515	202-225-5661	225-0285
Davis Danny (Rep D-IL) 2159 Rayburn Bldg *Web:* www.house.gov/davis	Washington	DC	20515	202-225-5006	225-5641
Ⓢ**Durbin Richard J (Sen D-IL)** 309 Hart Bldg *Web:* durbin.senate.gov	Washington	DC	20510	202-224-2152	228-0400
Emanuel Rahm (Rep D-IL) 1319 Longworth Bldg *Web:* www.house.gov/emanuel	Washington	DC	20515	202-225-4061	225-5603
Foster Bill (Rep D-IL) 2304 Rayburn Bldg *Web:* www.foster.house.gov	Washington	DC	20515	202-225-2976	225-0697
Gutierrez Luis V (Rep D-IL) 2266 Rayburn Bldg *Web:* luisgutierrez.house.gov	Washington	DC	20515	202-225-8203	225-7810
Hare Phil (Rep D-IL) 1118 Longworth Bldg *Web:* hare.house.gov	Washington	DC	20515	202-225-5905	225-5396
Jackson Jesse Jr (Rep D-IL) 2419 Rayburn Bldg *Web:* www.house.gov/jackson	Washington	DC	20515	202-225-0773	225-0899
Johnson Timothy V (Rep R-IL) 1207 Longworth Bldg *Web:* www.house.gov/timjohnson	Washington	DC	20515	202-225-2371	226-0791
Kirk Mark Steven (Rep R-IL) 1030 Longworth Bldg *Web:* www.house.gov/kirk	Washington	DC	20515	202-225-4835	225-0837
LaHood Ray (Rep R-IL) 1424 Longworth Bldg *Web:* www.house.gov/lahood	Washington	DC	20515	202-225-6201	225-9249
Lipinski Daniel (Rep D-IL) 1717 Longworth Bldg *Web:* www.lipinski.house.gov	Washington	DC	20515	202-225-5701	225-1012
Manzullo Donald (Rep R-IL) 2228 Rayburn Bldg *Web:* manzullo.house.gov	Washington	DC	20515	202-225-5676	225-5284
Ⓢ**Obama Barack (Sen D-IL)** 713 Hart Bldg *Web:* obama.senate.gov	Washington	DC	20510	202-224-2854	228-4260
Roskam Peter J (Rep R-IL) 507 Cannon Bldg *Web:* roskam.house.gov	Washington	DC	20515	202-225-4561	225-1166
Rush Bobby L (Rep D-IL) 2416 Rayburn Bldg *Web:* www.house.gov/rush	Washington	DC	20515	202-225-4372	226-0333
Schakowsky Janice D (Rep D-IL) 1027 Longworth Bldg *Web:* www.house.gov/schakowsky	Washington	DC	20515	202-225-2111	226-6890
Shimkus John (Rep R-IL) 2452 Rayburn Bldg *Web:* www.house.gov/shimkus	Washington	DC	20515	202-225-5271	225-5880
Weller Jerry (Rep R-IL) 108 Cannon Bldg *Web:* weller.house.gov	Washington	DC	20515	202-225-3635	225-3521

Indiana

				Phone	Fax
Ⓢ**Bayh Evan (Sen D-IN)** 131 Russell Bldg *Web:* bayh.senate.gov	Washington	DC	20510	202-224-5623	224-1377
Burton Dan (Rep R-IN) 2308 Rayburn Bldg *Web:* www.house.gov/burton	Washington	DC	20515	202-225-2276	225-0016
Buyer Steve (Rep R-IN) 2230 Rayburn Bldg *Web:* stevebuyer.house.gov	Washington	DC	20515	202-225-5037	225-2267
Carson Andre (Rep D-IN) 2455 Rayburn Bldg *Web:* carson.house.gov	Washington	DC	20515	202-225-4011	225-5633
Donnelly Joe (Rep D-IN) 1218 Longworth Bldg *Web:* donnelly.house.gov	Washington	DC	20515	202-225-3915	225-6798
Ellsworth Brad (Rep D-IN) 513 Cannon Bldg *Web:* ellsworth.house.gov	Washington	DC	20515	202-225-4636	225-3284
Hill Baron (Rep D-IN) 223 Cannon Bldg *Web:* baronhill.house.gov	Washington	DC	20515	202-225-5315	226-6866
Ⓢ**Lugar Richard G (Sen R-IN)** 306 Hart Bldg *Web:* lugar.senate.gov	Washington	DC	20510	202-224-4814	228-0360
Pence Mike (Rep R-IN) 1317 Longworth Bldg *Web:* mikepence.house.gov	Washington	DC	20515	202-225-3021	225-3382
Souder Mark (Rep R-IN) 2231 Rayburn Bldg *Web:* souder.house.gov	Washington	DC	20515	202-225-4436	225-3479
Visclosky Peter J (Rep D-IN) 2256 Rayburn Bldg *Web:* www.house.gov/visclosky	Washington	DC	20515	202-225-2461	225-2493

Iowa

				Phone	Fax
Boswell Leonard L (Rep D-IA) 1427 Longworth Bldg *Web:* www.house.gov/boswell	Washington	DC	20515	202-225-3806	225-5608
Braley Bruce (Rep D-IA) 1408 Longworth Bldg *Web:* braley.house.gov	Washington	DC	20515	202-225-2911	225-6666
Ⓢ**Grassley Charles E (Sen R-IA)** 135 Hart Bldg *Web:* grassley.senate.gov	Washington	DC	20510	202-224-3744	224-6020
Ⓢ**Harkin Tom (Sen D-IA)** 731 Hart Bldg *Web:* harkin.senate.gov	Washington	DC	20510	202-224-3254	224-9369
King Steve (Rep R-IA) 1609 Longworth Bldg *Web:* www.house.gov/steveking	Washington	DC	20515	202-225-4426	225-3193
Latham Tom (Rep R-IA) 2447 Rayburn Bldg *Web:* www.tomlatham.house.gov	Washington	DC	20515	202-225-5476	225-3301
Loebsack David (Rep D-IA) 1513 Longworth Bldg *Web:* loebsack.house.gov	Washington	DC	20515	202-225-6576	226-0757

Kansas

				Phone	Fax
Boyda Nancy (Rep D-KS) 1711 Longworth Bldg *Web:* boyda.house.gov	Washington	DC	20515	202-225-6601	225-7986
Ⓢ**Brownback Sam (Sen R-KS)** 303 Hart Bldg *Web:* brownback.senate.gov	Washington	DC	20510	202-224-6521	228-1265
Moore Dennis (Rep D-KS) 1727 Longworth Bldg *Web:* www.moore.house.gov	Washington	DC	20515	202-225-2865	225-2807
Moran Jerry (Rep R-KS) 2202 Rayburn Bldg *Web:* www.jerrymoran.house.gov	Washington	DC	20515	202-225-2715	225-5124
Ⓢ**Roberts Pat (Sen R-KS)** 109 Hart Bldg *Web:* roberts.senate.gov	Washington	DC	20510	202-224-4774	224-3514
Tiahrt Todd (Rep R-KS) 2441 Rayburn Bldg *Web:* www.house.gov/tiahrt	Washington	DC	20515	202-225-6216	225-3489

Kentucky

				Phone	Fax
Ⓢ**Bunning Jim (Sen R-KY)** 316 Hart Bldg *Web:* bunning.senate.gov	Washington	DC	20510	202-224-4343	228-1373
Chandler Ben (Rep D-KY) 1504 Longworth Bldg *Web:* chandler.house.gov	Washington	DC	20515	202-225-4706	225-2122
Davis Geoff (Rep R-KY) 1108 Longworth Bldg *Web:* geoffdavis.house.gov	Washington	DC	20515	202-225-3465	225-0003
Lewis Ron (Rep R-KY) 2418 Rayburn Bldg *Web:* www.house.gov/ronlewis	Washington	DC	20515	202-225-3501	226-2019
Ⓢ**McConnell Mitch (Sen R-KY)** 361A Russell Bldg *Web:* mcconnell.senate.gov	Washington	DC	20510	202-224-2541	224-2499
Rogers Harold (Rep R-KY) 2406 Rayburn Bldg *Web:* www.house.gov/rogers	Washington	DC	20515	202-225-4601	225-0940
Whitfield Ed (Rep R-KY) 2411 Rayburn Bldg *Web:* www.house.gov/whitfield	Washington	DC	20515	202-225-3115	225-3547
Yarmuth John (Rep D-KY) 319 Cannon Bldg *Web:* yarmuth.house.gov	Washington	DC	20515	202-225-5401	225-5776

Louisiana

				Phone	Fax
Alexander Rodney M (Rep R-LA) 316 Cannon Bldg *Web:* www.house.gov/alexander	Washington	DC	20515	202-225-8490	225-5639
Boustany Charles W Jr (Rep R-LA) 1117 Longworth Bldg *Web:* boustany.house.gov	Washington	DC	20515	202-225-2031	225-5724
Cazayoux Donald (Rep R-LA) 341 Cannon Bldg *Web:* www.cazayoux.house.gov	Washington	DC	20515	202-225-3901	225-7313
Jefferson William J (Rep D-LA) 2113 Rayburn Bldg *Web:* www.house.gov/jefferson	Washington	DC	20515	202-225-6636	225-1988
Ⓢ**Landrieu Mary (Sen D-LA)** 724 Hart Bldg *Web:* landrieu.senate.gov	Washington	DC	20510	202-224-5824	224-9735
McCrery Jim (Rep R-LA) 242 Cannon Bldg *Web:* mccrery.house.gov	Washington	DC	20515	202-225-2777	225-8039
Melancon Charlie (Rep R-LA) 404 Cannon Bldg *Web:* www.melancon.house.gov	Washington	DC	20515	202-225-4031	226-3944
Scalise Steve (Rep R-LA) 1205 Longworth Bldg *Web:* www.scalise.house.gov	Washington	DC	20515	202-225-3015	225-0739
Ⓢ**Vitter David (Sen R-LA)** 516 Hart Bldg *Web:* vitter.senate.gov	Washington	DC	20510	202-224-4623	228-5061

Maine

				Phone	Fax
Allen Thomas H (Rep D-ME) 1127 Longworth Bldg *Web:* tomallen.house.gov	Washington	DC	20515	202-225-6116	225-5590
Ⓢ**Collins Susan (Sen R-ME)** 413 Dirksen Bldg *Web:* collins.senate.gov	Washington	DC	20510	202-224-2523	224-2693
Michaud Mike (Rep D-ME) 1724 Longworth Bldg *Web:* michaud.house.gov	Washington	DC	20515	202-225-6306	225-2943
Ⓢ**Snowe Olympia J (Sen R-ME)** 154 Russell Bldg *Web:* snowe.senate.gov	Washington	DC	20510	202-224-5344	224-1946

Maryland

Name	City	State	Zip	Phone	Fax
Bartlett Roscoe G (Rep R-MD) 2412 Rayburn House Office Bldg. *Web:* www.bartlett.house.gov	Washington	DC	20515	202-225-2721	225-2193
Ⓢ**Cardin Benjamin L (Sen D-MD)** 509 Hart Bldg *Web:* cardin.senate.gov	Washington	DC	20510	202-224-4524	224-1651
Cummings Elijah (Rep D-MD) 2235 Rayburn Bldg *Web:* www.house.gov/cummings	Washington	DC	20515	202-225-4741	225-3178
Gilchrest Wayne T (Rep R-MD) 2245 Rayburn Bldg *Web:* gilchrest.house.gov	Washington	DC	20515	202-225-5311	225-0254
Hoyer Steny H (Rep D-MD) 1705 Longworth Bldg *Web:* www.hoyer.house.gov	Washington	DC	20515	202-225-4131	225-4300
Ⓢ**Mikulski Barbara A (Sen D-MD)** 503 Hart Bldg *Web:* mikulski.senate.gov	Washington	DC	20510	202-224-4654	224-8858
Ruppersberger Dutch (Rep D-MD) 1730 Longworth Bldg *Web:* dutch.house.gov	Washington	DC	20515	202-225-3061	225-3094
Sarbanes John P (Rep D-MD) 426 Cannon Bldg *Web:* sarbanes.house.gov	Washington	DC	20515	202-225-4016	225-9219
Van Hollen Christopher Jr (Rep D-MD) 1707 Longworth Bldg *Web:* www.house.gov/vanhollen	Washington	DC	20515	202-225-5341	225-0375
Wynn Albert R (Rep D-MD) 2470 Rayburn Bldg *Web:* wynn.house.gov	Washington	DC	20515	202-225-8699	225-8714

Massachusetts

Name	City	State	Zip	Phone	Fax
Capuano Michael E (Rep D-MA) 1530 Longworth Bldg *Web:* www.house.gov/capuano	Washington	DC	20515	202-225-5111	225-9322
Delahunt William (Rep D-MA) 2454 Rayburn Bldg *Web:* www.house.gov/delahunt	Washington	DC	20515	202-225-3111	225-5658
Frank Barney (Rep D-MA) 2252 Rayburn Bldg *Web:* www.house.gov/frank	Washington	DC	20515	202-225-5931	225-0182
Ⓢ**Kennedy Edward M (Sen D-MA)** 317 Russell Bldg *Web:* kennedy.senate.gov	Washington	DC	20510	202-224-4543	224-2417
Ⓢ**Kerry John F (Sen D-MA)** 304 Russell Bldg *Web:* kerry.senate.gov	Washington	DC	20510	202-224-2742	224-8525
Lynch Stephen F (Rep D-MA) 221 Cannon Bldg *Web:* www.house.gov/lynch	Washington	DC	20515	202-225-8273	225-3984
Markey Edward J (Rep D-MA) 2108 Rayburn Bldg *Web:* www.house.gov/markey	Washington	DC	20515	202-225-2836	226-0092
McGovern James P (Rep D-MA) 438 Cannon Bldg *Web:* www.house.gov/mcgovern	Washington	DC	20515	202-225-6101	225-5759
Neal Richard E (Rep D-MA) 2208 Rayburn Bldg *Web:* www.house.gov/neal	Washington	DC	20515	202-225-5601	225-8112
Olver John W (Rep D-MA) 1111 Longworth Bldg *Web:* www.house.gov/olver	Washington	DC	20515	202-225-5335	226-1224
Tierney John F (Rep D-MA) 2238 Rayburn Bldg *Web:* www.house.gov/tierney	Washington	DC	20515	202-225-8020	225-5915

Michigan

Name	City	State	Zip	Phone	Fax
Camp Dave (Rep R-MI) 137 Cannon Bldg *TF:* 800-342-2455 ■ *Web:* wwwc.house.gov/camp	Washington	DC	20515	202-225-3561	225-9679
Conyers John Jr (Rep D-MI) 2426 Rayburn Bldg *Web:* www.house.gov/conyers	Washington	DC	20515	202-225-5126	225-0072
Dingell John D (Rep D-MI) 2328 Rayburn Bldg *Web:* www.house.gov/dingell	Washington	DC	20515	202-225-4071	226-0371
Ehlers Vernon J (Rep R-MI) 2182 Rayburn Bldg *Web:* www.house.gov/ehlers	Washington	DC	20515	202-225-3831	225-5144
Hoekstra Peter (Rep R-MI) 2234 Rayburn Bldg *Web:* hoekstra.house.gov	Washington	DC	20515	202-225-4401	226-0779
Kildee Dale E (Rep D-MI) 2107 Rayburn Bldg *Web:* www.house.gov/kildee	Washington	DC	20515	202-225-3611	225-6393
Kilpatrick Carolyn C (Rep D-MI) 2264 Rayburn Bldg *Web:* www.house.gov/kilpatrick	Washington	DC	20515	202-225-2261	225-5730
Knollenberg Joe (Rep R-MI) 2349 Rayburn Bldg *Web:* www.knollenberg.house.gov	Washington	DC	20515	202-225-5802	226-2356
Ⓢ**Levin Carl (Sen D-MI)** 269 Russell Bldg *Web:* levin.senate.gov	Washington	DC	20510	202-224-6221	224-1388
Levin Sander M (Rep D-MI) 1236 Longworth Bldg *Web:* www.house.gov/levin	Washington	DC	20515	202-225-4961	226-1033
McCotter Thaddeus G (Rep R-MI) 1632 Longworth Bldg *Web:* mccotter.house.gov	Washington	DC	20515	202-225-8171	225-2667
Miller Candice S (Rep R-MI) 228 Cannon Bldg *Web:* candicemiller.house.gov	Washington	DC	20515	202-225-2106	226-1169
Rogers Mike (Rep R-MI) 133 Cannon Bldg *TF:* 877-333-6453 ■ *Web:* www.mikerogers.house.gov	Washington	DC	20515	202-225-4872	225-5820
Ⓢ**Stabenow Debbie (Sen D-MI)** 133 Hart Bldg *Web:* stabenow.senate.gov	Washington	DC	20510	202-224-4822	228-0325
Stupak Bart (Rep D-MI) 2352 Rayburn Bldg *Web:* www.house.gov/stupak	Washington	DC	20515	202-225-4735	225-4744
Upton Fred (Rep R-MI) 2183 Rayburn Bldg *Web:* www.house.gov/upton	Washington	DC	20515	202-225-3761	225-4986
Walberg Tim (Rep R-MI) 325 Cannon Bldg *Web:* walberg.house.gov	Washington	DC	20515	202-225-6276	225-6281

Minnesota

Name	City	State	Zip	Phone	Fax
Bachmann Michele (Rep R-MN) 412 Cannon Bldg *Web:* bachmann.house.gov	Washington	DC	20515	202-225-2331	225-6475
Ⓢ**Coleman Norm (Sen R-MN)** 320 Hart Bldg *TF:* 800-642-6041 ■ *Web:* coleman.senate.gov	Washington	DC	20510	202-224-5641	224-1152
Ellison Keith (Rep D-MN) 1130 Longworth Bldg *Web:* ellison.house.gov	Washington	DC	20515	202-225-4755	225-4886
Kline John P (Rep R-MN) 1429 Longworth Bldg *Web:* www.house.gov/kline	Washington	DC	20515	202-225-2271	225-2595
Ⓢ**Klobuchar Amy (Sen D-MN)** 302 Hart Bldg *Web:* klobuchar.senate.gov	Washington	DC	20510	202-224-3244	228-2186
McCollum Betty (Rep D-MN) 1714 Longworth Bldg *Web:* www.mccollum.house.gov	Washington	DC	20515	202-225-6631	225-1968
Oberstar James L (Rep D-MN) 2365 Rayburn Bldg *Web:* www.oberstar.house.gov	Washington	DC	20515	202-225-6211	225-0699
Peterson Collin C (Rep D-MN) 2211 Rayburn Bldg *Web:* collinpeterson.house.gov	Washington	DC	20515	202-225-2165	225-1593
Ramstad Jim (Rep R-MN) 103 Cannon Bldg *Web:* www.house.gov/ramstad	Washington	DC	20515	202-225-2871	225-6351
Walz Tim (Rep D-MN) 1529 Longworth Bldg *Web:* walz.house.gov	Washington	DC	20515	202-225-2472	225-3433

Mississippi

Name	City	State	Zip	Phone	Fax
Childers Travis (Rep D-MS) 2350 Rayburn Bldg	Washington	DC	20515	202-225-4306	225-3549
Ⓢ**Cochran Thad (Sen R-MS)** 113 Dirksen Bldg *Web:* cochran.senate.gov	Washington	DC	20510	202-224-5054	224-9450
Pickering Chip (Rep R-MS) 229 Cannon Bldg *Web:* www.house.gov/pickering	Washington	DC	20515	202-225-5031	225-5797
Taylor Gene (Rep D-MS) 2269 Rayburn Bldg *Web:* www.house.gov/genetaylor	Washington	DC	20515	202-225-5772	225-7074
Thompson Bennie G (Rep D-MS) 2432 Rayburn Bldg *Web:* benniethompson.house.gov	Washington	DC	20515	202-225-5876	225-5898
Ⓢ**Wicker Roger (Sen R-MS)** 487 Russell Bldg *Web:* wicker.senate.gov	Washington	DC	20510	202-224-6253	228-0378

Missouri

Name	City	State	Zip	Phone	Fax
Akin Todd (Rep R-MO) 117 Cannon Bldg *Web:* www.house.gov/akin	Washington	DC	20515	202-225-2561	225-2563
Blunt Roy (Rep R-MO) 217 Cannon Bldg *Web:* www.blunt.house.gov	Washington	DC	20515	202-225-6536	225-5604
Ⓢ**Bond Kit (Sen R-MO)** 274 Russell Bldg *Web:* bond.senate.gov	Washington	DC	20510	202-224-5721	224-8149
Carnahan Russ (Rep D-MO) 1710 Longworth Bldg *Web:* www.house.gov/carnahan	Washington	DC	20515	202-225-2671	225-7452
Clay William L (Rep D-MO) 434 Cannon Bldg *Web:* lacyclay.house.gov	Washington	DC	20515	202-225-2406	225-1725
Cleaver Emanuel (Rep D-MO) 1641 Longworth Bldg *Web:* www.house.gov/cleaver	Washington	DC	20515	202-225-4535	225-4403
Emerson Jo Ann (Rep R-MO) 2440 Rayburn Bldg *Web:* www.house.gov/emerson	Washington	DC	20515	202-225-4404	226-0326
Graves Sam (Rep R-MO) 1415 Longworth Bldg *Web:* www.house.gov/graves	Washington	DC	20515	202-225-7041	225-8221
Hulshof Kenny (Rep R-MO) 409 Cannon Bldg *Web:* hulshof.house.gov	Washington	DC	20515	202-225-2956	225-5712
Ⓢ**McCaskill Claire (Sen D-MO)** 717 Hart Bldg *Web:* mccaskill.senate.gov	Washington	DC	20510	202-224-6154	228-6326
Skelton Ike (Rep D-MO) 2206 Rayburn Bldg *Web:* www.house.gov/skelton	Washington	DC	20515	202-225-2876	225-2695

Montana

Name	City	State	Zip	Phone	Fax
Ⓢ**Baucus Max (Sen D-MT)** 511 Hart Bldg *Web:* baucus.senate.gov	Washington	DC	20510	202-224-2651	224-4700
Rehberg Dennis R (Rep R-MT) 516 Cannon Bldg *TF:* 888-232-2626 ■ *Web:* www.house.gov/rehberg	Washington	DC	20515	202-225-3211	225-5687
Ⓢ**Tester Jon (Sen D-MT)** 204 Russell Bldg *Web:* tester.senate.gov	Washington	DC	20510	202-224-2644	224-8594

Nebraska

Name	City	State	Zip	Phone	Fax
Fortenberry Jeff (Rep R-NE) 1517 Longworth Bldg *Web:* fortenberry.house.gov	Washington	DC	20515	202-225-4806	225-5686
Ⓢ**Hagel Charles (Sen R-NE)** 248 Russell Bldg *Web:* hagel.senate.gov	Washington	DC	20510	202-224-4224	228-5213
Ⓢ**Nelson Ben (Sen D-NE)** 720 Hart Bldg *Web:* bennelson.senate.gov	Washington	DC	20510	202-224-6551	228-0012
Smith Adrian M (Rep R-NE) 503 Cannon Bldg *Web:* adriansmith.house.gov	Washington	DC	20515	202-225-6435	225-0207
Terry Lee (Rep R-NE) 1524 Longworth Bldg *Web:* leeterry.house.gov	Washington	DC	20515	202-225-4155	226-5452

Nevada

Name	City	State	Zip	Phone	Fax
Berkley Shelley (Rep D-NV) 405 Cannon Bldg *TF:* 877-409-2488 ■ *Web:* berkley.house.gov	Washington	DC	20515	202-225-5965	225-3119
Ⓢ**Ensign John (Sen R-NV)** 119 Russell Bldg *Web:* ensign.senate.gov	Washington	DC	20510	202-224-6244	228-2193
Heller Dean (Rep R-NV) 1023 Longworth Bldg *Web:* heller.house.gov	Washington	DC	20515	202-225-6155	225-5679
Porter Jon (Rep R-NV) 218 Cannon Bldg *Web:* www.house.gov/porter	Washington	DC	20515	202-225-3252	225-2185
Ⓢ**Reid Harry (Sen D-NV)** 528 Hart Bldg *Web:* reid.senate.gov	Washington	DC	20510	202-224-3542	224-7327

New Hampshire

Name	City	State	Zip	Phone	Fax
Ⓢ**Gregg Judd (Sen R-NH)** 393 Russell Bldg *Web:* gregg.senate.gov	Washington	DC	20510	202-224-3324	224-4952
Hodes Paul (Rep D-NH) 506 Cannon House Office Bldg *Web:* hodes.house.gov	Washington	DC	20515	202-225-5206	225-2946
Shea-Porter Carol (Rep D-NH) 1508 Longworth Bldg *Web:* shea-porter.house.gov	Washington	DC	20515	202-225-5456	225-5822
Ⓢ**Sununu John E (Sen R-NH)** 111 Russell Bldg *Web:* sununu.senate.gov	Washington	DC	20510	202-224-2841	228-4131

New Jersey

Name	City	State	Zip	Phone	Fax
Andrews Robert E (Rep D-NJ) 2439 Rayburn Bldg *Web:* www.house.gov/andrews	Washington	DC	20515	202-225-6501	225-6583
Ferguson Mike (Rep R-NJ) 214 Cannon Bldg *Web:* www.house.gov/ferguson	Washington	DC	20515	202-225-5361	225-9460
Frelinghuysen Rodney (Rep R-NJ) 2442 Rayburn Bldg *Web:* frelinghuysen.house.gov	Washington	DC	20515	202-225-5034	225-3186
Garrett Scott (Rep R-NJ) 1318 Longworth Bldg *Web:* www.house.gov/garrett	Washington	DC	20515	202-225-4465	225-9048
Holt Rush (Rep D-NJ) 1019 Longworth Bldg *Web:* holt.house.gov	Washington	DC	20515	202-225-5801	225-6025
Ⓢ**Lautenberg Frank R (Sen D-NJ)** 324 Hart Bldg *Web:* lautenberg.senate.gov	Washington	DC	20510	202-224-3224	228-4054
LoBiondo Frank A (Rep R-NJ) 2427 Rayburn Bldg *Web:* www.house.gov/lobiondo	Washington	DC	20510	202-225-6572	225-3318
Ⓢ**Menendez Robert (Sen D-NJ)** 317 Hart Bldg *Web:* menendez.senate.gov	Washington	DC	20510	202-224-4744	228-2197

US Senators, Representatives, Delegates (Cont'd)

New Jersey (Cont'd)

				Phone	Fax
Pallone Frank Jr (Rep D-NJ) 237 Cannon Bldg *Web:* www.house.gov/pallone	Washington	DC	20515	202-225-4671	225-9665
Pascrell Bill (Rep D-NJ) 2464 Rayburn Bldg *Web:* www.pascrell.house.gov	Washington	DC	20515	202-225-5751	225-5782
Payne Donald M (Rep D-NJ) 2209 Rayburn Bldg *Web:* www.house.gov/payne	Washington	DC	20515	202-225-3436	225-4160
Rothman Steven R (Rep D-NJ) 2303 Rayburn Bldg *Web:* www.house.gov/rothman	Washington	DC	20515	202-225-5061	225-5851
Saxton Jim (Rep R-NJ) 2217 Rayburn Bldg *Web:* www.house.gov/saxton	Washington	DC	20515	202-225-4765	225-0778
Sires Albio (Rep D-NJ) 1024 Longworth Bldg *Web:* www.house.gov/sires	Washington	DC	20515	202-225-7919	226-0792
Smith Christopher H (Rep R-NJ) 2373 Rayburn Bldg *Web:* www.house.gov/chrissmith	Washington	DC	20515	202-225-3765	225-7768

New Mexico

				Phone	Fax
Ⓢ**Bingaman Jeff (Sen D-NM)** 703 Hart Bldg *Web:* bingaman.senate.gov	Washington	DC	20510	202-224-5521	224-2852
Ⓢ**Domenici Pete V (Sen R-NM)** 328 Hart Bldg *Web:* domenici.senate.gov	Washington	DC	20510	202-224-6621	228-3261
Pearce Steve (Rep R-NM) 1607 Longworth Bldg *Web:* pearce.house.gov	Washington	DC	20515	202-225-2365	225-9599
Udall Tom (Rep D-NM) 1410 Longworth Bldg *Web:* www.tomudall.house.gov	Washington	DC	20515	202-225-6190	226-1331
Wilson Heather (Rep R-NM) 442 Cannon Bldg *Web:* wilson.house.gov	Washington	DC	20515	202-225-6316	225-4975

New York

				Phone	Fax
Ackerman Gary L (Rep D-NY) 2243 Rayburn Bldg *Web:* www.house.gov/ackerman	Washington	DC	20515	202-225-2601	225-1589
Arcuri Michael (Rep D-NY) 327 Cannon Bldg *Web:* arcuri.house.gov	Washington	DC	20515	202-225-3665	225-1891
Bishop Timothy (Rep D-NY) 225 Cannon Bldg *Web:* timbishop.house.gov	Washington	DC	20515	202-225-3826	225-3143
Clarke Yvette D (Rep D-NY) 1029 Longworth Bldg *Web:* clarke.house.gov	Washington	DC	20515	202-225-6231	226-0112
Ⓢ**Clinton Hillary Rodham (Sen D-NY)** 476 Russell Bldg *Web:* clinton.senate.gov	Washington	DC	20510	202-224-4451	228-0282
Crowley Joseph (Rep D-NY) 2404 Rayburn Bldg *Web:* crowley.house.gov	Washington	DC	20515	202-225-3965	225-1909
Engel Eliot L (Rep D-NY) 2161 Rayburn Bldg *Web:* www.house.gov/engel	Washington	DC	20515	202-225-2464	225-5513
Fossella Vito J (Rep R-NY) 2453 Rayburn Bldg *Web:* www.house.gov/fossella	Washington	DC	20515	202-225-3371	226-1272
Gillibrand Kirsten (Rep D-NY) 120 Cannon Bldg *Web:* gillibrand.house.gov	Washington	DC	20515	202-225-5614	225-1168
Hall John J (Rep D-NY) 1217 Longworth Bldg *Web:* johnhall.house.gov	Washington	DC	20515	202-225-5441	225-3289
Higgins Brian M (Rep D-NY) 431 Cannon Bldg *Web:* www.house.gov/higgins	Washington	DC	20515	202-225-3306	226-0347
Hinchey Maurice D (Rep D-NY) 2431 Rayburn Bldg *Web:* www.house.gov/hinchey	Washington	DC	20515	202-225-6335	226-0774
Israel Steve (Rep D-NY) 432 Cannon Bldg *Web:* www.house.gov/israel	Washington	DC	20515	202-225-3335	225-4669
King Peter T (Rep R-NY) 339 Cannon Bldg *Web:* peteking.house.gov	Washington	DC	20515	202-225-7896	226-2279
Kuhl John R "Randy" Jr (Rep R-NY) 1505 Longworth Bldg *Web:* kuhl.house.gov	Washington	DC	20515	202-225-3161	226-6599
Lowey Nita M (Rep D-NY) 2329 Rayburn Bldg *Web:* www.house.gov/lowey	Washington	DC	20515	202-225-6506	225-0546
Maloney Carolyn B (Rep D-NY) 2331 Rayburn Bldg *Web:* www.house.gov/maloney	Washington	DC	20515	202-225-7944	225-4709
McCarthy Carolyn (Rep D-NY) 106 Cannon Bldg *Web:* carolynmccarthy.house.gov	Washington	DC	20515	202-225-5516	225-5758
McHugh John M (Rep R-NY) 2366 Rayburn Bldg *Web:* mchugh.house.gov	Washington	DC	20515	202-225-4611	226-0621
McNulty Michael R (Rep D-NY) 2210 Rayburn Bldg *Web:* www.house.gov/mcnulty	Washington	DC	20515	202-225-5076	225-5077
Meeks Gregory W (Rep D-NY) 2342 Rayburn Bldg *Web:* www.house.gov/meeks	Washington	DC	20515	202-225-3461	226-4169
Nadler Jerrold (Rep D-NY) 2334 Rayburn Bldg *Web:* www.house.gov/nadler	Washington	DC	20515	202-225-5635	225-6923
Rangel Charles B (Rep D-NY) 2354 Rayburn Bldg *Web:* www.house.gov/rangel	Washington	DC	20515	202-225-4365	225-0816
Reynolds Thomas M (Rep R-NY) 332 Cannon Bldg *Web:* www.house.gov/reynolds	Washington	DC	20515	202-225-5265	225-5910
Ⓢ**Schumer Charles E (Sen D-NY)** 313 Hart Bldg *Web:* schumer.senate.gov	Washington	DC	20510	202-224-6542	228-3027
Serrano Jose E (Rep D-NY) 2227 Rayburn Bldg *Web:* serrano.house.gov	Washington	DC	20515	202-225-4361	225-6001
Slaughter Louise M (Rep D-NY) 2469 Rayburn Bldg *Web:* www.slaughter.house.gov	Washington	DC	20515	202-225-3615	225-7822
Towns Edolphus (Rep D-NY) 2232 Rayburn Bldg *Web:* www.house.gov/towns	Washington	DC	20515	202-225-5936	225-1018
Velazquez Nydia M (Rep D-NY) 2466 Rayburn Bldg *Web:* www.house.gov/velazquez	Washington	DC	20515	202-225-2361	226-0327
Walsh James T (Rep R-NY) 2372 Rayburn Bldg *Web:* walsh.house.gov	Washington	DC	20515	202-225-3701	225-4042
Weiner Anthony D (Rep D-NY) 1122 Longworth Bldg *Web:* www.house.gov/weiner	Washington	DC	20515	202-225-6616	226-7253

North Carolina

				Phone	Fax
Ⓢ**Burr Richard (Sen R-NC)** 217 Russell Bldg *Web:* burr.senate.gov	Washington	DC	20510	202-224-3154	228-2981
Butterfield GK Jr (Rep D-NC) 413 Cannon Bldg *Web:* www.house.gov/butterfield	Washington	DC	20515	202-225-3101	225-3354
Coble Howard (Rep R-NC) 2468 Rayburn Bldg *Web:* coble.house.gov	Washington	DC	20515	202-225-3065	225-8611
Ⓢ**Dole Elizabeth H (Sen R-NC)** 555 Dirksen Bldg *Web:* dole.senate.gov	Washington	DC	20510	202-224-6342	228-1100
Etheridge Bob (Rep D-NC) 1533 Longworth Bldg *Web:* www.house.gov/etheridge	Washington	DC	20515	202-225-4531	225-5662
Foxx Virginia (Rep R-NC) 430 Cannon Bldg *Web:* www.virginiafoxx.com	Washington	DC	20515	202-225-2071	225-2995
Hayes Robin (Rep R-NC) 130 Cannon Bldg *Web:* www.hayes.house.gov	Washington	DC	20515	202-225-3715	225-4036
Jones Walter B (Rep R-NC) 2333 Rayburn Bldg *Web:* jones.house.gov	Washington	DC	20515	202-225-3415	225-3286
McHenry Patrick (Rep R-NC) 224 Cannon House Office Bldg *Web:* mchenry.house.gov	Washington	DC	20515	202-225-2576	225-0316
McIntyre Mike (Rep D-NC) 2437 Rayburn Bldg *Web:* www.house.gov/mcintyre	Washington	DC	20515	202-225-2731	225-5773
Miller Brad (Rep D-NC) 1722 Longworth Bldg *Web:* www.house.gov/bradmiller	Washington	DC	20515	202-225-3032	225-0181
Myrick Sue (Rep R-NC) 230 Cannon Bldg *Web:* myrick.house.gov	Washington	DC	20515	202-225-1976	225-3389
Price David (Rep D-NC) 2162 Rayburn Bldg *Web:* price.house.gov	Washington	DC	20515	202-225-1784	225-2014
Shuler Heath (Rep D-NC) 512 Cannon Bldg *Web:* shuler.house.gov	Washington	DC	20515	202-225-6401	226-6422
Watt Melvin L (Rep D-NC) 2236 Rayburn Bldg *Web:* www.house.gov/watt	Washington	DC	20515	202-225-1510	225-1512

North Dakota

				Phone	Fax
Ⓢ**Conrad Kent (Sen D-ND)** 530 Hart Bldg *Web:* conrad.senate.gov	Washington	DC	20510	202-224-2043	224-7776
Ⓢ**Dorgan Byron L (Sen D-ND)** 322 Hart Bldg *Web:* dorgan.senate.gov	Washington	DC	20510	202-224-2551	224-1193
Pomeroy Earl (Rep D-ND) 1501 Longworth Bldg *Web:* www.pomeroy.house.gov	Washington	DC	20515	202-225-2611	226-0893

Ohio

				Phone	Fax
Boehner John A (Rep R-OH) 1011 Longworth Bldg *Web:* johnboehner.house.gov	Washington	DC	20515	202-225-6205	225-0704
Ⓢ**Brown Sherrod (Sen D-OH)** 455 Russell Bldg *Web:* brown.senate.gov	Washington	DC	20510	202-224-2315	228-6321
Chabot Steve (Rep R-OH) 129 Cannon Bldg *Web:* www.house.gov/chabot	Washington	DC	20515	202-225-2216	225-3012
Hobson David L (Rep R-OH) 2346 Rayburn Bldg *Web:* hobson.house.gov	Washington	DC	20515	202-225-4324	225-1984
Jordan James D (Rep R-OH) 515 Cannon Bldg *Web:* jordan.house.gov	Washington	DC	20515	202-225-2676	226-0577
Kaptur Marcy (Rep D-OH) 2186 Rayburn Bldg *Web:* www.kaptur.house.gov	Washington	DC	20515	202-225-4146	225-7711
Kucinich Dennis (Rep D-OH) 2445 Rayburn Bldg *Web:* kucinich.house.gov	Washington	DC	20515	202-225-5871	225-5745
LaTourette Steve (Rep R-OH) 2371 Rayburn Bldg *Web:* www.house.gov/latourette	Washington	DC	20515	202-225-5731	225-3307
Pryce Deborah (Rep R-OH) 320 Cannon Bldg *Web:* www.house.gov/pryce	Washington	DC	20515	202-225-2015	225-3529
Regula Ralph (Rep R-OH) 2306 Rayburn Bldg *Web:* wwwc.house.gov/regula	Washington	DC	20515	202-225-3876	225-3059
Ryan Timothy J (Rep D-OH) 1421 Longworth Bldg *TF:* 800-856-4152 ■ *Web:* timryan.house.gov	Washington	DC	20515	202-225-5261	225-3719
Schmidt Jean (Rep R-OH) 238 Cannon Bldg *Web:* www.house.gov/schmidt	Washington	DC	20515	202-225-3164	225-1992
Space Zachary T (Rep D-OH) 315 Cannon Bldg *Web:* space.house.gov	Washington	DC	20515	202-225-6265	225-3394
Sutton Betty (Rep D-OH) 1721 Longworth Bldg *Web:* sutton.house.gov	Washington	DC	20515	202-225-3401	225-2266
Tiberi Patrick J (Rep R-OH) 113 Cannon Bldg *Web:* www.house.gov/tiberi	Washington	DC	20515	202-225-5355	226-4523
Tubbs Jones Stephanie (Rep D-OH) 1009 Longworth Bldg *Web:* www.house.gov/tubbsjones	Washington	DC	20515	202-225-7032	225-1339
Turner Michael (Rep R-OH) 1740 Longworth Bldg *Web:* www.house.gov/miketurner	Washington	DC	20515	202-225-6465	225-6754
Ⓢ**Voinovich George V (Sen R-OH)** 524 Hart Bldg *Web:* voinovich.senate.gov	Washington	DC	20510	202-224-3353	228-1382
Wilson Charles A (Rep D-OH) 226 Cannon Bldg *Web:* charliewilson.house.gov	Washington	DC	20515	202-225-5705	225-5907

Oklahoma

				Phone	Fax
Boren Dan (Rep D-OK) 216 Cannon Bldg *Web:* www.house.gov/boren	Washington	DC	20515	202-225-2701	225-3038
Ⓢ**Coburn Tom (Sen R-OK)** 172 Russell Bldg *Web:* coburn.senate.gov	Washington	DC	20510	202-224-5754	224-6008
Cole Tom (Rep R-OK) 236 Cannon Bldg *Web:* www.house.gov/cole	Washington	DC	20515	202-225-6165	225-3512
Fallin Mary (Rep R-OK) 1432 Longworth Bldg *Web:* fallin.house.gov	Washington	DC	20515	202-225-2132	226-1463
Ⓢ**Inhofe James M (Sen R-OK)** 453 Russell Bldg *Web:* inhofe.senate.gov	Washington	DC	20510	202-224-4721	228-0380
Lucas Frank D (Rep R-OK) 2311 Rayburn Bldg *Web:* www.house.gov/lucas	Washington	DC	20515	202-225-5565	225-8698
Sullivan John (Rep R-OK) 114 Cannon Bldg *Web:* sullivan.house.gov	Washington	DC	20515	202-225-2211	225-9187

Oregon

				Phone	Fax
Blumenauer Earl (Rep D-OR) 2267 Rayburn Bldg *Web:* blumenauer.house.gov	Washington	DC	20515	202-225-4811	225-8941
DeFazio Peter A (Rep D-OR) 2134 Rayburn Bldg *Web:* www.house.gov/defazio	Washington	DC	20515	202-225-6416	225-0032
Hooley Darlene (Rep D-OR) 2430 Rayburn Bldg *Web:* hooley.house.gov	Washington	DC	20515	202-225-5711	225-5699
Ⓢ**Smith Gordon (Sen R-OR)** 404 Russell Bldg *Web:* gsmith.senate.gov	Washington	DC	20510	202-224-3753	228-3997
Walden Greg (Rep R-OR) 1210 Longworth Bldg *Web:* www.walden.house.gov	Washington	DC	20515	202-225-6730	225-5774
Wu David (Rep D-OR) 2338 Rayburn Bldg *Web:* www.house.gov/wu	Washington	DC	20515	202-225-0855	225-9497
Ⓢ**Wyden Ron (Sen D-OR)** 223 Dirksen Bldg *Web:* wyden.senate.gov	Washington	DC	20510	202-224-5244	228-2717

Pennsylvania

				Phone	Fax
Altmire Jason (Rep D-PA) 1419 Longworth Bldg *Web:* altmire.house.gov	Washington	DC	20515	202-225-2565	226-2274

				Phone	Fax
Brady Robert A (Rep D-PA) 206 Cannon Bldg	Washington	DC	20515	202-225-4731	225-0088
Web: www.house.gov/robertbrady					
Carney Chris (Rep D-PA) 416 Cannon Bldg	Washington	DC	20515	202-225-3731	225-9594
Web: carney.house.gov					
Ⓢ**Casey Robert P Jr (Sen D-PA)** 383 Russell Bldg	Washington	DC	20510	202-224-6324	228-0604
Web: casey.senate.gov					
Dent Charles W (Rep R-PA) 116 Cannon Bldg	Washington	DC	20515	202-225-6411	226-0778
Web: dent.house.gov					
Doyle Mike (Rep D-PA) 401 Cannon Bldg	Washington	DC	20515	202-225-2135	225-3084
Web: www.house.gov/doyle					
English Phil (Rep R-PA) 2332 Rayburn Bldg	Washington	DC	20515	202-225-5406	225-3103
Web: www.house.gov/english					
Fattah Chaka (Rep D-PA) 2301 Rayburn Bldg	Washington	DC	20515	202-225-4001	225-5392
Web: www.house.gov/fattah					
Gerlach Jim (Rep R-PA) 308 Cannon Bldg	Washington	DC	20515	202-225-4315	225-8440
Web: gerlach.house.gov					
Holden Tim (Rep D-PA) 2417 Rayburn Bldg	Washington	DC	20515	202-225-5546	226-0996
Web: www.holden.house.gov					
Kanjorski Paul E (Rep D-PA) 2188 Rayburn Bldg	Washington	DC	20515	202-225-6511	225-0764
Web: kanjorski.house.gov					
Murphy Patrick (Rep D-PA) 1007 Longworth Bldg	Washington	DC	20515	202-225-4276	225-9511
Web: patrickmurphy.house.gov					
Murphy Timothy F (Rep R-PA) 322 Cannon Bldg	Washington	DC	20515	202-225-2301	225-1844
Web: murphy.house.gov					
Murtha John P (Rep D-PA) 2423 Rayburn Bldg	Washington	DC	20515	202-225-2065	225-5709
Web: www.house.gov/murtha					
Peterson John (Rep R-PA) 123 Cannon Bldg	Washington	DC	20515	202-225-5121	225-5796
Web: www.house.gov/johnpeterson					
Pitts Joseph R (Rep R-PA) 420 Cannon Bldg	Washington	DC	20515	202-225-2411	225-2013
Web: www.house.gov/pitts					
Platts Todd Russell (Rep R-PA) 1032 Longworth Bldg	Washington	DC	20515	202-225-5836	226-1000
Web: www.house.gov/platts					
Schwartz Allyson Y (Rep D-PA) 423 Cannon Bldg	Washington	DC	20515	202-225-6111	226-0611
Web: schwartz.house.gov					
Sestak Joseph (Rep D-PA) 1022 Longworth Bldg	Washington	DC	20515	202-225-2011	226-0280
Web: sestak.house.gov					
Shuster Bill (Rep R-PA) 204 Cannon Bldg	Washington	DC	20515	202-225-2431	225-2486
Web: www.house.gov/shuster					
Ⓢ**Specter Arlen (Sen R-PA)** 711 Hart Bldg	Washington	DC	20510	202-224-4254	228-1229
Web: specter.senate.gov					

Puerto Rico

				Phone	Fax
Fortuno Luis G (Rep R-PR) 126 Cannon Bldg	Washington	DC	20515	202-225-2615	225-2154
Web: www.house.gov/fortuno					

Rhode Island

				Phone	Fax
Kennedy Patrick (Rep D-RI) 407 Cannon Bldg	Washington	DC	20515	202-225-4911	225-3290
Web: www.patrickkennedy.house.gov					
Langevin James R (Rep D-RI) 109 Cannon Bldg	Washington	DC	20515	202-225-2735	225-5976
Web: www.house.gov/langevin					
Ⓢ**Reed Jack (Sen D-RI)** 728 Hart Bldg	Washington	DC	20510	202-224-4642	224-4680
Web: reed.senate.gov					
Ⓢ**Whitehouse Sheldon (Sen D-RI)** 502 Hart Bldg	Washington	DC	20510	202-224-2921	228-2853
Web: whitehouse.senate.gov					

South Carolina

				Phone	Fax
Barrett J Gresham (Rep R-SC) 439 Cannon Bldg	Washington	DC	20515	202-225-5301	225-3216
Web: www.house.gov/barrett					
Brown Henry E Jr (Rep R-SC) 1124 Longworth Bldg	Washington	DC	20515	202-225-3176	225-3407
TF: 888-868-0737 ■ *Web:* www.house.gov/henrybrown					
Clyburn James E (Rep D-SC) 2135 Rayburn Bldg	Washington	DC	20515	202-225-3315	225-2313
Web: www.house.gov/clyburn					
Ⓢ**DeMint Jim (Sen R-SC)** 340 Russell Bldg	Washington	DC	20510	202-224-6121	228-5143
Web: demint.senate.gov					
Ⓢ**Graham Lindsey (Sen R-SC)** 290 Russell Bldg	Washington	DC	20510	202-224-5972	224-3808
Web: lgraham.senate.gov					
Inglis Bob (Rep R-SC) 330 Cannon Bldg	Washington	DC	20515	202-225-6030	226-1177
Web: www.house.gov/inglis					
Spratt John M Jr (Rep D-SC) 1401 Longworth Bldg	Washington	DC	20515	202-225-5501	225-0464
Web: www.house.gov/spratt					
Wilson Joe (Rep R-SC) 212 Cannon Bldg	Washington	DC	20515	202-225-2452	225-2455
Web: joewilson.house.gov					

South Dakota

				Phone	Fax
Herseth Stephanie (Rep D-SD) 331 Cannon Bldg	Washington	DC	20515	202-225-2801	225-5823
Web: www.house.gov/herseth					
Ⓢ**Johnson Tim (Sen D-SD)** 136 Hart Bldg	Washington	DC	20510	202-224-5842	228-5765
Web: johnson.senate.gov					
Ⓢ**Thune John (Sen R-SD)** 493 Russell Bldg	Washington	DC	20510	202-224-2321	228-5429
Web: www.thune.senate.gov					

Tennessee

				Phone	Fax
Ⓢ**Alexander Lamar (Sen R-TN)** 455 Dirksen Bldg	Washington	DC	20510	202-224-4944	228-3398
Web: alexander.senate.gov					
Blackburn Marsha W (Rep R-TN) 509 Cannon Bldg	Washington	DC	20515	202-225-2811	225-3004
Web: www.house.gov/blackburn					
Cohen Steve (Rep D-TN) 1004 Longworth House Office Bldg	Washington	DC	20515	202-225-3265	225-5663
Web: cohen.house.gov					
Cooper Jim (Rep D-TN) 1536 Longworth Bldg	Washington	DC	20515	202-225-4311	226-1035
Web: www.cooper.house.gov					
Ⓢ**Corker Bob (Sen R-TN)** 185 Dirksen Bldg	Washington	DC	20510	202-224-3344	228-0566
Web: corker.senate.gov					
Davis David (Rep R-TN) 514 Cannon Bldg	Washington	DC	20515	202-225-6356	225-5714
Web: daviddavis.house.gov					
Davis Lincoln (Rep D-TN) 410 Cannon Bldg	Washington	DC	20515	202-225-6831	226-5172
Web: www.house.gov/lincolndavis					
Duncan John J Jr (Rep R-TN) 2207 Rayburn Bldg	Washington	DC	20515	202-225-5435	225-6440
Web: www.house.gov/duncan					
Gordon Bart (Rep D-TN) 2310 Rayburn Bldg	Washington	DC	20515	202-225-4231	225-6887
Web: gordon.house.gov					
Tanner John S (Rep D-TN) 1226 Longworth Bldg	Washington	DC	20515	202-225-4714	225-1765
Web: www.house.gov/tanner					

				Phone	Fax
Wamp Zach (Rep R-TN) 1436 Longworth Bldg	Washington	DC	20515	202-225-3271	225-3494
Web: www.house.gov/wamp					

Texas

				Phone	Fax
Barton Joe (Rep R-TX) 2109 Rayburn Bldg	Washington	DC	20515	202-225-2002	225-3052
Web: joebarton.house.gov					
Brady Kevin (Rep R-TX) 301 Cannon Bldg	Washington	DC	20515	202-225-4901	225-5524
Web: www.house.gov/brady					
Burgess Michael C (Rep R-TX) 1224 Longworth Bldg	Washington	DC	20515	202-225-7772	225-2919
Web: burgess.house.gov					
Carter John R (Rep R-TX) 408 Cannon Bldg	Washington	DC	20515	202-225-3864	225-5886
Web: www.house.gov/carter					
Conaway Mike (Rep R-TX) 511 Cannon Bldg	Washington	DC	20515	202-225-3605	225-1783
TF: 866-882-3811 ■ *Web:* conaway.house.gov					
Ⓢ**Cornyn John (Sen R-TX)** 517 Hart Bldg	Washington	DC	20510	202-224-2934	228-2856
Web: cornyn.senate.gov					
Cuellar Henry (Rep D-TX) 336 Cannon Bldg	Washington	DC	20515	202-225-1640	225-1641
Web: www.house.gov/cuellar					
Culberson John (Rep R-TX) 428 Cannon Bldg	Washington	DC	20515	202-225-2571	225-4381
Web: www.culberson.house.gov					
Doggett Lloyd (Rep D-TX) 201 Cannon Bldg	Washington	DC	20515	202-225-4865	225-3073
Web: www.house.gov/doggett					
Edwards Chet (Rep D-TX) 2369 Rayburn Bldg	Washington	DC	20515	202-225-6105	225-0350
Web: edwards.house.gov					
Gohmert Louie (Rep R-TX) 510 Cannon Bldg	Washington	DC	20515	202-225-3035	226-1230
TF: 866-535-6302 ■ *Web:* gohmert.house.gov					
Gonzalez Charles A (Rep D-TX) 303 Cannon Bldg	Washington	DC	20515	202-225-3236	225-1915
Web: gonzalez.house.gov					
Granger Kay (Rep R-TX) 440 Cannon Bldg	Washington	DC	20515	202-225-5071	225-5683
Web: kaygranger.house.gov					
Green Al (Rep D-TX) 425 Cannon Bldg	Washington	DC	20515	202-225-7508	225-2947
Web: www.house.gov/algreen					
Green Gene (Rep D-TX) 2335 Rayburn Bldg	Washington	DC	20515	202-225-1688	225-9903
Web: www.house.gov/green					
Hall Ralph M (Rep R-TX) 2405 Rayburn Bldg	Washington	DC	20515	202-225-6673	225-3332
Web: www.house.gov/ralphhall					
Hensarling Jeb (Rep R-TX) 132 Cannon Bldg	Washington	DC	20515	202-225-3484	226-4888
Web: www.house.gov/hensarling					
Hinojosa Ruben (Rep D-TX) 2463 Rayburn Bldg	Washington	DC	20515	202-225-2531	225-5688
Web: hinojosa.house.gov					
Ⓢ**Hutchison Kay Bailey (Sen R-TX)** 284 Russell Bldg	Washington	DC	20510	202-224-5922	224-0776
Web: hutchison.senate.gov					
Jackson Lee Sheila (Rep D-TX) 2435 Rayburn Bldg	Washington	DC	20515	202-225-3816	225-3317
Web: www.jacksonlee.house.gov					
Johnson Eddie Bernice (Rep D-TX) 1511 Longworth Bldg	Washington	DC	20515	202-225-8885	226-1477
Web: www.house.gov/ebjohnson					
Johnson Sam (Rep R-TX) 1211 Longworth Bldg	Washington	DC	20515	202-225-4201	225-1485
Web: www.samjohnson.house.gov					
Lampson Nick (Rep D-TX) 436 Cannon Bldg	Washington	DC	20515	202-225-5951	225-5241
Web: lampson.house.gov					
Marchant Kenny (Rep R-TX) 1037 Longworth Bldg	Washington	DC	20515	202-225-6605	225-0074
Web: www.marchant.house.gov					
McCaul Michael (Rep D-TX) 131 Cannon Bldg	Washington	DC	20515	202-225-2401	225-5955
Web: www.house.gov/mccaul					
Neugebauer Randy (Rep R-TX) 429 Cannon Bldg	Washington	DC	20515	202-225-4005	225-9615
Web: www.randy.house.gov					
Ortiz Solomon P (Rep D-TX) 2110 Rayburn Bldg	Washington	DC	20515	202-225-7742	226-1134
Web: www.house.gov/ortiz					
Paul Ron (Rep R-TX) 203 Cannon Bldg	Washington	DC	20515	202-225-2831	
Web: www.house.gov/paul					
Poe Ted (Rep R-TX) 1605 Longworth Bldg	Washington	DC	20515	202-225-6565	225-5547
TF: 866-425-6565 ■ *Web:* www.house.gov/poe					
Reyes Silvestre (Rep D-TX) 2433 Rayburn Bldg	Washington	DC	20515	202-225-4831	225-2016
Web: wwwc.house.gov/reyes					
Rodriguez Ciro D (Rep D-TX) 2458 Rayburn Bldg	Washington	DC	20515	202-225-4511	225-2237
Web: rodriguez.house.gov					
Sessions Pete (Rep R-TX) 1514 Longworth Bldg	Washington	DC	20515	202-225-2231	225-5878
Web: sessions.house.gov					
Smith Lamar (Rep R-TX) 2409 Rayburn Bldg	Washington	DC	20515	202-225-4236	225-8628
Web: lamarsmith.house.gov					
Thornberry Mac (Rep R-TX) 2457 Rayburn Bldg	Washington	DC	20515	202-225-3706	225-3486
Web: www.house.gov/thornberry					

Utah

				Phone	Fax
Ⓢ**Bennett Robert F (Sen R-UT)** 431 Dirksen Bldg	Washington	DC	20510	202-224-5444	228-1168
Web: bennett.senate.gov					
Bishop Rob (Rep R-UT) 124 Cannon Bldg	Washington	DC	20515	202-225-0453	225-5857
Web: www.house.gov/robbishop					
Cannon Christopher (Rep R-UT) 2436 Rayburn Bldg	Washington	DC	20515	202-225-7751	225-5629
Web: www.house.gov/cannon					
Ⓢ**Hatch Orrin G (Sen R-UT)** 104 Hart Bldg	Washington	DC	20510	202-224-5251	224-6331
Web: hatch.senate.gov					
Matheson Jim (Rep D-UT) 1323 Longworth Bldg	Washington	DC	20515	202-225-3011	225-5638
Web: matheson.house.gov					

Vermont

				Phone	Fax
Ⓢ**Leahy Patrick J (Sen D-VT)** 433 Russell Bldg	Washington	DC	20510	202-224-4242	224-3479
Web: leahy.senate.gov					
Ⓢ**Sanders Bernard (Sen I-VT)** 332 Dirksen Bldg	Washington	DC	20510	202-224-5141	228-0776
Web: sanders.senate.gov					
Welch Peter (Rep D-VT) 1404 Longworth Bldg	Washington	DC	20515	202-225-4115	225-6790
TF: 888-605-7270 ■ *Web:* welch.house.gov					

Virgin Islands

				Phone	Fax
Christensen Donna (Del D-VI) 1510 Longworth Bldg	Washington	DC	20515	202-225-1790	225-5517
Web: www.house.gov/christian-christensen					

Virginia

				Phone	Fax
Boucher Rick (Rep D-VA) 2187 Rayburn Bldg	Washington	DC	20515	202-225-3861	225-0442
Web: www.house.gov/boucher					
Cantor Eric (Rep R-VA) 329 Cannon Bldg	Washington	DC	20515	202-225-2815	225-0011
Web: cantor.house.gov					

US Senators, Representatives, Delegates (Cont'd)

Virginia (Cont'd)

Name / Address	City	State	Zip	Phone	Fax
Davis Tom (Rep R-VA) 2348 Rayburn Bldg *Web:* tomdavis.house.gov	Washington	DC	20515	202-225-1492	225-3071
Drake Thelma D (Rep R-VA) 1208 Longworth Bldg *Web:* drake.house.gov	Washington	DC	20515	202-225-4215	225-4218
Forbes J Randy (Rep R-VA) 307 Cannon Bldg *Web:* www.house.gov/forbes	Washington	DC	20515	202-225-6365	226-1170
Goode Virgil H Jr (Rep R-VA) 1520 Longworth Bldg *Web:* www.house.gov/goode	Washington	DC	20515	202-225-4711	225-5681
Goodlatte Robert W (Rep R-VA) 2240 Rayburn Bldg *Web:* www.house.gov/goodlatte	Washington	DC	20515	202-225-5431	225-9681
Moran James (Rep D-VA) 2239 Rayburn Bldg *Web:* moran.house.gov	Washington	DC	20515	202-225-4376	225-0017
Scott Robert C (Rep D-VA) 1201 Longworth Bldg *Web:* www.house.gov/scott	Washington	DC	20515	202-225-8351	225-8354
Ⓢ**Warner John (Sen R-VA)** 225 Russell Bldg *Web:* warner.senate.gov	Washington	DC	20510	202-224-2023	224-6295
Ⓢ**Webb Jim (Sen D-VA)** 144 Russell Bldg *Web:* webb.senate.gov	Washington	DC	20510	202-224-4024	228-6363
Wittman Rob (Rep R-VA) 1123 Longworth Bldg *Web:* www.wittman.house.gov	Washington	DC	20515	202-225-4261	225-4382
Wolf Frank R (Rep R-VA) 241 Cannon Bldg *Web:* www.house.gov/wolf	Washington	DC	20515	202-225-5136	225-0437

Washington

Name / Address	City	State	Zip	Phone	Fax
Baird Brian (Rep D-WA) 2443 Rayburn Bldg *Web:* www.house.gov/baird	Washington	DC	20515	202-225-3536	225-3478
Ⓢ**Cantwell Maria (Sen D-WA)** 511 Dirksen Bldg *Web:* cantwell.senate.gov	Washington	DC	20510	202-224-3441	228-0514
Dicks Norman D (Rep D-WA) 2467 Rayburn Bldg *Web:* www.house.gov/dicks	Washington	DC	20515	202-225-5916	226-1176
Hastings Doc (Rep R-WA) 1214 Longworth Bldg *Web:* hastings.house.gov	Washington	DC	20515	202-225-5816	225-3251
Inslee Jay (Rep D-WA) 403 Cannon Bldg *TF:* 800-422-5521 ■ *Web:* www.house.gov/inslee	Washington	DC	20515	202-225-6311	226-1606
Larsen Rick (Rep D-WA) 107 Cannon Bldg *Web:* www.house.gov/larsen	Washington	DC	20515	202-225-2605	225-4420
McDermott Jim (Rep D-WA) 1035 Longworth Bldg *Web:* www.house.gov/mcdermott	Washington	DC	20515	202-225-3106	225-6197
McMorris Cathy (Rep R-WA) 1708 Longworth House Office Bldg *Web:* www.mcmorris.house.gov	Washington	DC	20515	202-225-2206	225-3392
Ⓢ**Murray Patty (Sen D-WA)** 173 Russell Bldg *Web:* murray.senate.gov	Washington	DC	20510	202-224-2621	224-0238
Reichert Dave (Rep R-WA) 1223 Longworth Bldg *Web:* www.house.gov/reichert	Washington	DC	20515	202-225-7761	225-4282
Smith Adam (Rep D-WA) 2402 Rayburn Bldg *Web:* www.house.gov/adamsmith	Washington	DC	20515	202-225-8901	225-5893

West Virginia

Name / Address	City	State	Zip	Phone	Fax
Ⓢ**Byrd Robert C (Sen D-WV)** 311 Hart Bldg *Web:* byrd.senate.gov	Washington	DC	20510	202-224-3954	228-0002
Capito Shelley Moore (Rep R-WV) 1431 Longworth Bldg *Web:* capito.house.gov	Washington	DC	20515	202-225-2711	225-7856
Mollohan Alan B (Rep D-WV) 2302 Rayburn Bldg *Web:* www.house.gov/mollohan	Washington	DC	20515	202-225-4172	225-7564
Rahall Nick (Rep D-WV) 2307 Rayburn Bldg *Web:* www.rahall.house.gov	Washington	DC	20515	202-225-3452	225-9061
Ⓢ**Rockefeller Jay (Sen D-WV)** 531 Hart Bldg *Web:* rockefeller.senate.gov	Washington	DC	20510	202-224-6472	224-7665

Wisconsin

Name / Address	City	State	Zip	Phone	Fax
Baldwin Tammy (Rep D-WI) 2446 Rayburn Bldg *Web:* tammybaldwin.house.gov	Washington	DC	20515	202-225-2906	225-6942
Ⓢ**Feingold Russell D (Sen D-WI)** 506 Hart Bldg *Web:* feingold.senate.gov	Washington	DC	20510	202-224-5323	224-2725
Kagen Steve (Rep D-WI) 1232 Longworth Bldg *Web:* kagen.house.gov	Washington	DC	20515	202-225-5665	225-5729
Kind Ron (Rep D-WI) 1406 Longworth Bldg *Web:* www.house.gov/kind	Washington	DC	20515	202-225-5506	225-5739
Ⓢ**Kohl Herbert H (Sen D-WI)** 330 Hart Bldg *Web:* kohl.senate.gov	Washington	DC	20510	202-224-5653	224-9787
Moore Gwen (Rep D-WI) 1239 Longworth Bldg *Web:* www.house.gov/gwenmoore	Washington	DC	20515	202-225-4572	225-8135
Obey David R (Rep D-WI) 2314 Rayburn Bldg *Web:* obey.house.gov	Washington	DC	20515	202-225-3365	
Petri Thomas E (Rep R-WI) 2462 Rayburn Bldg *Web:* www.house.gov/petri	Washington	DC	20515	202-225-2476	225-2356
Ryan Paul (Rep R-WI) 1113 Longworth Bldg *Web:* www.house.gov/ryan	Washington	DC	20515	202-225-3031	225-3393
Sensenbrenner Jim Jr (Rep R-WI) 2449 Rayburn Bldg *Web:* sensenbrenner.house.gov	Washington	DC	20515	202-225-5101	225-3190

Wyoming

Name / Address	City	State	Zip	Phone	Fax
Ⓢ**Barrasso John (Sen R-WY)** 307 Dirksen Senate Office Bldg *Web:* barrasso.senate.gov/public/	Washington	DC	20510	202-224-6441	224-1724
Cubin Barbara (Rep R-WY) 1114 Longworth Bldg *Web:* www.house.gov/cubin	Washington	DC	20515	202-225-2311	225-3057
Ⓢ**Enzi Mike (Sen R-WY)** 379A Russell Bldg *Web:* enzi.senate.gov	Washington	DC	20510	202-224-3424	228-0359

346 GOVERNORS - STATE

Listings for governors are organized by state names.

Name / Address	City	State	Zip	Phone	Fax
Riley Robert (R) 600 Dexter Ave Suite N-104 *Web:* www.governor.state.al.us	Montgomery	AL	36130	334-242-7100	353-0004
Murkowski Frank (R) PO Box 110001 *Web:* www.gov.state.ak.us	Juneau	AK	99811	907-465-3500	465-3532
Tulafono Togiola (D) American Samoa Government *Web:* www.asg-gov.net	Pago Pago	AS	96799	684-633-4116	633-2269
Napolitano Janet (D) 1700 W Washington St Executive Tower 9th Fl *Web:* www.governor.state.az.us	Phoenix	AZ	85007	602-542-4331	542-7601
Huckabee Michael D (R) State Capitol Bldg Suite 250 *Web:* www.accessarkansas.org/governor	Little Rock	AR	72201	501-682-2345	682-1382
Schwarzenegger Arnold (R) State Capitol 1st Fl *Web:* www.governor.ca.gov	Sacramento	CA	95814	916-445-2841	445-4633
Owens Bill (R) 136 State Capitol Bldg *Web:* www.colorado.gov/governor	Denver	CO	80203	303-866-2471	866-2003
Rell M Jodi (R) 210 Capitol Ave *Web:* www.ct.gov/governorrell	Hartford	CT	06106	860-566-4840	524-7395
Minner Ruth Ann (D) 150 William Penn St 2nd Fl *Web:* www.state.de.us/governor	Dover	DE	19901	302-577-3210	739-2775
Bush Jeb (R) State Capitol *Web:* www.flgov.com	Tallahassee	FL	32399	850-488-4441	487-0801
Perdue Sonny (R) State Capitol Rm 203 *Web:* www.gov.state.ga.us	Atlanta	GA	30334	404-656-1776	657-7332
Camacho Felix (R) 238 Archbishop Flores St Suite 405 PO Box 2950 *Web:* www.nga.org/governors	Hagatna	GU	96910	671-472-8931	477-4826
Lingle Linda (R) State Capitol 415 S Beretania St *Web:* www.hawaii.gov/gov	Honolulu	HI	96813	808-586-0034	586-0006
Risch James E (R) State Capitol Bldg 2nd Fl *Web:* gov.idaho.gov	Boise	ID	83720	208-334-2100	334-3454
Blagojevich Rod R (D) State Capitol Bldg Rm 207 *Web:* www.illinois.gov/gov	Springfield	IL	62706	217-782-6830	782-1853
Daniels Mitch (R) State House 200 W Washington St Rm 206 *Web:* www.state.in.us/gov	Indianapolis	IN	46204	317-232-4567	232-3443
Vilsack Thomas J (D) State Capitol Bldg *Web:* www.governor.state.ia.us	Des Moines	IA	50319	515-281-5211	281-6611
Sebelius Kathleen (D) State Capitol Bldg 2nd Fl *Web:* www.ksgovernor.org	Topeka	KS	66612	785-296-3232	296-7973
Fletcher Ernie (R) State Capitol Bldg 700 Capitol Ave Rm 100 *Web:* governor.ky.gov	Frankfort	KY	40601	502-564-2611	564-2517
Jindal Bobby (R) PO Box 94004 *Web:* www.gov.state.la.us	Baton Rouge	LA	70804	225-342-7015	342-7099
Baldacci John (D) 1 State House Stn *Web:* www.maine.gov/governor	Augusta	ME	04333	207-287-3531	287-1034
Ehrlich Robert L Jr (R) State House 100 State Cir *TF:* 800-811-8336 ■ *Web:* www.gov.state.md.us	Annapolis	MD	21401	410-974-3901	974-3275
Romney Mitt (R) State House Executive Office Rm 360 *Web:* www.mass.gov	Boston	MA	02133	617-725-4000	727-9725
Granholm Jennifer (D) PO Box 30013 *Web:* www.michigan.gov/gov	Lansing	MI	48909	517-373-3400	335-6863
Pawlenty Tim (R) 130 State Capitol *TF:* 800-657-3717 ■ *Web:* www.governor.state.mn.us	Saint Paul	MN	55155	651-296-3391	296-2089
Barbour Haley (R) PO Box 139 *Web:* www.governorbarbour.com	Jackson	MS	39205	601-359-3150	359-3741
Blunt Matt (R) PO Box 720 *Web:* gov.missouri.gov	Jefferson City	MO	65102	573-751-3222	751-1495
Schweitzer Brian (D) PO Box 200801 *Web:* governor.mt.gov	Helena	MT	59620	406-444-3111	444-4151
Heineman David (R) PO Box 94848 *Web:* gov.nol.org	Lincoln	NE	68509	402-471-2244	471-6031
Guinn Kenny (R) 101 N Carson St *Web:* gov.state.nv.us	Carson City	NV	89701	775-684-5670	684-5683
Lynch John H (D) State House 107 N Main St Rm 208 *TF:* 800-852-3456 ■ *Web:* www.state.nh.us/governor	Concord	NH	03301	603-271-2121	271-7680
Corzine Jon (D) 125 W State St Box 001 *Web:* www.state.nj.us/governor	Trenton	NJ	08625	609-292-6000	292-3454
Richardson Bill (D) State Capitol Bldg 490 Old Santa Fe Trail Rm 400 *Web:* www.governor.state.nm.us	Santa Fe	NM	87501	505-827-3000	476-2226
Pataki George E (R) State Capitol Executive Chamber *Web:* www.state.ny.us/governor	Albany	NY	12224	518-474-8390	474-1513
Easley Michael F (D) 166 W Jones St 20301 MSC *Web:* www.governor.state.nc.us	Raleigh	NC	27699	919-733-5811	733-2120
Hoeven John (R) 600 E Boulevard Ave Dept 101 *Web:* governor.state.nd.us	Bismarck	ND	58505	701-328-2200	328-2205
Fitial Benigno (R) Office of the Governor CB 10007 Capitol Hill *Web:* net.saipan.com/cftemplates/executive	Saipan	MP	96950	670-664-2200	664-2211
Taft Bob (R) 77 S High St 30th Fl *Web:* governor.ohio.gov	Columbus	OH	43215	614-466-3555	466-9354
Henry Charles Bradford "Brad" (D) 2300 N Lincoln Blvd Rm 212 *Web:* www.gov.ok.gov	Oklahoma City	OK	73105	405-521-2342	521-3353
Kulongoski Ted (D) 900 Court St NE *Web:* www.governor.state.or.us	Salem	OR	97301	503-378-3111	378-6827
Rendell Edward G (D) 225 Main Capitol Bldg *Web:* www.governor.state.pa.us	Harrisburg	PA	17120	717-787-2500	772-8284
Acevedo-Vila Anibal (PPD) La Fortaleza *Web:* www.fortaleza.gobierno.pr	San Juan	PR	00901	787-725-7000	725-1472
Carcieri Don (R) State House *Web:* www.governor.state.ri.us	Providence	RI	02903	401-222-2080	273-5729
Sanford Mark (R) PO Box 12267 *Web:* www.scgovernor.com	Columbia	SC	29211	803-734-2100	734-5167
Rounds Mike (R) 500 E Capitol Ave *Web:* www.state.sd.us/governor	Pierre	SD	57501	605-773-3212	773-5844
Bredesen Phil (D) State Capitol 1st Fl *Web:* www.tennesseeanytime.org/governor	Nashville	TN	37243	615-741-2001	532-9711
Perry Rick (R) PO Box 12428 *Web:* www.governor.state.tx.us	Austin	TX	78711	512-463-2000	463-1849
Huntsman Jon M Jr (R) 210 State Capitol Complex Suite 220 *Web:* www.utah.gov/governor	Salt Lake City	UT	84114	801-538-1000	538-1528
Douglas James H (R) 109 State St 5th Fl *Web:* www.vermont.gov/governor	Montpelier	VT	05609	802-828-3333	828-3339
Turnbull Charles W (D) 21-22 Kongens Gade *Web:* www.nga.org	Saint Thomas	VI	00802	340-774-0001	774-1361
Kaine Tim (D) Patrick Henry Bldg 3rd Fl *Web:* www.governor.virginia.gov	Richmond	VA	23219	804-786-2211	371-6351
Gregoire Christine (D) 302 14th St SW PO Box 40002 *Web:* www.governor.wa.gov	Olympia	WA	98504	360-902-4111	753-4110
Manchin Joe III (D) State Capitol Bldg 1900 Kanawha Blvd E *Web:* www.wvgov.org	Charleston	WV	25305	304-558-2000	342-7025
Doyle Jim (D) State Capitol PO Box 7863 *Web:* www.wisgov.state.wi.us	Madison	WI	53707	608-266-1212	267-8983
Freudenthal David D (D) State Capitol 200 W 24th St Rm 124 *Web:* wyoming.gov/governor	Cheyenne	WY	82002	307-777-7434	632-3909

347 GRAPHIC DESIGN

SEE ALSO Typesetting & Related Services p. 2389

	City	State	Zip	Phone	Fax
3 Strikes Inc 1905 Elizabeth Ave	Rahway	NJ	07065	732-382-3820	382-4082
TF: 888-725-8483 ■ *Web:* www.3strikes.com					
Addis Group Inc 2515 9th St.	Berkeley	CA	94710	510-704-7500	704-7501
Web: www.addis.com					
Ambrosi & Assoc 200 W Jackson Blvd 6th Fl	Chicago	IL	60606	312-666-9200	666-8793
TF: 888-262-7674 ■ *Web:* www.ambrosi.com					
B & B Adcrafters Inc 1712 Marshall St NE	Minneapolis	MN	55413	612-788-9461	788-3253
TF: 888-788-9461 ■ *Web:* www.bbadcrafters.com					
Benchmark Imaging & Display 640 Busse Hwy	Park Ridge	IL	60068	847-292-5150	292-5159
TF: 800-626-3069 ■ *Web:* benchmarkimaging.com					
Bendsen Signs & Graphics Inc 2901 N Woodford St	Decatur	IL	62526	217-877-2345	877-2347
Web: www.bendsensigns.com					
BrandEquity International 2330 Washington St.	Newton	MA	02462	617-969-3150	969-1944
TF: 800-969-3150 ■ *Web:* www.brandequity.com					
Champion Awards Inc 3649 Winplace Rd.	Memphis	TN	38118	901-365-4830	365-2796
TF: 800-242-6781 ■ *Web:* www.champion-awards.com					
CMI Inc 1716 W Grand Ave.	Chicago	IL	60622	312-666-4000	666-4001
Web: www.cmiart.com					
Corporate Visions Inc 2000 M St NW 8th Fl	Washington	DC	20036	202-833-4333	833-4332
Web: www.corpvisions.com					
Creative Assoc 1 Snoopy Pl	Santa Rosa	CA	95403	707-546-7121	526-7361
Curran & Connors Inc 333 Marcus Blvd.	Hauppauge	NY	11788	631-435-0400	435-0422
Web: www.curran-connors.com					
Deskey Assoc Inc 120 E 8th St	Cincinnati	OH	45202	513-721-6800	639-7575
TF: 877-433-7539 ■ *Web:* www.deskey.com					
Dynamic Graphics Group 6000 N Forest Park Dr.	Peoria	IL	61614	309-688-8800	688-8809
TF: 800-255-8800 ■ *Web:* www.dynamicgraphics.com					
Flavia Publishing Inc 924 Anacapa St Suite B4	Santa Barbara	CA	93101	805-564-6907	966-9175
TF: 800-352-8424 ■ *Web:* www.flavia.com					
Girvin Inc 1601 2nd Ave 5th Fl.	Seattle	WA	98101	206-623-7808	674-7909
Web: www.girvindesign.com					
Great Lakes Graphics Inc 5555 W Howard St	Skokie	IL	60077	847-679-5757	679-6717
Web: www.glginc.com					
IDL Inc 420 Old William Penn Hwy	Monroeville	PA	15146	412-798-8180	793-1191
Web: www.idlpop.com					
Kane Graphical Corp 2255 W Logan Blvd	Chicago	IL	60647	773-384-1200	384-1207
TF: 800-992-2921 ■ *Web:* www.kanegraphical.com					
LSI Graphic Solutions 9260 Pleasantwood Ave NW	North Canton	OH	44720	330-494-9444	494-9991
Web: www.lsi-industries.com					
Mentus 6755 Mira Mesa Blvd Suite 123-137	San Diego	CA	92121	858-455-5500	455-6872
Web: www.mentusonline.com					
Metro Creative Graphics Inc 519 8th Ave	New York	NY	10018	212-947-5100	714-9139
TF: 800-223-1600 ■ *Web:* www.metrocreativegraphics.com					
NESCO Inc Service Group 6140 Parkland Blvd	Mayfield Heights	OH	44124	440-461-6000	449-3111
P & R Group 222 W Hubbard St	Chicago	IL	60610	312-329-9600	822-9592
Web: www.pandrgroup.com					
Payne Printery Inc 1101 Dallas Memorial Hwy	Dallas	PA	18612	570-675-1147	675-3159
TF: 800-724-3188					
Prism Studios Inc 2505 Kennedy St NE	Minneapolis	MN	55413	612-331-1000	331-4106
TF: 800-659-2001 ■ *Web:* www.prismstudios.com					
Signature Graphics Inc 1000 Signature Dr.	Porter	IN	46304	219-926-4994	926-7231
TF: 800-356-3235 ■ *Web:* www.signaturegraph.com					
Smith Design Assoc 205 Thomas St.	Glen Ridge	NJ	07028	973-429-2177	429-7119
Web: www.smithdesign.com					
Spire Inc 65 Bay St	Dorchester	MA	02125	617-426-3323	426-4114
TF: 800-653-3323 ■ *Web:* www.spire.net					
Subia Corp 6612 Gulton Ct NE	Albuquerque	NM	87109	505-345-2636	344-9177
TF: 800-275-2636 ■ *Web:* www.subia.com					
Unimac Graphics 350 Michele Pl	Carlstadt	NJ	07072	201-372-9650	372-9896
Web: www.unimacgraphics.com					
Vista Color Lab Inc 2048 Fulton Rd	Cleveland	OH	44113	216-651-2830	651-5004
TF: 800-890-0062 ■ *Web:* www.vistacolorimaging.com					
WBK Marketing & Design LLC					
537 E Pete Rose Way Suite 100	Cincinnati	OH	45202	513-784-0066	784-0986
Web: www.wbk.com					
Wesco Graphics Inc 410 E Grantline Rd Suite B	Tracy	CA	95376	209-832-1000	832-7800

348 GROCERY STORES

SEE ALSO Bakeries p. 1367; Convenience Stores p. 1559; Gourmet Specialty Shops p. 1692; Health Food Stores p. 1774; Ice Cream & Dairy Stores p. 1851; Wholesale Clubs p. 2415

	City	State	Zip	Phone	Fax
A & P 2 Paragon Dr.	Montvale	NJ	07645	201-573-9700	571-8820
Web: www.aptea.com					
Acme Markets Inc 75 Valley Stream Pkwy	Malvern	PA	19355	610-889-4000	889-3039
TF: 800-767-2312 ■ *Web:* www.acmemarkets.com					
Alaska Commercial Co 550 W 64th Ave Suite 200	Anchorage	AK	99518	907-273-4600	273-4800
TF: 800-478-4484 ■ *Web:* www.alaskacommercial.com					
Albany Public Markets 1000 S 2nd St.	Sunbury	PA	17801	570-286-4571	286-3286
TF: 800-662-5370					
Albertson's Inc 250 E Parkcenter Blvd	Boise	ID	83706	208-395-6200	395-6110*
NYSE: ABS ■ **Fax:* Mktg ■ *TF:* 888-746-7252 ■ *Web:* www.albertsons.com					
ALDI Inc 1200 N Kirk Rd	Batavia	IL	60510	630-879-8100	879-9901
TF: 800-388-2534 ■ *Web:* www.aldifoods.com					
Allen's of Hastings Inc 1115 W 2nd St	Hastings	NE	68901	402-463-5633	463-5730
Web: www.allensuperstore.com					
American Consumers Inc 55 Hannah Way	Rossville	GA	30741	706-861-3347	861-3364
TF: 800-742-3347					
Andronico's Market 1109 Washington Ave	Albany	CA	94706	510-559-2800	524-3601
Web: www.andronicos.com					
Atkinsons' Market Inc 451 4th St E.	Ketchum	ID	83340	208-726-5668	726-3603
Web: www.atkinsons.com					
Autry Greer & Sons Inc 2850 W Main St.	Prichard	AL	36612	251-457-8655	456-3744
TF: 800-477-9490 ■ *Web:* www.greers.com					
B & B Corporate Holdings Inc 927 US Hwy 301 S	Tampa	FL	33619	813-621-6411	626-4527*
**Fax:* Hum Res ■ *Web:* www.bnbch.com					
Baker's Supermarket Inc 5222 S 136th St.	Omaha	NE	68137	402-397-4321	331-1530
Balls Food Stores Inc 5300 Speaker Rd.	Kansas City	KS	66106	913-321-4223	551-8500
Web: www.henhouse.com					
Bashas Inc 22402 S Bashas Rd	Chandler	AZ	85248	480-895-9350	895-5292*
**Fax:* PR ■ *TF:* 800-755-7292 ■ *Web:* www.bashas.com					
BI-LO LLC PO Box 99.	Mauldin	SC	29662	864-213-5000	
Web: www.bi-lo.com					
Big Save Inc 4416 Waielo Rd PO Box 68	Eleele	HI	96705	808-335-3145	335-5049
Big Y Foods Inc 2145 Roosevelt Ave	Springfield	MA	01102	413-784-0600	732-8475
TF Cust Svc: 800-828-2688 ■ *Web:* www.bigy.com					
BiLo/Riverside Markets PO Box 607.	Du Bois	PA	15801	814-375-3663	375-2974
TF: 800-922-1026 ■ *Web:* www.bilofoods.com					
Bordner PJ Co Inc 2100 Wales Rd NE	Massillon	OH	44646	330-832-7522	832-9691
Bristol Farms 915 E 230th St	Carson	CA	90745	310-233-4700	233-4701
Web: www.bristolfarms.com					
Brookshire Brothers Ltd 1201 Ellen Trout Dr.	Lufkin	TX	75904	936-634-8155	633-4611
TF: 800-364-6690 ■ *Web:* www.brookshirebrothers.com					
Brookshire Grocery Co 1600 West SW Loop 323	Tyler	TX	75701	903-534-3000	
Web: www.brookshires.com					
Brown & Cole LLC 1331 Commercial St PO Box 9797	Bellingham	WA	98227	360-714-9797	
Web: www.brownandcole.com					
Brown & Cole Stores 1331 Commercial St.	Bellingham	WA	98225	360-714-9797	
TF: 800-743-0437 ■ *Web:* www.brownandcole.com					
Buehler Food Markets Inc 1401 Old Mansfield Rd	Wooster	OH	44691	330-264-4355	
Web: www.buehlers.com					
Buehler Foods Inc 1100 W 12th Ave	Jasper	IN	47547	812-482-1366	482-9806
Butera Finer Foods Inc 1 Clock Tower Plaza	Elgin	IL	60120	847-741-1010	741-9674
Web: www.buteramarket.com					
C & K Markets Inc DBA Ray's Food Place 615 5th St	Brookings	OR	97415	541-469-3113	469-6717
TF: 800-932-7297 ■ *Web:* www.ckmarket.com					
Calhoun Enterprises 4155 Lomac St Suite G	Montgomery	AL	36106	334-272-4400	272-7799
TF: 800-294-1995					
Camellia Foods 1300 Diamond Springs Rd Suite 500	Virginia Beach	VA	23445	757-855-3371	853-7405
Canada Safeway Ltd 1020 64th Ave NE	Calgary	AB	T2E7V8	403-730-3500	730-3902*
**Fax:* PR ■ *TF:* 888-310-1318 ■ *Web:* shop.safeway.com					
Capri IGA Foodliner 224 E Harris Ave	Greenville	IL	62246	618-664-0022	664-4629
Catalano's Stop & Shop 5612 Wilson Mills Rd	Highland Heights	OH	44143	440-442-8800	461-6759
TF: 800-991-5444 ■ *Web:* www.catalano.com					
Certi-Saver Supermarket 1 Certified Dr	Hodgkins	IL	60525	708-579-2100	354-7502
Web: www.certisaver.com					
Chief Super Market Inc 1340 W High St Suite E.	Defiance	OH	43512	419-782-0950	782-6047
City Market 555 Sandhill Ln	Grand Junction	CO	81503	970-241-0750	255-0941
Web: www.citymarket.com					
Clemens Markets Inc 1555 Bustard Rd PO Box 1555	Kulpsville	PA	19443	215-361-9000	393-9880*
**Fax:* Hum Res ■ *Web:* www.clemensmarkets.com					
Clines Corners Operating Co 1 Yacht Club Dr	Clines Corners	NM	87070	505-472-5488	472-5487
Coborn's Inc 1445 E Hwy 23	Saint Cloud	MN	56302	320-252-4222	252-0014
TF: 888-269-6201 ■ *Web:* www.cobornsinc.com					
Consun Food Industries Inc 123 N Gateway Blvd	Elyria	OH	44035	440-322-6301	322-8196
Cooke's Food Store Inc 3400 Keith St PO Box 2365	Cleveland	TN	37320	423-472-5034	479-6938
Covington Foods Inc 419 4th St PO Box 206	Covington	IN	47932	765-793-2470	793-0209
Crest Discount Foods Inc 249 N Douglas Blvd	Midwest City	OK	73130	405-733-2330	733-5126
Web: www.crestfoodsok.com					
Cub Foods Stores 421 S 3rd St PO Box 9	Stillwater	MN	55082	651-439-7200	779-2057
Web: www.cubfoods.com					
Dahl's Food Marts 4343 Merle Hay Rd	Des Moines	IA	50310	515-278-1657	278-0012
Dan's Supreme Supermarkets Inc 474 Fulton Ave	Hempstead	NY	11550	516-483-2400	483-1586
Decker's Food Center 631-A Commercial Dr	Gillette	WY	82716	307-682-5557	682-0402
Delsea Shop Rite 215 N Delsea Dr	Vineland	NJ	08360	856-691-9395	691-6167
Web: www.shoprite.com					
DeMoulas Super Markets Inc 875 East St	Tewksbury	MA	01876	978-851-8000	640-8390
Dierbergs Markets Inc 16690 Swingley Ridge Rd	Chesterfield	MO	63017	636-532-8884	812-1603
Web: www.dierbergs.com					
Dillon Cos Inc 2700 E 4th Ave	Hutchinson	KS	67501	620-665-5511	669-3169
TF: 877-283-6830					
Dominick's Finer Foods Inc 711 Jorie Blvd	Oak Brook	IL	60523	630-891-5000	891-5180*
**Fax:* PR ■ *TF:* 877-723-3929 ■ *Web:* www.dominicks.com					
Dorignac's Food Center Inc 710 Veterans Memorial Blvd	Metairie	LA	70005	504-837-4650	832-8944
Web: dorignacs.com					
Dorothy Lane Market Inc 2710 Far Hills Ave	Dayton	OH	45419	937-299-3561	299-3568
Web: www.dorothylane.com					
Double 8 Foods Inc 2201 E 46th St	Indianapolis	IN	46205	317-253-3417	257-0209
Web: www.double8foods.com					
Fareway Stores Inc 2300 E 8th St PO Box 70	Boone	IA	50036	515-432-2623	433-4416
Farmer Jack 18718 Borman Ave	Detroit	MI	48228	313-270-1226	
TF: 877-327-5225 ■ *Web:* www.farmerjack.com					
Felpausch Food Centers 127 S Michigan Ave	Hastings	MI	49058	269-945-3485	948-3499
TF: 800-648-6433 ■ *Web:* www.felpausch.com					
Fiesta Mart Inc 5235 Katy Fwy	Houston	TX	77007	713-869-5060	869-6197*
**Fax:* Cust Svc ■ *TF:* 877-256-5060 ■ *Web:* www.fiestamart.com					
Food City 22402 S Basha Rd PO Box 488	Chandler	AZ	85244	480-895-9350	895-5394*
**Fax:* Mktg ■ *TF:* 800-755-7292 ■ *Web:* www.myfoodcity.com					
Food Giant Supermarkets 120 Industrial Dr	Sikeston	MO	63801	573-471-3500	472-3135
TF: 800-388-3745					
Food Lion LLC 211 Executive Dr	Salisbury	NC	28147	704-633-8250	637-2581*
**Fax:* Hum Res ■ *Web:* www.foodlion.com					
Foodarama Supermarkets Inc 922 Hwy 33 Bldg 6 Suite 1	Freehold	NJ	07728	732-462-4700	294-2322
AMEX: FSM					
Foodland Super Market Ltd 3536 Harding Ave	Honolulu	HI	96816	808-732-0791	737-4583
Web: www.foodland.com					
Foodmaster Supermarkets Inc 100 Everett Ave Unit 12	Chelsea	MA	02150	617-660-1300	660-1399
Foods Inc 4343 Merle Hay Rd.	Des Moines	IA	50310	515-278-1657	278-0012
Four B Corp 5300 Speaker Rd.	Kansas City	KS	66106	913-321-4223	551-8500
Fred Meyer Inc PO Box 42121	Portland	OR	97242	503-232-8844	797-5395*
**Fax:* Cust Svc ■ *TF:* 800-858-9202 ■ *Web:* www.fredmeyer.com					
Fresh Brands Inc 2215 Union Ave PO Box 419	Sheboygan	WI	53081	920-457-4433	208-5000
TF: 800-530-7286 ■ *Web:* www.fresh-brands.com					
Fresh Encounter Inc 317 Main Cross St.	Findlay	OH	45840	419-422-8090	424-3932
Web: www.freshencounter.com					
FreshDirect Inc 23-30 Borden Ave	Long Island City	NY	11101	718-928-1000	928-1050
TF: 866-283-7674 ■ *Web:* www.freshdirect.com					
Fry's Food Stores of Arizona Inc 500 S 99th Ave	Tolleson	AZ	85353	623-936-2100	907-4966
TF: 800-828-5235 ■ *Web:* www.frysfood.com					
Gelson's Markets 2020 S Central Ave	Compton	CA	90220	310-638-2842	631-0950
Web: www.gelsons.com					
Genuardi's Family Markets Inc 301 E Germantown Pike	Norristown	PA	19401	610-277-6000	
TF Cust Svc: 877-723-3929 ■ *Web:* www.genuardis.com					
Gerland's Corp 3131 Pawnee St	Houston	TX	77054	713-746-3600	746-3621
Web: www.gerlands.com					
Giant Eagle Inc 101 Kappa Dr	Pittsburgh	PA	15238	412-963-6200	967-3700
TF Cust Svc: 800-553-2324 ■ *Web:* www.gianteagle.com					
Giant Food Inc 8301 Professional Pl Suite 115	Landover	MD	20785	301-341-4100	618-4998*
**Fax:* Cust Svc ■ *TF:* 888-469-4426 ■ *Web:* www.giantfood.com					
Giant Food Stores Inc 1149 Harrisburg Pike	Carlisle	PA	17013	717-249-4000	249-5871*
**Fax:* Mail Rm ■ *TF:* 800-814-4268 ■ *Web:* www.giantpa.com					
Golub Corp 501 Duanesburg Rd	Schenectady	NY	12306	518-355-5000	379-3515
Web: www.pricechopper.com					
Goodsons' Supermarkets Inc					
Rt 52 Premier Mountain PO Box 858	Welch	WV	24801	304-436-8482	436-6888
Grade A Markets Inc 563 Newfield Ave	Stamford	CT	06905	203-356-1662	961-8135
Great Atlantic & Pacific Co of Canada Ltd					
5559 Dundas St W.	Etobicoke	ON	M9B1B9	416-239-7171	234-6583*
**Fax:* Hum Res ■ *TF:* 800-268-2564 ■ *Web:* www.freshobsessed.com					

Company	City	State	ZIP	Phone	Fax
Great Atlantic & Pacific Tea Co Inc 2 Paragon Dr	Montvale	NJ	07645	201-573-9700	571-8820
NYSE: GAP ■ *Web:* www.aptea.com					
Gristede's Foods Inc 823 11th Ave	New York	NY	10019	212-956-5803	247-4509
Web: www.gristedes.com					
H-E-B Grocery Co 646 S Main Ave	San Antonio	TX	78204	210-938-8000	938-8169
Web: www.heb.com					
Haggen Inc PO Box 9704	Bellingham	WA	98227	360-733-8720	
Web: www.haggen.com					
Handy Andy Supermarkets 1500 S Zarzamora St Suite 512	San Antonio	TX	78207	210-227-8755	225-0991
Hannaford Bros Co 145 Pleasant Hill Rd	Scarborough	ME	04074	207-883-2911	
TF: 800-341-6393 ■ *Web:* www.hannaford.com					
Harmon City Inc 3540 S 4000 West Suite 500	West Valley City	UT	84120	801-969-8261	964-1299
Web: www.harmonsgrocery.com					
Harps Food Stores Inc 918 Gutensohn Rd	Springdale	AR	72762	479-751-7601	751-3625
TF: 877-772-8193 ■ *Web:* www.harpsfood.com					
Harris Teeter Inc 701 Crestdale Rd	Matthews	NC	28105	704-844-3100	
TF Cust Svc: 800-432-6111 ■ *Web:* www.harristeeter.com					
Harvest Foods 8109 I-30	Little Rock	AR	72209	501-570-0007	562-0792*
**Fax:* Hum Res ■ *Web:* www.harvestfoods.com					
HE Butt Grocery Co DBA H-E-B Grocery Co 646 S Main Ave	San Antonio	TX	78204	210-938-8000	938-8169
Web: www.heb.com					
Heinen's Inc 4540 Richmond Rd	Warrensville Heights	OH	44128	216-475-2300	514-4788
Web: www.heinens.com					
Hen House Market 5300 Speaker Rd	Kansas City	KS	66106	913-321-4223	551-8500
Web: www.henhouse.com					
HG Hill Stores Inc DBA S & C Foods 6604 Charlotte Ave	Nashville	TN	37209	615-352-6236	352-3749
Hi Nabor Supermarket Inc 7201 Winbourne Ave	Baton Rouge	LA	70805	225-357-1448	357-7109
Web: www.hinabor.com					
Hill HG Stores Inc DBA S & C Foods 6604 Charlotte Ave	Nashville	TN	37209	615-352-6236	352-3749
Homeland Stores 28 E 33rd St	Edmond	OK	73013	405-216-2200	216-2281
TF: 800-522-5658 ■ *Web:* www.homelandstores.com					
Hornbacher's 2510 N Broadway	Fargo	ND	58102	701-293-5444	293-8770
Web: www.hornbachers.com					
Houchens Industries Inc 700 Church St	Bowling Green	KY	42101	270-843-3252	
TF: 800-843-3252					
Huck's Convenient Food Stores 928 County Rd 1350 N	Carmi	IL	62821	618-382-2334	382-8956
TF: 800-876-2511 ■ *Web:* www.martinandbayley.com					
Hugo's 1925 13th Ave N	Grand Forks	ND	58203	701-772-5531	746-0913
Hy-Vee Inc 5820 Westown Pkwy	West Des Moines	IA	50266	515-267-2800	267-2817*
**Fax:* Mail Rm ■ *Web:* www.hy-vee.com					
Hyper Shoppes Inc 25 Whitney Dr Suite 122	Milford	OH	45150	513-248-9300	248-9731
IGA Inc 8725 W Higgins Rd Suite 725	Chicago	IL	60631	773-693-4520	693-1271
TF: 800-321-5442 ■ *Web:* www.iga.com					
Ingles Markets Inc 2913 US Hwy 70 W	Black Mountain	NC	28711	828-669-2941	669-3536
NASDAQ: IMKTA ■ *TF:* 800-635-5066 ■ *Web:* www.ingles-markets.com					
Inserra ShopRite 20 Ridge Rd	Mahwah	NJ	07430	201-529-5900	529-1189
Web: www.shoprite.com					
Jack Young's Supermarket Inc 3513 W Walnut Ave PO Box 3167	Visalia	CA	93278	559-625-9252	627-1945*
**Fax:* Acctg					
Jay C Food Stores 900-A Ave E	Seymour	IN	47274	812-522-1374	523-2103
JC Pace Ltd 420 Throckmorton St Suite 710	Fort Worth	TX	76102	817-332-1219	332-3296
Jerry Lee's Grocery Inc 1411 Hwy 90	Gautier	MS	39553	228-497-3281	497-1026
Jerry's Enterprises Inc 5101 Vernon Ave S	Minneapolis	MN	55436	952-922-8335	929-9281
Web: www.jerrysfoods.com					
Jewel Food Stores Inc 1955 W North Ave	Melrose Park	IL	60160	708-531-6000	531-6390*
**Fax:* Hum Res ■ *Web:* www.jewelosco.com					
K-VA-T Food Stores Inc 201 Trigg St	Abingdon	VA	24212	276-623-5100	623-5441
Web: www.foodcity.com					
Kash n' Karry Food Stores Inc 3801 Sugar Palm Dr	Tampa	FL	33619	813-620-1139	626-9550*
**Fax:* Mail Rm ■ *Web:* www.kashnkarry.com					
Kessler's Inc 621 6th Ave SE	Aberdeen	SD	57401	605-225-1692	225-0954
King Kullen Grocery Co Inc 185 Central Ave	Bethpage	NY	11714	516-733-7100	827-6325
Web: www.kingkullen.com					
Kirby Foods Inc 4102-B Fieldstone Rd PO Box 6268	Champaign	IL	61826	217-352-2600	352-9394
Web: www.kirbyfoods.com					
Kroger Co 1014 Vine St	Cincinnati	OH	45202	513-762-4000	762-1160*
NYSE: KR ■ **Fax:* Hum Res ■ *Web:* www.kroger.com					
KTA Super Stores 50 E Puainako St	Hilo	HI	96720	808-959-4575	959-8050
L & L Food Centers 4924 S ML King Jr Blvd	Lansing	MI	48910	517-887-1877	393-2477
Web: www.llfoodcenters.com/					
Loblaw Cos Ltd 22 St Clair Ave E	Toronto	ON	M4T2S7	416-922-8500	922-4395
TF: 877-525-4762 ■ *Web:* www.loblaw.com					
Logli Supermarkets 6410 E State St	Rockford	IL	61108	815-397-6080	397-9781
Web: www.logli.com					
Lowe's 1804 Hall Ave PO Box 1430	Littlefield	TX	79339	806-385-3366	385-8629
Web: www.lowesmarket.com					
Lowes Food Stores Inc 1381 Old Mill Cir Suite 200	Winston-Salem	NC	27103	336-659-0180	768-4702
TF: 800-669-5693 ■ *Web:* www.lowesfoods.com					
Mars Supermarkets Inc 3401 E Federal St	Baltimore	MD	21213	410-342-0197	
TF: 888-284-7773 ■ *Web:* www.marsfood.com					
Marsh Supermarkets Inc 9800 Crosspoint Blvd	Indianapolis	IN	46256	317-594-2100	594-2707
NASDAQ: MARSA ■ *Web:* www.marsh.net					
Martin & Bayley Inc DBA Huck's Convenient Food Stores 928 County Rd 1350 N	Carmi	IL	62821	618-382-2334	382-8956
TF: 800-876-2511 ■ *Web:* www.martinandbayley.com					
Martin's Marketplace 130 Tichenal Way	Cashmere	WA	98815	509-782-3801	782-2212
Web: www.martinsmarketplace.com					
Martin's SuperMarkets 760 W Cotter St	South Bend	IN	46613	574-234-5848	234-9827
TF: 800-910-7079 ■ *Web:* www.martins-supermarkets.com					
Mass Marketing Inc 401 Isom Rd Bldg 100	San Antonio	TX	78216	210-344-1960	341-6326
TF: 800-279-1149					
Meijer Inc 2929 Walker Ave NW	Grand Rapids	MI	49544	616-453-6711	453-6067
TF: 800-543-3704 ■ *Web:* www.meijer.com					
Meijer Stores Inc 2929 Walker Ave NW	Grand Rapids	MI	49544	616-453-6711	791-5131
TF: 800-543-3704 ■ *Web:* www.meijer.com					
Metro Inc 11011 boul Maurice Duplessis	Montreal	QC	H1C1V6	514-643-1000	
TF: 800-361-4681 ■ *Web:* www.metro.ca					
Meyer Fred Inc PO Box 42121	Portland	OR	97242	503-232-8844	797-5395*
**Fax:* Cust Svc ■ *TF:* 800-858-9202 ■ *Web:* www.fredmeyer.com					
Minyard Food Stores Inc 777 Freeport Pkwy	Coppell	TX	75019	972-393-8700	393-8550
Web: www.minyards.com					
Musser's Inc 35 Friendly Dr	Quarryville	PA	17566	717-284-4147	284-4145
Web: www.mussersmarket.com					
NETGROCER.com 14 Post Rd	Oakland	NJ	07436	201-337-3900	405-0578
TF: 888-638-4762 ■ *Web:* www.netgrocer.com					
Niemann Foods Inc 1501 N 12th St	Quincy	IL	62306	217-221-5600	221-5920
TF: 800-477-0156 ■ *Web:* www.discountfoods.com					
No Frills Supermarkets Inc 11163 Mills Alley Rd	Omaha	NE	68154	402-399-9244	399-0264
Nob Hill Foods 8420 Church St	Gilroy	CA	95020	408-842-6441	842-1583
TF: 800-725-3977 ■ *Web:* www.nobhill.com					
Nugget Markets 157 Main St	Woodland	CA	95695	530-662-5479	668-1246
Web: www.nuggetmarket.com					
Oleson's Food Stores 3860 N Long Lake Rd Suite A	Traverse City	MI	49684	231-947-6091	947-6548
Web: www.olesonsfoods.com					
O'Malia Food Markets Inc 9800 Crosspoint Blvd	Indianapolis	IN	46256	317-594-2100	594-2707
Web: www.omalias.com					
Overwaitea Food Group 19855 92A Ave	Langley	BC	V1M3B6	604-888-1213	
TF: 800-242-9229 ■ *Web:* www.owfg.com					
Owens RF Co Inc DBA Trucchi's Supermarkets 1062 Broadway	Raynham	MA	02767	508-824-7515	824-7576
Web: www.trucchis.com					
P & C Foods 1200 State Fair Blvd	Syracuse	NY	13209	315-457-9460	461-2353*
**Fax:* Mail Rm ■ *TF Cust Svc:* 800-724-0205 ■ *Web:* www.pandcfoods.com					
Pace JC Ltd 420 Throckmorton St Suite 710	Fort Worth	TX	76102	817-332-1219	332-3296
Pathmark Stores Inc 200 Milik St	Carteret	NJ	07008	732-499-3000	499-3072*
NASDAQ: PTMK ■ **Fax:* PR ■ *Web:* www.pathmark.com					
Peapod LLC 9933 Woods Dr	Skokie	IL	60077	847-583-9400	583-9494
TF: 800-573-2763 ■ *Web:* www.peapod.com					
Penn Traffic Co 1200 State Fair Blvd	Syracuse	NY	13209	315-453-7284	461-2387*
**Fax:* Acctg ■ *TF:* 800-275-9005 ■ *Web:* www.penntraffic.com					
Perlmart Inc 954 Rt 166	Toms River	NJ	08753	732-341-0700	240-9291
Piggly Wiggly Carolina Co Inc PO Box 118047	Charleston	SC	29423	843-554-9880	745-2730
TF: 800-243-9880 ■ *Web:* www.thepig.net					
Piggly Wiggly LLC 2605 Sagebrush Dr Suite 200	Flower Mound	TX	75028	972-410-2901	899-2905
TF: 800-800-8215 ■ *Web:* www.pigglywiggly.com					
Price Chopper Food Stores 5300 Speaker Rd	Kansas City	KS	66106	913-321-4223	551-8500
Web: www.mypricechopper.com					
Provigo Inc 400 St Croix Ave	Saint Laurent	QC	H4N3L4	514-383-3000	383-3100
TF: 800-261-1168 ■ *Web:* www.provigo.ca					
Publix Super Markets Inc 3300 Publix Corporate Pkwy	Lakeland	FL	33811	863-688-1188	284-5571*
**Fax:* Hum Res ■ *TF PR:* 800-342-1227 ■ *Web:* www.publix.com					
Pueblo International LLC 1300 NW 22nd St	Pompano Beach	FL	33069	954-977-2500	968-2648*
**Fax:* Hum Res ■ *Web:* www.puebloxtra.com					
Quality Food Centers Inc 10116 NE 8th St	Bellevue	WA	98004	425-455-3761	462-2162
TF: 800-335-0902 ■ *Web:* www.qfconline.com					
Quillin's Inc 700 N 3rd St Suite 105	La Crosse	WI	54601	608-785-1424	785-7175
Web: www.quillinsfoods.com					
Raley's 500 W Capitol Ave PO Cox 15618	Sacramento	CA	95852	916-373-3333	373-0881*
**Fax:* Cust Svc ■ *TF:* 800-925-9989 ■ *Web:* www.raleys.com					
Ralphs Grocery Co 1100 W Artesia Blvd	Compton	CA	90220	310-884-9000	884-2600
TF Cust Svc: 888-437-3496 ■ *Web:* www.ralphs.com					
Randalls Food Markets Inc PO Box 4506	Houston	TX	77210	713-268-3500	268-3602*
**Fax:* PR ■ *TF PR:* 877-475-3500 ■ *Web:* www.randalls.com					
Ray's Food Place 615 5th St	Brookings	OR	97415	541-469-3113	469-6717
TF: 800-932-7297 ■ *Web:* www.ckmarket.com					
Redner's Markets Inc 3 Quarry Rd	Reading	PA	19605	610-926-3700	926-6327
Web: www.rednersmarkets.com					
RF Owens Co Inc DBA Trucchi's Supermarkets 1062 Broadway	Raynham	MA	02767	508-824-7515	824-7576
Web: www.trucchis.com					
Rice Epicurean Markets Inc 5333 Gulfton St	Houston	TX	77081	713-662-7700	662-7757
Web: www.riceepicurean.com					
Riesbeck Food Markets Inc 48661 National Rd	Saint Clairsville	OH	43950	740-695-7050	695-7555
Web: www.riesbeckfoods.com					
Roberts Co Inc 1612 Adeline St	Hattiesburg	MS	39401	601-545-3411	545-1101
Roche Brothers Supermarkets Inc 70 Hastings St	Wellesley Hills	MA	02481	781-235-9400	235-3153
Web: www.rochebros.com					
Rosauers Super Markets Inc 1815 W Garland Ave	Spokane	WA	99205	509-326-8900	328-2483
Web: www.rosauers.com					
Roth's Family Markets 4895 Indian School Rd NE	Salem	OR	97305	503-393-7684	393-4456
TF: 800-722-7684 ■ *Web:* www.roths.com					
S & C Foods 6604 Charlotte Ave	Nashville	TN	37209	615-352-6236	352-3749
Safeway Inc 5918 Stoneridge Mall Rd	Pleasanton	CA	94588	925-467-3000	467-3321
NYSE: SWY ■ *Web:* www.safeway.com					
Save-A-Lot Ltd 100 Corporate Office Dr	Earth City	MO	63045	314-592-9100	592-9619
Web: www.save-a-lot.com					
Save Mart Supermarkets Inc PO Box 4278	Modesto	CA	95352	209-577-1600	577-3845*
**Fax:* Mktg ■ *Web:* www.savemart.com					
Schnuck Markets Inc 11420 Lackland Rd	Saint Louis	MO	63146	314-994-9900	994-4337
TF: 800-264-4400 ■ *Web:* www.schnucks.com					
Scolari's Food & Drug Co 255 S McCarran Blvd	Sparks	NV	89431	775-331-7700	331-0675
Web: www.scolaristores.com					
Scott's Food Stores Inc 4118 N Clinton St	Fort Wayne	IN	46805	260-483-9537	484-5034
Sedano's Supermarkets 3140 W 76th St	Hialeah	FL	33018	305-824-1034	556-6981
Web: www.sedanos.com					
Sentry Food Stores Inc 2304 W St Paul Ave	Waukesha	WI	53188	262-896-3640	896-3575
Web: www.sentryfoods.com					
Sherms Thunderbird Market Inc 753 S Grape St PO Box 1400	Medford	OR	97501	541-857-0850	857-0848
Shop 'n Save 10461 Manchester Rd	Kirkwood	MO	63122	314-984-0900	984-1390*
**Fax:* Hum Res ■ *TF:* 800-368-7052 ■ *Web:* www.shopnsave.com					
Shop-Rite Supermarkets Inc 55 Hannah Way PO Box 2328	Fort Oglethorpe	GA	30742	706-861-3347	861-3364
TF: 800-742-3347					
Shoppers Food & Pharmacy 4600 Forbes Blvd	Lanham	MD	20706	301-306-8600	
TF: 800-775-9888 ■ *Web:* www.shoppersfood.com					
ShopRite Supermarkets Inc 600 York St	Elizabeth	NJ	07207	908-527-3300	
TF: 800-746-7748 ■ *Web:* www.shoprite.com					
Smart & Final Inc 600 Citadel Dr	Commerce	CA	90040	323-869-7500	
NYSE: SMF ■ *TF:* 800-894-0511 ■ *Web:* www.smartandfinal.com					
Sobeys Inc 115 King St	Stellarton	NS	B0K1S0	902-752-8371	752-2960
TF Cust Svc: 888-944-0442 ■ *Web:* www.sobeys.ca					
Southern Family Markets 800 Lakeshore Pkwy	Birmingham	AL	35211	205-940-9400	912-4217*
**Fax:* Hum Res ■ *Web:* www.brunos.com					
Spartan Stores Inc 850 76th St SW PO Box 8700	Grand Rapids	MI	49518	616-878-2000	
NASDAQ: SPTN ■ *TF:* 800-343-4422 ■ *Web:* www.spartanstores.com					
Star Markets Ltd 1620 N School St	Honolulu	HI	96817	808-832-8400	832-8420
Web: www.star-markets.com					
Stater Bros Markets 21700 Barton Rd	Colton	CA	92324	909-783-5000	
Web: www.staterbros.com					
Stop Shop Save Food Markets 200 S Arlington Ave Suite 300	Baltimore	MD	21223	410-783-8180	783-8192
Stop & Shop Supermarket Co 1385 Hancock St	Quincy	MA	02169	781-380-8000	770-8190*
**Fax Area Code:* 617 ■ **Fax:* Hum Res ■ *Web:* www.stopandshop.com					
Sunset Food Mart Inc 1812 Green Bay Rd	Highland Park	IL	60035	847-432-5500	432-9335
Web: www.sunsetfoods.com					
Sunshine Market Inc 1492 Hwy 315	Wilkes-Barre	PA	18702	570-829-1392	829-6551
Web: www.sunshinesuperstore.com					
Super A Foods Inc 7200 Dominion Cir	Commerce	CA	90040	323-869-0600	869-0611
Web: www.superafoods.com					
SUPERVALU Inc 11840 Valley View Rd	Eden Prairie	MN	55344	952-828-4000	828-8998
NYSE: SVU ■ *TF Cust Svc:* 888-256-2800 ■ *Web:* www.supervalu.com					
Sure Save Supermarkets Ltd 16-586 Old Volcano Rd	Keaau	HI	96749	808-966-9009	966-6200
Web: www.suresave.com					
Tamura Superette Inc DBA Tamura Supermarket 86032 Farrington Hwy	Waianae	HI	96792	808-696-3321	696-8127
Tamura Supermarket 86032 Farrington Hwy	Waianae	HI	96792	808-696-3321	696-8127
Thruway Food Market & Shopping Center 78 Oak St	Walden	NY	12586	845-778-3535	778-3659
Web: www.shopthruway.com					
Times Super Market Ltd 3375 Koapaka St Suite D108	Honolulu	HI	96819	808-831-0811	831-0830
Web: timessupermarkets.com					
Tom's Food Markets Inc 1311 S Division St	Traverse City	MI	49684	231-946-6431	
Web: www.toms-foodmarkets.com					

	City	State	Zip	Phone	Fax
Tops Markets Inc PO Box 1027 *TF:* 800-522-2522 ■ *Web:* www.topsmarkets.com	Buffalo	NY	14240	716-635-5000	
Trader Joe's Co 800 S Shamrock Ave *Web:* www.traderjoes.com	Monrovia	CA	91016	626-599-3700	
Treasure Island Foods Inc 3460 N Broadway Ave	Chicago	IL	60657	773-327-4265	327-6337
Trucchi's Supermarkets 1062 Broadway *Web:* www.trucchis.com	Raynham	MA	02767	508-824-7515	824-7576
Ukrop's Super Markets Inc 2001 Maywill St Suite 100 **Fax:* Hum Res ■ *TF:* 800-868-2270 ■ *Web:* www.ukrops.com	Richmond	VA	23230	804-340-3000	340-5198*
United Supermarkets Ltd 7830 Orlando Ave *Web:* www.unitedtexas.com	Lubbock	TX	79423	806-791-0220	791-7491
United Supermarkets of Oklahoma Inc 1604 N Main St *Web:* www.unitedok.com	Altus	OK	73521	580-482-1414	480-3011
Uwajimaya Inc 600 5th Ave S *TF:* 800-889-1928 ■ *Web:* www.uwajimaya.com	Seattle	WA	98104	206-624-6248	405-2996
Valley Markets Inc DBA Hugo's 1925 13th Ave N	Grand Forks	ND	58203	701-772-5531	746-0913
Valu Discount Inc DBA Valu Market 315 Whittington Pkwy *Web:* www.valumarkets.com	Louisville	KY	40223	502-423-7110	426-3731
Valu Market 315 Whittington Pkwy *Web:* www.valumarkets.com	Louisville	KY	40223	502-423-7110	426-3731
Valueland 949 Four Mile Rd	Walker	MI	49544	616-784-3633	784-3899
Village Super Market Inc 733 Mountain Ave *NASDAQ: VLGEA*	Springfield	NJ	07081	973-467-2200	467-6582
Vons Cos Inc 618 Michillinda Ave *TF:* 877-723-3929 ■ *Web:* www.vons.com	Arcadia	CA	91007	626-821-7000	821-7000
Wayne Lee's Grocery & Market 1317 Telephone Rd	Pascagoula	MS	39567	228-762-4101	762-1438
Wegmans Food Markets Inc 1500 Brooks Ave **Fax:* Mail Rm ■ *TF:* 800-934-6267 ■ *Web:* www.wegmans.com	Rochester	NY	14624	585-328-2550	464-4626*
Weis Markets Inc 1000 S 2nd St *NYSE: WMK* ■ *Web:* www.weis.com	Sunbury	PA	17801	570-286-4571	286-3286
Western Beef Inc 47-05 Metropolitan Ave *Web:* www.westernbeef.com	Flushing	NY	11385	718-417-3770	628-2356
Western Supermarkets Inc 2614 19th St S *Web:* www.westernsupermarkets.com	Birmingham	AL	35209	205-879-3471	879-3476
White's Discount Food Market Corp 125 Lamont St	Johnson City	TN	37604	423-926-0779	926-9607
White's Fresh Foods Inc 125 Lamont St	Johnson City	TN	37604	423-926-0779	926-9607
Wilson Mills DBA Catalano's Stop & Shop 5612 Wilson Mills Rd *TF:* 800-991-5444 ■ *Web:* www.catalano.com	Highland Heights	OH	44143	440-442-8800	461-6759
WinCo Foods Inc 650 N Armstrong Pl *TF:* 800-635-5167 ■ *Web:* www.wincofoods.com	Boise	ID	83705	208-377-0110	377-0474
Winegars Super Markets Inc 574 W 3400 South	Bountiful	UT	84010	801-298-5407	298-5463
Winn-Dixie Stores Inc 5050 Edgewood Ct **Fax:* Mail Rm ■ *Web:* www.winn-dixie.com	Jacksonville	FL	32254	904-783-5000	783-5294*
Wyndall's Enterprises Inc 3232 Villa Point *Web:* www.wyndalls.com	Owensboro	KY	42303	270-684-9493	926-0407
Yokes Foods Inc 3426 S University Rd Suite 200 *Web:* www.yokesfoods.com	Spokane	WA	99206	509-921-2292	921-6801
Zallie Supermarkets 1230 Blackwood-Clementon Rd	Clementon	NJ	08021	856-627-6501	627-8650

349 GYM & PLAYGROUND EQUIPMENT

	City	State	Zip	Phone	Fax
American Athletic Inc 200 American Ave *TF:* 800-247-3978 ■ *Web:* www.americanathletic.com	Jefferson	IA	50129	515-386-3125	386-8737
American Playground Corp 6406 Production Dr *TF:* 800-541-1602 ■ *Web:* www.american-playground.com	Anderson	IN	46013	765-642-0288	649-7162
BCI Burke Co Inc 660 Van Dyne Rd *TF:* 800-356-2070 ■ *Web:* www.bciburke.com	Fond du Lac	WI	54937	920-921-9220	921-9566
Columbia Cascade Co 1975 SW 5th Ave *TF:* 800-547-1940 ■ *Web:* www.timberform.com	Portland	OR	97201	503-223-1157	223-4530
Draper Shade & Screen Co 411 S Pearl St *TF:* 800-238-7999 ■ *Web:* www.draperinc.com	Spiceland	IN	47385	765-987-7999	987-7142
Florida Playground & Steel Co 4701 S 50th St *TF:* 800-444-2655 ■ *Web:* www.fla-playground.com	Tampa	FL	33619	813-247-2812	247-1068
Game-Time Inc 150 Gametime Dr **Fax:* Hum Res ■ *TF Sales:* 800-235-2440 ■ *Web:* www.gametime.com	Fort Payne	AL	35968	256-845-5610	997-5408*
Grounds For Play Inc 1401 E Dallas St *TF:* 800-552-7529 ■ *Web:* www.groundsforplay.com	Mansfield	TX	76063	817-477-5482	477-1140
Howell Playground Equipment Inc 1714 E Fairchild *TF Orders:* 800-637-5075	Danville	IL	61832	217-442-0482	442-8944
Jaypro Sports Inc 976 Hartford Tpke *TF Cust Svc:* 800-243-0533 ■ *Web:* www.jaypro.com	Waterford	CT	06385	860-447-3001	444-1779
Koala Corp 7881 S Wheeling Ct *TF:* 888-733-3456 ■ *Web:* www.koala-corporation.com	Englewood	CO	80112	303-539-8300	539-8399
Landscape Structures Inc 601 7th St S *TF:* 800-328-0035 ■ *Web:* www.playlsi.com	Delano	MN	55328	763-972-3391	972-3185
Miracle Recreation Equipment Co 878 Hwy 60 *TF:* 800-523-4202 ■ *Web:* www.miracle-recreation.com	Monett	MO	65708	417-235-6917	235-3551
PlayCore Inc 430 Chestnut St Suite 300 **Fax Area Code:* 877 ■ *TF:* 888-404-5737 ■ *Web:* www.playcore.com	Chattanooga	TN	37402	423-756-0015	762-7565*
Playworld Systems Inc 1000 Buffalo Rd *TF:* 800-233-8404 ■ *Web:* www.playworldsystems.com	Lewisburg	PA	17837	570-522-9800	522-3030
PW Athletic Mfg Co 140 N Gilbert Rd *TF:* 800-687-5768 ■ *Web:* www.pwathletic.com	Mesa	AZ	85203	928-778-4232	962-5290
Recreation Creation Inc 215 W Mechanic St *TF Cust Svc:* 800-766-9458 ■ *Web:* www.rec-creations.com	Hillsdale	MI	49242	517-439-1591	439-1878
School-Tech Inc 745 State Cir Box 1941 **Fax Area Code:* 800 ■ *TF:* 800-521-2832 ■ *Web:* www.school-tech.com	Ann Arbor	MI	48106	734-761-5072	654-4321*
SportsPlay Equipment Inc 5642 Natural Bridge Ave *TF:* 800-727-8180 ■ *Web:* www.sportsplayinc.com	Saint Louis	MO	63120	314-389-4140	389-9034
Swing-N-Slide Corp 1212 Barberry Dr *TF:* 800-888-1232 ■ *Web:* www.swing-n-slide.com	Janesville	WI	53545	608-755-4777	755-4773
Ultra Play Systems Inc 1675 Locust St *TF:* 800-458-5872 ■ *Web:* www.ultraplay.com	Red Bud	IL	62278	618-282-8200	282-8202
WOW Playgrounds 2851 Polk St *TF:* 800-432-2283 ■ *Web:* www.wowplaygrounds.com	Hollywood	FL	33020	954-925-2800	925-0800

350 GYPSUM PRODUCTS

	City	State	Zip	Phone	Fax
American Gypsum Co 3811 Turtle Creek Blvd Suite 1200 *TF:* 866-439-5800 ■ *Web:* www.americangypsum.com	Dallas	TX	75219	214-530-5500	
BPB 2424 Lakeshore Rd W *TF:* 866-272-8722 ■ *Web:* www.westroc.com	Mississauga	ON	L5J1K4	905-823-9881	823-4860
BPB Gypsum 27442 Portola Pkwy Suite 100 *TF:* 800-426-3669 ■ *Web:* www.us.bpb-na.com/index2.html	Foothill Ranch	CA	92610	949-282-5300	282-5334
Canadian Gypsum Co Inc 350 Burnhamthorpe Rd W 5th Fl *Web:* www.cgcinc.com	Mississauga	ON	L5B3J1	905-803-5600	803-5688
Eagle Materials Inc 3811 Turtle Creek Blvd Suite 1100 *NYSE: EXP* ■ *TF:* 800-759-7625 ■ *Web:* www.eaglematerials.com	Dallas	TX	75219	214-432-2000	432-2100
G-P Gypsum Corp 133 Peachtree St NE **Fax:* Sales ■ *Web:* www.gp.com/gypsum	Atlanta	GA	30303	404-652-4000	586-8140*
Georgia-Pacific Corp 133 Peachtree St NE *Web:* www.gp.com	Atlanta	GA	30303	404-652-4000	230-5774
Hamilton Materials Inc 345 W Meats Ave *TF:* 800-331-5569 ■ *Web:* www.hamiltonmaterials.com	Orange	CA	92865	714-637-2770	627-9033
Lafarge North America Inc 12950 Worldgate Dr Suite 600 *NYSE: LAF* ■ *Web:* www.lafargenorthamerica.com	Herndon	VA	20170	703-480-3600	796-2214
National Gypsum Co 2001 Rexford Rd *TF:* 800-628-4662 ■ *Web:* www.national-gypsum.com	Charlotte	NC	28211	704-365-7300	365-7579
PABCO Gypsum 37849 Cherry St *TF:* 800-829-1577 ■ *Web:* pabcogypsum.paccoast.com	Newark	CA	94560	510-792-1577	797-8820
US Gypsum Co 125 S Franklin St *TF:* 800-621-9622	Chicago	IL	60606	312-606-4000	606-4093
USG Corp 125 S Franklin St *NYSE: USG* ■ *TF:* 800-621-9622 ■ *Web:* www.usg.com	Chicago	IL	60606	312-606-4000	606-4093

351 HAIRPIECES, WIGS, TOUPEES

	City	State	Zip	Phone	Fax
Afro World Hair Goods Inc 7276 Natural Bridge Rd *TF:* 800-228-9424 ■ *Web:* www.afroworld.com	Saint Louis	MO	63121	314-389-5194	389-8508
Alfieri Charles Studio 4390 N Federal Hwy Suite 203 *TF:* 800-321-2413 ■ *Web:* charlesalfieri.com	Fort Lauderdale	FL	33308	954-928-1755	928-1858
Alkinco 129 W 29th St *TF:* 800-424-7118 ■ *Web:* www.alkincohair.com	New York	NY	10001	212-719-3070	764-7804
Alternatives 2000 2175 California St PO Box 360 *Web:* www.onthetop.com	Sutter	CA	95982	530-673-8004	673-1471
Amekor Industries 500 Brook Rd Suite 100 *TF:* 800-345-6332 ■ *Web:* www.amekor.com	Conshohocken	PA	19428	610-825-6747	834-8427
Charles Alfieri Studio 4390 N Federal Hwy Suite 203 *TF:* 800-321-2413 ■ *Web:* charlesalfieri.com	Fort Lauderdale	FL	33308	954-928-1755	928-1858
Eva Gabor International Ltd 5900 Equitable Rd *TF:* 800-236-0326	Kansas City	MO	64120	816-231-3700	231-8030
Freeda Wigs 1524 Union St *Web:* www.freeda.com	Brooklyn	NY	11213	718-771-2000	756-1503
Headcovers Unlimited 35-B Tiffany Plaza *Web:* www.headcovers.com	Ardmore	OK	73401	580-226-5871	226-8632
Headstart Hair For Men Inc 3395 Cypress Gardens Rd *TF:* 800-645-6525 ■ *Web:* www.headstarthairformen.com	Winter Haven	FL	33884	863-324-5559	324-5673
Henry Margu Inc 540 Commerce Dr *TF:* 800-345-8284	Yeadon	PA	19050	610-622-0515	259-6541
HPH Corp 1529 SE 47th Terr *TF:* 800-654-9884 ■ *Web:* www.discounthairpiece.com	Cape Coral	FL	33904	239-540-0085	540-0892
Jacquelyn Wigs 15 W 37th St 4th Fl *TF:* 800-272-2424 ■ *Web:* www.jacquelynwigs.com	New York	NY	10018	212-302-2266	302-0991
Jean Paree Weegs Inc 4041 S 700 East Suite 2 *TF Orders:* 800-422-9447 ■ *Web:* www.jeanparee.com	Salt Lake City	UT	84107	801-328-9756	261-2047
Jon Renau Collection 2510 Island View Way *TF:* 800-462-9447 ■ *Web:* www.jonrenau.com	Vista	CA	92081	760-598-0067	598-1205
Knight Peggy Solutions Inc 180 Harbor Dr Suite 221 *TF:* 800-997-7753 ■ *Web:* www.peggyknight.com	Sausalito	CA	94965	415-289-1777	331-8839
Look of Love International 555-A N Michigan Ave *TF:* 800-526-7627 ■ *Web:* www.lookoflove.com	Kenilworth	NJ	07033	908-687-9502	687-9509
Louis Ferre Inc 302 5th Ave 10th Fl *TF:* 800-695-1061 ■ *Web:* www.louisferre.com	New York	NY	10001	212-239-1600	239-1601
National Fiber Technology LLC 300 Canal St *TF:* 800-842-2751 ■ *Web:* www.nftech.com	Lawrence	MA	01840	978-686-2964	686-1497
Peggy Knight Solutions Inc 180 Harbor Dr Suite 221 *TF:* 800-997-7753 ■ *Web:* www.peggyknight.com	Sausalito	CA	94965	415-289-1777	331-8839
Rene Of Paris 15551 Cabrito Rd *TF:* 800-353-7363 ■ *Web:* www.reneofparis.com	Van Nuys	CA	91406	818-908-3100	988-2496
TressAllure/General Wig 5800 NW 163rd St *TF:* 800-777-9447 ■ *Web:* www.tressallure.com	Miami Lakes	FL	33014	305-823-0600	823-0626
Troika International Inc 1555 Los Palos St *TF:* 800-787-6452 ■ *Web:* www.troikawig.com	Los Angeles	CA	90023	323-415-0199	415-0198
Wig America Co 265 McCone Ave *TF:* 800-338-7600 ■ *Web:* www.wigamerica.com	Hayward	CA	94545	510-887-9579	887-9574
World of Wigs 2305 E 17th St *TF:* 800-794-5572 ■ *Web:* www.worldofwigs.com	Santa Ana	CA	92705	714-547-4461	547-6063
Yaffa Wigs 4118 13th Ave *TF:* 800-233-0660 ■ *Web:* www.yaffawigs.com	Brooklyn	NY	11219	718-436-4280	436-1601
YK International Co 3246 W Montrose Ave *TF:* 800-621-0086	Chicago	IL	60618	773-583-5270	583-5272

352 HANDBAGS, TOTES, BACKPACKS

SEE ALSO Leather Goods - Personal p. 1889; Luggage, Bags, Cases p. 1923; Sporting Goods p. 2323; Tarps, Tents, Covers p. 2338

	City	State	Zip	Phone	Fax
Accurate Flannel Bag Co 35-37 36th St 6th Fl *TF:* 800-234-9200	Long Island City	NY	11106	718-784-7600	784-7647
Allegro Mfg Inc 7250 E Oxford Way *TF:* 800-833-5562 ■ *Web:* www.allegromfg.com	Commerce	CA	90040	323-724-0101	722-7341
Anchor Industries Inc 1100 Burch Dr *TF:* 800-544-4445 ■ *Web:* www.anchorinc.com	Evansville	IN	47725	812-867-2421	867-1429
Atchison Products Inc 201 Main St *Web:* www.atchisonbags.com	Atchison	KS	66002	913-367-6431	367-7353
Dow Cover Co Inc 373 Lexington Ave *TF:* 800-735-8877 ■ *Web:* www.dowcover.com	New Haven	CT	06513	203-469-5394	469-0742
Eastpak Corp PO Box 1817 *Web:* www.eastpak.com	Appleton	WI	54912	800-222-5725	
Etienne Aigner Group Inc 47 Brunswick Ave *TF:* 800-537-7463 ■ *Web:* www.etienneaigner.com	Edison	NJ	08818	732-248-9200	248-1296
Fabriko Inc 318 E Confederate Blvd **Fax Area Code:* 866 ■ *TF:* 800-558-0242 ■ *Web:* www.fabriko.com	Appomattox	VA	24522	434-352-7145	243-9862*
Gucci Group Inc 50 Hartz Way **Fax:* Hum Res ■ *Web:* www.guccigroup.com	Secaucus	NJ	07094	201-867-8800	617-2398*
Innovo Group Inc 2633 Kingston Pike Suite 100 *NASDAQ: INNO* ■ *TF:* 800-627-2621 ■ *Web:* www.innovogroup.com	Knoxville	TN	37919	865-546-1110	546-9277
JanSport Inc N 850 County Hwy CB *TF Cust Svc:* 800-346-8239 ■ *Web:* www.jansport.com	Appleton	WI	54914	920-734-5708	735-1933
Judith Leiber LLC 600 Madison Ave 17th Fl *Web:* www.judithleiber.com	New York	NY	10022	212-736-4244	736-4331
Kate Spade 48 W 25th St 7th Fl *Web:* www.katespade.com	New York	NY	10010	212-739-6550	

Company	City	State	Zip	Phone	Fax
LBU Inc 217 Brook Ave	Passaic	NJ	07055	973-773-4800	773-6005
TF: 800-678-4528 ■ *Web:* www.lbuinc.com					
LeSportsac Inc 358 5th Ave 8th Fl	New York	NY	10001	212-736-6262	643-8009
TF: 800-486-2247 ■ *Web:* www.lesportsac.com					
North Face Inc 2013 Farallon Dr	San Leandro	CA	94577	510-618-3500	618-3571*
**Fax:* Sales ■ *TF:* 800-535-3331 ■ *Web:* www.thenorthface.com					
Ohio Bag Corp 30 O'Connor Cir	West Orange	NJ	07052	973-669-0990	669-0991
Web: www.ohiobag.com					
Regal Bag Corp 302 N Water St	Newburgh	NY	12550	845-562-4922	565-0927
Salomon North America 5055 N Greeley Ave	Portland	OR	97217	971-234-2300	234-2450
TF: 877-272-5666 ■ *Web:* www.salomonsports.com					
SeamCraft Inc 932 W Dakin St	Chicago	IL	60613	773-281-5150	975-9200
TF: 800-322-2441 ■ *Web:* www.seamcraft.com					
Service Mfg Corp 5414 W Roosevelt Rd	Chicago	IL	60644	773-287-5500	287-5585
TF: 800-338-7082 ■ *Web:* www.servicemfg.com					
Spade Kate 48 W 25th St 7th Fl	New York	NY	10010	212-739-6550	
Web: www.katespade.com					
Vera Bradley Designs 2208 Production Rd	Fort Wayne	IN	46808	260-482-4673	484-2278
TF: 800-975-8372 ■ *Web:* www.verabradley.com					

353 HARDWARE - MFR

Company	City	State	Zip	Phone	Fax
Adams Rite Mfg Co 260 W Santa Fe St	Pomona	CA	91767	909-632-2300	632-2370
TF: 800-872-3267 ■ *Web:* www.adamsrite.com					
AdelWiggins Group 5000 Triggs St	Los Angeles	CA	90022	323-269-9181	269-3759
Web: www.adelwiggins.com					
AL Hansen Mfg Co 701 Pershing Rd	Waukegan	IL	60085	847-244-8900	244-7222
Web: www.alhansen.com					
Amerock Corp 6350 Stevens Forest Rd	Columbia	MD	21046	410-423-1600	423-1692*
**Fax:* Sales ■ *TF Cust Svc:* 800-435-6959 ■ *Web:* www.amerock.com					
AmerTac 1 Rt 17 S	Saddle River	NJ	07458	201-934-3224	934-3224
Web: www.amertac.com					
AmerTac DBA AmerTac 1 Rt 17 S	Saddle River	NJ	07458	201-934-3224	934-3224
Web: www.amertac.com					
Anderson Electrical Products Inc PO Box 455	Leeds	AL	35094	205-699-2411	699-5150
TF: 800-423-0730 ■ *Web:* www.hubbell.com					
Arrow Lock Co 100 Arrow Dr	New Haven	CT	06511	800-839-3157	421-6615
TF: 800-221-6529 ■ *Web:* www.arrowlock.com					
ASSA Inc 110 Sargent Dr	New Haven	CT	06511	203-603-5958	892-3256*
**Fax Area Code:* 800 ■ *TF:* 800-235-7482 ■ *Web:* www.assalock.com					
Atco Products Inc 189-V Frelinghuysen Ave	Newark	NJ	07114	973-242-5757	242-0131
Web: www.atcoproducts.com					
Attwood Corp 1016 N Monroe St	Lowell	MI	49331	616-897-9241	897-8358
Web: www.attwoodmarine.com					
Baldwin Hardware Corp 841 E Wyomissing Blvd	Reading	PA	19611	610-777-7811	796-4600
TF: 800-437-7448 ■ *Web:* www.baldwinhardware.com					
Band-It-IDEX Inc 4799 Dahlia St	Denver	CO	80216	303-320-4555	333-6549
TF: 800-525-0758 ■ *Web:* www.band-it-idex.com					
Baron Mfg Co 1200 Capitol Dr	Addison	IL	60101	630-628-9110	628-9141
TF: 800-368-8585 ■ *Web:* www.baronsnaps.com					
Basic Industries International Inc 302 S Milliken Ave Suite F	Ontario	CA	91761	909-390-6782	605-7647
Web: www.basicindustriesinc.com					
Belwith International Ltd 3100 Broadway Ave	Grandville	MI	49418	800-235-9484	858-2119
Web: www.belwith.com					
Best Lock Corp 6161 E 75th St	Indianapolis	IN	46250	317-849-2250	845-7651
Web: www.bestlock.com					
Bete Fog Nozzle Inc 50 Greenfield St	Greenfield	MA	01301	413-772-0846	772-6729
TF: 800-235-0049 ■ *Web:* www.bete.com					
Bomar Inc PO Box 1200	Charlestown	NH	03603	603-826-5794	826-4125
Web: www.pompanette.com/bomar					
Bommer Industries Inc PO Box 187	Landrum	SC	29356	864-457-3301	457-2487
TF: 800-334-1654 ■ *Web:* www.bommer.com					
Bourdon Forge Co Inc 99 Tuttle Rd	Middletown	CT	06457	860-632-2740	632-7247
Web: www.bourdonforge.com					
Brainerd Mfg Co Inc 140 Business Pk Dr	Winston-Salem	NC	27107	336-769-4077	771-6077*
**Fax:* Cust Svc ■ *TF:* 800-652-7277					
Breeze Industrial Products Corp 3582 Tunnelton Rd	Saltsburg	PA	15681	724-639-3571	639-3020
Web: www.breezeclamps.com					
Bronze Craft Corp 37 Will St	Nashua	NH	03060	603-883-7747	883-0222
TF: 800-488-7747 ■ *Web:* www.bronzecraft.com					
Chamberlain Group 845 Larch Ave	Elmhurst	IL	60126	630-279-3600	530-6091
TF: 800-282-6225 ■ *Web:* www.chamberlaingroup.com					
Charles Leonard Inc 145 Kennedy Dr	Hauppauge	NY	11788	631-273-4600	273-4222
TF: 800-999-7202 ■ *Web:* www.charlesleonard.com					
Charles Leonard Western Inc 235 W 140th St	Los Angeles	CA	90061	310-715-7464	715-7474
Charles Ramsey Co PO Box 2264	Kingston	NY	12402	845-338-1464	338-5751
Chicago Hardware & Fixture Co 9100 Parklane Ave	Franklin Park	IL	60131	847-455-6609	455-0012
Web: www.chicagohardware.com					
Collier-Keyworth Co PO Box 1109	Liberty	NC	27298	336-622-0120	622-0150
Colonial Bronze Co 511 Winsted Rd	Torrington	CT	06790	860-489-9233	482-8760
TF: 800-355-7894 ■ *Web:* www.colonialbronze.com					
Component Hardware Group Inc PO Box 2020	Lakewood	NJ	08701	732-363-4700	364-8110
TF: 800-526-3694 ■ *Web:* www.componenthardware.com					
CompX International Inc PO Box 200	Mauldin	SC	29662	864-297-6655	286-1698
NYSE: CIX ■ *Web:* www.compx.com					
Craft Inc PO Box 3049	South Attleboro	MA	02703	508-761-7917	399-7240
TF: 800-827-2388 ■ *Web:* www.craft-inc.com					
Daniel Edward W Co Inc 11700 Harvard Ave	Cleveland	OH	44105	216-295-2750	295-2758
TF Cust Svc: 800-338-2658 ■ *Web:* www.ewdaniel.com					
Dayton Superior Corp 7777 Washington Village Dr Suite 130	Dayton	OH	45459	937-428-6360	428-9115
TF: 877-632-9866 ■ *Web:* www.daytonsuperior.com					
DE-STA-CO 1025 Doris Rd	Auburn Hills	MI	48326	248-836-6700	836-6741*
**Fax:* Sales ■ *TF:* 888-337-8226 ■ *Web:* www.destaco.com					
Detmar Corp 2001 W Alexandrine Ave PO Box 08098	Detroit	MI	48208	313-831-1155	831-0624
Web: www.detmarcorp.com					
Dixie Industries PO Box 180600	Chattanooga	TN	37406	423-698-3323	622-3058
TF: 800-933-4943					
Dor-O-Matic Inc 121 W Railroad Ave	Princeton	IL	61356	815-875-3311	666-0472*
**Fax Area Code:* 800 ■ **Fax:* Sales ■ *TF:* 800-543-4635 ■ *Web:* www.doromatic.com					
DORMA Group North America Dorma Dr	Reamstown	PA	17567	717-336-3881	336-2106
TF: 800-523-8483					
Eastern Co 112 Bridge St	Naugatuck	CT	06770	203-729-2255	723-8653
AMEX: EML ■ *Web:* www.easterncompany.com					
Eberhard Mfg Co PO Box 368012	Cleveland	OH	44149	440-238-9720	572-2732
Web: www.eberhard.com					
Edward W Daniel Co Inc 11700 Harvard Ave	Cleveland	OH	44105	216-295-2750	295-2758
TF Cust Svc: 800-338-2658 ■ *Web:* www.ewdaniel.com					
Engineered Products Co PO Box 108	Flint	MI	48501	810-767-2050	767-5084
TF: 888-414-3726 ■ *Web:* www.epcohardware.com					
ER Wagner Mfg Co Inc 4611 N 32nd St	Milwaukee	WI	53209	414-871-5080	449-8228
TF: 800-558-5596 ■ *Web:* www.erwagner.com					
ESPE Mfg Co Inc 9220 Ivanhoe St	Schiller Park	IL	60176	847-678-8950	678-0253
TF Cust Svc: 800-367-3773 ■ *Web:* www.espemfg.com					
Faultless Caster Div FKI Industries 3438 Briley Park Blvd N	Nashville	TN	37207	615-687-6300	322-9329*
**Fax Area Code:* 800 ■ *TF Cust Svc:* 800-322-7359 ■ *Web:* www.faultlesscaster.com					
Federal Casters Corp 785 Harrison Ave	Harrison	NJ	07029	973-483-6700	483-5030
FKI Industries Faultless Caster Div 3438 Briley Park Blvd N	Nashville	TN	37207	615-687-6300	322-9329*
**Fax Area Code:* 800 ■ *TF Cust Svc:* 800-322-7359 ■ *Web:* www.faultlesscaster.com					
Folger Adam Security Inc 4634 S Presa St	San Antonio	TX	78223	210-533-1231	533-2211
TF: 800-966-6739					
Fortune Brands Home & Hardware Inc 520 Lake Cook Rd	Deerfield	IL	60015	847-484-4400	
Web: www.fortunebrands.com					
Fried Brothers Inc 467 N 7th St	Philadelphia	PA	19123	215-627-3205	592-1255
TF: 800-523-2924 ■ *Web:* www.fbisecurity.com					
Fulton Corp 303 8th Ave	Fulton	IL	61252	815-589-3211	589-4433
TF: 800-252-0002 ■ *Web:* www.fultoncorp.com					
Genie Co 22790 Lake Park Blvd	Alliance	OH	44601	330-821-5360	821-1927
TF Cust Svc: 800-654-3643 ■ *Web:* geniecompany.com					
Guard Security Hardware 1 S Middlesex Ave	Monroe Township	NJ	08831	609-860-9990	860-9991
TF Sales: 800-523-1268 ■ *Web:* www.hberger.com					
Guden HA Co Inc 99 Raynor Ave	Ronkonkoma	NY	11779	631-737-2900	737-2933
TF: 800-344-6437 ■ *Web:* www.guden.com					
Guerin PE Inc 23 Jane St	New York	NY	10014	212-243-5270	727-2290
Web: www.peguerin.com					
HA Guden Co Inc 99 Raynor Ave	Ronkonkoma	NY	11779	631-737-2900	737-2933
TF: 800-344-6437 ■ *Web:* www.guden.com					
Hager Co 139 Victor St	Saint Louis	MO	63104	314-772-4400	782-0149*
**Fax Area Code:* 800 ■ **Fax:* Sales ■ *TF:* 800-325-9995 ■ *Web:* www.hagerco.com					
Hamilton Caster & Mfg Co 1637 Dixie Hwy	Hamilton	OH	45011	513-863-3300	863-5508
Web: www.hamiltoncaster.com					
Hansen AL Mfg Co 701 Pershing Rd	Waukegan	IL	60085	847-244-8900	244-7222
Web: www.alhansen.com					
Hartwell Corp 900 S Richfield Rd	Placentia	CA	92870	714-993-4200	579-4419
Web: www.hartwellcorp.com					
HB Ives Co 50 Ives Pl	New Haven	CT	06511	203-772-4837	624-9005
TF: 877-613-8766 ■ *Web:* www.ivesharware.com					
Hickory Hardwood 3438 Briley Pk Rd	Nashville	TN	37207	615-687-6300	247-4110*
**Fax Area Code:* 616 ■ *TF:* 800-322-7359					
Hindley Mfg Co Inc PO Box 38	Cumberland	RI	02864	401-722-2550	722-3083
TF: 800-323-9031 ■ *Web:* www.hindley.com					
Holtz Jacob Co 2424 E York St	Philadelphia	PA	19125	215-423-2800	634-7454
Web: www.jacobholtz.com					
Howard James L & Co Inc 10 Britton Dr	Bloomfield	CT	06002	860-242-3581	242-9966
Hudson Lock Inc 81 Apsley St	Hudson	MA	01749	978-562-3481	562-9859
TF: 800-434-8960 ■ *Web:* www.hudsonlock.com					
Hydraflow Inc 1881 W Malvern Ave	Fullerton	CA	92833	714-773-2600	773-6351
Web: www.hydraflowusa.com					
Ideal Clamp 3200 Parker Dr	Saint Augustine	FL	32084	904-829-1000	825-1121
TF: 800-221-0100 ■ *Web:* www.idealclamp.com					
Ingersoll-Rand Co Von Duprin Exit Device Div 2720 Tobey Dr	Indianapolis	IN	46219	317-613-8944	999-0328*
**Fax Area Code:* 800 ■ *TF Cust Svc:* 800-999-0408 ■ *Web:* www.vonduprin.com					
Inwesco Inc 746 N Coney Ave	Azusa	CA	91702	626-334-9304	969-3404
TF: 800-266-9304 ■ *Web:* www.inwesco.com					
Ives HB Co 50 Ives Pl	New Haven	CT	06511	203-772-4837	624-9005
TF: 877-613-8766 ■ *Web:* www.iveshardware.com					
Jacknob Corp 290 Oser Ave	Hauppauge	NY	11788	631-231-9400	231-0330
TF: 888-231-9333 ■ *Web:* www.jacknob.com					
Jacob Holtz Co 2424 E York St	Philadelphia	PA	19125	215-423-2800	634-7454
Web: www.jacobholtz.com					
James L Howard & Co Inc 10 Britton Dr	Bloomfield	CT	06002	860-242-3581	242-9966
Jarvis Caster Co 881 Lower Brownsville Rd	Jackson	TN	38301	731-554-2138	881-5701*
**Fax Area Code:* 800 ■ *TF:* 800-995-9876 ■ *Web:* www.jarviscaster.com					
John Sterling Corp PO Box 469	Richmond	IL	60071	815-678-2031	678-4360
TF: 800-367-5726 ■ *Web:* www.johnsterling.com					
Johnson LE Products Inc 2100 Sterling Ave	Elkhart	IN	46516	574-293-5664	294-4697
TF: 800-837-5664 ■ *Web:* www.johnsonhardware.com					
Jonathan Engineered Solutions 410 Exchange St Suite 200	Irvine	CA	92602	714-665-4400	368-7002
Web: www.jonathanengr.com					
Kaba Ilco Corp 400 Jeffreys Rd	Rocky Mount	NC	27804	252-446-3321	446-4702
TF: 800-334-1381 ■ *Web:* www.kaba-ilco.com					
Kason Industries Inc 57 Amlajack Blvd	Shenandoah	GA	30265	770-251-1422	304-3030
TF: 800-935-2766 ■ *Web:* www.kasonind.com					
Keystone Electronics Corp 31-07 20th Rd	Astoria	NY	11105	718-956-8900	956-9040
TF: 800-221-5510 ■ *Web:* www.keyelco.com					
Knape & Vogt Mfg Co 2700 Oak Industrial Dr NE	Grand Rapids	MI	49505	616-459-3311	459-3290
NASDAQ: KNAP ■ *TF:* 800-253-1561 ■ *Web:* www.kv.com					
La Gard Inc 749 W Short St	Lexington	KY	40508	859-253-4744	255-2655
TF: 877-524-2732 ■ *Web:* www.lagard.com					
Larson Hardware Mfg Co PO Box E	Sterling	IL	61081	815-625-0503	625-8786
Web: www.larsonhdwe.com					
Lawrence Hardware Inc 4713 Hammermill Rd	Tucker	GA	30084	800-435-9568	892-7026
TF: 800-435-9568 ■ *Web:* www.lawrencehardware.com					
LE Johnson Products Inc 2100 Sterling Ave	Elkhart	IN	46516	574-293-5664	294-4697
TF: 800-837-5664 ■ *Web:* www.johnsonhardware.com					
Leonard Charles Inc 145 Kennedy Dr	Hauppauge	NY	11788	631-273-4600	273-4222
TF: 800-999-7202 ■ *Web:* www.charlesleonard.com					
Leonard Charles Western Inc 235 W 140th St	Los Angeles	CA	90061	310-715-7464	715-7474
Liberty Hardware Mfg Corp 140 Business Park Dr	Winston-Salem	NC	27107	336-769-4077	769-7306
TF: 800-542-3789 ■ *Web:* www.libertyhardware.com					
Master Lock Co 137 W Forest Hills Ave	Oak Creek	WI	53154	414-571-5625	308-9245*
**Fax Area Code:* 800 ■ *TF:* 800-308-9244 ■ *Web:* www.masterlock.com					
McKinney Products Inc 820 Davis St	Scranton	PA	18505	570-346-7551	541-1073*
**Fax Area Code:* 800 ■ **Fax:* Cust Svc ■ *TF:* 800-346-7707 ■					
Web: www.mckinneyhinge.com					
Medeco Security Locks Inc PO Box 3075	Salem	VA	24153	540-380-5000	421-6615*
**Fax Area Code:* 800 ■ *TF:* 800-839-3157 ■ *Web:* www.medeco.com					
Murray Corp 260 Schilling Cir	Hunt Valley	MD	21031	410-771-0380	771-5576
Web: www.murraycorp.com					
Nagel Chase Inc 2377 Delaney Rd	Gurnee	IL	60031	847-336-4494	336-6542
Web: www.paysoncasters.com/nagle					
National Mfg Co 1 1st Ave	Sterling	IL	61081	815-625-1320	625-1333
TF Cust Svc: 800-346-9445 ■ *Web:* www.natman.com					
Newell Rubbermaid Inc Tools & Hardware Group 10B Glenlake Pkwy Suite 600	Atlanta	GA	30328	770-407-3800	407-3970
Web: www.newellrubbermaid.com					
Nik-O-Lok Co 3130 N Mitthoeffer Rd	Indianapolis	IN	46235	317-899-6955	899-6977
TF: 800-428-4348					
No-Sag Products Corp 2225 Production Rd	Kendallville	IN	46755	260-347-2600	347-4764
TF: 800-345-0775					
Norton Industries Inc 20670 Corsair Blvd	Hayward	CA	94545	510-786-3638	786-3082
Nucor Corp Fastener Div PO Box 6100	Saint Joe	IN	46785	260-337-1600	337-1717
TF: 800-955-6826 ■ *Web:* www.nucor-fastener.com					
Paneloc Corp PO Drawer 547	Farmington	CT	06034	860-677-6711	677-8606
Web: www.paneloc.com					
Parker International Products 243 Stafford St	Worcester	MA	01603	508-791-7131	753-7928
TF: 800-225-9011 ■ *Web:* www.parkerinternationalproducts.com					

Phone | Fax

Payson Casters Inc 2323 N Delaney Rd ... Gurnee IL 60031 847-336-6200 336-6542
TF: 800-323-4552 ■ *Web:* www.paysoncasters.com
PE Guerin Inc 23 Jane St ... New York NY 10014 212-243-5270 727-2290
Web: www.peguerin.com
Perko Inc 16490 NW 13th Ave ... Miami FL 33169 305-621-7525 620-9978
Web: www.perko.com
PL Porter Co 3000 Winona Ave ... Burbank CA 91504 818-526-2600 842-6117
Polar Hardware Mfg Co 1813 W Montrose Ave ... Chicago IL 60613 773-935-8600 935-8749
Web: www.polarmfg.com
Pratt-Read Corp 1155 Railroad Ave ... Bridgeport CT 06605 203-366-4911 335-1802
TF: 800-677-0801 ■ *Web:* www.pratt-read.com
Precision Brand Products Inc 2250 Curtiss St ... Downers Grove IL 60515 630-969-7200 969-0310*
**Fax:* Sales ■ *TF:* 800-535-3727 ■ *Web:* www.precisionbrand.com
PrimeSource Building Products Inc 2115 E Beltline Rd ... Carrollton TX 75006 972-416-1976 416-8331
TF: 800-745-3341 ■ *Web:* www.primesourcebp.com
Qual-Craft Industries PO Box 559 ... Stoughton MA 02072 781-344-1000 344-0056
TF: 800-231-5647 ■ *Web:* www.qualcraft.com
Railway Specialties Corp PO Box 29 ... Bristol PA 19007 215-788-9242 788-9244
Web: www.railwayspecialties.com
Ramsey Charles Co PO Box 2264 ... Kingston NY 12402 845-338-1464 338-5751
Renosol Corp 1512 Woodland Dr ... Saline MI 48176 734-429-5418 429-5351
Web: www.renosol.com
Root Brothers Mfg & Supply Co 10317-25 S Michigan Ave ... Chicago IL 60628 773-264-5000 264-6365
Web: www.rootbrothers.com
RWM Casters Co PO Box 668 ... Gastonia NC 28053 704-866-8533 868-4205
TF: 800-634-7704 ■ *Web:* www.rwmcasters.com
S Parker Hardware Mfg Corp PO Box 9882 ... Englewood NJ 07631 201-569-1600 569-1082
TF: 800-772-7537 ■ *Web:* www.sparker.com
Sargent & Greenleaf Inc PO Box 930 ... Nicholasville KY 40340 859-885-9411 885-3063
TF: 800-826-7652 ■ *Web:* www.sglocks.com
Sargent Mfg Co 100 Sargent Dr ... New Haven CT 06511 203-562-2151 498-5677*
**Fax:* Sales ■ *Web:* www.sargentlock.com
Schlage Lock Co 11819 N Pennsylvania St ... Carmel IN 40632 317-810-3700
TF: 800-847-1864 ■ *Web:* www.schlagelock.com
Securitron Magnalock Corp 550 Vista Blvd ... Sparks NV 89434 775-355-5625 355-5636
TF Sales: 800-624-5625 ■ *Web:* www.securitron.com
Selby Furniture Hardware Co 321 Rider Ave ... Bronx NY 10451 718-993-3700 993-3143
TF: 800-224-0058 ■ *Web:* www.selbyhardware.com
Shelburne Corp 6221 Shelburne Rd ... Shelburne VT 05482 802-985-3321 985-8336
Simpson Strong-Tie Co Inc 5956 W Las Positas Blvd ... Pleasanton CA 94588 925-560-9000 847-1603
TF: 800-925-5099 ■ *Web:* www.strongtie.com
Solus Industrial Innovations LLC
30152 Aventura ... Rancho Santa Margarita CA 92688 949-589-3900 858-0300
TF Cust Svc: 800-825-8364 ■ *Web:* www.solusii.com
Southco Inc 210 N Brinton Lake Rd PO Box 0116 ... Concordville PA 19331 610-459-4000 459-4012
Web: www.southco.com
Southern Tool Mfg Co Inc PO Box 12008 ... Winston-Salem NC 27117 336-788-6321 785-0422
TF: 800-334-5262
Stanley Works 1000 Stanley Dr ... New Britain CT 06053 860-225-5111 827-3895
NYSE: SWK ■ *TF Cust Svc:* 800-262-2161 ■ *Web:* www.stanleyworks.com
Sterling John Corp PO Box 469 ... Richmond IL 60071 815-678-2031 678-4360
TF: 800-367-5726 ■ *Web:* www.johnsterling.com
Stimpson Co Inc 900 Sylvan Ave ... Bayport NY 11705 631-472-2000 472-2425
Web: www.stimpsonco.com
Trimco/Builders Brass Works PO Box 23277 ... Los Angeles CA 90023 323-262-4191 264-9018
TF: 800-637-8746 ■ *Web:* www.trimcobbw.com
Truth Hardware Inc 700 W Bridge St ... Owatonna MN 55060 507-451-5620 451-5655*
**Fax:* Cust Svc ■ *TF Cust Svc:* 800-866-7884 ■ *Web:* www.truth.com
Ultra Hardware Products LLC 1777 Hylton Rd ... Pennsauken NJ 08110 856-663-5050 858-7210*
**Fax Area Code:* 800 ■ *TF:* 800-426-6379 ■ *Web:* www.ultrahardware.com
Unicorp 291 Cleveland St ... Orange NJ 07050 973-674-1700 674-3803
TF: 800-526-1389 ■ *Web:* www.unicorpinc.com
United Fixtures Co 4300 Quality Dr ... South Bend IN 46628 574-282-8200 282-8280
TF: 800-468-8447 ■ *Web:* www.nationalstorefixtures.com
Universal Tool Co Inc 33 Rose Pl ... Springfield MA 01104 413-732-7738 733-6996
Von Duprin Exit Device Div Ingersoll-Rand Co
2720 Tobey Dr ... Indianapolis IN 46219 317-613-8944 999-0328*
**Fax Area Code:* 800 ■ *TF Cust Svc:* 800-999-0408 ■ *Web:* www.vonduprin.com
Wagner ER Mfg Co Inc 4611 N 32nd St ... Milwaukee WI 53209 414-871-5080 449-8228
TF: 800-558-5596 ■ *Web:* www.erwagner.com
Weber-Knapp Co PO Box 518 ... Jamestown NY 14701 716-484-9135 484-9142
Web: www.weber-knapp.com
Weiser Lock A Masco Co 19701 Da Vinci ... Lake Forest CA 92610 800-677-5625 713-7080
TF: 800-677-5625 ■ *Web:* www.weiserlock.com
Whistler Group Inc 13016 N Walton Blvd ... Bentonville AR 72712 479-273-6012 273-3188
TF Cust Svc: 800-531-0004 ■ *Web:* www.whistlergroup.com
Yale Norton Inc 1902 Airport Rd ... Monroe NC 28110 704-283-2101 338-0965*
**Fax Area Code:* 800 ■ *TF:* 800-438-1951
Yale Residential Security Products Inc
2725B Northwoods Pkwy ... Norcross GA 30071 678-728-7400 448-1102*
**Fax Area Code:* 770 ■ **Fax:* Cust Svc ■ *TF Cust Svc:* 800-542-7562 ■
Web: www.yaleresidential.com
Yale Security Group 1902 Airport Rd ... Monroe NC 28110 704-283-2101 338-0965*
**Fax Area Code:* 800 ■ *TF:* 800-438-1951 ■ *Web:* www.yalesecurity.com
Yardley Products Corp PO Box 357 ... Yardley PA 19067 215-493-2700 493-6796
TF: 800-457-0154 ■ *Web:* www.yardleyproducts.com

354 HARDWARE - WHOL

Phone | Fax

AB Wholesale Co 710 S College Ave ... Bluefield VA 24605 276-322-4686 326-1060
All-Pro Fasteners Inc 1916 Peyco Dr N ... Arlington TX 76001 817-467-5700 467-5365
TF: 800-361-6627 ■ *Web:* www.all-profasteners.com
Allied International 13207 Bradley Ave ... Sylmar CA 91342 818-364-2333 362-9066
TF: 800-533-8333 ■ *Web:* www.alliedtools.com
Amarillo Hardware Co PO Box 1891 ... Amarillo TX 79172 806-376-4722 374-5520
TF: 800-949-4722 ■ *Web:* www.ahcusa.com
Associated Steel Corp 18200 Miles Rd ... Cleveland OH 44128 216-475-8000 475-6067
TF: 800-441-9303 ■ *Web:* www.associatedsteel.com
B & T Wholesale Distributors Inc 846 Lind Ave SW ... Renton WA 98055 425-235-3592 235-3599
Baer Supply Co 909 Forest Edge Dr ... Vernon Hills IL 60061 847-913-2237 913-2230
TF: 800-944-2237 ■ *Web:* www.baerco.com
Barnett Inc 801 W Bay St ... Jacksonville FL 32204 904-384-6530 388-2723*
**Fax:* Mktg ■ *TF:* 800-288-2000 ■ *Web:* www.e-barnett.com
Berger Howard & Co Inc 1 S Middlesex Ave ... Monroe Township NJ 08831 609-860-9960 860-9991
TF: 800-523-1268
Blish-Mize Co 223 S 5th St ... Atchison KS 66002 913-367-1250 367-0667
TF: 800-995-0525 ■ *Web:* www.blishmize.com
Bostwick-Braun Co PO Box 912 ... Toledo OH 43697 419-259-3600 259-3959
TF: 800-777-9640
Bradley EB Co 5080 S Alameda St ... Los Angeles CA 90058 323-585-9201 585-5414
TF: 800-533-3030 ■ *Web:* www.ebbradley.com
Builders Hardware & Supply Co Inc PO Box C-79005 ... Seattle WA 98119 206-281-3700 281-3747
TF: 800-999-5158 ■ *Web:* www.builders-hardware.com

Phone | Fax

California Hardware Co 3601 E Jurupa St ... Ontario CA 91761 909-390-6100 390-8799
TF: 800-995-9223 ■ *Web:* www.daonline.com
Carlson Systems LLC 10840 Harney St PO Box 3036 ... Omaha NE 68103 402-593-5300 593-5366
TF: 800-325-8343 ■ *Web:* www.csystems.com
Cascade Wholesale Hardware Inc PO Box 1659 ... Hillsboro OR 97123 503-614-2600 629-5793*
**Fax Area Code:* 614 ■ *TF:* 800-877-9987 ■ *Web:* www.cascade.com
Dake Div JSJ Corp 724 Robbins Rd ... Grand Haven MI 49417 616-842-7110 842-0859
TF: 800-846-3253 ■ *Web:* www.dakecorp.com
Dillon Poe Supply Corp 215 Pelham Davis Cir ... Greenville SC 29615 864-213-9000 213-9700
TF: 800-849-4300 ■ *Web:* www.dillonsupply.com
Do it Best Corp PO Box 868 ... Fort Wayne IN 46801 260-748-5300 493-1245
Web: www.doitbest.com
Earnest Machine Products Co 12502 Plaza Dr ... Parma OH 44130 216-362-1100 362-9970
TF: 800-327-6378 ■ *Web:* www.earnestmachine.com
EB Bradley Co 5080 S Alameda St ... Los Angeles CA 90058 323-585-9201 585-5414
TF: 800-533-3030 ■ *Web:* www.ebbradley.com
Emhart Teknologies Inc 50 Shelton Technology Ctr PO Box 859 ... Shelton CT 06484 203-924-9341 925-3109
Web: www.emhart.com
Fastec Industrial Corp 23348 County Rd 6 ... Elkhart IN 46514 574-262-2505 262-8634*
**Fax:* Sales ■ *TF:* 800-837-2505 ■ *Web:* www.fastecindustrial.com
Fastenal Co PO Box 978 ... Winona MN 55987 507-454-5374 453-8049
NASDAQ: FAST ■ *TF:* 877-327-8362 ■ *Web:* www.fastenal.com
Faucet Queens Inc 650 Forest Edge Dr ... Vernon Hills IL 60061 847-821-0777 821-0277
Web: www.faucetqueen.com
General Fasteners Co 11820 Globe Rd ... Livonia MI 48150 734-452-2400 591-6387
TF: 800-945-2658 ■ *Web:* www.genfast.com
GM Industrial Inc PO Box 1346 ... Elkhart IN 46515 574-295-1080 262-1636
Grainger WW Inc 100 Grainger Pkwy ... Lake Forest IL 60045 847-535-1000
NYSE: GWW ■ *TF:* 888-361-8649 ■ *Web:* www.grainger.com
Handy Hardware Wholesale Inc 8300 Tewantin Dr ... Houston TX 77061 713-644-1495 644-3167
TF: 800-364-3835 ■ *Web:* www.handyhardware.com
Hans Johnsen Co 8901 Chancellor Row ... Dallas TX 75247 214-879-1550 879-1520
TF Sales: 800-879-1515 ■ *Web:* www.hjc.com
Hardware Distribution Warehouses Inc (HDW)
6900 Woolworth Rd ... Shreveport LA 71129 318-686-8527 686-8550
TF Cust Svc: 800-256-8527 ■ *Web:* www.hdwinc.com
HDW (Hardware Distribution Warehouses Inc)
6900 Woolworth Rd ... Shreveport LA 71129 318-686-8527 686-8550
TF Cust Svc: 800-256-8527 ■ *Web:* www.hdwinc.com
Heads & Threads International LLC 200 Kennedy Dr ... Sayreville NJ 08872 732-727-5800 727-5888
TF: 800-929-1950 ■ *Web:* www.headsandthreads.com
Hillman Group Inc 10590 Hamilton Ave ... Cincinnati OH 45231 513-851-4900 851-4997
TF: 800-800-4900 ■ *Web:* www.hillmangroup.com
Home Depot Supply 10641 Scripps Summit Ct ... San Diego CA 92131 858-831-2000 352-5354*
**Fax Area Code:* 800 ■ **Fax:* Sales ■ *TF:* 800-233-6166 ■ *Web:* hdsupply.com
House-Hasson Hardware Inc 3125 Water Plant Rd SE ... Knoxville TN 37914 865-525-0471 525-6178
TF: 800-333-0520 ■ *Web:* www.househasson.com
Howard Berger & Co Inc 1 S Middlesex Ave ... Monroe Township NJ 08831 609-860-9960 860-9991
TF: 800-523-1268
Integrated Logistics Solutions 23000 Euclid Ave ... Cleveland OH 44117 216-692-7100 692-7253
Web: www.ilsonline.com
Interline Brands Inc 801 W Bay St ... Jacksonville FL 32204 904-421-1400 288-2828*
NYSE: IBI ■ **Fax Area Code:* 800 ■ *TF:* 800-288-2000 ■ *Web:* www.interlinebrands.com
Jensen Distribution Services 314 W Riverside Ave ... Spokane WA 99201 509-624-1321 838-2432
TF: 800-234-1321 ■ *Web:* www.jensenonline.com
Johnsen Hans Co 8901 Chancellor Row ... Dallas TX 75247 214-879-1550 879-1520
TF Sales: 800-879-1515 ■ *Web:* www.hjc.com
JSJ Corp 700 Robbins Rd ... Grand Haven MI 49417 616-842-6350 847-3112
Web: www.jsjcorp.com
JSJ Corp Dake Div 724 Robbins Rd ... Grand Haven MI 49417 616-842-7110 842-0859
TF: 800-846-3253 ■ *Web:* www.dakecorp.com
Kentec Inc 3250 Centerville Hwy ... Snellville GA 30039 770-985-1907 985-6989
TF: 800-241-0148 ■ *Web:* www.kentec.com
Long-Lewis Hardware 430 9th St N ... Birmingham AL 35203 205-322-2561 322-2504
TF: 800-322-0492 ■ *Web:* www.long-lewis.com
Monroe Hardware Co PO Box 5015 ... Monroe NC 28111 704-289-3121 289-2838
TF: 800-222-1974 ■ *Web:* www.monroehardware.com
Moore-Handley Inc 3140 Pelham Pkwy ... Birmingham AL 35124 205-663-8011 663-8364
TF: 800-633-3848 ■ *Web:* www.moorehandley.com
Orgill Inc 3742 Tyndale Dr ... Memphis TN 38125 901-754-8850 752-8989
Web: www.orgill.com
Parts Assoc Inc 12420 Plaza Dr ... Parma OH 44130 216-433-7700 433-9051
TF: 800-321-1128 ■ *Web:* www.pai-net.com
Pentacon Inc 21123 Nordhoff St ... Chatsworth CA 91311 818-727-7800 727-8037
Web: www.pentacon.com
Pleasants Hardware Co 1010 Northwest Blvd ... Winston-Salem NC 27101 336-725-3067 725-6921
Web: www.pleasants.com
Porteous Fastener Co 1300 Morse Ave ... Elk Grove Village IL 60007 847-228-6313 228-6761
TF: 800-935-2002 ■ *Web:* www.porteousfastener.com
Ram Tool & Supply Co PO Box 320979 ... Birmingham AL 35232 205-591-2527 599-7053
TF: 800-292-6027 ■ *Web:* www.ram-tool.com
Reid Tool Supply Co Inc 2265 Black Creek Rd ... Muskegon MI 49444 231-777-3951 438-1145*
**Fax Area Code:* 800 ■ **Fax:* Sales ■ *TF Sales:* 800-253-0421 ■
Web: reidecom.reidtool.com/xephr/qbe/HOMEPAGE
Rock Island Corp 530 Oak Court Dr Suite 260 ... Memphis TN 38117 901-529-5700 526-6705
TF: 800-529-5701
Ryobi Technologies Inc 1428 Pearman Dairy Rd ... Anderson SC 29625 864-226-6511 261-9435
TF: 800-525-2579 ■ *Web:* www.ryobitools.com
Star Stainless Screw Co 30 West End Rd ... Totowa NJ 07511 973-256-2300 256-2423
TF: 800-631-3540
Techni-Tool Inc 1547 N Trooper Rd PO Box 1117 ... Worcester PA 19490 610-941-2400 828-5623
TF Cust Svc: 800-832-4866 ■ *Web:* www.techni-tool.com
Thruway Fasteners Inc 2910 Niagara Falls Blvd ... North Tonawanda NY 14120 716-694-1434 694-3865*
**Fax:* Sales ■ *TF:* 800-201-1619 ■ *Web:* www.thruwayfasteners.com
United Hardware Distributing Co PO Box 410 ... Minneapolis MN 55440 763-559-1800 559-5031
TF: 800-835-6560 ■ *Web:* www.unitedhardware.com
Wallace Hardware Co Inc PO Box 6004 ... Morristown TN 37815 423-586-5650 581-0766
TF: 800-776-0976 ■ *Web:* www.wallacehardware.com
Watters & Martin Inc 3800 Village Ave ... Norfolk VA 23502 757-857-0651 855-3991
TF: 800-446-8205 ■ *Web:* www.wattersandmartin.com
WBH Industries PO Box 98 ... Arlington TX 76004 817-649-5700 649-5701
WCL Co PO Box 3588 ... City of Industry CA 91744 626-968-5523 369-9805
TF: 800-331-3816 ■ *Web:* www.wclco.com
Wurth Adams Nut & Bolt 10100 85th Ave N PO Box 207 ... Maple Grove MN 55369 763-424-3374 493-0800
Web: www.adams-nutandbolt.com
Wurth Service Supply Inc 4935 W 86th St ... Indianapolis IN 46268 317-704-1000 704-8469*
**Fax:* Cust Svc ■ *TF:* 800-428-4686 ■ *Web:* www.servicesupply.com
WW Grainger Inc 100 Grainger Pkwy ... Lake Forest IL 60045 847-535-1000
NYSE: GWW ■ *TF:* 888-361-8649 ■ *Web:* www.grainger.com

355 HEALTH CARE PROVIDERS - ANCILLARY

SEE ALSO Home Health Services p. 1787; Hospices p. 1791; Vision Correction Centers p. 2405

				Phone	Fax
Amedisys Inc 5959 S Sherwood Forest Blvd Suite 300 *NASDAQ: AMED* ■ *TF:* 800-467-2662 ■ *Web:* www.amedisys.com	Baton Rouge	LA	70816	225-292-2031	292-8163
AmSurg Corp 20 Burton Hills Blvd 5th Fl *NASDAQ: AMSG* ■ *TF:* 800-945-2301 ■ *Web:* www.amsurg.com	Nashville	TN	37215	615-665-1283	665-0755
Apex Fitness Group 100 Camino Ruiz *TF:* 800-656-2739 ■ *Web:* www.apexfitness.com	Camarillo	CA	93012	805-449-1330	449-1370
Aptium Oncology 8201 Beverly Blvd *Web:* www.aptiumoncology.com	Los Angeles	CA	90048	323-966-3400	966-3597
BriteSmile Inc 460 N Wiget Ln *NASDAQ: BSML* ■ *TF:* 800-274-8376 ■ *Web:* www.britesmile.com	Walnut Creek	CA	94598	925-941-6260	941-6266
Curative Health Services Inc 150 Motor Pkwy 4th Fl *TF:* 800-966-5656 ■ *Web:* www.curative.com	Hauppauge	NY	11788	631-232-7000	232-9322
DaVita Inc 601 Hawaii St *NYSE: DVA* ■ *TF:* 800-310-4872 ■ *Web:* www.davita.com	El Segundo	CA	90245	310-536-2400	536-2675
Dialysis Corp of America 27 Miller St Suite 2 *NASDAQ: DCAI* ■ *TF:* 888-730-6164 ■ *Web:* www.dialysiscorporation.com	Lemoyne	PA	17043	717-730-6164	730-9133
Dynacq Healthcare Inc 10304 I-10 E Suite 369 *NASDAQ: DYII* ■ *Web:* www.dynacq.com	Houston	TX	77029	713-378-2000	378-3166
Elder Health Inc 3601 O'Donnell St *TF:* 800-557-0291 ■ *Web:* www.elderhealth.com	Baltimore	MD	21224	410-864-4400	864-4429
Elderhealth Northwest 800 Jefferson St *Web:* www.elderhealth.org	Seattle	WA	98104	206-467-7033	224-3779
Executive Health Group 10 Rockefeller Plaza 4th Fl **Fax:* Hum Res ■ *TF:* 800-362-8671	New York	NY	10020	212-332-3030	332-1170*
Fresenius Medical Care North America 95 Hayden Ave *NYSE: FMS* ■ **Fax:* Mail Rm ■ *TF:* 800-662-1237 ■ *Web:* www.fmcna.com	Lexington	MA	02420	781-402-9000	402-9731*
Gambro Healthcare Inc 5200 Virginia Way *TF:* 800-467-4736 ■ *Web:* www.gambrohealthcare.com	Brentwood	TN	37027	615-320-4200	320-4528
Hanger Orthopedic Group Inc 2 Bethesda Metro Ctr Suite 1200 *NYSE: HGR* ■ *TF:* 800-765-3822 ■ *Web:* www.hanger.com	Bethesda	MD	20814	301-986-0701	986-0702
Health Fitness Corp 3600 American Blvd West Suite 560 *TF:* 800-639-7913 ■ *Web:* www.hfit.com	Bloomington	MN	55431	952-831-6830	831-7264
HealthDrive Corp 25 Needham St *TF:* 888-964-6681 ■ *Web:* www.healthdrive.com	Newton	MA	02461	617-964-6681	964-0989
HealthSouth Corp 3660 Grandview Pkwy Suite 200 **Fax:* Hum Res ■ *TF:* 800-765-4772 ■ *Web:* www.healthsouth.com	Birmingham	AL	35243	205-967-7116	969-4740*
Healthtrax Inc 2345 Main St *Web:* www.healthtrax.com	Glastonbury	CT	06033	860-633-5572	652-7066
Healthways Inc 3841 Greenhills Village Dr Suite 300 *NASDAQ: HWAY* ■ *TF:* 800-327-3822 ■ *Web:* www.americanhealthways.com	Nashville	TN	37215	615-665-1122	665-7697
Hooper Holmes Inc 170 Mt Airy Rd *AMEX: HH* ■ *TF:* 800-782-7373 ■ *Web:* www.hooperholmes.com	Basking Ridge	NJ	07920	908-766-5000	766-5824
Med Tech 135 NW 100 Ave *TF:* 800-377-5869	Plantation	FL	33324	954-434-4341	434-0526
MedCath Inc 10720 Sikes Pl Suite 300 *NASDAQ: MDTH* ■ *Web:* www.medcath.com	Charlotte	NC	28277	704-708-6610	708-5035
Medstone International Inc 100 Columbia Suite 100 *TF:* 800-633-7866 ■ *Web:* www.medstone.com	Aliso Viejo	CA	92656	949-448-7700	448-7882
Midwest Medical Services 4280 Bluestem Rd **Fax Area Code:* 217 ■ *TF:* 888-850-7377 ■ *Web:* www.midwestmedicalservices.com	Charleston	IL	61920	888-850-7377	345-2601*
Miracle-Ear Inc 5000 Cheshire Ln N Suite 1 *TF:* 800-234-7714 ■ *Web:* www.miracle-ear.com	Plymouth	MN	55446	763-268-4000	268-4365
NovaCare Inc 680 American Ave **Fax:* Hum Res ■ *TF:* 800-331-8840 ■ *Web:* www.novacare.com	King of Prussia	PA	19406	610-992-7200	992-7264*
Orion HealthCorp Inc 1805 Old Alabama Rd Suite 350 *AMEX: ONH* ■ *Web:* www.orionhealthcorp.com	Roswell	GA	30076	678-832-1800	
PainCare Inc 1030 N Orange Ave Suite 105 *AMEX: PRZ* ■ *Web:* www.paincareinc.com	Orlando	FL	32801	407-367-0944	367-0950
Radiation Therapy Services Inc 2234 Colonial Blvd *NASDAQ: RTSX* ■ *TF:* 888-376-9729 ■ *Web:* www.rtsx.com	Fort Myers	FL	33907	239-931-7275	931-7380
Raytel Medical Corp 7 Waterside Crossing **Fax Area Code:* 800 ■ *TF:* 800-367-1095 ■ *Web:* www.raytel.com	Windsor	CT	06095	860-298-6100	562-4166*
RehabCare Group Inc 7733 Forsyth Blvd Suite 2300 *NYSE: RHB* ■ *TF:* 800-677-1238 ■ *Web:* www.rehabcare.com	Saint Louis	MO	63105	314-863-7422	863-0769
Renal Care Group Inc 2525 West End Ave Suite 600 *NYSE: RCI* ■ *Web:* www.renalcaregroup.com	Nashville	TN	37203	615-345-5500	345-5505
Sonus Corp 5000 Cheshire Ln N **Fax Area Code:* 763 ■ *Web:* www.sonus.com	Plymouth	MN	55446	800-432-7464	268-4353*
SunAlliance Healthcare Services Inc 9455 Farnham St Suite A	San Diego	CA	92123	858-576-7410	576-1661
SunDance Rehabilitation Corp 101 Sun Ave NE *TF:* 800-729-6600 ■ *Web:* www.sundancerehab.com	Albuquerque	NM	87109	505-821-3355	821-9440
SurgiCare Inc 6699 Chimney Rock Suite 105 *AMEX: SRG* ■ *Web:* www.surgicareinc.com	Houston	TX	77081	713-665-1406	665-8262
Symbion Inc 40 Burton Hills Blvd Suite 500 *NASDAQ: SMBI* ■ *Web:* www.symbion.com	Nashville	TN	37215	615-234-5900	234-5999
Theo & Alfred M Landon Center on Aging 3901 Rainbow Blvd *Web:* www2.kumc.edu/coa	Kansas City	KS	66160	913-588-1203	588-1201
United Surgical Partners International Inc 15305 Dallas Pkwy 1600 Lock Box 28 *NASDAQ: USPI* ■ *Web:* www.unitedsurgical.com	Addison	TX	75001	972-713-3500	713-3550
US Physical Therapy 1300 W Sam Houston Pkwy S Suite 300 *NASDAQ: USPH* ■ *TF:* 800-580-6285 ■ *Web:* www.usphysicaltherapy.com	Houston	TX	77042	713-297-7000	297-7090

356 HEALTH CARE SYSTEMS

SEE ALSO Hospitals - General Hospitals - US p. 1802

Health Care Systems are one or more hospitals owned, leased, sponsored, or managed by a central organization. Single-hospital systems are not included here; however, some large hospital networks or alliances may be listed.

				Phone	Fax
Adventist Health 2100 Douglas Blvd *Web:* www.adventisthealth.org	Roseville	CA	95661	916-781-2000	783-9146
Adventist Health System 111 N Orlando Ave *TF:* 800-327-9290 ■ *Web:* www.ahss.org	Winter Park	FL	32789	407-647-4400	975-1435
Advocate Health Care 2025 Windsor Dr *TF:* 800-323-8622 ■ *Web:* www.advocatehealth.com	Oak Brook	IL	60523	630-572-9393	572-9139
Albert Einstein Healthcare Network 5501 Old York Rd *TF:* 800-346-7834 ■ *Web:* www.einstein.edu	Philadelphia	PA	19141	215-456-7010	456-6199
Alexian Brothers Health System 3040 Salt Creek Ln *Web:* www.alexianhealthsystem.org	Arlington Heights	IL	60005	847-385-7100	483-7040
Allina Health System 710 E 24th St *Web:* www.allina.com	Minneapolis	MN	55404	612-775-5000	775-9733
Ancilla Systems Inc 1000 S Lake Pk Ave *Web:* www.ancilla.org	Hobart	IN	46342	219-947-8500	947-4037
Appalachian Regional Healthcare Service 2285 Executive Dr Suite 400 *Web:* www.arh.org	Lexington	KY	40505	859-226-2440	226-2586
Ardent Health Services LLC 1 Burton Hills Blvd Suite 250 *Web:* www.ardenthealth.com	Nashville	TN	37215	615-296-3000	296-6005
Ascension Health 4600 Edmundson Rd *Web:* www.ascensionhealth.org	Saint Louis	MO	63134	314-733-8000	733-8008
Aurora Health Care Inc 3000 W Montana St *Web:* www.aurorahealthcare.com	Milwaukee	WI	53234	414-647-3000	647-3494
Avera Health 3900 W Avera Dr *Web:* www.avera.org	Sioux Falls	SD	57108	605-322-4700	322-4799
Banner Health 1441 N 12th St *Web:* www.bannerhealth.com	Phoenix	AZ	85006	602-495-4000	495-4689
Baptist Health 9601 I-630 *Web:* www.baptist-health.com	Little Rock	AR	72205	501-202-2000	202-1159
Baptist Health System 3201 4th Ave S **Fax:* Hum Res ■ *Web:* www.bhsala.com	Birmingham	AL	35222	205-715-5000	715-5251*
Baptist Health Systems of South Florida 6855 Red Rd Suite 600 *TF:* 800-327-2491 ■ *Web:* www.baptisthealth.net	Coral Gables	FL	33143	786-662-7111	662-7334
Baptist Healthcare System 4007 Kresge Way *Web:* www.bhsi.com	Louisville	KY	40207	502-896-5000	896-5020
Baptist Hospital 2000 Church St *Web:* www.baptist-hosp.org	Nashville	TN	37236	615-284-5555	284-1592
Baptist Memorial Health Care Corp 6019 Walnut Grove Rd **Fax:* Admissions ■ *Web:* www.bmhcc.org	Memphis	TN	38120	901-227-2727	226-5661*
Baylor Health Care System 3500 Gaston Ave *Web:* www.baylorhealth.com	Dallas	TX	75246	214-820-0111	820-2594
Baystate Health Systems Inc 759 Chestnut St **Fax:* Hum Res ■ *Web:* baystatehealth.com	Springfield	MA	01199	413-784-0000	794-3325*
Benedictine Health System 503 E 3rd St Suite 400 *TF:* 800-833-7208 ■ *Web:* www.bhshealth.org	Duluth	MN	55805	218-786-2370	786-2373
BJC HealthCare 4444 Forest Park Ave Suite 500 *Web:* www.bjc.org	Saint Louis	MO	63108	314-286-2000	286-2060
Bon Secours Health System Inc 1505 Marriottsville Rd *Web:* www.bshsi.com	Marriottsville	MD	21104	410-442-5511	442-1082
Brim Healthcare Inc 105 Westwood Pl Suite 300 *Web:* www.brimhealthcare.com	Brentwood	TN	37027	615-309-6053	370-2859
CAMC Health System Inc 501 Morris St *Web:* www.camc.org	Charleston	WV	25301	304-388-7627	388-7696
CareGroup Inc 375 Longwood Ave 3rd Fl **Fax:* Hum Res ■ *Web:* www.caregroup.org	Boston	MA	02215	617-975-5000	632-9925*
Carilion Health System 1906 Belleview PO Box 13367 *Web:* www.carilion.com	Roanoke	VA	24033	540-981-7000	981-7670
Caritas Christi Health Care System 736 Cambridge St *Web:* www.caritaschristi.org	Brighton	MA	02135	617-789-2500	789-2124
Carolinas HealthCare System 1000 Blythe Blvd PO Box 32861 **Fax:* Mktg ■ *Web:* www.carolinas.org	Charlotte	NC	28232	704-355-2000	355-4084*
Cathedral Healthcare System Inc 219 Chestnut St *Web:* www.cathedralhealth.org	Newark	NJ	07105	973-690-3500	690-3601
Catholic Health East 4211 W Boy Scout Blvd Suite 160 *Web:* www.che.org	Tampa	FL	33607	813-874-0758	874-0710
Catholic Health Initiatives 1999 Broadway Suite 2600 *Web:* www.catholichealthinit.org	Denver	CO	80202	303-298-9100	298-9690
Catholic Healthcare Partners 615 Elsinore Pl **Fax:* Hum Res ■ *TF:* 800-367-9212 ■ *Web:* www.health-partners.org	Cincinnati	OH	45202	513-639-2800	639-2700*
Catholic Healthcare System 155 E 56th St 2nd Fl *Web:* www.catholichealthcaresystem.org	New York	NY	10022	212-752-7300	
Catholic Healthcare West 185 Berry St Suite 300 *Web:* www.chw.edu	San Francisco	CA	94107	415-438-5500	438-5724
Centra Health Inc 1920 Atherholt Rd *TF:* 800-777-4325 ■ *Web:* www.centrahealth.com	Lynchburg	VA	24501	434-947-4700	947-4892
Christiana Care Health System 501 W 14th St *Web:* www.christianacare.org	Wilmington	DE	19801	302-428-2203	428-2564
CHRISTUS Health 6363 N Hwy 161 Suite 450 *Web:* www.christushealth.org	Irving	TX	75038	214-492-8500	492-8540
CHRISTUS Schumpert Health System 1 St Mary Pl *TF:* 888-336-8115 ■ *Web:* www.christusschumpert.org	Shreveport	LA	71101	318-681-4500	681-4232
CHRISTUS Spohn Health System 1702 Santa Fe St *Web:* www.christusspohn.org	Corpus Christi	TX	78404	361-881-3400	885-0566
Clarent Hospital Corp 12337 Jones Rd Suite 218 *Web:* www.clarenthospital.com	Houston	TX	77070	281-970-5104	774-5120
Community Health Systems Inc 4000 Meridian Blvd *NYSE: CYH* ■ *TF:* 888-373-9600 ■ *Web:* www.chs.net	Franklin	TN	37067	615-465-7000	370-3548
Community Medical Centers 2823 Fresno St po bOX 1232 **Fax:* Admitting ■ *Web:* www.chsnet.com	Fresno	CA	93715	559-459-6000	459-2420*
Covenant Health System 3615 19th St *Web:* www.covenanthealth.org	Lubbock	TX	79410	806-725-1011	725-1055
Covenant Health Systems Inc 420 Bedford St *Web:* www.covenanths.com	Lexington	MA	02420	781-862-1634	862-5477
Crozer-Keystone Health System 100 W Sproul Rd Healthplex Pavilion 2 3rd Fl *Web:* www.crozer.org	Springfield	PA	19064	610-338-8200	338-8230
DCH Health System 809 University Blvd E *Web:* www.dchsystem.com	Tuscaloosa	AL	35401	205-759-7111	750-5541
Department of the Navy Medicine & Surgery Bureau 2300 'E' St NW *Web:* navymedicine.med.navy.mil	Washington	DC	20372	202-762-3218	
Detroit Medical Center 4201 St Antoine *Web:* www.dmc.org	Detroit	MI	48201	313-745-6035	578-3942
Dimensions Health Corp 3001 Hospital Dr *Web:* www.dimensionshealth.org	Cheverly	MD	20785	301-583-4000	618-2270
East Texas Medical Center Regional Healthcare System 1000 S Beckham Ave *Web:* www.etmc.org	Tyler	TX	75701	903-597-0351	596-3706
Eastern Maine Healthcare 43 Whiting Hill Rd *Web:* www.emh.org	Brewer	ME	04412	207-973-7050	973-7139
Empire Health Services 800 W 5th Ave PO Box 248 *Web:* www.empirehealth.org	Spokane	WA	99210	509-473-7960	473-7286
Fairview Hospital & Healthcare Services 2450 Riverside Ave S *TF:* 800-328-4661 ■ *Web:* fairview.org	Minneapolis	MN	55454	612-672-6000	672-7186
Franciscan Missionaries of Our Lady Health System 4200 Essen Ln *Web:* www.fmolhs.org	Baton Rouge	LA	70809	225-923-2701	926-4846
Franciscan Services Corp 6832 Convent Blvd *Web:* www.fscsylvania.org	Sylvania	OH	43560	419-882-8373	882-7360
Franciscan Sisters of Christian Charity HealthCare Ministry Inc 1415 S Rapids Rd *Web:* www.fhcm.org	Manitowoc	WI	54220	920-684-7071	684-6417
Geisinger Health System 100 N Academy Ave **Fax:* Mktg ■ *Web:* www.geisinger.org	Danville	PA	17822	570-271-6211	271-5636*
General Health System 3600 Florida Blvd *Web:* www.generalhealth.org	Baton Rouge	LA	70806	225-387-7767	237-1623

Phone Fax

Great Plains Health Alliance Inc 625 3rd St ... Phillipsburg KS 67661 785-543-2111
TF: 800-432-2779 ■ *Web:* www.gpha.com

Greenville Hospital System 701 Grove Rd ... Greenville SC 29605 864-455-7000 455-8434
TF: 800-472-8339 ■ *Web:* www.ghs.org

Guthrie Healthcare System 1 Guthrie Sq ... Sayre PA 18840 570-882-4312 882-5152
TF: 888-448-8474 ■ *Web:* www.guthrie.org

HCA Inc 1 Park Plaza ... Nashville TN 37203 615-344-9551 344-2830
NYSE: HCA ■ *TF:* 800-828-2561 ■ *Web:* www.hcahealthcare.com

HCA Midwest Div 903 E 104th St ... Kansas City MO 64131 816-508-4000 508-4036
Web: www.healthmidwest.org

Health Management Assoc Inc 5811 Pelican Bay Blvd Suite 500 ... Naples FL 34108 239-598-3131 597-5794
NYSE: HMA ■ *Web:* www.hma-corp.com

Healtheast 559 Capitol Blvd Suite 6-South ... Saint Paul MN 55103 651-232-2300 232-2315
Web: www.healtheast.org

Henry Ford Health System 1 Ford Pl ... Detroit MI 48202 313-916-2600 874-6380
TF: 800-999-4340 ■ *Web:* www.henryfordhealth.org

Hospital Sisters Health System
4936 Laverna Rd PO Box 19456 ... Springfield IL 62794 217-523-4747 523-0542
Web: www.hshs.org

IASIS Healthcare Corp 117 Seaboard Ln Bldg E ... Franklin TN 37067 615-844-2747 846-3006
Web: www.iasishealthcare.com

Infirmary Health System Inc
5 Mobile Infirmary Cir PO Box 2226 ... Mobile AL 36652 251-435-5500 435-2060
Web: www.mobileinfirmary.org

Inova Health System 8110 Gatehouse Rd ... Falls Church VA 22042 703-289-2069 289-2070
Web: www.inova.com

INTEGRIS Health Inc 3366 NW Expressway St Suite 800 ... Oklahoma City OK 73112 405-949-6066 951-2733
Web: www.integris-health.com

Intermountain Health Care Inc (IHC)
36 S State St 22nd Fl ... Salt Lake City UT 84111 801-442-2000 442-3327*
*Fax: Hum Res ■ *TF Hum Res:* 800-843-7820 ■ *Web:* www.ihc.com

Iowa Health System 1200 Pleasant St ... Des Moines IA 50309 515-241-6201 241-5994
Web: www.ihs.org

Jefferson Health System 259 N Radnor-Chester Rd Suite 290 ... Radnor PA 19087 610-225-6200 225-6260
Web: www.jeffersonhealth.org

Johns Hopkins Health System 600 N Wolfe St ... Baltimore MD 21287 410-955-5000 955-6575*
*Fax: Hum Res ■ *Web:* www.hopkinshospital.org

Kaiser Foundation Health Plan & Hospitals Inc
1 Kaiser Plaza 27th Fl ... Oakland CA 94612 510-271-5660 271-5820

Kindred Healthcare Inc 680 S 4th Ave ... Louisville KY 40202 502-596-7300 596-4052
NYSE: KND ■ *TF:* 800-545-0749 ■ *Web:* www.kindredhealthcare.com

Legacy Health System 1919 NW Lovejoy St ... Portland OR 97209 503-415-5600 415-5777
Web: www.legacyhealth.org

LifePoint Hospitals Inc 103 Powell Ct Suite 200 ... Brentwood TN 37027 615-372-8500
NASDAQ: LPNT ■ *Web:* www.lifepointhospitals.com

Los Angeles County Dept of Health Services
313 N Figueroa St Rm 912 ... Los Angeles CA 90012 213-240-8101 481-0503
Web: www.dhs.co.la.ca.us

Marian Health System Inc PO Box 4753 ... Tulsa OK 74159 918-742-9988 744-2716
Web: www.marianhealthsystem.com

Mayo Foundation 200 SW 1st St ... Rochester MN 55905 507-284-2511 284-0161

MedCath Inc 10720 Sikes Pl Suite 300 ... Charlotte NC 28277 704-708-6610 708-5035
NASDAQ: MDTH ■ *Web:* www.medcath.com

MedStar Health 5565 Sterrett Pl 5th Fl ... Columbia MD 21044 410-772-6500 715-3754
TF: 877-772-6505 ■ *Web:* www.medstarhealth.org

Memorial Health Services Inc 7677 Center Ave ... Huntington Beach CA 92647 562-933-1800 981-1336
Web: www.memorialcare.org

Memorial Health Systems 875 Sterthaus Ave ... Ormond Beach FL 32174 386-676-6000 676-6077*
*Fax: Admitting ■ *TF:* 888-647-0271 ■ *Web:* www.memorial-health.com

Memorial Hermann Healthcare System 7600 Beechnut St ... Houston TX 77074 713-776-5500 776-5144*
*Fax: Cust Svc ■ *Web:* www.memorialhermann.org

Mercy Health System 1 W Elm St ... Conshohocken PA 19428 610-567-6100 567-6444
Web: www.mercyhealth.org

Methodist Health Care System 6565 Fannin St ... Houston TX 77030 713-790-3311 793-1362*
*Fax: Admitting ■ *Web:* www.methodisthealth.com

Methodist Healthcare Inc 1265 Union Ave ... Memphis TN 38104 901-516-7000 516-2394
Web: www.methodisthealth.org

Methodist Hospitals of Dallas 1441 N Beckley Ave ... Dallas TX 75203 214-947-8181 947-6501
Web: www.methodisthealthsystem.org

MultiCare Health System 315 ML King Jr Way PO Box 5299 ... Tacoma WA 98415 253-403-1251 403-1180
Web: www.multicare.org

Munson Healthcare Inc 1105 6th St ... Traverse City MI 49684 231-922-9000 935-6859*
*Fax: Admitting ■ *TF:* 800-468-6766 ■ *Web:* www.munsonhealthcare.org

New York City Health & Hospitals Corp 125 Worth St ... New York NY 10013 212-788-3339 788-3348*
*Fax: PR ■ *Web:* www.ci.nyc.ny.us/html/hhc

New York-Presbyterian Healthcare System 622 W 168th St ... New York NY 10032 212-305-2500
TF: 877-697-9355 ■ *Web:* www.nyp.org/system

North Broward Hospital District 303 SE 17th St ... Fort Lauderdale FL 33316 954-355-5100 355-4966

North Mississippi Health Services 830 S Gloster St ... Tupelo MS 38801 662-377-3000 377-3990
Web: www.nmhs.net

North Shore-Long Island Jewish Health System
145 Community Dr ... Great Neck NY 11021 516-465-8000 465-2650*
*Fax: PR ■ *Web:* www.nslij.com

Norton Healthcare 415 E Broadway PO Box 35070 ... Louisville KY 40232 502-629-8025 629-8059
Web: www.nortonhealthcare.com

Novant Health Inc 3333 Silas Creek Pkwy ... Winston-Salem NC 27103 336-718-5000 297-1481
Web: www.novanthealth.org

Oakwood Health Services Corp
18101 Oakwood Blvd PO Box 2500 ... Dearborn MI 48123 313-593-7000 436-2049
TF: 800-543-9355 ■ *Web:* www.oakwood.org

OhioHealth Corporate Offices 1087 Dennison Ave 3rd Fl ... Columbus OH 43201 614-544-4485 544-5244
Web: www.ohiohealth.com

Orlando Regional Healthcare System 1414 Kuhl Ave ... Orlando FL 32806 407-841-5111 767-0896*
*Fax: Hum Res ■ *Web:* www.orlandoregional.org

OSF Healthcare System 800 NE Glen Oak Ave ... Peoria IL 61603 309-655-2850 655-6869
Web: www.osfhealthcare.org

Pacific Health Corp 14642 Newport Ave Suite 388 ... Tustin CA 92780 714-669-2085 669-2059

Palomar Pomerado Health System 15615 Pomerado Rd ... Poway CA 92064 858-613-4000 675-5467
TF: 800-628-2880 ■ *Web:* www.pphs.org

Partners HealthCare System Inc 800 Boylston St Suite 1150 ... Boston MA 02199 617-278-1000 278-1049
Web: www.partners.org

Premier Inc 12225 El Camino Real ... San Diego CA 92130 858-481-2727 481-8919
TF: 877-777-1552 ■ *Web:* www.premierinc.com

Presbyterian Healthcare Services 1100 Central Ave SE ... Albuquerque NM 87106 505-841-1234 841-1153
TF: 800-545-4030 ■ *Web:* www.phs.org

Provena Health 9223 W Saint Francis Rd ... Frankfort IL 60423 815-469-4888 469-4864
Web: www.provena.org

Providence Health & Services 9 E 9th Ave ... Spokane WA 99202 509-474-7337 474-4882
Web: www.prov-serv.com

Providence Health System 506 2nd Ave Suite 1200 ... Seattle WA 98104 206-464-3355 464-3038
Web: www.providence.org

Queen's Health Systems 1099 Alakea St Suite 1100 ... Honolulu HI 96813 808-532-6100 535-5415

Riverside Health System 701 Town Center Dr Suite 1000 ... Newport News VA 23606 757-534-7000 534-7087
Web: www.riverside-online.com

Rush System for Health
1653 W Congress Pkwy Kidston Bldg Suite 305 ... Chicago IL 60612 312-942-5000 942-5831
Web: www.rush.edu

Saint David's HealthCare 98 San Jacinto Blvd Suite 1800 ... Austin TX 78701 512-708-9700 482-4126*
*Fax: Mktg ■ *Web:* www.stdavids.com

Saint Francis Care 114 Woodland St ... Hartford CT 06105 860-714-4000 714-7809
Web: www.stfranciscare.org

Saint Joseph Health System 500 S Main St ... Orange CA 92868 714-347-7500 347-7501
Web: www.stjhs.org

Saint Mary's Good Samaritan Inc 605 N 12th St ... Mount Vernon IL 62864 618-242-4600 241-3810
TF: 800-310-0484 ■ *Web:* www.smgsi.com

Saint Vincent Catholic Medical Centers 170 W 12th St ... New York NY 10011 212-604-7000 558-2425*
*Fax Area Code: 718 ■ *Web:* www.svcmc.org

Scottsdale Healthcare 3621 N Wells Fargo Ave ... Scottsdale AZ 85251 480-481-4327 994-1597
Web: www.smhsi.com

Scripps Health 4275 Campus Point Ct ... San Diego CA 92121 858-678-6111 678-6767
TF: 800-727-4777 ■ *Web:* www.scrippshealth.org

Sentara Healthcare 6015 Poplar Hall Dr ... Norfolk VA 23502 757-455-7000 455-7964*
*Fax: Mktg ■ *Web:* www.sentara.com

Sharp Healthcare 8695 Spectrum Center Blvd ... San Diego CA 92123 858-499-4000 499-5237
Web: www.sharp.com

Shriners Hospitals for Children 2900 N Rocky Pt Dr ... Tampa FL 33607 813-972-2250 281-8113*
*Fax: Hum Res ■ *TF:* 800-237-5055 ■ *Web:* www.shrinershq.org/hospitals

Sisters of Charity of Leavenworth Health System
9801 Renner Blvd Suite 100 ... Lenexa KS 66219 913-895-2800 895-2900
Web: www.sclhsc.org

Sisters of Charity of Saint Augustine Health System
2351 E 22nd St ... Cleveland OH 44115 216-696-5560 696-2204
Web: www.csahealthsystem.org

Sisters of the Holy Family of Nazareth Sacred Heart Province
310 N River Rd ... Des Plaines IL 60016 847-298-6760 803-1941

Sisters of Mary of the Presentation Health System
1202 Page Drive SW PO Box 10007 ... Fargo ND 58106 701-237-9290 235-0906
Web: www.smphs.org

Sisters of Mercy Health System
14528 S Outer Forty Suite 100 ... Chesterfield MO 63017 314-579-6100 628-3723
Web: www.mercy.net

Sisters of Saint Francis Health Services Inc
1515 Dragoon Trail PO Box 1290 ... Mishawaka IN 46546 574-256-3935 256-0267
Web: www.ssfhs.org

Sisters of the Third Franciscan Order 2500 Grant Blvd ... Syracuse NY 13208 315-425-0115 425-0610
Web: www.osfsyr.org

Solaris Health System Inc 80 James St ... Edison NJ 08820 732-632-1501 632-1549
Web: www.solarishs.org

Southern Illinois Healthcare 1239 E Main St ... Carbondale IL 62902 618-457-5200 549-7522
TF: 866-744-2468 ■ *Web:* www.sih.net

Spartanburg Regional Healthcare System 101 E Wood St ... Spartanburg SC 29303 864-560-6000 560-6001*
*Fax: Mail Rm ■ *Web:* www.srhs.com

SSM Health Care 477 N Lindbergh Blvd ... Saint Louis MO 63141 314-994-7800 994-7900
Web: www.ssmhc.com

SunLink Health Systems Inc 900 Circle 75 Pkwy Suite 1120 ... Atlanta GA 30339 770-933-7000 933-7010
AMEX: SSY ■ *Web:* www.sunlinkhealth.com

Sutter Health 2200 River Plaza ... Sacramento CA 95833 916-733-8800 286-6611
TF: 800-606-7070 ■ *Web:* www.sutterhealth.org

Tenet Healthcare Corp 13737 Noel Rd ... Dallas TX 75240 469-893-2200 893-8600
NYSE: THC ■ *TF:* 800-743-6333 ■ *Web:* www.tenethealth.com

Texas Health Resources 611 Ryan Plaza Dr Suite 900 ... Arlington TX 76011 817-462-7900 462-6230
Web: www.texashealth.org

Triad Hospitals Inc 5800 Tennyson Pkwy ... Plano TX 75024 214-473-7000
NYSE: TRI ■ *TF:* 800-238-6006 ■ *Web:* www.triadhospitals.com

Trinity Health 27870 Cabot Dr ... Novi MI 48377 248-489-5004 489-6775
Web: www.trinity-health.org

Trinity Health System 380 Summit Ave ... Steubenville OH 43952 740-283-7000 283-7425
Web: www.trinityhealth.com

Truman Medical Center 2301 Holmes St ... Kansas City MO 64108 816-404-1000 404-2573
Web: www.trumed.org

United Health Services Hospitals 10-42 Mitchell Ave ... Binghamton NY 13903 607-762-2263 763-5186
Web: www.uhs.net

United Medical Corp 603 Main St ... Windermere FL 34786 407-876-2200 876-5959

Universal Health Services Inc 367 S Gulph Rd ... King of Prussia PA 19406 610-768-3300 768-3336
NYSE: UHS ■ *TF:* 800-347-7750 ■ *Web:* www.uhsinc.com

University of California Health System 1111 Franklin St ... Oakland CA 94607 510-987-0700 987-0894*
*Fax: Hum Res ■ *Web:* www.universityofcalifornia.edu/health

University Health Network 200 Elizabeth St ... Toronto ON M5G2C4 416-340-3388 340-4896*
*Fax: PR ■ *Web:* www.uhn.ca

University of Maryland Medical System 22 S Greene St ... Baltimore MD 21201 410-328-8667 328-2412
TF: 800-492-5538 ■ *Web:* www.umm.edu

University of Pittsburgh Medical Center Health System
200 Lothrop St ... Pittsburgh PA 15213 412-647-2345 647-4522*
*Fax: Hum Res ■ *TF:* 800-533-8762 ■ *Web:* www.upmc.edu

University of Texas System Office of Health Affairs
601 Colorado St ... Austin TX 78701 512-499-4224 499-4313
Web: www.utsystem.edu/hea

US Army Medical Command
2050 Worth Rd Bldg 2792 ... Fort Sam Houston TX 78234 210-221-6213
Web: www.armymedicine.army.mil

US Public Health Service Indian Health Service
801 Thompson Ave Suite 400 ... Rockville MD 20852 301-443-1083 443-0507*
*Fax: PR ■ *Web:* www.ihs.gov

Valley Health System 1117 E Devonshire Ave ... Hemet CA 92543 951-652-2811 925-6323
Web: www.valleyhealthsystem.com

Vanguard Health Systems Inc 20 Burton Hills Blvd Suite 100 ... Nashville TN 37215 615-665-6000 665-6099
Web: www.vanguardhealth.com

Veterans Health Administration 810 Vermont Ave NW ... Washington DC 20420 202-273-5400
Web: www1.va.gov/health

Via Christi Health System 3720 E Bayley St ... Wichita KS 67218 316-858-4939 858-4186
Web: www.via-christi.org

Vibra Healthcare 4550 Lena Dr ... Mechanicsburg PA 17055 717-591-5700 591-5710
Web: www.vibrahealthcare.com

Virginia Commonwealth University Health System
1250 E Marshall St ... Richmond VA 23219 804-828-9000 828-6727
Web: www.vcuhealth.org

Virtua Health 94 Brick Rd Suite 200 ... Marlton NJ 08053 856-355-0004 355-0012
Web: www.virtua.org

VistaCare Inc 4800 N Scottsdale Rd Suite 5000 ... Scottsdale AZ 85251 480-648-4545 648-4547
NASDAQ: VSTA ■ *TF:* 888-608-4665 ■ *Web:* www.vistacare.com

West Penn Allegheny Health System
320 E North Ave Suite 104 ... Pittsburgh PA 15212 412-359-8782 359-6516
Web: www.asri.edu

West Tennessee Healthcare 708 W Forest Ave ... Jackson TN 38301 731-541-5000 541-6802
Web: www.wth.net

Wheaton Franciscan Healthcare 26 W 171 Roosevelt Rd ... Wheaton IL 60187 630-462-9271 462-4977
Web: www.wheatonfranciscan.org

William Beaumont Hospital 3601 W 13-Mile Rd ... Royal Oak MI 48073 248-551-5000 898-0400*
*Fax: Admitting ■ *Web:* www.beaumonthospitals.com

357 HEALTH & FITNESS CENTERS

SEE ALSO Spas - Health & Fitness p. 2318; Weight Loss Centers & Services p. 2415

Company	City	State	Zip	Phone	Fax
24 Hour Fitness Worldwide Inc 12647 Alcosta Blvd 5th fl *TF:* 888-256-5485 ■ *Web:* www.24hourfitness.com	San Ramon	CA	94583	925-543-3100	543-3200
Anytime Fitness Inc 330 E Marie Ave. *TF:* 800-704-5004 ■ *Web:* www.anytimefitness.com	West Saint Paul	MN	55118	651-554-0144	554-0311
Bally Total Fitness Holding Corp 8700 W Bryn Mawr Ave *NYSE: BFT* ■ *Web:* www.ballyfitness.com	Chicago	IL	60631	773-399-1300	693-2982
Bel Air Athletic Club 8400 E Crescent Pkwy Suite 200 *TF:* 888-458-0489 ■ *Web:* www.baac.com	Greenwood Village	CO	80111	303-866-0800	
Boston Sports Clubs 10 Franklin St Suite 3 *Web:* www.bostonsportsclub.com	Boston	MA	02110	617-426-1058	
Brick Bodies Fitness Services Inc 201 Old Padonia Rd *TF:* 877-348-3861 ■ *Web:* www.brickbodies.com	Cockeysville	MD	21030	410-252-8058	560-3299
Butterfly Life 2404 San Ramon Valley Blvd Suite 200 **Fax Area Code: 925* ■ *Web:* www.butterflylife.com	San Ramon	CA	94583	800-288-8373	743-8820*
Capital City Club Inc 7 Harris St *Web:* www.capitalcityclub.org	Atlanta	GA	30303	404-523-8221	659-3498
Chelsea Piers Sports & Entertainment Complex W 23rd St & Hudson River *Web:* www.chelseapiers.com	New York	NY	10011	212-336-6666	336-6130
Club One Inc 555 Market St 13th fl *Web:* www.clubone.com	San Francisco	CA	94105	415-477-3000	477-3001
Clubsport of San Ramon 350 Bollinger Canyon Ln *Web:* www.clubsportsr.com	San Ramon	CA	94582	925-735-8500	735-7916
Contours Express Inc 156 Imperial Way *TF:* 877-227-2282 ■ *Web:* www.contoursexpress.com	Nicholasville	KY	40356	859-885-6441	241-2234
Court Sport 1 150 Clearbrook Rd *Web:* www.court-sports.com	Elmsford	NY	10523	914-592-3005	347-7432
Courthouse Athletic Club 495 State St 6th Fl *Web:* www.fitfx.com	Salem	OR	97301	503-364-1731	371-0773
Crunch Fitness International 11 E 26th St 5th Fl *TF:* 888-227-8624 ■ *Web:* www.crunch.com	New York	NY	10010	212-993-0300	993-0343
Curves International Inc 100 Ritchie Rd *TF:* 800-848-1096 ■ *Web:* www.curves.com	Waco	TX	76712	254-399-9285	399-9731
Cuts Fitness For Men 1120 Raritan Rd *Web:* www.cutsfitness.com	Clark	NJ	07066	732-381-9300	574-1130
Denver Athletic Club 1325 Glenarm Pl. *Web:* www.denverathleticclub.cc	Denver	CO	80204	303-534-1211	534-1125
Detroit Athletic Club 241 Madison St *Web:* www.thedac.com	Detroit	MI	48226	313-963-9200	963-8891
East Bank Club 500 N Kingsbury St *Web:* www.eastbankclub.com	Chicago	IL	60610	312-527-5800	527-5666
Equinox Fitness Holdings Inc 895 Broadway *TF:* 866-332-6549 ■ *Web:* www.equinoxfitness.com	New York	NY	10003	212-677-0180	777-9510
Fitcorp 800 Boylston St Prudential Ctr Suite 2475 *Web:* www.fitcorp.com	Boston	MA	02199	617-375-5600	262-2058
Fitness Center 2508 S Galen Dr *Web:* www.fitcen.com	Champaign	IL	61821	217-356-1616	356-7920
Fitness Co 2137 Hwy 35 N *Web:* www.thefitnesscompany.com	Holmdel	NJ	07733	732-203-1220	203-1660
Fitness Management Corp 7091 Orchard Lake Rd Suite 300 *Web:* www.fitnessusa.com	West Bloomfield	MI	48322	248-539-3800	932-3300
FitWorks 26391 Curtiss Wright Pkwy Suite 104 *TF:* 877-333-5348 ■ *Web:* www.fitworks.com	Richmond Heights	OH	44143	216-289-3100	289-3714
French Riviera Health Spa 3908 Veterans Memorial Blvd *Web:* www.frenchrivieraspa.com	Metairie	LA	70001	504-454-5855	454-7717
Gold's Gym International Inc 125 E John Carpenter Fwy Suite 1300 *TF:* 800-457-5375 ■ *Web:* www.goldsgym.com	Irving	TX	75062	214-574-4653	
GoodLife Fitness 355 Wellington St PO Box 23091 **Fax Area Code: 519* ■ *Web:* www.goodlifefitness.com	London	ON	N6A5N9	800-387-2524	438-7461*
Gorilla Sports 12440 E Imperial Hwy Suite 300 *TF:* 800-447-7457 ■ *Web:* www.gorillasports.com	Norwalk	CA	90651	562-484-2000	484-2444
Greenwood Athletic Club 5801 S Quebec St *Web:* www.greenwoodathleticclub.com	Greenwood Village	CO	80111	303-770-2582	850-9219
Greenwood Athletic Club 1330 Bypass 72 NE Piedmont Plaza *Web:* www.gwdac.com	Greenwood	SC	29649	864-229-7500	
Health Fitness Corp 3600 American Blvd West Suite 560 *TF:* 800-639-7913 ■ *Web:* www.hfit.com	Bloomington	MN	55431	952-831-6830	831-7264
Healthtrax Inc 2345 Main St. *Web:* www.healthtrax.com	Glastonbury	CT	06033	860-633-5572	652-7066
In-Shape Sports Club 1016 E Bianchi Rd Suite A-1 *Web:* www.inshapeclubs.com	Stockton	CA	95210	209-472-2231	474-7586
Kinderdance International Inc 1333 Gateway Dr Suite 1033 *TF:* 800-554-2334 ■ *Web:* www.kinderdance.com	Melbourne	FL	32901	321-984-4448	984-4490
LA Fitness International 8105 Irvine Ctr Dr Suite 200 **Fax Area Code: 800* ■ *TF:* 800-600-2540 ■ *Web:* www.lafitness.com	Irvine	CA	92618	949-255-7400	600-2539*
Lady of America Franchise Corp 500 E Broward Blvd Suite 1650 *TF:* 800-833-5239 ■ *Web:* www.ladyofamerica.com	Fort Lauderdale	FL	33394	954-527-5373	527-5436
Lake Shore Athletic Club Inc 2401 NW 94th St *Web:* www.lsac.com	Vancouver	WA	98665	360-574-1991	574-9233
Las Vegas Athletic Club 2655 S Maryland Pkwy Suite 201 *Web:* www.lvac.com	Las Vegas	NV	89109	702-734-8944	733-7771
Life Time Fitness 5525 Cedar Lake Rd. *Web:* www.lifetimefitness.com	Saint Louis Park	MN	55416	952-546-5474	525-2567
Life Time Fitness Inc 6442 City West Pkwy *NYSE: LTM* ■ *TF:* 888-430-5433 ■ *Web:* www.lifetimefitness.com	Eden Prairie	MN	55344	952-947-0000	947-0077
Little Gym International Inc 8970 E Raintree Dr Suite 200 *TF:* 888-228-2878 ■ *Web:* www.thelittlegym.com	Scottsdale	AZ	85260	480-948-2878	948-2765
Lucille Roberts Health Clubs Inc 4 E 80th St *Web:* www.lucilleroberts.com	New York	NY	10021	212-734-0616	734-4151
Milwaukee Athletic Club 758 N Broadway *Web:* www.macwi.org	Milwaukee	WI	53202	414-273-5080	273-4118
Multnomah Athletic Club 1849 SW Salmon St *Web:* www.themac.com	Portland	OR	97205	503-223-6251	525-8998
My Gym Enterprises Inc 15300 Ventura Blvd Suite 414 **Fax Area Code: 818* ■ *TF:* 800-426-4573 ■ *Web:* www.my-gym.com	Sherman Oaks	CA	91403	800-469-4967	907-0735*
New York Athletic Club Inc 180 Central Park S. *Web:* www.nyac.org	New York	NY	10019	212-247-5100	767-7137
New York Health & Racquet Club Inc 3 New York Plaza 8th Fl *TF:* 800-472-2378 ■ *Web:* www.nyhrc.com	New York	NY	10004	212-797-1500	837-4938
New York Sports Club 888 7th Ave 25th Fl *TF:* 800-301-1231 ■ *Web:* www.mysportsclubs.com	New York	NY	10106	212-246-6700	246-8422
Omni Fitness Club 40 E Norton St. *Web:* www.omnifitnessclub.com	Muskegon	MI	49444	231-739-3391	733-0156
Philadelphia Sports Clubs 888 7th Ave *TF:* 800-301-1231 ■ *Web:* www.mysportsclubs.com	New York	NY	10106	212-246-6700	246-8422
Pinnacle Fitness 12440 E Imperial Hwy Suite 300 *TF:* 800-447-7457 ■ *Web:* www.pinnaclefitness.com	Norwalk	CA	90651	562-484-2000	484-2444
Powerhouse Gym International 24385 Halsted Rd Suite 2000 *Web:* www.powerhousegym.com	Farmington Hills	MI	48335	248-476-2888	476-4732
Premier & Curzons Fitness Clubs 5100 Dixie Rd. *Web:* www.premierfitness.ca	Mississauga	ON	L4W1C9	905-602-9911	602-9922
Rivers Club Inc 1 Oxford Ctr 301 Grant St Suite 411 *Web:* www.riversclub.com	Pittsburgh	PA	15219	412-391-5227	391-5016
San Francisco Bay Club 150 Greenwich St *Web:* www.sfbayclub.com	San Francisco	CA	94111	415-433-2550	433-7161
Seattle Athletic Club 2020 Western Ave *Web:* www.sacdt.com	Seattle	WA	98121	206-443-1111	443-2632
Sports Club Co Inc 11151 Missouri Ave. *AMEX: SCY* ■ **Fax:* Hum Res ■ *Web:* www.thesportsclubla.com	Los Angeles	CA	90025	310-479-5200	479-8350*
StrollerFit Inc 100 E-Business Way Suite 290 *TF:* 866-222-9348 ■ *Web:* www.strollerfit.com	Cincinnati	OH	45241	513-489-2920	489-2964
Town Sports International Inc 888 7th Ave *TF:* 800-301-1231 ■ *Web:* www.mysportsclubs.com	New York	NY	10106	212-246-6700	246-8422
Washington Sports Clubs 888 7th Ave *TF:* 800-301-1231 ■ *Web:* www.mysportsclubs.com	New York	NY	10106	212-246-6700	246-8422
Wellbridge Co 8400 E Crescent Pkwy Suite 200 *TF:* 888-458-0489 ■ *Web:* www.wellbridge.com	Greenwood Village	CO	80111	303-866-0800	860-0440
Western Athletic Clubs 1 Lombard St *Web:* www.clubwest.com	San Francisco	CA	94111	415-781-1874	394-5570
World Gym International 226 E Palm Ave *TF:* 800-544-7441 ■ *Web:* www.worldgym.com	Burbank	CA	91502	818-955-8905	
YMCA Birmingham 5414 Hwy 280 Suite 200 *Web:* www.sportsfirst.com	Birmingham	AL	35243	205-981-0302	981-0660

358 HEALTH FOOD STORES

Company	City	State	Zip	Phone	Fax
Christopher Enterprises 155 W 250 N *TF:* 800-453-1406 ■ *Web:* www.drchristophers.com	Spanish Fork	UT	84660	801-794-6800	794-6801
Fresh Fields 6015 Executive Blvd **Fax:* Mktg	Rockville	MD	20852	301-984-3737	984-2072*
GNC Corp 300 6th Ave **Fax:* Cust Svc ■ *TF Cust Svc:* 888-462-2548 ■ *Web:* www.gnc.com	Pittsburgh	PA	15222	412-288-4600	338-8905*
Juice It Up! Franchise Corp 17915 Sky Park Cir Suite J *Web:* www.juiceitup.com	Irvine	CA	92614	949-475-0146	475-0137
Netrition Inc 20 Petra Ln *TF:* 888-817-2411 ■ *Web:* www.netrition.com	Albany	NY	12205	518-464-0765	456-9673
Pilgrims Fine Foods Inc PO Box 14686	Spokane	WA	99214	509-924-7781	924-1441
Ripple Creek USA LLC PO Box 1165 *Web:* www.ripplecreek.com	Southport	CT	06890	203-331-0363	382-0044
Smoothie King Franchises Inc 2400 Veterans Blvd Suite 110 *TF:* 800-577-4200 ■ *Web:* www.smoothieking.com	Kenner	LA	70062	504-467-4006	469-1274
Whole Foods Market Inc 550 Bowie St *NASDAQ: WFMI* ■ *Web:* www.wholefoodsmarket.com	Austin	TX	78703	512-477-4455	482-7000
Wild Oats Markets Inc 3375 Mitchell Ln *NASDAQ: OATS* ■ **Fax:* Mktg ■ *TF:* 877-542-9453 ■ *Web:* www.wildoats.com	Boulder	CO	80301	303-440-5220	938-8474*

359 HEALTH & MEDICAL INFORMATION - ONLINE

Company	City	State	Zip	Phone	Fax
ADAM Inc 1600 RiverEdge Pkwy Suite 100 *NASDAQ: ADAM* ■ *TF:* 800-755-2326 ■ *Web:* www.adam.com	Atlanta	GA	30328	770-980-0888	955-3088
AIDS Education Global Information System (AEGIS) 32234 Paseo Adelanto Suite B *Web:* www.aegis.com	San Juan Capistrano	CA	92675	949-248-5843	248-2839
Alternative Medicine.com 2995 Wilderness Pl Suite 205 **Fax Area Code: 415* ■ *TF:* 800-333-4325 ■ *Web:* www.alternativemedicine.com	Boulder	CO	80301	303-440-7402	789-1404*
At Health Inc 14241 NE Woodinville-Duvall Rd Suite 104 *TF:* 888-284-3258 ■ *Web:* www.athealth.com	Woodinville	WA	98072	360-668-3808	668-2216
BabyCenter LLC 163 Freelon St. *TF:* 866-241-2229 ■ *Web:* www.babycenter.com	San Francisco	CA	94107	415-537-0900	537-0909
Body The Body Health Resources Corp 250 W 57th St *Web:* www.thebody.com	New York	NY	10107	212-541-8500	541-4911
cancerfacts.com 1725 Westlake Ave N Suite 300 *TF Cust Svc:* 877-422-3228 ■ *Web:* www.cancerfacts.com	Seattle	WA	98109	206-270-0225	270-0229
drgreene.com 9000 Crow Canyon Rd Suite S220 *Web:* www.drgreene.com	Danville	CA	94506	925-964-1793	964-1794
eDiets.com Inc 1000 Corporate Dr *NASDAQ: DIET* ■ *TF:* 800-265-6170 ■ *Web:* www.ediets.com	Fort Lauderdale	FL	33334	954-360-9022	360-9095
eMedicine.com Inc 8420 W Dodge Rd Suite 402 *TF:* 866-363-3362 ■ *Web:* www.emedicine.com	Omaha	NE	68114	402-341-3222	341-3336
eMedicineHealth.com 8420 W Dodge Rd Suite 402 *TF:* 866-363-3362 ■ *Web:* www.emedicinehealth.com	Omaha	NE	68114	402-341-3222	341-3336
Food Allergy & Anaphylaxis Network (FAAN) 11781 Lee Jackson Hwy Suite 160 *TF:* 800-929-4040 ■ *Web:* www.foodallergy.org	Fairfax	VA	22033	703-691-3179	691-2713
HealthAtoZ 50 Millstone Rd Bldg 200 Suite 160 Windsor Corporate Park *Web:* www.healthatoz.com	East Windsor	NJ	08520	609-301-2189	426-4621
HealthBoards.com iCentric Corp 6601 Center Dr W 5th Fl *Web:* www.healthboards.com	Los Angeles	CA	90045	310-348-8120	348-8127
HealthCentral.com Inc 1655 N Ft Myer Dr Suite 400 *Web:* www.healthcentral.com	Arlington	VA	22209	703-302-1040	248-0830
Medem Inc 649 Mission St 2nd Fl *Web:* www.medem.com	San Francisco	CA	94105	415-644-3800	644-3950
Medicine Online Inc 18800 Delaware St Suite 650 *Web:* www.medicineonline.com	Huntington Beach	CA	92648	714-848-0444	242-1484
MedlinePlus National Library of Medicine 8600 Rockville Pike *TF:* 888-346-3656 ■ *Web:* medlineplus.gov	Bethesda	MD	20894	301-594-5983	402-1384
Medscape 669 River Dr Center 2 *TF:* 800-809-0703 ■ *Web:* www.medscape.com	Elmwood Park	NJ	07407	201-703-3400	703-3401
NIH SeniorHealth 9000 Rockville Pike Bldg 31 *TF:* 800-222-2225 ■ *Web:* nihseniorhealth.gov	Bethesda	MD	20892	301-496-1752	496-1072
OBGyn.net MediSpecialty.com Inc 1050 George St Suite 14-L *Web:* www.obgyn.net	New Brunswick	NJ	08901	732-828-6382	828-6385
Pain.com Dannemiller Memorial Educational Foundation 5711 NW Parkway Suite 100 *TF:* 800-328-2308 ■ *Web:* www.pain.com	San Antonio	TX	78249	210-641-8311	641-8329

				Phone	Fax
PubMed National Library of Medicine 8600 Rockville Pike *Web:* www.pubmed.gov	Bethesda	MD	20894	301-594-5983	402-1384
Quackwatch Inc PO Box 1747 *Web:* www.quackwatch.org	Allentown	PA	18105	610-437-1795	
WebMD 111 8th Ave *Web:* www.webmd.com	New York	NY	10011	212-624-3700	

HEATING EQUIPMENT - ELECTRIC

SEE Air Conditioning & Heating Equipment - Residential p. 1268

360 HEATING EQUIPMENT - GAS, OIL, COAL

SEE ALSO Air Conditioning & Heating Equipment - Commercial/Industrial p. 1267; Air Conditioning & Heating Equipment - Residential p. 1268; Boiler Shops p. 1387; Furnaces & Ovens - Industrial Process p. 1680

				Phone	Fax
Aerco International Inc 159 Paris Ave *TF:* 800-526-0288 ■ *Web:* www.aerco.com	Northvale	NJ	07647	201-768-2400	784-8073
Airtherm Mfg Inc 10805 Sunset Office Dr Suite L110 *Web:* www.airthermhvac.com	Saint Louis	MO	63127	314-835-9911	835-9692
Ajax Boiler Inc 2701 S Harbor Blvd *Web:* www.aboilerinc.com	Santa Ana	CA	92704	714-437-9050	437-9060
Aquatherm Industries Inc 1940 Rutgers University Blvd *TF:* 800-535-6307 ■ *Web:* www.warmwater.com	Lakewood	NJ	08701	732-905-0440	905-9899
Axeman-Anderson Co 300 E Mountain Ave *Web:* www.axeman-anderson.com	South Williamsport	PA	17702	570-326-9114	326-2152
Barnes & Jones Corp 91 Pacella Park Dr *Web:* www.barnesandjones.com	Randolph	MA	02368	781-963-8000	963-3322
Beckett RW Corp PO Box 1289 *TF:* 800-645-2876 ■ *Web:* www.beckettcorp.com	Elyria	OH	44036	440-327-1060	327-1064
Besicorp Ltd 1151 Flatbush Rd *Web:* www.besicorp.com	Kingston	NY	12401	845-336-7700	336-7172
BFS Industries LLC 200 Industrial Dr *Web:* www.bfs-ind.com	Butner	NC	27509	919-575-6711	575-4275
Burner Systems International Inc 3600 Cummings Rd *TF:* 800-251-6318 ■ *Web:* www.burnersystems.com	Chattanooga	TN	37419	423-822-3600	825-3710
Burnham Corp PO Box 3245 *TF:* 877-567-4328 ■ *Web:* www.burnham.com	Lancaster	PA	17603	717-397-4701	293-5827
Casso-Solar Corp 230 US Rt 202 PO Box 163 *TF:* 800-988-4455 ■ *Web:* www.cassosolar.com	Pomona	NY	10970	845-354-2500	362-1856
CFM Corp 410 Admiral Blvd *TF:* 800-525-1898 ■ *Web:* www.cfmcorp.com	Mississauga	ON	L5T2N6	905-670-7777	565-4690
Charles A Hones Inc 607 Albany Ave PO Box 518 *Web:* www.lbwhite.com	North Amityville	NY	11701	631-842-8886	842-9300
Country Flame Technologies 900 George St *Web:* www.countryflame.com	Marshfield	MO	65706	417-859-0990	859-0192
DESA International 2701 Industrial Dr *TF Cust Svc:* 800-432-5212 ■ *Web:* www.desaint.com	Bowling Green	KY	42101	270-781-9600	745-7800
Dunkirk Boilers 85 Middle Rd **Fax:* Cust Svc ■ *Web:* www.dunkirk.com	Dunkirk	NY	14048	716-366-5500	366-1209*
Ebner Furnaces Inc 224 Quadral Dr *Web:* www.ebnerfurnaces.com	Wadsworth	OH	44281	330-335-1600	335-1605
EFM Sales Co 302 S 4th St *TF:* 800-935-0933 ■ *Web:* www.efmheating.com	Emmaus	PA	18049	610-965-9041	967-6593
Electro-Flex Heat Inc 5 Northwood Rd *TF:* 800-585-4213 ■ *Web:* www.electroflexheat.com	Bloomfield	CT	06002	860-242-6287	242-7298
Embassy Industries Inc 300 Smith St *Web:* www.embassyind.com	Farmingdale	NY	11735	631-694-1800	694-1832
Empire Comfort Systems Inc 918 Freeburg Ave *TF:* 800-851-3153 ■ *Web:* www.empirecomfort.com	Belleville	IL	62222	618-233-7420	233-7097
Enercor Inc 6354 Pershing Ave **Fax Area Code:* 208	University City	MO	63130	314-381-1907	275-2416*
Erie Power Technologies Inc 5300 Knowledge Pkwy Suite 200 *TF:* 000-323-3743 ■ *Web:* www.eriepower.com	Erie	PA	16510	814-897-7000	897-1090
Fulton Cos 972 Centerville Rd PO Box 257 *Web:* www.fulton.com	Pulaski	NY	13142	315-298-5121	298-6390
Gordon-Piatt Group Inc PO Box 21220 **Fax Area Code:* 918	Tulsa	OK	74141	800-638-6940	234-1833*
Hago Mfg Co Inc 1120 Globe Ave *Web:* www.hagonozzles.com	Mountainside	NJ	07092	908-232-8687	232-7246
Hamworthy Peabody Combustion Inc 70 Shelton Technology Center *TF:* 877-732-2639 ■ *Web:* www.peabodyengineering.com	Shelton	CT	06484	203-922-1199	922-8866
Hayward Pool Products Inc 620 Division St *Web:* www.haywardnet.com	Elizabeth	NJ	07207	908-351-5400	351-4700
Hearth & Home Technologies Inc 20802 Kensington Blvd *TF:* 800-669-4328 ■ *Web:* www.hearthtech.com	Lakeville	MN	55044	952-985-6000	985-6001
Heat Controller Inc 1900 Wellworth Ave *Web:* www.heatcontroller.com	Jackson	MI	49203	517-787-2100	787-9341
Heatilator Inc 1915 W Saunders St *TF:* 800-669-4328 ■ *Web:* www.heatilator.com	Mount Pleasant	IA	52641	319-385-9211	986-4430
Hones Charles A Inc 607 Albany Ave PO Box 518 *Web:* www.lbwhite.com	North Amityville	NY	11701	631-842-8886	842-9300
John Zink Co LLC PO Box 21220 *TF:* 800-421-9242 ■ *Web:* www.johnzink.com	Tulsa	OK	74121	918-234-1800	234-2700
Johnston Boiler Co 300 Pine St **Fax:* Cust Svc ■ *TF:* 800-748-0295 ■ *Web:* www.johnstonboiler.com	Ferrysburg	MI	49409	616-842-5050	842-1854*
Knox Stove Works 1318 Proctor St PO Box 751	Knoxville	TN	37901	865-524-4113	637-2461
Koch Chemical Technology Group LLC 4111 E 37th St N *Web:* www.kochchemtech.com	Wichita	KS	67220	316-828-5500	828-4704
LB White Co Inc W 6636 LB White Rd *TF:* 800-345-7200 ■ *Web:* www.lbwhite.com	Onalaska	WI	54650	608-783-5691	783-6115
Lennox Hearth Products 1110 W Taft Ave **Fax Area Code:* 866 ■ *TF:* 800-854-0257 ■ *Web:* www.lennoxhearthproducts.com	Orange	CA	92865	714-921-6100	655-2008*
Meeder Equipment Co 12323 6th St *TF:* 800-423-3711 ■ *Web:* www.meeder.com/MeederEqCo.htm	Rancho Cucamonga	CA	91739	909-463-0600	463-0102
Messer Machine & Mfg Inc 1751 1st Ave PO Box 105	Windom	MN	56101	507-831-1904	831-1908
Mestek Inc 260 N Elm St *NYSE:* MCC ■ *Web:* www.mestek.com	Westfield	MA	01085	413-568-9571	562-7630
New Buck Corp 8000 Hwy 226 S PO Box 69 *Web:* www.buckstovecorp.com	Spruce Pine	NC	28777	828-765-6144	765-0462
New Yorker Boiler Co Inc 21 E Lincoln Ave Suite 100 *TF:* 800-535-4679 ■ *Web:* www.newyorkerboiler.com	Hatfield	PA	19440	215-855-8055	855-8229
North American Mfg Co Ltd 4455 E 71st St *TF:* 800-626-3477 ■ *Web:* www.namfg.com	Cleveland	OH	44105	216-271-6000	641-7852
P & F Industries Inc 300 Smith St *NASDAQ:* PFIN ■ *Web:* www.pfina.com	Farmingdale	NY	11735	631-694-1800	694-1836
Parker Boiler Co 5930 Bandini Blvd *Web:* www.parkerboiler.com	Los Angeles	CA	90040	323-727-9800	722-2848
Power Flame Inc 2001 S 21st St PO Box 974 *Web:* www.powerflame.com	Parsons	KS	67357	620-421-0480	421-0948
Powrmatic Inc 2906 Baltimore Blvd PO Box 439 *TF:* 800-966-9100 ■ *Web:* www.powrmatic.com	Finksburg	MD	21048	410-833-9100	833-7971
ProVision Technologies Inc 69 Railroad Ave Suite A-7 *Web:* www.provisiontechnologies.com	Hilo	HI	96720	808-969-3281	934-7462
Rasmussen Iron Works Inc 12028 E Philadelphia St *Web:* www.riwinc.com	Whittier	CA	90601	562-696-8718	698-3510
Raypak Inc 2151 Eastman Ave *TF:* 800-947-2975 ■ *Web:* www.raypak.com	Oxnard	CA	93030	805-278-5300	278-5468
Reimers Electra Steam Inc 4407 Martinsburg Pike PO Box 37 **Fax Area Code:* 800 ■ *TF:* 800-872-7562 ■ *Web:* www.reimersinc.com	Clear Brook	VA	22624	540-662-3811	726-4215*
Rite Engineering & Mfg Corp 9441 Washburn Rd	Downey	CA	90242	562-862-2135	861-9821
Roberts-Gordon Inc 1250 William St PO Box 44 *TF:* 800-828-7450 ■ *Web:* www.rg-inc.com	Buffalo	NY	14240	716-852-4400	852-0854
RW Beckett Corp PO Box 1289 *TF:* 800-645-2876 ■ *Web:* www.beckettcorp.com	Elyria	OH	44036	440-327-1060	327-1064
Schwank Inc 2 Schwank Way at Hwy 56N *TF:* 877-446-3727 ■ *Web:* www.schwankheaters.com	Waynesboro	GA	30830	706-554-6191	554-9390
Smith Cast Iron Boilers 260 N Elm St *Web:* www.smithboiler.com	Westfield	MA	01085	413-562-9631	562-3799
Spectrolab Inc 12500 Gladstone Ave *TF:* 800-936-4888 ■ *Web:* www.spectrolab.com	Sylmar	CA	91342	818-365-4611	898-7534
Taco Inc 1160 Cranston St **Fax:* Cust Svc ■ *TF:* 800-822-6007 ■ *Web:* www.taco-hvac.com	Cranston	RI	02920	401-942-8000	248-0046*
Temco Fireplace Products Inc 410 Admiral Blvd *Web:* www.temcofireplaces.com	Mississauga	ON	L5T2N6	905-670-7777	565-4690
Templeton Coal Co 701 Wabash Ave	Terre Haute	IN	47807	812-232-7037	232-3752
Temtex Industries Inc PO Box 5645	Riverside	CA	92517	951-779-6766	779-6768
US Stove Co Inc 400 Pedar Ave PO Box 151 *TF:* 800-750-2723 ■ *Web:* www.usstove.com	South Pittsburg	TN	37380	423-837-2100	837-2109
Utica Boilers Inc PO Box 4729 *TF:* 800-325-5479 ■ *Web:* www.uticaboilers.com	Utica	NY	13504	315-797-1310	797-3762
Vermont Castings Inc PO Box 501 *TF Prod Info:* 800-227-8683 ■ *Web:* www.vermontcastings.com	Bethel	VT	05032	802-234-2300	234-2340
Water Furnace International Inc 9000 Conservation Way **Fax:* Hum Res ■ *TF:* 800-222-5667 ■ *Web:* www.waterfurnace.com	Fort Wayne	IN	46809	260-478-5667	479-3284*
Wayne Combustion Systems 801 Glasgow Ave **Fax Area Code:* 800 ■ *TF:* 800-443-4625 ■ *Web:* www.waynecombustion.com	Fort Wayne	IN	46814	260-425-9200	345-0341*
Weil-McLain Co 500 Blaine St *Web:* www.weil-mclain.com	Michigan City	IN	46360	219-879-6561	879-4025
White LB Co Inc W 6636 LB White Rd *TF:* 800-345-7200 ■ *Web:* www.lbwhite.com	Onalaska	WI	54650	608-783-5691	783-6115
Williams Comfort Products 250 W Laurel St *Web:* www.williamscomfortprod.com	Colton	CA	92324	909-825-0993	370-0581
Zink John Co LLC PO Box 21220 *TF:* 800-421-9242 ■ *Web:* www.johnzink.com	Tulsa	OK	74121	918-234-1800	234-2700

361 HEAVY EQUIPMENT DISTRIBUTORS

SEE ALSO Farm Machinery & Equipment - Whol p. 1632; Industrial Equipment & Supplies (Misc) - Whol p. 1853

				Phone	Fax
Alban Tractor Co 8531 Pulaski Hwy **Fax:* Hum Res ■ *TF:* 800-492-6994 ■ *Web:* www.albancat.com	Baltimore	MD	21237	410-686-7777	780-3481*
Anderson Equipment Co 1000 Washington Pike **Fax:* Sales ■ *Web:* www.andersonequip.com	Bridgeville	PA	15017	412-343-2300	504-4251*
Anderson Machinery Co Inc 6535 Leopard St *TF:* 800-308-6043 ■ *Web:* www.andersonmachinerytexas.com	Corpus Christi	TX	78409	361-289-6043	289-6047
Aring Equipment Co Inc 13001 W Silver Spring Dr *Web:* www.aringequipment.com	Butler	WI	53007	262-781-3770	779-2737
Arnold Machinery Co 2975 W 2100 South *TF Cust Svc:* 800-821-0548 ■ *Web:* www.arnoldmachinery.com	Salt Lake City	UT	84119	801-972-4000	975-9749
Balzer Pacific Equipment Co 2136 SE 8th Ave *TF:* 800-442-0966 ■ *Web:* www.balzerpacific.com	Portland	OR	97214	503-232-5141	232-9556
Brandeis Machinery & Supply Co 1801 Watterson Trail *TF:* 800-274-7253 ■ *Web:* www.brandeismachinery.com	Louisville	KY	40299	502-493-4380	499-3180
Caspian Holdings of Delaware DBA Guyan Machinery Co PO Box 129 *TF:* 800-999-3888	Chapmanville	WV	25508	304-855-4501	855-8601
Chadwick-BaRoss Inc 160 Warren Ave *TF:* 800-477-4963 ■ *Web:* www.chadwick-baross.com	Westbrook	ME	04092	207-854-8411	854-8237
Cleveland Brothers Equipment Co Inc 5300 Paxton St *TF:* 800-482-2378 ■ *Web:* www.clevelandbrothers.com	Harrisburg	PA	17111	717-564-2121	564-6931
Conmaco/Rector LP 1602 Engineers Rd *Web:* www.conmaco.com	Belle Chasse	LA	70037	504-394-7330	393-8715
Cooke Sales & Service Co Inc Hwy 65 N PO Box 170	Chillicothe	MO	64601	660-646-1166	646-0381
Croushorn Equipment Co Inc PO Box 796 *TF:* 800-861-5070	Harlan	KY	40831	606-573-2454	573-2482
Dean Machinery Co 1201 W 31st St *Web:* www.deanmch.com	Kansas City	MO	64141	816-753-5300	753-6005
Doyle Equipment Co 20400 Rt 19 N *Web:* www.doyleequipment.com	Cranberry Township	PA	16066	724-776-3636	776-2450
Empire Southwest Co 1725 S Country Club Dr *TF:* 800-367-4731 ■ *Web:* empire.cat.com	Mesa	AZ	85210	480-633-4000	633-4489
Fabco Equipment Inc 11200 W Silver Spring Rd *Web:* www.fabco.com	Milwaukee	WI	53225	414-461-9100	461-8899
Fabick John Tractor Co 1 Fabick Dr *Web:* www.johnfabick.com	Fenton	MO	63026	636-343-5900	343-4910
Feenaughty Machinery Co 4800 NE Columbia Blvd *TF:* 800-875-2566 ■ *Web:* www.feenaughty.com	Portland	OR	97218	503-282-2566	282-1755
Foley Equipment Co 1550 S West St **Fax:* Sales ■ *Web:* www.foleyeq.com	Wichita	KS	67213	316-943-4211	943-0896*
General Equipment & Supplies Inc PO Box 2145 *TF:* 800-437-2924 ■ *Web:* www.genequip.com	Fargo	ND	58107	701-282-2662	281-9067
Guyan Machinery Co PO Box 129 *TF:* 800-999-3888	Chapmanville	WV	25508	304-855-4501	855-8601
Halton Co PO Box 3377 *TF:* 800-452-7676 ■ *Web:* www.haltonco.com	Portland	OR	97208	503-288-6411	281-9458
Heavy Machines Inc 3926 E Rains Rd *TF:* 800-238-5591 ■ *Web:* www.heavymachinesinc.com	Memphis	TN	38118	901-260-2200	260-2276
HO Penn Machinery Co Inc 122 Noxon Rd **Fax:* Mktg ■ *Web:* www.hopenn.com	Poughkeepsie	NY	12603	845-452-1200	452-3698*
Hoffman International Inc 300 S Randolphville Rd *TF:* 800-446-3362 ■ *Web:* www.hoffmanequip.com	Piscataway	NJ	08855	732-752-3600	968-8371
John Fabick Tractor Co 1 Fabick Dr *Web:* www.johnfabick.com	Fenton	MO	63026	636-343-5900	343-4910
MacAllister Machinery Co Inc 7515 E 30th St PO Box 1941 *TF:* 800-227-3228 ■ *Web:* www.macallister.com	Indianapolis	IN	46219	317-545-2151	860-3310

	City	State	ZIP	Phone	Fax
Martin Tractor Co Inc 1737 SW 42nd St *TF:* 800-666-5770 ■ *Web:* www.martintractor.com	Topeka	KS	66609	785-266-5770	267-3301
Milton CAT 554 Maple St *Web:* www.miltoncat.com	Hopkinton	NH	03229	603-746-4611	746-8686
Mississippi Valley Equipment Co Inc 1198 Pershall Rd *TF:* 800-325-8001	Saint Louis	MO	63137	314-869-8600	869-6862
Monroe Tractor & Implement Co Inc 1001 Lehigh Station Rd *Web:* www.monroetractor.com	Henrietta	NY	14467	585-334-3867	334-0001
Mustang Tractor & Equipment Co 12800 NW Fwy *TF:* 800-256-1001 ■ *Web:* www.mustangcat.com	Houston	TX	77040	713-460-2000	460-8473
Nortrax Equipment Co 310 Industrial Park Dr *TF:* 800-472-6685 ■ *Web:* www.nortrax.com	Ashland	WI	54806	715-682-5522	682-8476
Ohio Machinery Co 3993 E Royalton Rd *TF:* 800-837-6200 ■ *Web:* www.ohiomachinery.com	Broadview Heights	OH	44147	440-526-6200	526-9513
Patten Industries Inc 635 W Lake St *TF:* 877-688-2228 ■ *Web:* www.pattenindustries.com	Elmhurst	IL	60126	630-279-4400	279-7892
Phillips Victor L Co 4100 Gardner Ave *TF:* 800-878-9290 ■ *Web:* www.vlpco.com	Kansas City	MO	64120	816-241-9290	241-1738
Pioneer Machinery Co 3239 Sunset Blvd PO Box 3079 *TF:* 888-983-9990 ■ *Web:* www.pioneermachinery.com	West Columbia	SC	29171	803-936-9990	936-9415
Power Motive Corp 5000 Vasquez Blvd *TF:* 800-627-0087 ■ *Web:* www.powermotivecorp.com	Denver	CO	80216	303-355-5900	388-9328
Rasmussen Equipment Co 3333 W 2100 South *Web:* www.rasmussenequipment.com	Salt Lake City	UT	84119	801-972-5588	972-2215
RDO Equipment Co 700 7th St S *Web:* www.rdoequipment.com	Fargo	ND	58103	701-239-8730	271-6328
Ring Power Corp 500 World Commerce Pkwy *Web:* www.ringpower.com	Saint Augustine	FL	32092	904-737-7730	281-9110
Rish Equipment Co PO Box 330 *Web:* www.rish.com	Bluefield	WV	24701	304-327-5124	327-8821
Road Machinery Co 716 S 7th St *Web:* www.roadmachinery.com	Phoenix	AZ	85034	602-252-7121	253-9690
Roland Machinery Co 816 N Dirksen Pkwy *TF:* 800-252-2926 ■ *Web:* www.rolandmachinery.com	Springfield	IL	62702	217-789-7711	744-7314
Rudd Equipment Co 4344 Poplar Level Rd *TF:* 800-283-7833 ■ *Web:* www.ruddequipment.com	Louisville	KY	40213	502-456-4050	459-8695
Scott Machinery Co 4055 S 500 West *TF:* 800-734-7441 ■ *Web:* www.scottmachineryco.com	Salt Lake City	UT	84123	801-262-7441	261-1857
Sellers Tractor Co Inc 400 N Chicago St *Web:* www.sellersequipment.com	Salina	KS	67401	785-823-6378	823-8083
Southeastern Equipment Co Inc 10874 E Pike Rd *TF:* 800-798-5438 ■ *Web:* www.southeasternequip.com	Cambridge	OH	43725	740-432-6303	432-3303
Spreitzer Inc 3145 16th Ave SW *TF:* 800-823-0399 ■ *Web:* www.spreitzerinc.com	Cedar Rapids	IA	52404	319-365-9155	365-2525
Stowers Machinery Corp 6301 Old Rutledge Pike NE *Web:* stowers.cat.com	Knoxville	TN	37924	865-546-1414	595-1030
Stribling Equipment LLC 408 Hwy 49 S *Web:* www.striblingequipment.com	Richland	MS	39218	601-939-1000	932-3306
Toromont Industries Ltd 3131 Hwy 7 W *TSX: TIH* ■ *Web:* www.toromont.com	Concord	ON	L4K1B7	416-667-5511	667-5555
Tri-State Truck & Equipment Inc 5250 Midland Rd *TF:* 800-227-1132 ■ *Web:* www.tste.com	Billings	MT	59101	406-245-3188	238-1501
Tyler Equipment Corp 251 Shaker Rd *TF:* 800-292-6351 ■ *Web:* www.tylerequipment.com	East Longmeadow	MA	01028	413-525-6351	525-5909
Victor L Phillips Co 4100 Gardner Ave *TF:* 800-878-9290 ■ *Web:* www.vlpco.com	Kansas City	MO	64120	816-241-9290	241-1738
Wajax Ltd 3280 Wharton Way *TSX: WJX* ■ *Web:* www.wajax.com	Mississauga	ON	L4X2C5	905-212-3358	212-3350
West Side Tractor Sales Co 1400 W Ogden Ave *Web:* www.westsidetractorsales.com	Naperville	IL	60563	630-355-7150	355-7173
Western Power & Equipment 6407-B NE 117th Ave *TF:* 800-333-2346 ■ *Web:* www.wpec.com	Vancouver	WA	98662	360-253-2346	253-4830
Western States Equipment Co 500 E Overland Rd *TF:* 800-852-2287 ■ *Web:* www.wseco.com	Meridian	ID	83642	208-888-2287	884-2314
Wyoming Machinery Co 5300 Old West Yellowstone Hwy *Web:* www.wyomingcat.com	Casper	WY	82604	307-472-1000	261-4491

362 HELICOPTER TRANSPORT SERVICES

SEE ALSO Air Charter Services p. 1266; Ambulance Services p. 1277

	City	State	ZIP	Phone	Fax
Air Logistics of Alaska 1915 Donald Ave *Web:* www.olog.com	Fairbanks	AK	99701	907-452-1197	452-4539
Air Logistics Inc 4605 Industrial Dr *TF:* 800-365-6771 ■ *Web:* www.olog.com	New Iberia	LA	70560	337-365-6771	364-8222
Aircoastal Helicopters Inc 2615 Lantana Rd Suite J *Web:* www.aircoastal.com	Lantana	FL	33462	561-642-6840	642-5393
Biscayne Helicopters Inc 13955 SW 127th St Bldg 121 *Web:* www.biscaynehelicopters.com	Miami	FL	33186	305-252-3883	252-8154
Bristow Group Inc 224 Rue De Jean *NYSE: BRS* ■ *Web:* www.olog.com	Lafayette	LA	70508	337-233-1221	235-6678
Carson Helicopters 952 Blooming Glen Rd *TF:* 800-523-2335 ■ *Web:* www.carsonhelicopters.com	Perkasie	PA	18944	215-249-3535	249-1352
CHC Helicopter Corp 4740 Agar Dr *NYSE: FLI* ■ *Web:* www.chc.ca	Richmond	BC	V7B1A3	604-276-7500	
Coastal Helicopters Inc 8995 Yandukin Dr *TF:* 800-789-5610 ■ *Web:* www.coastalhelicopters.com	Juneau	AK	99801	907-789-5600	789-7076
Columbia Helicopters Inc 14452 Arndt Rd NE *Web:* www.colheli.com	Aurora	OR	97002	503-678-1222	678-5841
Corporate Helicopters of San Diego 3753 John J Montgomery Dr Suite 2 *TF:* 800-345-6737 ■ *Web:* www.corporatehelicopters.com	San Diego	CA	92123	858-505-5650	874-3038
Cougar Helicopters Inc Saint John's International Airport 40 Craig Dobbins' Way *Web:* www.cougar.ca	Saint John's	NL	A1A4Y3	709-758-4800	758-4850
Crescent Helicopters 1620 SW 75th Ave North Perry Airport *Web:* www.crescentair.com	Pembroke Pines	FL	33023	954-987-1900	987-1912
Era Helicopters Inc 6160 Carl Brady Dr *TF:* 800-843-1947 ■ *Web:* www.flyera.com	Anchorage	AK	99502	907-248-4422	266-8383
Evergreen Helicopters of Alaska Inc 1936 Merrill Field Dr *TF:* 800-958-2454 ■ *Web:* www.evergreenaviation.com	Anchorage	AK	99501	907-257-1500	279-6816
Evergreen International Aviation Inc 3850 Three Mile Ln *TF:* 800-472-9361 ■ *Web:* www.evergreenaviation.com	McMinnville	OR	97128	503-472-9361	472-1048
Gateway Helicopters Ltd PO Box 21028 Aviation Ln Hangar 4 *TF:* 888-474-4214 ■ *Web:* www.gatewayhelicopters.com	North Bay	ON	P1B9N8	705-474-4214	474-1813
Helicopter Express Inc 738 Briscoe Blvd Gwinnett County Airport Briscoe Field *Web:* www.helicopter-express.com	Lawrenceville	GA	30045	770-963-6889	963-7636
Helicopter Transport Services Inc 701 Wilson Pt Rd Box E *Web:* www.htshelicopters.com	Baltimore	MD	21220	410-391-7722	686-4507
Helicopter Transport Services Inc Construction Div 9980 N Rt 47	Morris	IL	60450	815-416-0100	416-0200
Heliflight Inc 2675 NW 56th St *Web:* www.heliflight.com	Fort Lauderdale	FL	33309	954-771-6969	938-9317
Helinet Aviation Services LLC 16425 Hart St Hangar 2 *TF:* 800-221-8389 ■ *Web:* www.helinetaviation.com	Van Nuys	CA	91406	818-902-0229	902-9278
Highland Helicopters Ltd 4240 Agar Dr *Web:* www.highland.ca	Richmond	BC	V7B1A3	604-273-6161	273-6088
Houston Helicopters Inc 3506 Lockheed St *Web:* www.houstonhelicopters.net	Pearland	TX	77581	281-485-1777	485-3701
Island Express Helicopter Service 1175 Queens Hwy S *TF:* 800-228-2566 ■ *Web:* www.islandexpress.com	Long Beach	CA	90802	310-510-2525	510-9671
Midwest Helicopter Airways Inc 525 Executive Dr *TF:* 800-323-7609 ■ *Web:* www.midwesthelicopter.com	Willowbrook	IL	60527	630-325-7860	325-3313
PHI Inc 2001 SE Evangeline Thwy *NASDAQ: PHII* ■ *TF:* 800-235-2452 ■ *Web:* www.phihelico.com	Lafayette	LA	70508	337-235-2452	235-3424
Saint Louis Helicopter LLC 18004 Edison Ave *TF:* 800-325-4046 ■ *Web:* www.stlouishelicopter.com	Chesterfield	MO	63005	636-532-1177	536-1714
San Joaquin Helicopters 1407 S Lexington St *Web:* www.sjhelicopters.com	Delano	CA	93215	661-725-1898	725-5401
Skydance Helicopters 2207 Bellanca St Suite B *TF:* 800-882-1651 ■ *Web:* www.skydanceheli.com	Minden	NV	89423	775-782-4040	782-0140
Skylane Helicopters LLC Decatur Municipal Airport PO Box 1110 *Web:* www.skylanehelicopters.com	Decatur	TX	76234	940-627-0895	627-0894
Tex-Air Helicopters Inc 8919 Paul B Koonce St *Web:* www.texairinc.com	Houston	TX	77061	713-649-6300	649-0572
VIH Helicopters Ltd 1962 Canso Rd *TF:* 866-844-4354 ■ *Web:* www.vih.com	North Saanich	BC	V8L5V5	250-656-3987	655-6839
VIH Logging Ltd 1962 Canso Rd *Web:* www.vih.com	North Saanich	BC	V8L5V5	250-656-1220	655-6839
Westcor Aviation Inc 7305 E Greenway Rd *Web:* www.westcoraviation.com	Scottsdale	AZ	85260	480-991-6558	991-7827
Wiggins Airways Inc 1 Garside Way *Web:* www.wiggins-air.com	Manchester	NH	03103	603-629-9191	665-9644
Yellowhead Helicopters Ltd 3010 Selwyn Rd *Web:* www.yellowheadheli.com	Valemount	BC	V0E2Z0	250-566-4401	566-4333

363 HOLDING COMPANIES

SEE ALSO Conglomerates p. 1527

A holding company is a company that owns enough voting stock in another firm to control management and operations by influencing or electing its board of directors.

363-1 Airlines Holding Companies

	City	State	ZIP	Phone	Fax
AirTran Holdings Inc 9955 AirTran Blvd *NYSE: AAI* ■ *Web:* www.airtran.com	Orlando	FL	32827	407-318-5600	318-5567
Alaska Air Group Inc 19300 International Blvd *NYSE: ALK* ■ *TF:* 800-451-0384 ■ *Web:* www.alaskaair.com	Seattle	WA	98188	206-392-5040	392-5860
AMR Corp 4333 Amon Carter Blvd *NYSE: AMR* ■ *Web:* www.aa.com	Fort Worth	TX	76155	817-963-1234	967-4162
ExpressJet Airlines 1600 Smith St *NYSE: XJT* ■ *TF:* 866-958-3932 ■ *Web:* www.expressjet.com	Houston	TX	77002	713-324-2639	324-4915
ExpressJet Holdings Inc DBA ExpressJet Airlines 1600 Smith St *NYSE: XJT* ■ *TF:* 866-958-3932 ■ *Web:* www.expressjet.com	Houston	TX	77002	713-324-2639	324-4915
Frontier Airlines Inc 7001 Tower Rd *NASDAQ: FRNT* ■ *TF:* 800-265-5505 ■ *Web:* www.frontierairlines.com	Denver	CO	80249	720-374-4200	374-4622
JetBlue Airways Corp 118-29 Queens Blvd *NASDAQ: JBLU* ■ *TF:* 800-538-2583 ■ *Web:* www.jetblue.com	Forest Hills	NY	11375	718-286-7900	709-3621
MAIR Holdings Inc 150 S 5th St Suite 1360 *NASDAQ: MAIR* ■ *Web:* www.mairholdings.com	Minneapolis	MN	55402	612-333-0021	333-0590
Mesa Air Group Inc 410 N 44th St Suite 700 *NASDAQ: MESA* ■ *TF:* 800-637-2247 ■ *Web:* www.mesa-air.com	Phoenix	AZ	85008	602-685-4000	685-4350
Midwest Air Group Inc 6744 S Howell Ave *AMEX: MEH* ■ *TF:* 800-452-2022 ■ *Web:* www.midwestairlines.com	Oak Creek	WI	53154	414-570-4000	570-0199
Northwest Airlines Corp 2700 Lone Oak Pkwy *TF:* 800-225-2525 ■ *Web:* www.nwa.com/corpinfo	Eagan	MN	55121	612-726-2111	726-0776
Republic Airways Holdings Inc 8909 Purdue Rd Suite 300 *NASDAQ: RJET* ■ *Web:* www.republicairways.com	Indianapolis	IN	46268	317-484-6000	484-6040
SkyWest Inc 444 S River Rd *NASDAQ: SKYW* ■ **Fax:* Cust Svc ■ *TF:* 888-717-9000 ■ *Web:* www.skywest.com	Saint George	UT	84790	435-634-3000	634-3405*
UAL Corp 1200 E Algonquin Rd *NASDAQ: UAUA* ■ *TF:* 800-241-6522 ■ *Web:* www.ual.com	Elk Grove Township	IL	60007	847-700-4000	700-2214
US Airways Group Inc 111 W Rio Salado Pkwy *NYSE: LCC* ■ *TF:* 800-428-4322 ■ *Web:* www.usairways.com	Tempe	AZ	85281	480-693-5050	
World Air Holdings Inc 101 World Dr HLH Bldg *NASDAQ: WLDA* ■ *Web:* www.worldair.com	Peachtree City	GA	30269	770-632-8000	

363-2 Bank Holding Companies

	City	State	ZIP	Phone	Fax
1st Constitution Bancorp 2650 Rte 130 & Dey Rd *NASDAQ: FCCY* ■ *Web:* www.1stconstitution.com	Cranbury	NJ	08512	609-655-4500	655-5653
1st Independence Financial Group Inc 104 S Chiles St *NASDAQ: FIFG* ■ *TF:* 800-776-3764 ■ *Web:* www.1stindependence.com	Harrodsburg	KY	40330	859-734-5452	734-7671
1st Source Corp 100 N Michigan St *NASDAQ: SRCE* ■ **Fax:* Hum Res ■ *TF Cust Svc:* 800-513-2360	South Bend	IN	46601	574-235-2000	235-2936*
Abigail Adams National Bancorp Inc 1130 Connecticut Ave NW Suite 200 *NASDAQ: AANB* ■ *Web:* www.adamsbank.com	Washington	DC	20036	202-772-3600	659-4980
Abington Community Bancorp Inc 180 Old York Rd *NASDAQ: ABBC* ■ *Web:* www.abingtonbankonline.com	Jenkintown	PA	19046	215-886-8280	887-4100
ABN AMRO Inc Park Ave Plaza 55 E 52nd St *NYSE: ABN* ■ *Web:* www.abnamro.com	New York	NY	10055	212-409-1000	
Access National Corp 1800 Robert Fulton Dr Suite 310 *NASDAQ: ANCX* ■ *Web:* www.accessnationalbank.com	Reston	VA	20191	703-871-2100	766-3386
Alabama National BanCorporation 1927 1st Ave N *NASDAQ: ALAB* ■ *TF:* 888-583-3200 ■ *Web:* www.alabamanational.com	Birmingham	AL	35203	205-583-3600	521-9307
Alliance Financial Corp 120 Madison St *NASDAQ: ALNC* ■ **Fax Area Code:* 315 ■ *TF:* 800-310-6275 ■ *Web:* www.alliancebankna.com	Syracuse	NY	13202	607-756-2831	475-4421*
Amarillo National Bancorp Inc 410 S Taylor St **Fax:* Hum Res ■ *TF:* 800-262-3733	Amarillo	TX	79101	806-378-8000	378-8066*

Company / Address	City	State	Zip	Phone	Fax
AMB Financial Corp 8230 Hohman Ave *Web:* www.ambfinancial.com	Munster	IN	46321	219-836-5870	836-5883
Amboy Bancorp 3590 US Hwy 9 S *TF:* 800-942-6269 ■ *Web:* www.amboybank.com	Old Bridge	NJ	08857	732-591-8700	591-0726
AMCORE Financial Inc 501 7th St *NASDAQ: AMFI* ■ **Fax:* Mktg ■ *TF:* 800-521-5150 ■ *Web:* www.amcore.com	Rockford	IL	61104	815-968-2241	961-7748*
Amegy Bancorp Inc 4400 Post Oak Pkwy **Fax:* Hum Res ■ *TF:* 800-324-6705	Houston	TX	77027	713-235-8800	571-5060*
Ameriana Bancorp 2118 Bundy Ave *NASDAQ: ASBI* ■ *TF:* 800-487-2118 ■ *Web:* www.ameriana.com	New Castle	IN	47362	765-529-2230	529-2232
American Bancorp of New Jersey Inc 365 Broad St *NASDAQ: ABNJ* ■ *Web:* www.americansavingsnj.com	Bloomfield	NJ	07003	973-748-3600	748-2047
American Bank Inc 4029 W Tilghman St *NASDAQ: AMBK* ■ *TF:* 888-366-6622 ■ *Web:* www.pcbanker.com	Allentown	PA	18104	610-366-1800	289-3326
American Community Bancshares Inc 2593 W Roosevelt Blvd *NASDAQ: ACBA* ■ **Fax:* Hum Res	Monroe	NC	28110	704-225-8444	291-2196*
American National Bankshares Inc 628 Main St *NASDAQ: AMNB* ■ *TF:* 800-240-8190 ■ *Web:* www.amnb.com	Danville	VA	24541	434-792-5111	792-1582
American River Bankshares 3100 Zinfandel Dr Suite 450 *NASDAQ: AMRB* ■ *Web:* www.amrb.com	Rancho Cordova	CA	95670	916-231-6701	851-1025
AmericanWest Bancorporation 41 W Riverside Ave Suite 400 *NASDAQ: AWBC* ■ *TF:* 800-772-5479 ■ *Web:* www.awbank.net	Spokane	WA	99201	509-467-6993	465-9681
Ameris Bancorp 24 2nd Ave SE *NASDAQ: ABCB* ■ *TF:* 888-556-2701 ■ *Web:* www.amerisbank.com	Moultrie	GA	31768	229-890-1111	890-2235
AmeriServe Financial Inc 216 Franklin St *NASDAQ: ASRV* ■ *TF Cust Svc:* 800-837-2265	Johnstown	PA	15901	814-533-5300	533-5427
Ames National Corp 405 5th St PO Box 846 *NASDAQ: ATLO* ■ *Web:* www.amesnational.com	Ames	IA	50010	515-232-6251	663-3033
AmSouth Bancorporation PO Box 11007 *NYSE: ASO* ■ *TF:* 800-267-6884 ■ *Web:* www.amsouth.com	Birmingham	AL	35288	205-320-7151	560-3879
Anchor BanCorp Wisconsin Inc 25 W Main St *NASDAQ: ABCW* ■ **Fax:* Hum Res ■ *TF:* 800-252-6246 ■ *Web:* www.anchorbank.com	Madison	WI	53707	608-252-8700	252-1889*
Annapolis Bancorp Inc 1000 Bestgate Rd Suite 400 *NASDAQ: ANNB* ■ *TF:* 800-582-2651 ■ *Web:* www.bankannapolis.com	Annapolis	MD	21401	410-224-4483	224-3132
Appalachian Bancshares Inc 822 Industrial Blvd *NASDAQ: APAB* ■ *Web:* www.appalachianbank.com	Ellijay	GA	30540	706-276-8000	276-8010
Arrow Financial Corp 250 Glen St *NASDAQ: AROW* ■ *Web:* www.arrowfinancial.com	Glens Falls	NY	12801	518-745-1000	761-6741
ASB Financial Corp 503 Chillicothe St *TF:* 866-866-3177	Portsmouth	OH	45662	740-354-3177	354-3170
Associated Banc-Corp 1200 Hansen Rd *NASDAQ: ASBC* ■ **Fax:* Hum Res ■ *TF PR:* 800-236-2722 ■ *Web:* www.associatedbank.com	Green Bay	WI	54304	920-491-7000	491-7180*
Astoria Financial Corp 1 Astoria Federal Plaza *NYSE: AF* ■ *Web:* www.asfc.com	Lake Success	NY	11042	516-327-3000	
Atlantic BancGroup Inc 1315 S 3rd St *NASDAQ: ATBC* ■ *Web:* www.oceansidebank.com	Jacksonville Beach	FL	32250	904-247-9494	247-9402
Atlantic Coast Federal Corp 505 Haines Ave *NASDAQ: ACFC* ■ *TF:* 800-342-2824 ■ *Web:* www.acfederal.net	Waycross	GA	31501	912-283-4711	284-2284
Auburn National Bancorporation Inc PO Box 3110 *NASDAQ: AUBN* ■ *TF:* 888-988-2162	Auburn	AL	36831	334-821-9200	887-2796
Bancorp Rhode Island PO Box 9488 *NASDAQ: BARI* ■ *Web:* www.bankri.com	Providence	RI	02940	401-456-5000	456-5154
BancorpSouth Inc 1 Mississippi Plaza *NYSE: BXS* ■ *TF:* 888-797-7711 ■ *Web:* www.bancorpsouth.com	Tupelo	MS	38802	662-680-2000	678-7299
Bancshares of Florida Inc 1185 Immokalee Rd *NASDAQ: BOFL* ■ *Web:* www.bankoffloridaonline.com	Naples	FL	34110	239-254-2100	254-2107
BancTrust Financial Group Inc 100 Saint Joseph St *NASDAQ: BTFG* ■ *TF:* 800-689-7929 ■ *Web:* www.banctrustfinancialgroupinc.com	Mobile	AL	36602	251-431-7800	431-7851
BancWest Corp PO Box 3200 *TF:* 888-844-4444 ■ *Web:* www.bancwestcorp.com	Honolulu	HI	96847	808-525-7000	525-5758
Bank of America Corp 100 N Tryon St Suite 200 Corporate Ctr *NYSE: BAC* ■ *TF:* 800-333-6262 ■ *Web:* www.bankofamerica.com	Charlotte	NC	28202	704-386-5681	386-6699
Bank of Commerce Holdings 1951 Churn Creek Rd *NASDAQ: BOCH* ■ *Web:* www.reddingbankofcommerce.com	Redding	CA	96002	530-224-3333	224-3337
Bank of Granite Corp 23 N Main St *NYSE: GRAN* ■ *Web:* www.bankofgranite.com	Granite Falls	NC	28630	828-496-2000	496-2116
Bank of Hawaii Corp 130 Merchant St *NYSE: BOH* ■ *TF:* 888-643-3888 ■ *Web:* www.boh.com	Honolulu	HI	96813	808-538-4007	
Bank Mutual Corp 4949 W Brown Deer Rd *NASDAQ: BKMU* ■ *TF:* 888-358-5070 ■ *Web:* www.bankmutual.com	Milwaukee	WI	53223	414-354-1500	354-5450
Bank of New York Co Inc 1 Wall St *NYSE: BK* ■ **Fax:* PR ■ *Web:* www.bankofny.com	New York	NY	10286	212-495-1784	635-1799*
Bank of the Ozarks Inc 12615 Chenal Pkwy Suite 3100 *NASDAQ: OZRK* ■ *TF:* 800-628-3552 ■ *Web:* www.bankozarks.com	Little Rock	AR	72211	501-978-2265	978-2224
Bank of South Carolina Corp 256 Meeting St *NASDAQ: BKSC* ■ *Web:* www.banksc.com	Charleston	SC	29401	843-724-1500	723-1513
BankAtlantic Bancorp Inc 2100 W Cypress Creek Rd *NYSE: BBX* ■ **Fax:* Hum Res ■ *TF:* 800-741-1700 ■ *Web:* www.bankatlanticbancorp.com	Fort Lauderdale	FL	33309	954-940-5000	940-5250*
BankFinancial Corp 15 W 60 N Frontage Rd *NASDAQ: BFIN* ■ **Fax Area Code:* 708 ■ *TF:* 800-894-6900 ■ *Web:* www.bankfinancial.com	Burr Ridge	IL	60527	630-242-7321	614-3090*
BankUnited Financial Corp 255 Alhambra Cir *NASDAQ: BKUNA* ■ *TF:* 800-440-9646 ■ *Web:* www.bankunitedfla.com	Coral Gables	FL	33134	305-569-2000	569-2026
Banner Corp PO Box 907 *NASDAQ: BANR* ■ **Fax:* Hum Res ■ *TF:* 800-272-9933	Walla Walla	WA	99362	509-527-3636	526-8717*
Bar Harbor Bankshares 82 Main St PO Box 400 *AMEX: BHB* ■ *TF:* 888-853-7100	Bar Harbor	ME	04609	207-288-3314	288-4560
BB & T Corp 200 W 2nd St *NYSE: BBT* ■ *TF:* 800-682-6902 ■ *Web:* www.bbandt.com	Winston-Salem	NC	27101	336-733-2000	
BCB Bancorp Inc 104-110 Ave C *NASDAQ: BCBP* ■ *Web:* www.bcbbancorp.com	Bayonne	NJ	07002	201-823-0700	339-0403
BCSB Bankcorp Inc 4111 E Joppa Rd Suite 300 *NASDAQ: BCSB*	Baltimore	MD	21236	410-256-5000	529-1672
Beach First National Bancshares Inc 3751 Grissom Pkwy Suite 100 *NASDAQ: BFNB* ■ *Web:* www.beachfirst.com	Myrtle Beach	SC	29577	843-626-2265	916-7818
Benjamin Franklin Bancorp Inc 58 Main St *NASDAQ: BFBC* ■ *TF:* 800-528-7000 ■ *Web:* www.benfranklinbank.com	Franklin	MA	02038	508-528-7000	520-8364
Berkshire Bancorp Inc 160 Broadway *NASDAQ: BERK*	New York	NY	10038	212-791-5362	791-5367
Berkshire Hills Bancorp Inc 24 North St *NASDAQ: BHLB* ■ *Web:* www.berkshirebank.com	Pittsfield	MA	01201	413-443-5601	443-3587
Beverly Hills Bancorp Inc 14523 SW Millikan Way Suite 200 *NASDAQ: BHBC*	Beaverton	OR	97005	503-223-5600	223-8799
Blue River Bancshares Inc 29 E Washington St *NASDAQ: BRBI* ■ *TF:* 800-298-3132 ■ *Web:* www.blueriverbancshares.com	Shelbyville	IN	46176	317-398-9721	421-4098
BNC Bancorp 831 Julian Ave *NASDAQ: BNCN* ■ *Web:* www.bankofnc.com	Thomasville	NC	27361	336-476-9200	476-5818
BNCCORP Inc 322 E Main Ave *NASDAQ: BNCC* ■ *Web:* www.bnccorp.com	Bismarck	ND	58501	701-250-3040	222-3653
BOE Financial Services of Virginia Inc 323 Prince St *NASDAQ: BSXT* ■ *TF:* 800-443-5524 ■ *Web:* www.bankofessex.com	Tappahannock	VA	22560	804-443-4343	443-9472
BofI Holding Inc 12777 High Bluff Dr Suite 100 *NASDAQ: BOFI* ■ *TF:* 877-541-2634 ■ *Web:* www.bofiholding.com	San Diego	CA	92130	858-350-6200	350-0443
BOK Financial Corp Bank of Oklahoma Tower PO Box 2300 *NASDAQ: BOKF* ■ *Web:* www.bokf.com	Tulsa	OK	74192	918-588-6000	588-6853
Boston Private Financial Holdings Inc 10 Post Office Sq *NASDAQ: BPFH* ■ *Web:* www.bostonprivate.com	Boston	MA	02109	617-912-1900	912-4551
BostonFed Bancorp Inc 17 New England Executive Pk *AMEX: BFD* ■ *Web:* www.bostonfed.com	Burlington	MA	01803	781-273-0300	273-5761
Bridge Capital Holdings 55 Almaden Blvd *NASDAQ: BBNK* ■ *Web:* www.bridgebank.com	San Jose	CA	95113	408-423-8500	423-8520
Bridge Street Financial Inc 300 State Rt 104 *NASDAQ: OCNB* ■ *TF:* 888-343-4101 ■ *Web:* www.ocnb.com	Oswego	NY	13126	315-343-4100	343-2481
Britton & Koontz Capital Corp 500 Main St *NASDAQ: BKBK* ■ *TF:* 866-425-2265 ■ *Web:* www4.bkbank.com	Natchez	MS	39120	601-445-5576	445-2488
Broadway Financial Corp 4800 Wilshire Blvd *NASDAQ: BYFC* ■ *TF:* 888-988-2265 ■ *Web:* www.broadwayfederalbank.com	Los Angeles	CA	90010	323-634-1700	634-1728
Brookline Bancorp Inc 160 Washington St *NASDAQ: BRKL* ■ *TF Cust Svc:* 877-668-2265 ■ *Web:* www.brooklinebank.com	Brookline	MA	02445	617-730-3500	730-3569
Brooklyn Federal Bancorp Inc 81 Court St *NASDAQ: BFSB* ■ *Web:* www.brooklynbank.com	Brooklyn	NY	11201	718-855-8500	858-5174
Brunswick Bancorp 439 Livingston Ave *AMEX: BRB* ■ *Web:* www.brunswickbank.com	New Brunswick	NJ	08901	732-247-5800	247-5990
Bryn Mawr Bank Corp 801 Lancaster Ave *NASDAQ: BMTC* ■ **Fax:* Cust Svc ■ *TF:* 888-732-2080 ■ *Web:* www.bmtc.com	Bryn Mawr	PA	19010	610-525-1700	526-2450*
BWC Financial Corp 1400 Civic Dr *NASDAQ: BWCF* ■ *TF:* 888-278-1079 ■ *Web:* www.bowc.com	Walnut Creek	CA	94596	925-932-5353	932-5439
C & F Financial Corp PO Box 391 *NASDAQ: CFFI* ■ *TF:* 800-296-6246	West Point	VA	23181	804-843-2360	843-3017
Cadence Financial Corp NBC Plaza 301 E Main St *AMEX: NBY* ■ **Fax:* Hum Res ■ *TF:* 888-622-7341 ■ *Web:* www.cadencebanking.com	Starkville	MS	39759	662-323-1341	338-5049*
CalFirst Bancorp 18201 Von Karman Ave Suite 700 *NASDAQ: CFNB* ■ *TF:* 800-496-4640 ■ *Web:* www.calfirstbancorp.com	Irvine	CA	92612	949-255-0500	255-0501
California First National Bancorp 18201 Von Karman Ave Suite 700 *NASDAQ: CFNB* ■ *TF:* 800-496-4640 ■ *Web:* www.calfirstbancorp.com	Irvine	CA	92612	949-255-0500	255-0501
Camco Financial Corp 6901 Glenn Hwy *NASDAQ: CAFI* ■ *Web:* www.advantagebank.com/site/camco.html	Cambridge	OH	43725	740-435-2020	435-2021
Camden National Corp 245 Commercial St *AMEX: CAC* ■ *TF:* 800-860-8821 ■ *Web:* www.camdennational.com	Rockport	ME	04856	207-236-8821	236-7889
Cape Fear Bank Corp 1117 Military Cutoff Rd *NASDAQ: CAPE* ■ *Web:* www.capefearbank.com	Wilmington	NC	28405	910-509-2000	256-4767
Capital Bank Corp 4901 Glenwood Ave *NASDAQ: CBKN* ■ *TF Cust Svc:* 800-308-3971 ■ *Web:* www.capitalbank-nc.com	Raleigh	NC	27612	919-645-6400	645-6499
Capital City Bank Group Inc 1860 Capital Cir NE *NASDAQ: CCBG* ■ *TF:* 888-671-0400 ■ *Web:* www.ccbg.com	Tallahassee	FL	32308	850-671-0400	878-9133
Capital Corp of the West 550 W Main St *NASDAQ: CCOW* ■ *Web:* www.ccow.com	Merced	CA	95340	209-725-2269	725-4550
CapitalSouth Bancorp 2340 Woodcrest Pl Suite 200 *NASDAQ: CAPB* ■ *Web:* www.capitalsouthbank.com	Birmingham	AL	35209	205-870-1939	879-3885
Capitol Bancorp Ltd 200 N Washington Sq *NYSE: CBC* ■ *Web:* www.cbcl.com	Lansing	MI	48933	517-487-6555	374-2576
Capitol Federal Financial 700 Kansas Ave *NASDAQ: CFFN* ■ *TF:* 888-822-7333 ■ *Web:* www.capfed.com	Topeka	KS	66603	785-235-1341	231-6216
Cardinal Financial Corp 8270 Greensboro Dr Suite 500 *NASDAQ: CFNL* ■ **Fax:* Hum Res ■ *TF:* 800-473-3247 ■ *Web:* www.cardinalbank.com/AboutUs.asp	McLean	VA	22102	703-584-3400	584-3518*
Carolina Bank Holdings Inc 2604 Lawndale Dr *NASDAQ: CLBH* ■ *Web:* www.carolinabank.com	Greensboro	NC	27408	336-288-1898	286-5553
Carolina National Corp 1350 Main St *NASDAQ: CNCP* ■ *Web:* www.carolinanationalbank.com	Columbia	SC	29201	803-779-0411	779-0722
Carrollton Bancorp 344 N Charles St *NASDAQ: CRRB* ■ *TF:* 800-222-6566 ■ *Web:* www.carrolltonbank.com	Baltimore	MD	21201	410-536-7386	737-7430
Carver Bancorp Inc 75 W 125th St *AMEX: CNY* ■ *Web:* www.carverbank.com	New York	NY	10027	212-876-4747	426-6214
Cascade Bancorp 1100 NW Wall St *NASDAQ: CACB* ■ *TF Cust Svc:* 877-617-3400	Bend	OR	97701	541-385-6205	382-8780
Cascade Financial Corp 2828 Colby Ave *NASDAQ: CASB* ■ **Fax:* Hum Res ■ *TF:* 800-326-8787	Everett	WA	98201	425-339-5500	259-8517*
Cathay General Bancorp Inc 777 N Broadway *NASDAQ: CATY* ■ *Web:* www.cathaybank.com	Los Angeles	CA	90012	213-625-4700	625-1368
Cavalry Bancorp Inc 114 W College St *NASDAQ: CAVB* ■ **Fax:* Hum Res	Murfreesboro	TN	37130	615-893-1234	849-2241*
CCF Holding Co 101 N Main St *NASDAQ: CCFH*	Jonesboro	GA	30236	770-478-8881	478-7597
Centennial Bank Holdings Inc 1331 17th St Suite 300 *NASDAQ: CBHI* ■ *Web:* www.cbhi.com	Denver	CO	80202	303-296-9600	
Center Bancorp Inc 2455 Morris Ave *NASDAQ: CNBC* ■ *TF:* 800-862-3683 ■ *Web:* www.centerbancorp.com	Union	NJ	07083	908-688-9500	810-7304
Center Financial Corp 3435 Wilshire Blvd Suite 700 *NASDAQ: CLFC* ■ *TF:* 888-699-7788	Los Angeles	CA	90010	213-251-2222	251-2204
Centerstate Banks of Florida 1101 1st St S Suite 202 *NASDAQ: CSFL*	Winter Haven	FL	33880	863-293-2600	297-8152
Central Bancorp Inc 399 Highland Ave *NASDAQ: CEBK* ■ *Web:* www.centralbk.com	Somerville	MA	02145	617-628-4000	629-4236
Central Federal Corp PO Box 345 *NASDAQ: CFBK* ■ *TF:* 888-273-8255	Wellsville	OH	43968	330-532-1517	532-3875
Central Jersey Bancorp 627 2nd Ave *NASDAQ: CJBK* ■ *Web:* www.cjbna.com	Long Branch	NJ	07740	732-571-1300	571-1037
Central Pacific Financial Corp PO Box 3590 *NYSE: CPF* ■ *TF:* 800-342-8422 ■ *Web:* www.cpbi.com	Honolulu	HI	96811	808-544-0500	544-0736
Central Valley Community Bancorp 600 Pollasky Ave *NASDAQ: CVCY* ■ *Web:* www.cvcb.com	Clovis	CA	93612	559-298-1775	221-4376
Central Virginia Bankshares Inc 2351 Anderson Hwy *NASDAQ: CVBK* ■ *TF:* 888-282-4030 ■ *Web:* www.centralvabank.com	Powhatan	VA	23139	804-598-4216	598-7672
Centrue Financial Corp 122 W Madison St *NASDAQ: TRUE* ■ *Web:* www.centrue.com	Ottawa	IL	61350	815-431-2720	
Century Bancorp Inc 400 Mystic Ave *NASDAQ: CNBKA* ■ *TF:* 800-442-1859 ■ *Web:* www.century-bank.com	Medford	MA	02155	781-391-4000	393-4077
CFS Bancorp Inc 707 Ridge Rd *NASDAQ: CITZ* ■ *Web:* www.cfsbancorp.com	Munster	IN	46321	219-836-5500	836-2950
Charter Financial Corp 1233 OG Skinner Dr *NASDAQ: CHFN* ■ *TF:* 800-763-4444	West Point	GA	31833	706-645-1391	645-1370
Chemical Financial Corp 333 E Main St *NASDAQ: CHFC* ■ *TF:* 800-722-6050 ■ *Web:* www.chemicalbankmi.com	Midland	MI	48640	989-839-5350	839-5255
Chittenden Corp PO Box 820 *NYSE: CHZ* ■ **Fax:* Mktg ■ *TF:* 800-642-3158 ■ *Web:* www.chittendencorp.com	Burlington	VT	05402	802-658-4000	660-1319*
Citizens Banking Corp 328 S Saginaw St *NASDAQ: CBCF* ■ *TF Cust Svc:* 800-825-7200 ■ *Web:* www.citizensonline.com	Flint	MI	48502	810-766-7500	768-4724
Citizens Financial Group Inc 1 Citizens Dr *TF:* 800-922-9999 ■ *Web:* www.citizensbank.com	Riverside	RI	02915	401-456-7000	455-5921
Citizens First Bancorp Inc 525 Water St *NASDAQ: CTZN* ■ *TF:* 800-922-5308 ■ *Web:* www.cfsbank.com	Port Huron	MI	48060	810-987-8300	987-7537
Citizens Holding Co 521 E Main St *AMEX: CIZ* ■ *Web:* www.thecitizensbankphila.com	Philadelphia	MS	39350	601-656-4692	656-4183
Citizens & Northern Corp 90-92 Main St *NASDAQ: CZNC* ■ *Web:* www.cnbankpa.com	Wellsboro	PA	16901	570-724-3411	723-8097
Citizens Republic Bancorp 1 Citizens Banking Center 328 S Saginaw St *NASDAQ: CRBC* ■ *Web:* www.citizensbanking.com	Flint	MI	48502	810-257-2506	

Bank Holding Companies (Cont'd)

Company	City	State	ZIP	Phone	Fax
Citizens South Banking Corp 519 S New Hope Rd	Gastonia	NC	28054	704-868-5200	868-2192*
NASDAQ: CSBC ■ **Fax:* Hum Res ■ *Web:* www.citizenssouth.com					
City Holding Co 25 Gatewater Rd	Cross Lanes	WV	25313	304-769-1100	769-1111
NASDAQ: CHCO ■ *TF:* 800-922-9236 ■ *Web:* www.cityholding.com					
City National Bancshares Inc 25 W Flagler St	Miami	FL	33130	305-577-7333	577-7495
TF: 800-435-8839 ■ *Web:* www.citynational.com					
City National Corp 400 N Roxbury Dr	Beverly Hills	CA	90210	310-888-6000	427-5020*
NYSE: CYN ■ **Fax Area Code:* 213 ■ **Fax:* Cust Svc ■ *TF:* 800-773-7100 ■ *Web:* www.cnb.com					
CKF Bancorp Inc PO Box 400	Danville	KY	40423	859-236-4181	236-4363
Clifton Savings Bancorp Inc 1433 Van Houten Ave PO Box 2149	Clifton	NJ	07015	973-473-2200	473-0451
NASDAQ: CSBK ■ *TF:* 888-562-6727 ■ *Web:* www.cliftonsavings.com					
CNB Financial Corp 1 S 2nd St	Clearfield	PA	16830	814-765-9621	765-0871
NASDAQ: CCNE ■ *TF:* 800-492-3221 ■ *Web:* www.bankcnb.com/					
Coast Financial Holdings Inc 1301 6th Ave W 3rd Fl	Bradenton	FL	34205	941-752-5900	345-1058
NASDAQ: CFHI ■ *Web:* www.coastbankflorida.com					
Coastal Financial Corp 2619 N Oak St	Myrtle Beach	SC	29577	843-205-2000	205-2481*
NASDAQ: CFCP ■ **Fax:* Hum Res ■ *TF:* 888-728-2265					
CoBiz Inc 821 17th St	Denver	CO	80202	303-293-2265	244-9700
NASDAQ: COBZ ■ *TF:* 800-574-4714 ■ *Web:* www.cobizinc.com					
Codorus Valley Bancorp Inc 105 Leader Heights Rd	York	PA	17403	717-846-1970	747-0633
NASDAQ: CVLY					
Colonial BancGroup Inc PO Box 1108	Montgomery	AL	36101	334-240-5000	240-5345
NYSE: CNB ■ *TF:* 888-285-5886 ■ *Web:* www.colonialbank.com					
Colonial Bankshares Inc 85 W Broad St	Bridgeton	NJ	08302	856-451-5800	451-5110
NASDAQ: COBK ■ *Web:* www.colonialbankfsb.com					
Colony Bankcorp Inc 115 S Grant St PO Box 989	Fitzgerald	GA	31750	229-426-6000	426-6039
NASDAQ: CBAN ■ *Web:* www.colonybankcorp.com					
Columbia Bancorp 7168 Columbia Gateway Dr	Columbia	MD	21046	410-423-8000	750-0105
TF: 888-822-2265 ■ *Web:* www.columbank.com					
Columbia Bancorp 401 E 3rd St Suite 200 PO Box 1030	The Dalles	OR	97058	541-298-6649	298-3157
NASDAQ: CBBO ■ *TF:* 877-272-3678 ■ *Web:* www.columbiariverbank.com					
Columbia Banking System Inc PO Box 2156	Tacoma	WA	98401	253-305-1900	304-0050
NASDAQ: COLB ■ *TF:* 800-305-1905 ■ *Web:* www.columbiabank.com					
Comerica Inc 500 Woodward Ave	Detroit	MI	48226	313-222-4000	964-3752*
NYSE: CMA ■ **Fax:* Hum Res ■ *TF:* 800-521-1190 ■ *Web:* www.comerica.com					
Comm Bancorp Inc 125 N State St	Clarks Summit	PA	18411	570-586-0377	587-3761
NASDAQ: CCBP ■ *TF:* 800-820-4642					
Commerce Bancorp Inc 1701 Rt 70 E	Cherry Hill	NJ	08034	856-751-9000	751-9260
NYSE: CBH ■ *TF Cust Svc:* 888-751-9000					
Commerce Bancshares Inc 1000 Walnut St	Kansas City	MO	64106	816-234-2000	234-2369
NASDAQ: CBSH ■ *TF:* 800-892-7100 ■ *Web:* www.commercebank.com/020.html					
Commercebank Holding Co 220 Alhambra Cir	Coral Gables	FL	33134	305-460-8701	460-4010*
**Fax:* Cust Svc ■ *Web:* www.commercebankfl.com					
CommerceFirst Bancorp Inc 1804 West St Suite 200	Annapolis	MD	21401	410-280-6695	280-8565
NASDAQ: CMFB ■ *Web:* www.commerce1st.com					
Commercial Bankshares Inc 1550 SW 57th Ave	Miami	FL	33144	305-267-1200	266-2939
NASDAQ: CLBK ■ *TF:* 800-752-7999 ■ *Web:* www.commercialbankfl.com					
Commercial National Financial Corp 900 Ligonier St	Latrobe	PA	15650	724-539-3501	539-0816*
NASDAQ: CNAF ■ **Fax:* Hum Res ■ *TF:* 800-803-2265					
Commonwealth Bankshares Inc 403 Boush St	Norfolk	VA	23510	757-446-6900	446-6929
NASDAQ: CWBS ■ *TF:* 888-446-9862 ■ *Web:* www.bankofthecommonwealth.com					
Community Bancorp 400 S 4th St Suite 215	Las Vegas	NV	89101	702-878-0700	947-3502
NASDAQ: CBON ■ *Web:* www.communitybanknv.com					
Community Bank Shares of Indiana Inc 101 W Spring St	New Albany	IN	47150	812-944-2224	949-6870
NASDAQ: CBIN ■ *TF:* 866-944-2004 ■ *Web:* www.cbinonline.com					
Community Bank System Inc 5790 Widewaters Pkwy	DeWitt	NY	13214	315-445-2282	445-2997*
NYSE: CBU ■ **Fax:* Acctg ■ *TF:* 800-724-2262 ■ *Web:* www.communitybankna.com					
Community Banks Inc 777 E Park Dr 2nd Fl	Harrisburg	PA	17111	717-920-1698	920-1683
NASDAQ: CMTY ■ *TF:* 800-331-8362 ■ *Web:* www.communitybanks.com					
Community Bankshares Inc PO Box 2086	Orangeburg	SC	29116	803-535-1060	535-1065
AMEX: SCB ■ *Web:* www.communitybankshares.com					
Community Capital Bancshares Inc PO Box 71269	Albany	GA	31708	229-446-2265	446-7030
NASDAQ: ALBY					
Community Capital Corp 1402C Hwy 72 W	Greenwood	SC	29649	864-941-8200	941-8283
NASDAQ: CPBK ■ *Web:* www.comcapcorp.com					
Community Central Bank Corp 100 N Main St	Mount Clemens	MI	48043	586-783-4500	783-9471
NASDAQ: CCBD ■ *TF:* 866-860-5349 ■ *Web:* www.communitycentralbank.com					
Community Financial Corp 38 N Central Ave	Staunton	VA	24401	540-886-0796	885-0643
NASDAQ: CFFC ■ *Web:* www.cbnk.com					
Community Investors Bancorp Inc 119 S Sandusky Ave	Bucyrus	OH	44820	419-562-7055	562-5516
TF: 800-222-4955 ■ *Web:* www.ffcb.com					
Community Shores Bank Corp 1030 W Norton Ave	Muskegon	MI	49441	231-780-1800	780-3006
NASDAQ: CSHB ■ *TF:* 888-853-6633 ■ *Web:* www.communityshores.com					
Community Trust Bancorp Inc 346 N Mayo Trail	Pikeville	KY	41501	606-432-1414	433-4637*
NASDAQ: CTBI ■ **Fax:* Hum Res ■ *TF:* 800-422-1090 ■ *Web:* www.ctbi.com					
Community West Bancshares 445 Pine Ave	Goleta	CA	93117	805-692-1862	692-8902
NASDAQ: CWBC ■ *Web:* www.communitywest.com					
CommunityBanks 1060 Main St	Blue Ball	PA	17506	866-255-2580	920-1683*
**Fax Area Code:* 717 ■ *TF:* 866-255-2580 ■ *Web:* www.communitybanks.com					
Compass Bancshares Inc 15 S 20th St	Birmingham	AL	35233	205-933-3000	297-3336*
NASDAQ: CBSS ■ **Fax:* Hum Res ■ *TF:* 800-239-2265 ■ *Web:* www.compassbank.com					
Connecticut Bank & Trust Co 58 State House Sq	Hartford	CT	06103	860-246-5200	
NASDAQ: CTBC ■ *Web:* thecbt.com					
Cooperative Bankshares Inc 201 Market St	Wilmington	NC	28401	910-343-0181	251-1652
NASDAQ: COOP ■ *TF:* 800-672-0443 ■ *Web:* www.coop-bank.com					
Corus Bankshares Inc 3959 N Lincoln Ave	Chicago	IL	60613	773-832-3462	388-3460*
NASDAQ: CORS ■ **Fax:* Cust Svc ■ *TF:* 800-555-5710 ■ *Web:* www.corusbank.com					
Cowlitz Bancorporation 927 Commerce Ave	Longview	WA	98632	360-423-9800	578-0918*
NASDAQ: CWLZ ■ **Fax:* Hum Res ■ *TF:* 800-340-8865 ■ *Web:* www.cowlitzbancorp.com					
Crazy Woman Creek Bancorp Inc PO Box 1020	Buffalo	WY	82834	307-684-5591	684-7854
TF: 800-348-8971					
Crescent Banking Co PO Box 668	Jasper	GA	30143	678-454-2265	454-2299
NASDAQ: CSNT ■ *TF:* 800-872-7941 ■ *Web:* www.crescentbank.com					
Crescent Financial Corp 1005 High House Rd	Cary	NC	27512	919-460-7770	460-2512
NASDAQ: CRFN ■ *Web:* www.crescentstatebank.com					
Cullen/Frost Bankers Inc 100 W Houston St	San Antonio	TX	78205	210-220-4011	220-4087*
NYSE: CFR ■ **Fax:* Mail Rm ■ *TF:* 800-562-6732 ■ *Web:* www.frostbank.com					
CVB Financial Corp PO Box 51000	Ontario	CA	91761	909-980-4030	481-2131*
NASDAQ: CVBF ■ **Fax:* Hum Res ■ *TF:* 888-222-5432 ■ *Web:* www.cbbank.com					
Dearborn Bancorp Inc 22290 Michigan Ave	Dearborn	MI	48124	313-274-1000	274-5050
NASDAQ: DEAR					
Dickinson Financial Corp 1100 Main St	Kansas City	MO	64105	816-472-5244	412-0024*
**Fax:* Hum Res					
Dime Community Bancshares Inc 209 Havemeyer St	Brooklyn	NY	11211	718-782-6200	486-7535*
NASDAQ: DCOM ■ **Fax:* Hum Res ■ *TF:* 800-321-3463					
Doral Financial Corp 1451 Franklin D Roosevelt Ave	Puerto Nuevo	PR	00920	787-474-6700	474-6882
NYSE: DRL ■ *Web:* www.doralfinancial.com					
Downey Financial Corp 3501 Jamboree Rd	Newport Beach	CA	92660	949-854-3100	854-8162
NYSE: DSL ■ *Web:* www.downeysavings.com					
Eagle Bancorp Inc 7815 Woodmont Ave	Bethesda	MD	20814	301-986-1800	986-8529
NASDAQ: EGBN ■ *TF:* 800-364-8313 ■ *Web:* www.eaglebankmd.com					
East West Bancorp Inc 1881 W Main St	Alhambra	CA	91801	626-308-2012	308-2034
NASDAQ: EWBC ■ *TF:* 888-895-5650 ■ *Web:* www.eastwestbank.com					
Eastern Bank Corp 265 Franklin St	Boston	MA	02110	617-897-1008	
TF Cust Svc: 800-327-8376 ■ *Web:* www.easternbank.com					
Eastern Virginia Bankshares Inc 330 Hospital Rd	Tappahannock	VA	22560	804-443-8400	445-1047
NASDAQ: EVBS ■ *Web:* www.evb.org					
ECB Bancorp Inc 35050 US Hwy 264 PO Box 337	Engelhard	NC	27824	252-925-9411	925-8491
NASDAQ: ECBE ■ *TF:* 800-849-2265 ■ *Web:* www.ecbbancorp.com					
EFC Bancorp Inc 1695 Larkin Ave	Elgin	IL	60123	847-741-3900	741-1655
AMEX: EFC ■ *TF:* 888-354-4632 ■ *Web:* www.efcbancorp.com					
Empire Financial Holding Co 2170 W SR 434 Suite 100	Longwood	FL	32779	407-774-1300	834-9995
AMEX: EFH ■ *TF:* 800-569-3337 ■ *Web:* www.empirenow.com					
Enterprise Bancorp Inc 222 Merrimack St	Lowell	MA	01852	978-459-9000	656-5813
NASDAQ: EBTC					
Enterprise Financial Services Corp 150 N Meramec Ave	Clayton	MO	63105	314-725-5500	721-6793
NASDAQ: EFSC ■ *Web:* www.enterprisebank.com					
ESB Financial Corp 600 Lawrence Ave	Ellwood City	PA	16117	724-758-5584	758-0576
NASDAQ: ESBF ■ *TF:* 800-533-4193 ■ *Web:* www.esbbank.com					
EuroBancshares Inc 270 Muñoz Rivera Ave	San Juan	PR	00918	787-751-7340	758-5611
NASDAQ: EUBK ■ *Web:* www.eurobankpr.com					
Evans Bancorp Inc 1 Grimsby Dr	Hamburg	NY	14075	716-549-1000	926-2005*
NASDAQ: EVBN ■ **Fax:* Hum Res ■ *Web:* www.evansbancorp.com					
Exchange National Bancshares Inc 132 E High St	Jefferson City	MO	65102	573-761-6100	761-6272
NASDAQ: EXJF ■ *TF:* 800-761-8362 ■ *Web:* www.exchangebancshares.com					
Farmers Capital Bank Corp 202 W Main St	Frankfort	KY	40601	502-227-1600	227-1692
NASDAQ: FFKT ■ *Web:* www.farmerscapital.com					
Fauquier Bankshares Inc 10 Courthouse Sq	Warrenton	VA	20186	540-347-2700	347-3392
NASDAQ: FBSS ■ *TF:* 800-638-3798					
FBOP Corp 11 W Madison St	Oak Park	IL	60302	708-386-5000	445-3165*
**Fax:* Hum Res ■ *Web:* www.fbopcorporation.com					
Federal Trust Corp 312 W 1st St	Sanford	FL	32772	407-645-1201	302-4704
AMEX: FDT					
FFD Financial Corp 321 N Wooster Ave	Dover	OH	44622	330-364-7777	364-7779
NASDAQ: FFDF ■ *Web:* www.ffsbd.com					
FFW Corp 1205 N Cass St	Wabash	IN	46992	260-563-3185	563-4841
TF: 800-377-4984 ■ *Web:* www.ffsbwabash.com					
Fidelity Bancorp Inc 1009 Perry Hwy	Pittsburgh	PA	15237	412-367-3300	364-6504
NASDAQ: FSBI ■ *TF:* 800-242-2500 ■ *Web:* www.fidelitybancorp-pa.com					
Fidelity Bankshares Inc 205 Datura St	West Palm Beach	FL	33401	561-514-9222	803-9968
NASDAQ: FFFL ■ *TF:* 800-422-3675 ■ *Web:* www.fidfedonline.com					
Fidelity Federal Bancorp 18 NW 4th St	Evansville	IN	47708	812-424-0921	473-9783
Web: www.ufb-ffed.com/bancorp					
Fidelity Southern Corp 3490 Piedmont Rd Suite 1550	Atlanta	GA	30305	404-639-6500	814-8060
NASDAQ: LION ■ *TF:* 888-248-5466 ■ *Web:* www.lionbank.com					
Fifth Third Bancorp 38 Fountain Sq Plaza	Cincinnati	OH	45263	513-579-5300	358-6020*
NASDAQ: FITB ■ **Fax:* Cust Svc ■ *TF:* 800-972-3030 ■ *Web:* www.53.com					
Financial Institutions Inc 220 Liberty St	Warsaw	NY	14569	585-786-1100	786-5254
NASDAQ: FISI ■ *TF:* 866-344-2677 ■ *Web:* www.fiiwarsaw.com					
First American Bank Corp 1650 Louis Ave	Elk Grove Village	IL	60009	847-952-3700	364-7467
Web: www.firstambank.com					
First Bancorp 341 N Main St	Troy	NC	27371	910-576-6171	576-1070
NASDAQ: FBNC ■ *TF:* 800-548-9377 ■ *Web:* secure.firstbancorp.com					
First BanCorp PO Box 9146	San Juan	PR	00908	787-729-8200	729-8205
NYSE: FBP ■ *Web:* www.firstbankpr.com					
First Bancorp of Indiana Inc 2200 W Franklin St	Evansville	IN	47712	812-423-3196	421-4107
NASDAQ: FBEI					
First Bancshares Inc 142 E 1st St	Mountain Grove	MO	65711	417-926-5151	926-4362
NASDAQ: FBSI					
First Banks Inc 135 N Meramec Ave	Clayton	MO	63105	314-854-4600	854-5454
TF: 800-760-2265 ■ *Web:* www.firstbanks.com					
First Busey Corp PO Box 17125	Urbana	IL	61803	217-365-4516	365-4592
NASDAQ: BUSE ■ *TF:* 800-672-8739 ■ *Web:* www.busey.com					
First Capital Inc 220 Federal Dr NW	Corydon	IN	47112	812-738-2198	738-2202
NASDAQ: FCAP ■ *TF:* 800-390-1465					
First Charter Corp PO Box 37937	Charlotte	NC	28237	704-688-4300	688-4475*
NASDAQ: FCTR ■ **Fax:* Hum Res ■ *TF:* 800-422-4650 ■ *Web:* www.firstcharter.com					
First Citizens Bancorporation Inc PO box 29	Columbia	SC	29202	803-771-8700	931-8519
TF: 888-612-4444 ■ *Web:* www.firstcitizensonline.com					
First Citizens BancShares Inc 3128 Smoketree Ct	Raleigh	NC	27604	888-323-4732	
NASDAQ: FCNCA ■ *Web:* www.firstcitizens.com					
First Commonwealth Financial Corp 22 N 6th St Old Courthouse Sq	Indiana	PA	15701	724-349-7220	463-5739*
NYSE: FCF ■ **Fax:* Hum Res ■ *TF:* 800-711-2265 ■ *Web:* www.fcfbank.com					
First Community Bancorp Inc 10250 Constellation Blvd	Los Angeles	CA	90067	619-233-5588	
NASDAQ: FCBP ■ *Web:* www.firstcommunitybancorp.com					
First Community Bank Corp 240 E Chestnut St	Olney	IL	62450	618-395-8676	392-4619
First Community Corp 5455 Sunset Blvd	Lexington	SC	29072	803-951-2265	951-1722*
NASDAQ: FCCO ■ **Fax:* Cust Svc ■ *TF:* 888-951-2265 ■ *Web:* www.firstcommunitysc.com					
First Defiance Financial Corp 601 Clinton St	Defiance	OH	43512	419-782-5015	784-3467*
NASDAQ: FDEF ■ **Fax:* Hum Res ■ *TF:* 800-472-6292 ■ *Web:* www.fdef.com					
First Federal Bancorporation PO Box 458	Bemidji	MN	56619	218-751-5120	751-5814
TF: 800-749-9606					
First Federal Bancshares of Arkansas Inc 1401 Hwy 62-65 N	Harrison	AR	72601	870-741-7641	365-8355
NASDAQ: FFBH ■ *TF:* 800-345-2539					
First Federal Bankshares Inc 329 Pierce St	Sioux City	IA	51101	712-277-0200	277-0377
NASDAQ: FFSX ■ *TF:* 800-352-4620 ■ *Web:* www.firstfederalbank.com					
First Federal Capital Corp 605 State St	La Crosse	WI	54601	608-784-8000	784-6807*
**Fax:* Cust Svc ■ *TF:* 800-657-4636 ■ *Web:* www.firstfed.com					
First Financial Bancorp 300 High St	Hamilton	OH	45011	513-867-4700	785-3434
NASDAQ: FFBC ■ *TF:* 800-543-2265 ■ *Web:* www.ffbc-oh.com					
First Financial Bankshares Inc PO Box 701	Abilene	TX	79604	325-627-7155	627-7393
NASDAQ: FFIN ■ *Web:* www.ffin.com					
First Financial Corp 1 First Financial Plaza	Terre Haute	IN	47807	812-238-6000	232-5336
NASDAQ: THFF ■ *TF:* 800-511-0045 ■ *Web:* www.first-online.com					
First Financial Holdings Inc PO Box 118068	Charleston	SC	29423	843-529-5933	529-5883*
NASDAQ: FFCH ■ **Fax:* Mktg ■ *Web:* www.firstfinancialholdings.com					
First Financial Service Corp 2323 Ring Rd	Elizabethtown	KY	42701	270-765-2131	737-1353
NASDAQ: FFKY ■ *TF:* 800-314-2265 ■ *Web:* www.ffsbky.com					
First Franklin Corp 4750 Ashwood Dr	Cincinnati	OH	45241	513-469-5352	469-5360
NASDAQ: FFHS					
First Horizon National Corp PO Box 84	Memphis	TN	38101	901-523-4444	523-4145*
NYSE: FHN ■ **Fax:* Mktg					
First Independence Corp PO Box 947	Independence	KS	67301	620-331-1660	331-1600
TF: 800-455-0744					
First Indiana Corp 135 N Pennsylvania St First Indiana Plaza Suite 1900	Indianapolis	IN	46204	317-269-1200	269-1341
NASDAQ: FINB ■ *TF Cust Svc:* 800-888-8586 ■ *Web:* www.firstindiana.com					
First Interstate Bancsystem Inc 401 N 31st St	Billings	MT	59101	406-255-5300	255-5213*
**Fax:* Hum Res					
First Keystone Financial Inc 22 W State St	Media	PA	19063	610-565-6210	892-5150
NASDAQ: FKFS ■ *TF:* 800-590-1414 ■ *Web:* www.firstkeystone.com					
First of Long Island Corp 10 Glen Head Rd	Glen Head	NY	11545	516-671-4900	656-3971*
NASDAQ: FLIC ■ **Fax:* Hum Res					
First M & F Corp 221 E Washington St	Kosciusko	MS	39090	662-289-5121	289-4801
NASDAQ: FMFC					
First Mariner Bancorp 1501 S Clinton St	Baltimore	MD	21224	410-342-2600	563-1594
NASDAQ: FMAR ■ *TF:* 888-561-2265					

Company	City	State	ZIP	Phone	Fax
First Merchants Corp 200 E Jackson St *NASDAQ: FRME* ■ **Fax: Mktg* ■ *TF:* 800-205-3464 ■ *Web:* www.firstmerchants.com	Muncie	IN	47305	765-747-1500	741-7283*
First Midwest Bancorp Inc 1 Pierce Pl Suite 1500 *NASDAQ: FMBI* ■ **Fax: Mktg* ■ *TF:* 800-322-3623	Itasca	IL	60143	630-875-7200	875-7396*
First Mutual Bancshares Inc 400 108th Ave NE *NASDAQ: FMSB* ■ *TF:* 800-735-7303	Bellevue	WA	98004	425-455-7300	453-5302
First National Lincoln Corp PO Box 940 *NASDAQ: FNLC* ■ *TF:* 800-564-3195 ■ *Web:* www.fnlc.com	Damariscotta	ME	04543	207-563-3195	563-3356
First National of Nebraska Inc 1 First National Ctr *TF:* 800-688-7070	Omaha	NE	68197	402-341-0500	342-4332
First Niagara Financial Group Inc 55 East Ave *NASDAQ: FNFG* ■ *TF:* 800-201-6621 ■ *Web:* www.fnfg.com	Lockport	NY	14095	716-625-7500	625-8952
First Niles Financial Inc 55 N Main St *NASDAQ: FNFI*	Niles	OH	44446	330-652-2539	652-0911
First Oak Brook Bancshares Inc 6111 N River Rd *NASDAQ: FOBB* ■ **Fax Area Code:* 847 ■ *TF:* 800-536-3000	Rosemont	IL	60018	888-422-6562	653-0085*
First Place Financial Corp 185 E Market St *NASDAQ: FPFC* ■ *TF:* 800-995-2646 ■ *Web:* www.firstplacebank.net	Warren	OH	44481	330-373-1221	393-5578
First Regional Bancorp 1801 Century Pk E Suite 800 *NASDAQ: FRGB*	Los Angeles	CA	90067	310-552-1776	552-1772
First Security Group Inc 817 Broad St *NASDAQ: FSGI* ■ *Web:* www.fsgbank.com	Chattanooga	TN	37402	423-266-2000	267-3383
First South Bancorp Inc 1311 Carolina Ave *NASDAQ: FSBK* ■ *TF:* 800-946-4178 ■ *Web:* www.firstsouthnc.com	Washington	NC	27889	252-946-4178	946-3873
First Southern Bancshares Inc 102 S Court St *TF:* 800-625-7131	Florence	AL	35630	256-764-7131	718-4260
First State Bancorporation 7900 Jefferson NE *NASDAQ: FSNM* ■ *TF:* 888-699-7500 ■ *Web:* www.fsbnm.com	Albuquerque	NM	87190	505-241-7500	241-7572
First State Financial Corp 22 S Links Ave *NASDAQ: FSTF* ■ *Web:* www.firststatefl.com	Sarasota	FL	34236	941-929-9000	951-6189
First United Corp 19 S 2nd St *NASDAQ: FUNC* ■ **Fax: Hum Res* ■ *TF:* 800-296-9471 ■ *Web:* www.mybankfirstunited.com	Oakland	MD	21550	301-334-9471	334-2061*
First West Virginia Bancorp Inc 1701 Warwood Ave *AMEX: FWV* ■ *TF:* 866-235-1923	Wheeling	WV	26003	304-277-1100	277-4705
Firstbank Corp 311 Woodworth Ave *NASDAQ: FBMI* ■ *Web:* www.firstbank-corp.com	Alma	MI	48801	989-463-3131	463-6438
FirstBank NW Corp 1300 16th Ave *NASDAQ: FBNW* ■ *Web:* www.fbnw.com	Clarkston	WA	99403	509-295-5100	295-5101
FirstFed Bancorp Inc 1630 4th Ave N *NASDAQ: FFDB* ■ *TF:* 800-436-5112 ■ *Web:* www.firstfedbessemer.com	Bessemer	AL	35020	205-428-8472	428-8652
FirstFed Financial Corp 401 Wilshire Blvd *NYSE: FED* ■ *TF:* 800-637-5540 ■ *Web:* www.firstfedca.com	Santa Monica	CA	90401	310-319-6000	319-5930
FirstMerit Corp 3 Cascade Plaza *NASDAQ: FMER* ■ **Fax: Mktg* ■ *TF:* 888-554-4362 ■ *Web:* www.firstmerit.com	Akron	OH	44308	330-996-6000	384-7008*
Flagstar Bancorp Inc 5151 Corporate Dr *NYSE: FBC* ■ **Fax: Hum Res* ■ *TF:* 800-945-7700 ■ *Web:* www.flagstar.com	Troy	MI	48098	248-312-2000	312-6842*
Flushing Financial Corp 1979 Marcus Ave Suite E-140 *NASDAQ: FFIC* ■ *Web:* www.flushingsavingsbank.com	Lake Success	NY	11042	718-961-5400	
FMS Financial Corp 3 Sunset Rd *NASDAQ: FMCO* ■ *Web:* www.fmsbank.net	Burlington	NJ	08016	609-386-2400	386-1979
FNB Corp 101 Sunset Ave *NASDAQ: FNBN* ■ *TF:* 800-873-1172 ■ *Web:* www.fnbnc.com	Asheboro	NC	27203	336-626-8300	626-8374
FNB Corp 1 FNB Blvd *NYSE: FNB* ■ *TF:* 888-981-6000 ■ *Web:* www.fnbcorporation.com	Hermitage	PA	16148	724-981-6000	983-3512
FNB Corp 105 Arbor Dr *NASDAQ: FNBP* ■ **Fax: Hum Res* ■ *TF:* 800-642-7416 ■ *Web:* www.fnbonline.com	Christiansburg	VA	24073	540-382-4951	381-2577*
FNB Financial Services Corp 202 S Main St PO Box 2037 *NASDAQ: FNBF*	Reidsville	NC	27323	336-342-3346	634-4771
Foothill Independent Bancorp Inc 510 S Grand Ave *NASDAQ: FOOT* ■ **Fax Area Code:* 626	Glendora	CA	91741	909-599-9351	914-5373*
Frontier Financial Corp PO Box 2215 *NASDAQ: FTBK*	Everett	WA	98213	425-514-0700	514-0718
Fulton Financial Corp 1 Penn Sq *NASDAQ: FULT* ■ **Fax: Mktg* ■ *TF:* 800-752-9580 ■ *Web:* www.fult.com	Lancaster	PA	17602	717-291-2411	295-2561*
Gateway Financial Holdings Inc PO Box 1908 *NASDAQ: GBTS* ■ *TF:* 800-597-0162	Elizabeth City	NC	27909	252-334-1511	334-1651
GB & T Bancshares Inc 500 Jesse Jewell Pkwy SE *NASDAQ: GBTB* ■ *Web:* www.gbtbancshares.com	Gainesville	GA	30501	770-532-1212	531-7368
German American Bancorp 711 Main St *NASDAQ: GABC* ■ *TF:* 800-482-1314 ■ *Web:* www.germanamericanbancorp.com	Jasper	IN	47546	812-482-1314	482-0758
GFSB Bancorp Inc 221 W Aztec Ave *NASDAQ: GUPB* ■ *TF:* 800-219-6201	Gallup	NM	87301	505-722-4361	722-9205
Glacier Bancorp Inc 49 Commons Loop *NASDAQ: GBCI* ■ *TF:* 800-735-4371 ■ *Web:* www.glacierbank.com	Kalispell	MT	59901	406-756-4200	751-4738
Golden West Financial Corp 1901 Harrison St *NYSE: GDW*	Oakland	CA	94612	510-446-6000	446-3786
Gouverneur Bancorp Inc 42 Church St *AMEX: GOV* ■ *Web:* www.gouverneurbank.com	Gouverneur	NY	13642	315-287-2600	287-4871
Great American Bancorp Inc 1311 S Neil St *Web:* www.greatamericanbancorp.com	Champaign	IL	61820	217-356-2265	356-2502
Great Lakes Bancorp Inc 2421 Main St *NYSE: GLK* ■ *Web:* www.greatlakesbancorp.com	Buffalo	NY	14214	716-961-1900	
Great Pee Dee Bancorp Inc 901 Chesterfield Hwy *NASDAQ: PEDE* ■ *Web:* www.sentrybankandtrust.com	Cheraw	SC	29520	843-537-7656	537-4436
Great Southern Bancorp Inc PO Box 9009GS *NASDAQ: GSBC* ■ *TF Cust Svc:* 800-749-7113 ■ *Web:* www.greatsouthernbank.com	Springfield	MO	65808	417-887-4400	895-4595
Greater Atlantic Financial Corp 10700 Parkridge Blvd Suite P50 *NASDAQ: GAFC* ■ *TF:* 800-296-5581	Reston	VA	20191	703-391-1300	391-1506
Greater Bay Bancorp 2860 W Bayshore Rd *NASDAQ: GBBK* ■ *TF:* 800-226-5262 ■ *Web:* www.gbbk.com	Palo Alto	CA	94301	650-813-8200	494-9220
Greater Community Bancorp 55 Union Blvd *NASDAQ: GFLS* ■ *Web:* www.greatercommunity.com	Totowa	NJ	07512	973-942-1111	942-9816
Greene County Bancorp Inc 302 Main St *NASDAQ: GCBC*	Catskill	NY	12414	518-943-2600	943-4431
GS Financial Corp 3798 Veterans Blvd *NASDAQ: GSLA* ■ *Web:* www.gsha.com	Metairie	LA	70002	504-457-6220	457-6227
Guaranty Bancshares Inc 100 W Arkansas St PO Box 1158 *TF:* 888-572-9881 ■ *Web:* www.gnty.com	Mount Pleasant	TX	75455	903-572-9881	572-5860
Guaranty Federal Bancshares Inc 1341 W Battlefield St *NASDAQ: GFED* ■ *Web:* www.gfed.com	Springfield	MO	65807	417-520-4333	
Guaranty Financial Group Inc 1300 S Mopac Expy *NYSE: GFG* ■ **Fax: Hum Res* ■ *TF:* 800-964-9420 ■ *Web:* www.guarantygroup.com	Austin	TX	78746	512-434-1000	434-8560*
Habersham Bancorp 282 Historic Hwy 441 N *NASDAQ: HABC* ■ *TF:* 800-822-0316 ■ *Web:* habcorp.com	Cornelia	GA	30531	706-778-1000	778-6886
Hancock Holding Co 2510 14th St *NASDAQ: HBHC* ■ *TF:* 800-522-6542 ■ *Web:* www.shareholder.com/hbhc/	Gulfport	MS	39501	228-868-4000	868-4627
Hanmi Financial Corp 3660 Wilshire Blvd Suite PH-A *NASDAQ: HAFC* ■ *Web:* www.hanmi.com	Los Angeles	CA	90010	213-382-2200	639-1789
Harbor Florida Bancshares Inc 100 S 2nd St *NASDAQ: HARB* ■ *TF:* 800-234-1959 ■ *Web:* www.harborfederal.com	Fort Pierce	FL	34950	772-461-2414	460-7001
Harleysville National Corp 483 Main St *NASDAQ: HNBC* ■ *TF:* 800-427-9300 ■ *Web:* www.hncbank.com	Harleysville	PA	19438	215-256-8851	256-1886
Harleysville Savings Financial Corp 271 Main St *NASDAQ: HARL* ■ *TF:* 888-256-8828 ■ *Web:* www.harleysvillesavings.com	Harleysville	PA	19438	215-256-8828	513-9393
Harrington West Financial Group Inc 610 Alamo Pintado Rd *NASDAQ: HWFG* ■ *TF:* 800-525-4959	Solvang	CA	93463	805-688-6644	688-4959
Harris Bankcorp Inc 111 W Monroe St *TF:* 888-340-2265	Chicago	IL	60603	312-461-2121	461-7646
Heartland Financial USA Inc 1398 Central Ave *NASDAQ: HTLF* ■ *TF:* 888-739-2100	Dubuque	IA	52001	563-589-2100	589-2090
Heritage Commerce Corp 150 Almaden Blvd *NASDAQ: HTBK* ■ *Web:* www.heritagecommercecorp.com	San Jose	CA	95113	408-947-6900	947-6910
Heritage Financial Corp 201 5th Ave SW *NASDAQ: HFWA* ■ *TF:* 800-455-6126 ■ *Web:* www.heritagebankwa.com/	Olympia	WA	98501	360-943-1500	352-0864
HF Financial Corp 225 S Main Ave *NASDAQ: HFFC* ■ *TF:* 800-244-2149 ■ *Web:* www.homefederal.com	Sioux Falls	SD	57104	605-333-7556	333-7621
HFB Financial Corp 1602 Cumberland Ave **Fax: Hum Res* ■ *TF:* 800-354-0182	Middlesboro	KY	40965	606-248-1095	242-1010*
High Country Bancorp Inc 7360 W Hwy 50 *TF:* 800-201-0557	Salida	CO	81201	719-539-2516	530-8880
HMN Financial Inc 1016 Civic Center Dr NW *NASDAQ: HMNF* ■ *TF:* 888-644-4142 ■ *Web:* www.justcallhome.com	Rochester	MN	55901	507-535-1200	346-1111
Home City Financial Corp PO Box 1288 *NASDAQ: HCFC*	Springfield	OH	45501	937-390-0470	322-5890
Home Federal Bancorp 501 Washington St *NASDAQ: HOMF* ■ *TF:* 800-876-4372 ■ *Web:* www.homf.com	Columbus	IN	47201	812-376-3323	378-4463
Home Financial Bancorp 279 E Morgan St PO Box 187 *TF:* 800-690-2095 ■ *Web:* www.hfbancorp.com/holding	Spencer	IN	47460	812-829-2095	829-3069
Home Loan Financial Corp 401 Main St *Web:* www.homeloansavingsbank.com	Coshocton	OH	43812	740-622-0444	623-6000
Home Street Bank Inc 601 Union St Suite 2000 **Fax: Mail Rm* ■ *TF:* 800-654-1075 ■ *Web:* www.homestreet.com	Seattle	WA	98101	206-623-3050	389-6351*
Homestead Bancorp Inc 195 N 6th St *Web:* www.homesteadbank.com	Ponchatoula	LA	70454	985-386-3379	386-2400
HopFed Bancorp Inc 2700 Fort Campbell Blvd *NASDAQ: HFBC*	Hopkinsville	KY	42240	270-885-1171	889-0313
Horizon Financial Corp 1500 Cornwall Ave *NASDAQ: HRZB* ■ *TF:* 800-955-9194 ■ *Web:* www.horizonbank.com	Bellingham	WA	98225	360-733-3050	733-7019
Horizon Financial Services Corp 301 1st Ave E *TF:* 800-659-2492 ■ *Web:* www.horizonfed.com	Oskaloosa	IA	52577	641-673-8328	673-3218
HSBC North America Holdings Inc 2700 Sanders Rd *TF:* 800-975-4722 ■ *Web:* www.hsbc.com	Prospect Heights	IL	60070	847-564-5000	205-7452
Hudson City Bancorp Inc W 80 Century Rd *NASDAQ: HCBK* ■ *TF:* 800-967-2200 ■ *Web:* www.hudsoncitysavingsbank.com	Paramus	NJ	07652	201-967-1900	967-0559
Hudson Valley Holding Corp 21 Scarsdale Rd *Web:* www.hudsonvalleybank.com	Yonkers	NY	10707	914-961-6100	961-7378
Huntington Bancshares Inc 41 S High St *NASDAQ: HBAN* ■ *TF:* 800-480-2265 ■ *Web:* www.huntington.com	Columbus	OH	43287	614-480-8300	480-5719
IBERIABANK Corp 1101 E Admiral Doyle Dr *NASDAQ: IBKC* ■ *TF:* 800-968-0801 ■ *Web:* www.iberiabank.com	New Iberia	LA	70560	337-365-2361	364-1171
IBT Bancorp Inc 309 Main St *AMEX: IRW*	Irwin	PA	15642	724-863-3100	863-3069
Independent Bank Corp 288 Union St *NASDAQ: INDB* ■ **Fax: Acctg* ■ *TF:* 800-826-6100	Rockland	MA	02370	781-878-6100	982-6130*
Independent Bank Corp 230 W Main St *NASDAQ: IBCP* ■ *TF:* 800-662-0102 ■ *Web:* www.independentbank.com	Ionia	MI	48846	616-527-2400	527-4004
IndyMac Bancorp Inc 155 N Lake Ave *NYSE: NDE* ■ *TF:* 800-669-2300 ■ *Web:* www.indymacbank.com	Pasadena	CA	91101	626-535-5901	
Integra Bank Corp PO Box 868 *NASDAQ: IBNK* ■ *TF:* 800-467-1928	Evansville	IN	47705	812-464-9800	464-9845
Interchange Financial Services Corp Park 80 W Plaza 2 *NASDAQ: IFCJ* ■ *TF:* 800-701-7718 ■ *Web:* www.interchangebank.com	Saddle Brook	NJ	07663	201-703-2265	384-3945
International Bancshares Corp 1200 San Bernardo Ave *NASDAQ: IBOC* ■ *Web:* www.ibc.com	Laredo	TX	78040	956-722-7611	726-6659
Intervest Bancshares Corp 1 Rockefeller Plaza Suite 400 *NASDAQ: IBCA* ■ *TF:* 877-226-5462 ■ *Web:* www.intervestnatbank.com	New York	NY	10020	212-218-2800	218-2808
INTRUST Financial Corp 105 N Main St *TF:* 800-895-2265 ■ *Web:* www.intrustbank.com	Wichita	KS	67202	316-383-1111	383-1828
Investors Financial Services Corp 200 Clarendon St *NASDAQ: IFIN* ■ *Web:* ir.ibtco.com	Boston	MA	02116	617-330-6700	937-1929
Irwin Financial Corp 500 Washington St PO Box 929 *NYSE: IFC* ■ *TF:* 888-879-5900 ■ *Web:* www.irwinfinancial.com	Columbus	IN	47202	812-376-1020	376-1709
ITLA Capital Corp 888 Prospect St Suite 110 *NASDAQ: ITLA* ■ *TF:* 888-551-4852 ■ *Web:* www.itlacapital.com	La Jolla	CA	92037	858-551-0511	551-1212
Jacksonville Bancorp Inc 100 N Laura St *NASDAQ: JAXB* ■ *TF:* 888-699-5292 ■ *Web:* www.jaxbank.com	Jacksonville	FL	32202	904-421-3040	421-3050
Jacksonville Bancorp Inc 1211 W Morton Ave *NASDAQ: JXSB* ■ *Web:* jacksonvillesavings.com	Jacksonville	IL	62650	217-245-4111	245-2010
Jeffersonville Bancorp 4866 SR 52 *NASDAQ: JFBC* ■ *TF:* 888-216-2265 ■ *Web:* www.jeffbank.com	Jeffersonville	NY	12748	845-482-4000	482-4140
Johnson Financial Group Inc 555 Main St Suite 400 *Web:* www.johnsonbank.com	Racine	WI	53403	262-619-2790	619-2795
JP Morgan Chase & Co 270 Park Ave *NYSE: JPM* ■ *TF:* 800-992-7169 ■ *Web:* www.jpmorganchase.com	New York	NY	10017	212-270-6000	
K-Fed Bancorp 1359 N Grand Ave *NASDAQ: KFED* ■ *TF:* 800-524-2274 ■ *Web:* www.k-fed.com	Covina	CA	91724	626-339-9663	858-5745
Kearny Financial Corp 120 Passaic Ave *NASDAQ: KRNY*	Fairfield	NJ	07004	973-244-4500	
Kentucky First Federal Bancorp 216 W Main St *NASDAQ: KFFB* ■ *TF:* 888-818-3372 ■ *Web:* www.ffsbfrankfort.com	Frankfort	KY	40601	502-223-1638	223-7136
KeyCorp 127 Public Sq *NYSE: KEY* ■ *TF Cust Svc:* 800-539-6070 ■ *Web:* www.key.com	Cleveland	OH	44114	216-689-3000	689-3403
KNBT Bancorp Inc 90 Highland Ave *NASDAQ: KNBT* ■ **Fax: Hum Res* ■ *TF:* 800-996-2062 ■ *Web:* www.knbt.com	Bethlehem	PA	18017	610-861-5000	867-5901*
Lakeland Bancorp Inc 250 Oak Ridge Rd *NASDAQ: LBAI* ■ *Web:* www.lakelandbank.com	Oak Ridge	NJ	07438	973-697-2000	697-8385
Lakeland Financial Corp 202 E Center St *NASDAQ: LKFN* ■ **Fax: Hum Res* ■ *TF:* 800-827-4522 ■ *Web:* www.lakecitybank.com	Warsaw	IN	46580	574-267-6144	267-9180*
Landmark Bancorp Inc 701 Poyntz Ave *NASDAQ: LARK* ■ *TF:* 800-322-6344 ■ *Web:* www.banklandmark.com	Manhattan	KS	66502	785-565-2000	537-0619
Laredo National Bancshares Inc 700 San Bernardo Ave **Fax: Mktg* ■ *TF Mktg:* 888-723-1151	Laredo	TX	78040	956-723-1151	764-1598*
LaSalle Bank Corp 135 S LaSalle St *TF:* 866-904-7222 ■ *Web:* www.lasallebank.com	Chicago	IL	60603	312-904-2000	904-6318
Leesport Financial Corp 1240 Broadcasting Rd *NASDAQ: FLPB* ■ *TF:* 888-238-3330 ■ *Web:* www.leesportfinancialcorp.com	Wyomissing	PA	19610	610-208-0966	372-5705
Lexington B & L Financial Corp 205 S 13th St PO Box 190 *Web:* www.bl-bank.com	Lexington	MO	64067	660-259-2247	259-4557
Lincoln Bancorp 1121 E Main St PO Box 510 *NASDAQ: LNCB* ■ *TF:* 888-895-6539 ■ *Web:* www.lincolnbankonline.com	Plainfield	IN	46168	317-839-6539	839-6775
LNB Bancorp Inc 457 Broadway *NASDAQ: LNBB* ■ *TF:* 800-860-1007 ■ *Web:* www.4lnb.com	Lorain	OH	44052	440-244-6000	244-4815
Logansport Financial Corp 723 E Broadway PO Box 569 *TF:* 800-541-9154 ■ *Web:* www.logansportsavings.com	Logansport	IN	46947	574-722-3855	722-3857
LSB Bancshares Inc 38 W 1st Ave *NASDAQ: LXBK* ■ **Fax: Acctg* ■ *TF:* 800-456-6505 ■ *Web:* www.lsbnc.com	Lexington	NC	27292	336-248-6500	248-6965*
LSB Corp 30 Massachusetts Ave *NASDAQ: LSBX* ■ *TF:* 800-730-9660 ■ *Web:* www.riverbk.com	North Andover	MA	01845	978-725-7500	725-7607
LSB Financial Corp 101 Main St *NASDAQ: LSBI* ■ *TF:* 800-704-3084	Lafayette	IN	47902	765-742-1064	742-1507

Bank Holding Companies (Cont'd)

				Phone	Fax
M & T Bank Corp 1 M & T Plaza 5th Fl NYSE: MTB ■ *Fax: Hum Res ■ TF: 800-724-2440 ■ Web: www.mandtbank.com	Buffalo	NY	14203	716-842-4200	842-5177*
Macatawa Bank Corp 10753 Macatawa Dr NASDAQ: MCBC ■ TF: 877-820-2265 ■ Web: www.macatawabank.com	Holland	MI	49422	616-820-1444	494-7644
Madison Bancshares Group Ltd 1767 Sentry Pkwy W TF: 800-848-9867 ■ Web: www.leesportfc.com	Blue Bell	PA	19422	215-641-1111	653-0699
MAF Bancorp Inc 55th St & Holmes Ave NASDAQ: MAFB ■ TF: 877-622-8700 ■ Web: www.mafbancorp.com	Clarendon Hills	IL	60514	630-325-7300	325-1193
Main Street Trust Inc 100 W University Ave Web: www.mainstreettrust.com	Champaign	IL	61824	217-351-6500	
MainSource Financial Group Inc 201 N Broadway PO Box 87 NASDAQ: MSFG ■ Web: www.mainsourcefinancial.com	Greensburg	IN	47240	812-663-0157	663-4812
Marquette Financial Corp 10000 W 151st St Web: www.emarquettebank.com	Orland Park	IL	60462	888-254-9500	
Marshall & Ilsley Corp 770 N Water St NYSE: MI ■ TF: 800-342-2265 ■ Web: www.mibank.com	Milwaukee	WI	53202	414-765-7801	765-7899
MASSBANK Corp 123 Haven St NASDAQ: MASB ■ TF: 800-447-1052 ■ Web: www.massbank.com	Reading	MA	01867	781-662-0100	942-8194
Matrix Bancorp Inc 700 17th St Suite 2100 NASDAQ: MTXC ■ *Fax Area Code: 720 ■ TF: 800-594-2079 ■ Web: www.matrixbancorp.com	Denver	CO	80202	303-595-9898	946-1217*
MB Financial Inc 6111 N River Rd NASDAQ: MBFI ■ *Fax Area Code: 773 ■ Web: www.mbfinancial.com	Rosemont	IL	60018	888-422-6562	278-4523*
MBT Financial Corp 102 E Front St NASDAQ: MBTF	Monroe	MI	48161	734-241-3431	242-2067
Mellon Financial Corp 500 Grant St 1 Mellon Center NYSE: MEL ■ *Fax: Hum Res ■ TF: 800-947-4748 ■ Web: www.mellon.com	Pittsburgh	PA	15258	412-234-5000	234-5466*
Mercantile Bancorp Inc 440 Maine St AMEX: MBR ■ Web: www.mercbanx.com	Quincy	IL	62301	217-223-7300	223-7340
Mercantile Bank Corp 310 Leonard St NW NASDAQ: MBWM ■ TF: 888-345-6296 ■ Web: www.mercbank.com	Grand Rapids	MI	49504	616-406-3000	454-5807
Mercantile Bankshares Corp 2 Hopkins Plaza NASDAQ: MRBK ■ Web: www.mercantile.net	Baltimore	MD	21201	410-237-5900	237-5979
Merchants Bancshares Inc PO Box 1009 NASDAQ: MBVT ■ *Fax: Cust Svc ■ TF: 800-322-5222 ■ Web: www.mbvt.com	Burlington	VT	05402	802-658-3400	865-1943*
Merrill Merchants Bancshares Inc 201 Main St NASDAQ: MERB ■ Web: www.merrillmerchants.com/	Bangor	ME	04401	207-942-4800	945-4712
Meta Financial Group Inc 121 E 5th St PO Box 1307 NASDAQ: CASH ■ TF: 800-792-6815 ■ Web: www.metacash.com	Storm Lake	IA	50588	712-732-4117	732-8122
MetroCorp Bancshares Inc 9600 Bellaire Blvd Suite 252 NASDAQ: MCBI ■ *Fax: Hum Res ■ TF: 888-414-3556	Houston	TX	77036	713-776-3876	414-3507*
MFB Corp 4100 Edison Lakes Pkwy NASDAQ: MFBC ■ *Fax: Hum Res ■ TF: 800-400-0433 ■ Web: www.mfbbankonline.com	Mishawaka	IN	46545	574-277-4200	273-7845*
MFB Financial 105 E Jefferson Blvd Suite 800	South Bend	IN	46601	574-239-7047	287-3116
Mid Penn Bancorp Inc 349 Union St AMEX: MBP ■ TF: 800-672-6843 ■ Web: www.midpennbank.com	Millersburg	PA	17061	717-692-2133	692-4861
Mid-State Bancshares PO Box 6002 NASDAQ: MDST ■ TF: 800-473-7788 ■ Web: www.midstatebank.com	Arroyo Grande	CA	93421	805-473-7710	473-7751
Midland Financial Co 501 NW Grand Blvd TF: 800-851-5041 ■ Web: www.midfirst.com	Oklahoma City	OK	73118	405-767-7000	843-6821
MidSouth Bancorp Inc 102 Versailles Blvd AMEX: MSL ■ TF: 800-213-2265 ■ Web: www.midsouthbank.com	Lafayette	LA	70501	337-237-8343	267-4316
Midwest Banc Holdings Inc 501 W North Ave NASDAQ: MBHI ■ TF: 800-471-4446 ■ Web: www.midwestbank.com	Melrose Park	IL	60160	708-865-1053	865-7013
MidWestOne Financial Group Inc 222 1st Ave E NASDAQ: OSKY ■ TF: 800-303-6740 ■ Web: www.midwestonefinancial.com	Oskaloosa	IA	52577	641-673-8448	673-7836
Millennium Bankshares Corp 1601 Washington Plaza NASDAQ: MBVA ■ Web: www.millenniumbankshares.com	Reston	VA	20190	703-464-0100	464-0064
Monroe Bancorp 210 E Kirkwood Ave NASDAQ: MROE ■ TF: 800-817-4622 ■ Web: www.monroebank.com	Bloomington	IN	47408	812-336-0201	331-3445
MutualFirst Financial Inc 110 E Charles St NASDAQ: MFSF ■ TF: 800-382-8031 ■ Web: www.mfsbank.com	Muncie	IN	47305	765-747-2800	213-2981
Nara Bancorp Inc 3701 Wilshire Blvd Suite 220 NASDAQ: NARA ■ Web: www.narabank.com	Los Angeles	CA	90010	213-389-2000	386-8425
NASB Financial Inc 12498 S 71st Hwy NASDAQ: NASB ■ TF: 800-677-6272 ■ Web: www.nasb.com/	Grandview	MO	64030	816-765-2200	316-4504
National Bankshares Inc 101 Hubbard St NASDAQ: NKSH ■ TF: 800-552-4123 ■ Web: www.nationalbankshares.com	Blacksburg	VA	24060	540-951-6300	951-6324
National City Corp 1900 E 9th St NYSE: NCC ■ TF: 800-622-8100 ■ Web: www.nationalcity.com	Cleveland	OH	44114	216-222-2000	222-2860
National Mercantile Bancorp 1880 Century Pk E Suite 800 NASDAQ: MBLA ■ Web: www.mnbla.com	Los Angeles	CA	90067	310-277-2265	282-6795
National Penn Bancshares Inc PO Box 547 NASDAQ: NPBC ■ TF: 800-822-3321	Boyertown	PA	19512	610-367-6001	369-6429
NBT Bancorp Inc 52 S Broad St NASDAQ: NBTB ■ *Fax: Hum Res ■ TF: 800-628-2265 ■ Web: www.nbtbank.com	Norwich	NY	13815	607-337-2265	336-5963*
New Hampshire Thrift Bancshares Inc 9 Main St NASDAQ: NHTB ■ TF: 800-281-5772 ■ Web: www.lakesunbank.com	Newport	NH	03773	603-863-5772	863-5250
New York Community Bancorp Inc 615 Merrick Ave NYSE: NYB ■ TF: 888-550-9888 ■ Web: www.mynycb.com	Westbury	NY	11590	516-683-4100	683-8360
NewAlliance Bancshares Inc 195 Church St NYSE: NAL ■ Web: www.newalliancebank.com	New Haven	CT	06510	203-787-1111	
Nexity Financial Corp 3500 Blue Lake Dr Suite 330 NASDAQ: NXTY ■ TF: 877-738-6391 ■ Web: www.nexitybank.com	Birmingham	AL	35243	205-298-6391	298-6395
North Central Bancshares Inc 825 Central Ave NASDAQ: FFFD ■ TF: 800-272-3445	Fort Dodge	IA	50501	515-576-7531	576-7962
North Fork Bancorp Inc 275 Broad Hollow Rd NYSE: NFB ■ TF: 877-694-9111 ■ Web: www.northforkbank.com	Melville	NY	11747	631-844-1000	694-0582
North Valley Bancorp 300 Park Marina Cir NASDAQ: NOVB ■ TF: 866-869-6673 ■ Web: www.novb.com	Redding	CA	96001	530-226-2900	221-4877
Northeast Bancorp 158 Court St AMEX: NBN ■ *Fax: Mktg ■ TF: 800-284-5989 ■ Web: www.northeastbank.com	Auburn	ME	04210	207-786-3245	777-5936*
Northeast Indiana Bancorp Inc 648 N Jefferson St TF: 800-550-3372	Huntington	IN	46750	260-356-3311	358-0036
Northeast Pennsylvania Financial Corp 12 E Broad St TF: 888-466-6745 ■ Web: www.ibank-1stfed.com	Hazleton	PA	18201	570-459-3700	459-3744
Northern States Financial Corp 1601 N Lewis Ave NASDAQ: NSFC ■ TF: 800-339-4432 ■ Web: www.bankofwaukegan.com/	Waukegan	IL	60085	847-244-6000	244-7485
Northern Trust Corp 50 S La Salle St NASDAQ: NTRS ■ Web: www.ntrs.com	Chicago	IL	60603	312-630-6000	630-1512
Northway Financial Inc PO Box 9 NASDAQ: NWFI ■ TF: 800-442-6666 ■ Web: www.berlincitybank.com	Berlin	NH	03570	603-752-1171	752-5009
Northwest Bancorp Inc 301 2nd Ave NASDAQ: NWSB ■ TF Cust Svc: 877-672-5678 ■ Web: www.northwestsavingsbank.com	Warren	PA	16365	814-726-2140	728-7736
Norwood Financial Corp 717 Main St NASDAQ: NWFL ■ TF: 800-598-5002	Honesdale	PA	18431	570-253-1455	253-3725
Oak Hill Financial Inc 14621 SR 93 NASDAQ: OAKF ■ Web: www.oakf.com	Jackson	OH	45640	740-286-3283	286-1224
Ocean Bankshares Inc 780 NW 42nd Ave TF: 877-310-2265 ■ Web: www.oceanbank.com	Miami	FL	33126	305-442-2660	446-2494
OceanFirst Financial Corp 975 Hooper Ave NASDAQ: OCFC ■ TF: 888-623-2633 ■ Web: www.oceanfirstonline.com	Toms River	NJ	08753	732-240-4500	349-5070
Ocwen Financial Corp 1661 Worthington Rd Suite 100 PO Box 24737 NYSE: OCN ■ *Fax: Hum Res ■ TF: 800-746-2936 ■ Web: www.ocwen.com	West Palm Beach	FL	33409	561-681-8000	682-8150*
Ohio Savings Financial Corp 1801 E 9th St Suite 200 TF: 800-860-2025	Cleveland	OH	44114	216-622-4100	588-4472
Ohio Valley Banc Corp 420 3rd Ave NASDAQ: OVBC ■ TF: 800-468-6682 ■ Web: www.ovbc.com	Gallipolis	OH	45631	740-446-2631	446-4643
Old National Bancorp 1 Main St NYSE: ONB ■ TF: 800-731-2265 ■ Web: www.oldnational.com	Evansville	IN	47708	812-464-1494	464-1567
Old Point Financial Corp 1 W Mellen St NASDAQ: OPOF ■ TF: 800-952-0051 ■ Web: www.oldpoint.com	Hampton	VA	23663	757-722-7451	728-1279
Old Second Bancorp Inc 37 S River St NASDAQ: OSBC ■ *Fax: Mktg ■ TF: 888-892-6565 ■ Web: www.o2bancorp.com	Aurora	IL	60506	630-892-0202	892-9630*
Omega Financial Corp 366 Walker Dr NASDAQ: OMEF ■ *Fax: Hum Res ■ TF: 877-861-7800 ■ Web: www.omegafinancial.com	State College	PA	16804	814-231-7680	231-6295*
Oneida Financial Corp 182 Main St NASDAQ: ONFC ■ TF: 800-211-0564 ■ Web: www.oneidabank.com	Oneida	NY	13421	315-363-2000	366-3709
Oriental Financial Group Inc 997 San Roberto St 9th Fl NYSE: OFG	San Juan	PR	00926	787-474-1993	474-1998
PAB Bankshares Inc 3250 N Valdosta Rd NASDAQ: PABK ■ TF: 800-394-2321 ■ Web: www.pabbankshares.com	Valdosta	GA	31604	229-241-2775	241-2774
Pacific Capital Bancorp 1 S Los Carneros Rd NASDAQ: PCBC ■ TF: 800-272-7200 ■ Web: www.pcbancorp.com	Goleta	CA	93117	805-564-6300	564-6232
Pacific Mercantile Bancorp 949 South Coast Dr 3rd Fl NASDAQ: PMBC ■ TF: 877-450-2265 ■ Web: www.pmbank.com	Costa Mesa	CA	92626	714-438-2500	438-1059
Pacific Premier Bancorp Inc 1600 Sunflower Ave 2nd Fl NASDAQ: PPBI ■ TF: 888-388-5433 ■ Web: www.pacificpremierbank.com	Costa Mesa	CA	92626	714-431-4000	433-3000
Pacific & Western Credit Corp 140 Fullarton St Suite 2002 TSX: PWC ■ Web: www.pwcorp.com	London	ON	N6A5P2	519-645-1919	645-2060
Pamrapo Bancorp Inc 611 Ave C PO Box 98 NASDAQ: PBCI ■ TF: 800-680-6872 ■ Web: www.pamrapo.com	Bayonne	NJ	07002	201-339-4600	437-9520
Park Bancorp Inc 5400 S Pulaski Rd NASDAQ: PFED ■ TF: 888-727-5333 ■ Web: www.parkfed.com	Chicago	IL	60632	773-582-8616	582-8657
Park National Corp 50 N 3rd St PO Box 3500 AMEX: PRK ■ TF: 800-762-2616 ■ Web: www.parknationalbank.com	Newark	OH	43058	740-349-8451	349-3931
Parkvale Financial Corp 4220 William Penn Hwy NASDAQ: PVSA	Monroeville	PA	15146	412-373-7200	374-9634
Partners Trust Financial Group Inc 233 Genessee St Web: www.partnerstrust.com	Utica	NY	13501	315-768-3000	738-4830
Pathfinder Bancorp Inc 214 W 1st St NASDAQ: PBHC ■ TF: 800-811-5620 ■ Web: www.pathfinderbancorpinc.com	Oswego	NY	13126	315-343-0057	342-9403
Patriot National Bancorp Inc 900 Bedford St NASDAQ: PNBK ■ TF: 800-762-7620 ■ Web: www.pnbk.com	Stamford	CT	06901	203-324-7500	324-8085
Peapack-Gladstone Financial Corp PO Box 178 AMEX: PGC ■ TF: 800-742-7595 ■ Web: www.pgbank.com	Gladstone	NJ	07934	908-234-0700	781-2046
PennFed Financial Service Inc 622 Eagle Rock Ave NASDAQ: PFSB ■ TF: 800-722-0351	West Orange	NJ	07052	973-669-7366	669-7374
Penns Woods Bancorp Inc 300 Market St NASDAQ: PWOD ■ TF: 888-412-5772	Williamsport	PA	17701	570-322-1111	320-2046
Pennsylvania Commerce Bancorp Inc 1249 Market St NASDAQ: COBH ■ TF: 800-937-2003 ■ Web: www.commercepc.com	Lemoyne	PA	17043	717-972-2875	975-9720
Peoples Bancorp 212 W 7th St NASDAQ: PFDC	Auburn	IN	46706	260-925-2500	925-8303
Peoples Bancorp Inc 138 Putnam St NASDAQ: PEBO ■ *Fax: Mail Rm ■ TF: 800-374-6123 ■ Web: www.peoplesbancorp.com	Marietta	OH	45750	740-373-3155	374-2020*
Peoples Bancorp of North Carolina Inc 518 W 'C' St NASDAQ: PEBK ■ TF: 800-948-7195 ■ Web: www.peoplesbanknc.com	Newton	NC	28658	828-464-5620	466-5043
Peoples BancTrust Co Inc 310 Broad St NASDAQ: PBTC ■ TF: 800-278-8725 ■ Web: www.peoplesbt.com	Selma	AL	36701	334-875-1000	875-1010
Peoples Community Bancorp Inc 6100 W Chester Rd NASDAQ: PCBI ■ TF: 888-815-3530 ■ Web: www.pcbionline.com	West Chester	OH	45069	513-870-3530	881-5933
People's First Properties Inc 1022 W 23rd St Suite 400 TF: 800-624-9699 ■ Web: www.peoplesfirst.com	Panama City	FL	32405	850-769-1111	770-7687
People's Mutual Holdings 850 Main St TF: 800-392-3009 ■ Web: www.peoples.com	Bridgeport	CT	06604	203-338-7171	338-3600
Peoples-Sidney Financial Corp 101 E Court St PO Box 727 TF: 800-235-8041	Sidney	OH	45365	937-492-6129	498-4554
PFF Bancorp Inc PO Box 1520 NYSE: PFB ■ TF: 888-733-5465 ■ Web: www.pffbank.com	Pomona	CA	91769	909-623-2323	620-0296
Pinnacle Bancshares Inc 1811 2nd Ave AMEX: PLE ■ Web: www.pinnaclebanc.com	Jasper	AL	35502	205-221-4111	221-8870
PNC Financial Services Group Inc 249 5th Ave 1 PNC Plaza NYSE: PNC ■ *Fax: Hum Res ■ TF: 877-762-2000 ■ Web: www.pnc.com	Pittsburgh	PA	15222	412-762-2000	762-3257*
Pocahontas Bancorp Inc 203 W Broadway NASDAQ: PFSL	Pocahontas	AR	72455	870-892-4595	892-8876
Popular Inc 209 Ponce de Leon Ave NASDAQ: BPOP ■ TF: 888-724-3650 ■ Web: www.bancopopular.com	San Juan	PR	00918	787-765-9800	753-9434
Premier Community Bankshares Inc 4095 Valley Pike NASDAQ: PREM ■ TF: 800-526-2265 ■ Web: www.premiercommunitybankshares.com	Winchester	VA	22602	540-869-6600	869-4994
Premier Financial Bancorp Inc 2883 5th Ave NASDAQ: PFBI ■ TF: 866-269-0298	Huntington	WV	25702	304-525-1600	525-9701
Princeton National Bancorp Inc 606 S Main St NASDAQ: PNBC ■ Web: www.pnbc-inc.com	Princeton	IL	61356	815-875-4444	872-0247
PrivateBancorp Inc 70 W Madison St Suite 200 NASDAQ: PVTB ■ Web: www.privatebk.com	Chicago	IL	60602	312-683-7100	683-7111
Prosperity Bancshares Inc 4295 San Felipe St NASDAQ: PRSP ■ Web: www.prosperitybanktx.com	Houston	TX	77027	713-693-9300	693-9309
Provident Bankshares Corp 114 E Lexington St NASDAQ: PBKS	Baltimore	MD	21202	410-277-7349	277-2887
Provident Community Bancshares Inc 2700 Celanese Rd NASDAQ: PCBS ■ TF: 888-427-9002 ■ Web: www.provcombank.com	Rock Hill	SC	29732	803-325-9400	
Provident Financial Holdings Inc 3756 Central Ave NASDAQ: PROV ■ TF: 800-442-5201	Riverside	CA	92506	951-686-6060	782-6132
Provident Financial Services Inc 830 Bergen Ave NYSE: PFS ■ TF: 800-742-2943 ■ Web: www.providentbanknj.com	Jersey City	NJ	07306	201-333-1000	
Provident New York Bancorp 400 Rella Blvd NASDAQ: PBNY ■ *Fax: Hum Res	Montebello	NY	10901	845-369-8040	369-8066*
Providian Financial Corp 201 Mission St *Fax: Hum Res ■ TF: 800-525-7557 ■ Web: www.providian.com	San Francisco	CA	94105	415-543-0404	278-6028*
PSB Bancorp Inc 1835 Market St 11 Penn Ctr Suite 2601 NASDAQ: PSBI ■ TF: 866-437-2265 ■ Web: www.firstpennbank.com	Philadelphia	PA	19103	215-979-7900	979-7979
Pulaski Financial Corp 12300 Olive Blvd NASDAQ: PULB ■ TF: 800-261-0113 ■ Web: www.pulaskibankstl.com	Saint Louis	MO	63141	314-878-2210	878-7130
PVF Capital Corp 30000 Aurora Rd NASDAQ: PVFC ■ TF: 800-676-2572 ■ Web: www.parkviewfederal.com/	Solon	OH	44139	440-248-7171	914-3658
QCR Holdings Inc 3551 7th St Suite 100 NASDAQ: QCRH ■ TF: 866-676-0551 ■ Web: www.qcbt.com	Moline	IL	61265	309-736-3580	743-7705
R & G Financial Corp PO Box 362394 NYSE: RGF ■ Web: www.rgonline.com/financial/more.html	Hato Rey	PR	00936	787-758-2424	766-6784
Rabobank 245 Park Ave Web: www.rabobankamerica.com	New York	NY	10167	212-916-7800	916-7993
Rainier Pacific Financial Group Inc 1498 Pacific Ave NASDAQ: RPFG ■ TF: 800-228-2858 ■ Web: www.rainierpac.com	Tacoma	WA	98402	253-926-4000	926-4070
RBC Centura Banks Inc PO Box 1220 Web: www.rbccentura.com	Rocky Mount	NC	27802	252-454-4400	
Regions Financial Corp 417 N 20th St NYSE: RF ■ TF: 800-734-4667 ■ Web: www.regionsbank.com	Birmingham	AL	35203	205-326-7100	326-7571

Phone Fax

Renasant Corp 209 Troy St. Tupelo MS 38802 662-680-1001 680-1448*
NASDAQ: RNST ■ **Fax:* Hum Res ■ *TF:* 800-680-1601 ■ *Web:* www.phcfc.com

Republic Bancorp Inc 601 W Market St. Louisville KY 40202 502-584-3600 561-7188
NASDAQ: RBCAA ■ *TF:* 888-540-5363 ■ *Web:* www.republicbank.com

Republic First Bancorp Inc 1608 Walnut St Suite 1000 Philadelphia PA 19103 215-735-4422 735-5373
NASDAQ: FRBK ■ *Web:* www.rfbkonline.com

River Valley Bancorp 430 Clifty Dr. Madison IN 47250 812-273-4949 265-6730*
NASDAQ: RIVR ■ **Fax:* Hum Res ■ *TF:* 800-994-4849 ■ *Web:* www.rvfbank.com

Riverview Bancorp Inc 900 Washington St Suite 900 Vancouver WA 98660 360-693-6650 693-6275
NASDAQ: RVSB ■ *Web:* www.riverviewbank.com

Rome Bancorp Inc 100 W Dominick St Rome NY 13440 315-336-7300 336-5440
NASDAQ: ROME ■ *TF:* 800-280-9315

Royal Bancshares of Pennsylvania Inc 732 Montgomery Ave Narberth PA 19072 610-668-4700 668-1185
NASDAQ: RBPAA ■ *TF:* 800-417-5198 ■ *Web:* www.royalbankpa.com/

S & T Bancorp Inc 43 S 9th St. Indiana PA 15701 724-349-1800 465-6874*
NASDAQ: STBA ■ **Fax:* Cust Svc ■ *TF:* 800-325-2265 ■ *Web:* www.stbank.com

Salisbury Bancorp Inc 5 Bissell St PO Box 1868 Lakeville CT 06039 860-435-9801 435-0631
AMEX: SAL ■ *Web:* www.salisburybank.com

Sandy Spring Bancorp Inc 17801 Georgia Ave. Olney MD 20832 301-774-6400 260-0600
NASDAQ: SASR ■ *TF:* 800-399-5919 ■ *Web:* www.sandyspringbank.com

Santander BanCorp 207 Ponce de Leon Ave San Juan PR 00918 787-777-4206 766-1437
NYSE: SBP ■ *Web:* www.santandernet.com

Savannah Bancorp Inc 25 Bull St. Savannah GA 31401 912-651-8200 651-4141*
NASDAQ: SAVB ■ **Fax:* Acctg ■ *Web:* www.savb.com

SCBT Financial Corp 950 John C Calhoun Dr Orangeburg SC 29115 803-534-2175 531-8744
NASDAQ: SCBT ■ *TF:* 800-277-2175 ■ *Web:* www.scbandt.com

Seacoast Banking Corp of Florida PO Box 9012. Stuart FL 34995 772-287-4000 288-6012
NASDAQ: SBCF ■ *TF:* 800-706-9991 ■ *Web:* www.seacoastbanking.net

Security Bank Corp 4219 Forsyth Rd Macon GA 31210 478-722-6200 722-6390
NASDAQ: SBKC ■ *Web:* www.securitybank.net

Shore Bancshares Inc 18 E Dover St Easton MD 21601 410-822-1400 820-4238
NASDAQ: SHBI ■ *Web:* www.shbi.net

Shore Financial Corp 25020 Shore Pkwy. Onley VA 23418 757-787-1335 789-3745
NASDAQ: SHBK ■ *TF:* 800-852-8176

Sierra Bancorp 86 N Main St Porterville CA 93257 559-782-4900 782-4994
NASDAQ: BSRR

Simmons First National Corp 501 Main St. Pine Bluff AR 71601 870-541-1000 541-1138*
NASDAQ: SFNC ■ **Fax:* Hum Res ■ *Web:* www.simmonsfirst.com

Sky Financial Group Inc 221 S Church St Bowling Green OH 43402 419-327-6300 327-6337*
NASDAQ: SKYF ■ **Fax:* Hum Res ■ *Web:* www.skyfi.com

Slade's Ferry Bancorp 100 Slade's Ferry Ave. Somerset MA 02726 508-675-2121 675-1751
NASDAQ: SFBC ■ *TF:* 800-643-7537 ■ *Web:* www.sladesferry.com

Sound Federal Bancorp 300 Mamaroneck Ave. Mamaroneck NY 10543 914-698-6400 698-5213
NASDAQ: SFFS

South Financial Group Inc 104 S Main St Greenville SC 29601 864-255-7900 239-6423
NASDAQ: TSFG ■ *TF Cust Svc:* 800-476-6400 ■ *Web:* www.thesouthgroup.com

South Street Financial Corp 155 W South St Albemarle NC 28001 704-982-9184 983-1308
NASDAQ: SSFC

Southern Banc Co Inc 221 S 6th St. Gadsden AL 35901 256-543-3860 543-3864
Web: www.sobanco.com

Southern Connecticut Bancorp Inc 215 Church St New Haven CT 06510 203-782-1100 787-5056
AMEX: SSE ■ *Web:* www.scbancorp.com

Southern Missouri Bancorp Inc 531 Vine St Poplar Bluff MO 63901 573-778-1800 686-2920
NASDAQ: SMBC

SouthFirst Bancshares Inc 126 N Norton Ave Sylacauga AL 35150 256-245-4365 245-6341
AMEX: SZB ■ *TF:* 800-239-1492 ■ *Web:* www.southfirst.com

Southside Bancshares Inc 1201 S Beckham Ave. Tyler TX 75701 903-531-7220 533-7383
NASDAQ: SBSI ■ *TF:* 800-962-4284 ■ *Web:* www.southside.com

Southwest Bancorp Inc 608 S Main St. Stillwater OK 74074 405-372-2230 742-1928*
NASDAQ: OKSB ■ **Fax:* Hum Res ■ *TF:* 888-762-4762

Southwest Georgia Financial Corp 201 1st St SE Moultrie GA 31768 229-985-1120 980-2211*
AMEX: SGB ■ **Fax:* Hum Res ■ *TF:* 888-683-2265 ■ *Web:* www.sgfc.com

Sovereign Bancorp Inc 1500 Market St Philadelphia PA 19102 610-320-8400 320-8448
NYSE: SOV ■ *TF:* 800-683-4663 ■ *Web:* www.sovereignbank.com

State Bancorp Inc 699 Hillside Ave New Hyde Park NY 11040 516-437-1000 465-2222
NASDAQ: STBC

State National Bancshares Inc
4500 Mercantile Plaza Dr Suite 300 Fort Worth TX 76137 817-547-1150
NASDAQ: SNBI ■ *Web:* www.statenationalbank.com

State Street Corp 1 Lincoln St Boston MA 02111 617-786-3000 664-3386*
NYSE: STT ■ **Fax:* Mktg ■ *Web:* www.statestreet.com

Sterling Bancorp 650 5th Ave. New York NY 10019 212-757-3300 490-8852
NYSE: STL ■ *Web:* www.sterlingbancorp.com

Sterling Bancshares Inc 2550 N Loop W Suite 200 Houston TX 77092 713-466-8300 466-3117
NASDAQ: SBIB ■ *TF:* 888-777-8735 ■ *Web:* www.banksterling.com

Sterling Financial Corp 1097 Commercial Ave. East Petersburg PA 17520 717-581-6030 581-6049
NASDAQ: SLFI ■ *Web:* www.sterlingfi.com

Sterling Financial Corp 111 N Wall St. Spokane WA 99201 509-624-4114 358-6161*
NASDAQ: STSA ■ **Fax:* Hum Res ■ *TF:* 800-772-7791

Suffolk Bancorp 4 W 2nd St PO Box 9000 Riverhead NY 11901 631-208-2350 727-3210
NASDAQ: SUBK ■ *Web:* www.scnb.com

Summit Bancshares Inc 3880 Hulen St Suite 300 Fort Worth TX 76107 817-336-6817 877-2672
NASDAQ: SBIT ■ *Web:* www.summitbank.net

Sun American Bancorp 3400 Coral Way. Miami FL 33145 305-421-6800 569-2087
AMEX: SBK ■ *Web:* www.panamericanbank.com

Sun Bancorp Inc 226 Landis Ave Vineland NJ 08360 856-691-7700 691-6763
NASDAQ: SNBC ■ *TF:* 800-691-7701 ■ *Web:* www.sunnb.com

Sun Bancshares Inc PO Box 1359 Murrells Inlet SC 29576 843-357-7007 652-5252

SunTrust Banks Inc 303 Peachtree St NE. Atlanta GA 30308 404-588-7711 335-2686
NYSE: STI ■ *TF:* 800-688-7878 ■ *Web:* www.suntrust.com

Superior Bancorp 17 N 20th St. Birmingham AL 35203 205-327-3547
NASDAQ: SUPR ■ *Web:* www.superiorbank.com

Susquehanna Bancshares Inc 24 N Cedar St PO Box 1000 Lititz PA 17543 717-626-4721 625-2701*
NASDAQ: SUSQ ■ **Fax:* Edit ■ *TF:* 800-311-3182 ■ *Web:* www.susqbanc.com

Sussex Bancorp 399 Rt 23 S Franklin NJ 07416 973-827-2914 827-2926
AMEX: SBB ■ *TF:* 800-511-9900 ■ *Web:* www.sussexbank.com

SVB Financial Group 3005 Tasman Dr. Santa Clara CA 95054 408-654-7282 496-2405
NASDAQ: SIVB ■ *Web:* www.svb.com

SVB Financial Services Inc 70 E Main St Somerville NJ 08876 908-541-9500 541-6464
TF: 800-991-4248

SY Bancorp Inc 1040 E Main St. Louisville KY 40206 502-582-2571 625-2431
NASDAQ: SYBT ■ *TF:* 800-625-9066 ■ *Web:* www.syb.com/

Synovus Financial Corp PO Box 120 Columbus GA 31902 706-649-5216
NYSE: SNV ■ *Web:* www.synovus.com

Taylor Capital Group Inc 9550 W Higgins Rd 5th Fl Rosemont IL 60018 847-653-7978 653-7890
NASDAQ: TAYC ■ *TF:* 800-727-2265 ■ *Web:* www.taylorcapitalgroup.com

TCF Financial Corp 801 Marquette Ave Minneapolis MN 55402 612-661-6500 661-8277*
NYSE: TCB ■ **Fax:* Hum Res ■ *TF:* 800-533-1723 ■ *Web:* www.tcfbank.com

TD Banknorth Inc 1 Portland Sq. Portland ME 04101 207-761-8500 761-8534
NYSE: BNK ■ *TF:* 800-462-6606 ■ *Web:* www.tdbanknorth.com

Team Financial Inc 8 W Peoria St Suite 200 PO Box 402 Paola KS 66071 913-294-9667 294-4406
NASDAQ: TFIN ■ *TF:* 800-880-6262 ■ *Web:* www.teamfinancialinc.com

Teche Holding Co 1120 Jefferson Terr Blvd. New Iberia LA 70560 337-365-0366 365-7130
AMEX: TSH ■ *TF:* 800-256-1500 ■ *Web:* www.teche.com

Temecula Valley Bancorp Inc
27710 Jefferson Ave Suite A100 Temecula CA 92590 951-694-9940 694-9194
NASDAQ: TMCV ■ *TF:* 800-939-3736 ■ *Web:* www.temvalbank.com

Texas Regional Bancshares Inc 3900 N 10th St 11th Fl. McAllen TX 78501 956-631-5400 631-5450
NASDAQ: TRBS ■ *Web:* www.trbsinc.com

TF Financial Corp 3 Penns Trail Newtown PA 18940 215-579-4000 579-4748
NASDAQ: THRD ■ *TF:* 888-918-4473 ■ *Web:* www.thirdfedbank.com

TIB Financial Corp 559 9th St N Naples FL 34102 239-263-3344 263-4543
NASDAQ: TIBB ■ *TF:* 800-233-6330 ■ *Web:* www.tibbank.com

TierOne Corporation 1235 'N' St PO Box 83009 Lincoln NE 68501 402-473-6250 435-0427
NASDAQ: TONE ■ *TF:* 800-288-0722 ■ *Web:* www.tieronebank.com/investor_relations

Timberland Bancorp Inc PO Box 697 Hoquiam WA 98550 360-533-4747 533-4743
NASDAQ: TSBK ■ *TF:* 800-562-8761

Tower Financial Corp 116 E Berry St. Fort Wayne IN 46802 260-427-7000 427-7180
NASDAQ: TOFC ■ *TF:* 877-427-7220 ■ *Web:* www.towerbank.net

TriCo Bancshares 63 Constitution Dr Chico CA 95973 530-898-0300 898-0310
NASDAQ: TCBK ■ *TF:* 800-922-8742 ■ *Web:* www.tcbk.com

Trustco Bank Corp NY PO Box 1082 Schenectady NY 12301 518-377-3311 381-3839
NASDAQ: TRST

Trustmark Corp PO Box 291 Jackson MS 39205 601-208-5111 944-5491*
NASDAQ: TRMK ■ **Fax:* Cust Svc ■ *TF:* 800-243-2524 ■ *Web:* www.trustmark.com

UCBH Holdings Inc 555 Montgomery St. San Francisco CA 94111 415-928-0700 346-2266
NASDAQ: UCBH ■ *TF:* 800-288-3899 ■ *Web:* www.unitedcb.com

UMB Financial Corp 1010 Grand Blvd Kansas City MO 64106 816-860-7000 860-4952
NASDAQ: UMBF ■ *TF:* 800-821-2171 ■ *Web:* www.umb.com

Umpqua Holdings Corp 1 SW Columbia St Suite 1200 Portland OR 97258 503-727-4100 544-3250*
NASDAQ: UMPQ ■ **Fax Area Code:* 971 ■ *TF:* 866-486-7782

Union Bankshares Corp 212 N Main St Bowling Green VA 22427 804-633-5031 633-1310
NASDAQ: UBSH ■ *TF:* 800-990-4828 ■ *Web:* www.ubsh.com

Union Bankshares Inc 20 Lower Main St. Morrisville VT 05661 802-888-6600 888-4921
AMEX: UNB ■ *TF:* 866-862-1891 ■ *Web:* www.unionbankvt.com

Union Community Bancorp 221 E Main St. Crawfordsville IN 47933 765-362-2400 364-9416
NASDAQ: UCBC ■ *Web:* www.unionfed.com

UnionBanCal Corp 400 California St 1st Fl San Francisco CA 94104 415-705-7000 765-3507*
NYSE: UB ■ **Fax:* PR

United Bancorp Inc 201 S 4th St. Martins Ferry OH 43935 740-633-0445 633-1448
NASDAQ: UBCP ■ *TF:* 888-275-5566 ■ *Web:* www.unitedbancorp.com

United Bancshares Inc 100 S High St PO Box 67 Columbus Grove OH 45830 419-659-2141 659-2069
NASDAQ: UBOH ■ *TF:* 800-837-8111 ■ *Web:* www.theubank.com

United Bankshares Inc 514 Market St Parkersburg WV 26101 304-424-8800 424-8833
NASDAQ: UBSI ■ *TF:* 800-345-4862 ■ *Web:* www.ubsi-wv.com

United Community Banks Inc 63 Hwy 515 Blairsville GA 30512 706-781-2265 745-8960
NASDAQ: UCBI ■ *TF:* 866-270-7200 ■ *Web:* www.ucbi.com

United Community Financial Corp 275 Federal Plaza W Youngstown OH 44503 330-742-0500 742-0593
NASDAQ: UCFC ■ *TF:* 888-822-4751 ■ *Web:* www.homesavings.com/about-corporate.asp

United PanAm Financial Corp
3990 Westerly Pl Suite 200 Newport Beach CA 92660 949-224-1917 224-1912
NASDAQ: UPFC ■ *TF:* 800-833-1940

United Security Bancshares Inc PO Box 249 Thomasville AL 36784 334-636-5424 636-9606
NASDAQ: USBI ■ *Web:* www.firstusbank.com

United Tennessee Bankshares Inc 170 W Broadway Newport TN 37821 423-623-6088 625-0301

Unity Bancorp Inc 64 Old Hwy 22 Clinton NJ 08809 908-730-7630 730-9430
NASDAQ: UNTY ■ *TF:* 800-618-2265 ■ *Web:* www.unitybank.com

University Bancorp Inc 2015 Washtenaw Ave Ann Arbor MI 48104 734-741-5858 741-5859
NASDAQ: UNIB ■ *TF:* 888-944-5004 ■ *Web:* www.university-bank.com

Univest Corp of Pennsylvania 14 N Main St PO Box 64197 Souderton PA 18964 215-721-2400 721-2433
NASDAQ: UVSP ■ *Web:* www.univest.net

US Bancorp 800 Nicollet Mall Minneapolis MN 55402 651-466-3000
NYSE: USB ■ *TF Cust Svc:* 800-872-2657 ■ *Web:* www.usbank.com

USB Holding Co Inc 100 Dutch Hill Rd. Orangeburg NY 10962 845-365-4600 365-4695
NYSE: UBH ■ *TF:* 800-616-3491 ■ *Web:* www.unionstate.com

Vail Banks Inc PO Box 6580. Avon CO 81620 970-476-2002 476-0200
NASDAQ: VAIL

Valley National Bancorp 1455 Valley Rd Wayne NJ 07470 973-305-8800 686-3491
NYSE: VLY ■ *TF:* 800-522-4100 ■ *Web:* www.valleynationalbank.com

Virginia Commerce Bancorp Inc 5350 Lee Hwy Arlington VA 22207 703-534-0700 534-7216
NASDAQ: VCBI ■ *Web:* www.vcbonline.com

Virginia Financial Group Inc 102 S Main St Culpeper VA 22701 540-825-4800 829-0299
NASDAQ: VFGI ■ *TF:* 800-825-4003 ■ *Web:* www.vfgi.net

W Holding Co Inc 19 W McKinley St Mayaguez PR 00680 787-834-8000 831-5958
NYSE: WHI

Wachovia Corp 301 S College St Charlotte NC 28202 704-374-6161 473-5879*
NYSE: WB ■ **Fax Area Code:* 877 ■ **Fax:* Hum Res ■ *TF:* 800-922-4684 ■
Web: www.wachovia.com

Washington Banking Co 321 SE Pioneer Way Oak Harbor WA 98277 360-679-3121 675-7282
NASDAQ: WBCO ■ *TF:* 800-290-6508

Washington Federal Inc 425 Pike St Seattle WA 98101 206-624-7930 467-0524
NASDAQ: WFSL ■ *TF:* 800-324-9375 ■ *Web:* www.washingtonfederal.com

Washington Trust Bancorp Inc 23 Broad St. Westerly RI 02891 401-348-1200 348-1470
NASDAQ: WASH ■ *TF:* 800-475-2265 ■ *Web:* www.washtrust.com

Wayne Savings Bancshares Inc 151 N Market St Wooster OH 44691 330-264-5767 264-5908
NASDAQ: WAYN ■ *TF:* 800-414-1103 ■ *Web:* www.waynesavings.com

Webster City Federal Bancorp 820 Des Moines St Webster City IA 50595 515-832-3071 832-3085
TF: 866-263-0293

Webster Financial Corp PO Box 10305 WFD 730 Waterbury CT 06726 800-325-2424 679-8989*
NYSE: WBS ■ **Fax Area Code:* 877 ■ *Web:* www.websteronline.com

Wells Fargo & Co 420 Montgomery St 12th Fl San Francisco CA 94104 800-869-3557 677-9075*
NYSE: WFC ■ **Fax Area Code:* 415 ■ **Fax:* Hum Res ■ *TF:* 800-333-0343 ■
Web: www.wellsfargo.com

Wells Financial Corp 53 1st St SW Wells MN 56097 507-553-3151 553-6295
TF: 800-944-5869 ■ *Web:* www.wellsfinancialcorp.com

WesBanco Inc 1 Bank Plaza Wheeling WV 26003 304-234-9000 234-9298
NASDAQ: WSBC ■ *TF:* 800-328-3369 ■ *Web:* www.wesbanco.com

West Bancorp Inc 1601 22nd St. West Des Moines IA 50266 515-222-2300 222-2346
NASDAQ: WTBA ■ *TF:* 800-810-2301

West Coast Bancorp 5335 Meadows Rd Suite 201 Lake Oswego OR 97035 503-598-3252 684-0781
NASDAQ: WCBO ■ *TF:* 800-895-3345 ■ *Web:* www.wcb.com

Westamerica Bancorp 4550 Mangels Blvd. Fairfield CA 94534 800-848-1088 863-6101*
NASDAQ: WABC ■ **Fax Area Code:* 707 ■ *Web:* www.westamerica.com

Westbank Corp 225 Park Ave 5th Fl. West Springfield MA 01089 413-747-1400 747-1456
NASDAQ: WBKC ■ *Web:* www.westbankcorponline.com

Westcorp Inc 23 Pasteur Irvine CA 92618 949-727-1000 727-2313
TF: 800-289-8004 ■ *Web:* www.westcorpinc.com

Western Alliance Bancorp 2700 W Sahara Ave Las Vegas NV 89102 702-248-4200 362-2026
NYSE: WAL ■ *TF:* 800-764-7619 ■ *Web:* www.westernalliancebancorp.com

Westfield Financial Inc 141 Elm St. Westfield MA 01085 413-568-1911 562-7939
AMEX: WFD ■ *TF:* 800-995-5734 ■ *Web:* www.westfieldbank.com

Westwood Holdings Group Inc 200 Crescent Ct Suite 1200 Dallas TX 75201 214-756-6900 756-6979
NYSE: WHG ■ *Web:* www.westwoodgroup.com

Whitney Holding Corp 228 St Charles Ave. New Orleans LA 70130 504-586-7272 586-3487*
NASDAQ: WTNY ■ **Fax:* Hum Res ■ *TF:* 800-383-6538

Wilber Corp The 245 Main St. Oneonta NY 13820 607-432-1700 433-4161
AMEX: GIW ■ *TF:* 800-374-7980 ■ *Web:* www.wilberbank.com

Willow Grove Bancorp Inc Welsh & Norristown Rds. Maple Glen PA 19002 215-646-1505 643-9413
NASDAQ: WGBC ■ *TF:* 800-647-5405 ■ *Web:* www.willowgrovebank.com/wgbancorp

Wilmington Trust Corp 1100 N Market St 1st Fl Wilmington DE 19890 302-651-1000 651-8937
NYSE: WL ■ *TF:* 800-523-2378 ■ *Web:* www.wilmingtontrust.com

Wintrust Financial Corp 727 N Bank Ln. Lake Forest IL 60045 847-615-4096 615-4091
NASDAQ: WTFC ■ *Web:* www.wintrust.com

Bank Holding Companies (Cont'd)

Phone Fax

WSFS Financial Corp 838 Market St. Wilmington DE 19801 302-792-6000 571-7102
NASDAQ: WSFS ■ *TF:* 888-973-7226 ■ *Web:* www.wsfsbank.com

WTB Financial Corp PO Box 2127 Spokane WA 99210 509-353-2265 353-6969*
**Fax:* Hum Res ■ *TF:* 800-788-4578 ■ *Web:* www.watrust.com

WVS Financial Corp 9001 Perry Hwy Pittsburgh PA 15237 412-364-1911 364-4120
NASDAQ: WVFC

Yardville National Bancorp 2465 Kuser Rd Hamilton NJ 08690 609-585-5100 584-8570
NASDAQ: YANB ■ *TF:* 888-443-5754 ■ *Web:* www.yanb.com

Zions Bancorp 1 S Main St Suite 1380 Salt Lake City UT 84111 801-974-8800 594-8402*
NASDAQ: ZION ■ **Fax:* Mktg ■ *TF:* 800-789-2265 ■ *Web:* www.zionsbank.com

363-3 Holding Companies (General)

Phone Fax

4Kids Entertainment Inc 1414 Ave of the Americas New York NY 10019 212-758-7666 980-0933
NYSE: KDE ■ *Web:* www.4kidsentertainment.com

A-Mark Financial Corp 100 Wilshire Blvd 3rd Fl Santa Monica CA 90401 310-319-0200 319-0279
Web: www.amark.com

Acuity Brands Inc 1170 Peachtree St NE Suite 2400 Atlanta GA 30309 404-853-1400 853-1411
NYSE: AYI ■ *Web:* www.acuitybrands.com

Advance Holding Corp 5673 Airport Rd Roanoke VA 24012 540-362-4911 561-1118
Web: www.advance-auto.com

Affiliated Managers Group Inc (AMG) 600 Hale St Prides Crossing MA 01965 617-747-3300 747-3380
NYSE: AMG ■ *Web:* www.amg.com

AG Edwards Inc 1 N Jefferson Ave Saint Louis MO 63103 314-955-3000 955-5612
NYSE: AGE ■ *TF:* 877-835-7877 ■ *Web:* www.agedwards.com

Ahold USA 13135 Lee Jackson Memorial Hwy Suite 210 Fairfax VA 22033 703-961-6000 961-6077*
**Fax:* Hum Res ■ *Web:* www.aholdusa.com

Alex Lee Inc 120 4th St SW Hickory NC 28602 828-323-4424 323-4435
Web: www.alexlee.com

Alliance Capital Management Holding LP
1345 Ave of the Americas New York NY 10105 212-969-1000 969-2229
NYSE: AC ■ *TF:* 800-221-5672 ■ *Web:* www.alliancecapital.com

Allied Holdings Inc 160 Clairemont Ave Decatur GA 30030 404-373-4285
Web: www.alliedholdings.com

Allied Sirva DBA Allied Worldwide 700 Oakmont Ln Westmont IL 60559 630-570-3000 570-3164

Alpine Group Inc 1 Meadowlands Plaza Suite 801 East Rutherford NJ 07073 201-549-4400 549-4428

American Standard Cos Inc 1 Centennial Ave Piscataway NJ 08854 732-980-6000 980-3335
NYSE: ASD ■ *TF:* 800-223-0068 ■ *Web:* www.americanstandard.com

AMETEK Inc 37 N Valley Rd Bldg 4 PO Box 1764 Paoli PA 19301 610-647-2121 323-9339*
NYSE: AME ■ **Fax Area Code:* 215 ■ *TF:* 800-473-1286 ■ *Web:* www.ametek.com

AMG (Affiliated Managers Group Inc) 600 Hale St Prides Crossing MA 01965 617-747-3300 747-3380
NYSE: AMG ■ *Web:* www.amg.com

AMIS Holdings Inc 2300 Buckskin Rd Pocatello ID 83201 208-233-4690 234-6796
NASDAQ: AMIS ■ *Web:* www.amis.com

Arden Group Inc PO Box 512256 Los Angeles CA 90051 310-638-2842 604-4896*
NASDAQ: ARDNA ■ **Fax:* Hum Res

Armor Holdings Inc 13386 International Pkwy Jacksonville FL 32218 904-741-5400 741-4756
NYSE: AH ■ *TF:* 800-428-0588 ■ *Web:* www.armorholdings.com

Armstrong Holdings Inc 2500 Columbia Ave Lancaster PA 17603 717-397-0611 396-6133*
**Fax:* Hum Res ■ *TF:* 800-446-8066 ■ *Web:* www.armstrong.com/corporatena

Atlas Copco North America Inc 34 Maple Ave Pine Brook NJ 07058 973-439-3400 439-9188
Web: www.atlascopco.com

Atlas World Group Inc 1212 St George Rd Evansville IN 47711 812-424-2222 421-7125
TF: 800-252-8885 ■ *Web:* www.atlasworldgroup.com

Augusta National Inc 2604 Washington Rd Augusta GA 30904 706-667-6000 736-2321

Austin Industries Inc 3535 Travis St Suite 300 Dallas TX 75204 214-443-5500 443-5581*
**Fax:* Acctg ■ *Web:* www.austin-ind.com

AuthentiDate Holding Corp 2165 Technology Dr Schenectady NY 12308 518-346-7799 346-1644
NASDAQ: ADAT ■ *TF:* 800-367-5906 ■ *Web:* www.authentidatehc.com

Banta Corp 225 Main St PO Box 8003 Menasha WI 54952 920-751-7777 751-7790
NYSE: BN ■ *Web:* www.banta.com

Bell Canada Enterprises Inc
1000 de la Gauchetiere St W Suite 3700 Montreal QC H3B4Y7 514-870-8777 870-4385
NYSE: BCE ■ *TF:* 888-932-6666 ■ *Web:* www.bce.ca

Bertelsmann Inc 1540 Broadway 24th Fl New York NY 10036 212-782-1000 782-1010
Web: www.bertelsmann.com

Bessemer Group Inc 100 Woodbridge Center Dr Woodbridge NJ 07095 732-855-0800 855-0196
Web: www.bessemer.com

BET Holdings II Inc 1235 W St NE Washington DC 20018 202-608-2000 608-2589*
**Fax:* PR ■ *TF:* 800-626-9911

Bing Group 11500 Oakland Ave Detroit MI 48211 313-867-3700 867-3897
Web: www.binggroup.com

Blount International Inc 4909 SE International Way Portland OR 97222 503-653-8881 653-4402*
NYSE: BLT ■ **Fax:* Hum Res ■ *Web:* www.blount.com

Blue Tee Corp 250 Park Ave S 2nd Fl New York NY 10003 212-598-0880 598-0896
Web: www.bluetee.com

Boca Resorts Inc 501 E Camino Real Boca Raton FL 33431 561-447-3000 447-3183
Web: www.bocaresortsinc.com

Boler Co 500 Park Blvd Suite 1000 Itasca IL 60143 630-773-9111 773-9121

Boral Industries Inc 200 Mansell Ct E Suite 310 Roswell GA 30076 770-645-4500 645-2888

Building Materials Holding Corp
4 Embarcadero Ctr Suite 3250 San Francisco CA 94111 415-627-9100 627-9119
NASDAQ: BMHC ■ *Web:* www.bmhc.com

Burlington Northern Santa Fe Corp 2650 Lou Menk Dr Fort Worth TX 76131 800-795-2673 352-7925*
NYSE: BNI ■ **Fax Area Code:* 817 ■ *Web:* www.bnsf.com

Cadmus Communications Corp 1801 Bayberry Ct Suite 200 Richmond VA 23226 804-287-5680 287-6267
NASDAQ: CDMS ■ *TF:* 877-422-3687 ■ *Web:* www.cadmus.com

California Sports Inc 555 N Nash St El Segundo CA 90245 310-426-6000 426-6115

Cardinal Health Inc 7000 Cardinal Pl Dublin OH 43017 614-757-5000 757-6000
NYSE: CAH ■ *TF:* 800-234-8701 ■ *Web:* www.cardinal.com

Carnival Corp 3655 NW 87th Ave Miami FL 33178 305-599-2600 406-4700
NYSE: CCL ■ *TF:* 800-438-6744 ■ *Web:* www.carnivalcorp.com

Cavs/Gund Arena Co 1 Center Ct Cleveland OH 44115 216-420-2000 420-2101
TF: 800-332-2287

CBRL Group Inc 305 Hartmann Dr Lebanon TN 37087 615-444-5533 443-9818
NASDAQ: CBRL ■ *TF:* 800-333-9566 ■ *Web:* www.cbrl.com

Celadon Group Inc 9503 E 33rd St Indianapolis IN 46235 317-972-7000 890-8099
NASDAQ: CLDN ■ *TF:* 800-235-2366 ■ *Web:* www.celadontrucking.com

CenturyTel Inc PO Box 4065 Monroe LA 71211 318-388-9000 388-9562
NYSE: CTL ■ *Web:* www.centurytel.com

CF Industries Holdings Inc 1 Salem Lake Dr Long Grove IL 60047 847-438-9500 438-0211
NYSE: CF ■ *Web:* www.cfindustries.com

Charles Schwab Corp 101 Montgomery St San Francisco CA 94104 415-636-7000 636-9820
NASDAQ: SCHW ■ *TF:* 800-435-4000 ■ *Web:* www.schwab.com

Charlotte Russe Holding Inc 4645 Morena Blvd San Diego CA 92117 858-587-1500 875-0336
NASDAQ: CHIC

Circuit City Stores Inc 9950 Mayland Dr Richmond VA 23233 804-527-4000 342-6482*
NYSE: CC ■ **Fax:* Cust Svc ■ *TF:* 800-251-2665 ■ *Web:* www.circuitcity.com

Citigroup Inc 399 Park Ave New York NY 10043 212-559-1000 559-5138*
NYSE: C ■ **Fax:* Hum Res ■ *Web:* www.citigroup.com

Clark Enterprises Inc 7500 Old Georgetown Rd Bethesda MD 20814 301-657-7100 657-7263
TF: 800-800-2242

Phone Fax

Clayton Holdings Inc 2 Corporate Dr Shelton CT 06484 203-926-5600 926-5750
NASDAQ: CLAY ■ *TF:* 888-449-4055 ■ *Web:* www.clayton.com

Clinical Data Inc 1 Gateway Ctr Suite 702 Newton MA 02458 617-527-9933 527-8230
NASDAQ: CLDA ■ *Web:* www.clda.com

Comcast Corp 1500 Market St Philadelphia PA 19102 215-665-1700 981-7790
NASDAQ: CMCSK ■ *Web:* www.comcast.com

ConAgra Foods Inc 1 ConAgra Dr Omaha NE 68102 402-595-4000 595-4707*
NYSE: CAG ■ **Fax:* Hum Res ■ *Web:* www.conagrafoods.com

Conning Corp 1 Financial Plaza Hartford CT 06103 860-527-1131 520-1240
TF: 888-266-6464 ■ *Web:* www.conning.com

CONSOL Energy Inc 1800 Washington Rd Pittsburgh PA 15241 412-831-4000 831-4004*
NYSE: CNX ■ **Fax:* Hum Res ■ *Web:* www.consolenergy.com

Consolidated Communications Holdings Inc 121 S 17th St Mattoon IL 61938 217-235-3311 258-7883
NASDAQ: CNSL ■ *Web:* www.consolidated.com

Consulier Engineering Inc 2391 Old Dixie Hwy Riviera Beach FL 33404 561-842-2492 845-3237
NASDAQ: CSLR ■ *Web:* www.consulier.com

Cookson America Inc 1 Cookson Pl Providence RI 02903 401-521-1000 521-5273
Web: www.cooksongroup.co.uk

Core-Mark Holding Co Inc
395 Oyster Point Blvd Suite 415 South San Francisco CA 94080 650-589-9445 952-4284
NASDAQ: CORE ■ *TF:* 800-622-1713 ■ *Web:* www.coremark.com

Covanta Holding Corp 40 Lane Rd Fairfield NJ 07004 973-882-9000 882-7076
NYSE: CVA ■ *Web:* www.covantaholding.com

Crown FZ Holding Corp PO Box 1168 Baltimore MD 21203 410-539-7400 659-4763

Dash Multi-Corp Inc 2500 Adie Rd Maryland Heights MO 63043 314-432-3200 432-3210
Web: www.dashmulticorp.com

DeBartolo Edward J Corp 7620 Marcus St Youngstown OH 44512 330-965-2000 965-2077
TF: 888-965-3532

Dectron International Inc 4300 Poirier Blvd Montreal QC H4R2C5 514-334-9609 334-9184
NASDAQ: DECT ■ *TF:* 888-332-8766 ■ *Web:* www.dectron.com

Delhaize America Inc 2110 Executive Dr PO Box 1330 Salisbury NC 28145 704-633-8250 637-2581*
NYSE: DEG ■ **Fax:* Hum Res ■ *Web:* 64.29.208.90

Deluxe Corp 3680 N Victoria St Shoreview MN 55126 651-483-7111
NYSE: DLX ■ *TF:* 800-328-7205 ■ *Web:* www.deluxe.com

Diamond Holding Corp 150 Marr Ave Marietta GA 30060 770-590-0152 590-0235
TF: 800-556-6211 ■ *Web:* www.diamondroller.com

DNP America LLC 335 Madison Ave 3rd Fl New York NY 10017 212-503-1060
Web: www.dnp.co.jp

Duchossois Industries Inc 845 Larch Ave Elmhurst IL 60126 630-279-3600 530-6091
TF: 800-282-6225

Dundee Bancorp Inc 1 Adelaide St E 28th Fl Toronto ON M5C2V9 416-863-6990 363-4536
TSX: DBCA ■ *Web:* www.dundeebancorp.com

DuPont EI de Nemours & Co Inc 1007 Market St Wilmington DE 19898 302-774-1000 999-4399
NYSE: DD ■ *TF:* 800-441-7515 ■ *Web:* www.dupont.com

Dwyer Group Inc 1010 N University Parks Dr Waco TX 76707 254-745-2400 745-2590
TF: 800-490-7501 ■ *Web:* www.dwyergroup.com

Edward J DeBartolo Corp 7620 Marcus St Youngstown OH 44512 330-965-2000 965-2077
TF: 888-965-3532

Edwards AG Inc 1 N Jefferson Ave Saint Louis MO 63103 314-955-3000 955-5612
NYSE: AGE ■ *TF:* 877-835-7877 ■ *Web:* www.agedwards.com

El DuPont de Nemours & Co Inc 1007 Market St Wilmington DE 19898 302-774-1000 999-4399
NYSE: DD ■ *TF:* 800-441-7515 ■ *Web:* www.dupont.com

Elecsys Corp 15301 W 109th St Lenexa KS 66219 913-647-0158 647-0132
AMEX: ASY ■ *Web:* www.elecsyscorp.com

Elvis Presley Enterprises Inc 3734 Elvis Presley Blvd Memphis TN 38186 901-332-3322 344-3116
TF: 800-238-2000 ■ *Web:* www.elvis.com

Emergency Medical Services LP
6200 S Syracuse Way Suite 200 Greenwood Village CO 80111 303-495-1200 495-1466
NYSE: EMS ■ *Web:* www.emsc.net

Eni Corp 485 Madison Ave New York NY 10022 646-264-2250
Web: www.eni.it/home/home_en.html

Enterprise GP Holdings LP 2727 N Loop W Suite 101 Houston TX 77008 713-426-4500
NYSE: EPE ■ *Web:* www.enterprisegp.com

Equitex Inc 7315 E Peakview Ave Englewood CO 80111 303-796-8940 796-9762
NASDAQ: EQTX ■ *Web:* www.equitex.net

ESCO Technologies Inc 9900 Clayton Rd Saint Louis MO 63124 314-213-7200 213-7250
NYSE: ESE ■ *TF:* 888-622-3726 ■ *Web:* www.escostl.com

EVCI Career Colleges Holding Corp 1 Van Der Donck St 2nd Fl Yonkers NY 10701 914-623-0700 964-8222
NASDAQ: EVCI ■ *Web:* www.evcinc.com

EXX Inc 1350 E Flamingo Rd Suite 689 Las Vegas NV 89119 702-598-3223
AMEX: EXX

FedEx Corp 942 S Shady Grove Road Memphis TN 38120 901-369-3600 434-9836
NYSE: FDX ■ *TF:* 800-463-3339 ■ *Web:* www.fedex.com

First Albany Cos Inc 677 Broadway Albany NY 12207 518-447-8500 447-8115*
NASDAQ: FACT ■ **Fax:* Hum Res ■ *TF:* 800-833-4168 ■ *Web:* www.firstalbany.com

Fluor Corp 1 Enterprise Dr Aliso Viejo CA 92656 949-349-2000 349-2585
NYSE: FLR ■ *Web:* www.fluor.com

Fortune Diversified Industries Inc 6402 Corporate Dr Indianapolis IN 46278 317-532-1374 532-1376
AMEX: FFI ■ *Web:* www.fdvi.net

Fresh Del Monte Produce Co 241 Sevilla Ave Coral Gables FL 33134 305-520-8400 567-0320
NYSE: FDP ■ *TF Cust Svc:* 800-950-3683 ■ *Web:* www.freshdelmonte.com

FTD Group Inc 3113 Woodcreek Dr Downers Grove IL 60515 630-719-7800 719-6183
NYSE: FTD ■ *TF:* 800-788-9000 ■ *Web:* www.ftd.com

G-I Holdings Inc 1361 Alps Rd Wayne NJ 07470 973-628-4032 628-3229
TF: 800-766-3411

Galardi Group Inc 4440 Von Karman Ave Suite 222 Newport Beach CA 92660 949-752-5800 851-2615

Genmar Holdings Inc 80 S 8th St Suite 2900 Minneapolis MN 55402 612-337-1956
TF: 800-328-5557 ■ *Web:* www.genmar.com

George Weston Ltd 22 St Clair Ave E Suite 1901 Toronto ON M4T2S7 416-922-2500 922-4395
TSX: WN ■ *Web:* www.weston.ca

Global Entertainment Corp 4909 E McDowell Rd Suite 104 Phoenix AZ 85008 480-994-0772 994-0759
AMEX: GEE ■ *Web:* www.globalentertainment2000.com

Golden Enterprises Inc 1 Golden Flake Dr Birmingham AL 35205 205-458-7316 458-7335
NASDAQ: GLDC ■ *TF:* 800-239-2447

Goodman Global Inc 2550 N Loop W Suite 400 Houston TX 77092 713-861-2500 861-3207
NYSE: GGL ■ *TF:* 888-593-9988 ■ *Web:* www.goodmanglobal.com

Goss Holdings Inc 3 Territorial Ct Bolingbrook IL 60440 630-755-9300 755-9301

GP Strategies Corp 777 Westchester Ave 4th Fl White Plains NY 10604 914-249-9700 249-9745*
NYSE: GPX ■ *Web:* www.gpstrategies.com

GSC Enterprises Inc PO Box 638 Sulphur Springs TX 75483 903-885-0829 885-6928
Web: www.grocerysupply.com

H Group Holding Co 200 W Madison St 39th Fl Chicago IL 60606 312-750-1234 750-8008

Hartmarx Corp 101 N Wacker Dr Chicago IL 60606 312-372-6300 444-2679*
NYSE: HMX ■ **Fax:* Hum Res ■ *Web:* www.hartmarx.com

Hartz Group 667 Madison Ave 24th Fl New York NY 10065 212-308-3336 644-5987
Web: www.hartz.com

Hickory Tech Corp 221 E Hickory St Mankato MN 56002 507-387-1151 625-9191
NASDAQ: HTCO ■ *TF:* 800-326-5789 ■ *Web:* www.hickorytech.com

Hitch Enterprises Inc 309 Northridge Cir PO Box 1308 Guymon OK 73942 580-338-8575 338-0132
TF: 800-634-8678 ■ *Web:* www.hitchok.com

Holberg Industries Inc 545 Steamboat Rd Greenwich CT 06830 203-661-2500 661-5756
Web: www.holberg.com

Home Capital Group Inc 145 King St W Suite 2300 Toronto ON M5H1J8 416-360-4663 363-7611
TSX: HCG ■ *TF:* 800-990-7881 ■ *Web:* www.homecapital.com

Huffy Corp 225 Byers Rd Miamisburg OH 45342 937-866-6251 865-5470
TF: 800-872-2453 ■ *Web:* www.huffy.com

Company	City	State	Zip	Phone	Fax
Hunt Consolidated Inc 1900 N Akard St Suite 1500	Dallas	TX	75201	214-978-8000	978-8888
TF: 800-435-7794 ■ *Web:* www.huntoil.com					
iGATE Corp 1000 Commerce Dr Parkridge 1	Pittsburgh	PA	15275	412-506-1131	494-9272
NASDAQ: IGTE ■ *TF:* 800-627-8323 ■ *Web:* www.igatecorp.com					
Impreso Inc 652 Southwestern Blvd	Coppell	TX	75019	972-462-0100	562-5357*
NASDAQ: ZCOM ■ **Fax Area Code:* 800 ■ *TF:* 800-521-8781					
Inergy Holdings LLC 2 Brush Creek Blvd Suite 200	Kansas City	MO	64112	816-842-8181	842-1904
NASDAQ: NRGP ■ *Web:* www.inergypropane.com					
International Specialty Holdings Inc 1361 Alps Rd	Wayne	NJ	07470	973-628-4000	628-3594
Web: www.ispcorp.com					
International Textile Group 804 Green Valley Rd Suite 300	Greensboro	NC	27408	336-379-6220	379-3310*
**Fax:* Hum Res					
Investors Capital Holdings Ltd 230 Broadway Suite 205	Lynnfield	MA	01940	781-593-8565	593-9464
AMEX: ICH ■ *TF:* 800-949-1422 ■ *Web:* www.investorscapital.com					
Investors Management Corp 5151 Glenwood Ave	Raleigh	NC	27612	919-781-9310	881-4686
TF: 800-284-5673					
INX Inc 6401 Southwest Fwy	Houston	TX	77074	713-795-2000	795-2001
AMEX: ISR ■ *Web:* www.i-sector.com					
ITOCHU International Inc 335 Madison Ave	New York	NY	10017	212-818-8000	818-8543*
**Fax:* Hum Res ■ *Web:* www.itochu.com					
James Richardson & Sons Ltd 1 Lombard Pl 30th Fl	Winnipeg	MB	R3B0Y1	204-953-7970	942-6339
Japan Railways Group 1 Rockefeller Plaza Suite 1410	New York	NY	10020	212-332-8686	332-8690
Web: www.japanrail.com					
Joy Global Inc 100 E Wisconsin Ave Suite 2780	Milwaukee	WI	53202	414-319-8500	319-8520
NASDAQ: JOYG ■ *Web:* www.joyglobal.com					
Kansas City Southern 427 W 12th St	Kansas City	MO	64105	816-983-1303	983-1297
NYSE: KSU ■ *TF:* 800-243-8624 ■ *Web:* www.kcsi.com					
Kawasaki Heavy Industries USA Inc 60 E 42nd St Suite 2501	New York	NY	10165	212-759-4950	759-6421
Web: www.khi.co.jp					
KCS International Inc 205 Charles St	Oconto	WI	54153	920-834-2211	834-2105*
**Fax:* Hum Res					
Kiewit Peter Sons' Inc 1000 Kiewit Plaza	Omaha	NE	68131	402-342-2052	271-2939*
**Fax:* Hum Res ■ *Web:* www.kiewit.com					
Kyocera International Inc 8611 Balboa Ave	San Diego	CA	92123	858-576-2600	569-9412
Web: global.kyocera.com					
Laidlaw International Inc 55 Shuman Blvd Suite 400	Naperville	IL	60563	630-848-3000	848-3151
NYSE: LI ■ *TF:* 800-524-3529 ■ *Web:* www.laidlaw.com					
Landmark Communications Inc 150 W Brambleton Ave	Norfolk	VA	23510	757-446-2010	446-2534
TF: 800-446-2004 ■ *Web:* www.landmarkcom.com					
Lanoga Corp 17946 NE 65th St	Redmond	WA	98052	425-883-4125	882-2959
Web: www.lanoga.com					
Lehman Brothers Holdings Inc 745 7th Ave	New York	NY	10019	212-526-7000	526-3738
NYSE: LEH ■ *TF:* 800-666-2388 ■ *Web:* www.lehman.com					
Levitt Corp 2200 W Cypress Creek Rd	Fort Lauderdale	FL	33309	954-958-1800	958-1968
NYSE: LEV ■ *Web:* www.levittcorporation.com					
Liberty Corp 135 Main St PO Box 502	Greenville	SC	29602	864-241-5400	241-5401*
**Fax:* Hum Res ■ *Web:* www.libertycorp.com					
Liberty Diversified Industries Inc 5600 Hwy 169 N	New Hope	MN	55428	763-536-6600	536-6685
TF: 800-421-1270 ■ *Web:* www.libertydiversified.com					
Liberty Media Holding Corp 12300 Liberty Blvd	Englewood	CO	80112	720-875-5400	875-7469
Web: www.libertymedia.com					
Lincoln Electric Holdings Inc 22801 Saint Clair Ave	Cleveland	OH	44117	216-481-8100	383-8385
NASDAQ: LECO ■ *TF:* 800-833-9353					
Lone Star Technologies Inc 15660 N Dallas Pkwy Suite 500	Dallas	TX	75248	972-386-3981	770-6471
NYSE: LSS ■ *TF:* 800-527-4615 ■ *Web:* www.lonestartech.com					
LVMH Moet Hennessy Louis Vuitton Inc 19 E 57th St	New York	NY	10022	212-931-2700	931-2737
Web: www.lvmh.com					
Magellan Midstream Holdings LP 1 Williams Center	Tulsa	OK	74172	918-574-7000	573-6714
NYSE: MGG ■ *TF:* 800-574-6671 ■ *Web:* www.mgglp.com					
Major Automotive Cos Inc 43-40 Northern Blvd	Long Island City	NY	11101	718-937-3700	
Marsh & McLennan Cos Inc 1166 Ave of the Americas	New York	NY	10036	212-345-5000	345-4808
NYSE: MMC ■ *Web:* www.marshmac.com					
Maxco Inc 1118 Centennial Way	Lansing	MI	48917	517-321-3130	321-1022
NASDAQ: MAXC ■ *Web:* www.maxc.com					
Maxcor Financial Group Inc 1 Seaport Plaza 19th Fl	New York	NY	10038	212-748-7000	778-8536
Web: www.maxf.com					
MCF Corp 600 California St 9th Fl	San Francisco	CA	94108	415-248-5600	274-5651
AMEX: MEM ■ *TF Sales:* 888-595-0999 ■ *Web:* www.merrimanco.com					
McKesson Corp 1 Post St	San Francisco	CA	94104	415-983-8300	983-8453
NYSE: MCK ■ *TF:* 800-482-3784 ■ *Web:* www.mckesson.com					
MDC Holdings Inc 4350 S Monaco St	Denver	CO	80237	303-773-1100	741-4134
NYSE: MDC					
Mitchel Group 1841 Ludlow Ave	Indianapolis	IN	46201	317-684-2600	532-9177
Web: www.tennscrewmach.com					
Mondial International Corp 101 Secor Ln PO Box 889	Pelham Manor	NY	10803	914-738-7411	738-7521
Web: www.mondialgroup.com					
Morgan Keegan Inc 50 N Front St 17th Fl	Memphis	TN	38103	901-524-4100	579-4406
TF: 800-366-7426					
Morton Industrial Group Inc 1021 W Birchwood St	Morton	IL	61550	309-266-7176	263-1866
Web: www.mortongroup.com					
Mpower Holding Corp 175 Sully's Trail Suite 300	Pittsford	NY	14534	585-218-6550	218-0881
AMEX: MPE ■ *Web:* www.mpowercom.com					
Natixis Capital Markets 9 W 57th St 35th Fl	New York	NY	10019	212-891-6100	891-6288
Web: www.ixiscm.com					
Navistar International Corp 4201 Winfield Rd	Warrenville	IL	60555	630-753-5000	753-3982
NYSE: NAV ■ *Web:* www.navistar.com					
NBC Universal Inc 30 Rockefeller Plaza	New York	NY	10112	212-664-4444	664-4085
Web: www.nbcuni.com					
NewMarket Corp 330 S 4th St	Richmond	VA	23219	804-788-5000	788-5688
NYSE: NEU ■ *TF:* 800-625-5191 ■ *Web:* www.newmarket.com					
NightHawk Radiology Holdings Inc					
250 Northwest Blvd Suite 202	Coeur d'Alene	ID	83814	208-676-8321	664-2720
NASDAQ: NHWK ■ *Web:* www.nighthawkrad.net					
North Pittsburgh Systems Inc 4008 Gibsonia Rd	Gibsonia	PA	15044	724-443-9600	443-9431
NASDAQ: NPSI ■ *TF:* 800-541-9225 ■ *Web:* www.northpittsburgh.com					
Oaks Group 11451 Katy Fwy Suite 505	Houston	TX	77079	713-722-8080	722-0880
Web: www.oaksgroup.com					
Omnicom Group Inc 437 Madison Ave	New York	NY	10022	212-415-3600	415-3530*
NYSE: OMC ■ **Fax:* Hum Res ■ *TF:* 800-332-3336 ■ *Web:* www.omnicomgroup.com					
OneTravel Holdings Inc 6836 Morrison Blvd Suite 200	Charlotte	NC	28211	704-366-5054	366-5056
AMEX: OTV ■ *Web:* www.onetravelholdings.com					
Orca Bay Sports & Entertainment 800 Griffiths Way	Vancouver	BC	V6B6G1	604-899-7400	899-7401
Web: www.canucks.com					
Otter Tail Corp 4334 18th Ave SW Suite 200	Fargo	ND	58106	701-232-6414	232-4108
NASDAQ: OTTR ■ *TF:* 866-410-8780 ■ *Web:* www.ottertail.com					
Pacer International Inc 2300 Clayton Rd Suite 1200	Concord	CA	94520	925-887-1400	887-1503
NASDAQ: PACR ■ *TF:* 877-917-2237 ■ *Web:* www.pacer-international.com					
Pamida Holdings Corp 8800 F St	Omaha	NE	68127	402-339-2400	596-7330
Pearson Inc 1330 Ave of the Americas 7th Fl	New York	NY	10019	212-641-2400	641-2500
Web: www.pearson.com					
Peter Kiewit Sons' Inc 1000 Kiewit Plaza	Omaha	NE	68131	402-342-2052	271-2939*
**Fax:* Hum Res ■ *Web:* www.kiewit.com					
Petters Group Worldwide LLC 4400 Baker Rd	Minnetonka	MN	55343	952-934-9918	936-5048
TF: 800-605-5364 ■ *Web:* www.pettersgroup.com					
Phazar Corp 101 SE 25th Ave	Mineral Wells	TX	76067	940-325-3301	325-0716
NASDAQ: ANTP ■ *Web:* www.phazar.com					
PHC Inc DBA Pioneer Behavioral Health					
200 Lake St Suite 102	Peabody	MA	01960	978-536-2777	536-2677
Web: www.phc-inc.com					
Price T Rowe Group Inc 100 E Pratt St	Baltimore	MD	21202	410-345-2000	345-2394*
NASDAQ: TROW ■ **Fax:* Hum Res ■ *TF:* 800-638-7890 ■ *Web:* www.troweprice.com					
Pro-Dex Inc 151 E Columbine Ave	Santa Ana	CA	92707	714-241-4411	513-7617
NASDAQ: PDEX ■ *TF:* 800-562-6204 ■ *Web:* www.pdex.com					
Pulte Homes Inc 100 Bloomfield Hills Pkwy Suite 300	Bloomfield Hills	MI	48304	248-647-2750	433-4598
NYSE: PHM ■ *TF:* 800-777-8583 ■ *Web:* www.pulte.com					
RAB Holdings Inc 444 Madison Ave Suite 601	New York	NY	10022	212-688-4500	888-5025
Ralcorp Holdings Inc 800 Market St PO Box 618	Saint Louis	MO	63188	314-877-7000	
NYSE: RAH ■ *Web:* www.ralcorp.com					
Red Apple Group Inc 823 11th Ave	New York	NY	10019	212-956-5803	247-4509
Resource America Inc 1845 Walnut St 10th Fl	Philadelphia	PA	19103	215-546-5005	546-5388
NASDAQ: REXI ■ *Web:* www.resourceamerica.com					
Restaurant Co 6075 Poplar Ave Suite 800	Memphis	TN	38119	901-766-6400	766-6482
Retail Ventures Inc 3241 Westerville Rd	Columbus	OH	43224	614-471-4722	478-2252
NYSE: RVI ■ *Web:* www.valuecity.com					
Reunion Industries Inc 11 Stanwix St Suite 1400	Pittsburgh	PA	15222	412-281-2111	281-4747
AMEX: RUN ■ *Web:* www.reunionindustries.com					
Revlon Inc 237 Park Ave	New York	NY	10017	212-527-4000	527-4995
NYSE: REV ■ *TF:* 800-473-8566 ■ *Web:* www.revlon.com					
Reyes Holdings LLC 9500 W Bryn Mawr Ave Suite 700	Rosemont	IL	60018	847-227-6500	671-4725
Web: www.reyesholdings.com					
Richardson James & Sons Ltd 1 Lombard Pl 30th Fl	Winnipeg	MB	R3B0Y1	204-953-7970	942-6339
Rockwood Holdings Inc 100 Overlook Ctr	Princeton	NJ	08540	609-514-0300	514-8720
NYSE: ROC ■ *Web:* www.rockwoodspecialties.com					
Rosen's Diversified Inc 1120 Lake Ave	Fairmont	MN	56031	507-238-4201	238-9966
Web: www.rosens.com					
RTI International Metals Inc 1000 Warren Ave	Niles	OH	44446	330-652-9951	544-7796*
NYSE: RTI ■ **Fax:* Sales ■ *Web:* www.rti-intl.com					
S & P Co 100 Shoreline Hwy Bldg B Suite 395	Mill Valley	CA	94941	415-332-0550	332-0567
Sabre Holdings Corp 3150 Sabre Dr	Southlake	TX	76092	682-605-1000	
NYSE: TSG ■ *Web:* www.sabre-holdings.com					
Sanders Morris Harris Group Inc 600 Travis St Suite 3100	Houston	TX	77002	713-224-3100	993-4677
NASDAQ: SMHG ■ *TF:* 800-538-0020 ■ *Web:* www.smhgroup.com					
Sandvik Inc 1702 Nevins Rd	Fair Lawn	NJ	07410	201-794-5000	794-5165
TF: 800-726-3845 ■ *Web:* www.sandvik.com					
Sara Lee Corp 70 W Madison St	Chicago	IL	60602	312-726-2600	558-4995*
NYSE: SLE ■ **Fax:* Hum Res ■ *TF:* 800-621-5235 ■ *Web:* www.saralee.com					
S&C Holdco 3 Inc 1770 Promontory Cir	Greeley	CO	80634	970-506-8000	506-8307
Web: www.swiftbrands.com					
Schering Berlin Inc 6 W Belt Rd	Wayne	NJ	07470	973-694-4100	487-2005
SCHOTT North America Inc 555 Taxter Rd	Elmsford	NY	10523	914-831-2200	831-2201
Web: www.us.schott.com					
Schuff International Inc 420 S 19th Ave	Phoenix	AZ	85009	602-252-7787	452-4468
TF: 800-528-0513 ■ *Web:* www.schuff.com					
Schwab Charles Corp 101 Montgomery St	San Francisco	CA	94104	415-636-7000	636-9820
NASDAQ: SCHW ■ *TF:* 800-435-4000 ■ *Web:* www.schwab.com					
Sears Holdings Corp 3333 Beverly Rd	Hoffman Estates	IL	60179	847-286-2500	286-7829
NASDAQ: SHLD ■ *Web:* www.searsholdings.com					
SGS North America Inc 201 State Rt 17 N	Rutherford	NJ	07070	201-508-3000	508-3193
TF: 800-747-9047 ■ *Web:* www.us.sgs.com					
Shenandoah Telecommunications Co PO Box 459	Edinburg	VA	22824	540-984-4141	984-4816
NASDAQ: SHEN ■ *TF:* 800-743-6835 ■ *Web:* www.shentel.com					
Siebert Financial Corp 885 3rd Ave Suite 1720	New York	NY	10022	212-644-2400	644-2741
NASDAQ: SIEB ■ *TF:* 800-872-0444 ■ *Web:* www.siebertnet.com					
Simpson Investment Co 917 E 11th St	Tacoma	WA	98421	253-779-6400	280-9000
Smiths Group Americas 101 Lindenwood Dr Suite 125	Malvern	PA	19355	610-578-9601	578-1445
Web: www.smiths-group.com					
Speedus Corp 9 Desbrosses St Suite 402	New York	NY	10013	888-773-3669	937-5230*
NASDAQ: SPDE ■ **Fax Area Code:* 212 ■ *Web:* www.speedus.com					
StanCorp Financial Group Inc 1100 SW 6th Ave	Portland	OR	97204	503-321-7000	321-5243
NYSE: SFG ■ *TF:* 800-642-9888 ■ *Web:* www.stancorpfinancial.com					
Sumitomo Canada Ltd 150 King St W Suite 2800	Toronto	ON	M5H1J9	416-860-3800	365-3141
Sumitomo Corp of America 600 3rd Ave 42nd Fl	New York	NY	10016	212-207-0700	207-0456
Web: www.sumitomocorp.com					
Suntory International Corp 7 Times Sq 21st Fl	New York	NY	10036	212-891-6600	891-6601
Web: www.suntory.com					
Superior Group Inc					
100 Front St Suite 525 1 Tower Bridge Bldg	West Conshohocken	PA	19428	610-397-2040	397-2720
Web: www.superior-group.com					
T Rowe Price Group Inc 100 E Pratt St	Baltimore	MD	21202	410-345-2000	345-2394*
NASDAQ: TROW ■ **Fax:* Hum Res ■ *TF:* 800-638-7890 ■ *Web:* www.troweprice.com					
Taylor Corp 1725 Roe Crest Dr	North Mankato	MN	56003	507-625-2828	
TF: 800-545-6620					
TD Ameritrade Holding Corp PO Box 3288	Omaha	NE	68103	402-331-2744	597-7759*
NASDAQ: AMTD ■ **Fax:* Hum Res ■ *TF:* 800-237-8692 ■					
Web: www.ameritradeholding.com					
Teijin Holdings USA 101 E 52nd St 27th Fl	New York	NY	10022	212-308-8744	308-8902
Web: www.teijin.co.jp/english					
Telephone & Data Systems Inc 30 N La Salle St Suite 4000	Chicago	IL	60602	312-630-1900	630-9299
AMEX: TDS ■ *Web:* www.teldta.com					
Terremark Worldwide Inc 2601 S Bayshore Dr Suite 900	Coconut Grove	FL	33133	305-856-3200	856-8190
AMEX: TWW ■ *Web:* www.terremark.com					
Thomson Corp 1 Station Pl Metro Ctr	Stamford	CT	06902	203-539-8000	539-7734
TF: 800-354-9706 ■ *Web:* www.thomson.com					
Thomson Corp PO Box 24 Toronto-Dominion Ctr Suite 2706	Toronto	ON	M5K1A1	416-360-8700	360-8812
NYSE: TOC ■ *Web:* www.thomson.com					
TIC Holdings Inc 2211 Elk River Rd	Steamboat Springs	CO	80487	970-879-2561	879-2380
Toyota Motor North America Inc 9 W 57th St Suite 4900	New York	NY	10019	212-223-0303	759-7670
TF: 800-331-4331 ■ *Web:* www.toyota.com					
TransDigm Group Inc 1301 E 9th St Suite 3710	Cleveland	OH	44114	216-706-2939	706-2937
NYSE: TDG ■ *Web:* www.transdigm.com					
Transtar Inc 1200 Penn Ave Suite 300	Pittsburgh	PA	15222	412-829-3390	829-6694*
**Fax:* Hum Res ■ *Web:* www.tstarinc.com					
Tredegar Corp 1100 Boulders Pkwy Suite 200	Richmond	VA	23225	804-330-1000	330-1177
NYSE: TG ■ *TF:* 800-411-7441 ■ *Web:* www.tredegar.com					
Trian Partners 280 Park Ave 41st Fl	New York	NY	10017	212-451-3000	451-3023*
**Fax:* Mail Rm ■ *TF:* 800-787-4272 ■ *Web:* www.triarc.com					
Trump Organization 725 5th Ave 26th Fl	New York	NY	10022	212-832-2000	935-0141
Turner Corp 901 Main St Suite 4900	Dallas	TX	75202	214-915-9600	915-9700
Web: www.turnerconstruction.com					
Unilever Canada Ltd 160 Bloor St E Suite 1500	Toronto	ON	M4W3R2	416-964-1857	964-8831
Web: www.unilever.ca					
Union Pacific Corp 1400 Douglas St	Omaha	NE	68179	402-544-5000	
NYSE: UNP ■ *TF:* 888-870-8777 ■ *Web:* www.up.com					
UST Inc 6 High Ridge Park Bldg A	Stamford	CT	06905	203-817-3000	
NYSE: UST ■ *TF:* 800-243-8536 ■ *Web:* www.ustinc.com					
Vector Group Ltd 100 SE 2nd St 32nd Fl	Miami	FL	33131	305-579-8000	579-8001
NYSE: VGR ■ *Web:* www.vectorgroupltd.com					
Versa Cos 867 Forest St	Saint Paul	MN	55106	651-778-3300	778-1321
Web: www.versaco.com					
Vivendi 800 3rd Ave	New York	NY	10022	212-572-7000	
Web: www.vivendiuniversal.com					
Vulcan International Corp 300 Delaware Ave Suite 1704	Wilmington	DE	19801	302-427-5804	
TF: 800-447-1146					

Holding Companies (General) (Cont'd)

	City	State	Zip	Phone	Fax
Warnaco Group Inc 501 7th Ave *NASDAQ: WRNC*	New York	NY	10018	212-287-8250	
Warren Equities Inc 27 Warren Way *Web:* www.warreneq.com	Providence	RI	02905	401-781-9000	461-7160
Waste Industries USA Inc 3301 Benson Dr Suite 601 *NASDAQ: WWIN* ■ *TF:* 800-647-9946 ■ *Web:* www.waste-ind.com	Raleigh	NC	27609	919-325-3000	325-4040
WebMD Health Holdings Inc 111 8th Ave 7th Fl *NASDAQ: WBMD* ■ *Web:* www.webmd.com	New York	NY	10011	212-624-3700	624-3800
Welch Allyn Inc 4341 State Street Rd **Fax:* Cust Svc ■ *TF Cust Svc:* 800-535-6663 ■ *Web:* www.welchallyn.com	Skaneateles Falls	NY	13153	315-685-4100	685-3361*
WESCO International Inc 225 W Station Sq Dr Suite 700 *NYSE: WCC* ■ *Web:* www.wescodist.com	Pittsburgh	PA	15219	412-454-2200	454-2505
Weston George Ltd 22 St Clair Ave E Suite 1901 *TSX: WN* ■ *Web:* www.weston.ca	Toronto	ON	M4T2S7	416-922-2500	922-4395
Williams Cos Inc 1 Williams Center *NYSE: WMB* ■ *TF:* 800-945-5426 ■ *Web:* www.williams.com	Tulsa	OK	74102	918-573-2000	573-6714
Williams Scotsman International Inc 8211 Town Center Dr *NASDAQ: WLSC* ■ *TF:* 800-782-1500 ■ *Web:* www.willscot.com	Baltimore	MD	21236	410-931-6000	931-6047
Worldwide Restaurant Concepts Inc 15301 Ventura Blvd Bldg B Suite 300 *Web:* www.wrconcepts.com	Sherman Oaks	CA	91403	818-662-9800	530-0189
Wyeth Corp 5 Giralda Farms *NYSE: WYE* ■ **Fax:* Hum Res ■ *TF:* 800-322-3129 ■ *Web:* www.wyeth.com	Madison	NJ	07940	973-660-5000	660-7026*
Xanser Corp 2435 N Central Expy Suite 700 *NYSE: XNR* ■ *TF:* 800-488-7973 ■ *Web:* www.xanser.com	Richardson	TX	75080	972-699-4000	699-4025
YRC Worldwide Inc 10990 Roe Ave *NASDAQ: YRCW* ■ **Fax:* Hum Res ■ *TF:* 800-458-3323 ■ *Web:* www.yellowroadway.com	Overland Park	KS	66211	913-696-6100	344-4717*

363-4 Insurance Holding Companies

	City	State	Zip	Phone	Fax
21st Century Holding Co PO Box 407193 *NASDAQ: TCHC* ■ *TF:* 800-333-3477	Fort Lauderdale	FL	33340	954-581-9993	584-0724
21st Century Insurance Group 6301 Owensmouth Ave *NYSE: TW* ■ *TF:* 800-443-3100 ■ *Web:* www.21st.com	Woodland Hills	CA	91365	818-704-3700	704-2961
AEGON USA Inc 4333 Edgewood Rd NE *Web:* www.aegonins.com	Cedar Rapids	IA	52499	319-398-8511	
Affirmative Insurance Holdings Inc 4450 Sojourn Dr Suite 500 *NASDAQ: AFFM* ■ *TF:* 800-877-0226 ■ *Web:* www.affirmativeinsurance.com	Addison	TX	75001	972-728-6300	991-0882
AFLAC Inc 1932 Wynnton Rd *NYSE: AFL* ■ **Fax:* Mktg ■ *TF:* 800-992-3522 ■ *Web:* www.aflac.com	Columbus	GA	31999	706-323-3431	660-7103*
AIG SunAmerica Inc 1 SunAmerica Ctr 37th Fl **Fax:* Cust Svc ■ *TF:* 800-445-7862 ■ *Web:* www.sunamerica.com	Los Angeles	CA	90067	310-772-6000	772-6699*
Alfa Insurance Corp PO Box 11000 *NASDAQ: ALFA* ■ **Fax:* Hum Res ■ *TF:* 888-964-2532 ■ *Web:* www.alfains.com	Montgomery	AL	36191	334-288-3900	613-4732*
Allstate Corp 2775 Sanders Rd Allstate Plaza *NYSE: ALL* ■ **Fax:* Hum Res ■ *TF:* 800-255-7828 ■ *Web:* www.allstate.com	Northbrook	IL	60062	847-402-5000	836-3998*
AMBAC Financial Group Inc 1 State Street Plaza 15th Fl *NYSE: ABK* ■ *TF:* 800-221-1854 ■ *Web:* www.ambac.com	New York	NY	10004	212-668-0340	509-9190
AmCOMP Inc 701 US Hwy 1 Suite 200 PO Box 88806 *NASDAQ: AMCP* ■ **Fax Area Code:* 800 ■ *TF:* 800-226-1898 ■ *Web:* www.amcomp.com	North Palm Beach	FL	33408	561-840-7171	226-1805*
American Equity Investment Life Holding Co 5000 Westown Pkwy Suite 440 *NYSE: AEL* ■ *TF:* 888-221-1234 ■ *Web:* www.american-equity.com	West Des Moines	IA	50266	515-221-0002	221-9947
American Family Insurance Group 6000 American Pkwy **Fax:* Mail Rm ■ *TF:* 800-374-0008 ■ *Web:* www.amfam.com	Madison	WI	53783	608-249-2111	243-4924*
American Fidelity Group 2000 N Classen Blvd **Fax:* Hum Res ■ *TF:* 800-654-8489 ■ *Web:* www.afadvantage.com	Oklahoma City	OK	73106	405-523-2000	523-5645*
American Financial Group Inc 1 E 4th St *NYSE: AFG* ■ *Web:* www.afginc.com	Cincinnati	OH	45202	513-579-2121	579-2580
American International Group Inc (AIG) 70 Pine St *NYSE: AIG* ■ *Web:* www.aig.com	New York	NY	10270	212-770-7000	949-1125
American Medical Security Group Inc 3100 AMS Blvd **Fax:* Hum Res ■ *TF:* 800-232-5432 ■ *Web:* www.eams.com	Green Bay	WI	54313	920-661-1111	661-5161*
American Physicians Capital Inc (APCapital) 1301 N Hagadorn Rd *NASDAQ: ACAP* ■ **Fax:* Investor Rel ■ *TF:* 800-748-0465 ■ *Web:* www.apcapital.com	East Lansing	MI	48823	517-351-1150	351-7866*
American Physicians Service Group Inc 1301 Capitol of Texas Hwy S Suite C-300 *NASDAQ: AMPH* ■ *TF:* 800-252-3628 ■ *Web:* www.amph.com	Austin	TX	78746	512-328-0888	314-4398
American Re Corp 555 College Rd E **Fax:* Mail Rm ■ *TF:* 800-255-5676 ■ *Web:* www.amre.com	Princeton	NJ	08543	609-243-4200	243-4257*
American Skandia Prudential Financial Co 1 Corporate Dr **Fax Area Code:* 877 ■ *TF:* 800-628-6039 ■ *Web:* www.americanskandia.prudential.com	Shelton	CT	06484	203-926-1888	207-7806*
American United Mutual Insurance Holding Co 1 American Sq *Web:* www.aul.com	Indianapolis	IN	46206	317-285-1111	
Americo Life Inc 1055 Broadway **Fax Area Code:* 800 ■ *TF Cust Svc:* 800-982-8144 ■ *Web:* www.americo.com	Kansas City	MO	64105	816-391-2000	395-9238*
Ameritas Holding Co 5900 O St *TF:* 800-311-7871 ■ *Web:* www.ameritas.com	Lincoln	NE	68510	402-467-1122	467-7790
AmerUS Annuity Group 555 S Kansas Ave *TF:* 800-255-2405 ■ *Web:* www.americaninvestors.com	Topeka	KS	66603	785-232-6945	295-4495
AmerUs Group Co 699 Walnut St *NYSE: AMH* ■ *TF:* 800-367-3669 ■ *Web:* www.amerus.com	Des Moines	IA	50309	515-362-3600	283-3434
Anthem Insurance Cos Inc 120 Monument Cir Suite 200 **Fax:* Hum Res ■ *TF:* 800-331-1476 ■ *Web:* www.anthem.com	Indianapolis	IN	46204	317-488-6000	488-6028*
Aon Corp 200 E Randolph St *NYSE: AOC* ■ *Web:* www.aon.com	Chicago	IL	60601	312-381-1000	
APCapital (American Physicians Capital Inc) 1301 N Hagadorn Rd *NASDAQ: ACAP* ■ **Fax:* Investor Rel ■ *TF:* 800-748-0465 ■ *Web:* www.apcapital.com	East Lansing	MI	48823	517-351-1150	351-7866*
Arch Capital Group Ltd 1 Liberty Plaza 53rd Fl *NASDAQ: ACGL* ■ *Web:* www.archcapgroup.com	New York	NY	10006	212-651-6500	651-6499
Argonaut Group Inc 10101 Reunion Pl Suite 500 *NASDAQ: AGII* ■ *TF:* 800-470-7958 ■ *Web:* www.argonautgroup.com	San Antonio	TX	78216	210-321-8400	377-2637
Assicurazioni Generali US Branch 1 Liberty Plaza 29th Fl *Web:* www.generali.com	New York	NY	10006	212-602-7600	587-9537
Assurant Group 11222 Quail Roost Dr *TF:* 800-852-2244 ■ *Web:* www.assurant.com	Miami	FL	33157	305-253-2244	252-6947
Assurant Inc 1 Chase Manhattan Plaza 41st Fl *NYSE: AIZ* ■ **Fax:* Hum Res ■ *TF:* 800-859-5676 ■ *Web:* www.assurant.com	New York	NY	10005	212-859-7000	859-7058*
Assurity Security Group Inc. 1526 K St *TF:* 800-747-7191 ■ *Web:* www.assurity.com	Lincoln	NE	68508	402-423-7191	423-7197
Atlantic American Corp PO Box 105185 *NASDAQ: AAME* ■ **Fax:* Mail Rm ■ *TF:* 800-241-1439 ■ *Web:* www.atlam.com	Atlanta	GA	30348	404-266-5500	266-5629*
Benfield Inc 500 N Akard St Suite 3700 *Web:* www.benfieldgroup.com	Dallas	TX	75201	214-756-7000	756-7001
Berkley WR Corp 475 Steamboat Rd *NYSE: BER* ■ *Web:* www.wrbc.com	Greenwich	CT	06830	203-629-3000	769-4098
Bexil Corp 11 Hanover Sq *AMEX: BXL* ■ *Web:* www.bexil.com	New York	NY	10005	212-785-0400	363-1101
Bristol West Holdings Inc 5701 Stirling Rd *NYSE: BRW* ■ *TF:* 888-888-0080 ■ *Web:* www.bristolwest.com	Davie	FL	33314	954-316-5200	316-5275
Capitol Transamerica Corp 1600 Aspen Commons **Fax:* Hum Res ■ *TF:* 800-475-4450 ■ *Web:* www.capitolindemnity.com	Middleton	WI	53562	608-829-4200	829-7409*
Chubb Corp 15 Mountain View Rd *NYSE: CB* ■ **Fax:* Mail Rm ■ *Web:* www.chubb.com	Warren	NJ	07059	908-903-2000	903-2027*
CIGNA Corp 1650 Market St 1 Liberty Pl *NYSE: CI* ■ *Web:* www.cigna.com	Philadelphia	PA	19192	215-761-1000	761-5597
Cincinnati Financial Corp 6200 S Gilmore Rd *NASDAQ: CINF* ■ *Web:* www.cinfin.com	Fairfield	OH	45014	513-870-2000	870-2911
Citizens Financial Corp 12910 Shelbyville Rd Suite 300 *NASDAQ: CNFL* ■ *TF:* 800-843-7752 ■ *Web:* www.citizensfinancialcorp.com	Louisville	KY	40243	502-244-2420	244-2439
Citizens Inc 400 E Anderson Ln *NYSE: CIA* ■ *TF:* 800-880-5044 ■ *Web:* www.citizensinc.com	Austin	TX	78752	512-837-7100	836-9785
CNA Financial Corp 333 S Wabash Ave *NYSE: CNA* ■ *TF:* 800-262-2000 ■ *Web:* www.cna.com	Chicago	IL	60604	312-822-5000	
Commerce Group Inc 11 Gore Rd *NYSE: CGI* ■ **Fax:* Hum Res ■ *TF:* 800-221-1605 ■ *Web:* www.commerceinsurance.com	Webster	MA	01570	508-943-9000	949-4921*
Connecticut General Corp 900 Cottage Grove Rd *TF:* 800-244-6224	Bloomfield	CT	06002	860-226-6000	226-2956
Conseco Inc 11825 N Pennsylvania St *NYSE: CNO* ■ **Fax:* Hum Res ■ *TF:* 800-541-2254 ■ *Web:* www.conseco.com	Carmel	IN	46032	317-817-6100	817-6721*
Cumberland Technologies Inc 4311 W Waters Ave Suite 401 *TF:* 800-723-0171 ■ *Web:* www.cumberlandtech.com	Tampa	FL	33614	813-885-2112	880-0901
CUNA Mutual Group 5910 Mineral Point Dr *TF:* 800-937-2644 ■ *Web:* www.cunamutual.com	Madison	WI	53705	608-238-5851	231-7875
Delphi Financial Group Inc 1105 N Market St Suite 1230 *NYSE: DFG* ■ *Web:* www.delphifin.com	Wilmington	DE	19801	302-478-5142	
Deutsche Bank Americas Holding Corp 60 Wall St *Web:* www.db.com	New York	NY	10005	212-250-2500	
Donegal Group Inc 1195 River Rd *NASDAQ: DGICB* ■ **Fax:* Hum Res ■ *TF:* 800-877-0600 ■ *Web:* www.donegalgroup.com	Marietta	PA	17547	717-426-1931	426-7030*
E-L Financial Corp Ltd 165 University Ave 10th Fl *TSX: ELF* ■ *Web:* www.sedar.com	Toronto	ON	M5H3B8	416-947-2578	362-2592
EMC Insurance Group Inc 717 Mulberry St *NASDAQ: EMCI* ■ *TF:* 800-362-2227 ■ *Web:* www.emcinsurance.com	Des Moines	IA	50309	515-280-2511	
Erie Insurance Group 100 Erie Insurance Pl *TF:* 800-458-0811 ■ *Web:* www.erie-insurance.com	Erie	PA	16530	814-870-2000	870-4408
Everest Re Group Ltd 477 Martinsville Rd *NYSE: RE* ■ *TF:* 800-551-6501 ■ *Web:* www.everestre.com	Liberty Corner	NJ	07938	908-604-3000	604-3450
Fairfax Financial Holdings Ltd 95 Wellington St W Suite 800 *Web:* fairfax.ca	Toronto	ON	M5J2N7	416-367-4941	367-4946
Farm Family Holdings Inc PO Box 656 *TF Cust Svc:* 800-843-3276 ■ *Web:* www.farmfamily.com	Albany	NY	12201	518-431-5000	431-5979
Farmers Insurance Group 4680 Wilshire Blvd *Web:* www.farmersinsurance.com	Los Angeles	CA	90010	323-932-3200	936-8479
FBL Financial Group Inc 5400 University Ave *NYSE: FFG* ■ *Web:* www.fblfinancial.com	West Des Moines	IA	50266	515-225-5400	226-6053
Federated Insurance Cos PO Box 328 **Fax:* Hum Res ■ *TF:* 800-533-0472 ■ *Web:* www.federatedinsurance.com	Owatonna	MN	55060	507-455-5200	444-6778*
Fidelity National Financial Inc 601 Riverside Avenue *NYSE: FNF* ■ **Fax Area Code:* 805 ■ *TF:* 888-934-3354 ■ *Web:* www.fnf.com	Jacksonville	FL	32204	904-854-8100	696-7823*
Financial Industries Corp 6500 River Place Blvd Bldg 1 *TF:* 800-925-6000 ■ *Web:* www.ficgroup.com	Austin	TX	78730	512-404-5000	404-5348
Financial Security Assurance Holdings Ltd 31 W 52nd St 13th Fl *TF:* 800-846-4372 ■ *Web:* www.fsa.com	New York	NY	10019	212-826-0100	
Firemans Fund Insurance Co 33 W Monroe St 12th Fl **Fax:* Mail Rm ■ *TF:* 800-255-2096 ■ *Web:* www.ffic.com	Chicago	IL	60603	312-346-6400	346-5748*
First Investors Corp 110 Fieldcrest Ave RARITAN Plaza I *TF:* 800-432-4026 ■ *Web:* www.firstinvestors.com	Edison	NJ	08837	732-855-2500	855-2579
Folksamerica Holding Co 1 Liberty Plaza 19th Fl *Web:* www.folksamerica.com	New York	NY	10006	212-312-2500	385-2279
Foremost Insurance Group PO Box 2450 *TF:* 800-527-3905 ■ *Web:* www.foremost.com	Grand Rapids	MI	49501	616-942-3000	956-8935
FPIC Insurance Group Inc 225 Water St Suite 1400 *NASDAQ: FPIC* ■ *TF:* 800-221-2101 ■ *Web:* www.fpic.com	Jacksonville	FL	32202	904-354-2482	475-1159
Fremont General Corp 2425 W Olympic Blvd 3rd Fl *NYSE: FMT* ■ *Web:* www.fremontgeneral.com	Santa Monica	CA	90404	310-315-5500	315-7016
GAINSCO Inc 3333 Lee Pkwy *AMEX: GAN* ■ *TF:* 800-810-9808 ■ *Web:* www.gainsco.com	Dallas	TX	75219	972-629-4301	629-4401
GEICO 1 GEICO Plaza *TF:* 800-824-5404 ■ *Web:* www.geico.com	Washington	DC	20076	301-986-2500	986-3757
General Re Corp 695 E Main St Financial Ctr *TF:* 800-431-9994 ■ *Web:* www.genre.com	Stamford	CT	06901	203-328-5000	328-6423
GMAC Insurance Holdings Inc 13736 Riverport Dr Suite 700 *TF:* 877-468-3466 ■ *Web:* www.gmacinsurance.com	Maryland Heights	MO	63043	314-493-8000	493-8113
Goran Capital Inc 2 Eva Rd Suite 200	Etobicoke	ON	M9C2A8	416-622-0660	622-8809
Great American Financial Resources Inc 250 E 5th St *NYSE: GFR* ■ *TF:* 800-438-3398 ■ *Web:* www.gafri.com	Cincinnati	OH	45202	513-333-5300	
Great-West Lifeco Inc 100 Osborne St N *Web:* www.greatwestlifeco.com	Winnepeg	MB	R3C3A5	204-946-8366	946-4139
Hallmark Financial Services Inc 777 Main St Suite 1000 *AMEX: HAF* ■ *Web:* www.hallmarkgrp.com	Fort Worth	TX	76102	817-348-1600	348-1815
Hanover Insurance Group Inc 440 Lincoln St *NYSE: THG* ■ *TF:* 800-533-7881 ■ *Web:* www.hanover.com/thg	Worcester	MA	01653	508-855-1000	853-6332
Harleysville Group Inc 355 Maple Ave *NASDAQ: HGIC* ■ **Fax:* Mktg ■ *TF:* 800-523-6344 ■ *Web:* www.harleysvillegroup.com	Harleysville	PA	19438	215-256-5000	256-5678*
Hartford Financial Services Group Inc 690 Asylum Ave *NYSE: HIG* ■ **Fax:* PR ■ *Web:* www.thehartford.com	Hartford	CT	06115	860-547-5000	547-3799*
HCC Insurance Holdings Inc 13403 Northwest Fwy *NYSE: HCC* ■ *Web:* www.hcch.com	Houston	TX	77040	713-690-7300	462-4210
HealthMarkets Inc 9151 Grapevine Hwy *TF:* 800-527-5504 ■ *Web:* www.healthmarkets.com	North Richland Hills	TX	76180	817-255-5200	255-8164
HM Insurance Group 120 5th Ave *TF:* 800-328-5433 ■ *Web:* www.hminsurancegroup.com	Pittsburgh	PA	15222	412-544-2000	544-1334
Horace Mann Educators Corp 1 Horace Mann Plaza *NYSE: HMN* ■ *TF:* 800-999-1030 ■ *Web:* www.horacemann.com	Springfield	IL	62715	217-789-2500	788-5161
Industrial Alliance Insurance & Financial Services Inc 1080 Grande Allee W PO Box 1907 Station Terminus *TSX: IAG* ■ *TF:* 800-463-6236 ■ *Web:* www.inalco.com	Quebec	QC	G1K7M3	418-684-5182	684-5106
ING Americas 5780 Powers Ferry Rd NW *Web:* www.ing-usa.com	Atlanta	GA	30327	770-980-5100	980-3301
InterContinental Life Corp 6500 River Place Blvd Bldg 1 *TF:* 800-925-6000	Austin	TX	78730	512-404-5000	404-5210
Interstate Insurance Group 33 W Monroe St 12th Fl *TF:* 800-255-2096	Chicago	IL	60603	312-346-6400	346-5748
Investors Title Co 121 N Columbia St *NASDAQ: ITIC* ■ **Fax Area Code:* 800 ■ *TF:* 800-326-4842 ■ *Web:* www.invtitle.com	Chapel Hill	NC	27514	919-968-2200	690-6105*
John Hancock Financial Services Inc 601 Congress St **Fax:* PR ■ *Web:* www.johnhancock.com	Boston	MA	02210	617-663-3000	663-4790*
Kansas City Life Insurance Co 3520 Broadway *NASDAQ: KCLI* ■ *TF:* 800-821-6164 ■ *Web:* www.kclife.com	Kansas City	MO	64111	816-753-7000	753-4902
Kingsway America Inc 150 NW Point Blvd *TF:* 877-717-5442 ■ *Web:* www.kingswayamerica.com	Elk Grove Village	IL	60007	847-871-6400	264-2700

Company	City	State	Zip	Phone	Fax
LandAmerica Financial Group Inc 101 Gateway Center Pkwy Gateway 1 *NYSE: LFG* ■ *TF:* 800-446-7086 ■ *Web:* www.landam.com	Richmond	VA	23235	804-267-8000	267-8616
Legal & General America Inc 1701 Research Blvd **Fax:* Cust Svc ■ *TF:* 800-638-8428 ■ *Web:* www.lgamerica.com	Rockville	MD	20850	301-279-4800	294-6960*
Liberty Mutual Holding Co Inc 175 Berkeley St *Web:* www.libertymutual.com	Boston	MA	02116	617-357-9500	350-7648
Lifetime Healthcare Cos 165 Court St *TF:* 800-847-1200 ■ *Web:* www.lifethc.com	Rochester	NY	14647	585-454-1700	238-4224
Lincoln Financial Group 1500 Market St Centre Sq West Tower Suite 3900 *NYSE: LNC* ■ **Fax:* PR ■ *TF:* 800-454-6265 ■ *Web:* www.lfg.com	Philadelphia	PA	19102	215-448-1400	448-3962*
Lincoln National Corp DBA Lincoln Financial Group 1500 Market St Centre Sq West Tower Suite 3900 *NYSE: LNC* ■ **Fax:* PR ■ *TF:* 800-454-6265 ■ *Web:* www.lfg.com	Philadelphia	PA	19102	215-448-1400	448-3962*
Lykes Bros Inc PO Box 2879 **Fax:* Hum Res ■ *TF:* 800-243-0494 ■ *Web:* www.lykes.com	Tampa	FL	33601	813-223-3911	221-1857*
MAMSI (Mid Atlantic Medical Services Inc) 4 Taft Ct *TF:* 800-331-2102 ■ *Web:* www.mamsiunitedhealthcare.com	Rockville	MD	20850	301-762-8205	360-8647
Mann Horace Educators Corp 1 Horace Mann Plaza *NYSE: HMN* ■ *TF:* 800-999-1030 ■ *Web:* www.horacemann.com	Springfield	IL	62715	217-789-2500	788-5161
Manulife Financial Corp 200 Bloor St E *NYSE: MFC* ■ *TF:* 800-795-9767 ■ *Web:* www.manulife.com	Toronto	ON	M4W1E5	416-926-3000	926-5454
Markel Corp 4521 Highwoods Pkwy *NYSE: MKL* ■ *TF:* 800-446-6671 ■ *Web:* www.markelcorp.com	Glen Allen	VA	23060	804-747-0136	965-1600
MBIA Inc 113 King St *NYSE: MBI* ■ **Fax:* Hum Res ■ *Web:* www.mbia.com	Armonk	NY	10504	914-273-4545	765-3299*
Meadowbrook Insurance Group Inc 26255 American Dr *NYSE: MIG* ■ *TF:* 800-482-2726 ■ *Web:* www.meadowbrookinsgrp.com	Southfield	MI	48034	248-358-1100	358-1614
MEEMIC Holdings Inc 1685 N Opdyke Rd PO Box 217019 *TF:* 888-463-3642 ■ *Web:* www.meemic.com	Auburn Hills	MI	48321	248-373-5700	377-8518
Merchants Group Inc 250 Main St *AMEX: MGP* ■ **Fax:* Hum Res ■ *TF:* 800-462-1077 ■ *Web:* www.merchantsgroup.com	Buffalo	NY	14202	716-849-3333	849-3388*
MGIC Investment Corp 250 E Kilbourn Ave *NYSE: MTG* ■ *TF:* 800-558-9900 ■ *Web:* www.mgic.com	Milwaukee	WI	53202	414-347-6480	347-6696
Mid Atlantic Medical Services Inc (MAMSI) 4 Taft Ct *TF:* 800-331-2102 ■ *Web:* www.mamsiunitedhealthcare.com	Rockville	MD	20850	301-762-8205	360-8647
Midland Co 7000 Midland Blvd *NASDAQ: MLAN* ■ *TF:* 800-759-9008 ■ *Web:* www.midlandcompany.com	Amelia	OH	45102	513-943-7100	
Mutual of Omaha Cos Mutual of Omaha Plaza *TF:* 800-775-6000 ■ *Web:* www.mutualofomaha.com	Omaha	NE	68175	402-342-7600	351-2775
National Atlantic Holdings Corp 4 Paragon Way *NASDAQ: NAHC*	Freehold	NJ	07728	732-665-1100	761-0243
Nationwide Financial Services Inc 5100 Rings Rd *NYSE: NFS* ■ **Fax Area Code:* 614 ■ *Web:* www.nationwidefinancial.com	Dublin	OH	43017	800-321-9332	249-8348*
Nationwide Insurance Enterprise 1 Nationwide Plaza *TF:* 800-882-2822 ■ *Web:* www.nationwide.com	Columbus	OH	43215	614-249-7111	249-6127
Navigators Group Inc 1 Penn Plaza 55th Fl *NASDAQ: NAVG* ■ *TF:* 800-496-2901 ■ *Web:* www.navigators-insurance.com	New York	NY	10119	212-244-2333	244-4077
NCRIC Group Inc 1115 30th St NW *TF:* 800-613-3615 ■ *Web:* www.ncric.com	Washington	DC	20007	202-969-1866	969-1881
NGL Insurance Group 2 E Gilman St **Fax Area Code:* 608 ■ *Web:* www.nationalguardian.com	Madison	WI	53703	800-548-2962	257-3940*
NYMAGIC Inc 919 3rd Ave 10th Fl *NYSE: NYM* ■ *TF:* 800-367-0224 ■ *Web:* www.nymagic.com	New York	NY	10022	212-551-0600	986-1310
Ohio Casualty Corp 9450 Seward Rd *NASDAQ: OCAS* ■ *TF:* 800-843-6446 ■ *Web:* www.ocas.com	Fairfield	OH	45014	513-603-2400	603-7900
Ohio National Financial Services Inc 1 Financial Way Suite 100 **Fax:* Hum Res ■ *TF:* 800-366-6654 ■ *Web:* www.ohionational.com	Cincinnati	OH	45242	513-794-6100	794-4504*
Old Republic International Corp 307 N Michigan Ave *NYSE: ORI* ■ *TF:* 800-621-0365 ■ *Web:* www.oldrepublic.com	Chicago	IL	60601	312-346-8100	726-0309
Pacific Mutual Holding Co 700 Newport Ctr Dr *TF:* 800-347-7787 ■ *Web:* www.pacificlife.com	Newport Beach	CA	92660	949-219-3011	219-5378
PAULA Financial 87 E Green St Suite 206 *NASDAQ: PFCO* ■ *Web:* www.paula.com	Pasadena	CA	91105	626-844-7500	844-7144
Penn-America Group Inc 420 S York Rd **Fax:* Claims ■ *Web:* www.penn-america.com	Hatboro	PA	19040	215-443-3600	443-3604*
Penn Treaty American Corp 3440 Lehigh St *NYSE: PTA* ■ *TF:* 800-222-3469 ■ *Web:* www.penntreaty.com	Allentown	PA	18103	610-965-2222	967-4616
Philadelphia Consolidated Holding Corp 1 Bala Plaza Suite 100 *NASDAQ: PHLY* ■ *TF:* 877-438-7459 ■ *Web:* www.phly.com	Bala Cynwyd	PA	19004	610-617-7900	617-7940
Phoenix Cos Inc 1 American Row PO Box 5056 *NYSE: PNX* ■ *TF:* 800-628-1936 ■ *Web:* www.phoenixwm.com	Hartford	CT	06102	860-403-5000	403-5629
PICO Holdings Inc 875 Prospect St Suite 301 *NASDAQ: PICO* ■ *TF:* 888-389-3222 ■ *Web:* www.picoholdings.com	La Jolla	CA	92037	858-456-6022	456-6480
PMA Capital Corp 380 Sentry Pkwy *NASDAQ: PMACA* ■ *Web:* www.pmacapital.com	Blue Bell	PA	19422	610-397-5298	397-5422
PMI Group Inc 3003 Oak Rd *NYSE: PMI* ■ *TF:* 800-288-1970 ■ *Web:* www.pmigroup.com	Walnut Creek	CA	94597	925-658-7878	658-6191
Power Financial Corp 751 Victoria Sq *TF:* 800-890-7440 ■ *Web:* www.powerfinancial.com	Montreal	QC	H2Y2J3	514-286-7400	286-7424
Preserver Group Inc 95 Rt 17 S *TF:* 800-242-0332 ■ *Web:* www.preserver.com	Paramus	NJ	07653	201-291-2000	291-2130
Presidential Life Corp 69 Lydecker St *NASDAQ: PLFE* ■ *TF:* 800-926-7599 ■ *Web:* www.presidentiallife.com	Nyack	NY	10960	845-358-2300	353-0273
Principal Financial Group Inc 711 High St *NYSE: PFG* ■ *TF:* 800-986-3343 ■ *Web:* www.principal.com	Des Moines	IA	50392	515-247-5111	247-5874
ProAssurance Corp 100 Brookwood Pl Suite 300 *NYSE: PRA* ■ **Fax:* Cust Svc ■ *TF:* 800-282-6242 ■ *Web:* www.proassurance.com	Birmingham	AL	35209	205-877-4400	802-4799*
Progressive Corp 6300 Wilson Mills Rd *NYSE: PGR* ■ **Fax:* Hum Res ■ *TF:* 800-321-9843 ■ *Web:* www1.progressive.com	Mayfield Village	OH	44143	440-461-5000	446-7436*
Protective Life Corp 2801 Hwy 280 S *NYSE: PL* ■ **Fax:* Hum Res ■ *TF:* 800-333-3418 ■ *Web:* www.protective.com	Birmingham	AL	35203	205-268-1000	268-3196*
Reinsurance Group of America Inc 1370 Timberlake Manor Pkwy *NYSE: RGA* ■ *TF:* 888-736-5445 ■ *Web:* www.rgare.com	Chesterfield	MO	63017	636-736-7000	736-7100
RLI Corp 9025 N Lindbergh Dr *NYSE: RLI* ■ *TF Cust Svc:* 800-331-4929 ■ *Web:* www.rlicorp.com	Peoria	IL	61615	309-692-1000	692-1068
SAFECO Corp 4333 Brooklyn Ave NE *NASDAQ: SAFC* ■ *TF:* 800-562-1018 ■ *Web:* www.safeco.com	Seattle	WA	98185	206-545-5000	545-5995
SCPIE Holdings Inc 1888 Century Park E Suite 800 *NYSE: SKP* ■ **Fax:* Hum Res ■ *TF:* 800-962-5549 ■ *Web:* www.scpie.com	Los Angeles	CA	90067	310-551-5900	551-5984*
SeaBright Insurance Holdings Inc 2101 4th Ave Suite 1600 *NASDAQ: SEAB* ■ *TF:* 888-636-1580 ■ *Web:* www.sbic.com	Seattle	WA	98121	206-269-8500	269-8903
Securian Financial Group Inc 400 Robert St N *Web:* www.securian.com	Saint Paul	MN	55101	651-665-3500	665-4488
Security Benefit Group of Cos 1 Security Benefit Pl **Fax:* Cust Svc ■ *TF:* 800-888-2461 ■ *Web:* www.securitybenefit.com	Topeka	KS	66636	785-438-3000	368-1772*
Selective Insurance Group Inc 40 Wantage Ave *NASDAQ: SIGI* ■ *TF:* 800-777-9656 ■ *Web:* www.selectiveinsurance.com	Branchville	NJ	07890	973-948-3000	948-0292
Sentry Insurance Group 1800 N Point Dr *TF:* 800-227-0201 ■ *Web:* www.sentry-insurance.com	Stevens Point	WI	54481	715-346-6000	346-6770
Southwestern Life Holdings Inc 8710 Freeport Pkwy Suite 150 **Fax Area Code:* 803	Irving	TX	75063	800-792-4368	333-7833*
StanCorp Financial Group Inc 1100 SW 6th Ave *NYSE: SFG* ■ *TF:* 800-642-9888 ■ *Web:* www.stancorpfinancial.com	Portland	OR	97204	503-321-7000	321-5243
State Auto Financial Corp 518 E Broad St *NASDAQ: STFC* ■ *TF:* 800-444-9950 ■ *Web:* www.stfc.com	Columbus	OH	43215	614-464-5000	464-5374
Summit Holding Southeast Inc PO Box 988 *TF:* 800-282-7648 ■ *Web:* www.summitholdings.com	Lakeland	FL	33802	863-665-6060	667-1528
Sun Life Financial Inc 150 King St W *NYSE: SLF* ■ **Fax Area Code:* 518 ■ *TF:* 877-786-5438 ■ *Web:* www.sunlife.com	Toronto	ON	M5H1J9	416-979-9966	888-2990*
Swiss Re Life & Health America Inc 175 King St **Fax:* Mail Rm ■ *TF:* 877-794-7773 ■ *Web:* www.swissre.com	Armonk	NY	10504	914-828-8500	828-7000*
Torchmark Corp 3700 S Stonebridge Dr *NYSE: TMK* ■ **Fax Area Code:* 205 ■ *Web:* www.torchmarkcorp.com	McKinney	TX	75070	972-569-5085	325-4110*
Transatlantic Holdings Inc 80 Pine St 9th Fl *NYSE: TRH* ■ *Web:* www.transre.com	New York	NY	10005	212-770-2000	785-7230
Travelers Cos Inc 385 Washington St *NYSE: TRV* ■ **Fax:* Hum Res ■ *TF:* 800-328-2189 ■ *Web:* www.travelers.com	Saint Paul	MN	55102	651-310-7911	310-2115*
Trenwick Group Ltd 1 Canterbury Green *Web:* www.trenwick.com	Stamford	CT	06901	203-353-5500	353-5555
ULLICO Inc 1625 Eye St NW *TF:* 800-431-5425 ■ *Web:* www.ullico.com	Washington	DC	20006	202-682-0900	
UNIFI Mutual Holding Co 5900 O St *TF:* 800-311-7871 ■ *Web:* www.unificompanies.com	Lincoln	NE	68510	402-467-1122	467-7939
United Fire Group 118 2nd Ave SE *TF:* 800-332-7977 ■ *Web:* www.unitedfiregroup.com	Cedar Rapids	IA	52401	319-399-5700	399-5499
United Trust Group Inc 5250 S 6th St *TF:* 800-323-0050 ■ *Web:* www.unitedtrustgroup.com	Springfield	IL	62703	217-241-6300	241-6578
UnitedHealthcare Co 9900 Bren Rd E *Web:* www.unitedhealthcare.com	Minnetonka	MN	55343	952-936-1300	936-7430
Unitrin Inc 1 E Wacker Dr *NYSE: UTR* ■ *Web:* www.unitrin.com	Chicago	IL	60601	312-661-4600	661-4690
Universal American Financial Corp 6 International Dr Suite 190 *NASDAQ: UHCO* ■ *TF:* 800-332-3377 ■ *Web:* www.uafc.com	Rye Brook	NY	10573	914-934-8300	934-9123
UnumProvident Corp 1 Fountain Sq *NYSE: UNM* ■ **Fax:* Investor Rel ■ *Web:* www.unum.com	Chattanooga	TN	37402	423-755-1011	755-3962*
Utica Mutual Insurance Co PO Box 530 *TF:* 800-274-1914 ■ *Web:* www.uticanational.com	Utica	NY	13503	315-734-2000	734-2680
Vesta Insurance Group Inc 3760 River Run Dr *NYSE: VTA* ■ **Fax Area Code:* 888 ■ *TF:* 800-444-2955 ■ *Web:* www.vesta.com	Birmingham	AL	35243	205-970-7000	286-9458*
Walshire Assurance Co 3501 Concord Rd PO Box 3709 *TF:* 800-876-3350	York	PA	17402	717-757-0000	751-0165
Western & Southern Financial Group 400 Broadway *TF:* 800-333-5222 ■ *Web:* www.westernsouthern.com	Cincinnati	OH	45202	513-629-1800	629-1212
White Mountains Insurance Group Ltd 80 S Main St *NYSE: WTM* ■ *Web:* www.whitemountains.com	Hanover	NH	03755	603-640-2200	643-4592
WR Berkley Corp 475 Steamboat Rd *NYSE: BER* ■ *Web:* www.wrbc.com	Greenwich	CT	06830	203-629-3000	769-4098
Zenith National Insurance Corp 21255 Califa St *NYSE: ZNT* ■ *TF:* 800-448-4356 ■ *Web:* www.znic.com	Woodland Hills	CA	91367	818-713-1000	592-0265

363-5 Utilities Holding Companies

Company	City	State	Zip	Phone	Fax
AGL Resources Inc 10 Peachtree Pl *NYSE: ATG* ■ **Fax:* Hum Res ■ *TF Cust Svc:* 800-427-5463 ■ *Web:* www.aglc.com	Atlanta	GA	30309	404-584-4000	584-4210*
Allegheny Energy Inc 800 Cabin Hill Dr *NYSE: AYE* ■ *TF Cust Svc:* 800-255-3443 ■ *Web:* www.alleghenyenergy.com	Greensburg	PA	15601	724-837-3000	830-5284
ALLETE Inc 30 W Superior St *NYSE: ALE* ■ **Fax:* Hum Res ■ *Web:* www.allete.com	Duluth	MN	55802	218-722-2641	723-3944*
Ameren Corp 1901 Chouteau Ave *NYSE: AEE* ■ *TF:* 800-552-7583 ■ *Web:* www.ameren.com	Saint Louis	MO	63103	314-621-3222	992-6755
American Electric Power Co Inc 1 Riverside Plaza *NYSE: AEP* ■ *TF Cust Svc:* 800-277-2177 ■ *Web:* www.aep.com	Columbus	OH	43215	614-716-1000	716-1823
American States Water Co 630 E Foothill Blvd *NYSE: AWR* ■ *TF:* 800-999-4033 ■ *Web:* www.aswater.com	San Dimas	CA	91773	909-394-3600	394-9708
American Water Works Co Inc 1025 Laurel Oak Rd *Web:* www.amwater.com	Voorhees	NJ	08043	856-346-8200	346-8360
Artesian Resources Corp 664 Churchmans Rd *NASDAQ: ARTNA* ■ *TF:* 800-332-5114	Newark	DE	19702	302-453-6900	453-6957
Atmos Energy Corp 5430 LBJ Fwy Suite 1800 *NYSE: ATO* ■ *TF:* 888-954-4321 ■ *Web:* www.atmosenergy.com	Dallas	TX	75240	972-934-9227	855-3040
BayCorp Holdings Ltd 1 New Hampshire Ave Suite 207 *AMEX: MWH*	Portsmouth	NH	03801	603-294-4850	457-6013
Black Hills Corp 625 9th St *NYSE: BKH* ■ **Fax:* Hum Res ■ *TF:* 800-843-8849 ■ *Web:* www.blackhillscorp.com	Rapid City	SD	57701	605-721-1700	721-2596*
CenterPoint Energy Inc 1111 Louisiana St *NYSE: CNP* ■ **Fax:* Hum Res ■ *TF Cust Svc:* 866-735-4268 ■ *Web:* www.centerpointenergy.com	Houston	TX	77002	713-207-1111	207-0050*
CH Energy Group Inc 284 South Ave *NYSE: CHG* ■ *Web:* www.chenergygroup.com	Poughkeepsie	NY	12601	845-452-2000	486-5415
Cleco Corp 2030 Donahue Ferry Rd *NYSE: CNL* ■ **Fax:* Cust Svc ■ *TF Cust Svc:* 800-622-6537 ■ *Web:* www.cleco.com	Pineville	LA	71360	318-484-7400	641-8196*
CMS Energy Corp 1 Energy Plaza *NYSE: CMS* ■ *TF:* 800-477-5050 ■ *Web:* www.cmsenergy.com	Jackson	MI	49201	517-788-0550	
Connecticut Water Service Inc 93 W Main St *NASDAQ: CTWS* ■ **Fax:* Cust Svc ■ *TF:* 800-286-5700 ■ *Web:* www.ctwater.com	Clinton	CT	06413	860-669-8636	664-8081*
Consolidated Edison Inc 4 Irving Pl *NYSE: ED* ■ **Fax:* Hum Res ■ *TF:* 800-752-6633 ■ *Web:* www.conedison.com	New York	NY	10003	212-460-4600	260-8647*
Constellation Energy Group Inc 750 E Pratt St *NYSE: CEG* ■ *Web:* www.constellationenergy.com	Baltimore	MD	21202	410-783-2800	783-3045
Dominion Resources Inc 120 Tredegar St *NYSE: D* ■ *TF:* 800-552-4034 ■ *Web:* www.dom.com	Richmond	VA	23219	804-819-2000	819-2233
DPL Inc 1065 Woodman Dr *NYSE: DPL* ■ *TF:* 800-322-9244 ■ *Web:* www.dplinc.com	Dayton	OH	45432	937-224-6000	259-7147
DTE Energy Co 2000 2nd Ave *NYSE: DTE* ■ **Fax:* Hum Res ■ *TF:* 800-477-4747 ■ *Web:* www.dteenergy.com	Detroit	MI	48226	313-235-4000	235-6830*
Duke Energy Corp 526 S Church St *NYSE: DUK* ■ **Fax:* Hum Res ■ *Web:* www.duke-energy.com	Charlotte	NC	28202	704-594-6200	382-3781*
Duquesne Light Holdings Inc 411 7th Ave *NYSE: DQE* ■ *TF:* 877-393-7800 ■ *Web:* www.dqe.com	Pittsburgh	PA	15219	412-393-6000	393-1414
Dynegy Inc 1000 Louisiana St Suite 5800 *NYSE: DYN* ■ *TF:* 800-922-2104 ■ *Web:* www.dynegy.com	Houston	TX	77002	713-507-6400	356-2105
Edison International 2244 Walnut Grove Ave *NYSE: EIX* ■ *TF Cust Svc:* 800-655-4555 ■ *Web:* www.edison.com	Rosemead	CA	91770	626-302-1212	
Emera Inc 1894 Barrington St *TSX: EMA* ■ *TF:* 800-358-1995 ■ *Web:* www.emera.com	Halifax	NS	B3J2W5	902-450-0507	428-6112
Enbridge Energy Management LLC 1100 Louisiana St Suite 3300 *NYSE: EEQ* ■ *TF:* 866-337-4636 ■ *Web:* www.enbridgemanagement.com	Houston	TX	77002	713-821-2000	821-2232
Energen Corp 605 Richard Arrington Blvd N *NYSE: EGN* ■ *TF:* 800-654-3206 ■ *Web:* www.energen.com	Birmingham	AL	35203	205-326-2700	326-2590
Energy East Corp 52 Farm View Dr *NYSE: EAS* ■ *Web:* www.energyeast.com	New Gloucester	ME	04260	207-688-6300	
EnergySouth Inc 2828 Dauphin St PO Box 2248 *NASDAQ: ENSI* ■ *Web:* www.energysouth.com	Mobile	AL	36652	251-450-4774	476-1745

Utilities Holding Companies (Cont'd)

Company	City	State	Zip	Phone	Fax
Entergy Corp 639 Loyola Ave	New Orleans	LA	70113	504-576-4000	576-4428
NYSE: ETR ■ *TF:* 800-368-3749 ■ *Web:* www.entergy.com					
Exelon Corp 10 S Dearborn St 37th Fl	Chicago	IL	60690	312-394-7398	394-3110
NYSE: EXC ■ *TF:* 800-334-7661 ■ *Web:* www.exeloncorp.com					
FirstEnergy Corp 76 S Main St	Akron	OH	44308	800-646-0400	761-2314*
NYSE: FE ■ **Fax Area Code:* 330 ■ *Web:* www.firstenergycorp.com					
FirstEnergy Corp 76 S Main St	Akron	OH	44308	800-646-0400	384-3866*
NYSE: FE ■ **Fax Area Code:* 330 ■ *Web:* www.firstenergycorp.com					
Fortis Inc 139 Water St Suite 201	Saint John's	NL	A1B3T2	709-737-2800	737-5307
TSX: FTS ■ *Web:* www.fortisinc.com					
FPL Group Inc 700 Universe Blvd	Juno Beach	FL	33408	561-694-4000	694-4620
NYSE: FPL ■ *Web:* www.fplgroup.com					
Great Plains Energy Inc 1201 Walnut St	Kansas City	MO	64106	816-556-2200	556-2884
NYSE: GXP ■ *Web:* www.greatplainsenergy.com					
Holly Energy Partners LP 100 Crescent Ct Suite 1600	Dallas	TX	75201	214-871-3555	871-3829
NYSE: HEP ■ *TF:* 800-453-5658 ■ *Web:* www.hollyenergy.com					
IDACORP Inc 1221 W Idaho St	Boise	ID	83702	208-388-2200	388-6914
NYSE: IDA ■ *Web:* www.idacorpinc.com					
Integrys Energy Group Inc 130 E Randolph Dr	Chicago	IL	60601	312-228-5400	
NYSE: TEG ■ *TF:* 800-699-1269 ■ *Web:* www.integrysgroup.com					
IPALCO Enterprises Inc PO Box 1595	Indianapolis	IN	46206	317-261-8261	630-5612
TF: 888-261-8222 ■ *Web:* www.ipalco.com					
ITC Holdings Corp 39500 Orchard Hill Pl Suite 200	Novi	MI	48375	248-374-7100	374-7136
NYSE: ITC ■ *Web:* www.itctransco.com					
KeySpan Corp DBA KeySpan Energy 1 MetroTech Ctr	Brooklyn	NY	11201	718-403-1000	403-2042*
NYSE: KSE ■ **Fax:* Investor Rel ■ *Web:* www.keyspanenergy.com					
KeySpan Energy 1 MetroTech Ctr	Brooklyn	NY	11201	718-403-1000	403-2042*
NYSE: KSE ■ **Fax:* Investor Rel ■ *Web:* www.keyspanenergy.com					
Laclede Group Inc 720 Olive St	Saint Louis	MO	63101	314-342-0500	588-0615*
NYSE: LG ■ **Fax:* Hum Res ■ *TF:* 800-887-4173 ■ *Web:* www.lacledegas.com					
LG & E Energy Corp 220 W Main St	Louisville	KY	40202	502-627-2000	627-3690
TF: 800-331-7370 ■ *Web:* www.lgeenergy.com					
MidAmerican Energy Holdings Co 666 Grand Ave PO Box 657	Des Moines	IA	50303	515-242-4300	281-2981
Web: www.midamerican.com					
National Fuel Gas Co 6363 Main St	Williamsville	NY	14221	716-857-7000	857-7206
NYSE: NFG ■ *TF Cust Svc:* 800-365-3234 ■ *Web:* www.nationalfuelgas.com					
National Grid 25 Research Dr	Westborough	MA	01582	508-389-2000	389-2028*
**Fax:* Hum Res ■ *TF:* 888-424-2113 ■ *Web:* www.nationalgridus.com					
New Jersey Resources Corp 1415 Wyckoff Rd	Wall	NJ	07719	732-938-1480	938-2134*
NYSE: NJR ■ **Fax:* Hum Res ■ *Web:* www1.njresources.com					
NiSource Inc 801 E 86th Ave	Merrillville	IN	46410	219-647-5990	647-5589*
NYSE: NI ■ **Fax:* Hum Res ■ *TF:* 800-464-7726 ■ *Web:* www.nisource.com					
Northeast Utilities 107 Selden St	Berlin	CT	06037	860-665-5000	665-5418*
NYSE: NU ■ **Fax:* Hum Res ■ *TF:* 800-286-5000 ■ *Web:* www.nu.com					
NorthWestern Corp 125 S Dakota Ave Suite 1100	Sioux Falls	SD	57104	605-978-2908	978-2910
NASDAQ: NWEC ■ *Web:* www.northwestern.com					
NSTAR 800 Boylston St	Boston	MA	02199	617-424-2000	441-8886*
NYSE: NST ■ **Fax Area Code:* 781 ■ *TF:* 800-592-2000 ■ *Web:* www.nstaronline.com					
OGE Energy Corp 321 N Harvey St	Oklahoma City	OK	73102	405-553-3000	553-3326
NYSE: OGE ■ *TF:* 800-272-9741 ■ *Web:* www.oge.com					
Peoples Energy Corp 130 E Randolph Dr	Chicago	IL	60601	312-240-4000	240-4697*
NYSE: PGL ■ **Fax:* Hum Res ■ *TF Cust Svc:* 866-556-6001 ■ *Web:* www.pecorp.com					
PG & E Corp 1 Market St	San Francisco	CA	94105	415-267-7000	817-8245*
NYSE: PCG ■ **Fax:* Hum Res ■ *TF:* 800-743-5000 ■ *Web:* www.pgecorp.com					
Pinnacle West Capital Corp 400 N 5th St	Phoenix	AZ	85004	602-250-1000	250-2741*
NYSE: PNW ■ **Fax:* Investor Rel ■ *TF:* 800-457-2983 ■ *Web:* www.pinnaclewest.com					
PNM Resources Inc Alvarado Sq	Albuquerque	NM	87158	505-848-2700	241-2365*
NYSE: PNM ■ **Fax:* Hum Res ■ *TF Cust Svc:* 800-687-7854 ■ *Web:* www.pnm.com					
PPL Corp 2 N 9th St	Allentown	PA	18101	610-774-5151	774-6043
NYSE: PPL ■ *TF:* 800-342-5775 ■ *Web:* www.pplweb.com					
Progress Energy Inc 410 S Wilmington St	Raleigh	NC	27602	919-546-6111	546-7784
NYSE: PGN ■ *TF:* 800-452-2777 ■ *Web:* www.progress-energy.com					
Public Service Enterprise Group Inc 80 Park Plaza	Newark	NJ	07102	973-430-7000	623-5389
NYSE: PEG ■ *TF Cust Svc:* 800-436-7734 ■ *Web:* www.pseg.com					
Puget Energy Inc 10885 NE 4th St	Bellevue	WA	98004	425-454-6363	424-6728
NYSE: PSD					
Questar Corp 180 E 100 South PO Box 45360	Salt Lake City	UT	84145	801-324-5000	324-3880
NYSE: STR ■ *TF:* 800-323-5517 ■ *Web:* www.questarcorp.com					
RGC Resources Inc 519 Kimball Ave	Roanoke	VA	24016	540-777-4427	777-3957*
NASDAQ: RGCO ■ **Fax:* Hum Res					
RGS Energy Group Inc 89 East Ave	Rochester	NY	14649	585-771-4444	724-8668
SCANA Corp 1426 Main St	Columbia	SC	29210	803-748-3000	786-4552
NYSE: SCG ■ *TF:* 800-251-7234 ■ *Web:* www.scana.com					
SEMCO Energy Inc 1411 3rd St Suite A	Port Huron	MI	48060	810-987-2200	987-7638
NYSE: SEN ■ *Web:* www.semcoenergy.com					
Sempra Energy Corp 101 Ash St	San Diego	CA	92101	619-696-2000	696-9202
NYSE: SRE ■ *TF:* 800-411-7343 ■ *Web:* www.sempra.com					
Sierra Pacific Resources 6226 W Sahara Ave	Las Vegas	NV	89146	702-367-5000	367-5053
NYSE: SRP ■ *TF:* 800-331-3103 ■ *Web:* www.sierrapacific.com					
SJW Corp 374 W Santa Clara St	San Jose	CA	95196	408-279-7900	279-7917
NYSE: SJW					
South Jersey Industries Inc Rt 54 1 S Jersey Plaza	Folsom	NJ	08037	609-561-9000	561-8225
NYSE: SJI ■ *TF Cust Svc:* 888-766-9900 ■ *Web:* www.sjindustries.com					
Southern Co 270 Peachtree St	Atlanta	GA	30303	404-506-5000	
NYSE: SO ■ *Web:* www.southernco.com					
Sprint Nextel Corp 2001 Edmund Halley Dr	Reston	VA	20191	703-433-4000	327-5182*
NYSE: S ■ **Fax Area Code:* 800 ■ *Web:* www.sprint.com					
Tokyo Gas Co Ltd 405 Lexington Ave 33rd Fl	New York	NY	10174	646-865-0577	865-0592
Web: www.tokyo-gas.co.jp/					
TOTAL America Services Inc 100 Pavonia Ave Suite 401	Jersey City	NJ	07310	201-626-3500	626-4004
TXU Corp 1601 Bryan St Energy Plaza	Dallas	TX	75201	214-812-4600	812-8419
NYSE: TXU ■ *Web:* www.txucorp.com					
UGI Corp 460 N Gulph Rd	King of Prussia	PA	19406	610-337-1000	992-3215*
NYSE: UGI ■ **Fax:* Hum Res ■ *Web:* www.ugicorp.com					
UIL Holdings Corp 157 Church St	New Haven	CT	06510	203-499-2000	499-3664
NYSE: UIL ■ *TF:* 800-722-5584 ■ *Web:* www.uil.com					
UniSource Energy Corp 1 S Church Ave	Tucson	AZ	85701	520-571-4000	884-3601
NYSE: UNS ■ *TF:* 800-328-8853 ■ *Web:* www.unisourceenergy.com					
United Water Resources Inc 200 Old Hook Rd	Harrington Park	NJ	07640	201-767-9300	767-7142*
**Fax:* Hum Res ■ *Web:* www.unitedwater.com					
Unitil Corp 6 Liberty Ln W	Hampton	NH	03842	603-772-0775	773-6605
AMEX: UTL ■ *Web:* www.unitil.com					
Vectren Corp 411 NW Riverside Dr	Evansville	IN	47708	812-491-4000	
NYSE: VVC ■ *TF:* 800-227-1376 ■ *Web:* www.vectren.com					
Westar Energy Inc 818 S Kansas Ave	Topeka	KS	66612	785-575-6300	575-8547*
NYSE: WR ■ **Fax:* Cust Svc ■ *TF Cust Svc:* 800-383-1183 ■ *Web:* www.wr.com					
WGL Holdings Inc 101 Constitution Ave NW	Washington	DC	20080	703-750-2000	750-4858
NYSE: WGL ■ *TF:* 800-752-7520 ■ *Web:* www.wglholdings.com					
Wisconsin Energy Corp 231 W Michigan St	Milwaukee	WI	53203	414-221-2345	221-4906*
NYSE: WEC ■ **Fax:* Mktg ■ *TF:* 800-558-3303 ■ *Web:* www.wisconsinenergy.com					

364 HOME FURNISHINGS - WHOL

Company	City	State	Zip	Phone	Fax
AA Importing Co Inc 7700 Hall St	Saint Louis	MO	63147	314-383-8800	383-2608
TF Cust Svc: 800-325-0602 ■ *Web:* www.aaimporting.com					
Acme Linen Co Inc 5136 E Triggs St	City of Commerce	CA	90022	323-266-4000	267-5771
TF: 800-255-2263 ■ *Web:* www.acmelinen.com					
Adleta Co 1645 Diplomat Dr Suite 200	Carrollton	TX	75006	972-620-5600	620-5666
TF: 800-423-5382 ■ *Web:* www.adleta.com					
Allure Home Creation Co Inc 85 Fulton St	Boonton	NJ	07005	973-402-8888	334-2383
American Accessories International Inc 301 E Church Ave	Knoxville	TN	37915	865-525-9100	525-0889
B & F System Inc 3920 S Walton Walker Blvd	Dallas	TX	75236	214-333-2111	333-2137
Web: www.bnfusa.com					
Baker Hospitality a Div of Dan River Inc 2291 Memorial Dr	Danville	VA	24541	804-799-7000	799-7276
TF: 877-622-5376					
Bishop Distributing Co 5200 36th St SE	Grand Rapids	MI	49512	616-942-9734	942-6073
TF Cust Svc: 800-748-0363 ■ *Web:* www.bishopdistributing.com					
Boston Warehouse Trading Corp 59 Davis Ave	Norwood	MA	02062	781-769-8550	769-9468
TF: 888-923-2982 ■ *Web:* www.bwtc.com					
BR Funsten & Co 825 Van Ness Ave Suite 201	San Francisco	CA	94109	415-674-0530	674-3452
TF: 800-999-9260 ■ *Web:* www.brfunsten.com					
CCA Global Partners 4301 Earth City Expy	Earth City	MO	63045	314-506-0000	291-6674
TF: 800-466-6984 ■ *Web:* www.ccaglobal.com					
CDC Distributors 10511 Medallion Dr	Cincinnati	OH	45241	513-771-3100	771-2920
Decorative Crafts Inc 50 Chestnut St	Greenwich	CT	06830	203-531-1500	531-1590
TF: 800-431-4455 ■ *Web:* www.decorativecrafts.com					
Decorize Inc 1938 E Phelps St	Springfield	MO	65802	417-879-3326	879-3330
AMEX: DCZ ■ *TF:* 877-669-3326 ■ *Web:* www.decorize.com					
Dimock Gould & Co 190 22nd St	Moline	IL	61265	309-797-0650	764-9922
TF: 800-274-4013					
Fabricut Inc 9303 E 46th St	Tulsa	OK	74145	918-622-7700	627-1916
TF: 800-999-8200 ■ *Web:* www.fabricut.com					
Florstar Sales Inc 1075 Taylor Rd	Romeoville	IL	60446	815-836-2800	836-2820
TF: 800-942-6285 ■ *Web:* www.florstar.com					
Hoboken Floors 5600 Bucknell Dr Sw	Atlanta	GA	30336	404-629-1425	349-9975
TF: 877-356-2687 ■ *Web:* www.hobokenfloors.com					
Interstate Supply Co 4445 Gustine Ave	Saint Louis	MO	63116	314-481-2222	481-8435
TF: 800-324-3535 ■ *Web:* www.interstatesupplyco.com					
Jacobs Trading Co 13505 Industrial Park Blvd	Plymouth	MN	55441	763-843-2000	843-2101
Web: www.jacobstrading.com					
James G Hardy & Co 249-19 148th Rd	Rosedale	NY	11422	212-689-6680	686-1827
TF: 800-847-4076 ■ *Web:* www.hardylinen.com					
Javic Wholesale Co 5400 S 27th St	Milwaukee	WI	53221	414-761-5404	761-5420
JJ Haines & Co Inc 6950 Aviation Blvd	Glen Burnie	MD	21061	410-760-4040	760-4045
TF: 800-922-9248 ■ *Web:* www.jjhaines.com					
Kinder-Harris Inc 203 E 22nd St	Stuttgart	AR	72160	870-673-1518	673-4319
TF: 800-688-8839 ■ *Web:* www.kinderharris.com					
KovalWilliamson 11208 47th Ave W	Mukilteo	WA	98275	425-347-4249	347-2368
TF: 800-972-4782 ■ *Web:* www.kwawest.com					
Kraus Floors 2785 Hwy 55	Eagan	MN	55121	651-454-1700	454-0316
TF: 800-328-2020					
Larson Distributing Co Inc 5925 N Broadway	Denver	CO	80216	303-296-7253	296-8583
TF: 800-736-3750 ■ *Web:* www.larsondistributing.com					
Longust Distributing Inc 2432 W Birchwood Ave	Mesa	AZ	85202	480-820-6244	345-0324
TF: 800-352-0521 ■ *Web:* www.longust.com					
Louis Bornstein & Co 321 Washington St	Somerville	MA	02143	617-776-3555	623-1913
TF Sales: 800-842-1111					
M Block & Sons Inc 5020 W 73rd St	Bedford Park	IL	60638	708-728-8400	728-0022
TF: 800-621-8845 ■ *Web:* www.mblock.com					
Momeni Inc 36 E 31st St 2nd Fl	New York	NY	10016	212-532-9577	779-9568
TF: 800-536-6778 ■ *Web:* www.momeni.com					
Mottahedeh & Co 41 Madison Ave	New York	NY	10010	212-685-3050	213-3978
TF: 800-242-3050 ■ *Web:* www.mottahedeh.com					
OneCoast Network LLC 2025 Monroe Dr	Atlanta	GA	30324	404-836-8900	836-8503
Web: www.onecoast.com					
Paterson Co Inc PO Box 7505	Mobile	AL	36670	251-443-6744	443-6746
Peking Handicraft Inc 1388 San Mateo Ave	South San Francisco	CA	94080	650-871-3788	871-3781
TF: 800-872-6888 ■ *Web:* www.pkhc.com					
Revere Mills Inc 3000 S River Rd	Des Plaines	IL	60018	847-759-6800	759-6840
TF: 800-367-8258					
Sobel Westex Inc 2670 Southwestern Ave	Las Vegas	NV	89109	702-735-4973	735-4957
TF: 800-282-3041 ■ *Web:* www.sobelwestex.com					
Stark Carpet Corp D & D Bldg 979 3rd Ave 11th Fl	New York	NY	10022	212-752-9000	758-4342
TF: 800-223-1224 ■ *Web:* www.starkcarpetcorp.com					
Trade Am International Inc 6580 Jimmy Carter Blvd	Norcross	GA	30071	770-263-6144	333-9448*
**Fax Area Code:* 800 ■ **Fax:* Cust Svc ■ *Web:* www.tradeam.com					
Wanke Cascade Co 6330 N Cutter Cir	Portland	OR	97217	503-289-8609	285-5640
TF: 800-365-5053 ■ *Web:* www.wanke.com					
WestPoint Home Inc Sales Div 28 E 28th St	New York	NY	10016	212-930-2000	679-2989
WMF/USA 85 Price Pkwy	Farmingdale	NY	11735	631-293-3990	293-3561
TF: 800-999-6347 ■ *Web:* www.wmf-usa.com					
Zak Designs Inc 1603 S Garfield Rd	Airway Heights	WA	99001	509-244-0555	244-0704
TF: 800-331-1089 ■ *Web:* www.zak.com					

365 HOME FURNISHINGS STORES

SEE ALSO Department Stores p. 1586; Furniture Stores p. 1685

Company	City	State	Zip	Phone	Fax
Altmeyer Home Stores Inc 6515 Rt 22	Delmont	PA	15626	724-468-3434	468-3233
TF: 800-394-6628 ■ *Web:* www.altmeyers.com					
Anna's Linens Inc 3550 Hyland Ave	Costa Mesa	CA	92626	714-850-0504	850-9170
Web: www.annaslinens.com					
Bazaar Home Fashions 7958 Ohio River Rd	Wheelersburg	OH	45694	740-574-0777	574-0779
TF: 877-764-0305 ■ *Web:* www.bazaarhomefashions.com					
Bed Bath & Beyond Inc 650 Liberty Ave	Union	NJ	07083	908-688-0888	688-6483
NASDAQ: BBBY ■ *TF:* 800-462-3966 ■ *Web:* www.bedbathandbeyond.com					
Besco Electric Supply Co 711 S 14th St	Leesburg	FL	34748	352-787-4542	365-0554
TF: 800-541-6618 ■ *Web:* www.bescoelectric.com					
Bridge Kitchenware Inc 711 3rd Ave	New York	NY	10017	212-688-4220	758-5387
TF: 800-274-3435 ■ *Web:* bridgekitchenware.com					
Bromberg & Co Inc 123 N 20th St	Birmingham	AL	35203	205-252-0221	458-0458
TF: 800-633-4616 ■ *Web:* www.brombergs.com					
Calvert Retail LP 100 W Rockland Rd Suite A PO Box 302	Montchanin	DE	19710	302-622-8811	622-8602
TF: 800-747-7224 ■ *Web:* www.calvertretail.com					
Carolina Pottery Inc 1000 Industrial Park Dr PO Box 2400	Smithfield	NC	27577	919-934-0309	989-6282
Web: www.carolinapotteryusa.com					
Chef's Catalog 5070 Centennial Blvd	Colorado Springs	CO	80919	972-969-3100	967-2433*
**Fax Area Code:* 800 ■ *TF Cust Svc:* 800-884-2433 ■ *Web:* www.chefscatalog.com					
Compleat Kitchen 240 Puuhale Rd Suite F	Honolulu	HI	96819	808-845-8444	841-5541
Web: www.compleatkitchen.com					

Company	City	State	Zip	Phone	Fax
Container Store 500 Freeport Pkwy	Coppell	TX	75019	972-538-6000	
TF: 800-733-3532 ■ *Web:* www.containerstore.com					
Cooking.com 2850 Ocean Park Blvd Suite 310	Santa Monica	CA	90405	310-450-3270	450-0615
TF: 800-663-8810 ■ *Web:* www.cooking.com					
Cost Plus World Market 200 4th St	Oakland	CA	94607	510-893-7300	893-3681
NASDAQ: CPWM ■ *TF:* 800-777-4665 ■ *Web:* www.worldmarket.com					
Cost Plus Inc DBA Cost Plus World Market 200 4th St	Oakland	CA	94607	510-893-7300	893-3681
NASDAQ: CPWM ■ *TF:* 800-777-4665 ■ *Web:* www.worldmarket.com					
Crate & Barrel 1250 Techny Rd	Northbrook	IL	60062	847-272-2888	272-5276
Web: www.crateandbarrel.com					
Dansk International Designs Ltd 1414 Radcliff St	Bristol PA	NJ	19007	267-525-7800	844-1576*
**Fax Area Code:* 609 ■ *TF Cust Svc:* 800-293-2675 ■ *Web:* www.dansk.com					
Design Within Reach Inc 225 Bush St 20th Fl	San Francisco	CA	94104	415-676-6500	676-6794
NASDAQ: DWRI ■ *TF:* 800-944-2233 ■ *Web:* www.dwr.com					
DirectBuy Inc 8450 Broadway	Merrillville	IN	46410	219-755-6211	755-6208
TF: 800-827-6400 ■ *Web:* www.directbuy.com					
EBSCO Industries Inc Military Service Co Div					
PO Box 1943	Birmingham	AL	35201	205-991-6600	408-4826
TF: 800-255-3722 ■ *Web:* www.militaryservicecompany.com					
Edward Joy Lighting & Electric Co 905 Canal St	Syracuse	NY	13217	315-474-3361	479-8604
Web: www.edwardjoyelectric.com					
Euromarket Designs Inc DBA Crate & Barrel					
1250 Techny Rd	Northbrook	IL	60062	847-272-2888	272-5276
Web: www.crateandbarrel.com					
Fina Michael C Inc 545 5th Ave	New York	NY	10017	212-557-2500	557-3862
TF: 800-289-3462 ■ *Web:* www.michaelcfina.com					
Flowerama of America Inc 3165 W Airline Hwy	Waterloo	IA	50703	319-291-6004	291-8676
TF: 800-728-6004 ■ *Web:* www.flowerama.com					
Foreside Co 33 Hutcherson Dr	Gorham	ME	04038	207-854-4000	854-3300
TF Cust Svc: 800-359-8380 ■ *Web:* www.foreside.com					
FurnitureFind.com Inc 311 W Jefferson Blvd	South Bend	IN	46601	574-299-2700	299-2645
TF: 800-362-7632 ■ *Web:* www.furniturefind.com					
Garden Ridge Corp 19411 Atrium Pl Suite 170	Houston	TX	77084	281-579-7901	578-5379
Web: www.gardenridge.com					
Geary's Stores Inc 351 N Beverly Dr	Beverly Hills	CA	90210	310-273-4741	859-8950
TF: 800-243-2797 ■ *Web:* www.gearys.com					
Glaze Supply Co Inc 117 W Cuyler St	Dalton	GA	30720	706-278-3663	278-7435
Gracious Home 1220 3rd Ave	New York	NY	10021	212-517-6300	249-1534
TF: 800-338-7809 ■ *Web:* www.gracioushome.com					
Granite City Electric Supply Co 19 Quincy Ave	Quincy	MA	02169	617-472-6500	472-8661
TF: 800-850-9400 ■ *Web:* www.granitecityelectric.com					
Gump's 135 Post St	San Francisco	CA	94108	415-982-1616	984-9374
TF: 800-766-7628 ■ *Web:* www.gumps.com					
Habitat Housewares					
3801 Old Seward Hwy Suite 7 University Center Mall	Anchorage	AK	99503	907-561-1856	563-5863
TF: 800-770-1856 ■ *Web:* www.habitathousewares.com					
Hammacher Schlemmer & Co 9307 N Milwaukee Ave	Niles	IL	60714	847-581-8600	581-8616
TF: 800-233-4800 ■ *Web:* www.hammacher.com					
Happi Stores Inc 6645 Poplar Ave Suite 105	Germantown	TN	38138	901-758-0034	758-8018
Home Accents Mart 2300 McFarland Blvd	Northport	AL	35476	205-339-6550	339-6553
HomeGoods Inc 770 Cochituate Rd	Framingham	MA	01701	508-390-3000	
Web: www.homegoods.com					
HomePortfolio Inc 288 Walnut St Suite 200	Newton	MA	02460	617-965-0565	965-4082
TF: 800-246-8136 ■ *Web:* www.homeportfolio.com					
International Cutlery Ltd 155 E 55th St Suite 6D	New York	NY	10022	212-924-7300	865-0806*
**Fax Area Code:* 646 ■ *TF:* 866-487-6164 ■ *Web:* www.internationalcutlery.com					
Jackalope Pottery 2820 Cerrillos Rd	Santa Fe	NM	87507	505-471-8539	471-6710
TF: 800-753-7757 ■ *Web:* www.jackalope.com					
Joy Edward Lighting & Electric Co 905 Canal St	Syracuse	NY	13217	315-474-3361	479-8604
Web: www.edwardjoyelectric.com					
Kirkland's Inc 805 N Parkway	Jackson	TN	38305	731-668-2444	664-9345
NASDAQ: KIRK ■ *TF:* 866-828-2444 ■ *Web:* www.kirklands.com					
Kitchen Collection Inc 71 E Water St	Chillicothe	OH	45601	740-773-9150	774-0590
TF: 800-292-9150 ■ *Web:* www.kitchencollection.com					
Kitchen Fantasy 27576 Ynez Rd Suite H9	Temecula	CA	92591	951-693-4264	693-4265
Web: www.kitchenfantasy.com					
Linens 'n Things Inc 6 Brighton Rd	Clifton	NJ	07015	973-778-1300	778-0822
TF: 866-568-7378 ■ *Web:* www.lnt.com					
Luxury Linens Corp 1830 Rt 130 N	Burlington	NJ	08016	609-387-7800	239-8242
Marburn Stores Inc 225 Walker St	Cliffside Park	NJ	07010	201-943-0222	943-0206
TF Cust Svc: 888-627-2876 ■ *Web:* www.marburn.com					
Mattress Firm Inc 5815 Gulf Fwy	Houston	TX	77023	713-923-1090	923-1096
Web: www.mattressfirm.com					
Michael C Fina Inc 545 5th Ave	New York	NY	10017	212-557-2500	557-3862
TF: 800-289-3462 ■ *Web:* www.michaelcfina.com					
Mikasa Inc 100 Plaza Dr	Secaucus	NJ	07094	201-867-9210	867-0580
TF Cust Svc: 800-833-4681 ■ *Web:* www.mikasa.com					
Military Service Co Div EBSCO Industries Inc					
PO Box 1943	Birmingham	AL	35201	205-991-6600	408-4826
TF: 800-255-3722 ■ *Web:* www.militaryservicecompany.com					
Pier 1 Imports Inc 100 Pier 1 Pl	Fort Worth	TX	76102	817-878-8000	
NYSE: PIR ■ *TF:* 800-245-4595 ■ *Web:* www.pier1.com					
Pottery Barn 151 Union St	San Francisco	CA	94111	415-421-7900	
Web: ww2.potterybarn.com					
Pratesi Linens Inc 381 Park Ave S Suite 1223	New York	NY	10016	212-689-3150	889-6721
TF: 800-332-6925 ■ *Web:* www.pratesi.com					
Replacements Ltd PO Box 26029	Greensboro	NC	27420	336-697-3000	697-3100
TF: 800-737-5223 ■ *Web:* www.replacements.com					
Restoration Hardware Inc 15 Koch Rd Suite J	Corte Madera	CA	94925	415-924-1005	927-9133
NASDAQ: RSTO ■ *Web:* www.restorationhardware.com					
Royal Doulton USA Inc 200 Cottontail Ln	Somerset	NJ	08873	732-356-7880	764-4974
TF: 800-682-4462 ■ *Web:* www.royaldoulton.com					
Seattle Lighting Fixture Co 222 2nd Ave Ext S	Seattle	WA	98104	206-622-1962	447-1660
TF Cust Svc: 800-689-1000 ■ *Web:* www.seattlelighting.com					
Shreve Crump & Low Co Inc 440 Boylston St	Boston	MA	02116	617-267-9100	247-6450
TF: 800-225-7088 ■ *Web:* www.shrevecrumpandlow.com					
Sultan & Sons 650 SW 9th Terr	Pompano Beach	FL	33069	954-782-6600	788-5847
TF: 800-299-6601 ■ *Web:* www.sultanandsons.com					
Sur La Table 5701 6th Ave S Suite 486	Seattle	WA	98108	206-682-7175	
TF: 800-243-0852 ■ *Web:* www.surlatable.com					
Syratech Corp 175 McClellan Hwy	East Boston	MA	02128	617-561-2200	568-9021
TF: 888-747-0475 ■ *Web:* www.syratech.com					
TJX Cos Inc 770 Cochituate Rd	Framingham	MA	01701	508-390-3000	390-5391*
NYSE: TJX ■ **Fax:* Hum Res ■ *Web:* www.tjx.com					
Villeroy & Boch Tableware Ltd 5 Vaughn Dr Suite 303	Princeton	NJ	08540	609-734-7800	734-7840
TF: 800-845-5376 ■ *Web:* www.villeroy-boch.com					
Waterford Wedgwood USA Inc 1330 Campus Pkwy	Wall	NJ	07719	732-938-5800	938-6915
Web: www.wwusa.com					
Welcome Home Inc 309 Raleigh St	Wilmington	NC	28412	910-791-4312	791-4945
TF: 800-348-4088					
William Glen Inc 2651 El Paseo Ln	Sacramento	CA	95821	916-485-3000	482-3562
TF: 800-842-3322 ■ *Web:* www.williamglen.com					
Williams-Sonoma Inc 3250 Van Ness Ave	San Francisco	CA	94109	415-421-7900	
NYSE: WSM ■ *TF Cust Svc:* 800-541-1262 ■ *Web:* www.williams-sonoma.com					
Williamsburg Pottery Factory Inc Rt 60 W	Lightfoot	VA	23090	757-564-3326	564-8241
TF: 800-768-8379 ■ *Web:* www.williamsburgpottery.com					
World Market DBA Cost Plus World Market 200 4th St	Oakland	CA	94607	510-893-7300	893-3681
NASDAQ: CPWM ■ *TF:* 800-777-4665 ■ *Web:* www.worldmarket.com					
Z Gallerie Inc 1855 W 139th St	Gardena	CA	90249	310-630-1200	527-2792
TF: 800-358-8288 ■ *Web:* www.zgallerie.com					
Zabar's & Co Inc 2245 Broadway	New York	NY	10024	212-787-2000	580-4477
TF: 800-697-6301 ■ *Web:* www.zabars.com					

366 HOME HEALTH SERVICES

SEE ALSO Hospices p. 1791

Company	City	State	Zip	Phone	Fax
Alacare Home Health & Hospice 2400 John Hawkins Pkwy	Birmingham	AL	35244	205-981-8000	981-8743
TF: 800-852-4724 ■ *Web:* www.alacare.com					
Allied Healthcare International Inc 245 Park AVe 24th Fl	New York	NY	10167	212-750-0064	750-7221
NASDAQ: AHCI					
Almost Family Inc 9510 Ormsby Station Rd Suite 300	Louisville	KY	40223	502-891-1000	891-8067
NASDAQ: AFAM ■ *TF:* 800-845-6987 ■ *Web:* www.almost-family.com					
Amedisys Inc 5959 S Sherwood Forest Blvd Suite 300	Baton Rouge	LA	70816	225-292-2031	292-8163
NASDAQ: AMED ■ *TF:* 800-467-2662 ■ *Web:* www.amedisys.com					
American HomePatient Inc 5200 Maryland Way Suite 400	Brentwood	TN	37027	615-221-8884	373-1947
TF: 800-890-7271 ■ *Web:* www.ahom.com					
Apria Healthcare Group Inc 26220 Enterprise Ct	Lake Forest	CA	92630	949-639-2000	
NYSE: AHG ■ *TF:* 800-277-4288 ■ *Web:* www.apria.com					
Arcadia Health Care 26777 Central Park Blvd Suite 200	Southfield	MI	48076	248-352-7530	352-7534
TF: 800-733-8427 ■ *Web:* www.arcadiaservices.com/homecare.htm					
Aroostook Home Health Services 658 Main St Suite 2	Caribou	ME	04736	207-492-8290	492-8245
TF: 877-688-9977 ■ *Web:* www.ahhs.net					
Ashtabula Regional Home Health Services PO Box 1428	Ashtabula	OH	44005	440-992-4663	992-0687
TF: 800-722-3330 ■ *Web:* www.neoseniorlink.org/Ashtabularegionalhomehealthservices					
Bayada Nurses Home Care Specialists 290 Chester Ave	Moorestown	NJ	08057	856-231-1000	231-1955
Web: www.bayada.com					
Building Blocks Pediatric Home Health Services					
9272 Jeronimo Rd Suite 106	Irvine	CA	92618	949-206-6899	206-6898
TF: 800-346-9490 ■ *Web:* www.care4kids.com					
Care Partners 68 Sweeten Creek Rd	Asheville	NC	28803	828-252-2255	252-9355
TF: 800-627-1533 ■ *Web:* www.carepartners.org					
CareSouth Homecare Professionals					
3626 Walton Way Ext Suite 2	Augusta	GA	30909	706-855-5533	854-7398
TF: 800-241-3363 ■ *Web:* www.caresouth.com					
Carter Healthcare 3105 S Meridian Ave	Oklahoma City	OK	73119	405-947-7700	947-7300
TF: 888-951-1112 ■ *Web:* www.carterhealthcare.com					
ComForcare Senior Services Inc					
2510 Telegraph Rd Suite 100	Bloomfield Hills	MI	48302	248-745-9700	745-9763
TF: 800-886-4044 ■ *Web:* www.comforcare.com					
Comfort Keepers Franchising Inc 6640 Poe Ave Suite 200	Dayton	OH	45414	937-264-1933	264-3103
TF: 800-387-2415 ■ *Web:* www.comfortkeepers.com					
Continucare Corp 7200 Corporate Center Dr Suite 600	Miami	FL	33126	305-500-2000	500-2080
AMEX: CNU ■ *TF:* 888-350-7515 ■ *Web:* www.continucare.com					
Coram Healthcare Corp 1675 Broadway Suite 900	Denver	CO	80202	303-292-4973	298-0043
TF: 800-267-2642 ■ *Web:* www.coramhc.com					
Gentiva Health Services Inc					
3 Huntington Quadrangle Suite 200S	Melville	NY	11747	631-501-7000	501-7144
NASDAQ: GTIV ■ *TF:* 866-436-8487 ■ *Web:* www.gentiva.com					
Griswold Special Care Inc 717 Bethlehem Pike Suite 300	Erdenheim	PA	19038	215-402-0200	402-0202
TF: 888-777-7630 ■ *Web:* www.griswoldspecialcare.com					
Help At Home Inc 1 N State St Suite 1500	Chicago	IL	60602	312-762-0900	704-0000
TF: 800-422-1755 ■ *Web:* www.helpathome.com					
Home Health Corp of America Inc					
620 Freedom Business Center Suite 105	King of Prussia	PA	19406	610-205-2440	205-2468
TF: 800-872-5230 ■ *Web:* www.hhcainc.com					
Home Helpers Inc 10700 Montgomery Rd	Cincinnati	OH	45242	513-563-8339	563-2691
TF: 800-216-4196 ■ *Web:* www.homehelpers.cc					
Home Instead Inc 13330 California St Suite 200	Omaha	NE	68154	402-498-4466	498-5757
TF: 888-484-5759 ■ *Web:* www.homeinstead.com					
Home IV Care & Nutritional Service PO Box 700	Stuarts Draft	VA	24477	540-932-3000	932-3028
TF: 800-552-6576 ■ *Web:* www.homeivcare.com					
HOMECALL Inc 1080 W Patrick St Suite 1043	Frederick	MD	21703	301-663-8818	644-2990*
**Fax Area Code:* 800 ■ *TF:* 800-444-0097 ■ *Web:* www.homecallinc.com					
Homewatch CareGivers 2865 S Colorado Blvd	Denver	CO	80222	303-758-7290	758-1724
TF: 800-777-9770 ■ *Web:* www.homewatchcaregivers.com					
Hospice Atlanta-Visiting Nurse Health System					
1244 Park Vista Dr	Atlanta	GA	30319	404-869-3000	869-3098
TF: 800-287-7849 ■ *Web:* www.vnhs.org					
Interim HealthCare Inc 1601 Sawgrass Corporate Pkwy	Sunrise	FL	33323	954-858-6000	858-2820
TF: 800-338-7786 ■ *Web:* www.interimhealthcare.com					
Kelly Home Care Services Inc 999 W Big Beaver Rd	Troy	MI	48084	248-362-4444	244-4922*
**Fax:* Hum Res ■ *TF:* 800-937-5355 ■ *Web:* www.kellyassistedliving.com					
Legum Home Health Care PO Box 700	Stuarts Draft	VA	24477	540-932-3000	932-3028
TF: 800-552-6576					
LHC Group LLC 420 W Pinhook Rd Suite A	Lafayette	LA	70503	337-233-1307	235-8037
NASDAQ: LHCG ■ *TF:* 800-489-1307 ■ *Web:* www.lhcgroup.com					
Lincare Holdings Inc 19387 US 19 N	Clearwater	FL	33764	727-530-7700	532-9692
NASDAQ: LNCR ■ *TF:* 800-284-2006 ■ *Web:* www.lincare.com					
Living Assistance Services Inc 28 W Eagle Rd Suite 204	Havertown	PA	19083	610-924-0630	924-9690
TF: 800-365-4189 ■ *Web:* www.livingassistance.com					
Maxim Healthcare Services 7227 Lee Deforest Dr	Columbia	MD	21046	410-910-1500	910-1600
TF: 800-796-2946 ■ *Web:* www.maxhealth.com					
Medical Center at Princeton Home Care 208 Bunn Dr	Princeton	NJ	08540	609-497-4900	497-4933
TF: 800-584-4153 ■ *Web:* www.princetonhcs.org					
Medical Services of America Inc 171 Monroe Ln	Lexington	SC	29072	803-957-0500	342-6190*
**Fax Area Code:* 888 ■ *TF:* 800-845-5850 ■ *Web:* www.msa-corp.com					
National Home Health Care Corp 700 White Plains Rd	Scarsdale	NY	10583	914-722-9000	722-9239
NASDAQ: NHHC ■ *Web:* www.nhhc.net					
New York Health Care Inc 1850 McDonald Ave	Brooklyn	NY	11223	718-375-6700	375-1555
Web: www.nyhc.com					
Option Care Inc 485 Half Day Rd Suite 300	Buffalo Grove	IL	60089	847-465-2100	913-8974
NASDAQ: OPTN ■ *TF:* 800-879-6137 ■ *Web:* www.optioncare.com					
Pediatric Services of America Inc 310 Technology Pkwy	Norcross	GA	30092	770-441-1580	417-3252*
NASDAQ: PSAI ■ **Fax:* Hum Res ■ *TF:* 800-950-1580 ■ *Web:* www.psakids.com					
Personal-Touch Home Care Inc 186-18 Hillside Ave	Jamaica	NY	11432	718-468-2500	264-5834*
**Fax:* Hum Res ■ *TF:* 800-937-4747 ■ *Web:* www.pthomecare.com					
Praxair Healthcare Services 2155 IH-10 E	Beaumont	TX	77701	409-835-3939	835-0382
TF: 800-871-1386 ■ *Web:* www.praxair.com					
Right at Home Inc 11949 Q St Suite 100	Omaha	NE	68137	402-697-7537	697-0289
TF: 877-697-7537 ■ *Web:* www.rightathome.net					
RoTech Medical Corp 3600 Timeland Rd Suite 114	Orlando	FL	32811	407-246-1226	841-1481
TF: 800-357-3835					
Selfhelp Community Services Inc 520 8th Ave 5th Fl	New York	NY	10018	212-971-7600	967-4784
Web: www.selfhelp.net					
Sentara Home Care Services					
535 Independence Pkwy Suite 200	Chesapeake	VA	23320	757-382-4980	382-4957
TF: 888-461-5649 ■ *Web:* www.sentara.com/facilities_services					

				Phone	Fax
Sta-Home Health Agency Inc 406 Briarwood Dr Bldg 200	Jackson	MS	39206	601-956-5100	956-3003
TF: 800-782-4663 ■ *Web:* www.sta-home.com					
Star MultiCare Services Inc					
33 Walt Whitman Rd Suite 302	Huntington Station	NY	11746	631-423-6689	427-5466
Web: www.starmulticare.com					
Tender Loving Care Health Care Services (TLC)					
1983 Marcus Ave Suite 200	Lake Success	NY	11042	516-358-1000	358-1034
Web: www.tlcathome.com					
Trinity Home Care 114-02 15th Ave	College Point	NY	11356	718-961-1634	762-8741
TF: 877-687-7369 ■ *Web:* www.trinityhomecare.com					
Ultra Care Home Medical 1815 Gardner Rd	Broadview	IL	60155	800-244-7404	450-1638*
*Fax Area Code: 708 ■ *TF:* 800-222-9444 ■ *Web:* www.ultracarehm.com					
Visiting Angels 28 W Eagle Rd Suite 204	Havertown	PA	19083	610-924-0630	924-9690
TF: 800-365-4189 ■ *Web:* www.livingassistance.com					
Visiting Nurse Corp of Colorado 390 Grant St	Denver	CO	80203	303-744-6363	698-6371
TF: 888-862-9693 ■ *Web:* www.vnacolorado.org					
VITAS Healthcare Corp 100 S Biscayne Blvd Suite 1500	Miami	FL	33131	305-374-4143	350-6784*
*Fax: Acctg ■ *TF:* 800-950-9200 ■ *Web:* www.vitas.com					
We Care Health Services Inc 151 Bloor St W Suite 602	Toronto	ON	M5S1S4	416-922-7601	922-6280
TF: 888-429-3227 ■ *Web:* www.wecare.ca					

367 HOME IMPROVEMENT CENTERS

SEE ALSO Construction Materials p. 1549

				Phone	Fax
Ace Hardware Corp 2200 Kensington Ct	Oak Brook	IL	60523	630-990-6600	990-6572*
*Fax: Mktg ■ *Web:* www.acehardware.com					
Alaska Industrial Hardware Inc 2192 Viking Dr	Anchorage	AK	99501	907-276-7201	258-3054
TF: 800-478-7201 ■ *Web:* www.aihalaska.com					
All American Home Center 7201 E Firestone Blvd	Downey	CA	90241	562-927-8666	928-0633
Web: www.aahc.com					
Arlington Coal & Lumber Co Inc 41 Park Ave	Arlington	MA	02476	781-643-8100	643-7414
TF: 800-649-8101 ■ *Web:* www.arlcoal.com					
Ashy Doug Building Materials Inc 4950 Johnston St	Lafayette	LA	70503	337-984-2110	989-9569
Web: www.dougashybuilding.com					
Aubuchon WE Co Inc 95 Aubuchon Dr	Westminster	MA	01473	978-874-0521	874-2096
TF: 800-282-4393 ■ *Web:* www.aubuchonhardware.com					
BGE Home Products & Services Inc 7161 Columbia Gateway	Columbia	MD	21046	410-720-6619	720-6244
TF: 888-243-4663 ■ *Web:* www.bgehome.com					
Big L Corp PO Box 134	Sheridan	MI	48884	989-291-3232	291-5751
Web: www.big-l-lumber.com					
BMC West Corp PO Box 70006	Boise	ID	83707	208-331-4300	331-4366
Web: www.bmcwest.com					
Busy Beaver Building Centers Inc					
3130 William Pitt Way Uparc Bldg A-6	Pittsburgh	PA	15238	412-828-2323	828-2395
Web: www.busybeaver.com					
Carter Cos 601 Tallmadge Rd	Kent	OH	44240	330-673-6100	678-6134
TF: 877-586-2374 ■ *Web:* www.carterlumber.com					
Carter-Jones Lumber Co 601 Tallmadge Rd	Kent	OH	44240	330-673-6100	678-6134
TF: 877-586-2374 ■ *Web:* www.carterlumber.com/main.asp?id=25					
Carter Lumber Co Inc 601 Tallmadge Rd	Kent	OH	44240	330-673-6100	678-6134
TF: 877-586-2374 ■ *Web:* www.carterlumber.com					
Choo Choo Build-it Mart 325 Commerce Loop	Vidalia	GA	30474	912-537-8964	537-4839
Web: www.choochoobuilditmart.com					
City Mill Co Ltd PO Box 1559	Honolulu	HI	96806	808-533-3811	524-8092*
*Fax: Hum Res ■ *Web:* www.citymill.com					
Contractor's Warehouse 3222 Winona Way Suite 201	North Highlands	CA	95660	916-331-5934	331-4658*
*Fax: Hum Res ■ *TF:* 800-789-8060 ■ *Web:* www.contractorswarehouse.com					
Cox Lumber Co 3300 Fairfield Ave S	Saint Petersburg	FL	33712	727-327-4503	327-5393
Web: www.coxlumber.com					
Dixieline Lumber Co Inc 3250 Sports Arena Blvd	San Diego	CA	92110	619-224-4120	225-8192
Web: www.dixieline.com					
Doug Ashy Building Materials Inc 4950 Johnston St	Lafayette	LA	70503	337-984-2110	989-9569
Web: www.dougashybuilding.com					
EBS Building Supplies 261 State St	Ellsworth	ME	04605	207-667-7134	667-6043
TF: 800-244-7134 ■ *Web:* www.ebsbuild.com					
EXPO Design Center 2455 Paces Ferry Rd	Atlanta	GA	30339	770-433-8211	384-2685*
*Fax: PR ■ *TF Cust Svc:* 800-553-3199 ■ *Web:* www.expo.com					
Ganahl Lumber Co 1220 E Ball Rd	Anaheim	CA	92805	714-772-5444	772-0639
Web: www.ganahl.com					
Grossman's Inc 90 Hawes Way	Stoughton	MA	02072	781-297-3300	297-0180
Web: www.bargain-outlets.com					
Grove Lumber & Hardware 2042 S Grove Ave	Ontario	CA	91761	909-947-0277	947-6917
Web: www.grovelumber.com					
H & E Do It Yourself Center Co 14021 Amargosa Rd	Victorville	CA	92392	760-241-7540	241-9084
Hacienda Home Centers Inc PO Box 30148	Albuquerque	NM	87190	505-884-8811	884-8959
Web: hacienda.doitbest.com					
Hayward Lumber Co 429 Front St	Salinas	CA	93901	831-755-8800	755-8821
Web: www.haywardlumber.com					
Home Depot Inc 2455 Paces Ferry Rd NW	Atlanta	GA	30339	770-433-8211	384-2356
NYSE: HD ■ *TF Cust Svc:* 800-553-3199 ■ *Web:* www.homedepot.com					
Lampert Yards Inc 1850 Como Ave	Saint Paul	MN	55108	651-695-3600	695-3601
Web: www.lampertyards.com					
Lester Building Supply 14 E Liberty St	Martinsville	VA	24112	276-638-8834	632-2117
Web: www.lestergroup.com/lhc/lhc.htm					
Lowe's Cos Inc 1000 Lowe's Blvd	Mooresville	NC	28117	704-758-1000	658-4766*
NYSE: LOW ■ *Fax Area Code: 336 ■ *TF:* 800-445-6937 ■ *Web:* www.lowes.com					
Lowe's Home Centers Inc PO Box 1111	North Wilkesboro	NC	28656	336-658-4000	658-4766
TF: 800-445-6937 ■ *Web:* www.lowes.com					
Lumbermens 3020 Willamette Dr NE	Lacey	WA	98516	360-456-1880	456-1884
TF: 800-842-8256 ■ *Web:* www.lumbermens-building.com					
MarJam Supply Co Inc 20 Rewe St	Brooklyn	NY	11211	718-388-6465	388-6737
TF: 800-462-7526 ■ *Web:* www.marjam.com					
McCoy's Building Supply Center Corp 1200 I-35 N	San Marcos	TX	78666	512-353-5400	395-6601
Web: www.mccoys.com					
Menard Inc 4777 Menard Dr	Eau Claire	WI	54703	715-876-5911	876-2868
Web: www.menards.com					
Mid-Cape Home Center 15 Main St	Orleans	MA	02653	508-255-0200	255-0599
National Home Centers Inc 1106 N Old Missouri Rd	Springdale	AR	72764	479-756-1700	927-5795
TF: 800-540-0529 ■ *Web:* www.nhci.com					
National Lumber 71 Maple St	Mansfield	MA	02048	508-339-8020	339-4518
TF: 800-370-9663 ■ *Web:* www.national-lumber.com					
Nickerson Lumber Co DBA Mid-Cape Home Center 15 Main St	Orleans	MA	02653	508-255-0200	255-0599
Northern Tool & Equipment Co 2800 Southcross Dr W	Burnsville	MN	55306	952-894-9510	894-1020
TF Cust Svc: 800-222-5381 ■ *Web:* www.northerntool.com					
Orchard Supply Hardware 6450 Via del Oro	San Jose	CA	95119	408-281-3500	365-2702*
*Fax: Mktg ■ *Web:* www.osh.com					
Ray Mart Inc PO Box 5548	Beaumont	TX	77726	409-835-4744	835-2208
RONA Inc 220 ch du Tremblay	Boucherville	QC	J4B8H7	514-599-5100	599-5137
Web: www.rona.ca					
Seigle's 1331 Davis Rd	Elgin	IL	60123	847-742-2000	697-6521
Web: www.seigles.com					
Spenard Builders Supply Inc 840 K St Suite 200	Anchorage	AK	99501	907-261-9120	261-9142
TF: 800-478-3141 ■ *Web:* www.sbsalaska.com					
Star Lumber & Supply Co Inc 325 S West St	Wichita	KS	67213	316-942-2221	941-0136
Web: www.starlumber.com					
Strober Organization Inc Furman St Pier 3	Brooklyn	NY	11201	718-875-9700	246-3080
Web: www.strober.com					
Sutherland Lumber Co 4000 Main St	Kansas City	MO	64111	816-756-3000	531-2930
TF: 800-821-2252 ■ *Web:* www.sutherlands.com					
True Value Co 8600 W Bryn Mawr Ave	Chicago	IL	60631	773-695-5000	695-6516
Web: www.truevaluecompany.com					
United Building Centers 125 W 5th St	Winona	MN	55987	507-452-2361	457-6780
Web: www.unitedbuildingcenters.com					
WE Aubuchon Co Inc 95 Aubuchon Dr	Westminster	MA	01473	978-874-0521	874-2096
TF: 800-282-4393 ■ *Web:* www.aubuchonhardware.com					
Youngdale's Inc 250 Market St	Turlock	CA	95380	209-632-3983	632-3032
Web: www.youngdales.com					

368 HOME INSPECTION SERVICES

				Phone	Fax
AmeriSpec Inc 889 Ridge Lake Blvd	Memphis	TN	38120	901-820-8500	820-8520
TF: 800-426-2270 ■ *Web:* www.amerispec.com					
BrickKicker Inc 849 N Ellsworth St	Naperville	IL	60563	630-420-9900	420-2270
TF: 800-821-1820 ■ *Web:* www.brickkicker.com					
HomeTeam Inspection Service Inc 575 Chamber Dr	Milford	OH	45150	513-831-1300	831-6010
TF: 800-598-5297 ■ *Web:* www.hometeaminspection.com					
HouseMaster 421 W Union Ave	Bound Brook	NJ	08805	732-469-6565	469-7405
TF: 800-526-3939 ■ *Web:* www.housemaster.com					
Kinship Inspection Service PO Box 251	Port Washington	WI	53074	262-284-7211	284-7220
LandAmerica Property Inspection Services					
925 North Point Pkwy Suite 400	Alpharetta	GA	30005	800-285-3001	344-1322
Web: www.inspectech.com					
National Property Inspections Inc (NPI) 9375 Burt St Suite 201	Omaha	NE	68114	402-333-9807	933-2508*
*Fax Area Code: 800 ■ *TF:* 800-333-9807 ■ *Web:* www.npiweb.com					
Pillar to Post Inc 13902 N Dale Mabry Hwy Suite 300	Tampa	FL	33618	813-962-4461	963-5301
TF: 800-294-5591 ■ *Web:* www.pillartopost.com					
WIN Home Inspections 6500 6th Ave NW	Seattle	WA	98117	206-728-8100	
TF: 800-967-8127 ■ *Web:* www.wini.com					
World Inspection Network International Inc 6500 6th Ave NW	Seattle	WA	98117	206-728-8100	
TF: 800-967-8127 ■ *Web:* www.wini.com					

369 HOME SALES & OTHER DIRECT SELLING

				Phone	Fax
1-800-Mattress 31-10 48th Ave	Long Island City	NY	11101	718-472-1200	472-1024
TF: 800-999-1000 ■ *Web:* www.mattress.com					
4Life Research 9850 S 300 West	Sandy	UT	84070	801-562-3600	533-3393*
*Fax Area Code: 800 ■ *TF Sales:* 888-454-3374 ■ *Web:* www.4-life.com					
Amway Corp 7575 Fulton St E	Ada	MI	49355	616-787-6000	682-4000
TF: 800-253-6500 ■ *Web:* www.amway.com					
Avon Products Inc 1251 Ave of the Americas	New York	NY	10020	212-282-5000	282-6825
NYSE: AVP ■ *TF Cust Svc:* 800-367-2866 ■ *Web:* www.avon.com					
BeautiControl Cosmetics Inc 2121 Midway Rd	Carrollton	TX	75006	972-458-0601	458-6904*
*Fax: Sales ■ *TF:* 800-232-8841 ■ *Web:* www.beauticontrol.com					
Color Me Beautiful Inc 7000 Infantry Ridge Rd Suite 200	Manassas	VA	20109	703-471-6400	471-0127
TF: 800-265-6763 ■ *Web:* www.colormebeautiful.com					
Colorado Prime Foods 500 Bi-County Blvd Suite 400	Farmingdale	NY	11735	631-694-1111	288-5938*
*Fax Area Code: 800 ■ *Fax: Cust Svc ■ *TF:* 800-365-2404 ■ *Web:* www.coloradoprimefoods.com					
Conklin Co Inc 551 Valley Park Dr	Shakopee	MN	55379	952-445-6010	496-4281
TF: 800-888-8838 ■ *Web:* www.conklin.com					
Cutco Cutlery Corp 322 Houghton Ave	Olean	NY	14760	716-373-6148	790-7184
TF: 800-828-0448 ■ *Web:* www.cutco.com					
Dial-A-Mattress Operating Corp DBA 1-800-Mattress					
31-10 48th Ave	Long Island City	NY	11101	718-472-1200	472-1024
TF: 800-999-1000 ■ *Web:* www.mattress.com					
Discovery Toys Inc 6400 Brisa St	Livermore	CA	94550	925-606-2600	447-0626
TF Cust Svc: 800-426-4777 ■ *Web:* www.discoverytoysinc.com					
Electrolux LLC 5420 LBJ Fwy Suite 800	Dallas	TX	75240	214-361-4300	378-7561
TF Cust Svc: 800-243-9078 ■ *Web:* www.electroluxusa.com					
Fuller Brush Co 1 Fuller Way	Great Bend	KS	67530	620-792-1711	792-1906
TF Cust Svc: 800-438-5537 ■ *Web:* www.fuller.com					
Golden Neo-Life Diamite International 3500 Gateway Blvd	Fremont	CA	94538	510-651-0405	440-2818
TF: 800-432-5848 ■ *Web:* www.gnld.com					
Goldshield Elite 1501 Northpoint Pkwy Suite 100	West Palm Beach	FL	33407	561-615-4701	423-3135*
*Fax Area Code: 800 ■ *TF:* 866-218-8142 ■ *Web:* www.goldshieldelite.com					
Herbalife International Inc 1800 Century Park E	Los Angeles	CA	90067	310-410-9600	557-3941*
*Fax: Hum Res ■ *TF:* 866-866-4744 ■ *Web:* www.herbalife.com					
Home Interiors & Gifts Inc 1649 Frankford Rd W	Carrollton	TX	75007	972-695-1000	490-7582*
*Fax Area Code: 214 ■ *Web:* www.homeinteriors.com					
Jafra Cosmetics International 2451 Townsgate Rd	Westlake Village	CA	91361	805-449-3000	449-3254
TF: 800-551-2345 ■ *Web:* www.jafra.com					
Mannatech Inc 600 S Royal Ln Suite 200	Coppell	TX	75019	972-471-7400	471-8135
NASDAQ: MTEX ■ *TF:* 800-281-4469 ■ *Web:* www.mannatech-inc.com					
Mary Kay Inc 16251 Dallas Pkwy	Addison	TX	75001	972-687-6300	687-1623*
*Fax: Cust Svc ■ *TF Cust Svc:* 800-627-9529 ■ *Web:* www.marykay.com					
Melaleuca Inc 3910 S Yellowstone Hwy	Idaho Falls	ID	83402	208-522-0700	528-2090*
*Fax Area Code: 888 ■ *TF Sales:* 800-282-3000 ■ *Web:* www.melaleuca.com					
Midwest Marketing Inc 239 Hwy 61 PO Box 125	Bloomsdale	MO	63627	573-483-2577	483-9747
TF: 800-662-7538 ■ *Web:* www.mwmktg.com					
Noevir USA Inc 1095 SE Main St	Irvine	CA	92614	949-660-1111	553-3224
TF: 800-872-8817 ■ *Web:* www.noevirusa.com					
North American Membership Group Inc					
12301 Whitewater Dr	Minnetonka	MN	55343	952-936-9333	988-7499
TF: 800-634-8598 ■ *Web:* www.namginc.com					
Nu Skin Enterprises Inc 75 W Center St	Provo	UT	84601	801-345-6100	345-5999
NYSE: NUS ■ *Web:* www.nuskin.com					
Nutrilite Products Inc 5600 Beach Blvd PO Box 5940	Buena Park	CA	90621	714-562-6200	736-7610
Web: www.nutrilite.com					
Pampered Chef Ltd 1 Pampered Chef Ln	Addison	IL	60101	630-261-8900	261-8992
TF: 888-687-2433 ■ *Web:* www.pamperedchef.com					
Partylite Gifts Inc 59 Armstrong Rd Suite A	Plymouth	MA	02360	508-830-3100	747-5508
Web: www.partylite.com					
Periodical Publishers Service Bureau 1 N Superior St	Sandusky	OH	44870	419-626-0623	621-4383
TF: 800-654-9204 ■ *Web:* www.ppsb.com					
Pola USA Inc 251 E Victoria St	Carson	CA	90746	310-527-9696	515-1195
TF: 800-222-6564 ■ *Web:* www.pola.com					
Princess House Inc 470 Miles Standish Blvd	Taunton	MA	02780	508-823-0711	823-5182
TF Sales: 800-622-0039 ■ *Web:* www.princesshouse.com					

	City	State	ZIP	Phone	Fax
Reliv International Inc 136 Chesterfield Industrial Blvd	Chesterfield	MO	63005	636-537-9715	537-9753
NASDAQ: RELV ■ *TF:* 800-735-4887 ■ *Web:* www.reliv.com					
Rena Ware International Inc PO Box 97050	Redmond	WA	98073	425-881-6171	882-7500
TF: 877-736-2245 ■ *Web:* www.renaware.com					
Rexair Inc 50 W Big Beaver Rd Suite 350	Troy	MI	48084	248-643-7222	643-7676
Web: www.rainbowsystem.com					
Rocher Yves Inc PO Box 1701	Champlain	NY	12919	800-321-3434	321-4909
TF: 888-909-0771 ■ *Web:* www.yvesrocherusa.com					
Saladmaster Inc 230 Westway Pl Suite 101	Arlington	TX	76018	817-633-3555	633-5544
TF: 800-765-5795 ■ *Web:* www.saladmaster.com					
Shaklee Corp 4747 Willow Rd	Pleasanton	CA	94588	925-924-2000	924-2862
TF: 800-742-5533 ■ *Web:* www.shaklee.com					
Specialty Merchandise Corp 996 Flower Glen St	Simi Valley	CA	93065	805-578-5500	584-8267
TF Orders: 800-877-7621 ■ *Web:* www.smcorp.com					
Stanley Home Products 1 Fuller Way	Great Bend	KS	67530	620-792-1711	792-1906
TF Cust Svc: 800-628-9032 ■ *Web:* www.shponline.com					
Success Motivation International Inc 4567 Lakeshore Dr	Waco	TX	76710	254-776-9966	776-1230
TF Sales: 888-391-0050 ■ *Web:* www.success-motivation.com					
Sunrider International 1625 Abalone Ave	Torrance	CA	90501	310-781-3808	222-6329*
**Fax:* Hum Res ■ *TF Orders:* 888-278-6743 ■ *Web:* www.sunrider.com					
Tupperware Corp 14901 S Orange Blossom Trail	Orlando	FL	32837	407-847-3111	826-8489
NYSE: TUP ■ *TF Cust Svc:* 800-772-4001 ■ *Web:* www.tupperware.com					
UndercoverWear Inc 30 Commerce Way Suite 2	Tewksbury	MA	01876	978-851-8580	640-2882
TF: 800-733-0007 ■ *Web:* www.undercoverwear.com					
Unicity Network Inc 1201 N 800 East	Orem	UT	84097	801-226-2224	864-2489*
**Fax Area Code:* 800 ■ *TF:* 800-748-4334 ■ *Web:* www.unicitynetwork.com					
University Subscription Service 1213 Butterfield Rd	Downers Grove	IL	60515	630-960-3233	960-3246
TF: 800-876-1213 ■ *Web:* www.ussmag.com					
Vector Marketing Co 322 Houghton Ave	Olean	NY	14760	716-373-6148	790-7173*
**Fax Area Code:* 585 ■ *TF:* 800-828-0448					
Vorwerk USA Co LP 1964 Corporate Sq	Longwood	FL	32750	407-830-9988	830-9958
TF: 888-867-9375 ■ *Web:* www.vorwerkusa.com					
Watkins Inc PO Box 5570 150 Liberty St	Winona	MN	55987	507-457-3300	452-6723
TF: 800-243-9423 ■ *Web:* www.watkinsonline.com					
World Book Inc 233 N Michigan Ave 20th Fl	Chicago	IL	60601	312-729-5800	729-5600
TF: 800-255-1750 ■ *Web:* www.worldbook.com					
Yves Rocher Inc PO Box 1701	Champlain	NY	12919	800-321-3434	321-4909
TF: 888-909-0771 ■ *Web:* www.yvesrocherusa.com					

370 HOME WARRANTY SERVICES

	City	State	ZIP	Phone	Fax
American Home Shield 889 Ridge Lake Blvd	Memphis	TN	38120	901-537-8000	537-8005
TF: 800-247-1644 ■ *Web:* ahswarranty.com					
Aon Warranty Group Inc 1000 Milwaukee Ave 6th Fl	Glenview	IL	60025	847-953-2025	765-1850*
**Fax Area Code:* 773 ■ *TF:* 800-747-5152 ■ *Web:* www.aon.com/us/					
Blue Ribbon Home Warranty Inc 95 S Wadsworth Blvd	Lakewood	CO	80226	303-986-3900	986-3152
TF: 800-571-0475 ■ *Web:* www.brhw.com					
Cross Country Group LLC 4040 Mystic Valley Pkwy	Medford	MA	02155	781-396-3700	391-7504
Web: www.ccgroup.com					
Cross Country Home Services					
1625 NW 136th Ave Suite 200	Fort Lauderdale	FL	33323	954-845-9100	845-2260
TF: 800-327-9787 ■ *Web:* www.cchs.com					
Fidelity National Home Warranty Inc 2950 Euskirk Ave	Walnut Creek	CA	94596	925-934-4450	308-1460*
**Fax Area Code:* 800 ■ *TF:* 800-862-6837 ■ *Web:* www.homewarranty.com					
First American Home Buyers Protection Corp					
7833 Haskell Ave PO Box 10180	Van Nuys	CA	91410	818-781-5050	772-1151*
**Fax Area Code:* 800 ■ *TF:* 800-444-9030 ■ *Web:* homewarranty.firstam.com					
HMS National Inc 1625 NW 136th Ave Suite 200	Fort Lauderdale	FL	33323	954-845-9100	845-2263
TF: 800-432-1033 ■ *Web:* www.hmsnet.com					
Home Buyers Warranty Corp 2675 S Abilene St	Aurora	CO	80014	303-368-4805	368-0529
Web: www.2-10.com					
Home Security of America Inc 310 N Midvale Blvd	Madison	WI	53705	608-231-0010	638-1741*
**Fax Area Code:* 877 ■ *TF:* 800-367-1448 ■ *Web:* www.onlinehsa.com					
Warrantech Corp Inc 2200 Hwy 121	Bedford	TX	76021	817-283-7267	
TF: 800-544-9510 ■ *Web:* www.warrantech.com					
Warrantech International Inc 2200 Hwy 121	Beford	TX	76021	817-283-7267	785-6151*
**Fax:* Hum Res ■ *TF:* 800-544-9510 ■ *Web:* www.warrantech.com					

371 HORSE BREEDERS

SEE ALSO Agricultural Services - Livestock Improvement Services p. 1265

	City	State	ZIP	Phone	Fax
Airdrie Stud Inc 2641 Old Frankfort Pike PO Box 487	Midway	KY	40347	859-873-7270	873-6140
Web: www.airdriestud.com					
Alex Trebek's Creston Farms 9010 Creston Rd	Paso Robles	CA	93446	805-239-0711	239-4473
Web: www.crestonfarms.com					
Ashford Stud 5095 Frankfort Rd PO Box 823	Versailles	KY	40383	859-873-7088	879-5756
Web: www.coolmore.com/america					
Calumet Farm 3301 Versailles Rd	Lexington	KY	40510	859-231-8272	254-4258
Web: www.calumetfarm.com					
Claiborne Farm PO Box 150	Paris	KY	40362	859-233-4252	987-0008
Web: www.clabornefarm.com					
Country Life Farm 319 Old Joppa Rd	Bel Air	MD	21014	410-879-1952	879-6207
Web: www.countrylifefarm.com					
Creston Farms 9010 Creston Rd	Paso Robles	CA	93446	805-239-0711	239-4473
Web: www.crestonfarms.com					
Darby Dan Farm 3225 Old Frankfort Pike	Lexington	KY	40510	859-254-0424	281-6612
Web: www.darbydan.com					
Gainesway Farm 3750 Paris Pike	Lexington	KY	40511	859-293-2676	299-9371
Web: www.gainesway.com					
Glencrest Farm 1576 Moores Mill Rd PO Box 4468	Midway	KY	40347	859-233-7032	233-9404
TF: 800-903-0136 ■ *Web:* www.glencrest.com					
Grant's Farm 10501 Gravois Rd	Saint Louis	MO	63123	314-843-1700	525-0822
Web: www.grantsfarm.com					
Jonabell Farm 3333 Bowman's Mill Rd	Lexington	KY	40513	859-255-8537	259-0040
Web: www.jonabell.com					
King Ranch Inc 2 Miles West of Hwy 141 PO Box 1090	Kingsville	TX	78364	361-592-6411	592-6885
TF: 800-375-6411 ■ *Web:* www.king-ranch.com					
Lane's End Farm 1500 Midway Rd PO Box 626	Versailles	KY	40383	859-873-7300	873-3746
Web: www.lanesend.com					
Margaux Farm LLC 596 Moores Mill Rd PO Box 4220	Midway	KY	40347	859-846-4433	846-4486
Web: www.margauxfarm.com					
Mill Ridge Farm 3414 Bowman Mill Rd	Lexington	KY	40513	859-231-0606	255-6010
Web: www.millridge.com					
Millford Farm 377 Weisenberger Mill Rd PO Box 4351	Midway	KY	40347	859-846-4705	846-4226
Web: www.millford.com					
Northview Stallion Station 55 Northern Dancer Dr	Chesapeake City	MD	21915	410-885-2855	
Web: www.northviewstallions.com					
Oak Spring Farms LLC 8540 Mill Reef Rd	Upperville	VA	20184	540-592-3211	592-3897
Old Frankfort Stud 3800 Old Frankfort Pike	Lexington	KY	40510	859-233-1717	233-1719
Web: www.oldfrankfortstud.com					
Overbrook Farm 2525 DeLong Rd	Lexington	KY	40515	859-273-1514	273-0034
Web: www.overbrookfarm.com					
Pin Oak Stud 830 Grassy Spring Rd PO Box 68	Versailles	KY	40383	859-873-1420	873-2391
Web: www.pinoakstud.com					
Stone Farm 200 Stoney Point Rd	Paris	KY	40361	859-987-3737	987-1474
Web: www.stonefarm.com					
Sugar Maple Farm 5 Sugar Ln	Poughquag	NY	12570	845-724-3500	724-5889
Web: www.sugarmaple-farm.com					
Three Chimneys Farm PO Box 114	Midway	KY	40347	859-873-7053	873-5723
Web: www.threechimneys.com					
Vinery Kentucky LLC DBA Vinery Ltd 4241 Spurr Rd	Lexington	KY	40511	859-455-9388	455-9588
Web: www.vinerykentucky.com					
Wafare Farm 3808 Old Frankfort Pike	Versailles	KY	40383	859-846-5202	846-5645
Web: www.wafarefarm.com					
Walmac International Stud Farm Inc 3395 Paris Pike	Lexington	KY	40511	859-299-0473	299-1259
Web: www.walmac.com					
Wimbledon Farm 1725 Walnut Hill Rd	Lexington	KY	40515	859-272-0636	271-1435
Web: www.wimbledonfarm.com					
Windfield Farms 2300 Simcoe St N PO Box 67	Oshawa	ON	L1H7K8	905-725-1195	579-7552
Web: www.windfields.com					
Windfields Farm 2525 DeLong Rd	Lexington	KY	40515	859-273-3050	273-3035
Web: www.windfields.com					
WinStar Farm LLC 3001 Pisgah Pike	Versailles	KY	40383	859-873-1717	873-1612
Web: www.winstarfarm.com					

372 HORTICULTURAL PRODUCTS GROWERS

SEE ALSO Garden Centers p. 1687; Seed Companies p. 2311

	City	State	ZIP	Phone	Fax
Ades & Gish Nurseries 875 Balour Dr	Encinitas	CA	92024	760-436-1377	436-8029
Web: www.agnurseries.com					
Aldershot of New Mexico Inc 4884 S Main St	Mesilla Park	NM	88047	505-523-8621	523-8688
TF: 888-768-6867					
Alex R Masson Inc 12819 198th St	Linwood	KS	66052	913-301-3281	301-3288
TF: 800-444-6210 ■ *Web:* www.armasson.com					
Altman Specialty Plants Inc 3742 Bluebird Canyon Rd	Vista	CA	92084	760-744-8191	744-8835
TF: 800-348-4881 ■ *Web:* www.livingtreasures.com					
B & H Flowers Inc 3516 Foothill Rd	Carpinteria	CA	93013	805-684-4550	684-1677
TF: 800-682-5666 ■ *Web:* www.bandhflowers.com					
Battlefield Farms Inc 23190 Clarks Mountain Rd	Rapidan	VA	22733	540-854-6485	854-6486
TF: 800-722-0744 ■ *Web:* www.battlefieldfarms.com					
Bay City Flower Co Inc					
2265 Cabrillo Hwy S PO Box 186	Half Moon Bay	CA	94019	650-726-5535	720-2004
TF Sales: 800-399-5858					
Bell Nursery Inc 3838 Bell Rd	Burtonsville	MD	20866	301-421-1500	421-4269
Web: www.bellnursery.com					
Bettinger Farms Inc 11602 Frankfort Rd	Swanton	OH	43558	419-829-2771	829-2147
Blue Ridge Growers Inc 1133 Ebenezer Church Rd	Rising Sun	MD	21911	410-658-6100	658-6698
TF: 800-637-2107					
Blue Ridge Growers Inc 21409 Germanna Hwy	Stevensburg	VA	22741	540-399-1636	399-9068
TF: 800-368-2030 ■ *Web:* www.blueridgegrowers.com					
Brand Flowers Inc 5300 Foothill Rd	Carpinteria	CA	93013	805-684-5531	684-1528
TF: 800-549-0089 ■ *Web:* www.brandflowers.com					
Burgett Floral Inc 2729 US Hwy 82	Mayhill	NM	88339	505-682-2667	
California Pajarosa 133 Hughes Rd PO Box 684	Watsonville	CA	95077	831-722-6374	722-1316
TF: 800-565-6374 ■ *Web:* www.pajarosa.com					
CD Ford & Sons Inc 16243 Ford Rd	Geneseo	IL	61254	309-944-4661	944-3703
TF: 800-383-4661 ■ *Web:* www.cdford.com					
Clearwater Nursery Inc 887 Mesa Rd PO Box 1170	Nipomo	CA	93444	805-929-3241	929-5421
Web: www.clearwaternursery.com					
Color Spot Nurseries Inc 2575 Olive Hill Rd	Fallbrook	CA	92028	760-695-1430	250-5135*
**Fax Area Code:* 800 ■ *TF:* 800-554-4065 ■ *Web:* www.colorspot.com					
Color Star Growers 14095 N Peyton Hwy	Peyton	CO	80831	719-749-2510	749-2512
TF: 800-971-1875					
Colorama Wholesale Nursery 1025 N Todd Ave	Azusa	CA	91720	626-969-3585	969-0481
Costa Nursery Farms Inc 22290 SW 162nd Ave	Goulds	FL	33170	305-247-3248	247-0591*
**Fax Area Code:* 786 ■ *TF:* 800-327-7074 ■ *Web:* www.costafarms.com					
Cuthbert Greenhouses Inc 4900 Hendron Rd	Groveport	OH	43125	614-836-3866	836-3767
TF: 800-321-1939					
Dallas Johnson Greenhouse Inc 2802 Twin City Dr	Council Bluffs	IA	51501	712-366-0407	366-4510
TF: 800-445-4794 ■ *Web:* www.djgreenhouse.com					
Dan Schantz Farm & Greenhouses LLC 8025 Spinnerstown Rd	Zionsville	PA	18092	610-967-2181	965-4506
TF: 800-451-3064 ■ *Web:* www.danschantz.com					
DeLeon's Bromeliads Co 13745 SW 216th St	Goulds	FL	33170	305-238-6028	235-2354
TF: 800-448-8649 ■ *Web:* www.deleons4color.com					
Delray Plants Inc 955 Old SR 8	Venus	FL	33960	863-465-1557	465-4365
TF: 800-854-5393					
Dramm & Echter Inc 1150 Quail Gardens Dr	Encinitas	CA	92024	760-436-0188	436-2974
TF: 800-854-7021 ■ *Web:* www.drammechter.com					
Ecke Paul Ranch Inc 441 Saxony Rd	Encinitas	CA	92024	760-753-1134	944-4000
TF: 800-468-3253 ■ *Web:* www.ecke.com					
El Modeno Gardens Inc 11911 Jeffrey Rd	Irvine	CA	92602	949-559-1234	559-6760
TF: 800-776-8111 ■ *Web:* elmodenogardens.com					
Engelmann Hermann Greenhouses Inc 2009 Marden Rd	Apopka	FL	32703	407-886-3434	886-0094
TF: 800-722-6435 ■ *Web:* www.exoticangel.com					
Ever-Bloom Inc 4701 Foothill Rd	Carpinteria	CA	93013	805-684-5566	684-7288
TF: 800-388-8112 ■ *Web:* www.ever-bloom.com					
Fernlea Nurseries Inc 294 Buck Blunt Rd	Quincy	FL	32351	850-442-6188	442-9566
TF: 800-428-9729					
Ford CD & Sons Inc 16243 Ford Rd	Geneseo	IL	61254	309-944-4661	944-3703
TF: 800-383-4661 ■ *Web:* www.cdford.com					
Garden State Growers 99 Locust Grove Rd	Pittstown	NJ	08867	908-730-8888	730-6676
TF: 800-288-8484 ■ *Web:* www.gardenstategrowers.com					
Geerlings Greenhouses Inc 496 Williams St	Piscataway	NJ	08854	732-752-2500	752-9691
Green Circle Growers Inc 15650 SR-511	Oberlin	OH	44074	440-775-1411	774-1465
TF: 800-533-4266					
Green Valley Floral Co 24999 Potter Rd	Salinas	CA	93908	831-424-7691	424-4473
TF: 800-228-1255 ■ *Web:* www.greenvalleyfloral.com					
Greenleaf Nursery Co 28406 Hwy 82	Park Hill	OK	74451	918-457-5172	457-5550
TF: 800-331-2982 ■ *Web:* www.glnsy.com					
Harts Nursery of Jefferson Inc 4049 Jefferson-Scio Rd	Jefferson	OR	97352	541-327-3366	327-1603
TF: 800-356-9335 ■ *Web:* www.hartsnursery.com					
Henry Mast Greenhouses Inc 2125 72nd St SW	Byron Center	MI	49315	616-878-3380	878-3610
Hermann Engelmann Greenhouses Inc 2009 Marden Rd	Apopka	FL	32703	407-886-3434	886-0094
TF: 800-722-6435 ■ *Web:* www.exoticangel.com					
Hines Horticulture Inc 12621 Jeffrey Rd	Irvine	CA	92620	949-559-4444	559-0668
NASDAQ: HORT ■ *TF:* 800-444-4499 ■ *Web:* www.hineshorticulture.com					

	City	State	Zip	Phone	Fax
Imperial Nurseries Inc 90 Salmon Brook St. *TF:* 800-343-3132 ■ *Web:* www.imperialnurseries.com	Granby	CT	06035	860-653-4541	653-2919
Ingleside Plantation Nurseries 5870 Leedstown Rd *Web:* www.inglesidenurseries.com	Oak Grove	VA	22443	804-224-7111	224-2032
Johannes Flowers Inc 4990 Foothill Rd *TF:* 800-365-9476 ■ *Web:* www.johannesflowers.com	Carpinteria	CA	93013	805-684-5686	566-2199
Johnsen Nurseries Inc 2897 Freedom Blvd *TF:* 800-322-6529 ■ *Web:* www.ameri-cal.com	Watsonville	CA	95076	831-728-4205	724-9281
Johnson Dallas Greenhouse Inc 2802 Twin City Dr. *TF:* 800-445-4794 ■ *Web:* www.djgreenhouse.com	Council Bluffs	IA	51501	712-366-0407	366-4510
Kerry's Bromeliad Nursery Inc 21840 SW 258th St. *TF:* 800-331-9127 ■ *Web:* www.kerrys.com	Homestead	FL	33031	305-247-7096	247-3392
Kitayama Brothers Inc 13239 Weld County Rd 4 *TF:* 800-829-5323	Brighton	CO	80601	303-659-8005	659-4022
Knox Nursery Inc 940 Avalon Rd *TF:* 800-441-5669 ■ *Web:* www.knoxnursery.com	Winter Garden	FL	34787	407-293-3721	290-1702
Kocher Flower Growers 950 Brittany Rd *TF:* 800-821-4421	Encinitas	CA	92024	760-436-1458	607-9105
Kurt Weiss Greenhouses Inc 95 Main St *TF:* 800-858-8555 ■ *Web:* kurtweiss.com	Center Moriches	NY	11934	631-878-2500	878-2553
Layser's Flowers Inc 501 W Washington Ave *Web:* www.laysersflowers.com	Myerstown	PA	17067	717-866-5746	866-6099
Mainland Nursery Inc J50 W Turner Rd. *TF:* 800-366-4048 ■ *Web:* www.mainlandnursery.com	Lodi	CA	95242	209-334-1680	333-0351
Masson Alex R Inc 12819 198th St *TF:* 800-444-6210 ■ *Web:* www.armasson.com	Linwood	KS	66052	913-301-3281	301-3288
Mast Henry Greenhouses Inc 2125 72nd St SW	Byron Center	MI	49315	616-878-3380	878-3610
Matsui Nursery Inc 1645 Old Stage Rd *TF:* 800-793-6433 ■ *Web:* www.matsuinursery.net	Salinas	CA	93908	831-422-6433	422-2387
McLellan Botanicals 688 Brannan St. *TF:* 800-467-2443 ■ *Web:* www.orchidexperts.com	San Francisco	CA	94107	415-546-4049	543-6836
Metrolina Greenhouses Inc 16400 Huntersville-Concord Rd *TF:* 800-222-2905 ■ *Web:* www.metrolinagreenhouses.com	Huntersville	NC	28078	704-875-1371	875-6741
Mid American Growers Inc 14240 Greenhouse Ave. *TF:* 800-892-6888	Granville	IL	61326	815-339-6831	339-2747
Milgro Nursery LLC 1085 N Victoria Ave. *TF:* 800-645-4769	Oxnard	CA	93030	805-383-3616	985-5860
Monrovia Nursery Growers 18331 E Foothill Blvd *TF:* 800-999-9321 ■ *Web:* www.monrovia.com	Azusa	CA	91702	626-334-9321	334-3126
Mount Arbor Nurseries 201 E Ferguson Rd *TF Sales:* 800-831-4125	Shenandoah	IA	51601	712-246-4250	246-1841
Mountain States Plants Corp 1421 W Gentile St. *TF:* 800-326-4490 ■ *Web:* www.msplants.com	Layton	UT	84041	801-544-8878	544-1175
Neal Robinson Wholesale Greenhouses PO Box 1337. *TF:* 800-874-2740	Los Fresnos	TX	78566	956-831-4656	233-5558
Nelson OF & Sons Nursery Inc 3207 Clarona Rd. *Web:* www.nelsonsfloridaroses.com	Apopka	FL	32703	407-886-3111	886-1489
NG Heimos Greenhouses Inc 12345 Eddie & Park Rd *TF:* 866-444-4590	Saint Louis	MO	63127	314-842-6900	849-1100
Nurserymen's Exchange 2651 N Cabrillo Hwy *TF:* 800-227-5229 ■ *Web:* www.bloomrite.com	Half Moon Bay	CA	94019	650-726-6361	712-4280
Ocean Breeze International 3910 N Via Real *TF:* 888-715-8888 ■ *Web:* www.oceanbreezeintl.com	Carpinteria	CA	93013	805-684-1747	684-0235
OF Nelson & Sons Nursery Inc 3207 Clarona Rd *Web:* www.nelsonsfloridaroses.com	Apopka	FL	32703	407-886-3111	886-1489
Oglevee Ltd 152 Oglevee Ln *TF:* 800-437-4733 ■ *Web:* www.oglevee.com	Connellsville	PA	15425	724-628-8360	628-7270
Pajaro Valley Greenhouses Inc 214 Lewis Rd. *TF Cust Svc:* 800-538-5922 ■ *Web:* www.pvflowers.com	Watsonville	CA	95076	831-722-2773	722-0124
Panzer Nursery Inc 17980 SW Baseline Rd *TF:* 888-212-5327 ■ *Web:* www.panzernursery.com	Beaverton	OR	97006	503-645-1185	629-9023
Parks Brothers Farm Inc 6733 Parks Rd *TF:* 800-334-5770 ■ *Web:* www.parksbrothers.com	Van Buren	AR	72956	479-474-1125	471-7051
Paul Ecke Ranch Inc 441 Saxony Rd. *TF:* 800-468-3253 ■ *Web:* www.ecke.com	Encinitas	CA	92024	760-753-1134	944-4000
Petitti Garden Centers 24964 Broadway Ave. *Web:* www.petittigardencenter.com	Oakwood Village	OH	44146	440-439-6511	439-7736
Post Gardens Inc 21189 Huron River Dr	Rockwood	MI	48173	734-379-9688	379-3008
Robinson Neal Wholesale Greenhouses PO Box 1337. *TF:* 800-874-2740	Los Fresnos	TX	78566	956-831-4656	233-5558
Rockwell Farms Inc 332 Rockwell Farms Rd. *TF:* 800-635-6576 ■ *Web:* www.rockwellfarms.com	Rockwell	NC	28138	704-279-5589	279-8573
Schantz Dan Farm & Greenhouses LLC 8025 Spinnerstown Rd *TF:* 800-451-3064 ■ *Web:* www.danschantz.com	Zionsville	PA	18092	610-967-2181	965-4506
Sedan Floral Inc 406 S School St PO Box 339 *Web:* www.sedanfloral.com	Sedan	KS	67361	620-725-3111	725-5257
Silver Terrace Nurseries Inc 501 North St. *TF:* 800-323-5977 ■ *Web:* www.citywreaths.com	Pescadero	CA	94060	650-879-2110	879-2164
Smith Gardens Inc 1265 Marine Dr. *TF:* 800-755-6256 ■ *Web:* www.northwestgrown.com	Bellingham	WA	98225	360-733-4671	647-1468
South Florida Growers 16885 SW 256th St *TF:* 866-948-3722 ■ *Web:* www.southfloridagrowers.com	Homestead	FL	33031	305-248-3722	248-9886
Speedling Inc 4300 Old 41 Hwy S PO box 7238 *TF:* 800-881-4769 ■ *Web:* www.speedling.com	Sun City	FL	33586	813-645-3221	645-0086
Sun Valley Floral Farms Inc 3160 Upper Bay Rd *TF:* 800-747-0396 ■ *Web:* www.sunvalleyfloral.com	Arcata	CA	95521	707-826-8700	826-8708
Sunshine Foliage World 2060 Steve Roberts Special *TF:* 800-872-0607 ■ *Web:* www.interiorscape.com/sfw	Zolfo Springs	FL	33890	863-735-0501	735-1810
Tagawa Greenhouses Inc 17999 Weld County Rd 4	Brighton	CO	80603	303-659-1260	659-4894
Ulery Greenhouse Co 2625 Old Clifton Rd *TF Cust Svc:* 800-722-5143 ■ *Web:* www.ulerygreenhouse.com	Springfield	OH	45502	937-325-5543	325-1824
Van Wingerden International Inc 1856 Jeffress Rd. *TF:* 800-226-3597	Fletcher	NC	28732	828-891-4116	891-8581
Watsonville Nurseries 110 Whiting Rd.	Watsonville	CA	95076	831-724-2487	724-0453
Weiss Kurt Greenhouses Inc 95 Main St *TF:* 800-858-8555 ■ *Web:* kurtweiss.com	Center Moriches	NY	11934	631-878-2500	878-2553
Wenke Greenhouses Co 2525 N 30th St *TF:* 800-311-7209 ■ *Web:* www.wenkegreenhouses.com	Kalamazoo	MI	49048	269-349-7882	349-1112
West Flower Growers Inc 3623 Etting Rd	Oxnard	CA	93033	805-488-0814	488-9433
Westerlay Orchids 3504 Via Real *TF:* 800-959-7673 ■ *Web:* www.westerlayorchids.com	Carpinteria	CA	93013	805-684-5411	684-5414
Westland Floral Co 1400 Cravens Lane *Web:* www.westlandfloral.com	Carpinteria	CA	93013	805-684-4011	684-0685
White's Nursery & Greenhouses Inc 3133 Old Mill Rd *TF:* 800-966-9969 ■ *Web:* www.whitesnursery.com	Chesapeake	VA	23323	757-487-1300	487-7845
Woodburn Nursery & Azaleas 13009 McKee School Rd *Web:* www.woodburnnursery.com	Woodburn	OR	97071	503-634-2231	634-2238
Worthington Farms Inc 3661 Ballards Crossroads Rd *Web:* www.worthingtonfarms.com	Greenville	NC	27834	252-756-3827	756-9442
Yoder Brothers Inc 115 3rd St SE *TF:* 800-321-9573 ■ *Web:* www.yoder.com	Barberton	OH	44203	330-745-2143	753-5294
Young's Plant Farm Inc 863 Airport Rd *TF:* 800-304-8609	Auburn	AL	36830	334-821-3500	821-3526

373 HOSE & BELTING - RUBBER OR PLASTICS

SEE ALSO Automotive Parts & Supplies - Mfr p. 1360

	City	State	Zip	Phone	Fax
American Hose & Industrial Rubber Inc 2545 N Broad St *TF:* 800-533-1134 ■ *Web:* www.americanhoseandrubber.com	Philadelphia	PA	19132	215-223-7710	223-7713
Ammeraal Beltech USA 7501 N St Louis Ave. *TF Cust Svc:* 800-323-4170 ■ *Web:* www.ammeraal-beltechusa.com	Skokie	IL	60076	847-673-6720	673-6373
Apache Hose & Belting Co Inc 4805 Bowling St SW *TF Cust Svc:* 800-553-5455 ■ *Web:* www.apachehb.com	Cedar Rapids	IA	52406	319-365-0471	365-2522
Aquapore Moisture Systems Inc 610 S 80th Ave *TF:* 800-426-8419	Tolleson	AZ	85353	623-936-8083	936-9040
Armstrong Industrial Hose Products LLC 96 Stokes Ave. *TF:* 800-275-6547 ■ *Web:* www.armstrongindustrialhose.com	Trenton	NJ	08638	609-883-3030	530-1023
Atco Rubber Products Inc 7101 Atco Dr *TF:* 800-877-3828 ■ *Web:* www.atcoflex.com	Fort Worth	TX	76118	817-595-2894	595-4634
Atcoflex Inc 14261 172nd Ave PO Box 118	Grand Haven	MI	49417	616-842-4661	842-4623
Belting Industries Co Inc 20 Boright Ave. *TF:* 800-843-2358 ■ *Web:* www.beltingindustries.com	Kenilworth	NJ	07033	908-272-8591	272-3825
Carlisle Power Transmission Products Inc 430 Southpointe Dr *TF:* 866-773-2926 ■ *Web:* www.cptbelts.com	Miamisburg	OH	45342	937-847-1500	847-1550
Chapin Watermatics Inc 740 Water St. *TF:* 800-242-7467 ■ *Web:* www.chapindrip.com	Watertown	NY	13601	315-782-1170	782-1490
Chemprene Inc 483 Fishkill Ave *TF:* 800-431-9981 ■ *Web:* www.chemprene.com	Beacon	NY	12508	845-831-2800	831-4639
Coilhose Pneumatics Inc 19 Kimberly Rd *TF:* 800-526-2100 ■ *Web:* www.coilhose.com	East Brunswick	NJ	08816	732-390-8480	390-9693
Colorite Plastics Co 101 Railroad Ave *TF:* 800-800-4673 ■ *Web:* www.coloriteplastics.com	Ridgefield	NJ	07657	201-941-2900	941-0308
Cooper Tire & Rubber Co 701 Lima Ave *NYSE: CTB* ■ *TF Cust Svc:* 800-854-6288 ■ *Web:* www.coopertires.com	Findlay	OH	45840	419-423-1321	424-4108
Copper State Rubber of Arizona Inc 750 S 59th Ave	Phoenix	AZ	85043	602-269-5927	269-8106
Cosmoflex Inc 4142 Industrial Dr PO Box 994	Hannibal	MO	63401	573-221-0242	221-9290
Couse & Bolten Co 90 South St *TF:* 800-360-1324	Newark	NJ	07114	973-344-6330	344-6335
Dynacraft Co 650 Milwaukee Ave N	Algona	WA	98001	253-333-3000	333-3041
Eaton Corp 1111 Superior Ave Eaton Center *NYSE: ETN* ■ *Web:* www.eaton.com	Cleveland	OH	44114	216-523-5000	523-4787
Fenner Drives 311 W Stiegel St *TF Sales:* 800-243-3374 ■ *Web:* www.fennerdrives.com	Manheim	PA	17545	717-665-2421	664-8214
Fenner Dunlop Conveyor Belting Americas 10125 S Tryon St *TF Cust Svc:* 800-922-1735 ■ *Web:* www.fennerdunlop.com	Charlotte	NC	28273	704-943-5669	334-7126
Flexaust Co 1510 Armstrong Rd. **Fax Area Code: 800* ■ *TF:* 800-343-0428 ■ *Web:* www.flexaust.com	Warsaw	IN	46580	574-267-7909	382-8464*
Flexfab LLC 1699 W M-43 Hwy *TF:* 800-331-0003 ■ *Web:* www.flexfab.com	Hastings	MI	49058	269-945-2433	945-4802
Flexon Industries Corp 1 Flexon Plaza *TF:* 800-327-4673 ■ *Web:* www.flexonhose.com	Newark	NJ	07114	973-824-5527	824-1208
Gates Corp 1551 Wewatta St *Web:* www.gates.com	Denver	CO	80202	303-744-1911	744-4000
Gates Interamerica 3609 N 29th Ave	Hollywood	FL	33020	954-926-4568	926-8024
Goodyear Tire & Rubber Co Industrial Rubber Products 13601 Industrial Pkwy *TF:* 800-235-8872	Marysville	OH	43040	937-644-8900	644-8969
Habasit ABT Inc 150 Industrial Park Rd *TF:* 800-522-2358 ■ *Web:* www.habasitabt.com	Middletown	CT	06457	860-632-2211	632-1710
Habasit Belting Inc 1400 Clinton St *TF:* 800-325-1585 ■ *Web:* www.habasitusa.com	Buffalo	NY	14206	716-824-8484	821-1316
HBD/Thermoid Inc 1301 W Sandusky Ave *TF:* 800-543-8070 ■ *Web:* www.hbdthermoid.com	Bellefontaine	OH	43311	937-593-5010	593-4354
Hi-Tech Duravent Inc 400 E Main St *TF:* 800-451-5985 ■ *Web:* www.hitechduravent.com	Georgetown	MA	01833	978-352-2077	352-2487
Hutchinson FTS Inc 1835 Technology Dr *Web:* www.hutchinsonfts.com	Troy	MI	48083	248-589-7710	589-7730
Jason Industrial Inc 340 Kaplan Dr *Web:* www.jasonindustrial.com	Fairfield	NJ	07004	973-227-4904	227-1651
JGB Enterprises Inc 115 Metropolitan Dr **Fax Area Code: 888* ■ *Web:* www.jgbhose.com	Liverpool	NY	13088	315-451-2770	451-6743*
Legg Co Inc 325 E 10th St *TF Sales:* 800-835-1003 ■ *Web:* www.leggbelting.com	Halstead	KS	67056	316-835-2256	835-3218
Lockwood Products Inc 5615 SW Willow Ln *TF:* 800-423-1625 ■ *Web:* www.loc-line.com	Lake Oswego	OR	97035	503-635-8113	635-2844
Mark IV Industries Inc 501 John James Audubon Pkwy *Web:* www.mark-iv.com	Amherst	NY	14226	716-689-4972	689-6098
MBL USA Corp 1040 N Ridge Ave	Lombard	IL	60148	630-620-1050	620-7538
Mercer Rubber Co 350 Rabro Dr *Web:* www.mercer-rubber.com	Hauppauge	NY	11788	631-582-1524	348-0279
Mulhern Belting Inc 148 Bauer Dr *TF:* 800-253-6300 ■ *Web:* www.mulhernbelting.com	Oakland	NJ	07436	201-337-5700	337-6540
NewAge Industries Inc Plastics Technology Group 145 James Way *TF:* 800-506-3924 ■ *Web:* www.newageindustries.com	Southampton	PA	18966	215-526-2300	526-2190
Novaflex Hose Inc 449 Trollingwood Rd. *TF Cust Svc:* 800-334-4270 ■ *Web:* www.novaflexhose.com	Haw River	NC	27258	336-578-2161	578-5554
Parker Fluid Connectors Group 6035 Parkland Blvd *TF:* 800-272-7537 ■ *Web:* www.parker.com/fcg	Cleveland	OH	44124	216-896-3000	896-4000
Performance Polymer Technologies Co 8801 Washington Blvd Suite 109 *Web:* www.pptech.com	Roseville	CA	95678	916-677-1414	677-1474
Ro-Lab American Rubber Co Inc 8830 W Linne Rd. *TF:* 888-276-2993 ■ *Web:* www.rolabamerican.com	Tracy	CA	95304	209-836-0965	836-0465
Salem-Republic Rubber Co 475 W California Ave *TF:* 800-686-4199 ■ *Web:* www.salem-republic.com	Sebring	OH	44672	330-938-9801	938-9809
Snap-Tite Hose Inc 217 Titusville Rd *Web:* www.snap-tite.com/divisions/sh/	Union City	PA	16438	814-438-7616	438-8163
Snap-Tite Inc 8325 Hessinger Dr *Web:* www.snap-tite.com	Erie	PA	16509	814-838-5700	833-0145
Sparks Belting Co 3800 Stahl Dr SE *TF:* 800-451-4537 ■ *Web:* www.sparksbelting.com	Grand Rapids	MI	49546	616-949-2750	949-8518
Standco Industries Inc 2701 Clinton Dr *TF:* 800-231-6018 ■ *Web:* www.standco.net	Houston	TX	77020	713-224-6311	229-9312
Tigerflex Corp 801 Estes Ave	Elk Grove Village	IL	60007	847-640-8366	640-8372
Titeflex Corp 603 Hendee St. *TF:* 800-765-2525 ■ *Web:* www.titeflex.com	Springfield	MA	01139	413-739-5631	271-8233
Unaflex Inc 3901 NE 12th Ave *TF:* 800-327-1286 ■ *Web:* www.unaflex.com	Pompano Beach	FL	33064	954-943-5002	941-7968
Voss Belting & Specialty Co 6965 N Hamlin Ave *TF:* 800-323-3935 ■ *Web:* www.vossbelting.com	Lincolnwood	IL	60712	847-673-8900	673-1408

374 HOSPICES

SEE ALSO Hospitals - Specialty Hospitals p. 1827

Alabama

	City	State	ZIP	Phone	Fax
Hospice of Cullman County 402 4th Ave NE	Cullman	AL	35055	256-739-5185	737-0985
Web: hospiceofcullmancounty.org					
Hospice of EAMC 665 Opelika Rd	Auburn	AL	36830	334-826-1899	826-0756
Hospice of Marshall County 408 Martling Rd	Albertville	AL	35951	256-891-7724	891-7754
TF: 888-334-9336 ■ *Web:* www.hospicemc.org					
Hospice of the Valley PO Box 2745	Decatur	AL	35602	256-350-5585	350-5567
TF: 877-260-3657 ■ *Web:* www.hospiceofthevalley.net					
Hospice of West Alabama 3851 Loop Rd	Tuscaloosa	AL	35404	205-523-0101	523-0102
TF: 877-362-7522 ■ *Web:* www.hospiceofwestalabama.org					
McAuley Hospice PO Box 1090	Daphne	AL	36526	251-626-2694	621-4424
Wiregrass Hospice PO Drawer 2127	Dothan	AL	36302	334-792-1100	794-0009
TF: 800-626-1101 ■ *Web:* www.wiregrasshospice.org					

Alaska

	City	State	ZIP	Phone	Fax
Hospice of Anchorage					
500 W International Airport Rd Suite C	Anchorage	AK	99518	907-561-5322	561-0334
Web: www.hospiceofanchorage.org					

Arizona

	City	State	ZIP	Phone	Fax
Banner Home Care & Hospice 1325 N Fiesta Blvd Suite 1	Gilbert	AZ	85233	480-497-5535	497-8250
TF: 800-293-6989					
Carondelet Hospice Services 630 N Alvernon Suite 361	Tucson	AZ	85711	520-205-7700	205-7598
Hospice of Arizona 2222 W Northern Ave Suite A100	Phoenix	AZ	85021	602-678-1313	242-2178
TF: 800-890-9046 ■ *Web:* www.hospiceaz.com					
Hospice Family Care 1550 S Alma School Rd Suite 102	Mesa	AZ	85210	480-461-3144	844-9711
Hospice Family Care 17220 N Boswell Blvd Suite 225-E	Sun City	AZ	85373	623-876-9100	876-9300
Hospice Family Care 6300 E El Dorado Plaza Suite A-100	Tucson	AZ	85715	520-790-9299	790-9211
TF: 800-839-3288					
Hospice of the Valley 777 W Southern Ave Suite 301	Mesa	AZ	85210	480-730-5980	730-6078
Hospice of the Valley 1510 E Flower St	Phoenix	AZ	85014	602-530-6900	530-6901
Web: www.hov.org					
Odyssey HealthCare Hospice 202 E Earll Dr Suite 160	Phoenix	AZ	85012	602-279-0677	279-1085
TF: 800-478-1682 ■ *Web:* www.odsyhealth.com					
RTA Hospice 511 S Mud Springs Rd	Payson	AZ	85541	928-472-6340	468-2120
TF: 800-450-9558 ■ *Web:* www.rtahospice.org					
Sun Health Hospice Care Services & Residence					
12740 N Plaza del Rio Blvd	Peoria	AZ	85381	623-815-2800	977-2868
TF: 800-858-9428					
Trinity Hospice 6245 N 24th Pkwy Suite 200-A	Phoenix	AZ	85016	602-351-2233	351-2288*
**Fax:* Admissions ■ *TF:* 888-763-0700 ■ *Web:* www.trinityhospice.com					
Tucson Medical Center Hospice 5301 E Grant Rd	Tucson	AZ	85712	520-324-2438	324-2432
TF: 800-526-5353					
VistaCare of Arizona 4800 N Scottsdale Rd Suite 3450	Phoenix	AZ	85251	602-648-6911	648-6912
Web: www.vistacare.com					

Arkansas

	City	State	ZIP	Phone	Fax
Arkansas Hospice 5600 W 12th St	Little Rock	AR	72204	501-748-3333	748-3334
TF: 877-257-3400 ■ *Web:* www.arkansashospice.org					
Baptist Hospice 11900 Colonel Glenn Rd Suite 2000	Little Rock	AR	72210	501-202-7474	202-7793
TF: 800-900-7474					
Hospice Home Care 1501 N University Ave Suite 340	Little Rock	AR	72207	501-666-9697	666-4616
TF: 800-479-2503					
Hospice of the Ozarks 701 Burnett Dr	Mountain Home	AR	72653	870-424-1771	
Web: www.baxterregional.org					
Peachtree Hospice 4300 Rogers Ave Suite 33	Fort Smith	AR	72903	479-494-0100	494-0102
TF: 800-752-0444 ■ *Web:* www.peachtreehospice.com					
Washington Regional Hospice 34 W Colt Square Dr Suite 1	Fayetteville	AR	72703	479-713-7385	444-7120
TF: 888-611-1094					

California

	City	State	ZIP	Phone	Fax
AseraCare Hospice - Orange 750 The City Dr Suite 120	Orange	CA	92868	714-980-0900	980-0910
TF: 877-508-0644 ■ *Web:* www.aserahospiceorange.com					
Citrus Valley Hospice 820 N Phillips Ave	West Covina	CA	91791	626-859-2263	974-0332
TF: 877-422-7301 ■ *Web:* www.cvhp.org/facilities/cvh/cvh_q&a.htm					
Community Hospice Inc 4368 Spyres Way	Modesto	CA	95356	209-578-6300	578-6391
TF: 866-645-4567 ■ *Web:* www.hospiceheart.org					
Desert Hospital Hospice of the Desert Communities					
1150 N Indian Canyon Dr	Palm Springs	CA	92263	760-323-6642	327-8086
TF: 800-962-3765					
Elizabeth Hospice 150 W Crest St	Escondido	CA	92025	760-737-2050	796-3788
TF: 800-797-2050 ■ *Web:* www.elizabethhospice.org					
Gentiva Health Services 4030 Moor Pk Ave Suite 251	San Jose	CA	95117	408-261-2801	261-9202
Hinds Hospice 1616 W Shaw Ave Suite B-6	Fresno	CA	93711	559-226-5683	226-1028
TF: 800-400-4677 ■ *Web:* www.hindshospice.com					
Hoffmann Hospice of the Valley 5300 California Ave Suite 1	Bakersfield	CA	93309	661-833-3900	716-1700
TF: 888-833-7900					
Hospice by the Bay 1540 Market St Suite 350	San Francisco	CA	94102	415-626-5900	626-7800
Web: www.hospicebythebay.citysearch.com					
Hospice Caring Project of Santa Cruz County 940 Disc Dr	Scotts Valley	CA	95066	831-430-3000	430-9272
Web: www.hospicesantacruz.org					
Hospice of the Central Coast					
2 Upper Ragsdale Dr Bldg D Suite 210	Monterey	CA	93941	831-649-7750	649-7751
Hospice of Marin 17 E Sir Francis Drake Blvd	Larkspur	CA	94939	415-927-2273	925-1004
Web: www.hospiceofmarin.org					
Hospice & Palliative Care of Contra Costa					
3470 Buskirk Ave	Pleasant Hill	CA	94523	925-609-1830	609-1841
Web: www.hospicecc.org					
Hospice of Presbyterian 15050 Imperial Hwy	La Mirada	CA	90638	562-944-1629	944-6169
Hospice of Redlands Community Hospital 350 Terracina Blvd	Redlands	CA	92373	909-335-5643	335-5648
Hospice of Saddleback Valley					
24022 Calle de la Plata Suite 200	Laguna Hills	CA	92653	949-598-3000	598-3030
Hospice of San Joaquin 3888 Pacific Ave	Stockton	CA	95204	209-957-3888	957-3986
Web: www.hospicesj.org					
Hospice Services of Santa Barbara					
222 E Canon Perdido St	Santa Barbara	CA	93101	805-965-5555	568-5178
Web: www.sbvna.org/html/hospice_services.html					
Hospice of the Valley 1150 S Bascom Ave Suite 7A	San Jose	CA	95128	408-947-1233	288-4172
Web: www.hov.org					
Kaiser Hayward Hospice Program 30116 Eigenbrodt Way	Union City	CA	94587	510-675-5777	675-5778
Kaiser Hospice 3174 Arden Way	Sacramento	CA	95825	916-486-5300	486-5301
Kaiser Permanente Hospital Hospice Dept					
280 W MacArthur Blvd	Oakland	CA	94611	510-752-6390	752-7734
Kaiser Permanente Los Angeles Hospice					
3699 Wilshire Blvd 3rd Fl	Los Angeles	CA	90010	323-783-7416	667-7455
Kaiser Walnut Creek Hospice 200 Muir Rd	Martinez	CA	94553	925-229-7800	229-7805
Livingston Memorial Visiting Nurse Assn Hospice					
1996 Eastman Ave Suite 101	Ventura	CA	93003	805-642-1608	642-0830
TF: 800-540-0543 ■ *Web:* www.lmvna.org					
Mercy Hospice 3400 Data Dr 1st Fl	Rancho Cordova	CA	95670	916-281-3900	281-3948
Mission Hospice Inc of San Mateo County					
1900 O'Farrell St Suite 200	San Mateo	CA	94403	650-554-1000	554-1001
Web: www.missionhospice.org					
Odyssey HealthCare Hospice					
7077 Orangewood Ave Suite 201	Garden Grove	CA	92841	714-934-4520	934-4515
TF: 800-797-2686 ■ *Web:* www.odsyhealth.com					
Optimal Hospice 4700 Stockdale Hwy Suite 120	Bakersfield	CA	93309	661-716-4000	716-4004
TF: 888-597-6115 ■ *Web:* www.optimalhs.com/hospice.html					
Paradise Hospice 1289 Bille Rd	Paradise	CA	95969	530-877-8755	877-4801
Ramona VNA & Hospice 890 W Stetson Ave Suite A	Hemet	CA	92543	951-658-9288	765-6229
TF: 800-588-7862 ■ *Web:* www.ramonavna.org					
Saint Agnes Hospice 1303 E Herndon Ave	Fresno	CA	93720	559-450-5600	449-5160
San Diego Hospice 4311 3rd Ave	San Diego	CA	92103	619-688-1600	688-9665
TF: 800-696-9474 ■ *Web:* www.sdhospice.com					
Sutter Hospice/Sacramento 2800 L St Suite 400	Sacramento	CA	95816	916-454-6525	454-6526
Web: www.sutterhealth.org					
Sutter VNA & Hospice 1 S Van Ness Ave	San Francisco	CA	94103	415-600-7500	600-7530
TF: 800-557-9777 ■ *Web:* www.suttervna.org					
Torrance Memorial Home Health & Hospice					
3330 Lomita Blvd Bldg 1 S	Torrance	CA	90505	310-784-3739	784-3717
Web: torrancememorial.org/helphome.htm					
TrinityCare Hospice 18331 Gridley Rd Suite F	Cerritos	CA	90703	562-809-2095	402-3336
TF: 866-210-1055					
TrinityCare Hospice 2601 Airport Dr Suite 230	Torrance	CA	90505	310-530-3800	534-5095
Web: www.trinitycarehospice.org					
UCD Hospice 3630 Business Dr Suite G	Sacramento	CA	95820	916-734-2458	736-3991
VITAS Healthcare Corp of California					
16830 Ventura Blvd Suite 315	Encino	CA	91436	818-385-0273	971-3580
TF: 800-757-4242 ■ *Web:* www.vitas.com					
VITAS Healthcare Corp of California 220 Commerce Suite 100	Irvine	CA	92602	714-921-2273	734-2780
TF: 800-486-6157 ■ *Web:* www.vitas.com					
VITAS Healthcare Corp of California					
9655 Granite Ridge Dr Suite 300	San Diego	CA	92123	858-499-8901	503-4785
TF: 800-966-8705 ■ *Web:* www.vitas.com					
VITAS Healthcare Corp of California					
990 W 190th St Suite 120	Torrance	CA	90502	310-324-2273	225-5959
TF: 800-966-7757 ■ *Web:* www.vitas.com					
VITAS Healthcare Corp of San Gabriel Cities 598 S Grand Ave	Covina	CA	91724	626-918-2273	960-8587
TF: 800-966-8709 ■ *Web:* www.vitas.com					
VNA Home Health Systems 2500 Red Hill Ave Suite 105	Santa Ana	CA	92705	949-263-4700	263-4807
Web: www.vnahhs.com					
VNA & Hospice of Northern California					
1900 Powell St Suite 300	Emeryville	CA	94608	510-450-8596	450-8532
TF: 888-600-7744 ■ *Web:* www.vnahnc.org					
VNA & Hospice of Southern California					
150 W 1st St Suite 270	Claremont	CA	91711	909-624-3574	624-1559
TF: 888-357-3574					
VNA of the Inland Counties 6235 River Crest Dr Suite L	Riverside	CA	92507	951-413-1200	656-0045
Web: www.vna-ic.org					

Colorado

	City	State	ZIP	Phone	Fax
Centura Home Care & Hospice 1391 Speer Blvd Suite 600	Denver	CO	80204	303-561-5100	561-5050
Web: www.centura.org					
Collier Hospice Center 3210 Lutheran Pkwy	Wheat Ridge	CO	80233	303-425-8000	467-4925
Hospice of Boulder County 2594 Trailridge Dr E	Lafayette	CO	80026	303-449-7740	449-6961
Web: www.hospiceboulder.org					
Hospice of Larimer County 305 Carpenter Rd	Fort Collins	CO	80525	970-663-3500	663-1180
Web: www.hlchospice.org					
Hospice of Metro Denver 501 S Cherry St Suite 700	Denver	CO	80246	303-321-2828	321-7171
Web: www.hospiceofmetrodenver.org					
Hospice & Palliative Care of Northern Colorado					
1801 16th St 4th Fl	Greeley	CO	80634	970-352-8487	475-0036
TF: 800-564-5563 ■ *Web:* www.northcoloradohospice.org					
Hospice & Palliative Care of Western Colorado					
2754 Compass Dr Suite 377	Grand Junction	CO	81506	970-241-2212	257-2400
TF: 866-310-8900 ■ *Web:* www.hospicewco.com					
Pikes Peak Hospice 825 E Pikes Peak Ave Suite 600	Colorado Springs	CO	80903	719-633-3400	633-3800
Web: www.pikespeakhospice.org					
Sangre de Cristo Hospice 1207 Pueblo Blvd Way	Pueblo	CO	81005	719-542-0032	542-1413

Connecticut

	City	State	ZIP	Phone	Fax
Abbott Terrace Health Center 44 Abbott Terr	Waterbury	CT	06702	203-755-4870	755-9016
Connecticut Hospice 100 Double Beach Rd	Branford	CT	06405	203-315-7500	315-7673*
**Fax:* Admissions ■ *TF:* 800-315-7654 ■ *Web:* www.hospice.com					
Hospice of Southeastern Connecticut Inc PO Box 902	Uncasville	CT	06382	860-848-5699	848-6898
TF: 877-654-4035 ■ *Web:* www.hospicesect.org					
Regional Hospice of Western Connecticut 405 Main St	Danbury	CT	06810	203-797-1685	792-1402
Web: www.danbury.org/hospice					
Visiting Nurse & Health Services of Connecticut Inc					
8 Keynote Dr	Vernon	CT	06066	860-872-9163	872-2419
Web: www.vnhsc.org					
Visiting Nurse & Hospice Care of Southwestern Connecticut					
1029 E Main St	Stamford	CT	06902	203-276-3000	276-3001
Web: www.vnhcsw.org					
VNA Health Care Hospice 103 Woodland St	Hartford	CT	06105	860-525-7001	278-0581
Web: www.vnastl.com					

Delaware

	City	State	ZIP	Phone	Fax
Compassionate Care Hospice of Delaware					
5610 Kirkwood Hwy	Wilmington	DE	19808	302-683-1000	683-1006
TF: 800-219-0092 ■ *Web:* www.cchnet.net					

District of Columbia

Name / Address	City	State	Zip	Phone	Fax
Hospice Care of the District of Columbia 4401 Connecticut Ave Suite 700 *TF:* 800-869-2136 ■ *Web:* www.capitalhospice.org	Washington	DC	20008	202-244-8300	244-1413

Florida

Name / Address	City	State	Zip	Phone	Fax
Bigbend Hospice 1723 Mahan Ctr Blvd *TF:* 800-772-5862 ■ *Web:* www.bigbendhospice.org	Tallahassee	FL	32308	850-878-5310	309-1638
Catholic Hospice 14875 NW 77th Ave Suite 100 *Web:* www.catholichospice.org	Miami Lakes	FL	33014	305-822-2380	824-0665
Community Hospice of Northeast Florida 580 W 8th St *Web:* www.communityhospice.com	Jacksonville	FL	32209	904-244-1651	244-1656
Comprehensive Home Health & Hospice Care 7270 NW 12th St PH 6	Miami	FL	33126	305-591-1606	591-1618
Covenant Hospice 5041 N 12th Ave *TF:* 800-541-3072 ■ *Web:* www.covenanthospice.org	Pensacola	FL	32504	850-433-2155	433-7212
Good Shepherd Hospice of Mid-Florida Inc 105 Arneson Ave *TF:* 800-753-1880 ■ *Web:* www.goodshepherdhospice.org	Auburndale	FL	33823	863-297-1880	965-5601
Gulfside Regional Hospice Inc 6117 Trouble Creek Rd *TF:* 800-561-4883 ■ *Web:* www.gulfsideregionalhospice.org	New Port Richey	FL	34653	727-845-5707	845-7254
Hernando Pasco Hospice 12107 Majestic Blvd *TF:* 800-486-8784 ■ *Web:* www.hphospice.org	Hudson	FL	34667	727-863-7971	868-9261
Hope Hospice 9470 HealthPark Cir *TF:* 800-835-1673 ■ *Web:* www.hopehospice.org	Fort Myers	FL	33908	239-482-4673	482-7298
Hospice of Citrus County PO Box 641270 *TF:* 866-642-0962 ■ *Web:* www.hospiceofcitruscounty.org	Beverly Hills	FL	34464	352-527-2020	527-0386
Hospice of the Comforter 480 W Central Pkwy *Fax: Admissions ■ *TF:* 800-767-9952 ■ *Web:* www.hospice-comforter.org	Altamonte Springs	FL	32714	407-682-0808	682-5787*
Hospice of the Florida Suncoast 5771 Roosevelt Blvd *Web:* www.thehospice.com	Clearwater	FL	33760	727-586-4432	523-2145
Hospice of Health First 1900 Dairy Rd	West Melbourne	FL	32904	321-952-0494	952-0382
Hospice of Lake & Sumter Inc 12300 Lane Park Rd *TF:* 888-728-6234 ■ *Web:* www.hospicels.com	Tavares	FL	32778	352-343-1341	343-6115
Hospice of Marion County PO Box 4860 *Web:* www.hospiceofmarion.com	Ocala	FL	34478	352-873-7434	873-7435
Hospice of Martin & Saint Lucie 1201 SE Indian St *TF:* 800-299-4677 ■ *Web:* www.tchospices.org	Stuart	FL	34997	772-403-4500	403-4518
Hospice of Naples 1095 Whippoorwill Ln *Web:* www.hospiceofnaples.org	Naples	FL	34105	239-261-4404	262-2429
Hospice of North Central Florida Inc 4200 NW 90th Blvd *TF:* 800-727-1889 ■ *Web:* www.hospice-cares.com	Gainesville	FL	32606	352-378-2121	379-6290
Hospice of Northeast Florida 4266 Sunbeam Rd *TF:* 800-658-8898 ■ *Web:* www.communityhospice.com	Jacksonville	FL	32257	904-268-5200	268-9795
Hospice of Palm Beach County 5300 East Ave *TF:* 800-287-4722 ■ *Web:* www.hpbc.com	West Palm Beach	FL	33407	561-848-5200	863-2044
Hospice of Saint Francis 1250-B Grumman Pl *TF:* 866-269-4240 ■ *Web:* www.nbbd.com/npr/hospice	Titusville	FL	32780	321-269-4240	269-5428
Hospice by the Sea 1531 W Palmetto Park Rd *Fax: Admissions ■ *TF:* 800-633-2577 ■ *Web:* www.hospicebytheseafl.org	Boca Raton	FL	33486	561-395-5031	368-6837*
Hospice of Southwest Florida 5955 Rand Blvd *TF:* 800-959-4291 ■ *Web:* www.hospice-swf.org	Sarasota	FL	34238	941-923-5822	925-0969
Hospice of the Treasure Coast 2500 Virginia Ave Suite 202 *TF:* 800-299-4677 ■ *Web:* www.hospicetc.org	Fort Pierce	FL	34981	772-465-0660	465-6309
Hospice & VNA of the Florida Keys 1319 William St *Web:* www.hospicevna.com	Key West	FL	33040	305-294-8812	292-9466
Hospice of Volusia/Flagler 3800 Woodbriar Trail *TF:* 800-272-2717 ■ *Web:* www.hfch.org/hospice	Port Orange	FL	32129	386-322-4701	322-4702
HospiceCare of Southeast Florida Inc 309 SE 18th St *TF:* 800-372-1757 ■ *Web:* www.hospicecareflorida.org	Fort Lauderdale	FL	33316	954-467-7423	524-6067
Lifepath Hospice 3010 W Azeele St *TF:* 800-209-2200 ■ *Web:* www.lifepath-hospice.org	Tampa	FL	33609	813-877-2200	872-7037
VITAS Healthcare Corp of Central Florida 5151 Adanson St Suite 200 *Web:* www.vitas.com	Orlando	FL	32804	407-875-0028	691-4517
VITAS Healthcare Corp of Florida 18001 Old Cutler Rd Suite 454 *TF:* 800-950-9200 ■ *Web:* www.vitas.com	Palmetto Bay	FL	33157	786-573-1379	573-7870
VITAS Innovative Hospice Care 100 S Biscayne Blvd Suite 1500 *Fax: Hum Res ■ *TF:* 800-950-9200 ■ *Web:* www.vitas.com	Miami	FL	33131	305-374-4143	350-6797*
VNA Hospice of IRC 1110 35th Ln *TF:* 800-749-5760 ■ *Web:* www.vnatc.com	Vero Beach	FL	32960	772-567-5551	567-9308
Wuesthoff Brevard Hospice 8060 Spyglass Hill Rd *TF:* 800-259-2007 ■ *Web:* www.wuesthoff.org	Viera	FL	32940	321-253-2222	255-8140

Georgia

Name / Address	City	State	Zip	Phone	Fax
Columbus Hospice 7020 Moon Rd *Web:* www.columbushospice.com	Columbus	GA	31909	706-569-7992	569-8560
Heyman HospiceCare PO Box 163 *TF:* 800-324-1078 ■ *Web:* www.floydmed.org	Rome	GA	30162	706-509-3200	509-3201
Hospice Atlanta-Visiting Nurse Health System 1244 Park Vista Dr *TF:* 800-287-7849 ■ *Web:* www.vnhs.org	Atlanta	GA	30319	404-869-3000	869-3098
Hospice of Central Georgia 3780 Eisenhower Pkwy *TF:* 800-211-1084	Macon	GA	31206	478-633-5660	781-3348
Hospice of NE Georgia Medical Center 2150 Limestone Pkwy Suite 222	Gainesville	GA	30501	770-533-8888	
Hospice Savannah Inc PO Box 13190 *TF:* 888-355-4911 ■ *Web:* www.hospicesavannah.org	Savannah	GA	31416	912-355-2289	355-2376
Hospice of Southwest Georgia 818 Gordon Ave *TF:* 800-290-6567	Thomasville	GA	31792	229-227-5520	227-5526
Peachtree Hospice 30 Perimeter Pk Suite 201	Atlanta	GA	30341	770-698-8785	698-9775
Trinity Hospital of Augusta 2260 Wrightsboro Rd *TF:* 800-533-3949 ■ *Web:* www.trinityofaugusta.com	Augusta	GA	30904	706-729-6000	729-6454
United Hospice-Atlanta 1626 Jeurgens Ct *TF:* 800-544-4788 ■ *Web:* www.united-hospice.com	Norcross	GA	30093	404-292-2081	297-4647
VITAS Hospice Care 5411 N Land Dr *TF:* 800-938-4827 ■ *Web:* www.vitas.com	Atlanta	GA	30342	404-250-1806	843-6510
Wellstar Community Hospice 4040 Hospital West Dr	Austell	GA	30106	770-732-6710	732-6732

Hawaii

Name / Address	City	State	Zip	Phone	Fax
Hospice Hawaii 860 Iwilei Rd *Web:* www.hospicehawaii.org	Honolulu	HI	96817	808-924-9255	922-9161
Hospice of Hilo 1011 Waianuenue Ave *Web:* www.hospiceofhilo.org	Hilo	HI	96720	808-969-1733	969-4863
Saint Francis Hospice Program 24 Puiwa Rd *Web:* www.stfrancishawaii.org/sfhs/	Honolulu	HI	96817	808-595-7566	595-3515

Idaho

Name / Address	City	State	Zip	Phone	Fax
Life's Doors Hospice PO Box 5754 *Web:* www.lifesdoors.com	Boise	ID	83705	208-344-6500	344-6590

Illinois

Name / Address	City	State	Zip	Phone	Fax
Advocate Hospice 1441 Branding Ave Suite 200 *Web:* www.advocatehealth.com	Downers Grove	IL	60515	630-963-6800	963-6877
Blessing Hospice Broadway at 14th St PO Box 7005 *TF:* 800-382-8833	Quincy	IL	62305	217-228-5521	223-8231
Carle Hospice 206-A W Anthony Dr *TF:* 800-239-3626 ■ *Web:* www.carle.com/default.asp	Champaign	IL	61822	217-383-3488	356-8672
CNS Home Health & Hospice 690 E North Ave Suite 100 *Web:* www.cnshomehealth.org	Carol Stream	IL	60188	630-665-7000	665-7371
Evanston Northwestern Healthcare Services Home Services Div 4901 Searle Pkwy Suite 130 *Web:* www.enh.org	Skokie	IL	60077	847-982-4300	982-4301
Family Hospice of Belleville Area 5110 W Main St *Web:* www.familyhospice.org	Belleville	IL	62226	618-277-1800	277-1074
Harbor Light Hospice 800 Roosevelt Rd Bldg C Suite 206 *TF:* 800-419-0542 ■ *Web:* www.hospiceharborlight.com	Glen Ellyn	IL	60137	630-942-0100	942-0118
Heartland Home Health Care & Hospice 4415 W Harrison Suite 401 *Web:* www.heartlandhomehealth.com	Hillside	IL	60162	708-234-2850	236-5150
Heartland Hospice 4415 Harrison St Suite 403	Hillside	IL	60162	708-234-2800	234-2828
Horizon Hospice 833 W Chicago Ave *TF:* 866-733-6028 ■ *Web:* www.horizonhospice.org	Chicago	IL	60622	312-733-2233	733-8952
Hospice of Lincolnland 700 Broadway E Suite 9	Mattoon	IL	61938	217-234-4075	348-6525
Hospice of Northeastern Illinois 410 S Hager Ave *TF:* 800-425-4444 ■ *Web:* www.hospiceanswers.org	Barrington	IL	60010	847-381-5599	381-1431
Hospice of Southern Illinois 305 S Illinois St *TF:* 800-233-1708 ■ *Web:* www.hospice.org	Belleville	IL	62220	618-235-1703	235-2828
Joliet Area Community Hospice 250 Water Stone Cir *TF:* 800-360-1817 ■ *Web:* www.joliethospice.org	Joliet	IL	60431	815-740-4104	740-4107
Little Company of Mary Home Based Services 9800 Southwest Hwy *Web:* www.lcmh.org	Oak Lawn	IL	60453	708-229-4663	499-5975
Methodist Medical Center of Illinois Hospice Services 221 NE Glen Oak Ave *Web:* www.methodistmedicalcenter.org	Peoria	IL	61636	309-672-5746	671-2168
Northern Illinois Hospice Assn 4215 Newburg Rd *Web:* www.northernillinoishospice.org	Rockford	IL	61108	815-398-0500	398-0588
OSF Hospice 2265 W Altorfer Dr	Peoria	IL	61615	309-683-7703	683-7824
Palliative CareCenter & Hospice of the North Shore 2050 Claire Ct *Web:* www.carecenter.org	Glenview	IL	60025	847-467-7423	556-1611
Provena Covenant Hospice 1400 W Park St *Web:* www.provena.org	Urbana	IL	61801	217-337-2470	337-2279
Rainbow Hospice 444 N Northwest Hwy Suite 145 *Web:* www.rainbowhospice.org	Park Ridge	IL	60068	847-685-9900	685-6390
Unity Hospice 439 E 31st St Suite 213 *TF:* 888-949-1188 ■ *Web:* www.unityhospice.com	Chicago	IL	60616	312-949-1188	949-0158
VITAS Healthcare Corp 600 Holiday Plaza Dr Suite 200 *Web:* www.vitas.com	Matteson	IL	60443	708-748-8777	748-8778
VITAS Healthcare Corp-North 700 N Sacramento Blvd Suite 201 *TF:* 800-938-4827	Chicago	IL	60612	773-533-2030	533-3166

Indiana

Name / Address	City	State	Zip	Phone	Fax
Covenant Hospice 1029 S 14th St *TF:* 877-757-1357 ■ *Web:* www.covenant-hospice.com	New Castle	IN	47362	765-529-6667	529-7094
Hospice of the Calumet Area 600 Superior Ave *Web:* www.hospicecalumet.org	Munster	IN	46321	219-922-2732	922-1947
Hospice & Palliative Care of Southern Indiana 624 E Market St *TF:* 800-895-5633 ■ *Web:* www.hospices.org/Southern_Indiana.htm	New Albany	IN	47150	812-945-4596	945-4733
Hospice of Saint Joseph County 111 Sunnybrook Ct *Web:* www.centerforhospice.org	South Bend	IN	46637	574-243-3100	243-3134
Hospice of South Central Indiana 2626 E 17th St	Columbus	IN	47201	812-314-8000	314-8151
Saint Vincent Hospice 8450 N Payne Rd Suite 100 *TF:* 888-780-7284 ■ *Web:* www.stvincent.org	Indianapolis	IN	46268	317-338-4040	338-4044
VistaCare Hospice 6431 S East St *TF:* 800-480-9408 ■ *Web:* www.vistacare.com	Indianapolis	IN	46227	317-788-0300	788-8760

Iowa

Name / Address	City	State	Zip	Phone	Fax
Cedar Valley Hospice 2101 Kimball Ave Suite 401 *TF:* 800-617-1972 ■ *Web:* www.cvhospice.org	Waterloo	IA	50702	319-272-2002	272-2071
Hospice of Central Iowa 401 Railroad Pl *TF:* 800-806-9934 ■ *Web:* www.hospice-iowa.org	West Des Moines	IA	50265	515-274-3400	271-1302
Hospice of North Iowa 232 2nd St SE *TF:* 800-297-4719	Mason City	IA	50401	641-422-6208	422-6244
Hospice of Siouxland 4300 Hamilton Blvd *TF:* 800-383-4545 ■ *Web:* www.hospiceofsiouxland.org	Sioux City	IA	51104	712-233-4100	233-1123
Mercy Hospice 638 S Bluff Blvd *TF:* 888-311-6702	Clinton	IA	52732	563-244-3666	244-3719

Kansas

Name / Address	City	State	Zip	Phone	Fax
Harry Hynes Memorial Hospice 313 S Market St *TF:* 800-767-4965 ■ *Web:* www.hynesmemorial.org	Wichita	KS	67202	316-265-9441	265-6066
Hospice Home Health of Olathe Medical Center 20333 W 151st St TDB 2 Suite 301 *TF:* 800-467-4451	Olathe	KS	66061	913-324-8515	324-8517
Hospice of Reno County 3 Compound Dr *TF:* 800-267-6891	Hutchinson	KS	67502	620-665-2473	669-5959
Hynes Harry Memorial Hospice 313 S Market St *TF:* 800-767-4965 ■ *Web:* www.hynesmemorial.org	Wichita	KS	67202	316-265-9441	265-6066
Midland Hospice Care 200 SW Frazier Cir *TF:* 800-491-3691 ■ *Web:* www.midlandhospice.org	Topeka	KS	66606	785-232-2044	232-5567

Kentucky

	City	State	ZIP	Phone	Fax
Community Hospice 1538 Central Ave	Ashland	KY	41101	606-329-1890	329-0018
TF: 800-926-6184 ■ *Web:* communityhospicecares.org					
Heritage Hospice 120 Enterprise Dr PO Box 1213	Danville	KY	40423	859-236-2425	236-6152
TF: 800-203-6633 ■ *Web:* www.heritagehospice.com					
Hospice Assn Inc 723 Harvard Dr	Owensboro	KY	42301	270-926-7565	926-1223
TF: 800-466-5348 ■ *Web:* www.hospiceohiovalley.org					
Hospice of the Bluegrass 2312 Alexandria Dr	Lexington	KY	40504	859-276-5344	223-0490
TF: 800-876-6005 ■ *Web:* www.hospicebg.com					
Hospice of Lake Cumberland 100 Pkwy Dr	Somerset	KY	42503	606-679-4389	678-0191
TF: 800-937-9596					
Hospice of Southern Kentucky 5872 Scottsville Rd	Bowling Green	KY	42104	270-782-3402	782-3496
TF: 800-344-9479					
Jessamine County Hospice PO Box 873	Nicholasville	KY	40356	859-887-2696	885-1474
TF: 800-279-0750					
Lourdes Homecare & Hospice 2855 Jackson St	Paducah	KY	42003	270-444-2262	444-2380
TF: 800-870-7460 ■ *Web:* elourdes.com					
Saint Anthony's Hospice 2410 S Green St	Henderson	KY	42420	270-826-2326	831-2169
Web: stanthonyshospice.org					
Saint Elizabeth Home Health Hospice 401 E 20th St	Covington	KY	41014	859-292-4256	292-4120
Web: www.stelizabeth.com					

Louisiana

	City	State	ZIP	Phone	Fax
Hospice of Acadiana 2600 Johnston St Suite 200	Lafayette	LA	70503	337-232-1234	232-1297
TF: 800-738-2226 ■ *Web:* www.hospiceacadiana.com					
Hospice of Baton Rouge 9063 Siegen Ln	Baton Rouge	LA	70810	225-767-4673	769-8113
TF: 800-349-8833 ■ *Web:* www.hospicebr.org					
Hospice of South Louisiana 6500 W Main St	Houma	LA	70360	985-868-3095	868-3910
North Oaks Hospice PO Box 2668	Hammond	LA	70404	985-230-7620	386-0184
Slidell Memorial Hospice 1045 Florida Ave Suite A	Slidell	LA	70458	985-847-0174	649-0671
TF: 888-643-2041					

Maine

	City	State	ZIP	Phone	Fax
HealthReach Homecare & Hospice PO Box 1568	Waterville	ME	04903	207-861-3400	861-3419
TF: 877-561-7299					

Maryland

	City	State	ZIP	Phone	Fax
Capital Hospice 9200 Basil Ct Suite 200	Largo	MD	20774	301-883-0866	883-0925
Web: www.capitalhospice.org					
Carroll Hospice 292 Stoner Ave	Westminster	MD	21157	410-871-8000	871-7216
TF: 888-224-2580 ■ *Web:* www.ccgh.com					
Coastal Hospice Inc 2604 Old Ocean City Rd	Salisbury	MD	21804	410-742-8732	548-5669
TF: 800-780-7886 ■ *Web:* www.coastalhospice.org					
Heartland Hospice Services 4 E Rolling Cross Rd Suite 307	Baltimore	MD	21228	410-719-8670	719-0241
TF: 888-332-6232 ■ *Web:* www.hcr-manorcare.com					
Hospice of Baltimore 6601 N Charles St	Baltimore	MD	21204	443-849-8200	849-6761
Hospice of the Chesapeake 445 Defense Hwy	Annapolis	MD	21401	410-987-2003	837-1505*
**Fax Area Code: 443* ■ *TF:* 800-745-6132 ■ *Web:* www.hospicechesapeake.org					
Montgomery Hospice Society 1355 Piccard Dr Suite 100	Rockville	MD	20850	301-921-4400	921-4433
Web: www.montgomeryhospice.org					
Richey Joseph Hospice 838 N Eutaw St	Baltimore	MD	21201	410-523-2150	523-1146
Web: www.josephricheyhospice.org					
Seasons Hospice 7008 Security Blvd Suite 300	Baltimore	MD	21244	410-594-9100	277-4251
TF: 888-523-6000 ■ *Web:* www.seasons.org					
Stella Maris Hospice Care Program 2300 Dulaney Valley Rd	Timonium	MD	21093	410-252-4500	560-9693
Web: www.stellamarisinc.com					

Massachusetts

	City	State	ZIP	Phone	Fax
Baystate VNA & Hospice 50 Maple St	Springfield	MA	01102	413-781-5070	781-3342
TF: 800-249-8298 ■ *Web:* www.baystatehealth.com					
Good Samaritan Hospice 310 Allston St	Brighton	MA	02135	617-566-6242	566-3055
HealthCare Dimensions 48 Woerid Ave Suite 102	Waltham	MA	02453	781-894-1100	736-0908
Hospice Care 100 Sylvan Rd	Woburn	MA	01801	781-279-4100	279-4677
TF: 866-279-7103 ■ *Web:* www.hospicecarema.org					
Hospice of Community Visiting Nurse Agency 10 Emory St	Attleboro	MA	02703	508-222-0118	226-8939
TF: 800-220-0110 ■ *Web:* www.communityvna.com					
Hospice Life Care 113 Hampden St	Holyoke	MA	01040	413-533-3923	536-4513
Hospice of the North Shore 10 Elm St	Danvers	MA	01923	978-774-7566	774-4389
Web: www.hns.org					
Hospice & Palliative Care of Cape Cod Inc 765 Attucks Way	Hyannis	MA	02601	508-957-0200	957-0229
TF: 800-642-2423 ■ *Web:* www.hospicecapecod.org					
Merrimack Valley Hospice 360 Merrimack St Bldg 9	Lawrence	MA	01843	978-552-4000	552-4544
TF: 800-933-5593 ■ *Web:* www.merrimackvalleyhospice.org					
Old Colony Hospice 1 Credit Union Way	Randolph	MA	02368	781-341-4145	297-7345
TF: 800-370-1322 ■ *Web:* www.oldcolonyhospice.org					
VNA Hospice Alliance 168 Industrial Dr	Northampton	MA	01060	413-584-1060	584-9615
TF: 800-244-1060					

Michigan

	City	State	ZIP	Phone	Fax
Angela Hospice Home Care 14100 Newburgh Rd	Livonia	MI	48154	734-464-7810	464-6930
TF: 800-467-7423 ■ *Web:* www.angelahospice.org					
Arbor Hospice & Home Care 2366 Oak Valley Dr	Ann Arbor	MI	48103	734-662-5999	662-2330
TF: 888-992-2273 ■ *Web:* www.arborhospice.org					
Community Hospice & Home Care Services 6639 Wayne Rd	Westland	MI	48185	734-522-4244	522-2099
TF: 800-444-0425					
Covenant VNA 500 S Hamilton St	Saginaw	MI	48602	989-799-6020	799-6062
TF: 800-862-4968					
Cranbrook Hospice Care 281 Enterprise Ct Suite 300	Bloomfield Hills	MI	48302	248-334-6700	334-7064
TF: 800-832-1155					
Genesys Hospice 7280 S State Rd	Goodrich	MI	48438	810-762-4370	762-4110
TF: 888-943-9690					
Good Samaritan Hospice Care 166 E Goodale Ave	Battle Creek	MI	49017	269-660-3600	660-3650
TF: 800-254-5939 ■ *Web:* www.lifespan4u.org					
Heartland Hospice 28588 Northwestern Hwy Suite 475	Southfield	MI	48034	248-948-1019	945-3333
Hospice Care of Southwest Michigan 222 N Kalamazoo Mall Suite 100	Kalamazoo	MI	49007	269-345-0273	345-8522
Web: www.hospiceswmi.org					
Hospice of Henry Ford Health System 655 W 13 Mile Rd 1st Fl	Madison Heights	MI	48071	248-585-5270	585-4210
Web: www.henryford.com					
Hospice of Holland Inc 270 Hoover Blvd	Holland	MI	49423	616-396-2972	396-2808
TF: 800-255-3522 ■ *Web:* www.hollandhospice.org					
Hospice at Home 4025 Health Park Ln	Saint Joseph	MI	49085	269-429-7100	428-3499
TF: 800-717-3811 ■ *Web:* www.hospiceathome.org					
Hospice of Lansing & Ionia Area Hospice 6035 Executive Dr Suite 103	Lansing	MI	48911	517-882-4500	882-3010
Web: www.hospiceoflansing.org					
Hospice of Michigan 400 Mack Ave	Detroit	MI	48201	313-578-5000	578-6385
TF: 888-466-5656 ■ *Web:* www.hom.org					
Hospice of North Ottawa Community 1515 S DeSpelder St	Grand Haven	MI	49417	616-846-2015	846-7227
TF: 800-670-7991 ■ *Web:* www.noch.org/hospice.html					
Karmanos Cancer Institute Hospice 24601 Northwestern Hwy	Southfield	MI	48075	248-827-1592	827-0972
TF: 800-527-6266 ■ *Web:* www.karmanos.org					
McLaren Hospice Service 1515 Cal Dr	Davison	MI	48423	810-496-8855	496-8775
TF: 800-206-4806					
Mid Michigan Hospice 3007 N Saginaw Rd	Midland	MI	48640	989-633-1400	633-1412
TF: 800-852-9350					
Munson Hospice 1105 6th St	Traverse City	MI	49684	231-935-6520	935-9142
TF: 800-252-2065 ■ *Web:* www.munsonhealthcare.com					
Saint Joseph Mercy Home Care & Hospice 806 Airport Blvd	Ann Arbor	MI	48108	734-327-3200	327-3274
TF: 888-884-6569					
Samaritan Care Hospice 24445 Northwestern Hwy Suite 105	Southfield	MI	48075	248-355-9900	355-5705
TF: 800-397-9360 ■ *Web:* www.samaritancarehospice.com					
VNA & Hospice of Southwest Michigan Hospice 348 N Burdick St	Kalamazoo	MI	49007	269-343-1396	382-8686
TF: 800-343-1396 ■ *Web:* www.borgess.com					

Minnesota

	City	State	ZIP	Phone	Fax
Allina Hospice & Palliative Care 1055 Westgate Dr Suite 100	Saint Paul	MN	55114	651-635-9173	628-2999
TF: 800-261-0879 ■ *Web:* www.allina.com					
Fairview Hospice 2450 26th Ave S	Minneapolis	MN	55406	612-728-2455	728-2400
TF: 800-285-5647 ■ *Web:* www.fairview.org					
Health Partners Hospice of the Lakes 8170 33rd Ave S	Minneapolis	MN	55425	952-883-6877	883-6883
Hospice of the Twin Cities 10405 6th Ave N Suite 250	Plymouth	MN	55441	763-531-2424	531-2422
Web: www.hospiceofthetwincities.com					
Mayo Hospice Program 200 1st St SW	Rochester	MN	55905	507-284-4002	284-0220
TF: 800-679-9084					
Methodist Homecare & Hospice 6500 Excelsior Blvd Box 650	Saint Louis Park	MN	55426	952-993-6087	993-5081
North Memorial Home Health & Hospice 3500 France Ave N Suite 101	Robbinsdale	MN	55422	763-520-5770	
Rice Hospice 301 SW Becker Ave	Willmar	MN	56201	320-231-4450	231-4864
TF: 800-336-7423					

Mississippi

	City	State	ZIP	Phone	Fax
Delta Area Hospice Care Ltd 522 Arnold Ave	Greenville	MS	38701	662-335-7040	335-7027
TF: 800-742-2641					
Hospice Ministries 450 Towne Center Blvd	Ridgeland	MS	39157	601-898-1053	898-4320
TF: 800-273-7724 ■ *Web:* www.hospiceministries.org					
North Mississippi Medical Center Hospice 422-A E President St	Tupelo	MS	38801	662-377-3612	377-2537
TF: 800-852-1610					
Sta-Home Hospice 406 Briarwood Dr Suite 500	Jackson	MS	39206	601-991-1933	991-3343
TF: 800-336-6557 ■ *Web:* www.sta-home.org					

Missouri

	City	State	ZIP	Phone	Fax
American Heartland Hospice 4372 Casa Brazilia Dr Suite 203	Saint Louis	MO	63129	314-894-8189	894-7334
Web: www.callmyhospice.com					
Hands of Hope Hospice 105 N Far West Dr Suite 100	Saint Joseph	MO	64506	816-271-7190	271-7672
TF: 800-443-1143					
Kansas City Hospice 9221 Ward Pkwy Suite 100	Kansas City	MO	64114	816-363-2600	523-0068
Web: www.kansascityhospice.org					
Odyssey Healthcare of Kansas City 800 E 101st Terr Suite 150	Kansas City	MO	64131	816-333-1980	333-2421
Web: www.odsyhealth.com/local/local_kansas.asp					
Saint John's Hospice Care 1378 E Republic Rd	Springfield	MO	65804	417-820-7550	820-7426
Saint Luke's Home Care & Hospice 3100 Broadway St Suite 1000	Kansas City	MO	64111	816-756-1160	756-0838
SSM Hospice 2 Harbor Bend Ct	Lake Saint Louis	MO	63367	636-695-2050	695-2060
TF: 800-835-1212 ■ *Web:* www.ssmhc.com					
Trinity Hospice 10805 Sunset Office Dr Suite 400	Sunset Hills	MO	63127	314-821-8826	821-2694
TF: 888-282-2273 ■ *Web:* www.trinityhospice.com					
Unity Health Hospice 1000 Des Peres Rd Suite 200B	Saint Louis	MO	63131	314-729-4400	729-4412
VNA Hospice Care 9450 Manchester Rd Suite 206	Saint Louis	MO	63119	314-918-7171	918-8054
TF: 800-392-4740 ■ *Web:* www.vnastl.com					

Montana

	City	State	ZIP	Phone	Fax
Peace Hospice of Montana 1101 26th St S	Great Falls	MT	59405	406-455-3040	455-3070

Nebraska

	City	State	ZIP	Phone	Fax
AseraCare Hospice - Lincoln 1600 S 70th St Suite 201	Lincoln	NE	68506	402-488-1363	488-5976
TF: 800-826-3841 ■ *Web:* www.aserahospicelincoln.com					
VNA of the Midlands Hospice 1941 S 42nd St Suite 225	Omaha	NE	68105	402-342-5566	342-9304
TF: 800-456-8869 ■ *Web:* www.vnaomaha.org					

Nevada

	City	State	ZIP	Phone	Fax
Adelson Nathan Hospice 4141 S Swenson St	Las Vegas	NV	89119	702-733-0320	938-3900
TF: 888-281-8646 ■ *Web:* www.nah.org					
Family Home Hospice 1701 W Charleston Blvd Suite 201	Las Vegas	NV	89102	702-383-0887	383-9826
TF: 800-999-2536					

Nevada (Cont'd)

				Phone	Fax
Nathan Adelson Hospice 4141 S Swenson St *TF:* 888-281-8646 ■ *Web:* www.nah.org	Las Vegas	NV	89119	702-733-0320	938-3900
Odyssey HealthCare of Las Vegas Inc 4011-A McLeod Dr *Web:* www.odsyhealth.com	Las Vegas	NV	89121	702-693-4904	693-4925
Saint Mary's Hospice of Northern Nevada 18653 Wedge Pkwy *TF:* 866-333-8059 ■ *Web:* www.saintmarysreno.com	Reno	NV	89511	775-770-3081	770-6904

New Hampshire

				Phone	Fax
Concord Regional Visiting Nurse Assoc Hospice Program 250 Pleasant St *TF:* 800-924-8620 ■ *Web:* www.crvna.org	Concord	NH	03302	603-224-4093	228-7360
Home Health & Hospice Care 22 Prospect St *TF:* 800-887-5973 ■ *Web:* www.hhhc.org	Nashua	NH	03060	603-882-2941	883-1515
Seacoast Hospice 10 Hampton Rd *TF:* 800-416-9207 ■ *Web:* www.seacoasthospice.org	Exeter	NH	03833	603-778-7391	418-0040
VNA of Manchester & Southern New Hampshire 33 S Commercial St Suite 401 *TF:* 800-624-6084	Manchester	NH	03101	603-622-3781	641-4074

New Jersey

				Phone	Fax
Atlantic City Medical Center Hospice 1406 Doughty Rd *TF:* 888-744-0523	Egg Harbor Township	NJ	08234	609-272-2424	272-2414
Center for Hope Hospice 1900 Raritan Rd *Web:* www.centerforhope.com	Scotch Plains	NJ	07076	908-889-7780	889-5172
Compassionate Care Hospice 140 Littleton Rd Suite 200 *TF:* 800-916-1494	Parsippany	NJ	07054	973-916-1400	402-4725
Compassionate Care Hospice 600 Highland Dr Suite 624 *TF:* 800-844-4774	West Hampton	NJ	08060	609-267-1178	267-7914
Home Health/Van Dyke Hospice 99 Rt 37 W *TF:* 800-338-3131	Toms River	NJ	08755	732-818-6800	818-6888
Hospice of New Jersey 400 Broadacres Dr 4th Fl *Web:* www.hospicenj.com	Bloomfield	NJ	07003	973-893-0818	893-0828
Hospice Program of Hackensack University Medical Center 30 Prospect Ave *Web:* www.humed.com/hospice	Hackensack	NJ	07601	201-342-7766	487-1982
Hunterdon Hospice 2100 Wescott Dr *Web:* www.hunterdonhealthcare.org	Flemington	NJ	08822	908-788-6600	788-6651
Karen Ann Quinlan Hospice 99 Sparta Ave *TF:* 800-882-1117 ■ *Web:* www.karenannquinlanhospice.org	Newton	NJ	07860	973-383-0115	383-6889
Lighthouse Hospice 1040 N Kings Hwy Suite 100 *TF:* 888-345-7742 ■ *Web:* www.lighthousehospice.net	Cherry Hill	NJ	08034	856-414-1155	414-1313
Quinlan Karen Ann Hospice 99 Sparta Ave *TF:* 800-882-1117 ■ *Web:* www.karenannquinlanhospice.org	Newton	NJ	07860	973-383-0115	383-6889
Saint Barnabas Hospice & Palliative Care Center 95 Old Short Hills Rd *Web:* www.sbhcs.com/hospitals/hospice/index.html	West Orange	NJ	07052	973-322-4800	322-4795
Samaritan Hospice 5 Eves Dr Suite 300 *TF:* 800-229-8183 ■ *Web:* www.samaritanhospice.org	Marlton	NJ	08053	856-596-1600	596-7881
South Jersey HealthCare HospiceCare 2848 S Delsea Dr *TF:* 800-584-1515 ■ *Web:* www.sjhs.com	Vineland	NJ	08360	856-794-1515	405-2870
VNA of Central Jersey 1100 Wayside Rd *TF:* 800-843-2220 ■ *Web:* www.vnacj.org	Tinton Falls	NJ	07712	732-695-4640	493-4256

New Mexico

				Phone	Fax
Mesilla Valley Hospice 299 E Montana Ave *Web:* www.mvhospice.org	Las Cruces	NM	88005	505-523-4700	527-2204
Presbyterian Hospice 8100 Constitution Pl NE 3rd Fl	Albuquerque	NM	87110	505-559-1122	559-6067
VistaCare Hospice 5639 Jefferson St NE *TF:* 888-605-1969 ■ *Web:* www.vistacare.com	Albuquerque	NM	87109	505-821-5404	821-5449
VistaCare Hospice 1515 W Calle Sur St *TF:* 800-658-6844	Hobbs	NM	88240	505-392-2060	392-2807

New York

				Phone	Fax
Cabrini Hospice 227 E 19th St *Web:* www.cabrininy.org/hospicecare.html	New York	NY	10003	212-995-6480	995-7015
Catskill Area Hospice & Palliative Care Inc 1 Birchwood Dr *TF:* 800-306-3870 ■ *Web:* www.cahpc.org	Oneonta	NY	13820	607-432-6773	432-7741
Community Hospice of Albany 445 New Karner Rd	Albany	NY	12205	518-724-0200	724-0299
East End Hospice 481 Westhampton-Riverhead Rd PO Box 1048 *Web:* www.eeh.org	Westhampton Beach	NY	11978	631-288-8400	288-8492
Good Shepherd Hospice 190 Motor Pkwy 1st Fl *Web:* www.goodshepherdhospice.chsli.org	Hauppauge	NY	11788	631-648-1255	648-1268
Good Shepherd Hospice 4747-20 Nesconset Hwy *Web:* www.goodshepherdhospice.chsli.org	Port Jefferson Station	NY	11776	631-474-4040	474-4058
Good Shepherd Hospice Nassau Branch 528 Mineola Ave	Carle Place	NY	11514	516-876-8485	876-8957
High Peaks Hospice PO Box 840 *TF:* 877-324-1686	Saranac Lake	NY	12983	518-891-0606	891-0657
HomeCare & Hospice 1225 W State St *TF:* 800-339-7011 ■ *Web:* www.communitycarewny.org	Olean	NY	14760	716-372-5735	372-4635
Hospicare of Tompkins County 172 E King Rd *Web:* www.hospicare.org	Ithaca	NY	14850	607-272-0212	272-0237
Hospice Care Inc 4277 Middle Settlement Rd *TF:* 800-317-5661 ■ *Web:* www.hospicecareinc.org	New Hartford	NY	13413	315-735-6484	793-8852
Hospice Care Network 99 Sunnyside Blvd *TF:* 800-246-7742 ■ *Web:* www.hospicecarenetwork.org	Woodbury	NY	11797	516-832-7100	832-7160
Hospice Care in Westchester & Putnam Inc 540 White Plains Rd Suite 300 *TF:* 800-298-6341 ■ *Web:* www.vnahv.org/1hospice.htm	Tarrytown	NY	10591	914-666-4228	666-0378
Hospice Chautauqua County 4840 W Lake Rd *Web:* hospicechautauqua.org	Mayville	NY	14757	716-753-5383	753-5253
Hospice Family Care 550 E Main St *Web:* www.homecare-hospice.org	Batavia	NY	14020	585-343-7596	343-7629
Hospice of Jefferson County 425 Washington St *Web:* www.jeffhospice.com	Watertown	NY	13601	315-788-7323	788-9653
Hospice at Lourdes 4102 Old Vestal Rd *Web:* www.lourdes.com	Vestal	NY	13850	607-798-5692	798-5345
Hospice of the North Country 43 Durkee St Suite 200 *TF:* 800-639-6430 ■ *Web:* www.hospicenc.com	Plattsburgh	NY	12901	518-561-8465	561-3182
Hospice of Orange & Sullivan Counties 800 Stony Brook Ct *TF:* 800-924-0157 ■ *Web:* www.hospiceoforange.com	Newburgh	NY	12550	845-561-6111	561-2179
Hospice & Palliative Care of Buffalo 225 Como Park Blvd *Web:* www.hospicebuffalo.org	Cheektowaga	NY	14227	716-686-1900	686-8181
Hospice of Saint Lawrence Valley 6805 State Hwy 11 *Web:* www.hospiceslv.org	Potsdam	NY	13676	315-265-3105	265-0323
Hospice of Westchester 95 S Broadway 4th Fl *Web:* www.hospiceofwestchester.com	White Plains	NY	10601	914-682-1484	682-9425
Jacob Perlow Hospice Beth Israel Medical Center 1775 Broadway Suite 300	New York	NY	10019	212-420-2844	420-2420
Jansen Memorial Hospice 69 Main St	Tuckahoe	NY	10707	914-961-2818	961-8654
Metropolitan Hospice of Greater New York 6323 7th Ave 3rd Fl *Web:* www.brooklynhospice.org	Brooklyn	NY	11220	718-921-7900	921-0752
Niagara Hospice 4675 Sunset Dr *TF:* 800-339-7011 ■ *Web:* www.niagarahospice.org	Lockport	NY	14094	716-439-4417	439-6035
Staten Island University Hospice 256 Mason Ave Bldg C *TF:* 866-799-2233 ■ *Web:* www.siuh.edu/hospice	Staten Island	NY	10305	718-226-6450	226-6607
United Hospice of Rockland 11 Stokum Ln *Web:* www.hospiceofrockland.org	New City	NY	10956	845-634-4974	634-7549
Visiting Nurse Service of New York Hospice Care 1250 Broadway 7th Fl *Web:* www.vnsny.org	New York	NY	10001	212-609-1900	290-3933
VNS Hospice of Suffolk 505 Main St	Northport	NY	11768	631-261-7200	261-1985

North Carolina

				Phone	Fax
Askins Kitty Hospice Center 107 Handley Park Ct *Web:* www.3hc.org	Goldsboro	NC	27534	919-735-5887	735-5948
Caldwell Hospice & Palliative Care 902 Kirkwood St NW *Web:* www.caldwellhospice.org	Lenoir	NC	28645	828-754-0101	757-3335
CarePartners Mountain Area Hospice PO Box 5779 *Web:* www.carepartners.org	Asheville	NC	28813	828-255-0231	255-2944
Duke Health Community Care 4321 Medical Park Dr Suite 101 *TF:* 800-599-9339	Durham	NC	27704	919-620-3853	620-9239
FirstHealth Hospice 5 Aviemore Dr *Web:* www.firsthealth.org	Pinehurst	NC	28374	910-715-6000	715-6032
Four Seasons Hospice & Palliative Care 571 S Allen Rd *Web:* www.nchospice.com	Flat Rock	NC	28731	828-692-6178	233-0351
Hospice of Alamance Caswell 914 Chapel Hill Rd *TF:* 800-588-8879 ■ *Web:* www.hospiceac.org	Burlington	NC	27215	336-532-0100	532-0060
Hospice of Burke County 1721 Enon Rd *Web:* www.burkehospice.org	Valdese	NC	28690	828-879-1601	879-3500
Hospice of Cabarrus County 5003 Hospice Ln *Web:* www.hpccc.org	Kannapolis	NC	28081	704-935-9434	935-9435
Hospice at Charlotte 1420 E 7th St *Web:* www.hospiceatcharlotte.com	Charlotte	NC	28204	704-375-0100	375-8623
Hospice of Cleveland County 951 Wendover Heights Dr *Web:* www.hospiceofclevelandcounty.org	Shelby	NC	28150	704-487-4677	481-8050
Hospice of Gaston County 258 E Garrison Blvd *Web:* www.gastonhospice.org	Gastonia	NC	28054	704-861-8405	865-0590
Hospice at Greensboro 2500 Summit Ave *Web:* www.hospicegso.org	Greensboro	NC	27405	336-621-2500	621-4516
Hospice & Palliative CareCenter 101 Hospice Ln *TF:* 888-876-3663 ■ *Web:* www.hospicecarecenter.org	Winston-Salem	NC	27103	336-768-3972	659-0461
Hospice of the Piedmont 1801 Westchester Dr *Web:* www.hospice-careconnection.org	High Point	NC	27262	336-889-8446	889-3450
Hospice of Randolph County 416 Vision Dr *Web:* www.hospiceofrandolph.org	Asheboro	NC	27203	336-672-9300	672-0868
Hospice of Rockingham County Inc PO Box 281 *Web:* www.hospiceofrockinghamcounty.com/	Wentworth	NC	27375	336-427-9022	427-9030
Hospice of Rutherford County PO Box 336 *Web:* www.hospiceofrutherford.com	Forest City	NC	28043	828-245-0095	248-1035
Hospice of Stanly County 960 N 1st St *TF:* 800-230-4236	Albemarle	NC	28001	704-983-4216	983-6662
Hospice of Union County 700 W Roosevelt Blvd *Web:* www.houc.org	Monroe	NC	28110	704-292-2100	292-2190
Hospice of Wake County Inc 1300 Saint Mary's St 4th Fl *TF:* 888-900-3959 ■ *Web:* www.hospiceofwake.org	Raleigh	NC	27605	919-828-0890	828-0664
Kitty Askins Hospice Center 107 Handley Park Ct *Web:* www.3hc.org	Goldsboro	NC	27534	919-735-5887	735-5948
Lower Cape Fear Hospice and Life Care 725-A Wellington Ave *TF:* 800-733-1476 ■ *Web:* www.hospiceandlifecarecenter.org	Wilmington	NC	28401	910-772-5444	762-9146
Palliative CareCenter & Hospice of Catawba Valley 3975 Robinson Rd *Web:* www.hospiceofcatawbavalley.org	Newton	NC	28658	828-466-0466	466-8862
Richmond County Hospice 1119 N US Hwy 1	Rockingham	NC	28379	910-997-4464	997-4484
Rowan Regional Home Health & Hospice 825A W Henderson St *TF:* 888-279-0304	Salisbury	NC	28144	704-637-7645	637-9901
University Hospice PO Box 272	Ahoskie	NC	27910	252-332-3392	332-5705

North Dakota

				Phone	Fax
Altru Hospice 1380 S Columbia Rd *TF:* 800-545-5615 ■ *Web:* www.altru.org	Grand Forks	ND	58206	701-780-5258	780-5849
Hospice of the Red River Valley 1701 38th St S Suite 101 *TF:* 800-237-4629 ■ *Web:* www.hrrv.org	Fargo	ND	58103	701-356-1500	356-1592

Ohio

				Phone	Fax
Bridge Home Health & Hospice 15100 Birchaven Ln *TF:* 800-982-3306 ■ *Web:* www.bvha.org/Facilities_Services/Bridge	Findlay	OH	45840	419-423-5351	423-8967
FairHope Hospice & Palliative Care Inc 1111 E Main St *TF:* 800-994-7077 ■ *Web:* www.fairhopehospice.org	Lancaster	OH	43130	740-654-7077	654-6321
Homereach Hospice 3595 Olentangy River Rd *TF:* 800-300-7075	Columbus	OH	43214	614-566-5377	566-4391
Hospice of Central Ohio 2269 Cherry Valley Rd *TF:* 800-804-2505 ■ *Web:* www.hospiceofcentralohio.org	Newark	OH	43055	740-344-0311	344-6577
Hospice of Cincinnati 4310 Cooper Rd *TF:* 800-691-7255 ■ *Web:* www.hospiceofcincinnati.org	Cincinnati	OH	45242	513-891-7700	792-6980
Hospice of the Cleveland Clinic 6801 Brecksville Rd Suite 10 *TF:* 800-263-0403	Independence	OH	44131	216-444-9819	520-1973
Hospice of Dayton 324 Wilmington Ave *TF:* 800-653-4490 ■ *Web:* www.hospicedayton.org	Dayton	OH	45420	937-256-4490	256-9802
Hospice of Medina County 797 N Court St *TF:* 800-700-4771 ■ *Web:* www.hospiceofmedina.org	Medina	OH	44256	330-722-4771	722-5266

Phone | Fax

Hospice of Miami County PO Box 502 .... Troy OH 45373 937-335-5191 335-8841
TF: 800-372-0009 ■ *Web:* homc.org

Hospice of North Central Ohio 1055 Dauch Dr .... Ashland OH 44805 419-281-7107 281-8427
TF: 800-952-2207 ■ *Web:* www.hospiceofnorthcentralohio.org

Hospice of Northwest Ohio 30000 E River Rd .... Perrysburg OH 43551 419-661-4001 661-4015
TF: 866-661-4001 ■ *Web:* www.hospicenwo.org

Hospice of Tuscarawas County 201 W 3rd St .... Dover OH 44622 330-343-7605 343-3542
TF: 800-947-7284 ■ *Web:* www.myhospice.org

Hospice of the Valley 5190 Market St .... Youngstown OH 44512 330-788-1992 788-1998
TF: 800-640-5180 ■ *Web:* www.hospiceofthevalley.com

Hospice of Visiting Nurse Service 3358 Ridgewood Rd .... Akron OH 44333 330-665-1455 668-4680
TF: 800-335-1455 ■ *Web:* www.vnsa.com

Hospice of Wayne County 2525 Back Orrville Rd .... Wooster OH 44691 330-264-4899 264-4874
TF: 800-884-6547 ■ *Web:* www.wchospice.org

Hospice of the Western Reserve 300 E 185th St .... Cleveland OH 44119 216-383-2222 383-3750
Web: www.hospicewr.org

Madison County Home Health Hospice 212 N Main St .... London OH 43140 740-845-7550 845-7551
TF: 866-357-4677 ■ *Web:* www.madisoncountyhospital.org

Mercy Home Care 2111 N Plum St Suite 4 .... Springfield OH 45504 937-328-5113 521-2304

Mercy Medical Center Hospice 7568 Whipple Ave NW .... Canton OH 44720 330-649-4380 649-4399

Mount Carmel Hospice 1144 Dublin Rd .... Columbus OH 43215 614-234-0200 234-0201

New Life Hospice 5255 N Abbe Rd .... Elyria OH 44035 440-934-1458 934-1567
TF: 800-770-5767

New Life Hospice Center of Saint Joseph 3700 Kolbe Rd .... Lorain OH 44053 440-960-4900 960-4904

Saint Rita's Hospice 959 W North St .... Lima OH 45801 419-226-9064 226-9281

Seasons of Life Hospice 9511 W Pleasant Valley Rd .... Cleveland OH 44130 440-743-7330 743-4905

State of the Heart Home Health & Hospice
1350 N Broadway .... Greenville OH 45331 937-548-2999 548-7144
TF: 800-417-7535 ■ *Web:* www.stateoftheheartcare.org

Stein Hospice Service 1200 Sycamore Line .... Sandusky OH 44870 419-625-5269 625-5761
TF: 800-625-5269 ■ *Web:* www.steinhospice.org

Universal Home Health & Hospice Care 701 S Main St .... Bellefontaine OH 43311 937-593-1605 592-1166
TF: 800-886-5936

Valley Hospice 380 Summit Ave .... Steubenville OH 43952 740-283-7487 284-4478
TF: 877-467-7423 ■ *Web:* www.valleyhospice.org

VistaCare Hospice 25 Whitney Dr Suite 102 .... Milford OH 45150 513-831-5800 831-5159
TF: 800-865-5980

VNA of Cleveland Hospice 2500 E 22nd St .... Cleveland OH 44115 216-931-1450 694-6355
TF: 800-862-5253

Oklahoma

Phone | Fax

Good Shepherd Hospice
4350 Will Rogers Pkwy Suite 400 .... Oklahoma City OK 73108 405-943-0903 943-0950
TF: 800-687-9808 ■ *Web:* www.goodshepherdhospice.com

Hospice of Oklahoma County
4334 NW Expressway Suite 106 .... Oklahoma City OK 73116 405-848-8884 841-4899
Web: www.hospiceokcounty.com

Mercy at Home Hospice 4401 W Memorial Rd Suite 143 .... Oklahoma City OK 73134 405-752-3890 752-3918

Saint Francis Hospice 6600 S Yale Ave Suite 350 .... Tulsa OK 74136 918-494-6465 491-5899

Trinity Hospice 12121 E 51st St Suite 102 .... Tulsa OK 74146 918-254-1727 254-1755
TF: 800-459-9671 ■ *Web:* www.trinityhospice.com

Oregon

Phone | Fax

Hospice of Bend-La Pine 2075 NE Wyatt Ct .... Bend OR 97701 541-383-3910 388-4221
Web: www.hospicebendlapine.org

Kaiser Permanente Hospice Care Program
2701 NW Vaughn St Suite 140 .... Portland OR 97210 503-499-5200 499-5220
TF: 800-448-0838

Legacy Visiting Nurses Assn Hospice PO Box 3426 .... Portland OR 97208 503-220-1000 225-6398
Web: www.legacyhealth.org

Lovejoy Hospice 939 SE 8th St .... Grants Pass OR 97526 541-474-1193 474-3035
TF: 888-758-8569 ■ *Web:* www.lovejoyhospice.org

Willamette Valley Hospice 1015 3rd St NW .... Salem OR 97304 503-588-3600 363-3891
TF: 800-555-2431 ■ *Web:* www.wvh.org

Pennsylvania

Phone | Fax

Albert Einstein Medical Center Hospice 5501 Old York Rd .... Philadelphia PA 19141 215-951-8260 951-8272

Berks VNA Hospice Program 1170 Berkshire Blvd .... Wyomissing PA 19610 610-378-0481 378-9762
TF: 800-346-7848 ■ *Web:* www.hhcminc.org

Chandler Hall Hospice 99 Barclay St .... Newtown PA 18940 215-860-4000 497-0802
TF: 888-603-1973 ■ *Web:* www.chandlerhall.org

Columbia Montour Home VNA Hospice
410 Glenn Ave Suite 200 .... Bloomsburg PA 17815 570-784-1723 784-8512
Web: www.cmhhh.org

Compassionate Care Hospice
3333 Street Rd Suite 235 Bldg 1 .... Bensalem PA 19020 215-245-3525 245-3540
TF: 800-584-8165

Einstein Albert Medical Center Hospice 5501 Old York Rd .... Philadelphia PA 19141 215-951-8260 951-8272

Family Hospice 50 Moffett St .... Pittsburgh PA 15243 412-572-8800 572-8827
TF: 800-513-2148 ■ *Web:* www.familyhospice.com

Forbes Hospice 115 S Neville St .... Pittsburgh PA 15213 412-325-7200 325-7303
TF: 800-381-8080 ■ *Web:* www.forbeshospice.com

Heartland Hospice 4070 Butler Pike Suite 100 .... Plymouth Meeting PA 19462 610-941-6700 941-6440
TF: 800-807-3738

Holy Redeemer Home Care & Hospice
12265 Townsend Rd Suite 400 .... Philadelphia PA 19154 215-671-9200 671-1950
Web: www.holyredeemer.com

Hospice Care of the VNA 468 N Hampton St .... Edwardsville PA 18704 570-819-0866 552-4039

Hospice of Central Pennsylvania PO Box 266 .... Enola PA 17025 717-732-1000 732-5348
TF: 866-779-7374 ■ *Web:* www.hospiceofcentralpa.org

Hospice Community Care 385 Wyoming Ave .... Kingston PA 18704 570-288-2288 288-7424
Web: www.hospice-homehealth.com

Hospice of Lancaster County 685 Good Dr PO Box 4125 .... Lancaster PA 17604 717-295-3900 391-9582
TF: 800-924-7610 ■ *Web:* www.hospiceoflancaster.org

Hospice Saint John 1201 N Church St Bldg B Suite 403 .... Hazleton PA 18202 570-459-6778 453-5202
TF: 877-438-3511

Lehigh Valley Hospice 2166 S 12th St Suite 101 .... Allentown PA 18103 610-969-0300 969-0454
TF: 800-944-4354 ■ *Web:* www.lvhhn.org/services/

Neighborhood Hospice 795 E Marshall St Suite 204 .... West Chester PA 19380 610-696-6511 344-7064
TF: 800-848-1155

Pinnacle Health Hospice 3705 Elmwood Dr .... Harrisburg PA 17110 717-782-2300 671-3713
TF: 800-889-1098

Samaritan Care Hospice 653 Skippack Pike .... Blue Bell PA 19422 215-653-7310 653-7340
TF: 800-764-6878 ■ *Web:* www.samaritancarehospice.com

SUN Home Health Services & Hospice 61 Duke St .... Northumberland PA 17857 570-473-8320 473-3070
TF: 888-478-6227 ■ *Web:* www.sunhomehealth.com

Phone | Fax

VITAS Healthcare Corp of Pennsylvania
1740 Walton Rd Suite 100 .... Blue Bell PA 19422 610-260-6020 238-4980
TF: 800-209-1080 ■ *Web:* www.vitas.com

VNA Hospice & Palliative Care Center 301 Delaware Ave .... Olyphant PA 18447 570-383-5180 383-5189
TF: 800-936-7671 ■ *Web:* www.vnahospice.org

VNA Hospice Western Pennsylvania 154 Hindman Rd .... Butler PA 16001 724-282-6806 282-1509
TF: 800-245-3042

Wissahickon Hospice 1 Presidential Blvd Suite 125 .... Bala Cynwyd PA 19004 610-617-2400 617-2409
TF: 800-700-8807

Rhode Island

Phone | Fax

Hospice Care of Rhode Island 169 George St .... Pawtucket RI 02860 401-727-7070 444-9080
TF: 800-338-6555 ■ *Web:* www.hhcri.org

VNS of Rhode Island Hospice Program
6 Blackstone Valley Pl Suite 515 .... Lincoln RI 02865 401-769-5670 762-2966
Web: www.vnsgri.org

South Carolina

Phone | Fax

Hospice Community Care PO Box 993 .... Rock Hill SC 29731 803-329-4663 329-5935
TF: 800-895-2273 ■ *Web:* www.hospicecommunitycare.org

Hospice of the Upstate 1835 Rogers Rd .... Anderson SC 29621 864-224-3358 224-9971
TF: 800-261-8636 ■ *Web:* hospicehouse.net

HospiceCare of the Piedmont 408 W Alexander Ave .... Greenwood SC 29646 864-227-9393 227-9377
Web: www.hospicepiedmont.org

McLeod Hospice 1203 E Cheves St .... Florence SC 29506 843-777-2564 777-5135
TF: 800-768-4556 ■ *Web:* www.mcleodhealth.org

Mercy Hospice of Horry County PO Box 50640 .... Myrtle Beach SC 29579 843-347-5500 347-5535
Web: www.mercyhospice.org

Open Arms Hospice 414-A Pettigru St .... Greenville SC 29601 864-233-5300 232-8598
TF: 800-277-2273

Palmetto Health Home Care & Hospice 1400 Pickens St .... Columbia SC 29202 803-296-3100 296-3320
TF: 800-238-1884 ■ *Web:* www.palmettohealth.org/community/homecare

South Dakota

Phone | Fax

Avera McKennan Hospice 800 E 21st St .... Sioux Falls SD 57117 605-322-7705 322-7713
Web: www.mckennan.org

Tennessee

Phone | Fax

Adventa Hospice 684 Hwy 91 Suite 1 .... Elizabethton TN 37643 423-547-0852 543-6449
TF: 800-774-1404

Adventa Hospice 1423 W Morris Blvd .... Morristown TN 37814 423-587-9484 587-9408
TF: 800-659-2633

Alive Hospice Inc 1718 Patterson St .... Nashville TN 37203 615-327-1085 321-8902
TF: 800-327-1085 ■ *Web:* www.alivehospice.org

Hospice of Chattanooga 4355 Hwy 58 Suite 101 .... Chattanooga TN 37416 423-267-6828 892-8301
TF: 800-267-6828 ■ *Web:* www.hospiceofchattanooga.org

Methodist Alliance Hospice 6423 Shelby View Dr Suite 103 .... Memphis TN 38134 901-516-1600 380-8170
TF: 800-968-8326

Trinity Hospice 1049 Cresthaven Rd .... Memphis TN 38119 901-767-6767 762-4627
TF: 800-727-6416 ■ *Web:* www.trinityhospice.com

Texas

Phone | Fax

American Hospice 1636 N Hampton Rd Suite 220 .... DeSoto TX 75115 972-228-2634 228-1698
TF: 800-689-1024

Ann's Haven VNA 216 W Mulberry St .... Denton TX 76201 940-349-5900 383-4000
TF: 800-383-5435

AseraCare Hospice - Austin 1212 Palm Valley Blvd .... Round Rock TX 78664 512-467-7423 218-9288
TF: 800-332-3982 ■ *Web:* www.aserahospiceaustin.com

Baptist Saint Anthony's Hospice PO Box 950 .... Amarillo TX 79105 806-212-8000 212-8031
TF: 800-315-6209

CHRISTUS Spohn Hospice
6200 Saratoga St Bldg 2 Suite 104 .... Corpus Christi TX 78414 361-994-3450 994-3495
TF: 800-341-1368 ■ *Web:* www.christusspohn.org/services_hospice.htm

CHRISTUS VNA 4415 Centerview Dr .... San Antonio TX 78228 210-785-5200 785-5803
Web: www.christushomecare.org

Community Hospice of Texas 6100 Western Pl Suite 500 .... Fort Worth TX 76107 817-870-2795 878-3717
TF: 800-226-0373 ■ *Web:* www.chot.org

Heart'sWay Hospice of Northeast Texas 1306 Pine Tree Rd .... Longview TX 75604 903-295-1680 295-1690
TF: 800-371-1016 ■ *Web:* www.heartswayhospice.org

Hendrick Hospice Care PO Box 1922 .... Abilene TX 79601 325-677-8516 675-5031
TF: 800-622-8516 ■ *Web:* www.hendrickhospice.org

Home Hospice of Grayson County PO Box 2306 .... Sherman TX 75091 903-868-9315 893-2772
Web: www.homehospice.org

Hope Hospice 611 N Walnut Ave .... New Braunfels TX 78130 830-625-7500 606-1388
Web: www.hopehospice.net

Hospice Austin 4107 Spicewood Springs Rd Suite 100 .... Austin TX 78759 512-342-4700 795-9053
TF: 800-445-3261 ■ *Web:* www.hospiceaustin.org

Hospice Brazos Valley 502 W 26th St .... Bryan TX 77803 979-821-2266 821-0041
TF: 800-824-2326 ■ *Web:* www.hospicebrazosvalley.org

Hospice Care Team 1708 Amburn Rd Suite C .... Texas City TX 77591 409-938-0070 938-1509
TF: 800-545-8738 ■ *Web:* www.hospicecareteam.org

Hospice of East Texas 4111 University Blvd .... Tyler TX 75701 903-581-5585 566-0291
TF: 800-777-9860 ■ *Web:* www.hospice-etex.com

Hospice of El Paso 1750 Curie Dr .... El Paso TX 79902 915-532-5699 532-7822
Web: www.hospiceelpaso.org

Hospice of Midland PO Box 2621 .... Midland TX 79702 432-682-2855 682-2989
TF: 800-646-6460 ■ *Web:* www.hospiceofmidland.org

Hospice Preferred Choice 1235 N Loop W Suite 215 .... Houston TX 77008 713-864-2626 864-9476
TF: 888-646-8696

Hospice of San Angelo 36 E Twohig St Suite 1100 .... San Angelo TX 76903 325-658-6524 658-8895
TF: 800-499-6524

Hospice of South Texas 605 E Locust Ave .... Victoria TX 77901 361-572-4300 570-1147
TF: 800-874-6908 ■ *Web:* www.hospiceofsouthtexas.org

Hospice at the Texas Medical Center 1905 Holcombe Blvd .... Houston TX 77030 713-467-7423 468-1397*
**Fax:* Admissions ■ *TF:* 800-630-7894 ■ *Web:* www.houstonhospice.org

Hospice of Wichita Falls 4909 Johnson Rd .... Wichita Falls TX 76310 940-691-0982 687-1294
Web: www.hospiceofwf.org

Odyssey Healthcare Hospice 6900 I 40 W Suite 150 .... Amarillo TX 79106 806-372-7696 372-2825

Odyssey HealthCare Inc 717 N Harwood St Suite 1500 .... Dallas TX 75201 214-922-9711 922-9752
NASDAQ: ODSY ■ *TF:* 888-922-9711 ■ *Web:* www.odyssey-healthcare.com

Texas (Cont'd)

	City	State	Zip	Phone	Fax
Samaritan Care Hospice 9535 Forest Ln Suite 211 TF: 800-473-2430 ■ Web: www.samaritancarehospice.com	Dallas	TX	75243	972-690-6632	690-0834
Trinity Hospice LLC 14180 Dallas Pkwy Suite 800 TF: 800-473-4368 ■ Web: www.trinityhospice.com	Dallas	TX	75254	214-306-4500	329-1963
VITAS Healthcare Corp 8585 N Stemmons Fwy Suite 700 South Tower TF: 800-664-2004 ■ Web: www.vitas.com	Dallas	TX	75247	972-661-2004	448-6542
VITAS Healthcare Corp 2501 Parkview Dr Suite 600 TF: 800-953-5855 ■ Web: www.vitas.com	Fort Worth	TX	76102	817-870-7000	870-7090
VITAS Healthcare Corp 18333 Egret Bay Suite 550 TF: 800-628-8081 ■ Web: www.vitas.com	Houston	TX	77058	281-335-3401	335-3450
VITAS Healthcare Corp 4828 Loop Central Dr Suite 890 TF: 800-628-8081 ■ Web: www.vitas.com	Houston	TX	77081	713-663-7777	663-4990
VITAS Healthcare Corp 5430 Fredericksburg Rd Suite 200 TF: 800-938-4827 ■ Web: www.vitas.com	San Antonio	TX	78229	210-348-4300	348-4383
VNA of Houston Hospice 601 Sawyer St Suite 750 TF: 800-375-6877	Houston	TX	77007	713-630-5591	630-5597

Utah

	City	State	Zip	Phone	Fax
IHC Home Care 2250 S 1300 W Suite A TF: 800-527-1118	Salt Lake City	UT	84119	801-977-9900	977-9956

Vermont

	City	State	Zip	Phone	Fax
Hospice VNA 331 Olcott Dr Suite U-1 TF: 800-858-1696 ■ Web: www.vnahospicevtnh.org	White River Junction	VT	05001	802-295-2604	295-6896

Virginia

	City	State	Zip	Phone	Fax
Adventa Hospice 154 W 4th St	Salem	VA	24153	540-378-5281	378-6005
Capital Hospice 6565 Arlington Blvd Suite 501 Web: www.capitalhospice.org	Falls Church	VA	22042	703-538-2065	538-2165
Capital Hospice Inc 6565 Arlington Blvd Web: www.capitalhospice.org	Falls Church	VA	22042	703-538-2065	538-2165
Crater Community Hospice 840 W Roslyn Rd Suite E Web: www.cratercommunityhospice.org	Colonial Heights	VA	23834	804-526-4300	526-4337
Good Samaritan Hospice 3825 Electric Rd SW Suite A TF: 888-466-7809 ■ Web: members.aol.com/goodsamhsp	Roanoke	VA	24018	540-776-0198	776-0841
Hospice of the Piedmont 2200 Old Ivy Rd Suite 2 TF: 800-975-5501 ■ Web: www.hopva.org	Charlottesville	VA	22903	434-817-6900	245-0187
Hospice of the Rapidan PO Box 1715 TF: 800-676-2012 ■ Web: www.hotr.org	Culpeper	VA	22701	540-825-4840	825-7752
Mary Washington Hospice 5012 Southpoint Pkwy Web: www.medicorp.org/hospice.mgi	Fredericksburg	VA	22407	540-741-3580	741-3581

Washington

	City	State	Zip	Phone	Fax
Evergreen Community Hospice 12822 124th Ln NE Web: www.evergreenhealthcare.org	Kirkland	WA	98034	425-899-1040	899-1033
Franciscan Hospice 2901 Bridgeport Way W TF: 800-338-8305	University Place	WA	98466	253-534-7000	534-7099
Hospice of Seattle 425 Pontius Ave N Suite 300 Web: www.providence.org	Seattle	WA	98109	206-320-4000	320-2280
Hospice of Spokane 121 S Arthur St TF: 888-459-0438 ■ Web: www.hospiceofspokane.org	Spokane	WA	99202	509-456-0438	458-0359
Providence Hospice & Home Care of Snohomish County 2731 Wetmore Ave Suite 500 TF: 800-825-0045	Everett	WA	98201	425-261-4800	261-4850
Providence Hospice of Seattle 425 Pontius Ave N Suite 300 Web: www.providence.org	Seattle	WA	98109	206-320-4000	320-2280
Providence Sound Home Care & Hospice PO Box 5008 TF: 800-869-7062	Lacey	WA	98509	360-459-8311	493-4657
Skagit Home Health & Hospice 2031-B Hospital Dr TF: 800-894-5877	Sedro Woolley	WA	98284	360-856-7770	856-7756
Tri-Cities Chaplaincy 2108 W Entiat Ave Web: www.tricitieschaplaincy.org	Kennewick	WA	99336	509-783-7416	735-7850
Whatcom Hospice 800 E Chestnut St Suite 1C Web: www.hospicehelp.org	Bellingham	WA	98225	360-733-5877	756-6884

West Virginia

	City	State	Zip	Phone	Fax
Hospice Care Corp Hwy 92 S PO Box 760 Web: www.hospicecarecorp.org	Arthurdale	WV	26520	304-864-0884	864-6306
Hospice of Huntington 1101 6th Ave TF: 800-788-5480 ■ Web: www.hospiceofhuntington.org	Huntington	WV	25701	304-529-4217	523-6051
Hospice of the Panhandle 122 Waverly Ct TF: 800-345-6538 ■ Web: www.hospiceotp.org	Martinsburg	WV	25401	304-264-0406	264-0409
Kanawha Hospice Care 1143 Dunbar Ave TF: 800-560-8523 ■ Web: www.kanawhahospice.org	Dunbar	WV	25064	304-768-8523	768-8627

Wisconsin

	City	State	Zip	Phone	Fax
AseraCare Hospice - Milwaukee 6737 W Washington Suite 3200 TF: 800-598-5132 ■ Web: www.aserahospicemilwaukee.com	West Allis	WI	53214	414-607-1782	607-6196
Aurora VNA Zilber Family Hospice 1155 Honey Creek Pkwy TF: 888-206-6955 ■ Web: www.aurorahealthcare.org	Wauwatosa	WI	53213	414-615-5900	615-5927
Beloit Regional Hospice 655 3rd St Suite 200 TF: 877-363-7421 ■ Web: www.beloitregionalhospice.com	Beloit	WI	53511	608-363-7200	363-7426
Comfort Care & Hospice Services 520 N 32nd Ave TF: 800-283-2881	Wausau	WI	54401	715-847-2702	847-2818
Franciscan Skemp Healthcare Hospice 212 S 11th St TF: 800-362-5454	La Crosse	WI	54601	608-791-9790	791-9548
Gundersen Lutheran at Home HomeCare & Hospice 914 Green Bay St TF: 800-362-9567 ■ Web: www.gundluth.org	La Crosse	WI	54601	608-775-8400	791-8440
Horizon Home Care & Hospice 8949 N Deerbrook Trail TF: 800-468-4660 ■ Web: www.hhch.net	Brown Deer	WI	53223	414-365-8300	365-8338
Hospice Alliance 10220 Prairie Ridge Blvd TF: 800-830-8344 ■ Web: www.hospicealliance.net	Pleasant Prairie	WI	53158	262-652-4400	652-4628
HospiceCare 5395 E Cheryl Pkwy TF: 800-553-4289 ■ Web: www.hospicecare.com	Madison	WI	53711	608-276-4660	276-4672
Ministry Home Care Hospice Services 611 Saint Joseph Ave Saint Joseph's Hospital TF: 800-397-0270 ■ Web: www.ministryhomecare.org	Marshfield	WI	54449	715-389-3802	387-9950
Saint Agnes Home Care Hospice 239 Trowbridge Dr TF: 800-236-4156	Fond du Lac	WI	54936	920-923-7950	923-7959
Theda Care at Home 3000 E College Ave TF: 800-984-5554 ■ Web: www.thedacare.org	Appleton	WI	54915	920-969-0919	969-0020
Unity Hospice 2366 Oak Ridge Cir TF: 800-990-9249 ■ Web: www.unityhospice.org	De Pere	WI	54115	920-338-1111	338-8111
VITAS Healthcare Corp 2675 N Mayfair Rd Suite 500 TF: 888-821-6500 ■ Web: www.vitas.com	Wauwatosa	WI	53226	414-257-2600	454-3133

Wyoming

	City	State	Zip	Phone	Fax
Central Wyoming Hospice Program 319 S Wilson St Web: www.cwhp.org	Casper	WY	82601	307-577-4832	577-4841

375 HOSPITAL HOSPITALITY HOUSES

	City	State	Zip	Phone	Fax
American Cancer Society Hope Lodge of Baltimore 636 W Lexington St TF: 888-227-6333 ■ Web: www.cancer.org	Baltimore	MD	21201	410-547-2522	539-8890
American Cancer Society Hope Lodge of Buffalo 197 Summer St Web: www.cancer.org	Buffalo	NY	14222	716-882-9244	822-4436
American Cancer Society Hope Lodge Burlington 211 East Ave Web: www.cancer.org	Burlington	VT	05401	802-652-0649	
American Cancer Society Hope Lodge of Charleston 269 Calhoun St TF: 800-282-4914 ■ Web: www.cancer.org	Charleston	SC	29401	843-958-0930	958-9054
American Cancer Society Hope Lodge of Marshfield 611 W Doege St Web: www.cancer.org	Marshfield	WI	54449	715-486-9100	486-9110
American Cancer Society Hope Lodge at Quality Hill Center 1120 Pennsylvania Ave Web: www.cancer.org	Kansas City	MO	64105	816-842-6427	842-5754
American Cancer Society Hope Lodge of Rochester 411 2nd St NW Web: www.cancer.org	Rochester	MN	55901	507-529-4673	529-4666
American Cancer Society Hope Lodge of Saint Louis 4215 Lindell Blvd Web: www.cancer.org	Saint Louis	MO	63108	314-286-8150	286-8155
American Cancer Society Hope Lodge Worcester 7 Oak St Web: www.cancer.org	Worcester	MA	01609	508-792-2985	753-3986
American Cancer Society Joe Lee Griffin Hope Lodge 1104 Ireland Way TF: 888-513-9933 ■ Web: www.cancer.org	Birmingham	AL	35205	205-558-7860	558-7862
American Cancer Society McConnell-Raab Hope Lodge 930 Wellness Dr	Greenville	NC	27834	252-695-6143	695-6557
American Cancer Society Winn-Dixie Hope Lodge 1552 Shoup Ct Web: www.cancer.org	Atlanta	GA	30033	404-327-9200	327-9808
American Cancer Society Winn-Dixie Hope Lodge at Gainesville 2121 SW 16th St Web: www.cancer.org	Gainesville	FL	32608	352-338-0601	378-7792
American Cancer Society Winn-Dixie Hope Lodge at Miami 1121 NW 14th St Web: www.cancer.org	Miami	FL	33136	305-547-2210	547-4187
Arbor House 300 Main St Web: www.cmmc.org	Lewiston	ME	04240	207-795-0111	795-2303
Arizona Transplant House 11600 N 84th St Web: www.aztransplanthouse.org	Scottsdale	AZ	85260	480-609-1324	609-7268
Arthur & Ruth Browne Lodge 6030 W 62nd St Web: www.cancer.org	Indianapolis	IN	46278	317-347-6670	347-6679
Atlanta Hospital Hospitality House 1815 Ponce de Leon Ave NE Web: atlhhh.org	Atlanta	GA	30307	404-377-6333	377-6398
Auxiliary Guest House 313 S Kline St	Aberdeen	SD	57401	605-622-5050	622-5266
Avera Queen of Peace 600 E 6th Ave	Mitchell	SD	57301	605-995-2468	995-2441
Bannister Family House 200 W Arbor Dr Web: health.ucsd.edu/bannister/default.asp	San Diego	CA	92103	619-543-7977	543-7937
Barnes Lodge 4520 Clayton Ave TF: 800-551-3492	Saint Louis	MO	63110	314-652-4319	535-2731
Baylor Plaza Hotel 3600 Gaston Ave Web: www.baylorhealth.com	Dallas	TX	75246	214-820-7000	820-7323
Beacon House 1301 N 3rd St Web: www.upbeaconhouse.org	Marquette	MI	49855	906-225-7100	225-4903
Blount Hospitality House 610 Madison St Web: blounthospitalityhouse.org	Huntsville	AL	35801	256-534-7014	512-5872
Brent House Hotel 1512 Jefferson Hwy TF: 800-535-3986 ■ Web: www.brenthouse.com	New Orleans	LA	70118	504-835-5411	842-4160
Brent's Place 1129 E 17th Ave Web: www.brentsplace.org	Denver	CO	80218	303-831-4545	831-4567
Browne Arthur & Ruth Lodge 6030 W 62nd St Web: www.cancer.org	Indianapolis	IN	46278	317-347-6670	347-6679
Caring House Inc 2625 Pickett Rd Web: caringhouse.com	Durham	NC	27705	919-490-5449	493-8044
Carolyn Scott Rainbow House 7815 Harney St Web: www.chsomaha.org	Omaha	NE	68114	402-955-7815	955-7805
Carpenter Hospitality House 121 5th Ave NE	Hickory	NC	28601	828-324-4544	324-6504
Casa Esperanza 1005 Yale NE Web: www.casaesperanzanm.org	Albuquerque	NM	87106	505-277-9880	277-9876
Cheney Francis Family Place 2882 State St Web: www.asante.org	Medford	OR	97504	541-789-5876	789-5841
Children's Hope House 7922 W Jefferson Blvd	Fort Wayne	IN	46804	260-459-8550	459-8551
Children's House at Johns Hopkins 1915 McElderry St Web: www.childrenshouse.org	Baltimore	MD	21205	410-614-2560	614-2568
Children's Inn at National Institutes Of Health 7 West Dr TF: 800-644-4660 ■ Web: www.childrensinn.org	Bethesda	MD	20892	301-496-5672	496-4421
Children's Miracle Network Family Guest House 1057 Patterson St	Eugene	OR	97401	541-685-1970	685-1962
Conine Clubhouse 921 N 35th Ave Web: www.jdch.com/conineclubhouse/ConineClubhouse.aspx	Hollywood	FL	33021	954-986-6323	985-2265
Connelly Hospitality House 710 S Lake	Farmington	NM	87401	505-324-2273	324-2271

	City	State	ZIP	Phone	Fax
Cross Travis & Beverly Guest Housing Center 9320 SW Barnes Rd	Portland	OR	97225	503-216-1575	216-6283
TF: 888-550-1575 ■ *Web:* www.providence.org/oregon					
Cynthia C & William E Perry Pavilion 9400 Turkey Lake Rd	Orlando	FL	32819	321-842-8844	842-8871
Web: orhs.org/comm_hosp/sand_lake/perry_pavilion.cfm					
Danielle House 160 Riverside Dr	Binghamton	NY	13905	607-724-1540	724-1540
Web: www.daniellehouse.org					
Devon Nicole House 21 Autumn St 5th Fl	Boston	MA	02215	617-355-8457	730-0223
Web: www.childrenshospital.org/dnh					
Edmond J Safra Family Lodge at National Institutes of Health 9000 Rockville Pike Bldg 65	Bethesda	MD	20892	301-496-6500	594-4589
Web: clinicalcenter.nih.gov/familylodge/index.shtml#referrals					
Ernest Eugenia Wyatt Guest House 317 Business Loop 70 W	Columbia	MO	65203	573-884-1825	884-2434
Family House Inc 1509 N Knoxville Ave	Peoria	IL	61603	309-685-5300	688-8324
Web: www.familyhousepeoria.org					
Fellowship Center 1901 Clinch Ave	Knoxville	TN	37916	865-541-1725	544-1760
Fisher House Inc 7323 Hwy 90 W Suite 107	San Antonio	TX	78227	210-673-7500	673-7579
Web: www.fisherhouseinc.org					
Fisher Zachary & Elizabeth House 3200 Vine St	Cincinnati	OH	45220	513-475-6571	487-6661
Francis Cheney Family Place 2882 State St	Medford	OR	97504	541-789-5876	789-5841
Web: www.asante.org					
Friendship Inn PO Box 3423	Kansas City	KS	66103	816-506-6339	
Gary's House 97 State St	Portland	ME	04101	207-773-9800	773-9888
Web: www.garys-house.org					
Gift of Life Transplant House 705 2nd St	Rochester	MN	55902	507-288-7470	281-9888
Web: www.gift-of-life.org					
Gross Pete House 525 Minor Ave N	Seattle	WA	98109	206-262-1000	262-1500
Web: www.fhcrc.org					
Hackerman-Patz House 1909 E Jefferson St	Baltimore	MD	21205	410-955-2304	
Web: www.hopkinskimmelcancercenter.org/kpr/theresidentialcareprogram.cfm					
Hanson House 380 E Paseo El Mirador	Palm Springs	CA	92262	760-416-5070	416-5071
Web: www.hansonhouse.org					
Holland's Rose 132 Griegos Rd NW	Albuquerque	NM	87107	505-345-2020	345-5464
Web: www.hollandsrose.com					
Home Away From Home 2600 E 18th St	Cheyenne	WY	82001	307-633-7212	633-7229
Hope Lodge Hershey Pennsylvania 125 Lucy Ave	Hummelstown	PA	17036	717-533-5111	533-2587
Web: www.cancer.org					
Hospital Hospitality House 342 S Limestone St	Lexington	KY	40508	859-254-8998	255-5185
Web: www.hospitalhospitalityhouse.org					
Hospital Hospitality House of Louisville 201 E Main St	Louisville	KY	40202	502-625-1360	625-1363
Web: www.hhhlouisville.org					
Hospital Hospitality House of Richmond Inc 612 E Marshall St PO Box 10090	Richmond	VA	23219	804-828-6901	828-6913
Web: www.hhhrichmond.org/hhh					
Hospital Hospitality House of Saginaw Inc 479 Shattuck Rd	Saginaw	MI	48604	989-752-8473	752-2769
Web: www.hhhofsaginaw.org					
Hospital Hospitality House of SW Michigan Inc 527 W South St	Kalamazoo	MI	49007	269-341-7811	341-7817
Web: www.hhhkz.org					
Hospital Hospitality Houses of Wilmington 1612 Medical Center Dr	Wilmington	NC	28401	910-763-3039	763-3141
Hospitality Homes PO Box 15265	Boston	MA	02115	617-482-4338	582-7980
TF: 888-595-4678 ■ *Web:* www.hosp.org					
Hospitality Homes of Cleveland 12704 Mapleleaf Dr	Cleveland	OH	44125	216-518-0404	
Web: www.hospitalityhomes.com					
Hospitality House of Charlotte PO Box 36891	Charlotte	NC	28236	704-384-6058	316-0349
Web: www.hospitalityhouseofcharlotte.org					
Hospitality House of Methodist Hospital Foundation 990 Oak Ridge Tpke PO Box 2529	Oak Ridge	TN	37830	865-481-5923	481-5403
Web: www.mmcoakridge.com					
Hospitality House of Tulsa PO Box 1988	Broken Arrow	OK	74013	918-694-8888	
Web: www.tulsahospitalityhouse.org					
Hotel Schmotel 2539 E Edison St	Tucson	AZ	85716	520-904-6333	795-3880
Web: www.hotelschmotel.com					
Hubbard House 29 W Miller St	Orlando	FL	32806	407-649-6886	849-6447
Web: www.orlandoregional.org/services/hubbardhouse/index.cfm					
Humility of Mary Guest House 427 Caroline Ave	Youngstown	OH	44504	330-480-2206	
Huntington Hospital Hospitality House 2801 S Staunton Rd	Huntington	WV	25702	304-522-1832	522-6706
Web: www.huntingtonhospitality.org					
Immanuel Auxiliary Hospitality House 7105 Newport Ave	Omaha	NE	68152	402-572-2828	572-3942
Inn at Cherry Hill 500 17th Ave	Seattle	WA	98122	206-320-2164	320-3526
Web: www.swedish.org					
Inn at Virginia Mason 1006 Spring St	Seattle	WA	98104	206-583-6453	625-7197
TF: 800-283-6453 ■ *Web:* www.innatvirginiamason.com					
Jenn's House Inc 3250 S Cedar Crest Blvd	Emmaus	PA	18049	610-965-1777	965-1777
Web: www.jennshouse.org					
Joanne Rockwell Memorial House 1910 E Jefferson St	Baltimore	MD	21205	410-955-2304	
Web: www.hopkinskimmelcancercenter.org/kpr/theresidentialcareprogram.cfm					
Joseph & Jeannette Silber American Cancer Society Hope Lodge 11432 Mayfield Rd	Cleveland	OH	44106	216-844-4673	844-2959
Web: www.cancer.org					
Kathy's House Inc 600 N 103 St	Milwaukee	WI	53226	414-453-8290	453-8292
Web: www.kathys-house.org					
Kelly's Place PO Box 54273	Cincinnati	OH	45254	513-771-7222	771-7344
Web: www.kellysplace.org					
Kevin Guest House 782 Ellicott St	Buffalo	NY	14203	716-882-1818	882-1291
Web: www.kevinguesthouse.com					
King's Daughters Hospitality House 2221 Central Ave	Ashland	KY	41101	606-326-7730	326-7748
Kohl's House at Children's Memorial Hospital 2422 N Orchard	Chicago	IL	60614	773-975-8881	880-3602
Web: www.childrensmemorial.org					
Lewis Rathbun Center 121 Sherwood Rd	Asheville	NC	28803	828-251-0595	251-0598
Web: www.lewisrathbuncenter.org					
Mario Pastega Guest House 3505 NW Samaritan Dr	Corvallis	OR	97330	541-768-4650	768-5124
Web: www.samhealth.org					
Massachusetts General Hospital Beacon House 19 Myrtle St	Boston	MA	02114	617-726-7679	918-5875
Masterson Place 2325 E Yellowstone Hwy	Casper	WY	82609	307-237-5933	237-5939
McDade House of Shreveport 1825 Warrington Pl	Shreveport	LA	71101	318-681-6560	681-6410
McRee Guest House 2721 S Washington	Lansing	MI	48910	517-372-6153	372-6554
Miracle House 80 8th Ave Suite 315	New York	NY	10011	212-989-7790	367-9281
Web: www.miraclehouse.org					
Molly's House 430 SE Osceola St	Stuart	FL	34994	772-223-6659	223-9990
Web: www.mollyshouse.org					
Morrison Rebecca A House 513 S 8th St	Salina	KS	67401	785-452-7500	452-7099
Web: www.srhc.com					
Munson Manor Hospitality House 1220 Medical Campus Dr	Traverse City	MI	49684	231-935-2300	935-2302
Web: www.munsonhealthcare.org					
Nebraska House 987600 Nebraska Medical Center	Omaha	NE	68198	402-559-2081	559-3232
Web: www.nebraskamed.com/transplant					
Nicole Devon House 21 Autumn St 5th Fl	Boston	MA	02215	617-355-8457	730-0223
Web: www.childrenshospital.org/dnh					
Nora's Home 910 Madison Ave	Memphis	TN	38103	901-682-4663	528-0194
Web: www.norashome.org					
Pastega Mario Guest House 3505 NW Samaritan Dr	Corvallis	OR	97330	541-768-4650	768-5124
Web: www.samhealth.org					
Pay It Forward House 719 Somonauk St	Sycamore	IL	60178	815-899-1106	
Web: www.payitforwardhouse.org					
Perry Cynthia C & William E Pavilion 9400 Turkey Lake Rd	Orlando	FL	32819	321-842-8844	842-8871
Web: orhs.org/comm_hosp/sand_lake/perry_pavilion.cfm					
Pete Gross House 525 Minor Ave N	Seattle	WA	98109	206-262-1000	262-1500
Web: www.fhcrc.org					
Prairie Lakes Caring Club House 401 9th Ave	Watertown	SD	57201	605-882-7725	882-7720
Web: www.prairielakes.com					
Providence House 3350 Providence Dr	Anchorage	AK	99508	907-261-4949	261-5628
Web: www.providence.org/alaska/facilities					
Quantum House 901 45th St	West Palm Beach	FL	33407	561-494-0515	494-0522
Web: www.quantumhouse.org					
Quincy Hospitality House 1129 Oak St	Quincy	IL	62301	217-228-3022	223-2569
Web: www.blessinghospital.org					
Rathbun Lewis Center 121 Sherwood Rd	Asheville	NC	28803	828-251-0595	251-0598
Web: www.lewisrathbuncenter.org					
Rathgeber Hospitality House 1615 12th St	Wichita Falls	TX	76301	940-764-2400	764-2456
Web: www.urhcs.org					
Rebecca A Morrison House 513 S 8th St	Salina	KS	67401	785-452-7500	452-7099
Web: www.srhc.com					
Renucci Hospitality House 100 Michigan St NE MC 172	Grand Rapids	MI	49503	616-391-1787	391-9300
River Oaks Hospitality House 1406 6th Ave N	Saint Cloud	MN	56303	320-251-2700	255-5803
Web: www.centracare.com					
Rockwell Joanne Memorial House 1910 E Jefferson St	Baltimore	MD	21205	410-955-2304	
Web: www.hopkinskimmelcancercenter.org/kpr/theresidentialcareprogram.cfm					
Rose Hill Hospitality House PO Box 1628	Grand Junction	CO	81506	970-243-7968	
Rosenbaum Family House PO Box 8228	Morgantown	WV	26506	304-598-6094	598-6412
Web: www.health.wvu.edu					
Safra Edmond J Family Lodge at National Institutes of Health 9000 Rockville Pike Bldg 65	Bethesda	MD	20892	301-496-6500	594-4589
Web: clinicalcenter.nih.gov/familylodge/index.shtml#referrals					
Saint Andrew's Lighthouse 1797 Beach Blvd	Jacksonville Beach	FL	32250	904-246-5606	246-9303
Web: www.standrewslighthouse.com					
Saint Joseph Inn 3310 E Grand	Wichita	KS	67218	316-689-6359	691-6763
Sarah House Inc 130 Roberts Ave	Syracuse	NY	13207	315-475-1747	
Web: www.sarahhouse.org					
Scott Carolyn Rainbow House 7815 Harney St	Omaha	NE	68114	402-955-7815	955-7805
Web: www.chsomaha.org					
Seton Guest Center 2131 W 3rd St	Los Angeles	CA	90057	213-484-7767	207-5816
Web: www.stvincentmedicalcenter.com					
Seton League House 3207 Wabash Ave	Austin	TX	78705	512-324-1999	324-1932
Web: seton.net					
Silber Joseph & Jeannette American Cancer Society Hope Lodge 11432 Mayfield Rd	Cleveland	OH	44106	216-844-4673	844-2959
Web: www.cancer.org					
Sowers Hospitality House 1701 S 17th St Suite 1H	Lincoln	NE	68502	402-438-2244	438-2426
Stanton Hospitality House 1617 Roxie Ave	Fayetteville	NC	28304	910-323-1771	485-3449
Steven's Hope for Children Inc 1014 W Foothill Blvd Suite B	Upland	CA	91786	909-373-0678	981-4578
Web: www.stevenshope.org					
Sumner Foundation Hospitality House 404 Steam Plant Rd	Gallatin	TN	37066	615-452-4009	452-0066
Web: www.sumner.org					
Sunshine House Guest Lodging 413 N Lilly Rd NE	Olympia	WA	98506	360-493-7940	493-5569
Taylor House 1431 N San Francisco St	Flagstaff	AZ	86001	928-226-0300	
Web: www.taylorhospitalityhouse.com					
Texoma Medical Center's Reba Ranch House 1100 Reba McEntire Ln	Denison	TX	75020	903-416-1500	416-1501
Web: www.thcs.org/reba					
Transplant House Inc 1500 NW 12th Ave 7th Fl	Miami	FL	33136	305-585-1500	585-1501
Web: www.transplantfoundation.org/house.htm					
Travis & Beverly Cross Guest Housing Center 9320 SW Barnes Rd	Portland	OR	97225	503-216-1575	216-6283
TF: 888-550-1575 ■ *Web:* www.providence.org/oregon					
Tree House at Liberty Hospital 2533 Glenn W Hendren Dr	Liberty	MO	64068	816-883-2088	883-2316
Web: www.libertyhospital.org					
University of Virginia Medical Center Hospital Hospitality House Inc Hospital Box 800703	Charlottesville	VA	22908	434-924-2285	924-1590
Web: www.healthsystem.virginia.edu					
Veterans Guest House 880 Locust St	Reno	NV	89502	775-324-6958	324-6071
Web: www.veteransguesthouse.org					
Walton Guest House PO Box 14001	Salem	OR	97302	503-561-5279	375-4828
Wesley Hospitality House Inc 1129 Horseshoe Rd	Elizabeth City	NC	27909	252-335-7117	335-7769
Web: www.whh-nc.org					
Yaffe House 3700 W 17th Ave	Denver	CO	80204	303-405-4275	405-4276
Zachary & Elizabeth Fisher House 3200 Vine St	Cincinnati	OH	45220	513-475-6571	487-6661

376 HOSPITAL HOSPITALITY HOUSES - RONALD MCDONALD HOUSE

Ronald McDonald House

	City	State	ZIP	Phone	Fax
Akron 245 Locust St	Akron	OH	44302	330-253-5400	253-5477
Web: www.akronchildrens.org/cms/site/226ef7b47b7e711f					
Albany 139 S Lake Ave	Albany	NY	12208	518-438-2655	459-6529
Web: www.rmhcofalbany.org					
Albuquerque 1011 Yale Ave NE	Albuquerque	NM	87106	505-842-8960	764-0412
Web: www.rmhc-nm.org					
Amarillo 1501 Streit Dr	Amarillo	TX	79106	806-358-8177	358-8170
Web: www.rmhofamarillo.org					
Ann Arbor 1600 Washington Heights	Ann Arbor	MI	48104	734-994-4442	994-4919
Web: rmh-annarbor.org					
Atlanta 792 Houston Mill Rd NE	Atlanta	GA	30329	404-315-1133	315-7873
Web: www.armh.com					
Atlanta 5420 Peachtree Dunwoody Rd	Atlanta	GA	30342	404-847-0760	250-4992
Web: www.armh.com					
Augusta 938 Greene St	Augusta	GA	30901	706-724-5901	722-0884
Web: www.mcghealth.org/Childrens_Medical_Center					
Austin 403 E 15th St	Austin	TX	78701	512-472-9844	472-5465
Web: www.rmhc-austin.org					
Baltimore 635 W Lexington St	Baltimore	MD	21201	410-528-1010	727-6177
Web: www.rmhbaltimore.com					
Bangor 654 State St	Bangor	ME	04401	207-942-9003	990-2984
Bend 1700 NE Purcell Blvd	Bend	OR	97701	541-318-4950	318-4994
Billings 1144 N 30th St	Billings	MT	59101	406-256-8006	256-0130
Birmingham 920 17th St S	Birmingham	AL	35205	205-933-0695	939-0035
Bismarck 609 N 7th St	Bismarck	ND	58501	701-258-8551	258-5076
Boise 101 Warm Springs Ave	Boise	ID	83712	208-336-5478	336-0587
Web: www.rmhidaho.org					
Boston 229 Kent St	Brookline	MA	02446	617-734-3333	734-5239
Web: www.ronaldmcdonaldhouseboston.org					
Buffalo 780 W Ferry St	Buffalo	NY	14222	716-883-1177	881-9312
Web: www.rmhbuffalo.org					
Burlington 16 S Winooski Ave	Burlington	VT	05401	802-862-4943	862-2175
Web: www.rmh-vermont.org					
Calgary 1921 28th St SW	Calgary	AB	T3E2H1	403-240-3000	240-9044
Web: www.rmhcalgary.org					
Camden 550 Mickle Blvd	Camden	NJ	08103	856-966-4663	966-1190
Web: www.ronaldhouse-snj.org					

	City	State	Zip	Phone	Fax
Chapel Hill 101 Old Mason Farm Rd	Chapel Hill	NC	27517	919-913-2040	966-7651
Web: www.chapelhillrmh.net					
Charleston 81 Gadsden St	Charleston	SC	29401	843-723-7957	722-2204
Web: www.charityadvantage.com/RonaldMcdonaldHouse					
Charleston 302 30th St	Charleston	WV	25304	304-346-0279	343-8385
Web: members.citynet.net/rmh					
Charlottesville 300 9th St SW	Charlottesville	VA	22903	434-295-1885	295-7735
Web: avenue.org/rmhc					
Chattanooga 200 Central Ave	Chattanooga	TN	37403	423-778-4300	778-4350
Web: www.rmhchattanooga.com					
Chicago 622 W Deming Pl	Chicago	IL	60614	773-348-5322	348-7619
Web: www.rmhchinorth.org					
Chicago 845 E 57th St	Chicago	IL	60637	773-324-5437	324-8029
Web: www.ronaldmcdonaldhouseuc.org					
Chicago PO Box 7002	Hines	IL	60141	708-327-2273	327-6000
Web: www.ronaldmcdonaldhouseuc.org					
Cincinnati 350 Erkenbrecher Ave	Cincinnati	OH	42229	513-636-7642	636-4887
Web: www.rmhcincinnati.org					
Cleveland 10415 Euclid Ave	Cleveland	OH	44106	216-229-5757	229-0556
Web: www.ronaldhousecle.org					
Colorado Springs 311 N Logan Ave	Colorado Springs	CO	80909	719-471-1814	471-7147
Web: www.rmhcs.org					
Columbia 1001 E Stadium Blvd	Columbia	MO	65201	573-443-7666	499-0131
Web: www.rmhccolumbia.org					
Columbia 2955 Colonial Dr	Columbia	SC	29203	803-254-3181	254-8688
Web: www.ronaldhouse.esmartweb.com					
Columbus 1959 Hamilton Rd	Columbus	GA	31904	706-321-0033	321-0034
Web: www.rmhcwga.org					
Columbus 555 Childrens Dr W	Columbus	OH	43205	614-227-3700	227-3765
Web: www.colrmhc.org					
Corpus Christi 3402 Fort Worth St	Corpus Christi	TX	78411	361-854-4073	854-9174
Web: www.corpuschristirmhc.org					
Dallas 5641 Medical Center Dr	Dallas	TX	75235	214-631-7354	631-1527
Web: www.rmhdallas.com					
Danville 100 N Academy Ave PO Box 300	Danville	PA	17821	570-271-6300	271-8182
Web: www.geisinger.org/about/ronald_mcdonald.shtml					
Denver 1300 E 21st Ave	Denver	CO	80905	303-832-6641	832-3802
Web: www.ronaldhouse.org					
Des Moines 1441 Pleasant St	Des Moines	IA	50314	515-243-2111	280-3111
Web: www.rmhdesmoines.org					
Detroit 3911 Beaubien Blvd	Detroit	MI	48201	313-745-5909	993-0399
Web: www.rmhdet.org					
Durham 506 Alexander Ave	Durham	NC	27705	919-286-9305	286-7307
Web: www.ronaldhousedurham.org					
Edmonton 7726 107th St	Edmonton	AB	T6E4K3	780-439-5437	433-6207
Web: www.rmhedmonton.ca					
El Paso 300 E California St	El Paso	TX	79902	915-542-1522	577-0678
Web: www.rmhc.org					
Falls Church 3312 Gallows Rd	Falls Church	VA	22042	703-698-7080	698-7745
Web: www.rmhc.greaterdc.org					
Fargo 1234 Broadway	Fargo	ND	58102	701-232-3980	234-9582
Web: www.rmhcfargo.org					
Fort Lauderdale 15 SE 15th St	Fort Lauderdale	FL	33316	954-828-1822	828-1824
Fort Myers 16100 Roserush Ct	Fort Myers	FL	33908	239-437-0202	437-3521
Web: www.ronaldmchouse.com/RMHFM					
Fort Worth 1004 7th Ave	Fort Worth	TX	76104	817-870-4942	870-0254
Web: www.ftworthrmh.org					
Gainesville 1600 SW 14th St	Gainesville	FL	32608	352-374-4404	335-5325
Web: www.rmhgainesville.com					
Galveston 301 14th St	Galveston	TX	77550	409-762-8770	762-9902
Web: www.rmhgalveston.org					
Grand Rapids 1323 Cedar St NE	Grand Rapids	MI	49503	616-776-1300	776-0368
Greenville 549 Moye Blvd	Greenville	NC	27834	252-830-0062	830-0298
Greenville 706 Grove Rd	Greenville	SC	29605	864-235-0506	235-2316
Web: www.rmhgreenville.org					
Halifax 1133 Tower Rd	Halifax	NS	B3H2Y7	902-429-4044	429-8650
Web: www.rmhatlantic.ca					
Hamilton 1510 Main St W	Hamilton	ON	L8S1E3	905-521-9983	521-9515
Web: www.rmhhamilton.ca					
Harlingen 1720 Treasure Hills Blvd	Harlingen	TX	78550	956-412-7200	412-6300
Web: www.rmhcrgv.org					
Hershey 745 W Governor Rd	Hershey	PA	17033	717-533-4001	533-1299
Web: www.ronaldshousehershey.org					
Honolulu 1970 Judd Hillside Rd	Honolulu	HI	96822	808-973-5683	955-8794
Houston 1907 Holcombe Blvd	Houston	TX	77030	713-795-3500	795-3595
Web: www.ronaldmcdonaldhousehouston.org/home.htm					
Huntington 1500 17th St	Huntington	WV	25701	304-529-1122	529-2970
Web: www.mchouse.org					
Indianapolis 435 Limestone St	Indianapolis	IN	46202	317-269-2247	267-0606
Web: www.rmh-indiana.org					
Iowa City 730 Hawkins Dr	Iowa City	IA	52246	319-356-3939	353-6873
Web: www.uihealthcare.com/depts/ronaldmcdonald					
Jackson 2524 N State St	Jackson	MS	39216	601-981-5683	981-3613
Jacksonville 824 Children's Way	Jacksonville	FL	32207	904-807-4663	807-4700
Web: www.rmhjax.org					
Johnson City 418 N State of Franklin Rd	Johnson City	TN	37604	423-975-5437	434-8989
Joplin 3402 S Jackson Ave PO Box 2688	Joplin	MO	64804	417-624-2273	624-0270
Web: www.rmhjoplin.org					
Kansas City 2502 Cherry St	Kansas City	MO	64108	816-842-8321	842-7033
Web: www.rmhckc.org					
Kansas City 2502 Cherry St	Kansas City	MO	64108	816-842-8321	421-7324
Web: www.rmhckc.org					
Knoxville 1705 W Clinch Ave	Knoxville	TN	37916	865-525-7933	525-7942
Web: www.knoxrmhc.org					
Lansing 121 S Holmes St	Lansing	MI	48912	517-485-9303	485-9810
Web: www.sparrow.org/childrenscenter/ccronald.asp					
Las Vegas 2323 Potosi St	Las Vegas	NV	89146	702-252-4663	252-7345
Web: www.rmhlv.com					
Lexington 1300 Ft Center Dr PO Box 22414	Lexington	KY	40502	859-268-0757	266-6771
Web: www.rmhclexington.com					
Little Rock 1009 Wolfe St	Little Rock	AR	72202	501-374-1956	374-2418
Loma Linda 11365 Anderson St	Loma Linda	CA	92354	909-558-8300	558-0300
Web: www.llrmh.org					
London 741 Base Line Rd E	London	ON	N6C2R6	519-685-3232	685-0703
Web: www.rmhlondon.ca					
Long Branch 131 Bath Ave	Long Branch	NJ	07740	732-222-8755	222-9363
Web: www.geocities.com/rmhoflb					
Los Angeles 4560 Fountain Ave	Los Angeles	CA	90029	323-666-6400	663-8550
Web: www.larmh.org					
Louisville 550 S 1st St	Louisville	KY	40202	502-581-1416	581-0037
Web: www.rmhlouisville.org					
Lubbock 1212 Indiana Ave	Lubbock	TX	79415	806-744-8877	744-3652
Web: www.rmhclubbock.com					
Macon 1160 Forsyth St	Macon	GA	31201	478-746-4090	746-0580
Web: www.ronaldhousecga.org					
Madera 9161 Randall Way	Madera	CA	93638	559-447-6770	447-6778
Web: www.ronald-mcdonaldhouse.com					

	City	State	Zip	Phone	Fax
Madison 2716 Marshall Ct	Madison	WI	53705	608-232-4660	232-4670
Web: www.rmhcmadison.org					
Marshfield 803 W North St	Marshfield	WI	54449	715-387-5899	389-5991
Web: www.rmhmarshfield.org					
Memphis 535 Alabama Ave	Memphis	TN	38105	901-529-4055	523-0315
Web: www.rmhmemphis.org					
Miami 1145 NW 14th Terr	Miami	FL	33136	305-324-5683	324-5689
Minneapolis 608 Ontario St SE	Minneapolis	MN	55414	612-331-5752	331-1255
Web: www.rmhmpls.com					
Missoula 3003 Ft Missoula Rd PO Box 1119	Missoula	MT	59804	406-541-7646	541-7642
Web: www.rmhmissoula.org					
Mobile 1626 Springhill Ave	Mobile	AL	36604	251-694-6873	438-2222
Monroe 200 S 3rd St	Monroe	LA	71202	318-387-7933	
Web: www.bayou.com/rmh					
Montreal 3201 Chemin de la Cote Sainte Catherine	Montreal	QC	H3T1C4	514-731-2871	739-8823
Morgantown 841 Country Club Dr	Morgantown	WV	26505	304-598-0050	599-0780
Web: www.rmhcmgtn.org					
Nashville 2144 Fairfax Ave	Nashville	TN	37212	615-343-4000	343-4004
Web: www.rmhnashville.com					
New Brunswick 145 Somerset St	New Brunswick	NJ	08901	732-249-1222	249-1439
Web: www.rmh-cnj.org					
New Haven 501 George St	New Haven	CT	06511	203-777-5683	777-3082
Web: www.ronaldmcdonaldhouse-ct.org					
New Hyde Park 267-07 76th Ave	New Hyde Park	NY	11042	718-343-5683	343-5798
Web: www.rmhlongisland.org					
New Orleans 4403 Canal St	New Orleans	LA	70119	504-486-6668	482-1666
New York 405 E 73rd St	New York	NY	10021	212-639-0100	472-0376
Web: www.rmdh.org					
Norfolk 404 Colley Ave	Norfolk	VA	23507	757-627-5386	622-0534
Web: www.rmhcnorfolk.com					
Oklahoma City 1301 NE 14th St	Oklahoma City	OK	73117	405-424-6873	424-0919
Web: www.rmhokc.org					
Omaha 620 S 38th Ave	Omaha	NE	68105	402-346-9377	346-9468
Web: www.rmhomaha.org					
Orange 383 S Batavia St	Orange	CA	92868	714-639-3600	516-3697
Web: www.ronaldhouseoc.org					
Orlando 2201 Alden Rd	Orlando	FL	32803	407-898-6127	896-3562
Web: www.rmhorlando.com					
Orlando 1630 Kuhl Ave	Orlando	FL	32806	407-581-1289	581-1392
Web: www.rmhorlando.com					
Ottawa 407 Smyth Rd	Ottawa	ON	K1H8M8	613-737-5523	737-5524
Web: www.rmhottawa.com					
Palo Alto 520 Sand Hill Rd	Palo Alto	CA	94304	650-470-6000	470-6018
Web: ronaldhouse-stanford.org					
Pasadena 763 S Pasadena Ave	Pasadena	CA	91105	626-585-1588	585-1688
Web: www.pasadenarmh.org					
Pensacola 5154 Bayou Blvd	Pensacola	FL	32503	850-477-2273	477-7607
Web: www.rmhpensacola.org					
Philadelphia 3925 Chestnut St	Philadelphia	PA	19104	215-387-8406	386-4977
Web: www.philarmh.org					
Phoenix 501 E Roanoke Ave	Phoenix	AZ	85004	602-264-2654	264-5670
Web: www.rmhcphoenix.com					
Pittsburgh 500 Shady Ave	Pittsburgh	PA	15206	412-362-3400	362-8540
Web: www.rmhcpgh.org					
Portland 250 Brackett St	Portland	ME	04102	207-780-6282	780-0198
Web: www.rmhportlandme.org					
Portland 3440 SW US Veterans Hospital Rd	Portland	OR	97239	503-494-5200	243-2969
Web: www.rmh-or.org					
Portland 2620 N Commercial Ave	Portland	OR	97227	503-287-7600	287-0001
Web: www.rmh-or.org					
Providence 45 Gay St	Providence	RI	02905	401-274-4447	751-3730
Web: www.providenceronaldmcdonaldhouse.org					
Richmond 2330 Monument Ave	Richmond	VA	23220	804-355-6517	358-3153
Web: richmondrmhc.homestead.com/richmondrmhc.html					
Roanoke 2224 S Jefferson St	Roanoke	VA	24014	540-857-0770	857-9584
Rochester 850 2nd St SW	Rochester	MN	55902	507-282-9632	252-2160
Web: ronhouserochmn.org					
Rochester 333 Westmoreland Dr	Rochester	NY	14620	585-442-5437	442-7330
Web: www.ronaldshouse.com					
Sacramento 2555 49th St	Sacramento	CA	95817	916-734-4230	734-4238
Web: www.rmhcnc.org					
Saint Louis 4381 W Pine Blvd	Saint Louis	MO	63108	314-531-6601	531-6353
Web: www.rmhcstl.com					
Saint Louis 3450 Park Ave	Saint Louis	MO	63104	314-773-1100	773-2053
Web: www.rmhcstl.com					
Saint Petersburg 401 7th Ave S	Saint Petersburg	FL	33701	727-821-8961	897-4836
Sainte-Foy 2747 boul Laurier	Sainte-Foy	QC	G1V2L9	418-651-1771	651-1772
Salt Lake City 935 E South Temple	Salt Lake City	UT	84102	801-363-4663	363-0092
Web: rmhslc.org					
San Antonio 227 Lewis St	San Antonio	TX	78212	210-223-6014	223-6138
San Antonio 4803 Sid Katz Dr	San Antonio	TX	78229	210-614-2554	614-2905
Web: www.sarmhc.com					
San Antonio 619 W Houston St	San Antonio	TX	78229	210-704-3860	704-3870
Web: www.christussantarosa.org/svc_other_mcdonald.htm					
San Diego 3101 Berger Ave	San Diego	CA	92123	858-292-7413	292-7357
Web: www.sdmcdonalds.com					
San Francisco 1640 Scott St	San Francisco	CA	94115	415-673-0891	673-1335
Web: www.ronaldhouse-sf.org					
Saskatoon 1011 University Dr	Saskatoon	SK	S7N0K4	306-244-5700	244-3099
Web: www.rmh.sk.ca					
Savannah 4710 Waters Ave	Savannah	GA	31404	912-356-5520	355-6877
Scranton 332 Wheeler Ave	Scranton	PA	18510	570-969-8998	969-8991
Web: www.rmhscranton.org					
Seattle 5000 40th Ave NE	Seattle	WA	98105	206-838-0600	838-0814
Web: www.rmhcseattle.org					
Seattle 5130 40th Ave NE	Seattle	WA	98105	206-838-0600	838-0650
Web: www.rmhcseattle.org					
Sioux City 2500 Nebraska St	Sioux City	IA	51104	712-255-4084	255-4281
Web: www.ronaldhouse-siouxcity.com					
Sioux Falls 2001 S Norton Ave	Sioux Falls	SD	57105	605-336-6398	339-2638
Spokane 1015 W 5th Ave	Spokane	WA	99204	509-624-0500	624-3267
Web: www.rmhspokane.org					
Springfield 610 N 7th St	Springfield	IL	62702	217-528-3314	528-6084
Web: www.rmhccentralil.org					
Springfield 34 Chapin Terr	Springfield	MA	01107	413-794-5683	794-8199
Web: www.ronmcdhouse.com					
Springfield 949 E Primrose St	Springfield	MO	65807	417-886-0225	882-7206
Web: www.ronaldmcdonaldhouse.org					
Syracuse 1027 E Genesee St	Syracuse	NY	13210	315-476-1027	476-5022
Web: www.cnyronaldmcdonaldhouse.org					
Tallahassee 712 E 7th Ave	Tallahassee	FL	32303	850-222-1706	222-0086
Web: www.tfn.net/RMHouse					
Tampa 35 Columbia Dr	Tampa	FL	33606	813-254-2398	254-8891
Web: www.rmhctampabay.com					
Temple 2415 S 47th St	Temple	TX	76504	254-770-0910	770-1622
Web: www.rmh-temple.com					

	City	State	ZIP	Phone	Fax
Toledo 3883 Monroe St	Toledo	OH	43606	419-471-4663	479-6961
Web: www.rmhctoledo.org					
Topeka 825 SW Buchanan St	Topeka	KS	66606	785-235-6852	235-3170
Web: www.ronaldmc.org					
Toronto 26 Gerrard St E	Toronto	ON	M5B1G3	416-977-0458	977-8807
Web: www.rmhtoronto.org					
Tucson 2230 E Speedway Blvd	Tucson	AZ	85719	520-326-0060	881-3314
Web: www.rmhctucson.org					
Tulsa 6102 S Hudson Ave	Tulsa	OK	74136	918-496-2727	496-2762
Web: www.rmhtulsa.org					
Vancouver 4116 Angus Dr	Vancouver	BC	V6J4H9	604-736-2957	736-5974
Web: www.ronaldmcdonaldhousebc.com					
Washington 1326 Quincy St NE	Washington	DC	20017	202-529-8204	635-3578
Web: www.rmhc.greaterdc.org					
Wauwatosa 8948 Watertown Plank Rd	Wauwatosa	WI	53226	414-475-5333	475-6342
Web: www.rmhcmilwaukee.com					
Wichita 520 N Rutan St	Wichita	KS	67208	316-687-2000	687-6654
Web: www.ronaldhousewichita.org					
Wichita 1110 N Emporia St	Wichita	KS	67214	316-269-4420	269-0665
Web: www.ronaldhousewichita.org					
Wilmington 1901 Rockland Rd	Wilmington	DE	19803	302-656-4847	658-6608
TF: 888-656-4847 ■ *Web:* www.rmhde.org					
Winnipeg 566 Bannatyne Ave	Winnipeg	MB	R3A0G7	204-774-4777	774-2160
Web: www.rmh.mb.ca					
Winston-Salem 419 S Hawthorne Rd	Winston-Salem	NC	27103	336-723-0228	723-0302
Web: www.wshouse.com					
Youngstown 2450 Goleta Ave	Youngstown	OH	44505	330-884-5220	884-5685
Ronald McDonald House Charities					
Dayton 555 Valley St	Dayton	OH	45404	937-224-0047	496-2476
Web: www.rmhdayton.org					
Reno 323 Maine St	Reno	NV	89502	775-322-4663	322-8670
Web: www.rmhc-reno.com					

377 HOSPITALS

SEE ALSO Health Care Providers - Ancillary p. 1772; Health Care Systems p. 1772; Hospices p. 1791; Veterans Nursing Homes - State p. 2403

377-1 Children's Hospitals

	City	State	ZIP	Phone	Fax
Alfred I duPont Hospital for Children 1600 Rockland Rd	Wilmington	DE	19803	302-651-4000	651-4224*
**Fax:* Admitting ■ *Web:* www.nemours.org					
All Children's Hospital 801 6th St S	Saint Petersburg	FL	33701	727-898-7451	767-8546*
**Fax:* Admitting ■ *TF:* 800-456-4543 ■ *Web:* www.allkids.org					
Arkansas Children's Hospital 800 Marshall St	Little Rock	AR	72202	501-364-1100	364-1452*
**Fax:* Admitting ■ *Web:* www.archildrens.org					
Arnold Palmer Hospital for Children & Women 92 W Miller St	Orlando	FL	32806	407-841-5111	649-6926
Web: www.arnoldpalmerhospital.org					
Bradley Hospital 1011 Veterans Memorial Pkwy	East Providence	RI	02915	401-432-1000	432-1500
Web: www.lifespan.org/bradley/					
Children's Care Hospital & School 2501 W 26th St	Sioux Falls	SD	57105	605-782-2300	782-2301
TF: 800-584-9294 ■ *Web:* www.cchs.org					
Children's Healthcare of Atlanta at Egleston					
1405 Clifton Rd NE	Atlanta	GA	30322	404-785-6000	325-6143*
**Fax:* Admitting ■ *TF:* 800-250-5437 ■ *Web:* www.choa.org					
Children's Healthcare of Atlanta at Scottish Rite					
1001 Johnson Ferry Rd NE	Atlanta	GA	30342	404-785-5252	785-4687*
**Fax:* Admitting ■ *TF:* 800-250-5437 ■ *Web:* www.choa.org					
Children's Hospital 1056 E 19th Ave	Denver	CO	80218	303-861-8888	837-4295*
**Fax:* Admitting ■ *TF:* 800-624-6553 ■ *Web:* www.thechildrenshospital.org					
Children's Hospital 200 Henry Clay Ave	New Orleans	LA	70118	504-899-9511	896-9708*
**Fax:* Admitting ■ *TF:* 800-299-9511 ■ *Web:* www.chnola.org					
Children's Hospital 8200 Dodge St	Omaha	NE	68114	402-354-5400	955-4046*
**Fax:* Admitting ■ *Web:* www.chsomaha.org					
Children's Hospital 700 Children's Dr	Columbus	OH	43205	614-722-2000	722-5995
TF: 800-792-8401 ■ *Web:* www.childrenscolumbus.org					
Children's Hospital of Alabama 1600 7th Ave S	Birmingham	AL	35233	205-939-9100	
Children's Hospital Boston 300 Longwood Ave	Boston	MA	02115	617-355-6000	
Web: www.childrenshospital.org					
Children's Hospital Central California 9300 Children's Pl	Madera	CA	93638	559-353-3000	353-5161*
**Fax:* Admitting ■ *TF:* 800-548-5435 ■ *Web:* www.childrenscentralcal.org					
Children's Hospital of the King's Daughters 601 Children's Ln	Norfolk	VA	23507	757-668-7000	668-8050*
**Fax:* Admitting ■ *Web:* www.chkd.org					
Children's Hospital of Los Angeles 4650 Sunset Blvd	Los Angeles	CA	90027	323-660-2450	668-1138*
**Fax:* Admitting ■ *Web:* www.childrenshospitalla.org					
Children's Hospital Medical Center of Akron 1 Perkins Sq	Akron	OH	44308	330-543-1000	543-3146*
**Fax:* Admitting ■ *TF:* 800-262-0333 ■ *Web:* www.akronchildrens.org					
Children's Hospital of Michigan 3901 Beaubien Blvd	Detroit	MI	48201	313-745-5437	966-5134*
**Fax:* Admitting ■ *Web:* www.dmc.org/chm					
Children's Hospital of Orange County 455 S Main St	Orange	CA	92868	714-997-3000	289-4559*
**Fax:* Admitting ■ *Web:* www.choc.org					
Children's Hospital of Philadelphia 3400 Civic Center Blvd	Philadelphia	PA	19104	215-590-1000	590-1413*
**Fax:* Admitting ■ *Web:* www.chop.edu					
Children's Hospital of Pittsburgh 3705 5th Ave	Pittsburgh	PA	15213	412-692-5325	692-8500
Web: www.chp.edu					
Children's Hospital & Regional Medical Center					
4800 Sand Point Way NE	Seattle	WA	98105	206-987-2000	987-5018*
**Fax:* Admitting ■ *TF:* 866-987-2000 ■ *Web:* www.chmc.org					
Children's Hospital & Research Center at Oakland					
747 52nd St	Oakland	CA	94609	510-428-3000	450-5884*
**Fax:* Admitting ■ *Web:* www.childrenshospitaloakland.org					
Children's Hospital of Wisconsin					
9000 W Wisconsin Ave PO Box 1997	Milwaukee	WI	53201	414-266-2000	266-2547*
**Fax:* Admitting ■ *Web:* www.chw.org					
Children's Hospitals & Clinics Minneapolis					
2525 Chicago Ave	Minneapolis	MN	55404	612-813-6100	813-6807
Web: www.childrenshc.org					
Children's Hospitals & Clinics Saint Paul 345 N Smith Ave	Saint Paul	MN	55102	651-220-6000	220-5147
Web: www.childrenshc.org					
Children's Institute of Pittsburgh 6301 Northumberland St	Pittsburgh	PA	15217	412-420-2400	420-2200
TF: 877-433-1109 ■ *Web:* www.amazingkids.org					
Children's Medical Center 1 Children's Plaza	Dayton	OH	45404	937-641-3000	641-3326*
**Fax:* Admitting ■ *Web:* www.cmc-dayton.org					
Children's Medical Center of Dallas 1935 Motor St	Dallas	TX	75235	214-456-7000	456-2197
Web: www.childrens.com					
Children's Memorial Hospital 2300 Children's Plaza	Chicago	IL	60614	773-880-4000	880-6986*
**Fax:* Admitting ■ *Web:* www.childrensmemorial.org					
Children's Mercy Hospital 2401 Gillham Rd	Kansas City	MO	64108	816-234-3000	
TF: 866-512-2168 ■ *Web:* www.cmh.edu					
Children's National Medical Center 111 Michigan Ave NW	Washington	DC	20010	202-884-5000	884-5561
Web: www.dcchildrens.com					
Children's Specialized Hospital 150 New Providence Rd	Mountainside	NJ	07092	908-233-3720	233-4176
TF: 888-224-5373 ■ *Web:* www.childrens-specialized.org					
Cincinnati Children's Hospital Medical Center					
3333 Burnet Ave	Cincinnati	OH	45229	513-636-4200	636-3733*
**Fax:* Admitting ■ *TF:* 800-344-2462 ■ *Web:* www.cincinnatichildrens.org					
Cleo Wallace Centers Westminster Campus					
8405 Church Ranch Blvd	Westminster	CO	80021	303-466-7391	466-0904*
**Fax:* Admitting ■ *TF:* 800-456-2536					
Cleveland Clinic Children's Hospital for Rehabilitation					
2801 ML King Jr Dr	Cleveland	OH	44104	216-721-5400	791-1012
Web: cms.clevelandclinic.org/childrenshospital					
Connecticut Children's Medical Center 282 Washington St	Hartford	CT	06106	860-545-9000	545-8560
Web: www.ccmckids.org					
Cook Children's Medical Center 801 7th Ave	Fort Worth	TX	76104	682-885-4000	885-4229
Web: www.cookchildrens.org					
Copper Hills Youth Center 5899 W Rivendell Dr	West Jordan	UT	84088	801-561-3377	569-2959
TF: 800-776-7116 ■ *Web:* www.copperhillsyouthcenter.com					
Covenant Children's Hospital 3615 19th St	Lubbock	TX	79410	806-725-1011	723-7189
Web: www.covenanthealth.org					
Crittenton Children's Center 10918 Elm Ave	Kansas City	MO	64134	816-765-6600	767-4101
Web: www.saintlukeshealthsystem.org					
CS Mott Children's Hospital 1500 E Medical Center Dr	Ann Arbor	MI	48109	734-936-4000	763-7736
TF: 800-211-8181 ■ *Web:* www.med.umich.edu/1libr/child/child01.htm					
Cumberland Hospital for Children & Adolescents					
9407 Cumberland Rd	New Kent	VA	23124	804-966-2242	966-5639
TF: 800-368-3472 ■ *Web:* www.cumberlandhospital.com					
Devereux Georgia Treatment Network 1291 Stanley Rd NW	Kennesaw	GA	30152	770-427-0147	424-9408
TF: 800-342-3357 ■ *Web:* www.devereuxga.org					
Devereux Hospital & Children's Center of Florida					
8000 Devereux Dr	Melbourne	FL	32940	321-242-9100	259-0786
DeVos Children's Hospital 100 Michigan St NE	Grand Rapids	MI	49503	616-391-9000	391-3105
Web: www.devoschildrens.org					
Driscoll Children's Hospital 3533 S Alameda St	Corpus Christi	TX	78411	361-694-5000	694-5317
TF: 800-324-5683 ■ *Web:* www.driscollchildrens.org					
DuPont Hospital for Children 1600 Rockland Rd	Wilmington	DE	19803	302-651-4000	651-4224*
**Fax:* Admitting ■ *Web:* www.nemours.org					
East Tennessee Children's Hospital 2018 Clinch Ave	Knoxville	TN	37916	865-541-8000	541-8289*
**Fax:* Claims ■ *Web:* www.etch.com					
Franciscan Children's Hospital 30 Warren St	Brighton	MA	02135	617-254-3800	779-1119
Web: www.fch.com					
Gillette Children's Specialty Healthcare					
200 E University Ave	Saint Paul	MN	55101	651-291-2848	229-3833
TF: 800-719-4040 ■ *Web:* www.gillettechildrens.org					
Gulf Coast Treatment Center 1015 Mar-Walt Dr	Fort Walton Beach	FL	32547	850-863-4160	863-8576
Hawthorn Center 18471 Haggerty Rd	Northville	MI	48167	248-349-3000	349-8259
TF: 800-434-2340					
Hospital for Sick Children 1731 Bunker Hill Rd NE	Washington	DC	20017	202-832-4400	529-1646
TF: 800-226-4444 ■ *Web:* www.hfscsite.org					
Inner Harbour Hospitals 4685 Dorsett Shoals Rd	Douglasville	GA	30135	770-942-2391	489-0406
TF: 800-255-8657 ■ *Web:* www.innerharbour.org					
JD McCarty Center for Children with Developmental Disabilities					
2002 E Robinson St	Norman	OK	73071	405-307-2800	307-2801
TF: 800-777-1272 ■ *Web:* www.jdmc.org					
Kennedy Krieger Institute 707 N Broadway	Baltimore	MD	21205	443-923-9200	923-9425
TF: 800-873-3377 ■ *Web:* www.kennedykrieger.org					
Larabida Children's Hospital & Research Center					
E 65th St at Lake Michigan	Chicago	IL	60649	773-363-6700	363-9554
Web: www.larabida.org					
Le Bonheur Children's Medical Center 50 N Dunlap	Memphis	TN	38103	901-287-5437	572-4568*
**Fax:* Admitting ■ *Web:* www.lebonheur.org					
Lucile Packard Children's Hospital 725 Welch Rd	Palo Alto	CA	94304	650-497-8000	497-8968*
**Fax:* Admitting ■ *Web:* www.lpch.org					
Mary Bridge Children's Hospital & Health Center					
317 ML King Way	Tacoma	WA	98405	253-403-1400	403-1247
TF: 800-552-1419 ■ *Web:* www.marybridge.org					
Massachusetts Hospital School 3 Randolph St	Canton	MA	02021	781-828-2440	821-4086
McCarty JD Center for Children with Developmental Disabilities					
2002 E Robinson St	Norman	OK	73071	405-307-2800	307-2801
TF: 800-777-1272 ■ *Web:* www.jdmc.org					
Medical University of South Carolina Children's Hospital					
165 Ashley Ave	Charleston	SC	29425	843-792-2300	792-8948
Web: www.musckids.com					
Miami Children's Hospital 3100 SW 62nd Ave	Miami	FL	33155	305-666-6511	663-8466
TF: 800-432-6837 ■ *Web:* www.mch.com					
Mott CS Children's Hospital 1500 E Medical Center Dr	Ann Arbor	MI	48109	734-936-4000	763-7736
TF: 800-211-8181 ■ *Web:* www.med.umich.edu/1libr/child/child01.htm					
Mount Washington Pediatric Hospital 1708 W Rogers Ave	Baltimore	MD	21209	410-578-8600	466-1715
Web: www.mwph.org					
National Hospital for Kids in Crisis 5300 Kids Peace Dr	Orefield	PA	18069	610-799-8800	799-7281*
**Fax:* Admitting ■ *TF:* 800-854-3123 ■ *Web:* www.kidspeace.org					
Phoenix Children's Hospital 1919 E Thomas Rd	Phoenix	AZ	85016	602-546-1000	546-0191
Web: www.phxchildrens.com					
Primary Children's Medical Center 100 N Medical Dr	Salt Lake City	UT	84113	801-588-2000	662-6202*
**Fax:* Admitting					
Queens Children's Psychiatric Center					
74-03 Commonwealth Blvd	Bellerose	NY	11426	718-264-4506	264-4954
Rady Children's Hospital 3020 Children's Way	San Diego	CA	92123	858-966-7474	966-4934*
**Fax:* Library ■ *Web:* www.rchsd.org					
Riverview Hospital for Children 915 River Rd	Middletown	CT	06457	860-704-4000	704-4032
Saint Christopher's Hospital for Children					
Erie Ave & Front St	Philadelphia	PA	19134	215-427-5000	427-6825*
**Fax:* Admitting ■ *Web:* www.stchristophershospital.com					
Saint Jude Children's Research Hospital 332 N Lauderdale St	Memphis	TN	38105	901-495-3300	495-5297*
**Fax:* Admitting ■ *TF:* 866-278-5833 ■ *Web:* www.stjude.org					
Saint Louis Children's Hospital 1 Children's Pl	Saint Louis	MO	63110	314-454-6000	454-2870
TF: 800-678-5437 ■ *Web:* www.stlouischildrens.org					
Schneider Children's Hospital 269-01 76th Ave	New Hyde Park	NY	11040	718-470-3000	
Web: www.schneiderchildrenshospital.org					
Searcy Hospital 725 E Coy Smith Hwy	Mount Vernon	AL	36560	251-662-6700	829-9075
Shriners Hospitals for Children Boston 51 Blossom St	Boston	MA	02114	617-722-3000	523-1684
TF: 800-255-1916 ■ *Web:* www.shrinershq.org/shc/boston					
Shriners Hospitals for Children Canada 1529 Cedar Ave	Montreal	QC	H3G1A6	514-842-4464	842-7553
Web: www.shrinershq.org/shc/canada					
Shriners Hospitals for Children Chicago 2211 N Oak Park Ave	Chicago	IL	60707	773-622-5400	385-5453*
**Fax:* Admitting ■ *TF:* 888-385-0161 ■ *Web:* www.shrinershq.org/shc/chicago					
Shriners Hospitals for Children Cincinnati 3229 Burnet Ave	Cincinnati	OH	45229	513-872-6000	872-6999
TF: 800-875-8580 ■ *Web:* www.shrinershq.org/shc/cincinnati					
Shriners Hospitals for Children Erie 1645 W 8th St	Erie	PA	16505	814-875-8700	875-8756
TF: 800-873-5437 ■ *Web:* www.shrinershq.org/shc/erie					
Shriners Hospitals for Children Galveston 815 Market St	Galveston	TX	77550	409-621-1366	621-1390
TF: 800-292-3938 ■ *Web:* www.shrinershq.org/shc/galveston					
Shriners Hospitals for Children Greenville 950 W Faris Rd	Greenville	SC	29605	864-271-3444	240-8175
Web: www.shrinershq.org/shc/greenville					
Shriners Hospitals for Children Honolulu 1310 Punahou St	Honolulu	HI	96826	808-941-4466	942-8573
TF: 888-888-6314 ■ *Web:* www.shrinershq.org/shc/honolulu					
Shriners Hospitals for Children Houston 6977 Main St	Houston	TX	77030	713-797-1616	793-3762*
**Fax:* Admitting ■ *Web:* www.shrinershq.org/shc/houston					

Children's Hospitals (Cont'd)

Name / Address	City	State	Zip	Phone	Fax
Shriners Hospitals for Children Intermountain Fairfax Rd & Virginia St	Salt Lake City	UT	84103	801-536-3500	536-3782
TF: 800-313-3745 ■ *Web:* www.shrinershq.org/shc/intermountain					
Shriners Hospitals for Children Lexington 1900 Richmond Rd	Lexington	KY	40502	859-266-2101	268-5636
TF: 800-668-4634 ■ *Web:* www.shrinershq.org/shc/lexington					
Shriners Hospitals for Children Los Angeles 3160 Geneva St	Los Angeles	CA	90020	213-388-3151	387-7528*
**Fax:* Admitting ■ *TF:* 888-486-5437 ■ *Web:* www.shrinershq.org/shc/losangeles					
Shriners Hospitals for Children Northern California 2425 Stockton Blvd	Sacramento	CA	95817	916-453-2000	453-2395*
**Fax:* Admitting ■ *Web:* www.shrinershq.org/shc/northerncalifornia					
Shriners Hospitals for Children Philadelphia 3551 N Broad St	Philadelphia	PA	19140	215-430-4000	430-4068*
**Fax:* Admitting ■ *TF:* 800-281-4050 ■ *Web:* www.shrinershq.org/shc/philadelphia					
Shriners Hospitals for Children Portland 3101 SW Sam Jackson Park Rd	Portland	OR	97239	503-241-5090	221-3475
Web: www.shrinershq.org/shc/portland					
Shriners Hospitals for Children Saint Louis 2001 S Lindbergh Blvd	Saint Louis	MO	63131	314-432-3600	432-2930
TF: 800-237-5055 ■ *Web:* www.shrinershq.org/shc/stlouis					
Shriners Hospitals for Children Shreveport 3100 Samford Ave	Shreveport	LA	71103	318-222-5704	424-7610
Web: www.shrinershq.org/shc/shreveport					
Shriners Hospitals for Children Spokane 911 W 5th Ave	Spokane	WA	99204	509-455-7844	623-0474*
**Fax:* Admitting ■ *Web:* www.shrinershq.org/shc/spokane					
Shriners Hospitals for Children Springfield 516 Carew St	Springfield	MA	01104	413-787-2000	787-2009
TF: 800-322-5905 ■ *Web:* www.shrinershq.org/shc/springfield					
Shriners Hospitals for Children Tampa 12502 N Pine Dr	Tampa	FL	33612	813-972-2250	975-7120*
**Fax:* Admitting ■ *TF:* 800-237-5055 ■ *Web:* www.shrinershq.org/shc/tampa					
Shriners Hospitals for Children Twin Cities 2025 E River Pkwy	Minneapolis	MN	55414	612-596-6100	339-5954
Web: www.shrinershq.org/shc/twincities					
SSM Cardinal Glennon Children's Hospital 1465 S Grand Blvd	Saint Louis	MO	63104	314-577-5600	
Web: www.cardinalglennon.com					
Stollery Children's Hospital 8440 112th St	Edmonton	AB	T6G2B7	780-407-8822	407-3301
Streamwood Behavioral Health Center 1400 E Irving Park Rd	Streamwood	IL	60107	630-837-9000	837-2639
TF: 800-272-7790 ■ *Web:* www.streamwoodhospital.com					
Texas Children's Hospital 6621 Fannin St	Houston	TX	77030	832-824-1000	825-3386
TF: 800-364-5437 ■ *Web:* www.texaschildrenshospital.org					
Texas Scottish Rite Hospital for Children 2222 Welborn St	Dallas	TX	75219	214-559-5000	559-7447
TF: 800-421-1121 ■ *Web:* www.tsrhc.org					
Wallace Cleo Centers Westminster Campus 8405 Church Ranch Blvd	Westminster	CO	80021	303-466-7391	466-0904*
**Fax:* Admitting ■ *TF:* 800-456-2536					
Wolfson Children's Hospital 800 Prudential Dr	Jacksonville	FL	32207	904-202-8000	202-8173
Web: www.wchjax.com					
Women's & Children's Hospital of Buffalo 219 Bryant St	Buffalo	NY	14222	716-878-7000	888-3979*
**Fax:* Admitting ■ *TF:* 800-388-9672 ■ *Web:* www.chob.edu					

377-2 General Hospitals - Canada

Name / Address	City	Prov	Postal Code	Phone	Fax
Aberbeen Hospital 835 E River Rd	New Glasgow	NS	B2H3S6	902-752-8311	752-4358
TF: 800-270-4776 ■ *Web:* www.aberdeenhospital.com					
Ajax & Pickering Health Center 580 Harwood Ave S	Ajax	ON	L1S2J4	905-683-2320	683-2618
Web: www.rougevalley.ca					
Arbutus Care Centre 4505 Valley Dr	Vancouver	BC	V6L2L1	604-261-4292	261-7849
Battlefords Union Hospital 1092 107th St	North Battleford	SK	S9A1Z1	306-446-6600	446-4114
Belleville General Hospital 265 Dundas St E	Belleville	ON	K8N5A9	613-969-7400	968-8234
Web: www.qhc.on.ca					
Bluewater Health 220 N Mitton St	Sarnia	ON	N7T6H6	519-464-4500	336-8780
Web: www.bluewaterhealth.ca					
Bluewater Health 89 Norman St	Sarnia	ON	N7T6S3	519-464-4400	336-8780
Web: www.bluewaterhealth.ca					
Brandon Regional Health Center 150 McTavish Ave E	Brandon	MB	R7A2B3	204-578-4000	578-4937
Web: www.brandonrha.mb.ca					
Brant Joseph Memorial Hospital 1230 N Shore Blvd	Burlington	ON	L7R4C4	905-632-3730	336-6480
Web: www.jbmh.com					
British Columbia's Women's Hospital & Health Centre 4500 Oak St	Vancouver	BC	V6H3N1	604-875-2424	875-3582
Web: www.cw.bc.ca/about_bcw.asp					
Brockville General Hospital 75 Charles St	Brockville	ON	K6V1S8	613-345-5645	345-8349
Web: www.bgh-on.ca					
Burnaby Hospital 3935 Kincaid St	Burnaby	BC	V5G2X6	604-434-4211	412-6170*
**Fax:* Mail Rm ■ *Web:* www.fraserhealth.ca					
Cambridge Memorial Hospital 700 Coronation Blvd	Cambridge	ON	N1R3G2	519-621-2330	740-4938
Web: www.cmh.org					
Campbell River Hospital 375 2nd Ave	Campbell River	BC	V9W3V1	250-287-7111	286-9675
Cape Breton Healthcare Complex 1482 George St	Sydney	NS	B1P1P3	902-567-8000	567-7921
Web: www.cbdha.nshealth.ca					
Centenary Health Centre 2867 Ellesmere Rd	Scarborough	ON	M1E4B9	416-284-8131	281-7323
Centre Hospitalier Affilie Pavillon Enfant-Jesus 1401 18th St	Quebec	QC	G1J1Z4	418-649-0252	649-5920*
**Fax:* Admissions					
Centre Hospitalier Affilie Universitaire de Quebec-Pavillon Saint-Sacrement 1050 ch de la Sainte-Foy	Quebec	QC	G1S4L8	418-682-7511	682-7877*
**Fax:* Admissions ■ *Web:* www.cha.quebec.qc.ca					
Centre Hospitalier Angrignon 8585 Terrasse Champlain	LaSalle	QC	H8P1C1	514-362-1000	362-2812
Centre Hospitalier Angrignon 4000 boul Lasalle	Verdun	QC	H4G2A3	514-362-1000	765-7306
Centre Hospitalier Anna-Laberge 200 boul Brisebois	Chateauguay	QC	J6K4W8	450-699-2425	699-2510*
**Fax:* Admissions ■ *TF:* 800-700-0621					
Centre Hospitalier Baie des Chaleurs 419 boul Perron	Maria	QC	G0C1Y0	418-759-3443	759-5333
Centre Hospitalier Beauce-Etchemin 1515 17e rue	Saint-Georges	QC	G5Y4T8	418-228-2031	227-9147*
**Fax:* Admissions					
Centre Hospitalier du Centre-de-la-Mauricie 50 118e rue	Shawinigan-Sud	QC	G9P5K1	819-536-7500	536-7687
Centre Hospitalier Chauveau 29 rue de l'Hopital	Loretteville	QC	G2A2T7	418-842-3651	842-8931
Centre Hospitalier d'Amqui 135 rue de l'Hopital	Amqui	QC	G5J2K5	418-629-2211	629-2211
Web: www.rqte.qc.ca					
Centre Hospitalier et Centre de Readaptation Antoine-Labelle 2561 ch de la Lievre S	Des Ruisseaux	QC	J9L3G3	819-623-1234	440-4376*
**Fax:* Admitting					
Centre Hospitalier Fleury 2180 Fleury St E	Montreal	QC	H2B1K3	514-381-9311	383-5287
Centre Hospitalier Le Gardeur 911 montee des Piommiers	Lachenaie	QC	J6V2H2	450-654-7525	470-2640
Web: www.chpierrelegardeur.ca					
Centre Hospitalier Granby 205 boul Leclerc	Grandby	QC	J2G1T7	450-372-5491	375-8037
Web: www.chgranby.qc.ca					
Centre Hospitalier Hotel-Dieu d'Amos 622 4e rue O	Amos	QC	J9T2S2	819-732-3341	732-7054
Centre Hospitalier Hotel-Dieu de Roberval 450 rue Brassard	Roberval	QC	G8H1B9	418-275-0110	275-6202
Centre Hospitalier Lac Megantic 3569 rue Laval	Lac-Megantic	QC	G6B1A5	819-583-0330	583-5364
Centre Hospitalier de Lachine 650 16th Ave	Lachine	QC	H8S3N5	514-637-2351	637-2570*
**Fax:* Admitting ■ *Web:* www.centrehospitalierdelachine.com					
Centre Hospitalier Laurentien 234 rue Saint-Vincent	Sainte-Agathe-des-Monts	QC	J8C2B8	819-324-4000	324-4001
Centre Hospitalier Mount Sinai 5690 Cavendish Blvd	Montreal	QC	H4W1S7	514-369-2222	369-2225
Centre Hospitalier Pierre Boucher 1333 boul Jacques-Cartier E	Longueuil	QC	J4M2A5	450-468-8111	468-8188
Centre Hospitalier de la Region de l'Amiante 1717 rue Notre-Dame N	Thetford Mines	QC	G6G2V4	418-338-7777	335-7616
Web: www.fondationchra.org					
Centre Hospitalier Regional 1750 prom Sunset	Bathurst	NB	E2A4L7	506-544-3000	544-2329
TF: 800-727-1699					
Centre Hospitalier Regional Baie-Comeau Pavillon Le Royer 635 boul Joliet	Baie-Comeau	QC	G5C1P1	418-589-3701	589-9654
Centre Hospitalier Regional du Grand Portage 75 rue Saint-Henri	Riviere-du-Loup	QC	G5R2A4	418-868-1010	868-1035
Centre Hospitalier Regional de Lanaudiere 1000 boul Sainte-Anne	Joliette	QC	J6E6J2	450-759-8222	759-5143
Centre Hospitalier Regional de Rimouski 150 ave Rouleau	Rimouski	QC	G5L5T1	418-723-7851	723-8616
Centre Hospitalier Regional de Sept-Iles 45 rue Père Divet	Sept-Iles	QC	G4R3N7	418-962-9761	962-2701
Centre Hospitalier Regional du Suroît 150 rue Saint-Thomas	Salaberry-de-Valleyfield	QC	J6T6C1	450-371-9920	371-7454*
**Fax:* Admissions ■ *Web:* www.chsuroit.qc.ca					
Centre Hospitalier Regional de Trois-Rivieres 731 rue Sainte-Julie	Trois-Rivieres	QC	G9A1X1	819-697-3333	372-3546
Centre Hospitalier de Rouyn-Noranda 4 9e rue	Rouyn-Noranda	QC	J9X2B2	819-764-5131	764-4211
Centre Hospitalier Saint-Eustache 520 boul Sauve	Saint-Eustache	QC	J7R5B1	450-473-6811	473-6966
Web: www.chse.qc.ca					
Centre Hospitalier Universitaire de Quebec 2705 Laurier Blvd	Sainte-Foy	QC	G1V4G2	418-656-4141	654-2247
Centre Hospitalier Universitaire de Quebec Pavillon Hotel-Dieu 11 Cote du Palais	Quebec	QC	G1R2J6	418-691-5151	691-5331
Centre Hospitalier de Val-d'Or 725 6e rue	Val-d'Or	QC	J9P3Y1	819-825-6711	825-7919
Centre Hospitalier des Vallees de l'Outaouais Pavillon de Gatineau 909 boul de la Verandrye O	Gatineau	QC	J8P7H2	819-561-8100	561-8306
Web: www.chvo.qc.ca					
Centre Le Jeannois Pavillon Hotel-Dieu d'Alma 300 boul Champlain S	Alma	QC	G8B5W3	418-669-2000	668-9695
Web: www.lejeannois.qc.ca					
Centre de sante Cloutier-du Rivage 155 rue Toupin	Cap-de-la-Madeleine	QC	G8T3Z8	819-370-2100	379-9644
Web: www.cloutier-durivage.qc.ca					
Centre de sante et de services sociaux de la Saint-Maurice 885 boul Ducharme	La Tuque	QC	G9X3C1	819-523-4581	523-9668
Web: www.csssm.ca					
Centre de sante Memphremagog 50 rue Saint-Patrice E	Magog	QC	J1X3X3	819-843-3381	843-8262
Centre de sante de la MRC de Maskinonge 41 boul Comtois	Louiseville	QC	J5V2H8	819-228-2731	228-8749
Web: www.medecinenmauricie.ca/Maskinonge					
Centre Universitaire de Sante de l'Estrie 580 rue Bowen S	Sherbrooke	QC	J1G2E8	819-346-1110	822-6780*
**Fax:* Admissions					
Chatham-Kent Health Alliance 80 Grand Ave W	Chatham	ON	N7L1B7	519-352-6400	436-2522
Web: www.ckha.on.ca					
CH/CHSLD de Papineau 500 rue Belanger	Buckingham	QC	J8L2M4	819-986-3341	986-4000
Web: www.chchsldpapineau.com					
Children's Hospital of Eastern Ontario 401 Smyth Rd	Ottawa	ON	K1H8L1	613-737-7600	738-4866
TF: 866-736-2436 ■ *Web:* www.cheo.on.ca					
Chilliwack General Hospital 45600 Menholm Rd	Chilliwack	BC	V2P1P7	604-795-4141	795-4110
Web: www.fraserhealth.ca					
CHSLD Centre de la Mauricie 1650 6e ave	Grand-Mere	QC	G9T2K4	819-533-2500	533-4998
Web: www.medecinenmauricie.ca					
Cite de la sante de Laval 1755 boul Rene Laennec	Laval	QC	H7M3L9	450-668-1010	975-5545
Web: www.citesante.laval.qc.ca					
Colchester Regional Hospital 207 Willow St	Truro	NS	B2N5A9	902-893-4321	893-5559
Web: www.cehha.nshealth.ca					
Complexe Hospitalier de la Sagamie 305 ave Saint-Vallier	Chicoutimi	QC	G7H5H6	418-541-1000	541-1168
Web: www.usherbrooke.ca/medecine/reseau/sagamie.html					
Complexe Sante et Services Sociaux Nicolet-Yamaska 675 rue Saint-Jean-Baptiste	Nicolet	QC	J3T1S4	819-293-2071	293-6160
Concordia Hospital 1095 Concordia Ave	Winnipeg	MB	R2K3S8	204-667-1560	667-1049
Web: www.concordiahospital.mb.ca					
Cornwall Community Hospital 840 McConnell Ave	Cornwall	ON	K6H5S5	613-938-4240	930-4502
Web: www.cornwallhospital.ca					
Cowichan District Hospital 3045 Gibbins Rd	Duncan	BC	V9L1E5	250-746-4141	746-4247
Credit Valley Hospital 2200 Eglinton Ave W	Mississauga	ON	L5M2N1	905-813-2200	813-4444
Web: www.cvh.on.ca					
Cypress Regional Hospital 499 4th Ave NE	Swift Current	SK	S9H2J9	306-778-9400	778-9409*
**Fax:* Admitting ■ *Web:* www.cypressrha.ca					
Dartmouth General Hospital 325 Pleasant St	Dartmouth	NS	B2Y4G8	902-465-8300	465-8537
Web: www.cdha.nshealth.ca					
Delta Hospital 5800 Mountain View Blvd	Delta	BC	V4K3V6	604-946-1121	946-3086
Web: www.fraserhealth.ca					
Dr Everett Chalmers Hospital 700 Priestman St	Fredericton	NB	E3B5N5	506-452-5400	452-5500
Web: www.rivervalleyhealth.nb.ca/english/aboutr3/list_en.htm					
Dr Georges L Dumont Regional Hospital 330 University Ave	Moncton	NB	E1C2Z3	506-862-4000	862-4256
TF: 888-826-9222					
Eagle Ridge Hospital & Health Care Centre 475 Guildford Way	Port Moody	BC	V3H3W9	604-461-2022	461-9972
Web: www.fraserhealth.ca					
East Kootenay Regional Hospital 13 24th Ave N	Cranbrook	BC	V1C3H9	250-426-5281	426-5285
TF: 866-288-8082 ■ *Web:* www.interiorhealth.ca					
Edmundston Regional Hospital 275 boul Hebert	Edmundston	NB	E3V4E4	506-739-2200	739-2248
Flin Flon General Hospital 50 Church St PO Box 340	Flin Flon	MB	R8A1N2	204-687-7591	687-8494
Foothills Medical Centre 1403 29th St NW	Calgary	AB	T2N2T9	403-670-1110	944-1663
Web: www.calgaryhealthregion.ca					
Glace Bay Healthcare Facility 300 South St	Glace Bay	NS	B1A1W5	902-849-5511	842-9775
Web: www.cbdha.nshealth.ca					
Grace General Hospital 300 Booth Dr	Winnipeg	MB	R3J3M7	204-837-8311	837-0029
Web: www.gracehospital.ca					
Grand River Hospital KW Health Centre 835 King St W PO Box 9056	Kitchener	ON	N2G1G3	519-749-4300	749-4208
Web: www.grandriverhospital.on.ca					
Greater Niagara General Hospital 5546 Portage Rd	Niagara Falls	ON	L2E6X2	905-358-0171	358-8435
Web: www.niagarahealth.on.ca					
Grey Bruce Health Services 1800 8th St E PO Box 1800	Owen Sound	ON	N4K6M9	519-376-2121	372-3942*
**Fax:* Admitting ■ *Web:* www.gbhs.on.ca					
Guelph General Hospital 115 Delhi St	Guelph	ON	N1E4J4	519-822-5350	822-2170
Web: www.guelphgeneralhospital.com					
Hamilton General Hospital 237 Barton St E	Hamilton	ON	L8L2X2	905-527-4322	525-3566
Hamilton Health Sciences 1200 Main St W	Hamilton	ON	L8N3Z5	905-521-2100	521-5067
Web: www.hamiltonhealthsciences.ca					
Headwaters Health Care Centre 100 Rolling Hills Dr	Orangeville	ON	L9W4X9	519-941-2410	942-0483
Web: www.headwatershealth.ca					
Health Sciences Centre 820 Sherbrook St	Winnipeg	MB	R3A1R9	204-774-6511	787-3341
Web: www.hsc.mb.ca					
High River Hospital 560 9th Ave W	High River	AB	T1V1B3	403-652-2200	652-0199
Hopital Brome Missisquoi-Perkins 950 rue Principale	Cowansville	QC	J2K1K3	450-266-4342	263-8669

Phone Fax

Hopital Charles LeMoyne 3120 boul Taschereau ... Greenfield Park QC J4V2H1 450-466-5000 466-5038
Web: www.hclm.qc.ca
Hopital d'Argenteuil 145 boul Providence ... Lachute QC J8H4C7 450-562-3761 566-3316
Hopital General de Montreal 1650 Cedar Ave ... Montreal QC H3G1A4 514-934-1934 934-8303
Web: www.muhc.ca/pfv/mgh
Hopital du Haut-Richelieu
920 boul du Seminaire N ... Saint-Jean-sur-Richelieu QC J3A1B7 450-359-5000 359-5137
Web: www.hhr.qc.ca
Hopital Jean-Talon 1385 Jean-Talon St E ... Montreal QC H2E1S6 514-495-6767 495-6771
Hopital Jeffery Hale 1250 ch Sainte-Foy ... Quebec QC G1S2M6 418-683-4471 683-8471
Hopital Laval 2725 ch Sainte-Foy ... Sainte-Foy QC G1V4G5 418-656-8711 656-4829
Hopital Maisonneuve-Rosemont 5415 de l'Assomption Blvd ... Montreal QC H1T2M4 514-252-3400 252-3569
Hopital Regional de Sudbury Emplacement Laurentien
41 Ramsey Lake Rd ... Sudbury ON P3E5J1 705-523-7100 523-7112
Web: www.hrsrh.on.ca
Hopital du Sacre-Coeur de Montreal 5400 Gouin Blvd W ... Montreal QC H4J1C5 514-338-2222 338-2384
Hopital Sainte-Anne-de-Beaupre 1100 rue Montagnards ... Beaupre QC G0A1E0 418-827-3726 827-3728
Hopital Sainte-Croix 570 rue Heriot ... Drummondville QC J2B1C1 819-478-6464 478-6410
Hopital Sainte-Justine 3175 cote Sainte-Catherine ... Montreal QC H3T1C5 514-345-4931 345-4882
Web: www.chu-sainte-justine.org/en/famille/accueil/Default.aspx
Hopital Santa Cabrini Ospedale 5655 Sainte-Zotique St E ... Montreal QC H1T1P7 514-252-6000 252-6453
Hotel-Dieu d'Arthabaska 5 rue des Hospitalières ... Victoriaville QC G6P6N2 819-357-2030 357-4314
Web: www.hda.ca
Hotel-Dieu Grace Hospital 1030 Ouellette Ave ... Windsor ON N9A1E1 519-973-4444 977-0018
Web: www.hdgh.org
Hotel Dieu Hospital 155 Ontario St ... Saint Catharines ON L2R5K3 905-682-6411 682-0663
Web: www.hdhsc.org
Hotel-Dieu de Levis 143 rue Wolfe ... Levis QC G6V3Z1 418-835-7121 835-7200
Web: www.hdl.qc.ca
Hotel-Dieu de Montmagny 350 boul Tache O ... Montmagny QC G5V3R8 418-248-0630 248-0947
Hotel-Dieu de Saint-Jerome 290 rue Montigny ... Saint-Jerome QC J7Z5T3 450-431-8200 431-8244
Hotel-Dieu de Sorel 400 ave Hotel-Dieu ... Sorel-Tracy QC J3P1N5 450-746-6000 746-6082
Web: www.hoteldieusorel.qc.ca
Humber River Regional Hospital 2111 Finch Ave W ... Toronto ON M3N1N1 416-744-2500 747-3882
Web: www.hrrh.on.ca
Innisfail Health Centre 5023 42nd St ... Innisfail AB T4G1A9 403-227-3381 227-7801
James Paton Memorial Hospital 125 Trans Canada Hwy ... Gander NL A1V1P7 709-256-2500 256-7800
Joseph Brant Memorial Hospital 1230 N Shore Blvd ... Burlington ON L7R4C4 905-632-3730 336-6480
Web: www.jbmh.com
Kelowna General Hospital 2268 Pandosy St ... Kelowna BC V1Y1T2 250-862-4000 862-4020
Web: www.interiorhealth.ca
Kingston General Hospital 76 Stuart St ... Kingston ON K7L2V7 613-548-3232 548-6042
Web: www.kgh.on.ca
Kootenay Boundary Regional Hospital 1200 Hospital Bench ... Trail BC V1R4M1 250-368-3311 364-3422
TF: 866-368-3314 ■ *Web:* www.interiorhealth.ca
Lacombe Hospital & Care Centre 5430 47th Ave ... Lacombe AB T4L1G8 403-782-3336 782-2818
Web: www.dthr.ab.ca
Lake of the Woods District Hospital 21 Sylvan St W ... Kenora ON P9N3W7 807-468-9861 468-3939
Web: www.lwdh.on.ca
Lakeridge Health Bowmanville 47 Liberty St S ... Bowmanville ON L1C2N4 905-623-3331 697-4685
Web: www.lakeridgehealth.on.ca
Lakeridge Health Oshawa 1 Hospital Ct ... Oshawa ON L1G2B9 905-576-8711 721-4736
Web: www.lakeridgehealth.on.ca
Lakeshore General Hospital 160 ch Stillview ... Pointe-Claire QC H9R2Y2 514-630-2225 630-2371
Web: www.lgh.qc.ca
Langley Memorial Hospital 22051 Fraser Hwy ... Langley BC V3A4H4 604-534-4121 534-8283
Web: www.fraserhealth.ca
Lethbridge Regional Hospital 960 19th St S ... Lethbridge AB T1J1W5 403-388-6111 382-6011
Web: www.chr.ab.ca
Lions Gate Hospital 231 E 15th St ... North Vancouver BC V7L2L7 604-988-3131 984-5838
TF: 800-984-1131 ■ *Web:* www.nscg.ca
London Health Sciences Centre 800 Commissioners Rd E ... London ON N6C6B5 519-685-8500 685-8127
Web: www.lhsc.on.ca
London Health Sciences Centre Victoria Campus
800 Commissioners Rd E ... London ON N6C6B5 519-685-8500 685-8127
Web: www.lhsc.on.ca
Markham Stouffville Hospital 381 Church St PO Box 1800 ... Markham ON L3P7P3 905-472-7000 472-7086
Web: www.msh.on.ca
Medicine Hat Regional Hospital 666 5th St SW ... Medicine Hat AB T1A4H6 403-529-8000 529-8998
Misericordia Community Hospital & Health Centre
16940 87th Ave ... Edmonton AB T5R4H5 780-735-2000 735-2774
Web: www.caritas.ab.ca
Mission Memorial Hospital 7324 Hurd St ... Mission BC V2V3H5 604-826-6261 826-9513
Web: www.fraserhealth.ca
Moncton Hospital 135 MacBeath Ave ... Moncton NB E1C6Z8 506-857-5111 857-5545
Web: www.serha.ca
Montfort Hospital 713 Montreal Rd ... Ottawa ON K1K0T2 613-746-4621 748-4914
Web: www.hopitalmontfort.com
Montreal Chest Institute 5655 Sainte-Zotique St E ... Montreal QC H1T1P7 514-252-6000 252-6453
Montreal Heart Institute 5000 Belanger St E ... Montreal QC H1T1C8 514-376-3330 593-2540
Web: www.icm-mhi.org
Moose Jaw Union Hospital 455 Fairford St E ... Moose Jaw SK S6H1H3 306-694-0200 694-0270
Mount Saint Joseph Hospital 3080 Prince Edward St ... Vancouver BC V5T3N4 604-874-1141
Mount Sinai Hospital 600 University Ave ... Toronto ON M5G1X5 416-596-4200 586-8544*
**Fax:* PR ■ *Web:* www.mtsinai.on.ca
Nanaimo Regional General Hospital 1200 Dufferin Crescent ... Nanaimo BC V9S2B7 250-754-2141 755-7633
Norfolk General Hospital 365 West St ... Simcoe ON N3Y1T7 519-426-0750 429-6998
Web: www.ngh.on.ca
North Bay General Hospital 750 Scollard St PO Box 2500 ... North Bay ON P1B5A4 705-474-8600 495-7981
Web: www.nbgh.on.ca
North York General Hospital 4001 Leslie St ... North York ON M2K1E1 416-756-6000 756-6738*
**Fax:* Hum Res ■ *Web:* www.nygh.on.ca
North York General Hospital 555 Finch Ave W ... North York ON M2R1N5 416-633-9420 635-2611
Web: www.nygh.on.ca
Northern Lights Regional Health Centre 7 Hospital St ... Fort McMurray AB T9H1P2 780-791-6161 791-6029
Web: www.nlrha.ab.ca
Oakville-Trafalgar Memorial Hospital 327 Reynolds St ... Oakville ON L6J3L7 905-845-2571 338-4636
Web: www.haltonhealthcare.com
Orillia Soldiers' Memorial Hospital 170 Colborne St W ... Orillia ON L3V2Z3 705-325-2201 325-7953*
**Fax:* Admissions ■ *Web:* www.osmh.on.ca
Pas Health Complex Inc 67 1st St W PO Box 240 ... The Pas MB R9A1K4 204-623-6431 623-9239
Paton James Memorial Hospital 125 Trans Canada Hwy ... Gander NL A1V1P7 709-256-2500 256-7800
Peace Arch Hospital 15521 Russell Ave ... White Rock BC V4B2R4 604-531-5512 541-5849
Web: www.fraserhealth.ca
Peace River Community Health Centre 10101 68th St ... Peace River AB T8S1T6 780-624-7500 618-3472
TF: 800-732-8981 ■ *Web:* www.pchr.ca
Pembroke Regional Hospital 705 MacKay St ... Pembroke ON K8A1G8 613-732-2811 732-9986
Web: www.pemgenhos.org
Penticton Regional Hospital 550 Carmi Ave ... Penticton BC V2A3G6 250-492-4000 492-9068
Web: www.interiorhealth.ca
Perth-Smiths Falls District Hospital 60 Cornelia St W ... Smiths Falls ON K7A2H9 613-283-2330 283-9342
Web: www.psfdh.on.ca
Peter Lougheed Centre 3500 26th Ave NE ... Calgary AB T1Y6J4 403-291-8555 943-4878
Web: www.calgaryhealthregion.ca
Peterborough Regional Health Ctr 1 Hospital Dr ... Peterborough ON K9J7C6 705-743-2121 876-5107
Web: www.prhc.on.ca

Phone Fax

Powell River General Hospital 5000 Joyce Ave ... Powell River BC V8A5R3 604-485-3211 485-3245
Web: www.vch.ca
Prince County Hospital 65 Roy Boapes Ave ... Summerside PE C1N6M8 902-438-4200 438-4511
Web: www.pchcare.com/inside.cfm
Prince George Regional Hospital 1475 Edmonton St ... Prince George BC V2M1S2 250-565-2000 565-2343
Queen Elizabeth Hospital 60 Riverside Dr PO Box 6600 ... Charlottetown PE C1A8T5 902-894-2111 894-2146
Queensway-Carleton Hospital 3045 Baseline Rd ... Ottawa ON K2H8P4 613-721-4700 721-2000
Web: www.qch.on.ca
Red Deer Regional Hospital Centre
3942 50th A Ave PO Bag 5030 ... Red Deer AB T4N4E7 403-343-4422 343-4866
Web: www.dthr.ab.ca
Reseau Sante Kamouraska 1201 6th Ave ... Lapocatiere QC G0R1Z0 418-856-7000 856-4737
Reseau Sante Richelieu-Yamaska
2750 boul Laframboise ... Saint-Hyacinthe QC J2S4Y8 450-771-3333 771-3289
Richmond Health Services 7000 Westminster Hwy ... Richmond BC V6X1A2 604-278-9711 244-5191
Web: www.richmondhealth.ca
Ridge Meadows Hospital & Health Care Centre
11666 Laity St PO Box 5000 ... Maple Ridge BC V2X5A3 604-463-4111 463-1888
Web: www.fraserhealth.ca
Rimbey Hospital & Care Centre 5228 50th Ave PO Box 440 ... Rimbey AB T0C2J0 403-843-2271 843-2506
Riverside Campus of Ottawa Hospital 1967 Riverside Dr ... Ottawa ON K1H7W9 613-738-7100 738-8522
Rockyview General Hospital 7007 14th St SW ... Calgary AB T2V1P9 403-541-3000 212-1242
Ross Memorial Hospital 10 Angeline St N ... Lindsay ON K9V4M8 705-324-6111 328-2817*
**Fax:* Mail Rm ■ *Web:* www.rmh.org
Royal Alexandra Hospital 10240 Kingsway Ave ... Edmonton AB T5H3V9 780-735-4111 735-5070
Web: www.capitalhealth.ca
Royal Columbian Hospital 330 E Columbia St ... New Westminster BC V3L3W7 604-520-4253 520-4827
Web: www.fraserhealth.ca
Royal Inland Hospital 311 Columbia St ... Kamloops BC V2C2T1 250-374-5111 314-2333
Royal University Hospital 103 Hospital Dr ... Saskatoon SK S7N0W8 306-655-1000 655-1586*
**Fax:* Admitting
Royal Victoria Hospital 201 Georgian Dr ... Barrie ON L4M6M2 705-728-9802 728-0892
Web: www.rvh.on.ca
Royal Victoria Hospital 687 Pine Ave W ... Montreal QC H3A1A1 514-934-1934 843-1661
Web: www.muhc.ca/pfv/rvh
Saint Boniface General Hospital 409 Tache Ave ... Winnipeg MB R2H2A6 204-233-8563 235-3695*
**Fax:* Hum Res ■ *Web:* www.sbgh.mb.ca
Saint Catharines General Hospital 142 Queenston St ... Saint Catharines ON L2R7C6 905-684-7271 688-8288*
**Fax:* Admitting ■ *Web:* www.niagarahealth.on.ca
Saint John Regional Hospital
400 University Ave PO Box 2100 ... Saint John NB E2L4L2 506-648-6000 648-6957
Web: www.ahsc.health.nb.ca/AboutUs/OurFacilities/facregional.shtml
Saint Joseph's General Hospital 2137 Comox Ave ... Comox BC V9M1P2 250-339-2242 339-1432
Web: www.stjosephs-comox.org
Saint Joseph's Health Centre
Guelph 100 Westmount Rd ... Guelph ON N1H5H8 519-824-6000 767-4156
Web: www.sjhh.guelph.on.ca
London 268 Grosvenor St ... London ON N6A4V2 519-646-6000 646-6603
Web: www.sjhc.london.on.ca
Toronto 30 The Queensway ... Toronto ON M6R1B5 416-530-6000 530-6603
Web: www.stjoe.on.ca
Saint Joseph's Healthcare Hamilton 50 Charlton Ave E ... Hamilton ON L8N4A6 905-522-4941 521-6140
Web: www.stjosham.on.ca
Saint Joseph's Lifecare Centre 99 Wayne Gretzky Pkwy ... Brantford ON N3S6T6 519-753-8641 753-7996
Web: www.sjlc.ca
Saint Mary's General Hospital 911 Queen's Blvd ... Kitchener ON N2M1B2 519-744-3311 749-6426
Web: www.smgh.ca
Saint Mary's Hospital Center 3830 Lacombe Ave ... Montreal QC H3T1M5 514-345-3511 734-2636
Web: www.smhc.qc.ca
Saint Michael's Hospital 30 Bond St ... Toronto ON M5B1W8 416-360-4000 864-5870
TF: 800-304-6394 ■ *Web:* www.stmichaelshospital.com
Saint Paul's Hospital 1702 20th St W ... Saskatoon SK S7M0Z9 306-655-5000 655-5555
Saint Thomas-Elgin General Hospital 189 Elm St ... Saint Thomas ON N5R5C4 519-631-2020 631-1825
Web: www.stegh.on.ca
Saskatoon City Hospital 701 Queen St ... Saskatoon SK S7K0M7 306-655-8000 655-8269
Web: www.saskatoonhealthregion.ca
Sault Area Hospitals 969 Queen St E ... Sault Sainte Marie ON P6A2C4 705-759-3434 759-3640
Web: www.sah.on.ca
Scarborough Hospital General Division
3050 Lawrence Ave E ... Scarborough ON M1P2V5 416-438-2911 431-8204
Web: www.tsh.to
Scarborough Hospital Grace Campus 3030 Birchmount Rd ... Scarborough ON M1W3W3 416-495-2400 495-2562
Web: www.tsh.to
Seven Oaks General Hospital 2300 McPhillips St ... Winnipeg MB R2V3M3 204-632-7133 697-2106
Web: www.sogh.mb.ca
Sir Mortimer B Davis Jewish General Hospital
3755 cote Sainte-Catherine ... Montreal QC H3T1E2 514-340-8222 340-7530
Web: www.jgh.ca
South Bruce Grey Health Centre 43 Queen St ... Kincardine ON 1G62Z2 519-396-3331 396-3699
Web: www.sbghc.on.ca
South Okanagan General Hospital RR 3 7139 362nd Ave ... Oliver BC V0H1T0 250-498-5000 498-5004
South Shore Regional Hospital 90 Glen Allan Dr ... Bridgewater NS B4V3S6 902-543-4603 527-5269
Southlake Regional Health Centre 596 Davis Dr ... Newmarket ON L3Y2P9 905-895-4521 853-2220
Web: www.southlakeregional.org
Stanton Regional Hospital 550 Byrne Rd PO Box 10 ... Yellowknife NT X1A2N1 867-669-4111 669-4102
Web: www.srhb.org
Stratford General Hospital 46 General Hospital Dr ... Stratford ON N5A2Y6 519-272-8210 272-8221
Web: www.hpha.ca
Sunnybrook & Women's College Health Sciences Centre
Sunnybrook Campus 2075 Bayview Ave ... Toronto ON M4N3M5 416-480-6100 480-6836
Web: www.sunnybrookandwomens.on.ca
Women's College Campus 76 Grenville St ... Toronto ON M5S1B2 416-323-6400 323-7331
Web: www.sunnybrookandwomens.on.ca
Surrey Memorial Hospital 13750 96th Ave ... Surrey BC V3V1Z2 604-581-2211 588-3320
Web: www.fraserhealth.ca
Thunder Bay Regional Health Sciences Centre
980 Olvier Rd ... Thunder Bay ON P7B6V4 807-343-7123 684-5890
Web: www.tbrh.net
Timmins & District Hospital 700 Ross Ave E ... Timmins ON P4N8P2 705-267-2131 267-6311
Web: www.tadh.com
Toronto General Hospital 200 Elizabeth St ... Toronto ON M5G2C4 416-340-3111 340-5191
Web: www.uhn.ca
Toronto Western Hospital 399 Bathurst St ... Toronto ON M5T2S8 416-603-2581 603-5434
Web: www.uhn.ca
Trillium Health Centre 100 Queensway W ... Mississauga ON L5B1B8 905-848-7100 848-7189
Web: www.trilliumhealthcentre.org
Trillium Health Centre Queensway Site 150 Sherway Dr ... Toronto ON M9C1A5 416-259-6671 849-5598*
**Fax Area Code:* 905 ■ *Web:* www.trilliumhealthcentre.org
University of Alberta Hospital 8440 112th St ... Edmonton AB T6G2B7 780-407-8822 407-7418
Web: www.capitalhealth.ca
Valley Regional Hospital 150 Exhibition St ... Kentville NS B4N5E3 902-678-7381 679-1904
Web: www.avdha.nshealth.ca
Vancouver General Hospital 899 W 12th Ave ... Vancouver BC V5Z1M9 604-875-4111 875-5701
Web: www.vanhosp.bc.ca
Vernon Jubilee Hospital 2101 32nd St ... Vernon BC V1T5L2 250-545-2211 545-5602
Web: www.interiorhealth.ca

General Hospitals - Canada (Cont'd)

Hospital	City	Prov	Postal Code	Phone	Fax
Victoria General Hospital 2340 Pembina Hwy *Web:* www.vgh.mb.ca	Winnipeg	MB	R3T2E8	204-269-3570	261-0223
Welland County General Hospital 65 3rd St *Web:* www.niagarahealth.on.ca/index2.html	Welland	ON	L3B4W6	905-732-6111	732-2628
West Coast General Hospital 3949 Port Alberni Hwy *Web:* www.viha.ca/facilities/central_island.htm	Port Alberni	BC	V9Y4S1	250-723-2135	724-8805
West Parry Sound Health Centre 6 Albert St *Web:* www.wpshc.com	Parry Sound	ON	P2A1T3	705-746-9321	746-4364
Western Memorial Regional Hospital 1 Brookfield Ave	Corner Brook	NL	A2H6J7	709-637-5000	637-5410
William Osler Health Centre					
Brampton Memorial Hospital Campus 20 Lynch St *Web:* www.williamoslerhc.on.ca	Brampton	ON	L6W2Z8	905-451-1710	451-8439
Etobicoke Hospital Campus 101 Humber College Blvd *Web:* www.williamoslerhc.on.ca	Etobicoke	ON	M9V1R8	416-747-3400	747-8608
Windsor Regional Hospital Metropolitan Campus 1995 Lens Ave *Web:* www.wrh.on.ca	Windsor	ON	N8W1L9	519-254-1661	254-3458
Windsor Regional Hospital Western Campus 1453 Prince Rd *Fax: Acctg ■ *Web:* www.wrh.on.ca	Windsor	ON	N9C3Z4	519-257-5100	254-3150*
Woodstock General Hospital 270 Riddell St *Fax: Admitting ■ *Web:* www.wgh.on.ca	Woodstock	ON	N4S6N6	519-421-4211	421-4238*
Yarmouth Regional Hospital 60 Vancouver St *Fax: Admitting ■ *Web:* www.swndha.nshealth.ca	Yarmouth	NS	B5A2P5	902-742-3541	749-1796*
York Central Hospital 10 Trench St *Web:* www.yorkcentral.com	Richmond Hill	ON	L4C4Z3	905-883-1212	883-2293
Yorkton Regional Health Centre 270 Bradbrooke Dr *Fax: Admitting ■ *Web:* www.shr.sk.ca	Yorkton	SK	S3N2K6	306-782-2401	786-0413*

377-3 General Hospitals - US

Alabama

Hospital	City	State	Zip	Phone	Fax
Andalusia Regional Hospital 849 S Three Notch St *Web:* www.andalusiaregional.com	Andalusia	AL	36420	334-222-8466	427-0349
Athens-Limestone Hospital 700 W Market St *Web:* www.alhosp.com	Athens	AL	35611	256-233-9292	233-9562
Baptist Medical Center-Princeton 701 Princeton Ave SW *Web:* www.bhsala.com/princeton/index.asp	Birmingham	AL	35211	205-783-3000	783-3758
Baptist Medical Center South 2105 E South Blvd *Fax: Admitting ■ *Web:* www.baptistfirst.org	Montgomery	AL	36116	334-288-2100	286-3511*
Baptist Shelby Medical Center 1000 1st St N *Web:* www.baptistmedical.org/shelby	Alabaster	AL	35007	205-620-8100	620-7003
Brookwood Medical Center 2010 Brookwood Medical Center Dr *Web:* www.bwmc.com	Birmingham	AL	35209	205-877-1000	877-1919
Bryan W Whitfield Memorial Hospital 105 US Hwy 80 E	Demopolis	AL	36732	334-289-4000	287-2594
Carraway Methodist Medical Center 1600 Carraway Blvd *Fax: Admitting ■ *Web:* www.carraway.org	Birmingham	AL	35234	205-502-6000	502-5268*
Citizens Baptist Medical Center 604 Stone Ave *Web:* www.bhsala.com/citizens/index.asp	Talladega	AL	35160	256-362-8111	761-4543
Cooper Green Hospital 1515 6th Ave S *Web:* www.coopergreenmercyhospital.org	Birmingham	AL	35233	205-930-3200	930-3497
Coosa Valley Medical Center 315 W Hickory St *Web:* www.cvhealth.net	Sylacauga	AL	35150	256-249-5000	249-5622
Crestwood Medical Center 1 Hospital Dr *Web:* crestwoodmedcenter.com	Huntsville	AL	35801	256-882-3100	880-4733
Cullman Regional Medical Center 1912 Alabama Hwy 157 *Web:* www.crmchospital.com	Cullman	AL	35058	256-737-2000	737-2596
DCH Regional Medical Center 809 University Blvd E *Web:* www.dchsystem.com/body.cfm?id=36926	Tuscaloosa	AL	35401	205-759-7111	759-6168
Decatur General Hospital 1201 7th St SE *Web:* www.decaturgeneral.org	Decatur	AL	35601	256-341-2000	341-2557
DeKalb Regional Medical Center 200 Medical Center Dr *Web:* www.dekalbregional.com	Fort Payne	AL	35968	256-845-3150	997-2512
East Alabama Medical Center 2000 Pepperell Pkwy *Web:* www.eamc.org	Opelika	AL	36801	334-749-3411	528-1509
Eliza Coffee Memorial Hospital 205 Marengo St *Web:* www.chgroup.org/main.html	Florence	AL	35630	256-768-9191	768-9420
Flowers Hospital 4370 W Main St *TF:* 800-824-6828 ■ *Web:* www.flowershospital.com	Dothan	AL	36305	334-793-5000	793-4613
Gadsden Regional Medical Center 1007 Goodyear Ave *Web:* www.gadsdenregional.com	Gadsden	AL	35903	256-494-4000	494-4474
Helen Keller Hospital 1300 S Montgomery Ave *Web:* www.helenkeller.com	Sheffield	AL	35660	256-386-4196	386-4559
Highlands Medical Center 380 Woods Cove Rd *Web:* www.highlandsmedcenter.com	Scottsboro	AL	35768	256-259-4444	218-3536
Huntsville Hospital 101 Sivley Rd SW *Web:* www.huntsvillehospital.org	Huntsville	AL	35801	256-265-1000	265-2585
Jackson Hospital 1725 Pine St *Fax: Admitting ■ *Web:* www.jackson.org	Montgomery	AL	36106	334-293-8000	293-8108*
Keller Helen Hospital 1300 S Montgomery Ave *Web:* www.helenkeller.com	Sheffield	AL	35660	256-386-4196	386-4559
Lanier Hospital & Health Services 4800 48th St *Web:* www.lanierhospital.com	Valley	AL	36854	334-756-1400	756-6698
Marshall Medical Center South 2505 US Hwy 431 N *Web:* www.mmcenters.com/mmcsouth.php	Boaz	AL	35957	256-593-8310	840-3647
Medical Center Enterprise 400 N Edwards St *TF:* 800-993-6837 ■ *Web:* www.mcehospital.com	Enterprise	AL	36330	334-347-0584	347-2080
Mobile Infirmary Medical Center 5 Mobile Infirmary Dr N *Fax: Admitting ■ *Web:* www.mimc.com	Mobile	AL	36607	251-435-2400	435-2543*
Northeast Alabama Regional Medical Center 400 E 10th St *Web:* www.rmccares.org	Anniston	AL	36207	256-235-5121	235-5608
Northport Medical Center 2700 Hospital Dr *Web:* www.dchsystem.com	Northport	AL	35476	205-333-4500	333-4522
Providence Hospital 6801 Airport Blvd *Fax: Admitting ■ *Web:* www.providencehospital.org	Mobile	AL	36608	251-633-1000	633-1679*
Riverview Regional Medical Center 600 S 3rd St *Web:* www.riverviewregional.com	Gadsden	AL	35901	256-543-5200	543-5888
Saint Vincent's East 50 Medical Park East Dr *Web:* www.stvhs.com/east/	Birmingham	AL	35235	205-838-3000	838-3065
Saint Vincent's Hospital 810 St Vincent's Dr *Fax: Admitting ■ *Web:* www.stv.org	Birmingham	AL	35205	205-939-7000	930-2259*
Southeast Alabama Medical Center 1108 Ross Clark Cir *TF:* 800-248-7047 ■ *Web:* www.samc.org	Dothan	AL	36301	334-793-8111	793-8751
Springhill Medical Center 3719 Dauphin St *Fax: Admissions ■ *Web:* www.springhillmedicalcenter.com	Mobile	AL	36608	251-344-9630	461-2439*
Thomas Hospital 750 Morphy Ave *TF:* 800-883-4309 ■ *Web:* www.thomashospital.com	Fairhope	AL	36532	251-928-2375	990-1497
Trinity Medical Center 800 Montclair Rd *Web:* www.trinitymedicalonline.com	Birmingham	AL	35213	205-592-1000	592-5927
UAB Hospital 619 S 19th St *Web:* www.health.uab.edu	Birmingham	AL	35294	205-934-9999	934-7779
UAB Medical West 995 9th Ave SW *TF:* 877-481-7001	Bessemer	AL	35022	205-481-7000	481-7595
University of South Alabama Children & Women's Hospital 1700 Center St *Fax: Admitting ■ *Web:* www.southalabama.edu/usacwh	Mobile	AL	36604	251-415-1000	415-1002*
University of South Alabama Medical Center 2451 Fillingim St *Fax: Admitting ■ *Web:* www.southalabama.edu/usamc	Mobile	AL	36617	251-471-7000	471-7275*
Vaughan Regional Medical Center 1015 Medical Center Pkwy *TF:* 800-498-8461 ■ *Web:* www.vaughanregional.com	Selma	AL	36701	334-418-4100	418-3599
Walker Baptist Medical Center 3400 Hwy 78 E *Web:* www.bhsala.com/walker/index.asp	Jasper	AL	35501	205-387-4000	387-4011

Alaska

Hospital	City	State	Zip	Phone	Fax
Alaska Native Medical Center (ANMC) 4315 Diplomacy Dr *TF Admitting:* 800-478-6661 ■ *Web:* www.anmc.org	Anchorage	AK	99508	907-563-2662	729-1984
Alaska Regional Hospital 2801 Debarr Rd *Web:* www.alaskaregional.com	Anchorage	AK	99508	907-276-1131	264-1179
Fairbanks Memorial Hospital 1650 Cowles St	Fairbanks	AK	99701	907-452-8181	458-5324
Providence Alaska Medical Center 3200 Providence Dr *Fax: Admitting ■ *Web:* www.providence.org/alaska/pamc	Anchorage	AK	99508	907-562-2211	261-6007*

Arizona

Hospital	City	State	Zip	Phone	Fax
Banner Baywood Medical Center 6644 E Baywood Ave *Web:* www.bannerhealth.com	Mesa	AZ	85206	480-981-2000	981-4198
Banner Desert Medical Center 1400 S Dobson Rd *Web:* www.bannerhealth.com	Mesa	AZ	85202	480-512-3000	512-8711
Banner Good Samaritan Medical Center 1111 E McDowell Rd *Web:* www.bannerhealth.com	Phoenix	AZ	85006	602-239-2000	239-5160
Banner Mesa Medical Center 1010 N Country Club Dr *Web:* www.bannerhealth.com/patients+and+visitors/facilities/arizona/mesa	Mesa	AZ	85201	480-834-1211	461-2090
Banner Thunderbird Medical Center 5555 W Thunderbird Rd *Web:* www.bannerhealth.com	Glendale	AZ	85306	602-588-5555	865-5930
Boswell Memorial Hospital 10401 W Thunderbird Blvd *Web:* www.sunhealth.org/boswell	Sun City	AZ	85351	623-977-7211	876-5795
Carondelet Saint Joseph's Hospital 350 N Wilmot Rd *Web:* www.carondelet.org/information/csj.htm	Tucson	AZ	85711	520-296-3211	873-3921
Carondelet Saint Mary's Hospital 1601 W St Mary's Rd *Web:* www.carondelet.org/information/csm.htm	Tucson	AZ	85745	520-622-5833	872-6641
Casa Grande Regional Medical Center 1800 E Florence Blvd *Web:* www.casagrandehospital.com	Casa Grande	AZ	85222	520-381-6300	381-6435
Chandler Regional Hospital 475 S Dobson Rd *TF:* 800-350-4677 ■ *Web:* www.chandlerregional.org	Chandler	AZ	85224	480-728-3000	728-3875
Del E Webb Memorial Hospital 14502 W Meeker Blvd *Web:* www.sunhealth.org/delwebb	Sun City West	AZ	85375	623-214-4000	214-4105
Flagstaff Medical Center 1200 N Beaver St *Web:* www.flagstaffmedicalcenter.com/pp_fmc/fmc_pp_home.htm	Flagstaff	AZ	86001	928-779-3366	947-3299
Havasu Regional Medical Center 101 Civic Center Ln *Web:* www.havasuregional.com	Lake Havasu City	AZ	86403	928-855-8185	505-5744
John C Lincoln Hospital North Mountain 250 E Dunlap Ave *Web:* www.jcl.com/northmountain	Phoenix	AZ	85020	602-943-2381	944-9610
Kingman Regional Medical Center 3269 Stockton Hill Rd *TF:* 877-757-2101 ■ *Web:* www.azkrmc.com	Kingman	AZ	86409	928-757-2101	757-0604
Lincoln John C Hospital North Mountain 250 E Dunlap Ave *Web:* www.jcl.com/northmountain	Phoenix	AZ	85020	602-943-2381	944-9610
Maricopa Medical Center 2601 E Roosevelt St *Web:* www.mihs.org	Phoenix	AZ	85008	602-344-5011	344-0719
Maryvale Hospital Medical Center 5102 W Campbell Ave *Web:* www.maryvalehospital.com	Phoenix	AZ	85031	623-848-5000	848-5553
Mayo Clinic Hospital 5777 E Mayo Blvd *Web:* www.mayoclinic.org/mchospital-sct	Phoenix	AZ	85054	480-515-6296	342-2525
Mesa General Hospital 515 N Mesa Dr *Web:* www.mesageneralhospital.com	Mesa	AZ	85201	480-969-9111	461-4433
Northwest Medical Center 6200 N La Cholla Blvd *Web:* www.northwestmedicalcenter.com	Tucson	AZ	85741	520-742-9000	469-8610
Paradise Valley Hospital 3929 E Bell Rd *Web:* www.paradisevalleyhospital.com	Phoenix	AZ	85032	602-923-5000	923-5707
Phoenix Baptist Hospital 2000 W Bethany Home Rd *Web:* www.baptisthealth.com	Phoenix	AZ	85015	602-249-0212	246-5979
Phoenix Memorial Hospital 1201 S 7th Ave *Web:* www.abrazohealthcare.com	Phoenix	AZ	85007	602-258-5111	824-3383
Saint Joseph's Hospital & Medical Center 350 W Thomas Rd *Web:* www.stjosephs-phx.org	Phoenix	AZ	85013	602-406-3000	406-7143
Saint Luke's Medical Center 1800 E Van Buren St *Web:* www.iasishealthcare.com/hospitals/az_slmed.htm	Phoenix	AZ	85006	602-251-8100	251-8685
Scottsdale Healthcare Osborn 7400 E Osborn Rd *Web:* www.shc.org	Scottsdale	AZ	85251	480-675-4000	882-4989
Scottsdale Healthcare Shea 9003 E Shea Blvd *Web:* www.shc.org	Scottsdale	AZ	85260	480-323-3000	323-3510
Tempe Saint Luke's Hospital 1500 S Mill Ave *Web:* www.tempestlukeshospital.com	Tempe	AZ	85281	480-968-9411	784-5539
Tucson Medical Center 5301 E Grant Rd *TF:* 800-526-5353 ■ *Web:* www.tmcaz.com	Tucson	AZ	85712	520-327-5461	
University Medical Center 1501 N Campbell Ave *Web:* www.azumc.com	Tucson	AZ	85724	520-694-0111	694-4085
University Physicians Healthcare Hospital at Kino Campus 2800 E Ajo Way *Web:* www.uph.org	Tucson	AZ	85713	520-874-2000	874-4042
US Public Health Service Phoenix Indian Medical Center 4212 N 16th St	Phoenix	AZ	85016	602-263-1200	263-1618
Yavapai Regional Medical Center 1003 Willow Creek Rd *TF:* 877-843-9762 ■ *Web:* www.yrmc.org	Prescott	AZ	86301	928-445-2700	771-5509
Yuma Regional Medical Center 2400 S Ave A *Web:* www.yumaregional.org	Yuma	AZ	85364	928-344-2000	336-7337

Arkansas

Hospital	City	State	Zip	Phone	Fax
Arkansas Methodist Medical Center 900 W Kingshighway *Web:* www.amhparagould.com	Paragould	AR	72450	870-239-7000	239-7400
Baptist Health Medical Center 3333 Spring Hill Dr *Web:* www.baptist-health.com	North Little Rock	AR	72117	501-202-3000	202-3813
Baptist Health Medical Center-Little Rock 9601 I-630 Exit 7 *Fax: Admitting ■ *TF:* 888-227-8478 ■ *Web:* www.baptist-health.org	Little Rock	AR	72205	501-202-2000	202-1226*
Baxter Regional Medical Center 624 Hospital Dr *Web:* www.baxterregional.org	Mountain Home	AR	72653	870-424-1000	424-2444

				Phone	Fax
Conway Regional Hospital 2302 College Ave	Conway	AR	72032	501-329-3831	450-2283
Web: www.conwayregional.org					
Crittenden Memorial Hospital 200 Tyler St	West Memphis	AR	72301	870-735-1500	732-7710
Web: www.crittendenmemorial.org					
Great River Medical Center PO Box 108	Blytheville	AR	72316	870-838-7300	838-7493
TF: 800-557-5591 ■ *Web:* www.greatrivermc.com					
Helena Regional Medical Center 1801 ML King Dr	Helena	AR	72342	870-338-5800	816-3909
Web: www.helenaregionalmedicalcenter.com					
Jefferson Regional Medical Center 1600 W 40th Ave	Pine Bluff	AR	71603	870-541-7100	541-7938
Web: www.jrmc.org					
Medical Center of South Arkansas 700 W Grove St	El Dorado	AR	71730	870-863-2000	863-5442
Web: www.mcsaeldo.com					
National Park Medical Center 1910 Malvern Ave	Hot Springs National Park	AR	71901	501-321-1000	620-1450
Web: www.nationalparkmedical.com					
NEA Medical Center 3024 Stadium Blvd	Jonesboro	AR	72401	870-972-7000	972-7051
TF: 800-999-4486 ■ *Web:* www.neamedicalcenter.com					
North Arkansas Regional Medical Center 620 N Willow St	Harrison	AR	72601	870-365-2000	365-2034
Web: www.narmc.com					
Northwest Medical Center 609 W Maple Ave	Springdale	AR	72764	479-751-5711	757-2908
Web: www.northwesthealth.com					
Ouachita County Medical Center 638 California St	Camden	AR	71701	870-836-1000	836-1358
Web: www.ouachitamedcenter.com					
Rebsamen Regional Medical Center 1400 Braden St	Jacksonville	AR	72076	501-985-7000	985-7407
Web: www.rebsamenmedicalcenter.com					
Saint Bernard's Medical Center 225 E Jackson Ave	Jonesboro	AR	72401	870-972-4100	974-5112
Web: www.sbrmc.com					
Saint Edward Mercy Medical Center 7301 Rogers Ave	Fort Smith	AR	72903	479-314-6000	314-1770
Web: www.stedwardmercy.com					
Saint Joseph's Mercy Health Center 300 Werner St	Hot Springs	AR	71913	501-622-1000	622-1199*
**Fax:* Admitting ■ *Web:* www.saintjosephs.com					
Saint Mary-Rogers Memorial Hospital 1200 W Walnut St	Rogers	AR	72756	479-636-0200	936-2906
Web: www.mercyhealthnwa.smhs.com					
Saint Mary's Regional Medical Center 1808 W Main St	Russellville	AR	72801	479-968-2841	968-8189
Web: www.saintmarysregional.com					
Saint Vincent Doctors Hospital 6101 St Vincent Cir	Little Rock	AR	72205	501-552-6000	552-5510
Saint Vincent Infirmary Medical Center 2 St Vincent Cir	Little Rock	AR	72205	501-552-3000	552-4241
Web: www.stvincenthealth.com/svimc					
Saline Memorial Hospital 1 Medical Park Dr	Benton	AR	72015	501-776-6000	776-6019
Web: www.salinememorial.org					
Southwest Regional Medical Center 11401 I-30	Little Rock	AR	72209	501-455-7100	455-7399
Web: www.southwestregional.com					
Sparks Regional Medical Center 1001 Towson Ave	Fort Smith	AR	72901	479-441-4000	441-5420
Web: www.sparks.org					
UAMS Medical Center 4301 W Markham St	Little Rock	AR	72205	501-686-7000	526-4282*
**Fax:* Admitting ■ *Web:* www.uams.edu/medcenter					
Washington Regional Medical Center 3215 N Northhills Blvd	Fayetteville	AR	72703	479-463-1000	463-5977
Web: www.wregional.com					
White County Medical Center 3214 E Race Ave	Searcy	AR	72143	501-268-6121	380-1011
TF: 888-562-7520 ■ *Web:* www.wcmc.org					
White River Medical Center 1710 Harrison St	Batesville	AR	72501	870-262-1200	262-1458
Web: www.wrmc.com					

California

				Phone	Fax
Alameda County Medical Center - Fairmont Hospital 15400 Foothill Blvd	San Leandro	CA	94578	510-667-7920	667-7852
Web: www.acmedctr.org					
Alameda County Medical Center-Highland Campus 1411 E 31st St	Oakland	CA	94602	510-437-4800	535-7722
Web: www.acmedctr.org					
Alta Bates Summit Medical Center 2450 Ashby Ave	Berkeley	CA	94705	510-540-4444	204-1883
Web: www.altabates.com					
Alvarado Hospital Medical Center 6655 Alvarado Rd	San Diego	CA	92120	619-287-3270	229-7020
Web: www.alvaradohospital.com					
Anaheim Memorial Medical Center 1111 W La Palma Ave	Anaheim	CA	92801	714-774-1450	999-6027*
**Fax:* Admitting ■ *Web:* www.memorialcare.com/anaheim					
Antelope Valley Hospital 1600 W Ave J	Lancaster	CA	93534	661-949-5000	949-5510
Web: www.avhospital.org					
Arrowhead Regional Medical Center 400 N Pepper Ave	Colton	CA	92324	909-580-1000	580-6214
TF: 877-873-2762 ■ *Web:* www.arrowheadmedcenter.org					
Bakersfield Memorial Hospital 420 34th St	Bakersfield	CA	93301	661-327-1792	327-2426*
**Fax:* Admitting ■ *Web:* www.bakersfieldmemorial.org					
Baldwin Park Medical Center 1011 Baldwin Park Blvd	Baldwin Park	CA	91706	626-851-1011	851-5101
Web: www.kaiserpermanente.org					
Beverly Hospital 309 W Beverly Blvd	Montebello	CA	90640	323-726-1222	725-4338
Web: www.beverly.org					
Brotman Medical Center 3828 Delmas Terr	Culver City	CA	90231	310-836-7000	202-4141
Web: www.brotmanmedicalcenter.com					
California Hospital Medical Center 1401 S Grand Ave	Los Angeles	CA	90015	213-748-2411	765-4078
Web: www.chmcla.org					
California Pacific Medical Center 3700 California St	San Francisco	CA	94118	415-600-6000	750-5007*
**Fax:* Admitting ■ *Web:* www.cpmc.org					
California Pacific Medical Center Davies Campus Castro & Duboce Sts	San Francisco	CA	94114	415-600-6000	565-6223
Web: www.cpmc.org					
California Pacific Medical Center Pacific Campus 2333 Buchanan St	San Francisco	CA	94115	415-563-4321	600-3679
Web: www.cpmc.org					
Cedars-Sinai Medical Center 8700 Beverly Blvd	Los Angeles	CA	90048	310-423-3277	123-0105*
**Fax:* Admitting ■ *TF:* 800-233-2771 ■ *Web:* www.csmc.edu					
Centinela Freeman Regional Medical Center 555 E Hardy St	Inglewood	CA	90301	310-673-4660	677-0535
Web: www.centinelafreeman.com					
Centinela Freeman Regional Medical Center-Marina Campus 4650 Lincoln Blvd	Marina del Rey	CA	90292	310-823-8911	574-7854
Centinela Freeman Regional Medical Center Memorial Campus 333 N Prairie Ave	Inglewood	CA	90301	310-674-7050	419-8273
TF: 800-455-1933 ■ *Web:* www.centinelafreeman.com					
Citrus Valley Medical Center Inter-Community Campus 210 W San Bernardino Rd	Covina	CA	91722	626-331-7331	859-5865
Web: www.cvhp.com/facilities/fac_icc.htm					
Citrus Valley Medical Center-Queen of the Valley Campus 1115 S Sunset Ave	West Covina	CA	91790	626-962-4011	813-7887
Web: www.cvhp.org/facilities/fac_qvc.htm					
City of Hope National Medical Center 1500 E Duarte Rd	Duarte	CA	91010	626-256-4673	
TF: 866-434-4673 ■ *Web:* www.cityofhope.org					
Coastal Communities Hospital 2701 S Bristol St	Santa Ana	CA	92704	714-754-5454	754-5556
Web: www.coastalcommhospital.com					
Community Hospital of Long Beach 1720 Termino Ave	Long Beach	CA	90804	562-498-1000	498-4434
Web: www.chlb.org					
Community Hospital of Los Gatos 815 Pollard Rd	Los Gatos	CA	95032	408-378-6131	866-4003
Web: www.communityhospitallg.com					
Community Hospital of the Monterey Peninsula 23625 Holman Hwy	Monterey	CA	93940	831-624-5311	625-4948
Web: www.chomp.org					
Community Hospital of San Bernardino 1805 Medical Center Dr	San Bernardino	CA	92411	909-887-6333	806-1035
Web: www.chsb.org					
Community Memorial Hospital 147 N Brent St	Ventura	CA	93003	805-652-5011	667-2895
Web: www.cmhhospital.com					
Community Regional Medical Center 2823 Fresno St	Fresno	CA	93721	559-459-6000	497-1835
Web: www.communitymedical.org					
Contra Costa Regional Medical Center 2500 Alhambra Ave	Martinez	CA	94553	925-370-5000	370-5138
Web: www.cchealth.org/medical_center					
Dameron Hospital 525 W Acacia St	Stockton	CA	95203	209-944-5550	461-3108
Web: www.dameronhospital.org					
Desert Regional Medical Center 1150 N Indian Canyon Dr	Palm Springs	CA	92262	760-323-6511	864-9577
TF: 800-962-3765 ■ *Web:* www.desertmedctr.com					
Doctors Medical Center 1441 Florida Ave	Modesto	CA	95350	209-578-1211	576-3680
Web: www.dmc-modesto.com					
Doctors Medical Center 2000 Vale Rd	San Pablo	CA	94806	510-970-5000	970-5730
Web: www.doctorsmedicalcenter.org					
Dominican Hospital 1555 Soquel Dr	Santa Cruz	CA	95065	831-462-7700	462-7555
Web: www.dominicanhospital.org					
Downey Regional Medical Center 11500 Brookshire Ave	Downey	CA	90241	562-904-5000	904-5309
Web: www.drmci.org					
Eden Medical Center 20103 Lake Chabot Rd	Castro Valley	CA	94546	510-537-1234	889-6506
Web: www.edenmedicalcenter.org					
Eisenhower Medical Center 39000 Bob Hope Dr	Rancho Mirage	CA	92270	760-340-3911	773-4396
Web: www.emc.org					
El Camino Hospital 2500 Grant Rd	Mountain View	CA	94040	650-940-7000	988-7862
Web: www.elcaminohospital.org					
El Centro Regional Medical Center 1415 Ross Ave	El Centro	CA	92243	760-339-7100	339-7345
Web: www.ecrmc.org					
Emanuel Medical Center 825 Delbon Ave	Turlock	CA	95382	209-667-4200	
Web: www.emanuelmedicalcenter.org					
Enloe Medical Center 1531 Esplanade	Chico	CA	95926	530-332-7300	899-2067
TF: 800-822-8102 ■ *Web:* www.enloe.org					
Feather River Hospital 5974 Pentz Rd	Paradise	CA	95969	530-877-9361	876-2160
Web: www.frhosp.org					
Foothill Presbyterian Hospital 250 S Grand Ave	Glendora	CA	91741	626-963-8411	857-3274
Web: www.cvhp.org					
Fountain Valley Regional Hospital & Medical Center 17100 Euclid St	Fountain Valley	CA	92708	714-966-7200	966-8039
Web: www.fountainvalleyhospital.com					
Fremont Medical Center 970 Plumas St	Yuba City	CA	95991	530-751-4000	751-4224
Web: www.frhg.org					
Garden Grove Hospital & Medical Center 12601 Garden Grove Blvd	Garden Grove	CA	92843	714-537-5160	741-3322
Web: www.gardengrovehospital.com					
Garfield Medical Center 525 N Garfield Ave	Monterey Park	CA	91754	626-573-2222	571-8972
Web: www.garfieldmedicalcenter.com					
Glendale Adventist Medical Center 1509 Wilson Terr	Glendale	CA	91206	818-409-8000	546-5600
Web: www.glendaleadventist.com					
Glendale Memorial Hospital & Health Center 1420 S Central Ave	Glendale	CA	91204	818-502-1900	
Web: www.glendalememorial.com					
Good Samaritan Hospital 1225 Wilshire Blvd	Los Angeles	CA	90017	213-977-2121	202-7452
Web: www.goodsam.org					
Good Samaritan Hospital 2425 Samaritan Dr	San Jose	CA	95124	408-559-2011	559-2675*
**Fax:* Admitting ■ *Web:* www.goodsamsj.org					
Greater El Monte Community Hospital 1701 Santa Anita Ave	South El Monte	CA	91733	626-579-7777	350-0368
Web: www.greaterelmonte.com					
Grossmont Hospital 5555 Grossmont Center Dr	La Mesa	CA	91942	619-465-0711	644-4140
Web: www.grossmonthealthcare.com					
Harbor-UCLA Medical Center 1000 W Carson St	Torrance	CA	90509	310-222-2345	328-7153
Web: www.humc.edu					
Hemet Valley Medical Center 1117 E Devonshire Ave	Hemet	CA	92543	951-652-2811	765-4988
Web: www.valleyhealthsystem.com/hemmain.htm					
Henry Mayo Newhall Memorial Hospital 23845 W McBean Pkwy	Valencia	CA	91355	661-253-8000	253-8897
Web: www.henrymayo.com					
Hoag Memorial Hospital Presbyterian 1 Hoag Dr	Newport Beach	CA	92663	949-645-8600	760-5593
Web: www.hoag.org					
Hollywood Presbyterian Medical Center 1300 N Vermont Ave	Los Angeles	CA	90027	323-913-4800	660-0446
Web: www.hollywoodpresbyterian.com					
Huntington Memorial Hospital 100 W California Blvd	Pasadena	CA	91109	626-397-5000	397-2995
Web: www.huntingtonhospital.com					
Irvine Regional Hospital & Medical Center 16200 Sand Canyon Ave	Irvine	CA	92618	949-753-2000	753-2289
Web: www.irvineregionalhospital.com					
John F Kennedy Memorial Hospital 47-111 Monroe St	Indio	CA	92201	760-347-6191	775-8014
Web: www.jfkmemorialhosp.com					
John Muir Medical Center 1601 Ygnacio Valley Rd	Walnut Creek	CA	94598	925-939-3000	947-3265
Web: www.jmmdhs.com/index.php/jmmdhs_jmmc.html					
Kaiser Permanente Fontana Medical Center 9961 Sierra Ave	Fontana	CA	92335	909-427-5000	427-4265
Kaiser Permanente Foundation Hospital 9400 E Rosecrans Ave	Bellflower	CA	90706	562-461-3000	461-4341
Kaiser Permanente Harbor City Medical Center 25825 S Vermont Ave	Harbor City	CA	90710	310-325-5111	517-2234
TF: 800-464-4000					
Kaiser Permanente Hayward Medical Center 27400 Hesperian Blvd	Hayward	CA	94545	510-784-4000	784-4722
Kaiser Permanente Hospital 441 N Lakeview Ave	Anaheim	CA	92807	714-279-4000	279-5590
TF: 800-464-4000					
Kaiser Permanente Los Angeles Medical Center 4867 Sunset Blvd	Los Angeles	CA	90027	323-783-4011	783-7227
Kaiser Permanente Medical Center 4647 Zion Ave	San Diego	CA	92120	619-528-5000	528-5317
Kaiser Permanente Medical Center 900 Kiely Blvd	Santa Clara	CA	95051	408-236-6400	236-4408
Web: www.kaisersantaclara.org					
Kaiser Permanente Medical Center 1200 El Camino Real	South San Francisco	CA	94080	650-742-2000	742-3046
TF: 800-660-1231					
Kaiser Permanente Medical Center Redwood City 1150 Veterans Blvd	Redwood City	CA	94063	650-299-2000	299-2421
TF: 800-464-4000					
Kaiser Permanente Medical Center San Francisco 2425 Geary Blvd	San Francisco	CA	94115	415-833-2000	833-2571*
**Fax:* Admitting					
Kaiser Permanente Medical Center-Santa Teresa 250 Hospital Pkwy	San Jose	CA	95119	408-972-7000	972-7156
Kaiser Permanente Medical Center-South Sacramento 6600 Bruceville Rd	Sacramento	CA	95823	916-688-2000	688-2978
TF: 800-464-4000					
Kaiser Permanente Medical Center-West Los Angeles 6041 Cadillac Ave	Los Angeles	CA	90034	323-857-2000	857-2307
Kaiser Permanente Panorama City Medical Center 13652 Cantara St	Panorama City	CA	91402	818-375-2000	

General Hospitals - US (Cont'd)

California (Cont'd)

Name / Address	City	State	Zip	Phone	Fax
Kaiser Permanente Riverside Medical Center 10800 Magnolia Ave	Riverside	CA	92505	951-353-2000	353-3055
TF Cust Svc: 800-464-4000					
Kaiser Permanente Sacramento Medical Center 2025 Morse Ave	Sacramento	CA	95825	916-973-5000	973-5717*
**Fax:* Admitting					
Kaiser Permanente San Rafael Medical Center 99 Montecillo Rd	San Rafael	CA	94903	415-444-2000	444-2492
TF: 800-464-4000 ■ *Web:* www.kaisersanrafael.org					
Kaiser Permanente Vallejo Medical Center 975 Sereno Dr	Vallejo	CA	94589	707-651-1000	651-2026
Kaiser Permanente Walnut Creek Medical Center 1425 S Main St	Walnut Creek	CA	94596	925-295-4000	
TF: 800-464-4000					
Kaiser Santa Rosa Medical Center 401 Bicentennial Way	Santa Rosa	CA	95403	707-571-4000	571-4556
Web: www.kaisersantarosa.org					
Kaweah Delta Hospital 400 W Mineral King Ave	Visalia	CA	93291	559-624-2000	635-4021
TF: 800-529-3244 ■ *Web:* www.kaweahdelta.org					
Kern Medical Center 1830 Flower St	Bakersfield	CA	93305	661-326-2000	326-2934*
**Fax:* Admitting ■ *Web:* www.kernmedicalcenter.com					
La Palma Intercommunity Hospital 7901 Walker St	La Palma	CA	90623	714-670-7400	670-6287
Web: www.lapalmaintercommunityhospital.com					
LAC-University of Southern California Medical Center 1200 N State St	Los Angeles	CA	90033	323-226-2622	226-6452
Lakewood Regional Medical Center 3700 E South St	Lakewood	CA	90712	562-531-2550	
Web: www.lakewoodregional.com					
Lancaster Community Hospital 43830 N 10th St West	Lancaster	CA	93534	661-948-4781	949-9783
Web: www.lancastercommunityhospital.net					
Little Company of Mary Hospital 4101 Torrance Blvd	Torrance	CA	90503	310-540-7676	540-8408
TF: 800-776-5264 ■ *Web:* www.lcmweb.org					
Little Company of Mary San Pedro Hospital 1300 W 7th St	San Pedro	CA	90732	310-832-3311	514-5314
Web: www.lcmhs.org/sp_facilities/index.html					
Lodi Memorial Hospital 975 S Fairmont Ave	Lodi	CA	95240	209-334-3411	339-7654
TF: 800-876-6750 ■ *Web:* www.lodihealth.org					
Loma Linda University Medical Center 11234 Anderson St	Loma Linda	CA	92354	909-558-4000	558-0308
TF: 877-558-6248 ■ *Web:* www.llu.edu/llumc					
Long Beach Memorial Medical Center 2801 Atlantic Ave	Long Beach	CA	90806	562-933-2000	933-1336
Web: www.memorialcare.com/long_beach					
Los Alamitos Medical Center 3751 Katella Ave	Los Alamitos	CA	90720	562-598-1311	493-2812
Web: www.losalamitosmedctr.com					
Los Angeles Community Hospital 4081 E Olympic Blvd	Los Angeles	CA	90023	323-267-0477	261-0809
Los Robles Regional Medical Center 215 W Janss Rd	Thousand Oaks	CA	91360	805-497-2727	370-4498
Web: www.losrobleshospital.com					
Madera Community Hospital 1250 E Almond Ave	Madera	CA	93637	559-673-5101	675-5509
Web: www.maderahospital.org					
Marian Medical Center 1400 E Church St	Santa Maria	CA	93454	805-739-3000	739-3060
Web: www.marianmedicalcenter.org					
Marin General Hospital 250 Bon Air Rd	Greenbrae	CA	94904	415-925-7000	925-7933
Web: www.maringeneral.com					
Memorial Medical Center 1700 Coffee Rd	Modesto	CA	95355	209-526-4500	521-6986*
**Fax:* Admitting ■ *Web:* www.memorialmedicalcenter.org					
Mercy General Hospital 4001 J St	Sacramento	CA	95819	916-453-4545	453-4295
Web: www.mercygeneral.org					
Mercy Hospital 2215 Truxtun Ave	Bakersfield	CA	93301	661-632-5000	327-2592
Web: www.mercybakersfield.org					
Mercy Medical Center Merced Community Campus 301 E 13th St	Merced	CA	95340	209-385-7000	385-7062
Web: www.mercymercedcares.org					
Mercy Medical Center Redding 2175 Rosaline Ave	Redding	CA	96001	530-225-6000	225-6125
TF: 800-521-6377 ■ *Web:* www.mercy.org					
Mercy San Juan Medical Center 6501 Coyle Ave	Carmichael	CA	95608	916-537-5000	537-5111
Web: www.mercysanjuan.org					
Methodist Hospital 7500 Hospital Dr	Sacramento	CA	95823	916-423-3000	423-6045
Web: www.methodistsacramento.org					
Methodist Hospital of Southern California 300 W Huntington Dr	Arcadia	CA	91007	626-445-4441	574-3767
Web: www.methodisthospital.org					
Mount Diablo Medical Center 2540 East St	Concord	CA	94520	925-682-8200	674-2009
Web: www.jmmdhs.com/index.php/jmmdhs_mdmc.html					
Natividad Medical Center 1441 Constitution Blvd	Salinas	CA	93906	831-755-4111	755-6254
Web: www.natividad.com					
Newhall Henry Mayo Memorial Hospital 23845 W McBean Pkwy	Valencia	CA	91355	661-253-8000	253-8897
Web: www.henrymayo.com					
Northbay Medical Center 1200 B Gale Wilson Blvd	Fairfield	CA	94533	707-429-3600	426-5287
TF: 888-294-3600 ■ *Web:* www.northbay.org					
Northridge Hospital Medical Center-Roscoe Blvd Campus 18300 Roscoe Blvd	Northridge	CA	91328	818-885-8500	885-5321
Web: www.northridgehospital.org					
O'Connor Hospital 2105 Forest Ave	San Jose	CA	95128	408-947-2500	947-2819
Web: www.oconnorhospital.org					
Olive View Medical Center 14445 Olive View Dr	Sylmar	CA	91342	818-364-1555	364-3011
Web: www.ladhs.org/hospitals/index.htm					
Olympia Medical Center 5900 W Olympic Blvd	Los Angeles	CA	90036	310-657-5900	932-5163*
**Fax Area Code:* 323 ■ *TF:* 800-827-8599 ■ *Web:* www.olympiamedicalcenter.com					
Orange Coast Memorial Medical Center 9920 Talbert Ave	Fountain Valley	CA	92708	714-962-4677	378-7079
Web: www.memorialcare.com/orange_coast					
Oroville Hospital 2767 Olive Hwy	Oroville	CA	95966	530-533-8500	532-8433
Web: www.orovillehospital.com					
Pacific Hospital of Long Beach 2776 Pacific Ave	Long Beach	CA	90806	562-595-1911	492-1363
Web: www.phlb.org					
Palomar Medical Center 555 E Valley Pkwy	Escondido	CA	92025	760-739-3000	739-3107
Web: www.pphs.org					
Parkview Community Hospital Medical Center 3865 Jackson St	Riverside	CA	92503	951-688-2211	352-5484
Web: www.pchmc.org					
Peninsula Hospital 1501 Trousdale Dr	Burlingame	CA	94010	650-696-5400	696-5279
Web: www.mills-peninsula.org					
Pioneers Memorial Health Care District 207 W Legion Rd	Brawley	CA	92227	760-351-3333	344-4401
Web: www.pmhd.org					
Pomerado Hospital 15615 Pomerado Rd	Poway	CA	92064	858-613-4000	613-5678
Web: www.pphs.org					
Pomona Valley Hospital Medical Center 1798 N Garey Ave	Pomona	CA	91767	909-865-9500	865-9796
Web: www.pvhmc.org					
Presbyterian Intercommunity Hospital 12401 Washington Blvd	Whittier	CA	90602	562-698-0811	698-1728
Web: www.whittierpres.com					
Providence Holy Cross Medical Center 15031 Rinaldi St	Mission Hills	CA	91345	818-365-8051	898-4688
Web: www.providence.org/LosAngeles/Facilities/Providence_Holy_Cross					
Providence Saint Joseph Medical Center 501 S Buena Vista St	Burbank	CA	91505	818-843-5111	
Web: www.providence.org/losangeles/facilities/providence_saint_joseph					
Queen of the Valley Medical Center 1000 Trancas St	Napa	CA	94558	707-252-4411	257-4032
Web: www.thequeen.org					
Regional Medical Center of San Jose 225 N Jackson Ave	San Jose	CA	95116	408-259-5000	729-2884
Web: www.regionalmedicalsanjose.com					
Rideout Memorial Hospital 726 4th St	Marysville	CA	95901	530-749-4300	751-4226
Riverside Community Hospital 4445 Magnolia Ave	Riverside	CA	92501	951-788-3000	788-3346
Web: www.rchc.org					
Riverside County Regional Medical Center 26520 Cactus Ave	Moreno Valley	CA	92555	951-486-4000	486-4260
Web: www.rcrmc.org					
Roseville Medical Center 1 Medical Plaza	Roseville	CA	95661	916-781-1000	781-1210
Web: www.sutterroseville.org					
Saddleback Memorial Medical Center 24451 Health Center Dr	Laguna Hills	CA	92653	949-837-4500	452-3467
Web: www.memorialcare.com/saddleback					
Saint Agnes Medical Center 1303 E Herndon Ave	Fresno	CA	93720	559-450-3000	450-3990
Web: www.samc.com					
Saint Bernardine Medical Center 2101 N Waterman Ave	San Bernardino	CA	92404	909-883-8711	881-4546
Web: www.stbernardinemedicalcenter.com					
Saint Francis Medical Center 3630 E Imperial Hwy	Lynwood	CA	90262	310-900-8900	900-4505*
**Fax:* Admitting ■ *Web:* www.stfrancismedicalcenter.org					
Saint Francis Memorial Hospital 900 Hyde St	San Francisco	CA	94109	415-353-6000	353-6203*
**Fax:* Admitting ■ *Web:* www.saintfrancismemorial.org					
Saint Helena Hospital 10 Woodland Rd	Saint Helena	CA	94574	707-963-3611	967-5712
Web: www.sthelenahospital.org					
Saint John's Hospital & Health Center 1328 22nd St	Santa Monica	CA	90404	310-829-5511	829-8295
Web: www.stjohns.org					
Saint John's Regional Medical Center 1600 N Rose Ave	Oxnard	CA	93030	805-988-2500	981-4440
Saint Joseph Hospital 2700 Dolbeer St	Eureka	CA	95501	707-445-8121	269-3897
Web: www.stjosepheureka.org					
Saint Joseph Hospital 1100 W Stewart Dr	Orange	CA	92868	714-633-9111	744-8784
Web: www.sjo.org					
Saint Joseph's Medical Center 1800 N California St	Stockton	CA	95204	209-943-2000	461-3299
Web: www.stjosephscares.org					
Saint Jude Medical Center 101 E Valencia Mesa Dr	Fullerton	CA	92835	714-871-3280	992-3029
Web: www.stjudemedicalcenter.org					
Saint Luke's Hospital 3555 Cesar Chavez St	San Francisco	CA	94110	415-647-8600	641-6899
Web: www.stlukes-sf.org					
Saint Mary Medical Center 1050 Linden Ave	Long Beach	CA	90813	562-491-9000	436-6378
Web: www.stmarymedicalcenter.org					
Saint Mary's Medical Center 450 Stanyan St	San Francisco	CA	94117	415-668-1000	668-4531
Web: www.stmarysmedicalcenter.com					
Saint Rose Hospital 27200 Calaroga Ave	Hayward	CA	94545	510-782-6200	887-7421
Web: www.strosehospital.org					
Saint Vincent Medical Center 2131 W 3rd St	Los Angeles	CA	90057	213-484-7111	484-9304
Web: www.stvincentmedicalcenter.com					
Salinas Valley Memorial Hospital 450 E Romie Ln	Salinas	CA	93901	831-757-4333	753-6296
TF: 888-755-7864 ■ *Web:* www.svmh.com					
San Antonio Community Hospital 999 San Bernardino Rd	Upland	CA	91786	909-985-2811	985-7659
Web: www.sach.org					
San Francisco General Hospital Medical Center 1001 Potrero Ave	San Francisco	CA	94110	415-206-8000	206-8440
Web: www.dph.sf.ca.us/chn/sfgh					
San Gabriel Valley Medical Center 438 W Las Tunas Dr	San Gabriel	CA	91776	626-289-5454	570-6555
Web: www.sgvmc.org					
San Joaquin General Hospital 500 W Hospital Rd	French Camp	CA	95231	209-468-6000	468-6659*
**Fax:* Admitting ■ *Web:* www.sjgeneralhospital.com					
Santa Barbara Cottage Hospital PO Box 689	Santa Barbara	CA	93102	805-682-7111	569-7561
Web: www.sbch.org					
Santa Clara Valley Medical Center 751 S Bascom Ave	San Jose	CA	95128	408-885-5000	793-1817
Web: www.scvmed.org					
Santa Monica UCLA Medical Center 1250 16th St	Santa Monica	CA	90404	310-319-4000	319-4821
Web: www.healthcare.ucla.edu/santa-monica					
Santa Rosa Memorial Hospital 1165 Montgomery Dr	Santa Rosa	CA	95405	707-546-3210	522-1543
Web: www.stjosephhealth.org/santarosa					
Scripps Green Hospital 10666 N Torrey Pines Rd	La Jolla	CA	92037	858-455-9100	554-2231
TF: 800-727-4777 ■ *Web:* www.scrippshealth.org/scripps_locations.asp					
Scripps Memorial Hospital-Chula Vista 435 H St	Chula Vista	CA	91910	619-691-7000	691-7522
Web: www.scrippshealth.org/hospitals/chula.html					
Scripps Memorial Hospital-Encinitas 354 Santa Fe Dr	Encinitas	CA	92024	760-753-6501	633-7356
Web: www.scrippshealth.org/Locations.asp?ID=3					
Scripps Memorial Hospital-La Jolla 9888 Genesee Ave	La Jolla	CA	92037	858-457-4123	626-6122
Web: www.scrippshealth.org					
Scripps Mercy Hospital 4077 5th Ave	San Diego	CA	92103	619-294-8111	686-3530
Web: www.scrippshealth.org/hospitals/mercy.html					
Sequoia Hospital 170 Alameda Ave	Redwood City	CA	94062	650-369-5811	367-5288
Web: www.sequoiahospital.org					
Seton Medical Center 1900 Sullivan Ave	Daly City	CA	94015	650-992-4000	991-6024
Web: www.setonmedicalcenter.org					
Sharp Chula Vista Medical Center 751 Medical Center Ct	Chula Vista	CA	91911	619-482-5800	482-3535
Web: www.sharp.com/hospital/index.cfm?id=915					
Sharp Memorial Hospital 7901 Frost St	San Diego	CA	92123	858-939-3400	939-3514
Web: www.sharp.com/hospital/index.cfm?id=919					
Shasta Regional Medical Center 1100 Butte St	Redding	CA	96001	530-244-5400	244-5119
Web: www.shastaregional.com					
Sherman Oaks Hospital & Health Center 4929 Van Nuys Blvd	Sherman Oaks	CA	91403	818-981-7111	907-4527
Web: www.shermanoakshospital.com					
Sierra Nevada Memorial Hospital 155 Glasson Way	Grass Valley	CA	95945	530-274-6000	274-6614
Web: www.snmh.org					
Sierra View District Hospital 465 W Putnam Ave	Porterville	CA	93257	559-784-1110	788-6135
Web: www.sierra-view.com					
Sierra Vista Regional Medical Center 1010 Murray Ave	San Luis Obispo	CA	93405	805-546-7600	546-7892
TF: 888-936-7200 ■ *Web:* www.sierravistaregional.com					
Simi Valley Hospital 2975 N Sycamore Dr	Simi Valley	CA	93065	805-955-6000	526-0837*
**Fax:* Admitting ■ *Web:* www.simivalleyhospital.com					
Sonora Regional Medical Center 1000 Greenly Rd	Sonora	CA	95370	209-536-5000	536-3500
Web: www.sonorahospital.org					
South Coast Medical Center 31872 Coast Hwy	Laguna Beach	CA	92651	949-499-1311	499-7529
Web: www.southcoastmedcenter.com					
Summit Medical Center 350 Hawthorne Ave	Oakland	CA	94609	510-655-4000	658-8593
Web: www.altabatessummit.com					
Sutter Auburn Faith Community Hospital 11815 Education St	Auburn	CA	95602	530-888-4500	886-6611
Web: www.sutterauburnfaith.org					
Sutter General Hospital 2801 L St	Sacramento	CA	95816	916-454-2222	733-3791
Web: www.sutterhealth.org					
Sutter Medical Center of Santa Rosa 3325 Chanate Rd	Santa Rosa	CA	95404	707-576-4000	576-4318
Web: www.suttersantarosa.org					
Sutter Memorial Hospital 5151 F St	Sacramento	CA	95819	916-454-3333	733-8135
Web: www.sutterhealth.org					
Sutter Solano Medical Center 300 Hospital Dr	Vallejo	CA	94589	707-554-4444	648-3227
Web: www.suttersolano.org					
Torrance Memorial Medical Center 3330 W Lomita Blvd	Torrance	CA	90505	310-325-9110	784-4801
Web: torrancememorial.org					

				Phone	Fax
Tri-City Medical Center 4002 Vista Way *Web:* www.tricitymed.org	Oceanside	CA	92056	760-724-8411	940-4050
Tri-City Regional Medical Center 21530 S Pioneer Blvd *Web:* www.tri-cityrmc.org	Hawaiian Gardens	CA	90716	562-860-0401	924-5871
Tulare District Hospital 869 N Cherry St *Web:* www.tdhs.org	Tulare	CA	93274	559-688-0821	685-3835
UCI Medical Center 101 The City Dr S *TF:* 877-824-3627 ■ *Web:* www.ucihealth.com	Orange	CA	92868	714-456-7001	456-7488
UCLA Medical Center 10833 Le Conte Ave *Web:* www.healthcare.ucla.edu	Los Angeles	CA	90095	310-825-9111	825-7271
UCSF Medical Center 505 Parnassus Ave *Web:* www.ucsfhealth.org	San Francisco	CA	94143	415-476-1000	
Ukiah Valley Medical Center 275 Hospital Dr *Web:* www.uvmc.org	Ukiah	CA	95482	707-462-3111	463-7384
University of California Davis Medical Center 2315 Stockton Blvd *Fax: Admitting ■ *Web:* www.ucdmc.ucdavis.edu	Sacramento	CA	95817	916-734-2011	734-8080*
University of California San Diego Medical Center 200 W Arbor Dr *TF:* 800-926-8273 ■ *Web:* health.ucsd.edu	San Diego	CA	92103	619-543-6222	543-7448
Valley Presbyterian Hospital 15107 Vanowen St *Web:* www.valleypres.org	Van Nuys	CA	91405	818-782-6600	902-3974
Verdugo Hills Hospital 1812 Verdugo Blvd *Web:* www.verdugohillshospital.org	Glendale	CA	91208	818-790-7100	952-4691
West Anaheim Medical Center 3033 W Orange Ave *Web:* www.westanaheimmedctr.com	Anaheim	CA	92804	714-827-3000	229-6813
Western Medical Center Anaheim 1025 S Anaheim Blvd *Web:* www.westernmedanaheim.com	Anaheim	CA	92805	714-533-6220	563-2859
Western Medical Center Santa Ana 1001 N Tustin Ave *TF:* 800-777-7464 ■ *Web:* www.westernmedicalcenter.com	Santa Ana	CA	92705	714-953-3500	953-3613
White Memorial Medical Center 1720 Cesar E Chavez Ave *Web:* www.whitememorial.com	Los Angeles	CA	90033	323-268-5000	881-8605
Whittier Hospital Medical Center 9080 Colima Rd *Web:* www.whittierhospital.com	Whittier	CA	90605	562-945-3561	693-6811
Woodland Healthcare 1325 Cottonwood St *Web:* www.woodlandhealthcare.org	Woodland	CA	95695	530-662-3961	666-7948

Colorado

				Phone	Fax
Arkansas Valley Regional Medical Center 1100 Carson Ave *Web:* www.avrmc.org	La Junta	CO	81050	719-384-5412	383-6005
Avista Adventist Hospital 100 Health Park Dr	Louisville	CO	80027	303-673-1000	673-1048
Boulder Community Hospital 1100 Balsam Ave *Fax: Admitting ■ *Web:* www.bch.org	Boulder	CO	80301	303-440-2273	440-2278*
Centura Saint Anthony Hospital North 2551 W 84th Ave *Web:* www.centura.org	Westminster	CO	80031	303-426-2151	426-2155
Denver Health Medical Center 777 Bannock St *Web:* www.denverhealth.org	Denver	CO	80204	303-436-6000	436-6243
Exempla Lutheran Medical Center 8300 W 38th Ave *Web:* www.exempla.org	Wheat Ridge	CO	80033	303-425-4500	425-8198
Exempla Saint Joseph Hospital 1835 Franklin St *Web:* www.exempla.org	Denver	CO	80218	303-837-7111	837-7123
Littleton Adventist Hospital 7700 S Broadway *Web:* www.mylittletonhospital.org	Littleton	CO	80122	303-730-8900	730-5867
Longmont United Hospital 1950 Mountain View Ave *Web:* www.luhcares.org	Longmont	CO	80501	303-651-5111	678-4050
McKee Medical Center 2000 Boise Ave *Fax: Admitting ■ *Web:* www.bannerhealth.com	Loveland	CO	80538	970-669-4640	635-4112*
Medical Center of Aurora 1501 S Potomac St *Web:* www.auroramed.com	Aurora	CO	80012	303-363-7200	337-9773
Memorial Hospital Central 1400 E Boulder St *Fax: Admissions ■ *Web:* www.memorialhealthsystem.com	Colorado Springs	CO	80909	719-365-5000	365-6884*
Mercy Medical Center 1010 Three Springs Blvd *TF:* 800-345-2516 ■ *Web:* www.mercydurango.org	Durango	CO	81301	970-247-4311	382-1065
North Colorado Medical Center 1801 16th St *Web:* www.bannerhealth.com	Greeley	CO	80631	970-352-4121	350-6644
North Suburban Medical Center 9191 Grant St *Web:* www.northsuburban.com	Thornton	CO	80229	303-451-7800	450-4588
Parkview Medical Center 400 W 16th St *TF:* 800-543-8984 ■ *Web:* www.parkviewmc.org	Pueblo	CO	81003	719-584-4000	584-4739
Penrose Hospital 2222 N Nevada Ave *Fax: Admitting ■ *Web:* www.penrosestfrancis.org/index.php?s=facility	Colorado Springs	CO	80907	719-776-5000	776-2442*
Porter Adventist Hospital 2525 S Downing St *Web:* www.porterhospital.org	Denver	CO	80210	303-778-1955	778-5252
Poudre Valley Hospital 1024 S Lemay Ave *TF:* 800-252-5784 ■ *Web:* www.pvhs.org	Fort Collins	CO	80524	970-495-7000	495-7601
Presbyterian-Saint Luke's Medical Center 1719 E 19th Ave *Web:* www.pslmc.com	Denver	CO	80218	303-839-6000	869-2428
Rose Medical Center 4567 E 9th Ave *TF:* 888-525-1253 ■ *Web:* www.rosemed.com	Denver	CO	80220	303-320-2121	320-2200
Saint Anthony Central Hospital 4231 W 16th Ave *Web:* www.stanthonyhosp.org	Denver	CO	80204	303-629-3511	629-2318
Saint Mary-Corwin Medical Center 1008 Minnequa Ave *Fax: Admitting ■ *TF:* 800-228-4039 ■ *Web:* www.stmarycorwin.org	Pueblo	CO	81004	719-557-4000	557-5529*
Saint Mary's Hospital & Medical Center 2635 N 7th St *TF:* 800-458-3888 ■ *Web:* www.stmarygj.com	Grand Junction	CO	81501	970-244-2273	244-7510
San Luis Valley Regional Medical Center 106 Blanca Ave *Web:* www.slvrmc.org	Alamosa	CO	81101	719-589-2511	587-1372
Swedish Medical Center 501 E Hampden Ave *Web:* www.swedishhospital.com	Englewood	CO	80113	303-788-5000	788-6265
University of Colorado Hospital 12605 E 16th Ave *Web:* www.uch.edu	Aurora	CO	80045	303-848-4011	

Connecticut

				Phone	Fax
Backus William W Hospital 326 Washington St *Web:* www.backushospital.org	Norwich	CT	06360	860-889-8331	823-6329
Bridgeport Hospital 267 Grant St *Web:* www.bridgeporthospital.org	Bridgeport	CT	06610	203-384-3000	384-3215
Bristol Hospital 41 Brewster Rd *Web:* www.bristolhospital.org	Bristol	CT	06010	860-585-3000	585-3058
Charlotte Hungerford Hospital 540 Litchfield St *Web:* www.charlottesweb.hungerford.org	Torrington	CT	06790	860-496-6666	482-8627
Danbury Hospital 24 Hospital Ave *TF:* 800-284-3262 ■ *Web:* www.danburyhospital.org	Danbury	CT	06810	203-737-7000	731-8030
Greenwich Hospital 5 Perryridge Rd *Web:* www.greenhosp.org	Greenwich	CT	06830	203-863-3000	863-3954
Griffin Hospital 130 Division St *Web:* www.griffinhealth.org	Derby	CT	06418	203-735-7421	732-7569
Hartford Hospital 80 Seymour St *Web:* www.harthosp.org	Hartford	CT	06102	860-545-5000	545-3622
Hospital of Saint Raphael 1450 Chapel St *TF:* 800-662-2366 ■ *Web:* www.srhs.org	New Haven	CT	06511	203-789-3000	867-5235
Johnson Memorial Hospital 201 Chestnut Hill Rd *Web:* www.johnsonhealthnetwork.com/jmhinc.htm	Stafford Springs	CT	06076	860-684-4251	684-8165
Lawrence & Memorial Hospital 365 Montauk Ave *TF:* 888-777-9539 ■ *Web:* www.lmhospital.org	New London	CT	06320	860-442-0711	444-3741
Manchester Memorial Hospital 71 Haynes St *Web:* www.echn.org/mmh.htm	Manchester	CT	06040	860-646-1222	522-3404
Middlesex Hospital 28 Crescent St *TF:* 800-664-5031 ■ *Web:* www.midhosp.org	Middletown	CT	06457	860-358-6000	346-5485
Milford Hospital 300 Seaside Ave *Web:* www.milfordhospital.org	Milford	CT	06460	203-876-4000	876-4198
New Britain General Hospital 100 Grand St *Web:* www.nbgh.org	New Britain	CT	06050	860-224-5011	224-5767
Norwalk Hospital 34 Maple St *Web:* www.norwalkhosp.org	Norwalk	CT	06856	203-852-2000	855-3780
Saint Francis Hospital & Medical Center 114 Woodland St *TF:* 800-993-4312 ■ *Web:* www.stfranciscare.org	Hartford	CT	06105	860-714-4000	714-8038
Saint Mary's Hospital 56 Franklin St *Web:* www.stmh.org	Waterbury	CT	06706	203-709-6000	709-3238
Saint Vincent's Medical Center 2800 Main St *Web:* www.stvincents.org	Bridgeport	CT	06606	203-576-6000	576-5345
Stamford Hospital 30 Shelburne Rd *Web:* www.stamhealth.org/tsh/tsh_about.html	Stamford	CT	06902	203-325-7000	276-7957
University of Connecticut Health Center John Dempsey Hospital 263 Farmington Ave *TF:* 800-535-6232 ■ *Web:* www.uchc.edu	Farmington	CT	06030	860-679-2000	679-1255
Waterbury Hospital 64 Robbins St *Web:* www.waterburyhospital.org	Waterbury	CT	06721	203-573-6000	573-6161
William W Backus Hospital 326 Washington St *Web:* www.backushospital.org	Norwich	CT	06360	860-889-8331	823-6329
Windham Community Memorial Hospital 112 Mansfield Ave *Web:* www.windhamhospital.org	Willimantic	CT	06226	860-456-9116	456-6838
Yale-New Haven Hospital 20 York St *Web:* www.ynhh.org	New Haven	CT	06504	203-688-4242	

Delaware

				Phone	Fax
Bayhealth Medical Center 21 W Clarke Ave *TF:* 800-990-4229 ■ *Web:* www.bayhealth.org	Milford	DE	19963	302-430-5738	430-5598
Beebe Medical Center 424 Savannah Rd *Web:* www.beebemed.org	Lewes	DE	19958	302-645-3300	645-3405
Christiana Hospital 4755 Ogletown-Stanton Rd *Fax: Admitting ■ *Web:* www.christianacare.org	Newark	DE	19718	302-733-1000	733-1313*
Kent General Hospital 640 S State St *TF:* 888-761-8300 ■ *Web:* www.bayhealth.org	Dover	DE	19901	302-674-4700	744-7181
Nanticoke Memorial Hospital 801 Middleford Rd *Web:* www.nanticoke.org	Seaford	DE	19973	302-629-6611	629-2493
Saint Francis Hospital 7th & Clayton St *Web:* www.stfrancishealthcare.org	Wilmington	DE	19805	302-421-4100	579-8320

District of Columbia

				Phone	Fax
George Washington University Hospital 900 23rd St NW *TF:* 888-449-4677 ■ *Web:* www.gwhospital.com	Washington	DC	20037	202-715-4000	
Georgetown University Hospital 3800 Reservoir Rd NW *Web:* gumc.georgetown.edu	Washington	DC	20007	202-784-2000	784-2875
Greater Southeast Community Hospital 1310 Southern Ave SE	Washington	DC	20032	202-574-6000	574-7188
Howard University Hospital 2041 Georgia Ave NW *Web:* www.huhosp.org	Washington	DC	20060	202-865-6100	865-1360
Providence Hospital 1150 Varnum St NE *Web:* www.provhosp.org	Washington	DC	20017	202-269-7000	269-7160
Sibley Memorial Hospital 5255 Loughboro Rd NW *Fax: Admissions ■ *Web:* www.sibley.org	Washington	DC	20016	202-537-4000	243-2246*
Washington Hospital Center 110 Irving St NW *Web:* www.whcenter.org	Washington	DC	20010	202-877-7000	877-7826

Florida

				Phone	Fax
Aventura Hospital 20900 Biscayne Blvd *Web:* www.aventurahospital.com	Aventura	FL	33180	305-682-7000	682-7105
Baptist Hospital 1000 W Moreno St *Web:* www.ebaptisthealthcare.org/BaptistHospital	Pensacola	FL	32501	850-434-4011	469-2307
Baptist Hospital of Miami 8900 N Kendall Dr *TF:* 800-327-2491 ■ *Web:* www.baptisthealth.net	Miami	FL	33176	786-596-1960	596-5960
Baptist Medical Center 800 Prudential Dr *TF:* 800-874-8567 ■ *Web:* www.e-baptisthealth.com	Jacksonville	FL	32207	904-202-2000	202-2285
Baptist Medical Center Beaches 1350 13th Ave S *Web:* www.e-baptisthealth.com	Jacksonville	FL	32250	904-627-2900	627-2901
Bay Medical Center 615 N Bonita Ave *TF:* 800-422-2418 ■ *Web:* www.baymedical.org	Panama City	FL	32401	850-769-1511	763-8827
Bayfront Medical Center 701 6th St S *Web:* www.bayfront.org	Saint Petersburg	FL	33701	727-823-1234	893-6930
Bethesda Memorial Hospital 2815 S Seacrest Blvd *Web:* www.bethesdaweb.com	Boynton Beach	FL	33435	561-737-7733	737-4534
Blake Medical Center 2020 59th St W *Web:* www.blakemedicalcenter.com	Bradenton	FL	34209	941-792-6611	798-6209
Boca Raton Community Hospital 800 Meadows Rd *Web:* www.brch.com	Boca Raton	FL	33486	561-395-7100	955-5040
Brandon Regional Hospital 119 Oakfield Dr *Web:* www.brandonhospital.com	Brandon	FL	33511	813-681-5551	654-7203
Brooksville Regional Hospital 17240 Cortez Blvd *Web:* www.brooksvilleregionalhospital.org	Brooksville	FL	34601	352-796-5111	544-5711
Broward General Medical Center 1600 S Andrews Ave *TF:* 866-293-7866 ■ *Web:* www.browardhealth.org	Fort Lauderdale	FL	33316	954-355-4400	355-4797
Cape Coral Hospital 636 Del Prado Blvd *Web:* www.leememorial.org	Cape Coral	FL	33990	239-574-2323	574-0079
Capital Regional Medical Center 2626 Capital Medical Blvd *Web:* www.tallahasseehospital.com	Tallahassee	FL	32308	850-325-5000	325-5198
Cedars Medical Center 1400 NW 12th Ave *Web:* www.cedarsmed.com	Miami	FL	33136	305-325-5511	325-4673
Central Florida Regional Hospital 1401 W Seminole Blvd *Web:* www.centralfloridaregional.com	Sanford	FL	32771	407-321-4500	324-4790
Charlotte Regional Medical Center 809 E Marion Ave *Web:* www.charlotteregional.com	Punta Gorda	FL	33950	941-639-3131	637-2579
Citrus Memorial Hospital 502 W Highland Blvd *Web:* www.citrusmh.com	Inverness	FL	34452	352-726-1551	344-6565
Cleveland Clinic Hospital 3100 Weston Rd *Web:* www.clevelandclinic.org/florida	Weston	FL	33331	954-689-5000	689-5165

General Hospitals - US (Cont'd)

Florida (Cont'd)

Name / Address	City	State	Zip	Phone	Fax
Columbia Hospital 2201 45th St *Web:* www.columbiahospital.com	West Palm Beach	FL	33407	561-842-6141	881-2650
Community Hospital 5637 Marine Pkwy *Web:* www.communityhospitalnpr.com	New Port Richey	FL	34652	727-848-1733	848-5136
Coral Gables Hospital 3100 Douglas Rd *Web:* www.coralgableshospital.com	Coral Gables	FL	33134	305-445-8461	441-6879
Coral Springs Medical Center 3000 Coral Hills Dr *Web:* www.browardhealth.org	Coral Springs	FL	33065	954-344-3000	344-3146
Delray Medical Center 5352 Linton Blvd *Web:* www.delraymedicalctr.com	Delray Beach	FL	33484	561-498-4440	495-3103
Doctors' Hospital 5000 University Dr *Web:* www.baptisthealth.net	Coral Gables	FL	33146	786-308-3000	308-3402
Doctors Hospital Sarasota 5731 Bee Ridge Rd *Web:* www.doctorsofsarasota.com	Sarasota	FL	34233	941-342-1100	379-8342
Edward White Hospital 2323 9th Ave N *Web:* www.edwardwhitehospital.com	Saint Petersburg	FL	33713	727-323-1111	328-6135
Ellis Helen Memorial Hospital 1395 S Pinellas Ave. *Web:* www.hemh.com	Tarpon Springs	FL	34689	727-942-5000	942-5161
Fawcett Memorial Hospital 21298 Olean Blvd *Web:* www.fawcetthospital.com	Port Charlotte	FL	33952	941-629-1181	627-6142
Flagler Hospital 400 Health Park Blvd *TF:* 866-834-3278 ■ *Web:* www.flaglerhospital.org	Saint Augustine	FL	32086	904-829-5155	819-4472
Florida Hospital DeLand 701 W Plymouth Ave **Fax:* Admitting ■ *Web:* www.fhdeland.org	DeLand	FL	32720	386-943-4522	943-3674*
Florida Hospital Heartland Medical Center 4200 Sun 'N Lake Blvd *Web:* www.flhosp-heartland.org	Sebring	FL	33871	863-453-7511	402-3110
Florida Hospital Oceanside 264 S Atlantic Ave *Web:* www.fhmd.com	Ormond Beach	FL	32176	386-672-4161	671-5072
Florida Hospital Orlando 601 E Rollins St *Web:* www.flhosp.org/locations/fhsouth/index.htm	Orlando	FL	32803	407-303-6611	
Florida Hospital Ormond Memorial 875 Sterthaus Ave *TF:* 888-647-0271 ■ *Web:* www.fhmd.com	Ormond Beach	FL	32174	386-676-6000	
Florida Hospital Zephyrhills 7050 Gall Blvd *Web:* www.fhzeph.org	Zephyrhills	FL	33541	813-788-0411	783-6196
Florida Medical Center 5000 W Oakland Park Blvd. *TF:* 800-222-9355 ■ *Web:* www.floridamedicalctr.com	Fort Lauderdale	FL	33313	954-735-6000	730-2805
Fort Walton Beach Medical Center 1000 Mar-Walt Dr *Web:* www.fwbmc.com	Fort Walton Beach	FL	32547	850-862-1111	862-9149
Gulf Coast Hospital 13681 Doctors Way *TF:* 800-440-4481 ■ *Web:* www.gulfcoasthospital.com	Fort Myers	FL	33912	239-768-5000	768-8379
Gulf Coast Medical Center 449 W 23rd St *Web:* www.egulfcoastmedical.com	Panama City	FL	32405	850-769-8341	747-7107
Halifax Medical Center 303 N Clyde Morris Blvd *Web:* www.hfch.org/hmc	Daytona Beach	FL	32114	386-254-4000	254-4375
Health Central 10000 W Colonial Dr. *Web:* www.health-central.org	Ocoee	FL	34761	407-296-1000	253-1675
Health First Cape Canaveral Hospital 701 W Cocoa Beach Causeway *TF:* 888-434-3730 ■ *Web:* www.health-first.org	Cocoa Beach	FL	32931	321-799-7111	799-8477
Helen Ellis Memorial Hospital 1395 S Pinellas Ave. *Web:* www.hemh.com	Tarpon Springs	FL	34689	727-942-5000	942-5161
Holmes Regional Medical Center 1350 S Hickory St *TF:* 888-434-3730 ■ *Web:* www.health-first.org	Melbourne	FL	32901	321-434-7000	434-7283
Holy Cross Hospital 4725 N Federal Hwy *Web:* www.holy-cross.com	Fort Lauderdale	FL	33308	954-771-8000	492-5741
Homestead Hospital 975 Baptist Way *Web:* www.baptisthealth.net	Homestead	FL	33033	786-243-8000	243-8557
Imperial Point Medical Center 6401 N Federal Hwy *Web:* www.nbhd.org	Fort Lauderdale	FL	33308	954-776-8500	776-8520
Indian River Medical Center 1000 36th St *TF:* 800-226-4764 ■ *Web:* www.irmc.cc	Vero Beach	FL	32960	772-567-4311	562-5628
Jackson Hospital 4250 Hospital Dr. *Web:* www.jacksonhosp.com	Marianna	FL	32446	850-526-2200	482-6374
Jackson Memorial Hospital 1611 NW 12th Ave *Web:* www.jhsmiami.org	Miami	FL	33136	305-585-1111	325-4262
JFK Medical Center 5301 S Congress Ave. *Web:* www.jfkmc.com	Atlantis	FL	33462	561-965-7300	548-3685
Jupiter Medical Center 1210 S Old Dixie Hwy *Web:* www.jupitermed.com	Jupiter	FL	33458	561-747-2234	744-4493
Kendall Regional Medical Center 11750 SW 40th St *Web:* www.kendallmed.com	Miami	FL	33175	305-223-3000	229-2481
Lakeland Regional Medical Center 1324 Lakeland Hills Blvd *Web:* www.lrmc.com	Lakeland	FL	33805	863-687-1100	687-1214
Largo Medical Center 201 14th St SW *Web:* www.largomedical.com	Largo	FL	33770	727-588-5200	588-5906
Lawnwood Regional Medical Center 1700 S 23rd St *Web:* www.lawnwoodmed.com	Fort Pierce	FL	34950	772-461-4000	460-1353
Lee Memorial Health Systems 2776 Cleveland Ave *Web:* www.leememorial.org	Fort Myers	FL	33901	239-332-1111	336-6170
Leesburg Regional Medical Center 600 E Dixie Ave *Web:* www.leesburgregional.org	Leesburg	FL	34748	352-365-4545	323-5009
Lower Keys Medical Center 5900 College Rd *Web:* www.lkmc.com	Key West	FL	33040	305-294-5531	294-8065
Manatee Memorial Hospital 206 2nd St E. *Web:* www.manateememorial.com	Bradenton	FL	34208	941-746-5111	745-6862
Martin Memorial Health Systems 200 SE Hospital Ave *Web:* www.mmhs.com	Stuart	FL	34994	772-287-5200	223-5946
Mease Countryside Hospital 3231 McMullen-Booth Rd. *Web:* www.measehospitals.com	Safety Harbor	FL	34695	727-725-6111	725-6181
Mease Dunedin Hospital 601 Main St *Web:* www.measehospitals.com	Dunedin	FL	34698	727-733-1111	734-6297
Memorial Hospital of Jacksonville 3625 University Blvd S. *Web:* www.memorialhospitaljax.com	Jacksonville	FL	32216	904-399-6111	391-1390
Memorial Hospital Miramar 1901 SW 172nd Ave *Web:* www.memorialmiramar.com	Miramar	FL	33029	954-538-5000	538-4818
Memorial Hospital Pembroke 7800 Sheridan St *Web:* www.memorialpembroke.com	Pembroke Pines	FL	33024	954-962-9650	963-8036
Memorial Hospital of Tampa 2901 W Swann Ave *Web:* www.memorialhospitaltampa.com	Tampa	FL	33609	813-873-6400	874-8685
Memorial Hospital West 703 N Flamingo Rd *Web:* www.memorialwest.com	Pembroke Pines	FL	33028	954-436-5000	433-7156
Memorial Regional Hospital 3501 Johnson St. *Web:* www.memorialregional.com	Hollywood	FL	33021	954-987-2000	985-3412
Mercy Hospital 3663 S Miami Ave *Web:* www.mercymiami.com	Miami	FL	33133	305-854-4400	285-2967
Metropolitan Hospital of Miami 5959 NW 7th St	Miami	FL	33126	305-264-1000	265-6536
Morton Plant Hospital 300 Pinellas St *Web:* www.mortonplant.com	Clearwater	FL	33756	727-462-7000	461-8101
Mount Sinai Medical Center 4300 Alton Rd *Web:* www.msmc.com	Miami Beach	FL	33140	305-674-2121	674-2007
Munroe Regional Medical Center 1500 SW 1st Ave *Web:* www.munroeregional.com	Ocala	FL	34474	352-351-7200	351-7336
Naples Community Hospital 350 7th St N *Web:* www.nchmd.org	Naples	FL	34102	239-436-5000	436-5914
North Broward Medical Center 201 E Sample Rd *Web:* www.browardhealth.org	Pompano Beach	FL	33064	954-941-8300	786-5174
North Florida Regional Medical Center 6500 Newberry Rd *Web:* www.nfrmc.com	Gainesville	FL	32605	352-333-4000	333-4800
North Okaloosa Medical Center 151 E Redstone Ave *Web:* www.northokaloosa.com	Crestview	FL	32539	850-682-9731	689-8484
North Ridge Medical Center 5757 N Dixie Hwy *Web:* www.northridgemedical.com	Fort Lauderdale	FL	33334	954-776-6000	493-5061
North Shore Medical Center 1100 NW 95th St *Web:* www.northshoremedical.com	Miami	FL	33150	305-835-6000	835-6163
Northside Hospital 6000 49th St N *Web:* www.northsidehospital.com	Saint Petersburg	FL	33709	727-521-4411	521-5007
Northwest Medical Center 2801 N SR 7 *Web:* www.northwestmed.com	Margate	FL	33063	954-978-4008	984-3721
Oakhill Hospital 11375 Cortez Blvd *Web:* www.oakhillhospital.com	Brooksville	FL	34613	352-596-6632	597-3024
Ocala Regional Medical Center 1431 SW 1st Ave *Web:* www.ocalaregional.com	Ocala	FL	34471	352-401-1000	401-1198
Orange Park Medical Center 2001 Kingsley Ave *Web:* www.opmedical.com	Orange Park	FL	32073	904-276-8500	213-2536
Orlando Regional Lucerne Hospital 818 Main Ln **Fax Area Code:* 321 ■ *Web:* www.orhs.org/comm_hosp/lucerne	Orlando	FL	32801	407-649-6111	841-4202*
Orlando Regional Medical Center 1414 Kuhl Ave *Web:* www.orhs.org/ormc	Orlando	FL	32806	407-841-5111	649-6845
Orlando Regional South Seminole Hospital 555 W State Rd 434 *Web:* www.orlandoregional.org	Longwood	FL	32750	407-767-1200	767-5801
Osceola Regional Medical Center 700 W Oak St *Web:* www.osceolaregional.com	Kissimmee	FL	34741	407-846-2266	518-3616
Palm Beach Gardens Medical Center 3360 Burns Rd. *Web:* www.pbgmc.com	Palm Beach Gardens	FL	33410	561-622-1411	694-7160
Palm Springs General Hospital 1475 W 49th St	Hialeah	FL	33012	305-558-2500	558-8679
Palmetto General Hospital 2001 W 68th St. *TF:* 888-222-2020 ■ *Web:* www.palmettogeneral.com	Hialeah	FL	33016	305-823-5000	362-0231
Palms of Pasadena Hospital 1501 Pasadena Ave S *Web:* www.palmspasadena.com	Saint Petersburg	FL	33707	727-381-1000	341-7629
Palms West Hospital 13001 Southern Blvd *TF:* 866-857-3936 ■ *Web:* www.palmswesthospital.com	Loxahatchee	FL	33470	561-798-3300	791-8108
Parrish Medical Center 951 N Washington Ave. *Web:* www.parrishmed.com	Titusville	FL	32796	321-268-6111	268-6231
Peace River Regional Medical Center 2500 Harbor Blvd *TF:* 800-226-4122 ■ *Web:* www.peaceriverregional.com	Port Charlotte	FL	33952	941-766-4122	766-4140
Plantation General Hospital 401 NW 42nd Ave *Web:* www.plantationgeneral.com	Plantation	FL	33317	954-587-5010	587-4597
Putnam Community Medical Center Hwy 20 W *Web:* www.pcmcfl.com	Palatka	FL	32177	386-328-5711	325-8178
Raulerson Hospital 1796 Hwy 441 N *Web:* www.raulersonhospital.com	Okeechobee	FL	34972	863-763-2151	824-2991
Regional Medical Center Bayonet Point 14000 Fivay Rd *Web:* www.rmchealth.com	Hudson	FL	34667	727-863-2411	869-5491
Sacred Heart Hospital of Pensacola 5151 N 9th Ave *TF:* 800-874-1026 ■ *Web:* www.sacred-heart.org	Pensacola	FL	32504	850-416-7000	416-6119
Saint Anthony's Hospital 1200 7th Ave N *Web:* www.stanthonys.com	Saint Petersburg	FL	33705	727-825-1000	825-1230
Saint Joseph's Hospital 3001 W ML King Jr Blvd *TF:* 800-347-2676 ■ *Web:* www.sjbhealth.org	Tampa	FL	33607	813-870-4000	870-4639
Saint Lucie Medical Center 1800 SE Tiffany Ave *Web:* www.stluciemed.com	Port Saint Lucie	FL	34952	772-335-4000	398-3608
Saint Luke's Hospital 4201 Belfort Rd *Web:* www.mayoclinic.org/stlukes-jax	Jacksonville	FL	32216	904-296-3700	296-4698
Saint Petersburg General Hospital 6500 38th Ave N *Web:* www.stpetegeneralhospital.com	Saint Petersburg	FL	33710	727-384-1414	341-4889
Saint Vincent's Medical Center 1800 Barrs St *Web:* jaxhealth.com	Jacksonville	FL	32204	904-308-7300	308-2992
Sarasota Memorial Hospital 1700 S Tamiami Trail *TF:* 800-764-8255 ■ *Web:* www.smh.com	Sarasota	FL	34239	941-917-9000	917-1716
Sebastian River Medical Center 13695 US Hwy 1 *Web:* www.srmcenter.com	Sebastian	FL	32958	772-589-3186	388-3689
Seven Rivers Regional Medical Center 6201 N Suncoast Blvd *Web:* www.srrmc.com	Crystal River	FL	34428	352-795-6560	795-8369
Shands at AGH Hospital 801 SW 2nd Ave *Web:* shands.org/hospitals/agh	Gainesville	FL	32601	352-733-0140	733-0151
Shands Hospital at the University of Florida 1600 SW Archer Rd *TF:* 800-749-7424 ■ *Web:* shands.org	Gainesville	FL	32610	352-265-0111	265-0363
Shands Jacksonville Medical Center 655 W 8th St *Web:* www.shandsjacksonville.com	Jacksonville	FL	32209	904-244-0411	244-2587
South Bay Hospital 4016 Sun City Center Blvd *Web:* www.southbayhospital.com	Sun City Center	FL	33573	813-634-3301	634-8712
South Florida Baptist Hospital 301 N Alexander St. *Web:* www.sjbhealth.org/home_south.cfm?id=587	Plant City	FL	33563	813-757-1200	757-8209
South Miami Hospital 6200 SW 73rd St **Fax Area Code:* 786 ■ *Web:* www.baptisthealth.net	Miami	FL	33143	305-661-4611	662-5302*
Southwest Florida Regional Medical Center 2727 Winkler Ave. *Web:* www.swfrmc.com	Fort Myers	FL	33901	239-939-1147	939-8260
Sun Coast Hospital 2025 Indian Rocks Rd *Web:* www.suncoasthealthcare.com	Largo	FL	33723	727-581-9474	587-7604
Tallahassee Memorial Hospital 1300 Miccosukee Rd *Web:* www.tmh.org	Tallahassee	FL	32308	850-431-1155	431-5883
Tampa General Hospital 2 Columbia Dr *Web:* www.tgh.org	Tampa	FL	33606	813-844-7000	844-4144
Town & Country Hospital 6001 Webb Rd *Web:* www.townandcountryhospital.com	Tampa	FL	33615	813-885-6666	887-5112
University Community Hospital 3100 E Fletcher Ave *Web:* www.uch.org	Tampa	FL	33613	813-971-6000	615-8100
University Community Hospital Carrollwood 7171 N Dale Mabry Hwy *Web:* www.uch.org	Tampa	FL	33614	813-932-2222	558-8011
University Hospital 7201 N University Dr *Web:* www.uhmchealth.com	Tamarac	FL	33321	954-721-2200	724-6575
Venice Regional Medical Center 540 The Rialto *Web:* www.veniceregional.com	Venice	FL	34285	941-485-7711	483-7699
West Boca Medical Center 21644 State Rd 7 *Web:* www.westbocamedctr.com	Boca Raton	FL	33428	561-488-8000	488-8105
West Florida Hospital 8383 N Davis Hwy *Web:* www.westfloridahospital.com	Pensacola	FL	32514	850-494-4000	494-5073
Westside Regional Medical Center 8201 W Broward Blvd *Web:* www.westsideregional.com	Plantation	FL	33324	954-473-6600	476-3974
Winter Haven Hospital 200 Ave F NE *Web:* www.winterhavenhospital.org	Winter Haven	FL	33881	863-293-1121	297-1867

Hospital	City	State	ZIP	Phone	Fax
Winter Park Memorial Hospital 200 N Lakemont Ave *Web:* www.wpmh.org	Winter Park	FL	32792	407-646-7000	646-7639
Wuesthoff Medical Center Rockledge 110 Longwood Ave *TF:* 800-742-9175 ■ *Web:* www.wuesthoff.org	Rockledge	FL	32956	321-636-2211	690-6645

Georgia

Hospital	City	State	ZIP	Phone	Fax
Athens Regional Medical Center 1199 Prince Ave *Web:* www.armc.org	Athens	GA	30606	706-475-7000	475-6775
Atlanta Medical Center 303 Parkway Dr NE *Web:* www.atlantamedcenter.com	Atlanta	GA	30312	404-265-4000	265-3903
Candler Hospital 5353 Reynolds St *Web:* www.sjchs.org	Savannah	GA	31405	912-819-6000	819-5887
Coffee Regional Medical Center 1101 Ocilla Rd *Web:* www.coffeeregional.org	Douglas	GA	31533	912-384-1900	389-2112
Coliseum Medical Center 350 Hospital Dr *Web:* www.coliseumhealthsystem.com	Macon	GA	31217	478-765-7000	742-1247
Colquitt Regional Medical Center 3131 S Main St *TF:* 888-262-2762 ■ *Web:* www.colquittregional.com	Moultrie	GA	31768	229-985-3420	891-9158
DeKalb Medical Center 2701 N Decatur Rd *Web:* www.dekalbmedicalcenter.org	Decatur	GA	30033	404-501-1000	501-1739
Doctors Hospital 3651 Wheeler Rd *Web:* www.doctors-hospital.net	Augusta	GA	30909	706-651-3232	651-2041
Doctors Hospital 616 19th St *Web:* www.doctorshospital.net	Columbus	GA	31901	706-494-4262	494-4156
Dodge County Hospital 901 Griffin Ave *Fax: Admitting ■ *Web:* www.dodgecountyhospital.com	Eastman	GA	31023	478-448-4000	374-9191*
East Georgia Regional Medical Center 1499 Fair Rd *Web:* www.egrmc.com	Statesboro	GA	30458	912-486-1000	871-2354
Emory Crawford Long Hospital 550 Peachtree St NE *Web:* www.emoryhealthcare.org/departments/ECLH/	Atlanta	GA	30308	404-686-4411	686-8956
Emory Eastside Medical Center 1700 Medical Way *Web:* www.emoryeastside.com	Snellville	GA	30078	770-979-0200	736-2395
Emory University Hospital 1364 Clifton Rd NE *Web:* www.emoryhealthcare.org	Atlanta	GA	30322	404-712-2000	686-8500
Fairview Park Hospital 200 Industrial Blvd *Web:* www.fairviewparkhospital.com	Dublin	GA	31021	478-275-2000	272-0211
Floyd Medical Center 304 Turner McCall Blvd *Web:* www.floyd.org	Rome	GA	30165	706-802-2000	509-6901
Grady Memorial Hospital 80 Jesse Hill Jr Dr SE *Web:* www.gradyhealthsystem.org	Atlanta	GA	30303	404-616-4307	616-6828
Gwinnett Medical Center 1000 Medical Center Blvd *Web:* www.gwinnetthealth.org/facilities/gmc.asp	Lawrenceville	GA	30045	770-995-4321	682-2257
Hamilton Medical Center 1200 Memorial Dr PO Box 1168 *Web:* www.hamiltonhealth.com	Dalton	GA	30720	706-278-2105	272-6111
Henry Medical Center 1133 Eagle's Landing Pkwy *Web:* www.henrymedical.com	Stockbridge	GA	30281	678-604-1000	604-5580
Houston Medical Center 1601 Watson Blvd *Web:* www.hhc.org	Warner Robins	GA	31093	478-922-4281	542-7955
Hutcheson Medical Center 100 Gross Crescent Cir *Web:* www.hutcheson.org	Fort Oglethorpe	GA	30742	706-858-2000	858-2111
John D Archbold Memorial Hospital PO Box 1018 *TF:* 800-341-1009 ■ *Web:* www.archbold.org	Thomasville	GA	31799	229-228-2000	551-8741
Meadows Regional Medical Center 1703 Meadows Ln *Web:* www.meadowsregional.org	Vidalia	GA	30474	912-537-8921	538-5366
Medical Center The 710 Center St *Web:* www.columbusregional.com/MedicalCenter	Columbus	GA	31901	706-571-1000	571-1216
Medical Center of Central Georgia 777 Hemlock St *Web:* www.mccg.org	Macon	GA	31201	478-633-1000	633-1702
Medical College of Georgia Hospital & Clinics 1120 15th St *TF:* 800-736-2273 ■ *Web:* www.mcghealth.org	Augusta	GA	30912	706-721-0211	721-1416
Memorial Health University Medical Center 4700 Waters Ave *Web:* www.memorialhealth.com	Savannah	GA	31404	912-350-8000	350-7073
Memorial Hospital of Adel 706 N Parrish Ave	Adel	GA	31620	229-896-8000	896-8001
Newnan Hospital 60 Hospital Rd *Web:* www.newnanhospital.org	Newnan	GA	30263	770-253-1912	254-3406
Newton Medical Center 5126 Hospital Dr NE *Web:* www.newtonmedical.com/	Covington	GA	30014	770-786-7053	385-4256
North Fulton Regional Hospital 3000 Hospital Blvd *Web:* www.northfultonregional.com	Roswell	GA	30076	770-751-2500	751-2912
Northeast Georgia Medical Center 743 Spring St NE *Web:* www.nghs.org	Gainesville	GA	30501	770-535-3553	718-5465
Northside Hospital 1000 Johnson Ferry Rd NE *Web:* www.northside.com	Atlanta	GA	30342	404-851-8000	250-1317
Oconee Regional Medical Center 821 N Cobb St *Web:* www.oconeeregional.com	Milledgeville	GA	31061	478-454-3500	454-3555
Palmyra Medical Centers 2000 Palmyra Rd *Web:* www.palmyramedicalcenters.com	Albany	GA	31701	229-434-2000	434-2563
Phoebe Putney Memorial Hospital 417 W 3rd Ave *TF:* 877-312-1167 ■ *Web:* www.phoebeputney.com	Albany	GA	31702	229-312-1000	312-4104
Piedmont Hospital 1968 Peachtree Rd NW *Web:* www.piedmonthospital.org	Atlanta	GA	30309	404-605-5000	609-6640
Redmond Regional Medical Center 501 Redmond Rd *Web:* www.redmondregional.com	Rome	GA	30165	706-291-0291	291-0971
Rockdale Medical Center 1412 Milstead Ave NE *Web:* www.rockdalemedicalcenter.org	Conyers	GA	30012	770-918-3000	918-3104
Saint Francis Hospital 2122 Manchester Expy *Web:* www.sfhga.com	Columbus	GA	31904	706-596-4000	596-4481
Saint Joseph Hospital 2260 Wrightsboro Rd *Fax: Admitting ■ *Web:* www.stjoshosp.org	Augusta	GA	30904	706-481-7000	481-7826*
Saint Joseph's Hospital 11705 Mercy Blvd *Web:* www.sjchs.org/	Savannah	GA	31419	912-819-4100	819-5188
Saint Joseph's Hospital of Atlanta 5665 Peachtree Dunwoody Rd NE *TF:* 800-678-5637 ■ *Web:* www.stjosephsatlanta.org	Atlanta	GA	30342	404-851-7001	851-7339
Saint Mary's Health Care System 1230 Baxter St *TF:* 800-233-7864 ■ *Web:* www.stmarysathens.org	Athens	GA	30606	706-389-3000	354-3197
South Georgia Medical Center 2501 N Patterson St *Web:* www.sgmc.org	Valdosta	GA	31602	229-333-1000	259-4136
Southeast Georgia Health System Brunswick Campus 2415 Parkwood Dr *Web:* www.sghs.org	Brunswick	GA	31520	912-466-7000	466-7013
Southern Regional Medical Center 11 Upper Riverdale Rd SW *Web:* www.southernregional.com	Riverdale	GA	30274	770-991-8000	909-2030
Spalding Regional Medical Center 601 S 8th St *Web:* www.spaldingregionalhosp.com	Griffin	GA	30224	770-228-2721	229-6953
Stephens County Hospital 2003 Falls Rd *Web:* www.stephenscountyhospital.com	Toccoa	GA	30577	706-282-4200	886-8045
Sumter Regional Hospital 100 Wheatley Dr *Web:* www.sumterregional.org	Americus	GA	31709	229-924-6011	924-1014
Tanner Medical Center 705 Dixie St *Web:* www.tanner.org	Carrollton	GA	30117	770-836-9666	838-8483
Tift Regional Medical Center 901 E 18th St *TF:* 800-648-1935 ■ *Web:* www.tiftregional.com	Tifton	GA	31794	229-382-7120	353-6192
University Health Care System 1350 Walton Way *Web:* universityhealth.org	Augusta	GA	30901	706-722-9011	774-4500
Upson Regional Medical Center 801 W Gordon St *Web:* www.urmc.org	Thomaston	GA	30286	706-647-8111	646-3310
Wayne Memorial Hospital 865 S 1st St *Web:* www.wmhweb.com	Jesup	GA	31545	912-427-6811	530-3495
Wellstar Cobb Hospital 3950 Austell Rd *Web:* www.wellstar.org	Austell	GA	30106	770-732-4000	732-3703
Wellstar Douglas Hospital 8954 Hospital Dr *Web:* www.wellstar.org	Douglasville	GA	30134	770-949-1500	920-6253
Wellstar Kennestone Hospital 677 Church St *Web:* www.wellstar.org	Marietta	GA	30060	770-793-5000	793-5918
West Georgia Medical Center 1514 Vernon Rd *TF:* 800-291-4418 ■ *Web:* www.wghs.org	LaGrange	GA	30240	706-882-1411	845-8918

Hawaii

Hospital	City	State	ZIP	Phone	Fax
Castle Medical Center 640 Ulukahiki St *Web:* www.castlemed.org	Kailua	HI	96734	808-263-5500	263-5143
Hilo Medical Center 1190 Waianuenue Ave *Web:* www.hmc.hhsc.org	Hilo	HI	96720	808-974-4700	974-4746
Kaiser Permanente Medical Center 3288 Moanalua Rd	Honolulu	HI	96819	808-432-0000	432-7736
Maui Memorial Hospital 221 Mahalani St *Web:* www.mmmc.hhsc.org	Wailuku	HI	96793	808-244-9056	243-4628
Queen's Medical Center 1301 Punchbowl St *Web:* www.queens.org	Honolulu	HI	96813	808-538-9011	537-7851
Saint Francis Medical Center 2230 Liliha St *Web:* www.stfrancishawaii.org/sfhs	Honolulu	HI	96817	808-547-6011	547-6611
Straub Clinic & Hospital 888 S King St *TF:* 800-232-9491 ■ *Web:* www.straubhealth.com	Honolulu	HI	96813	808-522-4000	522-4111
Wilcox Memorial Hospital 3420 Kuhio Hwy *Web:* www.wilcoxhealth.org/wilcox_hospital.html	Lihue	HI	96766	808-245-1100	245-1171

Idaho

Hospital	City	State	ZIP	Phone	Fax
Eastern Idaho Regional Medical Center 3100 Channing Way *Web:* www.eirmc.com	Idaho Falls	ID	83404	208-529-6111	529-7021
Kootenai Medical Center 2003 Lincoln Way *Web:* www.kmc.org	Coeur d'Alene	ID	83814	208-666-2000	666-3299
Magic Valley Regional Medical Center 650 Addison Ave W *TF:* 800-947-4852 ■ *Web:* www.mvrmc.com	Twin Falls	ID	83301	208-737-2000	737-2129
Mercy Medical Center 1512 12th Avenue Rd *Web:* www.mercynampa.org	Nampa	ID	83686	208-467-1171	463-5068
Portneuf Medical Center 651 Memorial Dr *Web:* www.portmed.org	Pocatello	ID	83201	208-239-1000	239-1934
Saint Alphonsus Regional Medical Center 1055 N Curtis Rd *TF:* 877-341-2121 ■ *Web:* www.saintalphonsus.org	Boise	ID	83706	208-367-2121	
Saint Joseph Regional Medical Center 415 6th St *Web:* www.sjrmc.org	Lewiston	ID	83501	208-743-2511	799-5528
Saint Luke's Regional Medical Center 190 E Bannock St *Web:* www.slrmc.org	Boise	ID	83712	208-381-2222	381-2861
West Valley Medical Center 1717 Arlington Ave *TF:* 800-937-8860 ■ *Web:* www.westvalleymedctr.com	Caldwell	ID	83605	208-459-4641	455-3717

Illinois

Hospital	City	State	ZIP	Phone	Fax
Advocate Bethany Hospital 3435 W Van Buren St *Web:* www.advocatehealth.com/beth	Chicago	IL	60624	773-265-7700	265-3605
Advocate Christ Medical Center 4440 W 95th St *Web:* www.advocatehealth.com/cmc/	Oak Lawn	IL	60453	708-684-8000	684-5012
Advocate Good Samaritan Hospital 3815 Highland Ave *Web:* www.advocatehealth.com/gsam	Downers Grove	IL	60515	630-275-5900	963-8605
Advocate Good Shepherd Hospital 450 W Hwy 22 *Web:* www.advocatehealth.com/gshp	Barrington	IL	60010	847-381-9600	381-8074
Advocate Illinois Masonic Medical Center 836 W Wellington Ave *Web:* www.advocatehealth.com/immc	Chicago	IL	60657	773-975-1600	296-5251
Advocate Lutheran General Hospital 1775 W Dempster St *Web:* www.advocatehealth.com/luth	Park Ridge	IL	60068	847-723-2210	723-2285
Advocate South Suburban Hospital 17800 S Kedzie Ave *Web:* www.advocatehealth.com/ssub	Hazel Crest	IL	60429	708-799-8000	213-0100
Advocate Trinity Hospital 2320 E 93rd St *Web:* www.advocatehealth.com/trin	Chicago	IL	60617	773-967-2000	967-4191
Alexian Brothers Medical Center 800 Biesterfield Rd *Web:* www.alexian.org	Elk Grove Village	IL	60007	847-437-5500	981-5774
Alton Memorial Hospital 1 Memorial Dr *Web:* www.altonmemorialhospital.org	Alton	IL	62002	618-463-7311	463-7723
Anderson Hospital 6800 SR 162 *Web:* www.andersonhospital.org	Maryville	IL	62062	618-288-5711	288-4088
Blessing Hospital Broadway at 11th St *Web:* www.blessinghospital.org	Quincy	IL	62301	217-223-5811	223-6891
BroMenn Regional Medical Center 1304 Franklin Ave *Web:* www.bromenn.org/bromennregional	Normal	IL	61761	309-454-1400	454-0103
Carle Foundation Hospital 611 W Park St *Web:* www.carle.com	Urbana	IL	61801	217-383-3311	383-3018
Centegra Memorial Medical Center 3701 Doty Road *TF:* 877-236-8347 ■ *Web:* www.centegra.org	Woodstock	IL	60098	815-338-2500	334-3948
Centegra Northern Illinois Medical Center 4201 Medical Ctr Dr *Web:* www.centegra.org	McHenry	IL	60050	815-344-5000	759-4387
Central DuPage Hospital 25 N Winfield Rd *TF:* 877-933-1600 ■ *Web:* www.cdh.org	Winfield	IL	60190	630-933-1600	933-2729
CGH Medical Center 100 E LeFevre Rd *Web:* www.cghmc.com	Sterling	IL	61081	815-625-0400	625-4825
Community Hospital of Ottawa 1100 E Norris Dr *Web:* www.chottawa.org	Ottawa	IL	61350	815-433-3100	431-5500
Condell Medical Center 801 S Milwaukee Ave *Web:* www.condell.org	Libertyville	IL	60048	847-362-2900	362-1721
Decatur Memorial Hospital 2300 N Edward St *Web:* www.dmhcares.org	Decatur	IL	62526	217-877-8121	876-2125
Delnor-Community Hospital 300 Randall Rd *TF:* 800-835-2696 ■ *Web:* www.delnor.com	Geneva	IL	60134	630-208-3000	208-3478
Edward Hospital 801 S Washington St *Web:* www.edward.org	Naperville	IL	60540	630-355-0450	
Elmhurst Memorial Hospital 200 Berteau Ave *Web:* www.emhc.org	Elmhurst	IL	60126	630-833-1400	782-7801
Evanston Hospital 2650 Ridge Ave *Web:* www.enh.org	Evanston	IL	60201	847-570-2000	570-2940
FHN Memorial Hospital 1045 W Stephenson St *TF:* 800-747-4131 ■ *Web:* www.fhn.org	Freeport	IL	61032	815-599-6000	599-6868

General Hospitals - US (Cont'd)

Illinois (Cont'd)

Hospital	City	State	ZIP	Phone	Fax
Galesburg Cottage Hospital 695 N Kellogg St *Web:* www.cottagehospital.com	Galesburg	IL	61401	309-343-8131	343-2393
Gateway Regional Medical Center 2100 Madison Ave *TF:* 800-559-9992 ■ *Web:* www.gatewayregional.net	Granite City	IL	62040	618-798-3000	798-3508
Genesis Medical Center Illini Campus 801 Illini Dr *TF:* 800-250-6020 ■ *Web:* www.genesishealth.com	Silvis	IL	61282	309-792-9363	792-4274
GlenOaks Hospital 701 Winthrop Ave *Web:* www.keepingyouwell.com/facilities/glenoaks	Glendale Heights	IL	60139	630-545-8000	545-3920
Gottlieb Memorial Hospital 701 W North Ave *Web:* www.gottliebhospital.org	Melrose Park	IL	60160	708-681-3200	450-5058
Graham Hospital 210 W Walnut St *Web:* www.grahamhospital.org	Canton	IL	61520	309-647-5240	649-5101
Herrin Hospital 201 S 14th St *Web:* www.herrinhospital.org	Herrin	IL	62948	618-942-2171	351-4929
Highland Park Hospital 777 Park Ave W *Web:* www.enh.org	Highland Park	IL	60035	847-432-8000	432-9305
Hinsdale Hospital 120 N Oak St *Web:* www.keepingyouwell.com/facilities/hinsdale	Hinsdale	IL	60521	630-856-9000	856-2021
Holy Cross Hospital 2701 W 68th St *Web:* www.holycrosshospital.org	Chicago	IL	60629	773-884-9000	884-8001
Holy Family Medical Center 100 N River Rd *Web:* www.reshealth.org	Des Plaines	IL	60016	847-297-1800	297-1863
Illinois Valley Community Hospital 925 West St *Web:* www.ivch.org	Peru	IL	61354	815-223-3300	780-3714
Ingalls Memorial Hospital 1 Ingalls Dr *Web:* www.ingalls.org	Harvey	IL	60426	708-333-2300	915-6136
John H Stoger Hospital of Cook County 1969 W Ogden St *Web:* www.ccbhs.org	Chicago	IL	60612	312-864-6000	864-3070
Katherine Shaw Bethea Hospital 403 E 1st St *Web:* www.ksbhospital.com	Dixon	IL	61021	815-288-5531	285-5859
Kenneth Hall Regional Hospital 129 N 8th St *Web:* www.khrh.org	East Saint Louis	IL	62201	618-274-1900	482-7014
Kishwaukee Community Hospital 626 Bethany Rd *TF:* 800-397-1521 ■ *Web:* www.kishhospital.org	DeKalb	IL	60115	815-756-1521	756-7665
La Grange Memorial Hospital 5101 S Willow Springs Rd *Web:* www.keepingyouwell.com/Facilities/lagrange	La Grange	IL	60525	708-245-9000	245-5646
Lake Forest Hospital 660 N Westmoreland Rd *Web:* www.lakeforesthospital.com	Lake Forest	IL	60045	847-234-5600	535-7846
Lincoln Park Hospital 550 W Webster Ave *Web:* www.lincolnparkhospital.com	Chicago	IL	60614	773-883-3800	883-5168
Little Company of Mary Hospital & Health Care Centers 2800 W 95th St *Web:* lcmh.org	Evergreen Park	IL	60805	708-422-6200	425-9756
Loretto Hospital 645 S Central Ave *Web:* www.lorettohospital.org	Chicago	IL	60644	773-626-4300	626-2613
Louis A Weiss Memorial Hospital 4646 N Marine Dr *Web:* www.weisshospital.org	Chicago	IL	60640	773-878-8700	564-7703
Loyola University Medical Center 2160 S 1st Ave *TF:* 888-584-7888 ■ *Web:* www.luhs.org	Maywood	IL	60153	708-216-9000	216-6791
MacNeal Hospital 3249 S Oak Park Ave *TF:* 888-622-6325 ■ *Web:* www.macneal.com	Berwyn	IL	60402	708-795-9100	783-3489
Memorial Hospital 4500 Memorial Dr *Web:* www.memhosp.com	Belleville	IL	62226	618-233-7750	257-5658
Memorial Hospital of Carbondale 405 W Jackson St *Web:* www.sih.net	Carbondale	IL	62902	618-549-0721	529-0449
Memorial Medical Center 701 N 1st St *Web:* www.memorialmedical.com	Springfield	IL	62781	217-788-3000	788-5591
Mercy Hospital & Medical Center 2525 S Michigan Ave *Web:* www.mercy-chicago.org	Chicago	IL	60616	312-567-2000	567-7054
Methodist Hospital of Chicago 5025 N Paulina St *Web:* www.methodistchicago.org	Chicago	IL	60640	773-271-9040	989-1321
Methodist Medical Center of Illinois 221 NE Glen Oak Ave *Web:* www.mymethodist.net	Peoria	IL	61636	309-672-5522	672-4230
Michael Reese Hospital 2929 S Ellis Ave *Web:* www.michaelreesehospital.com	Chicago	IL	60616	312-791-2000	791-5111
Morris Hospital 150 W High St *Web:* www.morrishospital.org	Morris	IL	60450	815-942-2932	942-3154
Mount Sinai Hospital Medical Center of Chicago 1500 S Fairfield St *Web:* www.sinai.org	Chicago	IL	60608	773-542-2000	257-6943
Northwest Community Hospital 800 W Central Rd *Web:* www.nch.org	Arlington Heights	IL	60005	847-618-1000	618-5009
Northwestern Memorial Hospital 251 E Huron St *Web:* www.nmh.org	Chicago	IL	60611	312-908-2000	926-8111
Norwegian-American Hospital 1044 N Francisco St *Web:* www.n-ahs.org	Chicago	IL	60622	773-292-8200	278-3531
OSF Saint Anthony Medical Center 5666 E State St *TF:* 800-343-3185 ■ *Web:* www.osfhealth.com	Rockford	IL	61108	815-226-2000	395-5449
OSF Saint Francis Medical Center 530 NE Glen Oak Ave *TF:* 888-627-5673 ■ *Web:* www.osfsaintfrancis.org	Peoria	IL	61637	309-655-2000	655-2347
OSF Saint Joseph Medical Center 2200 E Washington St *Web:* www.osfstjoseph.org	Bloomington	IL	61701	309-662-3311	662-7143
OSF Saint Mary Medical Center 3333 N Seminary St *Web:* www.osfstmary.org	Galesburg	IL	61401	309-344-3161	344-9498
Our Lady of Resurrection Medical Center 5645 W Addison St *Web:* www.reshealth.org	Chicago	IL	60634	773-282-7000	794-7651
Palos Community Hospital 12251 S 80th Ave *Web:* www.paloscommunityhospital.org	Palos Heights	IL	60463	708-361-4500	923-4620
Passavant Area Hospital 1600 W Walnut St *Web:* www.passavanthospital.com	Jacksonville	IL	62650	217-245-9541	479-5613
Pekin Hospital 600 S 13th St *Web:* www.pekinhospital.org	Pekin	IL	61554	309-347-1151	353-0908
Proctor Hospital 5409 N Knoxville Ave *Web:* www.proctor.org	Peoria	IL	61614	309-691-1000	691-4543
Provena Covenant Medical Center 1400 W Park St *TF:* 800-245-6697 ■ *Web:* www.provenacovenant.org	Urbana	IL	61801	217-337-2000	337-4541
Provena Mercy Center 1325 N Highland Ave	Aurora	IL	60506	630-859-2222	859-9014
Provena Saint Joseph Medical Center 333 N Madison St *Web:* www.provenasaintjoe.org	Joliet	IL	60435	815-725-7133	741-7579
Provena Saint Mary's Hospital 500 W Court St *Web:* www.provenastmarys.com	Kankakee	IL	60901	815-937-2490	937-8772
Provena United Samaritans Medical Center 812 N Logan Ave *Web:* www.provenausmc.com	Danville	IL	61832	217-443-5000	443-1965
Resurrection Medical Center 7435 W Talcott Ave *Web:* www.reshealth.org	Chicago	IL	60631	773-774-8000	594-7971
Riverside Medical Center 350 N Wall St *Web:* www.riversidehealthcare.org	Kankakee	IL	60901	815-933-1671	935-7823
Rockford Memorial Hospital 2400 N Rockton Ave *Web:* www.rhsnet.org	Rockford	IL	61103	815-971-5000	968-4795
Roseland Community Hospital 45 W 111th St	Chicago	IL	60628	773-995-3000	995-1052
Rush-Copley Medical Center 2000 Ogden Ave *Web:* www.rushcopley.com	Aurora	IL	60504	630-978-6200	978-6888
Rush North Shore Medical Center 9600 Gross Point Rd *Web:* www.rnsmc.org	Skokie	IL	60076	847-677-9600	933-6012
Rush Oak Park Hospital 520 S Maple Ave *Web:* www.oakparkhospital.org	Oak Park	IL	60304	708-383-9300	660-6658
Rush University Medical Center 1653 W Congress Pkwy *Web:* www.rush.edu	Chicago	IL	60612	312-942-5000	942-3212
Saint Alexius Medical Center 1555 Barrington Rd *Web:* www.stalexius.org	Hoffman Estates	IL	60169	847-843-2000	490-2570
Saint Anthony's Health Center 1 St Anthony's Way PO Box 340 *Web:* www.sahc.org	Alton	IL	62002	618-465-2571	465-4569
Saint Anthony's Memorial Hospital 503 N Maple St *Web:* www.stanthonyshospital.org	Effingham	IL	62401	217-342-2121	347-1563
Saint Bernard Hospital & Health Care Center 326 W 64th St *Web:* www.stbernardhospital.com	Chicago	IL	60621	773-962-3900	602-3849
Saint Elizabeth Hospital 1431 N Claremont Ave **Fax Area Code:* 312 ■ *Web:* www.reshealth.org	Chicago	IL	60622	773-278-2000	850-5970*
Saint Elizabeth's Hospital 211 S 3rd St *Web:* www.steliz.org	Belleville	IL	62222	618-234-2120	222-4650
Saint Francis Hospital of Evanston 355 Ridge Ave *Web:* www.reshealth.org	Evanston	IL	60202	847-492-4000	316-4500
Saint Francis Hospital & Health Center 12935 S Gregory St *Web:* www.stfrancisblueisland.com	Blue Island	IL	60406	708-597-2000	389-9480
Saint James Hospital & Health Centers 1423 Chicago Rd *Web:* www.stjameshospital.org	Chicago Heights	IL	60411	708-756-1000	756-6863
Saint James Hospital & Health Centers Olympia Fields Campus 20201 S Crawford Ave *Web:* www.stjameshospital.org	Olympia Fields	IL	60461	708-747-4000	503-3270
Saint John's Hospital 800 E Carpenter St *Web:* www.st-johns.org	Springfield	IL	62769	217-544-6464	535-3989
Saint Joseph Hospital 77 N Airlite St *Web:* www.provenasaintjoseph.com	Elgin	IL	60123	847-695-3200	931-5511
Saint Joseph Hospital & Health Care Center 2900 N Lake Shore Dr *Web:* www.reshealth.org	Chicago	IL	60657	773-665-3000	665-3861
Saint Mary of Nazareth Hospital Center 2233 W Division St *Web:* www.reshealth.org	Chicago	IL	60622	312-770-2000	770-3391
Saint Mary's Good Samaritan 400 N Pleasant Ave *Web:* www.smgsi.com	Centralia	IL	62801	618-532-6731	436-8024
Saint Mary's Hospital 1800 E Lake Shore Dr *Web:* www.stmarys-hospital.com	Decatur	IL	62521	217-464-2966	464-1616
Sarah Bush Lincoln Health Center 1000 Health Center Dr *Web:* www.sarahbush.org	Mattoon	IL	61938	217-258-2525	258-4117
Sherman Hospital 934 Center St *Web:* www.shermanhealth.com	Elgin	IL	60120	847-742-9800	429-2035
Silver Cross Hospital 1200 Maple Rd *Web:* www.silvercross.org	Joliet	IL	60432	815-740-1100	740-7047
South Shore Hospital 8012 S Crandon Ave *Web:* www.southshorehospital.com	Chicago	IL	60617	773-768-0810	768-8154
Swedish Covenant Hospital 5145 N California Ave *Web:* www.schosp.org	Chicago	IL	60625	773-878-8200	878-6152
SwedishAmerican Hospital 1401 E State St *TF:* 800-642-2790 ■ *Web:* www.swedishamerican.org	Rockford	IL	61104	815-968-4400	966-3999
Thorek Memorial Hospital 850 W Irving Park Rd *Web:* www.thorek.org	Chicago	IL	60613	773-525-6780	975-6703
Touchette Regional Hospital 5900 Bond Ave *Web:* www.touchette.org	Centreville	IL	62207	618-332-3060	332-5256
Trinity Medical Center West Campus 2701 17th St *Web:* www.trinityqc.com	Rock Island	IL	61201	309-793-2121	779-2303
University of Chicago Hospitals 5841 S Maryland Ave *TF:* 800-289-6333 ■ *Web:* www.uchospitals.edu	Chicago	IL	60637	773-702-1000	702-4846
University of Illinois Medical Center 1740 W Taylor St *Web:* uillinoismedcenter.org	Chicago	IL	60612	312-996-7000	996-7049
Vista Medical Center 1324 N Sheridan Rd *Web:* www.vistahealth.com/stmcvmh/index.htm	Waukegan	IL	60085	847-360-3000	360-4109
Vista West Center 2615 Washington St *Web:* www.vistahealth.com/stmcvmh/index.htm	Waukegan	IL	60085	847-249-3900	360-4109
Weiss Louis A Memorial Hospital 4646 N Marine Dr *Web:* www.weisshospital.org	Chicago	IL	60640	773-878-8700	564-7703
West Suburban Hospital Medical Center 3 Erie Ct *Web:* www.westsub.com	Oak Park	IL	60302	708-383-6200	383-3159
Westlake Hospital 1225 W Lake St *Web:* westlakehospital.reshealth.org	Melrose Park	IL	60160	708-681-3000	938-7975

Indiana

Hospital	City	State	ZIP	Phone	Fax
Ball Memorial Hospital 2401 W University Ave *Web:* accesschs.org	Muncie	IN	47303	765-747-3111	741-2848
Bloomington Hospital 601 W 2nd St *Web:* www.bhhs.org	Bloomington	IN	47403	812-336-6821	353-9339
Clark Memorial Hospital 1220 Missouri Ave *Web:* www.clarkmemorial.org	Jeffersonville	IN	47130	812-282-6631	283-2688
Columbus Regional Hospital 2400 E 17th St *TF:* 800-841-4938 ■ *Web:* www.crh.org	Columbus	IN	47201	812-379-4441	376-5001
Community Hospital 901 Macarthur Blvd **Fax:* Admitting ■ *Web:* www.comhs.org	Munster	IN	46321	219-836-1600	836-4073*
Community Hospital of Anderson & Madison Counties 1515 N Madison Ave *TF:* 800-430-4774 ■ *Web:* www.communityanderson.com	Anderson	IN	46011	765-298-4242	298-5848
Community Hospital East 1500 N Ritter Ave *Web:* www.ecommunity.com/east	Indianapolis	IN	46219	317-355-1411	355-1668
Deaconess Hospital 600 Mary St *Web:* www.deaconess.com	Evansville	IN	47747	812-450-5000	450-2155
Dunn Memorial Hospital 1600 23rd St *Web:* www.dunnmemorial.org	Bedford	IN	47421	812-275-3331	276-1211
Elkhart General Hospital 600 East Blvd *Web:* www.egh.org	Elkhart	IN	46514	574-294-2621	523-3495
Fayette Memorial Hospital 1941 Virginia Ave *Web:* www.fayettememorial.org	Connersville	IN	47331	765-825-5131	827-7886
Floyd Memorial Hospital 1850 State St *TF:* 800-423-1513 ■ *Web:* www.floydmemorial.org	New Albany	IN	47150	812-944-7701	949-5607
Good Samaritan Hospital 520 S 7th St *Web:* www.gshvin.org	Vincennes	IN	47591	812-882-5220	885-3737
Hendricks Regional Health Danville 1000 E Main St *Web:* www.hendrickshospital.org	Danville	IN	46122	317-745-4451	745-8400
Henry County Memorial Hospital 1000 N 16th St *Web:* www.hcmhcares.org	New Castle	IN	47362	765-521-0890	521-1555
Howard Regional Health System Main Campus 3500 S Lafountain St *Web:* www.howardregional.org	Kokomo	IN	46902	765-453-0702	453-8087
Indiana University Hospital 550 N University Blvd *Web:* www.clarian.org	Indianapolis	IN	46202	317-274-5000	274-1088
Johnson Memorial Hospital 1125 W Jefferson St *Web:* www.johnsonmemorial.org	Franklin	IN	46131	317-736-3300	736-2692
King's Daughters' Hospital 1 King's Daughters' Dr *TF:* 800-272-5341 ■ *Web:* www.kingsdaughtershospital.org	Madison	IN	47250	812-265-5211	265-0680

Hospital	City	State	ZIP	Phone	Fax
La Porte Hospital 1007 Lincolnway *Web:* www.laportehealth.org	La Porte	IN	46350	219-326-1234	325-5403
Lafayette Home Hospital 2400 South St *TF:* 800-654-9410 ■ *Web:* www.homehospital.com	Lafayette	IN	47904	765-447-6811	423-6364
Lutheran Hospital of Indiana 7950 W Jefferson Blvd *TF:* 800-444-2001 ■ *Web:* www.lutheran-hosp.com	Fort Wayne	IN	46804	260-435-7001	435-7632
Marion General Hospital 441 N Wabash Ave *Web:* www.mgh.net	Marion	IN	46952	765-662-1441	651-7351
Memorial Hospital & Health Care Center 800 W 9th St *Web:* www.mhhcc.org	Jasper	IN	47546	812-482-2345	482-0302
Memorial Hospital of South Bend 615 N Michigan St *Web:* www.qualityoflife.org	South Bend	IN	46601	574-234-9041	647-3670
Methodist Hospital 600 Grant St *Web:* www.methodisthospitals.org	Gary	IN	46402	219-886-4000	886-4688
Methodist Hospital of Indiana 1701 N Senate Blvd *TF:* 800-248-1199 ■ *Web:* www.clarian.org	Indianapolis	IN	46202	317-962-2000	
Parkview Hospital 2200 Randallia Dr *TF:* 888-856-2522 ■ *Web:* www.parkview.com	Fort Wayne	IN	46805	260-373-4000	373-3620
Porter-Valparaiso Hospital Campus 814 La Porte Ave *Web:* www.porterhealth.org	Valparaiso	IN	46383	219-465-4600	263-7067
Reid Hospital & Health Care Services 1401 Chester Blvd *Web:* www.reidhosp.com	Richmond	IN	47374	765-983-3000	983-3219
Riverview Hospital 395 Westfield Rd *TF:* 800-523-6001 ■ *Web:* www.riverviewhospital.com	Noblesville	IN	46060	317-773-0760	776-7134
Saint Anthony Medical Center 1201 S Main St *Web:* www.stanthonymedicalcenter.com	Crown Point	IN	46307	219-738-2100	757-6242
Saint Anthony Memorial Health Center 301 W Homer St *TF:* 888-879-8511 ■ *Web:* www.samhc.org	Michigan City	IN	46360	219-879-8511	877-1409
Saint Catherine Hospital 4321 Fir St *Web:* www.comhs.org/stcatherine	East Chicago	IN	46312	219-392-1700	392-7002
Saint Elizabeth Hospital Medical Center 1501 Hartford St *TF:* 800-371-6011 ■ *Web:* www.glhsi.org	Lafayette	IN	47904	765-423-6011	423-6364
Saint Francis Hospital & Health Centers 1600 Albany St *Web:* www.stfrancishospitals.org	Beech Grove	IN	46107	317-787-3311	782-6731
Saint John's Health System 2015 Jackson St *Web:* www.stjohnshealthsystem.org	Anderson	IN	46016	765-649-2511	646-8504
Saint Joseph Hospital 700 Broadway *TF:* 800-755-5266 ■ *Web:* www.lutheranhealthnetwork.com	Fort Wayne	IN	46802	260-425-3000	425-3108
Saint Joseph Regional Medical Center 801 E La Salle Ave *Web:* www.sjmed.com	South Bend	IN	46617	574-237-7111	237-7077
Saint Joseph Regional Medical Center Mishawaka 215 W 4th St *Web:* www.sjmed.com	Mishawaka	IN	46544	574-259-2431	257-2831
Saint Margaret Mercy Healthcare Centers 5454 Hohman Ave *Web:* www.smmhc.com	Hammond	IN	46320	219-932-2300	933-2585
Saint Mary Medical Center 1500 S Lake Park Ave *Web:* www.comhs.org/stmary	Hobart	IN	46342	219-942-0551	947-6037
Saint Mary's Medical Center of Evansville 3700 Washington Ave *Web:* www.stmarys.org	Evansville	IN	47750	812-485-4000	485-7080
Saint Vincent Indianapolis Hospital 2001 W 86th St *TF:* 866-338-2345 ■ *Web:* www.stvincent.org	Indianapolis	IN	46260	317-338-2345	338-7005
Schneck Medical Center 411 W Tipton St *TF:* 800-234-9222 ■ *Web:* www.yourhospital.org	Seymour	IN	47274	812-522-2349	522-0792
Terre Haute Regional Hospital 3901 S 7th St *TF:* 800-678-8474 ■ *Web:* www.regionalhospital.com	Terre Haute	IN	47802	812-232-0021	237-9514
Union Hospital 1606 N 7th St *Web:* www.unionhospitalhealthgroup.org/union	Terre Haute	IN	47804	812-238-7000	238-7113
Wishard Health Services 1001 W 10th St *Web:* www.wishard.edu	Indianapolis	IN	46202	317-639-6671	630-7678

Iowa

Hospital	City	State	ZIP	Phone	Fax
Allen Memorial Hospital 1825 Logan Ave *Web:* www.allenhospital.org	Waterloo	IA	50703	319-235-3941	235-3906
Broadlawns Medical Center 1801 Hickman Rd *TF:* 800-373-2806 ■ *Web:* www.broadlawns.org	Des Moines	IA	50314	515-282-2200	282-5785
Covenant Medical Center 3421 W 9th St *Web:* www.covhealth.com	Waterloo	IA	50702	319-272-8000	272-7313
Edmundson Jennie Memorial Hospital 933 E Pierce St *Web:* www.bestcare.org	Council Bluffs	IA	51503	712-328-6000	396-6288
Finley Hospital 350 N Grandview Ave *TF:* 800-582-1891 ■ *Web:* www.finleyhospital.org	Dubuque	IA	52001	563-582-1881	589-2562
Genesis Medical Center 1227 E Rusholme St *Web:* www.genesishealth.com	Davenport	IA	52803	563-421-6000	421-6500
Great River Medical Center 1221 S Gear Ave *Web:* www.greatrivermedical.org	West Burlington	IA	52655	319-768-1000	768-3266
Iowa Lutheran Hospital 700 E University Ave *Web:* www.ihsdesmoines.org/body.cfm?id=27	Des Moines	IA	50316	515-263-5612	263-2205
Iowa Methodist Medical Center 1200 Pleasant St *Web:* www.ihsdesmoines.org	Des Moines	IA	50309	515-241-6212	241-5994
Jennie Edmundson Memorial Hospital 933 E Pierce St *Web:* www.bestcare.org	Council Bluffs	IA	51503	712-328-6000	396-6288
Keokuk Area Hospital 1600 Morgan St *Web:* www.keokukhealthsystems.org	Keokuk	IA	52632	319-524-7150	524-5317
Marshalltown Medical & Surgical Center 3 S 4th Ave *Web:* www.everydaychampions.org	Marshalltown	IA	50158	641-754-5151	754-5181
Mary Greeley Medical Center 1111 Duff Ave *Web:* www.mgmc.org	Ames	IA	50010	515-239-2011	239-2007
Mercy Hospital 800 Mercy Dr *Web:* www.alegent.com/mercy	Council Bluffs	IA	51503	712-328-5000	325-2425
Mercy Hospital 500 E Market St *Web:* www.mercyic.org	Iowa City	IA	52245	319-339-0300	339-3788
Mercy Medical Center 701 10th St SE *Web:* www.mercycare.org	Cedar Rapids	IA	52403	319-398-6011	398-6912
Mercy Medical Center 1111 6th Ave *TF:* 800-637-2993 ■ *Web:* www.mercydesmoines.org	Des Moines	IA	50314	515-247-3121	247-4259
Mercy Medical Center 250 Mercy Dr *Web:* www.mercydubuque.com	Dubuque	IA	52001	563-589-8000	589-8073
Mercy Medical Center 801 5th St *Web:* www.mercysiouxcity.com	Sioux City	IA	51101	712-279-2010	279-2034
Mercy Medical Center North Iowa 1000 4th St SW *TF:* 800-433-3883 ■ *Web:* www.mercynorthiowa.com	Mason City	IA	50401	641-422-7000	422-7827
Ottumwa Regional Health Center 1001 Pennsylvania Ave *TF:* 800-933-6742 ■ *Web:* www.orhc.com	Ottumwa	IA	52501	641-682-7511	684-2324
Saint Luke's Hospital 1026 A Ave NE *Web:* www.crstlukes.com	Cedar Rapids	IA	52402	319-369-7211	369-8105
Saint Luke's Regional Medical Center 2720 Stone Park Blvd *TF:* 800-352-4660 ■ *Web:* www.stlukes.org	Sioux City	IA	51104	712-279-3500	279-7958
Trinity Regional Medical Center 802 Kenyon Rd *Web:* www.trmc.org	Fort Dodge	IA	50501	515-573-3101	573-8710
University of Iowa Hospitals & Clinics 200 Hawkins Dr *Web:* www.uihealthcare.com	Iowa City	IA	52242	319-356-1616	356-3862

Kansas

Hospital	City	State	ZIP	Phone	Fax
Central Kansas Medical Center 3515 Broadway St *Web:* www.ckmc.org	Great Bend	KS	67530	620-792-2511	786-6298
Coffeyville Regional Medical Center 1400 W 4th St *TF:* 800-540-2762 ■ *Web:* www.crmcinc.com	Coffeyville	KS	67337	620-251-1200	252-1651
Hays Medical Center 2220 Canterbury Dr *TF:* 800-248-0073 ■ *Web:* www.haysmed.com	Hays	KS	67601	785-623-5000	623-2291
Hutchinson Hospital 1701 E 23rd Ave *TF:* 800-794-7212 ■ *Web:* www.hutchinsonhospital.com	Hutchinson	KS	67502	620-665-2000	513-3811
Lawrence Memorial Hospital 325 Maine St *TF:* 800-749-4144 ■ *Web:* www.lmh.org	Lawrence	KS	66044	785-749-6100	749-6126
Menorah Medical Center 5721 W 119th St *Web:* www.menorahmedicalcenter.com	Overland Park	KS	66209	913-498-6000	345-3716
Mercy Health Center Fort Scott 401 Woodland Hills Blvd *TF:* 877-336-3729 ■ *Web:* www.mercykansas.com	Fort Scott	KS	66701	620-223-2200	223-5327
Mount Carmel Medical Center 1102 E Centennial St *Web:* www.mtcarmel.org	Pittsburg	KS	66762	620-231-6100	232-0493
Newman Regional Health 1201 W 12th Ave *Web:* www.newmanrh.org	Emporia	KS	66801	620-343-6800	341-7801
Olathe Medical Center 20333 W 151st St *Web:* www.ohsi.com/organizations/omci/index.php	Olathe	KS	66061	913-791-4200	791-4313
Overland Park Regional Medical Center 10500 Quivira Rd *Web:* www.oprmc.com	Overland Park	KS	66215	913-541-5000	541-5035
Providence Medical Center 8929 Parallel Pkwy	Kansas City	KS	66112	913-596-4000	596-4098
Saint Catherine Hospital 401 E Spruce St *Web:* www.stcath-hosp.org	Garden City	KS	67846	620-272-2222	272-2566
Saint Francis Health Center 1700 SW 7th St *TF:* 800-444-2954 ■ *Web:* www.stfrancistopeka.org	Topeka	KS	66606	785-295-8000	295-5479
Salina Regional Health Center 400 S Santa Fe Ave *Web:* www.srhc.com	Salina	KS	67401	785-452-7000	452-6963
Shawnee Mission Medical Center 9100 W 74th St *Web:* www.shawneemission.org	Shawnee Mission	KS	66204	913-676-2000	676-7792
Stormont-Vail Regional Health Center 1500 SW 10th Ave *TF:* 800-432-2951 ■ *Web:* www.stormontvail.org	Topeka	KS	66604	785-354-6000	354-6926
University of Kansas Hospital 3901 Rainbow Blvd *Web:* www.kumed.com	Kansas City	KS	66160	913-588-1270	588-1280
Via Christi Regional Medical Center 929 N Saint Francis St *Web:* www.via-christi.org	Wichita	KS	67214	316-268-5000	291-7999
Wesley Medical Center 550 N Hillside St *TF:* 800-362-0288 ■ *Web:* www.wesleymc.com	Wichita	KS	67214	316-962-2000	962-7076
Western Plains Medical Complex 3001 N Ave A *Web:* www.westernplainsmc.com	Dodge City	KS	67801	620-225-8400	225-8403

Kentucky

Hospital	City	State	ZIP	Phone	Fax
ARH Regional Medical Center 100 Medical Center Dr *Web:* www.arh.org	Hazard	KY	41701	606-439-1331	439-6682
Baptist Hospital East 4000 Kresge Way *Web:* www.baptisteast.com	Louisville	KY	40207	502-897-8100	897-8500
Baptist Regional Medical Center 1 Trillium Way *Web:* www.baptistregional.com	Corbin	KY	40701	606-528-1212	523-8726
Central Baptist Hospital 1740 Nicholasville Rd *Web:* www.centralbap.com	Lexington	KY	40503	859-275-6100	260-6119
Ephraim McDowell Regional Medical Center 217 S 3rd St *TF:* 800-686-4121 ■ *Web:* www.emrmc.org	Danville	KY	40422	859-239-1000	239-6709
Frankfort Regional Medical Center 299 King's Daughters Dr *Web:* www.frankfortregional.com	Frankfort	KY	40601	502-875-5240	226-7936
Greenview Regional Hospital 1801 Ashley Cir *Web:* www.greenviewhospital.com	Bowling Green	KY	42104	270-793-1000	793-5205
Hardin Memorial Hospital 913 N Dixie Ave *Web:* www.hmh.net/hardin	Elizabethtown	KY	42701	270-737-1212	706-1141
Harlan ARH Hospital 81 Ballpark Rd *Web:* www.arh.org/harlan.htm	Harlan	KY	40831	606-573-8100	573-8200
Highlands Regional Medical Center 5000 KY Rt 321 *TF:* 800-533-4762 ■ *Web:* www.hrmc.org	Prestonsburg	KY	41653	606-886-8511	886-1316
Jackson Purchase Medical Center 1099 Medical Center Cir *TF:* 800-251-1099 ■ *Web:* www.jacksonpurchase.com	Mayfield	KY	42066	270-251-4100	251-4507
Jennie Stuart Medical Center 320 W 18th St PO Box 400 *TF:* 800-887-5762 ■ *Web:* www.jsmc.org	Hopkinsville	KY	42241	270-887-0100	887-0223
Jewish Hospital 200 Abraham Flexner Way *Web:* www.jhhs.org	Louisville	KY	40202	502-587-4011	587-4088
Kindred Hospital Louisville 1313 St Anthony Pl *Web:* www.kindredlouisville.com	Louisville	KY	40204	502-587-7001	587-0060
King's Daughters Medical Center 2201 Lexington Ave *Web:* www.kdmc.com	Ashland	KY	41101	606-327-4000	327-7532
Lake Cumberland Regional Hospital 305 Langdon St *Web:* www.lcrh.ky	Somerset	KY	42503	606-679-7441	678-9919
Lourdes Hospital 1530 Lone Oak Rd *Web:* www.ehealthconnection.com/regions/lourdes	Paducah	KY	42003	270-444-2444	444-2980
Meadowview Regional Medical Center 989 Medical Park Dr *Web:* www.meadowviewregional.com	Maysville	KY	41056	606-759-5311	759-5616
Medical Center at Bowling Green 250 Park St *Web:* www.mcbg.org	Bowling Green	KY	42101	270-781-2150	842-0765
Methodist Hospital 1305 N Elm St *TF:* 800-467-7766 ■ *Web:* www.methodisthospital.net	Henderson	KY	42420	270-827-7700	827-7402
Middlesboro Appalachian Regional Hospital 3600 W Cumberland Ave *Web:* www.arh.org/middlesboro	Middlesboro	KY	40965	606-242-1100	248-1018
Muhlenberg Community Hospital 440 Hopkinsville St *Web:* www.mchky.org	Greenville	KY	42345	270-338-8000	338-8278
Murray-Calloway County Hospital 803 Poplar St *Web:* www.murrayhospital.org	Murray	KY	42071	270-762-1100	767-3600
Norton Audubon Hospital 1 Audubon Plaza Dr *Web:* www.nortonhealthcare.com	Louisville	KY	40217	502-636-7111	636-7216
Norton Hospital 200 E Chestnut St *Web:* www.nortonhealthcare.com	Louisville	KY	40202	502-629-8000	629-6060
Norton Suburban Hospital 4001 Dutchmans Ln *Web:* www.nortonhealthcare.com	Louisville	KY	40207	502-893-1000	899-6131
Our Lady of Bellefonte Hospital 1000 St Christopher Dr *Web:* www.olbh.com	Ashland	KY	41101	606-833-3333	833-3593
Owensboro Medical Health Systems 811 E Parish Ave *Web:* www.omhs.org	Owensboro	KY	42303	270-688-2000	688-1492
Pikeville Medical Center 911 Bypass Rd *Web:* www.medicalleader.org	Pikeville	KY	41501	606-437-3500	432-9479
Pineville Community Hospital 850 Riverview Ave	Pineville	KY	40977	606-337-3051	337-4284
Regional Medical Center 900 Hospital Dr *TF:* 800-998-5100 ■ *Web:* www.troverfoundation.org/about/about_rmc	Madisonville	KY	42431	270-825-5100	825-5204
Saint Claire Regional Medical Center 222 Medical Cir *Web:* www.st-claire.org	Morehead	KY	40351	606-783-6500	783-6503
Saint Elizabeth Medical Center-North 401 E 20th St *TF:* 800-888-7362 ■ *Web:* www.stelizabeth.com	Covington	KY	41014	859-292-4000	292-4487
Saint Joseph Hospital 1 St Joseph Dr **Fax:* Admitting ■ *Web:* www.sjhlex.org	Lexington	KY	40504	859-313-1000	313-3000*

General Hospitals - US (Cont'd)

Kentucky (Cont'd)

	City	State	Zip	Phone	Fax
Saint Joseph Hospital East 150 N Eagle Creek Dr	Lexington	KY	40509	859-967-5000	967-5332
Web: www.sjhlex.org					
Saint Luke Hospital East 85 N Grand Ave	Fort Thomas	KY	41075	859-572-3100	572-2349
TF: 800-345-7151 ■ *Web:* www.health-alliance.com/hospitals/index.html					
Saint Luke Hospital West 7380 Turfway Rd	Florence	KY	41042	859-212-5200	212-4411
TF: 800-345-7151 ■ *Web:* www.health-alliance.com/hospitals/index.html					
Saints Mary & Elizabeth Hospital 1850 Bluegrass Ave	Louisville	KY	40215	502-361-6000	361-6799
Web: www.caritas.com					
Samaritan Hospital 310 S Limestone St	Lexington	KY	40508	859-252-6612	226-7154
Web: www.samaritanhospital.com					
Taylor Regional Hospital 1700 Old Lebanon Rd	Campbellsville	KY	42718	270-465-3561	465-3465
Web: www.tchosp.org					
TJ Samson Community Hospital 1301 N Race St	Glasgow	KY	42141	270-651-4444	651-4848
TF: 800-651-5635 ■ *Web:* www.tjsamson.org					
University of Kentucky Chandler Medical Center 800 Rose St	Lexington	KY	40536	859-323-5000	323-2044
Web: www.mc.uky.edu					
University of Louisville Hospital 545 S Jackson St	Louisville	KY	40202	502-562-3000	562-4368
Web: www.uoflhealthcare.org					
Western Baptist Hospital 2501 Kentucky Ave	Paducah	KY	42003	270-575-2100	575-2164
Web: www.westernbaptist.com					
Whitesburg Appalachian Regional Hospital 240 Hospital Rd	Whitesburg	KY	41858	606-633-3500	633-3652
Web: www.arh.org/whitesburg.htm					
Williamson ARH Hospital 260 Hospital Dr	South Williamson	KY	41503	606-237-1700	237-1701
TF: 800-283-9375 ■ *Web:* www.arh.org/Williamson					

Louisiana

	City	State	Zip	Phone	Fax
American Legion Hospital 1305 Crowley Rayne Hwy	Crowley	LA	70526	337-783-3222	788-6413
Web: www.alh.org					
Baton Rouge General Medical Center 3600 Florida Blvd	Baton Rouge	LA	70806	225-387-7000	381-6165*
*Fax: Admissions ■ *Web:* www.brgeneral.org					
CHRISTUS Bossier Medical Center 2105 Airline Dr	Bossier City	LA	71111	318-848-8000	681-4215
Web: www.christushealth.org					
CHRISTUS Schumpert Highland 1453 E Bert Kouns	Shreveport	LA	71105	318-798-4300	798-4375
Web: www.christusschumpert.org/maphighland.htm					
CHRISTUS Schumpert St Mary Place 1 St Mary Pl	Shreveport	LA	71101	318-681-4500	681-4177
Web: www.christusschumpert.org					
Dauterive Hospital 600 N Lewis St	New Iberia	LA	70563	337-365-7311	374-4104
Web: www.dauterivehospital.com					
Doctors' Hospital of Opelousas 3983 I-49 S Service Rd	Opelousas	LA	70570	337-948-2100	948-2173
Web: www.doctorshospital.com					
EA Conway Medical Center 4864 Jackson St	Monroe	LA	71201	318-330-7000	330-7591
Web: www.conway.lsuhsc.edu					
Earl K Long Medical Center 5825 Airline Hwy	Baton Rouge	LA	70805	225-358-1000	
East Jefferson General Hospital 4200 Houma Blvd	Metairie	LA	70006	504-454-4000	456-8151
Web: www.ejgh.org					
Glenwood Regional Medical Center 503 McMillan Rd	West Monroe	LA	71291	318-329-4200	329-4710
Web: www.grmc.com					
Huey P Long Medical Center 352 Hospital Blvd PO Box 5352	Pineville	LA	71361	318-448-0811	473-6360
Web: www.lsuhsc.edu/hcsd/hpl					
Iberia Medical Center 2315 E Main St	New Iberia	LA	70560	337-364-0441	374-7641
Web: www.iberiamedicalcenter.com					
Kenner Regional Medical Center 180 W Esplanade Ave	Kenner	LA	70065	504-468-8600	464-8062
Web: www.kennerregional.com					
Lafayette General Medical Center 1214 Coolidge Blvd	Lafayette	LA	70505	337-289-7991	289-8671
Web: www.lafayettegeneral.org					
Lake Charles Memorial Hospital 1701 Oak Park Blvd	Lake Charles	LA	70601	337-494-3000	494-3299
Web: www.lcmh.com					
Lakeview Regional Medical Center 95 E Fairway Dr	Covington	LA	70433	985-867-3800	867-4449
Web: www.lakeviewregional.com					
Lane Regional Medical Center 6300 Main St	Zachary	LA	70791	225-658-4000	658-4234
Web: www.lanermc.org					
Leonard J Chabert Medical Center 1978 Industrial Blvd	Houma	LA	70363	985-873-2200	873-1262
Louisiana State Health Sciences Center 1541 Kings Hwy	Shreveport	LA	71130	318-675-5000	675-5666
Web: www.sh.lsuhsc.edu					
Minden Medical Center 1 Medical Plaza	Minden	LA	71055	318-377-2321	371-5606
Web: www.mindenmedicalcenter.com					
Natchitoches Parish Hospital 501 Keyser Ave	Natchitoches	LA	71457	318-214-4200	214-4455
Web: www.natchitocheshospital.org					
North Oaks Medical Center 15790 Paul Vega MD Drive	Hammond	LA	70403	985-345-2700	230-6482
Web: www.northoaks.org					
Northern Louisiana Medical Center 401 E Vaughn St	Ruston	LA	71270	318-254-2100	254-2728
Web: www.northernlouisianamedicalcenter.com					
NorthShore Regional Medical Center 100 Medical Center Dr	Slidell	LA	70461	985-649-7070	646-5552
Web: www.northshoremedctr.com					
Ochsner Clinic Foundation Hospital 1516 Jefferson Hwy	New Orleans	LA	70121	504-842-3000	842-2152
TF: 800-928-6247 ■ *Web:* www.ochsner.org					
Ochsner Medical Center Baton Rouge 17000 Medical Center Dr	Baton Rouge	LA	70816	225-752-2470	755-4891*
*Fax: Admissions ■ *Web:* www.ochsner.org					
Ochsner Medical Center West Bank 2500 Belle Chasse Hwy	Gretna	LA	70056	504-392-3131	391-5490
Web: www.ochsner.org					
Opelousas General Health System 1233 Wayne Gilmore Cir	Opelousas	LA	70570	337-948-3011	948-5126
Web: www.opelousasgeneral.com					
Our Lady of the Lake Regional Medical Center 5000 Hennessy Blvd	Baton Rouge	LA	70808	225-765-6565	765-5290*
*Fax: Admissions ■ *Web:* www.ololrmc.com					
Our Lady of Lourdes Regional Medical Center 611 Saint Landry St	Lafayette	LA	70506	337-289-2000	289-2574
Web: www.lourdes.net					
Rapides Regional Medical Center 211 4th St	Alexandria	LA	71301	318-473-3000	449-7575
Web: www.rapidesregional.com					
Saint Francis Medical Center 309 Jackson St	Monroe	LA	71201	318-327-4000	327-4142
Web: www.stfran.com					
Saint Francis North Hospital 3421 Medical Park Dr	Monroe	LA	71203	318-388-1946	388-7878
Web: www.stfran.com					
Saint Patrick Hospital of Lake Charles 524 S Ryan St	Lake Charles	LA	70601	337-436-2511	491-7157
Web: www.stpatrickhospital.org					
Saint Tammany Parish Hospital 1202 S Tyler St	Covington	LA	70433	985-898-4000	898-4491
Web: www.stph.org					
Savoy Medical Center 801 Poinciana Ave	Mamou	LA	70554	337-468-5261	468-3342
Web: www.savoymedical.com					
Slidell Memorial Hospital 1001 Gause Blvd	Slidell	LA	70458	985-643-2200	649-8626
Web: www.smhplus.org					
Teche Regional Medical Center 1125 Marguerite St	Morgan City	LA	70380	985-384-2200	380-4546
Web: www.techeregional.com					
Terrebonne General Medical Center 8166 Main St	Houma	LA	70360	985-873-4141	873-4640
TF: 800-456-9121 ■ *Web:* www.tgmc.com					
Thibodaux Regional Medical Center 602 N Acadia Rd	Thibodaux	LA	70301	985-447-5500	446-5033
TF: 800-822-8442 ■ *Web:* www.thibodaux.com					
Touro Infirmary 1401 Foucher St	New Orleans	LA	70115	504-897-7011	897-8769
Web: www.touro.com					
Tulane University Hospital & Clinic 1415 Tulane Ave	New Orleans	LA	70112	504-588-5263	988-7973
TF: 800-588-5800 ■ *Web:* www.tuhc.com					
University Hospital 2021 Perdido St	New Orleans	LA	70112	504-903-3000	903-6207
Web: www.mclno.org					
University Medical Center 2390 W Congress St	Lafayette	LA	70506	337-261-6000	261-6003
West Calcasieu Cameron Hospital 701 E Cypress St	Sulphur	LA	70663	337-527-7034	527-4164
Web: www.wcch.com					
West Jefferson Medical Center 1101 Medical Center Blvd	Marrero	LA	70072	504-347-5511	349-6299
Web: www.wjmc.org					
Willis-Knighton Medical Center 2600 Greenwood Rd	Shreveport	LA	71103	318-212-4000	212-4956
Web: www.wkmc.com/wik					

Maine

	City	State	Zip	Phone	Fax
Aroostook Medical Center 140 Academy St	Presque Isle	ME	04769	207-768-4900	768-4116
Web: www.tamc.org					
Central Maine Medical Center 300 Main St	Lewiston	ME	04240	207-795-0111	795-2303
Web: www.cmmc.org					
Eastern Maine Medical Center 489 State St	Bangor	ME	04401	207-973-7000	973-7348
Web: emmc.org/default.htm					
Maine General Medical Center 6 E Chestnut St	Augusta	ME	04330	207-626-1000	626-1549
Web: www.mainegeneral.org					
Maine Medical Center 22 Bramhall St	Portland	ME	04102	207-871-0111	662-6027
Web: www.mmc.org					
Brighton Campus 335 Brighton Ave	Portland	ME	04102	207-662-8000	662-8198
Mercy Hospital 144 State St	Portland	ME	04101	207-879-3000	879-3429
Web: www.mercyhospital.com					
Mid Coast Hospital 123 Medical Center Dr	Brunswick	ME	04011	207-729-0181	373-6195
TF: 877-729-0181 ■ *Web:* www.midcoasthealth.com					
Penobscot Bay Medical Center 6 Glen Cove Dr	Rockport	ME	04856	207-596-8000	593-5287
Web: www.penbayhealthcare.org					
Saint Joseph Hospital 360 Broadway	Bangor	ME	04401	207-262-1000	262-1240
Web: www.stjoseph-me.org					
Saint Mary's Regional Medical Center PO Box 291	Lewiston	ME	04243	207-777-8100	777-8800
Web: www.stmarysmaine.com					
Southern Maine Medical Center 1 Medical Center Dr	Biddeford	ME	04005	207-283-7000	283-7020
Web: www.smmc.org					

Maryland

	City	State	Zip	Phone	Fax
Anne Arundel Medical Center 2001 Medical Pkwy	Annapolis	MD	21401	443-481-1000	481-1313
Web: www.aahs.org					
Baltimore Washington Medical Center 301 Hospital Dr	Glen Burnie	MD	21061	410-787-4000	766-4036
Web: bwmc.umms.org					
Braddock Hospital Campus 900 Seton Dr	Cumberland	MD	21502	301-723-4200	723-5583
Web: www.wmhs.com					
Carroll Hospital Center 200 Memorial Ave	Westminster	MD	21157	410-848-3000	871-7474
Web: www.ccgh.com					
Civista Medical Center 701 E Charles St	La Plata	MD	20646	301-609-4000	609-4037
TF: 800-422-8585 ■ *Web:* www.civista.org					
Doctors Community Hospital 8118 Good Luck Rd	Lanham	MD	20706	301-552-8118	552-9306
Web: www.dchweb.org					
Franklin Square Hospital Center 9000 Franklin Square Dr	Baltimore	MD	21237	443-777-7000	777-7904
Web: www.medstarhealth.org					
Frederick Memorial Hospital 400 W 7th St	Frederick	MD	21701	240-566-3300	566-3666*
*Fax: Admitting ■ *Web:* www.fmh.org					
Good Samaritan Hospital of Maryland 5601 Loch Raven Blvd	Baltimore	MD	21239	410-532-8000	532-4599
Web: www.medstarhealth.org					
Greater Baltimore Medical Center 6701 N Charles St	Baltimore	MD	21204	443-849-2000	849-8679
Web: www.gbmc.org					
Harbor Hospital Center 3001 S Hanover St	Baltimore	MD	21225	410-350-3200	354-4440
Web: www.harborhospital.org					
Harford Memorial Hospital 501 S Union Ave	Havre de Grace	MD	21078	443-843-5000	
Web: www.uchs.org/hospitals/harfordmemorial.cfm					
Holy Cross Hospital 1500 Forest Glen Rd	Silver Spring	MD	20910	301-754-7000	754-7012
Web: www.holycrosshealth.org					
Howard County General Hospital 5755 Cedar Ln	Columbia	MD	21044	410-740-7890	740-7610
Web: www.hcgh.org					
Johns Hopkins Bayview Medical Center 4940 Eastern Ave	Baltimore	MD	21224	410-550-0100	550-7996
Web: www.hopkinsbayview.org					
Johns Hopkins Hospital 600 N Wolfe St	Baltimore	MD	21287	410-955-5000	502-5392
Web: www.hopkinsmedicine.org/hopkinshospital					
Laurel Regional Hospital 7300 Van Dusen Rd	Laurel	MD	20707	301-725-4300	497-7953
Web: www.dimensionshealth.org/lrh.shtml					
Maryland General Hospital 827 Linden Ave	Baltimore	MD	21201	410-225-8000	462-5834
Web: www.marylandgeneral.org					
Memorial Hospital at Easton 219 S Washington St	Easton	MD	21601	410-822-1000	822-7834
Web: www.shorehealth.org/about					
Mercy Medical Center 301 St Paul Pl	Baltimore	MD	21202	410-332-9000	962-1303
TF: 800-636-3729 ■ *Web:* www.mercymed.com					
Montgomery General Hospital 18101 Prince Philip Dr	Olney	MD	20832	301-774-8882	774-8886
Web: www.montgomerygeneral.com					
Northwest Hospital Center 5401 Old Court Rd	Randallstown	MD	21133	410-521-2200	521-7977
TF: 800-654-4677 ■ *Web:* www.lifebridgehealth.org/northwesthospital					
Peninsula Regional Medical Center 100 E Carroll St	Salisbury	MD	21801	410-546-6400	543-7102
TF: 800-543-7780 ■ *Web:* www.peninsula.org					
Prince George's Hospital Center 3001 Hospital Dr	Cheverly	MD	20785	301-618-2000	618-3966
Web: www.dimensionshealth.org/pghc.shtml					
Saint Agnes HealthCare 900 Caton Ave	Baltimore	MD	21229	410-368-6000	368-2109
TF: 800-875-8750 ■ *Web:* www.stagnes.org					
Saint Joseph Medical Center 7601 Osler Dr	Towson	MD	21204	410-337-1000	337-4860
Web: www.sjmcmd.org					
Saint Mary's Hospital 25500 Point Lookout Rd PO Box 527	Leonardtown	MD	20650	301-475-8981	475-5388
TF: 800-222-1764 ■ *Web:* www.smhwecare.com					
Shady Grove Adventist Hospital 9901 Medical Center Dr	Rockville	MD	20850	301-279-6000	217-5301
Web: www.adventisthealthcare.com/SGAH					
Sinai Hospital of Baltimore 2401 W Belvedere Ave	Baltimore	MD	21215	410-601-9000	601-8356
TF: 800-444-8233 ■ *Web:* www.sinai-balt.com					
Southern Maryland Hospital Center 7503 Surratts Rd	Clinton	MD	20735	301-868-8000	868-1368
Web: www.southernmarylandhospital.com					
Suburban Hospital 8600 Old Georgetown Rd	Bethesda	MD	20814	301-896-3100	897-1330
Web: www.suburbanhospital.org					
Union Hospital 106 Bow St	Elkton	MD	21921	410-398-4000	620-1494
Web: www.uhcc.com					
Union Memorial Hospital 201 E University Pkwy	Baltimore	MD	21218	410-554-2000	554-2652
Web: www.unionmemorial.org					
University of Maryland Medical Center 22 S Greene St	Baltimore	MD	21201	410-328-8667	
TF: 800-787-6363 ■ *Web:* www.umm.edu/center					

	City	State	Zip	Phone	Fax
Upper Chesapeake Medical Center 500 Upper Chesapeake Dr.	Bel Air	MD	21014	443-643-1000	643-1345
Web: www.uchs.org/hospitals/upperchesapeake.cfm					
Washington Adventist Hospital 7600 Carroll Ave	Takoma Park	MD	20912	301-891-7600	891-5991
Web: www.adventisthealthcare.com					
Washington County Hospital 251 E Antietam St	Hagerstown	MD	21740	301-790-8000	790-4980
Web: www.washingtoncountyhospital.com					
Western Maryland Health System Memorial Campus					
600 Memorial Ave	Cumberland	MD	21502	301-777-4000	723-4045
TF: 877-852-7400 ■ *Web:* www.wmhs.com					

Massachusetts

	City	State	Zip	Phone	Fax
Anna Jaques Hospital 25 Highland Ave	Newburyport	MA	01950	978-463-1000	463-1250
Web: www.ajh.org					
Baystate Medical Center 759 Chestnut St	Springfield	MA	01199	413-784-0000	794-2722
Web: www.baystatehealth.com/bmc					
Berkshire Medical Center 725 North St	Pittsfield	MA	01201	413-447-2000	447-2206
Web: www.berkshirehealthsystems.com/location_services.asp?ID=509					
Beth Israel Deaconess Medical Center 330 Brookline Ave	Boston	MA	02215	617-667-8000	754-2224
Web: www.bidmc.harvard.edu					
Beverly Hospital 85 Herrick St	Beverly	MA	01915	978-922-3000	921-7010
Web: www.beverlyhospital.com					
Boston Medical Center 1 Boston Medical Center Pl	Boston	MA	02118	617-638-8000	638-6905
Web: www.bmc.org					
Brockton Hospital 680 Centre St	Brockton	MA	02302	508-941-7000	941-6201
Web: www.brocktonhospital.com					
Cambridge Hospital 1493 Cambridge St	Cambridge	MA	02139	617-498-1000	665-1003
Web: www.challiance.org					
Cape Cod Hospital 27 Park St	Hyannis	MA	02601	508-771-1800	862-7337
Web: www.capecodhealth.org/capecodhospital					
Caritas Carney Hospital 2100 Dorchester Ave	Boston	MA	02124	617-296-4000	296-4033
Web: www.healthcaresource.com/CARNEY					
Caritas Norwood Hospital 800 Washington St	Norwood	MA	02062	781-769-4000	278-6810
Web: www.caritasnorwood.org					
Charlton Memorial Hospital 363 Highland Ave	Fall River	MA	02720	508-679-3131	679-7692
Web: www.southcoast.org/services/charlton.html					
Cooley Dickinson Hospital 30 Locust St	Northampton	MA	01060	413-582-2000	582-2867
Web: www.cooley-dickinson.org					
Emerson Hospital 133 ORNAC	Concord	MA	01742	978-369-1400	287-3655
Web: www.emersonhospital.org					
Falmouth Hospital 100 Ter Heun Dr	Falmouth	MA	02540	508-548-5300	457-3576
Web: www.capecodhealth.org/falmouthhospital					
Faulkner Hospital 1153 Centre St	Jamaica Plain	MA	02130	617-983-7000	524-8663
Web: www.faulknerhospital.org					
Franklin Medical Center 164 High St	Greenfield	MA	01301	413-772-0211	773-2693
Web: www.baystatehealth.com					
Good Samaritan Medical Center 235 N Pearl St	Brockton	MA	02301	508-427-3000	427-3010
Web: www.caritasgoodsam.org					
Harrington Memorial Hospital 100 South St	Southbridge	MA	01550	508-765-9771	765-3147
Web: www.harringtonhospital.org					
HealthAlliance Leominster Hospital 60 Hospital Rd	Leominster	MA	01453	978-537-4811	466-2200
Web: www.umassmemorial.org/ummhc/hospitals/alliance					
Heywood Hospital 242 Green St	Gardner	MA	01440	978-632-3420	630-6529
Web: www.heywood.org					
Holy Family Hospital & Medical Center 70 East St	Methuen	MA	01844	978-687-0151	688-7689
Web: www.holyfamilyhosp.org					
Holyoke Medical Center 575 Beech St	Holyoke	MA	01040	413-534-2500	534-2633
Web: www.holyokehealth.com					
Jordan Hospital 275 Sandwich St	Plymouth	MA	02360	508-746-2001	830-1131
Web: www.jordanhospital.org					
Lahey Clinic 41 Mall Rd	Burlington	MA	01805	781-744-5100	744-5210
TF: 800-524-3955 ■ *Web:* www.lahey.org					
Lawrence General Hospital 1 General St	Lawrence	MA	01842	978-683-4000	946-8199
Web: www.lawrencegeneral.org					
Lawrence Memorial Hospital of Medford 170 Governors Ave	Medford	MA	02155	781-306-6000	306-6361
Web: www.hallmarkhealth.org					
Lowell General Hospital 295 Varnum Ave	Lowell	MA	01854	978-937-6000	937-6103
Web: www.lowellgeneral.org					
Massachusetts General Hospital 55 Fruit St	Boston	MA	02114	617-726-2000	726-2093
Web: www.mgh.harvard.edu					
Melrose-Wakefield Hospital 585 Lebanon St	Melrose	MA	02176	781-979-3000	979-3015
Web: www.hallmarkhealth.org/melrose.php					
Mercy Medical Center 271 Carew St	Springfield	MA	01104	413-748-9000	781-7217
Web: www.mercycares.com					
Merrimack Valley Hospital 140 Lincoln Ave	Haverhill	MA	01830	978-374-2000	521-8138
Web: www.merrimackvalleyhospital.com					
MetroWest Medical Center 115 Lincoln St	Framingham	MA	01702	508-383-1000	383-1166
Web: www.mwmc.com					
Leonard Morse Campus 67 Union St	Natick	MA	01760	508-650-7000	650-7777
Web: www.mwmc.com					
Milford Regional Medical Center 14 Prospect St	Milford	MA	01757	508-473-1190	473-2744
Web: www.milfordregional.org					
Milton Hospital 199 Reedsdale Rd	Milton	MA	02186	617-696-4600	313-1565
Web: www.miltonhospital.org					
Morton Hospital & Medical Center 88 Washington St	Taunton	MA	02780	508-828-7000	824-6947
Web: www.mortonhospital.org					
Mount Auburn Hospital 330 Mt Auburn St	Cambridge	MA	02238	617-492-3500	499-5654
Web: www.mountauburn.caregroup.org					
New England Baptist Hospital 125 Parker Hill Ave	Boston	MA	02120	617-754-5800	754-6397
TF: 800-340-6324 ■ *Web:* www.nebh.org					
Newton-Wellesley Hospital 2014 Washington St	Newton	MA	02462	617-243-6000	243-6954
Web: www.nwh.org					
North Adams Regional Hospital 71 Hospital Ave	North Adams	MA	01247	413-663-3701	664-5197
Web: www.nbhealth.org					
North Shore Medical Center 81 Highland Ave	Salem	MA	01970	978-741-1200	
Web: www.nsmc.partners.org					
Quincy Medical Center 114 Whitwell St	Quincy	MA	02169	617-773-6100	376-1604
Web: www.quincymc.org					
Saint Anne's Hospital 795 Middle St	Fall River	MA	02721	508-674-5741	235-5647
Web: www.saintanneshospital.org					
Saint Elizabeth's Medical Center 736 Cambridge St	Brighton	MA	02135	617-789-3000	562-7568
Web: www.semc.org					
Saint Luke's Hospital of New Bedford 101 Page St	New Bedford	MA	02740	508-997-1515	979-8115
TF: 800-245-8537 ■ *Web:* www.southcoast.org/stlukes/					
Saint Vincent Hospital-Worcester Medical Center					
123 Summer St	Worcester	MA	01608	508-363-5000	363-5387
TF: 800-370-6300 ■ *Web:* www.stvincenthospital.com					
Saints Memorial Medical Center 1 Hospital Dr	Lowell	MA	01852	978-458-1411	934-8566
Web: www.saints-memorial.org					
South Shore Hospital 55 Fogg Rd	South Weymouth	MA	02190	781-340-8000	337-3768
TF: 800-472-3434 ■ *Web:* www.sshosp.org					
Sturdy Memorial Hospital 211 Park St	Attleboro	MA	02703	508-222-5200	236-8409
Web: www.sturdymemorial.org					
Tufts-New England Medical Center 750 Washington St	Boston	MA	02111	617-636-5000	636-7623
TF: 866-636-5001 ■ *Web:* www.nemc.org					
UMass Memorial Medical Center					
Memorial Campus 119 Belmont St	Worcester	MA	01605	508-334-1000	334-5049
Web: www.umassmemorial.org					
University Campus 55 Lake Ave N	Worcester	MA	01655	508-334-1000	856-1825
Web: www.umassmemorial.org					
Union Hospital 500 Lynnfield St	Lynn	MA	01904	781-581-9200	477-3840
Whidden Memorial Hospital 103 Garland St	Everett	MA	02149	617-389-6270	389-3883
Web: www.challiance.org/locations/locations.shtml					
Winchester Hospital 41 Highland Ave	Winchester	MA	01890	781-729-9000	756-2923
Web: www.winchesterhospital.org					

Michigan

	City	State	Zip	Phone	Fax
Alpena Regional Medical Center 1501 W Chisholm St	Alpena	MI	49707	989-356-7390	356-7305
Web: www.agh.org					
Battle Creek Health System Main Campus 300 North Ave	Battle Creek	MI	49008	269-966-8000	966-8010
Web: www.bchealth.com					
Bay Regional Medical Center 1900 Columbus Ave	Bay City	MI	48708	989-894-3000	894-3808
TF: 800-726-0666 ■ *Web:* www.baymed.org					
Bixby Medical Center 818 Riverside Ave	Adrian	MI	49221	517-263-0711	263-1839
Web: www.promedica.org					
Bon Secours Hospital 468 Cadieux Rd	Grosse Pointe	MI	48230	313-343-1000	343-1185
Web: bonsecourscottage.org					
Borgess Medical Center 1521 Gull Rd	Kalamazoo	MI	49048	269-226-7000	226-5966
Web: www.borgess.com					
Botsford General Hospital 28050 Grand River Ave	Farmington Hills	MI	48336	248-471-8000	471-8896
Web: www.botsfordsystem.org					
Bronson Methodist Hospital 601 John St	Kalamazoo	MI	49007	269-341-7654	341-8314
TF: 800-276-6766 ■ *Web:* www.bronsonhealth.com					
Chelsea Community Hospital 775 S Main St	Chelsea	MI	48118	734-475-1311	475-4066
Web: www.cch.org					
Community Health Center of Branch County					
274 E Chicago St	Coldwater	MI	49036	517-279-5400	279-7140
TF: 888-774-1471 ■ *Web:* www.chcbc.com					
Cottage Hospital 159 Kercheval Ave	Grosse Pointe Farms	MI	48236	313-640-1000	640-2507
Web: bonsecourscottage.org					
Covenant Medical Center Cooper 700 Cooper Ave	Saginaw	MI	48602	989-583-7080	583-6314*
**Fax:* Admitting ■ *Web:* www.covenanthealthcare.com					
Covenant Medical Center Harrison 1447 N Harrison St	Saginaw	MI	48602	989-583-4803	583-4784
Web: www.covenanthealthcare.com					
Crittenton Hospital 1101 W University Dr	Rochester Hills	MI	48307	248-652-5000	652-5424
Web: www.crittenton.com					
Detroit Receiving Hospital & University Health Center					
4201 St Antoine Blvd	Detroit	MI	48201	313-745-3100	745-3455
Web: www.drhuhc.org					
Dickinson County Healthcare System					
1721 S Stephenson Ave	Iron Mountain	MI	49801	906-774-1313	776-5427
Web: www.dchs.org					
Foote Health System 205 N East Ave	Jackson	MI	49201	517-788-4800	788-4829
Web: www.foote.com					
Ford Henry Hospital 2799 W Grand Blvd	Detroit	MI	48202	313-916-2600	916-8200
TF: 800-999-4340 ■ *Web:* www.henryfordhealth.org					
Ford Henry Wyandotte Hospital 2333 Biddle Ave	Wyandotte	MI	48192	734-284-2400	246-6904
Web: www.henryfordwyandotte.com					
Garden City Hospital 6245 Inkster Rd	Garden City	MI	48135	734-421-3300	421-3342
Web: www.gchosp.org					
Genesys Regional Medical Center 1 Genesys Pkwy	Grand Blanc	MI	48439	810-606-5000	606-6605
TF: 888-606-6556 ■ *Web:* www.genesys.org					
Gratiot Community Hospital 300 E Warwick Dr	Alma	MI	48801	989-463-1101	463-6948
Web: www.gratiothealth.com					
Hackley Hospital 1700 Clinton St	Muskegon	MI	49442	231-726-3511	722-0739
TF: 800-825-4677 ■ *Web:* www.hackley.org					
Harper University Hospital 3990 John R St	Detroit	MI	48201	313-745-8040	745-1520
Web: www.harperhospital.org					
Henry Ford Bi-County Hospital 13355 E Ten-Mile Rd	Warren	MI	48089	586-759-7300	759-7357
TF: 800-423-1948					
Henry Ford Hospital 2799 W Grand Blvd	Detroit	MI	48202	313-916-2600	916-8200
TF: 800-999-4340 ■ *Web:* www.henryfordhealth.org					
Henry Ford Macomb Hospital 15855 19-Mile Rd	Clinton Township	MI	48038	586-263-2300	263-2255
Web: www.stjoe-macomb.com					
Henry Ford Wyandotte Hospital 2333 Biddle Ave	Wyandotte	MI	48192	734-284-2400	246-6904
Web: www.henryfordwyandotte.com					
Holland Community Hospital 602 Michigan Ave	Holland	MI	49423	616-392-5141	394-3528
Web: www.hoho.org					
Hurley Medical Center 1 Hurley Plaza	Flint	MI	48503	810-257-9000	762-6585
TF: 800-336-8999 ■ *Web:* www.hurleymc.com					
Huron Valley Sinai Hospital 1 William Carls Dr	Commerce	MI	48382	248-937-3300	937-3378
Web: www.hvsh.org					
Ingham Regional Medical Center 401 W Greenlawn Ave	Lansing	MI	48910	517-334-2121	334-2939
Web: www.irmc.org					
Lakeland Hospital Saint Joseph 1234 Napier Ave	Saint Joseph	MI	49085	269-983-8300	982-4855
Web: www.lakelandhealth.org					
Lakeland Medical Center-Niles 31 N St Joseph Ave	Niles	MI	49120	269-683-5510	683-2337
Web: www.lakelandhealth.org					
Lapeer Regional Hospital 1375 N Main St	Lapeer	MI	48446	810-667-5500	667-5582
Web: www.lapeerregional.org					
Marquette General Hospital 580 W College Ave	Marquette	MI	49855	906-228-9440	225-3084
Web: www.mgh.org					
McLaren Regional Medical Center 401 S Ballenger Hwy	Flint	MI	48532	810-342-2000	342-2428
TF: 800-821-6517 ■ *Web:* www.mclaren.org					
Memorial Healthcare Center 826 W King St	Owosso	MI	48867	989-723-5211	725-7902
TF: 800-206-8706 ■ *Web:* www.memorialhealthcare.org					
Mercy General Health Partners					
Mercy Campus 1500 E Sherman Blvd	Muskegon	MI	49443	231-672-9341	672-3074
Web: www.mghp.com					
Muskegon Campus 1700 Oak Ave	Muskegon	MI	49442	231-672-3311	672-6255
Web: www.mghp.com					
Mercy Hospital 2601 Electric Ave	Port Huron	MI	48060	810-985-1500	985-1579
Web: www.mercyporthuron.com					
Mercy Hospital Cadillac 400 Hobart St	Cadillac	MI	49601	231-876-7200	876-7834
Web: www.munsonhealthcare.org					
Mercy Memorial Hospital 718 N Macomb St	Monroe	MI	48162	734-240-8400	240-4424
Web: www.mercymemorial.org					
Metro Health Hospital 1919 Boston St SE	Grand Rapids	MI	49506	616-252-7200	252-7307
TF: 800-968-0051 ■ *Web:* www.metrohealth.net					
MidMichigan Medical Center 4005 Orchard Dr	Midland	MI	48670	989-839-3000	839-1399
Web: www.midmichigan.org					
Mount Clemens General Hospital 1000 Harrington Blvd	Mount Clemens	MI	48043	586-493-8000	493-8700
Web: www.mcrmc.org					
Munson Medical Center 1105 6th St	Traverse City	MI	49684	231-922-9000	935-6548
TF: 800-468-6766 ■ *Web:* www.munsonhealthcare.org					
North Oakland Medical Center 461 W Huron St	Pontiac	MI	48341	248-857-7200	857-6801
Web: www.nomc.org					
Northern Michigan Hospital 416 Connable Ave	Petoskey	MI	49770	231-487-4000	487-7703
TF: 800-748-0466 ■ *Web:* www.northernhealth.org					

General Hospitals - US (Cont'd)

Michigan (Cont'd)

Hospital	City	State	Zip	Phone	Fax
Oakwood Annapolis Hospital 33155 Annapolis Rd *Web:* www.oakwood.org	Wayne	MI	48184	734-467-4000	467-4017
Oakwood Heritage Hospital 10000 S Telegraph Rd *Web:* www.oakwood.org	Taylor	MI	48180	313-295-5000	295-5085
Oakwood Hospital & Medical Center 18101 Oakwood Blvd *TF:* 800-543-9355 ■ *Web:* www.oakwood.org	Dearborn	MI	48124	313-593-7000	436-2042
Oakwood Southshore Medical Center 5450 Fort St. *Web:* www.oakwood.org	Trenton	MI	48183	734-671-3800	671-3891
POH Medical Center 50 N Perry St *Web:* www.pohmedical.org	Pontiac	MI	48342	248-338-5000	338-5667
Port Huron Hospital 1221 Pine Grove Ave *Web:* www.porthuronhosp.org	Port Huron	MI	48060	810-987-5000	985-2675
Providence Hospital 16001 W Nine-Mile Rd *Web:* www.providence-hospital.org	Southfield	MI	48075	248-849-3000	849-5399
Saint John Detroit Riverview Hospital 7733 E Jefferson Ave *Web:* www.stjohn.org/detroitriverview	Detroit	MI	48214	313-499-3000	499-4197
Saint John Hospital & Medical Center 22101 Moross Rd *Web:* stjohn.org	Detroit	MI	48236	313-343-4000	343-3607
Saint John Macomb Hospital 11800 E 12-Mile Rd *Web:* www.stjohn.org	Warren	MI	48093	586-573-5000	573-5541
Saint John Macomb-Oakland Hospital Oakland Center 27351 Dequindre Rd *Web:* www.stjohn.org	Madison Heights	MI	48071	248-967-7000	967-7619
Saint Joseph Mercy Hospital 5301 McAuley Dr. *Web:* www.sjmercyhealth.org	Ypsilanti	MI	48197	734-712-3456	712-2708
Saint Joseph Mercy Oakland 44405 Woodward Ave *Web:* www.stjoesoakland.org	Pontiac	MI	48341	248-858-3000	858-3155
Saint Mary Mercy Hospital 36475 Five-Mile Rd. *TF:* 800-464-7492 ■ *Web:* www.stmarymercy.org	Livonia	MI	48154	734-655-4800	655-3093
Saint Mary's Health Care 200 Jefferson St SE *Web:* www.smhealthcare.org	Grand Rapids	MI	49503	616-752-6090	752-4464
Saint Mary's Hospital 800 S Washington Ave *Web:* www.stmarysofmichigan.org	Saginaw	MI	48601	989-776-8000	776-1704
Sinai Grace Hospital 6071 W Outer Dr. *Web:* www.sinaigrace.org	Detroit	MI	48235	313-966-3300	966-3160
Sparrow Health System 1215 E Michigan Ave *TF:* 800-772-7769 ■ *Web:* www.sparrow.org	Lansing	MI	48912	517-364-1000	364-5050
Spectrum Health Blodgett Campus 1840 Wealthy St SE *TF:* 866-989-7999 ■ *Web:* www.spectrum-health.org	Grand Rapids	MI	49506	616-774-7444	391-1883
University Hospital 1500 E Medical Center Dr *Web:* www.med.umich.edu	Ann Arbor	MI	48109	734-936-4000	936-9437
War Memorial Hospital 500 Osborn Blvd *Web:* www.warmemorialhospital.org	Sault Sainte Marie	MI	49783	906-635-4460	635-4467
William Beaumont Hospital 3601 W 13-Mile Rd **Fax:* Admitting ■ *Web:* www.beaumonthospitals.com	Royal Oak	MI	48073	248-551-5000	898-0400*
William Beaumont Hospital Troy 44201 Dequindre Rd *TF:* 800-482-8767 ■ *Web:* www.beaumonthospitals.com	Troy	MI	48085	248-828-5100	964-8840

Minnesota

Hospital	City	State	Zip	Phone	Fax
Abbott Northwestern Hospital 800 E 28th St. *Web:* www.abbottnorthwestern.com	Minneapolis	MN	55407	612-863-4000	863-5667
Austin Medical Center 1000 1st Dr NW. *TF:* 888-609-4065 ■ *Web:* www.austinmedicalcenter.org	Austin	MN	55912	507-433-7351	434-1992
Cambridge Medical Center 701 S Dellwood St *Web:* www.cambridgemedicalcenter.com	Cambridge	MN	55008	763-689-7700	689-7941
Douglas County Hospital 111 17th Ave E. *Web:* www.dchospital.com	Alexandria	MN	56308	320-762-1511	762-6120
Fairview Ridges Hospital 201 Nicollet Blvd *Web:* www.ridges.fairview.org	Burnsville	MN	55337	952-892-2000	
Fairview Southdale Hospital 6401 France Ave S *Web:* www.southdale.fairview.org	Edina	MN	55435	952-924-5000	924-5382
Fairview-University Medical Center					
Riverside Campus 2450 Riverside Ave *Web:* www.fairview-university.fairview.org	Minneapolis	MN	55454	612-672-6000	273-4098
University Campus 500 Harvard St *TF:* 800-688-5252 ■ *Web:* www.fairview-university.fairview.org	Minneapolis	MN	55455	612-273-3000	273-1919
Fairview University Medical Center Mesabi 750 E 34th St *TF:* 888-870-8626 ■ *Web:* www.range.fairview.org/about	Hibbing	MN	55746	218-262-4881	362-6619
Hennepin County Medical Center 701 Park Ave *Web:* www.hcmc.org	Minneapolis	MN	55415	612-873-3000	904-4214
Immanuel-Saint Joseph's Hospital 1025 Marsh St *TF:* 800-327-3721 ■ *Web:* www.isj-mhs.net	Mankato	MN	56001	507-625-4031	345-2908
Lake Region Hospital 712 S Cascade St *Web:* www.lrhc.org	Fergus Falls	MN	56537	218-736-8000	736-8765
Mayo Clinic 200 1st St SW. *Web:* www.mayo.edu	Rochester	MN	55905	507-284-2511	284-0574
Mercy Hospital 4050 Coon Rapids Blvd *Web:* www.mercyunity.com/ahs/mercyunity.nsf	Coon Rapids	MN	55433	763-236-6000	236-8124
Methodist Hospital 6500 Excelsior Blvd *Web:* www.parknicollet.com/Methodist	Saint Louis Park	MN	55426	952-993-5000	993-5273
Miller-Dwan Medical Center 502 E 2nd St *Web:* www.miller-dwan.com	Duluth	MN	55805	218-727-8762	786-5892
North Country Regional Hospital 1300 Anne St NW *Web:* www.nchs.com/hospital.html	Bemidji	MN	56601	218-751-5430	333-5880
North Memorial Health Care 3300 Oakdale Ave N. *Web:* www.northmemorial.com	Robbinsdale	MN	55422	763-520-5200	520-1454
Regions Hospital 640 Jackson St *Web:* www.regionshospital.com	Saint Paul	MN	55101	651-254-3456	254-2194
Rice Memorial Hospital 301 Becker Ave SW. *Web:* www.ricehospital.com	Willmar	MN	56201	320-235-4543	231-4869
Ridgeview Medical Center 500 S Maple St *TF:* 800-967-4620 ■ *Web:* www.ridgeviewmedical.org	Waconia	MN	55387	952-442-2191	442-6524
Rochester Methodist Hospital 201 W Center St *Web:* www.mayoclinic.org/methodisthospital	Rochester	MN	55902	507-286-7890	266-7467
Saint Cloud Hospital 1406 6th Ave N. *TF:* 800-835-6652 ■ *Web:* www.centracare.com/sch	Saint Cloud	MN	56303	320-251-2700	255-5711
Saint John's Hospital 1575 Beam Ave *TF:* 866-257-4411 ■ *Web:* www.healtheast.org	Maplewood	MN	55109	651-232-7000	232-7697
Saint Joseph's Hospital 69 W Exchange St *Web:* www.healtheast.org	Saint Paul	MN	55102	651-232-3000	232-3518
Saint Joseph's Medical Center 523 N 3rd St **Fax:* Admitting ■ *TF:* 888-829-2861 ■ *Web:* www.sjmcmn.org	Brainerd	MN	56401	218-829-2861	828-3103*
Saint Luke's Hospital & Regional Trauma Center 915 E 1st St *TF:* 800-321-3790 ■ *Web:* www.slhduluth.com	Duluth	MN	55805	218-249-5555	249-3090
Saint Mary's Hospital 1216 2nd St SW *Web:* www.mayoclinic.org/saintmaryshospital	Rochester	MN	55902	507-255-5123	255-3125
Saint Mary's Medical Center 407 E 3rd St *Web:* www.smdc.org	Duluth	MN	55805	218-786-4000	786-4734
United Hospital 333 N Smith Ave *TF:* 800-869-1320 ■ *Web:* www.unitedhospital.com	Saint Paul	MN	55102	651-241-8000	241-5189
Unity Hospital 550 Osborne Rd *Web:* www.mercyunity.com/ahs/mercyunity.nsf	Fridley	MN	55432	763-236-5000	236-3516
Virginia Regional Medical Center 901 9th St N *Web:* www.vrmc.org	Virginia	MN	55792	218-741-3340	749-9427

Mississippi

Hospital	City	State	Zip	Phone	Fax
Anderson Jeff Regional Medical Center 2124 14th St *Web:* www.jarmc.org	Meridian	MS	39301	601-553-6000	553-6144
Baptist Medical Center 1225 N State St **Fax:* Admitting ■ *TF:* 800-948-6262 ■ *Web:* www.mbhs.org	Jackson	MS	39202	601-968-1000	968-1149*
Baptist Memorial Hospital DeSoto 7601 Southcrest Pkwy *Web:* www.bmhcc.org/facilities/desoto	Southaven	MS	38671	662-772-4000	772-2111
Baptist Memorial Hospital Golden Triangle 2520 5th St N. *TF:* 800-544-8762 ■ *Web:* www.bmhcc.org/services	Columbus	MS	39703	662-244-1000	244-1651
Baptist Memorial Hospital North Mississippi 2301 S Lamar Blvd *Web:* www.bmhcc.org	Oxford	MS	38655	662-232-8100	232-8391
Baptist Memorial Hospital Union County 200 Hwy 30 W *Web:* www.bmhcc.org/facilities/newalbany	New Albany	MS	38652	662-538-7631	538-2591
Biloxi Regional Medical Center 150 Reynoir St *Web:* www.hmabrmc.com	Biloxi	MS	39530	228-432-1571	436-1205
Bolivar Medical Center 901 Hwy 8 E PO Box 1380 *Web:* www.bolivarmedical.com	Cleveland	MS	38732	662-846-2496	846-2380
Central Mississippi Medical Center 1850 Chadwick Dr *TF:* 800-844-0919 ■ *Web:* www.centralmississippimedicalcenter.com	Jackson	MS	39204	601-376-1000	376-2821
Delta Regional Medical Center 1400 E Union St *Web:* www.deltaregional.com	Greenville	MS	38703	662-378-3783	334-2189
Forrest General Hospital 6051 US Hwy 49 *Web:* www.forrestgeneral.com	Hattiesburg	MS	39402	601-288-7000	288-4441
Gilmore Memorial Hospital 1105 Earl Frye Blvd *Web:* www.gilmorehealth.com	Amory	MS	38821	662-256-7111	256-6007
Greenwood Leflore Hospital 1401 River Rd. *Web:* www.glh.org	Greenwood	MS	38930	662-459-7000	459-2719
Grenada Lake Medical Center 960 Avent Dr *Web:* www.glmc.net	Grenada	MS	38901	662-227-7000	227-7021
Gulf Coast Medical Center 180-A Debuys Rd *Web:* www.gulfcoastmedicalcenter.com	Biloxi	MS	39531	228-388-6711	388-0486
Jeff Anderson Regional Medical Center 2124 14th St *Web:* www.jarmc.org	Meridian	MS	39301	601-553-6000	553-6144
King's Daughters Medical Center 427 Hwy 51 N *Web:* www.kdmc.org	Brookhaven	MS	39601	601-833-6011	833-2791
Magnolia Regional Health Center 611 Alcorn Dr *Web:* www.mrhc.org	Corinth	MS	38834	662-293-1000	293-7667
Memorial Hospital at Gulfport 4500 13th St *Web:* www.gulfportmemorial.com	Gulfport	MS	39501	228-863-1441	865-3000
Natchez Regional Medical Center 54 Sergeant S Prentiss Dr. *Web:* www.natchezregional.com	Natchez	MS	39120	601-443-2100	445-0362
North Mississippi Medical Center 830 S Gloster St *Web:* www.nmhs.net/tupelo	Tupelo	MS	38801	662-377-3000	377-3564
Northwest Mississippi Regional Medical Center 1970 Hospital Dr *Web:* www.nwmsregionalmedcenter.com	Clarksdale	MS	38614	662-627-3211	627-5440
Oktibbeha County Hospital 400 Hospital Rd *Web:* www.och.org	Starkville	MS	39759	662-323-4320	
Rankin Medical Center 350 Crossgates Blvd. *Web:* www.rankinmedcenter.com	Brandon	MS	39042	601-825-2811	824-8519
Riley Hospital 1102 Constitution Ave *Web:* www.rileyhosp.com	Meridian	MS	39302	601-693-2511	484-3130
River Oaks Hospital 1030 River Oaks Dr *Web:* www.riveroakshospital.org	Jackson	MS	39232	601-932-1030	936-2263
River Region Medical Center 2100 Hwy 61 N. *Web:* www.riverregion.com	Vicksburg	MS	39183	601-631-2131	883-5196
River Region West Campus 1111 N Frontage Rd. *TF:* 800-548-2419 ■ *Web:* www.riverregion.com	Vicksburg	MS	39180	601-636-2611	631-6094
Rush Foundation Hospital 1314 19th Ave *Web:* www.rushhealthsystems.org	Meridian	MS	39301	601-483-0011	703-4427
Saint Dominic-Jackson Memorial Hospital 969 Lakeland Dr *Web:* www.stdom.com	Jackson	MS	39216	601-200-2000	200-6800
Singing River Hospital 2809 Denny Ave. *Web:* www.srhshealth.com	Pascagoula	MS	39581	228-809-5000	809-5064
South Central Regional Medical Center 1220 Jefferson St. *Web:* www.scrmc.com	Laurel	MS	39440	601-426-4000	
Southwest Mississippi Regional Medical Center 215 Marion Ave *Web:* www.smrmc.com	McComb	MS	39648	601-249-5500	249-1709
University of Mississippi Medical Center 2500 N State St. *Web:* www.umc.edu	Jackson	MS	39216	601-984-1000	984-4125
Wesley Medical Center 5001 Hardy St *TF:* 800-622-8892 ■ *Web:* www.wesley.com	Hattiesburg	MS	39402	601-268-8000	268-5008

Missouri

Hospital	City	State	Zip	Phone	Fax
Audrain Medical Center 620 E Monroe St. *TF:* 800-748-7098 ■ *Web:* www.audrainmedicalcenter.com	Mexico	MO	65265	573-582-5000	582-3700
Barnes-Jewish Hospital 1 Barnes-Jewish Hospital Plaza *Web:* www.barnesjewish.org	Saint Louis	MO	63110	314-362-5000	362-3725
Barnes-Jewish Saint Peters Hospital 10 Hospital Dr. *Web:* www.bjc.org	Saint Peters	MO	63376	636-447-6600	916-9414
Boone Hospital Center 1600 E Broadway *Web:* www.boone.org	Columbia	MO	65201	573-815-8000	815-2638
Bothwell Regional Health Center 601 E 14th St *Web:* www.brhc.org	Sedalia	MO	65302	660-826-8833	
Capital Region Medical Center 1125 Madison St *Web:* www.crmc.org	Jefferson City	MO	65101	573-632-5000	632-5880
Centerpoint Medical Center 19600 E 39th st *Web:* www.centerpointmedical.com	Independence	MO	64057	816-698-7000	698-7003
Christian Hospital Northeast 11133 Dunn Rd **Fax:* Admissions ■ *Web:* www.christianhospital.org	Saint Louis	MO	63136	314-355-2300	653-4408*
Columbia Regional Hospital 404 Keene St. *Web:* www.columbiaregional.org	Columbia	MO	65201	573-875-9200	449-7588
Cox Hospital North 1423 N Jefferson Ave *Web:* www.coxhealth.com	Springfield	MO	65802	417-269-3000	269-8204
Cox Hospital South 3801 S National Ave *Web:* www.coxhealth.com	Springfield	MO	65807	417-269-6000	269-4108
DesPeres Hospital 2345 Dougherty Ferry Rd *TF:* 888-457-5203 ■ *Web:* www.desvereshospital.com	Saint Louis	MO	63122	314-966-9100	966-9274
Forest Park Hospital 6150 Oakland Ave *TF:* 877-249-8557 ■ *Web:* www.forestparkhospital.com	Saint Louis	MO	63139	314-768-3000	768-3990
Freeman Hospital & Health Systems 1102 W 32nd St *TF:* 800-477-6610 ■ *Web:* www.freemanhealth.com	Joplin	MO	64804	417-623-2801	347-6646

Hospital	City	State	ZIP	Phone	Fax
Golden Valley Memorial Hospital 1600 N 2nd St *TF:* 800-748-7681 ■ *Web:* www.gvmh.org	Clinton	MO	64735	660-885-5511	885-8496
Hannibal Regional Hospital 6000 Hospital Dr PO Box 551 *Web:* www.hrhonline.org	Hannibal	MO	63401	573-248-1300	248-5264
Heartland Hospital East 5325 Faraon St *TF:* 800-443-1143 ■ *Web:* www.heartland-health.com	Saint Joseph	MO	64506	816-271-6000	271-6659
Jefferson Memorial Hospital 1400 Hwy 61 S PO Box 350 *Web:* www.jeffersonmemorial.org	Crystal City	MO	63019	636-933-1000	933-1119
Kindred Hospital - Saint Louis 4930 Lindell Blvd *Web:* www.kindredstlouis.com/	Saint Louis	MO	63108	314-361-8700	361-1210
Lake Regional Health System 54 Hospital Dr *Web:* www.lakeregional.com	Osage Beach	MO	65065	573-348-8000	348-8309
Lee's Summit Hospital 2100 SE Blue Pkwy *Web:* www.leessummithospital.com	Lee's Summit	MO	64063	816-282-5000	282-5942
Liberty Hospital 2525 Glenn Hendren Dr *TF:* 888-610-7084 ■ *Web:* www.libertyhospital.org	Liberty	MO	64068	816-781-7200	792-7117
Mineral Area Regional Medical Center 1212 Weber Rd *Web:* www.marmc.net	Farmington	MO	63640	573-756-4581	756-6007
Missouri Baptist Medical Center 3015 N Ballas Rd *Web:* www.missouribaptistmedicalcenter.org	Saint Louis	MO	63131	314-432-1024	996-5373
Missouri Delta Medical Center 1008 N Main St *Web:* www.missouridelta.com	Sikeston	MO	63801	573-471-1600	472-7606
North Kansas City Hospital 2800 Clay Edwards Dr *Web:* www.nkch.org	North Kansas City	MO	64116	816-691-2000	346-7020
Ozarks Medical Center 1100 Kentucky Ave *Web:* www.ozarksmedicalcenter.com	West Plains	MO	65775	417-256-9111	257-6770
Parkland Health Center 1101 W Liberty St *Web:* www.parklandhealthcenter.org	Farmington	MO	63640	573-756-6451	760-8354
Phelps County Regional Medical Center 1000 W 10th St *TF:* 877-311-8899 ■ *Web:* www.pcrmc.com	Rolla	MO	65401	573-364-3100	458-8490
Poplar Bluff Regional Medical Center 2620 N Westwood Blvd *TF:* 800-327-0275 ■ *Web:* www.poplarbluffregional.com	Poplar Bluff	MO	63901	573-785-7721	727-2498
Poplar Bluff Regional Medical Center South Campus 621 WPine Blvd *TF:* 800-327-0275 ■ *Web:* www.poplarbluffregional.com	Poplar Bluff	MO	63901	573-686-4111	727-7462
Research Medical Center 2316 E Meyer Blvd	Kansas City	MO	64132	816-276-4000	276-4387
Saint Alexius Hospital Broadway Campus 3933 S Broadway *Web:* www.stalexiushospital.com	Saint Louis	MO	63118	314-865-3333	865-7938
Saint Anthony's Medical Center 10010 Kennerly Rd *Web:* www.stanthonysmedcenter.com	Saint Louis	MO	63128	314-525-1000	525-1228
Saint Francis Medical Center 211 St Francis Dr *Web:* www.sfmc.net	Cape Girardeau	MO	63703	573-331-3000	331-5009
Saint John's Hospital 1235 E Cherokee St *Web:* www.stjohns.com	Springfield	MO	65804	417-885-2000	820-2288
Saint John's Mercy Medical Center 615 S New Ballas Rd *Web:* www.stjohnsmercy.org	Saint Louis	MO	63141	314-251-6000	251-6910
Saint John's Regional Medical Center 2727 McClelland Blvd *Web:* www.stj.com	Joplin	MO	64804	417-781-2727	625-2910
Saint Joseph Health Center 1000 Carondelet Dr *Web:* www.carondelethealth.org	Kansas City	MO	64114	816-942-4400	943-3131
Saint Joseph Health Center 300 1st Capitol Dr *TF:* 800-835-1212 ■ *Web:* www.ssmstjoseph.com	Saint Charles	MO	63301	636-947-5000	947-5090
Saint Louis University Hospital 3635 Vista Ave *Web:* www.sluhospital.com	Saint Louis	MO	63110	314-577-8000	577-8003
Saint Luke's Hospital 232 S Woods Mill Rd *Web:* www.stlukes-stl.com	Chesterfield	MO	63017	314-434-1500	205-6865
Saint Luke's Hospital 4401 Wornall Rd *Web:* www.saintlukeshealthsystem.org	Kansas City	MO	64111	816-932-2000	932-5990
Saint Mary's Health Center 100 St Marys Medical Plaza *Web:* www.lethealingbegin.com	Jefferson City	MO	65101	573-761-7000	636-5733
Saint Mary's Health Center 6420 Clayton Rd *TF:* 800-468-7642 ■ *Web:* www.stmarys-stlouis.com	Richmond Heights	MO	63117	314-768-8000	768-8011
Saint Mary's Medical Center 201 NW RD Mize Rd *Web:* www.carondelethealth.org	Blue Springs	MO	64014	816-228-5900	655-5408
Skaggs Community Health Center 251 Skaggs Rd *Web:* www.skaggs.net	Branson	MO	65616	417-335-7000	334-1505
Southeast Missouri Hospital 1701 Lacey St *Web:* www.southeastmissourihospital.com	Cape Girardeau	MO	63701	573-334-4822	651-5850
SSM Saint Joseph Hospital of Kirkwood 525 Couch Ave *Web:* www.stjosephkirkwood.com	Kirkwood	MO	63122	314-966-1500	966-1681
Truman Medical Center Hospital Hill 2301 Holmes St *Web:* www.trumed.org	Kansas City	MO	64108	816-404-1000	404-2828
Twin Rivers Regional Medical Center 1301 1st St *Web:* www.twinriversmedctr.com	Kennett	MO	63857	573-888-4522	888-5525
University Hospital 1 Hospital Dr *Web:* www.muhealth.org/~hospital	Columbia	MO	65212	573-882-4141	884-4174
US Medical Center for Federal Prisoners 1900 W Sunshine St	Springfield	MO	65807	417-862-7041	837-1711

Montana

Hospital	City	State	ZIP	Phone	Fax
Benefis Health Care West Campus 500 15th Ave S *Web:* www.benefis.org	Great Falls	MT	59405	406-455-5000	455-2189
Benefis Healthcare East Campus 1101 26th St S *Web:* www.benefis.org	Great Falls	MT	59405	406-761-1200	455-4587
Billings Clinic 2800 10th Ave N *TF:* 800-332-7156 ■ *Web:* www.billingsclinic.com	Billings	MT	59101	406-657-4000	238-2785
Bozeman Deaconess Hospital 915 Highland Blvd *Web:* www.bozemandeaconess.org	Bozeman	MT	59715	406-585-5000	585-1070
Community Medical Center 2827 Fort Missoula Rd *Web:* www.communitymed.org	Missoula	MT	59804	406-728-4100	327-4501
Kalispell Regional Medical Center 310 Sunnyview Ln *TF:* 800-228-1574 ■ *Web:* www.krmc.org	Kalispell	MT	59901	406-752-5111	756-2703
Saint James Healthcare 400 S Clark St *Web:* stjameshealthcare.org	Butte	MT	59701	406-723-2500	723-2443
Saint Patrick Hospital 500 W Broadway St *Web:* www.saintpatrick.org	Missoula	MT	59802	406-543-7271	329-5693
Saint Peter's Hospital 2475 Broadway *Web:* www.stpetes.org	Helena	MT	59601	406-442-2480	444-2389
Saint Vincent Healthcare 1233 N 30th St *Web:* www.svh-mt.org	Billings	MT	59101	406-657-7000	237-3078

Nebraska

Hospital	City	State	ZIP	Phone	Fax
Bergen Mercy Medical Center 7500 Mercy Rd *Web:* www.alegent.com	Omaha	NE	68124	402-398-6060	398-6920
Bryan LGH Medical Center East 1600 S 48th St *TF:* 800-742-7844 ■ *Web:* www.bryanlgh.org	Lincoln	NE	68506	402-489-0200	481-8306
Bryan LGH Medical Center West 2300 S 16th St *TF:* 800-742-7844 ■ *Web:* www.bryanlgh.org	Lincoln	NE	68502	402-475-1011	481-5377
Creighton University Medical Center 601 N 30th St *Web:* health.creighton.edu	Omaha	NE	68131	402-449-4000	449-5020
Faith Regional Health Services 2700 W Norfolk Ave *Web:* www.frhs.org	Norfolk	NE	68701	402-371-4880	644-7468
Fremont Area Medical Center 450 E 23rd St *Web:* www.famc.org	Fremont	NE	68025	402-721-1610	727-3656
Good Samaritan Hospital 10 E 31st St *TF:* 800-658-4250 ■ *Web:* www.gshs.org	Kearney	NE	68847	308-865-7100	865-2913
Great Plains Regional Medical Center 601 W Leota St *TF:* 800-662-0011 ■ *Web:* www.gprmc.com	North Platte	NE	69101	308-696-8000	535-3410
Immanuel Medical Center 6901 N 72nd St *Web:* www.alegent.com	Omaha	NE	68122	402-572-2121	572-3177
Mary Lanning Memorial Hospital 715 N St Joseph Ave *Web:* www.mlmh.org	Hastings	NE	68901	402-463-4521	461-5321
Midlands Community Hospital 11111 S 84th St *Web:* www.alegent.com/body.cfm?id=2676	Papillion	NE	68046	402-593-3000	593-3100
Nebraska Methodist Hospital 8303 Dodge St *Web:* www.bestcare.org	Omaha	NE	68114	402-390-4000	354-8735
NHS University Hospital 600 S 42nd St *TF:* 800-642-1095 ■ *Web:* www.unmc.edu	Omaha	NE	68198	402-559-7416	559-7866
Regional West Medical Center 4021 Ave B *Web:* www.rwmc.net	Scottsbluff	NE	69361	308-635-3711	630-1815
Saint Elizabeth Regional Medical Center 555 S 70th St *Web:* www.saintelizabethonline.com	Lincoln	NE	68510	402-219-8000	219-8973
Saint Francis Medical Center 2620 W Faidley Ave *TF:* 800-353-4896 ■ *Web:* www.saintfrancisgi.org	Grand Island	NE	68803	308-384-4600	398-5589
The Nebraska Medical Center 4350 Dewey Ave *Web:* www.nebraskamed.com	Omaha	NE	68105	402-552-2000	552-3267
University of Nebraska Medical Center 600 S 42nd St *TF:* 800-642-1095 ■ *Web:* www.unmc.edu	Omaha	NE	68198	402-559-7416	559-7866

Nevada

Hospital	City	State	ZIP	Phone	Fax
Carson Tahoe Hospital 1600 Medical Pkwy *Web:* www.carsontahoehospital.com	Carson City	NV	89703	775-882-1361	887-4580
Desert Springs Hospital Medical Center 2075 E Flamingo Rd *Web:* www.desertspringshospital.net	Las Vegas	NV	89119	702-733-8800	369-7836
MountainView Hospital 3100 N Tenaya Way *Web:* www.mountainview-hospital.com	Las Vegas	NV	89128	702-255-5000	255-5074
Northern Nevada Medical Center 2375 E Prater Way *Web:* www.northernnvmed.com	Sparks	NV	89434	775-331-7000	356-4986
Renown Regional Medical Center 1155 Mill St *Web:* www.renown.org	Reno	NV	89502	775-982-4100	982-4111
Saint Mary's Regional Medical Center 235 W 6th St *Web:* www.saintmarysreno.com	Reno	NV	89503	775-770-3000	770-3621
Saint Rose Dominican Hospital 102 E Lake Mead Dr *Web:* www.strosecares.com	Henderson	NV	89015	702-616-5000	616-7549
Summerlin Hospital Medical Center 657 Town Center Dr *Web:* www.summerlinhospital.org	Las Vegas	NV	89144	702-233-7000	
Sunrise Hospital & Medical Center 3186 S Maryland Pkwy *Web:* www.sunrisehospital.com	Las Vegas	NV	89109	702-731-8000	731-8668
University Medical Center 1800 W Charleston Blvd *Web:* www.umc-cares.org	Las Vegas	NV	89102	702-383-2000	383-2067
Valley Hospital Medical Center 620 Shadow Ln *Web:* www.valleyhospital.net	Las Vegas	NV	89106	702-388-4000	388-4636

New Hampshire

Hospital	City	State	ZIP	Phone	Fax
Catholic Medical Center 100 McGregor St *TF:* 800-437-9666 ■ *Web:* www.catholicmedicalcenter.org	Manchester	NH	03102	603-668-3545	663-6989
Cheshire Medical Center 580 Court St *Web:* www.cheshire-med.com/tcmc.shtml	Keene	NH	03431	603-352-4111	354-5402
Concord Hospital 250 Pleasant St *Web:* www.crhc.org	Concord	NH	03301	603-225-2711	228-7020
Dartmouth-Hitchcock Medical Center 1 Medical Center Dr *Web:* www.dhmc.org	Lebanon	NH	03756	603-650-5000	650-8765
Elliot Hospital 1 Elliot Way *Web:* www.elliothospital.org	Manchester	NH	03103	603-669-5300	663-2777
Exeter Hospital 5 Alumni Dr *Web:* www.foreveryday.com/hospital/hospital.htm	Exeter	NH	03833	603-778-7311	580-6592
Frisbie Memorial Hospital 11 Whitehall Rd *Web:* www.frisbiehospital.com	Rochester	NH	03867	603-332-5211	335-8488
Lakes Region General Hospital 80 Highland St *Web:* www.lrgh.org	Laconia	NH	03246	603-524-3211	527-2887
Parkland Medical Center 1 Parkland Dr *Web:* www.parklandmedicalcenter.com	Derry	NH	03038	603-432-1500	421-2111
Portsmouth Regional Hospital 333 Borthwick Ave *TF:* 800-685-8282 ■ *Web:* www.portsmouthhospital.com	Portsmouth	NH	03801	603-436-5110	431-3783
Saint Joseph Hospital 172 Kinsley St *TF:* 877-899-6345 ■ *Web:* www.stjosephhospital.com	Nashua	NH	03060	603-882-3000	889-1651
Southern New Hampshire Medical Center 8 Prospect St *Web:* www.snhmc.org	Nashua	NH	03060	603-577-2000	577-5630
Wentworth-Douglass Hospital 789 Central Ave *TF:* 877-201-7100 ■ *Web:* www.wdhospital.com	Dover	NH	03820	603-742-5252	740-2242

New Jersey

Hospital	City	State	ZIP	Phone	Fax
Atlanticare Regional Medical Center 1925 Pacific Ave *Web:* www.atlanticare.org/armc	Atlantic City	NJ	08401	609-344-4081	569-7020
Barnert Hospital 680 Dr ML King Jr Way *Web:* www.barnerthosp.com	Paterson	NJ	07514	973-977-6600	742-6248
Bayonne Medical Center 29th St & Ave E *Web:* www.bayonnehospital.com	Bayonne	NJ	07002	201-858-5000	858-7355
Bayshore Community Hospital 727 N Beers St *Web:* www.bchs.com	Holmdel	NJ	07733	732-739-5900	739-5887
Bergen Regional Medical Center 230 E Ridgewood Ave *Web:* www.bergenregional.com	Paramus	NJ	07652	201-967-4000	967-4277
Cape Regional Medical Center 2 Stone Harbor Blvd *Web:* www.caperegional.com	Cape May Court House	NJ	08210	609-463-2000	465-9391
Capital Health System at Fuld 750 Brunswick Ave *Web:* www.capitalhealth.org	Trenton	NJ	08638	609-394-6000	394-6687
Capital Health System at Mercer 446 Bellevue Ave *Web:* www.capitalhealth.org	Trenton	NJ	08618	609-394-4000	394-4032
CentraState Medical Center 901 W Main St *Web:* www.centrastate.com	Freehold	NJ	07728	732-431-2000	462-5129
Chilton Memorial Hospital 97 W Parkway *Web:* www.chiltonmemorial.org	Pompton Plains	NJ	07444	973-831-5000	831-5183
Christ Hospital 176 Palisade Ave *Web:* www.christhospital.org	Jersey City	NJ	07306	201-795-8200	795-8758
Clara Maass Medical Center 1 Clara Maass Dr *Web:* www.saintbarnabas.com	Belleville	NJ	07109	973-450-2000	450-0181

General Hospitals - US (Cont'd)

New Jersey (Cont'd)

	City	State	ZIP	Phone	Fax
Columbus Hospital 495 N 13th St *Web:* www.columbushospital.org	Newark	NJ	07107	973-268-1400	268-1593
Community Medical Center 99 Hwy 37 W *Web:* www.sbhcs.com/hospitals/community_medical/index.html	Toms River	NJ	08755	732-240-8000	557-8935
Cooper University Hospital 1 Cooper Plaza *Web:* www.cooperhealth.org	Camden	NJ	08103	856-342-2000	342-3299
East Orange General Hospital 300 Central Ave *Web:* www.evh.org	East Orange	NJ	07017	973-672-8400	
Englewood Hospital & Medical Center 350 Engle St *Web:* www.englewoodhospital.com	Englewood	NJ	07631	201-894-3000	894-1345
Hackensack University Medical Center 30 Prospect Ave *Web:* www.humed.com	Hackensack	NJ	07601	201-996-2000	489-7275
Hoboken University Medical Center 308 Willow Ave *Web:* www.hobokenumc.com	Hoboken	NJ	07030	201-418-1000	418-1428
Holy Name Hospital 718 Teaneck Rd *Web:* www.holyname.org	Teaneck	NJ	07666	201-833-3000	833-3230
Hunterdon Medical Center 2100 Westcott Dr *Web:* www.hunterdonhealthcare.org	Flemington	NJ	08822	908-788-6100	788-6111
Irvington General Hospital 832 Chancellor Ave *Web:* www.saintbarnabas.com	Irvington	NJ	07111	973-399-6000	373-0799
Jersey City Medical Center 355 Grand St *Web:* www.libertyhealth.org	Jersey City	NJ	07302	201-915-2000	915-2559
Jersey Shore University Medical Center 1945 Rt 33 *Web:* www.meridianhealth.com/jsmc.cfm/index.cfm	Neptune	NJ	07754	732-775-5500	776-4836
JFK Medical Center 65 James St *Web:* jfkmc.org/index.htm	Edison	NJ	08818	732-321-7000	549-8532
Kennedy Health System-University Medical Center 2201 Chapel Ave W *Web:* www.kennedyhealth.org	Cherry Hill	NJ	08002	856-488-6500	488-6526
Kimball Medical Center 600 River Ave *Web:* www.saintbarnabas.com	Lakewood	NJ	08701	732-363-1900	886-4406
Lourdes Medical Center of Burlington County 218-A Sunset Rd *Web:* www.lourdesnet.org/burlington	Willingboro	NJ	08046	609-835-2900	835-3061
Maass Clara Medical Center 1 Clara Maass Dr *Web:* www.saintbarnabas.com	Belleville	NJ	07109	973-450-2000	450-0181
Meadowlands Hospital Medical Center 55 Meadowland Pkwy *Web:* www.libertyhealth.org/meadowlands.html	Secaucus	NJ	07096	201-392-3100	392-3527
Memorial Hospital Burlington County 175 Madison Ave *Web:* www.virtua.org	Mount Holly	NJ	08060	609-267-0700	702-9751
Memorial Hospital of Salem County 310 Woodstown Rd *Web:* www.mhschealth.com	Salem	NJ	08079	856-935-1000	935-3175
Monmouth Medical Center 300 2nd Ave *TF:* 888-661-7484 ■ *Web:* www.saintbarnabas.com	Long Branch	NJ	07740	732-222-5200	923-7544
Morristown Memorial Hospital 100 Madison Ave *Web:* www.atlantichealth.org	Morristown	NJ	07962	973-971-5000	290-7010
Mountainside Hospital 1 Bay Ave *Web:* www.atlantichealth.org	Montclair	NJ	07042	973-429-6000	429-6209
Muhlenberg Regional Medical Center Park Ave & Randolph Rd *Web:* www.muhlenberg.com/index.htm	Plainfield	NJ	07061	908-668-2000	226-4517
Newark Beth Israel Medical Center 201 Lyons Ave *Web:* www.saintbarnabas.com	Newark	NJ	07112	973-926-7000	923-2886
Newton Memorial Hospital 175 High St *Web:* www.nmhnj.org	Newton	NJ	07860	973-383-2121	383-8973
Ocean Medical Center 425 Jack Martin Blvd *Web:* www.meridianhealth.com/mcoc.cfm/index.cfm	Brick	NJ	08724	732-840-2200	840-3284
Our Lady of Lourdes Medical Center 1600 Haddon Ave *Web:* www.lourdesnet.org	Camden	NJ	08103	856-757-3500	757-3611
Overlook Hospital 99 Beauvoir Ave *Web:* www.atlantichealth.org	Summit	NJ	07901	908-522-2000	273-5134
Palisades Medical Center 7600 River Rd *Fax: Admitting ■ *Web:* www.palisadesmedical.org	North Bergen	NJ	07047	201-854-5000	854-5272*
Pascack Valley Hospital 250 Old Hook Rd *Fax: Admitting ■ *Web:* www.pvhospital.org	Westwood	NJ	07675	201-358-3000	358-3624*
PBI Regional Medical Center 70 Parker Ave *Web:* www.pbih.org	Passaic	NJ	07055	973-365-4300	471-5531
Raritan Bay Medical Center 530 New Brunswick Ave *Web:* www.rbmc.org	Perth Amboy	NJ	08861	732-442-3700	
Riverview Medical Center 1 Riverview Plaza *Web:* www.meridianhealth.com/rmc.cfm/index.cfm	Red Bank	NJ	07701	732-741-2700	224-8408
Robert Wood Johnson University Hospital 1 Robert Wood Johnson Pl *Web:* www.rwjuh.edu	New Brunswick	NJ	08901	732-828-3000	937-8730
Robert Wood Johnson University Hospital at Rahway 865 Stone St *Web:* www.rwjuhr.com	Rahway	NJ	07065	732-381-4200	499-6337
RWJ University Hospital at Hamilton 1 Hamilton Health Pl *Web:* www.rwjhamilton.org	Hamilton	NJ	08690	609-586-7900	584-6429
Saint Barnabas Medical Center 94 Old Short Hills Rd *Fax: Admitting ■ *TF:* 888-724-7123 ■ *Web:* www.sbhcs.com/hospitals/saint_barnabas	Livingston	NJ	07039	973-322-5000	322-8790*
Saint Clare's Hospital 25 Pocono Rd *Web:* www.saintclares.org	Denville	NJ	07834	973-625-6000	625-6184
Saint Francis Medical Center 601 Hamilton Ave *TF:* 800-950-2549 ■ *Web:* www.stfrancismedical.com	Trenton	NJ	08629	609-599-5000	695-2744
Saint James Hospital of Newark 155 Jefferson St *Web:* www.cathedralhealth.org	Newark	NJ	07105	973-589-1300	465-2590
Saint Joseph's Regional Medical Center 703 Main St *Web:* www.stjosephshealth.org	Paterson	NJ	07503	973-754-2000	754-2208
Saint Joseph's Wayne Hospital 224 Hamburg Tpke *Web:* www.sjwh.org	Wayne	NJ	07470	973-942-6900	389-4010
Saint Mary's Hospital 211 Pennington Ave *Web:* www.smh-passaic.org/smh/	Passaic	NJ	07055	973-470-3000	470-0184
Saint Michael's Medical Center 268 Dr ML King Jr Blvd *Web:* www.cathedralhealth.org	Newark	NJ	07102	973-877-5000	
Saint Peter's University Hospital 254 Easton Ave *Fax: Admitting ■ *Web:* www.saintpetersuh.com	New Brunswick	NJ	08901	732-745-8600	247-8159*
Shore Memorial Hospital 1 E New York Ave *Web:* www.shorememorial.org	Somers Point	NJ	08244	609-653-3500	927-8172
SJH Elmer Hospital 501 W Front St *Web:* www.sjhs.com	Elmer	NJ	08318	856-363-1000	358-3476
SJH Regional Medical Center 1505 W Sheman Ave *Web:* www.sjhealthcare.net	Vineland	NJ	08360	856-641-8000	451-7903
Somerset Medical Center 110 Rehill Ave *Web:* www.somersetmedicalcenter.com	Somerville	NJ	08876	908-685-2200	685-2894
Southern Ocean County Hospital 1140 Rt 72 W *Web:* www.soch.com	Manahawkin	NJ	08050	609-597-6011	978-8920
Trinitas Hospital 225 Williamson St *Web:* www.trinitashospital.com	Elizabeth	NJ	07207	908-994-5000	994-5756
Underwood-Memorial Hospital 509 N Broad St *Web:* www.umhospital.org	Woodbury	NJ	08096	856-845-0100	845-5322
Union Hospital 1000 Galloping Hill Rd *Web:* www.sbhcs.com/hospitals/union_hospital	Union	NJ	07083	908-687-1900	851-7281
University Medical Center at Princeton 253 Witherspoon St *Web:* www.princetonhcs.org/page1501.aspx	Princeton	NJ	08540	609-497-4000	497-4977
University of Medicine & Dentistry of New Jersey University Hospital 150 Bergen St Suite D347 *Web:* www.theuniversityhospital.com	Newark	NJ	07103	973-972-4300	972-6932
Valley Hospital 223 N Van Dien Ave *Web:* www.valleyhealth.com	Ridgewood	NJ	07450	201-447-8000	
Warren Hospital 185 Roseberry St *Web:* www.warrenhospital.org	Phillipsburg	NJ	08865	908-859-6700	213-1139
West Jersey Hospital Berlin 100 Townsend Ave *Web:* www.virtua.org/page.cfm?id=about_loc_berlin	Berlin	NJ	08009	856-322-3000	322-3201
West Jersey Hospital Marlton 90 Brick Rd *Web:* www.virtua.org/page.cfm?id=about_loc_marlton	Marlton	NJ	08053	856-355-6000	355-6201
West Jersey Hospital Voorhees 101 Carnie Blvd *Web:* www.virtua.org/page.cfm?id=about_loc_voorhees	Voorhees	NJ	08043	856-325-3000	325-3219

New Mexico

	City	State	ZIP	Phone	Fax
Albuquerque Regional Medical Center 601 ML King Jr Dr	Albuquerque	NM	87102	505-727-8000	727-7888
Carlsbad Medical Center 2430 W Pierce St *Web:* www.triadhospitals.com	Carlsbad	NM	88220	505-887-4100	887-4256
Eastern New Mexico Medical Center 405 W Country Club Rd *TF:* 800-437-9275 ■ *Web:* www.enmmc.com	Roswell	NM	88201	505-622-8170	624-8726
Espanola Hospital 1010 Spruce St *Web:* www.phs.org/espanola	Espanola	NM	87532	505-753-7111	367-0257
Gallup Indian Medical Center 516 E Nizhoni Blvd PO Box 1337	Gallup	NM	87301	505-722-1000	722-1397
Gerald Champion Memorial Hospital 2669 N Scenic Dr *Web:* www.gcrmc.org	Alamogordo	NM	88310	505-439-6100	443-7858
Gila Regional Medical Center 1313 E 32nd St *Web:* www.grmc.org	Silver City	NM	88061	505-538-4000	538-9714
Lea Regional Medical Center 5419 N Lovington Hwy *TF:* 877-492-8001 ■ *Web:* www.learegionalmedical.com	Hobbs	NM	88240	505-392-6581	492-5505
Lovelace Medical Center 5400 Gibson Blvd SE *TF:* 800-877-7526 ■ *Web:* www.lovelace.com	Albuquerque	NM	87108	505-262-7000	262-7729
Memorial Medical Center 2450 S Telshor Blvd *TF:* 800-829-8641 ■ *Web:* www.mmclc.org	Las Cruces	NM	88011	505-522-8641	521-5013
MountainView Regional Medical Center 4311 E Lohman Ave *TF:* 877-999-7604 ■ *Web:* www.mountainviewregional.com	Las Cruces	NM	88001	505-556-7600	556-7619
Plains Regional Medical Center 2100 ML King Blvd *TF:* 800-221-3706 ■ *Web:* www.phs.org	Clovis	NM	88101	505-769-2141	769-7337
Presbyterian Hospital 1100 Central Ave SE *TF:* 800-841-1861 ■ *Web:* www.phs.org	Albuquerque	NM	87106	505-841-1234	841-1861
Presbyterian Kaseman Hospital 8300 Constitution Ave NE *TF:* 800-432-4600 ■ *Web:* www.phs.org	Albuquerque	NM	87110	505-291-2000	291-2983
Rehoboth McKinley Christian Hospital 1901 Red Rock Dr *Web:* www.rmch.org	Gallup	NM	87301	505-863-7000	863-5806
Saint Vincent Regional Medical Center 455 St Michael's Dr *Web:* www.stvin.org	Santa Fe	NM	87505	505-983-3361	820-5210
San Juan Regional Medical Center 801 W Maple St *Web:* www.sanjuanregional.com	Farmington	NM	87401	505-325-5011	599-6249
University Hospital 2211 Lomas Blvd NE *Fax: Admitting ■ *Web:* hospitals.unm.edu/UNMH/Index.shtml	Albuquerque	NM	87106	505-272-2111	272-0122*

New York

	City	State	ZIP	Phone	Fax
Adirondack Medical Center 2233 SR-86 Lake Colby Dr *Web:* www.amccares.org	Saranac Lake	NY	12983	518-891-4141	891-1191
Albany Medical Center 43 New Scotland Ave *Fax: Admitting ■ *Web:* www.amc.edu	Albany	NY	12208	518-262-3125	262-3398*
Albany Memorial Hospital 600 Northern Blvd *Web:* www.nehealth.com	Albany	NY	12204	518-471-3221	449-4410
Alice Hyde Medical Center 133 Park St *Web:* www.alicehyde.com	Malone	NY	12953	518-483-3000	481-2320
Amsterdam Memorial Hospital 4988 State Hwy 30 *Web:* www.amsterdammemorial.org	Amsterdam	NY	12010	518-842-3100	841-3497
Arnot Ogden Medical Center 600 Roe Ave *Web:* www.aomc.org	Elmira	NY	14905	607-737-4100	737-4447
Auburn Memorial Hospital 17 Lansing St *Web:* www.auburnhospital.org	Auburn	NY	13021	315-255-7011	255-7382
Aurelia Osborn Fox Memorial Hospital 1 Norton Ave *Web:* www.aofoxhospital.com	Oneonta	NY	13820	607-432-2000	431-5006
Bayley Seton Hospital 75 Vanderbilt Ave *TF:* 800-273-1114 ■ *Web:* www.svcmc.org/bayleyseton	Staten Island	NY	10304	718-818-6000	818-6877
Bellevue Hospital Center 462 1st Ave	New York	NY	10016	212-562-4141	562-4036
Beth Israel Medical Center 1st Ave & 16th St *Web:* www.bethisraelny.org	New York	NY	10003	212-420-2000	844-1565
Kings Highway Div 3201 Kings Hwy *Web:* www.bethisraelny.org	Brooklyn	NY	11234	718-252-3000	951-2726
Bon Secours Community Hospital 160 E Main St *Web:* www.bonsecourscommunityhosp.org	Port Jervis	NY	12771	845-856-5351	858-7415
Bronx-Lebanon Hospital Center 1276 Fulton Ave *Web:* www.bronxcare.org	Bronx	NY	10456	718-590-1800	901-8247
Brookdale University Hospital & Medical Center 1 Brookdale Plaza *Web:* www.brookdalehospital.org	Brooklyn	NY	11212	718-240-5000	240-5577
Brookhaven Memorial Hospital Medical Center 101 Hospital Rd *Web:* www.brookhavenhospital.org	Patchogue	NY	11772	631-654-7100	447-3714
Brooklyn Hospital Center 121 DeKalb Ave *Web:* www.tbh.org	Brooklyn	NY	11201	718-250-8000	250-8902
Brooks Memorial Hospital 529 Central Ave *TF:* 800-366-0717 ■ *Web:* www.brookshospital.org	Dunkirk	NY	14048	716-366-1111	363-7288
Brunswick Hospital Center 366 Broadway *Web:* www.brunswickhospital.com	Amityville	NY	11701	631-789-7000	789-4929
Buffalo General Hospital 100 High St *TF:* 800-242-0055 ■ *Web:* www.kaleidahealth.org	Buffalo	NY	14203	716-859-5600	859-3323
Cabrini Medical Center 227 E 19th St *Web:* www.cabrininy.org	New York	NY	10003	212-995-6000	979-3476
Catskill Regional Medical Center 68 Harris-Bushville Rd *TF:* 800-633-3413 ■ *Web:* www.crmcny.org	Harris	NY	12742	845-794-3300	794-3240
Cayuga Medical Center 101 Dates Dr *Web:* www.cayugamed.org	Ithaca	NY	14850	607-274-4011	274-4527
Champlain Valley Physicians Hospital Medical Center 75 Beekman St *Web:* www.cvph.org	Plattsburgh	NY	12901	518-561-2000	561-0881
Claxton-Hepburn Medical Center 214 King St *Web:* www.chmed.org	Ogdensburg	NY	13669	315-393-3600	393-8506
Clifton Springs Hospital & Clinic 2 Coulter Rd *Web:* www.cliftonspringshospital.com	Clifton Springs	NY	14432	315-462-9561	462-3492

				Phone	Fax
Columbia Memorial Hospital 71 Prospect Ave	Hudson	NY	12534	518-828-7601	828-8525
Web: www.columbiamemorial.com					
Community General Hospital of Greater Syracuse 4900 Broad Rd	Syracuse	NY	13215	315-492-5011	492-5418
Web: www.cgh.org					
Coney Island Hospital 2601 Ocean Pkwy	Brooklyn	NY	11235	718-616-3000	616-4512
Web: www.ci.nyc.ny.us/html/hhc/html/facilities/coneyisland.shtml					
Corning Hospital 176 Denison Pkwy E	Corning	NY	14830	607-937-7200	937-7693
TF: 800-295-1122 ■ *Web:* www.corninghospital.com					
Cortland Memorial Hospital 134 Homer Ave	Cortland	NY	13045	607-756-3500	756-3590
Web: www.cortlandhospital.org					
Crouse Hospital 736 Irving Ave	Syracuse	NY	13210	315-470-7111	470-7014
Web: www.crouse.org					
De Graff Memorial Hospital 445 Tremont St	North Tonawanda	NY	14120	716-694-4500	690-2300
Web: www.kaleidahealth.org					
Ellis Hospital 1101 Nott St	Schenectady	NY	12308	518-243-4000	243-4668
Web: www.ellishospital.org					
Elmhurst Hospital Center 79-01 Broadway	Elmhurst	NY	11373	718-334-4000	334-5161
Erie County Medical Center 462 Grider St	Buffalo	NY	14215	716-898-3000	898-5178
Web: www.ecmc.edu					
Faxton Saint Luke's Healthcare					
Faxton Campus 1676 Sunset Ave	Utica	NY	13502	315-624-6000	624-4418
Web: www.faxtonstlukes.com					
Saint Luke's Campus 1656 Champlin Ave	New Hartford	NY	13413	315-624-6000	624-6269
Web: www.faxtonstlukes.com					
FF Thompson Hospital 350 Parrish St	Canandaigua	NY	14424	585-396-6000	396-6481
Web: www.thompsonhealth.com					
Flushing Hospital Medical Center 4500 Parsons Blvd	Flushing	NY	11355	718-670-5000	670-3077
Web: www.flushinghospital.org					
Forest Hills Hospital 102-01 66th Rd	Forest Hills	NY	11375	718-830-4000	830-4168
Web: www.northshorelij.com/body.cfm?ID=61					
Franklin Hospital 900 Franklin Ave	Valley Stream	NY	11580	516-256-6000	256-6503
Web: www.northshorelij.com/body.cfm?ID=58					
Geneva General Hospital 196 North St	Geneva	NY	14456	315-789-4222	787-4039
Web: www.flhealth.org					
Glen Cove Hospital 101 St Andrews Ln	Glen Cove	NY	11542	516-674-7300	674-7588
Web: www.northshorelij.com/body.cfm?ID=53					
Glens Falls Hospital 100 Park St	Glens Falls	NY	12801	518-926-1000	926-1919
TF: 800-836-3151 ■ *Web:* www.glensfallshospital.org					
Good Samaritan Hospital 255 Lafayette Ave	Suffern	NY	10901	845-368-5000	368-5430
Web: www.goodsamhosp.org					
Good Samaritan Hospital 1000 Montauk Hwy	West Islip	NY	11795	631-376-4005	376-4208
Web: www.good-samaritan-hospital.org					
Harlem Hospital Center 506 Lenox Ave	New York	NY	10037	212-939-1000	939-1974
Highland Hospital of Rochester 1000 South Ave	Rochester	NY	14620	585-473-2200	341-8350
Web: www.stronghealth.com/about/hospitals/highland.cfm					
Hudson Valley Hospital Center 1980 Crompond Rd	Cortlandt Manor	NY	10567	914-737-9000	
Web: www.hvhc.org					
Huntington Hospital 270 Park Ave	Huntington	NY	11743	631-351-2000	351-2586
Web: www.hunthosp.org					
Hyde Alice Medical Center 133 Park St	Malone	NY	12953	518-483-3000	481-2320
Web: www.alicehyde.com					
Interfaith Medical Center 1545 Atlantic Ave	Brooklyn	NY	11213	718-613-4000	613-4101
Web: www.interfaithmedical.com					
Jacobi Medical Center 1400 Pelham Pkwy S	Bronx	NY	10461	718-918-8141	918-4607
Web: www.nyc.gov/html/hhc/jacobi/home.html					
Jamaica Hospital Medical Center 8900 Van Wyck Expy	Jamaica	NY	11418	718-206-6000	657-0545
Web: www.jamaicahospital.org					
John T Mather Memorial Hospital 75 N Country Rd	Port Jefferson	NY	11777	631-473-1320	473-7367
Web: www.matherhospital.org					
Kenmore Mercy Hospital 2950 Elmwood Ave	Kenmore	NY	14217	716-879-6100	447-6090
Web: www.chsbuffalo.org/body.cfm?id=49					
Kings County Hospital Center 451 Clarkson Ave	Brooklyn	NY	11203	718-245-3131	613-8019
Web: home.nyc.gov/html/hhc/html/kings.html					
Kingsbrook Jewish Medical Center 585 Schenectady Ave	Brooklyn	NY	11203	718-604-5000	604-5243
Web: www.kingsbrook.org					
Lawrence Hospital 55 Palmer Ave	Bronxville	NY	10708	914-787-1000	787-3113
Web: www.lawrencehealth.org					
Lenox Hill Hospital 100 E 77th St	New York	NY	10021	212-434-2000	434-3205
Web: www.lenoxhillhospital.org					
Lincoln Medical & Mental Health Center 234 E 149th St	Bronx	NY	10451	718-579-5000	579-5319
Little Falls Hospital 140 Burwell St	Little Falls	NY	13365	315-823-1000	823-2516
Web: lfhny.org					
Lockport Memorial Hospital 521 East Ave	Lockport	NY	14094	716-514-5700	514-5783
Long Beach Medical Center 455 E Bay Dr	Long Beach	NY	11561	516-897-1000	897-1214
Web: www.lbmc.org					
Long Island College Hospital 339 Hicks St	Brooklyn	NY	11201	718-780-1000	780-1365
TF: 888-445-0338 ■ *Web:* www.lich.org					
Long Island Jewish Medical Center 270-05 76th Ave	New Hyde Park	NY	11040	718-470-7000	962-6759
Web: www.lij.edu					
Lutheran Medical Center 150 55th St	Brooklyn	NY	11220	718-630-7000	630-8228
Web: www.lmcmc.com					
Maimonides Medical Center 4802 10th Ave	Brooklyn	NY	11219	718-283-6000	635-8157
Web: www.maimonidesmed.org					
Mary Imogene Bassett Hospital 1 Atwell Rd	Cooperstown	NY	13326	607-547-3456	547-3921
TF: 800-227-7388 ■ *Web:* www.bassetthealthcare.org					
Mercy Hospital of Buffalo 565 Abbott Rd	Buffalo	NY	14220	716-826-7000	828-2700
Web: www.chsbuffalo.org/body.cfm?id=50					
Mercy Medical Center 1000 N Village Ave	Rockville Centre	NY	11570	516-705-1411	705-1406
Web: mercymedicalcenter.chsli.org					
Metropolitan Hospital Center 1901 1st Ave	New York	NY	10029	212-423-6262	423-8538
Millard Fillmore Gates Circle Hospital 3 Gates Cir	Buffalo	NY	14209	716-887-4600	887-4339
Web: www.kaleidahealth.org					
Montefiore Medical Center 111 E 210th St	Bronx	NY	10467	718-920-4321	920-8543
Web: www.montefiore.org					
Mount Saint Mary's Hospital 5300 Military Rd	Lewiston	NY	14092	716-297-4800	298-2001
Web: www.msmh.org					
Mount Sinai Hospital 1190 5th Ave	New York	NY	10029	212-241-6500	731-3418
Web: www.mountsinai.org					
Mount Sinai of Queens 25-10 30th Ave	Astoria	NY	11102	718-932-1000	278-1786
Web: www.mshq.org					
Mount Vernon Hospital 12 N 7th Ave	Mount Vernon	NY	10550	914-664-8000	664-2113
Web: www.ssmc.org/homepagemv.cfm?id=45					
Nassau University Medical Center 2201 Hempstead Tpke	East Meadow	NY	11554	516-572-0123	572-6252
Web: www.ncmc.edu					
New Island Hospital 4295 Hempstead Tpke	Bethpage	NY	11714	516-579-6000	579-0417
Web: www.newislandhospital.org					
New York Community Hospital 2525 Kings Hwy	Brooklyn	NY	11229	718-692-5300	692-8454
Web: www.nych.com					
New York Downtown Hospital 170 William St	New York	NY	10038	212-312-5000	312-5977
Web: www.downtownhospital.org					
New York Hospital Medical Center of Queens 56-45 Main St	Flushing	NY	11355	718-670-1021	661-7704
Web: www.nyhq.org					
New York Methodist Hospital 506 6th St	Brooklyn	NY	11215	718-780-3000	780-5975
Web: www.nym.org					
New York Presbyterian Hospital 525 E 68th St	New York	NY	10021	212-746-5454	746-4293
Web: www.nyp.org					
New York University Medical Center 560 1st Ave	New York	NY	10016	212-263-7300	263-8460
Web: www.med.nyu.edu					
Newark-Wayne Community Hospital 1250 Driving Park Ave PO Box 111	Newark	NY	14513	315-332-2022	332-2371
Web: www.viahealth.org/home_newarkwayne.cfm?id=25					
Niagara Falls Memorial Medical Center 621 10th St	Niagara Falls	NY	14302	716-278-4000	278-4054
Web: www.nfmmc.org					
North Central Bronx Hospital 3424 Kossuth Ave	Bronx	NY	10467	718-519-5000	519-3172
North Shore University Hospital 300 Community Dr	Manhasset	NY	11030	516-562-0100	562-4545
Web: www.northshorelij.com/body.cfm?ID=51					
North Shore University Hospital 888 Old Country Rd	Plainview	NY	11803	516-719-3000	719-2719
Web: www.northshorelij.com/visit/h_plainview.htm					
Northern Westchester Hospital 400 E Main St	Mount Kisco	NY	10549	914-666-1200	666-1055
Web: www.nwhc.net					
Nyack Hospital 160 N Midland Ave	Nyack	NY	10960	845-348-2000	348-3040
Web: www.nyackhospital.org					
Olean General Hospital 515 Main St	Olean	NY	14760	716-373-2600	375-6394
Web: www.ogh.org					
Oneida Healthcare Center 321 Genesee St	Oneida	NY	13421	315-363-6000	361-2043
Web: www.oneidahealthcare.org					
Orange Regional Medical Center 60 Prospect Ave	Middletown	NY	10940	845-343-2424	342-7514
Web: www.ormc.org					
Arden Hill Campus 4 Harriman Dr	Goshen	NY	10924	845-294-5441	294-2105
Web: www.ormc.org					
Oswego Hospital 110 W 6th St	Oswego	NY	13126	315-349-5511	349-5732
Web: oswegohealth.org/ohny/oh.tpl					
Our Lady of Lourdes Memorial Hospital 169 Riverside Dr	Binghamton	NY	13905	607-798-5111	798-7681
Web: www.lourdes.com					
Our Lady of Mercy Medical Center 600 E 233rd St	Bronx	NY	10466	718-920-9000	920-6829
Web: www.olmhs.org					
Park Ridge Hospital 1555 Long Pond Rd	Rochester	NY	14626	585-723-7000	368-3888
Web: www.unityhealth.org/parkridge.asp					
Parkway Hospital 70-35 113th St	Forest Hills	NY	11375	718-990-4100	261-2812
Peconic Bay Medical Center 1300 Roanoke Ave	Riverhead	NY	11901	631-548-6000	727-8890
Web: www.peconicbaymedicalcenter.org					
Peninsula Hospital Center 51-15 Beach Channel Dr	Far Rockaway	NY	11691	718-734-2000	734-2993
Phelps Memorial Hospital Center 701 N Broadway	Sleepy Hollow	NY	10591	914-366-3000	366-1017
Web: www.phelpshospital.org					
Putnam Hospital Center 670 Stoneleigh Ave	Carmel	NY	10512	845-279-5711	279-7482
Web: www.putnamhospital.org					
Queens Hospital Center 82-68 164th St	Jamaica	NY	11432	718-883-3000	883-6116
Richmond University Medical Center 355 Bard Ave	Staten Island	NY	10310	718-818-1234	818-3714
Rochester General Hospital 1425 Portland Ave	Rochester	NY	14621	585-922-4000	922-5105
Web: www.viahealth.org					
Rome Memorial Hospital 1500 N James St	Rome	NY	13440	315-338-7000	338-7695
Web: www.romehosp.org					
Saint Barnabas Hospital 4422 3rd Ave	Bronx	NY	10457	718-960-9000	960-5704
Web: www.stbarnabashospital.org					
Saint Catherine of Siena Medical Center 50 Rt 25 A	Smithtown	NY	11787	631-862-3000	862-3105
Web: stcatherines.chsli.org					
Saint Clare's Hospital of Schenectady 600 McClellan St	Schenectady	NY	12304	518-382-2000	347-5409
Web: www.stclares.org					
Saint Elizabeth Medical Center 2209 Genesee St	Utica	NY	13501	315-798-8100	734-3092
Web: www.stemc.org					
Saint Francis Hospital 241 North Rd	Poughkeepsie	NY	12601	845-483-5000	485-3762
Web: www.sfhhc.org					
Saint James Mercy Hospital 411 Canisteo St	Hornell	NY	14843	607-324-8000	324-8115
Web: www.stjamesmercy.org					
Saint John's Riverside Hospital ParkCare Pavilion 2 Park Ave	Yonkers	NY	10703	914-964-7300	964-7704
Web: www.riversidehealth.org					
Saint Joseph Hospital 2605 Harlem Rd	Cheektowaga	NY	14225	716-891-2400	891-2616
Web: www.chsbuffalo.org/body.cfm?id=52					
Saint Joseph's Hospital 555 E Market St	Elmira	NY	14901	607-733-6541	737-7837
Web: www.stjosephs.org					
Saint Joseph's Hospital Health Center 301 Prospect Ave	Syracuse	NY	13203	315-448-5111	448-6161
TF: 888-785-6371 ■ *Web:* www.sjhsyr.org					
Saint Joseph's Medical Center 127 S Broadway	Yonkers	NY	10701	914-378-7000	378-7130
Web: www.saintjosephs.org					
Saint Luke's Cornwall Hospital					
Cornwall Campus 19 Laurel Ave	Cornwall	NY	12518	845-534-7711	458-4811
Web: www.stlukescornwallhospital.org					
Newburgh Campus 70 Dubois St	Newburgh	NY	12550	845-561-4400	568-2919
Web: www.stlukescornwallhospital.org					
Saint Luke's-Roosevelt Hospital Center 1111 Amsterdam Ave	New York	NY	10025	212-523-4000	523-1981
Web: www.slrhc.org					
Saint Mary's Hospital 427 Guy Park Ave	Amsterdam	NY	12010	518-842-1900	841-7158
Web: www.smha.org					
Saint Mary's Hospital 1300 Massachusetts Ave	Troy	NY	12180	518-268-5000	268-5257
Web: www.setonhealth.org					
Saint Peter's Hospital 315 S Manning Blvd	Albany	NY	12208	518-454-1550	525-6327
Web: www.stpetershealthcare.org					
Saint Vincent's Hospital Manhattan 170 W 12th St	New York	NY	10011	212-604-7000	604-2100
Saint Vincent's Midtown Hospital 415 W 51st St	New York	NY	10019	212-586-1500	459-8127
Web: www.svcmc.org/midtown					
Samaritan Hospital 2215 Burdett Ave	Troy	NY	12180	518-271-3300	271-3203
Web: www.nehealth.com					
Samaritan Medical Center 830 Washington St	Watertown	NY	13601	315-785-4000	785-4343
TF: 877-888-6138 ■ *Web:* www.samaritanhealth.com					
Saratoga Hospital 211 Church St	Saratoga Springs	NY	12866	518-587-3222	580-4285
Web: www.saratogacare.org					
Sisters of Charity Hospital of Buffalo 2157 Main St	Buffalo	NY	14214	716-862-2000	862-1899
Web: www.chsbuffalo.org/body.cfm?id=53					
Sound Shore Medical Center of Westchester 16 Guion Pl	New Rochelle	NY	10802	914-632-5000	632-1976
Web: www.ssmc.org					
South Nassau Communities Hospital 1 Healthy Way	Oceanside	NY	11572	516-632-3000	336-2922
Web: www.southnassau.org					
Southampton Hospital 240 Meeting House Ln	Southampton	NY	11968	631-726-8200	726-8666
Web: www.southamptonhospital.org					
Southside Hospital 301 E Main St	Bay Shore	NY	11706	631-968-3000	968-3315
Web: www.southsidehospital.org					
Staten Island University Hospital 475 Seaview Ave	Staten Island	NY	10305	718-226-9000	226-8966
Web: www.siuh.edu					
Stony Brook University Hospital SUNY at Stony Brook	Stony Brook	NY	11794	631-689-8333	444-6649
Web: www.stonybrookhospital.com					
Strong Memorial Hospital 601 Elmwood Ave University of Rochester Medical Center	Rochester	NY	14642	585-275-2100	273-1118
Web: www.stronghealth.com/about/hospitals					
Syosset Hospital 221 Jericho Tpke	Syosset	NY	11791	516-496-6400	496-6487
Web: www.northshorelij.com/body.cfm?ID=62					
United Memorial Medical Center 127 North St	Batavia	NY	14020	585-343-6030	344-7434
Web: www.ummc.org					
University Hospital SUNY Upstate Medical University 750 E Adams St	Syracuse	NY	13210	315-464-5540	464-4841
TF: 877-464-5540 ■ *Web:* www.upstate.edu/uh					
University Hospital of Brooklyn 450 Clarkson Ave	Brooklyn	NY	11203	718-270-1000	221-6307
Web: www.uhb.org					

General Hospitals - US (Cont'd)

New York (Cont'd)

Hospital	City	State	Zip	Phone	Fax
Vassar Brothers Medical Center 45 Reade Pl *Web:* www.vassarbrothers.org	Poughkeepsie	NY	12601	845-454-8500	437-3120
Victory Memorial Hospital 699 92nd St *Web:* www.vmhny.org	Brooklyn	NY	11228	718-567-1234	567-1002
Westchester Medical Center 95 Grasslands Rd *Web:* www.wcmc.com	Valhalla	NY	10595	914-493-7000	493-2821
White Plains Hospital Center Davis Ave & E Post Rd *Web:* www.wphospital.org	White Plains	NY	10601	914-681-0600	681-2902
Winthrop University Hospital 259 1st St *Web:* www.winthrop.org	Mineola	NY	11501	516-663-0333	663-2953
Woodhull Medical & Mental Health Center 760 Broadway	Brooklyn	NY	11206	718-963-8000	963-8999

North Carolina

Hospital	City	State	Zip	Phone	Fax
Alamance Regional Medical Center 1240 Huffman Mill Rd *Web:* www.armc.com	Burlington	NC	27215	336-538-7000	538-7425
Albemarle Hospital 1144 North Road St *Web:* www.albemarlehosp.org	Elizabeth City	NC	27909	252-335-0531	384-4654
Annie Penn Hospital 618 S Main St *Web:* www.mosescone.com/body.cfm?id=414	Reidsville	NC	27320	336-951-4000	951-4561
Beaufort County Hospital 628 E 12th St *Web:* www.beaufortcountyhospital.org	Washington	NC	27889	252-975-4100	948-4800
Betsy Johnson Regional Hospital 800 Tilghman Dr *Web:* www.bjrh.org	Dunn	NC	28334	910-892-7161	891-6030
Caldwell Memorial Hospital 321 Malberry St *Web:* www.caldwellmemorial.org	Lenoir	NC	28645	828-757-5100	757-5512
Cape Fear Hospital 5301 Wrightsville Ave *Web:* www.nhhn.org	Wilmington	NC	28403	910-452-8100	452-8121
Cape Fear Valley Medical Center 1638 Owen Dr *Web:* www.capefearvalley.com	Fayetteville	NC	28304	910-609-4000	609-6160
Carolinas Medical Center 1000 Blythe Blvd *Web:* www.carolinashealthcare.org	Charlotte	NC	28203	704-355-2000	355-5577
Carolinas Medical Center Mercy 2001 Vail Ave *Web:* www.carolinas.org	Charlotte	NC	28207	704-379-5000	304-5695
Carolinas Medical Center Union 600 Hospital Dr *Web:* www.cmcunion.org/	Monroe	NC	28112	704-283-3100	296-4175
Carolinas Medical Center-University 8800 N Tryon St *Web:* www.carolinas.org	Charlotte	NC	28262	704-863-6000	863-6236
Carteret General Hospital 3500 Arendell St *Web:* www.ccgh.org	Morehead City	NC	28557	252-808-6000	808-6985
Catawba Valley Medical Center 810 Fairgrove Church Rd SE *Web:* www.catawbavalleymedical.org	Hickory	NC	28602	828-326-3000	326-3371
Central Carolina Hospital 1135 Carthage St *TF:* 800-292-2262 ■ *Web:* www.centralcarolinahosp.com	Sanford	NC	27330	919-774-2100	774-2295
Cleveland Regional Medical Center 201 E Grover St *Web:* www.clevelandregional.org	Shelby	NC	28150	704-487-3000	487-3790
Columbus County Hospital 500 Jefferson St *Web:* www.cchospital.com	Whiteville	NC	28472	910-642-8011	642-9305
Cone Moses H Memorial Hospital 1200 N Elm St *TF:* 866-391-2734 ■ *Web:* www.mosescone.com	Greensboro	NC	27401	336-832-7000	832-8192
Craven Regional Medical Center 2000 Neuse Blvd *Web:* www.cravenhealthcare.org	New Bern	NC	28560	252-633-8111	633-8144
Davis Regional Medical Center 218 Old Mocksville Rd *Web:* www.davisregional.com/drmc	Statesville	NC	28625	704-873-0281	838-7287
Duke Health Raleigh Hospital 3400 Wake Forest Rd *Web:* www.dukehealthraleigh.org	Raleigh	NC	27609	919-954-3000	954-3900
Duke University Hospital 2301 Erwin Rd *Web:* www.dukehealth.org/ServicesAndLocations/Locations/UniversityHospital/index	Durham	NC	27710	919-684-8111	
Durham Regional Hospital 3643 N Roxboro Rd *Web:* www.durhamregional.org	Durham	NC	27704	919-470-4000	470-6147
Forsyth Medical Center 3333 Silas Creek Pkwy *Web:* www.forsythmedicalcenter.org	Winston-Salem	NC	27103	336-718-5000	718-9258
Frye Regional Medical Center 420 N Center St *Web:* www.fryemedctr.com	Hickory	NC	28601	828-322-6070	315-3901
Gaston Memorial Hospital 2525 Court Dr *Web:* www.gastonhealthcare.org	Gastonia	NC	28054	704-834-2000	834-2500
Grace Hospital 2201 S Sterling St *TF:* 866-687-2747 ■ *Web:* www.blueridgehealth.org/our_facilities	Morganton	NC	28655	828-580-5000	580-5509
Halifax Regional Medical Center 250 Smith Church Rd *Web:* www.halifaxmedicalcenter.org	Roanoke Rapids	NC	27870	252-535-8011	535-8466
Harris Regional Hospital 68 Hospital Rd *TF:* 800-496-2362 ■ *Web:* www.westcare.org/About/Affiliates/Harris.html	Sylva	NC	28779	828-586-7000	586-7467
Heritage Hospital 111 Hospital Dr *Web:* www.uhseast.com/body.cfm?id=29	Tarboro	NC	27886	252-641-7700	641-7484
High Point Regional Hospital 601 N Elm St *TF:* 800-367-7066 ■ *Web:* www.highpointregional.com	High Point	NC	27262	336-878-6000	878-6158
Highsmith-Rainey Memorial Hospital 150 Robeson St *Web:* www.capefearvalley.com/facilities/hrmh.htm	Fayetteville	NC	28301	910-609-1000	609-1046
Hugh Chatham Memorial Hospital 180 Parkwood Dr *Web:* www.hughchatham.org	Elkin	NC	28621	336-835-3722	526-6056
Iredell Memorial Hospital 557 Brookdale Dr *Web:* www.iredellmemorial.org	Statesville	NC	28677	704-873-5661	872-7924
Johnston Memorial Hospital 509 N Bright Leaf Blvd *Web:* www.johnstonmemorial.org	Smithfield	NC	27577	919-934-8171	989-7297
Lake Norman Regional Medical Center 171 Fairview Rd *Web:* www.lnrmc.com	Mooresville	NC	28117	704-663-1113	660-4005
Lenoir Memorial Hospital 100 Airport Rd *Web:* www.lenoirmemorial.org	Kinston	NC	28501	252-522-7171	522-7007
Margaret R Pardee Memorial Hospital 800 N Justice St *Web:* www.pardeehospital.org	Hendersonville	NC	28791	828-696-1000	696-1128
Maria Parham Medical Center 566 Ruin Creek Rd PO Box 59 *Web:* www.mphosp.org	Henderson	NC	27536	252-438-4143	438-3690
Moore Regional Hospital 155 Memorial Dr *TF:* 800-672-6072 ■ *Web:* www.firsthealth.org	Pinehurst	NC	28374	910-715-1000	715-1462
Morehead Memorial Hospital 117 E King's Hwy *Web:* www.morehead.org	Eden	NC	27288	336-623-9711	623-7660
Moses H Cone Memorial Hospital 1200 N Elm St *TF:* 866-391-2734 ■ *Web:* www.mosescone.com	Greensboro	NC	27401	336-832-7000	832-8192
Nash General Hospital 2460 Curtis Ellis Dr *Web:* www.nhcs.org	Rocky Mount	NC	27804	252-443-8000	443-8877
New Hanover Regional Medical Center 2131 S 17th St *TF:* 877-228-8135 ■ *Web:* www.nhrmc.org	Wilmington	NC	28401	910-343-7000	343-7220
NorthEast Medical Center 920 Church St N *TF:* 800-842-6868 ■ *Web:* www.northeastmedical.org	Concord	NC	28025	704-783-3000	783-1409
Northern Hospital of Surry County 830 Rockford St *Web:* www.northernhospital.com	Mount Airy	NC	27030	336-719-7000	719-0302
Onslow Memorial Hospital 317 Western Blvd *Web:* www.onslowmemorial.org	Jacksonville	NC	28546	910-577-2345	577-2246
Pardee Margaret R Memorial Hospital 800 N Justice St *Web:* www.pardeehospital.org	Hendersonville	NC	28791	828-696-1000	696-1128
Pitt County Memorial Hospital 2100 Stantonsburg Rd *Web:* www.uhseast.com	Greenville	NC	27835	252-847-4100	847-5147
Presbyterian Hospital Charlotte 200 Hawthorne Ln *Web:* www.presbyterian.org	Charlotte	NC	28204	704-384-4000	384-5600
Randolph Hospital 364 White Oak St *Web:* www.randolphhospital.org	Asheboro	NC	27203	336-625-5151	626-7664
Rex Healthcare 4420 Lake Boone Trail *Web:* www.rexhealth.com	Raleigh	NC	27607	919-783-3100	781-7192
Richmond Memorial Hospital 925 Long Dr *Web:* www.firsthealth.org	Rockingham	NC	28379	910-417-3000	417-3709
Roanoke-Chowan Hospital 500 S Academy St *Web:* www.uhseast.com	Ahoskie	NC	27910	252-209-3000	209-3049
Rowan Regional Medical Center 612 Mocksville Ave *Web:* www.rowan.org	Salisbury	NC	28144	704-210-5000	210-5498
Rutherford Hospital 288 S Ridgecrest Ave *Web:* www.rutherfordhosp.org	Rutherfordton	NC	28139	828-286-5000	286-5207
Saint Joseph's Hospital 428 Biltmore Ave	Asheville	NC	28801	828-213-1111	213-0763
Sampson Regional Medical Center 607 Beaman St *Web:* www.sampsonrmc.org	Clinton	NC	28328	910-592-8511	590-2321
Scotland Memorial Hospital 500 Lauchwood Dr *TF:* 866-225-5764 ■ *Web:* scotland.fasthealth.com	Laurinburg	NC	28352	910-291-7000	291-7499
Southeastern Regional Medical Center 300 W 27th St *Web:* www.srmc.org	Lumberton	NC	28358	910-671-5000	671-5200
Stanly Memorial Hospital 301 Yadkin St *Web:* www.stanly.org	Albemarle	NC	28001	704-984-4000	983-3562
Thomasville Medical Center 207 Old Lexington Rd *TF:* 800-880-0110 ■ *Web:* www.thomasvillemedicalcenter.org	Thomasville	NC	27360	336-472-2000	476-2534
University of North Carolina Hospitals 101 Manning Dr *Web:* www.unchealthcare.org	Chapel Hill	NC	27514	919-966-4131	966-7772
Valdese General Hospital 720 Malcolm Blvd *Web:* www.carolinas.org	Valdese	NC	28690	828-874-2251	879-7544
Wake Forest University Baptist Medical Center Medical Center Blvd *Web:* www1.wfubmc.edu	Winston-Salem	NC	27157	336-716-2011	716-2067
WakeMed Raleigh Campus 3000 New Bern Ave *Web:* www.wakemed.org	Raleigh	NC	27610	919-350-8000	350-8868
Watauga Medical Center 336 Deerfield Rd *Web:* www.watamgamc.org	Boone	NC	28607	828-262-4100	262-4103
Wayne Memorial Hospital 2700 Wayne Memorial Dr *Web:* www.waynehealth.org	Goldsboro	NC	27534	919-736-1110	731-6966
Wesley Long Community Hospital 501 N Elam Ave *Web:* www.mosescone.com/body.cfm?id=41	Greensboro	NC	27403	336-832-1000	832-1742
Wilkes Regional Medical Center 1370 W 'D' St *Web:* www.wilkesregional.com	North Wilkesboro	NC	28659	336-651-8100	651-8465
Wilson Medical Center 1705 SW Tarboro St *Web:* www.wilmed.org	Wilson	NC	27893	252-399-8040	399-8778

North Dakota

Hospital	City	State	Zip	Phone	Fax
Altru Hospital 1200 S Columbia Rd *TF:* 800-732-4277 ■ *Web:* www.altru.org	Grand Forks	ND	58201	701-780-5000	780-5238
Medcenter One Hospital 300 N 7th St *TF:* 800-932-8758 ■ *Web:* www.medcenterone.com	Bismarck	ND	58501	701-323-6000	323-5221
MeritCare Medical Center 801 N Broadway PO Box MC **Fax:* PR ■ *TF:* 800-437-4010 ■ *Web:* www.meritcare.com/guidebook	Fargo	ND	58122	701-234-6000	234-6979*
Saint Alexius Medical Center 900 E Broadway Ave *Web:* www.saintalexius.org	Bismarck	ND	58501	701-224-7000	530-7612
Saint Joseph's Hospital & Health Center 30 7th St SW *TF:* 800-446-6215 ■ *Web:* www.stjoeshospital.org	Dickinson	ND	58601	701-456-4000	456-4800
Trinity Hospital Saint Joseph's 407 3rd St SE *TF:* 800-247-1316 ■ *Web:* www.trinityhealth.org	Minot	ND	58701	701-857-5000	857-5117
Trinity Medical Center 1 Burdick Expy W *Web:* www.trinityhealth.org	Minot	ND	58701	701-857-5000	857-5117

Ohio

Hospital	City	State	Zip	Phone	Fax
Adena Regional Medical Center 272 Hospital Rd *Web:* adena.org/Locations/armc.htm	Chillicothe	OH	45601	740-779-7500	779-7934
Affinity Medical Center 875 8th St NE *TF:* 800-346-4869 ■ *Web:* www.affinitymedicalcenter.com	Massillon	OH	44646	330-832-8761	837-6871
Akron General Medical Center 400 Wabash Ave **Fax:* Admitting ■ *TF:* 800-221-4601 ■ *Web:* www.agmc.org	Akron	OH	44307	330-344-6000	344-1752*
Alliance Community Hospital 200 E State St *Web:* www.achosp.org	Alliance	OH	44601	330-596-6000	596-7079
Ashtabula County Medical Center 2420 Lake Ave *Web:* www.acmchealth.org	Ashtabula	OH	44004	440-997-2262	997-6644
Aultman Hospital 2600 6th St SW *Web:* www.aultman.com	Canton	OH	44710	330-452-9911	438-6356
Barberton Citizens Hospital 155 5th St NE *TF:* 877-227-8745 ■ *Web:* www.barbhosp.com	Barberton	OH	44203	330-745-1611	848-7820
Bethesda Hospital 2951 Maple Ave *TF:* 800-322-4762	Zanesville	OH	43701	740-454-4000	454-4781
Bethesda North Hospital 10500 Montgomery Rd *Web:* www.trihealth.com	Cincinnati	OH	45242	513-745-1111	745-1441
Blanchard Valley Hospital 1900 S Main St *Web:* www.bvhealthsystem.org	Findlay	OH	45840	419-423-4500	423-5358
Bryan Hospital 433 W High St *Web:* www.chwchospital.com	Bryan	OH	43506	419-636-1131	636-3100
Charles F Kettering Memorial Hospital 3535 Southern Blvd *Web:* www.kmcnetwork.org	Kettering	OH	45429	937-298-4331	395-8423
CHP Regional Medical Center 3700 Kolbe Rd *TF:* 800-600-5275 ■ *Web:* www.ehealthconnection.com/regions/lorain	Lorain	OH	44053	440-960-3000	960-4630
Christ Hospital 2139 Auburn Ave *TF:* 800-527-8919 ■ *Web:* www.health-alliance.com/christ_control.html	Cincinnati	OH	45219	513-585-2000	585-3300
CHRISTUS Saint Elizabeth Health Center 1044 Belmont Ave *Web:* www.christusste.org	Youngstown	OH	44501	330-746-7211	480-2901
Clermont Mercy Hospital 3000 Hospital Dr	Batavia	OH	45103	513-732-8200	732-8550
Cleveland Clinic 9500 Euclid Ave *TF:* 800-223-2273 ■ *Web:* www.clevelandclinic.org	Cleveland	OH	44195	216-444-2200	444-0271
Clinton Memorial Hospital 610 W Main St *TF:* 800-803-9648 ■ *Web:* www.cmhregional.com	Wilmington	OH	45177	937-382-6611	283-9681
Community Hospital 2615 E High St *Web:* www.communityhospital.com	Springfield	OH	45505	937-325-0531	328-9600
Deaconess Hospital 311 Straight St *TF:* 800-398-5699 ■ *Web:* www.deaconess-healthcare.com	Cincinnati	OH	45219	513-559-2100	475-5251
Doctors Hospital 5100 W Broad St **Fax:* Admitting ■ *Web:* www.ohiohealth.com/facilities/doctors	Columbus	OH	43228	614-544-4000	544-1762*
Doctors Hospital of Stark County 400 Austin Ave NW *Web:* www.drshospital.com	Massillon	OH	44646	330-837-7200	830-1616

	City	State	Zip	Phone	Fax
East Liverpool City Hospital 425 W 5th St *Web:* www.elch.org	East Liverpool	OH	43920	330-385-7200	386-2074
East Ohio Regional Hospital 90 N 4th St *Web:* www.eastohioregionalhospital.com	Martins Ferry	OH	43935	740-633-1100	633-4512
EMH Regional Medical Center 630 E River St *Web:* www.emh-healthcare.org	Elyria	OH	44035	440-329-7500	329-7507
Euclid Hospital 18901 Lake Shore Blvd *Web:* www.euclidhospital.org	Euclid	OH	44119	216-531-9000	692-7488
Fairfield Medical Center 401 N Ewing St *TF:* 800-548-2627 ■ *Web:* www.fmchealth.org	Lancaster	OH	43130	740-687-8000	687-8115
Fairview Hospital 18101 Lorain Ave *TF:* 800-323-8434 ■ *Web:* www.fairviewhospital.org	Cleveland	OH	44111	216-476-7000	476-4064
Firelands Regional Medical Center 1101 Decatur St *TF:* 800-342-1177 ■ *Web:* www.firelands.com	Sandusky	OH	44870	419-557-7400	557-6977
Fisher-Titus Medical Center 272 Benedict Ave *TF:* 800-589-3862 ■ *Web:* www.ftmc.com	Norwalk	OH	44857	419-668-8101	663-6036
Flower Hospital 5200 Harroun Rd *Web:* www.promedica.org	Sylvania	OH	43560	419-824-1444	882-2342
Fort Hamilton Hospital 630 Eaton Ave *Web:* www.health-alliance.com/fort_control.html	Hamilton	OH	45013	513-867-2000	867-2119
Geauga Regional Hospital 13207 Ravenna Rd *Web:* www.uhhsgrh.com	Chardon	OH	44024	440-285-6000	286-7219
Good Samaritan Hospital 375 Dixmyth Ave *Web:* www.trihealth.com	Cincinnati	OH	45220	513-872-1400	872-1190
Good Samaritan Hospital 2222 Philadelphia Dr *Web:* www.goodsamdayton.org	Dayton	OH	45406	937-278-2612	276-8219
Good Samaritan Medical & Rehabilitation Center 800 Forest Ave *TF:* 800-322-4762	Zanesville	OH	43701	740-454-5843	
Grandview Medical Center 405 Grand Ave *Web:* www.kmcnetwork.org/hospitals/Grandview.cfm	Dayton	OH	45405	937-226-3200	226-3382
Grant Medical Center 111 S Grant Ave *Web:* www.ohiohealth.com/facilities/grant	Columbus	OH	43215	614-566-9000	566-8043
Greene Memorial Hospital 1141 N Monroe Dr *Web:* www.greenehealth.org/gmh	Xenia	OH	45385	937-372-8011	376-7381
Hillcrest Hospital 6780 Mayfield Rd *Web:* www.hillcresthospital.org	Mayfield Heights	OH	44124	440-449-4500	312-6407
Holzer Medical Center 100 Jackson Pike *Web:* www.holzer.org	Gallipolis	OH	45631	740-446-5000	446-5522
Huron Hospital 13951 Terrace Rd *Web:* www.huronhospital.org/	East Cleveland	OH	44112	216-761-3300	761-7476
Jewish Hospital 4777 E Galbraith Rd *Web:* www.jewishhospitalcincinnati.com	Cincinnati	OH	45236	513-686-3000	686-3003
Kaiser Permanente Parma Medical Center 12301 Snow Rd *TF:* 800-524-7372	Parma	OH	44130	216-362-2000	362-2093
Knox Community Hospital 1330 Coshocton Rd *Web:* www.knoxcommhosp.org	Mount Vernon	OH	43050	740-393-9000	399-3130
Lake Hospital System 10 E Washington St *Web:* www.lhs.net	Painesville	OH	44077	440-354-2400	354-1994
Lakewood Hospital 14519 Detroit Ave *TF:* 800-521-3955 ■ *Web:* www.lakewoodhospital.org	Lakewood	OH	44107	216-521-4200	529-7161
Licking Memorial Hospital 1320 W Main St *Web:* www.lmhealth.org	Newark	OH	43055	740-348-4000	348-4106
Lima Memorial Hospital 1001 Bellefontaine Ave *Web:* www.limamemorial.org	Lima	OH	45804	419-228-3335	226-5013
Lutheran Hospital 1730 W 25th St *Web:* www.lutheranhospital.org	Cleveland	OH	44113	216-696-4300	363-2082
Marietta Memorial Hospital 401 Matthew St *TF:* 800-523-3977 ■ *Web:* www.mmhospital.org	Marietta	OH	45750	740-374-1400	374-1412
Marion General Hospital 1000 McKinley Park Dr *Web:* www.mariongeneral.com	Marion	OH	43302	740-383-8400	383-8880
Marymount Hospital 12300 McCracken Rd *Web:* www.marymount.org	Garfield Heights	OH	44125	216-581-0500	587-8882
Medcentral Health System Mansfield Hospital 335 Glessner Ave *Web:* www.medcentral.org	Mansfield	OH	44903	419-526-8000	521-7960
Medical College of Ohio Hospital 3000 Arlington Ave *TF:* 800-321-8383	Toledo	OH	43614	419-383-4000	383-3850
Medina General Hospital 1000 E Washington St *TF:* 877-792-1001 ■ *Web:* www.medinahospital.org	Medina	OH	44256	330-725-1000	721-4906
Memorial Hospital 715 S Taft Ave *Web:* www.fremontmemorial.org	Fremont	OH	43420	419-332-7321	332-5875
Mercy Hospital Anderson 7500 State Rd *Web:* www.mercy.health-partners.org	Cincinnati	OH	45255	513-624-4500	624-3299
Mercy Hospital Fairfield 3000 Mack Rd *Web:* www.ehealthconnection.com/regions/cincinnati	Fairfield	OH	45014	513-870-7000	870-7065
Mercy Hospital Mount Airy 2446 Kipling Ave *Web:* www.mercy.health-partners.org	Cincinnati	OH	45239	513-853-5000	853-7865
Mercy Hospital Western Hills 3131 Queen City Ave *Web:* www.mercy.health-partners.org	Cincinnati	OH	45238	513-389-5000	389-5201
Mercy Medical Center 1320 Mercy Dr NW *TF:* 800-999-8662 ■ *Web:* www.thequalityhospital.com	Canton	OH	44708	330-489-1000	489-1312
Mercy Medical Center 1343 N Fountain Blvd *Web:* www.mercyhealth-partners.org	Springfield	OH	45501	937-390-5000	390-5527
MetroHealth Medical Center 2500 MetroHealth Dr *TF:* 800-554-5251 ■ *Web:* www.metrohealth.org	Cleveland	OH	44109	216-778-7800	
Miami Valley Hospital 1 Wyoming St *TF:* 800-544-0630 ■ *Web:* www.miamivalleyhospital.com	Dayton	OH	45409	937-223-6192	208-2225
Middletown Regional Hospital 105 McKnight Dr *TF:* 800-338-4057 ■ *Web:* www.middletownhospital.org	Middletown	OH	45044	513-424-2111	
Mount Carmel Saint Ann's Hospital 500 S Cleveland Ave *Web:* www.mountcarmelhealth.com/85.cfm	Westerville	OH	43081	614-898-4000	898-8668
Mount Carmel West Hospital 793 W State St *TF:* 800-225-9344 ■ *Web:* www.mountcarmelhealth.com/84.cfm	Columbus	OH	43222	614-234-5000	234-5740
Northside Medical Center 500 Gypsy Ln *Web:* www.forumhealth.org	Youngstown	OH	44501	330-884-1000	884-2589
Ohio State University Medical Center 410 W 10th Ave *Web:* medicalcenter.osu.edu	Columbus	OH	43210	614-293-8652	293-5677
Parma Community General Hospital 7007 Powers Blvd *TF:* 866-699-7244 ■ *Web:* www.parmahospital.org	Parma	OH	44129	440-743-3000	743-4386
Riverside Methodist Hospital 3535 Olentangy River Rd *TF:* 800-837-7555 ■ *Web:* www.ohiohealth.com/facilities/riverside	Columbus	OH	43214	614-566-5000	566-6760
Robinson Memorial Hospital 6847 N Chestnut St *Web:* robinsonmemorial.org	Ravenna	OH	44266	330-297-0811	297-2949
Saint Anne Mercy Hospital 3404 W Sylvania Ave *Web:* www.mercyweb.org	Toledo	OH	43623	419-407-2663	407-3888
Saint Charles Mercy Hospital 2600 Navarre Ave *TF:* 800-692-6363 ■ *Web:* www.mercyweb.org	Oregon	OH	43616	419-696-7200	696-7328
Saint John West Shore Hospital 29000 Center Ridge Rd *Web:* www.sjws.net	Westlake	OH	44145	440-835-8000	827-5015
Saint Joseph Health Center 667 Eastland Ave SE *Web:* www.ehealthconnection.com/regions/youngstown/content/show_facility.asp?facility_id=198	Warren	OH	44484	330-841-4000	841-4019
Saint Luke's Hospital 5901 Monclova Rd *Web:* www.stlukeshospital.com	Maumee	OH	43537	419-893-5911	891-8037
Saint Rita's Medical Center 730 W Market St *Web:* www.stritas.org	Lima	OH	45801	419-227-3361	226-9750
Saint Thomas Hospital 444 N Main St *Web:* www.summahealth.org	Akron	OH	44310	330-375-3000	375-3050
Saint Vincent Charity Hospital 2351 E 22nd St *TF:* 800-451-8128 ■ *Web:* www.svch.net	Cleveland	OH	44115	216-861-6200	363-2519
Saint Vincent Mercy Medical Center 2213 Cherry St *Web:* www.mercyweb.org	Toledo	OH	43608	419-321-3232	251-3810
Salem Community Hospital 1995 E State St *Web:* www.salemhosp.com	Salem	OH	44460	330-332-1551	332-7691
South Pointe Hospital 20000 Harvard Rd *Web:* www.southpointehospital.org	Warrensville Heights	OH	44122	216-491-6000	491-7193
Southeastern Ohio Regional Medical Center 1341 Clark St *Web:* www.seormc.org	Cambridge	OH	43725	740-439-3561	439-8175
Southern Ohio Medical Center 1805 27th St *Web:* www.somc.org	Portsmouth	OH	45662	740-354-5000	353-2981
Southwest General Health Center 18697 Bagley Rd *Web:* www.swgeneral.com	Middleburg Heights	OH	44130	440-816-8000	816-5348
Toledo Hospital 2142 N Cove Blvd *Fax: Admitting ■ *Web:* www.promedica.org	Toledo	OH	43606	419-291-4000	291-6901*
Trinity Medical Center West 4000 Johnson Rd *Web:* www.trinityhealth.com	Steubenville	OH	43952	740-264-8000	283-7104
Trumbull Memorial Hospital 1350 E Market St *Web:* www.trumhosp.org	Warren	OH	44482	330-841-9011	841-9281
Union Hospital 659 Boulevard *Web:* www.unionhospital.org	Dover	OH	44622	330-343-3311	365-3850
University Hospital 234 Goodman St *Web:* www.universityhospitalcincinnati.com	Cincinnati	OH	45219	513-584-1000	584-3779
University Hospital Bedford Medical Center 44 Blaine Ave *Web:* www.uhhsbmc.com	Bedford	OH	44146	440-735-3900	735-3631
University Hospital East 1492 E Broad St *Web:* www.medicalcenter.osu.edu	Columbus	OH	43205	614-257-3000	257-3439
University Hospitals of Cleveland 11100 Euclid Ave *Web:* www.uhhs.com	Cleveland	OH	44106	216-844-1000	844-2525
Upper Valley Medical Center 3130 N Dixie Hwy *Web:* www.uvmc.com	Troy	OH	45373	937-440-4000	440-7337
Wilson Memorial Hospital 915 W Michigan St *TF:* 800-589-9641 ■ *Web:* www.wilsonhospital.com	Sidney	OH	45365	937-498-2311	497-8251
Wood County Hospital 950 W Wooster St *Web:* www.wch.net	Bowling Green	OH	43402	419-354-8900	354-8957

Oklahoma

	City	State	Zip	Phone	Fax
Comanche County Memorial Hospital 3401 NW Gore Blvd *Web:* www.memorialhealthsource.com	Lawton	OK	73505	580-355-8620	585-5458
Deaconess Hospital 5501 N Portland Ave *Web:* www.deaconessokc.org	Oklahoma City	OK	73112	405-946-5581	604-6153
Duncan Regional Hospital 1407 Whisenant Dr *Web:* www.duncanregional.com	Duncan	OK	73533	580-252-5300	251-8559
Edmond Medical Center 1 S Bryant St *Web:* www.edmondmedctr.com	Edmond	OK	73034	405-341-6100	359-5500
Grady Memorial Hospital 2220 Iowa Ave *Web:* www.gradymem.org	Chickasha	OK	73018	405-224-2300	779-2413
Hillcrest Medical Center 1120 S Utica Ave *Web:* www.hillcrest.com	Tulsa	OK	74104	918-579-1000	584-0840
INTEGRIS Baptist Medical Center 3300 Northwest Expy *Fax: Admitting ■ *Web:* www.integris-health.com	Oklahoma City	OK	73112	405-949-3011	949-3998*
INTEGRIS Baptist Regional Health Center 200 2nd Ave SW *Web:* www.integris-health.com	Miami	OK	74354	918-542-6611	540-7605
INTEGRIS Bass Baptist Health Center 600 S Monroe St *Web:* www.integris-health.com	Enid	OK	73701	580-233-2300	548-1553
INTEGRIS Southwest Medical Center 4401 S Western St *Web:* www.integris-health.com	Oklahoma City	OK	73109	405-636-7000	636-7702
Jackson County Memorial Hospital 1200 E Pecan St *TF:* 800-250-9965 ■ *Web:* www.jcmh.com	Altus	OK	73521	580-482-4781	481-2345
Jane Phillips Medical Center 3500 SE Frank Phillips Blvd *Web:* www.jpmc.org	Bartlesville	OK	74006	918-333-7200	331-1529
McAlester Regional Health Center 1 Clark Bass Blvd *Web:* www.mrhcok.com	McAlester	OK	74501	918-426-1800	421-8066
Medical Center of Southeastern Oklahoma 1800 University Blvd *TF:* 888-280-6276 ■ *Web:* www.mcsohealth.com	Durant	OK	74701	580-924-3080	924-0422
Mercy Health Center 4300 W Memorial Rd *Web:* www.mercyok.net/mhc/default.asp	Oklahoma City	OK	73120	405-755-1515	936-5794
Mercy Memorial Health Center 1011 14th Ave NW *Web:* www.mercyok.com	Ardmore	OK	73401	580-223-5400	220-6580
Midwest Regional Medical Center 2825 Parklawn Dr *Web:* www.hma-corp.com/ok2.html	Midwest City	OK	73110	405-610-4411	610-1380
Muskogee Regional Medical Center 300 Rockefeller Dr *Web:* www.muskogeehealth.com	Muskogee	OK	74401	918-682-5501	684-2552
Norman Regional Hospital 901 N Porter St *Web:* www.normanregional.com	Norman	OK	73071	405-307-1000	307-1076
OSU Medical Center 744 W 9th St *TF:* 800-876-5664 ■ *Web:* www.tulsaregional.com	Tulsa	OK	74127	918-587-2561	599-5892
OU Medical Center 1200 Everett Dr *Web:* www.oumedcenter.com	Oklahoma City	OK	73104	405-271-5656	271-1773
Phillips Jane Medical Center 3500 SE Frank Phillips Blvd *Web:* www.jpmc.org	Bartlesville	OK	74006	918-333-7200	331-1529
Ponca City Medical Center 1900 N 14th St *Web:* www.poncamedcenter.com	Ponca City	OK	74601	580-765-3321	765-0341
Saint Anthony Hospital 1000 N Lee St *TF:* 800-227-6964 ■ *Web:* www.saintsok.com	Oklahoma City	OK	73101	405-272-7000	272-6592
Saint Anthony South 2129 SW 59th St *Web:* www.saintsok.com	Oklahoma City	OK	73119	405-685-6671	680-4149
Saint Francis Hospital 6161 S Yale Ave *TF:* 800-888-9599 ■ *Web:* www.saintfrancis.com	Tulsa	OK	74136	918-494-2200	494-1426
Saint John Medical Center 1923 S Utica Ave *Web:* www.sjmc.org	Tulsa	OK	74104	918-744-2345	744-2527
Saint Mary's Regional Medical Center 305 S 5th St *Web:* www.stmarysregional.com	Enid	OK	73701	580-233-6100	249-3982
SouthCrest Hospital 8801 S 101st East Ave *Web:* www.southcresthospital.com	Tulsa	OK	74133	918-294-4000	294-4809
Southwestern Medical Center 5602 SW Lee Blvd *Web:* www.swmconline.com	Lawton	OK	73505	580-531-4700	531-4702
Stillwater Medical Center 1323 W 6th St *Web:* www.stillwater-medical.org	Stillwater	OK	74074	405-372-1480	372-9552
Unity Health Center 1102 W MacArthur St *Web:* www.unityhealthcenter.com	Shawnee	OK	74804	405-273-2270	878-8101
Valley View Regional Hospital 430 N Monte Vista St *Web:* www.valleyviewregionalhospital.com	Ada	OK	74820	580-332-2323	421-6060

Oregon

	City	State	Zip	Phone	Fax
Adventist Medical Center 10123 SE Market St *Web:* www.adventisthealthnw.com	Portland	OR	97216	503-257-2500	261-6638

General Hospitals - US (Cont'd)

Oregon (Cont'd)

Hospital	City	State	Zip	Phone	Fax
Albany General Hospital 1046 6th Ave SW *Web:* www.samhealth.org/shs_facilities/agh	Albany	OR	97321	541-812-4000	812-4449
Bay Area Hospital 1775 Thompson Rd *Web:* www.bayareahospital.org	Coos Bay	OR	97420	541-269-8111	267-7057
Good Samaritan Regional Medical Center 3600 NW Samaritan Dr *TF:* 888-872-0760 ■ *Web:* www.samhealth.org/shs_facilities/gsrmc	Corvallis	OR	97330	541-757-5111	768-4776
Holy Rosary Medical Center 351 SW 9th St *TF:* 877-225-4762 ■ *Web:* www.holyrosary-ontario.org	Ontario	OR	97914	541-881-7000	881-7184
Kaiser Permanente Medical Center 10180 SE Sunnyside Rd *TF:* 800-813-2000	Clackamas	OR	97015	503-652-2880	571-2671
Legacy Emanuel Hospital & Health Center 2801 N Gantenbein Ave *TF:* 800-422-2509 ■ *Web:* www.legacyhealth.org	Portland	OR	97227	503-413-2200	413-2428
Legacy Good Samaritan Hospital 1015 NW 22nd Ave *TF:* 800-733-9959 ■ *Web:* www.legacyhealth.org	Portland	OR	97210	503-229-7711	413-6347
Legacy Meridian Park Hospital 19300 SW 65th Ave *Web:* www.legacyhealth.org	Tualatin	OR	97062	503-692-1212	692-2478
McKenzie-Willamette Hospital 1460 G St *Web:* www.mckweb.com	Springfield	OR	97477	541-726-4400	726-4540
Mercy Medical Center 2700 Stewart Pkwy *Web:* www.mercyrose.org	Roseburg	OR	97470	541-673-0611	677-4848
Oregon Health & Science University Hospital 3181 SW Sam Jackson Park Rd *Web:* www.ohsu.edu	Portland	OR	97239	503-494-8311	494-3400
Providence Medford Medical Center 1111 Crater Lake Ave *TF:* 877-541-0588 ■ *Web:* www.providence.org	Medford	OR	97504	541-773-6611	732-5872
Providence Portland Medical Center 4805 NE Glisan St *TF:* 800-833-8899 ■ *Web:* www.providence.org/oregon/facilities	Portland	OR	97213	503-215-1111	215-6858
Providence Saint Vincent Medical Center 9205 SW Barnes Rd *TF:* 800-677-6752 ■ *Web:* www.providence.org/oregon/facilities	Portland	OR	97225	503-216-1234	216-2468
Rogue Valley Medical Center 2825 E Barnett Rd *TF:* 800-944-7073 ■ *Web:* www.asante.org	Medford	OR	97504	541-789-7000	789-5931
Sacred Heart Medical Center 1255 Hilyard St *TF:* 800-288-7444 ■ *Web:* www.peacehealth.org	Eugene	OR	97401	541-686-7300	686-3699
Saint Charles Medical Center 2500 NE Neff Rd *Web:* www.scmc.org	Bend	OR	97701	541-382-4321	388-7723
Salem Hospital 665 Winter St SE *Web:* www.salemhospital.org	Salem	OR	97301	503-370-5200	561-4844
Sky Lakes Medical Center 2865 Daggett Ave *Web:* www.skylakes.org	Klamath Falls	OR	97601	541-882-6311	274-6725
Tuality Community Hospital 335 SE 8th Ave *Web:* www.tuality.org	Hillsboro	OR	97123	503-681-1111	681-1608
Willamette Falls Hospital 1500 Division St *Web:* www.willamettefallshospital.org	Oregon City	OR	97045	503-656-1631	650-6807

Pennsylvania

Hospital	City	State	Zip	Phone	Fax
Abington Memorial Hospital 1200 Old York Rd *Web:* www.amh.org	Abington	PA	19001	215-481-2000	481-4014
Albert Einstein Medical Center 5501 Old York Rd *TF:* 800-346-7834 ■ *Web:* www.einstein.edu	Philadelphia	PA	19141	215-456-7010	456-6242
Alle-Kiski Medical Center 1301 Carlisle St *Web:* www.wpahs.org/akmc	Natrona Heights	PA	15065	724-224-5100	226-7490
Allegheny General Hospital 320 E North Ave *Web:* www.wpahs.org/agh/index.html	Pittsburgh	PA	15212	412-359-3131	359-4108
Altoona Regional Health System Altoona Hospital 620 Howard Ave *TF:* 800-946-1902 ■ *Web:* www.altoonaregional.org	Altoona	PA	16601	814-889-2011	889-7808
Altoona Regional Health System Bon Secours Campus 2500 7th Ave *Web:* www.altoonaregional.org	Altoona	PA	16602	814-944-1681	889-7808
Armstrong County Memorial Hospital 1 Nolte Dr *Web:* www.acmh.org	Kittanning	PA	16201	724-543-8500	543-8535
Berwick Hospital Center 701 E 16th St *Web:* www.berwick-hospital.com	Berwick	PA	18603	570-759-5000	759-3473
Bradford Regional Medical Center 116 Interstate Pkwy *Web:* www.brmc.com	Bradford	PA	16701	814-368-4143	368-5722
Brandywine Hospital 201 Reeceville Rd *Web:* www.brandywinehospital.com	Coatesville	PA	19320	610-383-8000	383-8360
Bryn Mawr Hospital 130 S Bryn Mawr Ave *Web:* www.mainlinehealth.org/bmh	Bryn Mawr	PA	19010	610-526-3000	526-4488
Butler Memorial Hospital 911 E Brady St *Web:* www.butlerhealthsys.org	Butler	PA	16001	724-284-4413	284-4645
Canonsburg General Hospital 100 Medical Blvd *Web:* www.wpahs.org	Canonsburg	PA	15317	724-745-6100	873-5876
Carlisle Regional Medical Center 361 Alexander Spring Rd	Carlisle	PA	17015	717-249-1212	249-0770
Central Montgomery Medical Center 100 Medical Campus Dr *Web:* www.cmmc-uhs.com	Lansdale	PA	19446	215-368-2100	361-4933
Chambersburg Hospital 112 N 7th St *Web:* www.summithealth.org	Chambersburg	PA	17201	717-264-5171	267-7704
Charles Cole Memorial Hospital 1001 E 2nd St *Web:* www.charlescolehospital.com	Coudersport	PA	16915	814-274-9300	274-0884
Chester County Hospital 701 E Marshall St **Fax:* Admitting ■ *Web:* www.cchosp.com	West Chester	PA	19380	610-431-5000	430-2958*
Chestnut Hill Hospital 8835 Germantown Ave *Web:* www.chh.org	Philadelphia	PA	19118	215-248-8200	248-8330
Clarion Hospital 1 Hospital Dr *TF:* 800-522-0505 ■ *Web:* www.clarionhospital.org	Clarion	PA	16214	814-226-9500	226-1224
Clearfield Hospital 809 Turnpike Ave PO Box 992 *TF:* 888-313-0082 ■ *Web:* www.clearfieldhospital.org	Clearfield	PA	16830	814-765-5341	768-2421
Community Medical Center 1800 Mulberry St *Web:* www.cmchealthsys.org	Scranton	PA	18510	570-969-8000	969-8951
Crozer-Chester Medical Center 1 Medical Center Blvd *Web:* www.crozer.org	Upland	PA	19013	610-447-2000	447-2234
Delaware County Memorial Hospital 501 N Lansdowne Ave *Web:* www.crozer.org	Drexel Hill	PA	19026	610-284-8100	284-8993
Divine Providence Hospital 1100 Grampian Blvd	Williamsport	PA	17701	570-326-8181	321-7780
Doylestown Hospital 595 W State St *Web:* www.dh.org	Doylestown	PA	18901	215-345-2200	345-2532
DuBois Regional Medical Center 100 Hospital Ave *Web:* www.drmc.org	Du Bois	PA	15801	814-371-2200	375-3562
Easton Hospital 250 S 21st St *Web:* www.easton-hospital.com	Easton	PA	18042	610-250-4000	250-4078
Einstein at Elkins Park 60 E Township Line Rd *Web:* www.einstein.edu/facilities/article10068.html	Elkins Park	PA	19027	215-663-6000	663-6002
Elk Regional Health Center 763 Johnsonburg Rd *TF:* 877-391-6800 ■ *Web:* www.elkregional.org	Saint Marys	PA	15857	814-788-8000	788-8040
Ellwood City Hospital 724 Pershing St	Ellwood City	PA	16117	724-752-0081	752-0966
Ephrata Community Hospital 169 Martin Ave *Web:* www.ephratahospital.org	Ephrata	PA	17522	717-733-0311	738-6675
Evangelical Community Hospital 1 Hospital Dr *Web:* www.evanhospital.com	Lewisburg	PA	17837	570-522-2000	522-2500
Forbes Regional Hospital 2570 Haymaker Rd *Web:* www.wpahs.org/frh	Monroeville	PA	15146	412-858-2000	858-2088
Frankford Hospital Bucks County Campus 380 N Oxford Valley Rd *Web:* www.frankfordhospitals.org/about/article6459.html	Langhorne	PA	19047	215-949-5000	949-5105
Frankford Hospitals Frankford Campus 4900 Frankford Ave *Web:* www.frankfordhospitals.org	Philadelphia	PA	19124	215-831-2000	831-2331
Frick Hospital 508 S Church St	Mount Pleasant	PA	15666	724-547-1500	542-1815
Geisinger Medical Center 100 N Academy Ave *Web:* www.geisinger.org	Danville	PA	17822	570-271-6211	271-6927
Geisinger South Wilkes-Barre 25 Church St *Web:* www.geisinger.org	Wilkes-Barre	PA	18765	570-826-3100	831-8989
Geisinger Wyoming Valley Medical Center 1000 E Mountain Dr *Web:* www.geisinger.org/about/gwv.shtml	Wilkes-Barre	PA	18711	570-826-7300	826-7387
Gettysburg Hospital 147 Gettys St *Web:* www.gettysburghosp.org	Gettysburg	PA	17325	717-334-2121	338-3245
Gnaden Huetten Memorial Hospital 211 N 12th St *Web:* www.ghmh.org	Lehighton	PA	18235	610-377-1300	377-7000
Good Samaritan Hospital 252 S 4th St *Web:* www.gshleb.org	Lebanon	PA	17042	717-270-7500	272-4716
Good Samaritan Regional Medical Center 700 E Norwegian St *Web:* www.gsrmc.com	Pottsville	PA	17901	570-621-4000	622-7950
Grand View Hospital 700 Lawn Ave *Web:* www.gvh.org	Sellersville	PA	18960	215-453-4000	453-9151
Grove City Medical Center 631 N Broad St Ext *TF:* 877-459-5455 ■ *Web:* www.gcmcpa.org	Grove City	PA	16127	724-450-7000	450-7179
Hahnemann University Hospital 230 N Broad St **Fax:* Admitting ■ *Web:* www.hahnemannhospital.com	Philadelphia	PA	19102	215-762-7000	762-3272*
Hamot Medical Center 201 State St *Web:* www.hamot.org	Erie	PA	16550	814-877-6000	877-6104
Hanover Hospital 300 Highland Ave *TF:* 800-673-2426 ■ *Web:* www.hanoverhospital.org	Hanover	PA	17331	717-637-3711	633-3534
Harrisburg Hospital 111 S Front St *TF:* 888-782-5678 ■ *Web:* www.pinnaclehealth.org/body.cfm?id=771	Harrisburg	PA	17101	717-782-3131	782-5536
Hazleton General Hospital 700 E Broad St *Web:* www.ghha.org	Hazleton	PA	18201	570-450-4357	501-6203
Heart of Lancaster Regional Medical Center 1500 Highland Dr *Web:* www.heartoflancaster.com	Lititz	PA	17543	717-625-5000	625-5672
Holy Redeemer Hospital & Medical Center 1648 Huntingdon Pike *TF:* 800-818-4747 ■ *Web:* www.holyredeemer.com	Meadowbrook	PA	19046	215-947-3000	938-2023
Holy Spirit Hospital 503 N 21st St *Web:* www.hsh.org	Camp Hill	PA	17011	717-763-2100	763-2183
Hospital of the University of Pennsylvania 3400 Spruce St *Web:* www.pennhealth.com/hup	Philadelphia	PA	19104	215-662-4000	662-3645
Indiana Regional Medical Center 835 Hospital Rd *Web:* www.indianarmc.org	Indiana	PA	15701	724-357-7000	357-7449
Jameson Hospital 1211 Wilmington Ave *Web:* www.jamesonhealthsystem.com	New Castle	PA	16105	724-658-9001	656-4241
JC Blair Memorial Hospital 1225 Warm Springs Ave *Web:* www.jcblair.org	Huntingdon	PA	16652	814-643-2290	643-9718
Jeanes Hospital 7600 Central Ave *Web:* www.jeanes.com	Philadelphia	PA	19111	215-728-2000	728-3365
Jefferson Regional Medical Center 565 Coal Valley Rd *Web:* www.jeffersonregional.com	Pittsburgh	PA	15236	412-469-5000	469-7062
Lancaster General Hospital 555 N Duke St *Web:* www.lancastergeneral.org	Lancaster	PA	17604	717-290-5511	291-9657
Lancaster Regional Medical Center 250 College Ave *Web:* www.lancaster-regional.com	Lancaster	PA	17603	717-291-8211	291-8090
Lankenau Hospital 100 Lancaster Ave *Web:* www.mainlinehealth.org/lh	Wynnewood	PA	19096	610-645-2000	645-8007
Latrobe Area Hospital 1 Mellon Way *Web:* www.lah.com	Latrobe	PA	15650	724-537-1000	532-6073
Lehigh Valley Hospital 17th & Chew St PO Box 7017 **Fax:* Admitting ■ *TF:* 800-548-7247 ■ *Web:* www.lvh.com	Allentown	PA	18105	610-402-8000	402-1696*
Lehigh Valley Hospital Muhlenberg 2545 Schoenersville Rd **Fax Area Code:* 610 ■ *TF:* 800-548-7247 ■ *Web:* www.lvhhn.org/locations/muhlenberg	Bethlehem	PA	18017	484-884-2200	402-8061*
Lewistown Hospital 400 Highland Ave *TF:* 800-248-0505 ■ *Web:* www.lewistownhospital.org	Lewistown	PA	17044	717-248-5411	242-7132
Lower Bucks Hospital 501 Bath Rd *Web:* www.lowerbuckshospital.org	Bristol	PA	19007	215-785-9200	785-9175
Marian Community Hospital 100 Lincoln Ave *Web:* www.marianhospital.org/live	Carbondale	PA	18407	570-282-2100	282-7177
Meadville Medical Center 751 Liberty St *TF:* 800-283-8321 ■ *Web:* www.mmchs.org	Meadville	PA	16335	814-333-5000	333-9456
Medical Center The 1000 Dutch Ridge Rd	Beaver	PA	15009	724-728-7000	773-8210
Memorial Hospital 325 South Belmont St *TF:* 800-436-4326 ■ *Web:* www.mhyork.org	York	PA	17405	717-843-8623	849-5329
Memorial Medical Center 1086 Franklin St *Web:* www.conemaugh.org/locations/mmc/default.cfm	Johnstown	PA	15905	814-534-9000	539-0264
Mercy Hospital of Philadelphia 501 S 54th St *Web:* www.mercyhealth.org/mercyhosp	Philadelphia	PA	19143	215-748-9000	748-9339
Mercy Hospital of Pittsburgh 1400 Locust St *Web:* www.mercylink.org	Pittsburgh	PA	15219	412-232-8111	232-7380
Mercy Hospital of Scranton 746 Jefferson Ave *Web:* www.mercyhealthpartners.com	Scranton	PA	18510	570-348-7100	348-7639
Mercy Jeannette Hospital 600 Jefferson Ave **Fax:* Admitting ■ *Web:* www.jdmh.org	Jeannette	PA	15644	724-527-3551	527-9430*
Mercy Suburban Hospital 2701 De Kalb Pike *Web:* www.mercyhealth.org/suburban	Norristown	PA	19401	610-278-2000	272-4642
Methodist Hospital 2301 S Broad St *Web:* www.jeffersonhospital.org/methodist	Philadelphia	PA	19148	215-952-9000	952-9933
Millcreek Community Hospital 5515 Peach St *Web:* www.lecom.edu/millcreek%2Dcommunity%2Dhospital	Erie	PA	16509	814-864-4031	868-8249
Monongahela Valley Hospital 1163 Country Club Rd *Web:* www.monvalleyhospital.com	Monongahela	PA	15063	724-258-1000	258-1850
Montgomery Hospital 1301 Powell St *Web:* www.montgomeryhospital.org	Norristown	PA	19401	610-270-2000	270-2789
Moses Taylor Hospital 700 Quincy Ave *Web:* www.mth.org	Scranton	PA	18510	570-340-2100	969-2629
Mount Nittany Medical Center 1800 E Park Ave *TF:* 866-757-2317 ■ *Web:* www.mountnittany.org	State College	PA	16803	814-231-7000	231-7200
Nazareth Hospital 2601 Holme Ave *Web:* www.mercyhealth.org/nazareth	Philadelphia	PA	19152	215-335-6000	335-6363
Northeastern Hospital of Philadelphia 2301 E Allegheny Ave *Web:* www.health.temple.edu/northeastern.html	Philadelphia	PA	19134	215-291-3000	291-3418
Ohio Valley General Hospital 25 Heckel Rd *Web:* www.ohiovalleyhospital.org	McKees Rocks	PA	15136	412-777-6161	777-6131
Paoli Hospital 255 W Lancaster Ave *Web:* www.mainlinehealth.org/ph	Paoli	PA	19301	610-648-1000	647-0450

Phone Fax

Penn Presbyterian Medical Center 39th & Market Sts .... Philadelphia PA 19104 215-662-8000 662-9212
Web: www.pennhealth.com/presby
Penn State Milton S Hershey Medical Center
500 University Dr .... Hershey PA 17033 717-531-8521 531-4162
Web: www.hmc.psu.edu
Pennsylvania Hospital 800 Spruce St .... Philadelphia PA 19107 215-829-3000 829-6363
Web: www.uphs.upenn.edu/pahosp
Phoenixville Hospital 140 Nutt Rd .... Phoenixville PA 19460 610-983-1000 983-1488
Web: www.phoenixvillehospital.com
Pinnacle Health Hospital at Community General
4300 Londonderry Rd .... Harrisburg PA 17109 717-652-3000 782-5911
TF: 888-782-5678 ■ *Web:* www.pinnaclehealth.org/body.cfm?id=770
Pocono Medical Center 206 E Brown St .... East Stroudsburg PA 18301 570-421-4000 476-3469
Web: www.poconohealthsystem.org
Pottstown Memorial Medical Center 1600 E High St .... Pottstown PA 19464 610-327-7000 327-7432
Web: www.pottstownmemorial.com
Pottsville Hospital & Warne Clinic 420 S Jackson St .... Pottsville PA 17901 570-621-5000 622-8221
Web: www.pottsvillehospital.com
Reading Hospital & Medical Center PO Box 16052 .... Reading PA 19612 610-988-8000 988-5192
Web: www.readinghospital.org
Riddle Memorial Hospital 1068 W Baltimore Pike .... Media PA 19063 610-566-9400 891-3592
Web: www.riddlehospital.org
Robert Packer Hospital 1 Guthrie Sq .... Sayre PA 18840 570-888-6666 882-5091
TF: 888-448-8474 ■ *Web:* www.guthrie.org/AboutGuthrie/GuthrieFacilities/Packer
Roxborough Memorial Hospital 5800 Ridge Ave .... Philadelphia PA 19128 215-483-9900 487-4240
Web: www.roxboroughmemorial.com
Sacred Heart Hospital 421 Chew St .... Allentown PA 18102 610-776-4500 776-5352
TF: 800-694-4777 ■ *Web:* www.shh.org
Saint Clair Hospital 1000 Bower Hill Rd .... Pittsburgh PA 15243 412-561-4900 572-6580
Web: www.stclair.org
Saint Joseph Hospital 16th St at Girard Ave .... Philadelphia PA 19130 215-787-9000 787-2115
Web: www.nphs.com/stjo_home.html
Saint Joseph Medical Center 2500 Bernville Rd .... Reading PA 19605 610-378-2000 378-2798
Web: www.thefutureofhealthcare.org
Saint Luke's Hospital 801 Ostrum St .... Bethlehem PA 18015 610-954-4000
Web: www.slhn-lehighvalley.org
Saint Mary Medical Center 1201 Langhorne-Newtown Rd .... Langhorne PA 19047 215-710-2000 710-5971
Web: www.stmaryhealthcare.org
Saint Vincent Health Center 232 W 25th St .... Erie PA 16544 814-452-5000 455-1724
Web: www.saintvincenthealth.com
Sewickley Valley Hospital 720 Blackburn Rd .... Sewickley PA 15143 412-741-6600 749-7400
Web: www.heritagevalley.org
Sharon Regional Health System 740 E State St .... Sharon PA 16146 724-983-3911 983-3958
TF: 866-228-1055 ■ *Web:* www.sharonregional.com
Soldiers & Sailors Memorial Hospital 32-36 Central Ave .... Wellsboro PA 16901 570-724-1631 724-2126
TF: 888-294-9261 ■ *Web:* www.laurelhs.org/lhs-facilities/soldiers-sailors-memorial.asp
Somerset Hospital 225 S Center Ave .... Somerset PA 15501 814-443-5000 443-4937
Web: www.somersethospital.com
Sunbury Community Hospital 350 N 11th St .... Sunbury PA 17801 570-286-3333 286-3500
Web: www.schopc.org
Taylor Hospital 175 E Chester Pike .... Ridley Park PA 19078 610-595-6000 595-6198
Web: www.crozer.org
Temple University Hospital 3401 N Broad St .... Philadelphia PA 19140 215-707-2000 707-3679
Web: www.health.temple.edu/tuh
Temple University Hospital Episcopal Campus
100 E Lehigh Ave .... Philadelphia PA 19125 215-707-1200 707-0953
Web: www.templehealth.org
Thomas Jefferson University Hospital 111 S 11th St .... Philadelphia PA 19107 215-955-6000 955-6464
Web: www.jeffersonhospital.org
Uniontown Hospital 500 W Berkeley St .... Uniontown PA 15401 724-430-5000 430-3342
TF: 800-843-3121 ■ *Web:* www.uniontownhospital.com
University of Pittsburgh Medical Center
Braddock 400 Holland Ave .... Braddock PA 15104 412-636-5000 636-5605
Web: www.upmc.com
Horizon 110 N Main St .... Greenville PA 16125 724-588-2100 588-8902
TF: 888-447-1122 ■ *Web:* www.upmc.com
McKeesport 1500 5th Ave .... McKeesport PA 15132 412-664-2000 664-2309
Web: mckeesport.upmc.com
Northwest 100 Fairfield Dr .... Seneca PA 16346 814-676-7600 676-7150
Web: northwest.upmc.com
Passavant 9100 Babcock Blvd .... Pittsburgh PA 15237 412-367-6700 367-5498*
**Fax:* Admitting ■ *Web:* passavant.upmc.com
Presbyterian 200 Lothrop St .... Pittsburgh PA 15213 412-648-6000 647-3496
Web: www.upmc.edu/Presbyterian
Saint Margaret 815 Freeport Rd .... Pittsburgh PA 15215 412-784-4000 784-5384
Web: www.upmc.com
Shadyside 5230 Centre Ave .... Pittsburgh PA 15232 412-623-2121 623-1200
Web: shadyside.upmc.com
South Side 2000 Mary St .... Pittsburgh PA 15203 412-488-5550 488-5748
Web: www.upmc.com/Hospitals.htm
Warminster Hospital 225 Newtown Rd .... Warminster PA 18974 215-441-6600 441-5677
Web: www.warminsterhospital.com
Warren General Hospital 2 Crescent Park W .... Warren PA 16365 814-723-3300 723-2248
Web: www.wgh.org
Washington Hospital 155 Wilson Ave .... Washington PA 15301 724-225-7000 222-7316
Web: www.washingtonhospital.org
Wayne Memorial Hospital 601 Park St .... Honesdale PA 18431 570-253-8100 253-7312
Web: www.wmh.org
Western Pennsylvania Hospital 4800 Friendship Ave .... Pittsburgh PA 15224 412-578-5000 578-4321
Web: www.wpahs.org/wph/index.html
Westmoreland Regional Hospital 532 W Pittsburgh St .... Greensburg PA 15601 724-832-4000 830-8573
Web: www.westmoreland.org
Wilkes-Barre General Hospital 575 N River St .... Wilkes-Barre PA 18764 570-829-8111 552-3030*
**Fax:* Admitting ■ *Web:* www.wvhcs.org
Williamsport Hospital & Medical Center 777 Rural Ave .... Williamsport PA 17701 570-321-1000 321-3719
York Hospital 1001 S George St .... York PA 17405 717-851-2345 851-3020
Web: www.wellspan.org/AboutUs/York.htm

Rhode Island

Phone Fax

Kent Hospital 455 Toll Gate Rd .... Warwick RI 02886 401-737-7000 736-1000
Web: www.kentri.org
Landmark Medical Center 115 Cass Ave .... Woonsocket RI 02895 401-769-4100 766-5488
TF: 800-722-0175 ■ *Web:* www.landmarkmedical.org
Memorial Hospital of Rhode Island 111 Brewster St .... Pawtucket RI 02860 401-729-2000 722-0198
Web: mhriweb.org
Miriam Hospital 164 Summit Ave .... Providence RI 02906 401-793-2500 793-7587
Web: www.lifespan.org/partners/tmh
Newport Hospital 11 Friendship St .... Newport RI 02840 401-846-6400 848-6003
Web: www.lifespan.org/partners/nh
Our Lady of Fatima Hospital 200 High Service Ave .... North Providence RI 02904 401-456-3000 456-3028
Web: www.saintjosephri.com
Rhode Island Hospital 593 Eddy St .... Providence RI 02903 401-444-4000 444-4218
Web: www.lifespan.org/partners/rih
Roger Williams Medical Center 825 Chalkstone Ave .... Providence RI 02908 401-456-2000 456-2029
Web: www.rwmc.com
South County Hospital 100 Kenyon Ave .... Wakefield RI 02879 401-782-8000 789-9765
Web: www.schospital.com
Westerly Hospital 25 Wells St .... Westerly RI 02891 401-596-6000 348-3670
Web: www.westerlyhospital.org

South Carolina

Phone Fax

Aiken Regional Medical Centers 302 University Pkwy .... Aiken SC 29801 803-641-5000 641-5690
TF: 800-245-3679 ■ *Web:* www.aikenregional.com
Anderson Area Medical Center 800 N Fant St .... Anderson SC 29621 864-512-1000 260-3750
TF: 800-512-6688 ■ *Web:* www.anmed.com
Beaufort Memorial Hospital 955 Ribaut Rd .... Beaufort SC 29902 843-522-5200 522-5671
TF: 877-532-6472 ■ *Web:* www.bmhsc.org
Bon Secours Saint Francis Hospital
2095 Henry Tecklenburg Dr .... Charleston SC 29414 843-402-1000 402-1769
Web: www.ropersaintfrancis.com/bssf/
Carolina Pines Regional Medical Center
1304 W Bobo Newsome Hwy .... Hartsville SC 29550 843-339-2100 339-4116
Web: www.cprmc.com
Carolinas Hospital System 805 Pamplico Hwy .... Florence SC 29505 843-674-5000 674-2519
Web: www.carolinashospital.com
Colleton Medical Center 501 Robertson Blvd .... Walterboro SC 29488 843-549-6371 549-7562
Web: www.colletonmedical.com
Conway Medical Center 300 Singleton Ridge Rd .... Conway SC 29526 843-347-7111 347-8056
Web: www.conwaymedicalcenter.com
Georgetown Memorial Hospital 606 Black River Rd .... Georgetown SC 29440 843-527-7000 520-7887
Web: www.gmhsc.com
Grand Strand Regional Medical Center 809 82nd Pkwy .... Myrtle Beach SC 29572 843-692-1000 692-1109
TF: 800-222-1859 ■ *Web:* www.grandstrandmed.com
Greenville Memorial Hospital 701 Grove Rd .... Greenville SC 29605 864-455-7000 455-8921
Web: www.ghs.org/hospital/259
Hilton Head Regional Medical Center
25 Hospital Center Blvd .... Hilton Head Island SC 29926 843-681-6122 689-3670*
**Fax:* Admitting ■ *Web:* www.hiltonheadmedctr.com
Kershaw County Medical Center 1315 Roberts St .... Camden SC 29020 803-432-4311 713-6380
Web: www.kcmc.org
Lexington Medical Center 2720 Sunset Blvd .... West Columbia SC 29169 803-791-2000 791-2660
Web: www.lexmed.com
Marion County Medical Center PO Box 1150 .... Marion SC 29571 843-431-2000 431-2414
Web: www.marioncountymedical.com
Mary Black Memorial Hospital 1700 Skylyn Dr .... Spartanburg SC 29307 864-573-3000 573-3240
Web: www.maryblackhospital.org
McLeod Medical Center Dillon 301 E Jackson St .... Dillon SC 29536 843-774-4111 774-1563
Web: www.mcleodhealth.org
McLeod Regional Medical Center 555 E Cheves St .... Florence SC 29506 843-777-2000 777-5465
Web: www.mcleodhealth.org
Medical University of South Carolina Medical Center
169 Ashley Ave .... Charleston SC 29425 843-792-2300 792-3126
TF: 800-424-6872 ■ *Web:* www.musc.edu/medcenter
Oconee Memorial Hospital 298 Memorial Dr .... Seneca SC 29672 864-882-3351 882-3711
Web: www.oconeememorial.org
Palmetto Health Baptist Columbia 1330 Taylor St .... Columbia SC 29220 803-296-5010 296-5462
Web: www.palmettohealth.org
Palmetto Health Baptist Medical Center Easley
200 Fleetwood Dr .... Easley SC 29640 864-442-7200 442-7521
Web: www.palmettohealth.org
Palmetto Health Richland 5 Richland Medical Park .... Columbia SC 29203 803-434-7000 434-3571
Web: www.palmettohealth.org/facilities/richland
Piedmont Medical Center 222 S Herlong Ave .... Rock Hill SC 29732 803-329-1234 329-0979
Web: www.piedmonthealth.com
Providence Hospital 2435 Forest Dr .... Columbia SC 29204 803-256-5300 256-5935
Web: www.provhosp.com
Regional Medical Center of Orangeburg & Calhoun Counties
3000 Saint Matthews Rd .... Orangeburg SC 29118 803-395-2200 395-2304
TF: 800-476-3377
Roper Hospital 316 Calhoun St .... Charleston SC 29401 843-724-2000 724-2995
Web: www.ropersaintfrancis.com
Saint Francis Hospital 1 St Francis Dr .... Greenville SC 29601 864-255-1000 255-1137*
**Fax:* Hum Res
Self Regional Hospital 1325 Spring St .... Greenwood SC 29646 864-725-4111 725-4260
Web: www.selfregional.org
Spartanburg Regional Medical Center 101 E Wood St .... Spartanburg SC 29303 864-560-6000 560-6035
TF: 800-868-8784 ■ *Web:* www.srhs.com
Springs Memorial Hospital 800 W Meeting St .... Lancaster SC 29720 803-286-1481 286-1367
TF: 800-488-2567 ■ *Web:* www.springsmemorial.com
Trident Medical Center 9330 Medical Plaza Dr .... Charleston SC 29406 843-847-4000 847-4086
TF: 877-300-6062 ■ *Web:* www.tridenthealthsystem.com
Tuomey Regional Medical Center 129 N Washington St .... Sumter SC 29150 803-774-9000 774-9489
Web: www.tuomey.com
Upstate Carolina Medical Center 1530 N Limestone St .... Gaffney SC 29340 864-487-4271 489-0585
Web: www.upstatecarolina.org
Wallace Thomson Hospital 322 W South St .... Union SC 29379 864-427-0351 429-2653
Web: www.wallacethomson.com

South Dakota

Phone Fax

Avera McKennan Hospital & University Health Center
800 E 21st St .... Sioux Falls SD 57105 605-322-8000 322-7823*
**Fax:* Admitting ■ *Web:* www.mckennan.org
Avera Queen of Peace Hospital 525 N Foster St .... Mitchell SD 57301 605-995-2000 995-2441
TF: 888-531-1685 ■ *Web:* www.averaqueenofpeace.org
Avera Sacred Heart Hospital 501 Summit St .... Yankton SD 57078 605-668-8000 665-8840
Web: www.averasacredheart.com
Avera Saint Luke's Hospital 305 S State St .... Aberdeen SD 57401 605-622-5000 622-5127
TF: 800-225-8537 ■ *Web:* www.averastlukes.org
Huron Regional Medical Center 172 4th St SE .... Huron SD 57350 605-353-6200 353-6300
Web: www.huronregional.org
Prairie Lakes Hospital & Care Center 401 9th Ave NW .... Watertown SD 57201 605-882-7000 882-7607
TF: 877-917-7547 ■ *Web:* www.prairielakes.com
Rapid City Regional Hospital 353 Fairmont Blvd .... Rapid City SD 57701 605-719-1000 719-8988
Web: www.rcrh.org
Saint Mary's Healthcare Center 800 E Dakota Ave .... Pierre SD 57501 605-224-3100 224-3439
Web: www.st-marys.com
Sanford USD Medical Center 1305 W 18th St .... Sioux Falls SD 57117 605-333-1000 333-1531
Web: www.sanfordhealth.org

Tennessee

Phone Fax

Athens Regional Medical Center 1114 W Madison Ave .... Athens TN 37303 423-745-1411 744-3362
Web: www.athensrmc.com

General Hospitals - US (Cont'd)

Tennessee (Cont'd)

				Phone	Fax
Baptist Hospital 2000 Church St *Web:* www.baptist-hosp.org	Nashville	TN	37236	615-284-5555	284-1592
Baptist Hospital of East Tennessee 137 Blount Ave *Web:* www.bhset.org	Knoxville	TN	37920	865-632-5011	632-5086
Baptist Memorial Hospital Memphis 6019 Walnut Grove Rd *Web:* www.baptistonline.org/facilities/memphis	Memphis	TN	38120	901-226-5000	226-5618
Baptist Memorial Hospital Union City 1201 Bishop St *Web:* www.baptistonline.org/facilities/unioncity	Union City	TN	38261	731-885-2410	884-8603
Blount Memorial Hospital 907 E Lamar Alexander Pkwy *Web:* www.blountmemorial.org	Maryville	TN	37804	865-983-7211	981-2333
Bristol Regional Medical Center 1 Medical Park Blvd *Web:* www.wellmont.org/Facilities/Bristol/WBRMC/wbrmc.html	Bristol	TN	37620	423-968-1121	844-4204
Centennial Medical Center 2300 Patterson St *Web:* www.centennialmedctr.com	Nashville	TN	37203	615-342-1000	342-1045
Cookeville Regional Medical Center 142 W 5th St *Web:* www.crmchealth.org	Cookeville	TN	38501	931-528-2541	526-8814
Cumberland Medical Center 421 S Main St *Web:* www.cmchealthcare.org	Crossville	TN	38555	931-484-9511	707-8148
Delta Medical Center 3000 Getwell Rd *Web:* www.deltamedcenter.com	Memphis	TN	38118	901-369-8500	369-4603
Dyersburg Regional Medical Center 400 E Tickle St *Web:* www.dyersburgregionalmc.com	Dyersburg	TN	38024	731-285-2410	285-9545
Erlanger Medical Center 975 E 3rd St *TF:* 877-778-7001 ■ *Web:* www.erlanger.org	Chattanooga	TN	37403	423-778-7000	778-8068
Fort Sanders Regional Medical Center 1901 Clinch Ave SW *Web:* www.fsregional.com	Knoxville	TN	37916	865-541-1111	541-1262
Gateway Medical Center 1771 Madison St *Web:* www.ghsystem.com/aboutgateway.asp	Clarksville	TN	37043	931-552-6622	551-1027
Harton Regional Medical Center 1801 N Jackson St *TF:* 800-388-4278 ■ *Web:* www.hartonmedicalcenter.com	Tullahoma	TN	37388	931-393-3000	393-7855
HCA Southern Hills Medical Center 391 Wallace Rd *Web:* www.southernhills.com	Nashville	TN	37211	615-781-4000	781-4113
Henry County Medical Center 301 Tyson Ave *Web:* www.hcmc-tn.org	Paris	TN	38242	731-642-1220	642-9588
Holston Valley Hospital & Medical Center 130 W Ravine Rd *Web:* www.wellmont.org	Kingsport	TN	37660	423-224-4000	224-5037
Horizon Medical Center 111 Hwy 70 E *Web:* www.horizonmedctr.com	Dickson	TN	37055	615-446-0446	441-2514
Indian Path Medical Center 2000 Brookside Dr *Web:* www.msha.com/facility.cfm?id=50	Kingsport	TN	37660	423-392-7000	857-7109
Jackson-Madison County General Hospital 708 W Forest Ave *Web:* www.wth.net/body.cfm?id=121	Jackson	TN	38301	731-541-5000	541-3157
Johnson City Medical Center 400 N State of Franklin Rd *Web:* www.jcmc.com/facility.cfm?id=47	Johnson City	TN	37604	423-431-6111	431-3077
Lakeway Regional Hospital 726 McFarland St *Web:* www.lakewayregionalhospital.com	Morristown	TN	37814	423-586-2302	587-8548
Laughlin Memorial Hospital 1420 Tusculum Blvd *Web:* www.laughlinmemorial.org	Greeneville	TN	37745	423-787-5000	787-5083
Livingston Regional Hospital 315 Oak St *Web:* www.livingston-hospital.com	Livingston	TN	38570	931-823-5611	403-2334
Maury Regional Hospital 1224 Trotwood Ave *TF:* 800-799-5053 ■ *Web:* www.mauryregional.com	Columbia	TN	38401	931-381-1111	540-4160
Memorial Hospital 2525 Desales Ave *Web:* www.memorial.org	Chattanooga	TN	37404	423-495-2525	495-7726
Memorial North Park Hospital 2051 Hamill Rd *Web:* www.memorial.org/services/network/northpark.asp	Hixson	TN	37343	423-495-7100	495-7388
Methodist Hospital North 3960 New Covington Pike *Web:* www.methodisthealth.org/facility.asp	Memphis	TN	38128	901-516-5200	516-5323
Methodist Hospital South 1300 Wesley Dr *Web:* www.methodisthealth.org/facility.asp	Memphis	TN	38116	901-516-3700	516-3085
Methodist Medical Center of Oak Ridge 990 Oak Ridge Tpke *Web:* www.mmcoakridge.com	Oak Ridge	TN	37830	865-835-1000	835-4054
Middle Tennessee Medical Center 400 N Highland Ave *TF:* 800-596-3455 ■ *Web:* www.mtmc.org	Murfreesboro	TN	37130	615-849-4100	396-4659
Nashville General Hospital 1818 Albion St *Web:* www.nashville.gov/general_hospital	Nashville	TN	37208	615-341-4000	341-4493
Northcrest Medical Center 100 Northcrest Dr *Web:* www.northcrest.com	Springfield	TN	37172	615-384-2411	384-1509
Parkridge East Hospital 941 Spring Creek Rd *TF:* 800-605-1527 ■ *Web:* parkridgeeasthospital.com	Chattanooga	TN	37412	423-894-7870	855-3648
Parkridge Medical Center 2333 McCallie Ave *Web:* www.parkridgemedicalcenter.com	Chattanooga	TN	37404	423-698-6061	493-1208
Parkwest Medical Center 9352 Park West Blvd *Web:* www.covenanthealth.com	Knoxville	TN	37923	865-373-1000	373-1012
Regional Hospital of Jackson 367 Hospital Blvd *TF:* 800-454-9970	Jackson	TN	38305	731-661-2000	661-2187
Regional Medical Center at Memphis 877 Jefferson Ave *Web:* www.the-med.org	Memphis	TN	38103	901-545-7100	545-7037
Roane Medical Center 412 Devonia St *Web:* www.roanemedical.com	Harriman	TN	37748	865-882-1323	882-4343
Saint Francis Hospital 5959 Park Ave *Web:* www.saintfrancishosp.com	Memphis	TN	38119	901-765-1000	765-1799
Saint Mary's Medical Center 900 E Oak Hill Ave *Web:* www.ehealthconnection.com/regions/tennessee	Knoxville	TN	37917	865-545-8000	545-6732
Saint Thomas Hospital 4220 Harding Rd *Web:* www.saintthomas.org	Nashville	TN	37205	615-222-2111	222-6502
Skyline Madison Campus 500 Hospital Dr *Web:* www.skylinemadison.com/	Madison	TN	37115	615-865-2373	860-6378
Skyline Medical Center 3441 Dickerson Pike *TF:* 800-690-0096 ■ *Web:* www.skylinemedicalcenter.com	Nashville	TN	37207	615-769-2000	769-7102
SkyRidge Medical Center 2305 Chambliss Ave *Web:* www.skyridgemedicalcenter.net	Cleveland	TN	37311	423-559-6000	559-6653
Summit Medical Center 5655 Frist Blvd *Web:* www.summitmedctr.com	Hermitage	TN	37076	615-316-3000	316-4912
Sumner Regional Medical Center 555 Hartsville Pike *TF:* 800-728-4217 ■ *Web:* www.sumner.org	Gallatin	TN	37066	615-452-4210	328-5523
Takoma Regional Hospital 401 Takoma Ave *Web:* www.takoma.org	Greeneville	TN	37743	423-639-3151	636-2374
University Medical Center 1411 W Baddour Pkwy *Web:* www.hma-corp.com/tn2.html	Lebanon	TN	37087	615-444-8262	449-1215
University of Tennessee Medical Center 1924 Alcoa Hwy *Web:* www.utmedicalcenter.org	Knoxville	TN	37920	865-544-9000	544-9429
Vanderbilt University Medical Center 1211 22nd Ave S *Web:* www.mc.vanderbilt.edu	Nashville	TN	37232	615-322-5000	343-7317
Williamson Medical Center 2021 N Carothers Rd *Web:* www.williamsonmedicalcntr.org	Franklin	TN	37067	615-791-0500	435-5161

Texas

				Phone	Fax
Abilene Regional Medical Center 6250 S Hwy 83-84 *Web:* www.armc.info/armc/armchp.nsf	Abilene	TX	79606	325-695-9900	428-1029
Arlington Memorial Hospital 800 W Randol Mill Rd *Web:* www.texashealth.org	Arlington	TX	76012	817-548-6100	548-6357
Baptist Medical Center 111 Dallas St *Web:* www.baptisthealthsystem.com	San Antonio	TX	78205	210-297-7000	297-0700
Baylor All Saints Medical Center 1400 8th Ave *Web:* www.baylorhealth.com/locations/allsaints	Fort Worth	TX	76104	817-926-2544	927-6226
Baylor Medical Center at Garland 2300 Marie Curie Blvd *Web:* www.baylorhealth.com/Locations/garland	Garland	TX	75042	972-487-5000	485-3051
Baylor Medical Center at Irving 1901 N MacArthur Blvd *Web:* www.bhcs.com/Locations/Hospitals/Irving/	Irving	TX	75061	972-579-8100	579-5254
Baylor Regional Medical Center at Grapevine 1650 W College St *Web:* www.baylorhealth.com	Grapevine	TX	76051	817-488-7546	329-4812
Baylor University Medical Center at Dallas 3500 Gaston Ave *Web:* www.baylorhealth.com/Locations/Hospitals/BUMC	Dallas	TX	75246	214-820-0111	820-2411
Bayshore Medical Center 4000 Spencer Hwy *Web:* www.bayshoremedical.com	Pasadena	TX	77504	713-359-2000	359-1004
Bellaire Medical Center 5314 Dashwood Dr *Web:* www.bellairemedicalcenter.com	Houston	TX	77081	713-512-1200	512-1475
Ben Taub General Hospital 1504 Taub Loop *Web:* www.hchdonline.com	Houston	TX	77030	713-873-2000	873-2305
Brackenridge Hospital 601 E 15th St *Web:* www.seton.net	Austin	TX	78701	512-324-7000	324-7051
Brazosport Memorial Hospital 100 Medical Dr *Web:* www.brazosportmemorial.com	Lake Jackson	TX	77566	979-297-4411	297-6905
Brownwood Regional Medical Center 1501 Burnet Dr *Web:* www.brmc-cares.com	Brownwood	TX	76801	325-646-8541	646-5459
Central Texas Medical Center 1301 Wonder World Dr *TF:* 800-508-8515 ■ *Web:* www.ctmc.org	San Marcos	TX	78666	512-353-8979	753-3598
CHRISTUS Saint Elizabeth Hospital 2830 Calder Ave *Web:* www.christusste.org	Beaumont	TX	77702	409-892-7171	899-8191
CHRISTUS Saint John Hospital 18300 St John Dr *Web:* www.christusstjohn.org	Nassau Bay	TX	77058	281-333-5503	333-8891
CHRISTUS Saint Mary Hospital 3600 Gates Blvd *Web:* www.christusstmary.org	Port Arthur	TX	77642	409-985-7431	985-9404
CHRISTUS Saint Michael Health System 2600 Saint Michael Dr *Web:* www.christusstmichael.org	Texarkana	TX	75503	903-614-1000	614-2212
CHRISTUS Santa Rosa Hospital 333 N Santa Rosa St *Web:* www.christussantarosa.org	San Antonio	TX	78207	210-704-2011	704-3632
CHRISTUS Spohn Hospital Corpus Christi Shoreline 600 Elizabeth St *Web:* www.christushealth.org	Corpus Christi	TX	78404	361-881-3000	881-3149
CHRISTUS Spohn Hospital Corpus Christi-South 5950 Saratoga Blvd *Web:* www.christusspohn.org/locations_south.htm	Corpus Christi	TX	78414	361-985-5000	985-5173
CHRISTUS Spohn Hospital Kleberg 1311 General Cavazos Blvd *Web:* www.christusspohn.org	Kingsville	TX	78363	361-595-1661	595-5005
CHRISTUS Spohn Hospital Memorial 2606 Hospital Blvd *Web:* www.christusspohn.org	Corpus Christi	TX	78405	361-902-4000	902-4968
Citizens Medical Center 2701 Hospital Dr *Web:* www.citizensmedicalcenter.com	Victoria	TX	77901	361-573-9181	572-5070
Clear Lake Regional Medical Center 500 Medical Center Blvd *Web:* www.clearlakermc.com	Webster	TX	77598	281-332-2511	338-3352
Cleveland Regional Medical Center 300 E Crockett St *Web:* www.clevelandregionalmedicalcenter.com	Cleveland	TX	77327	281-593-1811	432-4370
College Station Medical Center 1604 Rock Prairie Rd *Web:* www.csmedcenter.com	College Station	TX	77845	979-764-5100	696-7373
Community Specialty Hospital 1111 Gallagher Dr *Web:* www.cshsherman.org	Sherman	TX	75090	903-870-7000	870-7599
Conroe Regional Medical Center 504 Medical Center Blvd *TF:* 888-633-2687 ■ *Web:* www.conroeregional.com	Conroe	TX	77304	936-539-1111	539-5620
Corpus Christi Medical Center 3315 S Alameda St *Web:* www.ccmedicalcenter.com	Corpus Christi	TX	78411	361-857-1501	761-1501
Corpus Christi Medical Center Bay Area 7101 S Padre Island Dr *Web:* www.ccmedicalcenter.com	Corpus Christi	TX	78412	361-761-1200	761-3670
Covenant Medical Center 3615 19th St *Web:* www.covenanthealth.org	Lubbock	TX	79410	806-725-1011	723-7188
Covenant Medical Lakeside 4000 24th St *Web:* www.covenanthealth.com	Lubbock	TX	79410	806-725-6000	723-6574
Cypress Fairbanks Medical Center 10655 Steepletop Dr *Web:* www.cyfairhospital.com	Houston	TX	77065	281-890-4285	890-5341
Del Sol Medical Center 10301 Gateway W *Web:* www.delsolmedicalcenter.com	El Paso	TX	79925	915-595-9000	595-7224
Denton Community Hospital 207 N Bonnie Brae St *Web:* www.dentonhospital.com	Denton	TX	76201	940-898-7000	898-7071
Denton Regional Medical Center 3535 S I-35 E *Web:* www.dentonregional.com	Denton	TX	76210	940-384-3535	384-4700
Detar Hospital Navarro 506 E San Antonio St *Web:* www.detar.com	Victoria	TX	77901	361-575-7441	788-6114
Detar Hospital North 101 Medical Dr *Web:* www.detar.com	Victoria	TX	77904	361-573-6100	788-2693
Doctors Hospital of Dallas 9440 Poppy Dr *Web:* www.doctorshospitaldallas.com	Dallas	TX	75218	214-324-6100	324-0612
Doctors Hospital of Laredo 10700 McPherson Rd *Web:* www.doctorshosplaredo.com	Laredo	TX	78045	956-523-2000	523-0444
Doctors Hospital Parkway 233 W Parker Rd	Houston	TX	77076	281-765-2600	765-7525
East Houston Regional Medical Center 13111 East Fwy *Web:* www.easthoustonrmc.com	Houston	TX	77015	713-393-2000	393-2714
East Texas Medical Center Athens 2000 S Palestine St *Web:* www.etmc.org	Athens	TX	75751	903-675-2216	676-3337
East Texas Medical Center Tyler 1000 S Beckham Ave *Web:* www.etmc.org	Tyler	TX	75701	903-597-0351	535-6334
Edinburg Regional Medical Center 1102 W Trenton Rd *TF:* 800-465-5585 ■ *Web:* www.edinburgregional.com	Edinburg	TX	78539	956-388-6000	388-6020
Fort Duncan Medical Center 3333 N Foster Maldonado Blvd *Web:* www.fortduncanmedicalcenter.com	Eagle Pass	TX	78852	830-773-5321	758-4851
Good Shepherd Medical Center 700 E Marshall Ave *Web:* www.gsmc.org	Longview	TX	75601	903-315-2000	315-2479
Gulf Coast Medical Center 1400 Hwy 59 *Web:* www.gulfcoastmedical.com	Wharton	TX	77488	979-532-2500	282-6190
Harris Methodist Fort Worth 1301 Pennsylvania Ave *Web:* www.texashealth.org	Fort Worth	TX	76104	817-882-2000	882-3169
Harris Methodist-HEB 1600 Hospital Pkwy *Web:* www.texashealth.org	Bedford	TX	76022	817-685-4000	685-4890
Harris Methodist Southwest 6100 Harris Pkwy *Web:* www.texashealth.org	Fort Worth	TX	76132	817-346-5050	433-6574
HCA Rio Grande Regional Hospital 101 E Ridge Rd *Web:* www.riograndereregionalhospital.com	McAllen	TX	78503	956-632-6000	632-6621
Hendrick Health System 1900 Pine St *Web:* www.hendrickhealth.org	Abilene	TX	79601	325-670-2000	670-2209

	City	State	Zip	Phone	Fax
Hillcrest Baptist Medical Center 3000 Herring Ave *Web:* www.hillcrest.net	Waco	TX	76708	254-202-2000	202-8978
Houston Northwest Medical Center 710 FM 1960 W *Web:* www.hnmc.com	Houston	TX	77090	281-440-1000	440-2666
Huguley Memorial Medical Center 11801 S Fwy *Web:* www.huguley.org	Burleson	TX	76028	817-293-9110	568-1298
Huntsville Memorial Hospital PO Box 4001 *Web:* www.huntsvillememorial.com	Huntsville	TX	77342	936-291-3411	291-4373
John Peter Smith Hospital 1500 S Main St *Web:* www.jpshealthnet.org	Fort Worth	TX	76103	817-921-3431	927-1604
Jones Wilson N Medical Center 500 N Highland Ave *TF:* 877-870-6696 ■ *Web:* www.wnj.org	Sherman	TX	75092	903-870-4611	891-2030
Kingwood Medical Center 22999 US Hwy 59 *Web:* www.kingwoodmedical.com	Kingwood	TX	77339	281-348-8000	348-8010
Knapp Medical Center 1401 E 8th St *Web:* www.knappmed.org	Weslaco	TX	78596	956-968-8567	969-2293
Lake Pointe Medical Center 6800 Senic Dr *Web:* www.lakepointemedical.com	Rowlett	TX	75088	972-412-2273	475-8345
Laredo Medical Center 1700 E Saunders Ave *Web:* www.laredomedical.com	Laredo	TX	78041	956-796-5000	796-3175
Las Colinas Medical Center 6800 N MacArthur Blvd *Web:* www.lascolinasmedical.com	Irving	TX	75039	972-969-2000	969-2080
Las Palmas Medical Center 1801 N Oregon St *Web:* www.laspalmashealth.com	El Paso	TX	79902	915-521-1200	544-5203
Longview Regional Medical Center 2901 N 4th St *Web:* www.longviewregional.com	Longview	TX	75605	903-758-1818	758-5167
Mainland Medical Center 6801 Emmett Lowry Expy *Web:* www.mainlandmedical.com	Texas City	TX	77591	409-938-5000	938-5001
Marshall Regional Medical Center 811 S Washington Ave *Web:* www.mrmc.net/	Marshall	TX	75670	903-935-9311	927-6101
McAllen Medical Center 301 W Expy 83 *Web:* www.mcallenmedicalcenter.com	McAllen	TX	78503	956-632-4000	632-4010
McKenna Memorial Hospital 600 N Union Ave *Web:* www.mckenna.org	New Braunfels	TX	78130	830-606-9111	620-0796
Medical Center of Arlington 3301 Matlock Rd *Web:* www.medicalcenterarlington.com	Arlington	TX	76015	817-465-3241	472-4878
Medical Center Hospital 500 W 4th St *Web:* www.odessamch.org	Odessa	TX	79761	432-640-4000	640-1118
Medical Center of Lewisville 500 W Main St *Web:* www.lewisvillemedical.com	Lewisville	TX	75057	972-420-1000	353-1789
Medical Center of Mesquite 1011 N Galloway Ave **Fax Area Code:* 972 ■ *Web:* www.mcmtx.com	Mesquite	TX	75149	214-320-7000	289-9468*
Medical Center of Plano 3901 W 15th St *Web:* www.medicalcenterofplano.com	Plano	TX	75075	972-596-6800	519-1409
Medical City Hospital 7777 Forest Ln *Web:* www.medicalcityhospital.com	Dallas	TX	75230	972-566-7000	566-5867
Memorial Hermann Baptist Beaumont Hospital 3080 College St *Web:* www.mhbh.org	Beaumont	TX	77701	409-212-5000	212-5001
Memorial Hermann Baptist Hospital 3080 College St *Web:* www.mhbh.org	Beaumont	TX	77701	409-212-5000	212-5022
Memorial Hermann Baptist Orange Hospital 608 Strickland Dr *Web:* www.mhbh.org	Orange	TX	77630	409-883-9361	883-1223
Memorial Hermann Hospital 6411 Fannin St *Web:* www.mhhs.org/locations/he.html	Houston	TX	77030	713-704-4000	704-5872
Memorial Hermann Katy Hospital 23900 Katy Fwy *Web:* www.memorialhermann.org/locations/K.html	Katy	TX	77494	281-644-7000	644-7090
Memorial Hermann Memorial City Hospital 921 Gessner Rd *TF:* 800-392-6370 ■ *Web:* www.mhhs.org/locations/mc.html	Houston	TX	77024	713-242-3000	242-4096
Memorial Hermann Southwest Hospital 7600 Beechnut St *Web:* www.mhhs.org/locations/sw.html	Houston	TX	77074	713-456-5000	456-8363
Memorial Medical Center of East Texas 1201 W Frank Ave *TF:* 800-348-5969 ■ *Web:* www.mymemorialhealth.org	Lufkin	TX	75904	936-634-8111	639-7004
Mesquite Community Hospital 3500 I-30 *Web:* www.mchtx.com	Mesquite	TX	75150	972-698-3300	698-2133
Methodist Charlton Medical Center 3500 W Wheatland Rd *Web:* www.methodisthealthsystem.org/facil_cmh.html	Dallas	TX	75237	214-947-7777	947-7525
Methodist Dallas Medical Center 1441 N Beckley Ave *Web:* www.methodisthealthsystem.org	Dallas	TX	75203	214-947-8181	947-3403
Methodist Diagnostic Hospital 6447 Main St *Web:* www.methodisthealth.com	Houston	TX	77030	713-790-0790	790-2605
Methodist Hospital 6565 Fannin St *Web:* www.methodisthealth.com	Houston	TX	77030	713-790-3311	790-2605
Methodist Hospital 7700 Floyd Curl Dr *Web:* mh.sahealth.com	San Antonio	TX	78229	210-575-4000	575-4410
Metroplex Hospital 2201 S Clear Creek Rd *Web:* www.mplex.org	Killeen	TX	76549	254-526-7523	526-3483
Metropolitan Methodist Hospital 1310 McCullough Ave *Web:* metro.sahealth.com	San Antonio	TX	78212	210-757-2200	757-2915
Midland Memorial Hospital 2200 W Illinois Ave *TF:* 800-833-2916 ■ *Web:* www.midland-memorial.com	Midland	TX	79701	432-685-1111	685-4970
Mission Hospital 900 S Bryan Rd *Web:* www.missionhospital.com	Mission	TX	78572	956-580-9000	580-9103
Mother Frances Hospital 800 E Dawson St *Web:* www.tmfhs.org	Tyler	TX	75701	903-593-8441	525-1201
Nacogdoches Medical Center 4920 NE Stallings Dr *TF:* 800-539-2772 ■ *Web:* www.nacmedicalcenter.com	Nacogdoches	TX	75965	936-569-9481	568-3400
Nacogdoches Memorial Hospital 1204 N Mound St *Web:* www.nacmem.org	Nacogdoches	TX	75961	936-564-4611	568-8588
Navarro Regional Hospital 3201 W Hwy 22 *Web:* www.navarrohospital.com	Corsicana	TX	75110	903-654-6800	654-6955
Nix Medical Center 414 Navarro St *Web:* www.nixhealth.com	San Antonio	TX	78205	210-271-1800	271-2023
North Austin Medical Center 12221 N Mopac Expy *TF:* 888-356-5315 ■ *Web:* northaustin.com	Austin	TX	78758	512-901-1000	901-1995
North Central Medical Center 4500 Medical Center Dr *Web:* www.ncentralmedical.com	McKinney	TX	75069	972-547-8000	547-8042
North Hills Hospital 4401 Booth Calloway Rd *Web:* www.northhillshospital.com	North Richland Hills	TX	76180	817-255-1000	255-1991
Northeast Baptist Hospital 8811 Village Dr *Web:* www.baptisthealthsystem.org/secondaryHome.aspx?siteid=8	San Antonio	TX	78217	210-297-2000	297-0200
Northeast Medical Center Hospital 18951 Memorial N *Web:* www.nemch.org	Humble	TX	77338	281-540-7700	540-7846
Northeast Methodist Hospital 12412 Judson Rd *Web:* nemh.sahealth.com	San Antonio	TX	78233	210-650-4949	757-5038
Northwest Texas Hospital 1501 S Coulter *Web:* www.nwtexashealthcare.com	Amarillo	TX	79106	806-354-1000	354-1122
OakBend Medical Center 1705 Jackson St *Web:* www.oakbendmedcenter.org	Richmond	TX	77469	281-342-2811	341-3056
Palestine Regional Medical Center 2900 S Loop 256 *Web:* www.palestineregional.com	Palestine	TX	75801	903-731-1000	731-2236
Pampa Regional Medical Center 1 Medical Plaza *TF:* 800-896-3684 ■ *Web:* www.prmctx.com	Pampa	TX	79065	806-665-3721	665-2361
Paris Regional Medical Center 820 Clarksville St *Web:* www.parisregional.com	Paris	TX	75460	903-785-4521	737-3848
Parkland Memorial Hospital 5201 Harry Hines Blvd **Fax:* Admitting ■ *Web:* www.pmh.org/medical_services/medicine.html	Dallas	TX	75235	214-590-8000	590-2713*

	City	State	Zip	Phone	Fax
Plaza Medical Center 900 8th Ave *Web:* www.plazamedicalcenter.com	Fort Worth	TX	76104	817-336-2100	347-5796
Presbyterian Hospital of Dallas 8200 Walnut Hill Ln *Web:* www.texashealth.org	Dallas	TX	75231	214-345-6789	345-4603
Presbyterian Hospital of Greenville 4215 Joe Ramsey Blvd *TF:* 800-984-9223 ■ *Web:* www.hmhd.org	Greenville	TX	75401	903-408-5000	408-1609
Providence Health Center 6901 Medical Pkwy *Web:* www.providence-waco.org	Waco	TX	76712	254-751-4000	751-4769
Providence Memorial Hospital 2001 N Oregon St *Web:* www.sphn.com	El Paso	TX	79902	915-577-6011	577-6549
RHD Memorial Medical Center 7 Medical Pkwy *Web:* www.rhdmemorial.com	Dallas	TX	75234	972-247-1000	888-7010
Richardson Regional Medical Center 401 W Campbell Rd *Web:* richardsonregional.com	Richardson	TX	75080	972-231-1441	498-4931
Round Rock Medical Center 2400 Round Rock Ave *Web:* www.roundrockmc.com	Round Rock	TX	78681	512-341-1000	238-1799
Saint Anthony's Baptist Health System 1600 Wallace Blvd *Web:* www.bsahs.org	Amarillo	TX	79106	806-212-2000	212-2919
Saint David's Medical Center 919 E 32nd St *Web:* www.stdavidsmc.com	Austin	TX	78705	512-476-7111	544-8102
Saint Joseph Medical Center 1401 St Joseph Pkwy *Web:* www.sjmctx.com	Houston	TX	77002	713-757-1000	657-7123
Saint Joseph Regional Health Center 2801 Franciscan Dr *Web:* www.st-joseph.org/sjrhc/default.htm	Bryan	TX	77802	979-776-3777	774-4590
Saint Luke's Episcopal Hospital 6720 Bertner Ave **Fax Area Code:* 832 ■ *Web:* www.sleh.com/sleh	Houston	TX	77030	713-785-8537	355-6812*
Saint Paul University Hospital 5909 Harry Hines Blvd *Web:* www.utsouthwestern.edu/utsw/home/pc/universityhospitals/index.html	Dallas	TX	75390	214-645-5555	634-7087
San Angelo Community Medical Center 3501 Knickerbocker Rd *Web:* www.sacmc.com	San Angelo	TX	76904	325-949-9511	947-6550
San Jacinto Methodist Hospital 4401 Garth Rd **Fax:* Admitting ■ *Web:* www.methodisthealth.com	Baytown	TX	77521	281-420-8600	420-8672*
Scott & White Memorial Hospital 2401 S 31st St *TF:* 800-792-3710 ■ *Web:* www.sw.org	Temple	TX	76508	254-724-2111	724-2786
Seton Medical Center 1201 W 38th St *Web:* www.seton.net	Austin	TX	78705	512-324-1000	324-1924
Shannon Medical Center 120 E Harris Ave *TF:* 888-653-6741 ■ *Web:* www.shannonhealth.com	San Angelo	TX	76903	325-653-6741	658-8295
Sid Peterson Memorial Hospital 710 Water St *Web:* www.spmh.com	Kerrville	TX	78028	830-896-4200	258-7833
Sierra Medical Center 1625 Medical Center Dr *Web:* www.sphn.com	El Paso	TX	79902	915-747-4000	747-2157
South Austin Hospital 901 W Ben White Blvd *Web:* www.southaustinhospital.com	Austin	TX	78704	512-447-2211	448-7326
Southeast Baptist Hospital 4214 E Southcross Blvd *Web:* www.baptisthealthsystem.com	San Antonio	TX	78222	210-297-3000	297-0300
Southwest General Hospital 7400 Barlite Blvd *Web:* www.swgeneralhospital.com	San Antonio	TX	78224	210-921-2000	921-3508
Southwestern General Hospital 1221 N Cotton St	El Paso	TX	79902	915-496-9600	496-9629
Spring Branch Medical Center 8850 Long Point St *Web:* www.springbranchmedical.com	Houston	TX	77055	713-467-6555	722-3771
Texoma Medical Center 1000 Memorial Dr *Web:* www.thcs.org	Denison	TX	75020	903-416-4000	416-4129
The Medical Center of Southeast Texas 2555 Jimmy Johnson Blvd *Web:* www.medicalcentersetexas.com	Port Arthur	TX	77640	409-724-7389	853-5910
Thomason Hospital 4815 Alameda Ave *Web:* www.thomasoncares.org	El Paso	TX	79905	915-544-1200	521-7612
Titus Regional Medical Center 2001 N Jefferson Ave *Web:* www.titusregional.com	Mount Pleasant	TX	75455	903-577-6000	577-6027
Tomball Regional Hospital 605 Holderrieth St *Web:* www.tomballhospital.org	Tomball	TX	77375	281-351-1623	351-4904
Trinity Medical Center 4343 N Josey Ln *Web:* www.trinitymedicalcenter.com	Carrollton	TX	75010	972-492-1010	492-9028
Twelve Oaks Medical Center 6700 Belaire Blvd *Web:* www.twelveoaksmedicalcenter.com	Houston	TX	77074	713-774-7611	778-2616
United Regional Health Care System					
Eighth Street Campus 1600 8th St *Web:* www.urhcs.org	Wichita Falls	TX	76301	940-764-7000	764-3041
Eleventh Street Campus 1600 11th St *Web:* www.urhcs.org	Wichita Falls	TX	76301	940-764-7000	764-3041
University Hospital 4502 Medical Dr *TF:* 800-256-2311 ■ *Web:* www.universityhealthsystem.com	San Antonio	TX	78229	210-358-4000	358-2837
University Medical Center 602 Indiana Ave *Web:* www.teamumc.org	Lubbock	TX	79415	806-775-8200	775-8611
University of Texas Health Center at Tyler 11937 US Hwy 271 *Web:* www.uthct.edu	Tyler	TX	75708	903-877-3451	877-7759
University of Texas Medical Branch Hospitals 301 University Blvd *Web:* www.utmb.edu	Galveston	TX	77555	409-772-1011	772-5119
Valley Baptist Medical Center 2101 Pease St *Web:* www.vbmc.org	Harlingen	TX	78550	956-389-1100	389-1632
Valley Baptist Medical Center Brownsville 1040 W Jefferson St **Fax:* Hum Res ■ *Web:* www.valleybaptist.net/brownsville	Brownsville	TX	78520	956-544-1400	541-0712*
Valley Regional Medical Center 100-A Alton Gloor Blvd *Web:* www.valleyregionalmedicalcenter.com	Brownsville	TX	78526	956-350-7000	350-7111
Wadley Regional Medical Center 1000 Pine St *Web:* www.wadleyhealth.com	Texarkana	TX	75501	903-793-4511	798-8030
West Houston Medical Center 12141 Richmond Ave *TF:* 800-558-7619	Houston	TX	77082	281-558-3444	596-5989
Wilson N Jones Medical Center 500 N Highland Ave *TF:* 877-870-6696 ■ *Web:* www.wnj.org	Sherman	TX	75092	903-870-4611	891-2030
Woodland Heights Medical Center 505 S John Redditt Dr *Web:* www.woodlandheights.net	Lufkin	TX	75904	936-634-8311	637-8600
Zale Lipshy University Hospital 5151 Harry Hines Blvd **Fax:* Admitting ■ *Web:* www.utsouthwestern.edu	Dallas	TX	75390	214-645-5555	545-4648*

Utah

	City	State	Zip	Phone	Fax
Alta View Hospital 9660 S 1300 East *Web:* intermountainhealthcare.org/xp/public/altaview	Sandy	UT	84094	801-501-2600	501-4327
American Fork Hospital 170 N 1100 East *Web:* intermountainhealthcare.org/xp/public/americanfork	American Fork	UT	84003	801-763-3300	855-3548
Cottonwood Hospital 5770 S Fashion Blvd 300 East *Web:* intermountainhealthcare.org/xp/public/cottonwood	Murray	UT	84107	801-314-5300	314-2272
Davis Hospital & Medical Center 1600 W Antelope Dr *Web:* www.davishospital.com	Layton	UT	84041	801-807-1000	807-7610
Dixie Regional Medical Center 544 S 400 East *Web:* intermountainhealthcare.org/xp/public/dixie	Saint George	UT	84770	435-251-1000	251-2115
Lakeview Hospital 630 E Medical Dr *Web:* www.lakeviewhospital.com	Bountiful	UT	84010	801-292-6231	299-2534
LDS Hospital 8th Ave & C St *TF:* 888-301-3880	Salt Lake City	UT	84143	801-408-1100	408-1665

General Hospitals - US (Cont'd)

Utah (Cont'd)

	City	State	Zip	Phone	Fax
Logan Regional Hospital 500 E 1400 N *Web:* www.loganregionalhospital.com	Logan	UT	84341	435-752-2050	716-5409
McKay-Dee Hospital Center 4401 S Harrison Blvd *Web:* intermountainhealthcare.org/xp/public/mckaydee	Ogden	UT	84403	801-627-2800	387-3725
Mountain View Hospital 1000 E 100 N *Web:* www.mvhpayson.com	Payson	UT	84651	801-465-7000	465-7170
Ogden Regional Medical Center 5475 S 500 East *TF:* 800-237-9194 ■ *Web:* www.ogdenregional.com	Ogden	UT	84405	801-479-2111	479-2091
Pioneer Valley Hospital 3460 S Pioneer Pkwy *Web:* www.pioneervalleyhospital.com	West Valley City	UT	84120	801-964-3100	964-3247
Saint Mark's Hospital 1200 East 3900 South *Web:* www.stmarkshospital.com	Salt Lake City	UT	84124	801-268-7111	270-3489
Salt Lake Regional Medical Center 1050 E South Temple *Web:* www.saltlakeregional.com	Salt Lake City	UT	84102	801-350-4111	350-4522
University of Utah Hospital & Clinics 50 N Medical Dr *Web:* www.med.utah.edu	Salt Lake City	UT	84132	801-581-2121	585-5280
Utah Valley Regional Medical Center 1034 N 500 West *Web:* intermountainhealthcare.org/xp/public/uvrmc	Provo	UT	84604	801-373-7850	357-7780

Vermont

	City	State	Zip	Phone	Fax
Central Vermont Medical Center 130 Fisher Rd *Web:* www.cvmc.hitchcock.org	Berlin	VT	05602	802-229-9121	371-4401
Fletcher Allen Health Care Medical Center Campus 111 Colchester Ave *Web:* www.fahc.org	Burlington	VT	05401	802-847-0000	847-5252
Northwestern Medical Center 133 Fairfield St *Web:* www.northwesternmedicalcenter.org	Saint Albans	VT	05478	802-524-5911	524-1088
Rutland Regional Medical Center 160 Allen St *TF:* 800-649-2187 ■ *Web:* www.rrmc.org	Rutland	VT	05701	802-775-7111	747-1620
Southwestern Vermont Medical Center 100 Hospital Dr *TF:* 800-543-1624 ■ *Web:* www.svhealthcare.org/hospital	Bennington	VT	05201	802-442-6361	447-5013
Springfield Hospital 25 Ridgewood Rd PO Box 2003 *Web:* www.springfieldhospital.org	Springfield	VT	05156	802-885-2151	885-7357

Virginia

	City	State	Zip	Phone	Fax
Alleghany Regional Hospital 1 ARH Ln PO Box 7 *Web:* www.alleghanyregional.com	Low Moor	VA	24457	540-862-6011	862-6589
Augusta Medical Center 78 Medical Center Dr PO Box 1000 *TF:* 800-932-0262 ■ *Web:* www.augustamed.com/amc.htm	Fishersville	VA	22939	540-932-4000	932-4809
Bon Secours DePaul Medical Center 150 Kingsley Ln *Web:* bonsecourshamptonroads.com	Norfolk	VA	23505	757-489-5000	889-5837
Bon Secours Maryview Medical Center 3636 High St **Fax:* Admitting ■ *Web:* bonsecourshamptonroads.com/facilities/maryview.html	Portsmouth	VA	23707	757-398-2200	398-2157*
Bon Secours Memorial Regional Medical Center 8260 Atlee Rd *TF:* 888-455-3766 ■ *Web:* bonsecours.org/richmond/mrmc.htm	Mechanicsville	VA	23116	804-764-6000	764-6420
Bon Secours Saint Francis Medical Center 13710 Saint Francis Blvd *TF:* 866-503-7369 ■ *Web:* www.bonsecours.com/	Midlothian	VA	23114	804-594-7300	
Bon Secours Saint Mary's Hospital 5801 Bremo Rd *TF:* 800-472-2011 ■ *Web:* bonsecours.org/richmond/smary.htm	Richmond	VA	23226	804-285-2011	285-8327
Buchanan General Hospital RR 5 Box 20 *Web:* www.bgh.org	Grundy	VA	24614	276-935-1000	935-4959
Carilion New River Valley Medical Center 2900 Lamb Cir *TF:* 800-432-7874 ■ *Web:* www.carilion.com/cnrv/index.html	Christiansburg	VA	24073	540-731-2000	731-2505
Carilion Roanoke Community Hospital 101 Elm Ave SE *Web:* www.carilion.com/crch	Roanoke	VA	24013	540-985-8000	224-4537
Carilion Roanoke Memorial Hospital 1906 Belleview Ave *Web:* www.carilion.com/crmh	Roanoke	VA	24014	540-981-7000	981-7670
Chesapeake General Hospital 736 Battlefield Blvd N *Web:* www.chesapeakehealth.com	Chesapeake	VA	23320	757-312-6100	312-6184
CJW Medical Center 7101 Jahnke Rd *TF:* 800-468-6620 ■ *Web:* www.cjwmedical.com	Richmond	VA	23225	804-320-3911	323-8049
Clinch Valley Medical Center 2949 W Front St *Web:* www.clinchvalleymedicalcenter.com	Richlands	VA	24641	276-596-6000	596-6009
Community Memorial Healthcenter 125 Buena Vista Cir PO Box 90 *Web:* www.cmh-sh.org	South Hill	VA	23970	434-447-3151	774-2401
Danville Regional Medical Center 142 S Main St *TF:* 800-688-3762 ■ *Web:* www.danvilleregional.org	Danville	VA	24541	434-799-2100	799-2260
Fauquier Hospital 500 Hospital Dr *Web:* www.fauquierhospital.org	Warrenton	VA	20186	540-347-2550	349-0572
Halifax Regional Hospital 2204 Wilborn Ave *Web:* www.hrhs.org	South Boston	VA	24592	434-517-3100	517-3626
Henrico Doctor's Hospital 1602 Skipwith Rd *Web:* www.henricodoctorshospital.com	Richmond	VA	23229	804-289-4500	289-4801
Inova Alexandria Hospital 4320 Seminary Rd *Web:* www.inova.com	Alexandria	VA	22304	703-504-3000	504-3700
Inova Fair Oaks Hospital 3600 Joseph Siewick Dr *Web:* www.inova.org/ifoh	Fairfax	VA	22033	703-391-3600	391-3273
Inova Fairfax Hospital 3300 Gallows Rd *Web:* www.inova.org	Falls Church	VA	22042	703-776-4001	776-3623
Inova Mount Vernon Hospital 2501 Parker's Ln *Web:* www.inova.org	Alexandria	VA	22306	703-664-7000	664-7235
John Randolph Medical Center 411 W Randolph Rd *TF:* 800-999-0374 ■ *Web:* www.johnrandolphmedicalcenter.com	Hopewell	VA	23860	804-541-1600	452-3346
Johnston Memorial Hospital 351 Court St NE *Web:* www.jmh.org	Abingdon	VA	24210	276-676-7000	676-2631
Lewis-Gale Medical Center 1900 Electric Rd *Web:* www.lewis-gale.com	Salem	VA	24153	540-776-4000	776-4785
Loudoun Hospital Center 44045 Riverside Pkwy *TF:* 888-542-8477 ■ *Web:* www.loudounhospital.org	Leesburg	VA	20176	703-858-6000	858-6610
Lynchburg General Hospital 1901 Tate Springs Rd	Lynchburg	VA	24501	434-947-3000	947-3271
Martha Jefferson Hospital 459 Locust Ave *Web:* www.marthajefferson.org	Charlottesville	VA	22902	434-982-7000	982-7324
Mary Immaculate Hospital 2 Bernardine Dr *Web:* www.bshsi.com	Newport News	VA	23602	757-886-6000	886-6751
Mary Washington Hospital 1001 Sam Perry Blvd *TF:* 800-468-1092 ■ *Web:* www.medicorp.org/mwh	Fredericksburg	VA	22401	540-741-1100	741-1420
MCV Hospital 1250 E Marshall St *Web:* www.vcuhealth.org	Richmond	VA	23219	804-828-9000	828-0170
Memorial Hospital 320 Hospital Dr *Web:* www.martinsvillehospital.org	Martinsville	VA	24115	276-666-7200	666-7600
Montgomery Regional Hospital 3700 S Main St *Web:* www.mrhospital.com	Blacksburg	VA	24060	540-951-1111	953-5295
Northern Virginia Community Hospital 601 S Carlin Springs Rd *Web:* www.nvchospital.com	Arlington	VA	22204	703-671-1200	578-2075
Norton Community Hospital 100 15th St NW *Web:* www.nchosp.org	Norton	VA	24273	276-679-9600	679-9664
Potomac Hospital 2300 Opitz Blvd *Web:* www.potomachospital.com	Woodbridge	VA	22191	703-670-1313	670-7643
Prince William Hospital 8700 Sudly Rd *Web:* www.pwhs.org	Manassas	VA	20110	703-369-8000	369-8010
Reston Hospital Center 1850 Town Center Pkwy *TF:* 800-695-9426 ■ *Web:* www.restonhospital.com	Reston	VA	20190	703-689-9000	689-0840
Retreat Hospital 2621 Grove Ave *TF:* 800-235-9091 ■ *Web:* www.retreathospital.com	Richmond	VA	23220	804-254-5100	254-5187
Riverside Regional Medical Center 500 J Clyde Morris Blvd *Web:* www.riverside-online.com/rrmc.htm	Newport News	VA	23601	757-594-2000	594-2084
Rockingham Memorial Hospital 235 Cantrell Ave *TF:* 800-543-2201 ■ *Web:* www.rmhonline.com	Harrisonburg	VA	22801	540-433-4100	433-4576
Sentara Careplex Hospital 3000 Colliseum Dr *TF:* 800-736-8272 ■ *Web:* www.sentara.com	Hampton	VA	23666	757-736-1000	736-2659
Sentara Leigh Hospital 830 Kempsville Rd *Web:* www.sentara.com/hospitals	Norfolk	VA	23502	757-261-6000	461-6796
Sentara Norfolk General Hospital 600 Gresham Dr **Fax:* Admitting ■ *Web:* www.sentara.com/hospitals	Norfolk	VA	23507	757-388-3000	388-4319*
Sentara Obici Hospital 2800 Godwin Blvd *TF:* 800-237-5788 ■ *Web:* www.sentara.com/	Suffolk	VA	23434	757-934-4000	934-4284
Sentara Virginia Beach General Hospital 1060 First Colonial Rd *TF:* 800-736-8272 ■ *Web:* www.sentara.com/hospitals	Virginia Beach	VA	23454	757-395-8000	395-6106
Sentara Williamsburg Regional Medical Center 100 Sentara Cir *Web:* www.sentara.com	Williamsburg	VA	23188	757-984-6000	984-8145
Shore Memorial Hospital 9507 Hospital Ave PO Box 17 *TF:* 800-834-7035 ■ *Web:* www.shorehealthservices.org	Nassawadox	VA	23413	757-414-8000	414-8633
Smyth County Community Hospital 565 Radio Hill Rd *Web:* www.scchosp.org	Marion	VA	24354	276-782-1234	782-1438
Southampton Memorial Hospital 100 Fairview Dr *Web:* www.smhfranklin.com	Franklin	VA	23851	757-569-6100	569-6390
Southside Community Hospital 800 Oak St *Web:* www.sch-farmville.org	Farmville	VA	23901	434-392-8811	392-7654
Southside Regional Medical Center 801 S Adams St *TF:* 866-434-9101 ■ *Web:* www.srmconline.com	Petersburg	VA	23803	804-862-5000	862-5948
Twin County Regional Hospital 200 Hospital Dr *TF:* 800-295-3342 ■ *Web:* www.tcrh.org	Galax	VA	24333	276-236-8181	236-1715
University of Virginia Medical Center 1215 Lee St *TF:* 800-251-3627 ■ *Web:* www.med.virginia.edu	Charlottesville	VA	22908	434-243-9318	982-3759
Virginia Baptist Hospital 3300 Rivermont Ave *TF:* 800-423-5535 ■ *Web:* www.centrahealth.com	Lynchburg	VA	24503	434-947-4000	947-7448
Virginia Hospital Center 1701 N George Mason Dr *Web:* www.virginiahospitalcenter.com	Arlington	VA	22205	703-558-5000	558-6583
Winchester Medical Center 1840 Amherst St *Web:* www.valleyhealthlink.com	Winchester	VA	22601	540-536-8000	536-8606

Washington

	City	State	Zip	Phone	Fax
Auburn Regional Medical Center 202 N Division St Plaza 1 *TF:* 800-303-7713 ■ *Web:* www.armcuhs.com	Auburn	WA	98001	253-833-7711	939-2376
Capital Medical Center 3900 Capital Mall Dr SW *TF:* 888-677-9757 ■ *Web:* www.capitalmedical.com	Olympia	WA	98502	360-754-5858	956-2574
Deaconess Medical Center 800 W 5th Ave *Web:* www.deaconess-spokane.org	Spokane	WA	99204	509-458-5800	473-7286
Eastside Hospital 2700 152nd Ave NE *Web:* www.ghc.org	Redmond	WA	98052	425-883-5151	883-5638
Evergreen Hospital Medical Center 12040 NE 128th St *Web:* www.evergreenhealthcare.org	Kirkland	WA	98034	425-899-1000	899-2624
Good Samaritan Hospital 407 14th Ave SE *Web:* www.goodsamhealth.org	Puyallup	WA	98372	253-848-6661	697-5656
Grays Harbor Community Hospital 920 Anderson Dr *Web:* www.ghchwa.org	Aberdeen	WA	98520	360-532-8330	537-5039
Harrison Memorial Hospital 2520 Cherry Ave *Web:* www.harrisonhospital.org	Bremerton	WA	98310	360-377-3911	792-6515
Highline Medical Center 16251 Sylvester Rd SW *Web:* www.hchnet.org	Burien	WA	98166	206-244-9970	246-5385
Holy Family Hospital 5633 N Lidgerwood St *Web:* www.holy-family.org	Spokane	WA	99208	509-482-0111	482-2456
Kadlec Medical Center 888 Swift Blvd *TF:* 800-780-6067 ■ *Web:* www.kadlecmed.org	Richland	WA	99352	509-946-4611	942-2679
Kennewick General Hospital 900 S Auburn St *Web:* www.kennewickgeneral.com	Kennewick	WA	99336	509-586-6111	586-5892
Legacy Salmon Creek Hospital 2211 NE 139th St *TF:* 877-397-9727 ■ *Web:* www.legacyhealth.org	Vancouver	WA	98686	360-487-1000	487-3459
Lourdes Medical Center 520 N 4th Ave *Web:* www.lourdeshealth.net	Pasco	WA	99301	509-547-7704	546-2291
Northwest Hospital 1550 N 115th St *Web:* www.nwhospital.org	Seattle	WA	98133	206-368-1700	368-1949
Olympic Medical Center 939 Caroline St *Web:* www.olympicmedical.org	Port Angeles	WA	98362	360-457-8513	417-7333
Overlake Hospital Medical Center 1035 116th Ave NE *Web:* www.overlakehospital.org	Bellevue	WA	98004	425-688-5000	688-5087
Providence Everett Medical Center 1321 Colby Ave *Web:* www.providence.org/everett	Everett	WA	98201	425-261-2000	261-4030
Providence Everett Medical Center Pacific Campus 916 Pacific Ave *Web:* www.providence.org/everett/facilities	Everett	WA	98201	425-258-7123	258-7734
Providence Hospital 914 S Scheuber Rd *TF:* 877-736-2803 ■ *Web:* www.providence.org/swsa/facilities/Centralia_Hospital/default.htm	Centralia	WA	98531	360-736-2803	330-8614
Providence Saint Peter Hospital 413 Lilly Rd NE *TF:* 888-492-9480 ■ *Web:* www.providence.org	Olympia	WA	98506	360-491-9480	493-4277
Sacred Heart Medical Center 101 W 8th Ave *TF:* 800-442-8534 ■ *Web:* www.shmc.org	Spokane	WA	99204	509-455-3131	474-4925
Saint Francis Hospital 34515 9th Ave S *Web:* www.fhshealth.org	Federal Way	WA	98003	253-838-9700	944-7913
Saint John Medical Center 1615 Delaware St *Web:* www.peacehealth.org/LowerColumbia/WhoWeAreSJMC.htm	Longview	WA	98632	360-423-1530	414-7500
Saint Joseph Hospital 2901 Squalicum Pkwy *TF:* 800-541-7209 ■ *Web:* www.peacehealth.org/Whatcom	Bellingham	WA	98225	360-734-5400	738-6393
Saint Joseph Medical Center 1717 S 'J' St *Web:* www.fhshealth.org	Tacoma	WA	98405	253-627-4101	426-6260
Saint Mary Medical Center 401 W Poplar St *TF:* 800-452-3320 ■ *Web:* www.smmc.com	Walla Walla	WA	99362	509-525-3320	522-5950
Skagit Valley Hospital 1415 E Kincaid St *Web:* www.skagitvalleyhospital.org	Mount Vernon	WA	98273	360-424-4111	428-2416
Southwest Washington Medical Center 420 NE Mother Joseph Pl *Web:* www.swmedicalcenter.com	Vancouver	WA	98664	360-514-2000	514-2006

Phone Fax

Stevens Memorial Hospital 21601 76th Ave W ... Edmonds WA 98026 425-640-4000 640-4010
Web: www.stevenshealthcare.org

Swedish Medical Center
Cherry Hill Campus 500 17th Ave ... Seattle WA 98122 206-320-2000 320-2140
Web: www.swedish.org
First Hill 747 Broadway ... Seattle WA 98122 206-386-6000 386-2277
Web: www.swedish.org

Tacoma General Hospital 315 MLK Jr Way ... Tacoma WA 98405 253-403-1000 403-1180
TF: 800-552-1419 ■ *Web:* www.multicare.org

University of Washington Medical Center 1959 NE Pacific St ... Seattle WA 98195 206-548-3300 598-2343
Web: www.washington.edu/medicine

Valley Hospital & Medical Center 12606 E Mission Ave ... Spokane WA 99216 509-924-6650 462-0502
Web: www.valleyhospital.org

Valley Medical Center 400 S 43rd St ... Renton WA 98055 425-228-3450 575-2593*
**Fax Area Code:* 206 ■ *TF:* 800-540-1814 ■ *Web:* www.valleymed.org

Virginia Mason Medical Center 925 Seneca St ... Seattle WA 98101 206-624-1144 223-6976
Web: www.virginiamason.org

Yakima Regional Medical & Heart Center 110 S 9th Ave ... Yakima WA 98902 509-575-5000 454-6193
Web: www.yakimaregional.org

Yakima Valley Memorial Hospital 2811 Tieton Dr ... Yakima WA 98902 509-575-8000 574-5800
Web: www.yakimamemorialhospital.org

West Virginia

Phone Fax

Beckley Appalachian Regional Hospital 306 Stanaford Rd ... Beckley WV 25801 304-255-3000 255-3544
Web: www.arh.org/beckley.htm

Bluefield Regional Medical Center 500 Cherry St ... Bluefield WV 24701 304-327-1100 327-1075
Web: www.bluefield.org

Cabell Huntington Hospital 1340 Hal Greer Blvd ... Huntington WV 25701 304-526-2000 526-2008
Web: www.cabellhuntington.org

Camden-Clark Memorial Hospital 800 Garfield Ave ... Parkersburg WV 26102 304-424-2111 424-2782
TF: 800-422-6437 ■ *Web:* www.ccmh.org

Charleston Area Medical Center 501 Morris St ... Charleston WV 25301 304-388-5432 388-3604
Web: www.camc.org

City Hospital PO Box 1418 ... Martinsburg WV 25402 304-264-1000 264-1255
Web: www.cityhospital.org

Davis Memorial Hospital Reed St & Gorman Ave PO Box 1484 ... Elkins WV 26241 304-636-3300 637-3184
Web: www.davishealthsystem.org

Fairmont General Hospital 1325 Locust Ave ... Fairmont WV 26554 304-367-7100 367-7167
Web: www.fghi.com

Greenbrier Valley Medical Center 202 Maplewood Ave ... Ronceverte WV 24970 304-647-4411 647-6010
Web: www.gvmc.com

Logan Regional Medical Center 20 Hospital Dr ... Logan WV 25601 304-831-1101 831-1871
Web: www.loganregionalmedicalcenter.com

Monongalia General Hospital 1200 JD Anderson Dr ... Morgantown WV 26505 304-598-1200 598-1987
TF: 800-992-7600 ■ *Web:* www.monhealthsys.org

Ohio Valley Medical Center 2000 Eoff St ... Wheeling WV 26003 304-234-0123 234-8229
Web: www.ohiovalleymedicalcenter.com

Pleasant Valley Hospital 2520 Valley Dr ... Point Pleasant WV 25550 304-675-4340 675-5243
Web: www.pvalley.org

Princeton Community Hospital 122 12th St ... Princeton WV 24740 304-487-7000 487-2161
Web: www.pchonline.org

Raleigh General Hospital 1710 Harper Rd ... Beckley WV 25801 304-256-4100 256-4009
TF: 800-368-8016 ■ *Web:* www.raleighgeneral.com

Reynolds Memorial Hospital 800 Wheeling Ave ... Glen Dale WV 26038 304-845-3211 843-3202
Web: www.reynoldsmemorial.com

Saint Francis Hospital 333 Laidley St ... Charleston WV 25301 304-347-6500 347-6885
Web: www.stfrancishospital.com

Saint Joseph's Hospital 1824 Murdock Ave ... Parkersburg WV 26101 304-424-4111 424-4807
Web: www.stjosephs-hospital.com

Saint Mary's Medical Center 2900 1st Ave ... Huntington WV 25701 304-526-1234 526-1538
TF: 800-978-6279 ■ *Web:* www.st-marys.org

Stonewall Jackson Memorial Hospital 230 Hospital Plaza ... Weston WV 26452 304-269-3000 269-8090
Web: www.stonewallhospital.com

Thomas Memorial Hospital 4605 MacCorkle Ave SW ... South Charleston WV 25309 304-766-3600 766-3477
Web: www.thomaswv.org

United Hospital Center 3 Hospital Plaza ... Clarksburg WV 26301 304-624-2121 624-2909
Web: www.uhcwv.org

Weirton Medical Center 601 Colliers Way ... Weirton WV 26062 304-797-6000 797-6176
TF: 800-243-4962 ■ *Web:* www.weirtonmedical.com

West Virginia University Hospitals Medical Center Dr ... Morgantown WV 26506 304-598-4200 598-4124
Web: www.health.wvu.edu

Wheeling Hospital 1 Medical Park ... Wheeling WV 26003 304-243-3000 243-3060
Web: www.wheelinghospital.com

Wisconsin

Phone Fax

All Saints Medical Center
Saint Luke's Campus 1320 Wisconsin Ave ... Racine WI 53403 262-636-2011 687-2115
TF: 800-526-9309 ■ *Web:* www.allsaintshealth.com
Saint Mary's Campus 3801 Spring St ... Racine WI 53405 262-687-4011 687-5116
TF: 800-526-9309 ■ *Web:* www.allsaintshealth.com

Appleton Medical Center 1818 N Meade St ... Appleton WI 54911 920-731-4101 738-6319
TF: 800-236-4101 ■ *Web:* www.thedacare.org

Aspirus Wausau Hospital 333 Pine Ridge Blvd ... Wausau WI 54401 715-847-2121 847-2108
TF: 800-283-2881 ■ *Web:* aspirus.org

Aurora Lakeland Medical Center W3985 County Rd NN ... Elkhorn WI 53121 262-741-2000 741-2759
Web: www.aurorahealthcare.org/facilities

Aurora Sinai Medical Center 945 N 12th St ... Milwaukee WI 53201 414-219-2000 219-6735
TF: 888-414-7762 ■ *Web:* www.aurorahealthcare.org

Bay Area Medical Center 3100 Shore Dr ... Marinette WI 54143 715-735-6621 735-8080
TF: 888-788-2070 ■ *Web:* www.bayareamedical.com

Beaver Dam Community Hospital 707 S University Ave ... Beaver Dam WI 53916 920-887-7181 887-7973
Web: www.bdch.com

Bellin Hospital 744 S Webster Ave ... Green Bay WI 54301 920-433-3500 431-5568
Web: www.bellin.org

Beloit Memorial Hospital 1969 W Hart Rd ... Beloit WI 53511 608-364-5011 364-5356
TF: 800-637-2641 ■ *Web:* www.beloitmemorialhospital.org

Columbia Saint Mary's Hospital 2025 E Newport Ave ... Milwaukee WI 53211 414-961-3300 961-8712
Web: www.columbia-stmarys.com

Community Memorial Hospital
W 180 N 8085 Town Hall Rd ... Menomonee Falls WI 53051 262-251-1000 253-7169
Web: www.communitymemorial.com

Elmbrook Memorial Hospital 19333 W North Ave ... Brookfield WI 53045 262-785-2000 785-2485
Web: www.wfhealthcare.org

Fort Atkinson Memorial Hospital 611 E Sherman Ave ... Fort Atkinson WI 53538 920-568-5000 568-5412
Web: www.forthealthcare.com

Franciscan Skemp Health Care 700 West Ave S ... La Crosse WI 54601 608-785-0940 791-9429

Froedtert Hospital 9200 W Wisconsin Ave ... Milwaukee WI 53226 414-259-3000 805-7790
Web: www.froedtert.com

Gundersen Lutheran Medical Center 1900 South Ave ... La Crosse WI 54601 608-785-0530 775-6334
TF: 800-362-9567 ■ *Web:* www.gundluth.org

Holy Family Memorial Medical Center 2300 Western Ave ... Manitowoc WI 54220 920-320-2011 320-1920
TF: 800-994-3662 ■ *Web:* www.hfmhealth.org

Phone Fax

Howard Young Medical Center 240 Maple St ... Woodruff WI 54568 715-356-8000 356-6097
Web: www.ministryhealth.org

Kenosha Medical Center 6308 8th Ave ... Kenosha WI 53143 262-656-2011 656-2124
Web: www.uhsi.org

Lakeview Medical Center 1100 N Main St ... Rice Lake WI 54868 715-234-1515 236-6342
Web: www.lakeviewmedical.com

Luther Hospital 1221 Whipple St Box 4105 ... Eau Claire WI 54702 715-838-3311 838-6688
Web: www.luthermidelfort.org

Memorial Medical Center 1615 Maple Ln ... Ashland WI 54806 715-682-4563 682-4022
Web: www.ashlandmmc.com

Mercy Hospital of Janesville 1000 Mineral Point Ave ... Janesville WI 53548 608-756-6000 756-6236
TF: 800-756-4147 ■ *Web:* www.mercyhealthsystem.com

Mercy Medical Center 500 S Oakwood Rd ... Oshkosh WI 54904 920-236-2000 223-0508
TF: 800-242-5650 ■ *Web:* www.affinityhealth.org

Meriter Hospital 202 S Park St ... Madison WI 53715 608-267-6000 267-6645
Web: www.meriter.com/mhs/index.htm

Monroe Clinic Hospital 515 22nd Ave ... Monroe WI 53566 608-324-1000 324-1114
TF: 800-338-0568 ■ *Web:* www.monroeclinic.org

Oconomowoc Memorial Hospital 791 Summit Ave ... Oconomowoc WI 53066 262-569-9400 569-0336
Web: www.oconomowocmemorial.org

Sacred Heart Hospital 900 W Clairemont Ave ... Eau Claire WI 54701 715-839-4121 839-8417
TF: 888-445-4554 ■ *Web:* www.sacredhearthospital-ec.org

Saint Agnes Hospital 430 E Division St ... Fond du Lac WI 54935 920-929-2300 926-4866
TF: 800-922-3400 ■ *Web:* www.agnesian.com

Saint Elizabeth Hospital 1506 S Oneida St ... Appleton WI 54915 920-738-2000 831-8948
TF: 800-223-7332 ■ *Web:* www.affinityhealth.org

Saint Francis Hospital 3237 S 16th St ... Milwaukee WI 53215 414-647-5000 647-5565
Web: www.covhealth.org

Saint Joseph's Community Hospital 3200 Pleasant Valley Rd ... West Bend WI 53095 262-334-5533 335-8152
Web: www.synergyhealth.org

Saint Joseph's Hospital 2661 County Hwy 'I' ... Chippewa Falls WI 54729 715-723-1811 726-3204
Web: www.stjoeschipfalls.com

Saint Joseph's Hospital 611 St Joseph Ave ... Marshfield WI 54449 715-387-1713 389-3939
Web: www.stjosephs-marshfield.org

Saint Joseph's Regional Medical Center
5000 W Chambers St ... Milwaukee WI 53210 414-447-2000
Web: www.covhealth.org

Saint Luke's Medical Center 2900 W Oklahoma Ave ... Milwaukee WI 53215 414-649-6000 649-8386
Web: www.aurorahealthcare.org/facilities

Saint Luke's South Hospital 5900 S Lake Dr ... Cudahy WI 53110 414-769-9000 489-4171
Web: www.aurorahealthcare.org

Saint Mary's Hospital 2323 N Lake Dr ... Milwaukee WI 53211 414-291-1000
Web: www.columbia-stmarys.com

Saint Mary's Hospital 2251 N Shore Dr ... Rhinelander WI 54501 715-361-2000 361-2011
TF: 800-578-0840 ■ *Web:* www.ministryhealth.org

Saint Mary's Hospital Medical Center 707 S Mills St ... Madison WI 53715 608-251-6100 258-6731
Web: www.stmarysmadison.com

Saint Mary's Hospital Ozaukee 13111 N Port Washington Rd ... Mequon WI 53097 262-243-7300
TF: 800-848-2844 ■ *Web:* www.columbia-stmarys.com

Saint Mary's Medical Center 1726 Shawano Ave ... Green Bay WI 54303 920-498-4200 498-1861
TF: 800-666-5606 ■ *Web:* www.stmgb.org

Saint Michael Hospital 2400 W Villard Ave ... Milwaukee WI 53209 414-527-8000 527-8510
Web: www.covhealth.org

Saint Michael's Hospital 900 Illinois Ave ... Stevens Point WI 54481 715-346-5000 346-5088
Web: www.ministryhealth.org

Saint Nicholas Hospital 3100 Superior Ave ... Sheboygan WI 53081 920-459-8300 457-4121
TF: 800-472-6710 ■ *Web:* www.stnicholashospital.org

Saint Vincent Hospital 835 S Van Buren St ... Green Bay WI 54301 920-433-0111 431-3215
TF: 800-236-3030 ■ *Web:* www.stvincenthospital.org

Sheboygan Memorial Medical Center 2629 N 7th St ... Sheboygan WI 53083 920-457-5033 451-5333
Web: www.aurorahealthcare.org

Theda Clark Medical Center 130 2nd St ... Neenah WI 54956 920-729-3100 729-3167
TF: 800-236-3122 ■ *Web:* www.thedacare.org

University of Wisconsin Hospital & Clinics 600 Highland Ave ... Madison WI 53792 608-263-6400 263-9830
TF: 800-323-8942 ■ *Web:* www.uwhealth.org

Waukesha Memorial Hospital 725 American Ave ... Waukesha WI 53188 262-928-1000 544-4995
TF: 800-326-2011 ■ *Web:* www.waukeshamemorial.org

West Allis Memorial Hospital 8901 W Lincoln Ave ... West Allis WI 53227 414-328-6000 328-8536
Web: www.aurorahealthcare.org

Wyoming

Phone Fax

Cheyenne Regional Medical Center 214 E 23rd St ... Cheyenne WY 82001 307-634-2273 633-3569
Web: www.crmcwy.com

Ivinson Memorial Hospital 255 N 30th St ... Laramie WY 82072 307-742-2141 742-0678
TF: 800-854-1115 ■ *Web:* www.ivinsonhospital.org

Memorial Hospital of Sheridan County 1401 W 5th St ... Sheridan WY 82801 307-672-1000 672-1007
Web: www.sheridanhospital.org

Memorial Hospital of Sweetwater County
1200 College Dr ... Rock Springs WY 82901 307-362-3711 352-8180
TF: 800-307-3711 ■ *Web:* www.minershospital.com

Wyoming Medical Center 1233 E 2nd St ... Casper WY 82601 307-577-7201 237-1703
TF: 800-822-7201 ■ *Web:* www.wmcnet.org

377-4 Military Hospitals

Phone Fax

Bayne-Jones Army Community Hospital 1585 3rd St Bldg 285 ... Fort Polk LA 71459 337-531-3118 531-3050

Brooke Army Medical Center
3851 Roger Brook Dr Bldg 3600 ... Fort Sam Houston TX 78234 210-916-6141 916-2100

Charleston Naval Hospital 3600 Rivers Ave ... North Charleston SC 29405 843-743-7000 743-7259
Web: www.nhchasn.med.navy.mil

Colonel Florence A Blanchfield Army Community Hospital
650 Joel Dr ... Fort Campbell KY 42223 270-798-8400 798-8812

Darnall Army Community Hospital Bldg 36000 ... Fort Hood TX 76544 254-288-8000 288-8827
TF: 800-611-2875

David Grant US Air Force Medical Center 101 Bodin Cir ... Travis AFB CA 94535 707-423-7300 423-7416
TF: 800-264-3462

Dewitt Army Community Hospital
9501 Farrell Rd Suite GC11 ... Fort Belvoir VA 22060 703-805-0510 805-0219

Dwight David Eisenhower Army Medical Center
Hospital Rd Bldg 300 ... Fort Gordon GA 30905 706-787-5811 787-5342*
**Fax:* Admitting ■ *Web:* www.ddeamc.amedd.army.mil

Ehrling Bergquist US Air Force Hospital 2501 Capehart Rd ... Offutt AFB NE 68113 402-294-9760 294-2816

Evans Army Community Hospital 1650 Cochran Cir ... Fort Carson CO 80913 719-526-7000 526-3776
Web: www.evans.amedd.army.mil/

General Leonard Wood Army Community Hospital
126 Missouri Ave ... Fort Leonard Wood MO 65473 573-596-1490 596-0030
Web: glwach.amedd.army.mil

Ireland Army Community Hospital 851 Ireland Loop ... Fort Knox KY 40121 502-624-9333 624-9604

Irwin Army Community Hospital 600 Caisson Hill Rd ... Fort Riley KS 66442 785-239-7000 239-7405

Keller Army Community Hospital 900 Washington Rd ... West Point NY 10996 845-938-3305 938-5164
Web: www.usma.edu/meddac/

Kimbrough Ambulatory Care Center 2480 Lewellyn Ave ... Fort Meade MD 20755 301-677-8392 677-8499

Military Hospitals (Cont'd)

				Phone	Fax
Lyster Army Health Clinic 301 Andrews St	Fort Rucker	AL	36362	334-255-7999	255-7710
Madigan Army Medical Center 9040 Jackson Ave	Tacoma	WA	98431	253-968-1110	968-1633*
*Fax: Admitting					
Martin Army Community Hospital					
7950 Martin Loop Bldg 9200	Fort Benning	GA	31905	706-544-2041	544-2407
McDonald Army Community Hospital 576 Jefferson Ave	Fort Eustis	VA	23604	757-878-7500	878-7661
TF: 800-304-9863					
Moncrief Army Community Hospital					
4500 Stuart St PO Box 500	Fort Jackson	SC	29207	803-751-2160	751-2471
National Naval Medical Center 8901 Wisconsin Ave	Bethesda	MD	20889	301-295-4611	295-6521
Web: www.dcmilitary.com/baseguides					
Naval Health Clinic Great Lakes 3001-A 6th St	Great Lakes	IL	60088	847-688-4560	688-5752
Naval Hospital Santa Margaritas St Bldg H-100	Camp Pendleton	CA	92055	760-725-1288	725-1689
Naval Hospital 2080 Child St	Jacksonville	FL	32214	904-542-7300	542-7281
Naval Hospital 6000 W Hwy 98	Pensacola	FL	32512	850-505-6601	505-6213
Web: psaweb.med.navy.mil					
Naval Hospital 100 Brewster Blvd	Camp Lejeune	NC	28547	910-450-4300	450-4012
Web: lej-www.med.navy.mil					
Naval Hospital Boone Rd	Bremerton	WA	98312	360-475-4000	475-4577
Web: nh_bremerton.med.navy.mil					
Naval Medical Center Portsmouth 620 John Paul Jones Cir	Portsmouth	VA	23708	757-953-5000	953-7935
Web: www-nmcp.med.navy.mil					
Naval Medical Center San Diego 34800 Bob Wilson Dr	San Diego	CA	92134	619-532-6400	
Web: www-nmcsd.med.navy.mil					
Raymond W Bliss Army Health Center 45001 Winrow St	Fort Huachuca	AZ	85613	520-533-9200	
Reynolds Army Community Hospital 4301 Mow Way Rd	Fort Sill	OK	73503	580-458-2000	458-3239
Web: wwwrach.sill.amedd.army.mil					
Tripler Army Medical Center 1 Jarrett White Rd Tripler AMC	Honolulu	HI	96859	808-433-6661	433-4899
Web: www.tamc.amedd.army.mil					
US Air Force 2nd Medical Group 243 Curtiss Rd	Barksdale AFB	LA	71110	318-456-6004	456-6112
US Air Force 6th Medical Group 8415 Bayshore Blvd	MacDill AFB	FL	33621	813-828-2273	828-5283
US Air Force 10th Medical Group					
4102 Pinion Dr Suite 100	USAF Academy	CO	80840	719-333-5111	333-5600
US Air Force 42nd Medical Group Hospital					
300 S Twining St	Maxwell AFB	AL	36112	334-953-7805	953-7270
US Air Force 56th Medical Group 7219 N Litchfield Rd	Luke AFB	AZ	85309	623-856-9100	
US Air Force 74th Medical Group					
4881 Sugar Maple Dr	Wright-Patterson AFB	OH	45433	937-257-9183	656-1767
TF: 800-941-4501					
US Air Force 82nd Medical Group 149 Hart St	Sheppard AFB	TX	76311	940-676-2010	676-6416
Web: www.sheppard.af.mil					
US Air Force 89th Medical Group 1050 W Perimeter	Andrews AFB	MD	20762	240-857-5911	857-8205
US Air Force 96th Medical Group 307 Boatner Rd Suite 114	Eglin AFB	FL	32542	850-883-8242	883-8222
US Air Force 355th Medical Group					
4175 S Alamo Ave	Davis-Monthan AFB	AZ	85707	520-228-3900	228-2901
US Air Force 375th Medical Group 310 W Losey St	Scott AFB	IL	62225	618-256-7500	256-7613
US Air Force Hospital 1st Medical Group 45 Pine Rd	Langley AFB	VA	23665	757-764-6969	764-9845
US Air Force Medical Center Keesler 81st Medical Group					
301 Fisher St	Keesler AFB	MS	39534	228-377-6550	377-9748
Web: www.keesler.af.mil					
Walter Reed Army Medical Center 6900 Georgia Ave NW	Washington	DC	20307	202-782-3501	782-9264*
*Fax: PR ■ Web: www.wramc.amedd.army.mil					
Wilford Hall US Air Force Medical Center					
2200 Bergquist Dr Suite 1 59MDW	Lackland AFB	TX	78236	210-292-7100	292-7983
William Beaumont Army Medical Center 5005 N Piedras St	El Paso	TX	79920	915-569-2121	569-2874
Winn Army Community Hospital 1061 Harmon Ave	Fort Stewart	GA	31314	912-435-6837	370-6546
Womack Army Medical Center Bldg 4-2817 Reilly Rd	Fort Bragg	NC	28310	910-907-6000	907-8473
Web: www.wamc.amedd.army.mil					

377-5 Psychiatric Hospitals

Listings here include state psychiatric facilities as well as private psychiatric hospitals.

				Phone	Fax
Alaska Psychiatric Institute 2800 Providence Dr	Anchorage	AK	99508	907-269-7100	269-7128
Web: health.hss.state.ak.us/dbh/API/					
Allentown State Hospital 1600 Hanover Ave	Allentown	PA	18109	610-740-3200	740-3413
TF: 800-256-3571					
Alton Mental Health Center 4500 College Ave	Alton	IL	62002	618-474-3200	474-3807
Ancora Psychiatric Hospital 301 Spring Garden Rd	Ancora	NJ	08037	609-561-1700	561-2509
Andrew McFarland Mental Health Center 901 Southwind Rd	Springfield	IL	62703	217-786-6900	786-7167
Anoka-Metro Regional Treatment Center 3301 7th Ave N	Anoka	MN	55303	763-712-4000	712-4013
Appalachian Behavioral Healthcare 100 Hospital Dr	Athens	OH	45701	740-594-5000	594-3006
Arbour Hospital 49 Robinwood Ave	Jamaica Plain	MA	02130	617-522-4400	390-1597
TF: 800-828-3934 ■ Web: www.arbourhealth.com					
Arizona State Hospital 2500 E Van Buren St	Phoenix	AZ	85008	602-244-1331	220-6292
TF: 877-588-5163					
Arkansas State Hospital 4313 W Markham St	Little Rock	AR	72205	501-686-9000	686-9483
Atascadero State Hospital 10333 S Camino Real	Atascadero	CA	93422	805-468-2000	466-6011
Austin State Hospital 4110 Guadalupe St	Austin	TX	78751	512-452-0381	419-2163
Banner Behavioral Health Hospital 7575 E Earll Dr	Scottsdale	AZ	85251	480-941-7500	994-5558
TF: 800-254-4357 ■ Web: www.bannerhealth.com					
Bellevue Hospital Center 462 1st Ave	New York	NY	10016	212-562-4141	562-4036
Belmont Center for Comprehensive Treatment					
4200 Monument Rd	Philadelphia	PA	19131	215-877-2000	581-9141*
*Fax: Admissions ■ Web: www.einstein.edu					
Big Spring State Hospital 1901 N Hwy 87	Big Spring	TX	79720	432-267-8216	268-7263
Brainerd Regional Human Services Center					
11800 State Hwy 18	Brainerd	MN	56401	218-828-2787	828-2207
Web: www.dhs.state.mn.us/SOS/default.htm					
Brentwood A Behavioral Health Co 1006 Highland Ave	Shreveport	LA	71101	318-678-7500	227-9296
TF: 877-678-7500					
Bridgewater State Hospital 20 Administration Rd	Bridgewater	MA	02324	508-279-4500	279-4832
Bronx Psychiatric Center 1500 Waters Pl	Bronx	NY	10461	718-931-0600	862-4858
Broughton Hospital 1000 S Sterling St	Morganton	NC	28655	828-433-2111	433-2292
Web: www.broughtonhospital.org					
Bryce Hospital 200 University Blvd	Tuscaloosa	AL	35401	205-759-0799	759-0895
BryLin Hospitals 1263 Delaware Ave	Buffalo	NY	14209	716-886-8200	886-1986
TF: 800-727-9546 ■ Web: www.brylin.com					
Buffalo Psychiatric Center 400 Forest Ave	Buffalo	NY	14213	716-885-2261	885-0710
Butler Hospital 345 Blackstone Blvd	Providence	RI	02906	401-455-6200	455-6532*
*Fax: Admitting ■ Web: www.butler.org					
Capital District Psychiatric Center 75 New Scotland Ave	Albany	NY	12208	518-447-9611	434-0041
Caritas Peace Center 2020 Newburg Rd	Louisville	KY	40205	502-451-3330	479-4350
TF: 800-451-3637 ■ Web: www.caritas.com					
Caro Center 2000 Chambers Rd	Caro	MI	48723	989-673-3191	673-6749
Carrier Clinic PO Box 147	Belle Mead	NJ	08502	908-281-1000	281-1680
TF: 800-933-3579 ■ Web: www.carrier.org					
Catawba Hospital PO Box 200	Catawba	VA	24070	540-375-4200	375-4394
Web: catawba.dmhmrsas.virginia.gov					
Cedar Springs Behavioral Health System					
2135 Southgate Rd	Colorado Springs	CO	80906	719-633-4114	578-0857
Web: www.psysolutions.com/facilities					
Cedarcrest Hospital 525 Russell Rd	Newington	CT	06111	860-666-4613	666-7642
CenterPointe Hospital 5931 Hwy 94 S	Saint Charles	MO	63304	636-441-7300	447-6001
TF: 800-345-5407 ■ Web: www.centerpointhospital.com					
Central Louisiana State Hospital PO Box 5031	Pineville	LA	71361	318-484-6200	484-6501
TF: 866-666-8335					
Central State Hospital 620 Broad St	Milledgeville	GA	31061	478-445-4575	445-6034
Web: www.centralstatehospital.org					
Central State Hospital 10510 LaGrange Rd	Louisville	KY	40223	502-253-7000	253-7044
Central State Hospital PO Box 4030	Petersburg	VA	23803	804-524-7000	524-7069
Web: www.csh.dmhmrsas.virginia.gov					
Central Washington Hospital PO Box 1887	Wenatchee	WA	98807	509-662-1511	665-6132
TF: 800-365-6428 ■ Web: www.cwhs.com					
Cherry Hospital 201 Stevens Mill Rd	Goldsboro	NC	27530	919-731-3200	731-3785
Chester Mental Health Center 1315 Lehman Dr PO Box 31	Chester	IL	62233	618-826-4571	826-3229
Chicago Lakeshore Hospital 4840 N Marine Dr	Chicago	IL	60640	773-878-9700	907-4607
TF: 800-888-0560					
Chicago-Read Mental Health Center 4200 N Oak Park Ave	Chicago	IL	60634	773-794-4000	794-4046
Choate Mental Health & Developmental Center 1000 N Main St	Anna	IL	62906	618-833-5161	833-4191
Clarks Summit State Hospital 1451 Hillside Dr	Clarks Summit	PA	18411	570-586-2011	587-7415
Clifton T Perkins Hospital Center 8450 Dorsey Run Rd	Jessup	MD	20794	410-724-3000	724-3009
Coastal Harbor Treatment Center 1150 Cornell Ave	Savannah	GA	31406	912-354-3911	355-1336
College Hospital 10802 College Pl	Cerritos	CA	90703	562-924-9581	865-1624
TF: 800-352-3301 ■ Web: www.collegehospitals.com					
College Hospital Costa Mesa 301 Victoria St	Costa Mesa	CA	92627	949-642-2734	574-3320
TF: 800-773-8001 ■ Web: www.collegehospitals.com					
Colorado Mental Health Institute at Fort Logan					
3520 W Oxford Ave	Denver	CO	80236	303-761-0220	866-7101*
*Fax: Hum Res ■ Web: www.cdhs.state.co.us/ODS/mif/index.html					
Colorado Mental Health Institute at Pueblo 1600 W 24th St	Pueblo	CO	81003	719-546-4000	546-4484
Community Behavioral Health Hospital					
1801 W Alcott Ave PO Box 478	Fergus Falls	MN	56537	218-332-5001	739-1329
Connecticut Valley Hospital PO Box 351	Middletown	CT	06457	860-262-5000	262-5989
Creedmoor Psychiatric Center 80-45 Winchester Blvd	Queens Village	NY	11427	718-464-7500	264-3635
Danville State Hospital 200 State Hospital Dr	Danville	PA	17821	570-271-4500	271-4694
TF: 888-796-3476					
Del Amo Hospital 23700 Camino Del Sol	Torrance	CA	90505	310-530-1151	539-5061
TF: 800-533-5266 ■ Web: www.delamohospital.com					
Delaware Psychiatric Center 1901 N Dupont Hwy	New Castle	DE	19720	302-255-2700	255-4422
Dominion Hospital 2960 Sleepy Hollow Rd	Falls Church	VA	22044	703-536-2000	533-9650
TF: 800-950-6463 ■ Web: www.dominionhospital.com					
Dorothea Dix Hospital 3601 MSC Ctr	Raleigh	NC	27699	919-733-5540	
Web: www.dhhs.state.nc.us/mhddsas/DIX/DDH.HTML					
Dorothea Dix Psychiatric Center 656 State St	Bangor	ME	04401	207-941-4000	941-4062
East Central Regional Hospital 3405 Mike Padgett Hwy	Augusta	GA	30906	706-792-7000	792-7138
Web: www.augustareg.dhr.state.ga.us					
East Louisiana State Hospital PO Box 498	Jackson	LA	70748	225-634-0100	634-4345
East Mississippi State Hospital PO Box 4128 West Stn	Meridian	MS	39304	601-482-6186	483-5543
Web: www.emsh.state.ms.us					
Eastern Louisiana Mental Health System Greenwell Springs Campus 23260 Greenwell Springs Rd PO Box 549	Greenwell Springs	LA	70739	225-262-2400	261-9080
Eastern State Hospital 627 W 4th St	Lexington	KY	40508	859-246-7000	246-7018*
*Fax: Hum Res					
Eastern State Hospital 4601 Iron Bound Rd	Williamsburg	VA	23187	757-253-5161	253-5065
Web: www.esh.state.va.us					
Eastern State Hospital PO Box 800	Medical Lake	WA	99022	509-299-3121	299-7015
Elgin Mental Health Center 750 S State St	Elgin	IL	60123	847-742-1040	429-4938
Elmira Psychiatric Center 100 Washington St	Elmira	NY	14901	607-737-4711	737-9080
Essex County Hospital Center 125 Fairview Ave	Cedar Grove	NJ	07009	973-228-8000	228-0674
Evansville State Hospital 3400 Lincoln Ave	Evansville	IN	47714	812-469-6800	469-6868
Fair Oaks Hospital 5440 Linton Blvd	Delray Beach	FL	33484	561-495-1000	495-3796
Fairfax Hospital 10200 NE 132nd St	Kirkland	WA	98034	425-821-2000	821-9010
TF: 800-435-7221 ■ Web: www.fairfaxhospital.com					
Fairmount Behavioral Health System 561 Fairthorne Ave	Philadelphia	PA	19128	215-487-4000	483-8187
TF: 800-235-0200 ■ Web: www.fairmountbhs.com					
Florida State Hospital PO Box 1000	Chattahoochee	FL	32324	850-663-7001	663-7303
Focus Healthcare of Georgia 2927 Demere Rd	Saint Simons Island	GA	31522	912-638-1999	638-2112
TF: 800-821-7224 ■ Web: www.focushealthcare.com					
Fort Lauderdale Hospital 1601 E Las Olas Blvd	Fort Lauderdale	FL	33301	954-463-4321	525-2584
TF: 800-585-7527 ■ Web: www.fortlauderdalehospital.org					
Four Winds Hospital 800 Cross River Rd	Katonah	NY	10536	914-763-8151	763-9597
TF: 800-528-6624 ■ Web: www.fourwindshospital.com					
Friends Hospital 4641 Roosevelt Blvd	Philadelphia	PA	19124	215-831-4600	831-7859
TF: 800-889-0548 ■ Web: www.friendshospitalonline.org					
Fulton State Hospital 600 E 5th St	Fulton	MO	65251	573-592-4100	592-3000
Web: www.dmh.missouri.gov/fulton					
GEO Care South Florida State Hospital					
800 E Cypress Dr	Pembroke Pines	FL	33025	954-392-3000	392-4304
Georgia Regional Hospital at Atlanta 3073 Panthersville Rd	Decatur	GA	30034	404-243-2100	212-5324
Web: www.atlantareg.dhr.state.ga.us					
Georgia Regional Hospital at Savannah 1915 Eisenhower Dr	Savannah	GA	31406	912-356-2011	356-2691
Gracie Square Hospital 420 E 76th St	New York	NY	10021	212-988-4400	434-5373
Web: www.nygsh.org					
Greater Binghamton Health Center 425 Robinson St	Binghamton	NY	13904	607-724-1391	773-4387
Green Oaks Hospital 7808 Clodus Fields Dr	Dallas	TX	75251	972-991-9504	789-1865
TF: 800-866-6554 ■ Web: www.greenoakspsych.com					
Greystone Park Psychiatric Hospital 1 Central Ave	Greystone Park	NJ	07950	973-538-1800	993-8782*
*Fax: Hum Res					
Griffin Memorial Hospital PO Box 151	Norman	OK	73070	405-321-4880	573-6652
TF: 877-580-5044					
H Douglas Singer Mental Health & Development Center					
4402 N Main St	Rockford	IL	61103	815-987-7096	987-7581
Hagedorn Psychiatric Hospital 200 Sanitorium Rd	Glen Gardner	NJ	08826	908-537-2141	537-3149
Hampstead Hospital 218 East Rd	Hampstead	NH	03841	603-329-5311	329-4746
Web: www.hampsteadhospital.com					
Harris County Psychiatric Center 2800 S MacGregor Way	Houston	TX	77021	713-741-5000	741-5939
Web: hcpc.uth.tmc.edu					
Hartgrove Hospital 520 N Ridgeway Ave	Chicago	IL	60624	773-722-3113	722-6361
TF: 800-478-4783 ■ Web: hartgrovehospital.com					
Havenwyck Hospital 1525 University Dr	Auburn Hills	MI	48326	248-373-9200	373-9077*
*Fax: Admitting ■ TF: 800-401-2727					
Hawaii State Hospital 45-710 Keaahala Rd	Kaneohe	HI	96744	808-247-2191	247-7335
Heartland Behavioral Healthcare 3000 S Erie St	Massillon	OH	44646	330-833-3135	833-6564
Hill Crest Behavioral Health Services 6869 5th Ave S	Birmingham	AL	35212	205-833-9000	838-2080
TF: 800-292-8553					
Holliswood Hospital 87-37 Palermo St	Holliswood	NY	11423	718-776-8181	776-8572*
*Fax: Admitting ■ TF: 800-486-3005					
Holly Hill Hospital 3019 Falstaff Rd	Raleigh	NC	27610	919-250-7000	231-3231
TF: 800-422-1840 ■ Web: www.psysolutions.com/facilities					
Horsham Clinic 722 E Butler Pike	Ambler	PA	19002	215-643-7800	654-1148*
*Fax: Admissions ■ TF: 800-237-4447 ■ Web: www.horshamclinic.com					
Hudson River Psychiatric Center 10 Ross Cir	Poughkeepsie	NY	12601	845-452-8000	452-8040
TF: 800-871-7910					
Hutchings Richard H Psychiatric Center 620 Madison St	Syracuse	NY	13210	315-426-3600	426-7751

				Phone	Fax
Intracare Medical Center Hospital 7601 Fannin St	Houston	TX	77054	713-790-0949	790-0456
Web: www.intracarehospital.com					
John J Madden Mental Health Center 1200 S 1st Ave	Hines	IL	60141	708-338-7400	338-7057
John Umstead Hospital 1003 12th St	Butner	NC	27509	919-575-7211	575-7013
Kalamazoo Psychiatric Hospital 1312 Oakland Dr	Kalamazoo	MI	49008	269-337-3000	337-3007*
**Fax:* Admitting					
Kerrville State Hospital 721 Thompson Dr	Kerrville	TX	78028	830-896-2211	792-4926
Kingsboro Psychiatric Center 681 Clarkson Ave	Brooklyn	NY	11203	718-221-7000	221-7633*
**Fax:* Admitting					
Lakeshore Mental Health Institute 5908 Lyons View Dr	Knoxville	TN	37919	865-584-1561	450-5203
Lakeside Behavioral Health System 2911 Brunswick Rd	Bartlett	TN	38133	901-377-4700	373-0912
Langley Porter Psychiatric Institute 401 Parnassus Ave	San Francisco	CA	94143	415-476-7000	476-7320
Web: psych.ucsf.edu					
Larned State Hospital RR 3 Box 89	Larned	KS	67550	620-285-2131	285-4359*
**Fax:* Hum Res					
Las Encinas Hospital 2900 E Del Mar Blvd	Pasadena	CA	91107	626-795-9901	
TF: 800-792-2345 ■ *Web:* www.lasencinashospital.com					
Lincoln Medical & Mental Health Center 234 E 149th St	Bronx	NY	10451	718-579-5000	579-5319
Lincoln Regional Center PO Box 94949	Lincoln	NE	68509	402-471-4444	479-5124
Logansport State Hospital 1098 SR 25 S	Logansport	IN	46947	574-722-4141	735-3414
Madden John J Mental Health Center 1200 S 1st Ave	Hines	IL	60141	708-338-7400	338-7057
Madison State Hospital 711 Green Rd	Madison	IN	47250	812-265-2611	265-7260
Manhattan Psychiatric Center-Ward's Island 600 E 125th St	New York	NY	10035	646-672-6767	672-6440
Mayview State Hospital 1601 Mayview Rd	Bridgeville	PA	15017	412-257-6500	257-6808
McFarland Andrew Mental Health Center 901 Southwind Rd	Springfield	IL	62703	217-786-6900	786-7167
McLean Hospital 115 Mill St	Belmont	MA	02478	617-855-2000	855-3735
Web: www.mclean.harvard.edu					
Meadows Psychiatric Center 132 Meadows Dr	Centre Hall	PA	16828	814-364-2161	364-9742
TF: 800-641-7529 ■ *Web:* www.themeadows.org					
Meadowview Psychiatric Hospital 595 County Ave	Secaucus	NJ	07094	201-319-3660	319-3616
Memorial Hermann Prevention & Recovery Center					
1550 La Concha Ln	Houston	TX	77054	713-578-3100	578-3106
TF: 800-464-7272 ■ *Web:* www.memorialhermann.org					
Mendota Mental Health Institute 301 Troy Dr	Madison	WI	53704	608-301-1000	301-1358*
**Fax:* Admissions ■ *Web:* www.dhfs.state.wi.us/MH_Mendota					
Menninger Clinic PO Box 809045	Houston	TX	77280	713-275-5000	275-5117
TF: 800-351-9058 ■ *Web:* www.menningerclinic.com					
Mental Health Institute 2277 Iowa Ave	Independence	IA	50644	319-334-2583	334-5252
MeritCare South University 1720 S University Dr	Fargo	ND	58103	701-280-4150	280-4819
Metropolitan Saint Louis Psychiatric Center					
5351 Delmar Blvd	Saint Louis	MO	63112	314-877-0500	877-0553
Metropolitan State Hospital 11401 Bloomfield Ave	Norwalk	CA	90650	562-863-7011	868-6920
Mid-Hudson Psychiatric Center Rt 17M Box 158	New Hampton	NY	10958	845-374-3171	374-3961
Middle Tennessee Mental Health Institute					
221 Stewarts Ferry Pike	Nashville	TN	37214	615-902-7400	902-7541
TF: 800-575-3506					
Milwaukee County Mental Health Complex					
9455 Watertown Plank Rd	Milwaukee	WI	53226	414-257-6995	257-5415*
**Fax:* Admissions					
Mississippi State Hospital PO Box 157A	Whitfield	MS	39193	601-351-8000	351-8228
Web: www.msh.state.ms.us					
Moccasin Bend Mental Health Institute					
100 Moccasin Bend Rd	Chattanooga	TN	37405	423-265-2271	785-3333
Mohawk Valley Psychiatric Center 1400 Noyes St	Utica	NY	13502	315-738-3800	738-4414
TF: 800-584-8640					
Montana State Hospital PO Box 300	Warm Springs	MT	59756	406-693-7000	693-7069
Moose Lake Regional Treatment Center 1111 Hwy 73	Moose Lake	MN	55767	218-485-5300	485-5316*
**Fax:* Hum Res					
Napa State Hospital 2100 Napa-Vallejo Hwy	Napa	CA	94558	707-253-5000	253-5513
New Hampshire Hospital 36 Clinton St	Concord	NH	03301	603-271-5200	271-5395
New Mexico Behavioral Health Institute					
3695 Hot Springs Blvd	Las Vegas	NM	87701	505-454-2100	454-2211*
**Fax:* Admissions ■ *TF:* 800-446-5970					
Norfolk Regional Center PO Box 1209	Norfolk	NE	68702	402-370-3400	370-3194
Norristown State Hospital 1001 Sterigere St	Norristown	PA	19401	610-313-1000	313-1013
North Coast Behavioral Health Care System North Campus					
1708 Southpoint Dr	Cleveland	OH	44109	216-787-0500	787-0446
North Dakota State Hospital 2605 Circle Dr	Jamestown	ND	58401	701-253-3650	253-3999
Northcoast Behavioral Healthcare System South Campus					
1756 Sagamore Rd PO Box 305	Northfield	OH	44067	330-467-7131	467-2420
Northwest Center for Behavioral Health PO Box 1	Fort Supply	OK	73841	580-766-2311	766-2017
Northwest Georgia Regional Hospital 1305 Redmond Cir	Rome	GA	30165	706-295-6246	802-5454
Northwest Missouri Psychiatric Rehabilitation Center					
3505 Frederick Ave	Saint Joseph	MO	64506	816-387-2300	387-2329*
**Fax:* Admitting					
Oklahoma Forensic Center PO Box 69	Vinita	OK	74301	918-256-7841	256-4491
Oregon State Hospital 2600 Center St NE	Salem	OR	97301	503-945-2800	945-2807
Osawatomie State Hospital 500 State Hospital Dr	Osawatomie	KS	66064	913-755-7000	755-7328*
**Fax:* Admitting					
Patton State Hospital 3102 E Highland Ave	Patton	CA	92369	909-425-7000	425-6370*
**Fax:* Admitting					
Peachford Behavioral Health System 2151 Peachford Rd	Atlanta	GA	30338	770-455-3200	455-2362
TF: 866-897-3224 ■ *Web:* www.peachfordbhs.com					
Pembroke Hospital 199 Oak St	Pembroke	MA	02359	781-826-8161	826-2061
TF Admissions: 800-222-2237					
Peninsula Hospital 2347 Jones Bend Rd	Louisville	TN	37777	865-970-9800	970-6317*
**Fax:* Admitting ■ *TF:* 800-526-8215 ■ *Web:* www.peninsula-hospital.org					
Perkins Clifton T Hospital Center 8450 Dorsey Run Rd	Jessup	MD	20794	410-724-3000	724-3009
Pilgrim Psychiatric Center 998 Crooked Hill Rd	West Brentwood	NY	11717	631-761-3500	761-2600
Pine Rest Christian Mental Health Services PO Box 165	Grand Rapids	MI	49501	616-455-5000	831-2608*
**Fax:* Hum Res ■ *TF:* 800-678-5500 ■ *Web:* www.pinerest.org					
Poplar Springs Hospital 350 Poplar Dr PO Box 3060	Petersburg	VA	23805	804-733-6874	862-6322*
**Fax:* Admitting ■ *Web:* www.poplarsprings.com					
Potomac Ridge Behavioral Health 14901 Broschart Rd	Rockville	MD	20850	301-251-4500	424-3841
TF: 800-204-8600 ■ *Web:* www.potomacridge.com					
Psychiatric Institute of Washington					
4228 Wisconsin Ave NW	Washington	DC	20016	202-885-5600	885-5614
TF: 800-369-2273 ■ *Web:* www.psychinstitute.com					
Research Psychiatric Center 2323 E 63rd St	Kansas City	MO	64130	816-444-8161	333-4495
Retreat Healthcare PO Box 803	Brattleboro	VT	05302	802-257-7785	258-3791*
**Fax:* Admissions ■ *TF:* 800-345-5550 ■ *Web:* www.retreathealthcare.org					
Reuther Walter P Psychiatric Hospital 30901 Palmer Rd	Westland	MI	48186	734-367-8400	722-5562*
**Fax:* Mail Rm					
Richard H Hutchings Psychiatric Center 620 Madison St	Syracuse	NY	13210	315-426-3600	426-7751
Richmond State Hospital 498 NW 18th St	Richmond	IN	47374	765-966-0511	966-4593
Web: www.richmondstatehospital.org					
Ridge Behavioral Health System 3050 Rio Dosa Dr	Lexington	KY	40509	859-269-2325	268-6451
TF: 800-753-4673 ■ *Web:* www.ridgebhs.com					
River Park Hospital 1230 6th Ave	Huntington	WV	25701	304-526-9111	526-9140
TF: 800-992-9101 ■ *Web:* www.riverparkhospital.net					
Riverview Psychiatric Center 250 Arsenal St	Augusta	ME	04330	207-287-7200	287-7127
Rochester Psychiatric Center 1111 Elmwood Ave	Rochester	NY	14620	585-241-1200	241-1424
Rockland Psychiatric Center 140 Old Orangeburg Rd	Orangeburg	NY	10962	845-359-1000	365-5569*
**Fax:* Admitting					
Rusk State Hospital PO Box 318	Rusk	TX	75785	903-683-3421	683-7101
Saint Elizabeths Hospital 2700 ML King Jr Ave SE	Washington	DC	20032	202-562-4000	645-7494
Saint Lawrence Psychiatric Center 1 Chimney Point Dr	Ogdensburg	NY	13669	315-541-2001	541-2013*
**Fax:* Admitting					
Saint Louis Psychiatric Rehabilitation Center					
5300 Arsenal St	Saint Louis	MO	63139	314-877-6500	877-5825
Saint Peter Regional Treatment Center 2100 Sheppard Dr	Saint Peter	MN	56082	507-931-7100	931-7711
San Antonio State Hospital 6711 S Braunfels Ave	San Antonio	TX	78223	210-532-8811	531-8171*
**Fax:* Admitting					
San Diego County Psychiatric Hospital 3853 Rosecrans St	San Diego	CA	92110	619-692-8232	542-4060
Searcy Hospital 725 E Coy Smith Hwy	Mount Vernon	AL	36560	251-662-6700	829-9075
Seton Shoal Creek Hospital 3501 Mills Ave	Austin	TX	78731	512-324-2000	324-2003
Web: www.seton.net/Wellness/BehavioralHealth543/index.asp					
Sharp-Mesa Vista Hospital 7850 Vista Hill Ave	San Diego	CA	92123	858-278-4110	715-8703
Web: www.sharp.com					
Sharpe William R Jr Hospital 936 Sharpe Hospital Rd	Weston	WV	26452	304-269-1210	269-6235
Sheppard Pratt at Ellicott City 4100 College Ave	Ellicott City	MD	21043	410-465-3322	461-7075
TF: 800-883-3322 ■ *Web:* www.sheppardpratt.org					
Sheppard Pratt Health System 6501 N Charles St	Baltimore	MD	21204	410-938-3000	938-3828*
**Fax:* Admissions ■ *TF:* 800-627-0330 ■ *Web:* www.sheppardpratt.org					
Singer H Douglas Mental Health & Development Center					
4402 N Main St	Rockford	IL	61103	815-987-7096	987-7581
South Beach Psychiatric Center 777 Seaview Ave	Staten Island	NY	10305	718-667-2300	667-2344
South Florida Evaluation & Treatment Center 2200 NW 7th Ave	Miami	FL	33127	305-637-2500	637-2650
South Oaks Hospital 400 Sunrise Hwy	Amityville	NY	11701	631-264-4000	264-5259
Southeast Louisiana Hospital 23515 Hwy 190	Mandeville	LA	70448	985-626-6300	626-6490*
**Fax:* Admitting					
Southeast Missouri Mental Health Center					
1010 W Columbia St	Farmington	MO	63640	573-218-6792	218-6785
Southwestern Virginia Mental Health Institute 340 Bagley Cir	Marion	VA	24354	276-783-1200	783-1216*
**Fax:* Admitting ■ *Web:* www.swvmhi.dmhmrsas.virginia.gov					
Spring Grove Hospital Center 55 Wade Ave	Catonsville	MD	21228	410-402-6000	402-7983
TF: 866-734-3337 ■ *Web:* www.springgrove.com					
Spring Harbor Hospital 123 Andover Rd	Westbrook	ME	04092	207-761-2200	761-2108
TF: 888-524-0080 ■ *Web:* www.springharbor.org					
Springfield Hospital Center 6655 Sykesville Rd	Sykesville	MD	21784	410-970-7000	970-7246
TF: 800-333-7564					
State Hospital South PO Box 400	Blackfoot	ID	83221	208-785-1200	785-8516
Summit Behavioral Healthcare 1101 Summit Rd	Cincinnati	OH	45237	513-948-3600	948-3080
Taunton State Hospital 60 Hodges Ave	Taunton	MA	02780	508-977-3000	977-3751
Terrell State Hospital 1200 E Brin St	Terrell	TX	75160	972-563-6452	551-8302*
**Fax:* Admitting					
Thomas B Finan Center					
10102 Country Club Rd SE PO Box 1722	Cumberland	MD	21501	301-777-2405	777-2364
TF: 888-854-0035					
Timberlawn Mental Health System 4600 Samuell Blvd	Dallas	TX	75228	214-381-7181	388-6306
TF: 800-426-4944 ■ *Web:* www.timberlawn.com					
Tinley Park Mental Health Center 7400 W 183rd St	Tinley Park	IL	60477	708-614-4000	614-4495
Torrance State Hospital SR 1014 PO Box 111	Torrance	PA	15779	724-459-8000	459-1212*
**Fax:* Admitting					
Trenton Psychiatric Hospital PO Box 7500	West Trenton	NJ	08628	609-633-1500	396-5701
Twin Valley Behavioral Healthcare 2200 W Broad St	Columbus	OH	43223	614-752-0333	752-0385
UCLA Neuropsychiatric Institute & Hospital					
760 Westwood Plaza	Los Angeles	CA	90095	310-825-0511	794-5098*
**Fax:* Admitting ■ *Web:* www.npi.ucla.edu					
University Behavioral Center 2500 Discovery Dr	Orlando	FL	32826	407-281-7000	282-7012
TF: 800-999-0807					
Utah State Hospital 1300 E Center St	Provo	UT	84606	801-344-4400	344-4291
Web: www.hsush.state.ut.us					
Walter P Reuther Psychiatric Hospital 30901 Palmer Rd	Westland	MI	48186	734-367-8400	722-5562*
**Fax:* Mail Rm					
Warren State Hospital 33 Main Dr	North Warren	PA	16365	814-723-5500	726-4377
Wernersville State Hospital PO Box 300	Wernersville	PA	19565	610-678-3411	670-4101
West Oaks Hospital 6500 Hornwood Dr	Houston	TX	77074	713-995-0909	778-5253
Westborough State Hospital Lyman St PO Box 288	Westborough	MA	01581	508-616-2100	616-2875*
**Fax:* Admissions					
Western Mental Health Institute 11100 Hwy 64 W	Bolivar	TN	38008	731-228-2000	658-2783
TF: 800-548-0635					
Western Missouri Mental Health Center 1000 E 24th St	Kansas City	MO	64108	816-512-7000	512-7509
Western State Hospital 2400 Russellville Rd	Hopkinsville	KY	42241	270-889-6025	886-4487
TF: 800-449-1189					
Western State Hospital PO Box 2500	Staunton	VA	24402	540-332-8000	332-8197
Web: www.healthsystem.virginia.edu/internet/dietetics/westernstate.cfm					
Western State Hospital 9601 Steilacoom Blvd SW	Tacoma	WA	98498	253-582-8900	756-2963
Westwood Lodge Hospital 45 Clapboardtree St	Westwood	MA	02090	781-762-7764	762-0550
TF: 800-222-2237 ■ *Web:* www.arbourhealth.com					
Wichita Falls State Hospital PO Box 300	Wichita Falls	TX	76307	940-692-1220	689-5538
William R Sharpe Jr Hospital 936 Sharpe Hospital Rd	Weston	WV	26452	304-269-1210	269-6235
William S Hall Psychiatric Institute 1800 Colonial Dr	Columbia	SC	29202	803-898-1693	898-2048
Willmar Regional Treatment Center 1550 Hwy 71 NE	Willmar	MN	56201	320-231-5100	231-5329
TF: 800-657-3898					
Winnebago Mental Health Institute					
1300 South Dr PO Box 9	Winnebago	WI	54985	920-235-4910	237-2047
Web: www.dhfs.state.wi.us/MH_Winnebago					
Wyoming State Hospital PO Box 177	Evanston	WY	82931	307-789-3464	789-7373
Web: mentalhealth.state.wy.us/hospital					

377-6 Rehabilitation Hospitals

				Phone	Fax
Allied Services Rehabilitation Hospital 475 Morgan Hwy	Scranton	PA	18508	570-348-1300	341-4548
Web: www.allied-services.org					
Bacharach Institute for Rehabilitation 61 W Jimmie Leads Rd	Pomona	NJ	08240	609-652-7000	652-7487
Web: www.bacharach.org					
Baptist Health Rehabilitation Institute of Arkansas					
9601 Interstate 630	Little Rock	AR	72205	501-202-7000	202-7259*
**Fax:* Admitting					
Baptist Rehabilitation Germantown 2100 Exeter Rd	Germantown	TN	38138	901-757-1350	757-3496
Web: www.baptistonline.org/facilities/germantown/					
Baylor Institute for Rehabilitation 909 N Washington Ave	Dallas	TX	75246	214-820-9300	818-8177
TF: 800-242-2334 ■ *Web:* www.baylorhealth.com					
Brooks Rehabilitation Hospital 3599 University Blvd S	Jacksonville	FL	32216	904-858-7600	858-7610
TF: 800-487-7342 ■ *Web:* www.brookshealth.org					
Bryn Mawr Rehabilitation Hospital 414 Paoli Pike	Malvern	PA	19355	610-251-5400	889-0943
TF: 888-734-2241 ■ *Web:* www.mainlinehealth.org/bmr					
Burke Rehabilitation Hospital 785 Mamaroneck Ave	White Plains	NY	10605	914-597-2500	597-0787
TF: 888-992-8753 ■ *Web:* www.burke.org					
Cardinal Hill Rehabilitation Hospital 2050 Versailles Rd	Lexington	KY	40504	859-254-5701	255-9303*
**Fax:* Admitting ■ *TF:* 800-843-1408 ■ *Web:* www.cardinalhill-northernky.org					
Charlotte Institute of Rehabilitation 1100 Blythe Blvd	Charlotte	NC	28203	704-355-4300	355-4231
TF: 800-634-2256 ■ *Web:* www.carolinas.org/services/rehab/cir					
Craig Hospital 3425 S Clarkson St	Englewood	CO	80113	303-789-8000	789-8219
Web: www.craighospital.org					
Crotched Mountain Rehabilitation Center 1 Verney Dr	Greenfield	NH	03047	603-547-3311	547-3232
Web: www.cmf.org					
Drake Center 151 W Galbraith Rd	Cincinnati	OH	45216	513-948-2500	948-2501
TF: 800-948-0003 ■ *Web:* www.drakecenter.com					

Rehabilitation Hospitals (Cont'd)

Phone | Fax

Edwin Shaw Rehab 1621 Flickinger Rd. Akron OH 44312 330-784-1271 784-1968
Web: www.edwinshaw.com

Fairlawn Rehabilitation Hospital 189 May St Worcester MA 01602 508-791-6351 753-2087
Web: www.fairlawnrehab.org

Frazier Rehabilitation Institute 220 Abraham Flexner Way. Louisville KY 40202 502-582-7400 582-7477

Gaylord Hospital 50 Gaylord Farms Rd PO Box 400 Wallingford CT 06492 203-284-2800 284-2894
TF: 866-429-5673 ■ *Web:* www.gaylord.org

Godhard Rehab & Northeast Specialty Hospital - Stoughton
909 Sumner St. Stoughton MA 02072 781-297-8200 297-8300*
*Fax: Admitting ■ *Web:* www.commonwealthcommunities.com

Good Shepherd Rehabilitation Hospital 501 Saint John St. Allentown PA 18103 610-776-3120 776-3503*
*Fax: Admitting ■ *TF:* 877-724-2247 ■ *Web:* www.goodshepherdrehab.org

Harmon Medical & Rehabilitation Hospital
2170 E Harmon Ave. Las Vegas NV 89119 702-794-0100 794-0041
Web: www.thicare.com/HarmonRehabHospital

HealthSouth Bakersfield Rehabilitation Hospital
5001 Commerce Dr Bakersfield CA 93309 661-323-5500 633-5254
Web: www.healthsouth.com

HealthSouth Braintree Rehabilitation Hospital 250 Pond St Braintree MA 02184 781-848-5353 356-2748
TF: 800-997-3422 ■ *Web:* www.healthsouth.com

HealthSouth Central Georgia Rehabilitation Hospital
3351 Northside Dr. Macon GA 31210 478-471-3536 471-6536
Web: www.healthsouth.com

HealthSouth Chattanooga Rehabilitation Hospital
2412 McCallie Ave Chattanooga TN 37404 423-698-0221 697-9124*
*Fax: Admissions ■ *TF:* 800-763-5189 ■ *Web:* www.healthsouth.com

HealthSouth City View Rehabilitation Hospital
6701 Oakmont Blvd Fort Worth TX 76132 817-370-4700 370-4986
Web: www.healthsouth.com

HealthSouth Dallas Rehab 2124 Research Row. Dallas TX 75235 214-904-6100 904-6144
Web: www.healthsouth.com

HealthSouth Deaconess Rehabilitation Hospital
4100 Covert Ave. Evansville IN 47714 812-476-9983 476-4270
TF: 800-677-3422 ■ *Web:* www.healthsouth.com

HealthSouth Harmarville Rehabilitation Hospital
320 Guys Run Rd PO Box 11460 Pittsburgh PA 15238 412-828-1300 828-6954*
*Fax: Admitting ■ *Web:* www.healthsouth.com

HealthSouth Hospital of Pittsburgh 2380 McGinley Rd. Monroeville PA 15146 412-856-2400 856-9320
TF: 800-695-4774 ■ *Web:* www.healthsouth.com

HealthSouth Houston Rehabilitation Institute
17506 Red Oak Dr. Houston TX 77090 281-580-1212 580-6714
Web: www.healthsouth.com

HealthSouth Humble Rehabilitation Hospital 19002 McKay Dr Humble TX 77338 281-446-6148 446-8022
Web: www.healthsouth.com

HealthSouth Kingsport Rehabilitation Hospital 113 Cassel Dr Kingsport TN 37660 423-246-7240 246-3441
Web: www.healthsouth.com

HealthSouth Lakeshore Rehabilitation Hospital
3800 Ridgeway Dr Homewood AL 35209 205-868-2000 868-2007
Web: www.healthsouth.com

HealthSouth Mountainview Regional Rehabilitation Hospital
1160 Van Voorhis Rd. Morgantown WV 26505 304-598-1100 598-1103
TF: 800-388-2451 ■ *Web:* www.healthsouth.com

HealthSouth New England Rehabilitation Hospital of Woburn
2 Rehabilitation Way Woburn MA 01801 781-935-5050 935-3555
Web: www.healthsouth.com

HealthSouth Nittany Valley Rehabilitation Hospital
550 W College Ave. Pleasant Gap PA 16823 814-359-3421 359-5898
TF: 800-842-6026 ■ *Web:* www.healthsouth.com

HealthSouth North Louisiana Rehabilitation Hospital
1401 Ezell St Ruston LA 71270 318-251-3126 251-1594
TF: 800-765-4772 ■ *Web:* www.healthsouth.com

HealthSouth Plano Rehabilitation Hospital 2800 W 15th St. Plano TX 75075 972-612-9000 423-4293
Web: www.healthsouth.com

HealthSouth Reading Rehabilitation Hospital
1623 Morgantown Rd Reading PA 19607 610-796-6000 796-6306
TF: 800-755-8027 ■ *Web:* www.healthsouth.com

HealthSouth Rehabilitation Hospital 7000 Jefferson St NE. Albuquerque NM 87109 505-344-9478 345-6722
Web: www.healthsouth.com

HealthSouth Rehabilitation Hospital of Altoona
2005 Valley View Blvd Altoona PA 16602 814-944-3535 944-6160
TF: 800-873-4220 ■ *Web:* www.healthsouth.com

HealthSouth Rehabilitation Hospital of Arlington
3200 Matlock Rd Arlington TX 76015 817-468-4000 468-3055
Web: www.healthsouth.com

HealthSouth Rehabilitation Hospital of Austin 1215 Red River Austin TX 78701 512-474-5700 479-3867
TF: 800-765-4772 ■ *Web:* www.healthsouth.com

HealthSouth Rehabilitation Hospital of Beaumont
3340 Plaza 10 Blvd Beaumont TX 77707 409-835-0835 835-1401
Web: www.healthsouth.com

HealthSouth Rehabilitation Hospital of Columbia
2935 Colonial Dr Columbia SC 29203 803-254-7777 401-1414
Web: www.healthsouth.com

HealthSouth Rehabilitation Hospital of Erie 143 E 2nd St. Erie PA 16507 814-878-1200 878-1399
TF: 800-234-4574 ■ *Web:* www.healthsouth.com

HealthSouth Rehabilitation Hospital of Fayetteville
153 E Monte Painter Dr. Fayetteville AR 72703 479-444-2200 444-2390
Web: www.healthsouth.com

HealthSouth Rehabilitation Hospital of Florence
900 E Cheves St. Florence SC 29506 843-679-9000 678-3767
Web: www.healthsouth.com

HealthSouth Rehabilitation Hospital of Fort Smith
1401 S 'J' St Fort Smith AR 72901 479-785-3300 785-8599
Web: www.healthsouth.com

HealthSouth Rehabilitation Hospital of Fort Worth
1212 W Lancaster Ave. Fort Worth TX 76102 817-870-2336 335-1202
Web: www.healthsouth.com

HealthSouth Rehabilitation Hospital of Jonesboro
1201 Fleming Ave Jonesboro AR 72401 870-932-0440 932-6792
Web: www.healthsouth.com

HealthSouth Rehabilitation Hospital of Largo
901 N Clearwater-Largo Rd Largo FL 33770 727-586-2999 588-3404
Web: www.healthsouth.com

HealthSouth Rehabilitation Hospital of Memphis
1282 Union Ave Memphis TN 38104 901-722-2000 729-5171
TF: 800-363-7342 ■ *Web:* www.healthsouth.com

HealthSouth Rehabilitation Hospital of Montgomery
4465 Narrow Lane Rd Montgomery AL 36116 334-284-7700 281-5136
Web: www.healthsouth.com

HealthSouth Rehabilitation Hospital of New Jersey
14 Hospital Dr Toms River NJ 08755 732-244-3100 244-7829*
*Fax: Hum Res ■ *Web:* www.healthsouth.com

HealthSouth Rehabilitation Hospital of North Alabama
107 Governors Dr Huntsville AL 35801 256-535-2300 428-2608
Web: www.healthsouth.com

HealthSouth Rehabilitation Hospital of Sarasota
3251 Proctor Rd Sarasota FL 34231 941-921-8600 922-6228
Web: www.healthsouth.com

HealthSouth Rehabilitation Hospital of Tallahassee
1675 Riggins Rd Tallahassee FL 32308 850-656-4800 656-4892
Web: www.healthsouth.com

HealthSouth Rehabilitation Hospital of Texarkana
515 W 12th St Texarkana TX 75501 903-793-0088 793-0899
Web: www.healthsouth.com

HealthSouth Rehabilitation Hospital of Tyler 3131 Troup Hwy Tyler TX 75701 903-510-7000 510-7005
Web: www.healthsouth.com

HealthSouth Rehabilitation Hospital of Utah 8074 S 1300 E Sandy UT 84094 801-561-3400 565-6576
Web: www.healthsouth.com

HealthSouth Rehabilitation Institute of Tucson
2650 N Wyatt Dr Tucson AZ 85712 520-325-1300 322-4400
Web: www.healthsouth.com

HealthSouth Rehabilitation of Mechanicsburg
175 Lancaster Blvd Mechanicsburg PA 17055 717-691-3700 697-6524
Web: www.healthsouth.com

HealthSouth Riosa 9119 Cinnamon Hill San Antonio TX 78240 210-691-0737 558-1297
Web: www.healthsouth.com

HealthSouth Sea Pines Rehabilitation Hospital
101 E Florida Ave. Melbourne FL 32901 321-984-4600 984-4627
Web: www.healthsouth.com

HealthSouth Sunrise Rehabilitation Hospital 4399 Nob Hill Rd Sunrise FL 33351 954-749-0300 746-1378
Web: www.healthsouth.com

HealthSouth Treasure Coast Rehabilitation Hospital
1600 37th St Vero Beach FL 32960 772-778-2100 562-9763
Web: www.healthsouth.com

HealthSouth Tustin Rehabilitation Hospital 14851 Yorba St Tustin CA 92780 714-832-9200 734-4851

Hebrew Rehabilitation Center 1200 Centre St. Roslindale MA 02131 617-325-8000 363-8911
Web: www.hebrewrehab.org

Helen Hayes Hospital Rt 9W. West Haverstraw NY 10993 845-947-3000 947-0036
TF: 888-707-3422 ■ *Web:* www.helenhayeshospital.org

Hillside Rehabilitation Hospital 8747 Squires Ln NE Warren OH 44484 330-841-3700 841-3647
Web: www.hillside-rehab.org

Hospital for Special Care 2150 Corbin Ave New Britain CT 06053 860-223-2761 827-4849
Web: www.hfsc.org

Howard Regional Health System West Campus Specialty Hospital
829 N Dixon Rd. Kokomo IN 46901 765-452-6700 452-7470
Web: www.howardregional.org

Idaho Elks Rehabilitation Hospital 600 N Robbins Rd Boise ID 83702 208-343-2583 489-4005
TF: 800-835-4514 ■ *Web:* www.idahoelksrehab.org

Institute for Rehabilitation & Research 1333 Moursund St. Houston TX 77030 713-799-5000 799-7095
TF: 800-447-3422 ■ *Web:* www.tirr.org

James H & Cecile C Quillen Rehabilitation Hospital
2511 Wesley St Johnson City TN 37601 423-283-0700 283-0906
Web: www.msha.com

JFK Johnson Rehabilitation Institute 65 James St. Edison NJ 08818 732-321-7050 632-1671
Web: www.njrehab.org

John Heinz Institute of Rehabilitation Medicine
150 Mundy St Wilkes-Barre PA 18702 570-826-3800 826-3898
TF: 877-727-3422

Kansas Rehabilitation Hospital 1504 SW 8th St. Topeka KS 66606 785-235-6600 232-8545
Web: www.kansasrehab.com

Kentfield Rehabilitation Hospital 1125 Sir Francis Drake Blvd. Kentfield CA 94904 415-456-9680 485-3601*
*Fax: Admissions ■ *Web:* www.kentfieldrehab.com

Kernan Hospital 2200 Kernan Dr Baltimore MD 21207 410-448-2500 448-2859
Web: www.kernan.org

Kessler Institute for Rehabilitation
1199 Pleasant Valley Way West Orange NJ 07052 973-731-3600
TF: 888-537-7537 ■ *Web:* www.kessler-rehab.com

Laguna Honda Hospital & Rehabilitation Center
375 Laguna Honda Blvd. San Francisco CA 94116 415-759-2300 759-2374

Madonna Rehabilitation Hospital 5401 South St Lincoln NE 68506 402-489-7102 486-8368
TF: 800-676-5448 ■ *Web:* www.madonna.org

Magee Rehabilitation Hospital
1513 Race St 6 Franklin Plaza. Philadelphia PA 19102 215-587-3000 568-1409*
*Fax: Admissions ■ *TF:* 800-966-2433 ■ *Web:* www.mageerehab.org

Marianjoy Rehabilitation Hospital 26 W 171 Roosevelt Rd Wheaton IL 60187 630-462-4000 462-4442
TF: 800-462-2371 ■ *Web:* www.marianjoy.org

Mary Free Bed Rehabilitation Hospital
235 Wealthy St SE. Grand Rapids MI 49503 616-242-0300 454-3939
TF: 800-528-8989 ■ *Web:* www.maryfreebed.com

Methodist Rehabilitation Center 1350 E Woodrow Wilson Dr Jackson MS 39216 601-981-2611 364-3465*
*Fax: Admitting ■ *TF:* 800-223-6672 ■ *Web:* www.mmrcrehab.org

Mid-America Rehabilitation Hospital 5701 W 110th St Overland Park KS 66211 913-491-2400 338-3762

Missouri Rehabilitation Center 600 N Main St Mount Vernon MO 65712 417-466-3711 461-5775
Web: www.muhealth.org

Montgomery Rehab Hospital Of Chestnut Hill
8601 Stenton Ave. Wyndmoor PA 19038 215-233-6200 233-6879
Web: www.montrehab.com

National Rehabilitation Hospital 102 Irving St NW. Washington DC 20010 202-877-1000 829-5180
Web: www.nrhrehab.org

New England Rehabilitation Hospital of Portland
335 Brighton Ave Portland ME 04102 207-775-4000 662-8446
Web: www.mainehealth.org/mmc_body.cfm?id=2169

New England Sinai Hospital & Rehabilitation Center
150 York St Stoughton MA 02072 781-344-0600 344-0128*
*Fax: Admitting ■ *Web:* newenglandsinai.org

North Valley Rehabilitation Hospital 8451 Pearl St Thornton CO 80229 303-288-3000 286-5163
Web: www.northvalleyrehab.com

Northeast Rehabilitation Hospital 70 Butler St Salem NH 03079 603-893-2900 893-1628
TF: 800-825-7292 ■ *Web:* www.northeastrehab.com

Pinecrest Rehabilitation Hospital 5360 Linton Blvd Delray Beach FL 33484 561-495-0400 499-6812
Web: www.pinecrestrehab.com

Quillen James H & Cecile C Rehabilitation Hospital
2511 Wesley St Johnson City TN 37601 423-283-0700 283-0906
Web: www.msha.com

Rancho Los Amigos National Rehabilitation Center
7601 E Imperial Hwy Downey CA 90242 562-401-7111 401-7022*
*Fax: Admitting ■ *TF:* 877-726-2461 ■ *Web:* www.rancho.org

Rehabilitation Hospital of Indiana 4141 Shore Dr Indianapolis IN 46254 317-329-2000 329-2600
TF: 800-933-0123 ■ *Web:* www.rhin.com

Rehabilitation Hospital of New Mexico 505 Elm St Albuquerque NM 87102 505-727-4700 727-4793

Rehabilitation Hospital of the Pacific 226 N Kuakini St. Honolulu HI 96817 808-531-3511 544-3335
TF: 800-973-4226 ■ *Web:* www.rehabhospital.org

Rehabilitation Institute of Chicago 345 E Superior St Chicago IL 60611 312-238-1000 238-1417*
*Fax: Admitting ■ *TF Admitting:* 800-354-7342 ■ *Web:* www.ric.org

Rehabilitation Institute of Michigan 261 Mack Blvd. Detroit MI 48201 313-745-1203 966-8294
Web: www.rimrehab.org

Roosevelt Warm Springs Institute for Rehabilitation
6135 Roosevelt Hwy Warm Springs GA 31830 706-655-5000 655-5258*
*Fax: Admissions ■ *Web:* www.rooseveltrehab.org

Sacred Heart Rehabilitation Institute 2025 E Newport Ave Milwaukee WI 53211 414-298-6700 298-6751

Saint Catherine's Rehabilitation Hospital
1050 NE 125th St North Miami FL 33161 305-891-8850 891-3361

Phone | Fax

Saint David's Rehabilitation Hospital 1005 E 32nd St — Austin TX 78705 512-867-5100 370-4439*
*Fax: Admissions ■ TF: 800-533-8545 ■ Web: www.stdavidsrehab.com
Saint Lawrence Rehabilitation Center
2381 Lawrenceville Rd — Lawrenceville NJ 08648 609-896-9500 895-0242
Web: www.slrc.org
Saint Luke's Rehabilitation Institute 711 S Cowley St — Spokane WA 99202 509-838-4771 473-6978
Web: www.st-lukes.org
Saint Vincent Rehabilitation Hospital 2201 Wildwood Ave — Sherwood AR 72120 501-834-1800 834-2227
San Joaquin Valley Rehabilitation Hospital 7173 N Sharon Ave — Fresno CA 93720 559-436-3600 436-3606
Web: www.sanjoaquinrehab.com
Santa Rosa Memorial Hospital - Sotoyome Campus
151 Sotoyome St — Santa Rosa CA 95405 707-543-2500 525-8413*
*Fax: Admitting
Schwab Rehabilitation Hospital & Care Network
1401 S California Blvd — Chicago IL 60608 773-522-2010 522-1177*
*Fax: Admitting
Shadyside Nursing & Rehabilitation Center 5609 5th Ave — Pittsburgh PA 15232 412-362-3500 362-1951
Shaughnessy-Kaplan Rehabilitation Hospital Dove Ave — Salem MA 01970 978-745-9000 741-1967
Web: www.nsmc.partners.org/whoweare/skrh1.html
Shepherd Center 2020 Peachtree Rd NW — Atlanta GA 30309 404-352-2020 350-7341
Web: www.shepherd.org
Sierra Providence Physical Rehabilitation Hospital
1740 Curie Dr — El Paso TX 79902 915-544-3399 541-7714
TF: 800-999-8392 ■ Web: www.sphn.com
Siskin Hospital for Physical Rehabilitation 1 Siskin Plaza — Chattanooga TN 37403 423-634-1200 634-1209
TF: 800-474-7546 ■ Web: www.siskinrehab.org
Southern Indiana Rehabilitation Hospital
3104 Blackiston Blvd — New Albany IN 47150 812-941-8300 941-6276
TF: 800-737-7090 ■ Web: www.sirh.org
Southern Kentucky Rehabilitation Hospital
1300 Campbell Ln — Bowling Green KY 42104 270-782-6900 782-7228
TF: 800-989-5775 ■ Web: www.skyrehab.com
Spalding Rehabilitation Hospital 900 Potomac St — Aurora CO 80011 303-367-1166 360-8208
TF: 800-367-3309 ■ Web: www.spaldingrehab.com
Spaulding Rehabilitation Hospital 125 Nashua St — Boston MA 02114 617-573-7000 573-7009
Web: www.spauldingrehab.com
SSM Rehab 6420 Clayton Rd Executive Offices — Saint Louis MO 63117 314-768-5300 768-5355
TF: 800-818-9494 ■ Web: www.ssmrehab.com
Sunnyview Hospital & Rehabilitation Center
1270 Belmont Ave — Schenectady NY 12308 518-382-4500 382-4533*
*Fax: Admitting ■ Web: www.sunnyview.org
Thoms Rehabilitation Hospital 68 Sweeten Creek Rd — Asheville NC 28803 828-274-2400 274-9452
TF: 800-627-1533 ■ Web: www.thoms.org
Trinity Neurological Rehabilitation Center 1400 Lindberg Dr — Slidell LA 70458 985-641-4985 646-0793
Via Christi Rehabilitation Center 1151 N Rock Rd — Wichita KS 67206 316-634-3400 634-1141
TF: 800-667-4241 ■ Web: www.viachristi.org
Walton Rehabilitation Hospital 1355 Independence Dr — Augusta GA 30901 706-724-7746 724-5752
TF: 866-492-5866 ■ Web: www.wrh.org
Warm Springs Rehabilitation Hospital 5101 Medical Dr — San Antonio TX 78229 210-616-0100 592-5457*
*Fax: Admitting ■ TF: 800-451-1350 ■ Web: www.warmsprings.org
Warm Springs Specialty Hospital 200 Memorial Dr — Luling TX 78648 830-875-8400 875-2080
TF: 800-792-9276 ■ Web: www.warmsprings.org
Wesley Rehabilitation Hospital 8338 W 13th St N — Wichita KS 67212 316-729-9999 729-8888
Whittier Rehabilitation Hospital 76 Summer St — Haverhill MA 01830 978-372-8000 374-4423
TF: 800-442-1717 ■ Web: www.whittierhealth.com
Youville Hospital & Rehabilitation Center
1575 Cambridge St — Cambridge MA 02138 617-876-4344 547-5501
Web: www.youville.org

377-7 Specialty Hospitals

Phone | Fax

Arthur G James Cancer Hospital & Richard J Solove Research Institute 300 W 10th Ave — Columbus OH 43210 614-293-5485 293-3132
TF: 888-293-5066 ■ Web: www.jamesline.com
Barbara Ann Karmanos Cancer Institute 4110 John R St — Detroit MI 48201 313-833-0710 831-6535
TF: 800-527-6266 ■ Web: www.karmanos.org
Bascom Palmer Eye Institute 900 NW 17th St — Miami FL 33136 305-326-6000 326-6374
TF: 800-329-7000 ■ Web: www.bpei.med.miami.edu
Bellevue Woman's Hospital 2210 Troy Rd — Miskayuna NY 12309 518-346-9400 346-9409
Web: www.bellevuewoman.com
Bone & Joint Hospital 1111 N Dewey Ave — Oklahoma City OK 73103 405-272-9671 552-9170*
*Fax: Admitting ■ Web: www.boneandjoint.com
Bordeaux Long-Term Care 1414 County Hospital Rd — Nashville TN 37218 615-862-7000 862-6960
Web: www.nashville.org/bordeaux
Brigham & Women's Hospital 75 Francis St — Boston MA 02115 617-732-5500 264-5181*
*Fax: Admitting ■ TF: 800-722-5520 ■ Web: www.brighamandwomens.org
Callahan Eye Foundation Hospital 1720 University Blvd — Birmingham AL 35233 205-325-8100 325-8587*
*Fax: Admitting ■ Web: www.health.uab.edu/eyes
Calvary Hospital 1740 Eastchester Rd — Bronx NY 10461 718-863-6900 518-2690*
*Fax: Hum Res ■ Web: www.calvaryhospital.org
City of Hope National Medical Center Beckman Research Institute
1500 E Duarte Rd — Duarte CA 91010 626-359-8111 930-5486
TF: 800-826-4673 ■ Web: bricoh.coh.org
Coler-Goldwater Specialty Hospital & Nursing Facility
1 Main St Franklin D Roosevelt Island — New York NY 10044 212-318-8000 318-4370
Web: www.coler-goldwater.org
Cornerstone Hospital of Austin 4207 Burnet Rd — Austin TX 78756 512-706-1900 706-1901
Dana-Farber Cancer Institute 44 Binney St — Boston MA 02115 617-632-3000 632-5520*
*Fax: PR ■ TF: 800-757-3324 ■ Web: www.dana-farber.org
Deborah Heart & Lung Center 200 Trenton Rd — Browns Mills NJ 08015 609-893-6611 893-1213
Web: www.deborah.org
Deer's Head Center PO Box 2018 — Salisbury MD 21802 410-543-4000 543-4151
Delaware Hospital for the Chronically Ill 100 Sunnyside Rd — Smyrna DE 19977 302-233-1000 223-1549*
*Fax: Admissions
Doheny Eye Institute 1450 San Pablo St — Los Angeles CA 90033 323-442-6300 442-6338
TF: 800-872-2273 ■ Web: www.usc.edu/hsc/doheny
Eleanor Slater Hospital 111 Howard Ave PO Box 8269 — Cranston RI 02920 401-462-3666 462-3679
Eye & Ear Clinic of Charleston 1306 Kanawha Blvd E — Charleston WV 25301 304-343-4371 353-0215
Web: www.wvha.com/web/eye.ear
Fox Chase Cancer Center 333 Cottman Ave — Philadelphia PA 19111 215-728-6900 728-2594
TF: 888-369-2427 ■ Web: www.fccc.edu
H Lee Moffitt Cancer Center & Research Institute
University of South Florida 12902 Magnolia Dr — Tampa FL 33612 813-972-4673 745-8495
TF: 800-456-3434 ■ Web: www.moffittcancercenter.com
Healtheast Bethesda Rehabilitation Hospital
559 Capitol Blvd — Saint Paul MN 55103 651-232-2000 232-2118
Web: www.healtheast.org
HealthSouth Rehabilitation Hospital of York 1850 Normandie Dr — York PA 17408 717-767-6941 764-1341
Web: www.healthsouth.com
Hebrew Hospital Home 801 Co-op City Blvd — Bronx NY 10475 718-239-6444 379-3790
Web: www.hhhinc.org
Hospice of Washington County Inc 747 Northern Ave — Hagerstown MD 21742 301-791-6360 791-6579
Web: www.hwc-md.org
Hospital for Special Surgery 535 E 70th St — New York NY 10021 212-606-1000 606-1930
Web: www.hss.edu

Phone | Fax

Hughston Orthopedic Hospital 100 Frist Ct — Columbus GA 31908 706-494-2100 494-2446
TF: 866-484-4786 ■ Web: www.hughstonsports.com
Jewish Memorial Hospital & Rehabilitation Center
59 Townsend St — Boston MA 02119 617-442-8760 989-8207
TF: 800-564-5868 ■ Web: www.jmhrc.com
Kapiolani Medical Center for Women & Children
1319 Punahou St — Honolulu HI 96826 808-983-6000 983-6173*
*Fax: Admitting ■ Web: www.kapiolani.org
Karmanos Barbara Ann Cancer Institute 4110 John R St — Detroit MI 48201 313-833-0710 831-6535
TF: 800-527-6266 ■ Web: www.karmanos.org
Kimmel Cancer Center 401 N Broadway Suite 1100 — Baltimore MD 21231 410-955-5222 955-6787
Web: www.hopkinskimmelcancercenter.org
Kindred Hospital Atlanta 705 Juniper St — Atlanta GA 30308 404-873-2871 873-4516
Web: www.kindredatlanta.com
Kindred Hospital Dallas 9525 Greenville Ave — Dallas TX 75243 214-355-2600 355-2630
Web: www.khdallas.com
Kindred Hospital Fort Worth Southwest 7800 Oakmont Blvd — Fort Worth TX 76132 817-346-0094 263-4071
Web: www.kindredhospitalfwsw.com
Kindred Hospital Kansas City 8701 Troost Ave — Kansas City MO 64131 816-995-2000 995-2171
Web: www.kindredhospitalkc.com
Kindred Hospital Northeast Braintree 2001 Washington St — Braintree MA 02184 781-848-2600 849-3290
Web: www.commonwealthcommunity.com
Kindred Hospital Park View 1400 State St — Springfield MA 01109 413-787-6700 726-6110
Lake Taylor Transitional Hospital 1309 Kempsville Rd — Norfolk VA 23502 757-461-5001 461-4282
Web: www.laketaylor.org
Lakeside Hospital 4700 I-10 Service Rd — Metairie LA 70001 504-885-3333 780-4336*
*Fax: Admitting ■ Web: www.lakesidehospital.com
Lawrence F Quigley Memorial Hospital 91 Crest Ave — Chelsea MA 02150 617-884-5660 884-1162
Leahi Hospital 3675 Kilauea Ave — Honolulu HI 96816 808-733-8000 733-7914
Web: www.leahi.hhsc.org
Life Care Hospital of Pittsburgh 225 Penn Ave — Pittsburgh PA 15221 412-247-2424 247-2333
Lombardi Comprehensive Cancer Center at Georgetown University 3800 Reservoir Rd NW — Washington DC 20007 202-444-2198 444-9429
Web: lombardi.georgetown.edu
Los Angeles County Central Jail Clinic 441 Bauchet St — Los Angeles CA 90012 213-974-4984 625-7361
Magee-Womens Hospital 300 Halket St — Pittsburgh PA 15213 412-641-1000 641-4343
Web: www.magee.edu
Mahelona Samuel Memorial Hospital 4800 Kawaihau Rd — Kapaa HI 96746 808-822-4961 823-4100
Web: www.smmh.hhsc.org
Massachusetts Eye & Ear Infirmary 243 Charles St — Boston MA 02114 617-523-7900 573-4017*
*Fax: Admitting ■ Web: www.meei.harvard.edu
Matheny Medical & Educational Center PO Box 339 — Peapack NJ 07977 908-234-0011 719-2137
Web: www.matheny.org
MD Anderson Cancer Center 1515 Holcombe Blvd — Houston TX 77030 713-792-2121 794-4915*
*Fax: Admitting ■ TF: 800-889-2094 ■ Web: www.mdanderson.org
Memorial Sloan-Kettering Cancer Center 1275 York Ave — New York NY 10021 212-639-2000 432-2331*
*Fax: Admitting ■ TF: 800-525-2225 ■ Web: www.mskcc.org
Miami Heart Institute 4701 N Meridian Ave — Miami Beach FL 33140 305-672-1111 674-3006
Web: www.miamiheart.com
Midwestern Regional Medical Center 2520 Elisha Ave — Zion IL 60099 847-872-4561 872-1591
TF: 800-322-9183 ■ Web: www.cancercenter.com
Monroe Community Hospital 435 E Henrietta Rd — Rochester NY 14620 585-760-6500 760-6026*
*Fax: Admitting ■ Web: www.monroehosp.org
National Jewish Medical & Research Center 1400 Jackson St — Denver CO 80206 303-388-4461
TF: 800-222-5864 ■ Web: www.njc.org
New York Eye & Ear Infirmary 310 E 14th St — New York NY 10003 212-979-4000 228-0664
TF: 800-449-4673 ■ Web: www.nyee.edu
New York University Hospital for Joint Diseases
301 E 17th St — New York NY 10003 212-598-6000 260-1203
TF: 800-372-2887 ■ Web: www.med.nyu.edu/hjd
Norris Comprehensive Cancer Center & Hospital
1441 Eastlake Ave — Los Angeles CA 90033 323-865-3000 865-3868
TF: 800-522-6237 ■ Web: ccnt.hsc.usc.edu
Oak Forest Hospital of Cook County 15900 S Cicero Ave — Oak Forest IL 60452 708-687-7200 687-7979
Oaks Treatment Center 1407 W Stassney Ln — Austin TX 78745 512-464-0200 464-0444
TF: 800-843-6257
Odessa Regional Hospital 520 E 6th St — Odessa TX 79761 432-582-8000 582-8901*
*Fax: Admitting ■ Web: www.odessaregionalhospital.com
Orthopaedic Hospital 2400 S Flower St — Los Angeles CA 90007 213-742-1000 742-1512
Web: www.orthohospital.org
Phillips Eye Institute 2215 Park Ave S — Minneapolis MN 55404 612-775-8800 870-0315*
*Fax: Admitting ■ Web: www.allina.com/ahs/pei.nsf
Piedmont Geriatric Hospital
5001 E Patrick Henry Hwy PO Box 427 — Burkeville VA 23922 434-767-4401 767-4500
Presbyterian Orthopaedic Hospital 1901 Randolph Rd — Charlotte NC 28207 704-316-2000 316-1803
Web: www.presbyterian.org
Princess Margaret Hospital 610 University Ave — Toronto ON M5G2M9 416-946-2000
Web: www.uhn.ca
Quigley Lawrence F Memorial Hosptial 91 Crest Ave — Chelsea MA 02150 617-884-5660 884-1162
River Oaks East-Woman's Pavilion 1026 N Flowood Dr — Flowood MS 39208 601-932-1000 932-4138*
*Fax: Admissions
Roswell Park Cancer Institute Elm & Carlton Sts — Buffalo NY 14263 716-845-2300 845-8335
TF: 877-275-7724 ■ Web: www.roswellpark.org
Runnells Specialized Hospital of Union County
40 Watchung Way — Berkeley Heights NJ 07922 908-771-5700 771-0376
Web: www.unioncountynj.org/runnells/
Saint Francis Health Care Center 401 N Broadway St — Green Springs OH 44836 419-639-2626 639-6225
TF: 800-248-2552 ■ Web: www.sfhcc.org
Saint Francis Hospital 100 Port Washington Blvd — Roslyn NY 11576 516-562-6000 562-6909
Web: www.stfrancisheartcenter.com
Saint Joseph's Women's Hospital Tampa
3030 W Dr ML King Blvd — Tampa FL 33607 813-879-4730 872-2912
Saint Jude Children's Research Hospital 332 N Lauderdale St — Memphis TN 38105 901-495-3300 495-5297*
*Fax: Admitting ■ TF: 866-278-5833 ■ Web: www.stjude.org
Saint Vincent Women's Hospital 8111 Township Line Rd — Indianapolis IN 46260 317-415-8111 415-7587*
*Fax: Admitting ■ TF: 877-664-4076 ■ Web: www.stvincent.org
Samuel Mahelona Memorial Hospital 4800 Kawaihau Rd — Kapaa HI 96746 808-822-4961 823-4100
Web: www.smmh.hhsc.org
Select Specialty Hospital Houston Heights 1917 Ashland St — Houston TX 77008 713-861-6161 802-8653
Sidney Kimmel Comprehensive Cancer Center at Johns Hopkins
401 N Broadway Suite 1100 — Baltimore MD 21231 410-955-5222 955-6787
Web: www.hopkinskimmelcancercenter.org
Siteman Cancer Center 4921 Parkview Pl — Saint Louis MO 63110 314-362-5196
TF: 800-600-3606 ■ Web: www.siteman.wustl.edu
Sloan-Kettering Cancer Center 1275 York Ave — New York NY 10021 212-639-2000 432-2331*
*Fax: Admitting ■ TF: 800-525-2225 ■ Web: www.mskcc.org
Specialty Hospital Jacksonville 4901 Richard St — Jacksonville FL 32207 904-737-3120 730-5991
TF: 800-378-9497 ■ Web: www.specialtyhospitaljax.com
Stanford Cancer Center 875 Lake Blake Wilbur Dr — Stanford CA 94305 650-498-6000 725-9113
Web: cancer.stanford.edu
Stony Point Surgical Center 8700 Stony Point Pkwy — Richmond VA 23235 804-775-4500 643-3542
TF: 800-328-7334 ■ Web: stonypointsc.com
Straith Hospital for Special Surgery 23901 Lahser Rd — Southfield MI 48034 248-357-3360 357-0915
Tewksbury Hospital 365 East St — Tewksbury MA 01876 978-851-7321 851-5648*
*Fax: Mail Rm ■ Web: www.mass.gov/dph/hosp/th.htm
Texas Center for Infectious Diseases 2303 SE Military Dr — San Antonio TX 78223 210-534-8857 531-4502
TF: 800-839-5864

Specialty Hospitals (Cont'd)

Phone Fax

Texas Orthopedic Hospital 7401 S Main St ... Houston TX 77030 713-799-8600 794-3580
TF: 800-678-4501 ■ *Web:* www.texasorthopedic.com
UC Davis Cancer Center 4501 X St ... Sacramento CA 95817 916-734-5800 703-5067
TF: 800-362-5566 ■ *Web:* www.ucdmc.ucdavis.edu/cancer
University of Michigan Trauma Burn Center
1500 E Medical Ctr Dr Rm 1C435-UH Box 0033 ... Ann Arbor MI 48109 734-936-9673 936-9657
University Specialty Hospital 601 S Charles St ... Baltimore MD 21230 410-547-8500 752-2920
Vanderbilt-Ingram Cancer Center 691 Preston Bldg ... Nashville TN 37232 615-936-5847
Web: www.vicc.org
Veterans Home & Hospital 287 West St ... Rocky Hill CT 06067 860-529-2571 721-5979*
**Fax:* Admitting
Villa Feliciana Chronic Disease Hospital 5002 Hwy 10 ... Jackson LA 70748 225-634-4000 634-4191
Wills Eye Hospital 840 Walnut St ... Philadelphia PA 19107 215-928-3000 928-0634
Web: www.willseye.org
Woman's Hospital 9050 Airlines Hwy ... Baton Rouge LA 70815 225-927-1300 924-8110
Web: www.womans.com
Woman's Hospital of Texas 7600 Fannin St ... Houston TX 77054 713-790-1234 790-0469
Web: www.womanshospital.com
Women & Infants Hospital of Rhode Island 101 Dudley St ... Providence RI 02905 401-274-1100 453-7666
Web: www.womenandinfants.com
Women's & Children's Hospital
4600 Ambassador Caffery Pkwy ... Lafayette LA 70508 337-521-9100 521-9102
Web: www.womens-childrens.com
Women's Christian Assn Hospital 207 Foote Ave ... Jamestown NY 14701 716-487-0141 644-8144*
**Fax:* Admitting ■ *Web:* www.wcahospital.org

377-8 Veterans Hospitals

Listings for veterans hospitals are organized by states, and then by city names within those groupings.

Phone Fax

Veterans Affairs Medical Center 700 S 19th St ... Birmingham AL 35233 205-933-8101 933-4498*
**Fax:* Admitting
VA Central Alabama Veterans Health Care System
215 Perry Hill Rd ... Montgomery AL 36109 334-272-4670 260-4115
TF: 800-214-8387
Veterans Affairs Medical Center 3701 Loop Rd E ... Tuscaloosa AL 35404 205-554-2000 554-2077
TF: 888-269-3045
Veterans Affairs Medical Center 2400 Hospital Rd ... Tuskegee AL 36083 334-727-0550 724-6825
TF: 800-214-8387
Carl T Hayden Veterans Affairs Medical Center
650 E Indian School Rd ... Phoenix AZ 85012 602-277-5551 222-6435
TF: 800-359-8262
Veterans Affairs Medical Center 500 Hwy 89 N ... Prescott AZ 86313 928-445-4860 776-6102
TF: 800-949-1005
Southern Arizona Veterans Healthcare System 3601 S 6th Ave ... Tucson AZ 85723 520-792-1450 629-4969*
**Fax:* Admissions
Veterans Affairs Medical Center 1100 N College Ave ... Fayetteville AR 72703 479-443-4301 444-5089
Veterans Affairs Medical Center 4300 W 7th St ... Little Rock AR 72205 501-257-1000 257-5404
Veterans Affairs Medical Center 2615 E Clinton Ave ... Fresno CA 93703 559-225-6100
Jerry L Pettis Memorial Veterans Affairs Medical Center
11201 Benton St ... Loma Linda CA 92357 909-825-7084 422-3140*
**Fax:* Admitting ■ *TF Mail Rm:* 800-741-8387 ■ *Web:* www.lom.med.va.gov
Veterans Affairs Medical Center 5901 E 7th St ... Long Beach CA 90822 562-826-8000 826-5906
TF: 888-769-8387 ■ *Web:* www.long-beach.med.va.gov
Veterans Affairs Medical Center 11301 Wilshire Blvd ... Los Angeles CA 90073 310-478-3711 268-3494
Web: www.gla.med.va.gov
Sepulveda Veterans Affairs Medical Center
16111 Plummer St ... North Hills CA 91343 818-891-7711
TF: 800-516-4567
Veterans Affairs Medical Center 3801 Miranda Ave ... Palo Alto CA 94304 650-493-5000 852-3228
Web: www.palo-alto.med.va.gov
Veterans Affairs Medical Center 3350 La Jolla Village Dr ... San Diego CA 92161 858-552-8585 642-3457*
**Fax:* Admitting ■ TF: 800-331-8387
Veterans Affairs Medical Center 4150 Clement St ... San Francisco CA 94121 415-221-4810 750-2177
Web: www.sf.med.va.gov
Veterans Affairs Medical Center 1055 Clermont St ... Denver CO 80220 303-399-8020 393-4656*
**Fax:* Mail Rm ■ TF: 888-336-8262
Veterans Affairs Medical Center 2121 North Ave ... Grand Junction CO 81501 970-242-0731 244-1323
Veterans Affairs Connecticut Health Care System
950 Campbell Ave ... West Haven CT 06516 203-932-5711 937-3966*
**Fax:* Admissions
Veterans Affairs Medical Center 1601 Kirkwood Hwy ... Wilmington DE 19805 302-994-2511
TF: 800-450-8262
Veterans Affairs Medical Center 50 Irving St NW ... Washington DC 20422 202-745-8000 745-2278*
**Fax:* Admissions
Veterans Affairs Medical Center
10000 Bay Pines Blvd PO Box 5005 ... Bay Pines FL 33744 727-398-6661 398-9442
TF: 888-820-0230 ■ *Web:* www.visn8.med.va.gov/baypines
Veterans Affairs Medical Center 1601 SW Archer Rd ... Gainesville FL 32608 352-376-1611 374-6113*
**Fax:* Mail Rm ■ TF: 800-324-8387 ■ *Web:* www.visn8.med.va.gov/nfsg
Veterans Affairs Medical Center 619 S Marion Ave ... Lake City FL 32025 386-755-3016 758-6005
Veterans Affairs Medical Center 1201 NW 16th St ... Miami FL 33125 305-324-4455 575-3420*
**Fax:* Admitting ■ TF: 888-276-1785
Veterans Affairs Medical Center 13000 Bruce B Downs Blvd ... Tampa FL 33612 813-972-2000 910-3020
Web: www.visn8.med.va.gov/Tampa
Veterans Affairs Medical Center
7305 N Military Trail ... West Palm Beach FL 33410 561-882-8262 422-8613
TF: 800-972-8262
Veterans Affairs Medical Center 1 Freedom Way ... Augusta GA 30904 706-733-0188 481-6726*
**Fax:* Admitting
Veterans Affairs Medical Center 1670 Clairmont Rd ... Decatur GA 30033 404-321-6111
TF: 800-944-9726
Carl Vinson Veterans Affairs Medical Center
1826 Veterans Blvd ... Dublin GA 31021 478-272-1210 277-2717*
**Fax:* Mail Rm ■ TF: 800-595-5229
Veterans Affairs Medical Center 500 W Fort St ... Boise ID 83702 208-422-1000 422-1148*
**Fax:* Admitting
Veterans Affairs Medical Center 820 S Damen Ave ... Chicago IL 60612 312-569-8387
Web: www.visn12.med.va.gov/chicago
Veterans Affairs Medical Center 1900 E Main St ... Danville IL 61832 217-554-3000 554-4856*
**Fax:* Admissions ■ *Web:* www1.va.gov/directory/guide/facility.asp?ID=36
Edward Hines Jr Veterans Affairs Hospital PO Box 5000 ... Hines IL 60141 708-202-8387 202-2506
Web: www.hines.med.va.gov
Veterans Affairs Medical Center 2401 W Main St ... Marion IL 62959 618-997-5311 993-4165*
**Fax:* Hum Res
Veterans Affairs Medical Center 3001 Green Bay Rd ... North Chicago IL 60064 847-688-1900 610-3280*
**Fax Area Code:* 224 ■ TF: 800-393-0865
Veterans Affairs Medical Center 2121 Lake Ave ... Fort Wayne IN 46805 260-426-5431 460-1332
TF: 800-360-8387

Phone Fax

Veterans Affairs Medical Center 1481 W 10th St ... Indianapolis IN 46202 317-554-0000
Web: www1.va.gov/directory/guide/facility.asp?ID=62
Veterans Affairs Medical Center 1700 E 38th St ... Marion IN 46953 765-674-3321 677-3188*
**Fax:* Admitting ■ TF: 800-498-8792
Veterans Affairs Medical Center 3600 30th St ... Des Moines IA 50310 515-699-5999 699-5862
TF: 800-294-8387 ■ *Web:* www1.va.gov/directory
Veterans Affairs Medical Center 601 Hwy 6 W ... Iowa City IA 52246 319-338-0581 339-7171
Web: www.iowa-city.med.va.gov
Veterans Affairs Medical Center 1515 W Pleasant St ... Knoxville IA 50138 641-842-3101 828-5066
TF: 800-816-8878 ■ *Web:* www1.va.gov/directory/guide/facility.asp?ID=66&dnum=ALL&map=1
Dwight D Eisenhower Veterans Affairs Medical Center
4101 S 4th St ... Leavenworth KS 66048 913-682-2000 758-4233
TF: 800-952-8387
Colmery-O'Neil Veterans Affairs Medical Center
2200 SW Gage Blvd ... Topeka KS 66622 785-350-3111 350-4336
TF: 800-574-8387
Veterans Affairs Medical Center 5500 E Kellogg St ... Wichita KS 67218 316-685-2221 651-3666
TF: 888-878-6881
Veterans Affairs Medical Center Lexington 1101 Veterans Dr ... Lexington KY 40502 859-233-4511 281-4953*
**Fax:* Admissions
Veterans Affairs Medical Center 800 Zorn Ave ... Louisville KY 40206 502-287-4000 287-6225*
**Fax:* Admitting
Veterans Affairs Medical Center
2495 Hwy 71 N PO Box 69004 ... Alexandria LA 71306 318-473-0010 483-5093*
**Fax:* Hum Res
Southeast Louisiana Veterans Healthcare System
1601 Perdido St ... New Orleans LA 70112 504-568-0811 310-6300
TF: 800-935-8387 ■ *Web:* www1.va.gov/new-orleans
Overton Brooks Veterans Affairs Medical Center
510 E Stoner Ave ... Shreveport LA 71101 318-221-8411 424-6156
TF: 800-863-7441 ■ *Web:* www.vba.va.gov/ro/new-orleans/vamcshrv.htm
Togus VA Medical Center 1 VA Center ... Augusta ME 04330 207-623-8411 623-5745*
**Fax:* Admissions ■ *Web:* www.visn1.med.va.gov/togus/index.asp
Veterans Affairs Medical Center 10 N Greene St ... Baltimore MD 21201 410-605-7000
TF: 800-463-6295
Edith Nourse Rogers Memorial Veterans Hospital
200 Springs Rd ... Bedford MA 01730 781-275-7500
Veterans Affairs Medical Center 940 Belmont St ... Brockton MA 02301 508-583-4500 895-0237
Web: www.visn1.med.va.gov/boston
Veterans Affairs Medical Center 150 S Huntington Ave ... Jamaica Plain MA 02130 617-232-9500 278-4410
Web: www.visn1.med.va.gov/boston
North Hampton Veterans Affairs Medical Center 421 N Main St ... Leeds MA 01053 413-584-4040 582-3185*
**Fax:* Admissions
Veterans Affairs Medical Center 2215 Fuller Rd ... Ann Arbor MI 48105 734-769-7100 761-5398*
**Fax:* Mail Rm
Veterans Affairs Medical Center 5500 Armstrong Rd ... Battle Creek MI 49015 269-966-5600 660-5021*
**Fax:* Admissions ■ TF: 888-214-1247
Veterans Affairs Medical Center 4646 John R St ... Detroit MI 48201 313-576-1000 576-1025
Veterans Affairs Medical Center 325 E 'H' St ... Iron Mountain MI 49801 906-774-3300 779-3108
TF: 800-215-8262 ■ *Web:* www.visn12.med.va.gov/ironmountain
Veterans Affairs Medical Center 1500 Weiss St ... Saginaw MI 48602 989-497-2500 791-2217
Web: www1.va.gov/directory
Veterans Affairs Medical Center 1 Veterans Dr ... Minneapolis MN 55417 612-725-2000 467-5531*
**Fax:* Admitting ■ TF: 866-414-5058
Veterans Affairs Medical Center 4801 Veterans Dr ... Saint Cloud MN 56303 320-252-1670 255-6494*
**Fax:* Mail Rm
Veterans Affairs Medical Center 400 Veterans Ave ... Biloxi MS 39531 228-523-5000 523-5701
Web: www.va.gov/biloxi
Veterans Affairs Medical Center 1500 E Woodrow Wilson Dr ... Jackson MS 39216 601-362-4471 368-3811*
**Fax:* Hum Res
Harry S Truman Memorial Veterans Hospital 800 Hospital Dr ... Columbia MO 65201 573-814-6000 814-6600
Veterans Affairs Medical Center 4801 E Linwood Blvd ... Kansas City MO 64128 816-861-4700 922-3331*
**Fax:* Hum Res ■ TF: 800-525-1483
John J Pershing Veterans Affairs Medical Center
1500 N Westwood Blvd ... Poplar Bluff MO 63901 573-686-4151 778-4559
Veterans Affairs Medical Center 915 N Grand Blvd ... Saint Louis MO 63106 314-487-0400
TF: 800-228-5459
Veterans Affairs Hospital 1892 Williams St ... Fort Harrison MT 59636 406-442-6410 447-7904
Veterans Affairs Medical Center 2201 N Broadwell Ave ... Grand Island NE 68801 308-382-3660 385-2712*
**Fax:* Admissions
Veterans Affairs Medical Center 600 S 70th St ... Lincoln NE 68510 402-489-3802 486-7840
TF: 866-851-6052
Veterans Affairs Medical Center 4101 Woolworth Ave ... Omaha NE 68105 402-346-8800 449-0697*
**Fax:* Admitting ■ TF: 800-451-5796
Sierra NV Healthcare Systems (VA Medical Center)
1000 Locust St ... Reno NV 89502 775-786-7200 328-1464*
**Fax:* Mail Rm ■ TF: 888-838-6256
Veterans Affairs Medical Center 718 Smyth Rd ... Manchester NH 03104 603-624-4366 626-6576
TF: 800-892-8384
Veterans Affairs Medical Center 385 Tremont Ave ... East Orange NJ 07018 973-676-1000 395-7148*
**Fax:* Hum Res ■ *Web:* www1.va.gov/visns/visn03/eorginfo.asp
Veterans Affairs Medical Center 151 Knollcroft Rd ... Lyons NJ 07939 908-647-0180 604-5245*
**Fax:* Admissions ■ *Web:* www1.va.gov/visns/visn03/lyonsinfo.asp
Veterans Affairs New Jersey Health Care System - Lyons Campus
151 Knollcroft Rd ... Lyons NJ 07939 908-647-0180 604-5245*
**Fax:* Admissions ■ *Web:* www1.va.gov/visns/visn03/lyonsinfo.asp
Veterans Affairs Medical Center 1501 San Pedro Dr SE ... Albuquerque NM 87108 505-265-1711 256-2855
Stratton Veterans Affairs Medical Center 113 Holland Ave ... Albany NY 12208 518-626-5000 626-6709*
**Fax:* Admitting ■ TF: 800-223-4810
Veterans Affairs Medical Center 222 Richmond Ave ... Batavia NY 14020 585-297-1000 344-3300
Veterans Affairs Medical Center 76 Veterans Ave ... Bath NY 14810 607-664-4000 664-4915*
**Fax:* Admissions ■ TF: 877-845-3247 ■ *Web:* www1.va.gov/visns/visn02/bath.html
James J Peters Veterans Affairs Medical Center
130 W Kingsbridge Rd ... Bronx NY 10468 718-584-9000 741-4571
Peters James J Veterans Affairs Medical Center
130 W Kingsbridge Rd ... Bronx NY 10468 718-584-9000 741-4571
Veterans Affairs Medical Center 800 Poly Pl ... Brooklyn NY 11209 718-836-6600 567-4029*
**Fax:* Admitting
Veterans Affairs Medical Center 3495 Bailey Ave ... Buffalo NY 14215 716-834-9200 862-8533
TF: 800-532-8387
Veterans Affairs Medical Center 400 Fort Hill Ave ... Canandaigua NY 14424 585-394-2000 393-8328
VA Hudson Valley Health Care System
Castle Point Campus 100 Rt 9 D ... Castle Point NY 12511 845-831-2000 838-5193
Web: www1.va.gov/visns/visn03/castinfo.asp
Franklin Delano Roosevelt Campus
2094 Albany Post Rd PO Box 100 ... Montrose NY 10548 914-737-4400 788-4244
TF: 800-269-8749 ■ *Web:* www1.va.gov/visns/visn03/mtrsinfo.asp
Veterans Affairs Medical Center 423 E 23rd St ... New York NY 10010 212-686-7500
Veterans Affairs Medical Center 79 Middleville Rd ... Northport NY 11768 631-261-4400 754-7952*
**Fax:* Admissions ■ TF: 800-827-1000
Veterans Affairs Medical Center 800 Irving Ave ... Syracuse NY 13210 315-425-4400 425-4375*
**Fax:* Admitting ■ TF: 800-792-4334
Veterans Affairs Medical Center 1100 Tunnel Rd ... Asheville NC 28805 828-298-7911 299-2502
TF: 800-932-6408
Veterans Affairs Medical Center 508 Fulton St ... Durham NC 27705 919-286-0411 286-6855

	City	State	Zip	Phone	Fax
Veterans Affairs Medical Center 2300 Ramsey St *TF:* 800-771-6106	Fayetteville	NC	28301	910-488-2120	
Hefner WG Bill Veterans Affairs Medical Center 1601 Brenner Ave *Fax: Admissions	Salisbury	NC	28144	704-638-9000	638-3319*
WG Bill Hefner Veterans Affairs Medical Center 1601 Brenner Ave *Fax: Admissions	Salisbury	NC	28144	704-638-9000	638-3319*
Veterans Affairs Medical Center 2101 Elm St N *TF:* 800-410-9723	Fargo	ND	58102	701-232-3241	239-3729
Veterans Affairs Medical Center 17273 SR-104	Chillicothe	OH	45601	740-773-1141	772-7023
Veterans Affairs Medical Center 3200 Vine St *TF:* 888-267-7873	Cincinnati	OH	45220	513-861-3100	
Veterans Affairs Medical Center 10701 East Blvd *TF:* 888-350-3100 ■ *Web:* www.cleveland.med.va.gov	Cleveland	OH	44106	216-791-3800	
Veterans Affairs Medical Center 4100 W 3rd St *Web:* www.dayton.med.va.gov	Dayton	OH	45428	937-268-6511	262-3383
Veterans Affairs Medical Center 1011 Honor Heights Dr *Fax: Admissions ■ *TF:* 888-397-8387	Muskogee	OK	74401	918-683-3261	680-3865*
Veterans Affairs Medical Center 921 NE 13th St *TF:* 866-835-5273	Oklahoma City	OK	73104	405-270-0501	270-5132
Veterans Affairs Medical Center 3710 SW US Veterans Hospital Rd *Fax: Admissions ■ *TF:* 888-233-8305	Portland	OR	97239	503-220-8262	402-2909*
Veterans Affairs Medical Center 913 NW Garden Valley Blvd *Web:* www1.va.gov/directory	Roseburg	OR	97470	541-440-1000	440-1225
James E Van Zandt Veterans Affairs Medical Center 2907 Pleasant Valley Blvd *TF:* 877-626-2500	Altoona	PA	16602	814-943-8164	940-7898
Veterans Affairs Medical Center 325 New Castle Rd *Fax: Hum Res ■ *TF:* 800-362-8262	Butler	PA	16001	724-287-4781	477-5019*
Veterans Affairs Medical Center 1400 Black Horse Hill Rd *Fax: Admissions ■ *TF:* 800-290-6172	Coatesville	PA	19320	610-384-7711	380-4333*
Veterans Affairs Medical Center 135 E 38th St *TF:* 800-274-8387	Erie	PA	16504	814-868-8661	860-2120
Veterans Affairs Medical Center 1700 S Lincoln Ave *Fax: Admissions ■ *TF:* 800-409-8771	Lebanon	PA	17042	717-272-6621	228-5944*
Veterans Affairs Medical Center 3900 Woodland Ave *Fax: Admissions ■ *TF:* 800-949-1001	Philadelphia	PA	19104	215-823-5800	823-5839*
Veterans Affairs Medical Center University Dr C *Web:* www.va.gov/pittsburgh	Pittsburgh	PA	15240	412-688-6000	688-6901
Veterans Affairs Medical Center 7180 Highland Dr *Web:* www.va.gov/pittsburgh/highland.htm	Pittsburgh	PA	15206	412-365-4900	365-5105
Veterans Affairs Medical Center 1111 E End Blvd	Wilkes-Barre	PA	18711	570-824-3521	
Veterans Affairs Medical Center 830 Chalkstone Ave *Fax: Hum Res	Providence	RI	02908	401-273-7100	457-3370*
Ralph H Johnson Veterans Affairs Medical Center 109 Bee St *Fax: Mail Rm	Charleston	SC	29401	843-577-5011	853-9167*
Veterans Affairs Medical Center 6439 Garners Ferry Rd *Fax: Mail Rm ■ *Web:* va.gov/columbiasc	Columbia	SC	29209	803-776-4000	695-6799*
Veterans Affairs Medical Center 113 Comanche Rd *TF:* 800-743-1070	Fort Meade	SD	57741	605-347-2511	347-7171
Veterans Affairs Medical Center 500 N 5th St *Fax: Admissions ■ *TF:* 800-764-5370	Hot Springs	SD	57747	605-745-2000	745-2093*
Royal C Johnson Veterans Memorial Hospital 2501 W 22nd St *TF:* 800-316-8387	Sioux Falls	SD	57105	605-336-3230	333-6872
Veterans Affairs Medical Center 1030 Jefferson Ave *Fax: Admissions	Memphis	TN	38104	901-523-8990	577-7533*
James H Quillen Veterans Affairs Medical Center Dogwood St Bldg 204 PO Box 4000	Mountain Home	TN	37684	423-926-1171	979-3519
Alvin C York Medical Center 3400 Lebanon Pike *Fax: Admitting	Murfreesboro	TN	37129	615-893-1360	867-5802*
Veterans Affairs Medical Center 1310 24th Ave S	Nashville	TN	37212	615-327-4751	
Thomas E Creek Veterans Affairs Medical Center 6010 Amarillo Blvd W *Fax: Admitting ■ *TF:* 800-687-8262	Amarillo	TX	79106	806-355-9703	354-7876*
Veterans Affairs Medical Center 300 Veterans Blvd *Fax: Admitting	Big Spring	TX	79720	432-263-7361	264-4816*
Veterans Affairs Medical Center 1201 E 9th St *TF:* 800-924-8387 ■ *Web:* www.north-texas.med.va.gov/bonhamgeninfo.htm	Bonham	TX	75418	903-583-2111	583-6600
Veterans Affairs Medical Center 4500 S Lancaster Rd *Fax: Admissions ■ *TF:* 800-849-3597 ■ *Web:* www.north-texas.med.va.gov	Dallas	TX	75216	214-742-8387	857-1171*
Veterans Affairs Medical Center 2002 Holcombe Blvd *Fax: Admitting ■ *TF:* 800-553-2278 ■ *Web:* www.houston.med.va.gov	Houston	TX	77030	713-791-1414	794-7218*
Audie L Murphy Memorial Veterans Hospital 7400 Merton Minter St	San Antonio	TX	78229	210-617-5300	
Veterans Affairs Medical Center 1901 Veterans Memorial Dr *Fax: Admissions ■ *Web:* www.central-texas.med.va.gov/main	Temple	TX	76504	254-778-4811	743-0691*
Veterans Affairs Medical Center 4800 Memorial Dr	Waco	TX	76711	254-752-6581	297-3077
Veterans Affairs Medical Center 500 S Foothill Dr *TF:* 800-827-1000 ■ *Web:* www.va.gov/visn19/slc.htm	Salt Lake City	UT	84148	801-582-1565	584-5624
Veterans Affairs Medical Center 215 N Main St *Web:* www.visn1.med.va.gov/wrj	White River Junction	VT	05009	802-295-9363	296-5138
Veterans Affairs Medical Center 100 Emancipation Dr *Fax: Admissions ■ *Web:* www1.va.gov/midatlantic/facilities/hampton.htm	Hampton	VA	23667	757-728-3100	728-3193*
Hunter Holmes McGuire Veterans Affairs Medical Center 1201 Broad Rock Blvd *TF:* 800-784-8381	Richmond	VA	23249	804-675-5000	675-5308
Veterans Affairs Medical Center 1970 Roanoke Blvd *Fax: Admitting	Salem	VA	24153	540-982-2463	983-1093*
Veterans Affairs Puget Sound Medical Center 1660 S Columbian Way *Fax: Admitting ■ *Web:* www.puget-sound.med.va.gov	Seattle	WA	98108	206-762-1010	764-2270*
Veterans Affairs Medical Center 4815 N Assembly St *Fax: Admitting	Spokane	WA	99205	509-434-7000	434-7131*
Veterans Affairs Medical Center 77 Wainwright Dr *Fax: Admissions	Walla Walla	WA	99362	509-525-5200	526-6207*
Veterans Affairs Medical Center 200 Veterans Ave *Web:* www1.va.gov/midatlantic/facilities/beckley.htm	Beckley	WV	25801	304-255-2121	255-2431
Louis A Johnson Veterans Affairs Medical Center 1 Medical Center Dr	Clarksburg	WV	26301	304-623-3461	626-7026
Veterans Affairs Medical Center 1540 Spring Valley Dr	Huntington	WV	25704	304-429-6741	429-0270
Veterans Affairs Medical Center 510 Butler Ave	Martinsburg	WV	25405	304-263-0811	264-3990
Veterans Affairs Medical Center 2500 Overlook Terr *Web:* www.madison.med.va.gov	Madison	WI	53705	608-256-1901	280-7116
Veterans Affairs Medical Center 5000 W National Ave *Fax: Admitting ■ *TF:* 888-469-6614	Milwaukee	WI	53295	414-384-2000	382-5388*
Veterans Affairs Medical Center 500 E Veterans St *Fax: Admissions ■ *TF:* 800-872-8662 ■ *Web:* www.visn12.med.va.gov/tomah	Tomah	WI	54660	608-372-3971	372-1692*
Veterans Affairs Medical Center 1898 Fort Rd *Fax: Admissions ■ *TF:* 800-370-0250	Sheridan	WY	82801	307-672-3473	672-1900*

HOSPITALS - DEVELOPMENTAL DISABILITIES

SEE Developmental Centers p. 1587

378 HOT TUBS, SPAS, WHIRLPOOL BATHS

	City	State	Zip	Phone	Fax
Alaglass Pools 165 Sweet Bay Rd *TF:* 877-655-7179 ■ *Web:* www.alaglass.com	Saint Matthews	SC	29135	803-655-7179	655-5680
Almost Heaven Group HC 67 Box 539 BB *Web:* www.almostheaven.net	Renick	WV	24966	304-497-2610	
American Whirlpool Products Corp 316 Vine St *Fax Area Code: 800 ■ *TF:* 800-327-1394 ■ *Web:* www.americanwhirlpool.com	Clifton	TN	38425	931-676-3195	398-5651*
Americh Corp 13212 Saticoy St *TF:* 800-453-1463 ■ *Web:* americh.com	North Hollywood	CA	91605	818-982-1711	982-2764
Apollo Marble Products 1355 White Dr	Titusville	FL	32780	321-268-0713	268-0905
Aqua Glass Corp 320 Industrial Park Dr *TF:* 800-632-0911 ■ *Web:* www.aquaglass.com	Adamsville	TN	38310	731-632-0911	632-4232
Aquatic Industries PO Box 889 *TF Cust Svc:* 800-928-3707 ■ *Web:* www.aquaticwhirlpools.com	Leander	TX	78646	512-259-2255	259-3633
Atlantic Whirlpools Inc 8721 Glenwood Ave *TF:* 800-849-8827 ■ *Web:* www.atlanticwhirlpools.com	Raleigh	NC	27617	919-783-7447	783-0146
Baker Mfg Corp 7460 Chancellor Dr *TF:* 800-881-2284	Orlando	FL	32809	407-816-9559	857-9240
Bath-Tec Inc PO Box 1118 *TF:* 800-526-3301 ■ *Web:* www.bathtec.com	Ennis	TX	75120	972-646-5279	646-5688
Bathroom World Mfg Co 3569 NW 10th Ave *TF:* 800-566-0541 ■ *Web:* www.bathroomworld.com	Fort Lauderdale	FL	33309	954-566-0451	561-8510
Best Bath Systems 4545 Enterprise St *TF:* 800-727-9907 ■ *Web:* www.best-bath.com	Boise	ID	83705	208-342-6823	342-6832
California Acrylic Industries Cal Spas 1462 E Ninth St *TF:* 800-225-7727 ■ *Web:* www.calspas.com	Pomona	CA	91766	909-623-8781	620-0751
Cameo Marble 540 Central Ct *TF:* 800-447-8558 ■ *Web:* www.cameomarble.com	New Albany	IN	47150	812-944-5055	944-5236
Clarke Products Inc 1170 109th St *TF:* 800-426-8964 ■ *Web:* www.clarkeproducts.com	Grand Prairie	TX	75050	972-660-1992	660-2259
Coleman Spas Inc 25605 S Arizona Ave *Web:* www.colemanspas.com	Chandler	AZ	85248	480-895-0598	895-7849
Dimension One Spas 2611 Business Park Dr *TF:* 800-345-7727 ■ *Web:* www.d1spas.com	Vista	CA	92081	760-727-7727	734-4225
DM Industries Ltd 2320 NW 147th St *TF:* 800-848-2772 ■ *Web:* www.vitabathandspa.com	Miami	FL	33054	305-685-5739	688-9415
Fox Pool Corp 3490 Board Rd *TF:* 800-723-1011 ■ *Web:* www.foxpool.com	York	PA	17402	717-764-8581	764-4293
Galaxy Aquatics Inc 1075 W Sam Houston Pkwy N Suite 210 *Web:* www.galaxy-aquatics.com	Houston	TX	77043	713-464-0303	464-0399
Gatsby Spas Inc 1003 S Alexander St Suite 7 *TF:* 800-393-7727 ■ *Web:* www.gatsby.com	Plant City	FL	33563	813-754-4122	752-5716
Hydra Baths 2100 S Fairview St *TF:* 800-854-8680 ■ *Web:* www.hydrabaths.com	Santa Ana	CA	92704	714-556-9133	708-0632
Hydro Systems Inc 29132 Ave Paine *TF:* 800-747-9990 ■ *Web:* www.hydrosystem.com	Valencia	CA	91355	661-775-0686	775-0668
Jason International Inc 8328 MacArthur Dr *TF:* 800-255-5766 ■ *Web:* www.jasoninternational.com	North Little Rock	AR	72118	501-771-4477	771-2333
Kallista Inc 1227 N 8th St Suite 2 *TF:* 888-452-5547 ■ *Web:* www.kallista.com	Sheboygan	WI	53081	920-457-4441	803-4867
Koral Industries Inc PO Box 1270 *TF:* 800-627-2441 ■ *Web:* www.koralco.com	Ennis	TX	75120	972-875-6555	875-9558
Lasco Bathware 8101 E Kaiser Blvd Suite 200 *Fax: Sales ■ *TF:* 800-877-2005 ■ *Web:* www.lascobathware.com	Anaheim	CA	92808	714-993-1220	998-3062*
MAAX Pearl 9224 73rd Ave N *TF:* 800-328-2531 ■ *Web:* www.maax.com/en/Products/Pearl.aspx?Brand=4	Brooklyn Park	MN	55428	763-424-3335	424-9808
Marquis Corp 596 Hoffman Rd *TF:* 800-275-0888 ■ *Web:* www.marquisspas.com	Independence	OR	97351	503-838-0888	838-3849
Oasis Industries Inc 1600 Mountain St *TF:* 800-323-2748 ■ *Web:* www.oasisbath.com	Aurora	IL	60505	630-898-3500	375-1500
Plastic Development Co Inc PO Box 4007 *TF:* 800-451-1420 ■ *Web:* www.pdcspas.com	Williamsport	PA	17701	570-323-3060	323-8485
Royal Baths Mfg Co 14635 Chrisman Rd *TF:* 800-826-0074 ■ *Web:* www.royalbaths.com	Houston	TX	77039	281-442-3400	442-1455
Spa Manufacturers 6060 Ulmerton Rd *TF:* 877-530-9493 ■ *Web:* www.spamanufacturers.com	Clearwater	FL	33760	727-530-9493	539-8151
Spurlin Industries Inc PO Box 707 *TF:* 800-749-4475 ■ *Web:* www.spurlinindustries.com	Palmetto	GA	30268	770-463-1644	463-2932
Thermo Spas Inc 155 East St *TF:* 800-876-0158 ■ *Web:* www.thermospas.com	Wallingford	CT	06492	203-265-6133	265-7133
Twirl Jet Spas Inc 3990 Industrial Ave *TF:* 800-854-4890 ■ *Web:* twirljetspas.com	Hemet	CA	92545	951-766-4306	766-4310
Watertech Whirlpool Bath & Spa 2507 Plymouth Rd *TF:* 800-289-8827 ■ *Web:* www.watertechtn.com	Johnson City	TN	37601	423-926-1470	926-6438
Watkins Mfg Corp 1280 Park Ctr Dr *TF:* 800-999-4688 ■ *Web:* www.hotspring.com	Vista	CA	92083	760-598-6464	598-8910

379 HOTEL RESERVATIONS SERVICES

	City	State	Zip	Phone	Fax
AC Central Reservations Inc 201 Tilton Rd London Square Mall Suite 17B *TF:* 888-227-6667 ■ *Web:* www.acrooms.com	Northfield	NJ	08225	609-383-8880	383-8801
Accommodations Plus 4230 Merrick Rd *TF:* 800-733-7666 ■ *Web:* www.hotelexpress.com	Massapequa	NY	11758	718-751-4000	995-6099
Advance Reservations Inn Arizona PO Box 950 *TF:* 800-456-0682 ■ *Web:* www.azres.com	Tempe	AZ	85280	480-990-0682	990-3390
Advanced Reservation Systems Inc 1059 1st Ave *TF:* 800-434-7894 ■ *Web:* www.aresdirect.com	San Diego	CA	92101	619-238-0900	374-2085
Alaska Sourdough Bed & Breakfast Assn 889 Cardigan Cir *Web:* www.alaskan.com/aksourdoughbba	Anchorage	AK	99503	907-563-6244	743-0664
Alberta Express Reservations Box 6295 *TF:* 800-884-8803 ■ *Web:* www.hotelforyou.com	Drayton Valley	AB	T7A1R7	780-621-2855	542-6505
All Around the Town 270 Lafayette St Suite 804 *TF:* 800-443-3800 ■ *Web:* www.newyorkcitybestbb.com	New York	NY	10012	212-334-2655	334-2654
Alliance Reservations Network 14435 N 7th St Suite 300-B *TF:* 800-892-2108 ■ *Web:* www.reservetravel.com	Phoenix	AZ	85022	602-952-2106	224-9896
American Country Collection of Bed & Breakfast Homes 1353 Union St *TF:* 800-810-4948 ■ *Web:* www.bandbreservations.com	Schenectady	NY	12308	518-370-4948	

Phone | Fax

AmeriRoom Casino & Hotel Reservations
22 Empire Dr Suite 2 ... West Atlantic NJ 08232 609-383-0303 645-1147
TF: 800-888-5825

Anchorage Alaska Bed & Breakfast Assn PO Box 242623 ... Anchorage AK 99524 907-272-5909 277-4034
TF: 888-584-5147 ■ Web: www.anchorage-bnb.com

Annapolis Accommodations 41 Maryland Ave ... Annapolis MD 21401 410-280-0900 263-1703
TF: 800-715-1000 ■ Web: www.stayannapolis.com

Atlantic City Toll-Free Reservations PO Box 665 ... Northfield NJ 08225 609-646-7070 646-8655
TF: 800-833-7070 ■ Web: www.actollfree.com

B & B Agency of Boston 47 Commercial Wharf #3 ... Boston MA 02110 617-720-3540 523-5761
TF: 800-248-9262 ■ Web: www.boston-bnbagency.com

Barclay International Group 6800 Jericho Tpke ... Syosset NY 11791 516-364-0064 364-4468
TF: 800-845-6636 ■ Web: www.barclayweb.com

Bed & Breakfast Accommodations Ltd PO Box 12011 ... Washington DC 20005 202-328-3510 332-3885
TF: 877-893-3233 ■ Web: bedandbreakfastdc.com

Bed & Breakfast Assn of Downtown Toronto
PO Box 190 Stn B ... Toronto ON M5T2W1 416-410-3938 483-8822
Web: www.bnbinfo.com

Bed & Breakfast Assoc Bay Colony Ltd
PO Box 57166 Babson Park Branch ... Boston MA 02457 781-449-5302 455-6745
TF: 888-486-6018 ■ Web: www.bnbboston.com

Bed & Breakfast Atlanta Reservation Services
790 North Ave Suite 202 ... Atlanta GA 30306 404-875-0525 876-6544
TF: 800-967-3224 ■ Web: www.bedandbreakfastatlanta.com

Bed & Breakfast Cape Cod PO Box 1312 ... Orleans MA 02653 508-255-3824 240-0599
TF: 800-541-6226 ■ Web: bedandbreakfastcapecod.com

Bed & Breakfast Directory for San Diego PO Box 3292 ... San Diego CA 92103 800-619-7666 299-6213*
*Fax Area Code: 619 ■ Web: www.sandiegobandb.com

Bed & Breakfast of Hawaii PO Box 449 ... Kapaa HI 96746 808-822-7771 822-2723
TF: 800-733-1632 ■ Web: www.bandb-hawaii.com

Bed & Breakfast Homes of Toronto Assn 287 Humberside Ave ... Toronto ON M6P1L4 416-363-6362
Web: www.bbcanada.com/associations/toronto2

Bed & Breakfast of Philadelphia PO Box 21 ... Devon PA 19333 610-687-3565 995-9524
TF: 800-448-3619 ■ Web: www.bnbphiladelphia.com

Bed & Breakfast Reservations 11A Beach Rd ... Gloucester MA 01930 978-281-9505 281-9426
TF: 800-832-2632 ■ Web: www.bbreserve.com

Bed & Breakfast San Francisco PO Box 420009 ... San Francisco CA 94142 415-899-0060 899-9923
TF: 800-452-8249 ■ Web: www.bbsf.com

Best Canadian Bed & Breakfast Network 1064 Balfour Ave ... Vancouver BC V6H1X1 604-738-7207 732-4998

Branson/Lakes Area Lodging Assn PO Box 430 ... Branson MO 65615 417-332-1400 239-1400
TF: 888-238-6782 ■ Web: www.bransonarealodging.com

Branson's Best Reservations 165 Expressway Ln ... Branson MO 65616 417-339-2204 339-4051
TF: 800-800-2019 ■ Web: www.bransonbest.com

Capital Area Bed & Breakfast Network 4938 Hampden Ln ... Bethesda MD 20814 703-549-3415
TF: 888-549-3415

Capitol Reservations
1730 Rhode Island Ave NW Suite 1210 ... Washington DC 20036 202-452-1270 452-0537
TF: 800-847-4832 ■ Web: www.visitdc.com

Central Reservation Service 200 Lookout Pl Suite 150 ... Maitland FL 32751 407-740-6442 740-8222
TF: 800-555-7555 ■ Web: www.reservation-services.com

Central Reservation Service of New England Inc
300 Terminal C Logan International Airport ... East Boston MA 02128 617-569-3800 561-4840
TF: 800-332-3026

Colonial Williamsburg Reservation Center PO Box 1776 ... Williamsburg VA 23187 757-253-2277 565-8797
TF: 800-447-8679 ■ Web: www.history.org

Colorado Resort Services 2955 Village Dr ... Steamboat Springs CO 80487 970-879-7654 879-3027
TF: 800-525-7654 ■ Web: www.crs-steamboat.com

DiscountHotels.com 1200 Lake Hearn Dr Suite 300 ... Atlanta GA 30319 404-256-6620
TF Cust Svc: 800-291-9960 ■ Web: www.discounthotels.com

Equity Corporate Housing 100 Northwoods Village Dr ... Casy NC 27513 919-468-5611 468-5499
TF: 800-533-2370 ■ Web: www.equitycorporatehousing.com

Eugene Area Bed & Breakfast Assn 1006 Taylor St ... Eugene OR 97402 541-302-3014
Web: www.eugene-lodging.com

Florida Hotels & Discount Guide
World Choice Travel 11300 US 1 Suite 300 ... North Palm Beach FL 33408 561-227-2181 845-5466
TF: 800-670-5445

Florida SunBreak 90 Alton Rd Suite 16 ... Miami Beach FL 33139 305-532-1516 532-0564
TF: 800-786-2732 ■ Web: www.floridasunbreak.com

Gites et Auberges du Passant
4545 Pierre-De Coubertin Ave CP 1000 Succursale M ... Montreal QC H1V3R2 514-252-3138 252-3173
Web: www.giteetaubergedupassant.com

Greater Miami & the Beaches Hotel Assn
407 Lincoln Rd Suite 10G ... Miami Beach FL 33139 305-531-3553 531-8954
TF: 800-531-3553 ■ Web: www.gmbha.org

Greater New Orleans Hotel & Lodging Assn
203 Carondelet St Suite 415 ... New Orleans LA 70130 504-525-2264 525-9327
Web: www.gnohla.com

Greek Hotel & Cruise Reservation Center
17280 Newhope St Suite 18 ... Fountain Valley CA 92708 714-429-7962 641-0303
TF: 800-736-5717 ■ Web: www.greekhotels.com

Greenville Area Central Reservations PO Box 10527 ... Greenville SC 29603 864-233-0461 421-0005
TF: 800-351-7180

Gulf Coast Hotel Reservations PO Box 116 ... Biloxi MS 39533 228-388-6117 388-8117
TF: 888-388-1006

Hawaii's Best Bed & Breakfasts PO Box 485 ... Laupahoehoe HI 96764 808-263-3100
TF: 800-262-9912 ■ Web: www.bestbnb.com

Hilton Head Vacation Rentals
430 William Hilton Pkwy Suite 504 ... Hilton Head Island SC 29926 843-689-3010 689-3011
TF: 800-732-7671 ■ Web: www.800beachme.com

Historic Charleston Bed & Breakfast Reservations Service
57 Broad St ... Charleston SC 29401 843-722-6606 722-9589
TF: 800-743-3583 ■ Web: historiccharlestonbedandbreakfast.com

Hot Rooms 1 E Erie St Suite 225 ... Chicago IL 60611 773-468-7666 649-0559*
*Fax Area Code: 312 ■ TF: 800-468-3500 ■ Web: www.hotrooms.com

Hotel Locators.com 919 Garnet Ave Suite 216 ... San Diego CA 92109 800-576-0003 581-1730*
*Fax Area Code: 858 ■ Web: www.hotellocators.com

HotelNetDiscount.com 3070 Windward Plaza Suite F-302 ... Alpharetta GA 30005 770-664-1316 664-1507
Web: www.hotelnetdiscount.com

Hotels.com 10440 N Central Expy Suite 800 ... Dallas TX 75231 214-361-7311
TF Sales: 800-964-6835 ■ Web: www.hotels.com

Jackson Hole Central Reservations 140 E Broadway Suite 24 ... Jackson WY 83001 307-733-4005 733-1286
TF: 800-443-6931 ■ Web: www.jacksonholewy.com

Jackson Hole Resort Reservations LLC PO Box 12739 ... Jackson WY 83002 307-733-6331 733-4728
TF: 800-329-9205 ■ Web: www.jacksonholeres.com

Key West Key 726 Passover Ln ... Key West FL 33040 305-294-4357 294-2974
TF: 800-881-7321 ■ Web: www.keywestkey.com

Know Before You Go Reservations
4720 W Irlo Bronson Memorial Hwy ... Kissimmee FL 34746 407-352-9813 396-8404
TF: 800-749-1993 ■ Web: www.knowbeforeugo.com

Leading Hotels of the World 99 Park Ave ... New York NY 10016 212-515-5600 515-5899
TF: 800-223-6800 ■ Web: www.lhw.com

Luxe Worldwide Hotels 11461 Sunset Blvd ... Los Angeles CA 90049 310-440-3090 440-0821
TF: 866-589-3411 ■ Web: www.luxehotels.com

Martha's Vineyard & Nantucket Reservations
73 Lagoon Pond Rd ... Vineyard Haven MA 02568 508-693-7200 693-1878
TF: 800-649-5671 ■ Web: www.mvreservations.com

Mi Casa Su Casa PO Box 950 ... Tempe AZ 85280 480-990-0682 990-3390
TF: 800-456-0682 ■ Web: www.azres.com

Myrtle Beach Reservation Service
1551 21st Ave N Suite 20 ... Myrtle Beach SC 29577 800-626-7477 448-8143*
*Fax Area Code: 843 ■ TF: 800-626-7477 ■ Web: www.mbhospitality.org

Nantucket Accommodations 4 Dennis Dr PO Box 217 ... Nantucket MA 02554 508-228-9559 325-7009
Web: www.nantucketaccommodation.com

National Reservation Bureau 3100 W Sahara Ave Suite 207 ... Las Vegas NV 89109 702-794-2820 794-3515
TF: 800-831-2754 ■ Web: www.nrbinc.com

New Mexico Central Reservations
800 20th St NW Suite B ... Albuquerque NM 87104 505-766-9770 247-8200
TF: 800-466-7829 ■ Web: www.nmtravel.com

New Orleans Accommodations Bed & Breakfast Service
828 Rue Royal Suite 259 ... New Orleans LA 70116 504-561-0447
TF: 888-240-0070 ■ Web: www.neworleansbandb.com

New Otani North America Reservation Center
120 S Los Angeles St ... Los Angeles CA 90012 213-629-1200 473-1416
TF: 800-421-8795

Ocean City Hotel-Motel-Restaurant Assn PO Box 340 ... Ocean City MD 21843 410-289-6733 289-5645
TF: 800-626-2326 ■ Web: www.ocvisitor.com/index.asp

Pacific Reservation Service 2520 Westlake Ave N ... Seattle WA 98109 206-439-7677 431-0932
TF: 800-684-2932 ■ Web: www.seattlebedandbreakfast.com

Private Lodging Service PO Box 18557 ... Cleveland OH 44118 216-291-1209

Quikbook 381 Park Ave S 3rd Fl ... New York NY 10016 212-779-7666 779-6120
TF: 800-789-9887 ■ Web: www.quikbook.com

Reservations USA 2713 North Pkwy ... Pigeon Forge TN 37863 865-453-6618 453-7484
TF: 800-251-4444 ■ Web: www.lodging4u.com

Resort 2 Me 2600 Garden Rd Suite 111 ... Monterey CA 93940 831-642-6622 642-6641
TF: 800-757-5646 ■ Web: www.resort2me.com

RSVP Martha's Vineyard PO Box 2042 ... Oak Bluffs MA 02557 508-693-9371 696-0431
TF: 866-778-7689 ■ Web: www.rsvpmarthasvineyard.com

San Diego Concierge 4379 30th St Suite 4 ... San Diego CA 92104 619-280-4121 280-4119
TF: 800-979-9091 ■ Web: www.sandiegoconcierge.com

San Diego Hotel Collection 1550 Hotel Cir N Suite 110 ... San Diego CA 92108 619-881-4700 881-4701
Web: www.comforthotelssandiego.com/

San Francisco Reservations 360 22nd St Suite 300 ... Oakland CA 94612 510-628-4444 628-9025
TF: 800-677-1550 ■ Web: www.hotelres.com

Scottsdale Resort Accommodations
7339 E Evans Rd Suite 100 ... Scottsdale AZ 85260 480-515-2300 505-7878
TF: 888-868-4378 ■ Web: www.scottsdale-resorts.com

Seattle Super Saver 701 Pike St Suite 800 ... Seattle WA 98101 206-461-5800 461-5855
TF: 800-535-7071 ■ Web: www.seeseattle.org/reservations

Southern Arizona Lodging & Resort Assn
3305 N Swan Rd Suite 109 ... Tucson AZ 85712 520-299-6787 299-6431
Web: www.salara.org

Stay Aspen Snowmass 425 Rio Grande Pl ... Aspen CO 81611 970-925-9000 925-9008
TF: 800-670-0792 ■ Web: www.stayaspensnowmass.com

Travel Planners Inc 381 Park Ave S ... New York NY 10016 212-532-1660 532-1556
TF: 800-221-3531 ■ Web: www.tphousing.com

Travelweb.com 2777 Stemmons Fwy Suite 675 ... Dallas TX 75207 800-818-0033 653-0023*
*Fax Area Code: 866 ■ Web: www.travelweb.com

Travelworm Inc 6280 S Valley View Blvd Suite 502 ... Las Vegas NV 89118 702-407-8000 407-8090
TF: 800-798-4955 ■ Web: www.travelworm.com

Turbotrip.com 4124 S McCann Ct ... Springfield MO 65804 800-473-7829 864-8811*
*Fax Area Code: 417 ■ Web: www.turbotrip.com

USA Hotel Guide 11300 Federal Hwy Suite 3 ... North Palm Beach FL 33408 561-227-2181 882-3954
TF: 888-729-7705 ■ Web: www.usahotelguide.com

USA Hotels 860 Wyckoff Ave ... Mahwah NJ 07430 201-847-9000 847-2170
TF: 800-343-8861 ■ Web: www.1800usahotels.com

Utell 8350 N Central Expy Suite 1900 ... Dallas TX 75206 214-234-4000 234-4040
TF: 800-223-6510 ■ Web: www.utell.com

Vacation Co 42 New Orleans Rd ... Hilton Head Island SC 29928 843-686-6100 686-3255
TF: 800-845-7018 ■ Web: www.vacationcompany.com

Washington DC Accommodations
2201 Wisconsin Ave NW Suite C-120 ... Washington DC 20007 202-289-2220 338-1365
TF: 800-554-2220 ■ Web: www.dcaccommodations.com

Winter Park Resort Travel Services PO Box 36 ... Winter Park CO 80482 970-726-5587 726-5993
TF: 800-525-3538 ■ Web: www.skiwinterpark.com

Worldhotels 152 W 57th St 33rd Fl ... New York NY 10019 212-956-0200 956-2555
Web: www.worldhotels.com

WorldRes USA DBA Web Reservations International
999 Baker Way Suite 290 ... San Mateo CA 94404 650-372-1700 372-1701
Web: www.worldres.com

Xanterra South Rim LLC PO Box 699 ... Grand Canyon AZ 86023 928-638-2631 638-9247*
*Fax: Mail Rm ■ TF: 888-297-2757 ■ Web: www.grandcanyonlodges.com

380 HOTELS - CONFERENCE CENTER

Phone | Fax

Aberdeen Woods Conference Center 201 Aberdeen Pkwy ... Peachtree City GA 30269 770-487-2666 487-1063
TF: 800-285-6338 ■ Web: www.awcc.com

ACE Conference Center & Country Club 800 Ridge Pike ... Lafayette Hill PA 19444 610-825-8000 940-4343
TF: 800-523-3000 ■ Web: www.aceconferencecenter.com

Airlie Conference Center 6809 Airlie Rd ... Warrenton VA 20187 540-347-1300 341-3207
TF: 800-288-9573 ■ Web: www.airlie.com

Allen James L Center 2169 Campus Dr ... Evanston IL 60208 847-864-9270 491-4323

Ashman Court Marriott Conference Hotel 111 W Main St ... Midland MI 48642 989-839-0500 837-6000
TF: 877-645-3643 ■ Web: www.marriott.com/property/propertypage/MBSAC

Aspen Wye River Conference Center 201 Wye Woods Way ... Queenstown MD 21658 410-827-7400 827-9295
Web: marriott.com/property/propertypage/bwiwy

Auburn University Hotel & Dixon Conference Center
241 S College St ... Auburn AL 36830 334-821-8200 826-8746
TF: 800-228-2876 ■ Web: www.auhcc.com

Babson Executive Conference Center
1 Woodland Hill Dr Babson Pk ... Wellesley MA 02457 781-239-4000 239-4026
Web: www.aramarkharrisonlodging.com/properties

Banff Centre 107 Tunnel Mountain Dr ... Banff AB T1L1H5 403-762-6100 762-6444
TF: 800-884-7574 ■ Web: www.banffcentre.ca

Biltmore Hotel & Conference Center of the Americas
1200 Anastasia Ave ... Coral Gables FL 33134 305-445-1926 913-3159
TF: 800-727-1926 ■ Web: www.biltmorehotel.com

Burkshire Marriott Conference Hotel 10 W Burke Ave ... Towson MD 21204 410-324-8100 616-3749
TF: 800-435-5986 ■ Web: www.marriott.com/property/propertypage/bwibu

Chaminade 1 Chaminade Ln ... Santa Cruz CA 95065 831-475-5600 476-4798
TF: 800-283-6569 ■ Web: www.chaminade.com

Chateau Elan Resort & Conference Center
100 rue Charlemagne ... Braselton GA 30517 678-425-0900 425-6000
TF: 800-233-9463 ■ Web: www.chateauelan.com

Chattanoogan The 1201 S Broad St ... Chattanooga TN 37402 423-756-3400 756-3404
TF: 877-756-1684 ■ Web: www.chattanooganhotel.com

Chauncey Conference Center 660 Rosedale Rd PO Box 6652 ... Princeton NJ 08541 609-921-3600 683-4958
Web: www.aramarkharrisonlodging.com/properties/chauncey

				Phone	Fax
Cheyenne Mountain Conference Resort					
3225 Broadmoor Valley Rd	Colorado Springs	CO	80906	719-538-4000	576-4186
TF: 800-428-8886 ■ *Web:* www.cheyennemountain.com					
Clarion Hotel & Conference Center Antietam Creek					
901 Dual Hwy.	Hagerstown	MD	21740	301-733-5100	733-9192
TF: 888-528-6738 ■ *Web:* www.clarionantietam.com					
Conference Center at Marlboro 280 Locke Dr.	Marlborough	MA	01752	508-263-5500	624-0130
Web: www.aramarkharrisonlodging.com/properties/marlborough					
Conference Center at NorthPointe 9243 Columbus Pike.	Lewis Center	OH	43035	614-880-4300	880-4167
TF: 866-233-9393 ■ *Web:* www.conferencecenteratnorthpointe.com					
Cook Hotel & Conference Center 3848 W Lakeshore Dr.	Baton Rouge	LA	70808	225-383-2665	383-4200
TF: 866-610-2665 ■ *Web:* www.thecookhotel.com					
Country Springs Hotel & Conference Center 2810 Golf Rd	Pewaukee	WI	53072	262-547-0201	547-0207
TF: 800-247-6640 ■ *Web:* www.countryspringshotel.com					
Crystal Mountain Resort 12500 Crystal Mountain Dr.	Thompsonville	MI	49683	231-378-2000	378-2998
TF: 800-968-7686 ■ *Web:* www.crystalmountain.com					
Delta Sherbrooke Hotel & Conference Centre					
2685 King St W	Sherbrooke	QC	J1L1C1	819-822-1989	822-8990
TF: 800-268-1133 ■ *Web:* www.deltahotels.com					
Dodgertown Sports & Conference Center 3901 26th St	Vero Beach	FL	32960	772-569-4900	562-5199
TF: 866-656-4900 ■ *Web:* www.dodgertownverobeach.com					
Dolce Hayes Mansion 200 Edenvale Ave	San Jose	CA	95136	408-226-3200	362-2377
TF: 800-420-3200 ■ *Web:* www.hayesmansion.com					
Doral Arrowwood Conference Resort 975 Anderson Hill Rd	Rye Brook	NY	10573	914-939-5500	323-5500
TF: 800-223-6725 ■ *Web:* www.arrowwood.com					
Doubletree Hotel & Executive Meeting Center Somerset					
200 Atrium Dr	Somerset	NJ	08873	732-469-2600	469-4617
TF: 800-222-8733 ■ *Web:* www.doubletreesomerset.com					
Dover Downs Hotel & Conference Center 1131 N DuPont Hwy	Dover	DE	19901	302-674-4600	857-2198
TF: 800-711-5882 ■ *Web:* www.doverdowns.com					
Edith Macy Conference Center 550 Chappaqua Rd.	Briarcliff Manor	NY	10510	914-945-8000	945-8009
TF: 800-442-6229 ■ *Web:* www.edithmacy.com					
Emory Conference Center Hotel 1615 Clifton Rd.	Atlanta	GA	30329	404-712-6000	712-6025
TF: 800-933-6679 ■ *Web:* www.emoryconferencecenter.com					
Evergreen Marriott Conference Resort					
4021 Lakeview Dr	Stone Mountain	GA	30083	770-879-9900	465-3264
TF: 800-228-9290 ■ *Web:* www.evergreenresort.com					
Fogelman Executive Conference Center					
330 Innovation Dr University of Memphis	Memphis	TN	38152	901-678-3700	678-5329
Web: www.wilsonhotels.com/properties/fec.html					
Founders Inn 5641 Indian River Rd	Virginia Beach	VA	23464	757-424-5511	366-0613
TF: 800-926-4466 ■ *Web:* www.foundersinn.com					
Four Points by Sheraton Norwood Hotel & Conference Center					
1125 Boston-Providence Tpke (Rt 1)	Norwood	MA	02062	781-769-7900	551-3552
Web: www.fourpointsnorwood.com					
Gaylord Opryland 2800 Opryland Dr	Nashville	TN	37214	615-889-1000	871-7741
Web: www.gaylordhotels.com					
Gaylord Palms Resort & Convention Center					
6000 W Osceola Pkwy	Kissimmee	FL	34746	407-586-0000	586-2199
Web: www.gaylordpalms.com					
Georgetown University Conference Center					
3800 Reservoir Rd NW	Washington	DC	20057	202-687-3200	687-3297
TF: 800-228-9290 ■ *Web:* marriott.com/property/propertyPage/WASGU					
Glen Cove Mansion Hotel & Conference Center					
200 Dosoris Ln	Glen Cove	NY	11542	516-671-6400	705-0147
Web: www.glencovemansion.com					
Grandover Resort & Conference Center 1000 Club Rd.	Greensboro	NC	27407	336-294-1800	856-9991
TF: 800-472-6301 ■ *Web:* www.grandoverresort.com					
Gurney's Inn Resort & Spa 290 Old Montauk Hwy	Montauk	NY	11954	631-668-2345	668-3576
TF: 800-848-7639 ■ *Web:* www.gurneys-inn.com					
Hamilton Park Hotel & Conference Center 175 Park Ave.	Florham Park	NJ	07932	973-377-2424	377-9560
TF: 800-321-6000 ■ *Web:* www.hamiltonparkhotel.com					
Heritage Hotel 522 Heritage Rd	Southbury	CT	06488	203-264-8200	264-5035
TF: 800-932-3466 ■ *Web:* www.heritagesouthbury.com					
Hickory Ridge Marriott Conference Hotel 1195 Summerhill Dr	Lisle	IL	60532	630-971-5000	971-6956
TF: 800-334-0344 ■ *Web:* www.marriott.com/property/propertypage/CHIHR					
Hidden Valley Resort & Conference Center					
1 Craighead Dr.	Hidden Valley	PA	15502	814-443-8000	443-1907
TF: 800-458-0175 ■ *Web:* www.hiddenvalleyresort.com					
Hilton Scranton & Conference Center 100 Adams Ave.	Scranton	PA	18503	570-343-3000	343-8415
Hilton Seattle Airport & Conference Center					
17620 Pacific Hwy S	Seattle	WA	98188	206-244-4800	248-4499
TF: 800-445-8667 ■ *Web:* www.hilton.com					
Hilton University of Florida Conference Center					
1714 SW 34th St.	Gainesville	FL	32607	352-371-3600	371-0306
TF: 800-774-1500 ■ *Web:* www.ufhotel.com					
Hotel Roanoke & Conference Center 110 Shenandoah Ave	Roanoke	VA	24016	540-985-5900	853-8264
TF: 866-594-4722 ■ *Web:* www.hotelroanoke.com					
IBM Palisades Conference Center 334 Rt 9 W	Palisades	NY	10964	845-732-6000	732-6175
TF: 800-426-0889 ■ *Web:* ibmpalisades.dolce.com					
Inn at Aspen 38750 Hwy 82	Aspen	CO	81611	970-925-1500	925-9037
TF: 800-952-1515					
Inn at Virginia Tech and Skelton Conference Center					
901 Prices Fork Rd MS 0104	Blacksburg	VA	24061	540-231-8000	231-0146
TF: 877-200-3360 ■ *Web:* www.innatvirginiatech.com					
InterContinental Hotel Cleveland 9801 Carnegie Ave	Cleveland	OH	44106	216-707-4100	707-4190
TF: 877-707-8999 ■ *Web:* www.cleveland-conferencecenter.intercontinental.com					
James L Allen Center 2169 Campus Dr	Evanston	IL	60208	847-864-9270	491-4323
John Hancock Hotel & Conference Center 40 Trinity Pl.	Boston	MA	02116	617-933-7700	933-7709
Web: www.jhcenter.com					
JR's Executive Inn Riverfront 1 Executive Blvd	Paducah	KY	42001	270-443-8000	444-5317
TF: 800-866-3636 ■ *Web:* www.jrsexecutiveinn.com					
Kingbridge Centre 12750 Jane St.	King City	ON	L7B1A3	905-833-3086	833-3075
TF: 800-827-7221 ■ *Web:* www.kingbridgecentre.com					
Kingsmill Resort & Spa 1010 Kingsmill Rd	Williamsburg	VA	23185	757-253-1703	253-8246
TF: 800-832-5665 ■ *Web:* www.kingsmill.com					
Lafayette Yard Marriott Conference Hotel 1 W Lafayette St	Trenton	NJ	08608	609-421-4000	421-4002
TF: 800-228-9290					
Lakeview Scanticon Resort & Conference Center					
1 Lakeview Dr	Morgantown	WV	26508	304-594-1111	594-9472
TF: 800-624-8300 ■ *Web:* www.lakeviewresort.com					
Lakeway Inn & Resort 101 Lakeway Dr	Austin	TX	78734	512-261-6600	261-7311
TF: 800-525-3929 ■ *Web:* lakeway.dolce.com					
Lansdowne Resort 44050 Woodridge Pkwy	Leesburg	VA	20176	703-729-8400	729-4096
TF: 800-541-4801 ■ *Web:* www.lansdowneresort.com					
Liberty Mountain Resort & Conference Center					
78 Country Club Trail	Carroll Valley	PA	17320	717-642-8282	742-6534
Web: www.libertymountainresort.com					
Lodge & Spa at Breckenridge 112 Overlook Dr.	Breckenridge	CO	80424	970-453-9300	453-0625
TF: 800-736-1607 ■ *Web:* www.thelodgeatbreck.com					
Macy Edith Conference Center 550 Chappaqua Rd.	Briarcliff Manor	NY	10510	914-945-8000	945-8009
TF: 800-442-6229 ■ *Web:* www.edithmacy.com					
Marietta Conference Center & Resort 500 Powder Springs St	Marietta	GA	30064	770-427-2500	819-3224*
**Fax Area Code:* 678 ■ *TF:* 888-685-2500 ■ *Web:* www.mariettaresort.com					
Marriott Conference Centers 1 Marriott Dr	Washington	DC	20058	301-380-3000	453-0309*
**Fax Area Code:* 800 ■ *Web:* www.marriott.com					
Marriott Kingsgate Conference Hotel at University of Cincinnati 151 Goodman St	Cincinnati	OH	45219	513-487-3800	487-3810
TF: 800-228-9290 ■ *Web:* www.marriott.com/cvgkg					
Marriott MeadowView Conference Resort & Convention Center					
1901 Meadowview Pkwy	Kingsport	TN	37660	423-578-6600	578-6630
TF: 800-820-5055 ■ *Web:* www.marriott.com/vanityredirect/TRICC/					
Marriott Montgomery Prattville at Capitol Hill					
2500 Legends Cir.	Prattville	AL	36066	334-290-1235	290-2222
TF: 888-250-3767 ■ *Web:* www.marriottcapitolhill.com					
Marriott Westfields Resort & Conference Center					
14750 Conference Center Dr	Chantilly	VA	20151	703-818-0300	818-3655
TF: 800-635-5666 ■ *Web:* www.marriotthotels.com/IADWF					
Marten House Hotel & Lilly Conference Center					
1801 W 86th St	Indianapolis	IN	46260	317-872-4111	415-5245
TF: 800-736-5634 ■ *Web:* www.martenhouse.com					
Meadowood Napa Valley 900 Meadowood Ln	Saint Helena	CA	94574	707-963-3646	963-3532
TF: 800-458-8080 ■ *Web:* www.meadowood.com					
Millennium Broadway Hotel New York 145 W 44th St	New York	NY	10036	212-768-4400	768-0847
TF: 800-622-5569 ■ *Web:* www.millenniumhotels.com					
National Center for Employee Development					
2801 E State Hwy 9	Norman	OK	73071	405-447-9100	366-1865
TF: 866-278-4434 ■ *Web:* www.nced.com					
NAV Canada Training & Conference Center 1950 Montreal Rd	Cornwall	ON	K6H6L2	613-936-5000	936-5046
TF: 877-832-6416 ■ *Web:* www.navcanada.ca					
New England Center					
15 Strafford Ave University of New Hampshire	Durham	NH	03824	603-862-2801	862-0692
TF: 800-590-4334 ■ *Web:* www.newenglandcenter.com					
North Maple Inn at Basking Ridge 300 N Maple Ave	Basking Ridge	NJ	07920	908-953-3000	953-3100
TF: 800-288-2687 ■ *Web:* www.northmapleinn.com					
Northland Inn & Executive Conference Center					
7025 Northland Dr	Minneapolis	MN	55428	763-536-8300	535-8221
TF: 800-441-6422 ■ *Web:* www.northlandinn.com					
Oak Brook Hills Resort & Conference Center					
3500 Midwest Rd.	Oak Brook	IL	60523	630-850-5555	850-5569
TF: 800-445-3315 ■ *Web:* www.marriott.com/property/propertypage/CHIMC					
Oak Ridge Conference Center 1 Oak Ridge Dr	Chaska	MN	55318	952-368-3100	368-1488
TF Sales: 800-737-9588 ■ *Web:* www.oakridgeconference.com					
Oasis Inn & Convention Center 2550 N Glenstone Ave	Springfield	MO	65803	417-866-5253	866-5292
TF: 888-532-4338 ■ *Web:* www.springfieldoasis.com					
Paul J Rizzo Conference Center 150 DuBose House Ln	Chapel Hill	NC	27517	919-913-2098	913-2099
Web: www.aramarkharrisonlodging.com/properties/rizzo					
Penn Stater Conference Center Hotel 215 Innovation Blvd	State College	PA	16803	814-863-5000	863-5002
TF: 800-233-7505 ■ *Web:* www2.pshs.psu.edu					
Pinehurst Co - The Club Corp 1 Carolina Vista	Pinehurst	NC	28374	910-235-8783	235-8705
R David Thomas Executive Conference Center 1 Science Dr	Durham	NC	27708	919-660-6400	660-3607
Web: aramarkharrisonlodging.mpoint.com					
Renaissance Portsmouth Hotel & Waterfront Conference Center 425 Water St	Portsmouth	VA	23704	757-673-3000	673-3030
TF: 888-839-1775 ■ *Web:* www.renaissancehotel.com/orfpt					
Renaissance Tulsa Hotel & Convention Center					
6808 S 107th East Ave	Tulsa	OK	74133	918-307-2600	307-2907
Web: www.renaissancehotel.com/tulbr					
Resort at Squaw Creek 400 Squaw Creek Rd	Olympic Valley	CA	96146	530-583-6300	581-6632
TF: 800-327-3353 ■ *Web:* www.squawcreek.com					
San Luis Resort Spa & Conference Center					
5222 Seawall Blvd	Galveston Island	TX	77551	409-744-1500	744-8452
TF: 800-445-0090 ■ *Web:* www.sanluisresort.com					
San Ramon Valley Conference Center					
3301 Crow Canyon Rd.	San Ramon	CA	94583	925-866-7500	866-7378
TF: 800-521-4335 ■ *Web:* www.sanramonvalleyconferencecenter.com					
Saratoga Hotel & Conference Center 534 Broadway.	Saratoga Springs	NY	12866	518-584-4000	584-7430
TF: 866-773-7070 ■ *Web:* www.thesaratogahotel.com					
Scottsdale Resort & Conference Center					
7700 E McCormick Pkwy	Scottsdale	AZ	85258	480-991-9000	596-7428
TF: 800-528-0293 ■ *Web:* www.scottsdale-resort.com					
Sheraton Meadowlands Hotel & Conference Center					
2 Meadowlands Plaza	East Rutherford	NJ	07073	201-896-0500	896-9696
TF: 800-325-3535 ■ *Web:* www.starwood.com/sheraton					
Sheraton New York Hotel & Towers 811 7th Ave	New York	NY	10019	212-581-1000	262-4410
TF: 800-223-6550 ■ *Web:* www.starwood.com/sheraton					
Skamania Lodge 1131 SW Skamania Lodge Way	Stevenson	WA	98648	509-427-7700	427-2547
TF: 800-221-7117 ■ *Web:* www.skamania.com					
Snowbird Ski & Summer Resort Hwy 210 PO Box 929000	Snowbird	UT	84092	801-742-2222	947-8227
TF: 800-453-3000 ■ *Web:* www.snowbird.com					
Snowmass Conference Center 76 Elbert Ln.	Snowmass Village	CO	81615	970-923-2000	923-5466
TF: 800-598-2006					
Spencer Conference Centre 551 Windermere Rd	London	ON	N5X2T1	519-679-4546	645-0733
TF: 800-983-6523 ■ *Web:* spencerconferencecentre.dolce.com					
Stoweflake Mountain Resort & Spa					
1746 Mountain Rd PO Box 369.	Stowe	VT	05672	802-253-7355	253-6858
TF: 800-253-2232 ■ *Web:* www.stoweflake.com					
Talaris Conference Center 4000 NE 41st St	Seattle	WA	98105	206-268-7000	268-7001
Web: www.talarisconferencecenter.com					
Tempe Mission Palms Hotel & Conference Center 60 E 5th St.	Tempe	AZ	85281	480-894-1400	968-7677
TF: 800-547-8705 ■ *Web:* www.missionpalms.com					
Thomas R David Executive Conference Center 1 Science Dr	Durham	NC	27708	919-660-6400	660-3607
Web: aramarkharrisonlodging.mpoint.com					
University Inn & Conference Center 2402 N Forest Rd.	Amherst	NY	14226	716-636-7500	636-8296
TF: 800-537-8483 ■ *Web:* www.universityinn.com					
University of Maryland University College Marriott Conference Center Hotel 3501 University Blvd E.	Adelphi	MD	20783	301-985-7303	985-7517
TF: 800-727-8622 ■ *Web:* www.conferencecenters.com/wasum					
University Place Conference Center & Hotel-Indianapolis					
850 W Michigan St	Indianapolis	IN	46202	317-269-9000	231-5168
TF: 800-627-2700 ■ *Web:* www.universityplace.iupui.edu					
University Plaza Hotel & Convention Center					
333 John Q Hammons Pkwy	Springfield	MO	65806	417-864-7333	831-5893
TF: 800-465-4329 ■ *Web:* www.upspringfield.com					
Valley Forge Scanticon Hotel & Conference Center					
1160 1st Ave	King of Prussia	PA	19406	610-265-1500	354-8100
TF: 800-333-3333 ■ *Web:* www.scanticonvalleyforge.com					
Whispering Woods Hotel & Conference Center					
11200 E Goodman Rd	Olive Branch	MS	38654	662-895-2941	895-1590
Web: www.wwconferencecenter.com					
White Oaks Conference Resort & Spa					
253 Taylor Rd	Niagara-on-the-Lake	ON	L0S1J0	905-688-2550	688-2220
TF: 800-263-5766 ■ *Web:* www.whiteoaksresort.com					
Woodlands Resort & Conference Center					
2301 N Millbend Dr	The Woodlands	TX	77380	281-367-1100	364-6275
TF: 800-433-2624 ■ *Web:* www.woodlandsresort.com					
Wyndham Peachtree Conference Center					
2443 Hwy 54 W	Peachtree City	GA	30269	770-487-2000	487-4428
TF: 800-996-3426 ■ *Web:* www.wyndham.com/hotels/ATLPT/main.wnt					

381 HOTELS - FREQUENT STAY PROGRAMS

Phone *Fax*

Adam's Mark Hotels Gold Mark Rewards 11330 Olive Blvd ...... Saint Louis MO 63141 314-567-9000 567-5324
TF: 800-444-2326 ■ *Web:* www.adamsmark.com

AmericInn Inn-Pressive Club 250 Lake Dr E .... Chanhassen MN 55317 952-294-5000 294-5001
Web: www.americinn.com/innpressive_club.aspx

Baymont Guest Ovations Program 100 E Wisconsin Ave......... Milwaukee WI 53202 414-905-2000 905-2957
TF: 866-464-2321 ■ *Web:* www.baymontinns.com

Best Traveler Program 13 Corporate Sq Suite 250 .... Atlanta GA 30329 404-321-4045 235-7465
TF: 800-237-8466 ■ *Web:* www.americasbestinns.com

Best Western Gold Crown Club International
20400 N 29th Ave .... Phoenix AZ 85027 800-237-8483 780-6988*
**Fax Area Code:* 623 ■ *Web:* www.goldcrownclub.com

CHIP Hospitality Traveller's Reward Program
1600-1030 W Georgia St................................ Vancouver BC V6E2Y3 604-646-2447 689-8167
TF: 800-431-0070 ■ *Web:* www.chiphospitality.com

Choice Privileges Reward Program 2697 US Hwy 50....... Grand Junction CO 81503 888-770-6800 257-1062*
**Fax Area Code:* 970 ■ *TF Cust Svc:* 800-521-2121 ■ *Web:* www.choiceprivileges.com

ClubHouse Rewards Program 3211 W Sencore Dr............. Sioux Falls SD 57107 605-334-2371 334-8480
Web: www.clubhouseinn.com

Concorde Hotels International Prestige Card
1 Penn Plaza Suite 2127 .... New York NY 10119 212-935-1045 752-8916
TF: 800-888-4747 ■ *Web:* www.concorde-hotels.com

Country Hearth Inn Country Club
4243 Don Woody Club Dr Suite 200.......................... Atlanta GA 30350 770-393-2662
TF: 888-635-2582 ■ *Web:* www.countryhearth.com/countryclub

Delta Hotels Privilege Program 100 Wellington St Suite 1200...... Toronto ON M5K1J3 416-874-2000 874-2001
TF: 888-321-3358 ■ *Web:* www.deltahotels.com/privilege

Drury Inns Gold Key Club PO Box 910.................. Cape Girardeau MO 63702 800-325-0581 334-6440*
**Fax Area Code:* 573 ■ *Web:* www.drurygoldkey.com

Exel Inns Insider's Program 4706 E Washington Ave .... Madison WI 53704 608-241-5271 241-3224
TF: 800-367-3935 ■ *Web:* www.exelinns.com/promotions.htm

Fairmont President's Club 650 California St 12th Fl......... San Francisco CA 94108 415-772-7800 772-7805
TF: 800-663-7575 ■ *Web:* www.fpcnews.com

Gold Points Reward Network PO Box 59159................. Minneapolis MN 55459 763-212-6900 212-5747
TF: 800-508-9000 ■ *Web:* www.goldpoints.com

GuestAwards Program 201 W North River Dr Suite 100 .... Spokane WA 99201 800-325-4000 459-6015*
**Fax Area Code:* 509 ■ *Web:* www.guestawards.com

Hilton HHonors Frequent Stay Program 2050 Chennault Dr .... Carrollton TX 75006 800-548-8690 788-1818*
**Fax Area Code:* 972 ■ *TF:* 800-548-8690 ■ *Web:* www.hiltonhhonors.com

Homestead Studio Suites Hotels SuiteOffers Program
100 Dunbar St .... Spartanburg SC 29306 864-573-1600 980-2311*
**Fax Area Code:* 770 ■ *Web:* www.homesteadhotels.com

Hospitality International INNcentive Card Program
1726 Montreal Cir .... Tucker GA 30084 800-247-4677 270-1077*
**Fax Area Code:* 770 ■ *Web:* www.bookroomsnow.com/inncentive.asp

Hyatt Gold Passport Program PO Box 27089........................ Omaha NE 68127 800-544-9288 593-9449*
**Fax Area Code:* 402 ■ *Web:* www.goldpassport.com

La Quinta Returns Club PO Box 2636....................... San Antonio TX 78299 800-642-4258 616-7616*
**Fax Area Code:* 210 ■ *Web:* www.lq.com/lq/returns

Leaders Club Services
Leading Hotels of the World 99 Park Ave.................. New York NY 10016 212-515-5600 515-5770
TF Resv: 800-223-6800 ■ *Web:* www.lhw.com/leaders_club

Lees Elite Club 130 N State St........................... North Vernon IN 47265 812-346-5072 346-7521
TF: 800-733-5337 ■ *Web:* www.leesinn.com/benefits.htm

Loews First Guest Recognition Program 2 2nd St Station Plaza......... Rye NY 10580 800-563-9712 563-9714
Web: www.loews-first.com/Loewsfirst.asp

Marriott Hotels Rewards Program 310 Bearcat Dr .... Salt Lake City UT 84115 800-249-0800 468-4033*
**Fax Area Code:* 801 ■ *TF Sales:* 800-450-4442 ■ *Web:* marriott.com/rewards

Masters Inn Preferred Guest Program PO Box 13069............ Savannah GA 31416 912-352-4493 352-0314
TF Resv: 800-633-3434 ■ *Web:* www.mastersinn.com/incentives.shtml

MicroPass Rewards Program 900 Skyline Dr Suite 100 .... Marion IL 62959 888-222-2142 998-2347*
**Fax Area Code:* 618 ■ *TF:* 888-222-2142 ■ *Web:* www.micro-pass.com

Omni Hotels Select Guest Program 11819 Miami St 3rd Fl.......... Omaha NE 68164 800-367-6664
TF Cust Svc: 877-440-6664 ■ *Web:* www.omnihotels.com/SelectGuestProgram.aspx

Prince Preferred Guest Program 100 Holomoana St............ Honolulu HI 96815 800-774-6234 943-4158*
**Fax Area Code:* 808 ■ *Web:* www.princepreferred.com

Priority Club Rewards PO Box 30320.................... Salt Lake City UT 84130 800-272-9273 725-8232
TF: 888-211-9874 ■ *Web:* www.ichotelsgroup.com/

Sandals Signature Guest Program 4950 SW 72nd Ave.............. Miami FL 33155 305-284-1300 666-5332*
**Fax:* PR ■ *TF:* 800-726-3257 ■ *Web:* www.sandals.com/ssg/index.cfm

Starwood Hotels Preferred Guest Program
111 Westchester Ave.................................. White Plains NY 10604 512-834-2426 834-0656
TF: 888-625-4988 ■ *Web:* www.starwoodhotels.com/preferredguest

TripRewards PO Box 4888 .... Aberdeen SD 57402 800-367-8747 306-0671
Web: www.triprewards.com

Wyndham ByRequest Program
1950 N Stemmons Fwy Suite 6001................................ Dallas TX 75207 214-863-1000 863-1342*
**Fax:* Hum Res ■ *TF:* 800-347-7559 ■ *Web:* www.wyndham.com

382 HOTELS & HOTEL COMPANIES

SEE ALSO Casino Companies p. 1409; Corporate Housing p. 1572; Hotel Reservations Services p. 1829; Hotels - Conference Center p. 1830; Hotels - Frequent Stay Programs p. 1832; Resorts & Resort Companies p. 2219

Phone *Fax*

5 Calgary Downtown Suites Hotel 618 5th Ave SW .... Calgary AB T2P0M7 403-263-0520 298-4888
TF: 800-661-1592 ■ *Web:* www.5calgary.com

21c Museum Hotel 700 W Main St............................ Louisville KY 40202 502-217-6300 217-6400
TF: 877-217-6400 ■ *Web:* www.21chotel.com

70 Park Avenue Hotel 70 Park Ave at 38th St.................. New York NY 10016 212-973-2400 973-2401
TF: 877-707-2752 ■ *Web:* www.70parkave.com

500 West Hotel 500 W Broadway.............................. San Diego CA 92101 619-234-5252 234-5272
TF: 866-500-7533 ■ *Web:* www.500westhotel.com

1859 Historic Hotels Ltd PO Box 59............................ Galveston TX 77553 409-763-8536 763-5304
Web: www.1859historichotels.com

Abraham Lincoln The - A Wyndham Historic Hotel
100 N 5th St .... Reading PA 19601 610-372-3700 372-2966
TF: 877-999-3223

Acadia Inn 98 Eden St.. Bar Harbor ME 04609 207-288-3500 288-8428
TF: 800-638-3636 ■ *Web:* www.acadiainn.com

Acapulco Hotel & Resort 2505 S Atlantic Ave........ Dayton Beach Shores FL 32118 386-761-2210 761-2216
TF: 800-245-3580 ■ *Web:* www.daytonahotels.com/Acapulco/index.php

Accent Inns Vancouver Airport 10551 St Edwards Dr........... Richmond BC V6X3L8 604-273-3311 273-9522
TF: 800-663-0298 ■ *Web:* www.accentinns.com/locations/airport.htm

Accent Inns Vancouver-Burnaby 3777 Henning Dr .... Burnaby BC V5C6N5 604-473-5000 473-5095
TF: 800-663-0298 ■ *Web:* www.accentinns.com/locations/burnaby.htm

Phone *Fax*

Accor North America 4001 International Pkwy................. Carrollton TX 75007 972-360-9000 360-5821
TF: 800-557-3435 ■ *Web:* www.accor-na.com

Accor North America Business & Leisure Div
Novotel 4001 International Pkwy .... Carrollton TX 75007 972-360-9000 360-2821
Web: www.novotel.com
Sofitel 4001 International Pkwy .... Carrollton TX 75007 972-360-9000 360-2821
Web: www.sofitel.com

Accor North America Economy Lodging Div
Motel 6 4001 International Pkwy........................... Carrollton TX 75007 972-360-9000 360-2821
TF: 800-466-8356 ■ *Web:* www.motel6.com
Red Roof Inn 4001 International Pkwy .... Carrollton TX 75007 972-360-9000 360-2821
TF: 800-733-7663 ■ *Web:* www.redroof.com
Studio 6 4001 International Pkwy .... Carrollton TX 75007 972-360-9000 360-2821
TF: 800-466-8356 ■ *Web:* www.staystudio6.com

Acqua Hotel 555 Redwood Hwy .... Mill Valley CA 94941 415-380-0400 380-9696
TF: 800-738-7477 ■ *Web:* www.marinhotels.com

Acqualina 17875 Collins Ave......................... Sunny Isles Beach FL 33160 305-918-8000 918-8100
Web: www.acqualinaresort.com

Adam's Mark Hotels & Resorts HBE Corp 11330 Olive Blvd...... Saint Louis MO 63141 314-567-9000 567-0602
TF: 800-444-2326 ■ *Web:* www.adamsmark.com

Adams Oceanfront Resort 4 Read St...................... Dewey Beach DE 19971 302-227-3030 227-1034
TF: 800-448-8080 ■ *Web:* www.adamsoceanfront.com

Admiral Benbow Inns of America Inc
51 Seven Hills Blvd PMB 300 .... Dallas GA 30132 770-529-7662 529-7661
TF: 800-451-1986 ■ *Web:* www.admiralbenbow.com

Admiral Fell Inn 888 S Broadway .... Baltimore MD 21231 410-522-7377 522-9602
TF: 800-292-4667 ■ *Web:* www.admiralfell.com

Admiral Hotel 2 Baltimore Ave .... Rehoboth Beach DE 19971 302-227-2103 227-3620
TF: 888-882-4188 ■ *Web:* www.admiralrehoboth.com/

Adolphus The 1321 Commerce St................................ Dallas TX 75202 214-742-8200 651-3588
TF: 800-221-9083 ■ *Web:* www.hoteladolphus.com

Adventureland Inn I-80 & Hwy 65 .... Des Moines IA 50316 515-265-7321 265-3506
TF: 800-910-5382 ■ *Web:* www.adventurelandpark.com/

Affina Dumont 150 E 34th St................................ New York NY 10016 212-481-7600 889-8856
TF: 866-233-4642 ■ *Web:* www.affinia.com

Affinia 50 155 E 50th St..................................... New York NY 10022 212-751-5710 753-1468
TF: 866-246-2203 ■ *Web:* www.affinia.com

Affinia Chicago 166 E Superior St .... Chicago IL 60611 312-787-6000 787-6133
TF: 866-246-2203 ■ *Web:* www.affinia.com

Affinia Gardens 215 E 64th St................................. New York NY 10065 212-355-1230 758-7858
TF: 800-637-8483 ■ *Web:* www.affinia.com

Affinia Hotels 500 W 37th St.................................. New York NY 10018 212-465-3700 465-3697
TF Resv: 866-246-2203 ■ *Web:* www.affinia.com

Affinia Manhattan 371 7th Ave .... New York NY 10001 212-563-1800 643-8028
TF: 866-246-2203 ■ *Web:* www.affinia.com

Airport Hotel Halifax 60 Sky Blvd Halifax International Airport .... Goffs NS B2T1K3 902-873-3000 873-3001
TF: 800-667-3333 ■ *Web:* www.airporthotelhalifax.com

Airport Regency Hotel 1000 NW Lejeune Rd .... Miami FL 33126 305-441-1600 443-0766
TF: 800-367-1039 ■ *Web:* www.airportregencyhotel.com

Airtel Plaza Hotel 7277 Valjean Ave.............................. Van Nuys CA 91406 818-997-7676 785-8864
TF: 800-224-7835 ■ *Web:* www.airtelplaza.com

Ala Moana Hotel 410 Atkinson Dr.............................. Honolulu HI 96814 808-955-4811 944-6839
TF: 800-367-6025 ■ *Web:* www.alamoanahotel.com

Alamo Inn 2203 E Commerce St.............................. San Antonio TX 78203 210-227-2203 222-2860
TF: 888-222-7666 ■ *Web:* www.alamoinnsa.com/

Albert at Bay Suite Hotel 435 Albert St........................... Ottawa ON K1R7X4 613-238-8858 238-1433
TF: 800-267-6644 ■ *Web:* www.albertatbay.com

Alberta Place Suite Hotel 10049 103rd St...................... Edmonton AB T5J2W7 780-423-1565 426-6260
TF: 800-661-3982 ■ *Web:* www.albertaplace.com

Albion Hotel 1650 James Ave.............................. Miami Beach FL 33139 305-913-1000 674-0507
TF: 888-665-0008

Alex The 205 E 45th St.. New York NY 10017 212-867-5100 867-7878
Web: www.thealexhotel.com

Alexander Hotel 5225 Collins Ave........................... Miami Beach FL 33140 305-865-6500 341-6553
TF: 800-327-6121 ■ *Web:* www.alexanderhotel.com

Alexander Palms Court 715 South St............................ Key West FL 33040 305-296-6413 292-3975
TF: 800-858-1943 ■ *Web:* www.alexanderpalms.com

Alexis Hotel 1007 1st Ave.. Seattle WA 98104 206-624-4844 621-9009
TF: 800-264-8482 ■ *Web:* www.alexishotel.com

Algonquin Hotel 59 W 44th St .... New York NY 10036 212-840-6800 944-1419
Web: www.thealgonquin.net

All Seasons Motor Inn 1199 Main St .... South Yarmouth MA 02664 508-394-7600 398-7160
TF: 800-527-0359 ■ *Web:* www.allseasons.com

Alpenhof Lodge 3255 W Village Dr........................ Teton Village WY 83025 307-733-3242 739-1516
TF: 800-732-3244 ■ *Web:* www.alpenhoflodge.com

Alta Peruvian Lodge PO Box 8017 Little Cottonwood Canyon........... Alta UT 84092 801-742-3000 742-3007
TF: 800-453-8488 ■ *Web:* www.altaperuvian.com

Alta Vista Hotel & Conference Center
260 Goodwin Crest Dr.................................. Birmingham AL 35209 205-290-8000 290-8001
TF: 888-290-8099 ■ *Web:* www.altavistahotel.com

Amalfi Hotel Chicago 20 W Kinzie St............................. Chicago IL 60610 312-395-9000 395-9001
TF: 877-262-5341 ■ *Web:* www.amalfihotelchicago.com

Amarillo Ritz Plaza Hotel 7909 I-40 E .... Amarillo TX 79118 806-373-3303 373-3353
TF: 800-274-5315 ■ *Web:* www.ritzcarlton.com

Ambassador Hotel 535 Tchoupitoulas St .... New Orleans LA 70130 504-527-5271 599-2107
TF: 800-455-3417 ■ *Web:* www.ambassadorhotelneworleans.com

Ambassador Hotel 3100 I-40 W .... Amarillo TX 79102 806-358-6161 358-9869
TF: 800-817-0521 ■ *Web:* www.ambassadoramarillo.com

Ambassador Hotel 2308 W Wisconsin Ave...................... Milwaukee WI 53233 414-342-8400 345-5001
Web: www.ambassadormilwaukee.com

Ambrosia House Tropical Lodging 615 Fleming St .... Key West FL 33040 305-296-9838 296-2425
TF: 800-535-9838 ■ *Web:* www.ambrosiakeywest.com

America's Best Franchising Inc
50 Glen Lake Pkwy NE Suite 350 .... Atlanta GA 30328 770-393-2662 393-2480
TF: 800-432-7992 ■ *Web:* www.buckheadamerica.com
America's Best Inns & Suites
50 Glen Lake Pkwy NE Suite 350 .... Atlanta GA 30328 770-393-2662 393-2480
TF: 800-432-7992 ■ *Web:* www.americasbestinns.com
Country Hearth Inn & Suites 50 Glen Lake Pkwy NE Suite 350..... Atlanta GA 30328 770-393-2662 393-2480
TF: 800-432-7992 ■ *Web:* www.countryhearth.com

America's Best Inns & Suites 50 Glen Lake Pkwy NE Suite 350 ..... Atlanta GA 30328 770-393-2662 393-2480
TF: 800-432-7992 ■ *Web:* www.americasbestinns.com

AmericInn International LLC 250 Lake Dr E................. Chanhassen MN 55317 952-294-5000 294-5001
TF Resv: 800-396-5007 ■ *Web:* www.americinn.com

AmeriHost Inn 1 Sylvan Way............................... Parsippany NJ 07054 973-428-9700
TF Resv: 800-889-8847 ■ *Web:* www.amerihostinn.com

Ameristar Casino & Hotel 3200 N Ameristar Dr .... Kansas City MO 64161 816-414-7000 414-7221*
**Fax:* Mktg ■ *TF:* 800-499-4961 ■ *Web:* www.ameristarcasino.com

Ameristar Casino Hotel Council Bluffs 2200 River Rd .... Council Bluffs IA 51501 712-328-8888 329-6984*
**Fax:* Mktg ■ *TF:* 877-462-7827 ■ *Web:* www.ameristarcasinos.com

AmeriSuites 700 Rt 46 E.. Fairfield NJ 07004 973-882-1010 882-7619*
**Fax:* Sales ■ *TF:* 800-833-1516 ■ *Web:* www.amerisuites.com

Ameritania Hotel New York 230 W 54th St...................... New York NY 10019 212-247-5000 247-3313
TF: 800-555-7555 ■ *Web:* www.ameritaniahotelnewyork.com

Ameritel Inn Boise Towne Square 7965 W Emerald St............... Boise ID 83704 208-378-7000 378-7040
TF: 800-600-6001 ■ *Web:* www.ameritelinns.com

	City	State	Zip	Phone	Fax
Ameritel Inn Pocatello 1440 Bench Rd	Pocatello	ID	83201	208-234-7500	234-0000
TF: 800-600-6001 ■ *Web:* www.ameritelinns.com					
Amsterdam Court Hotel 226 W 50th St	New York	NY	10019	212-459-1000	262-4170
TF: 888-664-6835 ■ *Web:* www.nychotels.com					
Amway Grand Plaza Hotel 187 Monroe Ave NW	Grand Rapids	MI	49503	616-774-2000	776-6489
TF: 800-253-3590 ■ *Web:* www.amwaygrand.com					
Anaheim Plaza Hotel 1700 S Harbor Blvd	Anaheim	CA	92802	714-772-5900	772-8386
TF: 800-532-4517 ■ *Web:* www.anaheimplazahotel.com					
Anastasia Inn 218 Anastasia Blvd	Saint Augustine	FL	32080	904-825-2879	825-2724
TF: 888-226-6181 ■ *Web:* www.anastasiainn.com					
Anchor-In 1 South St	Hyannis	MA	02601	508-775-0357	775-1313
Web: www.anchorin.com					
Anchorage Inn 26 Vendue Range	Charleston	SC	29401	843-723-8300	723-9543
TF: 800-421-2952 ■ *Web:* anchoragencharleston.com					
Anchorage Uptown Suites 234 E 2nd Ave	Anchorage	AK	99501	907-279-4232	279-4231
Web: portal.gci.net/anchorageuptownsuites/					
Andrews Hotel 624 Post St	San Francisco	CA	94109	415-563-6877	928-6919
TF: 800-926-3739 ■ *Web:* www.andrewshotel.com					
Angler's Inn 265 N Millward St PO Box 1247	Jackson	WY	83001	307-733-3682	733-8662
TF: 800-867-4667 ■ *Web:* anglersinn.net					
Ansonborough Inn 21 Hassell St	Charleston	SC	29401	843-723-1655	577-6888
TF: 800-522-2073 ■ *Web:* www.ansonboroughinn.com					
Antler Inn 43 W Pearl St PO Box 575	Jackson	WY	83001	307-733-2535	733-4158
TF: 800-483-8667 ■ *Web:* www.townsquareinns.com/antler-inn/					
Apollo Park Executive Suites					
805 S Circle Dr Suite 2B	Colorado Springs	CO	80910	719-634-0286	635-1539
TF: 800-279-3620 ■ *Web:* www.apollopark.com					
Apple Tree Inn 9508 N Division St	Spokane	WA	99218	509-466-3020	467-4377
TF: 800-323-5796 ■ *Web:* www.appletreeinnmotel.com					
Applewood Manor Inn 62 Cumberland Cir	Asheville	NC	28801	828-254-2244	254-0899
TF: 800-442-2197 ■ *Web:* www.applewoodmanor.com					
Aqua Bamboo 2425 Kuhio Ave	Honolulu	HI	96815	808-922-7777	922-9473
TF: 866-406-2782 ■ *Web:* www.aquaresorts.com					
Aqua Coconut Plaza Hotel 450 Lewers St	Honolulu	HI	96815	808-923-8828	923-3473
TF: 877-997-6667 ■ *Web:* www.aquaresorts.com/					
Aqua Hotel & Lounge 1530 Collins Ave	Miami Beach	FL	33139	305-538-4361	673-8109
Web: www.aquamiami.com					
Aqua Island Colony 445 Seaside Ave	Honolulu	HI	96815	808-923-2345	921-7105
TF: 800-367-5004 ■ *Web:* www.aquaresorts.com					
Aqua Waikiki Wave 2299 Kuhio Ave	Honolulu	HI	96815	808-922-1262	922-5048
TF: 866-406-2782 ■ *Web:* www.aquaresorts.com					
ARC The Hotel 140 Slater St	Ottawa	ON	K1P5H6	613-238-2888	238-0053
TF: 800-699-2516 ■ *Web:* www.arcthehotel.com					
Arena Hotel 817 The Alameda	San Jose	CA	95126	408-294-6500	294-6585
TF: 800-954-6835 ■ *Web:* www.pacifichotels.com					
Argonaut Hotel 495 Jefferson St	San Francisco	CA	94109	415-563-0800	563-2800
TF: 866-415-0704 ■ *Web:* www.argonauthotel.com					
Arizona Charlie's Boulder Casino & Hotel 4575 Boulder Hwy	Las Vegas	NV	89121	702-951-9000	951-1046
TF: 800-362-4040 ■ *Web:* www.arizonacharliesboulder.com					
Arizona Charlie's Decatur Casino & Hotel					
740 S Decatur Blvd	Las Vegas	NV	89107	702-258-5111	258-5192
TF: 800-342-2695 ■ *Web:* www.arizonacharliesdecatur.com					
Arizona Inn 2200 E Elm St	Tucson	AZ	85719	520-325-1541	881-5830
TF: 800-933-1093 ■ *Web:* www.arizonainn.com					
Arosa Suites Hotel 163 McLaren St	Ottawa	ON	K2P2G4	613-238-6783	238-5080
TF: 866-238-6783 ■ *Web:* www.arosahotel.com					
Ascot Inn 1025 S Tryon St	Charlotte	NC	28203	704-377-3611	
TF: 800-333-9417 ■ *Web:* www.boonelodging.com/ascot.html					
Ashland Springs Hotel 212 E Main St	Ashland	OR	97520	541-488-1700	488-0240
TF: 800-325-4000 ■ *Web:* www.ashlandspringshotel.com					
Ashmore Inn & Suites 4019 S Loop 289	Lubbock	TX	79423	806-785-0060	785-6001
TF: 800-785-0061 ■ *Web:* www.lubbocklegends.org/abc.html					
Ashton Hotel 610 Main St	Fort Worth	TX	76102	817-332-0100	332-0110
Web: www.slh.com/ashton					
Aspen Hotel & Suites 2900 S 68th St	Fort Smith	AR	72903	479-452-9000	484-0551
TF: 800-627-9417 ■ *Web:* www.aspenhotelandsuites.com					
Assiniboine Gordon Inn on the Park 1975 Portage Ave	Winnipeg	MB	R3J0J9	204-888-4806	897-9870
Web: www.gordonhotels.com/assiniboine.htm					
Associated Hotels LLC 29 S La Salle St Suite 705	Chicago	IL	60603	312-782-6008	782-2356
Web: www.associatedhotelsllc.com					
Asticou Inn 15 Peabody Dr	Northeast Harbor	ME	04662	207-276-3344	276-3373
TF: 800-258-3373 ■ *Web:* www.asticou.com					
Aston Pacific Inn Resort & Conference Centre					
1160 King George Hwy	Surrey	BC	V4A4Z2	604-535-1432	531-6979
TF: 800-667-2248 ■ *Web:* www.pacificinn.com					
Astor Crowne Plaza 739 Canal St	New Orleans	LA	70130	504-962-0500	962-0501
Web: www.astorcrowneplaza.com					
Astor Hotel The 924 E Juneau Ave	Milwaukee	WI	53202	414-271-4220	271-6370
TF: 800-558-0200 ■ *Web:* www.theastorhotel.com					
Atheneum Suite Hotel & Conference Center 1000 Brush Ave	Detroit	MI	48226	313-962-2323	962-2424
TF: 800-772-2323 ■ *Web:* www.atheneumsuites.com					
Atlantic The 601 N Fort Lauderdale Beach Blvd	Fort Lauderdale	FL	33304	954-567-8020	567-8040
Web: www.theatlantichotelfortlauderdale.com					
Atlantic Eyrie Lodge 6 Norman Rd	Bar Harbor	ME	04609	207-288-9786	288-8500
TF: 800-422-2883 ■ *Web:* www.atlanticeyrielodge.com/					
Atlantic Palace Suites Hotel 1507 Boardwalk	Atlantic City	NJ	08401	609-344-1200	345-0673
TF: 800-527-8483 ■ *Web:* www.atlanticpalacesuites.com					
Atlantic Sands Hotel 101 N Boardwalk	Rehoboth Beach	DE	19971	302-227-2511	227-9476
TF: 800-422-0600 ■ *Web:* www.atlanticsandshotel.com					
Atrium Hotel 18700 MacArthur Blvd	Irvine	CA	92612	949-833-2770	757-1228
TF: 800-854-3012 ■ *Web:* www.atriumhotel.com					
Atrium Suites Hotel Las Vegas 4255 S Paradise Rd	Las Vegas	NV	89169	702-369-4400	369-3770
TF: 800-330-7728 ■ *Web:* www.atriumsuiteshotel.com					
Auberge Saint-Antoine 8 Saint-Antoine St	Quebec	QC	G1K4C9	418-692-2211	692-1177
TF: 888-692-2211 ■ *Web:* www.saint-antoine.com					
Auberge du Soleil 180 Rutherford Hill Rd	Rutherford	CA	94573	707-963-1211	963-8764
TF: 800-348-5406 ■ *Web:* www.aubergedusoleil.com					
Auberge du Vieux-Port 97 de la Commune E	Montreal	QC	H2Y1J1	514-876-0081	876-8923
TF: 888-660-7678 ■ *Web:* www.aubergeduvieuxport.com					
Aurora Inn 51 Holland Ave	Bar Harbor	ME	04609	207-288-3771	
TF: 800-841-8925 ■ *Web:* www.aurorainn.com					
Austin Hotel & Spa 305 Malvern Ave	Hot Springs	AR	71901	501-623-6600	624-7160
TF: 877-623-6697 ■ *Web:* www.theaustinhotel.com					
Avalon Beverly Hills 9400 W Olympic Blvd	Beverly Hills	CA	90212	310-277-5221	277-4928
TF: 800-670-6183 ■ *Web:* www.avalonbeverlyhills.com					
Avalon Corporate Furnished Apartments 1553 Empire Blvd	Rochester	NY	14580	585-671-4421	671-9771
Web: www.rochesterfurnished.com					
Avalon Hotel 16 E 32nd St	New York	NY	10016	212-299-7000	299-7001
TF: 888-442-8256 ■ *Web:* www.avalonhotelnyc.com					
Avalon Hotel 16 W 10th St	Erie	PA	16501	814-459-2220	459-2322
TF: 800-822-5011 ■ *Web:* www.avalonerie.com					
Avalon Hotel & Spa 0455 SW Hamilton Ct	Portland	OR	97239	503-802-5800	802-5820
TF: 888-556-4402 ■ *Web:* www.avalonhotelandspa.com					
Avalon Majestic 700 Ocean Dr	Miami Beach	FL	33139	305-538-0133	534-0258
TF: 800-933-3306 ■ *Web:* www.southbeachhotels.com					
Avenue Inn & Spa 33 Wilmington Ave	Rehoboth Beach	DE	19971	302-226-2900	226-7549
TF: 800-433-5870 ■ *Web:* www.avenueinn.com					
Avenue Plaza Resort 2111 St Charles Ave	New Orleans	LA	70130	504-566-1212	525-6899
TF: 800-251-8736 ■ *Web:* www.avenueplazaresort.com					
Bahama House 2001 S Atlantic Ave	Daytona Beach Shores	FL	32118	386-248-2001	248-0991
TF: 800-571-2001 ■ *Web:* www.daytonabahamahouse.com					
Balance Rock Inn 21 Albert Meadow	Bar Harbor	ME	04609	207-288-2610	288-5534
TF: 800-753-0494 ■ *Web:* www.balancerockinn.com					
Balboa Park Inn 3402 Park Blvd	San Diego	CA	92103	619-298-0823	294-8070
TF: 800-938-8181 ■ *Web:* www.balboaparkinn.com					
Ballantines Hotels in Palm Springs					
1420 N Indian Canyon Dr	Palm Springs	CA	92262	760-320-1178	320-5308
TF: 800-485-2808 ■ *Web:* www.ballantineshotels.com					
Bally's Casino Tunica 1450 Bally's Blvd Casino Center	Robinsonville	MS	38664	662-357-1500	357-1756
TF: 800-382-2559 ■ *Web:* www.ballystunica.com					
Balmoral Inn 120 Balmoral Ave	Biloxi	MS	39531	228-388-6776	388-5450
TF: 800-393-9131 ■ *Web:* www.balmoralinn.com					
Bar Harbor Hotel-Bluenose Inn 90 Eden St	Bar Harbor	ME	04609	207-288-3348	288-2183
TF: 800-445-4077 ■ *Web:* www.bluenoseinn.com					
Barcelo Crestline Corp 8405 Greensboro Dr Suite 500	McLean	VA	22102	571-382-1700	382-1751
Web: www.barcelocrestline.com					
Barclay Hotel 1348 Robson St	Vancouver	BC	V5E1C5	604-688-8850	688-2534
Web: www.barclayhotel.com					
Barclay Towers 809 Atlantic Ave	Virginia Beach	VA	23451	757-491-2700	428-3790
TF: 800-344-4473 ■ *Web:* www.vbhotels.com/barclay					
Barnstead Inn 349 Bonnet St	Manchester Center	VT	05255	802-362-1619	362-0688
TF: 800-331-1619 ■ *Web:* www.barnsteadinn.com					
Baronne Plaza Hotel 201 Baronne St	New Orleans	LA	70112	504-522-0083	522-0053
TF: 888-756-0083 ■ *Web:* www.baronneplaza.com/					
Barrington Hotel & Suites 263 Shepherd of the Hills Expy	Branson	MO	65616	417-334-8866	336-2585
TF: 800-760-8866 ■ *Web:* barringtonhotel.com/					
Bavarian Inn PO Box 152	Custer	SD	57730	605-673-2802	673-4777
TF: 800-657-4312 ■ *Web:* www.bavarianinnsd.com					
Bay Club Hotel & Marina 2131 Shelter Island Dr	San Diego	CA	92106	619-224-8888	225-1604
TF: 800-672-0800 ■ *Web:* www.bayclubhotel.com					
Bay Harbor Inn & Suites 9660 E Bay Harbor Dr	Bay Harbor Island	FL	33154	305-868-4141	867-9094
Web: www.bayharborinn.com					
Bay Park Hotel 1425 Munras Ave	Monterey	CA	93940	831-649-1020	373-4258
TF: 800-338-3564 ■ *Web:* www.bayparkhotel.com					
Bayfront Inn 138 Avenida Menendez	Saint Augustine	FL	32084	904-824-1681	829-8721
TF: 800-558-3455 ■ *Web:* www.bayfrontinn.com					
Bayfront Inn on Fifth 1221 5th Ave S	Naples	FL	34102	239-649-5800	649-0523
TF: 800-382-7941 ■ *Web:* www.bayfrontinnnaples.com					
Baymont Inn & Suites 1 Sylvan Way	Parsippany	NJ	07054	973-753-6600	
TF Resv: 877-229-6668 ■ *Web:* www.baymontinns.com					
Beach Haven Inn 4740 Mission Blvd	San Diego	CA	92109	858-272-3812	272-3532
TF: 800-831-6323 ■ *Web:* www.beachhaveninn.com					
Beach House Suites by the Don Cesar 3400 Gulf Blvd	Saint Pete Beach	FL	33706	727-363-0001	363-5055
TF: 800-282-1116 ■ *Web:* www.beachhousesuites.com					
Beach Plaza Hotel 625 N Atlantic Blvd	Fort Lauderdale	FL	33304	954-566-7631	537-9358
TF: 800-451-4711 ■ *Web:* www.hotelbeachplaza.com					
Beachcomber Hotel 1340 Collins Ave	Miami Beach	FL	33139	305-531-3755	673-8609
Web: www.beachcombermiami.com					
Beacher's Lodge 6970 US Hwy A1A S	Saint Augustine	FL	32080	904-471-8849	471-3002
TF: 800-527-8849 ■ *Web:* www.beacherslodge.com					
Beachside Ocean Inn 905 S Atlantic Ave	Daytona Beach	FL	32118	386-255-5432	254-0885
TF: 888-558-5577					
Beacon Hotel 720 Ocean Dr	Miami Beach	FL	33139	305-674-8200	674-8976
TF: 800-426-7866 ■ *Web:* www.beacon-hotel.com					
Beacon Hotel & Corporate Quarters					
1615 Rhode Island Ave NW	Washington	DC	20036	202-296-2100	331-0227
TF: 800-821-4367 ■ *Web:* capitalhotelswdc.com/BeaconHotelWDC_com					
Beaver Creek Lodge 26 Avon Dale Ln	Beaver Creek	CO	81620	970-845-9800	845-8242
TF: 800-525-7280 ■ *Web:* www.beavercreeklodge.net					
Beechwood Hotel 363 Plantation St	Worcester	MA	01605	508-754-5789	752-2060
TF: 800-344-2589 ■ *Web:* www.beechwoodhotel.com					
Beekman Tower Hotel 3 Mitchell Pl	New York	NY	10017	212-355-7300	753-9366
TF: 866-298-4606 ■ *Web:* www.thebeekmanhotel.com					
Bel Age 1020 N San Vicente Blvd	West Hollywood	CA	90069	310-854-1111	
TF: 866-282-4560 ■ *Web:* www.belagehotel.com					
Belden-Stratford Hotel 2300 N Lincoln Park W	Chicago	IL	60614	773-281-2900	880-2039
TF: 866-589-3411 ■ *Web:* www.beldenstratford.com					
Bell Tower Hotel 300 S Thayer St	Ann Arbor	MI	48104	734-769-3010	769-4339
TF: 800-562-3559 ■ *Web:* www.belltowerhotel.com					
Bell Tower Inn 1235 2nd St SW	Rochester	MN	55902	507-289-2233	289-2233
TF: 800-448-7583 ■ *Web:* www.rochesterlodging.com/belltower/					
Bellasera Hotel 221 9th St S	Naples	FL	34102	239-649-7333	649-6233
TF: 888-627-1595 ■ *Web:* www.bellaseranaples.com					
Bellevue Club Hotel 11200 SE 6th St	Bellevue	WA	98004	425-454-4424	688-3101
TF: 800-579-1110 ■ *Web:* www.bellevueclub.com					
Bellmoor The 6 Christian St	Rehoboth Beach	DE	19971	302-227-5800	227-0323
TF: 800-425-2355 ■ *Web:* www.thebellmoor.com					
Belvedere Hotel 319 W 48th St	New York	NY	10036	212-245-7000	265-7778
TF: 888-468-3558 ■ *Web:* www.newyorkhotel.com					
Benchmark Hospitality International					
2170 Buckthorne Pl Suite 400	The Woodlands	TX	77380	281-367-5757	367-1407
Web: www.benchmark-hospitality.com					
Bendel Executive Suites 213 Bendel Rd	Lafayette	LA	70503	337-261-0604	233-4296
TF: 800-990-5708 ■ *Web:* www.bendelexec.com					
Benjamin The 125 E 50th St	New York	NY	10022	212-715-2500	715-2525
TF: 866-233-4642 ■ *Web:* www.thebenjamin.com					
Benson The 309 SW Broadway	Portland	OR	97205	503-228-2000	471-3920
TF: 800-426-0670 ■ *Web:* www.bensonhotel.com					
Bentley Beach Hotel 101 Ocean Dr	Miami Beach	FL	33139	305-938-4600	938-4601
TF: 866-236-8539 ■ *Web:* www.thebentleybeachhotel.com					
Bentley Hotel 510 Ocean Dr	Miami Beach	FL	33139	305-538-1700	532-4865
TF: 866-236-8539 ■ *Web:* www.thebentleyhotel.com					
Bentley Hotel New York 500 E 62nd St	New York	NY	10021	212-644-6000	207-4800
TF: 888-664-6235 ■ *Web:* www.hotelbentleynewyork.com					
Berkeley Hotel 1200 E Cary St	Richmond	VA	23219	804-780-1300	343-1885
TF: 888-780-4422 ■ *Web:* www.berkeleyhotel.com					
Bernards Inn 27 Mine Brook Rd	Bernardsville	NJ	07924	908-766-0002	766-4604
TF: 888-766-0002 ■ *Web:* www.bernardsinn.com					
Bernardus Lodge 415 Carmel Valley Rd	Carmel Valley	CA	93924	831-658-3400	659-8657
TF: 888-648-9463 ■ *Web:* www.bernardus.com					
Best Rest Inn 1206 W 2100 S	Ogden	UT	84401	801-393-8644	399-0954
TF: 800-343-8644					
Best Western The Academy Hotel					
8110 N Academy Blvd	Colorado Springs	CO	80920	719-598-5770	598-3434
TF: 800-333-3333 ■ *Web:* www.theacademyhotel.com					
Best Western Chincoteague Island					
7105 Maddox Blvd	Chincoteague Island	VA	23336	757-336-6557	336-6558
TF: 800-553-6117 ■ *Web:* www.bestwestern.com/chincoteagueisland					
Best Western International Inc 6201 N 24th Pkwy	Phoenix	AZ	85016	602-957-4200	957-5942*
**Fax:* Mktg ■ *TF:* 800-528-1234 ■ *Web:* www.bestwestern.com					
Best Western Laguna Brisas Spa Hotel					
1600 S Coast Hwy	Laguna Beach	CA	92651	949-497-7272	497-8306
TF: 877-503-1461 ■ *Web:* www.lagunabrisas.com					

Phone *Fax*

Betsy Hotel 1440 Ocean Dr . . . Miami Beach FL 33139 305-531-3934 531-9009
TF: 866-531-8950 ■ *Web:* www.thebetsyhotel.com
Beverly Garland's Holiday Inn at Universal Studios Hollywood 4222 Vineland Ave . . . North Hollywood CA 91602 818-980-8000 766-0112
TF: 800-238-3759 ■ *Web:* www.beverlygarland.com
Beverly Heritage Hotel 1820 Barber Ln . . . Milpitas CA 95035 408-943-9080 432-8617
TF: 800-443-4455 ■ *Web:* www.beverlyheritage.com
Beverly Hills Hotel 9641 Sunset Blvd . . . Beverly Hills CA 90210 310-276-2251 887-2887
TF: 800-283-8885 ■ *Web:* www.thebeverlyhillshotel.com
Beverly Hilton 9876 Wilshire Blvd . . . Beverly Hills CA 90210 310-274-7777 285-1313
TF: 800-445-8667 ■ *Web:* www.beverlyhilton.com
Beverly Wilshire - A Four Seasons Hotel 9500 Wilshire Blvd . . . Beverly Hills CA 90212 310-275-5200 274-2851
TF: 800-545-4000 ■ *Web:* www.fourseasons.com/beverlywilshire/
Bienville House Hotel 320 Decatur St . . . New Orleans LA 70130 504-529-2345 525-6079
TF: 800-535-7836 ■ *Web:* www.bienvillehouse.com
Billings Hotel & Convention Center 1223 Mullowney Ln . . . Billings MT 59101 406-248-7151 259-5338
TF: 800-537-7286 ■ *Web:* www.billingshotel.net
Bill's Gamblin' Hall & Saloon 3595 S Las Vegas Blvd . . . Las Vegas NV 89109 702-737-2100 894-9954
TF: 866-245-5748 ■ *Web:* www.billslasvegas.com
Biltmore Greensboro Hotel 111 W Washington St . . . Greensboro NC 27401 336-272-3474 275-2523
TF: 800-332-0303 ■ *Web:* www.biltmorehotelgreensboro.com/
Biltmore Hotel Oklahoma 401 S Meridian Ave . . . Oklahoma City OK 73108 405-947-7681 947-4253
TF: 800-522-6620 ■ *Web:* www.biltmoreokc.com/
Biltmore Hotel & Suites 2151 Laurelwood Rd . . . Santa Clara CA 95054 408-988-8411 988-0225
TF: 800-255-9925 ■ *Web:* www.hotelbiltmore.com
Biltmore Suites 205 W Madison St . . . Baltimore MD 21201 410-728-6550 728-5829
TF: 800-868-5064 ■ *Web:* www.biltmoresuites.com
Binion's Horseshoe Hotel & Casino 128 E Fremont St . . . Las Vegas NV 89101 702-382-1600 384-1574
TF: 800-237-6537 ■ *Web:* www.binions.com
Black Swan Inn 746 E Center St . . . Pocatello ID 83201 208-233-3051 478-8516
Web: www.blackswaninn.com
Blackfoot Inn 5940 Blackfoot Trail SE . . . Calgary AB T2H2B5 403-252-2253 252-3574
TF: 800-661-1151 ■ *Web:* www.blackfootinn.com
Blackwell The 2110 Tuttle Park Pl . . . Columbus OH 43210 614-247-4000 247-4040
TF: 866-247-4003 ■ *Web:* www.theblackwell.com
Blakely New York 136 W 55th St . . . New York NY 10019 212-245-1800 582-8332
TF: 800-735-0710 ■ *Web:* www.blakelynewyork.com
Blantyre 16 Blantyre Rd PO Box 995 . . . Lenox MA 01240 413-637-3556 637-4282
Web: www.blantyre.com
Blondell's Crown Square 1406 2nd St SW . . . Rochester MN 55902 507-282-9444 282-8683
TF: 800-441-5209 ■ *Web:* www.blondell.com
Blue Horizon Hotel 1225 Robson St . . . Vancouver BC V6E1C3 604-688-1411 688-4461
TF: 800-663-1333 ■ *Web:* www.bluehorizonhotel.com
Blue Moon Hotel 944 Collins Ave . . . Miami Beach FL 33139 305-673-2262 534-5399
TF: 800-724-1623 ■ *Web:* www.bluemoonhotel.com
Blue Parrot Inn 916 Elizabeth St . . . Key West FL 33040 305-296-0033 296-5697
TF: 800-231-2473 ■ *Web:* www.blueparrotinn.com
Bluenose Inn 636 Bedford Hwy . . . Halifax NS B3M2L8 902-443-3171 443-9368
TF: 800-565-2301 ■ *Web:* www.bluenoseinnandsuites.com
Boardwalk Inn 5757 Palm Blvd . . . Isle of Palms SC 29451 843-886-6000 886-2060
TF: 800-845-8880 ■ *Web:* www.wilddunes.com/accommodations.php
Boardwalk Plaza Hotel 2 Olive Ave . . . Rehoboth Beach DE 19971 302-227-7169 227-0561
TF: 800-332-3224 ■ *Web:* www.boardwalkplaza.com
Bodega Bay Lodge & Spa 103 Coast Hwy 1 . . . Bodega Bay CA 94923 707-875-3525 875-2428
TF: 800-368-2468 ■ *Web:* www.woodsidehotels.com/bodega
Bond Place Hotel 65 Dundas St E . . . Toronto ON M5B2G8 416-362-6061 360-6406
TF: 800-268-9390 ■ *Web:* www.bondplacehoteltoronto.com
Boomtown Hotel Casino 300 Riverside Dr . . . Bossier City LA 71111 318-746-0711 226-9434
TF: 877-862-4428 ■ *Web:* www.boomtownbossier.com
Boone Tavern Hotel of Berea College 100 Main St . . . Berea KY 40404 859-985-3700 985-3715
TF: 800-366-9358 ■ *Web:* www.boonetavernhotel.com
Borgata Hotel Casino & Spa 1 Borgata Way . . . Atlantic City NJ 08401 609-317-1000 317-1035
TF: 866-692-6742 ■ *Web:* www.theborgata.com
Boston Harbor Hotel 70 Rowes Wharf . . . Boston MA 02110 617-439-7000 330-9450
TF: 800-752-7077 ■ *Web:* www.bhh.com
Boston Park Plaza Hotel & Towers 50 Park Plaza . . . Boston MA 02116 617-426-2000 426-5545
TF: 800-225-2008 ■ *Web:* www.bostonparkplaza.com
Boulder Mountain Lodge 91 Four-Mile Canyon Rd . . . Boulder CO 80302 303-444-0882 541-0665
TF: 800-458-0882 ■ *Web:* www.boulderguide.com/Lodge
Boulder Station Hotel & Casino 4111 Boulder Hwy . . . Las Vegas NV 89121 702-432-7777 432-7744
TF: 800-683-7777 ■ *Web:* www.boulderstation.com
Bourbon Orleans - A Wyndham Historic Hotel 717 Orleans St . . . New Orleans LA 70116 504-523-2222 571-4666
TF: 866-527-1380 ■ *Web:* www.bourbonorleans.com
Bradley Boulder Inn 2040 16th St . . . Boulder CO 80302 303-545-5200 440-6740
TF: 800-858-5811 ■ *Web:* www.thebradleyboulder.com
Bradley Inn 3063 Bristol Rd . . . New Harbor ME 04554 207-677-2105 677-3367
TF: 800-942-5560 ■ *Web:* www.bradleyinn.com
Brandywine Suites Hotel 707 N King St . . . Wilmington DE 19801 302-656-9300 656-2459
TF: 800-756-0070 ■ *Web:* www.brandywinesuites.com
Brazilian Court Hotel 301 Australian Ave . . . Palm Beach FL 33480 561-655-7740 655-0801
TF: 800-552-0335 ■ *Web:* www.thebraziliancourt.com
Breakers Hotel 3rd St & Boardwalk . . . Ocean City MD 21843 410-289-9165
TF: 800-283-9165
Breakers Hotel & Suites 105 2nd St . . . Rehoboth Beach DE 19971 302-227-6688 227-2013
TF: 800-441-8009 ■ *Web:* www.thebreakershotel.com
Breakers at Waikiki 250 Beach Walk . . . Waikiki HI 96815 808-923-3181 923-7174
TF: 800-426-0494 ■ *Web:* www.breakers-hawaii.com
Breakwater Inn 1711 Glacier Ave . . . Juneau AK 99801 907-586-6303 463-4820
TF: 800-544-2250 ■ *Web:* www.breakwaterinn.com
Breckinridge Inn 2800 Breckinridge Ln . . . Louisville KY 40220 502-456-5050 451-1577
Web: www.breckinridgeinn.com
Brent House Hotel 1512 Jefferson Hwy . . . New Orleans LA 70118 504-835-5411 842-4160
TF: 800-535-3986 ■ *Web:* www.brenthouse.com
Briad Group 78 Okner Pkwy . . . Livingston NJ 07039 973-597-6433 597-6422
Web: www.briad.com
Bridgewater Hotel 723 1st Ave . . . Fairbanks AK 99701 907-452-6661 452-6126
TF: 800-528-4916 ■ *Web:* www.fountainheadhotels.com/bridgewater/bridgewater.htm
Bright Angel Lodge 1 Main St . . . Grand Canyon AZ 86023 928-638-2631 638-2876
Bristol Hotel 1055 1st Ave . . . San Diego CA 92101 619-232-6141 232-0118
TF: 800-662-4477 ■ *Web:* www.bristolhotelsandiego.com
Broadway Inn 264 W 46th St . . . New York NY 10036 212-997-9200 768-2807
TF: 800-826-6300 ■ *Web:* www.broadwayinn.com
Broker Inn 555 30th St . . . Boulder CO 80303 303-444-3330 444-6444
TF: 800-338-5407 ■ *Web:* www.boulderbrokerinn.com
Brookfield Suites Hotel & Convention Center 1200 S Moorland Rd . . . Brookfield WI 53008 262-782-2900 796-9159
TF: 800-444-6404 ■ *Web:* www.paragonhotels.com/brookfield.html
Brookshire Suites 120 E Lombard St . . . Baltimore MD 21202 410-625-1300 625-0912
TF: 866-583-4162 ■ *Web:* www.brookshiresuites.com
Brookstown Inn 200 Brookstown Ave . . . Winston-Salem NC 27101 336-725-1120 773-0147
TF: 800-845-4262 ■ *Web:* www.brookstowninn.com
Brookstreet Hotel 525 Legget Dr . . . Ottawa ON K2K2W2 613-271-1800 271-1850
TF: 888-826-2220 ■ *Web:* www.brookstreethotel.com
Brown County Inn 51 E State Rd 46 . . . Nashville IN 47448 812-988-2291 988-8312
TF: 800-772-5249 ■ *Web:* www.browncountyinn.com

Phone *Fax*

Brown Hotel The 335 W Broadway St . . . Louisville KY 40202 502-583-1234 587-7006
TF: 888-888-5252 ■ *Web:* www.thebrownhotel.com
Brown Palace Hotel 321 17th St . . . Denver CO 80202 303-297-3111 312-5900
TF: 800-321-2599 ■ *Web:* www.brownpalace.com
Brown's Wharf Inn 121 Atlantic Ave . . . Boothbay Harbor ME 04538 207-633-5440 633-5440
TF: 800-334-8110 ■ *Web:* www.brownswharfinn.com
Bryant Park Hotel 40 W 40th St . . . New York NY 10018 212-869-0100 869-4446
Web: www.bryantparkhotel.com
Buckingham Hotel 101 W 57th St . . . New York NY 10019 212-246-1500 262-0698
TF: 866-589-3411 ■ *Web:* www.buckinghamhotel.com/
Buckrail Lodge 110 E Karns Ave PO Box 23 . . . Jackson WY 83001 307-733-2079 734-1663
Web: www.buckraillodge.com
Budget Host International 2307-B Roosevelt Dr . . . Arlington TX 76016 817-861-6088 861-6089
Web: www.budgethost.com
Budget Suites of America 4640 S Eastern Ave . . . Las Vegas NV 89119 702-456-1606 456-8647
Web: www.budgetsuites.com
Buena Vista Suites 8203 World Center Dr . . . Orlando FL 32821 407-239-8588 239-1401
TF: 800-537-7737 ■ *Web:* www.buenavistasuites.com/
Bullock Hotel 633 Main St . . . Deadwood SD 57732 605-578-1745 578-1382
TF: 800-336-1876 ■ *Web:* www.heartofdeadwood.com/bh.htm
Burnside Hotel 739 Windmill Rd . . . Dartmouth NS B3B1C1 902-468-7117 468-1770
TF: 800-830-4656 ■ *Web:* www.burnsidehotel.ca
Burnsley Hotel 1000 Grant St . . . Denver CO 80203 303-830-1000 830-7676
TF: 800-231-3915 ■ *Web:* www.burnsley.com
Business Inn 180 MacLaren St . . . Ottawa ON K2P0L3 613-232-1121 232-8143
TF: 800-363-1777 ■ *Web:* www.thebusinessinn.com
Cabot Lodge Tallahassee North 2735 N Monroe St . . . Tallahassee FL 32303 850-386-8880 386-4254
TF: 800-223-1964 ■ *Web:* www.cabotlodge.com
Caesars Indiana Casino Hotel 11999 Ave of the Emperors . . . Elizabeth IN 47117 812-969-6000 969-6632
TF: 877-237-6626 ■ *Web:* www.harrahs.com
Caesars Palace Las Vegas 3570 Las Vegas Blvd S . . . Las Vegas NV 89109 702-731-7110 866-1700
TF: 800-634-6661 ■ *Web:* www.harrahs.com
California Hotel & Casino 12 Ogden Ave . . . Las Vegas NV 89101 702-385-1222 388-2660
TF: 800-634-6255 ■ *Web:* www.thecal.com
Camberley Hotel Co 4405 Northside Pkwy Suite 2124 . . . Atlanta GA 30327 404-261-9600 261-4278
TF: 800-555-8000 ■ *Web:* www.camberleyhotels.com
Cambria Suites 10750 Columbia Pike . . . Silver Spring MD 20901 301-592-5000 592-6157
TF: 800-424-6423 ■ *Web:* www.cambriasuites.com
Cambridge Suites Hotel Halifax 1583 Brunswick St . . . Halifax NS B3J3P5 902-420-0555 420-9379
TF: 800-565-1263 ■ *Web:* www.cambridgesuiteshotel.com/Halifax/
Cambridge Suites Hotel Toronto 15 Richmond St E . . . Toronto ON M5C1N2 416-368-1990 601-3753
TF: 800-463-1990 ■ *Web:* www.cambridgesuitestoronto.com
Camino Real El Paso 101 S El Paso St . . . El Paso TX 79901 915-534-3000 534-3024
TF: 800-769-4300 ■ *Web:* caminoreal.com/elpaso/
Campton Place Hotel 340 Stockton St . . . San Francisco CA 94108 415-781-5555 632-1670
TF: 800-235-4300 ■ *Web:* www.camptonplace.com
Campus Center Hotel 1 Campus Center Way University of Massachusetts . . . Amherst MA 01003 413-549-6000 545-1210
Web: www.aux.umass.edu/hotel/
Campus Inn & Suites 390 E Broadway . . . Eugene OR 97401 541-343-3376 485-9392
TF: 877-313-4137 ■ *Web:* www.campus-inn.com
Campus Tower Suite Hotel 11145 87th Ave . . . Edmonton AB T6G0Y1 780-439-6060 433-4410
TF: 888-962-2522 ■ *Web:* www.unlimitedreservationservices.com
Canad Inns - Club Regent Casino Hotel 1415 Regent Ave W . . . Winnipeg MB R2C3B2 204-667-5560 667-5913
TF: 888-332-2623 ■ *Web:* www.canadinns.com
Canad Inns Fort Garry 1824 Pembina Hwy . . . Winnipeg MB R3C2G2 204-261-7450 261-5433
TF: 888-332-2623 ■ *Web:* www.canadinns.com
Canad Inns Garden City 2100 McPhillips St . . . Winnipeg MB R2V3T9 204-633-0024 697-3377
TF: 888-332-2623 ■ *Web:* www.canadinns.com
Canad Inns Polo Park 1405 St Matthews Ave . . . Winnipeg MB R3G0K5 204-775-8791 783-4039
TF: 888-332-2623 ■ *Web:* www.canadinns.com
Canal Park Lodge 250 Canal Park Dr . . . Duluth MN 55802 218-279-6000 279-4055
TF: 800-777-8560 ■ *Web:* www.canalparklodge.com
Canandaigua Inn on the Lake 770 S Main St . . . Canandaigua NY 14424 585-394-7800 394-5003
TF: 800-228-2801 ■ *Web:* www.theinnonthelake.com
Candlewood Suites 3 Ravinia Dr Suite 100 . . . Atlanta GA 30346 770-604-2000 604-5403
Web: www.candlewoodsuites.com
Cannery Casino & Hotel 2121 E Craig Rd . . . North Las Vegas NV 89030 702-507-5700 507-5750
TF: 866-999-4899 ■ *Web:* www.cannerycasinos.com
Canoe Bay RR 2 PO Box 28 . . . Chetek WI 54728 715-924-4594 924-2078
Web: www.canoebay.com
Canterbury Hotel 123 S Illinois St . . . Indianapolis IN 46225 317-634-3000 685-2519
TF: 800-538-8186 ■ *Web:* www.canterburyhotel.com
Canterbury Inn 1900 Canterbury Rd . . . Sacramento CA 95815 916-927-3492 641-8594
Cape Cod Irish Village 512 Main St . . . West Yarmouth MA 02673 508-771-0100
TF: 800-244-9692 ■ *Web:* www.capecod-irishvillage.com
Cape Point Hotel Rte 28 . . . West Yarmouth MA 02673 508-778-1500 778-5516
TF: 800-323-9505 ■ *Web:* www.capepointhotel.com
Capital Hill Hotel & Suites 88 Albert St . . . Ottawa ON K1P5E9 613-235-1413 235-6047
TF: 800-463-7705 ■ *Web:* www.capitalhill.com
Capital Hotel 111 W Markham St . . . Little Rock AR 72201 501-374-7474 370-7091
TF: 877-637-0036 ■ *Web:* www.thecapitalhotel.com
Capitol Hill Suites 200 C St SE . . . Washington DC 20003 202-543-6000 547-2608
TF: 888-627-7811 ■ *Web:* www.capitolhillsuites.com
Capitol Plaza Hotel & Conference Center 100 State St . . . Montpelier VT 05602 802-223-5252 229-5427
TF: 800-274-5252 ■ *Web:* www.capitolplaza.com
Capitol Plaza Hotel Jefferson City 415 W McCarty St . . . Jefferson City MO 65101 573-635-1234 635-4565
TF: 800-338-8088 ■ *Web:* www.jqh.com
Capitol Plaza Hotel Topeka 1717 SW Topeka Blvd . . . Topeka KS 66612 785-431-7200 431-7206
TF: 800-579-7937 ■ *Web:* www.jqhhotels.com/home.aspx
Captain Bartlett Inn 1411 Airport Way . . . Fairbanks AK 99701 907-452-1888 452-7674
TF: 800-544-7528 ■ *Web:* www.captainbartlettinn.com
Captain Daniel Stone Inn 10 Water St . . . Brunswick ME 04011 207-725-9898 725-9898
TF: 877-573-5151 ■ *Web:* www.captaindanielstoneinn.com
Caribe Royale Orlando All-Suites Hotel & Convention Center 8101 World Center Dr . . . Orlando FL 32821 407-238-8000 238-8050
TF: 800-823-8300 ■ *Web:* www.cariberoyale.com
Carlson Hotels Worldwide PO Box 59159 . . . Minneapolis MN 55459 763-212-1000
Web: www.carlson.com
Country Inns & Suites by Carlson PO Box 59159 . . . Minneapolis MN 55459 763-212-1000
TF Resv: 800-456-4000 ■ *Web:* www.countryinns.com
Park Inn PO Box 59159 . . . Minneapolis MN 55459 763-212-1000 212-6631
TF Resv: 800-670-7275 ■ *Web:* www.parkinn.com
Park Plaza Hotels & Resorts PO Box 59159 . . . Minneapolis MN 55459 763-212-1000 212-6631
Web: www.carlsonhotelsmedia.tekgroup.com
Radisson Hotels & Resorts PO Box 59159 . . . Minneapolis MN 55459 763-212-5526 212-3400
TF: 800-333-3333 ■ *Web:* www.radisson.com
Regent International Hotels PO Box 59159 . . . Minneapolis MN 55459 763-212-3300 212-8197
Web: www.regenthotels.com
Carlton Arms 160 E 25th St . . . New York NY 10010 212-679-0680
Web: www.carltonarms.com
Carlton on Madison Ave 22 E 29th St . . . New York NY 10016 212-532-4100 889-8683
TF: 800-542-1502 ■ *Web:* www.carltonhotelny.com
Carlyle The 35 E 76th St . . . New York NY 10021 212-744-1600 717-4682
TF: 800-227-5737 ■ *Web:* www.thecarlyle.com
Carlyle Suites Hotel 1731 New Hampshire Ave NW . . . Washington DC 20009 202-234-3200 387-0085
TF: 800-964-5377 ■ *Web:* www.carlylesuites.com

	City	State	ZIP	Phone	Fax
Carmel River Inn Hwy 1 at Carmel River Bridge PO Box 221609	Carmel	CA	93922	831-624-1575	624-0290
TF: 800-882-8142 ■ *Web:* www.carmelriverinn.com					
Carnegie Hotel 1216 W State of Franklin Rd	Johnson City	TN	37604	423-979-6400	979-6424
TF: 866-757-8277 ■ *Web:* www.carnegiehotel.com					
Carolina Inn 211 Pittsboro St	Chapel Hill	NC	27516	919-933-2001	962-3400
TF: 800-962-8519 ■ *Web:* www.carolinainn.com					
Carousel Beachfront Hotel & Suites 11700 Coastal Hwy	Ocean City	MD	21842	410-524-1000	524-7766
TF: 800-641-0011 ■ *Web:* www.carouselhotel.com					
Carousel Inn & Suites 1530 S Harbor Blvd	Anaheim	CA	92802	714-758-0444	772-9960
TF: 800-854-6767 ■ *Web:* www.carouselinnandsuites.com					
Cartier Place Suite Hotel 180 Cooper St	Ottawa	ON	K2P2L5	613-236-5000	238-3842
TF: 800-236-8399 ■ *Web:* www.suitedreams.com					
Cartwright Hotel 524 Sutter St	San Francisco	CA	94102	415-421-2865	398-6345
TF: 800-794-7661 ■ *Web:* www.cartwrighthotel.com					
Casa Casuarina 1116 Ocean Dr	Miami Beach	FL	33139	305-672-6604	672-5930
Web: www.casacasuarina.com					
Casa de Estrellas 310 E Marcy St	Santa Fe	NM	87501	505-795-0278	989-7381
Web: casadeestrellas.com					
Casa Grande Suite Hotel 834 Ocean Dr	Miami Beach	FL	33139	305-672-7003	673-3669
TF: 866-420-2272 ■ *Web:* www.casagrandesuitehotel.com/					
Casa Madrona Hotel 801 Bridgeway	Sausalito	CA	94965	415-332-0502	288-0502
TF: 800-567-9524 ■ *Web:* www.casamadrona.com					
Casa Monica Hotel 95 Cordova St	Saint Augustine	FL	32084	904-827-1888	819-6065
TF: 888-472-6312 ■ *Web:* www.casamonica.com					
Casa Munras Hotel 700 Munras Ave	Monterey	CA	93940	831-375-2411	375-1365
TF: 800-222-2558 ■ *Web:* www.hotelcasamunras.com					
Casa Sirena Hotel & Marina 3605 Peninsula Rd	Oxnard	CA	93035	805-985-6311	985-4329
TF: 800-447-3529 ■ *Web:* www.casasirenahotel.com					
Casa Via Mar Inn & Tennis Club					
377 W Channel Islands Blvd	Port Hueneme	CA	93041	805-984-6222	984-9490
TF: 800-992-5522 ■ *Web:* www.casaviamar.com					
Casablanca Hotel 147 W 43rd St	New York	NY	10036	212-869-1212	391-7585
TF: 888-922-7225 ■ *Web:* www.casablancahotel.com					
Cascades Inn 3226 Shepherd of the Hills Expy	Branson	MO	65616	417-335-8424	334-1927
TF: 800-588-8424 ■ *Web:* www.cascadesinn.com					
Casino Aztar Hotel 421 NW Riverside Dr	Evansville	IN	47708	812-433-4444	433-4384
TF: 800-544-0120 ■ *Web:* www.casinoaztar.com					
Casino Royale Hotel 3411 Las Vegas Blvd S	Las Vegas	NV	89109	702-737-3500	650-4743
Web: www.casinoroyalehotel.com					
Casino Windsor Hotel 377 Riverside Dr E	Windsor	ON	N9A7H7	519-258-7878	985-5800
TF: 800-991-7777 ■ *Web:* www.harrahs.com					
Castle Group Inc Castle Resorts & Hotels					
500 Ala Moana Blvd Suite 555 3 Waterfront Plaza	Honolulu	HI	96813	808-524-0900	521-9994
TF: 800-733-7753 ■ *Web:* www.castleresorts.com					
Castle on the Hudson 400 Benedict Ave	Tarrytown	NY	10591	914-631-1980	631-4612
TF: 800-616-4487 ■ *Web:* www.castleonthehudson.com					
Castle Inn & Suites 1734 S Harbor Blvd	Anaheim	CA	92802	714-774-8111	956-4736
TF: 800-521-5653 ■ *Web:* www.castleinn.com					
Castle Resorts & Hotels					
500 Ala Moana Blvd Suite 555 3 Waterfront Plaza	Honolulu	HI	96813	808-524-0900	521-9994
TF: 800-733-7753 ■ *Web:* www.castleresorts.com					
Castle in the Sand Hotel 3701 Atlantic Ave	Ocean City	MD	21842	410-289-6846	289-9446
TF: 800-552-7263 ■ *Web:* www.castleinthesand.com					
Castleton Suites 9600 Southland Cir SW	Calgary	AB	T2V5A1	403-640-3900	253-4447
Web: www.castletonsuites.com					
Cathedral Hill Hotel 1101 Van Ness Ave	San Francisco	CA	94109	415-776-8200	441-2841
TF: 800-622-0855 ■ *Web:* www.cathedralhillhotel.com					
Cavalier Hotel 1320 Ocean Dr	Miami Beach	FL	33139	305-531-3555	531-5543
Web: www.cavaliermiami.com					
Celebration Hotel 700 Bloom St	Celebration	FL	34747	407-566-6000	566-6001
TF: 888-499-3800 ■ *Web:* www.celebrationhotel.com					
Centennial Hotel 96 Pleasant St	Concord	NH	03301	603-225-7102	225-5031
TF: 800-360-4839 ■ *Web:* www.thecentennialhotel.com					
Center Court Historic Inn & Cottages 915 Center St	Key West	FL	33040	305-296-9292	296-2561
TF: 800-797-8787 ■ *Web:* www.centercourtkw.com					
Century Hotel South Beach 140 Ocean Dr	Miami Beach	FL	33139	305-674-8855	538-5733
TF: 888-982-3688 ■ *Web:* www.centurysouthbeach.com					
Century House Inn 997 New Loudon Rd Rt 9	Latham	NY	12110	518-785-0931	785-3274
TF: 888-674-6873 ■ *Web:* www.thecenturyhouse.com					
Century Plaza Hotel & Spa 1015 Burrard St	Vancouver	BC	V6Z1Y5	604-687-0575	682-5790
TF: 800-663-1818 ■ *Web:* www.century-plaza.com					
Century Suites Hotel 300 SR-446	Bloomington	IN	47401	812-336-7777	336-0436
TF: 800-766-5446 ■ *Web:* www.centurysuites.com					
Chamberlain West Hollywood 1000 Westmount Dr	West Hollywood	CA	90069	310-657-7400	854-6744
TF: 800-201-9637 ■ *Web:* www.chamberlainwesthollywood.com					
Chambers Hotel 15 W 56th St	New York	NY	10019	212-974-5656	974-5657
TF: 866-204-5656 ■ *Web:* www.chambersnyc.com					
Chambers Hotel Minneapolis 901 Hennepin Ave	Minneapolis	MN	55403	612-767-6900	767-6801
TF: 877-767-6990 ■ *Web:* www.chambersminneapolis.com					
Chancellor Hotel on Union Square 433 Powell St	San Francisco	CA	94102	415-362-2004	362-1403
TF: 800-428-4748 ■ *Web:* www.chancellorhotel.com					
Chandler Inn 26 Chandler St	Boston	MA	02116	617-482-3450	542-3428
TF: 800-842-3450 ■ *Web:* www.chandlerinn.com					
Channel Inn Hotel 650 Water St SW	Washington	DC	20024	202-554-2400	863-1164
TF: 800-368-5668 ■ *Web:* www.channelinn.com					
Channel Islands Inn & Suites 1001 E Channel Islands Blvd	Oxnard	CA	93033	805-487-7755	486-1374
TF: 800-344-5998 ■ *Web:* www.channelislandsinn.com					
Charles Hotel Harvard Square 1 Bennett St	Cambridge	MA	02138	617-864-1200	864-5715
TF: 800-882-1818 ■ *Web:* www.charleshotel.com					
Charles Inn 20 Broad St	Bangor	ME	04401	207-992-2820	992-2826
Web: www.thecharlesinn.com					
Charleston Place 205 Meeting St	Charleston	SC	29401	843-722-4900	722-0728
TF: 800-611-5545 ■ *Web:* www.charlestonplace.com					
Charter at Beaver Creek 120 Offerson Rd PO Box 5310	Avon	CO	81620	970-949-6660	949-6709
TF: 800-525-6660 ■ *Web:* www.thecharter.com					
Chase Hotel at Palm Springs 200 W Arenas Rd	Palm Springs	CA	92262	760-320-8866	323-1501
TF: 877-532-4273 ■ *Web:* www.chasehotelpalmsprings.com					
Chase Park Plaza 212 N Kingshighway Blvd	Saint Louis	MO	63108	314-633-3000	633-3077
TF: 877-587-2427 ■ *Web:* www.chaseparkplaza.com					
Chase Suite Hotels by Woodfin					
12671 High Bluff Dr Suite 300	San Diego	CA	92130	858-794-2338	794-2348
TF: 800-237-8811 ■ *Web:* www.woodfinsuitehotels.com					
Chateau Bonne Entente 3400 ch Sainte-Foy	Sainte-Foy	QC	G1X1S6	418-653-5221	653-3098
TF: 800-463-4390 ■ *Web:* www.chateaubonneentente.com					
Chateau Dupre Hotel 131 Rue Decatur	New Orleans	LA	70130	504-569-0600	569-0606
TF: 800-211-3447 ■ *Web:* www.neworleansfinehotels.com/chateauduprehotel/					
Chateau Hotel & Conference Center 1601 Jumer Dr	Bloomington	IL	61704	309-662-2020	662-6522
TF: 866-690-4006 ■ *Web:* www.chateauhotel.biz					
Chateau on the Lake 415 N State Hwy 265	Branson	MO	65616	417-334-1161	339-5566
TF: 888-333-5253 ■ *Web:* www.chateauonthelakebranson.com					
Chateau Louis Hotel & Conference Centre 11727 Kingsway	Edmonton	AB	T5G3A1	780-452-7770	454-3436
TF: 800-661-9843 ■ *Web:* www.chateaulouis.com					
Chateau Marmont Hotel 8221 Sunset Blvd	Hollywood	CA	90046	323-656-1010	655-5311
TF: 800-242-8328 ■ *Web:* www.chateaumarmont.com					
Chateau Sonesta Hotel New Orleans 800 Iberville St	New Orleans	LA	70112	504-586-0800	586-1987
TF: 800-766-3782 ■ *Web:* www.sonesta.com/neworleans_chateau					

	City	State	ZIP	Phone	Fax
Chateau du Sureau 48688 Victoria Ln	Oakhurst	CA	93644	559-683-6860	683-0800
Web: www.chateausureau.com					
Chateau Vaudreuil Suites Hotel					
21700 Transcanada Hwy	Vaudreuil-Dorion	QC	J7V8P3	450-455-0955	455-6617
TF: 800-363-7896 ■ *Web:* www.chateau-vaudreuil.com					
Chateau Versailles 1659 Sherbrooke St W	Montreal	QC	H3H1E3	514-933-3611	933-7102
TF: 888-933-8111 ■ *Web:* www.versailleshotels.com					
Chelsea Savoy Hotel 204 W 23rd St	New York	NY	10011	212-929-9353	741-6309
TF: 866-929-9353 ■ *Web:* www.chelseasavoynyc.com					
Cheshire Lodge 6300 Clayton Rd	Saint Louis	MO	63117	314-647-7300	647-0442
TF: 800-325-7378 ■ *Web:* www.cheshirelodge.net					
Chesterfield Hotel 855 Collins Ave	Miami Beach	FL	33139	305-531-5831	535-9665
TF: 877-762-3477 ■ *Web:* www.thechesterfieldhotel.com					
Chesterfield Hotel 363 Cocoanut Row	Palm Beach	FL	33480	561-659-5800	659-6707
TF: 800-243-7871 ■ *Web:* www.chesterfieldpb.com					
Chestnut Hill Hotel 8229 Germantown Ave	Philadelphia	PA	19118	215-242-5905	242-8778
TF: 800-628-9744 ■ *Web:* www.chestnuthillhotel.com					
Chiltern Inn 3 Cromwell Harbor Rd	Bar Harbor	ME	04609	207-288-0114	288-0124
TF: 800-404-0114 ■ *Web:* www.chilterninn.com					
Chimo Hotel 1199 Joseph Cyr St	Ottawa	ON	K1J7T4	613-744-1060	744-7845
TF: 800-387-9779 ■ *Web:* www.chimohotel.com					
Choice Hotels International Inc 10750 Columbia Pike	Silver Spring	MD	20901	301-592-5000	592-6157
NYSE: CHH ■ *TF:* 800-424-6423 ■ *Web:* www.choicehotels.com					
Cambria Suites 10750 Columbia Pike	Silver Spring	MD	20901	301-592-5000	592-6157
TF: 800-424-6423 ■ *Web:* www.cambriasuites.com					
Choice Hotels Canada Inc 5090 Explorer Dr Suite 500	Mississauga	ON	L4W4T9	905-602-2222	624-7796
TF: 800-424-6423 ■ *Web:* www.choicehotels.ca					
Clarion Hotels 10750 Columbia Pike	Silver Spring	MD	20901	301-592-5000	592-6157
TF: 800-424-6423 ■ *Web:* www.clarionhotel.com					
Comfort Inns 10750 Columbia Pike	Silver Spring	MD	20901	301-592-5000	592-6157
TF: 800-424-6423 ■ *Web:* www.comfortinns.com					
Comfort Suites 10750 Columbia Pike	Silver Spring	MD	20901	301-592-5000	592-6157
TF: 800-424-6423 ■ *Web:* www.comfortsuites.com					
Econo Lodge 10750 Columbia Pike	Silver Spring	MD	20901	301-592-5000	592-6157
TF: 800-424-6423 ■ *Web:* www.econolodge.com					
MainStay Suites 10750 Columbia Pike	Silver Spring	MD	20901	301-592-5000	592-6157
TF: 800-424-6423 ■ *Web:* www.mainstaysuites.com					
Quality Inns Hotels & Suites 10750 Columbia Pike	Silver Spring	MD	20901	301-592-5000	592-6157
TF: 800-424-6423 ■ *Web:* www.qualityinn.com					
Rodeway Inns 10750 Columbia Pike	Silver Spring	MD	20901	301-592-5000	592-6157
TF: 800-424-6423 ■ *Web:* www.rodeway.com					
Sleep Inns 10750 Columbia Pike	Silver Spring	MD	20901	301-592-5000	592-6157
TF: 800-424-6423 ■ *Web:* www.sleepinn.com					
Suburban Extended Stay Hotel 10750 Columbia Pike	Silver Spring	MD	20901	301-592-5000	592-6157
TF Resv: 877-424-6423 ■ *Web:* www.suburbanhotels.com					
Christy Estates Suites 3942 Holly Rd	Corpus Christi	TX	78415	361-854-1091	854-4766
TF: 800-678-4836 ■ *Web:* www.christyestatesuites.com					
Chrysalis Inn & Spa 804 10th St	Bellingham	WA	98225	360-756-1005	647-0342
TF: 888-808-0005 ■ *Web:* www.thechrysalisinn.com					
Churchill Hotel 1914 Connecticut Ave NW	Washington	DC	20009	202-797-2000	462-0944
TF: 800-424-2464 ■ *Web:* www.thechurchillhotel.com					
Cincinnatian Hotel 601 Vine St	Cincinnati	OH	45202	513-381-3000	651-0256
TF: 800-942-9000 ■ *Web:* cincinnatianhotel.com					
Circa39 Hotel 3900 Collins Ave	Miami Beach	FL	33140	305-538-4900	538-4998
TF: 877-247-2239 ■ *Web:* www.circa39.com					
Circus Circus Hotel & Casino Reno 500 N Sierra St	Reno	NV	89503	775-329-0711	328-9652
TF: 800-648-5010 ■ *Web:* www.circusreno.com					
Circus Circus Hotel Casino & Theme Park Las Vegas					
2880 Las Vegas Blvd S	Las Vegas	NV	89109	702-734-0410	794-3816
TF Resv: 800-634-3450 ■ *Web:* www.circuscircus.com					
Citadel Halifax Hotel 1960 Brunswick St	Halifax	NS	B3J2G7	902-422-1391	429-6672
TF: 800-565-7162 ■ *Web:* www.citadelhalifax.com					
City Suites Hotel 933 W Belmont Ave	Chicago	IL	60657	773-404-3400	404-3405
TF: 800-248-9108 ■ *Web:* www.cityinns.com					
Civic Plaza Hotel 505 Pine St	Abilene	TX	79601	325-676-0222	676-0513
TF: 800-588-0222 ■ *Web:* www.civicplazahotel.com					
CJ Grand Hotel & Spa 67585 Hacienda Ave	Desert Hot Springs	CA	92240	760-329-4488	329-4570
Web: www.cjgrandhotel.com					
Clarendon Hotel & Suites 401 W Clarendon Ave	Phoenix	AZ	85013	602-252-7363	274-9009
Web: www.theclarendon.net					
Clarion Collection Sundance Plaza Hotel					
3050 University Pkwy	Winston-Salem	NC	27105	336-723-2911	714-4578
Web: www.clarionhotel.com					
Clarion Hotels 10750 Columbia Pike	Silver Spring	MD	20901	301-592-5000	592-6157
TF: 800-424-6423 ■ *Web:* www.clarionhotel.com					
Clayton on the Park 8025 Bonhomme Ave	Clayton	MO	63105	314-721-6543	721-8588
TF: 800-323-7500 ■ *Web:* www.claytononthepark.com					
Cleftstone Manor 92 Eden St	Bar Harbor	ME	04609	207-288-8086	288-2089
TF: 888-288-4951 ■ *Web:* www.cleftstone.com					
Cliff House at Pikes Peak 306 Canyon Ave	Manitou Springs	CO	80829	719-685-3000	685-3913
TF: 888-212-7000 ■ *Web:* www.thecliffhouse.com					
Clift The 495 Geary St	San Francisco	CA	94102	415-775-4700	441-4621
TF: 800-652-5438					
Clinton Inn Hotel 145 Dean Dr	Tenafly	NJ	07670	201-871-3200	871-3435
TF: 800-275-4411 ■ *Web:* www.clinton-inn.com					
Clocktower Inn Hotel 181 E Santa Clara St	Ventura	CA	93001	805-652-0141	643-1432
TF: 800-727-1027 ■ *Web:* www.clocktowerinn.com					
ClubHouse Inns of America Inc 3211 W Sencore Dr	Sioux Falls	SD	57107	605-334-2371	334-8480
Web: www.clubhouseinn.com					
C'mon Inn Billings 2020 Overland Ave	Billings	MT	59102	406-655-1100	652-7672
TF: 800-655-1170 ■ *Web:* www.cmoninn.com					
C'mon Inn Fargo 4338 20th Ave SW	Fargo	ND	58103	701-277-9944	277-9117
TF: 800-334-1570 ■ *Web:* www.cmoninn.com					
C'mon Inn Grand Forks 3051 32nd Ave S	Grand Forks	ND	58201	701-775-3320	780-8141
TF: 800-255-2323 ■ *Web:* www.cmoninn.com					
Coachman Inn 32959 SR-Hwy 20	Oak Harbor	WA	98277	360-675-0727	675-1419
TF: 800-635-0043 ■ *Web:* www.thecoachmaninn.com					
Coalson Plantation 301 Showboat Ln	Thomasville	GA	31792	229-226-2290	226-4585
TF: 888-920-3030 ■ *Web:* www.coalsonplantation.com/					
Coast Hotels & Resorts Canada					
1090 W Georgia St Suite 900	Vancouver	BC	V6E3V7	604-682-7982	682-7982
Web: www.coasthotels.com					
Coast Hotels & Resorts USA 2003 Western Ave Suite 500	Seattle	WA	98121	206-826-2700	826-2701
Web: www.coasthotels.com					
Coastal Hotel Group 2101 4th Ave Suite 1330	Seattle	WA	98121	206-388-0400	388-0401
Web: www.coastalhotel.com					
Coastal Inn Concorde 379 Windmill Rd	Dartmouth	NS	B3A1J6	902-465-7777	465-3956
TF: 800-565-1565 ■ *Web:* www.coastalinns.com/halifax.php					
Coastal Inns Inc 515 Kennedy St Unit 5	Dieppe	NB	E1A7R9	506-859-2486	857-1791
TF: 800-665-7829 ■ *Web:* www.coastalinns.com					
Cocca's Inn & Suites 2 Wolf Rd	Albany	NY	12205	518-459-2240	459-9758
TF: 888-426-2227 ■ *Web:* www.coccas.com					
Cohasset Harbor Inn 124 Elm St	Cohasset	MA	02025	781-383-6650	383-2872
TF: 800-252-5287					
Cohutta Lodge 500 Cochise Trail	Chatsworth	GA	30705	706-695-9601	695-0913
TF: 800-394-9790 ■ *Web:* www.cohuttalodge.com					

Phone Fax

Colby Hill Inn 33 The Oaks PO Box 779 ... Henniker NH 03242 603-428-3281 428-9218
TF: 800-531-0330 ■ *Web:* www.colbyhillinn.com

Colcord Hotel 15 N Robinson Ave ... Oklahoma City OK 73102 405-601-4300 208-4399
TF: 866-781-3800 ■ *Web:* www.colcordhotel.com

Colgate Inn 1 Payne St ... Hamilton NY 13346 315-824-2300 824-4500
Web: www.colgateinn.com

Collegiate Village Inn 2121 W Tennessee St ... Tallahassee FL 32304 850-576-6121 576-3508

Colonnade Hotel 120 Huntington Ave ... Boston MA 02116 617-424-7000 424-1717
TF: 800-962-3030 ■ *Web:* www.colonnadehotel.com

Colony The 1157 Chapel St ... New Haven CT 06511 203-776-1234 772-3929
Web: www.colonyatyale.com

Colony Hotel 155 Hammon Ave ... Palm Beach FL 33480 561-655-5430 832-7318
TF: 800-521-5525 ■ *Web:* www.thecolonypalmbeach.com

Colony Hotel & Cabana Club 525 E Atlantic Ave ... Delray Beach FL 33483 561-276-4123 276-0123
Web: www.thecolonyhotel.com

Colony South Hotel 7401 Surratts Rd ... Clinton MD 20735 301-856-4500 868-1439
TF: 800-537-1147 ■ *Web:* www.colonysouth.com

Colorado Belle Hotel & Casino 2100 S Casino Dr ... Laughlin NV 89029 702-298-4000 298-3697*
**Fax:* Hum Res ■ *TF Resv:* 800-477-4837 ■ *Web:* www.coloradobelle.com

Columbia Gorge Hotel 4000 Westcliff Dr ... Hood River OR 97031 541-386-5566 386-9141
TF: 800-345-1921 ■ *Web:* columbiagorgehotel.com/

Columbia Hospitality 2223 Alaskan Way Suite 200 ... Seattle WA 98121 206-239-1800 239-1801
Web: www.columbiahospitality.com

Columbia Sussex Corp 207 Grandview Dr ... Fort Mitchell KY 41017 859-331-0091 578-1190
Web: www.columbiasussex.com

Columns The 3811 St Charles Ave ... New Orleans LA 70115 504-899-9308 899-8170
TF: 800-445-9308 ■ *Web:* www.thecolumns.com

Comfort Inn & Suites Milwaukee 916 E State St ... Milwaukee WI 53202 414-276-8800 765-1919
TF: 888-522-9472

Comfort Inns 10750 Columbia Pike ... Silver Spring MD 20901 301-592-5000 592-6157
TF: 800-424-6423 ■ *Web:* www.comfortinns.com

Comfort Suites 10750 Columbia Pike ... Silver Spring MD 20901 301-592-5000 592-6157
TF: 800-424-6423 ■ *Web:* www.comfortsuites.com

Commander Hotel 1401 Atlantic Ave ... Ocean City MD 21842 410-289-6166 289-3998
TF: 888-289-6166 ■ *Web:* www.commanderhotel.com

Commonwealth Park Suites Hotel 901 Bank St ... Richmond VA 23219 804-343-7300 343-1025
TF: 888-343-7301 ■ *Web:* www.commonwealthparksuites.com

Conch House Heritage Inn 625 Truman Ave ... Key West FL 33040 305-293-0020 293-8447
TF: 800-207-5806 ■ *Web:* www.conchhouse.com

Conch House Marina Resort 57 Comares Ave ... Saint Augustine FL 32080 904-829-8646 829-5414
TF: 800-940-6256 ■ *Web:* www.conch-house.com

Concourse Hotel & Conference Center
4300 International Gateway ... Columbus OH 43219 614-237-2515 237-6134
TF: 800-541-4574 ■ *Web:* www.theconcoursehotel.com

Congress Plaza Hotel & Convention Center
520 S Michigan Ave ... Chicago IL 60605 312-427-3800 427-3972
TF: 800-635-1666 ■ *Web:* www.congressplazahotel.com

Conrad Hotels 9336 Civic Center Dr ... Beverly Hills CA 90210 310-278-4321 205-4613
TF: 800-445-8667 ■ *Web:* www.conradhotels.com

Conrad Miami 1395 Brickell Ave ... Miami FL 33131 305-503-6500 503-6599
Web: miami.conradmeetings.com

Continental Bayside Hotel 146 Biscayne Blvd ... Miami FL 33132 305-358-4555 371-5253
TF: 800-742-6331

Cooper Cos Cooper Hotels Div 1407 Union Ave Suite 400 ... Memphis TN 38104 901-725-9631 274-9169
Web: www.cooperhotels.com

Cooper Cos CSS Hotels Div 1407 Union Ave Suite 400 ... Memphis TN 38104 901-725-9631 274-9169
Web: www.cooperhotels.com

Copley Square Hotel 47 Huntington Ave ... Boston MA 02116 617-536-9000 267-3547
TF: 800-225-7062 ■ *Web:* www.copleysquarehotel.com

Coral Reef Resort 5800 Gulf Blvd ... Saint Pete Beach FL 33706 727-363-1604 363-6434
TF: 800-352-4874 ■ *Web:* www.vrivacations.com/resorts/crr

Cornhusker Hotel The 333 S 13th St ... Lincoln NE 68508 402-474-7474 474-1847
TF: 800-793-7474 ■ *Web:* www.thecornhusker.com

Cortina Inn & Resort 103 US Rt 4 ... Killington VT 05751 802-773-3333 773-8530
TF: 800-451-6108 ■ *Web:* www.cortinainn.com

Cosmopolitan Hotel 95 W Broadway ... New York NY 10007 212-566-1900 566-6909
TF: 888-895-9400 ■ *Web:* www.cosmohotel.com

Cosmopolitan Toronto Hotel 8 Colborne St ... Toronto ON M5E1E1 416-350-2000 350-2460
TF: 800-958-3488 ■ *Web:* www.cosmotoronto.com/

Country Hearth Inn & Suites 50 Glen Lake Pkwy NE Suite 350 ... Atlanta GA 30328 770-393-2662 393-2480
TF: 800-432-7992 ■ *Web:* www.countryhearth.com

Country Inn Lake Resort 1332 Airport Rd ... Hot Springs AR 71913 501-767-3535
TF: 800-822-7402 ■ *Web:* www.countryinnlakeresort.com

Country Inn at the Mall 936 Stillwater Ave ... Bangor ME 04401 207-941-0200 942-1167
TF: 800-244-3961 ■ *Web:* www.countryinnatthemall.net

Country Inn & Suites Albuquerque
7620 Pan American Fwy NE ... Albuquerque NM 87109 505-823-1300 823-2896
TF: 888-201-1746 ■ *Web:* www.countryinns.com

Country Inns & Suites by Carlson PO Box 59159 ... Minneapolis MN 55459 763-212-1000
TF Resv: 800-456-4000 ■ *Web:* www.countryinns.com

Courtyard Fort Lauderdale Beach 440 Seabreeze Blvd ... Fort Lauderdale FL 33316 954-524-8733 467-7489
TF: 888-236-2427 ■ *Web:* www.marriott.com/courtyard/travel.mi

Courtyard by Marriott 1 Marriott Dr ... Washington DC 20058 301-380-3000 380-3090
TF: 800-321-2211 ■ *Web:* www.marriott.com/courtyard

Cove Inn 900 Broad Ave S ... Naples FL 34102 239-262-7161 261-6905
TF: 800-255-4365 ■ *Web:* www.bestof.net/naples/hotels/coveinn/

Cowboy Village Resort 120 S Flat Creek Dr PO Box 8040 ... Jackson WY 83001 307-733-3121 739-1955
TF: 800-962-4988 ■ *Web:* www.cowboyvillage.com

Cozy Country Inn 103 Frederick Rd ... Thurmont MD 21788 301-271-4301 271-3107
Web: www.cozyvillage.com

Craftsman Inn 7300 E Genesee St ... Fayetteville NY 13066 315-637-8000 637-2440
TF: 800-797-4464 ■ *Web:* www.craftsmaninn.com

Creekside Inn 3400 El Camino Real ... Palo Alto CA 94306 650-493-2411 493-6787
TF: 866-589-3411 ■ *Web:* www.creekside-inn.com

Crescent Hotel 75 Prospect Ave ... Eureka Springs AR 72632 479-253-9766 253-5296
TF: 877-342-9766 ■ *Web:* www.crescent-hotel.com

Crescent Hotel 403 N Crescent Dr ... Beverly Hills CA 90210 310-247-0505 247-9053
TF: 800-451-1566 ■ *Web:* www.crescentbh.com

Crest Hotel & Suites 1670 James Ave ... Miami Beach FL 33139 305-531-0321 531-8180
Web: www.crestgrouphotels.com

Crestline Hotels & Resorts 8405 Greensboro Dr Suite 500 ... McLean VA 22102 571-382-1800 382-1860
Web: www.crestlinehotels.com

Crestwood Suites Extended Stay Hotels
4770 S Atlanta Rd Suite 200 ... Smyrna GA 30080 404-350-9990 350-8660
Web: www.crestwoodsuites.com

Crockett Hotel 320 Bonham St ... San Antonio TX 78205 210-225-6500 225-6251
TF: 800-292-1050 ■ *Web:* crockethotel.com/

Cross Creek Resort 3815 SR 8 ... Titusville PA 16354 814-827-9611 827-2062
TF: 800-461-3173 ■ *Web:* www.crosscreekresort.com

Crossland Economy Studios 100 Dunbar St ... Spartanburg SC 29306 864-573-1600 573-1695
TF: 877-276-7752 ■ *Web:* www.crosslandstudios.com

Crown Reef Resort 2913 S Ocean Blvd ... Myrtle Beach SC 29577 843-626-8077 916-0735
TF: 877-435-9125 ■ *Web:* www.crownreef.com/

Crowne Plaza Campbell House 1375 Harrodsburg Rd ... Lexington KY 40504 859-255-4281 254-4368
TF: 800-227-6963

Crowne Plaza Hotels & Resorts 3 Ravinia Dr Suite 100 ... Atlanta GA 30346 770-604-2000 604-5403
Web: www.crowneplaza.com

Crystal Beach Suites & Health Club 6985 Collins Ave ... Miami Beach FL 33141 305-865-9555 866-3514
TF: 800-435-0766 ■ *Web:* www.crystalbeachsuites.com

Crystal Inn Gulfport 9379 Canal Rd ... Gulfport MS 39503 228-822-9600 822-0666
TF: 888-822-9600 ■ *Web:* www.crystalinns.com/glfpt.html

Crystal Inn Salt Lake City Downtown 230 W 500 South ... Salt Lake City UT 84101 801-328-4466 328-4072
TF: 800-366-4466 ■ *Web:* www.crystalinns.com/slcdt.html

CSS Hotels Div Cooper Cos 1407 Union Ave Suite 400 ... Memphis TN 38104 901-725-9631 274-9169
Web: www.cooperhotels.com

Curtis The 1405 Curtis St ... Denver CO 80202 303-571-0300 825-4301
TF: 800-525-6651 ■ *Web:* www.thecurtis.com

Custom Hotel 8639 Lincoln Blvd ... Los Angeles CA 90045 310-645-0400 645-0700
TF: 866-589-3411 ■ *Web:* www.customhotel.com

Cypress Hotel 10050 S DeAnza Blvd ... Cupertino CA 95014 408-253-8900 253-3800
TF: 800-499-1408 ■ *Web:* www.thecypresshotel.com

Cypress Tree Inn 2227 N Fremont St ... Monterey CA 93940 831-372-7586 372-2940
TF: 800-446-8303 ■ *Web:* www.cypresstreeinn.com

Dahlmann Campus Inn 615 E Huron St ... Ann Arbor MI 48104 734-769-2200 769-6222
TF: 800-666-8693 ■ *Web:* www.campusinn.com

Dallas Plaza Hotel 1011 S Akard St ... Dallas TX 75215 214-421-1083 428-6827
Web: www.dallasplazahotel.com

Dan'l Webster Inn 149 Main St ... Sandwich MA 02563 508-888-3622 888-5156
TF: 800-444-3566 ■ *Web:* www.danlwebsterinn.com

Dauphine Orleans Hotel 415 Dauphine St ... New Orleans LA 70112 504-586-1800 586-1409
TF: 800-521-7111 ■ *Web:* www.dauphineorleans.com

Davenport Hotel 10 S Post St ... Spokane WA 99201 509-455-8888 624-4455
TF: 800-899-1482 ■ *Web:* www.thedavenporthotel.com

David William Hotel 700 Biltmore Way ... Coral Gables FL 33134 305-445-7821 913-1933
TF: 800-757-8073 ■ *Web:* www.davidwilliamhotel.com

Davidson Hotel Co 3340 Players Club Suite 200 ... Memphis TN 38125 901-761-4664 821-4104
Web: www.davidsonhotels.com

Days Hotel New York City Broadway 215 W 94th St ... New York NY 10025 212-866-6400 866-1357
TF: 800-834-2972 ■ *Web:* www.daysinn.com

Days Inn 1 Sylvan Way ... Parsippany NJ 07054 973-753-6600
TF Resv: 800-329-7466 ■ *Web:* www.daysinn.com

Daytona Beach Resort & Conference Center
2700 N Atlantic Ave ... Daytona Beach FL 32118 386-672-3770 673-7262
TF: 800-654-6216 ■ *Web:* www.daytonabeachresort.com

Daytona Inn Beach Resort 219 S Atlantic Ave ... Daytona Beach FL 32118 386-252-3626 255-3680
TF: 800-874-1822 ■ *Web:* www.bsrresorts.com/daytona-inn.htm

Dearborn Inn The - A Marriott Hotel 20301 Oakwood Blvd ... Dearborn MI 48124 313-271-2700 271-7464
TF: 800-228-9290 ■ *Web:* www.marriotthotels.com/DTWDI

Deer Path Inn 255 E Illinois Rd ... Lake Forest IL 60045 847-234-2280 234-3352
TF: 800-788-9480 ■ *Web:* www.dpihotel.com

Deerfoot Inn & Casino 11500 35th St SE ... Calgary AB T2Z3W4 403-236-7529 252-4767
TF: 877-236-5225 ■ *Web:* www.deerfootinn.com

Deerhaven Inn & Suites 740 Crocker Ave ... Pacific Grove CA 93950 831-373-1114 655-5048
TF: 800-525-3373 ■ *Web:* www.monterey.com/mcp/deerhaven/index.html

Del Monte Lodge - A Renaissance Hotel & Spa 41 N Main St ... Pittsford NY 14534 585-381-9900 381-9825
TF: 800-386-3376 ■ *Web:* marriott.com/hotels/travel/rocdl

DELAMAR Greenwich Harbor 500 Steamboat Rd ... Greenwich CT 06830 203-661-9800 661-2513
TF: 866-335-2627 ■ *Web:* www.slh.com/delamar

Delano Hotel 1685 Collins Ave ... Miami Beach FL 33139 305-672-2000 532-0099
TF: 800-697-1791 ■ *Web:* www.delano-hotel.com

Delta Hotels Ltd 100 Wellington St W Suite 1200 ... Toronto ON M5K1J3 416-874-2000 874-2001
TF Resv: 800-268-1133 ■ *Web:* www.deltahotels.com

Delta King Riverboat Hotel 1000 Front St ... Sacramento CA 95814 916-444-5464 447-5959
TF: 800-825-5464 ■ *Web:* www.deltaking.com

Denihan Hospitality Group LLC (DHG) Affinia Hotels
500 W 37th St ... New York NY 10018 212-465-3700 465-3697
TF Resv: 866-246-2203 ■ *Web:* www.affinia.com

DePalma Hotel Corp 700 Highlander Blvd Suite 400 ... Arlington TX 76015 817-557-1811 557-4333
Web: www.depalmahotels.com

Desert Inn Resort 900 N Atlantic Ave ... Daytona Beach FL 32118 386-258-6555 238-1635
TF: 800-826-1711 ■ *Web:* desertinnresort.com

Desmond Albany 660 Albany-Shaker Rd ... Albany NY 12211 518-869-8100 869-7659
TF: 800-448-3500 ■ *Web:* desmondhotelsalbany.com

Desmond Great Valley 1 Liberty Blvd ... Malvern PA 19355 610-296-9800 889-9869
TF: 800-575-1776 ■ *Web:* www.desmondgv.com

Destination Hotels & Resorts Inc
10333 E Dry Creek Rd Suite 450 ... Englewood CO 80112 303-799-3830 799-6011
TF: 800-633-8347 ■ *Web:* www.destinationhotels.com

Diamond Head Inn 605 Diamond St ... San Diego CA 92109 858-273-1900 273-8532
TF: 888-478-7829 ■ *Web:* diamond-head-inn.pacificahost.com

Dinah's Garden Hotel 4261 El Camino Real ... Palo Alto CA 94306 650-493-4542 856-4713
TF: 800-227-8220 ■ *Web:* www.dinahshotel.com

Disneyland Hotel 1150 W Magic Way ... Anaheim CA 92802 714-778-6600 956-6597
Web: disneyland.disney.go.com/dlr/index

Disney's Paradise Pier Hotel 1717 S Disneyland Dr ... Anaheim CA 92802 714-999-0990 776-5763
Web: disneyworld.disney.go.com

Disney's Saratoga Springs Resort & Spa
1960 Broadway St ... Lake Buena Vista FL 32830 407-827-1100 827-4444
Web: disneyworld.disney.go.com

Dockers Inn 3060 Green Mountain Dr ... Branson MO 65616 417-334-3600 334-8166
TF: 800-324-8748 ■ *Web:* www.dockersinn.com

Dolce International 28 W Grand Ave ... Montvale NJ 07645 201-307-8700 307-8837
TF: 888-993-6523 ■ *Web:* www.dolce.com

Dolphin Beach Resort 4900 Gulf Blvd ... Saint Pete Beach FL 33706 727-360-7011 367-5909
TF: 800-237-8916 ■ *Web:* www.dolphinbeach.com

Dolphin Inn 1705 Atlantic Ave ... Virginia Beach VA 23451 757-491-1420 425-8390
TF: 800-365-3467 ■ *Web:* www.vbeach.com/hotels/dolphin.htm

Don Hall's Guesthouse 1313 W Washington Center Rd ... Fort Wayne IN 46825 260-489-2524 489-7067
TF: 800-348-1999 ■ *Web:* www.donhalls.com

Donatello The 501 Post St ... San Francisco CA 94102 415-441-7100 885-8842
TF: 800-227-3184 ■ *Web:* www.thedonatello.com

Doral Tesoro Hotel & Golf Club 3300 Championship Pkwy ... Fort Worth TX 76177 817-961-0800 961-0900
TF: 866-983-7676 ■ *Web:* www.doraltesoro.com

Doubletree Claremont 555 W Foothill Blvd ... Claremont CA 91711 909-626-2411 624-0756
TF: 800-222-8733 ■ *Web:* doubletree1.hilton.com

Doubletree Hotel Downtown Wilmington Legal District
700 N King St ... Wilmington DE 19801 302-655-0400 655-0430
TF: 800-222-8733 ■ *Web:* doubletree1.hilton.com

Doubletree Hotels 9336 Civic Center Dr ... Beverly Hills CA 90210 310-278-4321 205-4613
TF: 800-222-8733 ■ *Web:* www.doubletree.com

Doubletree Inn at the Colonnade 4 W University Pkwy ... Baltimore MD 21218 410-235-5400 366-6734
TF: 800-222-8733 ■ *Web:* www.doubletree.com

Doubletree Marina Hotel 2800 Via Cabrillo Marina ... San Pedro CA 90731 310-514-3344 514-8945
TF: 800-222-8733 ■ *Web:* www.sanpedro.doubletree.com

Doubletree North Shore Hotel 9599 Skokie Blvd ... Skokie IL 60077 847-679-7000 679-9841
TF: 800-222-8733 ■ *Web:* doubletree1.hilton.com

Downtown Erie Hotel 18 W 18th St ... Erie PA 16501 814-456-2961 456-7067
Web: www.downtownetiehotel.com

Downtowner Inns 1726 Montreal Cir ... Tucker GA 30084 770-270-1180 270-1077
TF: 800-251-1962 ■ *Web:* www.bookroomsnow.com

Drake Hotel 140 E Walton Pl ... Chicago IL 60611 312-787-2200 787-1431
TF: 800-564-7602 ■ *Web:* www.thedrakehotel.com

Drawbridge Inn 2477 Royal Dr ... Fort Mitchell KY 41017 859-341-2800 341-5644
TF: 800-354-9793 ■ *Web:* www.drawbridgeinn.com

Name / Address	City	State	Zip	Phone	Fax
Dream 210 W 55th St	New York	NY	10019	212-247-2000	581-2248
TF: 866-437-3266 ■ *Web:* www.dreamny.com					
Driftwood Lodge 435 Willoughby Ave	Juneau	AK	99801	907-586-2280	586-1034
TF: 800-544-2239 ■ *Web:* www.driftwoodalaska.com					
Driftwood on the Oceanfront 1600 N Ocean Blvd	Myrtle Beach	SC	29578	843-448-1544	448-2917
TF: 800-942-3456 ■ *Web:* www.driftwoodlodge.com					
Driftwood Shores Resort 88416 1st Ave	Florence	OR	97439	541-997-8263	997-3253
TF: 800-422-5091 ■ *Web:* www.driftwoodshores.com					
Driskill Hotel 604 Brazos St	Austin	TX	78701	512-474-5911	474-2214
TF: 800-252-9367 ■ *Web:* www.driskillhotel.com					
Drury Inns Inc 721 Emerson Rd Suite 400	Saint Louis	MO	63141	314-429-2255	429-5166
TF: 800-378-7946 ■ *Web:* www.druryhotels.com					
Pear Tree Inns 721 Emerson Rd Suite 400	Saint Louis	MO	63141	314-429-2255	429-3679
Web: www.druryhotels.com					
Duane Street Hotel 130 Duane St	New York	NY	10013	212-964-4600	964-4800
TF: 866-589-3411 ■ *Web:* www.duanestreethotel.com/					
Dude Rancher Lodge 415 N 29th St	Billings	MT	59101	406-259-5561	259-0095
TF: 800-221-3302 ■ *Web:* www.duderancherlodge.com					
Duke Towers Residential Suites 807 W Trinity Ave	Durham	NC	27701	919-687-4444	683-1215
TF: 866-385-3869 ■ *Web:* www.duketower.com					
Duke's 8th Avenue Hotel 630 W 8th Ave	Anchorage	AK	99501	907-274-6213	272-6308
TF: 800-478-4837 ■ *Web:* www.dukesalaskahotel.com					
Dunes Manor Hotel 2800 Baltimore Ave	Ocean City	MD	21842	410-289-1100	289-4905
TF: 800-523-2888 ■ *Web:* www.dunesmanor.com					
Dunhill Hotel 237 N Tryon St	Charlotte	NC	28202	704-332-4141	376-4117
TF: 800-354-4141 ■ *Web:* www.dunhillhotel.com					
Dylan Hotel 52 E 41st St	New York	NY	10017	212-338-0500	338-0569
TF: 866-553-9526 ■ *Web:* www.dylanhotel.com					
Dynasty Suites 3735 Iowa Ave	Riverside	CA	92507	951-369-8200	341-6486
TF: 800-842-7899 ■ *Web:* www.dynastysuites.com					
Eagle Mountain House 179 Carter Notch Rd Box E	Jackson	NH	03846	603-383-9111	383-0854
TF: 800-966-5779 ■ *Web:* www.eaglemt.com					
Eagles Landing Hotel 12840 188th Ave SW	Rochester	WA	98579	360-273-8640	273-8670
TF: 800-370-8205 ■ *Web:* www.luckyeagle.com/hotel.htm					
East Canyon Hotel & Spa 288 E Camino Monte Vista	Palm Springs	CA	92262	760-320-1928	320-0599
TF: 877-324-6835 ■ *Web:* www.eastcanyonps.com					
Eastgate Tower 222 E 39th St	New York	NY	10016	212-687-8000	490-2634
TF: 866-233-4642 ■ *Web:* www.affinia.com					
Eastland Park Hotel 157 High St	Portland	ME	04101	207-775-5411	775-2872
TF: 888-671-8008 ■ *Web:* www.eastlandparkhotel.com					
Econo Lodge 10750 Columbia Pike	Silver Spring	MD	20901	301-592-5000	592-6157
TF: 800-424-6423 ■ *Web:* www.econolodge.com					
Eden House 1015 Fleming St	Key West	FL	33040	305-296-6868	294-1221
TF: 800-533-5397 ■ *Web:* www.edenhouse.com					
Edgewater The 666 Wisconsin Ave	Madison	WI	53703	608-256-9071	256-0910
TF: 800-922-5512 ■ *Web:* www.theedgewater.com					
Edgewater Beach Hotel 1901 Gulf Shore Blvd N	Naples	FL	34102	239-403-2000	403-2100
TF: 888-325-7711 ■ *Web:* www.edgewaternaples.com					
Edgewater Hotel 2411 Alaskan Way Pier 67	Seattle	WA	98121	206-728-7000	441-4119
TF: 800-624-0670 ■ *Web:* www.edgewaterhotel.com					
Edgewater Hotel & Casino 2020 S Casino Dr	Laughlin	NV	89028	702-298-2453	298-5606
TF: 800-677-4837 ■ *Web:* www.edgewater-casino.com					
Edgewater Resort 200 Edgewater Cir	Hot Springs	AR	71913	501-767-3311	
TF: 800-234-3687 ■ *Web:* www.ewresort.com					
Edgewater Resort & Waterpark 2400 London Rd	Duluth	MN	55812	218-728-3601	728-3727
TF: 800-777-7925 ■ *Web:* www.duluthwaterpark.com					
Edison Walthall Hotel 225 E Capitol St	Jackson	MS	39201	601-948-6161	948-0088
TF: 800-932-6161 ■ *Web:* www.edisonwalthallhotel.com					
Edmonds Harbor Inn & Suites 130 W Dayton	Edmonds	WA	98020	425-771-5021	672-2880
TF: 800-441-8033					
Edmonton House Suite Hotel 10205 100th Ave	Edmonton	AB	T5J4B5	780-420-4000	420-4364
TF: 800-663-1144 ■ *Web:* www.edmontonhouse.com					
EF Lane Hotel 30 Main St	Keene	NH	03431	603-357-7070	357-7075
TF: 888-300-5056 ■ *Web:* www.eflane.com					
Eisenhower Inn & Conference Center 2634 Emmitsburg Rd	Gettysburg	PA	17325	717-334-8121	334-6066
TF: 800-776-8349 ■ *Web:* www.eisenhower.com					
El Cortez Hotel & Casino 600 E Fremont St	Las Vegas	NV	89101	702-385-5200	474-3633
TF: 800-634-6703 ■ *Web:* www.elcortezhotelcasino.com					
El Encanto Hotel & Garden Villas 1900 Lasuen Rd	Santa Barbara	CA	93103	805-687-5000	687-3903
TF: 800-346-7039 ■ *Web:* www.elencantohotel.com					
El Rey Inn 1862 Cerillos Rd	Santa Fe	NM	87505	505-982-1931	989-9249
TF: 800-521-1349 ■ *Web:* www.elreyinnsantafe.com					
El Tovar Hotel PO Box 699	Grand Canyon	AZ	86023	928-638-2631	638-2855
TF: 888-297-2757 ■ *Web:* www.grandcanyonlodges.com					
Elan Hotel 8435 Beverly Blvd	Los Angeles	CA	90048	323-658-6663	658-6640
TF: 866-589-3411 ■ *Web:* www.elanhotel.com					
Elbow River Inn & Casino 218 18th Ave SE	Calgary	AB	T2G2H8	403-289-8880	290-1457
TF: 800-661-1463 ■ *Web:* www.elbowrivercasino.com					
Eldorado Hotel 309 W San Francisco St	Santa Fe	NM	87501	505-988-4455	995-4543
TF: 800-955-4455 ■ *Web:* www.eldoradohotel.com					
Eldorado Hotel Casino 345 N Virginia St	Reno	NV	89501	775-786-5700	322-7124
TF Resv: 800-648-5966 ■ *Web:* www.eldoradoreno.com					
Eldridge Hotel 701 Massachusetts St	Lawrence	KS	66044	785-749-5011	749-4512
TF: 800-527-0909 ■ *Web:* www.eldridgehotel.com					
Eliot Hotel 370 Commonwealth Ave	Boston	MA	02215	617-267-1607	536-9114
TF: 800-443-5468 ■ *Web:* www.eliothotel.com					
Elk Country Inn 480 W Pearl St PO Box 1255	Jackson	WY	83001	307-733-2364	733-4465
Web: www.townsquareinns.com/elk-country-inn/					
Elvis Presley's Heartbreak Hotel 3677 Elvis Presley Blvd	Memphis	TN	38116	901-332-1000	332-2107
TF: 877-777-0606 ■ *Web:* www.elvis.com/epheartbreakhotel					
Embarcadero Resort Hotel & Marina 1000 SE Bay Blvd	Newport	OR	97365	541-265-8521	265-7844
TF: 800-547-4779 ■ *Web:* www.embarcadero-resort.com					
Embassy Hotel 610 Polk St	San Francisco	CA	94102	415-673-1404	474-4188
Web: www.theembassyhotelsf.com					
Embassy Hotel & Suites 25 Cartier St	Ottawa	ON	K2P1J2	613-237-2111	563-1353
TF: 800-661-5495 ■ *Web:* www.embassyhotelottawa.com					
Embassy Suites Hotels 755 Crossover Ln	Memphis	TN	38117	901-374-5000	374-5948*
*Fax: Cust Svc ■ *TF:* 800-362-2779 ■ *Web:* www.embassysuites.com					
Embassy West Hotel 1400 Carling Ave	Ottawa	ON	K1Z7L8	613-729-4331	729-1600
TF: 800-267-8696 ■ *Web:* www.embassywesthotel.com					
Emerald Queen Hotel & Casino 5700 Pacific Hwy E	Tacoma	WA	98424	253-922-3555	922-3550
TF: 888-820-3555 ■ *Web:* www.emeraldqueencasino.com					
Emerson Resort & Spa 5368 Rt 28	Mount Tremper	NY	12457	845-688-7900	688-2789
TF: 877-688-2828 ■ *Web:* www.emersonresortandspa.com					
Emory Inn 1641 Clifton Rd	Atlanta	GA	30329	404-712-6720	712-6701
TF: 800-933-6679 ■ *Web:* www.emoryconferencecenter.com/accom.html					
Empire Landmark Hotel & Conference Centre					
1400 Robson St	Vancouver	BC	V6G1B9	604-687-0511	687-2801
TF: 800-830-6144 ■ *Web:* www.empirelandmarkhotel.com					
Empress Hotel 7766 Fay Ave	La Jolla	CA	92037	858-454-3001	454-6387
TF: 888-369-9900 ■ *Web:* www.empress-hotel.com					
Enclave Suites of Orlando 6165 Carrier Dr	Orlando	FL	32819	407-351-1155	351-2001
TF: 800-457-0077 ■ *Web:* www.enclavesuites.com					
Esplanade Hotel 95 S Broadway	White Plains	NY	10601	914-761-8100	761-9015
TF: 800-247-5322 ■ *Web:* www.esplanadecorporate.com					
Essex House Hotel & Convention Center 44916 N 10th St W	Lancaster	CA	93534	661-948-0961	945-3821
TF: 800-843-7739 ■ *Web:* www.essexhouse-hotel.com					
Ethan Allen Hotel 21 Lake Ave Ext	Danbury	CT	06811	203-744-1776	791-9673
TF: 800-742-1776 ■ *Web:* www.ethanallenhotel.com					
Euro-Suites Hotel 501 Chestnut Ridge Rd	Morgantown	WV	26505	304-598-1000	599-2736
TF: 800-678-1837 ■ *Web:* www.euro-suites.com					
Evergreen Lodge 250 South Frontage Rd W	Vail	CO	81657	970-476-7810	476-4504
TF: 800-284-8245 ■ *Web:* www.evergreenvail.com					
Ewa Hotel Waikiki 2555 Cartwright Rd	Honolulu	HI	96815	808-922-1677	923-8538
TF: 800-359-8639 ■ *Web:* www.ewahotel.com/e/					
Excalibur Hotel & Casino 3850 Las Vegas Blvd S	Las Vegas	NV	89109	702-597-7777	597-7009
TF Resv: 800-937-7777 ■ *Web:* www.excalibur.com					
Executive Hotel Vintage Court 650 Bush St	San Francisco	CA	94108	415-392-4666	433-4065
TF: 800-654-1100 ■ *Web:* www.vintagecourt.com					
Executive Hotels & Resorts					
Executive Pl Tower 8th Fl 1080 Howe St	Vancouver	BC	V6Z2T1	604-642-5250	642-5255
TSX: EIG ■ *Web:* www.executivehotels.net					
Executive Inn 978 Phillips Ln	Louisville	KY	40209	502-367-6161	366-2613
TF: 800-626-2706 ■ *Web:* www.executiveinnhotel.com					
Executive Inn Evansville 600 Walnut St	Evansville	IN	47708	812-424-8000	424-8999
TF: 877-424-0888 ■ *Web:* www.executiveinnevansville.com					
Executive Inn Group Corp Executive Hotels & Resorts					
Executive Pl Tower 8th Fl 1080 Howe St	Vancouver	BC	V6Z2T1	604-642-5250	642-5255
TSX: EIG ■ *Web:* www.executivehotels.net					
Executive Inn Rivermont 1 Executive Blvd	Owensboro	KY	42301	270-926-8000	926-8000
TF: 800-626-1936 ■ *Web:* www.executiveinnrivermont.com					
Executive Pacific Plaza Hotel 400 Spring St	Seattle	WA	98104	206-623-3900	623-2059
TF: 800-426-1165 ■ *Web:* www.pacificplazahotel.com					
Executive Suite Hotel 4360 Spenard Rd	Anchorage	AK	99517	907-243-6366	248-2161
TF: 800-770-6366 ■ *Web:* www.executivesuitehotel.com					
Executive West Hotel 830 Phillips Ln	Louisville	KY	40209	502-367-2251	363-2087
TF: 800-626-2708 ■ *Web:* www.executivewest.com					
Exel Inns of America Inc 4706 E Washington Ave	Madison	WI	53704	608-241-5271	241-3224
TF: 800-367-3935 ■ *Web:* www.exelinns.com					
Exel Management Assoc Exel Inns of America Inc					
4706 E Washington Ave	Madison	WI	53704	608-241-5271	241-3224
TF: 800-367-3935 ■ *Web:* www.exelinns.com					
Expressway Inn 1340 S 21st Ave	Fargo	ND	58103	701-235-3141	234-0474
TF: 800-437-0044 ■ *Web:* www.expresswayhotels.com/FargoInn.htm					
Expressway Suites 180 E Bismarck Expy	Bismarck	ND	58504	701-222-3311	222-3311
TF: 888-774-5566 ■ *Web:* www.expresswayhotels.com/BisSuites.htm					
Extended Stay Deluxe Studios 100 Dunbar St	Spartanburg	SC	29306	864-573-1600	573-1695
TF: 800-804-3724 ■ *Web:* www.extendedstaydeluxe.com					
Extended Stay Hotels c/o HVM LLC 100 Dunbar St	Spartanburg	SC	29306	864-573-1600	573-1695
Web: www.extendedstayhotels.com					
Crossland Economy Studios 100 Dunbar St	Spartanburg	SC	29306	864-573-1600	573-1695
TF: 877-276-7752 ■ *Web:* www.crosslandstudios.com					
Extended Stay Deluxe Studios 100 Dunbar St	Spartanburg	SC	29306	864-573-1600	573-1695
TF: 800-804-3724 ■ *Web:* www.extendedstaydeluxe.com					
Extended StayAmerica 100 Dunbar St	Spartanburg	SC	29306	864-573-1600	573-1695
TF: 800-398-7829 ■ *Web:* www.extendedstayamerica.com					
Homestead Studio Suites Hotels 100 Dunbar St	Spartanburg	SC	29306	864-573-1600	573-1695
TF: 800-804-3724 ■ *Web:* www.homesteadhotels.com					
StudioPLUS Deluxe Studios 100 Dunbar St	Spartanburg	SC	29306	864-573-1600	573-1695
TF: 888-788-3467 ■ *Web:* www.studioplus.com					
Extended StayAmerica 100 Dunbar St	Spartanburg	SC	29306	864-573-1600	573-1695
TF: 800-398-7829 ■ *Web:* www.extendedstayamerica.com					
Fairbanks Golden Nugget Hotel 900 Noble St	Fairbanks	AK	99701	907-452-5141	452-5458
Web: www.golden-nuggethotel.com					
Fairbanks Princess Riverside Lodge 4477 Pikes Landing Rd	Fairbanks	AK	99709	907-455-4477	455-4476
TF: 800-426-0500 ■ *Web:* www.princesslodges.com					
Fairfield Inn by Marriott 1 Marriott Dr	Washington	DC	20058	301-380-3000	380-3090
Web: www.marriott.com/fairfieldinn					
Fairmont Hotels & Resorts Inc 650 California St 12th Fl	San Francisco	CA	94108	415-772-7800	772-7805
Web: www.fairmont.com					
Fairmont Hotels & Resorts Inc					
100 Wellington St W TD Centre Suite 1600	Toronto	ON	M5K1B7	416-874-2600	874-2601
NYSE: FHR ■ *TF:* 800-866-5577 ■ *Web:* www.fairmont.com					
Fairmount Hotel The 401 S Alamo St	San Antonio	TX	78205	210-224-8800	475-0082
TF: 800-996-3426 ■ *Web:* www.thefairmounthotel-sanantonio.com					
Falmouth Inn 824 Main St	Falmouth	MA	02540	508-540-2500	540-9256
TF: 800-255-4157 ■ *Web:* www.falmouthinn.com					
Family Inn 208 S Old County Rd	Branson	MO	65616	417-334-2113	334-2234
Web: www.myfamilyinn.com					
Family Inns of America Inc PO Box 10	Pigeon Forge	TN	37868	865-453-4988	453-0220
TF: 800-251-9752 ■ *Web:* www.familyinnsofamerica.com					
Fantasyland Hotel 17700 87th Ave West Edmonton Mall	Edmonton	AB	T5T4V4	780-444-3000	444-3294
TF: 800-737-3783 ■ *Web:* www.fantasylandhotel.com					
Fearrington House 2000 Fearrington Village Center	Pittsboro	NC	27312	919-542-2121	542-4202
Web: www.fearringtonhouse.com					
Federal Square Suites 8781 Madison Blvd	Madison	AL	35758	256-772-8470	772-0620
TF: 800-458-1639 ■ *Web:* www.federalsquare.com					
Fenwick Inn 13801 Coastal Hwy	Ocean City	MD	21842	410-250-1100	250-0087
TF: 800-492-1873 ■ *Web:* www.fenwickinn.com					
Fiesta Henderson Casino Hotel 777 W Lake Mead Pkwy	Henderson	NV	89015	702-558-7000	567-7373
TF: 888-899-7770 ■ *Web:* henderson.fiestacasino.com					
Fiesta Inn Resort 2100 S Priest Dr	Tempe	AZ	85282	480-967-1441	967-0224
TF: 800-528-6481 ■ *Web:* www.fiestainnresort.com					
Fiesta Rancho Casino Hotel 2400 N Rancho Dr	Las Vegas	NV	89130	702-631-7000	638-3645
TF: 800-731-7333 ■ *Web:* www.fiestacasino.com					
Fifteen Beacon Hotel 15 Beacon St	Boston	MA	02108	617-670-1500	670-2525
TF: 877-982-3226 ■ *Web:* www.xvbeacon.com					
Fifth Season Inn 2219 S Waldron Rd	Fort Smith	AR	72903	479-452-4880	452-8653
TF: 877-452-4880					
Figueroa Hotel 939 S Figueroa St	Los Angeles	CA	90015	213-627-8971	689-0305
TF: 800-421-9092 ■ *Web:* www.figueroahotel.com					
Fiksdal Hotel & Suites 1215 2nd St SW	Rochester	MN	55902	507-288-2671	285-9325
TF: 800-366-3451 ■ *Web:* rochesterlodging.com/fiksdal					
Findlay Inn & Conference Center 200 E Main Cross St	Findlay	OH	45840	419-422-5682	422-5581
TF: 800-825-1455 ■ *Web:* www.findlayinn.com					
Fireside Inn & Suites 25 Airport Rd	West Lebanon	NH	03784	603-298-5906	298-0340
TF: 877-258-5900 ■ *Web:* www.afiresideinn.com					
First Gold Hotel 270 Main St	Deadwood	SD	57732	605-578-9777	578-3979
TF: 800-274-1876 ■ *Web:* www.firstgold.com					
First Interstate Inn 20 SE Wyoming Blvd	Casper	WY	82609	307-234-9125	265-0264
TF: 800-462-4667 ■ *Web:* www.1stinns.com					
Fisherman's Wharf Inn 22 Commercial St	Boothbay Harbor	ME	04538	207-633-5090	633-5092
TF: 800-628-6872					
Fitger's Inn 600 E Superior St	Duluth	MN	55802	218-722-8826	722-8826
TF: 888-348-4377 ■ *Web:* www.fitgers.com					
Fitzgerald Hotel 620 Post St	San Francisco	CA	94109	415-775-8100	775-1278
TF: 800-334-6835 ■ *Web:* www.fitzgeraldhotel.com					
Fitzgerald's Casino & Hotel Las Vegas 301 Fremont St	Las Vegas	NV	89101	702-388-2400	388-2183
TF: 800-274-5825 ■ *Web:* www.fitzgeraldslasvegas.com					
Fitzgeralds Casino & Hotel Reno 255 N Virginia St PO Box 40130	Reno	NV	89504	775-785-3300	785-3318
TF: 800-535-5825 ■ *Web:* www.fitzgeraldsreno.com					
Fitzgeralds Casino & Hotel Tunica 711 Lucky Ln	Robinsonville	MS	38664	662-363-5825	363-3579
TF: 888-766-5825 ■ *Web:* www.fitzgeraldstunica.com					

	City	State	Zip	Phone	Fax
Fitzpatrick Manhattan Hotel 687 Lexington Ave *TF:* 800-367-7701 ■ *Web:* www.fitzpatrickhotels.com	New York	NY	10022	212-355-0100	355-1371
Flagship All Suites Resort 60 N Maine Ave *TF:* 800-647-7890 ■ *Web:* www.flagshipresort.com	Atlantic City	NJ	08401	609-343-7447	347-9597
Flagship Hotel Over the Water 2501 Seawall Blvd *TF:* 800-392-6542 ■ *Web:* www.flagshiphotel.com	Galveston	TX	77550	409-762-9000	762-9040
Flamingo Hotel Tucson 1300 N Stone Ave *Web:* www.flamingohoteltucson.com	Tucson	AZ	85705	520-770-1910	770-0750
Flatotel International 135 W 52nd St *TF:* 800-352-8683 ■ *Web:* www.flatotel.com	New York	NY	10019	212-887-9400	887-9795
Foley Inn 14 W Hull St Chippewa Sq *TF:* 800-647-3708 ■ *Web:* www.foleyinn.com	Savannah	GA	31401	912-232-6622	231-1218
Foot of the Mountain Motel 200 W Arapahoe Ave *TF:* 866-773-5489 ■ *Web:* www.footofthemountainmotel.com	Boulder	CO	80302	303-442-5688	442-5719
Foothills Inn 1625 N La Crosse St *TF:* 877-428-5666 ■ *Web:* www.thefoothillsinn.com	Rapid City	SD	57701	605-348-5640	348-0073
Forest Manor Inn 866 Hendersonville Rd *TF:* 800-866-3531 ■ *Web:* www.forestmanorinn.com	Asheville	NC	28803	828-274-3531	274-3036
Fort Collins Mulberry Inn 4333 E Mulberry St *TF:* 800-234-5548 ■ *Web:* www.mulberry-inn.com	Fort Collins	CO	80524	970-493-9000	224-9636
Fort Garry The 222 Broadway *TF:* 800-665-8088 ■ *Web:* www.fortgarryhotel.com	Winnipeg	MB	R3C0R3	204-942-8251	956-2351
Fort Marcy Hotel Suites 320 Artist Rd *TF:* 800-745-9910 ■ *Web:* www.fortmarcy.com	Santa Fe	NM	87501	505-988-2800	992-1804
Forum Motor Inn 800-814 Atlantic Ave *Web:* www.theforuminoc.homestead.com	Ocean City	NJ	08226	609-399-8700	399-8704
Four Points by Sheraton 1111 Westchester Ave *TF Cust Svc:* 877-443-4585 ■ *Web:* www.starwood.com/fourpoints	White Plains	NY	10604	914-640-8100	640-8310
Four Points by Sheraton Charlotte 315 E Woodlawn Rd *TF:* 800-368-7764 ■ *Web:* www.starwoodhotels.com/fourpoints/	Charlotte	NC	28217	704-522-0852	522-1634
Four Queens Hotel & Casino 202 Fremont St *TF:* 800-634-6045 ■ *Web:* www.fourqueens.com	Las Vegas	NV	89101	702-385-4011	387-5133
Four Sails Resort Hotel 3301 Atlantic Ave *TF:* 800-227-4213 ■ *Web:* www.foursails.com	Virginia Beach	VA	23451	757-491-8100	491-0573
Four Seasons Hotels Inc 1165 Leslie St *NYSE: FS* ■ *TF:* 800-332-3442 ■ *Web:* www.fourseasons.com	Toronto	ON	M3C2K8	416-449-1750	441-4374
Francis Marion Hotel 387 King St *TF:* 877-756-2121 ■ *Web:* www.francismarioncharleston.com	Charleston	SC	29403	843-722-0600	723-4633
Franklin The 164 E 87th St *Web:* www.franklinhotel.com	New York	NY	10128	212-369-1000	369-8000
Fremont Hotel & Casino 200 E Fremont St *TF:* 800-634-6182 ■ *Web:* www.fremontcasino.com	Las Vegas	NV	89101	702-385-3232	385-6270
French Quarter Suites Hotel 2144 Madison Ave *TF:* 800-843-0353 ■ *Web:* www.memphisfrenchquarter.com	Memphis	TN	38104	901-728-4000	278-1262
Friday Harbor House 130 West St *TF:* 866-722-7356 ■ *Web:* www.fridayharborhouse.com	Friday Harbor	WA	98250	360-378-8455	378-8453
Galleria Park Hotel 191 Sutter St *TF:* 866-756-3036 ■ *Web:* www.galleriapark.com	San Francisco	CA	94104	415-781-3060	433-4409
Galt House Hotel 140 N 4th St *TF:* 800-626-1814 ■ *Web:* www.galthouse.com	Louisville	KY	40202	502-589-5200	589-3444
Garden City Hotel 45 7th St *TF:* 800-547-0400 ■ *Web:* www.gardencityhotel.com	Garden City	NY	11530	516-747-3000	747-1414
Garden Court Hotel 520 Cowper St *TF:* 800-824-9028 ■ *Web:* www.gardencourt.com	Palo Alto	CA	94301	650-322-9000	324-3609
Garden District Hotel 2203 St Charles Ave *TF:* 800-265-1856 ■ *Web:* www.thegardendistricthotel.com/	New Orleans	LA	70130	504-566-1200	581-1352
Garden Place Hotel 6615 Transit Rd *TF:* 800-427-3361 ■ *Web:* salvatores.net/garden_place/index.html	Williamsville	NY	14221	716-635-9000	635-9098
Gardens Hotel 526 Angela St *TF:* 800-526-2664 ■ *Web:* www.gardenshotel.com	Key West	FL	33040	305-294-2661	292-1007
Gardner Hotel 311 E Franklin Ave *Web:* www.gardnerhotel.com	El Paso	TX	79901	915-532-3661	532-0302
Garfield Suites Hotel 2 Garfield Pl *TF:* 800-367-2155 ■ *Web:* www.garfieldsuiteshotel.com	Cincinnati	OH	45202	513-421-3355	421-3729
Garrett's Desert Inn 311 Old Santa Fe Trail *TF:* 800-888-2145 ■ *Web:* www.garrettsdesertinn.com	Santa Fe	NM	87501	505-982-1851	989-1647
Gaslamp Plaza Suites 520 'E' St *TF:* 800-874-8770 ■ *Web:* www.gaslampplaza.com	San Diego	CA	92101	619-232-9500	238-9945
Gastonian The 220 E Gaston St *TF:* 800-322-6603 ■ *Web:* www.gastonian.com	Savannah	GA	31401	912-232-2869	232-0710
Gateways Inn 51 Walker St *TF:* 888-492-9466 ■ *Web:* www.gatewaysinn.com	Lenox	MA	01240	413-637-2532	637-1432
Gaylord Entertainment Co 1 Gaylord Dr *NYSE: GET* ■ *Web:* www.gaylordentertainment.com	Nashville	TN	37214	615-316-6000	316-6060
Gaylord Opryland 2800 Opryland Dr *Web:* www.gaylordhotels.com	Nashville	TN	37214	615-889-1000	871-7741
General Morgan Inn 111 N Main St *TF:* 800-223-2679 ■ *Web:* www.generalmorganinn.com	Greeneville	TN	37743	423-787-1000	787-1001
Genesee Grande Hotel 1060 E Genesee St *TF:* 800-365-4663 ■ *Web:* www.geneseegrande.com	Syracuse	NY	13210	315-476-4212	471-4663
Geneva on the Lake 1001 Lochland Rd *TF:* 800-343-6382 ■ *Web:* www.genevaonthelake.com	Geneva	NY	14456	315-789-7190	789-0322
George Washington Inn 500 Merrimac Trail *TF:* 800-666-8888	Williamsburg	VA	23185	757-220-1410	259-5500
George Washington University Inn 824 New Hampshire Ave NW *TF:* 800-426-4455 ■ *Web:* www.gwuinn.com	Washington	DC	20037	202-337-6620	298-7499
Georgetown Inn 1310 Wisconsin Ave NW *TF:* 888-587-2388 ■ *Web:* www.georgetowncollection.com	Washington	DC	20007	202-333-8900	625-1744
Georgian Court Hotel 773 Beatty St *TF:* 800-663-1155 ■ *Web:* www.georgiancourt.com	Vancouver	BC	V6B2M4	604-682-5555	682-8830
Georgian Hotel 1415 Ocean Ave *TF:* 800-538-8147 ■ *Web:* www.georgianhotel.com	Santa Monica	CA	90401	310-395-9945	451-3374
Georgian Resort 384 Canada St *TF:* 800-525-3436 ■ *Web:* www.georgianresort.com	Lake George	NY	12845	518-668-5401	668-5870
Georgian Terrace Hotel 659 Peachtree St NE *TF:* 800-651-2316 ■ *Web:* www.thegeorgianterrace.com	Atlanta	GA	30308	404-897-1991	724-9116
Gershwin Hotel 7 E 27th St *Web:* www.gershwinhotel.com	New York	NY	10016	212-545-8000	684-5546
Gideon Putnam Resort & Spa 24 Gideon Putnam Rd *TF:* 866-890-4171 ■ *Web:* www.gideonputnam.com	Saratoga Springs	NY	12866	518-584-3000	584-1354
Glacier Bay Country Inn 35 Tong Rd *TF:* 800-628-0912 ■ *Web:* www.glacierbayalaska.com	Gustavus	AK	99826	907-697-2288	697-2289
Glass House Inn 3202 W 26th St *TF:* 800-956-7222 ■ *Web:* www.glasshouseinn.com	Erie	PA	16506	814-833-7751	833-4222
Glen Grove Suites 2837 Yonge St *TF:* 800-565-3024 ■ *Web:* www.glengrove.com	Toronto	ON	M4N2J6	416-489-8441	440-3065
Glendorn 1000 Glendorn Dr *TF:* 800-843-8568 ■ *Web:* www.glendorn.com	Bradford	PA	16701	814-362-6511	368-9923
Glenerin Inn 1695 The Collegeway *TF:* 877-991-9971 ■ *Web:* www.glenerininn.com	Mississauga	ON	L5L3S7	905-828-6103	828-0891
Glenmore Inn 2720 Glenmore Trail SE *TF:* 800-661-3163 ■ *Web:* www.glenmoreinn.com	Calgary	AB	T2C2E6	403-279-8611	236-8035
Glidden House 1901 Ford Dr *TF:* 800-759-8358 ■ *Web:* www.gliddenhouse.com	Cleveland	OH	44106	216-231-8900	231-2130
Glorietta Bay Inn 1630 Glorietta Blvd *TF:* 800-283-9383 ■ *Web:* www.gloriettabayinn.com	Coronado	CA	92118	619-435-3101	435-6182
Gold Coast Hotel & Casino 4000 W Flamingo Rd *TF:* 888-402-6278 ■ *Web:* www.goldcoastcasino.com	Las Vegas	NV	89103	702-367-7111	367-8575
Gold Hill Hotel 1540 S Main St *Web:* www.goldhillhotel.net	Gold Hill	NV	89440	775-847-0111	847-0604
Gold Spike Hotel & Casino 400 E Ogden Ave *TF:* 877-467-7453 ■ *Web:* www.goldspikehotelcasino.com	Las Vegas	NV	89101	702-384-8444	382-5242
Gold Strike Casino Resort 1010 Casino Center Dr *TF Resv:* 888-245-7829 ■ *Web:* www.goldstrikemississippi.com	Tunica Resorts	MS	38664	662-357-1111	357-1306
Goldbelt Hotel Juneau 51 Egan Dr *TF:* 888-478-6909 ■ *Web:* www.goldbelt.com/subsidiaries/GBHJ.html	Juneau	AK	99801	907-586-6900	463-3567
Golden Eagle Resort 511 Mountain Rd PO Box 1090 *TF:* 800-626-1010 ■ *Web:* www.stoweagle.com	Stowe	VT	05672	802-253-4811	253-2561
Golden Hotel The 800 11th St *TF:* 800-233-7214 ■ *Web:* www.thegoldenhotel.com/	Golden	CO	80401	303-279-0100	279-9353
Goldener Hirsch Inn 7570 Royal St E *TF:* 800-252-3373 ■ *Web:* www.goldenerhirschinn.com	Park City	UT	84060	435-649-7770	649-7901
Good-Nite Inn Fremont 4135 Cushing Pkwy *TF:* 800-648-3466 ■ *Web:* www.goodnite.com	Fremont	CA	94538	510-656-9307	656-9110
Goodwin Hotel 1 Haynes St *TF:* 800-922-5006 ■ *Web:* www.goodwinhotel.com	Hartford	CT	06103	860-246-7500	247-4576
Gouverneur Hotel Montreal (Place-Dupuis) 1415 Saint-Hubert St *TF:* 888-910-1111 ■ *Web:* www.gouverneur.com	Montreal	QC	H2L3Y9	514-842-4881	842-8899
Gouverneur Hotels 1000 Sherbrooke St W Suite 2300 *Web:* www.gouverneur.com	Montreal	QC	H3A3R3	514-875-8822	875-0988
Governor Calvert House 58 State Cir *TF:* 800-847-8882 ■ *Web:* www.historicinnsofannapolis.com	Annapolis	MD	21401	410-263-2641	268-8041
Governor Hotel 614 SW 11th Ave *TF:* 800-554-3456 ■ *Web:* www.govhotel.com	Portland	OR	97205	503-224-3400	241-2122
Governor Hotel 621 S Capitol Way *TF:* 877-352-7701 ■ *Web:* www.olywagov.com	Olympia	WA	98501	360-352-7700	943-9349
Governor's House Hotel & Conference Center 2705 E South Blvd *TF:* 866-535-5392	Montgomery	AL	36116	334-288-2800	288-6472
Governor's Inn 210 Richards Blvd *TF:* 800-999-6689 ■ *Web:* governorsinnhotel.com	Sacramento	CA	95814	916-448-7224	448-7382
Governors Inn 209 S Adams St *Web:* www.thegovinn.com	Tallahassee	FL	32301	850-681-6855	222-3105
Governor's Inn 700 W Sioux Ave *TF:* 888-315-2378 ■ *Web:* www.govinn.com	Pierre	SD	57501	605-224-4200	
Graciela The Burbank 322 N Pass Ave *TF:* 888-956-1900 ■ *Web:* www.thegraciela.com	Burbank	CA	91505	818-842-8887	260-8999
Grafton on Sunset 8462 W Sunset Blvd *TF:* 800-821-3660 ■ *Web:* www.graftononsunset.com	West Hollywood	CA	90069	323-654-4600	654-5918
Gramercy Park Hotel 2 Lexington Ave *TF:* 800-221-4083 ■ *Web:* www.gramercyparkhotel.com	New York	NY	10010	212-475-4320	505-0535
Grand America Hotel 555 S Main St *TF:* 800-621-4505 ■ *Web:* www.grandamerica.com	Salt Lake City	UT	84111	801-258-6000	258-6911
Grand Beach Inn 198 E Grand Ave *TF:* 800-834-9696 ■ *Web:* www.oobme.com/Grand/gbihome.html	Old Orchard Beach	ME	04064	207-934-4621	934-3435
Grand Country Inn Grand Country Sq 1945 W Hwy 76 *TF:* 800-514-1088 ■ *Web:* www.grandcountry.com/hotel.asp	Branson	MO	65616	417-335-3535	336-6286
Grand Del Mar 5300 Grand Del Mar Ct *Web:* www.thegranddelmar.com/	San Diego	CA	92130	858-314-2000	314-2001
Grand Gateway Hotel 1721 N LaCrosse St *TF:* 866-742-1300 ■ *Web:* www.grandgatewayhotel.com	Rapid City	SD	57701	605-342-8853	342-0663
Grand Hotel The State Hwy 64 PO Box 3319 *TF:* 866-634-7263 ■ *Web:* the-grand-hotel-grand-canyon.pacificahost.com/	Grand Canyon	AZ	86023	928-638-3333	638-3131
Grand Hotel Edmonton 10266 103rd St *TF:* 888-422-6365 ■ *Web:* www.edmontongrandhotel.com	Edmonton	AB	T5J0Y8	780-422-6365	425-9070
Grand Hotel Minneapolis 615 2nd Ave S *TF:* 866-843-4726 ■ *Web:* www.grandhotelminneapolis.com	Minneapolis	MN	55402	612-339-3655	373-0407
Grand Hotel & Suites Toronto 225 Jarvis St *TF:* 877-324-7263 ■ *Web:* www.grandhoteltoronto.com	Toronto	ON	M5B2C1	416-863-9000	863-1100
Grand Hyatt Hotels 71 S Wacker Dr **Fax:* Mktg ■ *TF Resv:* 800-233-1234 ■ *Web:* www.hyatt.com	Chicago	IL	60606	312-750-1234	780-5289*
Grand Lodge Hotel 1700 American Blvd E *TF:* 866-472-6356 ■ *Web:* www.grandlodgemn.com	Bloomington	MN	55425	952-854-8700	854-8701
Grand Oaks Hotel 2315 Green Mountain Dr *TF:* 800-553-6423 ■ *Web:* www.grandoakshotel.net	Branson	MO	65616	417-336-6423	334-6264
Grand Summit Hotel 570 Springfield Ave *TF:* 800-346-0773 ■ *Web:* www.grandsummit.com	Summit	NJ	07901	908-273-3000	273-4228
Grande Colonial 910 Prospect St *Web:* www.thegrandecolonial.com	La Jolla	CA	92037	858-454-2181	454-5679
Grant Plaza Hotel 465 Grant Ave *TF:* 800-472-6899 ■ *Web:* www.grantplaza.com	San Francisco	CA	94108	415-434-3883	434-3886
Granville Island Hotel 1253 Johnston St *TF:* 800-663-1840 ■ *Web:* www.granvilleislandhotel.com	Vancouver	BC	V6H3R9	604-683-7373	683-3061
Graves 601 Hotel 601 1st Ave N *TF:* 866-523-1100 ■ *Web:* graves601hotel.com	Minneapolis	MN	55403	612-677-1100	677-1200
Graycote Inn 40 Holland Ave *Web:* www.graycoteinn.com	Bar Harbor	ME	04609	207-288-3044	288-2719
Great Divide Lodge 550 Village Rd *TF:* 800-321-8444 ■ *Web:* www.greatdividelodge.com	Breckenridge	CO	80424	970-453-4500	453-0212
Great Western Downtown Plaza 17 W 7th St *TF:* 800-585-5101 ■ *Web:* www.greatwesternhotels.com/tulsa.htm	Tulsa	OK	74119	918-585-5898	
Green Harbor Resort 182 Baxter Ave *Web:* www.greenharborresort.com	West Yarmouth	MA	02673	508-771-1126	771-0701
Green Mountain Inn 18 Main St PO Box 60 *TF:* 800-253-7302 ■ *Web:* www.greenmountaininn.com	Stowe	VT	05672	802-253-7301	253-5096
Green Park Inn 9239 Valley Blvd *TF:* 800-852-2462 ■ *Web:* www.greenparkinn.com	Blowing Rock	NC	28605	828-295-3141	295-3141
Green Valley Ranch Resort Casino & Spa 2300 Paseo Verde Pkwy *TF:* 866-617-0777 ■ *Web:* www.greenvalleyranchresort.com	Henderson	NV	89052	702-617-7777	617-7778
Greenwood Inn & Suites Calgary 3515 26th St NE *TF:* 888-233-6730 ■ *Web:* www.greenwoodinn.ca	Calgary	AB	T1Y7E3	403-250-8855	250-8050
Greenwood Inn & Suites Edmonton 4485 Gateway Blvd *TF:* 888-233-6730 ■ *Web:* www.greenwoodinn.ca	Edmonton	AB	T6H5C3	780-431-1100	437-3455
Greenwood Inn & Suites Winnipeg 1715 Wellington Ave *TF:* 888-233-6730 ■ *Web:* www.greenwoodinn.ca	Winnipeg	MB	R3H0G1	204-775-9889	775-4576
Grey Bonnet Inn 831 Rt 100 N *TF:* 800-342-2086 ■ *Web:* www.greybonnetinn.com	Killington	VT	05751	802-775-2537	775-3371
Greyfield Inn Box 900 *TF:* 888-241-6408 ■ *Web:* www.greyfieldinn.com	Fernandina Beach	FL	32035	904-261-6408	321-0666
Grove Hotel 245 S Capitol Blvd *TF:* 888-961-5000 ■ *Web:* www.grovehotelboise.com	Boise	ID	83702	208-333-8000	333-8800
Grove Isle Club & Resort 4 Grove Isle Dr *TF:* 800-884-7683 ■ *Web:* www.groveisle.com	Coconut Grove	FL	33133	305-858-8300	858-5908
Guest Inn 2533 N Piccoli Rd	Stockton	CA	95215	209-931-6675	931-8351
Guest Lodge at Cooper Aerobic Center Clinic 12230 Preston Rd *TF:* 800-444-5187 ■ *Web:* www.cooperaerobics.com/hotel	Dallas	TX	75230	972-386-0306	386-5415
GuestHouse International LLC 130 Maple Dr N **Fax Area Code:* 770 ■ *TF:* 800-214-8378 ■ *Web:* www.guesthouseintl.com	Hendersonville	TN	37075	615-264-8000	951-0307*
GulfStream Hotel 1 Lake Ave *TF:* 888-540-0669	Lake Worth	FL	33460	561-540-6000	582-6904

	City	State	ZIP	Phone	Fax
Habana Inn 2200 NW 39th Expy	Oklahoma City	OK	73112	405-528-2221	528-0496
TF: 800-988-2221 ■ *Web:* www.habanainn.com					
Habitat Suites 500 E Highland Mall Blvd	Austin	TX	78752	512-467-6000	452-6712
TF: 800-535-4663 ■ *Web:* habitatsuites.com					
Hacienda Hotel 525 N Sepulveda Blvd	El Segundo	CA	90245	310-615-0015	615-0217
TF: 800-421-5900 ■ *Web:* www.haciendahotel.com					
Hacienda The at Hotel Santa Fe 1501 Paseo del Peralta	Santa Fe	NM	87501	505-982-1200	955-7835
TF: 866-589-3411 ■ *Web:* www.hotelsantafe.com/the_hacienda/					
Halekulani Hotel 2199 Kalia Rd	Honolulu	HI	96815	808-923-2311	926-8004
TF: 800-367-2343 ■ *Web:* www.halekulani.com					
Half Moon Bay Lodge & Conference Center 2400 S Cabrillo Hwy	Half Moon Bay	CA	94019	650-726-9000	726-7951
TF: 800-710-0778 ■ *Web:* www.halfmoonbaylodge.com					
Halifax Marriott Harborfront Hotel 1919 Upper Water St	Halifax	NS	B3J3J5	902-421-1700	422-5805
TF: 866-425-4329 ■ *Web:* www.marriott.com					
Halliburton House Inn 5184 Morris St	Halifax	NS	B3J1B3	902-420-0658	423-2324
TF: 888-512-3344 ■ *Web:* www.thehalliburton.com					
Hallmark Resort 1400 S Hemlock	Cannon Beach	OR	97110	503-436-1566	436-0324
TF: 800-345-5676 ■ *Web:* www.hallmarkinns.com					
Hampshire Hotels & Resorts LLC 1251 Ave of the Americas Suite 934	New York	NY	10019	212-474-9800	474-9801
Web: www.hampshirehotels.com					
Hampton Hotels 755 Crossover Ln	Memphis	TN	38117	901-374-5000	374-5948*
*Fax: Cust Svc ■ *TF:* 800-362-2779 ■ *Web:* www.embassysuites.com					
Handlery Union Square Hotel 351 Geary St	San Francisco	CA	94102	415-781-7800	781-0216
TF: 800-843-4343 ■ *Web:* www.handlery.com					
Hanover Inn 2 S Main St	Hanover	NH	03755	603-643-4300	643-4433
TF: 800-443-7024 ■ *Web:* www.hanoverinn.com					
Harbor Court Hotel 165 Steuart St	San Francisco	CA	94105	415-882-1300	882-1313
TF: 800-346-0555 ■ *Web:* www.harborcourthotel.com					
Harbor Court Hotel 550 Light St	Baltimore	MD	21202	410-234-0550	659-5925
TF: 800-824-0076 ■ *Web:* www.harborcourt.com					
Harbor House 28 Pier 21	Galveston	TX	77550	409-763-3321	765-6421
TF: 800-874-3721 ■ *Web:* www.harborhousepier21.com					
Harbor House Resort 642 W Hawthorn St	San Diego	CA	92101	619-338-9966	
Harbor View Hotel 131 N Water St PO Box 7 Martha's Vineyard	Edgartown	MA	02539	508-627-7000	627-8417
TF: 800-225-6005 ■ *Web:* www.harbor-view.com					
Harborside Hotel & Marina 55 West St	Bar Harbor	ME	04609	207-288-5033	288-3661
TF: 800-328-5033 ■ *Web:* www.theharborsidehotel.com					
Harborside Inn 1 Christie's Landing	Newport	RI	02840	401-846-6600	849-8510
TF: 800-427-9444 ■ *Web:* www.newportharborsideinn.com					
Harborside Inn of Boston 185 State St	Boston	MA	02109	617-723-7500	670-6015
TF: 888-723-7565 ■ *Web:* www.harborsideinnboston.com					
Hard Rock Hotel & Casino Biloxi 777 Beach Blvd	Biloxi	MS	39530	228-276-7625	276-7007
TF: 877-877-6256 ■ *Web:* www.hardrockbiloxi.com					
Hard Rock Hotel San Diego 207 5th Ave	San Diego	CA	92101	619-702-3000	702-3007
TF: 866-751-7625 ■ *Web:* www.hardrockhotelsd.com/					
Harrah's Atlantic City 777 Harrah's Blvd	Atlantic City	NJ	08401	609-441-5000	340-8621
TF: 800-427-7247 ■ *Web:* www.harrahs.com/our_casinos/atl					
Harrah's Cherokee Casino & Hotel 777 Casino Dr	Cherokee	NC	28719	828-497-7777	497-5076
TF: 800-427-7247 ■ *Web:* www.harrahs.com/our_casinos/che					
Harrah's Council Bluffs 1 Harrah's Blvd	Council Bluffs	IA	51501	712-329-6000	329-6491
TF: 888-598-8451 ■ *Web:* www.harrahs.com/our_casinos/cou					
Harrah's Entertainment Inc 1 Harrah's Ct	Las Vegas	NV	89119	702-407-6000	407-6022
NYSE: HET ■ *TF:* 800-442-6443 ■ *Web:* www.harrahs.com					
Harrah's Joliet 151 N Joliet St	Joliet	IL	60432	815-740-7800	740-2223
TF: 800-427-7247 ■ *Web:* www.harrahs.com/our_casinos/jol					
Harrah's Lake Tahoe PO Box 8	Stateline	NV	89449	775-588-6611	586-6607
TF: 800-427-7247 ■ *Web:* www.harrahs.com/our_casinos/tah/					
Harrah's North Kansas City 1 Riverboat Dr	North Kansas City	MO	64116	816-472-7777	889-7116
TF: 800-427-7247 ■ *Web:* www.harrahs.com/our_casinos/nkc					
Harrah's Prairie Band Casino & Hotel 12305 150th Rd	Mayetta	KS	66509	785-966-7777	966-7799
TF: 800-427-7247 ■ *Web:* www.harrahs.com/our_casinos/top					
Harrah's Reno 219 N Center St	Reno	NV	89501	775-786-3232	788-2815
TF: 800-427-7247 ■ *Web:* www.harrahs.com/our_casinos/ren					
Harrah's Saint Louis Casino & Hotel 777 Casino Center Dr	Maryland Heights	MO	63043	314-770-8100	770-8399
TF: 800-427-7247 ■ *Web:* www.harrahs.com/our_casinos/stl					
Harraseeket Inn 162 Main St	Freeport	ME	04032	207-865-9377	865-1684
TF: 800-342-6423 ■ *Web:* www.harraseeketinn.com					
Harrison Plaza Suite Hotel 409 S Cole Rd	Boise	ID	83709	208-375-7666	376-3608
TF: 800-376-3608 ■ *Web:* www.harrisonhotelboise.com/					
Hartness House Inn 30 Orchard St	Springfield	VT	05156	802-885-2115	885-2207
TF: 800-732-4789 ■ *Web:* www.hartnesshouse.com					
Harvard Square Hotel 110 Mt Auburn St	Cambridge	MA	02138	617-864-5200	492-4896
TF: 800-458-5886 ■ *Web:* www.theinnatharvard.com					
Harvest Inn 1 Main St	Saint Helena	CA	94574	707-963-9463	963-4402
TF: 800-950-8466 ■ *Web:* www.harvestinn.com					
Harveys Resort Hotel & Casino Hwy 50 PO Box 128	Stateline	NV	89449	775-588-2411	588-6643
TF: 800-427-8397 ■ *Web:* www.harrahs.com/our_casinos/hlt/					
Hassayampa Inn 122 E Gurley St	Prescott	AZ	86301	928-778-9434	445-8590
TF: 800-322-1927 ■ *Web:* www.hassayampainn.com					
Hastings House 160 Upper Ganges Rd	Salt Spring Island	BC	V8K2S2	250-537-2362	537-5333
TF: 800-661-9255 ■ *Web:* www.hastingshouse.com					
Havana Libre Beach Resort 3010 Collins Ave	Miami Beach	FL	33140	305-531-7742	534-6158
TF: 800-528-0823					
Havana Riverwalk Inn 1015 Navarro St	San Antonio	TX	78205	210-222-2008	222-2717
TF: 888-224-2008 ■ *Web:* www.havanariverwalkinn.com					
Hawaiian Inn 2301 S Atlantic Ave	Daytona Beach Shores	FL	32118	386-255-5411	253-1209
TF: 800-457-0077 ■ *Web:* www.hawaiianinn.com					
Hawthorn Park Hotel 2431 N Glenstone Ave	Springfield	MO	65803	417-831-3131	831-9786
Web: www.hawthornparkhotel.com					
Hawthorn Suites 13 Corporate Sq Suite 250	Atlanta	GA	30329	404-321-4045	321-4482
TF: 800-527-1133 ■ *Web:* www.hawthorn.com					
Hawthorne Hotel 18 Washington Sq W	Salem	MA	01970	978-744-4080	745-9842
TF: 800-729-7829 ■ *Web:* www.hawthornehotel.com					
Hawthorne Inn & Conference Center 420 High St	Winston-Salem	NC	27101	336-777-3000	777-3282
TF: 800-972-3774 ■ *Web:* www.hawthorneinn.com					
Hay-Adams Hotel 800 16th St NW	Washington	DC	20006	202-638-6600	638-2716
TF: 800-424-5054 ■ *Web:* www.hayadams.com					
Haywood Park Hotel 1 Battery Park Ave	Asheville	NC	28801	828-252-2522	253-0481
TF: 800-228-2522 ■ *Web:* www.haywoodpark.com					
Hazelton Hotel The 118 Yorkville Ave	Toronto	ON	M5R1C2	416-963-6300	963-6399
TF: 866-473-6301 ■ *Web:* www.thehazeltonhotel.com/					
Heartland Inn Cedar Rapids 3315 Southgate Ct SW	Cedar Rapids	IA	52404	319-362-9012	362-9694
TF: 800-334-3277 ■ *Web:* www.heartlandinns.com/					
Heartland Inn Dubuque South 2090 Southpark Ct	Dubuque	IA	52003	563-556-6555	556-0542
TF: 800-334-3277 ■ *Web:* www.heartlandinns.com					
Heartland Inn Dubuque West 4025 McDonald Dr	Dubuque	IA	52003	563-582-3752	582-0113
TF: 800-334-3277 ■ *Web:* www.heartlandinns.com					
Heathman Hotel 1001 SW Broadway	Portland	OR	97205	503-241-4100	790-7110
TF: 800-551-0011 ■ *Web:* www.heathmanhotel.com					
Heathman Lodge 7801 NE Greenwood Dr	Vancouver	WA	98662	360-254-3100	254-6100
TF: 888-475-3100 ■ *Web:* www.heathmanlodge.com					
Helmsley Carlton House Hotel 680 Madison Ave	New York	NY	10021	212-838-3000	753-8575
TF: 800-221-4982 ■ *Web:* www.helmsleycarltonhouse.com					
Helmsley Enterprises Inc 230 Park Ave Suite 659	New York	NY	10169	212-679-3600	953-2180
Web: www.helmsleyhotels.com					
Helmsley Middletowne Hotel 148 E 48th St	New York	NY	10017	212-755-3000	832-0261
TF: 800-221-4982 ■ *Web:* www.helmsleymiddletowne.com					
Helmsley Park Lane Hotel 36 Central Park S	New York	NY	10019	212-371-4000	750-7279
TF: 800-221-4982 ■ *Web:* www.helmsleyparklane.com					
Helmsley Sandcastle Hotel 1540 Ben Franklin Dr	Sarasota	FL	34236	941-388-2181	388-2655
TF: 800-225-2181 ■ *Web:* www.helmsleysandcastle.com					
Hemstreet Development Corp 16100 NW Cornell Rd Suite 100	Beaverton	OR	97006	503-531-4000	531-4001
TF Resv: 800-443-7777 ■ *Web:* www.valuinn.com					
Henley Park Hotel 926 Massachusetts Ave NW	Washington	DC	20001	202-638-5200	638-6740
TF: 800-222-8474 ■ *Web:* www.henleypark.com					
Henlopen Hotel 511 N Boardwalk	Rehoboth Beach	DE	19971	302-227-2551	227-8147
TF: 800-441-8450 ■ *Web:* www.henlopenhotel.com					
Heritage Hotel 234 3rd Ave N	Saint Petersburg	FL	33701	727-822-4814	823-1644
Web: www.theheritagehi.com					
Heritage House Inn 5200 N Hwy 1	Little River	CA	95456	707-937-5885	937-0318
TF: 800-235-5885 ■ *Web:* www.heritagehouseinn.com					
Heritage Inn The 1350 Richmond Rd	Williamsburg	VA	23185	757-229-2455	229-0122
TF: 800-552-5571					
Heritage Inn & Golf Club 2 Postal Ln	Lewes	DE	19958	302-644-0600	644-8522
TF: 800-669-9399 ■ *Web:* www.heritageinnandgolf.com					
Hermitage Hotel 231 6th Ave N	Nashville	TN	37219	615-244-3121	254-6909
TF: 888-888-9414 ■ *Web:* www.thehermitagehotel.com					
Hermosa Inn 5532 N Palo Cristi Rd	Paradise Valley	AZ	85253	602-955-8614	955-8299
TF: 800-241-1210 ■ *Web:* www.hermosainn.com					
Hershey Entertainment & Resorts Co 27 W Chocolate Ave	Hershey	PA	17033	717-534-3131	534-3324
TF: 800-437-7439 ■ *Web:* www.hersheypa.com					
Hershey Lodge & Convention Center W Chocolate Ave & University Dr	Hershey	PA	17033	717-533-3311	533-9642
TF: 800-533-3131 ■ *Web:* www.hersheylodge.com					
HI Development Corp 111 W Fortune St	Tampa	FL	33602	813-229-6686	223-9734
Web: www.hidevelopment.com					
High Country Inn 1785 Hwy 105	Boone	NC	28607	828-264-1000	262-0073
TF: 800-334-5605 ■ *Web:* www.highcountryinn.com					
Highlander Inn 2 Highlander Way	Manchester	NH	03103	603-625-6426	625-6466
TF: 800-548-9248 ■ *Web:* www.highlanderinn.com/inn.html					
Highlands Inn 120 Highlands Dr	Carmel	CA	93923	831-624-3801	626-1574
TF: 800-682-4811 ■ *Web:* highlandsinn.hyatt.com/hyatt/hotels					
Hilgard House Hotel & Suites 927 Hilgard Ave	Los Angeles	CA	90024	310-208-3945	208-1972
TF: 800-826-3934 ■ *Web:* www.hilgardhouse.com					
Hilltop Inn of Vermont 3472 Airport Rd	Montpelier	VT	05602	802-229-5766	229-5766
Web: www.hilltopinnvt.net/					
Hilton Garden Inn 9336 Civic Center Dr	Beverly Hills	CA	90210	310-278-4321	205-4613
TF: 800-445-8667 ■ *Web:* www.hiltongardeninn.com					
Hilton Hotels 9336 Civic Center Dr	Beverly Hills	CA	90210	310-278-4321	205-4613
TF: 800-445-8667 ■ *Web:* www.hilton.com					
Hilton Hotels Corp 9336 Civic Center Dr	Beverly Hills	CA	90210	310-278-4321	205-4613
NYSE: HLT ■ *TF:* 800-445-8667 ■ *Web:* hiltonworldwide1.hilton.com					
Conrad Hotels 9336 Civic Center Dr	Beverly Hills	CA	90210	310-278-4321	205-4613
TF: 800-445-8667 ■ *Web:* www.conradhotels.com					
Doubletree Hotels 9336 Civic Center Dr	Beverly Hills	CA	90210	310-278-4321	205-4613
TF: 800-222-8733 ■ *Web:* www.doubletree.com					
Embassy Suites Hotels 755 Crossover Ln	Memphis	TN	38117	901-374-5000	374-5948*
*Fax: Cust Svc ■ *TF:* 800-362-2779 ■ *Web:* www.embassysuites.com					
Hampton Hotels 755 Crossover Ln	Memphis	TN	38117	901-374-5000	374-5948*
*Fax: Cust Svc ■ *TF:* 800-362-2779 ■ *Web:* www.embassysuites.com					
Hilton Garden Inn 9336 Civic Center Dr	Beverly Hills	CA	90210	310-278-4321	205-4613
TF: 800-445-8667 ■ *Web:* www.hiltongardeninn.com					
Hilton Hotels 9336 Civic Center Dr	Beverly Hills	CA	90210	310-278-4321	205-4613
TF: 800-445-8667 ■ *Web:* www.hilton.com					
Homewood Suites by Hilton 755 Crossover Ln	Memphis	TN	38117	901-374-5000	374-5760*
*Fax: Cust Svc ■ *TF:* 800-225-5466 ■ *Web:* www.homewood-suites.com					
Waldorf=Astoria Collection 9336 Civic Center Dr	Beverly Hills	CA	90210	310-278-4321	
Web: www.waldorfastoriacollection.com					
Historic French Market Inn 501 Rue Decatur	New Orleans	LA	70130	504-561-5621	569-0619
TF: 888-538-5651 ■ *Web:* www.frenchmarketinn.com					
Historic Inns of Annapolis 58 State Cir	Annapolis	MD	21401	410-263-2641	216-9122
TF: 800-847-8882 ■ *Web:* www.annapolisinns.com					
HLC Hotels Inc PO Box 13069	Savannah	GA	31416	912-352-4493	352-0314
TF: 800-358-6122 ■ *Web:* www.hlchotels.com					
Holiday Inn 301 Government St	Mobile	AL	36602	251-694-0100	694-0160
TF: 888-465-4329					
Holiday Inn Express 3 Ravinia Dr Suite 100	Atlanta	GA	30346	770-604-2000	604-5403
Web: www.hiexpress.com					
Holiday Inn Express DFW North 4550 W John Carpenter Fwy	Irving	TX	75063	972-929-4499	929-0774
TF: 888-465-4329 ■ *Web:* www.hiexpress.com					
Holiday Inn Express Vancouver 2889 E Hastings St	Vancouver	BC	V5K2A1	604-254-1000	253-1234
TF: 888-428-7486 ■ *Web:* www.hievancouver.com					
Holiday Inn Hotels & Resorts 3 Ravinia Dr Suite 100	Atlanta	GA	30346	770-604-2000	604-5403
Web: www.holidayinn.com					
Hollow Inn 278 S Main St	Barre	VT	05641	802-479-9313	476-5242
TF: 800-998-9444 ■ *Web:* www.hollowinn.com					
Hollywood Roosevelt Hotel 7000 Hollywood Blvd	Hollywood	CA	90028	323-466-7000	462-8056
TF: 800-950-7667					
Hollywood Standard Hotel 8300 Sunset Blvd	West Hollywood	CA	90069	323-650-9090	650-2820
Web: www.standardhotel.com					
Homestead Inn 420 Field Point Rd	Greenwich	CT	06830	203-869-7500	869-7502
Web: www.homesteadinn.com					
Homestead Studio Suites Hotels 100 Dunbar St	Spartanburg	SC	29306	864-573-1600	573-1695
TF: 800-804-3724 ■ *Web:* www.homesteadhotels.com					
Homewood Suites by Hilton 755 Crossover Ln	Memphis	TN	38117	901-374-5000	374-5760*
*Fax: Cust Svc ■ *TF:* 800-225-5466 ■ *Web:* www.homewood-suites.com					
Horizon Casino Hotel 1310 Mulberry St	Vicksburg	MS	39180	601-636-3423	630-2194
TF: 800-843-2343 ■ *Web:* www.horizonvicksburg.com					
Horton Grand Hotel 311 Island Ave	San Diego	CA	92101	619-544-1886	239-3823
TF: 800-542-1886 ■ *Web:* www.hortongrand.com					
Hospitality Inn 3709 NW 39th St	Oklahoma City	OK	73112	405-942-7730	948-6238
Hospitality Inn 4400 S 27th St	Milwaukee	WI	53221	414-282-8800	282-7713
TF: 800-825-8466 ■ *Web:* www.hospitalityinn.com					
Hospitality International Inc 1726 Montreal Cir	Tucker	GA	30084	770-270-1180	270-1077
TF: 800-251-1962 ■ *Web:* www.bookroomsnow.com					
Downtowner Inns 1726 Montreal Cir	Tucker	GA	30084	770-270-1180	270-1077
TF: 800-251-1962 ■ *Web:* www.bookroomsnow.com					
Master Hosts Inns & Resorts 1726 Montreal Cir	Tucker	GA	30084	770-270-1180	270-1077
TF: 800-247-4677 ■ *Web:* www.bookroomsnow.com					
Passport Inn 1726 Montreal Cir	Tucker	GA	30084	770-270-1180	270-1077
TF: 800-251-1962 ■ *Web:* www.bookroomsnow.com					
Red Carpet Inn 1726 Montreal Cir	Tucker	GA	30084	770-270-1180	270-1077
TF: 800-251-1962 ■ *Web:* www.bookroomsnow.com					
Scottish Inns 1726 Montreal Cir	Tucker	GA	30084	770-270-1180	270-1077
TF: 800-251-1962 ■ *Web:* www.bookroomsnow.com					
Hospitality Suites Resort 409 N Scottsdale Rd	Scottsdale	AZ	85257	480-949-5115	941-8014
TF: 800-445-5115 ■ *Web:* www.hospitalitysuites.com					
Host Airport Hotel 6945 Airport Blvd	Sacramento	CA	95837	916-922-8071	929-8636
TF: 800-903-4678 ■ *Web:* www.hostairporthotel.com					

Name / Address	City	State	Zip	Phone	Fax
Hostmark Hospitality Group 1111 Plaza Dr Suite 200 *Web:* www.hostmark.com	Schaumburg	IL	60173	847-517-9100	517-9797
Hot Springs Hotel & Spa 135 Central Ave *TF:* 888-624-5521 ■ *Web:* www.springshotelandspa.com	Hot Springs	AR	71901	501-624-5521	624-4635
Hotel 43 981 Grove St *TF:* 800-243-4622 ■ *Web:* www.hotel43.com/	Boise	ID	83702	208-342-4622	344-5751
Hotel 71 71 Saint-Pierre St *TF:* 888-692-1171 ■ *Web:* www.hotel71.ca/	Quebec City	QC	G1K4A4	418-692-1171	692-0669
Hotel 71 Chicago 71 E Wacker Dr *TF:* 888-621-4005 ■ *Web:* www.hotel71.com	Chicago	IL	60601	312-346-7100	346-1721
Hotel 140 140 Clarendon St *TF:* 800-714-0140 ■ *Web:* www.hotel140.com/	Boston	MA	02116	617-585-5600	585-5699
Hotel 373 373 5th Ave *TF:* 800-515-8373 ■ *Web:* www.hotel373.com/	New York	NY	10016	212-213-3388	
Hotel 1000 1000 1st Ave *TF:* 877-315-1088 ■ *Web:* www.hotel1000seattle.com	Seattle	WA	98104	206-957-1000	337-9457
Hotel The 801 Collins Ave *TF:* 800-727-5236 ■ *Web:* www.thehotelofsouthbeach.com	Miami Beach	FL	33139	305-531-2222	531-3222
Hotel Acadia 43 Sainte-Ursule St *TF:* 800-463-0280 ■ *Web:* hotelsnouvellefrance.com/fr/hotels_acadia.php	Quebec	QC	G1R4E4	418-694-0280	694-0458
Hotel Adagio 550 Geary St *TF:* 800-228-8830 ■ *Web:* www.thehoteladagio.com	San Francisco	CA	94102	415-775-5000	775-9388
Hotel Alex Johnson 523 6th St *TF:* 800-888-2539 ■ *Web:* www.alexjohnson.com	Rapid City	SD	57701	605-342-1210	342-7436
Hotel Allegro Chicago 171 W Randolph St *TF:* 800-643-1500 ■ *Web:* www.allegrochicago.com	Chicago	IL	60601	312-236-0123	236-3440
Hotel Ambassadeur 321 Sainte-Anne Blvd *TF:* 800-363-4619 ■ *Web:* www.hotelambassadeur.ca	Beauport	QC	G1E3L4	418-666-2828	666-2775
Hotel Ambassador 1324 S Main St *TF:* 888-408-8282 ■ *Web:* www.hotelambassador-tulsa.com	Tulsa	OK	74119	918-587-8200	587-8208
Hotel Andalucia 31 W Carrillo St *TF:* 877-468-3515 ■ *Web:* www.andaluciasb.com	Santa Barbara	CA	93101	805-884-0300	884-8153
Hotel Andra 2000 4th Ave *TF:* 877-448-8600 ■ *Web:* www.hotelandra.com	Seattle	WA	98121	206-448-8600	441-7140
Hotel Andrew Jackson 919 Royal St *TF:* 800-654-0224 ■ *Web:* www.andrewjacksonhotel.com/	New Orleans	LA	70116	504-561-5881	596-6769
Hotel Angeleno 170 N Church Ln *TF:* 866-264-3536 ■ *Web:* www.jdvhotels.com/angeleno	Los Angeles	CA	90049	310-476-6411	472-1157
Hotel de Anza 233 W Santa Clara St *TF:* 800-843-3700 ■ *Web:* www.hoteldeanza.com	San Jose	CA	95113	408-286-1000	286-0500
Hotel Astor 956 Washington Ave *TF:* 800-270-4981 ■ *Web:* www.hotelastor.com	Miami Beach	FL	33139	305-531-8081	531-3193
Hotel Avante 860 E El Camino Real *TF:* 800-538-1600 ■ *Web:* www.hotelavante.com	Mountain View	CA	94040	650-940-1000	968-7870
Hotel Baronette 27790 Novi Rd *TF:* 866-589-3411 ■ *Web:* www.hotelbaronette.com	Novi	MI	48377	248-349-7800	349-7467
Hotel Beacon 2130 Broadway *TF:* 800-572-4969 ■ *Web:* www.beaconhotel.com	New York	NY	10023	212-787-1100	724-0839
Hotel Bedford 118 E 40th St *TF:* 800-221-6881 ■ *Web:* www.bedfordhotel.com	New York	NY	10016	212-697-4800	697-1093
Hotel Bel-Air 701 Stone Canyon Rd *TF:* 800-648-4097 ■ *Web:* www.hotelbelair.com	Los Angeles	CA	90077	310-472-1211	476-5890
Hotel Ben Lomond 2510 Washington Blvd *TF:* 877-627-1900 ■ *Web:* www.benlomondsuites.com	Ogden	UT	84401	801-627-1900	394-5342
Hotel Bethlehem 437 Main St *TF:* 800-333-3333 ■ *Web:* www.radisson.com/bethlehempa	Bethlehem	PA	18018	610-625-5000	625-2218
Hotel Bijou 111 Mason St *TF:* 800-771-1022 ■ *Web:* www.jdvhotels.com/bijou/	San Francisco	CA	94102	415-771-1200	346-3196
Hotel Blake 500 S Dearborn St *Web:* www.hotelblake.com	Chicago	IL	60605	312-986-1234	939-2468
Hotel Le Bleu 370 4th Ave *Web:* www.hotellebleu.com	Brooklyn	NY	11215	718-625-1500	625-2600
Hotel Boulderado 2115 13th St *TF:* 800-433-4344 ■ *Web:* www.boulderado.com	Boulder	CO	80302	303-442-4344	442-4378
Hotel Britton 112 7th St *TF:* 800-444-5819	San Francisco	CA	94104	415-621-7001	621-4069
Hotel Burnham 1 W Washington St *TF:* 877-294-9712 ■ *Web:* www.burnhamhotel.com	Chicago	IL	60602	312-782-1111	782-0899
Hotel Cantlie Suites 1110 Sherbrooke St W *TF:* 800-567-1110 ■ *Web:* www.hotelcantlie.com	Montreal	QC	H3A1G9	514-842-2000	844-7808
Hotel Le Capitole 972 Saint-Jean St *TF:* 800-363-4040 ■ *Web:* www.lecapitole.com	Quebec	QC	G1R1R5	418-694-4040	694-9924
Hotel Captain Cook 939 W 5th Ave *TF:* 800-843-1950 ■ *Web:* www.captaincook.com	Anchorage	AK	99501	907-276-6000	343-2298
Hotel Carlton 1075 Sutter St *TF:* 800-738-7477 ■ *Web:* www.jdvhotels.com/carlton	San Francisco	CA	94109	415-673-0242	929-8788
Hotel Casa del Mar 1910 Ocean Way *TF:* 800-898-6999 ■ *Web:* www.hotelcasadelmar.com	Santa Monica	CA	90405	310-581-5533	581-5503
Hotel Chateau Bellevue 16 de la Porte St *TF:* 800-463-2617 ■ *Web:* www.vieux-quebec.com/Bellevue-English	Quebec	QC	G1R4M9	418-692-2573	692-4876
Hotel Chateau Laurier 1220 George V Pl W *TF:* 800-463-4453 ■ *Web:* www.vieux-quebec.com/Laurier-English	Quebec	QC	G1R5B8	418-522-8108	524-8768
Hotel Chelsea 944 Washington Ave *Web:* www.thehotelchelsea.com	Miami Beach	FL	33139	305-534-4069	672-6712
Hotel Le Cirque 2 Lee Circle *TF:* 800-684-9525 ■ *Web:* www.neworleansfinehotels.com/hotellecirque/	New Orleans	LA	70130	504-962-0900	962-0901
Hotel Clarendon 57 Sainte-Anne St *TF:* 888-554-6001 ■ *Web:* www.hotelclarendon.com	Quebec	QC	G1R3X4	418-692-2480	692-4652
Hotel Classique 2815 Laurier Blvd *TF:* 800-463-1885 ■ *Web:* www.hotelclassique.com	Sainte-Foy	QC	G1V4H3	418-658-2793	658-6816
Hotel Le Clos Saint-Louis 69 Saint-Louis St *TF:* 800-461-1311 ■ *Web:* www.clossaintlouis.com	Quebec	QC	G1R3Z2	418-694-1311	694-9411
Hotel Colorado 526 Pine St *TF:* 800-544-3998 ■ *Web:* www.hotelcolorado.com	Glenwood Springs	CO	81601	970-945-6511	945-7030
Hotel Commonwealth 500 Commonwealth Ave *TF:* 866-784-4000 ■ *Web:* www.hotelcommonwealth.com	Boston	MA	02215	617-933-5000	266-6888
Hotel Congress 311 E Congress St *TF:* 800-722-8848 ■ *Web:* www.hotelcongress.com	Tucson	AZ	85701	520-622-8848	792-6366
Hotel Contessa 306 W Market St *TF:* 866-435-0900 ■ *Web:* www.thehotelcontessa.com	San Antonio	TX	78205	210-229-9222	229-9228
Hotel Crescent Court 400 Crescent Ct *Web:* www.crescentcourt.com	Dallas	TX	75201	214-871-3200	871-3272
Hotel Deca 4507 Brooklyn Ave NE *TF:* 800-899-0251 ■ *Web:* www.hoteldeca.com	Seattle	WA	98105	206-634-2000	547-6029
Hotel Del Sol 3100 Webster St *TF:* 877-433-5765 ■ *Web:* www.jdvhotels.com/del_sol/	San Francisco	CA	94123	415-921-5520	931-4137
Hotel Deluxe 729 SW 15th Ave *TF:* 866-895-2094 ■ *Web:* www.hoteldeluxeportland.com	Portland	OR	97205	503-223-6311	219-2095
Hotel Derek 2525 West Loop S *TF:* 866-292-4100 ■ *Web:* www.hotelderek.com	Houston	TX	77027	713-961-3000	297-4392
Hotel DeVille 319 W Miller St *TF:* 800-392-3366 ■ *Web:* www.devillehotel.com	Jefferson City	MO	65101	573-636-5231	636-5260
Hotel Drisco 2901 Pacific Ave *TF:* 800-634-7277 ■ *Web:* www.hoteldrisco.com	San Francisco	CA	94115	415-346-2880	567-5537
Hotel Durant 2600 Durant Ave *TF:* 800-238-7268 ■ *Web:* www.jdvhotels.com/durant/	Berkeley	CA	94704	510-845-8981	486-8336
Hotel Edison 228 W 47th St *TF:* 800-637-7070 ■ *Web:* www.edisonhotelnyc.com	New York	NY	10036	212-840-5000	596-6868
Hotel Elysee 60 E 54th St *TF:* 800-535-9733 ■ *Web:* www.elyseehotel.com	New York	NY	10022	212-753-1066	980-9278
Hotel Encanto de Las Cruces 705 S Telshor Blvd	Las Cruces	NM	88011	505-522-4300	521-4707
Hotel du Fort 1390 du Fort St *TF:* 800-565-6333 ■ *Web:* www.hoteldufort.com	Montreal	QC	H3H2R7	514-938-8333	938-2078
Hotel Fort Des Moines 1000 Walnut St *TF:* 800-532-1466 ■ *Web:* www.hotelfortdm.com	Des Moines	IA	50309	515-243-1161	243-4317
Hotel Galvez - A Wyndham Historic Hotel 2024 Seawall Blvd *TF:* 800-996-3426 ■ *Web:* www.wyndham.com/hotels/GLSHG/main.wnt	Galveston	TX	77550	409-765-7721	765-5623
Hotel Gault 449 Sainte-Helene St *TF:* 866-904-1616 ■ *Web:* www.hotelgault.com/	Montreal	QC	H2Y2K9	514-904-1616	304-1717
Hotel George 15 'E' St NW *TF:* 800-576-8831 ■ *Web:* www.hotelgeorge.com	Washington	DC	20001	202-347-4200	347-4213
Hotel Le Germain 2050 Mansfield St *TF:* 877-333-2050 ■ *Web:* www.hotelgermain.com	Montreal	QC	H3A1Y9	514-849-2050	849-1437
Hotel Germain des Pres 1200 Germain-des-Pres Ave *TF:* 800-463-5253 ■ *Web:* www.germaindespres.com	Sainte-Foy	QC	G1V3M7	418-658-1224	658-8846
Hotel Le Germain Toronto 30 Mercer St *TF:* 866-345-9501 ■ *Web:* www.germaintoronto.com	Toronto	ON	M5V1H3	416-345-9500	345-9501
Hotel Giraffe 365 Park Ave S at 26th St *TF:* 877-296-0009 ■ *Web:* www.hotelgiraffe.com	New York	NY	10016	212-685-7700	685-7771
Hotel le Gite 5160 Wilfrid-Hamel Blvd W *TF:* 800-363-4906 ■ *Web:* www.hotellegite.com	Quebec	QC	G2E2G8	418-871-8899	872-8533
Hotel Gouverneur Sainte-Foy 3030 Laurier Blvd *TF:* 888-910-1111 ■ *Web:* www.gouverneursaintefoy.com	Sainte-Foy	QC	G1V2M5	418-651-3030	651-6797
Hotel Grand Pacific 463 Belleville St *TF:* 800-663-7550 ■ *Web:* www.hotelgrandpacific.com	Victoria	BC	V8V1X3	250-386-0450	380-4475
Hotel Grand Victorian 2325 W Hwy 76 *TF:* 800-324-8751 ■ *Web:* www.luxehotels.com	Branson	MO	65616	417-336-2935	336-1932
Hotel Granduca 1080 Uptown Park Blvd *TF:* 888-472-6382 ■ *Web:* www.granducahouston.com	Houston	TX	77056	713-418-1000	418-1001
Hotel Griffon 155 Steuart St *TF:* 800-321-2201 ■ *Web:* www.hotelgriffon.com	San Francisco	CA	94105	415-495-2100	495-3522
Hotel Group The (THG) 110 James St Suite 102 *Web:* www.thehotelgroup.com	Edmonds	WA	98020	425-771-1788	672-8280
Hotel Helix 1430 Rhode Island Ave NW *Web:* www.hotelhelix.com	Washington	DC	20005	202-462-9001	332-3519
Hotel Highland 1023 20th St S *TF:* 800-255-7304	Birmingham	AL	35205	205-933-9555	933-6918
Hotel Huntington Beach 7667 Center Ave *TF:* 877-891-0123 ■ *Web:* www.hotelhb.com	Huntington Beach	CA	92647	714-891-0123	895-4591
Hotel Icon 220 Main St *TF:* 800-970-4266 ■ *Web:* www.hotelicon.com	Houston	TX	77002	713-224-4266	223-3223
Hotel Indigo 3 Ravinia Dr Suite 100 **Fax Area Code: 770* ■ *Web:* www.hotelindigo.com	Atlanta	GA	30346	704-604-2000	604-5403*
Hotel Jerome 330 E Main St *TF:* 800-331-7213 ■ *Web:* www.hoteljerome.com	Aspen	CO	81611	970-920-1000	925-2784
Hotel La Jolla 7955 La Jolla Shores Dr *TF:* 800-666-0261 ■ *Web:* www.hotellajolla.com	La Jolla	CA	92037	858-459-0261	459-7649
Hotel Kabuki San Francisco 1625 Post St *TF:* 888-579-7711 ■ *Web:* www.miyakohotel.com	San Francisco	CA	94115	415-922-3200	614-5498
Hotel l'Appartement Montreal 455 Sherbrooke St W *TF:* 800-363-3010 ■ *Web:* www.appartementhotel.com	Montreal	QC	H3A1B7	514-284-3634	287-1431
Hotel Largo 9100 Basil Ct	Largo	MD	20774	301-773-0700	772-2016
Hotel Lawrence 302 S Houston St *TF:* 877-396-0334 ■ *Web:* www.hotellawrence.com	Dallas	TX	75202	214-761-9090	761-0740
Hotel Lombardy 2019 Pennsylvania Ave NW *TF:* 800-424-5486 ■ *Web:* www.hotellombardy.com	Washington	DC	20006	202-828-2600	872-0503
Hotel Lord-Berri 1199 Berri St *TF:* 888-363-0363 ■ *Web:* www.lordberri.com	Montreal	QC	H2L4C6	514-845-9236	849-9855
Hotel Los Gatos 210 E Main St *TF:* 866-335-1700 ■ *Web:* www.jdvhotels.com/los_gatos	Los Gatos	CA	95030	408-335-1700	335-1750
Hotel Lucia 400 SW Broadway *TF:* 877-225-1717 ■ *Web:* www.hotellucia.com	Portland	OR	97205	503-225-1717	225-1919
hotel Lumen 6101 Hillcrest Ave *TF:* 800-908-1140 ■ *Web:* www.hotellumen.com	Dallas	TX	75205	214-219-2400	219-2402
Hotel Lusso 1 N Post St *TF:* 800-525-4800 ■ *Web:* www.hotellusso.com	Spokane	WA	99201	509-747-9750	747-9751
Hotel Madera 1310 New Hampshire Ave NW *TF:* 800-368-5691 ■ *Web:* www.hotelmadera.com	Washington	DC	20036	202-296-7600	293-2476
Hotel Maison de Ville 727 Toulouse St *TF:* 800-634-1600 ■ *Web:* www.maisondeville.com	New Orleans	LA	70130	504-561-5858	528-9939
Hotel Majestic 1500 Sutter St *TF:* 800-869-8966 ■ *Web:* www.thehotelmajestic.com	San Francisco	CA	94109	415-441-1100	673-7331
Hotel Manoir Victoria 44 Cote du Palais *TF:* 800-463-6283 ■ *Web:* www.manoir-victoria.com	Quebec	QC	G1R4H8	418-692-1030	692-3822
Hotel Maritime Plaza 1155 Guy St *TF:* 800-363-6255 ■ *Web:* www.hotelmaritime.com	Montreal	QC	H3H2K5	514-932-1411	932-0446
Hotel Mark Twain 345 Taylor St *TF:* 877-854-4106 ■ *Web:* www.hotelmarktwain.com	San Francisco	CA	94102	415-673-2332	673-0529
Hotel Marlowe Cambridge 25 Edwind H Land Blvd *TF:* 800-825-7040 ■ *Web:* www.hotelmarlowe.com	Cambridge	MA	02141	617-868-8000	868-8001
Hotel Max 620 Stewart St *TF:* 866-833-6299 ■ *Web:* www.hotelmaxseattle.com	Seattle	WA	98101	206-441-4200	443-5754
Hotel Mead 451 E Grand Ave *TF:* 800-843-6323 ■ *Web:* www.hotelmead.com	Wisconsin Rapids	WI	54494	715-423-1500	422-7064
Hotel Mela 120 W 44th St *TF:* 877-452-6352 ■ *Web:* www.hotelmela.com	New York	NY	10036	212-710-7000	704-9680
Hotel Metro 411 E Mason St *TF:* 877-638-7620 ■ *Web:* www.hotelmetro.com	Milwaukee	WI	53202	414-272-1937	223-1158
Hotel Milano 55 5th St *TF:* 800-398-7555 ■ *Web:* hotelmilanosf.com	San Francisco	CA	94103	415-543-8555	543-8555
Hotel Monaco Chicago 225 N Wabash Ave *TF:* 800-397-7661 ■ *Web:* www.monaco-chicago.com	Chicago	IL	60601	312-960-8500	960-1883
Hotel Monaco Denver 1717 Champa St *TF:* 800-397-5380 ■ *Web:* www.monaco-denver.com	Denver	CO	80202	303-296-1717	296-1818
Hotel Monaco Portland 506 SW Washington at 5th Ave *TF:* 866-861-9514 ■ *Web:* www.monaco-portland.com	Portland	OR	97204	503-222-0001	
Hotel Monaco Salt Lake City 15 W 200 South *TF:* 877-294-9710 ■ *Web:* www.monaco-saltlakecity.com	Salt Lake City	UT	84101	801-595-0000	532-8500
Hotel Monaco San Francisco 501 Geary St *TF:* 866-622-5284 ■ *Web:* www.monaco-sf.com	San Francisco	CA	94102	415-292-0100	292-0111
Hotel Monaco Seattle 1101 4th Ave *TF:* 800-715-6513 ■ *Web:* www.monaco-seattle.com	Seattle	WA	98101	206-621-1770	621-7779
Hotel de la Montagne 1430 de la Montagne St *TF:* 800-361-6262 ■ *Web:* www.hoteldelamontagne.com	Montreal	QC	H3G1Z5	514-288-5656	288-9658
Hotel Monte Vista 100 N San Francisco St *TF:* 800-545-3068 ■ *Web:* www.hotelmontevista.com	Flagstaff	AZ	86001	928-779-6971	779-2904
Hotel Monteleone 214 Royal St *TF:* 800-535-9595 ■ *Web:* www.hotelmonteleone.com	New Orleans	LA	70130	504-523-3341	681-4413
Hotel Montgomery 211 S 1st St *TF:* 866-823-0530 ■ *Web:* www.jdvhotels.com/montgomery	San Jose	CA	95113	408-282-8800	282-8850
Hotel Monticello 1075 Thomas Jefferson St NW *TF:* 800-388-2410 ■ *Web:* www.monticellohotel.com	Washington	DC	20007	202-337-0900	333-6526

Phone Fax

Hotel Montreal Centrale 1586 Saint-Hubert St Montreal QC H2L3Z3 514-843-5739 904-0888
TF: 866-878-5739 ■ *Web:* www.hotelmontrealcentrale.com/
Hotel Murano 1320 Broadway Plaza Tacoma WA 98402 253-238-8000 627-3167
TF: 888-862-3255 ■ *Web:* www.hotelmuranotacoma.com/
Hotel Nikko San Francisco 222 Mason St San Francisco CA 94102 415-394-1111 394-1106
TF: 800-645-5687 ■ *Web:* www.hotelnikkosf.com
Hotel Normandin 4700 Pierre-Bertrand Blvd Quebec QC G2J1A4 418-622-1611 622-9277
TF: 800-463-6721 ■ *Web:* www.hotelnormandin.com
Hotel Northampton 36 King St Northampton MA 01060 413-584-3100 584-9455
TF: 800-547-3529 ■ *Web:* www.hotelnorthhampton.com
Hotel Ocean 1230 Ocean Dr Miami Beach FL 33139 305-672-2579 672-7665
TF: 800-783-1725 ■ *Web:* www.hotelocean.com
Hotel Oceana 202 W Cabrillo Blvd Santa Barbara CA 93101 805-965-4577 965-9937
TF: 800-965-9776 ■ *Web:* www.hoteloceana.com
Hotel Oceana 849 Ocean Ave Santa Monica CA 90403 310-393-0486 458-1182
TF: 800-777-0758 ■ *Web:* www.hoteloceana.com
Hotel at Old Town 830 E 1st St Wichita KS 67202 316-267-4800 267-4840
TF: 877-265-3869 ■ *Web:* www.hotelatoldtown.com
Hotel Omni Mont-Royal 1050 Sherbrooke St W Montreal QC H3A2R6 514-284-1110 845-3025
TF: 800-843-6664 ■ *Web:* www.omnihotels.com
Hotel Orrington 1710 Orrington Ave Evanston IL 60201 847-866-8700 866-8724
TF: 888-677-4648 ■ *Web:* www.hotelorrington.com
Hotel Pacific 300 Pacific St Monterey CA 93940 831-373-5700 373-6921
TF: 800-554-5542 ■ *Web:* www.hotelpacific.com
Hotel Palomar Arlington 1121 N 19th St Arlington VA 22209 703-351-9170 351-9175
TF: 866-505-1001 ■ *Web:* www.hotelpalomar-arlington.com/
Hotel Palomar Dallas 5300 E Mockingbird Ln Dallas TX 75206 214-520-7969 520-8025
TF: 888-253-9030 ■ *Web:* www.hotelpalomar-dallas.com
Hotel Palomar San Francisco 12 4th St San Francisco CA 94103 415-348-1111 348-0302
TF: 877-294-9711 ■ *Web:* www.hotelpalomar-sf.com
Hotel Parisi 1111 Prospect La Jolla CA 92037 858-454-1511 454-1531
TF: 877-472-7474 ■ *Web:* www.hotelparisi.com
Hotel Park City 2001 Park Ave Park City UT 84060 435-200-2000 940-5001
Web: www.hotelparkcity.com
Hotel Pere Marquette 501 Main St Peoria IL 61602 309-637-6500 637-6500
TF: 800-447-1676 ■ *Web:* www.hotelperemarquette.com
Hotel Phillips 106 W 12th St Kansas City MO 64105 816-221-7000 221-3477
TF: 800-433-1426 ■ *Web:* www.hotelphillips.com
Hotel Plaza Athenee 37 E 64th St New York NY 10065 212-734-9100 772-0958
TF: 800-447-8800 ■ *Web:* www.plaza-athenee.com
Hotel Plaza Quebec 3031 Laurier Blvd Sainte-Foy QC G1V2M2 418-658-2727 658-6587
TF: 800-567-5276 ■ *Web:* www.hotelsjaro.com/plazaquebec/index-en.aspx
Hotel Plaza Real 125 Washington Ave Santa Fe NM 87501 505-988-4900 983-9322
TF: 877-901-7666
Hotel du Pont 11th & Market Sts Wilmington DE 19801 302-594-3100 594-3108
TF: 800-441-9019 ■ *Web:* www.dupont.com/hotel
Hotel le Priori 15 du Sault-au-Matelot St Quebec QC G1K3Y7 418-692-3992 692-0883
TF: 800-351-3992 ■ *Web:* www.hotellepriori.com
Hotel Provincial 1024 Rue Chartres New Orleans LA 70116 504-581-4995 581-1018
TF: 800-535-7922 ■ *Web:* www.hotelprovincial.com
Hotel PUR 395 rue de la Couronne Quebec City QC G1K7X4 418-647-2611 640-0666
TF: 800-267-2002 ■ *Web:* www.hotelpur.com/
Hotel Quartier 2955 Laurier Blvd Sainte-Foy QC G1V2M2 418-650-1616 650-6611
Web: www.hotelquartier.com
Hotel Queen Mary 1126 Queens Hwy Long Beach CA 90802 562-435-3511 437-4531
TF: 800-437-2934 ■ *Web:* www.queenmary.com
Hotel Rex 562 Sutter St San Francisco CA 94102 415-433-4434 433-3695
TF: 800-433-4434 ■ *Web:* www.thehotelrex.com
Hotel Rodney 142 2nd St Lewes DE 19958 302-645-6466 645-7196
TF: 800-824-8754 ■ *Web:* www.hotelrodneydelaware.com
Hotel Roger Williams 131 Madison Ave New York NY 10016 212-448-7000 448-7007
TF Resv: 888-448-7788 ■ *Web:* www.hotelrogerwilliams.com
Hotel La Rose 308 Wilson St Santa Rosa CA 95401 707-579-3200 579-3247
TF: 800-527-6738 ■ *Web:* www.hotellarose.com
Hotel Rouge 1315 16th St NW Washington DC 20036 202-232-8000 667-9827
TF: 800-738-1202 ■ *Web:* www.rougehotel.com
Hotel Royal Palace 775 Honore Mercier Ave Quebec QC G1R6A5 418-694-2000 380-2553
TF: 800-567-5276 ■ *Web:* www.hotelsjaro.com/palaceroyal/index-en.aspx
Hotel Royal Plaza 1905 Hotel Plaza Blvd Lake Buena Vista FL 32830 407-828-2828 827-3977
TF: 800-248-7890 ■ *Web:* www.royalplaza.com
Hotel Ruby Foo's 7655 Decarie Blvd Montreal QC H4P2H2 514-731-7701 731-7158
TF: 800-361-5419 ■ *Web:* www.hotelrubyfoos.com
Hotel Saint Francis 210 Don Gaspar Ave Santa Fe NM 87501 505-983-5700 989-7690
TF: 800-529-5700 ■ *Web:* www.hotelstfrancis.com
Hotel Saint Germain 2516 Maple Ave Dallas TX 75201 214-871-2516 871-0740
TF: 800-683-2516 ■ *Web:* www.hotelstgermain.com
Hotel Saint Marie 827 Toulouse St New Orleans LA 70112 504-561-8951 571-2802
TF: 800-366-2743 ■ *Web:* www.hotelstmarie.com
Hotel Saint Pierre 911 Burgundy St New Orleans LA 70116 504-524-4401 593-9425
TF: 800-225-4040
Hotel Saint Regis Detroit 3071 W Grand Blvd Detroit MI 48202 313-873-3000 875-2035
Web: www.hotelstregisdetroit.com
Hotel San Carlos 202 N Central Ave Phoenix AZ 85004 602-253-4121 253-6668
TF: 866-253-4121 ■ *Web:* www.hotelsancarlos.com
Hotel Santa Barbara 533 State St Santa Barbara CA 93101 805-957-9300 962-2412
TF: 888-259-7700 ■ *Web:* www.hotelsantabarbara.com
Hotel Santa Fe 1501 Paseo de Peralta Santa Fe NM 87501 505-982-1200 984-2211
TF: 800-825-9876 ■ *Web:* www.hotelsantafe.com
Hotel Saranac 101 Main St Saranac Lake NY 12983 518-891-2200 891-5664
TF: 800-937-0211 ■ *Web:* www.hotelsaranac.com
Hotel Sax Chicago 333 N Dearborn St Chicago IL 60610 312-245-0333 923-2458
TF: 877-569-3742 ■ *Web:* www.loewshotels.com/hotels/chicago
Hotel Sepia 3135 ch St-Louis Sainte-Foy QC G1W1R9 418-653-4941 653-0774
TF: 800-463-6603 ■ *Web:* www.hotelsepia.ca
Hotel Shelley 844 Collins Ave Miami Beach FL 33139 305-531-3341 674-0811
TF: 877-762-3477 ■ *Web:* www.hotelshelley.com
Hotel Solamar 435 6th Ave San Diego CA 92101 619-531-8740 531-8742
TF: 877-230-0300 ■ *Web:* www.hotelsolamar.com
Hotel Le Soleil 567 Hornby St Vancouver BC V6C2E8 604-632-3000 632-3001
TF: 877-632-3030 ■ *Web:* www.lesoleilhotel.com
Hotel Le St-James 355 Saint-Jacques St Montreal QC H2Y1N9 514-841-3111 841-1232
TF: 866-841-3111 ■ *Web:* www.hotellestjames.com
Hotel St-Paul 355 McGill St Montreal QC H2Y2E8 514-380-2222 380-2202
TF: 866-380-2202 ■ *Web:* www.hotelstpaul.com
Hotel Strasburg 213 S Holliday St Strasburg VA 22657 540-465-9191 465-4788
TF: 800-348-8327 ■ *Web:* www.hotelstrasburg.com
Hotel Teatro 1100 14th St Denver CO 80202 303-228-1100 228-1101
TF: 888-727-1200 ■ *Web:* www.hotelteatro.com
Hotel Triton 342 Grant Ave San Francisco CA 94108 415-394-0500 394-0555
TF: 800-800-1299 ■ *Web:* www.hoteltriton.com
Hotel Universel 2300 ch Sainte-Foy Sainte-Foy QC G1V1S5 418-653-5250 653-4486
TF: 800-463-4495 ■ *Web:* www.hoteluniversel.qc.ca
Hotel Utica 102 Lafayette St Utica NY 13502 315-724-7829 733-7663
TF: 877-906-1912 ■ *Web:* www.hotelutica.com
Hotel Val-des-Neiges 201 Val-des-Neiges St Mont Sainte-Anne Beaupre QC G0A1E0 418-827-5711 827-5997
TF: 888-554-6005 ■ *Web:* www.hotelvaldesneiges.com/en

Phone Fax

Hotel Valencia Santana Row 355 Santana Row San Jose CA 95128 408-551-0010 551-0550
TF: 866-842-0100 ■ *Web:* sanjose.hotelvalencia.com/
Hotel Valley Ho 6850 Main St Scottsdale AZ 85251 480-248-2000 248-2002
TF: 866-882-4484 ■ *Web:* www.hotelvalleyho.com
Hotel Victoria 56 Yonge St Toronto ON M5E1G5 416-363-1666 363-7327
TF: 800-363-8228 ■ *Web:* www.hotelvictoria-toronto.com
Hotel Viking 1 Bellevue Ave Newport RI 02840 401-847-3300 848-4864
TF: 800-556-7126 ■ *Web:* www.hotelviking.com
Hotel Vintage Park 1100 5th Ave Seattle WA 98101 206-624-8000 623-0568
TF: 800-853-3914 ■ *Web:* www.hotelvintagepark.com
Hotel Vintage Plaza 422 SW Broadway Portland OR 97205 503-228-1212 228-3598
TF: 800-263-2305 ■ *Web:* www.vintageplaza.com
Hotel Vitale 8 Mission St San Francisco CA 94105 415-278-3700 278-3750
TF: 888-890-8688 ■ *Web:* www.hotelvitale.com/
Hotel Wales 1295 Madison Ave New York NY 10128 212-876-6000 860-7000
TF: 866-925-3746
Hotel Washington 515 15th St NW Washington DC 20004 202-638-5900 638-4275
TF: 800-424-9540 ■ *Web:* www.hotelwashington.com
Hotel Windsor 1700 Benjamin Franklin Pkwy Philadelphia PA 19103 215-981-5678 981-5684
Web: www.windsorhotel.com
Hotel Wolcott 4 W 31st St New York NY 10001 212-268-2900 563-0096
Web: www.wolcott.com
Hotel XIXe Siecle 262 Saint-Jacques St W Montreal QC H2Y1N1 514-985-0019 985-0059
TF: 877-553-0019 ■ *Web:* www.hotelxixsiecle.com/
Hotel ZaZa Dallas 2332 Leonard St Dallas TX 75201 214-468-8399 468-8397
TF: 800-597-8399 ■ *Web:* www.hotelzaza.com/dallas
Hotel ZaZa Houston 5701 Main St Houston TX 77005 713-526-1991 639-4545
TF Resv: 888-880-3244 ■ *Web:* www.hotelzaza.com/Houston
Houston Grand Plaza Hotel 8686 Kirby Dr Houston TX 77054 713-748-3221 796-9371
Web: www.houstongrandplaza.com
Howard Johnson 1 Sylvan Way Parsippany NJ 07054 973-753-6600
TF Resv: 800-446-4656 ■ *Web:* www.hojo.com
HTH Corp 2490 Kalakaua Ave Honolulu HI 96815 808-922-1233 923-2566*
**Fax:* Sales ■ *TF:* 800-367-6060 ■ *Web:* www.hthcorp.com
Hudson Hotel 356 W 58th St New York NY 10019 212-554-6000 554-6001
TF: 800-606-6090 ■ *Web:* www.morganshotelgroup.com
Humphrey's Half Moon Inn & Suites 2303 Shelter Island Dr San Diego CA 92106 619-224-3411 224-3478
TF: 800-542-7400 ■ *Web:* www.halfmooninn.com
Huntington Hotel & Nob Hill Spa 1075 California St San Francisco CA 94108 415-474-5400 474-6227
TF: 800-227-4683 ■ *Web:* www.huntingtonhotel.com
Hyannis Holiday Motel 131 Ocean St Hyannis MA 02601 508-775-1639 775-1672
TF: 800-423-1551 ■ *Web:* www.hyannisholiday.com
Hyannis Travel Inn 18 North St Hyannis MA 02601 508-775-8200 775-8200
TF: 800-352-7190 ■ *Web:* www.hyannistravelinn.com
Hyatt Hotels Corp 71 S Wacker Dr Chicago IL 60606 312-750-1234 750-8597*
**Fax:* Mktg ■ *TF:* 888-591-1234 ■ *Web:* www.hyatt.com
AmeriSuites 700 Rt 46 E Fairfield NJ 07004 973-882-1010 882-7619*
**Fax:* Sales ■ *TF:* 800-833-1516 ■ *Web:* www.amerisuites.com
Grand Hyatt Hotels 71 S Wacker Dr Chicago IL 60606 312-750-1234 780-5289*
**Fax:* Mktg ■ *TF Resv:* 800-233-1234 ■ *Web:* www.hyatt.com
Hyatt Place Hotels 71 S Wacker Dr Chicago IL 60606 312-750-1234 780-5289
TF Cust Svc: 888-492-8847 ■ *Web:* www.hyatt.com/hyatt/place
Hyatt Regency Hotels 71 S Wacker Dr Chicago IL 60606 312-750-1234 780-5289*
**Fax:* Mktg ■ *TF Resv:* 800-233-1234 ■ *Web:* www.hyatt.com
Hyatt Summerfield Suites 71 S Wacker Dr Chicago IL 60606 312-750-1234 780-5289
Web: www.hyatt.com/hyatt/summerfield
Park Hyatt Hotels 71 S Wacker Dr Chicago IL 60606 312-750-1234 780-5289*
**Fax:* Mktg ■ *TF Resv:* 800-233-1234 ■ *Web:* www.hyatt.com
US Franchise Systems Inc 13 Corporate Sq Suite 250 Atlanta GA 30329 404-321-4045 235-7465
TF: 888-225-5151 ■ *Web:* www.usfsi.com
Hyatt Place Hotels 71 S Wacker Dr Chicago IL 60606 312-750-1234 780-5289
TF Cust Svc: 888-492-8847 ■ *Web:* www.hyatt.com/hyatt/place
Hyatt Regency Hotels 71 S Wacker Dr Chicago IL 60606 312-750-1234 780-5289*
**Fax:* Mktg ■ *TF Resv:* 800-233-1234 ■ *Web:* www.hyatt.com
Hyatt Summerfield Suites 71 S Wacker Dr Chicago IL 60606 312-750-1234 780-5289
Web: www.hyatt.com/hyatt/summerfield
Iberville Suites 910 Iberville St New Orleans LA 70112 504-523-2400 524-1320
TF: 866-229-4351 ■ *Web:* www.ibervillesuites.com
Ilikai The 1777 Ala Moana Blvd Honolulu HI 96815 808-949-3811 947-4523
TF: 800-245-4524 ■ *Web:* www.ilikaihotel.com
Imperial Palace Hotel & Casino 3535 Las Vegas Blvd S Las Vegas NV 89109 702-731-3311 735-8328
TF: 800-634-6441 ■ *Web:* www.imperialpalace.com
Imperial Swan Hotel 7050 S Kirkman Rd Orlando FL 32819 407-351-2000 363-1835
TF: 800-327-3808 ■ *Web:* www.imperialswanorlando.com
Imperial of Waikiki 205 Lewers St Honolulu HI 96815 808-923-1827 921-7586
TF: 800-347-2582 ■ *Web:* www.imperialofwaikiki.com
Indian Creek Hotel 2727 Indian Creek Dr Miami Beach FL 33140 305-531-2727 531-5651
TF: 800-491-2772 ■ *Web:* www.indiancreekhotelmb.com
Indiana Memorial Union Hotel & Conference Center
900 E 7th St Bloomington IN 47405 812-855-2536 855-3426
TF: 800-209-8145 ■ *Web:* www.imu.indiana.edu
Indigo Inn 1 Maiden Ln Charleston SC 29401 843-577-5900 577-0378
TF: 800-845-7639 ■ *Web:* www.indigoinn.com
Ingleside Inn 200 W Ramon Rd Palm Springs CA 92264 760-325-0046 325-0710
TF: 800-772-6655 ■ *Web:* www.inglesideinn.com
Inlet Tower Suites 1200 L St Anchorage AK 99501 907-276-0110 258-4914
TF: 800-544-0786 ■ *Web:* www.inlettower.com
Inn on the Alameda 303 E Alameda St Santa Fe NM 87501 505-984-2121 986-8325
TF: 800-289-2122 ■ *Web:* www.inn-alameda.com
Inn of the Anasazi 113 Washington Ave Santa Fe NM 87501 505-988-3030 988-3277
TF: 800-688-8100 ■ *Web:* www.innoftheanasazi.com
Inn at the Ballpark 1520 Texas Ave Houston TX 77002 713-228-1520 228-1555
TF: 866-406-1520 ■ *Web:* www.innattheballpark.com
Inn on the Beach 1615 S Atlantic Ave Daytona Beach FL 32118 386-255-0921 255-3849
TF: 800-874-0975 ■ *Web:* www.innonthebeach.com
Inn on Biltmore Estate 1 Antler Hill Rd Asheville NC 28803 828-225-1600 225-1680
TF: 800-411-3812 ■ *Web:* www.biltmore.com
Inn on Bourbon - A Ramada Plaza Hotel 541 Bourbon St New Orleans LA 70130 504-524-7611 568-9427
TF: 800-535-7891 ■ *Web:* www.innonbourbon.com
Inn at Camachee Harbor 201 Yacht Club Dr Saint Augustine FL 32084 904-825-0003 825-0048
TF: 800-688-5379 ■ *Web:* www.camacheeinn.com
Inn of Chicago Magnificent Mile 162 E Ohio St Chicago IL 60611 312-787-3100 573-3159
TF: 800-557-2378 ■ *Web:* www.innofchicago.com/
Inn on the Creek 295 N Millward Ave PO Box 445 Jackson WY 83001 307-739-1565 734-9116
TF: 800-669-9534 ■ *Web:* www.innonthecreek.com
Inn at Essex 70 Essex Way Essex Junction VT 05452 802-878-1100 878-0063
TF: 800-727-4295 ■ *Web:* vtculinaryresort.com
Inn of Exeter 90 Front St Exeter NH 03833 603-772-5901 778-8757
TF: 800-782-8444
Inn on Fifth 699 5th Ave S Naples FL 34102 239-403-8777 403-8778
TF: 888-403-8778 ■ *Web:* innonfifth.com
Inn at the Forks 75 Forks Market Rd Winnipeg MB R3C0A2 204-942-6555 942-6979
TF: 877-377-4100 ■ *Web:* www.innforks.com
Inn at Gig Harbor 3211 56th St NW Gig Harbor WA 98335 253-858-1111 851-5402
TF: 800-795-9980 ■ *Web:* www.innatgigharbor.com
Inn on Gitche Gumee 8517 Congdon Blvd Duluth MN 55804 218-525-4979
TF: 800-317-4979 ■ *Web:* www.innongitchegumee.com

				Phone	Fax
Inn of the Governors 101 W Alameda St *TF*: 800-234-4534 ■ *Web*: www.innofthegovernors.com	Santa Fe	NM	87501	505-982-4333	989-9149
Inn at Harbour Town 11 Lighthouse Ln *TF*: 888-807-6873 ■ *Web*: www.seapines.com/accommodations/inn_at_harbour_town.cfm	Hilton Head Island	SC	29928	843-363-8100	363-8155
Inn at Harvard 1201 Massachusetts Ave *TF*: 800-458-5886 ■ *Web*: www.theinnatharvard.com	Cambridge	MA	02138	617-491-2222	520-3711
Inn at Henderson's Wharf 1000 Fell St *TF*: 800-522-2088 ■ *Web*: www.hendersonswharf.com	Baltimore	MD	21231	410-522-7777	522-7087
Inn at Jarrett Farm 38009 US Hwy 75 N *TF*: 877-371-1200 ■ *Web*: www.jarrettfarm.com	Ramona	OK	74061	918-371-1200	371-1300
Inn by the Lake 3300 Lake Tahoe Blvd *TF*: 800-877-1466 ■ *Web*: www.innbythelake.com	South Lake Tahoe	CA	96150	530-542-0330	541-6250
Inn on Lake Superior 350 Canal Park Dr *TF*: 888-668-4352 ■ *Web*: www.theinnonlakesuperior.com	Duluth	MN	55802	218-726-1111	727-3976
Inn at Lambertville Station 11 Bridge St *TF*: 800-524-1091 ■ *Web*: www.lambertvillestation.com/inn.html	Lambertville	NJ	08530	609-397-4400	397-9744
Inn at Langley 400 1st St *Web*: www.innatlangley.com/	Langley	WA	98260	360-221-3033	221-3033
Inn at Little Washington 309 Middle St PO Box 300 *Web*: www.theinnatlittlewashington.com	Washington	VA	22747	540-675-3800	675-3100
Inn of Long Beach 185 Atlantic Ave *TF*: 800-230-7500 ■ *Web*: www.innoflongbeach.com	Long Beach	CA	90802	562-435-3791	436-7510
Inn at Longshore 260 S Compo Rd *Web*: www.innatlongshore.com	Westport	CT	06880	203-226-3316	226-5723
Inn at the Market 86 Pine St *TF*: 800-446-4484 ■ *Web*: www.innatthemarket.com	Seattle	WA	98101	206-443-3600	448-0631
Inn at Mayo Clinic 4400 San Pablo Rd *TF*: 888-255-4458 ■ *Web*: www.mayoclinic.org/innatmayo-jax	Jacksonville	FL	32224	904-992-9992	992-4463
Inn at Montchanin Village Rte 100 & Kirk Rd *TF*: 800-269-2473 ■ *Web*: www.montchanin.com	Montchanin	DE	19710	302-888-2133	888-0389
Inn at Montpelier 147 Main St *Web*: www.innatmontpelier.com	Montpelier	VT	05602	802-223-2727	223-0722
Inn at Morro Bay 60 State Park Rd *TF*: 800-321-9566 ■ *Web*: www.innatmorrobay.com	Morro Bay	CA	93442	805-772-5651	772-4779
Inn on Mount Ada 398 Wrigley Rd PO Box 2560 *TF*: 800-608-7669 ■ *Web*: www.innonmtada.com	Avalon	CA	90704	310-510-2030	510-2237
Inn at Mystic 3 Williams Ave PO Box 216 *TF*: 800-237-2415 ■ *Web*: www.innatmystic.com	Mystic	CT	06355	860-536-9604	572-1635
Inn at National Hall 2 Post Rd W *TF*: 800-628-4255 ■ *Web*: www.innatnationalhall.com	Westport	CT	06880	203-221-1351	221-0276
Inn at Newport Beach 30 Wave Ave *TF*: 800-786-0310 ■ *Web*: www.innatnb.com	Middletown	RI	02842	401-846-0310	847-2621
Inn at Nichols Village 1101 Northern Blvd *TF*: 800-642-2215 ■ *Web*: www.nicholsvillage.com	Clarks Summit	PA	18411	570-587-1135	586-7140
Inn at the Opera 333 Fulton St *TF*: 800-325-2708 ■ *Web*: www.innattheopera.com	San Francisco	CA	94102	415-863-8400	861-0821
Inn at Otter Crest 301 Otter Crest Loop *TF*: 800-452-2101 ■ *Web*: www.innatottercrest.com	Otter Rock	OR	97369	541-765-2111	765-2047
Inn at Oyster Point 425 Marina Blvd *TF*: 800-642-2720 ■ *Web*: www.innatoysterpoint.com	South San Francisco	CA	94080	650-737-7633	737-0795
Inn at Palmetto Bluff 476 Mount Pelia Rd *TF*: 866-706-6565 ■ *Web*: www.palmettobluffresort.com	Blufton	SC	29910	843-706-6500	706-6550
Inn on the Paseo 630 Paseo de Peralta *TF*: 866-589-3411 ■ *Web*: www.innonthepaseo.com	Santa Fe	NM	87501	505-984-8200	955-7835
Inn at Pelican Bay 800 Vanderbilt Beach Rd *TF*: 800-597-8770 ■ *Web*: www.condohotelcenter.com/condo-hotels/featured-properties/pelican-bay.htm	Naples	FL	34108	239-597-8777	597-8012
Inn at Perry Cabin 308 Watkins Ln *TF*: 800-722-2949 ■ *Web*: www.perrycabin.com	Saint Michaels	MD	21663	410-745-2200	745-3348
Inn at Queen Anne 505 1st Ave N *TF*: 800-952-5043 ■ *Web*: www.innatqueenanne.com	Seattle	WA	98109	206-282-7357	217-9719
Inn at Reading 1040 N Park Rd *TF*: 800-383-9713 ■ *Web*: www.innatreading.com	Wyomissing	PA	19610	610-372-7811	372-4545
Inn at Saint John 939 Congress St *TF*: 800-636-9127 ■ *Web*: www.innatstjohn.com	Portland	ME	04102	207-773-6481	756-7629
Inn at Saint Mary's 53993 US Hwy 31-33 N *TF*: 800-947-8627 ■ *Web*: www.innatsaintmarys.com	South Bend	IN	46637	574-232-4000	289-0986
Inn at Sawmill Farm 7 Crosstown Rd PO Box 367 *TF*: 800-493-1133 ■ *Web*: www.theinnatsawmillfarm.com	West Dover	VT	05356	802-464-8131	464-1130
Inn of the Six Mountains 2617 Killington Rd *TF*: 800-228-4676 ■ *Web*: www.sixmountains.com	Killington	VT	05751	802-422-4302	422-4321
Inn & Spa at Loretto 211 Old Santa Fe Trail *TF*: 800-727-5531 ■ *Web*: www.innatloretto.com	Santa Fe	NM	87501	505-988-5531	984-7968
Inn at Spanish Head 4009 SW Hwy 101 *TF*: 800-452-8127 ■ *Web*: www.spanishhead.com	Lincoln City	OR	97367	541-996-2161	996-4089
Inn at Tallgrass 2280 N Tara Cir *TF*: 800-684-3466 ■ *Web*: www.theinnattallgrass.com	Wichita	KS	67226	316-684-3466	685-3466
Inn at the Tides PO Box 640 800 Hwy 1 *TF*: 800-541-7788 ■ *Web*: www.innatthetides.com	Bodega Bay	CA	94923	707-875-2751	875-2669
Inn at Union Square 440 Post St *TF*: 800-288-4346 ■ *Web*: www.unionsquare.com	San Francisco	CA	94102	415-397-3510	989-0529
Inn at Westminster Quay 900 Quayside Dr *TF*: 800-663-2001 ■ *Web*: www.innatwestminsterquay.com	New Westminster	BC	V3M6G1	604-520-1776	520-5645
Inns of America Suites 755 Raintree Dr *TF Resv*: 800-826-0778 ■ *Web*: www.innsofamerica.com	Carlsbad	CA	92009	760-438-6661	431-9212
Inns at Mill Falls 312 Daniel Webster Hwy *TF*: 800-622-6455 ■ *Web*: www.millfalls.com/	Meredith	NH	03253	603-279-7006	279-6797
InnSuites Hospitality Trust InnSuites Hotels Inc 1615 E Northern Ave Suite 102 *TF*: 800-842-4242 ■ *Web*: www.innsuites.com	Phoenix	AZ	85020	602-944-1500	678-0281
InnSuites Hotel Flagstaff/Grand Canyon 1008 E Rt 66 *TF*: 800-842-4242 ■ *Web*: flagstaff.innsuites.com/	Flagstaff	AZ	86001	928-774-7356	556-0130
InnSuites Hotel Tempe/Phoenix Airport 1651 W Baseline Rd *TF*: 800-841-4242 ■ *Web*: tempe.innsuites.com	Tempe	AZ	85283	480-897-7900	491-1008
InnSuites Hotel Tucson City Center 475 N Granada Ave *TF*: 877-446-6589 ■ *Web*: stmarys.innsuites.com	Tucson	AZ	85701	520-622-3000	623-8922
InnSuites Hotels Inc 1615 E Northern Ave Suite 102 *TF*: 800-842-4242 ■ *Web*: www.innsuites.com	Phoenix	AZ	85020	602-944-1500	678-0281
InterContinental Hotels Group					
Candlewood Suites 3 Ravinia Dr Suite 100 *Web*: www.candlewoodsuites.com	Atlanta	GA	30346	770-604-2000	604-5403
Crowne Plaza Hotels & Resorts 3 Ravinia Dr Suite 100 *Web*: www.crowneplaza.com	Atlanta	GA	30346	770-604-2000	604-5403
Holiday Inn Express 3 Ravinia Dr Suite 100 *Web*: www.hiexpress.com	Atlanta	GA	30346	770-604-2000	604-5403
Holiday Inn Hotels & Resorts 3 Ravinia Dr Suite 100 *Web*: www.holidayinn.com	Atlanta	GA	30346	770-604-2000	604-5403
Hotel Indigo 3 Ravinia Dr Suite 100 **Fax Area Code: 770* ■ *Web*: www.hotelindigo.com	Atlanta	GA	30346	704-604-2000	604-5403*
InterContinental Hotels Group (IHG) 3 Ravinia Dr Suite 100 *Web*: www.ichotelsgroup.com	Atlanta	GA	30346	770-604-2000	604-5403
InterContinental Hotels Group					
InterContinental Hotels & Resorts 3 Ravinia Dr Suite 100 *Web*: www.intercontinental.com	Atlanta	GA	30346	770-604-2000	604-5403
Staybridge Suites 3 Ravinia Dr Suite 100 *TF*: 800-465-4329 ■ *Web*: www.staybridge.com	Atlanta	GA	30346	770-604-2000	604-5403
InterContinental Hotels & Resorts 3 Ravinia Dr Suite 100 *Web*: www.intercontinental.com	Atlanta	GA	30346	770-604-2000	604-5403
International Hotel 20 SW 2nd Ave *TF*: 800-940-6811 ■ *Web*: www.internationalhotelmn.com	Rochester	MN	55902	507-328-8000	285-2701
International Hotel of Calgary 220 4th Ave SW *TF*: 800-637-7200 ■ *Web*: www.intlhotel.com	Calgary	AB	T2P0H5	403-265-9600	290-7879
International House Hotel 221 Camp St *TF*: 800-633-5770 ■ *Web*: www.ihhotel.com	New Orleans	LA	70130	504-553-9550	553-9560
Interstate Hotels & Resorts Inc 4501 N Fairfax Dr *NYSE: IHR* ■ *Web*: www.ihrco.com	Arlington	VA	22033	703-387-3100	387-3101
Iron Horse Resort 101 Iron Horse Way *TF*: 800-621-8190 ■ *Web*: www.ironhorse-resort.com	Winter Park	CO	80482	970-726-8851	726-2321
Iroquois New York 49 W 44th St *TF*: 800-332-7220 ■ *Web*: www.iroquoisny.com	New York	NY	10036	212-840-3080	719-0006
Island Hotel The 690 Newport Center Dr *TF*: 866-554-4620 ■ *Web*: www.islandhotel.com	Newport Beach	CA	92660	949-759-0808	759-0568
Isle of Capri Casino & Hotel 711 Isle of Capri Blvd *TF*: 800-843-4753 ■ *Web*: www.isleofcapricasino.com/Bossier_City	Bossier City	LA	71111	318-678-7777	424-1470
Isle of Capri Casino Resort 151 Beach Blvd *TF*: 800-843-4753 ■ *Web*: www.isleofcapricasino.com/Biloxi	Biloxi	MS	39530	228-435-5400	436-7834
Ivy Hotel 600 F St *TF*: 877-489-4489 ■ *Web*: www.ivyhotel.com	San Diego	CA	92101	619-814-1000	814-3636
Jack London Inn 444 Embarcadero W *TF*: 800-549-8780 ■ *Web*: www.jacklondoninn.com	Oakland	CA	94607	510-444-2032	834-3074
Jackson Hole Lodge 420 W Broadway PO Box 1805 *TF*: 800-604-9404 ■ *Web*: www.jacksonholelodge.com	Jackson	WY	83001	307-733-2992	739-2144
Jailhouse Inn 13 Marlborough St *TF*: 800-427-9444 ■ *Web*: www.historicinnsofnewport.com	Newport	RI	02840	401-847-4638	849-0605
James The Chicago 55 E Ontario *TF*: 877-526-3755 ■ *Web*: www.jameshotels.com	Chicago	IL	60611	312-337-1000	337-7217
James Gettys Hotel 27 Chambersburg St *TF*: 888-900-5275 ■ *Web*: www.jamesgettyshotel.com	Gettysburg	PA	17325	717-337-1334	334-2103
Jameson Inns 4770 S Atlanta Rd *TF*: 800-526-3766 ■ *Web*: www.jamesoninns.com	Smyrna	GA	30080	404-350-9990	350-6106
Janus Hotels & Resorts Inc 2300 Corporate Blvd NW Suite 232 *Web*: www.janushotels.com	Boca Raton	FL	33431	561-997-2325	997-5331
Jared Coffin House 29 Broad St *TF*: 800-248-2405 ■ *Web*: www.jaredcoffinhouse.com	Nantucket	MA	02554	508-228-2400	228-8549
Jefferson Hotel 101 W Franklin St *TF*: 800-424-8014 ■ *Web*: www.jeffersonhotel.com	Richmond	VA	23220	804-788-8000	225-0334
JHM Hotels Inc 60 Pointe Cir **Fax*: PR ■ *TF*: 800-763-1100 ■ *Web*: www.jhmhotels.com	Greenville	SC	29515	864-232-9944	232-6931*
John Q Hammons Hotel Management LLC 300 John Q Hammons Pkwy Suite 900 *Web*: www.jqhhotels.com	Springfield	MO	65806	417-864-4300	873-3540
Joie de Vivre Hospitality Inc 567 Sutter St *TF*: 800-738-7477 ■ *Web*: www.jdvhospitality.com	San Francisco	CA	94102	415-835-0300	835-0311
Jolly Hotel Madison Towers 22 E 38th St *TF*: 800-221-2626 ■ *Web*: www.jollymadison.com	New York	NY	10016	212-802-0600	447-0747
Jolly Roger Inn 640 W Katella Ave *TF*: 888-296-5986 ■ *Web*: www.jollyrogerhotel.com	Anaheim	CA	92802	714-782-7500	772-2308
Jorgenson's Inn & Suites 1714 11th Ave *TF*: 800-272-1770 ■ *Web*: www.jorgensonsinn.com	Helena	MT	59601	406-442-1770	449-0155
JR's Executive Inn Riverfront 1 Executive Blvd *TF*: 800-866-3636 ■ *Web*: www.jrsexecutiveinn.com	Paducah	KY	42001	270-443-8000	444-5317
Jumeirah Essex House 160 Central Park S *TF*: 888-637-5783 ■ *Web*: www.jumeirahessexhouse.com	New York	NY	10019	212-247-0300	315-1839
Juniper Inn 1315 N 27th St *TF*: 800-826-7530 ■ *Web*: juniperinn.uswestdex.com	Billings	MT	59101	406-245-4128	245-4128
Jury's Boston Hotel 350 Stuart St *TF*: 800-423-6953 ■ *Web*: www.jurysdoyle.com/boston-hotel	Boston	MA	02116	617-266-7200	266-7203
Jurys Washington Hotel 1500 New Hampshire Ave NW *TF*: 800-423-6953 ■ *Web*: www.jurys.com	Washington	DC	20036	202-483-6000	328-3265
JW Marriott Hotels & Resorts 1 Marriott Dr *TF*: 888-236-2427 ■ *Web*: marriott.com/jwmarriott	Washington	DC	20058	301-380-3000	
Kahala Mandarin Oriental Hotel Hawaii Resort 5000 Kahala Ave *TF*: 800-367-2525 ■ *Web*: www.mandarin-oriental.com/kahala	Honolulu	HI	96816	808-739-8888	739-8800
Kawada Hotel 200 S Hill St *TF*: 800-752-9232 ■ *Web*: www.kawadahotel.com	Los Angeles	CA	90012	213-621-4455	687-4455
Kellogg Hotel & Conference Center 55 S Harrison Rd Michigan State University Campus *TF*: 800-875-5090 ■ *Web*: www.hfs.msu.edu/kellogg	East Lansing	MI	48824	517-432-4000	353-1872
Kelly Inns Ltd 3205 W Sencore Dr *TF*: 800-635-3559 ■ *Web*: www.kellyinns.com	Sioux Falls	SD	57107	605-965-1440	965-1450
Kensington Court Ann Arbor 610 Hilton Blvd	Ann Arbor	MI	48108	734-761-7800	761-1040
Kensington Park Hotel 450 Post St *TF*: 800-553-1900 ■ *Web*: www.kensingtonparkhotel.com	San Francisco	CA	94102	415-788-6400	399-9484
Kensington Riverside Inn 1126 Memorial Dr NW *TF*: 877-313-3733 ■ *Web*: www.kensingtonriversideinn.com	Calgary	AB	T2N3E3	403-228-4442	228-9608
Kent The 1131 Collins Ave *TF*: 866-826-5368 ■ *Web*: www.thekenthotel.com	Miami Beach	FL	33139	305-604-5068	531-0720
Keswick Hall at Monticello 701 Club Dr *TF*: 800-274-5391 ■ *Web*: www.keswick.com	Keswick	VA	22947	434-979-3440	977-4171
Key Lime Inn 725 Truman Ave *TF*: 800-549-4430 ■ *Web*: www.keylimeinn.com	Key West	FL	33040	305-294-5229	294-9623
Keystone Lodge 0633 Tennis Townhouses Rd *Web*: www.preferredhotels.com	Keystone	CO	80435	970-496-2316	496-4215
Killington Grand Resort Hotel & Conference Center 228 E Mountain Rd *TF*: 800-621-6867 ■ *Web*: www.killington.com	Killington	VT	05751	802-422-5001	422-6881
Kimball Terrace Inn 10 Huntington Rd *TF*: 800-454-6225 ■ *Web*: www.kimballterraceinn.com	Northeast Harbor	ME	04662	207-276-3383	276-4102
Kimberly Hotel 145 E 50th St *TF*: 800-683-0400 ■ *Web*: www.kimberlyhotel.com	New York	NY	10022	212-755-0400	486-6915
Kimpton Hotel & Restaurant Group LLC 222 Kearny St Suite 200 *TF*: 800-546-2686 ■ *Web*: www.kimptonhotels.com	San Francisco	CA	94108	415-397-5572	296-8031
King Edward InnCommons Inn 5780-88 West St *TF*: 877-797-7999 ■ *Web*: www.commonsinn.ca	Halifax	NS	B3K1H8	902-484-3466	423-8910
King Kamehameha's Kona Beach Hotel 75-5660 Palani Rd *TF*: 800-367-2111 ■ *Web*: www.konabeachhotel.com	Kailua-Kona	HI	96740	808-329-2911	329-4602
King Pacific Lodge 255 W 1st St Suite 214 *TF*: 888-592-5464 ■ *Web*: www.kingpacificlodge.com	North Vancouver	BC	V7M3G8	604-987-5452	987-5472
Kings Island Resort & Conference Center 5691 Kings Island Dr *TF*: 800-704-2439 ■ *Web*: www.kingsislandresort.com	Mason	OH	45040	513-398-0115	398-1095
Kitano New York 66 Park Ave *TF*: 800-548-2666 ■ *Web*: www.kitano.com	New York	NY	10016	212-885-7000	885-7100
Knickerbocker on the Lake 1028 E Juneau Ave *Web*: www.knickerbockeronthelake.com	Milwaukee	WI	53202	414-276-8500	276-3668
Knights Inn 1 Sylvan Way *TF Resv*: 800-843-5644 ■ *Web*: www.knightsinn.com	Parsippany	NJ	07054	973-753-6600	
Knob Hill Inn 960 N Main St PO Box 800 *TF Resv*: 800-526-8010 ■ *Web*: www.knobhillinn.com	Ketchum	ID	83340	208-726-8010	726-2712
Koko Inn 5201 Ave Q *TF*: 800-782-3254 ■ *Web*: www.lubbockhospitality.net/Koko/	Lubbock	TX	79412	806-747-2591	747-2591

	City	State	Zip	Phone	Fax
Kona Kai Resort & Spa 1551 Shelter Island Dr	San Diego	CA	92106	619-221-8000	819-8101
TF: 800-566-2524 ■ *Web:* www.shelterpointe.com					
Kyoto Grand Hotel & Gardens 120 S Los Angeles St	Los Angeles	CA	90012	213-629-1200	622-0980
TF: 800-639-6826					
La Colombe D'Or Inn 3410 Montrose Blvd	Houston	TX	77006	713-524-7999	524-8923
Web: www.lacolombedor.com					
La Fonda 100 E San Francisco St	Santa Fe	NM	87501	505-982-5511	988-2952
TF: 800-523-5002 ■ *Web:* www.lafondasantafe.com					
La Pensione Hotel 606 W Date St	San Diego	CA	92101	619-236-8000	236-8088
TF: 800-232-4683 ■ *Web:* www.lapensionehotel.com					
La Playa Hotel & Cottages-by-the-Sea PO Box 900	Carmel	CA	93921	831-624-6476	624-7966
TF: 800-582-8900 ■ *Web:* www.laplayahotel.com					
La Posada de Albuquerque 125 2nd St NW	Albuquerque	NM	87102	505-242-9090	242-8664
TF: 800-777-5732 ■ *Web:* www.laposada-abq.com					
La Posada Hotel & Suites 1000 Zaragoza St	Laredo	TX	78040	956-722-1701	726-8524
TF: 800-444-2099 ■ *Web:* www.laposadahotel-laredo.com					
La Quinta Inn & Suites 909 Hidden Ridge Suite 600	Irving	TX	75038	214-492-6600	492-6785*
**Fax:* Mktg ■ *TF:* 877-204-9204 ■ *Web:* www.lq.com					
La Quinta Inn & Suites Secaucus Meadowlands					
350 Lighting Way	Secaucus	NJ	07094	201-863-8700	863-6209
TF: 800-531-5900 ■ *Web:* www.7719.lq.com/lq/index.jsp					
La Valencia Hotel 1132 Prospect St	La Jolla	CA	92037	858-454-0771	456-3921
TF: 800-451-0772 ■ *Web:* www.lavalencia.com					
Lafayette Hotel 600 St Charles Ave	New Orleans	LA	70130	504-524-4441	523-7327
Web: www.thelafayettehotel.com					
Lafayette Hotel 101 Front St	Marietta	OH	45750	740-373-5522	373-4684
TF: 800-331-9336 ■ *Web:* www.lafayettehotel.com					
Lafayette Hotel & Suites San Diego 2223 El Cajon Blvd	San Diego	CA	92104	619-296-2101	296-0512
TF: 800-468-3531 ■ *Web:* www.lafayettehotelsd.com					
Lafayette Park Hotel 3287 Mt Diablo Blvd	Lafayette	CA	94549	925-283-3700	284-1621
TF: 800-368-2468 ■ *Web:* www.lafayetteparkhotel.com					
Lajitas The Ultimate Hideout 100 Main St	Lajitas	TX	79852	432-424-5000	424-3277
TF: 877-525-4827 ■ *Web:* www.lajitas.com					
Lake Estes Inn & Suites 1650 Big Thompson Ave	Estes Park	CO	80517	970-586-3386	586-9000
TF: 800-332-6867 ■ *Web:* www.lakeestes.com					
Lake Louise Inn 210 Village Rd PO Box 209	Lake Louise	AB	T0L1E0	403-522-3791	522-2018
TF: 800-661-9237 ■ *Web:* www.lakelouiseinn.com					
Lake Lure Inn & Conference Center PO Box 10	Lake Lure	NC	28746	828-625-2525	625-9655
TF: 888-434-4970 ■ *Web:* www.lakelureinn.com					
Lake Merritt Hotel & Apartments 1800 Madison St	Oakland	CA	94612	510-832-2300	832-7150
TF: 800-933-4683 ■ *Web:* lakemerritthotel.com					
Lake Placid Lodge Whiteface Inn Ln	Lake Placid	NY	12946	518-523-2700	523-1124
TF: 877-523-2700 ■ *Web:* www.lakeplacidlodge.com					
Lake San Marcos Resort & Country Club					
1025 La Bonita Dr	Lake San Marcos	CA	92078	760-744-0120	744-0748
TF: 866-589-3411 ■ *Web:* www.lakesanmarcosresort.com					
Lakeside Inn 100 N Alexander St	Mount Dora	FL	32757	352-383-4101	385-1615
TF: 800-556-5016 ■ *Web:* www.lakeside-inn.com					
Lakeview on the Lake 8696 E Lake Rd	Erie	PA	16511	814-899-6948	
TF: 888-558-8439 ■ *Web:* www.lakevieweerie.com					
Lamothe House Hotel 621 Esplanade Ave	New Orleans	LA	70116	504-947-1161	218-4297
TF: 800-367-5858 ■ *Web:* www.lamothehouse.com					
Lamp Post Inn 2424 E Stadium Blvd	Ann Arbor	MI	48104	734-971-8000	971-7483
Web: www.lamppostinn.com					
Lamplighter Inn & Suites South 1772 S Glenstone Ave	Springfield	MO	65804	417-882-1113	882-8869
TF: 800-749-7275 ■ *Web:* www.lamplighter-sgf.com					
Lancaster Hotel 701 Texas St	Houston	TX	77002	713-228-9500	223-4528
TF: 800-231-0336 ■ *Web:* www.thelancaster.com					
Landmark Inn 230 N Front St	Marquette	MI	49855	906-228-2580	228-5676
TF: 800-752-6362 ■ *Web:* www.thelandmarkinn.com					
Lane Hospitality 1 Lane Center 1200 Shermer Rd	Northbrook	IL	60062	847-498-6650	498-6808
Web: www.lanehospitality.com					
Langdon Hall Country House Hotel & Spa 1 Langdon Dr	Cambridge	ON	N3H4R8	519-740-2100	740-8161
TF: 800-268-1898 ■ *Web:* www.langdonhall.ca					
Langham Hotel Boston 250 Franklin St	Boston	MA	02110	617-451-1900	423-2844
TF: 800-791-7781 ■ *Web:* www.langhamhotels.com					
Lantern Lodge Motor Inn 411 N College St	Myerstown	PA	17067	717-866-6536	866-8857
TF: 800-262-5564 ■ *Web:* www.thelanternlodge.com					
Larkspur Hotels & Restaurants Inc					
125 E Sir Francis Drake Blvd Suite 200	Larkspur	CA	94939	415-945-5000	945-5001
Web: www.larkspurhotels.com					
Las Vegas Club 18 E Fremont St	Las Vegas	NV	89101	702-385-1664	380-5793
TF: 800-634-6532 ■ *Web:* www.vegasclubcasino.net					
Las Vegas Sands Corp 3355 Las Vegas Blvd S	Las Vegas	NV	89109	702-733-5728	733-5620
NYSE: LVS ■ *Web:* www.lasvegassands.com					
LaSalle Hotel 120 S Main St	Bryan	TX	77803	979-822-2000	779-4343
TF: 866-822-2000 ■ *Web:* www.lasalle-hotel.com					
LaSalle Hotel Properties 3 Bethesda Metro Center Suite 1200	Bethesda	MD	20814	301-941-1500	941-1553
NYSE: LHO ■ *Web:* www.lasallehotels.com					
Latham Hotel 3000 M St NW	Washington	DC	20007	202-726-5000	337-4250
TF: 888-587-2377 ■ *Web:* georgetowncollection.com					
Latham Hotel Center City 135 S 17th St	Philadelphia	PA	19103	215-563-7474	568-0110
TF: 877-528-4261 ■ *Web:* www.lathamhotel.com					
Laurel Inn 444 Presidio Ave	San Francisco	CA	94115	415-567-8467	928-1866
TF: 800-552-8735 ■ *Web:* www.thelaurelinn.com					
Le Centre Sheraton Hotel & Towers Montreal					
1201 Rene-Levesque Blvd W	Montreal	QC	H3B2L7	514-878-2000	878-3958
TF: 888-627-7102 ■ *Web:* www.starwood.com/sheraton					
Le Chamois 4557 Blackcomb Way	Whistler	BC	V0N1B4	604-932-8700	932-4486
TF: 888-560-9453 ■ *Web:* www.whistler-lechamois.com					
Le Meridian 20 Sidney St	Cambridge	MA	02139	617-577-0200	494-8366
TF: 800-754-7130					
Le Meridien 1111 Westchester Ave	White Plains	NY	10604	914-640-8100	640-8310
TF: 800-625-5144 ■ *Web:* www.starwoodhotels.com/lemeridien					
Le Merigot - A JW Marriott Beach Hotel & Spa					
1740 Ocean Ave	Santa Monica	CA	90401	310-395-9700	395-9200
TF: 888-539-7899 ■ *Web:* www.lemerigotbeachhotel.com					
Le Montrose Suite Hotel 900 Hammond St	West Hollywood	CA	90069	310-855-1115	657-9192
TF: 800-776-0666 ■ *Web:* www.lemontrose.com					
Le Nouvel Montreal Hotel & Spa 1740 Rene-Levesque Blvd W	Montreal	QC	H3H1R3	514-931-8841	931-5581
TF: 800-363-6063 ■ *Web:* www.lenouvelhotel.com					
Le Parc Suite Hotel 733 N West Knoll Dr	West Hollywood	CA	90069	310-855-8888	659-7812
TF: 800-578-4837 ■ *Web:* www.leparcsuites.com					
Le Pavillon Hotel 833 Poydras St	New Orleans	LA	70112	504-581-3111	620-4130
Web: www.lepavillon.com					
Le Place D'armes Hotel & Suites 55 Saint-Jacques St	Montreal	QC	H2Y3X2	514-842-1887	842-6469
TF: 888-450-1887 ■ *Web:* www.hotelplacedarmes.com					
Le Port-Royal Hotel & Suites 144 Saint-Pierre St	Quebec	QC	G1K8N8	418-692-2777	692-2778
TF: 866-472-2777 ■ *Web:* www.hotelportroyalsuites.com/					
Le Richelieu Hotel 1234 Chartres St	New Orleans	LA	70116	504-529-2492	524-8179
TF: 800-535-9653 ■ *Web:* www.lerichelieuhotel.com					
Le Saint Sulpice 414 St Sulpice	Montreal	QC	H2Y2V5	514-288-1000	288-0077
TF: 877-785-7423 ■ *Web:* www.lesaintsulpice.com					
Ledgelawn Inn 66 Mt Desert St	Bar Harbor	ME	04609	207-288-4596	288-9968
TF: 800-274-5334 ■ *Web:* www.ledgelawninn.com					
Lees Inns of America Inc 130 N State St	North Vernon	IN	47265	812-346-5072	346-7521
TF Resv: 800-733-5337 ■ *Web:* www.leesinn.com					
Leisure Hotels LLC 4501 College Blvd Suite 275	Leawood	KS	66211	913-905-1460	905-1461
TF: 888-250-1618 ■ *Web:* www.leisurehotel.com					
Leisure Sports Inc 7077 Koll Center Pkwy Suite 110	Pleasanton	CA	94566	925-600-1966	600-1144
Web: www.leisuresportsinc.com					
Leland The 400 Bagley St	Detroit	MI	48226	313-962-2300	962-1045
L'Enfant Plaza Hotel 480 L'Enfant Plaza SW	Washington	DC	20024	202-484-1000	646-4456
TF: 800-635-5065 ■ *Web:* www.lenfantplazahotel.com					
Lenox Hotel 61 Exeter St	Boston	MA	02116	617-536-5300	267-1237
TF: 800-225-7676 ■ *Web:* www.lenoxhotel.com					
Leola Village Inn & Suites 38 Deborah Dr	Leola	PA	17540	717-656-7002	656-7648
TF: 877-669-5094 ■ *Web:* www.leolavillage.com					
Les Mars Hotel 27 North St	Healdsburg	CA	95448	707-433-4211	433-4611
Web: www.lesmarshotel.com					
Les Suites Hotel Ottawa 130 Besserer St	Ottawa	ON	K1N9M9	613-232-2000	232-1242
TF: 800-267-1989 ■ *Web:* www.les-suites.com					
L'Hotel Quebec 3115 des Hotels Ave	Sainte-Foy	QC	G1W3Z6	418-658-5120	658-4504
TF: 800-567-5276 ■ *Web:* www.hotelsjaro.com					
L'Hotel du Vieux-Quebec 1190 Saint-Jean St	Quebec	QC	G1R1S6	418-692-1850	692-5637
TF: 800-361-7787 ■ *Web:* www.hvq.com					
Library Hotel 299 Madison Ave	New York	NY	10017	212-983-4500	499-9099
TF: 877-793-7323 ■ *Web:* www.libraryhotel.com					
Lighthouse Club Hotel 201 60th St	Ocean City	MD	21842	410-524-5400	524-3928
TF: 888-371-5400					
Lighthouse Inn 6 Guthrie Pl	New London	CT	06320	860-443-8411	443-8411
TF: 888-600-5681 ■ *Web:* www.lighthouseinn-ct.com					
Lighthouse Lodge & Suites 1150 Lighthouse Ave	Pacific Grove	CA	93950	831-655-2111	655-4922
TF: 800-858-1249 ■ *Web:* www.lhls.com					
Lily Leon Hotel 855 Collins Ave	Miami Beach	FL	33139	305-535-9900	535-9665
TF: 877-762-3477 ■ *Web:* www.lilyleonhotel.com					
Linden Row Inn 100 E Franklin St	Richmond	VA	23219	804-783-7000	648-7504
TF: 800-348-7424 ■ *Web:* www.lindenrowinn.com					
Listel Vancouver Hotel 1300 Robson St	Vancouver	BC	V6E1C5	604-684-8461	684-7092
TF: 800-663-5491 ■ *Web:* www.thelistelhotel.com					
Litchfield Plantation Kings River Rd PO Box 290	Pawleys Island	SC	29585	843-237-9121	237-1688
TF: 800-869-1410 ■ *Web:* www.litchfieldplantation.com					
Little America Hotel Flagstaff 2515 E Butler Ave	Flagstaff	AZ	86004	928-779-2741	779-7983
TF: 800-352-4386 ■ *Web:* www.littleamerica.com/flagstaff					
Little America Hotel & Resort Cheyenne 2800 W Lincolnway	Cheyenne	WY	82001	307-775-8400	775-8425
TF: 888-709-8384 ■ *Web:* www.littleamerica.com/cheyenne					
Little America Hotel & Towers Salt Lake City					
500 S Main St	Salt Lake City	UT	84101	801-363-6781	596-5911
TF: 800-453-9450 ■ *Web:* www.littleamerica.com					
Little America Hotels & Resorts 500 S Main St	Salt Lake City	UT	84101	801-363-6781	596-5911
TF Resv: 800-453-9450 ■ *Web:* www.littleamerica.com					
Little America Wyoming PO Box 1	Little America	WY	82929	307-875-2400	872-2666
TF: 888-652-9042 ■ *Web:* www.littleamerica.com/wyoming/					
Little Inn by the Sea 4546 El Mar Dr	Lauderdale-by-the-Sea	FL	33308	954-772-2450	938-9354
TF: 800-492-0311 ■ *Web:* www.alittleinn.com					
Little Nell The 675 E Durant Ave	Aspen	CO	81611	970-920-4600	920-4670
TF: 888-843-6355 ■ *Web:* www.thelittlenell.com					
Lodge Alley Inn 195 E Bay St	Charleston	SC	29401	843-722-1611	577-7497
TF: 800-456-0009					
Lodge America 4700 S Atlanta Rd	Smyrna	GA	30080	404-350-9990	350-2240
Web: www.lodgeamerica.com					
Lodge on the Desert 306 N Alvernon Way	Tucson	AZ	85711	520-325-3366	327-5834
TF: 800-978-3598 ■ *Web:* www.lodgeonthedesert.com					
Lodge Hotel & Conference Center 900 Spruce Hills Dr	Bettendorf	IA	52722	563-359-7141	359-7141
TF: 800-285-8637 ■ *Web:* www.lodgehotel.biz					
Lodge at the Mountain Village 1415 Lowell Ave	Park City	UT	84060	435-649-0800	649-1464
TF: 888-727-5248 ■ *Web:* www.thelodgepc.com					
Lodge of the Ozarks 3431 W Hwy 76	Branson	MO	65616	417-334-7535	334-6861
TF: 800-213-2584 ■ *Web:* www.bransonlodging.net					
Lodge at Santa Fe 750 N St Francis Dr	Santa Fe	NM	87501	505-992-5800	992-5865
TF: 888-563-4373 ■ *Web:* hhandr.com/san_main.php					
Lodge & Spa at Breckenridge 112 Overlook Dr	Breckenridge	CO	80424	970-453-9300	453-0625
TF: 800-736-1607 ■ *Web:* www.thelodgeatbreck.com					
Lodge & Spa at Cordillera 2205 Cordillera Way	Edwards	CO	81632	970-926-2200	926-2486
TF: 800-877-3529 ■ *Web:* www.cordilleralodge.com					
LodgeWorks LP 8100 E 22nd St Bldg 500	Wichita	KS	67226	316-681-5100	681-0905
Web: www.lodgeworks.com					
Sierra Suites 8100 E 22nd St Bldg 500	Wichita	KS	67226	316-681-5100	681-0994
TF Resv: 888-695-7608 ■ *Web:* www.sierrasuites.com					
Lodgian Inc 3445 Peachtree Rd NE Suite 700	Atlanta	GA	30326	404-364-9400	364-0088
AMEX: LGN ■ *Web:* www.lodgian.com					
Lodging Unlimited Inc 344 Willowbrook Ln	West Chester	PA	19382	610-436-8400	436-8861
Web: www.lodgingunlimited.com					
Loews Hotels 667 Madison Ave	New York	NY	10021	212-521-2000	521-2994
TF: 800-235-6397 ■ *Web:* www.loewshotels.com					
Lofts Hotel & Suites 55 E Nationwide Blvd	Columbus	OH	43215	614-461-2663	461-2630
TF: 800-735-6387 ■ *Web:* www.55lofts.com					
Lombardy The Hotel 111 E 56th St	New York	NY	10022	212-753-8600	754-5683
TF: 800-223-5254 ■ *Web:* www.lombardyhotel.com					
London NYC The 151 W 54th St	New York	NY	10019	212-307-5000	765-6530
TF: 866-690-2029 ■ *Web:* www.thelondonnyc.com					
Lone Oak Lodge 2221 N Fremont St	Monterey	CA	93940	831-372-4924	372-4985
TF: 800-283-5663 ■ *Web:* www.loneoaklodge.com					
Long House Alaskan Hotel 4335 Wisconsin St	Anchorage	AK	99517	907-243-2133	243-6060
TF: 888-243-2133 ■ *Web:* www.longhousehotel.com					
Longhouse Hospitality 4770 S Atlanta Rd	Smyrna	GA	30080	404-350-9990	350-6106
TF Resv: 800-526-3766 ■ *Web:* longhousehospitality.com					
Crestwood Suites Extended Stay Hotels					
4770 S Atlanta Rd Suite 200	Smyrna	GA	30080	404-350-9990	350-8660
Web: www.crestwoodsuites.com					
Jameson Inns 4770 S Atlanta Rd	Smyrna	GA	30080	404-350-9990	350-6106
TF: 800-526-3766 ■ *Web:* www.jamesoninns.com					
Lodge America 4700 S Atlanta Rd	Smyrna	GA	30080	404-350-9990	350-2240
Web: www.lodgeamerica.com					
Signature Inns 4770 S Atlanta Rd	Smyrna	GA	30080	404-350-9990	601-6106
Web: www.signatureinns.com					
Sun Suites Extended Stay Hotels 4770 S Atlanta Rd Suite 200	Smyrna	GA	30080	404-350-9990	350-8660
Web: www.sunsuites.com					
Lonsdale Quay Hotel 123 Carrie Cates Ct	North Vancouver	BC	V7M3K7	604-986-6111	986-8782
TF: 800-836-6111 ■ *Web:* www.lonsdalequayhotel.com					
Lookout Inn 6901 Lookout Rd	Boulder	CO	80301	303-530-1513	530-4573
TF: 800-530-1513 ■ *Web:* www.guest-house.com					
Lord Elgin Hotel 100 Elgin St	Ottawa	ON	K1P5K8	613-235-3333	235-3223
TF: 800-267-4298 ■ *Web:* www.lordelginhotel.ca					
Lord Nelson Hotel & Suites 1515 South Park St	Halifax	NS	B3J2L2	902-423-6331	423-7148
TF: 800-565-2020 ■ *Web:* www.lordnelsonhotel.com					
Lord Stanley Suites on the Park 1889 Alberni St	Vancouver	BC	V6G3G7	604-688-9299	688-9297
TF: 888-767-7829 ■ *Web:* www.lordstanley.com					
Los Angeles Athletic Club 431 W 7th St	Los Angeles	CA	90014	213-625-2211	689-1194
TF: 800-421-8777 ■ *Web:* www.laac.com					
Los Willows Inn & Spa 530 Stewart Canyon Rd	Fallbrook	CA	92028	760-728-8121	728-3622
TF: 888-731-9400 ■ *Web:* www.loswillows.com					
Lowell The 28 E 63rd St	New York	NY	10065	212-838-1400	319-4230
TF: 800-221-4444 ■ *Web:* www.lowellhotel.com					

	City	State	Zip	Phone	Fax
Lowell Inn 102 N 2nd St *TF:* 888-569-3554 ■ *Web:* www.lowellinn.com	Stillwater	MN	55082	651-439-1100	439-0253
LQ Management LLC 909 Hidden Ridge Suite 600 *TF:* 866-832-6574 ■ *Web:* www.lq.com	Irving	TX	75038	214-492-6600	492-6785
La Quinta Inn & Suites 909 Hidden Ridge Suite 600 **Fax:* Mktg ■ *TF:* 877-204-9204 ■ *Web:* www.lq.com	Irving	TX	75038	214-492-6600	492-6785*
Lubbock Inn 3901 19th St *TF:* 800-545-8226 ■ *Web:* www.lubbockinn.com	Lubbock	TX	79410	806-792-5181	792-1319
Luxe Hotel Rodeo Drive 360 N Rodeo Dr *TF:* 800-468-3541 ■ *Web:* www.luxehotels.com	Beverly Hills	CA	90210	310-273-0300	859-8730
Luxe Hotel Sunset Boulevard 11461 Sunset Blvd *TF:* 800-468-3541 ■ *Web:* www.luxehotels.com	Los Angeles	CA	90049	310-476-6571	471-6310
Luxe Worldwide Hotels 11461 Sunset Blvd *TF:* 866-589-3411 ■ *Web:* www.luxehotels.com	Los Angeles	CA	90049	310-440-3090	440-0821
Luxor Hotel & Casino 3900 Las Vegas Blvd S *TF Resv:* 800-288-1000 ■ *Web:* www.luxor.com	Las Vegas	NV	89119	702-262-4000	262-4404
Luxury Collection 1111 Westchester Ave *TF Cust Svc:* 877-443-4585 ■ *Web:* www.starwood.com/luxury	White Plains	NY	10604	914-640-8100	640-8310
MacArthur Place 29 E MacArthur St *TF:* 800-722-1866 ■ *Web:* www.macarthurplace.com	Sonoma	CA	95476	707-938-2929	933-9833
Madison The - A Loews Hotel 1177 15th St NW *TF:* 866-563-9792 ■ *Web:* www.loewshotels.com	Washington	DC	20005	202-862-1600	785-1255
Madison Concourse Hotel & Governors Club 1 W Dayton St *TF:* 800-356-8293 ■ *Web:* www.concoursehotel.com	Madison	WI	53703	608-257-6000	257-5280
Madison Hotel 1 Convent Rd *TF:* 800-526-0729 ■ *Web:* www.themadisonhotel.com	Morristown	NJ	07960	973-285-1800	540-8566
Madison Hotel 79 Madison Ave *TF:* 888-636-7447 ■ *Web:* www.slh.com/madison	Memphis	TN	38103	901-333-1200	333-1299
Magnolia Hotel Dallas 1401 Commerce St *TF:* 888-915-1110 ■ *Web:* www.magnoliahotels.com/dallas.aspx	Dallas	TX	75201	214-915-6500	253-0053
Magnolia Hotel Denver 818 17th St *TF:* 888-915-1110 ■ *Web:* www.magnoliahoteldenver.com/denver.aspx	Denver	CO	80202	303-607-9000	607-0101
Magnolia Hotel Houston 1100 Texas Ave *TF:* 888-915-1110 ■ *Web:* www.magnoliahotelhouston.com	Houston	TX	77002	713-221-0011	221-0022
Magnolia Hotel & Spa 623 Courtney St *TF:* 877-624-6654 ■ *Web:* www.magnoliahotel.com	Victoria	BC	V8W1B8	250-381-0999	381-0988
Main Street Inn 2200 Main St *TF:* 800-471-3001 ■ *Web:* www.mainstreetinn.com	Hilton Head Island	SC	29926	843-681-3001	681-5541
Main Street Station Hotel & Casino 200 N Main St *TF:* 800-713-8933 ■ *Web:* www.mainstreetcasino.com	Las Vegas	NV	89101	702-387-1896	386-4421
MainStay Suites 10750 Columbia Pike *TF:* 800-424-6423 ■ *Web:* www.mainstaysuites.com	Silver Spring	MD	20901	301-592-5000	592-6157
Maison 140 Beverly Hills 140 Lasky Dr *TF:* 800-670-6182 ■ *Web:* www.maison140beverlyhills.com/	Beverly Hills	CA	90212	310-281-4000	281-4001
Maison Dupuy Hotel 1001 Toulouse St *TF:* 800-535-9177 ■ *Web:* www.maisondupuy.com	New Orleans	LA	70112	504-586-8000	648-6180
Majestic Hotel 528 W Brompton *TF:* 800-727-5108 ■ *Web:* www.cityinns.com	Chicago	IL	60657	773-404-3499	404-3495
Malaga Inn 359 Church St *TF:* 800-235-1586 ■ *Web:* www.malagainn.com	Mobile	AL	36602	251-438-4701	438-4701
Malibu Beach Inn 22878 Pacific Coast Hwy *TF:* 800-462-5428 ■ *Web:* www.malibubeachinn.com	Malibu	CA	90265	310-456-6444	456-1499
Mandarin Oriental Hotel Group (USA) 345 California St Suite 1250 *Web:* www.mandarinoriental.com	San Francisco	CA	94104	415-772-8800	782-3778
Mandarin Oriental Miami 500 Brickell Key Dr *TF:* 800-526-6566 ■ *Web:* www.mandarinoriental.com	Miami	FL	33131	305-913-8288	913-8300
Mandarin Oriental New York 80 Columbus Cir *TF:* 866-801-8880 ■ *Web:* www.mohg.com	New York	NY	10023	212-805-8800	805-8888
Mandarin Oriental San Francisco 222 Sansome St *TF:* 800-526-6566 ■ *Web:* www.mandarinoriental.com	San Francisco	CA	94104	415-276-9888	433-0289
Mandarin Oriental Washington DC 1330 Maryland Ave SW *TF:* 888-888-1778 ■ *Web:* www.mandarinoriental.com	Washington	DC	20024	202-554-8588	554-8999
Manor House Inn 106 West St *TF:* 800-437-0083 ■ *Web:* www.barharbormanorhouse.com	Bar Harbor	ME	04609	207-288-3759	288-2974
Mansfield The 12 W 44th St *TF:* 800-255-5167 ■ *Web:* www.mansfieldhotel.com	New York	NY	10036	212-944-6050	764-4477
Mansion on Forsyth Park 700 Drayton St *TF:* 888-711-5114 ■ *Web:* www.mansiononforsythpark.com	Savannah	GA	31401	912-238-5158	238-5146
Mansion on Turtle Creek 2821 Turtle Creek Blvd *TF:* 800-527-5432 ■ *Web:* www.mansiononturtlecreek.com	Dallas	TX	75219	214-559-2100	528-4187
Mansion View Inn & Suites 529 S 4th St *TF:* 800-252-1083 ■ *Web:* www.mansionview.com/	Springfield	IL	62701	217-544-7411	544-6211
Maple Hill Farm Bed & Breakfast Inn 11 Inn Rd *TF:* 800-622-2708 ■ *Web:* www.maplebb.com	Hallowell	ME	04330	207-622-2708	622-0655
Marcel Hotel The 201 E 24th St *TF:* 888-664-6235	New York	NY	10011	212-696-3800	696-0077
Marcus Corp 100 E Wisconsin Ave *NYSE:* MCS ■ *TF:* 800-274-0099 ■ *Web:* www.marcuscorp.com	Milwaukee	WI	53202	414-905-1000	905-2129
Marcus Hotels & Resorts 100 E Wisconsin Ave Suite 1900 *Web:* www.marcusresorts.com	Milwaukee	WI	53202	414-905-1200	905-2250
Marina Del Mar Resort & Marina 527 Caribbean Dr *TF:* 800-451-3483 ■ *Web:* www.marinadelmarkeylargo.com	Key Largo	FL	33037	305-451-4107	451-1891
Marina Dunes Resort 3295 Dunes Dr *TF:* 877-944-3863 ■ *Web:* www.marinadunes.com	Marina	CA	93933	831-883-9478	883-9477
Marina Inn at Grande Dunes 8121 Amalfi Pl *TF:* 877-913-1333 ■ *Web:* www.marinainnatgrandedunes.com	Myrtle Beach	SC	29572	843-913-1333	913-1334
Marine Surf Waikiki Hotel 364 Seaside Ave *TF:* 888-456-7873 ■ *Web:* www.marinesurf.com	Honolulu	HI	96815	808-931-2424	931-2454
Mariner's Point Resort 425 Grand Ave *Web:* www.marinerspointresort.com	Falmouth	MA	02540	508-457-0300	
Mark The 25 E 77th St *TF:* 800-843-6275 ■ *Web:* www.mandarinoriental.com	New York	NY	10021	212-744-4300	744-2749
Mark I Guest Suites 4321 Hale Parkway	Denver	CO	80220	303-331-7000	331-7171
Mark Spencer Hotel 409 SW 11th Ave *TF:* 800-548-3934 ■ *Web:* www.markspencer.com	Portland	OR	97205	503-224-3293	223-7848
Mark Twain Hotel 225 NE Adams St *TF:* 866-325-6351 ■ *Web:* www.marktwainhotel.com	Peoria	IL	61602	309-676-3600	636-6259
Market Pavilion Hotel 225 E Bay St *TF:* 877-440-2250 ■ *Web:* www.marketpavilion.com	Charleston	SC	29401	843-723-0500	723-4320
Maron Hotel & Suites 42 Lake Ave Ext Mill Plain Rd *Web:* www.maronhotel.com	Danbury	CT	06811	203-791-2200	791-2201
MarQueen Hotel 600 Queen Anne Ave N *TF:* 888-445-3076 ■ *Web:* www.marqueen.com	Seattle	WA	98109	206-282-7407	283-1499
Marquesa Hotel 600 Fleming St *TF:* 800-869-4631 ■ *Web:* www.marquesa.com	Key West	FL	33040	305-292-1919	294-2121
Marquette Hotel 710 Marquette Ave *TF:* 800-328-4782 ■ *Web:* www.marquettehotel.com	Minneapolis	MN	55402	612-333-4545	288-2188
Marquis Villas 140 Calle Encilia *TF:* 877-545-6211 ■ *Web:* www.marquis-villas.com	Palm Springs	CA	92262	760-322-2263	322-0515
Marriott Charleston Hotel 170 Lockwood Blvd *TF:* 888-236-2427 ■ *Web:* www.marriott.com	Charleston	SC	29403	843-723-3000	723-0276
Marriott Columbus 800 Front Ave *TF:* 800-445-9261 ■ *Web:* www.marriott.com/CSGMC	Columbus	GA	31901	706-324-1800	576-4413
Marriott Conference Centers 1 Marriott Dr *Web:* marriott.com/conferencecenters	Washington	DC	20058	301-380-3000	380-3090
Marriott Hotels & Resorts 1 Marriott Dr *TF:* 800-228-9290 ■ *Web:* marriott.com/marriott	Washington	DC	20058	301-380-3000	380-3090
Marriott International Inc 1 Marriott Dr *NYSE:* MAR ■ **Fax:* Mail Rm ■ *Web:* www.marriott.com	Washington	DC	20058	301-380-3000	380-3008*
Courtyard by Marriott 1 Marriott Dr *TF:* 800-321-2211 ■ *Web:* www.marriott.com/courtyard	Washington	DC	20058	301-380-3000	380-3090
Fairfield Inn by Marriott 1 Marriott Dr *Web:* www.marriott.com/fairfieldinn	Washington	DC	20058	301-380-3000	380-3090
JW Marriott Hotels & Resorts 1 Marriott Dr *TF:* 888-236-2427 ■ *Web:* marriott.com/jwmarriott	Washington	DC	20058	301-380-3000	
Marriott Conference Centers 1 Marriott Dr *Web:* marriott.com/conferencecenters	Washington	DC	20058	301-380-3000	380-3090
Marriott Hotels & Resorts 1 Marriott Dr *TF:* 800-228-9290 ■ *Web:* marriott.com/marriott	Washington	DC	20058	301-380-3000	380-3090
Renaissance Hotels & Resorts 1 Marriott Dr *Web:* marriott.com/renaissancehotels	Washington	DC	20058	301-380-3000	380-4055
Residence Inn by Marriott 1 Marriott Dr *TF:* 800-638-8108 ■ *Web:* www.marriott.com/residenceinn	Washington	DC	20058	301-380-3000	380-5197
Ritz-Carlton Hotel Co LLC 4445 Willard Ave Suite 800 *TF:* 800-241-3333 ■ *Web:* www.ritzcarlton.com	Chevy Chase	MD	20815	301-547-4700	547-4740
SpringHill Suites by Marriott 1 Marriott Dr *TF:* 800-228-9290 ■ *Web:* www.marriott.com/springhill	Washington	DC	20058	301-380-3000	380-3090
TownePlace Suites by Marriott 1 Marriott Dr *Web:* marriott.com/towneplace	Washington	DC	20058	301-380-3000	380-3090
Marseilles Hotel 1741 Collins Ave *TF:* 800-327-4739 ■ *Web:* www.marseilleshotel.com	Miami Beach	FL	33139	305-538-5711	673-1006
Marten House Hotel & Lilly Conference Center 1801 W 86th St *TF:* 800-736-5634 ■ *Web:* www.martenhouse.com	Indianapolis	IN	46260	317-872-4111	415-5245
Martha Washington Inn 150 W Main St *TF:* 888-999-8078 ■ *Web:* www.marthawashingtoninn.com	Abingdon	VA	24210	276-628-3161	628-8885
Maryland Inn 16 Church Circle *TF:* 800-847-8882 ■ *Web:* www.historicinnsofannapolis.com	Annapolis	MD	21401	410-263-2641	268-3613
Master Hosts Inns & Resorts 1726 Montreal Cir *TF:* 800-247-4677 ■ *Web:* www.bookroomsnow.com	Tucker	GA	30084	770-270-1180	270-1077
Masters Inns PO Box 13069 *TF:* 800-633-3434 ■ *Web:* www.mastersinn.com	Savannah	GA	31416	912-352-4493	352-0314
Matrix Hotel 10001 107th St *TF:* 866-456-8150 ■ *Web:* www.matrixedmonton.com/	Edmonton	AB	T5J1J1	780-429-2861	426-7225
Maumee Bay Resort & Conference Center 1750 Park Rd 2 *TF:* 800-282-7275 ■ *Web:* www.maumeebayresort.com	Oregon	OH	43618	419-836-1466	836-2438
Maxwell Hotel 386 Geary St *TF:* 800-553-1900 ■ *Web:* www.maxwellhotel.com	San Francisco	CA	94102	415-986-2000	397-2447
Mayfair Hotel & Spa 3000 Florida Ave *TF:* 800-433-4555 ■ *Web:* www.mayfairhotelandspa.com	Coconut Grove	FL	33133	305-441-0000	447-9173
Mayfield Inn & Suites 16615 109th Ave *TF:* 800-661-9804 ■ *Web:* www.mayfieldinnedmonton.com	Edmonton	AB	T5P4K8	780-484-0821	486-1634
Mayflower Inn 118 Woodbury Rd PO Box 1288 *Web:* www.mayflowerinn.com	Washington	CT	06793	860-868-9466	868-1497
Mayflower Park Hotel 405 Olive Way *TF:* 800-426-5100 ■ *Web:* www.mayflowerpark.com	Seattle	WA	98101	206-623-8700	382-6997
McCamly Plaza Hotel 50 Capital Ave SW *TF:* 888-622-2659 ■ *Web:* www.mccamlyplazahotel.com	Battle Creek	MI	49017	269-963-7050	963-4335
McKinley Grand Hotel 320 Market Ave S *TF:* 877-454-5008 ■ *Web:* www.mckinleygrandhotel.com	Canton	OH	44702	330-454-5000	454-5494
McLure House Hotel & Conference Center 1200 Market St	Wheeling	WV	26003	304-232-0300	
MCM Elegante Suites 4250 Ridgemont Dr *TF:* 888-897-9644 ■ *Web:* www.mcmelegantesuites.com/	Abilene	TX	79606	325-698-1234	698-2771
Mediterranean Inn 425 Queen Anne Ave N *TF:* 866-525-4700 ■ *Web:* www.mediterranean-inn.com	Seattle	WA	98109	206-428-4700	428-4699
Meeting Street Inn 173 Meeting St *TF:* 800-842-8022 ■ *Web:* www.meetingstreetinn.com	Charleston	SC	29401	843-723-1882	577-0851
Melrose Hotel Washington DC 2430 Pennsylvania Ave NW *TF:* 800-635-7673 ■ *Web:* www.melrosehotel.com	Washington	DC	20037	202-955-6400	955-5765
Mendocino Hotel & Garden Suites 45080 Main St *TF:* 800-548-0513 ■ *Web:* www.mendocinohotel.com	Mendocino	CA	95460	707-937-0511	937-0513
Menger Hotel 204 Alamo Plaza *TF:* 800-345-9285 ■ *Web:* mengerhotel.com/	San Antonio	TX	78205	210-223-4361	228-0022
Mercer Hotel 147 Mercer St *TF:* 888-918-6060 ■ *Web:* www.mercerhotel.com	New York	NY	10012	212-966-6060	965-3838
Mercury Resort 100 Collins Ave *TF:* 877-786-2732 ■ *Web:* www.mercuryresort.com	Miami Beach	FL	33139	305-398-3000	398-3001
Meridian Plaza Resort 2310 N Ocean Blvd *TF:* 800-323-3011 ■ *Web:* www.meridianplaza.com	Myrtle Beach	SC	29577	843-626-4734	448-4569
Metropolitan Hotel Toronto 108 Chestnut St *TF:* 800-668-6600 ■ *Web:* www.metropolitan.com/toronto/	Toronto	ON	M5G1R3	416-977-5000	977-9513
Metropolitan Hotel Vancouver 645 Howe St *TF:* 800-667-2300 ■ *Web:* www.metropolitan.com/vanc/	Vancouver	BC	V6C2Y9	604-687-1122	643-7267
Metterra Hotel on Whyte 10454 82nd Ave *TF:* 866-465-8150 ■ *Web:* www.metterra.com	Edmonton	AB	T6E4Z7	780-465-8150	465-8174
Meyer Crest Ltd 2515 Park Marina Dr Suite 201 *TF:* 800-626-1900 ■ *Web:* www.meyercrest.com	Redding	CA	96001	530-242-2010	247-3982
Meyer Jabara Hotels 1601 Belvedere Rd Suite 407 S *Web:* www.meyerjabarahotels.com	West Palm Beach	FL	33406	561-689-6602	689-4363
MGM Grand Detroit 1300 John C Lodge **Fax:* Hum Res ■ *TF:* 877-888-2121 ■ *Web:* www.mgmgranddetroit.com/	Detroit	MI	48226	313-393-7777	394-4210*
Miami International Airport Hotel NW 20th St & Le Jeune Rd *TF:* 800-327-1276 ■ *Web:* www.miahotel.com	Miami	FL	33122	305-871-4100	871-0800
Michelangelo Hotel 152 W 51st St *TF:* 800-237-0990 ■ *Web:* www.michelangelohotel.com	New York	NY	10019	212-765-1900	541-6604
Microtel Inns & Suites 13 Corporate Sq Suite 250 *TF:* 888-222-2142 ■ *Web:* www.microtelinn.com	Atlanta	GA	30329	404-321-4045	321-4482
Middlebury Inn 14 Courthouse Sq *TF:* 800-842-4666 ■ *Web:* www.middleburyinn.com	Middlebury	VT	05753	802-388-4961	388-4563
Midtown Hotel 220 Huntington Ave *TF:* 800-343-1177 ■ *Web:* www.midtownhotel.com	Boston	MA	02115	617-262-1000	262-8739
Mill Street Inn 75 Mill St *TF:* 800-392-1316 ■ *Web:* www.millstreetinn.com	Newport	RI	02840	401-849-9500	848-5131
Mill Valley Inn 165 Throckmorton Ave *TF:* 800-595-2100 ■ *Web:* www.marinhotels.com/mill_guestrooms.html	Mill Valley	CA	94941	415-389-6608	389-5051
Millennium Hotels & Resorts 6560 Greenwood Plaza Blvd Suite 300 *Web:* www.millenniumhotels.com	Greenwood Village	CO	80111	303-779-2000	779-2001
Mills House Hotel 115 Meeting St *TF:* 800-874-9600 ■ *Web:* www.millshouse.com	Charleston	SC	29401	843-577-2400	722-0623
Milner Hotel Boston 78 Charles St S *TF:* 800-453-1731 ■ *Web:* www.milner-hotels.com/boston.html	Boston	MA	02116	617-426-6220	350-0360
Milner Hotels Inc 1526 Centre St *TF:* 800-521-0592 ■ *Web:* www.milner-hotels.com	Detroit	MI	48226	313-962-5400	962-2116
Minto Place Suite Hotel 185 Lyons St *TF:* 800-267-3377 ■ *Web:* www.mintosuitehotel.com	Ottawa	ON	K1R7Y1	613-232-2200	232-6962
Mira Monte Inn & Suites 69 Mt Desert St *TF:* 800-553-5109 ■ *Web:* www.miramonte.com	Bar Harbor	ME	04609	207-288-4263	288-3115
Mirabeau Park Hotel 1100 N Sullivan Rd *Web:* www.mirabeauparkhotel.com	Spokane Valley	WA	99037	509-924-9000	922-4965
Miramar Hotel at Waikiki 2345 Kuhio St *TF:* 800-367-2303 ■ *Web:* www.miramarwaikiki.com	Honolulu	HI	96815	808-922-2077	926-3217

Phone Fax

Mirbeau Inn & Spa 851 W Genesee St ... Skaneateles NY 13152 315-685-5006 685-5150
TF: 877-647-2328 ■ *Web:* www.mirbeau.com

Mission Inn 3649 Mission Inn Ave ... Riverside CA 92501 951-784-0300 683-1342
TF: 800-843-7755 ■ *Web:* www.missioninn.com

Misty Harbor & Barefoot Beach Resort 118 Weirs Rd ... Gilford NH 03249 603-293-4500 293-0493
TF: 800-336-4789 ■ *Web:* www.mistyharbor.com

Miyako Inn & Spa 328 E 1st St ... Los Angeles CA 90012 213-617-2000 617-2700
TF: 800-228-6596 ■ *Web:* www.miyakoinn.com

MMI Hotel Group PO Box 320009 ... Jackson MS 39232 601-936-3666 939-5685
Web: www.mmihotelgroup.com

MODA Hotel 900 Seymour St ... Vancouver BC V6B3L9 604-683-4251 683-4256
Web: www.modahotel.ca/

Moderne Hotel The 243 W 55th St ... New York NY 10019 212-397-6767 397-8787
TF: 888-664-6235

Mojave A Desert Resort 73721 Shadow Mountain Dr ... Palm Desert CA 92260 760-346-6121 674-9072
TF: 800-391-1104 ■ *Web:* www.hotelmojave.com

Molokai Lodge & Beach Village 100 Maunaloa Hwy ... Maunaloa HI 96770 808-552-2741 552-2773
TF: 888-627-8082

Monarch Hotel & Conference Center 12566 SE 93rd Ave ... Clackamas OR 97015 503-652-1515 652-7509
TF: 800-492-8700 ■ *Web:* monarchhotel.citysearch.com

Mondrian Hotel 8440 Sunset Blvd ... West Hollywood CA 90069 323-650-8999 650-5215
TF: 800-525-8029 ■ *Web:* www.morganshotelgroup.com

Mondrian Scottsdale 7353 E Indian School Rd ... Scottsdale AZ 85251 480-308-1100 308-1200
TF: 800-697-1791 ■ *Web:* www.mondrianscottsdale.com

Monmouth Plantation 36 Melrose Ave ... Natchez MS 39120 601-442-5852 446-7762
TF: 800-828-4531 ■ *Web:* www.monmouthplantation.com

MontBleu Resort Casino & Spa 55 Hwy 50 PO Box 5800 ... Stateline NV 89449 775-588-3515 586-4695
TF: 800-648-3353 ■ *Web:* www.montbleuresort.com

Monte Carlo Inn-Airport Suites 5 Derry Rd ... Mississauga ON L5T2H8 905-564-8500 564-8400
TF: 800-363-6400 ■ *Web:* www.montecarloinns.com

Monterey Bay Inn 242 Cannery Row ... Monterey CA 93940 831-373-6242 373-7603
TF: 800-424-6242 ■ *Web:* www.montereybayinn.com

Monterey Hotel 406 Alvarado St ... Monterey CA 93940 831-375-3184 373-2899
TF: 800-727-0960 ■ *Web:* www.montereyhotel.com

Monterey Inn Resort & Conference Centre
2259 Prince of Wales Dr ... Ottawa ON K2E6Z8 613-226-5813 226-5900
TF: 800-288-3500 ■ *Web:* www.montereyinn.com

Monterey Plaza Hotel & Spa 400 Cannery Row ... Monterey CA 93940 831-646-1700 646-0285
TF: 800-334-3999 ■ *Web:* www.woodsidehotels.com

Monticello Inn 127 Ellis St ... San Francisco CA 94102 415-392-8800 398-2650
TF: 800-669-7777 ■ *Web:* www.monticelloinn.com

Moody Gardens Hotel 7 Hope Blvd ... Galveston TX 77554 409-741-8484 683-4937
TF: 888-388-8484 ■ *Web:* www.moodygardenshotel.com

Moorpark Hotel 4241 Moorpark Ave ... San Jose CA 95129 408-864-0300 864-0350
TF: 877-740-6622 ■ *Web:* www.moorparkhotel.com

Morgans Hotel 237 Madison Ave ... New York NY 10016 212-686-0300 779-8352
TF: 800-334-3408 ■ *Web:* www.morganshotel.com

Morgans Hotel Group Co 475 10th Ave ... New York NY 10018 212-277-4100 277-4260
NASDAQ: MHGC ■ *TF:* 800-697-1791 ■ *Web:* www.morganshotelgroup.com

Morris Inn Notre Dame Ave University of Notre Dame ... Notre Dame IN 46556 574-631-2000 631-2340
Web: morrisinn.nd.edu/

Morrison-Clark Inn 1101 11th St NW ... Washington DC 20001 202-898-1200 289-8576
TF: 800-222-8474 ■ *Web:* www.morrisonclark.com

Morrison House 116 S Alfred St ... Alexandria VA 22314 703-838-8000 684-6283
TF: 800-367-0800 ■ *Web:* www.morrisonhouse.com

Mosaic Hotel 125 S Spalding Dr ... Beverly Hills CA 90212 310-278-0303 278-1728
TF: 800-463-4466 ■ *Web:* www.mosaichotel.com

Mosser Hotel 54 4th St ... San Francisco CA 94103 415-986-4400 495-7653
TF: 800-227-3804 ■ *Web:* www.themosser.com

Motel 6 4001 International Pkwy ... Carrollton TX 75007 972-360-9000 360-2821
TF: 800-466-8356 ■ *Web:* www.motel6.com

Motel 6 Wichita 465 S Webb Rd ... Wichita KS 67207 316-684-6363 684-6363
TF: 800-466-8356 ■ *Web:* www.motel6.com

Mount View Hotel & Spa 1457 Lincoln Ave ... Calistoga CA 94515 707-942-6877 942-6904
TF: 800-816-6877 ■ *Web:* www.mountviewhotel.com

Mountain Haus 292 E Meadow Dr ... Vail CO 81657 970-476-2434 476-3007
TF: 800-237-0922 ■ *Web:* www.mountainhaus.com

Mountain Lake Hotel 115 Hotel Cir ... Pembroke VA 24136 540-626-7121 626-7172
TF: 800-346-3334 ■ *Web:* www.mtnlakehotel.com

Mountain Springs Cabins PO Box 6922 ... Asheville NC 28816 828-665-1004 667-1581
Web: www.mtnsprings.com

Mountain View Inn 121 Village Dr ... Greensburg PA 15601 724-834-5300 834-5304
TF: 800-537-8709 ■ *Web:* www.mountainviewinn.com

Mountain Villas 9525 W Skyline Pkwy ... Duluth MN 55810 218-624-5784 624-1949
TF: 866-688-4552 ■ *Web:* www.mtvillas.com

Movie Colony Hotel 726 N Indian Canyon Dr ... Palm Springs CA 92262 760-320-6340 320-1640
TF: 888-953-5700 ■ *Web:* www.moviecolonyhotel.com/

Mulberry Inn 601 E Bay St ... Savannah GA 31401 912-238-1200 236-2184
TF: 877-468-1200 ■ *Web:* www.savannahhotel.com

Muse The 130 W 46th St ... New York NY 10036 212-485-2400 485-2789
TF: 877-692-6873 ■ *Web:* www.themusehotel.com

Mutiny Hotel 2951 S Bayshore Dr ... Miami FL 33133 305-441-2100 441-2822
Web: www.mutinyhotel.com

Napa River Inn 500 Main St ... Napa CA 94559 707-251-8500 251-8504
TF: 877-251-8500 ■ *Web:* www.napariverinn.com

Nassau Inn The 10 Palmer Square ... Princeton NJ 08542 609-921-7500 921-9385
TF: 800-862-7728 ■ *Web:* www.nassauinn.com

Nathan Hale Inn & Conference Center 855 Bolton Rd ... Storrs CT 06268 860-427-7888 427-7850
Web: www.nathanhaleinn.com

National Hotel 1677 Collins Ave ... Miami Beach FL 33139 305-532-2311 534-1426
TF: 800-327-8370 ■ *Web:* www.nationalhotel.com

Nativo Lodge Hotel 6000 Pan American Fwy NE ... Albuquerque NM 87109 505-798-4300 798-4305
TF: 888-628-4861 ■ *Web:* hhandr.com/nat_main.php

New Haven Hotel 229 George St ... New Haven CT 06510 203-498-3100 498-0911
TF: 800-644-6835 ■ *Web:* www.newhavenhotel.com

New Haven Premier Suites Hotel 3 Long Wharf Dr ... New Haven CT 06511 203-777-5337 777-2808
TF: 866-458-0232 ■ *Web:* www.newhavensuites.com

New Otani Kaimana Beach Hotel 2863 Kalakaua Ave ... Honolulu HI 96815 808-923-1555 922-9404
TF: 800-356-8264 ■ *Web:* www.kaimana.com

New World Inn 265 33rd Ave ... Columbus NE 68601 402-564-1492 563-3989
TF: 800-433-1492 ■ *Web:* www.newworldinn.com

New York Helmsley Hotel 212 E 42nd St ... New York NY 10017 212-490-8900 986-4792
TF: 800-221-4982 ■ *Web:* www.newyorkhelmsley.com

New York New York Hotel & Casino 3790 Las Vegas Blvd S ... Las Vegas NV 89109 702-740-6969 740-6700
TF: 800-693-6763 ■ *Web:* www.nynyhotelcasino.com

New York Palace Hotel 455 Madison Ave ... New York NY 10022 212-888-7000 303-6000
TF: 800-697-2522 ■ *Web:* www.newyorkpalace.com

New Yorker Hotel 481 8th Ave ... New York NY 10001 212-971-0101 629-6536
TF: 800-764-4680 ■ *Web:* www.newyorkerhotel.com

New York's Hotel Pennsylvania 401 7th Ave ... New York NY 10001 212-736-5000 502-8712
TF: 800-223-8585 ■ *Web:* hotelpenn.com/thehotel.html

Newport Bay Club & Hotel 337 Thames St PO Box 1440 ... Newport RI 02840 401-849-8600 846-6857
Web: www.newportbayclub.com

Newport Beachside Hotel & Resort 16701 Collins Ave ... Miami Beach FL 33160 305-949-1300 947-5873
TF: 800-327-5476 ■ *Web:* www.newportbeachsideresort.com

Newport Gateway Hotel 31 W Main Rd ... Middletown RI 02842 401-847-2735 847-5434
TF: 800-427-9444 ■ *Web:* www.newportgatewayhotel.com

Newport Harbor Hotel & Marina 49 America's Cup Ave ... Newport RI 02840 401-847-9000 849-6380
TF: 800-955-2558 ■ *Web:* www.newporthotel.com

Nicollet Island Inn 95 Merriam St ... Minneapolis MN 55401 612-331-1800 331-5667
Web: www.nicolletislandinn.com

Nine Zero Hotel 90 Tremont St ... Boston MA 02108 617-772-5800 772-5810
TF: 866-646-9937 ■ *Web:* www.ninezerohotel.com

Nittany Lion Inn 200 W Park Ave ... State College PA 16803 814-865-8500 865-8501
TF: 800-233-7505 ■ *Web:* www.pshs.psu.edu/

Norwood Hotel 112 Marion St ... Winnipeg MB R2H0T1 204-233-4475 231-1910
TF: 888-888-1878 ■ *Web:* www.norwood-hotel.com

Novotel 4001 International Pkwy ... Carrollton TX 75007 972-360-9000 360-2821
Web: www.novotel.com

O Henry Hotel 624 Green Valley Rd ... Greensboro NC 27408 336-854-2000 854-2223
TF: 800-965-8259 ■ *Web:* www.o.henryhotel.com

O Hotel 819 S Flower St ... Los Angeles CA 90017 213-623-9904 614-8010
Web: www.ohotelgroup.com/

Oak Meadow Lodge 11503 Browning Rd ... Evansville IN 47725 812-867-6431 867-6400
TF: 800-933-1920 ■ *Web:* www.oakmeadowlodge.com

Oberlin Inn 7 N Main St ... Oberlin OH 44074 440-775-1111 775-6356
TF: 800-376-4173 ■ *Web:* www.oberlininn.com

O'Callaghan Annapolis Hotel 174 West St ... Annapolis MD 21401 410-263-7700 990-1400
TF: 866-782-9624 ■ *Web:* www.ocallaghanhotels.com

Occidental Hotels & Resorts 6303 Blue Lagoon Dr Suite 250 ... Miami FL 33126 305-262-5909 266-7845
TF: 800-858-2258 ■ *Web:* www.occidentalhotels.com

Ocean Five Hotel 436 Ocean Dr ... Miami Beach FL 33139 305-532-7093 534-7353
TF: 866-666-0505 ■ *Web:* www.oceanfivehotel.com

Ocean Forest Plaza 5523 N Ocean Blvd ... Myrtle Beach SC 29577 843-497-0044 497-3051
TF: 800-522-0818 ■ *Web:* www.sandsresorts.com

Ocean Hospitalities Inc 1000 Market St Bldg 1 Suite 300 ... Portsmouth NH 03801 603-559-2100 559-2195
Web: www.oceanhospitalities.com

Ocean Key Resort 424 Atlantic Ave ... Virginia Beach VA 23451 757-425-2200 491-1186
TF: 800-955-9700

Ocean Pointe Suites at Key Largo 500 Burton Dr ... Tavernier FL 33070 305-853-3000 853-3007
TF: 800-882-9464 ■ *Web:* www.oceanpointesuites.com

Ocean Resort Hotel Waikiki 175 Paoakalani Ave ... Honolulu HI 96815 808-922-3861 924-1982
TF: 800-367-2317 ■ *Web:* www.oceanresort.com

Ocean Sky Hotel & Resort 4060 Galt Ocean Dr ... Fort Lauderdale FL 33308 954-565-6611 564-7730
TF: 800-678-9022 ■ *Web:* www.oceanskyresort.com

Ocean Walk Resort 300 N Atlantic ... Daytona Beach FL 32118 386-323-4800 323-4810
TF: 800-347-9851 ■ *Web:* www.oceanwalk.com

Ocean Waters 2025 S Atlantic Ave ... Daytona Beach Shores FL 32118 386-257-1950 253-9935
TF: 800-874-7420 ■ *Web:* www.daytonahotels.com

Oceancliff Hotel & Resort 65 Ridge Rd ... Newport RI 02840 401-841-8868 849-3927
Web: www.newportexperience.com/oceancliff.htm

Ocotillo Lodge 1111 E Palm Canyon Dr ... Palm Springs CA 92264 760-416-0678 416-0599

OHANA Hotels & Resorts 2375 Kuhio Ave ... Honolulu HI 96815 808-921-6600
TF: 800-462-6262 ■ *Web:* www.ohanahotels.com

OHANA Waikiki Beachcomber Hotel 2300 Kalakaua Ave ... Honolulu HI 96815 808-922-4646 926-9973
TF: 800-622-4646 ■ *Web:* www.waikikibeachcomber.com

Old City House Inn 115 Cordova St ... Saint Augustine FL 32084 904-826-0113
Web: www.oldcityhouse.com

Old Mill Toronto Inn & Spa 21 Old Mill Rd ... Toronto ON M8X1G5 416-236-2641 236-2749
TF: 866-653-6455 ■ *Web:* www.oldmilltoronto.com/

Olympic Corporate Suites 400 Village Gardens SW ... Calgary AB T3H2L1 403-355-5175 697-3265
Web: www.olympicsuites.com

Omni Hotels 420 Decker Dr Suite 200 ... Irving TX 75062 972-730-6664 871-5665*
**Fax:* Mktg ■ *TF:* 800-843-6664 ■ *Web:* www.omnihotels.com

Omni La Mansion del Rio 112 College St ... San Antonio TX 78205 210-518-1000 226-0389
TF: 800-292-7300 ■ *Web:* www.lamansion.com

One Washington Circle Hotel 1 Washington Cir NW ... Washington DC 20037 202-872-1680 887-4989
TF: 800-424-9671 ■ *Web:* www.thecirclehotel.com

O'Neill Hotels & Resorts Management Ltd
401 W Georgia St Suite 1690 ... Vancouver BC V6B5A1 604-684-0444 684-0482
Web: www.oneillhotels.com

Onyx Hotel 155 Portland St ... Boston MA 02114 617-557-9955 557-0005
TF: 866-660-6699 ■ *Web:* www.onyxhotel.com

Opus Hotel 322 Davie St ... Vancouver BC V6B5Z6 604-642-6787 642-6787
TF: 866-642-6787 ■ *Web:* www.opushotel.com/

Opus Hotel Montreal 10 Sherbrooke St W ... Montreal QC H2X4C9 514-843-6000 843-6810
TF: 866-744-6346 ■ *Web:* www.opushotel.com/

Orchard Garden Hotel 466 Bush St ... San Francisco CA 94108 415-399-9807 393-9917
TF: 888-717-2881 ■ *Web:* www.theorchardgardenhotel.com/

Orchard Hotel 665 Bush St ... San Francisco CA 94108 415-362-8878 362-8088
TF: 888-717-2881 ■ *Web:* www.theorchardhotel.com

Orchards Hotel 222 Adams Rd ... Williamstown MA 01267 413-458-9611 458-3273
TF: 800-225-1517 ■ *Web:* www.orchardshotel.com

Orchards Inn of Sedona 254 Hwy N 89 A ... Sedona AZ 86336 928-282-2405 282-7818
Web: www.orchardsinn.com

Orient Express Hotels Inc 1114 Ave of the Americas 30th Fl ... New York NY 10036 212-302-5055 302-5203
NYSE: OEH ■ *TF:* 800-237-1236 ■ *Web:* www.orient-express.com

Orlando The 8384 W 3rd St ... Los Angeles CA 90048 323-658-6600 653-3464
TF: 800-624-6835 ■ *Web:* www.theorlando.com

Orleans Las Vegas Hotel & Casino 4500 W Tropicana Ave ... Las Vegas NV 89103 702-365-7111 365-7500
TF: 888-365-7111 ■ *Web:* www.orleanscasino.com

Outrigger Enterprises Group 2375 Kuhio Ave ... Honolulu HI 96815 808-921-6600 922-8509
TF: 800-462-6262 ■ *Web:* www.outriggerenterprisesgroup.com
OHANA Hotels & Resorts 2375 Kuhio Ave ... Honolulu HI 96815 808-921-6600
TF: 800-462-6262 ■ *Web:* www.ohanahotels.com
Outrigger Hotels & Resorts 2375 Kuhio Ave ... Honolulu HI 96815 808-921-6600 926-4368*
**Fax:* Sales ■ *TF:* 800-688-7444 ■ *Web:* www.outrigger.com

Outrigger Hotels & Resorts 2375 Kuhio Ave ... Honolulu HI 96815 808-921-6600 926-4368*
**Fax:* Sales ■ *TF:* 800-688-7444 ■ *Web:* www.outrigger.com

Outrigger Waikiki on the Beach 2335 Kalakaua Ave ... Honolulu HI 96815 808-923-0711 921-9749
TF: 800-688-7444 ■ *Web:* outrigger.com

Overlook Lodge ... Bear Mountain NY 10911 845-786-2731 786-2543
Web: www.bearmountaininn.com

Owyhee Plaza Hotel 1109 Main St ... Boise ID 83702 208-343-4611 336-3860
TF: 800-233-4611 ■ *Web:* www.owyheeplaza.com

Oxford Hotel 1600 17th St ... Denver CO 80202 303-628-5400 628-5413
TF: 800-228-5838 ■ *Web:* www.theoxfordhotel.com

Oxford Palace 745 S Oxford Ave ... Los Angeles CA 90005 213-389-8000 389-8500
TF: 800-532-7887 ■ *Web:* www.oxfordhotel.com

Oxford Suites Boise 1426 S Entertainment Ave ... Boise ID 38709 208-322-8000 322-8002
TF: 888-322-8001 ■ *Web:* www.oxfordsuitesboise.com

Oxford Suites Spokane-Downtown 115 W North River Dr ... Spokane WA 99201 509-353-9000 353-9164
TF: 800-774-1877 ■ *Web:* www.oxfordsuitesspokane.com

Oxford Suites Spokane Valley 15015 E Indiana Ave ... Spokane Valley WA 99216 509-847-1000 847-1001
TF: 866-668-7848 ■ *Web:* www.oxfordsuitesspokanevalley.com

Oyster Point Hotel Marina & Conference Center
146 Bodman Pl ... Red Bank NJ 07701 732-530-8200 747-1875
TF: 800-345-3484 ■ *Web:* www.mollypitcher-oysterpoint.com

Pacific Beach Hotel 2490 Kalakaua Ave ... Honolulu HI 96815 808-922-1233 922-0129
TF: 800-367-6060 ■ *Web:* www.pacificbeachhotel.com

Pacific Inn 600 Marina Dr ... Seal Beach CA 90740 562-493-7501 596-3448
TF: 866-466-0300 ■ *Web:* www.pacificinn-sb.com

Pacific Palisades Hotel 1277 Robson St ... Vancouver BC V6E1C4 604-688-0461 688-4374
TF: 800-663-1815 ■ *Web:* www.pacificpalisadeshotel.com

Name / Address	City	State	Zip	Phone	Fax
Pacific Shores Inn 4802 Mission Blvd	San Diego	CA	92109	858-483-6300	483-9276
TF: 888-478-7829 ■ *Web:* pacific-shores-inn.pacificahost.com					
Pacific Terrace Hotel 610 Diamond St	San Diego	CA	92109	858-581-3500	274-3341
TF: 800-344-3370 ■ *Web:* www.pacificterrace.com					
Pacifica Coast Hotels 1775 Hancock St Suite 100	San Diego	CA	92110	619-296-9000	296-9080
Web: www.pacificahost.com					
Pagoda Hotel 1525 Rycroft St	Honolulu	HI	96814	808-941-6611	955-5067
TF: 800-367-6060 ■ *Web:* www.pagodahotel.com					
Painted Buffalo Inn 400 W Broadway	Jackson	WY	83001	307-733-4340	733-7953
TF: 800-288-3866 ■ *Web:* www.paintedbuffaloinn.com					
Palace Casino 158 Howard Ave	Biloxi	MS	39530	228-432-8888	386-2314*
**Fax:* Mktg ■ *TF:* 800-725-2239 ■ *Web:* www.palacecasinoresort.com					
Palace Hotel 2 New Montgomery St	San Francisco	CA	94105	415-512-1111	543-0671
Web: www.sfpalace.com					
Palace Station Hotel & Casino 2411 W Sahara Ave	Las Vegas	NV	89102	702-367-2411	367-2478
TF: 800-634-3101 ■ *Web:* www.palacestation.com					
Palisades Extended-Stay Suites 101-1288 W Georgia St	Vancouver	BC	V6E4R3	604-891-6101	891-6151
Web: www.vancouverextendedstay.com					
Palmer House Hilton 17 E Monroe St	Chicago	IL	60603	312-726-7500	917-1707
TF: 800-445-8667 ■ *Web:* www.hiltonfamilychicago.com					
Palmer Inn The 3499 Rt 1 S	Princeton	NJ	08640	609-452-2500	452-1371
TF: 800-688-2500 ■ *Web:* www.palmerinnprinceton.com					
Palo Verde Inn & Suites 5251 S Julian Dr	Tucson	AZ	85706	520-294-5250	295-1058
TF: 800-272-6232 ■ *Web:* www.starbounding.com					
Palos Verdes Inn 1700 S Pacific Coast Hwy	Redondo Beach	CA	90277	310-316-4211	316-4863
TF: 800-421-9241 ■ *Web:* www.palosverdesinn.com					
Pan Pacific Hotel Vancouver 300-999 Canada Pl	Vancouver	BC	V6C3B5	604-662-8111	685-8690
TF: 800-937-1515 ■ *Web:* www.panpacific.com					
Pan Pacific Hotels & Resorts 500 Post St	San Francisco	CA	94102	415-732-7747	732-5800
TF: 800-327-8585 ■ *Web:* www.panpacific.com					
Pan Pacific Seattle 2125 Terry Ave	Seattle	WA	98121	206-264-8111	654-5049
Web: www.panpacific.com					
Pantages Suites Hotel & Spa 200 Victoria St	Toronto	ON	M5B1V8	416-362-1777	214-5618
TF: 866-852-1777 ■ *Web:* www.pantageshotel.com/					
Par-A-Dice Hotel 7 Blackjack Blvd	East Peoria	IL	61611	309-699-7711	699-9317
Web: www.par-a-dice.com					
Paradise Inn 819 Simonton St	Key West	FL	33040	305-293-8007	293-0807
TF: 800-888-9648 ■ *Web:* www.theparadiseinn.com					
Paragon Hotel Corp 5333 N 7th St Suite A-100	Phoenix	AZ	85014	602-248-0811	279-6765
Web: www.paragonhotels.com					
Paramount Hotel 235 W 46th St	New York	NY	10036	212-764-5500	354-5237
TF: 888-741-5600 ■ *Web:* www.solmelia.com					
Paramount Hotel 808 SW Taylor St	Portland	OR	97205	503-223-9900	223-7900
TF: 866-760-3174 ■ *Web:* www.portlandparamount.com					
Paramount Hotel 724 Pine St	Seattle	WA	98101	206-292-9500	292-8610
TF: 800-663-1144 ■ *Web:* www.paramounthotelseattle.com					
Paramount Hotel Group 710 Route 46 E Suite 206	Fairfield	NJ	07004	973-882-0505	882-0043
Web: www.paramounthotelgroup.com					
Parc 55 Hotel 55 Cyril Magnin St	San Francisco	CA	94102	415-392-8000	403-6602
Web: www.parc55hotel.com					
Paris Las Vegas 3655 Las Vegas Blvd S	Las Vegas	NV	89109	702-946-7000	946-4259
TF: 888-266-5687 ■ *Web:* www.harrahs.com					
Park Central The 640 Ocean Dr	Miami Beach	FL	33139	305-538-1611	534-7520
TF: 800-727-5236 ■ *Web:* www.theparkcentral.com					
Park Central Hotel 1010 Houston St	Fort Worth	TX	76102	817-336-2011	336-2011
TF: 800-848-7275 ■ *Web:* www.parkcentralhotel.com					
Park Central New York 870 7th Ave	New York	NY	10019	212-247-8000	707-5557
TF: 800-346-1359 ■ *Web:* www.parkcentralny.com					
Park Hyatt Hotels 71 S Wacker Dr	Chicago	IL	60606	312-750-1234	780-5289*
**Fax:* Mktg ■ *TF Resv:* 800-233-1234 ■ *Web:* www.hyatt.com					
Park Inn PO Box 59159	Minneapolis	MN	55459	763-212-1000	212-6631
TF Resv: 800-670-7275 ■ *Web:* www.parkinn.com					
Park Lane Hotel at Four Seasons 3005 High Point Rd	Greensboro	NC	27403	336-294-4565	294-0572
TF: 800-942-6556 ■ *Web:* www.park-lane-hotel.com					
Park Plaza Hotel Oakland 150 Hegenberger Rd	Oakland	CA	94621	510-635-5300	635-9661
TF: 800-635-5301 ■ *Web:* www.parkplazaoakland.com					
Park Plaza Hotels & Resorts PO Box 59159	Minneapolis	MN	55459	763-212-1000	212-6631
Web: www.carlsonhotelsmedia.tekgroup.com					
Park Shore Waikiki Hotel 2586 Kalakaua Ave	Honolulu	HI	96815	808-923-0411	923-0311
TF: 866-282-4773 ■ *Web:* www.parkshorewaikiki.com					
Park South Hotel 124 E 28th St	New York	NY	10016	212-448-0888	448-0811
TF: 800-315-4642 ■ *Web:* www.parksouthhotel.com					
Park Vista Resort Hotel					
705 Cherokee Orchard Rd PO Box 30	Gatlinburg	TN	37738	865-436-9211	430-7533
TF: 800-421-7275 ■ *Web:* www.parkvista.com					
Parkway Inn 125 N Jackson St PO Box 494	Jackson	WY	83001	307-733-3143	733-0955
TF: 800-247-8390 ■ *Web:* www.parkwayinn.com					
Parkway Plaza Hotel 123 W 'E' St	Casper	WY	82601	307-235-1777	235-8068
TF: 800-270-7829 ■ *Web:* www.parkwayplaza.net					
Partridge Inn 2110 Walton Way	Augusta	GA	30904	706-737-8888	731-0826
TF: 800-476-6888 ■ *Web:* www.partridgeinn.com					
Paso Robles Inn 1103 Spring St	Paso Robles	CA	93446	805-238-2660	238-4707
TF: 800-676-1713 ■ *Web:* www.pasoroblesinn.com					
Passport Inn 1726 Montreal Cir	Tucker	GA	30084	770-270-1180	270-1077
TF: 800-251-1962 ■ *Web:* www.bookroomsnow.com					
Peabody Hotel Group 5118 Park Ave Suite 245	Memphis	TN	38117	901-762-5400	762-5464
Web: www.peabodyhotelgroup.com					
Peabody Little Rock 3 Statehouse Plaza	Little Rock	AR	72201	501-906-4000	375-4721
TF: 800-527-1745 ■ *Web:* www.peabodylittlerock.com					
Peabody Memphis 149 Union Ave	Memphis	TN	38103	901-529-4000	529-3600
TF: 800-833-2548 ■ *Web:* www.peabodymemphis.com					
Peabody Orlando 9801 International Dr	Orlando	FL	32819	407-352-4000	351-9177
TF: 800-732-2639 ■ *Web:* www.peabodyorlando.com					
Peacock Suites Resort 1745 S Anaheim Blvd	Anaheim	CA	92805	714-535-8255	535-8914
TF: 800-522-6401 ■ *Web:* www.peacocksuitesresort.com					
Pear Tree Inns 721 Emerson Rd Suite 400	Saint Louis	MO	63141	314-429-2255	429-3679
Web: www.druryhotels.com					
Pearl Hotel The 1410 Rosecrans St	San Diego	CA	92106	619-226-6100	226-6161
TF: 877-732-7573 ■ *Web:* www.thepearlsd.com/					
Peery Hotel 110 W 300 South	Salt Lake City	UT	84101	801-521-4300	575-5014
TF: 800-331-0073 ■ *Web:* www.peeryhotel.com					
Pegasus International Hotel 501 Southard St	Key West	FL	33040	305-294-9323	294-4741
TF: 800-397-8148 ■ *Web:* www.pegasuskeywest.com					
Pelham Hotel 444 Common St	New Orleans	LA	70130	504-522-4444	539-9010
TF: 888-211-3447 ■ *Web:* www.thepelhamhotel.com					
Penguin Hotel 1418 Ocean Dr	Miami Beach	FL	33139	305-534-9334	604-0350
TF: 800-235-3296 ■ *Web:* www.penguinhotel.com					
Peninsula Beverly Hills 9882 S Santa Monica Blvd	Beverly Hills	CA	90212	310-551-2888	788-2319
TF: 800-462-7899 ■ *Web:* beverlyhills.peninsula.com					
Peninsula Chicago 108 E Superior St	Chicago	IL	60611	312-337-2888	751-2888
TF: 866-288-8889 ■ *Web:* chicago.peninsula.com					
Peninsula New York 700 5th Ave	New York	NY	10019	212-956-2888	903-3949
TF: 800-262-9467 ■ *Web:* newyork.peninsula.com					
Penn Tower Hotel 399 S 34th St	Philadelphia	PA	19104	215-387-8333	386-8306
Penn's View Hotel 14 N Front St	Philadelphia	PA	19106	215-922-7600	922-7642
TF: 800-331-7634 ■ *Web:* www.pennsviewhotel.com					
Peppermill Hotel & Casino 2707 S Virginia St	Reno	NV	89502	775-826-2121	826-5205
TF: 800-282-2444 ■ *Web:* www.peppermillreno.com					
Petite Auberge 863 Bush St	San Francisco	CA	94108	415-928-6000	673-7214
TF: 800-365-3004 ■ *Web:* www.jdvhotels.com/petite_auberge/					
Pfister Hotel 424 E Wisconsin Ave	Milwaukee	WI	53202	414-273-8222	273-5025
TF: 800-558-8222 ■ *Web:* www.pfisterhotel.com					
Phillips Beach Plaza Hotel 1301 Atlantic Ave	Ocean City	MD	21842	410-289-9121	289-3041
TF: 800-492-5834 ■ *Web:* www.phillipsbeachplaza.com					
Phoenix Grand Hotel Salem 201 Liberty St SE	Salem	OR	97301	503-540-7800	540-7830
TF: 877-540-7800 ■ *Web:* www.phoenixgrandhotel.com					
Phoenix Hotel 601 Eddy St	San Francisco	CA	94109	415-776-1380	885-3109
TF: 800-248-9466 ■ *Web:* www.jdvhotels.com/phoenix/					
Phoenix Park Hotel 520 North Capitol St NW	Washington	DC	20001	202-638-6900	393-3236
TF: 800-824-5419 ■ *Web:* www.phoenixparkhotel.com					
Piccadilly Inn Airport 5115 E McKinley Ave	Fresno	CA	93727	559-251-6000	251-6956
TF: 800-468-3587 ■ *Web:* www.piccadillyinn.com					
Piccadilly Inn Express 5113 E McKinley Ave	Fresno	CA	93727	559-456-1418	456-4643
TF: 800-445-2428 ■ *Web:* www.piccadillyinn.com/express.shtml					
Piccadilly Inn Shaw 2305 W Shaw Ave	Fresno	CA	93711	559-226-3850	226-2448
TF: 800-468-3587 ■ *Web:* www.piccadillyinn.com					
Piccadilly Inn University 4961 N Cedar St	Fresno	CA	93726	559-224-4200	227-2382
TF: 800-468-3587 ■ *Web:* www.piccadillyinn.com					
Pickwick Grand Heritage Hotel 85 5th St	San Francisco	CA	94103	415-421-7500	243-8066
TF: 800-227-3282 ■ *Web:* www.thepickwickhotel.com					
Pier 5 Hotel 711 Eastern Ave	Baltimore	MD	21202	410-539-2000	783-1469
TF: 866-583-4162 ■ *Web:* www.thepier5.com					
Pier Pointe Resort 4320 El Mar Dr	Lauderdale-by-the-Sea	FL	33308	954-776-5121	491-9084
TF: 800-331-6384 ■ *Web:* www.pier-pointe.com					
Pierpont Inn 550 Sanjon Rd	Ventura	CA	93001	805-643-6144	643-9167
TF: 800-285-4667 ■ *Web:* www.pierpontinn.com					
Pierre The 5th Ave at 61st St	New York	NY	10021	212-838-8000	940-8109
Web: www.tajhotels.com					
Pike Street Suites 1011 Pike St	Seattle	WA	98101	206-682-8282	682-5315
Web: www.pikestreetsuites.com					
Pillars Hotel at New River Sound 111 N Birch Rd	Fort Lauderdale	FL	33304	954-467-9639	763-2845
TF: 800-800-7666 ■ *Web:* www.pillarshotel.com					
Pine Crest Inn 85 Pine Crest Ln	Tryon	NC	28782	828-859-9135	859-9136
TF: 800-633-3001 ■ *Web:* www.pinecrestinn.com					
Pines Lodge 141 Scott Hill Rd	Avon	CO	81620	970-845-7900	845-7809
TF: 800-859-8242 ■ *Web:* pineslodge.rockresorts.com					
Pisgah Inn PO Box 749	Waynesville	NC	28786	828-235-8228	648-9719
Web: www.pisgahinn.com					
Pitcher Inn 275 Main St	Warren	VT	05674	802-496-6350	496-6354
TF: 888-867-4824 ■ *Web:* www.pitcherinn.com					
Place D'Armes Hotel 625 Saint Ann St	New Orleans	LA	70116	504-524-4531	571-2803
TF: 800-366-2743 ■ *Web:* www.placedarmes.com					
Place Louis Riel All-Suite Hotel 190 Smith St	Winnipeg	MB	R3C1J8	204-947-6961	947-3029
TF: 800-665-0569 ■ *Web:* www.placelouisriel.com					
Plains Hotel 1600 Central Ave	Cheyenne	WY	82001	307-638-3311	635-2022
TF: 866-275-2467 ■ *Web:* www.theplainshotel.com					
Plantation Inn of New England 295 Burnett Rd	Chicopee	MA	01020	413-592-8200	592-9671
TF: 800-248-8495 ■ *Web:* www.plantation-inn.com					
Planters Inn 29 Abercorn St	Savannah	GA	31401	912-232-5678	232-8893
TF: 800-554-1187 ■ *Web:* www.plantersinnsavannah.com					
Planters Inn 112 N Market St	Charleston	SC	29401	843-722-2345	577-2125
TF: 800-845-7082 ■ *Web:* www.plantersinn.com					
Platinum Hotel 211 E Flamingo Rd	Las Vegas	NV	89169	702-365-5000	365-5001
TF: 877-211-9111 ■ *Web:* www.theplatinumhotel.com/					
Plaza 500 Hotel 500 W 12th Ave	Vancouver	BC	V5Z1M2	604-873-1811	873-5103
TF: 800-473-1811 ■ *Web:* www.plaza500.com					
Plaza Hotel & Apartments 1007 N Cass St	Milwaukee	WI	53202	414-276-2101	276-0404
TF: 800-340-9590 ■ *Web:* www.shorelinerealestate.com/plaza					
Plaza Hotel & Casino 1 Main St	Las Vegas	NV	89101	702-386-2110	382-8281
TF: 800-634-6575 ■ *Web:* www.plazahotelcasino.com					
Plaza Inn 900 Medical Arts NE	Albuquerque	NM	87102	505-243-5693	843-6229
TF: 800-237-1307 ■ *Web:* www.plazainnabq.com					
Plaza on the River Resort Club Hotel 121 West St	Reno	NV	89501	775-786-2200	786-4861
TF: 800-628-5974					
Plaza Square Motor Lodge 2255 Central Blvd	Brownsville	TX	78520	956-546-5104	548-0243
Plaza Suite Hotel Resort 620 S Peters St	New Orleans	LA	70130	504-524-9500	524-2135
TF: 800-770-6721 ■ *Web:* www.plazaresort.com					
Plaza Suites Silicon Valley 3100 Lakeside Dr	Santa Clara	CA	95054	408-748-9800	748-1476
TF: 800-345-1554 ■ *Web:* www.theplazasuites.com					
Plim Plaza Hotel 2nd St & Boardwalk PO Box 160	Ocean City	MD	21843	410-289-6181	289-0714
TF: 800-837-3587 ■ *Web:* ocmdhotels.com/plimplaza					
Plump Jack's Squaw Valley Inn 1920 Squaw Valley Rd	Olympic Valley	CA	96146	530-583-1576	583-1734
TF: 800-323-7666 ■ *Web:* www.plumpjacksquawvalleyinn.com					
Point Plaza Suites & Conference Hotel					
950 J Clyde Morris Blvd	Newport News	VA	23601	757-599-4460	599-4336
TF: 800-841-1112 ■ *Web:* www.pointplazasuites.com					
Pollard The 2 N Broadway PO Box 650	Red Lodge	MT	59068	406-446-0001	446-0002
TF: 800-765-5273 ■ *Web:* www.thepollard.net					
Pontchartrain Hotel 2031 St Charles Ave	New Orleans	LA	70140	504-524-0581	529-1165
TF: 800-777-6193 ■ *Web:* www.pontchartrainhotel.com					
Port-O-Call Hotel 1510 Boardwalk	Ocean City	NJ	08226	609-399-8812	399-0387
TF: 800-334-4546 ■ *Web:* www.portocallhotel.com					
Portland Harbor Hotel 468 Fore St	Portland	ME	04101	207-775-9090	775-9990
TF: 888-798-9090 ■ *Web:* www.portlandharborhotel.com					
Portland Regency Hotel 20 Milk St	Portland	ME	04101	207-774-4200	775-2150
TF: 800-727-3436 ■ *Web:* www.theregency.com					
Portofino Hotel & Yacht Club 260 Portofino Way	Redondo Beach	CA	90277	310-379-8481	372-7329
TF: 800-468-4292 ■ *Web:* www.hotelportofino.com					
Portofino Inn & Suites Anaheim 1831 South Harbor Blvd	Anaheim	CA	92802	714-782-7600	782-7619
TF: 888-297-7143 ■ *Web:* www.portofinoinnanaheim.com					
Portola Plaza Hotel 2 Portola Plaza	Monterey	CA	93940	831-649-4511	372-0620
TF: 888-222-5851 ■ *Web:* www.portolaplazahotel.com					
Post Hotel 200 Pipestone Rd PO Box 69	Lake Louise	AB	T0L1E0	403-522-3989	522-3966
TF: 800-661-1586 ■ *Web:* www.posthotel.com					
Prairie Hotel 700 Prairie Park Ln PO Box 5210	Yelm	WA	98597	360-458-8300	458-8301
Web: www.prairiehotel.com					
Preferred Boutique 26 Corporate Plaza Suite 150	Newport Beach	CA	92660	949-719-3300	719-3301
Web: www.preferred-boutique.com					
Preferred Hotel Group 311 S Wacker Dr Suite 1900	Chicago	IL	60606	312-913-0400	913-5124
Web: www.preferredhotelgroup.com					
Preferred Boutique 26 Corporate Plaza Suite 150	Newport Beach	CA	92660	949-719-3300	719-3301
Web: www.preferred-boutique.com					
Preferred Hotels & Resorts Worldwide Inc					
311 S Wacker Dr Suite 1900	Chicago	IL	60606	312-913-0400	913-0444
TF: 800-323-7500 ■ *Web:* www.preferredhotels.com					
Sterling Hotels Corp 311 S Wacker Dr Suite 1900	Chicago	IL	60606	312-913-0400	913-5124
Web: www.sterlinghotels.com					
Summit Hotels & Resorts 311 S Wacker Dr Suite 1900	Chicago	IL	60606	312-913-0400	913-5124
TF: 800-457-4000 ■ *Web:* www.summithotels.com					
Preferred Hotels & Resorts Worldwide Inc					
311 S Wacker Dr Suite 1900	Chicago	IL	60606	312-913-0400	913-0444
TF: 800-323-7500 ■ *Web:* www.preferredhotels.com					

	City	State	Zip	Phone	Fax
Premier Hotel The 133 W 44th St	New York	NY	10036	212-789-7670	789-7673
TF: 800-622-5569					
Premier Suites 11601 W Markham Rd Suite D	Little Rock	AR	72211	501-221-7378	219-1920
TF: 800-735-2955 ■ *Web:* www.premiersuites.com					
Premiere Executive Suites 1479 Lower Water St Suite 190	Halifax	NS	B3J3Z4	902-420-1333	420-9600
TF: 866-844-1333 ■ *Web:* www.premieresuites.com					
Prescott Hotel 545 Post St	San Francisco	CA	94102	415-563-0303	563-6831
TF: 800-283-7322 ■ *Web:* www.prescotthotel.com					
President Abraham Lincoln Hotel & Conference Center 701 E Adams St	Springfield	IL	62701	217-544-8800	544-9607
TF: 866-208-9618 ■ *Web:* www.presidentabrahamlincolnhotel.com					
President Hotel 1423 Collins Ave	Miami Beach	FL	33139	305-538-2882	604-0350
TF: 800-235-3296 ■ *Web:* www.penguinhotel.com					
Priced Rite Suites 2327 University Ave	Green Bay	WI	54302	920-469-2130	
Web: www.pricedritesuites.com					
Prince Conti Hotel 830 Conti St	New Orleans	LA	70112	504-529-4172	636-1046
TF: 800-366-2743 ■ *Web:* www.princecontihotel.com					
Prince George Hotel 1725 Market St	Halifax	NS	B3J3N9	902-425-1986	429-6048
TF: 800-565-1567 ■ *Web:* www.princegeorgehotel.com					
Princess Bayside Beach Hotel & Golf Center 4801 Coastal Hwy	Ocean City	MD	21842	410-723-2900	723-0207
TF: 800-854-9785 ■ *Web:* www.princessbayside.com					
Princess Royale Oceanfront Hotel & Conference Center 9100 Coastal Hwy	Ocean City	MD	21842	410-524-7777	524-1623
TF: 800-476-9253 ■ *Web:* www.princessroyale.com					
Priory The 614 Pressley St	Pittsburgh	PA	15212	412-231-3338	231-4838
Web: www.thepriory.com					
Prospector Hotel 375 Whittier St	Juneau	AK	99801	907-586-3737	586-1204
TF: 800-331-2711 ■ *Web:* www.prospectorhotel.com					
Prospector Square Hotel & Conference Center 2200 Sidewinder Dr	Park City	UT	84060	435-649-7100	655-8377
Providence Biltmore Hotel Kennedy Plaza 11 Dorrance St	Providence	RI	02903	401-421-0700	455-3050
TF: 800-294-7709 ■ *Web:* www.providencebiltmore.com					
Publick House Historic Resort 295 Main St Rt 131	Sturbridge	MA	01566	508-347-3313	347-5073
TF: 800-782-5425 ■ *Web:* www.publickhouse.com					
Puffin Inn 4400 Spenard Rd	Anchorage	AK	99517	907-243-4044	248-6853
TF: 800-478-3346 ■ *Web:* www.puffininn.net					
Quail Run Lodge 1130 Bob Harman Rd	Savannah	GA	31408	912-964-1421	966-5646
TF: 800-627-7035 ■ *Web:* www.quailrunlodge.com					
Quality Inns Hotels & Suites 10750 Columbia Pike	Silver Spring	MD	20901	301-592-5000	592-6157
TF: 800-424-6423 ■ *Web:* www.qualityinn.com					
Quarterage Hotel 560 Westport Rd	Kansas City	MO	64111	816-931-0001	931-8891
TF: 800-942-4233 ■ *Web:* www.quarteragehotel.com					
Quarterpath Inn 620 York St	Williamsburg	VA	23185	757-220-0960	220-1530
TF: 800-446-9222 ■ *Web:* www.quarterpath.com					
Quebec Inn 7175 Hamel Blvd	Sainte-Foy	QC	G2G1B6	418-872-9831	872-1336
TF: 800-567-5276 ■ *Web:* www.hotelsjaro.com/					
Queen Anne Hotel 1590 Sutter St	San Francisco	CA	94109	415-441-2828	775-5212
TF: 800-227-3970 ■ *Web:* www.queenanne.com					
Queen & Crescent Hotel 344 Camp St	New Orleans	LA	70130	504-587-9700	587-9701
TF: 800-265-1856 ■ *Web:* www.queencrescenthotel.com/					
Queen Kapiolani Hotel 150 Kapahulu Ave	Honolulu	HI	96815	808-922-1941	922-2694
TF: 800-367-2317 ■ *Web:* www.queenkapiolani.com					
Quimby House Inn 109 Cottage St	Bar Harbor	ME	04609	207-288-5811	
TF: 800-344-5811 ■ *Web:* www.quimbyhouse.com					
Quincy Hotel 1823 L St NW	Washington	DC	20036	202-223-4320	293-4977
TF: 800-424-2970 ■ *Web:* www.thequincy.com					
Quorum Hotel Tampa 700 N Westshore Blvd	Tampa	FL	33609	813-289-8200	227-4466
TF: 877-478-6786 ■ *Web:* www.quorumtampa.com					
Quorum Hotels & Resorts 12770 Merit Dr Suite 700	Dallas	TX	75251	972-458-7265	991-5647
Web: www.quorumhotels.com					
Rabbit Hill Inn 48 Lower Waterford Rd	Lower Waterford	VT	05848	802-748-5168	748-8342
TF: 800-762-8669 ■ *Web:* www.rabbithillinn.com					
Radisson Butler Blvd 4700 Salisbury Rd	Jacksonville	FL	32256	904-281-9700	281-1957
TF: 888-201-1718 ■ *Web:* www.radisson.com					
Radisson Chicago-O'Hare Hotel 1450 E Touhy Ave	Des Plaines	IL	60018	847-296-8866	296-8268
TF: 888-201-1718 ■ *Web:* www.radisson.com					
Radisson Hotel Gateway Seattle-Tacoma Airport 18118 International Blvd S	Seattle	WA	98188	206-244-6666	244-6679
Web: www.radisson.com					
Radisson Hotels & Resorts PO Box 59159	Minneapolis	MN	55459	763-212-5526	212-3400
TF: 800-333-3333 ■ *Web:* www.radisson.com					
Radisson Milwaukee North Shore 7065 N Port Washington Rd	Milwaukee	WI	53217	414-351-6960	351-5194
Web: www.radisson.com					
Radnor Hotel 591 E Lancaster Ave	Saint Davids	PA	19087	610-688-5800	341-3299
TF: 800-537-3000 ■ *Web:* www.radnorhotel.com					
Raffaello Hotel 201 E Delaware Pl	Chicago	IL	60611	312-943-5000	924-9158
Web: www.chicagoraffaello.com					
Raffles L'Ermitage Beverly Hills 9291 Burton Way	Beverly Hills	CA	90210	310-278-3344	278-8247
TF: 800-800-2113 ■ *Web:* beverlyhills.raffles.com					
Railroad Pass Hotel & Casino 2800 S Boulder Hwy	Henderson	NV	89002	702-294-5000	294-0092
TF: 800-654-0877 ■ *Web:* www.railroadpass.com					
Ramada 1 Sylvan Way	Parsippany	NJ	07054	973-753-6600	
TF Resv: 800-272-6232 ■ *Web:* www.ramada.com					
Ramada Plaza & Conference Center 4900 Sinclair Rd	Columbus	OH	43229	614-846-0300	847-1022
TF: 800-272-6232 ■ *Web:* www.ramada.com					
Ranch Inn 45 E Pearl St	Jackson	WY	83001	307-733-6363	733-0623
TF: 800-348-5599 ■ *Web:* www.ranchinn.com					
Ranch at Steamboat 1800 Ranch Rd	Steamboat Springs	CO	80487	970-879-3000	879-5409
TF: 800-525-2002 ■ *Web:* www.ranch-steamboat.com					
Rancho Alegre Lodge 3600 S Park Loop Rd PO Box 998	Jackson	WY	83001	307-733-7988	734-0254
Web: www.ranchoalegre.com					
Rancho de San Juan PO Box 4140	Espanola	NM	87533	505-753-6818	753-6818
Web: www.ranchodesanjuan.com					
Raphael Kansas City 325 Ward Pkwy	Kansas City	MO	64112	816-756-3800	802-2131
TF: 800-821-5343 ■ *Web:* www.raphaelkc.com					
Red Carpet Inn 1726 Montreal Cir	Tucker	GA	30084	770-270-1180	270-1077
TF: 800-251-1962 ■ *Web:* www.bookroomsnow.com					
Red Jacket Beach Resort 1 S Shore Dr	South Yarmouth	MA	02664	508-398-6941	898-1214
TF: 800-227-3263 ■ *Web:* www.redjacketresorts.com					
Red Lion Hotels 201 W North River Dr Suite 100	Spokane	WA	99201	509-459-6100	325-7324
TF Resv: 800-733-5466 ■ *Web:* redlion.rdln.com					
Red Lion Hotels Corp 201 W North River Dr Suite 100	Spokane	WA	99201	509-459-6100	325-7324
NYSE: RLH ■ *TF Resv:* 800-325-4000 ■ *Web:* www.redlion.com					
Red Lion Hotels 201 W North River Dr Suite 100	Spokane	WA	99201	509-459-6100	325-7324
TF Resv: 800-733-5466 ■ *Web:* redlion.rdln.com					
WestCoast Hotel Partners					
Red Lion Hotel Corp 201 W North River Dr Suite 100	Spokane	WA	99201	509-459-6100	325-7324
TF: 800-325-4000 ■ *Web:* westcoast.rdln.com					
Red Lion Inn 30 Main St PO Box 954	Stockbridge	MA	01262	413-298-5545	298-5130
Web: www.redlioninn.com					
Red Rock Resort Spa & Casino 11011 W Charleston Blvd	Las Vegas	NV	89126	702-797-7777	797-7890
Web: www.redrocklasvegas.com					
Red Roof Inn 4001 International Pkwy	Carrollton	TX	75007	972-360-9000	360-2821
TF: 800-733-7663 ■ *Web:* www.redroof.com					
Redstone Inn 82 Redstone Blvd	Redstone	CO	81623	970-963-2526	963-2527
TF: 800-748-2524 ■ *Web:* www.redstoneinn.com/					
Redstone Inn & Suites 504 Bluff St	Dubuque	IA	52001	563-582-1894	
Web: www.theredstoneinn.com					
Regal Sun Resort at Walt Disney World Village 1850 Hotel Plaza Blvd	Lake Buena Vista	FL	32830	407-828-4444	828-8192
TF: 800-624-4109 ■ *Web:* www.regalsunresort.com					
Regency Fairbanks Hotel 95 10th Ave	Fairbanks	AK	99701	907-452-3200	452-6505
TF: 800-348-1340 ■ *Web:* www.regencyfairbankshotel.com					
Regency House Hotel 140 Rt 23 N	Pompton Plains	NJ	07444	973-696-0900	696-0201
TF: 800-696-0304 ■ *Web:* www.regencyhousehotel.com					
Regency Inn & Suites 3450 S Clack St	Abilene	TX	79606	325-695-7700	698-0546
TF: 800-676-7262					
Regency Suites Calgary 610 4th Ave SW	Calgary	AB	T2P0K1	403-231-1000	231-1012
TF: 800-468-4044 ■ *Web:* www.regencycalgary.com					
Regency Suites Green Bay 333 Main St	Green Bay	WI	54301	920-432-4555	432-0700
TF: 800-236-3330 ■ *Web:* www.regencygb.com					
Regency Suites Hotel Midtown Atlanta 975 W Peachtree St	Atlanta	GA	30309	404-876-5003	817-7511
TF: 800-642-3629 ■ *Web:* www.regencysuites.com					
Regent International Hotels PO Box 59159	Minneapolis	MN	55459	763-212-3300	212-8197
Web: www.regenthotels.com					
Remington Hotel Corp 14185 Dallas Pkwy Suite 1150	Dallas	TX	75254	972-980-2700	392-1929
Web: www.remingtonhospitalityservices.com					
Remington Suite Hotel 220 Travis St	Shreveport	LA	71101	318-425-5000	425-5011
TF: 800-444-6750 ■ *Web:* www.remingtonsuite.com					
Renaissance Hotels & Resorts 1 Marriott Dr	Washington	DC	20058	301-380-3000	380-4055
Web: marriott.com/renaissancehotels					
Reneson Hotel Group 121 7th St	San Francisco	CA	94103	415-626-0200	863-2529
TF: 800-444-5816 ■ *Web:* www.renesonhotels.com					
Rennaissance Syracuse 701 E Genesee St	Syracuse	NY	13210	315-479-7000	472-2700
TF: 800-468-3571					
Residence & Conference Centre - Toronto 1760 Finch Ave E	Toronto	ON	M2J5G3	416-491-8811	491-0486
TF: 877-225-8664 ■ *Web:* www.residenceconferencecentre.com/toronto					
Residence Inn by Marriott 1 Marriott Dr	Washington	DC	20058	301-380-3000	380-5197
TF: 800-638-8108 ■ *Web:* www.marriott.com/residenceinn					
Residences on Georgia 101-1288 W Georgia St	Vancouver	BC	V6E4R3	604-891-6101	891-6151
Web: www.respal.com					
ResidenSea 5200 Blue Lagoon Dr Suite 790	Miami	FL	33139	305-264-9090	269-1058
TF: 800-970-6601 ■ *Web:* www.residensea.com					
Resort at Port Ludlow 1 Heron Rd	Port Ludlow	WA	98365	360-437-7000	437-7410
TF: 877-805-0868 ■ *Web:* www.portludlowresort.com/					
ResortQuest Hawaii 2155 Kalakaua Ave Suite 500	Honolulu	HI	96815	808-931-1400	931-1565*
**Fax:* Hum Res ■ *TF:* 866-774-2924 ■ *Web:* www.resortquesthawaii.com					
ResortQuest Waikiki Circle Hotel 2464 Kalakaua Ave	Honolulu	HI	96815	808-923-1571	926-8024
TF: 866-774-2924 ■ *Web:* www.resortquesthawaii.com					
Resorts East Chicago 777 Resorts Blvd	East Chicago	IN	46312	219-378-3000	378-3498*
**Fax:* Hum Res ■ *TF:* 877-496-1777 ■ *Web:* www.resortseastchicago.com					
Resorts Tunica 1100 Casino Strip Blvd PO Box 750	Robinsonville	MS	38664	662-363-7777	357-2300
TF Resv: 866-797-7111 ■ *Web:* www.resorttunica.com					
Rhett House Inn 1009 Craven St	Beaufort	SC	29902	843-524-9030	524-1310
TF: 888-480-9530 ■ *Web:* www.rhetthouseinn.com					
Richardson Hotel 701 E Campbell Rd	Richardson	TX	75081	972-231-9600	907-2578
Web: www.therichardsonhotel.com					
Richfield Hospitality Services 7600 E Orchard Rd Suite 230-S	Greenwood Village	CO	80111	303-220-2000	220-2120
Web: www.richfield.com					
Richmond The 1757 Collins Ave	Miami Beach	FL	33139	305-538-2331	531-9021
TF: 800-327-3163 ■ *Web:* www.richmondhotel.com					
Richmond Hill Inn 87 Richmond Hill Dr	Asheville	NC	28806	828-252-7313	252-8726
TF: 888-742-4554 ■ *Web:* www.richmondhillinn.com					
Ridpath Hotel 515 W Sprague Ave	Spokane	WA	99201	509-838-2711	747-6970
TF: 800-325-4000 ■ *Web:* www.theridpathhotel.com					
Rittenhouse Hotel 210 W Rittenhouse Sq	Philadelphia	PA	19103	215-546-9000	732-3364
TF: 800-635-1042 ■ *Web:* www.rittenhousehotel.com					
Ritz-Carlton Dallas 2121 McKinney Ave	Dallas	TX	75201	214-922-0200	720-7575
TF: 800-960-7082 ■ *Web:* www.ritzcarlton.com					
Ritz-Carlton Hotel Co LLC 4445 Willard Ave Suite 800	Chevy Chase	MD	20815	301-547-4700	547-4740
TF: 800-241-3333 ■ *Web:* www.ritzcarlton.com					
Ritz Milner Hotel 813 S Flower St	Los Angeles	CA	90017	213-627-6981	623-9751
TF: 800-827-0411 ■ *Web:* www.milner-hotels.com/la.html					
Riu Hotel Florida Beach 3101 Collins Ave	Miami	FL	33140	305-673-5333	673-9335
TF: 888-666-8816 ■ *Web:* www.riu.com					
River Inn 924 25th St NW	Washington	DC	20037	202-337-7600	337-6520
TF: 800-424-2741 ■ *Web:* www.theriverinn.com					
River Street Inn 115 E River St	Savannah	GA	31401	912-234-6400	234-1478
TF: 800-253-4229 ■ *Web:* www.riverstreetinn.com					
Riveredge Resort Hotel 17 Holland St	Alexandria Bay	NY	13607	315-482-9917	482-5010
TF: 800-365-6987 ■ *Web:* www.riveredge.com					
RiverPlace Hotel 1510 SW Harbor Way	Portland	OR	97201	503-228-3233	295-6161
TF: 800-227-1333 ■ *Web:* www.riverplacehotel.com					
River's Edge Resort Cottages 4200 Boat St	Fairbanks	AK	99709	907-474-0286	474-3665
TF: 800-770-3343 ■ *Web:* www.riversedge.net					
Riverside Hotel 620 E Las Olas Blvd	Fort Lauderdale	FL	33301	954-467-0671	462-2148
TF: 800-325-3280 ■ *Web:* www.riversidehotel.com					
Riverside Inn 1 Fountain Ave	Cambridge Springs	PA	16403	814-398-4645	398-8161
TF: 800-964-5173 ■ *Web:* www.theriversideinn.com					
Riverstone Billings Inn 880 N 29th St	Billings	MT	59101	406-252-6800	252-6800
TF: 800-231-7782 ■ *Web:* www.billingsinn.com					
Riverview Plaza Hotel 64 S Water St	Mobile	AL	36602	251-438-4000	415-0123
TF: 800-444-2326 ■ *Web:* www.riverviewmobile.com					
Riviera Holdings Corp 2901 Las Vegas Blvd S	Las Vegas	NV	89109	702-734-5110	
AMEX: RIV ■ *TF:* 800-634-3420 ■ *Web:* www.rivierahotel.com					
Riviera Hotel 1431 Robson St	Vancouver	BC	V6G1C1	604-685-1301	685-1335
TF: 888-699-5222 ■ *Web:* www.rivieraonrobson.com					
Road King Inn Columbia Mall 3300 30th Ave S	Grand Forks	ND	58201	701-746-1391	746-8586
TF: 800-707-1391 ■ *Web:* www.roadkinginn.com					
Robert Johnson House 58 State Cir	Annapolis	MD	21401	410-263-2641	268-3613
TF: 800-847-8882 ■ *Web:* www.annapolisinns.com/robert-johnson-house.php					
Robert Treat Hotel 50 Park Pl	Newark	NJ	07102	973-622-1000	622-6410
TF: 800-569-2300 ■ *Web:* www.rthotel.com					
Roberts Mayfair The - A Wyndham Historic Hotel 806 Saint Charles St	Saint Louis	MO	63101	314-421-2500	421-6254
TF: 800-996-3426 ■ *Web:* www.wyndham.com/hotels/STLMF/main.wnt					
Rock View Resort 1049 Parkview Dr	Hollister	MO	65672	417-334-4678	334-1808
TF: 800-375-9530 ■ *Web:* www.rockviewresort.com					
Rocklin Park Hotel 5450 China Garden Rd	Rocklin	CA	95677	916-630-9400	630-9448
TF: 888-630-9400 ■ *Web:* www.rocklinpark.com					
Rodeway Inn & Suites 3033 Hilton Dr	Bossier City	LA	71111	318-747-2400	747-6822
TF: 800-424-6423 ■ *Web:* www.rodewayinn.com/					
Rodeway Inns 10750 Columbia Pike	Silver Spring	MD	20901	301-592-5000	592-6157
TF: 800-424-6423 ■ *Web:* www.rodeway.com					
Roger Sherman Inn 195 Oenoke Ridge	New Canaan	CT	06840	203-966-4541	966-0503
Web: www.rogershermaninn.com					
Roger Smith Hotel 501 Lexington Ave	New York	NY	10017	212-755-1400	758-4061
TF: 800-445-0277 ■ *Web:* www.rogersmith.com					
Roosevelt Hotel 45 E 45th St	New York	NY	10017	212-661-9600	885-6161
TF: 888-833-3969 ■ *Web:* www.theroosevelthotel.com					

Phone | Fax

Rose Hotel 807 Main St Pleasanton CA 94566 925-846-8802 846-2272
TF: 800-843-9540 ■ *Web:* www.rosehotel.net
Rosedale on Robson Suite Hotel 838 Hamilton St. Vancouver BC V6B6A2 604-689-8033 689-4426
TF: 800-661-8870 ■ *Web:* www.rosedaleonrobson.com
Rosellen Suites at Stanley Park 2030 Barclay St Vancouver BC V6G1L5 604-689-4807 684-3327
TF: 888-317-6648 ■ *Web:* www.rosellensuites.com
Rosen Centre Hotel 9840 International Dr Orlando FL 32819 407-996-9840 996-0865
TF: 800-204-7234 ■ *Web:* www.rosencentre.com
Rosen Hotels & Resorts Inc 9840 International Dr Orlando FL 32819 407-996-9840 996-0865
TF: 800-204-7234 ■ *Web:* www.rosenhotels.com
Rosen Plaza Hotel 9700 International Dr Orlando FL 32819 407-996-9700 354-5774
TF: 800-366-9700 ■ *Web:* www.rosenplaza.com
Rosen Shingle Creek 9939 Universal Blvd Orlando FL 32819 407-996-9939 996-9938
TF: 866-996-9939 ■ *Web:* www.rosenshinglecreek.com
Rosewood Hotels & Resorts 500 Crescent Ct Suite 300 Dallas TX 75201 214-880-4200 880-4201
TF: 888-767-3966 ■ *Web:* www.rosewoodhotels.com
Roslyn Claremont Hotel 1221 Old Northern Blvd Roslyn NY 11576 516-625-2700 625-2731
TF: 800-626-9005 ■ *Web:* www.roslynclaremonthotel.com
Rough Creek Lodge 5165 County Rd 2013 Glen Rose TX 76043 254-965-3700 918-2570
TF Resv: 800-864-4705 ■ *Web:* www.roughcreek.com
Royal Coachman Inn 5805 Pacific Hwy E Tacoma WA 98424 253-922-2500 922-6443
TF: 800-422-3051
Royal Garden at Waikiki Hotel 440 Olohana St Honolulu HI 96815 808-943-0202 946-8777
TF: 800-367-5666 ■ *Web:* www.royalgardens.com
Royal Holiday Beach Resort 1980 Beach Blvd Biloxi MS 39531 228-388-7553 388-8959
TF: 800-874-0402 ■ *Web:* www.condosinc.com
Royal Hotel South Beach 763 Pennsylvania Ave Miami Beach FL 33139 305-673-9009 673-9244
TF: 888-394-6835 ■ *Web:* www.royalhotelsouthbeach.com
Royal Palm Resort Hotel 1545 Collins Ave. Miami Beach FL 33139 786-276-0100
Web: www.royalpalmmiamibeach.com
Royal Plaza Hotel 425 E Main Rd. Middletown RI 02842 401-846-3555 846-3666
TF: 800-825-7072 ■ *Web:* www.royalplazahotel.net
Royal Regency Hotel 165 Tuckahoe Rd Yonkers NY 10710 914-476-6200 375-7017
TF: 800-215-3858 ■ *Web:* www.royalregencyhotelny.com
Royal Sonesta Hotel Boston 40 Edwin H Land Blvd Cambridge MA 02142 617-806-4200 806-4232
TF: 800-766-3782 ■ *Web:* www.sonesta.com/boston/
Royal Sonesta Hotel New Orleans 300 Bourbon St New Orleans LA 70130 504-586-0300 586-0335
TF: 800-766-3782 ■ *Web:* www.sonesta.com/neworleans_royal/
Royal Suite Lodge 3811 Minnesota Dr Anchorage AK 99503 907-563-3114 563-4296
TF: 800-282-3114
Royal Sun Inn 1700 S Palm Canyon Dr Palm Springs CA 92264 760-327-1564 323-9092
TF: 800-619-4786 ■ *Web:* www.royalsuninn.com
Royal Towers Hotel & Casino 140 6th St. New Westminster BC V3M1J4 604-524-3777 524-6673
TF: 800-663-0202 ■ *Web:* www.royaltowers.com
Royalton Hotel 44 W 44th St New York NY 10036 212-869-4400 869-8965
TF: 800-606-6090 ■ *Web:* www.royaltonhotel.com
Roycroft Inn 40 S Grove St East Aurora NY 14052 716-652-5552 655-5345
TF: 888-652-5552 ■ *Web:* www.roycroftinn.com
Rushmore View Inn 610 Hwy 16A Keystone SD 57751 605-666-4466 666-4425
TF: 800-888-2603 ■ *Web:* www.rushmoreviewinn.com
Saddleridge 44 Meadows Ln Beaver Creek CO 81620 970-845-5450 845-5459
TF: 800-859-8242 ■ *Web:* www.vbcrp.com
Sage Hospitality Resources LLC 1512 Larimer St Suite 800 Denver CO 80202 303-595-7200 595-7219
Web: www.sagehospitality.com
Sailport Resort 2506 Rocky Point Dr Tampa FL 33607 813-281-9599 281-9510
TF: 800-255-9599 ■ *Web:* www.sailportresort.com
Saint Ann/Marie Antoinette Hotel 717 Conti St New Orleans LA 70130 504-525-2300 524-8925
Web: www.stannmarieantoinette.com
Saint Anthony The - A Wyndham Historic Hotel
300 E Travis St San Antonio TX 78205 210-227-4392 227-0915
TF: 800-996-3426 ■ *Web:* www.wyndham.com/hotels/SATST/main.wnt
Saint Clair Inn 500 N Riverside Ave Saint Clair MI 48079 810-329-2222 329-7664
TF: 800-482-8327 ■ *Web:* www.stclairinn.com
Saint Gregory Luxury Hotel & Suites 2033 M Street NW Washington DC 20036 202-530-3600 466-6770
TF: 800-829-5034 ■ *Web:* capitalhotelswdc.com/StGregoryHotelWDC_com
Saint James Hotel 330 Magazine St New Orleans LA 70130 504-304-4000 304-4444
TF: 800-273-1889 ■ *Web:* www.saintjameshotel.com
Saint James Hotel 406 Main St Red Wing MN 55066 651-388-2846 388-5226
TF: 800-252-1875 ■ *Web:* www.st-james-hotel.com
Saint Julien Hotel & Spa 900 Walnut St Boulder CO 80302 720-406-9696 406-9668
TF: 877-303-0900 ■ *Web:* www.stjulien.com
Saint Louis Hotel 730 Bienville St New Orleans LA 70130 504-581-7300 679-5013
TF: 800-535-9111 ■ *Web:* www.stlouishotel.com
Saint Michaels Harbour Inn & Marina 101 N Harbor Rd Saint Michaels MD 21663 410-745-9001 745-9150
TF: 800-955-9001 ■ *Web:* www.harbourinn.com
Saint Paul Hotel 350 Market St Saint Paul MN 55102 651-292-9292 228-9506
TF: 800-292-9292 ■ *Web:* www.saintpaulhotel.com/
Saint Regis Hotel 602 Dunsmuir St Vancouver BC V6B1Y6 604-681-1135 683-1126
TF: 800-770-7929 ■ *Web:* www.stregishotel.com
Saint Regis Hotel Winnipeg 285 Smith St Winnipeg MB R3C1K9 204-942-0171 943-3077
TF: 800-663-7344 ■ *Web:* www.stregishotel.net
Saint Regis Hotels & Resorts 1111 Westchester Ave White Plains NY 10604 914-640-8100 640-8310
Web: www.starwood.com/stregis
Saint Tropez Hotel 455 E Harmon Ave Las Vegas NV 89109 702-369-5400 369-8901
TF: 800-666-5400 ■ *Web:* www.sttropezlasvegas.com
Sainte Claire The 302 S Market St San Jose CA 95113 408-295-2000 977-0403
TF: 866-870-0726 ■ *Web:* www.thesainteclaire.com
Salisbury Hotel 123 W 57th St New York NY 10019 212-246-1300 977-7752
TF: 888-692-5757 ■ *Web:* www.nycsalisbury.com
Sam's Town Hotel & Casino Shreveport
315 Clyde Fant Pkwy Shreveport LA 71101 318-424-7777 424-5658
TF: 877-429-0711 ■ *Web:* www.samstownshreveport.com
Sam's Town Hotel & Gambling Hall 5111 Boulder Hwy Las Vegas NV 89122 702-456-7777 454-8107
TF: 800-634-6371 ■ *Web:* www.samstownlv.com
San Carlos Hotel 150 E 50th St New York NY 10022 212-755-1800 688-9778
TF: 800-722-2012 ■ *Web:* www.sancarloshotel.com
San Joaquin Hotel 1309 W Shaw Ave Fresno CA 93711 559-225-1309 225-6021
TF: 800-775-1309 ■ *Web:* www.sjhotel.com
Sand Dollar Inn 755 Abrego St Monterey CA 93940 831-372-7551 372-0916
TF: 800-982-1986 ■ *Web:* www.sanddollarinn.com
Sandalwood Hotel & Suites 5050 Orbitor Dr Mississauga ON L4W4X2 905-238-9600 238-8502
TF: 800-387-3355 ■ *Web:* www.sandalwoodhotel.com
Sandman Hotels Inns & Suites 1755 W Broadway Suite 310 Vancouver BC V6J4S5 604-730-6600 730-4645
Web: www.sandmanhotels.com
Sands Beach Club All-Suite Resort Hotel 9400 Shore Dr Myrtle Beach SC 29572 843-449-1531 449-4021
TF: 800-845-6999 ■ *Web:* www.sandsresorts.com
Sands Central Inn 1525 Central Ave Hot Springs AR 71901 501-624-1258 624-2800
Sands Ocean Club Resort 9550 Shore Dr. Myrtle Beach SC 29572 843-449-6461 449-1837
TF: 800-845-6701 ■ *Web:* www.sandsresorts.com/resorts/oceanclub
Sands Regency Casino Hotel 345 N Arlington Ave Reno NV 89501 775-348-2200 348-2226
TF Resv: 800-648-3553 ■ *Web:* www.sandsregency.com
Sandwich Lodge & Resort 54 Rte 6A - Old King's Hwy Sandwich MA 02563 508-888-2275 888-8102
TF: 800-282-5353 ■ *Web:* www.sandwichlodge.com
Sandy Point Inn 6485 Twin Lakes Rd Boulder CO 80301 303-530-2939 530-9101
TF: 800-322-2939 ■ *Web:* www.sandypointinn.com
Sanibel Inn 937 E Gulf Dr Sanibel FL 33957 239-472-3181 472-5234
TF: 866-565-5480 ■ *Web:* www.sanibelcollection.com

Phone | Fax

Santa Barbara Inn 901 E Cabrillo Blvd Santa Barbara CA 93103 805-966-2285 966-6584
TF: 800-231-0431 ■ *Web:* www.santabarbarainn.com
Santa Maria Inn 801 S Broadway Santa Maria CA 93454 805-928-7777 928-5690
TF: 800-462-4276 ■ *Web:* www.santamariainn.com
Saratoga Hotel & Conference Center 534 Broadway Saratoga Springs NY 12866 518-584-4000 584-7430
TF: 866-773-7070 ■ *Web:* www.thesaratogahotel.com
Satellite Hotel 411 Lakewood Cir Colorado Springs CO 80910 719-596-6800 570-4499
TF: 800-423-8409
Saunders Hotel Group Ltd 240 Newbury St Boston MA 02116 617-425-0900 425-0901
Web: www.saundershotelgroup.net
Savoy Hotel 580 Geary St San Francisco CA 94102 415-441-2700 441-0124
TF: 800-227-4223 ■ *Web:* www.thesavoyhotel.com
Savoy on South Beach 425 Ocean Dr Miami Beach FL 33139 305-532-0200 534-7436
TF: 800-237-2869 ■ *Web:* www.savoymiami.com
Savoy Suites Georgetown 2505 Wisconsin Ave NW Washington DC 20007 202-337-9700 337-3644
TF: 800-944-5377 ■ *Web:* www.savoysuites.com
Scotsman Inn West 5922 W Kellogg St Wichita KS 67209 316-943-3800 943-3800
TF: 800-950-7268 ■ *Web:* www.scotsmaninn.com
Scottish Inns 1726 Montreal Cir Tucker GA 30084 770-270-1180 270-1077
TF: 800-251-1962 ■ *Web:* www.bookroomsnow.com
Sea Chambers Motel 67 Shore Rd Ogunquit ME 03907 207-646-9311 646-0938
Web: www.seachambers.com
Sea Gull Motel on the Beach 2613 Atlantic Ave Virginia Beach VA 23451 757-425-5711 425-5710
TF: 800-426-4855 ■ *Web:* www.seagullmotel.com
Sea Ranch Lodge 60 Sea Walk Dr The Sea Ranch CA 95497 707-785-2371 785-2917
TF: 800-732-7262 ■ *Web:* www.searanchlodge.com
Sea Turtle Inn 1 Ocean Blvd Atlantic Beach FL 32233 904-249-7402 247-1517
TF: 800-874-6000 ■ *Web:* www.seaturtle.com
Sea View Hotel 9909 Collins Ave Bal Harbour FL 33154 305-866-4441 866-1898
TF: 800-447-1010 ■ *Web:* www.seaview-hotel.com
Seacoast Inn 800 Seacoast Dr Imperial Beach CA 91932 619-424-5183 424-3090
TF: 800-732-2627 ■ *Web:* seacoast-inn-imperial-beach.pacificahost.com/
Seacoast Suites Hotel 5101 Collins Ave. Miami Beach FL 33140 305-865-5152 868-4090
TF: 800-969-6329 ■ *Web:* www.seacoastsuites.com
Seafarer of Chatham 2079 Main St Chatham MA 02633 508-432-1739 432-8969
TF: 800-786-2772
SeaGlass Tower 1400 N Ocean Blvd Myrtle Beach SC 29577 843-448-1441 626-6261
TF: 800-868-8886
Seaport Hotel & World Trade Center 1 Seaport Ln Boston MA 02210 617-385-4000 385-4001
TF: 877-732-7678 ■ *Web:* www.seaportboston.com
Seaport Marina Hotel 6400 E Pacific Coast Hwy Long Beach CA 90803 562-434-8451 598-6028
Web: www.seaportmarinahotel.com
Seascape Resort Monterey Bay 1 Seascape Resort Dr Aptos CA 95003 831-688-6800 685-0615
TF: 866-589-3411 ■ *Web:* www.seascaperesort.com
Seaside Inn 541 E Gulf Dr. Sanibel Island FL 33957 239-472-1400
TF: 866-565-5092 ■ *Web:* www.sanibelcollection.com
Seelbach Hilton Louisville 500 S 4th St Louisville KY 40202 502-585-3200 585-9239
TF: 800-333-3399 ■ *Web:* www.seelbachhilton.com
Select Franchising Inc Select Inn 1025 38th St SW Suite B Fargo ND 58103 701-282-6305 282-6308
Web: www.selectinn.com
Select Inn 1025 38th St SW Suite B Fargo ND 58103 701-282-6305 282-6308
Web: www.selectinn.com
Senate Luxury Suites 900 SW Tyler St. Topeka KS 66612 785-233-5050 233-1614
TF: 800-488-3188 ■ *Web:* www.senatesuites.com/
Seneca Hotel & Suites 200 E Chestnut St Chicago IL 60611 312-787-8900 988-4438
TF: 800-800-6261 ■ *Web:* www.senecahotel.com
Serene Hotel & Suites 12004 Coastal Hwy Ocean City MD 21842 410-250-4000 250-9014
TF: 800-542-4444 ■ *Web:* www.serenehotel.com
Serrano Hotel 405 Taylor St San Francisco CA 94102 415-885-2500 474-4879
TF: 877-294-9709 ■ *Web:* www.serranohotel.com
Setai The 2001 Collins Ave Miami Beach FL 33139 305-520-6000 520-6600
TF: 888-625-7500 ■ *Web:* www.setai.com
Settle Inn Airport 2620 S Packerland Dr Green Bay WI 54313 920-499-1900 499-1973
TF: 800-688-9052 ■ *Web:* www.settle-inn.com
Settle Inn Resort & Conference Center
3050 Green Mountain Dr Branson MO 65616 417-335-4700 335-3906
TF: 800-677-6906 ■ *Web:* www.bransonsettleinn.com
Seven Gables Inn 26 N Meramec Ave. Saint Louis MO 63105 314-863-8400 863-8846
TF: 800-433-6590 ■ *Web:* www.sevengablesinn.com
Shades of Green on Walt Disney World Resort
1950 W Magnolia Palm Dr. Lake Buena Vista FL 32830 407-824-3600 824-3665
TF: 888-593-2242 ■ *Web:* www.shadesofgreen.org
Shaner Hotel Group 1965 Waddle Rd State College PA 16803 814-234-4460 278-7295
Web: www.shanerhotels.com
Shawmut Inn 280 Friend St Boston MA 02114 617-720-5544 723-7784
Web: www.shawmutinn.com
Shelborne Beach Resort 1801 Collins Ave Miami Beach FL 33139 305-531-1271 531-2206
TF: 800-327-8757 ■ *Web:* www.shelborne.com
Shelburne Murray Hill 303 Lexington Ave New York NY 10016 212-689-5200 779-7068
TF: 866-233-4642 ■ *Web:* www.affinia.com
Shephard's Beach Resort 619 S Gulfview Blvd Clearwater Beach FL 33767 727-442-5107 446-4238
TF: 800-237-8477 ■ *Web:* www.shephards.com
Sheraton Colonial Hotel & Golf Club Boston North
1 Audubon Rd Wakefield MA 01880 781-245-9300 245-0842
Web: www.starwood.com/sheraton
Sheraton Delfina Santa Monica 530 W Pico Blvd Santa Monica CA 90405 310-399-9344 399-2504
TF: 888-627-8532 ■ *Web:* www.sheratonsantamonica.com/
Sheraton Detroit Riverside 2 Washington Blvd Detroit MI 48226 313-965-0200 262-5415
TF: 866-837-4212 ■ *Web:* www.starwoodhotels.com/sheraton/
Sheraton Gateway Hotel Los Angeles
6101 W Century Blvd Los Angeles CA 90045 310-642-1111 410-1267
TF: 800-325-3535 ■ *Web:* www.sheratonlosangeles.com/
Sheraton Hotels & Resorts 1111 Westchester Ave White Plains NY 10604 914-640-8100 640-8310
TF: 800-325-3535 ■ *Web:* www.starwood.com/sheraton
Sheridan Pond Executive Suites 8130 S Lakewood Pl Tulsa OK 74137 918-481-6598 492-6644
Web: www.sheridanpond.com
Sherry-Netherland Hotel 781 5th Ave New York NY 10022 212-355-2800 319-4306
TF: 877-743-7710 ■ *Web:* www.sherrynetherland.com
Shilo Inn Hotel Salt Lake City 206 S West Temple Salt Lake City UT 84101 801-521-9500 359-6527
TF: 800-222-2244 ■ *Web:* www.shiloinns.com
Shilo Inn Hotel Spokane 923 E 3rd Ave Spokane WA 99202 509-535-9000 535-5740
TF: 800-222-2244 ■ *Web:* www.shiloinns.com
Shilo Inn Suites Hotel Portland Airport
117707 NE Airport Way Portland OR 97220 503-252-7500 254-0794
TF: 800-222-2244 ■ *Web:* www.shiloinns.com
Shilo Inn Suites Salem 3304 Market St Salem OR 97303 503-581-4001 399-9385
TF: 800-222-2244 ■ *Web:* www.shiloinns.com
Shilo Inns Suites Hotels 11600 SW Shilo Ln Portland OR 97225 503-641-6565 644-0868*
**Fax:* Mktg ■ *TF:* 800-222-2244 ■ *Web:* www.shiloinns.com
Shore Club 1901 Collins Ave Miami FL 33139 305-695-3100 695-3299
Web: www.shoreclub.com
Shoreham Hotel 33 W 55th St New York NY 10019 212-247-6700 765-9741
TF: 800-553-3347 ■ *Web:* www.shorehamhotel.com
Shores Resort & Spa The 2637 S Atlantic Ave Daytona Beach Shores FL 32118 386-767-7350 760-3651
TF: 866-934-7467 ■ *Web:* www.shoresresort.com
Shutters on the Beach 1 Pico Blvd Santa Monica CA 90405 310-458-0030 458-4589
TF: 800-334-9000 ■ *Web:* www.shuttersonthebeach.com

Phone Fax

Siena Hotel 1505 E Franklin St Chapel Hill NC 27514 919-929-4000 968-8527
TF: 800-223-7379 ■ *Web:* sienahotel.com/

Sierra Suites 8100 E 22nd St Bldg 500 Wichita KS 67226 316-681-5100 681-0994
TF Resv: 888-695-7608 ■ *Web:* www.sierrasuites.com

Signature Inns 4770 S Atlanta Rd Smyrna GA 30080 404-350-9990 601-6106
Web: www.signatureinns.com

Silver Cloud Hotel Seattle Broadway 1100 Broadway Seattle WA 98122 206-325-1400 324-1995
TF: 800-590-1801 ■ *Web:* www.silvercloud.com

Silver Cloud Inn Seattle-Lake Union 1150 Fairview Ave N Seattle WA 98109 206-447-9500 812-4900
TF: 800-330-5812 ■ *Web:* www.scinns.com/lake.htm

Silver Cloud Inn University District 5036 25th Ave NE Seattle WA 98105 206-526-5200 522-1450
TF: 800-205-6940 ■ *Web:* www.silvercloud.com

Silver King Hotel 1485 Empire Ave Park City UT 84060 435-649-5500 649-6647
TF: 800-331-8652 ■ *Web:* www.silverkinghotel.com

Silver Smith Hotel & Suites 10 S Wabash Ave Chicago IL 60603 312-372-7696 372-7320
Web: www.silversmithhotel.com

Silverdale Beach Hotel 3073 NW Bucklin Hill Rd Silverdale WA 98383 360-698-1000 692-0932
TF: 800-544-9799 ■ *Web:* www.silverdalebeachhotel.com

Silverton Hotel & Casino 3333 Blue Diamond Rd Las Vegas NV 89139 702-263-7777 263-7002
TF: 800-588-7711 ■ *Web:* www.silvertoncasino.com

Silvertree Hotel 100 Elbert Ln Snowmass Village CO 81615 970-923-3520 923-5192
TF: 800-525-9402 ■ *Web:* www.silvertreehotel.com

Simonton Court Historic Inn & Cottages 320 Simonton St Key West FL 33040 305-294-6386 293-8446
TF: 800-944-2687 ■ *Web:* www.simontoncourt.com

Sir Francis Drake Hotel 450 Powell St San Francisco CA 94102 415-392-7755 391-8719
TF: 800-227-5480 ■ *Web:* www.sirfrancisdrake.com

Sise Inn 40 Court St Portsmouth NH 03801 603-433-1200 431-0200
TF: 877-747-3466 ■ *Web:* www.siseinn.com

Sixth Avenue Inn 2000 6th Ave Seattle WA 98121 206-441-8300 441-9903
TF: 800-648-6440 ■ *Web:* www.sixthaveinn.com

Sky Hotel 709 E Durant Ave Aspen CO 81611 970-925-6760 925-6778
TF: 800-882-2582 ■ *Web:* www.theskyhotel.com

Skyline Hotel 725 10th Ave New York NY 10019 212-586-3400 582-4604
TF: 800-433-1982 ■ *Web:* www.skylinehotelny.com

Sleep Inns 10750 Columbia Pike Silver Spring MD 20901 301-592-5000 592-6157
TF: 800-424-6423 ■ *Web:* www.sleepinn.com

Smoky Shadows Motel & Conference Center
4215 Parkway Pigeon Forge TN 37863 865-453-7155 453-0308
TF: 800-282-2121 ■ *Web:* www.smokyshadows.com

Snell House 21 Atlantic Ave Bar Harbor ME 04609 207-288-8004
TF: 866-763-5524 ■ *Web:* www.snellhouse.com

Snowbird Mountain Lodge 4633 Santeetlah Rd Robbinsville NC 28771 828-479-3433 479-3473
TF: 800-941-9290 ■ *Web:* www.snowbirdlodge.com

Snowy Owl Inn 4 Village Rd Waterville Valley NH 03215 603-236-8383 236-4890
TF: 800-766-9969 ■ *Web:* www.snowyowlinn.com

Sofia Hotel 132 W Broadway San Diego CA 92101 619-234-9200 544-9879
TF: 800-826-0009 ■ *Web:* www.thesofiahotel.com

Sofitel 4001 International Pkwy Carrollton TX 75007 972-360-9000 360-2821
Web: www.sofitel.com

SoHo Grand Hotel 310 W Broadway New York NY 10013 212-965-3000 965-3200
TF: 800-965-3000 ■ *Web:* www.sohogrand.com

SoHo Metropolitan Hotel 318 Wellington St W Toronto ON M5V3T4 416-599-8800 599-8801
TF: 866-764-6638 ■ *Web:* www.metropolitan.com/soho/

Somerset Hills Hotel 200 Liberty Corner Rd Warren NJ 07059 908-647-6700 647-8053
TF: 800-688-0700 ■ *Web:* www.shh.com

Somerset Inn 2601 W Big Beaver Rd Troy MI 48084 248-643-7800 643-2296
TF: 800-228-8769 ■ *Web:* www.somersetinn.com

Sonesta Hotel & Suites Coconut Grove
2889 McFarlane Rd Coconut Grove FL 33133 305-529-2828 529-2008
TF: 800-766-3782 ■ *Web:* www.sonesta.com/coconut_grove

Sonesta International Hotels Corp 116 Huntington Ave 9th Fl Boston MA 02116 617-421-5400 421-5402
NASDAQ: SNSTA ■ *TF:* 800-766-3782 ■ *Web:* www.sonesta.com

Song of the Sea 863 E Gulf Dr Sanibel Island FL 33957 239-472-2220
TF: 866-565-5101 ■ *Web:* www.sanibelcollection.com

Soniat House 1133 Chartres St New Orleans LA 70116 504-522-0570 522-7208
TF: 800-544-8808 ■ *Web:* www.soniathouse.com

Sophie Station Hotel 1717 University Ave Fairbanks AK 99709 907-479-3650 479-7951
TF: 800-528-4916 ■ *Web:* www.fountainheadhotels.com

Sorrento Hotel 900 Madison St Seattle WA 98104 206-622-6400 343-6155
TF: 800-426-1265 ■ *Web:* www.hotelsorrento.com

South Beach Marina Inn & Vacation Rentals
232 South Sea Pines Dr Hilton Head Island SC 29928 843-671-6498 671-7495
TF: 800-367-3909 ■ *Web:* www.sbinn.com

South Coast Hotel & Casino 9777 Las Vegas Blvd S Las Vegas NV 89123 702-796-7111 797-8041
TF: 866-796-7111 ■ *Web:* www.coastcasinos.com

South Pier Inn on the Canal 701 Lake Ave S Duluth MN 55802 218-786-9007 786-9015
TF: 800-430-7437 ■ *Web:* www.southpierinn.com

South Seas Hotel 1751 Collins Ave Miami Beach FL 33139 305-538-1411 532-9477
TF: 800-345-2678 ■ *Web:* www.southseashotel.com

Southampton Inn 91 Hill St Southampton NY 11968 631-283-6500 283-6559
TF: 800-832-6500 ■ *Web:* www.southamptoninn.com

Southernmost On the Beach 508 South St Key West FL 33040 305-296-5611 294-2108
TF: 800-354-4455 ■ *Web:* www.southernmostresorts.com

Southernmost Hotel 1319 Duval St Key West FL 33040 305-296-6577 294-8272
TF: 888-782-9722 ■ *Web:* www.southernmostresorts.com

Southfork Hotel 1600 N Central Expy Plano TX 75074 972-578-8555 578-2772
TF: 866-665-2680 ■ *Web:* www.southforkhotel.com

Southway Inn 2431 Bank St Ottawa ON K1V8R9 613-737-0811 737-3207
TF: 877-688-4929 ■ *Web:* www.southway.com

Spindrift Inn 652 Cannery Row Monterey CA 93940 831-646-8900 646-5342
TF: 800-841-1879 ■ *Web:* www.spindriftinn.com

Spring Creek Ranch 1800 Spirit Dance Rd Jackson WY 83001 307-733-8833 733-1964
TF: 800-443-6139 ■ *Web:* www.springcreekranch.com

SpringHill Suites by Marriott 1 Marriott Dr Washington DC 20058 301-380-3000 380-3090
TF: 800-228-9290 ■ *Web:* www.marriott.com/springhill

Springs Inn 2020 Harrodsburg Rd Lexington KY 40503 859-277-5751 277-3142
TF: 800-354-9503 ■ *Web:* www.springsinn.com

Stamford Suites 720 Bedford St Stamford CT 06901 203-359-7300 359-7304
TF: 866-394-4365 ■ *Web:* www.stamfordsuites.com

Stanford Court - A Renaissance Hotel 905 California St San Francisco CA 94108 415-989-3500 391-0513
TF: 800-227-4736 ■ *Web:* www.renaissancehotel.com/sfosc

Stanley Hotel 333 Wonderview Ave Estes Park CO 80517 970-586-3371 586-4964
TF: 800-976-1377 ■ *Web:* www.stanleyhotel.com

Stanyan Park Hotel 750 Stanyan St San Francisco CA 94117 415-751-1000 668-5454
Web: www.stanyanpark.com

Star Island Resort 5000 Avenue of the Stars Kissimmee FL 34746 407-997-8000 997-5252
TF: 800-513-2820 ■ *Web:* www.star-island.com

Starwood Hotels & Resorts Worldwide Inc
1111 Westchester Ave White Plains NY 10604 914-640-8100 640-8310
NYSE: HOT ■ *TF Cust Svc:* 877-443-4585 ■ *Web:* www.starwoodhotels.com

Four Points by Sheraton 1111 Westchester Ave White Plains NY 10604 914-640-8100 640-8310
TF Cust Svc: 877-443-4585 ■ *Web:* www.starwood.com/fourpoints

Le Meridien 1111 Westchester Ave White Plains NY 10604 914-640-8100 640-8310
TF: 888-625-5144 ■ *Web:* www.starwoodhotels.com/lemeridien

Luxury Collection 1111 Westchester Ave White Plains NY 10604 914-640-8100 640-8310
TF Cust Svc: 877-443-4585 ■ *Web:* www.starwood.com/luxury

Saint Regis Hotels & Resorts 1111 Westchester Ave White Plains NY 10604 914-640-8100 640-8310
Web: www.starwood.com/stregis

Sheraton Hotels & Resorts 1111 Westchester Ave White Plains NY 10604 914-640-8100 640-8310
TF: 800-325-3535 ■ *Web:* www.starwood.com/sheraton

W Hotels 1111 Westchester Ave White Plains NY 10604 914-640-8100 640-8310
TF: 877-443-4585 ■ *Web:* www.starwood.com/whotels/index.html

Westin Hotels & Resorts 1111 Westchester Ave White Plains NY 10604 914-640-8100 640-8310
TF: 877-443-4585 ■ *Web:* www.starwood.com/westin

State Plaza Hotel 2117 'E' St NW Washington DC 20037 202-861-8200 659-8601
TF: 800-424-2859 ■ *Web:* www.stateplaza.com

Staten Island Hotel 1415 Richmond Ave Staten Island NY 10314 718-698-5000 354-7071
TF: 800-532-3532 ■ *Web:* www.statenislandhotel.com

Staybridge Suites 3 Ravinia Dr Suite 100 Atlanta GA 30346 770-604-2000 604-5403
TF: 800-465-4329 ■ *Web:* www.staybridge.com

Sterling Hotel 1300 H St Sacramento CA 95814 916-448-1300 448-8066
TF: 800-365-7660 ■ *Web:* www.sterlinghotel.com

Sterling Hotels Corp 311 S Wacker Dr Suite 1900 Chicago IL 60606 312-913-0400 913-5124
Web: www.sterlinghotels.com

Stillwell Hotel 838 S Grand Ave Los Angeles CA 90017 213-627-1151 622-8940
TF: 800-553-4774 ■ *Web:* www.stillwell-la.com

Stockton Grand Hotel 2323 Grand Canal Blvd Stockton CA 95207 209-957-9090 473-0739
Web: stockton-grand-hotel.pacificahost.com/

Stockyards Hotel 109 E Exchange Ave Fort Worth TX 76106 817-625-6427 624-2571
TF: 800-423-8471 ■ *Web:* www.stockyardshotel.com

Stonebridge Inn 300 Carriage Way PO Box 5008 Snowmass Village CO 81615 970-923-2420 923-5889
TF: 800-922-7242 ■ *Web:* www.stonebridgeinn.com

Stonehedge Inn 160 Pawtucket Blvd Tyngsboro MA 01879 978-649-4400 649-9256
TF: 800-648-7070 ■ *Web:* www.stonehedgeinnandspa.com

Stoneleigh Hotel 2927 Maple Ave Dallas TX 75201 214-871-7111 871-9379
TF: 800-255-9299 ■ *Web:* www.stoneleighhotel.com

Stonewall Jackson Hotel & Conference Center
24 S Market St Staunton VA 24401 540-885-4848 885-4840
Web: www.stonewalljacksonhotel.com/

Stoney Creek Inn 101 Mariner's Way East Peoria IL 61611 309-694-1300 694-9303
TF: 800-659-2220 ■ *Web:* www.stoneycreekinn.com

Strater Hotel 699 Main Ave Durango CO 81301 970-247-4431 259-2208
TF: 800-247-4431 ■ *Web:* www.strater.com

Stratford Hotel 242 Powell St San Francisco CA 94102 415-397-7080 397-7087
TF: 888-504-6835 ■ *Web:* www.hotelstratford.com

Strathallan Hotel 550 East Ave Rochester NY 14607 585-461-5010 461-2503
TF: 800-678-7284 ■ *Web:* www.strathallan.com

Strathcona Hotel 919 Douglas St Victoria BC V8W2C2 250-383-7137 383-6893
Web: www.strathconahotel.com

Strathcona Hotel 60 York St Toronto ON M5J1S8 416-363-3321 363-4679
TF: 800-268-8304 ■ *Web:* www.thestrathconahotel.com

Stratosphere Tower Hotel & Casino 2000 S Las Vegas Blvd Las Vegas NV 89104 702-380-7777 383-4755*
**Fax:* Sales ■ *TF:* 800-998-6937 ■ *Web:* www.stratospherehotel.com

Studio 6 4001 International Pkwy Carrollton TX 75007 972-360-9000 360-2821
TF: 800-466-8356 ■ *Web:* www.staystudio6.com

StudioPLUS Deluxe Studios 100 Dunbar St Spartanburg SC 29306 864-573-1600 573-1695
TF: 888-788-3467 ■ *Web:* www.studioplus.com

Sturbridge Host Hotel & Conference Center 366 Main St Sturbridge MA 01566 508-347-7393 347-3944
TF: 800-582-3232 ■ *Web:* www.sturbridgehosthotel.com

Suburban Extended Stay Hotel 10750 Columbia Pike Silver Spring MD 20901 301-592-5000 592-6157
TF Resv: 877-424-6423 ■ *Web:* www.suburbanhotels.com

Sugar Magnolia 804 Edgewood Ave NE Atlanta GA 30307 404-222-0226 681-1067
Web: www.sugarmagnoliabb.com

Suites at Fisherman's Wharf 2655 Hyde St San Francisco CA 94109 415-771-0200 346-8058
TF: 800-227-3608 ■ *Web:* www.suitesatfishermanswharf.com

Suites Hotel in Canal Park The 325 Lake Ave S Duluth MN 55802 218-727-4663 722-0572
TF: 877-766-2665 ■ *Web:* www.thesuitesduluth.com

Summit Hotels & Resorts 311 S Wacker Dr Suite 1900 Chicago IL 60606 312-913-0400 913-5124
TF: 800-457-4000 ■ *Web:* www.summithotels.com

Summit Lodge & Spa 4359 Main St Whistler BC V0N1B4 604-932-2778 932-2716
TF: 888-913-8811 ■ *Web:* www.summitlodge.com

Sun Suites Extended Stay Hotels 4770 S Atlanta Rd Suite 200 Smyrna GA 30080 404-350-9990 350-8660
Web: www.sunsuites.com

Sun Viking Lodge 2411 S Atlantic Ave Daytona Beach Shores FL 32118 386-252-6252 252-5463
TF: 800-874-4469 ■ *Web:* www.sunviking.com

Sunburst Hospitality Corp 10770 Columbia Pike Silver Spring MD 20901 301-592-3800 592-3830
Web: www.sunbursthospitality.com

Suncoast Hotel & Casino 9090 Alta Dr Las Vegas NV 89145 702-636-7111 636-7288
TF: 877-677-7111 ■ *Web:* www.suncoastcasino.com

Sundial Boutique Hotel 4340 Sundial Crescent Whistler BC V0N1B4 604-932-2321 935-0554
TF: 800-661-2321 ■ *Web:* www.sundialhotel.com/

Sunrise Suites Resort 3685 Seaside Dr Key West FL 33040 305-296-6661 296-6968
TF: 888-723-5200 ■ *Web:* www.sunrisekeywest.com

Sunset Inn Travel Apartments 1111 Burnaby St Vancouver BC V6E1P4 604-688-2474 669-3340
TF: 800-786-1997 ■ *Web:* www.sunsetinn.com

Sunset Marquis Hotel & Villas 1200 N Alta Loma Rd West Hollywood CA 90069 310-657-1333 652-5300
TF: 800-858-9758 ■ *Web:* www.sunsetmarquishotel.com

Sunset Station Hotel & Casino 1301 W Sunset Rd Henderson NV 89014 702-547-7777 547-7744
TF: 888-786-7389 ■ *Web:* www.sunsetstation.com

Sunset Tower Hotel 8358 Sunset Blvd West Hollywood CA 90069 323-654-7100 654-9287
TF: 800-225-2637 ■ *Web:* www.sunsettowerhotel.com

Super 8 1 Sylvan Way Parsippany NJ 07054 973-753-6600
TF Resv: 800-800-8000 ■ *Web:* www.super8.com

Surf & Sand Resort 1555 South Coast Hwy Laguna Beach CA 92651 949-497-4477 494-2897
TF: 888-869-7569 ■ *Web:* www.surfandsandresort.com

Surfsand Resort 148 W Gower Rd Cannon Beach OR 97110 503-436-2274 436-9116
TF: 800-547-6100 ■ *Web:* www.surfsand.com

Surfside Inn 1211 Atlantic Ave Virginia Beach VA 23451 757-428-1183 428-2243
TF: 800-437-2497 ■ *Web:* www.virginiabeachsurfside.com

Surftides Beach Resort 2945 NW Jetty Ave Lincoln City OR 97367 541-994-2191 994-2727
TF: 800-452-2159 ■ *Web:* www.surftidesbeachresort.com

Surrey Hotel 20 E 76th St New York NY 10021 212-288-3700 628-1549
TF: 866-233-4642 ■ *Web:* www.affinia.com

Sutton Place Hotel Chicago 21 E Bellevue Pl Chicago IL 60611 312-266-2100 266-2103
TF: 800-606-8188 ■ *Web:* www.suttonplace.com/Chicago

Sutton Place Hotel Edmonton 10235 101st St Edmonton AB T5J3E9 780-428-7111 441-3098
TF: 800-263-9030 ■ *Web:* www.edmonton.suttonplace.com

Sutton Place Hotel Toronto 955 Bay St Toronto ON M5S2A2 416-924-9221 924-1778
TF: 800-268-3790 ■ *Web:* www.toronto.suttonplace.com

Sutton Place Hotel Vancouver 845 Burrard St Vancouver BC V6Z2K6 604-682-5511 642-2928
TF: 800-961-7555 ■ *Web:* www.vancouver.suttonplace.com

Swag The 2300 Swag Rd Waynesville NC 28785 828-926-0430 926-2036
TF: 800-789-7672 ■ *Web:* www.theswag.com

Sweden House 4605 E State St Rockford IL 61108 815-398-4130 398-9203
TF: 800-886-4138 ■ *Web:* www.swedenhouselodge.com

Taj Boston 15 Arlington St Boston MA 02116 617-536-5700 536-1335
TF: 877-482-5267 ■ *Web:* www.tajhotels.com

Talbott Hotel 20 E Delaware Pl Chicago IL 60611 312-944-4970 944-7241
TF: 800-825-2688 ■ *Web:* www.talbotthotel.com

Tarsadia Hotels 620 Newport Center Dr 14th Fl Newport Beach CA 92660 949-610-8000 610-8001
Web: www.tarsadia.com

Tazewell Hotel & Suites 245 Granby St Norfolk VA 23510 757-623-6200 457-1516
Web: www.thetazewell.com

				Phone	Fax
Terminal City Tower Hotel 837 W Hastings St *TF:* 888-253-8777 ■ *Web:* www.tctowerhotel.com	Vancouver	BC	V6C1B6	604-681-4121	488-8604
Teton Mountain Lodge 3385 W Village Dr *TF:* 800-801-6615 ■ *Web:* www.tetonlodge.com	Teton Village	WY	83025	307-734-7111	734-7999
Tharaldson Lodging Co 1202 Westrac Dr *Web:* www.tharaldson.com	Fargo	ND	58103	701-235-1060	232-6487
Thayer Hotel 674 Thayer Rd *TF:* 800-247-5047 ■ *Web:* www.thethayerhotel.com	West Point	NY	10996	845-446-4731	446-0338
The Tower Beverly Hills 1224 S Beverwil Dr *TF:* 800-421-3212 ■ *Web:* www.thetowerbeverlyhills.com	Los Angeles	CA	90035	310-277-2800	277-5470
Tickle Pink Inn at Carmel Highlands 155 Highland Dr *TF:* 800-635-4774 ■ *Web:* www.ticklepinkinn.com	Carmel	CA	93923	831-624-1244	626-9516
Tides The 1220 Ocean Dr *TF:* 866-438-4337 ■ *Web:* www.tidessouthbeach.com	Miami Beach	FL	33139	305-604-5070	503-3275
Tidewater Inn & Conference Center 101 E Dover St *TF:* 800-237-8775 ■ *Web:* www.tidewaterinn.com	Easton	MD	21601	410-822-1300	820-8847
Timbers Hotel The 4411 Peoria St *TF:* 800-844-9404 ■ *Web:* www.timbersdenver.com/	Denver	CO	80239	303-373-1444	373-1975
Time The 224 W 49th St *TF:* 877-846-3692 ■ *Web:* www.thetimeny.com	New York	NY	10019	212-246-5252	245-2305
Times Hotel & Suites 6515 Wilfrid-Hamel Blvd *Web:* timeshotel.ca	L'Ancienne-Lorette	QC	G2E5W3	418-877-7788	877-3333
Tivoli Lodge 386 Hanson Ranch Rd *TF:* 800-451-4756 ■ *Web:* www.tivolilodge.com	Vail	CO	81657	970-476-5615	476-6601
Topaz Hotel 1733 'N' St NW *TF:* 800-424-2950 ■ *Web:* www.topazhotel.com	Washington	DC	20036	202-393-3000	785-9581
TOWER23 Hotel 4551 Ocean Blvd *TF:* 866-869-3723 ■ *Web:* www.tower23hotel.com	San Diego	CA	92109	858-270-2323	274-2333
Town & Country Inn & Conference Center 2008 Savannah Hwy *TF:* 800-334-6660	Charleston	SC	29407	843-571-1000	766-9444
Town & Country Motor Inn Rt 2 PO Box 220 *TF:* 800-325-4386 ■ *Web:* www.townandcountryinn.com	Gorham	NH	03581	603-466-3315	466-3315
Town Inn Suites 620 Church St *TF:* 800-387-2755 ■ *Web:* www.towninn.com	Toronto	ON	M4Y2G2	416-964-3311	924-9466
TownePlace Suites by Marriott 1 Marriott Dr *Web:* marriott.com/towneplace	Washington	DC	20058	301-380-3000	380-3090
TownHouse Inn 1411 10th Ave S *TF:* 800-442-4667	Great Falls	MT	59405	406-761-4600	761-7603
Townsend Hotel 100 Townsend St *TF:* 800-548-4172 ■ *Web:* www.townsendhotel.com	Birmingham	MI	48009	248-642-7900	645-9061
Townsend Manor Inn 714 Main St *Web:* www.townsendmanorinn.com	Greenport	NY	11944	631-477-2000	
Tradewinds Carmel Mission St at 3rd Ave *TF:* 800-624-6665 ■ *Web:* www.tradewindscarmel.com	Carmel-by-the-Sea	CA	93921	831-624-2776	624-0634
TradeWinds Sandpiper Hotel & Suites 6000 Gulf Blvd *TF:* 800-237-0707 ■ *Web:* sandpiper.tradewindsresort.com	Saint Pete Beach	FL	33706	727-360-5551	363-2367
Travelodge 1 Sylvan Way *TF Resv:* 800-578-7878 ■ *Web:* www.travelodge.com	Parsippany	NJ	07054	973-753-6600	
Travelodge Virginia Beach 1909 Atlantic Ave *TF:* 800-578-7878 ■ *Web:* www.travelodge.com	Virginia Beach	VA	23451	757-425-0650	425-8898
Traymore Hotel 2445 Collins Ave *TF:* 800-445-1512 ■ *Web:* www.traymorehotel.com	Miami Beach	FL	33140	305-534-7111	538-2632
Treat Robert Hotel 50 Park Pl *TF:* 800-569-2300 ■ *Web:* www.rthotel.com	Newark	NJ	07102	973-622-1000	622-6410
Tremont Chicago 100 E Chestnut St *TF:* 800-621-8133 ■ *Web:* www.tremontchicago.com	Chicago	IL	60611	312-751-1900	751-8691
Tremont House - A Wyndham Historic Hotel 2300 Ship Mechanic Row *Web:* www.wyndham.com/hotels/GLSTH/main.wnt	Galveston	TX	77550	409-763-0300	763-1539
Tremont Park Hotel Baltimore 8 E Pleasant St *TF:* 800-873-6668 ■ *Web:* www.1800tremont.com	Baltimore	MD	21202	410-576-1200	244-1154
Tremont Plaza Hotel Baltimore 222 Saint Paul Pl *TF:* 800-873-6668 ■ *Web:* www.tremontsuitehotels.com	Baltimore	MD	21202	410-727-2222	685-4216
Trianon Old Naples 955 7th Ave S *TF:* 877-482-5228 ■ *Web:* www.trianon.com	Naples	FL	34102	239-435-9600	261-0025
Tribeca Grand Hotel 2 Avenue of the Americas *TF:* 800-965-3000 ■ *Web:* www.tribecagrand.com	New York	NY	10013	212-519-6600	519-6700
Trigild Inc 12707 High Bluff Dr Suite 300 *Web:* www.trigild.com	San Diego	CA	92130	858-720-6700	720-6707
Tropical Winds Oceanfront Hotel 1398 N Atlantic Ave *TF:* 800-245-6099	Daytona Beach	FL	32118	386-258-1016	255-6462
Tropicana Inn & Suites 1540 S Harbor Blvd *TF:* 800-828-4898 ■ *Web:* www.bei-hotels.com	Anaheim	CA	92802	714-635-4082	635-1535
Truman Hotel & Conference Center 1510 Jefferson St *TF:* 800-272-6232 ■ *Web:* www.trumanjeffersoncity.com	Jefferson City	MO	65109	573-635-7171	635-8006
Trump International Hotel & Tower 1 Central Park W *TF:* 888-448-7867 ■ *Web:* www.trumpintl.com	New York	NY	10023	212-299-1000	299-1150
Trump Marina Hotel & Casino Huron Ave & Brigantine Blvd *TF Resv:* 800-777-8477 ■ *Web:* www.trumpmarina.com	Atlantic City	NJ	08401	609-441-2000	345-7604
Trump Plaza Hotel & Casino 2225 Boardwalk *TF:* 800-677-7378 ■ *Web:* www.trumpplaza.com	Atlantic City	NJ	08401	609-441-6000	441-7881
Tudor Hotel & Suites 1111 Collins Ave *TF:* 800-843-2934 ■ *Web:* www.hoteltudor.com	Miami Beach	FL	33139	305-534-2934	534-1874
Tugboat Inn 80 Commercial St PO Box 267 *TF:* 800-248-2628 ■ *Web:* www.tugboatinn.com	Boothbay Harbor	ME	04538	207-633-4434	633-5892
Tuscany Suites & Casino 255 E Flamingo Rd *TF Resv:* 877-887-2261 ■ *Web:* www.sunsetstation.com	Las Vegas	NV	89109	702-893-8933	947-5994
TWELVE Atlantic Station 361 17th St *Web:* www.twelvehotels.com	Atlanta	GA	30363	404-961-1212	961-1221
TWELVE Centennial Park 400 W Peachtree St *Web:* www.twelvehotels.com	Atlanta	GA	30308	404-418-1212	418-1221
Twin Farms Stage Rd PO box 115 *TF:* 800-894-6327 ■ *Web:* www.twinfarms.com	Barnard	VT	05031	802-234-9999	234-9990
Twin Palms Hotel 225 E Apache Blvd *TF:* 800-367-0835 ■ *Web:* www.twinpalmshotel.com	Tempe	AZ	85281	480-967-9431	968-1877
Umstead Hotel & Spa 100 Woodland Pond *TF:* 866-877-4141 ■ *Web:* www.theumstead.com	Cary	NC	27513	919-447-4000	447-4100
Union Station - A Wyndham Historic Hotel 1001 Broadway St *TF:* 800-996-3426 ■ *Web:* www.wyndham.com/hotels/BNAUS/main.wnt	Nashville	TN	37203	615-726-1001	248-3554
University Inn Seattle 4140 Roosevelt Way NE *TF:* 800-733-3855 ■ *Web:* www.universityinnseattle.com	Seattle	WA	98105	206-632-5055	547-4937
University Place 310 SW Lincoln St *Web:* www.aux.pdx.edu/cegs/upl/	Portland	OR	97201	503-221-0140	226-6260
University Plaza Hotel & Conference Center 3110 Olentangy River Rd *TF:* 877-677-5292 ■ *Web:* www.universityplazaosu.com	Columbus	OH	43202	614-267-7461	263-5299
University Plaza Hotel & Convention Center 333 John Q Hammons Pkwy *TF:* 800-465-4329 ■ *Web:* www.upspringfield.com	Springfield	MO	65806	417-864-7333	831-5893
US Franchise Systems Inc 13 Corporate Sq Suite 250 *Fax: Mktg ■ *TF:* 888-225-5151 ■ *Web:* www.usfsi.com	Atlanta	GA	30329	404-321-4045	235-7465*
US Franchise Systems Inc 13 Corporate Sq Suite 250 *TF:* 888-225-5151 ■ *Web:* www.usfsi.com	Atlanta	GA	30329	404-321-4045	235-7465
Hawthorn Suites 13 Corporate Sq Suite 250 *TF:* 800-527-1133 ■ *Web:* www.hawthorn.com	Atlanta	GA	30329	404-321-4045	321-4482
Microtel Inns & Suites 13 Corporate Sq Suite 250 *TF:* 888-222-2142 ■ *Web:* www.microtelinn.com	Atlanta	GA	30329	404-321-4045	321-4482
US Grant The 326 Broadway *TF:* 800-237-5029 ■ *Web:* www.usgrant.net	San Diego	CA	92101	619-232-3121	232-3626
US Suites Portland 10220 SW Nimbus St *TF:* 800-877-8483 ■ *Web:* www.ussuites.com/portland.htm	Portland	OR	97223	503-443-2033	620-8593
Vacation Village Hotel 647 S Coast Hwy *TF:* 800-843-6895 ■ *Web:* www.vacationvillage.com	Laguna Beach	CA	92651	949-494-8566	494-1386
Vagabond Inns Inc 5933 W Century Blvd Suite 200 *TF:* 800-522-1555 ■ *Web:* www.vagabondinns.com	Los Angeles	CA	90045	310-410-5700	410-5777
Valhalla Inn Toronto 1 Valhalla Inn Rd *TF:* 800-268-2500 ■ *Web:* www.valhalla-inn.com	Toronto	ON	M9B1S9	416-239-2391	239-8764
Valley Park Hotel 2404 Stevens Creek Blvd *TF:* 800-954-6835 ■ *Web:* www.pacifichotels.com/valley/index.html	San Jose	CA	95128	408-293-5000	293-5287
Valley River Inn 1000 Valley River Way *TF:* 800-543-8266 ■ *Web:* www.valleyriverinn.com	Eugene	OR	97401	541-743-1000	683-5121
Vanderbilt Hall Hotel 41 Mary St *TF:* 888-826-4255 ■ *Web:* www.vanderbilthall.com	Newport	RI	02840	401-846-6200	847-7689
Varscona Hotel 8208 106th St *TF:* 888-515-3355 ■ *Web:* www.varscona.com	Edmonton	AB	T6E6R9	780-434-6111	439-1195
Velvet Cloak Inn 1505 Hillsborough St *TF:* 800-334-4372 ■ *Web:* www.velvetcloakinn.com	Raleigh	NC	27605	919-828-0333	828-2656
Vernon Manor Hotel 400 Oak St *TF:* 800-543-3999 ■ *Web:* www.vernonmanorhotel.com	Cincinnati	OH	45219	513-281-3300	281-8933
Viceroy Palm Springs 415 S Belardo Rd *TF:* 800-237-3687 ■ *Web:* www.viceroypalmsprings.com	Palm Springs	CA	92262	760-320-4117	323-3303
Viceroy Santa Monica 1819 Ocean Ave *TF:* 800-670-6185 ■ *Web:* www.viceroysantamonica.com	Santa Monica	CA	90401	310-260-7500	260-7515
Victoria Inn Winnipeg 1808 Wellington Ave *TF:* 877-842-4667 ■ *Web:* www.vicinn.com	Winnipeg	MB	R3H0G3	204-786-4801	786-1329
Victoria Regent Hotel 1234 Wharf St *TF:* 800-663-7472 ■ *Web:* www.victoriaregent.com	Victoria	BC	V8W3H9	250-386-2211	386-2622
Victorian Condo-Hotel & Conference Center 6300 Seawall Blvd *TF:* 800-231-6363 ■ *Web:* www.galveston.com/victorian	Galveston	TX	77551	409-740-3555	741-1676
Victorian Inn 487 Foam St *TF:* 800-232-4141 ■ *Web:* www.victorianinn.com/	Monterey	CA	93940	831-373-8000	373-4815
Villa Florence Hotel 225 Powell St *TF:* 800-553-4411 ■ *Web:* www.villaflorence.com	San Francisco	CA	94102	415-397-7700	397-1006
Villa Royale Inn 1620 Indian Trail *TF:* 800-245-2314 ■ *Web:* www.villaroyale.com	Palm Springs	CA	92264	760-327-2314	322-3794
Village Latch Inn 101 Hill St PO Box 3000 *Web:* www.villagelatch.com	Southampton	NY	11968	631-283-2160	283-3236
Village Suites at Ashland Hills 2525 Ashland St *TF:* 800-547-4747 ■ *Web:* www.windmillinns.com	Ashland	OR	97520	541-482-8310	488-1783
Villagio Inn & Spa 6481 Washington St *TF:* 800-351-1133 ■ *Web:* www.villagio.com	Yountville	CA	94599	707-944-8877	944-8855
Villamare 27-C Coligny Plaza *TF:* 800-854-6802	Hilton Head Island	SC	29928	843-842-6212	785-2147
Villas on the Bay 105 Marine St *Web:* www.thevillas.com	Saint Augustine	FL	32084	904-826-0575	
Villas de Santa Fe 400 Griffin St *TF:* 800-869-6790 ■ *Web:* www.villasdesantafe.com	Santa Fe	NM	87501	505-988-3000	988-4700
Vintage Inn Napa Valley 6541 Washington St *TF:* 800-351-1133 ■ *Web:* www.vintageinn.com	Yountville	CA	94599	707-944-1112	944-1617
Vintners Inn 4350 Barnes Rd *TF:* 800-421-2584 ■ *Web:* www.vintnersinn.com/	Santa Rosa	CA	95403	707-575-7350	575-1426
Virginian Lodge 750 W Broadway PO Box 1052 *TF:* 800-262-4999 ■ *Web:* www.virginianlodge.com	Jackson Hole	WY	83001	307-733-2792	733-9513
Virginian Suites 1500 Arlington Blvd *TF:* 800-275-2866 ■ *Web:* www.virginiansuites.com	Arlington	VA	22209	703-522-9600	525-4462
Viscount Gort Hotel 1670 Portage Ave *TF:* 800-665-1122 ■ *Web:* www.viscount-gort.com	Winnipeg	MB	R3J0C9	204-775-0451	772-2161
Viscount Suite Hotel 4855 E Broadway Blvd *TF:* 800-527-9666 ■ *Web:* www.viscountsuite.com	Tucson	AZ	85711	520-745-6500	790-5114
Vista Host Inc 10370 Richmond Ave Suite 150 *TF:* 800-688-4782 ■ *Web:* www.vistahost.com	Houston	TX	77042	713-267-5800	267-5820
Voyager Hotel 510 K St *TF:* 800-247-9070 ■ *Web:* www.voyagerhotel.com	Anchorage	AK	99501	907-277-9501	274-0333
Voyageur Inn 200 Viking Dr *TF:* 800-444-4493 ■ *Web:* www.voyageurinn.com	Reedsburg	WI	53959	608-524-6431	524-0036
Voyageur Lakewalk Inn 333 E Superior St *TF:* 800-258-3911 ■ *Web:* www.voyageurlakewalkinn.com	Duluth	MN	55802	218-722-3911	722-3124
W Hotels 1111 Westchester Ave *TF:* 877-443-4585 ■ *Web:* www.starwood.com/whotels/index.html	White Plains	NY	10604	914-640-8100	640-8310
Wagon Wheel Village 435 N Cache St *TF:* 800-323-9279	Jackson	WY	83001	307-733-2357	733-0568
Waikiki Gateway Hotel 2070 Kalakaua Ave *TF:* 800-247-1903 ■ *Web:* www.waikiki-gateway-hotel.com	Honolulu	HI	96815	808-955-3741	955-1313
Waikiki Joy Hotel 320 Lewers St *TF:* 800-321-2558 ■ *Web:* www.aston-hotels.com	Honolulu	HI	96815	808-923-2300	924-4010
Waikiki Parc Hotel 2233 Helumoa Rd *TF:* 800-422-0450 ■ *Web:* www.waikikiparchotel.com	Honolulu	HI	96815	808-921-7272	923-1336
Waikiki Resort Hotel 2460 Koa Ave *TF:* 800-367-5116 ■ *Web:* www.waikikiresort.com	Honolulu	HI	96815	808-922-4911	922-9468
Waldorf-Astoria 301 Park Ave *TF:* 800-925-3673 ■ *Web:* www.hilton.com/en/hi/waldorf/	New York	NY	10022	212-355-3000	872-7272
Waldorf Towers The 100 E 50th St *TF:* 800-445-8667 ■ *Web:* www.hilton.com	New York	NY	10022	212-355-3100	872-4799
Waldorf Towers Hotel 860 Ocean Dr *TF:* 800-933-2322 ■ *Web:* www.waldorftowers.com	Miami Beach	FL	33139	305-531-7684	672-6836
Waldorf=Astoria Collection 9336 Civic Center Dr *Web:* www.waldorfastoriacollection.com	Beverly Hills	CA	90210	310-278-4321	
Warwick Denver Hotel 1776 Grant St *TF:* 800-525-2888 ■ *Web:* www.warwickdenver.com	Denver	CO	80203	303-861-2000	832-0320
Warwick International Hotels Inc 65 W 54th St *TF:* 800-223-4099 ■ *Web:* www.warwickhotels.com	New York	NY	10019	212-247-2700	247-2725
Warwick Melrose Hotel 3015 Oak Lawn Ave *TF:* 800-521-7172 ■ *Web:* www.warwickmelrosedallas.com	Dallas	TX	75219	214-521-5151	521-2470
Warwick New York Hotel 65 W 54th St *Fax: Sales ■ *TF:* 800-223-4099 ■ *Web:* www.warwickhotelny.com	New York	NY	10019	212-247-2700	247-2725*
Warwick Regis Hotel San Francisco 490 Geary St *TF:* 800-827-3447 ■ *Web:* www.warwicksf.com	San Francisco	CA	94102	415-928-7900	441-8788
Warwick Seattle Hotel 401 Lenora St *TF:* 800-426-9280 ■ *Web:* www.warwickwa.com	Seattle	WA	98121	206-443-4300	448-1662
Washington Court Hotel 525 New Jersey Ave NW *TF:* 800-321-3010 ■ *Web:* www.washingtoncourthotel.com	Washington	DC	20001	202-628-2100	879-7918
Washington Duke Inn & Golf Club 3001 Cameron Blvd *TF:* 800-443-3853 ■ *Web:* www.washingtondukeinn.com	Durham	NC	27705	919-490-0999	688-0105
Washington Inn 495 10th St *Web:* www.thewashingtoninn.com	Oakland	CA	94607	510-452-1776	452-4436
Washington Plaza Hotel 10 Thomas Cir NW Massachusetts Ave at 14th St *TF:* 800-424-1140 ■ *Web:* www.washingtonplazahotel.com	Washington	DC	20005	202-842-1300	371-9602
Washington Square Hotel 103 Waverly Pl *TF:* 800-222-0418 ■ *Web:* www.wshotel.com	New York	NY	10011	212-777-9515	979-8373

	City	State	Zip	Phone	Fax
Washington Suites 100 S Reynolds St *TF:* 877-736-2500 ■ *Web:* www.washingtonsuitesalexandria.com	Alexandria	VA	22304	703-370-9600	370-0467
Washington Suites Georgetown 2500 Pennsylvania Ave NW *TF:* 877-736-2500 ■ *Web:* www.washingtonsuitesgeorgetown.com	Washington	DC	20037	202-333-8060	338-3818
Waterfront Plaza Hotel 10 Washington St *TF:* 800-729-3638 ■ *Web:* www.waterfrontplaza.com	Oakland	CA	94607	510-836-3800	832-5695
Waters Edge Hotel 25 Main St *TF:* 800-738-7477 ■ *Web:* www.marinhotels.com	Tiburon	CA	94920	415-789-5999	789-5888
Watertown Seattle 4242 Roosevelt Way NE *TF:* 866-944-4242 ■ *Web:* www.watertownseattle.com	Seattle	WA	98105	206-826-4242	315-4242
Wauwinet The PO Box 2580 Wauwinet Rd *TF:* 800-426-8718 ■ *Web:* www.wauwinet.com	Nantucket	MA	02584	508-228-0145	228-6712
WB Johnson Properties 100 W Paces Ferry Rd	Atlanta	GA	30305	404-237-7300	365-9800
Weatherford Hotel 23 N Leroux St *Web:* www.weatherfordhotel.com	Flagstaff	AZ	86001	928-774-2731	773-8951
Weber's Inn 3050 Jackson Rd *TF:* 800-443-3050 ■ *Web:* www.webersinn.com	Ann Arbor	MI	48103	734-769-2500	769-4743
Wedgewood Hotel 845 Hornby St *TF:* 800-663-0666 ■ *Web:* www.wedgewoodhotel.com	Vancouver	BC	V6Z1V1	604-689-7777	608-5348
Wedgewood Resort Hotel 212 Wedgewood Dr *TF:* 800-528-4916 ■ *Web:* www.fountainheadhotels.com/wedgewood/wedgewood.htm	Fairbanks	AK	99701	907-452-1442	451-8184
Wellington Hotel 871 7th Ave *TF:* 800-652-1212 ■ *Web:* www.wellingtonhotel.com	New York	NY	10019	212-247-3900	956-2381
Wellington Resort 551 Thames St *Web:* www.wellingtonresort.com	Newport	RI	02840	401-849-1770	847-6250
Wentworth Mansion 149 Wentworth St *TF:* 888-466-1886 ■ *Web:* www.wentworthmansion.com	Charleston	SC	29401	843-853-1886	720-5290
West Harvest Inn 17803 Stony Plain Rd *TF:* 800-661-6993 ■ *Web:* www.westharvest.ca	Edmonton	AB	T5S1B4	780-484-8000	486-6060
WestCoast Benson Hotel 309 SW Broadway *TF:* 800-426-0670 ■ *Web:* www.bensonhotel.com	Portland	OR	97205	503-228-2000	471-3920
WestCoast Hotel Partners Red Lion Hotel Corp 201 W North River Dr Suite 100 *TF:* 800-325-4000 ■ *Web:* westcoast.rdln.com	Spokane	WA	99201	509-459-6100	325-7324
Westford Regency Inn & Conference Center 219 Littleton Rd *TF:* 800-543-7801 ■ *Web:* www.westfordregency.com	Westford	MA	01886	978-692-8200	692-7403
Westgate Branson Woods 2201 Roark Valley Rd *TF:* 800-935-2345 ■ *Web:* www.wgbransonwoods.com	Branson	MO	65616	417-332-3550	334-0834
Westgate Hotel 1055 2nd Ave *TF:* 800-221-3802 ■ *Web:* www.westgatehotel.com	San Diego	CA	92101	619-238-1818	557-3737
Westgate Painted Mountain Golf Resort 6302 E McKellips Rd *TF:* 888-808-7410 ■ *Web:* www.wgpaintedmountain.com	Mesa	AZ	85215	480-654-3611	654-3613
Westgate Resort 1324 Richmond Rd *TF:* 800-782-3800 ■ *Web:* www.westgateresorts.com	Williamsburg	VA	23185	757-229-6220	229-2774
Westin Hotels & Resorts 1111 Westchester Ave *TF:* 877-443-4585 ■ *Web:* www.starwood.com/westin	White Plains	NY	10604	914-640-8100	640-8310
Westin San Francisco Market Street 50 3rd St *TF:* 888-627-8561 ■ *Web:* www.starwoodhotels.com/westin/	San Francisco	CA	94103	415-974-6400	543-8268
Westmark Hotels Inc 300 Elliott Ave W *TF:* 800-544-0970 ■ *Web:* www.westmarkhotels.com	Seattle	WA	98119	206-301-5223	285-7152
Westmont Hospitality Group Inc 5090 Explorer Dr Suite 700 *Web:* www.whg.com	Mississauga	ON	L4W4T9	905-629-3400	624-7805
Westmont Hospitality Group Inc 5847 San Felipe St Suite 4650 *TF:* 800-468-3512 ■ *Web:* www.whg.com	Houston	TX	77057	713-782-9100	782-9600
Westport Inn 1595 Post Rd E *TF:* 800-446-8997 ■ *Web:* www.westportinn.com	Westport	CT	06880	203-259-5236	254-8439
Wheatleigh Hawthorne Rd *Web:* www.wheatleigh.com	Lenox	MA	01240	413-637-0610	637-4507
Whiskey Pete's Hotel & Casino 100 W Primm Blvd *TF:* 800-386-7867 ■ *Web:* www.primmvalleyresorts.com	Primm	NV	89019	702-382-4388	679-5195
White Barn Inn 37 Beach Ave PO Box 560C *Web:* www.whitebarninn.com	Kennebunkport	ME	06046	207-967-2321	967-1100
White Elephant Inn & Cottages 50 Easton St *TF:* 800-475-2637 ■ *Web:* www.whiteelephanthotel.com	Nantucket	MA	02554	508-228-2500	325-1195
White Inn 52 E Main St *TF:* 888-373-3664 ■ *Web:* www.whiteinn.com	Fredonia	NY	14063	716-672-2103	672-2107
White Lodging Services Corp 1000 E 80th Pl Suite 600-N *Web:* www.whitelodging.com	Merrillville	IN	46410	219-769-3267	756-2902
White Swan Inn 845 Bush St *TF:* 800-999-9570 ■ *Web:* www.jdvhotels.com/white_swan_inn	San Francisco	CA	94108	415-775-1755	775-5717
Whitehall Hotel 105 E Delaware Pl *TF:* 800-948-4255 ■ *Web:* www.thewhitehallhotel.com	Chicago	IL	60611	312-944-6300	944-8552
Whitelaw Hotel 808 Collins Ave *Web:* www.whitelawhotel.com	Miami Beach	FL	33139	305-398-7000	398-7010
Whitney The - A Wyndham Historic Hotel 610 Poydras St *TF:* 800-996-3426 ■ *Web:* www.wyndham.com/hotels/MSYWW/main.wnt	New Orleans	LA	70130	504-581-4222	207-0101
Whitney Hotel 700 Woodrow St *TF:* 800-637-4008 ■ *Web:* www.whitneyhotel.com	Columbia	SC	29205	803-252-0845	771-0495
Wickaninnish Inn 500 Osprey Ln PO Box 250 *TF:* 800-333-4604 ■ *Web:* www.wickinn.com	Tofino	BC	V0R2Z0	250-725-3100	725-3110
Wild Palms Hotel 910 E Fremont Ave *TF:* 866-470-7062 ■ *Web:* www.jdvhotels.com/	Sunnyvale	CA	94087	408-738-0500	736-8302
Williamsburg Hospitality House 415 Richmond Rd *TF:* 800-932-9192 ■ *Web:* www.williamsburghosphouse.com	Williamsburg	VA	23185	757-229-4020	220-1560
Williamsburg Lodge 310 S England St *TF:* 800-447-8679 ■ *Web:* www.williamsburglodge.com	Williamsburg	VA	23185	757-229-1000	757-8243
Willows Historic Palm Springs Inn 412 W Tahquitz Canyon Way *TF:* 800-966-9597 ■ *Web:* www.thewillowspalmsprings.com	Palm Springs	CA	92262	760-320-0771	320-0780
Willows Hotel 555 W Surf St *TF:* 800-787-3108 ■ *Web:* www.cityinns.com	Chicago	IL	60657	773-528-8400	528-8483
Willows Lodge 14580 NE 145th St *TF:* 877-424-3930 ■ *Web:* www.willowslodge.com	Woodinville	WA	98072	425-424-3900	424-2585
Wilshire Grand Hotel & Center 930 Wilshire Blvd *TF:* 888-773-2888 ■ *Web:* www.wilshiregrand.com	Los Angeles	CA	90017	213-688-7777	612-3987
Wilson Hotel Management Co Inc 8700 Trail Lake Dr W Suite 300 *TF:* 800-945-7661 ■ *Web:* www.wilsonhotels.com	Memphis	TN	38125	901-346-8800	346-5808
Windmill Inn at Saint Philip's Plaza Tucson 4250 N Campbell Ave *TF:* 800-547-4747 ■ *Web:* www.windmillinns.com	Tucson	AZ	85718	520-577-0007	577-0045
Windsor Arms Hotel 18 Saint Thomas St *TF:* 877-999-2767 ■ *Web:* www.windsorarmshotel.com	Toronto	ON	M5S3E7	416-971-9666	921-9121
Windsor Capital Group Inc 3000 Ocean Park Blvd Suite 3010 *Web:* www.wcghotels.com	Santa Monica	CA	90405	310-566-1100	566-1199
Windsor Court Hotel 300 Gravier St *TF:* 800-262-2662 ■ *Web:* www.windsorcourthotel.com	New Orleans	LA	70130	504-523-6000	596-4513
Windsor Hotel 125 W Lamar St *TF:* 888-297-9567 ■ *Web:* www.windsor-americus.com	Americus	GA	31709	229-924-1555	924-1555
Winegardner & Hammons Inc 4243 Hunt Rd *Web:* www.whihotels.com	Cincinnati	OH	45242	513-891-1066	794-2590
Wingate by Wyndham 1 Sylvan Way *TF Resv:* 800-228-1000 ■ *Web:* www.wingateinns.com	Parsippany	NJ	07054	973-753-6600	
Wonder View Inn & Suites 50 Eden St PO Box 25 *TF:* 888-439-8439 ■ *Web:* www.wonderviewinn.com	Bar Harbor	ME	04609	207-288-3358	288-2005
Woodfin Suite Hotels LLC 12671 High Bluff Dr Suite 300 *TF:* 800-237-8811 ■ *Web:* www.woodfinsuitehotels.com	San Diego	CA	92130	858-794-2338	794-2348
Chase Suite Hotels by Woodfin 12671 High Bluff Dr Suite 300 *TF:* 800-237-8811 ■ *Web:* www.woodfinsuitehotels.com	San Diego	CA	92130	858-794-2338	794-2348
Woodmark Hotel on Lake Washington 1200 Carillon Point *TF:* 800-822-3700 ■ *Web:* www.thewoodmark.com	Kirkland	WA	98033	425-822-3700	822-3699
Wort Hotel 50 N Glenwood *TF:* 800-322-2727 ■ *Web:* www.worthotel.com	Jackson	WY	83001	307-733-2190	733-2067
Wyland Waikiki 400 Royal Hawaiian Ave *TF:* 866-346-4679	Honolulu	HI	96815	808-954-4000	954-4001
Wyndham Hotel Group 1 Sylvan Way *Web:* www.wyndhamworldwide.com	Parsippany	NJ	07054	973-753-6600	
AmeriHost Inn 1 Sylvan Way *TF Resv:* 800-889-8847 ■ *Web:* www.amerihostinn.com	Parsippany	NJ	07054	973-428-9700	
Baymont Inn & Suites 1 Sylvan Way *TF Resv:* 877-229-6668 ■ *Web:* www.baymontinns.com	Parsippany	NJ	07054	973-753-6600	
Days Inn 1 Sylvan Way *TF Resv:* 800-329-7466 ■ *Web:* www.daysinn.com	Parsippany	NJ	07054	973-753-6600	
Howard Johnson 1 Sylvan Way *TF Resv:* 800-446-4656 ■ *Web:* www.hojo.com	Parsippany	NJ	07054	973-753-6600	
Knights Inn 1 Sylvan Way *TF Resv:* 800-843-5644 ■ *Web:* www.knightsinn.com	Parsippany	NJ	07054	973-753-6600	
Ramada 1 Sylvan Way *TF Resv:* 800-272-6232 ■ *Web:* www.ramada.com	Parsippany	NJ	07054	973-753-6600	
Super 8 1 Sylvan Way *TF Resv:* 800-800-8000 ■ *Web:* www.super8.com	Parsippany	NJ	07054	973-753-6600	
Travelodge 1 Sylvan Way *TF Resv:* 800-578-7878 ■ *Web:* www.travelodge.com	Parsippany	NJ	07054	973-753-6600	
Wingate by Wyndham 1 Sylvan Way *TF Resv:* 800-228-1000 ■ *Web:* www.wingateinns.com	Parsippany	NJ	07054	973-753-6600	
Wyndham Hotels & Resorts 1 Sylvan Way *TF Resv:* 877-999-3223 ■ *Web:* www.wyndham.com	Parsippany	NJ	07054	973-753-6600	
Wyndham Hotels & Resorts 1 Sylvan Way *TF Resv:* 877-999-3223 ■ *Web:* www.wyndham.com	Parsippany	NJ	07054	973-753-6600	
Wyndham Worldwide Corp Wyndham Hotel Group 1 Sylvan Way *Web:* www.wyndhamworldwide.com	Parsippany	NJ	07054	973-753-6600	
Wynfrey Hotel 1000 Riverchase Galleria *TF:* 800-996-3739 ■ *Web:* www.wynfrey.com	Birmingham	AL	35244	205-987-1600	988-4597
Wynn Las Vegas 3131 Las Vegas Blvd S *TF:* 888-320-7123 ■ *Web:* www.wynnlasvegas.com	Las Vegas	NV	89109	702-770-7000	770-1571
Wyoming Inn of Jackson 930 W Broadway PO Box 8820 *Web:* www.wyoming-inn.com	Jackson	WY	83001	307-734-0035	734-0037
Yankee Inn 461 Pittsfield Lenox Rd *TF:* 800-835-2364 ■ *Web:* www.yankeeinn.com	Lenox	MA	01240	413-499-3700	499-3634
Yankee Peddler Inn 113 Touro St *TF:* 800-427-9444 ■ *Web:* www.historicinnsofnewport.com	Newport	RI	02840	401-846-1323	849-0426
Yarmouth Resort Rte 28 *Web:* www.yarmouthresort.com/	West Yarmouth	MA	02673	508-775-5155	
Yarrow Resort Hotel 1800 Park Ave *TF:* 800-927-7694 ■ *Web:* www.yarrowresort.com	Park City	UT	84060	435-649-7000	645-7007
Yogo Inn 211 E Main St *TF:* 800-860-9646 ■ *Web:* www.yogoinn.com	Lewistown	MT	59457	406-535-8721	535-8969
York Hotel 940 Sutter St *TF:* 800-553-1900 ■ *Web:* www.yorkhotel.com	San Francisco	CA	94109	415-885-6800	885-2115
York The Hotel 161 Donald St *TF:* 800-463-6400 ■ *Web:* www.yorkthehotel.com	Winnipeg	MB	R3C1M3	204-942-5300	943-7975
Yorktowne Hotel 48 E Market St *TF:* 800-233-9324 ■ *Web:* www.yorktowne.com	York	PA	17401	717-848-1111	854-7678

383 ICE - MANUFACTURED

	City	State	Zip	Phone	Fax
CV Ice Co Inc 83796 Date Ave *Web:* www.cvice.com	Indio	CA	92201	760-347-3529	347-4098
Dusing Bros Ice Mfg Co 3607 Dixie Hwy	Elsmere	KY	41018	859-727-2720	727-2780
Hanover Foods Corp 1550 York St PO Box 334 *TF:* 800-888-4646 ■ *Web:* www.hanoverfoods.com	Hanover	PA	17331	717-632-6000	632-6681
Happy Ice LLC 900 Turk Hill Rd *Web:* www.happyice.com	Fairport	NY	14450	585-388-0300	388-0185
Herrin Bros Co PO Box 5291	Charlotte	NC	28299	704-332-2193	376-3408
Icemakers Inc PO Box 321755 *TF:* 800-467-2181 ■ *Web:* www.icemakers.net	Birmingham	AL	35232	205-591-2791	591-2389
Jefferson Ice Co Inc 2248 N Natchez Ave *Web:* www.jeffersonice.com	Chicago	IL	60707	773-622-9400	622-7955
Lansdowne Beverage Inc 500 E Baltimore Pike *Web:* www.lansdownebeverage.com	Lansdowne	PA	19050	610-623-7000	623-7000
Maui Soda & Ice Works Ltd PO Box 1170	Wailuku	HI	96793	808-244-7951	244-4108
Mountain Water Ice Co 1107 E Walnut St	Santa Ana	CA	92701	714-835-8306	835-8448
National Cold Storage Inc 9948 W 87th St Suite A	Overland Park	KS	66212	913-385-9444	385-7979
Pelican Ice & Cold Storage Inc PO Box 2131	Kenner	LA	70063	504-525-4193	733-1271
Reddy Ice & Cassco Refrigerated Services 610 Pleasant Valley Rd PO Box 548 *TF:* 800-999-4231 ■ *Web:* www.reddyice.com	Harrisonburg	VA	22801	540-433-2751	433-7870
Reddy Ice Holdings Inc 8750 N Central Expy Suite 1800 *NYSE: FRZ* ■ *TF:* 800-683-4423 ■ *Web:* www.reddyice.com	Dallas	TX	75231	214-526-6740	528-0995
Union Ice Co 6100 E Sheila St	Los Angeles	CA	90040	323-890-3803	722-5394

384 ICE CREAM & DAIRY STORES

	City	State	Zip	Phone	Fax
All American Frozen Yogurt & Ice Cream Shops 812 SW Washington St Suite 1100 *Web:* www.allamericanicecream.com	Portland	OR	97205	503-224-6199	224-5042
Amy's Ice Creams 3500 Guadalupe St *Web:* www.amysicecreams.com	Austin	TX	78705	512-458-6895	458-4971
Bahama Buck's Original Shaved Ice Co 5123 69th St *Web:* www.bahamabucks.com	Lubbock	TX	79424	806-771-2189	771-2190
Baskin-Robbins Inc 130 Royall St *TF:* 800-859-5339 ■ *Web:* www.baskinrobbins.com	Canton	MA	02021	781-737-3000	
Ben & Jerry's Homemade Inc 30 Community Dr *Web:* www.benjerry.com	South Burlington	VT	05403	802-846-1500	846-1556
Braum's Ice Cream & Dairy Stores 3000 NE 63rd St *Web:* www.braums.com	Oklahoma City	OK	73121	405-478-1656	475-2460
Brigham's Inc 30 Mill St *TF:* 800-274-4426 ■ *Web:* www.brighams.com	Arlington	MA	02476	781-648-9000	646-0507

Company	City	State	ZIP	Phone	Fax
Bruster's Ice Cream Inc 730 Mulberry St *Web:* www.brusters.com	Bridgewater	PA	15009	724-774-4250	774-0666
Carvel Corp 175 Capital Blvd Suite 400 *TF:* 800-322-4848 ■ *Web:* www.carvel.com	Rocky Hill	CT	06067	860-257-4448	257-8859
Carvel Franchising 200 Glenridge Point Pkwy Suite 200 *TF:* 800-227-8353 ■ *Web:* www.carvel.com	Atlanta	GA	30342	404-255-3250	255-4978
CF Burger Creamery Co 8101 Greenfield Rd *TF:* 800-229-2322	Detroit	MI	48228	313-584-4040	584-9870
Cloverland Green Spring Dairy Inc 2701 Loch Raven Rd *TF Orders:* 800-876-6455 ■ *Web:* www.cloverlanddairy.com	Baltimore	MD	21218	410-235-4477	889-3690
Cold Stone Creamery Inc 9311 E Via De Ventura *TF Cust Svc:* 866-464-9467 ■ *Web:* www.coldstonecreamery.com	Scottsdale	AZ	85258	480-362-4800	362-4812
Crystal Cream & Butter Co 1013 D St *TF:* 800-272-7326 ■ *Web:* www.crystal-milk.com	Sacramento	CA	95814	916-444-7200	448-0284
Cumberland Farms Inc 777 Dedham St **Fax:* Hum Res ■ *TF:* 800-225-9702 ■ *Web:* www.cumberlandfarms.com	Canton	MA	02021	781-828-4900	828-9012*
Dairy Barn Stores Inc 544 Elwood Rd *TF:* 888-320-0246 ■ *Web:* www.dairybarn.com	East Northport	NY	11731	631-368-8050	266-2547
Dairy Queen 7505 Metro Blvd *TF:* 800-679-6556 ■ *Web:* www.dairyqueen.com	Minneapolis	MN	55439	952-830-0200	830-0480
Farm Stores 5800 NW 74th Ave *TF:* 800-726-3276 ■ *Web:* www.farmstores.com	Miami	FL	33166	305-471-5141	591-4243
Freshens Quality Brands 1750 The Exchange *TF:* 800-633-4519 ■ *Web:* www.freshens.com	Atlanta	GA	30339	678-627-5400	627-5454
Heritage Dairy Stores Inc 376 Jessup Rd *Web:* www.heritages.com	Thorofare	NJ	08086	856-845-2855	845-8392
Kilwin's Quality Confections 355 N Division Rd *TF:* 800-454-5946 ■ *Web:* www.kilwins.com	Petoskey	MI	49770	231-347-3800	347-6951
MaggieMoo's International LLC 10025 Governor Warfield Pkwy Suite 301 **Fax Area Code:* 410 ■ *Web:* www.maggiemoos.com	Columbia	MD	21044	800-949-8114	740-1500*
Marble Slab Creamery Inc 3100 S Gessner Suite 305 *Web:* www.marbleslab.com	Houston	TX	77063	713-780-3601	780-0264
Newport Creamery Inc 35 Stockanosset Rd *Web:* www.newportcreamery.com	Cranston	RI	02920	401-946-4000	946-4392
Parmalat/Sunnydale Farms Inc 400 Stanley Ave	Brooklyn	NY	11207	718-257-7600	257-7466
Rita's Water Ice Franchise Co LLC 1210 Northbrook Dr *TF:* 800-677-7482 ■ *Web:* www.ritasice.com	Trevose	PA	19053	215-876-9300	
Rosenberger's Dairies Inc 847 Forty Foot Rd PO Box 901 *TF:* 800-355-9074 ■ *Web:* www.rosenbergers.com	Hatfield	PA	19440	215-855-9074	855-6486
Royal Crest Dairy Inc 350 S Pearl St *Web:* www.royalcrestdairy.com	Denver	CO	80209	303-777-2227	744-9173
Stewart's Ice Cream Co Inc PO Box 435 *Web:* www.stewartshops.com	Saratoga Springs	NY	12866	518-581-1000	581-1209
Swensen's Ice Cream Co 4175 Veterans Memorial Hwy *TF:* 800-423-2763	Ronkonkoma	NY	11779	631-737-9898	737-9792
TCBY Enterprises Inc 2855 E Cottonwood Pkwy Suite 400 *TF:* 888-900-8229 ■ *Web:* www.tcby.com	Salt Lake City	UT	84121	801-736-5600	736-5970
Yogen Früz 8300 Woodbine Ave 5th Fl *Web:* www.yogenfruz.com	Markham	ON	L3R9Y7	905-479-8762	479-5235

385 IMAGING EQUIPMENT & SYSTEMS - MEDICAL

SEE ALSO Medical Instruments & Apparatus - Mfr p. 1953

Company	City	State	ZIP	Phone	Fax
4-D Neuroimaging Inc 9727 Pacific Heights Blvd *Web:* www.4dneuroimaging.com	San Diego	CA	92121	858-453-6300	453-4913
ACMI Corp 136 Turnpike Rd *TF:* 866-879-0640 ■ *Web:* www.acmicorp.com	Southborough	MA	01772	508-804-2600	804-2624
AFP Imaging Corp 250 Clearbrook Rd *TF:* 800-592-6666 ■ *Web:* www.afpimaging.com	Elmsford	NY	10523	914-592-6100	592-6148
Agfa Corp 100 Challenger Rd *TF:* 800-581-2432 ■ *Web:* www.agfa.com/usa	Ridgefield Park	NJ	07660	201-440-2500	342-4742
Applied Imaging Corp 120 Baytech Dr *TF:* 800-634-3622 ■ *Web:* www.aicorp.com	San Jose	CA	95134	408-719-6400	719-6401
Bio-Imaging Technologies Inc 826 Newtown-Yardley Rd Suite 101 *NASDAQ: BITI* ■ *TF:* 800-748-9032 ■ *Web:* www.bioimaging.com	Newtown	PA	18940	267-757-3000	757-3010
Bioscan Inc 4590 MacArthur Blvd NW *TF:* 800-255-7226 ■ *Web:* www.bioscan.com	Washington	DC	20007	202-338-0974	333-8514
BrainLAB Inc 3 Westbrook Corp Center Suite 400 *TF:* 800-784-7700 ■ *Web:* www.brainlab.com	Westchester	IL	60154	708-409-1343	409-1619
Camtronics Medical Systems 900 Walnut Ridge Dr *TF:* 800-634-5151 ■ *Web:* www.camtronics.com	Hartland	WI	53029	262-367-0700	367-0717
CIVCO Medical Instruments 102 1st St S *TF:* 800-445-6741 ■ *Web:* www.civcomedical.com	Kalona	IA	52247	319-656-4447	656-4451
Clarient Inc 33171 Paseo Cerveza *NASDAQ: CLRT* ■ *TF:* 888-443-3310 ■ *Web:* www.clarientinc.com	San Juan Capistrano	CA	92675	949-443-3355	443-3366
Del Global Technologies Corp 1 Commerce Park *Web:* www.delglobaltech.com	Valhalla	NY	10595	914-686-3650	686-0826
Dent-X Corp 250 Clearbrook Rd *TF:* 800-592-6666 ■ *Web:* www.dent-x.com	Elmsford	NY	10523	914-592-6100	592-6148
Dentsply International Inc 221 W Philadelphia St PO Box 872 *NASDAQ: XRAY* ■ *TF:* 800-877-0020 ■ *Web:* www.dentsply.com	York	PA	17405	717-845-7511	849-4762
Digirad Corp 13950 Stowe Dr *NASDAQ: DRAD* ■ *TF:* 800-947-6134 ■ *Web:* www.digirad.com	Poway	CA	92064	858-726-1600	726-1700
Dornier MedTech America Inc 1155 Roberts Blvd *TF:* 800-367-6437 ■ *Web:* www.dornier.com	Kennesaw	GA	30144	770-426-1315	426-6115
Eastman Kodak Co 343 State St *NYSE: EK* ■ *Web:* www.kodak.com	Rochester	NY	14650	800-698-3324	
Emageon Inc 1200 Corporate Dr Suite 200 *NASDAQ: EMAG* ■ *TF:* 866-362-4366 ■ *Web:* www.emageon.com	Birmingham	AL	35242	205-980-9222	980-9815
Fischer Imaging Corp 12300 N Grant St *TF:* 800-825-8434 ■ *Web:* www.fischerimaging.com	Denver	CO	80241	303-452-6800	450-4335
Fonar Corp 110 Marcus Dr *NASDAQ: FONR* ■ *Web:* www.fonar.com	Melville	NY	11747	631-694-2929	390-7766
GE Healthcare 3000 Grandview N **Fax:* Cust Svc ■ *TF:* 800-558-5102 ■ *Web:* www.gehealthcare.com	Waukesha	WI	53188	262-544-3011	548-2443*
GE OEC Medical Systems Inc 384 Wright Brothers Dr *TF:* 800-365-1366 ■ *Web:* www.gemedicalsystems.com/rad/xr	Salt Lake City	UT	84116	801-328-9300	328-4300
Given Imaging Ltd 5555 Oakbrook Pkwy Suite 355 *NASDAQ: GIVN* ■ *TF:* 800-448-3644 ■ *Web:* www.givenimaging.com	Norcross	GA	30093	770-662-0870	810-0006
Hitachi Medical Systems America Inc 1959 Summit Commerce Park *TF:* 800-800-3106 ■ *Web:* www.hitachimed.com	Twinsburg	OH	44087	330-425-1313	425-1410
Hologic Inc 35 Crosby Dr *NASDAQ: HOLX* ■ *TF:* 800-343-9729 ■ *Web:* www.hologic.com	Bedford	MA	01730	781-999-7300	280-0669
Holorad 2929 S Main St *Web:* www.holorad.com	Salt Lake City	UT	84115	801-983-6075	802-8004
iCAD Inc 4 Townsend W Suite 17 *NASDAQ: ICAD* ■ *TF:* 866-280-2239 ■ *Web:* www.icadmed.com	Nashua	NH	03063	603-882-5200	880-3843
Imaging Diagnostic Systems Inc 6531 NW 18th Ct *TF:* 800-992-9008 ■ *Web:* www.imds.com	Plantation	FL	33313	954-581-9800	581-0555
Immunicon Corp 3401 Masons Mill Rd Suite 100 *NASDAQ: IMMC* ■ *TF:* 877-822-0777 ■ *Web:* www.immunicon.com	Huntingdon Valley	PA	19006	215-830-0777	830-0751
IRIS International Inc 9172 Eton Ave *NASDAQ: IRIS* ■ *TF:* 800-776-4747 ■ *Web:* www.proiris.com	Chatsworth	CA	91311	818-709-1244	700-9661
iVOW Inc 2101 Faraday Ave *NASDAQ: IVOW* ■ *TF:* 800-510-8090 ■ *Web:* www.ivow.com	Carlsbad	CA	92008	760-603-9120	603-9170
Kodak Co 343 State St *NYSE: EK* ■ *Web:* www.kodak.com	Rochester	NY	14650	800-698-3324	
Mallinckrodt Pharmaceutical Products 675 McDonnell Blvd *TF:* 888-744-1414 ■ *Web:* www.mallinckrodt.com	Hazelwood	MO	63042	314-654-2000	654-6257
Medrad Inc 1 Medrad Dr **Fax:* Cust Svc ■ *TF Cust Svc:* 800-633-7237 ■ *Web:* www.medrad.com	Indianola	PA	15051	412-767-2400	767-4120*
Merge Technologies Inc 6737 W Washington St Suite 2250 *NASDAQ: MRGE* ■ *TF:* 877-446-3743 ■ *Web:* www.merge-efilm.com	Milwaukee	WI	53214	414-977-4000	977-4200
Minrad International Inc 847 Main St *AMEX: BUF* ■ *TF:* 800-832-3303 ■ *Web:* www.minrad.com	Buffalo	NY	14203	716-855-1068	855-1078
Neoprobe Corp 425 Metro Place N Suite 300 *TF:* 800-793-0079 ■ *Web:* www.neoprobe.com	Dublin	OH	43017	614-793-7500	793-7520
Nichols Institute Diagnostics 1311 Calle Batido *TF:* 800-286-4643 ■ *Web:* www.nicholsdiag.com	San Clemente	CA	92673	949-940-7200	940-7271
Novadaq Technologies Inc 2585 Skymark Ave Suite 306 *TF:* 888-728-4368 ■ *Web:* www.novadaq.com	Mississauga	ON	L4W4L5	905-629-3822	629-0282
Olympus America Inc 2 Corporate Center Dr **Fax:* Sales ■ *TF:* 800-446-5967 ■ *Web:* www.olympusamerica.com	Melville	NY	11747	631-844-5000	844-5110*
PerkinElmer Inc 45 William St *NYSE: PKI* ■ *Web:* www.perkinelmer.com	Wellesley	MA	02481	781-237-5100	237-9386
Philips Global PACS 5000 Marina Blvd Suite 100 *TF Cust Svc:* 877-328-2808 ■ *Web:* www.stentor.com	Brisbane	CA	94005	650-866-4100	228-5580
Philips Medical Systems 3000 Minuteman Rd *TF:* 866-246-7306 ■ *Web:* www.medical.philips.com	Andover	MA	01810	978-687-1501	689-8295
Philips Ultrasound 22100 Bothell Everett Hwy *TF Cust Svc:* 800-433-3246	Bothell	WA	98021	425-487-7000	487-7885
Positron Corp 1304 Langham Creek Dr Suite 300 *TF:* 800-766-2984 ■ *Web:* www.positron.com	Houston	TX	77084	281-492-7100	492-2961
Precision Optics Corp Inc 22 E Broadway *TF:* 800-447-2812 ■ *Web:* www.poci.com	Gardner	MA	01440	978-630-1800	630-1487
S & S Technology 10625 Telge Rd *TF:* 800-231-1747 ■ *Web:* www.ssxray.com	Houston	TX	77095	281-815-1300	815-1444
Shimadzu Medical Systems 20101 S Vermont Ave *TF:* 800-228-1429 ■ *Web:* www.shimadzumed.com	Torrance	CA	90502	310-217-8855	217-0661
Siemens Medical Solutions Inc 51 Valley Stream Pkwy *TF:* 866-872-9745 ■ *Web:* www.medical.siemens.com	Malvern	PA	19355	610-448-6300	219-3124
Siemens Medical Solutions Ultrasound Div 1230 Shorebird Way *TF:* 800-422-8766	Mountain View	CA	94043	650-969-9112	
Siemens Molecular Imaging Inc 810 Innovation Dr *TF:* 800-841-7226 ■ *Web:* www.medical.siemens.com	Knoxville	TN	37932	865-218-2000	218-3000
SonoSite Inc 21919 30th Dr SE *NASDAQ: SONO* ■ *TF:* 888-482-9449 ■ *Web:* www.sonosite.com	Bothell	WA	98021	425-951-1200	951-1201
Stereotaxis Inc 4320 Forest Park Ave *NASDAQ: STXS* ■ *Web:* www.stereotaxis.com	Saint Louis	MO	63108	314-615-6940	678-6110
Swissray International Inc 1180 McLester St Unit 2 *TF:* 800-903-5543 ■ *Web:* www.swissray.com	Elizabeth	NJ	07201	908-353-0971	353-1237
Topcon Medical Systems Inc 37 W Century Rd **Fax:* Cust Svc ■ *TF:* 800-223-1130 ■ *Web:* www.topcon.com/medical.html	Paramus	NJ	07652	201-261-9450	634-1365*
Toshiba America Inc 1251 Ave of the Americas Suite 4100 *TF:* 800-457-7777 ■ *Web:* www.toshiba.com	New York	NY	10020	212-596-0600	593-3875
Toshiba America Medical Systems Inc 2441 Michelle Dr *TF:* 800-421-1968 ■ *Web:* medical.toshiba.com	Tustin	CA	92780	714-730-5000	730-4022
Toshiba America MRI Inc 300 Utah Ave Suite 100 *TF:* 800-477-4674	South San Francisco	CA	94080	650-872-2722	871-0299
TriPath Imaging Inc 780 Plantation Dr *NASDAQ: TPTH* ■ *TF:* 800-426-2176 ■ *Web:* www.tripathimaging.com	Burlington	NC	27215	336-222-9707	290-8333
Varian Medical Systems Inc 3100 Hansen Way *NYSE: VAR* ■ **Fax:* Hum Res ■ *TF:* 800-544-4636 ■ *Web:* www.varian.com	Palo Alto	CA	94304	650-493-4000	424-4820*
Vision-Sciences Inc 9 Strathmore Rd *NASDAQ: VSCI* ■ *TF:* 800-874-9975 ■ *Web:* www.visionsciences.com	Natick	MA	01760	508-650-9971	650-9976
Wolf X-Ray Corp 100 W Industry Ct *TF Cust Svc:* 800-356-9729 ■ *Web:* www.wolfxray.com	Deer Park	NY	11729	631-242-9729	925-5003

386 IMAGING SERVICES - DIAGNOSTIC

Company	City	State	ZIP	Phone	Fax
Alliance Imaging Inc 1900 S State College Blvd Suite 600 *NYSE: AIQ* ■ *TF:* 800-544-3215 ■ *Web:* www.allianceimaging.com	Anaheim	CA	92806	714-688-7100	688-3333
Center for Diagnostic Imaging 5775 Wayzata Blvd Suite 400 *TF:* 877-566-6500 ■ *Web:* www.cdiradiology.com	Saint Louis Park	MN	55416	952-543-6500	847-1152
InfiMed Inc 121 Metropolitan Dr *TF:* 800-825-8845 ■ *Web:* www.infimed.com	Liverpool	NY	13088	315-453-4545	453-4550
InSight Health Services Corp 26250 Enterprise Ct Suite 100 *TF:* 800-874-8634 ■ *Web:* www.insighthealth.com	Lake Forest	CA	92630	949-282-6000	452-0203
Medical Resources Inc 1455 Broad St *TF:* 800-537-7272 ■ *Web:* www.mrii.com	Bloomfield	NJ	07003	973-707-1100	707-1118
Raytel Medical Corp 7 Waterside Crossing **Fax Area Code:* 800 ■ *TF:* 800-367-1095 ■ *Web:* www.raytel.com	Windsor	CT	06095	860-298-6100	562-4166*
Wendt-Bristol Health Services Corp 921-B Jasonway Ave	Columbus	OH	43214	614-221-6000	221-6168

387 INCENTIVE PROGRAM MANAGEMENT SERVICES

SEE ALSO Conference & Events Coordinators p. 1525

Many of the companies listed here provide travel as a reward for employees or corporate customers in order to boost sales or employee performance. Most of these companies are members of the Society of Incentive & Travel Executives. Some of the companies listed offer merchandise or other types of incentives as well.

Company	City	State	ZIP	Phone	Fax
ADI Meetings & Incentives Inc 1208 E Broadway Rd Suite 215 *TF:* 800-944-2359 ■ *Web:* www.adimi.com	Tempe	AZ	85282	480-350-9090	350-9393
Amorde Incentive Marketing 33161 Camino Capistrano Suite L *Web:* www.amordeincentivemktg.com	San Juan Capistrano	CA	92675	949-388-7078	388-7082
Beatty Group International 9800 SW Beaverton Hillsdale Hwy Suite 105 *TF:* 800-285-6215 ■ *Web:* www.beattygroup.com	Beaverton	OR	97005	503-644-3340	644-2219

				Phone	Fax
Brickell Incentives 569 Central Dr Suite 103 *Web:* www.brickellincentives.com	Virginia Beach	VA	23454	757-233-0076	368-0387
Destination Success 15 W Central Pkwy *TF:* 888-301-3866 ■ *Web:* www.destsuccess.com	Cincinnati	OH	45202	513-763-3070	763-3071
Don Jagoda Assoc Inc 100 Marcus Dr *Web:* www.dja.com	Melville	NY	11747	631-454-1800	454-1834
Eaton Incentives Inc 271 Rt 46 W Suite H-212 *Web:* www.eatonincentives.com	Fairfield	NJ	07004	973-882-7700	882-9825
Fennell Promotions Inc 951 Hornet Dr *Fax Area Code: 800 ■ *TF:* 800-495-9765 ■ *Web:* www.fennellpromotions.com	Hazelwood	MO	63042	314-592-3300	495-9845*
Fields Group Inc 9124 Technology Dr *TF:* 800-600-2969 ■ *Web:* www.thefieldsgroupinc.com	Fishers	IN	46038	317-578-4414	578-4411
Fraser & Hoyt Group Incentive Div 1505 Barrington St Suite 107 *TF:* 800-565-8747 ■ *Web:* www.fraserhoyt.com/incentives.asp	Halifax	NS	B3J3K5	902-421-1113	425-3756
Global Incentives Inc 2120 Main St Suite 130 *TF:* 800-292-7348 ■ *Web:* www.globalinc.net	Huntington Beach	CA	92648	714-960-2300	536-5308
Hospitality Marketing Concepts Inc 15751 Rockfield Blvd Suite 200 *TF:* 866-212-4462 ■ *Web:* www.clubhotel.com	Irvine	CA	92618	949-454-1800	454-1888
Impact Incentives & Meetings Inc 188 Rt 10 W Suite 204 *Web:* www.impactincentives.com	East Hanover	NJ	07936	973-952-9052	952-9062
Incentive Depot Inc 190 Port Augusta St Suite 200 *TF:* 866-943-3768 ■ *Web:* www.incentivedepot.com	Comox	BC	V9M2N1	250-890-0917	890-0938
Incentive Solutions 2337 Perimeter Park Dr Suite 220 *TF:* 800-463-5836 ■ *Web:* www.incentivesolutions.com	Atlanta	GA	30341	770-457-4597	457-4994
Incentive Travel & Meetings (ITM) 970 Clementstone Dr Suite 100 *Web:* www.usaitm.com	Atlanta	GA	30342	404-252-2728	252-8328
Incentive Travel Services Inc 805 Peachtree St NE Suite 602 *Web:* www.itstravel.com	Atlanta	GA	30308	404-872-6165	872-6695
Incentives Unlimited 1200 Woodruff Rd Suite C-27 *Web:* www.incentivesunlimited.com	Greenville	SC	29607	864-458-7694	458-7698
International Meeting Planners Ltd 4863 Hampshire Ct Suite 303 *Web:* www.internationalplanners.com	Naples	FL	34112	239-775-1467	775-1472
ITAGroup 4800 Westown Pkwy Suite 300 *TF:* 800-257-1985 ■ *Web:* www.itagroup.com	West Des Moines	IA	50266	515-224-3400	224-3552
ITM (Incentive Travel & Meetings) 970 Clementstone Dr Suite 100 *Web:* www.usaitm.com	Atlanta	GA	30342	404-252-2728	252-8328
Jagoda Don Assoc Inc 100 Marcus Dr *Web:* www.dja.com	Melville	NY	11747	631-454-1800	454-1834
Light Group Inc 1 Barker Ave Suite 215 *Web:* www.incentivesmotivate.com	White Plains	NY	10601	914-397-0800	397-8015
LMS Meetings & Incentives 300 Corporate Pointe Suite 310 *Web:* www.thelmscorp.com	Culver City	CA	90230	310-641-4222	641-5222
Maritz Travel Co 1395 N Highway Dr *TF:* 800-253-7562 ■ *Web:* www.maritztravel.com	Fenton	MO	63099	636-827-4000	
Marketing Innovators International Inc 9701 W Higgins Rd Suite 400 *TF:* 800-633-8747 ■ *Web:* www.marketinginnovators.com	Rosemont	IL	60018	847-696-1111	696-3194
Maxcel Co 6600 LBJ Fwy Suite 109 *Web:* www.maxcel.net	Dallas	TX	75240	972-644-0880	680-2488
Mayer Motivations Inc 2434 E Las Olas Blvd *TF:* 888-611-4376 ■ *Web:* www.mayermotivations.com	Fort Lauderdale	FL	33301	954-523-0074	523-0076
MotivAction 16355 36th Ave N Suite 100 *TF:* 800-326-2226 ■ *Web:* www.motivaction.com	Minneapolis	MN	55446	763-525-5200	525-5300
Motivation Through Incentives Inc 10400 W 103 St Suite 10 *TF:* 800-826-3464 ■ *Web:* www.miinc.com	Overland Park	KS	66214	816-942-0122	942-2252
Navigant Performance Group 86 Pleasant St *Web:* npg.navigant.com	Marlborough	MA	01752	508-460-1900	460-9996
Performance Strategies Inc 7420 Shadeland Station Way *Web:* www.performancestrategies.com	Indianapolis	IN	46256	317-842-0393	578-4711
Premier Incentives Inc 2 Market Sq *TF:* 888-255-0000 ■ *Web:* www.premierincentives.com	Marblehead	MA	01945	781-639-4444	639-4449
Premier Meetings & Incentives 2150 S Washburn St *TF:* 800-236-5095 ■ *Web:* www.gopmi.com	Oshkosh	WI	54903	920-236-8030	236-8006
Robbins Co 400 O'Neil Blvd *TF:* 800-343-3970 ■ *Web:* www.therobbinsco.com	Attleboro	MA	02703	508-222-2900	222-7089
S & H Solutions 1625 S Congress Ave *Web:* www.shsolutions.com	Delray Beach	FL	33445	561-454-7600	265-2493
Sperry & Hutchinson Co Inc 1625 S Congress Ave *Web:* www.shsolutions.com	Delray Beach	FL	33445	561-454-7600	265-2493
Student Advantage LLC 280 Summer St *TF:* 800-333-2920 ■ *Web:* www.studentadvantage.com	Boston	MA	02210	617-912-2011	912-2012
Sunbelt Motivation & Travel Inc 5215 N O'Connor Blvd Suite 950 *TF:* 800-558-0145 ■ *Web:* www.sunbeltmotivation.com	Irving	TX	75039	214-638-2400	630-6642
Travel Marketing Inc 4235 SW Corbett Ave *TF:* 800-283-1022 ■ *Web:* www.travelmarketing.org	Portland	OR	97239	503-222-1020	228-8767
Travelcorp 917 Duke St *TF:* 800-770-6910 ■ *Web:* www.travelcorpusa.com	Alexandria	VA	22314	703-299-9003	299-9012
United Incentives Inc 131 N 3rd St *TF:* 800-431-8497 ■ *Web:* www.unitedincentives.com	Philadelphia	PA	19106	215-625-2700	625-2502
Universal Odyssey Inc 1601 Dove St Suite 260 *Web:* www.universalodyssey.com	Newport Beach	CA	92660	949-263-1222	263-0983
USMotivation 7840 Roswell Rd Bldg 100 Suite 300 *TF:* 800-476-0496 ■ *Web:* www.usmotivation.com	Atlanta	GA	30350	770-290-4700	290-4701
Vertrue Inc 20 Glover Ave *NASDAQ: VTRU* ■ *TF:* 800-374-6135 ■ *Web:* www.vertrue.com	Norwalk	CT	06850	203-324-7635	674-7080
Viktor Incentives & Meetings 4020 Copper View Suite 130 *TF:* 800-748-0478 ■ *Web:* www.viktorwithak.com	Traverse City	MI	49684	231-947-0882	947-2532

388 INDUSTRIAL EQUIPMENT & SUPPLIES (MISC) - WHOL

				Phone	Fax
Abatix Corp 2400 Skyline Dr Suite 400 *NASDAQ: ABIX* ■ *TF:* 800-426-3983 ■ *Web:* www.abatix.com	Mesquite	TX	75149	214-381-1146	388-0443
Accurate Air Engineering Inc 16207 Carmenita Rd *TF:* 800-438-5577 ■ *Web:* www.accurateair.com	Cerritos	CA	90703	562-484-6370	484-6371
ACG Direct 14660 23-Mile Rd *TF:* 800-968-7101	Shelby Township	MI	48315	586-247-7100	247-6602
AIM Supply Co 7337 Bryan Dairy Rd *TF:* 800-999-0125 ■ *Web:* www.aimsupply.com	Largo	FL	33777	727-544-6114	544-6211
Aimco 10000 SE Pine St *TF:* 800-852-1368 ■ *Web:* www.aimco-global.com	Portland	OR	97216	503-255-7364	254-0036
Airgas Inc 6055 Rockside Woods Blvd *TF:* 800-554-8306 ■ *Web:* www.airgas.com	Independence	OH	44131	216-642-6600	573-7874
Airgas Inc 259 N Radnor-Chester Rd Suite 100 *NYSE: ARG* ■ *TF:* 800-255-2165 ■ *Web:* www.airgas.com	Radnor	PA	19087	610-687-5253	687-1052
Airgas North Central 3224 Cleveland Ave *Web:* www.airgas.com	Marinette	WI	54143	715-732-7950	732-7940
Alamo Iron Works Inc 943 AT&T Center Pkwy *TF Cust Svc:* 800-292-7817 ■ *Web:* www.aiwnet.com	San Antonio	TX	78219	210-223-6161	704-8351
Ames Supply Co 1936 University Ln *TF:* 800-323-3856 ■ *Web:* www.amessupply.com	Lisle	IL	60532	630-964-2440	964-0497
Applied Industrial Technologies Inc 1 Applied Plaza *NYSE: AIT* ■ *Fax: Hum Res ■ *Web:* web.applied.com	Cleveland	OH	44115	216-426-4000	426-4811*
Associated Packaging Inc 435 Calvert Dr *Web:* www.associatedpackaging.com	Gallatin	TN	37066	615-452-2131	452-7790
Barnes Distribution 1301 E 9th St Suite 700 *TF:* 800-726-9626 ■ *Web:* www.barnesdistribution.com	Cleveland	OH	44114	216-416-7200	430-6903
BC Bearing Group 8985 Fraserwood Ct *Web:* www.bearings.com	Burnaby	BC	V5J5E8	604-433-6711	433-5473
Bearing Distributors Inc 8000 Hub Pkwy *TF:* 888-435-7234 ■ *Web:* www.bdi-usa.com	Cleveland	OH	44125	216-642-9100	642-9573
Bearing Headquarters Co 2601 W Parkes Dr *Web:* www.bearingheadquarters.com	Broadview	IL	60155	708-681-4400	681-4462
Bearings & Drives Inc 607 Lower Poplar St PO Box 4325 *Web:* www.bearingsdrives.com	Macon	GA	31208	478-746-7623	742-7836
Berendsen Fluid Power 401 S Boston Ave 1200 Mid Continent Tower *TF:* 800-360-2327 ■ *Web:* www.bfpna.com	Tulsa	OK	74103	918-592-3781	581-5082
Berk O Co 3 Milltown Ct *TF:* 800-631-7392 ■ *Web:* www.oberk.com	Union	NJ	07083	908-851-9500	851-9367
Brake Supply Co Inc 5501 Foundation Blvd *TF:* 800-457-5788 ■ *Web:* www2.brake.com	Evansville	IN	47725	812-467-1000	429-9493
Briggs Equipment 2777 Stemmons Fwy Suite 1525 *TF:* 800-606-1833 ■ *Web:* www.briggsequipment.com	Dallas	TX	75207	214-630-0808	631-3560
Briggs Industrial Equipment 2777 Stemmons Fwy Suite 1525 *TF:* 800-606-1833 ■ *Web:* www.briggsindustrial.com	Dallas	TX	75207	214-630-0808	631-3560
C & H Distributors LLC 770 S 70th St *Fax Area Code: 800 ■ *TF Sales:* 800-558-9966 ■ *Web:* www.chdist.com	Milwaukee	WI	53214	414-443-1700	336-1331*
Canadian Bearings Ltd 1600 Drew Rd *TF:* 800-229-2327 ■ *Web:* www.canadianbearings.com	Mississauga	ON	L5S1S5	905-670-6700	670-0795
Carlson Systems LLC 10840 Harney St PO Box 3036 *TF:* 800-325-8343 ■ *Web:* www.csystems.com	Omaha	NE	68103	402-593-5300	593-5366
Carter Chambers LLC 6800 S Choctaw Dr *Web:* www.carterchambers.com	Baton Rouge	LA	70806	225-926-2236	926-1289
Cascade Machinery & Electric Inc 4600 E Marginal Way S PO Box 3575 *TF:* 800-289-0500 ■ *Web:* www.cascade-machinery.com	Seattle	WA	98124	206-762-0500	767-5122
Central Power Systems & Services 9200 W Liberty Dr *Fax: Sales ■ *Web:* www.cpower.com	Liberty	MO	64068	816-781-8070	781-2207*
CMC Construction Services 9103 E Almeda Rd *TF:* 877-297-9111 ■ *Web:* www.cmcconstructionservices.com	Houston	TX	77054	713-799-1150	799-8431
Connell Gatco Co 200 Connell Dr *TF:* 800-233-3240 ■ *Web:* www.connellco.com/GATCO.htm	Berkeley Heights	NJ	07922	908-673-3700	673-3800
Cross Co 4400 Piedmont Pkwy *TF:* 800-472-2767 ■ *Web:* www.crossco.com	Greensboro	NC	27410	336-856-6985	856-6999
Deacon Industrial Supply Co Inc 165 Boro Line Rd *Web:* www.deaconind.com	King of Prussia	PA	19406	610-265-5322	265-6470
Detroit Pump & Mfg Co 450 Fair St Bldg D *TF:* 800-686-1662 ■ *Web:* www.detroitpump.com	Ferndale	MI	48220	248-544-4242	544-4141
Dillon Supply Co 440 Civic Ave PO box 1111 *Web:* www.dillonsupply.com	Raleigh	NC	27602	919-832-7771	838-4251
DoALL Co 1480 S Wolf Rd *Web:* www.doall.com	Wheeling	IL	60090	847-495-6800	484-2045
Drago Supply Co 740 Houston Ave *Fax: Sales ■ *Web:* www.dragosupply.com	Port Arthur	TX	77640	409-983-4911	982-8240*
Duncan Industrial Solutions 3450 S MacArthur Blvd *TF:* 800-375-9470 ■ *Web:* www.duncanindustrial.com	Oklahoma City	OK	73179	405-688-2300	
DXP Enterprises Inc 7272 Pinemont Dr *NASDAQ: DXPE* ■ *TF:* 877-996-4700 ■ *Web:* www.dxpe.com	Houston	TX	77040	713-996-4700	996-4701
Eastern Lift Truck Co Inc 549 E Linwood Ave PO Box 307 *TF:* 888-779-8880 ■ *Web:* www.easternlifttruck.com	Maple Shade	NJ	08052	856-779-8880	482-8804
Edgen Corp 18444 Highland Rd *TF:* 866-334-3648 ■ *Web:* www.edgencorp.com	Baton Rouge	LA	70809	225-756-9868	756-7953
Ellison Machinery Co 9912 S Pioneer Blvd *TF:* 800-358-4828 ■ *Web:* www.ellisonmachinery.com	Santa Fe Springs	CA	90670	562-949-8311	949-9091
Endries International Inc 714 W Ryan St *TF:* 800-852-5821 ■ *Web:* www.endries.com	Brillion	WI	54110	920-756-2174	756-2925
Engman-Taylor Co Inc W142 N9351 Fountain Blvd *TF:* 800-236-1975 ■ *Web:* www.engman-taylor.com	Menomonee Falls	WI	53051	262-255-9300	255-6512
Exterran 8150 N Central Expy Suite 1550 *NYSE: HC* ■ *TF Sales:* 800-522-9270 ■ *Web:* www.exterran.com	Dallas	TX	75206	214-369-5554	378-5091
Fairmont Supply Co 401 Technology Dr *Web:* www.fairmontsupply.com	Canonsburg	PA	15317	724-514-3900	261-5310
FCx Performance Inc 3000 E 14th Ave *TF:* 800-253-6223 ■ *Web:* www.fcxperformance.com	Columbus	OH	43219	614-253-1996	253-2033
FD Stella Products Co 7000 Fenkell St *TF:* 800-447-7356 ■ *Web:* www.fdstella.com	Detroit	MI	48238	313-341-6400	342-8398
Forklifts of Minnesota Inc 501 W 78th St *TF:* 800-752-4300 ■ *Web:* www.forkliftsofmn.com	Bloomington	MN	55420	952-887-5400	881-3030
FUJIFILM Graphic System USA Inc 200 Summit Lake Dr *TF:* 800-755-3854 ■ *Web:* www.fujifilmgs.com	Valhalla	NY	10595	914-749-4800	749-4899
FW Webb 237 Albany St *TF:* 800-453-1100 ■ *Web:* www.fwwebb.com	Boston	MA	02118	617-227-2240	423-7858
Gas Equipment Co 1440 Lakes Pkwy Suite 300 *TF:* 800-241-4155	Lawrenceville	GA	30043	770-995-1131	995-1216
General Tool & Supply Co Inc 2705 NW Nicolai St *TF:* 800-783-3411 ■ *Web:* www.generaltool.com	Portland	OR	97210	503-226-3411	778-5518
Genuine Parts Co 2999 Circle 75 Pkwy *NYSE: GPC* ■ *Web:* www.genpt.com	Atlanta	GA	30339	770-953-1700	956-2211
Gosiger Inc 108 McDonough St *TF:* 800-888-4188 ■ *Web:* www.gosiger.com	Dayton	OH	45402	937-228-5174	228-5189
Grady W Jones Co 3965 Old Getwell Rd *TF:* 800-727-5118 ■ *Web:* www.gradyjones.com	Memphis	TN	38118	901-365-8830	368-5102
Hagemeyer North America Inc 1460 Tobias Gadson Blvd *TF:* 800-752-0007 ■ *Web:* www.hagemeyerna.com	Charleston	SC	29407	843-745-2400	745-6942
Haggard & Stocking Assoc 5318 Victory Dr *TF:* 800-622-4824 ■ *Web:* www.haggard-stocking.com	Indianapolis	IN	46203	317-788-4661	788-1645
Hahn Systems Co Inc 2401 Production Dr *TF:* 800-589-3796 ■ *Web:* www.hahnsystems.com	Indianapolis	IN	46241	317-243-3796	244-9079
Harrington Industrial Plastics LLC 14480 Yorba Ave *TF:* 800-669-8641 ■ *Web:* www.harringtonplastics.com	Chino	CA	91710	909-597-8641	597-9826
HD Supply Waterworks Ltd 1001 Washingtron Ave *TF:* 800-817-5355 ■ *Web:* www.nationalwaterworks.com	Waco	TX	76701	254-772-5355	772-5716
Herc-U-Lift Inc 5655 Hwy 12 W *TF:* 800-362-3500 ■ *Web:* www.herc-u-lift.com	Maple Plain	MN	55359	763-479-2501	479-2296
Hope Group 70 Bearfoot Rd *Web:* www.thehopegroup.com	Northborough	MA	01532	508-393-7660	393-8203
Hub Supply Inc 2546 S Leonine St *TF:* 800-482-8665 ■ *Web:* www.hubsupplyonline.com	Wichita	KS	67217	316-265-9608	265-6229
Hughes RS Co Inc 10639 Glenoaks Blvd *TF:* 877-774-8443 ■ *Web:* rshughes.com	Pacoima	CA	91331	818-686-9111	686-1973
Hull Lift Truck Inc 28747 Old US 33 W *TF:* 800-860-4855 ■ *Web:* www.hullifttruck.com	Elkhart	IN	46516	574-293-8651	293-9769
IBT Inc 9400 W 55th St *TF:* 800-332-2114 ■ *Web:* www.ibtinc.com	Merriam	KS	66203	913-677-3151	677-3752
Illinois Auto Electric Co 700 Enterprise St *TF:* 800-683-9312 ■ *Web:* www.illinoisautoelectric.com	Aurora	IL	60504	630-862-3300	862-3137

Phone *Fax*

Indoff Inc 11816 Lackland Rd Saint Louis MO 63146 314-997-1122 812-3931
TF: 800-486-7867 ■ *Web:* www.indoff.com
Indusco Group 1200 W Hamburg St Baltimore MD 21230 410-727-0665 727-2538
TF: 800-727-0665 ■ *Web:* www.induscowirerope.com
Industrial Controls Distributors Inc 1776 Bloomsbury Ave Wanamassa NJ 07712 732-918-9000 922-4417
TF: 800-631-2112 ■ *Web:* www.industrialcontrolsonline.com
Industrial Distribution Group Inc
950 E Paces Ferry Rd Suite 1575 Atlanta GA 30326 404-949-2100 949-2040
NASDAQ: IDGR ■ *Web:* www.idglink.com
Industrial Services of America Inc 7100 Grade Ln Louisville KY 40213 502-368-1661 368-1440
NASDAQ: IDSA ■ *TF:* 800-824-2144 ■ *Web:* www.isa-inc.com
Industrial Supply Solutions Inc 520 Elizabeth St Charleston WV 25311 304-346-5341 346-5347
TF: 800-346-5341 ■ *Web:* www.issimro.com
J & L Industrial Supply 20921 Lahser Rd Southfield MI 48034 800-521-9520 525-6817*
**Fax:* Cust Svc ■ *Web:* www.jlindustrial.com
Jabo Supply Corp 5164 Braley St Huntington WV 25705 304-736-8333 736-8551
TF: 800-334-5226 ■ *Web:* www.jabosupply.com
Jefferds Corp US Rt 35 W PO Box 757 Saint Albans WV 25177 304-755-8111 755-7544
TF: 800-735-8111 ■ *Web:* www.jefferds.com
Johnson & Towers Inc 2021 Briggs Rd Mount Laurel NJ 08054 856-234-6990 222-2414
TF: 800-394-6996 ■ *Web:* www.johnsontowers.com
Jones Grady W Co 3965 Old Getwell Rd Memphis TN 38118 901-365-8830 368-5102
TF: 800-727-5118 ■ *Web:* www.gradyjones.com
Kaman Industrial Technologies Inc 1 Waterside Crossing Windsor CT 06095 860-687-5000 687-5170
TF: 800-526-2626 ■ *Web:* www.kamandirect.com
Kennametal Inc 1600 Technology Way PO Box 231 Latrobe PA 15650 724-539-5000 539-8787
NYSE: KMT ■ *TF Cust Svc:* 800-446-7738 ■ *Web:* www.kennametal.com
Kimball Midwest 4800 Robert Rd Columbus OH 43228 614-219-6100 219-6101
TF: 800-233-1294 ■ *Web:* www.kimballmidwest.com
Kinecor 2200 52nd Ave Lachine QC H8T2Y3 514-636-3333 636-7777
TF: 866-336-7633 ■ *Web:* www.kinecor.com
Knickerbocker Russell Co Inc 4759 Campbells Run Pittsburgh PA 15205 412-494-9233 787-7991
Web: www.knickerbockerrussell.com
L & H Technologies Inc 11616 Wilmar Blvd Charlotte NC 28273 704-588-3670 588-5622
TF: 800-753-4576 ■ *Web:* www.lhtech.com
Lawson Products Inc 1666 E Touhy Ave Des Plaines IL 60018 847-827-9666 296-6309*
NASDAQ: LAWS ■ **Fax:* Sales ■ *TF:* 800-323-6312 ■ *Web:* www.lawsonproducts.com
Lewis Goetz & Co Inc 1571 Grandview Ave Paulsboro NJ 08066 856-579-1421 579-1429
TF: 800-562-8002 ■ *Web:* www.lewis-goetz.com
Lewis-Goetz & Co Inc 650 Washington Rd Suite 210 Pittsburgh PA 15228 412-341-7100 341-7192
TF: 800-289-1236 ■ *Web:* www.lewis-goetz.com
Lister-Petter Americas Inc 815 E 56 Hwy Olathe KS 66061 913-764-3512 764-5493
TF: 800-888-3512 ■ *Web:* www.lister-petter.com
Logan Corp 555 7th Ave Huntington WV 25706 304-526-4700 526-4747
TF: 888-853-4751 ■ *Web:* www.logancorp.com
Mac-Gray Corp 404 Wyman St Suite 404 Waltham MA 02451 781-487-7600 487-7601
NYSE: TUC ■ *TF:* 866-613-4411 ■ *Web:* www.mac-gray.com
Machine & Welding Supply Co 1660 Hwy 301 S PO Box 1708 Dunn NC 28335 910-892-4016 892-3575
Web: www.mwsc.com
Machinery Systems Inc 614 E State Pkwy Schaumburg IL 60173 847-882-8085 882-2894
TF: 800-347-8085 ■ *Web:* www.machinerysystems.com
Mahar Tool Supply Co Inc 112 Williams St Saginaw MI 48602 989-799-5530 799-0830
TF: 800-456-2427 ■ *Web:* www.mahartool.com
Martin Supply Co 200 Appleton Ave Sheffield AL 35660 256-383-3131 389-9447
TF: 800-828-8116 ■ *Web:* www.mscoinc.com
Material Handling Services Inc 650 W Grand Ave Elmhurst IL 60126 630-665-7200 665-4702
Web: www.mhs-lift.com
McJunkin Corp 835 Hillcrest Dr E Charleston WV 25311 304-348-5211 348-4938
TF: 800-624-8603 ■ *Web:* www.mcjunkin.com
Medart Inc 124 Manufacturers Dr Arnold MO 63010 636-282-2300 510-3100*
**Fax Area Code:* 888 ■ *TF:* 800-888-7181 ■ *Web:* www.medartinc.com
MEE Material Handling Equipment 11721 W Carmen Ave Milwaukee WI 53225 414-353-3300 353-6327
TF: 800-242-5452 ■ *Web:* www.meelift.com
Minnesota Supply Co Inc 6470 Flying Cloud Dr Eden Prairie MN 55344 952-828-7300 828-7301
TF: 800-869-1058 ■ *Web:* www.mnsupply.com
Mitsubishi International Corp 655 3rd Ave New York NY 10017 212-605-2000
Web: www.micusa.com
Modern Group Ltd 2501 Durham Rd Bristol PA 19007 215-943-9100 943-4978
TF: 800-223-3827 ■ *Web:* www.moderngroup.com
Morris Robert E Co 910 Gay Hill Rd Windsor CT 06095 860-687-3300 687-3301
TF: 800-223-0785 ■ *Web:* www.robertemorris.com
Motion Industries Inc 1605 Alton Rd Birmingham AL 35210 205-956-1122 951-1172
TF: 800-526-9328 ■ *Web:* www.motion-industries.com
MSC Industrial Direct Co 75 Maxess Rd Melville NY 11747 516-812-2000 255-5067*
NYSE: MSM ■ **Fax Area Code:* 800 ■ *TF:* 800-645-7270 ■ *Web:* www1.mscdirect.com
Multiquip Inc 18910 Wilmington Ave Carson CA 90746 310-537-3700 537-3927
TF: 800-421-1244 ■ *Web:* www.multiquip.com
National Welders Supply Co Inc 810 Gesco St Charlotte NC 28208 704-333-5475 342-0260
TF: 800-866-4422 ■ *Web:* www.nwsco.com
NC Machinery Co 17025 W Valley Hwy Tukwila WA 98188 425-251-9800 251-5886
TF: 800-562-4735 ■ *Web:* www.ncmachinery.com
Nebraska Machinery Co Inc 3501 S Jeffers St PO Box 809 North Platte NE 69103 308-532-3100 532-3173
TF: 800-494-9560 ■ *Web:* www.nebraska-machinery.com
Nelson-Jameson Inc 2400 E 5th St Marshfield WI 54449 715-387-1151 387-8746
TF: 800-826-8302 ■ *Web:* www.nelsonjameson.com
Newman's Inc 1300 Gazin St Houston TX 77020 713-675-8631 675-1589
TF: 800-231-3505 ■ *Web:* www.newcovalves.com
NSC International 7090 Central Ave Hot Springs AR 71913 501-525-0133 960-2727*
**Fax Area Code:* 800 ■ *TF:* 800-643-1520 ■ *Web:* www.binding.com
O Berk Co 3 Milltown Ct Union NJ 07083 908-851-9500 851-9367
TF: 800-631-7392 ■ *Web:* www.oberk.com
Ohio Transmission & Pump Co 1900 Jetway Blvd Columbus OH 43219 614-342-6123 342-6490
TF: 800-837-6827 ■ *Web:* www.otpnet.com
Pacific Power Products 600 S 56th Pl Ridgefield WA 98642 360-887-7400 887-7401
TF: 800-882-3860 ■ *Web:* www.pacificdda.com
Phenix Supply Co 5330 Dividend Dr Decatur GA 30035 770-981-2800 981-6462
TF: 800-688-3032 ■ *Web:* www.phenixsupply.com
Piping & Equipment Inc 9100 Canniff St Houston TX 77017 713-947-9393 948-9559
TF: 800-364-9384 ■ *Web:* www.pipingequipment.com
Pitman Co 721 Union Blvd Totowa NJ 07512 973-812-0400 812-1630
TF: 800-631-3128 ■ *Web:* www.pitmanco.com
Precision Industries Inc 4611 S 96th St Omaha NE 68127 402-593-7000 593-7054
TF: 800-373-7777 ■ *Web:* www.precisionind.com
Proctor Stanley Co 2016 Midway Dr Twinsburg OH 44087 330-425-7814 425-3222
TF: 800-352-0123 ■ *Web:* www.stanleyproctor.com
Production Tool Supply 8655 E Eight Mile Rd Warren MI 48089 586-755-7770 755-2151*
**Fax:* Sales ■ *TF:* 800-366-3600 ■ *Web:* www.pts-tools.com
R & M Energy Systems 301 Premier Rd Borger TX 79008 806-274-5293 274-3418
TF Sales: 800-858-4158 ■ *Web:* www.rmenergy.com
Red Man Pipe & Supply Co 8023 E 63rd Pl Suite 800 Tulsa OK 74133 918-250-8541 461-5376
TF: 800-666-3776 ■ *Web:* www.red-man.com
Rem Sales Inc 910 Gay Hill Rd Windsor CT 06095 860-687-3400 687-3401
TF: 800-808-1020 ■ *Web:* www.remsales.com
Rex Supply Co 3715 Harrisburg Blvd Houston TX 77003 713-222-2251 225-5739
TF: 800-369-0669 ■ *Web:* www.rex-supply.com
RHM Fluid Power Inc 375 Manufacturers Dr Westland MI 48186 734-326-5400 326-0339
Web: www.rhmfluidpower.com

Phone *Fax*

Robert E Morris Co 910 Gay Hill Rd Windsor CT 06095 860-687-3300 687-3301
TF: 800-223-0785 ■ *Web:* www.robertemorris.com
RS Hughes Co Inc 10639 Glenoaks Blvd Pacoima CA 91331 818-686-9111 686-1973
TF: 877-774-8443 ■ *Web:* rshughes.com
Ryan Herco Products Corp 3010 N San Fernando Blvd Burbank CA 91504 818-841-1141 973-2600
TF: 800-848-1141 ■ *Web:* www.ryanherco.com
Shively Brothers Inc 2919 S Grand Travers St PO Box 1520 Flint MI 48501 810-232-7401 232-3219
TF: 800-530-9352 ■ *Web:* www.shivelybros.com
Smith Power Products Inc 3065 W California Ave Salt Lake City UT 84104 801-415-5000 415-5700
TF: 800-658-5352 ■ *Web:* www.smithpowerproducts.com
Sooner Pipe LLC 1331 Lamar St Suite 970 4 Houston Center Houston TX 77010 713-759-1200 759-0442
TF: 800-888-9161 ■ *Web:* www.soonerpipe.com
Southern Pump & Tank Co 4800 N Graham St Charlotte NC 28269 704-596-4373 599-7700
TF Cust Svc: 800-477-2826 ■ *Web:* www.southernpump.com
Stanley M Proctor Co 2016 Midway Dr Twinsburg OH 44087 330-425-7814 425-3222
TF: 800-352-0123 ■ *Web:* www.stanleyproctor.com
Star CNC Machine Tool Corp 123 Powerhouse Rd Roslyn Heights NY 11577 516-484-0500 484-5820
TF: 800-377-4006 ■ *Web:* www.starcnc.com
Stella FD Products Co 7000 Fenkell St Detroit MI 48238 313-341-6400 342-8398
TF: 800-447-7356 ■ *Web:* www.fdstella.com
Strategic Distribution Inc 1414 Radcliffe St Suite 300 Bristol PA 19007 215-633-1900 633-4423
NASDAQ: STRD ■ *Web:* www.in-plantstore.com
SunSource Pabco Fluid Power Co Inc 5750 Hillside Ave Cincinnati OH 45233 513-941-6200 941-6452
TF: 800-727-2226 ■ *Web:* www.pabcofluidpower.com
Tate Engineering Systems Inc 1560 Caton Center Dr Baltimore MD 21227 410-242-8800 242-7777
TF: 800-800-8283 ■ *Web:* www.tate.com
Tencarva Machinery Co Inc 12200 Wilfong Ct Midlothian VA 23112 804-639-4646 639-2400
Web: www.tencarva.com
Texas Process Equipment Co 5880 Bingle Rd Houston TX 77092 713-460-5555 460-4807
TF: 800-828-4114 ■ *Web:* www.texasprocess.com
Travers Tool Co Inc 128-15 26th Ave Flushing NY 11354 718-886-7200 722-0703*
**Fax Area Code:* 800 ■ *TF Cust Svc:* 800-221-0270 ■ *Web:* www.travers.com
Valley National Gases LLC 67 43rd St PO Box 6628 Wheeling WV 26003 304-232-1541 233-2812
AMEX: VLG ■ *Web:* vngas.com
Valley Welders Supply 320 N 11th St Billings MT 59101 406-256-3330 256-3343
TF: 800-821-9470 ■ *Web:* www.valleywelders.com
Vellano Brothers Inc 7 Hemlock St Latham NY 12110 518-785-5537 785-5561
TF: 800-342-9855 ■ *Web:* www.vellano.com
Voto Manufacturers Sales Co 500 N 3rd St Steubenville OH 43952 740-282-3621 282-5441
TF: 800-848-4010 ■ *Web:* www.votosales.com
Wajax Ltd 3280 Wharton Way Mississauga ON L4X2C5 905-212-3358 212-3350
TSX: WJX ■ *Web:* www.wajax.com
Webb FW 237 Albany St Boston MA 02118 617-227-2240 423-7858
TF: 800-453-1100 ■ *Web:* www.fwwebb.com
Werres Corp 807 E South St Frederick MD 21701 301-620-4000 662-1028*
**Fax:* Sales ■ *TF:* 800-638-6563 ■ *Web:* www.werres.com
Western Branch Diesel Inc 3504 Shipwright St Portsmouth VA 23703 757-673-7000 673-7190
Web: www.wbdiesel.com
Wilson Supply Co 1301 Conti St Houston TX 77002 713-237-3700 237-3777
TF: 800-228-2893 ■ *Web:* www.wilsononline.com
Windsor Factory Supply Ltd 730 N Service Rd Windsor ON N8X3J3 519-966-2202 966-2740
TF: 800-387-2659 ■ *Web:* www.wfsltd.com
Wolseley Industrial Products Group 680 Davenport Rd Waterloo ON N2V2C3 519-885-6500 747-4133
Web: www.wolseleyinc.ca
Yamazen Inc 735 E Remington Rd Schaumburg IL 60173 847-882-8800 882-4296
TF: 800-882-8558 ■ *Web:* www.yamazen.com
Zatkoff Seals & Packings 23230 Industrial Park Dr Farmington Hills MI 48335 248-478-2400 478-3392
TF: 800-967-3257 ■ *Web:* www.zatkoff.com
Zuckerman-Honickman Inc 191 S Gulph Rd King of Prussia PA 19406 610-962-0100 962-1080
TF: 800-523-1475 ■ *Web:* www.zh-inc.com

389 INDUSTRIAL MACHINERY, EQUIPMENT, & SUPPLIES

SEE ALSO Conveyors & Conveying Equipment p. 1571; Food Products Machinery p. 1662; Furnaces & Ovens - Industrial Process p. 1680; Machine Shops p. 1923; Material Handling Equipment p. 1949; Packaging Machinery & Equipment p. 2042; Paper Industries Machinery p. 2047; Printing & Publishing Equipment & Systems p. 2141; Rolling Mill Machinery p. 2300; Textile Machinery p. 2361; Woodworking Machinery p. 2419

Phone *Fax*

3G Tech Inc 6920 Hayvenhurst Ave Suite 205 Van Nuys CA 91406 818-510-4709 510-4716
Web: www.hbsequipment.com
ABB Inc 501 Merritt 7 Norwalk CT 06851 203-750-2200 435-7365
TF Prod Info: 800-626-4999 ■ *Web:* www.abb.us
Adept Technology Inc 3011 Triad Dr Livermore CA 94551 925-245-3400 960-0592
NASDAQ: ADEP ■ *TF:* 800-292-3378 ■ *Web:* www.adept.com
Advanced Assembly Automation 313 Mound St Dayton OH 45402 937-222-3030 222-2931
Web: www.assembly-testww.com
Aeroglide Corp 100 Aeroglide Dr PO Box 29505 Raleigh NC 27626 919-851-2000 851-6029
TF: 800-722-7483 ■ *Web:* www.aeroglide.com
Alemite LLC 1057-521 Corporate Center Dr Suite 100 Fort Mill SC 29715 803-802-0001 802-0198
TF: 800-267-8022 ■ *Web:* www.alemite.com
Allen-Sherman-Hoff Co 185 Great Valley Pkwy Malvern PA 19355 610-647-9900 648-8679
TF: 888-274-7278 ■ *Web:* www.a-s-h.com
Allentown Equipment 421 Schantz Rd Allentown PA 18104 610-398-0451 398-9244
TF: 800-553-3414 ■ *Web:* www.allentownequipment.com
American Baler Co 800 E Centre St Bellevue OH 44811 419-483-5790 483-3815
TF: 800-843-7512 ■ *Web:* www.americanbaler.com
AO Smith Water Products Co 500 Tennessee Waltz Pkwy Ashland City TN 37015 615-792-4371 792-4371
TF: 800-365-8170 ■ *Web:* www.hotwater.com
Apache Stainless Equipment Corp
200 W Industrial Dr PO Box 538 Beaver Dam WI 53916 920-887-3721 887-0206
TF: 800-444-0398 ■ *Web:* www.apachestainless.com
Assembly Technology & Test 400 Florence St Saginaw MI 48602 989-791-6400 791-6486
Web: www.assembly-testww.com
Bagshaw WH Co Inc 1 Pine St Ext PO Box 766 Nashua NH 03061 603-883-7758 882-2651
TF: 800-343-7467 ■ *Web:* www.whbagshaw.com
Besser Co 801 Johnson St Alpena MI 49707 989-354-4111 354-3120
TF: 800-530-9980 ■ *Web:* www.besser.com
Besser Lithibar Co 13521 Quality Dr Holland MI 49424 616-399-5215 399-4026
TF: 800-626-0415 ■ *Web:* www.besser.com
Billco Mfg Inc 100 Halstead Blvd Zelienople PA 16063 724-452-7390 452-0217
Web: www.billco-mfg.com
BloApCo (Blower Application Co Inc)
N 114 W 19125 Clinton Dr Germantown WI 53022 262-255-5580 255-3446
TF: 800-959-0880 ■ *Web:* www.bloapco.com
Blower Application Co Inc (BloApCo)
N 114 W 19125 Clinton Dr Germantown WI 53022 262-255-5580 255-3446
TF: 800-959-0880 ■ *Web:* www.bloapco.com
Burke E Porter Machinery Co 730 Plymouth Ave NE Grand Rapids MI 49505 616-459-9531 459-1032
Web: www.bepco.com

Company	City	State	ZIP	Phone	Fax
Catalytica Energy Systems Inc 301 W Warner Rd Suite 132	Tempe	AZ	85284	480-556-5555	556-5500
NASDAQ: CESI ■ *Web:* www.catalyticaenergy.com					
Central Sprinkler Corp 451 N Cannon Ave	Lansdale	PA	19446	215-362-0700	362-4731
TF: 800-523-6512 ■ *Web:* www.tyco-central.com					
CFEE (Concrete Forming Equipment & Engineering Co) 305 S New Albany Ave	Sellersberg	IN	47172	812-246-8088	246-8833
TF: 800-590-2448 ■ *Web:* www.cfeeforms.com					
CHA Industries 4201 Business Center Dr	Fremont	CA	94538	510-683-8554	683-3848*
**Fax:* Sales ■ *Web:* www.chaindustries.com					
Charles Ross & Son Co 710 Old Willets Path	Hauppauge	NY	11788	631-234-0500	234-0691
TF: 800-243-7677 ■ *Web:* www.mixers.com					
Chemineer Inc 5870 Poe Ave	Dayton	OH	45414	937-454-3200	454-3379*
**Fax:* Sales ■ *TF:* 800-643-0641 ■ *Web:* www.chemineer.com					
Chemithon Corp 5430 West Marginal Way SW	Seattle	WA	98106	206-937-9954	932-3786
Web: www.chemithon.com					
Chief Automotive Systems Inc 1924 E 4th St	Grand Island	NE	68801	308-384-9747	384-8966*
**Fax:* Mktg ■ *TF:* 800-445-9262 ■ *Web:* www.chiefautomotive.com					
Cohesant Technologies Inc 5845 W 82nd St Suite 102	Indianapolis	IN	76278	317-875-5592	875-5456
NASDAQ: COHT ■ *Web:* www.cohesant.com					
Comau Pico 21000 Telegraph Rd	Southfield	MI	48034	248-353-8888	368-2511
Web: www.comaupico.com					
Concrete Forming Equipment & Engineering Co (CFEE) 305 S New Albany Ave	Sellersberg	IN	47172	812-246-8088	246-8833
TF: 800-590-2448 ■ *Web:* www.cfeeforms.com					
Corotec Corp 145 Hyde Rd	Farmington	CT	06032	860-678-0038	674-5229
TF: 800-423-0348 ■ *Web:* www.corotec.com					
CUNO Inc 400 Research Pkwy	Meriden	CT	06450	203-237-5541	238-8701
TF: 800-243-6894 ■ *Web:* www.cuno.com					
Davis-Standard LLC 1 Extrusion Dr	Pawcatuck	CT	06379	860-599-1010	599-6258
Web: www.davis-standard.com					
Despatch Industries Inc 8860 207th St W	Lakeville	MN	55044	952-469-5424	469-4513
Web: www.despatch.com					
Diamond Power International Inc 2600 E Main St	Lancaster	OH	43130	740-687-6500	687-4229
TF: 800-848-5086 ■ *Web:* www.diamondpower.com					
Dings Co 4740 W Electric Ave	Milwaukee	WI	53219	414-672-7830	672-5354
Web: www.dingsco.com					
Donaldson Co Inc 1400 W 94th St	Bloomington	MN	55431	952-887-3131	887-3155
NYSE: DCI ■ *Web:* www.donaldson.com					
Dorr-Oliver Eimco USA Inc 2850 S Decker Lake Dr	Salt Lake City	UT	84119	801-526-2000	526-2543
TF: 800-257-0552 ■ *Web:* www.glv.com					
Dresser-Rand Paul Clark Dr	Olean	NY	14760	716-375-3000	375-3178
NYSE: DRC ■ *Web:* www.dresser-rand.com					
Dusenbery John Co Inc 220 Franklin Rd	Randolph	NJ	07869	973-366-7500	366-7453
Web: www.dusenbery.com					
Easom Automation Systems 32471 Industrial Dr	Madison Heights	MI	48071	248-307-0650	307-0701
Web: www.easomeng.com					
Eaton Filtration 9151 Shaver Rd	Portage	MI	49024	269-323-1313	323-2403
TF: 800-525-4214 ■ *Web:* www.filtration.eaton.com					
Ecodyne Ltd 4475 Corporate Dr	Burlington	ON	L7L5T9	905-332-1404	332-6726
Web: www.ecodyne.com					
EFD Induction Inc 31511 Dequindre Rd	Madison Heights	MI	48071	248-658-0700	658-0701
Web: www.efd-induction.com					
Enerflex Systems Ltd 4700 47th St SE	Calgary	AB	T2B3R1	403-236-6800	720-4332
TSX: EFX ■ *TF:* 800-242-3178 ■ *Web:* www.enerflex.com					
Energy Sciences Inc 42 Industrial Way	Wilmington	MA	01887	978-694-9060	694-9046
Web: www.ebeam.com					
Engis Corp 105 W Hintz Rd	Wheeling	IL	60090	847-808-9400	808-9430
TF: 800-993-6447 ■ *Web:* www.engis.com					
Enterprise Co 616 S Santa Fe St	Santa Ana	CA	92705	714-835-0541	543-2856
Web: www.enterpriseco.com					
Entwistle Co 6 Bigelow St	Hudson	MA	01749	508-481-4000	481-4004
Web: www.entwistleco.com					
FANUC Robotics North America Inc 3900 W Hamlin Rd	Rochester Hills	MI	48309	248-377-7000	377-7832
TF: 800-477-6268 ■ *Web:* www.fanucrobotics.com					
Farrel Corp 25 Main St	Ansonia	CT	06401	203-736-5500	735-6267
TF: 800-800-7290 ■ *Web:* www.farrel.com					
Fluid Management Inc 1023 S Wheeling Rd	Wheeling	IL	60090	847-537-0880	537-5530
TF: 800-462-2466 ■ *Web:* www.fluidman.com					
Formaloy Corp 1080 W Jefferson St	Morton	IL	61550	309-266-5381	263-0366
Forward Technology Industries Inc 3050 Ranchview Ln N	Minneapolis	MN	55447	763-559-1785	559-3929
TF Cust Svc: 800-307-6040 ■ *Web:* www.forwardtech.com					
Foster Wheeler Energy International Inc Perryville Corporate Park	Clinton	NJ	08809	908-730-4000	730-5315
Web: www.fwc.com					
French Oil Mill Machinery Co 1035 W Greene St	Piqua	OH	45356	937-773-3420	773-3424
Web: www.frenchoil.com					
Fusion Inc 4658 E 355th St	Willoughby	OH	44094	440-946-3300	942-9083
TF: 800-626-9501 ■ *Web:* www.fusion-inc.com					
Galbreath Inc 461 E Rosser Dr	Winamac	IN	46996	574-946-6631	946-4579
TF: 800-285-0666 ■ *Web:* www.galbreath-inc.com					
Gamajet Cleaning Systems Inc 2485 Yellow Springs Rd	Malvern	PA	19355	610-408-9940	408-9945
TF Sales: 877-426-2538 ■ *Web:* www.gamajet.com					
GEA Niro Inc 9165 Rumsey Rd	Columbia	MD	21045	410-997-8700	997-5021
TF: 800-446-4231 ■ *Web:* www.niroinc.com					
General Equipment Co 620 Alexander Dr SW PO Box 334	Owatonna	MN	55060	507-451-5510	451-5511
TF Cust Svc: 800-533-0524 ■ *Web:* www.generalequip.com					
George Koch Sons LLC 10 S 11th Ave	Evansville	IN	47744	812-465-9600	465-9676*
**Fax:* Sales ■ *TF:* 888-873-5624 ■ *Web:* www.kochllc.com					
Gerber Scientific Inc 83 Gerber Rd	South Windsor	CT	06074	860-644-1551	643-7039
NYSE: GRB ■ *Web:* www.gerberscientific.com					
GL & V Inc 25 des Forges St Le Bourge du Fleuve Bldg Suite 420	Trois-Rivières	QC	G9A6A7	819-371-8265	373-4439
TSX: GLV ■ *Web:* www.glv.com					
Globe Products Inc 5051 Kitridge Rd	Dayton	OH	45424	937-233-0233	233-5290
Web: www.globe-usa.com					
Glunt Industries Inc 319 N River Rd NW	Warren	OH	44483	330-399-7585	393-0387
Web: www.glunt.com					
Gougler Industries Inc 705 Lake St	Kent	OH	44240	330-673-5821	673-5824
TF: 800-527-2282 ■ *Web:* www.gougler.com					
Graham Corp 20 Florence Ave	Batavia	NY	14020	585-343-2216	343-1097
AMEX: GHM ■ *TF Orders:* 800-828-8150 ■ *Web:* www.graham-mfg.com					
Groupe Laperrier & Verreault Inc 25 des Forges St Le Bourge du Fleuve Bldg Suite 420	Trois-Rivières	QC	G9A6A7	819-371-8265	373-4439
TSX: GLV ■ *Web:* www.glv.com					
Guzzler Mfg Inc 1621 S Illinois St	Streator	IL	61364	815-672-3171	672-2779*
**Fax:* Sales ■ *Web:* www.guzzler.com					
Hamon Research-Cottrell Inc 58 E Main St	Somerville	NJ	08876	908-685-4000	333-2152
TF: 800-722-7580 ■ *Web:* www.hamon-researchcottrell.com					
Hosokawa Micron Powder Systems 10 Chatham Rd	Summit	NJ	07901	908-273-6360	273-6344
Web: www.hosokawamicron.com					
Hosokawa Polymer Systems 63 Fuller Way	Berlin	CT	06037	860-828-0541	829-1313
TF: 800-233-6112 ■ *Web:* www.polysys.com					
Husky Injection Molding Systems Ltd 500 Queen St S	Bolton	ON	L7E5S5	905-951-5000	951-5384
TSX: HKY ■ *Web:* www.husky.ca					
ICS Inex Systems 13075 US Hwy 19 N	Clearwater	FL	33764	727-535-5502	532-8513
Web: www.inexvision.com					
Illinois Tool Works Inc (ITW) 3600 W Lake Ave	Glenview	IL	60026	847-724-7500	657-4261
NYSE: ITW ■ *TF:* 800-724-6166 ■ *Web:* www.itwinc.com					
Industrial Fabricators Inc 403 N Cemetery St	Thorp	WI	54771	715-669-5512	669-5514
Ingersoll-Rand Co 155 Chestnut Ridge Rd	Montvale	NJ	07645	201-573-0123	573-3172
NYSE: IR ■ *Web:* www.irco.com					
ITW (Illinois Tool Works Inc) 3600 W Lake Ave	Glenview	IL	60026	847-724-7500	657-4261
NYSE: ITW ■ *TF:* 800-724-6166 ■ *Web:* www.itwinc.com					
John Dusenbery Co Inc 220 Franklin Rd	Randolph	NJ	07869	973-366-7500	366-7453
Web: www.dusenbery.com					
KJ Brewco Collision Repair Systems Inc 309 Exchange Ave	Conway	AR	72032	501-450-1500	450-2085
TF: 800-582-5215 ■ *Web:* www.kansasjack.com					
Koch Chemical Technology Group LLC 4111 E 37th St N	Wichita	KS	67220	316-828-5500	828-4704
Web: www.kochchemtech.com					
Koch George Sons LLC 10 S 11th Ave	Evansville	IN	47744	812-465-9600	465-9676*
**Fax:* Sales ■ *TF:* 888-873-5624 ■ *Web:* www.kochllc.com					
Koch-Glitsch Inc 4111 East 37th St N	Wichita	KS	67220	316-828-5110	828-5263
Web: www.koch-glitsch.com					
Koch Membrane Systems Inc 850 Main St	Wilmington	MA	01887	978-694-7000	657-5208
TF: 800-343-0499 ■ *Web:* www.kochmembrane.com					
Komline-Sanderson Engineering Corp 12 Holland Ave	Peapack	NJ	07977	908-234-1000	234-9487
TF: 800-225-5457 ■ *Web:* www.komline.com					
Lawton Industries Inc 4353 Pacific St	Rocklin	CA	95677	916-624-7894	624-7898
TF: 800-692-2600 ■ *Web:* www.lawtonindustries.com					
Lee Industries Inc 50 W Pine St	Philipsburg	PA	16866	814-342-0461	342-5660
Web: www.leeind.com					
Lightnin 135 Mt Read Blvd	Rochester	NY	14611	585-436-5550	436-5589
Web: www.lightnin-mixers.com					
Lincoln Industrial Corp 1 Lincoln Way	Saint Louis	MO	63120	314-679-4200	424-5359*
**Fax Area Code:* 800 ■ **Fax:* Cust Svc ■ *Web:* www.lincolnindustrial.com					
Littleford Day Inc 7451 Empire Dr	Florence	KY	41042	859-525-7600	525-1446
TF: 800-365-8555 ■ *Web:* www.littleford.com					
Lynch Systems Inc 601 Independent St	Bainbridge	GA	39817	229-248-2345	243-0987
TF: 800-428-6333 ■ *Web:* www.lynchsystems.com					
Marathon Equipment Co 950 County Hwy 9 S PO Box 1798	Vernon	AL	35592	205-695-9105	695-8813
TF: 800-269-7237 ■ *Web:* www.marathon-equipment.com					
McKesson Automation Corp 500 Cranberry Wood Dr	Cranberry Township	PA	16066	724-741-8000	741-8002
TF: 800-700-8737 ■ *Web:* www.robot-rx.com					
McNeil & NRM Inc 96 E Crosier St	Akron	OH	44311	330-253-2525	253-5612
TF: 800-669-2525					
Mefiag Div Met-Pro Corp 1550 Industrial Dr	Owosso	MI	48867	989-725-8184	729-1013
Web: www.met-pro.com					
MEGTEC Systems Inc 830 Prosper Rd	De Pere	WI	54115	920-336-5715	336-3404
TF Cust Svc: 800-558-5535 ■ *Web:* www.megtec.com					
Met-Pro Corp 160 Cassell Rd PO Box 144	Harleysville	PA	19438	215-723-6751	723-6758
NYSE: MPR ■ *TF:* 800-722-3267 ■ *Web:* www.met-pro.com					
Met-Pro Corp Mefiag Div 1550 Industrial Dr	Owosso	MI	48867	989-725-8184	729-1013
Web: www.met-pro.com					
MFRI Inc 7720 N Lehigh Ave	Niles	IL	60714	847-966-1000	966-8563
NASDAQ: MFRI ■ *Web:* www.mfri.com					
Michigan Wheel Corp 1501 Buchanan Ave SW	Grand Rapids	MI	49507	616-452-6941	247-0227
TF: 800-369-4335 ■ *Web:* www.miwheel.com					
Micro-Poise Measurment Systems LLC 1624 Englewood Ave	Akron	OH	44305	330-784-1251	798-0250
Web: www.micropoise.com					
Milacron Inc 2090 Florence Ave	Cincinnati	OH	45206	513-487-5000	487-5615
NYSE: MZ ■ *Web:* www.milacron.com					
Minuteman International Inc 111 S Rohlwing Rd	Addison	IL	60101	630-627-6900	627-1130
TF: 800-323-9420 ■ *Web:* www.minutemanintl.com					
Mueller Paul Co 1600 W Phelps St	Springfield	MO	65802	417-831-3000	831-3528
TF: 800-641-2830 ■ *Web:* www.muel.com					
Mueller Steam Specialty 1491 NC Hwy 20 W	Saint Pauls	NC	28384	910-865-8241	865-8245
TF: 800-334-6259 ■ *Web:* www.muellersteam.com					
National Super Service Co Inc 3115 Frenchman Rd	Toledo	OH	43607	419-531-2121	531-3761
TF Cust Svc: 800-677-1663 ■ *Web:* www.nss.com					
Netzsch Inc 119 Pickering Way	Exton	PA	19341	610-363-8010	363-0971
Web: www.netzschusa.com					
Nilfisk-Advance Group 14600 21st Ave N	Plymouth	MN	55447	763-745-3500	745-3718*
**Fax:* Cust Svc ■ *TF Cust Svc:* 800-989-2235 ■ *Web:* www.nilfisk-advance.com					
Nordson Corp 28601 Clemens Rd	Westlake	OH	44145	440-892-1580	892-9507
NASDAQ: NDSN ■ *TF:* 800-321-2881 ■ *Web:* www.nordson.com					
Norwood Kingsley Machine Co 2538 Wisconsin Ave	Downers Grove	IL	60515	630-968-0647	968-7672
TF: 800-626-3464 ■ *Web:* www.kingsleymachine.com					
Pall Corp 2200 Northern Blvd	East Hills	NY	11548	516-484-5400	484-5228
NYSE: PLL ■ *TF:* 800-645-6532 ■ *Web:* www.pall.com					
Parkson Corp 2727 NW 62nd St	Fort Lauderdale	FL	33309	954-974-6610	974-6182
Web: www.parkson.com					
Paul Mueller Co 1600 W Phelps St	Springfield	MO	65802	417-831-3000	831-3528
TF: 800-641-2830 ■ *Web:* www.muel.com					
PDQ Mfg Inc 1698 Scheuring Rd	De Pere	WI	54115	920-983-8333	983-8330
TF: 800-227-3373 ■ *Web:* www.pdqinc.com					
Peerless Mfg Co 14651 N Dallas Pkwy Suite 500	Dallas	TX	75254	214-357-6181	351-0194
NASDAQ: PMFG ■ *Web:* www.peerlessmfg.com					
Peterson Machine Tool Inc 1100 N Union St	Council Grove	KS	66846	620-767-6721	676-6415
TF: 800-835-3528 ■ *Web:* www.petersonmachine.com					
Pfaudler Inc 1000 West Ave	Rochester	NY	14611	585-235-1000	235-6393
Web: www.pfaudler.com					
Pioneer/Eclipse Corp 1 Eclipse Rd	Sparta	NC	28675	336-372-8080	372-2895
TF Cust Svc: 800-367-3550 ■ *Web:* www.pioneer-eclipse.com					
Porter Burke E Machinery Co 730 Plymouth Ave NE	Grand Rapids	MI	49505	616-459-9531	459-1032
Web: www.bepco.com					
Porter International 131 Zapletal Way	Carthage	MO	64836	417-237-6244	237-6275
TF: 800-888-4569					
PPT Vision Inc 12988 Valleyview Rd	Eden Prairie	MN	55344	952-996-9500	996-9501
Web: www.pptvision.com					
Premier Mill Corp 1 Birchmont Dr	Reading	PA	19606	610-779-9500	779-9666
Web: www.premiermill.com					
PTI Technologies Inc 501 Del Norte Blvd	Oxnard	CA	93030	805-604-3700	604-3701
TF: 800-331-2701 ■ *Web:* www.ptitechnologies.com					
Pullman/Holt Corp 10702 N 46th St	Tampa	FL	33617	813-971-2223	971-6090
TF: 800-237-7582 ■ *Web:* www.pullmanholtcorp.com					
Quipp Inc 4800 NW 157th St	Miami	FL	33014	305-623-8700	623-0980
NASDAQ: QUIP ■ *TF:* 800-345-9680 ■ *Web:* www.quipp.com					
R-V Industries Inc 584 Poplar Rd	Honey Brook	PA	19344	610-273-2457	273-3361*
**Fax:* Sales ■ *Web:* www.rvii.com					
Retech Systems LLC 100 Henry Station Rd	Ukiah	CA	95482	707-462-6522	467-1708
Web: www.retechinc.com					
Roberts Sinto Corp 3001 W Main St	Lansing	MI	48917	517-371-2460	371-4930
Web: www.robertssinto.com					
Rotary Lift 2700 Lanier Dr	Madison	IN	47250	812-273-1622	273-3404
TF: 800-445-5438 ■ *Web:* www.rotarylift.com					
SAES Pure Gas Inc 4175 Santa Fe Rd	San Luis Obispo	CA	93401	805-541-9299	541-9399
Web: www.puregastechnologies.com					
Schutte & Koerting LLC 2510 Metropolitan	Trevose	PA	19053	215-639-0900	639-1597
TF: 800-752-8558 ■ *Web:* www.s-k.com					
Scott Fetzer Co 28800 Clemens Rd	Westlake	OH	44145	440-892-3000	892-3060

				Phone	Fax
Senior Flexonics Inc Metal Bellows Div 1075 Providence Hwy	Sharon	MA	02067	781-784-1400	784-1405
Web: www.metalbellows.com					
Shop-Vac Corp 2323 Reach Rd	Williamsport	PA	17701	570-326-0502	321-7089
Web: www.shopvac.com					
Smith AO Water Products Co 500 Tennessee Waltz Pkwy	Ashland City	TN	37015	615-792-4371	792-4371
TF: 800-365-8170 ■ *Web:* www.hotwater.com					
SPX Process Equipment 611 Sugar Creek Rd	Delavan	WI	53115	262-728-1900	252-5012*
*Fax Area Code: 800 ■ *TF:* 800-252-5200 ■ *Web:* www.spxpe.com					
Sterling Production Control Units 2280 W Dorothy Ln	Dayton	OH	45439	937-299-5594	299-3843
TF: 800-968-7728 ■ *Web:* www.sterlingpcu.com					
Strasbaugh 825 Buckley Rd	San Luis Obispo	CA	93401	805-541-6424	541-6425
Web: www.strasbaugh.com					
SunOpta Inc 2838 Bovaird Dr W	Brampton	ON	L7A0H2	905-455-1990	455-2529
NASDAQ: STKL ■ *Web:* www.sunopta.com					
Super Products LLC 17000 W Cleveland Ave	New Berlin	WI	53151	262-784-7100	784-9561
TF: 800-837-9711 ■ *Web:* www.superproductscorp.com					
Synventive Molding Solutions Inc 10 Centennial Dr	Peabody	MA	01960	978-750-8065	646-3600
TF: 800-367-5662 ■ *Web:* www.synventive.com					
Talley Defense Systems Inc 4051 N Higley Rd	Mesa	AZ	85215	480-898-2200	898-2358
TF: 800-444-8837 ■ *Web:* www.talleyds.com					
TCM Fork Lift Trucks 7950 Blankenship Dr	Houston	TX	77055	713-681-8888	681-8899
Web: www.tcmforklifttrucks.com					
Tennant Co 701 N Lilac Dr	Minneapolis	MN	55422	763-540-1200	540-1437
NYSE: TNC ■ *TF Cust Svc:* 800-553-8033 ■ *Web:* www.tennantco.com					
Terex Simplicity 212 S Oak St	Durand	MI	48429	989-288-3121	288-4113
Web: www.simplicityengineering.com					
Thermotron Industries Co 291 Kollen Park Dr	Holland	MI	49423	616-392-1491	392-5643
Web: www.thermotron.com					
Thomas Engineering Inc 575 W Central Rd	Hoffman Estates	IL	60195	847-358-5800	358-5817
TF: 800-634-9910 ■ *Web:* www.thomaseng.com					
Timesavers Inc 11123 89th Ave N	Maple Grove	MN	55369	763-488-6600	488-6601
TF: 800-537-3611 ■ *Web:* www.timesaversinc.com					
Unified Brands Inc 525 S Coldwater Rd	Weidman	MI	48893	989-644-3331	634-5369*
*Fax Area Code: 800 ■ *TF:* 800-621-8560 ■ *Web:* www.unifiedbrands.net					
United Silicone Inc 4471 Walden Ave	Lancaster	NY	14086	716-681-8222	681-8789
TF: 800-359-5995 ■ *Web:* www.unitedsilicone.com					
Universal Machine & Engineering Corp 645 Old Reading Pike	Stowe	PA	19464	610-323-1810	323-9756
Web: www.umc-oscar.com					
USM Corp 32 Stevens St	Haverhill	MA	01830	978-374-0303	373-7295
TF: 800-343-0772 ■ *Web:* www.usminternational.com					
Vactor Mfg Inc 1621 S Illinois St	Streator	IL	61364	815-672-3171	672-2779*
*Fax: Sales ■ *Web:* www.vactor.com					
Vacudyne Inc 375 E Joe Orr Rd	Chicago Heights	IL	60411	708-757-5200	757-7180
TF: 800-459-9591 ■ *Web:* www.vacudyne.com					
Van Air Systems Inc 2950 Mechanic St	Lake City	PA	16423	814-774-2631	774-3482
TF: 800-840-9906 ■ *Web:* www.vanairsystems.com					
VFP Fire Systems 1301 L'Orient St	Saint Paul	MN	55117	651-558-3300	558-3310
TF: 800-229-6263 ■ *Web:* www.vfpfire.com					
Videojet Technologies Inc 1500 Mittel Blvd	Wood Dale	IL	60191	630-860-7300	616-3657*
*Fax: Mktg ■ *TF Cust Svc:* 800-843-3610 ■ *Web:* www.videojet.com					
Vulcan Engineering Co 1 Vulcan Dr Helena Industrial Park	Helena	AL	35080	205-663-0732	663-9103
Web: www.vulcangroup.com					
Wastequip Inc 25800 Science Park Dr Suite 140	Cleveland	OH	44122	216-292-2554	292-0625
TF: 800-248-7717 ■ *Web:* www.wastequip.com					
Welex Inc 850 Jolly Rd	Blue Bell	PA	19422	215-542-8000	542-9841
Web: www.welex.com					
WH Bagshaw Co Inc 1 Pine St Ext PO Box 766	Nashua	NH	03061	603-883-7758	882-2651
TF: 800-343-7467 ■ *Web:* www.whbagshaw.com					
Williams Patent Crusher & Pulverizer Co 2701 N Broadway	Saint Louis	MO	63102	314-621-3348	436-2639
Web: www.williamscrusher.com					
Windsor Industries Inc 1351 W Stanford Ave	Englewood	CO	80110	303-762-1800	865-2800
TF: 800-444-7654 ■ *Web:* www.windsorind.com					
Wright Industries 1520 Elm Hill Pike	Nashville	TN	37210	615-361-6600	366-5978
Web: www.wrightind.com					

390 INFORMATION RETRIEVAL SERVICES (GENERAL)

SEE ALSO Investigative Services p. 1873

				Phone	Fax
Amigos Library Services 14400 Midway Rd	Dallas	TX	75244	972-851-8000	991-6061
TF: 800-843-8482 ■ *Web:* www.amigos.org					
BurrellesLuce 75 E Northfield Rd	Livingston	NJ	07039	973-992-6600	992-7675
TF: 800-631-1160 ■ *Web:* www.burrellesluce.com					
Cal Info 316 W 2nd St Suite 1102	Los Angeles	CA	90012	213-687-8710	687-8778
TF: 877-687-8710 ■ *Web:* calinfo.net					
Chemical Abstracts Service (CAS) PO Box 3012	Columbus	OH	43210	614-447-3600	447-3713
TF: 800-848-6538 ■ *Web:* info.cas.org					
CompetitivEdge 196 S Main St	Colchester	CT	06415	860-537-6731	537-6738
TF: 888-881-3343 ■ *Web:* www.clipresearch.com					
Data Transmission Network Corp 9110 W Dodge Rd Suite 200	Omaha	NE	68114	402-390-2328	390-7188
TF: 800-485-4000 ■ *Web:* www.dtn.com					
DataWorld Inc 15120 Enterprise Ct	Chantilly	VA	20151	703-227-9680	803-3299
TF: 800-368-5754 ■ *Web:* www.dataworld.com					
Dialog Corp 11000 Regency Pkwy Suite 10	Cary	NC	27511	919-462-8600	468-9890
TF: 800-334-2564 ■ *Web:* www.dialog.com					
EBSCO Information Services PO Box 1943	Birmingham	AL	35201	205-991-6600	991-1264
Web: www.ebsco.com					
Environmental Data Resources Inc 440 Wheelers Farms Rd	Milford	CT	06460	203-783-0300	231-6802*
*Fax Area Code: 800 ■ *TF:* 800-352-0050 ■ *Web:* www.edrnet.com					
FOI Services Inc 704 Quince Orchard Rd Suite 275	Gaithersburg	MD	20878	301-975-9400	975-0702
Web: www.foiservices.com					
FOIA Group Inc 1259 Connecticut Ave NW Suite 200	Washington	DC	20036	202-408-7028	461-3807*
*Fax Area Code: 703 ■ *Web:* www.foia.com					
FRANdata Corp 1655 N Fort Myer Dr Suite 410	Arlington	VA	22209	703-740-4707	740-4710
TF: 800-485-9570 ■ *Web:* www.frandata.com					
Guideline 625 Ave of the Americas 2nd Fl	New York	NY	10011	212-645-4500	645-7681
TF Cust Svc: 800-346-3688 ■ *Web:* www.guideline.com					
IHS Inc 15 Inverness Way E	Englewood	CO	80112	303-790-0600	754-3940
NYSE: IHS ■ *TF:* 800-525-7052 ■ *Web:* www.ihs.com					
Inform Research Services 250 Marquette Ave 4th Fl	Minneapolis	MN	55401	612-630-6020	630-6030
Web: www.mpls.lib.mn.us/inform.asp					
Infotrieve Inc 11755 Wilshire Blvd 19th Fl	Los Angeles	CA	90025	310-445-3001	445-3003
TF: 800-422-4633 ■ *Web:* www.infotrieve.com					
infoUSA Inc 5711 S 86th Cir	Omaha	NE	68127	402-593-4500	331-1505*
NASDAQ: IUSA ■ *Fax: Sales ■ *TF:* 800-321-0869 ■ *Web:* www.infousa.com					
Insurance Reference Systems Inc DBA SilverPlume					
2447 55th St Suite 201-B	Boulder	CO	80301	800-677-4442	449-1199*
*Fax Area Code: 303 ■ *Fax: Sales ■ *TF:* 800-677-4442 ■ *Web:* www.silverplume.com					
LexisNexis Group 9443 Springboro Pike	Miamisburg	OH	45342	937-865-6800	865-7476
TF: 800-227-9597 ■ *Web:* www.lexisnexis.com					
LexisNexis Martindale-Hubbell 121 Chanlon Rd	New Providence	NJ	07974	908-464-6800	464-3553*
*Fax: Edit ■ *TF:* 800-526-4902 ■ *Web:* www.martindale.com					
Marshall & Swift/Boeckh 2885 S Calhoun Rd	New Berlin	WI	53151	262-780-2800	860-6367
TF: 800-285-1288 ■ *Web:* www.msbinfo.com					
National Technical Information Service (NTIS)					
5285 Port Royal Rd	Springfield	VA	22161	703-605-6000	605-6900
TF Orders: 800-553-6847 ■ *Web:* www.ntis.gov					
Nelson Information 195 Broadway	New York	NY	10007	646-822-6499	
TF: 800-333-6357 ■ *Web:* www.nelsoninformation.com					
NERAC Inc 1 Technology Dr	Tolland	CT	06084	860-872-7000	875-1749
Web: www.nerac.com					
Newsbank Inc 4501 Tamiami Trail N Suite 316	Naples	FL	34103	239-263-6004	263-3004
TF Cust Svc: 800-243-7694 ■ *Web:* www.newsbank.com					
Ovid Technologies Inc 333 7th Ave 20th Fl	New York	NY	10001	646-674-6300	674-6301
TF: 800-950-2035 ■ *Web:* www.ovid.com					
ProQuest Co 300 N Zeeb Rd	Ann Arbor	MI	48103	734-761-4700	761-3940*
NYSE: PQE ■ *Fax: Cust Svc ■ *Web:* www.proquestcompany.com					
ProQuest Information & Learning Co 300 N Zeeb Rd	Ann Arbor	MI	48106	734-761-4700	997-4268*
*Fax: Hum Res ■ *TF:* 800-521-0600 ■ *Web:* www.il.proquest.com					
Questia Media America Inc 24 Greenway Plaza Suite 1050	Houston	TX	77046	713-358-2500	358-2601
TF: 888-950-2580 ■ *Web:* www.questia.com					
Research on Demand Inc PO Box 479	Santa Barbara	CA	93102	805-963-4095	564-4878*
*Fax Area Code: 877 ■ *TF:* 800-200-4095 ■ *Web:* www.researchondemand.com					
Research Wizard of Tulsa City-County Library 400 Civic Ctr	Tulsa	OK	74103	918-596-7991	596-2598
Web: www.researchwizard.org					
SilverPlume 2447 55th St Suite 201-B	Boulder	CO	80301	800-677-4442	449-1199*
*Fax Area Code: 303 ■ *Fax: Sales ■ *TF:* 800-677-4442 ■ *Web:* www.silverplume.com					
Sopheon Corp 3050 Metro Dr Suite 200	Minneapolis	MN	55425	952-851-7500	851-7599
TF: 800-367-8358 ■ *Web:* www.sopheon.com					
Thomson Financial 22 Thomson Pl	Boston	MA	02210	617-345-2000	856-5601*
*Fax: Hum Res ■ *TF:* 888-837-4636 ■ *Web:* www.thomson.com/financial					
Video Monitoring Services of America Inc					
6430 W Sunset Blvd Suite 400	Los Angeles	CA	90028	323-993-0111	467-7540
Web: www.vidmon.com					
VNU Inc 770 Broadway	New York	NY	10003	646-654-5000	654-5001
Web: www.vnu.com					
West Group 610 Opperman Dr	Eagan	MN	55123	651-687-7000	687-7551
TF Cust Svc: 800-328-4880 ■ *Web:* west.thomson.com					

391 INK

				Phone	Fax
3M Commercial Graphics Div					
3M General Offices Bldg 220-6W-06	Saint Paul	MN	55144	800-328-3908	737-9682*
*Fax Area Code: 651 ■ *Fax: Sales					
AJ Daw Printing Ink Co 3559 Greenwood Ave	Los Angeles	CA	90040	323-723-3253	725-7885
TF: 800-432-9465 ■ *Web:* www.dawink.com					
Alfa Ink Div Lakeland Laboratories 655 Washington Ave	Carlstadt	NJ	07072	201-939-1122	939-3328
American Inks & Coatings Corp 330 Pawlings Rd	Phoenixville	PA	19460	610-272-8866	933-2173
ANI Printing Inks 15500 28th Ave N	Plymouth	MN	55447	763-559-5911	559-0243
TF: 800-328-7838 ■ *Web:* www.aninks.com					
BASF Corp 100 Campus Dr	Florham Park	NJ	07932	973-245-6000	895-8002
NYSE: BF ■ *TF:* 800-526-1072 ■ *Web:* www.basf.com					
Bomark Inks Inc 601 S 6th Ave	City of Industry	CA	91746	626-968-1666	330-2373
TF: 800-323-5174 ■ *Web:* www.bomarkinks.com					
Braden Sutphin Ink Co 3650 E 93rd St	Cleveland	OH	44105	216-271-2300	271-0515
TF: 800-289-6872 ■ *Web:* www.bsink.com					
Central Ink Corp 1100 N Harvester Rd	West Chicago	IL	60185	630-231-6500	231-6554
TF: 800-345-2541 ■ *Web:* www.cicink.com					
Color Converting Industries Co 3535 SW 56th St	Des Moines	IA	50321	515-471-2100	471-2202
TF: 800-728-8200 ■ *Web:* www.color-converting.com					
Color Resolutions International 575 Quality Blvd	Fairfield	OH	45014	513-552-7200	552-1588
TF: 800-346-8570 ■ *Web:* www.colorresolutions.com					
Cudner & O'Connor Co 4035 W Kinzie St	Chicago	IL	60624	773-826-0200	826-0477
Web: www.candocinks.com					
Custom Chemicals Co 30 Paul Kohner Pl	Elmwood Park	NJ	07407	201-791-5100	791-2273
Daw AJ Printing Ink Co 3559 Greenwood Ave	Los Angeles	CA	90040	323-723-3253	725-7885
TF: 800-432-9465 ■ *Web:* www.dawink.com					
Del Val Ink & Color Inc PO Box 155	Riverton	NJ	08077	856-829-7474	829-8527
Flint Ink Corp 4600 Arrowhead Dr	Ann Arbor	MI	48105	734-622-6000	622-6131
Web: www.flintink.com					
Formulabs Inc 529 W 4th Ave	Escondido	CA	92025	760-741-2345	740-0593
TF: 800-642-2345 ■ *Web:* www.formulabs.com					
Gans Ink & Supply Co Inc 1441 Boyd St	Los Angeles	CA	90033	323-264-2200	264-2916
TF: 800-372-7410 ■ *Web:* www.gansink.com					
Gotham Ink & Color Co 19 Kay Fries Dr	Stony Point	NY	10980	845-947-4000	947-3270
Graphic Sciences Inc 7515 NE Ambassador Pl Suite L	Portland	OR	97220	503-460-0203	460-0225
TF: 888-546-4465 ■ *Web:* www.graphicsciences.com					
Handschy Industries Inc 120 25th Ave	Bellwood	IL	60104	708-547-9400	547-4774
Independent Ink Inc 13700 S Gramercy Pl	Gardena	CA	90249	310-523-4657	329-0943
TF: 800-446-5538 ■ *Web:* www.independentink.com					
International Coatings Co 13929 E 166th St	Cerritos	CA	90702	562-926-1010	926-9486
TF: 800-423-4103 ■ *Web:* www.iccink.com					
INX International Ink Co 651 Bonnie Ln	Elk Grove Village	IL	60007	847-981-9399	290-0037*
*Fax: Hum Res ■ *TF:* 800-631-7956 ■ *Web:* www.inxink.com					
Kerley Ink Engineers Inc 2700 S 12th Ave	Broadview	IL	60155	708-344-1295	865-5759
Web: www.kerleyink.com					
Keystone Printing Ink Co 2700 Roberts Ave	Philadelphia	PA	19129	215-228-8100	228-4743
TF: 800-523-0111 ■ *Web:* www.keystoneink.com					
Kohl & Madden Printing Ink Corp 651 Garden St	Carlstadt	NJ	07072	201-886-1203	886-8405
TF: 800-793-0022 ■ *Web:* www.kohlmadden.com					
Kramer Ink Co Inc 9900 Jordan Cir	Santa Fe Springs	CA	90670	562-946-8847	941-8828
TF: 800-543-8792					
Lakeland Laboratories Alfa Ink Div 655 Washington Ave	Carlstadt	NJ	07072	201-939-1122	939-3328
Miller-Cooper Co 5187 Merriam Dr	Merriam	KS	66203	913-312-5020	312-5033
TF: 800-289-6246 ■ *Web:* www.mcink.com					
Nazdar 8501 Hedge Lane Terr	Shawnee	KS	66227	913-422-1888	422-2296
TF: 800-767-9942 ■ *Web:* www.nazdar.com					
Nor-Cote International Inc 506 Lafayette Ave	Crawfordsville	IN	47933	765-362-9180	364-5408
TF: 800-488-9180 ■ *Web:* www.norcote.com					
Polypore Inc 4601 S 3rd Ave	Tucson	AZ	85714	520-889-3306	741-9647
Polytex Environmental Inks Ltd 820 E 140th St	Bronx	NY	10454	718-402-2000	402-2984
Web: www.polytexink.com					
Sensient Technologies Corp 777 E Wisconsin Ave 11th Fl	Milwaukee	WI	53202	414-271-6755	347-4783
NYSE: SXT ■ *TF:* 800-558-9892 ■ *Web:* www.sensient-tech.com					
Sericol Inc 1101 W Cambridge Dr	Kansas City	KS	66103	913-342-4060	342-4752
TF: 800-737-4265 ■ *Web:* www.sericol.com					
SICPA North America Inc 7145 Boone Ave N Suite 200	Brooklyn Park	MN	55428	763-535-7600	535-9034
Web: www.sicpa.com					
Spectrachem Corp 10 Dell Glen Ave Suite 3A	Lodi	NJ	07644	973-253-3553	253-3663
TF: 800-524-2806					
Sun Chemical Corp 35 Waterview Blvd	Parsippany	NJ	07054	973-404-6000	404-6001
Web: www.sunchemical.com					
Superior Printing Ink Co Inc 70 Bethune St	New York	NY	10014	212-741-3600	633-8283
Web: www.superiorink.com					

Phone | Fax

Toyo Ink America LLC 710 W Belden — Addison IL 60101 630-930-5100 628-1769
TF: 800-227-8696 ■ *Web:* www.toyoink.com

US Ink Corp 651 Garden St — Carlstadt NJ 07072 201-935-8666 933-3728*
**Fax:* Mktg ■ *TF:* 800-423-8838 ■ *Web:* www.usink.com

Van Son Holland Ink Corp of America 185 Oval Dr — Islandia NY 11749 800-645-4182 442-8744
TF: 800-645-4182 ■ *Web:* www.vansonink.com

Wikoff Color Corp 1886 Merritt Rd — Fort Mill SC 29715 803-548-2210 548-5728
Web: www.wikoff.com

392 INSULATION & ACOUSTICAL PRODUCTS

Phone | Fax

Acoustic Systems Inc 415 E St Elmo Rd — Austin TX 78745 512-444-1961 444-2282
TF: 800-749-1460 ■ *Web:* www.acousticsystems.com

Anco Products Inc 2500 S 17th St — Elkhart IN 46517 574-293-5574 295-6235
TF: 800-837-2626 ■ *Web:* www.ancoproductsinc.com

APi Group Inc Fabrication & Mfg Group 2366 Rose Pl — Saint Paul MN 55113 651-636-4320 636-0312
Web: www.apigroupinc.com/manufacturing.html

Applegate Insulation Mfg Inc 1000 Highview Dr — Webberville MI 48892 517-521-3545 521-3597
TF: 800-627-7536 ■ *Web:* www.applegateinsulation.com

CertainTeed Corp 750 E Swedesford Rd — Valley Forge PA 19482 610-341-7000 341-7797
TF Prod Info: 800-782-8777 ■ *Web:* www.certainteed.com

Claremont Sales Corp 35 Winsome Dr PO Box 430 — Durham CT 06422 860-349-4499 349-7977
TF: 800-222-4448 ■ *Web:* claremontcorporation.com

CTA Acoustics Inc 100 CTA Blvd PO Box 448 — Corbin KY 40702 606-528-8050 528-8074
Web: www.ctaacoustics.com

Dryvit Systems Inc 1 Energy Way — West Warwick RI 02893 401-822-4100 822-4510
TF: 800-556-7752 ■ *Web:* www.dryvit.com

Fibrex Insulations Inc 561 Scott Rd PO Box 2079 — Sarnia ON N7T7L4 519-336-7770 363-4440*
**Fax Area Code:* 800 ■ **Fax:* Cust Svc ■ *TF Cust Svc:* 800-265-7514 ■
Web: www.fibrex.on.ca

Hi-Temp Insulation Inc 4700 Calle Alto — Camarillo CA 93012 805-484-2774 484-7551
Web: www.hi-tempinsulation.com

ICA Inc 500 S 9th St — Lehighton PA 18235 610-377-4120 377-0788
Web: home.att.net/ICA_Inc

IIG (Industrial Insulation Group LLC) 1110 Sixteen Rd — Fruita CO 81521 970-858-3694 858-9641
Web: www.iig-llc.com

Industrial Acoustics Co Inc 1160 Commerce Ave — Bronx NY 10462 718-931-8000 863-1138
Web: www.industrialacoustics.com

Industrial Insulation Group LLC (IIG) 1110 Sixteen Rd — Fruita CO 81521 970-858-3694 858-9641
Web: www.iig-llc.com

Isolatek International Inc 41 Furnace St — Stanhope NJ 07874 973-347-1200 347-5131
TF: 800-631-9600 ■ *Web:* www.cafco.com

ITW Insulation Systems 919 N Trenton St — Ruston LA 71270 318-251-2920 251-1490
TF: 800-551-4866 ■ *Web:* www.itwinsulation.com

Johns Manville Corp 717 17th St PO Box 5108 — Denver CO 80217 303-978-2000 978-2041*
**Fax:* PR ■ *TF Prod Info:* 800-654-3103 ■ *Web:* www.jm.com

Johns Manville International Group Inc
717 17th St PO Box 5108 — Denver CO 80217 303-978-2000 978-2041*
**Fax:* PR ■ *TF:* 800-654-3101 ■ *Web:* www.jm.com

Knauf Insulation 1 Knauf Dr — Shelbyville IN 46176 317-398-4434 398-3675
TF: 800-825-4434 ■ *Web:* www.knauffiberglass.com

MAP of Easton Inc 3 Danforth Dr — Easton PA 18045 610-253-7135 253-1664
Web: www.map-easton.com

MIT International 9000 Railwood Dr — Houston TX 77078 713-675-0075 428-3777
TF: 800-275-6679 ■ *Web:* www.insulpad.com

Molded Acoustical Products of Easton Inc DBA MAP of Easton Inc
3 Danforth Dr — Easton PA 18045 610-253-7135 253-1664
Web: www.map-easton.com

Nu-Wool Co Inc 2472 Port Sheldon Rd — Jenison MI 49428 616-669-0100 669-2370
TF: 800-748-0128 ■ *Web:* www.nuwool.com

Owens Corning 1 Owens Corning Pkwy — Toledo OH 43659 419-248-8000 325-1538
Web: www.owenscorning.com

Pittsburgh Corning Corp 800 Presque Isle Dr — Pittsburgh PA 15239 724-327-6100 387-3806
TF: 800-245-1217 ■ *Web:* www.pittsburghcorning.com

Premier Mfg Corp 12117 Bennington Ave — Cleveland OH 44135 216-941-9700 941-9719
Web: www.premiermfg.com

Rock Wool Mfg Co 1400 7th Ct PO Box 506 — Leeds AL 35094 205-699-6121 699-3132
TF Sales: 800-874-7625 ■ *Web:* www.deltainsulation.com

S & S Industries Inc PO Box 17087 — Nashville TN 37217 615-754-8000 754-8011
TF: 800-445-6505

Saint-Gobain Corp 750 E Swedesford Rd — Valley Forge PA 19482 610-341-7000 341-7797
TF: 800-274-8530 ■ *Web:* www.saint-gobain.com/us

Scott Industries Inc 1573 Hwy 136 W PO Box 7 — Henderson KY 42419 270-831-2037 831-2039
TF: 800-951-9276 ■ *Web:* www.scott-mfg.com

Sloss Industries Corp 3500 35th Ave N — Birmingham AL 35207 205-808-7806 808-7715*
**Fax:* Sales ■ *Web:* www.sloss.com

Soundcoat Co Inc 1 Burt Dr — Deer Park NY 11729 631-242-2200 242-2246
TF: 800-394-8913 ■ *Web:* www.soundcoat.com

Thermafiber Inc 3711 W Mill St — Wabash IN 46992 260-563-2111 563-8979
TF: 888-834-2371 ■ *Web:* www.thermafiber.com

Thermoguard Insulation Co N 125 Dyer Rd — Spokane WA 99212 509-535-4600 535-8519
TF: 800-541-0579 ■ *Web:* www.thermoguard.net

Thermwell Products Co 420 Rt 17 S — Mahwah NJ 07430 201-684-4400 684-1214
TF: 800-526-5265 ■ *Web:* www.frostking.com

TIGHITCO Inc 1375 Seaboard Industrial Blvd — Atlanta GA 30318 404-355-1205 351-4458
TF: 800-223-1205 ■ *Web:* www.tighitco.com

Transco Products Inc 55 E Jackson Blvd Suite 2100 — Chicago IL 60604 312-427-2818 427-4975
Web: www.transcoproducts.com

Transonic Inc 2824 N Sylvania Ave — Fort Worth TX 76111 817-831-3119 831-3110

Unifrax Corp 2351 Whirlpool St — Niagara Falls NY 14305 716-278-3800 278-3904*
**Fax:* Cust Svc ■ *Web:* www.unifrax.com

USG Interiors Inc 125 S Franklin St — Chicago IL 60606 312-606-4000 606-4093
TF: 800-621-9622

Ward Process Inc 6 October Hill Rd — Holliston MA 01746 508-429-1165 429-8543
Web: www.aapusa.com

393 INSURANCE AGENTS, BROKERS, SERVICES

Phone | Fax

ABD Insurance & Financial Services 305 Walnut St — Redwood City CA 94063 650-839-6000 839-6050
TF: 800-542-7676 ■ *Web:* www.abdi.com

Acordia Inc 150 N Michigan Ave Suite 4100 — Chicago IL 60601 312-423-2500 423-2508
TF: 866-226-7342 ■ *Web:* www.acordia.com

Allied North America 390 N Broadway — Jericho NY 11753 516-733-9200 681-7390
TF: 800-861-9452 ■ *Web:* www.alliedna.com

ANCO Insurance 1733 Briarcrest Dr — Bryan TX 77802 979-776-2626 776-1308
TF: 800-749-1733 ■ *Web:* www.anco.com

Andreini & Co 220 W 20th Ave — San Mateo CA 94403 650-573-1111 378-4361
TF: 800-969-2522 ■ *Web:* www.andreini.com

Phone | Fax

Answer Financial Inc 15910 Ventura Blvd — Encino CA 91436 818-644-4000 644-4411
TF: 800-233-3028 ■ *Web:* www.answerfinancial.com

Aon Risk Services Inc 200 E Randolph St — Chicago IL 60601 312-381-4000 953-5390*
**Fax Area Code:* 847 ■ *TF:* 800-432-3672 ■ *Web:* www.aon.com

Arthur J Gallagher & Co 2 Pierce Pl — Itasca IL 60143 630-773-3800 285-4023
NYSE: AJG ■ *Web:* www.ajg.com

Associated Agencies Inc
1701 Golf Rd Tower 3 Suite 700 — Rolling Meadows IL 60008 847-427-8400 427-3559
TF: 800-443-2827 ■ *Web:* www.assocagencies.com

Automobile Protection Corp 6010 Atlantic Blvd — Norcross GA 30071 770-394-6610 394-2129
TF: 800-458-7071 ■ *Web:* www.easycare.com

BB & T Insurance Services Inc 3605 Glenwood Ave — Raleigh NC 27612 919-716-9777 716-9747
TF: 800-821-1284 ■ *Web:* www.bbandt.com

BMI Financial Group Inc 1320 S Dixie Hwy 6th Fl — Coral Gables FL 33146 305-443-2898 442-8486
Web: www.bmicos.com

Bollinger Insurance 101 JFK Pkwy — Short Hills NJ 07078 973-467-0444 921-2876
TF: 800-526-1379 ■ *Web:* www.bollingerinsurance.com

Bolton & Co 245 S Los Robles Ave Suite 105 — Pasadena CA 91101 626-799-7000 441-3233
TF: 888-700-1444 ■ *Web:* www.boltonco.com

Brown & Brown Inc 220 S Ridgewood Ave — Daytona Beach FL 32114 386-252-9601 239-5729
NYSE: BRO ■ *TF:* 800-877-2769 ■ *Web:* www.brown-n-brown.com

Burnham John Insurance Services PO Box 129077 — San Diego CA 92186 619-231-1010 326-9134
TF: 800-421-6744 ■ *Web:* www.johnburnham.com

BWD Group LLC 113 S Service Rd BWD Plaza — Jericho NY 11753 516-327-2700 327-2800
Web: www.bwdgroup.com

Calco Insurance Brokers & Agents Inc
2000 Alameda de las Pulgas — San Mateo CA 94403 650-295-4600 295-4622
TF: 800-282-2526 ■ *Web:* www.calco.com

CalSurance 681 S Parker St Suite 200 — Orange CA 92868 714-939-0800 939-1641
TF: 800-762-7800 ■ *Web:* www.calsurance.com

CBCA Inc 4150 International Plaza Suite 800 — Fort Worth TX 76109 817-737-1700 737-1781
TF: 800-759-0101 ■ *Web:* www.cbca.com

CBIZ Benefits and Insurance Services of Maryland Inc
44 Baltimore St — Cumberland MD 21502 301-777-1500 724-1643*
**Fax:* Sales ■ *TF Cust Svc:* 800-684-2474 ■ *Web:* www.bgsg.com

Charles L Crane Agency Co 100 S 4th St Suite 800 — Saint Louis MO 63102 314-241-8700 444-4970
Web: www.craneagency.com

Citizens Clair Insurance Group 2 W Lafayette St Suite 400 — Norristown PA 19401 610-825-5555 828-3349
TF: 800-220-3008 ■ *Web:* www.citizensclair.com

Coalition America Inc 4151 Ashford Dunwoody Rd Suite 615 — Atlanta GA 30319 404-459-7201 459-6645
Web: coalitionamerica.com

Commerce Insurance Services Inc
1701 Rt 70 E Commerce Atrium — Cherry Hill NJ 08034 856-489-7000 795-9783
TF: 888-751-9000 ■ *Web:* www.commerceonline.com

Crane Charles L Agency Co 100 S 4th St Suite 800 — Saint Louis MO 63102 314-241-8700 444-4970
Web: www.craneagency.com

Crawford & Co 5620 Glenridge Dr NE — Atlanta GA 30342 404-256-0830 847-3155*
NYSE: CRDa ■ **Fax:* Mktg ■ *TF:* 800-241-2541 ■ *Web:* www.crawfordandcompany.com

Crystal Frank & Co 32 Old Slip 17th Fl — New York NY 10005 212-344-2444 504-5989
TF: 800-221-5830 ■ *Web:* www.frankcrystal.com

Daniel & Henry Co 1001 Highlands Plaza Dr W Suite 500 — Saint Louis MO 63110 314-421-1525 444-1990
Web: www.danielandhenry.com

Dann Insurance 1500 S Lakeside Dr — Bannockburn IL 60015 847-444-1060 444-1065
TF: 800-323-0371 ■ *Web:* www.danninsurance.com

Davis J Rolfe Insurance Agency Inc
850 Concourse Pkwy S Suite 200 — Maitland FL 32751 407-691-9600 691-9718
TF: 800-896-0554 ■ *Web:* www.jrdavis.com

Detwiler Mitchell & Co 225 Franklin St — Boston MA 02110 617-451-0100 747-0800
Web: www.dmcos.com

Driver Alliant Insurance Services 1620 5th Ave — San Diego CA 92101 619-238-1828 699-1323
Web: www.driveralliant.com

Eagan Insurance Agency Inc 2629 N Causeway Blvd — Metairie LA 70002 504-836-9600 836-9621
TF: 888-882-9600 ■ *Web:* www.eaganins.com

Eastern Insurance Group LLC 233 W Central St — Natick MA 01760 508-651-7700 655-8853
TF: 800-333-7234 ■ *Web:* www.easterninsurance.com

Esurance Inc 747 Front St 4th Fl — San Francisco CA 94111 415-875-4500 875-4501
TF: 800-926-6012 ■ *Web:* www.esurance.com

First Acceptance Corp 3813 Green Hills Village Dr — Nashville TN 37215 615-844-2800 844-2835
NYSE: FAC ■ *Web:* www.firstacceptancecorp.com

Fortun Insurance Agency Inc 365 Palermo Ave — Coral Gables FL 33134 305-445-3535 447-9478
Web: www.fortuninsurance.com

Frank Crystal & Co 32 Old Slip 17th Fl — New York NY 10005 212-344-2444 504-5989
TF: 800-221-5830 ■ *Web:* www.frankcrystal.com

Fred A Moreton & Co 709 E South Temple — Salt Lake City UT 84102 801-531-1234 531-6117
TF: 800-594-8949 ■ *Web:* www.famoreton.com

Fred Loya Insurance 1800 Lee Trevino Suite 201 — El Paso TX 79936 915-590-5692 387-8220*
**Fax Area Code:* 800 ■ *TF:* 800-554-0595 ■ *Web:* www.fredloyainsurance.com

Frenkel & Co Inc 350 Hudson St — New York NY 10014 212-488-0200 488-1800
TF: 800-373-6535 ■ *Web:* www.frenkel.com

Fringe Benefits Management Co 3101 Sessions Rd — Tallahassee FL 32303 850-425-6200 425-6220
TF: 800-847-8286 ■ *Web:* www.fbmc-benefits.com

Frontier Adjusters of America Inc
45 E Monterey Way PO Box 7610 — Phoenix AZ 85011 602-264-1061 553-4799*
**Fax Area Code:* 800 ■ *TF:* 800-528-1187 ■ *Web:* www.frontieradjusters.com

Gallagher Arthur J & Co 2 Pierce Pl — Itasca IL 60143 630-773-3800 285-4023
NYSE: AJG ■ *Web:* www.ajg.com

Gallagher Healthcare Insurance Services Inc
2000 W Sam Houston Pkwy S Suite 2000 — Houston TX 77042 713-461-4000 461-4334
TF: 800-733-4474 ■ *Web:* www.ajg.com/healthcare

Graham Co 1 Penn Sq W Graham Bldg — Philadelphia PA 19102 215-567-6300 751-9518
TF: 888-472-4262 ■ *Web:* www.grahamco.com

Guaranty Insurance Services Inc 1300 S Mopac Expy — Austin TX 78746 512-434-8464 434-8304
TF: 800-331-8959 ■ *Web:* www.insurance.guarantygroup.com

Haas & Wilkerson Inc PO Box 2946 — Shawnee Mission KS 66201 913-432-4400 432-6159
TF: 800-821-7703 ■ *Web:* www.hwins.com

Hanafin Robert J Inc PO Box 509 — Endicott NY 13761 607-754-3500 754-9797
TF: 800-448-4826 ■ *Web:* www.hanafinbates.com

Hibbs Hallmark & Co PO Box 8357 — Tyler TX 75711 903-561-8484 581-5988
TF: 800-765-6767 ■ *Web:* www.hhccas.com

Hilb Rogal & Hobbs 4951 Lake Brook Dr Suite 500 — Glen Allen VA 23060 804-747-6500 747-6046
NYSE: HRH ■ *Web:* www.hrh.com

Holmes Murphy & Assoc Inc 3001 Westown Pkwy — West Des Moines IA 50266 515-223-6800 223-6944
TF: 800-247-7756 ■ *Web:* www.holmesmurphy.com

HUB International Ltd 55 E Jackson Blvd Suite 14A — Chicago IL 60604 877-402-6601 922-5358
NYSE: HBG ■ *TF:* 800-432-2558 ■ *Web:* www.hubinternational.com

Hub International Ltd 1065 Ave of the Americas — New York NY 10018 212-338-2000 338-2100
TF: 800-456-5293 ■ *Web:* www.hubinternational.com

Hylant Group 811 Madison Ave — Toledo OH 43624 419-255-1020 255-7557
TF: 800-449-5268 ■ *Web:* www.hylant.com

IMA Financial Group Inc 8200 E 32nd St N PO Box 2992 — Wichita KS 67226 316-267-9221 266-6254
TF: 800-333-8913 ■ *Web:* www.imacorp.com

Insurance & Risk Management 1111 Chestnut Hills Pkwy — Fort Wayne IN 46814 260-625-7500 625-7525
Web: www.insuranceriskmgmt.com

Insurance Services Office Inc (ISO) 545 Washington Blvd — Jersey City NJ 07310 201-469-2000 748-1472*
**Fax:* Hum Res ■ *TF:* 800-888-4476 ■ *Web:* www.iso.com

Insurance.com Insurance Agency LLC 29001 Solon Rd — Solon OH 44139 440-264-1120 498-1875
TF: 866-533-0227 ■ *Web:* www.insurance.com

	City	State	Zip	Phone	Fax
Interstate National Dealer Services Inc 333 Earle Ovington Blvd Suite 700 TF: 800-526-0929 ■ Web: www.inds.com	Uniondale	NY	11553	516-228-8600	222-1818
InterWest Insurance Services Inc 3636 American River Dr TF: 800-444-4134 ■ Web: www.iwins.com	Sacramento	CA	95864	916-488-3100	488-3492
ISO (Insurance Services Office Inc) 545 Washington Blvd *Fax: Hum Res ■ TF: 800-888-4476 ■ Web: www.iso.com	Jersey City	NJ	07310	201-469-2000	748-1472*
J Rolfe Davis Insurance Agency Inc 850 Concourse Pkwy S Suite 200 TF: 800-896-0554 ■ Web: www.jrdavis.com	Maitland	FL	32751	407-691-9600	691-9718
J Smith Lanier & Co 300 W 10th St TF: 800-226-4522 ■ Web: www.jsmithlanier.com	West Point	GA	31833	706-645-2211	643-0606
John Burnham Insurance Services PO Box 129077 TF: 800-421-6744 ■ Web: www.johnburnham.com	San Diego	CA	92186	619-231-1010	326-9134
John L Wortham & Son LP 2727 Allen Pkwy Web: www.jwortham.com	Houston	TX	77019	713-526-3366	526-2757
Keenan & Assoc 2355 Crenshaw Blvd Suite 200 PO Box 4328 TF: 800-654-8102 ■ Web: www.keenanassoc.com	Torrance	CA	90510	310-212-3344	328-6793
Kelter-Alliant Insurance Services Inc 101 Southfield TF: 800-888-9088 ■ Web: www.kelteralliant.com	Birmingham	MI	48009	248-540-3131	540-2002
Knox RC & Co 1 Goodwin Sq 24th Fl TF: 800-742-2765 ■ Web: www.rcknox.com	Hartford	CT	06103	860-524-7600	240-1599
Kraus-Anderson Insurance 420 Gateway Blvd TF: 800-207-9261 ■ Web: www.kainsurance.com	Burnsville	MN	55337	952-707-8200	890-0535
Lanier J Smith & Co 300 W 10th St TF: 800-226-4522 ■ Web: www.jsmithlanier.com	West Point	GA	31833	706-645-2211	643-0606
Lawley Service Insurance 120 Delaware Ave TF: 800-860-5741 ■ Web: www.lawleyinsurance.com	Buffalo	NY	14202	716-849-8618	849-8245
Leavitt Group 216 S 200 W PO Box 130 Web: www.leavitt.com	Cedar City	UT	84720	435-586-6553	586-1510
Lewer Agency Inc 4534 Wornall Rd TF: 800-821-7715 ■ Web: lewer.com	Kansas City	MO	64111	816-753-4390	561-6840
Lockton Cos 444 W 47th St Suite 900 Web: www.lockton.com	Kansas City	MO	64112	816-960-9000	960-9099
Loomis Co 850 Park Rd TF: 800-782-0392 ■ Web: www.loomisco.com	Wyomissing	PA	19610	610-374-4040	374-6578
Lovitt & Touche Inc 7202 E Rosewood St TF: 800-426-2756 ■ Web: www.lovitt-touche.com	Tucson	AZ	85710	520-722-3000	722-7245
Loya Fred Insurance 1800 Lee Trevino Suite 201 *Fax Area Code: 800 ■ TF: 800-554-0595 ■ Web: www.fredloyainsurance.com	El Paso	TX	79936	915-590-5692	387-8220*
Marsh Saldana 701 Ponce de Leon Ave Web: www.saldana.net	San Juan	PR	00907	787-721-2600	721-1093
Marshall & Sterling Inc 110 Main St TF: 800-333-3766 ■ Web: www.marshallsterling.com	Poughkeepsie	NY	12601	845-454-0800	454-0880
McGriff Seibels & Williams Inc 2211 7th Ave S PO Box 10265 TF: 800-476-2211 ■ Web: www.mcgriff.com	Birmingham	AL	35202	205-252-9871	581-9293
Mesirow Financial Insurance Services Div 350 N Clark St TF: 888-973-2323 ■ Web: www.mesirowfinancial.com	Chicago	IL	60610	312-595-6200	595-7205
Moreton Fred A & Co 709 E South Temple TF: 800-594-8949 ■ Web: www.famoreton.com	Salt Lake City	UT	84102	801-531-1234	531-6117
National Council on Compensation Insurance 901 Peninsula Corporate Cir *Fax: Cust Svc ■ TF Cust Svc: 800-622-4123 ■ Web: www.ncci.com	Boca Raton	FL	33487	561-893-1000	893-1191*
NCCI Holdings Inc 901 Peninsula Corporate Cir *Fax: Cust Svc ■ TF Cust Svc: 800-622-4123 ■ Web: www.ncci.com	Boca Raton	FL	33487	561-893-1000	893-1191*
NIA Group Inc 66 Rt 17 N *Fax Area Code: 866 ■ TF: 800-642-0106 ■ Web: www.niagroup.com	Paramus	NJ	07652	201-845-6600	795-1158*
Northwest Administrators Inc 2323 Eastlake Ave E TF: 800-552-7334	Seattle	WA	98102	206-329-4900	726-3209
Oswald Cos 1360 E 9th St Suite 600 TF: 800-466-0468 ■ Web: www.oswaldcompanies.com	Cleveland	OH	44114	216-367-8787	241-4520
Parker Smith & Feek Inc 2233 112th Ave NE TF: 800-457-0220 ■ Web: www.psfinc.com	Bellevue	WA	98004	425-709-3600	709-7460
POMCO 2425 James St TF: 800-766-2687 ■ Web: www.pomcoplus.com	Syracuse	NY	13206	315-432-9171	437-9466
Proctor Financial Inc 295 Kirts Blvd Suite 100 TF: 800-521-6800 ■ Web: www.pficmi.com	Troy	MI	48084	248-269-5700	269-5752
Protegrity Services Inc PO Box 914700 TF: 800-883-4000 ■ Web: www.protegritynow.com	Longwood	FL	32791	407-788-1717	788-0812
Quotesmith.com Inc 8205 S Cass Ave Suite 102 NASDAQ: QUOT ■ TF: 800-556-9393 ■ Web: www.insure.com	Darien	IL	60561	630-515-0170	515-0270
RC Knox & Co 1 Goodwin Sq 24th Fl TF: 800-742-2765 ■ Web: www.rcknox.com	Hartford	CT	06103	860-524-7600	240-1599
Rebsamen Insurance Inc 1500 Riverfront Dr TF: 800-542-0226 ■ Web: www.rebsamen.com	Little Rock	AR	72202	501-661-4800	666-9592
Rigg William Co 2001 Bryan St Suite 800 TF: 800-275-4449 ■ Web: www.wrigg.com	Dallas	TX	75201	214-979-6200	979-6215
Robert J Hanafin Inc PO Box 509 TF: 800-448-4826 ■ Web: www.hanafinbates.com	Endicott	NY	13761	607-754-3500	754-9797
Robertson Ryan & Assoc Inc 330 E Kilbourn Ave 2 Plaza East Suite 650	Milwaukee	WI	53202	414-271-3575	271-0196
Rutherfoord Thomas Inc 1 S Jefferson St TF: 800-283-1478 ■ Web: www.rutherfoord.com	Roanoke	VA	24011	540-982-3511	342-9747
Seitlin 9800 NW 41st St Suite 300 TF: 800-677-7348 ■ Web: www.seitlin.com	Miami	FL	33178	305-591-0090	593-6993
SilverStone Group 11516 Miracle Hills Dr Suite 102 TF: 800-288-5501 ■ Web: www.silverstonegroup.com	Omaha	NE	68154	402-964-5400	964-5454
Simkiss Cos 2 Paoli Office Pk PO Box 1787 Web: www.simkiss.com	Paoli	PA	19301	610-727-5300	727-5414
Star Casualty Insurance Co 3750 W Flagler St TF: 888-511-7722 ■ Web: www.starcasualty.com	Miami	FL	33134	305-443-2829	476-8586
Starkweather & Shepley Inc 60 Catamore Blvd TF: 800-854-4625 ■ Web: www.starkweathershepley.com	East Providence	RI	02914	401-435-3600	438-0150
Sullivan Curtis Monroe 2100 Main St 3rd Fl TF: 800-427-3253 ■ Web: www.sullivancurtismonroe.com	Irvine	CA	92614	949-250-7172	852-9762
Synaxis Group Inc 3401 West End Ave Suite 180 TF: 800-960-3560 ■ Web: www.synaxisgroup.com	Nashville	TN	37203	615-463-7800	463-7777
Talbot Financial Corp 7770 Jefferson St NE Suite 101 TF: 800-800-5661 ■ Web: www.talbotcorp.com	Albuquerque	NM	87109	505-828-4000	828-0732
Tanenbaum-Harber Co Inc 320 W 57th St 2nd Fl Web: www.tanhar.com	New York	NY	10019	212-603-0200	262-9470
Trover Solutions Inc 1930 Bishop Ln Suite 1500 TF: 800-456-7318 ■ Web: www.troversolutions.com	Louisville	KY	40218	502-454-1340	454-1291
UIC Inc 1 Park Way 3rd Fl Web: www.uici.com	Upper Saddle River	NJ	07458	201-661-5000	221-7529
USI Holdings Corp 555 Pleasantville Rd South Bldg Suite 160 NASDAQ: USIH ■ *Fax Area Code: 610 ■ Web: www.usi.biz	Briarcliff Manor	NY	10510	914-749-8500	537-4500*
Van Gilder Insurance Corp 700 Broadway Suite 1000 TF: 800-873-8500 ■ Web: www.vgic.com	Denver	CO	80204	303-837-8500	831-5295
VanBeurden Insurance Services Inc 1600 Draper St PO Box 67 Web: www.vanbeurden.com	Kingsburg	CA	93631	559-897-2975	897-4070
Wachovia Insurance Services 227 W Trade St 15th Fl TF: 800-868-8834 ■ Web: www.wachoviainsurance.com	Charlotte	NC	28202	704-335-4541	
Wells Fargo Insurance Inc 600 S Hwy 169 12th Fl TF: 800-328-2791 ■ Web: www.wellsfargo.com	Saint Louis Park	MN	55426	612-667-5600	667-2680
Wharton Group 101 S Livingston Ave TF: 800-521-2725 ■ Web: www.whartoninsurance.com/	Livingston	NJ	07039	973-992-5775	992-6660
William Rigg Co 2001 Bryan St Suite 800 TF: 800-275-4449 ■ Web: www.wrigg.com	Dallas	TX	75201	214-979-6200	979-6215
Willis Group Holdings Ltd 200 Liberty St 1 World Financial Center NYSE: WSH ■ TF: 800-234-8596 ■ Web: www.willis.com	New York	NY	10281	212-915-8888	915-8511
Willis of New York Inc 200 Liberty St 1 World Financial Center NYSE: WSH ■ TF: 800-234-8596 ■ Web: www.willis.com	New York	NY	10281	212-915-8888	915-8511
Wortham John L & Son LP 2727 Allen Pkwy Web: www.jwortham.com	Houston	TX	77019	713-526-3366	526-2757

394 INSURANCE COMPANIES

SEE ALSO Home Warranty Services p. 1789; Viatical Settlement Companies p. 2404

394-1 Animal Insurance

	City	State	Zip	Phone	Fax
Ark Agency Animal Insurance Services PO Box 223 TF: 800-328-8894 ■ Web: www.arkagency-naha.com	Paynesville	MN	56362	320-243-7250	243-7224
Canadian Livestock Insurance 480 University Ave Suite 412 TF: 800-727-1502 ■ Web: www.cdnlivestock.com	Toronto	ON	M5G1V2	416-510-8191	510-8186
Equisport Agency Inc PO Box 269 TF: 800-432-1215 ■ Web: www.equisportagency.com	Bloomfield Hills	MI	48303	248-644-1215	644-1404
Georgia Walker & Assoc Inc PO Box 584 TF: 800-385-2423 ■ Web: www.georgiawalker.com	Raymore	MO	64083	816-331-3211	331-4148
Henry Equestrian Insurance Brokers 28 Victoria St TF: 800-565-4321 ■ Web: www.hep.ca	Aurora	ON	L4G3L6	905-727-1144	727-4986
Markel Insurance Co 4600 Cox Rd TF: 800-431-1270 ■ Web: www.horseinsurance.com	Glen Allen	VA	23060	804-527-2700	527-7999
Merry Rama Insurance 4236 County Hwy 18 Web: www.cattlexchange.com/insurance.htm	Delhi	NY	13753	607-746-2226	746-2911
Petcare Insurance Brokers Ltd 710 Dorval Dr Suite 400 TF: 877-738-4584 ■ Web: www.petcareinsurance.com	Oakville	ON	L6K3V7	905-842-2615	842-1856
Pet's Health Plan 3840 Greentree Ave SW TF: 877-592-7387 ■ Web: www.petshealthplan.com	Canton	OH	44706	330-484-8179	484-8081
Veterinary Pet Insurance Inc 3060 Saturn St *Fax Area Code: 714 ■ Web: www.petinsurance.com	Brea	CA	92821	800-872-7387	985-0525*
Walker Georgia & Assoc Inc PO Box 584 TF: 800-385-2423 ■ Web: www.georgiawalker.com	Raymore	MO	64083	816-331-3211	331-4148

394-2 Life & Accident Insurance

	City	State	Zip	Phone	Fax
Abraham Lincoln Insurance Co 5250 S 6th St TF: 800-323-0050	Springfield	IL	62703	217-241-6300	241-6574
Acacia Life Insurance Co 7315 Wisconsin Ave *Fax: Cust Svc ■ TF: 800-444-1889	Bethesda	MD	20814	301-280-1000	280-1451*
Acacia National Life 7315 Wisconsin Ave TF: 800-444-1889	Bethesda	MD	20814	301-280-1000	280-1451
Aegon Special Markets Group Inc 20 Moores Rd TF: 800-523-7900 ■ Web: www.aegonsmg.com	Frazer	PA	19355	610-648-5000	648-5348
Aetna Inc 151 Farmington Ave NYSE: AET ■ TF: 800-872-3862 ■ Web: www.aetna.com	Hartford	CT	06156	860-273-0123	273-8909
AFLAC (American Family Life Assurance Co of Columbus) 1932 Wynnton Rd *Fax Area Code: 800 ■ *Fax: Cust Svc ■ TF: 800-992-3522 ■ Web: www.aflac.com	Columbus	GA	31999	706-323-3431	448-8922*
AGC Life Insurance Co 2000 American General Way TF: 800-888-2452	Brentwood	TN	37027	615-749-1000	749-1400
AIG American General 3051 Hollis Dr TF: 800-528-2011	Springfield	IL	62704	217-541-7700	
AIG American General 2727 A Allen Pkwy TF: 800-231-3655 ■ Web: www.aigag.com	Houston	TX	77019	713-522-1111	831-3028
AIG Life Insurance Co PO Box 2226 *Fax: Acctg ■ TF: 800-441-7468	Wilmington	DE	19899	302-594-2000	654-5436*
Alfa Insurance PO Box 11000 TF: 800-392-5705 ■ Web: www.alfains.com	Montgomery	AL	36191	334-288-3900	288-0905
Alfa Life Insurance Corp PO Box 11000 Web: www.alfains.com	Montgomery	AL	36191	334-288-3900	613-4849
Allegiance Life Insurance Co 1 Horace Mann Plaza TF: 800-999-1030	Springfield	IL	62715	217-789-2500	788-5161
Allianz Life Insurance Co of North America 5701 Golden Hills Dr *Fax: Mktg ■ TF: 800-328-5600 ■ Web: www.allianzlife.com	Minneapolis	MN	55416	763-765-6500	582-6407*
Allmerica Financial 440 Lincoln St TF: 800-533-7881 ■ Web: www.allmerica.com	Worcester	MA	01653	508-855-1000	853-6332
Allstate Life Insurance Co 3100 Sanders Rd Allstate West Plaza TF Cust Svc: 800-366-1411 ■ Web: www.allstate.com/products/life	Northbrook	IL	60062	847-402-5000	
Allstate Life Insurance Co of New York PO Box 80469	Lincoln	NE	68501	800-347-5433	255-1329
Amalgamated Life Insurance Co 730 Broadway Web: www.amalgamatedlife.com	New York	NY	10003	212-539-5000	
Amedex Insurance Co 7001 SW 97th Ave TF: 800-726-1203 ■ Web: www.amedex.com	Miami	FL	33173	305-275-1400	275-8484
Amedex Insurance Group 7001 SW 97th Ave TF: 800-726-1203 ■ Web: www.amedex.com	Miami	FL	33173	305-275-1400	275-8484
American Amicable Life Insurance Co PO Box 2549 TF: 800-736-7311 ■ Web: www.americanamicable.com	Waco	TX	76702	254-297-2777	297-2757
American Capitol Insurance Co 10555 Richmond Ave 2nd Fl TF: 800-527-2567	Houston	TX	77042	713-974-2242	953-7920
American Community Mutual Insurance Co 39201 Seven-Mile Rd TF: 800-991-2642 ■ Web: www.american-community.com	Livonia	MI	48152	734-591-9000	591-4628
American Equity Investment Life Insurance Co 5000 Westown Pkwy Suite 440 TF: 888-221-1234 ■ Web: www.american-equity.com	West Des Moines	IA	50266	515-221-0002	221-9947
American Family Life Assurance Co of Columbus (AFLAC) 1932 Wynnton Rd *Fax Area Code: 800 ■ *Fax: Cust Svc ■ TF: 800-992-3522 ■ Web: www.aflac.com	Columbus	GA	31999	706-323-3431	448-8922*

Phone | Fax

American Family Life Insurance Co 6000 American Pkwy .... Madison WI 53783 608-249-2111 243-4921
TF: 888-428-5433 ■ *Web:* www.amfam.com

American Family Mutual Insurance Co 6000 American Pkwy....... Madison WI 53783 608-249-2111 243-4921*
**Fax:* Hum Res ■ *TF Cust Svc:* 800-374-0008 ■ *Web:* www.amfam.com

American Fidelity Assurance Co 2000 N Classen Blvd .... Oklahoma City OK 73106 405-523-2000 523-5645
TF: 800-654-8489 ■ *Web:* www.afadvantage.com

American Fidelity Life Insurance Co 4060 Barrancas Ave .... Pensacola FL 32507 850-456-7401 453-5440
Web: www.americanfidelitylifeins.com

American Foreign Service Protective Assn 1716 'N' St NW..... Washington DC 20036 202-833-4910 833-4918
Web: www.afspa.org

American Founders Life Insurance Co PO Box 52121 .... Phoenix AZ 85072 480-425-5100 425-5150
TF: 800-531-5067 ■ *Web:* www.americanfounderslife.com

American General Life & Accident Insurance Co
2000 American General Way .... Brentwood TN 37027 615-749-1000 749-1400*
**Fax:* Hum Res ■ *TF:* 800-888-2452 ■ *Web:* www.aigag.com

American Health & Life Insurance Co
3001 Meacham Blvd Suite 200 .... Fort Worth TX 76137 817-348-7573 348-7167
TF: 800-711-3454

American Heritage Life Insurance Co
1776 American Heritage Life Dr.......................... Jacksonville FL 32224 904-992-1776 992-2747
TF: 800-521-3535 ■ *Web:* www.ahlcorp.com

American Income Life Insurance Co 1200 Wooded Acres .... Waco TX 76710 254-772-3050 751-8670
TF: 800-433-3405 ■ *Web:* www.ailins.com

American Investors Life Insurance Co 555 S Kansas Ave........... Topeka KS 66603 785-232-6945 295-4495
TF: 800-435-4884

American Life Insurance Co 600 King St 1 ALICO Plaza........ Wilmington DE 19801 302-594-2000 654-3154
TF: 800-441-7468

American National Insurance Co 1 Moody Plaza................ Galveston TX 77550 409-763-4661 766-6663
NASDAQ: ANAT ■ *Web:* www.anico.com

American Progressive Life & Health Insurance Co of New York
6 International Dr Suite 190.............................. Rye Brook NY 10573 914-934-8300 934-9123
TF: 800-332-3377 ■ *Web:* www.amerprog.com

American Republic Insurance Co 601 6th Ave .... Des Moines IA 50309 515-245-2000 247-2435
TF: 800-247-2190 ■ *Web:* www.americanrepublic.com

American Standard Insurance Co of Wisconsin
6000 American Pkwy.................................... Madison WI 53783 608-249-2111 243-4921
TF: 800-374-0008

American United Life Insurance Co
1 American Sq PO Box 368............................ Indianapolis IN 46206 317-285-1877 285-1855
TF: 800-537-6442 ■ *Web:* www.aul.com

Americo Financial Life & Annuity Insurance Co
PO Box 410288 .... Kansas City MO 64141 816-391-2000 391-2100
TF Cust Svc: 800-366-6565 ■ *Web:* www.americo.com

Ameritas Direct 5900 'O' St .... Lincoln NE 68510 402-467-1122 467-7935
TF: 800-552-3553 ■ *Web:* www.ameritasdirect.com

Ameritas Life Insurance Corp 5900 'O' St........................ Lincoln NE 68510 402-467-1122 467-7935*
**Fax:* Hum Res ■ *TF:* 800-283-9588 ■ *Web:* www.ameritas.com

Ameritas Variable Life Insurance Co 5900 'O' St.............. Lincoln NE 68510 402-467-1122 467-7935*
**Fax:* Hum Res ■ *TF:* 800-634-8353 ■ *Web:* www.overturelife.com

AmerUs Life Insurance Co 611 5th Ave .... Des Moines IA 50309 515-283-2371 557-2625
TF: 800-800-9882 ■ *Web:* www.ameruslife.com

Amica Life Insurance Co PO Box 6008 .... Providence RI 02940 800-242-6422 333-9360*
**Fax Area Code:* 401 ■ *TF:* 800-992-6422 ■ *Web:* www.amica.com

Annuity Investors Life Insurance Co 525 Vine St 7th Fl .... Cincinnati OH 45202 513-357-3300 357-3397
TF: 800-789-6771

Anthem Life Insurance Co 6740 N High St Suite 200 .... Worthington OH 43085 614-436-0688
TF: 800-551-7265 ■ *Web:* www.anthem.com

Assurant Employee Benefits 2323 Grand Blvd................ Kansas City MO 64108 816-474-2345 881-8996
TF: 800-733-7879 ■ *Web:* www.assurantemployeebenefits.com

Assurant Life Insurance Co 308 Maltbie St Suite 200............ Syracuse NY 13204 315-451-0066 453-2343
TF: 800-745-7100 ■ *Web:* www.assurant.com

Atlanta Life Insurance Co PO Box 2222 .... Decatur AL 35609 256-552-7011 552-7284
TF: 800-235-5422 ■ *Web:* www.atlantalife.com

Aurora National Life Assurance Co PO Box 4490................ Hartford CT 06147 800-265-2652 513-5390*
**Fax Area Code:* 860 ■ *Web:* www.auroralife.com

AUSA Life Insurance Co Inc 4333 Edgewood Rd NE.......... Cedar Rapids IA 52499 319-398-8511 369-2209
TF Cust Svc: 800-625-4213

Auto-Owners Life Insurance Co 6101 Anacapri Blvd .... Lansing MI 48917 517-323-1200 323-8796
TF: 800-288-8740 ■ *Web:* www.auto-owners.com

AXA Equitable Life Insurance Co 1290 Ave of the Americas....... New York NY 10104 212-554-1234
TF: 888-855-5100 ■ *Web:* www.axa-equitable.com

Baltimore Life Cos 10075 Red Run Blvd .... Owings Mills MD 21117 410-581-6600 654-0786*
**Fax:* Claims ■ *TF:* 800-628-5433 ■ *Web:* www.baltlife.com

Bank of America Insurance Services Inc PO Box 21848 .... Greensboro NC 27420 336-805-8800 805-2026
TF: 800-288-7647 ■ *Web:* www.bankofamerica.com/insurance

Bankers Fidelity Life Insurance Co 4370 Peachtree Rd .... Atlanta GA 30319 800-241-1439
Web: www.bflic.com

Bankers Insurance Co 360 Central Ave .... Saint Petersburg FL 33701 727-823-4000 898-1511
TF: 800-627-0000 ■ *Web:* www.bankersinsurance.com

Bankers Life & Casualty Co 222 Merchandise Mart Plaza........... Chicago IL 60654 312-396-6000 324-5060
TF: 800-621-3724 ■ *Web:* www.bankerslife.com

Banner Life Insurance Co 1701 Research Blvd .... Rockville MD 20850 301-279-4800 294-6961
TF: 800-638-8428 ■ *Web:* www.lgamerica.com/id00001.htm

Beneficial Financial Group 36 S State St .... Salt Lake City UT 84136 801-933-1100 531-3306
TF: 800-233-7979 ■ *Web:* www.beneficialfinancialgroup.com

Benevolent Life Insurance Co Inc 1624 Milam St.............. Shreveport LA 71103 318-425-1522 221-1761
TF: 800-435-1522

Berkshire Hathaway Life Insurance Co of Nebraska
3024 Harney St .... Omaha NE 68131 402-536-3000 536-3030
TF: 800-786-6426 ■ *Web:* www.bhln.com

Berkshire Life Insurance Co of America 700 South St............ Pittsfield MA 01201 413-499-4321 499-4831
TF: 800-819-2468 ■ *Web:* www.theberkshire.com

Booker T Washington Insurance Co PO Box 697 .... Birmingham AL 35201 205-328-5454 251-6873
TF: 800-228-4180

Boston Mutual Life Insurance Co 120 Royall St .... Canton MA 02021 781-828-7000 770-0490
TF: 800-669-2668 ■ *Web:* www.bostonmutual.com

Bristol West Insurance Group 5701 Stirling Rd...................... Davie FL 33314 954-316-5200 316-5275
Web: www.bristolwest.com

Canada Life Assurance Co 330 University Ave .... Toronto ON M5G1R8 416-597-1456 754-8849*
**Fax Area Code:* 866 ■ **Fax:* Claims ■ *Web:* www.canadalife.com

Catholic Family Life Insurance PO Box 11563 .... Milwaukee WI 53211 414-961-0500 961-0103*
**Fax:* Sales ■ *TF:* 800-227-2354 ■ *Web:* www.cfli.org

Central Benefits Mutual Insurance Co PO Box 850658 .... Richardson TX 75085 614-797-5200 797-5268
TF: 800-777-3377 ■ *Web:* www.centralbenefits.com

Central Security Life Insurance Co PO Box 833879 .... Richardson TX 75083 972-699-2770 699-2788
TF: 866-629-2677 ■ *Web:* www.cslic.com

Central States Health & Life Co of Omaha PO Box 34350.......... Omaha NE 68134 402-397-1111 399-3497
TF: 800-541-2363 ■ *Web:* www.cso.com

Chase Insurance Co 2500 Westfield Drive .... Elgin IL 60123 847-930-7000 874-0655
TF: 800-321-9313 ■ *Web:* www.chaseinsurancecompany.com

Chesapeake Life Insurance Co
1331 W Memorial Rd Suite 112 .... Oklahoma City OK 73114 405-848-0179 302-1486
TF: 800-725-7887 ■ *Web:* www.thechesapeakelife.com

CIGNA Reinsurance 900 Cottage Grove Rd......................... Hartford CT 06152 860-226-6000 226-4566
TF: 888-244-6237

Cincinnati Life Insurance Co PO Box 145496 .... Cincinnati OH 45250 513-870-2000 870-2911
TF: 800-783-4479

Citizens Insurance Co of America PO Box 149151.................. Austin TX 78714 512-836-9730 836-9785
TF: 800-880-5044 ■ *Web:* www.citizensinc.com

Citizens Security Life Insurance Co PO Box 436149 .... Louisville KY 40253 502-244-2420 244-2439
TF: 800-843-7752 ■ *Web:* www.citizenssecuritylife.com

CNA Valley Forge Life Insurance Co 100 CNA Dr .... Nashville TN 37214 615-871-1400 886-1883
TF: 800-437-8854

Colonial Life & Accident Insurance Co
1200 Colonial Life Blvd .... Columbia SC 29210 803-798-7000 731-2618
TF: 800-325-4368 ■ *Web:* www.coloniallife.com

Colonial Penn Life Insurance Co 399 Market St .... Philadelphia PA 19181 215-928-8000
TF: 800-523-9100 ■ *Web:* www.colonialpenn.com

Columbus Life Insurance Co 400 E 4th St PO Box 5737.......... Cincinnati OH 45201 513-361-6700 361-6939
TF: 800-677-8383 ■ *Web:* www.columbuslife.com

Combined Insurance Co of America 5050 N Broadway............ Chicago IL 60640 800-428-5466 765-1860*
**Fax Area Code:* 773 ■ *Web:* www.combined.com

Companion Life Insurance Co 3316 Farnam St .... Omaha NE 68175 800-775-6000 351-8679*
**Fax Area Code:* 402

Companion Life Insurance Co 7909 Parklane Rd Suite 200 .... Columbia SC 29223 803-735-1251 735-0736
TF: 800-753-0404 ■ *Web:* www.companionlife.com

Concord Group Insurance Cos 4 Bouton St .... Concord NH 03301 603-224-4086 225-5268*
**Fax:* Hum Res ■ *TF:* 800-852-3380 ■ *Web:* www.concordgroupinsurance.com

Connecticut General Life Insurance Co 900 Cottage Grove Rd ..... Hartford CT 06152 860-226-6000 226-4464*
**Fax:* Sales ■ *TF:* 800-444-2363

Conseco Annuity Assurance Co 11815 N Pennsylvania St .... Carmel IN 46032 317-817-6100 817-5704
TF: 800-541-2254 ■ *Web:* www.conseco.com

Conseco Health Insurance Co 11815 N Pennsylvania St............ Carmel IN 46932 317-817-6100 817-5704
TF: 800-541-2254 ■ *Web:* www.conseco.com

Conseco Insurance Co 11815 N Pennsylvania St.................. Carmel IN 46032 317-817-6300 817-3604
TF: 800-544-0467 ■ *Web:* www.conseco.com

Conseco Life Insurance Co 11815 N Pennsylvania St.............. Carmel IN 46032 317-817-6100 817-6721
Web: www.conseco.com

Conseco Medical Insurance Co 11815 N Pennsylvania St .... Carmel IN 46032 317-817-6100 817-6721
Web: www.conseco.com

Conseco Senior Health Insurance Co 11815 N Pennsylvania St...... Carmel IN 46032 317-817-6100 817-6721
Web: www.conseco.com

Conseco Variable Insurance Co 11815 N Pennsylvania St .... Carmel IN 46032 317-817-6100 817-6721
Web: www.conseco.com

Continental Assurance Co 333 S Wabash Ave.................... Chicago IL 60604 312-822-5000 822-6419
TF: 800-262-2000 ■ *Web:* www.cna.com

Continental General Insurance Co PO Box 247007................ Omaha NE 68124 402-397-3200 952-4325
TF: 800-545-8905 ■ *Web:* www.continentalgeneral.com

Cotton States Life Insurance Co 244 Perimeter Center Pkwy NE..... Atlanta GA 30346 770-391-8600 677-7264
TF: 800-282-6536 ■ *Web:* www.cottonstatesinsurance.com

COUNTRY Insurance & Financial Services
1701 Towanda Ave.................................. Bloomington IL 61701 309-557-3000 821-2501
TF: 888-211-2555 ■ *Web:* www.countryfinancial.com

Desjardins Financial Security Life Assurance Co
200 Ave des Commandeurs.................................. Levis QC G6V6R2 866-838-7553 833-0529*
**Fax Area Code:* 418 ■ *Web:* www.dsf-dfs.com

EMC National Life Co 4095 NW Urbandale Dr.................. Urbandale IA 50322 515-645-4000 645-4220
TF: 800-232-5818 ■ *Web:* www.emcnationallife.com

Empire General Life Assurance Corp
7400 W 130th St Suite 400............................... Overland Park KS 66213 913-897-9733 814-8720
TF: 800-688-3518 ■ *Web:* www.empiregeneral.com

Employers Insurance Co of Wausau A Mutual Co
2000 Westwood Dr .... Wausau WI 54401 715-845-5211 843-3847*
**Fax:* Hum Res ■ *TF:* 800-435-4401 ■ *Web:* www.wausau.com

Epic Life Insurance Co 1765 W Broadway...................... Madison WI 53713 608-223-2100 223-2159
TF Sales: 800-236-8809 ■ *Web:* www.epiclife.com

Equitable Distributors Inc 1290 Ave of the Americas .... New York NY 10104 212-554-1234 314-3141
TF: 888-855-5100 ■ *Web:* www.equidist.com

Equitable Life & Casualty Insurance Co
3 Triad Ctr Suite 200.............................. Salt Lake City UT 84180 801-521-2500 579-3790
TF Cust Svc: 800-352-5150 ■ *Web:* www.equilife.com

Erie Family Life Insurance Co 100 Erie Insurance Pl .... Erie PA 16530 814-870-2000 870-2095
TF: 800-458-0811 ■ *Web:* www.erieinsurance.com

Family Life Insurance Co 6500 River Place Blvd Bldg 1 .... Austin TX 78730 512-404-5000 404-5210
TF: 800-925-6000 ■ *Web:* www.ficgroup.com

Farm Bureau Life Insurance Co 5400 University Ave ..... West Des Moines IA 50266 515-225-5400 226-6053*
**Fax:* Hum Res ■ *TF:* 800-247-4170 ■ *Web:* www.fbfs.com

Farm Family Life Insurance Co PO Box 656 .... Albany NY 12201 518-431-5000 431-5979
TF: 800-948-3276 ■ *Web:* www.farmfamily.com

Farmers New World Life Insurance 3003 77th Ave SE .... Mercer Island WA 98040 206-232-8400 236-6642

Farmers & Traders Life Insurance Co
960 James St PO Box 1056............................... Syracuse NY 13201 315-471-5656 475-6612
TF: 800-347-0960 ■ *Web:* www.ftlife.com

Farmers Union Mutual Insurance Co PO Box 2020............. Jamestown ND 58402 701-252-2701 252-0404
TF: 800-366-6338

Federated Life Insurance Co PO Box 328 .... Owatonna MN 55060 507-455-5200 455-5997
TF: 800-533-0472 ■ *Web:* www.federatedinsurance.com

Federated Mutual Insurance Co PO Box 328 .... Owatonna MN 55060 507-455-5200 455-7808
TF: 800-533-0472 ■ *Web:* www.federatedinsurance.com

FEDUSA 1839 N Pine Island Rd.............................. Plantation FL 33322 954-475-0182 475-1058
Web: www.fedusa.com

FIC Insurance Group 6500 River Place Blvd Bldg 1.................. Austin TX 78730 512-404-5000 404-5213
TF: 800-925-6000 ■ *Web:* www.ficgroup.com

Fidelity & Guaranty Life Insurance Co 1001 Fleet St .... Baltimore MD 21202 410-895-0100 895-0132
TF Sales: 800-445-6758 ■ *Web:* www.omfn.com

Fidelity Investments Life Insurance Co 82 Devonshire St .... Boston MA 02109 617-563-7000 476-6105
TF: 800-544-2442

Financial Benefit Life Insurance Co 555 S Kansas Ave .... Topeka KS 66603 785-232-6945 276-3521
TF: 800-332-7732

First Alexander Hamilton Life Insurance Co PO Box 21008..... Greensboro NC 27420 336-691-3000 335-2692
TF: 800-487-1485

First Colony Life Insurance Co 3100 Albert Lankford Dr......... Lynchburg VA 24501 434-845-0911 948-5880*
**Fax:* Cust Svc ■ *TF:* 888-325-5433 ■ *Web:* www.firstcolonylife.com

First Investors Life Insurance Co Raritan Plaza 1 PO Box 7836...... Edison NJ 08818 732-855-2500 510-4209
TF: 800-832-7783 ■ *Web:* www.firstinvestorslife.com

First Penn-Pacific Life Insurance Co 10 N Martingale Rd ..... Schaumburg IL 60173 847-466-8000 466-3110*
**Fax:* Hum Res ■ *TF:* 800-450-3067 ■ *Web:* www.firstpenn.com

First UNUM Life Insurance Co 2211 Congress St .... Portland ME 04122 800-658-8686 328-8977*
**Fax Area Code:* 212 ■ *Web:* www.unumprovident.com

Forethought Financial Services Inc Forethought Ctr............. Batesville IN 47006 800-881-2430 934-8564*
**Fax Area Code:* 812 ■ *TF:* 800-881-2430 ■ *Web:* www.forethought.com

Fort Dearborn Life Insurance Co 1020 31st St .... Downers Grove IL 60515 800-633-3696 824-5418*
**Fax Area Code:* 630

Fremont Life Insurance Co PO Box 410288.................. Kansas City MO 64141 816-391-2000 391-2100
TF: 800-243-4651

Garden State Life Insurance Co
2450 S Shore Blvd Suite 401 .... League City TX 77573 281-538-1037 538-3705
TF: 800-638-8565 ■ *Web:* www.garden-state.com

General Reinsurance Corp 695 E Main St Financial Ctr........... Stamford CT 06901 203-328-5000 328-6423
TF: 800-431-9994 ■ *Web:* www.genre.com

Genworth Financial Inc 6620 W Broad St .... Richmond VA 23230 804-484-3821 484-7198
NYSE: GNW ■ *TF:* 888-436-9678 ■ *Web:* www.genworth.com

Gerber Life Insurance Co 1311 Mamaroneck Ave .... White Plains NY 10605 914-272-4000 272-4099
TF: 800-704-2180 ■ *Web:* www.gerberlife.com

Life & Accident Insurance (Cont'd)

Phone | Fax

Globe Life & Accident Insurance Co
204 N Robinson Ave Globe Life Ctr ... Oklahoma City OK 73102 405-270-1400 270-1496
TF: 800-654-5433 ■ *Web:* www.globeontheweb.com

Golden Rule Insurance Co 7440 Woodlands ... Indianapolis IN 46278 317-297-4123 298-0875
Web: www.goldenrule.com

Golden State Mutual Life Insurance Co
1999 W Adams Blvd ... Los Angeles CA 90018 323-731-1131 733-0320
TF: 800-225-5476 ■ *Web:* www.gsmlife.com

Grange Life Insurance Co 650 S Front St ... Columbus OH 43206 614-445-2900 445-2619
TF: 800-422-0550 ■ *Web:* www.grangeinsurance.com/Grange_Life

Great American Life Assurance Co of Puerto Rico Inc
PO Box 363786 ... San Juan PR 00936 787-758-4888 766-1985
TF: 800-980-7651 ■ *Web:* www.galifepr.com

Great American Life Insurance Co 525 Vine St 7th Fl ... Cincinnati OH 45202 513-357-3300 369-3839
TF: 800-854-3649 ■ *Web:* www.galic.com

Great Southern Life Insurance Co PO Box 410288 ... Kansas City MO 64141 816-391-2000 395-9238*
**Fax Area Code:* 800 ■ *TF:* 800-231-0801 ■ *Web:* www.greatsouthern.com

Great-West Life & Annuity Insurance Co
8515 E Orchard Rd ... Greenwood Village CO 80111 303-737-3000 737-3198
TF: 800-537-2033 ■ *Web:* www.gwla.com

Great-West Life Assurance Co PO Box 6000 ... Winnipeg MB R3C3A5 204-946-1190 946-4129*
**Fax:* Investor Rel ■ *Web:* www.gwl.ca

Group Variable Universal Life Insurance
190 Carondelet Plaza ... Saint Louis MO 63105 800-685-0124 862-5171*
**Fax Area Code:* 314 ■ *Web:* www.paragonlife.com

Guarantee Trust Life Insurance Co 1275 Milwaukee Ave ... Glenview IL 60025 847-699-0600 699-2355
TF: 800-338-7452 ■ *Web:* www.gtlic.com

Guardian Investor Services LLC 7 Hanover Sq ... New York NY 10004 212-598-8000 919-2170*
**Fax:* Hum Res ■ *TF:* 888-482-7342 ■ *Web:* www.guardianinvestor.com

Guardian Life Insurance Co of America 7 Hanover Sq ... New York NY 10004 212-598-8000 919-2762*
**Fax:* Hum Res ■ *TF:* 888-482-7342 ■ *Web:* www.guardianlife.com

GuideOne Mutual Insurance Co 1111 Ashworth Rd ... West Des Moines IA 50265 515-267-5000 267-5530*
**Fax:* Hum Res ■ *TF:* 877-448-4331 ■ *Web:* www.guideone.com

GuideOne Specialty Mutual Insurance Co
1111 Ashworth Rd ... West Des Moines IA 50265 515-267-5000 267-5530*
**Fax:* Hum Res ■ *TF:* 800-247-4181 ■ *Web:* www.guideone.com

Hannover Life Reassurance Co of America
800 N Magnolia Ave Suite 1400 ... Orlando FL 32803 407-649-8411 649-8322
TF: 800-327-1910 ■ *Web:* www.hlramerica.com

Harleysville Life Insurance Co 1440 Pennbrook Pkwy ... Lansdale PA 19446 800-222-1981
TF: 800-222-1981 ■ *Web:* www.harleysville.com

Harleysville Mutual Insurance Co 355 Maple Ave ... Harleysville PA 19438 215-256-5000 256-5601
TF: 800-523-6344 ■ *Web:* www.harleysville.com

Hartford Life & Accident Insurance Co 200 Hopmeadow St ... Simsbury CT 06089 860-525-8555
TF: 800-833-5575 ■ *Web:* www.thehartford.com

Harvey Watt & Co Atlanta Airport PO Box 20787 ... Atlanta GA 30320 404-767-7501 761-8326
TF: 800-241-6103 ■ *Web:* www.harveywatt.com

HealthExtras Inc 800 King Farm Blvd 4th Fl ... Rockville MD 20850 301-548-2900 548-2991
NASDAQ: HLEX ■ *TF:* 800-323-6640 ■ *Web:* www.healthextras.com

HM Benefits Administrators 5th Ave Pl 120 5th Ave ... Pittsburgh PA 15222 412-544-2000
TF: 800-833-1115 ■ *Web:* www.highmarklife.com

HM Life Insurance Co 1800 Center St ... Camp Hill PA 17089 717-731-8080 763-3815
TF: 800-345-3806 ■ *Web:* www.highmark.com

Horace Mann Insurance Co 1 Horace Mann Plaza ... Springfield IL 62715 217-789-2500 788-5161
TF: 800-999-1030 ■ *Web:* www.horacemann.com

Horace Mann Life Insurance Co 1 Horace Mann Plaza ... Springfield IL 62715 217-789-2500 788-5161
TF: 800-999-1030 ■ *Web:* www.horacemann.com

Humana Inc 500 W Main St ... Louisville KY 40202 502-580-1000 580-3690
NYSE: HUM ■ *TF:* 800-486-2620 ■ *Web:* www.humana.com

Illinois Mutual Life Insurance Co 300 SW Adams St ... Peoria IL 61634 309-674-8255 674-8637
TF: 800-380-6688 ■ *Web:* www.illinoismutual.com

Independence Holding Co 96 Cummings Point Rd ... Stamford CT 06902 203-358-8000 348-3103
NYSE: IHC ■ *Web:* www.independenceholding.com

Indiana Farm Bureau Insurance Co
225 S East St PO Box 1250 ... Indianapolis IN 46206 317-692-7200 692-7185*
**Fax:* Sales ■ *TF:* 800-723-3276 ■ *Web:* www.infarmbureau.com

Indianapolis Life Insurance Co
9200 Keystone Crossing Suite 800 ... Indianapolis IN 46240 317-927-6500 927-6510
TF: 800-457-3557 ■ *Web:* www.indianapolislife.com

Industrial-Alliance Life Insurance Co
1080 Grande Allee W PO Box 1907 Station Therminus ... Quebec City QC G1K7M3 418-684-5000 684-5106
TF: 800-463-6236 ■ *Web:* www.inalco.com

ING Financial Services Inc 151 Farmington Ave ... Hartford CT 06156 860-273-0123 636-2303
Web: www.ing-usa.com

ING Life of Georgia 5780 Powers Ferry Rd NW ... Atlanta GA 30327 770-980-5100 618-3819*
**Fax:* Hum Res ■ *TF:* 888-968-5433

ING Northern Annuity 2000 21st Ave NW ... Minot ND 58703 877-884-5050
Web: www.ing-usa.com/tsa

ING Southland Life Insurance Co 2000 21st Ave NW ... Minot ND 58703 701-858-2000 373-2090*
**Fax Area Code:* 877 ■ *TF:* 877-241-5050 ■ *Web:* www.ing-usa.com/southland

Insurance Companies at American General Financial
PO Box 59 ... Evansville IN 47701 812-424-8031 350-9582*
**Fax Area Code:* 800

Integrity Life Insurance Co 400 Broadway ... Cincinnati OH 45202 800-325-8583 220-2677*
**Fax Area Code:* 888 ■ *TF:* 800-325-8583 ■ *Web:* www.integritycompanies.com

Investors Guaranty Life Insurance Co PO Box 410288 ... Kansas City MO 64141 816-391-2000 391-2100
TF: 800-752-1387

Investors Heritage Life Insurance Co 200 Capital Ave ... Frankfort KY 40602 502-223-2361 875-7084
TF: 800-422-2011 ■ *Web:* www.investorsheritage.com

Investors Life Insurance Co of Indiana
6500 River Pl Blvd Bldg 1 ... Austin TX 78730 512-404-5000 404-5210
TF: 800-925-6000

Investors Life Insurance Co of North America
6500 River Pl Blvd Bldg 1 ... Austin TX 78730 512-404-5000 404-5210
TF: 800-925-6000 ■ *Web:* www.ficgroup.com

Investors Partner Life Insurance Co PO Box 111 ... Boston MA 02117 617-572-6000 572-7756
TF: 800-732-5543

Jackson National Life Insurance Co 1 Corporate Way ... Lansing MI 48951 517-381-5500 706-5515*
**Fax:* Hum Res ■ *TF:* 800-644-4565 ■ *Web:* www.jnl.com

Jefferson-Pilot LifeAmerica Insurance Co 100 N Greene St ... Greensboro NC 27401 336-691-3000 691-3311*
**Fax:* PR ■ *TF:* 800-487-1485

John Hancock Life Insurance Co PO Box 111 ... Boston MA 02117 617-572-6000 572-7756
TF: 800-732-5543 ■ *Web:* www.johnhancock.com

John Hancock New York 100 Summit Lake Dr 2nd Fl ... Valhalla NY 10595 914-773-0708 773-0709
TF: 800-551-2078 ■ *Web:* www.johnhancock.com

John Hancock Variable Life Insurance Co PO Box 111 ... Boston MA 02117 617-572-6000 572-7756
TF: 800-732-5543 ■ *Web:* www.johnhancock.com

Phone | Fax

Kanawha Insurance Co PO Box 610 ... Lancaster SC 29721 803-283-5300 283-5676*
**Fax:* Hum Res ■ *TF:* 800-635-4252 ■ *Web:* www.kanawha.com

Keyport Life Insurance Co 1 Sun Life Executive Pk ... Wellesley Hills MA 02481 781-237-6030 431-4959
TF: 800-225-3950

KMG America Corp 12600 Whitewater Dr Suite 150 ... Minnetonka MN 55343 952-930-4800 930-4802
NYSE: KMA ■ *TF:* 866-820-5642 ■ *Web:* www.kmgamerica.com

Knights of Columbus 1 Columbus Plaza ... New Haven CT 06510 203-752-4000 752-4100
TF: 800-524-3611 ■ *Web:* www.kofc.org

Lafayette Life Insurance Co PO Box 7007 ... Lafayette IN 47903 765-477-7411 477-3349
TF Cust Svc: 800-243-6631 ■ *Web:* www.llic.com

Liberty National Life Insurance Co PO Box 2612 ... Birmingham AL 35202 205-325-2722 325-4909
TF: 800-333-0637 ■ *Web:* www.libnat.com

Life Insurance Co of the Southwest PO Box 569080 ... Dallas TX 75356 214-638-7100 638-9162
TF: 800-543-3794 ■ *Web:* www.lifeofsouthwest.com

Life Investors Insurance Co of America
4333 Edgewood Rd NE ... Cedar Rapids IA 52499 319-398-8511 369-2209*
**Fax:* Cust Svc ■ *TF:* 800-625-4213

Lincoln National Life Insurance Co 1300 S Clinton St ... Fort Wayne IN 46802 260-455-2000 455-4268*
**Fax:* Hum Res ■ *TF:* 800-454-6265 ■ *Web:* www.lfg.com

London Insurance Group Corp PO Box 29045 ... Phoenix AZ 85038 800-433-8181 840-0969*
**Fax Area Code:* 602

London Life Insurance Co 255 Dufferin Ave ... London ON N6A4K1 519-432-5281 435-7555
TF: 800-667-3733 ■ *Web:* www.londonlife.com

Loyal American Life Insurance Co PO Box 559004 ... Austin TX 78755 800-633-6752 302-0913*
**Fax Area Code:* 512 ■ *Web:* www.loyalamerican.com

MAMSI Life & Health Insurance Co 4 Taft Ct ... Rockville MD 20850 301-762-8205 545-5389*
**Fax:* Hum Res ■ *TF:* 800-544-2853 ■ *Web:* www.mamsi.com

Mann Horace Insurance Co 1 Horace Mann Plaza ... Springfield IL 62715 217-789-2500 788-5161
TF: 800-999-1030 ■ *Web:* www.horacemann.com

Mann Horace Life Insurance Co 1 Horace Mann Plaza ... Springfield IL 62715 217-789-2500 788-5161
TF: 800-999-1030 ■ *Web:* www.horacemann.com

Manufacturers Life Insurance Co 200 Bloor St E ... Toronto ON M4W1E5 416-926-3000 926-5410
TF: 800-968-8761 ■ *Web:* www.manulife.ca

Manulife Financial 200 Bloor St E ... Toronto ON M4W1E5 416-926-3000 926-5410
Web: www.manulife.ca

Massachusetts Mutual Life Insurance Co 1295 State St ... Springfield MA 01111 413-788-8411 744-6005
TF: 800-272-2216 ■ *Web:* www.massmutual.com

Medico Life Insurance Co 1515 S 75th St ... Omaha NE 68124 402-391-6900 391-6489
TF: 800-228-6080

MEGA Life & Health Insurance Co
9151 Grapevine Hwy ... North Richland Hills TX 76180 817-255-3100 343-3702*
**Fax Area Code:* 800 ■ **Fax:* Cust Svc ■ *TF:* 800-527-2845 ■
Web: www.megainsurance.com

Merrill Lynch Life Insurance Co 4804 Deer Lake Dr E ... Jacksonville FL 32246 904-218-7000 218-7205*
**Fax:* Hum Res ■ *TF:* 800-535-5549

MetLife Inc 200 Park Ave ... New York NY 10166 212-578-2211 578-3320
NYSE: MET ■ *TF:* 800-638-5433 ■ *Web:* www.metlife.com

MetLife Investors Insurance Co 22 Corporate Plaza Dr ... Newport Beach CA 92660 949-629-1300 629-1687
TF: 800-848-3854 ■ *Web:* www.metlifeinvestors.com

Metropolitan Life Insurance Co
2701 Queens Plaza N Met Life Plaza ... Long Island City NY 11101 212-578-2211 689-1980*
**Fax:* Mail Rm ■ *TF:* 800-638-5433 ■ *Web:* www.metlife.com

Mid-Century Insurance Co 4680 Wilshire Blvd ... Los Angeles CA 90010 323-932-3200 932-3101
TF: 888-516-5656

Mid-West National Life Ins Co of Tennessee
9151 Grapevine Hwy ... North Richland Hills TX 76182 800-733-1110 377-4391*
**Fax Area Code:* 888 ■ *Web:* www.midwestlife.com

Middlesex Insurance Co 3 Carlisle Rd ... Westford MA 01886 978-392-7000 392-7033
TF: 800-225-1390

Midland National Life Insurance Co 1 Midland Plaza ... Sioux Falls SD 57193 605-335-5700 335-3621
TF: 800-923-3223 ■ *Web:* www.mnlife.com

Minnesota Life Insurance Co 400 Robert St N ... Saint Paul MN 55101 651-665-3500 665-4484
TF: 800-328-6124 ■ *Web:* www.minnesotalife.com

MML Bay State Life Insurance Co 1295 State St ... Springfield MA 01111 413-788-8411 329-4527*
**Fax Area Code:* 866 ■ *TF Cust Svc:* 800-767-1000 ■ *Web:* www.massmutual.com

Modern Woodmen of America 1701 1st Ave ... Rock Island IL 61201 309-786-6481 793-5506
TF: 800-447-9811 ■ *Web:* www.modernwoodmen.com

Monumental Life Insurance Co 2 E Chase St ... Baltimore MD 21202 410-685-2900 347-8653
TF: 800-638-3080 ■ *Web:* www.monlife.com

Motorists Life Insurance Co 471 E Broad St ... Columbus OH 43215 614-225-8211 225-8365
Web: www.motoristsgroup.com

Munich American Reassurance Co PO Box 3210 ... Atlanta GA 30302 770-394-5665 394-7744
Web: www.marclife.com

Mutual of America Life Insurance Co 320 Park Ave ... New York NY 10022 212-224-1600 224-2500*
**Fax:* Mail Rm ■ *TF:* 800-468-3785 ■ *Web:* www.mutualofamerica.com

Mutual of Omaha Insurance Co Mutual of Omaha Plaza ... Omaha NE 68175 402-342-7600 351-2775
TF: 800-775-6000 ■ *Web:* www.mutualofomaha.com

Mutual Protective Insurance Co 1515 S 75th St ... Omaha NE 68124 402-391-6900 391-6489
TF: 800-228-6080 ■ *Web:* www.mutualprotective.com

Mutual Savings Life Insurance Co 2801 Hwy 31 S ... Decatur AL 35603 256-552-7011 552-7284
TF Cust Svc: 800-239-6754 ■ *Web:* www.msldec.com

Mutual Trust Life Insurance Co 1200 Jorie Blvd ... Oak Brook IL 60522 630-990-1000 990-7083
TF: 800-323-7320 ■ *Web:* www.mutualtrust.com

National Benefit Life Insurance Co 333 W 34th St 10th Fl ... New York NY 10001 212-615-7500 615-7345
TF: 800-222-2062

National Guardian Life Insurance Co PO Box 1191 ... Madison WI 53701 608-257-5611 257-4308
TF: 800-548-2962 ■ *Web:* www.nationalguardian.com

National Health Insurance Co PO Box 619999 ... Dallas TX 75261 817-640-1900 640-3482
TF: 800-237-1900 ■ *Web:* www.nhic.com

National Life Insurance Co 1 National Life Dr ... Montpelier VT 05604 802-229-3333 229-9281
TF: 800-732-8939 ■ *Web:* www.nlv.com

National Mutual Benefit 6522 Grand Teton Plaza ... Madison WI 53719 608-833-1936 833-8714
TF: 800-779-1936 ■ *Web:* www.nmbfrat.org

National Security Life & Accident Insurance Co PO Box 149151 ... Austin TX 78714 512-837-7100 836-9785
TF: 800-880-5044

National Western Life Insurance Co 850 E Anderson Ln ... Austin TX 78752 512-836-1010 719-0104*
NASDAQ: NWLIA ■ **Fax:* Hum Res ■ *TF:* 800-531-5442 ■
Web: www.nationalwesternlife.com

Nationwide Life & Annuity Insurance Co 5100 Rings Rd ... Dublin OH 43017 614-249-7111 249-2205*
**Fax:* Hum Res ■ *TF:* 800-882-2822

Nationwide Life Insurance Co 5100 Rings Rd ... Dublin OH 43017 614-249-7111 249-2235
TF: 800-543-3747

Nationwide Provident 1000 Chesterbrook Blvd ... Berwyn PA 19312 610-889-1717 407-7357
TF: 800-523-4681 ■ *Web:* www.nationwideprovident.com

New England Financial 501 Boylston St ... Boston MA 02116 617-578-2000
TF Cust Svc: 800-388-4000 ■ *Web:* nef.metlife.com

New England Life Insurance Co 501 Boylston St ... Boston MA 02116 617-578-2000 536-2393*
**Fax:* Hum Res ■ *TF:* 800-388-4000

New York Life Insurance & Annuity Corp 51 Madison Ave ... New York NY 10010 212-576-7000 447-4292*
**Fax:* Hum Res ■ *TF:* 800-598-2019

New York Life Insurance Co 51 Madison Ave ... New York NY 10010 212-576-7000 448-1646
Web: www.newyorklife.com

Nippon Life Insurance Co of America 521 5th Ave 5th Fl ... New York NY 10175 212-682-3000 682-3002
TF: 877-252-7174 ■ *Web:* www.nlia.com

North American Co for Life & Health Insurance
525 W Van Buren St ... Chicago IL 60607 312-648-7600 648-7765
TF: 800-800-3656 ■ *Web:* www.nacolah.com

Phone | Fax

North Carolina Mutual Life Insurance Co 411 W Chapel Hill St Durham NC 27701 919-682-9201 683-1694
TF: 800-626-1899 ■ *Web:* www.ncmutuallife.com

Northwestern Mutual Life Insurance Co
720 E Wisconsin Ave Milwaukee WI 53202 414-271-1444 665-2690*
**Fax:* Hum Res ■ *Web:* www.nmfn.com

Ohio Life Insurance Co PO Box 410288 Kansas City MO 64141 816-391-2000 391-2100
TF: 800-456-6446

Ohio National Life Insurance Co 1 Financial Way Suite 100 Cincinnati OH 45242 513-794-6100 794-4730
TF: 800-366-6654 ■ *Web:* www.ohionational.com

Ohio State Life Insurance Co PO Box 410288 Kansas City MO 64141 816-391-2000 391-2100
TF: 800-752-1387 ■ *Web:* www.ohiostatelife.com

Old American Insurance Co 3520 Broadway Kansas City MO 64111 816-753-4900 753-4902
TF: 800-733-6242 ■ *Web:* www.oaic.com

OneAmerica Financial Partners Inc
1 American Sq PO Box 368 Indianapolis IN 46206 317-285-1111
Web: www.oneamerica.com

Oxford Life Insurance Co 2721 N Central Ave Phoenix AZ 85004 602-263-6666 277-5901
TF: 800-528-0463 ■ *Web:* www.oxfordlife.com

Ozark National Life Insurance Inc 500 E 9th St Kansas City MO 64106 816-842-6300 842-8373
Web: www.ozark-national.com

Pacific Life Insurance Co 700 Newport Ctr Dr Newport Beach CA 92660 949-219-3011 219-3483*
**Fax:* Hum Res ■ *TF:* 800-800-7646 ■ *Web:* www.pacificlife.com

Pan-American Life Insurance Co 601 Poydras St New Orleans LA 70130 504-566-1300 566-3381
TF Life Ins: 877-939-4550 ■ *Web:* www.panamericanlife.com

Partner Reinsurance Co of the US 1 Greenwich Plaza Greenwich CT 06830 203-485-4200 485-4300
TF: 800-261-3164 ■ *Web:* www.partnerre.com

Paul Revere Life Insurance Co 18 Chestnut St Worcester MA 01608 508-799-4441 751-7079*
**Fax:* Hum Res ■ *TF:* 800-799-0990

Pekin Life Insurance Co 2505 Court St Pekin IL 61558 309-346-1161 346-8512
TF: 800-322-0160 ■ *Web:* www.pekininsurance.com

Penn Insurance & Annuity Co 600 Dresher Rd Horsham PA 19044 215-956-8000 956-7950
TF Cust Svc: 800-523-0650

Penn Mutual Life Insurance Co 600 Dresher Rd Horsham PA 19044 215-956-8000 956-7699
TF Cust Svc: 800-523-0650 ■ *Web:* www.pennmutual.com

Penn Treaty Network America Insurance Co 3440 Lehigh St Allentown PA 18103 610-965-2222 967-4616
TF: 800-222-3469 ■ *Web:* www.penntreaty.com

Pharmacists Mutual Insurance Co
808 US Hwy 18 W PO Box 370 Algona IA 50511 515-295-2461 295-9306
TF: 800-247-5930 ■ *Web:* www.pharmacistsmutual.com

Phoenix Life Insurance Co 1 American Row Hartford CT 06115 860-403-5000 403-5534*
**Fax:* Hum Res ■ *TF Cust Svc:* 800-628-1936

Physicians Life Insurance Co 2600 Dodge St Omaha NE 68131 402-633-1000 633-1096
TF: 800-228-9100

Physicians Mutual Insurance Co 2600 Dodge St Omaha NE 68131 402-633-1000 633-1096
TF: 800-228-9100 ■ *Web:* www.physiciansmutual.com

Pioneer Mutual Life Insurance Co PO Box 2546 Fargo ND 58108 701-297-5700 297-5772
TF: 800-437-4692 ■ *Web:* www.pmlife.com

Presidential Life Insurance Co 69 Lydecker St Nyack NY 10960 845-358-2300 353-0273
TF: 800-926-7599 ■ *Web:* www.presidentiallife.com

Principal Life Insurance Co 711 High St Des Moines IA 50392 515-247-5111 247-5930
TF: 800-986-3343

Pro Assurance Corp 1115 30th St NW Washington DC 20007 202-969-1866 969-1881
TF: 800-613-3615 ■ *Web:* www.proassurance.com

Property-Owners Insurance Co PO Box 30660 Lansing MI 48909 517-323-1200 323-8796
TF: 800-288-8740

Protective Life & Annuity Insurance Co 2801 Hwy 280 S Birmingham AL 35223 205-879-9230 268-3196
TF: 800-866-3555 ■ *Web:* www.protective.com

Protective Life Insurance Co 2801 Hwy 280 S Birmingham AL 35223 205-879-9230 268-3196
TF: 800-866-3555 ■ *Web:* www.protective.com

Provident American Insurance Co Inc
10501 N Central Expy Suite 200 Dallas TX 75231 214-696-9091 696-4756
TF: 800-933-9456 ■ *Web:* www.providentamerican.com

Prudential Financial Inc 751 Broad St Newark NJ 07102 973-802-6000 367-6476
NYSE: PRU ■ *TF:* 800-843-7625 ■ *Web:* www.prudential.com

Pyramid Life Insurance Co PO Box 12922 Pensacola FL 32591 800-777-1126 432-7733*
**Fax Area Code:* 850 ■ *Web:* www.pyramidlife.com

RBC Insurance 2300 Main St Suite 450 Kansas City MO 64108 816-218-6500 218-6611
TF: 800-262-5433

RBC Liberty Insurance PO Box 789 Greenville SC 29602 864-609-8111 609-3581
TF: 800-551-8354 ■ *Web:* www.rbcinsurance.com

Reassure America Life Insurance Co PO box 360 Hartford CT 06141 800-323-8764

Reliable Life Insurance Co 100 King St W 11th Fl Hamilton ON L8N3K9 905-523-5587 528-8338*
**Fax:* Claims ■ *Web:* www.reliablelifeinsurance.com

Reliance Standard Life Insurance
2001 Market St Suite 1500 Philadelphia PA 19103 267-256-3500 256-3531*
**Fax:* Sales ■ *TF:* 800-351-7500 ■ *Web:* www.rsli.com

Reserve National Insurance Co PO Box 18448 Oklahoma City OK 73154 405-848-7931 254-2111
TF: 800-654-9106 ■ *Web:* www.reservenational.com

Security Benefit Life Insurance Co 1 Security Benefit Pl Topeka KS 66636 785-438-3000 438-5177*
**Fax:* Cust Svc ■ *TF:* 800-888-2461 ■ *Web:* www.securitybenefit.com

Security Financial Life Insurance Co 4000 Pine Lake Rd Lincoln NE 68516 402-434-9500 434-9634
TF: 800-284-8575 ■ *Web:* www.securityfinanciallife.com

Security Life Insurance Co of America 10901 Red Circle Dr Minnetonka MN 55343 952-544-2121 945-3419
TF: 800-328-4667 ■ *Web:* www.securitylifeinsurance.com

Security Mutual Life Insurance Co of New York
PO Box 1625 Binghamton NY 13902 607-723-3551 722-0598*
**Fax:* Cust Svc ■ *TF:* 800-346-7171 ■ *Web:* www.smlny.com

Sentry Life Insurance Co 1800 N Point Dr Stevens Point WI 54481 715-346-6000 346-7283
TF Cust Svc: 800-533-7827 ■ *Web:* www.sentry.com

Settlers Life Insurance Co PO Box 8600 Bristol VA 24203 276-645-4300 645-4399
TF: 800-523-2650 ■ *Web:* www.settlerslife.com

Shelter Life Insurance Co 1817 W Broadway Columbia MO 65218 573-445-8441 445-3199
TF Claims: 800-743-5837 ■ *Web:* www.shelterinsurance.com

Shenandoah Life Insurance Co 2301 Brambleton Ave Roanoke VA 24015 540-985-4400 985-4444
TF: 800-848-5433 ■ *Web:* www.shenlife.com

Sierra Health & Life Insurance Co PO Box 15645 Las Vegas NV 89114 702-242-7000 240-4829*
**Fax:* Hum Res ■ *TF:* 800-888-2264 ■ *Web:* www.sierrahealth.com

Southern Farm Bureau Life Insurance Co PO Box 78 Jackson MS 39205 601-981-7422 366-5808*
**Fax:* Hum Res ■ *Web:* www.sfbli.com

Southern Security Life Insurance Co
755 Rinehart Rd Suite 200 Lake Mary FL 32746 407-321-7113 323-9701
TF: 800-336-9558 ■ *Web:* www.southernsecuritylife.com

Southwestern Life Insurance Co 8710 Freeport Pkwy Suite 150 Irving TX 75063 800-792-4368 333-7833*
**Fax Area Code:* 803

Standard Insurance Co 1100 SW 6th Ave Portland OR 97204 503-248-2700 321-7757*
**Fax:* Hum Res ■ *TF:* 888-937-4783 ■ *Web:* www.standard.com

Standard Life & Accident Insurance Co PO Box 1800 Galveston TX 77553 888-350-1488 621-3096*
**Fax Area Code:* 409 ■ **Fax:* Cust Svc ■ *Web:* www.slaico.com

Standard Life Insurance Co of Indiana
10689 N Pennsylvania St Indianapolis IN 46280 317-574-6200 574-6278*
**Fax:* Mktg ■ *TF Mktg:* 800-767-7749 ■ *Web:* www.standard-usa.com

Standard Security Life Insurance Co of New York
485 Madison Ave 14th Fl New York NY 10022 212-355-4141 644-5786
Web: www.sslicny.com

State Farm Life & Accident Assurance Co
1 State Farm Plaza Bloomington IL 61710 309-766-2311 763-8777*
**Fax:* Mktg ■ *Web:* www.statefarm.com

State Farm Life Insurance Co 1 State Farm Plaza Bloomington IL 61710 309-766-2311 766-2621*
**Fax:* Hum Res ■ *Web:* www.statefarm.com/insuranc/life/life.htm

State Life Insurance Co 1 American Sq PO Box 368 Indianapolis IN 46206 317-285-2300 285-2380
TF: 800-428-9198 ■ *Web:* www.statelife.com

Stonebridge Life Insurance Co 2700 W Plano Pkwy Plano TX 75075 972-881-6000 881-6782
TF: 800-527-9027 ■ *Web:* www.stonebridge-jcp.com

Sun Life Assurance Co of Canada
1 Sun Life Executive Pk PO Box 9133 Wellesley Hills MA 02481 781-237-6030 431-4959*
**Fax:* Hum Res ■ *Web:* www.sunlife-usa.com

Sun Life Insurance & Annuity Co of New York
PO Box 9133 Wellesley Hills MA 02481 800-447-7569 304-5383*
**Fax Area Code:* 781

SunAmerica Life Insurance Co 1 SunAmerica Ctr Los Angeles CA 90067 310-772-6000 772-6361
TF: 800-445-7862 ■ *Web:* www.sunamerica.com

Sunset Life Insurance Co of America PO Box 219139 Kansas City MO 64121 800-678-6898 753-4902*
**Fax Area Code:* 816 ■ *Web:* www.sunsetlife.com

Texas Life Insurance Co PO Box 830 Waco TX 76703 254-752-6521 754-7629
TF: 800-283-9233 ■ *Web:* www.texaslife.com

Thrivent Financial for Lutherans 4321 N Ballard Rd Appleton WI 54919 920-734-5721 628-4757
TF: 800-847-4836 ■ *Web:* www.thrivent.com

TIAA-CREF 730 3rd Ave New York NY 10017 212-490-9000 914-8922*
**Fax Area Code:* 800 ■ *TF:* 800-842-2776 ■ *Web:* www.tiaa-cref.org

Transamerica Financial Life Insurance Co
4 Manhattanville Rd Purchase NY 10577 914-697-8000 697-8323*
**Fax:* Mktg ■ *TF:* 800-755-5801 ■ *Web:* www.tafinlife.com

Transamerica Life Insurance & Annuity Co
1150 S Olive St Los Angeles CA 90015 213-742-3111 741-7939*
**Fax:* Mail Rm ■ *TF:* 800-852-4678

Transamerica Occidental Life Insurance Co
1150 S Olive St Los Angeles CA 90015 213-742-2111 741-7939*
**Fax:* Mail Rm ■ *TF Cust Svc:* 800-852-4678

Travelers Indemnity Co 1 Tower Sq Hartford CT 06183 860-277-0111 277-1970*
**Fax:* Hum Res ■ *Web:* www.travelers.com

Travelers Life & Annuity Co 1 Cityplace Hartford CT 06103 860-308-1000
TF: 800-334-4298 ■ *Web:* www.travelerslife.com

Trustmark Insurance Co 400 Field Dr Lake Forest IL 60045 847-615-1500 615-3816
TF: 800-877-9077 ■ *Web:* www.trustmarkinsurance.com

Union Central Life Insurance Co 1876 Waycross Rd Cincinnati OH 45240 513-595-2200 595-2888
TF: 800-825-1551 ■ *Web:* www.unioncentral.com

Union Fidelity Life Insurance Co 500 Virginia Dr Fort Washington PA 19034 800-523-5758 468-4010*
**Fax Area Code:* 267

Union Labor Life Insurance Co 8403 Colesville Rd Silver Spring MD 20910 202-682-0900 682-4911
TF: 800-431-5425 ■ *Web:* www.ullico.com

United American Insurance Co Inc PO Box 8080 McKinney TX 75070 972-529-5085 569-3709
TF: 800-331-2512 ■ *Web:* www.unitedamerican.com

United Heritage Life Insurance Co PO Box 7777 Meridian ID 83680 208-466-7856 466-0825
TF: 800-657-6351 ■ *Web:* www.unitedheritage.com

United Insurance Co of America 1 E Wacker Dr Chicago IL 60601 312-661-4600 661-4731*
**Fax:* Hum Res

United Investors Life Insurance Co 2001 3rd Ave S Birmingham AL 35233 205-325-4300 325-2092*
**Fax:* Cust Svc ■ *TF:* 800-318-4542 ■ *Web:* www.uilic.com

United Life Insurance Co PO Box 73909 Cedar Rapids IA 52407 319-399-5700 399-5499
TF: 800-332-7977 ■ *Web:* www.unitedfiregroup.com

United of Omaha Life Insurance Co Mutual of Omaha Plaza Omaha NE 68175 402-342-7600 351-2775
TF: 800-775-6000 ■ *Web:* www.mutualofomaha.com

United World Life Insurance Co Mutual of Omaha Plaza Omaha NE 68175 402-342-7600 351-2775
TF: 800-775-6000 ■ *Web:* www.mutualofomaha.com

UnitedHealthcare Services Inc 9900 Bren Rd E Minnetonka MN 55343 952-936-1300 992-4182*
**Fax:* Sales ■ *TF:* 800-328-5979 ■ *Web:* www.unitedhealthcare.com

Unity Mutual Life Insurance Co PO Box 5000 Syracuse NY 13250 315-448-7000 448-7100
TF: 800-836-7100 ■ *Web:* www.unity-life.com

USAA Life Insurance Co 9800 Fredericksburg Rd San Antonio TX 78288 210-498-8000 531-8877*
**Fax Area Code:* 800 ■ **Fax:* Sales ■ *TF:* 800-531-8000 ■ *Web:* www.usaa.com

USG Annuity & Life Co 909 Locust St Des Moines IA 50309 515-698-7100 698-2001
TF: 800-369-3690

Utica National Insurance Group 180 Genesee St New Hartford NY 13413 315-734-2000 734-2680
TF: 800-274-1914 ■ *Web:* www.uticanational.com

Utica National Life Insurance Co 180 Genesee St New Hartford NY 13413 315-734-2000 734-2680
TF: 800-274-1914 ■ *Web:* www.uticalife.com

VALIC (Variable Annuity Life Insurance Co) 2929 Allen Pkwy Houston TX 77019 713-522-1111 831-4317*
**Fax:* Cust Svc ■ *TF:* 800-633-8960 ■ *Web:* www.aigvalic.com

Variable Annuity Life Insurance Co (VALIC) 2929 Allen Pkwy Houston TX 77019 713-522-1111 831-4317*
**Fax:* Cust Svc ■ *TF:* 800-633-8960 ■ *Web:* www.aigvalic.com

Wabash Life Insurance Co PO Box 1917 Carmel IN 46032 317-817-6100 817-6327
TF: 800-525-7662

Washington Booker T Insurance Co PO Box 697 Birmingham AL 35201 205-328-5454 251-6873
TF: 800-228-4180

Washington National Insurance Co 11815 N Pennsylvania St Carmel IN 46032 800-933-9301 817-4431*
**Fax Area Code:* 317 ■ **Fax:* Claims

Watt Harvey & Co Atlanta Airport PO Box 20787 Atlanta GA 30320 404-767-7501 761-8326
TF: 800-241-6103 ■ *Web:* www.harveywatt.com

Wawanesa Life Insurance Co 191 Broadway 2nd Fl Winnipeg MB R3C3P1 204-985-3811 985-3872
Web: www.wawanesalife.com

West Coast Life Insurance Co 343 Sansome St San Francisco CA 94104 415-591-8200 433-9477
TF: 800-366-9378 ■ *Web:* www.westcoastlife.com

Western American Life PO Box 833879 Richardson TX 75083 972-699-2770 699-2788
TF: 866-629-2677 ■ *Web:* www.cslic.com

Western Fraternal Life Assn 1900 1st Ave NE Cedar Rapids IA 52402 319-363-2653 363-8806
TF: 877-935-2467 ■ *Web:* www.wflains.com

Western Reserve Life Assurance Co of Ohio
570 Carillon Pkwy Saint Petersburg FL 33716 727-299-1800 299-1872*
**Fax:* Hum Res ■ *TF:* 800-851-9777 ■ *Web:* www.westernreserve.com

Western-Southern Life Assurance Co 400 Broadway Cincinnati OH 45202 513-629-1800 629-1212
TF: 800-333-5222 ■ *Web:* www.westernsouthernlife.com

Western & Southern Life Insurance Co 400 Broadway Cincinnati OH 45202 513-629-1800 629-1212*
**Fax:* Hum Res ■ *TF:* 800-333-5222 ■ *Web:* www.westernsouthernlife.com

Western United Life Assurance Co
929 W Sprague Ave PO Box 2290 Spokane WA 99210 509-835-2500 835-2468
TF: 800-247-2045 ■ *Web:* www.wula.com

William Penn Life Insurance Co of New York
100 Quentin Roosevelt Blvd Garden City NY 11530 516-794-3700 229-3004*
**Fax:* Hum Res ■ *TF:* 800-346-4773 ■ *Web:* www.lgamerica.com

Wisconsin National Life Insurance Co 2801 Hwy 280 S Birmingham AL 35223 205-879-9230 268-3684
TF: 800-955-4304

Woman's Life Insurance Society
1338 Military St PO Box 5020 Port Huron MI 48061 810-985-5191 985-6970
TF: 800-521-9292 ■ *Web:* www.womanslifeins.com

Woodmen Accident & Life Co 1526 K St Lincoln NE 68508 402-476-6500 437-4591
TF: 800-747-7191 ■ *Web:* www.walco.com

Woodmen of the World/Omaha Woodmen Life Insurance Society
1700 Farnam St Omaha NE 68102 402-342-1890 271-7269
TF: 800-225-3108 ■ *Web:* www.woodmen.com

394-3 Medical & Hospitalization Insurance

Companies listed here provide managed care and/or traditional hospital and medical service plans to individuals and/or groups. Managed care companies typically offer plans as Health Maintenance Organizations (HMOs), Preferred Provider Organizations (PPOs), Exclusive Provider Organizations (EPOs), and/or Point of Service (POS) plans. Other types of hospital and medical service plans offered by companies listed here include indemnity plans and medical savings accounts.

Phone *Fax*

AARP Health Care Options PO Box 1017 .... Montgomeryville PA 18936 800-523-5800 391-6259*
**Fax Area Code:* 610 ■ *Web:* www.aarphealthcare.com

Aetna Inc 151 Farmington Ave .... Hartford CT 06156 860-273-0123 273-8909
NYSE: AET ■ *TF:* 800-872-3862 ■ *Web:* www.aetna.com

Aetna US Healthcare Inc 980 Jolly Rd .... Blue Bell PA 19422 800-962-6842 775-6775*
**Fax Area Code:* 215 ■ **Fax:* Hum Res ■ *Web:* www.aetna.com

Alberta Blue Cross 10009 108th St NW .... Edmonton AB T5J3C5 780-498-8100 425-4627
TF: 800-661-6995 ■ *Web:* www.ab.bluecross.ca

Alliance PPO LLC 4 Taft Ct .... Rockville MD 20850 301-762-8205 545-5389*
**Fax:* Hum Res ■ *TF:* 800-544-2853 ■ *Web:* www.mamsi.com

Altius Health Plans 10421 S Jordan Gateway Suite 400 .... South Jordan UT 84095 801-355-1234 323-6400
TF: 800-365-1334 ■ *Web:* www.altiushealthplans.com

America Service Group Inc 105 Westpark Dr Suite 200 .... Brentwood TN 37027 615-373-3100 376-9862
NASDAQ: ASGRE ■ *TF:* 800-729-0069 ■ *Web:* www.asgr.com

American Community Mutual Insurance Co
39201 Seven-Mile Rd .... Livonia MI 48152 734-591-9000 591-4628
TF: 800-991-2642 ■ *Web:* www.american-community.com

American National Insurance Co 1 Moody Plaza .... Galveston TX 77550 409-763-4661 766-6663
NASDAQ: ANAT ■ *Web:* www.anico.com

American Specialty Health Plans 777 Front St .... San Diego CA 92101 619-297-8100 209-6233
TF: 800-848-3555 ■ *Web:* www.ashcompanies.com

American WholeHealth Networks Inc
46040 Center Oak Plaza Suite 130 .... Sterling VA 20166 703-547-5100 430-9638
TF: 800-274-7526 ■ *Web:* www.americanwholehealth.com

AMERIGROUP Corp 4425 Corporation Ln .... Virginia Beach VA 23462 757-490-6900 518-3600
NYSE: AGP ■ *TF:* 800-600-4441 ■ *Web:* www.amerigroupcorp.com

Ameritas Managed Dental Plan Inc 5900 'O' St .... Lincoln NE 68510 402-467-1122 467-7338
TF: 800-404-8019 ■ *Web:* group.ameritas.com

Anthem Blue Cross & Blue Shield 2015 Staples Mill Rd .... Richmond VA 23230 804-354-7000 354-3897
TF: 800-451-1527 ■ *Web:* www.anthem.com

Anthem Blue Cross Blue Shield Colorado 700 Broadway .... Denver CO 80273 303-831-2131 830-0887
TF: 800-654-9338 ■ *Web:* www.anthem.com

Anthem Blue Cross & Blue Shield of Connecticut
370 Bassett Rd .... North Haven CT 06473 203-239-4911 239-8495
TF: 800-922-1742 ■ *Web:* www.anthem.com

Anthem Blue Cross & Blue Shield of Maine
2 Gannett Dr .... South Portland ME 04106 207-822-7272 822-7375
TF Cust Svc: 800-482-0966 ■ *Web:* www.anthem.com

Anthem Blue Cross & Blue Shield of the Midwest
1351 William Howard Taft Rd .... Cincinnati OH 45204 513-872-8100 872-8174
TF: 888-426-8436

Anthem Blue Cross & Blue Shield of Nevada
6900 Westcliffe Dr Suite 600 .... Las Vegas NV 89145 702-228-2583 228-1259
TF Cust Svc: 800-992-6907

Anthem Blue Cross & Blue Shield of New Hampshire
3000 Goffs Falls Rd .... Manchester NH 03111 603-695-7000 695-7002*
**Fax:* Hum Res ■ *TF:* 800-225-2666

Anthem Blue Cross & Blue Shield of Virginia
277 Bendix Rd Suite 100 .... Virginia Beach VA 23452 757-326-5130 326-5186
TF: 800-640-0007 ■ *Web:* www.anthem.com

Arkansas Blue Cross Blue Shield PO Box 2181 .... Little Rock AR 72203 501-378-2000 378-2969
TF: 800-238-8379 ■ *Web:* www.arkbluecross.com

AvMed 4300 NW 89th Blvd .... Gainesville FL 32606 352-372-8400 337-8575*
**Fax:* Hum Res ■ *TF:* 800-346-0231 ■ *Web:* www.avmed.com

Blue Care Network of Michigan 20500 Civic Center Dr .... Southfield MI 48076 248-799-6400 799-6969*
**Fax:* Cust Svc ■ *TF:* 800-662-6667 ■ *Web:* www.mibcn.com

Blue Cross & Blue Shield of Alabama
450 Riverchase Pkwy E .... Birmingham AL 35244 205-988-2200 220-2902*
**Fax:* Hum Res ■ *TF:* 800-292-8868 ■ *Web:* www.bcbsal.org

Blue Cross Blue Shield of Arizona 2444 W Las Palmaritas Dr .... Phoenix AZ 85021 602-864-4400 864-4041*
**Fax:* Cust Svc ■ *TF:* 800-232-2345 ■ *Web:* www.bcbsaz.com

Blue Cross Blue Shield of Delaware PO Box 1991 .... Wilmington DE 19899 302-421-3000 421-3110*
**Fax:* Mktg ■ *TF:* 800-633-2563 ■ *Web:* www.bcbsde.com

Blue Cross & Blue Shield of Florida
4800 Deerwood Campus Pkwy PO Box 1798 .... Jacksonville FL 32231 904-791-6111 905-8126*
**Fax:* Hum Res ■ *TF:* 800-477-3736 ■ *Web:* www.bcbsfl.com

Blue Cross & Blue Shield of Florida Health Options Div
PO Box 1798 .... Jacksonville FL 32231 800-734-6656 363-4365*
**Fax Area Code:* 904

Blue Cross Blue Shield of Georgia 3350 Peachtree Rd NE .... Atlanta GA 30326 404-842-8000 842-8010
TF Cust Svc: 800-441-2273 ■ *Web:* www.bcbsga.com

Blue Cross Blue Shield of Illinois 300 E Randolph St .... Chicago IL 60601 312-653-6000 938-8847*
**Fax:* Hum Res ■ *Web:* www.bcbsil.com

Blue Cross Blue Shield of Kansas 1133 SW Topeka Blvd .... Topeka KS 66629 785-291-7000 291-6544
TF: 800-432-0216 ■ *Web:* www.bcbsks.com

Blue Cross & Blue Shield of Kansas City 2301 Main St .... Kansas City MO 64108 816-395-2222 395-2726*
**Fax:* Hum Res ■ *TF:* 800-892-6048 ■ *Web:* www.bcbskc.com

Blue Cross Blue Shield of Louisiana 5525 Reitz Ave .... Baton Rouge LA 70898 225-295-3307 295-2054
TF: 800-599-2583 ■ *Web:* www.bcbsla.com

Blue Cross Blue Shield of Massachusetts 401 Park Dr .... Boston MA 02215 800-262-2583 246-4832*
**Fax Area Code:* 617 ■ **Fax:* PR ■ *Web:* www.bcbsma.com

Blue Cross & Blue Shield of Michigan 600 Lafayette Blvd E .... Detroit MI 48226 313-225-9000 225-5629*
**Fax:* Hum Res ■ *Web:* www.bcbsm.com

Blue Cross Blue Shield of Minnesota PO Box 64560 .... Saint Paul MN 55164 651-662-8000 662-2727
TF: 800-382-2000 ■ *Web:* www.bluecrossmn.com

Blue Cross & Blue Shield of Mississippi PO Box 1043 .... Jackson MS 39215 601-932-3704 939-7035
TF: 800-222-8046 ■ *Web:* www.bcbsms.com

Blue Cross Blue Shield of Missouri 1831 Chestnut St .... Saint Louis MO 63103 314-923-4444 923-5002*
**Fax:* Sales ■ *TF:* 800-392-8740 ■ *Web:* www.bcbsmo.com

Blue Cross & Blue Shield of Montana 404 Fuller Ave .... Helena MT 59601 406-444-8200 442-6946*
**Fax:* Hum Res ■ *TF:* 800-447-7828 ■ *Web:* www.bcbsmt.com

Blue Cross Blue Shield of Nebraska 7261 Mercy Rd .... Omaha NE 68180 402-390-1820
TF: 800-642-8980 ■ *Web:* www.bcbsne.com

Blue Cross & Blue Shield of New Mexico PO Box 27630 .... Albuquerque NM 87125 505-291-3500 816-5011
TF: 800-835-8699 ■ *Web:* www.bcbsnm.com

Blue Cross & Blue Shield of North Carolina
1965 Ivory Creek Blvd .... Durham NC 27702 919-489-7431 765-3521*
**Fax:* Hum Res ■ *TF Cust Svc:* 800-446-8053 ■ *Web:* www.bcbsnc.com

Blue Cross Blue Shield of North Dakota 4510 13th Ave S .... Fargo ND 58121 701-282-1100 277-2216*
**Fax:* Hum Res ■ *TF:* 800-342-4718 ■ *Web:* www.bcbsnd.com

Blue Cross & Blue Shield of Oklahoma 1215 S Boulder Ave .... Tulsa OK 74119 918-560-3500 560-3060
TF Cust Svc: 800-942-5837 ■ *Web:* www.bcbsok.com

Blue Cross & Blue Shield of Rhode Island
444 Westminster St .... Providence RI 02903 401-459-1000 459-1996
TF: 800-637-3718 ■ *Web:* www.bcbsri.com

Phone *Fax*

Blue Cross & Blue Shield of South Carolina 4100 Percival Rd .... Columbia SC 29229 803-788-0222
TF: 800-288-2227 ■ *Web:* www.southcarolinablues.com

Blue Cross Blue Shield of Tennessee 801 Pine St .... Chattanooga TN 37402 423-755-5600
TF: 800-565-9140 ■ *Web:* www.bcbst.com

Blue Cross & Blue Shield of Texas Inc 901 S Central Expy .... Richardson TX 75080 972-766-6900 766-6060
TF Cust Svc: 800-521-2227 ■ *Web:* www.bcbstx.com

Blue Cross & Blue Shield of Vermont 445 Industrial Ln .... Montpelier VT 05602 802-223-6131 223-4229*
**Fax:* Hum Res ■ *TF:* 800-457-6648 ■ *Web:* www.bcbsvt.com

Blue Cross & Blue Shield of Western New York PO Box 80 .... Buffalo NY 14240 716-887-6900 887-7912
TF: 800-888-0757 ■ *Web:* www.healthnowny.com

Blue Cross Blue Shield of Wisconsin 401 W Michigan St .... Milwaukee WI 53203 414-226-5000 226-5059
TF: 800-558-1584 ■ *Web:* www.bcbswi.com

Blue Cross Blue Shield of Wyoming PO Box 2266 .... Cheyenne WY 82003 307-634-1393 778-8582
TF Cust Svc: 800-851-9145 ■ *Web:* www.bcbswy.com

Blue Cross of California 21555 Oxnard St .... Woodland Hills CA 91365 818-703-2345 703-2848
TF: 800-999-3643 ■ *Web:* www.bluecrossca.com

Blue Cross of Idaho 3000 E Pine Ave .... Meridian ID 83642 208-345-4550 331-7311
TF Cust Svc: 800-365-2345 ■ *Web:* www.bcidaho.com

Blue Cross of Northeastern Pennsylvania 19 N Main St .... Wilkes-Barre PA 18711 570-200-4300 200-6710
TF Cust Svc: 800-829-8599 ■ *Web:* www.bcnepa.com

Blue Shield of California 50 Beale St .... San Francisco CA 94105 415-229-5000 229-6222*
**Fax:* Hum Res ■ *Web:* www.mylifepath.com

BlueCross BlueShield of the Rochester Area 165 Court St .... Rochester NY 14647 585-454-1700 238-4400
TF: 800-847-1200 ■ *Web:* www.bcbsra.com

Capital Blue Cross 2500 Elmerton Ave .... Harrisburg PA 17110 610-820-2700
TF Cust Svc: 800-958-5558 ■ *Web:* www.capbluecross.com

Capital BlueCross 3815 Tecport Dr .... Harrisburg PA 17111 800-622-2843 703-8494*
**Fax Area Code:* 717 ■ *TF:* 800-622-2843 ■ *Web:* www.capbluecross.com

Capital District Physicians' Health Plan 1223 Washington Ave .... Albany NY 12206 518-641-3000 641-3507
TF: 800-777-2273 ■ *Web:* www.cdphp.com

Capital Health Plan 2140 Centerville Pl .... Tallahassee FL 32308 850-383-3333 383-3339
TF: 800-390-1434 ■ *Web:* www.capitalhealth.com

CareFirst BlueCross BlueShield 10455 Mill Run Cir .... Owings Mills MD 21117 410-581-3000 998-5576
Web: www.carefirst.com

Carelink Health Plans 500 Virginia St E Suite 400 .... Charleston WV 25301 304-348-2900 348-2064
TF: 800-348-2922 ■ *Web:* www.chccarelink.com

CarePlus Health Plans Inc 55 Alhambra Plaza 7th Fl .... Coral Gables FL 33134 305-441-9400 441-2294
TF: 800-577-1072 ■ *Web:* www.careplus-hp.com

Centene Corp 7711 Carondelet Ave Suite 800 .... Saint Louis MO 63105 314-725-4477 725-2065
NYSE: CNC ■ *TF:* 800-225-2573 ■ *Web:* www.centene.com

Central Reserve Life 17800 Royalton Rd .... Strongsville OH 44136 440-572-2400 572-8380
TF: 800-321-3997 ■ *Web:* www.centralreserve.com

Chiropractic Health Plan of California PO Box 190 .... Clayton CA 94517 925-672-0106 672-6657
TF: 800-995-2442 ■ *Web:* www.chpc.com

ChiroSource Inc 5356 Clayton Rd Suite 201 .... Concord CA 94521 925-844-3100 672-6657
TF: 800-680-9997 ■ *Web:* chpc.com

CIGNA Healthcare 900 Cottage Grove Rd .... Hartford CT 06152 860-226-6000
TF: 800-832-3211 ■ *Web:* www.cigna.com/health

CIGNA Healthcare of Arizona 11001 N Black Canyon Hwy .... Phoenix AZ 85029 602-942-4462 371-2526*
**Fax:* Hum Res ■ *TF:* 800-572-9990

CIGNA Healthcare of California 400 N Brand Blvd Suite 400 .... Glendale CA 91203 818-500-6262 500-6226*
**Fax:* Hum Res ■ *TF:* 800-344-7421

CIGNA Healthcare of Florida Inc Tampa
3101 W ML King Blvd Suite 200 .... Tampa FL 33607 813-353-4400 353-4411
TF: 800-832-3211

CIGNA Healthcare of New Hampshire 2 College Pk Dr .... Hooksett NH 03106 800-531-3121 268-7051*
**Fax Area Code:* 603

CIGNA Healthcare of North Carolina Inc
701 Corporate Center Dr .... Raleigh NC 27607 919-854-7000 854-7101*
**Fax:* Hum Res ■ *TF:* 800-849-9300 ■ *Web:* www.cigna.com

CIGNA Healthcare of San Diego 3636 Noble Dr Suite 150 .... San Diego CA 92122 858-625-5600 558-3710*
**Fax Area Code:* 800 ■ *TF:* 800-368-2471

Community Blue HMO of Blue Cross & Blue Shield of Western New York Inc PO Box 159 .... Buffalo NY 14240 716-884-2800 887-7912*
**Fax:* Cust Svc ■ *TF:* 800-544-2583 ■ *Web:* www.healthnowny.com

Community Care 218 W 6th St .... Tulsa OK 74119 918-594-5200 594-5209
TF: 800-278-7563 ■ *Web:* www.ccmhp.com

CompBenefits Corp 100 Mansell Ct E Suite 400 .... Roswell GA 30076 770-552-7101 998-6871*
**Fax:* Cust Svc ■ *TF:* 800-633-1262 ■ *Web:* www.compbenefits.com

Compcare Health Services Insurance Corp
20855 Watertown Rd Suite 140 .... Waukesha WI 53186 262-787-3402 787-3301
Web: www.bcbswi.com

CompcareBlue 20855 Watertown Rd Suite 140 .... Waukesha WI 53186 262-787-3402 787-3301
Web: www.bcbswi.com

Comprehensive Health Services Inc 8229 Boone Blvd Suite 700 .... Vienna VA 22182 703-760-0700 760-0894
TF: 800-638-8083 ■ *Web:* www.chsmedical.com/

ConnectiCare Inc 175 Scott Swamp Rd .... Farmington CT 06032 860-674-5700 674-5728
TF: 800-251-7722 ■ *Web:* www.connecticare.com

Consumer Health Network 3525 Quakerbridge Rd .... Hamilton NJ 08619 800-225-4246 631-0476*
**Fax Area Code:* 609 ■ *Web:* www.chnnetwork.com

Continental General Insurance Co PO Box 247007 .... Omaha NE 68124 402-397-3200 952-4325
TF: 800-545-8905 ■ *Web:* www.continentalgeneral.com

Coventry Health Care of Delaware Inc
2751 Centerville Rd Suite 400 .... Wilmington DE 19808 302-995-6100 633-4044
TF: 800-727-9951 ■ *Web:* www.chcde.com

Coventry Health Care of Georgia Inc
1100 Circle 75 Pkwy Suite 1400 .... Atlanta GA 30339 678-202-2100 202-2195
TF: 800-470-2004 ■ *Web:* www.chcga.com

Coventry Health Care Inc 6705 Rockledge Dr Suite 900 .... Bethesda MD 20817 301-581-0600 493-0705*
NYSE: CVH ■ **Fax:* Hum Res ■ *TF:* 800-843-7421 ■ *Web:* www.cvty.com

Coventry Health Care of Iowa Inc
4600 Westown Pkwy Regency 6 Suite 200 .... West Des Moines IA 50266 515-225-1234 223-0097
TF: 800-470-6352 ■ *Web:* www.chciowa.com

Coventry Health Care of Kansas Inc
8320 Ward Pkwy Suite 700 .... Kansas City MO 64114 816-221-8400 221-7709
TF: 800-468-1442 ■ *Web:* www.chckansas.com

Coventry Health Care of Louisiana Inc
3838 N Causeway Blvd Suite 3350 .... Metairie LA 70002 504-834-0840 834-2694
TF: 800-245-8327 ■ *Web:* www.chclouisiana.com

Coventry Health Care of Nebraska Inc
13305 Birch Dr Suite 100 .... Omaha NE 68164 402-498-9030 498-9706
TF: 800-471-0420 ■ *Web:* www.chcnebraska.com

Coventry HealthCare Management Corp 9881 Mayland Dr .... Richmond VA 23233 804-747-3700 747-8723
TF: 800-424-0077 ■ *Web:* www.cvty.com

DAKOTACARE 1323 S Minnesota Ave .... Sioux Falls SD 57105 605-334-4000 336-0270
TF: 800-325-5598 ■ *Web:* www.dakotacare.com

Davis Vision Inc 159 Express St .... Plainview NY 11803 516-932-9500 328-4761*
**Fax Area Code:* 888 ■ **Fax:* Claims ■ *TF:* 800-328-4728 ■ *Web:* idoc.davisvision.com

Dean Health Insurance Inc 1277 Deming Way .... Madison WI 53717 608-836-1400 827-4212
TF: 800-279-1301 ■ *Web:* www.deancare.com

Delta Dental of Alabama
1000 Mansell Exchange W Bldg 100 Suite 100 .... Alpharetta GA 30022 770-645-8700 518-4757
TF: 800-521-2651 ■ *Web:* www.deltadental.com

Delta Dental of Arizona PO Box 43026 .... Phoenix AZ 85080 800-352-6132 588-3636*
**Fax Area Code:* 602 ■ *Web:* www.deltadentalaz.com

Delta Dental of Arkansas 1513 Country Club Rd .... Sherwood AR 72120 501-835-3400 835-2733
TF: 800-462-5410 ■ *Web:* www.deltadentalar.com

Phone Fax

Delta Dental of California PO Box 7736 .... San Francisco CA 94120 415-972-8300 972-8424*
*Fax: Hum Res ■ TF: 888-335-8227 ■ Web: www.deltadentalca.org

Delta Dental of Colorado 4582 S Ulster St Suite 800 .... Denver CO 80237 303-741-9300 741-9338
TF: 800-233-0860 ■ Web: www.deltadentalco.com

Delta Dental of Connecticut PO Box 222 .... Parsippany NJ 07054 973-285-4000 285-4141
TF: 800-346-5377

Delta Dental of Delaware 1 Delta Dr .... Mechanicsburg PA 17055 717-766-8500 691-6653
TF: 800-932-0783 ■ Web: www2.midatlanticdeltadental.com

Delta Dental of Florida
1000 Mansell Exchange W Bldg 100 Suite 100................ Alpharetta GA 30022 770-645-8700 518-4757
TF: 800-521-2651

Delta Dental of Georgia
1000 Mansell Exchange W Bldg 100 Suite 100................ Alpharetta GA 30022 770-645-8700 518-4757
TF: 800-521-2651

Delta Dental of Idaho PO Box 2870.................................. Boise ID 83701 208-344-4546 344-4649
TF: 800-388-3490 ■ Web: www.deltadentalid.com

Delta Dental of Illinois PO Box 5402.................................. Lisle IL 60532 630-964-2400 964-2494
TF: 800-323-1743 ■ Web: www.deltadentalil.com

Delta Dental of Indiana PO Box 30416 .... Lansing MI 48909 800-524-0149
Web: www.deltadentalin.com

Delta Dental Insurance Co
1000 Mansell Exchange W Bldg 100 Suite 100................ Alpharetta GA 30022 770-645-8700 518-4757
TF: 800-521-2651 ■ Web: www.deltadental.com

Delta Dental Insurance Co of Alaska
257 E 200 South Suite 375............................ Salt Lake City UT 84111 801-575-5168 575-5171
TF: 800-521-2651 ■ Web: www.deltadentalins.com

Delta Dental of Iowa 2401 SE Tones Dr Suite 13 .... Ankeny IA 50021 515-261-5500 261-5577
TF: 800-532-1514 ■ Web: www.deltadentalia.com

Delta Dental of Kansas PO Box 49198......................... Wichita KS 67201 316-264-4511 462-3392
TF: 800-234-3375 ■ Web: www.deltadentalks.com

Delta Dental of Kentucky PO Box 242810.................. Louisville KY 40224 502-736-5000 736-4839
TF: 800-955-2030 ■ Web: www.ddpky.com

Delta Dental of Louisiana
1000 Mansell Exchange W Bldg 100 Suite 100................ Alpharetta GA 30023 770-645-8700 518-4757
TF: 800-521-2651

Delta Dental of Maine PO Box 2002 .... Concord NH 03302 603-223-1000 223-1199
TF: 800-537-1715 ■ Web: www.eligibility.nedelta.com

Delta Dental of Maryland 1 Delta Dr .... Mechanicsburg PA 17055 717-766-8500 691-6653
TF: 800-932-0783 ■ Web: www2.midatlanticdeltadental.com

Delta Dental of Massachusetts 465 Medford St.................. Boston MA 02129 617-886-1000 886-1199
TF Cust Svc: 800-872-0500 ■ Web: www.deltamass.com

Delta Dental of Michigan PO Box 30416..................... Lansing MI 48909 800-524-0149
Web: www.deltadentalmi.com

Delta Dental of Minnesota PO Box 330.................. Minneapolis MN 55440 651-406-5900
TF: 800-553-9536 ■ Web: www.deltadentalmn.org

Delta Dental of Mississippi
1000 Mansell Exchange W Bldg 100 Suite 100................ Alpharetta GA 30023 770-645-8700 518-4757
TF: 800-521-2651

Delta Dental of Missouri PO Box 8690 .... Saint Louis MO 63126 314-656-3000 656-2900
TF: 800-392-1167 ■ Web: www.deltadentalmo.com

Delta Dental of Montana
1000 Mansell Exchange W Bldg 100 Suite 100................ Alpharetta GA 30023 770-645-8700 518-4757
TF: 800-521-2651

Delta Dental of Nevada
1000 Mansell Exchange W Bldg 100 Suite 100................ Alpharetta GA 30023 770-645-8700 518-4757
TF: 800-521-2651

Delta Dental of New Hampshire 1 Delta Dr PO Box 2002........... Concord NH 03302 603-223-1000 223-1129*
*Fax: Cust Svc ■ TF: 800-537-1715

Delta Dental of New Jersey 1639 Rt 10 E.................... Parsippany NJ 07054 973-285-4000 285-4170*
*Fax: Hum Res ■ TF: 800-346-5377 ■ Web: www.deltadentalnj.org

Delta Dental of New Mexico
2500 Louisiana Blvd NE Suite 600 .... Albuquerque NM 87110 505-883-4777 883-7444
TF: 800-999-0963 ■ Web: www.deltadentalnm.com

Delta Dental of New York 1 Delta Dr.................... Mechanicsburg PA 17055 717-766-8500 691-6653
TF: 800-932-0783 ■ Web: www2.midatlanticdeltadental.com

Delta Dental of North Carolina 343 Six Forks Rd Suite 180......... Raleigh NC 27609 919-832-6015 832-6061*
*Fax: Cust Svc ■ TF: 800-662-8856

Delta Dental of Ohio PO Box 30416.............................. Lansing MI 48909 800-524-0149
Web: www.deltadentaloh.com

Delta Dental of Oklahoma 16 NW 63rd St Suite 301 .... Oklahoma City OK 73116 405-607-2100 607-2190
TF: 800-522-0188 ■ Web: www.deltadentalok.org

Delta Dental of Pennsylvania 1 Delta Dr................ Mechanicsburg PA 17055 717-766-8500 691-6653*
*Fax: Cust Svc ■ TF: 800-932-0783 ■ Web: www2.midatlanticdeltadental.com

Delta Dental Plan of Minnesota PO Box 330 .... Minneapolis MN 55440 651-406-5903
TF: 800-448-3815 ■ Web: www.deltadentalmn.org

Delta Dental of Rhode Island 10 Charles St .... Providence RI 02904 401-752-6100 752-6060*
*Fax: Cust Svc ■ TF: 800-843-3582 ■ Web: www.deltadentalri.com

Delta Dental of South Carolina PO Box 8690 .... Saint Louis MO 63126 314-656-3000 656-2900
TF: 800-392-1167

Delta Dental of South Dakota 720 N Euclid Ave PO Box 1157........ Pierre SD 57501 605-224-7345 224-0909
TF: 800-627-3961

Delta Dental of Tennessee 240 Venture Cir.................... Nashville TN 37228 615-255-3175 244-8108
TF: 800-223-3104 ■ Web: www.deltadentaltn.com

Delta Dental of Texas
1000 Mansell Exchange W Bldg 100 Suite 100................ Alpharetta GA 30022 770-645-8700 518-4757
TF: 800-521-2651

Delta Dental of Utah
1000 Mansell Exchange W Bldg 100 Suite 100................ Alpharetta GA 30022 770-645-8700 518-4757
TF: 800-521-2651

Delta Dental of Virginia 4818 Starkey Rd .... Roanoke VA 24014 540-989-8000 725-3890
TF: 800-367-3531 ■ Web: www.deltadentalva.com

Delta Dental of West Virginia 1 Delta Dr................ Mechanicsburg PA 17055 717-766-8500 691-6653
TF: 800-932-0783 ■ Web: www2.midatlanticdeltadental.com

Delta Dental of Wisconsin 2801 Hoover Rd PO Box 828 ...... Stevens Point WI 54481 715-344-6087 344-2446
TF: 800-236-3713 ■ Web: www.deltadentalwi.com

Delta Dental of Wyoming 320 W 25th St Suite 100 .... Cheyenne WY 82001 307-632-3313 632-7309
TF: 800-735-3379

Doral Dental USA LLC 12121 N Corporate Pkwy .... Mequon WI 53092 262-241-7140 241-7366*
*Fax: Hum Res ■ TF: 800-417-7140 ■ Web: www.doralusa.com

Empire Deluxe PPO 11 W 42nd St .... New York NY 10036 212-476-1000 476-1281*
*Fax: Hum Res ■ TF: 800-261-5962 ■ Web: www.empireblue.com

Excellus BlueCross BlueShield 12 Rhoads Dr...................... Utica NY 13502 800-544-1450 782-8349*
*Fax Area Code: 315 ■ *Fax: Cust Svc ■ Web: www.excellusbcbs.com

Excellus BlueCross BlueShield of Central New York
344 S Warren St .... Syracuse NY 13202 315-671-6400 448-4922*
*Fax: Cust Svc ■ TF: 800-633-6066 ■ Web: www.excellusbcbs.com

EyeMed Vision Care 4000 Luxottica Pl.............................. Mason OH 45040 888-439-3633 765-6050*
*Fax Area Code: 513 ■ Web: www.eyemedvisioncare.com

Fallon Community Health Plan Inc 10 Chestnut St .... Worcester MA 01608 508-799-2100 754-1931
TF: 800-333-2535 ■ Web: www.fchp.org

First Choice Health Plan 600 University St Suite 1400............. Seattle WA 98101 206-268-2406 268-2941*
*Fax: Cust Svc ■ TF: 800-783-7312 ■ Web: www.fchn.com

First Commonwealth Inc 550 W Jackson Blvd Suite 800 .... Chicago IL 60661 312-993-1000 279-5140
TF: 800-788-3384 ■ Web: www.firstcommonwealth.net

First Priority Health 19 N Main St......................... Wilkes-Barre PA 18711 800-822-8753 200-6730*
*Fax Area Code: 570 ■ Web: www.bcnepa.com

Phone Fax

Geisinger Health Plan 100 N Academy Ave .... Danville PA 17822 570-271-8760 271-5268
TF: 800-447-4000 ■ Web: www.thehealthplan.com

Golden Rule Insurance Co 7440 Woodlands .... Indianapolis IN 46278 317-297-4123 298-0875
Web: www.goldenrule.com

Golden West Dental & Vision Plan Inc PO Box 5347 .... Oxnard CA 93031 805-987-8941 389-1586*
*Fax: Mktg ■ TF: 800-995-4124 ■ Web: www.goldenwestdental.com

Great-West Healthcare 8515 E Orchard Rd.............. Greenwood Village CO 80111 800-537-2033 689-3198*
*Fax Area Code: 303 ■ Web: www.onehealthplan.com

Group Health Co-op 521 Wall St.................................. Seattle WA 98121 206-448-5600 448-2137
TF: 888-901-4636 ■ Web: www.ghc.org

Group Health Plan Inc 111 Corporate Office Dr Suite 400......... Earth City MO 63045 314-506-1700 506-1958
TF: 800-743-3901 ■ Web: www.ghp.com

Hanover Insurance Co 440 Lincoln St .... Worcester MA 01653 508-855-1000 853-6332
TF: 800-853-0456 ■ Web: www.hanover.com

Harvard Pilgrim Health Care Inc 93 Worcester St............... Wellesley MA 02481 617-509-1000 509-2515
TF: 888-888-4742 ■ Web: www.harvardpilgrim.org

Hawaii Dental Service 700 Bishop St Suite 700 .... Honolulu HI 96813 808-521-1431 529-9368
TF: 800-232-2533

Hawaii Medical Service Assn 818 Keeaumoku St .... Honolulu HI 96822 808-948-6111 948-5567*
*Fax: Cust Svc ■ TF: 800-776-4672 ■ Web: www.hmsa.com

Health Alliance Medical Plans 301 S Vine St..................... Urbana IL 61801 217-337-8400 337-8093
TF: 800-851-3379 ■ Web: www.healthalliance.org

Health Alliance Plan 2850 W Grand Blvd .... Detroit MI 48202 313-872-8100 664-8404*
*Fax: Hum Res ■ TF: 800-422-4641 ■ Web: www.hap.org

Health Care Savings Inc 4530 Park Rd Suite 110.............. Charlotte NC 28209 704-527-6261 527-5725
TF: 800-833-8464 ■ Web: www.healthcaresavings.com

Health Net Inc 21650 Oxnard St....................... Woodland Hills CA 91367 818-676-6000 676-5166*
NYSE: HNT ■ *Fax: Hum Res ■ TF: 800-291-6911 ■ Web: www.health.net

Health Options Div Blue Cross & Blue Shield of Florida
PO Box 1798 .... Jacksonville FL 32231 800-734-6656 363-4365*
*Fax Area Code: 904

Health Plan of Nevada Inc PO Box 15645.................... Las Vegas NV 89114 702-242-7200 242-7920
Web: www.healthplanofnevada.com

Health Plan of Upper Ohio Valley Inc
52160 National Rd E .... Saint Clairsville OH 43950 740-695-3585 695-5297
TF: 800-624-6961 ■ Web: www.healthplan.org

Health Services Group Inc 601 SW 2nd Ave .... Portland OR 97204 503-228-6554 243-3895
TF: 800-852-5195 ■ Web: www.odscompanies.com

HealthAmerica Pennsylvania Inc 3721 Tecport Dr .... Harrisburg PA 17111 717-540-4260 671-2407*
*Fax: Hum Res ■ TF: 800-788-6445 ■ Web: www.healthamerica.cvty.com

HealthCare USA 10 S Broadway Suite 1200.................. Saint Louis MO 63102 314-241-5300 241-8010
TF: 800-213-7792 ■ Web: www.chchcusa.com

HealthLink Inc 12443 Olive Blvd........................... Saint Louis MO 63141 314-989-6000 989-6301*
*Fax: Cust Svc ■ TF: 800-624-2356 ■ Web: www.healthlink.com

HealthPartners Inc PO Box 1309 .... Minneapolis MN 55440 952-883-5000 967-5666*
*Fax: Cust Svc ■ TF: 800-883-2177 ■ Web: www.healthpartners.com

Healthplex Inc 333 Earl Ovington Blvd........................ Uniondale NY 11553 516-794-3000 794-3186
TF: 800-468-0608 ■ Web: www.healthplex.com

HealthPlus of Michigan 2050 S Linden Rd .... Flint MI 48532 810-230-2000 230-2208
TF: 800-332-9161 ■ Web: www.healthplus.com

HealthSpring Inc 44 Vantage Way Suite 300 .... Nashville TN 37228 615-291-7000 291-2664
NYSE: HS ■ Web: www.myhealthspring.com

Heritage Summit HealthCare of Florida Inc PO Box 3623 .... Lakeland FL 33802 863-665-6629 665-5177
TF: 800-282-7644

Highmark Blue Cross Blue Shield 120 5th Ave Pl.............. Pittsburgh PA 15222 412-544-7000 544-8368*
*Fax: Hum Res ■ TF: 800-662-0849 ■ Web: www.highmark.com

Highmark Inc DBA Highmark Blue Cross Blue Shield
120 5th Ave Pl .... Pittsburgh PA 15222 412-544-7000 544-8368*
*Fax: Hum Res ■ TF: 800-662-0849 ■ Web: www.highmark.com

HIP Health Plans 7 W 34th St55 Water St..................... New York NY 10041 646-447-5000
TF: 800-447-8255 ■ Web: www.hipusa.com

Horizon Blue Cross Blue Shield of New Jersey 3 Penn Plaza E ...... Newark NJ 07105 973-466-4000 466-4317*
*Fax: Hum Res ■ TF: 800-466-2583 ■ Web: www.horizon-bcbsnj.com

Humana Inc 500 W Main St .... Louisville KY 40202 502-580-1000 580-3690
NYSE: HUM ■ TF: 800-486-2620 ■ Web: www.humana.com

Humana Military Healthcare Services 500 W Main St .... Louisville KY 40201 502-580-3200 580-2000
TF: 800-964-5482 ■ Web: www.humana-military.com

IHC Health Plans Inc PO Box 30192 .... Salt Lake City UT 84130 801-442-5000 442-3327*
*Fax: Hum Res ■ TF: 800-538-5038 ■ Web: www.ihc.com

Independence Blue Cross 1901 Market St................. Philadelphia PA 19103 215-241-2400 241-3237*
*Fax: Hum Res ■ TF: 800-227-3114 ■ Web: www.ibx.com

Independence Holding Co 96 Cummings Point Rd .... Stamford CT 06902 203-358-8000 348-3103
NYSE: IHC ■ Web: www.independenceholding.com

Independent Health Assn 511 Farber Lakes Dr .... Buffalo NY 14221 716-631-3001 631-2346*
*Fax: Hum Res ■ TF: 800-247-1466 ■ Web: www.independenthealth.com

Kaiser Foundation Health Plan & Hospitals Inc
1 Kaiser Plaza 27th Fl .... Oakland CA 94612 510-271-5660 271-5820

Kaiser Foundation Health Plan Inc 1 Kaiser Plaza 27th Fl .... Oakland CA 94612 510-271-5910 271-2383
TF: 800-464-4000

Kaiser Permanente 1 Kaiser Plaza 27th Fl....................... Oakland CA 94612 510-271-5910 271-2383
TF: 800-464-4000 ■ Web: www.kaiserpermanente.org

Kaiser Permanente California 1950 Franklin St.................. Oakland CA 94612 510-987-1000 873-5114*
*Fax: Hum Res ■ TF: 800-464-4000

Kaiser Permanente Colorado Denver/Boulder
10350 E Dakota Ave.. Denver CO 80231 303-338-3800 338-3444
TF: 800-632-9700

Kaiser Permanente Georgia
3495 Piedmont Rd NE Piedmont Ctr Bldg 9.................... Atlanta GA 30305 404-364-7000 364-4794*
*Fax: PR ■ TF: 800-611-1811

Kaiser Permanente Hawaii 711 Kapiolani Blvd .... Honolulu HI 96813 808-432-5955 432-5070
TF: 800-966-5955

Kaiser Permanente Mid-Atlantic States Inc
2101 E Jefferson St.. Rockville MD 20849 301-468-6000 879-6390*
*Fax: Cust Svc ■ TF: 800-368-5784 ■ Web: www.kp.org/locations/midatlantic

Kaiser Permanente Northwest 500 NE Multnomah St Suite 100..... Portland OR 97232 503-813-2800 813-4709*
*Fax: Hum Res ■ TF: 800-813-2000

Kaiser Permanente Ohio
1001 Lakeside Ave N Pt Tower Suite 1200.................. Cleveland OH 44114 216-621-5600 479-5663*
*Fax: Hum Res ■ TF: 888-571-4141

Kanawha Insurance Co PO Box 610.......................... Lancaster SC 29721 803-283-5300 283-5676*
*Fax: Hum Res ■ TF: 800-635-4252 ■ Web: www.kanawha.com

Keystone Health Plan East Inc 1901 Market St............... Philadelphia PA 19103 215-241-2400 761-0301
TF: 800-227-3114

Long Term Preferred Care Inc 801 Crescent Ctr Dr Suite 200 ...... Franklin TN 37067 800-742-1110 764-5632*
*Fax Area Code: 615 ■ Web: www.ltpc.com

Lovelace Health Plan 4101 Indian School Rd NE .... Albuquerque NM 87110 505-262-7363 262-7987*
*Fax: Hum Res ■ TF Hum Res: 800-877-7526 ■ Web: www.lovelacehealthplan.com

M-Care 2301 Commonwealth Blvd .... Ann Arbor MI 48105 734-747-8700 332-2071*
*Fax: Hum Res ■ TF: 800-658-8878 ■ Web: www.mcare.org

MAMSI Life & Health Insurance Co 4 Taft Ct .... Rockville MD 20850 301-762-8205 545-5389*
*Fax: Hum Res ■ TF: 800-544-2853 ■ Web: www.mamsi.com

MD IPA 4 Taft Ct .... Rockville MD 20850 301-762-8205 545-5389
TF: 800-638-8898 ■ Web: www.mamsi.com

MEDICA PO Box 9310.................................... Minneapolis MN 55440 952-992-2900 992-3700*
*Fax: Sales ■ TF Cust Svc: 800-952-3455 ■ Web: www.medica.com

Medical Mutual of Ohio 2060 E 9th St .... Cleveland OH 44115 216-687-7000 687-6444*
*Fax: Hum Res ■ TF: 800-700-2583 ■ Web: www.medmutual.com

Medical & Hospitalization Insurance (Cont'd)

Phone Fax

Memorial Health Partners
7135 Hodgson Memorial Dr Suite 13 Savannah GA 31406 912-350-6608 350-6420
TF: 800-566-6710 ■ *Web:* www.memorialhealth.com
MetLife Inc 200 Park Ave New York NY 10166 212-578-2211 578-3320
NYSE: MET ■ *TF:* 800-638-5433 ■ *Web:* www.metlife.com
Molina Healthcare Inc 1 Golden Shore Dr Long Beach CA 90802 562-435-3666 437-7235
NYSE: MOH ■ *TF:* 800-526-8196 ■ *Web:* www.molinahealthcare.com
Mountain State Blue Cross & Blue Shield 700 Market St Parkersburg WV 26102 304-424-7700 424-7730
TF: 800-344-5514 ■ *Web:* www.msbcbs.com
MVP Health Care 625 State St Schenectady NY 12305 518-370-4793 388-2603*
**Fax:* Hum Res ■ *TF:* 800-777-4793 ■ *Web:* www.mvphealthcare.com
Nationwide Health Plans 5525 Parkcenter Cir Dublin OH 43017 614-854-3001
TF: 800-372-0713 ■ *Web:* www.nationwidehealthplans.com
Neighborhood Health Partnership Inc 7600 Corporate Ctr Dr Miami FL 33126 305-715-2200 715-2220*
**Fax:* Hum Res ■ *TF:* 800-354-0222 ■ *Web:* www.neighborhood-health.com
Northeast Delta Dental 1 Delta Dr PO Box 2002 Concord NH 03302 603-223-1000 223-1199
TF: 800-537-1715 ■ *Web:* www.nedelta.com
ODS Companies DBA Health Services Group Inc
601 SW 2nd Ave Portland OR 97204 503-228-6554 243-3895
TF: 800-852-5195 ■ *Web:* www.odscompanies.com
OmniCare Health Plan 13333 Gratiot Ave Suite 400 Detroit MI 48207 866-316-3784 393-7944*
**Fax Area Code:* 313 ■ *TF:* 800-477-6664 ■ *Web:* www.omnicarehealthplan.com
Optima Health 4417 Corporation Ln Virginia Beach VA 23462 757-552-7400 687-6111
Web: www.optimahealth.com
Optima Health Services Inc 707 60th St Ct E Suite C Bradenton FL 34208 941-747-1585 745-1387
TF: 800-841-1585
Oxford Health Plans LLC 48 Monroe Tpke Trumbull CT 06611 203-459-9100 459-6464
TF: 800-444-6222 ■ *Web:* www.oxhp.com
Oxford Health Plans (NH) Inc 10 Tara Blvd Nashua NH 03062 603-891-7000 891-7050
TF: 800-889-7630
Oxford Health Plans (NJ) Inc 111 Wood Ave 2nd Fl Iselin NJ 08830 732-623-1000 623-1900
TF: 800-201-6920
Pacific Union Dental 1390 Willow Pass Rd Suite 800 Concord CA 94520 925-363-6000 363-6099
TF: 800-999-3367 ■ *Web:* www.pacificuniondental.com
PacifiCare of Arizona PO Box 52078 Phoenix AZ 85072 602-244-8200 681-7545
TF: 800-347-8600
PacifiCare of California 5701 Katella Ave Cypress CA 90630 714-952-1121 226-5990*
**Fax:* Hum Res ■ *TF:* 800-624-8822
PacifiCare of Colorado 6455 S Yosemite St Greenwood Village CO 80111 303-220-5800 714-3990
TF: 800-877-9777 ■ *Web:* www.pacificare.com
PacifiCare Dental & Vision Administrators PO Box 25187 Santa Ana CA 92704 800-622-6388 228-3384*
**Fax:* Cust Svc ■ *Web:* www.pacificare-dental.com
PacifiCare Health Systems Inc 5995 Plaza Dr Cypress CA 90630 714-952-1121 226-3584*
**Fax:* Hum Res ■ *TF Cust Svc:* 800-624-8822 ■ *Web:* www.pacificare.com
PacifiCare of Nevada 700 E Warm Springs Rd Las Vegas NV 89119 702-269-7500 269-2506
TF: 800-826-4347 ■ *Web:* www.pacificare.com
PacifiCare of Oklahoma 7666 E 61st St Suite 500 Tulsa OK 74133 918-459-1100 459-1450*
**Fax:* Hum Res ■ *TF:* 800-459-8890
PacifiCare of Oregon 5 Centerpointe Dr Suite 600 Lake Oswego OR 97035 800-922-1444 603-7373*
**Fax Area Code:* 503 ■ **Fax:* Hum Res
Pacificare of Texas 6200 NW Pkwy San Antonio TX 78249 210-474-5000
TF: 800-624-7272
Paramount Health Care 1901 Indian Wood Cir Maumee OH 43537 419-887-2525 887-2034*
**Fax:* Hum Res ■ *TF:* 800-462-3589 ■ *Web:* www.paramounthealthcare.com
Partners National Health Plans of North Carolina Inc
PO Box 17509 Winston-Salem NC 27116 336-760-4822 659-2963*
**Fax:* Cust Svc ■ *TF:* 800-942-5695 ■ *Web:* www.partnershealth.com
Physicians Health Plan Inc PO Box 30377 Lansing MI 48909 517-364-8400 364-8460
TF: 800-832-9186 ■ *Web:* www.phpmi.org
Physicians Plus Insurance Corp 22 E Mifflin St Suite 200 Madison WI 53701 608-282-8900 258-1908*
**Fax:* Hum Res ■ *TF:* 800-545-5015 ■ *Web:* www.pplusic.com
PlanVista Solutions 4010 Boy Scout Blvd Suite 200 Tampa FL 33607 813-353-2300 353-2310
TF: 866-318-6564 ■ *Web:* www.planvista.com
PMI Dental Health Plan 12898 Towne Ctr Dr Cerritos CA 90703 562-924-8311 924-8039
TF: 800-422-4234 ■ *Web:* www.deltadentalca.org
PPOM 28588 Northwestern Hwy Southfield MI 48034 248-357-7766 357-3169*
**Fax:* Cust Svc ■ *TF:* 800-831-1166 ■ *Web:* www.ppom.com
ppoNEXT Inc 400 Oceangate Suite 300 Long Beach CA 90802 866-776-6398 256-7299*
**Fax Area Code:* 562 ■ *Web:* www.pponext.com
Precis Inc 2040 N Hwy 360 Grand Prairie TX 75050 972-522-2000 606-9637
NASDAQ: PCIS ■ *TF:* 866-578-1665 ■ *Web:* www.precis-pcis.com
Preferred Care 259 Monroe Ave Rochester NY 14607 585-325-3920 325-3122
TF: 800-950-3224 ■ *Web:* www.preferredcare.org
Preferred CommunityChoice PPO 218 W 6th St Tulsa OK 74119 918-594-5200 594-5210
TF: 800-884-4776 ■ *Web:* www.ccmhp.com/prefppo.html
Preferred Health Systems Inc 8535 E 21st St N Wichita KS 67206 316-609-2345 609-2481
TF: 800-990-0345 ■ *Web:* www.phsystems.com
Premera Blue Cross 7001 220th St SW Mount Lake Terrace WA 98043 425-918-4000
TF: 800-722-1471 ■ *Web:* www.premera.com
Premera Blue Cross Blue Shield of Alaska
2550 Denali St Suite 1404 Anchorage AK 99503 907-258-5065
TF: 800-508-4722
Primary Health 800 Park Blvd Suite 760 Boise ID 83712 208-344-1811 433-4600*
**Fax:* Claims ■ *TF:* 800-688-5008 ■ *Web:* www.primaryhealth.com
Priority Health 1231 E Beltline Ave NE Grand Rapids MI 49525 616-942-0954 942-0145
TF: 800-942-0954 ■ *Web:* www.priority-health.com
Priority Health Managed Benefits Inc 1231 E Beltline NE Grand Rapids MI 49525 616-942-0954 942-0145
TF: 800-942-0954 ■ *Web:* www.priority-health.com
Prison Health Services 105 Westpark Dr Suite 200 Brentwood TN 37027 615-373-3100 376-9862
TF: 800-729-0069 ■ *Web:* www.prisonhealth.com
Providence Health System 1235 NE 47th St Suite 299 Portland OR 97213 503-215-4700 215-4703
TF: 800-833-8899 ■ *Web:* www.providence.org/oregon
Provident American Insurance Co Inc
10501 N Central Expy Suite 200 Dallas TX 75231 214-696-9091 696-4756
TF: 800-933-9456 ■ *Web:* www.providentamerican.com
Provider Networks of America Inc 4300 Center Way Pl Arlington TX 76018 800-462-7554 417-2839*
**Fax Area Code:* 817 ■ *Web:* www.providernetworks.com
QualChoice Health Plan Inc 6000 Parkland Blvd Cleveland OH 44124 440-460-0093 460-4005
TF: 800-460-9090
Regence Blue Cross Blue Shield of Oregon PO Box 1271 Portland OR 97207 503-225-5221 225-5274*
**Fax:* Hum Res ■ *TF:* 800-547-0939 ■ *Web:* www.or.regence.com
Regence Blue Shield 1800 9th Ave Seattle WA 98101 206-464-3600
TF: 800-544-4246 ■ *Web:* www.wa.regence.com
Regence Blue Shield of Idaho 1602 21st Ave Lewiston ID 83501 208-746-2671 798-2086*
**Fax:* Hum Res ■ *TF:* 800-632-2022 ■ *Web:* www.id.regence.com
Regence BlueCross BlueShield of Utah
2890 E Cottonwood Pkwy Salt Lake City UT 84121 801-333-2100 333-6506*
**Fax:* Hum Res ■ *TF Cust Svc:* 800-624-6519 ■ *Web:* www.ut.regence.com
Rocky Mountain Health Plans PO Box 10600 Grand Junction CO 81502 970-244-7760 244-7880
TF: 800-843-0719 ■ *Web:* www.rmhmo.org
SafeGuard Health Enterprises Inc 95 Enterprise Suite 100 Aliso Viejo CA 92656 949-425-4300 425-4565
TF: 800-880-1800 ■ *Web:* www.safeguard.net
Sagamore Health Network 11555 N Meridian St Suite 400 Carmel IN 46032 317-573-2886 573-2875
TF: 800-364-3469 ■ *Web:* www.sagamorehn.com

Phone Fax

Scott & White Health Plan 2401 S 31st St Temple TX 76508 254-298-3000 298-3011
TF: 800-321-7947 ■ *Web:* www.sw.org
Security Health Plan of Wisconsin Inc 1515 St Joseph Ave Marshfield WI 54449 715-387-5621 221-9500
TF: 800-472-2363 ■ *Web:* www.securityhealth.org
Sierra Health Services Inc PO Box 15645 Las Vegas NV 89114 702-242-7000 242-7920*
NYSE: SIE ■ **Fax:* Mktg ■ *Web:* www.sierrahealth.com
Sloans Lake Managed Care Inc
6501 S Fiddler's Green Cir Suite 300 Greenwood Village CO 80111 303-691-2200 504-5344*
**Fax:* Cust Svc ■ *TF:* 800-850-2249 ■ *Web:* www.sloanslake.com
Southern Health Services Inc 1000 Research Park Blvd Charlottesville VA 22911 434-975-1212 951-2552
TF: 800-424-0077 ■ *Web:* www.southernhealth.com
Spectera Inc 2811 Lord Baltimore Dr Baltimore MD 21244 410-265-6084 265-6260
TF: 800-638-3120 ■ *Web:* www.spectera.com
Spectera Vision 100 Corporate Pt Suite 380 Culver City CA 90230 310-242-6200 242-6222
TF: 800-305-0230 ■ *Web:* www.spectera.com/vision.html
STAR Human Resources Group Inc
2222 W Dunlap Ave Suite 350 Phoenix AZ 85021 602-956-4200 956-4238
TF: 800-308-5948 ■ *Web:* www.starbridge.com
Tufts Associated Health Plans Inc 333 Wyman St Waltham MA 02451 781-466-9400 466-8583
TF: 800-462-0224 ■ *Web:* www.tufts-healthplan.com
UHP Healthcare 3405 W Imperial Hwy Inglewood CA 90303 310-671-3465 673-9176
TF: 800-544-0088 ■ *Web:* www.uhphealthcare.com
Union Pacific Railroad Employees' Health Systems
795 N 400 West Salt Lake City UT 84103 801-595-4300 595-4399
TF: 800-547-0421 ■ *Web:* www.uphealth.com
United American Healthcare Corp 300 River Pl Suite 4950 Detroit MI 48207 313-393-4571 393-3394
NASDAQ: UAHC
United Concordia Cos Inc 3250 W Big Beaver Suite 327 Troy MI 48084 800-944-6432 458-1136*
**Fax Area Code:* 248 ■ *TF:* 800-944-6432 ■ *Web:* www.ucci.com
UnitedHealth Group Inc 9900 Bren Rd East Minnetonka MN 55343 952-936-1300 992-5210*
NYSE: UNH ■ **Fax:* Hum Res ■ *TF:* 800-328-5979 ■ *Web:* www.unitedhealthgroup.com
UnitedHealthcare 9900 Bren Rd E Minnetonka MN 55343 952-936-1300 992-5210*
**Fax:* Hum Res ■ *TF:* 800-328-5979 ■ *Web:* www.unitedhealthcare.com
UnitedHealthcare Services Co of the River Valley Inc
1300 River Dr Suite 200 Moline IL 61265 309-765-1200 765-0670*
**Fax:* Claims ■ *TF:* 800-224-6599 ■ *Web:* www.uhcrivervalley.com
Unity Health Insurance 840 Carolina St Sauk City WI 53583 608-643-2491 643-2564
TF: 800-362-3308 ■ *Web:* www.unityhealth.com
Univera Healthcare 205 Park Club Ln Buffalo NY 14221 716-847-1480 857-4543*
**Fax:* Hum Res ■ *TF:* 800-628-8451 ■ *Web:* www.univerahealthcare.com
Universal Care Inc 1600 E Hill St Signal Hill CA 90755 562-424-6200 427-6710*
**Fax:* Mktg ■ *TF:* 800-635-6668 ■ *Web:* www.universalcare.com
USA Managed Care Organization 7301 N 16th St Suite 201 Phoenix AZ 85020 800-872-0020 861-2805*
**Fax Area Code:* 602 ■ *TF:* 800-872-0020 ■ *Web:* www.usamco.com
Valley Health Plan Inc 2270 Eastridge Ctr Eau Claire WI 54701 715-836-1254 836-1298
TF: 800-472-5411 ■ *Web:* www.valleyhealth.biz/
Vision Service Plan (VSP) 3333 Quality Dr Rancho Cordova CA 95670 916-851-5000 851-4852
TF Cust Svc: 800-852-7600 ■ *Web:* www.vsp.com
Vista Health Plan 1340 Concrod Terr Sunrise FL 33323 954-858-3000
TF: 866-847-8235 ■ *Web:* www.vistahealthplan.com
Vytra Health Plans 395 N Service Rd Melville NY 11747 631-694-4000 694-5787*
**Fax:* Hum Res ■ *TF:* 800-448-2527 ■ *Web:* www.vytra.com
Washington Dental Service 9706 4th Ave NE Seattle WA 98115 206-522-1300 524-0913
TF: 800-367-4104 ■ *Web:* www.deltadentalwa.com
Well Path Community Health Plans
2801 Slater Rd Suite 200 Morrisville NC 27560 919-337-1800 337-1871
TF: 800-935-7284 ■ *Web:* www.wellpathonline.com
WellCare Group Inc 8735 Henderson Rd Rm 4 Tampa FL 33634 813-290-6200 675-2929
NYSE: WCG ■ *Web:* www.wellcare.com
WellCare of New York 1404 Rt 300 Newburgh NY 12550 800-288-5441 566-6056*
**Fax Area Code:* 845 ■ **Fax:* Cust Svc ■
Web: www.wellcare.com/HealthPlans/NewYork/Home.aspx
Wellmark Blue Cross & Blue Shield of Iowa
636 Grand Ave Des Moines IA 50309 515-245-4500 245-4698*
**Fax:* Hum Res ■ *TF:* 800-526-8995 ■ *Web:* www.wellmark.com
Wellmark Blue Cross & Blue Shield of South Dakota
1601 W Madison St Sioux Falls SD 57104 605-373-7200 373-7497
TF: 800-952-1976 ■ *Web:* www.wellmark.com
Wellmark Inc 636 Grand Ave Des Moines IA 50309 515-245-4500 245-4698
TF: 800-362-1697 ■ *Web:* www.wellmark.com
Wellmark of South Dakota Inc DBA Wellmark Blue Cross & Blue Shield of South Dakota 1601 W Madison St Sioux Falls SD 57104 605-373-7200 373-7497
TF: 800-952-1976 ■ *Web:* www.wellmark.com
WellPath Select Inc
6 Coliseum Ctr 2815 Coliseum Ctr Dr Suite 550 Charlotte NC 28217 704-357-1421 804-4807*
**Fax Area Code:* 866 ■ *TF:* 800-470-4523 ■ *Web:* www.wellpathonline.com
WellPoint Inc 120 Monument Cir Suite 200 Indianapolis IN 46204 317-488-6000 488-6304
NYSE: WLP ■ *TF:* 800-331-1476 ■ *Web:* www.anthem.com

394-4 Property & Casualty Insurance

Phone Fax

21st Century Casualty Co 6301 Owensmouth Ave Woodland Hills CA 91367 818-704-3700 329-9650*
**Fax Area Code:* 888 ■ *TF:* 800-443-3100
21st Century Insurance Co 6301 Owensmouth Ave Woodland Hills CA 91367 818-704-3700 329-9650*
**Fax Area Code:* 888 ■ *TF:* 800-443-3100 ■ *Web:* www.21st.com
Acceptance Insurance Cos Inc
300 W Broadway Suite 1600 Council Bluffs IA 51503 712-329-3600 329-3834
TF: 800-228-7217 ■ *Web:* www.aicins.com
Access Group PO Box 250367 Atlanta GA 30325 770-234-3600 234-3770
TF: 877-353-9837 ■ *Web:* www.accessgeneral.com
Accident Fund Co 232 S Capitol Ave Lansing MI 48901 517-342-4200 342-4268
TF: 800-888-0616 ■ *Web:* www.accidentfund.com
ACE USA 436 Walnut St Philadelphia PA 19101 215-640-1000 640-2489
Web: www.acelimited.com
Acuity Insurance PO Box 58 Sheboygan WI 53082 920-458-9131 458-1618
TF: 800-242-7666 ■ *Web:* www.acuity.com
Addison Insurance Co 118 2nd Ave SE Cedar Rapids IA 52401 319-399-5700 399-5499
TF: 800-332-7977 ■ *Web:* www.unitedfiregroup.com
Admiral Insurance Co 1255 Caldwell Rd Cherry Hill NJ 08034 856-429-9200 429-8611
Web: www.admiralins.com
Affirmative Insurance Services Inc PO Box 488 Bedford Park IL 60638 708-233-8290
TF: 800-255-4687 ■ *Web:* affirmativeinsurance.com
Ag States Agency 5500 Cenex Dr Inver Grove Heights MN 55077 651-355-3700 355-6359
TF: 800-548-1494 ■ *Web:* www.agstatesgroup.com
Alfa General Insurance Corp PO Box 11000 Montgomery AL 36191 334-288-3900 288-0905
Web: www.alfains.com
Alfa Insurance PO Box 11000 Montgomery AL 36191 334-288-3900 288-0905
TF: 800-392-5705 ■ *Web:* www.alfains.com
Allegiance Insurance Co 1 Horace Mann Plaza Springfield IL 62715 217-789-2500 788-5161
TF: 800-999-1030
Allianz Insurance Co 2350 Empire Ave Burbank CA 91504 818-260-7500 260-7207
TF: 800-421-0504 ■ *Web:* www.aic-allianz.com
ALLIED Group Inc 1100 Locust St Des Moines IA 50391 515-508-4211 280-4904
TF: 800-532-1436 ■ *Web:* www.alliedinsurance.com

				Phone	Fax
Allied Insurance 1601 Exposition Blvd *Fax: Claims ■ TF: 800-552-2437 ■ Web: www.alliedinsurance.com	Sacramento	CA	95815	916-924-4000	925-4933*
Allstate Indemnity Co 2775 Sanders Rd *Fax: Hum Res ■ TF: 800-366-2958	Northbrook	IL	60062	847-402-5000	836-3998*
Allstate Insurance Co 2775 Sanders Rd Allstate Plaza *Fax: Hum Res ■ TF: 800-366-2958 ■ Web: www.allstate.com	Northbrook	IL	60062	847-402-5000	836-3998*
American Agricultural Insurance Co 1501 E Woodfield Rd Suite 300 W Web: www.aaic.fb.com	Schaumburg	IL	60173	847-969-2900	969-2752
American Agrisurance Inc 300 W Broadway	Council Bluffs	IA	51503	712-329-3600	329-3834
American Alternative Insurance Corp 685 College Rd E TF: 800-305-4954	Princeton	NJ	08543	609-951-8295	951-8310
American Commerce Insurance Co 3590 Twin Creeks Dr TF: 800-848-2945 ■ Web: www.acilink.com	Columbus	OH	43204	614-272-6951	272-2130
American Family Mutual Insurance Co 6000 American Pkwy *Fax: Hum Res ■ TF Cust Svc: 800-374-0008 ■ Web: www.amfam.com	Madison	WI	53783	608-249-2111	243-4921*
American Federation Insurance Co 25400 US Hwy 19 N Suite 185 TF: 800-527-3907	Clearwater	FL	33763	727-712-2115	712-2114
American Fire & Casualty Co 9450 Seward Rd TF: 800-843-6446	Fairfield	OH	45014	513-867-3000	603-7900
American Hardware Mutual Insurance Co PO Box 15440 *Fax: Hum Res ■ TF: 800-227-4663	Minneapolis	MN	55440	952-935-1400	930-7348*
American Home Assurance Co 70 Pine St *Fax: Mail Rm	New York	NY	10270	212-770-7000	943-1125*
American Manufacturers Mutual Insurance Co 1 Kemper Dr TF: 800-833-0355	Long Grove	IL	60049	847-320-2000	320-5624
American Motorists Insurance Co 1 Kemper Dr *Fax: Hum Res ■ TF: 800-833-0355	Long Grove	IL	60049	847-320-2000	320-5335*
American National Property & Casualty Co 1949 E Sunshine St *Fax: Hum Res ■ TF: 800-333-2860 ■ Web: www.anpac.com	Springfield	MO	65899	417-887-0220	887-2814*
American Physicians Assurance Corp 1301 N Hagadorn Rd *Fax: Hum Res ■ TF: 800-748-0465 ■ Web: www.apcapital.com	East Lansing	MI	48823	517-351-1150	336-8496*
American Protection Insurance Co 1 Kemper Dr TF: 800-833-0355	Long Grove	IL	60049	847-320-2000	320-5624
American Reinsurance Co 555 College Rd E TF: 800-255-5676	Princeton	NJ	08543	609-243-4200	243-4257
American Road Insurance Co 4 Park Ln Blvd Suite 460 TF: 800-234-2722	Dearborn	MI	48126	313-845-5850	845-7367
American Southern Insurance Co 3715 Northside Pkwy NW Bldg 400 8th Fl TF: 800-241-1172 ■ Web: www.amsou.com	Atlanta	GA	30327	404-266-9599	266-8327
AMERISAFE Inc 2301 Hwy 190 W NASDAQ: AMSF ■ TF: 800-256-9052 ■ Web: www.amerisafe.com	DeRidder	LA	70634	337-463-9052	463-7298
Amerisure Insurance Co PO Box 2060 *Fax: Hum Res ■ TF: 800-257-1900 ■ Web: www.amerisure.com	Farmington Hills	MI	48333	248-615-9000	615-8548*
Amica Mutual Insurance Co 100 Amica Way *Fax Area Code: 401 ■ Web: www.amica.com	Lincoln	RI	02865	800-652-6422	334-4241*
Arbella Indemnity Insurance Co PO Box 699103 TF: 800-972-5348 ■ Web: www.arbella.com	Quincy	MA	02269	617-328-2800	328-2970
Arbella Mutual Insurance Co PO Box 699103 TF: 800-972-5348 ■ Web: www.arbella.com	Quincy	MA	02269	617-328-2800	328-2970
Arbella Protection Insurance Co PO Box 699103 TF: 800-972-5348 ■ Web: www.arbella.com	Quincy	MA	02269	617-328-2800	328-2970
Argonaut Insurance Co 250 Middlefield Rd TF: 800-222-7811	Menlo Park	CA	94025	650-326-0900	858-6508
Armed Forces Insurance Exchange (AFI) PO Box G TF: 800-828-7732 ■ Web: www.afi.org	Fort Leavenworth	KS	66027	913-651-5000	727-4686
Association Casualty Insurance Co PO Box 9728 TF: 800-252-9641 ■ Web: www.acic-armga.com	Austin	TX	78766	512-345-7500	345-1972
Association Risk Management General Agency PO Box 9728 Suite 160 TF: 800-252-9641	Austin	TX	78766	512-345-7500	345-1972
Atlantic Mutual Insurance Co 100 Wall St *Fax: Hum Res ■ Web: www.atlanticmutual.com	New York	NY	10005	212-943-1800	428-6566*
Atlantic Specialty Insurance Co 100 Wall St Web: www.atlanticmutual.com	New York	NY	10005	212-943-1800	428-6577
Audubon Insurance Group PO Drawer 15989 *Fax: Hum Res ■ TF: 800-274-9830	Baton Rouge	LA	70895	225-293-5900	295-3005*
Auto-Owners Insurance Co 6101 Anacapri Blvd TF: 800-346-0346 ■ Web: www.auto-owners.com	Lansing	MI	48917	517-323-1200	323-8796
Avemco Insurance Co 411 Aviation Way TF: 800-874-9125 ■ Web: www.avemco.com	Frederick	MD	21701	301-694-5700	694-4376
Avomark Insurance Co 9450 Seward Rd TF: 800-843-6446	Fairfield	OH	45014	513-603-7400	603-3219
AXA Canada Inc 2020 University St 6th Fl TF: 800-361-1594	Montreal	QC	H3A2A5	514-282-1914	282-9588
Baldwin & Lyons Inc 1099 N Meridian St Suite 700 NASDAQ: BWINB ■ TF: 800-231-6024 ■ Web: www.baldwinandlyons.com	Indianapolis	IN	46204	317-636-9800	632-9444
Bank of America Insurance Services Inc PO Box 21848 TF: 800-288-7647 ■ Web: www.bankofamerica.com/insurance	Greensboro	NC	27420	336-805-8800	805-2026
Bankers Insurance Co 360 Central Ave TF: 800-627-0000 ■ Web: www.bankersinsurance.com	Saint Petersburg	FL	33701	727-823-4000	898-1511
Berkshire Hathaway Group 3024 Harney St TF: 800-786-6426 ■ Web: www.brkdirect.com	Omaha	NE	68131	402-536-3000	536-3030
Berkshire Hathaway Homestates Cos 9290 W Dodge Rd Suite 300 TF: 800-488-2930 ■ Web: www.bh-hc.com	Omaha	NE	68114	402-393-7255	393-7619
Brooke Corp 10950 Grandview Dr Suite 600 NASDAQ: BXXX ■ TF: 800-642-1872 ■ Web: www.brookecorp.com	Overland Park	KS	66210	913-661-0123	451-3183
Brotherhood Mutual Insurance Co 6400 Brotherhood Way TF: 800-333-3735 ■ Web: www.brotherhoodmutual.com	Fort Wayne	IN	46825	260-482-8668	483-7525
California Automobile Insurance Co 4484 Wilshire Blvd TF: 800-431-6654	Los Angeles	CA	90010	323-937-1060	857-4936
California Casualty Insurance Group PO Box M *Fax: Hum Res ■ TF: 800-288-7765 ■ Web: www.calcas.com	San Mateo	CA	94403	650-574-4000	572-4608*
Canada Life Financial Corp 330 University Ave *Fax: Hum Res ■ TF: 888-252-1847 ■ Web: www.canadalife.com	Toronto	ON	M5G1R8	416-597-1456	597-6520*
Canal Insurance Co 400 E Stone Ave TF: 800-452-6911 ■ Web: www.canal-ins.com	Greenville	SC	29601	864-242-5365	232-5707
Capitol Indemnity Corp 1600 Aspen Commons TF: 800-475-4450 ■ Web: www.capitolindemnity.com	Middleton	WI	53562	608-829-4200	829-7419
Capitol Specialty Insurance Corp 1600 Aspen Commons TF: 800-475-4450	Middleton	WI	53562	608-829-4200	829-7411
Carolina Casualty Insurance Co 4600 Touchton Rd E Bldg 100 Suite 400 TF: 800-874-8053 ■ Web: www.carolinacas.com	Jacksonville	FL	32246	904-363-0900	363-8098
Centennial Insurance Co 7 Giralda Farms Suite 120 TF: 800-945-7461	Madison	NJ	07940	212-943-1800	618-6822
Central Insurance Cos 800 S Washington St *Fax: Claims ■ TF: 800-736-7000 ■ Web: www.central-insurance.com	Van Wert	OH	45891	419-238-1010	238-7626*
Century-National Insurance Co 12200 Sylvan St TF: 800-733-0880 ■ Web: www.cnico.com	North Hollywood	CA	91606	818-760-0880	781-3642
Chubb Group of Insurance Cos 15 Mountain View Rd Web: www.chubb.com	Warren	NJ	07059	908-903-2000	903-2027
Chubb & Son 15 Mountain View Rd TF: 800-252-4670 ■ Web: www.chubb.com	Warren	NJ	07059	908-903-2000	903-2027
Church Mutual Insurance Co 3000 Schuster Ln TF: 800-542-3465 ■ Web: www.churchmutual.com	Merrill	WI	54452	715-536-5577	539-4650
Cincinnati Indemnity Co 6200 S Gilmore Rd	Fairfield	OH	45014	513-870-2000	870-2093
Cincinnati Insurance Co 6200 S Gilmore Rd Web: www.cinfin.com	Fairfield	OH	45014	513-870-2000	870-2093
Citation Insurance Co 211 Main St	Webster	MA	01570	508-943-9000	949-4921
Citizens Insurance Co of America 645 W Grand River Ave TF: 800-388-1300	Howell	MI	48843	517-546-2160	546-2667
Civil Service Employees Insurance Co 50 California St Suite 2550 TF: 800-282-6848 ■ Web: www.cseinsurance.com	San Francisco	CA	94111	925-817-6300	817-6383
CNA 40 Wall St *Fax: Hum Res ■ TF: 800-331-6053 ■ Web: www.cna.com	New York	NY	10005	212-440-3000	440-7909*
CNA Insurance Co 333 S Wabash Ave TF: 800-262-2000 ■ Web: www.cna.com	Chicago	IL	60604	312-822-5000	822-6419
Commerce Insurance Co 211 Main St TF: 800-221-1605 ■ Web: www.commerceinsurance.com	Webster	MA	01570	508-943-9000	949-4921
Concord Group Insurance Cos 4 Bouton St *Fax: Hum Res ■ TF: 800-852-3380 ■ Web: www.concordgroupinsurance.com	Concord	NH	03301	603-224-4086	225-5268*
Conseco Insurance Co 11815 N Pennsylvania St TF: 800-544-0467 ■ Web: www.conseco.com	Carmel	IN	46032	317-817-6300	817-3604
Continental Casualty Co 333 S Wabash Ave TF: 800-262-2000 ■ Web: www.cna.com	Chicago	IL	60685	312-822-5000	822-6419
Continental Western Group 11201 Douglas Ave *Fax: Hum Res ■ TF: 800-235-2942 ■ Web: www.cwgins.com	Urbandale	IA	50322	515-473-3000	473-3021*
Converium 1 Canterbury Green *Fax: Hum Res ■ TF: 866-900-2762 ■ Web: www.converium.com	Stamford	CT	06901	203-965-8800	965-8865*
Coregis Insurance Co 525 W Van Buren St Suite 500 TF: 800-879-4428	Chicago	IL	60607	312-821-4000	821-4099
Cornhusker Casualty Co 9290 W Dodge Rd Suite 300 TF: 800-488-2930	Omaha	NE	68114	402-393-7255	393-7619
Cotton States Life Insurance Co 244 Perimeter Center Pkwy NE TF: 800-282-6536 ■ Web: www.cottonstatesinsurance.com	Atlanta	GA	30346	770-391-8600	677-7264
Cotton States Mutual Insurance Co 244 Perimeter Ctr Pkwy NE TF: 800-282-6536 ■ Web: www.cottonstatesinsurance.com	Atlanta	GA	30346	770-391-8600	391-8676
Country Casualty Insurance Co 1701 Towanda Ave TF: 888-211-2555	Bloomington	IL	61701	309-557-3000	557-3232
Country Mutual Insurance Co 1701 Towanda Ave TF: 888-211-2555	Bloomington	IL	61701	309-557-3000	557-3232
Crum & Forster Insurance Inc 305 Madison Ave PO Box 1973 *Fax: Hum Res ■ TF: 800-227-3745 ■ Web: www.cfins.com	Morristown	NJ	07962	973-490-6600	490-6940*
Cumberland Insurance Group 633 Shiloh Pike TF: 800-232-6992 ■ Web: www.cumberlandgroup.com	Bridgeton	NJ	08302	856-451-4050	455-8468
Cumberland Mutual Fire Insurance Co 633 Shiloh Pike TF: 800-232-6992	Bridgeton	NJ	08302	856-451-4050	455-8468
Dairyland Insurance Co 1800 N Point Dr TF: 800-526-4252	Stevens Point	WI	54481	715-346-6000	346-6770
DCAP Group Inc 1158 Broadway NASDAQ: DCAP ■ Web: www.dcapgroup.com	Hewlett	NY	11557	516-374-7600	295-7216
Direct General Corp 1281 Murfreesboro Rd NASDAQ: DRCT ■ *Fax Area Code: 800 ■ TF Cust Svc: 800-627-8006 ■ Web: www.direct-general.com	Nashville	TN	37217	615-399-4700	541-0856*
Donegal Mutual Insurance Co 1195 River Rd PO Box 302 TF: 800-877-0600 ■ Web: www.donegalgroup.com	Marietta	PA	17547	717-426-1931	426-7033
Dorinco Reinsurance Co 1320 Waldo Ave TF: 800-225-1350 ■ Web: www.dorinco.com	Midland	MI	48642	989-636-0047	638-9963
Economical Insurance Group 111 Westmount Rd S TF: 800-265-2180 ■ Web: www.economicalinsurance.com	Waterloo	ON	N2J4S4	519-570-8200	570-8389
Employers Insurance Co of Wausau A Mutual Co 2000 Westwood Dr *Fax: Hum Res ■ TF: 800-435-4401 ■ Web: www.wausau.com	Wausau	WI	54401	715-845-5211	843-3847*
Erie Indemnity Co 100 Erie Insurance Pl NASDAQ: ERIE ■ *Fax: Mail Rm ■ TF: 800-458-0811 ■ Web: www.erie-insurance.com	Erie	PA	16530	814-870-2000	870-3126*
Erie Insurance Co of New York 100 Erie Insurance Pl TF: 800-458-0811 ■ Web: www.erieinsurance.com	Erie	PA	16530	814-870-2000	870-4408
Erie Insurance Exchange 100 Erie Insurance Pl TF: 800-458-0811 ■ Web: www.erieinsurance.com	Erie	PA	16530	814-870-2000	870-4408
Erie Insurance Property & Casualty Co 100 Erie Insurance Pl TF: 800-458-0811 ■ Web: www.erieinsurance.com	Erie	PA	16530	814-870-2000	870-4408
Everest Reinsurance Co 477 Martinsville Rd TF: 800-269-6660 ■ Web: www.everestregroup.com	Liberty Corner	NJ	07938	908-604-3000	604-3450
Factory Mutual Insurance Co 1301 Atwood Ave TF: 800-343-7722 ■ Web: www.fmglobal.com	Johnston	RI	02919	401-275-3000	275-3029
Farm Family Casualty Insurance Co PO Box 656 TF: 800-843-3276 ■ Web: www.farmfamily.com	Albany	NY	12201	518-431-5000	431-5975
Farmers Alliance Mutual Insurance Co PO Box 1401 TF: 800-362-1075 ■ Web: www.fami.com	McPherson	KS	67460	620-241-2200	241-5482
Farmers Automobile Insurance Assn 2505 Court St TF: 800-322-0160	Pekin	IL	61558	309-346-1161	346-8512
Farmers Insurance Exchange 4680 Wilshire Blvd *Fax: Hum Res ■ TF: 888-516-5656 ■ Web: www.farmers.com	Los Angeles	CA	90010	323-932-3200	932-7496*
Farmers Mutual Hail Insurance Co of Iowa 6785 Westown Pkwy TF: 800-247-5248 ■ Web: www.fmh.com	West Des Moines	IA	50266	515-282-9104	282-1220
Farmers Mutual Insurance Co of Nebraska 1220 Lincoln Mall TF: 800-742-7433 ■ Web: www.fmne.com	Lincoln	NE	68508	402-434-8300	434-8385
Farmers Union Mutual Insurance Co PO Box 2020 TF: 800-366-6338	Jamestown	ND	58402	701-252-2701	252-0404
Farmland Mutual Insurance Co 1100 Locust St Dept 3000 TF: 800-228-6700 ■ Web: www.farmlandins.com	Des Moines	IA	50391	515-280-4211	508-4904
FCCI Insurance Group 6300 University Pkwy PO Box 58004 TF: 800-226-3224 ■ Web: www.fcci-group.com	Sarasota	FL	34232	941-907-3224	907-2709
Federal Insurance Co 15 Mountain View Rd TF: 800-252-4670	Warren	NJ	07059	908-903-2000	903-2027
Federated Mutual Insurance Co PO Box 328 TF: 800-533-0472 ■ Web: www.federatedinsurance.com	Owatonna	MN	55060	507-455-5200	455-7808
Federated Service Insurance Co PO Box 328 TF: 800-533-0472 ■ Web: www.federatedinsurance.com	Owatonna	MN	55060	507-455-5200	455-7808
FEDUSA 1839 N Pine Island Rd Web: www.fedusa.com	Plantation	FL	33322	954-475-0182	475-1058
FIC Insurance Group 6500 River Place Blvd Bldg 1 TF: 800-925-6000 ■ Web: www.ficgroup.com	Austin	TX	78730	512-404-5000	404-5213
Financial Indemnity Co 21650 Oxnard St Suite 1800 TF: 800-777-4342	Woodland Hills	CA	91367	818-313-8500	340-4881
Fireman's Fund Insurance Co 777 San Marin Dr *Fax: Mail Rm ■ TF: 800-227-1700 ■ Web: www.the-fund.com	Novato	CA	94998	415-899-2000	899-3600*
Fireman's Fund McGee Marine Underwriters 75 Wall St TF: 800-235-6029 ■ Web: www.firemansfund.com/marine	New York	NY	10005	212-524-8600	524-9362
Firemen's Insurance Co of Washington DC 4820 Lake Brook Dr TF: 800-283-1153	Glen Allen	VA	23060	804-285-2700	285-5717

Property & Casualty Insurance (Cont'd)

Phone | Fax

First Insurance Co of Hawaii Ltd
1100 Ward Ave PO Box 2866 Honolulu HI 96803 808-527-7777 527-3200
TF: 800-272-5202 ■ *Web:* www.ficoh.com

First National Insurance Co of America
4333 Brooklyn Ave NE Safeco Plaza Seattle WA 98185 206-545-5000 545-5651
TF: 800-332-3226

Florida Farm Bureau Casualty Insurance Co
5700 SW 34th St Gainesville FL 32608 352-378-1321 374-1577
Web: www.ffbic.com

Florida Farm Bureau General Insurance Co
5700 SW 34th St Gainesville FL 32608 352-378-1321 374-1577
Web: www.ffbic.com

Florida Farm Bureau Insurance Cos 5700 SW 34th St Gainesville FL 32608 352-378-1321 374-1577
Web: www.ffbic.com

FM Global 1301 Atwood Ave Johnston RI 02919 401-275-3000 275-3029
TF: 800-343-7722 ■ *Web:* www.fmglobal.com

Foremost Insurance Co PO Box 2450 Grand Rapids MI 49501 616-942-3000 956-3990
TF Cust Svc: 800-527-3905 ■ *Web:* www.foremost.com

Foremost Property & Casualty Insurance Co
PO Box 2450 Grand Rapids MI 49501 616-942-3000 956-3990
TF: 800-527-3905 ■ *Web:* www.foremost.com

Foremost Signature Insurance Co PO Box 2450 Grand Rapids MI 49501 616-942-3000 956-3990
TF: 800-527-3905 ■ *Web:* www.foremost.com

Frankenmuth Mutual Insurance Co 1 Mutual Ave Frankenmuth MI 48787 989-652-6121 652-3588
TF Cust Svc: 800-234-1133 ■ *Web:* www.fmins.com

Franklin Mutual Insurance Co PO Box 400 Branchville NJ 07826 973-948-3120 948-7190
TF: 800-842-0551 ■ *Web:* www.fmiweb.com

Frontier Insurance Group Inc 146 Rock Hill Dr Rock Hill NY 12775 845-794-3600 796-1906*
*Fax: Mktg ■ *Web:* www.frontier.com

GAINSCO County Mutual Insurance Co PO Box 199023 Dallas TX 75219 972-629-4301 629-4335

GEICO (Government Employees Insurance Co)
1 GEICO Plaza Washington DC 20076 301-986-3000 718-5239
TF: 800-841-3000 ■ *Web:* www.geico.com

GEICO Casualty Co 1 GEICO Plaza Washington DC 20076 301-986-2300 986-3225
TF: 800-841-3000 ■ *Web:* www.geico.com

GEICO General Insurance Co 1 GEICO Plaza Washington DC 20076 301-986-2300 986-2851
TF: 800-841-3000 ■ *Web:* www.geico.com

Gemini Insurance Co 200 W Madison St Suite 2700 Chicago IL 60606 312-553-4413 553-4416

General Casualty Co of Wisconsin 1 General Dr Sun Prairie WI 53596 608-837-4440 825-5125*
*Fax: Hum Res ■ *TF:* 800-362-5448 ■ *Web:* www.generalcasualty.com

General Reinsurance Corp 695 E Main St Financial Ctr Stamford CT 06901 203-328-5000 328-6423
TF: 800-431-9994 ■ *Web:* www.genre.com

General Star National Insurance Co
695 E Main St Financial Ctr Stamford CT 06901 203-328-5000 328-6423
TF: 800-431-9994 ■ *Web:* www.generalstar.com

Georgia Casualty & Surety Co 4370 Peachtree Rd NE Atlanta GA 30319 404-266-5500 266-5596
TF: 866-458-7506 ■ *Web:* www.georgiacasualty.com

Germania Farm Mutual Insurance Assn PO Box 645 Brenham TX 77834 979-836-5224 836-1977
TF: 800-392-2202 ■ *Web:* www.germania-ins.com

Globe Indemnity Co 9300 Arrowpoint Blvd Charlotte NC 28273 704-522-2000 522-3200
TF Cust Svc: 800-523-5451

GMAC Insurance 500 W 5th St Winston Salem NC 27152 336-770-2000 423-8325
TF: 877-468-3466 ■ *Web:* www.gmacinsurance.com

Golden Eagle Insurance Corp 525 B St San Diego CA 92101 619-744-6000 744-6511*
*Fax: Claims ■ *TF:* 800-688-8661 ■ *Web:* www.goldeneagle-ins.com

Gotham Insurance Co 919 3rd Ave 10th Fl New York NY 10022 212-551-0600 986-1310
TF: 800-367-0224 ■ *Web:* www.nymagic.com

Government Employees Insurance Co (GEICO)
1 GEICO Plaza Washington DC 20076 301-986-3000 718-5239
TF: 800-841-3000 ■ *Web:* www.geico.com

Grange Guardian 650 S Front St Columbus OH 43206 614-445-2900 445-2695*
*Fax: Hum Res ■ *TF:* 800-422-0550 ■ *Web:* www.grangeinsurance.com

Grange Mutual Casualty Co 650 S Front St Columbus OH 43206 614-445-2900 445-2337*
*Fax: Mktg ■ *TF:* 800-422-0550 ■ *Web:* www.grangeinsurance.com

Graphic Arts Mutual Insurance Co PO Box 530 Utica NY 13503 315-734-2000 734-2680
TF: 800-274-1914

Great American Insurance Co 580 Walnut St Cincinnati OH 45202 513-369-5000
Web: www.greatamericaninsurance.com

Great Central Insurance Co 3625 N Sheridan Rd Peoria IL 61633 309-688-8571 688-2738
TF: 800-447-1972 ■ *Web:* www.argonautgreatcentral.com

Great Northern Insurance Co 15 Mountain View Rd Warren NJ 07059 908-903-2000 903-2027
TF: 800-252-4670

Great West Casualty Co 1100 W 29th St South Sioux City NE 68776 402-494-2411 494-7450*
*Fax: Claims ■ *TF:* 800-228-8602 ■ *Web:* ssl.gwccnet.com

Grinnell Mutual Reinsurance Co 4215 Highway 146 Grinnell IA 50112 641-269-8000 236-2840
TF: 800-362-2041 ■ *Web:* www.gmrc.com

GuideOne Insurance Co 1111 Ashworth Rd West Des Moines IA 50265 515-267-5000 267-5530*
*Fax: Hum Res ■ *TF:* 877-448-4331 ■ *Web:* www.guideone.com

GuideOne Mutual Insurance Co 1111 Ashworth Rd West Des Moines IA 50265 515-267-5000 267-5530*
*Fax: Hum Res ■ *TF:* 877-448-4331 ■ *Web:* www.guideone.com

GuideOne Specialty Mutual Insurance Co
1111 Ashworth Rd West Des Moines IA 50265 515-267-5000 267-5530*
*Fax: Hum Res ■ *TF:* 800-247-4181 ■ *Web:* www.guideone.com

Hanover Insurance Co 440 Lincoln St Worcester MA 01653 508-855-1000 853-6332
TF: 800-853-0456 ■ *Web:* www.hanover.com

Harco National Insurance Co PO Box 68309 Schaumburg IL 60168 847-321-4800 321-4810
TF: 800-448-4642

Harleysville Atlantic Insurance Co
5901 Peachtree Dunwoody Rd NE Suite A-100 Atlanta GA 30328 770-391-1992 391-4364
TF: 800-543-6355 ■ *Web:* www.harleysvillegroup.com

Harleysville Insurance Co 7900 W 78th St Suite 400 Edina MN 55439 952-829-1400 829-1487
TF: 800-727-5353 ■ *Web:* www.harleysvilleinsurance.com

Harleysville Insurance Co of New Jersey
224 Strawbridge Dr Suite 301 Moorestown NJ 08057 856-642-1646 642-9415*
*Fax: Claims ■ *TF:* 888-595-9876 ■ *Web:* www.harleysvillegroup.com

Harleysville Insurance Co of New York 120 Washington St Watertown NY 13601 315-782-1160 782-4571*
*Fax: Hum Res ■ *TF:* 800-962-1006 ■ *Web:* www.harleysville.com

Harleysville Lake States Insurance Co
12935 S West Bay Shore Dr PO Box 352 Traverse City MI 49685 231-946-6390 946-0443
TF: 800-968-2090 ■ *Web:* www.harleysville.com

Harleysville Pennland Insurance Co 355 Maple Ave Harleysville PA 19438 215-256-5000 256-5602*
*Fax: Hum Res ■ *TF:* 800-523-6344 ■ *Web:* www.harleysville.com

Harleysville Preferred Insurance Co 355 Maple Ave Harleysville PA 19438 215-256-5000 256-5602*
*Fax: Hum Res ■ *TF:* 800-523-6344 ■ *Web:* www.harleysvillegroupinc.com

Harleysville Worcester Insurance Co 120 Front St Suite 400 Worcester MA 01608 508-751-8100 753-9366*
*Fax: Hum Res ■ *TF:* 800-225-7387 ■ *Web:* www.harleysvillegroup.com

Hartford Accident & Indemnity Co Hartford Plaza Hartford CT 06115 860-547-5000 547-5392
Web: www.thehartford.com

Hartford Casualty Insurance Co Hartford Plaza Hartford CT 06115 860-547-5000 547-2080
Web: www.thehartford.com

Hartford Fire Insurance Co Hartford Plaza Hartford CT 06115 860-547-5000 547-2680*
*Fax: Hum Res ■ *Web:* www.thehartford.com

Phone | Fax

Hartford Steam Boiler Inspection & Insurance Co
1 State St PO Box 5024 Hartford CT 06102 860-722-1866 722-5106
TF: 800-472-1866 ■ *Web:* www.hsb.com

Hartford's Omni Auto Plan PO Box 105440 Atlanta GA 30348 770-952-4500 983-3633*
*Fax Area Code: 800 ■ *TF:* 800-777-6664 ■ *Web:* www.thehartford.com

HealthLink Inc 12443 Olive Blvd Saint Louis MO 63141 314-989-6000 989-6301*
*Fax: Cust Svc ■ *TF:* 800-624-2356 ■ *Web:* www.healthlink.com

Hingham Mutual Fire Insurance Co 230 Beal St Hingham MA 02043 781-749-0841 749-4477
TF: 800-341-8200 ■ *Web:* www.hinghammutual.com

Home-Owners Insurance Co 6101 Anacapri Blvd Lansing MI 48909 517-323-1200 323-8796
TF: 800-288-8740

Horace Mann Insurance Co 1 Horace Mann Plaza Springfield IL 62715 217-789-2500 788-5161
TF: 800-999-1030 ■ *Web:* www.horacemann.com

Hortica Insurance PO Box 428 Edwardsville IL 62025 618-656-4240 656-7581
TF: 800-851-7740 ■ *Web:* www.hortica-insurance.com

HSB Group Inc 1 State St PO Box 5024 Hartford CT 06102 860-722-1866 722-5106
TF: 800-472-1866 ■ *Web:* www.hsb.com

ICW Group 11455 El Camino Real San Diego CA 92130 858-350-2400 350-2640
TF: 800-877-1111 ■ *Web:* www.icwgroup.com

IMT Insurance Co PO Box 1336 Des Moines IA 50305 515-327-2777 372-2892
TF: 800-274-3531 ■ *Web:* www.imtins.com

Indiana Farmers Mutual Insurance Group 10 W 106th St Indianapolis IN 46290 317-846-4211 848-8629
TF: 800-666-6460 ■ *Web:* www.indianafarmers.com

Infinity Insurance Co PO Box 830189 Birmingham AL 35283 205-870-4000 803-8406*
*Fax: Hum Res ■ *TF:* 800-334-1661 ■ *Web:* www.infinity-insurance.com

Infinity Property & Casualty Corp 11700 Great Oaks Way Alpharetta GA 30022 678-627-6000 627-7912
NASDAQ: IPCC ■ *TF:* 800-225-8930 ■ *Web:* www.ipacc.com

ING Canada Inc 700 University Ave Toronto ON M5G0A1 416-440-1000 440-4127*
*Fax: Claims ■ *TF:* 866-817-2138 ■ *Web:* www.ingcanada.com

Insurance Co of the West 11455 El Camino Real San Diego CA 92130 858-350-2400 350-2616
TF: 800-877-1111 ■ *Web:* www.icwgroup.com

Integrity Mutual Insurance Co 2121 E Capitol Dr PO Box 539 Appleton WI 54912 920-734-4511 730-5712
TF: 800-348-1741 ■ *Web:* www.integrityinsurance.com

Interstate Fire & Casualty Co 33 W Monroe St 14th Fl Chicago IL 60603 312-346-6400 346-5748
TF: 800-628-8574

Investors Underwriting Managers Inc 310 Hwy 35S Red Bank NJ 07701 732-224-0500 741-2266
TF: 800-243-6869 ■ *Web:* www.investorsunderwriters.com

Kemper Insurance Cos 1 Kemper Dr Long Grove IL 60049 847-320-2000 320-2494
TF: 800-833-0355 ■ *Web:* www.kemperinsurance.com

Kentucky Farm Bureau Mutual Insurance Co
9201 Bunsen Pkwy Louisville KY 40220 502-495-5000 495-5177
Web: www.kyfbins.com

Kingsway Financial Services Inc
5310 Explorer Dr Suite 200 Mississauga ON L4W5H8 905-629-7888 629-5008
NYSE: KFS ■ *TF:* 800-265-5458 ■ *Web:* www.kingsway-financial.com

KMG America Corp 12600 Whitewater Dr Suite 150 Minnetonka MN 55343 952-930-4800 930-4802
NYSE: KMA ■ *TF:* 866-820-5642 ■ *Web:* www.kmgamerica.com

Koch Supply & Trading LP 4111 E 37th St N Wichita KS 67220 316-828-5500 828-5752
TF: 800-245-2243 ■ *Web:* www.kochoil.com

Lafayette Insurance Co 2115 Winnie St Galveston TX 77550 409-766-4600 766-5531
TF: 800-580-2499

Leader Insurance Co 5205 N O'Connor Blvd Suite 700 Irving TX 75039 877-953-2337 532-3379
TF: 877-953-2337 ■ *Web:* www.leaderinsurance.com

Legion Insurance 1 Logan Sq Suite 1400 Philadelphia PA 19103 215-963-1200 963-7575
TF: 800-255-6738 ■ *Web:* www.legioninsurance.com

Lexington Insurance Co Inc 100 Summer St Boston MA 02110 617-330-1100 355-4891
TF: 800-355-4891 ■ *Web:* www.lexingtoninsurance.com

Liberty Mutual Group 175 Berkeley St Boston MA 02117 617-357-9500
Web: www.libertymutual.com

Lititz Mutual Insurance Co 2 N Broad St Lititz PA 17543 717-626-4751 626-0970
TF: 800-626-4751 ■ *Web:* www.lititzmutual.com

Lujan Manuel Insurance Inc PO Box 3727 Albuquerque NM 87190 505-266-7771 255-8140
TF: 888-652-7771 ■ *Web:* www.manuellujan.com

Lumbermen's Underwriting Alliance 2501 N Military Trail Boca Raton FL 33431 561-994-1900 997-9489*
*Fax: Hum Res ■ *TF:* 800-327-0630 ■ *Web:* www.ins-lua.com

Lykes Insurance Inc PO Box 2879 Tampa FL 33601 813-223-3911 221-1857
TF: 800-243-0491 ■ *Web:* www.lykesinsurance.com

Lynn Insurance Group 2501 N Military Trail Boca Raton FL 33431 561-994-1900 994-8362
TF: 800-327-0630

Magna Carta Co 1 Park Ave New York NY 10016 212-591-9500 591-9600
TF: 888-663-7275 ■ *Web:* www.mcarta.com

Main Street America Group 55 West St Keene NH 03431 603-352-4000 358-1173
TF: 800-258-5310 ■ *Web:* www.msagroup.com

Mann Horace Insurance Co 1 Horace Mann Plaza Springfield IL 62715 217-789-2500 788-5161
TF: 800-999-1030 ■ *Web:* www.horacemann.com

Manuel Lujan Insurance Inc PO Box 3727 Albuquerque NM 87190 505-266-7771 255-8140
TF: 888-652-7771 ■ *Web:* www.manuellujan.com

Markel Insurance Co 4600 Cox Rd Glen Allen VA 23060 804-527-2700 527-7999
TF: 800-431-1270 ■ *Web:* www.horseinsurance.com

Markel Insurance Co 4521 Highwoods Pkwy Glen Allen VA 23060 804-747-0136 965-1600
TF: 800-446-6671 ■ *Web:* www.markelcorp.com

Mendota Insurance Co 1285 Northland Dr Mendota Heights MN 55120 651-688-4100 688-4619
TF: 800-422-0792 ■ *Web:* www.mendota-insurance.com

Mercer Insurance Group Inc 10 N Hwy 31 PO Box 278 Pennington NJ 08534 609-737-0426 737-8719
NASDAQ: MIGP ■ *TF:* 800-223-0534 ■ *Web:* www.franklininsurance.com

Merchants Insurance Group PO Box 903 Buffalo NY 14240 716-849-3333 849-3246
TF: 800-462-1077 ■ *Web:* www.merchantsgroup.com

Mercury Casualty Co 555 W Imperial Hwy Brea CA 92821 714-671-6600 671-6603*
*Fax: Hum Res

Mercury General Corp 4484 Wilshire Blvd Los Angeles CA 90010 323-937-1060 857-7116
NYSE: MCY ■ *TF:* 800-431-6654 ■ *Web:* www.trustmercury.com

Mercury Insurance Co 555 W Imperial Hwy Brea CA 92821 714-671-6600 671-6603*
*Fax: Hum Res

MetLife Auto & Home Insurance Co 700 Quaker Ln Warwick RI 02886 401-827-2400 827-2358
TF: 800-422-4272 ■ *Web:* www.metlife.com

Michigan Millers Mutual Insurance Co PO Box 30060 Lansing MI 48909 517-482-6211 482-6245
TF: 800-888-1914 ■ *Web:* www.michiganmillers.com

Mico Insurance Co 471 E Broad St Columbus OH 43215 614-225-8211 225-8350
TF: 800-876-6426

Mid-Century Insurance Co 4680 Wilshire Blvd Los Angeles CA 90010 323-932-3200 932-3101
TF: 888-516-5656

Mid-Continent Casualty Co PO Box 1409 Tulsa OK 74101 918-587-7221 588-1293*
*Fax: Hum Res ■ *TF:* 800-722-4994 ■ *Web:* www.mcg-ins.com

Middlesex Insurance Co 3 Carlisle Rd Westford MA 01886 978-392-7000 392-7033
TF: 800-225-1390

Middlesex Mutual Assurance Co 213 Court St PO Box 891 Middletown CT 06457 860-347-4621 638-5260*
*Fax: Hum Res ■ *TF:* 800-899-0032 ■ *Web:* www.middlesexmutual.com

Midwest Employers Casualty Co
14755 N Outer 40 Dr Suite 300 Chesterfield MO 63017 636-449-7000 449-7199
TF: 877-632-2474 ■ *Web:* www.mwecc.com

Millers First Insurance Co 111 E 4th St Alton IL 62002 618-463-3636 463-2612*
*Fax: Cust Svc ■ *TF:* 800-558-0500 ■ *Web:* www.millersfirst.com

Millers Mutual Insurance Assn 111 E 4th St Alton IL 62002 618-463-3636 463-2612*
*Fax: Cust Svc ■ *TF:* 800-558-0500

Milwaukee Mutual Insurance Co
400 S Executive Dr Suite 200 Brookfield WI 50005 262-207-8500 754-9899*
*Fax: Hum Res ■ *TF:* 800-733-7366

	City	State	Zip	Phone	Fax
Montgomery Mutual Insurance Co					
6230 Old Dobbin Ln Suite 200	Columbia	MD	21045	410-953-8120	285-0837*
**Fax Area Code:* 443 ■ **Fax:* Hum Res ■ *TF:* 800-638-8933 ■					
Web: www.montgomery-ins.com					
Motorists Mutual Insurance Co 471 E Broad St	Columbus	OH	43215	614-225-8211	225-8407
Web: www.motoristsgroup.com:8080/cf					
Motors Insurance Corp 13736 Riverport Dr	Maryland Heights	MO	63043	314-493-8000	355-3800*
**Fax Area Code:* 800 ■ *TF:* 800-642-6464					
Mutual of Enumclaw Insurance Co 1460 Wells St	Enumclaw	WA	98022	360-825-2591	825-6885
TF: 800-366-5551 ■ *Web:* www.mutualofenumclaw.com					
National Farmers Union Property & Casualty Co					
5619 DTC Pkwy Suite 300	Greenwood Village	CO	80111	303-337-5500	200-7134
TF: 800-669-0622 ■ *Web:* www.nfuic.com					
National Fire & Marine Insurance Co 3024 Harney St	Omaha	NE	68131	402-536-3000	536-3030
National Grange Mutual Insurance Co 55 West St	Keene	NH	03431	603-352-4000	358-1173
TF: 800-258-5310					
National Indemnity Co 3024 Harney St	Omaha	NE	68131	402-536-3000	536-3030
Web: www.nationalindemnity.com					
National Interstate Corp 3250 Interstate Dr	Richfield	OH	44286	330-659-8900	659-8901
NASDAQ: NATL ■ *TF:* 800-929-1500 ■ *Web:* www.nationalinterstate.com					
National Union Fire Insurance Co of Pittsburgh Pennsylvania					
70 Pine St	New York	NY	10270	212-770-7000	943-1125*
**Fax:* Mail Rm					
Nationwide Mutual Fire Insurance Co 1 Nationwide Plaza	Columbus	OH	43215	614-249-7111	961-3064
TF: 800-882-2822 ■ *Web:* www.nationwide.com					
Nationwide Mutual Insurance Co 1 Nationwide Plaza	Columbus	OH	43215	614-249-7111	961-3064*
**Fax:* Cust Svc ■ *TF:* 800-882-2822 ■ *Web:* www.nationwide.com					
Nautilus Insurance Co 7273 E Butherus Dr	Scottsdale	AZ	85260	480-951-0905	951-9730
TF: 800-842-8972 ■ *Web:* www.nautilusinsgroup.com					
Navigator's Management Co Inc 1 Penn Plaza 55th Fl	New York	NY	10119	212-244-2333	244-4077
Web: www.navg.com					
New Jersey Manufacturers Insurance Co					
301 Sullivan Way	West Trenton	NJ	08628	609-883-1300	771-0384
TF: 800-232-6600 ■ *Web:* www.njm.com					
New York Central Mutual Fire Insurance Co					
1899 Central Plaza E	Edmeston	NY	13335	607-965-8321	965-2136
TF: 800-234-6926 ■ *Web:* www.nycm.com					
New York Marine & General Insurance Co					
919 3rd Ave 10th Fl	New York	NY	10022	212-551-0600	986-1310
TF: 800-367-0224 ■ *Web:* www.nymagic.com					
Nobel Insurance 12225 Greenville Ave Suite 750	Dallas	TX	75243	972-644-0434	644-0424
TF: 800-766-6235 ■ *Web:* www.nobelinsurance.com					
North American Specialty Insurance Co 650 Elm St 6th Fl	Manchester	NH	03101	603-644-6600	644-6613
TF: 800-542-9200					
North Carolina Farm Bureau Mutual Insurance Co					
PO Box 27427	Raleigh	NC	27611	919-782-1705	783-3593
Web: www.ncfbins.com					
North Pointe Insurance Co 28819 Franklin Rd	Southfield	MI	48034	248-358-1171	357-3895
Web: www.npic.com					
Northern Security Insurance Co PO Box 188	Montpelier	VT	05601	802-223-2341	229-7646
TF: 800-451-5000					
Northland Insurance Co PO Box 64816	Saint Paul	MN	55164	651-310-4100	310-4949
TF: 800-237-9334 ■ *Web:* www.northlandins.com					
Northwestern Pacific Indemnity Co 15 Mountain View Rd	Warren	NJ	07059	908-903-2000	903-2027
TF Claims: 800-252-4670					
Odyssey Re Holdings Corp 300 1st Stamford Pl	Stamford	CT	06902	203-977-8000	356-0196
NYSE: ORH ■ *TF:* 866-246-9945 ■ *Web:* www.odysseyre.com					
Ohio Casualty Insurance Co 9450 Seward Rd	Fairfield	OH	45014	513-603-2400	867-3215
TF: 800-843-6446 ■ *Web:* www.ocas.com					
Ohio Farmers Insurance Co 1 Park Cir	Westfield Center	OH	44251	330-887-0101	887-0840
TF: 800-243-0210 ■ *Web:* www.westfieldgrp.com					
Ohio Security Insurance Co 9450 Seward Rd	Fairfield	OH	45014	513-867-3000	603-3181
TF: 800-843-6446 ■ *Web:* www.ocas.com					
Oklahoma Farm Bureau Mutual Insurance Co					
2501 N Stiles Ave	Oklahoma City	OK	73105	405-523-2300	523-2362
Web: www.okfarmbureau.org					
Oklahoma Surety Co 1437 S Boulder Ave Suite 200	Tulsa	OK	74119	918-587-7221	588-1298
TF: 800-722-4994					
Old Dominion Insurance Co					
4601 Touchton Rd E Suite 330 PO Box 16100	Jacksonville	FL	32245	904-642-3000	730-9217
TF: 800-226-0875					
Old Republic Insurance Co PO Box 789	Greensburg	PA	15601	724-834-5000	834-4025
Web: www.oriconline.com					
Omaha Property & Casualty Insurance Co 3316 Farnam St	Omaha	NE	68131	402-342-7600	351-2650
TF: 800-788-9488 ■ *Web:* www.mutualofomaha.com					
OneBeacon Insurance Group 1 Beacon Ct	Canton	MA	02021	781-332-7000	332-7904
TF: 800-327-6286 ■ *Web:* www.onebeacon.com					
Oregon Mutual Insurance Co PO Box 808	McMinnville	OR	97128	503-472-2141	565-3846
TF: 800-888-2141 ■ *Web:* www.ormutual.com					
Oregon Mutual Insurance Group PO Box 808	McMinnville	OR	97128	503-472-2141	565-3846
TF: 800-888-2141 ■ *Web:* www.ormutual.com					
Owners Insurance Co 6101 Anacapri Blvd	Lansing	MI	48917	517-323-1200	323-8796
TF: 800-288-8740					
Patriot General Insurance Co 3 Carlisle Rd	Westford	MA	01886	978-392-7000	392-7033
Pekin Insurance Co 2505 Court St	Pekin	IL	61558	309-346-1161	346-8512
TF: 800-322-0160 ■ *Web:* www.pekininsurance.com					
Penn-America Insurance Co 420 S York Rd	Hatboro	PA	19040	215-443-3600	443-3604
Web: www.penn-america.com					
Penn National Insurance Co 2 N 2nd St Penn National Plaza	Harrisburg	PA	17101	717-234-4941	255-6850
TF: 800-388-4764 ■ *Web:* www.pennnationalinsurance.com					
Pennsylvania Manufacturers Assn Insurance Co					
380 Sentry Pkwy	Blue Bell	PA	19422	610-397-5000	397-5366*
**Fax:* Mail Rm ■ *TF:* 800-222-2749					
Permanent General Cos Inc 2636 Elm Hill Pike Suite 510	Nashville	TN	37214	615-242-1961	366-1718
TF: 800-280-1466 ■ *Web:* www.pgac.com					
Pharmacists Mutual Insurance Co					
808 US Hwy 18 W PO Box 370	Algona	IA	50511	515-295-2461	295-9306
TF: 800-247-5930 ■ *Web:* www.pharmacistsmutual.com					
Philadelphia Insurance Cos 1 Bala Plaza Suite 100	Bala Cynwyd	PA	19004	610-617-7900	617-7940
TF: 800-525-7662 ■ *Web:* www.phly.com					
Pinnacol Assurance PO Box 469011	Denver	CO	80246	303-361-4000	361-5000
TF: 800-873-7242 ■ *Web:* www.pinnacol.com					
PMA Reinsurance Corp 1735 Market St Mellon Bank Ctr	Philadelphia	PA	19103	215-665-5000	665-5099*
**Fax:* Mail Rm ■ *Web:* www.pmare.com					
Preferred Employers Group Inc 10800 Biscayne Blvd 10th Fl	Miami	FL	33161	305-893-4040	893-8659
TF: 800-433-5755 ■ *Web:* www.preferredemployers.com					
Preferred Employers Insurance Co PO Box 85478	San Diego	CA	92186	619-688-3900	688-3913
TF: 888-472-9224 ■ *Web:* www.preferredworkcomp.com					
Preferred Mutual Insurance Co 1 Preferred Way	New Berlin	NY	13411	607-847-6161	847-8046*
**Fax:* Mail Rm ■ *TF:* 800-333-7642 ■ *Web:* www.pminsco.com					
Preserver Insurance Co 95 Rt 17 S	Paramus	NJ	07652	201-291-2000	291-2127
TF: 800-242-0332 ■ *Web:* www.preserver.com					
Princeton Excess & Surplus Lines Insurance Co					
555 College Rd E	Princeton	NJ	08543	609-243-4200	243-4257
TF: 800-255-5676					
Princeton Insurance Cos 746 Alexander Rd	Princeton	NJ	08540	800-334-0588	734-8461*
**Fax Area Code:* 609 ■ *TF:* 800-433-0157 ■ *Web:* www.princetoninsurance.com					
ProCentury Corp 465 Cleveland Ave	Westerville	OH	43082	614-895-2000	895-2707
NASDAQ: PROS ■ *TF:* 800-878-7389 ■ *Web:* www.procentury.com					
Proformance Insurance Co 4 Paragon Way	Freehold	NJ	07728	732-665-1100	303-6770
TF: 800-298-5742 ■ *Web:* www.proinsureco.com					
Progressive Casualty Insurance Co					
6300 Wilson Mills Rd Campus E	Mayfield Village	OH	44143	440-461-5000	446-5372
TF: 800-321-9843 ■ *Web:* www1.progressive.com					
Protective Insurance Co 1099 N Meridian St Suite 700	Indianapolis	IN	46204	317-636-9800	632-9444
TF: 800-231-6024 ■ *Web:* www.baldwinandlyons.com					
Providence Mutual Fire Insurance Co 340 East Ave	Warwick	RI	02886	401-827-1800	822-1789
TF: 877-763-1800 ■ *Web:* www.providencemutual.com					
Providence Washington Insurance Co 88 Boyd Ave	East Providence	RI	02914	401-453-7000	453-7299
TF: 800-752-4549 ■ *Web:* www.provwash.com					
Prudential Financial Inc 751 Broad St	Newark	NJ	07102	973-802-6000	367-6476
NYSE: PRU ■ *TF:* 800-843-7625 ■ *Web:* www.prudential.com					
PXRE Corp 399 Thornall St 14th Fl	Edison	NJ	08837	732-906-8100	906-9157
Web: www.pxregroup.com					
PXRE Reinsurance Co 399 Thornall St 14th Fl	Edison	NJ	08837	732-906-8100	906-9157
QBE Reinsurance Corp 88 Pine St Wall St Plaza 16th Fl	New York	NY	10005	212-422-1212	422-1313
Web: www.qbe.com/americas/index.html					
Quincy Mutual Fire Insurance Co 57 Washington St	Quincy	MA	02169	617-472-8770	899-7790*
**Fax Area Code:* 800 ■ *TF:* 800-899-1116 ■ *Web:* www.quincymutual.com					
Ranger Insurance Co 10777 Westheimer Rd Suite 500	Houston	TX	77042	713-954-8100	954-8301*
**Fax:* Mktg ■ *TF:* 800-392-1970 ■ *Web:* www.rangerinsurance.com					
Republic Indemnity Co of America					
15821 Ventura Blvd Suite 370	Encino	CA	91436	818-990-9860	382-1252
TF: 800-821-4520 ■ *Web:* www.republicindemnity.com					
Republic Insurance Co Inc 5525 LBJ Fwy	Dallas	TX	75240	972-788-6220	788-6083
TF: 800-344-2275 ■ *Web:* www.republink.com					
Republic Western Insurance Co 2721 N Central Ave	Phoenix	AZ	85004	602-263-6755	745-6436
TF Claims: 800-528-7134 ■ *Web:* www.repwest.com					
Risk Planners Inc PO Box 240	Minneapolis	MN	55440	952-914-5777	914-5778
TF: 800-328-7475 ■ *Web:* www.riskplanners.com					
RLI Insurance Co 9025 N Lindbergh Dr	Peoria	IL	61615	309-692-1000	692-1068
TF: 800-331-4929 ■ *Web:* www.rlicorp.com					
Royal & SunAlliance Insurance Co of Canada					
10 Wellington St E	Toronto	ON	M5E1L5	416-366-7511	367-9869
TF: 800-268-8406 ■ *Web:* www.royalsunalliance.ca					
Royal & SunAlliance USA 9300 Arrowpoint Blvd	Charlotte	NC	28273	704-522-2000	522-3200
TF: 800-523-5451 ■ *Web:* www.royalsunalliance-usa.com					
RTW Inc 8500 Normandale Lake Blvd Suite 1400	Bloomington	MN	55437	952-893-0403	893-3700
NASDAQ: RTWI ■ *TF:* 800-789-2242 ■ *Web:* www.rtwi.com					
Safe Auto Insurance Co 3883 E Broad St	Columbus	OH	43213	614-231-0200	231-4690
TF: 800-723-3288 ■ *Web:* www.safeauto.com					
SAFECO Property & Casualty Insurance Cos					
4333 Brooklyn Ave NE Safeco Plaza	Seattle	WA	98185	206-545-5000	925-0165*
**Fax:* Hum Res ■ *Web:* www.safeco.com					
Safety Insurance Group Inc 20 Custom House St	Boston	MA	02110	617-951-0600	
NASDAQ: SAFT ■ *Web:* www.safetyinsurance.com					
Safety National Casualty Corp 2043 Woodland Pkwy	Saint Louis	MO	63146	314-995-5300	995-9921*
**Fax:* Mktg ■ *TF:* 800-289-7224 ■ *Web:* www.sncc.com					
Safeway Insurance Group 790 Pasquinelli Dr	Westmont	IL	60559	630-887-8300	887-8975*
**Fax:* Hum Res ■ *TF:* 800-273-0300 ■ *Web:* www.safewayinsurance.com					
Sagamore Insurance Co 1099 N Meridian St Suite 700	Indianapolis	IN	46204	317-636-9800	632-9444
TF: 800-231-6024 ■ *Web:* www.sagamoreinsurance.com					
Saint Paul Fire & Marine Insurance Co 385 Washington St	Saint Paul	MN	55102	651-310-7911	310-8294
TF: 800-328-2189 ■ *Web:* www.stpaul.com					
Savers Property & Casualty Insurance Co					
11880 College Blvd Suite 500	Overland Park	KS	66210	913-339-5000	339-5030
TF: 800-351-1411 ■ *Web:* www.meadowbrookinsgrp.com/savers.html					
Scottsdale Insurance Co 8877 N Gainey Ctr Dr	Scottsdale	AZ	85258	480-365-4000	483-6752
TF: 800-423-7675 ■ *Web:* www.scottsdaleins.com					
Secura Insurance Cos PO Box 819	Appleton	WI	54912	920-739-3161	739-6795
TF: 800-558-3405 ■ *Web:* www.secura.net					
Seibels Bruce Group Inc 1501 Lady St	Columbia	SC	29201	803-748-2000	748-8394*
**Fax:* Hum Res ■ *TF:* 800-525-8835 ■ *Web:* www.seibels.com					
Selective Insurance Co of America 40 Wantage Ave	Branchville	NJ	07890	973-948-3000	948-0292*
**Fax:* Hum Res ■ *TF:* 800-777-9656 ■ *Web:* www.selective.com					
Selective Way Insurance Co 40 Wantage Ave	Branchville	NJ	07890	973-948-3000	948-0292*
**Fax:* Hum Res ■ *TF:* 800-777-9656 ■ *Web:* www.selective.com					
Seneca Insurance Co Inc 160 Water St 16th Fl	New York	NY	10038	212-344-3000	344-4545
Web: www.senecainsurance.com					
Sentry Insurance A Mutual Co 1800 N Point Dr	Stevens Point	WI	54481	715-346-6000	346-6770*
**Fax:* Hum Res ■ *Web:* www.sentry.com					
Shand Morahan & Co Inc 10 Parkway N	Deerfield	IL	60015	847-572-6000	572-6137
Web: www.shand.com					
Shelter Mutual Insurance Co 1817 W Broadway	Columbia	MO	65218	573-445-8441	446-7318
TF: 800-743-5837 ■ *Web:* www.shelterins.com					
Signature Group 200 N Martingale Rd	Schaumburg	IL	60173	847-605-3000	605-4835*
**Fax:* Hum Res ■ *TF:* 800-621-0393					
Signet Star Reinsurance Co 475 Steamboat Rd	Greenwich	CT	06830	203-542-3800	542-3290
Sompo Japan Insurance Co of America					
2 World Financial Ctr 225 Liberty St 43rd Fl	New York	NY	10281	212-416-1200	
TF: 800-444-6870 ■ *Web:* www.sompo-japan-us.com					
Southern Farm Bureau Casualty Insurance Co					
1800 E County Line Rd Suite 400	Ridgeland	MS	39157	601-957-7777	957-4329
TF: 800-272-7977 ■ *Web:* www.sfbcic.com					
Southern Guaranty Insurance Co PO Box 235004	Montgomery	AL	36123	334-270-6000	270-6115
TF: 800-633-5606 ■ *Web:* www.sgic.com					
Southern-Owners Insurance Co 6101 Anacapri Blvd	Lansing	MI	48917	517-323-1200	323-8796
TF: 800-288-8740					
Specialty Underwriters' Alliance Inc					
222 S Riverside Plaza Suite 1600	Chicago	IL	60606	312-277-1600	577-0973
NASDAQ: SUAI ■ *TF:* 888-782-4672 ■ *Web:* www.suainsurance.com					
SS Nesbitt & Co Inc 2501 20th Pl S Suite 425	Birmingham	AL	35223	205-870-1316	870-3328
Web: www.ssnesbitt.com					
Star Insurance Co 26255 American Dr	Southfield	MI	48034	248-358-1100	358-1614
TF: 800-482-2726 ■ *Web:* www.meadowbrook.com/star.html					
State Auto National Insurance Co 518 E Broad St	Columbus	OH	43215	614-464-5000	464-5341*
**Fax:* Hum Res ■ *TF:* 800-444-9950 ■ *Web:* www.stateauto.com					
State Auto Property & Casualty Insurance Co					
518 E Broad St	Columbus	OH	43215	614-464-5000	464-5341*
**Fax:* Hum Res ■ *TF:* 800-444-9950 ■ *Web:* www.stateauto.com					
State Automobile Mutual Insurance Co 518 E Broad St	Columbus	OH	43215	614-464-5000	464-5341*
**Fax:* Hum Res ■ *TF:* 800-444-9950 ■ *Web:* www.stateauto.com					
State Farm Fire & Casualty Co 1 State Farm Plaza	Bloomington	IL	61710	309-766-2311	763-8777*
**Fax:* Mktg					
State Farm General Insurance Co 1 State Farm Plaza	Bloomington	IL	61710	309-766-2311	763-8777*
**Fax:* Mktg ■ *Web:* www.statefarm.com					
State Farm Indemnity Co 1 State Farm Plaza	Bloomington	IL	61710	309-766-2311	763-8777*
**Fax:* Mktg					
State Farm Insurance 333 First Commerce Dr	Aurora	ON	L4G8A4	905-750-4100	750-4716
Web: www.statefarm.ca					
State Farm Mutual Automobile Insurance Co					
1 State Farm Plaza	Bloomington	IL	61710	309-766-2311	763-8777*
**Fax:* Mktg ■ *Web:* www.statefarm.com					

Property & Casualty Insurance (Cont'd)

Company	City	State	Zip	Phone	Fax
STOPS Inc 8855 Grissom Pkwy *Fax Area Code: 800 ■ TF: 800-487-0521 ■ Web: www.stopsinc.com	Titusville	FL	32780	321-383-0499	383-4116*
Stratford Insurance Co 400 Parson's Pond Dr	Franklin Lakes	NJ	07417	201-847-8600	847-1010
Sumitomo Marine & Fire Insurance Co Ltd 15 Independence Blvd	Warren	NJ	07059	908-604-2900	
Swiss Re America Corp 175 King St TF: 877-794-7773 ■ Web: www.swissre.com	Armonk	NY	10504	914-828-8000	828-7000
Texas Pacific Indemnity Co 15 Mountain View Rd TF: 800-252-4670	Warren	NJ	07059	908-903-2000	903-2027
Toa Reinsurance Co of America 177 Madison Ave PO Box 1930 TF: 800-898-7977 ■ Web: www.toare.com	Morristown	NJ	07962	973-898-9480	898-9495
Tokio Marine Life 230 Park Ave TF: 800-628-2796 ■ Web: www.tokiomarine.us	New York	NY	10169	212-297-6600	297-6062
Topa Insurance Corp 1800 Ave of the Stars 12th Fl TF: 800-949-6505 ■ Web: www.topains.com	Los Angeles	CA	90067	310-201-0451	843-9409
Tower Group Inc 120 Broadway 14th Fl NASDAQ: TWGP ■ Web: www.twrgrp.com	New York	NY	10271	212-655-2000	655-2199
Transatlantic Reinsurance Co 80 Pine St 9th Fl Web: www.transre.com	New York	NY	10005	212-770-2000	269-6801
Transcontinental Insurance Co 333 S Wabash Ave CNA Ctr TF: 800-262-2000	Chicago	IL	60685	312-822-5000	822-6419
Transportation Insurance Co 333 S Wabash Ave TF: 800-262-2000	Chicago	IL	60604	312-822-5000	822-6419
Travelers Indemnity Co 1 Tower Sq *Fax: Hum Res ■ Web: www.travelers.com	Hartford	CT	06183	860-277-0111	277-1970*
Tri-State Insurance Co of Minnesota 10 Roundwind Rd PO Box 500 *Fax Area Code: 800 ■ TF: 800-533-0303 ■ Web: www.cwgcollectorcar.com	Luverne	MN	56156	507-283-9561	232-9925*
ULLICO Casualty Co 1625 Eye St NW TF: 800-431-5425 ■ Web: www.ullico.com	Washington	DC	20006	202-682-0900	682-4911
Underwriters MGA Inc PO Box 5488 TF: 888-560-3240 ■ Web: www.underwritersmga.com	McAllen	TX	78502	956-618-3862	631-6971
Underwriters Reinsurance Co 26050 Mureau Rd TF: 800-332-2801	Calabasas	CA	91302	818-878-9500	878-9535
Unigard Security Insurance Co 15805 NE 24th St *Fax: Mktg ■ TF: 800-777-1757 ■ Web: www.unigard.com	Bellevue	WA	98008	425-641-4321	644-5218*
Union National Fire Insurance Co 3636 S Sherwood Forest Blvd TF: 800-765-0550	Baton Rouge	LA	70816	225-292-7600	292-7614
Union Standard Insurance Co 122 W Carpenter Fwy Suite 350 TF: 800-444-0049 ■ Web: www.usic.com	Irving	TX	75039	972-719-2400	719-2401
United Casualty Insurance Co 12115 Lackland Rd TF: 800-777-8467	Saint Louis	MO	63146	314-819-4300	
United Fire & Casualty Co PO Box 73909 NASDAQ: UFCS ■ TF: 800-332-7977 ■ Web: www.unitedfiregroup.com	Cedar Rapids	IA	52407	319-399-5700	399-5499
United Heartland Inc PO Box 3026 TF: 800-258-2667 ■ Web: www.heartland.cobaltcorporation.com	Milwaukee	WI	53201	262-787-7700	787-7701
United National Group 3 Bala Plaza E Suite 300 TF: 800-333-0352 ■ Web: www.unitednat.com	Bala Cynwyd	PA	19004	610-664-1500	660-8882
United National Insurance Co 3 Bala Plaza E Suite 300 TF: 800-333-0352 ■ Web: www.unitednat.com	Bala Cynwyd	PA	19004	610-664-1500	660-8882
Unitrin Business Insurance 12790 Merit Dr TF: 800-777-2249 ■ Web: www.unitrinbusinessinsurance.com	Dallas	TX	75251	214-360-8000	
Universal Insurance Co PO Box 71338 *Fax: Claims	San Juan	PR	00936	787-793-7202	792-4788*
Universal Underwriters Group 7045 College Blvd TF: 800-821-7803 ■ Web: www.universalunderwriters.com	Overland Park	KS	66211	913-339-1000	339-1026
USA Workers' Injury Network 916 S Capital of Texas Hwy TF: 800-872-0820	Austin	TX	78746	512-306-0201	328-6785
USAA Property & Casualty Insurance Group 9800 Fredericksburg Rd Web: www.usaa.com	San Antonio	TX	78288	800-531-8169	531-8877
Utica National Insurance Group 180 Genesee St TF: 800-274-1914 ■ Web: www.uticanational.com	New Hartford	NY	13413	315-734-2000	734-2680
Valley Forge Insurance Co 100 CNA Dr TF: 800-437-8854	Nashville	TN	37214	615-871-1400	886-1883
Vermont Mutual Insurance Co PO Box 188 TF: 800-451-5000 ■ Web: www.vermontmutual.com	Montpelier	VT	05601	802-223-2341	229-7646
Vigilant Insurance Co 15 Mountain View Rd TF: 800-252-4670	Warren	NJ	07059	908-903-2000	903-2027
Viking Insurance 1800 N Point Dr PO Box 8026 *Fax Area Code: 715 ■ TF: 800-462-6342 ■ Web: www.vikinginsurance.com	Stevens Point	WI	54481	800-334-0090	346-9040*
Wausau Business Insurance Co 2000 Westwood Dr TF: 800-435-4401	Wausau	WI	54401	715-845-5211	843-3847
Wausau General Insurance Co 2000 Westwood Dr TF: 800-435-4401	Wausau	WI	54401	715-845-5211	843-3847
Wausau Service Corp 2000 Westwood Dr TF: 800-435-4401	Wausau	WI	54401	715-845-5211	843-3847
Wausau Underwriters Insurance Co 2000 Westwood Dr TF: 800-435-4401	Wausau	WI	54401	715-845-5211	843-3847
Wawanesa Mutual Insurance Co 191 Broadway Web: www.wawanesa.com	Winnipeg	MB	R3C3P1	204-985-3811	942-7724
Wesco-Financial Insurance Co 3024 Harney St	Omaha	NE	68131	402-536-3000	536-3030
West American Insurance Co 9450 Seward Rd TF: 800-843-6446 ■ Web: www.ocas.com	Fairfield	OH	45014	513-867-3000	603-7900
West Bend Mutual Insurance Co 1900 S 18th Ave TF: 800-236-5010 ■ Web: www.westbendmutual.com	West Bend	WI	53095	262-334-5571	338-7293
Western Agricultural Insurance Co 325 S Higley Rd	Higley	AZ	85236	480-635-3600	
Western Diversified Casualty Insurance Co 2345 Waukegan Rd Suite 210-E *Fax Area Code: 800 ■ TF: 800-323-5771	Bannockburn	IL	60015	847-948-8988	479-9375*
Western National Mutual Insurance Co 5350 W 78th St *Fax: Hum Res ■ TF: 877-862-8808 ■ Web: www.wnins.com	Edina	MN	55439	952-835-5350	921-3159*
Western Reserve Group 1685 Cleveland Rd *Fax: Hum Res ■ TF: 800-362-0426 ■ Web: www.wrg-ins.com	Wooster	OH	44691	330-262-9060	262-3259*
Westfield Cos PO Box 5001 TF: 800-368-3530 ■ Web: www.westfieldgrp.com	Westfield Center	OH	44251	330-887-0101	887-0840
Westfield Group 1 Park Cir PO Box 5001 TF: 800-243-0210 ■ Web: www.westfield-cos.com	Westfield Center	OH	44251	330-887-0101	887-0840
Westfield National Insurance Co PO Box 5001 TF: 800-368-3530 ■ Web: www.westfieldgrp.com	Westfield Center	OH	44251	330-887-0101	887-0840
Windsor Group 11700 Great Oak Way *Fax Area Code: 800 ■ TF: 800-852-8055	Atlanta	GA	30022	678-627-6000	228-8138*
XL Reinsurance America Inc 70 Sea View Ave Web: www.xlre.com	Stamford	CT	06902	203-964-5200	964-0763
Zenith Insurance Co PO Box 9055 TF: 800-448-4356 ■ Web: www.thezenith.com	Van Nuys	CA	91409	818-713-1000	883-3363
Zenithstar Insurance Co 1101 Capital of Texas Hwy S Bldg J PO Box 163510 *Fax: Claims ■ TF: 800-841-3987 ■ Web: www.zenithstar.com	Austin	TX	78716	512-306-1700	327-7145*

394-5 Surety Insurance

Company	City	State	Zip	Phone	Fax
ACMAT Corp 233 Main St Web: www.acmatcorp.com	New Britain	CT	06050	860-229-9000	229-1111
Acstar Insurance Co 233 Main St Web: www.acstarins.com	New Britain	CT	06050	860-224-2000	229-1111
Admiral Insurance Co 1255 Caldwell Rd Web: www.admiralins.com	Cherry Hill	NJ	08034	856-429-9200	429-8611
AMBAC Assurance Corp 1 State St Plaza 15th Fl TF: 800-221-1854 ■ Web: www.ambac.com	New York	NY	10004	212-668-0340	509-9190
American Bonding Co 8300 N Hayden Rd Suite A-205	Scottsdale	AZ	85258	480-948-5415	948-1829
American Fire & Casualty Co 9450 Seward Rd TF: 800-843-6446	Fairfield	OH	45014	513-867-3000	603-7900
American Healthcare Specialty Insurance Co 1888 Century Pk E Suite 800 *Fax: Mktg ■ TF: 800-962-5549	Los Angeles	CA	90067	310-551-5900	551-5945*
American Home Assurance Co 70 Pine St *Fax: Mail Rm	New York	NY	10270	212-770-7000	943-1125*
American Physicians Assurance Corp 1301 N Hagadorn Rd *Fax: Hum Res ■ TF: 800-748-0465 ■ Web: www.apcapital.com	East Lansing	MI	48823	517-351-1150	336-8496*
American Physicians Insurance Exchange (API) 1301 S Capitol of Texas Hwy Suite C-300 TF: 800-252-3628 ■ Web: www.apie.us	Austin	TX	78746	512-328-0888	314-4398
American Southern Insurance Co 3715 Northside Pkwy NW Bldg 400 8th Fl TF: 800-241-1172 ■ Web: www.amsou.com	Atlanta	GA	30327	404-266-9599	266-8327
API (American Physicians Insurance Exchange) 1301 S Capitol of Texas Hwy Suite C-300 TF: 800-252-3628 ■ Web: www.apie.us	Austin	TX	78746	512-328-0888	314-4398
Assurant Solutions 260 Interstate N Cir SE Web: www.assurantsolutions.com	Atlanta	GA	30339	770-763-1000	859-4403
Assured Guaranty Corp 1325 Ave of the Americas Web: www.assuredguaranty.com	New York	NY	10019	212-974-0100	581-3268
Balboa Life & Casualty Insurance Co 3349 Michelson Dr Suite 200 TF: 800-854-6115 ■ Web: www.balboainsurance.com	Irvine	CA	92612	949-222-8000	222-8716
Central Insurance Cos 800 S Washington St *Fax: Claims ■ TF: 800-736-7000 ■ Web: www.central-insurance.com	Van Wert	OH	45891	419-238-1010	238-7626*
Central States Indemnity Co of Omaha PO Box 34350 TF: 800-445-6500 ■ Web: www.csi-omaha.com	Omaha	NE	68134	402-997-8000	997-8010
Century Insurance Group 465 Cleveland Ave TF: 800-878-7389 ■ Web: www.centurysurety.com	Westerville	OH	43082	614-895-2000	895-7036
Chubb Specialty Insurance 82 Hopmeadow St TF: 800-432-8168 ■ Web: www.chubb.com	Simsbury	CT	06070	860-408-2000	408-2002
Cincinnati Casualty Co 6200 S Gilmore Rd Web: www.cinfin.com	Fairfield	OH	45014	513-870-2000	870-2093
Cincinnati Insurance Co 6200 S Gilmore Rd Web: www.cinfin.com	Fairfield	OH	45014	513-870-2000	870-2093
CMG Mortgage Insurance Co PO Box 7056 TF: 800-909-4264 ■ Web: www.cmgmi.com	San Francisco	CA	94120	415-284-2500	981-4601
CNA 40 Wall St *Fax: Hum Res ■ TF: 800-331-6053 ■ Web: www.cna.com	New York	NY	10005	212-440-3000	440-7909*
CNA Surety Corp 333 S Wabash Ave NYSE: SUR ■ TF: 877-672-6115 ■ Web: www.cnasurety.com	Chicago	IL	60604	312-822-5000	822-6419
Connecticut Medical Insurance Co PO Box 71 Web: www.ctmed.com	Glastonbury	CT	06033	860-633-7788	633-8237
Copic Insurance Co 7351 Lowry Blvd TF: 800-421-1834 ■ Web: callcopic.com/cic	Denver	CO	80230	720-858-6000	858-6001
Coregis Insurance Co 525 W Van Buren St Suite 500 TF: 800-879-4428	Chicago	IL	60607	312-821-4000	821-4099
Crum & Forster Insurance Inc 305 Madison Ave PO Box 1973 *Fax: Hum Res ■ TF: 800-227-3745 ■ Web: www.cfins.com	Morristown	NJ	07962	973-490-6600	490-6940*
Cumberland Casualty & Surety Co 4311 W Waters Ave Suite 401 TF: 800-723-0171 ■ Web: www.cumberlandtech.com	Tampa	FL	33614	813-885-2112	594-3323
Dentists Insurance Co 1201 K St 17th Fl Web: www.thedentists.com	Sacramento	CA	95814	916-443-4501	498-6162
Doctors' Co The 185 Greenwood Rd TF: 800-421-2368 ■ Web: www.thedoctors.com	Napa	CA	94558	707-226-0100	226-0165
Euler Hermes ACI 800 Red Brook Blvd 4th Fl TF: 877-883-3224	Owings Mills	MD	21117	410-753-0753	554-0883
Everest Reinsurance Co 477 Martinsville Rd TF: 800-269-6660 ■ Web: www.everestregroup.com	Liberty Corner	NJ	07938	908-604-3000	604-3450
Everhart JP & Co 1840 N Greenville Ave Suite 178 Web: www.texasnotaryonline.com	Richardson	TX	75081	972-808-9001	808-9012
Federated Mutual Insurance Co PO Box 328 TF: 800-533-0472 ■ Web: www.federatedinsurance.com	Owatonna	MN	55060	507-455-5200	455-7808
Financial Guaranty Insurance Co 125 Park Ave 6th Fl TF: 800-352-0001 ■ Web: www.fgic.com	New York	NY	10017	212-312-3000	312-3231
Financial Security Assurance Inc 31 W 52nd St 28th Fl TF: 800-846-4372 ■ Web: www.fsa.com	New York	NY	10019	212-826-0100	339-3575
Fireman's Fund Insurance Co 777 San Marin Dr *Fax: Mail Rm ■ TF: 800-227-1700 ■ Web: www.the-fund.com	Novato	CA	94998	415-899-2000	899-3600*
First Insurance Co of Hawaii Ltd 1100 Ward Ave PO Box 2866 TF: 800-272-5202 ■ Web: www.ficoh.com	Honolulu	HI	96803	808-527-7777	527-3200
First National Insurance Co of America 4333 Brooklyn Ave NE Safeco Plaza TF: 800-332-3226	Seattle	WA	98185	206-545-5000	545-5651
First Professionals Insurance Co 1000 Riverside Ave Suite 800 TF: 800-741-3742 ■ Web: www.fpicmedmal.com	Jacksonville	FL	32204	904-354-5910	358-6728
Frontier Insurance Group Inc 146 Rock Hill Dr *Fax: Mktg ■ Web: www.frontier.com	Rock Hill	NY	12775	845-794-3600	796-1906*
Genworth Financial Inc 6620 W Broad St NYSE: GNW ■ TF: 888-436-9678 ■ Web: www.genworth.com	Richmond	VA	23230	804-484-3821	484-7198
Genworth Mortgage Insurance Corp 6601 Six Forks Rd TF: 800-334-9270 ■ Web: www.ge-mi.com	Raleigh	NC	27615	919-846-4100	846-4434
Great American Insurance Co 580 Walnut St Web: www.greatamericaninsurance.com	Cincinnati	OH	45202	513-369-5000	
Hartford Accident & Indemnity Co Hartford Plaza Web: www.thehartford.com	Hartford	CT	06115	860-547-5000	547-5392
Hartford Fire Insurance Co Hartford Plaza *Fax: Hum Res ■ Web: www.thehartford.com	Hartford	CT	06115	860-547-5000	547-2680*
Hartford Underwriters Insurance Co Hartford Plaza *Fax: Hum Res ■ Web: www.thehartford.com	Hartford	CT	06115	860-547-5000	547-2680*
Heritage Insurance Managers Inc PO Box 659570 TF: 800-456-7480 ■ Web: www.heritage-ins.com	San Antonio	TX	78265	210-829-7467	822-4113
Illinois State Medical Inter-Insurance Exchange (ISMIE) 20 N Michigan Ave Suite 700 TF: 800-782-4767 ■ Web: www.ismie.com	Chicago	IL	60602	312-782-2749	782-2023
Indemnity Co of California 17780 Fitch Suite 200 TF: 800-782-1546 ■ Web: www.inscodico.com	Irvine	CA	92614	949-263-3300	553-8149
Insco Dico Group 17780 Fitch Suite 200 TF: 800-782-1546 ■ Web: www.inscodico.com	Irvine	CA	92614	949-263-3300	553-8149

	City	State	Zip	Phone	Fax
Insurance Co of the West 11455 El Camino Real *TF:* 800-877-1111 ■ *Web:* www.icwgroup.com	San Diego	CA	92130	858-350-2400	350-2616
International Fidelity Insurance Co 1 Newark Center 20th Fl **Fax:* Mktg ■ *TF:* 800-333-4167 ■ *Web:* www.ific.com	Newark	NJ	07102	973-624-7200	624-9048*
Investors Heritage Life Insurance Co 200 Capital Ave *TF:* 800-422-2011 ■ *Web:* www.investorsheritage.com	Frankfort	KY	40602	502-223-2361	875-7084
ISMIE (Illinois State Medical Inter-Insurance Exchange) 20 N Michigan Ave Suite 700 *TF:* 800-782-4767 ■ *Web:* www.ismie.com	Chicago	IL	60602	312-782-2749	782-2023
JP Everhart & Co 1840 N Greenville Ave Suite 178 *Web:* www.texasnotaryonline.com	Richardson	TX	75081	972-808-9001	808-9012
KaMMCO (Kansas Medical Mutual Insurance Co) 623 SW 10th Ave Suite 200 *TF:* 800-232-2259 ■ *Web:* www.kammco-msc.com	Topeka	KS	66612	785-232-2224	232-4704
Kansas Bankers Surety Co PO Box 1654	Topeka	KS	66601	785-228-0000	228-0079
Kansas Medical Mutual Insurance Co (KaMMCO) 623 SW 10th Ave Suite 200 *TF:* 800-232-2259 ■ *Web:* www.kammco-msc.com	Topeka	KS	66612	785-232-2224	232-4704
Lexington Insurance Co Inc 100 Summer St *TF:* 800-355-4891 ■ *Web:* www.lexingtoninsurance.com	Boston	MA	02110	617-330-1100	355-4891
Life of the South Insurance Co 100 W Bay St *TF:* 800-888-2738 ■ *Web:* www.life-south.com	Jacksonville	FL	32202	904-350-9660	354-4525
Louisiana Medical Mutual Insurance Co 1 Galleria Blvd Suite 700 *TF:* 800-452-2120 ■ *Web:* www.lammico.com	Metairie	LA	70001	504-831-3756	841-5300
Markel Insurance Co 4600 Cox Rd *TF:* 800-431-1270 ■ *Web:* www.horseinsurance.com	Glen Allen	VA	23060	804-527-2700	527-7999
MBIA Insurance Corp 113 King St *TF:* 800-765-6242 ■ *Web:* www.mbia.com	Armonk	NY	10504	914-273-4545	765-3163
Media/Professional Insurance Inc 2300 Main St Suite 800 *TF:* 866-282-0565 ■ *Web:* www.mediaprof.com	Kansas City	MO	64108	816-471-6118	471-6119
Medical Assurance 20 Allen Ave Suite 420	Saint Louis	MO	63119	314-961-7700	918-0530
Medical Assurance Inc 100 Brookwood Pl Suite 300 *TF:* 800-282-6242 ■ *Web:* www.proassurance.com	Birmingham	AL	35209	205-877-4400	802-4799
Medical Liability Mutual Insurance Co (MLMIC) 2 Park Ave 25th Fl *TF:* 800-275-6564 ■ *Web:* www.mlmic.com	New York	NY	10016	212-576-9800	725-0916
Medical Mutual Insurance Co of Maine PO Box 15275 *TF:* 800-942-2791 ■ *Web:* www.medicalmutual.com	Portland	ME	04112	207-775-2791	775-6576
Medical Mutual Liability Insurance Society of Maryland 225 International Cir *TF:* 800-492-0193	Hunt Valley	MD	21030	410-785-0050	785-2631
Medical Protective Co PO Box 15017 **Fax Area Code:* 800 ■ *TF:* 800-463-3776 ■ *Web:* www.medicalprotective.com	Fort Wayne	IN	46885	260-485-9622	398-6726*
MIIX Insurance Cos 102 Front St PO Box 39	Riverside	NJ	08075	866-670-6449	
Monumental General Insurance Co 520 Park Ave *TF:* 800-638-3080	Baltimore	MD	21201	410-685-5500	209-5914
Mortgage Guaranty Insurance Corp 270 E Kilbourn Ave *TF:* 800-558-9900 ■ *Web:* www.mgic.com	Milwaukee	WI	53202	414-347-6480	347-6696
National Union Fire Insurance Co of Pittsburgh Pennsylvania 70 Pine St **Fax:* Mail Rm	New York	NY	10270	212-770-7000	943-1125*
NCMIC Insurance Co 14001 University Ave **Fax Area Code:* 800 ■ *TF:* 800-769-2000 ■ *Web:* www.ncmic.com	Clive	IA	50325	515-313-4500	996-2642*
NCRIC Inc 1115 30th St NW *TF:* 800-613-3615 ■ *Web:* www.ncric.com	Washington	DC	20007	202-969-1866	969-1881
Nobel Insurance 12225 Greenville Ave Suite 750 *TF:* 800-766-6235 ■ *Web:* www.nobelinsurance.com	Dallas	TX	75243	972-644-0434	644-0424
Norcal Mutual Insurance Co Inc 560 Davis St *TF:* 800-652-1051 ■ *Web:* www.norcalmutual.com	San Francisco	CA	94111	415-397-9700	835-0800
Northwest Physicians Mutual Insurance Co 2965 Ryan Dr SE *TF:* 800-243-3503 ■ *Web:* www.npmic.com	Salem	OR	97301	503-371-8228	371-0087
OHIC Insurance Co 155 E Broad St 4th Fl *TF:* 800-666-6442 ■ *Web:* www.ohic.com	Columbus	OH	43215	614-221-7777	461-1120
Oklahoma Surety Co 1437 S Boulder Ave Suite 200 *TF:* 800-722-4994	Tulsa	OK	74119	918-587-7221	588-1298
Old Republic Insured Automotive Services Inc 8282 S Memorial Dr **Fax Area Code:* 800 ■ *TF:* 800-331-4065 ■ *Web:* www.orias.com	Tulsa	OK	74133	918-307-1000	874-9559*
Old Republic Surety 445 S Moorlands Rd Suite 301 *TF:* 800-217-1792 ■ *Web:* www.orsurety.com	Brookfield	WI	53005	262-797-2640	797-9495
Pekin Life Insurance Co 2505 Court St *TF:* 800-322-0160 ■ *Web:* www.pekininsurance.com	Pekin	IL	61558	309-346-1161	346-8512
Penn National Insurance Co 2 N 2nd St Penn National Plaza *TF:* 800-388-4764 ■ *Web:* www.pennnationalinsurance.com	Harrisburg	PA	17101	717-234-4941	255-6850
Pennsylvania Medical Society Liability Insurance Co PO Box 2080 *TF:* 800-445-1212 ■ *Web:* www.pmslic.com	Mechanicsburg	PA	17055	717-791-1212	796-8080
Pharmacists Mutual Insurance Co 808 US Hwy 18 W PO Box 370 *TF:* 800-247-5930 ■ *Web:* www.pharmacistsmutual.com	Algona	IA	50511	515-295-2461	295-9306
Physicians' Reciprocal Insurers 111 E Shore Rd PO Box 4300 *TF:* 800-632-6040 ■ *Web:* www.primedmal.com	Manhasset	NY	11030	516-365-6690	365-7522
PMI Mortgage Insurance Co 3003 Oak Rd *TF:* 800-288-1970 ■ *Web:* www.pmigroup.com	Walnut Creek	CA	94597	925-658-7878	658-6940
Podiatry Insurance Co of America DBA PICA Group 110 Westwood Pl Suite 100 *TF:* 866-742-2477 ■ *Web:* www.picagroup.com	Brentwood	TN	37027	615-371-8776	846-9486
Pre-Paid Legal Services Inc 1 Pre-Paid Way *NYSE:* PPD ■ **Fax:* Cust Svc ■ *TF:* 800-654-7757 ■ *Web:* www.prepaidlegal.com	Ada	OK	74820	580-436-1234	436-7565*
Princeton Insurance Cos 746 Alexander Rd **Fax Area Code:* 609 ■ *TF:* 800-433-0157 ■ *Web:* www.princetoninsurance.com	Princeton	NJ	08540	800-334-0588	734-8461*
Pro Insurance Co 2600 Professionals Dr *TF:* 800-292-1036 ■ *Web:* www.proassurance.com	Okemos	MI	48864	517-349-6500	349-8977
Progressive Casualty Insurance Co 6300 Wilson Mills Rd Campus E *TF:* 800-321-9843 ■ *Web:* www1.progressive.com	Mayfield Village	OH	44143	440-461-5000	446-5372
ProMutual Group 101 Arch St 4th Fl *TF:* 800-225-6168 ■ *Web:* www.promutualgroup.com	Boston	MA	02110	617-330-1755	330-1748
Protective Insurance Co 1099 N Meridian St Suite 700 *TF:* 800-231-6024 ■ *Web:* www.baldwinandlyons.com	Indianapolis	IN	46204	317-636-9800	632-9444
Radian Asset Assurance Inc 335 Madison Ave 25th Fl *TF:* 877-337-4925 ■ *Web:* www.radiangroupinc.com	New York	NY	10017	212-983-3100	682-5377
Radian Group Inc 1601 Market St *NYSE:* RDN ■ **Fax Area Code:* 888 ■ *TF:* 800-523-1988 ■ *Web:* www.radiangroupinc.com	Philadelphia	PA	19103	215-564-6600	262-2329*
Radian Guaranty Inc 1601 Market St **Fax Area Code:* 888 ■ *TF:* 800-523-1988 ■ *Web:* www.radiangroupinc.com	Philadelphia	PA	19103	215-564-6600	262-2329*
Radian Reinsurance Inc 335 Madison Ave 25th Fl *Web:* www.radiangroupinc.com	New York	NY	10017	212-983-3100	682-5377
Ranger Insurance Co 10777 Westheimer Rd Suite 500 **Fax:* Mktg ■ *TF:* 800-392-1970 ■ *Web:* www.rangerinsurance.com	Houston	TX	77042	713-954-8100	954-8301*
Reciprocal of America 4200 Innslake Dr	Glen Allen	VA	23060	804-747-8600	270-5281
Republic Mortgage Insurance Co 190 Oak Plaza Blvd **Fax:* Hum Res ■ *TF:* 800-999-7642 ■ *Web:* www.rmic.com	Winston-Salem	NC	27105	336-661-0015	661-3275*
RLI Insurance Co 9025 N Lindbergh Dr *TF:* 800-331-4929 ■ *Web:* www.rlicorp.com	Peoria	IL	61615	309-692-1000	692-1068
SAFECO Surety 1001 4th Ave Suite 1700 **Fax Area Code:* 425 ■ *Web:* www.safeco.com/surety/default.asp	Seattle	WA	98154	206-473-3799	376-6533*
Schinnerer Victor O & Co Inc 2 Wisconsin Cir Suite 1100 *TF:* 888-867-9327 ■ *Web:* www.schinnerer.com	Chevy Chase	MD	20815	301-961-9800	951-5444
Scottsdale Insurance Co 8877 N Gainey Ctr Dr *TF:* 800-423-7675 ■ *Web:* www.scottsdaleins.com	Scottsdale	AZ	85258	480-365-4000	483-6752
SCPIE Indemnity Co 1888 Century Pk E Suite 800 **Fax:* Sales ■ *TF Sales:* 800-962-5549 ■ *Web:* www.scpie.com	Los Angeles	CA	90067	310-551-5900	551-5945*
Securities Investors Protection Corp 805 15th St NW Suite 800 *Web:* www.sipc.org	Washington	DC	20005	202-371-8300	371-6728
Shand Morahan & Co Inc 10 Parkway N *Web:* www.shand.com	Deerfield	IL	60015	847-572-6000	572-6137
State Volunteer Mutual Insurance Co 101 W Park Dr Suite 300 *TF:* 800-342-2239 ■ *Web:* www.svmic.com	Brentwood	TN	37027	615-377-1999	370-1343
Surety Group Inc 1900 Emery St NW Suite 120 *TF:* 800-486-8211 ■ *Web:* www.suretygroup.com	Atlanta	GA	30318	404-352-8211	351-3237
Surety Specialists 4311 W Waters Ave Suite 401	Tampa	FL	33614	813-885-2112	594-3323
Texas Hospital Insurance Exchange 6300 La Calma Dr Suite 550 *TF:* 800-792-0060 ■ *Web:* www.thainsurance.com	Austin	TX	78752	512-451-5775	451-3101
Texas Lawyers Insurance Exchange 900 Congress Ave Suite 500 *Web:* www.tlie.org	Austin	TX	78701	512-480-9074	482-8738
Transatlantic Reinsurance Co 80 Pine St 9th Fl *Web:* www.transre.com	New York	NY	10005	212-770-2000	269-6801
Travelers Indemnity Co 1 Tower Sq **Fax:* Hum Res ■ *Web:* www.travelers.com	Hartford	CT	06183	860-277-0111	277-1970*
Triad Guaranty Insurance Corp 101 S Stratford Rd *TF Cust Svc:* 888-691-8074 ■ *Web:* www.tgic.com	Winston-Salem	NC	27104	336-723-1282	723-2824
Tudor Insurance Co 400 Parson's Pond Dr	Franklin Lakes	NJ	07417	201-847-8600	847-1010
ULLICO Casualty Co 1625 Eye St NW *TF:* 800-431-5425 ■ *Web:* www.ullico.com	Washington	DC	20006	202-682-0900	682-4911
United Guaranty Corp 230 N Elm St **Fax:* Hum Res ■ *TF:* 800-334-8966 ■ *Web:* www.ugcorp.com	Greensboro	NC	27401	336-373-0232	230-1946*
United National Group 3 Bala Plaza E Suite 300 *TF:* 800-333-0352 ■ *Web:* www.unitednat.com	Bala Cynwyd	PA	19004	610-664-1500	660-8882
Universal Insurance Co PO Box 71338 **Fax:* Claims	San Juan	PR	00936	787-793-7202	792-4788*
Universal Surety of America 5151 San Felipe Ave Suite 1800 *TF:* 888-736-9704 ■ *Web:* www.universalsurety.com	Houston	TX	77056	713-513-6300	513-6296
US Liability Insurance Group 190 S Warner Rd *TF:* 800-523-5545 ■ *Web:* www.usli.com	Wayne	PA	19087	610-688-2535	688-4391
Utica National Insurance Group 180 Genesee St *TF:* 800-274-1914 ■ *Web:* www.uticanational.com	New Hartford	NY	13413	315-734-2000	734-2680
Victor O Schinnerer & Co Inc 2 Wisconsin Cir Suite 1100 *TF:* 888-867-9327 ■ *Web:* www.schinnerer.com	Chevy Chase	MD	20815	301-961-9800	951-5444
Western World Insurance Co 400 Parson's Pond Dr *Web:* www.westernworld.com	Franklin Lakes	NJ	07417	201-847-8600	847-1010
Western World Insurance Group Inc 400 Parson's Pond Dr *Web:* www.westernworld.com	Franklin Lakes	NJ	07417	201-847-8600	847-1010
XL Specialty Insurance Co 20 N Martingale Rd Suite 200 *TF:* 800-394-3909	Schaumburg	IL	60173	847-517-2990	517-5240
Zurich North America 1400 American Ln **Fax Area Code:* 877 ■ **Fax:* Claims ■ *TF:* 800-382-2150 ■ *Web:* www.zurichna.com	Schaumburg	IL	60196	847-605-6000	962-2567*

394-6 Title Insurance

Most title insurance companies also provide other real estate services such as escrow, flood certification, appraisals, etc.

	City	State	Zip	Phone	Fax
Alamo Title Insurance 601 Riverside Ave *TF:* 800-292-5320 ■ *Web:* www.alamotitle.com	Jacksonville	FL	32204	904-854-8100	
AmeriPoint Title Inc 10101 Reunion Pl Suite 250 *Web:* www.ameripointtitle.com	San Antonio	TX	78216	210-340-2921	340-9640
Attorney's Title Insurance Fund Inc 6545 Corporate Ctr Blvd *TF:* 800-336-3863 ■ *Web:* www.thefund.com	Orlando	FL	32822	407-240-3863	240-1106
Capital Title Group Inc 14648 N Scottsdale Rd Suite 125 *NASDAQ:* CTGI ■ *Web:* www.capitaltitlegroup.com	Scottsdale	AZ	85254	480-624-4200	624-4201
Centex Corp Title Insurance & Escrow Operations 2728 N Harwood St	Dallas	TX	75201	214-981-5000	981-6840
Chicago Title Insurance Co 171 N Clark St **Fax:* Hum Res ■ *TF:* 800-621-1919 ■ *Web:* www.cmetro.ctic.com	Chicago	IL	60601	312-223-2000	223-5678*
Chicago Title Insurance Co of Oregon 10135 SE Sunnyside Rd Suite 130 *Web:* www.portland.ctic.com	Clackamas	OR	97015	503-653-7300	595-7924
Chicago Title & Trust Co 171 N Clark St **Fax:* Hum Res ■ *TF:* 800-621-1919 ■ *Web:* www.ctic.com	Chicago	IL	60601	312-223-2000	223-5627*
Commerce Title Co 1461 E Cooley Dr Suite 280 *TF:* 800-244-4322 ■ *Web:* www.commercetitlecompany.com	Colton	CA	92324	909-430-3218	433-0816
Commonwealth Land Title Insurance Co 101 Gateway Center Pkwy Gateway 1 **Fax:* Hum Res ■ *TF:* 800-388-8822 ■ *Web:* www.cltic.com	Richmond	VA	23235	804-267-8000	267-8836*
Community Title & Escrow Ltd 2600 State St Bldg D *TF:* 800-854-4049 ■ *Web:* www.communitytitle.net	Alton	IL	62002	618-466-7755	466-7782
Dakota Homestead Title Insurance Co 315 S Phillips Ave *TF:* 800-425-0388 ■ *Web:* www.dakotahomestead.com	Sioux Falls	SD	57104	605-336-0388	336-5649
Diversified Title & Escrow Services Co 222 S Harbor Blvd 8th Fl *TF:* 800-266-9488 ■ *Web:* www.todiversified.com	Anaheim	CA	92805	714-999-1800	999-1896
Fidelity National Title Group Inc 601 Riverside Ave *NYSE:* FNT ■ *TF:* 888-934-3354 ■ *Web:* www.fntg.com	Jacksonville	FL	32204	904-854-8100	357-1007
Fidelity National Title Insurance Co 10010 San Pedro Blvd Suite 700 *Web:* www.fntic.com	San Antonio	TX	78216	210-340-0456	336-2460
Fidelity National Title Insurance Co of Oregon 1001 SW 5th Ave *Web:* www.fntic.com	Portland	OR	97204	503-223-8338	796-6611
First American Corp 1 First American Way *NYSE:* FAF ■ *TF:* 800-854-3643 ■ *Web:* www.firstam.com	Santa Ana	CA	92707	714-558-3211	800-3135
First American Title Co of Los Angeles 520 N Central Ave **Fax:* Hum Res ■ *TF:* 800-328-2652 ■ *Web:* www.fatcola.com	Glendale	CA	91203	818-242-5800	242-0196*
First American Title Insurance Co 2 First American Way *TF:* 800-854-3643 ■ *Web:* www.firstam.com	Santa Ana	CA	92707	714-558-3211	800-4762
First American Title Insurance Co of Oregon 222 SW Columbia St Suite 400 *TF:* 800-929-3651 ■ *Web:* www.firstam.com/tri-counties	Portland	OR	97201	503-222-3651	790-1805
First American Title Insurance Co of Texas 1500 S Dairy Ashford St Suite 300 **Fax:* Hum Res ■ *TF:* 800-347-7826	Houston	TX	77077	281-588-2200	588-2236*
Gateway Title Co 1405 N San Fernando Blvd **Fax Area Code:* 800 ■ *TF:* 800-660-6992 ■ *Web:* www.gtc1.com	Burbank	CA	91504	818-953-2300	953-2377*

Title Insurance (Cont'd)

Company	City	State	Zip	Phone	Fax
Gracy Title Co 524 N Lamar Blvd Suite 200 *Web:* www.gracytitle.com	Austin	TX	78703	512-472-8421	478-6038
Greater Illinois Title Co 120 N La Salle St Suite900 *Web:* www.gitc.com	Chicago	IL	60602	312-236-7300	236-0284
Hanover Insurance Co 440 Lincoln St *TF:* 800-853-0456 ■ *Web:* www.hanover.com	Worcester	MA	01653	508-855-1000	853-6332
Investors Title Insurance Co 121 N Columbia St **Fax Area Code:* 800 ■ **Fax:* Claims ■ *TF:* 800-326-4842 ■ *Web:* www.invtitle.com	Chapel Hill	NC	27514	919-968-2200	690-6105*
Landamerica Lawyer's Title Insurance Corp 1555 E McAndrews Rd Suite 100	Medford	OR	97504	541-779-2811	772-6079
LandAmerica OneStop Inc 600 Clubhouse Dr **Fax Area Code:* 866 ■ *TF:* 866-226-8616 ■ *Web:* www.landam.com	Moon Township	PA	15108	412-507-2000	296-0095*
Lawyers Title Co 251 S Lake Ave Suite 400 *TF:* 800-347-7800	Pasadena	CA	91101	626-304-2700	795-0875
Lawyers Title Insurance Corp 101 Gateway Center Pkwy **Fax:* Hum Res ■ *TF:* 800-446-7086	Richmond	VA	23235	804-267-8000	267-8836*
Mississippi Valley Title Insurance Co 315 Tom Bigbee St *TF:* 800-647-2124 ■ *Web:* www.mvt.com	Jackson	MS	39201	601-969-0222	969-2215
Monroe Title Insurance Corp 47 W Main St *TF:* 800-966-6763 ■ *Web:* www.monroetitle.com	Rochester	NY	14614	585-232-4950	232-4988
North American Title Co 2185 N California Blvd Suite 575 *TF:* 800-869-3434 ■ *Web:* www.nat.com/nationalsite/default.asp	Walnut Creek	CA	94596	925-935-5599	933-4851
Ohio Bar Title Insurance Co 341 S 3rd St Suite 100 *TF:* 800-628-4853 ■ *Web:* www.ohiobartitle.com	Columbus	OH	43215	614-242-4300	242-4310
Old Republic National Title Insurance Co 400 2nd Ave S *TF:* 800-328-4441 ■ *Web:* www.oldrepnatl.com	Minneapolis	MN	55401	612-371-1111	371-1129
Old Republic Title Co 475 Sansome St Suite 1700 *Web:* www.ortc.com	San Francisco	CA	94111	415-421-3500	
Pacific Northwest Title Co of Washington Inc 215 Columbia St *TF:* 800-634-5544 ■ *Web:* www.pnwt.com	Seattle	WA	98104	206-622-1040	343-1334
Placer Title Co 455 Watt Ave *Web:* www.placertitle.com	Sacramento	CA	95864	916-973-1002	482-3049
Southland Title Co 7530 N Glenoaks Blvd *TF:* 800-747-7777 ■ *Web:* www.southlandtitle.com	Burbank	CA	91504	818-767-2000	768-5250
Stewart Information Services Corp 1980 Post Oak Blvd Suite 800 *NYSE:* STC ■ *TF:* 800-729-1900 ■ *Web:* www.stewart.com	Houston	TX	77056	713-625-8100	552-9523
Stewart REI Data Inc 1980 Post Oak Blvd Suite 800 **Fax Area Code:* 630 ■ *TF:* 888-534-4461 ■ *Web:* www.stewart.com	Houston	TX	77056	800-783-9278	705-9377*
Stewart Title Co 1980 Post Oak Blvd Suite 800 *TF:* 800-729-1900 ■ *Web:* www.stewart.com	Houston	TX	77056	713-625-8100	552-9523
Stewart Title Guaranty Co 1980 Post Oak Blvd Suite 800 *TF:* 800-729-1900 ■ *Web:* www.stewart.com	Houston	TX	77056	713-625-8100	552-9523
Stewart Title & Trust of Phoenix 244 W Osborn Rd **Fax:* Cust Svc ■ *Web:* www.stewartaz.com	Phoenix	AZ	85013	602-248-8444	241-7542*
Ticor Title Agency Co of Arizona 3131 E Camelback Rd Suite 220 *Web:* www.thenewticor.com	Phoenix	AZ	85016	602-200-6300	331-9001
Ticor Title Insurance Co 203 N LaSalle St Suite 2200 *TF:* 800-879-1167 ■ *Web:* www.ticortitle.com	Chicago	IL	60601	312-621-5000	621-5123
Title Guaranty of Hawaii Inc 235 Queen St *TF:* 800-548-2429 ■ *Web:* www.tghawaii.com	Honolulu	HI	96813	808-533-6261	532-3162
Title Resources Guaranty Co 8111 LBJ Fwy Suite 1200 *TF:* 800-526-8018 ■ *Web:* www.trgc.com	Dallas	TX	75251	972-644-6500	644-8141
Transnation Title Insurance Co 101 Gateway Ctr Pkwy Gateway 1 **Fax:* Hum Res ■ *TF:* 800-388-8822	Richmond	VA	23205	804-267-8000	267-8836*

394-7 Travel Insurance

Most of the companies listed here are insurance agencies and brokerages that specialize in selling travel insurance policies, rather than the insurers who underwrite the policies.

Company	City	State	Zip	Phone	Fax
Access America 2805 N Parham Rd *TF:* 800-729-6021 ■ *Web:* www.accessamerica.com	Richmond	VA	23294	804-285-3300	673-1586
All Aboard Benefits 6162 E Mockingird Ln Suite 104 *TF:* 800-462-2322 ■ *Web:* www.allaboardbenefits.com	Dallas	TX	75214	214-821-6677	821-6676
Continental Assurance Co 333 S Wabash Ave *TF:* 800-262-2000 ■ *Web:* www.cna.com	Chicago	IL	60604	312-822-5000	822-6419
CSA Travel Protection 5454 Ruffin Rd **Fax Area Code:* 800 ■ *TF:* 800-873-9855 ■ *Web:* www.csatravelprotection.com	San Diego	CA	92123	858-810-2000	336-6409*
Highway To Health Inc 1 Radnor Corporate Ctr Suite 100 *TF:* 888-243-2358 ■ *Web:* www.highwaytohealth.com	Radnor	PA	19087	610-254-8700	293-3529
Ingle International 460 Richmond St W Suite 701 *TF:* 800-360-3234 ■ *Web:* www.ingle-health.com	Toronto	ON	M5V1Y1	416-730-8488	730-1878
Insurance Co of the State of Pennsylvania 70 Pine St	New York	NY	10270	212-770-7000	
Insurance Consultants International 7405 Campstool Dr Suite 101 *TF:* 800-576-2674 ■ *Web:* www.globalhealthinsurance.com	Colorado Springs	CO	80922	719-573-9080	
International SOS Assistance Inc 3600 Horizon Blvd Suite 300 *TF:* 800-523-8930 ■ *Web:* www.internationalsos.com	Trevose	PA	19053	215-244-1500	942-8298
Lloyd's America Inc 25 W 53rd St 14th Fl *Web:* www.lloyds.com	New York	NY	10036	212-382-4060	382-4070
Pan-American Life Insurance Co 601 Poydras St *TF Life Ins:* 877-939-4550 ■ *Web:* www.panamericanlife.com	New Orleans	LA	70130	504-566-1300	566-3381
Travel Guard International 1145 Clark St **Fax Area Code:* 800 ■ *TF:* 800-826-1300 ■ *Web:* www.travelguard.com	Stevens Point	WI	54481	715-345-0505	955-8785*
Travel Insured International 52-S Oakland Ave PO Box 280568 *TF:* 800-243-3174 ■ *Web:* www.travelinsured.com	East Hartford	CT	06128	860-528-7663	528-8005
Travelex Insurance Services Inc 2121 N 117th Ave Suite 300 **Fax Area Code:* 800 ■ *TF:* 888-457-4602 ■ *Web:* www.travelex-insurance.com	Omaha	NE	68164	402-491-3200	867-9531*
Virginia Risk Co 9200 Keystone Crossing Suite 300 **Fax:* Claims ■ *TF:* 800-523-6944 ■ *Web:* www.virginiarisk.com	Indianapolis	IN	46240	317-818-2089	575-2659*
Wallach & Co Inc 107 W Federal St *TF:* 800-237-6615 ■ *Web:* www.wallach.com	Middleburg	VA	20117	540-687-3166	687-3172
World Access Inc 2805 N Parham Rd *TF:* 800-628-4908 ■ *Web:* www.worldaccess.com	Richmond	VA	23294	804-285-3300	673-1586

395 INTERCOM EQUIPMENT & SYSTEMS

Company	City	State	Zip	Phone	Fax
Anacom General Corp DBA Anacom-Medtek 1240 S Claudina St **Fax:* Sales ■ *TF:* 800-955-9540 ■ *Web:* www.anacom-medtek.com	Anaheim	CA	92805	714-774-8484	774-7388*
Clear-Com USA 850 Marina Village Pkwy *Web:* clearcom.com	Alameda	CA	94501	510-337-6600	
Clever Devices Ltd 137 Commercial St *TF:* 800-872-6129 ■ *Web:* www.cleverdevices.com	Plainview	NY	11803	516-433-6100	433-5088
Crest Healthcare Supply 195 S 3rd St *TF Cust Svc:* 800-328-8908 ■ *Web:* www.cresthealthcare.com	Dassel	MN	55325	320-275-3382	275-2306
David Clark Co Inc 360 Franklin St **Fax:* Sales ■ *TF Cust Svc:* 800-298-6235 ■ *Web:* www.davidclark.com	Worcester	MA	01615	508-751-5800	753-5827*
Lee Dan Communications Inc 155 Adams Ave *TF:* 800-231-1414 ■ *Web:* www.leedan.com	Hauppauge	NY	11788	631-231-1414	231-1498
Rauland-Borg Corp 3450 W Oakton St *TF:* 800-621-0087 ■ *Web:* www.rauland.com	Skokie	IL	60076	847-679-0900	679-1025

396 INTERIOR DESIGN

Company	City	State	Zip	Phone	Fax
Atlanta Architectural Textile 737 Miami Cir NE *TF:* 800-241-0178 ■ *Web:* www.curran-aat.com	Atlanta	GA	30324	404-237-4246	261-5141
Chambers H Co 1010 N Charles St	Baltimore	MD	21201	410-727-4535	727-6982
Cole Martinez Curtis & Assoc 4132A Del Rey Ave *Web:* www.cmcadesign.com	Marina del Rey	CA	90292	310-827-7200	822-5803
Curran Assoc 737 Miami Cir NE *TF:* 800-241-0178 ■ *Web:* www.curran-aat.com	Atlanta	GA	30324	404-237-4246	261-5141
Decor & You Inc 900 Main St South Bldg 2 *TF:* 800-477-3326 ■ *Web:* www.decorandyou.com	Southbury	CT	06488	203-264-3500	264-5095
Decorating Den Systems Inc DBA Interiors By Decorating Den 8659 Commerce Dr *TF:* 800-332-3367 ■ *Web:* www.decoratingden.com	Easton	MD	21601	410-822-9001	
Freeman Decorating Co 8801 Ambassador Row	Dallas	TX	75247	214-634-1463	634-2221
Gary Raub Assoc PO Box 26835	San Diego	CA	92196	858-565-2775	565-9035
H Chambers Co 1010 N Charles St	Baltimore	MD	21201	410-727-4535	727-6982
Hubbuch & Co 324 W Main St *Web:* www.hubbuch.com	Louisville	KY	40202	502-583-2713	582-7375
Interior Space International (ISI) 600 W Fulton St *Web:* www.epstein-isi.com	Chicago	IL	60661	312-454-9100	559-1217
Interiors By Decorating Den 8659 Commerce Dr *TF:* 800-332-3367 ■ *Web:* www.decoratingden.com	Easton	MD	21601	410-822-9001	
Kagan Vladimir Design Group 1185 Park Ave Suite 14G *Web:* www.vladimirkagan.com	New York	NY	10128	212-289-0031	360-7307
MGM Mirage Design Group Inc 3260 Industrial Rd *TF:* 800-477-5110	Las Vegas	NV	89109	702-792-4600	792-4790
Miller/Zell Inc 4715 Frederick Dr SW *Web:* www.millerzell.com	Atlanta	GA	30336	404-691-7400	699-2189
Omnifics Inc 5845 Richmond Hwy Suite 300 *Web:* www.omnifics.com	Alexandria	VA	22303	703-548-4040	
Peninsula Business Interiors Inc 4057 W Shaw Ave Suite 102 *Web:* www.pbioffice.com	Fresno	CA	93722	559-275-4111	275-0101
Raub Gary Assoc PO Box 26835	San Diego	CA	92196	858-565-2775	565-9035
TriMark Raygal 2719 White Rd *Web:* www.trimarkusa.com	Irvine	CA	92614	949-474-1000	474-7298
TriMark USA Inc 505 Collins St *TF:* 800-755-5580 ■ *Web:* www.trimarkusa.com	South Attleboro	MA	02703	508-399-2400	761-3600
Villa Lighting Supply Inc 1218 S Vandeventer Ave *TF:* 800-325-0963 ■ *Web:* www.villalighting.com	Saint Louis	MO	63110	314-531-2600	531-8720
Vladimir Kagan Design Group 1185 Park Ave Suite 14G *Web:* www.vladimirkagan.com	New York	NY	10128	212-289-0031	360-7307
Wilson Office Interiors 1540 Champion Dr *Web:* www.wilsonoi.com	Carrollton	TX	75006	972-488-4100	488-8815

397 INTERNET BACKBONE PROVIDERS

Companies that are, in effect, Internet service providers for Internet Service Providers (ISPs).

Company	City	State	Zip	Phone	Fax
AboveNet Communications Inc 360 Hamilton Ave *TF:* 866-859-6971 ■ *Web:* www.abovenet.com	White Plains	NY	10601	914-421-6700	421-6777
BT Infonet 2160 E Grand Ave *TF:* 877-325-2876 ■ *Web:* www.bt.infonet.com	El Segundo	CA	90245	310-335-2600	335-4507
Cogent Communications Group Inc 1015 31st St NW *NASDAQ:* CCOI ■ *TF:* 877-875-4432 ■ *Web:* www.cogentco.com	Washington	DC	20007	202-295-4200	338-8798
Global Crossing Ltd 200 Park Ave Suite 300 *NASDAQ:* GLBC ■ *Web:* www.globalcrossing.com	Florham Park	NJ	07932	973-410-8300	360-0148
IDT Corp 520 Broad St *NYSE:* IDT ■ *TF:* 800-225-5438 ■ *Web:* www.idt.net	Newark	NJ	07102	973-438-1000	438-1453
iPass Inc 3800 Bridge Pkwy *NASDAQ:* IPAS ■ *TF:* 877-674-7277 ■ *Web:* www.ipass.com	Redwood Shores	CA	94065	650-232-4100	232-4111
Level 3 Communications Inc 1025 Eldorado Blvd *NASDAQ:* LVLT ■ *TF:* 877-453-8353 ■ *Web:* www.level3.com	Broomfield	CO	80021	720-888-1000	
Megapath Inc 555 Anton Blvd *TF:* 888-443-7624 ■ *Web:* www.megapath.com	Costa Mesa	CA	92626	714-327-2000	327-2001
n|Frame Inc 701 Congressional Blvd Suite 100 *TF:* 888-223-8633 ■ *Web:* www.nframe.com	Carmel	IN	46032	317-805-3759	805-3757
NEON Communications Group Inc 2200 W Park Dr Suite 100 *AMEX:* NGI ■ *TF:* 800-891-5080 ■ *Web:* www.neoninc.com	Westborough	MA	01581	508-616-7800	616-7895
Qwest Communications International Inc 1801 California St *NYSE:* Q ■ *TF:* 800-899-7780 ■ *Web:* www.qwest.com	Denver	CO	80202	303-992-1400	992-1724
SAVVIS Inc 1 SAVVIS Pkwy *NASDAQ:* SVVS ■ *TF:* 800-728-8471 ■ *Web:* www.savvis.net	Town & Country	MO	63017	314-628-7000	
SunGard Availability Services 680 Swedesford Rd **Fax Area Code:* 610 ■ *TF:* 800-468-7483 ■ *Web:* www.availability.sungard.com	Wayne	PA	19087	484-582-2000	225-1120*
Verio Inc 8005 S Chester St Suite 200 *Web:* home.verio.com	Centennial	CO	80112	303-645-1900	792-3869
Verizon Business 1 Verizon Way *TF Cust Svc:* 866-232-4282 ■ *Web:* www.verizonbusiness.com	Basking Ridge	NJ	07920	800-339-9911	
VSNL International Inc 12010 Sunset Hills Rd 4th Fl *TF:* 800-465-8179 ■ *Web:* www.vsnlinternational.com	Reston	VA	20190	703-766-3100	766-3102
XO Communications Inc 11111 Sunset Hills Rd *TF:* 800-900-6398 ■ *Web:* www.xo.com	Reston	VA	20190	703-547-2000	547-2881

398 INTERNET BROADCASTING

Company	City	State	Zip	Phone	Fax
Atom Entertainment Inc 225 Bush St Suite 1200 *Web:* www.atomentertainment.com	San Francisco	CA	94104	415-503-2400	

				Phone	Fax
Audible Inc 65 Willowbrook Blvd 3rd Fl *NASDAQ: ADBL* ■ *TF:* 888-283-5051 ■ *Web:* www.audible.com	Wayne	NJ	07470	973-890-4070	890-2442
FeedRoom 205 Hudson St 8th Fl *Web:* www.feedroom.com	New York	NY	10013	212-219-0343	925-6471
IA Global Inc 550 N Reo St Suite 300 *AMEX: IAO* ■ *Web:* www.iaglobalinc.com	Tampa	FL	33609	813-261-5157	261-5158
IFILM Corp 1024 N Orange Dr *Web:* www.ifilm.com	Hollywood	CA	90038	323-308-3400	308-3595
LAUNCHcast 701 1st Ave *Web:* launch.yahoo.com/launchcast	Sunnyvale	CA	94089	408-349-3300	349-3301
Live365 Inc 950 Tower Ln Suite 400 *Web:* www.live365.com	Foster City	CA	94404	650-345-7400	345-7497
MSN WindowsMedia.com 1 Microsoft Way *Web:* www.windowsmedia.com	Redmond	WA	98052	425-882-8080	936-7329
Musicmatch Jukebox 16935 W Bernardo Dr Suite 270 *Web:* www.musicmatch.com	San Diego	CA	92127	858-485-4300	485-4301
OMT Inc 1555 Dublin Ave Unit 1 *TF:* 888-665-6501 ■ *Web:* www.omt.net	Winnipeg	MB	R3E3M8	204-786-3994	783-5805
ON24 Inc 799 Market St Suite 612 *Web:* www.on24.com	San Francisco	CA	94103	415-369-8000	369-8388
Trailervision Studios 6 Vista Rd *Web:* www.trailervision.com	Bolton West	QC	J0E2T0	450-242-2927	242-2313
WindowsMedia.com 1 Microsoft Way *Web:* www.windowsmedia.com	Redmond	WA	98052	425-882-8080	936-7329
Yahoo! LAUNCH 701 1st Ave *Web:* launch.yahoo.com/launchcast	Sunnyvale	CA	94089	408-349-3300	349-3301

399 INTERNET DOMAIN NAME REGISTRARS

				Phone	Fax
@Com Technology LLC 1353 Pine St Suite E *Web:* www.atcomtechnology.com	Walnut Creek	CA	94596	877-888-4424	
1Accredited 7 Shady Pond *Web:* www.1accredited.com	The Woodlands	TX	77382	936-321-3417	321-5567
4Domains.com 77-670 Springfield Ln Suite 11B *TF:* 877-777-6263 ■ *Web:* www.4domains.com	Palm Desert	CA	92211	760-360-4600	772-3654
123 Registration.com PO Box 2600 *Web:* www.123registration.com	Sarasota	FL	34230	941-954-5770	954-5771
A+Net Internet Services 10350 Barnes Canyon Rd **Fax Area Code:* 650 ■ *TF:* 877-275-8763 ■ *Web:* www.abac.com	San Diego	CA	92121	858-410-6929	475-8478*
Ace of Domains Inc 20 SW 27th Ave Suite 201 *TF:* 800-350-5476 ■ *Web:* www.aceofdomains.com	Pompano Beach	FL	33069	954-984-0923	
AITDomains.com 421 Maiden Ln **Fax Area Code:* 910 ■ *Web:* www.aitdomains.com	Fayetteville	NC	28301	877-549-2881	321-1390*
Alice's Registry Inc 704 Almar Ave *Web:* www.ar.com	Santa Cruz	CA	95060	831-423-8155	423-8255
Alldomains.com 391 N Ancestor Pl Suite 150 *TF:* 800-561-5131 ■ *Web:* www.alldomains.com	Boise	ID	83704	208-685-1888	685-1891
Annulet Inc 600 Preston Forest Suite 362 **Fax Area Code:* 214 ■ *Web:* www.annulet.com	Dallas	TX	75230	800-510-0853	739-6820*
AWRegistry Services 50 W 100 N *Web:* www.awregistry.com	Kamas	UT	84036	801-488-1200	466-1864
Best Registration Services Inc DBA BestRegistrar.com 1418 S 3rd St *TF:* 800-977-3475 ■ *Web:* www.bestregistrar.com	Louisville	KY	40208	502-637-4528	636-9157
BestRegistrar.com 1418 S 3rd St *TF:* 800-977-3475 ■ *Web:* www.bestregistrar.com	Louisville	KY	40208	502-637-4528	636-9157
BulkRegister.com 10 E Baltimore St Suite 1500 *TF:* 800-361-2682 ■ *Web:* www2.bulkregister.com	Baltimore	MD	21202	410-779-1400	
CVO.ca Corp 43 Auriga Dr *Web:* www.cvo.ca	Nepean	ON	K2E7Y8	613-768-5127	820-0777
directNIC 650 Poydras St Suite 1150 *Web:* www.directnic.com	New Orleans	LA	70130	504-679-5170	566-0484
Domain Bank Inc 23 W 4th St *TF:* 888-583-3382 ■ *Web:* www.domainbank.net	Bethlehem	PA	18015	610-317-9606	317-9570
Domain-It! 9525 Kenwood Rd Suite 328 *TF:* 866-927-3624 ■ *Web:* www.domainit.com	Cincinnati	OH	45242	513-351-4222	351-8222
Domain Registration Services DBA dotEarth.com PO Box 447 *Web:* www.dotearth.com	Palmyra	NJ	08065	888-339-9001	
Domainmonger 14128 126th Pl NE *Web:* www.domainmonger.com	Kirkland	WA	98034	425-821-8032	952-0172
DomainName.com PO Box 711 *Web:* domainname.com	Newburyport	MA	01950	978-462-5505	
DomainPeople Inc 550 Burrard St Suite 200 Bentall Tower 5 *TF:* 877-734-3667 ■ *Web:* www.domainpeople.com	Vancouver	BC	V6C2B5	604-639-1680	688-9013
DomainRegistry.com Inc 3554 Hulmeville Rd Suite 108 *Web:* www.domainregistry.com	Bensalem	PA	19020	215-244-6700	244-6605
Domainsatcost.ca 43 Auriga Dr *Web:* www.domainsatcost.ca	Ottawa	ON	K2E7Y8	613-768-5125	820-0777
DomainZoo.com Inc PO Box 36763 *Web:* www.domainzoo.com	Tucson	AZ	85740	520-531-1794	531-1859
dotEarth.com PO Box 447 *Web:* www.dotearth.com	Palmyra	NJ	08065	888-339-9001	
Dotster Inc 11807 NE 99th St Suite 1100 *Web:* www.dotster.com	Vancouver	WA	98682	360-253-2210	253-4234
Dynadot LLC PO Box 1072 **Fax Area Code:* 415 ■ *TF:* 866-652-2039 ■ *Web:* www.dynadot.com	Belmont	CA	94002	650-585-1961	869-2893*
easyDNS 219 Dufferin St Suite 304A *TF:* 888-677-4741 ■ *Web:* www.easydns.com	Toronto	ON	M6K3J1	416-535-8672	535-0237
eNameCo Inc 7 Shady Pond *Web:* www.enameco.com	The Woodlands	TX	77382	936-321-3417	321-5567
EnCirca Inc 400 W Cummings Pk Suite 1725-307 **Fax Area Code:* 781 ■ *Web:* www.encirca.biz	Woburn	MA	01801	800-366-1336	823-8911*
eNom Inc 2002 156th Ave NE Suite 300 *Web:* www.enom.com	Bellevue	WA	98007	425-883-8860	883-3553
Go Daddy Group Inc 14455 N Hayden Rd Suite 219 *Web:* www.godaddy.com	Scottsdale	AZ	85260	480-505-8899	505-8844
iHoldings.com Inc 13205 SW 137th Ave Suite 133 *Web:* www.iholdings.com	Miami	FL	33186	305-971-3440	971-3425
Misk 973 Main St Suite B *Web:* www.misk.com	Fishkill	NY	12524	845-896-4602	510-1878
Mobile Name Services 2002 156th Ave NE Suite 300 *Web:* www.mobilenameservices.com	Bellevue	WA	98007	425-788-9508	274-4519
Moniker Online Services LLC 20 SW 27th Ave Suite 201 *TF:* 800-841-7686 ■ *Web:* www.moniker.com	Pompano Beach	FL	33069	954-984-0923	
Name.com LLC 125 Rampart Way Suite 300 **Fax Area Code:* 303 ■ *Web:* www.name.com	Denver	CO	80230	720-249-2374	364-3646*
Namesbeyond.com 922 S Woodbourne Rd Suite 122 **Fax Area Code:* 215 ■ *TF:* 877-227-8870 ■ *Web:* www.namesbeyond.com	Levittown	PA	19057	267-573-1142	321-1970*
Namesdirect.com Inc 11807 NE 99th St Suite 1100 *Web:* www.namesdirect.com	Vancouver	WA	98682	360-253-2210	253-4234
NameSecure LLC PO Box 27096 *TF:* 800-299-1288 ■ *Web:* www.namesecure.com	Concord	CA	94527	925-609-1111	609-1112
Network Solutions LLC 13861 Sunrise Valley Dr Suite 300 *TF:* 800-638-9759 ■ *Web:* www.networksolutions.com	Herndon	VA	20171	703-742-0400	742-3386
Register.com Inc 575 8th Ave 11th Fl *TF:* 800-899-9724 ■ *Web:* www.register.com	New York	NY	10018	212-798-9100	594-9448
RegisterFly.com Inc 623 Eagle Rock Ave Suite 7 *Web:* www.registerfly.com	West Orange	NJ	07052	973-736-2545	736-1355
RegisterNames Inc PO Box 821066 **Fax Area Code:* 603 ■ *TF:* 888-295-7227 ■ *Web:* www.registernames.com	Vancouver	WA	98682	360-253-2210	462-4832*
Simply Named Inc 1829 US Hwy 64 *Web:* www.simplynamed.com	Marion	AR	72364	800-815-1654	
Stargate Holdings Corp 2805 Butterfield Rd Suite 100 *TF:* 800-282-6541 ■ *Web:* www.stargateinc.com	Oak Brook	IL	60523	630-572-2242	
The Registry at Info Avenue LLC PO Box 698 *TF:* 800-950-4726 ■ *Web:* www.iaregistry.com	Fort Mill	SC	29716	803-802-4600	802-4700
TierraNet Inc 9573 Chesapeake Dr 1st Fl *TF:* 877-843-7721 ■ *Web:* www.tierranet.com	San Diego	CA	92123	858-560-9416	560-9417
Tiger Technologies LLC PO Box 7596 **Fax Area Code:* 866 ■ *Web:* www.tigertech.net	Berkeley	CA	94707	510-527-3131	539-5032*
TUCOWS Inc 96 Mowat Ave *TF:* 800-371-6992 ■ *Web:* www.tucows.com	Toronto	ON	M6K3M1	416-535-0123	531-5584
Webnames.ca Inc 322 Water St 3rd Fl **Fax Area Code:* 604 ■ *Web:* www.webnames.ca	Vancouver	BC	V6B1B6	866-221-7878	633-3174*

400 INTERNET SEARCH ENGINES, PORTALS, DIRECTORIES

				Phone	Fax
555-1212.com Inc 1 Sansome St 39th Fl **Fax Area Code:* 925 ■ *Web:* www.555-1212.com	San Francisco	CA	94104	415-288-2440	476-1451*
About Inc 1440 Broadway *Web:* www.about.com	New York	NY	10018	212-204-4000	204-1521
AltaVista 74 N Pasadena Ave 3rd Fl *Web:* www.altavista.com	Pasadena	CA	91103	626-685-5601	
American Memory Library of Congress 101 Independence Ave SE *Web:* lcweb2.loc.gov/ammem	Washington	DC	20540	202-707-5000	707-5844
Ancestry.com 360 W 4800 North *TF Cust Svc:* 800-262-3787 ■ *Web:* www.ancestry.com	Provo	UT	84606	801-705-7000	705-7001
AnyWho Online Directory c/o AT & T Corp 1 AT & T Way *TF:* 800-222-0300 ■ *Web:* www.anywho.com	Bedminster	NJ	07921	908-221-2000	221-1211
AOL (America Online Inc) 22000 AOL Way *TF Orders:* 888-265-8002 ■ *Web:* www.aol.com	Dulles	VA	20166	703-265-1000	265-5769
Artcyclopedia 51 Tuscany Hills Terr NW *Web:* www.artcyclopedia.com	Calgary	AB	T3L2G7	403-547-9692	547-1506
ARTISTdirect Inc 10900 Wilshire Blvd Suite 1400 *Web:* www.artistdirect.com	Los Angeles	CA	90024	310-443-5360	443-5361
Ask.com 555 12th St Suite 500 *Web:* www.ask.com	Oakland	CA	94607	510-985-7400	985-7410
AudioGalaxy Inc 1135 W 6th St Suite 120 *Web:* www.audiogalaxy.com	Austin	TX	78703	512-482-8346	482-0336
Bankrate Inc 11760 US Hwy 1 Suite 500 *NASDAQ: RATE* ■ *TF:* 800-243-7720 ■ *Web:* www.bankrate.com/coinfo	North Palm Beach	FL	33408	561-630-2400	625-4540
Bio.com 1900 Powell St Suite 230 *TF:* 800-246-3010 ■ *Web:* www.bio.com	Emeryville	CA	94608	510-601-7194	601-1862
BioSpace Inc 564 Market St **Fax Area Code:* 239 ■ *TF:* 888-246-7722 ■ *Web:* www.biospace.com	San Francisco	CA	94104	732-528-3688	659-0111*
Buyer's Index Wired Markets Inc 1045 Via Mil Cumbres *Web:* www.buyersindex.com	Solana Beach	CA	92075	858-793-0085	793-0629
CEOExpress Co 1 Broadway 14th Fl *Web:* www.ceoexpress.com	Cambridge	MA	02142	617-482-1200	225-4440
citysearch.com 8833 W Sunset Blvd *Web:* www.citysearch.com	West Hollywood	CA	90069	213-739-3200	739-3299
Clickey Corp PO Box 19518 *Web:* www.clickey.com	Sacramento	CA	95819	916-451-0882	
CNET Search.com CNET Networks Inc 235 Second St *Web:* www.search.com	San Francisco	CA	94105	415-344-2000	
Congress.Org c/o Capitol Advantage 2751 Prosperity Ave Suite 600 *TF:* 800-659-8708 ■ *Web:* www.congress.org	Fairfax	VA	22031	703-289-4670	289-4678
d'ART 5202 Beech St Suite 100 *Web:* www.fine-art.com	Bellaire	TX	77401	713-592-8589	592-8905
Dictionary.com 65 Pine Ave Suite 319 *Web:* www.dictionary.com	Long Beach	CA	90802	562-432-3700	
Dine.com 445 Sherman Ave Suite C *Web:* www.dine.com	Palo Alto	CA	94306	650-847-3100	324-9379
Ditto.com 200 E 5th Ave Suite 112 *Web:* www.ditto.com	Naperville	IL	60563	630-904-7150	904-7151
Dogpile 601 108th Ave NE Suite 1200 *Web:* www.dogpile.com	Bellevue	WA	98004	425-201-6100	201-6150
Domainsearch.com 9525 Kenwood Rd Suite 328 *TF:* 866-927-3624 ■ *Web:* www.domainsearch.com	Cincinnati	OH	45242	513-351-4222	351-8222
EarthCam Inc 84 Kennedy St *Web:* www.earthcam.com	Hackensack	NJ	07601	201-488-1111	488-1119
Education Resource Organizations Directory (EROD) US Dept of Education 400 Maryland Ave SW *Web:* www.ed.gov/Programs/EROD	Washington	DC	20202	202-401-3000	260-7867
Encarta 1 Microsoft Way *TF:* 800-426-9400 ■ *Web:* encarta.msn.com	Redmond	WA	98052	425-882-8080	936-7329
Encyclopedia.com 360 N Michigan Ave Suite 1320 *Web:* www.encyclopedia.com	Chicago	IL	60601	312-782-3900	782-3901
EROD (Education Resource Organizations Directory) US Dept of Education 400 Maryland Ave SW *Web:* www.ed.gov/Programs/EROD	Washington	DC	20202	202-401-3000	260-7867
Essential Links Essentix Inc 13807 SE McLoughlin Suite 626 *TF:* 800-401-6970 ■ *Web:* www.el.com	Portland	OR	97222	503-659-0707	659-0700
Excite 1 Bridge St Suite 42 *Web:* www.excite.com	Irvington	NY	10053	914-591-2000	591-0205
Fact Monster Pearson Education 20 Park Plaza Suite 1220 *Web:* www.factmonster.com	Boston	MA	02116	781-455-1200	
Federal Resources for Educational Excellence (FREE) 400 Maryland Ave SW Rm 7W114 *TF:* 800-872-5327 ■ *Web:* www.ed.gov/free	Washington	DC	20202	202-401-3000	401-0596
FindLaw 610 Opperman Dr **Fax Area Code:* 800 ■ *Web:* www.findlaw.com	Eagan	MN	55123	651-687-7000	392-6206*
fine-art.com 5202 Beech St Suite 100 *Web:* www.fine-art.com	Bellaire	TX	77401	713-592-8589	592-8905
FREE (Federal Resources for Educational Excellence) 400 Maryland Ave SW Rm 7W114 *TF:* 800-872-5327 ■ *Web:* www.ed.gov/free	Washington	DC	20202	202-401-3000	401-0596
Genealogy.com 360 W 4800 North *TF:* 800-262-3787 ■ *Web:* www.genealogy.com	Provo	UT	84606	801-705-7000	705-7001
GoHip.com Inc 8306 Wilshire Blvd Suite 54 *TF:* 866-739-5517 ■ *Web:* www.gohip.com	Beverly Hills	CA	90211	213-596-6248	596-6249
Google Inc 1600 Amphitheatre Pkwy *NASDAQ: GOOG* ■ *Web:* www.google.com	Mountain View	CA	94043	650-253-0000	253-0001

				Phone	Fax
GourmetSpot StartSport Mediaworks Inc 1840 Oak Ave *Web:* www.gourmetspot.com	Evanston	IL	60201	847-866-1830	866-1880
GovSpot StartSpot Mediaworks Inc 1840 Oak Ave *Web:* www.govspot.com	Evanston	IL	60201	847-866-1830	866-1880
Great Web Sites for Kids American Library Assn 50 E Huron St *TF:* 800-545-2433 ■ *Web:* www.ala.org/parentspage/greatsites	Chicago	IL	60611	312-944-6780	
HighBeam Research Inc 65 E Wacker Pl Suite 400 *Web:* www.highbeam.com	Chicago	IL	60601	312-782-3900	782-3901
Hollywood Media Corp 2255 Glades Rd Suite 221A *NASDAQ: HOLL* ■ *TF:* 888-861-8898 ■ *Web:* www.hollywood.com	Boca Raton	FL	33431	561-998-8000	998-2974
HotBot 100 5th Ave *Web:* www.hotbot.com	Waltham	MA	02451	781-370-2700	370-2600
Hotelrooms.com Inc 108-18 Queens Blvd *TF:* 800-486-7000 ■ *Web:* www.hotelrooms.com	Forest Hills	NY	11375	718-730-6000	261-4598
HowStuffWorks Inc c/o Convex Group Inc 3350 Peachtree Rd Suite 1500 *Web:* www.howstuffworks.com	Atlanta	GA	30326	404-760-4729	
ImproveNet Inc 14023 Denver West Pkwy Bldg 64 Suite 200 *TF:* 800-474-1596 ■ *Web:* www.improvenet.com	Golden	CO	80401	303-963-7200	980-3003
Infoplease.com Pearson Education 20 Park Plaza Suite 1220 *Web:* www.infoplease.com	Boston	MA	02116	781-455-1200	
Information Outpost LLC 42 Holmes St *Web:* www.informationoutpost.com	Mystic	CT	06355	860-536-0028	
InfoSpace Inc 601 108th Ave NE Suite 1200 *NASDAQ: INSP* ■ *Web:* www.infospace.com	Bellevue	WA	98004	425-201-6100	201-6163
Internet Archive 116 Sheridan Ave PO Box 29244 *Web:* www.archive.org	San Francisco	CA	94129	415-561-6767	840-0391
Internet Public Library University of Michigan School of Information 304 West Hall *Web:* www.ipl.org	Ann Arbor	MI	48109	734-763-2285	764-2475
Jayde.com iEntry Inc 2549 Richmond Rd 2nd Fl *Web:* www.jayde.com	Lexington	KY	40509	859-514-2720	219-9065
KidsClick! Colorado State Library 201 E Colfax Ave Suite 309 *Web:* www.kidsclick.org	Denver	CO	80203	303-866-6900	866-6940
Law Engine c/o Goldberger & Assoc 920 Kline St Suite 304 *Web:* www.thelawengine.com	La Jolla	CA	92037	858-456-1234	454-3375
Law.com Inc 10 United Nations Plaza 3rd Fl **Fax Area Code:* 415 ■ *Web:* www.law.com	San Francisco	CA	94102	800-903-9872	558-9380*
LibrarySpot StartSpot Mediaworks Inc 1840 Oak Ave *Web:* www.libraryspot.com	Evanston	IL	60201	847-866-1830	
LookSmart Ltd 625 2nd St *NASDAQ: LOOK* ■ *TF:* 877-512-5665 ■ *Web:* www.looksmart.com	San Francisco	CA	94107	415-348-7000	348-7050
Lycos Inc 100 5th Ave *Web:* www.lycos.com	Waltham	MA	02451	781-370-2700	370-2600
MagPortal.com 275 Bryn Mawr Ave Suite M14 *Web:* www.magportal.com	Bryn Mawr	PA	19010	610-581-7702	
Mamma.com Inc 388 Saint Jacques St W 9th Fl *NASDAQ: MAMA* ■ *TF:* 888-841-2372 ■ *Web:* www.mamma.com	Montreal	QC	H2Y1S1	514-844-2700	844-3532
MetaCrawler 601 108th Ave NE Suite 1200 *TF:* 866-438-4677 ■ *Web:* www.metacrawler.com	Bellevue	WA	98004	425-201-6100	201-6150
MindEdge Inc 1601 Trapelo Rd Suite 170 *TF:* 877-592-8000 ■ *Web:* www.mindedge.com	Waltham	MA	02451	781-250-1805	250-1810
Miva Inc 5220 Summerlin Commons Blvd Suite 500 *NASDAQ: MIVA* ■ *TF:* 888-882-3178 ■ *Web:* www.miva.com/us	Fort Myers	FL	33907	239-561-7229	561-7224
MP3.com Inc 235 2nd St *Web:* www.mp3.com	San Francisco	CA	94105	415-344-2000	395-9207
MSN Encarta 1 Microsoft Way *TF:* 800-426-9400 ■ *Web:* encarta.msn.com	Redmond	WA	98052	425-882-8080	936-7329
MSN Search 1 Microsoft Way *TF:* 800-386-5550 ■ *Web:* search.msn.com	Redmond	WA	98052	425-882-8080	936-7329
MyFamily.com Inc 360 W 4800 North *TF:* 800-262-3787 ■ *Web:* www.myfamily.com	Provo	UT	84604	801-705-7000	705-7001
National Geographic For Kids National Geographic Society 1145 17th St NW *Web:* www.nationalgeographic.com/kids	Washington	DC	20036	202-857-7000	
Nerd World Media 8 New England Executive Pk *Web:* headlines.nerdworld.com	Burlington	MA	01803	781-272-6599	272-4855
NewsDirectory.com 96 Mowat Ave *Web:* www.newsd.com	Toronto	ON	M6K3M1	416-535-0123	531-5584
NewsHub 96 Mowat Ave *TF:* 800-371-6992 ■ *Web:* www.newshub.com	Toronto	ON	M6K3M1	416-535-0123	531-5584
NewzRoom Plesser Holland Assoc 20 W 22nd St Suite 903 *Web:* www.newzroom.com	New York	NY	10010	212-420-8383	727-2311
Nursing Center 323 Norristown Rd Suite 200 *TF:* 800-346-7844 ■ *Web:* www.nursingcenter.com	Ambler	PA	19002	215-646-8700	654-2585
PetFinder LLC PO Box 16385 *Web:* www.petfinder.com	Tucson	AZ	85732	520-321-1606	321-1625
PLANTS Database National Plant Data Ctr PO Box 74490 *Web:* plants.usda.gov	Baton Rouge	LA	70874	225-775-6280	775-8883
Pulp & Paper Network LLC 225 N Franklin Tpke *Web:* www.pulpandpaper.net	Ramsey	NJ	07446	201-818-4175	818-8720
Quickbrowse.com Inc 935 4th St *Web:* www.quickbrowse.com	Miami Beach	FL	33139	305-604-9500	468-6282
Quoteland.com Inc PO Box 600250 **Fax Area Code:* 781 ■ *Web:* www.quoteland.com	Newtonville	MA	02460	617-283-9296	235-0084*
Refdesk.com Inc 1006 Beaglin Park Dr Suite 102 *Web:* www.refdesk.com	Salisbury	MD	21804	410-546-5109	
Rhapsody.com 2012 16th St *TF:* 866-311-0228 ■ *Web:* www.rhapsody.com	San Francisco	CA	94103	415-934-2000	934-6720
RootsWeb.com 360 W 4800 North *TF:* 800-262-3787 ■ *Web:* www.rootsweb.com	Provo	UT	84606	801-705-7000	705-7001
Search.com CNET Networks Inc 235 Second St *Web:* www.search.com	San Francisco	CA*	94105	415-344-2000	
ServiceMagic Inc 14023 Denver W Pkwy Bldg 64 Suite 200 *TF:* 800-474-1596 ■ *Web:* www.servicemagic.com	Golden	CO	80401	303-963-7200	980-3003
ShoppingSpot 1840 Oak Ave *Web:* www.shoppingspot.com	Evanston	IL	60201	847-866-1830	866-1880
StartSpot Mediaworks Inc 1840 Oak Ave *Web:* www.startspot.com	Evanston	IL	60201	847-866-1830	866-1880
Switchboard Inc 134 Flanders Rd Suite 2 *TF:* 800-343-1511 ■ *Web:* www.switchboard.com	Westborough	MA	01581	508-983-1300	983-1301
Thinker ImageBase 233 Post St 6th Fl *Web:* www.thinker.org	San Francisco	CA	94108	415-750-3600	
Tours.com Inc 490 Post St Suite 1701 *Web:* www.tours.com	San Francisco	CA	94102	415-332-7916	332-7980
US/Canadian Parks About.com Inc 1440 Broadway 20th Fl *Web:* usparks.about.com	New York	NY	10018	212-204-4000	
USGS Education United States Geological Survey 12201 Sunrise Valley Dr MS 801 *Web:* education.usgs.gov	Reston	VA	20192	703-648-4000	648-4454
WebCrawler 601 108th Ave NE Suite 1200 *Web:* www.webcrawler.com	Bellevue	WA	98004	425-201-6100	201-6150
WebJunction Online Computer Library Center 6565 Frantz Rd *TF:* 800-848-5878 ■ *Web:* www.webjunction.org	Dublin	OH	43017	614-764-6000	764-6096
Wired News 660 3rd St 1st Fl *Web:* www.wired.com	San Francisco	CA	94107	415-276-8400	276-8500
Yahoo! Canada 207 Queens Key W Suite 801 *Web:* ca.yahoo.com	Toronto	ON	M5J1A7	416-341-8605	341-8800
Yahoo! Inc 701 1st Ave *NASDAQ: YHOO* ■ *Web:* www.yahoo.com	Sunnyvale	CA	94089	408-349-3300	349-3301
Yahoo! Search Marketing 74 N Pasadena Ave 3rd Fl *TF:* 888-811-4686 ■ *Web:* searchmarketing.yahoo.com	Pasadena	CA	91103	626-685-5600	685-5601
Yahooligans! 701 1st Ave *Web:* www.yahooligans.com	Sunnyvale	CA	94089	408-349-3300	349-3301
YELLOWPAGES.com LLC PO Box 567 **Fax Area Code:* 800 ■ *TF:* 877-647-6278 ■ *Web:* www.smartpages.com	Saint Louis	MO	63188	877-647-6278	303-3342*
YP.Com 4840 E Jasmine St Suite 105 *TF:* 800-300-3209 ■ *Web:* www.yp.com	Mesa	AZ	85205	480-654-9646	654-9727

401 INTERNET SERVICE PROVIDERS (ISPS)

				Phone	Fax
711.NET Inc 2063 N Lecanto Hwy *Web:* www.711online.net	Lecanto	FL	34461	866-558-6778	
A+Net Internet Services 10350 Barnes Canyon Rd **Fax Area Code:* 650 ■ *TF:* 877-275-8763 ■ *Web:* www.abac.com	San Diego	CA	92121	858-410-6929	475-8478*
ABT Internet 525 Northern Blvd Suite 302 *TF:* 800-367-3414 ■ *Web:* www.abt.net	Great Neck	NY	11021	516-829-5484	829-2955
Access US 712 N 2nd St Suite 300 *TF:* 800-638-6373 ■ *Web:* www.accessus.net	Saint Louis	MO	63102	314-655-7700	655-7701
America Online Inc (AOL) 22000 AOL Way *TF Orders:* 888-265-8002 ■ *Web:* www.aol.com	Dulles	VA	20166	703-265-1000	265-5769
America Online Latin America Inc 6600 N Andrews Ave Suite 300 *TF:* 800-827-6364 ■ *Web:* www.aola.com	Fort Lauderdale	FL	33309	954-689-3000	689-3200
AOL (America Online Inc) 22000 AOL Way *TF Orders:* 888-265-8002 ■ *Web:* www.aol.com	Dulles	VA	20166	703-265-1000	265-5769
AT & T Inc 175 E Houston St *NYSE: T* ■ **Fax:* Hum Res ■ *TF:* 888-875-6388 ■ *Web:* www.att.com	San Antonio	TX	78205	210-821-4105	351-2274*
ATX Communications Inc 2100 Renaissance Blvd *TF:* 800-220-2891 ■ *Web:* www.atx.com	King of Prussia	PA	19406	610-755-4000	755-3290
Aurora Cable Internet 350 Industrial Pkwy S *Web:* www.aci.on.ca	Aurora	ON	L4G3H3	905-727-1981	727-7407
BlueRibbon.com 625 Walnut Ridge Dr Suite 108 *TF:* 800-788-1298 ■ *Web:* www.blueribbon.com	Hartland	WI	53029	262-369-0600	369-0800
Cable One Inc 1314 N 3rd St 3rd Fl *Web:* www.cableone.net	Phoenix	AZ	85004	602-364-6000	364-6010
Cayuse Networks Inc 3019 117th Ave Ct E *Web:* www.cayuse.net	Edgewood	WA	98372	888-245-9691	
ChristianLiving.net 1302 Clear Springs Trace **Fax Area Code:* 502 ■ *TF Tech Supp:* 877-486-2660 ■ *Web:* www.christianliving.net	Louisville	KY	40223	888-772-7355	515-3710*
Cincinnati Bell Inc 221 E 4th St *NYSE: CBB* ■ *TF:* 800-422-1199 ■ *Web:* www.cincinnatibell.com	Cincinnati	OH	45202	513-397-9900	241-1264
ClearSail Communications LLC DBA Family.NET 5160 Timber Creek Rd *TF:* 888-905-0888 ■ *Web:* www.clearsail.net	Houston	TX	77017	713-230-2800	378-7550
CompuServe Interactive Services Inc 5000 Arlington Center Blvd *TF Cust Svc:* 800-848-8990 ■ *Web:* www.compuserve.com	Columbus	OH	43220	614-457-8600	457-0348
ConnectTo.Net 150 Professional Center Suite H *Web:* 1.connectto.net	Rohnert Park	CA	94928	800-603-3022	
Covad Communications Group Inc 110 Rio Robles *AMEX: DVW* ■ *TF Tech Supp:* 888-642-6823 ■ *Web:* www.covad.com	San Jose	CA	95134	408-952-6400	952-7687
Direct Internet Access PO Box 7263 **Fax Area Code:* 888 ■ *Web:* www.directinternet.net	Monroe	LA	71211	800-296-2249	835-2121*
DSL.net Inc 50 Barnes Park N *AMEX: BIZ* ■ *TF:* 800-455-5546 ■ *Web:* www.dsl.net	Wallingford	CT	06492	203-284-6100	284-6101
DSLextreme.com 20847 Sherman Way *TF:* 800-774-3379 ■ *Web:* www.dslextreme.com	Winnetka	CA	91306	818-902-4821	206-0326
EarthLink Inc 1375 Peachtree St NE *NASDAQ: ELNK* ■ **Fax:* Sales ■ *TF:* 800-332-4892 ■ *Web:* www.earthlink.net	Atlanta	GA	30309	404-815-0770	888-9210*
Expedient 1810 Parish St *TF:* 800-969-0099 ■ *Web:* www.expedient.com	Pittsburgh	PA	15220	412-316-7800	316-7899
Family.NET 5160 Timber Creek Rd *TF:* 888-905-0888 ■ *Web:* www.clearsail.net	Houston	TX	77017	713-230-2800	378-7550
FASTNET Corp 3864 Courtney St Suite 130 *TF:* 888-321-3278 ■ *Web:* www.fast.net	Bethlehem	PA	18017	610-954-5910	954-5925
Frontline Communications PO Box 98 *Web:* frontline.net	Orangeburg	NY	10962	888-376-6854	
HughesNet 11717 Exploration Ln *TF:* 800-347-3292 ■ *Web:* www.hughesnet.com	Germantown	MD	20876	301-428-5500	428-1868
Internet America Inc 350 N Saint Paul St 1 Dallas Ctr Suite 3000 *TF:* 800-232-4335 ■ *Web:* www.internetamerica.com	Dallas	TX	75201	214-861-2662	861-2663
Ionix Internet 266 Sutter St *TF:* 888-884-6649 ■ *Web:* www.ionix.net	San Francisco	CA	94108	415-288-9940	288-9942
iSelect Internet Inc 420 W Pine St *TF:* 888-677-8679 ■ *Web:* www.iselect.net	Lodi	CA	95240	209-334-0496	365-7390
J2 Interactive LLC 16 Harvard St *Web:* www.juniornet.com	Charlestown	MA	02129	617-241-7266	241-8636
MacConnect Inc 81 Larkfield Rd *TF:* 866-622-2666 ■ *Web:* www.macconnect.com	East Northport	NY	11731	866-622-2666	
MichTel Communications LLC 10 W Huron St *TF:* 888-244-6381 ■ *Web:* www.michtel.com	Pontiac	MI	48343	248-771-5000	776-1383
Microsoft Network (MSN) 1 Microsoft Way *TF Sales:* 800-426-9400 ■ *Web:* www.msn.com	Redmond	WA	98052	425-882-8080	936-7329
Millenicom 1735 SW Miles St Suite 2000 *TF:* 888-925-4221 ■ *Web:* www.millenicom.com	Portland	OR	97219	503-768-3063	
MSN (Microsoft Network) 1 Microsoft Way *TF Sales:* 800-426-9400 ■ *Web:* www.msn.com	Redmond	WA	98052	425-882-8080	936-7329
NetZero Inc 21301 Burbank Blvd *TF:* 888-340-0029 ■ *Web:* www.netzero.net	Woodland Hills	CA	91367	818-287-3000	287-3001
NeuStar Inc 46000 Center Oak Plaza *NYSE: NSR* ■ *Web:* www.neustar.biz	Sterling	VA	20166	571-434-5400	434-5459
New Edge Networks 3000 Columbia House Blvd Suite 106 *TF:* 877-725-3343 ■ *Web:* www.newedgenetworks.com	Vancouver	WA	98661	360-693-9009	
Newsguy Inc 824 Roosevelt Trail Suite 272 **Fax Area Code:* 408 ■ *Web:* www.newsguy.com	Windham	ME	04062	866-487-3638	720-7630*
Nova Internet Services Inc 12225 Greenville Ave Suite 230 *TF:* 877-668-2663 ■ *Web:* www.novaone.net	Dallas	TX	75243	214-904-9600	357-1431
PeoplePC Inc 100 Pine St Suite 1100 *TF:* 800-736-7537 ■ *Web:* www.peoplepc.com	San Francisco	CA	94111	415-732-4400	837-3857
ProtoSource Network 2511 W Shaw Ave Suite 102 *TF:* 866-490-8600 ■ *Web:* www.psnw.com	Fresno	CA	93711	559-486-8638	490-8630
Quik Internet 3151 Airway Ave Suite M-3 *Web:* www.quik.com	Costa Mesa	CA	92626	714-429-1040	429-1038
Road Runner Group 13241 Woodland Park Rd *Web:* www.rr.com	Herndon	VA	20171	703-345-2400	345-2517

				Phone	Fax
SafeBrowse.com Inc 315 Northpoint Pkwy Suite F	Acworth	GA	30102	877-944-7070	797-6492*
**Fax Area Code:* 678 ■ *Web:* www.safebrowse.com					
ServUsa Internet 305 S Main St PO Box 745	Laurinburg	NC	28353	910-276-1633	
Web: www.servusa.com					
Speakeasy Inc 1201 Western St	Seattle	WA	98121	206-728-9770	728-1500
TF: 800-556-5829 ■ *Web:* www.speakeasy.net					
TOAST.net 4841 Monroe St Suite 307	Toledo	OH	43623	419-292-2200	474-1762
TF: 888-862-7863 ■ *Web:* www.toast.net					
True Vine Online 50 Damsite Rd	Center Barnstead	NH	03225	877-878-3846	
Web: www.truevine.net					
United Online Inc 21301 Burbank Blvd	Woodland Hills	CA	91367	818-287-3000	287-3001
NASDAQ: UNTD ■ *Web:* www.unitedonline.net					
USURF America Inc 11101 W 120th Ave Suite 220	Broomfield	CO	80021	303-285-5379	861-7979
TF: 800-338-6919 ■ *Web:* www.usurf.com					
Verio Inc 8005 S Chester St Suite 200	Centennial	CO	80112	303-645-1900	792-3869
Web: home.verio.com					
Verizon Business 1 Verizon Way	Basking Ridge	NJ	07920	800-339-9911	
TF Cust Svc: 866-232-4282 ■ *Web:* www.verizonbusiness.com					
Verizon Communications Inc 140 West St	New York	NY	10036	212-395-2121	869-3265
NYSE: VZ ■ *Web:* www.verizon.com					
VIA NET.WORKS Inc 3575 Piedmont Rd Suite 710	Atlanta	GA	30305	404-926-3611	926-3612
TF: 800-749-1706 ■ *Web:* www.vianetworks.com					
WorldGate Communications Inc 3190 Tremont Ave	Trevose	PA	19053	215-354-5100	354-1040
NASDAQ: WGAT ■ *Web:* www.wgate.com					
ZDial Inc 119 High St PO Box 626	West Chester	PA	19380	610-692-9205	356-2250*
**Fax Area Code:* 302 ■ *TF:* 888-737-1001 ■ *Web:* www.zdial.com					

402 INVENTORY SERVICES

				Phone	Fax
Douglas-Guardian Services Corp 14800 St Mary's Ln	Houston	TX	77079	281-531-0500	531-1777
TF: 800-255-0552 ■ *Web:* www.douglasguardian.com					
MSI Inventory Service Corp PO Box 230129	Flowood	MS	39232	601-939-0130	939-0061
TF: 800-820-1460 ■ *Web:* www.msi-inv.com					
RGIS Inventory Specialists 2000 E Taylor Rd	Auburn Hills	MI	48326	248-651-2511	656-6609
TF: 800-521-3102 ■ *Web:* www.rgisinv.com					
WIS International 3770 Nashua Dr Suite 5	Mississauga	ON	L4V1M6	905-677-1947	677-1945
TF: 800-268-6848 ■ *Web:* www.wis.ca					

403 INVESTIGATIVE SERVICES

SEE ALSO Information Retrieval Services (General) p. 1856; Public Records Search Services p. 2146; Security & Protective Services p. 2310

				Phone	Fax
Advanced Investigations Inc 24 NW Racetrack Rd	Fort Walton Beach	FL	32547	850-863-3997	864-1733
Web: www.aiipi.com					
Alliance Investigations LLC 240 S Montezuma St Suite 100	Prescott	AZ	86303	928-717-1196	717-1366
TF: 800-717-1196 ■ *Web:* www.arizona-pi.com					
American Professional Services Inc 5350 S Western Ave Suite 700	Oklahoma City	OK	73109	405-636-4222	632-7667
TF: 800-219-9120 ■ *Web:* www.americanpi.net					
ASK Services Inc 42180 Ford Rd Suite 101	Canton	MI	48187	734-983-9040	983-9041
TF: 888-416-1313 ■ *Web:* www.ask-services.com					
Bishops Services Inc 20283 SR 7 Suite 400	Boca Raton	FL	33498	561-237-4242	237-4239
Web: www.bishopsservices.com					
Bombet Cashio & Assoc 11220 N Harrells Ferry Rd	Baton Rouge	LA	70816	225-275-0796	272-3631
TF: 800-256-5333 ■ *Web:* www.bombet.com					
Bontecou Investigative Services Inc 350 Broadway PO Box 2448	Jackson	WY	83001	307-733-2637	733-5873
TF: 877-733-2639 ■ *Web:* www.wyominginvestigator.com					
Brabston Legal Investigations Inc 3746 Halls Mills Rd	Mobile	AL	36693	251-666-5666	661-8807
TF: 800-239-4939					
Capitol Detective Agency 2922 N 18th Pl	Phoenix	AZ	85016	602-277-0770	264-9814
TF: 800-346-0347 ■ *Web:* www.capitoldetective.com					
Cleveland Process Support 40 Front St PO Box 5358	Central Point	OR	97502	541-665-5162	665-5182
TF: 800-888-6629					
Confidential Services PO Box 91034	Columbus	OH	43209	614-252-4646	252-4669
TF: 800-752-4581					
DataTrace Investigations Inc PO Box 95322	South Jordan	UT	84095	801-253-2400	253-2478
TF: 800-748-5335 ■ *Web:* www.datatraceonline.com					
Douglas Baldwin & Assoc PO Box 1249	La Canada	CA	91012	818-952-4433	790-4622
TF: 800-392-3950 ■ *Web:* www.baldwinpi.com					
EX-CEL Investigations PO Box 22124	Saint Petersburg	FL	33742	727-527-5440	527-2442
Web: www.ex-celpi.com					
Gietzen & Assoc Inc 1302 N Marion St	Tampa	FL	33602	813-223-3233	223-9717
TF: 888-779-2345 ■ *Web:* www.gietzen.com					
Gold Coast Agency Inc PO Box 51465	Sparks	NV	89435	775-324-1161	324-1163
Graymark Security Group 7301 NW 4th St Suite 110	Fort Lauderdale	FL	33317	954-581-5575	581-5750
TF: 800-881-3242 ■ *Web:* www.graymarksecurity.com					
Gregg Investigations Inc 6320 Monona Dr	Madison	WI	53716	608-256-1074	755-5853
TF: 800-866-1976 ■ *Web:* www.gregginvestigations.com					
Heartland Information Services Inc DBA Heartland Business Intelligence 527 Marquette Ave Suite 900	Minneapolis	MN	55402	612-371-9255	371-9262
TF: 800-967-1882 ■ *Web:* www.heartlandinfo.com					
Hoover Professional Investigations 3202 E 'M' St	Tacoma	WA	98404	253-272-5090	272-5090
Hrodey & Assoc PO Box 366	Woodstock	IL	60098	815-337-4636	337-4638
Web: www.hrodey.com					
ID Investigators & Adjustors Inc 31225 La Baya Dr Suite 111	Westlake Village	CA	91362	818-991-1122	991-3703
Web: www.idinvestigations.com					
International Investigators Inc 3216 N Pennsylvania St	Indianapolis	IN	46205	317-925-1496	926-1177
TF: 800-403-8111 ■ *Web:* www.iiiweb.net					
Internet Crimes Group Inc PO Box 3599	Princeton	NJ	08543	609-806-5000	806-5001
Web: www.icginc.com					
Intra-Lex Investigations Inc 505 6th St Suite 202	Sioux City	IA	51101	712-233-1639	255-1127
Investigative Services Inc PO Box 45143	Omaha	NE	68145	402-894-5625	896-0621
Johnson Rick & Assoc of Colorado 1649 Downing St	Denver	CO	80218	303-296-2200	296-3038
TF: 800-530-2300 ■ *Web:* www.denverpi.com					
Kansas Investigative Services Inc 970 N Santa Fe St	Wichita	KS	67214	316-267-1356	267-5476
TF: 888-889-3340					
Kessler International 45 Rockefeller Plaza Suite 2000	New York	NY	10111	212-286-9100	730-2433
TF: 800-932-2221 ■ *Web:* www.investigation.com					
Kroll Inc 900 3rd Ave 7th Fl	New York	NY	10022	212-593-1000	593-2631
TF: 800-675-3772 ■ *Web:* www.krollworldwide.com					
L & W Investigations Inc 23332 Mill Creek Dr Suite 130	Laguna Hills	CA	92653	949-305-7383	305-8928
Web: www.lwfranchise.com					
MacIntire & Assoc Inc 3906 W Ina Rd Suite 316	Tucson	AZ	85741	520-622-2737	363-6143*
**Fax Area Code:* 866 ■ *TF:* 800-641-2737 ■ *Web:* www.macintireandassociates.com					
Michael Ramey & Assoc Inc PO Box 744	Danville	CA	94526	925-820-8900	820-8082
TF: 800-321-0505 ■ *Web:* www.rameypi.com					
Niles Agency 350 Ward Ave Suite 106	Honolulu	HI	96814	808-254-8337	467-5980*
**Fax Area Code:* 888					
North Winds Investigations Inc PO Box 1654	Rogers	AR	72757	479-925-1612	925-2819
TF: 800-530-4514					
Northwest Location Services Inc DBA Legal Locate Services PO Box 948	Wauna	WA	98395	253-858-1984	238-0022
TF: 800-916-3724 ■ *Web:* www.nwlocation.com					
Owens & Assoc Investigations 2245 San Diego Ave Suite 225	San Diego	CA	92110	619-297-1343	297-7622
TF: 800-297-1343 ■ *Web:* www.owenspi.com					
PADIC Inc 1609 E Broadway	Gainesville	TX	76240	940-665-6130	665-7486
TF: 800-679-5727 ■ *Web:* www.padic.com					
Palmer Investigative Services 624 W Gurley St Suite A	Prescott	AZ	86305	928-778-2951	445-7204
TF: 800-280-2951 ■ *Web:* www.palmerinvestigative.com					
PI & Information Services LLC PO Box 157	Beaverton	OR	97075	503-643-4274	643-5474
TF: 800-649-7530 ■ *Web:* www.pi-info.com					
Port-O-Wild's Security Services PO Box 521	Bemidji	MN	56619	218-444-8200	
Ramey Michael & Assoc Inc PO Box 744	Danville	CA	94526	925-820-8900	820-8082
TF: 800-321-0505 ■ *Web:* www.rameypi.com					
Research Assoc Inc 27999 Clemens Rd	Westlake	OH	44145	440-892-1000	892-9439
TF: 800-255-9693 ■ *Web:* www.raiglobal.com					
Rick Johnson & Assoc of Colorado 1649 Downing St	Denver	CO	80218	303-296-2200	296-3038
TF: 800-530-2300 ■ *Web:* www.denverpi.com					
Shawver & Assoc 6262 Weber Rd Suite 112	Corpus Christi	TX	78413	361-880-8968	880-8971
TF: 800-364-2333 ■ *Web:* www.stxpi.com					
Southern Research Co Inc 2850 Centenary Blvd	Shreveport	LA	71104	318-227-9700	424-1801
TF: 888-772-6952 ■ *Web:* www.southernresearchinc.com					
Specialized Investigations 14530 Delano St	Van Nuys	CA	91411	818-909-9607	782-3012
TF: 800-714-3728 ■ *Web:* www.specialpi.com					
State Information Bureau 842 E Park Ave	Tallahassee	FL	32301	850-561-3990	561-3995
TF: 800-881-1742 ■ *Web:* www.sibflorida.com					
Stewart & Assoc Inc 50 W Douglas St Suite 1200	Freeport	IL	61032	815-235-3807	235-1290
TF: 800-442-3807 ■ *Web:* www.bwstewart.com					
VISTA Inc 29516 Southfield Rd Suite 104	Southfield	MI	48076	248-559-3500	559-4757
TF: 888-873-8478 ■ *Web:* www.vistapi.com					
VTS Investigations LLC PO Box 971	Elgin	IL	60121	847-888-4464	888-8588
TF: 800-538-4464 ■ *Web:* www.pichicago.com					
Wood & Tait Inc PO Box 6180	Kamuela	HI	96743	808-885-5090	630-0500*
**Fax Area Code:* 888 ■ *TF:* 800-774-8585 ■ *Web:* www.woodtait.com					

404 INVESTMENT ADVICE & MANAGEMENT

SEE ALSO Commodity Contracts Brokers & Dealers p. 1499; Investment Guides - Online p. 1876; Mutual Funds p. 2010; Securities Brokers & Dealers p. 2307

				Phone	Fax
Acadian Asset Management Inc 1 Post Office Sq 20th Fl	Boston	MA	02109	617-850-3500	850-3501
TF: 800-946-0166 ■ *Web:* www.acadian-asset.com					
Advent Capital Management LLC 1065 Ave of the Americas 31st Fl	New York	NY	10018	212-482-1600	480-9655
TF: 888-523-8368 ■ *Web:* www.adventcap.com					
AEW Capital Management LP 2 Seaport Ln World Trade Ctr E	Boston	MA	02210	617-261-9000	261-9555
Web: www.aew.com					
AGF Management Ltd 2920 Matheson Blvd E	Mississauga	ON	L4W5J4	905-214-8203	329-4243*
**Fax Area Code:* 888 ■ *TF:* 800-268-8583 ■ *Web:* www.agf.com					
Alger Fred Management Inc 30 Montgomery St 11th Fl	Jersey City	NJ	07302	201-547-3600	434-1459
TF: 800-223-3810 ■ *Web:* www.fredalger.com					
Allegiant Asset Management Co 1900 E 9th St	Cleveland	OH	44114	800-622-3863	692-2458*
**Fax Area Code:* 314 ■ *TF:* 800-646-3624 ■ *Web:* www.allegiantassetmanagement.com					
AllianceBernstein Holding LP 1345 Ave of the Americas	New York	NY	10105	212-969-1000	969-2229*
**Fax:* Hum Res ■ *TF Cust Svc:* 800-221-5672 ■ *Web:* www.alliancecapital.com					
Allianz of America Inc 55 Green Farms Rd PO Box 5160	Westport	CT	06881	203-221-8500	341-5722
Web: www.azoa.com					
Allianz Global Investors of America LP 680 Newport Ctr Dr Suite 250	Newport Beach	CA	92660	949-219-2200	
Web: www.allianzinvestors.com					
American Century Investments Inc 4500 Main St	Kansas City	MO	64111	816-531-5575	340-7962*
**Fax:* Cust Svc ■ *TF:* 800-345-2021 ■ *Web:* www.americancentury.com					
Amerindo Investment Advisors Inc 1 Embarcadero Ctr Suite 2300	San Francisco	CA	94111	415-362-0292	362-0533
TF: 888-832-4386 ■ *Web:* www.amerindo.com					
Ameriprise Financial Inc 55 Ameriprise Financial Center	Minneapolis	MN	55474	612-671-3131	671-8880
NYSE: AMP ■ *TF:* 800-328-8300 ■ *Web:* www.ameriprise.com					
Ameriprise Financial Services Inc 70100 Ameriprise Financial Center	Minneapolis	MN	55474	612-671-3131	671-8880
TF: 800-862-7919 ■ *Web:* www.ameriprise.com					
Amivest Capital Management 703 Market St 18th Fl	San Francisco	CA	94103	415-541-7744	541-9760
TF: 800-541-7774 ■ *Web:* www.wrapmanager.com					
AMR Investment Services Inc PO Box 619003 MD 2450	DFW Airport	TX	75261	817-967-3509	967-0768
TF: 800-967-9009 ■ *Web:* www.aafunds.com					
AmSouth Investment Services Inc (AIS) 250 Riverchase Pkwy E RCS 4th Fl	Birmingham	AL	35244	205-560-7998	560-7089
TF: 800-316-4009 ■ *Web:* www.amsouth.com/ais					
Analytic Investors Inc 500 S Grand Ave 23rd Fl	Los Angeles	CA	90071	213-688-3015	688-8856
TF: 800-618-1872 ■ *Web:* www.analyticinvestors.com					
Ariel Capital Management LLC 200 E Randolph Dr Suite 2900	Chicago	IL	60601	312-726-0140	726-7473
TF: 800-292-7435 ■ *Web:* www.arielmutualfunds.com					
Atalanta/Sosnoff Capital LLC 101 Park Ave 6th Fl	New York	NY	10178	212-867-5000	922-1820
Web: www.atalantasosnoff.com					
Atlantic Trust 100 E Pratt St Suite 1604	Baltimore	MD	21202	410-539-4660	539-4661
TF: 888-880-1621 ■ *Web:* www.atlantictrustco.com					
AXA Financial Inc 1290 Ave of the Americas	New York	NY	10104	212-554-1234	
Web: www.axa-financial.com					
AXA Rosenberg Investment Management LLC 4 Orinda Way Bldg E	Orinda	CA	94563	925-254-6464	253-0141
Web: www.axarosenberg.com					
Ayco Co LP 1 Wall St	Albany	NY	12205	518-464-2000	464-2122
Web: www.ayco.com					
Babson Capital Management Co 470 Atlantic Ave	Boston	MA	02210	617-225-3800	225-3801
TF: 877-766-0014 ■ *Web:* www.babsoncapital.com					
Bailard Biehl & Kaiser Group 950 Tower Ln Suite 1900	Foster City	CA	94404	650-571-5800	573-7128
TF: 800-882-8383 ■ *Web:* www.bailard.com					
Bank of Ireland Asset Management (US) Ltd 75 Holly Hill Ln	Greenwich	CT	06830	203-869-0111	869-0268
Web: www.biam.ie					
Barclays Global Investors 45 Fremont St 5th Fl	San Francisco	CA	94105	415-597-2000	597-2171
Web: www.barclaysglobal.com					
Baring Asset Management Co Inc 470 Atlantic Ave Independence Wharf	Boston	MA	02110	617-946-5200	946-5402
TF: 800-533-7432 ■ *Web:* www.baring-asset.com					
Barrow Hanley Mewhinney & Strauss Inc 2200 Ross Ave 31st Fl	Dallas	TX	75201	214-665-1900	665-1933*
**Fax:* Mktg ■ *Web:* www.barrowhanley.com					

Phone Fax

Bartlett & Co 36 E 4th St Suite 400 Cincinnati OH 45202 513-621-4612 621-6462
TF: 800-800-4612 ■ *Web:* www.bartlett1898.com

Batterymarch Financial Management Inc
200 Clarendon St 49th Fl Boston MA 02116 617-266-8300 266-0633
Web: www.batterymarch.com

Bernstein Investment Research & Management
1345 Ave of the Americas New York NY 10105 212-486-5800 756-1812*
**Fax:* Mktg ■ *Web:* www.bernstein.com

Bessemer Trust 630 5th Ave 6th Fl New York NY 10111 212-708-9100 265-5826
Web: www.bessemer.com

BlackRock Inc 40 E 52nd St New York NY 10022 212-754-5560
NYSE: BLK ■ *Web:* www.blackrock.com

BlackRock Realty Advisors Inc 300 Campus Dr Florham NJ 07932 973-264-2700
Web: www.ssrrealty.com

Boston Advisors Inc 1 Federal St 26th Fl Boston MA 02110 617-348-3100 348-0081
TF: 800-523-5903 ■ *Web:* www.bostonadvisors.com

Boston Financial Data Services 2 Heritage Dr North Quincy MA 02171 617-483-5000 483-2209
TF: 888-772-2337 ■ *Web:* www.bfds.com

Bramwell Capital Management 745 5th Ave 16th Fl New York NY 10151 212-308-0505 308-2551
TF: 800-272-6227 ■ *Web:* www.bramwell.com

Brandes Investment Partners LP
11988 El Camino Real Suite 500 San Diego CA 92130 858-755-0239 755-0916
TF: 800-237-7119 ■ *Web:* www.brandes.com

Brandywine Global Investment Management LLC
2929 Arch St 8th Fl Philadelphia PA 19104 215-609-3500 609-3501
TF: 800-348-2499 ■ *Web:* www.brandywineassetmgmtinc.com

Brazos Capital Management 5949 Sherry Ln Suite 1600 Dallas TX 75225 214-365-5200 706-5100
Web: www.brazosfunds.com

Bridgewater Assoc Inc 1 Glendinning Pl Westport CT 06880 203-226-3030 291-7300
Web: www.bridgewaterassociates.com

Brown Brothers Harriman & Co 140 Broadway New York NY 10005 212-483-1818 493-7287*
**Fax:* Hum Res ■ *Web:* www.bbh.com

Brown Capital Management Inc 1201 N Calvert St Baltimore MD 21202 410-837-3234 837-6525
TF: 800-809-3863 ■ *Web:* www.browncapital.com

Cadence Capital Management 265 Franklin St 11th Fl Boston MA 02110 617-624-3500 624-3591
TF: 800-298-2194 ■ *Web:* www.cadencecapital.com

Calamos Asset Management Inc 2020 Calamos Ct Naperville IL 60563 630-245-7200 245-6335
NASDAQ: CLMS ■ *TF:* 800-582-6959 ■ *Web:* www.calamos.com

Callan Assoc Inc 101 California St Suite 3500 San Francisco CA 94111 415-974-5060 291-4014
TF: 800-227-3288 ■ *Web:* www.callan.com

Cambiar Investors Inc 2401 E 2nd Ave Suite 400 Denver CO 80206 303-302-9000 302-9050
TF: 888-673-9950 ■ *Web:* www.cambiar.com

Capital Group Cos Inc 333 S Hope St Los Angeles CA 90071 213-486-9200 486-9217
TF: 800-421-8511 ■ *Web:* www.capgroup.com

Capital Growth Management LP 1 International Pl 45th Fl Boston MA 02110 617-737-3225 261-0572
TF: 800-334-6440

Capital Research & Management Co 333 S Hope St Los Angeles CA 90071 213-486-9200 486-9217

Capital Resource Advisors 200 W Adams Suite 1800 Chicago IL 60606 888-677-4272
Web: www.cradv.com

Cargill Asset Investment & Finance Group
12700 Whitewater Dr Minnetonka MN 55343 952-984-3444 984-3900
TF: 800-227-4455 ■ *Web:* www.cargill.com

CI Fund Management Inc 151 Yonge St 8th Fl Toronto ON M5C2W7 416-364-1145 364-6299
TSX: CIX ■ *TF:* 800-268-9374 ■ *Web:* www.cifunds.com

CIGNA Retirement & Investment Services 280 Trumbull St Hartford CT 06103 860-534-2000

Citigroup Asset Management 153 E 53rd St New York NY 10022 212-559-3706 559-1049
Web: www.citigroupam.com

Citigroup Global Markets Holdings Inc
300 First Stamford Pl 3rd Fl Stamford CT 06902 203-961-6000
TF Sales: 888-777-0102 ■ *Web:* www.citigroupcib.com

Cohen & Steers Inc 280 Park Ave 10th Fl New York NY 10017 212-832-3232 832-3498*
NYSE: CNS ■ **Fax:* Mktg ■ *TF:* 800-330-7348 ■ *Web:* www.cohenandsteers.com

Colony Capital Management 3060 Peachtree Rd NW Suite 1550 Atlanta GA 30305 404-365-5050 365-5070
TF: 877-365-5050 ■ *Web:* www.colonycapital.com

Columbia Funds Distributor Inc 1 Fincial Ctr Boston MA 02111 617-426-3750 781-3995*
**Fax Area Code:* 415 ■ *TF:* 800-225-2365 ■ *Web:* www.columbiafunds.com

Columbia Management Assoc Inc 1 Financial Ctr Boston MA 02111 617-426-3750 330-9701
TF: 800-225-2365 ■ *Web:* www.columbiamanagement.com

Columbia Management Group 1 Financial Ctr Boston MA 02111 617-426-3750 261-7350
TF: 800-225-2365 ■ *Web:* www.columbiamanagement.com

Columbus Circle Investors Inc 1 Station Pl Metro Ctr 8th Fl Stamford CT 06902 203-353-6000 406-5479
TF: 888-826-5247 ■ *Web:* www.columbuscircle.com

Connell Finance Co Inc 100 Connell Dr Suite 4000 Berkeley Heights NJ 07922 908-673-3700 673-3800
TF: 800-233-3240 ■ *Web:* www.connellco.com/CFC.htm

Connell Technologies Co LLC 350 Lindbergh Ave Livermore CA 94550 925-455-6790 455-6791
TF: 888-301-0300 ■ *Web:* www.connellco.com/CTL.htm

Conning Asset Management Co 1 Financial Plaza Hartford CT 06103 860-299-2000 299-2479
Web: www.conning.com/asset

Cooke & Bieler LP 1700 Market St Suite 3222 Philadelphia PA 19103 215-567-1101 567-1681
Web: www.cooke-bieler.com

CRA RogersCasey Inc 1 Parklands Dr Darien CT 06820 203-656-5900 656-2233
Web: www.crarogerscasey.com

Crown Financial Ministries 601 Broad St SE Gainesville GA 30501 770-534-1000 244-7519*
**Fax Area Code:* 678 ■ *TF:* 800-722-1976 ■ *Web:* www.crown.org

Dalton Greiner Hartman Maher & Co LLC
565 5th Ave Suite 2101 New York NY 10017 212-557-2445 557-4898
Web: www.dghm.net

Davis Hamilton Jackson & Assoc
1401 McKinney St Suite 1600 Houston TX 77010 713-853-2322 853-2308
TF: 800-594-0438 ■ *Web:* www.dhja.com

Dean Investment Assoc Kettering Tower Suite 2480 Dayton OH 45423 937-222-0282 227-9304
TF: 800-327-3656 ■ *Web:* www.chdean.com

Dearden Maguire Weaver & Barrett Inc
100 Front St 1 Tower Bridge Suite 560 West Conshohocken PA 19428 610-832-0277 832-0286
Web: www.dearden.com

Delaware Investments 2005 Market St Philadelphia PA 19103 215-255-1200 255-1002*
**Fax:* Hum Res ■ *TF:* 800-362-7500 ■ *Web:* www.delgroup.com

Denver Investment Advisors LLC 1225 17th St 26th Fl Denver CO 80202 303-312-5000 312-4900
Web: www.denveria.com

Dodge & Cox 555 California St 40th Fl San Francisco CA 94104 415-981-1710 986-8126
TF: 800-621-3979 ■ *Web:* www.dodgeandcox.com

Driehaus Capital Management Inc 25 E Erie St Chicago IL 60611 312-587-3800 587-3840
TF: 800-688-8819 ■ *Web:* www.driehaus.com

Duff & Phelps LLC 311 S Wacker Dr Suite 4200 Chicago IL 60606 312-697-4600 697-0115
Web: www.dufflic.com

DWS Scudder 222 S Riverside Plaza Chicago IL 60606 312-537-7000
Web: www.scudder.com

Eagle Asset Management 880 Carillon Pkwy Saint Petersburg FL 33716 727-573-2453 567-8020*
**Fax:* Mktg ■ *TF:* 800-237-3101 ■ *Web:* www.eagleasset.com

Earnest Partners LLC 1180 Peachtree St Suite 2300 Atlanta GA 30309 404-815-8772 815-8948
TF: 800-322-0068 ■ *Web:* www.earnestpartners.com

Eaton Vance Corp 255 State St Boston MA 02109 617-482-8260 482-2396*
NYSE: EV ■ **Fax:* Cust Svc ■ *TF:* 800-225-6265 ■ *Web:* www.eatonvance.com

Edgar Lomax Co 6564 Loisdale Ct Suite 310 Springfield VA 22150 703-719-0026
TF: 866-205-0524 ■ *Web:* www.edgarlomax.com

Phone Fax

Energy Investors Management Inc
63 Kendrick St 3 Charles River Pl Needham MA 02494 781-292-7000 292-7099
Web: www.eifgroup.com

Engemann Asset Management 600 N Rosemead Blvd Pasadena CA 91107 626-351-9686 351-4676
TF: 800-882-2855 ■ *Web:* www.eam.com

Essex Investment Management Co LLC 125 High St 29th Fl Boston MA 02110 617-342-3200 342-3280
TF: 800-342-3202 ■ *Web:* www.essexinvest.com

Fayez Sarofim & Co 2 Houston Ctr Suite 2907 Houston TX 77010 713-654-4484 654-8184
TF: 800-288-7125 ■ *Web:* www.sarofim.com

Federated Investors
1001 Liberty Ave Federated Investors Tower Pittsburgh PA 15222 412-288-1900 288-6751*
NYSE: FII ■ **Fax:* Hum Res ■ *TF:* 800-245-0242 ■ *Web:* www.federatedinvestors.com

Fidelity Investments 82 Devonshire St Boston MA 02109 617-563-7000
TF: 800-522-7297 ■ *Web:* www.fidelity.com

Fidelity Investments Institutional Services Co Inc
82 Devonshire St Boston MA 02109 617-563-7000
TF: 800-522-7297

Fiduciary Management Assoc LLC 55 W Monroe St Suite 2550 Chicago IL 60603 312-930-6850 641-2511
Web: www.fmausa.com

Fiduciary Management Inc of Milwaukee
100 E Wisconsin Ave Suite 2200 Milwaukee WI 53202 414-226-4545 226-4522
Web: www.fiduciarymgt.com

First Investors Management Co Inc 110 Wall St New York NY 10005 212-858-8000 858-8099
TF Cust Svc: 800-423-4026 ■ *Web:* www.firstinvestors.com

First Pacific Advisors Inc
11400 W Olympic Blvd Suite 1200 Los Angeles CA 90064 310-473-0225 996-5450
TF: 800-982-4372 ■ *Web:* www.fpafunds.com

Fischer Francis Trees & Watts Inc 200 Park Ave 46th Fl New York NY 10166 212-681-3000 681-3250
TF: 888-367-3389 ■ *Web:* www.fftw.com

Fisher Investments 13100 Skyline Blvd Woodside CA 94062 650-851-3334 851-3514
TF: 800-851-8845 ■ *Web:* www.fi.com

FMR Corp 82 Devonshire St Boston MA 02109 617-563-7000
TF: 800-522-7297 ■ *Web:* www.fidelity.com

Forest Investment Assoc 15 Piedmont Ctr Suite 1250 Atlanta GA 30305 404-261-9575 261-9574
Web: www.forestinvest.com

ForstmannLeff Assoc LLC 590 Madison Ave 39th Fl New York NY 10022 212-644-9888 588-0591*
**Fax:* Hum Res ■ *Web:* www.forstmannleff.com

Founders Asset Management LLC 210 University Blvd Suite 800 Denver CO 80206 303-394-4404 394-7870
TF: 800-525-2440 ■ *Web:* www.founders.com

Frank Russell Co PO Box 1616 Tacoma WA 98402 253-572-9500 591-3495
TF: 800-426-7969 ■ *Web:* www.russell.com

Franklin Resources Inc DBA Franklin Templeton Investments
1 Franklin Pkwy San Mateo CA 94403 650-312-2000 312-3655*
NYSE: BEN ■ **Fax:* Hum Res ■ *TF:* 800-342-5236 ■ *Web:* www.franklintempleton.com

Franklin Templeton Investments 1 Franklin Pkwy San Mateo CA 94403 650-312-2000 312-3655*
NYSE: BEN ■ **Fax:* Hum Res ■ *TF:* 800-342-5236 ■ *Web:* www.franklintempleton.com

Fred Alger Management Inc 30 Montgomery St 11th Fl Jersey City NJ 07302 201-547-3600 434-1459
TF: 800-223-3810 ■ *Web:* www.fredalger.com

Freedom Capital LLC 155 Federal St 16th Fl Boston MA 02110 617-722-4700 722-4714
TF: 800-861-8088 ■ *Web:* www.freedom-capital.com

GAMCO Investors Inc 1 Corporate Center Rye NY 10580 914-921-5000 921-5060
NYSE: GBL ■ *TF:* 800-422-3554 ■ *Web:* www.gabelli.com

Gannett Welsh & Kotler Inc 222 Berkeley St Suite 1500 Boston MA 02116 617-236-8900 236-1815
TF: 800-225-4236 ■ *Web:* www.gwkinc.com

Gartmore Morley Financial Services Inc
1300 SW 5th Ave Suite 3300 Portland OR 97201 503-620-7899 340-6573*
**Fax Area Code:* 614 ■ *TF:* 800-548-4806 ■ *Web:* www.gartmoremorley.com

Gemini Fund Services LLC 450 Wireless Blvd Hauppauge NY 11788 631-951-0500 951-0573
Web: www.geminifund.com

Glenmede Trust Co 1650 Market St Suite 1200 Philadelphia PA 19103 215-419-6000 419-6199
TF: 800-966-3200 ■ *Web:* www.glenmede.com

Goldman Sachs Asset Management 32 Old Slip 17th Fl New York NY 10005 212-902-1000
TF: 800-292-4726 ■ *Web:* www2.goldmansachs.com

Goode Investment Management Inc 50 Public Sq Suite 1700 Cleveland OH 44113 216-771-9000 771-1949
Web: www.goodeinvestment.com

Grantham Mayo Van Otterloo & Co LLC 40 Rowes Wharf Boston MA 02110 617-330-7500 261-0134
Web: www.gmo.com

Greenhill & Co Inc 300 Park Ave 23rd Fl New York NY 10022 212-389-1500 389-1700
NYSE: GHL ■ *Web:* www.greenhill-co.com

Guardian Investor Services LLC 7 Hanover Sq New York NY 10004 212-598-8000 919-2170*
**Fax:* Hum Res ■ *TF:* 888-482-7342 ■ *Web:* www.guardianinvestor.com

H & R Block Financial Advisors Inc 719 Griswold St Detroit MI 48226 313-628-1300 628-1288
TF: 800-521-1111 ■ *Web:* investment-center.hrblock.com

Harris Assoc LP 2 N La Salle St Suite 500 Chicago IL 60602 312-621-0600 621-0372
TF: 800-731-0700 ■ *Web:* www.harrisassoc.com

Harris myCFO Inc DBA myCFO 1700 Seaport Blvd 4th Fl Redwood City CA 94063 650-210-5000 210-5010
TF: 877-692-3609 ■ *Web:* www.mycfo.com

HD Vest Financial Services 6333 N State Hwy 161 4th Fl Irving TX 75038 972-870-6000 870-6128
TF: 800-821-8254 ■ *Web:* hdvest.com

Heitman LLC 191 N Wacker Dr Suite 2500 Chicago IL 60606 312-855-5700 849-4141
TF: 800-225-5435 ■ *Web:* www.heitman.com

Holland Capital Management LP 1 N Wacker Dr Suite 700 Chicago IL 60606 312-553-4830 553-4848
TF: 800-522-2711 ■ *Web:* www.hollandcap.com

HSBC Asset Management Inc 452 5th Ave New York NY 10018 212-525-5000
TF: 800-975-7722 ■ *Web:* www.banking.us.hsbc.com

Hughes Capital Management Inc 916 Prince St 3rd Fl Alexandria VA 22314 703-684-7222 684-7799

Hyperion Capital Management Inc
200 Vessey St 11th Fl 3 World Financial Center New York NY 10281 212-549-8400 549-8300
TF: 800-497-3746 ■ *Web:* www.hyperioncapital.com

ICM Asset Management Inc 601 W Main Ave Suite 600 Spokane WA 99201 509-455-3588 777-0999
TF: 800-488-4075 ■ *Web:* www.icmasset.com

IGM Financial Inc 447 Portage Ave 1 Canada Ctr Winnipeg MB R3C3B6 204-943-0361 956-7688
TSX: IGI ■ *Web:* www.investorsgroup.com

Independence Investment LLC 160 Federal St Boston MA 02110 617-228-8700 228-8894
Web: www.independence.com

INVESCO Capital Management Inc
1360 Peachtree St NE 1 Midtown Plaza Suite 100 Atlanta GA 30309 404-892-0896 439-4911
TF: 800-241-5477

InvestAmerica Investment Advisors Inc
101 2nd St SE Suite 800 Cedar Rapids IA 52401 319-363-8249 363-9683
Web: www.investamericaventuregroup.com

Investment Counselors of Maryland LLC 803 Cathedral St Baltimore MD 21201 410-539-3838 625-9016
Web: www.icomd.com

Investor Growth Capital Inc 630 5th Ave Suite 1965 New York NY 10111 212-515-9000 515-9009

IXIS Asset Management North America LP 399 Boylston St Boston MA 02116 617-449-2100 247-1447
TF: 800-225-5478 ■ *Web:* www.ixis-amna.com

J & W Seligman & Co Inc 100 Park Ave New York NY 10017 212-850-1864 922-5742
TF: 800-221-7844 ■ *Web:* www.seligman.com

John Hancock Funds 1 John Hancock Way Suite 1000 Boston MA 02217 800-225-5291 886-3561*
**Fax Area Code:* 617 ■ *TF Cust Svc:* 800-225-6020 ■ *Web:* www.jhfunds.com

Johnson Asset Management 555 Main St Suite 440 Racine WI 53403 262-681-4770 681-4792
TF: 800-407-5500 ■ *Web:* www.johnsonbank.com

Johnson Tom Investment Management Inc
204 N Robinson St Suite 2900 Oklahoma City OK 73102 405-236-2111 236-2008
Web: www.tjim.com

Phone Fax

Jones Heward Investment Counsel Inc
77 King St W Suite 4200 Toronto ON M5K1J5 416-359-5000 359-5040
Web: www.jonesheward.com
JPMorgan Fleming Asset Management PO Box 8528 Boston MA 02266 800-480-4111 471-3053*
**Fax Area Code:* 816 ■ *TF:* 800-348-4782 ■ *Web:* www.jpmorganfunds.com
Kopp Investment Advisors Inc 7701 France Ave S Suite 500 Edina MN 55435 952-841-0400 841-0411
TF: 800-333-9128 ■ *Web:* www.koppfunds.com
Leerink Swann & Co 1 Federal St 37th Fl Boston MA 02110 617-248-1601 918-4900
TF: 800-808-7525 ■ *Web:* www.leerink.com
Lehman Brothers Asset Management LLC
190 S La Salle St Suite 2400 Chicago IL 60603 312-325-7700 325-7722
TF: 800-764-9336
Loomis Sayles & Co Inc LP 1 Financial Ctr Boston MA 02111 617-482-2450 423-3065
TF: 800-343-2029 ■ *Web:* www.loomissayles.com
Lord Abbett & Co 90 Hudson St Jersey City NJ 07302 201-827-2000 888-4405*
**Fax Area Code:* 212 ■ *TF:* 800-874-3733 ■ *Web:* www.lordabbett.com
M & I Wealth Management 111 E Kilbourn Ave Milwaukee WI 53202 414-287-8700 287-7025
TF: 800-342-2265 ■ *Web:* www.mibank.com
Mackenzie Financial Corp 150 Bloor St W Suite M111 Toronto ON M5S3B5 416-922-5322 922-5660
TF: 888-653-7070 ■ *Web:* www.mackenziefinancial.com
Manning & Napier Advisors Inc 290 Woodcliff Dr Fairport NY 14450 585-325-6880 325-1984
Web: www.manning-napier.com
Marvin & Palmer Assoc Inc 1201 N Market St Suite 2300 Wilmington DE 19801 302-573-3570 573-2545
TF: 800-775-4259 ■ *Web:* www.marvinandpalmer.com
McGlinn Capital Management 850 N Wyomissing Blvd Wyomissing PA 19610 610-374-5125 371-1116
TF: 800-783-1478
McMorgan & Co 1 Bush St Suite 800 San Francisco CA 94104 415-788-9300 616-9300
Web: www.mcmorgan.com
MD Sass Investor Services Inc
1185 Ave of the Americas 18th Fl New York NY 10036 212-730-2000 764-0381
Web: www.mdsass.com
Mellon Capital Management Corp
595 Market St Suite 3000 San Francisco CA 94105 415-546-6056 777-5699
Web: www.mcm.com
MFS Investment Management 500 Boylston St Boston MA 02116 617-954-5000 654-3203*
**Fax Area Code:* 877 ■ *TF:* 800-637-2929 ■ *Web:* www.mfs.com
Moody's Corp 99 Church St New York NY 10007 212-553-0300 553-5376
NYSE: MCO ■ *Web:* www.moodys.com
Moore Capital Management Inc 1251 Ave of the Americas New York NY 10020 212-782-7000 782-7542
Web: www.moorecap.com
National Financial Partners Corp 787 7th Ave 11th Fl New York NY 10019 212-301-4000 301-4001
NYSE: NFP ■ *Web:* www.nfp.com
Navellier Securities Corp 1 E Liberty St 3rd Fl Reno NV 89501 775-785-2300 785-2321
TF: 800-887-8671 ■ *Web:* www.navellier.com
NCM Capital Management Group Inc
2634 Durham Chapel Hill Blvd Suite 206 Durham NC 27707 919-688-0620 683-1352*
**Fax:* Mktg ■ *Web:* www.ncmcapital.com
Nelson Benson & Zellmer Inc 3200 Cherry Creek S Dr Suite 730 Denver CO 80209 303-778-6800 778-7931
Neuberger Berman LLC 605 3rd Ave New York NY 10158 212-476-9000 476-9090
TF: 800-223-6448 ■ *Web:* www.nb.com
Nicholas-Applegate Capital Management
600 W Broadway 29th Fl San Diego CA 92101 619-687-8100 687-2979
TF: 800-656-6226 ■ *Web:* www.nacm.com
Northern Trust Co of Connecticut 300 Atlantic St Suite 400 Stamford CT 06901 203-977-7000 356-9341
TF: 800-722-4609 ■ *Web:* www.ntrs.com
Northern Trust Quantitative Advisors Inc 50 S La Salle St Chicago IL 60603 312-557-1426 557-1478*
**Fax:* Sales
Odlum Brown Ltd 250 Howe St Suite 1100 Vancouver BC V6C3S9 604-669-1600 681-8310
Web: www.odlumbrown.com
Payden & Rygel 333 S Grand Ave Los Angeles CA 90071 213-625-1900 628-8488
TF: 800-572-9336 ■ *Web:* www.payden.com
Peninsula Asset Management Inc 1111 3rd Ave W Suite 340 Bradenton FL 34205 941-748-8680 748-2654
TF: 800-269-6417 ■ *Web:* www.peninsulaasset.com
Phoenix Investment Partners Ltd 56 Prospect St Hartford CT 06115 860-403-5000
Web: www.phoenixinvestments.com
PLM International Inc 3988 N Central Expy Bldg 5 6th Fl Dallas TX 75204 214-887-7150 887-7411
TF: 800-626-7549 ■ *Web:* www.plm.com
Primerica Financial Services 3120 Breckinridge Blvd Duluth GA 30099 770-381-1000 564-6110*
**Fax:* PR ■ *TF:* 800-257-4725 ■ *Web:* ww4.primerica.com
Princor Financial Services Corp PO Box 10423 Des Moines IA 50306 515-247-5111 248-4745
TF: 888-774-6267 ■ *Web:* www.princor.com
Progress Investment Management Co
33 New Montgomery St Suite 1900 San Francisco CA 94105 415-512-3480 512-3475
Web: www.progressinvestment.com
Provident Investment Counsel 300 N Lake Ave Pasadena CA 91101 626-449-8500 356-0533
TF: 800-411-6387 ■ *Web:* www.provnet.com
Prudential Financial Inc 751 Broad St Newark NJ 07102 973-802-6000 367-6476
NYSE: PRU ■ *TF:* 800-843-7625 ■ *Web:* www.prudential.com
Pugh Capital Management Inc 1414 31st Ave S Suite 302 Seattle WA 98144 206-322-4985 322-3025
Web: www.pughcapital.com
Putnam Investments 1 Post Office Sq Boston MA 02109 617-292-1000
TF: 888-478-8626 ■ *Web:* www.putnam.com
Putnam Lovell NBF 65 E 55th St Park Ave Tower 34th Fl New York NY 10022 212-546-7500 644-2271
Web: www.putnamlovell.com
PVG Asset Management Corp 24918 Genesee Trail Rd Golden CO 80401 303-526-0548 526-1391
TF: 800-777-0818 ■ *Web:* www.pvgassetmanagement.com
RCM 4 Embarcadero Ctr San Francisco CA 94111 415-954-5474 954-8200
Web: www.rcm.com
Reed Conner & Birdwell Inc
11111 Santa Monica Blvd Suite 1700 Los Angeles CA 90025 310-478-4005 478-8496
TF: 877-478-4722 ■ *Web:* www.rcbinvest.com
Retirement System Group Inc 150 E 42nd St 27th Fl New York NY 10017 212-503-0100 503-0198
TF: 800-446-7774 ■ *Web:* www.rsgroup.com
Rhumbline Advisers Corp 30 Rowes Wharf Suite 350 Boston MA 02110 617-345-0434 345-0675
Web: www.rhumblineadvisers.com
Rice Hall James & Assoc LLC 600 W Broadway Suite 1000 San Diego CA 92101 619-239-9005
Web: www.ricehalljames.com
Rittenhouse Financial Services Inc
5 Radnor Corporate Ctr Suite 300 Radnor PA 19087 610-254-9600 225-3824*
**Fax:* PR ■ *TF:* 800-847-6369 ■ *Web:* www.nuveen.com/rittenhouse
RiverSource LLC 1737 Ameriprise Financial Center Minneapolis MN 55440 612-671-3131 671-8880
Web: www.riversource.com
RNC Capital Management LLC 11601 Wilshire Blvd 25th Fl Los Angeles CA 90025 310-477-6543 479-6406
TF: 800-877-7624 ■ *Web:* www.rnccapital.com
Royce & Assoc LLC 1414 Ave of the Americas 9th Fl New York NY 10019 212-486-1445 752-8875
TF: 800-348-1414 ■ *Web:* www.roycefunds.com
RREEF 101 California St 26th Fl San Francisco CA 94111 415-781-3300 986-6248
TF: 800-222-5885 ■ *Web:* www.rreef.com
Ruane Cunniff & Goldfarb Inc 767 5th Ave Suite 4701 New York NY 10153 212-832-5280 832-5298
Russell Investment Group 909 A St Tacoma WA 98402 800-787-7354 594-1889*
**Fax Area Code:* 253 ■ **Fax:* Mktg ■ *Web:* www.russell.com
Sarofim Fayez & Co 2 Houston Ctr Suite 2907 Houston TX 77010 713-654-4484 654-8184
TF: 800-288-7125 ■ *Web:* www.sarofim.com
SCM Advisors LLC 909 Montgomery St Suite 500 San Francisco CA 94133 415-486-6500 486-6780
TF: 800-828-1212 ■ *Web:* www.scmadv.com
Sears Investment Management Co 3333 Beverly Rd Hoffman Estates IL 60179 847-286-4766 286-4785

Phone Fax

SEI Investments Co 1 Freedom Valley Dr Oaks PA 19456 610-676-1000 676-4160*
NASDAQ: SEIC ■ **Fax:* Hum Res ■ *Web:* www.seic.com
Seligman J & W & Co Inc 100 Park Ave New York NY 10017 212-850-1864 922-5742
TF: 800-221-7844 ■ *Web:* www.seligman.com
Signalert Corp 150 Great Neck Rd Suite 301 Great Neck NY 11021 516-829-6444 829-9366
TF: 800-829-6229 ■ *Web:* www.systemsandforecasts.com
Simms Capital Management Inc 107 Elm St Suite 401 Stamford CT 06902 203-252-5700 252-5742
TF: 888-258-6365 ■ *Web:* www.simmscapital.com
Sit Investment Assoc Inc 80 S 8th St 3300 IDS Center Minneapolis MN 55402 612-332-3223 342-2018
Web: www.sitinvest.com
SKBA Capital Management
44 Montgomery St Suite 3500 San Francisco CA 94104 415-989-7852 989-2114
Web: www.skba.com
Smith Barney Consulting Group 222 Delaware Ave 7th Fl Wilmington DE 19801 302-888-4100 888-4199
Smith Graham & Co 600 Travis St Suite 6900 Houston TX 77002 713-227-1100 223-0844
TF: 800-739-4470 ■ *Web:* www.smith-graham.com
Standard & Poor's 55 Water St 45th Fl New York NY 10041 212-438-2000 438-3958*
**Fax:* Sales ■ *TF Cust Svc:* 800-344-3014 ■ *Web:* www.standardandpoors.com
Standish Mellon 1 Boston Pl Boston MA 02108 617-248-6000 248-6050
Web: www.standishmellon.com
StarMine Corp 49 Stevenson St 8th Fl San Francisco CA 94105 415-777-1147 536-0130
Web: www.starmine.com
State Street Global Advisors 1 Lincoln St Boston MA 02111 617-664-4738 654-6012
Web: www.ssga.com
Sterling Capital Management
2 Morrocroft Ctr 4064 Colony Rd Suite 300 Charlotte NC 28211 704-372-8670 376-8127
TF: 800-627-1156 ■ *Web:* www.sterling-capital.com
Strong Financial Corp PO Box 2936 Milwaukee WI 53201 414-359-1400 359-1013
TF: 800-368-1030
Swarthmore Group 1717 Arch St Suite 3810 Philadelphia PA 19103 215-557-9300 557-9305
Web: www.swarthmoregroup.com
Systematic Financial Management LP
300 Frank W Burr Blvd 7th Fl Glenpoint Ctr E Teaneck NJ 07666 201-928-1982 928-1984
TF: 800-258-0497 ■ *Web:* www.sfmlp.com
T Rowe Price Assoc Inc 100 E Pratt St Baltimore MD 21202 410-345-2000 345-6244*
**Fax:* Cust Svc ■ *TF:* 800-638-7890 ■ *Web:* www.troweprice.com
Thompson Siegel & Walmsley Inc
6806 Paragon Pl Suite 300 Richmond VA 23230 804-353-4500 353-0925
TF: 800-697-1056 ■ *Web:* www.tswinvest.com
Todd Investment Advisors Inc 101 S 5th St Suite 3160 Louisville KY 40202 502-585-3121 585-4203
TF: 888-544-8633 ■ *Web:* www.toddinvestment.com
Tom Johnson Investment Management Inc
204 N Robinson St Suite 2900 Oklahoma City OK 73102 405-236-2111 236-2008
Web: www.tjim.com
Torch Energy Advisors Inc 1221 Lamar St Suite 1175 Houston TX 77010 713-650-1246 655-1866
TF: 800-324-8672 ■ *Web:* www.teai.com
Transamerica Investment Management
11111 Santa Monica Blvd Suite 820 Los Angeles CA 90025 310-996-3200 477-9767
TF: 866-846-1800 ■ *Web:* www.timllc.com
Trinity Investment Management Corp 10 St James Ave Boston MA 02116 617-728-7200 728-7202
TF: 800-422-1854 ■ *Web:* www.trinityinvestment.com
Trusco Capital Management Inc 50 Hurt Plaza Suite 1400 Atlanta GA 30303 404-586-6450 575-2978
Web: www.truscocapital.com
Turner Investment Partners Inc 1205 Westlakes Dr Suite 100 Berwyn PA 19312 610-251-0268 251-0288
TF: 800-424-4865 ■ *Web:* www.turner-invest.com
UBS Global Asset Management Inc 51 W 52 St New York NY 10019 212-882-5000 882-5892
Web: us.ubs-globalam.com
UNC Partners 54 Burroughs St Boston MA 02130 617-522-2160 522-2176
Web: www.uncpartners.com
US Global Investors Inc PO Box 781234 San Antonio TX 78278 210-308-1234 308-1217
NASDAQ: GROW ■ *TF:* 800-873-8637 ■ *Web:* www.usfunds.com
US Trust Corp 114 W 47th St New York NY 10036 212-852-1000 852-3852
TF: 800-878-7878 ■ *Web:* www.ustrust.com
USAA Investment Management 9800 Fredericksburg Rd San Antonio TX 78288 210-498-8777 292-8177*
**Fax Area Code:* 800 ■ *TF:* 800-531-8448 ■ *Web:* www.usaa.com
Value Line Asset Management 220 E 42nd St New York NY 10017 212-907-1500 818-9781
TF: 800-634-3583 ■ *Web:* www.valueline.com
Value Line Inc 220 E 42nd St New York NY 10017 212-907-1500 818-9747
NASDAQ: VALU ■ *TF Cust Svc:* 800-634-3583 ■ *Web:* www.valueline.com
Van Kampen Investments Inc 1 Parkview Plaza Oakbrook Terrace IL 60181 630-684-6000 684-5997
TF: 800-225-2222 ■ *Web:* www.vankampen.com
Vanguard Group 455 Devon Park Dr Wayne PA 19087 610-669-1000 669-6551
TF: 800-662-7447 ■ *Web:* www.vanguard.com
Veritas Capital Fund LP 590 Madison Ave 41st Fl New York NY 10022 212-415-6700 688-9411
Web: www.veritascapital.com
Vest HD Financial Services 6333 N State Hwy 161 4th Fl Irving TX 75038 972-870-6000 870-6128
TF: 800-821-8254 ■ *Web:* hdvest.com
Vontobel Asset Management Inc 450 Park Ave 7th Fl New York NY 10022 212-415-7000 415-7087
TF: 800-445-8872 ■ *Web:* www.vusa.com
Voyageur Asset Management Inc 100 S 5th St Suite 2300 Minneapolis MN 55402 612-376-7000 376-7007
TF: 800-553-2143 ■ *Web:* www.voyageur.net
Waddell & Reed Financial Inc 6300 Lamar Ave Overland Park KS 66202 913-236-2000 236-5044
NYSE: WDR ■ *TF:* 888-923-3355 ■ *Web:* www.waddell.com
Washington Capital Management Inc 1301 5th Ave Suite 1500 Seattle WA 98101 206-382-0825 382-0950
Web: www.wcmadvisors.com
Wellington Management Co LLP 75 State St Boston MA 02109 617-951-5000 951-5250
Web: www.wellington.com
Wellington West Capital Inc
400 - 200 Waterfront Dr Suite 400 Winnipeg MB R3B3P1 204-925-2250 942-6194
TF: 800-461-6314 ■ *Web:* www.wellwest.ca
Wilshire Assoc Inc 1299 Ocean Ave Suite 700 Santa Monica CA 90401 310-451-3051 458-0520
Web: www.wilshire.com
Woodbury Financial Services Inc PO Box 64284 Saint Paul MN 55164 651-738-4000 738-5332
TF: 800-800-2000 ■ *Web:* www.woodburyfinancialservices.com
WP Stewart & Co Inc 527 Madison Ave 20th Fl New York NY 10022 212-750-8585 980-8039
NYSE: WPL ■ *Web:* www.wpstewart.com
Wright Investors' Service 440 Wheelers Farms Rd Milford CT 06461 203-783-4400 783-4401
TF: 800-232-0013 ■ *Web:* www.wisi.com
Yacktman Asset Management Co
6300 Bridgepoint Pkwy Bldg 1 Suite 320 Austin TX 78730 512-767-6700
TF: 800-356-6356 ■ *Web:* www.yacktman.com

405 INVESTMENT COMPANIES - SMALL BUSINESS

The companies listed here conform to the Small Business Administration's standards for investing.

Phone Fax

Agio Capital Partners I LP 5050 Lincoln Dr Suite 420 Edina MN 55436 952-938-1628 933-6066
Web: www.agio-capital.com
Allied Capital Corp 1919 Pennsylvania Ave NW 3rd Fl Washington DC 20006 202-721-6100 659-2053
NYSE: ALD ■ *TF:* 888-818-5298 ■ *Web:* www.alliedcapital.com

Phone Fax

Anthem Capital Management LLC 1414 Key Hwy Suite 300....... Baltimore MD 21230 410-625-1510 625-1735
Web: www.anthemcapital.com
Argentum Group 60 Madison Ave Suite 701.................... New York NY 10010 212-949-6262 949-8294
Web: www.argentumgroup.com
Atalanta Investment Co Inc PO Box 7718................. Incline Village NV 89452 775-833-1836 833-1890
BancBoston Ventures Inc 100 Federal St 19th Fl................. Boston MA 02110 617-434-2442 434-1153
TF: 800-841-4000 ■ *Web:* www.bancboscap.com
Bankers Capital Corp 3100 Gillham Rd...................... Kansas City MO 64109 816-531-1600 531-1334
Bankoh Investment Services Inc 130 Merchant St Suite 850...... Honolulu HI 96813 808-537-8500 538-4891
Web: www.boh.com
Blue Ridge Investors 300 N Greene St Suite 2100 .... Greensboro NC 27401 336-370-0576 274-4984
Capital for Business Inc 11 S Meramec Ave Suite 1430......... Saint Louis MO 63105 314-746-7427 746-8739
Web: www.capitalforbusiness.com
Capital Marketing Corp 4901 Bosque Blvd Suite 233 .... Waco TX 76710 254-741-1770 741-1777
Cedar Creek Partners LLC
10936 W Port Washington Rd Suite 180 .... Mequon WI 53092 414-272-5505 272-1029
Web: www.cedarllc.com
Center for Innovation
University of North Dakota PO Box 8372 .... Grand Forks ND 58202 701-777-3132 777-2339
Web: www.innovators.net
Charleston Capital Corp PO Box 328........................ Charleston SC 29402 843-723-6464 723-1228
CIP Capital LP 1200 Liberty Ridge Dr Suite 300 .... Wayne PA 19087 610-964-7860 964-8136
Domestic Capital Corp 815 Reservoir Ave..................... Cranston RI 02910 401-946-3310 943-6708
TF: 800-556-6600
Early Stage Enterprises 103 Carnegie Ctr Suite 100 .... Princeton NJ 08540 609-921-8896 921-8703
Web: www.esevc.com
East-West Mortgage 1568 Spring Hill Rd Suite 100 .... McLean VA 22102 703-442-0150 442-0156
TF: 800-844-1015 ■ *Web:* www.ewmortgage.com
El Dorado Ventures 2440 Sand Hill Rd Suite 200 .... Menlo Park CA 94025 650-854-1200 854-1202
Web: www.eldorado.com
Elk Assoc Funding Corp 747 3rd Ave 4th Fl.................... New York NY 10017 212-355-2449 759-3338
TF: 800-214-1047
Enterprise Venture Capital Corp of Pennsylvania
111 Market St .... Johnstown PA 15901 814-535-7597 535-8677
Eos Partners SBIC LP 320 Park Ave 9th Fl.................... New York NY 10022 212-832-5800 832-5815
Web: www.eospartners.com
Equitas LP 2000 Glen Echo Rd Suite 101...................... Nashville TN 37215 615-383-8673 383-8693
Forrest Binkley & Brown 19900 MacArthur Blvd Suite 570........... Irvine CA 92612 949-222-1987 222-1988
Web: www.fbbvc.com
Fostin Capital Corp 681 Andersen Dr........................ Pittsburgh PA 15220 412-928-8900 928-9635
Galliard Capital Management Inc
800 La Salle Ave Suite 2060 .... Minneapolis MN 55402 612-667-3210 667-3223
TF: 800-717-1617 ■ *Web:* www.galliard.com
GamePlan Financial Marketing LLC
300 ParkBrooke Pl Suite 200............................ Woodstock GA 30189 770-517-2765 517-0649
TF: 866-766-3855 ■ *Web:* www.gameplanfinancial.com
Gemini Investors LLC 20 William St Suite 250................... Wellesley MA 02481 781-237-7001 237-7233
Web: www.gemini-investors.com
Impact Seven Inc 147 Lake Almena Dr......................... Almena WI 54805 715-357-3334 357-6233
TF: 800-685-9353 ■ *Web:* www.impactseven.org
Kansas City Equity Partners 233 W 47th St .... Kansas City MO 64112 816-960-1771 960-1777
Web: www.kcep.com
Kansas Venture Capital Inc
6700 Antioch Plaza Suite 460 .... Overland Park KS 66204 913-262-7117 262-3509
Web: www.kvci.com
Kentucky Highlands Investment Corp PO Box 1738............... London KY 40743 606-864-5175 864-5194
Web: www.khic.org
Kline Hawkes & Co 11726 San Vicente Blvd Suite 300......... Los Angeles CA 90049 310-442-4700 442-4707
Web: www.klinehawkes.com
MACC Private Equities Inc 101 2nd St SE Suite 800 .... Cedar Rapids IA 52401 319-363-8249 363-9683
NASDAQ: MACC
Marwit Capital LLC 100 Bayview Cir Suite 550 .... Newport Beach CA 92660 949-861-3636 861-3637
Web: www.marwit.com
Mason Wells 411 E Wisconsin Ave Suite 1280 .... Milwaukee WI 53202 414-727-6400 727-6410
TF: 800-342-2265 ■ *Web:* www.masonwells.com
Mellon Ventures Inc 1 Mellon Center Suite 5210 .... Pittsburgh PA 15258 412-236-3594 236-3593
Web: www.mellonventures.com
Meridian Venture Partners 201 King of Prussia Rd Suite 240 .... Radnor PA 19087 610-254-2999 254-2996
Web: www.meridianventure.com
MorAmerica Capital Corp 101 2nd St SE Suite 800 .... Cedar Rapids IA 52401 319-363-8249 363-9683
Mountain Ventures Inc PO Box 1738.......................... London KY 40743 606-864-5175 864-5194
National City Equity Partners Inc 1900 E 9th St................ Cleveland OH 44114 216-222-2000 222-9965
Web: www.ncequitypartners.com
Northern Pacific Capital Corp PO Box 1658 .... Portland OR 97207 503-241-1255 299-6653
Novus Ventures LP 20111 Stevens Creek Blvd Suite 130.......... Cupertino CA 95014 408-252-3900 252-1713
Web: www.novusventures.com
RFE Investment Partners 36 Grove St .... New Canaan CT 06840 203-966-2800 966-3109
Web: www.rfeip.com
River Cities Capital Funds 221 E 4th St Suite 1900 .... Cincinnati OH 45202 513-621-9700 579-8939
Web: www.rccf.com
Rust Capital Ltd 327 Congress Ave Suite 350..................... Austin TX 78701 512-482-0806 474-1610
Seacoast Capital Partners 55 Ferncroft Rd...................... Danvers MA 01923 978-750-1351 750-1301
Web: www.seacoastcapital.com
Sorrento Assoc Inc 4370 La Jolla Village Dr Suite 1040......... San Diego CA 92122 858-452-3100 452-7607
Web: www.sorrentoventures.com
Spirit Enterprise LLP 481 E Division St Suite 800 .... Fond du Lac WI 54935 920-923-6335 923-4369
Web: www.spiritenterprise.com
Sprout Capital Corp 11 Madison Ave 13th Fl Tower .... New York NY 10010 212-538-3600 538-8245
Web: www.sproutgroup.com
Sterling/Carl Marks Capital Inc
175 Great Neck Rd Suite 408 .... Great Neck NY 11021 516-482-7374 487-0781
Web: www.sterlingcarlmarks.com
Stonehenge Capital Co LLC 236 3rd St .... Baton Rouge LA 70801 225-408-3000 408-3090
Web: www.stonehengecapital.com
Tappan Zee Capital Corp 201 Lower Notch Rd .... Little Falls NJ 07424 973-256-8280 256-2841
TD Capital (USA) Inc 111 Huntington Ave Suite 1400 .... Boston MA 02199 617-425-0800 425-0801
Web: www.tdcapital.com
UMB Capital Corp 1010 Grand Blvd .... Kansas City MO 64106 816-860-7914 860-7143
TF: 800-821-2171 ■ *Web:* www.umb.com
Vestor Partners LP 607 Cerrillos Rd Suite D2 .... Santa Fe NM 87505 505-988-9100 988-1958
Web: www.vestor.com
Virginia Capital Partners LLC 1801 Libbie Ave Suite 201 .... Richmond VA 23226 804-648-4802 648-4809
Web: www.vacapital.com
Wasatch Venture Corp 15 W South Temple St Suite 520...... Salt Lake City UT 84133 801-524-8939 524-8941
Web: www.wasatchvc.com
Waterside Capital Corp 500 E Main St Suite 800 .... Norfolk VA 23510 757-626-1111 626-0114
NASDAQ: WSCC ■ *Web:* www.watersidecapital.com
White Pines Ventures LLC 900 Victors Way Suite 280 .... Ann Arbor MI 48108 734-747-9401 747-9704
Web: www.whitepines.com
Winfield Capital Corp 237 Mamaroneck Ave .... White Plains NY 10605 914-949-2600 949-7195
Web: www.winfieldcapital.com

406 INVESTMENT COMPANIES - SPECIALIZED SMALL BUSINESS

Companies listed here conform to the Small Business Administration's requirements for investment in minority companies.

Phone Fax

Associated Southwest Investors Inc
6501 Americas Pkwy NE Suite 210....................... Albuquerque NM 87110 505-247-4050 888-5244
Bastion Capital Corp 1901 Ave of the Stars Suite 470 .... Los Angeles CA 90067 310-788-5700 277-7582
Continental SBIC 4141 N Henderson Rd Suite 8 .... Arlington VA 22203 703-527-5200 527-3700
Enterprise Ohio 8 N Main St...................................... Dayton OH 45402 937-461-6164 222-7035
Far East Capital Corp 350 S Grand Ave...................... Los Angeles CA 90071 213-687-1260 626-3884
TF: 800-753-8449
First American Capital Funding
10101 Slater Ave Suite 214.......................... Fountain Valley CA 92708 714-965-7190 965-7193
First County Capital Inc 40-48 Ming St Suite 301................ Flushing NY 11354 718-461-1778 461-1835
Fulcrum Venture Capital Corp
300 Corporate Pointe Suite 380.......................... Culver City CA 90230 310-645-1271 645-1272
Web: www.fulcrumventures.com
Greater Philadelphia Venture Capital Corp Inc
351 E Conestoga Rd .... Wayne PA 19087 610-688-6829 254-8958
Ibero American Investors Corp 104 Scio St.................... Rochester NY 14604 585-262-3440 262-3441
Web: www.iberoinvestors.com
Medallion Capital 3000 W County Rd 42 Suite 301 .... Burnsville MN 55337 952-831-2025 831-2945
Web: www.medallion.com
MESBIC Ventures Inc 2435 N Central Expy Suite 200........... Richardson TX 75080 972-991-1597 991-1647
Web: www.mvhc.com
Milestone Growth Fund 401 2nd Ave S Suite 1032............ Minneapolis MN 55401 612-338-0090 338-1172
Web: www.milestonegrowth.com
MMG Ventures LP 826 E Baltimore St .... Baltimore MD 21202 410-659-7850 333-2552
Web: www.mmggroup.com
Multimedia Broadcast Investment Corp 3101 South St NW..... Washington DC 20007 202-293-1166 293-1181
North Texas MESBIC 9500 4th Ln Suite 430 .... Dallas TX 75234 214-221-3565 221-3566
Opportunity Capital Corp 2201 Walnut Ave Suite 210............ Fremont CA 94538 510-795-7000 494-5439
Web: www.opportunitycapitalpartners.com
Pierre Funding Corp 805 3rd Ave 19th Fl...................... New York NY 10022 212-888-1515 687-0659
Polestar Capital Inc 180 N Michigan Ave Suite 1905 .... Chicago IL 60601 312-984-9090 984-9877
Web: www.polestarvc.com
Positive Enterprises Inc 1489 Webster St Suite 218......... San Francisco CA 94115 415-885-6600 928-6363
Rutgers Minority Investment Co 180 University Ave 3rd Fl.......... Newark NJ 07102 973-353-5627
Savant Group 6929 Sunrise Blvd Suite 109 .... Citrus Heights CA 95610 916-721-1400 721-7440
Web: www.thesavantgroup.com
Sun-Delta Capital Access Center Inc 819 Main St .... Greenville MS 38701 662-335-5291 335-5295
TF: 800-829-5338
Transportation Capital Corp 437 Madison Ave 38th Fl .... New York NY 10022 212-328-2100 328-2121
TF: 800-829-4867
Valley Capital Corp 535 Chestnut St Suite 161 .... Chattanooga TN 37402 423-265-1557 265-1588
West Tennessee Venture Capital Corp 5 N 3rd St Suite 2001..... Memphis TN 38103 901-523-1884 527-6091
Web: www.wtvcc.com
Women's Growth Capital Fund
1025 Thomas Jefferson NW Suite 305-W................... Washington DC 20007 202-342-1431 342-1203
TF: 888-640-8051

407 INVESTMENT GUIDES - ONLINE

SEE ALSO Buyer's Guides - Online p. 1403

Phone Fax

BestCalls.com 243 Old Adobe Rd........................... Los Gatos CA 95032 408-358-9540 370-1761
Web: www.bestcalls.com
BigCharts Inc 123 N 3rd St Suite 300 .... Minneapolis MN 55401 612-338-0049 338-0069
Web: bigcharts.marketwatch.com
Briefing.com Inc 555 S Airport Blvd Suite 150 .... Burlingame CA 94010 650-347-2220 347-2223
TF: 800-752-3013 ■ *Web:* www.briefing.com
ClearStation Inc 4500 Bohannon Dr......................... Menlo Park CA 94025 650-331-6000 331-6819
Web: clearstation.etrade.com
CNET Investor 1 Athenaeum St............................. Cambridge MA 02142 617-225-3200 225-3611
Web: investor.news.com
EarningsWhispers.com
c/o WebTools LLC 113 W Main St Suite 8 .... Jackson MO 63755 573-243-2734 243-2331
Web: www.earningswhispers.com
EDGAR Online Inc 50 Washington St 11th Fl .... Norwalk CT 06854 203-852-5666 852-5667*
NASDAQ: EDGR ■ **Fax:* Cust Svc ■ *TF:* 800-416-6651 ■ *Web:* www.edgar-online.com
eSignal 3955 Point Eden Way................................ Hayward CA 94545 510-266-6000 266-6100
TF Sales: 800-367-4670 ■ *Web:* www.esignal.com
FactSet Research Systems Inc 601 Merritt 7 3rd Fl .... Norwalk CT 06851 203-810-1000 810-1001
NYSE: FDS ■ *TF:* 877-322-8738 ■ *Web:* www.factset.com
FutureSource.com 208 S LaSalle St Suite 1444................. Chicago IL 60604 312-977-9067 977-9923
Web: www.futuresource.com
Harris myCFO Inc DBA myCFO 1700 Seaport Blvd 4th Fl...... Redwood City CA 94063 650-210-5000 210-5010
TF: 877-692-3609 ■ *Web:* www.mycfo.com
Hoover's Inc 5800 Airport Blvd.................................. Austin TX 78752 512-374-4500 374-4501
TF: 800-486-8666 ■ *Web:* www.hoovers.com
INVESTools Inc 3705 Haven Ave Suite 1..................... Menlo Park CA 94025 281-588-9700 588-9797
AMEX: IED ■ *Web:* www.investools.com
InvestorPlace.com
c/o Phillips Investment Resources LLC 2420A Gehman Ln ...... Lancaster PA 17602 800-219-8592 762-6776*
**Fax Area Code:* 301 ■ *Web:* www.investorplace.com
IPO Monitor 5200 W Century Blvd Suite 470................ Los Angeles CA 90045 800-266-0126 642-6933*
**Fax Area Code:* 310 ■ *Web:* www.ipomonitor.com
MarketCenter.com 3955 Point Eden Way......................... Hayward CA 94545 510-266-6000 266-6100
Web: www.marketcenter.com
MarketWatch Inc 825 Battery St....................... San Francisco CA 94111 415-733-0500 392-1972
Web: www.marketwatch.com
Motley Fool Inc 2000 Duke St 4th Fl .... Alexandria VA 22314 703-838-3665 254-1999
Web: www.fool.com
Prophet Financial Systems Inc 658 High St .... Palo Alto CA 94301 650-322-4183 322-4184
TF: 800-772-8040 ■ *Web:* www.prophet.net
Quote.com 3955 Point Eden Way .... Hayward CA 94545 510-266-6000 266-6100
TF: 800-498-8068 ■ *Web:* www.quote.com
Stockwatch 700 W Georgia St PO Box 10371 .... Vancouver BC V7Y1J6 604-687-1500 687-0541
TF: 800-268-6397 ■ *Web:* new.stockwatch.com
TheStreet.com Inc 14 Wall St 15th Fl .... New York NY 10005 212-321-5000 321-5016
NASDAQ: TSCM ■ *TF:* 800-562-9571 ■ *Web:* www.thestreet.com
Yahoo! Finance 701 1st Ave.................................. Sunnyvale CA 94089 408-349-3300 349-3301
Web: finance.yahoo.com

408 INVESTMENT (MISC)

SEE ALSO Banks - Commercial & Savings p. 1368; Commodity Contracts Brokers & Dealers p. 1499; Franchises p. 1672; Investment Guides - Online p. 1876; Mortgage Lenders & Loan Brokers p. 1397; Mutual Funds p. 2010; Newsletters - Investment Newsletters p. 2017; Real Estate Investment Trusts (REITs) p. 2201; Royalty Trusts p. 2300; Securities Brokers & Dealers p. 2307; Venture Capital Firms p. 2398

				Phone	Fax
ABRY Partners LLC 111 Huntington Ave 30th Fl *TF:* 800-578-2279 ■ *Web:* www.abry.com	Boston	MA	02199	617-859-2959	859-7205
Acacia Research Corp 500 Newport Center Dr Suite 700 *NASDAQ: ACTG* ■ *Web:* www.acaciaresearch.com	Newport Beach	CA	92660	949-480-8300	480-8301
Adams Express Co 7 Saint Paul St Suite 1140 *NYSE: ADX* ■ *TF:* 800-638-2479 ■ *Web:* www.adamsexpress.com	Baltimore	MD	21202	410-752-5900	659-0080
AEA Investors Inc 65 E 55th St *Web:* www.aeainvestors.com	New York	NY	10022	212-644-5900	888-1459
Anschutz Corp 555 17th St Suite 2400	Denver	CO	80202	303-298-1000	298-8881
Bancroft Fund Ltd 65 Madison Ave Suite 550 *AMEX: BCV* ■ *Web:* www.bancroftfund.com	Morristown	NJ	07960	973-631-1177	631-1313
BKF Capital Group Inc 1 Rockefeller Plaza 19th Fl *NYSE: BKF* ■ *TF:* 800-253-1891 ■ *Web:* www.bkfcapital.com	New York	NY	10020	212-332-8400	332-8487
CC Industries Inc 222 N La Salle St Suite 1000	Chicago	IL	60601	312-855-4000	236-7074
Central Securities Corp 630 5th Ave Suite 820 *AMEX: CET* ■ *TF:* 866-593-2507 ■ *Web:* www.centralsecurities.com	New York	NY	10111	212-698-2020	
Cerberus Capital Management LP 299 Park Ave *Web:* www.cerberuscapital.com	New York	NY	10171	212-891-2100	
Columbia Ventures Corp 203 SE Park Plaza Dr Suite 270 *TF:* 866-204-0747 ■ *Web:* www.colventures.com	Vancouver	WA	98684	360-816-1840	816-1841
Counsel Corp 40 King St W Suite 3200 *TSX: CXS* ■ *TF:* 800-879-9548 ■ *Web:* www.counselcorp.com	Toronto	ON	M5H3Y2	416-866-3000	866-3061
Danner Co 2 International Dr Suite 510	Nashville	TN	37217	615-367-9092	367-2156
Dundee Wealth Management Inc 1 Adelaide St E 27th Fl *TSX: DW* ■ *TF:* 888-332-2661 ■ *Web:* www.dundeewealth.com	Toronto	ON	M5C2V9	416-350-3250	350-5105
Energy Savings Income Fund 100 King St W Suite 2630 *TSX: SIF.UN* ■ *Web:* www.energysavingsincomefund.com	Toronto	ON	M5X1E1	416-367-2998	367-4749
Enerplus Resources Fund 333 7th Ave SW Suite 3000 *TSX: ERF.UN* ■ *TF:* 800-319-6462 ■ *Web:* www.enerplus.com	Calgary	AB	T2P2Z1	403-298-2200	298-2211
Enstar Group Inc 401 Madison Ave *NASDAQ: ESGR* ■ *Web:* www.enstargroup.com	Montgomery	AL	36104	334-834-5483	834-2530
Eureka Growth Capital 1717 Arch St 3420 Bell Atlantic Tower *Web:* www.eurekagrowth.com	Philadelphia	PA	19103	267-238-4200	238-4201
Fairmont Capital Inc 18200 Yorba Linda Blvd Suite 211 *Web:* www.fairmontcapital.com	Yorba Linda	CA	92886	714-524-4770	524-4775
Fairview Capital Partners Inc 10 Stanford Dr *Web:* www.fairviewcapital.com	Farmington	CT	06032	860-674-8066	678-5108
Fidelity Investments Charitable Gift Fund PO Box 55158 **Fax Area Code:* 617 ■ *Web:* www.charitablegift.org	Boston	MA	02205	800-682-4438	476-7206*
Forstmann Little & Co 767 5th Ave 44th Fl *Web:* www.forstmannlittle.com	New York	NY	10153	212-355-5656	759-9059
Fremont Group Inc 199 Fremont St *Web:* www.fremontgroup.com	San Francisco	CA	94105	415-284-8500	284-8191
General American Investors Co Inc 450 Lexington Ave Suite 3300 *NYSE: GAM* ■ *TF:* 800-436-8401 ■ *Web:* www.generalamericaninvestors.com	New York	NY	10017	212-916-8400	916-8490
Gores Technology Group 10877 Wilshire Blvd Suite 1805 *Web:* www.gores.com	Los Angeles	CA	90024	310-209-3010	209-3310
Gould Investors LP 60 Cutter Mill Rd Suite 303	Great Neck	NY	11021	516-466-3100	466-3132
Henry Crown & Co 222 N La Salle St Suite 2000	Chicago	IL	60601	312-236-6300	899-5039
Highland Capital Management LP 13455 Noel Rd 2 Galleria Tower Suite 800 *Web:* www.hcmlp.com	Dallas	TX	75240	972-628-4100	628-4147
Hillman Co 330 Grant St Suite 1900 *TF:* 800-445-5626	Pittsburgh	PA	15219	412-281-2620	338-3520
HM Capital Partners LLC 200 Crescent Ct Suite 1600 *Web:* www.hmcapital.com	Dallas	TX	75201	214-740-7300	720-7888
Hold Brothers On-Line Investment Services Inc 525 Washington Blvd 14th Fl *Web:* www.holdbrothers.com	Jersey City	NJ	07310	201-499-8700	499-8750
HomeVestors of America Inc 10670 N Central Expwy Suite 700 *Web:* www.homevestors.com	Dallas	TX	75231	972-761-0046	761-9022
ICV Capital Partners LLC 666 3rd Ave 29th Fl *Web:* www.icvcapital.com	New York	NY	10017	212-455-9600	455-9603
InvestPrivate.com 500 5th Ave 54th Fl *TF:* 877-669-4732 ■ *Web:* www.investprivate.com	New York	NY	10110	212-739-7700	655-0140
Lee Thomas H Partners 100 Federal St Suite 3500 *TF:* 800-227-1050	Boston	MA	02110	617-227-1050	227-3514
Lion Chemical Capital 535 Madison Ave 4th Fl *Web:* www.lionchemicalcapital.com	New York	NY	10022	212-355-5500	355-6283
Liquidnet Holdings Inc 498 7th Ave 12th Fl *Web:* www.liquidnet.com	New York	NY	10018	646-674-2000	674-2003
Marlin Holdings Inc 555 Theodore Fremd Ave Suite B-302	Rye	NY	10580	914-967-9400	967-9405
MassMutual Financial Group 140 Garden St *Web:* www.massmutual.com	Hartford	CT	06154	860-562-1000	
McCown De Leeuw & Co (MDC) 950 Tower Ln Suite 800 *Web:* www.mdcpartners.com	Foster City	CA	94404	650-854-6000	854-0853
MidCoast Financial Inc 1926 10th Ave N Suite 400 *Web:* www.midcoastfinancial.com	Lake Worth	FL	33461	561-540-6224	540-4226
Millennia Inc 2591 Dallas Pkwy Suite 102	Frisco	TX	75034	469-633-0100	633-0099
MML Investors Services Inc 1295 State St *TF:* 800-542-6767 ■ *Web:* www.massmutual.com/MMLISI	Springfield	MA	01111	413-737-8400	734-6581
Olympus Real Estate Corp 5080 Spectrum Dr Suite 1000E	Addison	TX	75001	972-980-2200	490-2800
Peacock Hislop Staley & Given Inc 2999 N 44th St Suite 100 *TF:* 800-999-1818 ■ *Web:* www.phsg.com	Phoenix	AZ	85018	602-952-6800	952-0924
Pembina Pipeline Income Fund 700 9th Ave SW Suite 2000 *TSX: PIF.UN* ■ *TF:* 888-428-3222 ■ *Web:* www.pembina.com	Calgary	AB	T2P3V4	403-231-7500	237-0254
Pennsylvania Early Stage Partners 1200 Liberty Ridge Dr Suite 310 *Web:* www.paearlystage.com	Wayne	PA	19087	610-293-4075	254-4240
Petroleum & Resources Corp 7 Saint Paul St Suite 1140 *NYSE: PEO* ■ *TF:* 800-638-2479 ■ *Web:* www.peteres.com	Baltimore	MD	21202	410-752-5900	659-0080
Platinum Equity Holdings 360 N Crescent Dr *Web:* www.peh.com	Beverly Hills	CA	90210	310-712-1850	712-1848
Potomac Capital Investment Corp 1801 K St NW Suite 900	Washington	DC	20006	202-775-4620	857-5760
Provender Capital Group LLC 17 State St *Web:* www.provender-capital.com	New York	NY	10004	212-271-8888	271-8875
Rand Capital Corp 2200 Rand Bldg *NASDAQ: RAND* ■ *Web:* www.randcapital.com	Buffalo	NY	14203	716-853-0802	854-8480
Safeguard International Fund LP 435 Devon Park Dr Bldg 400 *Web:* www.safeguardintl.com	Wayne	PA	19087	610-293-0838	293-0854
SCP Private Equity Partners 1200 Liberty Ridge Dr Suite 300 *Web:* www.scppartners.com	Wayne	PA	19087	610-995-2900	975-9546
Skinner Corp 1326 5th Ave Suite 717	Seattle	WA	98101	206-623-6480	623-2511
Smith Whiley & Co 242 Trumbull St 8th Fl *Web:* www.smithwhiley.com	Hartford	CT	06103	860-548-2513	548-2518
Sterling Capital Corp 100 Wall St 11th Fl *AMEX: SPR* ■ *TF:* 800-949-3456	New York	NY	10005	212-440-0821	440-0801
Superior Plus Income Fund 605 5th Ave SW Suite 2820 *TSX: SPF.UN* ■ *TF:* 866-490-7587 ■ *Web:* www.superiorplus.ca	Calgary	AB	T2P3H5	403-218-2970	218-2973
Technology Ventures Corp 1155 University Blvd SE *Web:* www.techventures.org	Albuquerque	NM	87106	505-246-2882	246-2891
Thomas H Lee Partners 100 Federal St Suite 3500 *TF:* 800-227-1050	Boston	MA	02110	617-227-1050	227-3514
Thomas Properties Group Inc 515 S Flower St 6th Fl *NASDAQ: TPGI* ■ *Web:* www.tpgre.com	Los Angeles	CA	90071	213-613-1900	633-4760
Tracinda Corp 150 Rodeo Dr Suite 250	Beverly Hills	CA	90212	310-271-0638	271-3416
Tri-Continental Corp 100 Park Ave 3rd Fl *NYSE: TY* ■ *TF:* 800-221-7844 ■ *Web:* www.tricontinental.com	New York	NY	10017	212-850-1864	922-5726
Vulcan Inc 505 5th Ave S Suite 900 *Web:* www.vulcan.com	Seattle	WA	98104	206-342-2000	342-3000
Welsh Carson Anderson & Stowe 320 Park Ave Suite 2500 *Web:* www.welshcarson.com	New York	NY	10022	212-893-9500	
Yucaipa Cos LLC 9130 W Sunset Blvd	Los Angeles	CA	90069	310-789-7200	789-7201

409 JANITORIAL & CLEANING SUPPLIES - WHOL

				Phone	Fax
American Sanitary Inc (AmSan) 3 Parkway N Suite 120 N *TF:* 888-468-1555 ■ *Web:* www.amsan.com	Deerfield	IL	60015	847-607-2300	607-2309
Brady Industries Inc 4175 S Arville St *TF:* 800-293-4698 ■ *Web:* www.bradyindustries.com	Las Vegas	NV	89103	702-876-3990	876-1580
EXSL/Ultra Labs Inc 30921 Wiegman Rd	Hayward	CA	94544	510-324-4567	324-8881
Fitch Co 2201 Russell St *TF:* 800-933-4824 ■ *Web:* www.fitchco.com	Baltimore	MD	21230	410-539-1953	727-2244
Florida Sanitary Suppliers 3031 N Andrews Ave Ext *TF:* 800-940-0900 ■ *Web:* www.florsan.com	Pompano Beach	FL	33064	954-972-1700	247-4301
Golden Products Co 5057 W Washington Blvd	Los Angeles	CA	90016	310-815-8283	815-8638
HP Products Corp 4220 Saguaro Trail *TF:* 800-382-5326 ■ *Web:* www.hpproducts.com	Indianapolis	IN	46268	317-298-9950	293-0459
I Janvey & Sons Inc 218 Front St *Web:* www.janvey.com	Hempstead	NY	11550	516-489-9300	486-3927
Industrial Soap Co 722 S Vandeventer Ave *Web:* www.industrialsoap.com	Saint Louis	MO	63110	314-241-6363	533-5556
Janvey I & Sons Inc 218 Front St *Web:* www.janvey.com	Hempstead	NY	11550	516-489-9300	486-3927
Kellermeyer Co 1025 Brown Ave *TF:* 800-462-9552 ■ *Web:* www.kellermeyer.com	Toledo	OH	43607	419-255-3022	255-2752
Kenway Distributors Inc PO Box 9347 *Web:* www.kenway.net	Louisville	KY	40209	502-367-2201	368-5519
Manny's Sanitary Supplies Inc 4866 Tchoupitoulas St *TF:* 800-256-2398	New Orleans	LA	70115	504-899-2358	891-7924
Rose Products & Services Inc 545 Stimmel Rd *TF:* 800-264-1568	Columbus	OH	43223	614-443-7647	443-2771
Sani-Clean Distributors 470 Riverside St	Portland	ME	04103	207-797-8240	878-3513
Unisource Maintenance Supply Systems Inc 13217 S Figueroa St *TF:* 888-242-1827	Los Angeles	CA	90061	310-527-3000	515-0269

410 JEWELERS' FINDINGS & MATERIALS

				Phone	Fax
Ampex Casting Corp 23 W 47th St 4th Fl	New York	NY	10036	212-719-1318	719-3493
ARC Traders Inc PO Box 3429 *TF:* 800-528-2374	Scottsdale	AZ	85271	480-945-0769	946-9089
BA Ballou & Co Inc 800 Waterman Ave *TF:* 800-729-3347 ■ *Web:* www.ballou.com	East Providence	RI	02914	401-438-7000	434-3336
Ballou BA & Co Inc 800 Waterman Ave *TF:* 800-729-3347 ■ *Web:* www.ballou.com	East Providence	RI	02914	401-438-7000	434-3336
Craftstones PO Box 847 *Web:* www.craftstones.com	Ramona	CA	92065	760-789-1620	789-3432
David H Fell & Co Inc 6009 Bandini Blvd *TF:* 800-822-1996 ■ *Web:* www.dhfco.com	Commerce	CA	90040	323-722-9992	722-6567
Fell David H & Co Inc 6009 Bandini Blvd *TF:* 800-822-1996 ■ *Web:* www.dhfco.com	Commerce	CA	90040	323-722-9992	722-6567
Findings Inc PO Box 462 *TF:* 800-343-0806 ■ *Web:* www.findingsinc.net	Keene	NH	03431	603-352-3717	352-5535
Gesswein Paul H & Co 255 Hancock Ave *TF:* 800-544-2043 ■ *Web:* www.gesswein.com	Bridgeport	CT	06605	203-366-5400	366-3953
Goldberg William Diamond Corp 589 5th Ave *Web:* www.williamgoldberg.com	New York	NY	10017	212-980-4343	980-6120
James A Murphy & Son Inc PO Box 3006 *TF:* 800-422-3237	South Attleboro	MA	02703	508-761-5060	761-4580
Kahan Jewelry Corp 36 W 47th St Rm 308	New York	NY	10036	212-719-1055	944-1715
Karbra Co 131 W 35th St 8th Fl *TF:* 800-527-2721	New York	NY	10001	212-736-9300	736-9303
Krohn Industries Inc 303 Veterans Blvd *TF:* 800-526-6299	Carlstadt	NJ	07072	201-933-9696	933-9684
Lazare Kaplan International Inc 19 W 44th St 16th Fl *AMEX: LKI* ■ *TF Cust Svc:* 800-554-3325 ■ *Web:* www.lazarediamonds.com	New York	NY	10036	212-972-9700	972-8561
Leach & Garner General Findings 57 John L Dietsch Sq PO Box 200 *TF:* 800-345-1105 ■ *Web:* www.leach-garner.com	North Attleboro	MA	02761	508-695-7800	699-4031
Lee's Mfg Co 160 Niantic Ave *TF:* 800-821-1700 ■ *Web:* www.leesmfg.com	Providence	RI	02907	401-353-1740	353-0740
Magic Novelty Inc 308 Dyckman St *Web:* www.magicnovelty.com	New York	NY	10034	212-304-2777	567-2809
MS Co PO Box 480 *TF:* 800-675-4657 ■ *Web:* mscompany.net	Attleboro	MA	02703	508-222-1700	222-6449
Murphy James A & Son Inc PO Box 3006 *TF:* 800-422-3237	South Attleboro	MA	02703	508-761-5060	761-4580
Paul H Gesswein & Co 255 Hancock Ave *TF:* 800-544-2043 ■ *Web:* www.gesswein.com	Bridgeport	CT	06605	203-366-5400	366-3953
Providence Chain 225 Carolina Ave *TF:* 800-783-1499 ■ *Web:* www.providencechain.com	Providence	RI	02905	401-781-1330	941-7932
Romanoff International Supply Corp 9 Deforest St *TF Cust Svc:* 800-221-7448 ■ *Web:* www.romanoff.com	Amityville	NY	11701	631-842-2400	842-0028
Stuller Settings Inc 302 Rue Louis XIV **Fax Area Code:* 337 ■ *Web:* www.stuller.com	Lafayette	LA	70598	800-877-7777	981-1655*
Tercat Tool & Die Co Inc 31 Delaine St	Providence	RI	02909	401-421-3371	351-2560
Victors 3-D Inc 25 Brook Ave	Maywood	NJ	07607	201-845-4433	712-0818
William Goldberg Diamond Corp 589 5th Ave *Web:* www.williamgoldberg.com	New York	NY	10017	212-980-4343	980-6120

411 JEWELRY - COSTUME

				Phone	Fax
1928 Jewelry Co 3000 W Empire Ave *TF:* 800-227-1928 ■ *Web:* www.1928.com	Burbank	CA	91504	818-841-1928	526-4558
A & Z Hayward Co 655 Waterman Ave *TF:* 800-556-7462 ■ *Web:* www.azhayward.com	East Providence	RI	02914	401-438-0550	438-6970
Accessories Assoc Inc 500 George Washington Hwy *TF:* 800-388-0258	Smithfield	RI	02917	401-231-3800	231-4625
Alan Jewelry Co Inc 1 Baker St	Providence	RI	02905	401-785-0900	461-8715
American Ring Co Inc 19 Grosvenor Ave	East Providence	RI	02914	401-438-9060	438-3806
Arden Jewelry Mfg Co 10 Industrial Ln *Web:* www.ardenjewelry.com	Johnston	RI	02919	401-274-9800	273-1862
Bazar Inc Sales Co 793 Waterman Ave	East Providence	RI	02914	401-434-2595	434-0814
C & J Jewelry Co Inc 100 Dupont Dr *TF:* 800-556-7494 ■ *Web:* www.candjjewelry.com	Providence	RI	02907	401-944-2200	944-7915
Carolee Designs Inc 19 E Elm St *TF:* 800-227-6533 ■ *Web:* www.carolee.com	Greenwich	CT	06830	203-629-1139	629-1872
Darlene Jewelry Mfg Co 93 Park Pl	Pawtucket	RI	02860	401-728-3300	722-4930
Donald Bruce & Co 3600 N Talman Ave	Chicago	IL	60618	773-477-8100	477-6293
Duchess Industries Inc 399 Main St	Lodi	NJ	07644	973-916-1122	916-0370
Gem-Craft Inc 1420 Elmwood Ave	Cranston	RI	02910	401-854-1200	854-1204
Howard Eldon Ltd 6654 NE 25th Ave *TF:* 800-685-1533	Ocala	FL	34479	352-629-2180	629-2750
Imperial-Deltah Inc 795 Waterman Ave *TF:* 800-556-7738	East Providence	RI	02914	401-434-2250	434-0814
Jewelry Fashions Inc 520 8th Ave 12th Fl	New York	NY	10018	212-947-7700	564-4829
Joan Rivers Worldwide 150 E 58th St 24th Fl *TF:* 800-337-4405	New York	NY	10155	212-751-2028	751-1967
Kirk's Folly 236 Chapman St *Web:* www.kirksfolly.com	Providence	RI	02905	401-941-4300	467-2360
Millard Wire 257 Industrial Dr *Web:* www.millardwire.com	Warwick	RI	02886	401-737-9330	737-9340
MJ Enterprises Inc 120 Railroad Ave *Web:* www.iopeners.com	Johnston	RI	02919	401-232-0200	232-7663
Monet Group Inc 1440 Broadway 3rd Fl	New York	NY	10018	212-626-5590	626-5487
Monet Group Inc Trifari Div 1440 Broadway 3rd Fl	New York	NY	10118	212-626-5590	626-5487
Museum Reproductions Inc 62 Harvard St *Web:* www.museumreproductions.com	Brookline	MA	02445	617-277-7707	277-3088
P & B Mfg Co Inc 655 Waterman Ave *TF:* 800-556-7462	East Providence	RI	02914	401-438-0550	438-6970
Plastic Craft Novelty Co Inc 12 Dunham St	Attleboro	MA	02703	508-222-1486	226-7295
Rivers Joan Worldwide 150 E 58th St 24th Fl *TF:* 800-337-4405	New York	NY	10155	212-751-2028	751-1967
Roman Research Inc 800 Franklin St *TF:* 800-225-8652	Hanson	MA	02341	781-618-2100	447-0995
Shira Accessories Ltd 30 W 36th St 5th Fl	New York	NY	10018	212-594-4455	594-4466
Speidel Corp 25 Fairmount Ave *TF:* 800-441-2200 ■ *Web:* www.speidel.com	East Providence	RI	02914	401-519-2000	519-2019
Swank Inc 656 Joseph Warner Blvd	Taunton	MA	02780	508-822-2527	977-4428
Swarovski Consumer Goods Ltd 1 Kenney Dr *TF:* 800-289-4900 ■ *Web:* www.swarovski.com	Cranston	RI	02920	401-463-6400	463-5257
Trifari Div Monet Group Inc 1440 Broadway 3rd Fl	New York	NY	10118	212-626-5590	626-5487
Uncas Mfg Co 150 Niantic Ave *TF Cust Svc:* 800-776-0980	Providence	RI	02907	401-944-4700	943-2951
Victoria & Co 10 New Rd	Rumford	RI	02916	401-435-9220	435-8481
Weingeroff Enterprises 1 Weingeroff Blvd *Web:* www.weingeroff.com	Cranston	RI	02910	401-467-2200	785-1320

412 JEWELRY - PRECIOUS METAL

				Phone	Fax
American Achievement Corp 7211 Circle S Rd *TF:* 800-531-5131 ■ *Web:* www.artcarved.com	Austin	TX	78745	512-444-0571	444-0065
Anthony Michael Jewelers Inc 124 S Terrace Ave *TF:* 800-966-8800 ■ *Web:* www.michaelanthony.com	Mount Vernon	NY	10550	914-699-0000	699-2335
Armbrust International Ltd 735 Allens Ave *Web:* www.armbrustintl.com	Providence	RI	02905	401-781-3300	781-2590
Aurafin OroAmerica 6701 N Nob Hill Rd *TF:* 800-327-1808 ■ *Web:* www.aurafin.com	Tamarac	FL	33321	954-718-3200	718-3208
Avery James Craftsman Inc 145 Avery Rd N *TF:* 800-283-1770 ■ *Web:* www.jamesavery.com	Kerrville	TX	78028	830-895-1122	895-6623
BA Ballou & Co Inc 800 Waterman Ave *TF:* 800-729-3347 ■ *Web:* www.ballou.com	East Providence	RI	02914	401-438-7000	434-3336
Balfour LG Co 7211 Circle S Rd *TF:* 888-225-3687 ■ *Web:* www.balfour.com	Austin	TX	78745	512-444-0571	
Ballou BA & Co Inc 800 Waterman Ave *TF:* 800-729-3347 ■ *Web:* www.ballou.com	East Providence	RI	02914	401-438-7000	434-3336
Black Hills Jewelry Mfg Co DBA Landstrom's Original Black Hills Gold Creations 405 Canal St *TF:* 800-343-0157 ■ *Web:* www.landstroms.com	Rapid City	SD	57701	605-343-0157	343-4683
Bondanza Michael Inc 10 W 46th St 12th Fl *TF:* 800-835-0041 ■ *Web:* www.michaelbondanza.com	New York	NY	10036	212-869-0043	921-2565
Brevard Designs 2304 Abbot Kinney Blvd PO Box 10999 *Web:* www.brevarddesign.com	Marina del Rey	CA	90295	310-577-1888	306-7736
Brogan Byard F Inc 124 S Keswick Ave *TF:* 800-232-7642 ■ *Web:* www.bfbrogan.com	Glenside	PA	19038	215-885-3550	885-1366
Cartier Inc 2 E 52nd St *TF Sales:* 800-227-8437 ■ *Web:* www.cartier.com	New York	NY	10022	212-753-0111	
Colibri Group 100 Niantic Ave *TF Cust Svc:* 800-556-7354 ■ *Web:* www.colibri.com	Providence	RI	02907	401-943-2100	946-5276
Cordova Inc PO Box 521831 *TF Cust Svc:* 800-221-0744	Flushing	NY	11352	718-961-1020	353-5753
Creed Rosary Mfg Inc 15 Kenneth Miner Dr *TF Orders:* 800-255-7439 ■ *Web:* www.creedrosary.com	Wrentham	MA	02093	508-384-7600	384-2626
Danecraft Inc 1 Baker St *Web:* www.danecraft.com	Providence	RI	02905	401-941-7700	461-8715
David Friedman & Sons 10 E 38th St	New York	NY	10016	212-532-3253	481-3394
David Yurman Designs Inc 24 Vestry St *TF:* 800-593-1597 ■ *Web:* www.davidyurman.com	New York	NY	10013	212-896-1550	
Diablo Mfg Co Inc 900 Golden Gate Terr PO Box 1108 *TF Sales:* 800-551-2233 ■ *Web:* www.diablosilver.com	Grass Valley	CA	95945	530-272-2241	272-2243
Eastern Silver Co 4901 16th Ave *Web:* www.easternsilver.com	Brooklyn	NY	11204	718-854-5600	854-0323
Erickson Gordon Co 13555 Grove Dr *TF:* 800-488-8443 ■ *Web:* www.gordonericksonjewelers.com	Maple Grove	MN	55311	763-416-3771	416-3773
Esposito Jewelry Inc 225 DuPont Dr *Web:* www.espositojewelry.com	Providence	RI	02907	401-943-1900	946-5860
Excell Mfg Co 49 Pearl St *TF:* 800-343-8410 ■ *Web:* www.excellmfg.com	Attleboro	MA	02703	508-222-9234	222-6531
F Byard Brogan Inc 124 S Keswick Ave *TF:* 800-232-7642 ■ *Web:* www.bfbrogan.com	Glenside	PA	19038	215-885-3550	885-1366
Fisher Robert S & Co Inc 280 Sheffield St *TF:* 800-526-8052 ■ *Web:* www.rsfisher.com	Mountainside	NJ	07092	908-928-0002	928-0092
Friedman David & Sons 10 E 38th St	New York	NY	10016	212-532-3253	481-3394
Fuller George H & Son Co 151 Exchange St *TF:* 800-237-0043 ■ *Web:* www.fullerfindings.com	Pawtucket	RI	02860	401-722-6530	723-1720
Garden Jewelry Co Inc 36 47th St Suite 900 *TF:* 800-321-0259	New York	NY	10036	212-840-5500	421-7813
Gem East Corp 2124 2nd Ave *TF:* 800-426-0605 ■ *Web:* www.gemeast.com	Seattle	WA	98121	206-441-1700	448-1801
Gemveto Jewelry Co Inc 16 E 52nd St *TF:* 800-221-4438	New York	NY	10022	212-755-2522	755-2027
George H Fuller & Son Co 151 Exchange St *TF:* 800-237-0043 ■ *Web:* www.fullerfindings.com	Pawtucket	RI	02860	401-722-6530	723-1720
Gold Lance Inc 148 E Broadway *TF:* 800-327-9381 ■ *Web:* www.goldlance.com	Owatonna	MN	55060	507-455-5033	455-6175
Gordon Erickson Co 13555 Grove Dr *TF:* 800-488-8443 ■ *Web:* www.gordonericksonjewelers.com	Maple Grove	MN	55311	763-416-3771	416-3773
Hallmark Sweet 49 Pearl St *TF:* 800-225-2706 ■ *Web:* www.hallmarksweet.com	Attleboro	MA	02703	508-222-9234	222-6531
Hammerman Brothers Inc 40 W 57th St *TF:* 800-223-6436 ■ *Web:* www.hammermanbrothers.com	New York	NY	10019	212-956-2800	956-2769
Harry Winston Inc 718 5th Ave *TF:* 800-988-4110 ■ *Web:* www.harrywinston.com	New York	NY	10019	212-245-2000	489-0016
Herff Jones Inc 4501 W 62nd St **Fax:* Hum Res ■ *TF:* 800-427-3393 ■ *Web:* www.herff-jones.com	Indianapolis	IN	46268	317-297-3740	329-3308*
Ira Green Inc 177 Georgia Ave *TF:* 800-663-7487 ■ *Web:* www.iragreen.com	Providence	RI	02905	401-467-4770	467-5557
J Jenkins Sons Co Inc 1801 Whitehead Rd *TF:* 800-296-3468 ■ *Web:* www.jjenkinssons.com	Baltimore	MD	21207	410-265-5200	298-4809
Jabel Inc 365 Coit St *TF:* 800-526-4597 ■ *Web:* www.jabel.com	Irvington	NJ	07111	973-374-6000	374-3141
Jacmel Jewelry Inc 30-00 47th Ave *Web:* www.jacmel.com	Long Island City	NY	11101	718-349-4300	349-4472
James Avery Craftsman Inc 145 Avery Rd N *TF:* 800-283-1770 ■ *Web:* www.jamesavery.com	Kerrville	TX	78028	830-895-1122	895-6623
Jenkins J Sons Co Inc 1801 Whitehead Rd *TF:* 800-296-3468 ■ *Web:* www.jjenkinssons.com	Baltimore	MD	21207	410-265-5200	298-4809
Jewel America Inc 119 W 40th St *TF:* 800-328-7173	New York	NY	10018	212-220-4222	220-7227
Johns R Ltd 7211 Circle S Rd **Fax Area Code:* 512 ■ *TF:* 800-531-5055	Austin	TX	78745	800-521-9493	440-1138*
Jostens Inc 3601 Minnesota Ave Suite 400 **Fax:* Hum Res ■ *TF:* 800-235-4774 ■ *Web:* www.jostens.com	Minneapolis	MN	55435	952-830-3300	830-3309*
Kaspar & Esh Inc 11-25 45th Ave *TF:* 800-223-2614	Long Island City	NY	11101	718-786-0771	786-4566
Kinsley & Sons Inc 24 S Church St **Fax Area Code:* 800 ■ *TF:* 800-468-4428 ■ *Web:* www.gothic-jewelry.com	Union	MO	60384	636-583-9966	841-1228*
Klitzner Industries Inc 44 Warren St *TF:* 800-556-6860 ■ *Web:* klitzner.com	Providence	RI	02907	401-751-7500	273-7474
Landstrom's Original Black Hills Gold Creations 405 Canal St *TF:* 800-343-0157 ■ *Web:* www.landstroms.com	Rapid City	SD	57701	605-343-0157	343-4683
Leach & Garner General Findings 57 John L Dietsch Sq PO Box 200 *TF:* 800-345-1105 ■ *Web:* www.leach-garner.com	North Attleboro	MA	02761	508-695-7800	699-4031
LG Balfour Co 7211 Circle S Rd *TF:* 888-225-3687 ■ *Web:* www.balfour.com	Austin	TX	78745	512-444-0571	
Loren Industries Inc 14051 NW 14th St *TF:* 800-772-8085 ■ *Web:* www.loren.com	Sunrise	FL	33023	954-835-0012	846-8819
Masters of Design 34 Extension St *TF:* 800-663-0501 ■ *Web:* www.mastersofdesign.com	Attleboro	MA	02703	508-695-0201	699-5996
Maui Divers of Hawaii Ltd 1520 Liona St *TF:* 800-462-4454 ■ *Web:* www.mauidivers.com	Honolulu	HI	96814	808-946-7979	946-0406
Mendelson & Assoc 2615 S Hill St *TF:* 800-421-0215	Los Angeles	CA	90007	213-746-0745	
Michael Anthony Jewelers Inc 124 S Terrace Ave *TF:* 800-966-8800 ■ *Web:* www.michaelanthony.com	Mount Vernon	NY	10550	914-699-0000	699-2335
Michael Bondanza Inc 10 W 46th St 12th Fl *TF:* 800-835-0041 ■ *Web:* www.michaelbondanza.com	New York	NY	10036	212-869-0043	921-2565
Novell Design Studio Inc 129 Chestnut St *TF:* 888-916-6835 ■ *Web:* www.novelldesignstudio.com	Roselle	NJ	07203	908-245-4200	245-5090
OC Tanner Co 1930 S State St *TF:* 800-453-7490 ■ *Web:* www.octanner.com	Salt Lake City	UT	84115	801-486-2430	483-8301
Oro-Cal Mfg Co Inc 1720 Bird St *TF:* 800-367-6225 ■ *Web:* www.orocal.com	Oroville	CA	95965	530-533-5085	533-5067
Ostbye & Anderson Inc 10055 51st Ave N **Fax Area Code:* 877 ■ *TF:* 800-328-4368 ■ *Web:* www.ostbye.com	Minneapolis	MN	55442	763-553-1515	553-1515*
Paris 1624 Knowlton St *Web:* www.paristiaras.com	Cincinnati	OH	45223	513-541-1888	542-8329
Plainville Stock Co Inc 104 South St PO Box 1628 *TF:* 800-343-2112 ■ *Web:* www.plainvillestock.com	Plainville	MA	02762	508-699-4434	695-0836
R Johns Ltd 7211 Circle S Rd **Fax Area Code:* 512 ■ *TF:* 800-531-5055	Austin	TX	78745	800-521-9493	440-1138*
Ring Specialty Co 2691 30th St *TF:* 800-328-6330 ■ *Web:* www.theringmakerinboulder.com	Boulder	CO	80301	303-440-5507	440-7617
Robert S Fisher & Co Inc 280 Sheffield St *TF:* 800-526-8052 ■ *Web:* www.rsfisher.com	Mountainside	NJ	07092	908-928-0002	928-0092
Rolyn Inc 189 Macklin St *TF:* 800-824-2683	Cranston	RI	02920	401-944-0844	944-5040
Sardelli International LLC 195 Dupont Dr *TF:* 800-327-4641 ■ *Web:* www.sardelli.com	Providence	RI	02907	401-944-8510	944-4493
Simco Mfg Jewelers Inc 62 W 47th St	New York	NY	10036	212-575-8390	768-0376
Stamper Black Hills Gold Jewelry 7201 S Hwy 16 *TF Cust Svc:* 800-523-7515 ■ *Web:* www.stamperbhg.com	Rapid City	SD	57702	605-342-0751	343-9783
Stanley Creations Inc 1414 Willow Ave *TF:* 800-220-1414 ■ *Web:* www.stanleycreations.com	Melrose Park	PA	19027	215-635-6200	635-2706
Sultan Co 3049 Ualena St 14th Fl *TF:* 800-260-3912 ■ *Web:* www.sultan.com	Honolulu	HI	96819	808-833-7772	837-1358
Tache USA Inc 44-40 11th St *TF:* 800-458-4300 ■ *Web:* www.tacheusa.com	Long Island City	NY	11101	718-706-8989	392-0774
Tanner OC Co 1930 S State St *TF:* 800-453-7490 ■ *Web:* www.octanner.com	Salt Lake City	UT	84115	801-486-2430	483-8301
Terryberry Co 2033 Oak Industrial Dr NE *TF:* 800-253-0882 ■ *Web:* www.terryberry.com	Grand Rapids	MI	49505	616-458-1391	458-5292
Tessler & Weiss Premesco Inc 2389 Vauxhall Rd	Union	NJ	07083	908-686-0513	686-9165
Tiara Corp 2425 Oakton St *TF:* 800-323-6510 ■ *Web:* www.tiaradirect.com	Evanston	IL	60202	847-570-4700	570-4708
Tiffany & Co 727 5th Ave *NYSE: TIF* ■ *TF Orders:* 800-526-0649 ■ *Web:* www.tiffany.com	New York	NY	10022	212-755-8000	605-4465
Trebor Enterprises Ltd PO Box 88	Freeport	IL	61032	815-235-1700	235-3900
Tru-Kay Mfg Co 2 Carol Dr *TF:* 800-795-2105 ■ *Web:* www.trukay.com	Lincoln	RI	02865	401-333-2105	334-0142
Uncas Mfg Co 150 Niantic Ave *TF Cust Svc:* 800-776-0980	Providence	RI	02907	401-944-4700	943-2951

				Phone	Fax
Wheeler Mfg 107 Main Ave PO Box 629	Lemmon	SD	57638	605-374-3848	374-3655
TF Orders: 800-843-1937 ■ *Web:* www.wheelermfg.com					
Winston Harry Inc 718 5th Ave	New York	NY	10019	212-245-2000	489-0016
TF: 800-988-4110 ■ *Web:* www.harrywinston.com					
Wright & Lato 800 Springdale Ave	East Orange	NJ	07017	973-674-8700	674-6964
TF: 800-724-1855 ■ *Web:* www.wlring.com					
Yurman David Designs Inc 24 Vestry St	New York	NY	10013	212-896-1550	
TF: 800-593-1597 ■ *Web:* www.davidyurman.com					

413 JEWELRY STORES

				Phone	Fax
Adler Coleman E & Sons Inc 722 Canal St	New Orleans	LA	70130	504-523-5292	568-0610
TF: 800-925-7912					
Albert S Smyth Co Inc 2020 York Rd	Timonium	MD	21093	410-252-6666	252-2355
TF: 800-638-3333 ■ *Web:* www.albertsmyth.com					
Argo & Lehne Jewelers Inc 3100 Tremont Rd	Columbus	OH	43221	614-457-6261	457-6716
Ashford.com 14001 NW 4th St	Sunrise	FL	33325	954-453-2874	835-2236
TF: 888-342-6663 ■ *Web:* www.ashford.com					
Bailey Banks & Biddle Div Zale Corp 901 W Walnut Hill Ln	Irving	TX	75038	972-580-4000	580-5907*
**Fax:* Mail Rm ■ *TF Cust Svc:* 800-651-4222 ■ *Web:* www.zalecorp.com					
Barr Brothers Inc 310 High St	Portsmouth	VA	23704	757-399-7424	
Ben Bridge Jeweler Inc PO Box 1908	Seattle	WA	98111	206-448-8800	448-7456
TF Cust Svc: 888-448-1912 ■ *Web:* www.benbridge.com					
Ben Moss Jewellers 300-201 Portage Ave	Winnipeg	MB	R3B3K6	204-947-6682	988-0148
TF: 888-236-6677 ■ *Web:* www.benmoss.com					
Blue Nile Inc 705 5th Ave S Suite 900	Seattle	WA	98104	206-336-6700	336-7950
NASDAQ: NILE ■ *TF:* 800-242-2728 ■ *Web:* www.bluenile.com					
Borsheim's Inc 120 Regency Pkwy	Omaha	NE	68114	402-391-0400	391-6694
TF: 800-642-4438 ■ *Web:* shop.borsheims.com					
Bridge Ben Jeweler Inc PO Box 1908	Seattle	WA	98111	206-448-8800	448-7456
TF Cust Svc: 888-448-1912 ■ *Web:* www.benbridge.com					
Brodkey Brothers Inc 12165 W Center Rd Suite 73	Omaha	NE	68144	402-330-9800	697-0603
Web: www.brodkeys.com					
Bromberg & Co Inc 123 N 20th St	Birmingham	AL	35203	205-252-0221	458-0458
TF: 800-633-4616 ■ *Web:* www.brombergs.com					
Carl Greve Jeweler Inc 731 SW Morrison St	Portland	OR	97205	503-223-7121	223-9754
TF: 800-284-2044 ■ *Web:* www.carlgreve.com					
Carlyle & Co Jewelers 4615 Dundas Dr	Greensboro	NC	27407	336-294-2450	679-6812*
**Fax Area Code:* 253 ■ *Web:* www.carlyleco.com					
Cartier Inc 2 E 52nd St	New York	NY	10022	212-753-0111	
TF Sales: 800-227-8437 ■ *Web:* www.cartier.com					
Coleman E Adler & Sons Inc 722 Canal St	New Orleans	LA	70130	504-523-5292	568-0610
TF: 800-925-7912					
Corbo Jewelers Inc 58 Park Ave	Rutherford	NJ	07070	201-438-4454	438-3108
Web: www.corbojewelers.com					
Crescent Jewelry Co 1101 Marina Village Pkwy	Alameda	CA	94501	510-523-9700	
TF: 800-588-4367 ■ *Web:* www.crescentjewelers.com					
De Von's Jewelers Inc 1910 29th St	Sacramento	CA	95816	916-451-6583	456-2514
Web: www.devonsjewelers.com					
DGSE Cos Inc 2817 Forest Ln	Dallas	TX	75234	972-484-3662	241-0646
NASDAQ: DGSE ■ *TF:* 800-527-5307 ■ *Web:* www.dgse.com					
Don Roberto Jewelers Inc 1020 Calle Recodo Suite 100	San Clemente	CA	92673	949-361-6700	498-9286
TF: 888-466-5300 ■ *Web:* www.donrobertojewelers.com					
Elegant Illusions Inc 542 Lighthouse Ave Suite 5	Pacific Grove	CA	93950	831-649-1814	649-1001
TF: 800-551-5045 ■ *Web:* www.elegantillusions.com					
Finks Jewelry Inc 3545 Electric Rd	Roanoke	VA	24018	540-342-2991	342-5916
TF: 800-699-7464 ■ *Web:* www.finks.com					
Finlay Enterprises Inc 529 5th Ave	New York	NY	10017	212-382-7400	
NASDAQ: FNLY ■ *Web:* www.finlayenterprises.com					
Firestone & Parson Inc 8 Newbury St	Boston	MA	02116	617-266-1858	
Foland Jewelry Brokers 630 E 11 Mile Rd	Royal Oak	MI	48067	248-336-6666	336-6667
TF: 877-365-2637 ■ *Web:* www.folands.com					
Fortunoff 70 Charles Lindbergh Blvd	Uniondale	NY	11553	516-832-9000	237-1703*
**Fax:* Hum Res ■ *TF Cust Svc:* 800-777-2807 ■ *Web:* www.fortunoff.com					
Fred Meyer Jewelers Inc 3800 SE 22nd Ave	Portland	OR	97202	503-797-5550	797-7616
TF: 800-858-9202 ■ *Web:* store.fredmeyerjewelers.com					
Freeman Jewelers Inc 76 Merchants Row	Rutland	VT	05701	802-773-2792	773-1685
TF: 800-949-2792 ■ *Web:* www.freeman-jewelers.com					
Friedman's Inc 171 Crossroads Pkwy	Savannah	GA	31407	912-233-9333	201-6604
TF: 800-545-9033 ■ *Web:* www.friedmans.com					
Gordon's Jewelers Div Zale Corp 901 W Walnut Hill Ln	Irving	TX	75038	972-580-4000	580-5523
TF Cust Svc: 888-467-3661 ■ *Web:* www.zalecorp.com					
Greve Carl Jeweler Inc 731 SW Morrison St	Portland	OR	97205	503-223-7121	223-9754
TF: 800-284-2044 ■ *Web:* www.carlgreve.com					
H Stern Jewelers Inc 645 5th Ave	New York	NY	10022	212-688-0300	888-5137
TF: 800-747-8376 ■ *Web:* www.hstern.net					
Haltoms Jewelers 317 Main St	Fort Worth	TX	76102	817-336-4051	336-0064
TF: 800-850-2303 ■ *Web:* www.haltoms.com					
Harry Ritchie's Jewelers Inc 956 Willamette St	Eugene	OR	97401	541-686-1787	485-8841
TF Cust Svc: 800-935-2850 ■ *Web:* www.harryritchies.com					
Harry Winston Inc 718 5th Ave	New York	NY	10019	212-245-2000	489-0016
TF: 800-988-4110 ■ *Web:* www.harrywinston.com					
Helzberg Diamonds 1825 Swift Ave	North Kansas City	MO	64116	816-842-7780	221-5002*
**Fax:* Sales ■ *TF:* 800-669-7780 ■ *Web:* www.helzberg.com					
JewelryWeb.com Inc 305 Northern Blvd Suite 101	Great Neck	NY	11021	516-482-3982	955-2520*
**Fax Area Code:* 800 ■ *TF:* 800-955-9245 ■ *Web:* www.jewelryweb.com					
Joseph S & Sons Inc DBA Josephs Jewelry 320 6th Ave	Des Moines	IA	50309	515-283-1961	283-0416
Web: www.josephsjewelers.com					
Josephs Jewelry 320 6th Ave	Des Moines	IA	50309	515-283-1961	283-0416
Web: www.josephsjewelers.com					
Karten's Jewelers 901 W Walnut Hill Ln	Irving	TX	75038	972-580-4000	
TF: 800-333-6739					
Kay Jewelers 375 Ghent Rd	Akron	OH	44333	330-668-5000	668-5184
TF: 800-681-8796 ■ *Web:* www.kay.com					
Krandall Sidney & Sons 755 W Big Beaver Rd Suite 103	Troy	MI	48084	248-362-4500	362-4509
Levy Jewelers Inc 101 E Broughton St	Savannah	GA	31401	912-233-1163	238-2110
TF: 800-237-5389 ■ *Web:* www.levyjewelers.com					
Lux Bond & Green Inc 46 Lasalle Rd	West Hartford	CT	06107	860-521-3015	521-8693
TF: 800-524-7336 ■ *Web:* www.lbgreen.com					
Mayor's Jewelers Inc 14051 NW 14th St Suite 200	Sunrise	FL	33323	954-846-8000	846-2787
TF: 800-223-6964 ■ *Web:* www.mayors.com					
Meyer Fred Jewelers Inc 3800 SE 22nd Ave	Portland	OR	97202	503-797-5550	797-7616
TF: 800-858-9202 ■ *Web:* store.fredmeyerjewelers.com					
Mondera.com 45 W 45th St 15th Fl	New York	NY	10036	212-997-9350	591-5207*
**Fax Area Code:* 917 ■ *TF:* 800-666-3372 ■ *Web:* www.mondera.com					
Morgan & Co 1131 Glendon Ave	Los Angeles	CA	90024	310-208-3377	208-6920
Web: www.morganjewellers.com					
Moss Ben Jewellers 300-201 Portage Ave	Winnipeg	MB	R3B3K6	204-947-6682	988-0148
TF: 888-236-6677 ■ *Web:* www.benmoss.com					
Odimo Inc 14001 NW 4th St	Sunrise	FL	33325	954-835-2233	835-2236
NASDAQ: ODMO ■ *TF:* 888-342-6663					
Osterman Jewelers 375 Ghent Rd	Akron	OH	44333	330-668-5000	668-5184
TF: 800-681-8796					
Reeds Jewelers Inc 2525 S 17th St	Wilmington	NC	28401	910-350-3100	350-3353
TF Orders: 877-406-3266 ■ *Web:* www.reeds.com					
Rogers Ltd 1050 Central Ave	Middletown	OH	45044	513-422-5407	420-8788
TF: 800-888-8805					
Ross Simons Jewelers Inc 9 Ross Simons Dr	Cranston	RI	02920	401-463-3100	463-8599
TF: 800-835-0919 ■ *Web:* www.ross-simons.com					
Samuels Jewelers Inc 2914 Montopolis Dr Suite 200	Austin	TX	78741	512-369-1400	369-1500
TF: 877-726-8357 ■ *Web:* www.samuelsjewelers.com					
Sherwood Management Co Inc DBA Daniels Jewelers PO Box 3750	Culver City	CA	90231	310-665-2100	665-2101
Web: www.danielsjewelers.com					
Sidney Krandall & Sons 755 W Big Beaver Rd Suite 103	Troy	MI	48084	248-362-4500	362-4509
Sterling Jewelers Inc 375 Ghent Rd	Akron	OH	44333	330-668-5000	668-5184*
**Fax:* Hum Res					
Stern H Jewelers Inc 645 5th Ave	New York	NY	10022	212-688-0300	888-5137
TF: 800-747-8376 ■ *Web:* www.hstern.net					
Sultan Co 3049 Ualena St 14th Fl	Honolulu	HI	96819	808-833-7772	837-1358
TF: 800-260-3912 ■ *Web:* www.sultan.com					
Tiffany & Co 727 5th Ave	New York	NY	10022	212-755-8000	605-4465
NYSE: TIF ■ *TF Orders:* 800-526-0649 ■ *Web:* www.tiffany.com					
Trabert & Hoeffer Inc 111 E Oak St	Chicago	IL	60611	312-787-1654	787-1446
Van Cleef & Arpels Inc 744 5th Ave	New York	NY	10019	212-644-9500	355-5697
TF: 800-822-5797 ■ *Web:* www.vancleef.com					
Watch Station 4000 Luxottica Pl	Mason	OH	45040	513-765-6000	
Web: www.watchstation.com					
Whitehall Jewellers Inc 155 N Wacker Dr Suite 500	Chicago	IL	60606	312-782-6800	782-8299
TF: 800-621-0771 ■ *Web:* www.whji.com					
Winston Harry Inc 718 5th Ave	New York	NY	10019	212-245-2000	489-0016
TF: 800-988-4110 ■ *Web:* www.harrywinston.com					
Zale Corp 901 W Walnut Hill Ln	Irving	TX	75038	972-580-4000	580-5907*
NYSE: ZLC ■ **Fax:* Mail Rm ■ *TF Cust Svc:* 800-866-9700 ■ *Web:* www.zalecorp.com					
Zale Corp Bailey Banks & Biddle Div 901 W Walnut Hill Ln	Irving	TX	75038	972-580-4000	580-5907*
**Fax:* Mail Rm ■ *TF Cust Svc:* 800-651-4222 ■ *Web:* www.zalecorp.com					
Zale Corp Gordon's Jewelers Div 901 W Walnut Hill Ln	Irving	TX	75038	972-580-4000	580-5523
TF Cust Svc: 888-467-3661 ■ *Web:* www.zalecorp.com					
Zale Corp Zales Jewelers Div 901 W Walnut Hill Ln	Irving	TX	75038	972-580-4000	580-5907
TF Cust Svc: 800-866-9700 ■ *Web:* www.zales.com					
Zales Jewelers Div Zale Corp 901 W Walnut Hill Ln	Irving	TX	75038	972-580-4000	580-5907
TF Cust Svc: 800-866-9700 ■ *Web:* www.zales.com					

414 JEWELRY, WATCHES, GEMS - WHOL

				Phone	Fax
A-Mark Precious Metals Inc 100 Wilshire Blvd 3rd Fl	Santa Monica	CA	90401	310-319-0200	319-0279
Web: www.amark.com					
Antwerp Diamond Distributors 6 E 45th St Suite 302	New York	NY	10017	212-319-3300	207-8168
TF: 800-223-0444					
Blank Joseph Inc 62 W 47th St Suite 808	New York	NY	10036	212-575-9050	302-8521
TF: 800-223-7666 ■ *Web:* www.josephblank.com					
Charles & Colvard Ltd 300 Perimiter Park Dr Suite A	Morrisville	NC	27560	919-468-0399	468-0486
NASDAQ: CTHR ■ *TF:* 800-210-4367 ■ *Web:* www.moissanite.com					
Charles Wolf Couture 579 5th Ave Suite 910	New York	NY	10017	212-371-6130	
Web: www.charleswolf.com					
Citra Trading Corp 590 5th Ave 14th Fl	New York	NY	10036	212-354-1000	382-2024
TF Orders: 800-223-6515 ■ *Web:* www.citra.com					
Continental Coin Corp 5627 Sepulveda Blvd	Van Nuys	CA	91411	818-781-4232	779-6320
TF: 888-367-9456					
Empire Diamond Corp 350 5th Ave Suite 7619	New York	NY	10118	212-564-4777	564-4960
TF: 800-728-3425 ■ *Web:* www.empirediamond.com					
Genender International Imports Inc 44 Century Dr	Wheeling	IL	60090	847-541-3333	541-4444
TF: 800-547-3333					
Gerson Co 1450 S Lone Elm St	Olathe	KS	66061	913-262-7400	262-3568
TF: 800-999-7401 ■ *Web:* www.gersoncompany.com					
Gilbert Ortega's Indian Art 3306 E Hwy 66	Gallup	NM	87301	505-863-7805	722-7794
Harry Winston Diamond Corp PO Box 4569 Station A	Toronto	ON	M5W4T9	416-362-2237	362-2230
Web: investor.harrywinston.com					
Heraeus PMM Inc 540 Madsion Ave	New York	NY	10022	212-752-2180	752-7141
HS Strygler & Co Inc 37 W 20th St Suite 1210	New York	NY	10011	212-758-4100	727-3700
Indian Trade Center Inc DBA Gilbert Ortega's Indian Art 3306 E Hwy 66	Gallup	NM	87301	505-863-7805	722-7794
Joseph Blank Inc 62 W 47th St Suite 808	New York	NY	10036	212-575-9050	302-8521
TF: 800-223-7666 ■ *Web:* www.josephblank.com					
Lazare Kaplan International Inc 19 W 44th St 16th Fl	New York	NY	10036	212-972-9700	972-8561
AMEX: LKI ■ *TF Cust Svc:* 800-554-3325 ■ *Web:* www.lazarediamonds.com					
Lyles-De Grazier Co 2050 Stemmons Suite 7943	Dallas	TX	75207	214-747-3558	741-3513
TF: 800-442-7125					
Paramount Sales Co Inc 10140 Gallows Point Dr	Knoxville	TN	37931	865-470-9977	470-9801
TF Cust Svc: 800-251-9183 ■ *Web:* www.paramountjewelry.com					
Roman Co 1201 Hanley Industrial Ct	Saint Louis	MO	63144	314-962-9750	968-5483
TF: 888-666-7744 ■ *Web:* www.romancompany.com					
Rothenberg & Schloss Inc 1450 S Lone Elm St	Olathe	KS	66061	913-262-7401	262-3568
SKL Co Inc 545 Island Rd	Ramsey	NJ	07446	201-825-6633	825-8009
Webster Watch Co Assoc 44 E 32nd St 7th Fl	New York	NY	10016	212-889-3560	213-2649*
**Fax:* Sales ■ *TF Orders:* 800-289-8963					
World Minerals Inc 130 Castilian Dr	Santa Barbara	CA	93117	805-562-0200	562-0298
TF: 800-893-4445 ■ *Web:* www.worldminerals.com					

415 JUVENILE DETENTION FACILITIES

SEE ALSO Correctional & Detention Management (Privatized) p. 1572; Correctional Facilities - Federal p. 1572; Correctional Facilities - State p. 1573

Listings are organized alphabetically by states.

				Phone	Fax
Bethel Youth Facility 950 State Hwy PO Box 1989	Bethel	AK	99559	907-543-5200	543-2710
Fairbanks Youth Facility 1502 Wilbur St	Fairbanks	AK	99701	907-451-2150	451-5152
Johnson Youth Center 3252 Hospital Dr	Juneau	AK	99801	907-586-9433	463-4933
TF: 800-478-9433					
Mat Su Youth Facility 581 Outer Springer Loop	Palmer	AK	99645	907-746-1630	761-7249
McLaughlin Youth Center 2600 Providence Dr	Anchorage	AK	99508	907-261-4399	261-4308
Nome Youth Facility 804 E 4th St	Nome	AK	99762	907-443-5434	443-7295
Arkansas Juvenile Access & Treatment Center 1501 Woody Dr	Alexander	AR	72002	501-682-9800	682-9801
Web: www.arkansas.gov/dhs/dys/dys_JCF_info.html					
Colt Juvenile Treatment Center 1388 SFC 118	Colt	AR	72326	870-633-6467	633-6732

Phone Fax

Jack Jones Jefferson County Juvenile Detention Center
301 E 2nd Ave Pine Bluff AR 71601 870-541-8502 541-8504
Web: www.jeffcoso.com
Northeast Arkansas Regional Juvenile Program
1800 Pine Grove Ln Harrisburg AR 72432 870-578-5886 578-9717
Northwest Arkansas Regional Juvenile Program PO Box 487 Mansfield AR 72944 479-928-0166 928-2060
DeWitt Nelson Youth Correctional Facility PO Box 213003 Stockton CA 95213 209-944-6113 465-2968
El Paso de Robles Youth Correctional Facility
4545 Airport Rd PO Box 7008 Paso Robles CA 93447 805-238-4040 227-2560
Web: www.cdcr.ca.gov
Heman G Stark Youth Correctional Facility 15180 S Euclid Ave Chino CA 91710 909-606-5000 606-5001
NA Chaderjian Youth Correctional Facility PO Box 213014 Stockton CA 95213 209-944-6401 547-0622
OH Close Youth Correctional Facility
7650 S Newcastle Rd PO Box 213001 Stockton CA 95213 209-944-6301 944-5612
Preston Youth Correctional Facility 201 Waterman Rd Ione CA 95640 209-274-8000 274-0276
Ventura Youth Correctional Facility 3100 Wright Rd Camarillo CA 93010 805-485-7951 485-2801
Adams Youth Services Center 1933 E Bridge St Brighton CO 80601 303-659-4450 637-0471
Gilliam Youth Services Center 2844 Downing St Denver CO 80205 303-291-8951 291-8990
Grand Mesa Youth Sevices Center 360 28th Rd Grand Junction CO 81501 970-242-1521 242-8127
Web: www.cdhs.state.co.us/dyc
Lookout Mountain Youth Services Center 2901 Ford St Golden CO 80401 303-273-2600 273-2622
Marvin W Foote Youth Services Center 13500 E Fremont Pl Englewood CO 80112 303-768-7520 768-7516
Mount View Youth Services Center 7862 W Mansfield Pkwy Denver CO 80235 303-987-4525 987-4538
Platte Valley Youth Services Center 2200 'O' St Greeley CO 80631 970-304-6220 304-6228
Pueblo Youth Services Center 1406 W 17th St Pueblo CO 81003 719-546-4915 546-4917
Spring Creek Youth Services Center 3190 E Las Vegas St Colorado Springs CO 80906 719-390-2788 390-2792
Zebulon Pike Youth Services Center
1427 W Rio Grande St Colorado Springs CO 80906 719-329-6924 635-2549
Connecticut Juvenile Training School 1225 Silver St Middletown CT 06457 860-638-2400 638-2410
Manson Youth Institution 42 Jarvis St Cheshire CT 06410 203-806-2500 699-1845
Ferris School 959 Centre Rd Wilmington DE 19805 302-993-3800 993-3820
New Castle County Detention Center 963 Centre Rd Wilmington DE 19805 302-633-3100 995-8393
Stevenson House Detention Center 750 N Dupont Hwy Milford DE 19963 302-422-1407 422-1535
Alachua Regional Juvenile Detention Center
3440 NE 39th Ave Gainesville FL 32609 352-955-2105 955-2105
Bay Regional Juvenile Detention Center 450 E 11th St Panama City FL 32401 850-872-4706 873-7099
Web: www.djj.state.fl.us/
Brevard Regional Juvenile Detention Center 5225 DeWitt Ave Cocoa FL 32927 321-690-3400 504-0907
Broward Regional Juvenile Detention Center
222 NW 22nd Ave Fort Lauderdale FL 33311 954-467-4563 327-6361
Dade Regional Juvenile Detention Center 3300 NW 27th Ave Miami FL 33142 305-637-4682 637-2812
Duval Regional Juvenile Detention Center 1241 E 8th St Jacksonville FL 32206 904-798-4820 798-4825
Escambia Regional Juvenile Detention Center
1800 W Saint Mary Ave Pensacola FL 32501 850-595-8820 595-8410
Hillsborough Regional Juvenile Detention Center East
9504 E Columbus Dr Tampa FL 33619 813-664-4100 664-4115
Hillsborough Regional Juvenile Detention Center West
3948 ML King Jr Blvd Tampa FL 33614 813-871-7650 673-4459
Leon Regional Juvenile Detention Center 2303 Ronellis Dr Tallahassee FL 32310 850-488-7672 922-2842
Manatee Regional Juvenile Detention Center 1803 5th St W Bradenton FL 34205 941-741-3023 741-3061
Marion Regional Juvenile Detention Center 3040 NW 10th St Ocala FL 34475 352-732-1450 732-1457
Okaloosa Regional Juvenile Detention Center
4448 Straight Line Rd Crestview FL 32439 850-689-7800 689-7970
Orange Regional Juvenile Detention Center 2800 S Bumby Ave Orlando FL 32806 407-897-2800 897-2856
Osceola Regional Juvenile Detention Center
2330 New Beginnings Rd Kissimmee FL 34744 407-943-3055 943-3064
Palm Beach Regional Juvenile Detention Center
1100 45th St Bldg A West Palm Beach FL 33407 561-881-5020 881-5019
Pasco Regional Juvenile Detention Center 28534 SR 52 San Antonio FL 33576 352-588-5900 588-5909
Pinellas Regional Juvenile Detention Center
5255 140th Ave N Clearwater FL 33760 727-538-7101 524-4352
Polk Regional Juvenile Detention Center 2155 Bob Phillips Rd Bartow FL 33830 863-534-7090 534-7024
Saint Lucie Regional Juvenile Detention Center 1301 Bell Ave Fort Pierce FL 34982 772-468-3940 468-4005
Seminole Regional Juvenile Detention Center 200 Bush Blvd Sanford FL 32773 407-330-6750 328-3947
Southwest Florida Juvenile Detention Center
2525 Ortiz Ave Fort Myers FL 33904 239-332-6927 332-6931
Volusia Regional Juvenile Detention Center
3840 Old Deland Rd Daytona Beach FL 32124 386-238-4780 238-4792
Hawaii Youth Correctional Facility 42-477 Kalanianaole Hwy Kailua HI 96734 808-266-9500 266-9506
Juvenile Corrections Center-Nampa 1650 11th Ave N Nampa ID 83687 208-465-8443 465-8484
Juvenile Corrections Center-Saint Anthony
2220 E 600 N PO Box 40 Saint Anthony ID 83445 208-624-3462 624-0973
Illinois Youth Center Chicago 136 N Western Ave Chicago IL 60612 312-633-5219 633-5229
Illinois Youth Center Harrisburg 1201 W Poplar St Harrisburg IL 62946 618-252-8681 252-2519
Illinois Youth Center Joliet 2848 W McDonough St Joliet IL 60436 815-725-1206 725-9819
Illinois Youth Center Pere Marquette 17808 State Hwy 100 W Grafton IL 62037 618-786-2371 786-2381
Illinois Youth Center Saint Charles
3825 Campton Hills Rd Saint Charles IL 60175 630-584-0506 584-1014
Illinois Youth Center Warrenville 30 W 200 Ferry Rd Warrenville IL 60555 630-983-6231 983-6231
Camp Summit Boot Camp 2407 N 500 W La Porte IN 46350 219-326-1188 326-9218
Indianapolis Juvenile Correctional Facility
2596 N Girls' School Rd Indianapolis IN 46214 317-244-3387 244-4670
Logansport Juvenile Correctional Facility 1118 S SR 25 Logansport IN 46947 574-753-7571 732-0729
Web: www.in.gov/indcorrection/facilites.htm
Northeast Juvenile Correctional Facility 7117 Venture Ln Fort Wayne IN 46818 260-497-7233 497-7543
Plainfield Re-Entry Educational Facility 501 W Main St Plainfield IN 46168 317-839-7751 838-7548
Web: www.in.gov/indcorrection/reentry/center
South Bend Juvenile Correctional Facility
4650 Old Cleveland Rd South Bend IN 46628 574-232-8808 232-9270
Iowa Juvenile Home 701 S Church St Toledo IA 52342 641-484-2560 484-2816
State Training School 3211 Edgington Ave Eldora IA 50627 641-858-5402 858-2416
Atchison Juvenile Correctional Facility
1900 N 2nd St PO Box 459 Atchison KS 66002 913-367-6590 367-2221
Web: jja.state.ks.us
Beloit Juvenile Correctional Facility
1720 N Hersey St PO Box 427 Beloit KS 67420 785-738-5735 738-3314
Larned Juvenile Correctional Facility 1301 Kansas Hwy 264 Larned KS 67550 620-285-0300 285-0301
Web: jja.state.ks.us/larned_index.htm
Topeka Juvenile Correctional Complex 1430 NW 25th St Topeka KS 66618 785-296-7709 354-9878
Web: jja.state.ks.us/topeka_index.htm
Maine Youth Center 675 Westbrook St South Portland ME 04106 207-822-0000 822-0042
Mountainview Youth Development Center 1182 Dover Rd Charleston ME 04422 207-285-0880 285-0836
Web: www.maine.gov/corrections/juvenile/mvydc.htm
Minnesota Correctional Facility-Red Wing 1079 Hwy 292 Red Wing MN 55066 651-267-3600 267-3761
Minnesota Correctional Facility - Togo 62741 County Rd 551 Togo MN 55723 218-376-4411 376-4489
Web: www.thistledewprograms.com
Thistledew Camp 62741 County Rd 551 Togo MN 55723 218-376-4411 376-4489
Web: www.thistledewprograms.com
Columbia Youth Complex 1730 Hwy 44 Columbia MS 39429 601-736-4591 736-5667
Oakley Training School Div of Youth Services
2375 Oakley Rd Raymond MS 39154 601-857-8031 857-8682
Pine Hills Youth Correctional Facility 4 N Haynes Ave Miles City MT 59301 406-232-1377 232-7432
Web: www.cor.state.mt.us
Riverside Youth Correctional Facility
2 Riverside Rd PO Box 88 Boulder MT 59632 406-225-4500 225-4511
Youth Transition Center 4212 3rd Ave S Great Falls MT 59405 406-452-1792 452-8745
Albert C Wagner Youth Correctional Facility PO Box 500 Bordentown NJ 08505 609-298-0500 298-3639

Phone Fax

Garden State Youth Correctional Facility PO Box 11401 Yardville NJ 08620 609-298-6300 324-0677
Mountainview Youth Correctional Facility 31 Petticoat Ln Annandale NJ 08801 908-638-6191 638-4423
SRP Boot Camp PO Box 360 Rt 72 New Lisbon NJ 08064 609-726-0804 726-0896
Alamogordo Reintegration Center PO Box 1966 Alamogordo NM 88310 505-434-0515 439-0321
Carlsbad Community Residential Facility 106 N Mesquite St Carlsbad NM 88220 505-885-8781 885-8683
Eagle Nest Reintegration Center PO Box 317 Eagle Nest NM 87718 505-377-6911 377-6911
New Mexico Boys' School PO Box 38 Springer NM 87747 505-483-2475 483-5030
Bridges Juvenile Center 1221 Spofford Ave Bronx NY 10474 718-764-2700 589-5406
Crossroads Juvenile Center 17 Bristol St Brooklyn NY 11212 718-495-8160 495-8254
Horizon Juvenile Center 560 Brook Ave Bronx NY 10455 718-292-0065 401-8109
Bladen Correctional Center 5853 US 701 N Elizabethtown NC 28337 910-862-3107 862-8563
Web: www.doc.state.nc.us
Foothills Correctional Institution 5150 Western Ave Morganton NC 28655 828-438-5585 438-5598
Morrison Youth Institution PO Box 169 Hoffman NC 28347 910-281-3161 281-0116
Western Youth Institution 5155 Western Ave Morganton NC 28655 828-438-6037 438-6076
Cuyahoga Hills Juvenile Correctional Facility
4321 Green Rd Highland Hills OH 44128 216-464-8200 464-3540
Web: www.dys.ohio.gov/dysweb/CHBSfacility.aspx
Indian River Juvenile Correctional Facility
2775 Indian River Rd SW Massillon OH 44648 330-837-4211 837-4740
Web: www.dys.ohio.gov/dysweb/IRSfacility.aspx
Mohican Juvenile Correctional Facility
1012 ODNR Mohican 51 Perrysville OH 44864 419-994-4127 994-3441
Web: www.dys.ohio.gov/dysweb/MYCfacility.aspx
Ohio River Juvenile Correctional Facility
4696 Gallia Pike Franklin Furnace OH 45629 740-354-7000 354-7022
Scioto Juvenile Correctional Facility 5993 Home Rd Delaware OH 43015 740-881-3250 881-6948
Web: www.dys.ohio.gov/dysweb/SJJCfacility.aspx
Central Oklahoma Detention Juvenile Center 700 S 9th St Tecumseh OK 74873 405-598-2135 598-8713
Web: www.ok.gov
Lloyd E Rader Center 13323 W Hwy 51 Sand Springs OK 74063 918-246-8000 241-0647
Southwest Oklahoma Juvenile Center 300 S Broadway Manitou OK 73555 580-397-3511 397-3491
Camp Florence 04859 S Jetty Rd Florence OR 97439 541-997-2076 997-4217
Camp Tillamook 6820 Barracks Cir Tillamook OR 97141 503-842-4243 842-1476
Corvallis House 330 NW 9th St Corvallis OR 97330 541-757-4144 758-0516
Eastern Oregon Youth Correctional Facility 1800 W Monroe St Burns OR 97720 541-573-3133 573-3665
Hillcrest Youth Correctional Facility 2450 Strong Rd SE Salem OR 97302 503-986-0400 986-0406
MacLaren Youth Correctional Facility 2630 N Pacific Hwy Woodburn OR 97071 503-981-9531 982-4439
OYA Riverbend 58231 Oregon Hwy 244 La Grande OR 97850 541-963-3611 663-9181
Web: www.oregon.gov/OYA/FACLTY/riverbend.shtml
Rogue Valley Youth Correctional Facility 2001 NE 'F' St Grants Pass OR 97526 541-471-2862 471-2861
Tillamook Youth Correctional Facility 6700 Officer Row Tillamook OR 97141 503-842-2565 842-4918
Web: www.oya.state.or.us/tycf.html
Young's Bay Juvenile Detention Center 1250 SE 19th St Warrenton OR 97146 503-861-0310 861-9247
Cresson Secure Treatment Unit
251 Corrections Rd PO Box 269 Cresson PA 16630 814-886-6903 886-6296
Loysville Secure Treatment Unit 10 Opportunity Dr Loysville PA 17047 717-789-4449 789-5538
Loysville Youth Development Center 10 Opportunity Dr Loysville PA 17047 717-789-3841 789-5538
New Castle Youth Development Center 1745 Frew Mill Rd New Castle PA 16101 724-656-7300 656-0999
North Central Secure Treatment Unit 13 Kirk Bride Dr Danville PA 17821 570-271-4700 271-4749
TF: 877-264-9782
South Mountain Secure Treatment Unit
1006 S Mountain Rd PO Box 374 South Mountain PA 17261 717-749-7904 749-7905
WINGS for Life - Pennsylvania 6710 Weaversville Rd Northampton PA 18067 610-262-1591 262-8164
Web: www.amikids.org/Schools/WINGS-PA.htm
Birchwood Institution 5000 Broad River Rd Columbia SC 29212 803-896-9104 896-6157
Willow Lane Institution 4650 Broad River Rd Columbia SC 29210 803-896-9225 896-9205
Brady Patrick Henry Boot Camp 12279 Brady Dr Custer SD 57730 605-673-2521 673-5875
STAR Academy 12279 Brady Dr Custer SD 57730 605-673-2521 673-5489
Web: www.state.sd.us/corrections/custer.htm
State Treatment & Rehabilitation Academy 12279 Brady Dr Custer SD 57730 605-673-2521 673-5489
Web: www.state.sd.us/corrections/custer.htm
Mountain View Youth Development Center 809 Peal Ln Dandridge TN 37725 865-397-0174 397-0738
Taft Youth Development Center 900 SR 301 Pikeville TN 37367 423-881-3201 881-4617
Wilder Youth Development Center
13870 Hwy 59 PO Box 639 Somerville TN 38068 901-465-7359 465-7363
Woodland Hills Youth Development Center 3965 Stewarts Ln Nashville TN 37218 615-532-2000 532-8402
Corsicana State Home 4000 W 2nd Ave Corsicana TX 75110 903-872-4821 872-6667
Web: www.tyc.state.tx.us
Crockett State School 1701 SW Loop 304 Crockett TX 75835 936-852-5000 544-2543
Evins Regional Juvenile Center 3801 E Monte Cristo Rd Edinburg TX 78541 956-289-5500 289-5577
Gainesville State School 1379 FM 678 Gainesville TX 76240 940-665-0701 665-0469
Web: www.tyc.state.tx.us
Giddings State School
2261 James A Thurman Rd PO Box 600 Giddings TX 78942 979-542-3686 542-0177
Web: www.tyc.state.tx.us
Ron Jackson State Juvenile Correctional Complex
PO Box 1267 Brownwood TX 76804 325-641-4200 646-7704
Sheffield Boot Camp 144 Main St Sheffield TX 79781 432-836-4624 836-4472
Victory Field Correctional Academy
FM 8407 433 W PO Box 2010 Vernon TX 76384 940-552-9347 553-1028
West Texas State School PO Box 415 Pyote TX 79777 432-389-5555 389-5522
Woodside Juvenile Rehabilitation Center 26 Woodside Dr E Colchester VT 05446 802-655-4990 655-3095
Beaumont Juvenile Correctional Center 3500 Beaumont Rd Beaumont VA 23014 804-556-3316 556-7288
Bon Air Juvenile Correctional Center 1900 Chatsworth Ave Bon Air VA 23235 804-323-2550 323-2440
Culpeper Juvenile Correctional Center 12240 Coffeewood Dr Mitchells VA 22729 540-727-3333 727-7117
Hanover Juvenile Correctional Center 7093 Broadneck Rd Hanover VA 23069 804-537-5316 537-5907
Natural Bridge Juvenile Correctional Center
1425 Arnold's Valley Rd Natural Bridge Station VA 24579 540-291-2129 291-2461
Oak Ridge Juvenile Correctional Center
1801 Old Bon Air Rd Richmond VA 23235 804-323-2335 323-2310
Greenhill School 375 SW 11th St Chehalis WA 98532 360-748-0131 740-3436
Maple Lane School 20311 Old Hwy 9 SW Centralia WA 98531 360-736-1361 273-0962
Naselle Youth Camp 11 Youth Camp Ln Naselle WA 98638 360-484-3236 484-7167
Davis Juvenile Correctional Center Blackwater Falls Rd Davis WV 26260 304-259-5241 259-4851
Web: www.wvdjs.state.wv.us
Ethan Allen School PO Box 900 Wales WI 53183 262-646-3341 646-3761
Web: www.wi-doc.com
Lincoln Hills School W4380 Copper Lake Rd Irma WI 54442 715-536-8386 536-8386
Prairie du Chien Correctional Institution
500 E Parrish St Prairie du Chien WI 53821 608-326-7828 326-5960
Web: www.wi-doc.com/prairie_du_chien.htm
Racine Youthful Offender Correctional Facility PO Box 2500 Racine WI 53404 262-638-1999 638-1777
Southern Oaks Girls School 21425-B Spring St Union Grove WI 53182 262-878-6500 878-6520
Regional Juvenile Detention Center Inc 201 N David St 3rd Fl Casper WY 82601 307-234-0057 268-8562
Web: www.fcs-inc.net/youth/jdc/services.htm

LABELS - FABRIC

SEE Textile Mills - Narrow Fabric Mills p. 2363

416 LABELS - OTHER THAN FABRIC

Company	City	State	ZIP	Phone	Fax
ACCO North America MACO Div 200 Sheffield St *Fax Area Code: 800 ■ Web: www.maco.com	Mountainside	NJ	07092	908-233-9190	793-9005*
Accurate Dial & Nameplate Inc 329 Mira Loma Ave *Fax Area Code: 818 ■ TF: 800-400-4455 ■ Web: www.accuratedial.com	Glendale	CA	91204	323-245-9181	243-6793*
Acro Labels Inc 2530 Wyandotte Rd TF: 800-355-2235 ■ Web: www.acrolabels.com	Willow Grove	PA	19090	215-657-5366	657-3325
Alcop Adhesive Label Co 826 Perkins Ln	Beverly	NJ	08010	609-871-4400	871-3017
AME Label Corp 25155 W Ave Stanford Web: www.amelabel.com	Valencia	CA	91355	661-257-2200	257-7981
American Law Label Inc 4135 S Pulaski Rd TF: 800-529-5223 ■ Web: www.americanlawlabel.com	Chicago	IL	60632	773-523-2222	523-3332
Arch Crown Tags Inc 177 Main St TF: 800-526-8353 ■ Web: www.archcrown.com	West Orange	NJ	07052	973-731-6300	731-2228
Art Style Printing Inc Dataware Div 7570 Renwick Dr TF: 800-426-4844 ■ Web: www.datawarelabels.com	Houston	TX	77081	713-432-1023	432-1385
Artisan Press 726 Jefferson Ave TF: 800-424-9364 ■ Web: www.artisanpress.net	Ashland	OR	97520	541-482-3373	482-3379
Atlas Tag & Label Inc 2361 Industrial Dr TF: 800-634-2705 ■ Web: www.atlas-tag.com	Neenah	WI	54956	920-722-1557	720-7900
Avery Dennison Automotive Products Div 15939 Industrial Pkwy Web: www.iapna.averydennison.com	Cleveland	OH	44135	216-267-8700	
Avery Dennison Business Media Div 685 Howard St TF: 800-777-2879 ■ Web: www.businessmedia.averydennison.com	Buffalo	NY	14206	716-852-2155	852-2175
Avery Dennison Corp 150 N Orange Grove Blvd NYSE: AVY ■ TF Cust Svc: 800-252-8379 ■ Web: www.averydennison.com	Pasadena	CA	91103	626-304-2000	304-2192
Avery Dennison Industrial Products Div 17700 Foltz Industrial Pkwy Web: www.iapna.averydennison.com	Strongsville	OH	44149	440-878-7000	878-7318
Avery Dennison Retail Information Services Div 3511 W Market St Suite 270 Web: www.ris.averydennison.com	Greensboro	NC	27403	336-856-8235	547-0031
Avery Dennison Tag & Label Div 3511 W Market St Suite 270	Greensboro	NC	27403	336-956-8235	547-0031
Best Label Co 2900 Faber St TF: 800-637-5333 ■ Web: www.bestlabel.com	Union City	CA	94587	510-489-5400	489-2914
Blue Ribbon Tag & Label Corp 4035 N 29th Ave TF: 800-433-4974 ■ Web: www.blueribbonlabel.com	Hollywood	FL	33020	954-922-9292	922-9977
Brady Corp 6555 W Good Hope Rd NYSE: BRC ■ *Fax Area Code: 800 ■ *Fax: Cust Svc ■ TF Cust Svc: 800-537-8791 ■ Web: www.bradycorp.com	Milwaukee	WI	53223	414-358-6600	292-2289*
Brady Identification Solutions 6555 W Good Hope Rd *Fax Area Code: 800 ■ *Fax: Cust Svc ■ TF Cust Svc: 800-537-8791 ■ Web: www.bradyid.com	Milwaukee	WI	53223	414-358-6600	292-2289*
CCL Label Inc 161 Worcester Rd Suite 502 Web: www.cclind.com/index_label.html	Framingham	MA	01701	508-872-4511	872-7671
Cellotape Inc 47623 Fremont Blvd TF: 800-231-0608 ■ Web: www.cellotape.com	Fremont	CA	94538	510-651-5551	651-8091
Chase Corp 26 Summer St AMEX: CCF ■ Web: www.chasecorp.com	Bridgewater	MA	02324	508-279-1789	697-6419
Chicago Decal Co 101 Tower Dr TF: 888-332-2577 ■ Web: www.chicagodecal.com	Burr Ridge	IL	60527	630-850-2122	850-7177
Clamp Swing Pricing Co Inc 8386 Capwell Dr TF: 800-227-7615 ■ Web: www.clampswing.com	Oakland	CA	94621	510-567-1600	567-1830
Continental Identification Products Inc PO Box 98 TF: 800-247-2499 ■ Web: www.continentalid.com	Sparta	MI	49345	616-887-7341	887-0154
Cortegra 6 Commerce Rd Web: www.cortegra.com	Fairfield	NJ	07004	973-808-8000	808-8010
Data Label Inc 1000 Spruce St TF: 800-457-0676 ■ Web: www.data-label.com	Terre Haute	IN	47807	812-232-0408	238-1847
Dataware Div Art Style Printing Inc 7570 Renwick Dr TF: 800-426-4844 ■ Web: www.datawarelabels.com	Houston	TX	77081	713-432-1023	432-1385
DeskTop Labels 7277 Boone Ave N TF: 800-241-9730 ■ Web: www.desktoplabels.com	Minneapolis	MN	55428	763-531-5800	531-5764
Discount Labels Inc 4115 Profit Ct *Fax Area Code: 800 ■ TF: 800-995-9500 ■ Web: www.discountlabels.com	New Albany	IN	47150	812-945-2617	995-9600*
East-West Label Co Inc 1000 E Hector St TF: 800-441-7333 ■ Web: www.ewlabel.com	Conshohocken	PA	19428	610-825-0410	825-6077
Ennis Tag & Label 118 W Main St *Fax Area Code: 800 ■ TF: 800-527-1008 ■ Web: www.ennistagandlabel.com	Wolfe City	TX	75496	903-496-2244	453-2674*
Fasson Roll North America 7670 Auburn Rd Web: na.fasson.com	Painesville	OH	44077	440-358-6000	358-6164
General Data Co Inc 4354 Ferguson Dr *Fax: Sales ■ TF: 800-733-5252 ■ Web: www.general-data.com	Cincinnati	OH	45245	513-752-7978	752-6947*
Gilbreth Packaging Systems 3001 State Rd TF: 800-758-5888 ■ Web: www.gilbrethusa.com	Croydon	PA	19021	215-785-3350	785-4046
Grand Rapids Label Co 2351 Oak Industrial Dr NE TF: 800-552-5215 ■ Web: www.grlabel.com	Grand Rapids	MI	49505	616-459-8134	459-4543
Graphic Technology Inc 301 Gardner Dr TF: 800-767-9930 ■ Web: www.graphic-tech.com	New Century	KS	66031	913-829-8000	829-1462
Green Bay Packaging Inc 1700 N Webster Ct TF: 800-558-4008 ■ Web: www.gbp.com	Green Bay	WI	54302	920-433-5111	
Harris Industries Inc 5181 Argosy Ave TF: 800-222-6866 ■ Web: www.harrisind.com	Huntington Beach	CA	92649	714-898-8048	898-7108
Hooven-Dayton Corp 8060 Technology Blvd TF: 800-621-9291 ■ Web: www.hoovendaytonlabels.com	Dayton	OH	45424	937-233-4473	233-9382
Impact Label Corp 3434 S Burdick St TF: 800-820-0362 ■ Web: www.impactlabel.com	Kalamazoo	MI	49001	269-381-4280	381-1055
International Label & Printing Co Inc 2550 United Ln TF: 800-244-1442 ■ Web: www.internationallabel.com	Elk Grove Village	IL	60007	630-595-1442	595-1747
International Playing Card & Label Co (IPC&L) 530 W Main St Web: www.ipcl.com	Rogersville	TN	37857	423-272-7644	272-2925
ITW Auto-Sleeve 2003 Case Pkwy S Unit 3 TF: 800-852-4571 ■ Web: www.itw-autosleeve.com	Twinsburg	OH	44087	330-487-2200	487-3700
Jordan Industries Inc Specialty Printing & Labeling Group 1751 Lake Cook Rd Suite 550 ArborLake Center Web: www.jordanindustries.com	Deerfield	IL	60015	847-945-5591	945-5698
Label Art 1 Riverside Way *Fax Area Code: 800 ■ *Fax: Cust Svc ■ TF: 800-258-1050 ■ Web: www.labelart.com	Wilton	NH	03086	603-654-6131	733-7800*
Label Craft Corp 5140 Firestone Pl Web: labelcraftusa.net	South Gate	CA	90280	323-564-5956	564-8510
Label Graphics Co Inc 1225 Carnegie St Suite 104B	Rolling Meadows	IL	60008	847-454-1005	454-1008
Labelmaster Co 5724 N Pulaski Rd TF: 800-621-5808 ■ Web: www.labelmaster.com	Chicago	IL	60646	773-478-0900	478-6054
Labeltape Inc 4489 E Paris Ave SE TF: 800-928-4537 ■ Web: www.labeltape-inc.com	Grand Rapids	MI	49512	616-698-1830	698-7831
Lancer Label 301 S 74th St TF Cust Svc: 800-228-7074 ■ Web: www.lancerlabel.com	Omaha	NE	68114	402-390-9119	390-9459
LGInternational 6700 SW Bradbury Ct TF: 800-345-0534 ■ Web: www.lgintl.com	Portland	OR	97224	503-620-0520	620-3296
MACO Div ACCO North America 200 Sheffield St *Fax Area Code: 800 ■ Web: www.maco.com	Mountainside	NJ	07092	908-233-9190	793-9005*
MACtac 4560 Darrow Rd TF: 800-762-2822 ■ Web: www.mactac.com	Stow	OH	44224	330-688-1111	688-2540
McCourt Label Co 20 Egbert Ln TF: 800-458-2390 ■ Web: www.mccourtlabel.com	Lewis Run	PA	16738	814-362-3851	362-4156
Mepco Label Systems PO Box 932 TF: 800-975-2235 ■ Web: www.mepcolabel.com	Stockton	CA	95201	209-946-0201	946-0164
Metro Label Corp 1395 Chattahoochee Ave NW TF: 800-235-8814 ■ Web: www.metro-label.com	Atlanta	GA	30318	404-351-5044	351-0646
Morgan Adhesives Co DBA MACtac 4560 Darrow Rd TF: 800-762-2822 ■ Web: www.mactac.com	Stow	OH	44224	330-688-1111	688-2540
MPI Label Systems Inc 450 Courtney Rd TF: 800-837-2134 ■ Web: www.mpilabels.com	Sebring	OH	44672	330-938-2134	938-9878
Multi-Color Corp 425 Walnut St Suite 1300 NASDAQ: LABL ■ Web: www.multicolorcorp.com	Cincinnati	OH	45202	513-381-1480	381-2813
Nashua Corp Label Products Div 3838 S 108th St TF: 800-533-8806 ■ Web: www.nashua.com/units/label/label.html	Omaha	NE	68144	402-397-3600	392-6080
National Label Co Inc 2025 Joshua Rd TF: 800-872-5223 ■ Web: www.nationallabel.com	Lafayette Hill	PA	19444	610-825-3250	834-8854
National Printing Converters Inc 18 S Murphy Ave *Fax Area Code: 800 ■ TF: 800-877-6724 ■ Web: www.npclabels.com	Brazil	IN	47834	812-448-2555	669-0329*
Northeast Data Services 1316 College Ave TF Cust Svc: 800-845-3720 ■ Web: www.artisticlabels.com	Elmira	NY	14901	607-733-5541	735-4540
Pamco Printed Tape & Label Co 2200 S Wolf Rd Web: www.pamcolabel.com	Des Plaines	IL	60018	847-803-2200	803-2209
Paxar Corp 105 Corporate Park Dr NYSE: PXR ■ TF: 888-447-2927 ■ Web: www.paxar.com	White Plains	NY	10604	914-697-6800	696-4128
Paxar Corp Systems Group 1 Wilcox St TF: 800-947-2927	Sayre	PA	18840	570-888-6641	888-4080
Pharmagraphics 1072 Boulder Rd Web: www.pharmagraphics.com	Greensboro	NC	27409	336-292-4555	292-1727
Precision Printing & Packaging Inc 801 Alfred Thun Rd	Clarksville	TN	37040	931-920-9000	920-9001
Print-O-Tape Inc 755 Tower Rd TF: 800-346-6311 ■ Web: www.printotape.com	Mundelein	IL	60060	847-362-1476	949-7449
Printed Systems 1271 Gillingham Rd *Fax: Sales ■ TF Sales: 800-352-2332 ■ Web: www.psdtag.com	Neenah	WI	54956	920-886-2000	886-2036*
Quikstik Label Mfg Co 210 Broadway TF: 800-225-3496 ■ Web: www.qsxlabels.com	Everett	MA	02149	617-389-7570	381-9280
Reidler Decal Corp 1 Reidler Rd St Clair Industrial Park TF: 800-628-7770 ■ Web: www.reidlerdecal.com	Saint Clair	PA	17970	570-429-1812	429-1528
Renaissance Mark 350 Southwood Ct Web: www.ren-mark.com	Bowling Green	KY	42101	270-745-0829	745-0810
Rydin Decal Co 660 Pond Dr TF: 800-448-1991 ■ Web: www.rydindecal.com	Wood Dale	IL	60191	630-766-8410	766-8459
Salem Label Co 1472 Salem Pkwy TF: 888-274-7465 ■ Web: www.salemlabel.com	Salem	OH	44460	330-332-1591	332-1563
Shamrock Scientific Specialty Systems Inc 34 Davis Dr *Fax Area Code: 800 ■ TF: 800-323-0249 ■ Web: www.shamrocklabels.com	Bellwood	IL	60104	708-547-9005	248-1907*
Smyth Cos Inc 1085 Snelling Ave N TF: 800-642-4544 ■ Web: www.smythco.com	Saint Paul	MN	55180	651-646-4544	646-8949
Sohn Mfg Inc 544 Sohn Dr Web: www.sohnmanufacturing.com	Elkhart Lake	WI	53020	920-876-3361	876-2952
Spear Inc 48 Powers St TF: 800-627-7327 ■ Web: www.spearinc.com	Milford	NH	03055	603-673-6353	672-8107
Spec Print Inc 1710 N Mt Juliet Rd TF: 800-989-3325 ■ Web: www.specprintinc.com	Mount Juliet	TN	37122	615-758-5913	758-5103
Spectrum Label Corp 30803 San Clemente St TF: 800-545-2235 ■ Web: www.spectrumlabel.com	Hayward	CA	94544	510-477-0707	477-0787
Spinnaker Coating Inc 518 E Water St TF: 800-543-9452 ■ Web: www.spinnakercoating.com	Troy	OH	45373	937-332-6500	335-2843
Spinnaker Industries Inc 4846 Jennings Ln Web: www.spinnakerindustries.com	Louisville	KY	40218	800-932-6210	903-7294
Strutz International Inc PO Box 509 Web: www.strutz.com	Mars	PA	16046	724-625-1501	625-3570
Tag-It Pacific Inc 21900 Burbank Blvd Suite 270 AMEX: TAG ■ TF: 800-335-4443 ■ Web: www.tagitpacific.com	Woodland Hills	CA	91367	818-444-4100	444-4105
Tape & Label Converters Inc 8231 Allport Ave TF: 888-285-2462 ■ Web: www.stickybiz.com	Santa Fe Springs	CA	90670	562-945-3486	696-8198
Tapecon Inc 10 Latta Rd TF: 800-333-2408 ■ Web: www.tapecon.com	Rochester	NY	14612	585-621-8400	621-1677
TAPEMARK Co 1685 Marthaler Ln TF: 800-535-1998 ■ Web: www.tapemark.com	West Saint Paul	MN	55118	651-455-1611	450-8403
United Ad Label Inc 30 Hazelwood Dr Suite 100 *Fax: Orders	Amherst	NY	14228	800-992-5755	962-0658*
Valmark Industries Inc 7900 National Dr TF: 800-770-7074 ■ Web: www.valmark.com	Livermore	CA	94550	925-960-9900	960-0900
Vitachrome Graphics Group Inc 11517 Los Nietos Rd Web: www.vitachrome.com	Santa Fe Springs	CA	90670	562-692-9200	692-9055
Weber Marking Systems Inc 711 W Algonquin Rd TF Sales: 800-225-0883 ■ Web: www.webermarking.com	Arlington Heights	IL	60005	847-364-8500	364-8575
West Coast Tag & Label Co PO Box 4099 *Fax Area Code: 800 ■ TF: 800-742-8247	West Hills	CA	91308	818-710-8484	458-8247*
Whitlam Label Co Inc 24800 Sherwood Ave TF: 800-755-2235 ■ Web: www.whitlam.com	Center Line	MI	48015	586-757-5100	757-1243
Wise Tag & Label Co Inc 7035 Central Hwy TF: 800-222-1327 ■ Web: www.wisetaglabel.com	Pennsauken	NJ	08109	856-663-2400	663-8610
Wright of Thomasville Corp 5115 Prospect St TF: 800-678-9019 ■ Web: www.wrightlabels.com	Thomasville	NC	27360	336-472-4200	476-8554
WS Packaging Group Inc 1102 Jefferson St TF: 800-236-3424 ■ Web: www.wspackaging.com	Algoma	WI	54201	920-487-3424	487-5644
YORK Label 405 Willow Springs Ln TF Cust Svc: 888-800-9675 ■ Web: www.yorklabel.com	York	PA	17402	717-266-9675	266-9835
Z International Inc 110 E 16th Ave TF: 800-528-4190 ■ Web: www.zintl.com	North Kansas City	MO	64116	816-474-8400	842-9179

417 LABOR UNIONS

Organization	City	State	ZIP	Phone	Fax
Actors' Equity Assn 165 W 46th St Web: www.actorsequity.org	New York	NY	10036	212-869-8530	719-9815
AFL-CIO (American Federation of Labor & Congress of Industrial Organizations) 815 16th St NW Web: www.aflcio.org	Washington	DC	20006	202-637-5000	637-5058
AFT Healthcare 555 New Jersey Ave NW TF: 800-238-1133 ■ Web: www.aft.org/healthcare	Washington	DC	20001	202-879-4491	393-5672
Air Line Pilots Assn 535 Herndon Pkwy TF: 800-359-2572 ■ Web: www.alpa.org	Herndon	VA	20170	703-689-2270	689-4177
Amalgamated Transit Union (ATU) 5025 Wisconsin Ave NW 3rd Fl TF: 888-240-1196 ■ Web: www.atu.org	Washington	DC	20016	202-537-1645	244-7824
American Federation of Government Employees 80 F St NW Web: www.afge.org	Washington	DC	20001	202-737-8700	639-6441

				Phone	Fax
American Federation of Labor & Congress of Industrial Organizations (AFL-CIO) 815 16th St NW	Washington	DC	20006	202-637-5000	637-5058
Web: www.aflcio.org					
American Federation of Musicians of the US & Canada (AFM) 1501 Broadway Suite 600	New York	NY	10036	212-869-1330	764-6134
TF: 800-762-3444 ■ *Web:* www.afm.org					
American Federation of State County & Municipal Employees 1625 L St NW	Washington	DC	20036	202-429-1000	429-1293
Web: www.afscme.org					
American Federation of Teachers (AFT) 555 New Jersey Ave NW	Washington	DC	20001	202-879-4400	879-4556*
**Fax:* PR ■ *TF:* 800-238-1133 ■ *Web:* www.aft.org					
American Federation of Television & Radio Artists (AFTRA) 260 Madison Ave 7th Fl	New York	NY	10016	212-532-0800	532-2242
Web: www.aftra.com					
American Postal Workers Union 1300 L St NW	Washington	DC	20005	202-842-4200	842-8500
Web: www.apwu.org					
American Train Dispatchers Assn (ATDA) 1370 Ontario St Suite 1040	Cleveland	OH	44113	216-241-2770	241-6286
Web: www.atdd.org					
Association of Civilian Technicians (ACT) 12620 Lake Ridge Dr	Woodbridge	VA	22192	703-494-4845	494-0961
Web: www.actnat.com					
Association of Flight Attendants 501 3rd St NW	Washington	DC	20001	202-434-1300	434-1319
Web: www.afanet.org					
Association of Professional Flight Attendants 1004 W Euless Blvd	Euless	TX	76040	817-540-0108	540-2077
TF: 800-395-2732 ■ *Web:* www.apfa.org					
Association of Western Pulp & Paper Workers PO Box 4566	Portland	OR	97208	503-228-7486	228-1346
Web: www.awppw.org					
Bakery Confectionery Tobacco Workers & Grain Millers International Union 10401 Connecticut Ave	Kensington	MD	20895	301-933-8600	946-8452
Web: www.bctgm.org					
Brotherhood of Locomotive Engineers & Trainmen 1370 Ontario St Mezzanine Level	Cleveland	OH	44113	216-241-2630	241-6516
Web: www.ble.org					
Brotherhood of Maintenance of Way Employees 2300 Civic Ctr Dr Suite 320	Southfield	MI	48076	248-948-1010	948-7150
Web: www.bmwe.org					
Brotherhood of Railroad Signalmen 917 Shenandoah Shores Rd	Front Royal	VA	22630	540-622-6522	622-6532
Web: www.brs.org					
Brotherhood Railway Carmen c/o Transportation Communications International Union 3 Research Pl	Rockville	MD	20850	301-948-4910	948-1369
Web: www.tcunion.org					
Canada Labour Congress 2841 Riverside Dr	Ottawa	ON	K1V8X7	613-521-3400	521-4655
Web: www.clc-ctc.ca					
Communications Workers of America (CWA) 501 3rd St NW	Washington	DC	20001	202-434-1100	434-1436*
**Fax:* Hum Res ■ *Web:* www.cwa-union.org					
Communications Workers of America Printing Publishing & Media Workers Sector 501 3rd St NW Suite 950	Washington	DC	20001	202-434-1238	434-1245
Congres du travail du Canada 2841 Riverside Dr	Ottawa	ON	K1V8X7	613-521-3400	521-4655
Web: www.clc-ctc.ca					
Directors Guild of America 7920 W Sunset Blvd	Los Angeles	CA	90046	310-289-2000	289-2029
TF: 800-421-4173 ■ *Web:* www.dga.org					
Distillery Wine & Allied Workers Div UFCW International Union 219 Paterson Ave	Little Falls	NJ	07424	973-237-1241	890-1956
Federal Education Assn 1201 16th St NW Suite 117	Washington	DC	20036	202-822-7850	822-7816
Web: www.feaonline.org					
Florida Education Assn 213 S Adams St	Tallahassee	FL	32301	850-201-2800	222-1840
TF: 888-807-8007 ■ *Web:* feaweb.org					
Glass Molders Pottery Plastics & Allied Workers International Union 608 E Baltimore Pike	Media	PA	19063	610-565-5051	565-0983
Web: www.gmpiu.org					
Graphic Artists Guild Inc 90 John St Suite 403	New York	NY	10038	212-791-3400	791-0333
Web: www.gag.org					
Graphic Communications International Union 1900 L St NW 9th Fl	Washington	DC	20036	202-462-1400	721-0600
Web: www.gciu.org					
Industrial Union of Marine & Shipbuilding Workers of America 719 E Fort Ave	Baltimore	MD	21230	410-837-0056	837-0058
Inlandboatmen's Union of the Pacific (IBU) 1711 W Nickerson St Suite D	Seattle	WA	98119	206-284-6001	284-5043
Web: www.ibu.org					
International Alliance of Theatrical Stage Employees Moving Picture Technicians (IATSE) 1430 Broadway 20th Fl	New York	NY	10018	212-730-1770	921-7699
TF: 800-223-6872 ■ *Web:* www.iatse-intl.org					
International Assn of Bridge Structural Ornamental & Reinforcing Iron Workers 1750 New York Ave NW Suite 400	Washington	DC	20006	202-383-4800	638-4856
TF: 800-368-0105 ■ *Web:* www.ironworkers.org					
International Assn of Fire Fighters (IAFF) 1750 New York Ave NW 3rd Fl	Washington	DC	20006	202-737-8484	737-8418
Web: www.iaff.org					
International Assn of Heat & Frost Insulators & Asbestos Workers 9602 ML King Jr Hwy	Lanham	MD	20706	301-731-9101	731-5058
Web: www.insulators.org					
International Assn of Machinists & Aerospace Workers 9000 Machinists Pl	Upper Marlboro	MD	20772	301-967-4500	967-4588
Web: www.goiam.org					
International Brotherhood of Boilermakers Iron Shipbuilders Blacksmiths Forgers & Helpers 753 State Ave Suite 570	Kansas City	KS	66101	913-371-2640	281-8101
Web: www.boilermakers.org					
International Brotherhood of Correctional Officers (IBCO) 159 Burgin Pkwy	Quincy	MA	02169	617-376-0220	376-0285
Web: www.ibco.org					
International Brotherhood of Electrical Workers 900 7th St NW	Washington	DC	20001	202-833-7000	467-6316
Web: www.ibew.org					
International Brotherhood of Police Officers 159 Burgin Pkwy	Quincy	MA	02169	617-376-0220	376-0285
Web: www.ibpo.org					
International Brotherhood of Teamsters 25 Louisiana Ave NW	Washington	DC	20001	202-624-6800	624-6918*
**Fax:* PR ■ *Web:* www.teamster.org					
International Chemical Workers Union Council 1799 Akron Peninsula Rd	Akron	OH	44313	330-926-1444	926-0816
Web: www.icwuc.org					
International Federation of Professional & Technical Engineers 8630 Fenton St Suite 400	Silver Spring	MD	20910	301-565-9016	565-0018
Web: www.ifpte.org					
International Longshore & Warehouse Union 1188 Franklin St 4th Fl	San Francisco	CA	94109	415-775-0533	775-1302
Web: www.ilwu.org					
International Longshoremen's Assn 17 Battery Pl Rm 930	New York	NY	10004	212-425-1200	425-2928
Web: www.ila2000.org					
International Organization of Masters Mates & Pilots 700 Maritime Blvd	Linthicum Heights	MD	21090	410-850-8700	850-0973
TF: 877-667-5522 ■ *Web:* www.bridgedeck.org					
International Union of Bricklayers & Allied Craftworkers (BAC) 1776 'I' St NW	Washington	DC	20006	202-783-3788	393-0219
TF: 888-880-8222 ■ *Web:* www.bacweb.org					
International Union of Electronic Electrical Salaried Machine & Furniture Workers 501 3rd St NW 6th Fl	Washington	DC	20001	202-434-1228	434-1250
Web: www.iue-cwa.org					
International Union of Elevator Constructors (IUEC) 7154 Columbia Gateway Dr	Columbia	MD	21046	410-953-6150	953-6169
Web: www.iuec.org					
International Union of Industrial Service Transport Health Employees 400 Market St 5th Fl	Newark	NJ	07105	973-344-3448	344-3449
TF: 800-331-1070					
International Union of Operating Engineers 1125 17th St NW	Washington	DC	20036	202-429-9100	778-2616
Web: www.iuoe.org					
International Union of Painters & Allied Trades 1750 New York Ave NW 8th Fl	Washington	DC	20006	202-637-0700	637-0771
Web: www.ibpat.org					
International Union of Petroleum & Industrial Workers 8131 E Rosecrans Ave	Paramount	CA	90723	562-630-6232	408-1073
TF: 800-624-5842					
International Union of Police Associations 1549 Ringling Blvd Suite 600	Sarasota	FL	34236	941-487-2560	487-2570
TF: 800-247-4872 ■ *Web:* www.iupa.org					
International Union Security Police & Fire Professionals of America (SPFPA) 25510 Kelly Rd	Roseville	MI	48066	586-772-7250	772-9644
TF: 800-228-7492 ■ *Web:* www.spfpa.org					
International Union United Automobile Aerospace & Agricultural Implement Workers of America (UAW) 8000 E Jefferson Ave	Detroit	MI	48214	313-926-5000	823-6016
Web: www.uaw.org					
Laborers' International Union of North America 905 16th St NW	Washington	DC	20006	202-737-8320	737-2754
Web: www.liuna.org					
Major League Baseball Players Assn (MLBPA) 12 E 49th St 24th Fl	New York	NY	10017	212-826-0808	752-4378
Web: mlbplayers.mlb.com/NASApp/mlb/pa/index.jsp					
Marine Engineers' Beneficial Assn (MEBA) 444 N Capitol St NW Suite 800	Washington	DC	20001	202-638-5355	638-5369
Web: www.d1meba.org					
NAGE (National Assn of Government Employees) 159 Burgin Pkwy	Quincy	MA	02169	617-376-0220	376-0285
Web: www.nage.org					
National Air Traffic Controllers Assn (NATCA) 1325 Massachusetts Ave NW	Washington	DC	20005	202-628-5451	628-5767
TF: 800-266-0895 ■ *Web:* www.natca.org					
National Alliance of Postal & Federal Employees 1628 11th St NW	Washington	DC	20001	202-939-6325	939-6389
Web: www.napfe.com					
National Assn of Broadcast Employees & Technicians-Communications Workers of America (NABET-CWA) 501 3rd St NW	Washington	DC	20001	202-434-1254	434-1426
Web: www.nabetcwa.org					
National Assn of Government Employees (NAGE) 159 Burgin Pkwy	Quincy	MA	02169	617-376-0220	376-0285
Web: www.nage.org					
National Assn of Letter Carriers 100 Indiana Ave NW	Washington	DC	20001	202-393-4695	737-1540
Web: www.nalc.org					
National Basketball Players Assn (NBPA) 310 Lennox Ave 3rd Fl	New York	NY	10027	212-655-0880	655-0881
Web: www.nbpa.com					
National Conference of Firemen & Oilers 1023 15th St NW 10th Fl	Washington	DC	20005	202-962-0981	872-1222
Web: www.ncfo.org					
National Education Assn (NEA) 1201 16th St NW	Washington	DC	20036	202-833-4000	822-7974
Web: www.nea.org					
National Federation of Federal Employees 805-15th St NW Suite 500	Washington	DC	20036	202-216-4420	862-4432
Web: www.nffe.org					
National Football League Players Assn (NFLPA) 2021 L St NW Suite 600	Washington	DC	20036	202-463-2200	857-0380
TF: 800-372-2000 ■ *Web:* www.nflpa.org					
National Hockey League Players Assn (NHLPA) 20 Bay St	Toronto	ON	M5J2N8	800-363-4625	
Web: www.nhlpa.com					
National League of Postmasters of the US 5904 Richmond Hwy Suite 500	Alexandria	VA	22303	703-329-4550	329-0466
Web: www.postmasters.org					
National Organization of Industrial Trade Unions 148-06 Hillside Ave	Jamaica	NY	11435	718-291-3434	526-2920
National Rural Letter Carriers' Assn 1630 Duke St 4th Fl	Alexandria	VA	22314	703-684-5545	548-8735
Web: www.nrlca.org					
National Treasury Employees Union 1750 H St NW 10th Fl	Washington	DC	20006	202-572-5500	572-5643
Web: www.nteu.org					
National Writers Union (NWU) 113 University Pl 6th Fl	New York	NY	10003	212-254-0279	254-0673
Web: www.nwu.org					
NBPA (National Basketball Players Assn) 310 Lennox Ave 3rd Fl	New York	NY	10027	212-655-0880	655-0881
Web: www.nbpa.com					
News Media Guild 424 W 33rd St Suite 260	New York	NY	10001	212-869-9290	840-0687
Web: www.newsmediaguild.org					
Newspaper Guild-Communications Workers of America 501 3rd St NW 6th Fl	Washington	DC	20001	202-434-7177	434-1472
TF: 800-585-5864 ■ *Web:* www.newsguild.org					
Office & Professional Employees International Union 265 W 14th St Suite 610	New York	NY	10011	212-675-3210	727-3466
TF: 800-346-7348 ■ *Web:* www.opeiu.org					
Operative Plasterers' & Cement Masons' International Assn of the US & Canada (OPCMIA) 11720 Beltsville Dr Suite 700	Beltsville	MD	20705	301-623-1000	623-1032
Web: www.opcmia.org					
Professional Security Officers Union 2201 Broadway Suite 101	Oakland	CA	94612	510-625-9913	625-0998
TF: 800-772-3326 ■ *Web:* www.seiu247.org					
Retail Wholesale & Department Store Union 30 E 29th St	New York	NY	10016	212-684-5300	779-2809
Web: www.rwdsu.org					
Rubber/Plastics Industry Conference of the United Steelworkers of America 5 Gateway Ctr 7th Fl	Pittsburgh	PA	15222	412-562-6971	562-6963
Screen Actors Guild (SAG) 5757 Wilshire Blvd	Los Angeles	CA	90036	323-954-1600	549-6775
Web: www.sag.org					
Seafarers International Union 5201 Auth Way	Camp Springs	MD	20746	301-899-0675	899-7355
TF: 800-252-4674 ■ *Web:* www.seafarers.org					
Service Employees International Union 1800 Massachusetts Ave NW	Washington	DC	20036	202-730-7000	429-5660
TF: 800-424-8592 ■ *Web:* www.seiu.org					
Sheet Metal Workers International Assn (SMWIA) 1750 New York Ave NW 6th Fl	Washington	DC	20006	202-783-5880	662-0894
TF: 800-457-7694 ■ *Web:* www.smwia.org					

Phone Fax

Transport Workers Union of America 80 West End Ave 6th Fl New York NY 10023 212-873-6000 579-3381
Web: www.twu.org
Transportation Communications International Union
3 Research Pl Rockville MD 20850 301-948-4910 948-1369
Web: www.goiam.org/tcunion.cfm
UFCW International Union Distillery Wine & Allied Workers Div
219 Paterson Ave Little Falls NJ 07424 973-237-1241 890-1956
UFCW Textile & Garment Council
4207 Lebanon Pike Suite 200 Hermitage TN 37076 615-889-9221 885-3102
TF: 888-462-4892 ■ *Web:* www.ufcw.org
Union of American Physicians & Dentists
180 Grand Ave Suite 1380 Oakland CA 94612 510-839-0193 763-8756
Web: www.uapd.com
UNITE HERE 275 7th Ave New York NY 10001 212-265-7000 265-3415
TF: 800-238-6483 ■ *Web:* www.unitehere.org
United Assn of Journeymen & Apprentices of the Plumbing Pipe Fitting Sprinkler Fitting Industry of the US & Canada 901 Massachusetts Ave NW Washington DC 20001 202-628-5823 628-5024
Web: www.ua.org
United Auto Workers 8000 E Jefferson Ave Detroit MI 48214 313-926-5000 823-6016
Web: www.uaw.org
United Brotherhood of Carpenters & Joiners of America
101 Constitution Ave NW Washington DC 20001 202-546-6206 543-5724
Web: www.carpenters.org
United Electrical Radio & Machine Workers of America
1 Gateway Ctr Suite 1400 Pittsburgh PA 15222 412-471-8919 471-8999
Web: www.ranknfile-ue.org
United Farm Workers of America (UFW)
29700 Woodford Techachpi Rd Keene CA 93531 661-822-5571 823-6174
Web: www.ufw.org
United Food & Commercial Workers International Union (UFCW) 1775 K St NW Washington DC 20006 202-223-3111 466-1562
TF: 800-551-4010 ■ *Web:* www.ufcw.org
United Mine Workers of America (UMWA) 8315 Lee Hwy Fairfax VA 22031 703-208-7200 208-7227
Web: www.umwa.org
United Scenic Artists 29 W 38th St 15th Fl New York NY 10018 212-581-0300 977-2011
Web: www.usa829.org
United Steel, Paper and Forestry, Rubber, Manufacturing, Energy, Allied-Industrial and Service Workers International Union (USW) 3340 Perimeter Hill Dr Nashville TN 37211 615-834-8590 834-7741
Web: www.usw.org
United Steelworkers of America (USWA) 5 Gateway Ctr Pittsburgh PA 15222 412-562-2400 562-2445
Web: www.uswa.org
United Steelworkers of America Rubber/Plastics Industry Conference 5 Gateway Ctr 7th Fl Pittsburgh PA 15222 412-562-6971 562-6963
United Transportation Union 14600 Detroit Ave Lakewood OH 44107 216-228-9400 228-5755
TF: 800-558-8842 ■ *Web:* www.utu.org
Utility Workers Union of America 815 16th St NW Washington DC 20006 202-974-8200 974-8201
Web: www.uwua.org
Writers Guild of America East (WGAE)
555 W 57th St Suite 1230 New York NY 10019 212-767-7800 582-1909
Web: www.wgaeast.org
Writers Guild of America West (WGAw) 7000 W 3rd St Los Angeles CA 90048 323-951-4000 782-4800
TF: 800-548-4532 ■ *Web:* www.wga.org

418 LABORATORIES - DENTAL

SEE ALSO Laboratories - Medical p. 1883

Phone Fax

Americus Dental Labs Inc 150-15 Hillside Ave Jamaica NY 11432 718-658-6655 657-8389
TF: 888-263-7428 ■ *Web:* www.americuslab.com
Boos Dental Laboratories 801 12th Ave N Minneapolis MN 55411 612-529-9655 529-6918
TF: 800-333-2667 ■ *Web:* www.dentalservices.net/boos
Dental Technologies Inc (DTI) 1638 W 3rd Ave Suite 300 Vancouver BC V6J1K2 604-873-2884 873-1671
Web: www.dtidental.com
Dentsply Friadent CeraMed 12860 W Cedar Dr Suite 110 Lakewood CO 80228 303-985-0800 989-5669
TF: 800-426-7836 ■ *Web:* www.ceramed.com
DTI (Dental Technologies Inc) 1638 W 3rd Ave Suite 300 Vancouver BC V6J1K2 604-873-2884 873-1671
Web: www.dtidental.com
Keller Laboratories Inc 160 Larkin Williams Industrial Ct Fenton MO 63026 636-717-1755 600-4396
TF: 800-325-3056 ■ *Web:* www.kellerlab.com
National Dentex Corp (NDX) 526 Boston Post Rd Suite 207 Wayland MA 01778 508-358-4422 358-6199
NASDAQ: NADX ■ *Web:* www.nationaldentex.com
NDX (National Dentex Corp) 526 Boston Post Rd Suite 207 Wayland MA 01778 508-358-4422 358-6199
NASDAQ: NADX ■ *Web:* www.nationaldentex.com
Posca Brothers Dental Laboratory Inc 641 W Willow St Long Beach CA 90806 562-427-1811 595-5821
TF: 800-338-1811 ■ *Web:* www.poscabrothers.com
Roe Dental Laboratory Inc 9565 Midwest Ave Garfield Heights OH 44125 216-663-2233 663-2237
TF: 800-228-6663 ■ *Web:* www.roedentallab.com

419 LABORATORIES - DRUG-TESTING

SEE ALSO Laboratories - Medical p. 1883

Phone Fax

Air Force Drug Testing Laboratory 2601 Ram Rd Suite 117 Brooks AFB TX 78235 210-536-3723 536-3219
Bio-Reference Laboratories Inc 481 Edward H Ross Dr Elmwood Park NJ 07407 201-791-2600 791-1941
NASDAQ: BRLI ■ *TF:* 800-229-5227 ■ *Web:* www.bioreference.com
Drug Detection Laboratories Inc
9700 Business Park Dr Suite 407 Sacramento CA 95827 916-366-3113 366-3917
Web: www.drugdetection.net
ElSohly Laboratories Inc 5 Industrial Park Dr Oxford MS 38655 662-236-2609 234-0253
Web: www.elsohly.com
Kroll Laboratory Specialists Inc 1111 Newton St Gretna LA 70053 504-361-8989 361-8298
TF: 800-433-3823 ■
Web: www.krollworldwide.com/services/screening/substance_abuse_testing
LabOne Inc 10101 Renner Blvd Lenexa KS 66219 913-888-1770 888-6374*
**Fax:* Sales ■ *TF:* 800-646-7788 ■ *Web:* www.labone.com
MecStat Laboratories 1700 S Mt Prospect Rd Des Plaines IL 60018 847-375-0770 375-0775
TF: 800-235-2367 ■ *Web:* www.usdtl.com
MEDTOX Scientific Inc 402 W County Rd D Saint Paul MN 55112 651-636-7466 636-5351
NASDAQ: MTOX ■ *TF:* 800-832-3244 ■ *Web:* www.medtox.com
SED Medical Laboratories 5601 Office Blvd Albuquerque NM 87109 505-727-6300 727-6244
TF: 800-999-5227 ■ *Web:* www.sedlabs.com
US Drug Testing Laboratories DBA MecStat Laboratories
1700 S Mt Prospect Rd Des Plaines IL 60018 847-375-0770 375-0775
TF: 800-235-2367 ■ *Web:* www.usdtl.com

420 LABORATORIES - GENETIC TESTING

SEE ALSO Laboratories - Medical p. 1883

Phone Fax

American Red Cross Pacific NorthWest Blood Service
3131 N Vancouver Ave Portland OR 97227 503-280-0210
Web: www.nwblood.redcross.org
Blood Systems Laboratories 2424 W Erie Dr Tempe AZ 85282 602-343-7000 343-7025
TF: 866-342-4275 ■ *Web:* www.bloodsystemslaboratories.org
BRT Laboratories Inc 400 W Franklin St Baltimore MD 21201 410-225-9595 383-0938
TF: 800-765-5170 ■ *Web:* www.brtlabs.com
Center for Genetic Testing at Saint Francis 6161 S Yale Ave Tulsa OK 74136 918-502-1720 502-1723
TF: 800-299-7919 ■ *Web:* www.sfh-lab.com
Clinical Testing & Research Inc 20 Wilsey Sq Ridgewood NJ 07450 201-652-2088 652-2775
TF: 888-837-5267 ■ *Web:* www.clinicaltesting.com
Commonwealth Biotechnologies Inc 601 Biotech Dr Richmond VA 23235 804-648-3820 648-2641
NASDAQ: CBTE ■ *TF:* 800-735-9224 ■ *Web:* www.cbi-biotech.com
DNA Diagnostics Center 1 DDC Way Fairfield OH 45014 513-881-7800 881-7803
TF: 800-362-2368 ■ *Web:* www.dnacenter.com
DNA Paternity Lab of Utah 2749 E Parleys Way Suite 100 Salt Lake City UT 84109 801-582-4200 582-8460
TF: 800-362-5559
Genecare Medical Genetics Center 201 Sage Rd Suite 300 Chapel Hill NC 27514 919-942-0021 967-9519
TF: 800-277-4363 ■ *Web:* www.genecare.com
Genelex Corp 3000 1st Ave Suite 1 Seattle WA 98121 206-382-9591 219-4000
TF: 800-523-6487 ■ *Web:* www.genelex.com
Genetic Profiles Corp 10675 Treena St Suite 103 San Diego CA 92131 858-623-0840 348-0048
TF: 800-551-7763 ■ *Web:* www.geneticprofiles.com
Genetica DNA Laboratories Inc 8740 Montgomery Rd Cincinnati OH 45236 513-985-9777 985-9983
TF: 800-433-6848 ■ *Web:* www.genetica.com
Genetics & IVF Institute 3015 Williams Dr Fairfax VA 22031 703-698-7355 698-1137
TF: 800-552-4363 ■ *Web:* www.givf.com
GenQuest DNA Analysis Laboratory
Univ of Nevada - Reno 1664 N Virginia St Reno NV 89557 775-784-4494 358-0657
TF: 877-362-5227 ■ *Web:* www.genquestdnalab.com
Genzyme Corp 500 Kendall St Cambridge MA 02142 617-252-7500 252-7600
NASDAQ: GENZ ■ *TF:* 800-326-7002 ■ *Web:* www.genzyme.com
Genzyme Genetics 3400 Computer Dr Westborough MA 01581 508-898-9001 389-5548
TF: 800-326-7002 ■ *Web:* www.genzymegenetics.com
Identigene Inc 5615 Kirby Dr Suite 800 Houston TX 77005 713-798-9510 798-9515
TF: 800-362-8973 ■ *Web:* www.identigene.com
Identity Genetics Inc 801 32nd Ave Brookings SD 57006 605-697-5300 697-5306
TF: 800-861-1054 ■ *Web:* www.identitygenetics.com
LabCorp (Laboratory Corp of America Holdings)
1447 York Ct Burlington NC 27215 336-584-5171 436-0609
NYSE: LH ■ *TF Cust Svc:* 800-334-5161 ■ *Web:* www.labcorp.com
Laboratories at Bonfils 717 Yosemite St 2nd Fl Denver CO 80230 303-365-9000 343-6666
TF: 800-321-6088 ■ *Web:* www.labsatbonfils.com
Laboratory Corp of America Holdings (LabCorp)
1447 York Ct Burlington NC 27215 336-584-5171 436-0609
NYSE: LH ■ *TF Cust Svc:* 800-334-5161 ■ *Web:* www.labcorp.com
Maxxam Analytics Inc 335 Laird Rd Unit 2 Guelph ON N1H6J3 519-836-2400 836-4218
TF: 877-706-7678 ■ *Web:* www.thednalab.com
Medical Genetics Consultants 910 Washington Ave Ocean Springs MS 39564 228-872-3680 872-1893
TF: 800-362-4363 ■ *Web:* www.legalgenetics.com
Memorial Blood Centers of Minnesota 737 Pelham Blvd Saint Paul MN 55114 651-332-7000 332-7001
Web: www.memorialbloodcenters.org
Molecular Pathology Laboratory Network Inc 250 E Broadway Maryville TN 37804 865-380-9746 380-9191
TF: 800-932-2943 ■ *Web:* www.molpath.net
NMS Labs 3701 Welsh Rd Willow Grove PA 19090 215-657-4900 657-2972
TF: 800-522-6671 ■ *Web:* www.nmslab.com
Orchid Cellmark Forensic DNA Testing
13988 Diplomat Dr Suite 100 Farmers Branch TX 75234 214-271-8400 271-8322
TF: 800-752-2774 ■ *Web:* www.orchid.com
Orchid Cellmark Inc 4390 US Rt 1 Princeton NJ 08540 609-750-2200 750-6400
NASDAQ: ORCH ■ *TF:* 888-398-9352 ■ *Web:* www.orchid.com
Paternity Testing Corp 300 Portland St Columbia MO 65201 573-442-9948 442-9870
TF: 888-837-8323 ■ *Web:* www.ptclabs.com
Pediatrix Screening 90 Emerson Ln Suite 1403 PO Box 219 Bridgeville PA 15017 412-220-2300 220-0784
TF: 866-463-6436 ■ *Web:* www.pediatrixscreening.com
RELIAGENE Technologies Inc 5525 Mounes St Suite 101 New Orleans LA 70123 504-734-9700 734-9787
TF: 800-256-4106 ■ *Web:* www.reliagene.com
Rhode Island Blood Center 405 Promenade St Providence RI 02908 401-453-8360 453-8557
TF: 800-283-8385 ■ *Web:* www.ribc.org
Saint Francis Medical Center Pathology Dept 2230 Liliha St Honolulu HI 96817 808-547-6536 547-6149
Scales Biological Laboratory Inc 220 Woodgate Dr S Brandon MS 39042 601-825-3211 825-1411
South Texas Blood & Tissue Center 6211 IH-10 W San Antonio TX 78201 210-731-5555 731-5501
TF: 800-292-5534 ■ *Web:* www.bloodntissue.org
State University of New York Upstate Medical University Tissue Typing Laboratory 750 E Adams St Syracuse NY 13210 315-464-4775 464-9557
University of North Texas DNA Identity Laboratory
3500 Camp Bowie Blvd Health Science Center Fort Worth TX 76107 817-735-5015 735-5016
TF: 800-687-5301 ■ *Web:* www.dnaidentitylab.com

421 LABORATORIES - MEDICAL

SEE ALSO Blood Centers p. 1384; Laboratories - Dental p. 1883; Laboratories - Drug-Testing p. 1883; Laboratories - Genetic Testing p. 1883; Organ & Tissue Banks p. 2041

Phone Fax

Bio-Reference Laboratories Inc 481 Edward H Ross Dr Elmwood Park NJ 07407 201-791-2600 791-1941
NASDAQ: BRLI ■ *TF:* 800-229-5227 ■ *Web:* www.bioreference.com
Calvert Laboratories Inc
100 Discovery Dr Scott Technology Park Olyphant PA 18447 570-586-2411 586-3450
TF: 800-300-8114 ■ *Web:* www.calvertlabs.com
Canadian Medical Laboratories Ltd 6560 Kennedy Rd Mississauga ON L5T2X4 905-565-0043 565-6704
TF: 800-263-0801 ■ *Web:* www.canmedlab.com
DIANON Systems Inc 200 Watson Blvd Stratford CT 06615 203-381-4000 380-4145
TF: 800-328-2666 ■ *Web:* www.dianon.com
Genova Diagnostics 63 Zillicoa St Asheville NC 28801 828-253-0621 252-9303*
**Fax:* Cust Svc ■ *TF:* 800-522-4762 ■ *Web:* www.gdx.net
LabCorp (Laboratory Corp of America Holdings)
1447 York Ct Burlington NC 27215 336-584-5171 436-0609
NYSE: LH ■ *TF Cust Svc:* 800-334-5161 ■ *Web:* www.labcorp.com
LabOne Inc 10101 Renner Blvd Lenexa KS 66219 913-888-1770 888-6374*
**Fax:* Sales ■ *TF:* 800-646-7788 ■ *Web:* www.labone.com

Phone Fax

Laboratory Corp of America Holdings (LabCorp)
1447 York Ct .... Burlington NC 27215 336-584-5171 436-0609
NYSE: LH ■ *TF Cust Svc:* 800-334-5161 ■ *Web:* www.labcorp.com
MDS Inc 2700 Matheson Blvd E Suite 300 W Tower .... Mississauga ON L4W4V9 416-675-6777 675-0688
NYSE: MDZ ■ *TF:* 877-675-6777 ■ *Web:* www.mdsintl.com
MDS Pharma Services Inc 2350 Cohen St .... Saint-Laurent QC H4R2N6 514-333-0033 333-8861
TF: 800-724-5941 ■ *Web:* www.mdsps.com
MEDTOX Scientific Inc 402 W County Rd D .... Saint Paul MN 55112 651-636-7466 636-5351
NASDAQ: MTOX ■ *TF:* 800-832-3244 ■ *Web:* www.medtox.com
Midwest Clinical Laboratories 11020 W Plank Ct Suite 100 .... Wauwatosa WI 53226 414-476-3400 256-5566
TF: 800-256-1522 ■ *Web:* www.midwestclinicallabs.com
Molecular Pathology Laboratory Network Inc 250 E Broadway .... Maryville TN 37804 865-380-9746 380-9191
TF: 800-932-2943 ■ *Web:* www.molpath.net
NMS Labs 3701 Welsh Rd .... Willow Grove PA 19090 215-657-4900 657-2972
TF: 800-522-6671 ■ *Web:* www.nmslab.com
Pathology Center 8303 Dodge St .... Omaha NE 68114 402-354-4540 354-4535
TF: 888-432-8980
Quest Diagnostics Inc 1290 Wall St W .... Lyndhurst NJ 07071 201-729-8980 729-8920*
NYSE: DGX ■ **Fax:* Cust Svc ■ *TF:* 800-631-1390 ■ *Web:* www.questdiagnostics.com
Quest Diagnostics at Nichols Institute
33608 Ortega Hwy .... San Juan Capistrano CA 92675 949-728-4000 728-4985*
**Fax:* Hum Res ■ *TF:* 800-642-4657
SED Medical Laboratories 5601 Office Blvd .... Albuquerque NM 87109 505-727-6300 727-6244
TF: 800-999-5227 ■ *Web:* www.sedlabs.com
South Bend Medical Foundation 530 N Lafayette Blvd .... South Bend IN 46601 574-234-4176 288-2262
TF: 800-950-7263 ■ *Web:* www.sbmflab.org
Specialty Laboratories Inc 27027 Tourney Rd .... Valencia CA 91355 661-799-6543 799-6634
TF Sales: 800-421-7110 ■ *Web:* www.specialtylabs.com
VCA Antech Inc 12401 W Olympic Blvd .... Los Angeles CA 90064 310-571-6500 571-6700
NASDAQ: WOOF ■ *TF:* 800-966-1822 ■ *Web:* www.vcaantech.com

422 LABORATORY ANALYTICAL INSTRUMENTS

SEE ALSO Glassware - Laboratory & Scientific p. 1691; Laboratory Apparatus & Furniture p. 1885

Phone Fax

Abaxis Inc 3240 Whipple Rd .... Union City CA 94587 510-675-6500 441-6150
NASDAQ: ABAX ■ *TF:* 800-822-2947 ■ *Web:* www.abaxis.com
Advanced Measurement Technology 801 S Illinois Ave .... Oak Ridge TN 37831 865-482-4411 483-0396
TF: 800-251-9750 ■ *Web:* www.ametek-online.com
Agilent Technologies Inc 5301 Stevens Creek Blvd .... Santa Clara CA 95051 877-424-4536 345-8474*
NYSE: A ■ **Fax Area Code:* 408 ■ *TF:* 877-424-4536 ■ *Web:* www.agilent.com
Airpax Corp 550 Highland St .... Frederick MD 21701 301-663-5141 698-0624
Web: www.airpax.net
Alltech Assoc Inc 2051 Waukegan Rd .... Deerfield IL 60015 847-948-8600 948-1078
TF Cust Svc: 800-255-8324 ■ *Web:* www.alltechweb.com
American Biologics 1180 Walnut Ave .... Chula Vista CA 91911 619-429-8200 429-8004
TF: 800-227-4473 ■ *Web:* americanbiologics.com
Applied Biosystems Group 850 Lincoln Ctr Dr .... Foster City CA 94404 650-570-6667 572-2743
NYSE: ABI ■ *TF:* 800-874-9868 ■ *Web:* www.appliedbiosystems.com
Arcturus Engineering Inc 400 Logue Ave .... Mountain View CA 94043 650-962-3020 962-3039
TF: 888-446-7911 ■ *Web:* www.arctur.com
Barnstead/Thermolyne Corp 2555 Kerper Blvd .... Dubuque IA 52001 563-556-2241 589-0516
TF: 800-446-6060 ■ *Web:* www.barnsteadthermolyne.com
BBI Source Scientific Inc 2144 Michelson Dr .... Irvine CA 92612 949-231-1706 231-5028
TF: 800-888-9285 ■ *Web:* www.bbii.com
BD Biosciences 2350 Qume Dr .... San Jose CA 95131 408-432-9475 954-2347
TF: 800-223-8226 ■ *Web:* www.bdbiosciences.com
Beckman Coulter Inc 4300 N Harbor Blvd .... Fullerton CA 92835 714-871-4848 773-8283
NYSE: BEC ■ *TF Cust Svc:* 800-742-2345 ■ *Web:* www.beckmancoulter.com
Bio-Rad Laboratories 1000 Alfred Nobel Dr .... Hercules CA 94547 510-724-7000 741-5824*
AMEX: BIO ■ **Fax:* Cust Svc ■ *Web:* www.biorad.com
Bioanalytical Systems Inc 2701 Kent Ave .... West Lafayette IN 47906 765-463-4527 497-1102
NASDAQ: BASI ■ *TF:* 800-845-4246 ■ *Web:* www.bioanalytical.com
Brinkmann Instruments Inc 1 Cantiague Rd PO Box 1019 .... Westbury NY 11590 516-334-7500 334-7506
TF: 800-645-3050 ■ *Web:* www.brinkmann.com
Bruker BioSciences Corp 40 Manning Rd .... Billerica MA 01821 978-663-3660 667-5993
NASDAQ: BRKR ■ *Web:* www.bdal.de
Buehler Ltd 41 Waukegan Rd .... Lake Bluff IL 60044 847-295-6500 295-7979
TF Sales: 800-283-4537 ■ *Web:* www.buehlerltd.com
Caliper Life Sciences Inc 68 Elm St .... Hopkinton MA 01748 508-435-9500 435-3439
NASDAQ: CALP ■ *Web:* www.caliperls.com
CDS Analytical Inc 465 Limestone Rd .... Oxford PA 19363 610-932-3636 932-4158
Web: www.cdsanalytical.com
Cellomics Inc 100 Technology Dr .... Pittsburgh PA 15219 412-770-2200 770-2201
Web: www.cellomics.com
CEM Corp PO Box 200 .... Matthews NC 28106 704-821-7015 821-7894
TF: 800-726-3331 ■ *Web:* www.cem.com
Cepheid 904 E Caribbean Dr .... Sunnyvale CA 94089 408-541-4191 541-4192
NASDAQ: CPHD ■ *TF:* 888-838-3222 ■ *Web:* www.cepheid.com
Cetac Technologies Inc 14306 Industrial Rd .... Omaha NE 68144 402-733-2829 733-5292
TF: 800-369-2822 ■ *Web:* www.cetac.com
CMI Inc 316 E 9th St .... Owensboro KY 42303 270-685-6545 685-6678
TF: 866-835-0690 ■ *Web:* www.alcoholtest.com
CompuMed Inc 5777 W Century Blvd Suite 1285 .... Los Angeles CA 90045 310-258-5000 645-5880
TF: 800-421-3395 ■ *Web:* www.compumed.net
Corning Inc Life Sciences Div 45 Nagog Park .... Acton MA 01720 978-635-2200 635-2476
TF: 800-492-1110 ■ *Web:* www.corning.com/lifesciences
Datacolor 5 Princess Rd .... Lawrenceville NJ 08648 609-924-2189 895-7472
TF: 800-433-1885 ■ *Web:* www.datacolor.com
Daxor Corp 350 5th Ave Suite 7120 .... New York NY 10118 212-244-0555 244-0806
AMEX: DXR ■ *Web:* www.daxor.com
DiaSys Corp 21 W Main St 4th Fl .... Waterbury CT 06702 203-755-5083 755-5105
AMEX: DYX ■ *TF:* 800-360-2003 ■ *Web:* www.diasys.com
Dionex Corp 1228 Titan Way .... Sunnyvale CA 94085 408-737-0700 736-4476
NASDAQ: DNEX ■ *TF Cust Svc:* 800-346-6390 ■ *Web:* www.dionex.com
EDAX Inc 91 McKee Dr .... Mahwah NJ 07430 201-529-4880 529-3156
Web: www.edax.com
FEI Co 5350 NE Dawson Creek Dr .... Hillsboro OR 97124 503-640-7500 640-7509
NASDAQ: FEIC ■ *TF:* 888-466-6455 ■ *Web:* www.feicompany.com
Fryer Co Inc 11177 Dundee Rd .... Huntley IL 60142 847-669-2000 669-2056
Web: www.fryerco.com
Gambro BCT 10811 W Collins Ave .... Lakewood CO 80215 303-232-6800 231-4032
TF: 877-339-4228 ■ *Web:* www.gambrobct.com
Gatan Inc 5933 Coronado Ln .... Pleasanton CA 94588 925-463-0200 463-0204
Web: www.gatan.com

Phone Fax

GE Healthcare Bone Densitometry 726 Heartland Trail .... Madison WI 53717 608-828-2663 826-7108
Web: www.gehealthcare.com/rad/bonedens
Genomic Solutions Inc 4355 Varsity Dr Suite E .... Ann Arbor MI 48108 734-975-4800 975-4808
TF: 877-436-6642 ■ *Web:* www.genomicsolutions.com
Gretag Macbeth LLC 617 Little Britain Rd .... New Windsor NY 12553 845-565-7660 565-0390
TF: 800-622-2384 ■ *Web:* www.gretagmacbeth.com
Hach Co PO Box 389 .... Loveland CO 80539 970-669-3050 669-2932
TF: 800-227-4224 ■ *Web:* www.hach.com
Harvard Bioscience Inc 84 October Hill Rd .... Holliston MA 01746 508-893-8999 429-5732
NASDAQ: HBIO ■ *TF:* 800-272-2775 ■ *Web:* www.harvardbioscience.com
Helena Laboratories Inc 1530 Lindbergh Dr .... Beaumont TX 77704 409-842-3714 842-3094
TF: 800-231-5663 ■ *Web:* www.helena.com
Hitachi High Technologies America Inc
10 N Martingale Rd Suite 500 .... Schaumburg IL 60173 847-273-4141 273-4407
Web: www.hii-hitachi.com
Horiba Instruments Inc 17671 Armstrong Ave .... Irvine CA 92614 949-250-4811 250-0924
TF: 800-446-7422 ■ *Web:* www.horiba.com
i-STAT Corp 104 Windsor Center Dr .... East Windsor NJ 08520 609-443-9300 443-9310
TF: 800-827-7828 ■ *Web:* www.i-stat.com
Illumina Inc 9885 Towne Centre Dr .... San Diego CA 92121 858-202-4500 202-4545
NASDAQ: ILMN ■ *TF:* 800-809-4566 ■ *Web:* www.illumina.com
Infolab Inc PO Box 1309 .... Clarksdale MS 38614 662-627-2283 627-1913
TF: 800-647-8222 ■ *Web:* www.infolabinc.com
Instrumentation Laboratory Inc 101 Hartwell Ave .... Lexington MA 02421 781-861-0710 861-1908
TF Sales: 800-955-9525 ■ *Web:* www.ilww.com
IRIS International Inc 9172 Eton Ave .... Chatsworth CA 91311 818-709-1244 700-9661
NASDAQ: IRIS ■ *TF:* 800-776-4747 ■ *Web:* www.proiris.com
Isco Inc 4700 Superior St PO Box 82531 .... Lincoln NE 68501 402-464-0231 465-3022*
**Fax:* Cust Svc ■ *TF:* 800-228-4250 ■ *Web:* www.isco.com
JEOL USA Inc 11 Dearborn Rd .... Peabody MA 01960 978-535-5900 536-2205
Web: www.jeol.com
LaMotte Co 802 Washington Ave .... Chestertown MD 21620 410-778-3100 778-6394
TF: 800-344-3100 ■ *Web:* www.lamotte.com
Leco Corp 3000 Lakeview Ave .... Saint Joseph MI 49085 269-985-5496 982-8977*
**Fax:* Sales ■ *TF:* 800-292-6141 ■ *Web:* www.leco.com
Luminex Corp 12212 Technology Blvd .... Austin TX 78727 512-219-8020 219-5195
NASDAQ: LMNX ■ *TF:* 888-219-8020 ■ *Web:* www.luminexcorp.com
Mandel Scientific Co Inc 2 Admiral Pl .... Guelph ON N1G4N4 519-763-2145 763-2005
TF: 888-883-3636 ■ *Web:* www.mandel.ca
Micromeritics Instrument Corp 1 Micromeritics Dr .... Norcross GA 30093 770-662-3620 662-3696
Web: www.micromeritics.com
Molecular Devices Corp 1311 Orleans Dr Suite 408 .... Sunnyvale CA 94089 408-747-1700 747-3601
NASDAQ: MDCC ■ *TF:* 800-635-5577 ■ *Web:* www.moleculardevices.com
Monogram Biosciences Inc 345 Oyster Point Blvd .... South San Francisco CA 94080 650-635-1100 624-4490
NASDAQ: MGRM ■ *TF:* 800-257-7121 ■ *Web:* www.monogrambio.com
MPD Inc 316 E 9th St .... Owensboro KY 42303 270-685-6200 685-6494
TF: 866-225-5673 ■ *Web:* www.mpdinc.com
Noran Instruments Inc 5225 Verona Rd .... Madison WI 53711 608-276-6100 273-5045
Nova Biomedical Corp 200 Prospect St Suite 3 .... Waltham MA 02454 781-894-0800 894-5915
TF: 800-458-5813 ■ *Web:* www.novabiomedical.com
OI Analytical 151 Graham Rd PO box 9010 .... College Station TX 77842 979-690-1711 690-0440
NASDAQ: OICO ■ *TF:* 800-653-1711 ■ *Web:* www.oico.com
OI Corp DBA OI Analytical 151 Graham Rd PO box 9010 .... College Station TX 77842 979-690-1711 690-0440
NASDAQ: OICO ■ *TF:* 800-653-1711 ■ *Web:* www.oico.com
Olis Inc 130 Conway Dr Suites A & B .... Bogart GA 30622 706-353-6547 353-1972
TF: 800-852-3504 ■ *Web:* www.olisweb.com
Olympus America Inc 2 Corporate Center Dr .... Melville NY 11747 631-844-5000 844-5110*
**Fax:* Sales ■ *TF:* 800-446-5967 ■ *Web:* www.olympusamerica.com
ONIX Systems Inc 9303 W Sam Houston Pkwy S .... Houston TX 77099 713-272-0404 272-2273
TF: 877-290-7422
Pall Life Sciences Inc 600 S Wagner Rd .... Ann Arbor MI 48103 734-665-0651 913-6114
TF: 800-521-1520 ■ *Web:* www.pall.com/laboratory
Panalaytical 12 Michigan Dr .... Natick MA 01760 508-647-1100 647-1115
TF: 800-279-7297 ■ *Web:* www.panalytical.com
Particle Measuring Systems Inc 5475 Airport Blvd .... Boulder CO 80301 303-443-7100 449-6870
TF Cust Svc: 800-238-1801 ■ *Web:* www.pmeasuring.com
PerkinElmer Inc 45 William St .... Wellesley MA 02481 781-237-5100 237-9386
NYSE: PKI ■ *Web:* www.perkinelmer.com
PerkinElmer Instruments Inc 710 Bridgeport Ave .... Shelton CT 06484 203-925-4600 925-4654
TF: 800-762-4000 ■ *Web:* las.perkinelmer.com
Pfeiffer Vacuum Inc 24 Trafalgar Sq .... Nashua NH 03063 603-578-6500 578-6550
TF Orders: 800-248-8254 ■ *Web:* www.balzers.com
Physical Electronics Inc 18725 Lake Dr E .... Chanhassen MN 55317 952-828-6100 828-6322
TF: 800-328-7515 ■ *Web:* www.phi.com
Response Biomedical Corp 1781 75th Ave W .... Vancouver BC V6O6T2 604-456-6010 456-6066
TF: 888-591-5577 ■ *Web:* www.responsebio.com
Roche Diagnostics Corp 9115 Hague Rd .... Indianapolis IN 46250 317-521-2000 521-2090
TF Cust Svc: 800-428-5076 ■ *Web:* www.roche-diagnostics.us
Rosetta Inpharmatics LLC 401 Terry Ave .... Seattle WA 98109 206-802-7000 802-6501
Web: www.rii.com
Sentry Equipment Corp 856 E Armour Rd .... Oconomowoc WI 53066 262-567-7256 567-4523
Web: www.sentry-equip.com
Shimadzu Scientific Instruments Inc 7102 Riverwood Dr .... Columbia MD 21046 410-381-1227 381-1222
TF: 800-477-1227 ■ *Web:* www.ssi.shimadzu.com
Smiths Detection 30 Hook Mountain Rd .... Pine Brook NJ 07058 973-830-2100 830-2200
TF: 800-536-2277 ■ *Web:* www.smithsdetection.com
Spectrum Laboratories Inc 18617 Broadwick St .... Rancho Dominguez CA 90220 310-885-4600 885-4666
TF: 866-634-3300 ■ *Web:* www.spectrapor.com
Spectrum Systems Inc 3410 W Nine-Mile Rd .... Pensacola FL 32526 850-944-3392 944-1011
TF: 877-837-6644 ■ *Web:* specsys.com
StatSpin Inc 85 Morse St .... Norwood MA 02062 781-551-0100 551-0036
TF: 800-782-8774 ■ *Web:* www.statspin.com
Stratagene Inc 11011 N Torrey Pines Rd .... La Jolla CA 92037 858-535-5400 535-0071
NASDAQ: STGN ■ *TF:* 800-894-1304 ■ *Web:* www.stratagene.com
Supelco Inc 595 N Harrison Rd .... Bellefonte PA 16823 814-359-3441 325-5052*
**Fax Area Code:* 800 ■ *TF:* 800-247-6628 ■ *Web:* www.sigmaaldrich.com
Teledyne Electronics & Communications
12964 Panama St .... Los Angeles CA 90066 310-822-8229 574-2092
Web: www.tet.com
Temptronic Corp 4 Commercial St .... Sharon MA 02067 781-688-2300 688-2301
TF Cust Svc: 800-558-5080 ■ *Web:* www.temptronic.com
Thermo Fisher Scientific 81 Wyman St PO Box 9046 .... Waltham MA 02454 781-622-1000 622-1207
NYSE: TMO ■ *TF:* 800-678-5599 ■ *Web:* www.thermofisher.com
Transgenomic Inc 12325 Emmet St .... Omaha NE 68164 402-452-5400 452-5401
NASDAQ: TBIO ■ *TF:* 888-233-9283 ■ *Web:* www.transgenomic.com
Varian Inc 3120 Hansen Way .... Palo Alto CA 94304 650-213-8000 213-8200
NASDAQ: VARI ■ *Web:* www.varianinc.com
Waters Corp 34 Maple St .... Milford MA 01757 508-478-2000 872-1990
NYSE: WAT ■ *TF:* 800-252-4752 ■ *Web:* www.waters.com
Westover Scientific Inc 18421 Bothell-Everett Hwy Suite 110 .... Bothell WA 98012 425-398-1298 398-0717
TF: 800-304-3202 ■ *Web:* www.westoverfiber.com
Whatman Inc 200 Park Ave Suite 210 .... Florham Park NJ 07932 973-245-8300 245-8301
TF: 800-942-8626 ■ *Web:* www.whatman.com

423 LABORATORY APPARATUS & FURNITURE

SEE ALSO Glassware - Laboratory & Scientific p. 1691; Laboratory Analytical Instruments p. 1884; Scales & Balances p. 2304

Company	City	State	ZIP	Phone	Fax
ABB Optical Inc 5360 NW 35th Ave	Fort Lauderdale	FL	33309	954-733-2300	735-4386
TF: 800-852-8089 ■ *Web:* www.abboptical.com					
Baker Co Inc 161 Gatehouse Rd PO Drawer E	Sanford	ME	04073	207-324-8773	324-3869
TF: 800-992-2537 ■ *Web:* www.bakerco.com					
Barnstead/Thermolyne Corp 2555 Kerper Blvd.	Dubuque	IA	52001	563-556-2241	589-0516
TF: 800-446-6060 ■ *Web:* www.barnsteadthermolyne.com					
Bel-Art Products Inc 6 Industrial Rd	Pequannock	NJ	07440	973-694-0500	694-7199
TF: 800-423-5278 ■ *Web:* www.bel-art.com					
Boekel Industries Inc 855 Pennsylvania Blvd.	Feasterville	PA	19053	215-396-8200	396-8264
TF: 800-336-6929 ■ *Web:* www.boekelsci.com					
Caliper Life Sciences Inc 68 Elm St	Hopkinton	MA	01748	508-435-9500	435-3439
NASDAQ: CALP ■ *Web:* www.caliperls.com					
Corning Inc Life Sciences Div 45 Nagog Park	Acton	MA	01720	978-635-2200	635-2476
TF: 800-492-1110 ■ *Web:* www.corning.com/lifesciences					
Durcon Co 8464 Ronda Dr	Canton	MI	48187	734-455-4520	455-5506
Web: www.durcon.com					
Edstrom Industries Inc 819 Bakke Ave	Waterford	WI	53185	262-534-5181	534-5184
TF: 800-558-5913 ■ *Web:* www.edstrom.com					
Fisher Hamilton LLC 1316 18th St	Two Rivers	WI	54241	920-793-1121	793-3084
Web: www.fisherhamilton.com					
Fisher Scientific International Inc 1 Liberty Ln	Hampton	NH	03842	603-926-5911	929-2379
NYSE: FSH ■ *Web:* www.fisherscientific.com					
Harlan Industries Inc 298 S Carroll Rd	Indianapolis	IN	46229	317-894-7521	894-1840
TF: 800-793-7287 ■ *Web:* www.harlan.com					
Infolab Inc PO Box 1309	Clarksdale	MS	38614	662-627-2283	627-1913
TF: 800-647-8222 ■ *Web:* www.infolabinc.com					
Kalamazoo Technical Furniture 6450 Valley Industrial Dr.	Kalamazoo	MI	49009	269-372-6000	
TF: 800-832-5227 ■ *Web:* www.teclab.com					
Kewaunee Scientific Corp 2700 W Front St PO Box 1842	Statesville	NC	28687	704-873-7202	873-5160*
NASDAQ: KEQU ■ **Fax:* Sales ■ *Web:* www.kewaunee.com					
Koch Modular Process Systems LLC 45 Eisenhower Dr	Paramus	NJ	07652	201-368-2929	368-8989
Web: www.modular-process.com					
Lab Fabricators Co 1802 E 47th St	Cleveland	OH	44103	216-431-5444	431-5447
TF: 888-431-5444 ■ *Web:* www.labfabricators.com					
Labconco Corp 8811 Prospect Ave	Kansas City	MO	64132	816-333-8811	363-0130
TF Cust Svc: 800-821-5525 ■ *Web:* www.labconco.com					
Lunaire Ltd 2821 Old Rt 15	New Columbia	PA	17856	570-538-7200	538-7383
Web: www.lunaire.com					
Millipore Corp 290 Concord Rd	Billerica	MA	01821	978-715-4321	645-5439*
NYSE: MIL ■ **Fax Area Code:* 800 ■ *TF:* 800-645-5476 ■ *Web:* www.millipore.com					
Nalge Nunc International 75 Panorama Creek Dr	Rochester	NY	14625	585-586-8800	899-7045
TF: 800-625-4327 ■ *Web:* www.nalgenunc.com					
New Brunswick Scientific Co Inc 44 Talmadge Rd	Edison	NJ	08818	732-287-1200	287-4222
NASDAQ: NBSC ■ *TF Cust Svc:* 800-631-5417 ■ *Web:* www.nbsc.com					
Omnicell Inc 1201 Charleston Rd	Mountain View	CA	94043	650-251-6100	251-6266
NASDAQ: OMCL ■ *TF:* 800-850-6664 ■ *Web:* www.omnicell.com					
Pacific Combustion Engineering Co 2107 Border Ave.	Torrance	CA	90501	310-212-6300	212-5333
TF: 800-342-4442 ■ *Web:* www.pacificcombustion.com					
Parr Instrument Co 211 53rd St	Moline	IL	61265	309-762-7716	762-9453
TF: 800-872-7720 ■ *Web:* www.parrinst.com					
Pfeiffer Vacuum Inc 24 Trafalgar Sq	Nashua	NH	03063	603-578-6500	578-6550
TF Orders: 800-248-8254 ■ *Web:* www.balzers.com					
Samco Scientific Corp 1050 Arroyo Ave	San Fernando	CA	91340	818-838-2400	838-2488
TF: 800-522-3359 ■ *Web:* www.samcosci.com					
Sargent-Welch 60 Pearce Ave	Tonawanda	NY	15150	716-874-4093	676-2540*
**Fax Area Code:* 800 ■ *TF:* 800-727-4368 ■ *Web:* www.sargentwelch.com					
Thermo Fisher Scientific 81 Wyman St PO Box 9046	Waltham	MA	02454	781-622-1000	622-1207
NYSE: TMO ■ *TF:* 800-678-5599 ■ *Web:* www.thermofisher.com					
ThermoGenesis Corp 2711 Citrus Rd	Rancho Cordova	CA	95742	916-858-5100	858-5199
NASDAQ: KOOL ■ *TF:* 800-783-8357 ■ *Web:* www.thermogenesis.com					
Thomas Scientific 1654 Highville Rd	Swedesboro	NJ	08085	856-467-2000	467-3087
TF: 800-345-2100 ■ *Web:* www.thomassci.com					
Valley City Mfg Co Ltd 64 Hatt St	Dundas	ON	L9H2G3	905-628-2255	628-4470
TF: 800-828-7628 ■ *Web:* www.valleycity.com					
Westfalia Separator Inc 100 Fairway Ct	Northvale	NJ	07647	201-767-3900	767-3416
TF: 800-722-6622 ■ *Web:* www.wsus.com					

424 LADDERS

Company	City	State	ZIP	Phone	Fax
ALACO Ladder Co 5167 G St	Chino	CA	91710	909-591-7561	591-7565
TF: 888-310-7040 ■ *Web:* www.alacoladder.com					
Ballymore Co 220 Garfield Ave	West Chester	PA	19380	610-696-3250	696-1217
TF: 800-762-8327 ■ *Web:* www.ballymore.com					
Cotterman Co PO Box 168	Croswell	MI	48422	810-679-4400	679-4510
TF: 800-552-3337 ■ *Web:* www.cotterman.com					
Duo-Safety Ladder Corp PO Box 497	Oshkosh	WI	54903	920-231-2740	231-2460
Web: www.duosafety.com					
Green Bull Inc 11225 Bluegrass Pkwy	Louisville	KY	40299	502-267-5577	267-6611
TF: 800-558-2855 ■ *Web:* www.greenbullladder.com					
Louisville Ladder Corp 7719 National Tpke Bldg A	Louisville	KY	40214	502-636-2811	636-1014
TF: 800-666-2811 ■ *Web:* www.louisvilleladder.com					
Lynn Ladder & Scaffolding Co Inc PO Box 346	Lynn	MA	01905	781-598-6010	593-7666
TF: 800-596-6717 ■ *Web:* www.lynnladder.com					
Putnam Rolling Ladder Inc 32 Howard St	New York	NY	10013	212-226-5147	941-1836
Web: www.putnamrollingladder.com					
Werner Co 93 Werner Rd	Greenville	PA	16125	724-588-2550	588-0315
Web: www.wernerco.com					
Wing Enterprises Inc PO Box 3100	Springville	UT	84663	801-489-3684	489-3685
TF: 800-453-1192 ■ *Web:* www.ladders.com					

425 LANDSCAPE DESIGN & RELATED SERVICES

Company	City	State	ZIP	Phone	Fax
AAA Landscape 3747 E Southern Ave.	Phoenix	AZ	85040	602-437-2690	437-2970
Web: www.aaalandscape.com					
Acres Group 170 N Garden Ave	Roselle	IL	60172	630-307-0700	307-0801
TF: 888-231-1300 ■ *Web:* www.acresgroup.com					
Annco Services Inc 8892 152nd Pl S	Delray Beach	FL	33446	561-638-2540	638-3993
Web: www.anncoservices.com					
Artistic Maintenance Inc 23676 Birtcher Dr	Lake Forest	CA	92630	949-581-9817	581-0436
TF: 800-698-9834 ■ *Web:* www.artisticmaintenance.com					
Brickman Group Ltd 375 S Flowers Mill Rd	Langhorne	PA	19047	215-757-9400	891-1259
TF: 800-451-7272 ■ *Web:* www.brickmangroup.com					
Cagwin & Dorward Inc 1565 S Novato Blvd Suite B	Novato	CA	94947	415-892-7710	892-7864
TF: 800-891-7710 ■ *Web:* www.cagwin.com					
Chapel Valley Landscape Co 3275 Jennings Chapel Rd PO Box 159	Woodbine	MD	21797	301-924-5400	854-6390
Web: chapelvalley.com					
Creative Environments Inc 2128 E Cedar St	Tempe	AZ	85281	480-777-9305	777-9296
Web: www.creativeenvironments.com					
D Schumacher Landscaping Inc 635 Manley St.	West Bridgewater	MA	02379	508-427-7707	427-7714
Web: www.dschumacher.com					
Davids Clarence & Co 22901 S Ridgeland Ave	Matteson	IL	60443	708-720-4100	720-4200
Web: www.clarencedavids.com					
EDAW Inc 150 Chestnut St	San Francisco	CA	94111	415-433-1484	788-4875
Web: www.edaw.com					
Environmental Earthscapes Inc DBA Groundskeeper The 5075 S Swan Rd	Tucson	AZ	85706	520-571-1575	750-7480
TF: 800-571-1575 ■ *Web:* www.groundskeeper.com					
Golden Bear International Inc 11780 US Hwy 1	North Palm Beach	FL	33408	561-626-3900	227-0302
Web: www.nicklaus.com					
Greeen View 2700 W Cedar Hills Dr.	Dunlap	IL	61525	309-243-7761	243-9353
Web: www.greenview.net					
Jensen Corp 10950 N Blaney Ave	Cupertino	CA	95014	408-446-1118	446-4881
Web: www.jensencorp.com					
Landscape Concepts Inc 31745 N Alleghany Rd	Grayslake	IL	60030	847-223-3800	223-0169
TF: 866-655-3800 ■ *Web:* www.landscapeconcepts.com					
Landscape Development Inc 28447 Witherspoon Pkwy.	Valencia	CA	91355	661-295-1970	295-1969
Web: www.landscapedevelopment.com					
Lied's Landscape Design & Construction N63 W22039 Hwy 74	Sussex	WI	53089	262-246-6901	246-3569
Web: www.lieds.com/design					
Lipinski Landscape & Irrigation Contractors Inc 100 Sharp Rd.	Marlton	NJ	08053	856-797-8000	983-0500
Web: www.lipinskiland.com					
LMI Landscapes Inc 1437 Halsey Way	Carrollton	TX	75007	972-446-0020	446-0028
Web: www.lmilandscapes.com					
Mariani Enterprises Inc 300 Rockland Rd	Lake Bluff	IL	60044	847-234-2172	234-2754
Web: www.marianilandscape.com					
Mariposa Horticultural Enterprises Inc 15529 Arrow Hwy	Irwindale	CA	91706	626-960-0196	960-8477
TF: 800-794-9458 ■ *Web:* www.mariposahorticultural.com					
McFall & Berry Landscape Management Co Inc PO Box 9185	McLean	VA	22102	703-255-9800	255-9080
Web: www.mcfallandberry.com					
Metroplex Garden Design Landscaping LP 2607 Walnut Hill Ln Suite 210	Dallas	TX	75229	214-366-2021	350-4203
Web: www.gardendesignlandscaping.com					
Mission Landscape Services Inc 536 Dyer Rd	Santa Ana	CA	92707	714-545-9962	668-0119
TF: 800-545-9963 ■ *Web:* www.missionlandscape.com					
Nicklaus Design 11780 US Hwy 1 Suite 500	North Palm Beach	FL	33408	561-626-3900	227-0302
Web: nicklaus.com/design					
Park West Cos Inc 22421 Gilberto Suite A	Rancho Santa Margarita	CA	92688	949-858-7006	858-7169
Web: www.parkwestlandscape.com					
Peoria Landscaping Co Inc DBA Greeen View 2700 W Cedar Hills Dr.	Dunlap	IL	61525	309-243-7761	243-9353
Web: www.greenview.net					
Schrickel Rollins & Assoc Inc 1161 Corporate Dr W Suite 200	Arlington	TX	76006	817-640-8212	649-7645
Web: www.sradesign.com					
Spectrum Care Landscape 27181 Burbank	Foothill Ranch	CA	92610	949-454-6900	454-6910
Web: www.spectrumcarelandscape.com					
Stiles Landscape Co 1080 SW 12 Ave	Pompano Beach	FL	33069	954-781-0247	
TF: 866-250-4074 ■ *Web:* www.stiles.com/landscape_about_us.htm					
Summit Landscape Services Inc 12452 Cutten Rd	Houston	TX	77066	281-583-7900	583-7994
Web: www.summitls.com					
Sun City Landscapes 4270 W Patrick Ln	Las Vegas	NV	89118	702-260-6309	260-6310
Web: www.suncityls.com					
Sungrow Landscape Services Inc 2007 Rutland Dr.	Austin	TX	78758	512-834-0123	834-0432
Web: www.sungrow.com					
SWA Group 2200 Bridgeway Blvd	Sausalito	CA	94965	415-332-5100	332-0719
Web: www.swagroup.com					
Synnestvedt & Assoc 24550 W Hwy 120	Round Lake	IL	60073	847-546-4700	
Web: www.synnestvedt.com					
Terrain Systems Inc 2960 E Elwood St	Phoenix	AZ	85040	602-304-0304	304-0321
Web: www.terrainlandscape.com					
Teufel Nursery Inc 12345 NW Barnes Rd.	Portland	OR	97229	503-646-1111	646-1112
TF: 800-483-8335 ■ *Web:* www.teufel.com					
TruGreen LandCare 860 Ridge Lake Blvd	Memphis	TN	38120	901-681-1800	681-1906
TF: 800-242-0442 ■ *Web:* www.trugreen.com					
Turf Management Systems Inc 2399 Royal Windsor	Mississauga	ON	L5J1K9	905-823-8550	823-4594
Web: www.weed-man.com					
Underwood Brothers DBA AAA Landscape 3747 E Southern Ave	Phoenix	AZ	85040	602-437-2690	437-2970
Web: www.aaalandscape.com					
US Lawns 4407 Vineland Rd Suite D-15	Orlando	FL	32811	800-875-2967	246-1623*
**Fax Area Code:* 407 ■ *Web:* www.uslawns.com					
ValleyCrest Cos 24151 Ventura Blvd	Calabasas	CA	91302	818-223-8500	223-8142
Web: www.valleycrest.com					
Vila & Son Landscaping Corp 20451 SW 216th St	Miami	FL	33170	305-255-9206	255-9207
Web: www.vila-n-son.com					

426 LANGUAGE SCHOOLS

SEE ALSO Translation Services p. 2378

Company	City	State	ZIP	Phone	Fax
Access International Business Institute 609 E Liberty St.	Ann Arbor	MI	48104	734-994-1456	994-7341
Web: www.accessesl.org					
AF International English School PO Box 6223	Westlake Village	CA	91362	805-496-6694	496-9622
Web: www.afint.com					
Agape English Language Institute 610 Pickens St	Columbia	SC	29201	803-799-7716	252-5500
TF: 877-476-2354 ■ *Web:* www.aeliusa.com					
American Academy of English 530 Golden Gate Ave.	San Francisco	CA	94102	415-567-0189	567-1475
Web: www.aae.edu					
American Language Communication Center 15 Penn Plaza	New York	NY	10001	212-736-2373	947-6403
Web: www.learnenglish.com					
AmeriSpan Unlimited PO Box 58129	Philadelphia	PA	19102	215-751-1100	751-1986
TF: 800-879-6640 ■ *Web:* www.amerispan.com					
Babel Fish 170 Laurier Ave W Suite 1000	Ottawa	ON	K1P5V5	613-233-8075	233-8589
Web: www.babelfish.com					
Berkeley English Academy 2161 Shattuck Ave Suite 313	Berkeley	CA	94704	510-549-9054	549-3357
Web: www.berkeleyenglishacademy.com					
Berlitz International Inc 400 Alexander Pk	Princeton	NJ	08540	609-514-9650	514-9648
TF: 800-257-9449 ■ *Web:* www.berlitz.com					
Boston Academy of English 59 Temple Pl 2nd Fl	Boston	MA	02111	617-338-6243	695-9349
Web: www.bostonacademyofenglish.com					

	City	State	Zip	Phone	Fax
Boston School of English 814 South St *Web:* www.bsml.com	Boston	MA	02131	617-325-2760	325-2763
Bouchereau Lingua International Inc 407 Saint-Laurent Blvd Suite 410 *Web:* www.bli.ca	Montreal	QC	H2Y2Y5	514-842-3847	842-3840
Brandon College 25 Kearny St 2nd Fl *Web:* www.brandoncollege.com	San Francisco	CA	94108	415-391-5711	391-3918
Centre Linguista 500 Rene-Levesque Blvd W Suite 802 *Web:* www.centrelinguista.com	Montreal	QC	H2Z1W7	514-397-1736	397-9007
Colorado School of English 331 14th St Suite 300 *Web:* www.englishamerica.com	Denver	CO	80202	720-932-8900	932-0315
Converse International School of Languages 636 Broadway Suite 210 *Web:* www.cisl.org	San Diego	CA	92101	619-239-3363	239-3778
Cultural Center for Language Studies 3191 Coral Way Suite 114 *TF:* 800-774-2227 ■ *Web:* www.cclscorp.com	Miami	FL	33145	305-529-8563	443-8538
Diplomatic Language Services LLC 1901 N Fort Myer Dr *TF:* 800-642-7974 ■ *Web:* www.dls-llc.com	Arlington	VA	22209	703-243-7884	243-7003
Diversified Language Institute 3525 Lomita Blvd Suite 102 *Web:* www.dliusa.com	Torrance	CA	90505	310-530-4009	530-2819
Educere International College 910 7th Ave SW Suite 1500 *Web:* www.educere.ca	Calgary	AB	T2P3N8	403-232-8551	233-0239
ELS Language Centers 400 Alexander Pk *TF:* 800-468-8978 ■ *Web:* www.els.edu	Princeton	NJ	08540	609-750-3500	750-3599
Embassy CES 330 7th Ave 2nd Fl *Web:* www.studygroup.com/embassyces	New York	NY	10001	212-497-0050	497-0045
English Connection Inc 77 Railroad Pl *Web:* www.englishconnection.com	Saratoga Springs	NY	12866	518-581-1478	581-1479
English for Internationals 575 Colonial Park Dr *Web:* www.eng4intl.com	Roswell	GA	30075	770-587-9640	587-0427
English Language Center 867 Boylston St *Web:* www.elcusa.com	Boston	MA	02116	617-536-9788	536-5789
ESL Instruction & Consulting Inc 42 Broad St NW *TF:* 877-342-4785 ■ *Web:* www.eslinstruction.com	Atlanta	GA	30303	404-577-2366	577-2360
Global Village English Centres 888 Cambie St *Web:* www.gvenglish.com	Vancouver	BC	V6B2P6	604-684-1118	684-1117
HablEspana 59 Temple Pl 2nd Fl *Web:* www.hablespana.com	Boston	MA	02111	617-426-4868	695-9349
Human International Academy 123 Camino de la Reina Suite W-200 *TF:* 866-486-2687 ■ *Web:* www.hiausa.com	San Diego	CA	92108	619-501-8091	501-9027
inlingua International 551 5th Ave 7th Fl *Web:* www.inlingua.com	New York	NY	10176	212-682-8585	599-0977
Intercultural Communications College 1601 Kapiolani Blvd Suite 1000 *Web:* www.icchawaii.edu	Honolulu	HI	96814	808-946-2445	946-2231
International Center for American English 1012 Prospect St Suite 200 *Web:* www.icae-lajolla.com	La Jolla	CA	92037	858-456-1212	456-1217
International Center for Language Studies Inc 1133 15th ST NW Suite 600 *Web:* www.icls.com	Washington	DC	20005	202-639-8800	783-6587
International English Institute 2755 E Shaw Ave Suite 101 *Web:* www.ieifresno.com	Fresno	CA	93710	559-294-1401	292-6231
International House Vancouver 1215 W Broadway Suite 200 *Web:* www.illc.com	Vancouver	BC	V6H1G7	604-739-9836	739-9839
International Language Institute 1137 Connecticut Ave NW 4th Fl *Web:* www.transemantics.com	Washington	DC	20005	202-362-2505	686-5603
International Language Institute 7071 Bayers Rd *Web:* www.ili-halifax.com	Halifax	NS	B3L2C2	902-429-3636	429-2900
Internexus 455 E 400 South Suite 202 *Web:* www.internexus.to	Salt Lake City	UT	84111	801-487-2499	487-2198
Intrax International Institute 600 California St 10th Fl *Web:* intraxinstitute.edu	San Francisco	CA	94108	415-434-1221	434-5404
Lado International College 2233 Wisconsin Ave NW *Web:* www.lado.com	Washington	DC	20007	202-223-0023	337-1118
Language Academy 300 NE 3rd Ave Suite 100 *Web:* www.languageacademy.com	Fort Lauderdale	FL	33301	954-462-8373	462-3738
Language Company 189 W 15th St *Web:* www.thelanguagecompany.com	Edmond	OK	73013	405-715-9996	715-1116
Language Door LLC 11870 Santa Monica Blvd Suite 202 *Web:* www.languagedoor.com	Los Angeles	CA	90025	310-826-4140	
Language Exchange International 500 NE Spanish River Blvd Suite 19 *TF:* 800-223-5836 ■ *Web:* www.languageexchange.com	Boca Raton	FL	33431	561-368-3913	368-9380
Language Pacifica 585 Glenwood Ave *Web:* www.languagepacifica.com	Menlo Park	CA	94025	650-321-1840	321-2510
Language Plus Inc 4110 Rio Bravo Suite 202 *Web:* www.languageplus.com	El Paso	TX	79902	915-544-8600	544-8640
Language Studies Canada 124 Eglinton Ave W Suite 400 *Web:* www.lsc-canada.com	Toronto	ON	M4R2G8	416-488-2200	488-2225
Language Studies International 1706 5th Ave 3rd Fl *Web:* www.lsi.edu	San Diego	CA	92101	619-234-2881	234-2883
Lingua School Inc 4188 S University Dr *Web:* www.linguaschool.com	Davie	FL	33328	954-577-9955	577-9977
Michigan Language Center 309 S State St *Web:* www.englishclasses.com	Ann Arbor	MI	48104	734-663-9415	663-9623
New England School of English 36 JFK St *Web:* www.nese.com	Cambridge	MA	02138	617-864-7170	864-7282
Nomen Global Language Centers 384 W Center St *TF:* 866-211-0689 ■ *Web:* www.nomenglobal.com	Provo	UT	84601	801-377-3223	377-3993
Olin Center 729 Boylston St *Web:* www.olincenter.com	Boston	MA	02116	617-247-3033	247-2959
OSULA Education Center 3921 Laurel Canyon Blvd *Web:* www.osula.com	Studio City	CA	91604	818-509-1484	753-3846
Pacific Language Institute 755 Burrard St Suite 300 *Web:* www.pli.ca	Vancouver	BC	V6Z1X6	604-688-8330	688-0638
POLY Languages Institute Inc 4221 Wilshire Blvd Suite 300-A *Web:* www.polylanguages.com	Los Angeles	CA	90010	323-933-9399	933-9361
Rennert Bilingual 216 E 45th St *Web:* www.rennert.com	New York	NY	10017	212-867-8700	867-7666
Rosemead College of English 8705 E Valley Blvd *Web:* www.rosemeadcollege.com	Rosemead	CA	91770	626-285-9668	285-1351
Saint Giles International San Francisco 785 Market St Suite 300 *Web:* www.stgiles-usa.com	San Francisco	CA	94103	415-788-3552	788-1923
SpringHills International Education Group 330 Bay St Suite 910 *Web:* www.springhillsgroup.com	Toronto	ON	M5H2S8	416-368-5118	361-2403
Tamwood International College 300-909 Burrard St *Web:* www.tamwood.com	Vancouver	BC	V6Z2N2	604-899-4480	899-4481
University Language Institute 2448 E 81st St Suite 1400 *Web:* www.uli.net	Tulsa	OK	74137	918-493-8088	493-8084
Wisconsin English as a Second Language Institute 19 N Pinckney St *Web:* www.wesli.com	Madison	WI	53703	608-257-4300	257-4346
Zoni Language Centers 22 W 34th St 3rd Fl *Web:* www.zoni.com	New York	NY	10001	212-736-9000	947-8030

427 LASER EQUIPMENT & SYSTEMS - MEDICAL

SEE ALSO Medical Instruments & Apparatus - Mfr p. 1953

	City	State	Zip	Phone	Fax
AMO Santa Clara 3400 Central Expy *TF:* 800-998-2020 ■ *Web:* www.visx.com	Santa Clara	CA	95051	408-733-2020	
BioLase Technology Inc 981 Calle Amanecer *NASDAQ: BLTI* ■ *TF:* 800-699-9462 ■ *Web:* www.biolase.com	San Clemente	CA	92673	949-361-1200	361-0204
Candela Corp 530 Boston Post Rd *NASDAQ: CLZR* ■ *TF:* 800-733-8550 ■ *Web:* www.candelalaser.com	Wayland	MA	01778	508-358-7400	358-5602
CardioGenesis Corp 26632 Towne Centre Dr Suite 320 *TF:* 800-238-2205 ■ *Web:* www.cardiogenesis.com	Foothill Ranch	CA	92610	714-649-5000	649-5100
Convergent Laser Technologies 1660 S Loop Rd *TF:* 800-848-8200 ■ *Web:* www.convergentlaser.com	Alameda	CA	94502	510-832-2130	832-1600
Cynosure Inc 5 Carlisle Rd *NASDAQ: CYNO* ■ *TF:* 800-886-2966 ■ *Web:* www.cynosurelaser.com	Westford	MA	01886	978-256-4200	256-6556
Diomed Holdings Inc 1 Dundee Pk *AMEX: DIO* ■ *Web:* www.diomedinc.com	Andover	MA	01810	978-475-7771	475-8488
IntraLase Corp 3 Morgan *NASDAQ: ILSE* ■ *TF:* 877-393-2020 ■ *Web:* www.intralase.com	Irvine	CA	92618	949-859-5230	461-3323
Iridex Corp 1212 Terra Bella Ave *NASDAQ: IRIX* ■ *TF Cust Svc:* 800-388-4747 ■ *Web:* www.iridex.com	Mountain View	CA	94043	650-940-4700	940-4710
Kigre Inc 100 Marshland Rd *Web:* www.kigre.com	Hilton Head Island	SC	29926	843-681-5800	681-4559
Lambda Physik USA Inc PO Box 54980 *TF:* 800-392-4637 ■ *Web:* www.lambdaphysik.com	Santa Clara	CA	95056	408-764-4000	764-4800
Laserscope 3070 Orchard Dr *NASDAQ: LSCP* ■ **Fax:* Sales ■ *TF:* 800-356-7600 ■ *Web:* www.laserscope.com	San Jose	CA	95134	408-943-0636	943-1051*
LaserSight Technologies Inc 6848 Stapoint Ct *TF:* 888-527-3235 ■ *Web:* www.lase.com	Winter Park	FL	32792	407-678-9900	678-9981
Lumenis Ltd 2400 Condensa St *TF:* 800-227-1914 ■ *Web:* www.lumenis.com	Santa Clara	CA	95051	408-764-3000	764-3999
Palomar Medical Technologies Inc 82 Cambridge St *NASDAQ: PMTI* ■ *TF:* 800-725-6627 ■ *Web:* www.palmed.com	Burlington	MA	01803	781-993-2300	993-2330
PhotoMedex Inc 147 Keystone Dr *NASDAQ: PHMD* ■ *TF:* 800-366-4758 ■ *Web:* www.photomedex.com	Montgomeryville	PA	18936	215-619-3600	619-3208
PLC Medical Systems Inc 10 Forge Pk *AMEX: PLC* ■ **Fax:* Sales ■ *TF:* 800-232-8422 ■ *Web:* www.plcmed.com	Franklin	MA	02038	508-541-8800	541-7944*
Spectranetics Corp 96 Talamine Ct *NASDAQ: SPNC* ■ *TF:* 800-633-0960 ■ *Web:* www.spectranetics.com	Colorado Springs	CO	80907	719-633-8333	633-2248
Trimedyne Inc 15091 Bake Pkwy *TF:* 800-733-5273 ■ *Web:* www.trimedyne.com	Irvine	CA	92618	949-559-5300	855-8206

428 LASERS - INDUSTRIAL

	City	State	Zip	Phone	Fax
AGL Corp 2202 Redmond Rd *TF:* 800-643-9696 ■ *Web:* www.agl-lasers.com	Jacksonville	AR	72076	501-982-4433	982-0880
Baublys Control Laser Corp 2419 Lake Orange Dr *Web:* www.controllaser.com	Orlando	FL	32837	407-926-3500	926-3590
Big Sky Laser Technologies Inc 601 Haggerty Ln *TF:* 800-224-4759 ■ *Web:* www.bigskylaser.com	Bozeman	MT	59715	406-586-0131	586-2924
Coherent Inc 5100 Patrick Henry Dr *NASDAQ: COHR* ■ *TF Sales:* 800-527-3786 ■ *Web:* www.cohr.com	Santa Clara	CA	95054	408-764-4000	764-4800
Continuum 3150 Central Expy *TF:* 800-956-7757 ■ *Web:* www.continuumlasers.com	Santa Clara	CA	95051	408-727-3240	727-3550
Cymer Inc 17075 Thornmint Ct *NASDAQ: CYMI* ■ *Web:* www.cymer.com	San Diego	CA	92127	858-385-7300	385-7100
Electro Scientific Industries Inc 13900 NW Science Pk Dr *NASDAQ: ESIO* ■ **Fax:* Claims ■ *TF Cust Svc:* 800-547-5746 ■ *Web:* www.elcsci.com	Portland	OR	97229	503-641-4141	671-5544*
Excel Technology Inc 41 Research Way *NASDAQ: XLTC* ■ *Web:* www.exceltechinc.com	East Setauket	NY	11733	631-784-6175	784-6195
GSI Group Inc 39 Manning Rd *NASDAQ: GSIG* ■ **Fax:* Sales ■ *TF:* 800-342-3757 ■ *Web:* www.gsilumonics.com	Billerica	MA	01821	978-439-5511	663-0131*
Ionatron Inc 3590 E Columbia St *NASDAQ: IOTN* ■ *Web:* www.ionatron.com	Tucson	AZ	85714	520-628-7415	622-3835
Isomet Corp 5263 Port Royal Rd *Web:* www.isomet.com	Springfield	VA	22151	703-321-8301	321-8546
Jodon Inc 62 Enterprise Dr *TF:* 800-989-5636 ■ *Web:* www.jodon.com	Ann Arbor	MI	48103	734-761-4044	761-3322
Kigre Inc 100 Marshland Rd *Web:* www.kigre.com	Hilton Head Island	SC	29926	843-681-5800	681-4559
Lambda Physik USA Inc PO Box 54980 *TF:* 800-392-4637 ■ *Web:* www.lambdaphysik.com	Santa Clara	CA	95056	408-764-4000	764-4800
Laserdyne Systems Div PRIMA North America Inc 8600 109th Ave N Suite 400	Champlin	MN	55316	763-433-3700	433-3701
Leica Geosystems LLC 3498 Kraft Ave *TF Sales:* 800-367-9453 ■ *Web:* www.leica-geosystems.com	Grand Rapids	MI	49512	616-949-7430	949-8693
Melles Griot Inc 2051 Talomar Airport Rd Suite 200 *TF Cust Svc:* 800-645-2737 ■ *Web:* www.mellesgriot.com	Carlsbad	CA	92009	760-438-5131	804-0049
Orthodyne Electronics 16700 Red Hill Ave *Web:* www.orthodyne.com	Irvine	CA	92606	949-660-0440	660-0444
OSI Laserscan 3259 Progress Dr *Web:* www.seo.com	Orlando	FL	32826	407-381-8117	381-2779
PRIMA North America Inc 711 E Main St *TF Cust Svc:* 800-722-1133 ■ *Web:* www.prima-na.com	Chicopee	MA	01020	413-598-5200	589-5201
PRIMA North America Inc Laserdyne Systems Div 8600 109th Ave N Suite 400	Champlin	MN	55316	763-433-3700	433-3701
PTR-Precision Technologies Inc 120 Post Rd *TF:* 888-478-7832 ■ *Web:* www.ptreb.com	Enfield	CT	06082	860-741-2281	745-7932
Rofin-Sinar Inc 40984 Concept Dr *NASDAQ: RSTI* ■ *Web:* www.rofin.com	Plymouth	MI	48170	734-455-5400	455-5587
Spectra-Physics Inc 1335 Terra Bella Ave *TF:* 800-456-2552 ■ *Web:* www.newport.com/spectralanding	Mountain View	CA	94043	650-961-2550	968-5215
STI Optronics Inc 2755 Northup Way *Web:* www.stioptronics.com	Bellevue	WA	98004	425-827-0460	828-3517
Synrad Inc 4600 Campus Pl *TF:* 800-796-7231 ■ *Web:* www.synrad.com	Mukilteo	WA	98275	425-349-3500	349-3667
TRUMPF Group 111 Hyde Rd *Web:* www.trumpf.com	Farmington	CT	06032	860-255-6000	677-4928

429 LAUNDRY & DRYCLEANING SERVICES

SEE ALSO Linen & Uniform Supply p. 1916

				Phone	Fax
1-800-DryClean LLC 3948 Ranchero Dr	Ann Arbor	MI	48108	866-822-6115	822-6888*
**Fax Area Code: 734* ■ *TF:* 800-379-2532 ■ *Web:* www.1-800-dryclean.com					
A Cleaner World Dry Cleaners					
2334 English Rd PO Box 6535	High Point	NC	27262	336-841-4188	841-4117
Web: www.acleanerworld.com					
ACW Management Corp DBA A Cleaner World Dry Cleaners					
2334 English Rd PO Box 6535	High Point	NC	27262	336-841-4188	841-4117
Web: www.acleanerworld.com					
Admiral Inc 4 N Taylor Ave	Annapolis	MD	21401	410-267-8381	263-4225
TF: 800-864-4429 ■ *Web:* www.admiralcleaners.com					
Al Phillips the Cleaner 3250 W Ali Baba Ln Suite C-F	Las Vegas	NV	89118	702-798-7333	798-1731
Web: www.alphillips-thecleaner.com					
Alaska Cleaners 610 W Fireweed Ln	Anchorage	AK	99503	907-265-4870	265-4812
AW Zengeler Cleaners 550 Dundee Rd	Northbrook	IL	60062	847-272-6550	272-5465
Web: www.zengelercleaners.com					
Certified Restoration DryCleaning Network LLC					
2060 Coolidge Hwy	Berkley	MI	48072	800-963-2736	246-7868*
**Fax Area Code: 248* ■ *Web:* www.restorationdrycleaning.com					
Coinmach Service Corp 303 SUnnyside Blvd Suite 70	Plainview	NY	11803	516-349-8555	349-9125
AMEX: DRA ■ *TF:* 800-747-9379 ■ *Web:* www.coinmachservicecorp.com					
Comet Cleaners 406 W Division St	Arlington	TX	76011	817-461-3555	861-4779
Web: www.cometcleaners.com					
Division Laundry & Cleaners Inc 6649 Old Hwy 90 W	San Antonio	TX	78227	210-674-5110	673-8510
Dry Cleaning Station 8301 Golden Valley Rd Suite 240	Minneapolis	MN	55427	763-541-0832	542-2246
TF: 800-655-8134 ■ *Web:* www.drycleaningstation.com					
Dryclean USA Inc 290 NE 68th St	Miami	FL	33138	305-758-0066	751-8390
AMEX: DCU ■ *TF:* 800-746-4583 ■ *Web:* www.drycleanusa.com					
Horlander Enterprises Inc DBA Nu-Yale Cleaners					
6300 Hwy 62	Jeffersonville	IN	47130	812-285-7400	285-7421
TF: 888-644-7400 ■ *Web:* www.nuyale.com					
Laundromax 411 Theodore Fremd Ave South Lobby	Rye	NY	10580	914-921-8240	
Martinizing Dry Cleaning 422 Wards Corner Rd	Loveland	OH	45140	513-351-6211	731-0818
TF: 800-827-0207 ■ *Web:* www.martinizing.com					
Max I Walkers Cleaners 4919 Underwood Ave	Omaha	NE	68132	402-558-3677	558-1957
Web: www.maxiwalker.com					
Nu-Yale Cleaners 6300 Hwy 62	Jeffersonville	IN	47130	812-285-7400	285-7421
TF: 888-644-7400 ■ *Web:* www.nuyale.com					
Pressed4Time Inc 8 Clock Tower Pl Suite 110	Maynard	MA	01754	978-823-8300	823-8301
TF: 800-423-8711 ■ *Web:* www.pressed4time.com					
Royal Airline Laundry Service Co 1107 Redford Ave	Far Rockaway	NY	11691	718-337-9390	337-9392
Salem Laundry Co 1 Lafayette St	Salem	MA	01970	978-744-1340	744-4216
Sloan's Dry Cleaning Inc 3001 N Main St	Los Angeles	CA	90031	323-225-1303	223-5358
Spic & Span Inc 4301 N Richards St	Milwaukee	WI	53212	414-964-5050	964-5042
Web: www.spicandspan.com					
Swan Super Cleaners Inc 1535 Bethel Rd	Columbus	OH	43220	614-442-5000	442-5007
Web: www.swancleaners.com					
Walker's Inc DBA Max I Walkers Cleaners					
4919 Underwood Ave	Omaha	NE	68132	402-558-3677	558-1957
Web: www.maxiwalker.com					
Westco Inc 3418 Americana Terr	Boise	ID	83706	208-342-3631	344-6423
Zengeler AW Cleaners 550 Dundee Rd	Northbrook	IL	60062	847-272-6550	272-5465
Web: www.zengelercleaners.com					

LAUNDRY EQUIPMENT - HOUSEHOLD

SEE Appliances - Major - Mfr p. 1279; Appliances - Whol p. 1280

430 LAUNDRY EQUIPMENT & SUPPLIES - COMMERCIAL & INDUSTRIAL

				Phone	Fax
Alliance Laundry Systems LLC PO Box 990	Ripon	WI	54971	920-748-3121	748-4429
Web: www.comlaundry.com					
American Dryer Corp 88 Currant Rd	Fall River	MA	02720	508-678-9000	678-9447
Web: www.amdry.com					
American Textile Processing LLC 422 Wards Corner Rd	Loveland	OH	45140	513-699-4280	699-4233
Bishop Freeman Co 1600 Foster St	Evanston	IL	60204	847-328-5200	328-0338
Braun GA Inc PO Box 70	Syracuse	NY	13205	315-475-3123	475-4130
TF: 800-432-7286 ■ *Web:* www.gabraun.com					
Chicago Dryer Co 2200 N Pulaski Rd	Chicago	IL	60639	773-235-4430	235-4439
Web: www.chidry.com					
Cissell Mfg Co 831 S 1st St	Louisville	KY	40203	502-587-1292	585-2333
TF: 800-882-6665 ■ *Web:* www.cissellmfg.com					
Coinmach Service Corp 303 SUnnyside Blvd Suite 70	Plainview	NY	11803	516-349-8555	349-9125
AMEX: DRA ■ *TF:* 800-747-9379 ■ *Web:* www.coinmachservicecorp.com					
Colmac Industries Inc PO Box 72	Colville	WA	99114	509-684-4506	684-4500
TF: 800-926-5622 ■ *Web:* www.colmacind.com					
Dexter Co 2211 W Grimes Ave	Fairfield	IA	52556	641-472-5131	472-6336
Web: www.dxtrco.com					
Edro Corp 37 Commerce St	East Berlin	CT	06023	860-828-0311	828-5984
TF Sales: 800-628-6434 ■ *Web:* www.edrodynawash.com					
Ellis Corp 1400 W Bryn Mawr Ave	Itasca	IL	60143	630-250-9222	250-9241
TF: 800-611-6806 ■ *Web:* www.elliscorp.com					
Forenta LP PO Box 607	Morristown	TN	37815	423-586-5370	586-3470
Web: www.forentausa.com					
GA Braun Inc PO Box 70	Syracuse	NY	13205	315-475-3123	475-4130
TF: 800-432-7286 ■ *Web:* www.gabraun.com					
Hoyt Corp 251 Forge Rd	Westport	MA	02790	508-636-8811	636-2088
TF: 800-343-9411 ■ *Web:* www.hoytcorp.com					
Marvel Petrol Dry 5922 San Pedro Ave	San Antonio	TX	78212	210-344-8551	344-3004
Web: www.marvelpetroldry.com					
Minnesota Chemical Co 2285 Hampden Ave	Saint Paul	MN	55114	651-646-7521	649-1101
TF: 800-328-5689 ■ *Web:* www.minnesotachemical.com					
Pellerin Milnor Corp 700 Jackson St	Kenner	LA	70062	504-467-9591	712-3783
Web: www.milnor.com					
Rema Dri-Vac Corp PO Box 86	Norwalk	CT	06852	203-847-2464	847-3609
Web: www.remadrivac.com					
Thermal Engineering of Arizona Inc 2250 W Wetmore Rd	Tucson	AZ	85705	520-888-4000	888-4457
TF: 866-832-7278 ■ *Web:* www.teatucson.com					
Washex Inc 5000 Central Fwy N	Wichita Falls	TX	76306	940-855-3990	855-9349
TF Sales: 800-433-0933 ■ *Web:* www.washex.com					

431 LAW FIRMS

SEE ALSO Arbitration Services - Legal p. 1283; Associations & Organizations - Professional & Trade - Legal Professionals Associations p. 1332; Bar Associations - State p. 1372; Litigation Support Services p. 1916

				Phone	Fax
Adorno & Yoss 2525 Ponce de Leon Blvd Suite 400	Miami	FL	33134	305-460-1000	460-1422
TF: 800-881-2064 ■ *Web:* www.adorno.com					
Akerman Senterfitt 1 SE 3rd Ave 25th Fl	Miami	FL	33131	305-374-5600	374-5095
Web: www.akerman.com					
Akin Gump Strauss Hauer & Feld LLP					
1333 New Hampshire Ave NW	Washington	DC	20036	202-887-4000	887-4288
Web: www.akingump.com					
Alston & Bird LLP 1201 W Peachtree St	Atlanta	GA	30309	404-881-7000	881-7777
Web: www.alston.com					
Andrews Kurth LLP 600 Travis St Chase Towers Suite 4200	Houston	TX	77002	713-220-4200	220-4285
Web: www.andrewskurth.com					
Arnold & Porter LLP 555 12th St NW	Washington	DC	20004	202-942-5000	942-5999
Web: www.arnoldporter.com					
Baker Botts LLP 910 Louisiana St 1 Shell Plaza	Houston	TX	77002	713-229-1234	229-1522
Web: www.bakerbotts.com					
Baker Donelson Bearman Caldwell & Berkowitz PC					
165 Madison Ave 1st Tennessee Bldg Suite 2000	Memphis	TN	38103	901-526-2000	577-2303
Web: www.bakerdonelson.com					
Baker Hostetler LLP					
1900 E 9th St National City Ctr Suite 3200	Cleveland	OH	44114	216-621-0200	696-0740
Web: www.bakerlaw.com					
Baker & McKenzie					
130 E Randolph Dr Suite 3500 1 Prudential Plaza	Chicago	IL	60601	312-861-8800	861-2899
Web: www.bakernet.com					
Ballard Spahr Andrews & Ingersoll LLP					
1735 Market St 51st Fl	Philadelphia	PA	19103	215-665-8500	864-8999
Web: www.ballardspahr.com					
Barnes & Thornburg 11 S Meridian St	Indianapolis	IN	46204	317-236-1313	231-7433
TF: 800-753-5139 ■ *Web:* www.btlaw.com					
Bingham McCutchen LLP 150 Federal St	Boston	MA	02110	617-951-8000	951-8736
Web: www.bingham.com					
Black Srebnick Kornspan & Stumpf PA					
201 S Biscayne Blvd Suite 1300	Miami	FL	33131	305-371-6421	
Web: www.royblack.com					
Blank Rome LLP 1 Logan Sq 130 N 18th St	Philadelphia	PA	19103	215-569-5500	569-5555
Web: www.blankrome.com					
Boies Schiller & Flexner LLP 5301 Wisconsin Ave NW	Washington	DC	20015	202-237-2727	237-6131
Web: www.boies-schiller.com					
Bracewell & Giuliani LLP 711 Louisiana St Suite 2300	Houston	TX	77002	713-223-2300	221-1212
Web: www.bracewellgiuliani.com					
Bryan Cave LLP					
1 Metropolitan Sq 211 N Broadway Suite 3800	Saint Louis	MO	63102	314-259-2000	259-2020
Web: www.bryancave.com					
Buchanan Ingersoll & Rooney PC					
301 Grant St 1 Oxford Ctr 20th Fl	Pittsburgh	PA	15219	412-562-8800	562-1041
TF: 800-444-6738 ■ *Web:* www.buchananingersoll.com					
Cadwalader Wickersham & Taft LLP 1 World Financial Center	New York	NY	10281	212-504-6000	504-6666
TF: 800-489-8682 ■ *Web:* www.cadwalader.com					
Chadbourne & Parke LLP 30 Rockefeller Plaza	New York	NY	10112	212-408-5100	541-5369
Web: www.chadbourne.com					
Christensen Glaser Fink Jacobs Weil & Shapiro LLP					
10250 Constellation Blvd 19th Fl	Los Angeles	CA	90067	310-553-3000	556-2920
Web: www.chrisglase.com					
Cleary Gottlieb Steen & Hamilton LLP 1 Liberty Plaza	New York	NY	10006	212-225-2000	225-3999
Web: www.cgsh.com					
Cochran Firm LLC 163 W Main St	Dothan	AL	36301	334-793-1555	793-8280
TF: 800-526-2472 ■ *Web:* www.cochranfirm.com					
Cooley Godward Kronish LLP					
5 Palo Alto Sq 3000 El Camino Real	Palo Alto	CA	94306	650-843-5000	849-7400
Web: www.cooley.com					
Covington & Burling LLP 1201 Pennsylvania Ave NW	Washington	DC	20004	202-662-6000	662-6291
Web: www.cov.com					
Cozen O'Connor 1900 Market St	Philadelphia	PA	19103	215-665-2000	665-2013
TF: 800-523-2900 ■ *Web:* www.cozen.com					
Cravath Swaine & Moore LLP 825 8th Ave Worldwide Plaza	New York	NY	10019	212-474-1000	474-3700
Web: www.cravath.com					
Davis Polk & Wardwell 450 Lexington Ave	New York	NY	10017	212-450-4000	450-3800
TF: 888-765-5529 ■ *Web:* www.dpw.com					
Davis Wright Tremaine LLP 1501 4th Ave Suite 2600	Seattle	WA	98101	206-622-3150	628-7699
Web: www.dwt.com					
Day Pitney LLP 242 Trumbull St	Hartford	CT	06103	860-275-0100	275-0343
Web: www.daypitney.com					
Debevoise & Plimpton LLP 919 3rd Ave	New York	NY	10022	212-909-6000	909-6836
Web: www.debevoise.com					
Dechert LLP 2929 Arch St Cira Center	Philadelphia	PA	19104	215-994-4000	994-2222
Web: www.dechert.com					
Dewey Ballantine LLP 1301 Ave of the Americas	New York	NY	10019	212-259-8000	259-6333
Web: www.deweyballantine.com					
Dickstein Shapiro LLP 1825 Eye St NW	Washington	DC	20006	202-420-2200	420-2201
Web: www.dicksteinshapiro.com					
DLA Piper 203 N LaSalle St Suite 1900	Chicago	IL	60601	312-368-4000	236-7516
Web: www.dlapiper.com					
Dorsey & Whitney LLP 50 S 6th St Suite 1500	Minneapolis	MN	55402	612-340-2600	340-2868
TF: 800-759-4929 ■ *Web:* www.dorsey.com					
Drinker Biddle & Reath LLP 18th & Cherry Sts 1 Logan Sq	Philadelphia	PA	19103	215-988-2700	988-2757
Web: www.drinkerbiddle.com					
Duane Morris LLP 30 S 17th St United Plaza	Philadelphia	PA	19103	215-979-1000	979-1020
Web: www.duanemorris.com					
Edwards Angell Palmer & Dodge LLP 111 Huntington Ave	Boston	MA	02199	617-239-0100	227-4420
Web: www.eapdlaw.com					
Epstein Becker & Green PC 250 Park Ave	New York	NY	10177	212-351-4500	661-0989
Web: www.ebglaw.com					
Faegre & Benson LLP 90 S 7th St 2200 Wells Fargo Bldg	Minneapolis	MN	55402	612-766-7000	766-1600
TF: 800-328-4393 ■ *Web:* www.faegre.com					
Fieger Fieger Kenney & Johnson PC 19390 W 10-Mile Rd	Southfield	MI	48075	248-355-5555	355-5148
Web: www.fiegerlaw.com					
Fish & Richardson PC 225 Franklin St 31st Fl	Boston	MA	02110	617-542-5070	542-8906
TF: 800-818-5070 ■ *Web:* www.fr.com					
Fitzpatrick Cella Harper & Scinto 30 Rockefeller Plaza	New York	NY	10112	212-218-2100	218-2200
Web: www.fitzpatrickcella.com					
Foley & Lardner LLP 777 E Wisconsin Ave	Milwaukee	WI	53202	414-271-2400	297-4900
TF: 800-558-1548 ■ *Web:* www.foley.com					
Fox Rothschild LLP 2000 Market St 10th Fl	Philadelphia	PA	19103	215-299-2000	299-2150
Web: www.foxrothschild.com					
Fried Frank Harris Shriver & Jacobson LLP 1 New York Plaza	New York	NY	10004	212-859-8000	859-4000
Web: www.ffhsj.com					
Frost Brown Todd LLC 201 E 5th St 2200 PNC Ctr	Cincinnati	OH	45202	513-651-6800	651-6981
Web: www.frostbrowntodd.com					

	City	State	ZIP	Phone	Fax
Fulbright & Jaworski LLP 1301 McKinney St Suite 5100	Houston	TX	77010	713-651-5151	651-5246
TF: 866-385-2744 ■ *Web:* www.fulbright.com					
Gary Williams Parenti Finney Lewis McManus Watson & Sperando PL Waterside Professional Bldg 221 E Osceola St	Stuart	FL	34994	772-283-8260	220-3343
TF: 800-329-4279 ■ *Web:* www.williegary.com					
Geragos & Geragos PC 644 S Figueroa St	Los Angeles	CA	90017	213-625-3900	625-1600
Web: www.geragos.com					
Gibbons PC 1 Gateway Ctr	Newark	NJ	07102	973-596-4500	596-0545
Web: www.gibbonslaw.com					
Gibson Dunn & Crutcher LLP 333 S Grand Ave Suite 4600	Los Angeles	CA	90071	213-229-7000	229-7520
TF: 800-822-7152 ■ *Web:* www.gibsondunn.com					
Goodwin Procter LLP 53 State St Exchange Pl	Boston	MA	02109	617-570-1000	523-1231
Web: www.goodwinprocter.com					
Greenberg Traurig LLP 1221 Brickell Ave 18th Fl	Miami	FL	33131	305-579-0500	579-0717
Web: www.gtlaw.com					
Haynes & Boone LLP 901 Main St Suite 3100	Dallas	TX	75202	214-651-5000	651-5940
Web: www.haynesboone.com					
Heller Ehrman LLP 333 Bush St Suite 3000	San Francisco	CA	94104	415-772-6000	772-6268
Web: www.hewm.com					
Hinshaw & Culbertson LLP 222 N LaSalle St Suite 300	Chicago	IL	60601	312-704-3000	704-3001
TF: 800-300-6812 ■ *Web:* www.hinshawlaw.com					
Hogan & Hartson LLP 555 13th St NW	Washington	DC	20004	202-637-5600	637-5910
Web: www.hhlaw.com					
Holland & Knight LLP 195 Broadway 24th Fl	New York	NY	10007	212-513-3200	385-9010
Web: www.hklaw.com					
Howrey LLP 1299 Pennsylvania Ave NW	Washington	DC	20004	202-783-0800	383-6610
TF: 800-727-1730 ■ *Web:* www.howrey.com					
Hughes Hubbard & Reed LLP 1 Battery Park Plaza	New York	NY	10004	212-837-6000	422-4726
Web: www.hugheshubbard.com					
Hunton & Williams LLP 951 E Byrd St Riverfront Plaza E Tower	Richmond	VA	23219	804-788-8200	788-8218
Web: www.hunton.com					
Irell & Manella LLP 1800 Ave of the Stars Suite 900	Los Angeles	CA	90067	310-277-1010	203-7199
Web: www.irell.com					
Jackson Lewis LLP 59 Maiden Ln 39th Fl	New York	NY	10038	212-697-8200	972-3213
Web: www.jacksonlewis.com					
Jenner & Block LLP 330 N Wabash Ave 40th Fl	Chicago	IL	60611	312-222-9350	527-0484
Web: www.jenner.com					
Jones Day 51 Louisiana Ave NW	Washington	DC	20001	202-879-3939	626-1700
Web: www.jonesday.com					
K & L Gates 535 Smithfield St Henry W Oliver Bldg	Pittsburgh	PA	15222	412-355-6500	355-6501
Web: www.klgates.com					
Katten Muchin Rosenman LLP 525 W Monroe St Suite 1300	Chicago	IL	60661	312-902-5200	902-1061
TF: 800-346-7400 ■ *Web:* www.kattenlaw.com					
Kaye Scholer LLP 425 Park Ave	New York	NY	10022	212-836-8000	836-8689
Web: www.kayescholer.com					
Kelley Drye & Warren LLP 101 Park Ave	New York	NY	10178	212-808-7800	808-7897
Web: www.kelleydrye.com					
Kilpatrick Stockton LLP 1100 Peachtree St Suite 2800	Atlanta	GA	30309	404-815-6500	815-6555
Web: www.kilpatrickstockton.com					
King & Spalding 1180 Peachtree St NE	Atlanta	GA	30309	404-572-4600	572-5100
Web: www.kslaw.com					
Kirkland & Ellis LLP 200 E Randolph Dr	Chicago	IL	60601	312-861-2000	861-2200
TF: 800-334-3133 ■ *Web:* www.kirkland.com					
Kirkpatrick & Lockhart Preston Gates Ellis LLP 535 Smithfield St Henry W Oliver Bldg	Pittsburgh	PA	15222	412-355-6500	355-6501
Web: www.klgates.com					
Kutak Rock LLP 1650 Farnam St	Omaha	NE	68102	402-346-6000	346-1148
Web: www.kutakrock.com					
Latham & Watkins LLP 885 3rd Ave	New York	NY	10022	212-906-1200	751-4864
Web: www.lw.com					
LeBoeuf Lamb Greene & MacRae LLP 125 W 55th St 12th Fl	New York	NY	10019	212-424-8000	424-8500
Web: www.llgm.com					
Lewis Brisbois Bisgaard & Smith LLP 221 N Figueroa St Suite 1200	Los Angeles	CA	90012	213-250-1800	250-7900
Web: www.lbbslaw.com					
Littler Mendelson PC 650 California St 20th Fl	San Francisco	CA	94108	415-433-1940	399-8490
TF: 888-548-8537 ■ *Web:* www.littler.com					
Locke Liddell & Sapp LLP 3400 JPMorgan Chase Tower 600 Travis	Houston	TX	77002	713-226-1200	223-3717
Web: www.lockeliddell.com					
Marshall Dennehey Warner Coleman & Goggin 1845 Walnut St 16th Fl	Philadelphia	PA	19103	215-575-2600	575-0856
Web: www.marshalldennehey.com					
Mayer Brown Rowe & Maw LLP 71 S Wacker Dr Suite 3200	Chicago	IL	60606	312-782-0600	701-7711
Web: www.mayerbrownrowe.com					
McCarter & English LLP 4 Gateway Center 100 Mulberry St	Newark	NJ	07102	973-622-4444	624-7070
Web: www.mccarter.com					
McDermott Will & Emery 227 W Monroe St Suite 4700	Chicago	IL	60606	312-372-2000	984-7700
Web: www.mwe.com					
McGuireWoods LLP 901 E Cary St One James Center	Richmond	VA	23219	804-775-1000	775-1061
Web: www.mcguirewoods.com					
McKenna Long & Aldridge LLP 303 Peachtree St Suite 5300	Atlanta	GA	30308	404-527-4000	527-4198
Web: www.mckennalong.com					
Milbank Tweed Hadley & McCloy LLP 1 Chase Manhattan Plaza	New York	NY	10005	212-530-5000	530-5219
Web: www.milbank.com					
Miller Canfield Paddock & Stone PLC 150 W Jefferson Ave Suite 2500	Detroit	MI	48226	313-963-6420	496-7500
Web: www.millercanfield.com					
Mintz Levin Cohn Ferris Glovsky & Popeo PC 1 Financial Center	Boston	MA	02111	617-542-6000	542-2241
Web: www.mintz.com					
Morgan Lewis & Bockius LLP 1701 Market St	Philadelphia	PA	19103	215-963-5000	963-5001
Web: www.morganlewis.com					
Morrison & Foerster LLP 425 Market St	San Francisco	CA	94105	415-268-7000	268-7522
TF: 800-669-5996 ■ *Web:* www.mofo.com					
Nelson Mullins Riley & Scarborough LLP 1320 Main St 17th Fl	Columbia	SC	29201	803-799-2000	256-7500
TF: 800-237-2000 ■ *Web:* www.nelsonmullins.com					
Nixon Peabody LLP 1300 Clinton Sq PO Box 31051	Rochester	NY	14603	585-263-1000	263-1600
Web: www.nixonpeabody.com					
O'Melveny & Myers LLP 400 S Hope St 10th Fl	Los Angeles	CA	90071	213-430-6000	430-6407
Web: www.omm.com					
Orrick Herrington & Sutcliffe LLP 666 5th Ave	New York	NY	10103	212-506-5000	506-5151
Web: www.orrick.com					
Patton Boggs LLP 2550 M St NW	Washington	DC	20037	202-457-6000	457-6315
Web: www.pattonboggs.com					
Paul Hastings Janofsky & Walker LLP 515 S Flower St 25th Fl	Los Angeles	CA	90071	213-683-6000	627-0705
TF: 888-745-9557 ■ *Web:* www.paulhastings.com					
Paul Weiss Rifkind Wharton & Garrison LLP 1285 Ave of the Americas	New York	NY	10019	212-373-3000	757-3990
Web: www.paulweiss.com					
Pepper Hamilton LLP 3000 Two Logan Sq 18th & Arch St	Philadelphia	PA	19103	215-981-4000	981-4750
Web: www.pepperlaw.com					
Perkins Coie LLP 1201 W 3rd Ave Suite 4800	Seattle	WA	98101	206-359-8000	359-9000
TF: 800-829-1177 ■ *Web:* www.perkinscoie.com					
Pillsbury Winthrop Shaw Pittman LLP 50 Fremont St	San Francisco	CA	94105	415-983-1000	983-1200
TF: 800-477-0770 ■ *Web:* www.pillsburylaw.com					
Polsinelli Shalton Flanigan Suelthaus PC 700 W 47th St Suite 1000	Kansas City	MO	64112	816-753-1000	753-1536
Web: www.polsinelli.com					
Proskauer Rose LLP 1585 Broadway	New York	NY	10036	212-969-3000	969-2900
Web: www.proskauer.com					
Quarles & Brady LLP 411 E Wisconsin Ave Suite 2040	Milwaukee	WI	53202	414-277-5000	271-3552
TF: 800-446-7545 ■ *Web:* www.quarles.com					
Reed Smith 435 6th Ave	Pittsburgh	PA	15219	412-288-3131	288-3063
Web: www.reedsmith.com					
Ropes & Gray LLP 1 International Pl	Boston	MA	02110	617-951-7000	951-7050
Web: www.ropesgray.com					
Schiff Hardin LLP 233 S Wacker Dr 6600 Sears Tower	Chicago	IL	60606	312-258-5500	258-5700
TF: 800-258-7799 ■ *Web:* www.schiffhardin.com					
Schulte Roth & Zabel LLP 919 3rd Ave	New York	NY	10022	212-758-0404	593-5955
TF: 800-346-9644 ■ *Web:* www.srz.com					
Sedgwick Detert Moran & Arnold LLP 1 Market Plaza Steuart Tower 8th Fl	San Francisco	CA	94105	415-781-7900	781-2635
TF: 800-826-3262 ■ *Web:* www.sdma.com					
Seyfarth Shaw LLP 131 S Dearborn St Suite 2400	Chicago	IL	60603	312-460-5000	460-7000
TF: 866-460-3476 ■ *Web:* www.seyfarth.com					
Shearman & Sterling LLP 599 Lexington Ave	New York	NY	10022	212-848-4000	848-7179
TF: 800-521-2918 ■ *Web:* www.shearman.com					
Sheppard Mullin Richter & Hampton LLP 333 S Hope St 48th Fl	Los Angeles	CA	90071	213-620-1780	620-1398
Web: www.sheppardmullin.com					
Sherman Richichi & Hickey LLC 27 5th St	Stamford	CT	06905	203-324-2296	348-7313
Web: www.srh-law.com					
Shook Hardy & Bacon LLP 2555 Grand Blvd	Kansas City	MO	64108	816-474-6550	421-5547
TF: 800-821-7962 ■ *Web:* www.shb.com					
Sidley Austin LLP 1 S Dearborn St	Chicago	IL	60603	312-853-7000	853-7036
Web: www.sidley.com					
Simpson Thacher & Bartlett LLP 425 Lexington Ave	New York	NY	10017	212-455-2000	455-2502
Web: www.stblaw.com					
Skadden Arps Slate Meagher & Flom LLP 4 Times Sq	New York	NY	10036	212-735-3000	735-2000
Web: www.skadden.com					
Snell & Wilmer LLP 400 E Van Buren St 1 Arizona Center	Phoenix	AZ	85004	602-382-6000	382-6070
TF: 800-322-0430 ■ *Web:* www.swlaw.com					
Sonnenschein Nath & Rosenthal LLP 233 S Wacker Dr 7800 Sears Tower	Chicago	IL	60606	312-876-8000	876-7934
Web: www.sonnenschein.com					
Spence Law Firm LLC PO Box 548 15 S Jackson St	Jackson	WY	83001	307-733-7290	733-5248
TF: 800-967-2117 ■ *Web:* www.spencelawyers.com					
Squire Sanders & Dempsey LLP 127 Public Sq 4900 Key Tower	Cleveland	OH	44114	216-479-8500	479-8780
TF: 800-743-2773 ■ *Web:* www.ssd.com					
Steptoe & Johnson LLP 1330 Connecticut Ave NW	Washington	DC	20036	202-429-3000	429-3902
Web: www.steptoe.com					
Sullivan & Cromwell LLP 125 Broad St	New York	NY	10004	212-558-4000	558-3588
Web: www.sullcrom.com					
Sutherland Asbill & Brennan LLP 999 Peachtree St NE	Atlanta	GA	30309	404-853-8000	853-8806
Web: www.sablaw.com					
Thelen Reid Brown Raysman & Steiner LLP 101 2nd St Suite 1800	San Francisco	CA	94105	415-371-1200	371-1211
Web: www.thelenreid.com					
Thompson Hine LLP 127 Public Sq 3900 Key Center	Cleveland	OH	44114	216-566-5500	566-5800
TF: 877-628-5500 ■ *Web:* www.thompsonhine.com					
Thompson & Knight LLP 1700 Pacific Ave Suite 3300	Dallas	TX	75201	214-969-1700	969-1751
Web: www.tklaw.com					
Troutman Sanders LLP 600 Peachtree St NE Suite 5200	Atlanta	GA	30308	404-885-3000	885-3900
TF: 800-255-8752 ■ *Web:* www.troutmansanders.com					
Venable LLP 575 7th St NW	Washington	DC	20004	202-344-4000	344-8300
Web: www.venable.com					
Vinson & Elkins LLP 1001 Fannin St First City Tower Suite 2500	Houston	TX	77002	713-758-2222	758-2346
Web: www.velaw.com					
Vorys Sater Seymour & Pease LLP 52 E Gay St	Columbus	OH	43216	614-464-6400	464-6350
Web: www.vssp.com					
Weil Gotshal & Manges LLP 767 5th Ave	New York	NY	10153	212-310-8000	310-8007
Web: www.weil.com					
White & Case LLP 1155 Ave of the Americas	New York	NY	10036	212-819-8200	354-8113
Web: www.whitecase.com					
Williams & Connolly LLP 725 12th St NW	Washington	DC	20005	202-434-5000	434-5029
Web: www.wc.com					
Willkie Farr & Gallagher LLP 787 7th Ave 2nd Fl	New York	NY	10019	212-728-8000	728-8111
Web: www.willkie.com					
Wilmer Cutler Pickering Hale & Dorr LLP 1875 Pennsylvania Ave	Washington	DC	20006	202-663-6000	663-6363
Web: www.wilmerhale.com					
WilmerHale 1875 Pennsylvania Ave	Washington	DC	20006	202-663-6000	663-6363
Web: www.wilmerhale.com					
Wilson Elser Moskowitz Edelman & Dicker LLP 150 E 42nd St	New York	NY	10017	212-490-3000	490-3038
Web: www.wilsonelser.com					
Wilson Sonsini Goodrich & Rosati 650 Page Mill Rd	Palo Alto	CA	94304	650-493-9300	493-6811
Web: www.wsgr.com					
Winston & Strawn LLP 35 W Wacker Dr 42nd Fl	Chicago	IL	60601	312-558-5600	558-5700
TF: 800-946-7866 ■ *Web:* www.winston.com					
Womble Carlyle Sandridge & Rice PLLC 1 W 4th St	Winston-Salem	NC	27101	336-721-3600	721-3660
Web: www.wcsr.com					

432 LAWN & GARDEN EQUIPMENT

SEE ALSO Farm Machinery & Equipment - Mfr p. 1631

	City	State	ZIP	Phone	Fax
American Biophysics Corp 140 Frenchtown Rd	North Kingstown	RI	02852	401-884-3500	884-6688
TF: 877-699-8727 ■ *Web:* www.mosquitomagnet.com					
American Lawn Mower Co 2100 N Grandville Ave	Muncie	IN	47303	765-288-6624	284-5263
Ames True Temper Inc 465 Railroad Ave	Camp Hill	PA	17011	717-737-1500	730-2550
TF: 800-393-1846 ■ *Web:* www.ames.com					
Ariens Co 655 W Ryan St	Brillion	WI	54110	920-756-2141	756-2407
Web: www.ariens.com					
Armatron International Inc 15 Highland Ave	Malden	MA	02148	781-321-2300	321-2309
TF: 800-343-3280					
Black & Decker Corp 701 E Joppa Rd	Towson	MD	21286	410-716-3900	716-2996*
NYSE: BDK ■ **Fax:* Mktg ■ *Web:* www.bdk.com					
Blount Inc Oregon Cutting Systems Div 4909 SE International Way	Portland	OR	97222	503-653-8881	653-4201
TF: 800-223-5168 ■ *Web:* www.oregonchain.com					
Blount Outdoor Products Group 4909 SE International Way	Portland	OR	97222	503-653-8881	653-4201
TF: 800-223-5168 ■ *Web:* www.blount.com/Cutsytm.html					

Phone | Fax

Bluemkes Inc 101 W Division ST PO Box 149 Rosendale WI 54974 920-872-2131 872-2134
TF: 800-236-2133 ■ *Web:* www.bluemkes.com

Brinly-Hardy Co 3230 Industrial Pkwy. Jeffersonville IN 47130 812-218-6080 218-6085
TF: 800-626-5329 ■ *Web:* www.brinly.com

California Flexrake Corp 9620 Gidley St Temple City CA 91780 626-443-4026 443-6887
TF: 800-266-4200 ■ *Web:* www.flexrake.com

CMD Products 1410 Flightline Dr Suite D Lincoln CA 95648 916-434-0228 434-0214
TF: 800-210-9949 ■ *Web:* www.cmdproducts.com

Commerce Corp 7603 Energy Pkwy Baltimore MD 21226 410-255-3500 360-6001*
**Fax:* Cust Svc ■ *TF:* 800-289-0982 ■ *Web:* www.commercecorp.com

Corona Clipper Inc 22440 Tomasco Canyon Rd. Corona CA 92879 951-737-6515 737-8657
TF: 800-847-7863 ■ *Web:* www.coronaclipper.com

Cub Cadet Corp 1620 Welch St Brownsville TN 38012 731-772-5600 779-5256
TF: 888-986-2288 ■ *Web:* www.cubcadet.com

Deere & Co John Deere Commercial & Residential Div
2000 John Deere Run PO Box 29533 Raleigh NC 27626 919-804-2000 804-2475
TF: 800-537-8233 ■ *Web:* www.deere.com

Dixon Industries Inc 2612 Hwy 169 N PO Box 1569 Coffeyville KS 67337 877-288-6673 251-4117*
**Fax Area Code:* 620 ■ *TF:* 877-288-6673 ■ *Web:* www.dixon-ztr.com

EarthWay Products Inc PO Box 547 Bristol IN 46507 574-848-7491 848-4249
TF: 800-678-0671 ■ *Web:* www.earthway.com

Echo Inc 400 Oakwood Rd Lake Zurich IL 60047 847-540-8400 540-8413
TF: 800-673-1558 ■ *Web:* www.echo-usa.com

Fiskars Brands Inc Garden Tools Div 780 Carolina St. Sauk City WI 53583 608-643-4389 643-4812
TF: 800-500-4849 ■ *Web:* gardening.fiskars.com

Frederick Mfg Corp 4840 E 12th St. Kansas City MO 64127 816-231-5007 541-2152*
**Fax Area Code:* 800 ■ *TF:* 800-743-3150

Giant Vac Inc 535 Macon St McDonough GA 30253 866-792-8223 792-8224
Web: www.giant-vac.com

Gilmour Mfg Group 492 Drum Ave Industrial Park Somerset PA 15501 814-443-4802 445-6605
TF Cust Svc: 800-458-0107 ■ *Web:* www.gilmour.com

Grasshopper Co 105 S Old Hwy 81 PO Box 637 Moundridge KS 67107 620-345-8621 345-2301
Web: www.grasshoppermower.com

Grassland Equipment & Irrigation Corp
250 Lake Ave PO Box 2060 Blasdell NY 14219 716-822-2020 822-8836
Web: www.grasslandcorp.com

Great States Corp 2100 Grandville Ave. Muncie IN 47303 765-288-6624 284-5263

Harnack Co 6016 Nordic Dr Cedar Falls IA 50613 319-277-0660 277-2275
TF Cust Svc: 800-772-2022 ■ *Web:* www.harnack.net

Hoffco/Comet Industries Inc 358 NW 'F' St. Richmond IN 47374 765-966-8161 935-2346
TF: 800-999-8161 ■ *Web:* www.hoffcocomet.com

HoffcoComet Industries Inc 358 NW 'F' St Richmond IN 47374 765-966-8161 935-2346
Web: www.hoffcocomet.com

Honda Power Equipment Mfg Inc
3721 Hwy 119 PO Box 37 Swepsonville NC 27359 336-578-5300 229-0768

Hound Dog Products Inc 465 Railroad Ave. Camp Hill PA 17011 800-694-6863 567-1904
TF: 800-694-6863 ■ *Web:* www.hound-dog.com

Howard Price Turf Equipment Inc 18155 Edison Ave Chesterfield MO 63005 636-532-7000 532-0201
Web: www.howardpriceturf.com

Husqvarna Turf Care Co 401 N Commerce St Beatrice NE 68310 402-223-2391 223-1053
TF: 877-368-8873 ■ *Web:* www.yazookees.com

Ingersoll Tractor Co 70 Ingersoll Dr. Portland ME 04103 207-878-5353 878-9109
TF: 800-760-1680 ■ *Web:* www.ingersolltractors.com

Jacobsen 3800 Arco Corporate Dr Suite 310 Charlotte NC 28273 704-504-6600 504-6661
TF: 866-522-6273 ■ *Web:* www.jacobsen.com

Janiak Mfg Inc 11 Machine Shop Hill Rd. South Windham CT 06266 860-423-7741 423-2654

John Deere Commercial & Residential Div Deere & Co
2000 John Deere Run PO Box 29533 Raleigh NC 27626 919-804-2000 804-2475
TF: 800-537-8233 ■ *Web:* www.deere.com

John Deere Landscapes 5610 McGinnis Ferry Rd Alpharetta GA 30005 770-442-8881 442-3214
Web: www.johndeerelandscapes.com

Kenney Corp 8420 Zionsville Rd Indianapolis IN 46268 317-872-4793 879-2331
TF: 800-878-8676 ■ *Web:* www.kmcturf.com

Lawn-Boy Inc 8111 S Lyndale Ave Bloomington MN 55420 952-888-8801 887-8258
TF: 800-526-6937 ■ *Web:* www.lawn-boy.com

Lawn & Golf Supply Co Inc 647 Nutt Rd PO Box 447 Phoenixville PA 19460 610-933-5801 933-8890
TF: 800-362-5650 ■ *Web:* www.lawn-golf.com

LESCO Inc 1301 E 9th St Suite 1300 Cleveland OH 44114 216-706-9250 706-5240*
NASDAQ: LSCO ■ **Fax:* Cust Svc ■ *TF:* 800-321-5325 ■ *Web:* www.lesco.com

LR Nelson Corp 1 Sprinkler Ln Peoria IL 61615 309-690-2200 692-5847
TF Sales: 800-635-7668 ■ *Web:* www.lrnelson.com

MacKissic Inc 1189 Old Schuylkill Rd. Parker Ford PA 19457 610-495-7181 495-5951
TF: 800-348-1117 ■ *Web:* www.mackissic.com

Master Mark Plastic Products Inc
30 E Railroad Ave PO Box 662 Albany MN 56307 320-845-2111 845-7093
TF Cust Svc: 800-535-4838 ■ *Web:* www.mastermark.com

Maxim Mfg Corp 16741 Hwy 21 PO Box 110 Sebastopol MS 39359 601-625-7471 625-8227
TF: 800-621-2789 ■ *Web:* www.maximmfg.com

McLane Mfg Inc 7110 E Rosecrans Ave. Paramount CA 90723 562-633-8158 602-0651
TF: 877-633-8158 ■ *Web:* www.mclanemower.com

Melnor Inc 3085 Shawnee Dr Winchester VA 22601 540-722-5600 411-2500*
**Fax Area Code:* 888 ■ *TF:* 877-283-0697 ■ *Web:* www.melnor.com

Mid West Products Inc PO Box 301 Phillipsburg OH 45354 937-337-3641 337-0755
Web: www.lambertmfg.com

Modern Line Products Co 801 Industrial Park Rd PO Box 110 Indianola MS 38751 662-887-4151 887-5200

MTD Products Inc 5903 Grafton Rd Valley City OH 44280 330-225-2600 273-4617*
**Fax:* Sales ■ *TF:* 800-800-7310 ■ *Web:* www.mtdproducts.com

National Mower Co 700 Raymond Ave. Saint Paul MN 55114 651-646-4079 646-2887
Web: www.nationalmower.com

Nelson LR Corp 1 Sprinkler Ln Peoria IL 61615 309-690-2200 692-5847
TF Sales: 800-635-7668 ■ *Web:* www.lrnelson.com

Oregon Cutting Systems Div Blount Inc
4909 SE International Way. Portland OR 97222 503-653-8881 653-4201
TF: 800-223-5168 ■ *Web:* www.oregonchain.com

Precision Products Inc 316 Limit St Lincoln IL 62656 217-735-1590 735-2435
TF Cust Svc: 800-225-5891 ■ *Web:* www.precisionprodinc.com

Price Howard Turf Equipment Inc 18155 Edison Ave Chesterfield MO 63005 636-532-7000 532-0201
Web: www.howardpriceturf.com

Rio Delmar Enterprises 8338 Elliott Rd PO Box 1409 Easton MD 21601 410-822-8866 822-9263
TF: 800-638-4402

Roeder Implement Co Inc 2804 Pembroke Rd. Hopkinsville KY 42240 270-886-3994 886-8752
TF: 800-844-3994 ■ *Web:* jddealer.deere.com/roederimplement/

Rotary Corp 801 W Barnart St PO Box 747 Glennville GA 30427 912-654-3433 654-3945
TF: 800-841-3989 ■ *Web:* www.rotarycorp.com

Rugg Mfg Co Inc 105 Newton St Greenfield MA 01302 413-773-5471 774-4354
TF: 800-633-8772 ■ *Web:* www.rugg.com

Simplicity Mfg Inc 500 N Spring St Port Washington WI 53074 262-284-8669 377-8202
Web: www.simplicitymfg.com

Snapper Inc 535 Macon St McDonough GA 30253 770-957-9141 957-7981
TF Cust Svc: 800-935-2967 ■ *Web:* www.snapperinc.com

Steiner Turf Equipment Inc 289 N Kurzen Rd Dalton OH 44618 330-828-0200 828-1008
Web: www.steinerturf.com

Stens Corp 2424 Cathy Ln. Jasper IN 47546 812-482-2526 482-1275
TF: 800-457-7444 ■ *Web:* www.stens.com

Stihl Inc 536 Viking Dr Virginia Beach VA 23452 757-486-9100 784-8576*
**Fax Area Code:* 888 ■ *TF Cust Svc:* 888-784-8575 ■ *Web:* www.stihlusa.com

Phone | Fax

Telsco Industries Inc Weathermatic 3301 W Kingsley Rd Garland TX 75041 972-278-6131 271-5710
TF: 888-484-3776 ■ *Web:* www.weathermatic.com

Toro Co 8111 Lyndale Ave. Bloomington MN 55420 952-888-8801 887-8258
NYSE: TTC ■ *TF:* 800-595-6841 ■ *Web:* www.toro.com

Toro Co Commercial Products Div 8111 Lyndale Ave Bloomington MN 55420 952-888-8801 887-8258
TF: 800-348-2424

Weathermatic 3301 W Kingsley Rd Garland TX 75041 972-278-6131 271-5710
TF: 888-484-3776 ■ *Web:* www.weathermatic.com

Westco Turf Supply 300 Technology Pk. Lake Mary FL 32746 407-333-3600 333-9246

Woods Equipment Co 2606 S Illinois Rt 2 Oregon IL 61061 815-732-2141 732-7580*
**Fax:* Sales ■ *TF:* 800-319-6637 ■ *Web:* www.woodsonline.com

433 LEATHER GOODS - PERSONAL

SEE ALSO Clothing & Accessories - Mfr p. 1449; Footwear p. 1665; Handbags, Totes, Backpacks p. 1769; Leather Goods (Misc) p. 1889; Luggage Stores p. XXXX; Luggage, Bags, Cases p. 1923

Phone | Fax

AD Sutton & Sons Inc 20 W 33rd St 2nd Fl. New York NY 10001 212-695-7070 695-8621
Web: www.adsutton.com

Berman Leather Co 2 Old New Milford Rd Suite 3-F Brookfield CT 06804 203-312-1300 312-1067
TF: 800-992-3762 ■ *Web:* www.bermanleather.com

Bosca Hugo Co Inc 1905 W Jefferson St Springfield OH 45506 937-323-5523 323-7063
TF: 800-732-6722 ■ *Web:* www.bosca.com

Bottega Veneta Inc 699 5th Ave New York NY 10022 212-371-5511 371-4361
TF: 877-362-1715 ■ *Web:* www.bottegaveneta.com

Buxton Co PO Box 1650 Springfield MA 01102 413-734-5900 785-1367
TF: 800-962-2813 ■ *Web:* www.buxton-dopp.com

California Optical Corp 2992 Alvarado St San Leandro CA 94577 510-352-4774 352-3714
TF: 800-523-5567 ■ *Web:* www.californiaoptical.com

Carroll Companies Inc PO Box 1549 Boone NC 28607 828-264-2521 264-2633
TF: 800-884-2521 ■ *Web:* www.clgco.com

Coach Inc 516 W 34th St New York NY 10001 212-594-1850 594-1682
NYSE: COH ■ *TF:* 800-444-3611 ■ *Web:* www.coach.com

Dooney & Bourke Inc 1 Regent St East Norwalk CT 06855 203-853-7515 838-7754
TF Cust Svc: 800-347-5000 ■ *Web:* www.dooney.com

Enger Kress Co 6510 Aurora Rd Suite C West Bend WI 53090 262-629-1553 629-1814
TF Cust Svc: 800-367-7547 ■ *Web:* www.engerkress.com

Etienne Aigner Group Inc 47 Brunswick Ave Edison NJ 08818 732-248-9200 248-1296
TF: 800-537-7463 ■ *Web:* www.etienneaigner.com

Hadley-Roma Watchband Corp 106 Corporate Pk Dr White Plains NY 10604 914-694-2000 694-1820
TF: 800-800-7662 ■ *Web:* www.hadleyroma.com

Humphreys Inc 2009 W Hastings St Chicago IL 60608 312-997-2358 997-2147
TF Cust Svc: 800-621-8541 ■ *Web:* www.humphreysinc.com

International Accessories 717 School St. Pawtucket RI 02860 401-725-4502 724-5180

Jaclyn Inc 197 W Spring Valley Ave Maywood NJ 07607 201-909-6000
AMEX: JLN ■ *Web:* www.jaclyninc.com

Louis Vuitton NA Inc 19 E 57th St New York NY 10022 212-931-2000 931-2097*
**Fax:* Mktg ■ *TF Cust Svc:* 866-884-8866 ■ *Web:* www.vuitton.com

Louis Vuitton US Mfg Inc 321 Covina Blvd San Dimas CA 91773 909-599-2411 394-0649
Web: www.louisvuitton.com

Penmar Inc PO Box 1235 Linden NJ 07038 908-523-0700
TF: 800-431-7890

Sharif Designs Ltd 34-12 36th Ave. Long Island City NY 11106 718-472-1100 937-2561

Stone Mountain Accessories 10 W 33rd St Suite 728 New York NY 10001 212-563-2500 564-2879
TF Cust Svc: 866-865-0786 ■ *Web:* www.stonemountainhandbags.com

Sutton AD & Sons Inc 20 W 33rd St 2nd Fl. New York NY 10001 212-695-7070 695-8621
Web: www.adsutton.com

Terner's of Miami Inc 3050 NW 40th St Miami FL 33142 305-638-7778 638-7712

TGL 300 Wilson Ave. Norwalk CT 06854 203-853-4747 853-0070

Trafalgar Ghurka Ltd 300 Wilson Ave. Norwalk CT 06854 203-853-4747 853-0070

Vuitton Louis US Mfg Inc 321 Covina Blvd San Dimas CA 91773 909-599-2411 394-0649
Web: www.louisvuitton.com

Westport Corp 40 E 34th St New York NY 10016 212-779-5900 779-3810
TF: 800-457-7782 ■ *Web:* www.mundiwestport.com

434 LEATHER GOODS (MISC)

Phone | Fax

Action Co 1425 N Tennessee St McKinney TX 75069 972-542-8700 562-7300
TF Sales: 800-937-3700 ■ *Web:* www.actioncompany.com

Auburn Leather Co 125 Caldwell St PO Box 338 Auburn KY 42206 270-542-4116 542-7107
TF: 800-635-0617 ■ *Web:* www.auburnleather.com

Brauer Brothers Mfg Co 345 Industrial Blvd McKinney TX 75069 314-231-2864 241-4952
TF: 800-527-2837 ■ *Web:* www.brauer-bros.com

Brockton Plastics Inc 230 Elliot St. Brockton MA 02302 508-587-2290 580-0524
Web: www.brocktonplastics.com

Capitol Saddlery 1614 Lavaca St Austin TX 78701 512-478-9309 474-2209
Web: www.capitolsaddlery.com

Carroll Companies Inc PO Box 1549 Boone NC 28607 828-264-2521 264-2633
TF: 800-884-2521 ■ *Web:* www.clgco.com

Chace Leather Products 507 Alden St Fall River MA 02723 508-678-7556 675-9666
TF: 800-272-4223 ■ *Web:* www.chaceleather.com

Champion Turf Equipment Inc 330 S Mission Rd Los Angeles CA 90033 323-264-0746 266-1244
TF: 800-421-6171

Circle Y of Yoakum Inc 201 W Morris St Yoakum TX 77995 361-293-5251 293-7192
TF: 800-531-3600 ■ *Web:* www.circley.com

Colorado Saddlery Co 1631 15th St PO Box 8538 Denver CO 80201 303-572-8350 692-7433*
**Fax Area Code:* 800 ■ *TF Cust Svc:* 800-521-2465 ■ *Web:* www.coloradosaddlery.com

Franklin Leddy Corp 2200 W Beauregard Ave San Angelo TX 76901 325-942-7655 942-7657

Garlin-Neumann Leathers Co Inc 66-D River Rd Hudson NH 03051 603-595-6319 881-9431
Web: garlinneumannleather.com

Gould & Goodrich Leather Inc 709 E McNeil St. Lillington NC 27546 910-893-2071 893-4742
TF: 800-277-0732 ■ *Web:* www.gouldusa.com

Hunter Co Inc 3300 W 71st Ave Westminster CO 80030 303-427-4626 428-3980
TF: 800-676-4868 ■ *Web:* www.huntercompany.com

Klein Tools Inc Fort Smith Div 5721-A S Zero St Fort Smith AR 72903 479-646-7347 648-1974
TF: 800-323-3664

Page Belting Co 24 Chenell Dr Concord NH 03301 603-225-5523 226-2790
TF: 800-258-3654 ■ *Web:* www.pagebelting.com

Robert F Lewis Inc 512 Woodstock Rd Woodstock VT 05091 802-457-1205

Safariland Ltd Inc 3120 E Mission Blvd. Ontario CA 91761 909-923-7300 923-7400
TF: 800-347-1200 ■ *Web:* www.safariland.com

Shoemaker Tex & Son Inc 714 W Cienega Ave San Dimas CA 91773 909-592-2071 592-2378
TF: 800-345-9959 ■ *Web:* www.texshoemaker.com

Simco Longhorn Leather Co Inc 1800 Daisy St Chattanooga TN 37406 423-624-3331 622-4096
TF Cust Svc: 800-251-6294 ■ *Web:* www.simcolonghorn.com

				Phone	Fax
Strong Group Inc 39 Grove St	Gloucester	MA	01930	978-281-3300	281-6321
TF Orders: 800-225-0724					
Tex Shoemaker & Son Inc 714 W Cienega Ave	San Dimas	CA	91773	909-592-2071	592-2378
TF: 800-345-9959 ■ *Web:* www.texshoemaker.com					
Tex Tan Western Leather Co 808 S US Hwy 77A	Yoakum	TX	77995	361-293-2314	293-2369
TF Cust Svc: 800-531-3608 ■ *Web:* www.textan.com					

435 LEATHER TANNING & FINISHING

				Phone	Fax
Bond Leather Co Inc 147 Summit St	Peabody	MA	01961	978-531-3227	531-2878
Carville National Leather Corp 10 Knox Ave PO Box 40	Johnstown	NY	12095	518-762-1634	762-8973
Web: www.carvillenational.com					
Cromwell Leather Co Inc 147 Palmer Ave	Mamaroneck	NY	10543	914-381-0100	381-0046
Web: www.cromwellgroup.com					
Cudahy Tanning Co Inc 5043 S Packard Ave PO Box 468	Cudahy	WI	53110	414-483-8100	483-2833
Web: www.cudahytanning.com					
Eagle Ottawa Leather Co LLC 2930 Auburn Rd	Rochester Hills	MI	48309	248-853-3122	853-6135
Web: www.eagleottawa.com					
Gloversville Embossing Corp 28-30 E 11th Ave	Gloversville	NY	12078	518-725-9116	725-8434
GST AutoLeather Inc 20 Oak Hollow Dr Suite 300	Southfield	MI	48034	248-436-2300	
Web: www.gstautoleather.com					
Gutmann Leather Co Inc 1511 W Webster Ave	Chicago	IL	60614	773-348-5300	348-7766
Hermann Oak Leather Co 4050 N 1st St	Saint Louis	MO	63147	314-421-1173	421-6152
TF: 800-325-7950 ■ *Web:* www.hermannoakleather.com					
Horween Leather Co 2015 N Elston Ave	Chicago	IL	60614	773-772-2026	772-9235
Web: www.horween.com					
Irving Tanning Co 9 Main St	Hartland	ME	04943	207-938-4491	938-2977*
**Fax:* Cust Svc ■ *Web:* www.irvingtanning.com					
North American Tanning Corp 224 W 35th St Suite 506	New York	NY	10001	212-643-1702	967-0068
Web: www.natanning.com					
Place WB LLC 368 W Sumner St	Hartford	WI	53027	262-673-3130	673-6233
TF: 800-826-4433 ■ *Web:* www.wbplace.com					
Salem Suede Inc 72 Flint St PO Box 708	Salem	MA	01970	978-744-1303	745-8044
Seidel Tanning Corp 1306 E Meinecke Ave	Milwaukee	WI	53212	414-562-4030	562-4445
Web: www.seideltanning.com					
Seton Co 1000 Madison Ave	Norristown	PA	19403	610-666-9600	666-1088
Simco Leather Corp 99 Pleasant Ave	Johnstown	NY	12095	518-762-7100	736-1514
Slip-Not Belting Corp 432 E Main St	Kingsport	TN	37660	423-246-8141	246-7728
Stahl USA 13 Corwin St	Peabody	MA	01961	978-531-0371	532-9062
Web: www.stahl.com					
WB Place LLC 368 W Sumner St	Hartford	WI	53027	262-673-3130	673-6233
TF: 800-826-4433 ■ *Web:* www.wbplace.com					
Wood & Hyde Leather Co Inc 68 Wood St	Gloversville	NY	12078	518-725-7105	725-5158
Web: www.woodandhyde.com					

436 LEGISLATION HOTLINES

				Phone	Fax
Legislative Information (LEGIS)	Washington	DC	20215	202-225-1772	
Alabama					
Bill Status-House State House 11 S Union St	Montgomery	AL	36130	334-242-7627	242-2489
Web: alisdb.legislature.state.al.us/acas					
Bill Status-Senate State House 11 S Union St Rm 716	Montgomery	AL	36130	334-242-7826	242-8819
TF: 800-499-3051 ■ *Web:* alisdb.legislature.state.al.us/acas					
Alaska Bill Status State Capitol MS 3100	Juneau	AK	99801	907-465-4648	465-2864
Web: www.legis.state.ak.us/basis					
Arizona Bill Status Capitol Complex 1700 W Washington St	Phoenix	AZ	85007	602-542-4900	542-4009
TF: 800-352-8404 ■ *Web:* www.azleg.state.az.us/legtext/bills.htm					
Arkansas					
Bill Status-House State Capitol Rm 350	Little Rock	AR	72201	501-682-7771	
Web: www.arkleg.state.ar.us					
Bill Status-Senate State Capitol Rm 320	Little Rock	AR	72201	501-682-5951	
Web: www.arkleg.state.ar.us					
California					
Bill Status-Assembly State Capitol Rm 3196	Sacramento	CA	95814	916-445-2323	
Web: www.leginfo.ca.gov/bilinfo.html					
Bill Status-Senate State Capitol Rm 3044	Sacramento	CA	95814	916-445-4251	445-4450
Web: www.leginfo.ca.gov/bilinfo.html					
Colorado Bill Status 200 E Colfax Ave	Denver	CO	80203	303-866-3055	866-4543
Web: www.leg.state.co.us					
Connecticut Bill Status Legislative Office Bldg	Hartford	CT	06106	860-240-0555	
Delaware Bill Status Legislative Hall PO Box 1401	Dover	DE	19903	302-739-4114	739-3895
Web: www.legis.state.de.us					
District of Columbia Bill Status					
1350 Pennsylvania Ave NW Suite 10	Washington	DC	20004	202-724-8050	
Web: www.dccouncil.washington.dc.us/lims/default.asp					
Florida Bill Status 111 W Madison St Rm 704	Tallahassee	FL	32399	850-488-4371	922-1534
TF: 800-342-1827 ■ *Web:* www.leg.state.fl.us					
Georgia					
Bill Status-House State Capitol Rm 309	Atlanta	GA	30334	404-656-5015	
Web: www.legis.state.ga.us					
Bill Status-Senate State Capitol Rm 353	Atlanta	GA	30334	404-656-5040	656-5043
Web: www.legis.state.ga.us					
Hawaii Bill Status 415 S Beretania St Rm 401	Honolulu	HI	96813	808-587-0478	587-0793
Web: www.capitol.hawaii.gov					
Idaho Bill Status PO Box 83720	Boise	ID	83720	208-334-2475	334-2125
Web: www3.state.id.us/legislat/legtrack.html					
Illinois Bill Status 705 Stratton Bldg	Springfield	IL	62706	217-782-3944	524-6059
Web: www.ilga.gov/legislation					
Indiana Bill Status					
State House 200 W Washington St Suite 301	Indianapolis	IN	46204	317-232-9856	
Web: www.in.gov/apps/lsa/session/billwatch					
Iowa Bill Status State Capitol Bldg Rm 16	Des Moines	IA	50319	515-281-5129	
Web: www.legis.state.ia.us/Bills.html					
Kansas Bill Status					
300 SW 10th Ave State Capitol Bldg Rm 343N	Topeka	KS	66612	785-296-3296	296-6650
Web: www.kslegislature.org					
Kentucky Bill Status					
State Capitol Bldg 700 Capitol Ave Rm 300	Frankfort	KY	40601	502-564-8100	564-6543
Web: www.lrc.state.ky.us/legislat/legislat.htm					
Louisiana Bill Status State Capitol 900 N 3rd St 13th Fl	Baton Rouge	LA	70804	225-342-2456	
TF: 800-256-3793 ■ *Web:* www.legis.state.la.us					
Maine Bill Status State House 100 State House Station	Augusta	ME	04333	207-287-1692	287-1580
Web: www.mainelegislature.org/legis/bills/					
Maryland Dept of Legislative Services 90 State Cir	Annapolis	MD	21401	410-946-5400	946-5405
TF: 800-492-7122 ■ *Web:* mlis.state.md.us					
Massachusetts Bill Status 1 Ashburton Pl Rm 1611	Boston	MA	02108	617-727-7030	742-4528
TF: 800-392-6090 ■ *Web:* www.mass.gov/legis/ltsform.htm					
Michigan Bill Status PO Box 30036	Lansing	MI	48909	517-373-0630	
Web: www.legislature.mi.gov					
Minnesota					
Bill Status-House 75 ML King Jr Blvd Rm 211	Saint Paul	MN	55155	651-296-6646	
Web: www.leg.state.mn.us/leg/legis.asp					
Bill Status-Senate 75 ML King Jr Blvd Rm 231	Saint Paul	MN	55155	651-296-2887	
Web: www.leg.state.mn.us/leg/legis.asp					
Mississippi Bill Status PO Box 1018	Jackson	MS	39215	601-359-3719	
Web: billstatus.ls.state.ms.us					
Missouri Bill Status 117A State Capitol	Jefferson City	MO	65101	573-751-4633	751-0130
Web: www.house.state.mo.us/jointsearch.asp					
Montana Legislative Services PO Box 201706	Helena	MT	59620	406-444-4800	444-3036
Web: leg.state.mt.us/css/bills					
Nebraska Bill Status 2018 State Capitol Bldg	Lincoln	NE	68509	402-471-2709	
Web: www.unicam.state.ne.us/					
Nevada Bill Status 401 S Carson St	Carson City	NV	89701	775-684-3360	
TF: 800-992-6761 ■ *Web:* www.leg.state.nv.us					
New Hampshire Bill Status 107 N Main St	Concord	NH	03301	603-271-3420	
Web: gencourt.state.nh.us					
New Jersey Bill Status State House Annex PO Box 068	Trenton	NJ	08625	609-292-4840	777-2440
TF: 800-792-8630 ■ *Web:* www.njleg.state.nj.us					
New Mexico Legislative Council Services					
490 Old Santa Fe Trail Rm 411	Santa Fe	NM	87501	505-986-4600	986-4680
Web: www.legis.state.nm.us					
New York (State) Bill Status 55 Elk St	Albany	NY	12210	518-455-7545	455-7681
TF: 800-342-9860 ■ *Web:* www.assembly.state.ny.us					
North Carolina Bill Status 16 W Jones St Rm 2226	Raleigh	NC	27601	919-733-7778	
Web: www.ncleg.net					
North Dakota Legislative Council Services					
State Capitol Bldg 600 E Boulevard Ave	Bismarck	ND	58505	701-328-2916	328-3615
Web: www.state.nd.us/lr					
Ohio Legislative Information Office 77 S High St	Columbus	OH	43215	614-466-8842	644-1721
TF: 800-282-0253 ■ *Web:* www.legislature.state.oh.us					
Oklahoma Legislation Service Bureau					
2300 N Lincoln Blvd Rm B30	Oklahoma City	OK	73105	405-521-4081	521-5507
Web: www.lsb.state.ok.us					
Oregon Publication & Distribution Services					
900 Court St NE Rm 49	Salem	OR	97310	503-986-1180	373-1527
Web: www.leg.state.or.us/bills_laws					
Pennsylvania Bill Status Main Capitol Bldg Rm 648	Harrisburg	PA	17120	717-787-2342	
Web: www.legis.state.pa.us					
Rhode Island Bill Status State House Rm 1	Providence	RI	02903	401-222-3580	
Web: www.rilin.state.ri.us					
South Carolina Bill Status PO Box 142	Columbia	SC	29201	803-212-6720	
Web: www.scstatehouse.net					
South Dakota Bill Status 500 E Capitol	Pierre	SD	57501	605-773-3251	
Web: legis.state.sd.us					
Tennessee Bill Status 320 6th Ave N 1st Fl	Nashville	TN	37243	615-741-3511	
Web: www.legislature.state.tn.us					
Texas Bill Status State Capitol 1100 Congress Ave Rm 2N-3	Austin	TX	78711	512-463-2182	475-4626
TF: 877-824-7038 ■ *Web:* www.capitol.state.tx.us					
Utah Bill Status 419 State Capitol	Salt Lake City	UT	84114	801-538-1588	538-1728
Web: le.utah.gov/Documents/bills.htm					
Vermont Bill Status 115 State St State House	Montpelier	VT	05633	802-828-2231	828-2424
Web: www.leg.state.vt.us					
Virginia Bill Status PO Box 406	Richmond	VA	23218	804-698-1500	786-3215
Web: legis.state.va.us					
Washington Bill Status PO Box 40600	Olympia	WA	98504	360-786-7573	
TF: 800-562-6000 ■ *Web:* www.leg.wa.gov					
West Virginia Bill Status State Capitol Rm MB27	Charleston	WV	25305	304-347-4831	347-4901
TF: 877-565-3447 ■ *Web:* www.legis.state.wv.us					
Wisconsin Bill Status 1 E Main St	Madison	WI	53708	608-266-9960	
TF: 800-362-9472 ■ *Web:* www.legis.state.wi.us					
Wyoming Legislative Service Office					
State Capitol Bldg Rm 213	Cheyenne	WY	82002	307-777-7881	777-5466
TF: 800-342-9570 ■ *Web:* legisweb.state.wy.us					

437 LIBRARIES

SEE ALSO Library Systems - Regional - Canadian p. 1912

437-1 Medical Libraries

				Phone	Fax
Alfred Taubman Medical Library					
University of Michigan 1135 E Catherine St Box 0726	Ann Arbor	MI	48109	734-764-1210	763-1473
Web: www.lib.umich.edu/taubman					
Allen Memorial Medical Library					
Case Western Reserve University 11000 Euclid Ave	Cleveland	OH	44106	216-368-3643	368-6396
Web: www.case.edu/chsl/allen.htm					
Allyn & Betty Taylor Library					
University of Western Ontario Natural Sciences Centre	London	ON	N6A5B7	519-661-3168	661-3435
Web: www.lib.uwo.ca/taylor					
Annette & Irwin Eskind Biomedical Library					
Vanderbilt University 2209 Garland Ave	Nashville	TN	37232	615-936-1400	936-1384
Web: www.mc.vanderbilt.edu/biolib					
Augustus C Long Health Sciences Library					
Columbia University 701 W 168th St	New York	NY	10032	212-305-3688	234-0595
Web: library.cpmc.columbia.edu/hsl/					
Bernard Becker Medical Library					
Washington University School of Medicine 660 S Euclid Ave CB 8132	Saint Louis	MO	63110	314-362-7080	454-6606
Web: becker.wustl.edu					
Bird Robert M Health Sciences Library					
University of Oklahoma Health Sciences Ctr 1000 Stanton L Young Blvd PO Box 26901	Oklahoma City	OK	73190	405-271-2285	271-3297
Web: library.ouhsc.edu					
Boston University School of Medicine Alumni Medical Library					
80 E Concord St	Boston	MA	02118	617-638-4232	638-4233
Web: med-libwww.bu.edu					
Bracken Health Sciences Library					
Queen's University Kingston Botterell Hall	Kingston	ON	K7L3N6	613-533-2510	533-6892
Web: library.queensu.ca/webmed					
Brown University Sciences Library 201 Thayer St Box 'I'	Providence	RI	02912	401-863-3333	863-2753
Web: www.brown.edu					
C Everett Koop Community Health Information Center					
College of Physicians of Philadelphia 19 S 22nd St	Philadelphia	PA	19103	215-563-3737	569-6477*
**Fax Area Code:* 205 ■ *Web:* www.collphyphil.org/chic.html					
Calder Louis Memorial Library					
University of Miami School of Medicine R-950 PO Box 016950	Miami	FL	33101	305-243-6648	325-9670
Web: calder.med.miami.edu					

Phone Fax

Carlson Loren D Health Sciences Library
University of California Davis 1 Shields Ave ... Davis CA 95616 530-752-1214 752-4718
Web: www.lib.ucdavis.edu/dept/hsl

Carpenter Coy C Library
Wake Forest University School of Medicine Medical Ctr Blvd ... Winston-Salem NC 27157 336-716-4691 716-2186
Web: www.wfubmc.edu/library

Chandler Medical Center Library
University of Kentucky 800 Rose St ... Lexington KY 40536 859-323-5727 323-1040
Web: www.mc.uky.edu/medlibrary

Charles A Dana Medical Library
University of Vermont Medical Education Center 81 Colchester Ave ... Burlington VT 05405 802-656-2201 656-0762
Web: library.uvm.edu/dana

Claude Moore Health Sciences Library
University of Virginia Health Science Ctr 1300 Jefferson Park Ave PO Box 800722 ... Charlottesville VA 22908 434-924-5444 982-4238

Cleveland Health Sciences Library
Case Western Reserve University Robbins Bldg 2109 Adelbert Rd ... Cleveland OH 44106 216-368-4540 368-3008
Web: www.case.edu/chsl/homepage.htm

Countway Francis A Library of Medicine
Harvard Medical School 10 Shattuck St ... Boston MA 02115 617-432-2136 432-4739
Web: www.countway.harvard.edu

Coy C Carpenter Library
Wake Forest University School of Medicine Medical Ctr Blvd ... Winston-Salem NC 27157 336-716-4691 716-2186
Web: www.wfubmc.edu/library

Creighton University Health Sciences Library
2500 California Plaza ... Omaha NE 68178 402-280-5108 280-5134
Web: www.hsl.creighton.edu

Crerar John Library University of Chicago 5730 S Ellis Ave ... Chicago IL 60637 773-702-7409 702-3317
Web: www.lib.uchicago.edu/e/crerar/home.html

Cushing Harvey/John Hay Whitney Medical Library
Yale University School of Medicine 333 Cedar St PO Box 208014 ... New Haven CT 06520 203-785-4356 785-5636
Web: www.med.yale.edu/library/

D Samuel Gottesman Library
Albert Einstein College of Medicine 1300 Morris Pk Ave ... Bronx NY 10461 718-430-3108 430-8795
Web: library.aecom.yu.edu

Dahlgren Memorial Library
Georgetown University Medical Ctr 3900 Reservoir Rd NW Box 571420 ... Washington DC 20057 202-687-1666 687-1862
Web: www.georgetown.edu/dml

Dana Biomedical Library Dartmouth College MS 6168 ... Hanover NH 03755 603-650-1658 650-1354
Web: www.dartmouth.edu/biomed

Dana Charles A Medical Library
University of Vermont Medical Education Center 81 Colchester Ave ... Burlington VT 05405 802-656-2201 656-0762
Web: library.uvm.edu/dana

Darling Louise M Biomedical Library
University of California Los Angeles 12-077 Ctr for the Health Sciences Box 951798 ... Los Angeles CA 90095 310-825-4904 825-0465
Web: www.library.ucla.edu/libraries/biomed

Del E Webb Memorial Library
Loma Linda University 11072 Anderson St ... Loma Linda CA 92354 909-558-4550 558-4188
Web: www.llu.edu/llu/library

Denison Memorial Library
University of Colorado Health Sciences Ctr 4200 E 9th Ave Box A-003 ... Denver CO 80262 303-315-7469 315-0294
Web: hsclibrary.uchsc.edu

Drexel University Library 245 N 15th St MS 449 ... Philadelphia PA 19102 215-762-7631 762-4028
Web: www.library.drexel.edu

Duke University Medical Center Library
103 Seeley Mudd Bldg DUMC 3702 ... Durham NC 27710 919-660-1150 681-7599
Web: www.mclibrary.duke.edu

Dykes Library
University of Kansas Medical Ctr 2100 W 39th Ave MS 1050 ... Kansas City KS 66160 913-588-7166 588-7304
Web: library.kumc.edu

Eccles Spencer S Health Sciences Library
University of Utah Health Sciences Ctr 10 N 1900 East Bldg 589 ... Salt Lake City UT 84112 801-581-8771 581-3632
TF: 866-581-5534 ■ *Web:* medlib.med.utah.edu

Edward G Miner Library
Univ of Rochester School of Medicine & Dentistry 601 Elmwood Ave ... Rochester NY 14642 585-275-3361 756-7762
Web: www.urmc.rochester.edu/hslt/miner

Edwin A Mirand Library
Roswell Pk Cancer Institute Elm & Carlton Sts ... Buffalo NY 14263 716-845-5966 845-8699
Web: www.roswellpark.org/document_120_97.html

Ehrman Medical Library
New York University Medical Ctr School of Medicine 550 1st Ave Rm 195 ... New York NY 10016 212-263-5393 263-6534
Web: library.med.nyu.edu

Eskind Annette & Irwin Biomedical Library
Vanderbilt University 2209 Garland Ave ... Nashville TN 37232 615-936-1400 936-1384
Web: www.mc.vanderbilt.edu/biolib

Falk Library of the Health Sciences
University of Pittsburgh 200 Scaife Hall ... Pittsburgh PA 15261 412-648-8866 648-9020
Web: www.hsls.pitt.edu/about/libraries/falk

Fordham Health Sciences Library
Wright State University 3640 Colonel Glenn Hwy ... Dayton OH 45435 937-775-2003 775-2232
Web: www.libraries.wright.edu/about/lochours/#fhsl

Francis A Countway Library of Medicine
Harvard Medical School 10 Shattuck St ... Boston MA 02115 617-432-2136 432-4739
Web: www.countway.harvard.edu

Galter Health Sciences Library
Northwestern University 303 E Chicago Ave Rm 2-212 ... Chicago IL 60611 312-503-8133 503-1204
Web: www.galter.northwestern.edu

George F Smith Library of the Health Sciences
Univ of Medicine & Dentistry of New Jersey 30 12th Ave Office C-932 ... Newark NJ 07103 973-972-8538 972-3870
Web: www.umdnj.edu/librweb/newarklib/library

George T Harrell Library
Pennsylvania State University College of Medicine 500 University Dr Milton S Hershey Medical Ctr H127 ... Hershey PA 17033 717-531-8626 531-8635
Web: www.hmc.psu.edu/library/

Gerstein Science Information Centre
University of Toronto 9 King's College Cir ... Toronto ON M5S1A5 416-978-2280 971-2848
Web: www.library.utoronto.ca/gerstein

Gibson D Lewis Library
University of North Texas Health Science Ctr 3500 Camp Bowie Blvd ... Fort Worth TX 76107 817-735-2380 735-5158
Web: library.hsc.unt.edu

Gottesman D Samuel Library
Albert Einstein College of Medicine 1300 Morris Pk Ave ... Bronx NY 10461 718-430-3108 430-8795
Web: library.aecom.yu.edu

Greenblatt Robert B MD Library
Medical College of Georgia 1459 Laney Walker Blvd ... Augusta GA 30912 706-721-3667 721-2018
Web: www.mcg.edu/library

Gustave L & Janet W Levy Library
Mt Sinai School of Medicine 1 Gustave L Levy Pl Box 1102 ... New York NY 10029 212-241-7892 241-4925
Web: www.mssm.edu/library

Hardin Library for the Health Sciences
University of Iowa 100 Hardin Library ... Iowa City IA 52242 319-335-9871 353-3752
Web: www.lib.uiowa.edu/hardin

Harrell George T Library
Pennsylvania State University College of Medicine 500 University Dr Milton S Hershey Medical Ctr H127 ... Hershey PA 17033 717-531-8626 531-8635
Web: www.hmc.psu.edu/library/

Harvey Cushing/John Hay Whitney Medical Library
Yale University School of Medicine 333 Cedar St PO Box 208014 ... New Haven CT 06520 203-785-4356 785-5636
Web: www.med.yale.edu/library/

Health Sciences Center Medical Library Shreveport
Louisiana State University Shreveport 1501 Kings Hwy ... Shreveport LA 71130 318-675-5445 675-5442
Web: lib.sh.lsuhsc.edu

Hill Lister Library of the Health Sciences
University of Alabama Birmingham 1530 3rd Ave S ... Birmingham AL 35294 205-934-2232 975-8313
Web: www.uab.edu/lister

Himmelfarb Health Sciences Library
George Washington University Medical Ctr 2300 Eye St NW ... Washington DC 20037 202-994-2850 994-4343
Web: www.gwumc.edu/library

Houston Academy of Medicine - Texas Medical Center Library
1133 John Freeman Blvd ... Houston TX 77030 713-795-4200 790-7052
Web: www.library.tmc.edu

Howard University Health Sciences Library 501 'W' St NW ... Washington DC 20059 202-884-1520 884-1506
Web: www.hsl.howard.edu

J Otto Lottes Health Sciences Library
University of Missouri Columbia Health Sciences Ctr 1 Hospital Dr HSL 327 ... Columbia MO 65212 573-882-4153 884-1421
Web: www.muhealth.org/library

John A Prior Health Sciences Library
Ohio State University 376 W 10th Ave ... Columbus OH 43210 614-292-4852 292-1920
Web: library.med.ohio-state.edu

John Crerar Library University of Chicago 5730 S Ellis Ave ... Chicago IL 60637 773-702-7409 702-3317
Web: www.lib.uchicago.edu/e/crerar/home.html

John W Scott Health Sciences Library
University of Alberta 2K3.28 Walter Mackenzie Center ... Edmonton AB T6G2R7 780-492-3899 492-6960
Web: www.library.ualberta.ca/aboutus/health

Kellogg WK Health Sciences Library
Dalhousie University 5850 College St Sir Charles Tupper Medical Bldg ... Halifax NS B3H1X5 902-494-2458 494-3750
Web: www.library.dal.ca/kellogg

Koop C Everett Community Health Information Center
College of Physicians of Philadelphia 19 S 22nd St ... Philadelphia PA 19103 215-563-3737 569-6477*
**Fax Area Code:* 205 ■ *Web:* www.collphyphil.org/chic.html

Kornhauser Health Sciences Library
University of Louisville 500 S Preston St ... Louisville KY 40202 502-852-5775 852-1631
Web: library.louisville.edu/kornhauser

Lamar Soutter Library
University of Massachusetts Medical School 55 Lake Ave N ... Worcester MA 01655 508-856-6099 856-5899
Web: library.umassmed.edu

Lane Medical Library
Stanford University Medical Ctr 300 Pasteur Dr Rm L-109 ... Stanford CA 94305 650-723-6831 725-7471
Web: lane.stanford.edu

Laupus William E Health Sciences Library
East Carolina University 600 Moye Blvd Health Sciences Bldg ... Greenville NC 27834 252-744-2230 744-3512
Web: www.ecu.edu/cs-dhs/laupuslibrary

Leon S McGoogan Library of Medicine
University of Nebraska Medical Ctr 986705 Nebraska Medical Ctr ... Omaha NE 68198 402-559-6221 559-5498
TF: 866-800-5209 ■ *Web:* www.unmc.edu/library

Levy Gustave L & Janet W Library
Mt Sinai School of Medicine 1 Gustave L Levy Pl Box 1102 ... New York NY 10029 212-241-7892 241-4925
Web: www.mssm.edu/library

Lewis Gibson D Library
University of North Texas Health Science Ctr 3500 Camp Bowie Blvd ... Fort Worth TX 76107 817-735-2380 735-5158
Web: library.hsc.unt.edu

Library of Rush University
Rush University Medical Center 600 S Paulina St 5th Fl ... Chicago IL 60612 312-942-5950 942-3143
Web: www.lib.rush.edu/library

Lilly Ruth Medical Library
Indiana University School of Medicine 975 W Walnut St Medical Research Bldg Rm 310 ... Indianapolis IN 46202 317-274-7182 278-2349
Web: www.medlib.iupui.edu

Lister Hill Library of the Health Sciences
University of Alabama Birmingham 1530 3rd Ave S ... Birmingham AL 35294 205-934-2232 975-8313
Web: www.uab.edu/lister

Lommen Health Sciences Library
University of South Dakota School of Medicine 414 E Clark St ... Vermillion SD 57069 605-677-5347 677-5124
Web: www.usd.edu/lhsl

Long Augustus C Health Sciences Library
Columbia University 701 W 168th St ... New York NY 10032 212-305-3688 234-0595
Web: library.cpmc.columbia.edu/hsl/

Loren D Carlson Health Sciences Library
University of California Davis 1 Shields Ave ... Davis CA 95616 530-752-1214 752-4718
Web: www.lib.ucdavis.edu/dept/hsl

Lottes J Otto Health Sciences Library
University of Missouri Columbia Health Sciences Ctr 1 Hospital Dr HSL 327 ... Columbia MO 65212 573-882-4153 884-1421
Web: www.muhealth.org/library

Louis Calder Memorial Library
University of Miami School of Medicine R-950 PO Box 016950 ... Miami FL 33101 305-243-6648 325-9670
Web: calder.med.miami.edu

Louise M Darling Biomedical Library
University of California Los Angeles 12-077 Ctr for the Health Sciences Box 951798 ... Los Angeles CA 90095 310-825-4904 825-0465
Web: www.library.ucla.edu/libraries/biomed

Loyola University Chicago Health Sciences Library
2160 S 1st Ave ... Maywood IL 60153 708-216-5301 216-6772
Web: library.luhs.org

Medical Libraries (Cont'd)

Phone | Fax

Lyman Maynard Stowe Library
University of Connecticut Health Ctr 263 Farmington Ave
PO Box 4003 … Farmington CT 06034 860-679-2839 679-1230
Web: library.uchc.edu

Maclean Neil John Health Sciences Library
University of Manitoba 770 Bannatyne Ave … Winnipeg MB R3E0W3 204-789-3464 789-3923
Web: www.umanitoba.ca/libraries/health/

Matthews-Fuller Health Sciences Library
Dartmouth College 1 Medical Center Dr MS 7300 … Lebanon NH 03756 603-650-7658 650-4372
Web: www.dartmouth.edu/~biomed

Mayo Foundation Mayo Medical Center Libraries
200 1st St SW … Rochester MN 55905 507-284-2061 284-1038
Web: www.mayo.edu/medlib

McGill University Life Sciences Library & Osler Library of the History of Medicine 3655 Sir William Osler Promenade
McIntyre Medical Sciences Bldg … Montreal QC H3G1Y6 514-398-4475 398-3890
Web: www.health.library.mcgill.ca

McGoogan Leon S Library of Medicine
University of Nebraska Medical Ctr 986705 Nebraska
Medical Ctr … Omaha NE 68198 402-559-6221 559-5498
TF: 866-800-5209 ■ *Web:* www.unmc.edu/library

McMaster University Health Sciences Library
1200 Main St W … Hamilton ON L8N3Z5 905-525-9140 528-3733
Web: hsl.mcmaster.ca

Medical University of South Carolina Library
171 Ashley Ave Suite 300 PO Box 250403 … Charleston SC 29425 843-792-2372 792-4900
Web: www.library.musc.edu

Meharry Medical College Library 1005 DB Todd Blvd … Nashville TN 37208 615-327-6318 327-6448
Web: library.mmc.edu

Memorial University of Newfoundland Health Sciences Library 300 Prince Philip Dr Health Science Ctr … Saint John's NL A1B3V6 709-777-6672 777-6866
Web: www.library.mun.ca/hsl/

Miner Edward G Library
Univ of Rochester School of Medicine & Dentistry 601
Elmwood Ave … Rochester NY 14642 585-275-3361 756-7762
Web: www.urmc.rochester.edu/hslt/miner

Mirand Edwin A Library
Roswell Pk Cancer Institute Elm & Carlton Sts … Buffalo NY 14263 716-845-5966 845-8699
Web: www.roswellpark.org/document_120_97.html

Moody Medical Library
University of Texas Medical Branch 301 University Blvd … Galveston TX 77555 409-772-2371 762-9782
Web: ar.utmb.edu/portals/mml_portal.asp

Moore Claude Health Sciences Library
University of Virginia Health Science Ctr 1300
Jefferson Park Ave PO Box 800722 … Charlottesville VA 22908 434-924-5444 982-4238

Mulford Raymon H Library
Medical College of Ohio Toledo 3045 Arlington Ave … Toledo OH 43614 419-383-4218 383-6146
Web: hsc.utoledo.edu/lib

National Institutes of Health (NIH)
Library 10 Center Dr MSC 1150 Bldg 10 … Bethesda MD 20892 301-496-5612 402-0254
Web: nihlibrary.nih.gov
National Library of Medicine
National Institutes of Health 8600 Rockville Pike Bldg 38 … Bethesda MD 20894 301-594-5983 402-1384
TF: 888-346-3656 ■ *Web:* www.nlm.nih.gov

Neil John Maclean Health Sciences Library
University of Manitoba 770 Bannatyne Ave … Winnipeg MB R3E0W3 204-789-3464 789-3923
Web: www.umanitoba.ca/libraries/health/

New York Academy of Medicine Library 1216 5th Ave … New York NY 10029 212-822-7315 423-0266
Web: www.nyam.org/library

New York Medical College Medical Sciences Library
95 Grasslands Rd Basic Science Bldg … Valhalla NY 10595 914-594-4200 594-3171
Web: library.nymc.edu

Norris Medical Library
University of Southern California 2003 Zonal Ave … Los Angeles CA 90089 323-442-1111 221-1235
Web: www.usc.edu/hsc/nml

Northeastern Ohio Universities College of Medicine Ocasek Library 4209 SR 44 PO Box 95 … Rootstown OH 44272 330-325-2511 325-6522
Web: www.neoucom.edu/audience/library

Oregon Health & Science University Library
3181 SW Sam Jackson Park Rd … Portland OR 97201 503-494-3460 494-3322
Web: www.ohsu.edu/library

Prior John A Health Sciences Library
Ohio State University 376 W 10th Ave … Columbus OH 43210 614-292-4852 292-1920
Web: library.med.ohio-state.edu

Raymon H Mulford Library
Medical College of Ohio Toledo 3045 Arlington Ave … Toledo OH 43614 419-383-4218 383-6146
Web: hsc.utoledo.edu/lib

Robert B Greenblatt MD Library
Medical College of Georgia 1459 Laney Walker Blvd … Augusta GA 30912 706-721-3667 721-2018
Web: www.mcg.edu/library

Robert M Bird Health Sciences Library
University of Oklahoma Health Sciences Ctr 1000
Stanton L Young Blvd PO Box 26901 … Oklahoma City OK 73190 405-271-2285 271-3297
Web: library.ouhsc.edu

Robert W Woodruff Health Sciences Center Library
Emory University 1462 Clifton Rd NE … Atlanta GA 30322 404-727-8727 727-5827
Web: www.healthlibrary.emory.edu

Rosalind Franklin University of Medicine & Science Learning Resource Center 3333 Green Bay Rd … North Chicago IL 60064 847-578-3242 578-3401
Web: www.rosalindfranklin.edu/lrc

Rowland Medical Library
University of Mississippi 2500 N State St … Jackson MS 39216 601-984-1231 984-1251
Web: library.umsmed.edu

Rutgers The State University of New Jersey Library of Science & Medicine 165 Bevier Rd … Piscataway NJ 08854 732-445-3854 445-5703
Web: www.libraries.rutgers.edu

Ruth Lilly Medical Library
Indiana University School of Medicine 975 W Walnut St
Medical Research Bldg Rm 310 … Indianapolis IN 46202 317-274-7182 278-2349
Web: www.medlib.iupui.edu

Saint Louis University Health Sciences Center Library
1402 S Grand Blvd … Saint Louis MO 63104 314-977-8800 977-5573
Web: www.slu.edu/libraries/hsc

Schaffer Library of the Health Sciences
Albany Medical College 47 New Scotland Ave … Albany NY 12208 518-262-5586 262-5820
Web: www.amc.edu/Academic/Schaffer

Scott John W Health Sciences Library
University of Alberta 2K3.28 Walter Mackenzie Center … Edmonton AB T6G2R7 780-492-3899 492-6960
Web: www.library.ualberta.ca/aboutus/health

Scott Memorial Library
Thomas Jefferson University 1020 Walnut St Rm 310 … Philadelphia PA 19107 215-503-8848 923-3203
Web: jeffline.jefferson.edu/sml/

Shiffman Medical Library Wayne State University 4325 Brush St … Detroit MI 48201 313-577-1088 577-6668
Web: www.lib.wayne.edu/shiffman

Phone | Fax

Shimberg Health Sciences Library
University of South Florida 12901 Bruce B Downs Blvd MDC
Box 31 … Tampa FL 33612 813-974-2243 974-4930
Web: hsc.usf.edu/library

Smith George F Library of the Health Sciences
Univ of Medicine & Dentistry of New Jersey 30 12th Ave
Office C-932 … Newark NJ 07103 973-972-8538 972-3870
Web: www.umdnj.edu/librweb/newarklib/library

Southern Illinois University School of Medicine Library
801 N Rutledge St PO Box 19625 … Springfield IL 62794 217-545-2122 545-0988
Web: www.siumed.edu/lib

Soutter Lamar Library
University of Massachusetts Medical School 55 Lake
Ave N … Worcester MA 01655 508-856-6099 856-5899
Web: library.umassmed.edu

Spencer S Eccles Health Sciences Library
University of Utah Health Sciences Ctr 10 N 1900 East
Bldg 589 … Salt Lake City UT 84112 801-581-8771 581-3632
TF: 866-581-5534 ■ *Web:* medlib.med.utah.edu

State University of New York at Buffalo Health Sciences Library
3435 Main St Abbott Hall Rm 102 … Buffalo NY 14214 716-829-3900 829-2211
Web: ublib.buffalo.edu/libraries/units/hsl

State University of New York Downstate Medical Center Medical Research Library of Brooklyn 450 Clarkson Ave
Box 14 … Brooklyn NY 11203 718-270-7401 270-7468
Web: servers.medlib.hscbklyn.edu

State University of New York Upstate Medical University Health Sciences Library 766 Irving Ave … Syracuse NY 13210 315-464-4582 464-7199
Web: www.upstate.edu/library

Stony Brook University Health Sciences Library
8034 SUNY HSC Level 3 Rm 136 … Stony Brook NY 11794 631-444-2512 444-6649
Web: www.hsclib.sunysb.edu

Stowe Lyman Maynard Library
University of Connecticut Health Ctr 263 Farmington Ave
PO Box 4003 … Farmington CT 06034 860-679-2839 679-1230
Web: library.uchc.edu

Taubman Alfred Medical Library
University of Michigan 1135 E Catherine St Box 0726 … Ann Arbor MI 48109 734-764-1210 763-1473
Web: www.lib.umich.edu/taubman

Taylor Allyn & Betty Library
University of Western Ontario Natural Sciences Centre … London ON N6A5B7 519-661-3168 661-3435
Web: www.lib.uwo.ca/taylor

Temple University Health Sciences Center Library
3440 N Broad St 2nd Fl Kresge Hall … Philadelphia PA 19140 215-707-4032 707-4135
Web: www.temple.edu/schools/libraries.html

Texas A & M University Medical Sciences Library
MS 4462 … College Station TX 77843 979-845-7428 845-7493

Texas Tech University Health Sciences Center Preston Smith Library of the Health Sciences 3601 4th St MS 7781 … Lubbock TX 79430 806-743-2203 743-2218
Web: www.ttuhsc.edu/libraries/

The Queen's Medical Center Hawaii Medical Library
1221 Punchbowl St … Honolulu HI 96813 808-547-4300 547-4019
Web: hml.org

Todd Wehr Library
Medical College of Wisconsin 8701 Watertown Plank Rd … Milwaukee WI 53226 414-456-8300 456-6532

Tompkins-McCaw Library
Virginia Commonwealth University 509 N 12th St PO
Box 980582 … Richmond VA 23298 804-828-0636 828-6089
Web: www.library.vcu.edu/tml

Tufts University Health Sciences Library 145 Harrison Ave … Boston MA 02111 617-636-6705 636-4039
Web: www.library.tufts.edu/hsl

Uniformed Services University of the Health Sciences Learning Resource Center 4301 Jones Bridge Rd … Bethesda MD 20814 301-295-3350 295-3795
Web: www.lrc.usuhs.mil

Universite Laval Bibliotheque Scientifique
Pavillon Alexandre-Vachon Cite Universitaire … Quebec QC G1K7P4 418-656-3967 656-7699
Web: www.bibl.ulaval.ca

Universite de Montreal
Bibliotheque de la Sante
2900 rue Edouard-Montpetit Rm L623 … Montreal QC H3C3J7 514-343-6826 343-2350
Web: www.bib.umontreal.ca/SA
Bibliotheque Paramedicale
2375 Cote Ste-Catherine Pavillion Marguerite d'Youville
Rm 2120 … Montreal QC H3T1A8 514-343-6180 343-2306
Web: www.bib.umontreal.ca

University of Arizona Arizona Health Sciences Library
1501 N Campbell Ave PO Box 245079 … Tucson AZ 85724 520-626-6121 626-2922
Web: www.ahsl.arizona.edu

University of Arkansas for Medical Sciences Medical Library
4301 W Markham St Slot 586 … Little Rock AR 72205 501-686-5980 686-6745
Web: www.library.uams.edu

University of Calgary Health Sciences Library
3330 Hospital Dr NW … Calgary AB T2N4N1 403-220-6855 282-7992
Web: library.ucalgary.ca/branches/healthscienceslibrary

University of California Irvine Science Library PO Box 19557 … Irvine CA 92623 949-824-3692 824-4851
Web: www.lib.uci.edu/libraries/science.html

University of California San Diego Biomedical Library
9500 Gilman Dr MC-0699 … La Jolla CA 92093 858-534-3253 534-6609
Web: scilib.ucsd.edu/bml

University of California San Diego Medical Center Library
216 W Dickinson St … San Diego CA 92103 619-543-6520 543-3289

University of California San Francisco Library & Center for Knowledge Management 530 Parnassus Ave Box 0840 … San Francisco CA 94143 415-476-8293 476-4653
Web: www.library.ucsf.edu

University of Cincinnati Medical Center Libraries
231 Albert Sabin Way PO Box 670574 … Cincinnati OH 45267 513-558-5656 558-2682
Web: aitl.uc.edu

University of Florida Health Science Center Library
1600 SW Archer Rd PO Box 100206 … Gainesville FL 32610 352-392-4016 392-2565
Web: www.library.health.ufl.edu

University of Illinois Chicago Library of the Health Sciences
1750 W Polk St MC 763 … Chicago IL 60612 312-996-8974 996-1899
Web: www.uic.edu/depts/lib/lhsc

University of Maryland Baltimore Health Sciences & Human Services Library 601 W Lombard St … Baltimore MD 21201 410-706-7928 706-8403
Web: www.hshsl.umaryland.edu

University of Minnesota Twin Cities Bio-Medical Library
505 Essex St SE 325 Diehl Hall … Minneapolis MN 55455 612-626-0998 626-5822
Web: www.biomed.lib.umn.edu

University of Nebraska Medical Center McGoogan Library of Medicine 986705 Nebraska Medical Ctr … Omaha NE 68198 402-559-4006 559-5498
Web: www.unmc.edu/library

University of North Carolina Chapel Hill Health Sciences Library CB 7585 … Chapel Hill NC 27599 919-962-0800 966-5592
Web: www.hsl.unc.edu

Name / Address	City	State	Zip	Phone	Fax
University of Ottawa Health Sciences Library 451 Smyth Rd Rm 1020 *Web:* www.biblio.uottawa.ca/health/	Ottawa	ON	K1H8M5	613-562-5407	562-5401
University of Pennsylvania Biomedical Library 3610 Hamilton Walk Johnson Pavilion *Web:* www.library.upenn.edu/biomed	Philadelphia	PA	19104	215-898-5817	573-4143
University of Saskatchewan Health Sciences Library 107 Wiggins Rd Suite B-205 *Web:* library.usask.ca/hsl	Saskatoon	SK	S7N5E5	306-966-5991	966-5918
University of South Carolina School of Medicine Library 6311 Garners Ferry Rd *Web:* uscm.med.sc.edu	Columbia	SC	29208	803-733-3344	733-1509
University of Tennessee Health Science Center Health Sciences Library & Biocommunications Center 877 Madison Ave *TF:* 877-747-0004 ■ *Web:* library.utmem.edu	Memphis	TN	38163	901-448-5404	448-7235
University of Texas Health Science Center San Antonio Libraries 7703 Floyd Curl Dr MSC 7940 *Web:* www.library.uthscsa.edu	San Antonio	TX	78229	210-567-2400	567-2490
University of Texas Southwestern Medical Center Dallas Library 5323 Harry Hines Blvd *Web:* www4.utsouthwestern.edu/library	Dallas	TX	75390	214-648-2626	648-2826
University of Washington Health Sciences Libraries & Information Center 1959 NE Pacific St Box 357155 *Web:* healthlinks.washington.edu/hsl	Seattle	WA	98195	206-543-3390	543-8066
University of Wisconsin Madison Ebling Library 750 Highland Ave *Web:* ebling.library.wisc.edu	Madison	WI	53705	608-262-2020	262-4732
Webb Del E Memorial Library Loma Linda University 11072 Anderson St *Web:* www.llu.edu/llu/library	Loma Linda	CA	92354	909-558-4550	558-4188
Wehr Todd Library Medical College of Wisconsin 8701 Watertown Plank Rd	Milwaukee	WI	53226	414-456-8300	456-6532
Weill Cornell Medical Library Weill Medical College of Cornell University 1300 York Ave Rm C115 *Web:* library.med.cornell.edu	New York	NY	10021	212-746-6050	746-6494
Welch William H Medical Library Johns Hopkins University 1900 E Monument St *Web:* www.welch.jhu.edu	Baltimore	MD	21205	410-955-3411	614-9555
West Virginia University Health Sciences Ctr Library PO Box 9801 *Web:* www.hsc.wvu.edu/library	Morgantown	WV	26506	304-293-2113	293-5995
William E Laupus Health Sciences Library East Carolina University 600 Moye Blvd Health Sciences Bldg *Web:* www.ecu.edu/cs-dhs/laupuslibrary	Greenville	NC	27834	252-744-2230	744-3512
William H Welch Medical Library Johns Hopkins University 1900 E Monument St *Web:* www.welch.jhu.edu	Baltimore	MD	21205	410-955-3411	614-9555
WK Kellogg Health Sciences Library Dalhousie University 5850 College St Sir Charles Tupper Medical Bldg *Web:* www.library.dal.ca/kellogg	Halifax	NS	B3H1X5	902-494-2458	494-3750
Woodruff Robert W Health Sciences Center Library Emory University 1462 Clifton Rd NE *Web:* www.healthlibrary.emory.edu	Atlanta	GA	30322	404-727-8727	727-5827
Woodward Biomedical Library University of British Columbia 2198 Health Sciences Mall *Web:* www.library.ubc.ca/woodward	Vancouver	BC	V6T1Z3	604-822-2883	822-5596

437-2 Presidential Libraries

Name / Address	City	State	Zip	Phone	Fax
Abraham Lincoln Presidential Library & Museum 112 N 6th St *TF:* 800-610-2094 ■ *Web:* www.alincoln-library.com	Springfield	IL	62701	217-524-7216	785-6250
Dwight D Eisenhower Presidential Library & Museum 200 SE 4th St *TF:* 877-746-4453 ■ *Web:* www.eisenhower.utexas.edu	Abilene	KS	67410	785-263-6700	263-6715
Franklin D Roosevelt Presidential Library & Museum 4079 Albany Post Rd *TF:* 800-337-8474 ■ *Web:* www.fdrlibrary.marist.edu	Hyde Park	NY	12538	845-229-8114	486-1147
George Bush Library & Museum 1000 George Bush Dr W *Web:* bushlibrary.tamu.edu	College Station	TX	77845	979-691-4000	691-4050
Gerald R Ford Library 1000 Beal Ave *Web:* www.fordlibrarymuseum.gov	Ann Arbor	MI	48109	734-205-0555	205-0571
Harry S Truman Presidential Library & Museum 500 W Hwy 24 *TF:* 800-833-1225 ■ *Web:* www.trumanlibrary.org	Independence	MO	64050	816-833-1400	833-4368
Herbert Hoover Presidential Library & Museum 210 Parkside Dr *Web:* www.hoover.archives.gov	West Branch	IA	52358	319-643-5301	643-5825
Jimmy Carter Library & Museum 441 Freedom Pkwy *Web:* www.jimmycarterlibrary.org	Atlanta	GA	30307	404-865-7100	865-7102
John F Kennedy Library & Museum Columbia Point *TF:* 866-535-1960 ■ *Web:* www.jfklibrary.org	Boston	MA	02125	617-514-1600	514-1652
Lyndon B Johnson Library & Museum 2313 Red River St *Web:* www.lbjlib.utexas.edu	Austin	TX	78705	512-721-0200	721-0170
Richard M Nixon Library & Birthplace 18001 Yorba Linda Blvd *Web:* www.nixonfoundation.org	Yorba Linda	CA	92886	714-993-5075	528-0544
Ronald Reagan Presidential Library & Museum 40 Presidential Dr *TF:* 800-410-8354 ■ *Web:* www.reagan.utexas.edu	Simi Valley	CA	93065	805-577-4000	577-4074
Rutherford B Hayes Presidential Center Spiegel Grove *TF:* 800-998-7737 ■ *Web:* www.rbhayes.org	Fremont	OH	43420	419-332-2081	332-4952
William J Clinton Presidential Center 1200 President Clinton Ave *Web:* www.clintonfoundation.org/cpc-index.htm	Little Rock	AR	72201	501-370-8000	375-0512
Woodrow Wilson Presidential Library 18-24 N Coalter St PO Box 24 *Web:* www.woodrowwilson.org	Staunton	VA	24402	540-885-0897	886-9874

437-3 Public Libraries

Listings for public libraries are alphabetized by city name within each state grouping.

Alabama

Name / Address	City	State	Zip	Phone	Fax
Aliceville Public Library 416 3rd Ave NE *Web:* home.nctv.com/apl	Aliceville	AL	35442	205-373-6691	373-3731
Public Library of Anniston & Calhoun County PO Box 308 *Web:* www.anniston.lib.al.us	Anniston	AL	36202	256-237-8501	238-0474
Escambia County Library System 700 E Church St	Atmore	AL	36502	251-368-4130	
Auburn Public Library 749 E Thach Ave *Web:* www.auburnalabama.org/library	Auburn	AL	36830	334-501-3190	
Bay Minette Public Library 205 W 2nd St *Web:* www.bayminettepubliclibrary.org	Bay Minette	AL	36507	251-580-1648	937-0339
Bessemer Public Library 701 9th Ave N *Web:* bessemer.lib.al.us	Bessemer	AL	35020	205-428-7882	428-7885
Birmingham Public Library 2100 Park Pl *Web:* www.bham.lib.al.us	Birmingham	AL	35203	205-226-3600	226-3731
Brewton Public Library 206 W Jackson St *Web:* www.apls.state.al.us	Brewton	AL	36426	251-867-4626	809-1749
Choctaw County Public Library 124 N Academy Ave *Web:* www.pinebelt.net/ccpl	Butler	AL	36904	205-459-2542	459-4122
Harrison Regional Library 50 Lester St *Web:* www.shelbycounty-al.org	Columbiana	AL	35051	205-669-3910	669-3940
Cullman County Public Library System 200 Clark St NE *Web:* www.ccpls.com	Cullman	AL	35055	256-734-1068	734-6902
Horseshoe Bend Regional Library 207 N West St *Web:* www.mindspring.com/~hbrl/hbrl.html	Dadeville	AL	36853	256-825-9232	825-4314
Wheeler Basin Regional Library PO Box 1766	Decatur	AL	35602	256-353-2993	350-6736
Florence-Lauderdale Public Library 350 N Wood Ave *Web:* www.flpl.lib.al.us	Florence	AL	35630	256-764-6564	764-6629
Gadsden Public Library 2829 W Meighan Blvd *Web:* www.library.gadsden.com	Gadsden	AL	35904	256-549-4699	549-4766
Guntersville Public Library 1240 O'Brig Ave *Web:* www.guntersvillelibrary.org	Guntersville	AL	35976	256-571-7595	571-7596
Cheaha Regional Library 935 Coleman St *Web:* www.cheaharegionallibrary.org	Heflin	AL	36264	256-463-7125	463-7128
Hoover Public Library 200 Municipal Dr *Web:* www.hoover.lib.al.us	Hoover	AL	35216	205-444-7800	444-7878
Hueytown Public Library 1372 Hueytown Rd *Web:* www.hueytown.com/htnlib.htm	Hueytown	AL	35023	205-491-1443	491-6319
Huntsville-Madison County Public Library 915 Monroe St *Web:* hpl.lib.al.us	Huntsville	AL	35801	256-532-5940	532-5997
Carl Elliott Regional Library 98 E 18th St	Jasper	AL	35501	205-221-2568	221-2584
Mobile Public Library 704 Government St *Web:* www.mplonline.org	Mobile	AL	36602	251-208-7076	208-7137
Montgomery City-County Public Library 245 High St *Web:* www.mccpl.lib.al.us	Montgomery	AL	36104	334-240-4999	240-4980
Lawrence County Public Library 401 College St *Web:* www.lawrencecountypublic.org	Moulton	AL	35650	256-974-0883	974-0890
Cross Trails Regional Library PO Box 770	Opp	AL	36467	334-493-9526	493-7503
Baldwin County Cooperative Library 22743 Milwaukee St PO Box 399 *Web:* www.gulftel.com/bclc	Robertsdale	AL	36567	251-947-7632	947-2651
Troy Public Library 300 N Three Notch St	Troy	AL	36081	334-566-1314	566-4392
Tuscaloosa Public Library 1801 Jack Warner Pkwy *Web:* www.tuscaloosa-library.org	Tuscaloosa	AL	35401	205-345-5820	758-1735
Bradshaw-Chambers County Public Library 3419 20th Ave *Web:* www.chamberscountylibrary.org	Valley	AL	36854	334-768-2161	768-7272

Alaska

Name / Address	City	State	Zip	Phone	Fax
ZJ Loussac Library 3600 Denali St *Web:* lexicon.ci.anchorage.ak.us	Anchorage	AK	99503	907-343-2975	343-2930
Big Lake Public Library PO Box 520829 *Web:* www.matsulibraries.org/biglake/	Big Lake	AK	99652	907-892-6475	892-6546
Fairbanks North Star Borough Public Library 1215 Cowles St *Web:* library.fnsb.lib.ak.us	Fairbanks	AK	99701	907-459-1020	459-1024
Homer Public Library 141 W Pioneer Ave *Web:* library.ci.homer.ak.us	Homer	AK	99603	907-235-3180	235-3136
Juneau Public Library 292 Marine Way *Web:* www.juneau.lib.ak.us/library/jpl.htm	Juneau	AK	99801	907-586-5324	586-3419

Arizona

Name / Address	City	State	Zip	Phone	Fax
Apache Junction Public Library 1177 N Idaho Rd *Web:* www.ajpl.org	Apache Junction	AZ	85219	480-983-0204	983-4540
Cochise County Library District PO Drawer AK *Web:* cochise.lib.az.us	Bisbee	AZ	85603	520-432-8930	432-7339
Chandler Public Library 22 S Delaware St *Web:* chandlerlibrary.org	Chandler	AZ	85225	480-782-2800	782-2823
Cottonwood Public Library 100 S 6th St	Cottonwood	AZ	86326	928-634-7559	634-0253
Flagstaff City-Coconino County Public Library System 300 W Aspen Ave *Web:* www.flagstaffpubliclibrary.org	Flagstaff	AZ	86001	928-779-7670	774-9573
Pinal County Library District 92 W Butte Ave *Web:* co.pinal.az.us/library/	Florence	AZ	85232	520-866-6457	866-6533
Southeast Regional Library 775 N Greenfield Rd	Gilbert	AZ	85234	480-539-5100	539-5159
Glendale Public Library 5959 W Brown St *Web:* www.glendaleaz.com/Library	Glendale	AZ	85302	623-930-3530	842-4209
Mesa Public Library 64 E 1st St *Web:* www.mesalibrary.org	Mesa	AZ	85201	480-644-2207	644-3490
Nogales City/Santa Cruz County Public Library 518 N Grand Ave	Nogales	AZ	85621	520-287-3343	287-4823
Page Public Library 479 Lake Powell Blvd *Web:* www.cityofpage.org	Page	AZ	86040	928-645-4270	645-5804
Peoria Public Library 8401 W Monroe Ave *Web:* www.peoriaaz.com/library.htm	Peoria	AZ	85345	623-773-7555	773-7567
Maricopa County Library District 17811 N 32nd St *Web:* www.maricopa.gov/library	Phoenix	AZ	85032	602-506-2950	506-4689
Phoenix Public Library 1221 N Central Ave *Web:* www.phoenixpubliclibrary.org	Phoenix	AZ	85004	602-534-2468	261-8836
Safford City - Graham County Library 808 7th Ave	Safford	AZ	85546	928-428-1531	348-3209
Scottsdale Public Library System 3839 N Drinkwater Blvd *Web:* library.ci.scottsdale.az.us	Scottsdale	AZ	85251	480-312-2474	312-7993
Tucson-Pima Public Library 101 N Stone Ave *Web:* www.library.pima.gov/index.cfm	Tucson	AZ	85701	520-791-4393	791-3213
Navajo Nation Library System PO Box 9040 *Web:* www.nnlib.org	Window Rock	AZ	86515	928-871-6526	871-7304

Arkansas

Name / Address	City	State	Zip	Phone	Fax
Arkansas River Valley Regional Library 501 N Front St *Web:* www.arvrls.com	Dardanelle	AR	72834	479-229-4418	229-2595
Barton Library 200 E 5th St	El Dorado	AR	71730	870-863-5447	862-3944
Washington County Library System 1080 W Clydesdale Dr *Web:* wcls.lib.ar.us	Fayetteville	AR	72701	479-442-6253	442-6812

Public Libraries (Cont'd)

Arkansas (Cont'd)

				Phone	Fax

Fort Smith Public Library 3201 Rogers Ave. Fort Smith AR 72903 479-783-0229 783-5129
Web: www.fspl.lib.ar.us
Southwest Arkansas Regional Library 500 S Elm St. Hope AR 71801 870-777-2957 777-2957
Crowley Ridge Regional Library 315 W Oak St Jonesboro AR 72401 870-935-5133 935-7987
Web: www.libraryinjonesboro.org
Central Arkansas Library System 100 Rock St Little Rock AR 72201 501-918-3000 375-7451
Web: www.cals.lib.ar.us
Baxter County Library 424 W 7th St. Mountain Home AR 72653 870-425-3598 425-7226
Web: www.baxtercountylibrary.org
William F Laman Public Library 2801 Orange St. North Little Rock AR 72114 501-758-1720 758-3539
Web: www.laman.net
Pope County Library System 116 E 3rd St. Russellville AR 72801 479-968-4368 968-3222
White County Public Library 113 E Pleasure St. Searcy AR 72143 501-268-2449 268-5682
West Memphis Public Library 213 N Avalon St. West Memphis AR 72301 870-732-7590 732-7636

California

				Phone	Fax

Alameda Free Library 2200A Central Ave. Alameda CA 94501 510-747-7777 337-1471
Web: www.ci.alameda.ca.us/library
Boys & Girls Library 2200A Central Ave. Alameda CA 94501 510-747-7705 337-1471
Alhambra Public Library 410 W Main St Alhambra CA 91801 626-570-5008 457-1104
Web: www.alhambralibrary.org
Anaheim Public Library 500 W Broadway Anaheim CA 92805 714-765-1880 765-1730
Web: www.anaheim.net/comm_svc/apl
Arcadia Public Library 20 W Duarte Rd. Arcadia CA 91006 626-821-5569 447-8050
Web: www.ci.arcadia.ca.us/home/index.asp?page=664
Placer County Library 350 Nevada St. Auburn CA 95603 530-886-4500 886-4555
Web: www.placer.ca.gov/library
Azusa City Library 729 N Dalton Ave Azusa CA 91702 626-812-5232 334-4868
Web: www.ci.azusa.ca.us/library
Beale Memorial Library 701 Truxtun Ave. Bakersfield CA 93301 661-868-0701 868-0799
Web: www.kerncountylibrary.org/beale.html
Beaumont Library District 125 E 8th St. Beaumont CA 92223 951-845-1357 845-6217
Web: www.bld.lib.ca.us
Benicia Public Library 150 E 'L' St Benicia CA 94510 707-746-4343 747-8122
Web: www.ci.benicia.ca.us/library.html
Berkeley Public Library 2090 Kittredge St. Berkeley CA 94704 510-981-6100 981-6111
Web: www.berkeleypubliclibrary.org
Beverly Hills Public Library 444 N Rexford Dr Beverly Hills CA 90210 310-288-2220 278-3387
Web: www.bhpl.org
Burbank Central Library 110 N Glenoaks Blvd. Burbank CA 91502 818-238-5600 238-5553
Web: www.burbank.lib.ca.us
Burlingame Public Library 480 Primrose Rd Burlingame CA 94010 650-342-1038 342-1948
Web: www.burlingame.org/library
Carlsbad City Library 1250 Carlsbad Village Dr Carlsbad CA 92008 760-434-2870 434-9975
Cerritos Public Library 18025 Bloomfield Ave Cerritos CA 90703 562-916-1350 916-1375
Web: www.ci.cerritos.ca.us/library/library.html
Chula Vista Public Library 365 F St. Chula Vista CA 91910 619-691-5069 427-4246
Web: www.chulavistalibrary.com
Colton Public Library 656 N 9th St Colton CA 92324 909-370-5083 422-0873
Corona Public Library 650 S Main St. Corona CA 92882 951-736-2382 736-2499
Web: www.coronapubliclibrary.org
Coronado Public Library 640 Orange Ave. Coronado CA 92118 619-522-7390 522-0326
Web: coronado.lib.ca.us
Covina Public Library 234 N 2nd Ave. Covina CA 91723 626-967-3935 915-8915
Daly City Public Library 40 Wembley Dr Daly City CA 94015 650-991-8025 991-8225
Web: www.dalycitylibrary.org
Dixon Public Library 230 N 1st St Dixon CA 95620 707-678-5447 678-3515
Web: www.dixonlibrary.com
Downey City Library 11121 Brookshire Ave Downey CA 90241 562-923-3256 923-3763
Web: www.downeylibrary.org
Los Angeles County Public Library 7400 E Imperial Hwy Downey CA 90242 562-940-8462 803-3032
Web: www.colapublib.org
El Centro Public Library 539 State St. El Centro CA 92243 760-337-4565 352-1384
Web: www.cityofelcentro.org/library
Imperial County Free Library 1125 Main St. El Centro CA 92243 760-482-4791 482-4792
Web: www.imperialcounty.net/library/
Escondido Public Library 239 S Kalmia St. Escondido CA 92025 760-839-4601 741-4255
Web: www.ci.escondido.ca.us/library
Humboldt County Library 1313 3rd St Eureka CA 95501 707-269-1900 269-1999
Web: www.humlib.org
Solano County Library 1150 Kentucky St Fairfield CA 94533 707-421-6510 421-7474
Web: www.solanolibrary.com
Alameda County Library 2450 Stevenson Blvd. Fremont CA 94538 510-745-1500 793-2987
Web: aclibrary.org
Fremont Main Library 2400 Stevenson Blvd. Fremont CA 94538 510-745-1400 797-6557
Web: www.aclibrary.org/siteindex.asp
Fresno County Free Library 2420 Mariposa St. Fresno CA 93721 559-488-3184 488-1971
Web: www.fresnolibrary.org
Fullerton Public Library 353 W Commonwealth Ave Fullerton CA 92832 714-738-6333 447-3280
Web: www.ci.fullerton.ca.us/library
Garden Grove Regional Library 11200 Stanford Ave Garden Grove CA 92840 714-530-0711
Web: www.ocpl.org
Glendale Public Library 222 E Harvard St Glendale CA 91205 818-548-2021 548-7225
Web: www.glendalepubliclibrary.org
Glendora Public Library & Cultural Center
140 S Glendora Ave. Glendora CA 91741 626-852-4891 852-4899
Web: www.ci.glendora.ca.us/library/
Kings County Library 401 N Douty St. Hanford CA 93230 559-582-0261 583-6163
Web: www.kingscountylibrary.org
Hayward Public Library 835 C St Hayward CA 94541 510-293-8685 733-6669
Web: www.library.ci.hayward.ca.us
Hemet Public Library 300 E Latham Ave Hemet CA 92543 951-765-2440 765-2446
San Benito County Free Library 470 5th St. Hollister CA 95023 831-636-4107 636-4099
Web: www.sanbenitofl.org
Huntington Beach Public Library 7111 Talbert Ave. Huntington Beach CA 92648 714-842-4481 375-5180
Web: www.hbpl.org
Inglewood Public Library 101 W Manchester Blvd Inglewood CA 90301 310-412-5397 412-8848
Amador County Library 530 Sutter St. Jackson CA 95642 209-223-6400 223-6303
Web: www.co.amador.ca.us/depts/library/index.htm
Lake County Library 1425 N High St Lakeport CA 95453 707-263-8816 263-6796
Livermore Public Library 1188 S Livermore Ave Livermore CA 94550 925-373-5500 373-5503
Web: www.livermore.lib.ca.us
Lodi Public Library 201 W Locust St Lodi CA 95240 209-333-5566 367-5944
Web: www.lodi.gov/library
Lompoc Public Library 501 E North Ave. Lompoc CA 93436 805-736-3477
Web: www.cityoflompoc.com/departments/library
Long Beach Public Library 101 Pacific Ave Long Beach CA 90822 562-570-7500 570-7408
Web: www.lbpl.org

				Phone	Fax

Braille Institute of America Library Services
741 N Vermont Ave Los Angeles CA 90029 323-660-3880 663-0867
Web: www.braillelibrary.org
Los Angeles Public Library 630 W 5th St Los Angeles CA 90071 213-228-7000 228-7369
Web: www.lapl.org
Los Gatos Public Library 110 E Main St. Los Gatos CA 95030 408-354-6891 399-5755
Web: library.town.los-gatos.ca.us
Madera County Library 121 N 'G' St. Madera CA 93637 559-675-7871 675-7998
Web: www.madera-county.com/library
Yuba County Library 303 2nd St. Marysville CA 95901 530-749-7380 741-3098
Web: www.co.yuba.ca.us/library
Menlo Park Public Library 800 Alma St. Menlo Park CA 94025 650-330-2501 327-7030
Web: www.menloparklibrary.org
Merced County Library 2100 'O' St Merced CA 95340 209-385-7643 726-7912
Web: web.co.merced.ca.us/library
Mill Valley Public Library 375 Throckmorton Ave. Mill Valley CA 94941 415-389-4292 388-8929
Web: www.millvalleylibrary.org
Stanislaus County Library 1500 'I' St. Modesto CA 95354 209-558-7800 529-4779
Web: www.stanislauslibrary.org
Monrovia Public Library 321 S Myrtle Ave. Monrovia CA 91016 626-256-8274 256-8255
Monterey Public Library 625 Pacific St Monterey CA 93940 831-646-3932 646-5618
Web: www.monterey.org/library
Bruggemeyer Memorial Library 318 S Ramona Ave Monterey Park CA 91754 626-307-1418 288-4251
Mountain View Public Library 585 Franklin St. Mountain View CA 94041 650-903-6335 962-0438
Web: library.ci.mtnview.ca.us
Napa City-County Library 580 Coombs St Napa CA 94559 707-253-4241 253-4615
Web: www.co.napa.ca.us/library
National City Public Library 1401 National City Blvd. National City CA 91950 619-470-5800 470-5880
Web: www.ci.national-city.ca.us
Nevada County Library 980 Helling Way. Nevada City CA 95959 530-265-7050 265-7241
Web: www.mynevadacounty.com/library
Newport Beach Public Library 1000 Avocado Ave. Newport Beach CA 92660 949-717-3800 640-5648
Web: www.city.newport-beach.ca.us/nbpl
Oakland Public Library 125 14th St. Oakland CA 94612 510-238-3144 238-2232
Web: www.oaklandlibrary.org
Oceanside Public Library 330 N Coast Hwy. Oceanside CA 92054 760-435-5600 435-5567
Web: www.library.ci.oceanside.ca.us
Ontario City Library 217 S Lemon Ave. Ontario CA 91761 909-395-2004 395-2043
Web: www.ci.ontario.ca.us/library
Orange Public Library 101 N Center St Orange CA 92866 714-288-2400 771-6126
Web: www.cityoforange.org/library/
Butte County Library 1820 Mitchell Ave. Oroville CA 95966 530-538-7641 538-7235
Web: www.buttecounty.net/bclibrary/
Oxnard Public Library 251 S 'A' St. Oxnard CA 93030 805-385-7500 385-7526
Web: www.oxnard.org
Palm Springs Public Library 300 S Sunrise Way. Palm Springs CA 92262 760-322-7323 320-9834
Web: www.palmspringslibrary.org
Palmdale City Library 700 E Palmdale Blvd Palmdale CA 93550 661-267-5600 267-5606
Web: www.palmdalelibrary.org
Palo Alto City Library 1213 Newell Rd. Palo Alto CA 94303 650-329-2436 327-2033
Web: www.cityofpaloalto.org//library
Metropolitan Cooperative Library System
3675 E Huntington Dr Suite 100 Pasadena CA 91107 626-683-8244 683-8097
Web: www.mcls.org
Pasadena Public Library 285 E Walnut St. Pasadena CA 91101 626-744-4052 585-8396
Web: cityofpasadena.net/library/
El Dorado County Library 345 Fair Ln. Placerville CA 95667 530-621-5540 622-3911
Web: www.eldoradolibrary.org
Contra Costa County Library 1750 Oak Park Blvd Pleasant Hill CA 94523 925-646-6423 646-6461
Web: www.ccclib.org
Pomona Public Library 625 S Garey Ave Pomona CA 91766 909-620-2043 620-3713
Web: www.youseemore.com/pomona/
Porterville Public Library 41 W Thurman Ave Porterville CA 93257 559-784-0177 781-4396
Rancho Cucamonga Public Library
7368 Archibald Ave Rancho Cucamonga CA 91730 909-477-2720 477-2721
Web: www.rcpl.lib.ca.us
Tehama County Library 645 Madison St. Red Bluff CA 96080 530-527-0604 527-1562
Shasta County Library 1855 Shasta St. Redding CA 96001 530-225-5769 241-7169
Web: www.shastacountylibrary.org
AK Smiley Public Library 125 W Vine St Redlands CA 92373 909-798-7565 798-7566
Web: www.akspl.org
Redondo Beach Public Library
303 N Pacific Coast Hwy Redondo Beach CA 90277 310-318-0675 318-3809
Redwood City Public Library 1044 Middlefield Rd. Redwood City CA 94063 650-780-7047 780-7008
Web: www.redwoodcity.org/library/index.html
Richmond Public Library 325 Civic Center Plaza Richmond CA 94804 510-620-6555 620-6850
Web: www.ci.richmond.ca.us/index.asp?NID=105
Riverside City Public Library 3581 Mission Inn Ave. Riverside CA 92501 951-826-5201 826-5407
Web: www.riversideca.gov/library
Roseville Public Library 225 Taylor St. Roseville CA 95678 916-774-5221 773-5594
Sacramento Public Library 828 'I' St Sacramento CA 95814 916-264-2770 264-2755
Web: www.saclibrary.org
Monterey County Free Libraries 26 Central Ave Salinas CA 93901 831-755-5838 755-5839
Web: www.co.monterey.ca.us/library
Salinas Public Library 350 Lincoln Ave Salinas CA 93901 831-758-7314 758-7336
Web: www.salinas.lib.ca.us
Calaveras County Library 891 Mountain Ranch Rd San Andreas CA 95249 209-754-6510 754-6512
Web: www.co.calaveras.ca.us/libraryinfo.asp
San Bernardino County Library 104 W 4th St San Bernardino CA 92415 909-387-5723 387-5724
Web: www.sbcounty.gov/library
San Bernardino Public Library 555 W 6th St. San Bernardino CA 92410 909-381-8201 381-8229
Web: www.sbpl.org
San Bruno Public Library 701 Angus Ave W San Bruno CA 94066 650-616-7078 876-0848
Web: sanbruno.ca.gov/city_services/library
San Diego County Library System
5555 Overland Ave Bldg 15 San Diego CA 92123 858-694-2415 495-5981
Web: www.sdcl.org
San Diego Public Library 820 'E' St San Diego CA 92101 619-236-5800 236-5878
Web: www.sandiego.gov/public-library/
San Francisco Public Library 100 Larkin St. San Francisco CA 94102 415-557-4400 557-4239
Web: www.sfpl.org
San Jose Public Library 130 E San Fernando St San Jose CA 95113 408-808-2000
Web: www.sjlibrary.org
Santa Clara County Library 1095 N 7th St. San Jose CA 95112 408-293-2326 287-9826
Web: www.santaclaracountylib.org
San Leandro Community Library 300 Estudillo Ave San Leandro CA 94577 510-577-3980 577-3967
San Luis Obispo City-County Library 995 Palm St. San Luis Obispo CA 93401 805-781-5991 781-1166
Web: www.slolibrary.org
Peninsula Library System 2471 Flores St. San Mateo CA 94403 650-349-5538 349-5089
Web: plsinfo.org
San Mateo County Library 25 Tower Rd San Mateo CA 94402 650-312-5258 312-5382
Web: www.smcl.org
Civic Center Library 3501 Civic Ctr Dr Administration Bldg. San Rafael CA 94903 415-499-6057 499-3726
Web: www.co.marin.ca.us/depts/LB/main/civic
Marin County Free Library 3501 Civic Center Dr Suite 414 San Rafael CA 94903 415-499-3220 499-3726
Web: www.co.marin.ca.us/depts/LB/main

Library / Address	City	State	Zip	Phone	Fax
San Rafael Public Library 1100 E St *Web:* www.srpubliclibrary.org	San Rafael	CA	94901	415-485-3323	485-3112
Orange County Public Library 1501 E St Andrew Pl	Santa Ana	CA	92705	714-566-3000	566-3042
Santa Ana Public Library 26 Civic Center Dr *Web:* www.ci.santa-ana.ca.us/library	Santa Ana	CA	92701	714-647-5250	647-5356
Santa Barbara Public Library 40 E Anapamu St *Web:* www.sbplibrary.org	Santa Barbara	CA	93101	805-962-7653	564-5660
Santa Clara City Library 2635 Homestead Rd *Web:* www.library.ci.santa-clara.ca.us	Santa Clara	CA	95051	408-615-2900	247-9657
Garfield Park Library 705 Woodrow Ave *Web:* www.santacruzpl.org/branches/gp/index.shtml	Santa Cruz	CA	95060	831-420-6344	420-6345
Santa Cruz City-County Public Library System 1543 Pacific Ave *Web:* www.santacruzpl.org	Santa Cruz	CA	95060	831-420-5600	420-5601
Santa Maria Public Library 420 S Broadway *Web:* www.ci.santa-maria.ca.us/210.html	Santa Maria	CA	93454	805-925-0994	928-7432
Santa Monica Public Library 1343 6th St *Web:* www.smpl.org	Santa Monica	CA	90401	310-458-8608	394-8951
Sonoma County Library 3rd & E Sts *Web:* www.sonoma.lib.ca.us	Santa Rosa	CA	95404	707-545-0831	575-0437
Tuolumne County Free Library 480 Greenley Rd	Sonora	CA	95370	209-533-5507	533-0936
South San Francisco Public Library 840 W Orange Ave	South San Francisco	CA	94080	650-829-3876	829-3866
Stockton-San Joaquin County Public Library 605 N El Dorado St *Web:* www.stockton.lib.ca.us	Stockton	CA	95202	209-937-8416	937-8683
Sunnyvale Public Library 665 W Olive Ave *Web:* www.ci.sunnyvale.ca.us/library	Sunnyvale	CA	94088	408-730-7300	735-8767
Thousand Oaks Library 1401 E Janss Rd *Web:* www.tol.lib.ca.us	Thousand Oaks	CA	91362	805-449-2660	373-6858
Belvedere-Tiburon Public Library 1501 Tiburon Blvd *Web:* bel-tib-lib.org	Tiburon	CA	94920	415-789-2665	789-2650
Torrance Public Library 3301 Torrance Blvd *Web:* www.torrnet.com/Library/5465.htm	Torrance	CA	90503	310-618-5950	618-5952
Tulare Public Library 113 N 'F' St *Web:* www.sjvls.org/tularepub/	Tulare	CA	93274	559-685-2341	685-2345
Mendocino County Library 105 N Main St *Web:* www.mendolibrary.org	Ukiah	CA	95482	707-463-4491	463-5472
Upland Public Library 450 N Euclid Ave *Web:* uplandpl.lib.ca.us	Upland	CA	91786	909-931-4200	931-4209
EP Foster Library 651 E Main St *Web:* www.vencolibrary.org/libraries/foster.html	Ventura	CA	93001	805-648-2716	648-3696
Ventura County Libraries 646 County Sq Dr Suite 150 *Web:* www.vencolibrary.org	Ventura	CA	93003	805-477-7331	477-7340
Tulare County Library System 200 W Oak Ave *Web:* www.tularecountylibrary.org	Visalia	CA	93291	559-733-6954	737-4586
Watsonville Public Library 310 Union St *Web:* www.watsonville.lib.ca.us	Watsonville	CA	95076	831-728-6040	763-4015
Whittier Public Library 7344 S Washington Ave *Web:* www.whittierch.org	Whittier	CA	90602	562-464-3450	464-3569
Woodland Public Library 250 1st St *Web:* www.cityofwoodland.org/library	Woodland	CA	95695	530-661-5981	666-5408
Yolo County Library 226 Buckeye St *Web:* www.yolocounty.org/org/library	Woodland	CA	95695	530-666-8005	666-8006
Yorba Linda Public Library 18181 Imperial Hwy *Web:* www.ylpl.lib.ca.us	Yorba Linda	CA	92886	714-777-2873	777-0640
Siskiyou County Library 719 4th St *Web:* www.snowcrest.net/siskiyoulibrary	Yreka	CA	96097	530-842-8175	842-7001
Sutter County Library 750 Forbes Ave	Yuba City	CA	95991	530-822-7137	671-6539

Colorado

Library / Address	City	State	Zip	Phone	Fax
Aurora Public Library 14949 E Alameda Pkwy *Web:* odyssey.aurora.lib.co.us	Aurora	CO	80012	303-739-6600	739-6638
Basalt Regional Library 99 Midland Ave	Basalt	CO	81621	970-927-4311	927-1351
Boulder Public Library 1000 Canyon Blvd *Web:* www.boulder.lib.co.us	Boulder	CO	80302	303-441-3100	442-1808
Eisenhower Mamie Doud Public Library 3 Community Park Rd *Web:* www.ci.broomfield.co.us/library	Broomfield	CO	80020	720-887-2300	887-1384
Mamie Doud Eisenhower Public Library 3 Community Park Rd *Web:* www.ci.broomfield.co.us/library	Broomfield	CO	80020	720-887-2300	887-1384
Arapahoe Library District Koebel Public Library 5955 S Holly St	Centennial	CO	80121	303-220-7704	220-1651
Pikes Peak Library District PO Box 1579 *Web:* www.ppld.org	Colorado Springs	CO	80901	719-531-6333	528-2810
Denver Public Library 10 W 14th Ave Pkwy *Web:* denverlibrary.org	Denver	CO	80204	720-865-1111	865-2085
Arapahoe Library District 12855 E Jamison Cir *Web:* www.arapahoelibraries.org	Englewood	CO	80112	303-798-2444	798-2485
Englewood Public Library 1000 Englewood Pkwy Englewood Civic Ctr	Englewood	CO	80110	303-762-2560	783-6890
Fort Collins Public Library 201 Peterson St *Web:* dalva.fcgov.com	Fort Collins	CO	80524	970-221-6740	221-6398
Weld Library District 1939 61st Ave *Web:* www.weld.lib.co.us	Greeley	CO	80634	970-506-8550	506-8551
Jefferson County Public Library 10200 W 20th Ave *Web:* jefferson.lib.co.us	Lakewood	CO	80215	303-232-9507	275-2234
Bemis Public Library 6014 S Datura St *Web:* www.littletongov.org/bemis	Littleton	CO	80120	303-795-3961	795-3996
Longmont Public Library 409 4th Ave *Web:* www.ci.longmont.co.us/library/index.htm	Longmont	CO	80501	303-651-8470	651-8911
Garfield County Public Library 402 W Main St *Web:* www.garfieldlibraries.org/new_castle.htm	New Castle	CO	81647	970-984-2347	984-2487
Pueblo Library District 100 E Abriendo Ave *Web:* pueblolibrary.org	Pueblo	CO	81004	719-562-5600	562-5610
Rangeview Library District 8992 Washington St *Web:* www.rangeviewld.org	Thornton	CO	80229	303-288-2001	287-5971
Westminster Public Library 7392 Irving St *Web:* www.ci.westminster.co.us	Westminster	CO	80030	303-430-2400	

Connecticut

Library / Address	City	State	Zip	Phone	Fax
Avon Free Public Library 281 Country Club Rd *Web:* www.avonctlibrary.info/	Avon	CT	06001	860-673-9712	675-6364
Bridgeport Public Library 925 Broad St *Web:* www.bportlibrary.org/	Bridgeport	CT	06604	203-576-7403	576-8255
Bristol Public Library PO Box 730	Bristol	CT	06011	860-584-7787	584-7696
Cheshire Public Library 104 Main St *Web:* www.cheshirelibrary.org	Cheshire	CT	06410	203-272-2245	272-7714
Danbury Public Library 170 Main St *Web:* danburylibrary.org	Danbury	CT	06810	203-797-4505	796-1518
East Hartford Public Library 840 Main St *Web:* www.ehtfdlib.info	East Hartford	CT	06108	860-289-6429	291-9166
Enfield Public Library 104 Middle Rd *Web:* www.enfieldpubliclibrary.org	Enfield	CT	06082	860-763-7510	763-7514
Fairfield Public Library 1080 Old Post Rd *Web:* www.fairfieldpubliclibrary.org	Fairfield	CT	06824	203-256-3155	256-3162
Welles-Turner Memorial Library 2407 Main St *Web:* www.wtmlib.com	Glastonbury	CT	06033	860-652-7719	652-7721
Groton Public Library 52 Newtown Rd Rt 117	Groton	CT	06340	860-441-6750	448-0363
Hamden Library 2901 Dixwell Ave *Web:* www.hamdenlibrary.org	Hamden	CT	06518	203-287-2686	287-2685
Hartford Public Library 500 Main St *Web:* www.hartfordpl.lib.ct.us	Hartford	CT	06103	860-695-6300	722-6900
Manchester Public Library 586 Main St *Web:* library.ci.manchester.ct.us	Manchester	CT	06040	860-643-2471	643-9453
Meriden Public Library 105 Miller St	Meriden	CT	06450	203-238-2344	238-3647
Milford Public Library 57 New Haven Ave	Milford	CT	06460	203-783-3290	877-1072
New Canaan Library 151 Main St *Web:* newcanaanlibrary.org	New Canaan	CT	06840	203-594-5000	594-5026
New Fairfield Free Public Library Brush Hill Rd PO Box F *Web:* www.newfairfieldlibrary.org	New Fairfield	CT	06812	203-312-5679	312-5685
New Haven Free Public Library 133 Elm St *Web:* www.cityofnewhaven.com/library/	New Haven	CT	06510	203-946-8130	946-8140
Lucy Robbins Welles Library 95 Cedar St *Web:* www.newington.lib.ct.us	Newington	CT	06111	860-665-8730	667-1255
Norwalk Public Library 1 Belden Ave *Web:* www.norwalklib.org	Norwalk	CT	06850	203-899-2780	866-7982
Plumb Memorial Library 65 Wooster St *Web:* www.plumblibrary.org	Shelton	CT	06484	203-924-1580	924-8422
Simsbury Public Library 725 Hopmeadow St *Web:* www.simsburylibrary.info	Simsbury	CT	06070	860-658-7663	658-6732
Southington Public Library 255 Main St *Web:* www.southingtonlibrary.org	Southington	CT	06489	860-628-0947	628-0488
Ferguson Library 1 Public Library Plaza *Web:* www.fergusonlibrary.org	Stamford	CT	06904	203-964-1000	357-9098
Wallace Willoughby Memorial Library 146 Thimble Islands Rd *Web:* www.wwml.org	Stony Creek	CT	06405	203-488-8702	315-3347
Willoughby Wallace Memorial Library 146 Thimble Islands Rd *Web:* www.wwml.org	Stony Creek	CT	06405	203-488-8702	315-3347
Trumbull Library 33 Quality St *Web:* www.trumbullct-library.org	Trumbull	CT	06611	203-452-5197	452-5125
Silas Bronson Library 267 Grand St *Web:* www.bronsonlibrary.org	Waterbury	CT	06702	203-574-8222	574-8055
West Hartford Public Library 20 S Main St *Web:* www.west-hartford.com/library	West Hartford	CT	06107	860-523-3279	523-3236
Wethersfield Public Library 515 Silas Deane Hwy *Web:* www.wethersfieldlibrary.org	Wethersfield	CT	06109	860-721-2985	721-2991
Windsor Public Library 323 Broad St *Web:* www.windsorlibrary.com	Windsor	CT	06095	860-285-1910	285-1889

Delaware

Library / Address	City	State	Zip	Phone	Fax
Dover Public Library 45 S State St *Web:* www.lib.de.us	Dover	DE	19901	302-736-7030	736-5087
Kent County Library 2319 S Dupont Hwy *Web:* www.co.kent.de.us/Departments/CommunitySvcs/Library	Dover	DE	19901	302-698-6440	698-6441
Hockessin Public Library 87 Reads Way	New Castle	DE	19720	302-239-5160	239-1519
Kirkwood Highway Public Library 87 Reads Way	New Castle	DE	19720	302-995-7663	995-7687
New Castle Public Library 424 Delaware St *Web:* www.newcastlepublic.lib.de.us	New Castle	DE	19720	302-328-1995	328-4412
Newark Free Library 750 Library Ave	Newark	DE	19711	302-731-7550	731-4019
Rehoboth Beach Public Library 226 Rehoboth Ave *Web:* www.rehobothlibrary.org	Rehoboth Beach	DE	19971	302-227-8044	227-0597
Concord Pike Public Library 1300 Foulk Rd	Wilmington	DE	19803	302-478-7961	478-2461
Wilmington Public Library 10th & Market Sts *Web:* www.wilmlib.org	Wilmington	DE	19801	302-571-7400	654-9132

District of Columbia

Library / Address	City	State	Zip	Phone	Fax
Library of Congress 101 Independence Ave SE *Web:* www.loc.gov	Washington	DC	20540	202-707-5000	
Martin Luther King Jr Memorial Library 901 G St NW *Web:* dclibrary.org	Washington	DC	20001	202-727-1111	
National Library of Education 400 Maryland Ave SW *TF:* 800-424-1616 ■ *Web:* ies.ed.gov/ncee/projects/nat_ed_library.asp	Washington	DC	20202	202-205-5015	260-7364

Florida

Library / Address	City	State	Zip	Phone	Fax
Altamonte Springs City Library 281 N Maitland Ave	Altamonte Springs	FL	32701	407-830-3895	263-3716
DeSoto County Library 125 N Hillsboro Ave *Web:* www.heartlineweb.org/des	Arcadia	FL	34266	863-993-4851	491-4095
Citrus County Library System 425 W Roosevelt Blvd *Web:* www.cclib.org	Beverly Hills	FL	34465	352-746-9077	746-9493
Boca Raton Public Library 200 NW Boca Raton Blvd *Web:* www.bocalibrary.org	Boca Raton	FL	33432	561-393-7852	393-7823
Boynton Beach City Library 208 S Seacrest Blvd *Web:* coala.org/boynton	Boynton Beach	FL	33435	561-742-6390	742-6381
Manatee County Public Library System 1301 Barcarrota Blvd W *Web:* www.co.manatee.fl.us/library/master.html	Bradenton	FL	34205	941-748-5555	749-7191
Hernando County Public Library System 238 Howell Ave *Web:* www.hcpl.lib.fl.us	Brooksville	FL	34601	352-754-4043	754-4044
Seminole County Public Library 215 N Oxford Rd *Web:* www.seminolecountyfl.gov/lls/library	Casselberry	FL	32707	407-339-4000	339-7931
Clearwater Public Library 100 N Osceola Ave *Web:* www.clearwater-fl.com/cpl	Clearwater	FL	33755	727-562-4970	562-4977
Clewiston Public Library System 120 W Osceola Ave *Web:* www.hendrylibraries.org/clewiston.htm	Clewiston	FL	33440	863-983-1493	983-9194
Central Brevard Library 308 Forest Ave *Web:* www.brev.org	Cocoa	FL	32922	321-633-1792	633-1806
Volusia County Public Library 105 E Magnolia Ave *Web:* merlin.vcpl.lib.fl.us	Daytona Beach	FL	32114	386-257-6036	257-6026
Walton-De Funiak Library 3 Circle Dr	De Funiak Springs	FL	32435	850-892-3624	892-4438
Delray Beach Library 29 SE 4th Ave *Web:* www.delraylibrary.org	Delray Beach	FL	33483	561-266-0194	266-9757
Broward County Library 100 S Andrews Ave *Web:* www.browardlibrary.org	Fort Lauderdale	FL	33301	954-357-7444	
Lee County Library 2050 Central Ave *Web:* www.lee-county.com/library	Fort Myers	FL	33901	239-338-3155	479-4634

Public Libraries (Cont'd)

Florida (Cont'd)

Library	City	State	Zip	Phone	Fax
Saint Lucie County Library System 101 Melody Ln *Web:* www.st-lucie.lib.fl.us	Fort Pierce	FL	34950	772-462-1615	462-2750
Alachua County Library District 401 E University Ave *Web:* www.acld.lib.fl.us	Gainesville	FL	32601	352-334-3934	334-3918
Gulfport Public Library 5501 28th Ave S *Web:* www.tblc.org/gpl	Gulfport	FL	33707	727-893-1074	893-1072
John F Kennedy Library 190 W 49th St *Web:* www.ci.hialeah.fl.us/library	Hialeah	FL	33012	305-821-2700	818-9144
Pasco County Library System 8012 Library Rd *Web:* www.pascolibraries.org	Hudson	FL	34667	727-861-3020	861-3025
Monroe County Public Library System 700 Fleming St	Key West	FL	33040	305-292-3595	295-3626
Osceola County Library System 211 E Dakin Ave *Web:* osceolalibrary.org	Kissimmee	FL	34741	407-935-0777	935-0676
Columbia County Public Library 308 NW Columbia Ave *Web:* www.columbia.lib.fl.us	Lake City	FL	32055	386-758-2101	758-2135
Lake Worth Public Library 15 N 'M' St *Web:* www.lakeworth.org/index.asp?Type=B_BASIC&SEC={D4A82210-BB5D-4782-A298-DEA0789605CB}	Lake Worth	FL	33460	561-533-7354	586-1651
Lakeland Public Library 100 Lake Morton Dr *Web:* www.lakelandgov.net/library/home.html	Lakeland	FL	33801	863-834-4270	834-4293
Leesburg Public Library 204 N 5th St *Web:* www.leesburgflorida.gov/library/	Leesburg	FL	34748	352-728-9790	728-9794
Miami-Dade Public Library 101 W Flagler St *Web:* www.mdpls.org	Miami	FL	33130	305-375-2665	375-3048
Collier County Public Library 650 Central Ave *Web:* www.collier-lib.org	Naples	FL	34102	239-262-4130	649-1293
North Miami Public Library 835 NE 132nd St	North Miami	FL	33161	305-891-5535	892-0843
North Miami Beach Public Library 1601 NE 164th St	North Miami Beach	FL	33162	305-948-2970	787-6007
Oakland Park Library 1298 NE 37th St *Web:* www.oaklandparkfl.org/library.htm	Oakland Park	FL	33334	954-561-6287	561-6146
Ocala Public Library 2720 E Silver Springs Blvd *Web:* www.marioncountyfl.org/library/li_home.htm	Ocala	FL	34470	352-671-8551	368-4545
Okeechobee County Library 206 SW 16th St *Web:* www.heartlineweb.org/oke	Okeechobee	FL	34974	863-763-3536	763-5368
Clay County Public Library System 1895 Town Ctr Blvd *Web:* ccpl.lib.fl.us	Orange Park	FL	32003	904-278-4745	278-4747
Orange County Library System 101 E Central Blvd *Web:* www.ocls.lib.fl.us	Orlando	FL	32801	407-835-7323	835-7650
Putnam County Library System 601 College Rd *TF:* 800-231-4045 ■ *Web:* www.putnam-fl.com/lib/	Palatka	FL	32177	386-329-0126	329-1240
Flagler County Public Library 2500 Palm Coast Pkwy NW *Web:* www.flaglerlibrary.org	Palm Coast	FL	32137	386-446-6763	446-6773
Bay County Public Library 25 W Government St Box 59625 *Web:* www.nwrls.lib.fl.us	Panama City	FL	32412	850-872-7500	872-7507
Northwest Regional Library System 25 W Government St *Web:* www.nwrls.com	Panama City	FL	32401	850-872-7500	872-7507
West Florida Regional Library 200 W Gregory St *Web:* www.cityofpensacola.com/library	Pensacola	FL	32501	850-436-5060	436-5039
Helen B Hoffman Plantation Library 501 N Fig Tree Ln	Plantation	FL	33317	954-797-2140	797-2767
Gadsden County Public Library 341 E Jefferson St	Quincy	FL	32351	850-627-7106	627-7775
Riviera Beach Public Library 600 W Blue Heron Blvd	Riviera Beach	FL	33404	561-845-4195	881-7308
Saint Johns County Public Library 1960 N Ponce de Leon Blvd *Web:* www.sjcpls.org	Saint Augustine	FL	32084	904-827-6940	827-6945
Saint Petersburg Public Library 3745 9th Ave N *Web:* st-petersburg-library.org	Saint Petersburg	FL	33713	727-893-7724	892-5432
Seminole County Public Library - North Branch 150 N Palmetto Ave *Web:* www.seminolecountyfl.gov/lls/library	Sanford	FL	32771	407-330-3737	330-3120
Sarasota County Public Library System 6700 Clark Rd *Web:* suncat.co.sarasota.fl.us	Sarasota	FL	34241	941-316-1172	316-1227
Selby Public Library 1331 1st St *Web:* www.sclibs.net/Default.aspx	Sarasota	FL	34236	941-861-1100	316-1188
Heartland Library Cooperative 319 W Center Ave *Web:* www.heartlineweb.org	Sebring	FL	33870	863-402-6716	402-6743
Martin County Public Library 2351 SE Monterey Rd *Web:* www.library.martin.fl.us	Stuart	FL	34996	772-288-5702	219-4959
Leon County Public Library System 200 W Park Ave *Web:* www.leoncountylibrary.org	Tallahassee	FL	32301	850-487-2665	487-1793
Tampa-Hillsborough County Public Library System 900 N Ashley Dr *Web:* www.thpl.org	Tampa	FL	33602	813-273-3652	272-5640
Lake County Library System 312 W Main St *Web:* www.lakeline.lib.fl.us	Tavares	FL	32778	352-253-6180	253-6184
Indian River County Library 1600 21st St *Web:* indian-river.lib.fl.us	Vero Beach	FL	32960	772-770-5060	770-5066
Palm Beach County Public Library System 3650 Summit Blvd *Web:* www.pbclibrary.org	West Palm Beach	FL	33406	561-233-2600	233-2622
West Palm Beach Public Library 100 Clematis St *Web:* www.wpbpl.com	West Palm Beach	FL	33401	561-868-7700	835-7020
Winter Haven Public Library 325 Avenue A NW *Web:* www.pclc.lib.fl.us/winterhaven	Winter Haven	FL	33881	863-291-5880	298-7708

Georgia

Library	City	State	Zip	Phone	Fax
Dougherty County Public Library 300 N Pine Ave *Web:* www.docolib.org	Albany	GA	31701	229-420-3200	
Athens/Clarke County Library 2025 Baxter St *Web:* www.clarke.public.lib.ga.us	Athens	GA	30606	706-613-3650	613-3660
Atlanta-Fulton Public Library 1 Margaret Mitchell Sq *Web:* www.af.public.lib.ga.us	Atlanta	GA	30303	404-730-1700	730-1990
Southeastern Library Network 1438 W Peachtree St NW Suite 200 *TF:* 800-999-8558 ■ *Web:* www.solinet.net	Atlanta	GA	30309	404-892-0943	892-7879
Augusta-Richmond County Library 902 Greene St *Web:* www.ecgrl.public.lib.ga.us	Augusta	GA	30901	706-821-2600	724-6762
Brunswick-Glynn County Regional Library 208 Gloucester St	Brunswick	GA	31520	912-267-1212	267-9597
West Georgia Regional Library 710 Rome St *Web:* www.wgrl.org	Carrollton	GA	30117	770-836-6711	836-4787
Bartow County Public Library 429 W Main St *Web:* www.bartowlibraryonline.org	Cartersville	GA	30120	770-382-4203	386-3056
Columbus Public Library 3000 Macon Rd *Web:* www.thecolumbuslibrary.org	Columbus	GA	31906	706-243-2669	
Northwest Georgia Regional Library 310 Cappes St *Web:* www.ngrl.org	Dalton	GA	30720	706-876-1360	272-2977
DeKalb County Public Library 215 Sycamore St *Web:* www.dekalblibrary.org	Decatur	GA	30030	404-370-3070	370-3073
Flint River Regional Library 800 Memorial Dr	Griffin	GA	30223	770-412-4770	412-4771
Clayton County Library System 865 Battle Creek Rd *Web:* www.clayton.public.lib.ga.us	Jonesboro	GA	30236	770-473-3850	473-3858
LaFayette-Walker County Library 305 S Duke St *Web:* www.chrl.org	La Fayette	GA	30728	706-638-2992	638-4028
Gwinnett County Public Library 1001 Lawrenceville Hwy *Web:* www.gwinnettpl.org	Lawrenceville	GA	30045	770-822-4522	822-5379
Middle Georgia Regional Library System 1180 Washington Ave *Web:* www.co.bibb.ga.us/library	Macon	GA	31201	478-744-0841	744-0840
Cobb County Public Library System 266 Roswell St *Web:* www.cobbcat.org	Marietta	GA	30060	770-528-2320	528-2349
Henry County Public Library System 1001 Florence McGarity Blvd *Web:* www.henry.public.lib.ga.us	McDonough	GA	30252	770-954-2806	954-2808
Sara Hightower Regional Library 205 Riverside Pkwy NE *Web:* www.floyd.public.lib.ga.us	Rome	GA	30161	706-236-4600	236-4631
Live Oak Public Libraries 2002 Bull St *Web:* www.liveoakpl.org	Savannah	GA	31401	912-652-3600	652-3638
South Georgia Regional Library 300 Woodrow Wilson Dr *Web:* www.sgrl.org	Valdosta	GA	31602	229-333-0086	333-7669

Idaho

Library	City	State	Zip	Phone	Fax
Boise Public Library 715 S Capitol Blvd *Web:* www.boisepubliclibrary.org	Boise	ID	83702	208-384-4238	384-4025
Coeur d'Alene Public Library 702 E Front *Web:* www.cdalibrary.org	Coeur d'Alene	ID	83814	208-769-2315	769-2381
Idaho Falls Public Library 457 W Broadway *Web:* www.ifpl.org	Idaho Falls	ID	83402	208-529-1450	612-8467
Lewiston City Library 428 Thain Rd *Web:* www.cityoflewiston.org/library	Lewiston	ID	83501	208-743-6519	798-4446
Nampa Public Library 101 11th Ave S *Web:* www.nampalibrary.org	Nampa	ID	83651	208-465-2263	465-2277
Marshall Public Library 113 S Garfield St *Web:* www.marshallpl.org/	Pocatello	ID	83204	208-232-1263	232-9266
Twin Falls Public Library 201 4th Ave E *Web:* www.twinfallspubliclibrary.org	Twin Falls	ID	83301	208-733-2964	733-2965

Illinois

Library	City	State	Zip	Phone	Fax
Addison Public Library 2 Friendship Plaza *Web:* www.addisonlibrary.org	Addison	IL	60101	630-543-3617	543-7275
Arlington Heights Memorial Library 500 N Dunton Ave *Web:* www.ahml.info	Arlington Heights	IL	60004	847-392-0100	506-2650
Aurora Public Library 1 E Benton St *Web:* www.aurora.lib.il.us	Aurora	IL	60505	630-264-4100	896-3209
Belleville Public Library 121 E Washington St	Belleville	IL	62220	618-234-0441	234-9474
Bensenville Community Public Library 200 S Church Rd *Web:* www.bensenville.lib.il.us	Bensenville	IL	60106	630-766-4642	766-0788
Berwyn Public Library 2701 S Harlem Ave *Web:* www.berwynlibrary.net	Berwyn	IL	60402	708-795-8000	795-8102
Bloomington Public Library 205 E Olive St Box 3308 *Web:* www.bloomingtonlibrary.org	Bloomington	IL	61702	309-828-6091	828-7312
Fountaindale Public Library 300 W Briarcliff Rd *Web:* www.fountaindale.lib.il.us	Bolingbrook	IL	60440	630-759-2102	759-9519
Metropolitan Library System 125 Tower Dr *TF:* 866-734-2004 ■ *Web:* www.mls.lib.il.us	Burr Ridge	IL	60527	630-734-5000	734-5050
Calumet City Public Library 660 Manistee Ave *Web:* www.calumetcitypl.org	Calumet City	IL	60409	708-862-6220	862-0872
Carbondale Public Library 405 W Main St *Web:* www.carbondale.lib.il.us	Carbondale	IL	62901	618-457-0354	457-0353
Carol Stream Public Library 616 Hiawatha Dr *Web:* www.cslibrary.org	Carol Stream	IL	60188	630-653-0755	653-6809
Champaign Public Library 505 S Randolph St *Web:* www.champaign.org	Champaign	IL	61820	217-356-7243	
Lincoln Trail Libraries System 1704 W Interstate Dr *Web:* www.ltls.org	Champaign	IL	61822	217-352-0047	352-7153
Chicago Public Library 400 S State St *Web:* www.chipublib.org	Chicago	IL	60605	312-747-4999	747-4968
Gerber/Hart Library & Archives 1127 W Granville Ave *Web:* www.gerberhart.org	Chicago	IL	60660	773-381-8030	381-8030
Chicago Heights Free Public Library 25 W 15th St *Web:* www2.sls.lib.il.us/CHS	Chicago Heights	IL	60411	708-754-0323	754-0325
Cicero Public Library 5225 W Cermak Rd	Cicero	IL	60804	708-652-8084	652-1668
Crystal Lake Public Library 126 Paddock St *Web:* www.crystallakelibrary.org	Crystal Lake	IL	60014	815-459-1687	459-5845
Danville Public Library 319 N Vermilion St *Web:* www.danville.lib.il.us	Danville	IL	61832	217-477-5220	477-5230
Decatur Public Library 130 N Franklin St *Web:* www.decatur.lib.il.us	Decatur	IL	62523	217-424-2900	233-4071
DeKalb Public Library 309 Oak St *Web:* www.dkpl.org	DeKalb	IL	60115	815-756-9568	756-7837
Des Plaines Public Library 1501 Ellinwood Ave *Web:* www.dppl.org	Des Plaines	IL	60016	847-827-5551	827-7974
Downers Grove Public Library 1050 Curtiss St *Web:* www.downersgrovelibrary.org	Downers Grove	IL	60515	630-960-1200	960-9374
Alliance Library System 600 High Point Ln Suite 1 *TF:* 800-700-4857 ■ *Web:* www.alliancelibrarysystem.com	Eask Peoria	IL	61611	309-694-9200	694-9230
East Saint Louis Public Library 5300 State St *Web:* www.eaststlouislibrary.org	East Saint Louis	IL	62203	618-397-0991	397-1260
Elk Grove Village Public Library 1001 Wellington Ave *Web:* www.egvpl.org	Elk Grove Village	IL	60007	847-439-0447	439-0475
Elmhurst Public Library 125 S Prospect Ave *Web:* www.elmhurstpubliclibrary.org	Elmhurst	IL	60126	630-279-8696	279-0636
Evanston Public Library 1703 Orrington Ave *Web:* www.evanston.lib.il.us/library/library.html	Evanston	IL	60201	847-866-0300	866-0313
Freeport Public Library 100 E Douglas St *Web:* www.freeportpubliclibrary.org	Freeport	IL	61032	815-233-3000	297-8236
Galesburg Public Library 40 E Simmons St *Web:* www.galesburglibrary.org	Galesburg	IL	61401	309-343-6118	343-4877
DuPage Library System 127 S 1st St *Web:* www.dupagels.lib.il.us	Geneva	IL	60134	630-232-8457	232-0699
Glenview Public Library 1930 Glenview Rd *Web:* www.glenviewpl.org	Glenview	IL	60025	847-729-7500	729-7682
Grande Prairie Public Library 3479 W 183rd St *Web:* www.grandeprairie.org	Hazel Crest	IL	60429	708-798-5563	798-5874
Highland Park Public Library 494 Laurel Ave *Web:* www.hplibrary.org	Highland Park	IL	60035	847-432-0216	432-9139
Joliet Public Library 150 N Ottawa St *Web:* www.joliet.lib.il.us	Joliet	IL	60432	815-740-2660	740-6161
Kankakee Public Library 201 E Merchant St *Web:* www.lions-online.org	Kankakee	IL	60901	815-939-4564	939-9057

	City	State	ZIP	Phone	Fax
Ela Area Public Library District 275 Mohawk Trail	Lake Zurich	IL	60047	847-438-3433	438-9290
Web: www.eapl.org					
Lewis O Flom Lansing Public Library 2750 Indiana Ave	Lansing	IL	60438	708-474-2447	474-9466
Web: www.lansing.lib.il.us					
Helen M Plum Memorial Library 110 W Maple St	Lombard	IL	60148	630-627-0316	627-0336
Web: www.plum.lib.il.us					
Maywood Public Library 121 S 5th Ave	Maywood	IL	60153	708-343-1847	343-2115
Web: www.maywood.org					
Moline Public Library 504 17th St	Moline	IL	61265	309-762-6883	797-0484
Web: www.molinelibrary.com					
Morton Grove Public Library 6140 Lincoln Ave	Morton Grove	IL	60053	847-965-4220	965-7903
Web: www.webrary.org/mgplhome.html					
Mount Prospect Public Library 10 S Emerson St	Mount Prospect	IL	60056	847-253-5675	253-5677
Web: www.mppl.org					
Naperville Public Libraries 200 W Jefferson Ave	Naperville	IL	60540	630-961-4100	637-4870
Web: www.naperville-lib.org					
Normal Public Library 206 W College	Normal	IL	61761	309-452-1757	452-5312
Web: www.normal-library.org					
North Chicago Public Library 2100 Argonne Dr	North Chicago	IL	60064	847-689-0125	689-9117
Web: www.northchicagopubliclibrary.org					
Northbrook Public Library 1201 Cedar Ln	Northbrook	IL	60062	847-272-6224	498-0440
Oak Lawn Public Library 9427 S Raymond Ave	Oak Lawn	IL	60453	708-422-4990	442-5061
Web: www.lib.oak-lawn.il.us					
Oak Park Public Library 834 Lake St	Oak Park	IL	60301	708-383-8200	383-6384
Web: www.oppl.org					
Orland Park Public Library 14921 Ravinia Ave	Orland Park	IL	60462	708-349-8138	349-8322
Web: www.orlandparklibrary.org					
Park Forest Public Library 400 Lakewood Blvd	Park Forest	IL	60466	708-748-3731	748-8829
Web: www.pfpl.org					
Park Ridge Public Library 20 S Prospect Ave	Park Ridge	IL	60068	847-825-3123	825-0001
Web: www.parkridgelibrary.org					
Pekin Public Library 301 S 4th St	Pekin	IL	61554	309-347-7111	347-6587
Web: www.pekin.net/library/					
Peoria Public Library 107 NE Monroe St	Peoria	IL	61602	309-672-8835	674-0116
Web: www.peoriapubliclibrary.org					
Quincy Public Library 526 Jersey St	Quincy	IL	62301	217-223-1309	222-3052
Web: www.quincylibrary.org					
Rock Island Public Library 401 19th St	Rock Island	IL	61201	309-732-7323	732-7342
Web: ripl.lib.il.us					
Prairie Area Library System 4021 Morsay Dr	Rockford	IL	61107	815-229-0330	229-6843
TF: 877-542-7257 ■ *Web:* www.palsnet.info					
Rockford Public Library 215 N Wyman St	Rockford	IL	61101	815-965-6731	965-6735
Web: www.rockfordpubliclibrary.org					
Schaumburg Township District Library 130 S Roselle Rd	Schaumburg	IL	60193	847-985-5860	923-3335
Web: www.stdl.org					
Shorewood-Troy Public Library District 650 Deerwood Dr	Shorewood	IL	60431	815-725-1715	725-1722
Web: www.shorewood.lib.il.us					
Skokie Public Library 5215 W Oakton St	Skokie	IL	60077	847-673-7774	673-7797
Web: www.skokielibrary.org					
Lincoln Library 326 S 7th St	Springfield	IL	62701	217-753-4900	753-5329
Web: www.lincolnlibrary.info					
Tinley Park Public Library 17101 S 71st Ave	Tinley Park	IL	60477	708-532-0160	532-2981
Web: www.tplibrary.org					
Urbana Free Library 210 W Green St	Urbana	IL	61801	217-367-4057	367-4061
Web: urbanafreelibrary.org					
Waukegan Public Library 128 N County St	Waukegan	IL	60085	847-623-2041	623-2092
Web: www.waukeganpl.org					
Wheaton Public Library 225 N Cross St	Wheaton	IL	60187	630-668-1374	668-8950
Web: www.wheaton.lib.il.us/library					
North Suburban Library System 200 W Dundee Rd	Wheeling	IL	60090	847-459-1300	459-0380
TF: 800-374-7134 ■ *Web:* www.nsls.info					
Woodridge Public Library 3 Plaza Dr	Woodridge	IL	60517	630-964-7899	964-0175
Web: www.woodridgelibrary.org					

Indiana

	City	State	ZIP	Phone	Fax
Anderson Public Library 111 E 12th St	Anderson	IN	46016	765-641-2456	641-2197
Web: www.and.lib.in.us					
Batesville Memorial Public Library 131 N Walnut St	Batesville	IN	47006	812-934-4706	934-6288
Web: www.bmpl.cnz.com					
Bedford Public Library 1323 K St	Bedford	IN	47421	812-275-4471	277-1145
Web: www.bedlib.org					
Monroe County Public Library 303 E Kirkwood Ave	Bloomington	IN	47408	812-349-3050	349-3051
Web: www.monroe.lib.in.us					
Wells County Public Library 200 W Washington St	Bluffton	IN	46714	260-824-1612	824-3129
Web: www.wellscolibrary.org					
Carmel Clay Public Library 55 4th Ave SE	Carmel	IN	46032	317-844-3361	571-4285
Web: www.carmel.lib.in.us					
Charlestown Clark County Public Library 51 Clark Rd	Charlestown	IN	47111	812-256-3337	256-3890
Bartholomew County Public Library 536 5th St	Columbus	IN	47201	812-379-1255	379-1275
Web: www.barth.lib.in.us					
Fayette County Public Library 828 N Grand Ave	Connersville	IN	47331	765-827-0883	825-4592
Web: www.fcplibrary.lib.in.us					
East Chicago Public Library 2401 E Columbus Dr	East Chicago	IN	46312	219-397-2453	397-6715
Web: www.ecpl.org					
Evansville Vanderburgh Public Library 200 SE ML King Jr Blvd	Evansville	IN	47713	812-428-8218	428-8397
Web: www.evpl.org					
Allen County Public Library 900 Library Plaza	Fort Wayne	IN	46802	260-421-1200	421-1386
Web: www.acpl.lib.in.us					
Frankfort Community Public Library 208 W Clinton St	Frankfort	IN	46041	765-654-8746	654-8747
Web: www.accs.net/fcpl					
Johnson County Public Library 401 S State St	Franklin	IN	46131	317-738-2833	738-9635
Web: www.jcplin.org					
Gary Public Library 220 W 5th Ave	Gary	IN	46402	219-886-2484	886-6829
Web: www.gary.lib.in.us					
Putnam County Public Library 103 E Poplar St PO Box 116	Greencastle	IN	46135	765-653-2755	653-2756
Web: www.putnam.lib.in.us					
Hammond Public Library 564 State St	Hammond	IN	46320	219-931-5100	931-3474
Web: www.hammond.lib.in.us					
Indianapolis-Marion County Public Library 202 N Alabama St	Indianapolis	IN	46202	317-269-1700	269-1768
Web: www.imcpl.org					
Jasper-Dubois County Public Library 1116 Main St	Jasper	IN	47546	812-482-2712	482-7123
Kokomo-Howard County Public Library 220 N Union St	Kokomo	IN	46901	765-457-3242	457-3683
Web: www.kokomo.lib.in.us					
La Porte County Public Library 904 Indiana Ave	La Porte	IN	46350	219-362-6156	362-6158
Web: www.lapcat.org					
Tippecanoe County Public Library 627 South St	Lafayette	IN	47901	765-429-0100	429-0150
Web: www.tcpl.lib.in.us					
LaGrange County Public Library 203 W Spring St	LaGrange	IN	46761	260-463-2841	
Web: www.lagrange.lib.in.us					
Logansport-Cass County Public Library 616 E Broadway	Logansport	IN	46947	574-753-6383	722-5889
Web: www.logan.lib.in.us					
Madison-Jefferson County Public Library 420 W Main St	Madison	IN	47250	812-265-2744	265-2217
Web: www.madison-jeffco.lib.in.us					
Marion Public Library 600 S Washington St	Marion	IN	46953	765-668-2900	668-2911
Web: www.marion.lib.in.us					
Morgan County Public Library 110 S Jefferson St	Martinsville	IN	46151	765-342-3451	342-9992
Web: morg.lib.in.us					
Lake County Public Library 1919 W 81st Ave	Merrillville	IN	46410	219-769-3541	769-0690
Web: www.lakeco.lib.in.us					
Mooresville Public Library 220 W Harrison St	Mooresville	IN	46158	317-831-7323	831-7383
Web: www.mooresvillelib.org					
New Albany-Floyd County Public Library 180 W Spring St	New Albany	IN	47150	812-944-8464	949-3734
Web: www.nafclibrary.org					
New Castle-Henry County Public Library 376 S 15th St PO Box J	New Castle	IN	47362	765-529-0362	521-3581
Web: www.nchcpl.lib.in.us					
Morrisson-Reeves Public Library 80 N 6th St	Richmond	IN	47374	765-966-8291	962-1318
Web: www.mrl.lib.in.us					
Jackson County Public Library 303 W 2nd St	Seymour	IN	47274	812-522-3412	522-5456
Web: www.japl.lib.in.us					
Shelbyville-Shelby County Public Library 57 W Broadway	Shelbyville	IN	46176	317-398-7121	398-4430
Web: www.sscpl.lib.in.us					
Saint Joseph County Public Library 304 S Main St	South Bend	IN	46601	574-282-4630	280-2763
Web: sjcpl.lib.in.us					
Vigo County Public Library 1 Library Sq	Terre Haute	IN	47807	812-232-1113	232-3208
Web: www.vigo.lib.in.us					
Valparaiso Public Library 103 Jefferson St	Valparaiso	IN	46383	219-462-0524	477-4867
Web: www.pcpls.lib.in.us/Branches/brvalpo.htm					
Knox County Public Library 502 N 7th St	Vincennes	IN	47591	812-886-4380	886-0342
Web: www.kcpl.lib.in.us					
West Lafayette Public Library 200 Northwestern Ave	West Lafayette	IN	47906	765-743-2261	743-2063
Web: www.wlaf.lib.in.us					

Iowa

	City	State	ZIP	Phone	Fax
Ames Public Library 515 Douglas Ave	Ames	IA	50010	515-239-5630	232-4571
Web: www.amespubliclibrary.org					
Kirkendall Public Library 1210 NW Prairie Ridge Dr	Ankeny	IA	50021	515-965-6460	965-6474
Web: www.ci.ankeny.ia.us/Library					
Bettendorf Public Library 2950 Learning Campus Dr	Bettendorf	IA	52722	563-344-4175	344-4185
Web: www.bettendorflibrary.com					
Burlington Public Library 501 N 4th St	Burlington	IA	52601	319-753-1647	229-0406
Web: www.burlington.lib.ia.us					
Cedar Falls Public Library 524 Main St	Cedar Falls	IA	50613	319-273-8643	273-8648
Web: www.cedarfallspubliclibrary.org					
Cedar Rapids Public Library 500 1st St SE	Cedar Rapids	IA	52401	319-398-5123	398-0476
Web: www.crlibrary.org					
East Central Regional Library 222 3rd St SE Suite 402	Cedar Rapids	IA	52401	319-365-0521	365-0194
Clinton Public Library 306 8th Ave S	Clinton	IA	52732	563-242-8441	242-8162
Council Bluffs Public Library 400 Willow Ave	Council Bluffs	IA	51503	712-323-7553	323-1269
Web: www.cbpl.lib.ia.us					
Davenport Public Library 321 Main St	Davenport	IA	52801	563-326-7832	326-7809
Web: www.davenportlibrary.com					
Des Moines Public Library 1000 Grand Ave	Des Moines	IA	50309	515-283-4152	237-1654
Web: www.desmoineslibrary.com					
Carnegie-Stout Public Library 360 W 11th St	Dubuque	IA	52001	563-589-4225	589-4217
Web: www.dubuque.lib.ia.us					
Scott County Library 200 N 6th Ave	Eldridge	IA	52748	563-285-4794	285-4743
Fayette Community Library PO Box 107	Fayette	IA	52142	563-425-3344	425-3344
Web: www.fayetteia.com/Library.htm					
Fort Dodge Public Library 424 Central Ave	Fort Dodge	IA	50501	515-573-8167	573-5422
Web: www.fortdodgeiowa.org/department/index.asp?fDD=11-0					
Iowa City Public Library 123 S Linn St	Iowa City	IA	52240	319-356-5200	356-5494
Web: www.icpl.org					
Marion Public Library 1095 6th Ave	Marion	IA	52302	319-377-3412	377-0113
Web: www.cityofmarion.org/library					
Marshalltown Public Library 36 N Center St	Marshalltown	IA	50158	641-754-5738	754-5708
Web: www.marshalltownlibrary.org					
Mason City Public Library 225 2nd St SE	Mason City	IA	50401	641-421-3668	423-2615
Web: www.mcpl.org					
Muscatine Public Library 304 Iowa Ave	Muscatine	IA	52761	563-263-3068	264-1033
Web: www.muscatinelibrary.us/					
Newton Public Library 100 N 3rd Ave W PO Box 746	Newton	IA	50208	641-792-4108	791-0729
Web: www.iren.net/newtonpl					
Ottumwa Public Library 102 W 4th St	Ottumwa	IA	52501	641-682-7563	682-4970
Sioux City Public Library 529 Pierce St	Sioux City	IA	51101	712-255-2933	279-6432
Web: www.siouxcitylibrary.org					
Urbandale Public Library 3520 86th St	Urbandale	IA	50322	515-278-3945	278-3918
Web: www.urbandalelibrary.org					
Waterloo Public Library 415 Commercial St	Waterloo	IA	50701	319-291-4521	291-6736
Web: www.wplwloo.lib.ia.us					
West Des Moines Public Library 4000 Mills Civic Pkwy	West Des Moines	IA	50265	515-222-3400	222-3401
Web: www.wdm.lib.ia.us					

Kansas

	City	State	ZIP	Phone	Fax
Belleville Public Library 1327 19th St	Belleville	KS	66935	785-527-5305	527-5305
Web: www.bellevillelibrary.org					
Emporia Public Library 110 E 6th Ave	Emporia	KS	66801	620-342-6524	340-6444
Web: skyways.lib.ks.us/library/emporia					
Finney County Public Library Garden City 605 E Walnut St	Garden City	KS	67846	620-272-3680	272-3682
Hutchinson Public Library 901 N Main St	Hutchinson	KS	67501	620-663-5441	663-9506
Web: www.hutchpl.org					
Dorothy Bramlage Public Library Junction City 230 W 7th St	Junction City	KS	66441	785-238-4311	238-7873
Web: www.jclib.org					
Kansas City Kansas Public Library 625 Minnesota Ave	Kansas City	KS	66101	913-551-3280	279-2032
Web: www.kckpl.lib.ks.us					
Lawrence Public Library 707 Vermont St	Lawrence	KS	66044	785-843-3833	843-3368
Web: www.lawrence.lib.ks.us					
Leavenworth Public Library 417 Spruce St	Leavenworth	KS	66048	913-682-5666	682-1248
Web: skyways.lib.ks.us/library/leavenworth/					
Manhattan Public Library 629 Poyntz Ave	Manhattan	KS	66502	785-776-4741	776-1545
TF: 800-432-2796 ■ *Web:* www.manhattan.lib.ks.us					
Olathe Public Library 201 E Park St	Olathe	KS	66061	913-764-2259	971-6809
Web: olathe.lib.ks.us					
Salina Public Library 301 W Elm St	Salina	KS	67401	785-825-4624	823-0706
Web: www.salpublib.org					
Johnson County Library PO Box 2933	Shawnee Mission	KS	66201	913-495-2400	495-2460
Web: www.jocolibrary.org					
Topeka & Shawnee County Public Library 1515 SW 10th Ave	Topeka	KS	66604	785-580-4400	580-4496
Web: www.tscpl.org					
Wichita Public Library 223 S Main St	Wichita	KS	67202	316-261-8500	262-4540
Web: www.wichita.lib.ks.us					

Public Libraries (Cont'd)

Kentucky

Library	City	State	Zip	Phone	Fax
Boyd County Public Library 1740 Central Ave	Ashland	KY	41101	606-329-0518	329-0578
Web: www.thebookplace.org					
Bowling Green Public Library 1225 State St	Bowling Green	KY	42101	270-781-4882	781-3699
Web: www.bgpl.org					
Kenton County Public Library 502 Scott Blvd	Covington	KY	41011	859-962-4060	962-4096
Web: www.kenton.lib.ky.us					
Boyle County Public Library 307 W Broadway	Danville	KY	40422	859-236-8466	236-7692
Hardin County Public Library 100 Jim Owen Dr	Elizabethtown	KY	42701	270-769-6337	769-0437
Web: www.hcpl.info					
Paul Sawyier Public Library 319 Wapping St	Frankfort	KY	40601	502-352-2665	227-2250
Web: www.pspl.org					
Sawyier Paul Public Library 319 Wapping St	Frankfort	KY	40601	502-352-2665	227-2250
Web: www.pspl.org					
Lexington Public Library 140 E Main St	Lexington	KY	40507	859-231-5504	231-5598
Web: www.lexpublib.org					
Louisville Free Public Library 301 York St	Louisville	KY	40203	502-574-1600	574-1666
Web: lfpl.org					
Daviess County Public Library 450 Griffith Ave	Owensboro	KY	42301	270-684-0211	684-0218
Web: dcplibrary.org					
McCracken County Public Library 555 Washington St	Paducah	KY	42003	270-442-2510	
Web: www.mclib.net					
Pulaski County Public Library 107 N Main St	Somerset	KY	42501	606-679-8401	679-1779
Web: www.pulaskipubliclibrary.org					

Louisiana

Library	City	State	Zip	Phone	Fax
Vermilion Parish Library 405 E Saint Victor	Abbeville	LA	70510	337-893-2655	898-0526
Rapides Parish Library 411 Washington St	Alexandria	LA	71301	318-445-2411	445-6478
Web: www.rpl.org					
Tangipahoa Parish Library 739 W Oak St	Amite	LA	70422	985-748-7151	748-5476
Web: www.tangipahoa.lib.la.us					
Morehouse Parish Library PO BOX 232	Bastrop	LA	71221	318-281-3683	
Web: www.youseemore.com/morehouse					
East Baton Rouge Parish Library 7711 Goodwood Blvd	Baton Rouge	LA	70806	225-231-3700	231-3759
Web: www.ebr.lib.la.us					
Bossier Parish Library 2206 Beckett St	Bossier City	LA	71111	318-746-1693	746-7768
Web: www.bossierlibrary.org					
Plaquemines Parish Library 35572 Hwy 11 S	Buras	LA	70041	504-657-7121	657-6175
Saint Bernard Parish Library 1125 E St Bernard Hwy	Chalmette	LA	70043	504-279-0448	277-3645
Saint Tammany Parish Library 310 W 21st Ave	Covington	LA	70433	985-893-6282	893-6283
Acadia Parish Library PO Box 1509	Crowley	LA	70527	337-788-1880	788-3759
Web: www.acadia.lib.la.us					
Beauregard Parish Library 205 S Washington Ave	DeRidder	LA	70634	337-463-6217	462-5434
Web: www.beau.lib.la.us					
Ascension Parish Library 500 Mississippi St	Donaldsonville	LA	70346	225-473-8052	473-9522
Web: www.ascension.lib.la.us/apl					
Saint Mary Parish Library 206 Iberia St	Franklin	LA	70538	337-828-1624	828-2329
TF: 800-732-8698					
Washington Parish Library 825 Free St	Franklinton	LA	70438	985-839-7805	839-7808
Web: www.wplib.org					
Terrebonne Parish Library 424 Roussell St	Houma	LA	70360	985-876-5861	876-5864
Web: www.terrebonne.lib.la.us					
Jefferson Davis Parish Library 118 W Plaquemine St	Jennings	LA	70546	337-824-1210	824-5444
Web: www.jefferson-davis.lib.la.us					
Lafayette Parish Public Library 301 W Congress St	Lafayette	LA	70501	337-261-5775	261-5782
Calcasieu Parish Public Library System 301 W Claude St	Lake Charles	LA	70605	337-475-8798	475-8806
Web: www.calcasieu.lib.la.us					
Saint John the Baptist Parish Library 2920 Hwy 51	LaPlace	LA	70068	985-652-6857	652-2144
Web: www.stjohn.lib.la.us					
Vernon Parish Library 1401 Nolan Trace	Leesville	LA	71446	337-239-2027	238-0666
TF: 800-737-2231 ■ *Web:* www.vernon.lib.la.us					
Livingston Parish Library 13986 Florida Blvd PO Drawer 397	Livingston	LA	70754	225-686-2436	686-3888
Web: www.livingston.lib.la.us					
Saint Charles Parish Library 105 Lakewood Dr	Luling	LA	70070	985-785-8464	785-8499
Web: www.stcharles.lib.la.us					
DeSoto Parish Library 109 Crosby St	Mansfield	LA	71052	318-872-6100	872-6120
Avoyelles Parish Library 104 N Washington St	Marksville	LA	71351	318-253-7559	253-6361
Web: www.avoyelles.lib.la.us					
Jefferson Parish Library 4747 W Napoleon Ave	Metairie	LA	70001	504-838-1100	838-1117
Web: www.jefferson.lib.la.us					
Webster Parish Library 521 East & West Sts	Minden	LA	71055	318-371-3080	371-3081
Web: www.webster.lib.la.us					
Ouachita Parish Public Library 1800 Stubbs Ave	Monroe	LA	71201	318-327-1490	327-1373
Web: www.oplib.org					
Natchitoches Parish Library 450 2nd St	Natchitoches	LA	71457	318-357-3280	357-7073
Web: www.youseemore.com/Natchitoches					
Iberia Parish Library 445 E Main St	New Iberia	LA	70560	337-373-0075	373-0086
Web: www.iberia.lib.la.us					
Opelousas-Eunice Public Libraries 212 E Grolee St	Opelousas	LA	70570	337-948-3693	948-5200
Iberville Parish Library 24605 J Gerald Berret Blvd	Plaquemine	LA	70765	225-687-2520	687-9719
Web: www.iberville.lib.la.us					
Lincoln Parish Library 910 N Trenton St	Ruston	LA	71270	318-251-5030	251-5045
Web: www.lincoln.lib.la.us					
Saint Martin Parish Library 201 Porter St	Saint Martinville	LA	70582	337-394-2207	394-2248
Web: www.stmartin.lib.la.us					
Shreve Memorial Library 424 Texas St	Shreveport	LA	71101	318-226-5897	226-4780
Web: www.shreve-lib.org					
Lafourche Parish Library 303 W 5th St	Thibodaux	LA	70301	985-446-1163	446-3848
Web: www.lafourche.org					
Evangeline Parish Library 242 W Main St	Ville Platte	LA	70586	337-363-1369	363-2353
Web: www.evangeline.lib.la.us					

Maine

Library	City	State	Zip	Phone	Fax
Auburn Public Library 49 Spring St	Auburn	ME	04210	207-333-6640	333-6644
Web: www.auburn.lib.me.us					
Lithgow Public Library 45 Winthrop St	Augusta	ME	04330	207-626-2415	626-2419
Web: www.lithgow.lib.me.us					
Bangor Public Library 145 Harlow St	Bangor	ME	04401	207-947-8336	945-6694
TF: 800-427-8336 ■ *Web:* www.bpl.lib.me.us					
Jessup Memorial Library 34 Mt Desert St	Bar Harbor	ME	04609	207-288-4245	288-9067
Camden Public Library 55 Main St	Camden	ME	04843	207-236-3440	236-6673
Web: www.camden.lib.me.us					
Lewiston Public Library 200 Lisbon St	Lewiston	ME	04240	207-784-0135	784-3011
Web: www.lplonline.org					
Portland Public Library 5 Monument Sq	Portland	ME	04101	207-871-1700	871-1715
Web: www.portlandlibrary.com					

Maryland

Library	City	State	Zip	Phone	Fax
Anne Arundel County Public Library 5 Harry S Truman Pkwy	Annapolis	MD	21401	410-222-7371	222-7188
Web: web.aacpl.lib.md.us					
Enoch Pratt Free Library 400 Cathedral St	Baltimore	MD	21201	410-396-5430	396-1351
Web: www.prattlibrary.org					
Harford County Public Library 1221-A Brass Mill Rd Riverside Business Pk	Belcamp	MD	21017	410-575-6761	273-5606
Web: www.hcplonline.info					
Dorchester County Public Library 303 Gay St	Cambridge	MD	21613	410-228-7331	228-6313
Web: www.dorchesterlibrary.org					
Queen Anne's County Free Library 121 S Commerce St	Centreville	MD	21617	410-758-0980	758-0614
Web: www.quan.lib.md.us					
Howard County Central Library 10375 Little Patuxent Pkwy	Columbia	MD	21044	410-313-7800	313-7742
Web: www.hclibrary.org					
Allegany County Public Library System 31 Washington St	Cumberland	MD	21502	301-777-1200	777-7299
Web: lib.allconet.org					
Caroline County Public Library 100 Market St	Denton	MD	21629	410-479-1343	479-1443
Web: www.carolib.org/library					
Talbot County Free Library 100 W Dover St	Easton	MD	21601	410-822-1626	820-8217
Web: www.talb.lib.md.us/library					
Cecil County Public Library 301 Newark Ave	Elkton	MD	21921	410-996-5600	996-5604
Web: www.ebranch.cecil.lib.md.us					
Frederick County Public Library 110 E Patrick St	Frederick	MD	21701	301-694-1630	631-3789
Web: www.fcpl.org					
Washington County Free Library 100 S Potomac St	Hagerstown	MD	21740	301-739-3250	739-7603
Web: www.wc-link.org/wcfl/					
Prince George's County Memorial Library 6532 Adelphi Rd	Hyattsville	MD	20782	301-699-3500	699-0122
Web: www.prge.lib.md.us					
Charles County Public Library 2 Garrett Ave	La Plata	MD	20646	301-934-9001	934-2297
Web: www.somd.lib.md.us/CHAS/Libraries					
Laurel Library 507 7th St	Laurel	MD	20707	301-776-6790	
Saint Mary's County Memorial Library 23250 Hollywood Rd	Leonardtown	MD	20650	301-475-2846	884-4415
Web: www.stmalib.org					
Ruth Enlow Library 6 N 2nd St	Oakland	MD	21550	301-334-3996	334-4152
Web: www.relib.net					
Ocean City Branch Library 200 14th St	Ocean City	MD	21842	410-289-7297	289-5577
Web: www.worcesterlibrary.org/					
Calvert County Public Library PO Box 405	Prince Frederick	MD	20678	410-535-0291	535-3022
Web: www.calvert.lib.md.us					
Montgomery County Dept of Public Libraries 99 Maryland Ave	Rockville	MD	20850	240-777-0001	777-0014
Wicomico County Free Library 122 S Division St	Salisbury	MD	21801	410-749-3612	548-2968
Web: www.wicomicolibrary.org					
Worcester County Library 307 N Washington St	Snow Hill	MD	21863	410-632-2600	632-1159
Web: www.worc.lib.md.us/library/home.html					
Baltimore County Public Library 320 York Rd	Towson	MD	21204	410-887-6100	887-6103
Web: www.bcplonline.org					
Carroll County Public Library 115 Airport Dr	Westminster	MD	21157	410-386-4500	386-4509
Web: library.carr.org					

Massachusetts

Library	City	State	Zip	Phone	Fax
Agawam Public Library 750 Cooper St	Agawam	MA	01001	413-789-1550	789-1552
Jones Library Inc 43 Amity St	Amherst	MA	01002	413-256-4090	256-4096
Web: www.joneslibrary.org					
Memorial Hall Library Elm Sq	Andover	MA	01810	978-623-8400	623-8407
Web: www.mhl.org					
Robbins Library 700 Massachusetts Ave	Arlington	MA	02476	781-316-3200	
Attleboro Public Library 74 N Main St	Attleboro	MA	02703	508-222-0157	226-3326
Web: www.sailsinc.org/Attleboro/apl.htm					
Sturgis Library 3090 Main St	Barnstable	MA	02630	508-362-6636	362-5467
Web: www.sturgislibrary.org					
Bedford Free Public Library 7 Mudge Way	Bedford	MA	01730	781-275-9440	275-3590
Web: www.bedfordlibrary.net					
Bellingham Public Library 100 Blackstone St	Bellingham	MA	02019	508-966-1660	966-3189
Web: www.bellinghamma.org/Library					
Beverly Public Library 32 Essex St	Beverly	MA	01915	978-921-6062	922-8329
Web: www.noblenet.org/beverly					
Billerica Public Library 15 Concord Rd	Billerica	MA	01821	978-671-0948	667-4242
Web: www.billericalibrary.org					
Boston Public Library 700 Boylston St Copley Sq	Boston	MA	02116	617-536-5400	236-4306
Web: www.bpl.org					
Thayer Public Library 798 Washington St	Braintree	MA	02184	781-848-0405	356-5447
Web: www.thayerpubliclibrary.org					
Brockton Public Library 304 Main St	Brockton	MA	02301	508-580-7890	580-7898
Web: www.brocktonpubliclibrary.org					
Brookline Public Library 361 Washington St	Brookline	MA	02445	617-730-2360	730-2160
Web: www.brooklinelibrary.com					
Burlington Public Library 22 Sears St	Burlington	MA	01803	781-270-1690	229-0406
Web: burlingtonpubliclibrary.org					
Cambridge Public Library 449 Broadway	Cambridge	MA	02138	617-349-4036	349-4428
Web: www.ci.cambridge.ma.us/~CPL					
Centerville Public Library 585 Main St	Centerville	MA	02632	508-790-6220	790-6218
Web: www.centervillelibrary.org					
Chelmsford Public Library 25 Boston Rd	Chelmsford	MA	01824	978-256-5521	256-8511
Web: www.chelmsfordlibrary.org					
Chelsea Public Library 569 Broadway	Chelsea	MA	02150	617-889-8330	889-8364
Chicopee Public Library 449 Front St	Chicopee	MA	01013	413-594-1800	594-1819
Web: www.chicopeepubliclibrary.org					
Cotuit Library PO Box 648	Cotuit	MA	02635	508-428-8141	428-4636
Web: www.library.cotuit.ma.us					
Dartmouth Public Libraries 732 Dartmouth St	Dartmouth	MA	02748	508-999-0726	992-9914
Web: dartmouthpubliclibraries.org					
Moses Greeley Parker Memorial Library 28 Arlington St	Dracut	MA	01826	978-454-5474	454-9120
Web: www.dracutlibrary.org					
Parlin Memorial Library 410 Broadway	Everett	MA	02149	617-394-2300	389-1230
Web: www.noblenet.org/everett					
Millicent Library PO Box 30	Fairhaven	MA	02719	508-992-5342	993-7288
Web: www.millicentlibrary.org					
Fall River Public Library 104 N Main St	Fall River	MA	02720	508-324-2700	324-2707
Web: www.sailsinc.org/fallriver/main.htm					
Falmouth Public Library 123 Katharine Lee Bates Rd	Falmouth	MA	02540	508-457-2555	457-2559
Web: www.falmouthpubliclibrary.org					
Fitchburg Public Library 610 Main St	Fitchburg	MA	01420	978-345-9635	345-9631

Phone Fax

Framingham Public Library 49 Lexington St ... Framingham MA 01702 508-879-3570 820-7210
Web: www.framinghamlibrary.org
Sawyer Free Library 2 Dale Ave ... Gloucester MA 01930 978-281-9763 281-9770
Web: www.sawyerfreelibrary.org
Holmes Public Library 470 Plymouth St ... Halifax MA 02338 781-293-2271 294-8518
Web: www.sailsinc.org/halifax
Haverhill Public Library 99 Main St ... Haverhill MA 01830 978-373-1586 373-8466
Web: www.haverhillpl.org
Holyoke Public Library 335 Maple St ... Holyoke MA 01040 413-322-5640 532-4230
Web: www.holyokelibrary.org
Hyannis Public Library 401 Main St ... Hyannis MA 02601 508-775-2280 790-0087
Web: www.hyannislibrary.org
Lawrence Public Library 51 Lawrence St ... Lawrence MA 01841 978-682-1727 688-3142
Web: www.lawrencefreelibrary.org
Leominster Public Library 30 West St ... Leominster MA 01453 978-534-7522
Web: www.leominsterlibrary.org
Cary Memorial Library 1874 Massachusetts Ave ... Lexington MA 02420 781-862-6288 862-7355
Web: www.carylibrary.org
Pollard Memorial Library 401 Merrimack St ... Lowell MA 01852 978-970-4120 970-4117
Web: www.pollardml.org
Lynn Public Library 5 N Common St ... Lynn MA 01902 781-595-0567 592-5050
Web: www.noblenet.org/lynn
Malden Public Library 36 Salem St ... Malden MA 02148 781-324-0218 324-4467
Web: www.maldenpubliclibrary.org
Marlborough Public Library 35 W Main St ... Marlborough MA 01752 508-624-6900 485-1494
Web: www.marlborough-ma.gov/gen/MarlboroughMA_PubLibrary/index
Ventress Library 15 Library Plaza ... Marshfield MA 02050 781-834-5535 837-8362
Web: www.ventresslibrary.org
Marstons Mills Public Library 2160 Main St ... Marstons Mills MA 02648 508-428-5175 420-5194
Web: www.mmpl.org
Medford Public Library 111 High St ... Medford MA 02155 781-395-7950 391-2261
Web: www.medfordlibrary.org
Melrose Public Library 69 W Emerson St ... Melrose MA 02176 781-665-2313 662-4229
Web: www.melrosepubliclibrary.org
Milford Town Library 80 Spruce St ... Milford MA 01757 508-473-2145 473-8651
Web: www.milfordtownlibrary.org
Milton Public Library 476 Canton Ave ... Milton MA 02186 617-698-5757 698-0441
Web: www.miltonlibrary.org
Morse Institute Library 14 E Central St ... Natick MA 01760 508-647-6520 647-6527
Web: www.morseinstitute.org
Needham Free Public Library 1139 Highland Ave ... Needham MA 02494 781-455-7559 455-7591
Web: www.town.needham.ma.us/Library
New Bedford Free Public Library 613 Pleasant St ... New Bedford MA 02740 508-991-6279 979-1481
Web: www.ci.new-bedford.ma.us
Newton Free Library 330 Homer St ... Newton Center MA 02459 617-796-1360 965-8457
Web: www.ci.newton.ma.us/Library
Norfolk Public Library 139 Main St ... Norfolk MA 02056 508-528-3380 528-6417
Web: users.rcn.com/npl
Richards Memorial Library 118 N Washington St ... North Attleboro MA 02760 508-699-0122 699-0122
Forbes Library 20 West St ... Northampton MA 01060 413-584-8550 587-1015
Web: www.forbeslibrary.org
Northborough Free Library 34 Main St ... Northborough MA 01532 508-393-5025 393-5027
Morrill Memorial Library 33 Walpole St PO Box 220 ... Norwood MA 02062 781-769-0200
Web: www.ci.norwood.ma.us/library/
Osterville Free Library 43 Wianno Ave ... Osterville MA 02655 508-428-5757 428-5557
Web: www.ostervillefreelibrary.org
Peabody Institute Library 82 Main St ... Peabody MA 01960 978-531-0100 532-1797
Web: www.peabodylibrary.org
Berkshire Athenaeum 1 Wendell Ave ... Pittsfield MA 01201 413-499-9480 499-9489
Web: www.berkshire.net/PittsfieldLibrary/
Plymouth Public Library 132 South St ... Plymouth MA 02360 508-830-4250 830-4258
Web: www.plymouthpubliclibrary.org
Provincetown Public Library 330 Commercial St ... Provincetown MA 02657 508-487-7094 487-7096
Thomas Crane Public Library 40 Washington St ... Quincy MA 02169 617-376-1300 376-1308
Web: ci.quincy.ma.us/tcpl
Turner Free Library 2 N Main St ... Randolph MA 02368 781-961-0932 961-0933
Reading Public Library 64 Middlesex Ave ... Reading MA 01867 781-944-0840 942-9106
Web: www.readingpl.org
Revere Public Library 179 Beach St ... Revere MA 02151 781-286-8380 286-8382
Salem Public Library 370 Essex St ... Salem MA 01970 978-744-0860 745-8616
Saugus Free Public Library 295 Central St ... Saugus MA 01906 781-231-4168 231-4169
Web: www.noblenet.org/saugus/
Sharon Public Library 11 N Main St ... Sharon MA 02067 781-784-1578 784-4728
Web: www.townofsharon.net/Public_Documents
Central Massachusetts Regional Library System
8 Flagg Rd ... Shrewsbury MA 01545 508-757-4110 757-4370
TF: 800-922-8326 ■ *Web:* www.cmrls.org
Somerville Public Library 79 Highland Ave ... Somerville MA 02143 617-623-5000 628-4052
Web: www.somervillepubliclibrary.org
Bacon Free Library 58 Eliot St ... South Natick MA 01760 508-653-6730 651-7013
Springfield City Library 220 State St ... Springfield MA 01103 413-263-6828 263-6817
Web: www.springfieldlibrary.org
Stoughton Public Library 84 Park St ... Stoughton MA 02072 781-344-2711 344-7340
Taunton Public Library 12 Pleasant St ... Taunton MA 02780 508-821-1411 821-1414
Web: www.tauntonlibrary.org
Tewksbury Public Library 300 Chandler St ... Tewksbury MA 01876 978-640-4490
Web: www.tewksburypl.org
Upton Town Library 2 Main St ... Upton MA 01568 508-529-6272 529-2453
Web: webpages.charter.net/uptonlib
Lucius Beebe Memorial Library 345 Main St ... Wakefield MA 01880 781-246-6334 246-6385
Web: www.wakefieldlibrary.org
Walpole Public Library 65 Common St ... Walpole MA 02081 508-660-7340 660-2714
Web: www.walpole.ma.us/library.htm
Metrowest Massachusetts Regional Library System
135 Beaver St ... Waltham MA 02452 781-398-1819 398-1821
Web: www.mmrls.org
Waltham Public Library 735 Main St ... Waltham MA 02451 781-314-3425 647-5873
Web: www.waltham.lib.ma.us
Watertown Free Public Library 30 Common St ... Watertown MA 02472 617-972-6431 926-4375
Web: www.watertownlib.org
Wayland Free Public Library 5 Concord Rd ... Wayland MA 01778 508-358-2311 358-5249
Web: www.wayland.ma.us/library
Wellesley Free Library 530 Washington St ... Wellesley MA 02482 781-235-1610 237-4875
Web: www.ci.wellesley.ma.us/library
Whelden Memorial Library PO Box 147 ... West Barnstable MA 02668 508-362-2262 362-1344
Web: home.comcast.net/whelden
West Falmouth Library Inc PO Box 1209 ... West Falmouth MA 02574 508-548-4709 457-9534
West Springfield Public Library 200 Park St ... West Springfield MA 01089 413-736-4561 736-6469
Web: www.wspl.org
Westfield Athenaeum 6 Elm St ... Westfield MA 01085 413-568-7833 568-0988
Web: www.westath.org
Tufts Library 46 Broad St ... Weymouth MA 02188 781-337-1402 682-6123
Western Massachusetts Regional Library System
4 Industrial Dr ... Whately MA 01093 413-665-9898 665-8877
Web: www.wmrls.org
David & Joyce Milne Public Library 1095 Main St ... Williamstown MA 01267 413-458-5369 458-3085
Web: www.milnelibrary.org
Woburn Public Library 45 Pleasant St ... Woburn MA 01801 781-933-0148 938-7860
Web: www.woburnpubliclibrary.org
Woods Hole Public Library
581 Woods Hole Rd PO Box 185 ... Woods Hole MA 02543 508-548-8961 540-1969

Michigan

Phone Fax

Lenawee County Library 4459 W US 223 ... Adrian MI 49221 517-263-1011
Web: www.lenawee.lib.mi.us
Alpena County George N Fletcher Public Library 211 N 1st Ave ... Alpena MI 49707 989-356-6188 356-2765
Web: www.alpenalib.org
Ann Arbor District Library 343 S 5th Ave ... Ann Arbor MI 48104 734-994-2333 327-8309
Web: www.aadl.org
Bay County Library System 307 Lafayette Ave ... Bay City MI 48708 989-894-2837 894-2021
Web: baycountylibrary.org
Benton Harbor Public Library 213 E Wall St ... Benton Harbor MI 49022 269-926-6139 926-1674
Web: www.geocities.com/bhlibrary
Baldwin Public Library 300 W Merrill St ... Birmingham MI 48009 248-647-1700 644-7297
Web: www.baldwinlib.org
Bloomfield Township Public Library 1099 Lone Pine Rd ... Bloomfield Hills MI 48302 248-642-5800 642-4175
Web: www.btpl.org
Cadillac-Wexford County Public Library 411 S Lake St ... Cadillac MI 49601 231-775-6541 775-1749
Web: www.cadillaclibrary.org
Canton Public Library 1200 S Canton Ctr Rd ... Canton MI 48188 734-397-0999 397-1130
Web: www.cantonpl.org
Macomb County Library 16480 Hall Rd ... Clinton Township MI 48038 586-286-6660 412-5958
Web: www.libcoop.net/mcl/
Kent District Library 814 W River Center Dr NE ... Comstock Park MI 49321 616-784-2007 647-9211
Web: www.kdl.org
Henry Ford Centennial Library 16301 Michigan Ave ... Dearborn MI 48126 313-943-2330 943-3063
Web: www.dearborn.lib.mi.us
Detroit Public Library 5201 Woodward Ave ... Detroit MI 48202 313-833-1000 832-0877
Web: www.detroit.lib.mi.us
East Lansing Public Library 950 Abbott Rd ... East Lansing MI 48823 517-351-2420 351-9536
Web: www.elpl.org
Eastpointe Memorial Library 15875 Oak St ... Eastpointe MI 48021 586-445-5096 775-0150
Web: ci.eastpointe.mi.us/library
Escanaba Public Library 400 Ludington St ... Escanaba MI 49829 906-786-4463 786-0942
Web: www.uproc.lib.mi.us
Ferndale Public Library 222 E Nine-Mile Rd ... Ferndale MI 48220 248-546-2504 545-5840
Web: www.ferndale.lib.mi.us
Flint Public Library 1026 E Kearsley St ... Flint MI 48502 810-232-7111 249-2635
Web: www.flint.lib.mi.us/fpl.html
Genesee District Library G-4195 W Pasadena Ave ... Flint MI 48504 810-732-0110 732-3146
Web: www.thegdl.org
Garden City Public Library 2012 Middlebelt Rd ... Garden City MI 48135 734-793-1830 793-1831
Web: garden-city.lib.mi.us
Loutit District Library 407 Columbus St ... Grand Haven MI 49417 616-842-5560 847-0570
Web: www.loutitlibrary.org
Grand Rapids Public Library 111 Library St NE ... Grand Rapids MI 49503 616-988-5400 988-5429
Web: www.grapids.lib.mi.us
Herrick District Library 300 S River Ave ... Holland MI 49423 616-355-1400 355-1426
Web: www.herrickdl.org
Dickinson County Library 401 Iron Mountain St ... Iron Mountain MI 49801 906-774-1218 774-4079
Web: www.dcl-lib.org
Jackson District Library 244 W Michigan Ave ... Jackson MI 49201 517-788-4087 782-8635
Web: www.jackson.lib.mi.us
Georgetown Township Library 1525 Baldwin St ... Jenison MI 49428 616-457-9620 457-3666
Web: www.gtwp.com/library.htm
Kalamazoo Public Library 315 S Rose St ... Kalamazoo MI 49007 269-342-9837 553-7921
Web: www.kpl.gov
Orion Township Public Library 825 Joslyn Rd ... Lake Orion MI 48362 248-693-3000 693-3009
Web: www.orion.lib.mi.us
Capital Area District Library 401 S Capitol Ave ... Lansing MI 48933 517-367-6300 374-1068
Web: www.cadl.org
Lapeer District Library 201 Village West Dr S ... Lapeer MI 48446 810-664-9521 664-8527
Web: www.library.lapeer.org
Livonia Public Library 32777 Five Mile Rd ... Livonia MI 48154 734-466-2491 458-6011
Web: livonia.lib.mi.us
Madison Heights Public Library
240 W Thirteen Mile Rd ... Madison Heights MI 48071 248-588-2029 588-2470
Peter White Public Library 217 N Front St ... Marquette MI 49855 906-228-9510 226-1783
Web: www.uproc.lib.mi.us/pwpl
White Peter Public Library 217 N Front St ... Marquette MI 49855 906-228-9510 226-1783
Web: www.uproc.lib.mi.us/pwpl
Grace A Dow Memorial Library 1710 W St Andrews Rd ... Midland MI 48640 989-837-3430 837-3468
Web: www.midland-mi.org/gracedowlibrary
Monroe County Library System 3700 S Custer Rd ... Monroe MI 48161 734-241-5277 241-4722
TF: 800-462-2050 ■ *Web:* monroe.lib.mi.us
Veterans Memorial Library 301 S University Ave ... Mount Pleasant MI 48858 989-773-3242 772-3280
Muskegon Area District Library 4845 Airline Rd ... Muskegon MI 49444 231-737-6248 737-6307
Web: www.madl.org
Niles District Library 620 E Main St ... Niles MI 49120 269-683-8545 683-0075
Web: www.nileslibrary.com
Novi Public Library 45245 W 10 Mile Rd ... Novi MI 48375 248-349-0720 349-6520
Web: novi.lib.mi.us
Oak Park Public Library 14200 Oak Park Blvd ... Oak Park MI 48237 248-691-7480 691-7155
Web: www.oak-park.lib.mi.us
Owosso Public Library 502 W Main St ... Owosso MI 48867 989-725-5134 723-5444
Pontiac Public Library 60 E Pike St ... Pontiac MI 48342 248-758-3942 758-3990
Web: pontiac.lib.mi.us
Saint Clair County Library System 210 McMorran Blvd ... Port Huron MI 48060 810-987-7323 987-7874
Web: www.sccl.lib.mi.us
Portage District Library 300 Library Ln ... Portage MI 49002 269-329-4544 324-9222
Web: www.portagelibrary.info
Rochester Hills Public Library 500 Olde Towne Rd ... Rochester MI 48307 248-656-2900 650-7131
Web: www.rhpl.org
Roseville Public Library 29777 Gratiot Ave ... Roseville MI 48066 586-445-5407 445-5499
Web: www.libcoop.net/roseville/
Royal Oak Public Library 222 E Eleven Mile Rd ... Royal Oak MI 48067 248-246-3700 545-6220
Public Libraries of Saginaw 505 Janes St ... Saginaw MI 48607 989-755-0904 755-9828
Web: www.saginawlibrary.org
Saint Clair Shores Public Library 22500 11-Mile Rd ... Saint Clair Shores MI 48081 586-771-9020 771-8935
Web: www.libcoop.net/stclairshores/
Bayliss Public Library 541 Library Dr ... Sault Sainte Marie MI 49783 906-632-9331 632-3117
Web: www.uproc.lib.mi.us/bpl
Shelby Township Library 51680 Van Dyke Hwy ... Shelby Township MI 48316 586-739-7414 726-0535
Web: www.libcoop.net/shelby/
Southfield Public Library 26300 Evergreen Rd ... Southfield MI 48076 248-796-4200 354-5319
Web: www.sfldlib.org
Library Network The 13331 Reeck Rd ... Southgate MI 48195 734-281-3830 281-1905
Web: tln.lib.mi.us
Sterling Heights Public Library 40255 Dodge Park Rd ... Sterling Heights MI 48313 586-446-2665 276-4067
Web: www.shpl.net
Troy Public Library 510 W Big Beaver Rd ... Troy MI 48084 248-524-3538 524-0112
Web: www.libcoop.net/troy

Public Libraries (Cont'd)

Michigan (Cont'd)

Library	City	State	ZIP	Phone	Fax
Warren Public Library 5460 Arden *Web:* www.libcoop.net/warren/	Warren	MI	48092	586-751-5377	264-2811
Waterford Township Public Library 5168 Civic Ctr Dr *Web:* www.waterford.lib.mi.us	Waterford	MI	48329	248-674-4831	674-1910
West Bloomfield Township Public Library 4600 Walnut Lake Rd *Web:* www.wblib.org	West Bloomfield	MI	48323	248-682-2120	232-2333

Minnesota

Library	City	State	ZIP	Phone	Fax
Albert Lea Public Library 211 E Clark St *Web:* www.city.albertlea.org/library.htm	Albert Lea	MN	56007	507-377-4350	377-4339
Douglas County Library 720 Fillmore St *Web:* www.douglascountylibrary.org	Alexandria	MN	56308	320-762-3014	762-3036
Anoka County Library 711 County Rd 10 NE *Web:* www.anoka.lib.mn.us	Blaine	MN	55434	763-717-3267	717-3259
East Central Regional Library 244 S Birch St *Web:* ecrl.lib.mn.us	Cambridge	MN	55008	763-689-7390	689-7389
Carver County Library 4 City Hall Plaza *Web:* www.carverlib.org	Chaska	MN	55318	952-448-9395	448-9392
Duluth Public Library 520 W Superior St *Web:* www.duluth.lib.mn.us	Duluth	MN	55802	218-730-3800	723-3822
Dakota County Library System 1340 Wescott Rd *Web:* www.co.dakota.mn.us/library	Eagan	MN	55123	651-688-1500	688-1530
Buckham Memorial Library 11 E Division St *Web:* www.ci.faribault.mn.us/lib	Faribault	MN	55021	507-334-2089	
Minneapolis Public Library 300 Nicollet Mall *Web:* www.mplib.org	Minneapolis	MN	55401	612-630-6000	630-6210
Hennepin County Library 12601 Ridgedale Dr *Web:* www.hennepin.lib.mn.us	Minnetonka	MN	55305	952-847-8500	847-8600
Lake Agassiz Regional Library 118 S 5th St *Web:* www.larl.org	Moorhead	MN	56561	218-233-3757	233-7556
Owatonna Public Library 105 N Elm St *Web:* www.owatonna.lib.mn.us	Owatonna	MN	55060	507-444-2460	444-2465
Rochester Public Library 101 2nd St SE *Web:* www.rochesterpubliclibrary.org	Rochester	MN	55904	507-285-8000	287-1910
Great River Regional Library 405 W Saint Germain St *Web:* www.griver.org	Saint Cloud	MN	56301	320-650-2500	650-2501
Saint Paul Public Library 90 W 4th St *Web:* www.sppl.org	Saint Paul	MN	55102	651-266-7000	266-7060
Scott County Library System 13090 Alabama Ave S *Web:* www.scott.lib.mn.us	Savage	MN	55378	952-707-1770	707-1775
Ramsey County Public Library 4570 N Victoria St *Web:* ramsey.lib.mn.us	Shoreview	MN	55126	651-486-2200	486-2220
Pioneerland Library System 410 SW 5th St *Web:* www.pioneerland.lib.mn.us	Willmar	MN	56201	320-235-6106	214-0187
Winona Public Library 151 W 5th St PO Box 1247 *Web:* www.selco.lib.mn.us/winona	Winona	MN	55987	507-452-4582	452-5842
Washington County Library 8595 Central Pk Pl *Web:* www.co.washington.mn.us/info_for_residents/library	Woodbury	MN	55125	651-275-8500	275-8509
Nobles County Library 407 12th St	Worthington	MN	56187	507-372-2981	372-2982

Mississippi

Library	City	State	ZIP	Phone	Fax
Hancock County Library 312 Hwy 90 *Web:* www.hancock.lib.ms.us	Bay Saint Louis	MS	39520	228-467-5282	467-5503
Madison County-Canton Public Library 102 Priestley St *Web:* www.mad.lib.ms.us	Canton	MS	39046	601-859-3202	859-2728
Carnegie Public Library 114 Delta Ave *Web:* www.cplclarksdale.lib.ms.us	Clarksdale	MS	38614	662-624-4461	627-4344
Bolivar County Library 104 S Leflore Ave *TF:* 888-268-8076 ■ *Web:* www.bolivar.lib.ms.us	Cleveland	MS	38732	662-843-2774	843-4701
Columbus-Lowndes County Library 314 N 7th St *Web:* www.lowndes.lib.ms.us	Columbus	MS	39701	662-329-5300	329-5156
Washington County Library 341 S Main St	Greenville	MS	38701	662-335-2331	390-4758
Greenwood-Leflore Public Library 405 W Washington St	Greenwood	MS	38930	662-453-3634	453-0683
Harrison County Library System 47 Maples Dr Trailer 1 *Web:* www.harrison.lib.ms.us	Gulfport	MS	35907	228-871-7171	
Library of Hattiesburg Petal & Forrest County 329 Hardy St *Web:* www.hpfc.lib.ms.us	Hattiesburg	MS	39401	601-582-4461	582-5338
First Regional Library 370 W Commerce St	Hernando	MS	38632	662-429-4439	429-8853
Marshall County Library 109 E Gholson Ave	Holly Springs	MS	38635	662-252-3823	252-3066
Sunflower County Library 201 Cypress Dr	Indianola	MS	38751	662-887-2298	887-1618
Jackson/Hinds Library System 300 N State St *TF:* 800-968-5803 ■ *Web:* www.jhlibrary.com	Jackson	MS	39201	601-968-5811	968-5817
Laurel-Jones County Library 530 Commerce St *Web:* www.laurel.lib.ms.us	Laurel	MS	39440	601-428-4313	428-4314
Meridian-Lauderdale County Public Library 2517 7th St *Web:* www.meridian.lib.ms.us	Meridian	MS	39301	601-693-6771	486-2260
Jackson-George Regional Library System 3214 S Pascagoula St *Web:* www.jgrls.org	Pascagoula	MS	39567	228-769-3060	769-3113
Pearl River County Library System 900 Goodyear Blvd *Web:* www.pearlriver.lib.ms.us	Picayune	MS	39466	601-798-5081	798-5082
Starkville Public Library 326 University Dr *Web:* www.starkville.lib.ms.us	Starkville	MS	39759	662-323-2766	323-9140
Lee County Library 219 N Madison St	Tupelo	MS	38804	662-841-9027	840-7615
Warren County-Vicksburg Public Library 700 Veto St *Web:* www.warren.lib.ms.us	Vicksburg	MS	39180	601-636-6411	634-4809

Missouri

Library	City	State	ZIP	Phone	Fax
Taneyhills Community Library 200 S 4th St	Branson	MO	65616	417-334-1418	
Camden County Library District 89 Rodeo Rd PO Box 1320 *Web:* www.camden.lib.mo.us	Camdenton	MO	65020	573-346-5954	346-1263
Cape Girardeau Public Library 711 N Clark St *Web:* capelibrary.org	Cape Girardeau	MO	63701	573-334-5279	334-8334
Daniel Boone Regional Library 100 W Broadway *TF:* 800-324-4806 ■ *Web:* www.dbrl.org	Columbia	MO	65203	573-443-3161	443-3281
Cass County Public Library 400 E Mechanic St *Web:* www.casscolibrary.org	Harrisonville	MO	64701	816-884-6223	884-2301
Mid-Continent Public Library 15616 E 24 Hwy *Web:* www.mcpl.lib.mo.us	Independence	MO	64050	816-836-5200	521-7253
Missouri River Regional Library 214 Adams St *Web:* www.mrrl.org	Jefferson City	MO	65101	573-634-2464	634-7028
Joplin Public Library 300 S Main St *Web:* www.joplinpubliclibrary.org	Joplin	MO	64801	417-623-7953	624-5217
Kansas City Public Library 14 W 10th St *Web:* www.kclibrary.org	Kansas City	MO	64105	816-701-3400	701-3401
Linda Hall Library 5109 Cherry St *TF:* 800-662-1545 ■ *Web:* www.lindahall.org	Kansas City	MO	64110	816-363-4600	926-8790
Dunklin County Library 209 N Main St	Kennett	MO	63857	573-888-3561	888-6393
Kirkwood Public Library 140 E Jefferson Ave *Web:* kpl.lib.mo.us	Kirkwood	MO	63122	314-821-5770	822-3755
Christian County Library 1005 N 4th Ave *Web:* christiancounty.lib.mo.us	Ozark	MO	65721	417-581-2432	581-8855
Saint Louis County Library 1640 S Lindbergh Blvd *Web:* www.slcl.lib.mo.us	Saint Louis	MO	63131	314-994-3300	997-7602
Saint Louis Public Library 1301 Olive St *Web:* www.slpl.lib.mo.us	Saint Louis	MO	63103	314-241-2288	539-0393
Saint Charles City County Library District 77 Boone Hill Dr Box 529 *Web:* www.win.org/library	Saint Peters	MO	63376	636-441-2300	441-3132
Springfield-Greene County Library 4623 S Campbell *Web:* thelibrary.springfield.missouri.org	Springfield	MO	65810	417-874-8120	874-8121
University City Public Library 6701 Delmar Blvd *Web:* www.ucpl.lib.mo.us	University City	MO	63130	314-727-3150	727-6005

Montana

Library	City	State	ZIP	Phone	Fax
Parmly Billings Library 510 N Broadway *Web:* www.billings.lib.mt.us	Billings	MT	59101	406-657-8257	657-8293
Bozeman Public Library 220 E Lamme St *Web:* www.bozemanlibrary.org	Bozeman	MT	59715	406-582-2400	
Butte-Silver Bow Public Library 226 W Broadway	Butte	MT	59701	406-723-3361	782-1825
Great Falls Public Library 301 2nd Ave N *Web:* www.greatfallslibrary.org	Great Falls	MT	59401	406-453-0349	453-0181
Lewis & Clark Library 120 S Last Chance Gulch *Web:* www.lewisandclarklibrary.org	Helena	MT	59601	406-447-1690	447-1687
Flathead County Library 247 1st Ave E *Web:* www.flatheadcountylibrary.org	Kalispell	MT	59901	406-758-5819	758-5868
Missoula Public Library 301 E Main St *Web:* www.missoula.lib.mt.us	Missoula	MT	59802	406-721-2665	728-5900

Nebraska

Library	City	State	ZIP	Phone	Fax
Bellevue Public Library 1003 Lincoln Rd	Bellevue	NE	68005	402-293-3157	293-3163
Columbus Public Library 2504 14th St *Web:* www.columbuslibrary.info	Columbus	NE	68601	402-564-7116	563-3378
Edith Abbott Memorial Library 211 N Washington St *Web:* www.gi.lib.ne.us	Grand Island	NE	68801	308-385-5333	385-5339
Hastings Public Library 517 W 4th St *Web:* www.hastings.lib.ne.us	Hastings	NE	68901	402-461-2346	461-2359
Kearney Public Library & Information Center 2020 1st Ave *Web:* cityofkearney.org/index.asp?ID=6	Kearney	NE	68847	308-233-3282	233-3291
Lincoln City Libraries 136 S 14th St *Web:* www.ci.lincoln.ne.us/city/library	Lincoln	NE	68508	402-441-8500	441-8586
North Platte Public Library 120 W 4th St	North Platte	NE	69101	308-535-8036	535-8296
Omaha Public Library 215 S 15th St *Web:* www.omaha.lib.ne.us	Omaha	NE	68102	402-444-4800	444-4504

Nevada

Library	City	State	ZIP	Phone	Fax
Carson City Library 900 N Roop St	Carson City	NV	89701	775-887-2247	887-2273
Las Vegas-Clark County Library District 833 Las Vegas Blvd N *Web:* www.lvccld.org	Las Vegas	NV	89101	702-734-7323	507-3598
Douglas County Library PO Box 337	Minden	NV	89423	775-782-9841	782-5754
North Las Vegas Public Library 2300 Civic Center Dr	North Las Vegas	NV	89030	702-633-1070	649-2576
Washoe County Library 301 S Center St *Web:* www.washoe.lib.nv.us	Reno	NV	89501	775-327-8300	327-8390

New Hampshire

Library	City	State	ZIP	Phone	Fax
Amherst Town Library 14 Main St *Web:* www.amherst.lib.nh.us	Amherst	NH	03031	603-673-2288	672-6063
Concord Public Library 45 Green St *Web:* www.ci.concord.nh.us/Library/default.asp	Concord	NH	03301	603-225-8670	230-3693
Derry Public Library 64 E Broadway *Web:* www.derry.lib.nh.us	Derry	NH	03038	603-432-6140	432-6128
Dover Public Library 73 Locust St *Web:* www.dover.lib.nh.us	Dover	NH	03820	603-516-6050	516-6053
Taylor Library 49 E Derry Rd	East Derry	NH	03041	603-432-7186	432-0985
Howe Library 13 E South St *Web:* www.thehowe.org	Hanover	NH	03755	603-643-4120	643-0725
Hollis Social Library 2 Monument Sq *Web:* www.hollis.nh.us/library	Hollis	NH	03049	603-465-7721	465-3507
Manchester City Library 405 Pine St *Web:* www.manchester.lib.nh.us	Manchester	NH	03104	603-624-6550	624-6559
Nashua Public Library 2 Court St *Web:* www.nashualibrary.org	Nashua	NH	03060	603-589-4600	594-3457
Rochester Public Library 65 S Main St *Web:* www.rpl.lib.nh.us	Rochester	NH	03867	603-332-1428	335-7582
Kelley Library 234 Main St *Web:* www.salem.lib.nh.us	Salem	NH	03079	603-898-7064	898-8583

New Jersey

Library	City	State	ZIP	Phone	Fax
Atlantic City Free Public Library 1 N Tennessee Ave *Web:* www.acfpl.org	Atlantic City	NJ	08401	609-345-2269	345-5570
Bayonne Free Public Library 697 Ave C *Web:* www.bayonnenj.org/library	Bayonne	NJ	07002	201-858-6970	437-6928
Belleville Public Library 221 Washington Ave *Web:* www.bellepl.org	Belleville	NJ	07109	973-450-3434	759-6731
Warren County Library 199 Hardwick St *Web:* www.warrenlib.com	Belvidere	NJ	07823	908-475-6322	475-6359
Bloomfield Public Library 90 Broad St	Bloomfield	NJ	07003	973-566-6200	566-6217
Cumberland County Library 800 E Commerce St *Web:* www.clueslibs.org	Bridgeton	NJ	08302	856-453-2210	451-1940

Library	City	State	ZIP	Phone	Fax
Somerset County Library 1 Vogt Dr	Bridgewater	NJ	08807	908-526-4016	526-5221
Web: somerset.lib.nj.us					
Camden Free Public Library 418 Federal St	Camden	NJ	08101	856-757-7640	757-7631
Cape May County Library 30 W Mechanic St	Cape May Court House	NJ	08210	609-463-6350	465-3895
Web: www.cape-may.county.lib.nj.us					
Cherry Hill Public Library 1100 Kings Hwy N	Cherry Hill	NJ	08034	856-667-0300	667-4937
Web: www.cherryhill.lib.nj.us					
Clark Public Library 303 Westfield Ave	Clark	NJ	07066	732-388-5999	388-7866
Web: www.clarklibrary.org					
Clifton Public Library 292 Piaget Ave	Clifton	NJ	07011	973-772-5500	772-2926
Web: www.cliftonpl.org					
East Brunswick Public Library 2 Jean Walling Civic Ctr	East Brunswick	NJ	08816	732-390-6950	390-6869
Web: www.ebpl.org					
East Orange Public Library 21 S Arlington Ave	East Orange	NJ	07018	973-266-5600	674-1991
Web: www.eopl.org					
Edison Township Free Public Library 340 Plainfield Ave	Edison	NJ	08817	732-287-2298	819-9134
Web: www.lmxac.org/edisonlib					
Elizabeth Public Library 11 S Broad St	Elizabeth	NJ	07202	908-354-6060	354-5845
Web: www.elizpl.org					
Englewood Public Library 31 Engle St	Englewood	NJ	07631	201-568-2215	568-6895
Web: www.englewoodlibrary.org					
Maurice M Pine Free Public Library 10-01 Fair Lawn Ave	Fair Lawn	NJ	07410	201-796-3400	794-6344
Web: www.bccls.org/fairlawn					
Hunterdon County Library 314 SR 12	Flemington	NJ	08822	908-788-1444	806-4862
Web: www.hclibrary.us					
Fort Lee Free Public Library 320 Main St	Fort Lee	NJ	07024	201-592-3614	585-0375
Web: www.bccls.org/fortlee					
Garfield Free Public Library 500 Midland Ave	Garfield	NJ	07026	973-478-3800	478-7162
Web: www.bccls.org/garfield					
Johnson Public Library 275 Moore St	Hackensack	NJ	07601	201-343-4169	343-1395
Web: www.bccls.org/hackensack					
Hamilton Township Public Library 1 Municipal Dr	Hamilton	NJ	08619	609-581-4060	581-4067
Web: www.hamiltonpl.org					
Hoboken Public Library 500 Park Ave	Hoboken	NJ	07030	201-420-2346	420-2299
Margaret E Heggan Public Library 208 E Holly Ave	Hurffville	NJ	08080	856-589-3334	582-2042
Web: www.hegganlibrary.org					
Irvington Public Library Civic Sq	Irvington	NJ	07111	973-372-6400	372-6860
Web: www.irvingtonpubliclibrary.org					
Jersey City Public Library 472 Jersey Ave	Jersey City	NJ	07302	201-547-4500	547-4584
Kearny Public Library 318 Kearny Ave	Kearny	NJ	07032	201-998-2666	998-1141
Web: www.kearnylibrary.org					
Lakewood Public Library 301 Lexington Ave	Lakewood	NJ	08701	732-363-1435	363-1438
Mercer County Library 2751 Brunswick Pike	Lawrenceville	NJ	08648	609-989-6916	538-1208
Web: www.mcl.org					
Linden Public Library 31 E Henry St	Linden	NJ	07036	908-298-3830	486-2636
Web: www.lindenpl.org					
Livingston Public Library 10 Robert H Harp Dr	Livingston	NJ	07039	973-992-4600	994-2346
Web: www.bccls.org/livingston					
Long Branch Free Public Library 328 Broadway	Long Branch	NJ	07740	732-222-3900	222-3799
Web: www.lmxac.org/longbranch					
Monmouth County Library 125 Symmes Rd	Manalapan	NJ	07726	732-431-7220	409-2556
Web: www.monmouth.lib.nj.us					
Atlantic County Library-Mays Landing 40 Farragut Ave	Mays Landing	NJ	08330	609-646-8699	625-8143
Web: www.atlanticlibrary.org					
Middletown Township Library 55 New Monmouth Rd	Middletown	NJ	07748	732-671-3700	671-5839
Web: www.mtpl.org					
South Brunswick Public Library 110 Kingston Ln	Monmouth Junction	NJ	08852	732-329-4000	329-0573
Web: www.lmxac.org/sobr					
Montclair Public Library 50 S Fullerton Ave	Montclair	NJ	07042	973-744-0500	744-5268
Web: www.montlib.com					
Mount Arlington Public Library 404 Howard Blvd	Mount Arlington	NJ	07856	973-398-1516	398-0171
Web: www.gti.net/mountarlington					
Mount Laurel Library 100 Walt Whitman Ave	Mount Laurel	NJ	08054	856-234-7319	234-6916
Web: www.mtlaurel.lib.nj.us					
Gloucester County Library System 389 Wolfert Stn Rd	Mullica Hill	NJ	08062	856-223-6000	223-6039
Web: www.gcls.org					
Neptune Public Library 25 Neptune Blvd	Neptune	NJ	07753	732-775-8241	774-1132
Web: neptunepubliclibrary.org					
New Brunswick Free Public Library 60 Livingston Ave	New Brunswick	NJ	08901	732-745-5108	846-0226
Web: www.lmxac.org/nbfpl/					
Newark Public Library 5 Washington St	Newark	NJ	07101	973-733-7784	733-5919
Web: www.npl.org					
Sussex County Library 125 Morris Tpke	Newton	NJ	07860	973-948-3660	948-2071
Web: www.sussexcountylibrary.org					
North Bergen Free Public Library 8411 Bergenline Ave	North Bergen	NJ	07047	201-869-4715	868-0968
North Brunswick Public Library 880 Hermann Rd	North Brunswick	NJ	08902	732-246-3545	246-1341
Web: www.lmxac.org/northbrunswick					
Nutley Free Public Library 93 Booth Dr	Nutley	NJ	07110	973-667-0405	667-0408
Web: www.bccls.org/nutley					
Ocean City Public Library 1735 Simpson Ave	Ocean City	NJ	08226	609-399-2434	398-8944
Web: www.oceancitylibrary.org					
Old Bridge Public Library 1 Old Bridge Plaza	Old Bridge	NJ	08857	732-607-7921	607-4816
Orange Public Library 348 Main St	Orange	NJ	07050	973-673-0153	673-1847
Web: www.orangepl.org					
Sayreville Free Public Library 1050 Washington Rd	Parlin	NJ	08859	732-727-0212	553-0776
Web: www.lmxac.org/sayreville/					
Parsippany-Troy Hills Public Library 292 Parsippany Rd	Parsippany	NJ	07054	973-887-8907	887-0062
Web: www.parsippanylibrary.org					
Passaic Public Library 195 Gregory Ave	Passaic	NJ	07055	973-779-0474	779-0889
Web: www.bccls.org/passaic					
Paterson Free Public Library 250 Broadway	Paterson	NJ	07501	973-321-1223	321-1205
Web: www.patersonpl.org					
Pennsauken Free Public Library 5605 Crescent Blvd	Pennsauken	NJ	08110	856-665-5959	486-0142
Web: www.pennsaukenlibrary.org					
Perth Amboy Public Library 196 Jefferson St	Perth Amboy	NJ	08861	732-826-2600	324-8079
John F Kennedy Library 500 Hoes Ln	Piscataway	NJ	08854	732-463-1633	463-9022
Web: www.piscatawaylibrary.org/kennedy.html					
Plainfield Public Library 8th St & Park Ave	Plainfield	NJ	07060	908-757-1111	754-0063
Rahway Public Library 2 City Hall Plaza	Rahway	NJ	07065	732-340-1551	340-0393
Web: www.lmxac.org/rahway					
Franklin Township Public Library 485 DeMott Ln	Somerset	NJ	08873	732-873-8700	873-0746
Web: www.franklintwp.org					
Teaneck Public Library 840 Teaneck Rd	Teaneck	NJ	07666	201-837-4171	837-0410
Web: www.teaneck.org					
Ocean County Library 101 Washington St	Toms River	NJ	08753	732-349-6200	473-1356
Web: www.oceancountylibrary.org					
Trenton Public Library 120 Academy St	Trenton	NJ	08608	609-392-7188	396-8631
Web: www.trenton.lib.nj.us					
Union Township Public Library 1980 Morris Ave	Union	NJ	07083	908-851-5450	851-4671
Web: www.uplnj.org					
Union City Public Library 324 43rd St	Union City	NJ	07087	201-866-7500	866-0962
Vineland Public Library 1058 E Landis Ave	Vineland	NJ	08360	856-794-4244	691-0366
Web: www.vineland.lib.nj.us					
Camden County Library 203 Laurel Rd	Voorhees	NJ	08043	856-772-1636	772-6105
Web: www.camden.lib.nj.us					
Wayne Public Library 461 Valley Rd	Wayne	NJ	07470	973-694-4272	692-0637
Web: www.waynepubliclibrary.org					

Library	City	State	ZIP	Phone	Fax
West Milford Township Library 1490 Union Valley Rd	West Milford	NJ	07480	973-728-2820	728-2106
Web: www.wmtl.org					
West New York Public Library 425 60th St	West New York	NJ	07093	201-295-5135	662-1473
West Orange Public Library 46 Mt Pleasant Ave	West Orange	NJ	07052	973-736-0198	736-1655
Web: www.wopl.lib.nj.us					
Burlington County Library 5 Pioneer Blvd	Westampton	NJ	08060	609-267-9660	267-4091
Web: www.bcls.lib.nj.us					
Westfield Memorial Library 550 E Broad St	Westfield	NJ	07090	908-789-4090	789-0921
Web: www.wmlnj.org					
Morris County Free Library 30 E Hanover Ave	Whippany	NJ	07981	973-285-6934	285-6973
Web: www.gti.net/mocolib1/MCL.html					
Monroe Township Free Public Library 306 S Main St	Williamstown	NJ	08094	856-629-1212	875-0191
Web: www.monroetownshiplibrary.org					
Willingboro Public Library 220 Willingboro Pkwy	Willingboro	NJ	08046	609-877-6668	835-1699
Web: www.willingboro.org					
Woodbridge Public Library George Frederick Plaza	Woodbridge	NJ	07095	732-634-4450	634-1569
Web: www.woodbridge.lib.nj.us					

New Mexico

Library	City	State	ZIP	Phone	Fax
Alamogordo Public Library 920 Oregon Ave	Alamogordo	NM	88310	505-439-4140	439-4108
Rio Grande Valley Library System 501 Copper Ave NW	Albuquerque	NM	87102	505-768-5141	768-5191
Web: www.cabq.gov/library					
Artesia Public Library 306 W Richardson Ave	Artesia	NM	88210	505-746-4252	746-3075
Web: www.pvtnetworks.net/apublib					
Carlsbad Public Library 101 S Halagueno	Carlsbad	NM	88220	505-885-6776	885-8809
Web: www.cityofcarlsbadnm.com/community%5Fdevelopment/library					
Clovis-Carver Public Library 701 Main St	Clovis	NM	88101	505-769-7840	769-7842
Web: www.library.cityofclovis.org					
Marshall Memorial Library 301 S Tin St	Deming	NM	88030	505-546-9202	546-9649
Web: www.zianet.com/demingpl					
Espanola Public Library 314-A N Paseo de Onate	Espanola	NM	87532	505-747-6087	753-5543
Web: www.youseemore.com/espanola					
Farmington Public Library 2101 Farmington Ave	Farmington	NM	87401	505-599-1270	599-1257
Hobbs Public Library 509 N Shipp St	Hobbs	NM	88240	505-397-9328	397-1508
Web: hobbspublib.leaco.net					
Thomas Branigan Memorial Library 200 E Picacho Ave	Las Cruces	NM	88001	505-528-4000	528-4030
Web: library.las-cruces.org					
Esther Bone Memorial Library 950 Pinetree Rd SE	Rio Rancho	NM	87124	505-891-5013	891-7246
Web: www.ci.rio-rancho.nm.us/library.htm					
Roswell Public Library 301 N Pennsylvania Ave	Roswell	NM	88201	505-622-7101	622-7107
Web: www.roswellpubliclibrary.org					
Santa Fe Public Library 145 Washington Ave	Santa Fe	NM	87501	505-955-6780	955-6676
Web: www.ci.santa-fe.nm.us/sfpl					
Socorro Public Library 401 Park St	Socorro	NM	87801	505-835-1114	835-1182
Web: www.adobelibrary.org					

New York

Library	City	State	ZIP	Phone	Fax
Albany Public Library 161 Washington Ave	Albany	NY	12210	518-449-3380	449-3386
Web: www.albanypubliclibrary.org					
Amherst Public Library 350 John James Audubon Pkwy	Amherst	NY	14228	716-689-4922	689-6116
Baldwinsville Public Library 33 E Genesee St	Baldwinsville	NY	13027	315-635-5631	635-6760
Web: www.bville.lib.ny.us					
Suffolk Co-op Library System 627 N Sunrise Service Rd	Bellport	NY	11713	631-286-1600	286-1647
Web: www.suffolk.lib.ny.us					
Broome County Public Library 185 Court St	Binghamton	NY	13901	607-778-6451	778-6429
Web: www.bclibrary.info					
Brentwood Public Library 2nd Ave & 4th St	Brentwood	NY	11717	631-273-7883	435-8094
Web: brentwood.suffolk.lib.ny.us					
Bronx Library Center 310 E Kings Bridge Rd	Bronx	NY	10458	718-579-4244	579-4264
Brooklyn Public Library Grand Army Plaza	Brooklyn	NY	11238	718-230-2100	230-2097
Web: www.brooklynpubliclibrary.org					
Buffalo & Erie County Public Library 1 Lafayette Sq	Buffalo	NY	14203	716-858-8900	858-6211
Web: www.buffalolib.org					
Reinstein Public Library 2580 Harlem Rd	Cheektowaga	NY	14225	716-892-8089	
East Rochester Public Library 111 W Elm St	East Rochester	NY	14445	585-586-8302	
Web: mcls.rochester.lib.ny.us/erochester					
Steele Memorial Library 101 E Church St	Elmira	NY	14901	607-733-9173	733-9176
Web: www.steele.lib.ny.us					
Hamburg Public Library 102 Buffalo St	Hamburg	NY	14075	716-649-4415	649-4160
Hempstead Public Library 115 Nichols Ct	Hempstead	NY	11550	516-481-6990	481-6719
Web: www.nassaulibrary.org					
Finger Lakes Library System 119 E Green St	Ithaca	NY	14850	607-273-4074	273-3618
TF: 800-909-3557 ■ *Web:* www.flls.org					
Tompkins County Public Library 101 E Green St	Ithaca	NY	14850	607-272-4557	272-8111
Web: www.tcpl.org					
Queens Borough Public Library 89-11 Merrick Blvd	Jamaica	NY	11432	718-990-0700	658-2919*
**Fax:* Hum Res ■ *Web:* www.queenslibrary.org					
Chautauqua-Cattaraugus Library System 106 W 5th St	Jamestown	NY	14701	716-484-7135	483-6880
Web: www.cclslib.org					
Town of Tonawanda Public Library Kenmore Branch 160 Delaware Rd	Kenmore	NY	14217	716-873-2842	873-8416
Web: www.buffalolib.org/libraries/kenmore					
Lancaster Public Library 5466 Broadway	Lancaster	NY	14086	716-683-1120	686-0749
William K Sanford Town Library 629 Albany Shaker Rd	Loudonville	NY	12211	518-458-9274	438-0988
Web: www.colonie.org/library					
Ramapo Catskill Library System 619 Rt 17-M	Middletown	NY	10940	845-343-1131	343-1205
Web: www.rcls.org					
Mount Vernon Public Library 28 S 1st Ave	Mount Vernon	NY	10550	914-668-1840	668-1018
Web: www.mountvernonpubliclibrary.org					
New York Public Library 476 5th Ave	New York	NY	10018	212-930-0800	930-0572
Web: www.nypl.org					
Niagara Falls Public Library 1425 Main St	Niagara Falls	NY	14305	716-286-4894	286-4885
Web: www.niagarafallspubliclib.org					
Penfield Public Library 1985 Baird Rd	Penfield	NY	14526	585-383-0500	340-8748
Web: www.penfieldlibrary.org					
Clinton-Essex-Franklin Library System 33 Oak St	Plattsburgh	NY	12901	518-563-5190	563-0421
Web: www.cefls.org					
Mid-Hudson Library System 103 Market St	Poughkeepsie	NY	12601	845-471-6060	454-5940
Web: midhudson.org					
Brighton Memorial Library 2300 Elmwood Ave	Rochester	NY	14618	585-784-5300	784-5333
Web: www.brightonlibrary.org					
Central Library of Rochester & Monroe County 115 South Ave	Rochester	NY	14604	585-428-8100	428-8353
Web: www.rochester.lib.ny.us/central					
Chili Public Library 3333 Chili Ave	Rochester	NY	14624	585-889-2200	889-5819
Web: www.libraryweb.org/chili/					
Gates Public Library 1605 Buffalo Rd	Rochester	NY	14624	585-247-6446	426-5733
Web: www.gateslibrary.org					
Greece Public Library 2 Vince Tofany Blvd	Rochester	NY	14616	585-225-8951	225-2777
Web: www.rochester.lib.ny.us/greece					

Public Libraries (Cont'd)

New York (Cont'd)

Library	City	State	ZIP	Phone	Fax
Henrietta Public Library 455 Calkins Rd *Web:* www.hpl.org	Rochester	NY	14623	585-359-7093	334-6369
Irondequoit Public Library 45 Cooper Rd. *Web:* www.libraryweb.org/irondequoit/	Rochester	NY	14617	585-336-6062	336-6066
Schenectady County Public Library System 99 Clinton St *Web:* www.scpl.org	Schenectady	NY	12305	518-388-4500	386-2241
John C Hart Memorial Library 1130 E Main St	Shrub Oak	NY	10588	914-245-5262	245-5936
Saint George Library Center 5 Central Ave.	Staten Island	NY	10301	718-442-8560	447-2703
Onondaga County Public Library 447 S Salina St *Web:* www.ocpl.lib.ny.us	Syracuse	NY	13202	315-435-1800	435-8533
Nassau Library System 900 Jerusalem Ave *Web:* www.nassaulibrary.org	Uniondale	NY	11553	516-292-8920	481-4777
Mid-York Library System 1600 Lincoln Ave *Web:* www.midyork.org	Utica	NY	13502	315-735-8328	735-0943
Henry Waldinger Memorial Library 60 Verona Pl. *Web:* www.nassaulibrary.org/valleyst	Valley Stream	NY	11582	516-825-6422	825-6551
Four County Library System 304 Clubhouse Rd. *Web:* www.4cls.org	Vestal	NY	13850	607-723-8236	723-1722
Vestal Public Library 320 Vestal Pkwy E	Vestal	NY	13850	607-754-4243	754-7936
Albert Wisner Public Library 2 Colonial Ave *Web:* www.albertwisnerlibrary.org	Warwick	NY	10990	845-986-1047	987-1228
North Country Library System 22072 CR 190 *Web:* www.nc3r.org/ncls	Watertown	NY	13601	315-782-5540	782-6883
Roswell P Flower Memorial Library 229 Washington St. *Web:* www.flowermemoriallibrary.org	Watertown	NY	13601	315-788-2352	788-2584
Webster Public Library Webster Plaza 980 Ridge Rd *Web:* www.websterlibrary.org	Webster	NY	14580	585-872-7075	872-7073
West Islip Public Library 3 Higbie Ln. *Web:* www.wipublib.org	West Islip	NY	11795	631-661-7080	661-7137
West Seneca Public Library 1300 Union Rd	West Seneca	NY	14224	716-674-2928	
White Plains Public Library 100 Martine Ave *Web:* www.whiteplainslibrary.org	White Plains	NY	10601	914-422-1400	422-1462
Yonkers Public Library 1 Larkin Center *Web:* www.ypl.org	Yonkers	NY	10701	914-337-1500	376-3676

North Carolina

Library	City	State	ZIP	Phone	Fax
Stanly County Public Library 133 E Main St *Web:* www.stanlylib.org	Albemarle	NC	28001	704-986-3759	983-6713
Randolph Public Library 201 Worth St. *Web:* www.randolphlibrary.org	Asheboro	NC	27203	336-318-6800	318-6823
Asheville-Buncombe Library System 67 Haywood St. *Web:* www.buncombecounty.org/governing/depts/Library/	Asheville	NC	28801	828-250-4746	255-5213
Transylvania County Library 105 S Broad St *Web:* transylvania.lib.nc.us	Brevard	NC	28712	828-884-3151	877-4230
Pender County Public Library 103 S Cowan St *Web:* tlc.library.net/pender	Burgaw	NC	28425	910-259-1234	259-0656
Central North Carolina Regional Library 342 S Spring St. *Web:* www.cncrl.com	Burlington	NC	27215	336-229-3588	229-3592
Chapel Hill Public Library 100 Library Dr *Web:* townhall.townofchapelhill.org/library/	Chapel Hill	NC	27514	919-968-2780	968-2838
Public Library of Charlotte & Mecklenburg County 310 N Tryon St *Web:* www.plcmc.org	Charlotte	NC	28202	704-336-2725	336-2002
Sampson-Clinton Public Library 217 Graham St	Clinton	NC	28328	910-592-4153	590-3504
Durham County Library 300 N Roxboro St *Web:* www.durhamcountylibrary.org	Durham	NC	27701	919-560-0220	560-0106
Rockingham County Public Library 527 Boone Rd *Web:* www.rcpl.org	Eden	NC	27288	336-627-1106	623-1258
Bladen County Public Library 111 N Cypress St	Elizabethtown	NC	28337	910-862-6990	862-8777
Northwestern Regional Library 111 N Front St *Web:* www.nwrl.org	Elkin	NC	28621	336-835-4894	526-2270
Cumberland County Public Library 300 Maiden Ln *Web:* www.cumberland.lib.nc.us	Fayetteville	NC	28301	910-483-1580	486-5372
Gaston County Public Library 1555 E Garrison Blvd *Web:* www.glrl.lib.nc.us	Gastonia	NC	28054	704-868-2164	853-0609
Greensboro Public Library PO Box 3178 *Web:* www.greensborolibrary.org	Greensboro	NC	27402	336-373-2474	333-6781
Halifax County Library System PO Box 97	Halifax	NC	27839	252-583-3631	583-8661
Leslie H Perry Memorial Library 134 Rose Ave	Henderson	NC	27536	252-438-3316	438-3744
Henderson County Public Library 301 N Washington St *Web:* www.henderson.lib.nc.us	Hendersonville	NC	28739	828-697-4725	692-8449
High Point Public Library 901 N Main St *Web:* www.hipopl.org	High Point	NC	27262	336-883-3660	883-3636
Onslow County Public Library 58 Doris Ave E *Web:* www.co.onslow.nc.us/library	Jacksonville	NC	28540	910-455-7350	455-1661
Duplin County Library PO Box 930	Kenansville	NC	28349	910-296-2117	296-2172
Caldwell County Public Library 120 Hospital Ave *Web:* www.ccpl.us	Lenoir	NC	28645	828-757-1288	757-1413
Davidson County Public Library System 602 S Main St *Web:* www.ils.unc.edu/nclibs/davidson	Lexington	NC	27292	336-242-2064	249-8161
Harnett County Public Library PO Box 1149 *Web:* www.harnett.org/library	Lillington	NC	27546	910-893-3446	893-3001
Franklin County Library 906 N Main St	Louisburg	NC	27549	919-496-2111	496-1339
Robeson County Public Library 101 N Chestnut	Lumberton	NC	28359	910-738-4859	739-8321
McDowell County Public Library 90 W Court St *Web:* main.nc.us/libraries/mcdowell	Marion	NC	28752	828-652-3858	652-2098
Davie County Public Library 371 N Main St. *Web:* www.co.davie.nc.us	Mocksville	NC	27028	336-751-2023	751-1370
Union County Public Library 316 E Windsor St *Web:* www.union.lib.nc.us	Monroe	NC	28112	704-283-8184	282-0657
Burke County Public Library 204 S King St *Web:* www.bcpls.org	Morganton	NC	28655	828-437-5638	433-1914
New Bern-Craven County Public Library 400 Johnson St *Web:* newbern.cpclib.org	New Bern	NC	28560	252-638-7800	638-7817
Catawba County Library 115 W 'C' St *Web:* library.co.catawba.nc.us	Newton	NC	28658	828-464-2421	465-8293
Appalachian Regional Library 215 10th St *Web:* www.arlibrary.org	North Wilkesboro	NC	28659	336-838-2818	667-2638
Richard H Thornton Public Library 210 Main St *Web:* www.granville.lib.nc.us	Oxford	NC	27565	919-693-1121	693-2244
Wake County Public Library System 4020 Carya Dr *Web:* www.wakegov.com/county/libraries/	Raleigh	NC	27610	919-250-1200	250-1209
Rowan Public Library PO Box 4039 *Web:* www.rowanpubliclibrary.org	Salisbury	NC	28145	704-638-3000	638-3002
Lee County Library 107 Hawkins Ave	Sanford	NC	27330	919-774-6045	775-1832
Public Library of Johnston County & Smithfield 305 Market St	Smithfield	NC	27577	919-934-8146	934-8084
Brunswick County Library 109 W Moore St *Web:* library.brunsco.net	Southport	NC	28461	910-457-6237	457-6977
Rutherford County Library 255 Callahan Koon Rd	Spindale	NC	28160	828-287-6117	287-6119
Iredell County Library PO Box 1810 *Web:* www.iredell.lib.nc.us	Statesville	NC	28687	704-878-3090	878-5449
Edgecombe County Memorial Library 909 Main St *Web:* www.edgecombelibrary.org	Tarboro	NC	27886	252-823-1141	823-7699
Alexander County Library 77 1st Ave SW *Web:* www.alexanderlibrary.org	Taylorsville	NC	28681	828-632-4058	632-1094
Haywood County Public Library 678 S Haywood St *Web:* www.haywoodlibrary.org	Waynesville	NC	28786	828-452-5169	452-6746
Columbus County Public Library 407 N Powell Blvd	Whiteville	NC	28472	910-642-3116	642-3839
New Hanover County Public Library 201 Chestnut St *Web:* www.nhcgov.com/LIB/LIBmain.asp	Wilmington	NC	28401	910-798-6320	798-6312
Wilson County Public Library 249 W Nash St *Web:* www.wilson-co.com/library.html	Wilson	NC	27893	252-237-5355	243-4311
Forsyth County Public Library 660 W 5th St *Web:* www.forsyth.cc/library/	Winston-Salem	NC	27101	336-703-2665	727-2549
Gunn Memorial Public Library 161 Main St E	Yanceyville	NC	27379	336-694-9673	694-9846

North Dakota

Library	City	State	ZIP	Phone	Fax
Bismarck Veterans Memorial Public Library 515 N 5th St *Web:* www.bismarcklibrary.org	Bismarck	ND	58501	701-222-6410	221-6854
Fargo Public Library 408 Robert St *Web:* www.cityoffargo.com/library/	Fargo	ND	58102	701-241-1491	241-8581
Carnegie Regional Library 49 W 7th St *TF:* 800-568-5964	Grafton	ND	58237	701-352-2754	352-2757
Grand Forks Public Library 2110 Library Cir *Web:* www.grandforksgov.com/library	Grand Forks	ND	58201	701-772-8116	772-1379
Minot Public Library 516 2nd Ave SW *Web:* www.minotlibrary.org	Minot	ND	58701	701-852-1045	852-2595

Ohio

Library	City	State	ZIP	Phone	Fax
Akron-Summit County Public Library 60 S High St *Web:* www.ascpl.lib.oh.us	Akron	OH	44326	330-643-9000	643-9033
Rodman Public Library 215 E Broadway St *Web:* www.rodmanlibrary.com	Alliance	OH	44601	330-821-2665	821-5053
Ashtabula County District Library 335 W 44th St *Web:* www.ashtabula.lib.oh.us	Ashtabula	OH	44004	440-997-9341	992-7714
Clermont County Public Library System 326 Broadway St *Web:* www.clermont.lib.oh.us	Batavia	OH	45103	513-732-2736	732-3177
Logan County District Library 220 N Main St *Web:* www.loganco.lib.oh.us	Bellefontaine	OH	43311	937-599-4189	599-5503
Bexley Public Library 2411 E Main St *Web:* www.bexlib.org	Bexley	OH	43209	614-231-2793	231-0794
Wood County District Public Library 251 N Main St *Web:* wcdpl.lib.oh.us	Bowling Green	OH	43402	419-352-5104	354-0405
Guernsey County District Public Library 800 Steubenville Ave *Web:* www.gcdpl.lib.oh.us	Cambridge	OH	43725	740-432-5946	432-7142
Stark County District Library 715 Market Ave N *Web:* www.stark.lib.oh.us	Canton	OH	44702	330-452-0665	452-0403
Carroll County District Library 70 2nd St NE *Web:* www.carroll.lib.oh.us	Carrollton	OH	44615	330-627-2613	627-2523
Geauga County Public Library 12701 Ravenwood Dr *Web:* www.geauga.lib.oh.us	Chardon	OH	44024	440-286-6811	286-7419
Chillicothe & Ross County Public Library 140-146 S Paint St *Web:* www.chillicothe.lib.oh.us	Chillicothe	OH	45601	740-702-4145	702-4156
Public Library of Cincinnati & Hamilton County 800 Vine St *Web:* www.cincinnatilibrary.org	Cincinnati	OH	45202	513-369-6900	369-3123
Pickaway County District Public Library 1160 N Court St *TF:* 888-268-3756 ■ *Web:* www.pickawaylib.org	Circleville	OH	43113	740-477-1644	474-2855
Cleveland Public Library 325 Superior Ave *Web:* www.cpl.org	Cleveland	OH	44114	216-623-2800	623-7015
Cleveland Heights-University Heights Public Library 2345 Lee Rd *Web:* www.heightslibrary.org	Cleveland Heights	OH	44118	216-932-3600	932-0932
Columbus Metropolitan Library 96 S Grant Ave *Web:* www.columbuslibrary.org	Columbus	OH	43215	614-645-2275	645-2050
Coshocton Public Library 655 Main St. *Web:* www.coshocton.lib.oh.us	Coshocton	OH	43812	740-622-0956	622-4331
Dayton Metro Library 215 E 3rd St *Web:* www.daytonmetrolibrary.org	Dayton	OH	45402	937-227-9500	227-9524
Defiance Public Library 320 Fort St *Web:* www.defiance.lib.oh.us	Defiance	OH	43512	419-782-1456	782-6235
Delaware County District Library 84 E Winter St *Web:* www.delawarelibrary.org	Delaware	OH	43015	740-362-3861	369-0196
Brooke-Gould Memorial Library 450 S Barron St *TF:* 800-241-7731 ■ *Web:* www.pcdl.lib.oh.us/locations/eaton.html	Eaton	OH	45320	937-456-4331	456-4774
Findlay Hancock County District Public Library 206 Broadway *Web:* www.findlaylibrary.org	Findlay	OH	45840	419-422-1712	422-0638
Birchard Public Library of Sandusky County 423 Croghan St. *Web:* www.birchard.lib.oh.us	Fremont	OH	43420	419-334-7101	334-4788
Dr Samuel L Bossard Memorial Library 7 Spruce St *Web:* www.bossard.lib.oh.us	Gallipolis	OH	45631	740-446-7323	446-1701
Portage County District Library 10482 South St *TF:* 800-500-5179 ■ *Web:* www.portagecounty.lib.oh.us	Garrettsville	OH	44231	330-527-4378	527-4370
Lane Public Library 300 N 3rd St *Web:* www.lanepl.org	Hamilton	OH	45011	513-894-7156	894-2718
Highland County District Library 10 Willettsville Pike	Hillsboro	OH	45133	937-393-3114	393-2985
Briggs Lawrence County Public Library 321 S 4th St *Web:* www.briggslibrary.com	Ironton	OH	45638	740-532-1124	532-4948
Lakewood Public Library 15425 Detroit Ave *Web:* www.lkwdpl.org	Lakewood	OH	44107	216-226-8275	521-4327
Fairfield County District Library 219 N Broad St *Web:* www.fairfield.lib.oh.us	Lancaster	OH	43130	740-653-2745	653-4199
Lebanon Public Library 101 S Broadway	Lebanon	OH	45036	513-932-2665	932-7323
Lima Public Library 650 W Market St *Web:* www.limalibrary.com	Lima	OH	45801	419-228-5113	228-0955
Logan-Hocking County District Library 230 E Main St *Web:* www.hocking.lib.oh.us	Logan	OH	43138	740-385-2348	385-9093
Lorain Public Library System 351 6th St *TF:* 800-322-7323 ■ *Web:* www.lorain.lib.oh.us	Lorain	OH	44052	440-244-1192	244-4888
Mansfield-Richland County Public Library 43 W 3rd St *Web:* www.mrcpl.org	Mansfield	OH	44902	419-521-3100	525-4750
Washington County Public Library 615 5th St *Web:* www.wcplib.lib.oh.us	Marietta	OH	45750	740-373-1057	373-2860
Medina County District Library 210 S Broadway *Web:* www.mcdl.info	Medina	OH	44256	330-725-0588	725-2053
Middletown Public Library 125 S Broad St *Web:* www.middletownlibrary.org	Middletown	OH	45044	513-424-1251	424-6585

Phone Fax

Holmes County District Public Library 3102 Glen Dr . . . Millersburg OH 44654 330-674-5972 674-1938
Web: www.holmes.lib.oh.us
Mount Vernon & Knox County Public Library
201 N Mulberry St . . . Mount Vernon OH 43050 740-392-2665 397-3866
Web: www.knox.net
Perry County District Library 117 S Jackson St . . . New Lexington OH 43764 740-342-4195 342-4204
Web: www.pcdl.org
Tuscarawas County Public Library 121 Fair Ave NW . . . New Philadelphia OH 44663 330-364-4474 364-8217
Web: www.tusclibrary.org
Newark Public Library 101 W Main St . . . Newark OH 43055 740-349-5500 349-5575
Web: www.newarklibrary.info
Putnam County District Library 525 N Thomas St . . . Ottawa OH 45875 419-523-3747 523-6477
Web: www.putnamco.lib.oh.us
Morely Library 184 Phelps St . . . Painesville OH 44077 440-352-3383 352-9079
Web: www.morleylibrary.org
Cuyahoga County Public Library 2111 Snow Rd . . . Parma OH 44134 216-398-1800 749-9479
TF: 800-749-5560 ■ *Web:* www.cuyahogalibrary.org
Paulding County Carnegie Library 205 S Main St . . . Paulding OH 45879 419-399-2032 399-2114
Web: pauldingcountylibrary.org
Portsmouth Public Library 1220 Gallia St . . . Portsmouth OH 45662 740-354-5688 353-3483
Web: www.portsmouth.lib.oh.us
Clark County Public Library 201 S Fountain Ave . . . Springfield OH 45501 937-328-6903 328-6908
Web: www.ccpl.lib.oh.us
Public Library of Steubenville & Jefferson County
407 S 4th St . . . Steubenville OH 43952 740-282-9782 282-2919
Web: www.steubenville.lib.oh.us
Tiffin-Seneca Public Library 77 Jefferson St . . . Tiffin OH 44883 419-447-3751 447-3045
Web: www.tiffinsen.lib.oh.us
Toledo-Lucas County Public Library 325 N Michigan St . . . Toledo OH 43604 419-259-5200 259-5119
Web: www.toledolibrary.org
Troy-Miami County Public Library 419 W Main St . . . Troy OH 45373 937-339-0502 335-4880
Web: www.troypubliclibrary.org
Upper Arlington Public Library 2800 Tremont Rd . . . Upper Arlington OH 43221 614-486-9621 486-4530
Web: ualibrary.org
Brumback Library 215 W Main St . . . Van Wert OH 45891 419-238-2168 238-3180
Web: www.brumbacklib.com
Warren-Trumbull County Public Library 444 Mahoning Ave NW . . . Warren OH 44483 330-399-8807 395-3988
Web: www.wtcpl.lib.oh.us
Carnegie Public Library 127 S North St . . . Washington Court House OH 43160 740-335-2540 335-2928
Web: www.carnegie.lib.oh.us
Garnet A Wilson Public Library of Pike County
207 N Market St . . . Waverly OH 45690 740-947-4921 947-2918
Web: www.pike.lib.oh.us
Westerville Public Library 126 S State St . . . Westerville OH 43081 614-882-7277 882-4160
Web: www.wpl.lib.oh.us
Wayne County Public Library 304 N Market St . . . Wooster OH 44691 330-262-0916 262-7313
Web: www.wayne.lib.oh.us
Greene County Public Library 76 E Market St . . . Xenia OH 45385 937-376-2996 372-4673
Web: www.gcpl.lib.oh.us
Public Library of Youngstown & Mahoning County
305 Wick Ave . . . Youngstown OH 44503 330-744-8636 744-2258
Web: www.ymc.lib.oh.us
Muskingum County Library System 220 N 5th St . . . Zanesville OH 43701 740-453-0391 455-6357
Web: www.muskingumlibrary.org

Oklahoma

Phone Fax

Bartlesville Public Library 600 S Johnstone Ave . . . Bartlesville OK 74003 918-337-5353 337-5338
Web: www.bartlesville.lib.ok.us
Enid-Public Library of Enid & Garfield County 120 W Maine St . . . Enid OK 73701 580-234-6313 233-2948
Lawton Public Library 110 SW 4th St . . . Lawton OK 73501 580-581-3450 248-0243
Web: www.cityof.lawton.ok.us/library
Southeastern Public Library System 401 N 2nd St . . . McAlester OK 74501 918-426-0456 426-0543
Web: www.sepl.lib.ok.us
Eastern Oklahoma District Library System
814 W Okmulgee St . . . Muskogee OK 74401 918-683-2846 683-0436
Web: www.eodls.lib.ok.us
Pioneer Library System 225 N Webster Ave . . . Norman OK 73069 405-321-1481 701-2608
Web: www.pioneer.lib.ok.us
Metropolitan Library of Oklahoma County 300 Park Ave . . . Oklahoma City OK 73102 405-231-8650 232-5493
Web: www.mls.lib.ok.us
Ponca City Library 515 E Grand Ave . . . Ponca City OK 74601 580-767-0345 767-0377
Stillwater Public Library 1107 S Duck St . . . Stillwater OK 74074 405-372-3633 624-0552
Web: www.stillwater.lib.ok.us
Tulsa City-County Library 400 Civic Center . . . Tulsa OK 74103 918-596-7977 596-7990
Web: www.tulsalibrary.org

Oregon

Phone Fax

Beaverton City Library 12375 SW 5th St . . . Beaverton OR 97005 503-644-2197 526-2636
Web: www.wilinet.wccls.lib.or.us
Bend Public Library 601 NW Wall St . . . Bend OR 97701 541-385-3244 389-2982
Web: www.dpls.lib.or.us
Coos Bay Public Library 525 W Anderson Ave . . . Coos Bay OR 97420 541-269-1101 269-7567
Web: bay.cooslibraries.org
Corvallis-Benton County Library 645 NW Monroe Ave . . . Corvallis OR 97330 541-766-6928 766-6915
Web: library.ci.corvallis.or.us
Eugene Public Library 100 W 10th Ave . . . Eugene OR 97401 541-682-5450 682-5898
Josephine County Library System 200 NW 'C' St . . . Grants Pass OR 97526 541-474-5482 474-5485
Hillsboro Public Library 775 SE 10th St . . . Hillsboro OR 97123 503-615-6500 615-6501
Web: www.ci.hillsboro.or.us/Library
Klamath County Library 126 S 3rd St . . . Klamath Falls OR 97601 541-882-8894 882-6166
Lake Oswego Public Library 706 4th St . . . Lake Oswego OR 97034 503-636-7628 635-4171
Web: www.ci.oswego.or.us/library/library.htm
McMinnville Public Library 225 NW Adams St . . . McMinnville OR 97128 503-435-5555 435-5560
Web: www.maclibrary.org
Jackson County Library System 205 S Central Ave . . . Medford OR 97501 541-774-6427 774-6748
Web: www.jcls.org
Ledding Library 10660 SE 21st Ave . . . Milwaukie OR 97222 503-659-3911 659-9497
Web: www.milwaukie.lib.or.us
Clackamas County Library 16201 SE McLoughlin Blvd . . . Oak Grove OR 97267 503-655-8543
Web: library.co.clackamas.or.us/lib/index.html
Oregon City Public Library 362 Warner Milne Rd . . . Oregon City OR 97045 503-657-8269 657-3702
Web: www.oregoncity.lib.or.us
Multnomah County Library 801 SW 10th Ave . . . Portland OR 97205 503-988-5123 988-5226
Web: www.multcolib.org
Douglas County Library System 1409 NE Diamond Lake Blvd . . . Roseburg OR 97470 541-440-4311 440-4315
Web: www.co.douglas.or.us/library/
Salem Public Library 585 Liberty St SE . . . Salem OR 97301 503-588-6071 588-6055
Web: www.cityofsalem.net/departments/library
Springfield Public Library 225 5th St . . . Springfield OR 97477 541-726-3766 726-3747
Web: library.ci.springfield.or.us

Phone Fax

Tigard Public Library 13500 SW Hall Blvd . . . Tigard OR 97223 503-684-6537 598-7515
Web: www.ci.tigard.or.us/library

Pennsylvania

Phone Fax

Allentown Public Library 1210 W Hamilton St . . . Allentown PA 18102 610-820-2400 820-0640
Web: www.allentownpl.org
Altoona Area Public Library 1600 5th Ave . . . Altoona PA 16602 814-946-0417 946-3230
Web: www.altoonalibrary.org
Bethlehem Area Public Library 11 W Church St . . . Bethlehem PA 18018 610-867-3761 867-2767
Web: www.bapl.org
Bucks County Free Library 150 S Pine St . . . Doylestown PA 18901 215-348-0332 348-4760
Web: www.buckslib.org
Erie County Library System 160 E Front St . . . Erie PA 16507 814-451-6900 451-6969
Web: www.erielibrary.org
Raymond M Blasco MD Memorial Library 160 E Front St . . . Erie PA 16507 814-451-6900 451-6969
Web: www.erielibrary.org
Chester County Library 450 Exton Sq Pkwy . . . Exton PA 19341 610-280-2600 280-2694
Web: www.ccls.org
Adams County Public Library 140 Baltimore St . . . Gettysburg PA 17325 717-334-5716 334-7992
Web: www.adamslibrary.org
Dauphin County Library System 101 Walnut St . . . Harrisburg PA 17101 717-234-4961 234-7479
Web: dcls.org
Cambria County Library System 248 Main St . . . Johnstown PA 15901 814-536-5131 536-6905
Web: www.cclib.lib.pa.us
Lancaster Public Library 125 N Duke St . . . Lancaster PA 17602 717-394-2651 394-3083
Web: www.lancaster.lib.pa.us
Lebanon Community Library 125 N 7th St . . . Lebanon PA 17046 717-273-7624 273-2719
Web: www.lebanoncountylibraries.org/lebanon
Monessen Public Library & District Center 326 Donner Ave . . . Monessen PA 15062 724-684-4750 684-7077
Web: www.monpldc.org
Montgomery County-Norristown Public Library
1001 Powell St . . . Norristown PA 19401 610-278-5100 278-5110
Web: mnl.mclinc.org
Oil Creek District Library Center 2 Central Ave . . . Oil City PA 16301 814-678-3054 676-0359
TF: 888-645-2489 ■ *Web:* www.oilcitylibrary.org
Osceola Mills Public Library 600 Lingle St . . . Osceola Mills PA 16666 814-339-7229 339-7719
Free Library of Philadelphia 1901 Vine St . . . Philadelphia PA 19103 215-686-5322 563-3628
Web: www.library.phila.gov
Carnegie Library of Pittsburgh 4400 Forbes Ave . . . Pittsburgh PA 15213 412-622-3131 622-6278
Web: www.carnegielibrary.org
Pottsville Free Public Library 215 W Market St . . . Pottsville PA 17901 570-622-8880 622-2157
Web: www.pottsvillelibrary.org
Reading Public Library 100 S 5th St . . . Reading PA 19602 610-655-6355 655-6609
Web: www.reading.lib.pa.us
Albright Memorial Library 500 Vine St . . . Scranton PA 18509 570-348-3000 348-3020
Web: www.albright.org
Osterhout Free Library 71 S Franklin St . . . Wilkes-Barre PA 18701 570-823-0156 823-5477
Web: www.osterhout.lib.pa.us
James V Brown Library of Williamsport & Lycoming County
19 E 4th St . . . Williamsport PA 17701 570-326-0536 326-1671
Web: www.jvbrown.edu
Martin Memorial Library 159 E Market St . . . York PA 17401 717-846-5300 848-2330
Web: www.yorklibraries.org
York County Library System 118 Pleasant Acres Rd 2nd Fl . . . York PA 17402 717-840-7435 751-0741
Web: www.yorklibraries.org

Rhode Island

Phone Fax

Coventry Public Library 1672 Flat River Rd . . . Coventry RI 02816 401-822-9100 822-9133
Web: www.coventrylibrary.org
Cranston Public Library 140 Sockanosset Cross Rd . . . Cranston RI 02920 401-943-9080 946-5079
Web: www.cranstonlibrary.org
Cumberland Public Library 1464 Diamond Hill Rd . . . Cumberland RI 02864 401-333-2552 334-0578
Web: www.cumberlandlibrary.org
East Providence Public Library 41 Grove Ave . . . East Providence RI 02914 401-434-2453 434-3324
Web: www.eastprovidencelibrary.com
Marian J Mohr Memorial Library 1 Memorial Ave . . . Johnston RI 02919 401-231-4980 231-4984
Newport Public Library 300 Spring St . . . Newport RI 02840 401-847-8720 842-0841
North Providence Union Free Library
1810 Mineral Spring Ave . . . North Providence RI 02904 401-353-5600 353-1794
Web: 131.109.225.131/nprlib
Pawtucket Public Library 13 Summer St . . . Pawtucket RI 02860 401-725-3714 728-2170
Web: web.provlib.org/pawlib
Providence Public Library 150 Empire St . . . Providence RI 02903 401-455-8000 455-8080
Web: www.provlib.org
Warwick Public Library 600 Sandy Ln . . . Warwick RI 02886 401-739-5440 732-2055
Web: wpl.lib.ri.us
West Warwick Public Library System 1043 Main St . . . West Warwick RI 02893 401-828-3750 828-8493
Web: www.wwlibrary.org
Westerly Public Library 44 Broad St . . . Westerly RI 02891 401-596-2877 596-5600
Web: www.westerlylibrary.org
Woonsocket Harris Public Library 303 Clinton St . . . Woonsocket RI 02895 401-769-9044 767-4140
Web: www.woonsocketlibrary.org

South Carolina

Phone Fax

ABBE Regional Library 314 Chesterfield St SW . . . Aiken SC 29801 803-642-7575 642-7597
Web: www.abbe-lib.org
Aiken-Bamberg-Barnwell-Edgefield Regional Library System
314 Chesterfield St SW . . . Aiken SC 29801 803-642-7575 642-7597
Web: www.abbe-lib.org
Anderson County Library PO Box 4047 . . . Anderson SC 29622 864-260-4500 260-4510
Web: www.andersonlibrary.org
Lexington County Circulating Library 203 Armory St . . . Batesburg SC 29006 803-532-9223 359-0185
Web: www.lex.lib.sc.us
Beaufort County Library 311 Scott St . . . Beaufort SC 29902 843-470-6500 470-6542
Web: www.co.beaufort.sc.us/bftlib
Marlboro County Library 200 John Corry Rd . . . Bennettsville SC 29512 843-479-5630 479-5645
Web: www.marlborocountylibrary.org
Kershaw County Library 1304 Broad St . . . Camden SC 29020 803-425-1508 425-7180
Web: www.kershaw.lib.sc.us
Charleston County Library System 68 Calhoun St . . . Charleston SC 29401 843-805-6801 727-3741
Web: www.ccpl.org
Chester County Library 100 Center St . . . Chester SC 29706 803-377-8145 377-8146
Web: www.chesterlibsc.org
Chesterfield County Library 119 W Main St . . . Chesterfield SC 29709 843-623-7489 623-3295
Richland County Public Library 1431 Assembly St . . . Columbia SC 29201 803-799-9084
Web: www.richland.lib.sc.us
Horry County Public Library 1008 5th Ave . . . Conway SC 29526 843-248-1543 248-1548
Web: www.horry.lib.sc.us

Public Libraries (Cont'd)

South Carolina (Cont'd)

Library	City	State	ZIP	Phone	Fax
Darlington County Library 204 N Main St	Darlington	SC	29532	843-398-4940	398-4942
Web: darlington-lib.org					
Dillon County Library 600 E Main St	Dillon	SC	29536	843-774-0330	774-0733
Pickens County Library 304 Biltmore Rd	Easley	SC	29640	864-850-7077	850-7088
Florence County Library 509 S Dargan St	Florence	SC	29506	843-662-8424	661-7544
Web: www.florencelibrary.org					
Cherokee County Public Library 300 E Rutledge Ave	Gaffney	SC	29340	864-487-2711	487-2752
Greenville County Library 25 Heritage Green Pl	Greenville	SC	29601	864-242-5000	235-8375
Web: www.greenvillelibrary.org					
Greenwood-Abbeville Regional Library 106 N Main St	Greenwood	SC	29646	864-941-4650	941-4651
Hilton Head Library 11 Beach City Rd	Hilton Head Island	SC	29926	843-342-9200	342-9220
Williamsburg County Library 215 N Jackson St	Kingstree	SC	29556	843-355-9486	355-9991
Web: www.wlbg.lib.sc.us					
Lancaster County Library 313 S White St	Lancaster	SC	29720	803-285-1502	285-6004
Web: www.lanclib.org					
Laurens County Library 1017 W Main St	Laurens	SC	29360	864-681-7323	681-0598
Web: www.lcpl.org					
Harvin Clarendon County Library 215 N Brooks St	Manning	SC	29102	803-435-8633	435-8101
Web: www.hccl.lib.sc.us					
Marion County Library 101 E Court St	Marion	SC	29571	843-423-8300	423-8302
Web: www.co.marion.sc.us/colibrary.html					
Berkeley County Library 100 Library St	Moncks Corner	SC	29461	843-719-4223	719-4732
Web: www.berkeley.lib.sc.us					
Chapin Memorial Library 400 14th Ave N	Myrtle Beach	SC	29577	843-918-1275	918-1288
Web: www.cityofmyrtlebeach.com/library.html					
Orangeburg County Library PO Box 1367	Orangeburg	SC	29116	803-531-4636	533-5860
Web: www.orangeburgcounty.org/library/					
York County Library 138 E Black St	Rock Hill	SC	29730	803-324-3055	328-9290
Web: www.yclibrary.org					
Dorchester County Library 506 N Parler Ave	Saint George	SC	29477	843-563-9189	563-7823
Web: www.dcl.lib.sc.us					
Spartanburg County Public Library 151 S Church St	Spartanburg	SC	29306	864-596-3507	596-3518
Web: www.infodepot.org					
Sumter County Library 111 N Harvin St	Sumter	SC	29150	803-773-7273	773-4875
Web: www.midnet.sc.edu/sumtercls					
Union County Carnegie Library 300 E South St	Union	SC	29379	864-427-7140	427-5155
Web: www.unionlibrary.org					
Oconee County Library 501 W South Broad St	Walhalla	SC	29691	864-638-4133	638-4132
Web: www.ocplibrary.org					
Colleton County Memorial Library 600 Hampton St	Walterboro	SC	29488	843-549-5621	549-5122
Web: www.colletonlibrary.org					

South Dakota

Library	City	State	ZIP	Phone	Fax
Brookings Public Library 515 3rd St	Brookings	SD	57006	605-692-9407	692-9386
Web: www.brookingslibrary.org					
RE Rawlins Municipal Library 1000 E Church St	Pierre	SD	57501	605-773-7421	773-7423
Web: rplib.sdln.net					
Rapid City Public Library 610 Quincy St	Rapid City	SD	57701	605-394-4171	394-4064
Web: www.rapidcitylibrary.org					
Siouxland Libraries 201 N Main Ave	Sioux Falls	SD	57104	605-367-8700	367-4312
Web: www.siouxlandlib.org					

Tennessee

Library	City	State	ZIP	Phone	Fax
Cheatham County Public Library					
188 County Services Dr Suite 200	Ashland City	TN	37015	615-792-4828	792-2054
EG Fisher Public Library 1289 Ingleside Ave	Athens	TN	37303	423-745-7782	745-1763
Sullivan County Public Library 1655 Blountville Blvd PO 510	Blountville	TN	37617	423-279-2714	279-2836
Web: www.wrlibrary.org/sullivan/					
Chattanooga-Hamilton County Bicentennial Library					
1001 Broad St	Chattanooga	TN	37402	423-757-5310	757-4994
Web: www.lib.chattanooga.gov					
Clarksville Montgomery County Public Library					
350 Pageant Ln Suite 501	Clarksville	TN	37040	931-648-8826	648-8831
Web: www.clarksville.org					
Cleveland Public Library 795 N Church St	Cleveland	TN	37311	423-472-2163	339-9791
Web: www.clevelandlibrary.org					
Clinton Public Library 118 S Hicks St	Clinton	TN	37716	865-457-0519	457-4233
Blue Grass Regional Library 104 E 6th St	Columbia	TN	38401	931-388-9282	388-1762
Maury County Public Library 211 W 8th St	Columbia	TN	38401	931-388-6332	388-6371
Web: www.maurycountylibrary.org					
Putnam County Library 50 E Broad St	Cookeville	TN	38501	931-526-2416	372-8517
Web: www.pclibrary.org					
Tipton County Public Library 300 W Church Ave	Covington	TN	38019	901-476-8289	476-0008
Art Circle Public Library 154 E 1st St	Crossville	TN	38555	931-484-6790	484-2350
Web: www.artcircle.crossville.com					
Dickson County Public Library 206 Henslee Dr	Dickson	TN	37055	615-446-8293	446-9130
Web: www.dicksonpubliclibrary.org					
McIver's Grant Public Library 204 N Mill Ave	Dyersburg	TN	38024	731-285-5032	285-9332
Elizabethton-Carter County Public Library					
201 N Sycamore St	Elizabethton	TN	37643	423-547-6360	
Web: www.eccpl.org					
Fayetteville-Lincoln County Public Library					
400 Rocky Knob Ln	Fayetteville	TN	37334	931-433-3286	433-0063
Williamson County Public Library 611 W Main St	Franklin	TN	37064	615-794-3105	595-1245
Web: lib.williamson-tn.org					
EW Carmack-Sumner County Public Library 658 Hartsville Pike	Gallatin	TN	37066	615-452-1722	451-3319
Greeneville-Greene County Public Library 210 N Main St	Greeneville	TN	37745	423-638-5034	638-3841
Web: www.ggcpl.org					
Martin Curtis-Hendersonville Public Library					
116 Dunn St PO Box 1099	Hendersonville	TN	37077	615-824-0656	824-3112
Jacksboro Public Library 585 Main St Suite 201	Jacksboro	TN	37757	423-562-3675	562-9587
Web: www.jacksboropubliclibrary.org					
Jackson-Madison County Library 433 E Lafayette St	Jackson	TN	38301	731-425-8600	425-8609
Web: www.jmcl.tn.org					
Johnson City Public Library 100 W Millard St	Johnson City	TN	37604	423-434-4450	434-4469
Web: www.jcpl.net					
Washington County-Jonesborough Library 200 Sabin Dr	Jonesborough	TN	37659	423-753-1800	753-1802
Web: www.wrlibrary.org/libraries/washco.htm					
Kingsport Public Library 400 Broad St	Kingsport	TN	37660	423-224-2559	224-2558
Web: www.kingsportlibrary.org					
Knox County Public Library System 500 W Church Ave	Knoxville	TN	37902	865-215-8700	
Web: www.knoxcounty.org/library					
Lawrence County Public Library 519 E Gaines St	Lawrenceburg	TN	38464	931-762-4627	766-1597
Lebanon-Wilson County Public Library 108 S Hatton St	Lebanon	TN	37087	615-444-0632	444-0535
Web: www.lebanonlibrary.net					
Lenoir City Public Library PO Box 1156	Lenoir City	TN	37771	865-986-3210	
Reelfoot Regional Library Center PO Box 168	Martin	TN	38237	731-587-2347	587-0027
Blount County Public Library 508 N Cusick St	Maryville	TN	37804	865-982-0981	977-1142
Web: www.discoveret.org/bcpl					
WH & Edgar Magness Community House & Library					
118 W Main St	McMinnville	TN	37110	931-473-2428	473-6778
Memphis/Shelby County Public Library 3030 Poplar Ave	Memphis	TN	38111	901-415-2700	323-7107
Web: www.memphislibrary.lib.tn.us					
Morristown-Hamblen Public Library 417 W Main St	Morristown	TN	37814	423-586-6410	587-6226
Nolichucky Regional Library Center 315 McCrary Dr	Morristown	TN	37814	423-586-6251	586-7741
Web: state.tn.us/tsla/regional/regional.htm					
Highland Rim Regional Library Center 2118 E Main St	Murfreesboro	TN	37130	615-893-3380	895-6727
TF: 800-257-7323					
Linebaugh Public Library 105 W Vine St	Murfreesboro	TN	37130	615-893-4131	848-5038
Web: www.linebaugh.org					
Ben West Public Library 615 Church St	Nashville	TN	37219	615-862-5800	880-2119
Web: www.library.nashville.org					
Nashville Public Library 615 Church St	Nashville	TN	37219	615-862-5800	880-2119
Web: www.library.nashville.org					
Stokely Memorial Library 383 E Broadway	Newport	TN	37821	423-623-3832	623-3832
Oak Ridge Public Library 1401 Oak Ridge Tpke	Oak Ridge	TN	37830	865-425-3455	425-3429
Web: www.ci.oak-ridge.tn.us/lib-html/orlib.htm					
WG Rhea Library 400 W Washington St	Paris	TN	38242	731-642-1702	642-1777
Giles County Public Library 122 S 2nd St	Pulaski	TN	38478	931-363-2720	424-7032
Web: www.gilescountylibrary.org					
Hawkins County Public Library 407 E Main St	Rogersville	TN	37857	423-272-8710	272-9261
Sevier County Public Library 321 Court Ave	Sevierville	TN	37862	865-453-3532	908-6108
Web: www.sevierlibrary.org					
Argie Cooper Public Library 100 S Main St	Shelbyville	TN	37160	931-684-7323	685-4848
Web: www.acolibrary.com					
Somerville-Fayette County Library 216 W Market St	Somerville	TN	38068	901-465-5248	465-5271
Gorham MacBane Public Library 405 White St	Springfield	TN	37172	615-384-5123	384-0106
Barbara Reynolds Carr Memorial Library					
1304 Old Knoxville Rd	Tazewell	TN	37879	423-626-5414	626-9481
Obion County Public Library 1221 E Reelfoot Ave	Union City	TN	38261	731-885-7000	885-9638
Web: www.oclibrary.org					
Franklin County Library 105 S Porter St	Winchester	TN	37398	931-967-3706	962-1477

Texas

Library	City	State	ZIP	Phone	Fax
Abilene Public Library 202 Cedar St	Abilene	TX	79601	325-677-2474	738-8082
Web: www.abilenetx.com/apl					
Alice Public Library 401 E 3rd St	Alice	TX	78332	361-664-9506	668-3248
Amarillo Public Library 413 E 4th Ave	Amarillo	TX	79101	806-378-3054	
Web: www.amarillolibrary.org					
Brazoria County Library System					
111 E Locust St Bldg A Suite 250	Angleton	TX	77515	979-864-1505	864-1298
Web: www.bcls.lib.tx.us					
Arlington Public Library 101 E Abram St	Arlington	TX	76010	817-459-6900	459-6902
Web: www.pub-lib.ci.arlington.tx.us					
George W Hawkes Central Library 101 E Abram St	Arlington	TX	76010	817-459-6900	459-6902
Web: www.pub-lib.ci.arlington.tx.us					
Hawkes George W Central Library 101 E Abram St	Arlington	TX	76010	817-459-6900	459-6902
Web: www.pub-lib.ci.arlington.tx.us					
Henderson County CW Murchison Memorial Library					
121 S Prairieville St	Athens	TX	75751	903-677-7295	677-7275
Austin Public Library 800 Guadalupe St	Austin	TX	78701	512-974-7400	499-7403
Web: www.ci.austin.tx.us/library					
Sterling Municipal Library Mary Elizabeth Wilbanks Ave	Baytown	TX	77520	281-427-7331	420-5347
Web: www.sml.lib.tx.us					
Beaumont Public Library System 801 Pearl St	Beaumont	TX	77701	409-838-6606	838-6838
Bedford Public Library 1805 L Don Dodson Dr	Bedford	TX	76021	817-952-2335	952-2396
Web: www.bedfordlibrary.org					
Howard County Library 500 S Main St	Big Spring	TX	79720	432-264-2260	264-2263
Web: www.howard-county.lib.tx.us					
Hutchinson County Library 625 N Weatherly St	Borger	TX	79007	806-273-0126	273-0128
Nancy Carol Roberts Memorial Library 100 W Academy St	Brenham	TX	77833	979-337-7201	
Web: www.ci.brenham.tx.us/html/body_library.html					
Brownsville Public Library 2600 Central Blvd	Brownsville	TX	78520	956-548-1055	548-0684
Web: www.bpl.us					
Brownwood Public Library 600 Carnegie Blvd	Brownwood	TX	76801	325-646-0155	646-6503
Bryan Public Library 201 E 26th St	Bryan	TX	77803	979-209-5600	209-5610
Web: www.bcslibrary.org					
Van Zandt County Library 317 1st Monday Ln	Canton	TX	75103	903-567-4276	567-6981
Carrollton Public Library 4220 N Josey Ln	Carrollton	TX	75010	972-466-4800	466-4722
Web: www.cityofcarrollton.com/library					
Montgomery County Library 104 I-45 N	Conroe	TX	77301	936-788-8360	788-8398
Web: www.countylibrary.org					
Corpus Christi Public Libraries 805 Comanche St	Corpus Christi	TX	78401	361-880-7070	880-7046
Web: www.library.ci.corpus-christi.tx.us					
Corsicana Public Library 100 N 12th St	Corsicana	TX	75110	903-654-4810	654-4814
Web: www.ci.corsicana.tx.us/library.html					
J Eric Jonsson Central Library 1515 Young St	Dallas	TX	75201	214-670-1400	670-1684
Web: dallaslibrary.org/central.htm					
Deer Park Public Library 3009 Center St	Deer Park	TX	77536	281-478-7208	478-7212
Val Verde County Library 300 Spring St	Del Rio	TX	78840	830-774-7595	774-7607
Web: www.vvcl.org					
Denison Public Library 300 W Gandy St	Denison	TX	75020	903-465-1797	465-1130
Web: www.barr.org/denison.htm					
Denton Public Library 502 Oakland St	Denton	TX	76201	940-349-8565	349-8260
Web: www.cityofdenton.com/pages/library.cfm					
DeSoto Public Library 211 E Pleasant Run Rd Suite C	DeSoto	TX	75115	972-230-9656	230-5797
Web: www.desotolibrary.info					
Duncanville Public Library 201 James Collins Blvd	Duncanville	TX	75116	972-780-5050	780-4958
Web: www.youseemore.com/duncanville/					
Eagle Pass Public Library 589 Main St	Eagle Pass	TX	78852	830-773-2516	773-4204
Web: www.eaglepass.lib.tx.us					
Edinburg Public Library 401 E Cano St	Edinburg	TX	78539	956-383-6246	292-2026
Web: www.edinburg.lib.tx.us					
Euless Public Library 201 N Ector Dr	Euless	TX	76039	817-685-1482	267-1979
Web: www.euless.org/library/					
El Paso County Library PO Box 788	Fabens	TX	79838	915-764-3635	764-3468
Fort Worth Public Library 500 W 3rd St	Fort Worth	TX	76102	817-871-7701	871-7734
Web: www.fortworthlibrary.org					
Friendswood Public Library 416 S Friendswood Dr	Friendswood	TX	77546	281-482-7135	482-2685
Web: www.friendswood.lib.tx.us					
Cooke County Library 200 S Weaver St	Gainesville	TX	76240	940-665-2401	665-5885
Rosenberg Library 2310 Sealy Ave	Galveston	TX	77550	409-763-8854	763-1064
Web: www.rosenberg-library.org					
Nicholson Memorial Library System 625 Austin St	Garland	TX	75040	972-205-2543	205-2523
Web: www.nmls.lib.tx.us					
Upshur County Library 702 W Tyler St	Gilmer	TX	75644	903-843-5001	843-3995
Hood County Library 222 N Travis St	Granbury	TX	76048	817-573-3569	573-3969
Grapevine Public Library 1201 Municipal Way	Grapevine	TX	76051	817-410-3410	410-3080
Web: www.ci.grapevine.tx.us/IndividualDepartments/Library/tabid/101/Default.aspx					

Library	City	State	ZIP	Phone	Fax
W Walworth Harrison Public Library 1 Lou Finney Ln. *Web:* www.youseemore.com/harrison	Greenville	TX	75401	903-457-2992	457-2961
Haltom City Public Library 3201 Friendly Ln *Web:* www.haltomcitytx.com/library	Haltom City	TX	76117	817-222-7786	834-1446
Harlingen Public Library 410 76th Dr.	Harlingen	TX	78550	956-430-6650	430-6654
Rusk County Library 106 E Main St *Web:* www.rclib.org	Henderson	TX	75652	903-657-8557	657-7637
Harris County Public Library System 8080 El Rio St. *Web:* www.hcpl.net	Houston	TX	77054	713-749-9000	749-9090
Houston Public Library 500 McKinney St. *Fax Area Code: 832 ■ *Web:* www.houstonlibrary.org	Houston	TX	77002	713-236-1313	393-1324*
Hurst Public Library 901 Precinct Line Rd *Web:* www.ci.hurst.tx.us/lib/index.htm	Hurst	TX	76053	817-788-7300	590-9515
Irving Public Library System 801 W Irving Blvd *Web:* www.irving.lib.tx.us	Irving	TX	75060	972-721-2606	721-2463
Butt-Holdsworth Memorial Library 505 Water St. *Web:* www.bhmlibrary.org	Kerrville	TX	78028	830-257-8422	792-5552
Killeen Public Library 205 E Church St	Killeen	TX	76541	254-526-6527	526-8737
Robert J Kleberg Public Library 220 N 4th St. *Web:* www.kleberglibrary.com	Kingsville	TX	78363	361-592-6381	
Laredo Public Library 1120 E Calton Rd *Web:* www.laredolibrary.org	Laredo	TX	78041	956-795-2400	795-2403
Helen Hall Library 100 W Walker St. *Web:* www.leaguecitylibrary.org	League City	TX	77573	281-554-1111	
Lewisville Public Library 1197 W Main St. *Web:* library.cityoflewisville.com	Lewisville	TX	75067	972-219-3571	219-5094
Longview Public Library 222 W Cotton St. *Web:* www.longview.lib.tx.us	Longview	TX	75601	903-237-1351	237-1327
Lubbock Public Library 1306 9th St. *Web:* www.lubbocklibrary.com	Lubbock	TX	79401	806-775-2835	775-2827
Marshall Public Library 300 S Alamo St *Web:* www.marshallpubliclibrary.org	Marshall	TX	75670	903-935-4465	935-4463
McAllen Memorial Library 601 N Main St. *Web:* www.mcallen.lib.tx.us	McAllen	TX	78501	956-688-3300	
Mesquite Public Library 300 W Grubb Dr *Web:* www.cityofmesquite.com/library/index.php	Mesquite	TX	75149	972-216-6220	216-6740
Midland County Public Library 301 W Missouri Ave. *Web:* www.co.midland.tx.us/Library/default.asp	Midland	TX	79701	432-688-4320	688-4939
Speer Memorial Library 801 E 12th St. *Web:* www.mission.lib.tx.us	Mission	TX	78572	956-580-8750	580-8756
Nacogdoches Public Library 1112 North St. *Web:* npl.sfasu.edu	Nacogdoches	TX	75961	936-559-2970	569-8282
New Braunfels Public Library 700 E Common St *Web:* www.nbpl.lib.tx.us	New Braunfels	TX	78130	830-608-2150	608-2151
North Richland Hills Public Library 6720 NE Loop 820 *Web:* www.library.nrhtx.com	North Richland Hills	TX	76180	817-427-6800	427-6808
Ector County Library 321 W 5th St *Web:* www.ector.lib.tx.us	Odessa	TX	79761	432-337-2501	337-6502
Palestine Public Library 1101 N Cedar St *Web:* www.youseemore.com/palestine/	Palestine	TX	75801	903-729-4121	729-4062
Pasadena Public Library 1201 Jeff Ginn Memorial Dr. *Web:* www.ci.pasadena.tx.us/library/home.html	Pasadena	TX	77506	713-477-0276	473-9640
Pharr Memorial Library 121 E Cherokee St *Web:* www.pharr.lib.tx.us	Pharr	TX	78577	956-787-3966	787-3345
Unger Memorial Library 825 Austin St. *Web:* www.texasonline.net/unger	Plainview	TX	79072	806-296-1148	291-1245
Plano Public Library System 5024 Custer Rd *Web:* www.plano.gov/Departments/Libraries	Plano	TX	75023	972-769-4200	769-4256
Port Arthur Public Library 4615 9th Ave *Web:* www.pap.lib.tx.us	Port Arthur	TX	77642	409-985-8838	985-5969
Richardson Public Library 900 Civic Ctr Dr *Web:* www.cor.net/library	Richardson	TX	75080	972-744-4350	744-5806
George Memorial Library 1001 Golfview Dr. *Web:* www.fortbend.lib.tx.us	Richmond	TX	77469	281-342-4455	341-2689
Starr County Public Library 700 E Canales St	Rio Grande City	TX	78582	956-487-4389	487-7390
Round Rock Public Library 216 E Main St. *Web:* www.ci.round-rock.tx.us	Round Rock	TX	78664	512-218-7001	218-7061
Tom Green County Library System 113 W Beauregard Ave *Web:* www.tgclibrary.com	San Angelo	TX	76903	325-655-7321	659-4027
Daughters of the Republic of Texas Library PO Box 1401 *Web:* www.drtl.org	San Antonio	TX	78295	210-225-1071	212-8514
San Antonio Public Library 600 Soledad St. *Web:* www.sanantonio.gov/library/	San Antonio	TX	78205	210-207-2500	207-2603
San Benito Public Library 101 W Rose St. *Web:* www.cityofsanbenito.com/library.htm	San Benito	TX	78586	956-361-3860	361-3867
San Marcos Public Library 625 E Hopkins St *Web:* www.ci.san-marcos.tx.us/library.htm	San Marcos	TX	78666	512-393-8200	754-8131
Sherman Public Library 421 N Travis St *Web:* www.barr.org/sherman1.htm	Sherman	TX	75090	903-892-7240	892-7101
Taylor Public Library 400 Porter St *Web:* www.ci.taylor.tx.us/taylorpl/homepage.html	Taylor	TX	76574	512-352-3434	352-8080
Temple Public Library 100 W Adams Ave	Temple	TX	76501	254-298-5555	298-5328
Terrell Public Library 301 N Rockwell Ave.	Terrell	TX	75160	972-551-6663	551-6662
Texarkana Public Library 600 W 3rd St.	Texarkana	TX	75501	903-794-2149	794-2139
Moore Memorial Public Library 1701 9th Ave N *Web:* www.texascity-library.org	Texas City	TX	77590	409-643-5979	948-1106
The Colony Public Library 6800 Main St. *Web:* www.ci.the-colony.tx.us/depts/library/lib.html	The Colony	TX	75056	972-625-1900	624-2245
Tyler Public Library 201 S College Ave *Web:* www.tylerlibrary.com	Tyler	TX	75702	903-593-7323	531-1329
Victoria Public Library 302 N Main St. *Web:* victoriapubliclibrary.org	Victoria	TX	77901	361-572-2704	572-2779
Waco-McLennan County Library 1717 Austin Ave *Web:* www.waco-texas.com	Waco	TX	76701	254-750-5941	750-5940
Watauga Public Library 7109 Whitley Rd. *Web:* www.cowtx.org/library/libindex.htm	Watauga	TX	76148	817-514-5855	581-3910
Weatherford Public Library 1014 Charles St	Weatherford	TX	76086	817-598-4150	598-4161
Weslaco Public Library 525 S Kansas Ave. *Web:* www.weslaco.lib.tx.us	Weslaco	TX	78596	956-968-4533	969-4069
Wharton County Library 1920 N Fulton St *Web:* www.whartonco.lib.tx.us	Wharton	TX	77488	979-532-8080	532-2792
Wichita Falls Public Library 600 11th St. *Web:* www.wfpl.net	Wichita Falls	TX	76301	940-767-0868	720-6672

Utah

Library	City	State	ZIP	Phone	Fax
Davis County Library 38 S 100 E PO Box 115 *Web:* www.co.davis.ut.us/library	Farmington	UT	84025	801-451-2322	451-9561
Logan Library 255 N Main St *Web:* www.logan.lib.ut.us	Logan	UT	84321	435-716-9123	716-9145
Murray Public Library 166 E 5300 S *Web:* murray.lib.ut.us	Murray	UT	84107	801-264-2574	264-2586
Weber County Library 2464 Jefferson Ave *TF:* 888-618-0564 ■ *Web:* www.weberpl.lib.ut.us	Ogden	UT	84401	801-337-2617	337-2615
Orem Public Library 58 N State St *Web:* lib.orem.org	Orem	UT	84057	801-229-7050	229-7130
Provo City Library 550 N University Ave. *Web:* www.provo.lib.ut.us	Provo	UT	84601	801-852-6650	852-6688
Washington County Public Library 50 S Main St. *Web:* library.washco.utah.gov	Saint George	UT	84770	435-634-5737	634-5798
Salt Lake City Public Library 210 E 400 South *Web:* www.slcpl.lib.ut.us	Salt Lake City	UT	84111	801-524-8200	322-8196
Salt Lake County Library System 2197 E Fort Union Blvd. *Web:* www.slco.lib.ut.us	Salt Lake City	UT	84121	801-943-4636	942-6323

Vermont

Library	City	State	ZIP	Phone	Fax
Fletcher Free Public Library 235 College St *Web:* www.fletcherfree.org	Burlington	VT	05401	802-863-3403	865-7227
Kellogg-Hubbard Library 135 Main St. *Web:* www.kellogghubbard.org/	Montpelier	VT	05602	802-223-3338	223-3338

Virginia

Library	City	State	ZIP	Phone	Fax
Washington County Public Library 205 Oak Hill St *Web:* www.wcpl.net	Abingdon	VA	24210	276-676-6222	676-6235
Alexandria Library 717 Queen St *Web:* www.alexandria.lib.va.us	Alexandria	VA	22314	703-838-4555	838-5021
Amherst County Public Library 382 S Main St *Web:* www.acpl.us	Amherst	VA	24521	434-946-9388	946-9348
Arlington County Central Library 1015 N Quincy St *Web:* www.arlingtonva.us/Departments/Libraries/LibrariesMain.aspx	Arlington	VA	22201	703-228-5990	228-7720
Bristol Public Library 1400 Euclid Ave. *Web:* www.wrlibrary.org/libraries/brpage.html	Bristol	VA	24201	276-669-9444	669-5593
Jefferson-Madison Regional Library 201 E Market St. *Web:* jmrl.org	Charlottesville	VA	22902	434-979-7151	971-7035
Pittsylvania County Public Library 24 Military Dr *Web:* www.pcplib.org	Chatham	VA	24531	434-432-3271	432-1405
Chesapeake Public Library 298 Cedar Rd *Web:* www.chesapeake.lib.va.us	Chesapeake	VA	23322	757-382-6576	382-8567
Chesterfield County Public Library 9501 Lori Rd *Web:* www.library.co.chesterfield.va.us	Chesterfield	VA	23832	804-748-1601	751-4679
Montgomery-Floyd Regional Library 125 Sheltman St. *Web:* www.mfrl.org	Christiansburg	VA	24073	540-382-6965	382-6964
Culpeper County Library 271 Southgate Shopping Ctr. *Web:* tlc.library.net/culpeper	Culpeper	VA	22701	540-825-8691	825-7486
Danville Public Library 511 Patton St *Web:* www.danvillelibrary.org	Danville	VA	24541	434-799-5195	972-5172
Shenandoah County Library 514 Stoney Creek Blvd *Web:* www.shenandoah.co.lib.va.us	Edinburg	VA	22824	540-984-8200	984-8207
Fairfax County Public Library 12000 Government Ctr Pkwy Suite 324 *Web:* www.fairfaxcounty.gov/library/	Fairfax	VA	22035	703-324-3100	222-3193
Augusta County Library 1759 Jefferson Hwy *Web:* www.lib.co.augusta.va.us	Fishersville	VA	22939	540-949-6354	
Samuels Public Library 538 Villa Ave. *Web:* www.shentel.net/library/samuels	Front Royal	VA	22630	540-635-3153	635-7229
Gloucester Library 6920 Main St	Gloucester	VA	23061	804-693-2998	693-1477
Buchanan County Public Library RR 2 Box 3 *Web:* www.bcplnet.org	Grundy	VA	24614	276-935-6581	935-6292
Hampton Public Library 4207 Victoria Blvd *Web:* www.hamptonpubliclibrary.org	Hampton	VA	23669	757-727-1154	727-1152
Massanutten Regional Library 174 S Main St *TF:* 877-695-4272 ■ *Web:* www.mrlib.org	Harrisonburg	VA	22801	540-434-4475	434-4382
Russell County Public Library 203 NW Main St PO Box 247 *Web:* www.russell.lib.va.us	Lebanon	VA	24266	276-889-8063	889-8045
Loudoun County Public Library Administration 908-A Trailview Blvd SE *Web:* www.lcpl.lib.va.us	Leesburg	VA	20175	703-777-0368	771-5238
Lynchburg Public Library 2315 Memorial Ave *Web:* www.lynchburgva.gov/publiclibrary	Lynchburg	VA	24501	434-847-1577	845-1479
Newport News Public Library 110 Main St. *Web:* www.newportnewslib.org	Newport News	VA	23601	757-591-4858	591-7425
Newport News Public Library System 700 Town Center Dr Suite 300 *Web:* www.nngov.com/library/	Newport News	VA	23606	757-926-1350	926-1365
Kirn Memorial Public Library 301 E City Hall Ave *Web:* www.npl.lib.va.us	Norfolk	VA	23510	757-664-7323	664-7320
Norfolk Public Library 301 E City Hall Ave. *Web:* www.npl.lib.va.us	Norfolk	VA	23510	757-664-7323	664-7320
Petersburg Public Library 137 S Sycamore St. *Web:* www.ppls.org	Petersburg	VA	23803	804-733-2387	733-7972
Portsmouth Public Library 601 Court St	Portsmouth	VA	23704	757-393-8501	393-5107
Prince William Public Library System 13083 Chinn Pk Dr *Web:* www.pwcgov.org/library	Prince William	VA	22192	703-792-6100	792-4875
Pulaski County Library 60 W 3rd St. *Web:* www.pclibs.org	Pulaski	VA	24301	540-980-7770	980-7775
County of Henrico Public Library System 1001 N Laburnum Ave. *Web:* www.co.henrico.va.us/library	Richmond	VA	23223	804-222-1643	222-5566
Richmond Public Library 101 E Franklin St *Web:* www.richmondpubliclibrary.org	Richmond	VA	23219	804-646-4256	646-7685
Roanoke City Public Libraries 706 S Jefferson St. *Web:* www.roanokegov.com	Roanoke	VA	24016	540-853-2475	853-1781
Roanoke County Public Library 3131 Electric Rd SW *Web:* www.roanokecountyva.gov/Departments/Library	Roanoke	VA	24018	540-772-7507	989-3129
Franklin County Public Library 355 Franklin St.	Rocky Mount	VA	24151	540-483-3098	483-6652
Campbell County Public Library PO Box 310. *Web:* tlc.library.net/campbell	Rustburg	VA	24588	434-332-9560	332-9697
Suffolk Public Library System 443 W Washington St *Web:* www.suffolk.lib.va.us	Suffolk	VA	23434	757-934-7686	
Tazewell County Public Library 310 E Main St	Tazewell	VA	24651	276-988-3639	988-5980
Virginia Beach Public Library 4100 Virginia Beach Blvd *Web:* www.vbgov.com/dept/library	Virginia Beach	VA	23452	757-385-0150	
Fauquier County Public Library 11 Winchester St.	Warrenton	VA	20186	540-347-8750	349-3278
Williamsburg Regional Library 7770 Croaker Rd *Web:* www.wrl.org	Williamsburg	VA	23188	757-259-4050	259-4079
Lonesome Pine Regional Library 124 Library St *Web:* www.lprlibrary.org	Wise	VA	24293	276-328-8061	328-1739
York County Public Library 8500 George Washington Memorial Hwy *Web:* www.yorkcounty.gov/library	Yorktown	VA	23692	757-890-3377	890-2956

Washington

Library	City	State	ZIP	Phone	Fax
Anacortes Public Library 1220 10th St	Anacortes	WA	98221	360-293-1910	293-1929

Public Libraries (Cont'd)

Washington (Cont'd)

Library	City	State	ZIP	Phone	Fax
Auburn Library 1102 Auburn Way S *Web:* www.kcls.org/auburn/aubhome.cfm	Auburn	WA	98002	253-931-3018	735-5005
Bellingham Public Library 210 Central Ave *Web:* www.bellinghampubliclibrary.org	Bellingham	WA	98225	360-676-6860	676-7795
Kitsap Regional Library 1301 Sylvan Way *TF:* 877-883-9900 ■ *Web:* www.krl.org	Bremerton	WA	98310	360-405-9110	405-9156
Everett Public Library 2702 Hoyt Ave *Web:* www.epls.org	Everett	WA	98201	425-257-8010	257-8016
King County Library System 960 Newport Way NW *Web:* www.kcls.org	Issaquah	WA	98027	425-369-3224	369-3214
Longview Public Library 1600 Louisiana St *Web:* www.longviewlibrary.org	Longview	WA	98632	360-442-5300	442-5954
Sno-Isle Regional Library 7312 35th Ave NE *Web:* www.sno-isle.org	Marysville	WA	98271	360-659-8447	651-7151
Puyallup Public Library 324 S Meridian *Web:* www.cityofpuyallup.org/page.php?id=334	Puyallup	WA	98371	253-841-5454	841-5483
Renton Public Library 100 Mill Ave S	Renton	WA	98055	425-235-2610	430-6833
Richland Public Library 955 Northgate Dr *Web:* www.richland.lib.wa.us	Richland	WA	99352	509-942-7450	942-7447
Seattle Public Library 1000 4th Ave *Web:* www.spl.org	Seattle	WA	98104	206-386-4100	386-4119
Spokane County Library District 4322 N Argonne Rd *Web:* www.scld.org	Spokane	WA	99212	509-924-4122	928-4157
Spokane Public Library 906 W Main Ave *Web:* www.spokanelibrary.org	Spokane	WA	99201	509-444-5300	444-5365
Pierce County Library System 3005 112th St E *Web:* www.piercecountylibrary.org	Tacoma	WA	98446	253-536-6500	537-4600
Tacoma Public Library 1102 Tacoma Ave S *Web:* www.tpl.lib.wa.us	Tacoma	WA	98402	253-591-5666	591-5470
Timberland Regional Library 415 Tumwater Blvd SW *Web:* www.timberland.lib.wa.us	Tumwater	WA	98501	360-943-5001	586-6838
Fort Vancouver Regional Library 1007 E Mill Plain Blvd *Web:* www.fvrl.org	Vancouver	WA	98663	360-695-1561	693-2681
Walla Walla Public Library 238 E Alder St *Web:* www.walnet.walla-walla.wa.us	Walla Walla	WA	99362	509-527-4388	527-3748
North Central Regional Library 238 Olds Stn Rd *Web:* www.ncrl.org	Wenatchee	WA	98801	509-663-1117	662-8060
Yakima Valley Regional Library 102 N 3rd St *Web:* www.yvrl.org	Yakima	WA	98901	509-452-8541	575-2093

West Virginia

Library	City	State	ZIP	Phone	Fax
Raleigh County Public Library 221 N Kanawha St	Beckley	WV	25801	304-255-0511	255-9161
Craft Memorial Library 600 Commerce St	Bluefield	WV	24701	304-325-3943	325-3702
Kanawha County Public Library 123 Capital St *Web:* kanawha.lib.wv.us	Charleston	WV	25301	304-343-4646	348-6530
Mingo County Public Library Helena Ave	Delbarton	WV	25670	304-475-2749	475-3970
Cabell County Public Library 455 9th St Plaza *Web:* cabell.lib.wv.us	Huntington	WV	25701	304-528-5700	528-5701
Ceredo-Kenova Public Library 1200 Oak St *Web:* www.wcpl.lib.wv.us	Kenova	WV	25530	304-453-2462	453-2462
Martinsburg-Berkeley County Public Library 101 W King St *Web:* www.youseemore.com/martinsburgberkeley	Martinsburg	WV	25401	304-267-8933	267-9720
Morgantown Public Library 373 Spruce St *Web:* morgantown.lib.wv.us	Morgantown	WV	26505	304-291-7425	291-7437
Miracle Valley Regional Library System 700 5th St	Moundsville	WV	26041	304-845-6911	845-6912
Fayette County Public Library 531 Summit St *Web:* fayette.lib.wv.us	Oak Hill	WV	25901	304-465-0121	465-5664
Parkersburg & Wood County Public Library 3100 Emerson Ave	Parkersburg	WV	26104	304-420-4587	420-4589
Wyoming County Public Library Castlerock Ave PO Box 130	Pineville	WV	24874	304-732-6899	732-6899
Mason County Public Library 508 Viand St	Point Pleasant	WV	25550	304-675-0894	675-0895
Jackson County Public Library 208 N Church St *Web:* jackson.park.lib.wv.us	Ripley	WV	25271	304-372-5343	372-7935
Mary H Weirton Public Library 3442 Main St *Web:* weirton.lib.wv.us	Weirton	WV	26062	304-797-8510	797-8526
McDowell Public Library 90 Howard St	Welch	WV	24801	304-436-3070	436-8079
Ohio County Public Library 52 16th St *Web:* wheeling.weirton.lib.wv.us	Wheeling	WV	26003	304-232-0244	232-6848

Wisconsin

Library	City	State	ZIP	Phone	Fax
Appleton Public Library 225 N Oneida St *Web:* www.apl.org	Appleton	WI	54911	920-832-6179	832-6182
Northern Waters Library Service 3200 E Lakeshore Dr *TF:* 800-228-5684 ■ *Web:* www.nwls.lib.wi.us	Ashland	WI	54806	715-682-2365	685-2704
Beaver Dam Community Library 311 N Spring St *Web:* www.beaverdam.lib.wi.us	Beaver Dam	WI	53916	920-887-4631	887-4633
Beloit Public Library 409 Pleasant St *Web:* www.als.lib.wi.us/BPL	Beloit	WI	53511	608-364-2905	364-2907
Brookfield Public Library 1900 N Calhoun Rd *Web:* www.brookfieldlibrary.com	Brookfield	WI	53005	262-782-4140	796-6670
Chippewa Falls Public Library 105 W Central St *Web:* www.chippewafallslibrary.org	Chippewa Falls	WI	54729	715-723-1146	720-6922
Indianhead Federated Library System 1538 Truax Blvd *Web:* www.ifls.lib.wi.us	Eau Claire	WI	54703	715-839-5082	839-5151
LE Phillips Memorial Public Library 400 Eau Claire St *Web:* www.eauclaire.lib.wi.us	Eau Claire	WI	54701	715-839-1648	839-3822
Phillips LE Memorial Public Library 400 Eau Claire St *Web:* www.eauclaire.lib.wi.us	Eau Claire	WI	54701	715-839-1648	839-3822
Southwest Wisconsin Library System 1775 4th St *Web:* www.swls.org	Fennimore	WI	53809	608-822-3393	822-6251
Fond du Lac Public Library 32 Sheboygan St *Web:* www.fdlpl.org	Fond du Lac	WI	54935	920-929-7080	929-7082
Germantown Community Library N112 W16957 Mequon Rd *Web:* www.hnet.net/duer	Germantown	WI	53022	262-253-7760	253-7763
Grafton Public Library 1620 11th Ave *Web:* www.grafton.lib.wi.us/	Grafton	WI	53024	262-375-5315	375-5317
Brown County Library 515 Pine St *Web:* www.co.brown.wi.us/library	Green Bay	WI	54301	920-448-4400	448-4388
Greenfield Public Library 7215 W Coldspring Rd *Web:* www.greenfieldlibrary.org	Greenfield	WI	53220	414-321-9595	321-8595
La Crosse County Library PO Box 220 *Web:* www.lacrossecountylibrary.com	Holmen	WI	54636	608-526-9600	526-3299
Arrowhead Library System 210 Dodge St *Web:* als.lib.wi.us	Janesville	WI	53548	608-758-6690	758-6689
Hedberg Public Library 316 S Main St *Web:* www.hedbergpubliclibrary.org	Janesville	WI	53545	608-758-6600	758-6583
Kenosha Public Library PO Box 1414 *Web:* www.kenosha.lib.wi.us	Kenosha	WI	53141	262-564-6100	564-6370
La Crosse Public Library 800 Main St *Web:* www.lacrosselibrary.org	La Crosse	WI	54601	608-789-7100	789-7106
Madison Public Library 201 W Mifflin St *Web:* www.madisonpubliclibrary.org	Madison	WI	53703	608-266-6300	266-4338
Manitowoc-Calumet Library System 707 Quay St *Web:* www.manitowoc.lib.wi.us	Manitowoc	WI	54220	920-683-4863	683-4873
Marinette County Consolidated Public Library 1700 Hall Ave	Marinette	WI	54143	715-732-7570	732-7575
Marshfield Public Library 211 E 2nd St *Web:* www.marshfieldlibrary.org	Marshfield	WI	54449	715-387-8494	387-6909
Mid-Wisconsin Federated Library System 201 N Main St *Web:* www.mwfls.org	Mayville	WI	53050	920-387-7284	387-7288
Menasha Public Library 440 1st St *Web:* www.menashalibrary.org	Menasha	WI	54952	920-967-5166	967-5159
Menomonee Falls Public Library W156 N8436 Pilgrim Rd *Web:* www.mf.lib.wi.us	Menomonee Falls	WI	53051	262-532-8900	532-8939
Menomonie Public Library 600 Wolske Bay Rd *Web:* www.menomonielibrary.org	Menomonie	WI	54751	715-232-2164	232-2324
Middleton Public Library 7425 Hubbard Ave *Web:* www.midlibrary.org/library/default.asp	Middleton	WI	53562	608-831-5564	836-5724
Milwaukee Public Library 814 W Wisconsin Ave *Web:* www.mpl.org	Milwaukee	WI	53233	414-286-3000	286-2798
Neenah Public Library 240 E Wisconsin Ave *Web:* www.neenahlibrary.org	Neenah	WI	54956	920-751-4722	866-6324
New Berlin Public Library 14750 W Cleveland Ave *Web:* www.wcfls.lib.wi.us/newberlin/	New Berlin	WI	53151	262-785-4980	785-4984
Oshkosh Public Library 106 Washington Ave *Web:* www.oshkoshpubliclibrary.org	Oshkosh	WI	54901	920-236-5200	236-5227
Winnefox Library System 106 Washington Ave *Web:* www.winnefox.org	Oshkosh	WI	54901	920-236-5220	236-5228
Oxford Public Library 129 S Franklin Ave *Web:* www.oxfordlibrary.org	Oxford	WI	53952	608-586-4458	586-4559
Racine Public Library 75 7th St *Web:* www.racinelib.lib.wi.us	Racine	WI	53403	262-636-9170	636-9260
Mead Public Library 710 N 8th St *Web:* www.sheboygan.lib.wi.us	Sheboygan	WI	53081	920-459-3400	459-4336
Portage County Public Library 1001 Main St *Web:* library.uwsp.edu/pcl/pcpl.htm	Stevens Point	WI	54481	715-346-1544	346-1239
Door County Library 107 S 4th Ave *Web:* www.dcl.lib.wi.us	Sturgeon Bay	WI	54235	920-743-6578	743-6697
Superior Public Library 1530 Tower Ave *Web:* www.ci.superior.wi.us/library/	Superior	WI	54880	715-394-8860	394-8870
Lakeshores Library System 106 W Main St *Web:* www.lakeshores.lib.wi.us	Waterford	WI	53185	262-514-4500	514-4544
Watertown Public Library 100 S Water St *Web:* www.watertown.lib.wi.us	Watertown	WI	53094	920-262-4090	261-8943
Waukesha Public Library 321 Wisconsin Ave *Web:* www.waukesha.lib.wi.us	Waukesha	WI	53186	262-524-3680	524-3677
Marathon County Public Library 300 N 1st St *Web:* www.mcpl.lib.wi.us	Wausau	WI	54403	715-261-7200	261-7219
Wauwatosa Public Library 7635 W North Ave *Web:* tpublib.fp.execpc.com	Wauwatosa	WI	53213	414-471-8484	479-8984
West Allis Public Library 7421 W National Ave *Web:* www.ci.west-allis.wi.us/library/library_services.htm	West Allis	WI	53214	414-302-8500	302-8545
West Bend Community Memorial Library 630 Poplar St *Web:* www.west-bendlibrary.org	West Bend	WI	53095	262-335-5151	335-5150
McMillan Memorial Library 490 E Grand Ave *Web:* www.mcmillanlibrary.org	Wisconsin Rapids	WI	54494	715-423-1040	423-2665

Wyoming

Library	City	State	ZIP	Phone	Fax
Natrona County Public Library 307 E 2nd St *Web:* www.natronacountylibrary.org/	Casper	WY	82601	307-237-4935	266-3734
Laramie County Public Library 2200 Pioneer Ave *Web:* www.lclsonline.org	Cheyenne	WY	82001	307-634-3561	634-2082
Campbell County Public Library 2101 S 4-J Rd *Web:* www.ccpls.org	Gillette	WY	82718	307-682-3223	686-4009
Sweetwater County Library System 300 N 1st East St *Web:* www.sweetwaterlibraries.com	Green River	WY	82935	307-875-3615	872-3203
Teton County Public Library 125 Virginian Ln *Web:* www.tclib.org	Jackson	WY	83001	307-733-2164	733-4568
Fremont County Library System 451 N 2nd St	Lander	WY	82520	307-332-5194	332-3909
Albany County Public Library 310 S 8th St *Web:* acpl.lib.wy.us	Laramie	WY	82070	307-721-2580	721-2584

437-4 Special Collections Libraries

Library	City	State	ZIP	Phone	Fax
Academy of Motion Picture Arts & Sciences Herrick Library 333 S La Cienega Blvd *Web:* www.oscars.org/mhl	Beverly Hills	CA	90211	310-247-3020	657-5193
Academy of Natural Sciences Stewart Library 1900 Benjamin Franklin Pkwy *Web:* www.ansp.org/library	Philadelphia	PA	19103	215-299-1000	
Adirondack Museum Library PO Box 99 *Web:* www.adirondackmuseum.net/research/research_library.shtml	Blue Mountain Lake	NY	12812	518-352-7311	352-7653
African American Museum & Library in Oakland 659 14th St *Web:* www.oaklandlibrary.org/AAMLO	Oakland	CA	94612	510-637-0200	637-0204
AIDS Library 1233 Locust St 2nd Fl *Web:* www.aidslibrary.org	Philadelphia	PA	19107	215-985-4851	985-4492
American Antiquarian Society (AAS) 185 Salisbury St *Web:* www.americanantiquarian.org	Worcester	MA	01609	508-755-5221	753-3311
American Craft Council Library 72 Spring St *Web:* www.craftcouncil.org	New York	NY	10012	212-274-0630	274-0650
American Film Institute Mayer Library 2021 N Western Ave *Web:* www.afi.com/about/library.aspx	Los Angeles	CA	90027	323-856-7654	467-4578
American Kennel Club Library 260 Madison Ave 4th Fl *Web:* www.akc.org/about/library	New York	NY	10016	212-696-8245	696-8281
American Library Assn Library 50 E Huron St **Fax Area Code: 312* ■ *Web:* www.ala.org/ala/alalibrary	Chicago	IL	60611	800-545-2433	280-3255*
American Museum of Natural History Library Central Park W at 79th St *Web:* library.amnh.org	New York	NY	10024	212-769-5400	769-5009
American Numismatic Society Library 96 Fulton St *Web:* www.numismatics.org/library	New York	NY	10038	212-571-4470	571-4479
American Philatelic Research Library (APRL) 100 Match Factory Pl *Web:* www.stamps.org/TheLibrary/lib_AbouttheAPRL.htm	Bellefonte	PA	16823	814-237-3803	237-6128

Phone | Fax

APRL (American Philatelic Research Library)
100 Match Factory Pl. . . . Bellefonte PA 16823 814-237-3803 237-6128
Web: www.stamps.org/TheLibrary/lib_AbouttheAPRL.htm

Association for Research & Enlightenment Library
215 67th St . . . . Virginia Beach VA 23451 757-428-3588 422-6921
Web: www.edgarcayce.org/visit_are/are_library.htm

Athenaeum of Philadelphia 219 S 6th St. . . . Philadelphia PA 19106 215-925-2688 925-3755
Web: www.philaathenaeum.org

Basketball Hall of Fame Hickox Library
1000 W Columbus Ave . . . . Springfield MA 01105 413-231-5524 781-1939
Web: www.hoophall.com/library/library.htm

Beinecke Rare Book & Manuscript Library at Yale
121 Wall St Yale University . . . . New Haven CT 06511 203-432-2977 432-4047
Web: www.library.yale.edu/beinecke

Bentley Historical Library 1150 Beal Ave. . . . Ann Arbor MI 48109 734-764-3482 936-1333
Web: bentley.umich.edu

Boston Athenaeum 10 1/2 Beacon St. . . . Boston MA 02108 617-227-0270 227-5266
Web: www.bostonathenaeum.org

Brookings Institution Library 1775 Massachusetts Ave NW . . . . Washington DC 20036 202-797-6240 797-2970
Web: www.brookings.edu

Center for Migration Studies of New York Inc Library & Archives 209 Flagg Pl . . . . Staten Island NY 10304 718-351-8800 667-4598
Web: cmsny.library.net

Cullman Library
Smithsonian Institution NHB CE-G15 MRC 154 PO Box 37012 . . . . Washington DC 20013 202-633-1184 633-0219
Web: www.sil.si.edu/libraries/cullman

Dibner Library of the History of Science & Technology
Smithsonian Institution NMAH 1041 MRC 672 PO Box 37012 . . . . Washington DC 20013 202-633-3872 633-9102
Web: www.sil.si.edu/libraries/dibner

Ernie Pyle Library 900 Girard Blvd SE . . . . Albuquerque NM 87106 505-256-2065 256-2069

Folger Shakespeare Library 201 East Capitol St SE . . . . Washington DC 20003 202-544-4600 544-4623
Web: www.folger.edu

Frank Lloyd Wright Preservation Trust Special Collections
931 Chicago Ave . . . . Oak Park IL 60302 708-848-1976 848-1248
Web: www.wrightplus.org/museum/special.html

George E Brown Jr Library of the National Academies
500 5th St NW. . . . Washington DC 20001 202-334-2125 334-1651
Web: www7.nationalacademies.org/nrclibrary

George Eastman House Menschel Library 900 East Ave . . . . Rochester NY 14607 585-271-3361 271-3970
Web: eastmanhouse.org/inc/visit/research.php#

George Peabody Library 17 E Mount Vernon Pl. . . . Baltimore MD 21202 410-659-8179 659-8137
Web: www.library.jhu.edu/collections

Gettysburg National Military Park Library & Research Center
97 Taneytown Rd. . . . Gettysburg PA 17325 717-334-1124 334-1997
Web: www.nps.gov/gett/library/libmain.htm

Gorgas Memorial Library . . . . Silver Spring MD 20910 301-319-9555
Web: wrair-www.army.mil/Resources.asp

Harriet Beecher Stowe House & Library 77 Forest St. . . . Hartford CT 06105 860-525-9317 522-9259
Web: www.harrietbeecherstowecenter.org

Harry Library of Fishes 300 Gulf Stream Way . . . . Dania Beach FL 33004 954-927-2628 924-4299
Web: www.igfa.org/lib.asp

Herrick Library 333 S La Cienega Blvd. . . . Beverly Hills CA 90211 310-247-3020 657-5193
Web: www.oscars.org/mhl

Hickox Library 1000 W Columbus Ave . . . . Springfield MA 01105 413-231-5524 781-1939
Web: www.hoophall.com/library/library.htm

Huntington Library-Art Collections & Botanical Gardens
1151 Oxford Rd . . . . San Marino CA 91108 626-405-2100 405-0225
Web: www.huntington.org

International Game Fish Assn Harry Library of Fishes
300 Gulf Stream Way. . . . Dania Beach FL 33004 954-927-2628 924-4299
Web: www.igfa.org/lib.asp

Juilliard School Wallace Library 60 Lincoln Center Plaza . . . . New York NY 10023 212-799-5000 769-6421
Web: www.juilliard.edu/library

Karpeles Manuscript Library 453 Porter Ave. . . . Buffalo NY 14201 716-885-4139 885-4139
Web: www.rain.org/~karpeles/

Library Co of Philadelphia 1314 Locust St . . . . Philadelphia PA 19107 215-546-3181 546-5167
Web: www.librarycompany.org

Lincoln Memorial Shrine 125 W Vine St . . . . Redlands CA 92373 909-798-7632 798-7566
Web: www.lincolnshrine.org

Mayer Library 2021 N Western Ave . . . . Los Angeles CA 90027 323-856-7654 467-4578
Web: www.afi.com/about/library.aspx

Menschel Library 900 East Ave . . . . Rochester NY 14607 585-271-3361 271-3970
Web: eastmanhouse.org/inc/visit/research.php#

Moon Library & Civil Rights Archives 4805 Mt Hope Dr. . . . Baltimore MD 21215 410-358-8900 486-9255
TF: 877-622-2798 ■ *Web:* www.naacp.org/programs/library/library_index.html

National Assn for the Advancement of Colored People Moon Library & Civil Rights Archives 4805 Mt Hope Dr. . . . Baltimore MD 21215 410-358-8900 486-9255
TF: 877-622-2798 ■ *Web:* www.naacp.org/programs/library/library_index.html

National Baseball Hall of Fame & Museum Library
25 Main St . . . . Cooperstown NY 13326 607-547-0330 547-4094
Web: www.baseballhalloffame.org/library

National Steinbeck Center 1 Main St. . . . Salinas CA 93901 831-796-3833 796-3828
Web: www.steinbeck.org

Portsmouth Athenaeum 9 Market Sq . . . . Portsmouth NH 03801 603-431-2538 431-7180
Web: www.portsmouthathenaeum.org

Providence Athenaeum 251 Benefit St. . . . Providence RI 02903 401-421-6970 421-2860
Web: www.providenceathenaeum.org

Redwood Library & Athenaeum 50 Bellevue Ave . . . . Newport RI 02840 401-847-0292 847-0192
Web: www.redwoodlibrary.org

Rosenbach Museum & Library 2008 DeLancey Pl . . . . Philadelphia PA 19103 215-732-1600 545-7529
Web: www.rosenbach.org

Salem Athenaeum 337 Essex St. . . . Salem MA 01970 978-744-2540 744-7536
Web: www.salemathenaeum.net

Schomburg Center for Research in Black Culture
515 Malcolm X Blvd. . . . New York NY 10037 212-491-2200
Web: www.nypl.org/research/sc/sc.html

Smithsonian Institution
Cullman Library
Smithsonian Institution NHB CE-G15 MRC 154 PO Box 37012 . . . . Washington DC 20013 202-633-1184 633-0219
Web: www.sil.si.edu/libraries/cullman
Dibner Library of the History of Science & Technology
Smithsonian Institution NMAH 1041 MRC 672 PO Box 37012 . . . . Washington DC 20013 202-633-3872 633-9102
Web: www.sil.si.edu/libraries/dibner

Stewart Library 1900 Benjamin Franklin Pkwy . . . . Philadelphia PA 19103 215-299-1000
Web: www.ansp.org/library

US Dept of Transportation Library
1200 New Jersey Ave Se Rm W12-300 . . . . Washington DC 20590 202-366-0746 366-7779
Web: dotlibrary.dot.gov

US Holocaust Memorial Museum Library
100 Raoul Wallenburg Pl SW . . . . Washington DC 20024 202-488-0400 488-2613
Web: www.ushmm.org/research/library

Vietnam Archive Texas Tech University MS 1041 . . . . Lubbock TX 79409 806-742-9010 742-0496
Web: www.vietnam.ttu.edu

Wallace Library 60 Lincoln Center Plaza . . . . New York NY 10023 212-799-5000 769-6421
Web: www.juilliard.edu/library

Walter Reed Army Institute of Research Gorgas Memorial Library . . . . Silver Spring MD 20910 301-319-9555
Web: wrair-www.army.mil/Resources.asp

437-5 State Libraries

Phone | Fax

Alabama Public Library Service 6030 Monticello Dr . . . . Montgomery AL 36130 334-213-3900 213-3993
Web: www.apls.state.al.us

Alaska State Library PO Box 110571 . . . . Juneau AK 99811 907-465-2910 465-2151
Web: www.library.state.ak.us

Arizona State Library 1700 W Washington St Rm 200 . . . . Phoenix AZ 85007 602-542-4035 542-4972
Web: www.lib.az.us

Arkansas State Library 1 Capitol Mall 5th Fl . . . . Little Rock AR 72201 501-682-1527 682-1529
Web: www.asl.lib.ar.us

California State Library 914 Capitol Mall. . . . Sacramento CA 95814 916-654-0261 654-0241
Web: www.library.ca.gov

Colorado State Library 201 E Colfax Ave Rm 309 . . . . Denver CO 80203 303-866-6900 866-6940
Web: www.cde.state.co.us/index_library.htm

Connecticut State Library 231 Capitol Ave . . . . Hartford CT 06106 860-757-6510 757-6503
Web: www.cslib.org

Delaware Div of Libraries 43 S DuPont Hwy . . . . Dover DE 19901 302-739-4748 739-6787
Web: www.lib.de.us

Georgia Public Library Services 1800 Century Pl Suite 150 . . . . Atlanta GA 30345 404-982-3560 982-3563
Web: www.georgialibraries.org

Hawaii State Public Library 478 S King St . . . . Honolulu HI 96813 808-586-3505
Web: www.hcc.hawaii.edu/hspls

Idaho Commission for Libraries 325 W State St . . . . Boise ID 83702 208-334-2150 334-4016
Web: libraries.idaho.gov/

Illinois State Library 300 S 2nd St. . . . Springfield IL 62701 217-782-2994 785-4326
Web: www.cyberdriveillinois.com/departments/library/home.html

Indiana State Library 140 N Senate Ave. . . . Indianapolis IN 46204 317-232-3675 232-3728
Web: www.statelib.lib.in.us

Iowa State Library 112 E Grand Ave. . . . Des Moines IA 50319 515-281-4105 281-6191
Web: www.statelibraryofiowa.org

Kansas State Library 300 SW 10th Ave Capitol Bldg Rm 343 N . . . . Topeka KS 66612 785-296-3296 296-6650
Web: skyways.lib.ks.us

Kentucky Dept for Libraries & Archives 300 Coffee Tree Rd . . . . Frankfort KY 40602 502-564-8300 564-5773
Web: www.kdla.ky.gov

Library of Michigan 702 W Kalamazoo St PO Box 30007 . . . . Lansing MI 48909 517-373-5504 373-1580
Web: www.libofmich.lib.mi.us

Library of Virginia 800 E Broad St . . . . Richmond VA 23219 804-692-3500 692-3594
Web: www.lva.lib.va.us

Louisiana State Library 701 N 4th St. . . . Baton Rouge LA 70821 225-342-4915 219-4725
Web: www.state.lib.la.us

Maine State Library 64 State House Stn . . . . Augusta ME 04333 207-287-5600 287-5615
Web: www.state.me.us/msl

Massachusetts Board of Library Commissioners
98 N Washington St. . . . Boston MA 02114 617-725-1860 421-9833
Web: mblc.state.ma.us

Mississippi Library Commission 1221 Ellis Ave. . . . Jackson MS 39209 601-961-4111 354-4181
TF: 800-647-7542 ■ *Web:* www.mlc.lib.ms.us

Missouri State Library 600 W Main St PO Box 387 . . . . Jefferson City MO 65102 573-751-3615 526-1142
Web: www.sos.mo.gov/library

Montana State Library 1515 E 6th Ave PO Box 201800 . . . . Helena MT 59620 406-444-3115 444-0266
Web: msl.state.mt.us

Nebraska State Library PO Box 98931 . . . . Lincoln NE 68509 402-471-3189 471-1011
Web: www.nlc.state.ne.us

Nevada State Library & Archives 100 N Stewart St . . . . Carson City NV 89701 775-684-3360 684-3330
Web: dmla.clan.lib.nv.us/docs/nsla

New Hampshire State Library 20 Park St. . . . Concord NH 03301 603-271-2144 271-2205
Web: www.nh.gov/nhsl

New Jersey State Library 185 N State St PO Box 520 . . . . Trenton NJ 08625 609-292-6200 292-2746
Web: www.state.nj.us/statelibrary/njlib.htm

New York State Library Empire State Plaza . . . . Albany NY 12230 518-474-5355 474-5786
Web: www.nysl.nysed.gov

North Carolina State Library 109 E Jones St. . . . Raleigh NC 27699 919-807-7400 733-8748
Web: statelibrary.dcr.state.nc.us

North Dakota State Library 604 East Blvd Dept 250 . . . . Bismarck ND 58505 701-328-2492 328-2040
Web: ndsl.lib.state.nd.us

Oklahoma Dept of Libraries 200 NE 18th St . . . . Oklahoma City OK 73105 405-521-2502 525-7804
TF: 800-522-8116 ■ *Web:* www.odl.state.ok.us

Oregon State Library 250 Winter NE State Library Bldg. . . . Salem OR 97301 503-378-4243 588-7119
Web: oregon.gov/OSL

Pennsylvania Commonwealth Libraries 333 Market St . . . . Harrisburg PA 17126 717-787-2646 772-3265
Web: www.statelibrary.state.pa.us

Rhode Island Office of Library & Information Services
1 Capitol Hill 4th Fl . . . . Providence RI 02908 401-222-2726 222-4195
Web: www.olis.state.ri.us

South Carolina State Library PO Box 11469 . . . . Columbia SC 29211 803-734-8666 734-8676
Web: www.state.sc.us/scsl

South Dakota State Library 800 Governors Dr. . . . Pierre SD 57501 605-773-3131 773-4950
TF: 800-423-6665 ■ *Web:* www.sdstatelibrary.com

State Library of Florida 500 S Bronough St . . . . Tallahassee FL 32399 850-245-6600 245-6651
Web: dlis.dos.state.fl.us/stlib

State Library of Ohio 274 E 1st Ave. . . . Columbus OH 43201 614-644-7061 466-3584
TF: 800-686-1532 ■ *Web:* winslo.state.oh.us

Tennessee State Library & Archives 403 7th Ave N . . . . Nashville TN 37243 615-741-2764 741-6471
Web: state.tn.us/tsla

Texas State Library 1201 Brazos . . . . Austin TX 78701 512-463-5460 463-5436
Web: www.tsl.state.tx.us

Utah State Library 250 N 1950 West Suite A. . . . Salt Lake City UT 84116 801-715-6777 715-6767
Web: library.utah.gov

Vermont Dept of Libraries 109 State St. . . . Montpelier VT 05609 802-828-3261 828-2199
Web: dol.state.vt.us

Washington State Library 6880 Capitol Blvd S . . . . Olympia WA 98504 360-704-5200 586-7575
Web: www.secstate.wa.gov/library

West Virginia Library Commission 1900 Kanawha Blvd E . . . . Charleston WV 25305 304-558-2041 558-2044
Web: www.librarycommission.lib.wv.us

Wisconsin Dept of Public Instruction Library Services Div
125 S Webster St PO Box 7841 . . . . Madison WI 53707 608-266-3390 267-1052
TF: 800-441-4563 ■ *Web:* www.dpi.state.wi.us/

Wyoming State Library 2301 Capitol Ave . . . . Cheyenne WY 82002 307-777-6333 777-6289
Web: www-wsl.state.wy.us

437-6 University Libraries

Listings for university libraries are arranged by states.

Phone | Fax

Alabama Agricultural & Mechanical University Drake Memorial Learning Resources Center 4900 Meridian St . . . . Huntsville AL 35810 256-372-4747
Web: www.aamu.edu

University Libraries (Cont'd)

Library	City	State	ZIP	Phone	Fax
Auburn University Draughon Library 231 Mell St *Web:* www.lib.auburn.edu	Auburn University	AL	36849	334-844-4500	844-4424
Tuskegee University Ford Motor Co Library/Learning Resource Center Hollis Burke Frissell Library Bldg *Web:* www.tuskegee.edu	Tuskegee	AL	36088	334-727-8894	727-9282
University of Alabama Gorgas Library PO Box 870266 *Web:* www.lib.ua.edu/libraries/gorgas	Tuscaloosa	AL	35487	205-348-6047	348-0760
University of Alaska Anchorage Consortium Library 3211 Providence Dr *Web:* www.lib.uaa.alaska.edu	Anchorage	AK	99508	907-786-1848	
University of Alaska Fairbanks Rasmuson Library PO Box 756800 *Web:* www.uaf.edu/library	Fairbanks	AK	99775	907-474-7481	474-6841
Arizona State University Hayden Library PO Box 871006 *Web:* www.asu.edu/lib/libraries/hayden	Tempe	AZ	85287	480-965-3417	965-9169
Northern Arizona University Cline Library PO Box 6022 *TF:* 800-247-3380 ■ *Web:* www.nau.edu/library/	Flagstaff	AZ	86011	928-523-6802	523-3770
University of Arizona Library 1510 E University Blvd *Web:* www.library.arizona.edu	Tucson	AZ	85721	520-621-3430	621-9733
University of Arkansas Libraries 365 McIlroy Ave MULN 206 *Web:* dante.uark.edu	Fayetteville	AR	72701	479-575-6702	575-6656
University of Central Arkansas Torreyson Library 201 Donaghey Ave *Web:* library.uca.edu	Conway	AR	72035	501-450-3129	450-5208
California Institute of Technology Library 1200 E California Blvd MC I-32 *Web:* library.caltech.edu	Pasadena	CA	91125	626-395-6405	792-7540
California Lutheran University Pearson Library 60 W Olsen Rd *Web:* www.callutheran.edu	Thousand Oaks	CA	91360	805-493-3250	493-3842
California Polytechnic State University Kennedy Library 1 Grand Ave *Web:* www.lib.calpoly.edu	San Luis Obispo	CA	93407	805-756-2029	756-2346
California State Polytechnic University Library 3801 W Temple Ave *Web:* www.csupomona.edu/~library	Pomona	CA	91768	909-869-3074	869-6922
California State University Bakersfield Stiern Library 9001 Stockdale Hwy *Web:* www.lib.csubak.edu	Bakersfield	CA	93311	661-664-3172	654-3238
California State University Chico Meriam Library *Web:* www.csuchico.edu/library	Chico	CA	95929	530-898-6502	898-4443
California State University Dominguez Hills Library 1000 E Victoria St *Web:* library.csudh.edu	Carson	CA	90747	310-243-3715	516-4219
California State University Fresno Madden Library 5200 N Barton Ave M/S ML 34 *Web:* lib.csufresno.edu	Fresno	CA	93740	559-278-2596	278-6952
California State University Fullerton Pollak Library PO Box 4150 *Web:* www.library.fullerton.edu	Fullerton	CA	92834	714-278-2633	278-2439
California State University Long Beach University Library 1250 Bellflower Blvd *Web:* www.csulb.edu/library	Long Beach	CA	90840	562-985-4047	985-1703
California State University Los Angeles Kennedy Memorial Library 5151 State University Dr *Web:* www.calstatela.edu/library	Los Angeles	CA	90032	323-343-3988	343-6401
California State University Northridge Oviatt Library 18111 Nordhoff St *Web:* library.csun.edu	Northridge	CA	91330	818-677-2285	677-2676
California State University Sacramento Library 2000 State University Dr E *Web:* library.csus.edu	Sacramento	CA	95819	916-278-6708	278-5917
California State University San Bernardino Pfau Library 5500 University Pkwy *Web:* www.lib.csusb.edu	San Bernardino	CA	92407	909-537-5000	537-7079
California State University San Marcos Library 333 S Twin Oaks Valley Rd *Web:* library.csusm.edu	San Marcos	CA	92096	760-750-4340	
California State University Stanislaus Library 801 W Monte Vista Ave *Web:* www.library.csustan.edu	Turlock	CA	95382	209-667-3234	667-3164
Humboldt State University Library 1 Harpst St *Web:* library.humboldt.edu	Arcata	CA	95521	707-826-3431	826-3440
John F Kennedy University Fisher Library 100 Ellinwood Way *Web:* www.library.jfku.edu	Pleasant Hill	CA	94523	925-969-3100	
Occidental College Clapp Library 1600 Campus Rd *Web:* departments.oxy.edu/library	Los Angeles	CA	90041	323-259-2640	341-4991
Pepperdine University Payson Library 24255 Pacific Coast Hwy *Web:* library.pepperdine.edu	Malibu	CA	90263	310-506-4252	506-4117
San Francisco State University Leonard Library 1630 Holloway Ave *Web:* www.library.sfsu.edu	San Francisco	CA	94132	415-338-1854	
Sonoma State University University Library 1801 E Cotati Ave *Web:* libweb.sonoma.edu	Rohnert Park	CA	94928	707-664-2375	664-2090
Stanford University Green Library 557 Escondido Mall *Web:* library.stanford.edu/depts/green	Stanford	CA	94305	650-723-9108	725-6874
University of California Berkeley Library *Web:* www.lib.berkeley.edu	Berkeley	CA	94720	510-642-6657	643-0315
University of California Davis Shields Library 100 NW Quad *Web:* www.lib.ucdavis.edu	Davis	CA	95616	530-752-6561	752-7815
University of California Irvine Library PO Box 19557 *Web:* www.lib.uci.edu	Irvine	CA	92623	949-824-6836	824-3644
University of California Los Angeles Library System Charles E Young Research Library PO Box 951575 *Web:* www.library.ucla.edu	Los Angeles	CA	90095	310-825-1201	206-4109
University of California Riverside Libraries PO Box 5900 *Web:* library.ucr.edu	Riverside	CA	92517	951-827-3220	827-3281
University of California San Diego Libraries 9500 Gilman Dr Suite 0175 *Web:* libraries.ucsd.edu	La Jolla	CA	92093	858-534-3336	
University of California San Francisco Kalmanovitz Library 530 Parnassus Ave *Web:* www.library.ucsf.edu	San Francisco	CA	94143	415-476-8293	476-4653
University of California Santa Barbara Davidson Library *Web:* www.library.ucsb.edu	Santa Barbara	CA	93106	805-893-2478	
University of California Santa Cruz McHenry Library 1156 High St *Web:* library.ucsc.edu	Santa Cruz	CA	95064	831-459-2076	459-8206
University of San Francisco Gleeson Library 2130 Fulton St *Web:* www.usfca.edu/library	San Francisco	CA	94117	415-422-2660	422-2233
University of Southern California Doheny Memorial Library 3550 Trousdale Pkwy University Pk Campus *Web:* www.usc.edu/isd/libraries	Los Angeles	CA	90089	213-740-4039	
Colorado State University Morgan Library *Web:* lib.colostate.edu	Fort Collins	CO	80523	970-491-1833	491-1195
University of Colorado at Boulder Libraries 1720 Pleasant St 184 UCB *Web:* ucblibraries.colorado.edu	Boulder	CO	80309	303-492-8705	492-1881
University of Colorado at Colorado Springs Kraemer Family Library PO Box 7150 *Web:* web.uccs.edu/library	Colorado Springs	CO	80933	719-262-3286	528-5227
University of Denver Westminster Law Library 2255 E Evans Ave *Web:* www.law.du.edu/library	Denver	CO	80208	303-871-6190	871-6999
University of Northern Colorado Michener Library *Web:* www.unco.edu/library	Greeley	CO	80634	970-351-2601	351-2963
Central Connecticut State University Burritt Library 1615 Stanley St *Web:* library.ccsu.edu/lib	New Britain	CT	06050	860-832-2055	832-3409
Connecticut College Shain Library 270 Mohegan Ave *Web:* www.conncoll.edu/is/info-resources	New London	CT	06320	860-439-2655	439-2871
Eastern Connecticut State University Smith Library 83 Windham St *Web:* www.easternct.edu/smithlibrary	Willimantic	CT	06226	860-465-4506	465-5522
Southern Connecticut State University Buley Library 501 Crescent St *Web:* library.scsu.ctstateu.edu	New Haven	CT	06515	203-392-5750	392-5775
Trinity College Raether Library 300 Summit St *Web:* www.trincoll.edu/depts/library	Hartford	CT	06106	860-297-2268	297-2251
University of Connecticut Babbidge Library 369 Fairfield Rd Unit 2005 *Web:* www.lib.uconn.edu	Storrs	CT	06269	860-486-2219	486-0584
Wesleyan University Olin Library 252 Church St *Web:* www.wesleyan.edu/libr	Middletown	CT	06459	860-685-2660	685-2661
Western Connecticut State University Haas Library 181 White St *Web:* library.wcsu.edu	Danbury	CT	06810	203-837-9100	837-9108
Yale University Sterling Memorial Library PO Box 208240 *Web:* www.library.yale.edu	New Haven	CT	06520	203-432-1775	432-1294
University of Delaware Library 181 S College Ave *Web:* www.lib.udel.edu	Newark	DE	19717	302-831-2965	831-1046
American University Bender Library 4400 Massachusetts Ave NW *Web:* www.library.american.edu	Washington	DC	20016	202-885-3200	885-3226
Catholic University of America Mullen Library 620 Michigan Ave NE Rm308 *Web:* libraries.cua.edu	Washington	DC	20064	202-319-5060	319-4735
Gallaudet University Library 800 Florida Ave NE *Web:* library.gallaudet.edu	Washington	DC	20002	202-651-5217	651-5213
George Washington University Gelman Library 2130 H St NW *Web:* www.gwu.edu/gelman	Washington	DC	20052	202-994-6558	463-1340
Georgetown University Lauinger Library 3700 'O' St NW Box 57174 *Web:* www.library.georgetown.edu	Washington	DC	20057	202-687-7452	687-1215
Barry University Barry Memorial Library 11300 NE 2nd Ave *Web:* www.barry.edu/libraryservices	Miami	FL	33161	305-899-3760	899-4792
Florida A & M University Coleman Memorial Library 1500 S Martin Luther King Blvd *Web:* www.famu.edu/library	Tallahassee	FL	32307	850-599-3370	561-2293
Florida Atlantic University Wimberly Library 777 Glades Rd *Web:* www.fau.edu/library	Boca Raton	FL	33431	561-297-3760	297-2189
Florida International University Libraries University Park Campus *Web:* weblib.fiu.edu	Miami	FL	33199	305-348-2451	348-6579
Florida State University Strozier Library Rm 314 *Web:* www.lib.fsu.edu	Tallahassee	FL	32306	850-644-5211	644-5016
Stetson University duPont-Ball Library 421 N Woodland Blvd Unit 8418 *Web:* www.stetson.edu/departments/library	DeLand	FL	32720	386-822-7183	822-7199
University of Central Florida Library PO Box 162666 *Web:* library.ucf.edu	Orlando	FL	32816	407-823-2564	823-2529
University of Florida Libraries PO Box 117001 *Web:* www.uflib.ufl.edu	Gainesville	FL	32611	352-392-0342	392-7251
University of Miami Richter Library PO Box 248214 *Web:* www.library.miami.edu	Coral Gables	FL	33124	305-284-3551	284-4027
University of North Florida Carpenter Library 4567 St Johns Bluff Rd S Bldg 12 *Web:* www.unf.edu/library	Jacksonville	FL	32224	904-620-2616	620-2719
University of South Florida Libraries 4202 E Fowler Ave LIB 122 *Web:* www.lib.usf.edu	Tampa	FL	33620	813-974-2721	974-5153
Emory University Woodruff Library 540 Asbury Cir *Web:* www.emory.edu/libraries.cfm	Atlanta	GA	30322	404-727-6861	727-0805
Georgia Institute of Technology Library 225 North Ave NW *Web:* www.library.gatech.edu	Atlanta	GA	30332	404-894-4500	894-0399
Georgia Southern University Henderson Library PO Box 8074 *Web:* library.georgiasouthern.edu	Statesboro	GA	30460	912-681-5115	681-0093
Georgia State University Library 100 Decatur St SE *Web:* www.library.gsu.edu	Atlanta	GA	30303	404-651-2172	651-2476
Mercer University Tarver Library 1300 Edgewood Ave *Web:* tarver.mercer.edu	Macon	GA	31207	478-301-2960	301-2111
University of Georgia Library 320 S Jackson St *Web:* www.libs.uga.edu	Athens	GA	30602	706-542-0621	542-4144
Valdosta State University Odum Library 1500 N Patterson St *Web:* books.valdosta.edu	Valdosta	GA	31698	229-333-5860	259-5055
Hawaii Pacific University Meader Library 1060 Bishop St *Web:* www.hpu.edu	Honolulu	HI	96813	808-544-0210	521-7998
University of Hawaii at Hilo Mookini Library 200 W Kawili St *Web:* library.uhh.hawaii.edu	Hilo	HI	96720	808-974-7346	
University of Hawaii at Manoa Hamilton Library 2550 McCarthy Mall *Web:* libweb.hawaii.edu	Honolulu	HI	96822	808-956-7205	956-5968
Boise State University Albertsons Library 1910 University Dr *Web:* library.boisestate.edu	Boise	ID	83725	208-426-1204	426-1885
Idaho State University Oboler Library 850 South 9th Ave Bldg 50 Campus Box 8089 *Web:* www.isu.edu/library	Pocatello	ID	83209	208-282-2958	282-5847
University of Idaho Library Box 442350 *Web:* www.lib.uidaho.edu	Moscow	ID	83844	208-885-6534	
Bradley University Cullom-Davis Library 1501 W Bradley Ave *Web:* library.bradley.edu	Peoria	IL	61625	309-677-2825	677-2558
DePaul University Loop Campus Library 1 E Jackson Blvd 10th Fl *Web:* www.lib.depaul.edu	Chicago	IL	60605	312-362-8433	362-6186

Library	City	State	ZIP	Phone	Fax
Illinois Institute of Technology Galvin Library 35 W 33rd St *Web:* www.gl.iit.edu	Chicago	IL	60616	312-567-6847	567-3955
Illinois State University Milner Library 201 N School St *Web:* www.library.ilstu.edu	Normal	IL	61790	309-438-3451	438-3676
Knox College Seymour Library 2 E South St *Web:* library.knox.edu	Galesburg	IL	61401	309-341-7246	341-7799
Loyola University Chicago Cudahy Library 6525 N Sheridan Rd *Web:* libraries.luc.edu/about/cudahy.shtml	Chicago	IL	60626	773-508-2658	508-2993
Northeastern Illinois University Williams Library 5500 N St Louis Ave *Web:* www.neiu.edu/neiulib	Chicago	IL	60625	773-442-4470	442-4531
Northern Illinois University University Libraries 180 W Stadium Dr *Web:* www.niulib.niu.edu	DeKalb	IL	60115	815-753-1094	753-9803
Northwestern University Library 1970 Campus Dr *Web:* www.library.northwestern.edu	Evanston	IL	60208	847-491-7658	491-8306
Quincy University Brenner Library 1800 College Ave *Web:* www.quincy.edu/library	Quincy	IL	62301	217-228-5345	228-5354
Southern Illinois University Carbondale Morris Library 605 Agriculture Dr MC 6632 *Web:* www.lib.siu.edu	Carbondale	IL	62901	618-453-2522	453-3440
Southern Illinois University Edwardsville Lovejoy Library PO Box 1063 *Web:* www.library.siue.edu/lib	Edwardsville	IL	62026	618-650-2172	650-2717
University of Chicago Library 1100 E 57th St *Web:* www.lib.uchicago.edu	Chicago	IL	60637	773-702-8740	702-6623
University of Illinois Chicago Daley Library 801 S Morgan St Rm 1-280 *Web:* www.uic.edu/depts/lib	Chicago	IL	60607	312-996-2716	413-0424
University of Illinois Springfield Brookens Library 1 University Plaza MS BRK 140 *Web:* library.uis.edu	Springfield	IL	62703	217-206-6633	206-6208
University of Illinois Urbana-Champaign Library 1408 W Gregory Dr MC-522 *Web:* www.library.uiuc.edu	Urbana	IL	61801	217-333-2290	333-2214
Western Illinois University Malpass Library 1 University Cir *Web:* www.wiu.edu/library	Macomb	IL	61455	309-298-2762	298-2791
Ball State University Bracken Library 2000 University Ave *Web:* www.bsu.edu/library	Muncie	IN	47306	765-285-5143	
Butler University Irwin Library 4600 Sunset Ave *Web:* www.butler.edu/library	Indianapolis	IN	46208	317-940-9227	940-9711
DePauw University West Library 11 E Larabee St *Web:* www.depauw.edu/library	Greencastle	IN	46135	765-658-4420	658-4445
Indiana State University Cunningham Memorial Library 650 Sycamore St *TF:* 800-851-4279 ■ *Web:* odin.indstate.edu	Terre Haute	IN	47809	812-237-2580	237-2567
Indiana University Bloomington Libraries 1320 E 10th St *Web:* www.libraries.iub.edu	Bloomington	IN	47405	812-855-8028	855-2576
Indiana University Northwest Library 3400 Broadway *Web:* www.iun.edu/lib	Gary	IN	46408	219-980-6580	980-6558
Indiana University-Purdue University Fort Wayne Helmke Library 2101 E Coliseum Blvd *Web:* www.lib.ipfw.edu	Fort Wayne	IN	46805	260-481-6514	481-6509
Indiana University-Purdue University Indianapolis Library 755 W Michigan St *Web:* www.ulib.iupui.edu	Indianapolis	IN	46202	317-274-0462	278-2300
Indiana University South Bend Schurz Library 1700 Mishawaka Ave PO Box 7111 *Web:* www.iusb.edu/libg	South Bend	IN	46634	574-527-4440	520-4472
Purdue University Libraries ADMN 504 W State St *Web:* www.lib.purdue.edu	West Lafayette	IN	47907	765-494-2900	494-0156
University of Notre Dame Hesburgh Library *Web:* www.library.nd.edu	Notre Dame	IN	46556	574-631-5252	631-6772
Drake University Cowles Library 28th St & University Ave *Web:* www.lib.drake.edu	Des Moines	IA	50311	515-271-2111	271-3933
Grinnell College Burling Library *Web:* www.lib.grin.edu	Grinnell	IA	50112	641-269-3350	269-4283
Iowa State University Parks Library Osborn Dr & Morrill Rd *Web:* www.lib.iastate.edu	Ames	IA	50011	515-294-3642	294-5525
Saint Ambrose University O'Keefe Library 518 W Locust St *TF:* 888-272-8542 ■ *Web:* library.sau.edu	Davenport	IA	52803	563-333-6245	333-6248
University of Iowa Libraries 100 Main Library *Web:* www.lib.uiowa.edu	Iowa City	IA	52242	319-335-5299	335-5900
Kansas State University Hale Library 137 Hale Library Mid-Campus Dr *Web:* www.lib.ksu.edu	Manhattan	KS	66506	785-532-3014	532-7415
MidAmerica Nazarene University Mabee Library 2030 E College Way *Web:* www.mnu.edu/academics/mabee	Olathe	KS	66062	913-791-3485	791-3285
Pittsburg State University Axe Library 1701 S Broadway *Web:* library.pittstate.edu	Pittsburg	KS	66762	620-235-4882	235-4090
University of Kansas Watson Library 1425 Jayhawk Blvd *Web:* www.lib.ku.edu/	Lawrence	KS	66045	785-864-3956	864-8986
Wichita State University Ablah Library 1845 Fairmount St Box 68 *Web:* library.wichita.edu	Wichita	KS	67260	316-978-3582	978-3048
Berea College Hutchins Library 100 Campus Dr *Web:* www.berea.edu/hutchinslibrary	Berea	KY	40404	859-985-3364	985-3912
Kentucky State University Blazer Library 400 E Main St *Web:* www.kysu.edu/academics/library	Frankfort	KY	40601	502-597-6852	597-5068
Northern Kentucky University Steely Library *Web:* library.nku.edu	Highland Heights	KY	41099	859-572-5457	572-5390
University of Kentucky Young Library 500 S Limestone St *Web:* www.uky.edu/Libraries/wty.html	Lexington	KY	40506	859-257-0500	257-0505
University of Louisville Ekstrom Library 2301 S 3rd St *Web:* library.louisville.edu/ekstrom	Louisville	KY	40292	502-852-6745	852-7394
Western Kentucky University Libraries 1906 College Heights Blvd Suite 11067 *Web:* www.wku.edu/Library	Bowling Green	KY	42101	270-745-2904	745-6422
Grambling State University Lewis Memorial Library 100 Johnson St *Web:* www.gram.edu/library	Grambling	LA	71245	318-274-2568	274-3268
Louisiana State University Middleton Library *Web:* www.lib.lsu.edu	Baton Rouge	LA	70803	225-578-8875	578-6825
Louisiana Tech University Prescott Memorial Library PO Box 10408 *Web:* www.latech.edu/library	Ruston	LA	71272	318-257-3555	257-2447
Loyola University Monroe Library 6363 St Charles Ave *Web:* library.loyno.edu	New Orleans	LA	70118	504-864-7051	864-7247
McNeese State University Frazar Memorial Library PO Box 91445 *TF:* 800-622-3352 ■ *Web:* www.library.mcneese.edu	Lake Charles	LA	70609	337-475-5725	475-5719
Nicholls State University Ellender Memorial Library 906 E 1st St *Web:* www.nicholls.edu/library	Thibodaux	LA	70301	985-448-4646	448-4925
Northwestern State University Watson Memorial Library 913 University Pkwy **Fax Area Code: 318* ■ *Web:* www.nsula.edu/watson_library/index.html	Natchitoches	LA	71497	888-540-9657	357-4470*
Southeastern Louisiana University Sims Memorial Library SLU 10896 *Web:* www.selu.edu/library	Hammond	LA	70402	985-549-3860	549-3995
Tulane University Howard-Tilton Memorial Library 7001 Freret St *Web:* library.tulane.edu	New Orleans	LA	70118	504-865-5131	865-6773
University of Louisiana at Lafayette Dupre Library 302 E Saint Mary Blvd *Web:* library.louisiana.edu	Lafayette	LA	70504	337-482-6025	482-5841
University of New Orleans Long Library 2000 Lakeshore Dr *Web:* library.uno.edu	New Orleans	LA	70148	504-280-6556	280-7277
Xavier University of Louisiana Library 1 Drexel Dr *Web:* www.xula.edu/library	New Orleans	LA	70125	504-520-7304	520-7917
Bates College Ladd Library 48 Campus Ave *Web:* abacus.bates.edu/library	Lewiston	ME	04240	207-786-6263	786-6055
Bowdoin College Hawthorne-Longfellow Library 3000 College Stn *Web:* library.bowdoin.edu	Brunswick	ME	04011	207-725-3280	725-3083
Colby College Miller Library 5100 Mayflower Hill *Web:* www.colby.edu/academics_cs/library	Waterville	ME	04901	207-859-5147	859-5105
University of Maine Fogler Library 5729 Fogler Library *Web:* www.library.umaine.edu	Orono	ME	04469	207-581-1666	581-1653
Bowie State University Marshall Library 14000 Jericho Park Rd *Web:* www.bowiestate.edu/research/libraries	Bowie	MD	20715	301-860-3850	860-3848
Frostburg State University Ort Library 1 Stadium Dr *Web:* www.frostburg.edu/dept/library	Frostburg	MD	21532	301-687-4395	687-7069
Johns Hopkins University Sheridan Libraries 3400 N Charles St *Web:* www.library.jhu.edu	Baltimore	MD	21218	410-516-8325	516-5080
Salisbury University Blackwell Library 1101 Camden Ave *Web:* www.salisbury.edu/library	Salisbury	MD	21801	410-543-6130	543-6203
Towson University Cook Library 8000 York Rd *Web:* cooklibrary.towson.edu	Towson	MD	21252	410-704-2461	704-3292
University of Baltimore Langsdale Library 1420 Maryland Ave *Web:* langsdale.ubalt.edu	Baltimore	MD	21201	410-837-4260	837-4248
University of Maryland McKeldin Library McKeldin Library *Web:* www.lib.umd.edu	College Park	MD	20742	301-405-9075	
University of Maryland Baltimore county Kuhn Library 1000 Hilltop Cir *Web:* www.umbc.edu/aok	Baltimore	MD	21250	410-455-2232	
Amherst College Frost Library PO Box 5000 *Web:* www.amherst.edu/library	Amherst	MA	01002	413-542-2373	542-2662
Boston College Libraries 140 Commonwealth Ave *Web:* www.bc.edu/libraries	Chestnut Hill	MA	02467	617-552-4472	552-0599
Boston University Mugar Memorial Library 771 Commonwealth Ave *Web:* www.bu.edu/library/	Boston	MA	02215	617-353-3710	353-2084
Brandeis University Library Box 549110 MS 045 *Web:* lts.brandeis.edu	Waltham	MA	02454	781-736-4700	736-4719
Bridgewater State College Maxwell Library 10 Shaw Rd *Web:* www.bridgew.edu/library	Bridgewater	MA	02325	508-531-1392	531-1349
College of the Holy Cross Dinand Library 1 College St *Web:* www.holycross.edu	Worcester	MA	01610	508-793-2642	793-2372
Harvard University Widener Library Wadsworth House 1341 Massachusetts Ave *Web:* hul.harvard.edu	Cambridge	MA	02138	617-495-3650	496-8740
Massachusetts Institute of Technology Libraries 77 Massachusetts Ave Rm 14S-216 *Web:* libraries.mit.edu	Cambridge	MA	02139	617-253-5651	253-8894
Mount Holyoke College Williston Memorial Library 50 College St *Web:* www.mtholyoke.edu/lits/library	South Hadley	MA	01075	413-538-2230	538-2370
Northeastern University Snell Library 360 Huntington Ave *Web:* www.lib.neu.edu	Boston	MA	02115	617-373-2350	373-5409
Simmons College Beatley Library 300 The Fenway *Web:* my.simmons.edu/library	Boston	MA	02115	617-521-2786	521-3093
Suffolk University Sawyer Library 8 Ashburton Pl *Web:* www.suffolk.edu/sawlib	Boston	MA	02108	617-573-8535	573-8756
Tufts University Tisch Library 35 Professors Row *Web:* www.library.tufts.edu/tisch	Medford	MA	02155	617-627-3345	627-3002
University of Massachusetts Amherst Du Bois Library 154 Hicks Way *Web:* www.library.umass.edu	Amherst	MA	01003	413-545-0284	545-6873
University of Massachusetts Boston Healey Library 100 Morrissey Blvd *Web:* www.lib.umb.edu	Boston	MA	02125	617-287-5900	287-5955
University of Massachusetts Dartmouth Library 285 Old Westport Rd *Web:* www.lib.umassd.edu	North Dartmouth	MA	02747	508-999-8675	999-9142
University of Massachusetts Lowell Lydon Library 84 University Ave *Web:* library.uml.edu	Lowell	MA	01854	978-934-3205	934-3014
Andrews University White Library 1400 Grove Ave *TF:* 800-253-2874 ■ *Web:* www.andrews.edu/library	Berrien Springs	MI	49104	269-471-3267	471-6166
Calvin College Hekman Library 1855 Knollcrest Cir *Web:* www.calvin.edu/library	Grand Rapids	MI	49546	616-957-7197	526-6470
Central Michigan University Library 300 E Preston St Park Library Rm 142 *Web:* www.lib.cmich.edu	Mount Pleasant	MI	48859	989-774-3352	774-2160
Eastern Michigan University Halle Library 955 W Circle Dr *Web:* www.emich.edu/halle	Ypsilanti	MI	48197	734-487-0020	487-8861
Ferris State University FLITE Library 1010 Campus Dr *Web:* www.ferris.edu/library	Big Rapids	MI	49307	231-591-3602	591-3724
Grand Valley State University Zumberge Library 1 Campus Dr *TF:* 800-879-0581 ■ *Web:* www.gvsu.edu/library	Allendale	MI	49401	616-331-3252	331-3504
Hope College Van Wylen Library 53 Graves Pl *TF:* 800-968-7850 ■ *Web:* www.hope.edu/lib	Holland	MI	49423	616-395-7790	395-7965
Kalamazoo College Upjohn Library 1200 Academy St *Web:* www.kzoo.edu/is/library	Kalamazoo	MI	49006	269-337-7153	337-7143
Lake Superior State University Shouldice Library 906 Ryan Ave *Web:* www.lssu.edu/library	Sault Sainte Marie	MI	49783	906-635-2815	635-2193
Michigan State University Library 100 Library *TF:* 800-500-1554 ■ *Web:* www.lib.msu.edu	East Lansing	MI	48824	517-353-8700	432-1191
Michigan Technological University Van Pelt Library 1400 Townsend Dr *Web:* www.lib.mtu.edu	Houghton	MI	49931	906-487-2508	487-2357
Saginaw Valley State University Zahnow Library 7400 Bay Rd *TF:* 800-968-9500 ■ *Web:* www.svsu.edu/library	University Center	MI	48710	989-964-4240	964-4383
University of Michigan Libraries 920 S University Ave *Web:* www.lib.umich.edu	Ann Arbor	MI	48109	734-764-9356	763-5080

University Libraries (Cont'd)

Library	City	State	ZIP	Phone	Fax
University of Michigan Dearborn Mardigian Library 4901 Evergreen Rd *Web:* libraryweb.umd.umich.edu	Dearborn	MI	48128	313-593-5445	593-5561
Wayne State University Libraries 5150 Anthony Wayne Dr Suite 1210 *Web:* www.lib.wayne.edu	Detroit	MI	48202	313-577-4023	577-5265
Western Michigan University Waldo Library 1903 W Michigan Ave MS 5353 *Web:* www.wmich.edu/library/about	Kalamazoo	MI	49008	269-387-5202	387-5077
Bemidji State University Clark Library 1500 Birchmont Dr NE *Web:* www.bemidjistate.edu/library	Bemidji	MN	56601	218-755-3345	
Bethel University Library 3900 Bethel Dr *Web:* library.bethel.edu	Saint Paul	MN	55112	651-638-6222	635-1971
Carleton College Gould Library 1 N College St *Web:* apps.carleton.edu/campus/library	Northfield	MN	55057	507-646-4260	646-4087
College of Saint Benedict Clemens Library 37 S College Ave *Web:* www.csbsju.edu/library	Saint Joseph	MN	56374	320-363-5611	363-5197
Hamline University Bush Memorial Library 1536 Hewitt Ave *Web:* www.hamline.edu/bushlibrary	Saint Paul	MN	55104	651-523-2375	523-2199
Macalester College Wallace Library 1600 Grand Ave *Web:* www.macalester.edu/library	Saint Paul	MN	55105	651-696-6346	696-6617
Minnesota State University Mankato Memorial Library PO Box 8419 *Web:* lib.mnsu.edu	Mankato	MN	56002	507-389-5952	389-5155
Minnesota State University Moorhead Lord Library 1104 7th Ave S *Web:* www.mnstate.edu/library	Moorhead	MN	56563	218-477-2922	477-5924
Saint Cloud State University Library 720 4th Ave S *Web:* lrs.stcloudstate.edu	Saint Cloud	MN	56301	320-308-2022	308-4778
Saint John's University Alcuin Library PO Box 2000 *Web:* www.csbsju.edu/library	Collegeville	MN	56321	320-363-2122	363-2126
Saint Olaf College Libraries 1510 Saint Olaf Ave *Web:* www.stolaf.edu/library	Northfield	MN	55057	507-646-3224	646-3734
University of Minnesota Crookston UMC Library 2900 University Ave *Web:* library.umcrookston.edu	Crookston	MN	56716	218-281-8399	281-8080
University of Minnesota Duluth UMD Library 416 Library Dr *Web:* www.d.umn.edu/lib	Duluth	MN	55812	218-726-8102	726-8019
University of Minnesota Morris Briggs Library 600 E 4th St *Web:* www.morris.umn.edu/library	Morris	MN	56267	320-589-6176	589-6168
University of Minnesota Twin Cities Wilson Library 309 19th Ave S *Web:* wilson.lib.umn.edu	Minneapolis	MN	55455	612-624-0303	626-9353
University of Saint Thomas O'Shaughnessy-Frey Library 2115 Summit Ave MS 5004 *Web:* www.stthomas.edu/libraries	Saint Paul	MN	55105	651-962-5494	962-5406
Winona State University Krueger Library PO Box 5838 *Web:* www.winona.edu/library	Winona	MN	55987	507-457-5140	457-5594
Mississippi State University Library PO Box 5408 *Web:* library.msstate.edu	Mississippi State	MS	39762	662-325-7667	325-3560
University of Mississippi Williams Library *TF:* 800-653-6577 ■ *Web:* www.olemiss.edu/depts/general_library	University	MS	38677	662-915-7091	915-5734
University of Central Missouri Kirkpatrick Library 601 S Missouri *Web:* library.ucmo.edu	Warrensburg	MO	64093	660-543-4565	543-8001
University of Missouri Columbia Ellis Library *Web:* mulibraries.missouri.edu	Columbia	MO	65201	573-882-4701	882-8044
University of Missouri Kansas City Nichols Library 5100 Rockhill Rd *Web:* www.umkc.edu/lib/MNL	Kansas City	MO	64110	816-235-1534	333-5584
University of Missouri Saint Louis Jefferson Library 1 University Blvd *Web:* www.umsl.edu/services/tjl	Saint Louis	MO	63121	314-516-5060	516-5853
Washington University in Saint Louis Olin Library 1 Brookings Dr CB 1061 *Web:* library.wustl.edu	Saint Louis	MO	63130	314-935-5400	935-4045
Montana State University Library Renne Library PO Box 173320 *Web:* www.lib.montana.edu	Bozeman	MT	59717	406-994-3171	994-2851
University of Montana Missoula Mansfield Library 32 Campus Dr *Web:* www.lib.umt.edu	Missoula	MT	59812	406-243-6860	243-4067
University of Montana Western Carson Library 710 S Atlantic St *Web:* www.umwestern.edu/library	Dillon	MT	59725	406-683-7541	683-7493
Peru State College Library 600 Hoyt St *Web:* www.umbc.edu/aok	Peru	NE	68421	402-872-2218	872-2298
University of Nebraska Lincoln Love Memorial Library PO Box 88410 *Web:* iris.unl.edu	Lincoln	NE	68588	402-472-2848	472-5131
University of Nebraska Omaha University Library 6001 Dodge St *Web:* library.unomaha.edu	Omaha	NE	68182	402-554-2640	554-3215
University of Nevada Las Vegas Lied Library 4505 S Maryland Pkwy Box 7001 *Web:* library.nevada.edu	Las Vegas	NV	89154	702-895-2286	895-2287
University of Nevada Reno Getchell Library 1664 N Virginia St MS 322 *Web:* www.library.unr.edu	Reno	NV	89557	775-784-6508	784-4529
Dartmouth College Baker-Berry Library HB 6025 *Web:* library.dartmouth.edu	Hanover	NH	03755	603-646-2236	646-3702
Keene State College Mason Library 229 Main St *Web:* www.keene.edu/library	Keene	NH	03435	603-358-2711	
Plymouth State University Lamson Library Highland Ave *Web:* www.plymouth.edu/library	Plymouth	NH	03264	603-535-2258	535-2445
University of New Hampshire Dimond Library 18 Library Way *Web:* www.library.unh.edu	Durham	NH	03824	603-862-1540	862-0247
Princeton University Library 1 Washington Rd *Web:* library.princeton.edu	Princeton	NJ	08544	609-258-4820	258-4105
Rider University Moore Library 2083 Lawrenceville Rd *Web:* library.rider.edu/moore	Lawrenceville	NJ	08648	609-896-5111	896-8029
Rutgers The State University of New Jersey Libraries 169 College Ave *Web:* www.libraries.rutgers.edu	New Brunswick	NJ	08901	732-932-7505	932-1101
William Paterson University Cheng Library 300 Pompton Rd *Web:* www.wpunj.edu/library	Wayne	NJ	07470	973-720-2541	720-2585
Eastern New Mexico University Golden Library Station 32 *Web:* www.enmu.edu/academics/library	Portales	NM	88130	505-562-2624	562-2647
New Mexico Institute of Mining & Technology Skeen Library 801 Leroy Pl *Web:* www.nmt.edu/about/snaps/tour/gallery/pages/neast/library.htm	Socorro	NM	87801	505-835-5614	835-6666
New Mexico State University Library 2911 McFie Cir Box 30006 Dept 3475 *Web:* lib.nmsu.edu	Las Cruces	NM	88003	505-646-6928	646-7477
University of New Mexico Zimmerman Library 1 University of New Mexico MSC 05 3020 *Web:* elibrary.unm.edu/zimmerman	Albuquerque	NM	87131	505-277-4241	
Bard College Stevenson Library PO Box 5000 *Web:* www.bard.edu/library	Annandale-on-Hudson	NY	12504	845-758-6822	758-5801
Baruch College Newman Library 151 E 25th St *Web:* newman.baruch.cuny.edu	New York	NY	10010	646-312-1600	
Brooklyn College Library 2900 Bedford Ave *Web:* library.brooklyn.cuny.edu	Brooklyn	NY	11210	718-951-5336	951-4540
Buffalo State College EH Butler Library 1300 Elmwood Ave *Web:* www.buffalostate.edu/library	Buffalo	NY	14222	716-878-6314	878-4316
Butler EH Library 1300 Elmwood Ave *Web:* www.buffalostate.edu/library	Buffalo	NY	14222	716-878-6314	878-4316
City College of New York Cohen Library NAC Bldg *Web:* www.ccny.cuny.edu/library	New York	NY	10031	212-650-7155	650-7604
Colgate University Case Library 13 Oak Dr *Web:* www.colgate.edu	Hamilton	NY	13346	315-228-7300	228-7934
Columbia University Butler Library 535 W 114th St *Web:* www.columbia.edu/cu/lweb	New York	NY	10027	212-854-2271	854-9099
Cornell University Olin Library *Web:* www.library.cornell.edu/olinuris	Ithaca	NY	14853	607-255-4144	255-6788
Fordham University Walsh Library 441 E Fordham Rd *Web:* www.library.fordham.edu	Bronx	NY	10458	718-817-3570	817-3582
Hamilton College Burke Library 198 College Hill Rd *Web:* www.hamilton.edu/library	Clinton	NY	13323	315-859-4475	859-4578
Hofstra University Axinn Library 123 Hofstra University *Web:* www.hofstra.edu/libraries	Hempstead	NY	11549	516-463-5940	463-6387
Hunter College Library 695 Park Ave *Web:* library.hunter.cuny.edu	New York	NY	10021	212-772-4179	772-4142
Ithaca College Library 1201 Gannett Ctr *Web:* www.ithaca.edu/library	Ithaca	NY	14850	607-274-3206	274-1539
Jewish Theological Seminary Library 3080 Broadway *Web:* www.jtsa.edu/library	New York	NY	10027	212-678-8075	678-8891
Lehman College Library 250 Bedford Park Blvd W *Web:* www.lehman.edu/provost/library	Bronx	NY	10468	718-960-8577	960-8952
New York University Bobst Library 70 Washington Sq S *Web:* library.nyu.edu	New York	NY	10012	212-998-2500	995-4829
Niagara University Library Lewison Rd *Web:* www.niagara.edu/library	Niagara University	NY	14109	716-286-8020	286-8030
Pace University Birnbaum Library 1 Pace Plaza *Web:* pace.edu/library	New York	NY	10038	212-346-1332	346-1516
Rensselaer Polytechnic Institute Folsom Library 110 8th St *Web:* library.rpi.edu	Troy	NY	12180	518-276-8310	276-8559
Rochester Institute of Technology Wallace Library 90 Lomb Memorial Dr *Web:* wally.rit.edu	Rochester	NY	14623	585-475-2562	475-7007
Rockefeller University Library 1230 York Ave Box 263 *Web:* www.rockefeller.edu/library	New York	NY	10021	212-327-8915	327-7840
State University of New York College at Cortland Memorial Library PO Box 2000 *Web:* library.cortland.edu	Cortland	NY	13045	607-753-2590	753-5669
State University of New York College at Geneseo Milne Library 1 College Cir *Web:* www.geneseo.edu	Geneseo	NY	14454	585-245-5594	245-5769
Syracuse University Bird Library 222 Waverly Ave *Web:* library.syr.edu	Syracuse	NY	13244	315-443-2093	443-9510
University at Albany University Libraries 1400 Washington Ave *Web:* library.albany.edu	Albany	NY	12222	518-442-3568	442-3567
University at Buffalo University Libraries Capen Hall Rm 432 *Web:* ublib.buffalo.edu/libraries	Buffalo	NY	14260	716-645-2965	645-3844
University of Rochester Rhees Library 755 Library Rd RC Box 270055 *Web:* www.lib.rochester.edu	Rochester	NY	14627	585-275-4461	273-5309
Vassar College Library 124 Raymond Ave Box 20 *Web:* library.vassar.edu	Poughkeepsie	NY	12604	845-437-5760	437-5864
Wells College Long Library Main St *Web:* www.wells.edu/LIBRARY/welcome.htm	Aurora	NY	13026	315-364-3351	364-3412
Appalachian State University Belk Library 218 College St PO Box 32026 *Web:* www.library.appstate.edu	Boone	NC	28608	828-262-2300	262-3001
Duke University Perkins Library PO Box 90193 *Web:* library.duke.edu	Durham	NC	27708	919-660-5800	660-5923
East Carolina University Joyner Library E 5th St *Web:* www.ecu.edu/cs-lib	Greenville	NC	27858	252-328-6518	328-4834
North Carolina State University Libraries Campus Box 7111 *Web:* www.lib.ncsu.edu	Raleigh	NC	27695	919-515-2843	515-3628
University of North Carolina Chapel Hill Davis Library CB 3922 *Web:* www.lib.unc.edu	Chapel Hill	NC	27514	919-962-1356	843-8936
University of North Carolina Charlotte Atkins Library 9201 University City Blvd *Web:* www.library.uncc.edu/	Charlotte	NC	28223	704-687-2030	687-3050
University of North Carolina Greensboro Jackson Library PO Box 26170 *Web:* library.uncg.edu	Greensboro	NC	27402	336-334-5880	334-5399
University of North Carolina Wilmington Randall Library 601 S College Rd *Web:* library.uncwil.edu	Wilmington	NC	28403	910-962-3272	962-3078
Wake Forest University Reynolds Library PO Box 7777 *Web:* zsr.wfu.edu	Winston-Salem	NC	27109	336-758-4931	758-5605
Minot State University Olson Library 500 University Ave W *Web:* www.minotstateu.edu/library	Minto	ND	58701	701-858-3200	
North Dakota State University Library Box 5599 *Web:* www.lib.ndsu.nodak.edu	Fargo	ND	58105	701-231-8888	231-7138
University of North Dakota Chester Fritz Library PO Box 9000 *Web:* www.library.und.edu	Grand Forks	ND	58202	701-777-2189	777-3319
Ashland University Library 509 College Ave *Web:* www.ashland.edu/library	Ashland	OH	44805	419-289-5400	289-5422
Bowling Green State University Jerome Library *Web:* www.bgsu.edu/colleges/library	Bowling Green	OH	43403	419-372-2051	372-0475
Case Western Reserve University Smith Library 11055 Euclid Ave *Web:* library.case.edu/ksl	Cleveland	OH	44106	216-368-3506	368-3669
Cedarville University Centennial Library 251 N Main St *TF:* 800-233-2784 ■ *Web:* www.cedarville.edu/academics/library	Cedarville	OH	45314	937-766-7700	766-2337
Cleveland State University University Library 2121 Euclid Ave Rhodes Tower *Web:* www.ulib.csuohio.edu	Cleveland	OH	44115	216-687-5300	687-5098
Denison University Doane Library 400 W Loop PO Box L *Web:* www.denison.edu/library	Granville	OH	43023	740-587-6235	587-6285
Kent State University Libraries PO Box 5190 *Web:* www.library.kent.edu	Kent	OH	44242	330-672-2962	672-4811
Miami University King Library *Web:* www.lib.muohio.edu	Oxford	OH	45056	513-529-2883	529-1719
Oberlin College Library 148 W College St *Web:* www.oberlin.edu/library/	Oberlin	OH	44074	440-775-8285	775-8739

Library	City	State	Zip	Phone	Fax
Ohio Northern University Heterick Memorial Library 525 S Main St	Ada	OH	45810	419-772-2181	772-1927
Web: www.onu.edu/library					
Ohio State University Libraries 1858 Neil Ave Mall	Columbus	OH	43210	614-292-6175	292-7859
Web: library.osu.edu					
Ohio University Alden Library Park Pl	Athens	OH	45701	740-593-2703	593-0138
Web: www.library.ohiou.edu					
Shawnee State University Clark Memorial Library 940 2nd St	Portsmouth	OH	45662	740-351-3267	351-3432
Web: www.shawnee.edu/off/cml					
University of Akron Bierce Library 315 Buchtel Common Rm 161	Akron	OH	44325	330-972-7497	972-5106
Web: www.uakron.edu/libraries					
University of Cincinnati Langsam Library PO Box 210033	Cincinnati	OH	45221	513-556-1515	556-0325
Web: www.libraries.uc.edu					
University of Toledo Carlson Library 2801 W Bancroft St MS 509	Toledo	OH	43606	419-530-2324	530-2726
Web: www.cl.utoledo.edu					
Wittenberg University Thomas Library PO Box 7207	Springfield	OH	45501	937-327-7511	327-6139
Web: www6.wittenberg.edu/lib					
Wright State University Dunbar Library 3640 Colonel Glenn Hwy Rm 126	Dayton	OH	45435	937-775-4125	775-2356
Web: www.libraries.wright.edu					
Xavier University McDonald Memorial Library 3800 Victory Pkwy	Cincinnati	OH	45207	513-745-3884	745-1932
Web: www.xavier.edu/library					
Youngstown State University Maag Library 1 University Plaza	Youngstown	OH	44555	330-941-3675	941-3734
Web: www.maag.ysu.edu					
East Central University Linscheid Library 1100 E 14th St	Ada	OK	74820	580-310-5376	436-3242
Web: www.ecok.edu					
Northeastern State University Vaughan Library 711 N Grand Ave	Tahlequah	OK	74464	918-456-3235	458-2197
Web: library.nsuok.edu/index.html					
Oklahoma State University Low Library	Stillwater	OK	74078	405-744-9729	744-7579
Web: www.library.okstate.edu					
Oral Roberts University Library 7777 S Lewis Ave	Tulsa	OK	74171	918-495-6723	495-6893
Web: www.oru.edu/university/library					
University of Oklahoma Bizzell Memorial Library 401 W Brooks St	Norman	OK	73019	405-325-4142	325-7550
Web: libraries.ou.edu					
University of Tulsa McFarlin Library 2933 E 6th St	Tulsa	OK	74104	918-631-2352	631-3791
Web: www.lib.utulsa.edu					
Eastern Oregon University Pierce Library 1 University Blvd	La Grande	OR	97850	541-962-3864	962-3335
Web: pierce.eou.edu					
Lewis & Clark College Watzek Library 0615 SW Palatine Hill Rd.	Portland	OR	97219	503-768-7270	768-7282
Web: library.lclark.edu					
Oregon State University Valley Library 121 Valley Library	Corvallis	OR	97331	541-737-3411	737-3453
Web: osulibrary.oregonstate.edu					
Pacific University Library 2043 College Way	Forest Grove	OR	97116	503-352-1400	352-1416
Web: www.pacificu.edu/library					
Portland State University Millar Library 1875 SW Park Ave.	Portland	OR	97201	503-725-4424	725-4524
Web: www.pdx.edu/library					
Reed College Library 3203 SE Woodstock Blvd	Portland	OR	97202	503-777-7702	777-7786
Web: library.reed.edu					
Southern Oregon University Hannon Library 1250 Siskiyou Blvd	Ashland	OR	97520	541-552-6441	552-6429
Web: www.sou.edu/library					
University of Oregon Knight Library 1299 University of Oregon	Eugene	OR	97403	541-346-3053	346-3485
Web: libweb.uoregon.edu					
Western Oregon University Hamersly Library 345 N Monmouth Ave	Monmouth	OR	97361	503-838-8418	838-8645
Web: www.wou.edu/provost/library					
Willamette University Hatfield Library 900 State St	Salem	OR	97301	503-370-6312	370-6141
Web: library.willamette.edu					
Bloomsburg University Andruss Library 400 E 2nd St	Bloomsburg	PA	17815	570-389-4205	389-3895
Web: library.bloomu.edu					
Bucknell University Bertrand Library Moore Ave.	Lewisburg	PA	17837	570-577-1882	577-3313
Web: www.bucknell.edu/isr					
California University of Pennsylvania Manderino Library 250 University Ave	California	PA	15419	724-938-4091	938-5901
Web: www.library.cup.edu					
Carnegie Mellon University Libraries 4909 Frew St	Pittsburgh	PA	15213	412-268-2446	268-2793
Web: www.library.cmu.edu					
Dickinson College Waidner-Spahr Library PO Box 1773	Carlisle	PA	17013	717-245-1397	245-1439
Web: lis.dickinson.edu					
Drexel University Hagerty Library 33rd St & Market St	Philadelphia	PA	19104	215-895-2767	895-2070
Web: www.library.drexel.edu					
Duquesne University Gumberg Library 915 Locust St	Pittsburgh	PA	15282	412-396-6130	396-1658
Web: www.library.duq.edu					
East Stroudsburg University Kemp Library 200 Prospect St	East Stroudsburg	PA	18301	570-422-3465	422-3151
Web: www.esu.edu/library					
Edinboro University of Pennsylvania Baron-Forness Library 200 Tartan Rd	Edinboro	PA	16444	814-732-2273	732-2883
Web: www.edinboro.edu/cwis/Library/Menu.html					
Franklin & Marshall College Shadek-Fackenthal Library 450 College Ave	Lancaster	PA	17604	717-291-4184	291-4160
Web: www.library.fandm.edu					
Haverford College Magill Library 370 Lancaster Ave.	Haverford	PA	19041	610-896-1163	896-1102
Web: www.haverford.edu/library					
Indiana University of Pennsylvania Stapleton Library 431 S 11th St.	Indiana	PA	15705	724-357-2330	357-4891
Web: www.lib.iup.edu					
Kutztown University Rohrbach Library 15200 Kutztown Rd Bldg 5	Kutztown	PA	19530	610-683-4480	683-4483
Web: www.kutztown.edu/library					
La Salle University Connelly Library 1900 W Olney Ave	Philadelphia	PA	19141	215-951-1287	951-1595
Web: alpha.lasalle.edu/library					
Lafayette College Skillman Library 710 Sullivan Rd	Easton	PA	18042	610-330-5151	252-0370
Web: www.library.lafayette.edu					
Lehigh University Fairchild-Martindale Library 8A E Packer Ave.	Bethlehem	PA	18015	610-758-3025	758-3004
Web: www.lehigh.edu/library					
Mansfield University North Hall Library	Mansfield	PA	16933	570-662-4670	662-4993
Web: lib.mansfield.edu					
Pennsylvania State University Libraries 510 Paterno Library	University Park	PA	16802	814-865-0401	865-3665
Web: www.libraries.psu.edu					
Swarthmore College McCabe Library 500 College Ave	Swarthmore	PA	19081	610-328-8477	328-7329
Web: www.swarthmore.edu/Library					
Temple University Paley Library 1210 W Berks St MS 017-00	Philadelphia	PA	19122	215-204-8231	204-5201
Web: www.library.temple.edu					
University of Pennsylvania Van Pelt Library 3420 Walnut St	Philadelphia	PA	19104	215-898-7091	898-0559
Web: www.library.upenn.edu/vanpelt					
University of Pittsburgh Hillman Library 3960 Forbes Ave	Pittsburgh	PA	15260	412-648-7710	648-7887
Web: www.library.pitt.edu					
Villanova University Falvey Memorial Library 800 Lancaster Ave	Villanova	PA	19085	610-519-4270	519-5018
Web: library.villanova.edu					
West Chester University Green Library 29 W Rosedale Ave	West Chester	PA	19383	610-436-2747	738-0555
Web: www.wcupa.edu/library.fhg					
Brown University Rockefeller Library 10 Prospect St	Providence	RI	02912	401-863-2162	863-1272
Web: www.brown.edu					
Bryant University Krupp Library 1150 Douglas Pike	Smithfield	RI	02917	401-232-6125	232-6126
Web: www.bryant.edu/bryant/library.jsp					
Salve Regina University McKillop Library 100 Ochre Pt Ave	Newport	RI	02840	401-341-2291	341-2951
Web: library.salve.edu					
University of Rhode Island Libraries 15 Lippitt Rd	Kingston	RI	02881	401-874-2672	874-4608
Web: www.uri.edu/library					
Clemson University Library Box 343001	Clemson	SC	29634	864-656-3026	656-0758
Web: www.lib.clemson.edu					
Francis Marion University Rogers Library PO Box 100547	Florence	SC	29501	843-661-1310	661-1309
Web: www.fmarion.edu/academics/library					
University of South Carolina Cooper Library 1322 Greene St	Columbia	SC	29208	803-777-3142	777-4661
Web: www.sc.edu/library/tcl.html					
Dakota State University Mundt Library 820 N Washington Ave	Madison	SD	57042	605-256-5203	256-5208
Web: www.departments.dsu.edu/library					
South Dakota State University Briggs Library N Campus Dr Box 2115	Brookings	SD	57007	605-688-5106	688-6133
TF: 800-786-2038 ■ *Web:* www3.sdstate.edu/academics/library					
University of South Dakota Weeks Library 414 E Clark St	Vermillion	SD	57069	605-677-5371	677-5488
Web: www.usd.edu/library					
Austin Peay State University Woodward Library PO Box 4595	Clarksville	TN	37044	931-648-7346	221-7296
Web: library.apsu.edu					
Middle Tennessee State University Walker Library PO Box 13	Murfreesboro	TN	37132	615-898-2772	904-8505
Web: www.mtsu.edu/library					
Rhodes College Barret Library 2000 N Pkwy	Memphis	TN	38112	901-843-3900	843-3404
Web: www.rhodes.edu					
University of Memphis McWherter Library 126 Ned R McWherter Library	Memphis	TN	38152	901-678-2201	678-8218
Web: www.lib.memphis.edu					
University of Tennessee Chattanooga Lupton Library 615 McCallie Ave	Chattanooga	TN	37403	423-425-4501	425-4775
Web: www.lib.utc.edu					
University of Tennessee Knoxville Hodges Library 1015 Volunteer Blvd.	Knoxville	TN	37996	865-974-4351	974-0555
Web: www.lib.utk.edu					
University of Tennessee Martin Meek Library	Martin	TN	38238	731-881-7061	881-7074
Web: www.utm.edu/library.php					
Vanderbilt University Heard Library 419 21st Ave S	Nashville	TN	37240	615-322-7100	343-8279
Web: www.library.vanderbilt.edu					
Abilene Christian University Brown Library PO Box ACU29208	Abilene	TX	79699	325-674-2316	674-2202
Web: www.acu.edu/academics/library					
Angelo State University Henderson Library 2025 S Johnson St ASU Stn Box 11013	San Angelo	TX	76909	325-942-2051	942-2198
Web: www.angelo.edu/services/library					
Baylor University Moody Memorial Library & Jones Library PO Box 97148	Waco	TX	76798	254-710-2112	752-5332
Web: www.baylor.edu/lib					
Hardin-Simmons University Richardson Library HSU Box 16195	Abilene	TX	79698	325-670-1236	677-8351
Web: rupert.alc.org/library					
Lamar University Gray Library 211 Redbird Ln	Beaumont	TX	77705	409-880-8118	880-2318
Web: biblos.lamar.edu					
McMurry University Jay-Rollins Library PO Box 218	Abilene	TX	79697	325-793-4692	793-4930
Web: www.mcm.edu/academic/depts/library/libraryhome.htm					
Rice University Fondren Library 6100 Main St MS 44	Houston	TX	77005	713-348-4022	348-5258
Web: www.rice.edu/fondren					
Sam Houston State University Gresham Library 1830 Bobby K Marks Dr	Huntsville	TX	77340	936-294-1614	294-3615
Web: library.shsu.edu					
Sixth Floor Museum 411 Elm St Suite 120 Dealey Plaza	Dallas	TX	75202	214-747-6660	747-6662
TF: 888-485-4854 ■ *Web:* www.jfk.org					
Southern Methodist University Central University Libraries 6414 Hilltop Ln	Dallas	TX	75205	214-768-2401	768-3815
Web: www.smu.edu/libraries/					
Stephen F Austin State University Steen Library 1936 North St PO Box 13055	Nacogdoches	TX	75962	936-468-4101	468-7610
Web: libweb.sfasu.edu					
Texas A & M University					
Evans Library 5000 Tamu	College Station	TX	77843	979-845-8111	845-6238
Web: library.tamu.edu					
Libraries 5000 TAMU	College Station	TX	77843	979-845-8111	845-6238
Web: library.tamu.edu					
Texas Christian University Burnett Library 2913 W Lowden St Box 298400	Fort Worth	TX	76129	817-257-7106	257-7282
Web: libnt4.lib.tcu.edu					
Texas State University San Marcos Alkek Library 601 University Dr	San Marcos	TX	78666	512-245-2133	245-3002
Web: www.library.txstate.edu					
Texas Tech University Libraries 18th & Boston Ave Box 40002	Lubbock	TX	79409	806-742-2261	742-0737
Web: library.ttu.edu/ul					
Texas Woman's University Blagg-Huey Library PO Box 425528	Denton	TX	76204	940-898-2665	898-3764
Web: www.twu.edu/library					
Trinity University Coates Library 1 Trinity Pl.	San Antonio	TX	78212	210-999-8127	999-8021
Web: lib.trinity.edu					
University of Houston Anderson Library 114 University Libraries	Houston	TX	77204	713-743-9800	743-9811
Web: info.lib.uh.edu					
University of North Texas Libraries PO Box 305190	Denton	TX	76203	940-565-2413	369-8760
TF: 877-872-0264 ■ *Web:* www.library.unt.edu					
University of Texas Libraries PO Box P	Austin	TX	78713	512-495-4250	495-4347
Web: www.lib.utexas.edu					
Brigham Young University Lee Library 2060 HBLL	Provo	UT	84602	801-422-2905	422-0466
Web: www.lib.byu.edu					
University of Utah Marriott Library Marriott Library 295 S 1500 East	Salt Lake City	UT	84112	801-581-8558	585-3464
Web: www.lib.utah.edu					
Utah State University Merrill-Cazier Library 3000 Old Main Hill	Logan	UT	84322	435-797-2631	797-2880
Web: library.usu.edu					
Weber State University Stewart Library 2901 University Cir.	Ogden	UT	84408	801-626-6403	626-7045
TF: 877-306-3140 ■ *Web:* library.weber.edu					
Middlebury College Library 110 Storrs Ave	Middlebury	VT	05753	802-443-5494	443-5698
Web: www.middlebury.edu/academics/lis/lib					
University of Vermont Bailey/Howe Library Bailey-Howe Library	Burlington	VT	05405	802-656-2023	656-4038
Web: library.uvm.edu					
Christopher Newport University Smith Library 1 University Pl	Newport News	VA	23606	757-594-7133	594-7776
Web: library.cnu.edu					

University Libraries (Cont'd)

	City	State	Zip	Phone	Fax
College of William & Mary Swem Library PO Box 8794 *Web:* www.swem.wm.edu	Williamsburg	VA	23187	757-221-3067	221-2635
Emory & Henry College Kelly Library 30480 Armbrister Dr PO Box 948 *Web:* www.library.ehc.edu	Emory	VA	24327	276-944-6208	944-4592
George Mason University Fenwick Library 4400 University Dr *Web:* library.gmu.edu	Fairfax	VA	22030	703-993-2240	
James Madison University Carrier Library MSC 1704 *Web:* www.lib.jmu.edu/carrier	Harrisonburg	VA	22807	540-568-6150	568-6339
Radford University McConnell Library PO Box 6881 *Web:* lib.radford.edu	Radford	VA	24142	540-831-5471	831-6138
Regent University Library 1000 Regent University Dr *Web:* www.regent.edu/general/library	Virginia Beach	VA	23464	757-226-4150	226-4167
Sweet Briar College Cochran Library 134 Chapel Rd *Web:* www.cochran.sbc.edu	Sweet Briar	VA	24595	434-381-6138	381-6173
University of Richmond Boatwright Memorial Library 28 Westhampton Way *Web:* library.richmond.edu	Richmond	VA	23173	804-289-8454	287-1840
University of Virginia Clemons Library PO Box 400710 *Web:* www.lib.virginia.edu/clemons	Charlottesville	VA	22904	434-924-3684	924-7468
Virginia Commonwealth University Cabell Library 901 Park Ave Box 842033 *Web:* www.library.vcu.edu/jbc	Richmond	VA	23284	804-828-1105	828-0151
Virginia Polytechnic Institute & State University Libraries PO Box 90001 *Web:* www.lib.vt.edu	Blacksburg	VA	24062	540-231-5593	231-7808
Central Washington University Brooks Library 400 E University Way *Web:* www.lib.cwu.edu	Ellensburg	WA	98926	509-963-3682	963-3684
Evergreen State College Evans Library 2700 Evergreen Pkwy NW *Web:* www.evergreen.edu/library	Olympia	WA	98505	360-867-6250	866-6790
Gonzaga University Foley Library 502 E Boone Ave *TF:* 800-498-5941 ■ *Web:* www.gonzaga.edu/Campus+Resources	Spokane	WA	99258	509-323-5931	323-5904
Pacific Lutheran University Mortvedt Library 12180 Park Ave S *Web:* www.plu.edu/~libr	Tacoma	WA	98447	253-535-7500	535-7315
Seattle University Lemieux Library 900 Broadway *Web:* www.seattleu.edu/lemlib	Seattle	WA	98122	206-296-6233	296-2572
University of Washington Libraries Box 352900 *Web:* www.lib.washington.edu	Seattle	WA	98195	206-543-0242	
Washington State University Holland Library PO Box 645610 *Web:* www.wsulibs.wsu.edu/holland/holhp.htm	Pullman	WA	99164	509-335-9671	335-1889
Marshall University Drinko Library 400 Hal Greer Blvd *Web:* www.marshall.edu/library	Huntington	WV	25755	304-696-2321	696-5858
West Virginia University Libraries PO Box 6069 *Web:* www.libraries.wvu.edu	Morgantown	WV	26506	304-293-2440	293-6638
Lawrence University Mudd Library PO Box 599 *Web:* www.lawrence.edu/library	Appleton	WI	54911	920-832-6750	832-6967
Marquette University Raynor Memorial Library 1355 W Wisconsin Ave *Web:* www.marquette.edu/library	Milwaukee	WI	53233	414-288-7556	288-5324
University of Wisconsin La Crosse Murphy Library 1631 Pine St *Web:* www.uwlax.edu/murphylibrary	La Crosse	WI	54601	608-785-8505	785-8639
University of Wisconsin Eau Claire McIntyre Library 105 Garfield Ave *TF:* 877-267-1384 ■ *Web:* www.uwec.edu/library	Eau Claire	WI	54702	715-836-3715	836-2949
University of Wisconsin Green Bay Cofrin Library 2420 Nicolet Dr *Web:* www.uwgb.edu/library	Green Bay	WI	54311	920-465-2333	465-2388
University of Wisconsin Madison Libraries 728 State St *Web:* www.library.wisc.edu	Madison	WI	53706	608-262-3193	265-2754
University of Wisconsin Milwaukee Golda Meir Library 2311 E Hartford Ave *Web:* www.uwm.edu/Library	Milwaukee	WI	53211	414-229-4785	
University of Wisconsin Oshkosh Polk Library 800 Algoma Blvd *Web:* www.uwosh.edu/library	Oshkosh	WI	54901	920-424-3334	424-7338
University of Wisconsin Parkside Library 900 Wood Rd *Web:* www.uwp.edu/departments/library/	Kenosha	WI	53141	262-595-2360	595-2545
University of Wisconsin River Falls Davee Library 410 S 3rd St *Web:* www.uwrf.edu/library	River Falls	WI	54022	715-425-3321	425-3590
University of Wisconsin Stevens Point University Library 900 Reserve St *Web:* library.uwsp.edu	Stevens Point	WI	54481	715-346-2540	346-2367
University of Wisconsin Stout Library 315 10th Ave E *TF:* 800-787-8688 ■ *Web:* www.uwstout.edu/lib	Menomonie	WI	54751	715-232-1215	232-1783
University of Wisconsin Superior Library PO Box 2000 *TF:* 877-232-1727 ■ *Web:* library.uwsuper.edu	Superior	WI	54880	715-394-8343	394-8462
University of Wisconsin Whitewater Andersen Library 800 W Main St *Web:* library.uww.edu	Whitewater	WI	53190	262-472-5511	472-5727
University of Wyoming Libraries PO Box 3334 *Web:* www-lib.uwyo.edu	Laramie	WY	82071	307-766-3190	766-2510

438 LIBRARY ASSOCIATIONS - STATE & PROVINCE

	City	State	Zip	Phone	Fax
Alabama Library Assn (ALLA) 400 S Union St Suite 395 *TF:* 877-563-5146 ■ *Web:* allanet.org	Montgomery	AL	36104	334-263-1272	265-1281
Alaska Library Assn (AkLA) PO Box 81084 *Web:* www.akla.org	Fairbanks	AK	99708	907-563-2944	
Library Assn of Alberta (LAA) 80 Baker Crescent NW *TF:* 877-522-5550 ■ *Web:* www.laa.ca	Calgary	AB	T2L1R4	403-284-5818	282-6646
Arizona Library Assn (AzLA) 2302 N 3rd St Suite F *Web:* www.azla.org	Phoenix	AZ	85004	602-712-9822	252-5265
Arkansas Library Assn (ArLA) 9 Shackleford Plaza Suite 1 *Web:* www.arlib.org	Little Rock	AR	72211	501-228-0775	228-5535
British Columbia Library Assn (BCLA) 900 Howe St Suite 150 *Web:* www.bcla.bc.ca	Vancouver	BC	V6Z2M4	604-683-5354	609-0707
California Library Assn (CLA) 717 20th St Suite 200 *Web:* www.cla-net.org	Sacramento	CA	95814	916-447-8541	447-8394
Colorado Library Assn (CLA) 4350 Wadsworth Blvd Suite 340 *Web:* www.cla-web.org	Wheat Ridge	CO	80033	303-463-6400	431-9752
Connecticut Library Assn (CLA) PO Box 85 *Web:* cla.uconn.edu	Willimantic	CT	06226	860-465-5006	465-5004
District of Columbia Library Assn PO Box 14177 *Web:* www.dcla.org	Washington	DC	20044	202-872-1112	
Florida Library Assn (FLA) 1133 W Morse Blvd Suite 201 *Web:* www.flalib.org	Winter Park	FL	32789	407-647-8839	629-2502
Georgia Library Assn (GLA) PO Box 793 *Web:* gla.georgialibraries.org	Rex	GA	30273	770-961-3520	961-3712
Illinois Library Assn (ILA) 33 W Grand Ave Suite 301 *Web:* www.ila.org	Chicago	IL	60610	312-644-1896	644-1899
Indiana Library Federation (ILF) 941 E 86th St Suite 260 *Web:* www.ilfonline.org	Indianapolis	IN	46240	317-257-2040	257-1389
Iowa Library Assn (ILA) 3636 Westown Pkwy Suite 202 *TF:* 800-452-5507 ■ *Web:* www.iowalibraryassociation.org	West Des Moines	IA	50266	515-273-5322	273-5323
Kansas Library Assn (KLA) 901 N Main St *Web:* skyways.lib.ks.us/KLA	Hutchinson	KS	67501	620-663-5441	663-9506
Kentucky Library Assn (KLA) 1501 Twilight Trail *Web:* www.kylibasn.org	Frankfort	KY	40601	502-223-5322	223-4937
Louisiana Library Assn (LLA) 421 S 4th St *Web:* www.llaonline.org	Eunice	LA	70535	337-550-7890	550-7846
Maine Library Assn (MLA) 331 State St *Web:* www.mainelibraries.org	Augusta	ME	04330	207-623-8428	626-5947
Manitoba Library Assn (MLA) 606-100 Arthur St *Web:* www.mla.mb.ca	Winnipeg	MB	R3B1H3	204-943-4567	942-1555
Maryland Library Assn (MLA) 1401 Hollins St *Web:* www.mdlib.org	Baltimore	MD	21223	410-947-5090	947-5089
Massachusetts Library Assn (MLA) PO Box 1445 *Web:* www.masslib.org	Marstons Mills	MA	02648	508-428-5865	428-5865
Michigan Library Assn (MLA) 1407 Rensen St Suite 2 *Web:* www.mla.lib.mi.us	Lansing	MI	48910	517-394-2774	394-2675
Minnesota Library Assn (MLA) 1619 Dayton Ave Suite 314 *TF:* 877-867-0982 ■ *Web:* mnlibraryassociation.org	Saint Paul	MN	55104	651-641-0982	649-3169
Mississippi Library Assn (MLA) PO Box 20448 *Web:* www.misslib.org	Jackson	MS	39289	601-352-3917	352-4240
Missouri Library Assn (MLA) 1306 Business Rt 63 S Suite B *Web:* molib.org	Columbia	MO	65201	573-449-4627	449-4655
Nebraska Library Assn (NLA) PO Box 98 *Web:* www.nebraskalibraries.org	Crete	NE	68333	402-826-2636	
New Jersey Library Assn (NJLA) PO Box 1534 *Web:* www.njla.org	Trenton	NJ	08607	609-394-8032	394-8164
New Mexico Library Assn (NMLA) PO Box 26074 *Web:* www.nmla.org	Albuquerque	NM	87125	505-400-7309	899-7600
New York Library Assn (NYLA) 252 Hudson Ave *TF:* 800-252-6952 ■ *Web:* www.nyla.org	Albany	NY	12210	518-432-6952	427-1697
North Carolina Library Assn (NCLA) 1811 Capital Blvd *Web:* www.nclaonline.org	Raleigh	NC	27604	919-839-6252	839-6253
Ohio Library Council (OLC) 2 Easton Oval Suite 525 *TF:* 800-436-5423 ■ *Web:* www.olc.org	Columbus	OH	43215	614-416-2258	416-2270
Oklahoma Library Assn (OLA) 300 Hardy Dr *Web:* www.oklibs.org	Edmond	OK	73013	405-348-0506	348-1629
Ontario Library Assn (OLA) 50 Wellington St *TF:* 866-873-9867 ■ *Web:* www.accessola.org	Toronto	ON	M5E1C8	416-363-3388	941-9581
Oregon Library Assn (OLA) PO Box 2042 *Web:* www.olaweb.org	Salem	OR	97308	503-370-7019	587-8063
Pennsylvania Library Assn (PaLA) 220 Cumberland Pkwy Suite 10 *Web:* www.palibraries.org	Mechanicsburg	PA	17055	717-766-7663	766-5440
Quebec Library Assn (ABQLA) PO Box 1095 *Web:* www.abqla.qc.ca	Pointe-Claire	QC	H9S4H9	514-697-0146	
Saskatchewan Library Assn (SLA) 2010 7th Ave Suite 15 *Web:* www.lib.sk.ca/sla	Regina	SK	S4R1C2	306-780-9413	780-9447
South Carolina Library Assn (SCLA) PO Box 1763 *Web:* www.scla.org	Columbia	SC	29202	803-252-1087	252-0589
South Dakota Library Assn (SDLA) 610 Quincy St *Web:* www.sdlibraryassociation.org	Rapid City	SD	57709	605-394-4171	394-6626
Tennessee Library Assn (TLA) PO Box 241074 *Web:* www.tnla.org	Memphis	TN	38124	901-485-6952	
Texas Library Assn (TLA) 3355 Bee Cave Rd Suite 401 *TF:* 800-580-2852 ■ *Web:* www.txla.org	Austin	TX	78746	512-328-1518	328-8852
Virginia Library Assn (VLA) PO Box 8277 *Web:* www.vla.org	Norfolk	VA	23503	757-583-0041	583-5041
Wisconsin Library Assn (WLA) 5250 E Terrace Dr Suite A-1 *Web:* www.wla.lib.wi.us	Madison	WI	53718	608-245-3640	245-3646

439 LIBRARY SYSTEMS - REGIONAL - CANADIAN

	City	Prov	Postal Code	Phone	Fax
Albert-Westmorland-Kent Regional Library 644 Main St Suite 201	Moncton	NB	E1C1E2	506-869-6032	869-6022
Annapolis Valley Regional Library 26 Bay Rd *Web:* www.valleylibrary.ca	Bridgetown	NS	B0S1C0	902-665-2995	665-4899
Bibliotheque Regionale Du Haut-Saint-Jean 540 Principale St	Saint-Basile	NB	E7C1J5	506-263-3423	263-3425
Cape Breton Regional Library 50 Falmouth St	Sydney	NS	B1P6X9	902-562-3279	564-0765
Cariboo Regional Library District 180-D N 3rd Ave Suite D *Web:* www.cln.bc.ca	Williams Lake	BC	V2G2A4	250-392-3630	392-2812
Centre Regional de Services Aux Bibliotheques Publiques du Bas-Saint-Laurent Inc 465 rue Saint-Pierre	Riviere-du-Loup	QC	G5R4T6	418-867-1682	867-3434
Centre Regional de Services Aux Bibliotheques Publiques du Centre-du-Quebec de Lanaudiere et de la Mauricie Inc 3125 rue Girard	Trois-Rivieres	QC	G8Z2M4	819-375-9623	375-0132
Centre Regional de Services Aux Bibliotheques Publiques de la Cote-Nord Inc 59 rue Napoleon *Web:* www.crsbpcn.qc.ca	Sept-Iles	QC	G4R5C5	418-962-1020	962-5124
Centre Regional de Services Aux Bibliotheques Publiques de L'Abitibi-Temiscamingue Nord du Quebec Inc 20 boul Quebec *Web:* www.crsbpat.qc.ca	Rouyn-Noranda	QC	J9X2E6	819-762-4305	762-5309
Centre Regional de Services Aux Bibliotheques Publiques des Laurentides Inc 29 rue Brissette *Web:* www.crsbpl.qc.ca	Sainte-Agathe-des-Monts	QC	J8C3L1	819-326-6440	326-0885
Centre Regional de Services Aux Bibliotheques Publiques de L'Estrie Inc 4155 rue Brodeur *Web:* www.crsbpe.qc.ca	Sherbrooke	QC	J1L1K4	819-565-9744	565-9157
Centre Regional de Services Aux Bibliotheques Publiques de L'Outaouais Inc 2295 rue Saint-Louis	Gatineau	QC	J8T5L8	819-561-6008	561-6767
Centre Regional de Services Aux Bibliotheques Publiques de la Monteregie Inc 275 rue Conrad-Pelletier *Web:* crsbp.org	La Prairie	QC	J5R4V1	450-444-5433	659-3364
Centre Regional de Services Aux Bibliotheques Publiques Regions de Quebec et Chaudiere-Appalaches Inc 3189 rue Albert-Demers *Web:* www.crsbp-qca.qc.ca	Charny	QC	G6X3A1	418-832-6166	832-6168

Name / Address	City	State	Postal	Phone	Fax
Chaleur Regional Library 113-A Roseberry St	Campbellton	NB	E3N2G7	506-789-6599	789-7318
Chinook Arch Regional Library System 2902 7th Ave N	Lethbridge	AB	T1H5C6	403-380-1500	380-3550
Web: www.chinookarch.ab.ca					
Chinook Regional Library 1240 Chaplin St W	Swift Current	SK	S9H0G8	306-773-3186	773-0434
Web: www.city.swift-current.sk.ca					
Colchester-East Hants Public Library 754 Prince St	Truro	NS	B2N1G9	902-895-4183	895-7149
Web: cehlibrary.ednet.ns.ca					
Cumberland Regional Library 21 Acadia St PO Box 220	Amherst	NS	B4H3Z2	902-667-2549	667-1360
Web: crl.library.ns.ca					
Eastern Counties Regional Library 390 Murray St	Mulgrave	NS	B0E2G0	902-747-2597	747-2500
Web: ecrl.library.ns.ca					
Evergreen Regional Library 65 1st Ave	Gimli	MB	R0C1B0	204-642-7912	642-8319
Fraser Valley Regional Library 34589 Delair Rd	Abbotsford	BC	V2S5Y1	604-859-7141	852-5701
Web: www.fvrl.bc.ca					
Halifax Regional Library 60 Alderney Dr	Dartmouth	NS	B2Y4P8	902-490-5744	490-5762
Web: www.halifaxpubliclibraries.ca					
Lakeland Library Region 1302 100th St	North Battleford	SK	S9A0V8	306-445-6108	445-5717
Web: www.lakeland.lib.sk.ca					
Lakeland Regional Library 318 Williams Ave	Killarney	MB	R0K1G0	204-523-4949	523-7460
Marigold Library System 710 2nd St	Strathmore	AB	T1P1K4	403-934-5334	934-5331
Web: www.marigold.ab.ca					
Northern Lights Library System PO Bag 8	Elk Point	AB	T0A1A0	780-724-2596	724-2597
Web: www.nlls.ab.ca					
NWT Library Services 75 Woodland Dr	Hay River	NT	X0E1G1	867-874-6531	874-3321
Web: www.nwtpls.gov.nt.ca					
Okanagan Regional Library 1430 KLO Rd	Kelowna	BC	V1W3P6	250-860-4033	861-8696
Web: www.orl.bc.ca					
Ontario Library Service North - Sudbury 334 Regent St	Sudbury	ON	P3C4E2	705-675-6467	675-2285
Palliser Regional Library 366 Coteau St W	Moose Jaw	SK	S6H5C9	306-693-3669	692-5657
Web: www.palliser.lib.sk.ca					
Parkland Regional Library 5404 56th Ave	Lacombe	AB	T4L1G1	403-782-3850	782-4650
TF: 800-567-9024 ■ *Web:* www.prl.ab.ca					
Parkland Regional Library 504 Main St N	Dauphin	MB	R7N1C9	204-638-6410	638-9483
Web: www.parklandlib.mb.ca					
Parkland Regional Library PO Box 5049	Yorkton	SK	S3N3Z4	306-783-7022	782-2844
Web: www.parkland.lib.sk.ca					
Peace Library System 8301 110th St	Grande Prairie	AB	T8W6T2	780-538-4656	539-5285
Web: www.peacelibrarysystem.ab.ca					
Pictou-Antigonish Regional Library 182 Dalhousie St	New Glasgow	NS	B2H5E3	902-755-6031	755-6775
Web: www.parl.ns.ca					
Prince Edward Island Provincial Library Service					
89 Red Head Rd	Morell	PE	C0A1S0	902-961-7320	961-7322
Web: www.library.pe.ca					
Provincial Information & Library Resources Board					
Central Div 6 Bell Pl	Gander	NL	A1V1X2	709-651-5354	256-2194
Eastern Div Arts & Culture Ctr	Saint John's	NL	A1B3A3	709-737-3508	737-3571
Web: www.nlpubliclibraries.ca					
West Newfoundland-Labrador Div 5 Union St	Corner Brook	NL	A2H5M7	709-634-7333	634-7313
Web: www.nlpubliclibraries.ca					
Public Library InterLINK 7252 Kings Way	Burnaby	BC	V5E1G3	604-517-8441	517-8410
Saint John Regional Library 1 Market Sq	Saint John	NB	E2L4Z6	506-643-7220	643-7225
Shortgrass Library System 2375 10th Ave SW	Medicine Hat	AB	T1A8G2	403-529-0550	528-2473
Web: www.shortgrass-lib.ab.ca					
South Central Regional Library 160 Main St	Winkler	MB	R6W1B4	204-325-7174	325-5915
Web: www.scrlibrary.mb.ca					
South Shore Regional Library PO Box 34	Bridgewater	NS	B4V2W6	902-543-2548	543-8191
Web: ssrl.library.ns.ca					
Southeast Regional Library 49 Bison Ave	Weyburn	SK	S4H0H9	306-848-3100	842-2665
Web: www.southeast.lib.sk.ca					
Southern Ontario Library Service 111 Peter St Suite 902	Toronto	ON	M5V2H1	416-961-1669	961-5122
TF: 800-387-5765 ■ *Web:* www.library.on.ca/solsindex.html					
Southwestern Manitoba Regional Library PO Box 670	Melita	MB	R0M1L0	204-522-3923	522-3421
Web: www.mts.net/swmblib					
Thompson-Nicola Regional District Library System					
465 Victoria St Suite 100	Kamloops	BC	V2C2A9	250-372-5145	374-8355
Web: www.tnrdlib.bc.ca					
Vancouver Island Regional Library 6250 Hammond Bay Rd	Nanaimo	BC	V9R5N3	250-758-4697	758-2482
Web: www.virl.bc.ca					
Wapiti Regional Library 145 12th St E	Prince Albert	SK	S6V1B7	306-764-0712	922-1516
Web: www.panet.pa.sk.ca					
Western Counties Regional Library 405 Main St	Yarmouth	NS	B5A1G3	902-742-2486	742-6920
Web: www.westerncounties.ca					
Western Manitoba Regional Library 710 Rosser Ave Unit 1	Brandon	MB	R7A0K9	204-727-6648	727-4447
Web: www.wmrlibrary.mb.ca					
Wheatland Regional Library 806 Duchess St	Saskatoon	SK	S7K0R3	306-652-5077	931-7611
Web: www.wheatland.sk.ca					
Yellowhead Regional Library 433 King St	Spruce Grove	AB	T7X2Y1	780-962-2003	962-2770
Web: www.yrl.ab.ca					
York Regional Library 4 Carleton St	Fredericton	NB	E3B5P4	506-453-5380	457-4878

440 LIGHT BULBS & TUBES

Name / Address	City	State	Zip	Phone	Fax
Advanced Lighting Technologies Inc 32000 Aurora Rd	Solon	OH	44139	440-248-3510	836-7030
TF: 800-338-6161 ■ *Web:* www.adlt.com					
AETEK UV Systems 1200 Windham Pkwy	Romeoville	IL	60446	630-226-4200	226-4215
TF Sales: 800-333-2304 ■ *Web:* www.fusionuv.com					
American Power Products Inc 1169 Sherborn Rd	Corona	CA	92879	951-284-7400	284-7410
TF: 800-533-2929 ■ *Web:* www.applighting.com					
Amglo Kemlight Laboratories Inc 215 Gateway Rd	Bensenville	IL	60106	630-350-9470	350-9474
Web: www.amglo.com					
Carley Lamps Inc 1502 W 228th St	Torrance	CA	90501	310-325-8474	534-2912
Web: www.carleylamps.com					
EGL Co Inc 100 Industrial Rd	Berkeley Heights	NJ	07922	908-508-1111	508-1122
Web: www.egl-neon.com					
Emess Design Group LLC 1 Early St	Ellwood City	PA	16117	724-758-0707	758-7530
TF: 800-688-2579 ■ *Web:* www.emessdesign.com					
Eye Lighting International NA 9150 Hendricks Rd	Mentor	OH	44060	440-350-7000	350-7001
TF: 888-665-2677 ■ *Web:* www.eyelighting.com					
Frameworks Inc 1 High St	Antrim	NH	03440	603-464-5190	464-7373
GE Consumer Products Appliance Park Rm 129	Louisville	KY	40225	502-452-4311	452-0054*
**Fax:* Cust Svc ■ *TF:* 800-626-2000 ■ *Web:* www.geconsumerproducts.com					
GE Lighting 1975 Noble Rd	East Cleveland	OH	44112	216-266-2121	
Web: www.gelighting.com					
General Electric Canada Inc 2300 Meadowvale Blvd	Mississauga	ON	L5N5P9	905-858-5100	
Web: www.ge.com/canada					
Hanovia Corp 825 Lehigh Ave	Union	NJ	07083	908-688-0050	686-8404
TF: 800-229-3666 ■ *Web:* hanovia-uv.com					
HH Fluorescent Parts Inc 104 Beecher Ave	Cheltenham	PA	19012	215-379-2750	379-2756
Interlectric Corp 1401 Lexington Ave	Warren	PA	16365	814-723-6061	723-1074
TF: 800-722-2184 ■ *Web:* www.interlectric.com					
LCD Lighting Inc 37 Robinson Blvd	Orange	CT	06477	203-795-1520	795-2874
TF: 800-245-4458 ■ *Web:* www.lcdl.com					
Ledtronics Inc 23105 Kashiwa Ct	Torrance	CA	90505	310-534-1505	534-1424
TF: 800-579-4875 ■ *Web:* www.led.net					
Light Sources Inc 37 Robinson Blvd	Orange	CT	06477	203-799-7877	795-5267
TF: 800-245-4458 ■ *Web:* www.light-sources.com					
Litetronics International Inc 4101 W 123rd St	Alsip	IL	60803	708-389-8000	371-0627
TF: 800-860-3392 ■ *Web:* www.litetronics.com					
OSRAM Sylvania Glass Technologies 131 Portsmouth Ave	Exeter	NH	03833	603-772-4331	778-0674
TF: 800-258-8290 ■ *Web:* www.sylvania.com/pmc/glass					
OSRAM Sylvania Inc 100 Endicott St	Danvers	MA	01923	978-777-1900	750-2152
Web: www.sylvania.com					
PerkinElmer Inc 45 William St	Wellesley	MA	02481	781-237-5100	237-9386
NYSE: PKI ■ *Web:* www.perkinelmer.com					
Philips Lighting Co 200 Franklin Sq Dr	Somerset	NJ	08875	732-563-3000	563-3200
TF: 800-555-0050 ■ *Web:* www.nam.lighting.philips.com/us					
Rogers Corp Durel Div 2225 W Chandler Blvd	Chandler	AZ	85224	480-917-6000	917-6049
Web: www.rogerscorporation.com/durel					
Ross Lighting Corp 395 Project St	Jesup	GA	31598	912-530-8200	530-9366
TF: 800-737-4334					
Sun Ergoline Inc 1 Walter Kratz Dr	Jonesboro	AR	72401	870-935-1130	935-3618
TF: 800-643-0086 ■ *Web:* www.sundash.com					
Technical Consumer Products Inc 300 Lena Dr	Aurora	OH	44202	330-995-6111	995-6188
TF: 800-324-1496 ■ *Web:* www.tcpi.com					
Trojan Inc 198 Trojan St PO Box 850	Mount Sterling	KY	40353	859-498-0526	498-0528
TF: 800-264-0526 ■ *Web:* www.trojaninc.com					
Ushio America Inc 5440 Cerritos Ave	Cypress	CA	90630	714-236-8600	776-3641*
**Fax Area Code:* 800 ■ **Fax:* Mktg ■ *TF:* 800-326-1960 ■ *Web:* www.ushio.com					
UVP Inc 2066 W 11th St	Upland	CA	91786	909-946-3197	946-3597
TF: 800-452-6788 ■ *Web:* www.uvp.com					
Venture Lighting International Inc 32000 Aurora Rd	Solon	OH	44139	440-248-3510	836-7030
TF: 800-338-6161 ■ *Web:* www.venturelighting.com					
Welch Allyn Inc Lighting Products Div					
4619 Jordan Rd	Skaneateles Falls	NY	13153	315-685-4347	685-2854
Westinghouse Lighting Corp 12401 McNulty Rd	Philadelphia	PA	19154	215-671-2000	464-4115
TF Orders: 800-999-2226 ■ *Web:* www.westinghouselighting.com					

441 LIGHTING EQUIPMENT - VEHICULAR

Name / Address	City	State	Zip	Phone	Fax
Astronics Corp 130 Commerce Way	East Aurora	NY	14052	716-805-1599	655-0309
NASDAQ: ATRO ■ *Web:* www.astronics.com					
ATC Lighting & Plastics Inc 107 N Eagle St	Geneva	OH	44041	440-466-7670	466-0186
TF: 800-543-1943 ■ *Web:* www.atc-lighting-plastics.com					
Aurora Cord & Cable Co 325 S Union St	Aurora	IL	60505	630-851-1616	851-1626
Web: www.auroracord.com					
Avtec Inc 6 Industrial Park	Cahokia	IL	62206	618-337-7800	337-7976
TF: 800-552-8832 ■ *Web:* www.avtec-inc.com					
Bruce Industries Inc 101 Evans Ave	Dayton	NV	89403	775-246-0101	246-0451
Web: www.bruceind.com					
CML Innovative Technologies 147 Central Ave	Hackensack	NJ	07601	800-575-1030	575-1040*
**Fax Area Code:* 877 ■ *Web:* www.cml-it.com					
Delphi Safety & Interior Systems 1401 Crooks Rd	Troy	MI	48084	248-813-2000	813-2108
Federal Signal Corp Emergency Products Div					
2645 Federal Signal Dr	University Park	IL	60466	708-534-3400	534-9050
Web: www.fedsig.com					
Guide Corp 600 Corporation Dr	Pendleton	IN	46064	765-221-7000	221-6776
Web: www.guidecorp.com					
JW Speaker Corp					
W 185 N 11315 Whitney Dr PO Box 1011	Germantown	WI	53022	262-251-6660	251-2918
TF: 800-558-7288 ■ *Web:* www.jwspeaker.com					
Luminator 1200 E Plano Pkwy	Plano	TX	75074	972-881-5483	881-8900
TF: 800-388-8205 ■ *Web:* www.luminatorusa.com					
North American Lighting Inc 20 Industrial Pk	Flora	IL	62839	618-662-4483	662-8143
Web: www.nal.com					
Nova Electronics Inc 36 Doctor Foote Rd	Colchester	CT	06415	860-537-3471	537-0656
Web: www.strobe.com					
OSRAM Sylvania Automotive Lighting Div 275 W Main St	Hillsboro	NH	03244	603-464-5533	464-0259
TF: 800-729-3777 ■ *Web:* www.sylvania.com/auto					
Peterson Mfg Co 4200 E 135th St	Grandview	MO	64030	816-765-2000	761-6693
TF: 800-821-3490 ■ *Web:* www.pmlights.com					
Pyramid Technologies Inc 48 Elm St	Meriden	CT	06450	203-238-0550	634-1696
TF: 888-479-7264 ■ *Web:* www.pyramid-technologies.com					
Sate-Lite Mfg Co 6230 Gross Point Rd	Niles	IL	60714	847-647-1515	647-6719
Web: www.sate-lite.com					
Sidler Inc 1155 E Whitcomb Ave	Madison Heights	MI	48071	248-583-2710	583-2723
Web: www.sidler.com					
Soderberg Mfg Co Inc 20821 Currier Rd	Walnut	CA	91789	909-595-1291	
Web: www.soderberg-mfg.com					
Speaker JW Corp					
W 185 N 11315 Whitney Dr PO Box 1011	Germantown	WI	53022	262-251-6660	251-2918
TF: 800-558-7288 ■ *Web:* www.jwspeaker.com					
Teledyne Lighting & Display Products 12964 Panama St	Los Angeles	CA	90066	310-574-2001	574-2070
Web: www.teledynelighting.com					
Trans-Lite Inc 120 Wampus Ln	Milford	CT	06460	203-878-8567	877-2630
Web: www.trans-liteinc.com					
Truck-Lite Co Inc 310 E Elmwood Ave	Falconer	NY	14733	716-665-6214	665-6403
TF Cust Svc: 800-562-5012 ■ *Web:* www.truck-lite.com					
Unity Mfg Co 1260 N Clybourn Ave	Chicago	IL	60610	312-943-5200	943-5681
Web: www.unityusa.com					
Valeo Sylvania 1231 A Ave	North Seymour	IN	47274	812-523-5200	524-5316
Web: www.valeosylvania.com					
Vehicle Safety Mfg LLC 408 Central Ave	Newark	NJ	07107	973-643-3000	643-2167
TF: 800-832-7233 ■ *Web:* www.vehiclesafetymfg.com					
Whelen Engineering Co Inc Winthrop Rd & Rt 145	Chester	CT	06412	860-526-9504	526-4078
Web: www.whelen.com					

442 LIGHTING FIXTURES & EQUIPMENT

Name / Address	City	State	Zip	Phone	Fax
Acuity Brands Lighting 1170 Peachtree St NE	Atlanta	GA	30309	404-853-1400	
Web: www.acuitybrandslighting.com					
Adjusta-Post Lighting Co 3960 Summit Rd	Norton	OH	44203	330-745-1692	745-9746
TF: 800-321-2132 ■ *Web:* www.aplighting.com					
ALP Lighting Components Inc 6333 Gross Point Rd	Niles	IL	60714	773-774-9550	594-3874
TF: 877-257-5841 ■ *Web:* www.alp-ltg.com					
Altman Lighting Inc 57 Alexander St	Yonkers	NY	10701	914-476-7987	966-1980
TF: 800-367-2586 ■ *Web:* www.altmanltg.com					
American Fluorescent Corp 2345 N Ernie Krueger Cir	Waukegan	IL	60087	847-249-5970	249-2618
TF: 800-873-2326 ■ *Web:* www.americanfluorescent.com					
American Louver Co 7700 Austin Ave	Skokie	IL	60077	847-470-3300	470-0420
TF: 800-323-4250 ■ *Web:* www.americanlouver.com					

Company / Address	City	State	Zip	Phone	Fax
Amerillum Corp 2835 La Mirada Dr *Web:* www.amerillum.com	Vista	CA	92083	760-727-7675	727-7695
Antique Street Lamps Inc 2011-B W Rundberg Ln *Web:* www.antiquestreetlamps.com	Austin	TX	78758	512-977-8444	832-1869
Ashley Lighting Inc 405 Industrial Dr *TF:* 800-343-5267 ■ *Web:* www.ashley-lighting.com	Trumann	AR	72472	870-483-6181	483-7140
Automatic Power Inc 213 Hutchinson St *Web:* www.automaticpower.com	Houston	TX	77003	713-228-5208	228-3717
Baldinger Louis & Sons Inc 19-02 Steinway St *Web:* www.baldinger.com	Astoria	NY	11105	718-204-5700	721-4986
Ballantyne of Omaha Inc 4350 McKinley St *AMEX: BTN* ■ *TF:* 800-262-5016 ■ *Web:* www.ballantyne-omaha.com	Omaha	NE	68112	402-453-4444	453-7238
Bieber Lighting Corp 626 S Isis Ave *TF:* 800-243-2375 ■ *Web:* www.bieberlighting.com	Inglewood	CA	90301	310-645-6789	216-0333
Big Beam Emergency Systems Inc 290 E Prairie St PO Box 518 *Web:* www.bigbeam.com	Crystal Lake	IL	60039	815-459-6100	459-6126
Boyd Lighting Co 944 Folsom St *Web:* www.boydlighting.com	San Francisco	CA	94107	415-778-4300	778-4319
Brinkmann Corp 4215 McEwen Rd *TF:* 800-527-0717 ■ *Web:* www.brinkmann.net	Dallas	TX	75244	972-387-4939	770-8515
Bronzelite Commercial Landscape Lighting 100 Craftway *TF:* 800-273-1569 ■ *Web:* www.bronzelite.com	Littlestown	PA	17340	717-359-7131	359-9289
Burton Medical Products Inc 21100 Lassen St *TF Cust Svc:* 800-444-9909 ■ *Web:* www.burtonmedical.com	Chatsworth	CA	91311	818-701-8700	701-8725
Canlyte Inc 3015 Louis Amos *TF:* 800-565-5486 ■ *Web:* www.canlyte.com	Lachine	QC	H8T1C4	514-636-0670	636-8498
Carlisle & Finch Co 4562 W Mitchell Ave *Web:* www.carlislefinch.com	Cincinnati	OH	45232	513-681-6080	681-6226
Catalina & Tensor Lighting 18191 NW 68th Ave *TF:* 800-872-5267 ■ *Web:* www.catalinaltg.com	Miami	FL	33015	305-558-4777	558-3024
Chapman Mfg Co Inc PO Box 359 *Web:* www.chapmanco.com	Avon	MA	02322	508-588-3200	587-7592
Chloride Systems 272 W Stag Park Service Rd **Fax Area Code:* 800 ■ *Web:* www.chloridesys.com	Burgaw	NC	28425	910-259-1000	258-8803*
Color Kinetics Inc 10 Milk St Suite 1100 *NASDAQ: CLRK* ■ *TF:* 888-385-5742 ■ *Web:* www.colorkinetics.com	Boston	MA	02108	617-423-9999	423-9998
Columbia Lighting Inc 3808 N Sullivan Rd Bldg 29 *Web:* www.columbia-ltg.com	Spokane	WA	99216	509-924-7000	921-7566
Commercial Lighting Industries 30643 Front St *TF:* 800-755-0155 ■ *Web:* www.commercial-lighting.net	Thousand Palms	CA	92276	760-343-2704	262-3041
Con-Tech Lighting 2783 Shermer Rd *TF:* 800-728-0312 ■ *Web:* www.con-techlighting.com	Northbrook	IL	60062	847-559-5500	559-5505
Cooper Frederick Lamp LLC 5750 W Bloomingdale Ave *Web:* www.frederickcooper.com	Chicago	IL	60639	773-384-0800	384-7526
Cooper Industries 600 Travis St Suite 5800 *NYSE: CBE* ■ *Web:* www.cooperindustries.com	Houston	TX	77002	713-209-8400	209-8995
Cooper Lighting Inc 1121 Hwy 74 S **Fax:* Mktg ■ *Web:* www.cooperlighting.com	Peachtree City	GA	30269	770-486-4800	486-4801*
Corbett Lighting Inc 14625 E Clark Ave **Fax Area Code:* 800 ■ *TF:* 800-533-8769 ■ *Web:* www.corbettlighting.com	City of Industry	CA	91745	626-336-4511	544-8769*
Coronet Lighting 16210 S Avalon Blvd *TF:* 800-421-2748 ■ *Web:* www.coronetlighting.com	Gardena	CA	90248	310-327-6700	532-8092
Crouse-Hinds Airport Lighting Products 1200 Kennedy Rd *Web:* www.chalp.com	Windsor	CT	06095	860-683-4300	683-4354
Crownlite Mfg Corp 1546 Ocean Ave	Bohemia	NY	11716	631-589-9100	589-4584
CW Cole & Co Inc 2560 N Rosemead Blvd *Web:* www.colelighting.com	South El Monte	CA	91733	626-443-2473	443-9253
Day-Brite/Capri/Omega 776 S Green St **Fax:* Hum Res ■ *TF:* 800-955-5352 ■ *Web:* www.dcolighting.com	Tupelo	MS	38804	662-842-7212	841-5509*
Dazor Mfg Corp 11721 Dunlap Industrial Dr *TF:* 800-345-9103 ■ *Web:* www.dazor.com	Maryland Heights	MO	63043	314-652-2400	652-2069
Dinico Products Inc 3960 Summit Rd *TF:* 800-321-2132 ■ *Web:* www.dinico.com	Norton	OH	44203	330-745-1692	745-9746
Doane LC Co 110 Pond Meadow Rd PO Box 700 *TF:* 800-447-5006 ■ *Web:* www.lcdoane.com	Ivoryton	CT	06442	860-767-8295	767-1397
Dual-Lite Inc 101 Corporate Dr **Fax:* Cust Svc ■ *Web:* www.dual-lite.com	Spartanburg	SC	29303	864-599-6000	699-1428*
Duray Fluorescent Mfg Co 2050 W Balmoral Ave *Web:* www.durayinc.com	Chicago	IL	60625	773-271-2800	271-4410
Edison Price Lighting Inc 41-50 22nd St *TF:* 800-275-8548 ■ *Web:* www.epl.com	Long Island City	NY	11101	718-685-0700	786-8530
El Products 55 2nd St *Web:* www.limelite.com	Maxwell	TX	78656	512-357-2776	357-2786
Electrix Inc 45 Spring St *Web:* www.electrix.com	New Haven	CT	06519	203-776-5577	624-7545
Energy Focus Inc 32000 Aurora Rd *NASDAQ: EFOI* ■ *TF:* 800-327-7877 ■ *Web:* www.energyfocusinc.com	Solon	OH	44139	440-715-1300	715-1314
Entourage LA 100 Wilshire Blvd Suite 800 *Web:* www.entouragela.com	Santa Monica	CA	90401	310-656-0499	656-0269
ExceLine 2345 Vauxhall Rd *TF:* 800-334-2212 ■ *Web:* www.exceline.com	Union	NJ	07083	908-964-7000	964-0968
Forecast 1600 Fleetwood Dr *TF:* 800-234-0416 ■ *Web:* www.forecastltg.com	Elgin	IL	60123	847-622-0416	622-2542
Frederick Cooper Lamp LLC 5750 W Bloomingdale Ave *Web:* www.frederickcooper.com	Chicago	IL	60639	773-384-0800	384-7526
Fulton Industries Inc 135 E Linfoot St PO Box 377 *TF:* 800-537-5012 ■ *Web:* www.fultonindoh.com	Wauseon	OH	43567	419-335-3015	335-3215
Gardco Lighting 1611 Clovis Barker Rd *TF:* 800-227-0758 ■ *Web:* www.gardcolighting.com	San Marcos	TX	78666	512-753-1000	753-7851
Garrity Industries Inc 14 New Rd *TF:* 800-872-5483 ■ *Web:* www.garritylites.com	Madison	CT	06443	203-245-8383	245-4734
GE Lighting 1975 Noble Rd *Web:* www.gelighting.com	East Cleveland	OH	44112	216-266-2121	
GE Lighting Systems Inc 3010 Spartanburg Hwy *TF:* 877-798-6702 ■ *Web:* www.ge-lightingsystems.com	East Flat Rock	NC	28726	828-693-2000	693-2103
Genlyte Group Inc 10350 Ormsby Park Pl Suite 601 *NASDAQ: GLYT* ■ **Fax:* Sales ■ *TF:* 800-365-4448 ■ *Web:* www.genlyte.com	Louisville	KY	40223	502-420-9500	420-9540*
Guth Lighting 1324 Washington Ave Suite 200 PO Box 7079 *Web:* www.guth.com	Saint Louis	MO	63177	314-533-3200	533-9127
Hadco Lighting 100 Craftway *TF:* 800-331-4185 ■ *Web:* www.hadcolighting.com	Littlestown	PA	17340	717-359-7131	359-9289
Hanover Lantern Inc 350 Kindig Ln *TF:* 800-233-7196 ■ *Web:* www.hanoverlantern.com	Hanover	PA	17331	717-632-6464	632-5039
HE Williams Inc 831 W Fairview Ave *TF:* 800-358-4064 ■ *Web:* www.hew.com	Carthage	MO	64836	417-358-4065	358-6015
High End Systems Inc 2105 Gracy Farms Ln *TF:* 800-890-8989 ■ *Web:* www.highend.com	Austin	TX	78758	512-836-2242	837-5290
High Q Lighting Inc 11439 E Lakewood Blvd *Web:* www.hql.net	Holland	MI	49424	616-396-3591	396-8863
Hinkley Lighting 12600 Berea Rd *TF:* 800-446-5539 ■ *Web:* www.hinkleylighting.com	Cleveland	OH	44111	216-671-3300	671-4537
Holophane 214 Oakwood Ave PO Box 3004 *TF:* 866-465-6742 ■ *Web:* www.holophane.com	Newark	OH	43058	740-345-9631	349-4426
Honeywell Airport Systems 2121 Union Pl *TF:* 800-581-5591 ■ *Web:* www.airportsystems.honeywell.com	Simi Valley	CA	93065	805-581-5591	522-1624
Hubbell Lighting Inc 701 Millennium Blvd *TF:* 800-328-7480 ■ *Web:* www.hubbelllighting.com	Greenville	SC	29607	864-678-1000	678-1065
Hunter Lighting Group 11660 Central Pkwy *Web:* www.hunterltg.com	Jacksonville	FL	32224	904-642-4340	642-4150
Hydrel 12881 Bradley Ave *TF:* 800-750-9773 ■ *Web:* www.hydrel.com	Sylmar	CA	91342	818-362-9465	362-6548
Indy Lighting Inc 12001 Exit 5 Pkwy *TF:* 800-428-5212 ■ *Web:* www.indylighting.com	Fishers	IN	46037	317-849-1233	576-8006
International Lighting 1825 N 19th St *TF:* 800-325-7050 ■ *Web:* www.inlite.com	Saint Louis	MO	63106	314-621-0600	621-6944
Jimco Lamp & Mfg Co 11759 Hwy 63 N PO Box 490 *TF:* 800-643-0092 ■ *Web:* www.jimcolamp.com	Bono	AR	72416	870-935-6820	935-6822
JJI Lighting Group 11500 Melrose Ave *Web:* www.jjilightinggroup.com	Franklin Park	IL	60131	847-451-0700	455-0954
Juno Lighting Group 1300 S Wolf Rd *TF:* 800-323-5068 ■ *Web:* www.junolighting.com	Des Plaines	IL	60017	847-827-9880	827-2925
Justice Design Group Inc 261 S Figueroa St Suite 450 **Fax Area Code:* 800 ■ *TF Cust Svc:* 800-533-4799 ■ *Web:* www.jdg.com	Los Angeles	CA	90012	213-437-0102	533-2911*
Kenall Mfg 1020 Lakeside Dr *TF:* 800-453-6255 ■ *Web:* www.kenall.com	Gurnee	IL	60031	847-360-8200	360-1781
Kichler Lighting 7711 E Pleasant Valley Rd PO Box 318010 **Fax Area Code:* 888 ■ **Fax:* Cust Svc ■ *TF:* 888-659-8809 ■ *Web:* www.kichler.com	Cleveland	OH	44131	216-573-1000	659-8808*
Kim Lighting Inc 16555 E Gale Ave *Web:* www.kimlighting.com	City of Industry	CA	91745	626-968-5666	330-3861
Kirlin Co 3401 E Jefferson Ave *Web:* www.kirlinlighting.com	Detroit	MI	48207	313-259-6400	259-3121
Koehler-Bright Star Inc 380 Stewart Rd *TF Cust Svc:* 800-631-3814 ■ *Web:* www.flashlight.com	Hanover Township	PA	18706	570-825-1900	825-1984
Kurt Versen Co 10 Charles St *Web:* www.kurtversen.com	Westwood	NJ	07675	201-664-8200	664-4801
Kurtzon Lighting Inc 1420 S Talman Ave *TF:* 800-837-8937 ■ *Web:* www.kurtzon.com	Chicago	IL	60608	773-277-2121	277-9164
Lamplight Farms Inc 4900 N Lilly Rd *TF:* 800-645-5267 ■ *Web:* www.lamplightfarms.com	Menomonee Falls	WI	53051	262-781-9590	781-6774
LC Doane Co 110 Pond Meadow Rd PO Box 700 *TF:* 800-447-5006 ■ *Web:* www.lcdoane.com	Ivoryton	CT	06442	860-767-8295	767-1397
Ledalite Architectural Products 19750-92A Ave *Web:* www.ledalite.com	Langley	BC	V1M3B2	604-888-6811	888-2003
Legion Lighting Co Inc 221 Glenmore Ave *TF:* 800-453-4466 ■ *Web:* www.legionlighting.com	Brooklyn	NY	11207	718-498-1770	498-0128
Lightguard 272 W Stag Park Service Rd **Fax Area Code:* 800 ■ *Web:* www.lightguard.com	Burgaw	NC	28425	910-259-1000	258-8803*
Lightolier 631 Airport Rd *TF:* 800-215-1068 ■ *Web:* www.lightolier.com	Fall River	MA	02720	508-679-8131	674-4710
Lights of America 611 Reyes Dr *TF Cust Svc:* 800-321-8100 ■ *Web:* www.lightsofamerica.com	Walnut	CA	91789	909-594-7883	594-6758
Lite Energy 189 Bullock Dr *TF:* 800-463-5456 ■ *Web:* www.liteenergy.com	Markham	ON	L3P1W4	905-294-9570	294-6644
Litecontrol 100 Hawks Ave *Web:* www.litecontrol.com	Hanson	MA	02341	781-294-0100	293-2849
Lithonia Lighting 1400 Lester Rd *TF Cust Svc:* 800-858-7763 ■ *Web:* www.lithonia.com	Conyers	GA	30012	770-922-9000	483-2635
Louis Baldinger & Sons Inc 19-02 Steinway St *Web:* www.baldinger.com	Astoria	NY	11105	718-204-5700	721-4986
LSI Industries Inc 10000 Alliance Rd *NASDAQ: LYTS* ■ *TF:* 800-765-3454 ■ *Web:* www.lsi-industries.com	Cincinnati	OH	45242	513-793-3200	984-1335
LSI Lighting Solutions 500 Hudson Valley Ave *Web:* www.lsi-industries.com	New Windsor	NY	12553	845-562-5500	562-3082
Lumax Industries Inc Chestnut Ave & 4th St PO Box 991 *Web:* www.lumaxlighting.com	Altoona	PA	16603	814-944-2537	944-6413
Lumec Inc 640 Cure-Boivin *Web:* www.lumec.com	Boisbriand	QC	J7G2A7	450-430-7040	430-1453
Luxo Corp 200 Clearbrook Rd **Fax:* Sales ■ *TF:* 800-222-5896 ■ *Web:* www.luxous.com	Elmsford	NY	10523	914-345-0067	345-0068*
Mag Instrument Inc 2001 S Hillman Ave **Fax Area Code:* 775 ■ *TF:* 800-289-6241 ■ *Web:* www.maglite.com	Ontario	CA	91761	909-947-1006	719-4586*
Manning Lighting 1810 North Ave PO Box 1063 *Web:* www.manningltg.com	Sheboygan	WI	53083	920-458-2184	458-2491
Mario Industries Inc 2490 Patterson Ave SW *TF:* 800-458-1244 ■ *Web:* www.marioindustries.com	Roanoke	VA	24016	540-342-1111	345-4813
Mark Architectural Lighting 3 Kilmer Rd *TF:* 800-526-6280 ■ *Web:* www.marklighting.com	Edison	NJ	08817	732-985-2600	985-8441
Mark IV Industries Inc 501 John James Audubon Pkwy *Web:* www.mark-iv.com	Amherst	NY	14226	716-689-4972	689-6098
Mercury Lighting Products Co Inc 20 Audrey Pl *TF:* 800-637-2879 ■ *Web:* www.mercltg.com	Fairfield	NJ	07004	973-244-9444	244-2584
Minka Group 1151 W Bradford Ct *TF:* 800-221-7977 ■ *Web:* www.minkagroup.net	Corona	CA	92882	951-735-9220	735-9758
Mole-Richardson Co Inc 937 N Sycamore Ave *Web:* www.mole.com	Hollywood	CA	90038	323-851-0111	851-5593
Mule Lighting Inc 46 Baker St *TF:* 800-556-7690 ■ *Web:* www.mulelighting.com	Providence	RI	02905	401-941-4446	941-2929
Multi-Electric Mfg Inc 4223 W Lake St *Web:* www.multielectric.com	Chicago	IL	60624	773-722-1900	722-5694
Musco Lighting 100 1st Ave W *TF:* 800-825-6020 ■ *Web:* www.musco.com	Oskaloosa	IA	52577	641-673-0411	673-4852
National Lighting Co Inc 522 Cortlandt St *Web:* www.natltg.com	Belleville	NJ	07109	973-751-1600	751-4931
Nightscaping 1705 E Colton Ave *TF:* 800-544-4840 ■ *Web:* www.nightscaping.com	Redlands	CA	92374	909-794-2121	389-9088
North Star Lighting Inc 2150 Parkes Dr *TF:* 800-229-4330 ■ *Web:* www.nslights.com	Broadview	IL	60155	708-681-4330	681-4006
Norwell Mfg Inc 82 Stevens St *TF:* 800-822-2831 ■ *Web:* www.norwellinc.com	East Taunton	MA	02718	508-822-5854	823-9431
Nulco Lighting 30 Beecher St PO Box 1328 *TF:* 800-668-5269 ■ *Web:* www.nulcolighting.com	Pawtucket	RI	02862	401-728-5200	728-8210
Omniglow LLC 91 Pinevale St *TF Cust Svc:* 866-783-3799 ■ *Web:* www.omniglow.com	Indian Orchard	MA	01151	413-241-6010	543-5470
OSRAM Sylvania Inc 100 Endicott St *Web:* www.sylvania.com	Danvers	MA	01923	978-777-1900	750-2152
Pacific Coast Lighting Inc 20310 Plummer St *TF:* 800-709-9004 ■ *Web:* www.pacificcoastlighting.com	Chatsworth	CA	91311	818-886-9751	886-5751
Paraflex Industries 2006 Inc 141 Lanza Ave *Web:* www.paraflex.com	Garfield	NJ	07026	973-340-6040	340-6043
Paramount Industries Inc 304 N Howard St *TF:* 800-521-5405 ■ *Web:* www.paramount-lighting.com	Croswell	MI	48422	810-679-2551	679-4045
Pauluhn Electric Mfg LLP 1616 N Main St *Web:* www.pauluhn.com	Pearland	TX	77581	281-485-4311	485-4398
Peerless Lighting Corp 2246 5th St *Web:* www.peerless-lighting.com	Berkeley	CA	94710	510-845-2760	845-2776
Pieri Creations LLC 100 W Oxford St *Web:* www.piericreations.net	Philadelphia	PA	19122	215-634-0700	634-5525
Prescolite Inc 101 Corporate Dr *Web:* www.prescolite.com	Spartanburg	SC	29303	864-599-6000	599-6153
Progress Lighting Co 101 Corporate Dr *Web:* www.progresslighting.com	Spartanburg	SC	29303	864-599-6000	

				Phone	Fax
Prudential Lighting Corp 1774 E 21st St	Los Angeles	CA	90058	213-746-0360	746-8838
Web: www.prulite.com					
Quality Lighting 2930 S Fairview St	Santa Ana	CA	92704	714-371-2394	668-1107
TF: 800-545-1326 ■ *Web:* www.qualitylighting.com					
Quoizel Inc 6 Corporate Pkwy	Goose Creek	SC	29445	843-553-6700	553-1002
Web: www.quoizelonline.com					
RAB Lighting 170 Ludlow Ave	Northvale	NJ	07647	201-784-8600	784-0077
TF: 800-938-1010 ■ *Web:* www.rabweb.com					
Rangaire Co 501 S Wilhite St	Cleburne	TX	76031	817-556-6500	556-6549
Rejuvenation Inc 2550 NW Nicolai St	Portland	OR	97210	503-231-1900	526-7329*
**Fax Area Code:* 800 ■ *TF:* 888-401-1900 ■ *Web:* www.rejuvenation.com					
Renova Lighting Systems Inc 300 High Point Ave	Portsmouth	RI	02871	401-682-1850	682-1860
TF: 800-635-6682 ■ *Web:* www.renova.com					
Schonbek Worldwide Lighting Inc 61 Industrial Blvd	Plattsburgh	NY	12901	518-563-7500	563-4228
TF: 800-836-1892 ■ *Web:* www.schonbek.com					
Sea Gull Lighting Products LLC A Generations Brands Co					
301 W Washington St	Riverside	NJ	08075	856-764-0500	764-6308
TF: 800-347-5483 ■ *Web:* www.seagulllighting.com					
Sentry Electric 185 Buffalo Ave	Freeport	NY	11520	516-379-4660	378-0624
Web: www.sentrylighting.com					
Shaper Lighting 1141 Marina Way S	Richmond	CA	94804	510-234-2370	234-2371
Web: www.shaperlighting.com					
Siemens Airfield Solutions Inc 977 Gahanna Pkwy	Columbus	OH	43230	614-861-1304	864-2069
TF: 800-545-4157 ■ *Web:* www.sas.siemens.com					
SIMKAR Corp 700 Ramona Ave	Philadelphia	PA	19120	215-831-7700	831-7703*
**Fax:* Cust Svc ■ *TF:* 800-523-3602 ■ *Web:* www.simkar.com					
Specialty Lighting 639 Washburn Switch Rd PO Box 1680	Shelby	NC	28151	704-482-3416	484-0818
Web: www.specialtylighting.com					
Spectrolab Inc 12500 Gladstone Ave	Sylmar	CA	91342	818-365-4611	898-7534
TF: 800-936-4888 ■ *Web:* www.spectrolab.com					
Spectrum Brands Inc 601 Rayovac Dr	Madison	WI	53711	608-275-3340	275-4577
NYSE: SPC ■ *TF:* 800-237-7000 ■ *Web:* www.rayovac.com					
Spring City Electrical Mfg Co PO Box 19	Spring City	PA	19475	610-948-4000	948-5577
Web: www.springcity.com					
Stonco Lighting 2345 Vauxhall Rd	Union	NJ	07083	908-964-7000	964-0968
TF: 800-334-2212 ■ *Web:* www.stoncolighting.com					
Strand Lighting Inc 6603 Darin Way	Cypress	CA	90630	714-230-8200	899-0042
TF: 800-733-0564 ■ *Web:* www.strandlight.com					
Stylecraft Lamps Inc					
325 Kapik Industrial Dr Hwy 51 N PO Box 347	Hernando	MS	38632	662-429-5279	662-5279*
**Fax Area Code:* 601					
Swivelier Co Inc 600 Bradley Hill Rd	Blauvelt	NY	10913	845-353-1455	353-1512
Web: www.swivelier.com					
Tech Lighting LLC 7400 Linda Ave	Skokie	IL	60076	847-410-4400	410-4500
TF: 800-522-5315 ■ *Web:* www.techlighting.com					
Thomas Lighting Canada 189 Bullock Dr	Markham	ON	L3P1W4	905-294-9570	294-9811
TF: 800-463-5456 ■ *Web:* www.thomaslightingcanada.com					
TIR Systems Ltd 7700 Riverfront Gate	Burnaby	BC	V5J5M4	604-294-8477	294-3733
TSX: TIR ■ *TF:* 800-663-2036 ■ *Web:* www.tirsys.com					
Translite Sonoma 22678 Broadway Suite 1	Sonoma	CA	95476	707-996-6906	996-6926
TF: 888-999-4540 ■ *Web:* www.translite.com					
Tri-Lite Inc 1642 Besley Ct	Chicago	IL	60622	773-384-7765	384-5115
TF: 800-322-5250 ■ *Web:* www.triliteinc.com					
Troy-CSL Lighting Inc 14625 E Clark Ave	City of Industry	CA	91745	626-336-4511	330-4266
TF: 800-533-8769 ■ *Web:* www.troy-lighting.com					
Uspar Enterprises Inc 13404 S Monte Vista Ave	Chino	CA	91710	909-591-7506	590-3220
TF: 800-251-4612 ■ *Web:* www.uspar.com					
Versen Kurt Co 10 Charles St	Westwood	NJ	07675	201-664-8200	664-4801
Web: www.kurtversen.com					
Western Reflections 261 Commerce Way	Gallatin	TN	37066	615-451-9700	452-0283
TF Cust Svc: 800-507-8302 ■ *Web:* www.western-reflections.com					
Westinghouse Lighting Corp 12401 McNulty Rd	Philadelphia	PA	19154	215-671-2000	464-4115
TF Orders: 800-999-2226 ■ *Web:* www.westinghouselighting.com					
Wide-Lite Corp 1611 Clovis Barker Rd PO Box 606	San Marcos	TX	78667	512-392-5821	753-1122
TF: 800-235-2314 ■ *Web:* www.wide-lite.com					
Wildwood Lamps & Accents 516 Paul St PO Box 672	Rocky Mount	NC	27803	252-446-3266	977-6669
Web: www.wildwoodlamps.com					
Williams HE Inc 831 W Fairview Ave	Carthage	MO	64836	417-358-4065	358-6015
TF: 800-358-4064 ■ *Web:* www.hew.com					
Wilshire Mfg Co 645 Myles Standish Blvd	Taunton	MA	02780	508-824-1970	822-7046
TF: 800-443-4695 ■ *Web:* www.wilshiremfg.com					

443 LIME

				Phone	Fax
Carmeuse North America 11 Stanwix St 11th Fl	Pittsburgh	PA	15222	412-995-5500	995-5570
TF: 800-445-3930 ■ *Web:* www.carmeusena.com					
Cemex Puerto Rico Inc					
RT 165 KM 2.7 Industrial Amelia Park	Bucahna Guaynabo	PR	00968	787-783-3000	781-8850
Web: www.cemex.com					
Chemical Lime Co PO Box 985004	Fort Worth	TX	76185	817-732-8164	732-8564
Web: www.chemicallime.com					
Cheney Lime & Cement 478 Graystone Rd	Allgood	AL	35013	205-625-3031	625-3032
TF: 800-752-8282 ■ *Web:* www.cheneylime.com					
Graymont Inc 10991 Shellbridge Way Suite 200	Richmond	BC	V6X3C6	604-276-9331	276-9337
Web: www.graymont.com					
LWB Refractories Co PO Box 1189	York	PA	17405	717-848-1501	848-2294
TF: 800-233-1991					
Martin Limestone Inc PO Box 550	Blue Ball	PA	17506	717-354-1300	766-0202*
**Fax Area Code:* 814 ■ *Web:* www.martinlimestone.com					
Martin Marietta Materials Inc 2710 Wycliff Rd	Raleigh	NC	27607	919-781-4550	
NYSE: MLM ■ *Web:* www.martinmarietta.com					
Mercer Lime & Stone Co 50 Abele Rd Suite 1006	Bridgeville	PA	15017	412-220-0316	220-0347
Web: www.mercerlime.com					
Minerals Technologies Inc 405 Lexington Ave 20th Fl	New York	NY	10174	212-878-1800	878-1801
NYSE: MTX ■ *Web:* www.mineralstech.com					
Mississippi Lime Co 3870 S Lindberg Suite 200	Saint Louis	MO	63127	314-543-6300	543-6570
TF: 800-437-5463 ■ *Web:* www.mississippilime.com					
Oglebay Norton Co 1001 Lakeside Ave 15th Fl	Cleveland	OH	44114	216-861-3300	861-8709
TF: 800-321-4230 ■ *Web:* www.oglebaynorton.com					
Rockwell Lime Co Inc 4110 Rockwood Rd	Manitowoc	WI	54220	920-682-7771	682-7972
TF: 800-558-7711 ■ *Web:* www.rockwelllime.com					
Schildberg Construction Co PO Box 358	Greenfield	IA	50849	641-743-2131	
Texas Industries Inc 1341 W Mockingbird Ln Suite 700W	Dallas	TX	75247	972-647-6700	647-3878
NYSE: TXI ■ *Web:* www.txi.com					
Texas Lime Co PO Box 851	Cleburne	TX	76033	817-641-4433	556-0905
TF Orders: 800-772-8000					
US Lime & Minerals Inc 5429 LBJ Fwy Suite 230	Dallas	TX	75240	972-991-8400	385-1340
NASDAQ: USLM ■ *TF:* 800-991-5463 ■ *Web:* www.uslm.com					
Western Lime Corp PO Box 57	West Bend	WI	53095	262-334-3005	334-2874
TF: 800-433-0036 ■ *Web:* www.westernlime.com					

444 LIMOUSINE SERVICES

				Phone	Fax
1st Corporate Limousine DBA Carey Executive Limousine					
245 University Ave SW	Atlanta	GA	30315	770-933-9000	933-9937
TF: 800-241-3943 ■ *Web:* www.careyatlanta.com					
A Family Limousine 6311 Stirling Rd	Davie	FL	33314	954-522-7455	522-7403
TF: 877-599-5466 ■ *Web:* www.afamilylimo.com					
A1 Worldwide Limousine Inc 69 Yorkville Ave Suite 205	Toronto	ON	M5R1B8	416-922-5466	922-4748
TF: 877-537-5466 ■ *Web:* www.a1worldwidelimo.com					
Advantage Limousine Services Inc DBA ALS Transportation Inc					
6529 Cunningham Rd Suite 2303	Houston	TX	77041	713-355-5466	983-9959
TF: 888-983-9991 ■ *Web:* www.advantagelimos.com					
Air Brook Limousine Inc 18 Overlook Ave	Rochelle Park	NJ	07662	201-843-6100	845-4480
TF: 800-800-1990 ■ *Web:* www.airbrook.com					
AirportsPickup.com PO Box 652	New York	NY	10040	212-927-7152	591-8290*
**Fax Area Code:* 917 ■ *TF:* 877-800-6500 ■ *Web:* www.airportspickup.com					
Alliance Limousine Inc 14553 Delano St Unit 210	Van Nuys	CA	91411	323-465-9406	786-8810*
**Fax Area Code:* 818 ■ *TF:* 800-954-5466 ■ *Web:* www.alliancelimo.net					
ALS Transportation Inc 6529 Cunningham Rd Suite 2303	Houston	TX	77041	713-355-5466	983-9959
TF: 888-983-9991 ■ *Web:* www.advantagelimos.com					
Ambassador Limousine 3215 Cinder Ln	Las Vegas	NV	89103	702-362-6200	889-0080
TF: 888-519-5466 ■ *Web:* www.ambassadorlasvegas.com					
American Coach Limousine 1433 W Jeffrey Dr	Addison	IL	60101	630-629-0001	629-0002
TF: 888-709-5466 ■ *Web:* www.americancoachlimousine.com					
AnyPointLimo.com PO Box 242	Drexel Hill	PA	19026	610-626-9091	628-0782
Web: www.anypointlimo.com					
Arizona Limousines Inc 8900 N Central Ave Suite 101	Phoenix	AZ	85020	602-267-7097	870-3388
TF: 800-678-0033 ■ *Web:* www.arizonalimos.com					
Bayview Limousine Service 15701 Nelson Pl S	Seattle	WA	98188	206-824-6200	277-5895*
**Fax Area Code:* 425 ■ *TF:* 800-606-7880 ■ *Web:* www.bayviewlimo.com					
Bethany Limousine & Bus 2120 West Virginia Ave NE	Washington	DC	20002	202-857-0440	857-7826
TF: 800-424-2971 ■ *Web:* www.blslimos.com					
BostonCoach 69 Norman St	Everett	MA	02149	617-394-3900	381-8725
TF: 800-672-7676 ■ *Web:* www.bostoncoach.com					
Broward Limousine & Airport Service Inc 9342 NW 5th St	Plantation	FL	33317	954-791-3000	791-7363
TF: 800-276-9273 ■ *Web:* www.browardlimo.com					
Burgundy Global 336 W Passaic St 2nd Fl	Rochelle Park	NJ	07662	201-291-4290	291-9497
TF: 800-546-6236 ■ *Web:* www.burgundyglobal.com					
Carefree Lifestyle Inc 1031 5th St	Miami Beach	FL	33139	305-534-3531	534-3819
TF: 866-589-8796 ■ *Web:* www.carefreelifestyle.net					
Carey Executive Limousine 245 University Ave SW	Atlanta	GA	30315	770-933-9000	933-9937
TF: 800-241-3943 ■ *Web:* www.careyatlanta.com					
Carey International Inc 4530 Wisconsin Ave NW 5th Fl	Washington	DC	20016	202-895-1200	895-1201
TF: 800-336-4646 ■ *Web:* www.ecarey.com					
Classic Transportation Group 1600 Locust Ave	Bohemia	NY	11716	631-567-5100	567-3722
TF: 800-666-4949 ■ *Web:* www.classictrans.com					
Connecticut Limousine LLC 230 Old Gate Ln	Milford	CT	06460	203-878-6867	783-6997
TF: 800-472-5466 ■ *Web:* www.ctlimo.com					
Cosmopolitan Limousine 1601 S Preston St	Louisville	KY	40217	502-634-5466	214-7409
TF: 800-603-6594 ■ *Web:* www.cosmolimoky.com					
Dav El Chauffeured Transportation Network 200 2nd St	Chelsea	MA	02150	617-887-0900	887-0902
TF: 800-922-0343 ■ *Web:* www.davel.com					
DispatchOne 2835 Belvidere Rd Suite 309 PO Box 8787	Waukegan	IL	60079	847-662-8802	662-9975
Web: www.dispatchone.com					
Elite Limousine Service Inc 1059 12th Ave Suite E	Honolulu	HI	96816	808-735-2431	735-5159
TF: 800-776-2098 ■ *Web:* www.elitelimohawaii.com					
Empire International Ltd 55 Walnut St	Norwood	NJ	07648	201-784-1200	784-1729
TF: 800-451-5466 ■ *Web:* www.empireint.com					
Executive Transportation Brokers Inc DBA AirportsPickup.com					
PO Box 652	New York	NY	10040	212-927-7152	591-8290*
**Fax Area Code:* 917 ■ *TF:* 877-800-6500 ■ *Web:* www.airportspickup.com					
Executive Transportation Service Inc					
7108 DeSoto Ave Suite 204	Canoga Park	CA	91303	818-716-7727	347-4633
TF: 800-348-4010 ■ *Web:* www.execlimoservice.com					
Four Seasons Limousine Co					
2432 W Peoria Ave Bldg 8 Suite 1144	Phoenix	AZ	85029	602-443-2200	443-2202
TF: 877-548-1612 ■ *Web:* www.fourseasonslimocompany.com					
Gateway Limousines 1550 Gilbreth Rd	Burlingame	CA	94010	650-345-7077	697-7739
TF: 800-486-7077 ■ *Web:* www.gatewaylimousine.com					
International Chauffeured Service Worldwide					
53 E 34th St 4th Fl	New York	NY	10016	212-213-0302	266-5254*
**Fax Area Code:* 877 ■ *TF:* 800-266-5254 ■ *Web:* www.bookalimo.com					
Leros First Class 6 Skyline Dr	Hawthorne	NY	10532	914-747-2300	747-2917
TF: 800-825-3767 ■ *Web:* www.leroslimo.com					
Limo One 1342 Shoulder Creek Ln	San Bruno	CA	94066	415-531-6180	240-0138*
**Fax Area Code:* 650 ■ *TF:* 877-490-5466 ■ *Web:* www.sflimousine.com					
Marriton Limousine 13900 N IH-35 Suite J	Austin	TX	78728	512-329-7007	989-7217
TF: 800-940-7007 ■ *Web:* www.marritonlimo.com					
Mears Transportation Group 324 W Gore St	Orlando	FL	32806	407-422-4561	422-6923
TF: 800-759-5219 ■ *Web:* www.mearstransportation.com					
Olympic Airporter 5005 Rts 33 & 34	Farmingdale	NJ	07727	732-938-6666	938-4015
TF: 800-822-9797 ■ *Web:* www.olympicairporter.com					
Omni Limousine Inc 3935 W Reno Ave Suite A	Las Vegas	NV	89118	702-367-1000	871-6496
TF: 800-325-8003 ■ *Web:* www.omnilimo.com					
Park Cities Limousine 619 S Hill Ave	Dallas	TX	75223	214-824-0011	827-0136
TF: 888-559-0708 ■ *Web:* www.limodfw.com					
PHL Limousine 101 Rt 130 Suite 6	Cinnaminson	NJ	08077	856-786-7151	
TF: 866-264-5466 ■ *Web:* www.phl-limo.com/index.php					
Pioneer Limousine Service 15643 Sherman Way Suite 410	Van Nuys	CA	91406	818-609-1566	780-8310
TF: 800-640-0700 ■ *Web:* www.pioneerlimos.com					
Pontarelli Limousine Service 2225 W Hubbard St	Chicago	IL	60612	312-226-5466	226-1300
TF: 800-322-5466 ■ *Web:* www.pontarelliischicago.com					
Regency Limousine International 23-57 83rd St	East Elmhurst	NY	11370	718-507-4000	507-8283
TF: 866-302-2201 ■ *Web:* www.rlilimo.com					
Royal Coachman Worldwide 88 Ford Rd Unit 26	Denville	NJ	07834	973-400-4000	675-4365
TF: 800-472-7433 ■ *Web:* www.royalcoachman.com					
Seattle Limousine Service PO Box 80205	Seattle	WA	98108	206-762-3339	762-3394
TF: 800-274-3339 ■ *Web:* www.seattlelimo.com					
SecureCar Worldwide 55 Walnut St	Norwood	NJ	07648	201-784-8326	784-3792
TF: 866-227-1481 ■ *Web:* www.securecarworldwide.com					
Starlite Limousines LLC 15111 N Hayden Rd Suite 300	Scottsdale	AZ	85260	480-905-1234	422-4396
TF: 877-474-4847 ■ *Web:* www.starlitelimos.com					
SuperShuttle International Inc					
14500 N Northsight Blvd Suite 329	Scottsdale	AZ	85260	480-609-3000	607-9317
Web: www.supershuttle.com					
US Coachways Inc 87 Ellis St Suite 4	Staten Island	NY	10307	718-477-4242	477-9009
TF: 800-359-5991 ■ *Web:* www.uscoachways.com					
VIPride.com 15111 N Hayden Rd Suite 300	Scottsdale	AZ	85260	480-905-1234	422-4396
TF: 877-474-4847 ■ *Web:* www.vipride.com					
Winn Transportation 1831 Westwood Ave	Richmond	VA	23227	804-358-9466	353-2606
TF: 800-296-9466 ■ *Web:* www.winnbus.com					

445 LINEN & UNIFORM SUPPLY

				Phone	Fax
AAA Uniform Service 4120 Truman Rd. *TF:* 800-366-0564 ■ *Web:* www.aaauniform.com	Kansas City	MO	64127	816-231-5737	231-3550
Ace-Tex Enterprises 7601 Central St *TF:* 800-444-3800 ■ *Web:* www.ace-tex.com	Detroit	MI	48210	313-834-4000	834-0260
Alsco Inc 711 E Vermont St *TF:* 888-297-8049 ■ *Web:* alsco.com	Indianapolis	IN	46202	317-263-5260	264-5143
Alsco Inc 505 E South Temple St. *TF:* 877-328-8831 ■ *Web:* www.alsco.com	Salt Lake City	UT	84102	801-328-8831	363-5680
AmeriPride Services Inc 10801 Wayzata Blvd *TF Cust Svc:* 800-595-3913 ■ *Web:* www.ameripride.com	Minnetonka	MN	55305	952-738-4200	738-4252
Amertex Service Group Inc 370 Orchard Lake Rd	Pontiac	MI	48341	248-454-8300	454-9750
Angelica Corp 424 S Woods Mill Rd *NYSE: AGL* ■ *TF:* 800-235-8410 ■ *Web:* www.angelica.com	Chesterfield	MO	63017	314-854-3800	854-3890
Apparelmaster 123 Harrison Ave *TF:* 877-543-1678 ■ *Web:* www.apparelmaster.net	Harrison	OH	45030	513-202-1600	202-1660
Arrow Uniform Rental Inc 6400 Monroe Blvd *TF:* 800-552-7769 ■ *Web:* www.arrowuniform.com	Taylor	MI	48180	313-299-5000	299-5093
Associated Textile Rental Services Inc 3993 Oneida St.	New Hartford	NY	13413	315-797-2600	797-1612
Capitol Uniform & Linen Service PO Box 1414 *TF:* 800-323-1511	Dover	DE	19903	302-674-1511	674-1558
Christian WH & Sons Inc 22-28 Franklin St *Web:* www.whchristian.com	Brooklyn	NY	11222	718-389-7000	389-9644
Cintas Corp PO Box 625737 *NASDAQ: CTAS* ■ *TF:* 800-786-4367 ■ *Web:* www.cintas-corp.com	Cincinnati	OH	45262	513-459-1200	
Continental Linen Services 4200 Manchester Rd *TF:* 800-875-4636 ■ *Web:* www.clsimage.com	Kalamazoo	MI	49001	269-343-2551	343-7246
Coyne Textile Services Inc 140 Cortland Ave *TF:* 800-672-6963 ■ *Web:* www.coynetextileservices.com	Syracuse	NY	13202	315-475-1626	475-2140
Domestic Linen Supply & Laundry Inc 3800 18th St. *TF:* 800-430-0871 ■ *Web:* www.domesticuniform.com	Detroit	MI	48208	313-831-6700	831-2617
G & K Services fInc 324 Taylor St *TF:* 800-255-8391 ■ *Web:* www.gkservices.com	Manchester	NH	03103	603-625-9722	625-5413
G & K Services Inc 5995 Opus Pkwy Suite 500 *NASDAQ: GKSRA* ■ *TF:* 800-452-2737 ■ *Web:* www.gkservices.com	Minnetonka	MN	55343	952-912-5500	912-5999
G & K Services Inc 2117 Berry St *TF:* 800-214-5614 ■ *Web:* www.gkservices.com	Kingsport	TN	37664	423-247-4101	247-9244
Healthcare Services Group Inc 3220 Tillman Dr Suite 300 *NASDAQ: HCSG* ■ *TF:* 800-523-2248 ■ *Web:* www.hcsgcorp.com	Bensalem	PA	19020	215-639-4274	
Hospital Laundry Services Inc 45 W Hintz Rd *Web:* www.hlschicago.com	Wheeling	IL	60090	847-229-0900	537-9198
Industrial Towel & Uniform Inc 2700 S 160th St *TF:* 800-767-2487 ■ *Web:* www.itu-at.com	New Berlin	WI	53151	262-782-1950	782-1802
Iron City Uniform Rental 6640 Frankstown Ave *TF:* 800-532-2010 ■ *Web:* www.ironcityuniform.com	Pittsburgh	PA	15206	412-661-2001	661-9356
Linens of the Week 713 Lamont St NW *TF:* 800-355-8874 ■ *Web:* www.linensoftheweek.com	Washington	DC	20010	202-291-9200	291-6485
Mickey's Linen & Towel Supply 4601 W Addison St	Chicago	IL	60641	773-545-7211	545-9111
Mission Linen Supply PO Box 1299 *TF Hum Res:* 800-944-5539 ■ *Web:* www.missionlinen.com	Santa Barbara	CA	93102	805-963-1841	730-3718
Model Coverall Service Inc 100 28th St SE *TF:* 800-968-6491 ■ *Web:* www.modelcoverall.com	Grand Rapids	MI	49548	616-241-6491	241-0677
Morgan Services Inc 323 N Michigan Ave *TF:* 888-966-7426 ■ *Web:* www.morganservices.com	Chicago	IL	60601	312-346-3181	346-0144
Nixon Uniform Service Inc 2925 Northeast Blvd *TF Sales:* 888-649-6687 ■ *Web:* www.uniformservice.com	Wilmington	DE	19802	302-764-7550	764-7543
Overall Laundry Service Inc 7200 Hardeson Rd *TF:* 800-683-7255 ■ *Web:* www.overallservices.com	Everett	WA	98203	425-353-0800	290-6519
Prudential Overall Supply PO Box 11210 *TF:* 800-767-5536 ■ *Web:* www.pos-clean.com	Santa Ana	CA	92711	949-250-4855	261-1947
Roscoe Co 3535 W Harrison St *TF Cust Svc:* 800-722-5010	Chicago	IL	60624	773-722-5000	722-3338
S & R Uniforms Inc 1833 14th St W *TF:* 800-553-4065 ■ *Web:* www.sruniforms.com	Bradenton	FL	34205	941-748-1245	747-4699
Sitex Corp 1300 Commonwealth Dr *TF:* 800-278-3537 ■ *Web:* www.sitex-corp.com	Henderson	KY	42420	270-827-3537	826-5567
Spirit Services 1021 Ware St *TF:* 888-774-7484	Albany	GA	31705	229-436-1811	435-3560
Superior Linen Service 1012 S Center St.	Tacoma	WA	98409	253-383-2636	383-1061
Textile Care Services Inc 225 Wood Lake Dr SE *TF:* 800-422-0945 ■ *Web:* www.textilecs.com	Rochester	MN	55904	507-288-1861	252-7550
UniFirst Corp 68 Jonspin Rd *NYSE: UNF* ■ *TF:* 800-347-7888 ■ *Web:* www.unifirst.com	Wilmington	MA	01887	978-658-8888	657-5663
Unitech Services Group 295 Parker St *Web:* www.u1st.com	Springfield	MA	01151	413-543-6911	543-6989
Valiant Products Corp 2727 5th Ave W *TF Cust Svc:* 800-347-2727 ■ *Web:* www.valiantproducts.com	Denver	CO	80204	303-892-1234	892-5535
Western Uniform & Towel Service Inc 1707 N Mosley St *TF:* 800-214-2342 ■ *Web:* www.westernuniform.com	Wichita	KS	67214	316-264-2342	264-9042
WH Christian & Sons Inc 22-28 Franklin St *Web:* www.whchristian.com	Brooklyn	NY	11222	718-389-7000	389-9644

446 LIQUOR STORES

				Phone	Fax
21st Amendment Inc 1158 W 86th St	Indianapolis	IN	46260	317-846-1678	846-5687
67 Liquors Inc 5360 N Federal Hwy	Lighthouse Point	FL	33064	954-428-6255	725-0837
ABC Fine Wines & Spirits 8989 S Orange Ave. *TF:* 800-854-7283 ■ *Web:* www.abcfinewineandspirits.com	Orlando	FL	32824	407-851-0000	857-5500
Berbiglia Inc 1114 W 103 St *Web:* www.berbiglia.com	Kansas City	MO	64114	816-942-0070	942-1777
Beverages & more! 1470 Enea Cir Suite 1600 *Web:* www.bevmo.com	Concord	CA	94520	925-609-6000	609-7011
Bevmax Wines & Liquors 808 E Main St *Web:* www.bevmax.com	Stamford	CT	06902	203-357-9151	359-9967
BK Miller Co Inc 4501 B Auth Place *TF:* 800-801-7632 ■ *Web:* www.bkmiller.com	Suitland	MD	20746	301-423-6200	423-0251
Chalet Wine & Cheese Shops 5100 W Dempster St *Web:* www.binnys.com	Skokie	IL	60077	847-674-4200	674-4207
Crown Liquors of Fort Lauderdale 910 NW 10th Pl. *TF:* 888-563-9463 ■ *Web:* www.crownwineandspirits.com	Fort Lauderdale	FL	33311	954-763-6831	462-0125
Don's & Ben's Inc 10903 Industry Dr.	San Antonio	TX	78217	210-646-9992	646-6145
Flanigan's Enterprises Inc 5059 NE 18th Ave *AMEX: BDL* ■ *Web:* www.flanigans.net	Fort Lauderdale	FL	33334	954-377-1961	377-1980
Gold Standard Enterprises Inc DBA Chalet Wine & Cheese Shops 5100 W Dempster St *Web:* www.binnys.com	Skokie	IL	60077	847-674-4200	674-4207
Goody-Goody Liquors Inc 10301 Harry Hines Blvd *Web:* www.goodygoody.com	Dallas	TX	75229	214-350-5806	350-4258
Kings Liquor Inc 2810 W Berry St *Web:* www.kingsliquor.com	Fort Worth	TX	76109	817-923-3737	927-0021
Maggiore Cos 2927 Harrisburg Rd NE	Canton	OH	44705	330-454-7913	454-7978
MGM Liquor Stores Inc 1124 Larpenteur Ave W	Saint Paul	MN	55113	651-487-1006	487-9401
Mozingo Liquors Inc 120 S 6th St	Hartsville	SC	29550	843-332-6554	332-6921
Pinkie's Inc 1426 E 8th St *Web:* www.pinkiesonline.com	Odessa	TX	79761	432-580-0439	580-0918
Richard's Liquors & Fine Wines 1701 Brun St Suite 200 *Web:* www.richardsliquors.com	Houston	TX	77219	713-529-6266	529-3884
SavWay Liquors Inc 3821 S York Rd	Oak Brook	IL	60523	630-986-0500	986-0059
Sherry-Lehmann Inc 679 Madison Ave *Web:* www.sherry-lehmann.com	New York	NY	10021	212-838-7500	838-9285
Shop 'N Save Liquors 20 Independence Ave.	Quincy	MA	02169	617-773-2060	786-9797
Sigel's Beverages LP 2960 Anode Ln. *Web:* www.sigels.com	Dallas	TX	75220	214-350-1271	357-3490
Spec's Wines Spirits & Finer Foods 2410 Smith St *TF:* 888-526-8787 ■ *Web:* www.specsonline.com	Houston	TX	77006	713-526-8787	526-6129
Touring & Tasting 207 E Victoria St *TF:* 800-850-4370 ■ *Web:* www.touringandtasting.com	Santa Barbara	CA	93101	805-965-2813	965-2873
Wine Club 2110 E McFadden Ave Suite E *TF:* 800-966-5432 ■ *Web:* www.thewineclub.com	Santa Ana	CA	92705	714-835-6485	835-5062
Wine.com Inc 114 Sansome St 6th Fl **Fax Area Code: 415* ■ *Web:* www.wine.com	San Francisco	CA	94104	877-289-6886	291-9599*
WineStyles Inc 5100 W Copans Rd Suite 310 *TF:* 866-424-9463 ■ *Web:* winestyles.net	Margate	FL	33063	954-984-0070	984-0074
Zachys Wine & Liquor Inc 16 East Pkwy *TF:* 800-723-0241 ■ *Web:* www.zachys.com	Scarsdale	NY	10583	914-723-0241	723-1033

447 LITERARY AGENTS

				Phone	Fax
Aaron M Priest Literary Agency 708 3rd Ave 23rd FL	New York	NY	10017	212-818-0344	573-9417
Browne & Miller Literary Assoc LLC 410 S Michigan Ave Suite 460 *Web:* www.browneandmiller.com	Chicago	IL	60605	312-922-3063	922-1905
Carol Mann Agency 55 5th Ave *Web:* www.carolmannagency.com	New York	NY	10003	212-206-5635	675-4809
David Black Literary Agency 156 5th Ave Suite 608	New York	NY	10010	212-242-5080	924-6609
Dominick Abel Literary Agency Inc 146 W 82nd St Suite 1B	New York	NY	10024	212-877-0710	595-3133
Don Congdon Assoc Inc 156 5th Ave Suite 625	New York	NY	10010	212-645-1229	727-2688
Donadio & Olsen Inc 121 W 27th St Suite 704	New York	NY	10001	212-691-8077	633-2837
Dystel & Goderich Literary Management 1 Union Sq W Suite 904 *Web:* www.dystel.com	New York	NY	10003	212-627-9100	627-9313
Elaine Markson Literary Agency 44 Greenwich Ave	New York	NY	10011	212-243-8480	691-9014
Fifi Oscard Agency 110 W 40th St Suite 2100 *Web:* www.fifioscard.com	New York	NY	10018	212-764-1100	840-5019
Frances Collin Literary Agent PO Box 33 *Web:* www.francescollin.com	Wayne	PA	19087	610-254-0555	254-5029
Garon PinderLANE & Jay-Brooke Assoc 159 W 53rd St Suite 14-C	New York	NY	10019	212-489-0880	489-7104
George Borchardt Inc 136 E 57th St	New York	NY	10022	212-753-5785	838-6518
Harold Ober Assoc Inc 425 Madison Ave 10th Fl.	New York	NY	10017	212-759-8600	759-9428
Harvey Klinger Inc 300 W 55th St *Web:* www.harveyklinger.com	New York	NY	10019	212-581-7068	315-3823
IMG Literary 825 7th Ave 9th Fl *Web:* www.imgworld.com	New York	NY	10019	212-489-5400	246-1118
InkWell Management 521 5th Ave Suite 2600 *Web:* www.inkwellmanagement.com	New York	NY	10175	212-922-3500	922-0535
Jane Rotrosen Agency 318 E 51st St	New York	NY	10022	212-593-4330	935-6985
Jean V Naggar Literary Agency Inc 216 E 75th St Suite 1E *Web:* www.jvnla.com	New York	NY	10021	212-794-1082	794-3605
Jeff Herman Literary Agency Inc PO Box 1522	Stockbridge	MA	01262	413-298-0077	298-8188
Joan Daves Agency 21 W 26th St	New York	NY	10010	212-685-2663	685-1781
John Hawkins & Assoc Inc 71 W 23rd St Suite 1600 *Web:* www.jhalit.com	New York	NY	10010	212-807-7040	807-9555
Joy Harris Literary Agency 156 5th Ave Suite 617	New York	NY	10010	212-924-6269	924-6609
Lescher & Lescher Ltd 47 E 19th St	New York	NY	10003	212-529-1790	529-2716
Loretta Barrett Books Inc 101 5th Ave 11th Fl *Web:* www.lorettabarrettbooks.com	New York	NY	10003	212-242-3420	807-9579
Lowenstein-Yost Assoc Inc 121 W 27th St Suite 601 *Web:* www.lowensteinyost.com	New York	NY	10001	212-206-1630	727-0280
Manus & Assoc Literary Agency Inc 425 Sherman Ave Suite 200 *Web:* www.manuslit.com	Palo Alto	CA	94306	650-470-5151	470-5159
Michael Larsen/Elizabeth Pomada Literary Agents 1029 Jones St *Web:* www.larsenpomada.com	San Francisco	CA	94109	415-673-0939	
Nancy Love Literary Agency 250 E 65th St Suite 4A	New York	NY	10021	212-980-3499	308-6405
New England Publishing Assoc Inc 59 Parker Hill Rd *Web:* www.nepa.com	Higganum	CT	06441	860-345-7323	345-3660
Nolan/Lehr Group Betsy Nolan Literary Agency Div 214 W 29th St Suite 1002	New York	NY	10001	212-967-8200	967-7292
Peter Rubie Literary Agency 240 W 35th St Suite 500 *Web:* www.prlit.com	New York	NY	10001	212-279-1776	279-0927
Richard Curtis Assoc Inc 171 E 74th St 2nd Fl *Web:* www.curtisagency.com	New York	NY	10021	212-772-7363	772-7393
Roslyn Targ Literary Agency 105 W 13th St	New York	NY	10011	212-206-9390	989-6233
Sandra Dijkstra Literary Agency 1155 Camino Del Mar PMB 515	Del Mar	CA	92014	858-755-3115	794-2822
Sanford J Greenburger Assoc Inc 55 5th Ave 15th Fl *Web:* www.greenburger.com	New York	NY	10003	212-206-5600	463-8718
Sarah Jane Freymann Literary Agency 59 W 71st St Suite 9B *Web:* www.sarahjanefreymann.com	New York	NY	10023	212-362-9277	501-8240
Sheree Bykofsky Assoc Inc 16 W 36th St 13th Fl *Web:* users.rcn.com/sheree.interport/	New York	NY	10018	212-244-4144	244-0129
Trident Media Group 41 Madison Ave 36th Fl *Web:* www.tridentmediagroup.com	New York	NY	10010	212-333-1517	262-4849
Wallace Literary Agency 301 E 79th St Suite 14-J	New York	NY	10021	212-570-9090	772-8979
William Morris Agency 1 William Morris Pl *Web:* www.wma.com	Beverly Hills	CA	90212	310-859-4000	859-4462
William Morris Agency 1325 Ave of the Americas *Web:* www.wma.com	New York	NY	10019	212-586-5100	246-3583
Writers House 21 W 26th St *Web:* www.writershouse.com	New York	NY	10010	212-685-2400	685-1781

448 LITIGATION SUPPORT SERVICES

				Phone	Fax
Al Betz & Assoc PO Box 665 *Web:* albetzreporting.com	Westminster	MD	21158	410-752-1733	875-2857

Phone | Fax

Alderson Reporting Co 1111 14th St NW Suite 400 Washington DC 20005 202-289-2260 289-2221
TF: 800-367-3376 ■ *Web:* www.aldersonreporting.com
Allied Court Reporters Inc 115 Phenix Ave Cranston RI 02920 401-946-5500 946-9228
TF: 888-443-3767 ■ *Web:* www.alliedcourtreporters.com
Atkinson-Baker Inc 500 N Brand Blvd 3rd Fl Glendale CA 91203 818-551-7300 551-7330
TF: 800-288-3376 ■ *Web:* www.depo.com/abtabi.htm
Betz Al & Assoc PO Box 665 Westminster MD 21158 410-752-1733 875-2857
Web: albetzreporting.com
Compex Legal Services Inc 325 S Maple Ave Torrance CA 90503 310-782-1801 479-3365*
**Fax Area Code:* 800 ■ *TF Cust Svc:* 800-426-6739 ■ *Web:* www.compexlegal.com
Compulit 4460 44th St SE Suite D Grand Rapids MI 49512 616-285-9590 285-9603
TF: 800-858-4536 ■ *Web:* www.compulit.com
Courtroom Sciences Inc
4950 N O'Connor Rd Corporate Plaza 1 1st Fl Irving TX 75062 972-717-1773 717-3985
Web: www.courtroomsciences.com
CT Corp 111 8th Ave New York NY 10011 518-451-8000 938-8343*
**Fax Area Code:* 800 ■ *TF:* 800-624-0909 ■ *Web:* ctadmin.ctadvantage.com
DecisionQuest 21535 Hawthorne Blvd Suite 310 Torrance CA 90503 310-618-9600 618-1122
TF: 800-327-2449 ■ *Web:* www.decisionquest.com
Depobook Reporting Services 1600 G St Suite 101 Modesto CA 95354 209-544-6466 544-6566
TF: 800-830-8885 ■ *Web:* www.depobook.com
DepoNet 25 A Vreeland Rd Florham Park NJ 07932 800-337-6638 355-3094*
**Fax Area Code:* 973 ■ *Web:* www.deponet.com
DOAR Litigation Consulting 170 Earle Ave Lynbrook NY 11563 516-823-4000 823-4400
Web: www.doar.com
Esquire Deposition Services LLC
25A Vreeland Rd Suite 200 Florham Park NJ 07932 973-377-7750 377-7121
Web: www.esquirecom.com
First Advantage Corp 100 Carillon Pkwy Saint Petersburg FL 33716 727-214-3411 214-3410
TF: 800-321-4473 ■ *Web:* www.fadv.com
FTI Consulting Inc 900 Bestgate Rd Suite 100 Annapolis MD 21401 410-224-8770 224-8378
NYSE: FCN ■ *TF:* 800-334-5701 ■ *Web:* www.fticorp.com
Hahn & Bowersock Corp 151 Kalmus Dr Suite L-1 Costa Mesa CA 92626 714-549-3700 549-3641
TF: 800-660-3187 ■ *Web:* www.hahnbowersock.com
Hutchings Court Reporters LLC
6055 E Washington Blvd 8th Fl Los Angeles CA 90040 323-888-6300 888-6333
TF: 800-697-3210 ■ *Web:* www.hutchings.com
Jane Rose Reporting 74 5th Ave New York NY 10011 715-472-4631 825-9055*
**Fax Area Code:* 800 ■ *TF:* 800-825-3341 ■ *Web:* www.janerose.net
Jury Research Institute 2617 Danville Blvd PO Box 100 Alamo CA 94507 925-932-5663 932-8409
TF: 800-233-5879 ■ *Web:* www.jri-inc.com
LECG LLC 2000 Powell St Suite 600 Emeryville CA 94608 510-985-6700 653-9898
NASDAQ: XPRT ■ *Web:* www.lecg.com
LegaLink 101 Arch St 3rd Fl Boston MA 02110 617-542-0039 542-2119
TF: 800-662-1466 ■ *Web:* www.legalink.com
National Forensic Center PO Box 270529 San Diego CA 92198 858-487-0300 487-7747
Professional Shorthand Reporters Inc
601 Poydras St Suite 1615 New Orleans LA 70130 504-529-5255 529-5257
TF: 800-536-5255 ■ *Web:* www.psrdepo.com
Ralph Rosenberg Court Reporters Inc
1001 Bishop St Suite 2460 American Savings Bank Tower Honolulu HI 96813 808-524-2090 524-2596
TF: 888-524-5888 ■ *Web:* www.hawaii-court-reporters.com
Starr Litigation Services Inc 1201 Grand Ave West Des Moines IA 50265 515-224-1616 224-4863
TF: 800-627-8277 ■ *Web:* www.starrlit.com
Trial Behavior Consulting Inc
505 Sansome St Suite 1701 San Francisco CA 94111 415-781-5879 362-8775
Web: www.trialbehavior.com
TrialGraphix Inc 3300 Corporate Way Miramar FL 33025 305-576-5400 576-0188
TF: 800-334-5403 ■ *Web:* www.trialgraphix.com
US Legal Support Inc 363 N Sam Houston Pkwy E Suite 900 Houston TX 77060 713-653-7100 653-7171
TF: 800-567-8757 ■ *Web:* www.uslegalsupport.com
Verdict Systems LLC 1400 E Southern Ave Suite 710 Tempe AZ 85282 480-627-2430 627-2431
Web: www.verdictsystems.com
Veritext LLC 25 B Vreeland Rd Suite 301 Florham Park NJ 07932 973-410-4040 410-1313
Web: www.veritextllc.com
Z-Axis Corp 5445 DTC Pkwy Suite 450 Greenwood Village CO 80111 303-713-0200 713-0299
TF: 800-827-2947 ■ *Web:* www.zaxis.com

449 LIVESTOCK - WHOL

SEE ALSO Agricultural Products - Cattle Ranches, Farms, Feedlots (Beef Cattle) p. 1262; Agricultural Products - Hog Farms p. 1263

Phone | Fax

Alabama Livestock Auction Inc 700 Hwy 80 E Uniontown AL 36786 334-628-2371 628-6268
Barber Eugene & Sons Inc 395 Lisle Industrial Ave Lexington KY 40511 859-255-8751 253-2815
Blackfoot Livestock Auction 93 Rich Ln PO Box 830 Blackfoot ID 83221 208-785-0500 785-0503
Web: www.blackfootlivestockauction.com
Blue Grass Stockyard 375 Lisle Industrial Ave PO Box 1023 Lexington KY 40588 859-255-7701 255-5495
TF: 800-621-3972 ■ *Web:* www.bgstockyards.com
Capital Land & Livestock Co 4651 E FM 487 Schwertner TX 76573 254-527-3342 527-4400
Web: www.cllnet.com
Central Livestock Assn 310 Market Ln South Saint Paul MN 55075 651-451-1844 451-1774
TF: 800-733-1844 ■ *Web:* www.crinet.com
Chillicothe Livestock Market Inc Old Hwy 36 E PO Box 948 Chillicothe MO 64601 660-646-1621 646-1269
Web: www.chillicothelivestock.com
D & S Cattle Co 2167 SR 66 PO Box 172 Zolfo Springs FL 33890 863-735-1112 735-1282
TF: 800-522-0534
Delta Sales Yard 700 W 5th St Delta CO 81416 970-874-4612 874-3087
Empire Livestock Marketing LLC 5001 Brittonfield Pkwy East Syracuse NY 13035 315-433-9129 431-1328
TF: 800-462-8802 ■ *Web:* www.empirelivestock.com
Equity Co-op Livestock Sales Assn E 10890 Penny Ln Baraboo WI 53913 608-356-8311 356-0117
TF: 800-362-3989 ■ *Web:* www.equitycoop.com
Eugene Barber & Sons Inc 395 Lisle Industrial Ave Lexington KY 40511 859-255-8751 253-2815
Farmers Livestock Auction Inc 1581 E Emma Ave Springdale AR 72764 479-751-5727 751-5896
Farmers Livestock Marketing Assn
840 IL Rt 127 PO Box 435 Greenville IL 62246 618-664-1432 664-2868
TF: 800-743-9110 ■ *Web:* www.farmerslivestock.com
Finger Lakes Livestock Exchange Inc 3865 Rt 5 & 20 Canandaigua NY 14424 585-394-1515 394-9151
Web: www.fingerlakeslivestockex.com
Four States Livestock Sales 501 E 1st St Hagerstown MD 21741 301-733-8120 733-7318
High Plains Livestock Exchange LLC 28601 Hwy 34 PO Box 158 Brush CO 80723 970-842-5115 842-5088
TF: 866-842-5115 ■ *Web:* www.hplivestock.com
Keoco Auction Co Inc 603 S Warren St Sigourney IA 52591 641-622-3535 622-3429
Kidron Auction Inc 4885 Kidron Rd Kidron OH 44636 330-857-2641 857-2507
TF: 800-589-9749
Lewiston Sales Inc 21241 Dutchmans Crossing Rd Lewiston MN 55952 507-523-2112 523-2400
TF: 800-732-6334
Lynch Livestock Inc 331 3rd St NW Waucoma IA 52171 563-776-6861 776-3095
Web: www.lynchlivestock.com
Midwest Land & Cattle Co Inc PO Box 816 Olathe KS 66051 913-782-6677 782-7883
Miller Livestock Markets Inc 100 Sale Barn Rd Dequincy LA 70633 337-786-2995 786-3270

Phone | Fax

Mo-Kan Livestock Markets Inc RR 2 Box 152 Butler MO 64730 660-679-6535 679-6540
TF: 800-887-8156 ■ *Web:* www.mokanlivestock.com
O & S Cattle Co 100 Stockyards Rd Suite 106 South Saint Paul MN 55075 651-455-1102 455-8394
TF: 800-328-0124
Pipestone Livestock Auction Market 1500 7th St SE Pipestone MN 56164 507-825-3306 825-3308
Web: www.pipestonelivestock.com
Prairie Livestock LLC 3464 Barton Ferry Rd West Point MS 39773 662-494-5651 494-2672
TF: 800-647-6350 ■ *Web:* www.prairielivestock.net
Producers Livestock Auction Co 1131 N Bell St San Angelo TX 76903 325-653-3371 653-3370
Web: www.producersandcargile.com
Producers Livestock Marketing Assn 4809 S 114th St Omaha NE 68137 402-597-9189 597-9505
TF: 800-257-4046 ■ *Web:* www.plmcoop.com
Rich Prairie Livestock Exchange 96 Hwy 27 W Pierz MN 56364 320-468-2514 468-6373
Robert Winner Sons Inc 8544 SR 705 Yorkshire OH 45388 419-582-4321 582-3013
Web: www.winnersmeats.com
Sennett Sales Inc 3180 Turnpike Rd Sennett NY 13021 315-253-3579 253-3579
Sheridan Livestock Auction Co Inc PO Box 378 Rushville NE 69360 308-327-2406 327-2383
Stockmen's Livestock Market Inc E Hwy 50 PO Box 280 Yankton SD 57078 605-665-9641 665-9644
TF: 800-532-0952 ■ *Web:* www.livestock-marketing.com
Thomas Cattle Buying Services 14451 NE 20th St Williston FL 32696 352-528-4518 528-2510
TF: 800-654-1871
Topeka Auction & Marketing Inc DBA Topeka Livestock Auction
601 E Lake St Topeka IN 46571 260-593-2522 593-2258
Topeka Livestock Auction 601 E Lake St Topeka IN 46571 260-593-2522 593-2258
Torrington Livestock Markets LLC 626 W Valley Rd Torrington WY 82240 307-532-3333 532-2040
Web: www.torringtonlive.com
Turner County Stockyard 1315 US Hwy 41 S Ashburn GA 31714 229-567-3371
United Producers Inc 5909 Cleveland Ave Columbus OH 43231 614-890-6666 890-4776
TF: 800-456-3276 ■ *Web:* www.uproducers.com
Vintage Sales Stables Inc 3451 Lincoln Hwy E Paradise PA 17562 717-442-4181 442-8031
Wayland Hopkins Livestock 3634 10th St Wayland MI 49348 269-792-2296 792-8055
Wiechman Pig Co Inc 725 Schneider Fremont NE 68025 402-721-5115 727-1919
TF: 800-727-5153
Winner Livestock Auction Co 31690 Livestock Barn Rd Winner SD 57580 605-842-0451 842-3562
TF: 800-201-0451 ■ *Web:* www.winnerlivestock.com
Winner Robert Sons Inc 8544 SR 705 Yorkshire OH 45388 419-582-4321 582-3013
Web: www.winnersmeats.com
Winter Livestock Inc 11802 W Owen K Garriott Rd Enid OK 73703 580-796-2150 796-2154
Web: www.winterlivestock.com
Wisconsin Livestock Brokers Inc PO Box 13125 Green Bay WI 54307 920-865-7404 865-4001

450 LIVESTOCK & POULTRY FEEDS - PREPARED

Phone | Fax

Acco Feeds Inc 1025 China St Abilene TX 79602 325-672-3271 672-1704
TF: 800-592-4476 ■ *Web:* www.accofeeds.com
ADM Alliance Nutrition Inc 1000 N 30th St Quincy IL 62301 217-222-7100 222-4069
TF: 800-292-3333 ■ *Web:* www.admani.com
AG Partners Inc 512 S 8th St PO Box 467 Lake City MN 55041 651-345-3328 345-2212
TF: 800-772-2990
Ag Processing Inc 12700 W Dodge Rd PO Box 2047 Omaha NE 68103 402-496-7809 498-5548
TF: 800-247-1345 ■ *Web:* www.agp.com
Agri-King Inc 18246 Waller Rd Fulton IL 61252 815-589-2525 589-4700
TF: 800-435-9560 ■ *Web:* www.agriking.com
Ahrberg Milling Co 200 S Depot St PO Box 968 Cushing OK 74023 918-225-0267 225-0275
TF: 800-324-0267 ■ *Web:* www.ahrbergmilling.com
AL Gilbert Co 304 N Yosemite Ave Oakdale CA 95361 209-847-1721 847-3542
TF: 800-847-1721
Alabama Farmers Co-op Inc 121 Somerville Rd NE Decatur AL 35601 256-353-6843 350-1770
TF: 800-737-6843 ■ *Web:* www.alafarm.com
Albion Laboratories Inc 101 N Main St Clearfield UT 84015 801-773-4631 773-4633
TF: 800-453-2406 ■ *Web:* www.albion-an.com
Alderman Cave Feeds 158 N Main St PO Box 217 Winters TX 79567 325-754-4546 754-4549
TF: 800-588-3333 ■ *Web:* www.acfeeds.com
American Proteins Inc 4705 Leland Dr Cumming GA 30041 770-886-2250 886-2296
TF: 800-346-7476 ■ *Web:* www.americanproteins.com
Bagdad Roller Mills Inc 5740 Elmburg Rd PO Box 7 Bagdad KY 40003 502-747-8968 747-8960
TF: 800-928-3333 ■ *Web:* bagdadrollermills.com
Baker HJ & Bros Inc 228 Saugatuck Ave Westport CT 06880 203-682-9200 227-8351
Web: www.bakerbro.com
Belstra Milling Co Inc 424 15th St PO Box 460 Demotte IN 46310 219-987-4343 987-5227
TF: 800-276-2789 ■ *Web:* www.belstramilling.com
BioZyme Inc 6010 Stockyards Expy Saint Joseph MO 64504 816-238-3326 238-7549
TF: 800-821-3070 ■ *Web:* www.biozymeinc.com
Blair Milling & Elevator Co 1000 Main St PO Box 437 Atchison KS 66002 913-367-2310 367-3220
TF: 800-633-2931
Blue Seal Feeds Inc 15 Buttrick Rd Londonderry NH 03053 603-437-3400 437-3403
TF Cust Svc: 800-367-2730 ■ *Web:* www.blueseal.com
Buckeye Nutrition 330 E Schultz Ave PO Box 505 Dalton OH 44618 330-828-2251 828-2309
TF: 800-417-6460 ■ *Web:* www.buckeyenutrition.com
Cargill Inc Animal Nutrition Div 12900 Whitewater Dr Minnetonka MN 55343 952-984-1920
TF: 800-227-4455 ■ *Web:* www.cargillanimalnutrition.com
Cargill Inc North America 15407 McGinty Rd Wayzata MN 55391 952-742-7575
TF: 800-227-4455
Central AG Services 209 N Bridge St Clarissa MN 56440 218-756-2112 756-2451
Circle S Ranch Inc 1604 Circle S Ranch Rd Monroe NC 28112 704-764-7414 764-7646
Co-op Sampo Inc 14 Birch Ave SE PO Box 220 Menahga MN 56464 218-564-4534 564-4534
Cumberland Valley Co-op Assn 908 Mt Rock Rd Shippensburg PA 17257 717-532-2191 532-4353
TF: 800-488-2197
Cutler-Dickerson Co Inc 507 College Ave Adrian MI 49221 517-265-5191 263-4213
TF: 800-968-5191
Dairymen's Feed & Supply Co-op 323 E Washington St Petaluma CA 94952 707-763-1585 763-5239
TF: 800-862-4699
Darling International Inc 251 O'Connor Ridge Blvd Suite 300 Irving TX 75038 972-717-0300 717-1588
AMEX: DAR ■ *TF:* 800-800-4841 ■ *Web:* www.darlingii.com
DeKalb Feeds Inc 105 Dixon Ave Rock Falls IL 61071 815-625-4546
DSM Food Specialties Inc 45 Waterview Blvd Parsippany NJ 07054 800-662-4478 257-8265*
**Fax Area Code:* 973 ■ *TF:* 800-662-4478 ■ *Web:* www.dsm.com/dfs
Eagle Roller Mill Co 1101 Airport Rd Shelby NC 28150 704-487-5061 482-1263
TF: 800-223-9108 ■ *Web:* www.eaglerollermill.com
Eastern Farmers Co-op 401 S Railroad Ave Jasper MN 56144 507-348-3911 348-8835
TF: 800-865-2773
Effingham Equity Inc 201 W Roadway Ave Effingham IL 62401 217-342-4101 347-7601
TF: 800-223-1337 ■ *Web:* www.effinghamequity.com
Elenbaas Co 411 W Front St Sumas WA 98295 360-988-5811 988-0411
TF: 800-808-6954 ■ *Web:* www.elenbaasco.com
Farm Service Elevator Co 3939 County Rd 5 SW PO Box 933 Willmar MN 56201 320-235-8870 235-8879
TF: 800-328-8847
Farmer's Co-op 201 E Orin St Gordon NE 69343 308-282-0898 282-0046
TF: 800-252-0898
Farmers Co-op Elevator Co 109 Isabella St Radcliffe IA 50230 515-899-2101 899-2105
Web: www.radcliffecoop.com
Farmers Co-op Elevator Co 177 W Main St PO Box 108 Cottonwood MN 56229 507-423-5412 423-5551

Company	City	State	Zip	Phone	Fax
Farmers Union Co-op 14610 240th St E	Hastings	MN	55033	651-437-8333	
Feed Products Inc 1000 W 47th Ave	Denver	CO	80211	303-455-3646	477-6206
TF: 800-332-8285					
First Cooperative Assn 113 S Lewis Ave	Cleghorn	IA	51014	712-436-2224	436-2655
TF: 800-594-9424 ■ *Web:* www.firstcoop.com					
FL Emmert Co Inc 2007 Dunlap St	Cincinnati	OH	45214	513-721-5808	721-6087
TF: 800-441-3343 ■ *Web:* www.emmert.com					
Flint River Mills Inc 1100 Dothan Rd PO Box 280	Bainbridge	GA	39818	229-246-2232	243-7376*
**Fax:* Cust Svc ■ *TF Cust Svc:* 800-841-8502					
FM Brown's Sons Inc 127 S Furnace St PO Box 67	Birdsboro	PA	19508	610-582-2741	
TF: 800-362-6455 ■ *Web:* www.fmbrown.com					
Form-A-Feed Inc 740 Bowman St	Stewart	MN	55385	320-562-2413	562-2125
TF: 800-422-3649 ■ *Web:* www.formafeed.com					
Franklin Feed & Supply Co 1977 Philadelphia Ave	Chambersburg	PA	17201	717-264-6148	264-7865
TF: 800-722-2074					
Friona Industries LP 500 S Taylor St Suite 601	Amarillo	TX	79101	806-374-1811	374-1324
TF: 800-658-6014 ■ *Web:* www.frionaind.com					
Furst-McNess Co 120 E Clark St	Freeport	IL	61032	815-235-6151	232-9724
TF: 800-435-5131 ■ *Web:* www.mcness.com					
Goldsboro Milling Co 938 Millers Chapel Rd	Goldsboro	NC	27534	919-778-3130	778-8111
TF: 800-768-7823					
Grange Co-op Supply Assn 89 Alder St	Central Point	OR	97502	541-664-1261	664-1246
TF: 800-888-6317 ■ *Web:* www.grangecoop.com					
Griffin Industries 4221 Alexandria Pike	Cold Spring	KY	41076	859-781-2010	572-2575
TF: 800-743-7413 ■ *Web:* www.griffinind.com					
H Rockwell & Son 164 Troy St	Canton	PA	17724	570-673-5148	673-5150
TF: 888-654-6626					
Harvest Land Co-op 711 Front St	Morgan	MN	56266	507-249-3196	641-2179
TF: 800-245-5819 ■ *Web:* www.harvestland.com					
HJ Baker & Bros Inc 228 Saugatuck Ave	Westport	CT	06880	203-682-9200	227-8351
Web: www.bakerbro.com					
Hogslat Midwest Inc 200 N & Meridian Rd	Camden	IN	46917	574-967-4145	967-4742
TF: 800-735-4135					
Hubbard Feeds Inc 424 N Riverfront Dr	Mankato	MN	56001	507-388-9400	388-9453
TF: 800-869-7219 ■ *Web:* www.hubbardfeeds.com					
Hunt & Behrens Inc 30 Lakeville St	Petaluma	CA	94952	707-762-4594	762-9164
Island Dehy Inc 120 E 6th St PO Box 88	Cozad	NE	69130	308-784-2115	784-2268
J & H Milling Co Inc 101 W Mills St	Walstonburg	NC	27888	252-753-4290	753-4290
JBS United Inc 4310 W SR 38 PO Box 108	Sheridan	IN	46069	317-758-4495	758-9016
Web: www.jbsunited.com					
JD Heiskell & Co 116 W Cedar St	Tulare	CA	93274	559-685-6100	686-8697
TF: 800-366-1886 ■ *Web:* www.heiskell.com					
John A Van Den Bosch Co 4511 Holland Ave	Holland	MI	49424	616-848-2000	848-2100
TF Cust Svc: 800-968-6477 ■ *Web:* www.vbosch.com					
Kay Dee Feed Co Inc 1919 Grand Ave	Sioux City	IA	51106	712-277-2011	279-1946
TF: 800-831-4815					
Keith Smith Co Inc 130 K-Tech Ln	Hot Springs	AR	71914	501-760-0100	760-9199
Web: www.keith-smith.com					
Kemin Industries Inc 2100 Maury St	Des Moines	IA	50317	515-266-2111	559-5223
TF: 800-777-8307 ■ *Web:* www.kemin.com					
Kent Feeds Inc 1600 Oregon St	Muscatine	IA	52761	563-264-4211	264-4318*
**Fax:* Hum Res ■ *TF:* 800-552-9620					
Lackawanna Products Corp 8545 Main St	Williamsville	NY	14221	716-633-1940	634-8139
Lakeland Animal Nutrition 2725 S Combee Rd	Lakeland	FL	33803	863-682-4995	686-9427
TF: 800-682-6144 ■ *Web:* www.lanutrition.com					
Land O'Lakes Farmland Feed LLC 4001 Lexington Ave N	Arden Hills	MN	55126	651-481-2222	
TF: 800-328-9680 ■ *Web:* www.landolakesinc.com					
Land O'Lakes Inc Western Feed Div 2407 Warren Ave	Twin Falls	ID	83301	208-459-3689	454-0012
TF: 800-328-6616					
Lucta USA Inc 1829 Stanley St	Northbrook	IL	60062	847-272-6650	272-2090
TF: 800-323-5341 ■ *Web:* www.lucta.com					
Madison County Co-op 323 W Fulton St	Canton	MS	39046	601-859-1271	859-1272
Manna Pro Corp 707 Spirit 40 Park Dr Suite 150	Chesterfield	MO	63005	636-681-1700	681-1799
TF: 800-690-9908 ■ *Web:* www.mannapro.com					
Mark Hershey Farms Inc 479 Horseshoe Pike	Lebanon	PA	17042	717-867-4624	867-4313
TF: 888-801-3301 ■ *Web:* www.markhersheyfarms.com					
Merrick's Inc 2415 Parview Rd PO Box 620307	Middleton	WI	53562	608-831-3440	836-8943
TF: 800-637-7425 ■ *Web:* www.merricks.com					
MFA Inc 201 Ray Young Dr	Columbia	MO	65201	573-874-5111	876-5430
Web: www.mfaincorporated.com					
Milk Specialties Co 260 S Washington St	Carpentersville	IL	60110	847-426-3411	426-4121
TF: 800-323-5424 ■ *Web:* www.milkspecialties.com					
Modesto Tallow Co 925 Crows Landing Rd	Modesto	CA	95351	209-522-7224	575-0278
Morgan Grain & Feed Co 260 Front St PO Box 248	Morgan	MN	56266	507-249-3157	249-3507
TF: 800-449-3157					
Moroni Feed Co 15 E 1900 S PO Box 368	Moroni	UT	84646	435-436-8221	436-8101
Mountaire Corp 204 E 4th St	North Little Rock	AR	72114	501-372-6524	372-3972
Web: www.mountaire.com					
Mountaire Farms of North Carolina 203 Morris Farm Rd	Candor	NC	27229	910-974-3232	974-3165
TF: 800-284-4528					
Moyer & Son Inc 113 E Reliance Rd	Souderton	PA	18964	215-723-6000	721-2814
TF: 800-345-0419 ■ *Web:* www.emoyer.com					
Novus International Inc 530 Maryville Center Dr Suite 100	Saint Louis	MO	63141	314-576-8886	576-2148
TF: 888-906-6887 ■ *Web:* www.novusint.com					
Oberbeck Grain Co 700 Walnut St	Highland	IL	62249	618-654-2387	654-5862
TF: 800-632-2012					
OMCO Inc 214 E Mill St	Odon	IN	47562	812-636-7362	636-4777
TF: 800-274-0203					
Pennfield Corp 711 Rohrerstown Rd	Lancaster	PA	17604	717-299-2561	295-8783
TF: 800-732-0467 ■ *Web:* www.dairyfeed.com					
Pied Piper Mills Inc 423 E Lake Dr	Hamlin	TX	79520	325-576-3684	576-3460
TF: 800-338-4610 ■ *Web:* www.piedpiperpetfood.net					
Pine Manor Inc 2704 S Main St	Goshen	IN	46526	574-533-4186	533-6954
Prairie Lakes Co-op 524 Pulp St PO Box 580	Starbuck	MN	56381	320-239-2226	239-2227
TF: 800-808-1626					
Preble Feed & Grain Inc Werling Dr PO Box 52	Preble	IN	46782	260-547-4452	
TF: 800-566-4452					
Prince Agri Products Inc 1 Prince Plaza PO Box 1009	Quincy	IL	62306	217-222-8854	222-5098
Web: www.princeagri.com					
Prince Mfg Co 229 Radio Rd	Quincy	IL	62305	646-747-4200	228-0466*
**Fax Area Code:* 217 ■ *Web:* www.princemfg.com					
Producers Co-op Assoc 300 E Buffalo St PO Box 323	Girard	KS	66743	620-724-8241	724-8243
Web: www.girardcoop.com					
Quali Tech Inc 318 Lake Hazeltine Dr	Chaska	MN	55318	952-448-5151	448-3603
Web: www.qualitechco.com					
Ragland Mills Inc 14079 Hammer Rd	Neosho	MO	64850	417-451-2510	451-7499
Web: www.raglandmills.com					
Ralco Nutrition Inc 1600 Hahn Rd	Marshall	MN	56258	507-532-5748	532-5740
TF: 800-533-5306 ■ *Web:* www.ralconutrition.com					
Rangen Inc 115 13th Ave S	Buhl	ID	83316	208-543-6421	543-6090
TF: 800-657-6446 ■ *Web:* www.rangen.com					
Rivard's Quality Seeds Inc 103 Main St PO Box 303	Argyle	MN	56713	218-437-6638	437-6392
TF: 888-543-6638 ■ *Web:* www.rivards.com					
RMC Inc 1040 S High St	Harrisonburg	VA	22801	540-434-5333	434-7090
SCE 1380 Hwy 63	New Sharon	IA	50207	641-637-4097	637-4292
Web: www.scecoop.com					
Seminole Stores Inc 335 NE Watula Ave PO Box 940	Ocala	FL	34478	352-732-4143	732-5968
TF: 800-683-1881 ■ *Web:* www.seminolefeed.com					
Star Milling Co 24067 Water St	Perris	CA	92570	951-657-3143	657-3114
TF: 800-733-6455 ■ *Web:* www.starmilling.com					
Stillwater Milling Co 512 E 6th St	Stillwater	OK	74074	405-372-3445	743-3730
TF: 800-364-6804 ■ *Web:* www.stillwatermill.com					
Texas Farm Products Co 915 S Fredonia St	Nacogdoches	TX	75964	936-564-3711	560-8200
TF: 800-392-3110 ■ *Web:* www.texasfarm.com					
Triple Crown Nutrition Inc 319 Barry Ave S Suite 303	Wayzata	MN	55391	952-473-6330	473-6571
TF: 800-451-9916 ■ *Web:* www.triplecrownfeed.com					
Triple F Inc 10104 Douglas Ave	Des Moines	IA	50322	515-254-1200	276-5749
TF: 800-383-5406 ■ *Web:* www.triplef.us					
Trouw Nutrition 115 Executive Dr	Highland	IL	62249	618-654-2070	654-7012
TF: 800-365-1357 ■ *Web:* www.trouw-nutritionusa.com					
United Co-op 202 N Main St	Monona	IA	52159	563-539-2001	539-2004
TF: 800-727-5890					
United Co-op Farmers Inc 22 Kimball Pl	Fitchburg	MA	01420	978-345-4103	345-7187
TF: 800-545-6655 ■ *Web:* www.ucf-inc.com					
Ursa Farmers Co-op Inc 202 W Maple Ave PO Box 8	Ursa	IL	62376	217-964-2111	964-2260
Web: www.ursacoop.com					
Valley Proteins Inc 151 Valpro Dr	Winchester	VA	22603	540-877-2590	877-3215
Web: valleyproteins.com					
Van Den Bosch John A Co 4511 Holland Ave	Holland	MI	49424	616-848-2000	848-2100
TF Cust Svc: 800-968-6477 ■ *Web:* www.vbosch.com					
Vita Plus Corp 1508 W Badger Rd	Madison	WI	53713	608-256-1988	283-7990
TF: 800-362-8334 ■ *Web:* www.vitaplus.com					
Western Stockmens Inc 223 Rodeo Ave	Caldwell	ID	83605	208-459-0777	455-4859
TF: 800-624-9425					
Wolfkill Feed & Fertilizer Corp 217 E Stretch St PO Box 578	Monroe	WA	98272	360-794-7065	704-3561
TF: 800-525-4539					
Zeigler Brothers Inc 400 Gardner Station Rd	Gardners	PA	17324	717-677-6181	677-6826
TF: 800-841-6800 ■ *Web:* www.zeiglerfeed.com					
Zephyr Feed Co 40140 Lynbrook Dr	Zephyrhills	FL	33540	813-782-1578	788-4265

451 LOGGING

Company	City	State	Zip	Phone	Fax
B & S Logging Inc 1110 NE Laughlin Rd	Prineville	OR	97754	541-447-3175	447-7141
Barclay Contractors 612 N Brooks Camp Rd	Sisters	OR	97759	541-549-3666	549-1179
Bowater Inc Forest Products Div 5020 Hwy 11 S	Calhoun	TN	37309	423-336-2211	336-7330
Web: www.bowater.com/en/divisionsCanadianProducts.shtml					
Canal Wood LLC 2430 N Main St	Conway	SC	29528	843-488-9663	488-3515
TF: 866-587-1460 ■ *Web:* www.canalwood.com					
Crane Mills Inc 22938 South Ave	Corning	CA	96021	530-824-5427	824-3157
Croman Corp 801 Ave C	White City	OR	97503	541-826-4455	826-7430
Freres Lumber Co Inc PO Box 276	Lyons	OR	97358	503-859-2121	859-2112
Greif Inc 425 Winter Rd	Delaware	OH	43015	740-549-6000	549-6100
NYSE: GEF ■ *TF:* 800-354-7343 ■ *Web:* www.greif.com					
Harold Barclay Logging Co Inc DBA Barclay Contractors					
612 N Brooks Camp Rd	Sisters	OR	97759	541-549-3666	549-1179
Herbert C Haynes Inc 40 Rt 168 PO Box 96	Winn	ME	04495	207-736-3412	736-2900
TF: 800-432-7867					
Hopkes Logging Co Inc 2235 Hadley Rd N	Tillamook	OR	97141	503-842-2491	842-9858
Huffman & Wright Logging Inc 801 SE 3rd St PO Box 910	Canyonville	OR	97417	541-839-4251	839-6463
Web: www.huffman-wright.com					
International Forest Products Ltd (Interfor)					
1055 Sunsmuir St Suite 3500	Vancouver	BC	V7X1H7	604-689-6800	688-0313
Web: www.interfor.com					
Klukwan Inc 425 Sawmill Rd	Haines	AK	99827	907-766-2211	766-2973
TF: 800-558-5926 ■ *Web:* www.klukwan.com					
MAXXAM Group Inc 5847 San Felipe St Suite 2600	Houston	TX	77057	713-975-7600	267-3703
Midwest Walnut Co 1914 Postevin St	Council Bluffs	IA	51503	712-325-9191	325-0156
TF: 800-592-5688 ■ *Web:* www.midwestwalnut.com					
Pacific Lumber Co 125 Main St PO Box 37	Scotia	CA	95565	707-764-2222	764-4171
Web: www.palco.com					
Plum Creek Timber Co Inc 999 3rd Ave Suite 4300	Seattle	WA	98104	206-467-3600	467-3795
NYSE: PCL ■ *Web:* www.plumcreek.com					
Roseburg Forest Products Co PO Box 1088	Roseburg	OR	97470	541-679-3311	
TF: 800-548-5275 ■ *Web:* www.rfpco.com					
Sealaska Corp 1 Sealaska Plaza Suite 400	Juneau	AK	99801	907-586-1512	586-8191
Web: www.sealaska.com					
Sierra Pacific Industries 19794 Riverside Ave	Anderson	CA	96007	530-378-8000	378-8109
Web: www.sierrapacificind.com					
Squires Timber Co 143 NC Hwy 53 PO Box 549	Elizabethtown	NC	28337	910-862-3533	862-6441
Web: www.squirestimber.com					
Western Forest Products Inc 435 Trunk Rd 3rd Fl	Duncan	BC	V9L2P9	250-748-3711	748-6630
TSX: WEF ■ *Web:* www.westernforest.com					
Yeomans Wood & Timber Inc 714 Empire Expy PO Box 658	Swainsboro	GA	30401	478-237-9940	237-5098

452 LOGISTICS SERVICES (TRANSPORTATION & WAREHOUSING)

SEE ALSO Freight Forwarders p. 1676; Marine Services p. 1946; Rail Transport Services p. 2196; Trucking Companies p. 2386; Warehousing & Storage - Commercial Warehousing p. 2411

Company	City	State	Zip	Phone	Fax
A Duie Pyle Inc 650 Westtown Rd PO Box 564	West Chester	PA	19381	610-696-5800	696-3768
TF: 800-523-5020 ■ *Web:* www.pyleco.com					
ABX Logistics Inc 8200 Roberts Dr Suite 200	Atlanta	GA	30350	770-353-4200	698-0695
Web: www.abxusa.com					
Access Business Group 7575 Fulton St E	Ada	MI	49355	616-787-5358	
TF Cust Svc: 800-253-6500 ■ *Web:* www.accessbusinessgroup.com					
AIMS Logistics 311 Moore Ln	Collierville	TN	38017	901-854-5777	854-5775
TF: 877-406-9966 ■ *Web:* www.aimslogistics.com					
American Port Services 198 Gulfstream Rd PO Box 193	Savannah	GA	31402	912-966-2198	966-2791
Web: www.amportserv.com					
AN Deringer Inc 64 N Main St	Saint Albans	VT	05478	802-524-8110	524-5970
TF: 800-448-8108 ■ *Web:* www.anderinger.com					
APL Logistics Inc 1111 Broadway	Oakland	CA	94607	510-272-8000	272-7011
TF: 800-999-7733 ■ *Web:* www.apllogistics.com					
Associated Global Systems Inc					
3333 New Hyde Park Rd	New Hyde Park	NY	11042	516-627-8910	627-8851
TF Cust Svc: 800-645-8300 ■ *Web:* www.agsystems.com					
BAX Global Inc 440 Exchange	Irvine	CA	92602	714-442-4500	442-2850
TF: 800-225-5229 ■ *Web:* www.baxglobal.com					
BDP International Inc 510 Walnut St	Philadelphia	PA	19106	215-629-8900	629-8940
TF: 888-999-2379 ■ *Web:* www.bdpinternational.com					

				Phone	Fax
Bekins Co 330 S Mannheim Rd *Web:* www.bekins.com	Hillside	IL	60162	708-547-2000	
Bender Group 345 Parr Cir *TF:* 800-621-9402 ■ *Web:* www.bendergroup.com	Reno	NV	89512	775-788-8800	788-8811
BFS Global 3101 Towercreek Pkwy Suite 170 **Fax Area Code:* 678 ■ *TF:* 800-847-3865 ■ *Web:* www.bfsglobal.com	Atlanta	GA	30339	770-956-1990	560-7077*
CaseStack Inc 2850 Ocean Park Blvd Suite 100 *TF:* 866-828-7120 ■ *Web:* www.casestack.com	Santa Monica	CA	90405	310-473-8885	943-4137
Caterpillar Logistics Services Inc 500 N Morton Ave *TF:* 800-447-6434 ■ *Web:* www.catlogistics.com	Morton	IL	61550	309-266-3591	
CH Robinson Worldwide Inc 8100 Mitchell Rd Suite 200 *NASDAQ: CHRW* ■ *TF:* 800-247-5644 ■ *Web:* www.chrobinson.com	Eden Prairie	MN	55344	952-937-8500	937-6714
Clipper Exxpress Inc 9014 Heritage Pkwy Suite 300 *TF:* 800-678-2547 ■ *Web:* www.clippergroup.com	Woodridge	IL	60517	630-739-0700	739-1817
Crowley Logistics Inc 9487 Regency Sq Blvd *TF:* 800-874-6769 ■ *Web:* www.crowley.com	Jacksonville	FL	32225	904-727-2200	727-4062
CSX Intermodal Inc 301 W Bay St *TF:* 800-542-2754 ■ *Web:* www.csxi.com	Jacksonville	FL	32202	904-633-1000	633-1102
Daniel F Young Inc 1235 Westlakes Dr Suite 255 *Web:* www.dfyoung.com	Berwyn	PA	19312	610-725-4000	725-0570
Deringer AN Inc 64 N Main St *TF:* 800-448-8108 ■ *Web:* www.anderinger.com	Saint Albans	VT	05478	802-524-8110	524-5970
DHL Logistics 3435 Airborne Rd *TF:* 800-637-5502 ■ *Web:* www.dhl-usa.com/logisticsSol	Wilmington	OH	45177	937-382-6565	382-3573
Dixie Warehouse Services 6001 National Tpke PO Box 36158 *Web:* www.dixiewarehouse.com	Louisville	KY	40233	502-368-6564	366-6133
DSC Logistics 1750 S Wolf Rd *TF:* 800-372-1960 ■ *Web:* www.dsclogistics.com	Des Plaines	IL	60018	847-390-6800	390-7276
Eagle Global Logistics 15350 Vickery Dr *NASDAQ: EAGL* ■ *TF:* 800-821-9956 ■ *Web:* www.eaglegl.com	Houston	TX	77032	281-618-3100	618-3223
EGL Inc DBA Eagle Global Logistics 15350 Vickery Dr *NASDAQ: EAGL* ■ *TF:* 800-821-9956 ■ *Web:* www.eaglegl.com	Houston	TX	77032	281-618-3100	618-3223
Elston-Richards Inc 3701 Patterson Ave SE *Web:* www.elstonrichards.com	Grand Rapids	MI	49512	616-698-2698	698-8090
Exel 570 Polaris Pkwy *TF:* 800-272-1052 ■ *Web:* www.exel.com	Westerville	OH	43082	614-865-8500	865-8877
Expeditors International of Washington Inc 1015 3rd Ave 12th Fl *NASDAQ: EXPD* ■ *TF:* 800-284-7474 ■ *Web:* www.expeditors.com	Seattle	WA	98104	206-674-3400	682-9777
Express-1 Expedited Solutions Inc 429 Post Rd *AMEX: XPO* ■ *TF:* 800-800-5161 ■ *Web:* www.express-1.com	Buchanan	MI	49107	269-695-2700	695-7458
FedEx Supply Chain Services Inc 5455 Darrow Rd **Fax:* Hum Res ■ *TF:* 800-588-3020 ■ *Web:* www.fedex.com/us/supplychain/main	Hudson	OH	44236	330-342-3000	342-8037*
FedEx Trade Networks 850 SW 7th St Suite 100 *Web:* www.ftn.fedex.com	Renton	WA	98057	425-793-1900	793-8600
GeoLogistics Corp 1251 E Dyer Rd Suite 200 *Web:* www.geo-logistics.com	Santa Ana	CA	92705	714-513-3000	
Global Transporation Services Inc 1930 6th Ave S Suite 400 *TF:* 800-580-6779 ■ *Web:* www.globalcontainerline.com	Seattle	WA	98134	206-624-4354	624-2116
Griffin Transport Services Inc PO Box 11245 *TF:* 800-361-5028 ■ *Web:* www.griffintransport.com	Reno	NV	99510	775-331-8010	331-6745
Hankyu International Transport (USA) Inc 1561 Beachey Pl *Web:* www.hankyu-usa.com	Carson	CA	90746	310-884-2400	884-3777
Hanson Logistics 2900 S State St Suite 4 E *TF:* 888-772-1197 ■ *Web:* www.hansonlogisticsgroup.com	Saint Joseph	MI	49085	269-982-1390	982-1506
Highway Transport Inc PO Box 50068 *Web:* www.hytt.com	Knoxville	TN	37950	865-584-8631	584-2851
Horizon Air Freight 152-15 Rockaway Blvd *TF:* 800-221-6028 ■ *Web:* www.haf.com	Jamaica	NY	11434	718-528-3800	949-0655
Hub Group Inc 3050 Highland Pkwy Suite 100 *NASDAQ: HUBG* ■ *TF:* 800-964-2515 ■ *Web:* www.hubgroup.com	Downers Grove	IL	60515	630-271-3600	964-6475
Hunt JB Transport Services Inc 615 JB Hunt Corporate Dr *NASDAQ: JBHT* ■ **Fax:* Hum Res ■ *TF:* 800-643-3622 ■ *Web:* www.jbhunt.com	Lowell	AR	72745	479-820-0000	820-8249*
James Group International 4335 W Fort St *Web:* www.jamesgroupintl.com	Detroit	MI	48209	313-841-0070	841-5074
JB Hunt Transport Services Inc 615 JB Hunt Corporate Dr *NASDAQ: JBHT* ■ **Fax:* Hum Res ■ *TF:* 800-643-3622 ■ *Web:* www.jbhunt.com	Lowell	AR	72745	479-820-0000	820-8249*
Kenco Group Inc 2001 Riverside Dr *TF:* 800-365-7189 ■ *Web:* www.kencogroup.com	Chattanooga	TN	37406	423-756-5552	756-1529
Kintetsu World Express USA Inc 100 Jericho Quadrangle Suite 326 *TF:* 800-275-4045 ■ *Web:* www.kweusa.com	Jericho	NY	11753	516-933-7100	933-7731
Kom International 300 St-Sacrement Suite 307 *Web:* www.komintl.com	Montreal	QC	H2Y1X4	514-849-4000	849-8888
Kuehne & Nagel Inc 10 Exchange Pl 19th Fl *Web:* www.kn-portal.com	Jersey City	NJ	07302	201-413-5500	413-5777
L & L Oil Gas Services 3421 N Causeway Blvd Suite 502 *TF:* 800-445-6482 ■ *Web:* www.lloil.com/	Metairie	LA	70002	504-832-8600	832-8620
Landstar Logistics Inc 13410 Sutton Park Dr S **Fax Area Code:* 800 ■ *TF:* 800-872-9400 ■ *Web:* www.landstar.com	Jacksonville	FL	32224	904-399-8909	872-8574*
Leicht Transfer & Storage Co 1401 State St PO Box 2447 *TF:* 800-338-5665 ■ *Web:* www.leichtgb.com	Green Bay	WI	54306	920-432-8632	432-4130
Matson Integrated Logistics Inc 1815 S Meyers Rd Suite 700 *TF:* 866-640-6050 ■ *Web:* www.matson.com	Villa Park	IL	60181	630-203-3500	916-4931
McLean Cargo Specialists Inc 1310 Rankin Rd *Web:* www.mclean-cargo.com	Houston	TX	77073	281-443-2777	443-3777
Menlo Worldwide Inc 2855 Campus Dr Suite 300 *TF:* 800-227-1981 ■ *Web:* www.menloworldwide.com	San Mateo	CA	94403	650-378-5200	357-9160
Meridian IQ 10990 Roe Ave *TF:* 877-246-4909 ■ *Web:* www.meridianiq.com	Overland Park	KS	66211	913-906-6800	906-6996
MHF Logistical Solutions Inc 800 Cranberry Woods Dr Suite 450 *TF:* 877-452-9300 ■ *Web:* www.mhfls.com	Cranberry Township	PA	16066	724-772-9800	772-9850
Mitsui & Co (USA) Inc 200 Park Ave 36th Fl *NASDAQ: MITSY* ■ *Web:* www.mitsui.com	New York	NY	10166	212-878-4000	878-4800
National Freight Inc 71 W Park Ave *TF:* 800-922-5088 ■ *Web:* www.natlfreight.com	Vineland	NJ	08360	856-691-7000	
Navis Logistics Network 5675 DTC Blvd Suite 280 *TF:* 800-525-6309 ■ *Web:* www.gonavis.com	Greenwood Village	CO	80111	303-741-6626	741-6653
Pacer Global Logistics 6805 Perimeter Dr *TF:* 800-837-7584 ■ *Web:* www.pacerglobal.com	Dublin	OH	43016	614-923-1400	923-1410
Pacific CMA Inc 153-04 Rockaway Blvd *AMEX: PAM* ■ *Web:* www.pacificcma.com	Jamaica	NY	11434	212-247-0049	247-0245
Panalpina 1776 On-the-Green 67 E Park Pl *TF:* 866-202-0377 ■ *Web:* www.panalpina.com	Morristown	NJ	07960	973-683-9000	254-5799
Park-Ohio Holdings Corp 23000 Euclid Ave *NASDAQ: PKOH* ■ *Web:* www.pkoh.com	Cleveland	OH	44117	216-692-7200	692-7174
PBB Global Logistics 33 Walnut St *Web:* www.pbb.com	Fort Erie	ON	L2A1S7	905-871-6500	871-6066
Penske Logistics Rt 10 Pheasant Rd PO box 563 **Fax:* Sales ■ *Web:* www.penskelogistics.com	Reading	PA	19603	610-775-6000	856-7056*
Pierce Distribution Services Co 2028 E Riverside Blvd PO Box 15600 *TF:* 800-466-7397 ■ *Web:* www.piercedistribution.com	Loves Park	IL	61132	815-636-5650	636-5660
Pilot Air Freight Corp 314 N Middletown Rd *TF Cust Svc:* 800-447-4568 ■ *Web:* www.pilotair.com	Lima	PA	19037	610-891-8100	565-4267
Progistix-Solutions Inc 20 Norelco Dr Suite 100 *TF:* 800-277-6447 ■ *Web:* www.progistix.com	Toronto	ON	M9L1S2	416-401-7000	401-7151
Pyle A Duie Inc 650 Westtown Rd PO Box 564 *TF:* 800-523-5020 ■ *Web:* www.pyleco.com	West Chester	PA	19381	610-696-5800	696-3768
ROACO Logistics Services 500 Country Club Dr *Web:* www.roaco.com	Bensenville	IL	60106	630-379-0958	993-2355
Robinson CH Worldwide Inc 8100 Mitchell Rd Suite 200 *NASDAQ: CHRW* ■ *TF:* 800-247-5644 ■ *Web:* www.chrobinson.com	Eden Prairie	MN	55344	952-937-8500	937-6714
Ryder System Inc 11690 NW 105th St *NYSE: R* ■ *TF:* 800-327-3399 ■ *Web:* www.ryder.com	Miami	FL	33178	305-500-3726	500-4599
Saddle Creek Corp 3010 Saddle Creek Rd *Web:* www.saddlecrk.com	Lakeland	FL	33801	863-665-0966	667-1813
Schenker Inc 150 Albany Ave *Web:* www.schenkerusa.com	Freeport	NY	11520	516-377-3000	377-3092
Schneider Logistics Inc 3101 S Packerland Dr *TF:* 800-525-9358 ■ *Web:* www.schneiderlogistics.com	Green Bay	WI	54306	920-592-2000	592-2517
Seko Worldwide Inc 1100 Arlington Heights Rd *TF:* 800-323-1235 ■ *Web:* www.sekoworldwide.com	Itasca	IL	60143	630-919-4800	773-9179
SOS (Store Opening Solutions) 800 Middle Tennessee Blvd *TF:* 877-388-9262 ■ *Web:* www.store-solutions.com	Murfreesboro	TN	37129	615-867-0858	867-4740
Store Opening Solutions (SOS) 800 Middle Tennessee Blvd *TF:* 877-388-9262 ■ *Web:* www.store-solutions.com	Murfreesboro	TN	37129	615-867-0858	867-4740
Thoroughbred Direct Intermodal Services 2260 Butler Pike Suite 400 *TF:* 877-250-2902 ■ *Web:* www.ns-direct.com	Plymouth Meeting	PA	19462	610-567-3360	567-3389
Titan Global Distribution 1100 Corporate Sq Suite 150 *TF:* 800-325-4074 ■ *Web:* www.titanglobal.com	Saint Louis	MO	63132	314-817-0051	817-0070
TNT Logistics North America 10751 Deerwood Park Blvd Suite 200 *TF:* 888-564-4789 ■ *Web:* www.tntlogistics.com	Jacksonville	FL	32256	904-928-1400	928-1410
TRANSFLO Corp 6735 Southpoint Dr S MC J975 *Web:* www.transflo.net	Jacksonville	FL	32216	904-279-6310	245-2136
TransMontaigne Inc 1670 Broadway Suite 3100 *NYSE: TMG* ■ *Web:* www.transmontaigne.com	Denver	CO	80217	303-626-8200	626-8228
TransOceanic Shipping Co Inc 3850 N Causeway Blvd Suite 1330 *Web:* www.transoceanic.com	Metairie	LA	70002	504-465-1000	465-1023
Transplace 5800 Granite Pkwy Suite 1000 *Web:* www.transplace.com	Plano	TX	75024	972-731-4500	731-4501
Unitrans International Corp 709 S Hindry Ave *Web:* www.unitrans-us.com	Inglewood	CA	90301	310-410-7676	410-1719
UPS Supply Chain Solutions 12380 Morris Rd **Fax Area Code:* 770 ■ *TF:* 800-982-9170 ■ *Web:* www.ups-scs.com	Alpharetta	GA	30005	678-746-4100	994-3125*
UTi Worldwide Inc 230-39 International Airport Center Blvd Suite 1000 *NASDAQ: UTIW* ■ *Web:* www.go2uti.com	Springfield Gardens	NY	11413	516-394-6200	
Vimich Traffic Logistics 12201 Tecumseh Rd E *TF:* 800-284-1045 ■ *Web:* www.vimich.com	Tecumseh	ON	N8N1M3	519-735-6933	735-4309
Weber Distribution Inc 13530 Rosecrans Ave *Web:* www.weberdistribution.com	Santa Fe Springs	CA	90670	562-802-8802	802-9792
Young Daniel F Inc 1235 Westlakes Dr Suite 255 *Web:* www.dfyoung.com	Berwyn	PA	19312	610-725-4000	725-0570

453 LONG-TERM CARE FACILITIES

SEE ALSO Long-Term Care Facilities Operators p. 1922; Retirement Communities p. 2297; Veterans Nursing Homes - State p. 2403

Free-standing facilities accredited by the Joint Commission on Accreditation of Healthcare Organizations. Listings in this category are organized alphabetically by states.

				Phone	Fax
Canterbury Health Facility 1720 Knowles Rd	Phenix City	AL	36869	334-291-0485	297-5816
Laurelton Rehabilitation & Nursing Center 850 NW 9th St	Alabaster	AL	35007	205-663-3859	663-9791
Mercy Medical 101 Villa Dr *Web:* www.mercymedical.com	Daphne	AL	36526	251-626-2694	621-4463
Northside Health Care 700 Hutchins Ave	Gadsden	AL	35901	256-543-7101	543-2367
Catalina Care Center 2611 N Warren Ave	Tucson	AZ	85719	520-795-9574	321-4983
Coronado Care Center 11411 N 19th Ave	Phoenix	AZ	85029	602-256-7500	943-7697
East Mesa Care Center 51 S 48th St	Mesa	AZ	85206	480-832-8333	830-2466
La Mesa Rehabilitation & Care Center 2470 S Arizona Ave	Yuma	AZ	85364	928-344-8541	344-0823
Osborn Health & Rehabilitation 3333 N Civic Center Plaza	Scottsdale	AZ	85251	480-994-1333	990-3895
Calistoga Gardens 1715 Washington St	Calistoga	CA	94515	707-942-6253	942-6288
Casa Colina Center for Rehabilitation 255 E Bonita Ave *TF:* 800-926-5462 ■ *Web:* www.casacolina.org	Pomona	CA	91769	909-596-7733	596-7845
Chapman Harbor Skilled Nursing Facility 12232 Chapman Ave	Garden Grove	CA	92840	714-971-5517	748-7851
Clear View Sanitarium & Convalescent Center 15823 S Western Ave	Gardena	CA	90247	310-538-2323	538-3509
Covina Rehabilitation Center 261 W Badillo St **Fax:* Admitting	Covina	CA	91723	626-967-3874	967-5724*
Driftwood Health Care Center 4109 Emerald St	Torrance	CA	90503	310-371-4628	214-1882
Encinitas Nursing & Rehabilitation Center 900 Santa Fe Dr	Encinitas	CA	92024	760-753-6423	753-4979
English Oaks Nursing & Rehabilitation Center 2633 W Rumble Rd	Modesto	CA	95350	209-577-1001	577-0366
Evergreen Convalescent Hospital & Rehabilitation Center 1527 Springs Rd	Vallejo	CA	94591	707-643-2793	554-2876
Evergreen Rehabilitation & Care Center 2030 Evergreen Ave *Web:* www.evergreencare.com	Modesto	CA	95350	209-577-1055	550-3615
Extended Care Hospital Westminster 206 Hospital Cir	Westminster	CA	92683	714-891-2769	893-1014
Fairfield Nursing & Rehabilitation Center 1255 Travis Blvd	Fairfield	CA	94533	707-425-0623	425-0704
French Park Care Center 600 E Washington Ave *Web:* www.frenchparkcenter.com	Santa Ana	CA	92701	714-973-1656	836-4349
Gateway Care & Rehabilitation Center 26660 Patrick Ave	Hayward	CA	94544	510-782-1845	782-9913
Gladstone Care & Rehabilitation Center 435 E Gladstone St *Web:* www.gladstonecare.com	Glendora	CA	91740	626-963-5955	963-8683
Grand Terrace Healthcare Center 12000 Mt Vernon Ave	Grand Terrace	CA	92313	909-825-5221	783-4811
Hanford Nursing & Rehabilitation Hospital 1007 W Lacey Blvd	Hanford	CA	93230	559-582-2871	582-5853
Heritage Rehabilitation Center 21414 S Vermont Ave	Torrance	CA	90502	310-320-8714	320-1809
Huntington Valley Health Care Center 8382 Newman Ave	Huntington Beach	CA	92647	714-842-5551	848-5359
La Jolla Nursing & Rehabilitation Center 2552 Torrey Pines Rd	La Jolla	CA	92037	858-453-5810	452-4301
La Mariposa Care & Rehabilitation 1244 Travis Blvd	Fairfield	CA	94533	707-422-7750	422-7818
New Orange Hills 5017 E Chapman Ave *Web:* www.neworangehills.com	Orange	CA	92869	714-997-7090	997-4631
Orinda Convalescent Hospital 11 Altarinda Rd	Orinda	CA	94563	925-254-6500	254-9063

				Phone	Fax
Pacific Coast Manor 1935 Wharf Rd	Capitola	CA	95010	831-476-0770	476-0737
Pacifica Nursing & Rehabilitation Center 385 Esplanade Ave	Pacifica	CA	94044	650-993-5576	359-9388
Park Anaheim HealthCare Center 3435 W Ball Rd	Anaheim	CA	92804	714-827-5880	827-4015
Park Regency Care Center 1770 W La Habra Blvd	La Habra	CA	90631	562-691-8810	697-8478
Web: parkcentercare.com					
Sea Cliff Health Care Center 18811 Florida St	Huntington Beach	CA	92648	714-847-3515	847-2852
Seton Medical Center Coastside 600 Marine Blvd	Moss Beach	CA	94038	650-728-5521	728-5314
Web: www.dochs.org					
Subacute Saratoga Children's Hospital 13425 Sousa Ln	Saratoga	CA	95070	408-378-8875	378-7419
Web: www.subacutesaratoga.com					
SunBridge Brittany Care Center 3900 Garfield Ave	Carmichael	CA	95608	916-481-6455	481-6489
SunBridge Care & Rehabilitation for Carmichael 8336 Fair Oaks Blvd	Carmichael	CA	95608	916-944-3100	944-4202
SunBridge Care & Rehabilitation for Tustin 2210 E 1st St	Santa Ana	CA	92705	714-547-7091	547-4516
SunBridge Heritage Care Center 9107 N Davis Rd	Stockton	CA	95209	209-478-6488	952-1782
Tulare Nursing & Rehabilitation 680 E Merritt Ave	Tulare	CA	93274	559-686-8581	686-5393
Tunnell Center for Rehabilitation and Healthcare 1359 Pine St	San Francisco	CA	94109	415-673-8405	563-2174
Web: www.tunnellrehab.com					
Villa Maria Care Center 425 E Barcellus Ave	Santa Maria	CA	93454	805-922-3558	922-5548
Village Square Nursing & Rehabilitation Center 1586 W San Marcos Blvd	San Marcos	CA	92078	760-471-2986	471-5176
Windsor Rehabilitation Care Center 3806 Clayton Rd	Concord	CA	94521	925-689-2266	689-0509
Web: www.windsorcares.com					
Boulder Manor 4685 Baseline Rd	Boulder	CO	80303	303-494-0535	494-0162
Ashlar of Newtown 139 Totey Hill Rd PO Box 5505	Newtown	CT	06470	203-426-5847	364-3160
Avon Health Center Inc 652 W Avon Rd	Avon	CT	06001	860-673-2521	675-1101
Branford Hills Health Care Center 189 Alps Rd	Branford	CT	06405	203-481-6221	483-1893
Web: www.bhhcc.com					
Brook Hollow Health Care Center 55 Kondracki Ln	Wallingford	CT	06492	203-265-6771	284-3883
Web: www.brookhollowhealthcarecenter.com					
Cedar Lane Rehabilitation & Health Care Center 128 Cedar Ave	Waterbury	CT	06705	203-757-9271	753-3672
Web: www.cedarlanerehabilitationandhealthcarecenter.com					
Clifton House Rehabilitation Center 181 Clifton St	New Haven	CT	06513	203-467-1666	469-7213
Connecticut Health of Southport 930 Mill Hill Terr	Southport	CT	06890	203-259-7894	254-3720
Web: www.cthealthfacilities.com/southport/southport_home.html					
Danbury Health Care Center 107 Osborne St	Danbury	CT	06810	203-792-8102	791-1441*
*Fax: Admitting					
Darien Health Care Center 599 Boston Post Rd	Darien	CT	06820	203-655-7727	655-6718
Elim Park Baptist Home Inc 140 Cook Hill Rd	Cheshire	CT	06410	203-272-3547	271-7794
Web: www.elimpark.org					
Golden Hill Health Care Center 2028 Bridgeport Ave	Milford	CT	06460	203-877-0371	877-6185
Harborside Healthcare - Glen Hill 1 Glen Hill Rd	Danbury	CT	06811	203-744-2840	792-1521
Web: www.harborsidehealthcare.com					
Haven Health Center of Danielson 111 Westcott Rd	Danielson	CT	06239	860-774-9540	774-9703
Web: www.havenhealthcare.com					
Haven Health Center of Sound View 1 Care Ln	West Haven	CT	06516	203-934-7955	934-1038
Web: www.havenhealthcare.com					
Haven Health Center of Waterford 171 Rope Ferry Rd	Waterford	CT	06385	860-443-8357	447-8351
Web: www.havenhealthcare.com					
Haven Health Center of Windham 595 Valley St	Willimantic	CT	06226	860-423-2597	450-7070
Web: www.havenhealthcare.com					
Health Center of Greater Waterbury 177 Whitewood Rd	Waterbury	CT	06708	203-757-9491	575-1714
Hebrew Home & Hospital 1 Abrahms Blvd	West Hartford	CT	06117	860-523-3800	523-3949
Web: www.hebrew-home-hospital.org					
Highlands Health Care Center 745 Highland Ave	Cheshire	CT	06410	203-272-7285	250-6068*
*Fax: Admitting					
Jewish Home for the Elderly of Fairfield County 175 Jefferson St	Fairfield	CT	06825	203-365-6400	374-8082
Web: www.jhe.org					
Kent Ltd 46 Maple St	Kent	CT	06757	860-927-5368	927-1594
TF: 800-353-5368					
Manchester Manor 385 W Center St	Manchester	CT	06040	860-646-0129	645-0313
Web: www.manchestermanorct.com					
Mariner Health Care at Bride Brook 23 Liberty Way	Niantic	CT	06357	860-739-4007	739-3880
Masonic Healthcare Center 22 Masonic Ave	Wallingford	CT	06492	203-679-5900	679-6459
Web: www.masonicare.org					
Miller Memorial Community 360 Broad St	Meriden	CT	06450	203-237-8815	630-3714
Web: www.emmci.org					
Montowese Health & Rehabilitation Center Inc 163 Quinnipiac Ave	North Haven	CT	06473	203-624-3303	789-4433
Web: www.montowesehealth.com					
Newington Health Care Center 240 Church St	Newington	CT	06111	860-667-2256	667-6367
Noble Horizons 17 Cobble Rd	Salisbury	CT	06068	860-435-9851	435-0636
Web: www.noblehorizons.org					
Pendleton Health & Rehabilitation Center 44 Maritime Dr	Mystic	CT	06355	860-572-1700	572-7830
River Glen Health Care Center 162 S Britain Rd	Southbury	CT	06488	203-264-9600	264-9603
Sharon Health Care Center 27 Hospital Hill Rd	Sharon	CT	06069	860-364-1002	364-0237
Subacute Center of Bristol 23 Fair St	Forestville	CT	06010	860-589-2923	589-3148
Summit at Plantsville 261 Summit St	Plantsville	CT	06479	860-628-0364	628-9166
Valerie Manor Inc 1360 Torringford St	Torrington	CT	06790	860-489-1008	496-9252
Vernon Manor Health Care Center 180 Regan Rd	Vernon	CT	06066	860-871-0385	871-9098
Watrous Nursing Center 9 Neck Rd	Madison	CT	06443	203-245-9483	245-4668
Waveny Care Center 3 Farm Rd	New Canaan	CT	06840	203-594-5200	594-5327
Web: www.waveny.org					
West Hartford Health & Rehabilitation Center 130 Loomis Dr	West Hartford	CT	06107	860-521-8700	521-7452
Web: www.westhartfordhealth.com					
West River Health Care Center 245 Orange Ave	Milford	CT	06460	203-876-5123	876-5129
Westport Health Care Center 1 Burr Rd	Westport	CT	06880	203-226-4201	221-4766
Wethersfield Health Care Center 341 Jordan Ln	Wethersfield	CT	06109	860-563-0101	257-6107
Armed Forces Retirement Home - Washington 3700 N Capitol St NW	Washington	DC	20011	202-730-3011	730-3155
Web: www.afrh.gov					
Bay Pointe Nursing Pavilion 4201 31st St S	Saint Petersburg	FL	33712	727-867-1104	867-9837
Bayside Rehabilitation & Health Center 811 Jackson St N	Saint Petersburg	FL	33705	727-896-3651	821-2453
Boca Raton Rehabilitation Center 755 Meadows Rd	Boca Raton	FL	33486	561-391-5200	391-0685
Web: www.flcare.com					
Consulate Health Care of Brandon 701 Victoria St	Brandon	FL	33510	813-681-4220	689-5685
Web: www.tandemhealthcare.com					
Consulate Health Care at Lake Parker 2020 W Lake Parker Dr	Lakeland	FL	33805	863-682-7580	683-9564
Web: www.tandemhealthcare.com					
Consulate Health Care of Tallahassee 1650 Phillips Rd	Tallahassee	FL	32308	850-942-9868	942-1074
Web: www.tandemhealthcare.com					
Harmony Health Center at Greenbriar 9820 N Kendall Dr	Miami	FL	33176	305-271-6311	274-5880
Heartland Health Care Center Boynton Beach 3600 Old Boynton Rd	Boynton Beach	FL	33436	561-736-9992	364-9527
Heartland Health Care Center Miami Lakes 5725 NW 186th St	Hialeah	FL	33015	305-625-9857	625-1988
TF: 800-427-4397					
Heartland Health Care & Rehabilitation Center 7225 Boca Del Mar Dr	Boca Raton	FL	33433	561-362-9644	391-8295
Heartland Health Care & Rehabilitation Center 5401 Sawyer Rd	Sarasota	FL	34233	941-925-3427	925-8469
Heartland South Jacksonville 3648 University Blvd S	Jacksonville	FL	32216	904-733-7440	448-9425
Leesburg Health & Rehabilitation LLC 715 E Dixie Ave	Leesburg	FL	34748	352-728-3020	728-6071
ManorCare Health Services - Carrollwood 3030 W Bearss Ave	Tampa	FL	33618	813-968-8777	961-5189
Web: www.hcr-manorcare.com					
Moody Manor Inc 7150 Holatee Trail	Southwest Ranches	FL	33330	954-434-2016	434-0561

				Phone	Fax
Palmetto Health Center 6750 W 22nd Ct	Hialeah	FL	33016	305-823-3119	825-8255
River Garden Hebrew Home for the Aged 11401 Old St Augustine Rd	Jacksonville	FL	32258	904-260-1818	260-9733
Web: www.rivergarden.org					
Southern Pines Nursing Center 6140 Congress St	New Port Richey	FL	34653	727-842-8402	841-8060
Tandem Health Care of Orange Park 1215 Kingsley Ave	Orange Park	FL	32073	904-269-8922	269-1346
Web: www.tandemhealthcare.com					
Woods of Manatee Springs 5627 9th St E	Bradenton	FL	34203	941-753-8941	753-7576
Briarcliff Haven Healthcare & Rehabiliation Center 1000 Briarcliff Rd NE	Atlanta	GA	30306	404-875-6456	874-4606
Web: www.thicare.com/BriarcliffHavenHealthcare					
Family Life Enrichment Centers Inc PO Box 10	High Shoals	GA	30645	706-769-7738	769-5944
Web: www.familylifecare.org					
Oak Manor & Pine Manor Nursing Homes Inc PO Box 9696	Columbus	GA	31908	706-324-0387	324-0927
Island Nursing Home 1205 Alexander St	Honolulu	HI	96826	808-946-5027	947-6202
Kula Hospital 100 Keokea Pl	Kula	HI	96790	808-878-1221	878-1791
Web: www.kula.hhsc.org					
Alma Nelson Manor Inc 550 S Mulford Rd	Rockford	IL	61108	815-399-4914	484-1024
Anchorage of Bensenville 111 E Washington St	Bensenville	IL	60106	630-766-5800	766-5473
Apostolic Christian Restmor Inc 935 E Jefferson St	Morton	IL	61550	309-266-7141	266-7877
Ballard Healthcare Residence 9300 Ballard Rd	Des Plaines	IL	60016	847-294-2300	299-4012
Web: www.ballardhealthcare.com					
Barton W Stone Christian Home 873 Grove St	Jacksonville	IL	62650	217-479-3400	243-8553
Bethany Terrace Nursing Centre 8425 N Waukegan Rd	Morton Grove	IL	60053	847-965-8100	965-0114
Web: www.bethanyterrace.org					
Brentwood North Nursing & Rehabilitation Center 3705 Deerfield Rd	Riverwoods	IL	60015	847-459-1200	947-9005
Web: www.boulevardhealthcare.com					
Brentwood Subacute Rehabilitation Center 5400 W 87th St	Burbank	IL	60459	708-423-1200	423-8405
Community Nursing & Rehabilitation Center 1136 N Mill St	Naperville	IL	60563	630-355-3300	355-1417
Web: www.cnrcllc.com					
Douglas Rehabilitation & Care Center 3516 Powell Ln	Mattoon	IL	61938	217-234-6401	258-3300
Evenglow Lodge Inc 215 E Washington St	Pontiac	IL	61764	815-844-6131	842-3558
Web: www.evenglowlodge.org					
Fairview Baptist Home 250 Village Dr	Downers Grove	IL	60516	630-769-6200	769-6226
Heartland Health Care Center Canton 2081 N Main St	Canton	IL	61520	309-647-6135	647-6141
John C Proctor Endowment 2724 W Reservoir Blvd	Peoria	IL	61615	309-685-6580	566-4292
Web: www.proctorendowment.org					
Lieberman Geriatric Health Centre 9700 Gross Point Rd	Skokie	IL	60076	847-674-7210	674-6366
ManorCare Health Services - Arlington Heights 715 W Central Rd	Arlington Heights	IL	60005	847-392-2020	392-0174
ManorCare Health Services - Homewood 940 Maple Ave	Homewood	IL	60430	708-799-0244	799-1505
TF: 800-427-4012					
ManorCare Health Services - Oak Lawn East 9401 S Kostner Ave	Oak Lawn	IL	60453	708-423-7882	423-7947
TF: 800-427-1902					
Norridge Health Care & Rehabilitation Center 7001 W Cullom Ave	Norridge	IL	60706	708-457-0700	457-8852
Web: www.norridgecare.com					
North Adams Home Inc 2259 E 1100th St	Mendon	IL	62351	217-936-2137	936-2818
Oakton Pavilion Healthcare Facility Inc 1660 Oakton Pl	Des Plaines	IL	60018	847-299-5588	493-6525
OSF Saint Clare Home 5533 N Galena Rd	Peoria Heights	IL	61616	309-682-5428	682-8478
Web: www.osfhealthcare.org/scnh					
Piatt County Nursing Home 1111 N State St	Monticello	IL	61856	217-762-2506	762-6325
Pinecrest Manor 414 S Wesley Ave	Mount Morris	IL	61054	815-734-4103	734-7318
Plymouth Place Inc 315 N LaGrange Rd	La Grange Park	IL	60526	708-354-0340	482-6847
Web: www.plymouthplace.org					
Proctor John C Endowment 2724 W Reservoir Blvd	Peoria	IL	61615	309-685-6580	566-4292
Web: www.proctorendowment.org					
Regency Nursing Centre 6631 N Milwaukee Ave	Niles	IL	60714	847-647-7444	647-6403
Web: www.regencyhealthcare.com					
Sherman West Court 1950 Larkin Ave	Elgin	IL	60123	847-742-7070	742-7248
Sherwin Manor Nursing Center 7350 N Sheridan Rd	Chicago	IL	60626	773-274-1000	274-2353
Web: www.sherwinmanornursing.com					
Cambridge Manor 8530 Township Line Rd	Indianapolis	IN	46260	317-876-9955	876-6016
Canterbury Nursing & Rehabilitation Center 2827 Northgate Blvd	Fort Wayne	IN	46835	260-485-9691	492-1699
Heritage Center 1201 W Buena Vista Rd	Evansville	IN	47710	812-429-0700	429-1849
TF: 800-704-0700 ■ *Web:* www.holidayhealthcare.com					
Miller's Merry Manor 1500 Grant St	Huntington	IN	46750	260-356-5713	356-8671
Web: www.millersmerrymanor.com					
Miller's Merry Manor 200 26th St PO Box 480	Logansport	IN	46947	574-722-4006	753-8753
Web: www.millersmerrymanor.com					
Miller's Merry Manor 612 E 11th St	Rushville	IN	46173	765-932-4127	932-3054
Northwest Manor Health Care Center 6440 W 34th St	Indianapolis	IN	46224	317-293-4930	291-1543
Saint Vincent Pediatric Rehabilitation Center 1707 W 86th St	Indianapolis	IN	46260	317-415-5500	415-5595
TF: 866-338-2345 ■ *Web:* www.stvincent.org					
Vermillion Convalescent Center 1705 S Main St	Clinton	IN	47842	765-832-3573	832-3420
Waters of Covington 1600 E Liberty St	Covington	IN	47932	765-793-4818	793-5047
Web: www.thewaters.net					
Anamosa Care Center 1209 E 3rd St	Anamosa	IA	52205	319-462-4356	462-5038
Bettendorf Health Care Center 2730 Crow Creek Rd PO Box 1026	Bettendorf	IA	52722	563-332-7463	332-3656
Danville Care Center 401 S Birch St	Danville	IA	52623	319-392-4259	392-8350
Edgewood Convalescent Home PO Box 39	Edgewood	IA	52042	563-928-6461	928-6462
Great River Care Center 1400 W Main St PO Box 370	McGregor	IA	52157	563-873-3527	873-3723
Lone Tree Health Care Center 501 E Pioneer Rd	Lone Tree	IA	52755	319-629-4255	629-4505
Monticello Nursing & Rehabilitation Center 500 Pinehaven Dr	Monticello	IA	52310	319-465-5415	465-3205
New Hampton Nursing & Rehabilitation Center 703 S 4th Ave	New Hampton	IA	50659	641-394-4153	394-5483
New London Nursing & Rehabilitation Center 100 Care Cir PO Box 136	New London	IA	52645	319-367-5753	367-2003
Saint Luke's Living Center East 1220 5th Ave SE	Cedar Rapids	IA	52403	319-366-8701	366-8702
Web: www.livingcentereast.com					
Saint Luke's Living Center West 1050 4th Ave SE	Cedar Rapids	IA	52403	319-366-8714	366-8854
State Center Nursing & Rehabilitation Center 702 3rd St NW	State Center	IA	50247	641-483-2812	483-2675
Wheatland Manor Inc PO Box 369	Wheatland	IA	52777	563-374-1295	374-1107
Christopher East Health Care Center 4200 Brown's Ln	Louisville	KY	40220	502-459-8900	459-5026
Web: www.hcr-manorcare.com					
Winchester Centre for Health & Rehabilitation 200 Glenway Rd	Winchester	KY	40391	859-744-1800	744-0285
Brewer Rehabilitation & Living Center 74 Parkway S	Brewer	ME	04412	207-989-7300	989-4240
Russell Park Manor 158 Russell St	Lewiston	ME	04240	207-786-0691	782-8094
Fox Chase Rehabilitation & Nursing Center 2015 E West Hwy	Silver Spring	MD	20910	301-587-2400	587-2404
Web: www.foxchaserehabilitationandnursingcenter.com					
FutureCare Canton Harbor 1300 S Ellwood Ave	Baltimore	MD	21224	410-342-6644	327-3949
Web: www.futurecarehealth.com					
Keswick Multi-Care Center 700 W 40th St	Baltimore	MD	21211	410-235-8860	235-7425
Web: www.keswick-multicare.org					
Levindale Hebrew Geriatric Center & Hospital 2434 W Belvedere Ave	Baltimore	MD	21215	410-466-8700	601-2890
Web: www.lifebridgehealth.org/levindale					
ManorCare Health Services - Rossville 6600 Ridge Rd	Baltimore	MD	21237	410-574-4950	391-4386

Facility	City	State	Zip	Phone	Fax
ManorCare Health Services - Ruxton 7001 N Charles St	Towson	MD	21204	410-821-9600	337-8313
Woodside Center 9101 2nd Ave	Silver Spring	MD	20910	301-588-5544	588-5547
Braintree Landing Skilled Nursing & Rehabilitation Center 95 Commercial St	Braintree	MA	02184	781-848-3678	356-8559
Briarwood Healthcare Nursing Center 150 Lincoln St	Needham	MA	02492	781-449-4040	449-4129
Brook Farm Rehabilitation & Nursing Center 1190 VFW Pkwy	West Roxbury	MA	02132	617-325-1688	469-5673
Brookline Health Care Center 99 Park St	Brookline	MA	02446	617-731-1050	731-6516
Cedar Hill Health Care Center 49 Thomas Patten Dr	Randolph	MA	02368	781-961-1160	963-5744
Chestnut Hill Rehabilitation & Nursing Center 32 Chestnut St	East Longmeadow	MA	01028	413-525-1893	525-8261
Colonial Nursing & Rehabilitation Inc 125 Broad St	Weymouth	MA	02188	781-337-3121	337-9831
Eastpointe Rehabilitation & Skilled Care Center 255 Central Ave	Chelsea	MA	02150	617-884-5700	884-7005
Essex Park Nursing & Rehabilitation Center 265 Essex St	Beverly	MA	01915	978-927-3260	922-8347
Fairview Commons Nursing & Rehabilitation Center 151 Christian Hill Rd	Great Barrington	MA	01230	413-528-4560	528-5691
Web: www.fairviewcommons.org					
Harrington House Nursing & Rehabilitation Center 160 Main St	Walpole	MA	02081	508-660-3080	660-1634
Holyoke Rehabilitation Center 260 Easthampton Rd	Holyoke	MA	01040	413-538-9733	538-9919
TF: 800-394-9733					
Jewish Nursing Home of Western Massachusetts Inc 770 Converse St	Longmeadow	MA	01106	413-567-6211	567-2477*
**Fax:* Admitting					
JML Care Center 184 Ter Heun Dr	Falmouth	MA	02540	508-457-4621	457-1218
Web: www.capecodhealthcare.org					
John Scott House Nursing & Rehabilitation Center 233 Middle St	Braintree	MA	02184	781-843-1860	843-8834
Lexington Health Care Center 178 Lowell St	Lexington	MA	02420	781-862-7400	862-5021
Web: www.lexingtonhcc.com					
Lowell Health Care Center 19 Varnum St	Lowell	MA	01850	978-454-5644	459-6520
TF: 800-966-5644					
Marlborough Hills Healthcare Center 121 Northboro Rd E	Marlborough	MA	01752	508-485-4040	481-5585
Meadow Green Nursing & Rehabilitation Center 45 Woburn St	Waltham	MA	02452	781-899-8600	899-3124
Web: www.meadowgreen.org					
Methuen Health & Rehabilitation Center 480 Jackson St	Methuen	MA	01844	978-686-3906	687-6007
Middleboro Skilled Care Center 23 Isaac St	Middleboro	MA	02346	508-947-9295	947-7974
Mount Saint Vincent Nursing Home Inc 35 Holy Family Rd	Holyoke	MA	01040	413-532-3246	532-0309
Newton Health Care Center 2101 Washington St	Newton	MA	02462	617-969-4660	964-4622
North Adams Common Nursing Home 175 Franklin St	North Adams	MA	01247	413-664-4041	662-3490
Web: www.northadamscommons.org					
Peabody Glen Health Care Center 199 Andover St	Peabody	MA	01960	978-531-0772	532-4134
Web: www.peabodyglenhcc.com					
Port Health Care 113 Low St	Newburyport	MA	01950	978-462-7373	462-6510
Radius Healthcare Center at Danvers 56 Liberty St	Danvers	MA	01923	978-777-2700	774-4463
Redstone Rehabilitation & Nursing Center 135 Benton Dr	East Longmeadow	MA	01028	413-525-3336	525-9814
Sacred Heart Nursing Home 359 Summer St	New Bedford	MA	02740	508-996-6751	996-5189
Scott John House Nursing & Rehabilitation Center 233 Middle St	Braintree	MA	02184	781-843-1860	843-8834
Senior Healthcare of Harwich 111 Headwaters Dr	Harwich	MA	02645	508-430-1717	432-1809
Sherrill House Inc 135 S Huntington Ave	Jamaica Plain	MA	02130	617-731-2400	731-8671
Web: www.sherrillhouse.org					
SunBridge Care & Rehabilitation for Milford 10 Veteran's Memorial Dr	Milford	MA	01757	508-473-6414	473-9974
TF: 800-729-6600					
Williamstown Commons Nursing & Rehabilitation Center 25 Adams Rd	Williamstown	MA	01267	413-458-2111	458-3156
TF: 800-869-6675					
Wilmington Health Care Center 750 Woburn St	Wilmington	MA	01887	978-988-0888	658-6470
Worcester Skilled Care Center 59 Acton St	Worcester	MA	01604	508-791-3147	753-6267
Web: www.wingatehealthcare.com					
Bay County Medical Care Facility 564 W Hampton Rd	Essexville	MI	48732	989-892-3591	892-6991
Clarkston Specialty Healthcare Center 4800 Clintonville Rd	Clarkston	MI	48346	248-674-0903	674-3431
Web: www.thicare.com/ClarkstonSpecialty					
Crestmont Health Care Center 111 Trealout Dr	Fenton	MI	48430	810-629-4105	629-7538
Farmington HealthCare Center 34225 Grand River Ave	Farmington	MI	48335	248-477-7373	477-2888
Web: www.fivestarqualitycare.com					
Golden Oaks Medical Care Facility 1200 N Telegraph Rd Bldg 32E	Pontiac	MI	48341	248-858-1415	858-4026
Grand Blanc Rehabilitation & Nursing Center 11941 Belsay Rd	Grand Blanc	MI	48439	810-694-1970	694-4081
Heartland Health Care Center Georgian Bloomfield 2975 N Adams Rd	Bloomfield Hills	MI	48304	248-645-2900	433-1415
TF: 800-427-1902					
Heartland Health Care Center University 28550 Five Mile Rd	Livonia	MI	48154	734-427-8270	427-2135
Web: www.hcr-manorcare.com					
Howell Care Center 3003 W Grand River	Howell	MI	48843	517-546-4210	546-9495
Web: www.fivestarqualitycare.com					
Isabella County Medical Care Facility 1222 North Dr	Mount Pleasant	MI	48858	989-772-2957	772-3669
Martha T Berry Memorial Medical Care Facility 43533 Elizabeth Rd	Mount Clemens	MI	48043	586-469-5265	466-7418
Web: macombcountymi.gov/marthatberry					
Mercy Bellbrook 873 W Avon Rd	Rochester Hills	MI	48307	248-656-3239	656-8160
Web: www.mercybellbrook.org					
Mercy Pavilion of Battle Creek 80 N 20th St	Battle Creek	MI	49015	269-964-5400	964-5559
Shore Haven A Mercy Living Center 900 S Beacon Blvd	Grand Haven	MI	49417	616-846-1850	846-0971
Web: www.mercyshorehaven.org					
Tendercare Clare 600 SE 4th St	Clare	MI	48617	989-386-7723	386-4100
Web: www.tendercare.net					
Big Bend Woods Health Care Center 110 Highland Ave	Valley Park	MO	63088	636-225-5144	225-8427
Elder Care of the Valley 6768 N Hwy 67	Florissant	MO	63034	314-741-9101	741-4936
Riverside Nursing & Rehabilitation Center 4700 NW Cliffview Dr	Riverside	MO	64150	816-741-5105	746-1301
Sunset Hills Health & Rehabilitation Center 10954 Kennerly Rd	Saint Louis	MO	63128	314-843-4242	843-4031
Web: www.thicare.com/SunsetHills					
Village North Health Center 11160 Village North Dr	Saint Louis	MO	63136	314-355-8010	653-4880
Web: www.bjc.org					
Good Shepherd Rehabilitation & Nursing Center 20 Plantation Dr	Jaffrey	NH	03452	603-532-8762	593-0006
Greenbriar Terrace Healthcare 55 Harris Rd	Nashua	NH	03062	603-888-1573	888-5089
Web: www.greenbriarterrace.com					
Hackett Hill Healthcare Center 191 Hackett Hill Rd	Manchester	NH	03102	603-668-8161	622-2584
Mount Carmel Nursing Home 235 Myrtle St	Manchester	NH	03104	603-627-3811	626-4696
Pleasant Valley Nursing Center 8 Peabody Rd	Derry	NH	03038	603-434-1566	434-2299
Saint Ann Healthcare Center 195 Dover Point Rd	Dover	NH	03820	603-742-2612	743-3055
Saint Francis Healthcare Center 406 Court St	Laconia	NH	03246	603-524-0466	527-0884
Saint Teresa Healthcare Center 519 Bridge St	Manchester	NH	03104	603-668-2373	668-0059
Saint Vincent dePaul Healthcare Center 29 Providence Ave	Berlin	NH	03570	603-752-1820	752-7149
Camden County Health Services Center 20 N Woodbury Turnersville Rd	Blackwood	NJ	08012	856-374-6600	
Web: www.cchsc.com					
Daughters of Miriam Center/Gallen Institute 155 Hazel St	Clifton	NJ	07015	973-772-3700	253-5389
Web: www.daughtersofmiriamcenter.org					
Dunroven Health Care Center 221 County Rd	Cresskill	NJ	07626	201-567-9310	541-9224
Web: www.care-one.com					
Linwood Convalescent Center 201 New Rd & Central Ave	Linwood	NJ	08221	609-927-6131	927-5899
Web: www.brandycare.com					
Manor The 689 W Main St	Freehold	NJ	07728	732-431-5200	409-2446
ManorCare Health Services - Mountainside 1180 Rt 22 W	Mountainside	NJ	07092	908-654-0020	654-8661
Web: www.hcr-manorcare.com					
ManorCare Health Services - West Deptford 550 Jessup Rd	West Deptford	NJ	08066	856-848-9551	848-1817
Morris View Nursing Home PO Box 437	Morris Plains	NJ	07950	973-285-2820	285-6062
Somerset Valley Rehabilitation & Nursing Center 1621 Rt 22 W	Bound Brook	NJ	08805	732-469-2000	469-8917
South Jersey Health Care Center 2 Cooper Plaza	Camden	NJ	08103	856-342-7600	968-0250
Valley Health Care Center 300 Old Hook Rd	Westwood	NJ	07675	201-664-8888	263-0545
Web: www.care-one.com					
Voorhees Pediatric Facility 1304 Laurel Oak Rd	Voorhees	NJ	08043	856-346-3300	435-4223
TF: 888-877-3100 ■ *Web:* www.forkidcare.com					
Willow Creek Rehabilitation & Care Center 1165 Easton Ave	Somerset	NJ	08873	732-246-4100	246-3926
Woodcrest Healthcare Center 800 River Rd	New Milford	NJ	07646	201-967-1700	967-0327*
**Fax:* Admitting					
Bainbridge Nursing & Rehabilitation Center 3518 Bainbridge Ave	Bronx	NY	10467	718-655-1991	655-3903
Clove Lakes Health Care & Rehabilitation Center 25 Fanning St	Staten Island	NY	10314	718-289-7900	761-8701
Web: www.clovelakes.com					
Dumont Masonic Home 676 Pelham Rd	New Rochelle	NY	10805	914-632-9600	632-4766
Web: www.dumontmasonichome.org					
East Haven Nursing Home 2323 Eastchester Rd	Bronx	NY	10469	718-655-2848	515-8249
Golden Gate Rehabilitation & Health Care Center 191 Bradley Ave	Staten Island	NY	10314	718-698-8800	698-5536
Grace Plaza of Great Neck Inc 15 St Paul's Pl	Great Neck	NY	11021	516-466-3001	466-7624
Web: www.graceplaza.com					
Haven Manor Health Care Center 1441 Gateway Blvd	Far Rockaway	NY	11691	718-471-1500	471-9606
Margaret Tietz Center for Nursing Care 164-11 Chapin Pkwy	Jamaica	NY	11432	718-298-7800	262-8839
Web: www.mtcnc.org					
Mosholu Parkway Nursing & Rehabilitation Center 3356 Perry Ave	Bronx	NY	10467	718-655-3568	547-8295
Northwoods of Cortland 28 Kellogg Rd	Cortland	NY	13045	607-753-9631	756-2968
Web: www.northwoodshealth.net					
Northwoods at Hilltop 1805 Providence Ave	Niskayuna	NY	12309	518-374-2212	374-4330
TF: 800-697-5374 ■ *Web:* www.northwoodshealth.net					
Northwoods at Rosewood Gardens 284 Troy Rd	Rensselaer	NY	12144	518-286-1621	286-1691
Web: www.northwoodshealth.net					
Northwoods at Troy 100 New Turnpike Rd	Troy	NY	12182	518-235-1410	235-1632
Web: www.northwoodshealth.net					
Palm Gardens Center for Nursing & Rehabilitation 615 Ave C	Brooklyn	NY	11218	718-633-3300	853-8680
Promenade Rehabilitation & Health Care Center 140 Beach 114th St	Rockaway Park	NY	11694	718-945-4600	634-8237
Providence Rest 3304 Waterbury Ave	Bronx	NY	10465	718-931-3000	863-0185
Web: www.providencerest.org					
Robert L Yeager Health Center 50 Sanatorium Rd	Pomona	NY	10970	845-364-2745	364-2708
Robinson Terrace 28652 State Hwy 23	Stamford	NY	12167	607-652-7521	652-3362
Web: www.robinsonterrace.com					
Saint Mary's Hospital for Children Inc 29-01 216th St	Bayside	NY	11360	718-281-8800	281-8523
Web: www.stmaryskids.org					
Sea View Hospital Rehabilitation Center & Home 460 Brielle Ave	Staten Island	NY	10314	718-317-3221	351-7898
Web: www.nyc.gov/html/hhc/seaview/					
Victory Lake Nursing Center 419 Quaker Ln	Hyde Park	NY	12538	845-229-9177	229-9819
Wayne Center for Nursing & Rehabilitation 3530 Wayne Ave	Bronx	NY	10467	718-655-1700	515-5650
Wesley Group Inc 3 Upton Pk	Rochester	NY	14607	585-241-2100	241-2180
Web: www.thewesleycommunity.com					
Blue Ridge Health Care Center 3830 Blue Ridge Rd	Raleigh	NC	27612	919-781-4900	571-2583
Cypress Pointe Rehabilitation & HealthCare Center 2006 S 16th St	Wilmington	NC	28401	910-763-6271	251-9803
Erwin Garden Rehabilitation 3100 Erwin Rd	Durham	NC	27705	919-383-1546	383-0862
Web: www.thicare.com/durham					
Kindred Hospital Greensboro 2401 Southside Blvd	Greensboro	NC	27406	336-271-2800	271-2734
TF: 877-836-2671 ■ *Web:* www.kindredhospitalgreensboro.com					
North Carolina Special Care Center 4761 Ward Blvd	Wilson	NC	27893	252-399-2112	399-2132
Valley Nursing Center 581 NC Hwy 16 S	Taylorsville	NC	28681	828-632-8146	635-0300
Arbors at Canton 2714 13th St NW	Canton	OH	44708	330-456-2842	456-5343
Arbors at Delaware 2270 Warrensburg Rd	Delaware	OH	43015	740-369-9614	
Arbors East Subacute Nursing & Rehabilitation Center 5500 E Broad St	Columbus	OH	43213	614-575-9003	575-9101
Arbors at Marietta 400 7th St	Marietta	OH	45750	740-373-3597	373-3915
Arbors at Toledo Subacute & Rehabilitation Center 2920 Cherry St	Toledo	OH	43608	419-242-7458	242-6514
Arbors West 375 W Main St	West Jefferson	OH	43162	614-879-7661	879-7604
Aurora Manor Special Care Centre 101 S Bissell Rd	Aurora	OH	44202	330-562-5000	562-5181
Cedarwood Plaza 12504 Cedar Rd	Cleveland Heights	OH	44106	216-371-3600	371-6766
Columbus Rehabilitation & Subacute Institute 44 S Souder Ave	Columbus	OH	43222	614-228-5900	228-3989
Community Multicare Center 908 Symmes Rd	Fairfield	OH	45014	513-868-6500	868-7150
Web: www.communitymulticarecenter.com					
Gateway Health Care Center 3 Gateway Dr	Euclid	OH	44119	216-486-4949	481-5155
Web: www.gatewaypathways.com					
Heartland of Beavercreek 1974 N Fairfield Rd	Dayton	OH	45432	937-429-1106	429-0902
Heartland of Centerburg 212 Fairview Ave	Centerburg	OH	43011	740-625-5774	625-7426
Heartland of Marysville 755 S Plum St	Marysville	OH	43040	937-644-8836	644-1811
Heartland of Perrysburg 10540 Fremont Pike	Perrysburg	OH	43551	419-874-3578	874-7753
Hennis Care Centre 1720 Cross St	Dover	OH	44622	330-364-8849	364-2128
Web: www.henniscarecentre.com					
Horizon Village Nursing & Rehabilitation Center 2473 North Rd NE	Warren	OH	44483	330-372-2251	372-6419
ManorCare Health Services - Akron 1211 W Market St	Akron	OH	44313	330-867-8530	867-9159
ManorCare Health Services - North Olmsted 23225 Lorain Rd	North Olmsted	OH	44070	440-779-6900	779-8166
TF: 888-427-6999 ■ *Web:* www.hcr-manorcare.com					
Miami Shores of Moraine Nursing Center 3421 Pinnacle Rd	Dayton	OH	45418	937-268-3488	267-5021
Middlebury Manor 974 E Market St	Akron	OH	44305	330-762-9066	762-4004
Newark Healthcare Centre 75 McMillen Dr	Newark	OH	43055	740-344-0357	344-0452
Saint Augustine Manor 7801 Detroit Ave	Cleveland	OH	44102	216-634-7400	939-7577*
**Fax:* Admitting					
University Hospitals Health System Heather Hill 12340 Bass Lake Rd	Chardon	OH	44024	440-285-4040	285-7743
Web: www.heatherhill.com					
Villa Angela Nursing Rehabilitation Center 5700 Karl Rd	Columbus	OH	43229	614-846-5420	854-7830
Village of Westerville 1060 Eastwind Dr	Westerville	OH	43081	614-895-1038	895-1094
Walton Manor Health Care Center 19859 Alexander Rd	Walton Hills	OH	44146	440-439-4433	439-0691
Waterford Commons Nursing Center 955 Garden Lake Pkwy	Toledo	OH	43614	419-382-2200	381-0188
ManorCare Health Services - Northwest 5301 N Brookline St	Oklahoma City	OK	73112	405-946-3351	948-6132
Oklahoma Veterans Center Norman PO Box 1668	Norman	OK	73070	405-360-5600	364-8432
Web: www.odva.state.ok.us					
Cascade Terrace Nursing Center 5601 SE 122nd Ave	Portland	OR	97236	503-761-3181	761-5956

	City	State	Zip	Phone	Fax
Beverly Healthcare Western Reserve 1521 W 54th St	Erie	PA	16509	814-864-0671	866-5681
TF: 877-823-8375					
Colonial Manor Nursing Home 970 Colonial Ave	York	PA	17403	717-845-2661	845-3101
Golden Living Center 350 Old Gilkeson Rd	Pittsburgh	PA	15228	412-257-4444	257-8226
Greenery of Canonsburg 2200 Hill Church-Houston Rd	Canonsburg	PA	15317	724-745-8000	746-8780
Web: www.thicare.com/GreeneryofCanonsburg					
Hanover Hall Nursing & Rehabilitation Center 267 Frederick St	Hanover	PA	17331	717-637-8937	637-3939
Integrated Health Services of Greater Pittsburgh 890 Weatherwood Ln	Greensburg	PA	15601	724-837-8076	837-3152
Jefferson Manor Health Center 417 Rt 28	Brookville	PA	15825	814-849-8026	849-3889
Web: www.jeffersonmanor.com					
Kindred Hospital Philadelphia 6129 Palmetto St	Philadelphia	PA	19111	215-722-8555	725-8998
Web: www.kindredphila.com					
Kindred Hospital Pittsburgh 7777 Steubenville Pike	Oakdale	PA	15071	412-494-5500	494-5511
Web: www.kindredhospitalpittsburgh.com					
Laurel Center 125 Holly Rd	Hamburg	PA	19526	610-562-2284	562-0775
Liberty Nursing & Rehabilitation Center 535 N 17th St	Allentown	PA	18104	610-432-4351	435-4470
Presbyterian SeniorCare-Southminster Place 880 S Main St	Washington	PA	15301	724-222-4300	250-4998
Web: www.srcare.org					
Presbyterian SeniorCare-Westminster Place 1215 Hulton Rd	Oakmont	PA	15139	412-828-5600	826-6059
TF: 877-772-6500 ■ *Web:* www.srcare.org					
Quincy United Methodist Home & Village 6596 Orphanage Rd	Quincy	PA	17247	717-749-3151	749-2013
Web: www.quincyhome.com					
Redstone Highlands Health Care Center 6 Garden Center Dr	Greensburg	PA	15601	724-832-8400	836-3710
Web: www.redstonehighlands.org					
Rest Haven-York 1050 S George St	York	PA	17403	717-843-9866	846-5894
Web: www.resthavenyork.com					
Saint John Specialty Care Center 500 Wittenberg Way	Mars	PA	16046	724-625-1571	625-0087
TF: 800-641-7788					
South Mountain Restoration Center 10058 S Mountain Rd	South Mountain	PA	17261	717-749-3121	749-3946
TF: 877-765-0331					
Sterling Healthcare & Rehabilitation Center 318 S Orange St	Media	PA	19063	610-566-1400	566-1585
Web: www.sterlinghcr.com					
Susquehanna Valley Nursing & Rehabilitation Center 745 Old Chiques Hill Rd	Columbia	PA	17512	717-684-7555	684-3677
TF: 800-840-9075					
Twinbrook Medical Center 3805 Field St	Erie	PA	16511	814-898-5600	899-9829
TF: 800-427-9149					
Woodhaven Care Center 2400 McGinley Rd	Monroeville	PA	15146	412-856-4770	856-6856
Oak Hill Nursing & Rehabilitation Center 544 Pleasant St	Pawtucket	RI	02860	401-725-8888	727-6731*
**Fax:* Admitting ■ *Web:* www.oakhillrehab.com					
Saint Elizabeth Home 1 St Elizabeth Way	East Greenwich	RI	02818	401-471-6060	471-6072
Web: www.stelizabethcommunity.com					
CM Tucker Jr Nursing Care Center 2200 Harden St	Columbia	SC	29203	803-737-5300	737-5342
Driftwood Rehabilitation & Nursing Center 2375 Baker Hospital Blvd	North Charleston	SC	29405	843-744-2750	747-0406
Heartland Health Care Center Charleston 1800 Eagle Landing Blvd	Hanahan	SC	29406	843-553-0656	553-9773
Allen Morgan Health Center 177 N Highland Ave	Memphis	TN	38111	901-325-4003	325-4011
Briarcliff Health Care Center 100 Elmhurst Dr	Oak Ridge	TN	37830	865-481-3367	482-5961
Manor House of Dover PO Box 399	Dover	TN	37058	931-232-6902	232-4256
Hearthstone of Round Rock 401 Oakwood Blvd	Round Rock	TX	78681	512-388-7494	388-2166
Web: www.hearthstonehealth.com					
Heartland Health Care Center Austin 11406 Rustic Rock Dr	Austin	TX	78750	512-335-5028	335-0709
Heartland Health Care Center Bedford 2001 Forest Ridge Dr	Bedford	TX	76021	817-571-6804	267-4176
Heartland of San Antonio 1 Heartland Dr	San Antonio	TX	78247	210-653-1219	653-8977
Kindred Hospital Fort Worth 815 8th Ave	Fort Worth	TX	76104	817-332-4812	332-8843
Plum Creek Healthcare Center 5601 Plum Creek Dr	Amarillo	TX	79124	806-351-1000	355-9650
Treemont Nursing & Rehabilitation Center 5550 Harvest Hill Rd Suite 500	Dallas	TX	75230	972-661-1862	980-6731
South Davis Community Hospital 401 South 400 E	Bountiful	UT	84010	801-295-2361	295-1398
TF: 877-913-2847 ■ *Web:* www.sdch.com					
Sunshine Terrace Foundation Inc 225 N 200 W	Logan	UT	84321	435-752-0411	752-1318
Web: www.sunshineterrace.com					
Bay Pointe Medical & Rehabilitation Center 1148 First Colonial Rd	Virginia Beach	VA	23454	757-481-3321	481-4413
Berkshire Health Care Center 705 Clearview Dr	Vinton	VA	24179	540-982-6691	985-4899
Harbour Pointe Medical & Rehabilitation Center 1005 Hampton Blvd	Norfolk	VA	23507	757-623-5602	623-4646
HCR Manor Care Health Services 550 S Carlin Springs Rd	Arlington	VA	22204	703-379-7200	578-5788
Web: www.hcr-manorcare.com					
James River Convalescent Center 540 Aberthaw Ave	Newport News	VA	23601	757-595-2273	595-2271
Lucy Corr Village 6800 Lucy Corr Blvd	Chesterfield	VA	23832	804-748-1511	706-4967
Web: www.lucycorrvillage.com					
Lynchburg Health & Rehabilitation Center 5615 Seminole Ave	Lynchburg	VA	24502	434-239-2657	239-4062
ManorCare Health Services - Fair Oaks 12475 Lee Jackson Memorial Hwy	Fairfax	VA	22033	703-352-7172	352-1455
Riverside Regional Convalescent Center 1000 Old Denbigh Blvd	Newport News	VA	23602	757-875-2000	875-2036
The Laurels of University Park 2420 Pemberton Rd	Richmond	VA	23233	804-747-9200	747-1574
Ballard Care & Rehabilitation 820 NW 95th St	Seattle	WA	98117	206-782-0100	781-1448
Seattle Medical & Rehabilitation Center 555 16th Ave	Seattle	WA	98122	206-324-8200	324-0780
Glenwood Park Retirement Village 1924 Glenwood Park Rd	Princeton	WV	24740	304-425-8128	425-9711*
**Fax:* Admitting ■ *Web:* www.gwpinc.org					
Brewster Village 3300 W Brewster St	Appleton	WI	54914	920-832-5400	832-4922
Web: www.co.outagamie.wi.us/Brewster					
Clement Manor 3939 S 92nd St	Greenfield	WI	53228	414-321-1800	546-7357
Web: www.clementmanor.com					
Franciscan Villa 3601 S Chicago Ave	South Milwaukee	WI	53172	414-764-4100	764-0706
Web: www.franciscanvilla.org					
Middleton Village Nursing & Rehabilitation Center 6201 Elmwood Ave	Middleton	WI	53562	608-831-8300	831-4253
Mount Carmel Health & Rehabilitation Center 5700 W Layton Ave	Greenfield	WI	53220	414-281-7200	281-0744

454 LONG-TERM CARE FACILITIES OPERATORS

	City	State	Zip	Phone	Fax
Active Services Corp 400 Redland Ct Suite 114	Owings Mills	MD	21117	443-548-2260	548-2260
TF: 800-805-7430 ■ *Web:* www.activeservices.com					
Advocat Inc DBA Diversicare Management Services 1621 Galleria Blvd	Brentwood	TN	37027	615-771-7575	
Web: www.diversicaremanagement.com					
Aegis Assisted Living 17602 NE Union Hill Rd	Redmond	WA	98052	425-861-9993	861-7278
TF: 888-252-3447 ■ *Web:* www.aegisal.com					
American Religious Town Hall Inc 745 N Buckner Blvd	Dallas	TX	75218	214-328-9828	328-3042
TF: 800-783-9828 ■ *Web:* www.americanreligious.org					
Americare Systems Inc 214 N Scott St	Sikeston	MO	63801	573-471-1113	471-8235
Web: www.americareusa.net					
Assisted Living Concepts Inc 1349 Empire Central Suite 999	Dallas	TX	75247	214-424-4000	424-4100
Web: www.alcco.com					
Atria Senior Living Group 401 S 4th St Suite 1900	Louisville	KY	40202	502-779-4700	
Web: www.atriaseniorliving.com					
Balanced Care Corp 1215 Manor Dr	Mechanicsburg	PA	17055	717-796-6100	796-6150
TF: 888-227-3145					
Brookdale Senior Living Inc 330 N Wabash Ave Suite 1400	Chicago	IL	60611	312-977-3700	977-3701
NYSE: BKD ■ *Web:* www.brookdaleliving.com					
CabelTel International Corp 1755 Wittington Pl Suite 340	Dallas	TX	75234	972-407-8400	407-8436
AMEX: GBR ■ *TF:* 888-407-8400 ■ *Web:* www.cabeltel.us					
Cardinal Ritter Senior Services 7601 Watson Rd	Saint Louis	MO	63119	314-961-8000	961-1934
Web: www.ccstl.org/crss					
Comprehensive Systems Inc 1700 Clark St	Charles City	IA	50616	641-228-4842	228-4675
Diversicare Management Services 1621 Galleria Blvd	Brentwood	TN	37027	615-771-7575	
Web: www.diversicaremanagement.com					
Elder Living Concepts Inc 51 Summer St	Rowley	MA	01969	978-948-7383	948-2718
ElderWood Senior Care 7 Limestone Dr	Williamsville	NY	14221	716-633-3900	633-1153
TF: 888-826-9663 ■ *Web:* www.elderwood.com					
Emeritus Corp 3131 Elliott Ave Suite 500	Seattle	WA	98121	206-298-2909	301-4500
AMEX: ESC ■ *TF:* 800-429-4828 ■ *Web:* www.emeritus.com					
Extendicare Inc 3000 Steeles Ave E	Markham	ON	L3R9W2	905-470-4000	470-5588
NYSE: EXE ■ *Web:* www.extendicare.com					
Five Star Quality Care Inc 400 Centre St	Newton	MA	02458	617-796-8387	796-8385
AMEX: FVE ■ *Web:* www.fivestarqualitycare.com					
Genesis HealthCare Corp 101 E State St	Kennett Square	PA	19348	610-444-6350	925-4000
NASDAQ: GHCI ■ *TF:* 800-699-1520 ■ *Web:* www.genesishcc.com					
Golden Ventures 1000 Fianna Way	Fort Smith	AR	72919	479-201-2000	201-1101
TF: 877-823-8375 ■ *Web:* www.goldenven.com					
Harborside Healthcare Corp 1 Beacon St Suite 1100	Boston	MA	02108	617-646-5400	646-5454
Web: www.harborsidehealthcare.com					
HCF Inc 1100 Shawnee Rd	Lima	OH	45805	419-999-2010	999-6284
TF: 800-999-2110 ■ *Web:* www.hcfinc.com					
HCR Manor Care 333 N Summit St PO Box 10086	Toledo	OH	43699	419-252-5500	252-5510*
NYSE: HCR ■ **Fax:* Hum Res ■ *TF:* 800-422-2098 ■ *Web:* www.hcr-manorcare.com					
Kindred Healthcare Inc 680 S 4th Ave	Louisville	KY	40202	502-596-7300	596-4052
NYSE: KND ■ *TF:* 800-545-0749 ■ *Web:* www.kindredhealthcare.com					
Lexington Healthcare Group 665 W North Ave	Lombard	IL	60148	630-458-4700	458-4797
Web: www.lexingtonhealth.com					
Life Care Centers of America Inc 3001 Keith St NW	Cleveland	TN	37312	423-472-9585	339-8332
Web: www.lifecarecenters.com					
Manor Care Inc 333 N Summit St PO Box 10086	Toledo	OH	43699	419-252-5500	252-5510*
NYSE: HCR ■ **Fax:* Hum Res ■ *TF:* 800-422-2098 ■ *Web:* www.hcr-manorcare.com					
Mariner Health Care Inc 1 Ravinia Dr Suite 1500	Atlanta	GA	30346	678-443-7000	393-8054*
**Fax Area Code:* 770 ■ *TF:* 800-929-4762 ■ *Web:* www.marinerhealth.com					
Mid-America Health Centers Inc 200 W Douglas Suite 600	Wichita	KS	67202	316-262-4206	262-1358
National HealthCare Corp 100 Vine St PO Box 1398	Murfreesboro	TN	37133	615-890-2020	890-0123
AMEX: NHC ■ *Web:* www.nhccare.com					
Odyssey HealthCare Inc 717 N Harwood St Suite 1500	Dallas	TX	75201	214-922-9711	922-9752
NASDAQ: ODSY ■ *TF:* 888-922-9711 ■ *Web:* www.odyssey-healthcare.com					
Royal Management Corp DBA Lexington Healthcare Group 665 W North Ave	Lombard	IL	60148	630-458-4700	458-4797
Web: www.lexingtonhealth.com					
Salem Senior Housing 1105 Brooktown Ave	Winston-Salem	NC	27101	336-724-1000	724-9955
TF: 800-721-8182					
Skilled Healthcare LLC 27442 Portola Pkwy Suite 200	Foothill Ranch	CA	90610	949-282-5800	282-5870
Web: www.skilledhealthcare.com					
Sun Health Corp 13180 N 103rd Dr	Sun City	AZ	85351	623-876-5352	876-5310
Web: www.sunhealth.org					
Sun Healthcare Group Inc 101 Sun Ave NE	Albuquerque	NM	87109	505-821-3355	468-2501
NASDAQ: SUNH ■ *TF:* 800-856-2512 ■ *Web:* www.sunh.com					
Sun Healthcare Group Inc Inpatient Services 101 Sun Ave NE	Albuquerque	NM	87109	505-821-3355	468-2501
TF: 800-729-6600 ■ *Web:* www.sunh.com					
SunBridge Assisted Living Residences 101 Sun Ave NE	Albuquerque	NM	87109	505-821-3355	468-6210
TF: 800-729-6600					
SunBridge Healthcare Corp 101 Sun Ave NE	Albuquerque	NM	87109	505-821-3355	468-2501
TF: 800-729-6600 ■ *Web:* www.sunh.com					
Sunrise Senior Living Inc 7902 Westpark Dr	McLean	VA	22102	703-273-7500	744-1601
NYSE: SRZ ■ *TF:* 800-929-4124 ■ *Web:* www.sunriseseniorliving.com					
Tandem Health Care Inc 800 Concourse Pkwy S Suite 200	Maitland	FL	32751	407-571-1550	571-1599
Web: www.tandemhealthcare.com					

455 LOTTERIES, GAMES, SWEEPSTAKES

SEE ALSO Games & Gaming p. 1686

	City	State	Zip	Phone	Fax
Arizona Lottery 4740 E University Dr	Phoenix	AZ	85034	480-921-4400	921-5512
Web: www.arizonalottery.com					
Atlantic Lottery Corp 922 Main St	Moncton	NB	E1C8W6	506-867-5800	867-5555
TF: 800-561-3942 ■ *Web:* www.alc.ca					
British Columbia Lottery Corp 74 W Seymour St	Kamloops	BC	V2C1E2	250-828-5500	828-5631
Web: www.bclc.com					
California State Lottery Commission 600 N 10th St	Sacramento	CA	95814	916-323-7095	323-7087
Web: www.calottery.com					
Colorado Lottery 212 W 3rd St Suite 210	Pueblo	CO	81003	719-546-2400	546-5208
TF: 800-999-2959 ■ *Web:* www.coloradolottery.com					
Connecticut Lottery Corp 270 John Downey Dr	New Britain	CT	06051	860-348-4000	348-4015
Web: www.ctlottery.org					
Delaware State Lottery 1575 McKee Rd Suite 102	Dover	DE	19904	302-739-5291	739-6706
TF: 800-338-6200 ■ *Web:* lottery.state.de.us					
District of Columbia Lottery & Charitable Games Control Board 2101 ML King Jr Ave SE	Washington	DC	20020	202-645-8000	645-8077
Web: www.dclottery.com					
Email-Lotto W 2605 Hwy 23	Fond du Lac	WI	54935	920-924-9527	
Web: www.email-lotto.com					
Florida Lottery Dept 250 Marriott Dr	Tallahassee	FL	32301	850-487-7777	487-7796*
**Fax:* Hum Res ■ *Web:* www.flalottery.com					
FreeLotto c/o PlasmaNet Inc 420 Lexington Ave Suite 2435	New York	NY	10170	212-931-6760	931-6761
Web: www.freelotto.com					
Gamesville Inc 100 5th Ave	Waltham	MA	02451	781-370-2700	370-2600
Web: www.gamesville.com					
Georgia Lottery Corp 250 Williams St NW Suite 3000	Atlanta	GA	30303	404-215-5000	215-8871
Web: www.galottery.com					
Hoosier Lottery 201 S Capitol Ave Suite 1100	Indianapolis	IN	46225	317-264-4800	264-4933
TF: 800-955-6886 ■ *Web:* www.in.gov/hoosierlottery					
Idaho Lottery 1199 Shoreline Ln Suite 100	Boise	ID	83702	208-334-2600	334-2610
TF: 800-432-5688 ■ *Web:* www.idaholottery.com					
Illinois Lottery 101 W Jefferson St	Springfield	IL	62702	217-524-5155	558-2468
TF: 800-252-1775 ■ *Web:* www.illinoislottery.com					
Iowa Lottery 2323 Grand Ave	Des Moines	IA	50312	515-281-7900	281-7882*
**Fax:* Hum Res ■ *Web:* www.ialottery.com					

				Phone	Fax
iWin.com Inc 10940 Wilshire Blvd	Los Angeles	CA	90024	310-264-4300	264-4399
Web: www.iwin.com					
iWon Inc 555 12th St Suite 500	Oakland	CA	94607	510-985-7400	985-7410
Web: www.iwon.com					
Jackpot.com					
c/o Vendare Media 2101 Rosecrans Ave Suite 2000	El Segundo	CA	90245	310-647-6000	647-6001
Web: www.jackpot.com					
Kansas Lottery 128 N Kansas Ave	Topeka	KS	66603	785-296-5700	296-5712
TF: 800-544-9467 ■ *Web:* www.kslottery.com					
Kentucky Lottery Corp 1011 W Main St	Louisville	KY	40202	502-560-1500	560-1532
TF: 800-937-8946 ■ *Web:* www.kylottery.com					
Loto-Quebec 500 Sherbrooke St W Suite 2000	Montreal	QC	H3A3G6	514-282-8000	873-3721
Web: www.loto-quebec.com					
Louisiana Lottery Corp 555 Laurel St	Baton Rouge	LA	70801	225-297-2000	297-2005
Web: www.louisianalottery.com					
Maine State Lottery 8 State House Stn	Augusta	ME	04333	207-287-3721	287-6769
Web: www.mainelottery.com					
Maryland State Lottery 1800 Washington Blvd Suite 330	Baltimore	MD	21230	410-230-8790	230-8728
Web: www.mdlottery.com					
Massachusetts State Lottery Commission 60 Columbian St	Braintree	MA	02184	781-849-5555	849-5546
Web: www.masslottery.com					
Michigan State Lottery 101 E Hillsdale St PO Box 30023	Lansing	MI	48909	517-335-5600	335-5644
Web: www.michigan.gov/lottery					
Minnesota State Lottery 2645 Long Lake Rd	Roseville	MN	55113	651-297-7456	
Web: www.mnlottery.com					
Missouri Lottery PO Box 1603	Jefferson City	MO	65102	573-751-4050	751-5188
Web: www.molottery.state.mo.us					
Montana Lottery 2525 N Montana Ave	Helena	MT	59601	406-444-5825	444-5830
Web: www.montanalottery.com					
Multi-State Lottery Assn 4400 NW Urbandale Dr	Urbandale	IA	50322	515-453-1400	453-1420
Web: www.musl.com					
Nebraska Lottery PO Box 98901	Lincoln	NE	68509	402-471-6100	471-6108
TF: 800-587-5200 ■ *Web:* www.nelottery.com					
New Hampshire Lottery Commission 14 Integra Dr	Concord	NH	03301	603-271-3391	271-6289
Web: www.nhlottery.org					
New Jersey Lottery PO Box 041	Trenton	NJ	08625	609-599-5800	599-5935
Web: www.njlottery.net					
New Mexico Lottery PO Box 93190	Albuquerque	NM	87199	505-342-7600	342-7511
Web: www.nmlottery.com					
New York (State) State Lottery PO Box 7500	Schenectady	NY	12301	518-388-3300	388-3403*
**Fax:* PR ■ *Web:* www.nylottery.org					
North Dakota Lottery 600 E Boulevard Ave Dept 125	Bismark	ND	58505	701-328-1574	328-1580
Web: www.ndlottery.org					
Ohio Lottery Commission 615 W Superior Ave	Cleveland	OH	44113	216-787-3200	787-3313
Web: www.ohiolottery.com					
Ontario Lottery & Gaming Corp 4120 Yonge St Suite 420	Toronto	ON	M2P2B8	416-224-1772	224-7000
TF: 800-387-0098 ■ *Web:* www.olg.ca					
Oregon Lottery 500 Airport Rd SE	Salem	OR	97301	503-540-1000	540-1001
Web: www.oregonlottery.org					
Pennsylvania State Lottery 2850 Turnpike Industrial Dr	Middletown	PA	17057	717-986-4699	986-4767
TF: 800-692-7481 ■ *Web:* www.palottery.com					
pogo.com					
c/o Electronic Arts Inc 209 Redwood Shores Pkwy	Redwood City	CA	94065	650-628-1500	628-1414
TF: 800-804-0836 ■ *Web:* www.pogo.com					
Rhode Island Lottery 1425 Pontiac Ave	Cranston	RI	02920	401-463-6500	463-5008
Web: www.rilot.com					
South Carolina Education Lottery 1333 Main St 4th Fl	Columbia	SC	29201	803-737-2002	737-2005
Web: www.sceducationlottery.com					
South Dakota Lottery PO Box 7107	Pierre	SD	57501	605-773-5770	773-5786
Web: www.sdlottery.org					
Tennessee Lottery 200 Athens Way Suite 200	Nashville	TN	37228	615-324-6500	
Web: www.tnlottery.com					
Texas Lottery Commission PO Box 16630	Austin	TX	78761	512-344-5000	478-3682
TF: 800-375-6886 ■ *Web:* www.txlottery.org					
TroppoLotto c/o Trancos Inc 1450 Veterans Blvd 3rd Fl	Redwood City	CA	94063	650-364-3110	364-3184
Web: www.troppolotto.com					
Uproar Inc					
c/o Vendare Media 2101 Rosecrans Ave Suite 2000	El Segundo	CA	90245	310-647-6000	647-6001
Web: www.uproar.com					
Vermont Lottery Commission 1311 US Route 302 Suite 100	Barre	VT	05641	802-479-5686	479-4294
Web: www.vtlottery.com					
Virginia Lottery 900 E Main St	Richmond	VA	23219	804-692-7777	692-7775
Web: www.valottery.com					
Washington State Lottery PO Box 43000	Olympia	WA	98504	360-664-4720	664-2630
Web: www.walottery.com					
West Virginia Lottery PO Box 2067	Charleston	WV	25327	304-558-0500	558-0129
TF: 800-982-4946 ■ *Web:* www.wvlottery.com					
Western Canada Lottery Corp 125 Garry St 10th Fl	Winnipeg	MB	R3C4J1	204-942-8217	946-1442
Web: www.wclc.com					
Wisconsin Lottery PO Box 8941	Madison	WI	53708	608-261-8800	264-6644
Web: www.wilottery.com					
Youbet.com Inc 5901 DeSoto Ave	Woodland Hills	CA	91367	818-668-2100	668-2101
NASDAQ: UBET ■ *TF:* 888-968-2388 ■ *Web:* www.youbet.com					

456 LUGGAGE, BAGS, CASES

SEE ALSO Handbags, Totes, Backpacks p. 1769; Leather Goods - Personal p. 1889

				Phone	Fax
Ace Products Group 11 5th St Suite 106	Petaluma	CA	94952	707-765-1500	762-1899
TF: 800-950-1095 ■ *Web:* www.aceproducts.com					
Airway Industries Inc/Atlantic Products Corp					
10th & Factory Ave Airway Park	Ellwood City	PA	16117	724-752-0012	752-3444
TF Cust Svc: 800-245-1750 ■ *Web:* www.atlanticluggage.com					
AJ Siris Corp Inc 10 Essex St PO Box AV	Paterson	NJ	07509	973-684-7700	684-3251
TF: 800-526-5300 ■ *Web:* www.ajsiris.com					
Alfred Freistat Case Co 14900 NW 24th Ct	Opa Locka	FL	33054	305-688-2577	685-2291
Anvil Cases 15730 Salt Lake Ave	City of Industry	CA	91745	626-968-4100	968-1703
TF: 800-359-2684 ■ *Web:* www.anvilcase.com					
Award Winner Group 202 W 3rd St	Mount Vernon	NY	10550	914-664-7134	668-2858
Web: www.awardwinnergroup.com					
Bergman Luggage Co 401 NE Northgate Way Suite 937	Seattle	WA	98125	503-282-3264	
Web: www.bergmanluggage.com					
Bottega Veneta Inc 699 5th Ave	New York	NY	10022	212-371-5511	371-4361
TF: 877-362-1715 ■ *Web:* www.bottegaveneta.com					
Brewer-Cantelmo Co Inc 350 7th Ave 4th Fl	New York	NY	10001	212-244-4600	244-1640
Web: www.brewer-cantelmo.com					
Calzone Case Co 225 Black Rock Ave	Bridgeport	CT	06605	203-367-5766	336-4406
TF Cust Svc: 800-243-5152 ■ *Web:* www.calzonecase.com					
CH Ellis Co Inc 2432 Southeastern Ave	Indianapolis	IN	46201	317-636-3351	635-5140
TF Sales: 800-466-3351 ■ *Web:* www.chellis.com					
Coach Inc 516 W 34th St	New York	NY	10001	212-594-1850	594-1682
NYSE: COH ■ *TF:* 800-444-3611 ■ *Web:* www.coach.com					
Crouch & Fitzgerald 400 Madison Ave	New York	NY	10017	212-755-5888	832-6461
TF: 800-627-6824 ■ *Web:* www.crouchandfitzgerald.com					
Delsey Luggage 6735 Business Pkwy Suite A	Elkridge	MD	21075	410-796-5655	796-4192
TF: 800-558-3344 ■ *Web:* www.delsey.com					
Eagle Creek Inc 3055 Enterprise Ct	Vista	CA	92081	760-599-6500	599-4722
TF Cust Svc: 800-874-9925 ■ *Web:* www.eaglecreek.com					
Fendi NA Inc 720 5th Ave 5th Fl	New York	NY	10019	212-920-8100	767-0545
TF: 800-336-3469 ■ *Web:* www.fendi.com					
Forward Industries Inc 1801 Green Rd Suite E	Pompano Beach	FL	33064	954-419-9544	419-9735
NASDAQ: FORD ■ *TF:* 800-872-3935 ■ *Web:* www.forwardindustries.com					
Freistat Alfred Case Co 14900 NW 24th Ct	Opa Locka	FL	33054	305-688-2577	685-2291
Gucci Group Inc 50 Hartz Way	Secaucus	NJ	07094	201-867-8800	617-2398*
**Fax:* Hum Res ■ *Web:* www.guccigroup.com					
Hartmann Luggage 1301 Hartmann Dr	Lebanon	TN	37087	615-444-5000	443-4619
TF: 800-331-0613 ■ *Web:* www.hartmann.com					
High Sierra Sport Co 880 Corporate Woods Pkwy	Vernon Hills	IL	60061	847-913-1100	913-1145
TF: 800-323-9590 ■ *Web:* www.hssc.com					
Jameslee Corp 3500 N Kostner Ave	Chicago	IL	60641	773-427-9999	
Johnston Mfg 753 Arrow Grand Cir	Covina	CA	91722	626-967-1511	331-9725
TF: 877-891-8899 ■ *Web:* www.johnstonmfg.com					
LC Industries 401 N Western Ave	Chicago	IL	60612	312-455-0500	265-6569*
**Fax Area Code:* 800 ■ *TF:* 800-539-6255					
Leather Specialty Co 1088 Business Ln	Naples	FL	34110	239-333-1000	333-1004
TF: 888-771-0200 ■ *Web:* www.leatherspecialty.com					
LeSportsac Inc 358 5th Ave 8th Fl	New York	NY	10001	212-736-6262	643-8009
TF: 800-486-2247 ■ *Web:* www.lesportsac.com					
Louis Vuitton NA Inc 19 E 57th St	New York	NY	10022	212-931-2000	931-2097*
**Fax:* Mktg ■ *TF Cust Svc:* 866-884-8866 ■ *Web:* www.vuitton.com					
Louis Vuitton US Mfg Inc 321 Covina Blvd	San Dimas	CA	91773	909-599-2411	394-0649
Web: www.louisvuitton.com					
Mercury Luggage Mfg Co DBA Mercury Luggage/Seward					
Trunk 4843 Victor St	Jacksonville	FL	32207	904-733-9595	733-9671
TF: 800-874-1885 ■ *Web:* www.mercuryluggage.com					
Mercury Luggage/Seward Trunk 4843 Victor St	Jacksonville	FL	32207	904-733-9595	733-9671
TF: 800-874-1885 ■ *Web:* www.mercuryluggage.com					
Monarch Luggage Co Inc 2580 Prospect Ct	Aurora	IL	60504	630-585-6030	585-6380
TF: 800-747-2802					
Pedro Companies 106 E 10th St	Saint Paul	MN	55101	651-224-9491	224-8674
TF: 800-328-9284 ■ *Web:* www.pedrocompanies.com					
Platt Luggage Inc 4051 W 51st St	Chicago	IL	60632	773-838-2000	838-2010
TF: 800-222-1555 ■ *Web:* www.plattluggage.com					
RJ Singer International Inc 4801 W Jefferson Blvd	Los Angeles	CA	90016	323-735-1717	735-3753
Web: www.rjsinger.com					
Robert Mfg Co Inc 4000 E 10th Ct	Hialeah	FL	33013	305-691-5311	696-3949
TF: 800-478-0199					
Royal Case Co Inc 315 S Montgomery St	Sherman	TX	75090	903-868-0288	893-7984
Web: www.royalcase.com					
Samsonite Corp 11200 E 45th Ave	Denver	CO	80239	303-373-2000	373-6300
TF: 800-223-7267 ■ *Web:* www.samsonite.com					
Singer RJ International Inc 4801 W Jefferson Blvd	Los Angeles	CA	90016	323-735-1717	735-3753
Web: www.rjsinger.com					
Siris AJ Corp Inc 10 Essex St PO Box AV	Paterson	NJ	07509	973-684-7700	684-3251
TF: 800-526-5300 ■ *Web:* www.ajsiris.com					
SKB Corp 434 W Levers Pl	Orange	CA	92867	714-637-1252	637-0491
TF: 800-410-2024 ■ *Web:* www.skbcases.com					
Skyway Luggage Co Inc 30 Wall St	Seattle	WA	98121	206-441-5300	441-5306
Web: www.skywayluggage.com					
Targus Inc 1211 N Miller St	Anaheim	CA	92806	714-765-5555	765-5599
TF: 800-950-5122 ■ *Web:* www.targus.com					
TGL 300 Wilson Ave	Norwalk	CT	06854	203-853-4747	853-0070
Travelpro USA 700 Banyan Trail	Boca Raton	FL	33431	561-998-2824	998-8487
TF: 888-741-7471 ■ *Web:* www.travelpro.com					
Vera Bradley Designs 2208 Production Rd	Fort Wayne	IN	46808	260-482-4673	484-2278
TF: 800-975-8372 ■ *Web:* www.verabradley.com					
Vuitton Louis US Mfg Inc 321 Covina Blvd	San Dimas	CA	91773	909-599-2411	394-0649
Web: www.louisvuitton.com					
Zero Mfg Inc 500 W 200 North	North Salt Lake	UT	84054	801-298-5900	292-9450
TF: 800-545-1030 ■ *Web:* www.zerocases.com					

457 MACHINE SHOPS

SEE ALSO Precision Machined Products p. 2133

				Phone	Fax
Acme Industries Inc 55 E Bradrock Dr	Des Plaines	IL	60018	847-296-3346	296-8622
Web: www.acmeind.com					
Advance Mfg Co Inc 8 Tpke Industrial Rd PO Box 726	Westfield	MA	01085	413-568-2411	568-6011
Web: www.advancemfg.com					
AJR Industries Inc 117 Gordon St	Elk Grove Village	IL	60007	847-439-0380	439-0230
Web: www.ajrindustries.com					
Alken-Ziegler Inc 406 S Park Dr	Kalkaska	MI	49646	231-258-4906	258-8062
Web: www.alken-ziegler.com					
Allied Engineering & Production Corp 2421 Blanding Ave	Alameda	CA	94501	510-522-1500	522-2868
Web: www.alliedeng.com					
American Grinding & Machine Co 2000 N Mango Ave	Chicago	IL	60639	773-889-4343	889-3781
TF: 877-988-4343 ■ *Web:* www.americangrinding.com					
Anderson Tool & Engineering Co Inc					
1735 W 53 St PO Box 1158	Anderson	IN	46015	765-643-6691	643-5022
Web: www.ateinc.com					
Bob Inc 8740 49th Ave N	New Hope	MN	55428	763-533-2261	533-1735
Web: www.bobinc.com					
Chalmers & Kubeck Inc 150 Commerce Dr	Aston	PA	19014	610-494-4300	485-1484
TF: 800-242-5637 ■ *Web:* www.candk.com					
Craft Machine Works Inc 2102 48th St	Hampton	VA	23661	757-380-8615	380-9120
TF: 888-350-6006 ■ *Web:* www.craftmachine.com					
Dechert Dynamics Corp 713 W Main St	Palmyra	PA	17078	717-838-1326	838-1525
Web: www.decherts.com					
Downey Grinding Co PO Box 583	Downey	CA	90241	562-803-5556	803-3237
Web: www.downeygrinding.com					
Ebtec Corp 120 Shoemaker Ln	Agawam	MA	01001	413-786-0393	789-2851
Web: www.ebteccorp.com					
EBW Inc 3760 Marsh Rd	Madison	WI	53718	608-838-8786	838-6433
TF: 800-475-5151 ■ *Web:* www.ebw.com					
Electro-Tech Machining 2000 W Gaylord St	Long Beach	CA	90813	562-436-9281	437-5421
Web: www.etm-lb.com					
Femco Machine Co 754 S Main St Ext	Punxsutawney	PA	15767	814-938-9763	938-8332
TF: 800-458-3445 ■ *Web:* www.femcomach.com					
Fluid Energy Processing & Equipment Co					
153 Penn Ave Box 200	Hatfield	PA	19440	215-368-2510	412-7245
Web: www.fluidenergype.com					

Company	City	State	ZIP	Phone	Fax
Framingham Welding & Engineering Corp 120 Leland St PO Box 112 *Web:* www.framinghamwelding.com	Framingham	MA	01702	508-875-3563	626-4234
Fraser Mfg Corp 7235 Boyington St	Lexington	MI	48450	810-359-5338	359-8731
Furmanite America 101 Old Underwood Rd Suite F *TF:* 800-444-5572 ■ *Web:* www.furmaniteusa.com	La Porte	TX	77571	281-842-5100	842-5111
Grand Valley Mfg Co 220 S Washington St *Web:* www.gvmco.com	Titusville	PA	16354	814-827-2707	827-4349
Granite State Mfg Co 124 Joliette St *Web:* www.gsmai.com	Manchester	NH	03102	603-668-1900	668-1906
GT Sales & Mfg Inc PO Box 9408 *Web:* www.gtsales.com	Wichita	KS	67277	316-943-2171	943-4800
Highway Machine Co Inc (HMC) RR 1 Box 208A *TF:* 800-803-0112 ■ *Web:* www.hmcgears.com	Princeton	IN	47670	812-385-3639	385-8186
Hitachi High Technologies America Inc 10 N Martingale Rd Suite 500 *Web:* www.hii-hitachi.com	Schaumburg	IL	60173	847-273-4141	273-4407
Howard Engineering Co Inc 687 Wooster St PO Box 1315 *Web:* www.howardengineering.com	Naugatuck	CT	06770	203-729-5213	729-3843
Hughes RS Co Inc Saunders Div 975 N Todd Ave *TF Sales:* 888-932-8836 ■ *Web:* www.saunderscorp.com	Azusa	CA	91702	626-691-1111	691-0116
Illinois Machine & Tool Works 1961 Edgewater Dr *Web:* www.illmachtool.com	North Pekin	IL	61554	309-382-3045	382-2644
Indiana Tool/Indiana Gear 6100 Michigan Rd PO Box 399 *Web:* www.itamco.com	Plymouth	IN	46563	574-936-2112	936-7224
Industrial Tool Inc 9210 52nd Ave N *TF Sales:* 800-776-4455 ■ *Web:* www.industrial-tool.com	Minneapolis	MN	55428	763-533-7244	533-1712
JF Fredericks Tool Co Inc 25 Spring Ln *Web:* www.jfftool.com	Farmington	CT	06032	860-677-2646	674-8679
Johnson Technology Corp 2034 Latimer Dr	Muskegon	MI	49442	231-777-2685	773-1397
K & M Machine-Fabricating Inc 20745 M-60 E PO Box 218 **Fax:* Sales ■ *Web:* www.k-mm.com	Cassopolis	MI	49031	269-445-2495	445-3002*
Kewaunee Fabrications LLC 520 N Main St *Web:* www.kewauneefabrications.com	Kewaunee	WI	54216	920-388-2000	388-0263
Keystone Honing Co PO Box 187 *TF:* 800-458-3847 ■ *Web:* www.keystonehoning.com	Titusville	PA	16354	814-827-9641	827-6678
Kurt Mfg Co 5280 Main St NE *TF:* 800-458-7811 ■ *Web:* www.kurt.com	Minneapolis	MN	55421	763-572-1500	572-9878
LaVezzi Precision Inc 999 Regency Dr *TF:* 800-323-1772 ■ *Web:* www.lavezzi.com	Glendale Heights	IL	60139	630-582-1230	582-1238
Lemco Tool Corp 1850 Metzger Ave *TF:* 800-233-8713 ■ *Web:* www.lemco-tool.com	Cogan Station	PA	17728	570-494-0620	494-0860
Lindquist Machine Corp PO Box 2327 *TF:* 888-499-0831 ■ *Web:* www.lmc-corp.com	Green Bay	WI	54306	920-713-4100	499-8482
Lith-O-Roll Corp 9521 Telstar Ave **Fax Area Code:* 800 ■ *TF:* 800-423-4176 ■ *Web:* www.lithoroll.com	El Monte	CA	91731	626-579-0340	548-4676*
Logan Machine Co 1405 Home Ave *Web:* www.loganmachine.com	Akron	OH	44310	330-633-6163	633-6362
Major Tool & Machine Inc 1458 E 19th St *Web:* www.majortool.com	Indianapolis	IN	46218	317-636-6433	634-9420
Manor Tool & Mfg Co 9200 Ivanhoe St *Web:* www.manortool.com	Schiller Park	IL	60176	847-678-2020	678-6937
Marine Exhaust Systems of Alabama Inc 757 Nichols Ave *Web:* www.mesamarine.com	Fairhope	AL	36532	251-928-1234	928-1234
McBride & Shoff Inc 503 N Niles St *Web:* www.mcbrideandshoff.com	Metamora	IL	61548	309-367-4193	367-2552
Merit Gage Inc 3954 Meadowbrook Rd *Web:* www.meritgage.com	Saint Louis Park	MN	55426	952-935-0113	935-2641
Meyer Tool Inc 3055 Colerain Ave *TF:* 800-286-7362 ■ *Web:* www.meyertool.com	Cincinnati	OH	45225	513-681-7362	853-4439
Micro Instrument Corp 1199 Emerson St *TF:* 800-200-3150 ■ *Web:* www.microinstrument.com	Rochester	NY	14606	585-458-3150	254-0922
Myrmo & Sons Inc 3600 Franklin Blvd *TF:* 800-683-7040 ■ *Web:* www.myrmo.com	Eugene	OR	97403	541-747-4561	747-6832
Nassau Tool Works Inc 34 Lamar St	West Babylon	NY	11704	631-643-5000	643-5062
Nu Tech Industries Inc 4020 E 138th St *Web:* www.ntihc.com	Grandview	MO	64030	816-763-8600	763-9177
Numerical Precision Inc 2204 S Foster Ave *Web:* www.numericalprecision.com	Wheeling	IL	60090	847-394-3610	394-3962
Ohio Fabricators Co 111 N 14th St *Web:* www.ohfab.com	Coshocton	OH	43812	740-622-5922	622-3307
Onamac Industries Inc 11504 Airport Rd Bldg G *TF:* 877-742-2718 ■ *Web:* www.onamac.com	Everett	WA	98204	425-743-6676	742-2718
OP Schuman & Sons Inc 2001 County Line Rd *Web:* www.opschuman.com	Warrington	PA	18976	215-343-1530	343-1633
PCI Energy Services 1 Energy Dr *TF:* 800-345-6108 ■ *Web:* www.pci-energy.com	Lake Bluff	IL	60044	847-680-8100	680-7140
Peko Precision Products Inc 1400 Emerson St *Web:* www.pekoprecision.com	Rochester	NY	14606	585-647-3010	647-1366
PEMCO-Naval Engineering Works Inc 3614 Frederic St *Web:* www.pemco-inc.com	Pascagoula	MS	39567	228-769-7081	769-6520
Precision Gears Inc N 13 W 24705 Bluemound Rd *Web:* www.precisiongears.com	Pewaukee	WI	53072	262-542-4261	542-1592
Precision Metal Products Inc 307 Pepe's Farm Rd *Web:* www.pmpinc.biz	Milford	CT	06460	203-877-4258	878-8353
Precision Screw Thread Corp S 82 W 19275 Apollo Dr *TF:* 800-828-3431 ■ *Web:* www.precisionscrewthread.com	Muskego	WI	53150	262-679-9000	679-9004
Process Equipment Co 6555 S SR-202 *TF:* 800-424-0325 ■ *Web:* www.processeq.com	Tipp City	OH	45371	937-667-4451	667-4798
Process Industries 3860 N River Rd *TF:* 800-860-1631 ■ *Web:* www.processgear.com	Schiller Park	IL	60176	847-671-1631	671-6840
Prototype Machine Co 818 Prototype Rd PO Box 249	Flatonia	TX	78941	361-865-3579	865-3235
Quality Engineering & Tool Co Inc 380 S Wheatfield St *Web:* www.qualityengineeringandtool.com	York	PA	17403	717-854-3875	843-0297
Saegertown Mfg Corp 1 Crawford St *Web:* www.smcmfg.com	Saegertown	PA	16433	814-763-2655	763-2069
Saunders Div RS Hughes Co Inc 975 N Todd Ave *TF Sales:* 888-932-8836 ■ *Web:* www.saunderscorp.com	Azusa	CA	91702	626-691-1111	691-0116
Schaffer Grinding Co 848 S Maple Ave *Web:* www.schaffergrinding.com	Montebello	CA	90640	323-724-4476	724-2635
Scheirer Machine Co Inc 3200 Industrial Blvd *TF:* 800-448-4590 ■ *Web:* www.scheirer.com	Bethel Park	PA	15102	412-833-6500	833-8110
Scheu & Kniss Inc PO Box 2947 *TF:* 800-635-6303 ■ *Web:* www.scheu-kniss.com	Louisville	KY	40201	502-635-6303	635-7850
Schmiede Corp 1865 Riley Creek Rd PO Box 1630 *TF:* 800-535-1851 ■ *Web:* www.schmiedecorp.com	Tullahoma	TN	37388	931-455-4801	455-1703
Schobers Machine & Engineering 705 S Electric Ave *Web:* www.schobers.com	Alhambra	CA	91803	626-576-0685	576-8895
Schuman OP & Sons Inc 2001 County Line Rd *Web:* www.opschuman.com	Warrington	PA	18976	215-343-1530	343-1633
Schwartz Industries Inc 6909 E 11-Mile Rd *Web:* www.schwartzind.com	Warren	MI	48092	586-759-1777	759-0808
SMF Inc 1550 Industrial Pk PO Box 157 *Web:* www.smf-inc.com	Minonk	IL	61760	309-432-2586	432-2390
Smith West Inc 404 W Guadalupe Rd *Web:* www.smithwest.com	Tempe	AZ	85283	480-839-0501	838-2054
South Side Machine Works Inc 3761 Eiler St *Web:* www.southsidemachine.net	Saint Louis	MO	63116	314-481-7171	481-9271
Special Projects Mfg Co 7601 Wyatt Dr *TF:* 800-342-7458 ■ *Web:* www.spmflo.com	Fort Worth	TX	76108	817-246-2461	246-6324
Standard Locknut Inc 1045 E 169th St *TF:* 800-783-6887 ■ *Web:* www.stdlocknut.com	Westfield	IN	46074	317-867-0100	867-4231
Sterling Engineering Corp 236 Newhartford Rd *Web:* www.sterlingeng.com	Barkhamsted	CT	06063	860-379-3366	379-3278
Steward Machine Co Inc 3911 13th Ave N *TF:* 800-394-6461 ■ *Web:* www.stewardmachine.com	Birmingham	AL	35234	205-841-6461	849-8029
Tell Tool Inc PO Box 1278 *Web:* www.telltool.com	Westfield	MA	01086	413-568-1671	562-7237
TurboCare Chicopee 2140 Westover Rd *TF:* 800-887-2622 ■ *Web:* www.turbocare.com	Chicopee	MA	01022	413-593-0500	593-3424
Twin City EDM 7940 Rancher Rd NE *TF:* 800-269-8919 ■ *Web:* www.twincityedm.com	Fridley	MN	55432	763-783-7808	783-7842
Vaga Industries Inc 2505 Loma Ave *Web:* www.vaga.com	South El Monte	CA	91733	626-442-7436	442-4330
Van Dusen & Meyer Inc 50 Parrott Dr *TF:* 800-760-6242 ■ *Web:* www.naiad.com	Shelton	CT	06484	203-929-6355	929-3594
Vescio Threading Co 14002 Anson Ave *TF:* 800-361-4218 ■ *Web:* www.vesciothreading.com	Santa Fe Springs	CA	90670	562-802-1868	802-2073
Walco Tool & Engineering Co 18954 Airport Rd *TF:* 800-808-9365 ■ *Web:* www.walcotool.com	Lockport	IL	60441	815-834-0225	838-6046
Washington Tool & Machine Co 1 S Baird Ave PO Box 873 *Web:* www.washtool.com	Washington	PA	15301	724-225-7470	225-7484
Weaver Industries Inc 425 S 4th St *TF:* 800-292-7670 ■ *Web:* www.weaverind.com	Denver	PA	17517	717-336-7507	336-4182
Wesel Mfg Co 710 Layton Rd *Web:* www.weselmach.com	Clark Summit	PA	18411	570-585-2976	585-2976
West Engineering Co Inc 10106 Louistown Rd *Web:* www.west-engineering.net	Ashland	VA	23005	804-798-3966	798-8590
Will-Burt Co PO Box 900 *Web:* www.willburt.com	Orrville	OH	44667	330-682-7015	684-5257
WSI Industries Inc 213 Chelsea Rd *NASDAQ: WSCI* ■ *Web:* www.wsci.com	Monticello	MN	55362	763-295-9202	295-9212
Xtek Inc 11451 Reading Rd *TF:* 888-332-9835 ■ *Web:* www.xtek.com	Cincinnati	OH	45241	513-733-7800	733-7939

458 MACHINE TOOLS - METAL CUTTING TYPES

SEE ALSO Machine Tools - Metal Forming Types p. 1925; Metalworking Devices & Accessories p. 1967

Company	City	State	ZIP	Phone	Fax
Abbco Inc 26 N Garden Ave *TF:* 866-986-6546	Bensenville	IL	60106	630-595-7115	595-6431
Accurate Boring Co 17420 Malyn Blvd *Web:* www.accurateboring.com	Fraser	MI	48026	586-294-7555	294-2530
Acme Mfg Co 4240 N Atlantic Blvd *TF:* 888-340-2263 ■ *Web:* www.acmemfg.com	Auburn Hills	MI	48326	248-393-7300	393-4060
Airtronics Gage & Machine Co 516 Slade Ave *Web:* www.airtronicsgage.com	Elgin	IL	60120	847-695-0911	695-8745
Allen Chas G Co Inc 25 Williamsville Rd *Web:* www.chasgallen.com	Barre	MA	01005	978-355-2911	355-2917
Allied Tool Products 9334 N 107th St *TF:* 800-558-5147 ■ *Web:* www.atptools.com	Milwaukee	WI	53224	414-355-8280	355-8297
Amada Cutting Technologies Inc 14849 E Northam St *TF:* 800-877-4729 ■ *Web:* www.amadabandsaw.com	La Mirada	CA	90638	714-670-1704	670-2017
American Broach & Machine Co 4600 Jackson Rd *Web:* www.americanbroach.com	Ann Arbor	MI	48103	734-761-5021	761-7626
American GFM Corp 1200 Cavalier Blvd *Web:* www.agfm.com	Chesapeake	VA	23323	757-487-2442	487-5274
American Heller Corp 15285 Leone Dr *TF:* 800-950-2487 ■ *Web:* www.americanheller.com	Macomb	MI	48042	586-677-2300	677-2292
Ann Arbor Machine 5800 Sibley Rd *Web:* www.aam-ch.com	Chelsea	MI	48118	734-475-0505	475-4336
Automatic Tooling Corp 521 Saint Jean St	Detroit	MI	48214	313-822-9250	822-0192
Automation Assoc Inc 416 Campus Dr *TF:* 800-927-7348 ■ *Web:* www.autoinc.com	Arlington Heights	IL	60004	847-255-4500	255-9648
Babin Machine Works Inc 2510 N 9th St PO Box 2007 *TF:* 800-269-1274	Beaumont	TX	77704	409-892-1231	892-1236
Bader Stephen Co Inc 10 Charles St PO Box 297 *Web:* www.stephenbader.com	Valley Falls	NY	12185	518-753-4456	753-4962
Bardons & Oliver Inc 5800 Harper Rd *Web:* www.bardonsoliver.com	Solon	OH	44139	440-498-5800	498-2001
Barnes International Inc 814 Chestnut St PO Box 1203 *TF:* 800-435-4877 ■ *Web:* www.barnesintl.com	Rockford	IL	61105	815-964-8661	964-5074
Bor-o Tools Corp 2525 Industrial Row	Troy	MI	48084	248-280-1600	280-1603
Bourn & Koch Inc 2500 Kishwaukee St *TF:* 800-248-8120 ■ *Web:* www.bourn-koch.com	Rockford	IL	61104	815-965-4013	965-0019
Bryant Grinder 65 Pearl St *Web:* www.bryantgrinder.com	Springfield	VT	05156	802-885-5161	885-9444
Burr Oak Tool & Gauge Co Inc PO Box 338 *Web:* www.burroak.com	Sturgis	MI	49091	269-651-9393	651-4324
Carlson Tool & Machine Co 2300 Gary Ln *Web:* www.carlsontoolandmachine.com	Geneva	IL	60134	630-232-2460	232-2016
Chas G Allen Co Inc 25 Williamsville Rd *Web:* www.chasgallen.com	Barre	MA	01005	978-355-2911	355-2917
Cincinnati Lamb 2200 Litton Ln *TF:* 800-934-0735 ■ *Web:* www.cincinnatilamb.com	Hebron	KY	41048	859-534-4600	534-4997
Cincinnati Lamb 13900 Lakeside Cir *TF:* 800-521-0166 ■ *Web:* www.cincinnatilamb.com	Sterling Heights	MI	48313	586-566-2400	532-3102
Continental Machines Inc 5505 W 123rd St	Savage	MN	55378	952-890-3300	895-6450
Cook RF Mfg Co 4585 Allen Rd *Web:* www.rfcook.com	Stow	OH	44224	330-923-9797	923-8641
Crafts Technologies 91 Joey Dr *TF:* 800-323-6802 ■ *Web:* www.craftstech.net	Elk Grove Village	IL	60007	847-758-3100	758-0162
Cross Huller 13900 Lakeside Cir *TF:* 800-521-0166 ■ *Web:* www.crosshuller.com	Sterling Heights	MI	48313	586-566-2400	586-3726
Darex 210 E Hersey St PO Box 730 *TF:* 800-547-0222 ■ *Web:* www.darex.com	Ashland	OR	97520	541-488-2224	488-2229
Davenport Machine Inc 167 Ames St *TF:* 800-344-5748 ■ *Web:* www.davenportmachine.com	Rochester	NY	14611	585-235-4545	235-7997
Davis & Thompson Co N 58 W 14630 Shawn Cir *Web:* entrusttool.com/davisandthompson.htm	Menomonee Falls	WI	53051	262-252-3686	252-4075
Dayton Machine Tool Co 1314 Webster St *Web:* www.dmtnet.com	Dayton	OH	45404	937-222-6444	222-6448
Detroit Broach Co 2750 Paldan Dr *TF:* 800-383-6978 ■ *Web:* www.dbcbroach.com	Auburn Hills	MI	48326	248-370-0600	370-9110
DoALL Co 1480 S Wolf Rd *Web:* www.doall.com	Wheeling	IL	60090	847-495-6800	484-2045

Company	City	State	Zip	Phone	Fax
DS Technology Inc 7861 Palace Dr *TF:* 800-531-0135 ■ *Web:* www.ds-technologie.de	Cincinnati	OH	45249	513-247-2590	247-2599
Dynetics Corp 30 Nashua St *Web:* www.dyneticscorp.com	Woburn	MA	01801	781-933-2680	933-9028
Eagle Tool Co 101 Woodward Ave	Iron Mountain	MI	49801	906-774-0284	774-0342
EH Wachs Co 600 Knightsbridge Pkwy **Fax:* Sales ■ *TF:* 800-323-8185 ■ *Web:* www.wachsco.com	Lincolnshire	IL	60069	847-537-8800	520-1168*
Entrust Tool & Design Co Inc N 58 W 14630 Shawn Cir *Web:* www.entrusttool.com	Menomonee Falls	WI	53051	262-252-3802	252-4075
Everite Machine Products Co 501 E Erie Ave *Web:* www.everite.net	Philadelphia	PA	19134	215-425-3750	426-7768
Ex-Cell-O Machine Tools 13900 Lakeside Cir *TF:* 800-837-6277 ■ *Web:* www.ex-cell-o.com	Sterling Heights	MI	48313	586-566-2400	586-3726
Extrude Hone Corp 1 Industry Blvd *TF:* 800-367-1109 ■ *Web:* www.extrudehone.com	Irwin	PA	15642	724-863-5900	863-8759
Flow International Corp 23500 64th Ave S *NASDAQ:* FLOW ■ *TF:* 800-446-3569 ■ *Web:* www.flowcorp.com	Kent	WA	98032	253-850-3500	813-3285
General Machine & Tool Works Inc 313 W Chestnut St	Chicago	IL	60610	312-337-2177	337-0244
GF AgieCharmilles 560 Bond St *TF:* 800-282-1336 ■ *Web:* us.gfac.com	Lincolnshire	IL	60069	847-913-5300	913-5340
Giddings & Lewis LLC 142 Doty St PO Box 590 **Fax:* Sales ■ *TF:* 800-343-2847 ■ *Web:* www.giddings.com	Fond du Lac	WI	54936	920-921-9400	906-2075*
Giddings & Lewis Machine Tools 142 Doty St PO Box 590 *Web:* www.glmachinetools.com	Fond du Lac	WI	54936	920-921-9400	906-2522
Gleason Corp 1000 University Ave *TF:* 800-280-0825 ■ *Web:* www.gleason.com	Rochester	NY	14607	585-473-1000	264-9765
Grob Inc 1731 10th Ave *TF:* 800-225-6481 ■ *Web:* www.grobinc.com	Grafton	WI	53024	262-377-1400	377-2106
Hammond Roto-Finish 1600 Douglas Ave *TF:* 800-253-9896 ■ *Web:* www.hammondmach.com	Kalamazoo	MI	49007	269-345-7151	345-1710
Hanchett Mfg Inc 906 N State St *TF:* 800-454-7463 ■ *Web:* www.hanchett.com	Big Rapids	MI	49307	231-796-7678	796-4851
Hardinge Inc 1 Hardinge Dr *NASDAQ:* HDNG ■ *TF:* 800-843-8801 ■ *Web:* www.hardinge.com	Elmira	NY	14905	607-734-2281	732-4925
Harig Products Inc 1875 Big Timber Rd *Web:* www.harigproducts.com	Elgin	IL	60123	847-695-1000	695-1043
Harrington Tool Co PO Box 280 *Web:* www.harringtontool.com	Ludington	MI	49431	231-843-3445	845-7477
Hause Machines 809 S Pleasant St *TF:* 800-932-8665 ■ *Web:* www.hausemachines.com	Montpelier	OH	43543	419-485-3158	485-3146
Hausermann Abrading Process Co 300 W Laura Dr *Web:* www.hausermann.net	Addison	IL	60101	630-543-6688	543-6689
Hetran Inc 70 Pinedale Industrial Rd *Web:* www.hetraninc.com	Orwigsburg	PA	17961	570-366-1411	366-1829
Hudson Machinery Worldwide PO Box 831 *TF:* 800-343-0772 ■ *Web:* www.hudsonmachinery.com	Haverhill	MA	01831	978-374-0303	373-7295
Huffman Corp 1050 Huffman Way *TF:* 888-483-3626 ■ *Web:* www.huffmancorp.com	Clover	SC	29710	803-222-4561	222-7599
Hurco Cos Inc 1 Technology Way *NASDAQ:* HURC ■ *TF Sales:* 800-634-2416 ■ *Web:* www.hurco.com	Indianapolis	IN	46268	317-293-5309	298-2621
Hydromat Inc 11600 Adie Rd **Fax:* Sales ■ *TF:* 888-432-0070 ■ *Web:* www.hydromat.com	Saint Louis	MO	63043	314-432-4644	432-7552*
Hypertherm Inc 21 Great Hollow Rd PO Box 5010 *TF:* 800-643-0030 ■ *Web:* www.hypertherm.com	Hanover	NH	03755	603-643-3441	643-5352
Hypneumat Inc 5900 W Franklin Dr *Web:* www.hypneumat.com	Franklin	WI	53132	414-423-7400	423-7414
Industrial Metal Products Corp 3417 W Saint Joseph St **Fax:* Sales ■ *Web:* www.impco.com	Lansing	MI	48917	517-484-9411	484-0502*
Industrial Steel & Machine Sales Inc 2712 Lackland Dr *Web:* www.is-ms.net	Waterloo	IA	50702	319-296-1816	296-3630
ITW Heartland 3600 W Lake Ave *TF:* 800-724-6166 ■ *Web:* www.itwinc.com	Glenview	IL	60026	847-724-7500	657-4261
Jasco Cutting Tools 1390 Mt Read Blvd *TF:* 800-868-1074 ■ *Web:* www.jascotools.com	Rochester	NY	14606	585-546-1254	254-2655
Johann A Krause Inc 901 Doris Rd *Web:* www.jakrauseinc.com	Auburn Hills	MI	48326	248-340-8000	340-8001
John J Adams Die Corp 10 Nebraska St *TF:* 800-356-0110 ■ *Web:* johnjadamscuttingdies.com	Worcester	MA	01604	508-757-3894	753-8016
Kasper Machine Co 29275 Stephenson Hwy *Web:* www.kaspermachine.com	Madison Heights	MI	48071	248-547-3150	547-1293
Kaufman Mfg Co 547 S 29th St PO Box 1056 *Web:* www.kaufmanmfg.com	Manitowoc	WI	54221	920-684-6641	686-4103
Kennametal Inc 1600 Technology Way PO Box 231 *NYSE:* KMT ■ *TF Cust Svc:* 800-446-7738 ■ *Web:* www.kennametal.com	Latrobe	PA	15650	724-539-5000	539-8787
Kingsbury Corp 80 Laurel St *Web:* www.kingsburycorp.com	Keene	NH	03431	603-352-5212	352-8789
Kitamura Machinery of USA Inc 78 E Century Dr *Web:* www.kitamura-machinery.com	Wheeling	IL	60090	847-520-7755	520-7763
Klingelhofer Corp 165 Mill Ln *Web:* www.klingelhofer.com	Mountainside	NJ	07092	908-232-7200	232-1841
Koike Aronson Inc 635 W Main St PO Box 307 *TF:* 800-252-5232 ■ *Web:* www.koike.com	Arcade	NY	14009	585-492-2400	457-3517
Komatsu America Corp Cutting Technologies Div 92 Cummings Park *TF:* 800-707-2767 ■ *Web:* www.fineplasma.com	Woburn	MA	01801	781-782-0505	782-0506
Krause Johann A Inc 901 Doris Rd *Web:* www.jakrauseinc.com	Auburn Hills	MI	48326	248-340-8000	340-8001
Kyocera Tycom Corp 17862 Fitch Ave **Fax Area Code:* 949 ■ *TF:* 800-537-0294 ■ *Web:* www.kyoceratycom.com	Irvine	CA	92614	800-537-0294	955-0874*
Landis Grinding Systems 20 E 6th St *Web:* www.landisgardner.com	Waynesboro	PA	17268	717-762-2161	765-5140
Leader Tool Co 630 N Huron PO Box 66	Harbor Beach	MI	48441	989-479-3281	479-3307
Lucas Precision LP 13020 Saint Clair Ave *Web:* www.lucasprecision.com	Cleveland	OH	44108	216-451-5588	451-5174
Makino Inc 7680 Innovation Way *TF:* 888-625-4661 ■ *Web:* www.makino.com	Mason	OH	45040	513-573-7200	573-7360
Manchester Tool Co 5142 Manchester Rd *TF Cust Svc:* 800-237-8789 ■ *Web:* www.manchestertools.com	Akron	OH	44319	330-644-8853	644-6139
McLean Inc 3409 E Miraloma Ave *TF Cust Svc:* 800-451-2424 ■ *Web:* www.mcleanlathe.com	Anaheim	CA	92806	714-996-5451	996-5453
Metal Cutting Corp 89 Commerce Rd *Web:* www.metalcutting.com	Cedar Grove	NJ	07009	973-239-1100	239-6651
Metl-Saw Systems Inc 2950 Bay Vista Ct *Web:* www.metlsaw.com	Benicia	CA	94510	707-746-6200	746-5085
Meyers WF Co 1017 14th St PO Box 426 *TF:* 800-457-4055 ■ *Web:* www.wfmeyers.com	Bedford	IN	47421	812-275-4485	275-4488
MG Systems & Welding Inc W 141 N 9427 Fountain Blvd *Web:* www.mg-systems-welding.com	Menomonee Falls	WI	53051	262-255-5520	255-5170
Mitsubishi Materials USA Corp 17401 Eastman St *TF:* 800-523-0800	Irvine	CA	92614	949-862-5100	862-5169
Monarch Lathes LP 615 N Oaks Ave PO Box 4609 *Web:* www.lucasprecision.com/monarch	Sidney	OH	45365	937-492-4111	492-7958
Morgood Tools Inc 940 Millstead Way *Web:* www.morgood.com	Rochester	NY	14624	585-436-8828	436-2426
Nachi Machining Technology Co 17500 23-Mile Rd *Web:* www.nachimtc.com	Macomb	MI	48044	586-263-0100	263-4571
NNT Corp 1320 Norwood Ave *TF:* 800-556-9999 ■ *Web:* www.nntcorp.com	Itasca	IL	60143	630-875-9600	875-8899
Normac Inc 10 Loop Rd PO Box 69 *Web:* www.normac.com	Arden	NC	28704	828-684-1002	209-9001
North American Products Corp 1180 Wernsing Rd **Fax Area Code:* 800 ■ *TF Cust Svc:* 800-634-8665 ■ *Web:* www.naptools.com	Jasper	IN	47546	812-482-2000	457-7458*
Ohio Broach & Machine Co 35264 Topps Industrial Pkwy **Fax:* Sales ■ *Web:* www.ohiobroach.com	Willoughby	OH	44094	440-946-1040	946-0725*
Okuma America Corp 11900 W Hall Dr *Web:* www.okumaamerica.com	Charlotte	NC	28278	704-588-7000	588-6503
Oliver of Adrian 831 Division St PO Box 189 *TF:* 877-668-0885 ■ *Web:* www.oliverinstrument.com	Adrian	MI	49221	517-263-2132	265-8698
P & R Industries Inc 1524 Clinton Ave N	Rochester	NY	14621	585-266-6725	266-0075
Parker Majestic Inc 300 N Pike Rd *TF:* 866-572-7537 ■ *Web:* www.parkermajestic.com	Sarver	PA	16055	724-352-1551	353-1196
Peddinghaus Corp 300 N Washington Ave *TF:* 800-786-2448 ■ *Web:* www.peddinghaus.com	Bradley	IL	60915	815-937-3800	937-4003
Pioneer Broach Co 6434 Telegraph Rd *TF:* 800-621-1945 ■ *Web:* www.pioneerbroach.com	Los Angeles	CA	90040	323-728-1263	722-1699
PMC Industries Inc 29100 Lakeland Blvd *Web:* www.pmcindustries.com	Wickliffe	OH	44092	440-943-3300	944-1974
Reno Machine Co Inc 170 Pane Rd *Web:* www.reno-machine.com	Newington	CT	06111	860-666-5641	667-4496
Republic-Lagun Machine Tool Co 1000 E Carson St *TF:* 800-421-2105 ■ *Web:* www.lagun.com	Carson	CA	90745	310-518-1100	830-0923
Rex-Buckeye Co Inc 1230-A W 58th St *TF:* 800-932-0011 ■ *Web:* www.rexbuckeye.com	Cleveland	OH	44102	216-939-9000	939-3300
RF Cook Mfg Co 4585 Allen Rd *Web:* www.rfcook.com	Stow	OH	44224	330-923-9797	923-8641
Rockford Ettco 3445 Lonergan Dr *Web:* www.ettco.com	Rockford	IL	61109	815-874-4753	874-9425
Rothenberger USA 4455 Boeing Dr **Fax Area Code:* 800 ■ *TF:* 800-435-0786 ■ *Web:* www.rothenberger-usa.com	Rockford	IL	61109	815-397-7617	451-2632*
Rottler Mfg 8029 S 200th St *TF:* 800-452-0534 ■ *Web:* www.rottlermfg.com	Kent	WA	98032	253-872-7050	395-0230
Royal Master Grinders Inc 143 Bauer Dr *Web:* www.royalmaster.com	Oakland	NJ	07436	201-337-8500	337-2324
RP Machine Enterprises Inc 820 Cochran St *Web:* www.rpmachine.com	Statesville	NC	28677	704-872-8888	872-5777
S & M Machine Service Inc 109 E Highland Dr *TF:* 800-323-1579 ■ *Web:* www.snmmachine.com	Oconto Falls	WI	54154	920-846-8130	846-4803
S & S Machinery Co 140 53rd St *TF:* 800-540-9723 ■ *Web:* www.sandsmachinery.com	Brooklyn	NY	11232	718-492-7400	439-3930
Saginaw Machine Systems Inc 800 N Hamilton St *Web:* www.saginawmachine.com	Saginaw	MI	48602	989-753-8465	758-5575
Sandvik Coromant Co 1702 Nevins Rd *TF Cust Svc:* 800-726-3845 ■ *Web:* www.sandvik.com	Fair Lawn	NJ	07410	201-794-5000	794-5165
Savage Saws 100 Indel Ave PO Box 156 *TF:* 877-779-8763 ■ *Web:* www.savagesaws.com	Rancocas	NJ	08073	609-267-8501	267-1366
Seneca Falls Technology Group 314 Fall St *Web:* www.sftg.com	Seneca Falls	NY	13148	315-568-5804	568-5800
Servo Products Co 34940 Lakeland Blvd *TF:* 800-521-7359 ■ *Web:* www.servoproductsco.com	East Lake	OH	44095	440-942-9999	942-9100
Setco Sales Co 5880 Hillside Ave *TF:* 800-543-0470 ■ *Web:* www.setcousa.com	Cincinnati	OH	45233	513-941-5110	941-6913
SGS Tool Co 55 S Main St **Fax:* Hum Res ■ *Web:* www.sgstool.com	Munroe Falls	OH	44262	330-688-6667	686-2128*
Simmons Machine Tool Corp 1700 N Broadway	Albany	NY	12204	518-462-5431	462-0371
Snappy Air Distribution Products 1011 11th Ave SE *TF:* 800-328-2044	Detroit Lakes	MN	56501	218-847-9258	847-6322
South Bend Lathe 1735 N Bendix Dr *Web:* www.southbendlathe.com	South Bend	IN	46628	574-289-0293	289-0906
Southwestern Industries Inc 2615 Homestead Pl *TF:* 800-421-6875 ■ *Web:* www.southwesternindustries.com	Rancho Dominguez	CA	90220	310-608-4422	764-2668
Stephen Bader Co Inc 10 Charles St PO Box 297 *Web:* www.stephenbader.com	Valley Falls	NY	12185	518-753-4456	753-4962
Sunnen Products Co 7910 Manchester Ave **Fax:* Cust Svc ■ *TF:* 800-325-3670 ■ *Web:* www.sunnen.com	Saint Louis	MO	63143	314-781-2100	781-2268*
Technidrill Systems Inc 429 Portage Blvd *TF:* 800-914-5863 ■ *Web:* www.technidrillsystems.com	Kent	OH	44240	330-678-9980	678-9981
Thermal Dynamics Corp 82 Benning St *TF:* 800-752-7621 ■ *Web:* www.thermal-dynamics.com	West Lebanon	NH	03784	603-298-5711	298-0558
Thurston Mfg Co Inc 14 Thurber Blvd *Web:* www.thurstonmfg.com	Smithfield	RI	02917	401-232-9100	232-9101
Tornos Technologies US Corp 70 Pocono Rd *TF:* 800-243-5027 ■ *Web:* www.tornos.ch	Brookfield	CT	06804	203-775-4319	775-4281
Toyoda Machinery USA Inc 316 W University Dr *TF:* 800-257-2985 ■ *Web:* www.toyodausa.com	Arlington Heights	IL	60004	847-253-0340	577-4680
TRI-CAM Inc 2730 Eastrock Dr PO Box 5046 *Web:* www.tricaminc.com	Rockford	IL	61125	815-226-9200	226-0661
Turmatic Systems Inc 11600 Adie Rd *TF:* 888-432-0070 ■ *Web:* www.turmatic.com	Saint Louis	MO	63043	314-993-0600	993-0676
US Tool Grinding Inc 701 S Desloge Dr *TF:* 800-775-8665 ■ *Web:* www.ustg.net	Desloge	MO	63601	573-431-3856	431-6655
Valenite LLC 1675 Whitcomb Ave **Fax Area Code:* 800 ■ *TF Cust Svc:* 800-488-9112 ■ *Web:* www.valenite.com	Madison Heights	MI	48071	248-589-1000	488-0695*
Vernon Tool Co Ltd 503 Jones Rd *TF:* 800-452-1542 ■ *Web:* www.vernontool.com	Oceanside	CA	92054	760-433-5860	757-2233
Wachs EH Co 600 Knightsbridge Pkwy **Fax:* Sales ■ *TF:* 800-323-8185 ■ *Web:* www.wachsco.com	Lincolnshire	IL	60069	847-537-8800	520-1168*
Wells WF Inc 16645 Heimbach Rd *Web:* www.wfwells.com	Three Rivers	MI	49093	269-279-5123	279-6337
WF Meyers Co 1017 14th St PO Box 426 *TF:* 800-457-4055 ■ *Web:* www.wfmeyers.com	Bedford	IN	47421	812-275-4485	275-4488
WF Wells Inc 16645 Heimbach Rd *Web:* www.wfwells.com	Three Rivers	MI	49093	269-279-5123	279-6337
Whitney Tool Co Inc 906 R St PO Box 545 *TF:* 800-536-1971 ■ *Web:* www.whitney-tool.com	Bedford	IN	47421	812-275-4491	275-6458
Wisconsin Machine Tool Corp 3225 Gateway Rd Suite 100 *TF:* 800-243-3078 ■ *Web:* www.machine-tool.com	Brookfield	WI	53045	262-317-3048	317-3049

459 MACHINE TOOLS - METAL FORMING TYPES

SEE ALSO Machine Tools - Metal Cutting Types p. 1924; Metalworking Devices & Accessories p. 1967; Rolling Mill Machinery p. 2300; Tool & Die Shops p. 2369

Company	City	State	Zip	Phone	Fax
Advanced Hydraulics Inc 13568 Vintage Pl *TF:* 888-581-8079	Chino	CA	91710	909-590-7644	590-7049

Phone Fax

Ajax Technologies 1441 Chardon Rd ... Cleveland OH 44117 216-531-1010 481-6369

Alva Allen Industries Inc 1001-15 N 3rd St PO Box 427 ... Clinton MO 64735 660-885-3331 885-3333
TF Cust Svc: 800-343-5657 ■ *Web:* www.alvaallenind.com

Amada America Inc 7025 Firestone Blvd ... Buena Park CA 90621 714-739-2111 739-4099
TF: 800-626-6612 ■ *Web:* www.amada.com

American Actuator Corp PO Box 113096 ... Stamford CT 06911 203-324-6334 324-4471
Web: www.americanactuator.com

Anderson Cook Inc 17650 15-Mile Rd ... Fraser MI 48026 586-293-0800 293-0833
Web: www.andersoncook.com

Atlas Technologies Inc 3100 Cotter Ave ... Fenton MI 48430 810-629-6663 629-8145
TF: 800-536-3162 ■ *Web:* www.atlastechnologies.com

Badge A Minit Ltd 345 N Lewis Ave ... Oglesby IL 61348 815-883-8822 883-9696
TF: 800-223-4103 ■ *Web:* www.badgeaminit.com

Beatty Machine & Mfg Co Inc 940 150th St ... Hammond IN 46327 219-931-3000 937-1662

Bedco Inc 4600 Bree Rd ... East China MI 48054 810-329-2292 329-4017
Web: www.bedcoinc.com

Bliss Clearing Niagara 1004 E State St ... Hastings MI 49058 269-948-3300 948-3313
TF: 800-642-5477 ■ *Web:* www.blissclearingniagara.com

Bradbury Co Inc PO Box 667 ... Moundridge KS 67107 620-345-6394 345-6381
TF: 800-397-6394 ■ *Web:* www.bradburygroup.net/brad.cfm

Bruderer Inc 1200 Hendricks Causeway ... Ridgefield NJ 07657 201-941-2121 886-2010
Web: www.bruderer.com

Burr Oak Tool & Gauge Co Inc PO Box 338 ... Sturgis MI 49091 269-651-9393 651-4324
Web: www.burroak.com

CA Lawton Co Inc 1950 Enterprise Way ... De Pere WI 54115 920-558-4422 337-2477
TF: 800-842-6888 ■ *Web:* www.calawton.com

California Aircraft Tool Co 821 W Olive St ... Inglewood CA 90301 323-670-2536 670-6862*
**Fax Area Code:* 310 ■ *Web:* www.californiaaircrafttool.com

Chicago Dreis & Krump Mfg Co 7400 S Loomis Blvd ... Chicago IL 60636 773-874-1200 874-2622
Web: www.dreis-krump.com

Cincinnati Inc 7420 Kilby Rd ... Harrison OH 45030 513-367-7100 367-7552
Web: www.e-ci.com

CJ Winter Machine Technologies Inc 167 Ames St ... Rochester NY 14611 585-429-5000 429-5095
TF: 800-288-7655 ■ *Web:* www.cjwinter.com

Cyril Bath Co 1610 Airport Rd ... Monroe NC 28110 704-289-8531 289-3932
TF: 800-801-1418 ■ *Web:* www.cyrilbath.com

DR Sperry & Co 623 Rathbone Ave ... North Aurora IL 60506 630-892-4361 892-1664
TF: 888-997-9297 ■ *Web:* www.drsperry.com

EB Automation Industries Ltd 116 Toledo St ... Farmingdale NY 11735 631-752-1642 752-1644

Edwards Mfg Co 1107 Sykes St PO Box 166 ... Albert Lea MN 56007 507-373-8206 373-9433
TF: 800-373-8206 ■ *Web:* www.edwardsironworkers.com

Eitel Presses Inc 97 Pinedale Industrial Rd ... Orwigsburg PA 17961 570-366-0585 366-2536
TF: 800-458-2218 ■ *Web:* www.eitelpresses.com

Erie Press Systems 1253 W 12th St PO Box 4061 ... Erie PA 16512 814-455-3941 456-4819*
**Fax:* Mktg ■ *TF:* 800-222-3608 ■ *Web:* www.eriepress.com

Feintool Cincinnati 11280 Cornell Park Dr ... Cincinnati OH 45242 513-247-0110 247-0060
Web: www.feintool-usa.com

FH Peterson Machine Corp 143 South St ... Stoughton MA 02072 781-341-4930 341-6022
Web: www.fhpetersonmachine.com

GEMCOR Corp 100 GEMCOR Dr ... West Seneca NY 14224 716-674-9300 674-3171
Web: www.gemcor.com

General Broach Co Spline Rolling Div 307 Salisbury St ... Morenci MI 49256 517-458-7555 458-6821
Web: www.generalbroach.com

Grant Assembly Technologies 90 Silliman Ave ... Bridgeport CT 06605 203-366-4557 366-0370
TF: 800-227-2150 ■ *Web:* www.grantriveters.com

Greenerd Press & Machine Co Inc 41 Crown St ... Nashua NH 03060 603-889-4101 889-7601
TF: 800-877-9110 ■ *Web:* www.greenerd.com

Grob Inc 1731 10th Ave ... Grafton WI 53024 262-377-1400 377-2106
TF: 800-225-6481 ■ *Web:* www.grobinc.com

H & H Tooling Inc 30505 Clemens Rd ... Westlake OH 44145 440-250-3204 250-3205
TF: 800-808-6840 ■ *Web:* www.hhtooling.com

Heim LP 6360 W 73rd St ... Chicago IL 60638 708-496-7450 496-7428
Web: www.theheimgroup.com

Hess Engineering Inc 2950 Redfield Rd ... Niles MI 49120 269-683-4182 683-1775
Web: www.hess-eng.com

HPM Div Taylor's Industrial Services LLC 820 Marion Rd ... Mount Gilead OH 43338 419-946-0222 946-2473
Web: www.taylorsind.com/2003/hpm/index.php

Hudson Machinery Worldwide PO Box 831 ... Haverhill MA 01831 978-374-0303 373-7295
TF: 800-343-0772 ■ *Web:* www.hudsonmachinery.com

JD Phillips Corp 181 N Industrial Hwy ... Alpena MI 49707 989-356-2279 356-6081
Web: www.jdphillipscorp.com

JF Helmold & Brothers Inc 901 Morse Ave ... Elk Grove Village IL 60007 847-437-7085 437-6033
TF: 800-323-8898 ■ *Web:* www.helmold.com

Kinefac Corp 156 Goddard Memorial Dr ... Worcester MA 01603 508-754-6891 756-5342
TF: 800-458-5941 ■ *Web:* www.kinefac.com

Koppy Corp 199 Kay Industrial Dr ... Orion MI 48359 248-373-5200 373-5201
Web: www.koppycorp.com

L & F Industries Corp Div of Erie Press Systems
1253 W 12th St PO Box 4061 ... Erie PA 16512 814-455-3941 456-4819
TF: 800-222-3608 ■ *Web:* www.lfindustries.com

Lawton CA Co Inc 1950 Enterprise Way ... De Pere WI 54115 920-558-4422 337-2477
TF: 800-842-6888 ■ *Web:* www.calawton.com

Leader Tool Co 630 N Huron PO Box 66 ... Harbor Beach MI 48441 989-479-3281 479-3307

Lockformer Co 711 Ogden Ave ... Lisle IL 60532 630-964-8000 964-5685
Web: www.lockformer.com

Magnum Integrated Technologies 4 Thomas Dr Unit 5 ... Westbrook ME 04092 207-854-9791 896-1905*
**Fax Area Code:* 800 ■ *TF:* 800-830-0642 ■ *Web:* www.magnum-integrated.com

Manor Industries Inc 24400 Maplehurst ... Clinton Township MI 48036 586-463-4604 463-3905
Web: www.manorindustries.com

Mate Precision Tooling Inc 1295 Lund Blvd ... Anoka MN 55303 763-421-0230 421-0285
TF: 800-328-4492 ■ *Web:* www.matept.com

Met-Coil Systems Corp 5460 6th St SW ... Cedar Rapids IA 52404 319-363-6566 362-0225
Web: www.metcoil.com

Minster Machine Co 240 W 5th St PO Box 120 ... Minster OH 45865 419-628-2331 628-3517
Web: www.minster.com

Murata Machinery USA Inc 2120 Queen City Dr ... Charlotte NC 28208 704-875-9280 392-6541
TF: 800-428-8469 ■ *Web:* www.muratec-usa.com

National Diecasting Machinery & Kard Trim Presses
33 Plan Way Bldg 7 ... Warwick RI 02886 401-737-3005 739-2528
TF: 800-242-1253 ■ *Web:* www.nationalkard.com

National Machinery LLC 161 Greenfield St ... Tiffin OH 44883 419-447-5211 443-2379
Web: www.nationalmachinery.com

NFM Welding Engineers 577 Oberlin Rd SW ... Massillon OH 44647 330-837-3868 837-2230
Web: www.nfmwe.com

Oak Products Inc 504 Wade St ... Sturgis MI 49091 269-651-8513 659-4625
Web: www.oakproducts.biz

Pacific Press Technologies 714 Walnut St ... Mount Carmel IL 62863 618-262-8666 262-7000
TF: 800-851-3586 ■ *Web:* www.pacific-press.com

Pacific Roller Die Co 1321 W Winton Ave ... Hayward CA 94545 510-782-7242 887-5639
TF: 800-253-6463 ■ *Web:* www.prdcompany.com

PCC Specialty Products Inc Reed-Rico Div 28 Sword St ... Auburn MA 01501 508-753-6530 753-0127
TF Cust Svc: 800-343-6068 ■ *Web:* www.reedrico.com

Peterson FH Machine Corp 143 South St ... Stoughton MA 02072 781-341-4930 341-6022
Web: www.fhpetersonmachine.com

PHI Inc 14955 E Salt Lake Ave ... City of Industry CA 91746 626-968-9680 333-3610
Web: www.phi-tulip.com

Phillips JD Corp 181 N Industrial Hwy ... Alpena MI 49707 989-356-2279 356-6081
Web: www.jdphillipscorp.com

Presses Inc 6360 W 73rd St ... Chicago IL 60638 708-496-7400 496-7428
Web: www.theheimgroup.com

QPI Multipress Inc 2222 S 3rd St ... Columbus OH 43207 614-228-0185 228-2358
Web: www.multipress.com

Reed-Rico Div PCC Specialty Products Inc 28 Sword St ... Auburn MA 01501 508-753-6530 753-0127
TF Cust Svc: 800-343-6068 ■ *Web:* www.reedrico.com

Reno Machine Co Inc 170 Pane Rd ... Newington CT 06111 860-666-5641 667-4496
Web: www.reno-machine.com

Rimrock Corp 1700 Jetway Blvd ... Columbus OH 43219 614-471-5926 471-7388
Web: www.rimrockcorp.com

Rogers Assoc Machine Tool Corp 15 Saint James St ... Rochester NY 14606 585-647-2230 647-1161
Web: www.ramtc.com

Roper Whitney of Rockford Inc 2833 Huffman Blvd ... Rockford IL 61103 815-962-3011 962-2227*
**Fax:* Sales ■ *Web:* www.roperwhitney.com

Royle Systems Group 1000 Cannonball Rd ... Pompton Lakes NJ 07442 973-839-8118 839-7327
Web: roylesystems.com

Sandvik Hard Materials Co 1600 Freeway Blvd ... Brooklyn Center MN 55430 763-560-4600 560-4611
Web: www.technicaltooling.com

Sonnet Tool Co 12822 Simms Ave ... Hawthorne CA 90250 310-973-4114 973-0573

Sperry DR & Co 623 Rathbone Ave ... North Aurora IL 60506 630-892-4361 892-1664
TF: 888-997-9297 ■ *Web:* www.drsperry.com

Strippit/LVD 12975 Clarence Ctr Rd ... Akron NY 14001 716-542-4511 542-5957
TF: 800-828-1527 ■ *Web:* www.strippit.com

Taylor's Industrial Services LLC HPM Div 820 Marion Rd ... Mount Gilead OH 43338 419-946-0222 946-2473
Web: www.taylorsind.com/2003/hpm/index.php

Tetrahedron Assoc Inc PO Box 710157 ... San Diego CA 92171 619-661-0552 661-0559
TF: 800-958-3872 ■ *Web:* www.tetrahedronassociates.com

Threaded Rod Co Inc 1929 Columbia Ave ... Indianapolis IN 46202 317-921-3000 921-3011
TF: 800-354-3330 ■ *Web:* www.threadedrod.com

Tishken Products Co 26800 Bedford Heights ... Bedford OH 44146 216-591-2180 292-6581
Web: www.tishken.com

Tools for Bending Inc 194 W Dakota Ave ... Denver CO 80223 303-777-7170 777-4749
TF Cust Svc: 800-873-3305 ■ *Web:* www.toolsforbending.com

US Baird Corp 1700 Stratford Ave PO Box 9706 ... Stratford CT 06615 203-375-3361 378-6006
Web: www.usbaird.com

US Machine Tools Corp 70 Horizon Dr ... Bristol CT 06010 860-953-8306 953-0364
TF: 800-664-0013 ■ *Web:* www.usmt.com

Vamco International 555 Epsilon Dr ... Pittsburgh PA 15238 412-963-7100 963-7160
Web: www.vamcointernational.com

WA Whitney Co 650 Race St ... Rockford IL 61101 815-964-6771 964-3175
TF: 800-435-2823 ■ *Web:* www.wawhitney.com

Wabash MPI 1569 Morris St PO Box 298 ... Wabash IN 46992 260-563-1184 563-1396
Web: www.wabashmpi.com

Williams White & Co 600 River Dr ... Moline IL 61265 309-797-7650 797-7677
TF: 877-797-7650 ■ *Web:* www.williamswhite.com

Winter CJ Machine Technologies Inc 167 Ames St ... Rochester NY 14611 585-429-5000 429-5095
TF: 800-288-7655 ■ *Web:* www.cjwinter.com

Wrentham Steel Products Co 30 Kendrick St ... Wrentham MA 02093 508-384-2166 384-7466
TF: 800-251-2166 ■ *Web:* www.wrenthamsteel.com

Wysong & Miles Co Inc 4820 US 29 N ... Greensboro NC 27405 336-621-3960 375-6187
TF: 800-299-7664 ■ *Web:* www.wysongmiles.com

460 MAGAZINES & JOURNALS

SEE ALSO Publishing Companies - Periodicals Publishers p. 2156

460-1 Agriculture & Farming Magazines

Phone Fax

Alfa News 2108 E South Blvd ... Montgomery AL 36116 334-288-3900 284-3957

American Agriculturist 1685 Baltimore Pike PO Box 4475 ... Gettysburg PA 17325 717-334-4300 334-3129
Web: www.americanagriculturist.com

American Quarter Horse Journal PO Box 200 ... Amarillo TX 79168 806-376-4811 349-6400
TF: 800-291-7323 ■ *Web:* www.aqha.com/showing/index.html

Beef 7900 International Dr Suite 300 ... Minneapolis MN 55425 952-851-9329 851-4601
TF Cust Svc: 800-722-5334 ■ *Web:* www.beef-mag.com

Beef Today Magazine 555 SW Peak Rd ... Polo MO 64671 816-586-5555
Web: www.agweb.com/beeftoday.asp

Breeders Journal 1525 River Rd ... DeForest WI 53532 608-846-6211 846-6434
TF: 800-356-5331

Buckeye Farm News PO Box 182383 ... Columbus OH 43218 614-246-8240 249-2200

Cooperative Farmer PO Box 26234 ... Richmond VA 23260 804-281-1369 281-1119

Cooperative Partners PO Box 64089 ... Saint Paul MN 55164 651-355-5151 282-7861
TF: 800-867-6747 ■ *Web:* www.mbrservices.com/coopartners/subscribe.cfm

Dairy Herd Management Magazine 10901 W 84th Terr ... Lenexa KS 66214 913-438-8700 438-0695
TF: 800-255-5113 ■ *Web:* www.dairyherd.com

Dairy Today 261 E Broadway PO Box 1167 ... Monticello MN 55362 763-271-3363 271-3360
Web: www.agweb.com/dairytoday.asp

Farm Bureau News 600 Maryland Ave SW Suite 800 ... Washington DC 20024 202-484-3600 406-3606
Web: www.fb.org/fbn

Farm Bureau Press 10720 Kanis Rd ... Little Rock AR 72211 501-224-4400 228-1557
Web: www.arfb.com

Farm Industry News 7900 International Dr Suite 300 ... Minneapolis MN 55425 952-851-9329 851-4601
TF Cust Svc: 800-722-5334 ■ *Web:* www.farmindustrynews.com

Farm Journal 1818 Market St 31st Fl ... Philadelphia PA 19103 215-557-8900 568-5012
TF: 800-523-1538 ■ *Web:* www.agweb.com/farmjournal.asp

Farm & Ranch Living 5400 S 60th St ... Greendale WI 53129 414-423-0100 423-8463
TF: 800-344-6913 ■ *Web:* www.farmandranchliving.com

Farm Show PO Box 1029 ... Lakeville MN 55044 952-469-5572 469-5575
TF: 800-834-9665 ■ *Web:* www.farmshow.com

Floridagriculture PO Box 147030 ... Gainesville FL 32614 352-374-1521 374-1530
Web: www.floridagriculture.org

Georgia Farm Bureau News 1620 Bass Rd ... Macon GA 31210 478-474-8411 474-8750
TF: 800-342-1192 ■ *Web:* www.gfb.org/gfbnews/gfbnews.html

Hoard's Dairyman 28 Milwaukee Ave W PO Box 801 ... Fort Atkinson WI 53538 920-563-5551 563-7298
Web: www.hoards.com

Hoosier Farmer PO Box 1290 ... Indianapolis IN 46206 317-692-7822 692-7854

Iowa Farm Bureau Spokesman 5400 University Ave ... West Des Moines IA 50266 515-225-5413 225-5419
TF: 800-442-3276

Kansas Living 2627 KFB Plaza ... Manhattan KS 66503 785-587-6000 587-6914
TF: 800-406-3053 ■ *Web:* www.kfb.org

Neighbors Magazine 2108 E South Blvd ... Montgomery AL 36116 334-288-3900 284-3957
Web: www.alfafarmers.org/neighbors/index.phtml

Pork Report PO Box 9114 ... Des Moines IA 50306 515-223-2600 223-2646
TF: 800-456-7675 ■ *Web:* www.pork.org

Progressive Farmer 2100 Lakeshore Dr ... Birmingham AL 35209 205-445-6000 877-6450
TF: 800-366-4712 ■ *Web:* www.progressivefarmer.com

Soybean Digest 7900 International Dr Suite 300 ... Minneapolis MN 55425 952-851-4667 851-4601
TF Cust Svc: 800-722-5334 ■ *Web:* www.cornandsoybeandigest.com

	City	State	Zip	Phone	Fax
Successful Farming 1716 Locust St	Des Moines	IA	50309	515-284-3000	284-3127
TF Cust Svc: 800-374-3276 ■ *Web:* www.agriculture.com/sfonline/index.html					
Tennessee Farm Bureau News PO Box 313	Columbia	TN	38402	931-388-7872	388-5818
Web: www.tnfarmbureau.org					
Texas Agriculture PO Box 2689	Waco	TX	76702	254-772-3030	772-1766
TF: 800-772-6535 ■ *Web:* www.txfb.org					
Texas Neighbors PO Box 2689	Waco	TX	76702	254-751-2251	772-1766
Web: www.txfb.org					
Top Producer 1818 Market St 31st Fl	Philadelphia	PA	19103	215-557-8964	568-3989
TF: 800-523-1538					

460-2 Art & Architecture Magazines

	City	State	Zip	Phone	Fax
American Artist Magazine 770 Broadway	New York	NY	10003	646-654-5500	654-5514
Web: www.myamericanartist.com					
AmericanStyle Magazine 3000 Chestnut Ave Suite 304	Baltimore	MD	21211	410-889-3093	243-7089
Web: www.americanstyle.com					
Architectural Digest 6300 Wilshire Blvd 11th Fl	Los Angeles	CA	90048	323-965-3700	965-4978
Web: www.architecturaldigest.com					
Architectural Record 2 Penn Plaza 9th Fl	New York	NY	10121	212-904-2594	904-4256
TF Cust Svc: 888-867-6395 ■ *Web:* archrecord.construction.com					
Architectural West Magazine 546 Court St	Reno	NV	89501	775-333-1080	333-1081
Web: www.architecturalwest.com					
Architecture 770 Broadway	New York	NY	10003	646-654-4482	654-5817
TF: 800-562-2706 ■ *Web:* www.architecturemag.com					
Art in America Magazine 575 Broadway	New York	NY	10012	212-941-2800	941-2819*
**Fax:* Cust Svc ■ *TF Cust Svc:* 800-925-8059 ■ *Web:* www.artinamericamagazine.com					
Art & Antiques Magazine 3500 Lenox Rd NE Suite 680	Atlanta	GA	30326	404-201-2500	201-2501
Web: www.artandantiques.net					
Art & Auction Magazine 111 8th Ave	New York	NY	10011	212-447-9555	447-5221
Web: www.artandauction.com					
Art Calendar PO Box 970	Dunnellon	FL	34432	866-427-8225	749-9626*
**Fax Area Code:* 410 ■ *TF:* 866-427-8225 ■ *Web:* www.artcalendar.com					
Artforum International Magazine 350 7th Ave 19th Fl	New York	NY	10001	212-475-4000	529-1257
TF: 800-966-2783 ■ *Web:* www.artforum.com					
Artist's Magazine The 4700 E Galbraith Rd	Cincinnati	OH	45236	513-531-2690	891-7153
TF: 800-283-0963 ■ *Web:* www.artistsmagazine.com					
ARTnews Magazine 48 W 38th St 9th Fl	New York	NY	10018	212-398-1690	819-0394
TF: 800-284-4625 ■ *Web:* www.artnewsonline.com					
Bomb Magazine 80 Hanson Pl Suite 703	Brooklyn	NY	11217	718-636-9100	636-9200
Web: www.bombsite.com					
Design Journal 1431 7th St Suite 205	Santa Monica	CA	90401	310-394-4394	394-0966
Web: www.designjournalmag.com					
Design/Build Business 1233 Janesville Ave	Fort Atkinson	WI	53538	920-563-6388	563-1706
TF: 800-547-7377 ■ *Web:* www.rdbmagazine.com					
Gallery Guide 97 Grayrock Rd PO Box 5541	Clinton	NJ	08809	908-638-5255	638-8737
Web: www.galleryguide.com					
HOW Design 4700 E Galbraith Rd	Cincinnati	OH	45036	513-531-2690	891-7153
TF Cust Svc: 800-333-1115 ■ *Web:* www.howdesign.com					
Inland Architect 3550 W Peterson Ave Suite 100	Chicago	IL	60659	773-866-9900	866-9881
TF: 888-641-3169 ■ *Web:* www.inlandarchitectmag.com					
Interior Design Magazine PO Box 5662	Harlan	IA	51593	800-900-0804	733-8019*
**Fax Area Code:* 712 ■ *Web:* www.interiordesign.net					
Landscape Architecture Magazine 636 'I' St NW	Washington	DC	20001	202-898-2444	898-1185
Web: www.asla.org/nonmembers/lam.cfm					
Metropolis Magazine 61 W 23rd St 4th Fl	New York	NY	10010	212-627-9977	627-9988
TF: 800-344-3046 ■ *Web:* www.metropolismag.com					
Modernism Magazine 199 George St	Lambertville	NJ	08530	609-397-4104	397-4409
Web: www.modernismmagazine.com					
Pastel Journal 4700 E Galbraith Rd	Cincinnati	OH	45236	513-531-2690	891-7153
TF: 800-283-0963 ■ *Web:* pasteljournal.com/index.asp					
Preservation Magazine 1785 Massachusetts Ave NW	Washington	DC	20036	202-588-6000	588-6266
TF: 800-944-6847 ■ *Web:* www.nationaltrust.org/Magazine/					
Southwest Art Magazine 5444 Westheimer Rd Suite 1440	Houston	TX	77056	713-296-7900	850-1314*
**Fax:* Edit ■ *TF:* 800-621-3963 ■ *Web:* www.southwestart.com					
Step Inside Design Magazine 6000 N Forest Park Dr	Peoria	IL	61614	309-688-8800	688-8515
TF: 800-255-8800 ■ *Web:* www.dgusa.com					
Studio Photography & Design Magazine					
3 Huntington Quad Suite 301-N	Melville	NY	11747	631-845-2700	845-7109
TF: 800-308-6397 ■ *Web:* www.imaging-info.com					
Sunshine Artist Magazine 4075 LB McLeod Rd Suite E	Orlando	FL	32811	407-648-7479	648-7454
Web: www.sunshineartist.com					
Watercolor Magic 4700 E Galbraith Rd	Cincinnati	OH	45236	513-531-2690	891-7153
TF Cust Svc: 800-811-9834 ■ *Web:* www.watercolormagic.com					
Wildlife Art Magazine 611 Main St PO Box 219	Ramona	CA	92065	760-788-9453	788-9454
TF: 800-221-6547 ■ *Web:* www.wildlifeartmag.com					

460-3 Automotive Magazines

	City	State	Zip	Phone	Fax
4-Wheel & Off-Road Magazine 6420 Wilshire Blvd	Los Angeles	CA	90048	323-782-2000	782-2467
TF: 800-436-6520 ■ *Web:* www.primedia.com					
American Iron Magazine 1010 Summer St	Stamford	CT	06905	203-425-8777	425-8775
TF Cust Svc: 877-693-3572 ■ *Web:* www.americanironmagazine.com					
American Motorcyclist 13515 Yarmouth Dr	Pickerington	OH	43147	614-856-1900	856-1920
TF: 800-262-5646 ■ *Web:* www.ama-cycle.org/magazine/					
Automobile Magazine 120 E Liberty St	Ann Arbor	MI	48104	734-994-3500	994-1153
Web: www.automobilemag.com					
AutoWeek 1155 Gratiot Ave	Detroit	MI	48207	313-446-6000	446-0347
TF Circ: 888-288-6954 ■ *Web:* www.autoweek.com					
Backroads Magazine 160 County Rd 521	Newton	NJ	07860	973-948-4176	948-0823
Web: www.backroadsusa.com					
Canadian Biker 735 Market St	Victoria	BC	V8T2E2	250-384-0333	384-1832
TF: 800-667-5667 ■ *Web:* www.canadianbiker.com					
Car Craft 6420 Wilshire Blvd	Los Angeles	CA	90048	323-782-2000	782-2263
TF: 800-436-6520 ■ *Web:* www.carcraft.com					
Car & Driver 2002 Hogback Rd	Ann Arbor	MI	48105	734-971-3600	971-9188
TF: 800-666-9485 ■ *Web:* www.caranddriver.com					
Car Stereo Review 1633 Broadway 45th Fl	New York	NY	10019	212-767-6000	767-5615
TF: 800-498-1993 ■ *Web:* www.soundandvisionmag.com					
Chevy Outdoors 30400 Van Dyke Ave	Warren	MI	48093	586-574-9100	447-7566*
**Fax Area Code:* 248					
Classic Trucks Magazine 2400 E Katella Ave 11th Fl	Anaheim	CA	92806	714-939-2240	978-6390
Web: www.classictrucksweb.com					
Cycle World 1499 Monrovia Ave	Newport Beach	CA	92663	949-720-5300	631-0651
TF: 800-876-8316 ■ *Web:* www.cycleworld.com					
Dirt Rider 6420 Wilshire Blvd	Los Angeles	CA	90048	323-782-2000	782-2372
TF Orders: 800-800-3478					
Dirt Wheels 25233 Anza Dr	Valencia	CA	91355	661-295-1910	295-1278
Web: www.dirtwheelsmag.com					
Easyriders 28210 Dorothy Dr	Agoura Hills	CA	91301	818-889-8740	889-1252
TF: 800-247-6246					
Four Wheeler 6420 Wilshire Blvd	Los Angeles	CA	90048	323-782-2000	782-2704
TF: 800-777-0555					
Friction Zone Magazine 60166 Hop Patch Spring Rd	Mountain Center	CA	92561	951-659-9500	659-8182
TF: 877-713-9700 ■ *Web:* www.friction-zone.com					
Grassroots Motorsports 310 Division Ave	Ormond Beach	FL	32174	386-673-4148	673-6040
TF: 888-676-9747 ■ *Web:* www.grassrootsmotorsports.com					
Hemmings Motor News 222 Main St	Bennington	VT	05201	802-442-3101	447-1561
TF: 800-227-4373 ■ *Web:* www.hemmings.com					
Hot Rod Magazine 6420 Wilshire Blvd	Los Angeles	CA	90048	323-782-2000	782-2223
TF Orders: 800-800-4681 ■ *Web:* www.hotrod.com					
Lowrider Magazine 2400 E Katella Ave 11th Fl	Anaheim	CA	92806	714-939-2400	978-6390
Web: www.lowridermagazine.com					
Motor Age Magazine 7500 Old Oak Blvd	Cleveland	OH	44130	440-243-8100	
TF: 800-822-6678 ■ *Web:* www.motorage.com/motorage					
Motor Trend 6420 Wilshire Blvd 7th Fl	Los Angeles	CA	90048	323-782-2000	782-2355
TF: 800-800-6848 ■ *Web:* www.motortrend.com					
Motorcycle Consumer News 3 Burroughs	Irvine	CA	92618	949-855-8822	855-0654
Web: www.mcnews.com/mcnews					
Motorcyclist 6420 Wilshire Blvd	Los Angeles	CA	90048	323-782-2000	666-5629*
**Fax Area Code:* 800 ■ *TF:* 800-800-7433 ■ *Web:* www.motorcyclistonline.com					
NASCAR Winston Cup Illustrated					
120 W Morehead St Suite 320	Charlotte	NC	28202	704-973-1300	973-1303
TF: 800-883-7323 ■ *Web:* www.scenedaily.com					
National Speed Sport News PO Box 1210	Harrisburg	NC	28075	704-455-2531	455-2605
TF: 866-455-2531 ■ *Web:* www.nationalspeedsportnews.com					
Off-Road 2400 E Katella Ave Suite 1100	Anaheim	CA	92806	714-939-2400	978-6390
Web: www.off-roadweb.com					
Popular Hot Rodding 774 S Placentia Ave	Placentia	CA	92870	714-939-2400	572-1864
Web: www.popularhotrodding.com					
Road King Magazine 28 White Bridge Rd Suite 209	Nashville	TN	37205	615-373-8838	
Web: www.roadking.com					
Road & Track 1499 Monrovia Ave	Newport Beach	CA	92663	949-720-5300	631-2757
TF Cust Svc: 800-876-8316 ■ *Web:* www.roadandtrack.com					
Sport Compact Car Magazine 2400 E Katella Ave 11th Fl	Anaheim	CA	92806	714-939-2400	978-6390
Web: www.sportcompactcarweb.com					
Sport Rider Magazine 6420 Wilshire Blvd	Los Angeles	CA	90048	323-782-2584	782-2372
Web: www.sportrider.com					
Sports Car 16842 Von Karman Ave Suite 125	Irvine	CA	92606	949-417-6700	417-6750
TF: 800-722-7140 ■ *Web:* www.sportscarmag.com					
Stock Car Racing 9036 Brittany Way	Tampa	FL	33619	813-675-3500	675-3559
Web: www.stockcarracing.com					
Super Chevy Magazine 774 S Placentia Ave 2nd Fl	Placentia	CA	92870	714-939-2559	572-1864
Web: www.superchevy-web.com					
Truck Trend Magazine 6420 Wilshire Blvd	Los Angeles	CA	90048	323-782-2000	782-2313
Web: www.trucktrend.com					
Vette 774 S Placentia Ave 2nd Fl	Placentia	CA	92870	714-939-2559	572-1864
Web: www.vetteweb.com					

460-4 Boating Magazines

	City	State	Zip	Phone	Fax
48 Degrees North 6327 Seaview Ave N	Seattle	WA	98107	206-789-7350	789-6392
Web: www.48north.com					
Blue Water Sailing Magazine Box 268	Newport	RI	02840	401-847-7612	845-8580
TF: 888-800-7245 ■ *Web:* www.bwsailing.com					
Boating 1633 Broadway 41st Fl	New York	NY	10019	212-767-6041	767-4831
Web: www.boatingmag.com					
Boating Life Magazine 460 N Orlando Ave Suite 200	Winter Park	FL	32789	407-628-4802	628-7061
Web: www.boatinglifemag.com					
Boating World 2100 Powers Ferry Rd Suite 300	Atlanta	GA	30339	770-955-5656	952-0669
Web: www.boatingworldonline.com					
Cruising World 55 Hammarlund Way	Middletown	RI	02842	401-845-5100	845-5180
Web: www.cruisingworld.com					
Go Boating Magazine 17782 Cowan Suite A	Irvine	CA	92614	949-660-6150	660-6172
Web: www.goboatingamerica.com					
Good Old Boat Magazine 7340 Niagara Ln N	Maple Grove	MN	55311	763-420-8923	420-8921
Web: www.goodoldboat.com					
Lakeland Boating 727 S Dearborn St Suite 812	Chicago	IL	60605	312-276-0610	276-0619
Web: www.lakelandboating.com					
Motor Boating & Sailing 18 Marshall St Suite 114	South Norwalk	CT	06834	203-299-5950	299-5951
TF: 800-888-9123 ■ *Web:* www.motorboating.com					
PassageMaker Magazine 105 Eastern Ave Suite 203	Annapolis	MD	21403	410-990-9086	990-9094
TF: 888-487-2953 ■ *Web:* www.passagemaker.com					
Power & Motoryacht 260 Madison Ave 8th Fl	New York	NY	10016	917-256-2200	256-2282
TF: 800-284-8036 ■ *Web:* www.powerandmotoryacht.com					
SAIL Magazine 98 N Washington St 2nd Fl	Boston	MA	02114	617-720-8600	723-0911
TF: 800-745-7245 ■ *Web:* www.sailmag.com					
Sailing World 55 Hammarlund Way	Middletown	RI	02842	401-845-5100	845-5180
TF Cust Svc: 866-436-2460 ■ *Web:* www.sailingworld.com					
Sea Magazine 17782 Cowan St Suite A	Irvine	CA	92614	949-660-6150	660-6172
TF: 800-873-7327 ■ *Web:* www.seamagazine.com					
Showboats International 910 SE 17th St Suite 400	Fort Lauderdale	FL	33316	954-525-8626	525-7954
TF: 800-325-2695 ■ *Web:* www.showboats.com					
Yachting 18 Marshall St Suite 114	South Norwalk	CT	06854	203-299-5900	299-5901
TF: 800-999-0869 ■ *Web:* www.yachtingnet.com					

460-5 Business & Finance Magazines

	City	State	Zip	Phone	Fax
ABA Banking Journal 345 Hudson St	New York	NY	10014	212-620-7200	633-1165
Web: www.ababj.com					
Accounting Today PO Box 4871	Chicago	IL	60694	800-260-2793	
Web: www.webcpa.com					
Active Trader Magazine 150 S Wacker Dr Suite 880	Chicago	IL	60606	312-775-5421	775-5423
Web: www.activetradermag.com					
Advertising Age 360 N Michigan Ave	Chicago	IL	60601	312-649-5200	649-5331
TF: 800-678-2724 ■ *Web:* www.adage.com					
Adweek 770 Broadway	New York	NY	10003	646-654-5500	654-5835
TF: 800-722-6658 ■ *Web:* www.adweek.com					
AHA News 1 N Franklin St Suite 2800	Chicago	IL	60606	312-893-6800	422-4500
TF: 800-621-6902 ■ *Web:* www.ahanews.com					
Alaska Business Monthly					
501 W Northern Lights Blvd Suite 100	Anchorage	AK	99503	907-276-4373	279-2900
TF: 800-770-4373 ■ *Web:* www.akbizmag.com					
American Agent & Broker 1801 Park 270 Dr Suite 550	Saint Louis	MO	63146	314-824-5500	824-5640
TF: 888-772-8926 ■ *Web:* www.agentandbroker.com					
American Banker 1 State Street Plaza	New York	NY	10004	212-803-8200	843-9600
TF: 800-221-1809 ■ *Web:* www.americanbanker.com					
American Journalism Review					
University of Maryland 1117 Journalism Bldg					
Room 2116	College Park	MD	20742	301-405-8803	405-8323
TF: 800-827-0771 ■ *Web:* www.ajr.org					
American Statistician 732 N Washington St	Alexandria	VA	22314	703-684-1221	684-2037*
**Fax:* Cust Svc ■ *TF:* 888-231-3473 ■ *Web:* www.amstat.org/publications/tas					
Appraisal Journal 550 W Van Buren St Suite 1000	Chicago	IL	60607	312-335-4100	335-4400
Web: www.appraisalinstitute.org/publications					

Business & Finance Magazines (Cont'd)

Phone | Fax

Area Development 400 Post Ave Suite 304 .... Westbury NY 11590 516-338-0900 338-0100
TF: 800-735-2732 ■ Web: www.area-development.com
Arkansas Business Journal 122 E 2nd St .... Little Rock AR 72203 501-372-1443 375-7933
TF: 888-322-6397 ■ Web: www.arkansasbusiness.com
ASID Professional Designer 608 Massachusetts Ave NE .... Washington DC 20002 202-546-3480 546-3240
TF: 800-775-2743
Association Management 1575 'I' St NW .... Washington DC 20005 202-371-0940 371-8825
Web: www.asaecenter.org
Atlanta Business Chronicle 3423 Piedmont Rd Suite 400........... Atlanta GA 30305 404-249-1000 249-1048
Web: www.bizjournals.com/atlanta
Austin Business Journal 111 Congress Ave Suite 750..............Austin TX 78701 512-494-2500 494-2525*
*Fax: Edit ■ TF: 888-819-4126 ■ Web: www.bizjournals.com/austin
Baltimore Business Journal 111 Market Pl Suite 720 .... Baltimore MD 21202 410-576-1161 752-3112
Web: www.bizjournals.com/baltimore
Banking Strategies Magazine 1 N Franklin St Suite 1000.......... Chicago IL 60606 312-553-4600 683-2415
Web: www.bai.org/bankingstrategies/about.asp
Barron's The Dow Jones Business & Financial Weekly
200 Liberty St ....New York NY 10281 212-416-2700 416-2829
TF: 800-544-0422 ■ Web: online.barrons.com
Best's Review Ambest Rd.................................. Oldwick NJ 08858 908-439-2200 439-3363
Web: www.ambest.com/review
Birmingham Business Journal 2140 11th Ave S Suite 205 ...... Birmingham AL 35205 205-322-0000 322-0040
Web: www.bizjournals.com/birmingham
Black Enterprise Magazine 130 5th Ave ....New York NY 10011 212-242-8000 886-9610
TF Cust Svc: 800-727-7777 ■ Web: www.blackenterprise.com
Bloomberg Magazine PO Box 840 .... Princeton NJ 08540 609-279-3000 897-8394
Web: www.bloomberg.com
Blue Ridge Business Journal 302 2nd St 4th Fl ....Roanoke VA 24016 540-777-6460 777-6471
Web: bizjournal.com
Boston Business Journal 160 Federal St 12th Fl .... Boston MA 02110 617-330-1000 330-1016
Web: www.bizjournals.com/boston
Boulder County Business Report 3180 Sterling Cir Suite 201....... Boulder CO 80301 303-440-4950 440-8954
Web: www.bcbr.com
Brandweek 770 Broadway.................................New York NY 10003 646-654-5000 654-5375
Web: www.brandweek.com
Broadcasting & Cable 360 Park Ave S.........................New York NY 10010 646-746-6965 746-7097
TF: 800-554-5729 ■ Web: www.broadcastingcable.com
Building Online Business 3300 N Central Ave Suite 300........... Phoenix AZ 85012 480-990-1101 990-0819
Business 2.0 1 California St 29th Fl...................... San Francisco CA 94111 415-293-4800 293-5900
Web: money.cnn.com/magazines/business2
Business Credit 8840 Columbia 100 Pkwy..................... Columbia MD 21045 410-740-5560 740-5574
TF: 800-955-8815 ■ Web: www.fcibglobal.com/services/bcm.html
Business Examiner 1517 S Fawcett Ave Suite 350................ Tacoma WA 98402 253-404-0891 404-0892
TF: 800-540-8322 ■ Web: www.businessexaminer.com
Business Facilities 44 Apple St Suite 3..................... Tinton Falls NJ 07724 732-842-7433 758-6634
TF: 800-524-0337 ■ Web: www.facilitycity.com/busfac
Business First 501 S 4th St Suite 130...................... Louisville KY 40202 502-583-1731 587-1703
TF: 800-704-3757 ■ Web: www.bizjournals.com/louisville
Business First 465 Main St.................................. Buffalo NY 14203 716-854-5822 854-3394
Web: www.bizjournals.com/buffalo
Business Insurance 360 N Michigan Ave .... Chicago IL 60601 312-649-5200 280-3174
TF: 800-678-2724 ■ Web: www.businessinsurance.com
Business Journal The 25 E Boardman St....................Youngstown OH 44501 330-744-5023 744-5838
TF: 800-837-6397 ■ Web: www.business-journal.com
Business Journal of Milwaukee 600 W Virginia St Suite 500..... Milwaukee WI 53204 414-278-7788 278-7028
Web: www.bizjournals.com/milwaukee
Business Journal of Phoenix 101 N 1st Ave Suite 2300........... Phoenix AZ 85003 602-230-8400 230-0955
Web: www.bizjournals.com/phoenix
Business Journal of Portland 851 SW 6th Ave Suite 500..........Portland OR 97204 503-274-8733 219-3450
Web: www.bizjournals.com/portland
Business Journal of San Jose 96 N 3rd St Suite 100............ San Jose CA 95112 408-295-3800 295-5028
Web: www.bizjournals.com/sanjose
Business Journal of Tampa Bay 4350 W Cypress St Suite 800 ...... Tampa FL 33607 813-873-8225 876-1827
Web: tampabay.bizjournals.com/tampabay
Business Leader 3801 Wake Forest Rd Suite 215.................Raleigh NC 27609 919-872-7077 872-1590
TF: 877-693-5999 ■ Web: www.businessleader.com
Business Magazine 1450 Don Mills Rd .... Toronto ON M3B3R5 416-383-2300 383-2443
TF: 800-668-7678
Business Opportunities Journal PO Box 60762................ San Diego CA 92166 800-809-1763 263-1763*
*Fax Area Code: 619 ■ Web: www.boj.com
Business Press 3509 Hulen St Suite 201......................Fort Worth TX 76107 817-336-8300 332-3038
Web: www.fwbusinesspress.com
Business Standards Magazine 12110 Sunset Hills Rd Suite 200 ..... Reston VA 20190 703-437-9000 437-9001
TF: 800-862-4977 ■ Web: www.businessstandards.com
Business in Vancouver 102 E 4th Ave .... Vancouver BC V5T1G2 604-688-2398 688-1963
TF: 800-208-2011 ■ Web: www.biv.com
BusinessWeek 1221 Ave of the Americas.....................New York NY 10020 212-512-2511 512-4045
TF Cust Svc: 800-635-1200 ■ Web: www.businessweek.com
California Real Estate 525 S Virgil Ave.....................Los Angeles CA 90020 213-739-8320 480-7724
Web: car.org/index.php?id=MjU4NA==
Canadian Business 1 Mt Pleasant Rd 11th Fl.................... Toronto ON M4Y2Y5 416-764-1200 764-1255
TF: 800-465-0700 ■ Web: www.canadianbusiness.com
Capital District Business Review PO Box 15081................. Albany NY 12212 518-437-9855 640-6801
Web: www.bizjournals.com/albany
Central New York Business Journal 231 Walton St.............. Syracuse NY 13202 315-472-3104 472-3644
TF: 800-836-3539 ■ Web: www.cnybj.com
CFO 253 Summer St .... Boston MA 02210 617-345-9700 951-4090
TF: 800-877-5416 ■ Web: www.cfo.com
Charlotte Business Journal 1100 S Tryon St Suite 100 .... Charlotte NC 28203 704-973-1100 973-1101*
*Fax: Edit ■ TF: 800-948-5323 ■ Web: www.bizjournals.com/charlotte
Chief Executive 110 Summit Ave........................... Montvale NJ 07645 201-930-5959 930-5956
Web: www.chiefexecutive.net
Cincinnati Business Courier 101 W 7th St ....Cincinnati OH 45202 513-621-6665 621-2462
Web: www.bizjournals.com/cincinnati
CIO 492 Old Connecticut Path.............................Framingham MA 01701 508-872-8200 879-7784
TF: 800-788-4605 ■ Web: www.cio.com
Columbia Journalism Review
Columbia University 2950 Broadway Journalism Bldg ....New York NY 10027 212-854-1881 854-8580
Web: www.cjr.org
Columbus Business First 303 W Nationwide Blvd ....Columbus OH 43215 614-461-4040 365-2980
Web: www.bizjournals.com/columbus
Communications News 2500 N Tamiami Trail ....Nokomis FL 34275 941-966-9521 966-2590
TF: 800-226-6113 ■ Web: www.comnews.com
Contract Design 770 Broadway...............................New York NY 10003 646-654-5500 654-7212
TF: 800-950-1314 ■ Web: www.contractmagazine.com
Corporate Logo 3300 N Central Ave Suite 300.................. Phoenix AZ 85012 480-990-1101 990-0819
Web: www.corporatelogo.com
CPA Journal 3 Park Ave 18th Fl ....New York NY 10016 212-719-8300 719-4755
TF: 800-633-6320 ■ Web: www.cpaj.com
Crain's Chicago Business 360 N Michigan Ave.................. Chicago IL 60601 312-649-5200
TF: 800-678-2724 ■ Web: chicagobusiness.com
Crain's Cleveland Business 700 W St Clair Ave Suite 310 .... Cleveland OH 44113 216-522-1383 694-4264
TF: 888-909-9111 ■ Web: www.crainscleveland.com

Phone | Fax

Crain's Detroit Business 1155 Gratiot Ave........................ Detroit MI 48207 313-446-6000 446-1687
TF: 888-909-9111 ■ Web: www.crainsdetroit.com
Crain's New York Business 711 3rd Ave Suite 300..............New York NY 10017 212-210-0100 210-0799*
*Fax: Edit ■ TF: 800-283-2724 ■ Web: www.newyorkbusiness.com
Credit Union Magazine 5710 Mineral Pt Rd.....................Madison WI 53705 608-231-4000 231-4263
TF Cust Svc: 800-356-9655 ■ Web: www.cuna.org
Daily Business Review 1 SE 3rd Ave Suite 900....................Miami FL 33131 305-377-3721 347-6626*
*Fax: Edit ■ TF: 800-777-7300 ■ Web: www.dailybusinessreview.com
Dallas Business Journal 12801 N Central Expy Suite 800............Dallas TX 75243 214-696-5959 361-4045*
*Fax: Edit ■ Web: www.bizjournals.com/dallas
Denver Business Journal 1700 Broadway Suite 515 .... Denver CO 80290 303-837-3500 837-3535
Web: www.bizjournals.com/denver
Des Moines Business Record 100 4th St.................... Des Moines IA 50309 515-288-3336 288-0309
Web: www.businessrecord.com
Drug Topics 5 Paragon Dr.................................. Montvale NJ 07645 201-358-7200 722-2490*
*Fax: Cust Svc ■ TF: 800-232-7379 ■ Web: www.drugtopics.com
E-Commerce Times 15821 Ventura Blvd Suite 625 .... Encino CA 91436 818-461-9700 461-9710
TF: 877-328-5500 ■ Web: www.ecommercetimes.com
Eastern Pennsylvania Business Journal
65 E Elizabeth Ave Suite 700............................. Bethlehem PA 18018 610-807-9619 807-9612
TF: 800-328-1026 ■ Web: www.epbj.com
Economist The 111 W 57th St 8th Fl ....New York NY 10019 212-541-0500 541-9378
TF: 800-456-6086 ■ Web: www.economist.com
Editor & Publisher 770 Broadway...........................New York NY 10003 646-654-5000 654-5370
TF: 800-783-4903 ■ Web: www.editorandpublisher.com
Electronic Business Today 225 Wyman St ....Waltham MA 02451 781-734-8000 734-8076
TF Cust Svc: 800-446-6551 ■ Web: reed-electronics.com/eb-mag/
Electronic Publishing 1421 S Sheridan Rd .... Tulsa OK 74112 918-835-3161 831-9497
TF: 800-331-4463 ■ Web: ep.pennnet.com/home.cfm
Employee Benefit News 1325 G St NW Suite 970............ Washington DC 20005 202-504-1122 772-1448
TF: 888-280-4820 ■ Web: www.benefitnews.com
Enterprise Magazine 136 S Main St Suite 721 ....Salt Lake City UT 84101 801-533-0556 533-0684
Web: www.slenterprise.com
Entrepreneur Magazine 2445 McCabe Way Suite 400............... Irvine CA 92614 949-261-2325 261-7729
TF: 800-274-6229 ■ Web: www.entrepreneur.com
Expansion Management 1300 E 9th St........................ Cleveland OH 44114 216-931-9860 696-6023
TF: 800-539-7263 ■ Web: www.expansionmanagement.com
Fairfield County Business Journal 3 Gannett Dr..............White Plains NY 10604 914-694-3600 694-3680
TF: 800-784-4564 ■ Web: www.fairfieldcountybusinessjournal.com
Fast Company 375 Lexington Ave............................New York NY 10017 212-499-2000 389-5496
TF: 800-542-6029 ■ Web: www.fastcompany.com
Finance & Commerce
730 2nd Ave S US Trust Bldg Suite 100.................. Minneapolis MN 55402 612-333-4244 333-3243
TF: 800-397-4348 ■ Web: www.finance-commerce.com
Financial Planning Magazine 1 State Street Plaza 27th Fl ....New York NY 10004 888-280-4820 843-9608*
*Fax Area Code: 212 ■ Web: www.financial-planning.com
Fleet Owner 11 Riverbend Dr S PO Box 4211 .... Stamford CT 06907 203-358-9900 358-5819
TF: 800-776-1246 ■ Web: www.fleetowner.com
Forbes 60 5th Ave ....New York NY 10011 212-620-2200 620-1873*
*Fax: Edit ■ TF: 800-888-9896 ■ Web: www.forbes.com
Fortune Rockefeller Ctr Time & Life Bldg.....................New York NY 10020 212-522-1212 467-0579
TF: 800-621-8000 ■ Web: money.cnn.com/magazines/fortune
Foundation News & Commentary 1828 L St NW Suite 300...... Washington DC 20036 202-467-0445 785-3926
TF: 800-771-8187 ■ Web: www.foundationnews.org
Franchising World 1501 K St NW Suite 350 .... Washington DC 20005 202-628-8000 628-0812
TF: 800-543-1038 ■ Web: www.franchise.org
FSB Rockefeller Ctr 1271 Ave of the Americas 4th Fl.............New York NY 10020 212-522-3263 522-8717
TF Cust Svc: 800-771-1444 ■ Web: money.cnn.com/magazines/fsb
Futures 833 W Jackson Blvd 7th Fl .... Chicago IL 60607 312-846-4600 846-4638
TF: 800-972-9316 ■ Web: www.futuresmag.com
Global Finance 411 5th Ave 7th Fl ....New York NY 10016 212-447-7900 447-7750
Web: www.gfmag.com
Grand Rapids Business Journal 549 Ottawa Ave NW ....Grand Rapids MI 49503 616-459-0555 459-4800
Web: www.grbj.com/GRBJ/Homepage.htm
Graphic Arts Monthly 360 Park Ave S ....New York NY 10010 646-746-7321
Web: www.gammag.com
Greater Baton Rouge Business Report
445 North Blvd Suite 210 .... Baton Rouge LA 70802 225-928-1700 926-1329*
*Fax: Sales ■ Web: www.businessreport.com
Greater Lansing Business Monthly
120 N Washington Sq Suite 800............................ Lansing MI 48933 517-487-1714 487-9597
Web: www.lansingbusinessmonthly.com
Greenville Magazine 614 N Main St.........................Greenville SC 29601 864-271-1105 271-1165
Web: www.greenvillemagazine.com
Harvard Business Review 60 Harvard Way...................... Boston MA 02163 617-783-7500 783-7555*
*Fax: Cust Svc ■ TF: 800-274-3214 ■
Web: harvardbusinessonline.hbsp.harvard.edu/b02/en/hbr/hbr_home.jhtml
Health Facilities Management 1 N Franklin Suite 2800 .... Chicago IL 60606 312-893-6800 422-4500
TF: 800-621-6902 ■ Web: www.hospitalconnect.com/hfmmagazine/jsp/currentissue.jsp
Health Supplement Retailer 3300 N Central Ave Suite 300......... Phoenix AZ 85012 480-990-1101 990-0819
Web: www.hsrmagazine.com
Healthcare Informatics PO Box 2178.......................... Skokie IL 60079 847-763-9291 963-9287
TF Cust Svc: 800-525-5003 ■ Web: www.healthcare-informatics.com
Hispanic Business 425 Pine Ave.......................... Santa Barbara CA 93117 805-964-4554 964-6139
TF Sales: 888-447-7287 ■ Web: www.hispanicbusiness.com
Hospitals & Health Networks 1 N Franklin Suite 2700 .... Chicago IL 60606 312-893-6800 422-4500
TF: 800-621-6902
Hotels 2000 Clearwater Dr.............................. Oak Brook IL 60523 630-288-8000 288-8265
Web: www.hotelsmag.com
Houston Business Journal 1233 West Loop S Suite 1300..........Houston TX 77027 713-688-8811 963-0482*
*Fax: Edit ■ Web: www.bizjournals.com/houston
HRMagazine 1800 Duke St .... Alexandria VA 22314 703-548-3440 836-0367
TF: 800-283-7476 ■ Web: www.shrm.org/hrmagazine/
Human Resource Executive 747 Dresher Rd Suite 500........... Horsham PA 19044 215-784-0860 784-0870
TF: 800-341-7874 ■ Web: www.workindex.com
In Business Magazine 200 River Pl Suite 250.................Madison WI 53716 608-204-9655 204-9656
Web: www.inbusinessmagazine.com
Inc 7 World Trade Center ....New York NY 10007 212-389-5300 389-5398
TF: 800-234-0999 ■ Web: www.inc.com/magazine
Independent Agent 127 S Peyton St........................ Alexandria VA 22314 703-683-4422 683-7556
TF: 800-221-7917 ■ Web: www.iamagazine.com
Indiana Business Magazine 1100 Waterway Blvd .... Indianapolis IN 46202 317-692-1200 692-4250
TF: 800-473-2526 ■ Web: www.indianabusiness.com
Indianapolis Business Journal
41 E Washington St Suite 200.......................... Indianapolis IN 46204 317-634-6200 263-5406*
*Fax: Edit ■ TF: 800-968-1225 ■ Web: www.ibj.com
Inside Collin County Business
2222 W Spring Creek Pkwy Suite 114 .... Plano TX 75023 972-612-2425 612-9329
Web: www.insidetxbiz.com
Institutional Investor 225 Park Ave S ....New York NY 10003 212-224-3300 224-3171*
*Fax: Edit ■ TF: 800-715-9197 ■ Web: www.dailyii.com
Internal Auditor 247 Maitland Ave .... Altamonte Springs FL 32701 407-937-1100 937-1101
Web: www.theiia.org/iia/index.cfm?doc_id=540
Jacksonville Business Journal
1200 River Pl Blvd Suite 201............................Jacksonville FL 32207 904-396-3502 396-5706
Web: www.bizjournals.com/jacksonville

	City	State	Zip	Phone	Fax
Journal of Accountancy					
201 Plaza III Harborside Financial Ctr	Jersey City	NJ	07311	201-938-3000	938-3329
TF: 888-777-7077 ■ *Web:* www.aicpa.org/pubs/jofa/joahome.htm					
Journal of Business 429 E 3rd Ave	Spokane	WA	99202	509-456-5257	456-0624
Web: www.spokanejournal.com					
Journal of Financial Planning 4100 E Mississippi Ave Suite 400	Denver	CO	80246	303-759-4900	759-0749
TF: 800-322-4237 ■ *Web:* www.fpanet.org/journal					
Journal of Housing & Community Development					
630 'I' St NW	Washington	DC	20001	202-289-3500	289-8181
TF: 877-866-2476 ■ *Web:* www.nahro.org					
Journal of Property Management 430 N Michigan Ave 7th Fl	Chicago	IL	60611	312-329-6000	661-0217
TF: 800-837-0706 ■ *Web:* www.irem.org/sechome.cfm?sec=jpm					
Kansas City Business Journal 1100 Main St Suite 210	Kansas City	MO	64105	816-421-5900	472-4010
Web: www.bizjournals.com/kansascity					
Las Vegas Business Press 1385 Pama Ln Suite 111	Las Vegas	NV	89119	702-871-6780	220-5481
Web: www.lvbusinesspress.com					
Law Enforcement Technology 1233 Janesville Ave	Fort Atkinson	WI	53538	920-563-6388	563-1701
TF: 800-547-7377 ■ *Web:* www.officer.com					
Leadership 465 Gundersen Dr	Carol Stream	IL	60188	630-260-6200	260-0114
TF: 800-777-3136 ■ *Web:* www.christianitytoday.com/leaders					
Life Assn News 2901 Telestar Ct	Falls Church	VA	22042	703-770-8477	770-8212
TF: 800-247-4074 ■ *Web:* www.advisortoday.com					
Life Insurance Selling 1801 Park 270 Dr Suite 550	Saint Louis	MO	63146	314-824-5500	824-5640
TF: 888-772-8926 ■ *Web:* www.lifeinsuranceselling.com					
Lodging 385 Oxford Valley Rd Suite 420	Yardley	PA	19067	215-321-9662	321-5124
Web: www.lodgingmagazine.com					
Los Angeles Business Journal					
5700 Wilshire Blvd Suite 170	Los Angeles	CA	90036	323-549-5225	549-5255
Web: www.labusinessjournal.com					
Manage 2210 Arbor Blvd	Dayton	OH	45439	937-294-0421	294-2374
Management Accounting Quarterly 10 Paragon Dr	Montvale	NJ	07645	201-573-9000	573-0639
TF Cust Svc: 800-638-4427 ■ *Web:* www.imanet.org/ima					
Marketing News 311 S Wacker Dr Suite 5800	Chicago	IL	60606	312-542-9000	922-3763
TF: 800-262-1150 ■ *Web:* www.marketingpower.com					
Materials Management in Health Care					
1 N Franklin St Suite 2700	Chicago	IL	60606	312-893-6800	422-4500
TF: 800-621-6902					
Meeting News 770 Broadway	New York	NY	10003	646-654-4420	654-7212
TF: 800-950-1314 ■ *Web:* www.mimegasite.com/mimegasite/meeting_news.jsp					
Meetings & Conventions 500 Plaza Dr	Secaucus	NJ	07094	201-902-2000	319-1796
TF: 800-446-6551 ■ *Web:* www.meetings-conventions.com					
Memphis Business Journal 80 Monroe Ave Suite 600	Memphis	TN	38103	901-523-1000	526-5240
Web: www.bizjournals.com/memphis					
Mergers & Acquisitions 1 State Street Plaza	New York	NY	10004	212-803-6051	747-1154
TF Cust Svc: 800-455-5844 ■ *Web:* www.majournal.com					
Miami Business 200 SE 1st St Suite 601	Miami	FL	33131	305-379-1118	379-1119
Midlands Business Journal 1324 S 119th St	Omaha	NE	68144	402-330-1760	758-9315
Web: www.mbj.com					
Minneapolis-Saint Paul Business Journal					
120 S 6th St Suite 900	Minneapolis	MN	55402	612-288-2100	288-2121
TF: 800-704-3757 ■ *Web:* twincities.bizjournals.com/twincities/					
Minority Business Entrepreneur 3528 Torrance Blvd Suite 101	Torrance	CA	90503	310-540-9398	792-8263
Web: www.mbemag.com					
Mississippi Business Journal 5120 Galaxie Dr	Jackson	MS	39206	601-364-1000	364-1007
TF: 800-283-4625 ■ *Web:* www.msbusiness.com					
Modern Healthcare 360 N Michigan Ave	Chicago	IL	60601	312-649-5200	280-3189
TF: 800-678-9595 ■ *Web:* www.modernhealthcare.com					
Nashville Business Journal 344 4th Ave N	Nashville	TN	37219	615-248-2222	248-6246
Web: nashville.bizjournals.com/nashville					
National Notary 9350 DeSoto Ave	Chatsworth	CA	91311	818-739-4000	700-1942
TF Cust Svc: 800-876-6827 ■ *Web:* www.nationalnotary.org					
National Real Estate Investor					
6151 Powers Ferry Rd NW Suite 200	Atlanta	GA	30339	770-955-2500	618-0348
Web: www.nreionline.com					
National Underwriter 3341 Newark St	Hoboken	NJ	07030	201-963-2300	526-1260
TF: 800-543-0874 ■ *Web:* cms.nationalunderwriter.com/cms/NUPC/website/Home					
New Accountant 3550 W Peterson Ave Suite 100	Chicago	IL	60659	773-866-9900	866-9981
Web: www.newaccountantusa.com					
New Castle Business Ledger 168 Elkton Rd Suite 206	Newark	DE	19711	302-737-0923	737-9019
Web: www.ledgerdelaware.com					
New Jersey Business Magazine 310 Passaic Ave Suite 201	Fairfield	NJ	07004	973-882-5004	882-4648
Web: www.njbmagazine.com					
New Mexico Business Journal					
1720 Louisiana Blvd NE Suite 202	Albuquerque	NM	87107	505-830-2043	255-1094
Web: www.nmbiz.com					
New Orleans City Business					
111 Veterans Memorial Blvd Suite 1440	Metairie	LA	70005	504-834-9292	832-3550
Web: www.neworleanscitybusiness.com					
Northern Colorado Business Report 141 S College Ave	Fort Collins	CO	80524	970-221-5400	221-5432
TF: 800-440-3506 ■ *Web:* www.ncbr.com					
Office Systems 99 252 N Main St Suite 200 PO Box 1028	Mount Airy	NC	27030	336-783-0000	783-0045
Web: www.os-od.com					
Orange County Business Journal 2600 Michelson Dr Suite 170	Irvine	CA	92612	949-833-8373	833-8751
Web: www.ocbj.com					
Orlando Business Journal 315 E Robinson St Suite 250	Orlando	FL	32801	407-649-8470	649-8469
TF: 888-649-6251 ■ *Web:* www.bizjournals.com/orlando					
Ottawa Business Journal 5300 Canotek Rd Unit 30	Ottawa	ON	K1J8R7	613-744-4800	744-8232
Web: www.ottawabusinessjournal.com					
Palm Beach Daily Business Review					
324 Datura St Suite 140	West Palm Beach	FL	33401	561-820-2060	820-2077
TF: 800-777-7300 ■ *Web:* www.dailybusinessreview.com					
Pensions & Investments 711 3rd Ave	New York	NY	10017	212-210-0115	210-0117
TF Cust Svc: 888-446-1422 ■ *Web:* www.pionline.com					
Pharmaceutical Representative 2 Northfield Plaza Suite 300	Northfield	IL	60093	847-441-3700	441-3701
TF: 800-451-7838 ■ *Web:* www.pharmrep.com					
Philadelphia Business Journal 400 Market St Suite 1200	Philadelphia	PA	19106	215-238-1450	238-9489
TF: 800-220-3202 ■ *Web:* www.bizjournals.com/philadelphia					
Pittsburgh Business Times 424 S 27th St Suite 211	Pittsburgh	PA	15203	412-481-6397	481-9956
Web: www.bizjournals.com/pittsburgh					
Potentials 50 S 9th St	Minneapolis	MN	55402	612-333-0471	333-6526
TF Cust Svc: 800-328-4329 ■ *Web:* www.potentialsmag.com					
Practical Accountant 1 State Street Plaza	New York	NY	10004	212-803-8200	292-5216
Print 38 E 29th St 3rd Fl	New York	NY	10016	212-447-1400	447-5231
TF: 877-860-9145 ■ *Web:* www.printmag.com					
Providence Business News 220 W Exchange St Suite 210	Providence	RI	02903	401-273-2201	274-6580*
**Fax:* Hum Res ■ *Web:* www.pbn.com					
Puget Sound Business Journal 801 2nd Ave Suite 210	Seattle	WA	98104	206-583-0701	447-8510
Web: www.bizjournals.com/seattle					
Purchasing Magazine 225 Wyman St	Waltham	MA	02451	781-734-8203	734-8076
TF Cust Svc: 800-446-6551 ■ *Web:* www.manufacturing.net/pur					
Red Herring 19 Davis Dr	Belmont	CA	94002	650-428-2900	428-2901
Web: www.redherring.com					
Registered Representative 249 W 17th St	New York	NY	10011	212-462-3580	206-3622*
**Fax:* Edit ■ *TF:* 866-505-7173 ■ *Web:* registeredrep.com					
Restaurant Business 770 Broadway 4th Fl	New York	NY	10003	646-654-5000	654-7390
Web: www.restaurantbiz.com					
Rio Grande Valley Business Journal 1300 Wild Rose Ln	Brownsville	TX	78520	956-546-5113	546-0903*
**Fax:* Sales ■ *TF:* 800-556-9876					
Risk Management 1065 Ave of the Americas 13th Fl	New York	NY	10018	212-286-9292	986-9716
Web: www.rmmag.com					
Rochester Business Journal 45 East Ave Suite 500	Rochester	NY	14604	585-546-8303	546-3398
Web: www.rbj.net					
Rough Notes 11690 Technology Dr	Carmel	IN	46032	317-582-1600	816-1000
TF: 800-428-4384 ■ *Web:* www.roughnotes.com					
Sacramento Business Journal 1400 X St	Sacramento	CA	95818	916-447-7661	444-7779
Web: www.bizjournals.com/sacramento					
Saint Louis Business Journal 815 Olive St Suite 100	Saint Louis	MO	63101	314-421-6200	621-5031
Web: www.bizjournals.com/stlouis					
Sales & Marketing Management 770 Broadway	New York	NY	10003	646-654-4500	654-7616
Web: www.salesandmarketing.com					
San Antonio Business Journal 8200 IH 10 W Suite 820	San Antonio	TX	78230	210-341-3202	341-3031
Web: www.bizjournals.com/sanantonio					
San Diego Business Journal					
4909 Murphy Canyon Rd Suite 200	San Diego	CA	92123	858-277-6359	277-2149
TF: 888-425-7325 ■ *Web:* www.sdbj.com					
San Francisco Business Times Magazine					
275 Battery St Suite 940	San Francisco	CA	94111	415-989-2522	398-2494
Web: www.bizjournals.com/sanfrancisco					
Self Employed America PO Box 612067	Dallas	TX	75261	800-232-6273	551-4446
Web: www.nase.org					
Selling Power 1140 International Pkwy	Fredericksburg	VA	22406	540-752-7000	752-7001
TF: 800-752-7355 ■ *Web:* www.sellingpower.com					
Signal 4400 Fair Lakes Ct	Fairfax	VA	22033	703-631-6100	631-6188
TF: 800-336-4583 ■ *Web:* www.afcea.org/signal					
Sloan Management Review 77 Massachusetts Ave E60-100	Cambridge	MA	02139	617-253-7170	258-9739
TF: 800-876-5764 ■ *Web:* sloanreview.mit.edu/smr					
Small Business Opportunities 1115 Broadway 8th Fl	New York	NY	10010	212-807-7100	924-8416
Web: www.sbomag.com					
South Florida Business Journal					
1000 E Hillsboro Blvd Suite 103	Deerfield Beach	FL	33441	954-949-7600	949-7591
Web: www.bizjournals.com/southflorida					
South Sound Business Examiner 1517 S Fawcett St Suite 350	Tacoma	WA	98402	253-404-0891	404-0892
TF: 800-540-8322 ■ *Web:* www.businessexaminer.com					
Springfield Business Journal 313 Park Central W	Springfield	MO	65806	417-831-3238	831-5478
Web: www.sbj.net					
Strategic Finance Magazine 10 Paragon Dr	Montvale	NJ	07645	201-573-9000	573-0639
TF: 800-638-4427 ■ *Web:* www.imanet.org/publications_sfm.asp					
Successful Meetings 770 Broadway	New York	NY	10003	646-654-5049	654-7473
Web: www.mimegasite.com					
Tempdigest 7474 S Kirkwood Suite 108	Houston	TX	77072	281-498-2913	530-7082
TF: 800-444-0674 ■ *Web:* www.staffdigest.com					
Today's Realtor 430 N Michigan Ave 9th Fl	Chicago	IL	60610	312-329-8458	329-5978
TF: 800-874-6500 ■ *Web:* www.realtor.org/rmodaily.nsf					
Toledo Business Journal PO Box 1206	Toledo	OH	43537	419-865-0972	865-2429
Web: www.toledobiz.com					
Training & Development Magazine 1640 King St	Alexandria	VA	22313	703-683-8100	683-8103
Web: www.astd.org/astd/publications/td_magazine					
Training Magazine 50 S 9th St	Minneapolis	MN	55402	612-333-0471	333-6526
TF Cust Svc: 800-328-4329 ■ *Web:* www.trainingmag.com					
Tri Cities Business Journal PO Box 643	Blountville	TN	37617	423-323-7111	323-1479
Web: www.bjournal.com					
Triangle Business Journal 1305 Navaho Dr Suite 100	Raleigh	NC	27609	919-878-0010	790-6885
Web: triangle.bizjournals.com					
US Banker 1 State St 27th Fl	New York	NY	10004	212-967-7000	695-8172
TF: 800-221-1809 ■ *Web:* www.us-banker.com/usb/m_usb3.shtml					
Utah Business Magazine 859 W 10600 South Suite 101	South Jordan	UT	84095	801-568-0114	568-0812
TF: 800-823-0038 ■ *Web:* www.utahbusiness.com					
Vancouver Business Journal 1251 Officers Row	Vancouver	WA	98661	360-695-2442	695-3056
Web: www.vbjusa.com					
Virginia Business Magazine 333 E Franklin St	Richmond	VA	23219	804-649-6999	649-6311
Web: virginiabusiness.com					
Washington Business Journal 1555 Wilson Blvd Suite 400	Arlington	VA	22209	703-258-0800	258-0802
Web: washington.bizjournals.com/washington					
Wichita Business Journal 121 N Mead St Suite 100	Wichita	KS	67202	316-267-6406	267-8570
Web: www.bizjournals.com/wichita					
Women in Business 9100 Ward Pkwy PO Box 8728	Kansas City	MO	64114	816-361-6621	361-4991
Workforce Management Magazine 4 Executive Cir Suite 185	Irvine	CA	92614	949-255-5340	221-8964
Web: www.workforce.com					
Your Church 465 Gundersen Dr	Carol Stream	IL	60188	630-260-6200	260-0114
Web: www.christianitytoday.com					

460-6 Children's & Youth Magazines

	City	State	Zip	Phone	Fax
American Girl Magazine 8400 Fairway Pl	Middleton	WI	53562	608-836-4848	
TF: 800-360-1861 ■ *Web:* www.americangirl.com					
AppleSeeds Magazine 30 Grove St Suite C	Peterborough	NH	03458	603-924-7209	924-7380
TF: 800-821-0115 ■ *Web:* www.cobblestonepub.com/magazine/APP					
Archie Comics 325 Fayette Ave	Mamaroneck	NY	10543	914-381-5155	381-2335
Web: www.archiecomics.com					
Ask Magazine 30 Grove St Suite C	Peterborough	NH	03458	603-924-7209	924-7380
TF: 800-821-0115 ■ *Web:* www.cobblestonepub.com/magazine/ASK					
Babybug Magazine 30 Grove St Suite C	Peterborough	NH	03458	603-924-7209	924-7380
TF: 800-821-0115 ■ *Web:* www.cobblestonepub.com/magazine/BBB					
Boys' Life 1325 W Walnut Hill Ln	Irving	TX	75038	972-580-2000	580-2502
Web: www.boyslife.org					
Calliope Magazine 30 Grove St Suite C	Peterborough	NH	03458	603-924-7209	924-7380
TF: 800-821-0115 ■ *Web:* www.cobblestonepub.com/magazine/CAL					
Child Life Magazine					
Children's Better Health Institute 1100 Waterway Blvd	Indianapolis	IN	46202	317-636-8881	684-8094
TF: 800-558-2376 ■ *Web:* cbhi.org/magazines/childlife					
Children's Digest					
Children's Better Health Institute 1100 Waterway Blvd	Indianapolis	IN	46202	317-636-8881	684-8094
TF: 800-558-2376 ■ *Web:* cbhi.org/magazines/childrensdigest					
Children's Playmate Magazine					
Children's Better Health Institute 1100 Waterway Blvd	Indianapolis	IN	46202	317-636-8881	684-8094
TF: 800-558-2376 ■ *Web:* cbhi.org/magazines/childrensplaymate					
Cicada Magazine 30 Grove St Suite C	Peterborough	NH	03458	603-924-7209	924-7380
TF: 800-821-0115 ■ *Web:* www.cobblestonepub.com/magazine/CIC					
Click Magazine 30 Grove St Suite C	Peterborough	NH	03458	603-924-7209	924-7380
TF: 800-821-0115 ■ *Web:* www.cobblestonepub.com/magazine/CLK					
Cobblestone Magazine 30 Grove St Suite C	Peterborough	NH	03458	603-924-7209	924-7380
TF: 800-821-0115 ■ *Web:* www.cobblestonepub.com/magazine/COB					
CosmoGIRL! 224 W 57th St	New York	NY	10019	212-649-3570	
Web: www.cosmogirl.com					
Creative Kids Magazine PO Box 8813	Waco	TX	76714	254-756-3337	756-3339
TF: 800-998-2208 ■ *Web:* www.prufrock.com					
Cricket Magazine 30 Grove St Suite C	Peterborough	NH	03458	603-924-7209	924-7380
TF: 800-821-0115 ■ *Web:* www.cobblestonepub.com/magazine/CKT					
DECA Dimensions 1908 Association Dr	Reston	VA	20191	703-860-5000	860-4013
Web: www.deca.org					

Children's & Youth Magazines (Cont'd)

Phone | Fax

Dig Magazine 30 Grove St Suite C .... Peterborough NH 03458 603-924-7209 924-7380
TF: 800-821-0115 ■ *Web:* www.cobblestonepub.com/magazine/DIG

Disney Adventures 114 5th Ave .... New York NY 10011 212-633-4400 633-5929
TF Cust Svc: 800-829-5146 ■ *Web:* disney.go.com/DisneyAdventures

Faces Magazine About People 30 Grove St Suite C .... Peterborough NH 03458 603-924-7209 924-7380
TF: 800-821-0115 ■ *Web:* www.cobblestonepub.com/magazine/FAC

FamilyFun 114 5th Ave .... New York NY 10011 212-633-3620 633-5929*
**Fax:* Hum Res ■ *TF:* 800-829-5146 ■ *Web:* family.go.com

Girl's Life Magazine 4517 Hartford Rd .... Baltimore MD 21214 410-426-9600 254-0991
TF: 888-999-3222 ■ *Web:* www.girlslife.com

Highlights for Children 1800 Watermark Dr .... Columbus OH 43215 614-486-0631 324-1630
TF Cust Svc: 800-255-9517 ■ *Web:* www.highlights.com

Humpty Dumpty's Magazine 1100 Waterway Blvd .... Indianapolis IN 46202 317-636-8881 684-8094
TF: 800-558-2376 ■ *Web:* www.cbhi.org/magazines/humptydumpty/index.shtml

Insights 11250 Waples Mill Rd .... Fairfax VA 22030 703-267-1000 267-3971

Jack & Jill 1100 Waterway Blvd .... Indianapolis IN 46202 317-636-8881 684-8094
TF: 800-558-2376 ■ *Web:* www.cbhi.org/magazines/jackandjill/index.shtml

Ladybug Magazine 30 Grove St Suite C .... Peterborough NH 03458 603-924-7209 924-7380
TF: 800-821-0115 ■ *Web:* www.cobblestonepub.com/magazine/LYB

Muse Magazine 30 Grove St Suite C .... Peterborough NH 03458 603-924-7209 924-7380
TF: 800-821-0115 ■ *Web:* www.cobblestonepub.com/magazine/MUS

National Geographic World 1145 17th St NW .... Washington DC 20036 202-857-7000 775-6141
TF: 800-647-5463 ■ *Web:* www.nationalgeographic.com

New Expression 600 S Michigan Ave Columbia College .... Chicago IL 60605 312-922-7150 922-7151
Web: www.newexpression.org

New Moon Magazine 2 W 1st St Suite 101 .... Duluth MN 55802 218-728-5507 728-0314
TF: 800-381-4743 ■ *Web:* www.newmoon.org

New Youth Connections 224 W 29th St 2nd Fl .... New York NY 10001 212-279-0708 279-8856

Nickelodeon Magazine 1633 Broadway 7th Fl .... New York NY 10019 212-654-7707 654-4870
TF: 800-947-7052 ■ *Web:* www.nick.com/all_nick/nick_mag/index.jhtml

Odyssey 30 Grove St Suite C .... Peterborough NH 03458 603-924-7209 924-7380
TF: 800-821-0115 ■ *Web:* www.odysseymagazine.com

Owl Magazine 10 Lower Spadina Ave Suite 400 .... Toronto ON M5V2Z2 416-340-2700 340-9769
TF: 800-551-6957 ■ *Web:* www.owlkids.com

Ranger Rick 11100 Wildlife Ctr Dr .... Reston VA 20190 800-822-9919
Web: www.nwf.org/gowild

Sesame Street 1 Lincoln Plaza 2nd Fl .... New York NY 10023 212-595-3456 875-6105

Seventeen 959 8th Ave .... New York NY 10019 800-388-1749
TF: 800-388-1749 ■ *Web:* www.seventeen.com

Spider Magazine 30 Grove St Suite C .... Peterborough NH 03458 603-924-7209 924-7380
TF: 800-821-0115 ■ *Web:* www.cobblestonepub.com/magazine/SDR

Sports Illustrated for Kids 1271 Avenue of the Americas .... New York NY 10020 212-522-1212 522-0660
TF Cust Svc: 800-992-0196 ■ *Web:* www.sikids.com

Stone Soup Magazine PO Box 83 .... Santa Cruz CA 95063 831-426-5557 426-1161
TF: 800-447-4569 ■ *Web:* www.stonesoup.com

Teen 3000 Ocean Pk Blvd Suite 3048 .... Santa Maria CA 90405 310-664-2950 664-2959
Web: www.teenmag.com

Teen People 1271 6th Ave Time & Life Bldg .... New York NY 10020 212-522-1212 522-0601*
**Fax:* Edit ■ *TF:* 800-284-0200 ■ *Web:* www.teenpeople.com

Teen Voices Magazine PO Box 120-027 .... Boston MA 02112 888-882-8336
Web: www.teenvoices.com

TeenVogue Magazine 4 Times Sq .... New York NY 10036 212-286-2860 286-8169
Web: www.teenvogue.com/magazine

Turtle Magazine 1100 Waterway Blvd .... Indianapolis IN 46202 317-636-8881 684-8094
TF: 800-558-2376 ■ *Web:* www.cbhi.org/magazines/turtle/index.shtml

Twist 270 Sylvan Ave .... Englewood Cliffs NJ 07632 201-569-6699 569-4458
TF Cust Svc: 800-757-7053 ■ *Web:* www.twistmag.com

US Kids Magazine 1100 Waterway Blvd .... Indianapolis IN 46202 317-636-8881 684-8094
TF: 800-558-2376 ■ *Web:* www.cbhi.org/magazines/uskids/index.shtml

Wild Animal Baby 8925 Leesburg Pike .... Vienna VA 22184 800-611-1599
Web: www.nwf.org/wildanimalbaby

Writing Magazine 3001 Cindel Dr .... Delran NJ 08075 856-786-5500 786-3360
TF: 800-446-3355

Your Big Backyard 8925 Leesburg Pike .... Vienna VA 22184 800-611-1599 442-7332*
**Fax Area Code:* 703 ■ *TF:* 800-611-1599 ■ *Web:* www.nwf.org/yourbigbackyard

Your Prom Magazine 750 3rd Ave 4th Fl .... New York NY 10017 212-630-4000 630-5890
Web: www.yourprom.com/magazine

460-7 Computer & Internet Magazines

Phone | Fax

2600 Magazine PO Box 752 .... Middle Island NY 11953 631-751-2600 474-2677
Web: www.2600.com

Boardwatch Magazine 23 Leonard St .... New York NY 10013 212-925-0020 925-3324

BYTE.com 600 Community Dr .... Manhasset NY 11030 516-562-5000 562-5196
TF: 800-645-6278 ■ *Web:* www.byte.com

Computer 10662 Los Vaqueros Cir .... Los Alamitos CA 90720 714-821-8380 821-4010
TF Orders: 800-272-6657 ■ *Web:* www.computer.org/computer/

Computer Graphics World 98 Spit Brook Rd .... Nashua NH 03062 603-891-0123 891-0539
TF: 800-331-4463 ■ *Web:* cgw.pennnet.com/home.cfm

Computer Shopper Magazine 460 Park Ave S 9th Fl .... New York NY 10016 917-326-8700
TF: 800-274-6384

Computer Telephony 11 W 19th St 3rd Fl .... New York NY 10011 212-600-3000
TF: 888-824-9793 ■ *Web:* www.callcentermagazine.com

Computers in Libraries 143 Old Marlton Pike .... Medford NJ 08055 609-654-6266 654-4309
TF: 800-300-9868 ■ *Web:* www.infotoday.com/cilmag

ComputerUser Magazine 220 S 6th St Suite 500 .... Minneapolis MN 55402 612-339-7571 339-5806
Web: www.computeruser.com

Computerworld 1 Speen St .... Framingham MA 01701 508-879-0700 875-3701*
**Fax:* Mktg ■ *TF:* 800-343-6474 ■ *Web:* www.computerworld.com

Darwin Magazine 492 Old Connecticut Path .... Framingham MA 01701 508-872-0080 875-4489
TF: 800-942-4672 ■ *Web:* www.darwinmag.com

DB2 Magazine 2800 Campus Dr .... San Mateo CA 94403 650-513-4300 513-4613
Web: www.db2mag.com

DM Review 220 Regency Ct Suite 210 .... Brookfield WI 53045 262-784-0444 782-9489
Web: www.dmreview.com

Dr Dobb's Journal 2800 Campus Dr .... San Mateo CA 94403 650-513-4300 513-4618
TF: 800-289-9839 ■ *Web:* www.ddj.com

DV: Digital Video Magazine 7300 N Linder Ave .... Skokie IL 60076 847-763-9581 763-9522
TF: 888-776-7002 ■ *Web:* www.dv.com/magazine

e-doc 1100 Wayne Ave Suite 1100 .... Silver Spring MD 20910 301-587-8202 587-2711
TF: 800-477-2446 ■ *Web:* www.edocmagazine.com

eContent 88 Danbury Rd Suite 1-D .... Wilton CT 06897 203-761-1466 761-1444
TF: 800-248-8466 ■ *Web:* www.econtentmag.com

eWEEK Magazine 28 E 28th St 8th Fl .... New York NY 10016 212-503-3500 503-5317
TF: 888-663-8438 ■ *Web:* www.eweek.com

Federal Computer Week 3141 Fairview Park Dr Suite 777 .... Falls Church VA 22042 703-876-5100 876-5101
Web: www.fcw.com

Government Computer News 10 G St NE Suite 500 .... Washington DC 20002 202-772-2500 772-2516*
**Fax:* Edit ■ *TF:* 866-447-6864 ■ *Web:* www.gcn.com

Hotwired 100 5th Ave .... Waltham MA 02451 781-370-2700 370-2600
Web: hotwired.wired.com

Phone | Fax

IEEE Computer Graphics & Applications
10662 Los Vaqueros Cir .... Los Alamitos CA 90720 714-821-8380 821-4010
TF: 800-272-6657 ■ *Web:* www.computer.org/cga

IEEE Micro 10662 Los Vaqueros Cir .... Los Alamitos CA 90720 714-821-8380 821-4010
TF: 800-272-6657 ■ *Web:* www.computer.org/micro

Information Today Magazine 143 Old Marlton Pike .... Medford NJ 08055 609-654-6266 654-4309
TF: 800-300-9868 ■ *Web:* www.infotoday.com

InformationWeek 600 Community Dr .... Manhasset NY 11030 516-562-7911 562-5036
TF: 800-645-6278 ■ *Web:* www.informationweek.com

InfoWorld 501 2nd St Suite 120 .... San Francisco CA 94107 415-243-4344 978-3120
TF: 800-227-8365 ■ *Web:* www.infoworld.com

Intelligent Enterprise 2800 Campus Dr .... San Mateo CA 94403 650-513-4300 513-4610
TF Cust Svc: 800-289-9839 ■ *Web:* www.intelligententerprise.com

IT Architect 600 Harrison St .... San Francisco CA 94107 415-947-6000 947-6022
Web: www.networkmagazine.com

Law Technology News 345 Park Ave S .... New York NY 10010 212-779-9200 696-1848
TF Cust Svc: 800-274-2893 ■ *Web:* www.lawtechnews.com

MacHome 200 Folsom St Suite 150 .... San Francisco CA 94105 415-957-1911 882-9502
TF: 800-800-6542 ■ *Web:* www.machome.com

Macworld Magazine 501 2nd St Suite 120 .... San Francisco CA 94107 415-243-4141 442-3543
TF Cust Svc: 800-873-4941 ■ *Web:* www.macworld.com

Manufacturing Systems 2000 Clearwater Dr .... Oak Brook IL 60523 630-320-7000 288-8764
TF: 800-662-7776 ■ *Web:* www.mbtmag.com

Maximum PC Magazine
400 Shoreline Ct Suite 400 .... South San Francisco CA 94080 650-872-1642 872-2207
Web: www.maximumpc.com

MultiMedia Schools 143 Old Marlton Pike .... Medford NJ 08055 609-654-6266 654-4309
TF: 800-300-9868 ■ *Web:* www.infotoday.com/MMSchools

Network Computing 600 Community Dr .... Manhasset NY 11030 516-562-5000 562-7293
Web: www.networkcomputing.com

Network World 118 Turnpike Rd .... Southborough MA 01772 508-875-6400 490-6417
TF: 800-622-1108 ■ *Web:* www.networkworld.com

Online 143 Old Marlton Pike .... Medford NJ 08055 609-654-6266 654-4309
TF: 800-300-9868 ■ *Web:* www.onlinemag.net

Oracle Magazine PO Box 1263 .... Skokie IL 60076 847-647-9635 647-0226*
**Fax:* Cust Svc ■ *Web:* www.oracle.com/oramag/index.html

PC Magazine 28 E 28th St .... New York NY 10016 212-503-5100 503-5799
TF: 800-289-0429 ■ *Web:* www.pcmag.com

PC World Magazine 501 2nd St Suite 600 .... San Francisco CA 94107 415-243-0500 442-1891
TF: 800-234-3498 ■ *Web:* www.pcworld.com

Publish c/o Ziff Davis Media Inc 462 Boston St .... Topsfield MA 01983 978-887-2246 887-6117
Web: www.publish.com

Scientific Computing & Instrumentation Magazine
100 Enterprise Dr Suite 600 .... Rockaway NJ 07866 973-920-7000 920-7551
TF: 800-662-7776 ■ *Web:* www.scientificcomputing.com

Searcher: The Magazine for Database Professionals
143 Old Marlton Pike .... Medford NJ 08055 609-654-6266 654-4309
TF: 800-300-9868 ■ *Web:* www.infotoday.com/searcher

Software Magazine 233 Needham St Suite 300 .... Newton MA 02464 508-668-1150
Web: www.softwaremag.com

SupplyChain Manufacturing & Logistics Magazine
PO Box 332 .... Newton Upper Falls MA 02464 617-527-4626 527-8102
Web: www.scml-mag.com

Wired Magazine 520 3rd St 3rd Fl .... San Francisco CA 94107 415-276-5000 276-5100
TF: 800-769-4733 ■ *Web:* www.wired.com/wired/current.html

460-8 Education Magazines & Journals

Phone | Fax

Academe 1012 14th St NW Suite 500 .... Washington DC 20005 202-737-5900 737-5526
TF: 800-424-2973

Access Learning 214 Lincoln St Suite 112 .... Allston MA 02134 617-254-9481 254-9776
Web: www.ciconline.com

Advocate 100 E Edwards St .... Springfield IL 62704 217-544-0706 544-6423
TF: 800-252-8076

AEA Advocate 345 E Palm Ln .... Phoenix AZ 85004 602-264-1774 240-6887
TF: 800-352-5411 ■ *Web:* www.arizonaea.org

Alabama School Journal PO Box 4177 .... Montgomery AL 36103 334-834-9790 262-8377
TF: 800-392-5839 ■ *Web:* www.myaea.org

American Educator 555 New Jersey Ave NW .... Washington DC 20001 202-879-4400 879-4534
TF: 800-238-1133 ■ *Web:* www.aft.org/american_educator

American Libraries 50 E Huron St .... Chicago IL 60611 312-944-6780 440-0901
TF: 800-545-2433 ■ *Web:* www.ala.org/alonline

American Teacher 555 New Jersey Ave NW .... Washington DC 20001 202-879-4400 783-2014
TF: 800-238-1133 ■ *Web:* www.aft.org/publications/american_teacher

Arkansas Educator 1500 W 4th St .... Little Rock AR 72201 501-375-4611 375-4620

California Educator 1705 Murchison Dr .... Burlingame CA 94010 650-697-1400 552-5002

Chronicle of Higher Education 1255 23rd St NW Suite 700 .... Washington DC 20037 202-466-1000 452-1033
TF Sales: 800-728-2803 ■ *Web:* chronicle.com

Colorado School Journal 1500 Grant St .... Denver CO 80203 303-837-1500 837-9006
TF: 800-332-5939

Dance Teacher Magazine 110 William St 23rd Fl .... New York NY 10038 800-362-6765 265-8908*
**Fax Area Code:* 212 ■ *Web:* www.dance-teacher.com

Education Center Inc 3515 W Market St Suite 200 .... Greensboro NC 27403 336-854-0309 547-1587
TF: 800-714-7991 ■ *Web:* www.theeducationcenter.com

Education Digest PO Box 8623 .... Ann Arbor MI 48107 734-975-2800 975-2787
TF: 800-530-9673 ■ *Web:* www.eddigest.com

Education Week 6935 Arlington Rd .... Bethesda MD 20814 301-280-3100 280-3250
TF: 800-346-1834 ■ *Web:* www.edweek.org

Educational Leadership 1703 N Beauregard St .... Alexandria VA 22311 703-578-9600 575-5400
TF: 800-933-2723 ■ *Web:* www.ascd.org

Educators' Advocate 411 E Capitol Ave .... Pierre SD 57501 605-224-9263 224-5810
TF: 800-529-0090 ■ *Web:* www.sdea.org

FOCUS 1529 18th St NW .... Washington DC 20036 202-387-5200 265-2384
TF: 800-741-9415 ■ *Web:* www.maa.org/pubs/focus.html

Harvard Educational Review 8 Story St 1st Fl .... Cambridge MA 02138 617-495-3432 496-3584
TF: 800-513-0763 ■ *Web:* www.gse.harvard.edu/~hepg/her.html

IEA Reporter PO Box 2638 .... Boise ID 83701 208-344-1341 336-6967
Web: www.idahoea.org

Instructor 557 Broadway .... New York NY 10012 212-343-6100 343-6930
TF: 800-544-2917 ■ *Web:* teacher.scholastic.com

ISTA Advocate 150 W Market St Suite 900 .... Indianapolis IN 46204 317-263-3400 655-3700
TF: 800-382-4037

Journal of Physical Education Recreation & Dance
1900 Association Dr .... Reston VA 20191 703-476-3477 476-9527
Web: www.aahperd.org

KEA News 401 Capital Ave .... Frankfort KY 40601 502-875-2889 227-8062
TF: 800-231-4532 ■ *Web:* www.kea.org/news

LAE News PO Box 479 .... Baton Rouge LA 70821 225-343-9243 343-9272
Web: www.lae.org

Library Journal 360 Park Ave S .... New York NY 10010 646-746-6819 746-6734
Web: libraryjournal.com

Mailbox Bookbag 3515 W Market St Suite 200 .... Greensboro NC 27403 336-854-0309 547-1587
TF: 800-714-7991 ■ *Web:* www.theeducationcenter.com

Mailbox Teacher 3515 W Market St Suite 200 .... Greensboro NC 27403 336-854-0309 547-1590
TF: 800-714-7993 ■ *Web:* www.themailbox.com

				Phone	Fax
Maine Educator 35 Community Dr	Augusta	ME	04330	207-622-5866	623-2129
TF: 800-452-8709					
MEA Voice PO Box 2573	East Lansing	MI	48826	517-332-6551	337-5414
TF: 800-292-1934 ■ *Web:* www.mea.org					
Minnesota Educator 41 Sherburne Ave	Saint Paul	MN	55103	651-227-9541	292-4802
TF: 800-652-9073					
Mississippi Educator 775 N State St	Jackson	MS	39202	601-354-4463	352-7054
TF: 800-530-7998					
MTA Today Magazine 20 Ashburton Pl	Boston	MA	02108	617-742-7950	742-7046
TF: 800-392-6175					
NCAE News Bulletin PO Box 27347	Raleigh	NC	27611	919-832-3000	829-1626
TF: 800-662-7924 ■ *Web:* www.ncae.org					
NCTM News Bulletin 1906 Association Dr	Reston	VA	20191	703-620-9840	476-2970
Web: www.nctm.org/news					
NEA Today 1201 16th St NW	Washington	DC	20036	202-822-7207	822-7206
TF: 800-229-4200 ■ *Web:* www.nea.org/neatoday					
New Hampshire Educator 103 N State St	Concord	NH	03301	603-224-7751	224-2648
Web: www.neanh.org					
New York Teacher 800 Troy-Schenectady Rd	Latham	NY	12110	518-213-6000	213-6415
Web: nysut.org/newyorkteacher					
NJEA Review 180 W State St	Trenton	NJ	08607	609-599-4561	392-6321
Web: www.njea.org					
NSEA Voice 605 S 14th St	Lincoln	NE	68508	402-475-7611	475-2630
TF: 800-742-0047 ■ *Web:* www.nsea.org					
OEA Focus PO Box 18485	Oklahoma City	OK	73154	405-528-7785	524-0350
TF: 800-522-8091					
Ohio Schools 225 E Broad St PO Box 2550	Columbus	OH	43216	614-228-4526	228-8771
On Campus 555 New Jersey Ave NW	Washington	DC	20001	202-879-4400	783-2014
TF: 800-238-1133 ■ *Web:* www.aft.org/publications/on_campus					
Oregon Education 6900 SW Atlanta St Bldg 1	Portland	OR	97223	503-684-3300	684-8063
Web: www.oregoned.org					
Reading Teacher The PO Box 8139	Newark	DE	19711	302-731-1600	731-1057
Web: www.reading.org/publications/rt/					
Scholastic Coach 557 Broadway	New York	NY	10012	212-343-6100	343-6930
TF: 800-724-6527 ■ *Web:* www.scholastic.com/coach					
School & Community PO Box 458	Columbia	MO	65205	573-442-3127	443-5079
TF: 800-392-0532					
School Library Journal 360 Park Ave S	New York	NY	10010	646-746-6759	746-6689
Web: www.schoollibraryjournal.com					
Teacher Magazine 6935 Arlington Rd Suite 100	Bethesda	MD	20814	301-280-3100	280-3150
TF: 800-346-1834 ■ *Web:* www.edweek.org/tm/					
Teaching Exceptional Children 1110 N Glebe Rd Suite 300	Arlington	VA	22201	703-620-3660	715-8412
TF: 888-232-7733					
Teaching K-8 40 Richards Ave	Norwalk	CT	06854	203-855-2650	855-2656
TF Cust Svc: 800-678-8793 ■ *Web:* www.teachingk-8.com					
Teaching Tolerance 400 Washington Ave	Montgomery	AL	36104	334-956-8200	956-8486
Web: www.tolerance.org/teach/magazine/index.jsp					
TSTA Advocate 316 W 12th St	Austin	TX	78701	512-476-5355	486-7049
TF: 800-324-5355 ■ *Web:* www.tsta.org					
Vermont NEA Today 10 Wheelock St	Montpelier	VT	05602	802-223-6375	223-1253
TF: 800-649-6375 ■ *Web:* www.vtnea.org					
Virginia Journal of Education 116 S 3rd St	Richmond	VA	23219	804-648-5801	775-8379
TF: 800-552-9554 ■ *Web:* www.veaweteach.org/articles_vje.asp					
Voice 400 N 3rd St PO Box 1724	Harrisburg	PA	17105	717-255-7000	255-7124
TF: 800-944-7732					
WEA News 115 E 22nd St Suite 1	Cheyenne	WY	82001	307-634-7991	778-8161
TF: 800-442-2395 ■ *Web:* westfield.massteacher.org/newspg.html					
West Virginia School Journal 1558 Quarrier St	Charleston	WV	25311	304-346-5315	346-4325
TF: 800-642-8261 ■ *Web:* www.wvea.org					
Young Children Magazine 1313 L St NW Suite 500	Washington	DC	20005	202-232-8777	328-1846
Web: www.journal.naeyc.org					

460-9 Entertainment & Music Magazines

				Phone	Fax
American Cinematographer Magazine 1782 N Orange Dr	Hollywood	CA	90028	323-969-4333	876-4973
TF: 800-448-0145 ■ *Web:* www.theasc.com					
American Songwriter Magazine 1303 16th Ave S 2nd Fl	Nashville	TN	37212	615-321-6096	321-6097
Web: www.americansongwriter.com					
Amusement Business 5055 Wilshire Blvd	Los Angeles	CA	90036	323-525-2350	525-2372
TF: 800-745-8922 ■ *Web:* www.amusementbusiness.com					
Back Stage Magazine 770 Broadway	New York	NY	10003	646-654-5500	654-5835
TF Subscription: 800-437-3183 ■ *Web:* www.backstage.com					
Bass Player 2800 Campus Dr	San Mateo	CA	94403	650-513-4300	513-4642
TF Cust Svc: 800-234-1831 ■ *Web:* www.bassplayer.com					
Billboard Magazine 770 Broadway	New York	NY	10003	646-654-5500	654-5835
TF Cust Svc: 800-437-3183 ■ *Web:* www.billboard-online.com					
Black Talent News Magazine					
8306 Wilshire Blvd Suite 2057	Beverly Hills	CA	90211	310-203-1336	943-2326
Web: www.blacktalentnews.com					
Boxoffice Magazine 155 S El Molino Ave Suite 100	Pasadena	CA	91101	626-396-0250	396-0248
Web: www.boxoff.com					
Broadcast Engineering Magazine 9800 Metcalf Ave	Overland Park	KS	66212	913-341-1300	
Web: broadcastengineering.com					
Cadence Cadence Bldg	Redwood	NY	13679	315-287-2852	287-2860
Web: www.cadencebuilding.com					
Canadian Musician Magazine 23 Hanover Dr	Saint Catharines	ON	L2W1A3	905-641-3471	641-1648
Web: www.canadianmusician.com					
Casino Player 8025 Black Horse Pike Suite 470	West Atlantic City	NJ	08232	609-484-8866	645-1661
TF: 800-969-0711 ■ *Web:* www.casinoplayer.com					
Country Song Roundup 210 Rt 4 E Suite 211	Paramus	NJ	07652	201-843-4004	
Country Weekly 118 16th Ave S Suite 230	Nashville	TN	37203	615-259-1111	255-1110
Web: www.countryweekly.com					
Creative Screenwriting Magazine					
6404 Hollywood Blvd Suite 415	Los Angeles	CA	90028	323-957-1405	957-1406
Web: www.creativescreenwriting.com					
Dance Magazine 333 7th Ave 11th Fl	New York	NY	10001	212-979-4814	674-0102*
**Fax Area Code:* 646 ■ *TF:* 800-331-1750 ■ *Web:* www.dancemagazine.com					
Down Beat 102 N Haven Rd	Elmhurst	IL	60126	630-941-2030	941-3210
TF: 800-535-7496 ■ *Web:* www.downbeat.com					
Dramatics 2343 Auburn Ave	Cincinnati	OH	45219	513-421-3900	421-7077
Web: www.etassoc.org/publications/dramatics.asp					
Emmy Magazine 5220 Lankershim Blvd	North Hollywood	CA	91601	818-754-2800	761-2827
Web: www.emmys.com/emmymag/index.php					
Entertainment Weekly 1675 Broadway 29th Fl	New York	NY	10019	212-522-5600	522-0074
TF: 800-828-6882 ■ *Web:* www.ew.com/ew/					
Film Comment 70 Lincoln Center Plaza	New York	NY	10023	212-875-5610	875-5636
TF Cust Svc: 800-783-4903 ■ *Web:* www.filmlinc.com/fcm/fcm.htm					
GamePro 555 12th St Suite 1100	Oakland	CA	94607	510-768-2700	768-2701
TF: 800-678-9097 ■ *Web:* www.gamepro.com					
Grammy Magazine 3402 Pico Blvd	Santa Monica	CA	90405	310-392-3777	392-9262
TF: 800-423-2017 ■ *Web:* www.grammy.com					
Guitar Player 2800 Campus Dr	San Mateo	CA	94403	650-513-4300	513-4616
TF Cust Svc: 800-289-9839 ■ *Web:* www.guitarplayer.com					
Hit Parader 210 Rt 4 E Suite 211	Paramus	NJ	07652	201-843-4004	843-8636
Web: www.hitparader.com					
Hollywood Reporter 5055 Wilshire Blvd Suite 600	Los Angeles	CA	90036	323-525-2000	525-2377*
**Fax:* Edit ■ *Web:* www.hollywoodreporter.com					
Hollywood Scriptwriter Magazine PO Box 11163	Carson	CA	90749	310-283-1630	926-2060*
**Fax Area Code:* 562 ■ *Web:* www.hollywoodscriptwriter.com					
International Musician 1501 Broadway Suite 600	New York	NY	10036	212-869-1330	764-6134
TF: 800-762-3444					
Jazziz					
2650 N Military Trail Suite 140 Fountain Square II Bldg	Boca Raton	FL	33431	561-893-6868	893-6867
TF: 800-742-3252 ■ *Web:* www.jazziz.com					
JazzTimes 8737 Colesville Rd 9th Fl	Silver Spring	MD	20910	301-588-4114	588-5531
TF: 800-866-7664 ■ *Web:* www.jazztimes.com					
Keyboard Magazine 2800 Campus Dr	San Mateo	CA	94403	650-513-4300	513-4661
TF Cust Svc: 800-289-9919 ■ *Web:* www.keyboardmag.com					
Las Vegas Magazine 2290 Corporate Circle Suite 250	Henderson	NV	89074	702-383-7185	383-1089
TF: 800-746-9484 ■ *Web:* www.lvshowbiz.com					
Le Lundi 7 Bates Rd	Montreal	QC	H2V4V7	514-848-7000	848-9547
Live Design 249 W 17th St	New York	NY	10011	212-204-1813	204-1823
TF Sales: 800-827-0315 ■ *Web:* livedesignonline.com					
Metal Edge 333 7th Ave 11th Fl	New York	NY	10001	212-780-3500	979-4825
TF: 800-741-1289 ■ *Web:* www.metaledgemag.com					
Movieline Magazine 10537 Santa Monica Blvd Suite 250	Los Angeles	CA	90025	310-234-9501	234-0332
Web: www.movieline.com					
Multichannel News 360 Park Ave S	New York	NY	10010	646-746-6400	746-6700
TF Cust Svc: 888-343-5563 ■ *Web:* www.multichannel.com					
OnSat PO Box 2347	Shelby	NC	28151	704-482-9673	484-6976
TF Cust Svc: 800-234-0021 ■ *Web:* www.onsat.com					
Opera News 70 Lincoln Center Plaza 6th Fl	New York	NY	10023	212-769-7070	769-7007
Web: www.metoperafamily.org/operanews					
Playbill 525 7th Ave Suite 1801	New York	NY	10018	212-557-5757	682-2932
TF: 800-533-4330 ■ *Web:* www.playbill.com					
Pollstar 4697 W Jacquelyn Ave	Fresno	CA	93722	559-271-7900	271-7979*
**Fax:* Edit ■ *TF:* 800-344-7383 ■ *Web:* www.pollstar.com					
Premiere 1633 Broadway	New York	NY	10019	212-767-6000	767-5450
TF Cust Svc: 800-274-4027 ■ *Web:* www.premieremag.com					
Road Gear 1633 Broadway	New York	NY	10019	212-767-6000	767-5600
Web: www.roadgearmag.com					
Rolling Stone 1290 Ave of the Americas 2nd Fl	New York	NY	10104	212-484-1616	767-8203
TF: 800-568-7655 ■ *Web:* www.rollingstone.com					
Satellite Direct PO Box 310156	Newington	CT	06131	206-262-8183	262-8187
TF: 800-234-4220 ■ *Web:* www.directmagazine.com					
Satellite Orbit 701 5th Ave 42nd Fl	Seattle	WA	98104	206-262-8183	262-8187
TF: 800-234-4220 ■ *Web:* www.orbitmagazine.com					
Sheet Music Magazine 2 Depot Plaza Suite 301	Bedford Hills	NY	10507	914-244-8500	244-8560
TF Claims: 800-759-3036 ■ *Web:* www.sheetmusicmagazine.com					
Singing News 330 University Hall Dr	Boone	NC	28607	828-264-3700	264-4621
TF: 800-255-2810 ■ *Web:* www.singingnews.com					
Soap Opera Digest 261 Madison Ave 10th Fl	New York	NY	10016	212-716-2700	661-2560
TF: 800-829-9095 ■ *Web:* www.soapoperadigest.com					
Soap Opera Weekly 261 Madison Ave 9th Fl	New York	NY	10016	212-716-8400	661-1825
TF: 800-829-9096 ■ *Web:* www.soapopera.com					
Spin 205 Lexington Ave 3rd Fl	New York	NY	10016	212-231-7400	231-7300
TF Cust Svc: 800-274-7597 ■ *Web:* www.spin.com					
Take One 86 Elm St	Peterborough	NH	03458	603-924-7271	924-7013
TF: 800-677-8847					
The Source 11 Broadway Suite 360	New York	NY	10004	212-253-3700	253-9344
Web: www.thesource.com					
TV Guide 100 Matsonford Rd 4 Radnor Corp Ctr	Radnor	PA	19088	610-293-8500	293-4849
TF Cust Svc: 800-866-1400 ■ *Web:* www.tvguide.com					
TV Hebdo 7 Bates Rd	Montreal	QC	H2V4V7	514-848-7000	848-0945
Web: tvhebdo.infinit.net					
Variety 5700 Wilshire Blvd Suite 120	Los Angeles	CA	90036	323-857-6600	857-0742
TF: 800-552-3632 ■ *Web:* www.variety.com					
Vibe Magazine 215 Lexington Ave 6th Fl	New York	NY	10016	212-448-7300	448-7400
TF: 800-477-3974 ■ *Web:* www.vibe.com					
Video Age International Magazine 216 E 75th St	New York	NY	10021	212-288-3933	734-9033
Web: www.videoageinternational.com					
Video Event 86 Elm St	Peterborough	NH	03458	603-924-7271	924-7013
TF: 800-677-8847					
Videomaker Magazine 1350 E 9th St	Chico	CA	95928	530-891-8410	891-8443
TF: 800-284-3226 ■ *Web:* www.videomaker.com					

460-10 Fraternal & Special Interest Magazines

				Phone	Fax
AARP Modern Maturity 601 'E' St NW	Washington	DC	20049	202-434-6880	434-6883
TF: 888-687-2277 ■ *Web:* www.aarpmagazine.org					
AAUW Outlook 1111 16th St NW	Washington	DC	20036	202-785-7700	872-1425
TF: 800-326-2289 ■ *Web:* www.aauw.org					
Adoptive Families Magazine 39 W 37th St	New York	NY	10018	646-366-0830	366-0842
TF: 800-372-3300 ■ *Web:* www.adoptivefamilies.com					
American Legion Auxiliary National News					
777 N Meridian St 3rd Fl	Indianapolis	IN	46204	317-955-3845	955-3884
Web: www.legion-aux.org					
American Legion Magazine PO Box 1055	Indianapolis	IN	46206	317-630-1200	630-1280
Web: www.legion.org/pubs/publica.htm#mag					
American Scholar 1606 New Hampshire Ave NW	Washington	DC	20009	202-265-3808	986-1601
TF: 800-821-4567 ■ *Web:* www.pbk.org					
American Spirit 1776 D St NW	Washington	DC	20006	202-628-1776	879-8283
Web: www.dar.org/natsociety/magazine.cfm					
Civitan Magazine 1 Civitan Pl PO Box 130744	Birmingham	AL	35213	205-591-8910	592-6307
TF: 800-248-4826					
Columbia 1 Columbus Plaza	New Haven	CT	06510	203-752-4000	752-4109
TF: 800-380-9995 ■ *Web:* www.kofc.org					
Commentary 165 E 56th St	New York	NY	10022	212-891-1400	891-6700
TF: 800-829-6270 ■ *Web:* www.commentarymagazine.com					
Disabled American Veterans Magazine					
3725 Alexandria Pike	Cold Spring	KY	41076	859-441-7300	441-1416
TF: 877-426-2838 ■ *Web:* www.dav.org/magazine/index.html					
Eagle Magazine 1623 Gateway Cir S	Grove City	OH	43123	614-883-2200	883-2201
Web: www.foe.com/magazine					
Elks Magazine 425 W Diversey Pkwy	Chicago	IL	60614	773-755-4700	755-4745
Web: www.elks.org/elksmag					
Empire State Mason 71 W 23rd St	New York	NY	10010	212-741-4500	633-2639
TF: 800-362-7664					
Gettysburg Review 300 N Washington St	Gettysburg	PA	17325	717-337-6000	357-6145
TF: 800-431-0803 ■ *Web:* www.gettysburg.edu/academics/gettysburg_review					
Girl Scout Leader 420 5th Ave	New York	NY	10018	212-852-8000	852-6511
TF: 800-223-0624					
Hispanic 6355 NW 36th St	Miami	FL	33166	305-774-3546	774-3578
TF Cust Svc: 800-251-2688 ■ *Web:* www.hispaniconline.com					
Irish America 875 Ave of the Americas Suite 2100	New York	NY	10001	212-244-3344	274-3344
TF: 800-582-6642 ■ *Web:* www.irishamerica.com					
Journal Francais 944 Market St Suite 210	San Francisco	CA	94102	415-981-9088	981-9177
TF Cust Svc: 800-232-1549 ■ *Web:* www.journalfrancais.com					
Kiwanis Magazine 3636 Woodview Trace	Indianapolis	IN	46268	317-875-8755	879-0204
TF: 800-549-2647 ■ *Web:* www.kiwanis.org/magazine					

Fraternal & Special Interest Magazines (Cont'd)

Name / Address	City	State	Zip	Phone	Fax
Lion Magazine 300 W 22nd St *TF Circ:* 800-710-7822 ■ *Web:* www.lionsclubs.org/EN/content/news_magazine.shtml	Oak Brook	IL	60523	630-571-5466	571-8890
Mensa Bulletin 1229 Corporate Dr W *TF:* 800-294-8035	Arlington	TX	76006	817-607-0060	649-5232
Military History Magazine 741 Miller Dr SE Suite D2 **Fax:* Edit ■ *TF:* 800-829-3340	Leesburg	VA	20175	703-771-9400	779-8345*
Modern Woodmen 1701 1st Ave *TF:* 800-447-9811	Rock Island	IL	61201	309-786-6481	793-5507
Moose Magazine 155 S International Dr *Web:* www.mooseintl.org/public/moose_Magazine.aspx	Mooseheart	IL	60539	630-859-2000	859-6620
Only Child Magazine 137 N Larchmont Blvd Suite 556 *Web:* www.onlychild.com	Los Angeles	CA	90004	323-937-6815	
Optimist Magazine 4494 Lindell Blvd *TF:* 800-500-8130	Saint Louis	MO	63108	314-371-6000	371-6006
Phi Delta Kappan PO Box 789 *TF:* 800-766-1156 ■ *Web:* www.pdkintl.org	Bloomington	IN	47402	812-339-1156	339-0018
Plus Magazine 793 Higuera St Suite 10 *Web:* plus.maths.org	San Luis Obispo	CA	93401	805-544-8711	546-8827
Poets & Writers 72 Spring St *Web:* www.pw.org	New York	NY	10012	212-226-3586	226-3963
Police Times 6350 Horizon Dr *Web:* www.aphf.org/pt.html	Titusville	FL	32780	321-264-0911	264-0033
Quill & Scroll University of Iowa E346 Adler Journalism Bldg *Web:* www.uiowa.edu/quill-sc	Iowa City	IA	52242	319-335-3457	335-3989
Retirement Life 606 N Washington St	Alexandria	VA	22314	703-838-7760	838-7781
Rotarian 1560 Sherman Ave Rotary International Headquarters *Web:* www.rotary.org/newsroom/rotarian/index.shtml	Evanston	IL	60201	847-866-3000	328-8554
Royal Neighbor 230 16th St *TF:* 800-627-4762 ■ *Web:* www.royalneighbors.com/MemberBenefits/rnmagazine.cfm	Rock Island	IL	61201	309-788-4561	788-9234
Sample Case 632 N Park St *TF:* 800-848-0123	Columbus	OH	43215	614-228-3276	228-1898
Scouting Magazine PO Box 152079 *Web:* www.scoutingmagazine.org	Irving	TX	75015	972-580-2000	580-2502
Tikkun 2342 Shattuck Ave Suite 1200 *Web:* www.tikkun.org	Berkeley	CA	94704	510-644-1200	644-1255
Twins Magazine 11211 E Arapahoe Rd Suite 101 *TF:* 888-558-9467 ■ *Web:* www.twinsmagazine.com	Centennial	CO	80112	303-290-8500	290-9025
VFW Auxiliary 406 W 34th St *Web:* www.ladiesauxvfw.com/magazine.html	Kansas City	MO	64111	816-561-8655	931-4753
VFW Magazine 406 W 34th St *Web:* www.vfw.org/index.cfm?fa=news.mag&did=578	Kansas City	MO	64111	816-756-3390	968-1169
WOODMEN 1700 Farnam St *TF:* 800-225-3108 ■ *Web:* www.woodmen.com/about/woodmag.cfm	Omaha	NE	68102	402-342-1890	271-7269

460-11 General Interest Magazines

Name / Address	City	State	Zip	Phone	Fax
Adventure 1145 17th St NW *TF:* 800-647-5463 ■ *Web:* www.nationalgeographic.com/adventure	Washington	DC	20036	202-857-7000	775-6141
Alfred Hitchcock Mystery Magazine 475 Park Ave S 11th Fl *TF:* 800-333-3311 ■ *Web:* www.themysteryplace.com	New York	NY	10016	212-686-7188	686-7414
Allure 4 Times Sq *TF:* 800-223-0780 ■ *Web:* www.allure.com	New York	NY	10036	212-286-2860	286-2690
American Baby 375 Lexington Ave **Fax:* Edit ■ *TF:* 800-678-1208 ■ *Web:* www.americanbaby.com	New York	NY	10017	212-557-6600	499-1590*
American Profile 341 Cool Springs Blvd Suite 400 *TF:* 800-720-6323 ■ *Web:* www.americanprofile.com	Franklin	TN	37067	615-468-6000	468-6100
Asimov's Science Fiction 475 Park Ave S 11th Fl *TF:* 800-333-4108 ■ *Web:* www.asimovs.com	New York	NY	10016	212-686-7188	686-7414
Atlantic Monthly 600 New Hampshire Ave NW *TF Cust Svc:* 800-234-2411 ■ *Web:* www.theatlantic.com	Washington	DC	20037	202-266-6000	266-7001
Avenue 79 Madison Ave 16th Fl *Web:* www.avenuemagazine.com	New York	NY	10016	212-268-8600	268-0503
BabyTalk Rockefeller Center Time & Life Bldg **Fax:* Sales ■ *TF:* 800-234-0847 ■ *Web:* www.parenting.com/parenting/babytalk/index.html	New York	NY	10020	212-522-1212	522-3611*
Barron's The Dow Jones Business & Financial Weekly 200 Liberty St *TF:* 800-544-0422 ■ *Web:* online.barrons.com	New York	NY	10281	212-416-2700	416-2829
Better Homes & Gardens 1716 Locust St *TF:* 800-374-4244 ■ *Web:* www.bhg.com	Des Moines	IA	50309	515-284-3000	284-3763
Better Investing PO Box 220 *TF:* 877-275-6242 ■ *Web:* www.betterinvesting.org/bimagazine	Royal Oak	MI	48068	248-583-6242	583-4880
Black Collegian 140 Carondelet St *Web:* www.black-collegian.com	New Orleans	LA	70130	504-523-0154	523-0271
Black Enterprise Magazine 130 5th Ave *TF Cust Svc:* 800-727-7777 ■ *Web:* www.blackenterprise.com	New York	NY	10011	212-242-8000	886-9610
Bon Appetit 6300 Wilshire Blvd 10th Fl *TF:* 800-765-9419 ■ *Web:* www.epicurious.com/bonappetit	Los Angeles	CA	90048	323-965-3400	937-1206
Booklist 50 E Huron St *TF:* 800-545-2433 ■ *Web:* www.ala.org/ala/booklist/booklist.htm	Chicago	IL	60611	312-944-6780	337-6787
Brain Child Magazine PO Box 714 **Fax Area Code:* 928 ■ *Web:* www.brainchildmag.com	Lexington	VA	24450	888-304-6667	441-4827*
Bridal Guide 330 7th Ave 10th Fl *TF:* 800-472-7744 ■ *Web:* www.bridalguide.com	New York	NY	10001	212-838-2570	308-7165
Bride's 750 3rd Ave 4th Fl *TF:* 800-777-5786 ■ *Web:* www.brides.com	New York	NY	10017	212-630-5900	630-5889
BusinessWeek 1221 Ave of the Americas *TF Cust Svc:* 800-635-1200 ■ *Web:* www.businessweek.com	New York	NY	10020	212-512-2511	512-4045
Campus Life 465 Gundersen Dr *TF Cust Svc:* 800-678-6083 ■ *Web:* www.christianitytoday.com/teens	Carol Stream	IL	60188	630-260-6200	260-0114
Canadian Living 25 Sheppard Ave W Suite 100 *TF:* 800-387-6332 ■ *Web:* www.canadianliving.com	Toronto	ON	M2N6S7	416-733-7600	733-3398
Capper's 1503 SW 42nd St *TF:* 800-678-5779 ■ *Web:* www.cappers.com	Topeka	KS	66609	785-274-4300	274-4305
Chatelaine 1 Mt Pleasant Rd 8th Fl *TF:* 800-268-9119 ■ *Web:* www.chatelaine.com	Toronto	ON	M4Y2Y5	416-764-1888	764-2431
Child 375 Lexington Ave 9th Fl **Fax:* Edit ■ *TF:* 800-777-0222 ■ *Web:* www.child.com	New York	NY	10017	212-499-2000	499-2038*
Chocolatier 45 W 34th St Suite 600 *Web:* www.bakingshop.com/magazine/chocolatier.htm	New York	NY	10001	212-239-0855	967-4184
College Outlook & Career Opportunities 20 E Gregory Blvd *TF:* 800-274-8867 ■ *Web:* www.collegeoutlook.net	Kansas City	MO	64114	816-361-0616	361-6164
Conde Nast House & Garden 4 Times Sq **Fax:* Edit	New York	NY	10036	212-286-2860	286-8533*
Consumer Reports 101 Truman Ave *TF Orders:* 800-288-7898 ■ *Web:* www.consumerreports.org	Yonkers	NY	10703	914-378-2000	378-2900
Consumers Digest 520 Lake Cook Rd Suite 500	Deerfield	IL	60015	847-607-3000	607-3009
Cook's Illustrated 17 Station St *TF Circ:* 800-526-8442 ■ *Web:* www.cooksillustrated.com	Brookline	MA	02445	617-232-1000	232-1572
Cosmopolitan 300 W 57th St *TF:* 800-888-2676 ■ *Web:* www.cosmomag.com	New York	NY	10019	212-649-2000	307-6563
Country 5400 S 60th St *TF:* 800-344-6913 ■ *Web:* www.country-magazine.com	Greendale	WI	53129	414-423-0100	423-1143
Country Home 1716 Locust St *TF Cust Svc:* 800-374-9431 ■ *Web:* www.countryhome.com	Des Moines	IA	50309	515-284-3000	284-2552
Country Living 300 W 57th St *TF:* 800-888-0128 ■ *Web:* www.countryliving.com	New York	NY	10019	212-649-2000	956-3857
Coup de Pouce 2001 ave University Suite 900 *TF:* 800-528-3836 ■ *Web:* www.coupdepouce.com	Montreal	QC	H3A2A6	514-499-0561	499-1844
Cuisine 2200 Grand Ave *TF:* 800-333-5441 ■ *Web:* www.cuisinemagazine.com	Des Moines	IA	50312	515-282-7000	283-2003
Delicious! 1401 Pearl St Suite 200 *TF:* 800-431-1255 ■ *Web:* www.deliciouslivingmag.com	Boulder	CO	80302	303-939-8440	938-1621
Details 750 3rd Ave 3rd Fl *TF:* 800-627-6367 ■ *Web:* men.style.com/details	New York	NY	10017	212-630-4000	630-3815
Diversion 300 W 57th St *Web:* www.diversionmag.com	New York	NY	10019	212-969-7500	969-7563
Ebony 820 S Michigan Ave *TF:* 800-999-5954 ■ *Web:* www.ebony.com	Chicago	IL	60605	312-322-9200	
Economist The 111 W 57th St 8th Fl *TF:* 800-456-6086 ■ *Web:* www.economist.com	New York	NY	10019	212-541-0500	541-9378
Elegant Bride 750 3rd Ave 4th Fl *TF:* 800-353-9118 ■ *Web:* www.brides.com	New York	NY	10017	212-630-4000	630-5890
Elle 1633 Broadway 44th Fl *TF:* 800-876-8775 ■ *Web:* www.elle.com	New York	NY	10019	212-767-5800	489-4216
Elle Decor 1633 Broadway 41st Fl *TF:* 800-274-4687 ■ *Web:* www.elledecor.com	New York	NY	10019	212-767-5800	489-4216
Ellery Queen Mystery Magazine 475 Park Ave S 11th Fl *Web:* www.themysteryplace.com/eqmm/index.shtml	New York	NY	10016	212-686-7188	686-7414
Entrepreneur Magazine 2445 McCabe Way Suite 400 *TF:* 800-274-6229 ■ *Web:* www.entrepreneur.com	Irvine	CA	92614	949-261-2325	261-7729
Esquire 300 W 57th St *TF:* 800-888-5400 ■ *Web:* www.esquire.com	New York	NY	10019	212-649-2000	977-3158
Essence Magazine 135 W 50th St 4th Fl **Fax Area Code:* 212 ■ *TF:* 800-274-9398 ■ *Web:* www.essence.com	New York	NY	10020	800-274-9398	921-5173*
Expecting 375 Lexington Ave 10th Fl	New York	NY	10017	212-499-2000	499-2083
Family Circle 375 Lexington Ave 9th Fl *TF:* 800-627-4444 ■ *Web:* www.familycircle.com	New York	NY	10017	212-499-2000	499-1987
First For Women 270 Sylvan Ave *TF:* 800-938-8312 ■ *Web:* www.bauerpublishing.com	Englewood Cliffs	NJ	07632	201-569-6699	569-6264
Food & Wine 1120 Ave of the Americas *TF:* 800-333-6569 ■ *Web:* www.foodandwine.com	New York	NY	10036	212-382-5600	764-2177
For the Bride Magazine 222 W 37th St *Web:* www.demetriosbride.com	New York	NY	10018	212-967-5222	967-1682
Forbes 60 5th Ave **Fax:* Edit ■ *TF:* 800-888-9896 ■ *Web:* www.forbes.com	New York	NY	10011	212-620-2200	620-1873*
Fortune Rockefeller Ctr Time & Life Bldg *TF:* 800-621-8000 ■ *Web:* money.cnn.com/magazines/fortune	New York	NY	10020	212-522-1212	467-0579
Franchise Handbook 1020 N Broadway Suite 111 *TF:* 800-272-0246 ■ *Web:* www.franchise1.com	Milwaukee	WI	53202	414-272-9977	272-9973
Futurist 7910 Woodmont Ave Suite 450 *TF:* 800-989-8274 ■ *Web:* www.wfs.org	Bethesda	MD	20814	301-656-8274	951-0394
Glamour 4 Times Sq *TF:* 800-274-7410 ■ *Web:* www.glamour.com	New York	NY	10036	212-286-2860	286-6928
Globe 1000 American Media Way *TF:* 800-749-7733	Boca Raton	FL	33467	561-997-7733	989-1275
Good Housekeeping 300 W 57 St *TF:* 800-888-7788 ■ *Web:* www.goodhousekeeping.com	New York	NY	10019	212-649-2000	265-3307
Gourmet 4 Times Sq *TF:* 800-365-2454 ■ *Web:* www.epicurious.com/gourmet	New York	NY	10036	212-286-2860	286-2672
GQ: Gentlemen's Quarterly 4 Times Sq *TF:* 800-289-9330 ■ *Web:* men.style.com/gq	New York	NY	10036	212-286-2860	286-7093
Grit 1503 SW 42nd St *TF:* 866-803-7096 ■ *Web:* www.grit.com	Topeka	KS	66609	785-274-4300	274-4305
Harper's Bazaar 300 W 57th St **Fax:* Edit ■ *TF:* 800-888-3045 ■ *Web:* www.harpersbazaar.com	New York	NY	10019	212-903-5000	262-7101*
Harper's Magazine 666 Broadway *TF:* 800-444-4653 ■ *Web:* www.harpers.org	New York	NY	10012	212-420-5720	228-5889
Hispanic Business 425 Pine Ave *TF Sales:* 888-447-7287 ■ *Web:* www.hispanicbusiness.com	Santa Barbara	CA	93117	805-964-4554	964-6139
Home Magazine 1633 Broadway 42nd Fl *TF:* 800-950-7370 ■ *Web:* www.homemag.com	New York	NY	10019	212-767-6000	489-4576
House Beautiful 300 W 57th St **Fax:* Edit ■ *TF:* 800-444-6873 ■ *Web:* www.housebeautiful.com	New York	NY	10019	212-903-5000	586-3439*
In Touch Weekly Magazine 270 Sylvan Ave *TF:* 800-938-8312 ■ *Web:* intouchweekly.hollywood.com	Englewood Cliffs	NJ	07632	201-569-6699	569-2510
Inc 7 World Trade Center *TF:* 800-234-0999 ■ *Web:* www.inc.com/magazine	New York	NY	10007	212-389-5300	389-5398
InStyle Rockefeller Ctr Time & Life Bldg *Web:* www.instyle.com	New York	NY	10020	212-522-1212	522-0325
Interview 575 Broadway 5th Fl *TF:* 800-925-9574 ■ *Web:* www.interviewmagazine.com	New York	NY	10012	212-941-2900	941-2819
Jet 820 S Michigan Ave *TF:* 800-999-2617 ■ *Web:* www.jetmag.com	Chicago	IL	60605	312-322-9200	322-0951
Kiplinger's Personal Finance Magazine 1729 H St NW *TF:* 800-544-0155 ■ *Web:* www.kiplinger.com/magazine	Washington	DC	20006	202-887-6400	778-8976
Ladies' Home Journal 125 Park Ave *TF:* 800-374-4545 ■ *Web:* www.lhj.com	New York	NY	10017	212-557-6600	455-1010
Latina 1500 Broadway Suite 700 *Web:* www.latina.com	New York	NY	10036	212-642-0200	997-2553
Lucky 4 Times Sq *TF:* 800-223-0780 ■ *Web:* www.luckymag.com	New York	NY	10036	212-286-2860	286-8083
Mad Magazine 1700 Broadway *TF:* 800-462-3624 ■ *Web:* www.dccomics.com/mad/	New York	NY	10019	212-506-4850	506-4848
Marie Claire 300 W 57th St **Fax Area Code:* 646 ■ *TF:* 800-777-3287 ■ *Web:* www.marieclaire.com	New York	NY	10019	212-841-8400	280-1089*
Martha Stewart Living 11 W 42nd St *TF:* 800-999-6518 ■ *Web:* www.marthastewart.com	New York	NY	10036	212-827-8000	827-8149
Maxim 1040 Avenue of the Americas 16th Fl *TF:* 800-829-5572 ■ *Web:* www.maximonline.com	New York	NY	10018	212-302-2626	302-2635
Men's Journal 1290 Ave of the Americas 2nd Fl *TF:* 800-677-6367 ■ *Web:* www.mensjournal.com	New York	NY	10104	212-484-1616	484-3435
Metropolitan Home 1633 Broadway 41st Fl *TF:* 800-374-4638	New York	NY	10019	212-767-4500	767-5636
Modern Bride 750 3rd Ave 4th Fl *TF Cust Svc:* 800-777-5786 ■ *Web:* www.brides.com/modernbride	New York	NY	10017	212-630-5900	630-5889
Money Rockefeller Ctr Time & Life Bldg *TF:* 800-633-9970 ■ *Web:* money.cnn.com/magazines/moneymag	New York	NY	10020	212-522-1212	522-0189
More 375 Lexington Ave **Fax:* Edit ■ *TF:* 888-699-4036 ■ *Web:* www.more.com	New York	NY	10017	212-557-6600	499-1794*
Ms 1600 Wilson Blvd Suite 801 *TF:* 866-672-6363 ■ *Web:* www.msmagazine.com	Arlington	VA	22209	703-522-4201	522-2219
National Business Woman 1900 M St NW Suite 310 *Web:* www.bpwusa.org	Washington	DC	20036	202-293-1100	861-0298
National Examiner 1000 American Media Way *TF:* 800-749-7733	Boca Raton	FL	33467	561-997-7733	997-5595
National Geographic Adventure 1145 17th St NW *TF:* 800-647-5463 ■ *Web:* www.nationalgeographic.com/adventure	Washington	DC	20036	202-857-7000	775-6141
National Geographic Magazine 1145 17th St NW *TF:* 800-647-5463 ■ *Web:* www.nationalgeographic.com/media/ngm	Washington	DC	20036	202-857-7000	775-6141

	City	State	Zip	Phone	Fax
New York Review of Books 1755 Broadway 5th Fl *TF:* 800-354-0050 ■ *Web:* www.nybooks.com	New York	NY	10019	212-757-8070	333-5374
Newsweek 251 W 57th St **Fax:* Edit ■ *TF Cust Svc:* 800-631-1040 ■ *Web:* www.newsweek.com	New York	NY	10019	212-445-4000	445-4425*
North Light 4700 E Galbraith Rd *TF Orders:* 800-289-0963	Cincinnati	OH	45236	513-531-2690	531-4082
Nylon 110 Greene St Suite 607 *Web:* www.nylonmag.com	New York	NY	10012	212-226-6454	226-7738
O The Oprah Magazine 300 W 57th St *TF:* 888-446-4438 ■ *Web:* www.oprah.com/omagazine	New York	NY	10019	212-649-2000	
Onion The 536 Broadway 10th Fl *Web:* www.theonion.com	New York	NY	10012	212-627-1972	627-1711
Parade 711 3rd Ave *Web:* www.parade.com	New York	NY	10017	212-450-7000	450-7284
Parenting Rockefeller Center Time & Life Bldg *TF Circ:* 800-234-0847 ■ *Web:* www.parenting.com/parenting	New York	NY	10020	212-522-1212	522-8750
Parents 375 Lexington Ave 10th Fl **Fax:* Edit ■ *TF:* 800-727-3682 ■ *Web:* www.parents.com	New York	NY	10017	212-499-2000	499-2083*
Penthouse 2 Penn Plaza Suite 1125 *TF:* 800-289-7368 ■ *Web:* www.penthouse.com	New York	NY	10121	212-702-6000	702-6262
People Rockefeller Ctr Time & Life Bldg *TF:* 800-541-9000 ■ *Web:* people.aol.com/people	New York	NY	10020	212-522-1212	522-0331
People en Espanol Magazine Rockefeller Ctr Time & Life Bldg *TF:* 800-950-8100	New York	NY	10020	212-522-1212	467-2945
Personal Excellence Magazine 1806 N 1120 West *TF:* 877-250-1983 ■ *Web:* www.eep.com	Provo	UT	84604	801-375-4060	377-5960
Playboy 680 N Lake Shore Dr *TF:* 800-999-4438 ■ *Web:* www.playboy.com/magazine	Chicago	IL	60611	312-751-8000	751-2818
Playgirl 801 2nd Ave 9th Fl *TF:* 800-877-6139 ■ *Web:* www.playgirl.com	New York	NY	10017	212-661-7878	697-6343
Psychology Today 115 E 23 St 9th Fl **Fax:* Edit ■ *TF:* 800-234-8361 ■ *Web:* www.psychologytoday.com	New York	NY	10010	212-260-7210	260-7445*
Publishers Weekly 360 Park Ave S 13th Fl *TF:* 800-278-2991 ■ *Web:* publishersweekly.reviewsnews.com	New York	NY	10010	646-746-6758	746-6631
Quick Cooking 5400 S 60th St *TF:* 800-344-6913 ■ *Web:* www.bestsimplerecipes.com	Greendale	WI	53129	414-423-0100	423-1143
Reader's Digest Reader's Digest Rd *TF Cust Svc:* 800-234-9000 ■ *Web:* www.rd.com	Pleasantville	NY	10570	914-238-1000	244-7653
Real Simple Magazine Rockefeller Ctr Time & Life Bldg *Web:* www.realsimple.com	New York	NY	10020	212-522-1212	522-0601
Redbook 300 W 57th St *TF:* 800-888-0008 ■ *Web:* www.redbookmag.com	New York	NY	10019	212-649-2000	581-8114
Reminisce 5400 S 60th St *TF:* 800-344-6913 ■ *Web:* www.reminisce.com	Greendale	WI	53129	414-423-0100	423-8463
Remodeling Ideas 1716 Locust St	Des Moines	IA	50309	515-284-3000	284-3697
Saturday Evening Post 1100 Waterway Blvd *TF:* 800-558-2376 ■ *Web:* www.saturdayeveningpost.com	Indianapolis	IN	46202	317-634-1100	637-0126
Saveur 15 E 32nd St 12th Fl *Web:* www.saveur.com	New York	NY	10016	212-219-7400	
Scholastic Parent & Child 557 Broadway *TF:* 800-724-6527 ■ *Web:* www.scholastic.com/earlylearner/parentandchild	New York	NY	10012	212-343-6100	343-6620
Self 4 Times Sq *TF:* 800-274-6111 ■ *Web:* www.self.com	New York	NY	10036	212-286-2860	286-8110
SmartMoney 1755 Broadway 2nd Fl *TF:* 800-444-4204 ■ *Web:* www.smartmoney.com	New York	NY	10019	212-765-7323	830-9292
Smithsonian 750 9th St NW Suite 7100 *TF:* 800-766-2149 ■ *Web:* www.smithsonianmag.si.edu	Washington	DC	20001	202-633-6090	275-1972
Star Magazine 1000 American Media Way *TF:* 800-749-7733 ■ *Web:* www.starmagazine.com	Boca Raton	FL	33464	561-997-7733	
Starlog Magazine 475 Park Ave S 11th Fl *Web:* www.starlog.com	New York	NY	10016	212-689-2830	686-7414
Sun 1000 American Media Way *TF:* 800-749-7733	Boca Raton	FL	33467	561-997-7733	998-0798
Sunset Magazine 80 Willow Rd *TF:* 800-777-0117 ■ *Web:* www.sunset.com/sunset	Menlo Park	CA	94025	650-321-3600	327-7537
Surface Magazine 1663 Mission St Suite 700 *Web:* www.surfacemag.com	San Francisco	CA	94103	415-575-3100	575-3105
Taste Of Home 5400 S 60th St *TF:* 800-344-6913 ■ *Web:* www.tasteofhome.com	Greendale	WI	53129	414-423-0100	423-8463
Television Week 6500 Wilshire Blvd Suite 2300 **Fax:* Edit ■ *TF:* 888-446-1422 ■ *Web:* www.tvweek.com	Los Angeles	CA	90048	323-370-2400	653-4425*
The New Yorker 4 Times Sq **Fax:* Edit ■ *TF:* 800-825-2510 ■ *Web:* www.newyorker.com	New York	NY	10036	212-286-5400	286-5735*
This Old House 1185 Ave of the Americas 27th Fl *Web:* www.thisoldhouse.com/toh/magazines	New York	NY	10036	212-522-9465	522-9436
Time Rockefeller Ctr Time & Life Bldg *TF:* 800-541-2000 ■ *Web:* www.time.com/time/	New York	NY	10020	212-522-1212	522-0023
Town & Country 300 W 57th St **Fax:* Edit ■ *TF:* 800-289-8696 ■ *Web:* magazines.ivillage.com/townandcountry	New York	NY	10019	212-903-5000	262-7107*
Traditional Home 1716 Locust St **Fax:* Edit ■ *TF Circ:* 800-374-8791 ■ *Web:* www.traditionalhome.com	Des Moines	IA	50309	515-284-3000	284-2083*
True Confessions 200 Madison Ave Suite 2000 *TF:* 800-666-8783 ■ *Web:* www2.trueromancemag.com/indextc.asp	New York	NY	10016	212-725-8811	
True Romance 200 Madison Ave Suite 2000 *TF:* 800-666-8783 ■ *Web:* www2.trueromancemag.com	New York	NY	10016	212-725-8811	
True Story 200 Madison Ave Suite 2000 *TF:* 800-666-8783 ■ *Web:* www2.truestorymail.com/index.asp	New York	NY	10016	212-725-8811	
Upscale 600 Bronner Brothers Way *Web:* www.upscalemagazine.com	Atlanta	GA	30310	404-758-7467	755-9892
Us Weekly Magazine 1290 Ave of the Americas 2nd Fl *TF Cust Svc:* 800-283-3956 ■ *Web:* www.usmagazine.com	New York	NY	10104	212-484-1616	651-7890
USA Weekend 535 Madison Ave 21st Fl *TF Edit:* 800-487-2956 ■ *Web:* www.usaweekend.com	New York	NY	10022	212-715-2100	935-5576
Utne Reader 12 N 12th St Suite 400 *TF Cust Svc:* 800-736-8863 ■ *Web:* www.utne.com	Minneapolis	MN	55403	612-338-5040	338-6043
Vanity Fair 4 Times Sq **Fax:* Edit ■ *TF:* 800-690-6115 ■ *Web:* www.vanityfair.com	New York	NY	10036	212-286-2860	286-6707*
Vogue 4 Times Sq **Fax:* Edit ■ *TF:* 800-690-6115 ■ *Web:* www.style.com/vogue	New York	NY	10036	212-286-2860	286-8169*
W 750 3rd Ave 7th Fl *TF:* 800-289-0390 ■ *Web:* www.style.com/w	New York	NY	10017	212-630-4000	630-3566
Weekly World News 1000 American Media Way *TF:* 800-749-7733	Boca Raton	FL	33467	561-997-7733	241-5689
Western Living 2608 Granville St Suite 560 *TF:* 800-363-3272 ■ *Web:* www.westernlivingmagazine.com	Vancouver	BC	V6H3V3	604-877-7732	877-4848
Wilson Quarterly 1300 Pennsylvania Ave NW 1 Woodrow Wilson Plaza *TF Orders:* 800-829-5108 ■ *Web:* wwics.si.edu	Washington	DC	20004	202-691-4000	691-4036
Woman's Day 1633 Broadway 42nd Fl *TF:* 800-234-2960 ■ *Web:* www.womansday.com	New York	NY	10019	212-767-6000	767-5610
Woman's World 270 Sylvan Ave *TF:* 800-216-6981 ■ *Web:* www.bauerpublishing.com	Englewood Cliffs	NJ	07632	201-569-0006	569-3584
Women's Wear Daily 750 3rd Ave 5th Fl *TF:* 800-289-0273 ■ *Web:* www.wwd.com	New York	NY	10017	212-630-3520	630-3566
Working Mother 60 E 42nd St 27th Fl *TF:* 800-627-0690 ■ *Web:* www.workingmother.com	New York	NY	10165	212-351-6400	351-6487
Worth Magazine 1177 Ave of the Americas 10th Fl *TF Circ:* 800-777-1851 ■ *Web:* www.worth.com	New York	NY	10036	212-223-3100	230-0201
Your Money 520 Lake Cook Rd Suite 500 *TF:* 800-777-0025	Deerfield	IL	60015	847-607-3000	607-3009

460-12 Government & Military Magazines

	City	State	Zip	Phone	Fax
Air Force Magazine 1501 Lee Hwy *TF:* 800-727-3337 ■ *Web:* www.afa.org/magazine/aboutmag.asp	Arlington	VA	22209	703-247-5800	247-5853
Air Force Times 6883 Commercial Dr *TF:* 800-368-5718 ■ *Web:* www.airforcetimes.com	Springfield	VA	22159	703-750-9000	750-8601
Airman Magazine 203 Norton St *Web:* www.af.mil/news/airman/indxflas.html	San Antonio	TX	78226	210-925-7757	925-7219
ARMY Magazine 2425 Wilson Blvd *TF:* 800-336-4570 ■ *Web:* www.ausa.org/www/armymag.nsf	Arlington	VA	22201	703-841-4300	525-9039
Army Times 6883 Commercial Dr *TF:* 800-368-5718 ■ *Web:* www.armytimes.com	Springfield	VA	22159	703-750-9000	658-8314
Governing 1100 Connecticut Ave NW Suite 1300 *TF:* 800-944-0922 ■ *Web:* www.governing.com	Washington	DC	20036	202-862-8802	862-0032
Government Executive 600 New Hampshire Ave NW Suite 400 *TF:* 800-207-8001 ■ *Web:* www.govexec.com	Washington	DC	20037	202-266-7300	266-7350
Government Product News 1300 E 9th St Penton Media Bldg *Web:* www.govpro.com	Cleveland	OH	44114	216-696-7000	696-7658
Government Standard 80 F St NW	Washington	DC	20001	202-737-8700	639-6441
Military & Aerospace Electronics 98 Spit Brook Rd *TF:* 800-225-0556 ■ *Web:* mae.pennnet.com	Nashua	NH	03062	603-891-0123	891-9294
Military Engineer 607 Prince St *TF:* 800-336-3097	Alexandria	VA	22314	703-549-3800	548-6153
Naval Affairs 125 N West St *Web:* www.fra.org/navalaffairs	Alexandria	VA	22314	703-683-1400	549-6610
Navy Times 6883 Commercial Dr *TF:* 800-368-5718 ■ *Web:* www.navytimes.com	Springfield	VA	22159	703-750-9000	750-8767
Public Employee 1625 L St NW *Web:* www.afscme.org	Washington	DC	20036	202-429-1130	429-1120
Retired Officer Magazine 201 N Washington St *TF:* 800-245-8762 ■ *Web:* www.troa.org/Magazine	Alexandria	VA	22314	703-549-2311	838-8179
Soldier of Fortune 5735 Arapahoe Ave Suite A-5 *TF:* 800-800-7630 ■ *Web:* www.sofmag.com	Boulder	CO	80303	303-449-3750	444-5617

460-13 Health & Fitness Magazines

	City	State	Zip	Phone	Fax
American Fitness 15250 Ventura Blvd Suite 200 *TF:* 800-446-2322 ■ *Web:* www.afaa.com	Sherman Oaks	CA	91403	818-905-0040	990-5468
Arthritis Today 1330 W Peachtree St Suite 100 *TF:* 800-283-7800 ■ *Web:* www.arthritis.org/resources/arthritistoday	Atlanta	GA	30309	404-872-7100	965-7575
Cooking Light 2100 Lakeshore Dr *TF:* 800-366-4712 ■ *Web:* www.cookinglight.com	Birmingham	AL	35209	205-445-6000	445-6600
Diabetes Forecast 1701 N Beauregard St *TF:* 800-676-4065 ■ *Web:* www.diabetes.org	Alexandria	VA	22311	703-549-1500	549-6995
Diabetes Self-Management 150 W 22nd St *TF Circ:* 800-234-0923 ■ *Web:* www.diabetes-self-mgmt.com	New York	NY	10011	212-989-0200	989-4786
Fitness 375 Lexington Ave *TF:* 800-888-1181 ■ *Web:* www.fitnessmagazine.com	New York	NY	10012	212-499-2000	499-1697
Fitness Rx for Men Magazine 690 Rt 25A Suite 8 PO Box 834 *Web:* www.fitnessrxformen.com	East Setauket	NY	11733	631-751-9696	751-9699
Fitness Rx for Women Magazine 690 Rt 25A Suite 8	East Setauket	NY	11733	631-751-9696	
FitPregnancy Magazine 21100 Erwin St *Web:* www.fitpregnancy.com	Woodland Hills	CA	91367	818-884-6800	884-6800
Flex 21100 Erwin St *TF:* 800-423-5590 ■ *Web:* www.flexonline.com	Woodland Hills	CA	91367	818-884-6800	884-6733
Health & You 780 Township Line Rd	Yardley	PA	19067	267-685-2800	685-2995
Ironman Magazine 1701 Ives Ave *TF:* 800-447-0008 ■ *Web:* www.ironmanmagazine.com	Oxnard	CA	93033	805-385-3500	385-3515
Let's Live 11050 Santa Monica Blvd 3rd Fl *Web:* www.letsliveonline.com	Los Angeles	CA	90025	310-445-7500	445-7583
Men's Fitness 1 Park Ave 3rd Fl *Web:* www.mensfitness.com	New York	NY	10016	212-545-4800	
Men's Health 400 S 10th St *TF:* 800-666-2303 ■ *Web:* www.menshealth.com	Emmaus	PA	18098	610-967-5171	967-7725
Monster Muscle Magazine PO Box 2561 *TF:* 800-268-2248 ■ *Web:* www.powermagonline.com	Spokane	WA	99220	509-868-2192	
Ms Fitness Magazine PO Box 2490 *Web:* www.msfitness.com	White City	OR	97503	541-830-0400	830-0410
Muscle & Fitness 21100 Erwin St *TF Orders:* 800-423-5590 ■ *Web:* www.muscleandfitness.com	Woodland Hills	CA	91367	818-884-6800	595-0463
Muscle & Fitness Hers Magazine 21100 Erwin St *Web:* www.muscleandfitnesshers.com	Woodland Hills	CA	91367	818-884-6800	
Natural Health Magazine 1 Park Ave 3rd Fl *Web:* www.naturalhealthmag.com	New York	NY	10016	800-268-4968	
Prevention 400 S Kent St *TF:* 800-813-8070 ■ *Web:* www.prev.com	Emmaus	PA	18098	610-967-5171	967-7654
Rodale's Heart & Soul 1 N Charles St 25th Fl *Web:* www.heartandsoul.com	Baltimore	MD	21202	410-576-9199	576-8298
Runner's World 400 S Kent St *TF Cust Svc:* 800-666-2828 ■ *Web:* www.runnersworld.com	Emmaus	PA	18098	610-967-5171	967-7948
Shape 21100 Erwin St *Web:* www.shape.com	Woodland Hills	CA	91367	818-595-0593	
Vegetarian Times 300 N Continental Blvd Suite 650 *TF:* 800-423-4880 ■ *Web:* www.vegetariantimes.com	El Segundo	CA	90245	310-356-4104	356-4110
Vibrant Life Magazine 55 W Oak Ridge Dr *Web:* www.vibrantlife.com	Hagerstown	MD	21740	301-393-4019	393-4055
Vim & Vigor 1010 E Missouri Ave *TF:* 800-282-5850	Phoenix	AZ	85014	602-395-5850	395-5853
Yoga Journal Magazine 475 Sansome St Suite 850 *Web:* www.yogajournal.com	San Francisco	CA	94111	415-591-0555	591-0733

460-14 Hobby & Personal Interests Magazines

	City	State	Zip	Phone	Fax
Air Classics 9509 Vassar Ave Suite A *TF:* 800-562-9182	Chatsworth	CA	91311	818-700-6868	700-6282
American History Illustrated 140 Terry Dr Suite 103 *Web:* www.historynet.com/ah	Newtown	PA	18940	215-968-5020	579-8053
American Photo 1633 Broadway 43rd Fl *TF:* 800-274-4514 ■ *Web:* www.popphoto.com	New York	NY	10019	212-767-6006	333-2439
American Square Dance Magazine 34 E Main St *TF:* 888-588-2362 ■ *Web:* www.americansquaredance.com	Apopka	FL	32703	407-886-7151	886-8464
Antique Trader 700 E State St *TF:* 800-258-0929 ■ *Web:* www.krause.com/static/antreview.htm	Iola	WI	54990	715-445-2214	445-4087

Hobby & Personal Interests Magazines (Cont'd)

				Phone	Fax
Antiques 575 Broadway 5th Fl *TF Cust Svc:* 800-925-9271 ■ *Web:* www.magazineantiques.com	New York	NY	10012	212-941-2800	941-2897
AOPA Pilot 421 Aviation Way *TF:* 800-872-2672 ■ *Web:* www.aopa.org	Frederick	MD	21701	301-695-2000	695-2180
Aquarium Fish 3 Burroughs *TF Cust Svc:* 800-365-4421 ■ *Web:* www.aquariumfish.com	Irvine	CA	92618	949-855-8822	855-3045
Arabian Horse World 1316 Tamson Drive Suite 101 *TF:* 800-955-9423 ■ *Web:* www.ahwmagazine.com	Cambria	CA	94328	805-771-2300	927-6522
Astronomy 21027 Crossroads Cir **Fax:* Cust Svc ■ *TF Cust Svc:* 800-553-6644 ■ *Web:* www.astronomy.com/content/static/magazine	Waukesha	WI	53186	262-796-8776	796-1615*
Autograph Collector Magazine 3629 W MacArthur Blvd Suite 210 *TF:* 800-996-3977 ■ *Web:* www.autographcollector.com	Santa Ana	CA	92704	714-557-1995	557-2105
Backpacker 475 Sansome St Suite 850 **Fax Area Code:* 610 ■ *TF Subcriptions:* 800-666-3434	San Francisco	CA	94111	800-666-3454	967-8181*
Bead & Button Magazine 21027 Crossroads Cir **Fax:* Cust Svc ■ *TF Cust Svc:* 800-533-6644 ■ *Web:* www.beadandbutton.com	Waukesha	WI	53186	262-796-8776	796-1615*
BeadStyle Magazine 21027 Crossroads Cir **Fax:* Cust Svc ■ *TF Cust Svc:* 800-533-6644 ■ *Web:* www.beadstylemag.com	Waukesha	WI	53186	262-796-8776	796-1615*
Beadwork Magazine 201 E 4th St *TF Cust Svc:* 800-272-2193 ■ *Web:* www.interweave.com/bead/default.asp	Loveland	CO	80537	970-669-7672	669-6117
Better Homes & Gardens WOOD Magazine 1716 Locust St **Fax Area Code:* 515 ■ **Fax:* Edit ■ *Web:* www.woodmagazine.com	Des Moines	IA	50309	800-374-9663	284-2115*
Bicycling 135 N 6th St **Fax:* Edit ■ *TF Cust Svc:* 800-666-2806 ■ *Web:* www.bicycling.com	Emmaus	PA	18098	610-967-5171	967-8960*
Bike PO Box 1028 *Web:* www.bikemag.com	Dana Point	CA	92629	949-496-5922	496-7849
Bird Talk 3 Burroughs *TF Cust Svc:* 800-365-4421 ■ *Web:* www.animalnetwork.com/birdtalk	Irvine	CA	92618	949-855-8822	855-3045
Birder's World Magazine 21027 Crossroads Cir **Fax:* Cust Svc ■ *TF Cust Svc:* 800-533-6644 ■ *Web:* www.birdersworld.com	Waukesha	WI	53186	262-796-8776	796-1615*
Birds & Blooms 5400 S 60th St **Fax:* Edit ■ *TF:* 800-344-6913 ■ *Web:* www.birdsandblooms.com	Greendale	WI	53129	414-423-0100	423-8463*
Blood-Horse PO Box 911088 *TF:* 800-866-2361 ■ *Web:* www.bloodhorse.com	Lexington	KY	40591	859-278-2361	276-4450
British Heritage 140 Terry Dr Suite 103 *TF:* 800-829-3340 ■ *Web:* www.historynet.com/bh/	Newtown	PA	18940	215-968-5020	579-8053
Camcorder & ComputerVideo Magazine 290 Maple Ct Suite 232 *Web:* www.candcv.com/index.shtml	Ventura	CA	93003	805-644-3824	644-3875
Cat Fancy 3 Burroughs *TF Cust Svc:* 800-365-4421 ■ *Web:* www.catchannel.com	Irvine	CA	92618	949-855-8822	855-3045
Ceramics Monthly 735 Ceramics Pl Suite 100 *TF:* 800-342-3594 ■ *Web:* www.ceramicsmonthly.org	Westerville	OH	43081	614-895-4213	891-8960
Chess Life PO Box 3967 *TF Sales:* 800-903-8723 ■ *Web:* www.uschess.org	Crossville	TN	38557	931-787-1234	787-1200
Cigar Aficionado 387 Park Ave S 8th Fl *TF Sales:* 800-992-2442 ■ *Web:* www.cigaraficionado.com	New York	NY	10016	212-684-4224	481-0722
Classic Toy Trains 21027 Crossroads Cir **Fax:* Cust Svc ■ *TF Cust Svc:* 800-533-6644 ■ *Web:* www.trains.com/maghomepage/maghomepage.asp?idMagazine=4	Waukesha	WI	53186	262-796-8776	796-1615*
Classic Trains Magazine 21027 Crossroads Cir **Fax:* Cust Svc ■ *TF Cust Svc:* 800-533-6644 ■ *Web:* www.trains.com/maghomepage/maghomepage.asp?idMagazine=2	Waukesha	WI	53186	262-796-8776	796-1615*
Coin Prices 700 E State St *TF:* 866-700-2986 ■ *Web:* www.krause.com/static/coins.htm	Iola	WI	54990	715-445-2214	445-4087
Coin World PO Box 150 *TF Cust Svc:* 866-222-3621 ■ *Web:* www.coinworld.com	Sidney	OH	45365	937-498-0800	498-0812
COINage Magazine 290 Maple Ct Suite 232 *Web:* www.coinagemag.com	Ventura	CA	93003	805-644-3824	644-3875
Computer Gaming World Magazine 28 E 28th St 11th Fl **Fax Area Code:* 212 ■ *TF:* 800-827-4450 ■ *Web:* cgw.1up.com	New York	NY	10016	800-827-4450	503-3995*
Country Decorating Ideas Magazine 1115 Broadway 8th Fl *Web:* www.countrydecoratingideas.com	New York	NY	10010	212-807-7100	463-9958
Country Sampler Magazine 707 Kautz Rd *Web:* www.sampler.com	Saint Charles	IL	60174	630-377-8000	377-8194
Country Woman Magazine 5400 S 60th St **Fax:* Edit ■ *TF:* 800-344-6913 ■ *Web:* www.countrywomanmagazine.com	Greendale	WI	53129	414-423-0100	423-8463*
Crafts 'n Things PO Box 4821 **Fax Area Code:* 937 ■ *TF:* 800-444-0441 ■ *Web:* www.craftsnthings.com	Sidney	OH	45365	866-222-3621	498-0876*
Creating Keepsakes Magazine 14850 Pony Express Rd *TF:* 888-247-5282 ■ *Web:* www.creatingkeepsakes.com	Bluffdale	UT	84065	801-816-8300	816-8301
Crochet World Magazine 306 E Parr Rd *Web:* www.crochet-world.com	Berne	IN	46711	260-589-4000	589-8093
Daily Racing Form 100 Broadway 7th Fl *TF Cust Svc:* 800-306-3676 ■ *Web:* www.drf.com	New York	NY	10005	212-366-7600	366-7738
Decorative Artist's Workbook 4700 E Galbraith Rd *TF Cust Svc:* 800-333-0888 ■ *Web:* www.decorativeartist.com	Cincinnati	OH	45236	513-531-2690	891-7153
Digital Photographer Magazine 290 Maple Ct Suite 232 *Web:* www.digiphotomag.com	Ventura	CA	93003	805-644-3824	644-3875
Dog Fancy 3 Burroughs *TF Cust Svc:* 800-365-4421 ■ *Web:* www.dogchannel.com	Irvine	CA	92618	949-855-8822	855-3045
Dog World 3 Burroughs *TF:* 800-365-4421 ■ *Web:* www.dogchannel.com	Irvine	CA	92618	949-855-8822	855-3045
Doll Crafter Magazine PO Box 5000 *Web:* www.dollccmag.com	Iola	WI	54945	715-445-5000	445-4053
Dollhouse Miniatures PO Box 595 *TF:* 800-437-5828 ■ *Web:* www.dhminiatures.com	Boston	MA	02117	617-536-0100	536-0102
Equus 656 Quince Orchard Rd Suite 600 *TF Cust Svc:* 800-829-5910 ■ *Web:* www.equisearch.com/magazines/Equus/	Gaithersburg	MD	20878	301-977-3900	990-9015
Family Handyman Magazine 2915 Commerce Dr Suite 700 *TF:* 800-285-4961 ■ *Web:* www.rd.com/familyhandyman	Eagan	MN	55121	651-454-9200	994-2250
Family Tree Magazine 4700 E Galbraith Rd *TF Cust Svc:* 888-403-9008 ■ *Web:* www.familytreemagazine.com	Cincinnati	OH	45236	513-531-2690	891-7153
Fine Cooking Magazine 63 S Main St *TF:* 800-283-7252 ■ *Web:* www.taunton.com/finecooking	Newtown	CT	06470	203-426-8171	426-3434
Fine Woodworking 63 S Main St PO Box 5506 *TF:* 800-283-7252 ■ *Web:* www.taunton.com/finewoodworking	Newtown	CT	06470	203-426-8171	270-6753
FineScale Modeler 21027 Crossroads Cir **Fax:* Cust Svc ■ *TF Cust Svc:* 800-533-6644 ■ *Web:* www2.finescale.com/fsm	Waukesha	WI	53186	262-796-8776	796-1615*
Flyer PO Box 39099 *TF:* 800-426-8538 ■ *Web:* www.generalaviationnews.com	Lakewood	WA	98439	253-471-9888	471-9911
Flying Magazine 1633 Broadway 43rd Fl *TF Cust Svc:* 800-274-6793 ■ *Web:* www.flyingmag.com	New York	NY	10019	212-767-6000	767-5600
Garden Railways Magazine 21027 Crossroads Cir *TF:* 800-533-6644 ■ *Web:* www.trains.com/maghomepage/maghomepage.asp?idMagazine=5	Waukesha	WI	53186	262-796-8776	796-1615
Growing Edge Magazine PO Box 1027 *TF:* 800-888-6785 ■ *Web:* www.growingedge.com/magazine	Corvallis	OR	97339	541-757-8477	757-0028
HauteDoll Magazine 5711 8th Ave *Web:* www.barbiebazaar.com/hautedoll.htm	Kenosha	WI	53140	262-658-1004	658-0433
Horse Illustrated 3 Burroughs *TF:* 800-365-4421 ■ *Web:* www.horseillustrated.com	Irvine	CA	92618	949-855-8822	855-3045
Horse & Rider 261 Madison Ave 4th Fl **Fax Area Code:* 972 ■ *TF:* 877-717-8928 ■ *Web:* www.primedia.com/divisions/enthusiastmedia/horseandrider	New York	NY	10016	877-717-8928	309-5670*
Horticulture The Magazine of American Gardening 98 N Washington St *Web:* www.hortmag.com	Boston	MA	02114	617-742-5600	367-6364
Jewelry Crafts Magazine 290 Maple Ct Suite 232 *Web:* www.jewelrycraftsmag.com/index.shtml	Ventura	CA	93003	805-644-3824	644-3875
Knitting World Magazine 306 E Parr Rd *Web:* www.knittingdigest.com	Berne	IN	46711	260-589-4000	589-8093
Lapidary Journal 300 Chesterfield Pkwy Suite 100 **Fax:* Edit ■ *TF:* 800-676-4336 ■ *Web:* www.lapidaryjournal.com	Malvern	PA	19355	610-232-5700	232-5756*
McCall Patterns 120 Broadway *Web:* www.mccall.com	New York	NY	10271	212-465-6800	465-6814
McCall's Quilting Magazine 741 Corporate Cir Suite A **Fax Area Code:* 303 ■ *TF:* 800-944-0736 ■ *Web:* www.mccallsquilting.com	Golden	CO	80401	800-944-0736	277-0370*
Memory Makers magazine 4700 E Galbraith Rd *Web:* www.memorymakersmagazine.com	Cincinnati	OH	45236	513-531-2690	891-7196
Model Airplane News 20 Westport Rd *TF:* 800-877-5160 ■ *Web:* www.modelairplanenews.com	Wilton	CT	06897	203-431-9000	761-8744
Model Railroader Magazine 21027 Crossroads Cir **Fax:* Cust Svc ■ *TF Cust Svc:* 800-533-6644	Waukesha	WI	53186	262-796-8776	796-1615*
Mountain Bike 135 N 6th St **Fax:* Mktg ■ *TF:* 800-666-1817 ■ *Web:* www.mountainbike.com	Emmaus	PA	18098	610-967-5171	967-7522*
Nuts & Volts Magazine 430 Princeland Ct *TF Orders:* 800-783-4624 ■ *Web:* www.nutsvolts.com	Corona	CA	92879	951-371-8497	371-3052
Organic Gardening 400 S 10th St *TF Circ:* 800-666-2206 ■ *Web:* www.organicgardening.com	Emmaus	PA	18098	610-967-5171	967-7722
Outdoor Life 2 Park Ave *TF:* 800-227-2224 ■ *Web:* www.outdoorlife.com	New York	NY	10016	212-779-5004	779-5468
Outdoor Photographer 12121 Wilshire Blvd Suite 1200 *TF Cust Svc:* 800-283-4410 ■ *Web:* www.outdoorphotographer.com	Los Angeles	CA	90025	310-820-1500	826-5008
Outside 400 Market St *TF:* 800-688-7433 ■ *Web:* www.outsidemag.com	Santa Fe	NM	87501	505-989-7100	989-4700
Paper Crafts Magazine 14850 Pony Express Rd *TF:* 800-727-2387 ■ *Web:* www.papercraftsmag.com	Bluffdale	UT	84065	801-816-8300	816-8301
PC Gamer Magazine 4000 Shoreline Ct Suite 400 *TF:* 800-898-7159 ■ *Web:* www.pcgamer.com	South San Francisco	CA	94080	650-872-1642	872-2207
Plane & Pilot 12121 Wilshire Blvd Suite 1200 *TF:* 800-283-4330 ■ *Web:* www.planeandpilotmag.com	Los Angeles	CA	90025	310-820-1500	826-5008
Popular Mechanics 300 W 57th St **Fax Area Code:* 646 ■ *TF:* 800-333-4948 ■ *Web:* www.popularmechanics.com	New York	NY	10019	212-649-2000	280-1081*
Popular Photography 1633 Broadway 43rd Fl *TF:* 800-876-6636 ■ *Web:* www.popphoto.com	New York	NY	10019	212-767-6000	767-5600
Popular Woodworking 4700 E Galbraith Rd *TF Cust Svc:* 877-860-9140 ■ *Web:* www.popularwoodworking.com	Cincinnati	OH	45236	513-531-2690	891-7196
Practical Horseman 665 Quince Orchard Rd Suite 600 *TF Cust Svc:* 877-717-8929 ■ *Web:* www.primedia.com/divisions/enthusiastmedia/practicalhorseman	Gaithersburg	MD	20878	301-977-3900	990-9015
QST 225 Main St *Web:* www.arrl.org/qst	Newington	CT	06111	860-594-0200	594-0259
Quick Quilts Magazine 741 Corporate Cir Suite A **Fax Area Code:* 303 ■ *TF:* 800-277-0370 ■ *Web:* www.quickquilts.com	Golden	CO	80401	800-277-0370	277-0370*
Quilter Magazine 7 Waterloo Rd *TF:* 800-940-6593 ■ *Web:* www.thequiltermag.com	Stanhope	NJ	07874	973-347-6900	347-6909
Quilter's Newsletter Magazine 741 Corporate Cir Suite A **Fax Area Code:* 303 ■ *TF:* 800-477-6089 ■ *Web:* www.qnm.com	Golden	CO	80401	800-477-6089	277-0370*
Quiltmaker Magazine 741 Corporate Cir Suite A **Fax Area Code:* 303 ■ *TF:* 800-388-7023 ■ *Web:* www.quiltmaker.com	Golden	CO	80401	800-388-7023	277-0370*
Radio Control Boat Modeler 20 Westport Rd *TF:* 800-877-5160 ■ *Web:* www.rcboatmodeler.com	Wilton	CT	06897	203-431-9000	761-8744
Reptiles 3 Burroughs *TF:* 800-365-4421 ■ *Web:* www.animalnetwork.com/reptiles/	Irvine	CA	92618	949-855-8822	855-3045
Rock & Gem Magazine 290 Maple Ct Suite 232 *Web:* www.rockngem.com	Ventura	CA	93003	805-644-3824	644-3875
Rubber Stamper Magazine 207 Commercial Ct *TF:* 800-969-7176 ■ *Web:* www.rubberstamper.com	Morganville	NJ	07751	732-536-5160	536-5761
Rug Hooking Magazine 5067 Ritter Rd *TF:* 800-732-3669 ■ *Web:* www.rughookingonline.com	Mechanicsburg	PA	17055	717-796-0411	796-0412
Scale Auto Magazine 21027 Crossroads Cir **Fax:* Cust Svc ■ *TF Cust Svc:* 800-533-6644 ■ *Web:* www.scaleautomag.com	Waukesha	WI	53186	262-796-8776	796-1615*
Sew Beautiful Magazine 149 Old Big Cove Rd *Web:* www.sewbeautiful.com	Brownsboro	AL	35741	256-533-9586	533-9630
Shutterbug 1419 Chaffee Dr Suite 1 *TF:* 800-829-3340 ■ *Web:* www.shutterbug.net	Titusville	FL	32780	321-269-3212	225-3149
Smoke Magazine 26 Broadway Suite 9-M *Web:* www.smokemag.com	New York	NY	10004	212-391-2060	827-0945
Threads Magazine 63 S Main St PO Box 5506 *TF:* 800-283-7252 ■ *Web:* www.taunton.com/threads/index.asp	Newtown	CT	06470	203-426-8171	270-6753
Trains 21027 Crossroads Cir **Fax:* Cust Svc ■ *TF Cust Svc:* 800-533-6644 ■ *Web:* www.trains.com	Waukesha	WI	53186	262-796-8776	796-1615*
Western Horseman 3850 N Nevada Ave *Web:* www.westernhorseman.com	Colorado Springs	CO	80907	719-633-5524	473-0997
Wine Spectator 387 Park Ave S 8th Fl *TF Orders:* 800-752-7799 ■ *Web:* www.winespectator.com	New York	NY	10016	212-684-4224	481-0722
Woodshop News 10 Bokum Rd *TF:* 800-444-7686 ■ *Web:* www.woodshopnews.com	Essex	CT	06426	860-767-8227	767-0645
Woodsmith 2200 Grand Ave *TF Cust Svc:* 800-333-5075 ■ *Web:* www.woodsmith.com	Des Moines	IA	50312	515-282-7000	282-6741
Workbench 2200 Grand Ave *TF Cust Svc:* 800-311-3991 ■ *Web:* www.workbenchmagazine.com	Des Moines	IA	50312	515-282-7000	282-6741

460-15 Law Magazines & Journals

				Phone	Fax
@Law 314 E 3rd St Suite 210	Tulsa	OK	74120	918-582-5188	582-5907
ABA Journal 321 N Clark St *TF:* 800-285-2221 ■ *Web:* www.abanet.org/journal	Chicago	IL	60610	312-988-5000	988-5528
Advocate PO Box 895	Boise	ID	83701	208-334-4500	334-4515
Alabama Lawyer 415 Dexter Ave	Montgomery	AL	36104	334-269-1515	261-6310
Alaska Bar Rag PO Box 100279	Anchorage	AK	99510	907-272-7469	279-1037
American Lawyer 345 Park Ave S *TF:* 800-888-8300 ■ *Web:* www.americanlawyer.com	New York	NY	10010	212-779-9200	696-4514
Arizona Attorney 4201 N 24th St Suite 200 *Web:* www.myazbar.org/AZAttorney	Phoenix	AZ	85016	602-252-4804	271-4930
Arkansas Lawyer 400 W Markham St *Web:* www.arkbar.com	Little Rock	AR	72201	501-375-4606	375-4901
Banking Law Journal 807 Las Cimas Pkwy Suite 300 *TF Cust Svc:* 800-456-2340 ■ *Web:* www.sheshunoff.com/store/819.html	Austin	TX	78746	512-472-2244	305-6575
Bench & Bar of Minnesota 600 Nicollet Mall Suite 380 *Web:* www2.mnbar.org/benchandbar	Minneapolis	MN	55402	612-333-1183	333-4927
California Bar Journal 180 Howard St *Web:* www.calbar.ca.gov/state/calbar/	San Francisco	CA	94105	415-538-2504	538-2247
California Lawyer 44 Montgomery St Suite 250 *Web:* www.dailyjournal.com	San Francisco	CA	94104	415-296-2400	296-2440

	City	State	Zip	Phone	Fax
Colorado Lawyer 1900 Grant St Suite 900 *Web:* www.cobar.org/tcl/index.cfm	Denver	CO	80203	303-860-1118	894-0821
Compleat Lawyer 321 N Clark St *TF:* 800-285-2221 ■ *Web:* www.abanet.org/genpractice/magazine/archives.html	Chicago	IL	60610	312-988-5000	988-5528
Connecticut Lawyer PO Box 350 *Web:* www.ctbar.org/article/articleview/24	New Britain	CT	06050	860-223-4400	223-0538
Family Advocate 321 N Clark St *TF:* 800-285-2221 ■ *Web:* www.abanet.org/family/advocate/home.html	Chicago	IL	60610	312-988-5000	988-5528
Florida Bar Journal 651 E Jefferson St *TF:* 800-342-8060 ■ *Web:* www.floridabar.org	Tallahassee	FL	32399	850-561-5600	681-3859
Georgia Bar Journal 104 Marietta St NW Suite 100 *Web:* www.gabar.org/gabarjournal.asp?Header=gabarjournal	Atlanta	GA	30303	404-527-8700	527-8717
Harvard Law Review 1511 Massachusetts Ave Gannett House *Web:* www.harvardlawreview.org	Cambridge	MA	02138	617-495-4650	495-2748
Hawaii Bar Journal 1132 Bishop St Suite 906	Honolulu	HI	96813	808-537-1868	521-7936
Illinois Bar Journal 424 S 2nd St *TF:* 800-252-8908 ■ *Web:* www.isba.org/IBJ/home.asp	Springfield	IL	62701	217-525-1760	525-0712
In Re: 301 N Market St	Wilmington	DE	19801	302-658-5279	658-5212
InsideCounsel 222 S Riverside Plaza Suite 620 *Web:* www.insidecounsel.com	Chicago	IL	60606	312-654-3500	654-3525
Iowa Lawyer 521 E Locust St 3rd Fl *Web:* www.iowabar.org/main.nsf	Des Moines	IA	50309	515-243-3179	243-2511
Journal of the Kansas Bar Assn 1200 SW Harrison St *Web:* www.ksbar.org	Topeka	KS	66612	785-234-5696	234-3813
Journal of the Missouri Bar 326 Monroe St PO Box 119 *Web:* www.mobar.org/7b2e21b5-eb97-4f01-91da-1ff2beb5bb45.aspx	Jefferson City	MO	65102	573-635-4128	635-2811
Kentucky Bench & Bar 514 W Main St	Frankfort	KY	40601	502-564-3795	564-3225
Lawyers Journal 20 West St *Web:* www.massbar.org/publications/lawyersjournal/	Boston	MA	02111	617-338-0500	338-0650
Legal Management: Journal of the Assn of Legal Administrators 75 Tri State International Suite 222 *Web:* www.alanet.org	Lincolnshire	IL	60069	847-267-1252	267-1329
Los Angeles Lawyer 261 S Figueroa St Suite 300 *Web:* www.lacba.org/showpage.cfm?pageid=40	Los Angeles	CA	90012	213-896-6503	896-6500
Louisiana Bar Journal 601 St Charles Ave *Web:* www.lsba.org/Benefits/louisiana_bar_journal.html	New Orleans	LA	70130	504-566-1600	566-0930
Maine Bar Journal 124 State St PO Box 788 *TF:* 800-475-7523 ■ *Web:* www.mainebar.org	Augusta	ME	04332	207-622-7523	623-0083
Maryland Bar Journal 520 W Fayette St *TF:* 800-492-1964 ■ *Web:* www.msba.org/departments	Baltimore	MD	21201	410-685-7878	837-0518
Michigan Bar Journal 306 Townsend St *Web:* www.michbar.org/journal	Lansing	MI	48933	517-346-6300	482-6248
Mississippi Lawyer 643 N State St *Web:* www.msbar.org	Jackson	MS	39202	601-948-4471	355-8635
Montana Lawyer 7 W 6th Ave Suite 2B *Web:* www.montanabar.org	Helena	MT	59601	406-442-7660	442-7763
National Jurist PO Box 939039 *TF:* 800-465-3462 ■ *Web:* www.nationaljurist.com	San Diego	CA	92913	858-503-7572	503-7583
National Law Journal 345 Park Ave S *TF:* 800-888-8300 ■ *Web:* www.law.com/jsp/nlj/index.jsp	New York	NY	10010	212-779-9200	696-4514
Nevada Lawyer 600 E Charleston Blvd *Web:* www.nvbar.org/Publications/Publications.htm	Las Vegas	NV	89104	702-382-2200	385-2878
New Hampshire Bar News 2 Pillsbury St Suite 300 *Web:* www.nhbar.org	Concord	NH	03301	603-224-6942	224-2910
New Jersey Lawyer Magazine 1 Cragwood Rd *Web:* www.njsba.com/magazine/	South Plainfield	NJ	07080	908-226-0052	226-0139
New York Law Journal 345 Park Ave S *TF:* 800-888-8300 ■ *Web:* www.law.com/jsp/nylj/index.jsp	New York	NY	10010	212-779-9200	696-4514
New York State Bar News 1 Elk St *Web:* www.nysba.org	Albany	NY	12207	518-463-3200	463-4276
Ohio Lawyer PO Box 16562 *TF:* 800-282-6556	Columbus	OH	43216	614-487-2050	487-1008
Oklahoma Bar Journal 1901 Lincoln Blvd *Web:* www.okbar.org/obj	Oklahoma City	OK	73105	405-524-2365	416-7001
Oregon State Bar Bulletin 5200 SW Meadows Rd *TF:* 800-452-8260 ■ *Web:* www.osbar.org/publications/bulletin/bulletin.html	Lake Oswego	OR	97035	503-620-0222	684-1366
Pennsylvania Bar News 100 South St *TF:* 800-932-0311 ■ *Web:* www.pabar.org/barnews.shtml	Harrisburg	PA	17101	717-238-6715	238-7182
Practical Lawyer 4025 Chestnut St *TF:* 800-253-6397	Philadelphia	PA	19104	215-243-1600	243-1664
Practical Real Estate Lawyer 4025 Chestnut St *TF:* 800-253-6397	Philadelphia	PA	19104	215-243-1600	243-1664
Rhode Island Bar Journal 115 Cedar St *Web:* www.ribar.com/aboutus/barjournal.asp	Providence	RI	02903	401-421-5740	421-2703
South Carolina Lawyer 950 Taylor St	Columbia	SC	29201	803-799-6653	799-4118
Student Lawyer 321 N Clark ST *TF:* 800-285-2221 ■ *Web:* www.abanet.org/lsd/studentlawyer/	Chicago	IL	60610	312-988-5000	988-5528
Tennessee Bar Journal 221 4th Ave N Suite 400 *Web:* www.tba.org/Journal_Current/tbj-200404.html	Nashville	TN	37219	615-383-7421	297-8058
Texas Bar Journal 1414 Colorado St Suite 312 *Web:* www.texasbar.com	Austin	TX	78701	512-463-1463	463-1475
Trial 1050 31st St NW *TF:* 800-424-2725	Washington	DC	20007	202-965-3500	965-0030
Washington Lawyer 1250 H St NW Suite 600 *Web:* www.dcbar.org	Washington	DC	20005	202-737-4700	626-3471
Washington State Bar News 2101 4th Ave 4th Fl *TF:* 800-945-9722 ■ *Web:* www.wsba.org	Seattle	WA	98121	206-727-8215	727-8320
West Virginia Lawyer 2006 Kanawha Blvd E *Web:* www.wvbar.org/barinfo/lawyer/magtext.htm	Charleston	WV	25311	304-558-2456	558-2467
Wisconsin Lawyer 5302 Eastpark Blvd *TF:* 800-728-7788 ■ *Web:* www.wisbar.org/wislawmag	Madison	WI	53718	608-250-6127	257-5502
Wyoming Lawyer 500 Randall Ave	Cheyenne	WY	82001	307-632-9061	632-3737
Yale Law Journal PO Box 208215 *Web:* www.yale.edu/yalelj/	New Haven	CT	06520	203-432-1666	432-7482

460-16 Medical Magazines & Journals

	City	State	Zip	Phone	Fax
Academic Physician & Scientist 333 7th Ave 20th Fl	New York	NY	10001	646-674-6536	674-6503
Access Magazine 444 N Michigan Ave Suite 3400 *TF:* 800-243-2342 ■ *Web:* www.adha.org/publications/index.html	Chicago	IL	60611	312-440-8900	440-6780
Alabama MD 19 S Jackson St *TF:* 800-239-6272	Montgomery	AL	36104	334-263-6441	269-5200
Alaska Medicine 4107 Laurel St	Anchorage	AK	99508	907-562-0304	561-2063
American Dental Assn News 211 E Chicago Ave *TF:* 800-621-1099 ■ *Web:* www.ada.org/prof/resources/pubs/adanews/index.asp	Chicago	IL	60611	312-440-2500	440-7494
American Family Physician 11400 Tomahawk Creek Pkwy *TF:* 800-274-2237 ■ *Web:* www.aafp.org/afp.xml	Leawood	KS	66211	913-906-6000	906-6080
American Journal of Nursing 333 7th Ave 20th Fl *TF:* 800-777-2295 ■ *Web:* www.nursingworld.org/ajn	New York	NY	10001	212-886-1200	886-1206
American Journal of Psychiatry 1000 Wilson Blvd Suite 1825 *TF:* 800-368-5777 ■ *Web:* ajp.psychiatryonline.org	Arlington	VA	22209	703-907-7300	907-1085
American Medical News 515 N State St *Web:* www.ama-assn.org/amednews	Chicago	IL	60610	312-464-4429	464-4445
American Nurse 8515 Georgia Ave Suite 400 *TF:* 800-274-4262 ■ *Web:* www.nursingworld.org	Silver Spring	MD	20910	301-628-5000	628-5001
American Psychologist 750 1st St NE *TF:* 800-374-2721 ■ *Web:* www.apa.org/journals/amp.html	Washington	DC	20002	202-336-5500	336-6091
Annals of Internal Medicine 190 North Independence Mall W *TF:* 800-523-1546 ■ *Web:* www.annals.org	Philadelphia	PA	19106	215-351-2400	351-2644
Arizona Medicine 810 W Bethany Home Rd *Web:* www.azmedassn.org	Phoenix	AZ	85013	602-246-8901	242-6283
Assisted Living Success 3300 N Central Ave Suite 300 *Web:* www.alsuccess.com	Phoenix	AZ	85012	480-990-1101	990-0819
CA-A Cancer Journal for Clinicians 1599 Clifton Rd NE *Web:* caonline.amcancersoc.org	Atlanta	GA	30329	404-929-6824	327-6404
Clinician Reviews 1515 Broad St *Web:* www.medscape.com/viewpublication/95_index	Bloomfield	NJ	07003	973-916-1000	916-1919
Compendium of Continuing Education in Dentistry 103 College Rd E *Web:* www.dentallearning.com	Princeton	NJ	08540	609-524-9500	524-9658
Connecticut Medicine 160 Saint Ronan St *TF:* 800-635-7740 ■ *Web:* www.csms.org	New Haven	CT	06511	203-865-0587	865-4997
Contemporary Esthetics & Restorative Practice 103 College Rd E *Web:* www.dentallearning.com	Princeton	NJ	08540	609-524-9500	524-9658
Contemporary OB/GYN 5 Paragon Dr *TF:* 888-581-8052 ■ *Web:* www.contemporaryobgyn.net	Montvale	NJ	07645	973-944-7777	847-5340
Contemporary Pediatrics 5 Paragon Dr *TF:* 888-581-8052 ■ *Web:* www.contemporarypediatrics.com/contpeds/	Montvale	NJ	07645	973-944-7777	944-7892
Contemporary Urology 5 Paragon Dr *TF:* 888-581-8052 ■ *Web:* www.contemporaryurology.com/conturo/	Montvale	NJ	07645	973-944-7777	944-7892
Cortlandt Forum 114 W 26th St 3rd Fl *Web:* www.cortlandtforum.com	New York	NY	10001	646-638-6000	638-6117
Delaware Medical Journal 131 Continental Dr Suite 405 *Web:* www.medsocdel.org	Newark	DE	19713	302-658-7596	658-9669
Dental Economics 1421 S Sheridan Rd *TF:* 800-331-4463 ■ *Web:* de.pennnet.com	Tulsa	OK	74112	918-835-3161	831-9497
Dental Practice Report 2 Northfield Plaza Suite 300 *TF:* 800-323-3337 ■ *Web:* www.dentalproducts.net	Northfield	IL	60093	847-441-3700	441-3702
Dental Products Report 2 Northfield Plaza Suite 300 *TF:* 800-323-3337 ■ *Web:* www.dentalproducts.net	Northfield	IL	60093	847-441-3700	441-3702
Diabetes Advisor 1701 N Beauregard St *TF:* 800-342-2383	Alexandria	VA	22311	703-549-1500	549-6995
Emergency Medicine 7 Century Dr Suite 302 *TF:* 800-976-4040 ■ *Web:* www.emedmag.com	Parsippany	NJ	07054	973-206-3434	701-8895
EyeNet Magazine 655 Beach St *TF:* 866-561-8558 ■ *Web:* www.aao.org/news/eyenet	San Francisco	CA	94109	415-561-8500	561-8533
Family Practice Management 11400 Tomahawk Creek Pkwy *TF:* 800-274-2237 ■ *Web:* www.aafp.org/fpm.xml	Leawood	KS	66211	913-906-6000	906-6080
Female Patient 7 Century Dr Suite 302 *TF:* 800-976-4040	Parsippany	NJ	07054	973-206-3434	206-9378
Hospital Physician 125 Strafford Ave Suite 220	Wayne	PA	19087	610-975-4541	975-4564
Infection Control Today 3300 N Central Ave Suite 300 *Web:* www.infectioncontroltoday.com	Phoenix	AZ	85012	480-990-1101	990-0819
Internal Medicine News 5635 Fishers Ln Suite 6000 *TF:* 800-445-6975 ■ *Web:* www.einternalmedicinenews.com	Rockville	MD	20852	240-221-4500	221-4400
Internal Medicine World Report 241 Forsgate Dr *Web:* www.imwronline.com	Jamesburg	NJ	08831	732-656-1140	656-1142
Iowa Medicine 1001 Grand Ave *TF:* 800-747-3070 ■ *Web:* www.iowamedical.org	West Des Moines	IA	50265	515-223-1401	223-8420
JAMA (Journal of the American Medical Assn) 515 N State St *TF:* 800-262-2350 ■ *Web:* jama.ama-assn.org	Chicago	IL	60610	312-464-5000	464-4184
Journal of the American Dental Assn 211 E Chicago Ave *TF:* 800-621-8099 ■ *Web:* www.ada.org/prof/pubs/jada/	Chicago	IL	60611	312-440-2740	440-2550
Journal of the American Dietetic Assn 120 S Riverside Plaza Suite 2000 *TF:* 800-877-1600 ■ *Web:* www.adajournal.org	Chicago	IL	60606	312-899-0040	899-4790
Journal of the American Medical Assn (JAMA) 515 N State St *TF:* 800-262-2350 ■ *Web:* jama.ama-assn.org	Chicago	IL	60610	312-464-5000	464-4184
Journal of the American Pharmacists Assn 2215 Constitution Ave NW *TF:* 800-237-2742 ■ *Web:* www.aphanet.org	Washington	DC	20037	202-429-7557	628-5425
Journal of the American Veterinary Medical Assn 1931 N Meacham Rd Suite 100 *TF:* 800-248-2862	Schaumburg	IL	60173	847-925-8070	925-1329
Journal of the Arkansas Medical Society PO Box 55088 *TF:* 800-524-1058	Little Rock	AR	72215	501-224-8967	224-6489
Journal of the Florida Medical Assn 123 S Adams St *TF:* 800-762-0233	Tallahassee	FL	32301	850-224-6496	222-8030
Journal of Kentucky Medical Assn 4965 US Hwy 42 KMA Bldg Suite 2000 *Web:* www.kyma.org	Louisville	KY	40222	502-426-6200	426-6877
Journal of the Louisiana State Medical Society 6767 Perkins Rd *TF:* 800-375-9508 ■ *Web:* www.lsms.org	Baton Rouge	LA	70808	225-763-8500	763-2332
Journal of the Medical Assn of Georgia 1330 W Peachtree St NW Suite 500 *TF:* 800-282-0224	Atlanta	GA	30309	404-876-7535	881-5021
Journal of the Mississippi State Medical Assn PO Box 2548 *TF:* 800-898-0251 ■ *Web:* www.msmaonline.com	Ridgeland	MS	39158	601-853-6733	853-6746
Journal of Oklahoma State Medical Assn 601 NW Grand Blvd *TF:* 800-522-9452 ■ *Web:* www.okmed.org	Oklahoma City	OK	73118	405-843-9571	842-1834
Journal of Practical Nursing PO Box 25647 *Web:* www.napnes.org	Alexandria	VA	22313	703-933-1003	940-4089
Journal of the South Carolina Medical Assn 132 W Park Blvd *TF:* 800-327-1021 ■ *Web:* www.scmanet.org	Columbia	SC	29210	803-798-6207	772-6783
Laboratory Medicine 330 W Monroe St Suite 1600 *TF:* 800-621-4142	Chicago	IL	60603	312-541-4999	541-4998
Mayo Clinic Proceedings 200 1st St SW Siebens Bldg 770 *TF:* 800-707-7040 ■ *Web:* www.mayoclinicproceedings.com	Rochester	MN	55905	507-284-2094	284-0252
Medical Economics 5 Paragon Dr *TF:* 888-581-8052 ■ *Web:* www.memag.com	Montvale	NJ	07645	973-944-7777	847-5390
Medicine & Health/Rhode Island 235 Promenade St Suite 500 Box 20 *Web:* www.rimed.org	Providence	RI	02908	401-331-3207	751-8050
Michigan Medicine 120 W Saginaw St	East Lansing	MI	48823	517-337-1351	337-2490
Michigan Medicine 1300 Godward St NE Suite 2500 *TF:* 800-342-5662 ■ *Web:* www.mmaonline.net/publications/mn-med.cfm	Minneapolis	MN	55413	612-378-1875	378-3875
Missouri Medicine PO Box 1028 *Web:* msma.org	Jefferson City	MO	65102	573-636-5151	636-8552
Monitor on Psychology 750 1st Ave NE *Web:* www.apa.org/monitor	Washington	DC	20002	202-336-5500	336-6103
NASW News 750 1st St NE Suite 700 *TF:* 800-638-8799 ■ *Web:* www.naswpress.org	Washington	DC	20002	202-408-8600	336-8312
NCMS Bulletin 222 N Person St *TF:* 800-722-1350	Raleigh	NC	27601	919-833-3836	833-2023

Medical Magazines & Journals (Cont'd)

Phone | Fax

New England Journal of Medicine 10 Shattuck St ... Boston MA 02115 617-734-9800 739-9864
TF: 800-843-6356 ■ *Web:* www.nejm.org
New Jersey Medicine 2 Princess Rd ... Lawrenceville NJ 08648 609-896-1766 896-1368
Web: www.msnj.org
News of New York 420 Lakeville Rd PO Box 5404 ... Lake Success NY 11042 516-488-6100 328-1982
Web: www.mssny.org
Nurseweek 6860 Santa Teresa Blvd ... San Jose CA 95119 408-249-5877 249-3756
TF: 800-859-2091 ■ *Web:* www.nurseweek.com
Nursing 2004 323 Norristown Rd Suite 200 ... Ambler PA 19002 215-646-8700 653-0826
TF: 800-346-7844 ■ *Web:* www.nursing2005.com
Nursing Management 323 Norristown Rd Suite 200 ... Ambler PA 19002 215-646-8700 646-1083
TF: 800-346-7844 ■ *Web:* www.nursingmanagement.com
Nursing Spectrum Greater New York/New Jersey Metro
900 Merchants Concourse Suite 216 ... Westbury NY 11590 516-222-0909 222-0131
Web: www.nursingspectrum.com
Ohio Medicine 3401 Mill Run Dr ... Hilliard OH 43026 614-527-6762 527-6763
TF: 800-766-6762
Patient Care 5 Paragon Dr ... Montvale NJ 07645 973-944-7777 847-5330
TF: 888-581-8052 ■ *Web:* www.patientcareonline.com
Pharmacy Today 2215 Constitution Ave NW ... Washington DC 20037 202-429-7557 628-5425
TF: 800-327-2742 ■ *Web:* www.pharmacy-today.co.nz
Physician & Sportsmedicine 149 5th Ave 10th Fl ... New York NY 10010 212-812-8427 228-1308
Web: www.physsportsmed.com
Postgraduate Medicine 149 5th Ave 10th Fl ... New York NY 10010 212-812-8427 228-1308
Web: www.postgradmed.com
Psychotherapy Networker 7705 13th St NW ... Washington DC 20012 202-829-2452 726-7983
TF: 888-883-3782 ■ *Web:* www.psychotherapynetworker.org
RN 5 Paragon Dr ... Montvale NJ 07645 973-944-7777 847-5350
TF: 888-581-8052 ■ *Web:* www.rnweb.com
Social Work 750 1st St NE Suite 700 ... Washington DC 20002 202-408-8600 336-8312
TF: 800-638-8799 ■ *Web:* www.naswpress.org
South Dakota Medicine 1323 S Minnesota Ave ... Sioux Falls SD 57105 605-336-1965 336-0270
Web: www.sdsma.org/aboutsdsma/publications/index.cfm
Southern Medical Journal 35 Lakeshore Dr ... Birmingham AL 35209 205-945-1840 945-1548
TF: 800-423-4992 ■ *Web:* www.sma.org/smj/index.cfm
Tennessee Medicine PO Box 120909 ... Nashville TN 37212 615-385-2100 312-1959
Texas Medicine 401 W 15th St ... Austin TX 78701 512-370-1300 370-1693
TF: 800-880-1300 ■ *Web:* www.texmed.org/ata/nrm/tme/texmed_mag.asp
US Pharmacist 100 Ave of the Americas 9th Fl ... New York NY 10013 212-274-7000 219-7835
TF: 877-529-1746 ■ *Web:* www.uspharmacist.com
Veterinary Economics 8033 Flint St ... Lenexa KS 66214 913-492-4300 492-4157
TF: 800-255-6864 ■ *Web:* www.vetecon.com
Veterinary Medicine 8033 Flint St ... Lenexa KS 66214 913-492-4300 492-4157
TF: 800-255-6864 ■ *Web:* www.vetmedpub.com/vetmed
Virginia Medical News 2924 Emerywood Pkwy Suite 300 ... Richmond VA 23294 804-353-2721 355-6189
TF: 800-746-6768
West Virginia Medical Journal PO Box 4106 ... Charleston WV 25364 304-925-0342 925-0345
Web: www.wvsma.com
Wisconsin Medical Journal 330 E Lakeside St ... Madison WI 53715 608-257-6781 283-5401
TF: 800-362-9080

460-17 Political & Current Events Magazines

Phone | Fax

7 Jours 7 Bates Rd ... Montreal QC H2V4V7 514-848-7000 848-7070
American Prospect 2000 L St NW Suite 717 ... Washington DC 20036 202-776-0730 776-0740
Web: www.prospect.org
American Spectator 1611 N Kent St Suite 901 ... Arlington VA 22209 703-807-2011 807-2013
TF: 800-524-3469 ■ *Web:* www.spectator.org
Commonweal 475 Riverside Dr Suite 405 ... New York NY 10115 212-662-4200 662-4183
TF: 888-495-6755 ■ *Web:* www.commonwealmagazine.org
Criminal Politics Magazine PO Box 37432 ... Cincinnati OH 45222 513-475-0100 475-6014
TF: 800-543-0486 ■ *Web:* www.criminalpolitics.com
Foreign Affairs 58 E 68th St ... New York NY 10021 212-434-9525 861-1849*
**Fax: Edit* ■ *TF:* 800-829-5539 ■ *Web:* www.foreignaffairs.org
Foreign Policy Magazine 1779 Massachusetts Ave NW ... Washington DC 20036 202-939-2230 483-4430
Web: www.foreignpolicy.com
Freeman The 30 S Broadway ... Irvington-on-Hudson NY 10533 914-591-7230 591-8910
TF Sales: 800-960-4333 ■ *Web:* www.fee.org/publications/the-freeman
Human Events 1 Massachusetts Ave NW Suite 600 ... Washington DC 20001 202-216-0600 216-0615
TF Cust Svc: 800-787-7557 ■ *Web:* www.humaneventsonline.com
Indian Affairs Newsletter 966 Hungerford Dr Suite 12-B ... Rockville MD 20850 240-314-7155 314-7159
Web: www.indian-affairs.org
Maclean's Magazine 1 Mt Pleasant Rd 11th Fl ... Toronto ON M4Y2Y5 416-764-1300 764-1301
TF: 800-268-9119 ■ *Web:* www.macleans.ca
Mother Jones 222 Sutter St Suite 600 ... San Francisco CA 94108 415-321-1700 665-6696
TF: 800-438-6656 ■ *Web:* www.motherjones.com
Moving Ideas Network 1100 15th St NW Suite 600 ... Washington DC 20005 202-903-0348 903-0344
Web: www.movingideas.org
Nation 33 Irving Pl 8th Fl ... New York NY 10003 212-209-5400 982-9000
TF Cust Svc: 800-333-8536 ■ *Web:* www.thenation.com
National Journal 600 New Hampshire Ave NW ... Washington DC 20037 202-266-7230 266-7240
TF: 800-356-4838 ■ *Web:* nationaljournal.com
National Review 215 Lexington Ave 4th Fl ... New York NY 10016 212-679-7330 849-2835
Web: www.nationalreview.com
National Voter 1730 'M' St NW Suite 1000 ... Washington DC 20036 202-429-1965 429-0854
Web: www.lwv.org/elibrary/national_voter.html
New Perspectives Quarterly (NPQ)
10951 W Pico Blvd Suite 315 ... Los Angeles CA 90064 310-474-0011 474-8064
Web: www.digitalnpq.org
New Republic 1331 H St NW Suite 700 ... Washington DC 20005 202-508-4444 628-9383
Web: www.tnr.com
Newsweek 251 W 57th St ... New York NY 10019 212-445-4000 445-4425*
**Fax: Edit* ■ *TF Cust Svc:* 800-631-1040 ■ *Web:* www.newsweek.com
NPQ (New Perspectives Quarterly)
10951 W Pico Blvd Suite 315 ... Los Angeles CA 90064 310-474-0011 474-8064
Web: www.digitalnpq.org
Reason 3415 S Sepulveda Blvd Suite 400 ... Los Angeles CA 90034 310-391-2245 391-4395
TF Cust Svc: 888-732-7668 ■ *Web:* www.reason.com
Slate Magazine 1800 M St Suite 330 ... Washington DC 20036 202-261-1310 261-1310
Web: slate.com
Slate Magazine 251 W 57th St ... New York NY 10019 212-445-5330 445-5318
Web: slate.com
Time Rockefeller Ctr Time & Life Bldg ... New York NY 10020 212-522-1212 522-0023
TF: 800-541-2000 ■ *Web:* www.time.com/time/
US News & World Report 6420 Wilshire Blvd ... Los Angeles CA 90048 202-955-2000 955-2685
TF: 800-436-6520 ■ *Web:* www.usnews.com
Washington Monthly 1319 F St NW Suite 710 ... Washington DC 20004 202-393-5155 393-2444
Web: www.washingtonmonthly.com
Weekly Standard 1150 17th St NW Suite 505 ... Washington DC 20036 202-293-4900 293-4901
TF Cust Svc: 800-274-7293 ■ *Web:* www.weeklystandard.com
World Press Review 735 Mulberry Pl ... North Woodmere NY 11581 516-791-6788 791-1007
TF: 888-757-3238 ■ *Web:* www.worldpress.org

Phone | Fax

WorldNetDaily.com PO Box 1627 ... Medford OR 97501 541-474-1776 474-1770
TF: 877-366-1776 ■ *Web:* www.worldnetdaily.com

460-18 Religious & Spiritual Magazines

Phone | Fax

Biblical Archaeology Review 4710 41st St NW ... Washington DC 20016 202-364-3300 364-2636
TF: 800-221-4644 ■ *Web:* www.bib-arch.org
Body & Soul 42 Pleasant St ... Watertown MA 02472 617-926-0200 926-5021
TF: 800-755-1178 ■ *Web:* www.marthastewart.com
Catholic Digest PO Box 6015 ... New London CT 06320 860-437-3012 437-3013
TF: 800-678-2836 ■ *Web:* www.catholicdigest.org
Charisma 600 Rinehart Rd ... Lake Mary FL 32746 407-333-0600 333-7100
TF: 800-829-3346 ■ *Web:* www.charismamag.com
Christian Reader 465 Gundersen Dr ... Carol Stream IL 60188 630-260-6200 260-0114
TF Cust Svc: 800-223-3161 ■ *Web:* www.christianitytoday.com/spiritual
Christianity Today 465 Gundersen Dr ... Carol Stream IL 60188 630-260-6200 260-0114
TF: 800-999-1704 ■ *Web:* www.christianitytoday.com/ctmag
Church Business 3300 N Central Ave Suite 300 ... Phoenix AZ 85012 480-990-1101 990-0819
Web: www.churchbusiness.com
Episcopal Life 815 2nd Ave Episcopal Church Ctr ... New York NY 10017 212-716-6009 949-8059
TF: 800-334-7626 ■ *Web:* www.episcopal-life.org
Gospel Today Magazine 286 Hwy 314 Suite C ... Fayetteville GA 30214 770-719-4825 716-2660
Web: www.gospeltoday.com
Guideposts Magazine 39 Seminary Hill Rd ... Carmel NY 10512 845-225-3681 684-0679*
**Fax Area Code:* 212 ■ *TF:* 800-431-2344 ■ *Web:* www.guideposts.com
Hadassah Magazine 50 W 58th St ... New York NY 10019 212-451-6289 451-6257
International Jewish Monthly 2020 'K' St NW 7th Fl ... Washington DC 20006 202-857-6600
Web: www.bnaibrith.org
Jewish Family & Life Magazine
90 Oak St PO Box 9129 ... Newton Upper Falls MA 02464 617-965-7700 965-7772
TF: 888-458-8535 ■ *Web:* www.jewishfamily.com
Kashrus Magazine PO Box 204 ... Brooklyn NY 11204 718-336-8544 336-8550
Web: www.kashrusmagazine.com
Lutheran 8765 W Higgins Rd ... Chicago IL 60631 773-380-2540 380-2751
TF: 800-638-3522 ■ *Web:* www.thelutheran.org
Marriage Partnership Magazine 465 Gundersen Dr ... Carol Stream IL 60188 630-260-6200 260-0114
Web: www.christianitytoday.com/marriage
Ministries Today Magazine 600 Rinehart Rd ... Lake Mary FL 32746 407-333-0600 333-7100
Web: www.ministriestoday.com
Moment Magazine 4115 Wisconsin Ave NW Suite 102 ... Washington DC 20016 202-363-6422 362-2514
Web: www.momentmag.com
New Man 600 Rinehart Rd ... Lake Mary FL 32746 407-333-0600 333-7100
TF: 800-829-3346 ■ *Web:* www.newmanmag.com
Presbyterians Today 100 Witherspoon St ... Louisville KY 40202 502-569-5637 569-8632
Reform Judaism 633 3rd Ave 7th Fl ... New York NY 10017 212-650-4240 650-4249
Web: reformjudaismmag.org
Saint Anthony Messenger 28 W Liberty St ... Cincinnati OH 45202 513-241-5616 241-1197
TF: 800-488-0488 ■ *Web:* www.americancatholic.org/messenger
SpiritLed Woman Magazine 600 Rinehart Rd ... Lake Mary FL 32746 407-333-0600 333-7100
Web: www.spiritledwoman.com
Today's Christian Woman 465 Gundersen Dr ... Carol Stream IL 60188 630-260-6200 260-0114
TF Orders: 800-365-9484 ■ *Web:* www.christianitytoday.com/women
US Catholic Magazine 205 W Monroe ... Chicago IL 60606 312-236-7782 236-8207
TF Cust Svc: 800-328-6515 ■ *Web:* uscatholic.claretians.org
Woman's Touch Magazine 1445 N Boonville Ave ... Springfield MO 65802 417-862-2781 862-0503
Web: womanstouch.ag.org

460-19 Science & Nature Magazines

Phone | Fax

AIR (Annals of Improbable Research) PO Box 380853 ... Cambridge MA 02238 617-491-4437 661-0927
Web: www.improbable.com
American Forests 734 15th St NW Suite 800 ... Washington DC 20005 202-737-1944 737-2457
TF: 800-368-5748 ■ *Web:* www.americanforests.org
American Laboratory 30 Controls Dr ... Shelton CT 06484 203-926-9300 926-9310*
**Fax: Edit* ■ *Web:* www.iscpubs.com
American Scientist PO Box 13975 ... Research Triangle Park NC 27709 919-549-0097 549-0090
TF: 800-282-0444 ■ *Web:* www.americanscientist.org
Annals of Improbable Research (AIR) PO Box 380853 ... Cambridge MA 02238 617-491-4437 661-0927
Web: www.improbable.com
Archaeology Magazine 36-36 33rd St ... Long Island City NY 11106 718-472-3050 472-3051*
**Fax: Cust Svc* ■ *Web:* www.archaeology.org
Audubon Magazine 700 Broadway 5th Fl ... New York NY 10003 212-979-3000 477-9069
TF Cust Svc: 800-274-4201 ■ *Web:* magazine.audubon.org
Aviation Week & Space Technology
1200 G St NW Suite 922 ... Washington DC 20005 202-383-2314 383-2347*
**Fax: Edit* ■ *Web:* www.aviationnow.com
BioScience 1444 'I' St NW Suite 200 ... Washington DC 20005 202-628-1500 628-1509
TF: 800-992-2427 ■ *Web:* www.aibs.org/bioscience
BioTechniques 1 Research Dr Suite 400A ... Westborough MA 01581 508-614-1414 616-2930
Web: www.biotechniques.com
California Wild Magazine
California Academy of Sciences 875 Howard St ... San Francisco CA 94103 415-321-8000 321-8610
Web: www.calacademy.org/calwild
Defenders Magazine 1130 17th St NW ... Washington DC 20036 202-682-9400 682-1331
TF: 800-798-2172 ■ *Web:* www.defenders.org/defendersmag
Discover Magazine 90 5th Ave 11th Fl ... New York NY 10011 800-829-9132 246-1020*
**Fax Area Code:* 515 ■ **Fax: Cust Svc* ■ *TF Circ:* 800-829-9132 ■
Web: discovermagazine.com
Earth Island Journal 300 Broadway Suite 28 ... San Francisco CA 94133 415-788-3666 788-7324
Web: www.earthisland.org/eijournal
E/The Environmental Magazine PO Box 5098 ... Westport CT 06881 203-854-5559 866-0602
TF: 800-967-6572 ■ *Web:* www.emagazine.com
Friends of the Earth Magazine
1717 Massachusetts Ave Suite 600 ... Washington DC 20036 202-783-7400 783-0444
TF: 877-843-8687 ■ *Web:* www.foe.org
Garden Compass 1450 Front St ... San Diego CA 92101 619-239-2202 239-4621
Web: www.gardencompass.com
International Laboratory 30 Controls Dr PO Box 870 ... Shelton CT 06484 203-926-9300 926-9310
Web: www.internationallaboratory.com
NASA Tech Briefs 1466 Broadway Suite 910 ... New York NY 10036 212-490-3999 986-7864
TF: 800-944-6272 ■ *Web:* www.nasatech.com
National Parks Magazine 1300 19th St NW Suite 300 ... Washington DC 20036 202-223-6722 659-0650
TF: 800-628-7275 ■ *Web:* www.npca.org/magazine
National Wildlife Magazine 11100 Wildlife Ctr Dr ... Reston VA 22190 703-438-6000 438-6040
TF Cust Svc: 800-822-9919 ■ *Web:* www.nwf.org/nationalwildlife
Natural History Magazine
American Museum of Natural History 175-208 Central
Pk W ... New York NY 10024 212-769-5500 246-1020*
**Fax Area Code:* 515 ■ **Fax: Cust Svc* ■ *TF:* 800-234-5252 ■
Web: www.naturalhistorymag.com
Nature National Press Bldg 529 14th St NW Suite 968 ... Washington DC 20045 202-737-2355 628-1609
TF: 800-524-0384 ■ *Web:* www.nature.com

Name / Address	City	State	Zip	Phone	Fax
Orion Magazine 187 Main St. *TF:* 888-909-6568 ■ *Web:* www.orionoline.org/index2.html	Great Barrington	MA	01230	413-528-4422	528-0676
Physics Today 1 Physics Ellipse *TF:* 800-344-6902 ■ *Web:* www.aip.org/pt	College Park	MD	20740	301-209-3040	209-0842
Popular Science Magazine 2 Park Ave 9th Fl *TF Cust Svc:* 800-289-9399 ■ *Web:* www.popsci.com	New York	NY	10016	212-779-5000	779-5108
R & D Magazine 100 Enterprise Dr Suite 600 Box 912 *TF:* 800-222-0289 ■ *Web:* www.rdmag.com	Rockaway	NJ	07866	973-920-7000	920-7542
Science 1200 New York Ave NW *TF:* 800-731-4939 ■ *Web:* www.sciencemag.org	Washington	DC	20005	202-326-6500	289-5762
Science Illustrated 8428 Holly Leaf Dr	McLean	VA	22102	703-356-1688	
Science News 1719 'N' St NW *TF Sales:* 800-552-4412 ■ *Web:* www.sciencenews.org	Washington	DC	20036	202-785-2255	659-0365
Sciences 81 Stage Point Rd PO Box 1770	Manomet	MA	02345	508-224-6521	224-6521
Scientific American Magazine 415 Madison Ave *Fax Area Code: 515 ■ *Fax: Cust Svc ■ *Web:* www.sciam.com	New York	NY	10017	800-333-1199	246-1020*
Scientist The 400 Market St Suite 1250 *Web:* www.the-scientist.com	Philadelphia	PA	19106	215-351-1660	351-1143
Sierra Magazine 85 2nd St 2nd Fl *Web:* www.sierraclub.org/sierra/	San Francisco	CA	94105	415-977-5500	977-5794
Sky & Telescope Magazine 49 Bay State Rd *TF:* 800-253-0245 ■ *Web:* skyandtelescope.com	Cambridge	MA	02138	617-864-7360	864-6117
Smithsonian Air & Space Magazine 750 9th St NW Suite 7100 *TF Cust Svc:* 800-766-2149 ■ *Web:* www.airspacemag.com	Washington	DC	20013	202-275-1230	275-1886
Technology Review Magazine 1 Main St 7th Fl *Web:* www.techreview.com	Cambridge	MA	02142	617-475-8000	475-8042
Wildlife Conservation Magazine 2300 Southern Blvd *TF:* 800-786-8226 ■ *Web:* www.wildlifeconservation.org	Bronx	NY	10460	718-220-6876	584-2625

460-20 Sports Magazines

Name / Address	City	State	Zip	Phone	Fax
American Hunter 11250 Waples Mill Rd *TF:* 800-672-3888	Fairfax	VA	22030	703-267-1300	267-3971
American Rifleman 11250 Waples Mill Rd *TF:* 800-672-3888	Fairfax	VA	22030	703-267-1379	267-3971
Baseball America Magazine PO Box 2089 *Web:* www.baseballamerica.com/today	Durham	NC	27702	919-682-9635	682-2880
Basketball Digest 990 Grove St 4th Fl *TF Cust Svc:* 800-877-5893 ■ *Web:* www.centurysports.net/basketball	Evanston	IL	60201	847-491-6440	491-0867
Bassmaster Magazine PO Box 10000 *TF:* 877-277-7872 ■ *Web:* espn.go.com/outdoors/bassmaster	Lake Buena Vista	FL	32830	407-566-2277	566-2072
Beckett Baseball Card Monthly 15850 Dallas Pkwy *Web:* www.beckett.com	Dallas	TX	75248	972-991-6657	991-8930
Beckett Football Card Monthly 15850 Dallas Pkwy *Web:* www.beckett.com	Dallas	TX	75248	972-991-6657	991-8930
Bowhunting World 14505 21st Ave N Suite 202 *TF:* 800-766-0039 ■ *Web:* www.bowhuntingworld.com	Plymouth	MN	55447	763-473-5800	473-5801
Climbing Magazine 0326 Hwy 133 Suite 190 *TF:* 800-493-4569 ■ *Web:* www.climbing.com	Carbondale	CO	81623	970-963-9449	963-9442
Competitor Magazine 444 S Cedros Ave Suite 185 *Web:* www.competitor.com	Solana Beach	CA	92075	858-793-2711	793-2710
Discovery YMCA 101 N Wacker Dr *TF:* 800-872-9622	Chicago	IL	60606	312-977-0031	977-4809
Ducks Unlimited Magazine 1 Waterfowl Way *TF:* 800-453-8257 ■ *Web:* www.ducks.org/media/magazine	Memphis	TN	38120	901-758-3825	758-3850
ESPN Magazine 19 E 34th St *TF Cust Svc:* 888-267-3684 ■ *Web:* espn.go.com/magazine	New York	NY	10016	212-515-1000	515-1285
Field & Stream 2 Park Ave *TF Cust Svc:* 800-999-0869 ■ *Web:* www.fieldandstream.com	New York	NY	10016	212-779-5000	725-3836
Florida Sports 605 Belvedere Rd Suite 9 *Web:* www.floridasports.com	West Palm Beach	FL	33405	561-838-9060	838-9037
Florida Sportsman 2700 S Kanner Hwy *Web:* www.flsportsman.com	Stuart	FL	34994	772-219-7400	219-6900
Game & Fish Magazine 2250 New Market Pkwy Suite 110 *Web:* www.gameandfishmag.com	Marietta	GA	30067	770-953-9222	933-9510
Golf Digest 20 Westport Rd PO Box 850 *TF:* 800-962-5513 ■ *Web:* www.golfdigest.com	Wilton	CT	06897	203-761-5100	761-5129
Golf Magazine 2 Park Ave *TF:* 800-227-2224 ■ *Web:* www.golfonline.com/golfonline	New York	NY	10016	212-779-5000	
Golf Tips Magazine 12121 Wilshire Blvd Suite 1200 *TF:* 800-283-4330 ■ *Web:* www.golftipsmag.com	Los Angeles	CA	90025	310-820-1500	826-5008
Golf for Women 750 3rd Ave 3rd Fl *TF:* 800-205-1008 ■ *Web:* www.golf.com/women	New York	NY	10017	212-630-2700	630-3299
Golf World 210 Westport Rd PO Box 850 *TF:* 800-962-5513 ■ *Web:* www.golfdigest.com/newsandtour	Wilton	CT	06897	203-761-5100	761-5131
Gun World 265 S Anita Dr Suite 120 *Web:* www.gunworld.com	Orange	CA	92868	714-939-9991	939-9909
Guns & Ammo 6420 Wilshire Blvd 14th Fl *TF:* 800-800-2666 ■ *Web:* www.gunsandammomag.com	Los Angeles	CA	90048	323-782-2563	782-2477
Hockey News 100-25 Sheppard Ave W *TF:* 888-361-9768 ■ *Web:* www.thn.com	Toronto	ON	M2N6S7	416-733-7600	733-3566
Hooked On the Outdoors Magazine 4830 River Green Pkwy Suite 150 *Web:* www.hookedontheoutdoors.com	Duluth	GA	30396	770-396-4320	390-9498
In-Fisherman 7819 Highland Scenic Rd *TF:* 800-441-1740 ■ *Web:* www.in-fisherman.com	Baxter	MN	56425	218-829-1648	829-3091
Journal of the Philosophy of Sport 1607 N Market St *TF:* 800-747-4457 ■ *Web:* www.humankinetics.com	Champaign	IL	61820	217-351-5076	351-1549
Journal of Sport & Social Issues 2455 Teller Rd *TF:* 800-818-7243	Thousand Oaks	CA	91320	805-499-0721	499-0871
Links Magazine PO Box 7628 *Web:* www.linksmagazine.com	Hilton Head Island	SC	29938	843-842-6200	842-6233
North American Fisherman 12301 Whitewater Dr Suite 260 *TF:* 800-843-6232	Minnetonka	MN	55343	952-936-9333	936-9755
North American Hunter 12301 Whitewater Dr Suite 260 *TF:* 800-922-4868	Minnetonka	MN	55343	952-936-9333	936-9755
Paddler Magazine 735 Oak St *Web:* www.paddlermagazine.com	Steamboat Springs	CO	80477	970-879-1450	870-1404
Paintball Sports Magazine 2090 5th Ave Suite 2 *Web:* www.paintballsportsinc.com	Ronkonkoma	NY	11779	631-580-7772	580-3725
Petersen's Hunting 6420 Wilshire Blvd *TF:* 800-800-8326 ■ *Web:* www.huntingmag.com	Los Angeles	CA	90048	323-782-2563	782-2467
Powder The Skier's Magazine PO Box 1028 *Web:* www.powdermag.com	Dana Point	CA	92629	949-496-5922	496-7849
Rocky Mountain Sports 2525 15th St Suite 1A *Web:* www.rockymountainsports.com	Denver	CO	80211	303-477-9770	477-9747
Salt Water Sportsman 2 Park Ave *TF:* 800-759-2127 ■ *Web:* www.saltwatersportsman.com/saltwater	New York	NY	10016	212-779-5179	779-5999
Shooting Times 2 News Plaza 2nd Fl *TF Orders:* 800-521-2885 ■ *Web:* www.shootingtimes.com	Peoria	IL	61614	309-682-6626	682-7394
Ski Magazine 2 Park Ave *TF:* 800-227-2224 ■ *Web:* www.skimag.com	New York	NY	10016	212-779-5000	779-5469
Skiing Magazine 2 Park Ave *TF:* 800-227-2224 ■ *Web:* www.skiingmag.com/skiing	New York	NY	10016	212-779-5000	779-5466
Snowboarder PO Box 1028 *TF Orders:* 800-955-9120 ■ *Web:* www.snowboardermag.com	Dana Point	CA	92629	949-496-5922	496-7849
Snowmobile 6420 Sycamore Ln Suite 100 *TF Cust Svc:* 800-848-6247 ■ *Web:* www.snowmobilenews.com	Maple Grove	MN	55369	763-383-4400	383-4499
Sport Aviation 3000 Poberezny Rd *Web:* www.eaa.org/benefits/sportaviation	Oshkosh	WI	54902	920-426-4800	426-4828
Sport Fishing Magazine 460 N Orlando Ave Suite 200 *Web:* www.sportfishingmag.com	Orlando	FL	32789	407-628-4802	628-7061
Sporting Classics PO Box 23707 *TF:* 800-849-1004 ■ *Web:* www.sportingclassics.net	Columbia	SC	29224	803-736-2424	736-3404
Sporting News 14500 S Outer 40 Suite 300 *TF:* 800-443-1886 ■ *Web:* www.sportingnews.com	Chesterfield	MO	63017	314-485-6412	485-6364
Sports Afield Magazine 15621 Chemical Ln *TF:* 800-451-4788 ■ *Web:* www.sportsafield.com	Huntington Beach	CA	92649	714-373-4910	894-4949
Sports Business Daily 120 W Morehead St Suite 310 *TF:* 800-829-9839 ■ *Web:* www.sportsbizdaily.com	Charlotte	NC	28202	704-973-1500	973-1501
Sports Illustrated 1271 Avenue of the Americas *TF:* 800-541-1000 ■ *Web:* sportsillustrated.cnn.com	New York	NY	10020	212-522-1212	
Sports Spectrum PO Box 2037 *Fax Area Code: 866 ■ *TF:* 866-821-2971 ■ *Web:* www.sportsspectrum.com	Indian Trail	NC	28079	704-821-2971	875-2669*
Surfer PO Box 420235 *TF:* 800-289-0636 ■ *Web:* www.surfermag.com	Palm Coast	FL	32142	386-447-6383	447-2321
Surfing 950 Calle Amanecer Suite C *Web:* www.surfingthemag.com	San Clemente	CA	92673	949-492-7873	498-6485
T & L Golf 1120 Avenue of the Americas *TF:* 800-947-7961 ■ *Web:* www.travelandleisure.com/tlgolf	New York	NY	10036	212-382-5600	382-5670
Tennis 79 Madison Ave 8th Fl *TF:* 800-666-8336 ■ *Web:* www.tennis.com	New York	NY	10016	212-636-2700	636-2720
TransWorld SNOWboarding 353 Airport Rd *TF:* 800-788-7072 ■ *Web:* www.transworldsnowboarding.com/snow	Oceanside	CA	92054	760-722-7777	722-0653
TransWorld Surf 353 Airport Rd *TF:* 800-788-7072 ■ *Web:* www.transworldsurf.com	Oceanside	CA	92054	760-722-7777	722-0653
VeloNews 1830 N 55th St *Web:* www.velonews.com	Boulder	CO	80301	303-440-0601	444-6788

460-21 Trade & Industry Magazines

Name / Address	City	State	Zip	Phone	Fax
AAPG Explorer 1444 S Boulder Ave *TF:* 800-364-2274 ■ *Web:* www.aapg.org/explorer/index.cfm	Tulsa	OK	74119	918-584-2555	560-2636
Aerospace America 1801 Alexander Bell Dr Suite 500 *TF:* 800-639-2422 ■ *Web:* www.aiaa.org/aerospace	Reston	VA	20191	703-264-7500	264-7551
Air Conditioning Heating & Refrigeration News 2401 W Big Beaver Rd Suite 700 *TF:* 800-837-8337 ■ *Web:* www.achrnews.com	Troy	MI	48084	248-362-3700	362-0317
Air Transport World 8380 Colesville Rd Suite 700 *TF:* 800-366-1901 ■ *Web:* www.atwonline.com	Silver Spring	MD	20910	301-650-2420	650-2434
American Salon 757 3rd Ave 5th Fl *TF:* 800-342-8244 ■ *Web:* www.americansalonmag.com	New York	NY	10017	212-895-8200	895-8210
American Trucker 7355 Woodland Dr *TF:* 800-827-7468 ■ *Web:* www.trucker.com	Indianapolis	IN	46278	317-297-5500	299-1356
ASCE News 1801 Alexander Bell Dr *TF:* 800-548-2723 ■ *Web:* www.pubs.asce.org/news/newnews.html	Reston	VA	20191	703-295-6215	295-6277
Automotive Executive 8400 Westpark Dr *TF:* 800-252-6232 ■ *Web:* www.aemag.com	McLean	VA	22102	703-821-7150	821-7234
Automotive News 1155 Gratiot Ave *TF:* 800-678-9595 ■ *Web:* www.autonews.com	Detroit	MI	48207	313-446-6000	446-0383
Bartender Magazine PO Box 158 *Fax: Edit ■ *TF Sales:* 800-463-7465 ■ *Web:* www.bartender.com	Liberty Corner	NJ	07938	908-766-6006	766-6607*
Boating Industry 6420 Sycamore Ln Suite 100 *TF:* 800-848-6247 ■ *Web:* www.boating-industry.com	Maple Grove	MN	55369	763-383-4400	383-4499
Builder 1 Thomas Cir NW Suite 600 *TF:* 800-636-0336 ■ *Web:* www.builderonline.com	Washington	DC	20005	202-452-0800	785-1974
Building Design & Construction 2000 Clearwater Dr *Web:* www.bdcnetwork.com	Oak Brook	IL	60523	630-288-8000	288-8155
Business & Commercial Aviation 54 Danbury Rd *TF Cust Svc:* 800-525-5003 ■ *Web:* www.awgnet.com/bca/	Ridgefield	CT	06817	203-826-7134	
Chain Pharmacy 425 Park Ave 6th Fl *Fax: Edit ■ *TF:* 800-453-2427	New York	NY	10022	212-756-5220	756-5250*
Chemical Engineering 110 William St 11th Fl *Web:* www.che.com	New York	NY	10038	212-621-4900	621-4685
Chemical & Engineering News 1155 16th St NW *Fax Area Code: 610 ■ *TF:* 800-227-5558 ■ *Web:* pubs.acs.org/cen/index.html	Washington	DC	20036	800-227-5558	964-8071*
Chemical Equipment 100 Enterprise Dr Suite 600 Suite 600 *TF Cust Svc:* 800-547-7377 ■ *Web:* www.chem.info	Rockaway	NJ	07866	973-920-7000	920-7542
Chemical Processing 555 W Pierce Rd Suite 301 *TF:* 800-984-7644 ■ *Web:* www.chemicalprocessing.com	Itasca	IL	60143	630-467-1300	467-1109
Chemical Week PO Box 749 *TF Cust Svc:* 800-774-5733 ■ *Web:* www.chemweek.com	Mount Morris	IL	61054	815-734-5806	734-1223
Civil Engineering 1801 Alexander Bell Dr Suite 100 *Fax: Edit ■ *TF:* 800-548-2723 ■ *Web:* www.pubs.asce.org	Reston	VA	20191	703-295-6000	295-6278*
Contract Employment Weekly c/o CE Publications Inc PO Box 3006 *Web:* www.ceweekly.com	Bothell	WA	98041	425-806-5200	806-5585
Control 555 W Pierce Rd Suite 301 *TF:* 800-984-7644 ■ *Web:* www.controlmagazine.com	Itasca	IL	60143	630-467-1300	467-1124
Control Engineering 2000 Clearwater Dr *Web:* www.manufacturing.net/ctl	Oak Brook	IL	60523	630-288-8000	288-8580
Controller PO Box 85310 *TF:* 800-247-4890 ■ *Web:* www.controller.com	Lincoln	NE	68501	402-479-2143	479-2135
Convenience Store News 770 Broadway 4th Fl *Web:* www.csnews.com	New York	NY	10003	646-654-4500	654-7676
DaySpa Magazine 7628 Densmore Ave *TF:* 800-442-5667 ■ *Web:* www.dayspamagazine.com	Van Nuys	CA	91406	818-782-7328	782-7450
Design News 225 Wyman St *TF:* 800-283-3666 ■ *Web:* www.designnews.com	Waltham	MA	02451	781-734-8000	
Designfax 2500 Tamiami Trail N *Web:* www.manufacturingcenter.com/dfx	Nokomis	FL	34275	941-966-9521	966-2590
Digital Content Producer 9800 Metcalf Ave *TF:* 800-814-9511 ■ *Web:* digitalcontentproducer.com	Overland Park	KS	66212	913-341-1300	
EC & M 9800 Metcalf Ave *TF Acctg:* 800-814-9511 ■ *Web:* www.ecmweb.com	Overland Park	KS	66212	913-341-1300	
EDN 225 Wyman St *TF Orders:* 800-283-3666 ■ *Web:* www.reed-electronics.com/ednmag	Waltham	MA	02451	781-734-8000	
EE Times 600 Community Dr *TF:* 800-645-6278 ■ *Web:* www.eet.com	Manhasset	NY	10030	516-562-5000	562-5325
Electronic Component News 100 Enterprise Dr Suite 600 *TF:* 800-547-7000 ■ *Web:* www.reed-electronics.com/ecnmag	Rockaway	NJ	07866	973-920-7000	920-7542
Electronic News 1101 S Winchester Blvd *Web:* www.reed-electronics.com/electronicnews/	San Jose	CA	91528	408-243-8838	345-4400
Electronic Products 50 Charles Lindbergh Blvd Suite 100 *Web:* www.hearstcorp.com	Uniondale	NY	11553	516-227-1300	227-1444
ENR/Engineering News-Record 2 Penn Plaza 9th Fl *TF:* 800-525-5003 ■ *Web:* enr.construction.com	New York	NY	10121	212-904-2000	904-2007
EPRI Journal 3420 Hillview Ave *TF:* 800-313-3774 ■ *Web:* www.epri.com/journal	Palo Alto	CA	94304	650-855-2000	855-2900

Trade & Industry Magazines (Cont'd)

				Phone	Fax
Equipment Today 1233 Janesville Ave	Fort Atkinson	WI	53538	920-563-6388	563-1700
TF: 800-547-7377					
FDM Magazine 1350 E Touhy Ave Suite 105-W	Des Plaines	IL	60018	847-390-6700	390-7100
Web: www.fdmonline.com					
Fine Homebuilding 63 S Main St	Newtown	CT	06470	203-426-8171	270-6753
TF: 800-283-7252 ■ *Web:* www.taunton.com/finehomebuilding					
Food Management 1300 E 9th St	Cleveland	OH	44114	216-696-7000	696-0836
Food Processing 555 W Pierce Rd Suite 301	Itasca	IL	60143	630-467-1300	467-1179
TF: 800-984-7644 ■ *Web:* www.foodprocessing.com					
Furniture/Today Box 2754	High Point	NC	27261	336-605-0121	605-1143
Web: www.furnituretoday.com					
Giftware News 20 W Kinzie St 12th Fl	Chicago	IL	60610	312-849-2220	849-2174
TF: 800-229-1967 ■ *Web:* www.talcott.com					
Glass Magazine 8200 Greensboro Dr Suite 302	McLean	VA	22102	703-442-4890	442-0630
Web: www.glass.org/magazine/index.htm					
Gourmet Retailer 3301 Ponce de Leon Blvd Suite 300	Coral Gables	FL	33134	305-446-3388	446-2868
TF: 800-397-1137 ■ *Web:* www.gourmetretailer.com/gourmetretailer/index.jsp					
Graphicommunicator 1900 L St NW	Washington	DC	20036	202-462-1400	721-0600
Healthcare Foodservice PO Box 470067	Celebration	FL	34747	407-566-1700	566-0055
TF: 800-525-2015 ■ *Web:* www.healthcarefoodservice.ws/magazine.asp					
Heavy Duty Trucking 38 Executive Pk Suite 300	Irvine	CA	92614	949-261-1636	261-2904
TF: 800-233-1911 ■ *Web:* www.heavydutytrucking.com					
Home Media Retailing 201 E Sandpointe Ave Suite 500	Santa Ana	CA	92707	714-338-6751	338-6710*
**Fax:* Sales ■ *TF:* 800-371-6897 ■ *Web:* www.homemediaretailing.com					
IEEE Spectrum 3 Park Ave 17th Fl	New York	NY	10016	212-419-7760	419-7589
Web: www.spectrum.ieee.org					
Industrial Equipment News 5 Penn Plaza 8th Fl	New York	NY	10001	212-695-0500	629-1585
Web: www.thomaspublishing.com					
Industrial Maintenance & Plant Operation					
100 Enterprise Dr Suite 600	Rockaway	NJ	07866	973-920-7000	920-7542
TF: 800-547-7377 ■ *Web:* www.impomag.com					
IndustryWeek 1300 E 9th St	Cleveland	OH	44114	216-696-7000	696-7670
Web: www.industryweek.com					
Inside Self Storage 3300 N Central Ave Suite 3000	Phoenix	AZ	85012	480-990-1101	990-0819
Web: www.insideselfstorage.com					
JEMS Communications Inc 525 B St Suite 1900	San Diego	CA	92101	619-687-3272	699-6396
TF Cust Svc: 800-266-5367 ■ *Web:* www.jems.com					
Job Shop Technology Magazine 16 Waterbury Rd	Prospect	CT	06712	203-758-4474	758-4475
TF: 800-317-0474 ■ *Web:* www.jobshoptechnology.com					
Journal of Petroleum Technology 222 Palisades Creek Dr	Richardson	TX	75080	972-952-9393	952-9435
TF: 800-456-6863 ■ *Web:* www.spe.org					
Journal of Protective Coatings & Linings					
2100 Wharton St Suite 310	Pittsburgh	PA	15203	412-431-8300	431-5428
TF: 800-837-8303 ■ *Web:* www.paintsquare.com					
Laboratory Equipment 100 Enterprise Dr Suite 600 Box 912	Rockaway	NJ	07866	973-920-7000	920-7542
TF: 800-547-7377 ■ *Web:* www.labequipmag.com					
Land Line 1 NW OOIDA Dr	Grain Valley	MO	64029	816-229-5791	443-2227
TF: 800-444-5791 ■ *Web:* www.landlinemag.com					
Looking Fit 3300 N Central Ave Suite 3000	Phoenix	AZ	85012	480-990-1101	990-0819
Web: www.lookingfit.com					
Machine Design 1300 E 9th St	Cleveland	OH	44114	216-696-7000	696-0177
Web: www.machinedesign.com					
Make-Up Artist Magazine 4018 NE 112 Ave Suite D-8	Vancouver	WA	98682	360-882-3488	885-1836
TF: 800-805-6648 ■ *Web:* www.makeupmag.com					
Manufacturing Engineering 1 SME Dr PO Box 930	Dearborn	MI	48121	313-271-1500	425-3400
TF Cust Svc: 800-733-4763 ■ *Web:* www.sme.org/cgi-bin/find-issues.pl?&&ME&SME&					
Material Handling Management 1300 E 9th St	Cleveland	OH	44114	216-696-7000	696-7658
Web: www.mhmanagement.com					
Mechanical Engineering 3 Park Ave	New York	NY	10016	212-591-7000	591-7739
TF Cust Svc: 800-843-2763 ■ *Web:* www.memagazine.org					
Mediaweek 770 Broadway 7th Fl	New York	NY	10003	646-654-5500	654-5368
Web: www.mediaweek.com					
Modern Car Care 3300 N Central Ave Suite 3000	Phoenix	AZ	85012	480-990-1101	990-0819
Web: www.moderncarcare.com					
Modern Machine Shop 6915 Valley Ave	Cincinnati	OH	45244	513-527-8800	527-8801
TF: 800-950-8020 ■ *Web:* www.mmsonline.com					
Modern Materials Handling 225 Wyman St	Waltham	MA	02451	781-734-8000	
TF: 800-283-3666 ■ *Web:* www.mmh.com					
Modern Plastics 11444 W Olympic Blvd Suite 900	Los Angeles	CA	90064	310-445-4200	
TF: 800-257-9402 ■ *Web:* www.modplas.com					
Modern Salon 400 Knightsbridge Pkwy	Lincolnshire	IL	60069	847-634-2600	634-4379
TF: 800-621-2845 ■ *Web:* www.modernsalon.com					
Motor 50 Charles Lindbergh Blvd Suite 100	Uniondale	NY	11553	516-227-1404	227-1901
Web: www.motor.com					
Motor Age 2 Northfield Plaza Suite 300	Northfield	IL	60093	847-441-3700	441-3777
Web: www.motorage.com/motorage/					
Motorcycle Industry Magazine 1521 Church St	Gardnerville	NV	89410	775-782-0222	782-0266
TF: 800-576-4624 ■ *Web:* www.mimag.com					
MRO Today 730 Madison Ave PO Box 470	Fort Atkinson	WI	53538	920-563-5225	563-4269
TF: 800-932-7732 ■ *Web:* www.mrotoday.com					
Nailpro Magazine 7628 Densmore Ave	Van Nuys	CA	91406	818-782-7328	782-7450
TF: 800-442-5667 ■ *Web:* www.nailpro.com					
Nails Magazine 3520 Challenger St	Torrance	CA	90507	310-533-2400	533-2507
Web: www.nailsmag.com					
National Clothesline 801 Easton Rd Suite 2	Willow Grove	PA	19090	215-830-8467	830-8490
Web: www.natclo.com					
National Fisherman 121 Free St	Portland	ME	04101	207-842-5600	842-5603
TF: 800-959-5073 ■ *Web:* www.nationalfisherman.com					
National Fitness Trade Journal PO Box 2490	White City	OR	97503	541-830-0400	830-0410
Web: www.msfitness.com/NationalFitness/TradeJournal/nftj.html					
National Jeweler 770 Broadway	New York	NY	10003	646-708-7300	654-4948
TF: 800-250-2430 ■ *Web:* www.national-jeweler.com					
Nation's Restaurant News 425 Park Ave 6th Fl	New York	NY	10022	212-756-5000	486-1148*
**Fax:* Mktg ■ *TF:* 800-944-4676 ■ *Web:* www.nrn.com					
Natural Products Industry Insider					
3300 N Central Ave Suite 3000	Phoenix	AZ	85012	480-990-1101	990-0819
Web: www.naturalproductsinsider.com					
New Equipment Digest 1300 E 9th St	Cleveland	OH	44114	216-696-7000	696-1309
Web: www.newequipment.com					
Oil & Gas Journal PO Box 1260	Tulsa	OK	74101	918-835-3161	831-9497
TF: 800-331-4463 ■ *Web:* www.ogj.com/index.cfm					
Overdrive 3200 Rice Mine Rd NE	Tuscaloosa	AL	35406	205-349-2990	349-6359
TF: 800-633-5953 ■ *Web:* www.etrucker.com					
Packaging Digest 2000 Clearwater Dr	Oak Brook	IL	60523	630-288-8000	288-8750
Web: www.packagingdigest.com					
Phoenix: Voice of the Scrap Recycling Industries					
1615 L St NW Suite 6000	Washington	DC	20036	202-737-1770	626-0900
Web: www.isri.org					
Phone+ 3300 N Central Ave Suite 3000	Phoenix	AZ	85012	480-990-1101	990-0819
Web: www.phoneplusmag.com					
Phone+ International 3300 N Central Ave Suite 3000	Phoenix	AZ	85012	480-990-1101	990-0819
Web: www.phoneplusmag.com					
Photo Insider 11 Vreeland Rd	Florham Park	NJ	07932	973-377-1003	377-2679
TF: 800-631-0300 ■ *Web:* www.photoinsider.com					
Plant Engineering 2000 Clearwater Dr	Oak Brook	IL	60523	630-288-8000	288-8781
Web: www.manufacturing.net/ple					
Plant Services 555 W Pierce Rd Suite 301	Itasca	IL	60143	630-467-1300	467-1120
TF: 800-984-7644 ■ *Web:* www.plantservices.com					
Plastics Technology 7 Penn Plaza Suite 1002	New York	NY	10001	646-827-4848	527-8801*
**Fax Area Code:* 513 ■ *Web:* www.plasticstechnology.com					
Power 2 Penn Plaza	New York	NY	10121	212-904-2000	904-3232
Pro Lights & Staging News Magazine					
6000 S Eastern Suite 14-J	Las Vegas	NV	89119	702-932-5585	932-5584
TF: 866-776-2003 ■ *Web:* www.plsn.com					
Proceedings of the IEEE 445 Hoes Ln	Piscataway	NJ	08855	732-562-5478	562-5456
Web: www.ieee.org					
Processing 555 W Pierce Rd Suite 301	Itasca	IL	60143	630-467-1300	467-1123
Web: www.processingmagazine.com					
Product Design & Development 100 Enterprise Dr Suite 600	Rockaway	NJ	07866	973-920-7000	920-7531
TF: 800-547-7377					
Professional Builder 2000 Clearwater Dr	Oak Brook	IL	60523	630-288-8000	288-8145
Web: www.housingzone.com/pb/index.asp					
Professional Surveyor 100 Tuscanny Dr Suite B1	Frederick	MD	21702	301-682-6101	682-6105
Web: www.profsurv.com					
Progressive Grocer 770 Broadway 5th Fl	New York	NY	10003	646-708-0300	654-7463
Web: www.progressivegrocer.com					
Publishers Weekly 360 Park Ave S 13th Fl	New York	NY	10010	646-746-6758	746-6631
TF: 800-278-2991 ■ *Web:* publishersweekly.reviewsnews.com					
Qualified Remodeler 1233 Janesville Ave	Fort Atkinson	WI	53538	920-563-6388	563-1707
TF: 800-547-7377 ■ *Web:* www.qrmagazine.com					
Quality Progress PO Box 3005	Milwaukee	WI	53201	414-272-8575	272-1734
TF: 800-248-1946 ■ *Web:* www.asq.org/pub/qualityprogress					
RCR Wireless News 1746 Cole Blvd Suite 150	Golden	CO	80401	303-733-2500	733-9941
Web: www.rcrnews.com					
Remodeling 1 Thomas Cir NW Suite 600	Washington	DC	20005	202-452-0800	785-1974
TF: 888-269-8410 ■ *Web:* www.remodeling.hw.net					
Restaurant Hospitality 1300 E 9th St	Cleveland	OH	44114	216-696-7000	696-0836
Restaurants & Institutions 2000 Clearwater Dr	Oak Brook	IL	60523	630-288-8000	288-8215
Web: www.rimag.com					
Retail Pharmacy Management 545 W 45th St 8th Fl	New York	NY	10036	212-957-5300	957-7230
Web: www.retailpharmacynews.com					
Shopping Center World 249 W 17th St	New York	NY	10011	212-204-4200	514-9050*
**Fax Area Code:* 914 ■ *Web:* retailtrafficmag.com					
Street & Smith's SportsBusiness Journal					
120 W Morehead St Suite 310	Charlotte	NC	28202	704-973-1410	973-1401
Web: www.sportsbusinessjournal.com					
Sun Wellness 3300 N Central Ave Suite 3000	Phoenix	AZ	85012	480-990-1101	990-0819
Web: www.sun-wellness.com					
Supermarket News PO Box 155548 10th Fl	North Hollywood	CA	91616	800-424-8698	630-3768*
**Fax Area Code:* 212 ■ *Web:* www.supermarketnews.com					
Telecommunications 685 Canton St	Norwood	MA	02062	781-769-9750	762-9077
TF: 800-225-9978 ■ *Web:* www.telecoms-mag.com					
Telephony Magazine 330 N Wabash Ave Suite 2300	Chicago	IL	60611	312-595-1080	595-0295
TF: 800-458-0479 ■ *Web:* telephonyonline.com					
Transportation & Distribution 1300 E 9th St	Cleveland	OH	44114	216-696-7000	696-2737
Web: www.logisticstoday.com					
Travel Weekly Crossroads 100 Lighting Way	Secaucus	NJ	07094	201-902-2000	902-1916
TF: 800-742-7076 ■ *Web:* www.travelweekly.com					
Trucker's Connection 5960 Crooked Creek Rd Suite 15	Norcross	GA	30092	770-416-0927	416-1734
Web: www.truckersconnection.com					
UA Journal PO Box 37800	Washington	DC	20013	202-628-5823	628-5024
United Mine Workers Journal 8315 Lee Hwy	Fairfax	VA	22031	703-208-7200	208-7227
Web: www.umwa.org/journal/journal.shtml					
Urban Call 4265 Brownsboro Rd Suite 225	Winston-Salem	NC	27106	336-759-7477	759-7212
Web: www.urbancall.com					
VARBusiness 600 Community Dr	Manhasset	NY	11030	516-562-5000	562-5325*
**Fax:* Edit ■ *Web:* www.cmp.com					
Videography Magazine 810 7th Ave 27th Fl	New York	NY	10019	212-378-0400	378-0470
Web: www.videography.com					
Water & Wastes Digest					
3030 W Salt Creek Ln Suite 201	Arlington Heights	IL	60005	847-391-1000	390-0408
TF: 800-220-7851 ■ *Web:* www.waterinfocenter.com					
Women's Wear Daily 750 3rd Ave 5th Fl	New York	NY	10017	212-630-3520	630-3566
TF: 800-289-0273 ■ *Web:* www.wwd.com					
Writer's Digest 4700 E Galbraith Rd	Cincinnati	OH	45236	513-531-2690	531-4744
TF Cust Svc: 800-888-6880 ■ *Web:* www.writersdigest.com					
X-Change 3300 N Central Ave Suite 3000	Phoenix	AZ	85012	480-990-1101	990-0819
Web: www.x-changemag.com					

460-22 Travel & Regional Interest Magazines

				Phone	Fax
AAA World 1 River Pl	Wilmington	DE	19801	888-222-4252	230-2758*
**Fax Area Code:* 302					
Alaska 301 Arctic Slope Ave Suite 300	Anchorage	AK	99518	907-272-6070	275-2117
TF: 800-458-4010 ■ *Web:* www.alaskamagazine.com					
Alaska Airlines Magazine 2701 1st Ave Suite 250	Seattle	WA	98121	206-441-5871	448-6939
Web: www.alaskaair.com/www2/magazine/Magazines.asp					
American Way 4333 Amon Carter Blvd MD 5374	Fort Worth	TX	76155	817-967-1804	967-1571
Web: www.americanwaymag.com					
Arizona Highways 2039 W Lewis Ave	Phoenix	AZ	85009	602-712-2000	254-4505
TF: 800-543-5432 ■ *Web:* www.arizonahighways.com					
Atlanta Magazine 260 Peachtree St Suite 300	Atlanta	GA	30303	404-527-5500	527-5575
Web: www.atlantamagazine.com					
Attache (US Airways) 1301 Carolina St	Greensboro	NC	27401	336-378-6065	275-2864
Web: www.attachemag.com					
Baltimore Magazine 1000 Lancaster St Suite 400	Baltimore	MD	21202	410-752-4200	625-0280
TF Cust Svc: 800-935-0838 ■ *Web:* www.baltimoremagazine.net					
Beverly Hills 213 9171 Wilshire Blvd Suite 310	Beverly Hills	CA	90210	310-275-8850	275-1341
Web: www.beverlyhills213.com					
Boston Magazine 300 Massachusetts Ave	Boston	MA	02115	617-262-9700	262-4925
TF: 800-333-2003 ■ *Web:* www.bostonmagazine.com					
Buffalo Spree 6215 Sheridan Dr	Williamsville	NY	14221	716-634-0820	810-0075
Web: www.buffalospree.com					
Business Travel News 770 Broadway	New York	NY	10003	646-654-4500	654-4456
TF Cust Svc: 800-950-1314 ■ *Web:* www.btnmag.com					
Cape Cod Life 270 Communications Way Bldg 6	Hyannis	MA	02601	508-775-9800	775-9801
TF: 800-698-1717 ■ *Web:* www.capecodlife.com					
Caribbean Travel & Life 460 N Orlando Ave Suite 200	Winter Park	FL	32789	407-628-5662	628-7061
TF Circ: 800-588-1689 ■ *Web:* www.worldpub.net					
Carnegie Magazine 4400 Forbes Ave	Pittsburgh	PA	15213	412-622-3131	622-6258
Web: www.carnegiemuseums.org/cmag					
Chesapeake Bay Magazine 1819 Bay Ridge Ave Suite 180	Annapolis	MD	21403	410-263-2662	267-6924
TF: 800-584-5066 ■ *Web:* www.cbmmag.net					
Chicago 435 N Michigan Ave Suite 1100	Chicago	IL	60611	312-222-8999	222-0699*
**Fax:* Edit ■ *TF:* 800-999-0879 ■ *Web:* www.chicagomag.com					
Chicago Life PO Box 11311	Chicago	IL	60611	773-528-2737	
Web: www.chicagolife.net					
Cincinnati 441 Vine St Suite 200	Cincinnati	OH	45202	513-421-4300	562-2746
TF Cust Svc: 800-846-4333 ■ *Web:* www.cincinnatimagazine.com					

	City	State	ZIP	Phone	Fax
Cleveland Magazine 1422 Euclid Ave Suite 730 *TF:* 800-210-7293 ■ *Web:* www.clevelandmagazine.com	Cleveland	OH	44115	216-771-2833	781-6318
Coastal Living 2100 Lakeshore Dr *TF Cust Svc:* 888-252-3529 ■ *Web:* www.coastalliving.com	Birmingham	AL	35209	205-445-6000	445-6990
Columbus Monthly 5255 Sinclair Rd *Web:* www.columbusmonthly.com	Columbus	OH	43229	614-888-4567	848-3838
Conde Nast Traveler 4 Times Sq *TF:* 800-223-0780 ■ *Web:* www.concierge.com/cntraveler	New York	NY	10036	212-286-2860	286-2190
Connecticut 35 Nutmeg Dr *TF:* 800-974-2001 ■ *Web:* www.connecticutmag.com	Trumbull	CT	06611	203-380-6600	380-6610
Continental 99 Bedford St 5th Fl	Boston	MA	02111	617-451-1700	338-7767
Cruise Travel 990 Grove St Suite 400 *TF:* 800-877-5893 ■ *Web:* www.travel.org/CruiseTravel	Evanston	IL	60201	847-491-6440	491-6203
Delta Air Lines Sky 1301 Carolina St *Web:* www.delta-sky.com	Greensboro	NC	27401	336-378-6065	275-2864
Departures Magazine 1120 Ave of the Americas 11th Fl *TF:* 800-333-7483 ■ *Web:* www.departures.com	New York	NY	10036	212-382-5600	827-6413
Down East: The Magazine of Maine 680 Commercial St *TF:* 800-727-7422 ■ *Web:* www.downeast.com	Rockport	ME	04856	207-594-9544	594-7215
Endless Vacation 9998 N Michigan Rd *Web:* www.evmediakit.com	Carmel	IN	46032	317-805-9000	
Exclusively Yours Magazine 740 N Plankinton Ave Suite 500 *Web:* www.eymag.com	Milwaukee	WI	53203	414-271-4270	271-0383
Family Motor Coaching 8291 Clough Pike *TF:* 800-543-3622 ■ *Web:* www.fmca.com	Cincinnati	OH	45244	513-474-3622	474-2332
Frequent Flyer 3025 Highland Pkwy Suite 200 *TF:* 800-525-1138 ■ *Web:* www.frequentflyer.oag.com	Downers Grove	IL	60515	630-515-5300	515-3251
GO Magazine 6600 AAA Dr *TF:* 800-477-4222 ■ *Web:* www.aaacarolinas.com	Charlotte	NC	28212	704-377-3600	569-7815
Going Places 1515 N Westshore Blvd *Web:* www.aaagoingplaces.com	Tampa	FL	33607	813-289-5000	289-6245
Gotham Magazine 257 Park Ave S 5th Fl **Fax Area Code:* 212 ■ *TF:* 800-566-3622 ■ *Web:* www.gotham-magazine.com	New York	NY	10010	646-835-5200	760-0003*
Guest Informant 21200 Erwin St *TF:* 800-275-5885	Woodland Hills	CA	91367	818-716-7484	716-7583
Hamptons Magazine 67 Hampton Rd Suite 5 *Web:* www.hamptons-magazine.com	Southampton	NY	11968	631-283-7125	283-7854
Hana Hou (Hawaiian Airlines) 3465 Waialae Ave Suite 340 *TF:* 888-733-3336 ■ *Web:* www.hanahou.com	Honolulu	HI	96816	808-733-3333	733-3340
Hemispheres 1301 Carolina St *Web:* www.hemispheresmagazine.com	Greensboro	NC	27401	336-378-6065	275-2864
Home & Away Nebraska 10703 J St *TF:* 800-842-7294 ■ *Web:* www.homeandawaymagazine.com	Omaha	NE	68127	402-592-5000	331-5194
Honolulu Magazine 1000 Bishop St Suite 405 *TF:* 800-788-4230 ■ *Web:* www.honolulumagazine.com	Honolulu	HI	96813	808-537-9500	537-6455
Horizon Air Magazine 2701 1st Avenue Suite 250 *Web:* www.alaskaair.com/www2/magazine/Magazines.asp	Seattle	WA	98121	206-441-5871	448-6939
Houston LifeStyle 10707 Corporate Dr Suite 170 *Web:* www.houstonlifestyles.com	Stafford	TX	77477	281-240-2445	240-5079
Hudson Valley 22 IBM Rd Suite 108 *TF:* 800-274-7844 ■ *Web:* www.hvmag.com	Poughkeepsie	NY	12601	845-463-0542	463-1544
Indianapolis Monthly 40 Monument Cir Suite 100 *TF Circ:* 888-403-9005 ■ *Web:* www.indianapolismonthly.com	Indianapolis	IN	46204	317-237-9288	684-2080
Inland Empire Magazine 3769 Tibbetts St Suite A *TF:* 877-357-2005 ■ *Web:* www.inlandempiremagazine.com	Riverside	CA	92506	951-682-3026	682-0246
InsideFlyer Magazine 1930 Frequent Flyer Point *TF:* 800-767-8896 ■ *Web:* www.insideflyer.com	Colorado Springs	CO	80915	719-597-8889	597-6855
Islands 460 N Orlando Ave Suite 200 *TF:* 800-250-2153 ■ *Web:* www.islands.com	Winter Park	FL	32789	407-628-4802	628-7061
Jacksonville 1261 King St *TF Circ:* 800-962-0214 ■ *Web:* www.jacksonvillemag.com	Jacksonville	FL	32204	904-389-3622	389-3628
Journeys The 815 Farmington Ave **Fax:* PR	West Hartford	CT	06119	860-236-3261	523-1797*
Key Magazine PO Box 111266 *Web:* keymagazine.com	Memphis	TN	38111	901-458-3912	458-5723
Key: This Week in Chicago 226 E Ontario St Suite 300	Chicago	IL	60611	312-943-0838	664-6113
Leisure Travel News 770 Broadway *TF Cust Svc:* 800-950-1314 ■ *Web:* www.ltn.com	New York	NY	10003	646-654-4500	654-4456
Los Angeles Confidential Magazine 8500 Wilshire Blvd Suite 1006 *TF:* 800-566-3622 ■ *Web:* www.la-confidential-magazine.com	Beverly Hills	CA	90211	310-289-7300	289-0444
Los Angeles Magazine 5900 Wilshire Blvd 10th Fl **Fax:* Edit ■ *TF Cust Svc:* 800-876-5222 ■ *Web:* www.lamag.com	Los Angeles	CA	90036	323-801-0100	801-0105*
Louisville Magazine 137 W Muhammad Ali Blvd Suite 101 *Web:* www.louisville.com/loumag	Louisville	KY	40202	502-625-0100	625-0107
Manhattan 330 W 56th St Suite 3G *Web:* www.manhattanbride.com	New York	NY	10019	212-265-7970	265-8052
Memphis 460 Tennessee St Suite 200 *Web:* www.memphismagazine.com	Memphis	TN	38103	901-521-9000	521-0129
Michigan Living 1 Auto Club Dr	Dearborn	MI	48126	313-336-1330	336-0993
Michigan Out-of-Doors PO Box 30235 *TF:* 800-777-6720 ■ *Web:* www.mucc.org	Lansing	MI	48909	517-371-1041	371-1505
Midwest Living 1716 Locust St *TF:* 800-678-8093 ■ *Web:* www.midwestliving.com	Des Moines	IA	50309	515-284-2662	284-3836
Midwest Motorist 12901 N 40th Dr *TF:* 800-222-7623	Saint Louis	MO	63141	314-523-7350	523-6982
Milwaukee Magazine 417 E Chicago St *TF:* 800-662-4818 ■ *Web:* www.milwaukeemagazine.com	Milwaukee	WI	53202	414-273-1101	273-0016
Minneapolis-Saint Paul 220 S 6th St Suite 500 *TF:* 800-788-0204 ■ *Web:* www.mspmag.com	Minneapolis	MN	55402	612-339-7571	339-5806
Mississippi 5 Lakeland Cir *TF:* 800-844-8418 ■ *Web:* www.mississippimagazine.com	Jackson	MS	39216	601-982-8418	982-8447
MotorHome 2575 Vista Del Mar Dr *TF Cust Svc:* 800-678-1201 ■ *Web:* www.motorhome.com	Ventura	CA	93001	805-667-4100	667-4484
Motorist 4100 E Arkansas Ave *TF:* 877-244-9790	Denver	CO	80222	303-753-8800	758-8515
National Geographic Traveler 1145 17th St NW *TF:* 800-647-5463 ■ *Web:* www.nationalgeographic.com	Washington	DC	20036	202-857-7000	775-6141
Nevada Magazine 401 N Carson St *TF:* 800-495-3281 ■ *Web:* www.nevadamagazine.com	Carson City	NV	89701	775-687-5416	687-6159
New Jersey Monthly 55 Park Pl PO Box 920 *TF Cust Svc:* 888-419-0419 ■ *Web:* www.njmonthly.com	Morristown	NJ	07963	973-539-8230	538-2953
New Mexico Magazine PO Box 12002 *TF:* 800-898-6639 ■ *Web:* www.nmmagazine.com	Santa Fe	NM	87504	505-476-0202	827-6496
New Orleans Magazine 110 Veterans Memorial Blvd Suite 123 *TF Edit:* 877-221-3512 ■ *Web:* www.neworleansmagazine.com	Metairie	LA	70005	504-828-1380	828-1385
New York 444 Madison Ave *TF Circ:* 800-678-0900 ■ *Web:* www.newyorkmetro.com	New York	NY	10022	212-508-0700	
Newport Beach 714 1901 Westcliff Dr Suite 11 *Web:* www.newportbeach714.com	Newport Beach	CA	92660	949-722-1286	722-6632
Nob Hill Gazette 5 3rd St Hearst Bldg Suite 222 *Web:* www.nobhillgazette.com	San Francisco	CA	94103	415-227-0190	974-5103
North Shore 3701 W Lake Ave **Fax:* Edit ■ *Web:* www.northshoremag.com	Glenview	IL	60026	847-486-0600	486-7427*
Northwest Airlines World Traveler 9655 SW Sunshine Ct Suite 500	Beaverton	OR	97005	503-520-1955	520-1975
NWA World Traveler 9655 SW Sunshine Ct Suite 500 *Web:* www.nwaworldtraveler.com	Beaverton	OR	97005	503-520-1955	520-1275
Ohio Magazine 1422 Euclid Ave Suite 730 *TF:* 800-210-7293 ■ *Web:* www.ohiomagazine.com	Cleveland	OH	44115	216-771-2833	771-2654
Ohio Motorist 5700 Brecksville Rd	Independence	OH	44131	216-606-6700	606-6710
Orange Coast Magazine 3701 Birch St Suite 100 *TF:* 888-881-5861 ■ *Web:* www.orangecoast.com	Newport Beach	CA	92660	949-862-1133	862-0133
Oregon Coast Magazine 4969 Hwy 101 Suite 2 *TF:* 800-348-8401 ■ *Web:* www.northwestmagazines.com	Florence	OR	97439	541-997-8401	997-1124
Orlando Magazine 801 N Magnolia Ave Suite 201 *Web:* www.orlandomagazine.com	Orlando	FL	32803	407-318-7251	237-6258
Palm Beach Illustrated 1000 N Dixie Hwy Suite C *TF:* 800-308-7346 ■ *Web:* www.palmbeachillustrated.com	West Palm Beach	FL	33401	561-659-0210	659-1736
Palm Springs Life Magazine 303 N Indian Canyon *TF:* 800-775-7256 ■ *Web:* www.desert-resorts.com/indexps.html	Palm Springs	CA	92262	760-325-2333	325-7008
Philadelphia Magazine 1818 Market St 36th Fl *TF:* 800-777-1003 ■ *Web:* www.phillymag.com	Philadelphia	PA	19103	215-564-7700	656-3500
Phoenix Magazine 8501 E Princess Dr Suite 190 *Web:* www.phoenixmag.com	Scottsdale	AZ	85255	480-664-3960	664-3962
Pittsburgh Magazine 4802 5th Ave *TF Sales:* 800-495-7323	Pittsburgh	PA	15213	412-622-6440	622-7066
Porthole Cruise Magazine 4517 NW 31st Ave *TF:* 888-774-4768 ■ *Web:* www.porthole.com	Fort Lauderdale	FL	33309	954-377-7777	377-7000
San Diego Magazine 1450 Front St *TF:* 800-600-2489 ■ *Web:* www.sandiego-online.com	San Diego	CA	92101	619-230-9292	230-0490
San Francisco 243 Vallejo St *Web:* www.sanfran.com	San Francisco	CA	94111	415-398-2800	398-6777
Savannah Magazine 1375 Chatham Pkwy *Web:* www.savannahmagazine.com	Savannah	GA	31405	912-652-0423	525-0611
Southern Accents 2100 Lakeshore Dr *TF:* 800-366-4712 ■ *Web:* www.southernaccents.com	Birmingham	AL	35209	205-445-6000	445-6990
Southern Living 2100 Lakeshore Dr *TF:* 800-366-4712 ■ *Web:* www.southernliving.com	Birmingham	AL	35209	205-445-6000	445-6085
Southwest Airlines Spirit 4333 Amon Carter Blvd MD 4374 *Web:* www.spiritmag.com	Fort Worth	TX	76155	817-967-1803	931-3015
Spirit of Aloha 707 Richards St Suite 525 *Web:* www.spiritofaloha.com	Honolulu	HI	96813	808-524-7400	531-2306
Sun Life PO Box 10187	Glendale	AZ	85318	623-878-2210	
Texas Monthly 701 Brazos St Suite 1600 *TF:* 800-759-2000 ■ *Web:* www.texasmonthly.com	Austin	TX	78701	512-320-6900	476-9007
Today's Chicago Woman Magazine 150 E Huron St Suite 1001 *Web:* www.todayschicagowoman.com	Chicago	IL	60611	312-951-7600	951-9083
Toronto Life 111 Queen St E Suite 320 *Web:* www.torontolife.com	Toronto	ON	M5C1S2	416-364-3333	861-1169
Trailer Life 2575 Vista Del Mar Dr *TF:* 800-765-1912 ■ *Web:* www.trailerlife.com	Ventura	CA	93001	805-667-4100	667-4484
Travel + Leisure 1120 Ave of the Americas 10th Fl **Fax:* Edit ■ *TF:* 800-888-8728 ■ *Web:* www.travelandleisure.com	New York	NY	10036	212-382-5600	382-5877*
Travel Agent Magazine 757 3rd Ave 5th Fl *TF:* 800-895-8210 ■ *Web:* www.travelagentcentral.com/travelagentcentral	New York	NY	10017	212-895-8200	895-8210
Travel Holiday 1633 Broadway *TF Circ:* 800-937-9241 ■ *Web:* www.travelholiday.com	New York	NY	10019	212-767-6000	767-5115
TravelAge West 11400 W Olympic Blvd Suite 325 *Web:* www.travelagewest.com	Los Angeles	CA	90064	310-954-2510	954-2525
Travelhost 10701 N Stemmons Fwy *TF:* 800-527-1782 ■ *Web:* www.travelhost.com	Dallas	TX	75220	972-556-0541	432-8729
Tucson Lifestyle Magazine 7000 E Tanque Verde Rd Suite 11 *Web:* www.tucsonlifestyle.com	Tucson	AZ	85715	520-721-2929	721-8665
US Airways Magazine c/o Pace Communications Inc 1301 Carolina St *Web:* usairwaysmag.com	Greensboro	NC	27401	336-378-6065	
Vermont Life 6 Baldwin St *TF:* 800-284-3243 ■ *Web:* www.vtlife.com	Montpelier	VT	05602	802-828-3241	455-3399
VIA 150 Van Ness Ave *Web:* www.viamagazine.com	San Francisco	CA	94102	415-565-2451	863-4726
Washingtonian 1828 L St NW Suite 200 **Fax:* Edit ■ *TF:* 877-532-6083 ■ *Web:* www.washingtonian.com	Washington	DC	20036	202-296-3600	785-1822*
Waterway Guide 326 1st St Suite 400 *TF:* 800-233-3359 ■ *Web:* www.waterwayguide.com	Annapolis	MD	21403	443-482-9377	482-9422
Western Outdoors 185 Avenida La Plata *TF Cust Svc:* 800-290-2929	San Clemente	CA	92673	949-366-0030	366-0309
Westways 3333 Fairview Rd *Web:* www.aaa-calif.com	Costa Mesa	CA	92626	714-885-2388	885-2335
Where Baltimore 575 S Charles St Suite 503 *Web:* www.wheremagazine.com	Baltimore	MD	21201	410-783-7520	783-1763
Where Boston 45 Newbury St Suite 506 *TF:* 800-233-1339 ■ *Web:* www.wheremagazine.com	Boston	MA	02116	617-701-2100	262-2474
Where Chicago 1165 N Clark St Suite 302 *Web:* www.wheremagazine.com	Chicago	IL	60610	312-642-1896	642-5467
Where Los Angeles 3679 Motor Ave Suite 300 *Web:* www.wherela.com	Los Angeles	CA	90034	310-280-2880	280-2890
Where New Orleans 528 Wilkinson Row *Web:* www.wheremagazine.com	New Orleans	LA	70130	504-522-6468	522-0018
Where New York 79 Madison Ave *TF:* 800-666-8336	New York	NY	10016	212-636-2700	636-2787
Where Philadelphia 301 S 19th St Suite 1-S	Philadelphia	PA	19103	215-893-5100	893-5105
Where Saint Louis 1750 S Brentwood Blvd Suite 511	Saint Louis	MO	63144	314-968-4940	968-0813
Where San Francisco 555 Montgomery St Suite 803 *Web:* www.wheresf.com	San Francisco	CA	94111	415-901-6260	901-6261
Where Scottsdale 3295 N Drinkwater Blvd Suite 5	Scottsdale	AZ	85251	480-481-9981	481-9979
Where Seattle 1904 3rd Ave Suite 623 *Web:* www.where-seattle.com	Seattle	WA	98101	206-826-2665	826-2676
Where Washington 1720 'I' St NW Suite 600	Washington	DC	20006	202-463-4550	463-4553
Wisconsin Trails 10 E Doty St Suite 200 *TF:* 800-236-8088 ■ *Web:* www.wistrails.com	Madison	WI	53703	608-256-9106	
Yankee 1121 Main St PO Box 520 *TF:* 800-288-4284 ■ *Web:* www.yankeemagazine.com	Dublin	NH	03444	603-563-8111	563-8252

461 MAGNETS - PERMANENT

	City	State	ZIP	Phone	Fax
Arnold Magnetic Technologies Corp 300 N West St *TF:* 800-545-4578 ■ *Web:* www.arnoldmagnetics.com	Marengo	IL	60152	815-568-2000	568-2228
Bangor Electronics Co 100 Industrial Park Dr *Web:* www.bangorelectronics.com	Bangor	MI	49013	269-427-7944	
Dexter Magnetic Technologies Inc 1050 Morse Ave *Web:* www.dextermag.com	Elk Grove Village	IL	60007	847-956-1140	956-8205
Electron Energy Corp 924 Links Ave *TF:* 800-824-2735 ■ *Web:* www.electronenergy.com	Landisville	PA	17538	717-898-2294	898-0660
Eneflux Armtek Magnetics Inc 700 Hicksville Rd Suite 110 *Web:* www.eamagnetics.com	Bethpage	NY	11714	516-349-0022	

				Phone	Fax
Flexmag Industries Inc 107 Industry Rd *TF:* 800-543-4426 ■ *Web:* www.arnoldmagnetics.com/plants/flexmag/	Marietta	OH	45750	740-374-8024	374-5068
Hitachi Magnetics Corp 7800 Neff Rd *TF:* 800-955-9321	Edmore	MI	48829	989-427-5151	427-5571
Jobmaster Corp 1505 Serpentine Rd *TF Cust Svc:* 800-642-1400 ■ *Web:* www.jobmaster.com	Baltimore	MD	21209	410-655-1400	521-5461
Magnaworks Technology Inc 36 Carlough Rd *Web:* www.magnaworkstechnology.com	Bohemia	NY	11716	631-218-3431	218-3432
Magnet Technology Inc 1599 Kingsview Dr *Web:* www.magtech.cc	Lebanon	OH	45036	513-932-4416	932-4502
Magnetic Component Engineering Inc 2830 Lomita Blvd **Fax Area Code:* 310 ■ *Web:* www.mceproducts.com	Torrance	CA	90505	800-989-5656	784-3192*
National Magnetics Group Inc 1210 Win Dr *Web:* www.magneticsgroup.com	Bethlehem	PA	18017	610-867-7600	867-0200
Permanent Magnet Co Inc 4437 Bragdon St *TF:* 800-547-1336	Indianapolis	IN	46226	317-547-1336	549-9259
Thomas & Skinner Inc 1120 E 23rd St *Web:* www.thomas-skinner.com	Indianapolis	IN	46205	317-923-2501	923-5919

462 MAIL ORDER HOUSES

SEE ALSO Art Supply Stores p. 1286; Book, Music, Video Clubs p. 1388; Checks - Personal & Business p. 1440; Computer Stores p. 1520; Seed Companies p. 2311

				Phone	Fax
1-800 Contacts Inc 66 E Wadsworth Park Dr *NASDAQ: CTAC* ■ *TF:* 800-266-8228 ■ *Web:* www.1800contacts.com	Draper	UT	84020	801-924-9800	924-9905
Aerobic Life Industries Inc 2800 E Chambers St Suite 700 *TF Orders:* 800-798-0707 ■ *Web:* www.aerobiclife.com	Phoenix	AZ	85040	602-283-0755	283-0760
Allied Marketing Group Inc 1555 Regal Row **Fax:* Mktg ■ *TF Cust Svc:* 800-762-3302 ■ *Web:* www.alliedmarketinggroup.com	Dallas	TX	75247	214-915-7000	915-7458*
American Blind & Wallpaper Factory 909 N Sheldon Rd *TF Cust Svc:* 800-575-9019 ■ *Web:* www.abwf.com	Plymouth	MI	48170	734-207-5800	207-0947
America's Hobby Center Inc 8300 Tonnelle Ave *TF:* 800-242-1931 ■ *Web:* www.ahc1931.com	North Bergen	NJ	07047	201-662-8500	662-1450
Backcountry.com 2607 S 3200 West Suite A *TF Orders:* 800-409-4502 ■ *Web:* www.backcountry.com	West Valley City	UT	84119	801-973-4553	746-7581
Barrie Pace Catalog 101 N Wacker Dr *TF:* 800-441-6011 ■ *Web:* www.barriepace.com	Chicago	IL	60606	312-372-6300	357-5876
Bean LL Inc 15 Casco St *TF Cust Svc:* 800-341-4341 ■ *Web:* www.llbean.com	Freeport	ME	04033	207-865-4761	552-2802
Bedford Fair Lifestyles 421 Landmark Dr **Fax Area Code:* 520 ■ *Web:* www.bedfordfair.com	Wilmington	NC	28410	800-964-9030	750-6767*
Blair Corp 220 Hickory St *AMEX: BL* ■ *TF Cust Svc:* 800-458-6057 ■ *Web:* www.blair.com	Warren	PA	16366	814-723-3600	726-6079
Boston Proper 6500 Park of Commerce Blvd *Web:* www.bostonproper.com	Boca Raton	FL	33487	561-241-1700	241-1055
Brawn of California Inc 1500 Harbor Blvd *TF:* 800-293-9333	Weehawken	NJ	07086	201-272-3368	
Campmor Inc 28 Parkway *TF Orders:* 800-526-4784 ■ *Web:* www.campmor.com	Upper Saddle River	NJ	07458	201-825-8300	236-3601
Chadwick's of Boston 35 United Dr *TF:* 800-525-6650 ■ *Web:* www.chadwicks.com	West Bridgewater	MA	02379	508-583-8110	587-8327
Childcraft Education Corp 1156 Four Star Dr **Fax Area Code:* 888 ■ *TF:* 800-631-5652 ■ *Web:* www.childcrafteducation.com	Mount Joy	PA	17552	717-653-7500	532-4453*
Cinmar LP 5566 W Chester Rd *TF:* 800-436-2100 ■ *Web:* www.frontgate.com	West Chester	OH	45069	513-603-1000	603-1270
Coldwater Creek Inc 1 Coldwater Creek Dr *NASDAQ: CWTR* ■ *TF Cust Svc:* 800-262-0040 ■ *Web:* www.coldwater-creek.com	Sandpoint	ID	83864	208-263-2266	263-1582
Company Store 500 Company Store Rd **Fax Area Code:* 800 ■ *TF:* 800-285-3696 ■ *Web:* www.thecompanystore.com	La Crosse	WI	54601	608-791-6000	238-0271*
Cornerstone Brands Inc 5568 West Chester Rd *TF:* 800-436-2100 ■ *Web:* www.cornerstonebrands.com	West Chester	OH	45069	513-603-1400	603-1270
Crest Fruit Co 100 N Tower Rd *TF:* 800-695-2253	Alamo	TX	78516	956-787-9971	787-7161
Crutchfield Corp 1 Crutchfield Park *TF Sales:* 800-955-3000 ■ *Web:* www.crutchfield.com	Charlottesville	VA	22911	434-817-1000	817-1010
Current USA Inc 1005 E Woodmen Rd *TF Cust Svc:* 800-525-7170 ■ *Web:* currentcatalog.com	Colorado Springs	CO	80920	719-594-4100	531-2820
dELiA*s Inc 435 Hudson St 3rd Fl *NASDAQ: DLIA* ■ *TF:* 800-335-4269 ■ *Web:* www.delias.com	New York	NY	10014	212-807-9060	590-3600
Digi-Key Corp 701 Brooks Ave S *TF:* 800-344-4539 ■ *Web:* www.digikey.com	Thief River Falls	MN	56701	218-681-6674	681-3380
Eastbay Inc 500 N 72nd Ave PO Box 8066 **Fax:* Cust Svc ■ *TF:* 800-826-2205 ■ *Web:* www.eastbay.com	Wausau	WI	54402	800-628-6301	991-4920*
ET Wright & Co Inc 1356 Williams St **Fax Area Code:* 800 ■ *TF:* 800-934-1022 ■ *Web:* www.etwright.com	Chippewa Falls	WI	54729	715-723-1871	446-2329*
Everglades Direct 720 International Pkwy *TF:* 800-999-9111 ■ *Web:* www.evergladesdirect.com	Sunrise	FL	33325	954-846-8899	846-0777
Figi's Inc 3200 S Maple Ave *TF:* 800-422-3444 ■ *Web:* www.figis.com	Marshfield	WI	54449	715-387-1771	384-1597
Fingerhut Cos Inc 7777 Golden Triangle Dr *Web:* www.fingerhut.com	Eden Prairie	MN	55344	952-656-4037	656-4117
Forestry Suppliers Inc 205 W Rankin St *TF Cust Svc:* 800-752-8460 ■ *Web:* www.forestry-suppliers.com	Jackson	MS	39201	601-354-3565	292-0165
Franklin Mint Corp 105 Commerce Dr *TF:* 800-523-7622 ■ *Web:* www.franklinmint.com	Aston	PA	19014	610-459-6000	459-6880
Gaiam Inc 360 Interlocken Blvd Suite 300 *NASDAQ: GAIA* ■ *TF:* 800-869-3446 ■ *Web:* www.gaiam.com	Broomfield	CO	80021	303-464-3600	222-3700
Geerlings & Wade Inc 960 Turnpike St **Fax Area Code:* 800 ■ *TF:* 800-782-9463 ■ *Web:* www.geerwade.com	Canton	MA	02021	781-821-4152	329-8466*
Gump's 135 Post St *TF:* 800-766-7628 ■ *Web:* www.gumps.com	San Francisco	CA	94108	415-982-1616	984-9374
Hammacher Schlemmer & Co 9307 N Milwaukee Ave *TF:* 800-233-4800 ■ *Web:* www.hammacher.com	Niles	IL	60714	847-581-8600	581-8616
Hanna Andersson Corp 1010 NW Flanders St *TF Cust Svc:* 800-222-0544 ■ *Web:* www.hannaandersson.com	Portland	OR	97209	503-242-0920	222-0544
Hanover Direct Inc 1500 Harbor Blvd *Web:* www.hanoverdirect.com	Union City	NJ	07086	201-863-7300	272-3191
Harry & David Holdings Inc 2500 S Pacific Hwy **Fax Area Code:* 877 ■ *TF Cust Svc:* 800-345-5655 ■ *Web:* www.harryanddavid.com	Medford	OR	97501	541-776-2121	233-2300*
HearthSong 3700 Wyse Rd **Fax Area Code:* 800 ■ **Fax:* Orders ■ *TF Orders:* 800-533-4397 ■ *Web:* www.hearthsong.com	Dayton	OH	45414	540-948-7100	638-5102*
Hello Direct Inc 75 Northeastern Blvd **Fax Area Code:* 800 ■ *TF:* 800-444-3556 ■ *Web:* www.hello-direct.com	Nashua	NH	03062	603-579-5300	456-2566*
Helm Inc 14310 Hamilton Ave *TF:* 800-448-8631 ■ *Web:* www.helminc.com	Highland Park	MI	48203	313-865-5000	865-2457
Highsmith Inc W 5527 SR 106 PO Box 800 *TF:* 800-558-3899 ■ *Web:* www.highsmith.com	Fort Atkinson	WI	53538	920-563-9571	563-7395
Houston Numismatic Exchange Inc 2486 Times Blvd *TF:* 800-231-3650 ■ *Web:* www.hnex.com	Houston	TX	77005	713-528-2135	528-7618
HSN Catalog Services 5201 Richmond Rd *TF:* 800-944-8870 ■ *Web:* www.improvementscatalog.com	Bedford	OH	44146	216-831-6191	831-4026
iPrint Systems DBA iPrint.com 1475 Veterans Blvd *Web:* www102.iprint.com	Redwood City	CA	94063	650-474-3939	474-3990
J Crew Group Inc 770 Broadway *TF:* 800-932-0043 ■ *Web:* www.jcrew.com	New York	NY	10003	212-209-2500	209-2666
J Jill Group Inc The 4 Batterymarch Park *NASDAQ: JILL* ■ *TF:* 800-430-3661 ■ *Web:* www.jjillgroup.com	Quincy	MA	02169	617-376-4300	769-0177
Jackson & Perkins 2500 S Pacific Hwy PO Box 1028 *TF Cust Svc:* 800-872-7673 ■ *Web:* www.jacksonandperkins.com	Medford	OR	97501	541-776-2000	864-2194
JC Whitney 761 Progress Pkwy **Fax Area Code:* 800 ■ *TF:* 800-529-4486 ■ *Web:* www.jcwhitney.com	La Salle	IL	61301	815-667-4486	537-2700*
JDR Microdevices Inc 1330 Kifer Rd **Fax Area Code:* 800 ■ *TF Sales:* 800-538-5000 ■ *Web:* www.jdr.com	Sunnyvale	CA	94086	408-736-1450	538-5005*
Johnny Appleseed's Inc 30 Tozer Rd *TF Cust Svc:* 800-767-6666 ■ *Web:* www.appleseeds.com	Beverly	MA	01915	978-922-2040	922-7001
Kimball Miles Co 250 City Center Bldg *TF:* 800-546-2255 ■ *Web:* www.mileskimball.com	Oshkosh	WI	54906	920-231-3800	231-4804
Lands' End Inc 1 Lands' End Ln **Fax Area Code:* 800 ■ *TF Orders:* 800-345-3696 ■ *Web:* www.landsend.com	Dodgeville	WI	53595	608-935-9341	332-0103*
Levenger 420 S Congress Ave *TF Cust Svc:* 800-544-0880 ■ *Web:* www.levenger.com	Delray Beach	FL	33445	561-276-2436	272-1553
Lillian Vernon Corp 2600 International Pkwy *TF:* 800-505-2250 ■ *Web:* www.lillianvernon.com	Virginia Beach	VA	23452	757-427-7700	427-7819
LL Bean Inc 15 Casco St *TF Cust Svc:* 800-341-4341 ■ *Web:* www.llbean.com	Freeport	ME	04033	207-865-4761	552-2802
Mary Maxim Inc 2001 Holland Ave PO Box 5019 *TF:* 800-962-9504 ■ *Web:* www.marymaxim.com	Port Huron	MI	48061	810-987-2000	987-5056
MBI Inc 47 Richards Ave **Fax:* Cust Svc ■ *TF:* 800-243-5160 ■ *Web:* www.mbi-inc.com	Norwalk	CT	06857	203-853-2000	866-1716*
McMaster-Carr Supply Co 600 County Line Rd *Web:* www.mcmaster.com	Elmhurst	IL	60126	630-834-9600	834-9427
MediaBay Inc 2 Ridgedale Ave Suite 300 *NASDAQ: MBAY* ■ *TF:* 800-688-8780 ■ *Web:* www.mediabay.com	Cedar Knolls	NJ	07927	973-539-9528	539-1273
Miles Kimball Co 250 City Center Bldg *TF:* 800-546-2255 ■ *Web:* www.mileskimball.com	Oshkosh	WI	54906	920-231-3800	231-4804
Movies Unlimited Inc 3015 Darnell Rd *TF:* 800-668-4344 ■ *Web:* www.moviesunlimited.com	Philadelphia	PA	19154	215-637-4444	637-2429
NASCO International Inc 901 Janesville Ave *TF Orders:* 800-558-9595 ■ *Web:* www.enasco.com	Fort Atkinson	WI	53538	920-563-2446	563-8296
National Wholesale Co Inc 400 National Blvd *TF:* 800-480-4673 ■ *Web:* www.shopnational.com	Lexington	NC	27292	336-248-5904	248-2880
Newport News Inc 711 3rd Ave 4th Fl *TF Sales:* 800-894-9639 ■ *Web:* www.newport-news.com	New York	NY	10017	212-986-2585	916-8281
Norm Thompson Outfitters Inc 3188 NW Aloclek Dr *TF:* 800-547-1160 ■ *Web:* www.normthompson.com	Hillsboro	OR	97124	503-614-4600	614-4601
Northeast Data Services 1316 College Ave *TF Cust Svc:* 800-845-3720 ■ *Web:* www.artisticlabels.com	Elmira	NY	14901	607-733-5541	735-4540
NRC Sports Inc 603 Pleasant St *TF:* 800-243-5033 ■ *Web:* www.nrcsports.com	Paxton	MA	01612	508-852-8206	852-8206
Oriental Trading Co Inc 5455 S 90th St *TF:* 800-225-6440 ■ *Web:* www.orientaltrading.com	Omaha	NE	68127	402-596-1200	596-2322
Patagonia Inc 259 W Santa Clara Dr PO Box 150 *TF Cust Svc:* 800-638-6464 ■ *Web:* www.patagonia.com	Ventura	CA	93001	805-643-8616	653-6355
Pets Unlimited LLC 1 Maplewood Dr *TF Cust Svc:* 800-367-3647 ■ *Web:* www.dog.com	Hazleton	PA	18201	570-384-5555	384-4833
PETsMART Direct 1989 Transit Way *TF:* 800-785-0504 ■ *Web:* www.petsmart.com	Brockport	NY	14420	585-637-7508	637-7625
Popular Club 20 Commerce Way *TF:* 800-767-2582 ■ *Web:* www.popularclub.com	Totowa	NJ	07512	973-470-3800	200-7033
Professional Cutlery Direct LLC 242 Branford Rd **Fax Area Code:* 800 ■ *TF:* 800-859-6994 ■ *Web:* www.cutlery.com	North Branford	CT	06471	203-871-1000	296-8039*
Publishers Clearing House 382 Channel Dr *TF:* 800-682-3124 ■ *Web:* www.pch.com	Port Washington	NY	11050	516-883-5432	944-5601
Real Goods Trading Corp 360 Interlocken Blvd Suite 300 *TF:* 800-762-7325 ■ *Web:* www.realgoods.com	Broomfield	CO	80021	303-222-3600	222-3700
Redcats USA 463 7th Ave *Web:* www.redcatsusa.com	New York	NY	10018	212-613-9500	613-9590
Roaman's 2300 Southeastern Ave *Web:* www.roamans.com	Indianapolis	IN	46283	800-459-1025	268-2657
S & S Worldwide Inc 75 Mill St *TF Orders:* 800-243-9232 ■ *Web:* www.ssww.com	Colchester	CT	06415	860-537-3451	537-2563
ShopNBC 6740 Shady Oak Rd **Fax:* Hum Res ■ *TF:* 800-676-5523 ■ *Web:* www.shopnbc.com	Eden Prairie	MN	55344	952-943-6000	943-6711*
SkyMall Inc 1520 E Pima St *TF:* 800-759-6255 ■ *Web:* www.skymall.com	Phoenix	AZ	85034	602-254-9777	254-6075
Specialty Catalog Corp 400 Manley St *TF:* 800-472-4017 ■ *Web:* www.scdirect.com	West Bridgewater	MA	02379	508-238-0199	894-0181
Spiegel Inc 1 Spiegel Ave **Fax Area Code:* 757 ■ *TF:* 800-345-4500 ■ *Web:* www.spiegel.com	Hampton	VA	23630	800-345-4500	334-3994*
Sportsman's Guide Inc 411 Farwell Ave *NASDAQ: SGDE* ■ **Fax:* Hum Res ■ *TF Cust Svc:* 800-888-5222 ■ *Web:* www.sportsmansguide.com	South Saint Paul	MN	55075	651-451-3030	552-5258*
Sunnyland Farms Inc 2314 Willson Rd *Web:* www.sunnylandfarms.com	Albany	GA	31705	229-436-5654	888-8332
Swiss Colony Inc 1112 7th Ave *Web:* www.swisscolony.com	Monroe	WI	53566	608-328-8400	328-8457
Thompson Norm Outfitters Inc 3188 NW Aloclek Dr *TF:* 800-547-1160 ■ *Web:* www.normthompson.com	Hillsboro	OR	97124	503-614-4600	614-4601
Tog Shop Inc 30 Tozer Rd **Fax Area Code:* 800 ■ *TF Cust Svc:* 800-262-8888 ■ *Web:* www.togshop.com	Beverly	MA	01915	978-922-2040	755-7557*
TravelSmith Outfitters Inc 60 Leveroni Ct **Fax Area Code:* 800 ■ *TF:* 800-950-1600 ■ *Web:* www.travelsmith.com	Novato	CA	94949	415-382-1855	950-1656*
Unicover Corp 1 Unicover Center *TF Cust Svc:* 800-443-4225 ■ *Web:* www.unicover.com	Cheyenne	WY	82008	307-771-3000	771-3134
Van Dyke Supply Co 39771 Hwy 34 E *TF:* 800-843-3320 ■ *Web:* www.vandykes.com	Woonsocket	SD	57385	605-796-4425	796-4085
Victorian Trading Co 15600 W 99th St **Fax Area Code:* 800 ■ *TF Cust Svc:* 800-700-2035 ■ *Web:* www.victoriantradingco.com	Lenexa	KS	66219	913-438-3995	724-7697*
Victoria's Secret Direct LLC 3425 Morse Crossing *TF:* 800-888-1500 ■ *Web:* www.victoriassecret.com	Columbus	OH	43219	614-337-5000	337-5075
Whitney JC 761 Progress Pkwy **Fax Area Code:* 800 ■ *TF:* 800-529-4486 ■ *Web:* www.jcwhitney.com	La Salle	IL	61301	815-667-4486	537-2700*
Williams-Sonoma Inc 3250 Van Ness Ave *NYSE: WSM* ■ *TF Cust Svc:* 800-541-1262 ■ *Web:* www.williams-sonoma.com	San Francisco	CA	94109	415-421-7900	
Willow Ridge 421 Landmark Dr **Fax Area Code:* 910 ■ *Web:* www.willowridgecatalog.com	Wilmington	NC	28410	800-388-2012	798-2000*
Wintersilks Inc 212 E Washington Ave 4th Fl *TF:* 800-648-7455 ■ *Web:* www.wintersilks.com	Madison	WI	53703	608-280-9000	280-9448
Woodcraft Supply LLC 1177 Rosemar Rd PO Box 1686 *TF Cust Svc:* 800-535-4482 ■ *Web:* www.woodcraft.com	Parkersburg	WV	26105	304-422-5412	428-8271

Phone | Fax

Wright ET & Co Inc 1356 Williams St .... Chippewa Falls WI 54729 715-723-1871 446-2329*
*Fax Area Code: 800 ■ TF: 800-934-1022 ■ Web: www.etwright.com

Zappos.com 271 Omega Pkwy Suite 104 .... Shepherdsville KY 40165 502-543-7200 543-5223
TF: 800-927-7671 ■ Web: www.zappos.com

463 MALLS - SHOPPING

Phone | Fax

Ala Moana Shopping Center 1450 Ala Moana Blvd .... Honolulu HI 96814 808-955-9517 955-2193
Web: www.alamoanacenter.com

Allen Premium Outlets 820 W Stacy Rd .... Allen TX 75013 972-678-7000 678-7011
Web: www.premiumoutlets.com/allen

Altamonte Mall 451 E Altamonte Dr .... Altamonte Springs FL 32701 407-830-4422 215-5125
Web: www.altamontemall.com

Arizona Mills 5000 Arizona Mills Cir .... Tempe AZ 85282 480-491-7300 491-7400
Web: www.arizonamills.com

Arrowhead Towne Center 7700 W Arrowhead Towne Center .... Glendale AZ 85308 623-979-7777 979-4447
Web: www.arrowheadtownecenter.com

Arsenal Mall 485 Arsenal St .... Watertown MA 02472 617-923-4700 924-0741
Web: www.simon.com

Arundel Mills 7000 Arundel Mills Cir .... Hanover MD 21076 410-540-5110 540-5120
Web: www.arundelmillsmall.com

Aspen Grove Lifestyle Center 7301 S Santa Fe Dr .... Littleton CO 80120 303-794-0640 798-0238
Web: www.shopaspengrove.com

Augusta Mall 3450 Wrightsboro Rd .... Augusta GA 30909 706-733-1001 733-7980
Web: www.augustamall.com

Aventura Mall 19501 Biscayne Blvd .... Aventura FL 33180 305-935-1110 935-0829
Web: www.shopaventuramall.com

Avenues Mall 10300 Southside Blvd .... Jacksonville FL 32256 904-363-3054 363-3058
Web: www.simon.com

Bannister Mall 5600 E Bannister Rd .... Kansas City MO 64137 816-763-6900 767-1247
Web: www.shopbannister.com

Barton Creek Square Mall 2901 S Capital of Texas Hwy .... Austin TX 78746 512-327-7040 328-0923
Web: www.simon.com

Battlefield Mall 2825 S Glenstone Ave .... Springfield MO 65804 417-883-7777 883-2641
Web: www.simon.com

Bellevue Square 575 Bellevue Sq .... Bellevue WA 98004 425-454-2431 455-3631
Web: www.bellevuesquare.com

Block at Orange 20 City Blvd W .... Orange CA 92868 714-769-4000 769-4010
Web: www.theblockatorange.com

Bloomington Antique Mall 311 W 7th St .... Bloomington IN 47401 812-332-2290 333-1335
Web: www.bloomingtonantiquemall.com

Boulevard Mall 3528 S Maryland Pkwy .... Las Vegas NV 89169 702-735-8268 732-9197
Web: www.blvdmall.com

Boulevard Mall 730 Alberta Dr .... Amherst NY 14226 716-834-8600 836-6127
Web: www.boulevard-mall.com

Boynton Beach Mall 801 N Congress Ave .... Boynton Beach FL 33426 561-736-7902 736-7907
Web: www.simon.com

Brea Mall 1065 Brea Mall .... Brea CA 92821 714-990-2732 990-5048
Web: www.simon.com

Briarwood Mall 100 Briarwood Cir .... Ann Arbor MI 48108 734-769-9610 769-2531
Web: www.shopbriarwood.com

Broward Mall 8000 W Broward Blvd .... Plantation FL 33388 954-473-8100 472-1389
Web: westfield.com/broward/

Buena Park Downtown 8308 On The Mall .... Buena Park CA 90620 714-828-7722 527-0723
Web: www.buenaparkdowntown.com

Burbank Town Center 201 E Magnolia Blvd .... Burbank CA 91501 818-566-8556 566-7936
Web: www.burbanktowncenter.com

Burlington Mall 75 Middlesex Tpke .... Burlington MA 01803 781-272-8667 229-0420
Web: www.simon.com

Burnsville Center 1178 Burnsville Center .... Burnsville MN 55306 952-435-8182 892-5073
Web: www.burnsvillecenter.com

Camarillo Premium Outlets 740 E Ventura Blvd .... Camarillo CA 93010 805-445-8520 445-8522
Web: www.premiumoutlets.com

Carlsbad Premium Outlets 5620 Paseo del Norte .... Carlsbad CA 92008 760-804-9000 804-9044
Web: www.premiumoutlets.com

Carolina Place Mall 11025 Carolina Place Pkwy .... Pineville NC 28134 704-543-9300 543-6355
Web: www.shopcarolinaplace.com

Carousel Center 9090 Carousel Center Dr .... Syracuse NY 13290 315-466-7000 466-5405
Web: www.carouselcenter.com

Carousel Mall 295 Carousel Mall .... San Bernardino CA 92401 909-884-0106 885-6893

Cary Towne Center 1105 Walnut St .... Cary NC 27511 919-460-1053 467-5509
Web: www.shopcarytownecentermall.com

Casino Factory Shoppes LLC 13118 US Hwy 61 N .... Tunica Resorts MS 38664 662-363-1940 363-1941
Web: www.casinofactoryshoppes.com

Castleton Square Mall 6020 E 82nd St .... Indianapolis IN 46250 317-849-9993 849-4689
Web: www.simon.com

Centre at Salisbury 2300 N Salisbury Blvd .... Salisbury MD 21801 410-548-1600 749-4256
Web: www.centreatsalisbury.com

Century III Mall 3075 Clairton Rd .... West Mifflin PA 15123 412-653-1220 655-0202
Web: www.simon.com

Chapel Hills Mall 1710 Briargate Blvd .... Colorado Springs CO 80920 719-594-0111 594-6439
Web: www.chapelhillsmall.com

Cherry Creek Shopping Center 3000 E 1st Ave .... Denver CO 80206 303-388-3900 377-7359
Web: www.shopcherrycreek.com

Chicago Premium Outlets 1650 Premium Outlets Blvd .... Aurora IL 60504 630-585-2200 236-0036

Christiana Mall 715 Christiana Mall Rd .... Newark DE 19702 302-731-9815 731-9950
Web: www.shopchristianamall.com

Cielo Vista Mall 8401 Gateway Blvd W .... El Paso TX 79925 915-779-7070 772-4926
Web: www.simon.com

Cincinnati Mills 600 Cincinnati Mills Dr .... Cincinnati OH 45240 513-671-2929 671-7502
Web: www.cincinnatimills.com

Citadel Mall 750 Citadel Dr E .... Colorado Springs CO 80909 719-591-2900 597-4839
Web: www.shopthecitadel.com

Citadel Mall 2070 Sam Rittenberg Blvd .... Charleston SC 29407 843-766-8511 763-8534
Web: www.shopcitadel-mall.com

City Centre 1420 5th Ave .... Seattle WA 98101 206-624-8800

Clackamas Town Center 12000 SE 82nd Ave .... Portland OR 97086 503-653-6913 653-7357*
*Fax: Cust Svc ■ TF: 800-969-7820 ■ Web: www.clackamastowncenter.com

Coliseum Mall 1800 W Mercury Blvd .... Hampton VA 23666 757-838-1505 827-9166
Web: www.coliseummall.com

Collin Creek Mall 811 N Central Expy .... Plano TX 75075 972-422-1070 881-1642
Web: www.collincreekmall.com

Colonial Mall Bel Air 3299 Bel Air Mall .... Mobile AL 36606 251-473-8623 476-5722
Web: www.colonialmallbelair.com

Colonie Center 131 Colonie Center .... Albany NY 12205 518-459-9020 459-2147
Web: www.shopatcoloniecenter.com

Colorado Mills 14500 W Colfax .... Lakewood CO 80401 303-384-3000 384-3010
Web: www.coloradomills.com

Phone | Fax

Columbia Gorge Premium Outlets 450 NW 257th Way .... Troutdale OR 97060 503-669-8060 666-3062
Web: www.premiumoutlets.com

Columbia Place 7201 Two Notch Rd .... Columbia SC 29223 803-788-4678 736-9168
TF: 800-699-2857 ■ Web: www.shopcolumbiaplace.com

Columbus City Center 111 S 3rd St .... Columbus OH 43215 614-221-4900 469-5093
TF: 800-882-4900

Commons at Federal Way 1928 S Commons .... Federal Way WA 98003 253-839-6151 946-1413

Complexe Les Ailes 677 Sainte-Catherine St W .... Montreal QC H3B5K3 514-288-3759 288-3779
Web: www.complexelesailes.com

Concord Mills 8111 Concord Mills Blvd .... Concord NC 28027 704-979-3000 979-5050
TF: 877-626-4557 ■ Web: www.concordmillsmall.com

CoolSprings Galleria 1800 Galleria Blvd Suite 2075 .... Franklin TN 37067 615-771-2050 771-2127
Web: www.coolspringsgalleria.com

Coral Ridge Mall 1451 Coral Ridge Ave .... Coralville IA 52241 319-625-5500 625-5501
Web: www.coralridgemall.com

Coronado Center 6600 Menaul St NE Suite 1 .... Albuquerque NM 87110 505-881-4600 881-0145
Web: www.coronadocenter.com

Countryside Mall 27001 US 19 N .... Clearwater FL 33761 727-796-1079 791-8470
Web: westfield.com/countryside/

Crabtree Valley Mall 4325 Glenwood Ave .... Raleigh NC 27612 919-787-2506 787-7108
Web: www.crabtree-valley-mall.com

Cross County Shopping Center 6K Mall Walk .... Yonkers NY 10704 914-968-9570 423-7760

Crossgates Mall 1 Crossgates Mall Rd .... Albany NY 12203 518-869-9565 869-9683
TF: 800-439-2011 ■ Web: www.shopcrossgates.com

Crossroads Mall 7000 Crossroads Blvd .... Oklahoma City OK 73149 405-631-4421 634-1503
Web: www.shopcrossroadsmall.com

Cumberland Mall 1000 Cumberland Mall .... Atlanta GA 30339 770-435-2206 438-0432
Web: www.cumberlandmall.com

Dadeland Mall 7535 N Kendall Dr .... Miami FL 33156 305-665-6226 665-5012
Web: www.simon.com

Dallas Galleria 13350 N Dallas Pkwy .... Dallas TX 75240 972-702-7100 702-7130
Web: www.dallasgalleria.com

Dayton Mall 2700 Miamisburg Centerville Rd .... Dayton OH 45459 937-433-9833 433-5289
Web: www.daytonmall.net

DCOTA (Design Center of the Americas) 1855 Griffin Rd .... Dania Beach FL 33004 954-920-7997 920-8066
TF: 800-573-2682 ■ Web: www.dcota.com

Deerbrook Mall 20131 Hwy 59 N .... Humble TX 77338 281-446-5300 446-6626
Web: www.shopdeerbrookmall.com

Del Amo Fashion Center 3525 Carson St .... Torrance CA 90503 310-542-8525 793-9235
Web: www.themills.com

Design Center of the Americas (DCOTA) 1855 Griffin Rd .... Dania Beach FL 33004 954-920-7997 920-8066
TF: 800-573-2682 ■ Web: www.dcota.com

Dixie Outlet Mall 1250 S Service Rd .... Mississauga ON L5E1V4 905-278-3494 278-4283
Web: dixieoutletmall.shopping.ca

Dolphin Mall 11401 NW 12 St .... Miami FL 33172 305-365-7446 436-9000
Web: www.shopdolphinmall.com

Domain The 11410 Century Oaks Terr .... Austin TX 78758 512-795-4230
Web: www.simon.com

East Towne Mall 89 E Towne Mall .... Madison WI 53704 608-244-1501 244-8306
Web: www.shopeasttowne-mall.com

Eastern Shore Centre 30500 State Hwy 181 .... Spanish Fort AL 36527 251-625-0060 625-0039
Web: www.easternshorecentre.com

Eastfield Mall 1655 Boston Rd .... Springfield MA 01129 413-543-8000 543-4221
Web: www.eastfieldmall.com

Eastland Mall 800 N Green River Rd .... Evansville IN 47715 812-477-4848 474-1691
Web: www.simon.com

Eastland Mall 5471 Central Ave .... Charlotte NC 28212 704-537-2626 568-0291
Web: www.eastlandmall.com

Eastmont Town Center 1 Eastmont Mall .... Oakland CA 94605 510-632-1131 636-1727

Eastridge Mall 2200 Eastridge Mall .... San Jose CA 95122 408-238-3600 274-9684
Web: www.eastridgecenter.com

Eastwood Mall 5555 Youngstown-Warren Rd .... Niles OH 44446 330-652-6980 544-5929
Web: www.eastwoodmall.net

Eastwood Towne Center 3003 Preyde Blvd .... Lansing MI 48912 517-316-9209 316-9214
Web: www.shopeastwoodtownecenter.com

Echelon Mall 1285 Echelon Mall .... Voorhees NJ 08043 856-772-1950 772-2831
Web: www.shopechelonmall.com

Edmonton City Centre 2000 10025-102A Ave .... Edmonton AB T5J2Z2 780-426-8444 441-4700

El Con Mall 3601 E Broadway Blvd Suite 5B .... Tucson AZ 85716 520-795-9958 323-1856
Web: www.shopelcon.com

Emerald Square Mall 999 S Washington St .... North Attleboro MA 02760 508-699-7979 695-6684
Web: www.simon.com

Empire Mall 5000 Empire Mall .... Sioux Falls SD 57106 605-361-3300 362-0283
Web: www.theempiremall.com

Essex Shoppes & Cinema 21 Essex Way Suite 107 .... Essex VT 05451 802-878-4200 879-5080
TF: 800-657-2777 ■ Web: www.essexshoppes.com

Evergreen Plaza 9730 S Western Ave .... Evergreen Park IL 60805 708-422-5454 422-9780
Web: www.evergreenplaza.com

Factory Stores of America 12101 S Factory Outlet Dr .... Draper UT 84020 801-571-2933

Factory Stores at North Bend 461 South Fork Ave SW .... North Bend WA 98045 425-888-4505 888-4514

Fair Oaks Shopping Center 11750 Fair Oaks .... Fairfax VA 22030 703-359-8300 273-0547
Web: www.shopfairoaksmall.com

Fairlane Town Center 18900 Michigan Ave .... Dearborn MI 48126 313-593-3330 593-0572
TF: 800-992-9500 ■ Web: www.shopfairlane.com

Fallbrook Center 9301 Tampa Ave .... Northridge CA 91324 818-885-9700 340-0206

Fashion Island Shopping Center 401 Newport Center Dr .... Newport Beach CA 92660 949-721-2000 720-3350
TF: 800-495-4753 ■ Web: www.shopfashionisland.com

Fashion Place 6191 S State St .... Murray UT 84107 801-262-9447 261-0660
Web: www.fashionplace.com

Fashion Valley Mall 7007 Friars Rd .... San Diego CA 92108 619-688-9113 294-8291
Web: www.simon.com

Fayette Mall 3401 Nicholasville Rd Suite 303 .... Lexington KY 40503 859-272-3493 273-6376
Web: www.shopfayette-mall.com

Festival Bay Mall at International Drive
5250 International Dr Suite 650 .... Orlando FL 32819 407-351-7718 351-7734
TF: 800-481-1944 ■ Web: www.belz.com

Fiesta Mall 1445 W Southern Ave Suite 2104 .... Mesa AZ 85202 480-833-4121 834-8462
Web: www.shopfiesta.com

First Colony Mall 16535 Southwest Fwy Suite 1 .... Sugar Land TX 77479 281-265-6123 265-6124
Web: www.firstcolonymall.com

Florida Mall 8001 S Orange Blossom Trail .... Orlando FL 32809 407-851-6255 855-1827
Web: www.simon.com

Foothill Village 1400 Foothill Dr .... Salt Lake City UT 84108 801-487-6670
Web: www.foothillvillage.com

Fort Worth Town Center 4200 South Fwy Suite 2500 .... Fort Worth TX 76115 817-922-8888 927-1833

Four Seasons Town Centre 400 Four Seasons Town Centre ..... Greensboro NC 27427 336-299-9200 299-9923
Web: www.shopfourseasons.com

Fox River Mall 4301 W Wisconsin Ave .... Appleton WI 54913 920-739-4100 739-8210
TF: 800-876-6255 ■ Web: www.foxrivermall.com

Franklin Mills 1455 Franklin Mills Cir .... Philadelphia PA 19154 215-632-1500 632-7888
TF: 800-336-6255 ■ Web: www.franklinmills.com/index2.html

Freehold Raceway Mall 3710 Rt 9 Suite 1000 .... Freehold NJ 07728 732-577-1300 577-6809
Web: www.freeholdracewaymall.com

Galleria The 5085 Westheimer Rd Suite 4850 .... Houston TX 77056 713-621-1907 966-3596
Web: www.simon.com

Galleria at Fort Lauderdale 2414 E Sunrise Blvd .... Fort Lauderdale FL 33304 954-564-1015 566-9976
Web: www.galleriamall-fl.com

Name / Address	City	State	Zip	Phone	Fax
Galleria at Sunset 1300 W Sunset Rd Suite 1400	Henderson	NV	89014	702-434-2409	434-0259
Web: www.galleriaatsunset.com					
Galleria at Tyler 1299 Galleria at Tyler St	Riverside	CA	92503	951-351-3112	351-3139
Web: www.galleriatyler.com					
Galleria at White Plains 100 Main St	White Plains	NY	10601	914-682-0111	682-1609
Web: www.galleriaatwhiteplains.com					
Gallery at Market East 9th & Market Sts	Philadelphia	PA	19107	215-925-7162	440-0116
Web: www.galleryatmarketeast.com					
Garden State Plaza 1 Garden State Plaza	Paramus	NJ	07652	201-843-2404	843-1716
Web: www.westfield.com/gardenstateplaza					
Gardens Mall The 3101 PGA Blvd	Palm Beach Gardens	FL	33410	561-622-2115	694-9380
Web: www.thegardensmall.com					
Genesee Valley Center 3341 Linden Rd S	Flint	MI	48507	810-732-4000	732-4343
Web: www.geneseemall.com					
Glenbrook Square 4201 Coldwater Rd	Fort Wayne	IN	46805	260-483-2119	483-7756
Web: www.glenbrooksquaremall.com					
Glendale Galleria 2148 Glendale Galleria	Glendale	CA	91210	818-240-9481	240-0587
Web: www.glendalegalleria.com					
Golf Mill Shopping Center 239 Golf Mill Center	Niles	IL	60714	847-699-1070	699-1593
Web: www.golfmill.com					
Governor's Square 1500 Apalachee Pkwy	Tallahassee	FL	32301	850-671-4636	942-0136
Web: www.governorssquare.com					
Grapevine Mills 3000 Grapevine Mills Pkwy	Grapevine	TX	76051	972-724-4900	724-4920
Web: www.grapevinemills.com/index2.html					
Great Lakes Mall 7850 Mentor Ave	Mentor	OH	44060	440-255-6900	255-0509
Web: www.simon.com					
Great Mall of the Bay Area 447 Great Mall Dr	Milpitas	CA	95035	408-945-4022	945-4027
Web: www.greatmallbayarea.com					
Great Mall of the Great Plains 20700 W 151st St	Olathe	KS	66061	913-829-3509	829-6748
TF: 888-386-6255 ■ *Web:* www.greatmallgreatplains.com					
Green Acres Mall 2034 Green Acres Mall	Valley Stream	NY	11581	516-561-7360	561-3870
Web: www.greenacresmallonline.com					
Greenspoint Mall 208 Greenspoint Mall	Houston	TX	77060	281-875-4201	873-7144
Web: www.greenspointmall.com					
Greenwood Park Mall 1251 US Hwy 31 N	Greenwood	IN	46142	317-881-6758	887-8606
Web: www.simon.com					
Grove The 189 The Grove Dr	Los Angeles	CA	90036	323-900-8000	900-8001
TF: 888-315-8883 ■ *Web:* www.thegrovela.com					
Gurnee Mills 6170 W Grand Ave	Gurnee	IL	60031	847-263-7500	263-2423
TF: 800-937-7467 ■ *Web:* www.gurneemills.com					
Gwinnett Place Mall 2100 Pleasant Hill Rd	Duluth	GA	30096	770-476-5160	476-9355
Web: www.simon.com					
Halifax Shopping Centre 7001 Mumford Rd	Halifax	NS	B3L4N9	902-453-1752	454-6908
Web: www.halifaxshoppingcentre.com					
Hamilton Mall 4403 Black Horse Pike	Mays Landing	NJ	08330	609-646-8326	645-7837
Web: www.shophamilton.com					
Hamilton Place 2100 Hamilton Place Blvd	Chattanooga	TN	37421	423-894-7177	892-0765
Web: www.hamiltonplace.com					
Hanes Mall 3320 Silas Creek Pkwy Suite 264	Winston-Salem	NC	27103	336-765-8323	765-3738
TF: 800-443-6255 ■ *Web:* www.shophanesmall.com					
Hawthorn Center 122 Hawthorn Center	Vernon Hills	IL	60061	847-362-2600	362-2689
Haywood Mall 700 Haywood Rd	Greenville	SC	29607	864-288-0511	297-6018
Web: www.simon.com					
Hickory Hollow Mall 5252 Hickory Hollow Pkwy	Antioch	TN	37013	615-731-3500	731-1034
Web: www.hickoryhollowmall.com					
Highland Mall 6001 Airport Blvd	Austin	TX	78752	512-451-2920	452-1463
Hillsdale Shopping Center 60 31st Ave	San Mateo	CA	94403	650-345-8222	573-5457
Web: www.shophillsdale.com					
Hilltop Mall 2200 Hilltop Mall Rd	Richmond	CA	94806	510-223-6900	223-1453
Web: www.shophilltop.com					
Holt Renfrew Centre 50 Bloor St W	Toronto	ON	M5W3L8	905-793-4682	793-4722
Holyoke Mall at Ingleside 50 Holyoke St	Holyoke	MA	01040	413-536-1440	536-5740
Web: www.holyokemall.com					
Horizon Outlet Center at Monroe La Plaisance Rd	Monroe	MI	48161	734-241-4813	241-3745
Independence Center 2035 Independence Center Dr	Independence	MO	64057	816-795-8600	795-7836
Web: www.simon.com					
Independence Mall 3500 Oleander Dr	Wilmington	NC	28403	910-392-1776	392-1176
Web: www.westfield.com					
Ingram Park Mall 6301 NW Loop 410	San Antonio	TX	78238	210-523-1228	681-4614
Web: www.simon.com					
Irving Mall 3880 Irving Mall	Irving	TX	75062	972-255-0571	570-7310
Web: www.simon.com					
Jefferson Mall 4801 Outerloop Rd	Louisville	KY	40219	502-968-4101	969-0882
Web: www.shopjefferson-mall.com					
Jefferson Valley Mall 650 Lee Blvd	Yorktown Heights	NY	10598	914-245-4200	245-3479
Web: www.simon.com					
Jersey Gardens 651 Kapkowski Rd	Elizabeth	NJ	07201	908-354-5900	436-3029
Web: www.jerseygardens.com					
Katy Mills 5000 Katy Mills Cir	Katy	TX	77494	281-644-5000	644-5001
Web: www.katymills.com					
Kenwood Towne Center 7875 Montgomery Rd	Cincinnati	OH	45236	513-745-9100	745-9974
Web: www.kenwoodcentre.com					
King of Prussia Mall 160 N Gulph Rd	King of Prussia	PA	19406	610-265-5727	265-1640
Web: www.kingofprussiamall.com					
Lafayette Square Mall 3919 Lafayette Rd	Indianapolis	IN	46254	317-291-6390	291-1897
Web: www.simon.com					
Lakeland Factory Outlet Mall 3536 Canada Rd	Lakeland	TN	38002	901-386-3180	
Lakeline Mall 11200 Lakeline Mall Dr	Cedar Park	TX	78613	512-257-7467	257-0522
Web: www.shopsimon.com					
Lakeside Mall 14000 Lakeside Cir	Sterling Heights	MI	48313	586-247-4131	247-0762
TF: 800-334-5573 ■ *Web:* www.shop-lakesidemall.com					
Lakewood Center Mall 500 Lakewood Center	Lakewood	CA	90712	562-633-0437	633-1452
Web: www.shoplakewoodcenter.com					
Las Vegas Premium Outlets 875 S Grand Central Pkwy	Las Vegas	NV	89106	702-474-7500	676-1184
Web: www.premiumoutlets.com					
Lehigh Valley Mall 250 Lehigh Valley Mall	Whitehall	PA	18052	610-264-5511	264-5957
Web: www.lehighvalleymall.com					
Lenox Square Mall 3393 Peachtree Rd NE	Atlanta	GA	30326	404-233-6767	233-7868
Web: www.simon.com					
Liberty Tree Mall 100 Independence Way	Danvers	MA	01923	978-777-0794	777-9857
Web: www.simon.com					
Lincoln Mall 208 Lincoln Mall Dr	Matteson	IL	60443	708-747-5600	747-5629
Web: www.lincoln-mall.com					
Lloyd Center 2201 Lloyd Center	Portland	OR	97232	503-282-2511	280-9407
Web: www.lloydcenter.com					
Los Cerritos Center 239 Los Cerritos Center	Cerritos	CA	90703	562-860-0341	860-5289
Web: www.shoploscerritos.com					
Lynnhaven Mall 701 Lynnhaven Pkwy Suite 1068	Virginia Beach	VA	23452	757-340-9340	463-8150
Web: www.lynnhavenmall.com					
Macon Mall 3661 Eisenhower Pkwy	Macon	GA	31206	478-477-8840	474-5238
Web: www.shopmaconmall.com					
Maine Mall 364 Maine Mall Rd	South Portland	ME	04106	207-774-0303	774-6813
Web: www.mainemall.com					
Mall of America 60 E Broadway	Bloomington	MN	55425	952-883-8810	883-8866
Web: www.mallofamerica.com					
Mall at Cortana 9401 Cortana Pl	Baton Rouge	LA	70815	225-923-1412	928-7920
Web: www.cortanamall.com					
Mall del Norte 5300 San Dario Suite 206C	Laredo	TX	78041	956-724-8191	724-9583
Web: www.malldelnorte.com					
Mall at Fairfield Commons 2727 Fairfield Commons	Beavercreek	OH	45431	937-427-4300	427-3668
Web: www.mallatfairfieldcommons.com					
Mall at Greece Ridge Center 271 Greece Ridge Center Dr	Rochester	NY	14626	585-225-1140	227-2525
Mall of Louisiana 6401 Bluebonnet Blvd	Baton Rouge	LA	70836	225-761-7228	761-7225
Web: www.mallofllouisiana.com					
Mall at Millenia 4200 Conroy Rd	Orlando	FL	32839	407-363-3555	363-6877
Web: www.mallatmillenia.com					
Mall at Robinson 100 Robinson Centre Dr	Pittsburgh	PA	15205	412-788-0816	788-1156
Web: www.shoprobinsonmall.com					
Mall Saint Matthews 5000 Shelbyville Rd Suite 50	Louisville	KY	40207	502-893-0311	897-5849
Web: www.mallstmatthews.com					
Mall at Short Hills 1200 Morris Tpke	Short Hills	NJ	07078	973-376-7350	376-2976
Web: www.shopshorthills.com					
Mall at Wellington Green 10300 W Forest Hill Blvd	Wellington	FL	33414	561-227-6900	227-0832
Web: www.shopwellingtongreen.com					
Marketplace Mall 1 Miracle Mile Dr	Rochester	NY	14623	585-424-6220	427-2745
Web: www.themarketplacemall.com					
Memorial City Mall 900 Gessner Rd Suite 303	Houston	TX	77024	713-464-8640	464-7845
Web: www.shopmemorialcity.com					
Merle Hay Mall 3800 Merle Hay Rd	Des Moines	IA	50310	515-276-8551	276-9227
Web: www.merlehaymall.com					
Metro North Mall 400 NW Barry Rd	Kansas City	MO	64155	816-436-7800	436-9952
Web: www.metronorthmallkc.com					
Metrocenter Mall 9617 N Metro Pkwy W Suite 1001	Phoenix	AZ	85051	602-997-2641	870-9983
Web: www.metrocentermall.com					
Metrocenter Mall 1395 Metrocenter	Jackson	MS	39209	601-969-7633	969-6820
Web: www.metromalljackson.com					
Mic Mac Mall 21 MicMac Blvd	Dartmouth	NS	B3A4N3	902-463-5891	469-5268
Web: micmacmall.shopping.ca					
Midtown Plaza 211 Midtown Plaza	Rochester	NY	14604	585-530-2000	325-2576
Web: www.midtownrochester.com					
Midway Mall 3343 Midway Mall Blvd	Elyria	OH	44035	440-324-6610	324-7276
Web: www.midwaymallshopping.com					
Mill Creek Mall 654 Mill Creek Mall	Erie	PA	16565	814-868-9000	864-1193
Web: www.millcreekmall.net					
Mission Valley Center 1640 Camino del Rio N Suite 351	San Diego	CA	92108	619-296-6375	692-0555
Web: westfield.com/missionvalley/					
Monroeville Mall 200 Mall Blvd	Monroeville	PA	15146	412-243-8511	372-0205
Web: www.monroevillemall.com					
Montclair Plaza 5060 Montclair Plaza Ln	Montclair	CA	91763	909-626-2442	624-6195
Web: www.montclairplaza.com					
Montebello Town Center 2134 Montebello Town Center Dr	Montebello	CA	90640	323-722-1776	722-1268
Web: www.montebellotowncenter.com					
Moreno Valley Mall 22500 Town Cir	Moreno Valley	CA	92553	951-653-1177	653-1171
Natick Mall 1245 Worcester St	Natick	MA	01760	508-655-4800	650-9945
Web: www.natickmall.com					
Newpark Mall 2086 Newpark Mall	Newark	CA	94560	510-794-5522	796-7968
Web: www.newparkmall.com					
North County Fair 272 E Via Rancho Pkwy	Escondido	CA	92025	760-489-2332	489-7158
Web: www.westfield.com/northcounty					
North East Mall 1101 Melbourne Rd Suite 1000	Hurst	TX	76053	817-284-3427	595-4471
Web: www.simon.com					
North Idaho Outlets 4300 W Riverbend Ave	Post Falls	ID	83854	208-773-4555	773-4556
TF: 888-678-9847					
North Star Mall 7400 San Pedro Ave Suite 2000	San Antonio	TX	78216	210-342-2325	342-7023
Web: www.northstarmall.com					
North Town Mall 4750 N Division St	Spokane	WA	99207	509-482-0178	483-0360
Web: www.northtownmall.com					
Northbrook Court 2171 Northbrook Ct	Northbrook	IL	60062	847-498-1770	498-5194
Web: www.northbrookcourt.com					
Northgate Mall 9501 Colerain Ave	Cincinnati	OH	45251	513-385-5600	385-5603
Web: www.mynorthgatemall.com					
Northgate Mall 401 NE Northgate Way Suite 210	Seattle	WA	98125	206-362-4777	361-8760
Web: www.simon.com					
NorthPark Center 8687 N Central Expy	Dallas	TX	75225	214-363-7441	363-0195
Web: www.northparkcenter.com					
Northpoint Mall 1000 Northpoint Cir	Alpharetta	GA	30022	770-740-9273	442-8295
Web: www.northpointmall.com					
Northridge Fashion Center 9301 Tampa Ave	Northridge	CA	91324	818-885-9700	885-0029
Web: www.northridgefashioncenter.com					
Northridge Mall 796 Northridge Mall	Salinas	CA	93906	831-449-7226	449-6756
Web: www.shop-northridge-mall.com					
Northshore Mall 210 Andover St	Peabody	MA	01960	978-531-3440	532-9115
Web: www.simon.com					
Northwoods Mall 2150 Northwoods Blvd Unit 60	North Charleston	SC	29406	843-797-3060	797-8363
Web: www.shopnorthwoods-mall.com					
Oak Park Mall 11461 W 95th St	Overland Park	KS	66214	913-888-4400	599-5839
Web: www.thenewoakparkmall.com					
Oakbrook Shopping Center 100 Oakbrook Center	Oak Brook	IL	60523	630-573-0250	573-0710
Web: www.oakbrookcenter.com					
Oaks The 222 W Hillcrest Dr	Thousand Oaks	CA	91360	805-495-4628	495-9656
Web: www.shoptheoaksmall.com					
Oakwood Center 197 Westbank Expy	Gretna	LA	70056	504-361-1550	
Web: www.oakwoodcenter.com					
Ohio Valley Mall 67800 Mall Rd	Saint Clairsville	OH	43950	740-695-4526	695-1451
Web: www.ohiovalleymall.net					
Old Orchard Center 66 Old Orchard Center Suite F-66	Skokie	IL	60077	847-674-7070	674-7083
Web: westfield.com					
Ontario Mills 1 Mills Cir Suite 1	Ontario	CA	91764	909-484-8300	476-0241
TF: 888-526-4557 ■ *Web:* www.ontariomills.com/index2.html					
Opry Mills 433 Opry Mills Dr	Nashville	TN	37214	615-514-1100	514-1120
TF: 877-746-7386 ■ *Web:* www.oprymills.com					
Orland Square 288 Orland Sq	Orland Park	IL	60462	708-349-6936	349-8419
Web: www.simon.com					
Orlando Fashion Square 3201 E Colonial Dr	Orlando	FL	32803	407-896-1131	894-8381
Web: www.orlandofashionsquare.com					
Orlando Premium Outlets 8200 Vineland Ave	Orlando	FL	32821	407-238-7787	238-7649
Web: www.premiumoutlets.com/orlando					
Outlet Shoppes at El Paso 7051 S Desert Blvd	Canutillo	TX	79835	915-877-3208	
Outlets at Loveland 5661 McWhinney Blvd	Loveland	CO	80538	970-663-1717	663-2421
TF: 888-255-1273 ■ *Web:* www.outletsatloveland.com					
Oxford Valley Mall 2300 E Lincoln Hwy	Langhorne	PA	19047	215-752-0222	750-0469
Web: www.oxfordvalleymall.com					
Padre-Staples Mall 5488 S Padre Island Dr	Corpus Christi	TX	78411	361-991-3755	993-5631
Palm Beach Mall 1801 Palm Beach Lakes Blvd	West Palm Beach	FL	33401	561-683-9186	683-9266
Web: www.simon.com					
Paradise Valley Mall 4568 E Cactus Rd	Phoenix	AZ	85032	602-996-8840	494-1991
Web: paradisevalleymall.westcor.com					

Name / Address	City	State	ZIP	Phone	Fax
Park City Center 142 Park City Center	Lancaster	PA	17601	717-393-3851	392-8577
Web: www.parkcitycenter.com					
Park Meadows Retail Resort 8401 Park Meadows Center Dr	Littleton	CO	80124	303-792-2533	792-3360
Web: www.parkmeadows.com					
Park Meadows Town Center 8401 Park Meadows Ctr Dr	Littleton	CO	80124	303-792-2533	792-3360
Web: www.parkmeadows.com					
Park Place 5870 E Broadway Blvd	Tucson	AZ	85711	520-747-7575	571-7622
Web: www.parkplacemall.com					
Parks at Arlington 3811 S Cooper St Suite 2206	Arlington	TX	76015	817-467-0200	468-5356
Web: www.theparksatarlington.com					
Parkway Place 2801 Memorial Pkwy SW	Huntsville	AL	35801	256-533-0700	533-5637
Web: www.parkwaycitymall.com					
Parkway Plaza 415 Parkway Plaza	El Cajon	CA	92020	619-579-9932	579-1280
Web: www.westfield.com/parkway					
Parmatown Mall 7899 W Ridgewood Dr	Parma	OH	44129	440-885-5506	884-9330
Web: www.parmatown.com					
Pearlridge Center 231 Pearlridge Center	Aiea	HI	96701	808-488-0981	488-9456
Web: www.pearlridgeonline.com					
Pembroke Lakes Mall 11401 Pines Blvd Suite 546	Pembroke Pines	FL	33026	954-436-3520	436-7992
Web: www.pembrokelakesmall.com					
Penn Square Mall 1901 Northwest Expy	Oklahoma City	OK	73118	405-842-4424	842-4676
Web: www.simon.com					
Perimeter Mall 4400 Ashford-Dunwoody Rd Suite 1360	Atlanta	GA	30346	770-394-4270	396-4732
Web: www.perimetermall.com					
Phoenix Spectrum Mall 1703 W Bethany Home Rd	Phoenix	AZ	85015	602-249-0670	246-8690
Pittsburgh Mills 590 Pittsburgh Mills Cir	Tarentum	PA	15084	724-904-9010	904-9020
Web: www.pittsburghmills.com					
Place de la Cite 2600 Laurier Blvd	Sainte-Foy	QC	G1V4T3	418-657-7015	657-6924
Web: www.placedelacite.com					
Polaris Fashion Place 1500 Polaris Pkwy Suite 3000	Columbus	OH	43240	614-846-1500	846-4617
Web: www.polarisfashionplace.com					
Potomac Mills 2700 Potomac Mills Cir Suite 307	Prince William	VA	22192	703-496-9301	643-1054
Web: www.potomacmills.com/index2.html					
Prime Outlets at Birch Run 12240 S Beyer Rd	Birch Run	MI	48415	989-624-6226	624-6125
TF: 877-466-8853 ■ *Web:* www.primeoutlets.com					
Prime Outlets Ellenton 5461 Factory Shops Blvd	Ellenton	FL	34222	941-723-1150	723-9437
TF: 888-260-7608 ■ *Web:* www.primeoutlets.com					
Prime Outlets at Lebanon 1 Outlet Village Blvd	Lebanon	TN	37090	615-444-0433	444-6933
TF: 800-617-2588 ■ *Web:* www.primeoutlets.com					
Prime Outlets Orlando Designer Centre 5211 International Dr	Orlando	FL	32819	407-352-9600	351-3873
Web: www.primeretail.com					
Prime Outlets Saint Augustine 500 Belz Outlet Blvd	Saint Augustine	FL	32084	904-826-1311	826-4470
Web: www.primeoutlets.com					
Prime Outlets San Marcos 3939 S IH-35	San Marcos	TX	78666	512-396-2200	396-2232
TF: 800-628-9465 ■ *Web:* www.primeretail.com					
Provo Towne Centre 1200 Towne Centre Blvd	Provo	UT	84601	801-852-2400	852-2405
Web: www.shopprovotownecentre.com					
Puente Hills Mall 1600 Azusa Ave	City of Industry	CA	91748	626-912-8777	913-2719
Quail Springs Mall 2501 W Memorial Rd	Oklahoma City	OK	73134	405-755-6530	751-8344
Web: www.quailspringsmall.com					
Quaker Bridge Mall 150 Quaker Bridge Mall	Lawrenceville	NJ	08648	609-799-8177	275-6523
Web: www.quakerbridgemall.com					
Randall Park Mall 20801 Miles Rd	Cleveland	OH	44128	216-663-1250	663-8750
Web: www.randallparkmall.net					
Randhurst Shopping Center 999 N Elmhurst Rd	Mount Prospect	IL	60056	847-259-0500	259-0228
Web: www.randhurstmall.com					
Redmond Town Center 16495 NE 74th St	Redmond	WA	98052	425-867-0808	867-1577
Web: www.redmondtowncenter.com					
Regency Mall 5538 Durand Ave	Racine	WI	53406	262-554-7979	554-7477
Web: www.shopregency-mall.com					
Regency Square Mall 9501 Arlington Expy Suite 100	Jacksonville	FL	32225	904-725-3830	724-7109
Web: www.regencysquaremall.com					
Ridgedale Center 12401 Wayzata Blvd	Minnetonka	MN	55305	952-541-4864	540-0154
Web: www.ridgedalecenter.com					
Ridgmar Mall 1888 Green Oaks Rd	Fort Worth	TX	76116	817-731-0856	763-5146
Web: www.ridgmar.com					
River Oaks Center 96 River Oaks Dr	Calumet City	IL	60409	708-868-0600	868-1402
Web: www.simon.com					
Riverchase Galleria 3000 Riverchase Galleria Suite 400	Birmingham	AL	35244	205-985-3039	985-3040
Web: www.riverchasegalleria.com					
Rivergate Mall 1000 Rivergate Pkwy Suite 1	Goodlettsville	TN	37072	615-859-3456	851-9656
Web: www.rivergate-mall.com					
RiverTown Crossings 3700 Rivertown Pkwy SW	Grandville	MI	49418	616-257-5000	257-0507
Web: www.rivertowncrossings.com					
Rockaway Townsquare Mall 301 Mt Hope Ave	Rockaway	NJ	07866	973-361-4070	361-1561
Web: www.simon.com					
Rolling Oaks Mall 6909 N Loop 1604 E	San Antonio	TX	78247	210-651-5513	651-6326
Web: www.simon.com					
Roosevelt Field Mall 630 Old Country Rd	Garden City	NY	11530	516-742-8001	742-8004
Web: www.simon.com					
Rosedale Center 10 Rosedale Center	Roseville	MN	55113	651-638-3553	638-3599
Web: www.myrosedale.com					
Ross Park Mall 1000 Ross Park Mall Dr	Pittsburgh	PA	15237	412-369-4400	369-4408
Web: www.simon.com					
Saint Clair Square 134 St Clair Sq	Fairview Heights	IL	62208	618-632-7567	632-4452
Web: www.stclairsquare.com					
Saint Louis Mills 5555 St Louis Mills Blvd	Hazelwood	MO	63042	314-227-5555	227-5901
Web: www.stlouismills.com					
San Jacinto Mall 1496 San Jacinto Mall	Baytown	TX	77521	281-421-4533	421-7377
Web: www.sanjacintomall.com					
Sawgrass Mills 12801 W Sunrise Blvd	Sunrise	FL	33323	954-846-2300	846-2312
Web: www.sawgrassmillsmall.com					
Seattle Premium Outlets 10600 Quil Ceda Blvd	Tulalip	WA	98271	360-654-3000	654-3901
Web: www.premiumoutlets.com/seattle					
Security Square Mall 6901 Security Blvd	Baltimore	MD	21244	410-265-6000	281-1473
Web: www.securitysquare.com					
Seminole Towne Center 200 Towne Center Cir	Sanford	FL	32771	407-323-2262	323-2464
Web: www.simon.com					
Sharpstown Mall 7500 Bellaire Blvd Suite 201	Houston	TX	77036	713-777-1111	777-7924
Shops at Briargate 1885 Briargate Pkwy	Colorado Springs	CO	80920	719-265-6264	268-0738
Web: www.theshopsatbriargate.com					
Shops at La Cantera 15900 La Cantera Pkwy Suite 6698	San Antonio	TX	78256	210-582-6255	582-6699
Web: www.theshopsatlacantera.com					
Shops at Riverwoods 4801 N University Ave	Provo	UT	84604	801-802-8430	802-8431
Web: www.shopsatriverwoods.com					
Shops at Tanforan 1150 El Camino Real	San Bruno	CA	94066	650-873-2000	873-4210
Web: www.theshopsattanforan.com					
Shops at Willow Bend 6121 W Park Blvd Suite 1000	Plano	TX	75093	972-202-7115	202-1122
Web: www.shopwillowbend.com					
Shops at Woodlake 725 Woodlake Rd Suite Q	Kohler	WI	53044	920-459-1713	208-2363
Web: www.destinationkohler.com/shops/shops.html					
Six Flags Mall 2911 E Division St	Arlington	TX	76011	817-640-1641	649-1825
Solomon Pond Mall 601 Donald Lynch Blvd	Marlborough	MA	01752	508-303-6255	303-0206
Web: www.simon.com					
South Bay Galleria 1815 Hawthorne Blvd Suite 201	Redondo Beach	CA	90278	310-371-7546	371-0103
Web: www.southbaygalleria.com					
South Coast Plaza 3333 Bristol St	Costa Mesa	CA	92626	714-435-2000	540-7334
Web: www.southcoastplaza.com					
South Mall 3300 Lehigh St	Allentown	PA	18103	610-791-0606	797-4065
Web: www.shopsouthmall.com					
South Park Mall 2310 SW Military Dr	San Antonio	TX	78224	210-921-0534	921-0628
Web: www.visitsouthpark.com					
South Plains Mall 6002 Slide Rd	Lubbock	TX	79414	806-792-4653	799-2331
Web: www.southplainsmall.com					
South Shore Plaza 250 Granite St	Braintree	MA	02184	781-843-8200	843-4708
Web: www.simon.com					
Southcenter Mall 633 Southcenter Mall	Seattle	WA	98188	206-246-7400	244-8607
Web: westfield.com/southcenter/					
Southdale Center 6610 Southdale Center	Edina	MN	55435	952-925-7874	925-7856
Web: www.southdalecenter.com					
Southern Park Mall 7401 Market St	Youngstown	OH	44512	330-758-4511	726-2719
Web: www.simon.com					
Southlake Mall 1000 Southlake Mall	Morrow	GA	30260	770-961-1050	961-1113
Web: www.shopsouthlakemall.com					
Southland Mall 1 Southland Mall Dr	Hayward	CA	94545	510-782-5050	887-9619
Web: www.southlandmall.com					
Southland Mall 20505 S Dixie Hwy	Miami	FL	33189	305-235-8562	235-7956
Web: www.mysouthlandmall.com					
SouthPark Mall 4400 Sharon Rd	Charlotte	NC	28211	704-364-4411	364-4913
TF: 888-364-4411 ■ *Web:* www.simon.com					
SouthPointe Pavilions 2910 Pine Lake Rd Suite Q	Lincoln	NE	68516	402-421-2114	421-2191
Web: www.southpointeshopping.com					
Southridge Mall 1111 E Army Post Rd	Des Moines	IA	50315	515-287-3880	287-0983
Web: www.shopsouthridgemall.com					
Southridge Mall 5300 S 76th St	Greendale	WI	53129	414-421-1102	421-0492
Web: www.shopsouthridge.com					
Southwest Center Mall 3662 W Camp Wisdom Rd	Dallas	TX	75237	972-296-1491	296-4220
Southwest Plaza Regional Shopping Center 8501 W Bowles Ave	Littleton	CO	80123	303-973-5300	972-9516
Web: www.southwestplaza.com					
Spring Hill Mall 1072 Spring Hill Mall	West Dundee	IL	60118	847-428-2200	428-2219
Web: www.springhillmall.com					
Springfield Mall 6500 Springfield Mall	Springfield	VA	22150	703-971-3600	922-5018
Web: www.springfieldmall.com					
Square One Mall 1201 Broadway	Saugus	MA	01906	781-233-8787	231-9787
Web: www.simon.com					
Stanford Shopping Center 680 Stanford Shopping Center	Palo Alto	CA	94304	650-617-8200	617-8227
TF: 800-772-9332 ■ *Web:* www.simon.com					
Staten Island Mall 2655 Richmond Ave	Staten Island	NY	10314	718-761-6800	494-6766
Web: www.statenisland-mall.com					
Stonebriar Centre 2601 Preston Rd	Frisco	TX	75034	972-668-6255	668-6151
Web: www.shopstonebriar.com					
Stoneridge Shopping Center 1 Stoneridge Mall	Pleasanton	CA	94588	925-463-2778	463-1467
Web: www.shopstoneridge.com					
Stratford Square Mall 152 Stratford Sq	Bloomingdale	IL	60108	630-351-9400	351-9769
Web: www.stratfordmall.com					
Summit Sierra 13925 S Virginia St Suite 212	Reno	NV	89511	775-853-7800	
Web: www.thesummitonline.com/					
Sunrise Mall 6041 Sunrise Mall	Citrus Heights	CA	95610	916-961-7150	961-7326
Web: www.sunrisemallonline.com					
Sunvalley Mall 1 Sunvalley Mall	Concord	CA	94520	925-825-0400	825-1392
Web: www.shopsunvalley.com					
SuperMall of the Great Northwest 1101 SuperMall Way	Auburn	WA	98001	253-833-9500	833-9006
TF: 800-729-8258 ■ *Web:* www.supermall.com					
Tacoma Mall 4502 S Steele St	Tacoma	WA	98409	253-475-4565	472-3413
Web: www.shopsimon.com					
Tallahassee Mall 2415 N Monroe St	Tallahassee	FL	32303	850-385-7145	385-6203
Web: www.shoptallahasseemall.com					
Tanger Outlet Center San Marcos 4015 S IH-35 Suite 319	San Marcos	TX	78666	512-396-7446	396-7449
TF: 800-408-8424 ■ *Web:* www.tangeroutlet.com					
Topanga Plaza 6600 Topanga Canyon Blvd	Canoga Park	CA	91303	818-594-8740	999-0878
Web: www.westfield.com/topanga/					
Town Center at Boca Raton 6000 Glades Rd	Boca Raton	FL	33431	561-368-6000	338-0891
Web: www.simon.com					
Town Center at Cobb 400 Ernest Barrett Pkwy NW	Kennesaw	GA	30144	770-424-9486	424-7917
Web: www.simon.com					
Town East Mall 2063 Town East Mall	Mesquite	TX	75150	972-270-4431	686-8974
Web: www.towneastmall.com					
Tri-County Mall 11700 Princeton Pike	Cincinnati	OH	45246	513-671-0120	671-2931
Web: www.tri-countymall.com					
Trumbull Shopping Park 5065 Main St	Trumbull	CT	06611	203-372-4500	372-0197
Web: www.westfield.com/trumbull					
Tucson Mall 4500 N Oracle Rd	Tucson	AZ	85705	520-293-7330	293-0543
Web: www.shoptucsonmall.com					
Tulsa Promenade 4107 S Yale Ave	Tulsa	OK	74135	918-627-9224	663-9385
Web: www.tulsapromenade.com					
Tyrone Square 6901 Tyrone Sq	Saint Petersburg	FL	33710	727-345-0126	345-5699
Web: www.simon.com					
Tysons Corner Center 1961 Chain Bridge Rd	McLean	VA	22102	703-893-9400	893-2632
TF: 888-289-7667 ■ *Web:* www.shoptysons.com					
University Mall 2200 E Fowler Ave	Tampa	FL	33612	813-971-3465	971-0923
Web: www.universitymalltampa.com					
University Park Mall 6501 N Grape Rd	Mishawaka	IN	46545	574-277-2223	272-5924
Web: www.simon.com					
Vallco Fashion Park 10123 N Wolfe Rd	Cupertino	CA	95014	408-255-5660	725-0370
Web: www.vallcomall.com					
Valley Fair Shopping Center 2855 Stevens Creek Blvd Suite 2178	Santa Clara	CA	95050	408-248-4451	248-8614
Web: westfield.com/valleyfair/					
Valley Plaza Mall 2701 Ming Ave	Bakersfield	CA	93304	661-832-2436	832-4312
Web: www.valleyplazamall.com					
Valley View Antique Mall 7281 Sharon-Warren Rd	Brookfield	OH	44403	330-448-6866	448-2570
Web: www.valleyviewinc.com					
Valley View Center Mall 13331 Preston Rd	Dallas	TX	75240	972-661-2425	239-1344
Web: www.shopvalleyviewcenter.com					
Valley View Mall 4802 Valley View Blvd	Roanoke	VA	24012	540-563-4400	366-8742
TF: 800-321-1711 ■ *Web:* www.valleyviewmall.com					
Vaughan Mills 1 Bass Pro Mills Dr	Vaughan	ON	L4K5W4	905-879-2110	879-1888
Web: www.vaughanmills.com					
Viejas Outlet Center 5005 Willows	Alpine	CA	91901	619-659-2070	659-2077
Web: www.shopviejas.com					
Vintage Faire Mall 3401 Dale Rd	Modesto	CA	95356	209-527-3401	527-3428
Web: www.shopvintagefairemall.com					
Virginia Center Commons 10101 Brook Rd Suite 765	Glen Allen	VA	23059	804-266-9000	266-9148
Web: www.simon.com					
Vista Ridge Mall 2401 S Stemmons Fwy	Lewisville	TX	75067	972-315-0015	315-3725
Web: www.vistaridgemall.com					
Volusia Mall 1700 W International Speedway Blvd	Daytona Beach	FL	32114	386-253-6783	254-8256
Web: www.volusiamall.net					

				Phone	Fax
Waccamaw Factory Shoppes 3071 Waccamaw Blvd TF: 800-444-8258	Myrtle Beach	SC	29579	843-236-8200	236-8748
Walden Galleria 1 Walden Galleria Web: www.waldengalleria.com	Buffalo	NY	14225	716-681-7600	681-1773
Warwick Mall 400 Bald Hill Rd Suite 100 Web: www.warwickmall.com	Warwick	RI	02886	401-739-7500	732-6052
Washington Square Mall 10202 E Washington St Web: www.simon.com	Indianapolis	IN	46229	317-899-4567	897-9428
Washington Square Shopping Center 9585 SW Washington Square Rd Web: www.shopwashingtonsquare.com	Tigard	OR	97281	503-639-8860	620-5612
West Oaks Mall 9401 W Colonial Dr Web: www.westoaksmall.com	Ocoee	FL	34761	407-294-2775	294-6051
West Oaks Mall 1000 West Oaks Mall Web: www.shopwestoaksmall.com	Houston	TX	77082	281-531-1332	531-1579
West Ridge Mall 1801 SW Wanamaker Rd Web: www.simon.com	Topeka	KS	66604	785-272-5119	272-1483
West Shore Plaza 250 West Shore Blvd Web: www.westshoreplaza.com	Tampa	FL	33609	813-286-0790	286-1250
West Town Mall 7600 Kingston Pike Web: www.simon.com	Knoxville	TN	37919	865-693-0292	531-0503
West Towne Mall 66 West Towne Way TF: 800-833-6330 ■ Web: www.shopwesttowne-mall.com	Madison	WI	53719	608-833-1544	833-5065
Westchester The 125 Westchester Ave Suite 925 Web: www.simon.com	White Plains	NY	10601	914-421-1333	421-1475
Westfarms Mall 500 Westfarms Mall Web: www.shopwestfarms.com	Farmington	CT	06032	860-561-3420	521-8682
Westfield Citrus Park 8021 Citrus Park Town Center Web: www.westfield.com/citruspark/	Tampa	FL	33625	813-926-4644	926-4601
Westfield Crestwood 109 Crestwood Plaza Suite 100 Web: westfield.com/crestwood/	Saint Louis	MO	63126	314-962-2395	962-2384
Westfield Franklin Park 5001 Monroe St Suite 700 Web: westfield.com/franklinpark/	Toledo	OH	43623	419-473-3317	473-0199
Westfield MainPlace 2800 N Main St Web: westfield.com/mainplace	Santa Ana	CA	92705	714-547-7000	547-2643
Westfield Mid Rivers Mall 1600 Mid Rivers Mall Web: www.westfield.com/midrivers	Saint Peters	MO	63376	636-970-2610	970-2950
Westfield Montgomery 7101 Democracy Blvd Web: westfield.com/montgomery/	Bethesda	MD	20817	301-469-6000	469-7612
Westfield North Bridge 520 N Michigan Ave	Chicago	IL	60611	312-327-2300	327-2310
Westfield San Francisco Centre 865 Market St Box A Web: www.sanfranciscoshopping.com	San Francisco	CA	94103	415-512-6776	512-6770
Westfield Santa Anita 400 S Baldwin Ave Web: westfield.com/santaanita/	Arcadia	CA	91007	626-445-3116	446-9320
Westfield Sarasota Square US Hwy 41 & Beneva Rd Web: westfield.com/sarasota/	Sarasota	FL	34238	941-922-9609	921-2632
Westfield Shoppingtown Annapolis 2002 Annapolis Mall Web: westfield.com/annapolis/	Annapolis	MD	21401	410-266-5432	266-3572
Westfield Shoppingtown Fashion Square 14006 Riverside Dr Web: www.westfield.com/fashionsquare	Sherman Oaks	CA	91423	818-783-0550	783-5955
Westfield Shoppingtown SouthPark 500 Southpark Center Web: www.westfield.com/southpark	Strongsville	OH	44136	440-238-9000	846-8323
Westfield Shoppingtown UTC 4545 La Jolla Village Dr Web: westfield.com/utc/	San Diego	CA	92122	858-546-8858	552-9065
Westfield South County Mall 18 S County Centerway Web: westfield.com/southcounty	Saint Louis	MO	63129	314-892-5203	892-0006
Westfield Southgate 3501 S Tamiami Trail Web: www.westfield.com	Sarasota	FL	34239	941-955-0900	954-3087
Westfield West County Center 80 W County Center Web: www.westfield.com/westcounty	Des Peres	MO	63131	314-288-2020	288-2030
Westfield West Covina 112 Plaza Dr Web: www.westfield.com/westcovina	West Covina	CA	91790	626-960-1881	337-3337
WestGate Mall 205 W Blackstock Rd Suite 1 Web: www.westgate-mall.com	Spartanburg	SC	29301	864-574-0263	587-8363
Westlake Center 400 Pine St Web: www.westlakecenter.com	Seattle	WA	98101	206-467-1600	467-1603
Westland Shopping Center 35000 W Warren Rd Web: www.westlandcenter.com	Westland	MI	48185	734-425-5001	425-9205
Westminster Mall 1025 Westminster Mall Web: www.simon.com	Westminster	CA	92683	714-898-2558	892-8824
Westminster Mall 5433 W 88th Ave Web: www.shopwestminstermall.com	Westminster	CO	80031	303-428-5634	757-1604
Westmoreland Mall Rt 30 E Web: www.westmorelandmall.com	Greensburg	PA	15601	724-836-5025	836-4825
White Marsh Mall 8200 Perry Hall Blvd Web: www.whitemarshmall.com	Baltimore	MD	21236	410-931-7100	931-7120
Willowbrook Mall 1400 Willowbrook Mall Web: www.willowbrook-mall.com	Wayne	NJ	07470	973-785-1616	785-8632
Willowbrook Mall 2000 Willowbrook Mall Web: www.shopwillowbrookmall.com	Houston	TX	77070	281-890-8000	890-3109
Windsor Park Mall 7900 IH-35 N	San Antonio	TX	78218	210-654-9084	654-4850
Wolfchase Galleria 2760 N Germantown Pkwy Web: www.simon.com	Memphis	TN	38133	901-381-2769	388-5542
Woodbridge Center 250 Woodbridge Ctr Dr Web: www.woodbridgecenter.com	Woodbridge	NJ	07095	732-636-4600	636-0417
Woodburn Company Stores 1001 Arney Rd TF: 888-664-7467 ■ Web: www.woodburncompanystores.com	Woodburn	OR	97071	503-981-1900	982-7434
Woodfield Mall 5 Woodfield Mall Web: www.shopwoodfield.com	Schaumburg	IL	60173	847-330-1537	330-0251
Woodland Hills Mall 7021 S Memorial Dr Suite 225B Web: www.simon.com	Tulsa	OK	74133	918-250-1449	250-9084
Woodland Mall 3195 28th St SE Web: www.shopwoodlandmall.com	Grand Rapids	MI	49512	616-949-0010	949-7348
Worthington Square 150 W Wilson Bridge Rd Web: www.worthingtonsquare.com	Worthington	OH	43085	614-841-1110	841-1109
Yorktown Shopping Center 203 Yorktown Center Web: www.yorktowncenter.com	Lombard	IL	60148	630-629-7330	629-7334

464 MALTING PRODUCTS

SEE ALSO Breweries p. 1397

				Phone	Fax
Briess Malting Co 625 S Irish Rd Web: www.briess.com	Chilton	WI	53014	920-849-7711	849-4277
Cargill Malt - Specialty Products Group 704 S 15th St TF Sales: 800-669-6258 ■ Web: www.specialtymalts.com	Sheboygan	WI	53081	920-459-4148	458-9034
Froedtert Malting Co PO Box 712 TF: 800-646-6258 ■ Web: www.imc-world.com	Milwaukee	WI	53201	414-671-1166	671-1385
Gambrinus Malting Corp 1101 Industrial Dr	Armstrong	BC	V0E1B6	250-546-8911	546-8798
JE Siebel Sons' Co Div Quest International 5115 Sudge Blvd	Hoffman Estates	IL	60192	847-645-7400	645-7062
LE Cooke Co 26333 Rd 140	Visalia	CA	93292	559-732-9146	732-3702
Premier Malt Products Inc 25760 Groesbeck Hwy Suite 103 TF Cust Svc: 800-521-1057 ■ Web: www.premiermalt.com	Warren	MI	48089	586-443-3355	443-4580
Quest International JE Siebel Sons' Co Div 5115 Sudge Blvd	Hoffman Estates	IL	60192	847-645-7400	645-7062
Rahr Malting Co Inc 301 4th Ave S Suite 567	Minneapolis	MN	55415	612-332-5161	332-6841
United Canadian Malt Ltd 843 Park St S	Peterborough	ON	K9J3V1	705-876-9110	876-9118
Yakima Brewing & Malting Co 1803 Presson Pl	Yakima	WA	98903	509-575-1900	457-6782

465 MANAGED CARE - BEHAVIORAL HEALTH

				Phone	Fax
Allen Group 2965 W State Rd 434 Suite 100 TF: 800-272-7252 ■ Web: www.theallengroup.com	Longwood	FL	32779	407-788-8822	862-1477
American Behavioral Benefits Managers 550 Montgomery Hwy Suite 300 TF: 800-677-4544 ■ Web: www.americanbehavioral.com	Birmingham	AL	35216	205-871-7814	868-9600
American Psych Systems 8403 Colesville Rd Suite 1600 TF: 800-305-3720 ■ Web: www.apscare.com	Silver Spring	MD	20910	301-571-0633	493-0776
APC Hegeman 50 Dietz St Suite K TF: 800-327-0085	Oneonta	NY	13820	607-432-9039	432-7029
APS Healthcare Inc 8403 Colesville Rd TF: 800-305-3720 ■ Web: www.apshealthcare.com	Silver Spring	MD	20910	301-563-5633	563-7348
Associated Behavioral Health Care Inc 4700 42nd Ave SW Suite 480 TF: 800-858-6702 ■ Web: www.abhc.com	Seattle	WA	98116	206-935-1282	937-1380
Baxter Assistance Services Inc 2800 E Broadway Suite C-416 Web: www.bas-employeeassistance.com	Pearland	TX	77581	866-443-0005	910-1600
Bensinger DuPont & Assoc 20 N Wacker Dr Suite 920 TF: 800-227-8620 ■ Web: www.bensingerdupont.com	Chicago	IL	60606	312-726-8620	726-1061
CIGNA Behavioral Health Inc 11095 Viking Dr Suite 350 TF: 800-433-5768 ■ Web: www.cignabehavioral.com	Eden Prairie	MN	55344	952-996-2000	
Comprehensive Behavioral Care Inc 204 S Hoover Blvd Suite 200 TF: 800-435-5348 ■ Web: www.comprehensivecare.com	Tampa	FL	33609	813-288-4808	288-4844
Comprehensive EAP 5 Militia Dr TF: 800-344-1011 ■ Web: www.compeap.com	Lexington	MA	02421	781-863-8283	860-9839
ComPsych Corp 455 N City Front Plaza Dr NBC Tower 13th Fl TF: 800-272-7255 ■ Web: www.compsych.com	Chicago	IL	60611	312-595-4000	595-4029
Contact Behavioral Health Services 1400 E Southern Ave Suite 800 TF: 800-888-1477 ■ Web: www.contactbhs.com	Tempe	AZ	85282	480-730-3023	730-5528
COPE Inc 1120 G St NW Suite 550 TF: 800-247-3054 ■ Web: www.cope-inc.com	Washington	DC	20005	202-628-5100	628-5111
CorpCare Assoc Inc 7000 Peachtree Dunwoody Rd Bldg 4 Suite 300 TF: 800-728-9444 ■ Web: www.corpcareeap.com	Atlanta	GA	30328	770-396-5253	396-9522
CorpHealth Inc 1300 Summit Ave Suite 600 TF: 800-240-8388 ■ Web: www.corphealth.com	Fort Worth	TX	76102	817-332-2519	335-9100
Corporate Care Works 8665 Baypine Rd Suite 100 TF: 800-327-9757 ■ Web: www.corporatecareworks.com	Jacksonville	FL	32256	904-296-9436	296-1511
EAP Consultants Inc 3901 Roswell Rd Suite 340 TF: 800-869-0276 ■ Web: www.eapconsultants.com	Marietta	GA	30062	770-951-8021	953-3174
EAP Systems 500 W Cummings Park Suite 6000 TF: 800-327-6721 ■ Web: www.eapsystems.com	Woburn	MA	01801	781-935-8850	935-2594
FEI Behavioral Health 11700 W Lake Park Dr TF: 800-782-1948 ■ Web: www.feinet.com	Milwaukee	WI	53224	414-359-1055	359-1973
FHC Health Systems 240 Corporate Blvd TF: 800-451-3581 ■ Web: www.fhchealthsystems.com	Norfolk	VA	23502	757-459-5100	459-5219
Holman Group 21050 Vanowen St TF: 800-321-2843 ■ Web: www.holmangroup.com	Canoga Park	CA	91303	818-704-1444	704-9339
Horizon EAP 9370 Sky Park Ct Suite 140 TF: 800-372-4472 ■ Web: www.integratedinsights.com	San Diego	CA	92123	858-571-1698	571-1868
Horizon Health Corp 1500 Waters Ridge Dr NASDAQ: HORC ■ TF: 800-931-4646 ■ Web: www.hmhm.com	Lewisville	TX	75057	972-420-8200	420-8287
Human Management Services Inc 1463 Dunwoody Dr TF: 800-343-2186 ■ Web: www.hmsincorp.com	Westchester	PA	19380	610-644-6000	644-1134
Hurst Place 555 Sanatorium Rd TF: 888-521-8300 ■ Web: www.hurstplace.com	Hamilton	ON	L8N3Z5	905-521-8300	521-8166
Interface EAP Inc 10370 Richmond Ave Suite 1100 *Fax Area Code: 800 ■ TF: 800-324-4327 ■ Web: www.ieap.com	Houston	TX	77042	713-781-3364	304-4838*
Interpersonal Dynamics Inc 2265 Teton Plaza TF: 800-658-3837 ■ Web: www.idynamic.com	Idaho Falls	ID	83404	208-529-1737	529-1757
Lexington Group 1200 Boston Post Rd *Fax Area Code: 860 ■ TF: 800-571-0197 ■ Web: www.the-lexington-group.com	Guilford	CT	06437	800-571-0197	606-9800*
Magellan Health Services Inc 6950 Columbia Gateway Dr NASDAQ: MGLN ■ TF: 800-458-2740 ■ Web: www.magellanhealth.com	Columbia	MD	21046	410-953-1000	953-5200
Managed Health Network Inc 1600 Los Gamos Dr Suite 300 TF: 800-327-2133 ■ Web: www.mhn.com	San Rafael	CA	94903	818-676-6775	
Mental Health Network Inc (MHNet Inc) 9606 N MoPac Exwy Suite 600 Web: www.mhnet.com	Austin	TX	78759	512-347-7900	347-1810
MHNet Inc (Mental Health Network Inc) 9606 N MoPac Exwy Suite 600 Web: www.mhnet.com	Austin	TX	78759	512-347-7900	347-1810
Midwest EAP Solutions Inc 1010 W Saint Germain St Suite 580 TF: 800-383-1908 ■ Web: www.midwesteap.com	Saint Cloud	MN	56301	320-253-1909	240-1501
National Employee Assistance Services Inc N 17 W 24100 Riverwood Dr Suite 300 TF: 800-634-6433 ■ Web: www.neas.com	Waukesha	WI	53188	262-574-2500	798-3928
National MENTOR Inc DBA MENTOR 313 Congress St TF: 800-388-5150 ■ Web: www.mentormpn.com	Boston	MA	02210	617-790-4800	790-4848
New Directions Behavioral Health LLC PO Box 6729 TF: 800-528-5763 ■ Web: www.ndbh.com	Leawood	KS	66206	913-982-8200	982-8401
PacifiCare Behavioral Health Inc 3120 Lake Center Dr TF: 800-357-5850 ■ Web: www.pbhi.com	Santa Ana	CA	92704	714-445-0300	513-6602
Perspectives Ltd 20 N Clark St Suite 2650 TF: 800-866-7556 ■ Web: www.perspectivesltd.com	Chicago	IL	60602	312-558-1560	558-1570
Preferred Mental Health Management Inc 401 E Douglas Ave Suite 300 TF: 800-776-4357 ■ Web: www.pmhm.com	Wichita	KS	67202	316-262-0444	262-0003
Providence Service Corp 620 N Craycroft Rd NASDAQ: PRSC ■ TF: 800-489-0064 ■ Web: www.provcorp.com	Tucson	AZ	85711	520-748-7108	745-1707
Psychiatric Solutions Inc 840 Crescent Center Dr Suite 460 NASDAQ: PSYS ■ Web: www.psysolutions.com	Franklin	TN	37067	615-312-5700	312-5711
Stuecker & Assoc Inc 1169 Eastern Pkwy Suite 2243 TF: 800-799-9327 ■ Web: www.stueckerandassoc.com	Louisville	KY	40217	502-452-9227	452-1529
United Behavioral Health Inc 425 Market St 27th Fl TF: 800-888-2998 ■ Web: www.unitedbehavioralhealth.com	San Francisco	CA	94105	415-547-5000	547-6200
ValueOptions Inc 12369 Sunrise Valley Dr Suite C TF: 866-221-0644 ■ Web: www.valueoptions.com	Reston	VA	20191	703-390-6800	390-6810

Phone | Fax

Wellpoint Behavioral Health/Blue Cross
9655 Granite Ridge Dr 6th Fl. San Diego CA 92123 858-571-8300 278-7822
TF: 800-999-7222 ■ *Web:* www.wellpoint.com

466 MANAGEMENT SERVICES

SEE ALSO Association Management Companies p. 1287; Educational Institution Operators & Managers p. 1594; Facilities Management Services p. 1630; Hotels & Hotel Companies p. 1832; Incentive Program Management Services p. 1852; Investment Advice & Management p. 1873; Pharmacy Benefits Management Services p. 2112

Phone | Fax

2 Places At 1 Time Inc 739 Travert Ave Suite E Atlanta GA 30318 404-815-9980 815-9277
TF: 877-275-2237 ■ *Web:* www.2placesat1time.com
Access Systems Inc 11710 Plaza America Dr Suite 900 Reston VA 20190 703-464-6900 464-6990
Web: www.accsys-inc.com
AimNet Solutions Inc 401 Merritt Seven Norwalk CT 06851 203-840-5700 849-9776
TF: 800-553-6006 ■ *Web:* www.aimnetsolutions.com
Ajilon Services Inc 210 W Pennsylvania Ave 5th Fl Towson MD 21204 410-821-0435 828-0106
TF: 800-626-8082 ■ *Web:* www.ajilon.com
American Claims Evaluation Inc 1 Jericho Plaza 1st Fl Jericho NY 11753 516-938-8000 938-0405
NASDAQ: AMCE
American Dental Partners Inc 201 Edgewater Dr Suite 285 Wakefield MA 01880 781-224-0880 224-4216
NASDAQ: ADPI ■ *TF:* 877-252-7414 ■ *Web:* www.amdpi.com
American Imaging Management 5040 Lake Cook Rd Deerfield IL 60015 847-564-8500 559-6900
TF: 800-340-0010 ■ *Web:* www.americanimaging.net
AmerInd Inc 3060 Williams Dr Suite 600 Fairfax VA 22031 703-752-8400 560-1396
Web: www.amerind.com
AmeriPath Inc 7111 Fairway Dr Suite 400 Palm Beach Gardens FL 33418 561-845-1850 845-0129
TF: 800-330-6565 ■ *Web:* www.ameripath.com
Aspen Systems Corp 2277 Research Blvd Rockville MD 20850 301-519-5000 519-5299
TF: 800-685-6867 ■ *Web:* www.aspensys.com
Atrilogy Solutions Group Inc
15375 Barranca Pkwy Suite 201 Bldg B Irvine CA 92618 949-754-0500 203-8766
Web: www.atrilogy.com
AVIDYN Inc 12750 Merit Dr Suite 500 Dallas TX 75251 972-447-6447 447-6444
Web: www.avidyn.com
Birner Dental Management Services Inc
3801 E Florida Ave Suite 508 Denver CO 80210 303-691-0680 691-0889
NASDAQ: BDMS ■ *Web:* www.bdms-perfectteeth.com
Capgemini US LLC 750 7th Ave Suite 1800 New York NY 10036 917-934-8000 934-8001
Web: www.us.capgemini.com
Care Choices 34605 12-Mile Rd Farmington Hills MI 48331 248-489-6203 489-6280
TF Sales: 800-261-3452 ■ *Web:* www.carechoices.com
Castle Dental Centers Inc 3701 Kriby Dr Suite 550 Houston TX 77098 281-999-9999
TF: 800-867-6453 ■ *Web:* www.castledental.com
Catapult Technology Ltd 7500 Old Georgetown Rd 11th Fl Bethesda MD 20814 240-482-2100 986-8688*
**Fax Area Code:* 301 ■ *Web:* www.catapulttechnology.com
Central Management Co Inc PO Box 1438 Winnfield LA 71483 318-628-4116 628-1141
Web: www.centralmanagement.com
Ceridian 3311 E Old Shakopee Rd Minneapolis MN 55425 952-853-8100 614-4600*
**Fax Area Code:* 248 ■ *Web:* www.ceridian.com/myceridian
Ceridian Canada Ltd 125 Garry St Winnipeg MB R3C3P2 204-946-0770 956-4026
TF: 866-975-1808 ■ *Web:* www.ceridian.ca
Coast Dental Services Inc 2502 N Rocky Point Rd Suite 1000 Tampa FL 33607 813-288-1999 281-9284
TF: 800-983-3848 ■ *Web:* www.coastdental.com
Commodity Sourcing Group 19730 Ralston St Detroit MI 48203 313-366-0660 366-0110
Web: www.csgbuy.com
Comprehensive Care Corp 3405 W ML King Hwy Suite 101 Tampa FL 33609 813-288-4808 288-4844
Web: www.compcare.com
Computer Sciences Corp Healthcare Group
1160 W Swedesford Rd Suite 200 Berwyn PA 19312 610-251-0660 647-4912
Web: www.csc.com/industries/healthservices
Concentra Inc 5080 Spectrum Dr Suite 1200 W Addison TX 75001 972-364-8000 387-0019
TF: 800-232-3550 ■ *Web:* www.concentra.com
Connell Purchasing Services 55 Shuman Blvd Suite 500 Naperville IL 60563 630-210-7450 579-9123
Web: www.connellpurchasing.com
Correctional Medical Services Inc 12647 Olive Blvd Saint Louis MO 63141 800-325-4809
TF: 800-325-4809 ■ *Web:* www.cmsstl.com
CorVel Corp 2010 Main St Suite 600 Irvine CA 92614 949-851-1473 851-1469
NASDAQ: CRVL ■ *Web:* www.corvel.com
CRAssociates Inc 8580 Cinderbed Rd Suite 2400 Newington VA 22122 703-550-8145 272-8966*
**Fax Area Code:* 877 ■ *TF:* 877-272-8960 ■ *Web:* www.crassoc.com
Cross Country Group LLC 4040 Mystic Valley Pkwy Medford MA 02155 781-396-3700 391-7504
Web: www.ccgroup.com
Dental Care Alliance Inc 1 S School Ave Suite 1000 Sarasota FL 34237 941-955-3150 330-0765
eLoyalty Corp 150 Field Dr Suite 250 Lake Forest IL 60045 847-582-7000 582-7001
NASDAQ: ELOY ■ *TF:* 877-235-6925 ■ *Web:* www.eloyalty.com
EmCare 1717 Main St Suite 5200 Dallas TX 75201 214-712-2000 712-2444
TF: 800-527-2145 ■ *Web:* www.emcare.com
Emdeon Practice Services 2202 N West Shore Blvd Suite 300 Tampa FL 33607 813-202-5000
TF: 877-932-6301 ■ *Web:* www.emdeonps.com
Emergency Consultants Inc 4075 Copper Ridge Dr Traverse City MI 49684 231-946-8970 946-1730
TF: 800-253-1795 ■ *Web:* www.eci-med.cc
File Keepers LLC 6277 E Slauson Ave Los Angeles CA 90040 323-728-3151 728-1349
TF: 800-332-3453 ■ *Web:* www.filekeepers.com
First Health Group Corp 3200 Highland Ave Downers Grove IL 60515 630-737-7900 719-0076
TF: 800-445-1425 ■ *Web:* www.firsthealth.com
First Health Services Corp 4300 Cox Rd Glen Allen VA 23060 804-965-7400 965-7416
TF: 800-884-2822 ■ *Web:* www.fhsc.com
Focus Healthcare Management Inc
720 Cool Springs Blvd Suite 300 Franklin TN 37067 615-778-4000 778-0814
TF: 800-873-0055 ■ *Web:* www.focus-ppo.com
Fortune Practice Management
9888 Carroll Centre Rd Suite 100 San Diego CA 92126 858-535-6287 535-6387
TF: 800-628-1052 ■ *Web:* www.fortunepractice.com
Franchise Co The 5397 Eglinton Ave W Suite 108 Etobicoke ON M9C5K6 416-620-4700 620-9955
Web: www.thefranchisecompany.com
Genscape Inc 445 E Main St Suite 200 Louisville KY 40202 502-583-3435 583-3464
Web: www.genscape.com
Group Management Services Inc 3296 Columbia Rd Suite 101 Richfield OH 44286 330-659-0100 659-0150
TF: 800-456-2885 ■ *Web:* www.groupmgmt.com
Hawthorne Corp PO Box 61000 Charleston SC 29419 843-797-8484 797-5258
Web: www.hawthornecorp.com
HealthAxis Inc 5215 N O'Connor Blvd Irving TX 75039 972-443-5000 556-0572
NASDAQ: HAXS ■ *Web:* www.healthaxis.com
Healthrisk Group Inc 505 City Pkwy W Suite 100 Orange CA 92868 714-704-0100 704-0111
TF: 800-955-9600 ■ *Web:* www.hrgi-online.com
Hill Physicians Medical Group Inc PO Box 5080 San Ramon CA 94583 925-820-8300 820-8252
TF: 800-445-5747 ■ *Web:* www.hillphysicians.com

Phone | Fax

HyperSoft Inc 4 E Washington Ave Athens TN 37303 423-744-7071 744-3012
Web: www.hypersoft.net
Infocrossing Inc 2 Christie Heights St Leonia NJ 07605 201-840-4700 840-7250
NASDAQ: IFOX ■ *TF:* 800-431-1912 ■ *Web:* www.infocrossing.com
Ingenix Inc 12125 Technology Dr Eden Prairie MN 55344 952-833-7100 833-7201
TF: 888-445-8745 ■ *Web:* www.ingenix.com
IntegraMed America Inc 2 Manhattanville Rd Purchase NY 10577 914-253-8000 253-8008
NASDAQ: INMD ■ *Web:* www.integramed.com
Integreo Inc 400 Perimeter Center Terr Suite 249 Atlanta GA 30346 770-280-2630 280-2631
TF: 800-350-5781 ■ *Web:* www.integreo.com
InterDent Inc 222 N Sepulveda Blvd Suite 740 El Segundo CA 90245 310-765-2400 765-2456
Web: www.interdent.com
International Health Partners Inc 1 Yorkdale Rd Suite 320 Toronto ON M6A3A1 403-264-7664 264-7640
Web: www.ihp.ca
(i)Structure Inc 11800 Ridge Pkwy Suite 200 Broomfield CO 80021 888-757-7501 965-5866*
**Fax Area Code:* 402 ■ *TF:* 888-757-7501 ■ *Web:* www.i-structure.com
Jardon & Howard Technologies Inc
13501 Ingenuity Dr Suite 300 Orlando FL 32826 407-381-7797 381-0017
TF: 888-657-2727 ■ *Web:* www.jht.com
Johnson & Johnson Health Care Systems Inc 425 Hoes Ln Piscataway NJ 08854 732-562-3000 562-3299
TF: 800-255-2500
Juniper Group Inc 60 Cutter Mill Suite 611 Great Neck NY 11021 516-829-4670 829-4691
Web: www.junipergroup.com
Management & Engineering Technologies International Inc
(METI) 8600 Boeing Dr El Paso TX 79925 915-772-4975 772-2253
Web: www.meticorp.com
Matria Healthcare Inc 1850 Parkway Pl 12th Fl Marietta GA 30067 770-767-4500 767-8849
NASDAQ: MATR ■ *TF:* 800-456-4060 ■ *Web:* www.matria.com
Med-Emerg International Inc
6711 Mississauga Rd Suite 404 Mississauga ON L5N2W3 905-858-1368 858-1399
TF: 800-265-3429 ■ *Web:* www.med-emerg.com
Medcor Inc PO Box 550 McHenry IL 60051 815-363-9500 363-9696
Web: www.medcor.com
MEDSTAT Group 777 E Eisenhower Pkwy Ann Arbor MI 48108 734-996-1180 913-3600*
**Fax:* Hum Res ■ *Web:* www.medstat.com
METI (Management & Engineering Technologies International
Inc) 8600 Boeing Dr El Paso TX 79925 915-772-4975 772-2253
Web: www.meticorp.com
Metropolitan Health Networks Inc
250 Australian Ave S Suite 400 West Palm Beach FL 33401 561-805-8500 805-8501
AMEX: MDF ■ *TF:* 888-663-8227 ■ *Web:* www.metcare.com
MHM Services Inc 1593 Spring Hill Rd Suite 610 Vienna VA 22182 703-749-4600 749-4604
TF: 800-416-3649 ■ *Web:* www.mhm-services.com
MicroSource Inc 6161 S Syracuse Way Greenwood Village CO 80111 303-706-0990 706-1861
Web: www.microsource.com
Modis Inc 1 Independent Dr Suite 215 Jacksonville FL 32202 904-360-2300 360-2323
TF: 800-372-2788 ■ *Web:* www.modisit.com
Monarch Dental Corp 650 International Pkwy Suite 100 Richardson TX 75081 972-702-7446 671-0139
Web: www.monarchdental.com
National Flood Services Inc PO Box 2057 Kalispell MT 59903 406-756-8656 257-2008
TF: 888-888-2170 ■ *Web:* www.nfsmt.com
OCA Inc 3850 N Causeway Blvd Suite 800 Metairie LA 70002 504-834-4392 834-3663
TF: 866-765-8583 ■ *Web:* www.ocai.com
Occupational Health & Rehabilitation Inc
175 Derby St Suite 36 Hingham MA 02043 781-741-5175 741-5499
TF: 800-622-4584 ■ *Web:* www.ohplus.com
OrthAlliance Inc 21535 Hawthorne Blvd Suite 200 Torrance CA 90503 310-792-1300 792-1350
Web: www.orthalliance.com
Orthodontic Centers of America
3850 N Causeway Blvd Suite 800 Metairie LA 70002 504-834-4392 834-3663
TF: 866-765-8583 ■ *Web:* www.ocai.com
Paradigm Health Corp 1001 Galaxy Way Suite 300 Concord CA 94520 925-676-2300 676-0640
TF: 800-676-6777 ■ *Web:* www.paradigmhealth.com
Patricia Seybold Group 210 Commercial St Boston MA 02109 617-742-5200 742-1028
TF: 800-826-2424 ■ *Web:* www.psgroup.com
Pediatrix Medical Group Inc PO Box 559001 Fort Lauderdale FL 33355 954-384-0175 233-3192*
NYSE: PDX ■ **Fax:* Hum Res ■ *TF:* 800-243-3839 ■ *Web:* www.pediatrix.com
Per-Se Technologies Inc 1145 Sanctuary Pkwy Suite 200 Alpharetta GA 30004 770-237-4300 237-4317
NASDAQ: PSTI ■ *TF:* 877-736-3773 ■ *Web:* www.per-se.com
PFSweb Inc 500 N Central Expwy Suite 500 Plano TX 75074 972-881-2900 426-8616
NASDAQ: PFSW ■ *TF:* 888-330-5504 ■ *Web:* www.pfsweb.com
Pitney Bowes Management Services 90 Park Ave 11th Fl New York NY 10016 212-808-3800
TF: 800-669-0800 ■ *Web:* www.pb.com
Prospect Medical Holdings Inc 400 Corporate Pointe Culver City CA 90230 310-338-8677 338-1109
AMEX: PZZ
Provell Inc 11100 Mayzata Blvd Suite 680 Minnetonka MN 55305 952-258-2000 258-2100*
**Fax:* Hum Res ■ *Web:* www.provell.com
Radiation Management Consultants 3019 Darnell Rd Philadelphia PA 19154 215-824-1300 824-1371
TF: 800-793-1304 ■ *Web:* www.rmcmedical.com
Radiologix Inc 2200 Ross Ave Suite 3600 Dallas TX 75201 214-303-2776 303-2778
AMEX: RGX ■ *TF:* 800-908-9302 ■ *Web:* www.radiologix.com
Restaurant Partners Inc 112 E Concord St Orlando FL 32801 407-839-5070 839-3388
Web: www.restaurantpartnersinc.com
Select Medical Corp 4716 Old Gettysburg Rd Mechanicsburg PA 17055 717-972-1100 972-1042
TF: 888-735-6332 ■ *Web:* www.selectmedicalcorp.com
Sentry Hospitality Ltd 136 E 57th St New York NY 10022 212-753-5347 688-2772
Web: www.sentryhospitality.com
Sheridan Healthcare Inc
1613 N Harrison Pkwy Bldg C Suite 200 Sunrise FL 33323 954-838-2371 851-1715*
**Fax:* Mktg ■ *TF:* 800-437-2672 ■ *Web:* www.sheridanhealthcare.com
SHPS Inc 11405 Bluegrass Pkwy Louisville KY 40299 502-267-4900 263-5610
TF: 888-421-7477 ■ *Web:* www.shps.com
Shred First LLC 380 Carolina Dr Roebuck SC 29376 864-577-9645 577-9647
TF: 800-387-2009 ■ *Web:* www.shredfirst.net
SJB Group Inc PO Box 1751 Baton Rouge LA 70821 225-769-3400 769-3596
Web: www.sjbgroup.com
Sourcecorp Inc 3232 McKinney Ave Suite 1000 Dallas TX 75204 214-740-6500 740-6556
NASDAQ: SRCP ■ *TF:* 888-339-4462 ■ *Web:* www.srcp.com
Specialized Services Inc 23077 Greenfield Rd Suite 470 Southfield MI 48075 248-557-1030 557-0755
TF: 866-774-2004 ■ *Web:* www.ssi-inc.com
Spectrum Healthcare Resources Inc
12647 Olive Blvd Suite 600 Saint Louis MO 63141 314-744-4100 744-4180*
**Fax:* Hum Res ■ *TF:* 800-325-3982 ■ *Web:* www.shrusa.com
StarTek Inc 44 Cook St 4th Fl Denver CO 80206 303-361-6000 388-9970
NYSE: SRT ■ *Web:* www.startek.com
Sterling Healthcare 1000 Park Forty Plaza Suite 500 Durham NC 27713 919-383-0355 806-5180
TF: 800-476-4587 ■ *Web:* www.sterling-healthcare.com
Stream International Inc
2220 Campbell Creek Blvd Suite 100 Richardson TX 75080 469-624-5000
TF: 888-284-5834 ■ *Web:* www.stream.com
Sun Solution Consulting 101 Sun Ave NE Albuquerque NM 87109 505-821-3355 798-5076
TF: 800-729-6600
Surgical Services Inc 5776 Hoffner Ave Suite 200 Orlando FL 32822 407-249-1946 275-9192
TF: 800-349-4374 ■ *Web:* www.surgicalservices.com
Transcend Services Inc 945 E Paces Ferry Rd NE Suite 1475 Atlanta GA 30326 404-836-8000 364-8009
NASDAQ: TRCR ■ *Web:* www.transcendservices.com
UCI Medical Affiliates Inc 4416 Forest DR Columbia SC 29206 803-782-4278 252-8077

Phone Fax

US Energy Services Inc 1000 Superior Blvd Suite 201 .... Wayzata MN 55391 952-745-4300 473-1224
Web: www.usenergyservices.com
US Oncology Inc 16825 Northchase Dr Suite 1300 .... Houston TX 77060 832-601-8766
TF: 800-381-2637 ■ *Web:* www.usoncology.com
vCustomer Corp 570 Kirkland Way .... Kirkland WA 98033 206-802-0200 802-0201
Web: www.vcustomer.com
Vercuity Solutions Inc
5889 S Greenwood Plaza Blvd Suite 300 .... Greenwood Village CO 80111 303-218-5300 218-5301
TF: 888-372-8489 ■ *Web:* www.vercuity.com
VHA Inc 220 E Las Colinas Blvd .... Irving TX 75039 972-830-0000 830-0012
TF: 800-842-5146 ■ *Web:* www.vha.com
VisionQuest National Ltd 600 N Swan Rd .... Tucson AZ 85711 520-881-3950 881-3269
Web: www.vq.com
Volt VIEWtech Inc 5109 E La Palma Suite D .... Anaheim CA 92807 714-695-3300 701-9893
TF: 800-998-8658 ■ *Web:* www.voltviewtech.com
VTA Management Services Inc 1901 Emmons Ave Suite 200 .... Brooklyn NY 11235 718-615-0049 615-1972
TF: 800-874-3469
Walker Financial Corp 990 Stewart Ave Suite 60-A .... Garden City NY 11530 516-832-7000 832-7979
X-Sells Inc 1 Edgewater Dr Suite 110 .... Norwood MA 02062 781-270-4050 278-4060
Web: www.x-sells.com
Xand Corp 11 Skyline Dr .... Hawthorne NY 10532 914-592-8282 592-3482
TF: 800-522-2823 ■ *Web:* www.xand.com

467 MANNEQUINS & DISPLAY FORMS

Phone Fax

Barnhart Display 174 W Hudson Ave .... Englewood NJ 07631 201-569-2569 569-6992
Web: www.barnhartdisplay.com
Goldsmith New York at Studio 350 601 W 26th St Suite 350 ...... New York NY 10001 212-366-9040
Web: www.goldsmith-inc.com
Ronis Brothers 39 Harriet Pl .... Lynbrook NY 11563 516-887-5266 887-5288
Web: www.ronis.com
Siegel & Stockman USA 126 W 25th St .... New York NY 10001 212-633-0138 366-0575
TF: 888-515-8949 ■ *Web:* www.siegel-stockman.com
Silvestri Studio Inc 8125 Beach St .... Los Angeles CA 90001 323-277-4420 585-0861
TF: 800-647-8874 ■ *Web:* www.silvestricalifornia.com

468 MARINE SERVICES

SEE ALSO Freight Transport - Deep Sea (Domestic Ports) p. 1677; Freight Transport - Deep Sea (Foreign Ports) p. 1677; Freight Transport - Inland Waterways p. 1677; Logistics Services (Transportation & Warehousing) p. 1918

Phone Fax

Allied Towing Corp 500 E Indian River Rd .... Norfolk VA 23523 757-545-7301 545-5692
TF: 800-446-8241
American Port Service Inc 2901 Childs St .... Baltimore MD 21226 410-350-0400 354-8812
Web: www.amports.com
Andrie Inc 561 E Western Ave .... Muskegon MI 49442 231-728-2226 726-6747
Web: www.andrie.com
Bay Houston Towing Co 2243 Milford St .... Houston TX 77098 713-529-3755 529-2591
TF: 800-324-3755 ■ *Web:* www.bayhouston.com
Bisso Towboat Co Inc 8237 Oak St .... New Orleans LA 70178 504-861-1411 861-9298
Web: www.bissotowing.com
Boston Towing & Transportation Co LP 36 New St .... East Boston MA 02128 617-567-9100 567-2583
TF: 800-836-8847
Brown Marine Service Inc 40 Audusson Ave .... Pensacola FL 32507 850-453-3471 457-1662
Web: www.brownmarine.com
Candies Otto LLC 17271 Hwy 90 .... Des Allemands LA 70030 504-469-7700 469-7740
TF: 800-535-4563 ■ *Web:* www.ottocandies.com
Cargo Express Inc 1790 Yardley-Langhorne Rd Suite 202 .... Yardley PA 19067 215-493-2662 493-4430
Web: www.cargoexpressinc.com
Cenac Towing Co Inc PO Box 2617 .... Houma LA 70361 985-872-2413 851-1761
TF: 800-942-5476
Coastal Tug & Barge Inc 1020 Port Blvd Suite 2 .... Miami FL 33132 305-579-5013 371-3041
TF: 800-323-2495
Cooper/T Smith Stevedoring Co
118 N Royal St Commerce Bldg Suite 1100 .... Mobile AL 36602 251-431-6100 431-6150
TF: 800-239-8484 ■ *Web:* www.coopertsmith.com
Crescent Towing & Salvage Co Inc 1240 Patterson St .... New Orleans LA 70130 504-366-1521 361-9038
TF: 800-843-3930
Crowley Maritime Corp 555 12th St Suite 2130 .... Oakland CA 94607 510-251-7500 251-7510
TF: 800-276-9539 ■ *Web:* www.crowley.com
Det Norske Veritas USA Inc 16340 Park Ten Pl Suite 100 .... Houston TX 77084 281-721-6600 721-6900
Dix Industries Inc 5500 RL Ostos Rd .... Brownsville TX 78521 956-831-4228 831-2559
Web: www.dixshipping.com
Donjon Marine Co Inc 1250 Liberty Ave .... Hillside NJ 07205 908-964-8812 964-7426
Web: www.donjon.com
Dunlap Towing Co PO Box 593 .... La Conner WA 98257 360-466-3114 466-3116
TF: 800-476-3114 ■ *Web:* www.dunlaptowing.com
Eagle Marine Industries Inc 1 Riverview Ave .... Sauget IL 62201 618-875-1153 875-1505
East Coast Terminal Co Inc 102 Marine Terminal Dr .... Savannah GA 31402 912-236-1531 235-4837
Eastwind Maritime SA Inc 444 Madison Ave Suite 200 .... New York NY 10022 212-838-1113 838-8439
Web: www.eastwind@eastwindgroup.com
Eckstein Marine Services LLC 5135 Storey St .... Harahan LA 70123 504-733-5845 733-7637
TF: 800-735-5845
Edison Chouest Offshore LLC 16201 E Main St .... Galliano LA 70354 985-632-7144 632-2282
TF: 800-417-7144 ■ *Web:* www.chouest.com
Eller & Co Inc 1850 Eller Dr Suite 403 .... Fort Lauderdale FL 33316 954-525-3381 524-2644
Eller-ITO Stevedoring Co LLC 899 S America Way .... Miami FL 33132 305-379-3700 371-9969
Web: www.ellerito.com
Foss Maritime Co 660 W Ewing St .... Seattle WA 98119 206-281-3800 281-4702
TF: 800-426-2885 ■ *Web:* www.foss.com
G & H Towing Co Inc PO Drawer 2270 .... Galveston TX 77553 409-744-6311 740-2575
General Steamship Corp Ltd 575 Redwood Hwy Suite 200 .... Mill Valley CA 94941 415-389-5200 389-9020
Web: www.gensteam.com
Global Material Services LLC PO Box 13286 .... Memphis TN 38113 901-775-0500 775-0415
Web: www.globalmat.com
Golden Stevedoring Co Inc PO Box 869 .... Mobile AL 36601 251-433-3726 433-0379
Great Lakes Towing Co 4500 Division Ave .... Cleveland OH 44102 216-621-4854 621-7616
TF: 800-321-3663 ■ *Web:* www.thegreatlakesgroup.com
Hawaii Stevedores Inc PO Box 2160 .... Honolulu HI 96805 808-527-3400 527-3448
Hawaiian Tug & Barge PO Box 3288 .... Honolulu HI 96801 808-543-9311 543-9477
TF: 800-572-2743 ■ *Web:* www.htbyb.com
Higman Marine Services 1980 Post Oak Blvd Suite 1101 .... Houston TX 77056 713-552-1101 552-0732
Hornbeck Offshore Services Inc
103 Northpark Blvd Suite 300 .... Covington LA 70433 985-727-2000 727-2006
NYSE: HOS ■ *TF:* 800-535-5843 ■ *Web:* www.hornbeckoffshore.com

Phone Fax

International Marine Terminals Partnership
18559 Hwy 23 .... Port Sulphur LA 70083 504-656-7341 656-2626
International Transportation Service Inc 1281 Pier J Ave ...... Long Beach CA 90802 562-435-7781 491-1935
James Marine Paducah River Service PO Box 2305 .... Paducah KY 42002 270-898-7392 898-7881
Web: www.jamesmarine.com
K-Sea Transportation LLC 2700 W Commodore Way .... Seattle WA 98199 206-443-9418 343-0424
Kinder Morgan 5807 Navigation .... Houston TX 77011 713-923-6678 923-3128
Kinder Morgan Bulk Terminals Inc 7116 Hwy 22 .... Sorrento LA 70778 225-675-5387 675-5923
TF: 800-535-8170 ■ *Web:* www.kindermorgan.com
Kinder Morgan/Pinney Dock & Transport LLC PO Box 41 .... Ashtabula OH 44005 440-964-7186 964-5210
Web: www.pinneydock.com
Lambert's Point Docks PO Box 89 .... Norfolk VA 23501 757-446-1212 446-1245
Leboeuf Brothers Towing Co Inc PO Box 9036 .... Houma LA 70361 985-594-6692 594-5253
TF: 800-256-5088
Loop LLC PO Box 7250 .... Metairie LA 70010 504-368-5667
Web: www.loopllc.com/f1.htm
Marine Terminals Corp 3 Embarcadero Center Suite 550 ..... San Francisco CA 94111 415-646-8100 981-9540
TF: 800-676-5252 ■ *Web:* www.mtcorp.com
McAllister Towing & Transportation Co Inc
17 Battery Pl Suite 1200 .... New York NY 10004 212-269-3200 509-1147
Web: www.mcallistertowing.com
McCabe Hamilton & Renny Co Ltd PO Box 210 .... Honolulu HI 96810 808-524-3255 545-3101
Web: www.mhrhawaii.com
MEMCO Barge Line 16090 Swingley Ridge Rd Suite 600 .... Chesterfield MO 63017 636-530-2100 530-4100
TF: 800-207-8011 ■ *Web:* www.memcobarge.com
Murphy Marine Services Inc 11 Gist Rd 1st Fl .... Port of Wilmington DE 19801 302-571-4700 571-4702
Nassau Terminals LLC 501 N 3rd St .... Fernandina Beach FL 32034 904-261-0048 261-4407
New Haven Terminal Inc 100 Waterfront St .... New Haven CT 06512 203-468-0805 469-6374
New York State Canal Corp 200 Southern Blvd .... Albany NY 12201 518-471-5010
TF: 800-422-6254 ■ *Web:* www.canals.state.ny.us
Nicholson Terminal & Dock Co PO Box 18066 .... River Rouge MI 48218 313-842-4300 843-1091
Web: www.nicholson-terminal.com
North Star Terminal & Stevedore Co LLC
790 Ocean Dock Rd .... Anchorage AK 99501 907-272-7537 272-8927
Web: www.northstarak.com
Odyssey Marine Exploration Inc 5215 W Laurel St .... Tampa FL 33607 813-876-1776 876-1777
AMEX: OMR ■ *Web:* www.odysseymarine.com
Otto Candies Inc 17271 Hwy 90 .... Des Allemands LA 70030 504-469-7700 469-7740
TF: 800-535-4563 ■ *Web:* www.ottocandies.com
P & O Ports North America Inc 99 Wood Ave S Level 8 Suite 804 .... Iselin NJ 08830 732-603-2630 635-3874
Web: www.poportsna.com
Parker Towing Co Inc PO Box 20908 .... Tuscaloosa AL 35402 205-349-1677 758-0061
TF: 800-329-1677 ■ *Web:* www.parkertowing.com
Port Arthur Towing Co PO Box 966 .... Groves TX 77619 409-962-8536 962-1923
Port of Miami Terminal Operating Co LC
1007 N America Way Suite 400 .... Miami FL 33132 305-416-7600 374-6724
Web: www.pomtoc.com
RMS Titanic Inc 3340 Peachtree Rd NE Suite 2250 .... Atlanta GA 30326 404-842-2600 842-2626
Web: www.rmstitanic.net
Rukert Terminals Corp 2021 S Clinton St .... Baltimore MD 21224 410-276-1013 522-1031
Web: www.rukert.com
Sause Brothers 3710 NW Front Ave .... Portland OR 97210 503-222-1811 222-2010
TF: 800-488-4167 ■ *Web:* www.sause.com
Sea Tow Services International Inc
1560 Youngs Ave PO Box 1178 .... Southold NY 11971 631-765-3660 765-5208
TF: 800-473-2869 ■ *Web:* www.seatow.com
SEACOR Holdings Inc 460 Park Ave 12th Fl .... New York NY 10022 212-307-6633 582-8522
NYSE: CKH ■ *Web:* www.seacorsmit.com
Southern Stevedoring Co LP PO Box 1052 .... Channelview TX 77530 713-453-3388 453-3458
SSA Marine 1131 SW Klickitat Way .... Seattle WA 98134 206-623-0304 623-0179
TF: 800-422-3505 ■ *Web:* www.ssamarine.com
Teco Barge Line 100 Scott St .... Metropolis IL 62960 618-524-3100 524-8680
TF: 800-455-5731 ■ *Web:* www.tecobargeline.com
Texas American Shipping Corp 24800 Pitkin Rd Suite B .... Spring TX 77386 281-367-7010 367-7056
Tidewater Inc 601 Poydras St Suite 1900 .... New Orleans LA 70130 504-568-1010 566-4580
NYSE: TDW ■ *TF:* 800-678-8433 ■ *Web:* www.tdw.com
Trans Pacific Container Service Corp
920 W Harry Bridges Blvd .... Wilmington CA 90744 310-830-2000 513-7400
Web: www.trapac.com
Trico Marine Services Inc 250 N American Ct .... Houma LA 70363 985-851-3833 851-4321
NASDAQ: TRMA ■ *Web:* www.tricomarine.com
Trimodal Inc 8009 34th Ave S Suite 300 .... Minneapolis MN 55425 952-253-6900 253-6901
Web: www.trimodalinc.com
Virginia International Terminals Inc PO Box 1387 .... Norfolk VA 23501 757-440-7000 440-7221
TF: 800-541-2431 ■ *Web:* www.vit.org
Waxler Towing Co Inc PO Box 253 .... Memphis TN 38101 901-946-1607 947-1230
Web: www.waxler.com
Western Towboat Co Inc 617 NW 40th St .... Seattle WA 98107 206-789-9000 789-9755
TF: 800-932-9651 ■ *Web:* www.westerntowboat.com

469 MARKET RESEARCH FIRMS

Phone Fax

Abacus Direct 2550 Crescent Dr .... Layfayette CO 80026 303-410-5100 410-5300
Web: www.abacus-direct.com
Abt Assoc Inc 55 Wheeler St .... Cambridge MA 02138 617-492-7100 492-5219
Web: www.abtassociates.com
ACNielsen BASES 50 W Rivercenter Blvd Suite 600 .... Covington KY 41011 859-905-4000 905-5000
TF: 800-544-7373 ■ *Web:* www.bases.com
ACNielsen Corp 770 Broadway .... New York NY 10003 646-654-5000 654-5002
Web: acnielsen.com
Arbitron Inc 9705 Patuxent Woods Dr .... Columbia MD 21046 410-312-8000 312-8607*
NYSE: ARB ■ **Fax:* Hum Res ■ *TF:* 800-272-4876 ■ *Web:* www.arbitron.com
B/R/S Group Inc 901 'E' St Suite 300 .... San Rafael CA 94901 415-526-2040 526-2075
TF: 800-552-0810 ■ *Web:* www.brsgroup.com
Burke Inc 805 Central Ave 5th Fl .... Cincinnati OH 45202 513-241-5663 684-7500
Web: www.burke.com
C & R Research Services Inc 500 N Michigan Ave Suite 1200 ...... Chicago IL 60611 312-828-9200 527-3113
TF: 800-621-5022 ■ *Web:* www.cr-research.com
Cheskin Research 255 Shoreline Dr Suite 350 .... Redwood City CA 94065 650-802-2100 593-1125
TF: 888-969-3284 ■ *Web:* www.cheskin.com
comScore Inc 11465 Sunset Hills Rd Suite 200 .... Reston VA 20190 703-438-2000 438-2051
Web: www.comscore.com
Data Development Worldwide 120 5th Ave 9th Fl .... New York NY 10011 212-633-1100 633-6499
Web: www.datadw.com
Directions Research Inc 401 E Court St Suite 200 .... Cincinnati OH 45202 513-651-2990 651-2998
Web: www.directionsrsch.com
Forrester Research Inc 400 Technology Sq .... Cambridge MA 02139 617-497-7090 613-5000
NASDAQ: FORR ■ *TF:* 866-367-7378 ■ *Web:* www.forrester.com
Gallup Organization 901 F St NW .... Washington DC 20004 202-715-3030 715-3041
TF: 877-242-5587 ■ *Web:* www.gallup.com
Gartner Inc 56 Top Gallant Rd .... Stamford CT 06904 203-316-1111 316-6300
NYSE: IT ■ *TF:* 800-328-2776 ■ *Web:* www.gartner.com

Company	City	State	Zip	Phone	Fax
GFK Custom Research Inc 8401 Golden Valley Rd PO Box 27900	Minneapolis	MN	55427	763-542-0800	542-0864
TF: 800-328-6784					
Greenfield Consulting Group 274 Riverside Ave 4th Fl	Westport	CT	06880	203-221-0411	221-0791
TF: 888-816-9901 ■ *Web:* www.greenfieldgroup.com					
Greenfield Online Inc 21 River Rd Suite 2000	Wilton	CT	06897	203-834-8585	834-8686
NASDAQ: SRVY ■ *TF:* 888-291-9997 ■ *Web:* www.greenfield.com					
Harris Interactive Inc 60 Corporate Woods	Rochester	NY	14623	585-272-8400	272-7258
NASDAQ: HPOL ■ *TF:* 800-866-7655 ■ *Web:* www.harrisinteractive.com					
IDC (International Data Corp) 5 Speen St	Framingham	MA	01701	508-872-8200	935-4015
TF: 800-343-4935 ■ *Web:* www.idcresearch.com					
Ideas International Inc 800 Westchester Ave Suite S620	Rye Brook	NY	10573	914-937-4302	937-2485
TF: 800-253-1799 ■ *Web:* www.ideasinternational.com					
IMS Health Inc 901 Main Ave Suite 612	Norwalk	CT	06851	203-845-5200	845-5299
NYSE: RX ■ *Web:* www.imshealth.com					
In-Stat 225 Wyman St	Waltham	MA	02451	781-734-8000	
TF: 800-283-3666 ■ *Web:* www.instat.com					
Information Resources Inc 150 N Clinton St	Chicago	IL	60661	312-726-1221	
Web: us.infores.com					
International Communications Research 53 W Baltimore Pike	Media	PA	19063	484-840-4300	840-4599
TF Cust Svc: 800-633-1986 ■ *Web:* www.icrsurvey.com					
International Data Corp (IDC) 5 Speen St	Framingham	MA	01701	508-872-8200	935-4015
TF: 800-343-4935 ■ *Web:* www.idcresearch.com					
Ipsos-ASI Inc 301 Merritt 7 Corporate Pk	Norwalk	CT	06851	203-840-3400	840-3490
Web: www.ipsos-asi.com					
JD Power & Assoc 2625 Townsgate Rd Suite 100	West Lake Village	CA	91361	805-418-8000	418-8900
TF: 800-274-5372 ■ *Web:* www.jdpower.com					
Kantar Group 501 Kings Hwy E 4th Fl	Fairfield	CT	06825	203-330-5200	330-5201
Web: www.kantargroup.com					
Knowledge Networks 1350 Willow Rd Suite 102	Menlo Park	CA	94025	650-289-2000	289-2001
Web: www.knowledgenetworks.com					
Lieberman Research 98 Cutter Mill Rd Suite 359-S	Great Neck	NY	11021	516-829-8880	829-9419
Web: www.liebermanresearch.com					
Macro International Inc 11785 Beltsville Dr Suite 300	Calverton	MD	20705	301-572-0200	572-0999
Web: www.macrointernational.com/					
M/A/R/C Group 1660 Westridge Cir	Irving	TX	75038	972-983-0400	983-0404
TF: 800-527-2680 ■ *Web:* www.marcresearch.com					
Maritz Inc 1375 N Highway Dr	Fenton	MO	63099	636-827-4000	827-4336*
**Fax:* Hum Res ■ *Web:* www.maritz.com					
Maritz Research Inc 1355 N Highway Dr	Fenton	MO	63099	636-827-4000	827-2487
Web: www.maritzresearch.com					
Market Decisions Inc 75 Washington Ave Suite 206	Portland	ME	04101	207-767-6440	767-8158
TF: 800-293-1538 ■ *Web:* www.marketdecisions.com					
Market Strategies Inc 20255 Victor Pkwy Suite 400	Livonia	MI	48152	734-542-7600	542-7620
Web: www.marketstrategies.com					
Marketing Analysts Inc 176 Croghan Spur Rd Suite 100	Charleston	SC	29407	843-797-8900	797-1075
TF: 800-513-4247 ■ *Web:* www.mairesearch.com					
Marketing & Planning Systems 201 Jones Rd	Waltham	MA	02451	781-642-6277	642-9508
TF: 800-696-6605 ■ *Web:* www.mapsnet.com					
Marketing Research Services Inc 720 E Pete Rose Way Suite 200	Cincinnati	OH	45202	513-579-1555	562-8819
TF: 800-729-6774 ■ *Web:* www.mrsi.com					
Marketing Workshop Inc 3725 Da Vinci Ct Suite 200	Norcross	GA	30092	770-449-6767	449-6739
TF: 800-284-7707 ■ *Web:* www.mwshop.com					
MarketVision Research Inc 10300 Alliance Rd Suite 200	Cincinnati	OH	45242	513-791-3100	794-3500
TF: 800-232-4250 ■ *Web:* www.marketvisionresearch.com					
Millward Brown Group 4950 Yonge St Suite 600	North York	ON	M2N6K1	416-221-9200	221-7681
Web: www.millwardbrown.com					
Millward Brown IntelliQuest 1250 Capital of Texas Hwy Bldg 1 Suite 600	Austin	TX	78746	512-329-0808	329-0888
TF: 800-283-9608 ■ *Web:* www.millwardbrown.com					
MORPACE International Inc 31700 Middlebelt Rd Suite 200	Farmington Hills	MI	48334	248-737-5300	737-5326
TF: 800-878-7223 ■ *Web:* www.morpace.com					
National Research Corp 1245 Q St	Lincoln	NE	68508	402-475-2525	475-9061
NASDAQ: NRCI ■ *Web:* www.nationalresearch.com					
NetRatings Inc 890 Hillview Ct Suite 300	Milpitas	CA	95035	408-941-2900	942-9114
NASDAQ: NTRT ■ *TF:* 888-634-1222 ■ *Web:* www.netratings.com					
Nielsen Co 770 Broadway	New York	NY	10003	646-654-5000	654-5001
Nielsen Co 1 N Lexington Ave 14th Fl	White Plains	NY	10601	914-684-5500	684-5680
Nielsen Media Research Inc 770 Broadway	New York	NY	10003	646-654-8300	654-8990
Web: www.nielsenmedia.com					
NPD Group Inc 900 W Shore Rd	Port Washington	NY	11050	516-625-0700	625-2444
Web: www.npd.com					
Opinion Research Corp 600 College Rd E 4th Fl	Princeton	NJ	08540	609-452-5400	419-1892
NASDAQ: ORCI ■ *TF:* 800-444-4672 ■ *Web:* www.opinionresearch.com					
Power JD & Assoc 2625 Townsgate Rd Suite 100	West Lake Village	CA	91361	805-418-8000	418-8900
TF: 800-274-5372 ■ *Web:* www.jdpower.com					
Pretesting Co Inc 38 Franklin St	Tenafly	NJ	07670	201-569-4800	569-4842
Web: www.pretesting.com					
RDA Group 450 Enterprise Ct	Bloomfield Hills	MI	48302	248-332-5000	332-4168
TF: 800-669-7324 ■ *Web:* www.rdagroup.com					
Reis Inc 530 5th Ave 5th Fl	New York	NY	10036	212-921-1122	921-2533
TF: 800-366-7347 ■ *Web:* www.reis.com					
Research International USA 222 Merchandise Mart Plaza Suite 275	Chicago	IL	60654	312-787-4060	787-4156
Web: www.riusa.com					
Savitz Research Solutions 13747 Montfort Dr Suite 330	Dallas	TX	75240	972-386-4050	661-3198
Web: www.savitzresearch.com					
Schulman Ronca & Bucuvalas Inc 275 7th Ave Suite 2700	New York	NY	10001	212-779-7700	779-7785
Web: www.srbi.com					
Simmons Market Research Bureau Inc 1501 FAU Research Park Blvd Suite 100	Deerfield Beach	FL	33441	954-427-4104	427-3760
Web: www.smrb.com					
Synovate Inc 222 S Riverside Plaza	Chicago	IL	60606	312-526-4000	526-4099
TF: 800-745-4267 ■ *Web:* www.synovate.com					
TeleSight Inc 820 N Franklin St	Chicago	IL	60610	312-640-2500	944-7872
TF: 800-608-3651 ■ *Web:* www.telesight.com					
TNS Intersearch 410 Horsham Rd	Horsham	PA	19044	215-442-9000	442-9040
TF: 800-350-8356 ■ *Web:* www.tns-global.com					
Verispan LLC 650 Dresher Rd	Horsham	PA	19044	215-347-6800	347-6970
Web: www.verispan.com					
Walker Information Inc 301 Pennsylvania Pkwy	Indianapolis	IN	46280	317-843-3939	843-8904
TF: 800-334-3939 ■ *Web:* www.walkerinfo.com					
Westat Inc 1650 Research Blvd	Rockville	MD	20850	301-251-1500	294-2040
TF: 800-937-8281 ■ *Web:* www.westat.com					
Yankelovich Inc 400 Meadowmont Village Cir Suite 431	Chapel Hill	NC	27517	919-932-8858	932-8829
TF: 800-926-5356 ■ *Web:* www.yankelovich.com					

470 MARKING DEVICES

Company	City	State	Zip	Phone	Fax
American Marking Systems Inc 1015 Paulison Ave PO Box 1677	Clifton	NJ	07015	973-478-5600	478-0039
TF: 800-782-6766 ■ *Web:* www.ams-stamps.com					
Automark Marking Systems 13475 Lakefront Dr	Earth City	MO	63045	314-739-0430	739-1483
TF: 888-777-2303 ■ *Web:* www.automark.com					
Cable Markers Co Inc 22600-F Lambert St Suite 1204	Lake Forest	CA	92630	949-699-1636	699-1642
TF: 800-746-7655 ■ *Web:* www.cablemarkers.com					
Carco Inc 10333 Shoemaker PO Box 13859	Detroit	MI	48213	313-925-9000	925-9602
Web: www.carcousa.com					
CH Hanson Co 2000 N Aurora Rd	Naperville	IL	60563	630-848-2000	848-2515
TF: 800-827-3398 ■ *Web:* www.chhanson.com					
Cosco Industries Inc 7220 W Wilson Ave	Harwood Heights	IL	60706	708-457-2410	323-0275*
**Fax Area Code:* 800 ■ *TF:* 800-323-0253 ■ *Web:* www.cosco2000.com					
DM Stamps & Specialties Inc 1609 N Riverfront Dr	Mankato	MN	56001	507-387-4444	658-7171*
**Fax Area Code:* 800 ■ *Web:* www.dmpolystamps.com					
Excelsior Marking Products 888 W Waterloo Rd	Akron	OH	44314	330-745-2300	745-2333
TF: 800-433-3615 ■ *Web:* www.excelsiormarking.com					
GB Products International Corp 5650 Imhoff Dr Suite B	Concord	CA	94520	925-825-3040	798-1468
TF: 800-650-0341 ■ *Web:* www.gbproductsintl.com					
Hampton Technologies LLC 19 Industrial Blvd	Medford	NY	11763	631-924-1335	924-1669
TF: 800-229-1019 ■ *Web:* www.hamptontech.net					
Hitt Marking Devices Inc 3231 W MacArthur Blvd	Santa Ana	CA	92704	714-979-1405	979-1407
TF: 800-969-6699 ■ *Web:* www.hittmarking.com					
Huntington Park Rubber Stamp 2761 E Slauson Ave	Huntington Park	CA	90255	323-582-6461	582-8046
TF: 800-882-0129 ■ *Web:* www.hprubberstamp.com					
Industrial Marking Products 1415 Grovenburg Rd	Holt	MI	48842	517-699-2160	699-1505
Web: www.industrialmarking.com					
Jackson Marking Products Co 9105 N Rainbow Ln	Mount Vernon	IL	62864	618-242-1334	242-7732
TF: 800-782-6722 ■ *Web:* www.rubber-stamp.com					
JP Nissen Co 2544 Fairhill Ave PO Box 339	Glenside	PA	19038	215-886-2025	886-0707
Web: www.nissenmarkers.com					
La-Co/Markal Co 1201 Pratt Blvd	Elk Grove Village	IL	60007	847-956-7600	448-5436*
**Fax Area Code:* 800 ■ *TF:* 800-621-4025 ■ *Web:* www.laco.com					
M & R Marking Systems Inc 100 Springfield Ave	Piscataway	NJ	08855	732-562-9500	272-8550*
**Fax Area Code:* 800 ■ *Web:* www.mrmarking.com					
Mark Master Inc 11111 N 46th St	Tampa	FL	33617	813-988-6000	985-6860
TF: 800-441-6275 ■ *Web:* www.mmstamp.com					
Markem Corp 150 Congress St PO Box 2100	Keene	NH	03431	603-352-1130	357-5871
TF: 800-462-7536 ■ *Web:* www.markem.com					
Matthews International Corp Marking Products Div 6515 Penn Ave	Pittsburgh	PA	15206	412-665-2500	665-2550
TF: 800-775-7775 ■ *Web:* www.matthewsmarking.com					
MECCO Marking & Traceability Rochester Rd PO Box 307	Ingomar	PA	15127	412-369-9199	366-3048
TF: 888-369-9199 ■ *Web:* www.meccomark.com					
Menke Marking Devices 13253 Alondra Blvd PO Box 2986	Santa Fe Springs	CA	90670	562-921-1380	921-1184
TF: 800-231-6023 ■ *Web:* www.menkemarking.com					
Meyercord Revenue 475 Village Dr	Carol Stream	IL	60188	630-682-6200	682-6269
TF: 800-223-6923 ■ *Web:* www.meyercord.com					
New Method Steel Stamps Inc 31313 Kendall Ave	Fraser	MI	48026	586-293-0200	908-6677*
**Fax Area Code:* 888 ■ *TF:* 888-318-6677 ■ *Web:* www.newmethod.com					
Norwood Marking Systems 2538 Wisconsin Ave	Downers Grove	IL	60515	630-968-0646	968-7672
TF: 800-626-3464 ■ *Web:* www.itw-norwood.com					
Paterson Stamp Works 1015 Paulison Ave PO Box 1677	Clifton	NJ	07015	973-478-5600	478-0039
TF: 800-782-6766					
Saint Paul Stamp Works Inc 87 Empire Dr	Saint Paul	MN	55103	651-222-2100	228-1314
Web: www.stpaulstamp.com					
Samoss Group Ltd Moss Samuel H Div 213 W 35th St 13th Fl	New York	NY	10001	212-239-6677	239-0041
Web: www.samuelhmoss.com					
Schwaab Inc 11415 W Burleigh St	Milwaukee	WI	53222	414-771-4150	771-7165
TF: 800-935-9877 ■ *Web:* www.schwaab.com					
Schwerdtle Stamp Co 166 Elm St	Bridgeport	CT	06604	203-330-2750	330-2760
TF: 800-535-0004 ■ *Web:* www.schwerdtle.com					
Signet Marking Devices 3121 Red Hill Ave	Costa Mesa	CA	92626	714-549-0341	549-0972
TF: 800-421-5150 ■ *Web:* www.signetmarking.com					
Stamp-Rite Inc 154 S Larch St	Lansing	MI	48912	517-487-5071	487-6211
TF: 800-328-1988 ■ *Web:* www.stamprite.com					
Tacoma Rubber Stamp Co 919 Market St	Tacoma	WA	98402	253-383-5433	383-0649
TF: 800-544-7281 ■ *Web:* www.tacomarubberstamp.com					
Telesis Technologies Inc 740 Welch Rd	Commerce Township	MI	48390	248-624-4249	624-4431
TF Sales: 800-654-5696 ■ *Web:* www.telesis.com					
Volk Corp 23936 Industrial Park Dr	Farmington Hills	MI	48335	248-477-6700	478-6884
TF Cust Svc: 800-521-6799 ■ *Web:* www.volkcorp.com					
Wendell's Inc 6601 Bunker Lake Blvd NW	Ramsey	MN	55303	763-576-8200	576-0995
TF: 800-936-3355 ■ *Web:* www.wendellsinc.com					

471 MASS TRANSPORTATION (LOCAL & SUBURBAN)

SEE ALSO Bus Services - Intercity & Rural p. 1400

Company	City	State	Zip	Phone	Fax
AC Transit 1600 Franklin St	Oakland	CA	94612	510-891-4777	891-4818*
**Fax:* Cust Svc ■ *Web:* www.actransit.org					
Alameda-Contra Costa Transit District 1600 Franklin St	Oakland	CA	94612	510-891-4777	891-4818*
**Fax:* Cust Svc ■ *Web:* www.actransit.org					
Alaska Marine Highway System	Juneau	AK	99801	907-465-3941	465-2476
TF: 800-642-0066 ■ *Web:* www.dot.state.ak.us/amhs					
Altamont Commuter Express (ACE) 949 E Channel St	Stockton	CA	95202	800-411-7245	944-6273*
**Fax Area Code:* 209 ■ *TF:* 800-411-7245 ■ *Web:* www.acerail.com					
Ann Arbor Transportation Authority 2700 S Industrial Hwy	Ann Arbor	MI	48104	734-973-6500	973-6338
Web: www.theride.org					
Bay Area Rapid Transit District 300 Lakeside Dr	Oakland	CA	94612	510-464-6000	464-7175*
**Fax:* Mktg ■ *Web:* www.bart.gov					
BC Transit PO Box 610	Victoria	BC	V8W2P3	250-385-2551	995-5639
Web: www.bctransit.com					
Bi-State Development Agency 707 N 1st St	Saint Louis	MO	63102	314-982-1400	923-3019*
**Fax:* Cust Svc ■ *Web:* www.metrostlouis.org					
Bus The 811 Middle St	Honolulu	HI	96819	808-848-4500	848-4419
Web: www.thebus.org					
Cape Cod Regional Transit Authority (CCRTA) PO Box 1988	Hyannis	MA	02601	508-775-8504	775-8513
TF: 800-352-7155 ■ *Web:* www.capecodtransit.org					
Capital District Transportation Authority (CDTA) 110 Watervliet Ave	Albany	NY	12206	518-482-8822	446-0675
Web: www.cdta.org					
Capital Metropolitan Transportation Authority 2910 E 5th St	Austin	TX	78702	512-389-7400	389-1283
Web: www.capmetro.org					
Catalina Express Berth 95	San Pedro	CA	90731	310-519-1212	548-8425
TF Resv: 800-481-3470 ■ *Web:* www.catalinaexpress.com					
Central New York Regional Transportation Authority 200 Cortland Ave	Syracuse	NY	13205	315-442-3400	442-3337
Web: www.centro.org					
Central Ohio Transit Authority (COTA) 1600 McKinley Ave	Columbus	OH	43222	614-228-1776	275-5933
Web: www.cota.com					
Central Puget Sound Regional Transit Authority 401 S Jackson St	Seattle	WA	98104	206-398-5000	689-4918*
**Fax:* Hum Res ■ *Web:* www.soundtransit.org					

	City	State	ZIP	Phone	Fax
Champaign-Urbana Mass Transit District 1101 E University Ave *Web:* www.cumtd.com	Urbana	IL	61802	217-384-8188	384-8215
Charleston Area Regional Transportation Authority (CARTA) 36 John St *Web:* www.ridecarta.com	Charleston	SC	29403	843-724-7420	720-1985
Chicago Transit Authority (CTA) PO Box 3555 **Fax:* Cust Svc ■ *Web:* www.transitchicago.com	Chicago	IL	60654	312-664-7200	432-7185*
Citizens Area Transit 600 S Grand Central Pkwy Suite 350 *Web:* www.rtcsouthernnevada.com	Las Vegas	NV	89106	702-455-7433	676-1518
Connecticut Transit 100 Leibert Rd *Web:* www.cttransit.com	Hartford	CT	06141	860-522-8101	247-1810
CTA (Chicago Transit Authority) PO Box 3555 **Fax:* Cust Svc ■ *Web:* www.transitchicago.com	Chicago	IL	60654	312-664-7200	432-7185*
Dallas Area Rapid Transit Authority (DART) PO Box 660163 *TF:* 888-557-6669 ■ *Web:* www.dart.org	Dallas	TX	75266	214-749-3278	749-3661
Delaware Transit Corp 119 Lower Beach St Suite 100 *TF:* 800-652-3278 ■ *Web:* www.dartfirststate.com	Wilmington	DE	19805	302-576-6000	577-6066
Erie Metropolitan Transit Authority (EMTA) 127 E 14th St *Web:* www.emtaerie.com	Erie	PA	16503	814-459-4287	456-9032
Escambia County Area Transit (ECAT) 1515 W Fairfield Dr *Web:* www.goecat.com	Pensacola	FL	32501	850-595-3228	595-3222
Fort Wayne Public Transportation Corp 801 Leesburg Rd *Web:* www.fwcitilink.com	Fort Wayne	IN	46808	260-432-4546	436-7729
Fresno Area Express 2223 G St *Web:* www.fresno.gov/fax	Fresno	CA	93706	559-621-7433	488-1065
GO Transit 20 Bay St Suite 600 *Web:* www.gotransit.com	Toronto	ON	M5J2W3	416-869-3200	869-3525
Gold Coast Transit (GCT) 301 E 3rd St *Web:* www.goldcoasttransit.org	Oxnard	CA	93030	805-487-4222	487-0925
Golden Empire Transit District 1830 Golden State Ave *Web:* www.getbus.org	Bakersfield	CA	93301	661-324-9874	869-6394
Greater Cleveland Regional Transit Authority (RTA) 1240 W 6th St **Fax:* Hum Res ■ *Web:* www.gcrta.org	Cleveland	OH	44113	216-566-5100	781-4483*
Greater Peoria Mass Transit District 2105 NE Jefferson St *Web:* www.gptransit.org	Peoria	IL	61603	309-676-4040	676-8373
Greater Portland Transit District 114 Valley St *Web:* www.transportme.org	Portland	ME	04102	207-774-0351	774-6241
Greater Vancouver Transportation Authority 4720 Kingsway Suite 1600 *Web:* www.translink.bc.ca	Burnaby	BC	V5H4N2	604-453-4500	453-4626
GRTC Inc 101 S Davis Ave *Web:* www.ridegrtc.com	Richmond	VA	23220	804-358-3871	342-1933
Honolulu Dept of Transportation Services 650 S King St 3rd Fl *Web:* www.co.honolulu.hi.us/dts	Honolulu	HI	96813	808-523-4125	523-4730
Inter-Urban Transit Partnership 300 Ellsworth St SW *Web:* www.ridetherapid.org	Grand Rapids	MI	49503	616-776-1100	456-1941
King County Dept of Transportation 201 S Jackson St *Web:* transit.metrokc.gov	Seattle	WA	98104	206-684-1481	689-3187
Mass Transit Administration of Maryland (MTA) 6 Saint Paul St *Web:* www.mtamaryland.com	Baltimore	MD	21202	410-539-5000	333-3279
Massachusetts Bay Transportation Authority (MBTA) 10 Park Plaza **Fax:* Mktg ■ *Web:* www.mbta.com	Boston	MA	02116	617-222-5000	222-3340*
Memphis Area Transit Authority (MATA) 1370 Levee Rd *Web:* www.matatransit.com	Memphis	TN	38108	901-722-7100	722-7123
Metra 547 W Jackson Blvd **Fax:* Mktg ■ *Web:* www.metrarail.com	Chicago	IL	60661	312-322-6777	322-6747*
Metro 707 N 1st St **Fax:* Cust Svc ■ *Web:* www.metrostlouis.org	Saint Louis	MO	63102	314-982-1400	923-3019*
Metro 201 S Jackson St *Web:* transit.metrokc.gov	Seattle	WA	98104	206-684-1481	689-3187
Metro Transit 560 6th Ave N **Fax:* Mktg ■ *Web:* www.metrotransit.org	Minneapolis	MN	55411	612-349-7332	349-7675*
Metro Transit 200 Ilsley Ave *Web:* www.halifax.ca/metrotransit	Dartmouth	NS	B3B1V1	902-490-4000	490-6688
Metro Transit 300 SW 7th St *Web:* www.okladot.state.ok.us/transit/okcg.htm	Oklahoma City	OK	73109	405-235-7433	297-2111
Metrolink 700 S Flower St Suite 2600 *TF:* 800-371-5465 ■ *Web:* www.metrolinktrains.com	Los Angeles	CA	90017	213-452-0200	452-0429
Metropolitan Atlanta Rapid Transit Authority (MARTA) 2424 Piedmont Rd NE *Web:* www.itsmarta.com	Atlanta	GA	30324	404-848-5000	
Metropolitan Transit Authority of Harris County 1900 Maine *Web:* www.hou-metro.harris.tx.us	Houston	TX	77002	713-739-4000	739-3769
Metropolitan Transit Commission 560 6th Ave N *Web:* www.metrotransit.org	Minneapolis	MN	55411	612-349-7400	349-7675
Metropolitan Transportation Authority 347 Madison Ave **Fax:* Mktg ■ *Web:* www.mta.nyc.ny.us	New York	NY	10017	212-878-7000	878-0150*
Metropolitan Transportation Authority (MTA) 1 Gateway Plaza *TF:* 800-266-6883 ■ *Web:* www.mta.net	Los Angeles	CA	90012	213-922-2000	922-3929
Miami-Dade Transit (MDTA) 111 NW 1st St Suite 910 *Web:* www.co.miami-dade.fl.us/transit	Miami	FL	33128	305-375-5675	375-4605
Milwaukee County Transit System 1942 N 17th St **Fax:* Hum Res ■ *Web:* www.ridemcts.com	Milwaukee	WI	53205	414-344-4550	344-2876*
Monterey-Salinas Transit 1 Ryan Ranch Rd *Web:* www.mst.org	Monterey	CA	93940	831-899-2555	899-3805
MTA (Metropolitan Transportation Authority) 1 Gateway Plaza *TF:* 800-266-6883 ■ *Web:* www.mta.net	Los Angeles	CA	90012	213-922-2000	922-3929
Muni 401 Van Ness Ave *Web:* www.sfmuni.com	San Francisco	CA	94102	415-554-4166	554-4174
MV Transportation Inc 360 Campus Ln Suite 201 *Web:* www.mvtransit.com	Fairfield	CA	94534	707-863-8980	863-8944
New Jersey Transit Corp 1 Penn Plaza E **Fax:* Cust Svc ■ *TF Cust Svc:* 800-772-3606 ■ *Web:* www.njtransit.com	Newark	NJ	07105	973-491-7000	491-7567*
New Orleans Regional Transit Authority (RTA) 2817 Canal St *Web:* www.norta.com	New Orleans	LA	70118	504-827-8300	248-3637
New York City Transit Authority 370 Jay St *Web:* www.mta.nyc.ny.us/nyct/	Brooklyn	NY	11201	718-330-3000	243-3283
Niagara Frontier Transit Metro System Inc 181 Ellicott St Suite 1 *Web:* www.nfta.com/metro	Buffalo	NY	14202	716-855-7211	855-7657
North County Transit District (NCTD) 810 Mission Rd *Web:* www.gonctd.com	Oceanside	CA	92054	760-967-2828	722-1490
Northeast Illinois Regional Commuter Railroad Corp 547 W Jackson Blvd **Fax:* Mktg ■ *Web:* www.metrarail.com	Chicago	IL	60661	312-322-6777	322-6747*
Northern Indiana Commuter Transportation District 33 E US Hwy 12 *TF:* 800-356-2079 ■ *Web:* www.nictd.com	Chesterton	IN	46304	219-926-5744	929-4438
Norwalk Transit District 275 Wilson Ave *Web:* www.norwalktransit.com	Norwalk	CT	06854	203-852-0000	853-6761
Oahu Transit Services 811 Middle St *Web:* www.thebus.org	Honolulu	HI	96819	808-848-4500	848-4419
OC Transpo 1500 St Laurent Blvd *Web:* www.octranspo.com	Ottawa	ON	K1G0Z8	613-741-6440	230-6543
Orange County Transportation Authority 550 S Main St PO Box 14184 *Web:* www.octa.net	Orange	CA	92863	714-560-6282	560-5899
Pace Suburban Bus 550 W Algonquin Rd **Fax:* Cust Svc ■ *Web:* www.pacebus.com	Arlington Heights	IL	60005	847-364-8130	364-7236*
Pierce Transit 3701 96th St SW PO Box 99070 *TF:* 800-562-8109 ■ *Web:* www.ptbus.pierce.wa.us	Lakewood	WA	98499	253-581-8000	581-8075
Port Authority of Allegheny County 345 6th Ave 3rd Fl **Fax:* Cust Svc ■ *Web:* www.portauthority.org	Pittsburgh	PA	15222	412-566-5500	566-5406*
rabbittransit 1230 Roosevelt Ave *TF:* 800-632-9063 ■ *Web:* www.rabbittransit.org	York	PA	17404	717-846-5562	848-4853
Regional Transit Service Inc 1372 E Main St *Web:* www.rgrta.org	Rochester	NY	14609	585-654-0200	654-0293
Regional Transit System (RTS) 100 SE 10th Ave *Web:* www.go-rts.com	Gainesville	FL	32601	352-334-2600	334-2607
Regional Transportation Authority 175 W Jackson Blvd Suite 1550 *Web:* www.rtachicago.com	Chicago	IL	60604	312-913-3200	913-3118
Regional Transportation Commission of Southern Nevada 600 S Grand Central Pkwy Suite 350 *Web:* www.rtcsouthernnevada.com	Las Vegas	NV	89106	702-455-7433	676-1518
Regional Transportation District (RTD) 1600 Blake St *TF:* 800-877-7433 ■ *Web:* www.rtd-denver.com	Denver	CO	80202	303-628-9000	299-2015
Rhode Island Public Transit Authority 265 Melrose St *Web:* www.ripta.com	Providence	RI	02907	401-781-9400	784-9595
Riverside Transit Agency (RTA) 1825 3rd St PO Box 59968 *TF:* 800-800-7821 ■ *Web:* www.rrta.com	Riverside	CA	92517	951-682-1234	684-1007
RTA (Greater Cleveland Regional Transit Authority) 1240 W 6th St **Fax:* Hum Res ■ *Web:* www.gcrta.org	Cleveland	OH	44113	216-566-5100	781-4483*
RTA (New Orleans Regional Transit Authority) 2817 Canal St *Web:* www.norta.com	New Orleans	LA	70118	504-827-8300	248-3637
RTS (Regional Transit System) 100 SE 10th Ave *Web:* www.go-rts.com	Gainesville	FL	32601	352-334-2600	334-2607
Sacramento Regional Transit District 1400 29th St *Web:* www.sacrt.com	Sacramento	CA	95816	916-321-2800	444-2156
San Diego Metropolitan Transit Development Board 1255 Imperial Ave Suite 1000 *Web:* www.sdcommute.com	San Diego	CA	92101	619-231-1466	234-3407
San Diego Transit Corp 100 16th St *Web:* www.sdcommute.com	San Diego	CA	92101	619-238-0100	696-8159
San Francisco Municipal Railway 401 Van Ness Ave *Web:* www.sfmuni.com	San Francisco	CA	94102	415-554-4166	554-4174
San Joaquin Regional Transit District 1533 E Lindsay St *Web:* www.sanjoaquinrtd.com	Stockton	CA	95205	209-948-5566	525-6507
San Mateo County Transit District 1250 San Carlos Ave *TF:* 800-660-4287 ■ *Web:* www.caltrain.com	San Carlos	CA	94070	650-508-6200	508-6443
Santa Barbara Metropolitan Transit District 550 Olive St *Web:* www.sbmtd.gov	Santa Barbara	CA	93101	805-963-3364	962-4794
Santa Clara Valley Transportation Authority (VTA) 3331 N 1st St **Fax:* PR ■ *TF:* 800-894-9908 ■ *Web:* www.vta.org	San Jose	CA	95134	408-321-5555	955-0893*
SMART (Suburban Mobility Authority for Regional Transportation) 660 Woodward Ave First National Bldg **Fax Area Code:* 313 ■ **Fax:* Hum Res ■ *Web:* www.smartbus.org	Detroit	MI	48226	866-962-5515	223-2370*
Societe de Transport de Montreal (STM) 800 rue Gauchetiere O CP 2000 *Web:* www.stcum.qc.ca	Montreal	QC	H5A1K6	514-288-6287	280-5888
Sonoma County Transit 355 W Robles Ave *TF:* 800-345-7433 ■ *Web:* www.sctransit.com	Santa Rosa	CA	95407	707-585-7516	585-7713
Sound Transit 401 S Jackson St **Fax:* Hum Res ■ *Web:* www.soundtransit.org	Seattle	WA	98104	206-398-5000	689-4918*
Southeastern Pennsylvania Transportation Authority (SEPTA) 1234 Market St *Web:* www.septa.org	Philadelphia	PA	19107	215-580-4000	
Southern California Regional Rail Authority 700 S Flower St Suite 2600 *TF:* 800-371-5465 ■ *Web:* www.metrolinktrains.com	Los Angeles	CA	90017	213-452-0200	452-0429
Springfield Area Transit Co 2840 Main St	Springfield	MA	01107	413-732-2161	736-6345
Steamship Authority 1 Railroad Ave *Web:* www.steamshipauthority.com	Woods Hole	MA	02543	508-548-5011	548-8410
Suburban Mobility Authority for Regional Transportation (SMART) 660 Woodward Ave First National Bldg **Fax Area Code:* 313 ■ **Fax:* Hum Res ■ *Web:* www.smartbus.org	Detroit	MI	48226	866-962-5515	223-2370*
Toronto Transit Commission 1900 Yonge St **Fax:* PR ■ *Web:* www.ttc.ca	Toronto	ON	M4S1Z2	416-393-4000	338-0128*
Transit Authority of River City (TARC) 1000 W Broadway **Fax:* Cust Svc ■ *Web:* www.ridetarc.com	Louisville	KY	40203	502-585-1234	213-3243*
TransLink 4720 Kingsway Suite 1600 *Web:* www.translink.bc.ca	Burnaby	BC	V5H4N2	604-453-4500	453-4626
Tri-County Commuter Rail Authority 800 NW 33rd St Suite 100 *Web:* www.tri-rail.com	Pompano Beach	FL	33064	954-942-7245	788-7878
Tri-County Metropolitan Transportation District of Oregon 4012 SE 17th Ave **Fax:* Mktg ■ *Web:* www.trimet.org	Portland	OR	97202	503-962-3000	962-6469*
Triangle Transit Authority PO Box 13787 *Web:* www.ridetta.org	Research Triangle Park	NC	27709	919-549-9999	485-7441
Utah Transit Authority 3600 South 700 W PO Box 30810 **Fax:* Cust Svc ■ *TF:* 800-743-3882 ■ *Web:* www.utabus.com	Salt Lake City	UT	84130	801-262-5626	287-4522*
VIA Metropolitan Transit 800 W Myrtle St **Fax:* Cust Svc ■ *TF:* 866-362-4200 ■ *Web:* www.viainfo.net	San Antonio	TX	78212	210-362-2000	362-2563*
Virginia Railway Express (VRE) 1500 King St Suite 202 *TF:* 800-743-3873 ■ *Web:* www.vre.org	Alexandria	VA	22314	703-684-1001	684-1313
VPSI Inc 1220 Rankin St *Web:* www.vpsiinc.com	Troy	MI	48083	248-597-3500	597-3501
Washington Metropolitan Area Transit Authority 600 5th St NW *Web:* www.wmata.com	Washington	DC	20001	202-637-7000	962-1420
Westchester County Dept of Transportation 100 E 1st St *Web:* www.co.westchester.ny.us/transportation	Mount Vernon	NY	10550	914-813-7777	813-7735
Worcester Regional Transit Authority 287 Grove St **Fax:* Cust Svc ■ *Web:* www.therta.com	Worcester	MA	01605	508-791-9782	752-3153*
York County Transportation Authority 1230 Roosevelt Ave *TF:* 800-632-9063 ■ *Web:* www.rabbittransit.org	York	PA	17404	717-846-5562	848-4853

472 MATCHES & MATCHBOOKS

Company	City	State	ZIP	Phone	Fax
Atlantis Match Co 524 Center Rd *Web:* www.matchbooks.com	Frankfort	IL	60423	815-464-2187	469-7089
Atlas Match LLC 1801 S Airport Cir *TF:* 800-628-2426 ■ *Web:* www.atlasmatch.com	Euless	TX	76040	817-267-1500	354-7478
DD Bean & Sons Co 207 Peterborough St **Fax:* Sales ■ *TF:* 800-326-8311 ■ *Web:* www.ddbean.com	Jaffrey	NH	03452	603-532-8311	532-6001*
Diamond Brands Div Jarden Home Brands 345 S High St Suite 201 *TF Cust Svc:* 800-392-2575 ■ *Web:* www.diamondbrands.com	Muncie	IN	47305	765-281-5000	281-5450
Jarden Home Brands Diamond Brands Div 345 S High St Suite 201 *TF Cust Svc:* 800-392-2575 ■ *Web:* www.diamondbrands.com	Muncie	IN	47305	765-281-5000	281-5450
Maryland Match Corp 605 Alluvion St *TF:* 800-423-0013 ■ *Web:* www.marylandmatch.com	Baltimore	MD	21230	410-752-8164	752-3441
Universal Creative Concepts Corp 13700 State Rd *Web:* www.uccadv.com	North Royalton	OH	44133	440-230-1366	230-1919

473 MATERIAL HANDLING EQUIPMENT

SEE ALSO Conveyors & Conveying Equipment p. 1571

Company	City	State	ZIP	Phone	Fax
4Front Engineered Solutions Inc 1612 Hutton Dr Suite 140 *TF:* 866-691-1377 ■ *Web:* www.4frontes.com	Carrollton	TX	75006	972-466-0707	323-2661
Abell-Howe Crane Inc 375 W South Frontage Rd Suite A *TF:* 800-366-0068 ■ *Web:* www.abellhowe.com	Bolingbrook	IL	60440	630-626-5520	626-5229
Acco Material Handling Solutions PO Box 792 *TF:* 800-967-7333 ■ *Web:* www.accochain.com	York	PA	17405	717-741-4863	741-8507
Advance Lifts Inc 701 S Kirk Rd *TF:* 800-843-3625 ■ *Web:* www.advancelifts.com	Saint Charles	IL	60174	630-584-9881	584-9405
Air Technical Industries 7501 Clover Ave *TF:* 800-321-9680 ■ *Web:* www.airtechnical.com	Mentor	OH	44060	440-951-5191	953-9237
American Crane & Equipment Corp 531 Old Swede Rd *TF:* 877-877-6778 ■ *Web:* www.americancrane.com	Douglassville	PA	19518	610-385-6061	385-4876
American Lifts 601 W McKee St **Fax:* Hum Res ■ *TF:* 800-426-9772 ■ *Web:* www.americanlifts.com	Greensburg	IN	47240	812-663-4085	663-4173*
American Power Pull Corp PO Box 109 *TF:* 800-808-5922 ■ *Web:* www.americanpowerpull.com	Wauseon	OH	43567	419-335-7050	335-7070
Autoquip Corp PO Box 1058 *TF:* 888-811-9876 ■ *Web:* www.autoquip.com	Guthrie	OK	73044	405-282-5200	282-8105
Bayhead Products Corp 173 Crosby Rd *TF:* 800-603-0053 ■ *Web:* bayheadproducts.com	Dover	NH	03820	603-742-3000	743-4701
Berns Co 1250 W 17th St *TF:* 800-421-3773 ■ *Web:* www.thebernsco.com	Long Beach	CA	90813	562-437-0471	436-1074
Breeze-Eastern Corp 700 Liberty Ave *TF Sales:* 800-929-1919 ■ *Web:* www.breeze-eastern.com	Union	NJ	07083	908-686-4000	686-9292
Busse/SJI Corp 124 N Columbus St *TF:* 800-882-4995 ■ *Web:* www.arrowheadsystems.com	Randolph	WI	53956	920-326-3131	326-3134
Cannon Equipment Co 15100 Business Pkwy *TF:* 800-825-8501 ■ *Web:* www.cannonequipment.com	Rosemount	MN	55068	651-322-6300	322-1583
Cascade Corp PO Box 20187 *NYSE:* CAE ■ *TF:* 800-227-2233 ■ *Web:* www.cascorp.com	Portland	OR	97294	503-669-6300	669-6716
Charnstrom WA Co 5391 12th Ave E **Fax Area Code:* 800 ■ *TF Cust Svc:* 800-328-2962 ■ *Web:* www.charnstrom.com	Shakopee	MN	55379	952-403-0303	916-3215*
Clark Material Handling Co 700 Enterprise Dr *TF:* 866-252-5275 ■ *Web:* www.clarkmhc.com	Lexington	KY	40510	859-422-6400	
Clyde Machines Inc PO Box 194 *Web:* www.clydemachines.com	Glenwood	MN	56334	320-634-4504	634-4506
Columbus McKinnon Corp 140 John James Audubon Pkwy *NASDAQ:* CMCO ■ *TF:* 800-888-0985 ■ *Web:* www.cmworks.com	Amherst	NY	14228	716-689-5400	639-4250
Cozzini Inc 4300 W Bryn Mawr Ave *TF:* 800-227-4447 ■ *Web:* www.cozzini.com	Chicago	IL	60646	773-478-9700	478-8689
Crane Tech Solutions LLC 2030 Ponderosa St *TF:* 800-996-6355 ■ *Web:* www.cranetechsolutions.com	Portsmouth	VA	23701	757-405-0311	405-0313
Craneveyor Corp 1524 N Potrero Ave PO Box 3727 *TF:* 800-423-4180	South El Monte	CA	91733	626-442-1524	442-7308
Crosby McKissick PO Box 3128 *TF:* 800-772-1500 ■ *Web:* www.thecrosbygroup.com	Tulsa	OK	74101	918-834-4611	832-0940
Crown Equipment Corp 44 S Washington St **Fax:* Hum Res ■ *Web:* www.crownlift.com	New Bremen	OH	45869	419-629-2311	629-2145*
Crysteel Mfg Inc 52182 Ember Rd *TF Orders:* 800-533-0494 ■ *Web:* www.crysteel.com	Lake Crystal	MN	56055	507-726-2728	726-2442
Deco Corp PO Box 632	Columbus	IN	47202	812-342-4451	342-4452
Dematic 507 Plymouth Ave NE *TF Cust Svc:* 800-530-9153 ■ *Web:* www.dematic.us/	Grand Rapids	MI	49505	616-913-6200	913-7701
Detroit Hoist Co 6650 Sterling Dr N *TF:* 800-521-9126 ■ *Web:* www.detroithoist.com	Sterling Heights	MI	48312	586-268-2600	268-0044
Downs Crane & Hoist Co Inc 8827 S Juniper St *TF:* 800-748-5994 ■ *Web:* www.downscrane.com	Los Angeles	CA	90002	323-589-6061	589-6066
Drake-Scruggs Equipment Inc 2000 S Dirksen Pkwy *Web:* www.drake-scruggs.com	Springfield	IL	62703	217-753-3871	753-2760
Drexel Industries Inc 1900 North St *Web:* www.drexeltrucks.com	Marysville	KS	66508	785-562-5381	562-4853
Eaton Aerospace Aurora 2501 Dallas St **Fax:* Cust Svc ■ *Web:* www.stanleyaviation.com	Aurora	CO	80010	303-340-5200	340-5337*
Ederer LLC 3701 S Norfolk St Suite 301 *Web:* www.par.com/our_companies_ederer.php	Seattle	WA	98124	206-622-4421	623-8583
Elwell-Parker Ltd 6499 W 65th St *TF Cust Svc:* 800-367-5600 ■ *Web:* www.elwellparker.com	Bedford Park	IL	60638	708-458-2200	458-1176
Escalera Inc 708 S Industrial Dr *TF:* 800-622-1359 ■ *Web:* www.escalera.com	Yuba City	CA	95993	530-673-6318	673-6376
Excalibur Equipment LLC Gregory Industrial Trucks 285 Eldridge Rd *Web:* www.exforklifts.com	Fairfield	NJ	07004	973-808-8399	808-8398
Excellon Automation Inc 20001 S Rancho Way *TF:* 800-392-3556 ■ *Web:* www.excellon.com	Rancho Dominguez	CA	90220	310-668-7700	668-7800
FL Smidth Inc 2040 Ave C *TF:* 800-523-9482 ■ *Web:* www.flsmidth.com	Bethlehem	PA	18017	610-264-6011	264-6701
Flexible Material Handling 9501 Granger Rd *TF:* 800-669-1501	Cleveland	OH	44125	216-587-1575	587-2833
Gaffey Inc 9655 Alawhe Dr *TF:* 800-331-3916 ■ *Web:* www.gaffey.com	Claremore	OK	74019	918-343-1191	343-1199
Genie Industries Inc PO Box 97030 *TF Sales:* 800-536-1800 ■ *Web:* www.genielift.com	Redmond	WA	98073	425-881-1800	883-3475
Grove Worldwide LLC PO Box 21 *Web:* www.groveworldwide.com	Shady Grove	PA	17256	717-597-8121	597-4062
Gunnebo-Johnson Corp 1240 N Harvard Ave **Fax:* Cust Svc ■ *TF Sales:* 800-331-5460 ■ *Web:* www.gunnebojohnson.com	Tulsa	OK	74115	918-832-8933	834-0984*
Harlan Materials Handling Corp PO Box 15159 *TF:* 800-255-4262 ■ *Web:* www.harlan-corp.com	Kansas City	KS	66115	913-342-5650	321-5802
Harlo Corp PO Box 129 *TF:* 800-391-4151 ■ *Web:* www.harlo.com	Grandville	MI	49468	616-538-0550	538-0554
Heyl & Patterson Inc PO Box 36 *Web:* www.heylpatterson.com	Pittsburgh	PA	15230	412-788-9810	788-9822
Hilman Inc 12 Timber Ln *TF Cust Svc:* 888-276-5548 ■ *Web:* www.hilmanrollers.com	Marlboro	NJ	07746	732-462-6277	462-6355
Hoist Equipment Co 26161 Cannon Rd *Web:* www.hoistequipment.com	Bedford Heights	OH	44146	440-232-0300	232-3366
Indusco Group 1200 W Hamburg St *TF:* 800-727-0665 ■ *Web:* www.induscowirerope.com	Baltimore	MD	21230	410-727-0665	727-2538
Industrial Vehicles International Inc 6737 E 12th St *Web:* www.indvehicles.com	Tulsa	OK	74112	918-836-6516	838-9529
Interlake Material Handling Inc 1230 E Diehl Rd Suite 400 *TF Sales:* 800-282-8032 ■ *Web:* www.interlake.com	Naperville	IL	60563	630-245-8800	245-8906
Iowa Mold Tooling Co Inc (IMT) 500 Hwy 18 W *TF:* 800-247-5958 ■ *Web:* www.imt.com	Garner	IA	50438	641-923-3711	923-2424
ITW BGK Finishing Systems 4131 Pheasant Ridge Dr NE *Web:* www.itwbgk.com/homepageFRAMES.html	Minneapolis	MN	55449	763-784-0466	784-1362
James Walker Co 7109 Milford Industrial Rd	Baltimore	MD	21208	410-486-3950	486-5176
Jervis B Webb Co 34375 W 12-Mile Rd *TF:* 800-526-9322 ■ *Web:* www.jervisbwebb.com	Farmington Hills	MI	48331	248-553-1220	553-1200
Jungheinrich Lift Truck Corp 5701 Eastport Blvd *Web:* www.jungheinrich-us.com	Richmond	VA	23231	804-737-7400	737-9050
Kalmar Industries Corp 415 E Dundee St *TF:* 888-229-6300 ■ *Web:* www.kalmarind-northamerica.com	Ottawa	KS	66067	785-242-2200	242-6117
Kelly Systems Inc 422 N Western Ave *Web:* www.kellytubesystems.com	Chicago	IL	60612	312-733-3224	733-6971
Key Handling Systems Inc 137 W Commercial Ave *Web:* www.keyhandling.com	Moonachie	NJ	07074	201-933-9333	933-5732
Konecranes America 7300 Chippewa Blvd *TF:* 800-231-0241 ■ *Web:* www.kciamericas.com	Houston	TX	77086	281-445-2225	445-9355
Kornylak Corp 400 Heaton St *TF:* 800-837-5676 ■ *Web:* www.kornylak.com	Hamilton	OH	45011	513-863-1277	863-7644
KWD Mfg Co 2230 W Southcross Blvd	San Antonio	TX	78211	210-924-5999	924-6799
Landoll Corp 1900 North St **Fax:* Sales ■ *TF Cust Svc:* 800-446-5175 ■ *Web:* www.landoll.com	Marysville	KS	66508	785-562-5381	562-4893*
Leebaw Mfg Co Inc PO Box 553 *TF:* 800-841-8083 ■ *Web:* www.leebaw.com	Canfield	OH	44406	330-533-3368	533-3917
Lift-All Co Inc 1909 McFarland Dr **Fax:* Cust Svc ■ *TF:* 800-909-1964 ■ *Web:* www.lift-all.com	Landisville	PA	17538	717-898-6615	898-1215*
Lift-Tech International 414 W Broadway Ave **Fax Area Code:* 800 ■ *TF Cust Svc:* 800-955-5541	Muskegon	MI	49443	231-733-0821	742-9270*
Liftex Inc 1230 Old York Rd Suite 101 *TF:* 800-448-3079 ■ *Web:* www.liftex.com	Warminster	PA	18974	215-957-0810	957-9180
Linde Hydraulics Corp 5089 W Western Reserve Rd *Web:* www.lindeamerica.com	Canfield	OH	44406	330-533-6801	
Linvar LLC 245 Hamilton St *TF:* 800-282-5288	Hartford	CT	06106	860-951-3818	951-3547
Lodi Metal Tech Inc 213 S Kelly St *Web:* www.lodirack.com	Lodi	CA	95240	209-334-2500	334-1259
Lovegreen Industrial Services Inc 2280 Sibley Ct *Web:* www.lovegreen.com	Eagan	MN	55122	651-890-1166	890-8370
Luker Inc 514 National Ave *TF:* 800-982-9534 ■ *Web:* www.lukerinc.com	Augusta	GA	30901	706-724-0244	724-1050
MacCabe Electric Conductors Inc 426 Stump Rd *Web:* www.maccabeelectric.com	Montgomeryville	PA	18936	215-368-9420	368-9220
Magline Inc 503 S Mercer St *TF:* 800-624-5463 ■ *Web:* www.magliner.com	Pinconning	MI	48650	989-879-2411	879-5399
Manitou North America 6401 Imperial Dr *TF Cust Svc:* 800-433-3304 ■ *Web:* www.manitou-na.com	Waco	TX	76712	254-799-0232	799-4433
Matot Inc 2501 Van Buren St *TF:* 800-369-1070 ■ *Web:* www.matot.com	Bellwood	IL	60104	708-547-1888	547-1608
Maxon Industries Inc 11921 Slauson Ave **Fax Area Code:* 888 ■ *TF:* 800-227-4116 ■ *Web:* www.maxonlift.com	Santa Fe Springs	CA	90670	562-464-0099	771-7713*
Mazzella Lifting Technologies 21000 Aerospace Pkwy *TF:* 800-362-4601 ■ *Web:* www.mazzellalifting.com	Cleveland	OH	44142	440-239-7000	239-7010
Mertz Mfg LLC 1701 N Waverly St *TF:* 800-654-6433 ■ *Web:* www.mertzok.com	Ponca City	OK	74601	580-762-5646	767-8411
Mitsubishi Caterpillar Forklift America Inc 2121 W Sam Houston Pkwy N *Web:* www.mcfa.com	Houston	TX	77043	713-365-1000	365-1441
Morris Material Handling Inc 315 W Forest Hill Ave *Web:* www.morriscranes.com	Oak Creek	WI	53154	414-764-6200	570-2779
NACCO Materials Handling Group Inc 650 NE Holladay St Suite 1600 *Web:* www.nmhg.com	Portland	OR	97232	503-721-6000	721-1352
Nestaway 9501 Granger Rd *Web:* www.nestawaywire.com	Cleveland	OH	44125	216-587-1500	587-2774
Nissan Forklift Corp North America (NFC) 240 N Prospect St *TF:* 800-871-5438 ■ *Web:* www.nissanforklift.com	Marengo	IL	60152	815-568-0061	568-8340
NMC-Wollard Inc 2021 Truax Blvd *TF:* 800-656-6867 ■ *Web:* www.nmc-wollard.com	Eau Claire	WI	54703	715-835-3151	835-6625
North American Industries Inc 80 Holton St *TF:* 800-847-8470 ■ *Web:* www.naicranes.com	Woburn	MA	01801	781-721-4446	729-3343
Nutting 505 W Airport Dr *TF:* 800-533-0337 ■ *Web:* www.acconutting.com/	Watertown	SD	57201	605-882-3000	882-4226
Ohio Magnetics Inc 5400 Dunham Rd *TF:* 800-486-6446 ■ *Web:* www.ohiomagnetics.com/ohio.htm	Maple Heights	OH	44137	216-662-8484	662-2911
P & H Mining Equipment 4400 W National Ave *Web:* www.phmining.com	Milwaukee	WI	53214	414-671-4400	671-7604
Paceco Corp 25503 Whitesell St *Web:* www.pacecocorp.com	Hayward	CA	94545	510-264-9288	264-9280
Paragon Technologies Inc 600 Kuebler Rd *AMEX:* PTG ■ *Web:* www.paragontechnologiesinc.com	Easton	PA	18040	610-252-3205	252-3102
Pettibone Michigan LLC 1100 Superior Ave *TF:* 800-467-3884 ■ *Web:* www.pettibone-mi.com	Baraga	MI	49908	906-353-6611	353-6325
Philadelphia Tramrail Co 2207 E Ontario St *TF:* 800-523-3654 ■ *Web:* www.philadelphiatramrail.com	Philadelphia	PA	19134	215-533-5100	537-8536
Phillips Mine & Mill Inc PO Box 409 *Web:* www.phillipsmineandmill.com	Irwin	PA	15642	724-864-8900	864-8909
Positech Corp 191 N Rush Lake Rd *TF:* 800-831-6026 ■ *Web:* www.positech-solutions.com	Laurens	IA	50554	712-841-4548	841-4765
Powell Systems Inc 162 Churchill-Hubbard Rd *Web:* www.powellsystems.com	Youngstown	OH	44505	330-759-9220	759-9434
Production Equipment Co 401 Liberty St *TF:* 800-758-5697	Meriden	CT	06450	203-235-5795	237-5391
Progressive Crane Inc 21000 Aero Space Pkwy *TF:* 800-832-7263 ■ *Web:* www.progressivecrane.com	Cleveland	OH	44142	440-239-7000	239-7010
Proserv Anchor Crane Group 2020 E Grauwyler Rd *TF:* 800-275-2624 ■ *Web:* www.proservanchor.com	Irving	TX	75061	972-438-5100	438-3428
Pucel Enterprises Inc 1440 E 36th St *TF:* 800-336-4986 ■ *Web:* www.pucel-grizzly.com	Cleveland	OH	44114	216-881-4604	881-6731
Raymond Corp 8-20 S Canal St *TF:* 800-235-7200 ■ *Web:* www.raymondcorp.com	Greene	NY	13778	607-656-2311	656-9005

Phone *Fax*

RKI Inc 2301 Central Pkwy . . . Houston TX 77092 713-688-4414 688-5776
Web: www.rki-us.com
Royal Tractor Co Inc 109 Overland Park Pl . . . New Century KS 66031 913-782-2598 782-4588
Web: www.royaltractor.com
Shepard Niles 220 N Genesee St . . . Montour Falls NY 14865 607-535-7111 535-7323
TF: 800-481-2260 ■ *Web:* www.shepard-niles.com
Sherman & Reilly Inc PO Box 11267 . . . Chattanooga TN 37401 423-756-5300 756-2948
TF Sales: 800-251-7780 ■ *Web:* www.sherman-reilly.com
Smidth FL Inc 2040 Ave C . . . Bethlehem PA 18017 610-264-6011 264-6701
TF: 800-523-9482 ■ *Web:* www.flsmidth.com
Spandeck Inc 129 Confederate Dr . . . Franklin TN 37064 615-794-4556 790-6803
TF: 800-272-3325 ■ *Web:* www.mantiscranes.com
Stinar Corp 3255 Sibley Memorial Hwy . . . Saint Paul MN 55121 651-454-5112 454-5143
Web: www.stinar.com
Stock Fairfield Corp PO Box 420 . . . Marion OH 43302 740-387-3327 387-4869
TF: 800-827-3364 ■ *Web:* www.fairfieldengineering.com
Streator Dependable Mfg Co 1705 N Shabbona St . . . Streator IL 61364 815-672-0551 672-7631
TF: 800-795-0551 ■ *Web:* www.streatordependable.com
Taylor-Dunn Mfg Co Inc 2114 W Ball Rd . . . Anaheim CA 92804 714-956-4040 956-3130
TF: 800-688-8680 ■ *Web:* www.taylor-dunn.com
TC/American Monorail Inc 12070 43rd St NE . . . Saint Michael MN 55376 763-497-7000 497-7001
Web: www.tcamerican.com
Terex Corp 500 Post Rd E Suite 320 . . . Westport CT 06880 203-222-7170 222-7976
NYSE: TEX ■ *Web:* www.terex.com
Terex Corp Crane Div 202 Raleigh St . . . Wilmington NC 28412 910-395-8500 395-8551*
**Fax:* Hum Res ■ *TF:* 800-250-2726 ■ *Web:* www.terex.com
Terex-Telelect Inc 500 Oakwood Rd PO Box 1150 . . . Watertown SD 57201 605-882-4000 882-1842
Web: www.telelect.com
Thern Inc 5712 Industrial Park Rd . . . Winona MN 55987 507-454-2996 454-5282
TF: 800-843-7648 ■ *Web:* www.thern.com
Tiffin Parts 235 Miami St . . . Tiffin OH 44883 419-447-6545 447-7527
TF: 800-219-6354 ■ *Web:* www.tiffinparts.com
Toyoshima Special Steel USA 735 S Saint Paul St . . . Indianapolis IN 46203 317-638-3511 631-7729
TF: 800-428-4599
Trambeam Corp 206 Lee St . . . Attalla AL 35954 256-538-9983 538-8818
Web: www.trambeam.com
TransTechnology Corp 700 Liberty Ave . . . Union NJ 07083 908-903-1600 903-1616
Web: www.transtechnology.com
Triple/S Dynamics Inc PO Box 151027 . . . Dallas TX 75315 214-828-8600 828-8688
TF: 800-527-2116 ■ *Web:* www.sssdynamics.com
UpRight Inc 2686 S Maple Ave . . . Fresno CA 93725 559-443-6600 268-2433
TF Cust Svc: 800-926-5438 ■ *Web:* www.upright.com
Valley Craft Inc 2001 S Hwy 61 . . . Lake City MN 55041 651-345-3386 345-3606
TF Cust Svc: 800-328-1480 ■ *Web:* www.valleycraft.com
Vibra Screw Inc 755 Union Blvd . . . Totowa NJ 07512 973-256-7410 256-7567
Web: www.vibrascrewinc.com
WA Charnstrom Co 5391 12th Ave E . . . Shakopee MN 55379 952-403-0303 916-3215*
**Fax Area Code:* 800 ■ *TF Cust Svc:* 800-328-2962 ■ *Web:* www.charnstrom.com
Waldon Manufacturing LLC 201 W Oklahoma Ave . . . Fiarview OK 73737 580-227-3711
TF: 866-283-2165 ■ *Web:* www.waldonequipment.com
Walker James Co 7109 Milford Industrial Rd . . . Baltimore MD 21208 410-486-3950 486-5176
Waste Technology Corp 5400 Rio Grande Ave . . . Jacksonville FL 32254 904-355-5558 358-7013
TF: 800-231-9286
Wayne Engineering Corp 701 Performance Dr . . . Cedar Falls IA 50613 319-266-1721 266-8207
Web: www.wayneusa.com
WB McGuire Co PO Box 309 . . . Germantown WI 53022 262-255-1510 255-4199
TF: 800-624-8473 ■ *Web:* www.wbmcguire.com
Webb Jervis B Co 34375 W 12-Mile Rd . . . Farmington Hills MI 48331 248-553-1220 553-1200
TF: 800-526-9322 ■ *Web:* www.jervisbwebb.com
Wesco Industrial Products Inc PO Box 47 . . . Lansdale PA 19446 215-699-7031 699-3836
TF: 800-445-5681 ■ *Web:* www.wescomfg.com
Western Hoist Inc 1839 Cleveland Ave . . . National City CA 91950 619-474-3361 474-8261
TF: 888-994-6478 ■ *Web:* www.westernhoist.com
Whiting Corp 26000 Whiting Way . . . Monee IL 60449 708-587-2000 587-2001
TF: 800-255-8594 ■ *Web:* www.whitingcorp.com
Wiggins Lift Co Inc PO Box 5187 . . . Oxnard CA 93031 805-485-7821 485-5230
TF: 800-350-7821 ■ *Web:* www.wigginslift.com
Yale Materials Handling Corp 1400 Sullivan Dr Caller 12011 . . . Greenville NC 27834 252-931-5100 931-7873
Web: northamerica.yale.com

474 MATTRESSES & ADJUSTABLE BEDS

SEE ALSO Furniture - Mfr - Household Furniture p. 1682

Phone *Fax*

Ackerman Mfg Co/Spring Air 4140 Park Ave . . . Saint Louis MO 63110 314-771-3052 771-6013
TF: 800-264-3052 ■ *Web:* www.springair.com
Aero Products International Inc
1834 Walden Office Sq 3rd Fl . . . Schaumburg IL 60173 847-485-3200 485-3290
TF Cust Svc: 888-462-4468 ■ *Web:* www.thinkaero.com
American Bedding Industries 500 S Falkenburg Rd . . . Tampa FL 33619 813-651-2233 657-9763
TF: 800-780-1084 ■ *Web:* www.springair.com
Ark-Ell Springs Div Leggett & Platt Inc
101 Industrial Rd PO Box 308 . . . Houlka MS 38850 662-568-3393 568-3325
Bechik Products Inc 1140 Homer St . . . Saint Paul MN 55116 651-698-0364 698-1009
TF: 800-328-6569 ■ *Web:* www.bechik.com
Bowles Mattress Co Inc 1220 Watt St . . . Jeffersonville IN 47130 812-288-8614 288-8650
TF: 800-223-7509 ■ *Web:* www.bowlesmattress.com
Chittenden & Eastman Co 100 New Rand Rd . . . Sweet Springs MO 65351 319-753-2811
TF Cust Svc: 800-553-5623
Classic Sleep Products Inc 8214 Wellmoor Ct . . . Jessup MD 20794 410-904-0006 498-6149*
**Fax Area Code:* 301 ■ *TF:* 877-707-7533 ■ *Web:* www.classicmattress.com
Clearwater Mattress Inc 1185 Gooden Crossing . . . Largo FL 33778 727-539-1600 539-8064
TF: 800-274-6288 ■ *Web:* www.clearwatermattress.com
Comfortex Inc 1680 Wilkie Dr PO Box 850 . . . Winona MN 55987 507-454-6579 454-6581
TF: 800-445-4007 ■ *Web:* www.comfortexinc.com
Continental Silverline Products Inc 710 N Drennan St . . . Houston TX 77003 713-222-7394 222-1934
TF: 800-392-9205 ■ *Web:* www.restonic.com
Corsicana Bedding Inc PO Box 1050 . . . Corsicana TX 75151 903-872-2591 983-2663*
**Fax Area Code:* 800 ■ *TF:* 800-323-4349 ■ *Web:* www.corsicanabedding.com
Cotton Belt Inc 401 E Sater St . . . Pinetops NC 27864 252-827-4192 827-5683
TF: 800-849-4192 ■ *Web:* www.edgecombe.com
Craftmatic Organization Inc 2500 Interplex Dr . . . Trevose PA 19053 215-639-1310 639-9941
TF Cust Svc: 800-677-8200 ■ *Web:* www.craftmatic.com
Diamond Mattress Co Inc 3112 Las Hermanas St E . . . Compton CA 90221 323-774-6840 638-2005*
**Fax Area Code:* 310 ■ *Web:* www.diamondmattress.com
Dreamline Mfg Inc 1514 S 2nd St PO Box 1250 . . . Cabot AR 72023 501-843-3585 843-2990
TF: 800-888-3585 ■ *Web:* www.dreamlinebedding.com
Flexi-Mat Corp 14420 Van Dyke Rd . . . Plainfield IL 60544 815-609-4600 609-4671
TF: 800-338-7392 ■ *Web:* www.fleximat.com
Fraenkel Co Inc 10600 S Choctaw Dr PO Box 15385 . . . Baton Rouge LA 70895 225-275-8111 272-7319
TF: 800-847-2580 ■ *Web:* www.fraenkel.com

Phone *Fax*

Gold Bond Mattress Co 261 Weston St . . . Hartford CT 06120 860-549-2000 527-3101
TF: 800-873-8498 ■ *Web:* www.goldbondmattress.com
Herr Mfg Div Serta Inc 18 Prestige Ln . . . Lancaster PA 17603 717-392-4168 392-6154
TF: 800-626-6249
Home-Style Industries Inc 1323 11th Ave N PO Box 1500 . . . Nampa ID 83653 208-466-8481 467-9942
Web: www.home-style.com
IBC Group Inc 730 W McNab Rd . . . Fort Lauderdale FL 33309 954-968-2333 974-7070
TF: 800-776-1166 ■ *Web:* www.ibcgroup.com
Imperial Bedding Co 720 11th St PO Box 5347 . . . Huntington WV 25703 304-529-3321 525-5317
TF: 800-529-3321 ■ *Web:* www.imperialbedding.com
Jackson Mattress Co Inc 3154 Camden Rd PO Box 64609 . . . Fayetteville NC 28306 910-425-0131 425-1602
TF: 800-763-7378
Jamison Bedding Inc PO Box 681948 . . . Franklin TN 37068 615-794-1883 794-2254
TF: 800-255-1883 ■ *Web:* www.jamisonbedding.com
King Koil Licensing Co Inc 15 Salt Creek Ln Suite 210 . . . Hinsdale IL 60521 630-230-9744 230-9749
TF: 800-525-8331 ■ *Web:* www.kingkoil.com
Kingsdown Inc 126 W Holt St PO Box 388 . . . Mebane NC 27302 919-563-3531 563-6730*
**Fax:* Cust Svc ■ *TF Cust Svc:* 800-354-5464 ■ *Web:* www.kingsdown.com
Kolcraft Enterprises Inc 10832 NC Hwy 211 E . . . Aberdeen NC 28315 910-944-9345
TF Cust Svc: 800-453-7673 ■ *Web:* www.kolcraft.com
Leggett & Platt Inc PO Box 757 . . . Carthage MO 64836 417-358-8131 358-5840*
NYSE: LEG ■ **Fax:* Hum Res ■ *TF:* 800-888-4569 ■ *Web:* www.leggett.com
Leggett & Platt Inc Ark-Ell Springs Div
101 Industrial Rd PO Box 308 . . . Houlka MS 38850 662-568-3393 568-3325
Lemoyne Sleeper Co Inc 57 S 3rd St PO Box 227 . . . Lemoyne PA 17043 717-763-1630 763-1634
TF: 800-382-1217 ■ *Web:* www.lemoynesleeper.com
Meridian Mattress Factory Inc 200 Rubush Rd PO Box 5127 . . . Meridian MS 39302 601-693-3875 693-5462
TF: 800-844-3875
National Bedding Co 61 Leona Dr . . . Middleboro MA 02346 508-946-4700 946-5217
TF: 800-343-1006
National Bedding Co Div Serta Inc 1500 Lee Lane . . . Beloit WI 53511 608-365-6266 365-9362
TF: 800-767-6267 ■ *Web:* www.serta.com
Northwest Bedding Co 6102 S Hayford Rd . . . Spokane WA 99224 509-244-3000 244-9905
TF: 800-456-7686
Omaha Bedding Co 4011 S 60th St PO Box 27396 . . . Omaha NE 68127 402-733-8600 733-0586
TF: 800-279-9018
Paramount Industrial Cos Inc 1112 Kingwood Ave . . . Norfolk VA 23502 757-855-3321 855-2029
TF: 800-777-5337
Peerless Mattress & Furniture Co G-3437 Miller Rd . . . Flint MI 48507 810-230-7440 230-0143
TF: 800-253-0937 ■ *Web:* www.peerlessfurn.com
Penfield Mfg Co 1710 N Salina St . . . Syracuse NY 13208 315-471-7145 471-7140
TF: 800-724-1868
Restonic Mattress Corp 1540 E Dundee Rd Suite 102 . . . Palatine IL 60074 847-241-1130 241-1136
TF: 800-898-6075 ■ *Web:* www.restonic.com
Restonic New Albany 901 Park Place . . . New Albany IN 47150 812-945-4122 945-4469
TF: 800-234-4422 ■ *Web:* www.restonic.com
Riverside Mattress Co Inc 225 Dunn Rd . . . Fayetteville NC 28312 910-483-0461 484-2334
TF: 888-288-5195
Royal Bedding Co 11650 Lakeside Crossing Ct . . . Saint Louis MO 63146 314-647-5200 645-6528
TF: 800-875-1517
Sanitary Mattress Co Inc 5808 Berry Brook Dr . . . Houston TX 77017 713-227-0121 227-8159
TF: 800-603-3375
Sealy Corp 1 Office Pkwy at Sealy Dr . . . Trinity NC 27370 336-861-3500 861-3501
NYSE: ZZ ■ *TF Cust Svc:* 800-697-3259 ■ *Web:* www.sealy.com
Select Comfort Corp 6105 Trenton Ln N . . . Plymouth MN 55442 763-551-7000 551-7826*
NASDAQ: SCSS ■ **Fax:* Cust Svc ■ *TF:* 800-472-7185 ■ *Web:* www.selectcomfort.com
Serta Inc Herr Mfg Div 18 Prestige Ln . . . Lancaster PA 17603 717-392-4168 392-6154
TF: 800-626-6249
Serta Inc National Bedding Co Div 1500 Lee Lane . . . Beloit WI 53511 608-365-6266 365-9362
TF: 800-767-6267 ■ *Web:* www.serta.com
Serta International Inc 5401 Trillium Blvd . . . Hoffman Estates IL 60192 847-645-0200 645-0205
TF: 888-557-3782 ■ *Web:* www.serta.com
Serta Mattress/AW Inc 8415 Ardmore Rd . . . Landover MD 20785 301-322-1000 341-4639
TF: 800-638-0520 ■ *Web:* www.serta.com
Simmons Co 1 Concourse Pkwy Suite 800 . . . Atlanta GA 30328 770-512-7700 392-2560
Web: www.simmons.com
Sleep Products Inc 901 Park Place . . . New Albany IN 47150 812-945-4122 945-4469
TF: 800-234-4422 ■ *Web:* www.restonic.com
Southerland Inc 1973 Southerland Dr . . . Nashville TN 37207 615-226-9650 650-2653
TF: 888-226-9009 ■ *Web:* www.southerlandsleep.com
Spring Air Co 1111 Nicholas Blvd . . . Elk Grove Village IL 60007 847-439-4399 439-4322
Web: www.springair.com
Standard Mattress Co Inc 261 Weston St . . . Hartford CT 06120 860-549-2000 527-3101
TF: 800-873-8498 ■ *Web:* www.goldbondmattress.com
Stearns & Foster Bedding Co 1 Office Pkwy at Sealy Dr . . . Trinity NC 27370 336-861-3500 861-3506
TF: 800-867-3259 ■ *Web:* www.stearnsandfoster.com
Symbol Mattress Co 4901 Fitzhugh Ave . . . Richmond VA 23230 804-353-8965 353-8762
TF: 800-446-2791 ■ *Web:* www.symbolmattress.com
Taylor Bedding Inc 1133 MacArthur Ave . . . New Orleans LA 70058 504-341-0059 341-5633
Tempur-Pedic International Inc 1713 Jaggie Fox Way . . . Lexington KY 40511 859-259-0754 259-9843
NYSE: TPX ■ *Web:* www.tempurpedic.com
Therapedic Inc 103 College Rd E . . . Princeton NJ 08540 609-720-0700 720-0797
TF: 800-322-1054 ■ *Web:* www.therapedic.com
United Sleep Products Inc 412 Oak St PO Box 256 . . . Denver PA 17517 717-336-2846 336-2048
TF: 800-447-2119 ■ *Web:* www.unitedsleepproducts.com
Western Mattress & Furniture Co 117 E Concho Ave . . . San Angelo TX 76903 325-653-4507 653-8323
TF: 800-880-4507 ■ *Web:* www.westernmattressandfurniture.com
White Dove Ltd 3201 Harvard Ave . . . Cleveland OH 44105 216-341-0200 341-3399
Web: www.whitedoveusa.com
Winston-Salem Industries for the Blind
7730 N Point Dr . . . Winston-Salem NC 27106 336-759-0551 759-0990
Web: www.wsifb.com
World Sleep Products Inc 12 Esquire Rd . . . North Billerica MA 01862 978-667-6648 667-6683
TF: 800-370-8700

475 MEASURING, TESTING, CONTROLLING INSTRUMENTS

SEE ALSO Electrical Signals Measuring & Testing Instruments p. 1607

Phone *Fax*

AAI Corp 404 Industrial Rd Suite 1 . . . Choctaw MS 39350 601-389-5300 389-5336
Web: www.aaicorp.com
ABB Inc 501 Merritt 7 . . . Norwalk CT 06851 203-750-2200 435-7365
TF Prod Info: 800-626-4999 ■ *Web:* www.abb.us
Adcole Corp 669 Forest St . . . Marlborough MA 01752 508-485-9100 481-6142
TF: 800-858-5802 ■ *Web:* www.adcole.com
Aero Systems Engineering Inc 358 E Fillmore Ave . . . Saint Paul MN 55107 651-227-7515 227-0519
TF: 800-321-0288 ■ *Web:* www.aerosysengr.com
AGR International Inc 615 Whitestown Rd . . . Butler PA 16001 724-482-2163 482-2767
Web: www.agrintl.com
Air Gage Co 12170 Globe Rd . . . Livonia MI 48150 734-853-9220 853-2454
Web: www.airgage.com

Company	City	State	ZIP	Phone	Fax
AMETEK Aerospace 50 Fordham Rd *Fax: Cust Svc ■ Web: www.ametek.com/aerospace	Wilmington	MA	01887	978-988-4101	988-4944*
AMETEK Inc Test & Calibration Instruments Div 8600 Somerset Dr TF: 800-527-9999 ■ Web: www.ametekcalibration.com	Largo	FL	33773	727-536-7831	539-6882
AMETEK US Gauge 820 Pennsylvania Blvd TF: 888-625-5895 ■ Web: www.ametekusg.com	Feasterville	PA	19053	215-355-6900	354-1802
AMETEK US Gauge PMT Products Div 820 Pennsylvania Blvd TF: 888-625-5895 ■ Web: www.ametekusg.com	Feasterville	PA	19053	215-355-6900	354-1800
APA Enterprises Inc 2950 NE 84th Ln NASDAQ: APAT ■ Web: www.apaenterprises.com	Blaine	MN	55449	763-784-4995	784-2038
Bently Nevada Corp 1631 Bently Pkwy S *Fax: Cust Svc ■ TF: 800-227-5514 ■ Web: www.bently.com	Minden	NV	89423	775-782-3611	215-2873*
Beta LaserMike Inc 8001 Technology Blvd TF: 800-886-9935 ■ Web: www.betalasermike.com	Dayton	OH	45424	937-233-9935	233-7284
Bruel & Kjaer Instruments Inc 2815-A Colonnades Ct. TF: 800-241-9188 ■ Web: www.bkhome.com	Norcross	GA	30071	770-209-6907	448-3246
Canberra Industries Inc 800 Research Pkwy TF: 800-243-4422 ■ Web: www.canberra.com	Meriden	CT	06450	203-238-2351	235-1347
Clayton Industries 17477 Hurley St TF: 800-423-4585 ■ Web: www.claytonindustries.com	City of Industry	CA	91744	626-435-1200	435-0180
Control Screening LLC 2 Gardner Rd TF: 800-231-6414 ■ Web: www.controlscreening.com	Fairfield	NJ	07004	973-276-6161	276-6162
Crane Nuclear Inc 2825 Cobb International Blvd TF: 800-795-8013 ■ Web: www.cranenuclear.com	Kennesaw	GA	30152	770-424-6343	429-4750
Cubic Transportation Systems Inc 5650 Kearny Mesa Rd. Web: www.cubic.com/cts	San Diego	CA	92111	858-268-3100	292-9987
Danaher Corp 2099 Pennsylvania Ave NW 12th Fl NYSE: DHR ■ Web: www.danaher.com	Washington	DC	20006	202-828-0850	828-0860
Davis Instrument Corp 3465 Diablo Ave. TF: 800-678-3669 ■ Web: www.davisnet.com	Hayward	CA	94545	510-732-9229	670-0589
Dresser Inc 15455 Dallas Pkwy Suite 1100 Web: www.dresser.com	Addison	TX	75001	972-361-9800	361-9903
Dynisco LLC 38 Forge Pkwy TF: 800-332-2215 ■ Web: www.dynisco.com	Franklin	MA	02038	508-541-9400	541-6206
Eagle Test Systems Inc 2200 Millbrook Dr NASDAQ: EGLT ■ Web: www.eagletest.com	Buffalo Grove	IL	60089	847-367-8282	367-8640
Emerson Process Management CSI 835 Innovation Dr TF: 800-675-4726 ■ Web: www.compsys.com	Knoxville	TN	37932	865-675-2110	218-1401
Endevco Corp 30700 Rancho Viejo Rd TF: 800-982-6732 ■ Web: www.endevco.com	San Juan Capistrano	CA	92675	949-493-8181	661-7231
Enidine Inc 7 Centre Dr. TF: 800-852-8508 ■ Web: www.enidine.com	Orchard Park	NY	14127	716-662-1900	662-1909
Fairfield Industries Inc 14100 Southwest Frwy Suite 600 TF: 800-231-9809 ■ Web: www.fairfield.com	Sugar Land	TX	77478	281-275-7500	275-7550
FARO Technologies Inc 125 Technology Park NASDAQ: FARO ■ TF: 800-736-0234 ■ Web: www.faro.com	Lake Mary	FL	32746	407-333-9911	333-4181
Fiber Instruments Sales Inc 161 Clear Rd TF Sales: 800-500-0347 ■ Web: www.fiberinstrumentsales.com	Oriskany	NY	13424	315-736-2206	736-2285
Fisher Research Laboratory Inc 1465 Henry Brennan Suite H TF: 800-672-6738 ■ Web: www.fisherlab.com	El Paso	TX	79936	915-633-8354	633-8529
Fluke Biomedical Radiation Management Services 6045 Cochran Rd TF: 800-850-4608 ■ Web: global.flukebiomedical.com	Solon	OH	44139	440-248-9300	349-2307
Garrett Metal Detectors 1881 W State St TF: 800-234-6151 ■ Web: www.garrett.com	Garland	TX	75042	972-494-6151	494-1881
GE Infrastructure Security 205 Lowell St. *Fax Area Code: 866 ■ TF: 800-433-5346 ■ Web: www.gesecurity.com	Wilmington	MA	01887	978-658-3767	249-9105*
GE Ion Track 205 Lowell St. *Fax Area Code: 866 ■ TF: 800-433-5346 ■ Web: www.gesecurity.com	Wilmington	MA	01887	978-658-3767	249-9105*
GE Reuter-Stokes 8499 Darrow Rd. Web: www.gepower.com/dhtml/reuterstokes/en_us	Twinsburg	OH	44087	330-425-3755	963-2462
General Monitors Inc 26776 Simpatica Cir. TF: 866-686-0741 ■ Web: www.generalmonitors.com	Lake Forest	CA	92630	949-581-4464	581-1151
Geometrics Inc 2190 Fortune Dr. Web: www.geometrics.com	San Jose	CA	95131	408-954-0522	954-0902
George Risk Industries Inc 802 S Elm St. TF Sales: 800-523-1227 ■ Web: www.grisk.com	Kimball	NE	69145	308-235-4645	235-2609
GFI Genfare 751 Pratt Blvd Web: www.gfigenfare.com	Elk Grove Village	IL	60007	847-593-8855	593-1824
Gleason M & M Precision Systems Corp 300 Progress Rd. Web: www.gleason.com	Dayton	OH	45449	937-859-8273	859-4452
Goodrich Corp 2730 W Tyvola Rd 4 Coliseum Ctr NYSE: GR ■ TF: 800-784-7009 ■ Web: www.goodrich.com	Charlotte	NC	28217	704-423-7000	423-7002
Goodrich Corp Fuel & Utility Systems Div 100 Patton Rd. TF: 800-722-7251 ■ Web: www.fus.goodrich.com	Vergennes	VT	05491	802-877-2111	877-4111
GSE Tech-motive Tool 1525 Fairlane Cir. TF: 800-795-7875 ■ Web: www.gsetechmotive.com	Allen Park	MI	48101	313-253-1300	253-1327
Hamilton Sundstrand Sensor Systems 2771 N Garey Ave Web: www.hssensorsystems.com	Pomona	CA	91767	909-593-3581	392-3205
Herman H Sticht Co Inc 45 Main St Suite 701 TF: 800-221-3203 ■ Web: www.stichtco.com	Brooklyn	NY	11201	718-852-7602	852-7915
Hexagon Metrology Inc 660 S Military Rd PO Box 1658 TF Cust Svc: 800-535-1236 ■ Web: www.sheffieldmeasurement.com	Fond du Lac	WI	54936	920-906-7700	906-7701
Howell Instruments Inc 3479 W Vickery Blvd Web: www.howellinst.com	Fort Worth	TX	76107	817-336-7411	336-7874
Industrial Dynamics Co Ltd 3100 Fujita St. TF: 888-434-5832 ■ Web: www.filtec.com	Torrance	CA	90505	310-325-5633	530-1000
Input/Output Inc 12300 Parc Crest Dr NYSE: IO ■ Web: www.i-o.com	Stafford	TX	77477	281-933-3339	879-3532
Instron Corp 825 University Ave Web: www.instron.com	Norwood	MA	02062	781-828-2500	575-5750
Instron Corp Wilson Instruments Div 825 University Ave TF: 800-695-4273 ■ Web: www.instron.com/hardness/index.asp	Norwood	MA	02062	781-575-6000	575-5770
Instron Industrial Products Group 900 Liberty St TF: 800-726-8378 ■ Web: www.satec.com	Grove City	PA	16127	724-458-9610	458-9614
Interface Inc 7401 E Butherus Dr. TF: 800-947-5598 ■ Web: www.interfaceforce.com	Scottsdale	AZ	85260	480-948-5555	948-1924
Isra Surface Vision Inc 4470 Peachtree Lakes Dr Web: www.lasorsystronics.com	Duluth	GA	30096	770-449-7776	449-0399
Kahn & Co Inc 885 Wells Rd Web: www.kahn.com	Wethersfield	CT	06109	860-529-8643	529-1895
Kavlico Corp 14501 Princeton Ave Web: www.kavlico.com	Moorpark	CA	93021	805-523-2000	523-7125
Kinemetrics Inc 222 Vista Ave Web: www.kinemetrics.com	Pasadena	CA	91107	626-795-2220	795-0868
Kistler Instrument Corp 75 John Glenn Dr TF: 888-547-8537 ■ Web: www.kistler.com	Amherst	NY	14228	716-691-5100	691-5226
Konica Minolta Sensing Americas Inc 101 Williams Dr TF: 888-473-2656 ■ Web: se.konicaminolta.us	Ramsey	NJ	07446	201-825-4000	
Ktech Corp 1300 Eubank Blvd SE TF: 877-998-5830 ■ Web: www.ktech.com	Albuquerque	NM	87123	505-998-5830	998-5848
L-3 Avionics Systems 5353 52nd St SE *Fax: Hum Res ■ TF: 800-253-9525 ■ Web: www.as.l-3com.com	Grand Rapids	MI	49512	616-949-6600	285-4457*
Leica Geosystems LLC 3498 Kraft Ave TF Sales: 800-367-9453 ■ Web: www.leica-geosystems.com	Grand Rapids	MI	49512	616-949-7430	949-8693
Link Engineering Co Inc 43855 Plymouth Oaks Blvd Web: www.linkeng.com	Plymouth	MI	48170	734-453-0800	453-0802
Lockheed Martin Sippican 7 Barnabas Rd Web: www.sippican.com	Marion	MA	02738	508-748-1160	748-3626
Ludlum Measurements Inc 501 Oak St. TF: 800-622-0828 ■ Web: www.ludlums.com	Sweetwater	TX	79556	325-235-5494	235-4672
Magnetic Analysis Corp 535 S 4th Ave TF: 800-463-8622 ■ Web: www.mac-ndt.com	Mount Vernon	NY	10550	914-699-9450	699-9837
Marposs Corp 3300 Cross Creek Pkwy TF: 800-627-7677 ■ Web: www.marposs.com	Auburn Hills	MI	48326	248-370-0404	370-0990
Mason Industries Inc 350 Rabro Dr Web: www.mason-ind.com	Hauppauge	NY	11788	631-348-0282	348-0279
Meteorlogix LLC 11400 Rupp Dr. TF: 800-328-2278 ■ Web: www.meteorlogix.com	Burnsville	MN	55337	952-890-0609	882-4500
Metrix Instrument Co 8824 Fallbrook Dr TF: 800-638-7494 ■ Web: www.metrix1.com	Houston	TX	77064	713-461-2131	559-9417
Metrosonics 1060 Corporate Center Dr TF: 800-245-0779 ■ Web: www.metrosonics.com	Oconomowoc	WI	53066	262-567-9157	567-4047
Metrotech Corp 3251 Olcott St. TF: 800-446-3392 ■ Web: www.metrotech.com	Santa Clara	CA	95054	408-734-1400	734-1415
Morcom International Inc 3656 Centerview Dr Unit 1 Web: www.morcom.com	Chantilly	VA	20151	703-263-9305	263-9308
MTS Systems Corp 14000 Technology Dr. NASDAQ: MTSC ■ TF Cust Svc: 800-328-2255 ■ Web: www.mts.com	Eden Prairie	MN	55344	952-937-4000	937-4515
Mustang Dynamometer 2300 Pinnacle Pkwy TF: 888-468-7826 ■ Web: www.mustangdyne.com	Twinsburg	OH	44087	330-963-5400	425-3310
Nanometrics Inc 1550 Buckeye Dr NASDAQ: NANO ■ TF: 800-955-6266 ■ Web: www.nanometrics.com	Milpitas	CA	95035	408-435-9600	232-5910
Nextest Systems Corp 1901 Monterey Rd NASDAQ: NEXT ■ Web: www.nextest.com	San Jose	CA	95112	408-817-7200	817-7210
Ohmart/VEGA Corp 4241 Allendorf Dr. TF: 800-543-8668 ■ Web: www.ohmartvega.com	Cincinnati	OH	45209	513-272-0131	272-0133
Olympus NDT NW 421 N Quay St *Fax: Sales ■ Web: www.olympusndt.com	Kennewick	WA	99336	509-735-7550	735-4672*
On-Site Analysis Inc 7108 Fairway Dr Suite 130 TF: 800-285-7708 ■ Web: www.on-siteanalysis.com	Palm Beach Gardens	FL	33418	561-775-5756	691-5220
Oxford Instruments Measurement Systems 945 Busse Rd. TF: 800-678-1117 ■ Web: www.oxford-instruments.com	Elk Grove Village	IL	60007	847-439-4404	439-4425
OYO Geospace Corp 7007 Pinemont Dr NASDAQ: OYOG ■ Web: www.oyogeospace.com	Houston	TX	77040	713-986-4444	986-4445
Panalaytical 12 Michigan Dr. TF: 800-279-7297 ■ Web: www.panalytical.com	Natick	MA	01760	508-647-1100	647-1115
Perceptron Inc 47827 Halyard Dr. NASDAQ: PRCP ■ TF: 800-333-7753 ■ Web: www.perceptron.com	Plymouth	MI	48170	734-414-6100	414-4700
Princeton Gamma-Tech Instruments Inc 303-C College Rd E TF: 800-229-7484 ■ Web: www.pgt.com	Princeton	NJ	08540	609-924-7310	924-1729
Radiation Monitoring Devices 44 Hunt St Suite 2 TF: 800-532-3763 ■ Web: www.rmdinc.com	Watertown	MA	02472	617-926-1167	926-9980
Rochester Gauges Inc of Texas 11616 Harry Hines Blvd TF: 800-821-1829 ■ Web: www.rochestergauges.com	Dallas	TX	75229	972-241-2161	620-1403
Rudolph Technologies Inc 550 Clark Dr PO Box 1000 NASDAQ: RTEC ■ TF: 877-467-8365 ■ Web: www.rudolphtech.com	Budd Lake	NJ	07828	973-691-1300	426-1483
Saint-Gobain Crystals 12345 Kinsman Rd TF: 800-472-5656 ■ Web: www.bicron.com	Newbury	OH	44065	440-564-2251	564-8047
Schenck Pegasus Corp 2890 John R Rd TF: 800-899-5119 ■ Web: www.schenckpegasuscorp.com	Troy	MI	48083	248-689-9000	689-8578
Schmitt Industries Inc 2765 NW Nicolai St NASDAQ: SMIT ■ Web: www.schmitt-ind.com	Portland	OR	97210	503-227-7908	223-1258
Sensor Systems LLC 2800 Anvil St N TF: 800-688-2181 ■ Web: www.vsensors.com	Saint Petersburg	FL	33710	727-347-2181	347-7520
Sercel Inc 17200 Park Row Web: www.sercel.com	Houston	TX	77084	281-492-6688	579-6555
Setra Systems Inc 159 Swanson Rd. TF: 800-257-3872 ■ Web: www.setra.com	Boxborough	MA	01719	978-263-1400	264-0292
Smiths Detection 2202 Lakeside Blvd. Web: www.smithsdetection.com	Edgewood	MD	21040	410-510-9100	510-9490
Sorrento Electronics Inc 4949 Greencraig Ln TF: 800-252-1180 ■ Web: www.sorrento.com	San Diego	CA	92123	858-522-8300	522-8301
SPECTRO Analytical Instruments Inc 1515 N Hwy 281 TF: 800-580-6608 ■ Web: www.spectro-ai.com	Marble Falls	TX	78654	830-798-8786	798-8467
Sticht Herman H Co Inc 45 Main St Suite 701 TF: 800-221-3203 ■ Web: www.stichtco.com	Brooklyn	NY	11201	718-852-7602	852-7915
SuperFlow Technologies Group 3512 N Tejon St. TF: 800-471-7701 ■ Web: www.superflow.com	Colorado Springs	CO	80907	719-471-1746	471-1490
Taber Industries 455 Bryant St. Web: www.taberindustries.com	North Tonawanda	NY	14120	716-694-4000	694-1450
Taylor Hobson Inc 1725 Western Dr. TF: 800-872-7265 ■ Web: www.taylor-hobson.com	West Chicago	IL	60185	630-621-3099	231-1739
Tel-Instrument Electronics Corp 728 Garden St AMEX: TIK ■ Web: www.telinst.com	Carlstadt	NJ	07072	201-933-1600	933-7340
Testing Machines Inc 2 Fleetwood Ct TF: 800-678-3221 ■ Web: www.testingmachines.com	Ronkonkoma	NY	11749	631-439-5400	439-5420
Thermo Fisher Scientific 81 Wyman St PO Box 9046 NYSE: TMO ■ TF: 800-678-5599 ■ Web: www.thermofisher.com	Waltham	MA	02454	781-622-1000	622-1207
Thermo Fisher Scientific Inc 10010 Mesa Rim Rd TF: 800-488-4399 ■ Web: www.thermofisher.com	San Diego	CA	92121	858-450-9811	546-1734
Tinius Olsen Testing Machine Co Inc 1065 Easton Rd PO Box 1009 Web: www.tiniusolsen.com	Horsham	PA	19044	215-675-7100	441-0899
Topcon Positioning Systems Inc 7400 National Dr Web: www.topconpositioning.com	Livermore	CA	94551	925-245-8300	245-8599
Unilux Inc 59 N 5th St. TF: 800-522-0801 ■ Web: www.unilux.com	Saddle Brook	NJ	07663	201-712-1266	712-1366
Uster Technologies Inc 456 Troy Cir PO Box 51270 Web: www.uster.com	Knoxville	TN	37919	865-588-9716	588-0914
Vaisala-GAI 2705 E Medina Rd. TF: 800-294-3520 ■ Web: thunderstorm.vaisala.com	Tucson	AZ	85706	520-741-2838	741-2848
Vaisala Inc 10-D Gill St. TF: 888-824-7252 ■ Web: www.vaisala.com	Woburn	MA	01801	781-933-4500	933-8029
Veri-Tek International Corp 50120 Pontiac Trail AMEX: VCC ■ Web: www.veri-tek.com	Wixom	MI	48393	248-560-1000	560-2000
Verity Instruments Inc 2901 Eisenhower St. Web: www.verityinst.com	Carrollton	TX	75007	972-446-9990	446-9586
Vishay Measurements Group Inc PO Box 27777 Web: www.vishay.com/brands/measurements_group	Raleigh	NC	27611	919-365-3800	365-3945
Vishay Micro Measurements PO Box 27777 Web: www.vishay.com/brands/measurements_group	Raleigh	NC	27611	919-365-3800	365-3945
White's Electronics Inc 1011 Pleasant Valley Rd TF Sales: 800-547-6911 ■ Web: www.whitesdetectors.com	Sweet Home	OR	97386	541-367-6121	367-6629

476 MEAT PACKING PLANTS

SEE ALSO Poultry Processing p. 2132

Company / Address	City	State	Zip	Phone	Fax
Abbott's Meat Inc 3623 Blackington Ave	Flint	MI	48532	810-232-7128	232-7960
Abbyland Foods Inc 502 E Linden St PO Box 69	Abbotsford	WI	54405	715-223-6386	223-6388
Web: www.abbyland.com					
Academy Packing Co Inc 2881 Wyoming St	Dearborn	MI	48120	313-841-4900	841-9760
Allen Brothers Inc 3737 S Halsted St	Chicago	IL	60609	773-890-5100	890-9377
TF: 800-548-7777 ■ *Web:* www.allenbrothers.com					
Alpine Packing Co 9900 Lower Sacramento Rd	Stockton	CA	95210	209-477-2691	477-1994
TF: 800-399-6328 ■ *Web:* www.alpinemeats.com					
American Foods Group Inc PO Box 8547	Green Bay	WI	54308	920-437-6330	436-6510
TF: 800-345-0293 ■ *Web:* www.americanfoodsgroup.com					
Atlantic Veal & Lamb Inc 275 Morgan Ave	Brooklyn	NY	11211	718-599-6400	599-6404
Best Packers Inc 1122 Bronson St	Palatka	FL	32177	386-328-5127	325-1239
TF Sales: 800-771-9378					
Bicara Ltd 4215 Exchange Ave	Los Angeles	CA	90058	323-582-7401	582-1813
Birchwood Foods 6009 Goshen Springs Rd	Norcross	GA	30071	770-448-9101	447-0459
Web: www.bwfoods.com					
Brown Packing Co Inc 1 Dutch Valley Dr	South Holland	IL	60473	708-849-7990	849-8094
TF: 800-832-8325					
Buchy Charles G Packing Co 1050 Progress St	Greenville	OH	45331	937-548-2128	548-6880
TF: 800-762-1060					
Cargill Meat Solutions 151 N Main PO Box 2519	Wichita	KS	67201	316-291-2500	291-2547*
**Fax:* Hum Res					
Carolina Packers Inc 2999 Brightless Blvd PO Box 1109	Smithfield	NC	27577	919-934-2181	989-6794
TF: 800-682-7675 ■ *Web:* www.carolinapackers.com					
Cattleman's Meat Co 1825 Scott St	Detroit	MI	48207	313-833-2700	833-7164
TF: 800-766-5699					
Caviness Packing Co 3255 W Hwy 60	Hereford	TX	79045	806-357-2443	357-2277
Central Beef Industry LLC 571 W Kings Hwy PO Box 399	Center Hill	FL	33514	352-793-3671	793-2227
Central Nebraska Packing Inc 2800 E 8th St	North Platte	NE	69103	308-532-1250	532-2744
TF Cust Svc: 800-445-2881 ■ *Web:* www.nebraskabrand.com					
Charles G Buchy Packing Co 1050 Progress St	Greenville	OH	45331	937-548-2128	548-6880
TF: 800-762-1060					
Cherry Meat Packers Inc 4750 S California Ave	Chicago	IL	60632	773-927-1200	927-1520
Chiappetti Wholesale Meat Inc 3900 S Emerald Ave	Chicago	IL	60609	773-847-1556	847-3837
Web: chiappettilambandveal.com					
Chip Steak & Provision Co 232 Dewey St	Mankato	MN	56001	507-388-6277	388-6279
TF: 888-244-7783					
Chisesi Brothers Meat Packing Co 5221 Jefferson Hwy	Harahan	LA	70123	504-822-3550	822-3916
TF: 800-966-3550					
Cimpl Meats Inc 1000 Cattle Dr PO Box 80	Yankton	SD	57078	605-665-1665	665-8908
Clougherty Packing Co DBA Farmer John Meats					
3049 E Vernon Ave	Los Angeles	CA	90058	323-583-4621	584-1699
TF Sales: 800-432-7637 ■ *Web:* www.farmerjohn.com					
Comer Packing 1000 Poplar St PO Box 33	Aberdeen	MS	39730	662-369-9325	369-9375
TF: 800-748-8916					
ConAgra Foods Retail Products Co Deli Foods Group					
215 W Field Rd	Naperville	IL	60563	630-857-1000	512-1124
TF: 800-325-7424					
Conti Packing Co Inc					
2299 Brighton Henritta Town Line Rd PO box 23025	Rochester	NY	14692	585-424-2500	424-2504
Cougle Commission Co 345 N Aberdeen St	Chicago	IL	60607	312-666-7861	666-6434
Web: www.couglecommission.com					
Cudahy Patrick Inc 1 Sweet Apple-Wood Ln	Cudahy	WI	53110	414-744-2000	744-4213
TF: 800-486-6900 ■ *Web:* www.patrickcudahy.com					
Curtis Packing Co 2416 Randolph Ave	Greensboro	NC	27406	336-275-7684	275-1901
TF: 800-852-7890 ■ *Web:* www.curtispackingcompany.com					
Dallas City Packing Inc 3049 Morrell St	Dallas	TX	75203	214-948-3901	942-2039
TF: 800-876-6328					
Demakes Enterprises Inc DBA Old Neighborhood Foods					
37 Waterhill St	Lynn	MA	01905	781-595-1557	595-7523
TF: 800-628-3529					
DL Lee & Sons Inc 927 Hwy 32 E	Alma	GA	31510	912-632-4406	632-8298
TF Cust Svc: 800-673-9339					
EA Miller Inc 410 N 200 West	Hyrum	UT	84319	435-245-6456	245-6634
TF: 800-873-0939 ■ *Web:* www.eamiller.com					
Eddy Packing Co Inc 404 Airport Dr	Yoakum	TX	77995	361-293-2361	293-2254
TF: 800-292-2361 ■ *Web:* www.eddypacking.com					
EE Mucke & Sons Inc 2326 Main St	Hartford	CT	06120	860-246-5609	
Esskay Inc PO Box 587	Riderwood	MD	21139	410-823-2100	823-3058
TF: 800-638-7350 ■ *Web:* www.esskaymeat.com					
Fair Oaks Farms Inc 7600 95th St	Pleasant Prairie	WI	53158	262-947-0320	947-0340
TF: 800-528-8615 ■ *Web:* www.fairoaksfarms.com					
Falter Herman Packing Co Inc 384 Greenlawn Ave	Columbus	OH	43223	614-444-1141	445-3915
TF: 800-325-6328					
Farm Boy Meats 2751 N Kentucky Ave PO Box 996	Evansville	IN	47706	812-425-5231	428-8432
TF: 800-852-3976 ■ *Web:* www.farmboyfoodservice.com					
Farmer John Meats 3049 E Vernon Ave	Los Angeles	CA	90058	323-583-4621	584-1699
TF Sales: 800-432-7637 ■ *Web:* www.farmerjohn.com					
Fort Pitt Brand Meat Co PO Box F	Evans City	PA	16033	724-538-3160	538-3262
Web: www.isalys.com					
Frankel L Packing Co Inc 230 N Peoria St	Chicago	IL	60607	312-421-3200	421-6049
Freirich Foods Inc 815 W Kerr St PO Box 1529	Salisbury	NC	28145	704-636-2621	636-4650
TF: 800-554-4788 ■ *Web:* www.freirich.com					
Fresh Mark Inc 1888 Southway St SE	Massillon	OH	44646	330-832-7491	830-3174
TF: 800-860-6777 ■ *Web:* www.freshmark.com					
Gibbon Packing Inc 218 E Hwy 30 PO Box 730	Gibbon	NE	68840	308-468-5771	468-5262
TF: 800-652-1910					
Glaziers Packing Co Inc 3140 State Hwy 11	Malone	NY	12953	518-483-4990	483-8300
Golden State Foods 18301 Von Karman Ave Suite 1100	Irvine	CA	92612	949-252-2000	252-2080
Web: www.goldenstatefoods.com					
Greater Omaha Packing Co 3001 L St PO Box 7566	Omaha	NE	68107	402-731-3480	731-7542
TF: 800-747-5400 ■ *Web:* www.greateromaha.com					
Gwaltney of Smithfield Ltd 601 N Church St	Smithfield	VA	23430	757-357-3131	
TF: 800-888-7521 ■ *Web:* www.gwaltneyfoods.com					
Hahn Brothers Inc 440 Hahn Rd PO Box 395	Westminster	MD	21158	410-848-4200	848-1247
TF: 800-227-7675					
Hansel 'n Gretel Brand Inc 79-36 Cooper Ave	Glendale	NY	11385	718-326-0041	326-2069
TF: 800-635-3354					
Harris Ranch Beef Co 16277 S McCall Ave PO Box 220	Selma	CA	93662	559-896-3081	896-3095
TF: 800-742-1955 ■ *Web:* www.harrisranch.com					
Hatfield Quality Meats Inc 2700 Funks Rd PO Box 902	Hatfield	PA	19440	215-368-2500	
TF: 800-523-5291 ■ *Web:* www.hatfieldqualitymeats.com					
Hausman Sam Meat Packer Inc					
4261 Beacon St PO Box 2422	Corpus Christi	TX	78403	361-883-5521	883-0512
TF: 800-364-5521 ■ *Web:* www.samhausman.com					
Herman Falter Packing Co Inc 384 Greenlawn Ave	Columbus	OH	43223	614-444-1141	445-3915
TF: 800-325-6328					
JF O'Neill Packing Co Inc 3120 G St	Omaha	NE	68107	402-733-1200	733-1724
JH Routh Packing Co Inc 4413 W Bogart Rd	Sandusky	OH	44870	419-626-2251	625-4782
TF: 800-446-6759					
John Morrell & Co 805 E Kemper Rd	Cincinnati	OH	45246	513-346-3540	346-7552*
**Fax:* Cust Svc ■ *TF:* 800-445-2013 ■ *Web:* www.johnmorrell.com					
Kenosha Beef International Ltd 3111 152nd Ave PO Box 639	Kenosha	WI	53141	262-859-2272	859-2078
TF: 800-541-1685					
King Meat Co Inc 4215 Exchange Ave	Los Angeles	CA	90058	323-582-7401	582-1813
L Frankel Packing Co Inc 230 N Peoria St	Chicago	IL	60607	312-421-3200	421-6049
L & H Packing Co 647 Steves Ave PO Box 831368	San Antonio	TX	78283	210-532-3241	532-9819
TF: 800-999-3241 ■ *Web:* www.lhpacking.com					
Land O'Frost Inc 16850 Chicago Ave	Lansing	IL	60438	708-474-7100	474-9329
TF: 800-323-3308 ■ *Web:* www.landofrost.com					
Long Prairie Packing Co 10 Riverside Dr	Long Prairie	MN	56347	320-732-2171	732-2914
Mariah Foods 1333 Indiana Ave	Columbus	IN	47201	812-378-3366	372-6943*
**Fax:* Sales ■ *TF:* 800-227-6328					
Martin's Abattoir & Wholesale Meats Inc 1600 Martin Rd	Godwin	NC	28344	910-567-6102	567-5241
Web: www.martinmeats.com					
Miller EA Inc 410 N 200 West	Hyrum	UT	84319	435-245-6456	245-6634
TF: 800-873-0939 ■ *Web:* www.eamiller.com					
Morrell John & Co 805 E Kemper Rd	Cincinnati	OH	45246	513-346-3540	346-7552*
**Fax:* Cust Svc ■ *TF:* 800-445-2013 ■ *Web:* www.johnmorrell.com					
Morrilton Packing Co Inc 51 Blue Diamond Dr	Morrilton	AR	72110	501-354-2474	354-2283
TF: 800-264-2475					
National Beef Packing Co LLC 12200 Ambassador Dr	Kansas City	MO	64163	816-713-8500	
TF: 800-449-2333 ■ *Web:* www.nationalbeef.com					
New City Packing & Provision 2600 Church Rd	Aurora	IL	60504	630-851-8800	898-3030
TF: 800-621-0397 ■ *Web:* www.newcitypacking.com					
Ohio Packing Co 1340 Emig Rd	Columbus	OH	43223	614-239-1600	237-0885
TF: 800-282-6403 ■ *Web:* www.ohiopacking.com					
Old Neighborhood Foods 37 Waterhill St	Lynn	MA	01905	781-595-1557	595-7523
TF: 800-628-3529					
Olymel LP 2200 Pratte Ave Pratte	Saint-Hyacinthe	QC	J2S4B6	450-771-0400	771-0519
Web: www.olymel.com					
OSI Industries LLC 1225 Corporate Blvd	Aurora	IL	60504	630-851-6600	851-8223
Web: www.osigroup.com					
Palo Duro Meat 4206 Amarillo Blvd E PO Box 31117	Amarillo	TX	79120	806-372-5781	372-1215
TF: 800-624-4785					
Pearl Meat Packing Co Inc 227 York Ave	Randolph	MA	02368	781-228-5100	228-5123
TF: 800-462-3022 ■ *Web:* www.pearlmeat.com					
Plumrose USA Inc 7 Lexington Ave	East Brunswick	NJ	08816	732-257-6600	257-6644
TF: 800-526-4909 ■ *Web:* www.plumroseusa.com					
Premium Standard Farms Inc					
805 Pennsylvania Ave Suite 200	Kansas City	MO	64105	816-472-7675	843-1450
NASDAQ: PORK ■ *Web:* www.psfarms.com					
Quality Meats & Seafoods 700 Center St	West Fargo	ND	58078	701-282-0202	282-0583
TF: 800-959-4250 ■ *Web:* www.qualitymeats.com					
Raber Packing Co 1413 N Raber Rd	Peoria	IL	61604	309-673-0721	673-6308
TF: 800-331-0545					
Rineharts Meat Processing Inc 133 Bell Rd PO Box 6880	Branson	MO	65615	417-334-2070	334-2059
RL Ziegler Co Inc PO Box 1640	Tuscaloosa	AL	35403	205-758-3621	758-0185
TF: 800-392-6328 ■ *Web:* www.zmeats.com					
Robbins Packing Co Inc 229 Stockyard Rd	Statesboro	GA	30458	912-764-7503	489-2823
TF: 800-487-2705					
Rochelle Foods Inc 1001 S Main St Box 45	Rochelle	IL	61068	815-562-4141	562-4149
Rose Packing Co Inc 65 S Barrington Rd	South Barrington	IL	60010	847-381-5700	381-9436*
**Fax:* Cust Svc ■ *TF:* 800-323-7363 ■ *Web:* www.rosepacking.com					
Routh JH Packing Co Inc 4413 W Bogart Rd	Sandusky	OH	44870	419-626-2251	625-4782
TF: 800-446-6759					
Sam Hausman Meat Packer Inc					
4261 Beacon St PO Box 2422	Corpus Christi	TX	78403	361-883-5521	883-0512
TF: 800-364-5521 ■ *Web:* www.samhausman.com					
Sam Kane Beef Processors Inc 9001 Leopard St	Corpus Christi	TX	78409	361-241-5000	242-2999
TF: 800-242-4142 ■ *Web:* www.samkanebeef.com					
Schenk Packing Co Inc 8204 288th St NW	Stanwood	WA	98292	360-629-3939	629-4451
Schwab & Co Inc 1111 Linwood Blvd	Oklahoma City	OK	73106	405-235-2377	236-4694
TF Cust Svc: 888-508-8668 ■ *Web:* www.schwabmeat.com					
Sioux-Preme Packing Co 4241 US 75th Ave PO Box 255	Sioux Center	IA	51250	712-722-2555	722-2666
TF: 800-735-7675 ■ *Web:* www.siouxpreme.com					
Skylark Meats Inc 4430 S 110th St	Omaha	NE	68137	402-592-0300	592-1414
Web: www.skylarkmeats.com					
Smithfield Beef Group 2580 University Ave PO Box 23000	Green Bay	WI	54305	920-468-4000	468-7140
TF: 800-753-7724 ■ *Web:* www.smithfieldbeef.com					
Smithfield Foods Inc 200 Commerce St	Smithfield	VA	23430	757-365-3000	365-3017*
NYSE: SFD ■ **Fax:* Cust Svc ■ *TF:* 800-276-6158 ■ *Web:* www.smithfieldfoods.com					
Smithfield Packing Co Inc 501 N Church St	Smithfield	VA	23430	757-357-4321	357-1366*
**Fax:* Hum Res ■ *TF:* 800-444-9180 ■ *Web:* www.smithfieldfoods.com					
Square H Brands 2731 S Soto St	Los Angeles	CA	90023	323-267-4600	261-7350
TF Cust Svc: 800-424-6339 ■ *Web:* www.squarehbrands.com					
Superior Packing Co 1477 Drew Ave Suite 101	Davis	CA	95616	530-758-3091	758-3152
TF: 800-228-5262					
T & J Meat Packing Co 635 Glenwood Dyer Rd	Chicago Heights	IL	60411	708-758-6748	758-8688
Taylor Excel Rt 706 PO Box 188	Wyalusing	PA	18853	570-746-3000	746-3888
TF: 800-828-9527					
Thompson Packers Inc 550 Carnation St	Slidell	LA	70460	985-641-6640	645-2112
TF: 800-989-6328 ■ *Web:* www.thompack.com					
Travis Meats Inc 7210 Clinton Hwy PO Box 670	Powell	TN	37849	865-938-9051	938-9211
TF: 800-247-7606 ■ *Web:* www.travismeats.com					
Tyson Fresh Meats Inc 800 Stevens Port Dr	Dakota Dunes	SD	57049	605-235-2061	235-2068
TF: 800-416-2272 ■ *Web:* www.tyson.com/Corporate/B2B/FreshMeats					
Washington Beef LLC 201 Elmwood Rd PO Box 832	Toppenish	WA	98948	509-865-2121	865-2827
TF: 800-289-2333 ■ *Web:* www.wabeef.com					
Wolverine Packing Co Inc 2535 Rivard St	Detroit	MI	48207	313-259-7500	568-1909
TF: 800-521-1390 ■ *Web:* www.wolverinepacking.com					
Zeigler RL Co Inc PO Box 1640	Tuscaloosa	AL	35403	205-758-3621	758-0185
TF: 800-392-6328 ■ *Web:* www.zmeats.com					

477 MEDICAL ASSOCIATIONS - STATE

SEE ALSO Associations & Organizations - Professional & Trade - Health & Medical Professionals Associations p. 1326

Association / Address	City	State	Zip	Phone	Fax
Alabama Medical Assn 19 S Jackson St	Montgomery	AL	36104	334-263-6441	269-5200
TF: 800-239-6272 ■ *Web:* www.masalink.org					
Alaska State Medical Assn 4107 Laurel St	Anchorage	AK	99508	907-562-0304	561-2063
Arizona Medical Assn 810 W Bethany Home Rd	Phoenix	AZ	85013	602-246-8901	242-6283
TF: 800-482-3480 ■ *Web:* www.armadoc.com					
Arkansas Medical Society PO Box 55088	Little Rock	AR	72215	501-224-8967	224-6489
TF: 800-542-1058 ■ *Web:* www.arkmed.org					
California Medical Assn 1201 J St Suite 200	Sacramento	CA	95814	415-882-5100	882-3349
Web: www.cmanet.org					
Colorado Medical Society 7351 Lowry Blvd	Denver	CO	80230	720-859-1001	859-7509
TF: 800-654-5653 ■ *Web:* www.cms.org					
Connecticut State Medical Society 160 Saint Ronan St	New Haven	CT	06511	203-865-0587	865-4997
TF: 800-635-7740 ■ *Web:* www.csms.org					

Phone | Fax

Delaware Medical Society 131 Continental Dr Suite 405 .... Newark DE 19713 302-658-7596 658-9669
TF: 800-348-6800 ■ *Web:* www.medsocdel.org

Florida Medical Assn 123 S Adams St .... Tallahassee FL 32301 850-224-6496 224-6627
TF: 800-762-0233 ■ *Web:* www.fmaonline.org

Georgia Medical Assn 1330 W Peachtree St NW Suite 500 .... Atlanta GA 30309 404-876-7535 881-5021
TF: 800-282-0224 ■ *Web:* www.mag.org

Hawaii Medical Assn 1360 S Beretania St Suite 200 .... Honolulu HI 96814 808-536-7702 528-2376
TF: 866-536-8666 ■ *Web:* www.hmaonline.net

Idaho Medical Assn 305 W Jefferson St .... Boise ID 83702 208-344-7888 344-7903
Web: www.idmed.org

Illinois State Medical Society 20 N Michigan Ave Suite 700 .... Chicago IL 60602 312-782-1654 782-2023
Web: www.isms.org

Indiana State Medical Assn 322 Canal Walk .... Indianapolis IN 46202 317-261-2060 261-2076
TF: 800-257-4762 ■ *Web:* www.ismanet.org

Iowa Medical Society 1001 Grand Ave .... West Des Moines IA 50265 515-223-1401 223-0590
TF: 800-747-3070 ■ *Web:* www.iowamedicalsociety.org

Kansas Medical Society 623 SW 10th Ave .... Topeka KS 66612 785-235-2383 235-5114
TF: 800-332-0156 ■ *Web:* www.kmsonline.org

Kentucky Medical Assn
4965 US Hwy 42 KMA Bldg Suite 2000 .... Louisville KY 40222 502-426-6200 426-6877
TF: 800-686-9923 ■ *Web:* www.kyma.org

Louisiana State Medical Society
6767 Perkins Rd Suite 100 .... Baton Rouge LA 70808 225-763-8500 763-6122
TF: 800-375-9508 ■ *Web:* www.lsms.org

Maine Medical Assn 30 Association Dr .... Manchester ME 04351 207-622-3374 622-3332
TF: 800-772-0815 ■ *Web:* www.mainemed.com

Maryland State Medical Society 1211 Cathedral St .... Baltimore MD 21201 410-539-0872 547-0915
TF: 800-492-1056 ■ *Web:* www.medchi.org

Massachusetts Medical Society 860 Winter St .... Waltham MA 02451 781-893-4610 893-8009
TF: 800-322-2303 ■ *Web:* www.massmed.org

Medical Society of the District of Columbia
1115 30th St NW Suite 1002 .... Washington DC 20007 202-466-1800 452-1542
Web: www.msdc.org

Michigan State Medical Society 120 W Saginaw St .... East Lansing MI 48823 517-337-1351 337-2490
Web: www.msms.org

Minnesota Medical Assn 1300 Godward St NE Suite 2500 .... Minneapolis MN 55413 612-378-1875 378-3875
TF: 800-342-5662 ■ *Web:* www.mnmed.org

Mississippi State Medical Assn 408 W Parkway Pl .... Ridgeland MS 39157 601-853-6733 853-6746
TF: 800-898-0251

Missouri State Medical Assn 113 Madison St .... Jefferson City MO 65101 573-636-5151 636-8552
TF: 800-869-6762 ■ *Web:* www.msma.org

Montana Medical Assn 2021 11th Ave Suite 1 .... Helena MT 59601 406-443-4000 443-4042
TF: 877-443-4000 ■ *Web:* www.mmaoffice.com

Nebraska Medical Assn 233 S 13th St Suite 1512 .... Lincoln NE 68508 402-474-4472 474-2198
Web: www.nebmed.org

Nevada State Medical Assn 3660 Baker Ln Suite 101 .... Reno NV 89509 775-825-6788 825-3202
Web: www.nsmadocs.org

New Hampshire Medical Society 7 N State St .... Concord NH 03301 603-224-1909 226-2432
TF: 800-564-1909 ■ *Web:* www.nhms.org

New Jersey Medical Society 2 Princess Rd .... Lawrenceville NJ 08648 609-896-1766 896-1368
TF: 800-322-6765 ■ *Web:* www.msnj.org

New Mexico Medical Society 7770 Jefferson NE Suite 400 .... Albuquerque NM 87109 505-828-0237 828-0336
TF: 800-748-1596 ■ *Web:* www.swcp.com/nmms

New York State Medical Society
420 Lakeville Rd PO Box 5404 .... Lake Success NY 11042 516-488-6100 488-1267
TF: 800-523-4405 ■ *Web:* www.mssny.org

North Carolina Medical Society 222 N Person St .... Raleigh NC 27601 919-833-3836 833-2023
TF: 800-722-1350 ■ *Web:* www.ncmedsoc.org

North Dakota Medical Assn 1622 E Interstate Ave .... Bismarck ND 58503 701-223-9475 223-9476
Web: www.ndmed.com

Ohio State Medical Assn 3401 Mill Run Dr .... Hilliard OH 43026 614-527-6762 527-6763
TF: 800-766-6762 ■ *Web:* www.osma.org

Oklahoma State Medical Assn 601 NW Grand Blvd .... Oklahoma City OK 73118 405-843-9571 842-1834
TF: 800-522-9452 ■ *Web:* www.osmaonline.org

Oregon Medical Assn 5210 SW Corbett Ave .... Portland OR 97239 503-226-1555 241-7148
Web: www.theoma.org

Pennsylvania Medical Society 777 E Park Dr .... Harrisburg PA 17111 717-558-7750 558-7840
Web: www.pamedsoc.org

Rhode Island Medical Society 235 Promenade St Suite 500 .... Providence RI 02908 401-331-3207 751-8050
Web: www.rimed.org

South Carolina Medical Assn 132 W Park Blvd .... Columbia SC 29210 803-798-6207 772-6783
TF: 800-327-1021 ■ *Web:* www.scmanet.org

South Dakota State Medical Assn 1323 S Minnesota Ave .... Sioux Falls SD 57105 605-336-1965 336-0270
Web: www.sdsma.org

Tennessee Medical Assn 2301 21st Ave A .... Nashville TN 37212 615-385-2100 383-5918
TF: 800-659-1862 ■ *Web:* www.medwire.org

Texas Medical Assn 401 W 15th St .... Austin TX 78701 512-370-1300 370-1693
TF: 800-880-1300 ■ *Web:* www.texmed.org

Utah Medical Assn 540 E 500 South .... Salt Lake City UT 84102 801-355-7477 532-1550
Web: www.utahmed.org

Vermont Medical Society 134 Main St .... Montpelier VT 05601 802-223-7898 223-1201
TF: 800-640-8767 ■ *Web:* www.vtmd.org

Virginia Medical Society 4205 Dover Rd .... Richmond VA 23221 804-353-2721 355-6189
TF: 800-746-6768 ■ *Web:* www.msv.org

Washington State Medical Assn 2033 6th Ave Suite 1100 .... Seattle WA 98121 206-441-9762 441-5863
TF: 800-552-0612 ■ *Web:* www.wsma.org

West Virginia State Medical Assn 4301 MacCorkle Ave .... Charleston WV 25364 304-925-0342 925-0345
TF: 800-257-4747 ■ *Web:* www.wvsma.com

Wisconsin State Medical Society 330 E Lakeside St .... Madison WI 53701 608-257-6781 442-3802
TF: 866-442-3800 ■ *Web:* www.wisconsinmedicalsociety.org

Wyoming Medical Society 1920 Evans Ave .... Cheyenne WY 82001 307-635-2424 632-1973
Web: www.wyomed.org

478 MEDICAL & DENTAL EQUIPMENT & SUPPLIES - WHOL

Phone | Fax

Buffalo Hospital Supply Co Inc 4039 Genesee St .... Buffalo NY 14225 716-626-9400 626-4307
TF: 800-724-0530 ■ *Web:* www.buffalohospital.com

Burkhart Dental Supply Co 2502 S 78th St .... Tacoma WA 98409 253-474-7761 472-4773
TF Cust Svc: 800-828-2089 ■ *Web:* www.burkhartdental.com

Burrows Co 230 W Palatine Rd .... Wheeling IL 60090 847-537-7300 537-7786
Web: www.burrowsco.com

Butler Animal Health Supply LLC 5600 Blazer Pkwy .... Dublin OH 43017 614-761-9095 646-4507*
**Fax Area Code:* 651 ■ *TF PR:* 800-848-5983 ■ *Web:* www.accessbutler.com

Caligor Medical & Office Supplies Inc
846 Pelham Pkwy .... Pelham Manor NY 10803 914-738-8400 738-9539*
**Fax:* Cust Svc ■ *TF:* 800-225-9906 ■ *Web:* www.caligor.com

Chindex International Inc 7201 Wisconsin Ave Suite 703 .... Bethesda MD 20814 301-215-7777 215-7719
NASDAQ: CHDX ■ *Web:* www.chindex.com

Derma Sciences Inc 214 Carnegie Center Suite 100 .... Princeton NJ 08540 609-514-4744 514-8554
TF: 800-825-4325 ■ *Web:* www.dermasciences.com

Estorge Surgical Supplies 112 S Pierce St .... Lafayette LA 70501 337-232-8920 235-6071
TF: 800-256-8990

Evans-Sherratt Co 13050 Northend Ave .... Oak Park MI 48237 248-584-5500 584-5510
TF: 800-248-3826 ■ *Web:* www.evans-sherratt.com

Grogans Health Care Supply Inc 1016 S Broadway St .... Lexington KY 40504 859-254-6661 254-6666
TF: 800-365-1020 ■ *Web:* www.grogans.com

Gulf South Medical Supply Inc 173 E Marketridge Dr .... Ridgeland MS 39157 601-856-5900 827-2002*
**Fax Area Code:* 800 ■ *TF:* 800-347-2456 ■ *Web:* www.gsms.com

Henry Schein Inc 135 Duryea Rd .... Melville NY 11747 631-843-5500 843-5652
NASDAQ: HSIC ■ *TF:* 800-582-2702 ■ *Web:* www.henryschein.com

Iowa Veterinary Supply Co 124 Country Club Rd .... Iowa Falls IA 50126 641-648-2529 648-9224
TF: 800-392-5636 ■ *Web:* www.iowavet.com

Kentec Medical Inc 17871 Fitch .... Irvine CA 92614 949-863-0810 724-8923
TF: 800-825-5996 ■ *Web:* www.kentecmedical.com

Laboratory Supply Co 250 Ottawa Ave .... Louisville KY 40209 502-363-1891 364-1609*
**Fax:* Acctg ■ *TF Cust Svc:* 800-888-5227 ■ *Web:* www.labsco.com

Leeches USA Ltd 300 Shames Dr .... Westbury NY 11590 516-333-2570 997-4948
TF: 800-645-3569 ■ *Web:* www.leechesusa.com

Liberty Medical Supply Inc 10045 SE Federal Hwy .... Port Saint Lucie FL 34952 772-398-5800 762-0826*
**Fax Area Code:* 800 ■ *TF:* 800-633-2001 ■ *Web:* www.libertymedical.com

LXU Healthcare 3708 E Columbia St .... Tucson AZ 85714 520-512-1100 512-8019
TF: 888-842-6999 ■ *Web:* www.lxuhc.com

Mabis Healthcare Inc 1931 Norman Dr .... Waukegan IL 60085 847-680-6811 680-9646
TF: 800-728-6811 ■ *Web:* www.mabis.net

MacGill William V & Co 1000 N Lombard Rd .... Lombard IL 60148 630-889-0500 727-3433*
**Fax Area Code:* 800 ■ *TF:* 800-323-2841 ■ *Web:* www.macgill.com

McKesson Medical Group Extended Care
8121 10th Ave N .... Golden Valley MN 55427 763-595-6000 595-6677
TF: 800-328-8111 ■ *Web:* www.mckesson.com/ext_care.html

McKesson Medical-Surgical 8741 Landmark Rd .... Richmond VA 23228 804-264-7500 264-7679
TF: 800-446-3008 ■ *Web:* www.mckgenmed.com

Medicore Inc 2337 W 76th St .... Hialeah FL 33016 305-558-4000 825-0961
TF: 800-327-8894

Mesa Laboratories Inc 12100 W 6th Ave .... Lakewood CO 80228 303-987-8000 987-8989
NASDAQ: MLAB ■ *TF Sales:* 800-992-6372 ■ *Web:* www.mesalabs.com

Micro Bio-Medics Inc 846 Pelham Pkwy .... Pelham Manor NY 10803 914-738-8400 738-8999
TF: 800-431-2743

Midland Hospital Supply Inc 2011 Great Northern Dr .... Fargo ND 58102 701-235-4451 235-7920
TF: 800-747-4450 ■ *Web:* www.midlandhs.com

Midwest Veterinary Supply Inc 11965 Larc Industrial Blvd .... Burnsville MN 55337 952-894-4350 894-5407
TF: 800-328-2975 ■ *Web:* www.midwestveterinarysupply.com

Moore Medical Corp 389 John Downey Dr .... New Britain CT 06050 860-826-3600 223-2382
TF Sales: 800-234-1464 ■ *Web:* www.mooremedical.com

National Logistics Services LLC 11445 G Cronridge Dr .... Owings Mills MD 21117 410-581-1800 581-1809
TF: 800-638-8672 ■ *Web:* www.nlsanimalhealth.com

NLS Animal Health 11445 G Cronridge Dr .... Owings Mills MD 21117 410-581-1800 581-1809
TF: 800-638-8674 ■ *Web:* www.nlsanimalhealth.com

Oakworks Inc 923 E Wellspring Rd .... New Freedom PA 17349 717-235-6807 562-4787*
**Fax Area Code:* 877 ■ *TF:* 800-558-8850 ■ *Web:* www.oakworks-inc.com

Omron Healthcare Inc 1200 Lakeside Dr .... Bannockburn IL 60015 847-680-6200 637-6763*
**Fax Area Code:* 800 ■ **Fax:* Cust Svc ■ *TF:* 800-323-1482 ■
Web: www.omronhealthcare.com

Owens & Minor Inc 9120 Lockwood Blvd .... Mechanicsville VA 23116 804-723-7000 723-7100
NYSE: OMI ■ *Web:* www.owens-minor.com

Patterson Cos Inc 1031 Mendota Heights Rd .... Saint Paul MN 55120 651-686-1600 686-9331
NASDAQ: PDCO ■ *TF:* 800-328-5536 ■ *Web:* www.pattersondental.com

PolyMedica Corp 11 State St .... Woburn MA 01801 781-933-2020 933-7992
NASDAQ: PLMD ■ *TF:* 800-886-4050 ■ *Web:* www.polymedica.com

PracticeWares Dental Supply 11291 Sunrise Park Dr .... Rancho Cordova CA 95742 916-638-8020 344-6710*
**Fax Area Code:* 800 ■ *TF:* 800-800-4939 ■ *Web:* www.practicewares.com

PSS World Medical Inc 4345 Southpoint Blvd .... Jacksonville FL 32216 904-332-3000 332-3213*
NASDAQ: PSSI ■ **Fax:* Hum Res ■ *Web:* www.pssd.com

Radiometer America Inc 810 Sharon Dr .... Westlake OH 44145 440-871-8900 871-8117
TF: 800-736-0600 ■ *Web:* www.radiometer.com

Sammons Preston Inc 4 Sammons Ct .... Bolingbrook IL 60440 630-226-1300 547-4333*
**Fax Area Code:* 800 ■ *TF:* 800-323-5547 ■ *Web:* www.sammonspreston.com

Schein Henry Inc 135 Duryea Rd .... Melville NY 11747 631-843-5500 843-5652
NASDAQ: HSIC ■ *TF:* 800-582-2702 ■ *Web:* www.henryschein.com

Somagen Diagnostics Inc 9220 25th Ave .... Edmonton AB T6N1E1 780-702-9500 438-6595
TF: 800-661-9993 ■ *Web:* www.somagen.com

Southern Prosthetic Supply Co 6025 Shiloh Rd Suite A .... Alpharetta GA 30005 678-455-8888 869-7776*
**Fax Area Code:* 800 ■ *TF Cust Svc:* 800-767-7776 ■ *Web:* www.spsco.com

Sullivan-Schein Dental 10920 W Lincoln Ave .... West Allis WI 53227 414-321-8881 321-8865
TF: 800-648-6684 ■ *Web:* www.henryschein.com

Sun Healthcare Group Inc Pharmaceutical Services
101 Sun Ave NE .... Albuquerque NM 87109 505-468-4168 468-4344
TF: 800-729-6600 ■ *Web:* www.sunh.com

Tetra Medical Supply Corp 6364 W Gross Pt Rd .... Niles IL 60714 847-647-0590 647-9034
TF Cust Svc: 800-621-4041 ■ *Web:* www.tetramed.com

VWR International 1310 Goshen Pkwy .... West Chester PA 19380 610-431-1700 431-9174
TF: 800-932-5000 ■ *Web:* www.vwrsp.com

William V MacGill & Co 1000 N Lombard Rd .... Lombard IL 60148 630-889-0500 727-3433*
**Fax Area Code:* 800 ■ *TF:* 800-323-2841 ■ *Web:* www.macgill.com

Wise El Santo Co Inc 11000 Linpage Pl .... Saint Louis MO 63132 314-428-3100 428-7017
TF: 800-727-8541 ■ *Web:* www.wiseelsanto.com

Zee Medical Inc 22 Corporate Park .... Irvine CA 92606 949-252-9500 252-9649
TF: 800-841-8417 ■ *Web:* www.zeemedical.com

MEDICAL FACILITIES

SEE Developmental Centers p. 1587; Health Care Providers - Ancillary p. 1772; Hospices p. 1791; Hospitals p. 1799; Imaging Services - Diagnostic p. 1852; Substance Abuse Treatment Centers p. 2335

479 MEDICAL INSTRUMENTS & APPARATUS - MFR

SEE ALSO Imaging Equipment & Systems - Medical p. 1852; Medical Supplies - Mfr p. 1955

Phone | Fax

3M Medical Specialties & OEM Products Div
3M Health Care Ctr Bldg 275-4 W-02 .... Saint Paul MN 55144 800-228-3957 772-2547

Abbott Laboratories 100 Abbott Park Rd .... Abbott Park IL 60064 847-937-6100
NYSE: ABT ■ *TF:* 800-323-9100 ■ *Web:* www.abbott.com

Accurate Surgical & Scientific Instruments Corp
300 Shames Dr .... Westbury NY 11590 516-333-2570 997-4948
TF: 800-645-3569 ■ *Web:* www.accuratesurgical.com

Acme United Corp 60 Round Hill Rd .... Fairfield CT 06824 203-254-6060 254-6019
AMEX: ACU ■ *TF:* 800-835-2263 ■ *Web:* www.acmeunited.com

AESCULAP Inc 3773 Corporate Pkwy .... Center Valley PA 18034 800-282-9000 791-6886*
**Fax Area Code:* 610 ■ *TF:* 800-282-9000 ■ *Web:* www.aesculapusa.com

	City	State	Zip	Phone	Fax
Akorn Inc 2500 Millbrook Dr *AMEX:* AKN ■ *TF:* 800-932-5676 ■ *Web:* www.akorn.com	Buffalo Grove	IL	60089	847-279-6100	279-6123
Aksys Ltd 2 Marriott Dr *NASDAQ:* AKSY ■ *TF:* 877-229-5700 ■ *Web:* www.aksys.com	Lincolnshire	IL	60069	847-229-2020	229-2080
ALARIS Medical Systems Inc 10221 Wateridge Cir *TF:* 800-854-7128 ■ *Web:* www.alarismed.com	San Diego	CA	92121	858-458-7000	458-7760
Alcon Laboratories Inc Surgical Div 6201 South Fwy **Fax Area Code:* 800 ■ *TF:* 800-862-5266 ■ *Web:* www.alconlabs.com/us/aa/Surgical	Fort Worth	TX	76134	817-293-0450	241-0677*
Allied Healthcare Products Inc 1720 Sublette Ave *NASDAQ:* AHPI ■ **Fax Area Code:* 800 ■ **Fax:* Cust Svc ■ *TF:* 800-444-3940 ■ *Web:* www.alliedhpi.com	Saint Louis	MO	63110	314-771-2400	477-7701*
American Medical Instruments Inc 8 Ledgewood Blvd *Web:* www.amiinc.com	Dartmouth	MA	02747	508-985-9900	985-9911
AngioDynamics Inc 603 Queensbury Ave *NASDAQ:* ANGO ■ *TF:* 800-772-6446 ■ *Web:* www.angiodynamics.com	Queensbury	NY	12804	518-798-1215	798-1360
Angiotech Pharmaceuticals Inc 1618 Station St *NASDAQ:* ANPI ■ *Web:* www.angiotech.com	Vancouver	BC	V6A1B6	604-221-7676	221-2330
Antares Pharma Inc 13755 1st Ave N Suite 100 *AMEX:* AIS ■ *TF:* 800-328-3077 ■ *Web:* www.antarespharma.com	Minneapolis	MN	55441	763-475-7700	476-1009
Aradigm Corp 3929 Point Eden Way *NASDAQ:* ARDM ■ *Web:* www.aradigm.com	Hayward	CA	94545	510-265-9000	265-0277
Arrow International Inc 2400 Bernville Rd *NASDAQ:* ARRO ■ *TF:* 800-233-3187 ■ *Web:* www.arrowintl.com	Reading	PA	19605	610-378-0131	374-5360
ATEK Medical Mfg 620 Watson St SW *TF:* 800-690-2365 ■ *Web:* www.atekmedical.com	Grand Rapids	MI	49504	616-643-5200	643-1482
Atrion Corp 1 Allentown Pkwy *NASDAQ:* ATRI ■ *TF:* 800-627-0226 ■ *Web:* www.atrioncorp.com	Allen	TX	75002	972-390-9800	396-7581
B Braun of America Inc 824 12th Ave *TF:* 800-523-9676 ■ *Web:* www.bbraunusa.com	Bethlehem	PA	18018	610-691-5400	691-2202
Bard Access Systems Inc 5425 W Amelia Earhart Dr *TF:* 800-443-5505 ■ *Web:* www.bardaccess.com	Salt Lake City	UT	84116	801-595-0700	595-4907
Bard CR Inc 730 Central Ave *NYSE:* BCR ■ *Web:* www.crbard.com	Murray Hill	NJ	07974	908-277-8000	
Bard CR Inc Medical Div 8195 Industrial Blvd **Fax Area Code:* 800 ■ **Fax:* Cust Svc ■ *TF:* 800-526-4455 ■ *Web:* www.bardmedical.com	Covington	GA	30014	770-784-6100	852-1339*
Bard CR Inc Peripheral Vascular Div PO Box 1740 **Fax Area Code:* 800 ■ **Fax:* Cust Svc ■ *TF:* 800-321-4254	Tempe	AZ	85281	480-894-9515	440-5316*
Bard CR Inc Urological Div 8195 Industrial Blvd **Fax:* Mktg ■ *TF:* 800-526-4455 ■ *Web:* www.bardurological.com	Covington	GA	30014	770-786-9051	784-6908*
Bausch & Lomb Surgical Inc 180 Via Verde Dr **Fax Area Code:* 800 ■ **Fax:* Hum Res ■ *TF Cust Svc:* 800-338-2020 ■ *Web:* www.bausch.com/us/resource/surgical	San Dimas	CA	91773	909-971-5100	362-7006*
Baxter Healthcare Corp 1 Baxter Pkwy *Web:* www.baxter.com	Deerfield	IL	60015	847-948-2000	948-3948
Baxter International Inc 1 Baxter Pkwy *NYSE:* BAX ■ *Web:* www.baxter.com	Deerfield	IL	60015	847-948-2000	948-3948
Bayer Healthcare 511 Benedict Ave *TF:* 800-431-1970 ■ *Web:* www.bayerdiag.com	Tarrytown	NY	10591	914-631-8000	524-2132
BD Medical 9450 S State St *TF:* 888-237-2762 ■ *Web:* www.bd.com/aboutbd/wwbusinesses/#medical	Sandy	UT	84070	801-565-2300	565-2740
Becton Dickinson & Co 1 Becton Dr *NYSE:* BDX ■ **Fax:* Cust Svc ■ *TF Cust Svc:* 888-237-2762 ■ *Web:* www.bd.com	Franklin Lakes	NJ	07417	201-847-6800	847-4882*
Becton Dickinson Consumer Healthcare 1 Becton Dr *TF:* 888-237-2762 ■ *Web:* www.bd.com/consumer	Franklin Lakes	NJ	07417	201-847-6800	847-4882
Becton Dickinson Pharmaceutical Systems 1 Becton Dr *TF:* 888-237-2762 ■ *Web:* www.bd.com/pharmaceuticals	Franklin Lakes	NJ	07417	201-847-6800	847-4847
Beere Precision Medical Instruments Inc 5307 95th Ave *TF:* 800-295-8505 ■ *Web:* www.beeremedical.com	Kenosha	WI	53144	262-657-2800	657-2801
Best Vascular 4350 International Blvd Suite E *TF:* 800-668-6783 ■ *Web:* www.bestvascular.com	Norcross	GA	30093	770-717-0904	717-1283
BG Sulzle Inc 1 Needle Ln *Web:* www.bgsulzle.com	North Syracuse	NY	13212	315-454-3221	454-9879
Bioject Medical Technologies Inc 20245 SW 95 Ave *NASDAQ:* BJCT ■ *TF:* 800-683-7221 ■ *Web:* www.bioject.com	Tualatin	OR	97062	503-692-8001	692-6698
BioMerieux Inc 595 Anglum Rd **Fax Area Code:* 800 ■ *TF:* 800-638-4835 ■ *Web:* www.biomerieux.com	Hazelwood	MO	63042	314-731-8500	325-1598*
Biosense Webster Inc 3333 Diamond Canyon Rd *TF:* 800-729-9010 ■ *Web:* www.biosensewebster.com	Diamond Bar	CA	91765	909-839-8500	468-3841
Boston Scientific Corp 1 Boston Scientific Pl *NYSE:* BSX ■ **Fax Area Code:* 888 ■ **Fax:* Cust Svc ■ *TF:* 800-272-3737 ■ *Web:* www.bsci.com	Natick	MA	01760	508-650-8000	272-9444*
Boston Scientific Corp 4100 Hamline Ave N *TF:* 800-405-9611 ■ *Web:* www.guidant.com	Saint Paul	MN	55112	651-582-4000	582-4166
Braemar Inc 1285 Corporate Center Dr *TF:* 800-328-2719 ■ *Web:* www.braemarinc.com	Eagan	MN	55121	651-286-8620	286-8630
Cambridge Heart Inc 1 Oak Park Dr *TF:* 888-226-9283 ■ *Web:* www.cambridgeheart.com	Bedford	MA	01730	781-271-1200	275-8431
Cantel Medical Corp 150 Clove Rd 9th Fl *NYSE:* CMN ■ *Web:* www.cantelmedical.com	Little Falls	NJ	07424	973-890-7220	890-7270
Cardica Inc 900 Saginaw Dr *NASDAQ:* CRDC ■ *Web:* www.cardica.com	Redwood City	CA	94063	650-364-9975	364-3134
Cardima Inc 47266 Benicia St *TF:* 888-354-0300 ■ *Web:* www.cardima.com	Fremont	CA	94538	510-354-0300	657-4476
Cardinal Health Automation & Information Services 3750 Torrey View Ct *TF:* 800-367-9947 ■ *Web:* www.cardinal.com/content/businesses	San Diego	CA	92130	858-480-6000	480-6329
CardioTech International Inc 229 Andover St *AMEX:* CTE ■ *Web:* www.cardiotech-inc.com	Wilmington	MA	01887	978-657-0075	657-0074
CAS Medical Systems Inc 44 E Industrial Rd *NASDAQ:* CASM ■ *TF:* 800-227-4414 ■ *Web:* www.casmed.com	Branford	CT	06405	203-488-6056	488-9438
Celsion Corp 10220-L Old Columbia Rd *AMEX:* CLN ■ *TF:* 800-262-0394 ■ *Web:* www.celsion.com	Columbia	MD	21046	410-290-5390	290-5394
Chad Therapeutics Inc 21622 Plummer St *AMEX:* CTU ■ *TF:* 800-423-8870 ■ *Web:* www.chadtherapeutics.com	Chatsworth	CA	91311	818-882-0883	882-1809
Clinical Data Inc 1 Gateway Ctr Suite 702 *NASDAQ:* CLDA ■ *Web:* www.clda.com	Newton	MA	02458	617-527-9933	527-8230
CNS Inc 7615 Smetana Ln *NASDAQ:* CNXS ■ *TF:* 800-441-0417 ■ *Web:* www.cns.com	Eden Prairie	MN	55347	952-229-1500	229-1700
Codman & Shurtleff Inc 325 Paramount Dr *TF:* 800-225-0460 ■ *Web:* www.jnjcodman.com	Raynham	MA	02767	508-880-8100	880-8122
Conceptus Inc 331 E Evelyn Ave *NASDAQ:* CPTS ■ *TF:* 800-434-7240 ■ *Web:* www.conceptus.com	Mountainview	CA	94041	650-962-4000	962-5200
CONMED Corp 525 French Rd *NASDAQ:* CNMD ■ **Fax Area Code:* 800 ■ **Fax:* Cust Svc ■ *TF:* 800-448-6506 ■ *Web:* www.conmed.com	Utica	NY	13502	315-797-8375	438-3051*
CONMED Endoscopic Technologies 129 Concord Rd Bldg 3 *TF:* 800-225-1332 ■ *Web:* www.conmed.com/EndoTechnologies.php	Billerica	MA	01821	978-663-8989	262-4802
CONMED Linvatec 11311 Concept Blvd **Fax:* Cust Svc ■ *TF:* 800-325-5900 ■ *Web:* www.linvatec.com	Largo	FL	33773	727-392-6464	399-5256*
Cook Critical Care 750 Daniels Way **Fax Area Code:* 800 ■ *TF:* 800-457-4500 ■ *Web:* www.cookcriticalcare.com	Bloomington	IN	47404	812-339-2235	554-8335*
Cook Endoscopy 4900 Bethania Stn Rd *TF:* 800-245-4717 ■ *Web:* www.wilsoncook.com	Winston-Salem	NC	27105	336-744-0157	744-1147
Cook Inc PO Box 489 **Fax Area Code:* 800 ■ *TF:* 800-457-4500 ■ *Web:* www.cookincorporated.com	Bloomington	IN	47402	812-339-2235	554-8335*
Cook OB/GYN 1100 W Morgan St **Fax Area Code:* 800 ■ *TF:* 800-541-5591 ■ *Web:* www.cookobgyn.com	Spencer	IN	47460	812-829-6500	837-4130*
Cook Surgical PO Box 489 **Fax Area Code:* 800 ■ *TF:* 800-457-4500 ■ *Web:* www.cooksurgical.com	Bloomington	IN	47402	812-339-2235	554-8335*
Cook Urological Inc 1100 W Morgan St *TF:* 800-457-4500 ■ *Web:* www.cookurological.com	Spencer	IN	47460	812-829-4891	829-1801
Cook Vascular Inc 1186 Montgomery Ln *TF:* 800-245-4715 ■ *Web:* www.cookvascular.com	Vandergrift	PA	15690	724-845-8621	845-2848
Cooper Cos Inc 21062 Bake Pkwy Suite 100 *NYSE:* COO ■ *TF:* 888-822-2660 ■ *Web:* www.coopercos.com	Lake Forest	CA	92630	949-597-4700	597-0662
CooperSurgical Inc 95 Corporate Dr **Fax Area Code:* 800 ■ **Fax:* Cust Svc ■ *TF:* 800-645-3760 ■ *Web:* www.coopersurgical.com	Trumbull	CT	06611	203-929-6321	262-0105*
Cordis Corp PO Box 025700 **Fax:* Mail Rm ■ *TF:* 800-327-2490 ■ *Web:* www.cordis.com	Miami	FL	33102	786-313-2000	313-2080*
Covidien Ltd 15 Hampshire St *NYSE:* COV ■ *Web:* www.covidien.com	Mansfield	MA	02048	508-261-8000	261-8062
CR Bard Inc 730 Central Ave *NYSE:* BCR ■ *Web:* www.crbard.com	Murray Hill	NJ	07974	908-277-8000	
CR Bard Inc Medical Div 8195 Industrial Blvd **Fax Area Code:* 800 ■ **Fax:* Cust Svc ■ *TF:* 800-526-4455 ■ *Web:* www.bardmedical.com	Covington	GA	30014	770-784-6100	852-1339*
CR Bard Inc Peripheral Vascular Div PO Box 1740 **Fax Area Code:* 800 ■ **Fax:* Cust Svc ■ *TF:* 800-321-4254	Tempe	AZ	85281	480-894-9515	440-5316*
CR Bard Inc Urological Div 8195 Industrial Blvd **Fax:* Mktg ■ *TF:* 800-526-4455 ■ *Web:* www.bardurological.com	Covington	GA	30014	770-786-9051	784-6908*
Criticare Systems Inc 20925 Crossroads Cir Suite 100 *AMEX:* CMD ■ *TF:* 800-458-4615 ■ *Web:* www.csiusa.com	Waukesha	WI	53186	262-798-8282	798-8290
CryoCor Inc 9717 Pacific Heights Blvd *NASDAQ:* CRYO ■ *TF:* 866-909-2796 ■ *Web:* www.cryocor.com	San Diego	CA	92121	858-909-2200	909-2300
Cutera Inc 3240 Bayshore Blvd *NASDAQ:* CUTR ■ *TF:* 888-428-8372 ■ *Web:* www.cutera.com	Brisbane	CA	94005	415-657-5500	330-2444
Daig Corp 14901 DeVeau Pl *TF:* 800-328-3873	Minnetonka	MN	55345	952-933-4700	933-0307
Datascope Corp 14 Philips Pkwy *NASDAQ:* DSCP ■ *TF:* 800-288-2121 ■ *Web:* www.datascope.com	Montvale	NJ	07645	201-391-8100	307-5400
Davol Inc 100 Sockanossett Crossroad PO Box 8500 **Fax Area Code:* 800 ■ *TF:* 800-556-6756 ■ *Web:* www.davol.com	Cranston	RI	02920	401-463-7000	463-3142*
Deltec Inc 1265 Grey Fox Rd *TF:* 800-426-2448 ■ *Web:* www.deltec.com	Saint Paul	MN	55112	651-633-2556	628-7459
Dolphin Medical Inc 12525 Chadron Ave *TF:* 866-588-9539 ■ *Web:* www.dolphinmedical.com	Hawthorne	CA	90250	310-978-3073	978-1816
Electro-Optical Sciences Inc 3 W Main St Suite 201 *NASDAQ:* MELA ■ *Web:* www.eo-sciences.com	Irvington	NY	10533	914-591-3783	591-3701
Empi Inc 599 Cardigan Rd **Fax Area Code:* 800 ■ *TF:* 800-328-2536 ■ *Web:* www.empi.com	Saint Paul	MN	55126	651-415-9000	450-3593*
Encision Inc 6797 Winchester Cir *AMEX:* ECI ■ *TF:* 800-998-0986 ■ *Web:* www.encision.com	Boulder	CO	80301	303-444-2600	444-2693
Endocare Inc 201 Technology Dr *TF:* 800-683-8938 ■ *Web:* www.endocare.com	Irvine	CA	92618	949-450-5400	450-5300
Endologix Inc 11 Studebaker *NASDAQ:* ELGX ■ **Fax Area Code:* 877 ■ *TF:* 800-983-2284 ■ *Web:* www.endologix.com	Irvine	CA	92618	949-457-9546	843-1500*
Enpath Medical Inc 2300 Berkshire Ln N *NASDAQ:* NPTH ■ *TF:* 800-559-2613 ■ *Web:* www.enpathmedical.com	Plymouth	MN	55441	763-951-8181	951-0148
EP Technologies 2710 Orchard Pkwy *TF Cust Svc:* 800-552-6700	San Jose	CA	95134	408-895-3500	895-3501
Escalon Medical Corp 565 E Swedesford Rd Suite 200 *NASDAQ:* ESMC ■ *Web:* www.escalonmed.com	Wayne	PA	19087	610-688-6830	688-3641
Ethicon Endo-Surgery Inc 4545 Creek Rd *TF:* 800-556-8451 ■ *Web:* www.ethiconendo.com	Cincinnati	OH	45242	513-337-7000	
ev3 Inc 9600 54th Ave N Suite 100 *NASDAQ:* EVVV ■ *TF:* 800-716-6700 ■ *Web:* www.ev3.net	Plymouth	MN	55442	763-398-7000	398-7200
Fisher Scientific International Inc 1 Liberty Ln *NYSE:* FSH ■ *Web:* www.fisherscientific.com	Hampton	NH	03842	603-926-5911	929-2379
G & G Instrument Corp 466 Saw Mill River Rd *TF:* 800-882-2288 ■ *Web:* www.datacut.com/gg/	Ardsley	NY	10502	914-693-6000	693-6738
Gaymar Industries Inc 10 Centre Dr **Fax Area Code:* 800 ■ **Fax:* Cust Svc ■ *TF:* 800-828-7341 ■ *Web:* www.gaymar.com	Orchard Park	NY	14127	716-662-2551	993-7890*
Getinge USA Inc 1777 E Henrietta Rd **Fax Area Code:* 800 ■ *TF Cust Svc:* 800-950-9912 ■ *Web:* www.getingeusa.com	Rochester	NY	14623	585-475-1400	950-2570*
Gettig Technologies Inc 1 Streamside Pl *Web:* www.gettig.com	Spring Mills	PA	16875	814-422-8892	422-8011
GF Health Products Inc 2935 Northeast Pkwy **Fax Area Code:* 800 ■ *TF:* 800-235-4661 ■ *Web:* www.grahamfield.com	Atlanta	GA	30360	770-447-1609	726-0601*
Gyrus Medical Inc 6655 Wedgwood Rd Suite 160 *TF:* 800-852-9361 ■ *Web:* www.gyrusgroup.com/medical	Maple Grove	MN	55311	763-416-3000	416-3070
Haemonetics Corp 400 Wood Rd *NYSE:* HAE ■ **Fax Area Code:* 800 ■ **Fax:* Cust Svc ■ *TF:* 800-225-5242 ■ *Web:* www.haemonetics.com	Braintree	MA	02184	781-848-7100	860-1512*
HemoSense Inc 651 River Oaks Pkwy *AMEX:* HEM ■ *TF:* 877-436-6444 ■ *Web:* www.hemosense.com	San Jose	CA	95134	408-719-1393	719-1184
Hill-Rom Services Inc 1069 SR 46 E **Fax:* Hum Res ■ *Web:* www.hill-rom.com	Batesville	IN	47006	812-934-7777	931-3592*
HNS International Inc 4992 E Hunter Ave *TF:* 877-474-6539 ■ *Web:* www.injex.com	Anaheim	CA	92807	714-777-5111	777-5150
Hoggan Health Industries Inc 8020 S 1300 West *TF:* 800-678-7888 ■ *Web:* www.hogganhealth.com	West Jordan	UT	84088	801-572-6500	572-6514
Hospira Inc 275 N Field Dr *NYSE:* HSP ■ *TF:* 877-946-7747 ■ *Web:* www.hospira.com	Lake Forest	IL	60045	224-212-2000	
Hypertension Diagnostics Inc 2915 Waters Rd Suite 108 *TF:* 888-785-7392 ■ *Web:* www.hdi-pulsewave.com	Eagan	MN	55121	651-687-9999	687-0485
Implant Sciences Corp 107 Audubon Rd #5 *AMEX:* IMX ■ *Web:* www.implantsciences.com	Wakefield	MA	01880	781-246-0700	246-1167
Integra LifeSciences Holdings Corp 311 Enterprise Dr *NASDAQ:* IART ■ *TF:* 800-654-2873 ■ *Web:* www.integra-ls.com	Plainsboro	NJ	08536	609-275-0500	799-3297
Intuitive Surgical Inc 950 Kifer Rd *NASDAQ:* ISRG ■ *TF:* 888-868-4647 ■ *Web:* www.intuitivesurgical.com	Sunnyvale	CA	94086	408-523-2100	523-1390
Invacare ICCG 1644 Lotsie Blvd *TF:* 800-347-5440 ■ *Web:* www.invacare-ccg.com	Saint Louis	MO	63132	314-253-5440	253-3463
Inverness Corp 17-10 Willow St *TF:* 800-631-0860 ■ *Web:* www.invernesscorp.com	Fair Lawn	NJ	07410	201-794-3400	794-6814
Jenckes Machine Co PO Box 364 *TF:* 866-941-1455	Warren	RI	02885	401-247-1999	247-4575
Johnson Matthey Medical Products 1401 King Rd *TF:* 800-442-1405 ■ *Web:* www.jmmedical.com	West Chester	PA	19380	610-648-8000	648-8105
Jordan Industries Inc Healthcare Products Group 1751 Lake Cook Rd ArborLake Ctr Suite 550	Deerfield	IL	60015	847-945-5591	945-5698
Kensey Nash Corp 735 Pennsylvania Dr *NASDAQ:* KNSY ■ *TF:* 800-524-1984 ■ *Web:* www.kenseynash.com	Exton	PA	19341	484-713-2100	713-2900
Kimberly-Clark/Ballard Medical Products 1400 Holcomb Bridge Rd **Fax Area Code:* 801 ■ *TF:* 800-528-5591 ■ *Web:* www.kchealthcare.com	Roswell	GA	30076	800-524-3577	572-6999*
Lake Region Mfg Co Inc 340 Lake Hazeltine Dr *Web:* www.lakergn.com	Chaska	MN	55318	952-448-5111	448-3441
Mallinckrodt Inc 675 McDonnell Blvd **Fax:* Hum Res ■ *TF:* 888-744-1414 ■ *Web:* www.mallinckrodt.com	Hazelwood	MO	63042	314-654-2000	654-6257*

Phone | Fax

Manan Medical Products Inc 241 W Palatine Rd ... Wheeling IL 60090 847-637-3333 637-3334
TF: 800-424-6779 ■ *Web:* www.manan.com

McKinley Medical LLP 4080 Youngfield St ... Wheat Ridge CO 80033 303-420-9569 420-4545
TF: 800-578-0555 ■ *Web:* www.mckinleymed.com

Medrad Inc 1 Medrad Dr ... Indianola PA 15051 412-767-2400 767-4120*
**Fax:* Cust Svc ■ *TF Cust Svc:* 800-633-7237 ■ *Web:* www.medrad.com

Medtronic Inc 710 Medtronic Pkwy NE ... Minneapolis MN 55432 763-514-4000 514-4879
NYSE: MDT ■ *TF Cust Svc:* 800-328-2518 ■ *Web:* www.medtronic.com

Medtronic Neurosurgery 125 Cremona Dr ... Goleta CA 93117 805-968-1546 968-5038
TF Cust Svc: 800-468-9710

Medtronic Perfusion Systems 7611 Northland Dr ... Brooklyn Park MN 55428 763-391-9000 391-9100
TF: 800-328-3320 ■ *Web:* www.medtronic.com

Medtronic Powered Surgical Solutions 4620 N Beach St ... Fort Worth TX 76137 817-788-6400 788-6401*
**Fax:* Orders ■ *TF:* 800-433-7639 ■ *Web:* www.medtronic.com/neuro/midasrex

Medtronic Vascular 3576 Unocal Pl ... Santa Rosa CA 95403 707-525-0111 525-0114
TF: 800-308-7868 ■ *Web:* www.medtronic.com/vascular

Medwave Inc 435 Newbury St Suite 206 ... Danvers MA 01923 800-894-7601 762-8908*
NASDAQ: MDWV ■ **Fax Area Code:* 978 ■ *TF:* 800-894-7601 ■ *Web:* www.mdwv.com

Meridian Medical Technologies Inc
6350 Stevens Forest Rd Suite 301 ... Columbia MD 21046 443-259-7800 259-7801
TF: 800-638-8093 ■ *Web:* www.meridianmeds.com

Merit Medical Systems Inc 1600 W Merit Pkwy ... South Jordan UT 84095 801-253-1600 253-1652
NASDAQ: MMSI ■ *TF:* 800-356-3748 ■ *Web:* www.merit.com

Micro-Tube Fabricators Inc 250 Lackland Dr ... Middlesex NJ 08846 732-469-7420 469-4314

MicroAire Surgical Instruments Inc 1641 Edlich Dr ... Charlottesville VA 22911 434-975-8000 975-4144
TF: 800-538-5561 ■ *Web:* www.microaire.com

Minntech Corp 14605 28th Ave N ... Minneapolis MN 55447 763-553-3300 551-2688
TF: 800-328-3345 ■ *Web:* www.minntech.com

Nephros Inc 3960 Broadway ... New York NY 10032 212-781-5113 781-5166
AMEX: NEP ■ *Web:* www.nephros.com

Novosci 2828 N Crescent Ridge Dr ... The Woodlands TX 77381 281-363-4950 570-4009*
**Fax Area Code:* 888 ■ *TF:* 800-322-2273 ■ *Web:* www.novosci.us

NuVasive Inc 4545 Towne Centre Ct ... San Diego CA 92121 858-909-1800 909-2000
NASDAQ: NUVA ■ *TF:* 800-455-1476 ■ *Web:* www.nuvasive.com

NxStage Medical Inc 439 S Union St 5th Fl ... Lawrence MA 01843 978-687-4700 687-4809
NASDAQ: NXTM ■ *TF:* 866-697-8243 ■ *Web:* www.nxstage.com

Ortho-Clinical Diagnostics Inc 1001 US Rt 202 N PO Box 350 ... Raritan NJ 08869 908-218-1300 453-3660*
**Fax Area Code:* 585 ■ **Fax:* Cust Svc ■ *TF:* 800-828-6316 ■
Web: www.orthoclinical.com

Osteomed Corp 3885 Arapaho Rd ... Addison TX 75001 972-677-4600 677-4601
TF Cust Svc: 800-456-7779 ■ *Web:* www.osteomedcorp.com

Osteometer MediTech Inc 12525 Chadron Ave ... Hawthorne CA 90250 310-978-3073 676-0948
TF: 866-421-7762 ■ *Web:* www.osteometer.com

PerkinElmer Inc 45 William St ... Wellesley MA 02481 781-237-5100 237-9386
NYSE: PKI ■ *Web:* www.perkinelmer.com

Pilling Surgical 2917 Weck Dr ... Research Triangle Park NC 27709 919-544-8000 332-2308*
**Fax Area Code:* 800 ■ *TF Cust Svc:* 800-523-6507 ■ *Web:* www.pillingsurgical.com

Possis Medical Inc 9055 Evergreen Blvd NW ... Minneapolis MN 55433 763-780-4555 780-2227
NASDAQ: POSS ■ *TF:* 800-810-7677 ■ *Web:* www.possis.com

PreMD Inc 4211 Yonge St Suite 615 ... Toronto ON M2P2A9 416-222-3449 222-4533
AMEX: PME ■ *Web:* www.premdinc.com

Propper Mfg Co Inc 36-04 Skillman Ave ... Long Island City NY 11101 718-392-6650 482-8909
TF Cust Svc: 800-832-4300 ■ *Web:* www.proppermfg.com

ResMed Inc 14040 Danielson St ... Poway CA 92064 858-746-2400 746-2900
NYSE: RMD ■ *TF:* 800-424-0737 ■ *Web:* www.resmed.com

Rochester Medical Corp 1 Rochester Medical Dr ... Stewartville MN 55976 507-533-9600 533-4232
NASDAQ: ROCM ■ *TF:* 800-243-3315 ■ *Web:* www.rocm.com

Siemens Medical Solutions Inc 51 Valley Stream Pkwy ... Malvern PA 19355 610-448-6300 219-3124
TF: 866-872-9745 ■ *Web:* www.medical.siemens.com

Signalife Inc 531 S Main St Suite 301 ... Greenville SC 29601 864-233-2300 233-2100
AMEX: SGN ■ *Web:* www.signalife.com

Smith & Nephew Inc Endoscopy Div 150 Minuteman Rd ... Andover MA 01810 978-749-1000 749-1599
TF: 800-343-8386 ■ *Web:* www.smith-nephew.com/what/endoscopy.jsp

Smiths Medical MD Inc 1265 Grey Fox Rd ... Saint Paul MN 55112 651-633-2556 628-7459
TF: 800-258-5361 ■ *Web:* www.smiths-medical.com

Sorin Group USA Inc 14401 W 65th Way ... Arvada CO 80004 303-425-5508 467-6584
TF: 800-221-7943 ■ *Web:* www.soringroup-usa.com

Specialized Health Products International Inc (SHPI)
585 W 500 South ... Bountiful UT 84010 801-298-3360 298-1759
TF: 800-306-3360 ■ *Web:* www.shpi.com

SpectruMedix Corp 2124 Old Gatesburg Rd ... State College PA 16803 814-867-8600 867-4513
Web: www.spectrumedix.com

SS White Medical Products Inc 151 Old New Brunswick Rd ... Piscataway NJ 08854 732-752-8300 752-8315
TF Cust Svc: 888-779-4483 ■ *Web:* www.sswhitemedical.com

STERIS Corp 5960 Heisley Rd ... Mentor OH 44060 440-354-2600 639-4450*
NYSE: STE ■ **Fax:* Cust Svc ■ *TF:* 800-548-4873 ■ *Web:* www.steris.com

Stryker Corp 2725 Fairfield Rd ... Kalamazoo MI 49002 269-385-2600 385-1062
NYSE: SYK ■ *TF:* 800-726-2725 ■ *Web:* www.strykercorp.com

Stryker Instruments 4100 E Milham Ave ... Kalamazoo MI 49001 269-323-7700 324-5367
TF Cust Svc: 800-253-3210 ■ *Web:* www.stryker.com/instruments

Sulzle BG Inc 1 Needle Ln ... North Syracuse NY 13212 315-454-3221 454-9879
Web: www.bgsulzle.com

Sunrise Medical Continuing Care Group 5001 Joerns Dr ... Stevens Point WI 54481 715-341-3600 341-3962
TF: 800-972-7581

Symmetry Medical Inc 220 W Market St ... Warsaw IN 46580 574-268-2252 267-4551
NYSE: SMA ■ *Web:* www.symmetrymedical.com

Teleflex Medical Group 2917 Weck Dr ... Research Triangle Park NC 27709 919-544-8000 932-5329*
**Fax Area Code:* 800 ■ *TF:* 800-334-9751 ■ *Web:* www.teleflexmedical.com

Terumo Cardiovascular Systems Corp 6200 Jackson Rd ... Ann Arbor MI 48103 734-663-4145 292-6551*
**Fax Area Code:* 800 ■ **Fax:* Cust Svc ■ *TF:* 800-262-3304 ■ *Web:* www.terumo-us.com

Terumo Medical Corp 2101 Cottontail Ln ... Somerset NJ 08873 732-302-4900 302-3083
TF: 800-283-7866 ■ *Web:* www.terumomedical.com

TFX Medical Inc 50 Plantation Dr ... Jaffrey NH 03452 603-532-7706 532-8211
TF: 800-548-6600 ■ *Web:* www.tfxmedical.com

Topcon Medical Systems Inc 37 W Century Rd ... Paramus NJ 07652 201-261-9450 634-1365*
**Fax:* Cust Svc ■ *TF:* 800-223-1130 ■ *Web:* www.topcon.com/medical.html

Urologix Inc 14405 21st Ave N ... Minneapolis MN 55447 763-475-1400 475-1443
NASDAQ: ULGX ■ *TF:* 800-475-1403 ■ *Web:* www.urologix.com

Uroplasty Inc 5420 F Elta Rd ... Minnetonka MN 55343 612-378-1180 378-2027
AMEX: UPI ■ *Web:* www.uroplasty.com

US Surgical Corp 150 Glover Ave ... Norwalk CT 06856 203-845-1000 544-8772*
**Fax Area Code:* 800 ■ **Fax:* Cust Svc ■ *TF:* 800-722-8772 ■ *Web:* www.ussurg.com

Utah Medical Products Inc 7043 S 300 West ... Midvale UT 84047 801-566-1200 566-2062
NASDAQ: UTMD ■ *TF:* 800-533-4984 ■ *Web:* www.utahmed.com

vasamed 7615 Golden Triangle Dr Suite C ... Eden Prairie MN 55344 952-944-5857 944-6022
TF: 800-695-2737 ■ *Web:* www.vasamed.com

Vascular Solutions Inc 6464 Sycamore Ct ... Maple Grove MN 55369 763-656-4300 656-4250
NASDAQ: VASC ■ *Web:* www.vascularsolutions.com

Ventana Medical Systems Inc 1910 Innovation Pk Dr ... Tucson AZ 85755 520-887-2155 887-2558
NASDAQ: VMSI ■ *TF:* 800-227-2155 ■ *Web:* www.ventanamed.com

ViaCirq 400 South Point Blvd Bldg 501 Suite 230 ... Canonsburg PA 15317 724-745-2362 745-2728
TF Cust Svc: 877-952-6100 ■ *Web:* www.viacirq.com

VIASYS Healthcare Inc 227 Washington St Suite 200 ... Conshohocken PA 19428 610-862-0800 862-0836
NYSE: VAS ■ *Web:* www.viasyshealthcare.com

Vital Signs Inc 20 Campus Rd ... Totowa NJ 07512 973-790-1330 790-3307
NASDAQ: VITL ■ *TF:* 800-932-0760 ■ *Web:* www.vital-signs.com

VNUS Medical Technologies Inc 5799 Fontanoso Way ... San Jose CA 95138 408-360-7200 365-8480
NASDAQ: VNUS ■ *TF:* 888-797-8346 ■ *Web:* www.vnus.com

Walco International Inc 7 Village Cir Suite 200 ... Westlake TX 76262 817-859-3000 859-3099
TF: 877-289-9252 ■ *Web:* www.walcoinc.com

White SS Medical Products Inc 151 Old New Brunswick Rd ... Piscataway NJ 08854 732-752-8300 752-8315
TF Cust Svc: 888-779-4483 ■ *Web:* www.sswhitemedical.com

ZLB Behring LLC 1020 1st Ave PO Box 61501 ... King of Prussia PA 19406 610-878-4000 878-4009
TF: 800-683-1288 ■ *Web:* www.zlbbehring.com

480 MEDICAL SUPPLIES - MFR

SEE ALSO Personal Protective Equipment & Clothing p. 2105

Phone | Fax

3M Health Care Solutions 3M Ctr ... Saint Paul MN 55144 651-733-1110
TF Prod Info: 800-364-3577 ■ *Web:* www.3m.com/US/healthcare

3M Medical Specialties & OEM Products Div
3M Health Care Ctr Bldg 275-4 W-02 ... Saint Paul MN 55144 800-228-3957 772-2547

Abbott Vascular 400 Saginaw Dr ... Redwood City CA 94063 650-474-3000 474-3010
TF: 800-587-7965 ■ *Web:* www.abbottvascular.com

Adhesives Research Inc 400 Seaks Run Rd PO Box 100 ... Glen Rock PA 17327 717-235-7979 235-8320
TF: 800-445-6240 ■ *Web:* www.adhesivesresearch.com

Advanced Sterilization Products 33 Technology Dr ... Irvine CA 92618 949-581-5799 450-6800
TF: 800-595-0200 ■ *Web:* www.cidex.com

AESCULAP Inc 3773 Corporate Pkwy ... Center Valley PA 18034 800-282-9000 791-6886*
**Fax Area Code:* 610 ■ *TF:* 800-282-9000 ■ *Web:* www.aesculapusa.com

Allergan 2525 Dupont Dr ... Irvine CA 92612 805-683-6761 967-5839
TF: 800-624-4261 ■ *Web:* www.allergan.com

Allied Healthcare Products Inc 1720 Sublette Ave ... Saint Louis MO 63110 314-771-2400 477-7701*
NASDAQ: AHPI ■ **Fax Area Code:* 800 ■ **Fax:* Cust Svc ■ *TF:* 800-444-3940 ■
Web: www.alliedhpi.com

American Medical Systems Holdings Inc 10700 Bren Rd W ... Minnetonka MN 55343 952-933-4666 930-6157
NASDAQ: AMMD ■ *TF:* 800-328-3881 ■ *Web:* www.visitams.com

Animas Corp 200 Lawrence Dr ... West Chester PA 19380 610-644-8990 644-8717
TF: 877-937-7867 ■ *Web:* www.animascorp.com

Arizant Inc 10393 W 70th St ... Eden Prairie MN 55344 952-947-1200 947-1400
TF: 800-800-4346 ■ *Web:* www.arizant.com

Armstrong Medical Industries Inc 575 Knightsbridge Pkwy ... Lincolnshire IL 60069 847-913-0101 913-0138
TF Cust Svc: 800-323-4220 ■ *Web:* www.armstrongmedical.com

Arthrex Inc 1370 Creekside Blvd ... Naples FL 34108 239-643-5553 591-6980
TF: 800-934-4404 ■ *Web:* www.arthrex.com

Aspen Surgical 6945 Southbelt Dr SE ... Caledonia MI 49316 616-698-7100 364-5381*
**Fax Area Code:* 888 ■ *TF:* 888-364-7004 ■ *Web:* www.aspensurgical.com

ATS Medical Inc 3905 Annapolis Ln Suite 105 ... Minneapolis MN 55447 763-553-7736 557-2244
NASDAQ: ATSI ■ *TF:* 866-287-6331 ■ *Web:* www.atsmedical.com

Avery Dennison Corp 150 N Orange Grove Blvd ... Pasadena CA 91103 626-304-2000 304-2192
NYSE: AVY ■ *TF Cust Svc:* 800-252-8379 ■ *Web:* www.averydennison.com

Avitar Inc 65 Dan Rd ... Canton MA 02021 781-821-2440 821-4458
AMEX: AVR ■ *TF:* 800-255-0511 ■ *Web:* www.avitarinc.com

Bard CR Inc 730 Central Ave ... Murray Hill NJ 07974 908-277-8000
NYSE: BCR ■ *Web:* www.crbard.com

Bard CR Inc Urological Div 8195 Industrial Blvd ... Covington GA 30014 770-786-9051 784-6908*
**Fax:* Mktg ■ *TF:* 800-526-4455 ■ *Web:* www.bardurological.com

Battle Creek Equipment Co 307 W Jackson St ... Battle Creek MI 49017 269-962-6181 962-8058
TF Cust Svc: 800-253-0854

Bausch & Lomb Surgical Inc 180 Via Verde Dr ... San Dimas CA 91773 909-971-5100 362-7006*
**Fax Area Code:* 800 ■ **Fax:* Hum Res ■ *TF Cust Svc:* 800-338-2020 ■
Web: www.bausch.com/us/resource/surgical

Baxter International Inc 1 Baxter Pkwy ... Deerfield IL 60015 847-948-2000 948-3948
NYSE: BAX ■ *Web:* www.baxter.com

Becton Dickinson & Co 1 Becton Dr ... Franklin Lakes NJ 07417 201-847-6800 847-4882*
NYSE: BDX ■ **Fax:* Cust Svc ■ *TF Cust Svc:* 888-237-2762 ■ *Web:* www.bd.com

Becton Dickinson Consumer Healthcare 1 Becton Dr ... Franklin Lakes NJ 07417 201-847-6800 847-4882
TF: 888-237-2762 ■ *Web:* www.bd.com/consumer

Beiersdorf North America 187 Danbury Rd ... Wilton CT 06897 203-563-5800 854-8112*
**Fax:* Hum Res ■ *TF:* 800-233-2340 ■ *Web:* www.beiersdorf.com

Beltone Electronics Corp 2601 Patriot Blvd ... Glenview IL 60026 847-832-3300 832-3201
TF: 800-235-8663 ■ *Web:* www.beltone.com

BioCore Medical Technologies Inc
6030 M Marshalee Dr Suite 512 ... Elkridge MD 21075 301-740-1893 740-1899
TF: 888-565-5243 ■ *Web:* www.biocore.com

BioHorizons Implant Systems Inc
One Perimeter Pk S Suite 230 S ... Birmingham AL 35243 205-967-7880 870-0304
TF: 888-246-8338 ■ *Web:* www.biohorizons.com

Biomet Inc 56 E Bell Dr ... Warsaw IN 46582 574-267-6639 267-8137
NASDAQ: BMET ■ *TF:* 800-348-9500 ■ *Web:* www.biomet.com

Bristol-Myers Squibb Co 345 Park Ave ... New York NY 10154 212-546-4000 546-4020
NYSE: BMY ■ *Web:* www.bms.com

BSN Medical Inc 5825 Carnegie Blvd ... Charlotte NC 28209 704-554-9933 551-8581*
**Fax:* Sales ■ *TF:* 800-221-7573 ■ *Web:* www.jobst-usa.com

BSN Medical Inc 5825 Carnegie Blvd ... Charlotte NC 28209 704-331-0600 331-8785
TF: 800-552-1157 ■ *Web:* www.bsnmedical.com

Burke Mobility Products Inc 1800 Merriam Ln ... Kansas City KS 66106 913-722-5658 722-2614
TF Sales: 800-255-4147

CarboMedics Inc 1300 E Anderson Ln ... Austin TX 78752 512-435-3200 435-3306
TF: 800-648-1579 ■ *Web:* www.carbomedics.com

Chattanooga Group 4717 Adams Rd ... Hixson TN 37343 423-870-2281 870-7402
TF: 800-592-7329 ■ *Web:* www.chattgroup.com

CMS Industries Ltd 1320 Alberta Ave ... Saskatoon SK S7K1R5 306-955-8821 955-3090
TF: 800-668-8821 ■ *Web:* www.redimedic.com

Codman & Shurtleff Inc 325 Paramount Dr ... Raynham MA 02767 508-880-8100 880-8122
TF: 800-225-0460 ■ *Web:* www.jnjcodman.com

Conor Medsystems Inc 1003 Hamilton Ct ... Menlo Park CA 94025 650-614-4100 614-4125
NASDAQ: CONR ■ *Web:* www.conormed.com

Covidien Ltd 15 Hampshire St ... Mansfield MA 02048 508-261-8000 261-8062
NYSE: COV ■ *Web:* www.covidien.com

CR Bard Inc 730 Central Ave ... Murray Hill NJ 07974 908-277-8000
NYSE: BCR ■ *Web:* www.crbard.com

CR Bard Inc Urological Div 8195 Industrial Blvd ... Covington GA 30014 770-786-9051 784-6908*
**Fax:* Mktg ■ *TF:* 800-526-4455 ■ *Web:* www.bardurological.com

Cramer Products Inc PO Box 1001 ... Gardner KS 66030 913-856-7511 884-5626
TF: 800-345-2231 ■ *Web:* www.cramersportsmed.com

Cyberonics Inc Cyberonics Bldg 100 Cyberonics Blvd ... Houston TX 77058 281-228-7200 218-9332
NASDAQ: CYBX ■ *TF:* 800-332-1375 ■ *Web:* www.cyberonics.com

Davol Inc 100 Sockanossett Crossroad PO Box 8500 ... Cranston RI 02920 401-463-7000 463-3142*
**Fax:* Cust Svc ■ *TF:* 800-556-6756 ■ *Web:* www.davol.com

Depuy Companies 325 Paramount Dr ... Raynham MA 02767 508-880-8100 828-3192*
**Fax:* Hum Res ■ *TF:* 800-451-2006

DePuy Inc 700 Orthopedic Dr ... Warsaw IN 46581 574-267-8143 371-4847
TF: 800-473-3789 ■ *Web:* www.depuy.com

DeRoyal Industries Inc 200 DeBusk Ln ... Powell TN 37849 865-938-7828 362-1245*
**Fax:* Hum Res ■ *TF:* 800-251-9864 ■ *Web:* www.deroyal.com

Company	City	State	ZIP	Phone	Fax
dj Orthopedics Inc 1430 Decision St	Vista	CA	92081	760-727-1280	734-3595
NYSE: DJO ■ *TF:* 800-321-9549 ■ *Web:* www.djortho.com					
EBI Medical Systems LP 100 Interpace Pkwy	Parsippany	NJ	07054	973-299-9300	524-0457*
**Fax Area Code:* 800 ■ *TF:* 800-526-2579 ■ *Web:* www.ebimedical.com					
Electric Mobility Corp 1 Mobility Plaza	Sewell	NJ	08080	856-468-0270	468-3426
TF Cust Svc: 800-257-7955 ■ *Web:* www.electricmobility.com					
Environmental Tectonics Corp 125 James Way	Southampton	PA	18966	215-355-9100	357-4000
AMEX: ETC ■ *Web:* www.etcusa.com					
Ergodyne Corp 1410 Energy Park Dr Suite 1	Saint Paul	MN	55108	651-642-9889	642-1882
TF: 800-225-8238 ■ *Web:* www.ergodyne.com					
Ethicon Inc US Hwy 22 W PO Box 151	Somerville	NJ	08876	908-218-0707	
Web: www.ethiconinc.com					
Everest & Jennings 2935 Northeast Pkwy	Atlanta	GA	30360	770-447-1609	726-0601*
**Fax Area Code:* 800 ■ *TF:* 800-235-4661					
Exactech Inc 2320 NW 66th Ct	Gainesville	FL	32653	352-377-1140	378-2617
NASDAQ: EXAC ■ *TF:* 800-392-2832 ■ *Web:* www.exac.com					
Female Health Co 515 N State St Suite 2225	Chicago	IL	60610	312-595-9123	595-9122
TF: 800-635-0844 ■ *Web:* www.femalehealth.com					
Ferno-Washington Inc 70 Weil Way	Wilmington	OH	45177	937-382-1451	382-1191
TF: 800-733-3766 ■ *Web:* www.ferno.com					
Freeman Mfg Co 900 W Chicago Rd PO Box J	Sturgis	MI	49091	269-651-2371	651-8248
TF: 800-253-2091 ■ *Web:* www.freemanmfg.com					
Gambro Renal Products 10810 W Collins Ave	Lakewood	CO	80215	303-232-6800	231-4032*
**Fax:* Mktg ■ *TF:* 800-525-2623 ■ *Web:* www.usa-gambro.com					
Genzyme Biosurgery 55 Cambridge Pkwy	Cambridge	MA	02142	617-494-8484	252-7600
TF: 800-326-7002 ■ *Web:* www.genzymebiosurgery.com					
Genzyme Corp 500 Kendall St	Cambridge	MA	02142	617-252-7500	252-7600
NASDAQ: GENZ ■ *TF:* 800-326-7002 ■ *Web:* www.genzyme.com					
GF Health Products Inc 2935 Northeast Pkwy	Atlanta	GA	30360	770-447-1609	726-0601*
**Fax Area Code:* 800 ■ *TF:* 800-235-4661 ■ *Web:* www.grahamfield.com					
Gish Biomedical Inc 22942 Arroyo Vista	Rancho Santa Margarita	CA	92688	949-635-6200	635-6292
TF: 800-938-0531 ■ *Web:* www.gishbiomedical.com					
GN ReSound Corp 8001 Bloomington Fwy	Bloomington	MN	55420	952-769-8000	469-8001
TF: 800-248-4327 ■ *Web:* www.gnresound-group.com					
Gore WL & Assoc Inc 551 Papermill Rd	Newark	DE	19711	302-738-4880	738-7710
Web: www.gore.com					
Gyrus Medical Inc ENT Div 2925 Appling Rd	Bartlett	TN	38133	901-373-0200	373-0237
TF: 800-262-3540 ■ *Web:* www.gyrus-ent.com					
Hanger Orthopedic Group Inc 2 Bethesda Metro Ctr Suite 1200	Bethesda	MD	20814	301-986-0701	986-0702
NYSE: HGR ■ *TF:* 800-765-3822 ■ *Web:* www.hanger.com					
Hanger Prosthetics & Orthopedics Inc 2 Bethesda Metro Center Suite 1200	Bethesda	MD	20814	301-986-0701	986-0702
TF: 877-442-6437 ■ *Web:* www.hanger.com					
HearUSA Inc 1250 Northpoint Pkwy	West Palm Beach	FL	33407	561-478-8770	684-3695
AMEX: EAR ■ *TF Cust Svc:* 800-731-3277 ■ *Web:* www.hearx.com					
Helvoet Pharma Inc 9012 Pennsauken Hwy	Pennsauken	NJ	08110	856-663-2202	663-2636
TF: 800-874-3586 ■ *Web:* www.helvoetpharma.com					
Hightech American Industrial Laboratories Inc 320 Massachusetts Ave	Lexington	MA	02420	781-862-9884	860-7722
Web: www.hailabs.com					
Hollister Inc 2000 Hollister Dr	Libertyville	IL	60048	847-680-1000	918-3446*
**Fax:* Hum Res ■ *TF:* 800-323-4060 ■ *Web:* www.hollister.com					
Hospira Inc 275 N Field Dr	Lake Forest	IL	60045	224-212-2000	
NYSE: HSP ■ *TF:* 877-946-7747 ■ *Web:* www.hospira.com					
Hoveround Corp 2151 Whitfield Industrial Way	Sarasota	FL	34243	941-739-6200	727-8686
TF: 800-701-3021 ■ *Web:* www.hoveround.com					
Hy-Tape International Inc PO Box 540	Patterson	NY	12563	845-878-4848	878-4104
TF: 800-248-0101 ■ *Web:* www.hytape.com					
I-Flow Corp 20202 Windrow Dr	Lake Forest	CA	92663	949-206-2700	206-2600
NASDAQ: IFLO ■ *TF:* 800-448-3569 ■ *Web:* www.iflo.com					
ICU Medical Inc 951 Calle Amanecer	San Clemente	CA	92673	949-366-2183	366-8368
NASDAQ: ICUI ■ *TF:* 800-824-7890 ■ *Web:* www.icumed.com					
Ideal Tape Co 1400 Middlesex St	Lowell	MA	01851	978-458-6833	458-0302
TF: 800-284-3325 ■ *Web:* www.idealtape.com					
Independence Technology LLC 45 Technology Dr	Warren	NJ	07059	908-755-8300	412-2299
TF: 888-463-3000 ■ *Web:* www.independencenow.com					
International Technidyne Corp 8 Olsen Ave	Edison	NJ	08820	732-548-5700	548-2419
TF: 800-631-5945 ■ *Web:* www.itcmed.com					
Interpore Spine Ltd 181 Technology Dr	Irvine	CA	92618	949-453-3200	453-3225
TF: 800-722-4489 ■ *Web:* www.interpore.com					
Invacare Corp 1 Invacare Way	Elyria	OH	44036	440-329-6000	619-7996*
NYSE: IVC ■ **Fax Area Code:* 877 ■ *TF:* 800-333-6900 ■ *Web:* www.invacare.com					
Johnson & Johnson Consumer Products Co 199 Grandview Rd	Skillman	NJ	08558	908-874-1000	
TF: 800-526-3967 ■ *Web:* www.johnsonsbaby.com					
Johnson & Johnson Inc 7101 Notre-Dame E	Montreal	QC	H1N2G4	514-251-5100	251-6233
TF: 800-361-8990 ■ *Web:* www.jnjcanada.com					
Jordan Industries Inc Healthcare Products Group 1751 Lake Cook Rd ArborLake Ctr Suite 550	Deerfield	IL	60015	847-945-5591	945-5698
K-Tube Corp 13400 Kirkham Way	Poway	CA	92064	858-513-9229	705-8823*
**Fax Area Code:* 800 ■ **Fax:* Cust Svc ■ *TF:* 800-394-0058 ■ *Web:* www.k-tube.com					
Kimberly-Clark PO Box 619100	Dallas	TX	75261	972-281-1200	577-7777*
**Fax Area Code:* 817 ■ *TF:* 800-321-1435 ■ *Web:* www.kimberly-clark.com					
Kimberly-Clark Corp Professional Health Care Business 1400 Holcomb Bridge Rd	Roswell	GA	30076	770-587-8000	587-7718
Web: www.kchealthcare.com					
Kimberly-Clark/Ballard Medical Products 1400 Holcomb Bridge Rd	Roswell	GA	30076	800-524-3577	572-6999*
**Fax Area Code:* 801 ■ *TF:* 800-528-5591 ■ *Web:* www.kchealthcare.com					
Kinetic Concepts Inc (KCI Inc) 8023 Vantage Dr	San Antonio	TX	78230	210-524-9000	255-6992*
NYSE: KCI ■ **Fax:* Hum Res ■ *TF:* 800-531-5346 ■ *Web:* www.kci1.com					
Kyphon Inc 1221 Crossman Ave	Sunnyvale	CA	94089	408-548-6500	548-6501
NASDAQ: KYPH ■ *TF:* 877-459-7466 ■ *Web:* www.kyphon.com					
Langer Inc 450 Commack Rd	Deer Park	NY	11729	631-667-1200	667-1203
NASDAQ: GAIT ■ *TF:* 800-233-2687 ■ *Web:* www.langerbiomechanics.com					
Leisure Lift 1800 Merriam Ln	Kansas City	KS	66106	913-722-5658	722-2614
TF: 800-255-0285 ■ *Web:* www.pacesaver.com					
LPS Industries Inc 10 Caesar Pl	Moonachie	NJ	07074	201-438-3515	438-0040
TF Sales: 800-275-4577 ■ *Web:* www.lpsind.com					
Ludlow Tape 25 Forge Pkwy	Franklin	MA	02038	800-343-7875	328-4844
TF: 800-445-5025 ■ *Web:* covalenceadhesives.com					
M & C Specialties Co 90 James Way	Southampton	PA	18966	215-322-1600	322-1620
TF Cust Svc: 800-441-6996 ■ *Web:* www.mcspecialties.com					
Martech Medical Products Inc 1500 Delp Dr	Harleysville	PA	19438	215-256-8833	256-8837
Web: www.martechmedical.com					
Medegen Medical Products 209 Medegen Dr	Gallaway	TN	38036	901-867-2951	867-8954
TF Cust Svc: 800-233-1987 ■ *Web:* www.medegen.com					
Medical Action Industries Inc 800 Prime Pl	Hauppauge	NY	11788	631-231-4600	231-3075
NASDAQ: MDCI ■ *TF:* 800-645-7042 ■ *Web:* www.medical-action.com					
Medline Industries Inc 1 Medline Pl	Mundelein	IL	60060	847-949-5500	643-3126
TF Cust Svc: 800-633-5463 ■ *Web:* www.medline.com					
Medrad Inc 1 Medrad Dr	Indianola	PA	15051	412-767-2400	767-4120*
**Fax:* Cust Svc ■ *TF Cust Svc:* 800-633-7237 ■ *Web:* www.medrad.com					
Medtronic Inc 710 Medtronic Pkwy NE	Minneapolis	MN	55432	763-514-4000	514-4879
NYSE: MDT ■ *TF Cust Svc:* 800-328-2518 ■ *Web:* www.medtronic.com					
Medtronic Inc Heart Valve Div 1851 E Deere Ave	Santa Ana	CA	92705	949-474-3943	474-3953
TF: 800-326-3330 ■ *Web:* www.medtronic.com					
Medtronic MiniMed Inc 18000 Devonshire St	Northridge	CA	91325	818-362-5958	
TF: 800-933-3322 ■ *Web:* www.minimed.com					
Medtronic Powered Surgical Solutions 4620 N Beach St	Fort Worth	TX	76137	817-788-6400	788-6401*
**Fax:* Orders ■ *TF:* 800-433-7639 ■ *Web:* www.medtronic.com/neuro/midasrex					
Medtronic Sofamor Danek Inc 1800 Pyramid Pl	Memphis	TN	38132	901-396-3133	344-1555*
**Fax:* Hum Res ■ *TF:* 800-763-2667 ■ *Web:* www.sofamordanek.com					
Medtronic Xomed Inc 6743 Southpoint Dr N	Jacksonville	FL	32216	904-296-9600	279-7593*
**Fax:* Hum Res ■ *TF:* 800-874-5797 ■ *Web:* www.xomed.com					
Mentor Corp 201 Mentor Dr	Santa Barbara	CA	93111	805-879-6000	
NYSE: MNT ■ *TF:* 800-525-0245 ■ *Web:* www.mentorcorp.com					
Microtek Medical Holdings Inc 13000 Deerfield Pkwy Suite 300	Alpharetta	GA	30004	678-896-4400	896-4297
NASDAQ: MTMD ■ *TF:* 800-777-7977 ■ *Web:* www.microtekmed.com					
Microtek Medical Inc 512 Lehmberg Rd	Columbus	MS	39702	662-327-1863	327-5921
TF: 800-824-3027 ■ *Web:* www.microtekmed.com					
Milestone Scientific Inc 220 S Orange Ave	Livingston	NJ	07039	973-535-2717	535-2829
AMEX: MSS ■ *TF:* 800-862-1125 ■ *Web:* www.milestonescientific.com					
Miracle-Ear Inc 5000 Cheshire Ln N Suite 1	Plymouth	MN	55446	763-268-4000	268-4365
TF: 800-234-7714 ■ *Web:* www.miracle-ear.com					
Mitek Products 325 Paramount Dr	Raynham	MA	02767	508-880-8100	382-4697*
**Fax Area Code:* 800 ■ *TF:* 800-382-4682 ■ *Web:* www.jnjgateway.com					
National Fab 9561 Satellite Blvd Suite 350	Orlando	FL	32837	407-852-6170	852-6171
TF: 877-265-1491					
NELCO Inc 800 W Cummings Park Suite 3950	Woburn	MA	01801	781-933-1940	933-4763
TF: 800-635-2613 ■ *Web:* www.nelco-usa.com					
Nice-Pak Products Inc 2 Nice-Pak Pk	Orangeburg	NY	10962	845-365-1700	365-1717
TF: 800-999-6423 ■ *Web:* www.nicepak.com					
NMT Medical Inc 27 Wormwood St	Boston	MA	02210	617-737-0930	737-0924
NASDAQ: NMTI ■ *TF:* 800-666-6484 ■ *Web:* www.nmtmedical.com					
NorMed 4310 S 131 Pl	Seattle	WA	98168	206-242-8228	242-3315
TF: 800-288-8200 ■ *Web:* www.normed.com					
Ortho Development Corp 12187 S Business Park Dr	Draper	UT	84020	801-553-9991	553-9993
TF: 800-429-8339 ■ *Web:* www.odev.com					
Orthofix Inc 1720 Bray Central Dr	McKinney	TX	75069	469-742-2500	742-2556
TF: 800-527-0404 ■ *Web:* www.orthofix.com					
OrthoLogic Corp 1275 W Washington St	Tempe	AZ	85281	602-286-5520	926-2616
NASDAQ: OLGC ■ *TF:* 800-937-5520 ■ *Web:* www.orthologic.com					
Orthovita Inc 45 Great Valley Pkwy	Malvern	PA	19355	610-640-1775	666-2555*
NASDAQ: VITA ■ **Fax Area Code:* 888 ■ **Fax:* Cust Svc ■ *TF:* 800-676-8482 ■ *Web:* www.orthovita.com					
Osteomed Corp 3885 Arapaho Rd	Addison	TX	75001	972-677-4600	677-4601
TF Cust Svc: 800-456-7779 ■ *Web:* www.osteomedcorp.com					
Perma-Type Co Inc 83 Northwest Dr	Plainville	CT	06062	860-747-9999	747-1986
TF: 800-243-4234 ■ *Web:* www.perma-type.com					
Phonic Ear Inc 2080 Lakeville Hwy	Petaluma	CA	94954	707-769-1110	781-9415
TF: 800-227-0735 ■ *Web:* www.phonicear.com					
Posey Co 5635 Peck Rd	Arcadia	CA	91006	626-443-3143	767-3933*
**Fax Area Code:* 800 ■ *TF:* 800-447-6739 ■ *Web:* www.posey.com					
Precision Dynamics Corp 13880 Del Sur St	San Fernando	CA	91340	818-897-1111	899-4045
TF: 800-847-0670 ■ *Web:* www.pdcorp.com					
Precision Technology Inc 50 Maple St	Norwood	NJ	07648	201-767-1600	767-6739
Web: www.ptiplastics.com					
Rehab Plus Therapeutics Products Inc 105 Industrial Dr	Wolfforth	TX	79382	806-791-2288	791-2290
TF: 800-288-8059 ■ *Web:* www.rehabplus.com					
Retractable Technologies Inc 511 Lobo Ln	Little Elm	TX	75068	972-294-1010	294-4400
AMEX: RVP ■ *TF:* 888-806-2626 ■ *Web:* www.vanishpoint.com					
Rockford Medical & Safety Co 2420 Harrison Ave	Rockford	IL	61108	815-394-4809	394-0320
TF: 800-541-2528 ■ *Web:* www.firensafety.com					
Rusch Inc 2917 Weck Dr	Research Triangle Park	NC	27009	919-544-8000	399-1028*
**Fax Area Code:* 800 ■ *TF:* 800-514-7234 ■ *Web:* www.myrusch.com					
Saint Jude Medical Inc 1 Lillehei Plaza	Saint Paul	MN	55117	651-483-2000	482-8318
NYSE: STJ ■ *TF:* 800-328-9634 ■ *Web:* www.sjm.com					
SCOOTER Store Inc 1650 Independence Dr	New Braunfels	TX	78132	830-626-5600	620-4598
TF: 800-723-4535 ■ *Web:* www.thescooterstore.com					
Seattle Systems Inc 26296 Twelve Trees Ln NW	Poulsbo	WA	98370	360-697-5656	697-5879
TF: 800-248-6463					
Siemens Hearing Instruments Inc 10 Constitution Ave	Piscataway	NJ	08855	732-562-6600	562-6696
TF: 800-766-4500 ■ *Web:* www.siemens-hearing.com					
Smith & Nephew Inc 1450 E Brooks Rd	Memphis	TN	38116	901-396-2121	396-9929
TF Cust Svc: 800-238-7538 ■ *Web:* www.smith-nephew.com					
Smith & Nephew Inc Orthopaedic Div 1450 Brooks Rd	Memphis	TN	38116	901-396-2121	621-6924*
**Fax Area Code:* 800 ■ *TF:* 800-821-5700 ■ *Web:* www.smith-nephew.com/what/orthopaedics.jsp					
Smith & Nephew Inc Wound Management Div 11775 Starkey Rd	Largo	FL	33773	727-392-1261	392-6914
TF Cust Svc: 800-876-1261 ■ *Web:* www.smith-nephew.com/what/wound.jsp					
Smiths Medical ASD Inc 160 Weymouth St	Rockland	MA	02370	781-878-8011	878-8201
TF: 800-553-8352 ■ *Web:* www.smiths-medical.com					
Smiths Medical MD Inc 1265 Grey Fox Rd	Saint Paul	MN	55112	651-633-2556	628-7459
TF: 800-258-5361 ■ *Web:* www.smiths-medical.com					
Smiths Medical Respiratory Support Products 9255 Custom House Plaza Suite N	San Diego	CA	92154	619-710-1000	
TF: 800-258-5361					
Sonic Innovations Inc 2795 E Cottonwood Pkwy Suite 660	Salt Lake City	UT	84121	801-365-2800	365-3000
NASDAQ: SNCI ■ *TF Cust Svc:* 888-576-6424 ■ *Web:* www.sonici.com					
Sorin Group USA Inc 14401 W 65th Way	Arvada	CO	80004	303-425-5508	467-6584
TF: 800-221-7943 ■ *Web:* www.soringroup-usa.com					
Span-America Medical Systems Inc 70 Commerce Ctr	Greenville	SC	29615	864-288-8877	288-8692
NASDAQ: SPAN ■ *TF:* 800-888-6752 ■ *Web:* www.spanamerica.com					
SpectRx Inc 4955 Avalon Ridge Pkwy Suite 300	Norcross	GA	30071	770-242-8723	242-8639
Web: www.spectrx.com					
Spenco Medical Corp 6301 Imperial Dr	Waco	TX	76712	254-772-6000	772-6536
TF: 800-877-3626 ■ *Web:* www.spenco.com					
SRI/Surgical Express Inc 12425 Race Track Rd	Tampa	FL	33626	813-891-9550	925-8388
NASDAQ: STRC ■ *TF:* 877-478-7439 ■ *Web:* www.srisurgical.com					
SSL Americas Inc 3585 Engineering Dr Suite 200	Norcross	GA	30092	770-582-2222	582-2233
TF: 888-387-3927 ■ *Web:* www.ssl-international.com					
Standard Textile Co Inc 1 Knollcrest Dr	Cincinnati	OH	45237	513-761-9255	761-0467
TF: 800-888-5000 ■ *Web:* www.standardtextile.com					
Starkey Laboratories Inc 6700 Washington Ave S	Eden Prairie	MN	55344	952-941-6401	828-6972
TF: 800-328-8602 ■ *Web:* www.starkey.com					
STERIS Corp 5960 Heisley Rd	Mentor	OH	44060	440-354-2600	639-4450*
NYSE: STE ■ **Fax:* Cust Svc ■ *TF:* 800-548-4873 ■ *Web:* www.steris.com					
Stryker Corp 2725 Fairfield Rd	Kalamazoo	MI	49002	269-385-2600	385-1062
NYSE: SYK ■ *TF:* 800-726-2725 ■ *Web:* www.strykercorp.com					
Sunrise Medical Inc 2382 Faraday Ave Suite 200	Carlsbad	CA	92008	760-930-1500	930-1585
TF: 800-278-6747 ■ *Web:* www.sunrisemedical.com					
Sunrise Medical Respiratory Div 100 DeVilbiss Dr	Somerset	PA	15501	814-443-4881	443-7572
TF: 800-333-4000					
Surgical Appliance Industries Inc 3960 Rosslyn Dr	Cincinnati	OH	45209	513-271-4594	309-9055*
**Fax Area Code:* 800 ■ *TF:* 800-888-0458 ■ *Web:* www.surgicalappliance.com					
Symmetry Medical Inc 220 W Market St	Warsaw	IN	46580	574-268-2252	267-4551
NYSE: SMA ■ *Web:* www.symmetrymedical.com					
Synovis Life Technologies Inc 2575 University Ave W Suite 180	Saint Paul	MN	55114	651-796-7300	642-9018
NASDAQ: SYNO ■ *TF:* 800-487-9627 ■ *Web:* www.synovislife.com					
Synthes USA 1302 Wrights Ln E	West Chester	PA	19380	610-719-5000	251-5046*
**Fax:* Hum Res					
TAPEMARK Co 1685 Marthaler Ln	West Saint Paul	MN	55118	651-455-1611	450-8403
TF: 800-535-1998 ■ *Web:* www.tapemark.com					

				Phone	Fax
Tefron USA Inc 720 W Main St. *TF:* 800-554-5541 ■ *Web:* www.tefron.com	Valdese	NC	28690	828-879-6500	879-6579
Therakos Inc 437 Creamery Way *Web:* www.therakos.com	Exton	PA	19341	610-280-1000	280-1087
TIDI Products LLC 570 Enterprise Dr *TF:* 800-215-5464 ■ *Web:* www.tidiproducts.com	Neenah	WI	54956	920-751-4300	751-4370
Tillotson Healthcare Corp 8-10 Glenshaw St. *TF:* 800-445-6830 ■ *Web:* www.thcnet.com	Orangeburg	NY	10962	845-365-8200	365-8201
Tri-State Hospital Supply Corp 301 Catrell Dr *TF:* 800-248-4058 ■ *Web:* www.tshsc.com	Howell	MI	48843	517-546-5400	546-9388
Utah Medical Products Inc 7043 S 300 West *NASDAQ: UTMD* ■ *TF:* 800-533-4984 ■ *Web:* www.utahmed.com	Midvale	UT	84047	801-566-1200	566-2062
Venture Tape Corp 30 Commerce Rd *TF:* 800-343-1076 ■ *Web:* www.venturetape.com	Rockland	MA	02370	781-331-5900	871-0065
Vital Signs Inc 20 Campus Rd *NASDAQ: VITL* ■ *TF:* 800-932-0760 ■ *Web:* www.vital-signs.com	Totowa	NJ	07512	973-790-1330	790-3307
West Pharmaceutical Services Inc 101 Gordon Dr. *NYSE: WST* ■ *TF:* 800-345-9800 ■ *Web:* www.westpharma.com	Lionville	PA	19341	610-594-2900	594-3000
WL Gore & Assoc Inc 551 Papermill Rd. *Web:* www.gore.com	Newark	DE	19711	302-738-4880	738-7710
Wright Medical Group Inc 5677 Airline Rd *NASDAQ: WMGI* ■ *TF:* 800-238-7188 ■ *Web:* www.wmt.com	Arlington	TN	38002	901-867-9971	867-9534
Wright Medical Technology Inc 5677 Airline Rd. **Fax:* Cust Svc ■ *TF:* 800-238-7188 ■ *Web:* www.wmt.com	Arlington	TN	38002	901-867-9971	867-9534*
Young Innovations Inc 13705 Shoreline Ct E. *NASDAQ: YDNT* ■ **Fax Area Code:* 314 ■ *TF:* 800-325-1881 ■ *Web:* www.yiinc.com	Earth City	MO	63045	847-458-5400	344-0021*
ZEVEX International Inc 4314 ZEVEX Pk Ln. *NASDAQ: ZVXI* ■ *TF:* 800-970-2337 ■ *Web:* www.zevex.com	Salt Lake City	UT	84123	801-264-1001	264-1051
Zimmer Holdings Inc 1800 W Center St *NYSE: ZMH* ■ *TF:* 800-613-6131 ■ *Web:* www.zimmer.com	Warsaw	IN	46580	574-267-6131	372-4988

481 MEDICAL TRANSCRIPTION SERVICES

Companies listed here have a national or regional clientele base.

				Phone	Fax
MED-TECH Resource Inc 2053 Franklin Way *TF:* 800-538-7498 ■ *Web:* www.med-tech.net	Marietta	GA	30067	770-955-7292	951-0408
Medifax Inc 10003 Roberts Rd. *Web:* www.medifax.net	Palos Hills	IL	60465	708-741-5947	741-5954
MediGrafix Inc 11205 Wright Cir Suite 120 *TF:* 877-284-5147 ■ *Web:* www.medigrafix.com	Omaha	NE	68144	402-333-3323	333-1939
MedQuist Inc 1000 Bishops State Blvd Suite 300 *TF:* 800-233-3030 ■ *Web:* www.medquist.com	Mount Laurel	NJ	08054	856-206-4000	206-4020
Mid-South Transcription Center 1765-A Lelia Dr Suite 103	Jackson	MS	39216	601-982-1750	981-2416
Perfect Word Processing Inc 475 High Mountain Rd Suite 6 *Web:* www.pwp-mt.com	North Haledon	NJ	07508	973-238-0023	238-0021
Rapid Transcript Inc 4311 Wilshire Blvd Suite 209 *Web:* www.rapidtranscript.com	Los Angeles	CA	90010	323-964-0400	964-0412
Spheris 720 Cool Springs Blvd Suite 200 *TF:* 800-368-1717 ■ *Web:* www.spheris.com	Franklin	TN	37067	615-261-1500	261-1790
Thomas Transcription Services Inc 550 Balmoral Cir Suite 201 *TF:* 888-878-2889 ■ *Web:* www.thomastx.com	Jacksonville	FL	32218	904-751-5058	751-5240
TMT Medical Services 8404 83rd Ave Sw Suite I *Web:* www.tmtmedicalservices.com	Lakewood	WA	98498	253-584-3177	581-6542
Transcend Services Inc 945 E Paces Ferry Rd NE Suite 1475 *NASDAQ: TRCR* ■ *Web:* www.transcendservices.com	Atlanta	GA	30326	404-836-8000	364-8009
Webmedx Inc 564 Alpha Dr. *TF:* 888-932-6339 ■ *Web:* webmedx.com	Pittsburgh	PA	15238	412-968-9244	968-9144

482 MEDICINAL CHEMICALS & BOTANICAL PRODUCTS

SEE ALSO Biotechnology Companies p. 1380; Diagnostic Products p. 1587; Pharmaceutical Companies p. 2109; Pharmaceutical Companies - Generic Drugs p. 2111; Vitamins & Nutritional Supplements p. 2405

Companies listed here manufacture medicinal chemicals and botanical products in bulk for sale to pharmaceutical, vitamin, and nutritional product companies.

				Phone	Fax
Acic Fine Chemicals Inc 81 Saint Claire Blvd *TF:* 800-265-6727 ■ *Web:* www.acic.com	Brantford	ON	N3S7X6	519-751-3668	751-1378
Adams Respiratory Therapeutics Inc 14801 Sovereign Rd. *NASDAQ: ARXT* ■ *TF:* 800-770-5270 ■ *Web:* www.adamslaboratories.com	Fort Worth	TX	76155	817-786-1200	786-1150
Advitech Inc 1165 boul Lebourgneuf Suite 140. *Web:* www.advitech.com	Quebec	QC	G2K2C9	418-686-7498	686-2446
AF-Zeta Inc 163 Madison Ave. *Web:* www.af-zeta.com	Morristown	NJ	07960	973-267-2205	267-2208
Alpharma Inc Human Pharmaceutical Div 1 Executive Dr 4th Fl. *TF:* 800-645-4216 ■ *Web:* www.alpharma.com	Fort Lee	NJ	07024	201-947-7774	947-0795
AM Todd Co 1717 Douglas Ave. *TF:* 800-968-2603 ■ *Web:* www.amtodd.com	Kalamazoo	MI	49007	269-343-2603	343-3399
American Laboratories Inc 4410 S 102nd St. *TF Cust Svc:* 800-445-5989 ■ *Web:* www.americanlaboratories.com	Omaha	NE	68127	402-339-2494	339-0801
Anika Therapeutics Inc 236 W Cummings Park *NASDAQ: ANIK* ■ *Web:* www.anikatherapeutics.com	Woburn	MA	01801	781-932-6616	932-9735
Apotex Fermentation Inc 40 Scurfield Blvd *TF:* 800-667-4708 ■ *Web:* www.apoferm.mb.ca	Winnipeg	MB	R3Y1G4	204-989-6830	488-4063
Apotex Pharmachem Inc 34 Spalding Dr *Web:* www.apotexpharmachem.com	Brantford	ON	N3T6B8	519-756-8942	753-3051
Array BioPharma Inc 3200 Walnut St. *NASDAQ: ARRY* ■ *TF:* 877-633-2436 ■ *Web:* www.arraybiopharma.com	Boulder	CO	80301	303-381-6600	449-5376
Bachem Bioscience Inc 3700 Horizon Dr. *TF:* 800-634-3183 ■ *Web:* www.bachem.com	King of Prussia	PA	19406	610-239-0300	239-0800
Balchem Corp 52 Sunrise Park Rd PO Box 600 *AMEX: BCP* ■ *Web:* www.balchem.com	New Hampton	NY	10958	845-355-5300	326-5742
BASF Corp 100 Campus Dr. *NYSE: BF* ■ *TF:* 800-526-1072 ■ *Web:* www.basf.com	Florham Park	NJ	07932	973-245-6000	895-8002
Baxter Bioscience 1978 W Winton Ave *TF:* 800-423-2090 ■ *Web:* www.biosciencecms.com	Hayward	CA	94545	510-786-9744	887-1388
BCN Chemicals Inc 1320 Rt 9 *TF:* 800-661-1226 ■ *Web:* www.bcnchem.com	Champlain	NY	12919	514-630-1044	697-0201
Bedford Laboratories Inc 300 Northfield Rd *TF:* 800-562-4797 ■ *Web:* www.bedfordlabs.com	Bedford	OH	44146	440-232-3320	232-2772
Ben Venue Laboratories Inc 300 Northfield Rd *TF:* 800-562-4797 ■ *Web:* www.benvenue.com	Bedford	OH	44146	440-232-3320	232-2772
Betachem Inc 58 Ware Rd	Upper Saddle River	NJ	07458	201-327-4100	327-9366
Biddle Sawyer Corp 360 W 31st St 21 Penn Plaza Suite 1102 *TF:* 800-654-7001 ■ *Web:* www.biddlesawyer.com	New York	NY	10001	212-736-1580	239-1089
Bio-Botanica Inc 75 Commerce Dr. *TF:* 800-645-5720 ■ *Web:* www.bio-botanica.com	Hauppauge	NY	11788	631-231-5522	231-7332
Blessed Herbs Inc 109 Barre Plains Rd *TF:* 800-489-4372 ■ *Web:* www.blessedherbs.com	Oakham	MA	01068	508-882-3839	882-3755
Boehringer Ingelheim Chemicals Inc 2820 N Normandy Dr *TF:* 800-820-6015 ■ *Web:* www.bichemicals.com	Petersburg	VA	23805	804-504-8700	504-8685
Botanicals International Inc 2550 El Presidio St. *Web:* www.botanicals.com	Long Beach	CA	90810	310-637-9566	637-3644
Cambrex Charles City Inc 1205 11th St. *TF:* 800-247-1833 ■ *Web:* www.cambrex.com	Charles City	IA	50616	641-257-1000	228-4152
Cambrex Corp 1 Meadowlands Plaza 15th Fl *NYSE: CBM* ■ *TF:* 800-638-8174 ■ *Web:* www.cambrex.com	East Rutherford	NJ	07073	201-804-3000	804-9852
Cambrex North Brunswick Inc 661 Hwy 1 *TF Sales:* 866-286-9133 ■ *Web:* www.cambrex.com	North Brunswick	NJ	08902	732-447-1900	447-1910
Carrington Laboratories Inc 2001 Walnut Hill Ln *NASDAQ: CARN* ■ *TF Cust Svc:* 800-527-5216 ■ *Web:* www.carringtonlabs.com	Irving	TX	75038	972-518-1300	518-1020
Cedarburg Pharmaceuticals Inc 870 Badger Cir *Web:* www.cedarburglabs.com	Grafton	WI	53024	262-376-1467	376-1068
Chemical Co The 19 Narragansett Ave *Web:* www.thechemco.com	Jamestown	RI	02835	401-423-3100	423-3102
ChemWerth Inc 1764 Litchfield Tpke *Web:* www.chemwerth.com	Woodbridge	CT	06525	203-387-7794	387-8132
Contract Pharmacal Corp 135 Adams Ave. *Web:* www.contractpharmacal.com	Hauppauge	NY	11788	631-231-4610	231-4156
Cyanotech Corp 73-4460 Queen Kaahumanu Hwy Suite 102 *NASDAQ: CYAN* ■ *TF Sales:* 800-453-1187 ■ *Web:* www.cyanotech.com	Kailua-Kona	HI	96740	808-326-1353	329-4533
DSM Pharmaceuticals Inc 5900 NW Greenville Blvd *Web:* www.dsm.com	Greenville	NC	27835	252-758-3436	707-7050
Elge Inc 1000 Cole Ave. *Web:* www.elgeinc.com	Rosenberg	TX	77471	281-232-0463	232-0476
Ferro Pfanstiehl Laboratories Inc 1219 Glen Rock Ave *TF:* 800-383-0126 ■ *Web:* www.ferro.com/our+products/pharmaceuticals	Waukegan	IL	60085	847-623-0370	623-9173
Flavine North America Inc 10 Reuten Dr. *Web:* www.flavine.com	Closter	NJ	07624	201-768-4190	768-2854
Fytokem Products Inc 110 Research Dr Suite 101 *Web:* www.fytokem.com	Saskatoon	SK	S7N3R3	306-668-2552	978-2436
Garden State Nutritionals 8 Henderson Dr. *TF:* 800-526-9095 ■ *Web:* www.gardenstatenutritionals.com	West Caldwell	NJ	07006	973-575-9200	575-6782
George Uhe Co Inc 219 River Dr *TF:* 800-850-4075 ■ *Web:* www.uhe.com	Garfield	NJ	07026	201-843-4000	843-7517
Greer Laboratories Inc 639 Nuway Cir. *TF Cust Svc:* 800-378-3906 ■ *Web:* www.greerlabs.com	Lenoir	NC	28645	828-754-5327	754-5320
GYMA Laboratories of America Inc 135 Cantiague Rock Rd. *Web:* www.gyma.com	Westbury	NY	11590	516-933-0900	933-1075
ICC Industries Inc 460 Park Ave. *TF:* 800-422-1720 ■ *Web:* www.iccchem.com	New York	NY	10022	212-521-1700	521-1794
Interchem Corp 120 Rt 17 N. *Web:* www.interchem.com	Paramus	NJ	07652	201-261-7333	261-7339
JB Laboratories Inc 13295 Reflections Dr *Web:* www.jblabs.com	Holland	MI	49424	616-738-8500	738-8709
Johnson Matthey Inc Pharmaceutical Materials Div 2003 Nolte Dr. *TF:* 800-444-8544 ■ *Web:* www.jmpharma.com	West Deptford	NJ	08066	856-853-8000	384-7186
Johnson Matthey Pharma Services 25 Patton Rd *Web:* www.jmpharmaservices.com	Devens	MA	01434	978-784-5000	784-5500
Lannett Co Inc 9000 State Rd. *AMEX: LCI* ■ *TF:* 800-325-9994 ■ *Web:* www.lannett.com	Philadelphia	PA	19136	215-333-9000	333-9004
Libby Laboratories Inc 1700 6th St *Web:* www.libbylabs.com	Berkeley	CA	94710	510-527-5400	527-8687
Long Wing International 2021 Midwest Rd Suite 200 *Web:* www.longwing.net	Oak Brook	IL	60523	630-734-0570	
LycoRed Corp 377 Crane St *TF:* 800-631-3424 ■ *Web:* www.lycored.com	Orange	NJ	07051	973-882-0322	882-0323
Mallinckrodt Baker Inc 222 Red School Ln. **Fax:* Cust Svc ■ *TF:* 800-582-2537 ■ *Web:* www.mallbaker.com	Phillipsburg	NJ	08865	908-859-2151	859-6905*
Mallinckrodt Inc 675 McDonnell Blvd **Fax:* Hum Res ■ *TF:* 888-744-1414 ■ *Web:* www.mallinckrodt.com	Hazelwood	MO	63042	314-654-2000	654-6257*
Multisorb Technologies Inc 325 Harlem Rd *TF Cust Svc:* 800-445-9890 ■ *Web:* www.multisorb.com	West Seneca	NY	14224	716-824-8900	824-4091
Naturex Inc 375 Huyler St. *Web:* www.naturex.com	South Hackensack	NJ	07606	201-440-5000	342-8000
NHK Laboratories Inc 12230 E Florience Ave *TF:* 877-645-5227 ■ *Web:* www.nhklabs.com	Santa Fe Springs	CA	90670	562-944-5400	944-0266
Norac Technologies Inc 9110 23rd Ave *TF:* 800-621-7521 ■ *Web:* www.noractech.com	Edmonton	AB	T6N1H9	780-414-9595	450-1016
Nutraceutix Inc 9609 153rd Ave NE *TF:* 800-548-3222 ■ *Web:* www.nutraceutix.com	Redmond	WA	98052	425-883-9518	869-1020
NutriScience Innovations LLC 2450 Reservoir Ave *Web:* www.nutriscienceusa.com	Trumbull	CT	06611	203-372-8877	372-9977
Nutrition 21 Inc 4 Manhattanville Rd *NASDAQ: NXXI* ■ *TF:* 800-699-3533 ■ *Web:* www.nutrition21.com	Purchase	NY	10577	914-701-4500	696-0860
Paddock Laboratories Inc 3940 Quebec Ave N *TF Orders:* 800-328-5113 ■ *Web:* www.paddocklabs.com	Minneapolis	MN	55427	763-546-4676	546-4842
Patheon Inc 2100 Syntex Ct *TF:* 888-728-4366 ■ *Web:* www.patheon.com	Mississauga	ON	L5N7K9	905-821-4001	812-6709
PendoPharm Inc 5950 chemin Cote-de-Liesse *TF:* 866-384-6516 ■ *Web:* www.pendopharm.com	Mont Royal	QC	H4T1E2	514-340-5045	733-9684
Pharma Tech Industries Inc 1310 Stylemaster Dr *Web:* www.pharma-tech.net	Union	MO	63084	636-583-8664	583-5373
Sabinsa Corp 70 Ethel Rd W Suite 6 *Web:* www.sabinsa.com	Piscataway	NJ	08854	732-777-1111	777-1443
Savient Pharmaceuticals Inc 1 Tower Center Blvd 14th Fl *NASDAQ: SVNT* ■ *TF:* 800-284-2480 ■ *Web:* www.savientpharma.com	East Brunswick	NJ	08816	732-418-9300	418-9235
Scientific Protein Laboratories Inc 700 E Main St PO Box 158 *TF:* 800-334-4775 ■ *Web:* www.spl-pharma.com	Waunakee	WI	53597	608-849-5944	849-4053
SICOR Inc 19 Hughes. *TF:* 800-806-4226 ■ *Web:* www.gensiasicor.com	Irvine	CA	92618	949-455-4700	855-8210
Siegfried USA Inc 33 Industrial Park Rd. *TF Cust Svc:* 877-763-8630 ■ *Web:* www.ganes.com	Pennsville	NJ	08070	856-678-3601	678-4008
Sigma-Aldrich Corp 3050 Spruce St. *NASDAQ: SIAL* ■ **Fax Area Code:* 800 ■ *TF:* 800-325-3010 ■ *Web:* www.sigmaaldrich.com	Saint Louis	MO	63103	314-771-5765	325-5052*
SPI Pharma 321 Cherry Ln *TF:* 800-789-9755 ■ *Web:* www.spipharma.com	New Castle	DE	19720	302-576-8554	576-8569
SST Corp 635 Brighton Rd. *TF:* 800-222-0921 ■ *Web:* www.sst-corp.com	Clifton	NJ	07012	973-473-4300	473-4326
Starwest Botanicals Inc 11253 Trade Center Dr *TF:* 800-800-4372 ■ *Web:* www.starwestherb.com	Rancho Cordova	CA	95742	916-638-8100	853-9673
Tapestry Pharmaceuticals Inc 4840 Pearl E Cir Suite 300W *NASDAQ: TPPH* ■ *TF:* 800-976-2776 ■ *Web:* www.tapestrypharma.com	Boulder	CO	80301	303-516-8500	530-1296

Phone Fax

Terry Laboratories Inc 390 N Wickham Rd Suite F .... Melbourne FL 32935 321-259-1630 242-0625
TF: 800-367-2563 ■ Web: www.terrylabs.com

Tri-K Industries Inc 151 Veterans Dr .... Northvale NJ 07647 201-750-1055 750-9785
TF: 800-526-0372 ■ Web: www.tri-k.com

Truett Laboratories Inc 798 N Coney Ave .... Azusa CA 91702 626-334-5106 969-3026
Web: www.truettlaboratories.com

TSI Health Sciences Inc 7168 Expressway..................... Missoula MT 59808 406-549-9123 549-6139
TF: 877-549-9123 ■ Web: www.tsiinc.com

Uhe George Co Inc 219 River Dr .... Garfield NJ 07026 201-843-4000 843-7517
TF: 800-850-4075 ■ Web: www.uhe.com

United-Guardian Inc 230 Marcus Blvd PO Box 18050..........Hauppauge NY 11788 631-273-0900 273-0858
AMEX: UG ■ TF: 800-645-5566 ■ Web: www.u-g.com

Vinchem Inc 301 Main St ....Chatham NJ 07928 973-635-4841 635-1459
Web: www.vinchem.com

Wilcox Emporium Warehouse 161 Howard St ....Boone NC 28607 828-262-1221 264-1408
Web: www.wilcoxemporium.com

Xechem International Inc
100 Jersey Ave Bldg B Suite 310 .... New Brunswick NJ 08901 732-247-3300 247-4090
TF: 800-858-5854 ■ Web: www.xechem.com

483 METAL - STRUCTURAL (FABRICATED)

Phone Fax

Aerospace America Inc 900 Harry Truman Pkwy PO Box 189 ...... Bay City MI 48707 989-684-2121 684-4486
TF: 800-237-6414 ■ Web: www.aerospaceamerica.com

Afco Mfg Corp 428 Cogshall St PO Box 230 ....Holly MI 48442 248-634-4415 634-6301
TF: 800-743-4415 ■ Web: www.afcomfg.com

Afco Steel Inc 1423 E 6th St .... Little Rock AR 72202 501-340-6200 340-6333
Web: www.afcosteel.com

Amerimax Building Products Inc 5208 Tennyson Pkwy Suite 100 ..... Plano TX 75024 469-366-3200 366-3260
TF: 800-258-6295 ■ Web: www.amerimaxbp.com

Amerimax Home Products Inc 450 Richardson Dr...............Lancaster PA 17603 717-299-3711 299-3014
TF: 800-347-2586 ■ Web: www.amerimax.com

APi Group Inc Fabrication & Mfg Group 2366 Rose Pl.......... Saint Paul MN 55113 651-636-4320 636-0312
Web: www.apigroupinc.com/manufacturing.html

Barker Steel Co Inc 55 Sumner St.............................. Milford MA 01757 508-473-8484 473-8512
TF: 800-370-0132 ■ Web: www.barker.com

Berlin Steel Construction Co 76 Depot Rd PO Box 428 ....Kensington CT 06037 860-828-3531 828-5253
Web: www.berlinsteel.com

Bethesda Iron Works Inc 650 Lofstrand Ln.................... Rockville MD 20850 301-762-9100 279-0052
TF: 800-762-1383

Braden Mfg LLC 5199 N Mingo Rd............................ Tulsa OK 74117 918-272-5371 272-7414
TF: 800-272-3360 ■ Web: www.braden.com

BW Fabricators LP 4140 Reilly Rd .... Wichita Falls TX 76305 940-855-2710 855-2833
TF: 800-508-2710 ■ Web: www.bwenv.com

Canam Steel Corp 4010 Clay St.........................Point of Rocks MD 21777 301-874-5141 874-5685
TF: 800-638-4293 ■ Web: www.canamsteel.com

Carolina Steel Corp 1451 S Elm Eugene St................. Greensboro NC 27406 336-275-9711 691-5772
TF: 800-632-0286 ■ Web: www.carolinasteel.com

Central Texas Iron Works Inc 1000 Winchell St PO Box 2555 .... Waco TX 76702 254-776-8000 776-8844
Web: www.ctiw.com

CENTRIA 1005 Beaver Grade Rd ....Moon Township PA 15108 412-299-8000 299-8051*
*Fax: Hum Res ■ TF: 800-759-7474 ■ Web: www.centria.com

Chart Denver 5995 N Washington St .... Denver CO 80216 303-296-0105 295-2207
Web: www.cryenco.com

Cives Steel Co 210 Cives Ln.............................Winchester VA 22603 540-667-3480 662-2680
Web: www.cives.com

Clark Western Building System 101 Clark Blvd............. Middle Town OH 45044 513-539-2900 539-2901
TF: 800-882-7883 ■ Web: www.clarksteel.com

Clermont Steel Fabricators LLC 2565 Old SR 32 .... Batavia OH 45103 513-732-6033 732-5344
Web: www.clermontsteel.com

CMC Alamo Steel Co 2784 Old Dallas Rd............................ Waco TX 76705 254-799-2471 799-6227
TF: 800-810-3166 ■ Web: www.cmcalamosteel.com

CMC Capitol City Steel 14501 I-35 ....Buda TX 78610 512-282-8820 295-2500
TF: 800-333-8820 ■ Web: www.cmc.com

CMC Joist & Deck 25 DeForest Ave........................... Summit NJ 07901 908-277-1617 277-1619
TF: 800-631-1215 ■ Web: www.cmcjoist.com

CMC Rebar Carolinas 2528 N Chester St.......................Gastonia NC 28052 704-865-8571 865-2713
TF: 800-476-6975 ■ Web: www.cmc.com

CMC Rebar Georgia 251 Hosea Rd.........................Lawrenceville GA 30045 770-963-6251 339-6623
Web: www.cmc.com

CMC South Carolina Steel 113 E Warehouse Ct ....Taylors SC 29687 864-244-2860 244-8776
Web: www.cmcscs.com

Dietrich Industries Inc 500 Grant St Suite 2226 .... Pittsburgh PA 15219 412-281-2805
Web: www.dietrichindustries.com

Eastern Bridge LLC 386 River Rd .... Claremont NH 03743 603-542-5202 542-5317

Economy Forms Corp 1800 NE Broadway.................... Des Moines IA 50313 515-266-1141 313-4424
TF: 888-289-3326 ■ Web: www.efco-usa.com

Enco Materials Inc 110 N 1st St .... Nashville TN 37213 615-256-3199 259-3589
TF: 800-876-3626 ■ Web: www.encomaterials.com

Euramax International Inc 5445 Triangle Pkwy Suite 350......... Norcross GA 30092 770-449-7066
Web: www.euramax.com

Fabral Inc 3449 Hempland Rd .... Lancaster PA 17601 717-397-2741 397-1040
TF: 800-477-2741 ■ Web: www.fabral.com

Frey John S Enterprises Inc 1900 E 64th St..................Los Angeles CA 90001 323-583-4061 582-1015
TF: 800-377-3322

General Steel Fabricators 927 Schifferdecker Rd .... Joplin MO 64801 417-623-2224 623-2204
TF: 800-820-8644 ■ Web: www.generalsteelfabricators.com

Glenco Steel Corp 8657 Live Oak Ave .... Fontana CA 92335 909-854-9000 854-9008
Web: www.glencometalbuildings.com

Harris Structural Steel Co Inc 1640 New Market Ave .... South Plainfield NJ 07080 732-752-6070 752-1158

Hirschfeld Steel Co Inc 112 W 29th St .... San Angelo TX 76903 325-486-4201 486-4380
TF: 800-375-3216 ■ Web: www.hirschfeld.com

Hogan Mfg Inc 1638 Main St PO Box 398.......................... Escalon CA 95320 209-838-7323 838-8648
Web: www.hoganmfg.com

Hunt Rodney Co Inc 46 Mill St............................... Orange MA 01364 978-544-2511 544-7204
TF: 800-448-8860 ■ Web: www.rodneyhunt.com

Hyspan Precision Products Inc 1685 Brandywine Ave...........Chula Vista CA 91911 619-421-1355 421-1702
Web: www.hyspan.com

InterLock Industries Inc 445 E Market St Suite 310 .... Louisville KY 40202 502-569-2007 569-2016
Web: www.interlockindustries.com

JH Industries Inc 1981 E Aurora Rd.......................... Twinsburg OH 44087 330-963-4105 963-4111
TF: 800-321-4968 ■ Web: www.copperloy.com

John S Frey Enterprises Inc 1900 E 64th St...................Los Angeles CA 90001 323-583-4061 582-1015
TF: 800-377-3322

Johnson Brothers Metal Forming Co 5520 McDermott Dr ....Berkeley IL 60163 708-449-7050 449-0042
Web: www.johnsonrollforming.com

LeJeune Steel Co 118 W 60th St........................... Minneapolis MN 55419 612-861-3321 861-2724
Web: www.lejeunesteel.com

Lichtenwald-Johnston Iron Works Corp
7840 Lehigh St PO Box 1328 .... Morton Grove IL 60053 847-966-1100 966-1159

LSI Metal Fabrication Inc 3871 Turkeyfoot Rd .... Erlanger KY 41018 859-342-9944 342-2275
TF: 800-546-1513

Phone Fax

M & J Materials Inc 7561 Gadsden Hwy PO Box 428........... Trussville AL 35173 205-655-7451 655-4100

Mark Steel Corp 1230 W 200 South.......................Salt Lake City UT 84104 801-521-0670 303-2040
Web: www.marksteel.net

McElroy Metal Mill Inc 1500 Hamilton Rd...................Bossier City LA 71111 318-747-8000 752-5017
TF: 800-950-6531 ■ Web: www.mcelroymetal.com

Miller Metal Fabricators Inc 345 National Ave PO Box 3165...... Staunton VA 24402 540-886-5575

Mound Technologies Inc 25 Mound Park Dr.................Springboro OH 45066 937-748-2937 748-9763
Web: moundtechnologies.com

Norlen Inc 900 Grossman Dr .... Schofield WI 54476 715-359-0506 359-0901
TF: 800-648-6594 ■ Web: www.norlen.com

Nucor Corp 1915 Rexford Rd .... Charlotte NC 28211 704-366-7000 362-4208
NYSE: NUE ■ Web: www.nucor.com

Nucor Corp Vulcraft Div 1501 W Darlington St.................Florence SC 29501 843-662-0381 662-3132
Web: www.vulcraft.com

Ornamental Metal Works Inc 2100 N Woodford St.............. Decatur IL 62526 217-428-3446 424-2326

Owen Industries Inc 501 Ave H .... Carter Lake IA 51510 712-347-5500 347-6166
TF: 800-831-9252 ■ Web: www.owenind.com

Owen Steel Co 727 Mauney Dr............................ Columbia SC 29201 803-251-7680 251-7613
TF: 800-922-5134 ■ Web: www.owensteel.com

Owens Corning Fabricating Solutions 426 N Main St.............. Elkhart IN 46516 574-522-8473 522-5451
TF: 877-632-2935

Paxton & Vierling Steel Co 501 Ave H...................... Carter Lake IA 51510 712-347-5500 347-6166
TF: 800-831-9252 ■ Web: www.pvsteel.com

PDM Bridge Corp 211 Comfort Rd .... Palatka FL 32177 386-328-4683 328-2804
Web: www.pdmbridge.com

Progressive Power Technologies 100 Precision Dr.............. Harmony PA 16037 724-452-6065 452-6540

PSP Industries 300 Montague Expy Suite 200.................... Milpitas CA 95035 408-942-1155 262-5388
Web: www.pspindustries.com

Ranor Inc 1 Bella Dr ....Westminster MA 01473 978-874-0591 874-2748
TF: 800-225-9552 ■ Web: www.ranor.com

Rodney Hunt Co Inc 46 Mill St................................. Orange MA 01364 978-544-2511 544-7204
TF: 800-448-8860 ■ Web: www.rodneyhunt.com

Schuff Steel Inc 1920 Ledo Rd .... Albany GA 31707 229-883-4506 438-8316
TF: 800-528-0513 ■ Web: www.schuff.com

Shape Corp 1900 Hayes St.............................. Grand Haven MI 49417 616-846-8700 846-3464
Web: www.shapecorp.com

Southeastern Steel Co 211 N Koppers Rd......................Florence SC 29506 843-662-5236 662-6261
TF: 800-476-7372 ■ Web: www.sesteel.com

Standard Iron Inc 2516 Vance Ave.........................Chattanooga TN 37404 423-756-0940 756-0944
Web: www.standardiron.com

Steel Fabricators LLC 721 NE 44th St.................. Fort Lauderdale FL 33334 954-772-0440 938-7527*
*Fax: Sales ■ Web: www.steelfabflorida.com

Structural Metals Inc 1 Steel Mill Dr.......................... Seguin TX 78156 830-372-8200 379-8567
TF Sales: 800-227-6489

Structural Steel Services
6215 Saint Louis St South Industrial Park ....Meridian MS 39307 601-482-8181 482-1520

Stupp Brothers Inc 3800 Weber Rd ....Saint Louis MO 63125 314-638-5000 638-5439
TF: 800-899-1856 ■ Web: www.stupp.com

Tarpon Industries Inc 2420 Wills St.........................Marysville MI 48040 810-364-7421 364-5610
AMEX: TPO ■ Web: www.tarponind.com

Trinity Structural Towers Inc 2525 N Stemmons Fwy.............Dallas TX 75207 214-631-4420 589-8640
TF: 800-631-8501 ■ Web: www.trinitytowers.com

Union Metal Corp 1432 Maple Ave NE.......................... Canton OH 44705 330-456-7653 456-0196
Web: www.unionmetal.com

Unistrut Corp 4205 Elizabeth St .... Wayne MI 48184 734-721-4040 721-4106
TF Cust Svc: 800-521-7730 ■ Web: www.unistrut.com

Vulcraft Div Nucor Corp 1501 W Darlington St.................Florence SC 29501 843-662-0381 662-3132
Web: www.vulcraft.com

W & W Steel Co 1730 W Reno Ave .... Oklahoma City OK 73106 405-235-3621 236-4842
Web: www.wwsteel.com

Will-Burt Co PO Box 900...................................... Orrville OH 44667 330-682-7015 684-5257
Web: www.willburt.com

Wisconsin Structural Steel Co Hwy 63 N .... Barronett WI 54813 715-822-2647 822-2906

484 METAL COATING, PLATING, ENGRAVING

Phone Fax

Alcoa Inc 201 Isabella St .... Pittsburgh PA 15212 412-553-4545 553-4498
NYSE: AA ■ Web: www.alcoa.com

All Metals Processing of Orange County Inc
8401 Standustrial St .... Stanton CA 90680 714-828-8238 828-4552
TF: 800-894-4489 ■ Web: www.allmetalsprocessing.com

Aluminum Coil Anodizing Corp 501 E Lake St................Streamwood IL 60107 630-837-4000 837-0814
Web: www.acacorp.com

American Nickeloid Co 2900 W Main St .... Peru IL 61354 815-223-0373 223-5344
TF: 800-645-5643 ■ Web: www.nickeloid.com

Andal Corp 630 5th Ave ....New York NY 10111 212-218-2811 218-2822

Apollo Metals Ltd 1001 14th Ave.............................. Bethlehem PA 18018 610-867-5826 867-7594
TF: 800-338-0199 ■ Web: www.corusspecialstrip.com/apollo/

Archer Wire International Corp 7300 S Narragansett Ave...... Bedford Park IL 60638 708-563-1700 563-1740
Web: www.archerwire.com

Bredero Shaw A ShawCor Co
3838 N Sam Houston Pkwy E Suite 500........................ Houston TX 77032 281-886-2350 886-2353
Web: www.brederoshaw.com

Canfield Metal Coating Corp 460 W Main St PO Box 556 .... Canfield OH 44406 330-533-3311 533-5741
TF: 877-264-5262 ■ Web: www.coilcoat.com

Chicago Metallic Corp 4849 S Austin Ave..................... Chicago IL 60638 708-563-4600
TF: 800-323-7164 ■ Web: www.chicago-metallic.com

Decorated Products Inc 1 Arch Rd.......................... Westfield MA 01086 413-568-0944 568-1875
TF: 800-639-4909 ■ Web: www.decorated.com

Deposition Sciences Inc 3300 Coffey Ln.................... Santa Rosa CA 95403 707-573-6700 579-0731
TF: 866-433-7724 ■ Web: www.depsci.com

Donham Craft Inc 15 E Waterbury Rd .... Naugatuck CT 06770 203-729-8244 729-8487
TF: 800-739-1919 ■ Web: www.donhamcraft.com

DS Mfg Co 67 5th St NE....................................Pine Island MN 55963 507-356-8322 356-8436

Electric Coating Technologies (ECT) 8687 S 77th Ave..........Bridgeview IL 60455 708-598-5100 598-6990
TF: 800-752-9957 ■ Web: ect.esmark.com

Foster LB Co 415 Holiday Dr............................... Pittsburgh PA 15220 412-928-3400 928-3427*
NASDAQ: FSTR ■ *Fax: Sales ■ TF: 800-255-4500 ■ Web: www.lbfoster.com

General Extrusions Inc 4040 Lake Park Rd ....Youngstown OH 44512 330-783-0270 788-1250
Web: www.genext.com

GM Nameplate Inc 2040 15th Ave W .... Seattle WA 98119 206-284-2200 284-3705
TF: 800-366-7668 ■ Web: www.gmnameplate.com

Hytek Finishes Co 8127 S 216th St.............................. Kent WA 98032 253-872-7160 872-7214
Web: www.hytekfinishes.com

Interplex Engineered Products 231 Ferris Ave.............East Providence RI 02916 401-434-6543 399-7655*
*Fax Area Code: 508 ■ Web: www.interplex.com

IonBond LLC 200 Roundhill Dr ....Rockaway NJ 07866 973-586-4700 586-4729
Web: www.ionbond.com

KNS Cos Inc 475 Randy Rd............................. Carol Stream IL 60188 630-665-9010 665-1819
Web: www.knscompanies.com

LB Foster Co 415 Holiday Dr.............................. Pittsburgh PA 15220 412-928-3400 928-3427*
NASDAQ: FSTR ■ *Fax: Sales ■ TF: 800-255-4500 ■ Web: www.lbfoster.com

Company	City	State	ZIP	Phone	Fax
Lorin Industries 1265 E Keating Ave *TF:* 800-678-1215 ■ *Web:* www.lorin.com	Muskegon	MI	49443	231-722-1631	728-3139
Magnetic Metals Corp 1900 Hayes Ave *TF:* 800-257-8174 ■ *Web:* www.magmet.com	Camden	NJ	08105	856-964-7842	963-8569
Master Finish Co 2020 Nelson Ave SE *TF:* 888-372-2913 ■ *Web:* www.masterfinishco.com	Grand Rapids	MI	49507	616-245-1228	245-0039
Material Sciences Corp 2200 E Pratt Blvd *NYSE: MSC* ■ *TF:* 800-877-9078 ■ *Web:* www.matsci.com	Elk Grove Village	IL	60007	847-439-2210	439-0737
Metal Cladding Inc 230 S Niagara St *TF:* 800-432-5513 ■ *Web:* www.metalcladding.com	Lockport	NY	14094	716-434-5513	439-4010
MetoKote Corp 1340 Neubrecht Rd *Web:* www.metokote.com	Lima	OH	45801	419-227-1100	996-7801
Mills Cos Inc 5201 Gershwin Ave N *TF:* 800-367-9045 ■ *Web:* www.millsawards.com	Saint Paul	MN	55128	651-770-6660	770-0224
Nor-Ell Inc 851 Hubbard Ave *Web:* www.nor-ell.com	Saint Paul	MN	55104	651-487-1441	488-1626
North American Galvanizing & Coatings Inc 5314 S Yale Ave Suite 1000 *AMEX: NGA* ■ *Web:* www.nagalv.com	Tulsa	OK	74135	918-494-0964	488-8172
Northern Engraving Corp 803 S Black River St *Web:* www.norcorp.com	Sparta	WI	54656	608-269-6911	269-6735
Passaic Engraving Co Inc 41 Brook Ave *Web:* www.passaicengraving.com	Passaic	NJ	07055	973-777-0621	777-7791
Plastene Supply Div Siegel-Robert Inc 101 Meatte St	Portageville	MO	63873	573-379-3857	379-5677
Porcelen Ltd 333 Welton St *TF:* 800-243-6256	Hamden	CT	06517	203-248-6346	248-8489
Porter Process Co 1600 Industry Rd *TF:* 800-618-4701 ■ *Web:* www.porterprocess.com	Hatfield	PA	19440	215-855-9916	855-3570
Precision Graphics Inc 21 County Line Rd *Web:* www.precisiongraphics.us	Somerville	NJ	08876	908-707-8880	707-8884
Precoat Metals Div Sequa Corp 1310 Papin St 3rd Fl *Web:* www.precoatmetals.com	Saint Louis	MO	63103	314-436-7010	436-7050
Premier Die Casting Co 1177 Rahway Ave *TF:* 800-394-3006 ■ *Web:* www.diecasting.com	Avenel	NJ	07001	732-634-3000	634-0590
Providence Metallizing Co Inc 51 Fairlawn Ave *Web:* www.provmet.com	Pawtucket	RI	02860	401-722-5300	724-3410
Rimex Metals (USA) Inc 2850 Woodbridge Ave *Web:* www.rimexmetals.com	Edison	NJ	08837	732-549-3800	549-6435
Roehlen Engraving 5901 Lewis Rd *Web:* www.roehlenengraving.com	Sandston	VA	23150	804-222-2821	226-3462
Roesch Inc 100 N 24th St *TF:* 800-423-6243 ■ *Web:* www.roeschinc.com	Belleville	IL	62222	618-233-2760	233-1186
Roll Coater Inc 8440 Woodfield Crossing Bldg 2 Suite 500 *Web:* www.rollcoater.com	Indianapolis	IN	46240	317-462-7761	467-7323
Rome Metals Inc 499 Delaware Ave *Web:* www.romemetals.com	Rochester	PA	15074	724-775-1664	775-1668
Royal Silver Mfg Co Inc 3300 Chesapeake Blvd	Norfolk	VA	23513	757-855-6004	855-0017
S & S Procelain Inc 1410 S 13th St	Louisville	KY	40210	502-635-7421	634-9800
Sapa Inc 7933 NE 21st Ave *TF:* 800-547-0790 ■ *Web:* www.sapagroup.com	Portland	OR	97211	503-972-1404	802-3060
Savon Plating & Powder Coating Inc 15523 Illinois Ave	Paramount	CA	90723	562-634-6189	602-0690
Sequa Corp Precoat Metals Div 1310 Papin St 3rd Fl *Web:* www.precoatmetals.com	Saint Louis	MO	63103	314-436-7010	436-7050
Siegel-Robert Inc 8645 S Broadway *Web:* www.srob.com	Saint Louis	MO	63111	314-638-8300	638-5832
Siegel-Robert Inc Plastene Supply Div 101 Meatte St	Portageville	MO	63873	573-379-3857	379-5677
Standex International Corp Engraving Group 5901 Lewis Rd *Web:* www.standexengraving.com	Sandston	VA	23150	804-222-2821	226-3462
State Plating 450 N 9th St *TF:* 800-428-6340 ■ *Web:* www.stateplating.com	Elwood	IN	46036	765-552-5047	552-6980
Sumco Inc 1351 S Girls School Rd	Indianapolis	IN	46231	317-241-7600	248-2352
Summit Corp of America 1430 Waterbury Rd *TF:* 800-854-0176 ■ *Web:* www.scact.com	Thomaston	CT	06787	860-283-4391	283-4010
Towne Technologies Inc 6-10 Bell Ave *Web:* www.townetech.com	Somerville	NJ	08876	908-722-9500	722-8394
Unicote Corp 33165 Groesbeck Hwy *Web:* www.unicotecorporation.com	Fraser	MI	48026	586-296-0700	296-3155
US Chrome Corp 175 Garfield Ave *TF:* 800-637-9019 ■ *Web:* www.uschrome.com	Stratford	CT	06615	203-378-9622	386-0067
Vapor Technologies Inc 6400 Dry Creek Pkwy *Web:* www.vaportech.com	Longmont	CO	80503	303-652-8500	652-8600

485 METAL FABRICATING - CUSTOM

Company	City	State	ZIP	Phone	Fax
Afco Industries Inc 3400 Roy Ave *TF:* 800-551-6576 ■ *Web:* www.afco-ind.net	Alexandria	LA	71302	318-448-1651	443-5158
Aldine Metal Products Corp 566 Danbury Rd Unit 1 *TF:* 877-775-2551 ■ *Web:* www.aldinemetal.com	New Milford	CT	06776	860-350-2552	350-1061
Alpha Sintered Metals Inc 95 Mason Run Rd *Web:* www.alphasintered.com	Ridgway	PA	15853	814-773-3191	776-1009
American Aluminum Co 230 Sheffield St *TF:* 800-315-3977 ■ *Web:* www.amalco.com	Mountainside	NJ	07092	908-233-3500	233-3241
Angell & Giroux Inc 2727 Alcazar St *Web:* www.angellandgiroux.com	Los Angeles	CA	90033	323-269-8596	269-0454
Applied Engineering Inc 2008 E Hwy 50 *Web:* www.appliedeng.com	Yankton	SD	57078	605-665-4425	665-1479
Aquarius Metal Products Corp 2475 Millennium Dr *Web:* www.aquariusmetal.com	Elgin	IL	60123	847-841-1400	841-8424
Ascension Industries 1254 Erie Ave *Web:* www.asmfab.com	North Tonawanda	NY	14120	716-695-2040	693-9882
Associated Steel Workers Ltd PO Box 488	Aiea	HI	96701	808-682-5588	682-7392
Autoswage Products Inc 726 River Rd *Web:* www.autoswage.com	Shelton	CT	06484	203-929-1401	929-6187
Brakewell Steel Fabricator Inc 55 Leone Ln *TF:* 888-914-9131 ■ *Web:* www.brakewell.com	Chester	NY	10918	845-469-9131	469-7618
Capital Engineering & Mfg Co 5837 S Ashland Ave	Chicago	IL	60636	773-737-8000	925-3628
Cerro Fabricated Products Inc 300 Triangle Dr *Web:* www.cerrofabricated.com	Weyers Cave	VA	24486	540-234-9252	234-8416
Chandler Industries Inc 1654 N 9th St *Web:* www.chandlerindustries.com	Montevideo	MN	56265	320-269-8893	269-5827
Chicago Metal Fabricators Inc 3724 S Rockwell St *Web:* www.chicagometal.com	Chicago	IL	60632	773-523-5755	523-8680
Clark Western Building System 101 Clark Blvd *TF:* 800-882-7883 ■ *Web:* www.clarksteel.com	Middle Town	OH	45044	513-539-2900	539-2901
CMW Inc 70 S Gray St *Web:* www.cmwinc.com	Indianapolis	IN	46201	317-634-8884	630-2159
Compax Inc 1210 N Blue Gum St *Web:* www.compaxinc.com	Anaheim	CA	92806	714-630-3670	632-1344
Cross Brothers Inc 5255 Sheila St *Web:* www.crossbrothersinc.com	Los Angeles	CA	90040	323-266-2000	266-2106
CSM Metal Fabricating & Engineering Inc 1800 S San Pedro St *TF:* 800-272-4806 ■ *Web:* www.csmworks.com	Los Angeles	CA	90015	213-748-7321	749-5106
D & S Mfg Inc PO Box 279 *Web:* www.dsmfg.com	Black River Falls	WI	54615	715-284-5376	284-4084
Daniel Tanney Co Inc 3268 Clive Ave	Bensalem	PA	19020	215-639-3131	638-3333
Demsey Mfg Co 78 New Wood Rd *TF:* 800-533-6739 ■ *Web:* www.demseyelets.com	Watertown	CT	06795	860-274-6209	274-0186
Diez Group 8111 Tireman Ave *Web:* www.diezgroup.com	Dearborn	MI	48126	313-491-1200	491-6210
Dynamic Materials Corp 5405 Spine Rd *NASDAQ: BOOM* ■ *TF:* 800-821-2666 ■ *Web:* www.dynamicmaterials.com	Boulder	CO	80301	303-665-5700	604-1893
East Windsor Welding & Fabricating Inc PO Box 357	East Windsor Hill	CT	06028	860-528-7107	291-9542
Fabricated Components Inc PO Box 431 *TF:* 800-233-8163 ■ *Web:* www.fabricatedcomponents.com	Stroudsburg	PA	18360	570-421-4110	421-2553
GKN Sinter Metals Inc 3300 University Dr *Web:* www.gknsintermetals.com	Auburn Hills	MI	48326	248-371-0800	371-0809
Gordon Mfg Div Leggett & Platt Inc 5250 52nd St SE	Grand Rapids	MI	49512	616-698-6060	698-0231
Harford Systems Inc 2225 Pulaski Hwy PO Box 700 *TF:* 800-664-7620 ■ *Web:* www.harfordsystems.com	Aberdeen	MD	21001	410-272-3400	273-7892
Harris Mfg Inc 4775 E Vine Ave *Web:* www.harrismfg.com	Fresno	CA	93725	559-268-7422	268-2846
Hurtt Fabricating Corp PO Box 128 *TF:* 800-844-3010	Marceline	MO	64658	660-376-3501	376-2015
Industrial & Detention Fabricators Inc PO Box 190337	Mobile	AL	36619	251-653-7656	653-8442
Johnson Matthey Noble Metals 1401 King Rd *TF:* 800-441-8159 ■ *Web:* www.noble.matthey.com	West Chester	PA	19380	610-648-8000	648-8105
Lafayette Quality Products PO Box 5827	Lafayette	IN	47903	765-447-3106	448-6788
Leggett & Platt Inc Gordon Mfg Div 5250 52nd St SE	Grand Rapids	MI	49512	616-698-6060	698-0231
Liquidmetal Technologies Inc 30452 Esperanza *Web:* www.liquidmetal.com	Rancho Santa Margarita	CA	92688	949-635-2100	635-2188
Lucasey Mfg Corp PO Box 14023 *TF:* 800-582-2739 ■ *Web:* www.lucasey.net	Oakland	CA	94614	510-534-1435	534-6828
Manufacturers Industrial Group LLC 659 Natchez Trace Dr *Web:* www.migllc.com	Lexington	TN	38351	731-967-0001	968-3320
MarathonNorco Aerospace Inc 8301 Imperial Dr *Web:* www.mnaerospace.com	Waco	TX	76712	254-776-0650	776-6558
Master Metal Products Co 495 Emory St *Web:* www.mastermetalproducts.com	San Jose	CA	95110	408-275-1210	275-0523
Matthews Industries 23 2nd St SW *Web:* www.matthewsindustries.com	Decatur	AL	35601	256-353-0271	353-3850
Metal Fabricating Corp 10408 Berea Rd *Web:* www.metalfabricatingcorp.com	Cleveland	OH	44102	216-631-2480	631-2453
MP Metal Products Inc PO Box 170 *Web:* www.mpmetals.com	Ixonia	WI	53036	920-261-9650	261-9652
National Sintered Alloys Inc PO Box 332 *Web:* www.pm-nsa.com	Clinton	CT	06413	860-669-8653	669-5428
Newbrook Machines Inc PO Box 231	Silver Creek	NY	14136	716-934-2651	934-0453
Nor-Cal Metal Fabricators 1121 3rd St *Web:* www.nc-mf.com	Oakland	CA	94607	510-836-1451	208-2838
Peterson Enterprises Inc 10728 Prospect Ave Suite G	Santee	CA	92071	619-448-8484	448-8680
Progressive Mfg Co Inc PO Box 5334	Kansas City	KS	66119	913-621-5700	621-7039
Progressive Tool & Mfg Co PO Box 668 *Web:* www.ptmmn.com	Pine Island	MN	55963	507-356-8345	356-4557
Pulley-Kellam Co Inc 245 Erie St	Huntington	IN	46750	260-356-6326	356-1928
Right Manufacturing 7949 Stromesa Ct Suite G *Web:* www.rightmfg.com	San Diego	CA	92126	858-566-7002	566-7623
Rose Metal Products Inc 1955 E Division St *Web:* www.rosemetalproducts.com	Springfield	MO	65803	417-865-1676	865-7673
Sioux Mfg Corp PO Box 400 *Web:* www.siouxmanufacturing.com	Fort Totten	ND	58335	701-766-4211	766-4359
Sommer Metalcraft Corp 315 Poston Dr *TF:* 800-654-3124 ■ *Web:* www.sommermetalcraft.com	Crawfordsville	IN	47933	765-362-6200	359-4202
Sorini Mfg Co 2524 S Blue Island Ave	Chicago	IL	60608	773-247-5858	247-7186
Southwire Co Machinery Div 401 Fertilla St *TF:* 800-444-1700 ■ *Web:* www.southwire.com	Carrollton	GA	30117	770-832-4242	832-5228
Tanney Daniel Co Inc 3268 Clive Ave	Bensalem	PA	19020	215-639-3131	638-3333
Tomax Fabricating Inc 5449 Peck Rd	Arcadia	CA	91006	626-443-1796	443-1798
TPI Powder Metallurgy Inc 12030 Beaver Rd *Web:* www.tpipm.com	Saint Charles	MI	48655	989-865-9921	865-9924
Uni-Form Components Co 16969 Old Beaumont Hwy 90 *TF:* 800-231-3272 ■ *Web:* www.uniformcomponents.com	Houston	TX	77049	281-456-9310	456-0245
Unifab Corp 3030 Kersten Ct *TF:* 800-648-9569 ■ *Web:* www.unifabcorp.com	Kalamazoo	MI	49048	269-382-2803	382-2825
Weldments Inc 10720 N 2nd St	Rockford	IL	61115	815-633-3393	633-2524
White River Distributors Inc PO Box 2037 *TF:* 800-548-7219 ■ *Web:* www.lpgbobtails.com	Batesville	AR	72503	870-793-2374	793-8230
Wire Products Mfg Corp PO Box 407	Merrill	WI	54452	715-536-7144	536-1476
Young Custom Metal Fabrication 6205 Saint Louis St *Web:* www.theyounggroup.net	Meridian	MS	39307	601-483-6281	693-6529

486 METAL FORGINGS

Company	City	State	ZIP	Phone	Fax
Alcoa Wheel Products International 1600 Harvard Ave *TF:* 800-242-9898 ■ *Web:* www.alcoawheels.com	Cleveland	OH	44105	216-641-3600	641-4032
Aluminum Precision Products Inc 3333 W Warner St *TF:* 800-411-8983 ■ *Web:* www.aluminumprecision.com	Santa Ana	CA	92704	714-546-8125	540-8862
Ameri-Forge Group Inc 13770 Industrial Rd *Web:* www.ameriforge.com	Houston	TX	77015	713-393-4200	455-8366
AMSTED Industries Inc 180 N Stetson St Suite 1800 **Fax: Hum Res* ■ *Web:* www.amsted.com	Chicago	IL	60601	312-645-1700	819-8504*
Anchor-Harvey Components Inc 600 W Lamm Rd *TF:* 888-367-4464 ■ *Web:* www.forgings.com	Freeport	IL	61032	815-235-4400	235-3587
Ball Chain Mfg Co Inc 741 S Fulton Ave *Web:* www.ballchain.com	Mount Vernon	NY	10550	914-664-7500	664-7460
Berkeley Forge & Tool Inc 1331 East Shore Hwy *Web:* www.berkforge.com	Berkeley	CA	94710	510-526-5034	525-9014
Bharat Forge America 2807 S ML King Jr Blvd *TF:* 800-968-2932 ■ *Web:* www.bharatforgeamerica.com	Lansing	MI	48910	517-393-5300	393-6256
Buchanan Metal Forming Inc 103 W Smith St *TF:* 800-253-0585 ■ *Web:* www.bmfcorp.com	Buchanan	MI	49107	269-695-3836	695-3830
Canton Drop Forge Inc 4575 Southway St SW *Web:* www.cantondropforge.com	Canton	OH	44706	330-477-4511	477-2046
Carlton Forge Works Inc 7743 E Adams St	Paramount	CA	90723	562-633-1131	531-8896
Clifford-Jacobs Forging Co 2410 N 5th St PO Box 830 *Web:* www.clifford-jacobs.com	Champaign	IL	61822	217-352-5172	352-4629
Columbus McKinnon Corp Midland Forge Div 101 50th Ave SW *TF:* 800-888-0985	Cedar Rapids	IA	52404	319-362-1111	362-4492
Commercial Forged Products Div Wozniak Industries Inc 5757 W 65th St *TF:* 800-637-2695 ■ *Web:* www.commercialforged.com	Bedford Park	IL	60638	708-458-1220	458-9346
Consolidated Industries Inc PO Box 280 *Web:* www.forgemetal.com	Cheshire	CT	06410	203-272-5371	272-5672
Cornell Forge Co 6666 W 66th St *TF:* 800-356-0204 ■ *Web:* www.cornellforge.com	Chicago	IL	60638	708-458-1582	728-9883

Company	City	State	Zip	Phone	Fax
Corry Forge Co 441 E Main St *Web:* www.elwd.com/corry.htm	Corry	PA	16407	814-664-9664	664-9452
Coulter Forge Technology Inc 1494 67th St PO Box 8008 *TF:* 800-648-4884 ■ *Web:* www.coulter-forge.com	Emeryville	CA	94662	510-420-3500	420-3555
Crow W Pat Forgings Inc 200 Luxton St *Web:* www.wpatcrow.com	Fort Worth	TX	76104	817-536-2861	531-2196
DeKalb Forge Co 1832 Pleasant St *Web:* www.dekalbforge.com	DeKalb	IL	60115	815-756-3538	756-6958
Doncasters Storms Forge Div 160 Cottage St *Web:* www.doncasters-stormsforge.com	Springfield	MA	01104	413-785-1801	785-5680
Ellwood City Forge 800 Commercial Ave PO Box 31 *TF:* 800-843-0166 ■ *Web:* www.ellwoodgroup.com/ecf.htm	Ellwood City	PA	16117	724-752-0055	752-3449
Enterprise Automotive Systems 21445 Hoover Rd *Web:* www.think-eas.com	Warren	MI	48089	586-755-3180	759-3540
Erie Forge & Steel Inc 1341 W 16th St *Web:* www.erieforge.com	Erie	PA	16502	814-452-2300	459-9170
Federal Flange 4014 Pinemont St *TF:* 800-231-0150 ■ *Web:* www.federalflange.com	Houston	TX	77018	713-681-0606	681-3005
Forged Products Inc 6505 N Houston Rosslyn Rd *TF:* 800-876-3416 ■ *Web:* www.fpitx.com	Houston	TX	77091	713-462-3416	460-9404
Forged Vessel Connections Inc 2525 DeSoto St *TF Cust Svc:* 800-231-2701 ■ *Web:* www.forgedvesselconn.com	Houston	TX	77091	713-688-9705	688-7954
Green Bay Drop Forge 1341 S State St PO Box 11797 *TF:* 800-824-4896 ■ *Web:* www.greenbaydropforge.com	Green Bay	WI	54307	920-432-6401	432-0859
Griffin Wheel Co 200 W Monroe St *TF:* 800-604-6061 ■ *Web:* www.griffinwheel.com	Chicago	IL	60606	312-346-3300	346-3373
H & L Tooth Co Inc 10055 E 56 St N *TF:* 800-458-6684 ■ *Web:* www.hltooth.com	Tulsa	OK	74117	918-272-0951	272-0163
Hammond & Irving Inc 254 North St *Web:* www.hammond-irving.com	Auburn	NY	13021	315-253-6265	253-3136
Hirschvogel Inc 2230 S 3rd St *TF:* 866-367-4464	Columbus	OH	43207	614-445-6060	445-7335
Impact Forge Group Inc 2805 Norcross Dr PO Box 1847 *TF:* 800-367-1433 ■ *Web:* www.impactforge.com	Columbus	IN	47201	812-342-4437	342-4553
Independent Forge Co 692 N Batavia St *Web:* www.independentforge.com	Orange	CA	92868	714-997-7337	997-7546
Jernberg Industries Inc 328 W 40th Pl *Web:* www.jernberg.com	Chicago	IL	60609	773-268-3004	268-3220
Kerkau Mfg Co 910 Harry S Truman Pkwy *TF:* 800-248-5060 ■ *Web:* www.kerkau.com	Bay City	MI	48706	989-686-0350	686-0399
Keystone Forging Co 215 Duke St PO Boxs 269 *Web:* www.keystoneforging.com	Northumberland	PA	17857	570-473-3524	473-7273
KomTeK Technologies 40 Rockdale St *TF:* 800-756-6835 ■ *Web:* www.komtektech.com	Worcester	MA	01606	508-853-4500	853-2753
Kropp Forge 5301 W Roosevelt Rd *Web:* www.kroppforge.com	Cicero	IL	60804	708-652-6691	652-6696
Ladish Co Inc 5481 S Packard Ave PO Box 8902 *NASDAQ: LDSH* ■ *Web:* www.ladish.com	Cudahy	WI	53110	414-747-2611	747-3540
Lake City Industries LLC Forging Div 4150 N Wolcott Rd	Lake City	MI	49651	231-839-7102	839-4022
Lakeview Forge Co PO Box 1030 *Web:* www.lakeviewforge.com	Erie	PA	16512	814-454-4518	455-5875
Lefere Forge & Machine Co 665 Hupp Ave *Web:* www.lefereforge.com	Jackson	MI	49203	517-784-7109	784-0929
Lehigh Heavy Forge Corp 1275 Daly Ave *Web:* www.lhforge.com	Bethlehem	PA	18015	610-332-8100	332-8101
Lenape Forged Products Corp 1334 Lenape Rd *Web:* www.lenapeforge.com	West Chester	PA	19382	610-793-5090	793-3070
Liberty Forge Inc 1507 Fort Worth St PO Drawer 1210 *TF:* 800-231-2377 ■ *Web:* www.libertyforgeinc.com	Liberty	TX	77575	936-336-5785	336-2740
Louisville Forge & Gear Works LLC 596 Triport Rd *Web:* www.louisvilleforge.com	Georgetown	KY	40324	502-863-7575	863-4928
Machine Specialty & Mfg Inc 215 Rousseau Rd *TF:* 800-256-1292 ■ *Web:* www.machine-specialty.com	Youngsville	LA	70592	337-837-0020	837-0062
McKees Rocks Forgings 75 Nichol Ave *TF:* 800-223-2818 ■ *Web:* www.mckeesrocksforgings.com	McKees Rocks	PA	15136	412-778-2020	778-2025
McKenzie Valve & Machining Co 145 Airport Rd *Web:* www.mckenzievalve.com	McKenzie	TN	38201	731-352-5027	352-3029
McWilliams Forge Co Inc 387 Franklin Ave *Web:* www.mcwilliamsforge.com	Rockaway	NJ	07866	973-627-0200	625-9316
Meadville Forging Co 15309 Baldwin St PO Box 459 *Web:* www.meadforge.com	Meadville	PA	16335	814-724-1280	333-4657
Metal Forming & Coining Corp 1007 Illinois Ave *Web:* www.mfccorp.com	Maumee	OH	43537	419-893-8748	893-6828
Metalist International Inc 1159 S Pennsylvania Ave *Web:* www.metalist.com	Lansing	MI	48912	517-371-2940	371-3027
Mid-West Forge Corp 17301 St Clair Ave *Web:* www.mid-westforge.com	Cleveland	OH	44110	216-481-3030	481-7288
Midland Forge Div Columbus McKinnon Corp 101 50th Ave SW *TF:* 800-888-0985	Cedar Rapids	IA	52404	319-362-1111	362-4492
Millennium Forge Inc 990 W Ormsby Ave *Web:* www.millenniumforge.com	Louisville	KY	40210	502-635-3350	635-3028
Modern Drop Forge Co 13810 S Western Ave *Web:* www.modernforge.com	Blue Island	IL	60406	708-388-1806	597-3633
Modern Forge/Tennessee Inc 501 Rock Ln *Web:* www.modernforge.com	Piney Flats	TN	37686	423-282-0327	538-8185
Moline Forge Inc 4101 4th Ave *Web:* www.molineforge.com	Moline	IL	61265	309-762-5506	762-5508
National Flame & Forge Inc 330 W 25th St *Web:* www.nationalflame.com	Houston	TX	77008	713-869-5724	869-7737
National Flange & Fitting Co 4420 Creekmont St *TF:* 800-231-1424	Houston	TX	77091	713-688-2515	688-0205
Nonferrous Products Inc PO Box 349 *TF:* 800-423-5612 ■ *Web:* www.nonferrousproducts.com	Franklin	IN	46131	317-738-2558	738-2685
Norforge & Machining Inc 195 N Dean St *TF:* 800-457-7699 ■ *Web:* www.norforge.com	Bushnell	IL	61422	309-772-3124	772-9206
Nortrak Inc DBA VAE Nortrak North America Inc 3422 1st Ave S *TF:* 800-638-4657 ■ *Web:* www.nortrak.com	Seattle	WA	98134	206-622-0125	621-9626
Ohio Star Forge Co 4000 Mahoning Ave NW *Web:* www.ohiostar.com	Warren	OH	44483	330-847-6360	847-6368
Pacific Forge Inc 10641 Etiwanda Ave *Web:* www.pacificforge.com	Fontana	CA	92337	909-390-0701	390-0708
Parish International Inc PO Box 468 *TF:* 877-496-8378 ■ *Web:* www.parishforge.com	Hempstead	TX	77445	979-826-8222	826-8224
Patriot Forge Co 1802 Cranberry St *TF:* 877-495-9542 ■ *Web:* www.patriotforge.com	Erie	PA	16502	814-456-2088	456-4395
Phoenix Forging Co Inc 800 Front St *TF:* 800-444-3674 ■ *Web:* www.phoenixforge.com	Catasauqua	PA	18032	610-264-2861	266-0530
Pioneer Forge Div Powers & Sons LLC 101 Industrial Ave PO Box 598 *Web:* www.letts.com/pioneer	Pioneer	OH	43554	419-737-2373	737-2978
Portland Forge PO Box 905 *Web:* www.portlandforge.com	Portland	IN	47371	260-726-8121	726-8021
Powers & Sons LLC Pioneer Forge Div 101 Industrial Ave PO Box 598 *Web:* www.letts.com/pioneer	Pioneer	OH	43554	419-737-2373	737-2978
Precision Metal Products Inc 850 W Bradley Ave *Web:* www.pmp-elcajon.com	El Cajon	CA	92020	619-448-2711	448-2005
Presrite Corp 3665 E 78th St *Web:* www.presrite.com	Cleveland	OH	44105	216-441-5990	441-2644
Randall Bearings Inc 1046 Greenlawn Ave PO Box 1258 *Web:* www.randallbearings.com	Lima	OH	45802	419-223-1075	228-0200
Rockford Drop Forge & Machine Co 2011 10th St	Rockford	IL	61104	815-963-9611	963-7950
Saint Croix Forge Inc 5195 Scandia Trail *TF:* 800-966-3668 ■ *Web:* www.stcroixforge.com	Forest Lake	MN	55025	651-464-8967	464-8213
Scot Forge Co 8001 Winn Rd PO Box 8 *TF:* 800-435-6621 ■ *Web:* www.scotforge.com	Spring Grove	IL	60081	815-675-1000	675-4100
Standard Steel Div Freedom Forge Corp 500 N Walnut St *Web:* www.standardsteel.com	Burnham	PA	17009	717-248-4911	248-8050
Standard Steel LLC 500 N Walnut St *Web:* www.standardsteel.com	Burnham	PA	17009	717-248-4911	248-8050
Steel Industries Inc 12600 Beech-Daly Rd *TF:* 877-783-3599 ■ *Web:* www.steelindustriesinc.com	Redford	MI	48239	313-535-8505	534-2165
Storms Forge Div Doncasters 160 Cottage St *Web:* www.doncasters-stormsforge.com	Springfield	MA	01104	413-785-1801	785-5680
Sypris Technologies 2820 W Broadway PO Box 32160 *TF:* 800-626-5655 ■ *Web:* www.tubeturns.com	Louisville	KY	40232	502-774-6011	774-6300
T & W Forge Inc 562 W Ely St *Web:* www.twforge.com	Alliance	OH	44601	330-821-5740	821-7309
TECT Corp 1211 Old Albany Rd *TF:* 800-298-0333 ■ *Web:* www.tectcorp.com	Thomasville	GA	31792	229-228-2600	228-8949
Texas Metal Works Inc 13770 Industrial Rd *Web:* www.texmet.com	Houston	TX	77015	713-393-4200	455-8366
TFO Tech Co Ltd 221 State St	Jeffersonville	OH	43128	740-426-6381	426-6511
Thermal Structures Inc 2362 Railroad St *TF:* 888-800-5811 ■ *Web:* www.thermalstructures.com	Corona	CA	92880	951-736-9911	736-1064
Thoro'Bred Inc 5020 E La Palma Ave *TF:* 800-854-6059 ■ *Web:* www.horseshoes.com/thorobred	Anaheim	CA	92807	714-779-2581	779-1582
ThyssenKrupp Gerlach Co 1000 Lynch Rd *Web:* www.thyssenkruppgerlach.com	Danville	IL	61834	217-431-0060	431-8934
Trinity Forge Inc 947 Trinity Dr *Web:* www.trinityforge.com	Mansfield	TX	76063	817-473-1515	473-6743
Turbine Engine Components Technologies Corp DBA TECT Corp 1211 Old Albany Rd *TF:* 800-298-0333 ■ *Web:* www.tectcorp.com	Thomasville	GA	31792	229-228-2600	228-8949
Unit Drop Forge Co Inc 1903 S 62nd St PO Box 340350 *Web:* www.unitforgings.com	West Allis	WI	53234	414-545-3000	545-6318
United Brass Manufacturers Inc 35030 Goddard Rd PO Box 74095	Romulus	MI	48174	734-941-0700	941-0640
VAE Nortrak North America Inc 3422 1st Ave S *TF:* 800-638-4657 ■ *Web:* www.nortrak.com	Seattle	WA	98134	206-622-0125	621-9626
W Pat Crow Forgings Inc 200 Luxton St *Web:* www.wpatcrow.com	Fort Worth	TX	76104	817-536-2861	531-2196
Walker Forge Inc 222 E Erie St Suite 300 *Web:* www.walkerforge.com	Milwaukee	WI	53202	414-223-2000	223-2019
Webb Forging Co Inc 34375 W 12 Mile Rd *TF:* 800-526-9322 ■ *Web:* www.jervisbwebb.com	Farmington Hills	MI	48331	248-553-1000	553-1228
Weber Metals Inc 16706 Garfield Ave *Web:* www.webermetals.com	Paramount	CA	90723	562-602-0260	602-0468
Western Forge & Flange Co PO Box 1788 *TF:* 800-352-6433 ■ *Web:* www.western-forge.com	Cleveland	TX	77328	281-727-7000	727-7060
Wilton Precision Steel Co 320 W 1st St *Web:* www.wps01.com	Wilton	IA	52778	563-732-3363	732-3365
Wozniak Industries Inc 2 Mid America Plaza Suite 706 *Web:* www.wozniakindustries.com	Oakbrook Terrace	IL	60181	630-954-3400	954-3605
Wozniak Industries Inc Commercial Forged Products Div 5757 W 65th St *TF:* 800-637-2695 ■ *Web:* www.commercialforged.com	Bedford Park	IL	60638	708-458-1220	458-9346
Wyman-Gordon Co 244 Worcester St *TF:* 800-343-6070 ■ *Web:* www.wyman-gordon.com	North Grafton	MA	01536	508-839-4441	839-7500

487 METAL HEAT TREATING

Company	City	State	Zip	Phone	Fax
Aerocraft Heat Treating Co Inc 15701 Minnesota Ave *Web:* www.aerocraft-ht.com	Paramount	CA	90723	562-634-3311	633-0364
Ajax Metal Processing Inc 4651 Bellevue St *Web:* www.ajaxmetal.com	Detroit	MI	48207	313-267-2100	267-2110
Alfred Heller Heat Treating Co 5 Wellington St *TF:* 800-946-8847 ■ *Web:* www.alfredheller.com	Clifton	NJ	07015	973-772-4200	772-0433
Atmosphere Annealing Inc 209 W Mount Hope Ave *Web:* www.atmosphereannealing.com	Lansing	MI	48910	517-485-5090	482-7240
Burke Forging & Heat Treating Inc 30 Sherer St	Rochester	NY	14611	585-235-6060	235-6068
Commercial Steel Treating Corp 31440 Stephenson Hwy *Web:* www.commercialsteel.com	Madison Heights	MI	48071	248-588-3300	588-3534
Curtiss-Wright Corp 4 Becker Farm Rd 3rd Fl *NYSE: CW* ■ *Web:* www.curtisswright.com	Roseland	NJ	07068	973-597-4700	597-4799
Dayton Forging & Heat Treating Co 215 N Findlay St *Web:* www.daytonforging.com	Dayton	OH	45403	937-253-4126	253-0409
Fisher-Barton Inc 201 Fredrick St	Watertown	WI	53094	920-261-0131	261-4549
Flame Metals Processing Corp 7317 W Lake St	Minneapolis	MN	55426	952-929-7815	925-0572
FPM LLC 1501 S Lively Blvd *TF:* 800-875-3316 ■ *Web:* www.fpmht.com	Elk Grove Village	IL	60007	847-228-2525	228-5912
Gibraltar Industries Inc 3556 Lakeshore Rd *NASDAQ: ROCK* ■ **Fax:* Sales ■ *TF:* 800-777-0675 ■ *Web:* www.gibraltar1.com	Buffalo	NY	14219	716-826-6500	826-1589*
Heat Treat Corp of America 1120 W 119th St	Chicago	IL	60643	773-264-1234	264-4321
Heller Alfred Heat Treating Co 5 Wellington St *TF:* 800-946-8847 ■ *Web:* www.alfredheller.com	Clifton	NJ	07015	973-772-4200	772-0433
HI TecMetal Group Inc 1101 E 55th St *TF:* 877-484-2867 ■ *Web:* www.htg.cc	Cleveland	OH	44103	216-881-8100	881-6811
Hi-Temp Inc 75 E Lake St *Web:* www.bluewaterthermal.com	Northlake	IL	60164	708-410-8000	
Industrial Steel Treating Inc 613 Carroll St *Web:* www.indstl.com	Jackson	MI	49204	517-787-6312	787-5441
MACSTEEL 1 Jackson Sq Suite 500 **Fax:* Sales ■ *TF Sales:* 800-888-7833 ■ *Web:* www.macsteel.com	Jackson	MI	49201	517-782-0415	782-8736*
Maxco Inc 1118 Centennial Way *NASDAQ: MAXC* ■ *Web:* www.maxc.com	Lansing	MI	48917	517-321-3130	321-1022
Metal Improvement Co LLC 10 Forest Ave *Web:* www.metalimprovement.com	Paramus	NJ	07652	201-843-7800	843-3460
Milastar Corp 7317 W Lake St *TF:* 877-888-8874	Minneapolis	MN	55426	952-929-7815	925-0572
Miller Consolidated Industries Inc 2221 Arbor Blvd *TF:* 800-589-4133	Dayton	OH	45439	937-294-2681	296-7986
Modern Industries Inc 613 W 11th St *Web:* www.mi-erie.com	Erie	PA	16501	814-455-8061	453-4382
Nitrex Metal Inc 3474 Poirier Blvd *Web:* www.nitrex.com	Saint-Laurent	QC	H4R2J5	514-335-7191	335-4160

	City	State	ZIP	Phone	Fax
Paulo Products Co 5620 W Park Ave	Saint Louis	MO	63110	314-647-7500	647-7582
Web: www.paulo.com					
Quanex Corp 1900 West Loop S Suite 1500	Houston	TX	77027	713-961-4600	439-1016
NYSE: NX ■ *TF:* 800-231-8176 ■ *Web:* www.quanex.com					
Rex Heat Treat 8th St & Valley Forge Rd PO Box 270	Lansdale	PA	19446	215-855-1131	855-2028
TF: 800-220-6053 ■ *Web:* www.rexheattreat.com					
Riverdale Plating & Heat Treating Inc 680 W 134th St	Riverdale	IL	60827	708-849-2050	849-6010
Web: www.rpht.com					
Robert Wooler Co 1755 Susquehanna Rd	Dresher	PA	19025	215-542-7600	542-0250
Web: www.robertwooler.com					
Specialty Steel Treating Inc 34501 Commerce Rd	Fraser	MI	48026	586-293-5355	293-5390
Web: www.specialtysteeltreating.com					
Sun Steel Treating Inc 55 N Mill St	South Lyon	MI	48178	248-471-0844	437-3140
TF: 877-471-0844 ■ *Web:* www.sunsteeltreating.com					
TC Industries Inc 3703 S Rt 31	Crystal Lake	IL	60012	815-459-2400	459-3303
ThyssenKrupp Stahl Co 11 E Pacific PO Box 6	Kingsville	MO	64061	816-597-3322	597-3485
TF: 888-395-1042 ■ *Web:* www.stahlspecialty.com					
Tri-City Heat Treat Co 2020 5th St	Rock Island	IL	61201	309-786-2689	786-2691
Trutec Industries Inc 4700 Gateway Blvd	Springfield	OH	45502	937-323-8833	323-9192
TF: 800-933-8832 ■ *Web:* www.parkerionics.com					
Wall Colmonoy Corp 30261 Stephenson Hwy	Madison Heights	MI	48071	248-585-6400	585-7960
TF: 800-521-2412 ■ *Web:* www.wallcolmonoy.com					
Ward Aluminum Casting Co 642 Growth Ave	Fort Wayne	IN	46808	260-426-8700	420-1919
TF: 866-427-8700 ■ *Web:* www.wardcorp.com					
Wooler Robert Co 1755 Susquehanna Rd	Dresher	PA	19025	215-542-7600	542-0250
Web: www.robertwooler.com					

488 METAL INDUSTRIES (MISC)

SEE ALSO Foundries - Investment p. 1669; Foundries - Iron & Steel p. 1669; Foundries - Nonferrous (Castings) p. 1670; Metal Heat Treating p. 1960; Metal Tube & Pipe p. 1964; Steel - Mfr p. 2333; Wire & Cable p. 2415

	City	State	ZIP	Phone	Fax
Alcan Inc 1188 Sherbrooke St W	Montreal	QC	H3A3G2	514-848-8000	848-8115
NYSE: AL ■ *Web:* www.alcan.com					
Alcoa Inc 201 Isabella St	Pittsburgh	PA	15212	412-553-4545	553-4498
NYSE: AA ■ *Web:* www.alcoa.com					
Alcoa Mill Products 4879 State St	Riverdale	IA	52722	563-459-3000	459-3021
TF: 800-237-3254 ■ *Web:* www.millproducts-alcoa.com					
Alcoa Primary Metals					
900 S Gay St Riverview Tower Suite 1100	Knoxville	TN	37902	865-594-4700	594-4790*
**Fax:* Sales ■ *TF:* 800-852-0238 ■ *Web:* www.alcoa.com/primary_na					
Allegheny Ludlum Corp 1357 E Rodney French Blvd	New Bedford	MA	02744	508-996-5691	984-8900
Web: www.alleghenyrodney.com					
Allegheny Technologies Inc 6 PPG Pl Suite 1000	Pittsburgh	PA	15222	412-394-2800	395-2804*
NYSE: ATI ■ **Fax:* Hum Res ■ *TF Sales:* 800-258-3586 ■ *Web:* www.alleghenytechnologies.com					
Allvac Inc 2020 Ashcraft Ave	Monroe	NC	28110	704-289-4511	289-4018*
**Fax:* Sales ■ *TF:* 800-841-5491 ■ *Web:* www.allvac.com					
Altech LLC 242 America Pl	Jeffersonville	IN	47130	812-282-8256	280-6070
TF: 800-264-8256					
AMETEK Inc Specialty Metal Products Div					
1085 Rt 519 PO Box 427	Eighty Four	PA	15330	724-225-8400	225-6622
Web: www.ametekmetals.com					
AMETEK Specialty Metal Products 21 Toelles Rd	Wallingford	CT	06492	203-265-6731	294-0196
Web: www.ametekmetals.com					
Ampco Metal Inc 1117 E Algonquin Rd	Arlington Heights	IL	60005	847-437-6000	437-6008
TF: 800-437-6100 ■ *Web:* www.ampcometal.com					
Anaheim Extrusion Co Inc 1330 N Kraemer Blvd	Anaheim	CA	92806	714-630-3111	630-1823
TF: 800-660-3318 ■ *Web:* www.anaheimextrude.com					
Ansonia Copper & Brass Inc 75 Liberty St	Ansonia	CT	06401	203-732-6600	735-3787
TF Cust Svc: 800-521-1703 ■ *Web:* www.ansoniacb.com					
Arkansas Aluminum Alloys Inc 4400 Malvern Rd	Hot Springs	AR	71901	501-262-3420	262-3555
TF Cust Svc: 800-643-1302 ■ *Web:* www.arkalumalloys.com					
Arvinyl Metal Laminates Corp 233 N Sherman Ave	Corona	CA	92882	951-371-7800	371-7118
TF: 800-278-4695 ■ *Web:* www.arvinyl.com					
Audubon Metals LLC 3055 Ohio Dr	Henderson	KY	42420	270-830-6622	830-9594
Web: www.audubonmetals.com					
Big River Zinc Corp 2401 Mississippi Ave	Sauget	IL	62201	618-274-5000	274-4444
TF: 800-274-4002 ■ *Web:* www.bigriverzinc.com					
Bolton Metal Products Co 2022 Axemann Rd PO Box 388	Bellefonte	PA	16823	814-355-6330	355-6227*
**Fax:* Sales ■ *Web:* www.boltonmetals.com					
Bonnell William L Co 25 Bonnell St	Newnan	GA	30263	770-253-2020	254-7711
Web: www.bonlalum.com					
Broco Inc 10868 Bell Ct	Rancho Cucamonga	CA	91730	909-483-3222	483-3233
TF: 800-845-7259 ■ *Web:* www.brocoinc.com					
Bunting Magnetics Co 500 S Spencer Ave	Newton	KS	67114	316-284-2020	283-4975
TF Cust Svc: 800-835-2526 ■ *Web:* www.bunting-magnetics.com					
Cabot Supermetals 1223 County Line Rd PO Box 1608	Boyertown	PA	19512	610-367-1500	369-8259*
**Fax:* Sales ■ *TF:* 800-531-3676 ■ *Web:* www.cabot-corp.com					
Cannon-Muskegon Corp 2875 Lincoln St	Muskegon	MI	49441	231-755-1681	755-4975
TF: 800-253-0371 ■ *Web:* www.c-mgroup.com					
Cardinal Aluminum Co 6910 Preston Hwy	Louisville	KY	40219	502-969-9302	968-4269
TF Cust Svc: 800-398-7833 ■ *Web:* www.1800extrude.com					
CCMA LLC 450 Corporate Pkwy Suite 100	Amherst	NY	14226	716-446-8800	446-8809
TF: 800-828-6621 ■ *Web:* www.ccmetals.com					
Century Aluminum Co 2511 Garden Rd Bldg A Suite 200	Monterey	CA	93940	831-642-9300	642-9399
NASDAQ: CENX ■ *TF:* 888-642-9300 ■ *Web:* centuryca.com					
Century Aluminum Co Century Rd PO Box 98	Ravenswood	WV	26164	304-273-6241	273-6286
TF: 800-258-6686 ■ *Web:* www.centuryca.com					
Century Aluminum of Kentucky					
1627 State Route 271 N PO Box 500	Hawesville	KY	42348	270-685-2493	852-2886
Certified Alloy Products Inc 3245 Cherry Ave	Long Beach	CA	90807	562-595-6621	427-8667
TF: 800-421-3763					
Chase Brass & Copper Co					
14212 County Rd M 50 PO Box 152	Montpelier	OH	43543	419-485-3193	485-4850*
**Fax:* Mail Rm ■ *TF:* 800-537-4291 ■ *Web:* www.chasebrass.com					
Chicago Extruded Metals Co 1601 S 54th Ave	Cicero	IL	60804	708-656-7900	780-3479
TF Cust Svc: 800-323-8102 ■ *Web:* www.csm.com					
Clarion Sintered Metals PO Box S	Ridgway	PA	15853	814-773-3124	776-5775
Colonial Metals Co 217 Linden St PO Box 311	Columbia	PA	17512	717-684-2311	684-9555
Web: www.colonialmetalsco.com					
Cookson Electronics Assembly Materials 600 Rte 440	Jersey City	NJ	07304	201-434-6778	434-7508
TF: 800-367-5460 ■ *Web:* www.alphametals.com					
Croft LLC 107 Oliver Emmerich Dr	McComb	MS	39648	601-684-6121	684-5134
TF: 800-222-3195 ■ *Web:* www.croftllc.com					
Custom Aluminum Products Inc 414 W Division St	South Elgin	IL	60177	847-741-6333	741-2266
TF: 800-745-6333 ■ *Web:* www.custom-aluminum.com					
Danaher Motion 1500 Mittel Blvd	Wood Dale	IL	60191	630-860-7300	694-3305
TF: 866-993-2624 ■ *Web:* www.danahermotion.com					
Deringer-Ney Inc 616 Atrium Dr Suite 100	Vernon Hills	IL	60061	847-566-4100	367-6029
Web: www.deringerney.com					
Doe Run Co 1801 Park 270 Dr Suite 300	Saint Louis	MO	63146	314-453-7110	453-7180
TF: 800-356-3786 ■ *Web:* www.doerun.com					
Dynamet Inc 195 Museum Rd	Washington	PA	15301	724-228-1000	229-4195
TF: 800-237-9655 ■ *Web:* www.dynamet.com					
Eastern Alloys Inc 11 Henry Henning Dr PO Box 317	Maybrook	NY	12543	845-427-2151	427-5185
TF: 800-456-1496 ■ *Web:* www.eazall.com					
Elkem Metals Co 2700 Lake Rd E PO Box 40	Ashtabula	OH	44004	440-993-2300	993-2393
TF: 800-848-9795					
Elmet Technologies Inc 1560 Lisbon St	Lewiston	ME	04240	207-784-3591	786-8924
TF: 800-343-8008 ■ *Web:* www.elmettechnologies.com					
Empire Resources Inc 1 Parker Plaza	Fort Lee	NJ	07024	201-944-2200	944-2226
AMEX: ERS ■ *Web:* www.empireresources.com					
Erie Coke Corp 925 E Bay Dr PO Box 6180	Erie	PA	16512	814-454-0177	454-2331
Web: www.eriecoke.com					
Extruded Metals Inc 302 Ashfield St	Belding	MI	48809	616-794-1200	794-1544
TF: 800-428-7296 ■ *Web:* www.extrudedmetals.com					
Futura Industries Freeport Center Bldg H-11 PO Box 160350	Clearfield	UT	84016	801-773-6282	774-3271*
**Fax:* Hum Res ■ *TF Cust Svc:* 800-824-2049 ■ *Web:* www.futuraind.com					
GARMCO USA 55 Triangle St	Danbury	CT	06810	203-743-2731	743-8838
TF: 800-722-3645 ■ *Web:* www.garmco.com					
General Extrusions Inc 4040 Lake Park Rd	Youngstown	OH	44512	330-783-0270	788-1250
Web: www.genext.com					
Glines & Rhodes Inc 189 East St	Attleboro	MA	02703	508-226-2000	226-7136
TF: 800-343-1196 ■ *Web:* www.glinesandrhodes.com					
Globe Metallurgical Corp 2401 Old Montgomery Hwy	Selma	AL	36703	334-872-3491	874-2098
Gulf Reduction Corp 6020 Navigation Blvd	Houston	TX	77011	713-926-1705	923-1783
TF: 800-899-1705 ■ *Web:* www.uszinc.com					
H Kramer & Co 1345 W 21st St	Chicago	IL	60608	312-226-6600	226-4713
TF: 800-621-2305					
Handy & Harman 555 Theodore Fremd Ave	Rye	NY	10580	914-921-5200	925-4496
Web: www.handyharman.com					
Haynes International Inc 1020 W Park Ave PO Box 9013	Kokomo	IN	46904	765-456-6000	456-6905
TF: 800-354-0806 ■ *Web:* www.haynesintl.com					
HC Starck Inc 45 Industrial Pl	Newton	MA	02461	617-630-5800	630-4888
Web: www.hcstarck.com					
Hoeganaes Corp 1001 Taylors Ln	Cinnaminson	NJ	08077	856-829-2220	303-2720*
**Fax:* Hum Res ■ *Web:* www.hoeganaes.com					
Hoover Precision Products Inc 2200 Pendley Rd	Cumming	GA	30041	770-889-9223	889-0828
Web: www.hooverprecision.com					
Hoover & Strong Inc 10700 Trade Rd	Richmond	VA	23236	804-794-3700	616-9997*
**Fax Area Code:* 800 ■ *TF Cust Svc:* 800-759-9997 ■ *Web:* hooverandstrong.com					
Horsehead Corp 300 Frankfort Rd	Monaca	PA	15061	724-774-1020	773-2299
TF Cust Svc: 800-648-8897 ■ *Web:* www.horsehead.net					
Hussey Copper Ltd 100 Washington St	Leetsdale	PA	15056	724-251-4200	251-4243
TF: 800-733-8866 ■ *Web:* www.husseycopper.com					
Hydro Aluminum North America					
801 International Dr Suite 200	Linthicum	MD	21090	410-487-4500	487-8053
TF: 888-935-5752 ■ *Web:* www.hydroaluminumna.com					
Hydro Aluminum Rockledge Inc 100 Gus Hipp Blvd	Rockledge	FL	32955	321-636-8147	632-1486*
**Fax:* Sales ■ *Web:* www.hydro.com					
IMC Group 165 Township Line Rd 1 Pitcairn Pl Suite 1200	Jenkintown	PA	19046	215-517-6000	517-6050
TF: 800-220-6800 ■ *Web:* www.imc-group.com					
Indalex Aluminum Solutions Group					
75 Tri State International Dr	Lincolnshire	IL	60069	847-810-3000	295-3845
TF: 877-276-1802 ■ *Web:* www.indalex.com					
Industrial Tectonics Inc 7222 W Huron River Dr	Dexter	MI	48130	734-426-4681	426-4701
TF: 800-482-2255 ■ *Web:* www.itiball.com					
Intalco Aluminum Corp 4050 Mountain View Rd	Ferndale	WA	98248	360-384-7061	384-6185
TF: 800-752-0852					
Johnson Matthey Inc 435 Devon Park Dr Suite 600	Wayne	PA	19087	610-971-3000	971-3022
Web: www.matthey.com					
JW Aluminum 1100 Richmond St	Jackson	TN	38301	731-424-2000	422-7805
Web: www.jwaluminum.com					
JW Aluminum Co 435 Old Mount Holly Rd	Goose Creek	SC	29445	843-572-1100	572-3546*
**Fax:* Sales ■ *TF:* 800-568-1100 ■ *Web:* www.jwaluminum.com					
Kaiser Aluminum & Chemical Corp					
27422 Portola Pkwy Suite 350	Foothill Ranch	CA	92610	949-614-1740	614-1930
Web: www.kaiseral.com					
Kaiser Aluminum Corp 27422 Portola Pkwy Suite 350	Foothill Ranch	CA	92610	949-614-1740	614-1930
Web: www.kaiseral.com					
Keymark Corp 1188 Cayadutta Rd	Fonda	NY	12068	518-853-3421	853-3130
TF: 800-833-1609 ■ *Web:* www.keymarkcorp.com					
Keystone Powdered Metal Co 251 State St	Saint Marys	PA	15857	814-781-1591	781-7648
Web: www.keystonepm.com					
Kramer H & Co 1345 W 21st St	Chicago	IL	60608	312-226-6600	226-4713
TF: 800-621-2305					
Light Metals Corp 2740 Prairie St SW	Wyoming	MI	49509	616-538-3030	538-2713
Web: www.light-metals.com					
Linemaster Switch Corp 29 Plaine Hill Rd	Woodstock	CT	06281	860-974-1000	974-3668*
**Fax Area Code:* 800 ■ *Web:* www.linemaster.com					
Loxcreen Co Inc 1630 Old Dunbar Rd	West Columbia	SC	29172	803-822-8200	822-8547
TF: 800-394-8667 ■ *Web:* www.loxcreen.com					
Lucas-Milhaupt Inc 5656 S Pennsylvania Ave	Cudahy	WI	53110	414-769-6000	769-1093
TF: 800-558-3856 ■ *Web:* www.lucas-milhaupt.com					
Luvata Appleton LLC 553 Carter Ct	Kimberly	WI	54136	920-749-3820	749-3850
TF: 800-747-2912 ■ *Web:* www.luvata.com					
Luvata Buffalo Inc 70 Sayre St	Buffalo	NY	14207	716-879-6700	879-6988
TF Sales: 800-828-7426 ■ *Web:* www.luvata.com					
Luvata Ohio Inc 801 Pittsburgh Dr	Delaware	OH	43015	740-363-1981	363-3847
Web: www.luvata.com					
Magnat-Fairview Inc					
Westover Industrial Park 1102 Sheridan St	Chicopee	MA	01022	413-593-5742	593-9451
TF: 800-569-1286 ■ *Web:* magnatfairview.com					
Magnesium Elektron 1001 College St	Madison	IL	62060	618-452-5190	452-3190
TF Sales: 800-851-3145 ■ *Web:* www.magnesium-elektron.com					
Magnetech Industrial Services Inc 551 W Merrill St	Indianapolis	IN	46225	317-266-1659	637-5744
TF: 800-944-0141 ■ *Web:* www.magnetech.com					
Magnode Corp 400 E State St	Trenton	OH	45067	513-988-6351	988-6357
Web: www.magnode.com					
Magotteaux Inc 724 Cool Springs Blvd Suite 200	Franklin	TN	37067	615-385-3055	297-6743
Web: www.magotteaux.com					
Memry Corp 3 Berkshire Blvd	Bethel	CT	06801	203-739-1100	798-6363
AMEX: MRY ■ *TF:* 866-466-3679 ■ *Web:* www.memry.com					
Metal Conversions Ltd Crawford Rd PO Box 787	Mansfield	OH	44901	419-525-0011	525-4961
Metallurgical Products Co 810 Lincoln Ave PO Box 598	West Chester	PA	19381	610-696-6770	430-8431
TF: 800-659-4672 ■ *Web:* www.metprodco.com					
Metglas Inc 440 Allied Dr	Conway	SC	29526	843-349-7319	349-6815
TF: 800-581-7654 ■ *Web:* www.metglas.com					
Midland Industries Inc 1424 N Halsted St	Chicago	IL	60622	312-664-7300	664-7371
TF: 800-662-8228 ■ *Web:* www.zincbig.com					
Miller Co 275 Pratt St	Meriden	CT	06450	203-235-4474	639-6924
Web: www.themillerco.com					
Mueller Brass Co 2199 Lapeer Ave	Port Huron	MI	48060	810-987-7770	987-9108
TF: 800-553-3336					
Mueller Industries Inc 8285 Tournament Dr Suite 150	Memphis	TN	38125	901-753-3200	753-3251
NYSE: MLI ■ *TF:* 800-348-8464 ■ *Web:* www.muellerindustries.com					

				Phone	Fax
NetShape Technologies Inc 31005 Solon Rd *TF:* 866-429-5724 ■ *Web:* www.netshapetech.com	Solon	OH	44139	440-248-5456	248-5807
New England Miniature Ball Inc 163 Greenwood Rd W PO Box 585 *Web:* www.nemb.com	Norfolk	CT	06058	860-542-5543	542-5058
Nichols Aluminum 1725 Rockingham Rd *TF:* 800-553-5508 ■ *Web:* www.nicholsal.com	Davenport	IA	52802	563-324-2121	324-7911
NN Inc 2000 Waters Edge Dr Bldg 3 Suite 12 *NASDAQ: NNBR* ■ *TF:* 800-733-9151 ■ *Web:* www.nnbr.com	Johnson City	TN	37604	423-743-9151	743-8870
Noranda Aluminum Inc 801 Crescent Center Dr Suite 600 *TF:* 800-344-7522	Franklin	TN	37067	615-771-5700	771-5701
Norandal USA Inc 1709 Jake Alexander Blvd S	Salisbury	NC	28146	704-633-6020	637-4582
Norandal USA Inc 400 Bill Brooks Dr	Huntingdon	TN	38344	731-986-5011	986-2739
Novelis Inc 3399 Peachtree Rd NE Suite 1500 *NYSE: NVL* ■ *Web:* www.novelis.com	Atlanta	GA	30326	404-814-4200	814-4219
Novelis North America 6060 Parkland Blvd *Web:* www.novelis.com	Cleveland	OH	44124	440-423-6600	423-6601
Nyrstar Clarksville 1800 Zinc Plant Rd PO Box 1104 *Web:* www.nyrstar.com	Clarksville	TN	37041	931-552-4200	552-0471
Olin Corp Brass Div 427 N Shamrock St **Fax:* Hum Res ■ *Web:* www.olinbrass.com	East Alton	IL	62024	618-258-2000	258-2938*
Ormet Corp 43840 State Rt 7 PO Box 176 *TF:* 800-282-9701 ■ *Web:* www.ormet.com	Hannibal	OH	43931	740-483-1381	483-2622
Ormet Primary Aluminum Corp 43840 State Rd 7 PO Box 176 *TF:* 800-282-9701 ■ *Web:* www.ormet.com	Hannibal	OH	43931	740-483-1381	483-2622
Pacal LLC 2500 W County Rd B **Fax:* Sales ■ *TF:* 800-328-9836 ■ *Web:* www.pacal.com	Roseville	MN	55113	651-631-1111	631-9268*
Patrick Industries Inc Patrick Metals Div 5020 Lincolnway E *TF:* 800-922-9692 ■ *Web:* www.patrickmetals.com	Mishawaka	IN	46544	574-255-9692	256-6577
Patrick Metals Div Patrick Industries Inc 5020 Lincolnway E *TF:* 800-922-9692 ■ *Web:* www.patrickmetals.com	Mishawaka	IN	46544	574-255-9692	256-6577
Penn Aluminum International Inc 1117 N 2nd St PO Box 490 *TF:* 800-445-7366 ■ *Web:* www.pennaluminum.com	Murphysboro	IL	62966	618-684-2146	684-2463
Phelps Dodge Refining Corp 897 Hawkins Blvd	El Paso	TX	79915	915-778-9881	782-7783
Piper Metal Forming Corp 795 Sam Barkley Dr *Web:* www.piperimpact.com	New Albany	MS	38652	662-534-5046	538-6561
Polymetallurgical Corp 262 Broad St *Web:* www.polymer.com	North Attleboro	MA	02760	508-695-9312	695-7512
Profile Extrusion Co 100 Anderson Rd *Web:* www.profile-extrusion.com	Rome	GA	30161	706-234-7558	234-7649
Quanex Corp 1900 West Loop S Suite 1500 *NYSE: NX* ■ *TF:* 800-231-8176 ■ *Web:* www.quanex.com	Houston	TX	77027	713-961-4600	439-1016
Revere Copper Products Inc 1 Revere Park **Fax:* Sales ■ *TF:* 800-448-1776 ■ *Web:* www.reverecopper.com	Rome	NY	13440	315-338-2022	338-2224*
RMI Titanium Co 1000 Warren Ave **Fax:* Sales	Niles	OH	44446	330-652-9951	544-7796*
Ross Metals Corp 54 W 47th St *TF:* 800-654-7677	New York	NY	10036	212-869-4433	768-3018
RSR Corp 2777 Stemmons Fwy Suite 1800	Dallas	TX	75207	214-631-6070	631-6146
Sanders Lead Co 1 Sanders Rd PO Box 707 *TF:* 800-633-8744	Troy	AL	36081	334-566-1563	566-0107
Sandvik Special Metals Corp 43507 S Piert Rd *Web:* www.smt.sandvik.com	Kennewick	WA	99337	509-586-4131	582-3552
Shieldalloy Metallurgical Corp 545 Beckett Rd Suite 201 *TF:* 800-762-2020 ■ *Web:* www.shieldalloy.com	Swedesboro	NJ	08085	856-692-4200	241-4655
Simcala Inc 1940 Ohio Ferro Rd PO Box 68 *TF:* 800-321-9828	Mount Meigs	AL	36057	334-215-7560	215-8969
Sipi Metals Corp 1720 N Elston Ave *Web:* www.sipimetals.com	Chicago	IL	60622	773-276-0070	276-7014
Southern Metals Co 111 N Raleigh Ave PO Box 471 *TF:* 800-843-2771 ■ *Web:* www.sometco.com	Sheffield	AL	35660	256-383-3261	383-5204
Southwire Co 1 Southwire Dr *TF:* 800-444-1700 ■ *Web:* www.southwire.com	Carrollton	GA	30119	770-832-4242	838-6462
Special Metals Corp 4317 Middle Settlement Rd **Fax:* Sales ■ *TF:* 800-334-8351 ■ *Web:* www.specialmetals.com	New Hartford	NY	13413	315-798-2900	798-2016*
Spectro Alloys Corp 13220 Doyle Path *TF:* 800-328-9321 ■ *Web:* www.spectroalloys.com	Rosemount	MN	55068	651-437-2815	438-3714
Starck HC Inc 45 Industrial Pl *Web:* www.hcstarck.com	Newton	MA	02461	617-630-5800	630-4888
Taber Extrusions LP 915 S Elmira Ave *TF:* 800-563-6853 ■ *Web:* www.taberextrusions.com	Russellville	AR	72802	479-968-1021	968-8645
Tifton Aluminum Co Inc 250 Southwell Blvd *TF Sales:* 800-841-2030	Tifton	GA	31794	229-382-7330	388-6707
Titanium Metals Corp (TIMET) 224 Valley Creek Blvd Suite 200 *NYSE: TIE* ■ *TF:* 800-753-1550 ■ *Web:* www.timet.com	Exton	PA	19341	610-968-1284	968-1318
Tower Extrusions Ltd Hwy 79 S PO Box 218 *Web:* www.towerextrusion.com	Olney	TX	76374	940-564-5681	564-5033
Tree Island Industries 3933 Boundary Rd *TF:* 800-663-8757 ■ *Web:* www.treeisland.com/	New Westminster	BC	V3L4Y1	604-524-3744	524-2362
Universal Molding Co Inc 10807 Stanford Ave *TF:* 888-437-1750 ■ *Web:* www.universalmold.com	Lynwood	CA	90262	310-886-1750	632-7775
US Bronze Powders Inc 408 Rt 202 N *TF:* 800-544-0186 ■ *Web:* www.usbronzepowders.com	Flemington	NJ	08822	908-782-5454	782-3489
US Magnesium LLC 238 N 2200 West *Web:* www.usmagnesium.com	Salt Lake City	UT	84116	801-532-2043	534-1407
Valmont Industries Inc 1 Valmont Plaza *NYSE: VMI* ■ *TF:* 800-825-6668 ■ *Web:* www.valmont.com	Omaha	NE	68154	402-963-1000	963-1100
Victory White Metal Co 6100 Roland Ave *TF:* 800-635-5050 ■ *Web:* www.vwmc.com	Cleveland	OH	44127	216-271-1400	271-6430
Wabash Alloys LLC PO Box 466 *TF:* 800-348-0571 ■ *Web:* www.wabashalloys.com	Wabash	IN	46992	260-563-7461	563-5997
Wah Chang 1600 Old Salem Rd NE *TF:* 888-926-4211 ■ *Web:* www.wahchang.com	Albany	OR	97321	541-926-4211	812-7030
William L Bonnell Co 25 Bonnell St *Web:* www.bonlalum.com	Newnan	GA	30263	770-253-2020	254-7711
Williams Advanced Materials 2978 Main St *TF:* 800-327-1355 ■ *Web:* www.williams-adv.com	Buffalo	NY	14214	716-837-1000	833-2926

489 METAL PRODUCTS - HOUSEHOLD

				Phone	Fax
Acme International Enterprises Inc 1006 Chancellor Ave *Web:* www.acme-usa.com	Maplewood	NJ	07040	973-416-0400	416-0499
All-Clad Metalcrafters LLC 424 Morganza Rd *TF Cust Svc:* 800-255-2523 ■ *Web:* www.allclad.com	Canonsburg	PA	15317	724-745-8300	746-5035
Calphalon Corp PO Box 583 **Fax:* Sales ■ *TF:* 800-809-7267 ■ *Web:* www.calphalon.com	Toledo	OH	43697	419-666-8700	666-2859*
Chantal Cookware Corp 5425 N Sam Houston Pkwy W *TF:* 800-365-4354 ■ *Web:* www.chantalcookware.com	Houston	TX	77086	281-587-7800	444-1253
CM Packaging 800 Ela Rd *TF:* 800-323-0422 ■ *Web:* www.cmpackaging.com	Lake Zurich	IL	60047	847-438-2171	438-0369
Farberware Div Lifetime Brands Inc 1000 Stewart Ave *TF:* 800-252-3390 ■ *Web:* www.farberware.com	Garden City	NY	11530	516-683-6000	683-6161
G & S Metal Products Co Inc 3330 E 79th St *Web:* www.gsmetal.com	Cleveland	OH	44127	216-441-0700	441-0736
Heuck ME Co Inc 1111 Western Row Rd *TF Cust Svc:* 866-634-3825 ■ *Web:* www.heuck.com	Mason	OH	45040	513-573-9918	573-9919
Hoffritz Div Lifetime Brands Inc 1000 Stewart Ave *TF:* 800-252-3390 ■ *Web:* www.hoffritz.com	Garden City	NY	11530	516-683-6000	683-6161
Kitchen-Quip Inc PO Box 548 *Web:* www.kqcasting.com	Waterloo	IN	46793	260-837-8311	837-7919
Le Creuset of America Inc 114 Bob Gifford Blvd *TF:* 800-827-1798 ■ *Web:* www.lecreuset.com	Early Branch	SC	29916	803-943-4308	943-0241
Lifetime Brands Inc 1000 Stewart Ave *NASDAQ: LCUT* ■ *TF:* 800-252-3390 ■ *Web:* www.lifetime.hoan.com	Garden City	NY	11530	516-683-6000	683-6161
Lifetime Brands Inc Farberware Div 1000 Stewart Ave *TF:* 800-252-3390 ■ *Web:* www.farberware.com	Garden City	NY	11530	516-683-6000	683-6161
Lifetime Brands Inc Hoffritz Div 1000 Stewart Ave *TF:* 800-252-3390 ■ *Web:* www.hoffritz.com	Garden City	NY	11530	516-683-6000	683-6161
ME Heuck Co Inc 1111 Western Row Rd *TF Cust Svc:* 866-634-3825 ■ *Web:* www.heuck.com	Mason	OH	45040	513-573-9918	573-9919
Meyer Corp 525 Curtola Pkwy **Fax:* PR ■ *TF Cust Svc:* 800-888-3883 ■ *Web:* www.meyer.com	Vallejo	CA	94590	707-551-2800	551-2953*
Newell Rubbermaid Inc Home & Family Group 10B Glenlake Pkwy Suite 300 *TF:* 800-434-4314 ■ *Web:* www.newellrubbermaid.com	Atlanta	GA	30328	770-407-3800	407-3970
Nordic Products Inc DBA Norpro 2215 Merrill Creek Pkwy *TF:* 800-722-0202 ■ *Web:* www.norpro.com	Everett	WA	98203	425-261-1000	261-1001
Nordic Ware Inc 5005 Hwy 7 *TF:* 800-328-4310 ■ *Web:* www.nordicware.com	Minneapolis	MN	55416	952-920-2888	924-9668
Northland Aluminum Products Inc DBA Nordic Ware Inc 5005 Hwy 7 *TF:* 800-328-4310 ■ *Web:* www.nordicware.com	Minneapolis	MN	55416	952-920-2888	924-9668
OXO International 75 9th Ave 5th Fl *TF:* 800-545-4411 ■ *Web:* www.oxo.com	New York	NY	10011	212-242-3333	242-3336
Regal Ware Inc 1675 Reigle Dr *Web:* www.regalware.com	Kewaskum	WI	53040	262-626-2121	626-8565
Rena Ware International Inc PO Box 97050 *TF:* 877-736-2245 ■ *Web:* www.renaware.com	Redmond	WA	98073	425-881-6171	882-7500
Saladmaster Inc 230 Westway Pl Suite 101 *TF:* 800-765-5795 ■ *Web:* www.saladmaster.com	Arlington	TX	76018	817-633-3555	633-5544
Swing-A-Way Mfg 4100 Beck Ave	Saint Louis	MO	63116	314-773-1487	773-5187
T-Fal Corp 1 Boland Dr Suite 101 *TF:* 800-395-8325 ■ *Web:* www.t-falusa.com	West Orange	NJ	07052	973-736-0300	736-9078
Wilton Armetale Co PO Box 600 *TF:* 800-553-2048 ■ *Web:* www.armetale.com	Mount Joy	PA	17552	717-653-4444	653-6573
Wilton Industries Inc 2240 W 75th St **Fax:* Sales ■ *TF:* 800-794-5866 ■ *Web:* www.wilton.com	Woodridge	IL	60517	630-963-7100	963-7196*
World Kitchen Inc 11911 Freedom Dr Suite 600 *TF Cust Svc:* 800-999-3436 ■ *Web:* www.worldkitchen.com	Reston	VA	20190	703-456-4700	456-2020
Zyliss USA Corp 1 Post Suite 100 *TF:* 888-794-7623 ■ *Web:* www.zylissusa.com	Irvine	CA	92618	949-699-1884	699-1788

490 METAL PRODUCTS (MISC)

				Phone	Fax
Accuride International Inc 12311 Shoemaker Ave *Web:* www.accuride.com	Santa Fe Springs	CA	90670	562-903-0200	903-0232
Alwin Mfg Co Inc 1206 Velp Ave *Web:* www.alwin.com	Green Bay	WI	54303	920-499-1424	499-7254
Amatom Electronic Hardware LLC 5 Pasco Hill Rd *TF:* 800-243-6032 ■ *Web:* www.amatom.com	Cromwell	CT	06416	860-828-0847	526-2057
Bead Industries Inc 11 Cascade Blvd *TF:* 800-297-4851 ■ *Web:* www.beadindustries.com	Milford	CT	06460	203-301-0270	301-0280
Bobrick Washroom Equipment Inc 11611 Hart St *Web:* www.bobrick.com	North Hollywood	CA	91605	818-764-1000	765-2700
Lechler Inc 445 Kautz Rd **Fax Area Code:* 800 ■ *TF Cust Svc:* 800-777-2926 ■ *Web:* www.lechler.com	Saint Charles	IL	60174	630-377-6611	444-7069*
Muza Metal Products Corp 606 E Murdock Ave *Web:* www.muzametal.com	Oshkosh	WI	54901	920-236-3535	236-3520
Parmatech Corp 2221 Pine View Way *Web:* www.parmatech.com	Petaluma	CA	94954	707-778-2266	778-2262
Polar Ware Co Inc PO Box 211 *TF Cust Svc:* 800-237-3655 ■ *Web:* www.polarware.com	Sheboygan	WI	53082	920-458-3561	458-2205
Precision Valve Corp PO Box 309 *TF:* 800-431-2697 ■ *Web:* www.precision-valve.com	Yonkers	NY	10702	914-969-6500	966-4428
Spirol International Corp 30 Rock Ave *Web:* www.spirol.com	Danielson	CT	06239	860-774-8571	774-2048
Spraying Systems Co PO Box 7900 *TF:* 800-957-7729 ■ *Web:* www.spray.com	Wheaton	IL	60189	630-665-5000	260-0842
Trinity Industries Inc Head Div 2525 N Stemmons Fwy *Web:* www.trinityheads.com	Dallas	TX	75207	214-631-4420	589-8501

491 METAL STAMPINGS

SEE ALSO Closures - Metal or Plastics p. 1448; Electronic Enclosures p. 1612; Metal Stampings - Automotive p. 1964

				Phone	Fax
Accurate Perforating Co 3636 S Kedzie Ave *TF:* 800-621-0273 ■ *Web:* www.accurateperforating.com	Chicago	IL	60632	773-254-3232	254-9453
Acme Metal Cap Inc Co 33-53 62nd St *TF:* 800-338-3581 ■ *Web:* www.acmepans.com	Woodside	NY	11377	718-335-3000	335-3037
Admiral Craft Equipment Corp 940 S Oyster Bay Rd *TF:* 800-223-7750 ■ *Web:* www.admiralcraft.com	Hicksville	NY	11801	516-433-3535	447-7751
Admiral Tool & Mfg Co 3700 N Talman Ave *Web:* www.admiraltool.com	Chicago	IL	60618	773-477-4300	477-1356
AK Stamping Inc 1159 US Rt 22 *TF Cust Svc:* 800-227-3258 ■ *Web:* www.akstamping.com	Mountainside	NJ	07092	908-232-7300	232-4729
Albest Metal Stamping Corp 1 Kent Ave *Web:* www.albest.com	Brooklyn	NY	11211	718-388-6000	388-0404
Alcoa Inc 201 Isabella St *NYSE: AA* ■ *Web:* www.alcoa.com	Pittsburgh	PA	15212	412-553-4545	553-4498
Alinabal Inc 28 Woodmont Rd *TF:* 800-254-6763 ■ *Web:* www.alinabal.com	Milford	CT	06460	203-877-3241	874-5063
All New Stamping Co 10801 Lower Azusa Rd **Fax Area Code:* 800 ■ *TF:* 800-877-7775 ■ *Web:* www.allnewstamping.com	El Monte	CA	91731	626-443-8813	877-8121*
American Metalcraft Inc 2074 George St *TF:* 800-333-9133 ■ *Web:* www.amnow.com	Melrose Park	IL	60160	708-345-1177	345-5758

Phone | Fax

American Trim 1005 W Grand Ave .... Lima OH 45801 419-228-1145 996-4850
Web: www.amtrim.com
APG Cash Drawer Div Upper Midwest Industries Inc
5250 Industrial Blvd NE .... Minneapolis MN 55421 763-571-5000 571-5771
Web: www.apgcd.com
Aranda Tooling Inc 15301 Springdale St .... Huntington Beach CA 92649 714-379-6565 379-6570
Web: www.arandatooling.com
Argo Products Co 3500 Goodfellow Blvd .... Saint Louis MO 63120 314-385-1803 385-1808
Web: www.argoproducts.com
Arrow Tru-Line Inc 2211 S Defiance St .... Archbold OH 43502 419-446-2785 445-2068
TF: 877-285-7253 ■ *Web:* www.arrowtruline.com
Assurance Mfg Co 9010 Evergreen Blvd .... Coon Rapids MN 55433 763-780-4252 780-8847
Web: www.assurancemfg.com
BAE Industries Inc 24400 Sherwood Ave .... Center Line MI 48015 586-754-3000 754-3007
Web: www.baeind.com
Banner Stamping Co 1308 Holly Ave .... Columbus OH 43212 614-291-3105 291-3125
Web: www.bannerstamping.com
Bazz Houston Co 12700 Western Ave .... Garden Grove CA 92841 714-898-2666 898-1389
TF: 800-385-9608 ■ *Web:* www.bazz-houston.com
Behrens Mfg Co 471 W 3rd St .... Winona MN 55987 507-454-4664 452-2106
Web: www.behrensmfg.com
Bermo Inc 4501 Ball Rd NE .... Circle Pines MN 55014 763-786-7676 785-2159
TF: 800-695-7676 ■ *Web:* www.bermo.com
Beta Shim Co 11 Progress Dr .... Shelton CT 06484 203-926-1150 929-5509
Web: www.betashim.com
Bettcher Amherst Metal Stamping 16000 Commerce Park Dr .... Cleveland OH 44142 216-267-0850 267-7654
Web: www.bettcherllc.com
Bi-Link Metal Specialties Inc 391 S Glen Ellyn Rd .... Bloomingdale IL 60108 630-858-5900 858-5995
Web: www.bi-link.net
Bopp-Busch Mfg Co PO Box 589 .... Au Gres MI 48703 989-876-7121 876-6555
Web: www.boppbusch.com
Brainin Advance Industries Inc 48 Frank Mossberg Dr .... Attleboro MA 02703 508-222-3151 226-8703
Web: www.brainin.com
Buhrke Industries LLC 511 W Algonquin Rd .... Arlington Heights IL 60005 847-981-7550 981-0772
Web: www.buhrke.com
Burnside Industries LLC 6830 Grand Haven Rd .... Spring Lake MI 49456 231-798-3394 798-2316
Capitol Stampings Corp 2700 W North Ave .... Milwaukee WI 53208 414-372-3500 372-3535
Web: www.capitolstampings.com
Chilton Products Div Western Industries Inc 300 E Breed St .... Chilton WI 53014 920-849-2381 849-4947
TF: 877-671-7063
Cly-Del Mfg Co 151 Sharon Rd .... Waterbury CT 06705 203-574-2100 753-3326
Web: www.cly-del.com
Connecticut Stamping & Bending Co 206 Newington Ave .... New Britain CT 06051 860-225-4637 229-4328
TF: 800-966-6964
Cooper Mfg Co 410 S 1st Ave .... Marshalltown IA 50158 641-752-6736 752-7476
Crest Mfg Co 5 Hood Dr PO Box 368 .... Lincoln RI 02865 401-333-1350 333-0821
TF: 800-652-7378 ■ *Web:* www.crestmfg.com
Custom Stamping & Mfg Inc 1340 SE 9th St .... Portland OR 97214 503-238-3700 238-3742
Web: www.customstampingmfg.com
Danco Precision Inc Wheatland & Mellon Sts .... Phoenixville PA 19460 610-933-8981 935-2011
Web: www.dancoprecision.com
Danville Metal Stamping Co Inc 20 Oakwood Ave .... Danville IL 61832 217-446-0647 446-3751
Web: www.danvillemetal.com
Dayton Rogers Mfg Co 8401 W 35 'W' Service Dr .... Blaine MN 55449 763-784-7714 784-8209
TF: 800-677-8881 ■ *Web:* www.daytonrogers.com
De Biasi Group 1555 Enterprise Rd .... Mississauga ON L4W4L4 905-670-1555 670-3415
Web: www.debiasi.com
Dee Zee Inc 1572 NE 58th Ave .... Des Moines IA 50313 515-265-7331 265-7926
TF: 800-779-2102 ■ *Web:* www.deezee.com
Defiance Metal Products 21 Seneca St .... Defiance OH 43512 419-784-5332 782-0148
Web: www.defiancemetal.com
Delta Consolidated Industries Inc PO Box 1846 .... Jonesboro AR 72403 870-935-3711 935-4994
TF: 800-643-0084 ■ *Web:* www.deltastorage.com
Diamond Mfg Co 243 W 8th St .... Wyoming PA 18644 570-693-0300 693-3500
TF: 800-233-9601 ■ *Web:* www.diamondman.com
Diamond Perforated Metals Inc 7300 W Sunnyview Ave .... Visalia CA 93291 559-651-1889 651-1815
TF: 800-642-4334 ■ *Web:* www.diamondperf.com
Dixie Seal & Stamp Co 755 North Ave NE .... Atlanta GA 30306 404-875-8883 872-3504
Web: www.dixieseal.com
DORMA Architectural Hardware 1003 W Broadway PO Box 8 .... Steeleville IL 62288 618-965-3491 965-9022
Web: www.dorma-usa.com
Dove Die & Stamping Co 15665 Brookpark Rd .... Cleveland OH 44142 216-267-3720 267-7250
Web: www.dovedie.com
Dubuque Stamping & Mfg Inc PO Box 798 .... Dubuque IA 52004 563-583-5716 556-8729
Web: www.dbqstamp.com
Dudek & Bock Spring Mfg Co 5100 W Roosevelt Rd .... Chicago IL 60644 773-379-4100 379-4715
Web: www.dudek-bock.com
DureX Inc 5 Stahuber Ave .... Union NJ 07083 908-688-0800 688-0718
Web: www.durexinc.com
East Moline Metal Products Co 1201 7th St .... East Moline IL 61244 309-752-1350 752-1380
TF Sales: 800-325-4151 ■ *Web:* www.emmetal.com
Eclipse Mfg Co 1828 Oakland Ave .... Sheboygan WI 53081 920-457-2311 457-4935
Web: www.eclipsemfg.com
Elmira Stamping & Mfg Corp 1704 Cedar St .... Elmira NY 14904 607-734-2058 732-0573
Web: www.elmirastamping.com
Florence Corp 40 Shuman Blvd Suite 290 .... Naperville IL 60563 630-369-7040 428-1886
TF: 800-275-1747 ■ *Web:* www.auth-florence.com
Fraen Corp 80 Newcrossing Rd .... Reading MA 01867 781-942-2223 942-2426
TF: 800-370-0078 ■ *Web:* www.fraen.com
Fuller Box Co 150 Chestnut St .... North Attleboro MA 02760 508-695-2525 695-2187
Web: www.fullerbox.com
Fulton Industries Inc 135 E Linfoot St PO Box 377 .... Wauseon OH 43567 419-335-3015 335-3215
TF: 800-537-5012 ■ *Web:* www.fultonindoh.com
Gasser & Sons Inc 440 Moreland Rd .... Commack NY 11725 631-543-6600 543-6649
Web: www.gasser.com
General Machine & Tool Works Inc 313 W Chestnut St .... Chicago IL 60610 312-337-2177 337-0244
General Press & Fabricating Co 1500 W Saint Paul Ave .... Milwaukee WI 53233 414-272-6000 272-1558
Web: www.generalpress.biz
Gilco Inc 16000 Common Rd .... Roseville MI 48066 586-779-5850 778-7190
TF: 800-424-4526 ■ *Web:* www.gilco.com
GMP Metal Products Inc 3883 Delor St .... Saint Louis MO 63116 314-481-0300 481-1379
TF: 800-325-9808 ■ *Web:* www.gmpmetal.com
Griffiths Corp 2727 Niagara Ln N .... Minneapolis MN 55447 763-557-8935 559-5290
Grigoleit Co PO Box 831 .... Decatur IL 62525 217-429-5411
Guarantee Specialties Inc 9401 Carr Ave .... Cleveland OH 44108 216-451-9744 451-3332
Web: www.gsi-garvin.com
Hannibal Industries Inc 3851 S Santa Fe Ave .... Los Angeles CA 90058 323-588-4261 589-5640
TF: 800-433-3166 ■ *Web:* www.hannibalindustries.com
Harvey Vogel Mfg Co 425 Weir Dr .... Woodbury MN 55125 651-739-7373 739-8666
Web: www.harveyvogel.com
HEB Mfg Co Inc 67 Vermont Rt 110 PO Box 188 .... Chelsea VT 05038 802-685-4821 685-7755
TF: 800-639-4187 ■ *Web:* www.hebmfg.com
Hendrick Mfg Co 1 7th Ave .... Carbondale PA 18407 570-282-1010 282-1506*
*Fax: Sales ■ *TF Cust Svc:* 800-225-7373 ■ *Web:* www.hendrickmfg.com
Heyco Products 1800 Industrial Way North .... Toms River NJ 08755 732-286-1800 244-8843
TF: 800-526-4182 ■ *Web:* www.heyco.com

HMC Holdings LLC 720 Dartmouth Ln .... Buffalo Grove IL 60089 847-541-5070 541-0096
TF: 800-874-6625 ■ *Web:* www.homakmfg.com
Hobson & Motzer Inc 30 Air Line Dr PO Box 427 .... Durham CT 06422 860-349-1756 349-3602
TF: 800-476-5111 ■ *Web:* www.hobsonmotzer.com
HPL Stampings Inc 425 Enterprise Pkwy .... Lake Zurich IL 60047 847-540-1400 540-1422
Web: www.hplstampings.com
Hudson Tool & Die Co 1327 N US 1 .... Ormond Beach FL 32174 386-672-2000 676-6212*
*Fax: Sales ■ *Web:* www.hudsontool.com
Innovative Stamping Corp 2068 Gladwick St .... Compton CA 90220 310-537-6996 537-0312
TF: 800-400-0047 ■ *Web:* www.innovative-sys.com
Kendale Industries Inc 7600 Hub Pkwy .... Cleveland OH 44125 216-524-5400 524-6750
TF: 800-321-9308 ■ *Web:* www.kendaleinc.com
Kennedy Mfg Co 520 E Sycamore St .... Van Wert OH 45891 419-238-2442 238-5644
TF: 800-413-8665 ■ *Web:* www.kennedymfg.com
Keystone Friction Hinge Co 520 Matthews Blvd .... South Williamsport PA 17702 570-323-9479 326-0217
Kilmartin Industries DBA Roger Williams Mint 79 Walton St .... Attleboro MA 02703 508-226-3310 226-2033
TF: 800-225-2734 ■ *Web:* www.mintusa.com
KMC Stampings 1221 S Park St .... Port Washington WI 53074 262-284-3424 284-9774
Web: www.kmcstampings.com
Knaack Mfg Co 420 E Terra Cotta Ave .... Crystal Lake IL 60014 815-459-6020 459-9097
TF: 800-456-7865 ■ *Web:* www.knaack.com
Kromet International Inc 200 Sheldon Dr .... Cambridge ON N1R7K1 519-623-2511 624-9729
Web: www.kromet.com
Lacey Mfg Co Inc 1146 Barnum Ave .... Bridgeport CT 06610 203-336-0121 336-1774
Web: www.laceymfg.com
Larson Tool & Stamping Co 90 Olive St .... Attleboro MA 02703 508-222-0897 226-7407
Web: www.larsontool.com
Mass Precision Sheetmetal Inc 2110 Oakland Rd .... San Jose CA 95131 408-954-0200 954-0288
Web: www.massprecision.com
McAlpin Industries Inc 255 Hollenbeck St .... Rochester NY 14621 585-266-3060 266-8091
Web: www.mcalpin-ind.com
Mercury Aircraft Inc 15-17 Wheeler Ave .... Hammondsport NY 14840 607-569-4200 569-4634
Web: www.mercuryaircraftinc.com
Metal Box International 11600 W King St .... Franklin Park IL 60131 847-455-8500 455-6030
Metal Components Inc
3281 Roger B Chaffee Memorial Blvd SE .... Grand Rapids MI 49548 616-252-1900 252-1970
Micro Stamping Corp 140 Belmont Dr .... Somerset NJ 08873 732-302-0800 302-0436
Web: www.microstamping.com
Midwest Wire Products LLC
649 S Lansing Ave PO Box 770 .... Sturgeon Bay WI 54235 920-743-6591 743-3777
TF: 800-445-0225 ■ *Web:* www.wireforming.com
MJ Celco Inc 3900 Wesley Terr .... Schiller Park IL 60176 847-671-1900 671-1978
Web: www.mjcelco.com
Morgal Machine Tool Co Inc 2100 S Yellow Springs St .... Springfield OH 45506 937-325-5561 325-1957
Web: www.morgal.com
MPI International 2129 Austin Ave .... Rochester Hills MI 48309 248-853-9010 853-5107
Web: www.mpi-int.com
New Standard Corp 74 Commerce Way .... York PA 17406 717-653-1811 757-2312
Web: www.newstandard.com
Northern Stamping Corp 6600 Chapek Pkwy .... Cuyahoga Heights OH 44125 216-883-8888 883-8237
Oakland Tool & Mfg Co Inc 34700 Commerce Dr .... Fraser MI 48026 586-294-0100 294-6139
Web: www.oaklandtool.com
Oberg Industries Inc 2301 Silverville Rd .... Freeport PA 16229 724-295-2121 295-2588
TF: 800-286-1275 ■ *Web:* www.oberg.com
Okay Industries Inc 200 Ellis St .... New Britain CT 06051 860-225-8707 225-7047
Web: www.okayind.com
P & G Steel Products Co Inc 54 Gruner Rd .... Buffalo NY 14227 716-896-7900 896-4129
TF: 800-952-3696 ■ *Web:* www.pgsteel.com
Parkview Metal Products Inc 1275 Ensell Rd .... Lake Zurich IL 60047 847-540-2323 540-8648
Web: www.parkviewmetal.com
Parkview South Dakota LLC 316 E Industrial Ave .... Lennox SD 57039 605-647-6000 647-6003
Web: www.parkviewmetal.com/south_dakota.html
Peerless Industries Inc 1980 Hawthorne Ave .... Melrose Park IL 60160 708-865-8870 865-0760
TF: 800-729-0307 ■ *Web:* www.peerlessindustries.com
Pelham Products Inc 46 Payne Rd .... Bethel CT 06801 203-792-1515 798-1892
Web: www.pelhamproducts.com
Penn United Technology Inc 799 N Pike Rd .... Cabot PA 16023 724-352-1507 352-4970
Web: www.pennunited.com
Perfection Spring & Stamping Corp
1449 E Algonquin Rd .... Mount Prospect IL 60056 847-437-3900 437-1322
Web: www.pss-corp.com
Plainfield Cos 1351 N Division St .... Plainfield IL 60544 815-436-5671 439-2970
Web: www.plainfieldcompanies.com
Precision Resource 25 Forest Pkwy .... Shelton CT 06484 203-925-0012 926-9010
Web: www.precisionresource.com
Premium Allied Tool Inc 5680 Old Hwy 54 .... Philpot KY 42366 270-729-4242 729-4332
Prestige Stamping Inc 23513 Groesbeck Hwy .... Warren MI 48089 586-773-2700 773-2298
Web: www.prestigestamping.com
Punch Press Products Inc 2035 E 51st St .... Vernon CA 90058 323-581-7151 581-0341
Web: www.punch-press.com
Quality Perforating Inc 166 Dundaff St .... Carbondale PA 18407 570-282-4344 282-4627
TF: 800-872-7373 ■ *Web:* www.qualityperf.com
Quality Tool & Stamping Co Inc 2642 Mcilwraith St .... Muskegon MI 49444 231-733-2538 733-0983
Web: www.qtstamping.com
Ramcel Engineering Co 2926 MacArthur Blvd .... Northbrook IL 60062 847-272-6980 272-7196
Web: www.ramcel.com
RES Mfg Co Inc 7801 N 73rd St .... Milwaukee WI 53223 414-354-4530 354-9027
TF: 800-334-8044 ■ *Web:* www.resmfg.com
Roger Williams Mint 79 Walton St .... Attleboro MA 02703 508-226-3310 226-2033
TF: 800-225-2734 ■ *Web:* www.mintusa.com
Saunders Mfg Co Inc 61 Nickerson Hill Rd .... Readfield ME 04355 207-685-3385 685-9918
TF Cust Svc: 800-341-4674 ■ *Web:* www.saunders-usa.com
Slidematic Products Co 4520 W Addison St .... Chicago IL 60641 773-545-4213 545-0797
Web: www.slidematicproducts.com
Small Parts Inc 600 Humphrey St PO Box 23 .... Logansport IN 46947 574-753-6323 753-6660
Web: www.smallpartsinc.com
Sons Tool Inc 460 Thompson Rd .... Woodville WI 54028 715-698-2471 698-2335
Web: www.sonstool.com
Spindustries LLC 1301 La Salle St .... Lake Geneva WI 53147 262-248-6601 248-1277
Web: www.lgspin.com
Stack-On Products Co PO Box 489 .... Wauconda IL 60084 847-526-1611 526-6599
TF: 800-323-9601 ■ *Web:* www.stack-on.com
Stamtex Metal Stampings 112 Erie St .... Niles OH 44446 330-652-2558 652-7369
Web: www.stamtexmetalproducts.com
Stanco Metal Products Inc 2101 168th Ave .... Grand Haven MI 49417 616-842-5000 842-9080
TF: 800-530-9655 ■ *Web:* www.stancometal.com
Stanley Spring & Stamping Corp 5050 W Foster Ave .... Chicago IL 60630 773-777-2600 777-3894
Web: www.stanleyspring.com
Steel City Corp 190 N Meridian Rd .... Youngstown OH 44501 330-792-7663 792-7951
TF: 800-321-0350 ■ *Web:* www.scity.com
Stewart EFI LLC 45 Old Waterbury Rd .... Thomaston CT 06787 860-283-8213 283-5610
TF: 800-393-5387 ■ *Web:* www.stewartefi.com
Stiglitz Corp 1747 Mellwood Ave .... Louisville KY 40206 502-897-1543 893-1669
Web: www.stiglitz.com
T & D Metal Products Co 602 E Walnut St .... Watseka IL 60970 815-432-4938 432-6271
TF: 800-634-7267 ■ *Web:* www.tdmetal.com

Phone *Fax*

Tempco Mfg Co Inc 2475 Hwy 55 .... Mendota Heights MN 55120 651-452-1441 452-1125
Web: www.tempcomfg.com
Thomas Engineering Co 7024 Northland Dr .... Brooklyn Park MN 55428 763-533-1501 533-8091
Web: www.thomasengineering.com
Trans-Matic Mfg Co 300 E 48th St ....Holland MI 49423 616-820-2500 820-2702
TF: 866-467-7267 ■ *Web:* www.transmatic.com
Triad Metal Products Co 12990 Snow Rd .... Parma OH 44130 216-676-6505 676-6510
Web: www.triadmetal.com
Trine Products Corp 1430 Ferris Pl ....Bronx NY 10461 718-828-5200 828-4052
TF: 800-223-8075 ■ *Web:* www.trinecorp.com
Triton Industries Inc 1020 N Kolmar Ave...................... Chicago IL 60651 773-384-3700 384-8748
Web: www.tritonindustries.com
Truelove & MacLean Inc 984 Waterville St .... Waterbury CT 06704 203-574-2240 753-1085
Web: www.trumac.com
UMI Co Inc 1520 S 5th St.................................. Hopkins MN 55343 952-935-8431 935-6631
Upper Midwest Industries Inc APG Cash Drawer Div
5250 Industrial Blvd NE.............................. Minneapolis MN 55421 763-571-5000 571-5771
Web: www.apgcd.com
Vogel Harvey Mfg Co 425 Weir Dr......................... Woodbury MN 55125 651-739-7373 739-8666
Web: www.harveyvogel.com
Wallace Metal Products
1804 Hillyer Robinson Industrial Pkwy......................Anniston AL 36207 256-831-4826 831-7908
TF: 888-831-9675
Waterloo Industries Inc 100 E 4th St......................... Waterloo IA 50703 319-235-7131 232-3924
TF: 800-833-8851 ■ *Web:* www.waterlooindustries.com
Wauconda Tool & Engineering 821 W Algonquin Rd ....Algonquin IL 60102 847-658-4588 658-0788
Web: www.wauconda.com
Weiss-Aug Co Inc 220 Merry Ln.......................... East Hanover NJ 07936 973-887-7600 887-8109
Web: www.weiss-aug.com
Western Industries Inc W 156 N 9073 Pilgrim Rd ....Menomonee Falls WI 53051 262-251-1915 251-6727
Web: www.westernind.com
Western Industries Inc Chilton Products Div 300 E Breed St........ Chilton WI 53014 920-849-2381 849-4947
TF: 877-671-7063
Winzeler Stamping Co 129 Wabash Ave...................... Montpelier OH 43543 419-485-3147 485-5039
Web: www.winzelerstamping.com
Wisconsin Tool & Stamping Co 9521 W Ainslie St .... Schiller Park IL 60176 847-678-7573 678-2950
Wolverine Metal Stamping Inc 3600 Tennis Ct............. Saint Joseph MI 49085 269-429-6600 429-6657
Web: www.wms-inc.com
Wozniak Industries Inc
2 Mid America Plaza Suite 706......................Oakbrook Terrace IL 60181 630-954-3400 954-3605
Web: www.wozniakindustries.com
Wrico Stamping Co 2727 Niagara Ln N .... Minneapolis MN 55447 763-559-2288 553-7976
Web: www.wrico-net.com
York Stamping 620 S 'J' St.................................. Richmond IN 47374 765-966-1576 935-0348
York Stamping DBA Wallace Metal Products
1804 Hillyer Robinson Industrial Pkwy......................Anniston AL 36207 256-831-4826 831-7908
TF: 888-831-9675

492 METAL STAMPINGS - AUTOMOTIVE

SEE ALSO Automotive Parts & Supplies - Mfr p. 1360

Phone *Fax*

Acemco Automotive 7297 Enterprise Dr..................... Spring Lake MI 49456 231-799-8612 799-9904
Web: www.acemco.com
Ada Metal Products Inc 7120 Capital Dr .... Lincolnwood IL 60712 847-673-1190 673-4860
Web: www.adametal.com
Advance Engineering Co 12025 Dixie Ave .... Redford MI 48239 313-537-3500 537-7389
AJ Rose Mfg Co 38000 Chester Rd ....Avon OH 44011 440-934-7700 934-2802
Web: www.ajrose.com
American Metal & Plastics Inc 450 32nd St SW ....Grand Rapids MI 49548 616-452-6061 452-3835
Web: www.ampi-gr.com
AMG Industries Inc 200 Commerce Dr.................... Mount Vernon OH 43050 740-397-4044 397-3092*
**Fax:* Mail Rm ■ *Web:* www.amgindustries.com
Bayloff Stamped Products 8091 SR 5 ....Kinsman OH 44428 330-876-4511 876-4632
Web: www.bayloff.com
Benteler Automotive 1780 Pond Run.......................Auburn Hills MI 48326 248-377-9999 364-7125
Web: www.benteler.de
Bing Metals Group Stamp & Assembly 11500 Oakland Ave .... Detroit MI 48211 313-867-3700 867-3897
Web: www.binggroup.com
Brown Corp of America Inc 401 S Steele St ....Ionia MI 48846 616-527-4050 527-3385
TF: 800-530-9570 ■ *Web:* www.browncorp.com
Buhrke Industries LLC 511 W Algonquin Rd ....Arlington Heights IL 60005 847-981-7550 981-0772
Web: www.buhrke.com
Burkland Inc 6520 S State Rd .... Goodrich MI 48438 810-636-2233 636-7525
C Cowles & Co Inc 83 Water St...............................New Haven CT 06511 203-865-3117 773-1019
TF: 800-624-4483 ■ *Web:* www.ccowles.com
Center Mfg Inc 990 84th St .... Byron Center MI 49315 616-878-3324 878-3477
Web: www.centermfg.com
Central Mfg Inc 601 S Main St PO Box 508 ....Parker City IN 47368 765-468-7133 468-8170
Checker Motors Corp 2016 N Pitcher St .... Kalamazoo MI 49007 269-343-6121 343-6823
Clark Metal Products Co 100 Serell Dr .... Blairsville PA 15717 724-459-7550 459-0207
Web: www.clark-metal.com
Concord Tool & Mfg Co Inc 106 N Groesbeck Hwy......... Mount Clemens MI 48043 586-465-6537 465-2556
Web: www.concordtool.com
Cooper-Standard Automotive Inc 39550 Orchard Hill Place Dr......... Novi MI 48375 248-596-5900 596-6540*
**Fax:* Hum Res ■ *Web:* www.cooperstandard.com
Cowles C & Co Inc 83 Water St...............................New Haven CT 06511 203-865-3117 773-1019
TF: 800-624-4483 ■ *Web:* www.ccowles.com
Decoma International Inc 50 Casmir Ct......................... Concord ON L4K4J5 905-669-2888 669-4992
TF: 800-461-3967 ■ *Web:* www.decoma.com
DGS Stamping LLC 10302 Madison Ave .... Cleveland OH 44102 216-961-4172 651-2409
Dixien LLC PO Box 337 .... Forest Park GA 30298 404-366-7427 366-2403
Web: www.dixien.com
Duffy Tool & Stamping LLC 3401 W 8th St ....Muncie IN 47302 765-288-1931 288-4784
Web: www.duffytool.com
F & B Mfg Co Inc 4316 N 39th Ave .... Phoenix AZ 85019 602-272-3900 272-3326
Web: www.fbmfg.com
Fisher Corp 1625 W Maple Rd ....Troy MI 48084 248-280-0808 280-0725
Web: www.fisherco.com
Florida Production Engineering Co 2 Tower Cir E.........Ormond Beach FL 32174 386-677-2566 673-1130
Web: www.fpe-inc.com
Genco Stamping & Mfg Co 2001 Genco Dr ....Cookeville TN 38506 931-528-5574 528-8379
Gerstenslager Co 1425 E Bowman St PO Box 6011 .... Wooster OH 44691 330-262-2015 262-4009*
**Fax:* Sales ■ *Web:* www.worthingtonindustries.com
GHSP Co 1250 S Beechtree St.......................... Grand Haven MI 49417 616-842-5500 842-7230
Web: www.ghsp.com
Gill Tool & Die 5801 Clay Ave SW ....Grand Rapids MI 49548 616-531-5620 531-7730
Grant Industries Inc 33415 Groesbeck Hwy.......................Fraser MI 48026 586-293-9200 293-9346
Web: www.grantgrp.com
Hamlin Steel Products LLC 2741 Wingate Ave......................Akron OH 44314 330-753-7791 753-5577
Web: www.hamlinsteel.com

Phone *Fax*

Industrial Components Inc 2250 NW 102nd Ave ....Miami FL 33172 305-477-0387 594-7332
Web: www.icassemblies.com
ITW Drawform 500 Fairview Rd.................................. Zeeland MI 49464 616-772-1910 772-9572
Web: www.drawform.com
ITW Highland 1240 Wolcott St PO Box 1858 .... Waterbury CT 06722 203-574-3200 754-4019
Web: www.itwhighland.com
Lapeer Metal Stamping Co
130 N Groesbeck PO Box 407........................ Mount Clemens MI 48046 586-307-3003 468-8401
Web: www.lapeermetal.com
Lapeer Metal Stamping Cos Inc 930 S Saginaw St................ Lapeer MI 48446 810-664-8588 664-9810
Web: www.lapeermetal.com
LMC Industries Inc 100 Manufacturers Dr .... Arnold MO 63010 636-282-8080 282-7114
Web: www.lmcindustries.com
Logghe Stamping Co 16711 E 13-Mile Rd ....Fraser MI 48026 586-293-2250 293-7202
Luitink Mfg Co W 140 N 8700 Lily Rd PO Box 366........Menomonee Falls WI 53052 262-251-8800 251-8804
Web: www.luitink.com
Manter Technology Corp 7177 Marine City Hwy .... Marine City MI 48039 810-765-8000 765-3373
Web: www.mantertech.com
Marquette Tool & Die Co 3185 S Kingshighway Blvd ....Saint Louis MO 63139 314-771-8509 771-7964
Martinrea Fabco Hot Stamping 19200 Glendale Ave.............. Detroit MI 48223 313-272-8400 272-9360
Mayflower Vehicle Systems 60581 SR 7....................... Shadyside OH 43947 740-676-6542 676-9273
McKechnie Vehicle Components 5440 Corporate Dr Suite 100 .... Troy MI 48098 248-641-4700 641-4731
Web: www.mvcusa.com
Means Industries Inc 1860 S Jefferson Ave.................... Saginaw MI 48601 989-754-3300 754-3301
TF: 800-869-1433 ■ *Web:* www.meansindustries.com
Midway Products Group Inc 1 Lyman E Hoyt Dr................ Monroe MI 48161 734-241-7242 241-7511*
**Fax:* Sales ■ *Web:* www.midwayproducts.com
Midwest Stamping Inc 3455 Briarfield Blvd Suite A............Maumee OH 43537 419-724-6970 724-6972
Modern Metal Products Co 726 Beacon St ....Loves Park IL 61111 815-877-9571 877-6384
Web: www.modernmetal.net
Modineer Co 2190 Industrial Dr PO Box 640..........................Niles MI 49120 269-683-2550 683-7984
Web: www.modineer.com
Moroso Performance Products Inc 80 Carter Dr................. Guilford CT 06437 203-453-6571 453-6906*
**Fax:* Cust Svc ■ *Web:* www.moroso.com
MPI International 2129 Austin Ave..................... Rochester Hills MI 48309 248-853-9010 853-5107
Web: www.mpi-int.com
NAS Interplex Inc 1434 110th St Suite 301 ....College Point NY 11356 718-961-6212 886-0573
Noble Metal Processing Inc 28207 Van Dyke Ave.................Warren MI 48092 586-751-5300 751-5301
ODM Tool & Mfg Co 9550 Joliet Rd............................. McCook IL 60525 708-485-6130 485-6540
Web: www.odmtool.com
Ogihara America Corp 1480 W McPherson Park Dr .... Howell MI 48843 517-548-4900 548-6036
Web: www.ogihara.com
Olson International Ltd 50 W North Ave .... Lombard IL 60148 630-629-9494
Web: www.metalstamper.com
Plainfield Cos 1351 N Division St .... Plainfield IL 60544 815-436-5671 439-2970
Web: www.plainfieldcompanies.com
Pridgeon & Clay Inc 50 Cottage Grove St SW...............Grand Rapids MI 49507 616-241-5675 281-1799
Web: www.pridgeonandclay.com
Q3 Industries Inc 777 Manor Park Dr.........................Columbus OH 43228 614-870-0195 870-0196
Web: www.q3inds.com
Quality Metalcraft Inc 33355 Glendale St ....Livonia MI 48150 734-261-6700 261-5180
Web: www.qualitymetalcraft.com
Radar Industries 27101 Grosbeck Hwy..........................Warren MI 48089 586-779-0300 779-0355
TF: 800-779-0300 ■ *Web:* www.radarind.com
Republic Die & Tool Co 45000 Van Born Rd PO Box 339..........Belleville MI 48112 734-699-3400 699-4081
Riviera Tool Co 5460 Executive Pkwy SE...................Grand Rapids MI 49512 616-698-2100 698-2470
AMEX: RTC ■ *Web:* www.rivieratool.com
Rose AJ Mfg Co 38000 Chester Rd ....Avon OH 44011 440-934-7700 934-2802
Web: www.ajrose.com
S & Z Tool & Die Co Inc 3180 Berea Rd .... Cleveland OH 44111 216-252-4250 252-7270
Web: www.sztool.com
Sanderson Industries Inc 3550 Atlanta Industrial Pkwy NW .... Atlanta GA 30331 404-699-2022 696-3956
Web: www.sndrsn.com
Shiloh Industries Corp 5389 W 130th St .... Cleveland OH 44130 216-267-2600 265-4244
NASDAQ: SHLO ■ *Web:* www.shiloh.com
Sky-Tek LLC 35588 Veronica St ....Livonia MI 48150 734-464-3811 542-3710
Web: www.skyteklic.com
Stamco Industries Inc 26650 Lakeland Blvd ....Euclid OH 44132 216-731-9333 731-9338
Stanco Metal Products Inc 2101 168th Ave .... Grand Haven MI 49417 616-842-5000 842-9080
TF: 800-530-9655 ■ *Web:* www.stancometal.com
Steel Parts Corp 801 Berryman Pike ....Tipton IN 46072 765-675-2191 675-4232
Stewart EFI LLC 45 Old Waterbury Rd ....Thomaston CT 06787 860-283-8213 283-5610
TF: 800-393-5387 ■ *Web:* www.stewartefi.com
Syracuse Stamping Co 1054 S Clinton St...................... Syracuse NY 13202 315-476-5306 474-8876
TF: 800-581-5555 ■ *Web:* www.syraco.com
Taber Bushnell 7709 Winpark Dr ....Minneapolis MN 55427 763-546-0994 546-4469
TF: 800-811-9362 ■ *Web:* www.taberbushnell.com
TFO Tech Co Ltd 221 State St...............................Jeffersonville OH 43128 740-426-6381 426-6511
Thiel Tool & Engineering Co Inc
4622 Bulwer Ave PO Box 470007.........................Saint Louis MO 63147 314-241-6121 241-7857
TF: 800-862-4145 ■ *Web:* www.thieltool.com
Thomas Engineering Co 7024 Northland Dr................ Brooklyn Park MN 55428 763-533-1501 533-8091
Web: www.thomasengineering.com
ThyssenKrupp Budd Co 3155 W Big Beaver Rd PO Box 2601.......... Troy MI 48007 248-643-3500 643-3593
Web: www.buddcompany.com
Toledo Technologies PO Box 596............................. Toledo OH 43697 419-661-1333 661-1337
Web: www.toledotech.com
Tower Automotive 27175 Haggerty Rd............................. Novi MI 48377 248-675-6000 675-6200
Web: www.towerautomotive.com
Triad Metal Products Co 12990 Snow Rd .... Parma OH 44130 216-676-6505 676-6510
Web: www.triadmetal.com
United Metal Products Corp 8101 Lyndon St .... Detroit MI 48238 313-933-8750 933-1001
Web: www.unitedmetalproducts.com
Varbros LLC 16025 Brookpark Rd......................... Cleveland OH 44142 216-267-5200 267-5205
Web: www.varbroscorp.com
Versatube Corp 4755 Rochester Rd .... Troy MI 48085 248-689-7373 689-8293
Web: www.versatubecorp.com
Welarco Fabrications Inc 7400 W Plank Rd ....Peoria IL 61604 309-697-9400 697-2400
TF: 800-447-6464
Wellington Industries Inc 39555 S I-94 Service Dr...............Belleville MI 48111 734-942-1060 942-9430
Web: www.wellingtonind.com
Wisconsin Metal Products Co 1807 DeKovin Ave .... Racine WI 53403 262-633-6301 633-8962
Web: www.wmpco.com
Wolverine Metal Specialties 1013 Thorrez Rd .... Jackson MI 49201 517-750-3414 750-1644

493 METAL TUBE & PIPE

Phone *Fax*

AK Tube LLC 30400 E Broadway...........................Walbridge OH 43465 419-661-4150 661-4380
TF: 800-955-8031 ■ *Web:* www.aktube.com
Allied Tube & Conduit Inc 16100 S Lathrop Ave.................. Harvey IL 60426 708-339-1610 339-9838*
**Fax:* Hum Res ■ *TF:* 800-882-5543 ■ *Web:* www.alliedtube.com
American Cast Iron Pipe Co (ACIPCO) 2916 16th St N......... Birmingham AL 35207 205-325-7701 307-2747
TF: 800-442-2347 ■ *Web:* www.acipco.com

				Phone	Fax
Atlas Tube 1855 122nd St *TF:* 800-733-5683 ■ *Web:* www.atlastube.com	Chicago	IL	60633	773-646-4500	646-6128
Avis Industrial Corp 1909 S Main St *Web:* www.avisindustrial.com	Upland	IN	46989	765-998-8100	998-8111
Beck Industries 28707 La Rue St	Elkhart	IN	46517	574-294-5621	294-5628
Berg Steel Pipe Corp 5315 W 19th St *TF:* 800-874-0384 ■ *Web:* www.bergpipe.com	Panama City	FL	32401	850-769-2273	763-9683
Bristol Metals LP 390 Bristol Metals Rd *Web:* www.brismet.com	Bristol	TN	37620	423-968-2151	989-4742
Bull Moose Tube Co 1819 Clarkson Rd Suite 100 **Fax:* Sales ■ *TF:* 800-325-4467 ■ *Web:* www.bullmoosetube.com	Chesterfield	MO	63017	636-537-2600	537-5848*
California Steel & Tube 16049 Stephens St *TF:* 800-338-8823	City of Industry	CA	91745	626-968-5511	369-9660
Camdel Metals Corp 12244 Willow Grove Rd *Web:* www.camdelmetals.com	Camden	DE	19934	302-697-9521	697-9620
Cerro Flow Products Inc PO Box 66800 *TF:* 888-237-7611 ■ *Web:* www.cerroflow.com	Saint Louis	MO	63166	618-337-6000	337-6958
Charlotte Pipe & Foundry Co 2109 Randolph Rd *TF:* 800-432-6172 ■ *Web:* www.charlottepipe.com	Charlotte	NC	28207	704-372-5030	348-6450
Crucible Materials Corp Trent Tube Div 2015 Energy Dr **Fax:* Sales ■ *TF:* 800-558-2260 ■ *Web:* www.trenttube.com	East Troy	WI	53120	262-642-7321	642-9571*
CTP 3750 Shelby St *Web:* www.tubeproc.com/CTP/CTP.htm	Indianapolis	IN	46227	317-787-5747	782-9489
Dekoron Unitherm Inc 1531 Commerce Creek Blvd *TF:* 800-633-5015 ■ *Web:* www.unithermcc.com	Cape Coral	FL	33909	239-995-8111	995-8027
Earle M Jorgensen Co 10650 S Alameda St *NYSE: JOR* ■ *TF:* 800-336-5365 ■ *Web:* www.emjmetals.com	Lynwood	CA	90262	323-567-1122	563-5500
Elano Corp 2455 Dayton-Xenia Rd *Web:* www.elanocorp.com	Dayton	OH	45434	937-426-0621	426-7181
Eugene Welding Co 2420 Wills St *TF:* 800-959-0857 ■ *Web:* www.ewco.net	Marysville	MI	48040	810-364-7421	364-4347
Felker Brothers Corp 22 N Chestnut Ave *TF:* 800-826-2304 ■ *Web:* www.felkerbrothers.com	Marshfield	WI	54449	715-384-3121	387-6837
Handy & Harman Tube Co Inc 1244 Willow Grove Rd *TF:* 800-766-8823 ■ *Web:* www.handytube.com	Camden	DE	19934	302-697-9521	697-9620
Hanna Steel Corp 3812 Commerce Ave *TF:* 800-633-8252 ■ *Web:* www.hannasteel.com	Fairfield	AL	35064	205-780-1111	783-8290
Hannibal Industries Inc 3851 S Santa Fe Ave *TF:* 800-433-3166 ■ *Web:* www.hannibalindustries.com	Los Angeles	CA	90058	323-588-4261	589-5640
Hofmann Industries Inc 3145 Shillington Rd *Web:* www.hofmann.com	Sinking Spring	PA	19608	610-678-8051	670-2221
Howell Metal Co 574 Depot Rd PO Box 218 *TF:* 800-247-2048 ■ *Web:* www.howellmetal.com	New Market	VA	22844	540-740-3111	740-9568
Hydro Aluminum North America 801 International Dr Suite 200 *TF:* 888-935-5752 ■ *Web:* www.hydroaluminumna.com	Linthicum	MD	21090	410-487-4500	487-8053
Indiana Tube Corp 2100 Lexington Ave	Evansville	IN	47720	812-424-9028	424-0340
International Metal Hose Co 520 Goodrich Rd *TF:* 800-458-6855 ■ *Web:* www.metalhose.com	Bellevue	OH	44811	419-483-7690	483-8225
John Maneely Co 900 Haddon Ave Suite 500 *TF:* 800-257-8182	Collingswood	NJ	08108	856-854-5400	858-5578
Keystone Tube Co 3400 N Wolf Rd *TF Cust Svc:* 800-323-9493	Franklin Park	IL	60131	708-841-2450	841-3724
LeFiell Mfg Co 13700 Firestone Blvd *TF:* 800-451-5971 ■ *Web:* www.lefiell.com	Santa Fe Springs	CA	90670	562-921-3411	921-5480
Lock Joint Tube Inc 515 W Ireland Rd **Fax:* Sales ■ *TF:* 800-257-6859 ■ *Web:* www.ljtube.com	South Bend	IN	46614	574-299-5326	299-3464*
Maneely John Co 900 Haddon Ave Suite 500 *TF:* 800-257-8182	Collingswood	NJ	08108	856-854-5400	858-5578
Marcegaglia USA Inc 1001 E Waterfront Dr **Fax:* Sales ■ *Web:* www.gruppomarcegaglia.com	Munhall	PA	15120	412-462-2185	462-6059*
Maverick Tube Corp 16401 Swingley Ridge Rd Suite 700 *NYSE: MVK* ■ *TF:* 888-628-8823 ■ *Web:* www.maverick-tube.com	Chesterfield	MO	63017	636-733-1600	733-1676
Morris Coupling Co 2240 W 15th St *TF:* 800-426-1579 ■ *Web:* www.morriscoupling.com	Erie	PA	16505	814-459-1741	453-5155
National Metalwares Inc 900 N Russell Ave *Web:* www.nationalmetalwares.com	Aurora	IL	60506	630-892-9000	892-2573
Northwest Pipe Co 200 SW Market St Suite 1800 *NASDAQ: NWPX* ■ *TF:* 800-989-9631 ■ *Web:* www.nwpipe.com	Portland	OR	97201	503-946-1200	978-2561
Oakley Industries Inc 3211 W Bear Creek Dr *Web:* www.oakleyindustries.com	Englewood	CO	80110	303-761-1835	781-7307
Outokumpu Stainless Pipe Inc 1101 N Main St **Fax Area Code:* 800 ■ *TF:* 800-731-7473 ■ *Web:* www.outokumpu.com	Wildwood	FL	34785	352-748-1313	416-7473*
Pipe Fabricating & Supply Co 1235 N Kraemer Blvd *Web:* www.pipefab.com	Anaheim	CA	92806	714-630-5200	630-1277
Plymouth Tube Co 29 W 150 Warrenville Rd *TF:* 800-323-9506 ■ *Web:* www.plymouth.com	Warrenville	IL	60555	630-393-3550	393-3551
PTC Alliance Copperleaf Corporate Center 6051 Wallace Rd Ext Suite 200 *TF:* 888-299-8823 ■ *Web:* www.ptcalliance.com	Wexford	PA	15090	412-299-7900	299-2619
Quanex Corp 1900 West Loop S Suite 1500 *NYSE: NX* ■ *TF:* 800-231-8176 ■ *Web:* www.quanex.com	Houston	TX	77027	713-961-4600	439-1016
Reading Tube Corp 86 Tube Dr PO Box 14026 *TF:* 800-523-8263	Reading	PA	19612	610-926-4141	926-7317
Sharon Tube Co 134 Mill St *TF:* 800-245-8115 ■ *Web:* www.sharontube.com	Sharon	PA	16146	724-981-5200	983-1031
Small Tube Products Co Inc PO Box 1674	Altoona	PA	16603	814-695-4491	695-4304
Southern Metals Co 111 N Raleigh Ave PO Box 471 *TF:* 800-843-2771 ■ *Web:* www.sometco.com	Sheffield	AL	35660	256-383-3261	383-5204
Stupp Corp 12555 Ronaldson Rd *TF:* 800-535-9999 ■ *Web:* www.stuppcorp.com	Baton Rouge	LA	70807	225-775-8800	775-7610
Superior Tube Co 3900 Germantown Pike *TF:* 800-658-8600 ■ *Web:* www.superiortube.com	Collegeville	PA	19426	610-489-5200	489-5252
Swepco Tube Corp 1 Clifton Blvd *Web:* www.swepcotube.com	Clifton	NJ	07015	973-778-3000	778-9289
Synalloy Corp 2155 W Croft Cir *NASDAQ: SYNL* ■ *TF Orders:* 800-763-1001 ■ *Web:* www.synalloy.com	Spartanburg	SC	29302	864-585-3605	596-1501
Tarpon Industries Inc 2420 Wills St *AMEX: TPO* ■ *Web:* www.tarponind.com	Marysville	MI	48040	810-364-7421	364-5610
Tex-Tube Co 1503 N Post Oak Rd *TF:* 800-839-7473 ■ *Web:* www.tex-tube.com	Houston	TX	77055	713-686-4351	685-3222
Troxel Co 11495 Hwy 57 *Web:* www.troxel.com	Moscow	TN	38057	901-877-6875	877-3439
Tube Processing Corp 604 E Le Grande Ave *TF:* 800-776-4119 ■ *Web:* www.tubeproc.com	Indianapolis	IN	46203	317-787-1321	787-5384
United Industries Inc 1546 Henry Ave *Web:* www.unitedindustries.com	Beloit	WI	53511	608-365-8891	365-1259
UNR-Leavitt 1717 W 115th St *TF:* 800-532-8488 ■ *Web:* www.leavitt-tube.com	Chicago	IL	60643	773-239-7700	239-1023
Valmont Industries Inc 1 Valmont Plaza *NYSE: VMI* ■ *TF:* 800-825-6668 ■ *Web:* www.valmont.com	Omaha	NE	68154	402-963-1000	963-1100
Van Leeuwen Pipe & Tube Inc 2875 64th Ave *Web:* www.vanleeuwen.com	Edmonton	AB	T6P1R1	780-469-7410	466-5970
Webco Industries Inc 9101 W 21st St *Web:* www.webcoindustries.com	Sand Springs	OK	74063	918-241-1000	245-0306
Western Tube & Conduit Corp 2001 E Dominguez St *Web:* www.westerntube.com	Long Beach	CA	90810	310-537-6300	604-9785
Wheatland Tube Co 900 Haddon Ave Suite 500 *TF:* 800-257-8182 ■ *Web:* www.wheatland.com	Collingswood	NJ	08108	856-854-5400	854-0616
Wolverine Tube Inc 200 Clinton Ave W Suite 1000 *NYSE: WLV* ■ *TF:* 800-633-3972 ■ *Web:* www.wlv.com	Huntsville	AL	35801	256-890-0460	890-0470

494 METAL WORK - ARCHITECTURAL & ORNAMENTAL

				Phone	Fax
2nd Ave Design 737 W 2nd Ave *TF:* 800-843-1602 ■ *Web:* www.2ndave.com	Mesa	AZ	85210	480-464-8366	835-7385
AEP-Span Corp 5100 E Grand Ave *TF:* 800-527-2503 ■ *Web:* www.aep-span.com	Dallas	TX	75223	214-827-1740	828-1394
Airflex Industrial Corp 965 Conklin St *Web:* www.airflexind.com	Farmingdale	NY	11735	631-752-1234	752-1309
Airolite Co 27855 State Route 7 *TF:* 800-247-6548 ■ *Web:* www.airolite.com	Marietta	OH	45750	740-373-7676	373-6666
Alabama Metal Industries Corp (AMICO) 3245 Fayette Ave **Fax:* Sales ■ *TF:* 800-366-2642 ■ *Web:* www.amico-online.com	Birmingham	AL	35208	205-787-2611	780-7838*
Aluma Systems 55 Costa Rd *TF:* 888-284-9897 ■ *Web:* www.aluma.com	Toronto	ON	L4K1M8	905-669-5282	660-8062
Alvarado Mfg Co Inc 12660 Colony St *TF:* 800-423-4143 ■ *Web:* www.alvaradomfg.com	Chino	CA	91710	909-591-8431	628-1403
American Stair Corp Inc 642 Forestwood Dr *TF:* 800-872-7824 ■ *Web:* www.americanstair.com	Romeoville	IL	60446	815-886-9600	372-3683
AMICO (Alabama Metal Industries Corp) 3245 Fayette Ave **Fax:* Sales ■ *TF:* 800-366-2642 ■ *Web:* www.amico-online.com	Birmingham	AL	35208	205-787-2611	780-7838*
ATAS International Inc 6612 Snowdrift Rd *TF:* 800-468-1441 ■ *Web:* www.atas.com	Allentown	PA	18106	610-395-8445	395-9342
BETCO (Builders Equipment & Tool Co) 1617 Enid St *TF:* 800-847-5722 ■ *Web:* www.scaffold.com	Houston	TX	77009	713-869-3491	869-6541
Bil-Jax Inc 125 Taylor Pkwy *TF:* 800-537-0540 ■ *Web:* www.biljax.com	Archbold	OH	43502	419-445-8915	445-0367
Brand Energy & Infrastructure Services Inc 2505 S Main St **Fax Area Code:* 770 ■ *TF:* 888-842-7263 ■ *Web:* www.brandscaffold.com	Kennesaw	GA	30144	678-285-1498	514-0285*
Builders Equipment & Tool Co (BETCO) 1617 Enid St *TF:* 800-847-5722 ■ *Web:* www.scaffold.com	Houston	TX	77009	713-869-3491	869-6541
Cherokee Metals Co Inc 4648 S Old Peachtree Rd *TF:* 877-656-1900 ■ *Web:* www.cherokeemetals.com	Norcross	GA	30071	770-449-1444	559-4933
Chicago Metallic Corp 4849 S Austin Ave *TF:* 800-323-7164 ■ *Web:* www.chicago-metallic.com	Chicago	IL	60638	708-563-4600	
Construction Specialties Inc 3 Werner Way *TF:* 800-972-7214	Lebanon	NJ	08833	908-236-0800	236-0801
Custom Enclosures Inc 500 Harvester Ct #4	Wheeling	IL	60090	847-520-5511	520-5588
Duvinage Corp 60 W Oak Ridge Dr *TF:* 800-541-2645 ■ *Web:* www.duvinage.com	Hagerstown	MD	21740	301-733-8255	791-7240
Fisher & Ludlow Tru-Weld Grating 2000 Corporate Dr Suite 400 *TF:* 800-445-7093 ■ *Web:* fisherludlow.com	Wexford	PA	15090	724-934-5320	934-5348
Forms & Surfaces 30 Pine St *TF:* 800-553-7722 ■ *Web:* www.forms-surfaces.com	Pittsburgh	PA	15223	412-781-9003	781-7840
Gadsden Scaffold Co Inc 137 Ewing Ave *TF:* 800-538-1780 ■ *Web:* www.gadsdenscaffold.com	Gadsden	AL	35901	256-547-6918	549-5502
GS Metals Corp 3764 Longspur Rd **Fax:* Sales ■ *TF:* 800-851-9341 ■ *Web:* www.gsmetals.com	Pinckneyville	IL	62274	618-357-5353	357-3605*
Hapco Inc 26252 Hillman Hwy *TF:* 800-368-7171 ■ *Web:* www.hapco.com	Abingdon	VA	24210	276-628-7171	623-2594
Hart & Cooley Inc 500 E 8th St **Fax Area Code:* 800 ■ *TF:* 800-435-6341 ■ *Web:* www.hartandcooley.com	Holland	MI	49423	616-392-7855	223-8461*
Hunter Douglas Architectural Products Inc 5015 Oakbrook Pkwy Suite 100 *TF:* 800-366-4327 ■ *Web:* www.hunterdouglasceilings.com	Norcross	GA	30093	770-806-9557	806-0214
IKG Industries 1514 S Sheldon Rd *TF Cust Svc:* 800-324-8417 ■ *Web:* www.ikgindustries.com	Channelview	TX	77530	281-452-6637	
Irvine Access Floors Inc 9425 Washington Blvd Suite Y-WW *TF:* 800-969-8870 ■ *Web:* www.intandem.com/IrvineAccessFloors	Laurel	MD	20723	301-617-9333	617-9907
Jackburn Mfg Inc 438 Church St *Web:* www.jackburn.com	Girard	PA	16417	814-774-3573	774-2854
Laurel Steel Products Co 18 Mount Pleasant Rd *TF:* 800-426-1983 ■ *Web:* www.marwas.com	Scottdale	PA	15683	724-887-8090	887-7723
Lawrence Metal Products Inc 260 Spur Dr S PO Box 400-M *TF Sales:* 800-441-0019 ■ *Web:* www.lawrencemetal.com	Bay Shore	NY	11706	631-666-0300	666-0336
Livers Bronze Co 4621 E 75th Terr *Web:* www.liversbronze.com	Kansas City	MO	64132	816-300-2828	300-0864
LL Building Products Inc 295 McKoy Rd *Web:* www.llbuildingproducts.com	Burgaw	NC	28425	910-815-2600	259-6383
Marwas Steel Co DBA Laurel Steel Products Co 18 Mount Pleasant Rd *TF:* 800-426-1983 ■ *Web:* www.marwas.com	Scottdale	PA	15683	724-887-8090	887-7723
McGregor Industries Inc 46 Line St *TF:* 800-326-6786 ■ *Web:* www.mcgregorindustries.com	Dunmore	PA	18512	570-343-2436	343-4915
Milgo Industrial Inc 68 Lombardi St *Web:* www.milgo-bufkin.com	Brooklyn	NY	11222	718-388-4363	963-0614
Morton Mfg Co 700 Liberty Dr *Web:* www.mortonmfg.com	Libertyville	IL	60048	847-362-5400	362-5434
Moultrie Mfg Co 1403 Georgia Hwy 133 S PO Box 2948 *TF:* 800-841-8674 ■ *Web:* www.moultriemanufacturing.com	Moultrie	GA	31776	229-985-1312	890-7245
Overly Mfg Co 574 W Otterman St *TF:* 800-979-7300 ■ *Web:* www.overly.com	Greensburg	PA	15601	724-834-7300	830-2871
Patent Construction Systems 1 Mack Centre Dr *TF:* 800-969-5600 ■ *Web:* www.pcshd.com	Paramus	NJ	07652	201-261-5600	261-5544
Perry Mfg Co Inc 1233 W 18th St *TF:* 800-428-7200 ■ *Web:* www.perryscaffolds.com	Indianapolis	IN	46202	317-231-9037	231-9161
Spider Staging Corp 365 Upland Dr *TF:* 800-428-7887 ■ *Web:* www.spiderstaging.com	Tukwila	WA	98188	206-575-6445	575-6240
Steel Ceilings Inc 451 E Coshocton St *TF:* 800-848-0496 ■ *Web:* www.steelceilings.com	Johnstown	OH	43031	740-967-1063	967-1478
Superior Aluminum Products Inc 555 E Main St PO Box 430 *Web:* www.superioraluminum.com	Russia	OH	45363	937-526-4065	526-3904
Tate Access Floors Inc 7510 Montevideo Rd *TF:* 800-231-7788 ■ *Web:* www.tateaccessfloors.com	Jessup	MD	20794	410-799-4200	799-4207
Universal Builders Supply Inc 27 Horton Ave *TF:* 800-582-0070 ■ *Web:* www.ubs1.com	New Rochelle	NY	10801	914-699-2400	699-2609
Universal Mfg Corp 550 W New Castle St PO Box 220 *TF:* 800-836-8780	Zelienople	PA	16063	724-452-8300	452-0576
Velux-Greenwood Inc 450 Old Brickyard Rd *TF:* 800-688-3589 ■ *Web:* www.velux-america.com	Greenwood	SC	29648	864-941-4700	941-4870
Vicwest Corp 1296 South Service Rd W *TF:* 800-265-6583 ■ *Web:* www.vicwest.com	Oakville	ON	L6L5T7	905-825-2252	825-2272
Waco Scaffolding & Equipment Co 4545 Spring Rd PO Box 318028 *TF:* 800-901-2282 ■ *Web:* www.wacoscaf.com	Cleveland	OH	44131	216-749-8900	741-8486
Wooster Products Inc 1000 Spruce St *TF:* 800-321-4936 ■ *Web:* www.wooster-products.com	Wooster	OH	44691	330-264-2844	262-4151

Phone | Fax

Worthington Armstrong Venture (WAVE)
9 Old Lincoln Hwy Suite 200 ... Malvern PA 19355 610-722-1200 722-1247

495 METALS SERVICE CENTERS

Phone | Fax

ABC Metals Inc 500 W Clinton St ... Logansport IN 46947 574-753-0471 753-6110
TF: 800-238-8470 ■ *Web:* www.abcmetals.com

Alamo Iron Works Inc 943 AT&T Center Pkwy ... San Antonio TX 78219 210-223-6161 704-8351
TF Cust Svc: 800-292-7817 ■ *Web:* www.aiwnet.com

Alaskan Copper & Brass Co 3223 6th Ave S ... Seattle WA 98134 206-623-5800 382-7335
TF: 800-552-7661 ■ *Web:* www.alascop.com

Alcoa Inc 201 Isabella St ... Pittsburgh PA 15212 412-553-4545 553-4498
NYSE: AA ■ *Web:* www.alcoa.com

Alro Steel Corp 3100 E High St ... Jackson MI 49203 517-787-5500 787-6390
TF: 800-877-2576 ■ *Web:* www.alro.com

AM Castle & Co 3400 N Wolf Rd ... Franklin Park IL 60131 847-455-7111 455-0587*
AMEX: CAS ■ **Fax:* Sales ■ *TF:* 800-289-2785 ■ *Web:* www.amcastle.com

American Steel LLC 4033 NW Yeon Ave ... Portland OR 97210 503-226-1511 225-0211
TF: 800-547-9032 ■ *Web:* www.americansteel.com

American Strip Steel Inc 400 Metuchen Rd ... South Plainfield NJ 07080 201-991-1500
TF: 800-526-1216 ■ *Web:* www.americanstrip.com

AMI Metals Inc 1738 General George Patton Dr ... Brentwood TN 37027 615-377-0400 377-0103
TF: 800-727-1903 ■ *Web:* www.amimetals.com

Art Iron Inc 860 Curtis St ... Toledo OH 43609 419-241-1261 242-9768
TF: 800-472-1113 ■ *Web:* www.artiron.com

Bing Metals Group Steel Processing Div 1500 E Euclid St ... Detroit MI 48211 313-875-2022 875-2328
TF: 800-521-1564 ■ *Web:* www.binggroup.com

Bobco Metals Co 2000 S Alameda St ... Los Angeles CA 90058 800-262-2605 748-5824*
**Fax Area Code:* 213 ■ *TF:* 800-262-2605 ■ *Web:* www.bobcomall.com

Bohler-Uddeholm North America 2505 Millenium Dr ... Elgin IL 60124 630-883-3100 883-3101
TF: 800-638-2520 ■ *Web:* www.bucorp.com

Bralco Metals Div Reliance Steel & Aluminum Co
15090 Northam St ... La Mirada CA 90638 714-736-4800 736-4840
TF: 800-628-1864 ■ *Web:* www.bralco.com

Brown-Strauss Steel 2495 Uravan St ... Aurora CO 80011 303-371-2200 375-8122
TF Sales: 800-677-2778 ■ *Web:* www.brown-strauss.com

Cambridge-Lee Industries Inc 1340 Soldiers Field Rd ... Brighton MA 02135 617-783-3100 746-1169*
**Fax:* Sales ■ *TF:* 800-225-4378 ■ *Web:* www.camlee.com

Cambridge Street Metal Co Inc 500 Lincoln St ... Allston MA 02134 617-254-7580 254-3552
Web: www.cambridgestreetmetal.com

Castle AM & Co 3400 N Wolf Rd ... Franklin Park IL 60131 847-455-7111 455-0587*
AMEX: CAS ■ **Fax:* Sales ■ *TF:* 800-289-2785 ■ *Web:* www.amcastle.com

Castle Metals Inc 2505 Millenium Dr ... Elgin IL 60124 630-883-3100 883-3101
TF: 800-289-2785 ■ *Web:* www.castlemetals.com

Central Steel & Wire Co 3000 W 51st St ... Chicago IL 60632 773-471-3800 232-9279*
**Fax Area Code:* 800 ■ *TF:* 800-621-8510 ■ *Web:* www.centralsteel.com

Chatham Steel Corp 501 W Boundary St ... Savannah GA 31402 912-233-4182 944-0265*
**Fax:* Hum Res ■ *TF:* 800-546-2650 ■ *Web:* www.chathamsteel.com

Chicago Tube & Iron Co 1 Chicago Tube Dr ... Romeoville IL 60446 815-834-2500 588-3958
TF Cust Svc: 800-972-0217 ■ *Web:* www.chicagotube.com

Clayton Metals Inc 546 Clayton Ct ... Wood Dale IL 60191 800-323-7628 860-1053*
**Fax Area Code:* 630 ■ *Web:* www.claytonmetals.com

CMC Joist & Deck 25 DeForest Ave ... Summit NJ 07901 908-277-1617 277-1619
TF: 800-631-1215 ■ *Web:* www.cmcjoist.com

CMC Rebar 4846 Singleton Blvd ... Dallas TX 75712 214-631-5250 637-1110
Web: www.cmc.com

Coilplus Pennsylvania Inc 5135 Bleigh St ... Philadelphia PA 19136 215-331-5200 331-9538
TF: 800-355-5200

Columbia Pipe & Supply Co 1120 W Pershing Rd ... Chicago IL 60609 773-927-6600 927-8415
TF: 888-361-7700 ■ *Web:* www.columbiapipe.com

Commercial Metals Co (CMC) 6565 N MacArthur Blvd Suite 800 ... Irving TX 75039 214-689-4300 689-5886
NYSE: CMC ■ *Web:* www.commercialmetals.com

Commercial Metals Co Dallas Trading Div
6565 N MacArthur Blvd Suite 800 ... Irving TX 75039 214-689-4300 689-5886
Web: www.commercialmetals.com/daltrade.asp

Commonwealth Metal Corp 2200 Fletcher Ave ... Fort Lee NJ 07024 201-569-2000 569-8628
TF: 800-772-2119

Consolidated Pipe & Supply Inc 1205 Hilltop Pkwy ... Birmingham AL 35204 205-323-7261 251-7838
TF Sales: 800-467-7261 ■ *Web:* www.consolidatedpipe.com

Contractors Steel Co 36555 A,rjeo, Rd ... :ovpmoa MI 48150 734-464-4000 452-3939*
**Fax:* Sales ■ *TF:* 800-521-3946 ■ *Web:* www.contractorssteel.com

Copper & Brass Sales 22355 W 11 Mile Rd ... Southfield MI 48033 248-233-5600 233-5699
TF: 800-926-2600 ■ *Web:* www.copperandbrass.com

Coral Sales Co 9838 SE 17th Ave ... Milwaukie OR 97222 503-655-6351 657-9649
TF: 800-538-7245 ■ *Web:* www.coralsales.com

Corus America Inc 475 N Martingale Rd Suite 400 ... Schaumburg IL 60173 847-619-0400 619-0468
TF: 800-542-6244 ■ *Web:* www.corusgroup.com

Decker Steel & Supply Inc 4500 Train Ave ... Cleveland OH 44102 216-281-7900 281-1441
TF: 800-321-6100 ■ *Web:* www.deckersteel.com

Duhig & Co Inc PO Box 226966 ... Los Angeles CA 90022 323-263-7161 263-3891
Web: www.duhig.com

East Coast Metal Distributors Inc 1313 S Briggs Ave ... Durham NC 27703 919-598-5030 598-1404
Web: www.ecmdi.com

Eaton Steel Corp 10221 Capital Ave ... Oak Park MI 48237 248-398-3434 398-1434
TF: 800-527-3851 ■ *Web:* www.eatonsteel.com

Edgcomb Metals Co 555 State Rd ... Bensalem PA 19020 215-639-4000 245-3373*
**Fax:* Sales ■ *TF:* 800-562-6777

Energy & Process Corp 2146B Flintstone Dr ... Tucker GA 30084 770-934-3101 938-8903
TF: 800-241-9460 ■ *Web:* www.energyandprocess.com

Farwest Steel Corp 2000 Henderson Ave ... Eugene OR 97403 541-686-2000 681-7241*
**Fax:* Hum Res ■ *TF:* 800-542-5091 ■ *Web:* www.farweststeel.com

Feralloy Corp 8755 W Higgins Rd Suite 970 ... Chicago IL 60631 773-380-1500 380-1535
Web: www.feralloy.com

Friedman Industries Inc PO Box 21147 ... Houston TX 77226 713-672-9433 672-7043
AMEX: FRD ■ *TF:* 800-899-7695 ■ *Web:* www.friedmanindustries.com

Future Metals Inc 10401 State St ... Tamarac FL 33321 954-724-1400 721-5050
TF: 800-733-0960 ■ *Web:* www.futuremetals.com

Gerber Metal Supply Co 2 Boundary Rd ... Somerville NJ 08876 908-823-9150 823-9160
TF: 800-836-4672 ■ *Web:* www.gerbermetal.com

Gibbs Wire & Steel Co Inc PO Box 520 ... Southington CT 06489 860-621-0121 628-7780
TF: 800-800-4422 ■ *Web:* www.gibbswire.com

Gibraltar Metals Corp 1050 Military Rd ... Buffalo NY 14217 716-875-7920 875-7381
TF: 800-873-6322

Hanna Steel Corp 3812 Commerce Ave ... Fairfield AL 35064 205-780-1111 783-8290
TF: 800-633-8252 ■ *Web:* www.hannasteel.com

Hickman Williams & Co 250 E 5th St Suite 300 ... Cincinnati OH 45202 513-621-1946 621-0024
Web: www.hicwilco.com

Hummelstein Iron & Metal Inc PO Box 1580 ... Jonesboro AR 72403 870-932-8361 935-4044
Web: www.hummelstein.com

Independent Steel Co 615 Liverpool Dr ... Valley City OH 44280 330-225-7741 273-6265
Web: www.independentsteel.com

Infra-Metals 400 Northridge Rd Suite 850 ... Atlanta GA 30350 770-641-6460 641-6495
Web: www.infra-metals.com

Phone | Fax

Kane Steel Co PO Box 829 ... Millville NJ 08332 856-825-2200 327-0762
TF: 800-223-5263 ■ *Web:* www.kanesteel.com

Ken-Mac Metals Inc 17901 Englewood Dr ... Cleveland OH 44130 440-234-7500 234-4459
TF: 800-831-9503 ■ *Web:* www.kenmacmetals.com

Kenwal Steel Corp 8223 W Warren Ave ... Dearborn MI 48126 313-739-1000 739-1001
TF: 800-521-7522 ■ *Web:* www.kenwal.com

Kerry Steel Inc 31731 Northwestern Hwy Suite 200 ... Farmington Hills MI 48334 248-352-0000 352-2589
Web: www.kerrysteel.com

Klein Steel Service 105 Vanguarden Pkwy ... Rochester NY 14606 585-328-4000 328-0470
TF: 800-477-6789 ■ *Web:* www.kleinsteel.com

Kreher Steel Co LLC 1550 N 25th Ave ... Melrose Park IL 60160 708-345-8180 345-8293
TF: 800-323-0745 ■ *Web:* www.kreher.com

LaBarge Pipe & Steel Co 500 N Broadway Suite 1600 ... Saint Louis MO 63102 314-231-3400 982-9395*
**Fax:* Sales ■ *TF:* 800-325-3363 ■ *Web:* www.labargepipe.com

Lapham-Hickey Steel Corp 5500 W 73rd St ... Chicago IL 60638 708-496-6111 496-8504
TF Cust Svc: 800-323-8443 ■ *Web:* www.lapham-hickey.com

Lexington Steel Corp 5443 W 70th Pl ... Bedford Park IL 60638 708-594-9200 594-5233
Web: www.lexsteel.com

Lindquist Steels Inc 1050 Woodend Rd ... Stratford CT 06615 203-377-2828 386-0132
TF: 800-243-9637 ■ *Web:* www.lindquiststeels.com

Lyon Conklin & Co 7030 Troy Hill Dr Suite 700A ... Elkridge MD 21075 410-540-2800 796-1087
TF: 800-759-5966

Maas-Hansen Steel Corp 2435 E 37th St ... Vernon CA 90058 323-583-6321 586-9535
TF: 800-647-8335 ■ *Web:* www.maashansen.com

Macsteel Service Centers USA
888 San Clemente Dr Suite 250 ... Newport Beach CA 92660 949-219-9000 219-9009
TF: 866-622-7833 ■ *Web:* www.macsteelusa.com

Majestic Steel USA 5300 Majestic Pkwy ... Bedford Heights OH 44146 440-786-2666 786-0576
TF: 800-321-5590 ■ *Web:* www.majesticsteel.com

Marmon/Keystone Corp PO Box 992 ... Butler PA 16003 724-283-3000 283-0558
TF: 800-544-1748 ■ *Web:* www.marmonkeystone.com

McNichols Co 2502 N Rocky Point Dr Suite 950 ... Tampa FL 33607 813-282-3828 287-1066
TF: 800-237-3828 ■ *Web:* www.mcnichols.com

Merit USA 620 Clark Ave ... Pittsburg CA 94565 925-427-2500 427-6427
TF: 800-445-6374 ■ *Web:* www.meritsteel.com

MetalCenter Inc 12034 S Greenstone Ave ... Santa Fe Springs CA 90670 562-944-3322 944-1346
TF: 800-448-0001

Metals USA Inc 1 Riverway Suite 1100 ... Houston TX 77056 713-965-0990 965-0067
TF: 888-871-8701 ■ *Web:* www.metalsusa.com

Metrolina Steel Inc PO Box 790465 ... Charlotte NC 28206 704-598-7007 598-9135
TF: 800-849-7835 ■ *Web:* www.metrolinasteel.com

Mineral & Pigment Solutions Inc 1000 Coolidge St ... South Plainfield NJ 07080 908-561-6100 253-5041*
**Fax Area Code:* 800 ■ *TF:* 800-732-0562 ■ *Web:* www.mp-solutionsinc.com

Mitsubishi International Corp 655 3rd Ave ... New York NY 10017 212-605-2000
Web: www.micusa.com

Namasco Corp 500 Colonial Center Pkwy Suite 500 ... Roswell GA 30076 678-259-8800 259-8873
Web: www.namasco.com

National Material LP 1965 Pratt Blvd ... Elk Grove Village IL 60007 847-806-4700 806-7220
Web: www.nmlp.com

New Process Steel Corp 5800 Westview Dr ... Houston TX 77055 713-686-9631 686-3236
TF: 800-392-4989 ■ *Web:* www.newprocesssteel.com

Nippon Steel USA Inc 780 3rd Ave 34th Fl ... New York NY 10017 212-486-7150 593-3049
TF: 800-345-6477 ■ *Web:* www.nsc.co.jp

Okaya USA Inc 140 E Ridgewood Ave ... Paramus NJ 07652 201-734-7000 734-7500

Olympic Steel Inc 5080 Richmond Rd ... Bedford Heights OH 44146 216-292-3800 292-3513*
NASDAQ: ZEUS ■ **Fax:* Sales ■ *TF:* 800-321-6290 ■ *Web:* www.olysteel.com

O'Neal Steel Inc 744 41st St N ... Birmingham AL 35222 205-599-8000 599-8211*
**Fax:* Sales ■ *TF:* 800-292-4090 ■ *Web:* www.onealsteel.com

Owen Industries Inc 501 Ave H ... Carter Lake IA 51510 712-347-5500 347-6166
TF: 800-831-9252 ■ *Web:* www.owenind.com

Pacesetter Steel Service Inc 3300 Town Point Dr ... Kennesaw GA 30144 770-919-8000 581-8880*
**Fax Area Code:* 678 ■ *TF:* 800-749-6505 ■ *Web:* www.teampacesetter.com

Pacific Steel & Recycling 1401 3rd St NW ... Great Falls MT 59404 406-771-7222 453-4269
TF: 800-889-6264 ■ *Web:* www.pacific-recycling.com

Peterson Steel Corp 61 W Mountain St ... Worcester MA 01606 508-853-3630 853-7485
TF: 800-325-3245 ■ *Web:* www.petersonsteel.com

Petroleum Pipe & Supply Inc 516 Industry Way ... Heidelberg PA 15106 412-279-7710 279-9029

Phoenix Metals Co PO Box 805 ... Norcross GA 30091 770-447-4211 246-8166
TF: 800-241-2290 ■ *Web:* www.phoenixmetals.net

Pipe Distributors Inc 5400 Mesa Dr ... Houston TX 77028 713-635-4200 635-8465
TF: 800-989-7473

Precision Steel Warehouse Inc 3500 N Wolf Rd ... Franklin Park IL 60131 847-455-7000 455-1341
TF: 800-323-0740 ■ *Web:* www.precisionsteel.com

Premier Pipe LP 654 N Sam Houston Pkwy Suite 300 ... Houston TX 77060 832-300-8100 300-8198
Web: www.prempipe.com

Rancocas Metals Corp 35 Indel Ave ... Rancocas NJ 08073 609-267-4120 267-5690
TF: 800-762-6382 ■ *Web:* www.rancocasmetals.com

Reliance Steel & Aluminum Co
350 S Grand Ave Suite 5100 ... Los Angeles CA 90071 213-687-7700 687-8792
NYSE: RS ■ *Web:* www.rsac.com

Reliance Steel & Aluminum Co Bralco Metals Div
15090 Northam St ... La Mirada CA 90638 714-736-4800 736-4840
TF: 800-628-1864 ■ *Web:* www.bralco.com

Rolled Alloys Inc 125 W Sterns Rd ... Temperance MI 48182 734-847-0561 847-6917
TF: 800-521-0332 ■ *Web:* www.rolledalloys.com

Russel Metals Bahcall Group PO Box 1054 ... Appleton WI 54912 920-734-9271 730-5858
TF Sales: 800-236-0500

Russel Metals Inc 1900 Minnesota Ct Suite 210 ... Mississauga ON L5N3C9 905-819-7777 819-7409
TSX: RUS ■ *TF:* 800-268-0750 ■ *Web:* www.russelmetals.com

Ryerson PO Box 4725 ... Norcross GA 30091 770-368-4311 368-4230
TF: 800-243-8855

Ryerson Inc 2621 W 15th Pl ... Chicago IL 60608 773-762-2121 762-2194*
NYSE: RYI ■ **Fax:* Hum Res ■ *Web:* www.ryerson.com

Ryerson Inc 455 85th Ave NW ... Minneapolis MN 55433 763-717-9000 717-7168
TF: 800-328-7800 ■ *Web:* www.ryerson.com

Sabel Steel Industries Inc PO Box 4747 ... Montgomery AL 36103 334-265-6771 263-7949
TF Sales: 800-392-5754 ■ *Web:* www.sabelsteel.com

Service Steel & Pipe Inc 1130 Fullerton St ... Shreveport LA 71107 318-222-9462 424-6641
TF: 800-256-8598

Shamrock Steel Sales Inc 238 W County Rd S ... Odessa TX 79763 432-337-2317 337-5049
TF: 800-299-2317 ■ *Web:* shamrocksteelsales.com

Shane Steel Processing Inc 17495 Malyn St ... Fraser MI 48026 586-296-1990 296-2255
Web: www.shanesteel.com

Siskin Steel & Supply Co Inc PO Box 1191 ... Chattanooga TN 37401 423-756-3671 265-4758*
**Fax:* Mktg ■ *TF Sales:* 800-756-3671 ■ *Web:* www.siskin.com

Smith Pipe & Steel Inc 735 N 19th Ave ... Phoenix AZ 85009 602-257-9494 253-8770
TF Cust Svc: 800-352-4596

SOS Metals Inc PO Box 8712 ... West Chester OH 45071 513-896-2700 785-2350
Web: www.sossteel.com

State Pipe & Supply Inc 9615 S Norwalk Blvd ... Santa Fe Springs CA 90670 562-695-5555 692-1054
TF: 800-733-6410 ■ *Web:* www.statepipe.com

Staub Metals Corp PO Box 1425 ... Paramount CA 90723 562-602-2200 602-1358
TF: 800-447-8282 ■ *Web:* www.staubmetals.com

Steel Engineers Inc 716 W Mesquite Ave ... Las Vegas NV 89106 702-386-0023 386-6723
TF: 800-838-4043 ■ *Web:* www.steelengineers.com

Steel & Pipe Supply Co 555 Poyntz Ave ... Manhattan KS 66502 785-537-2222 587-5176
TF: 800-521-2345 ■ *Web:* www.spsci.com

Company	City	State	ZIP	Phone	Fax
Steel Warehouse Co Inc 2722 W Tucker Dr *TF:* 800-348-2529 ■ *Web:* www.steelwarehouse.com	South Bend	IN	46619	574-236-5100	236-5154
Texas Pipe & Supply Co Inc 2330 Holmes Rd *TF:* 800-233-8736 ■ *Web:* www.texaspipe.com	Houston	TX	77051	713-799-9235	799-8701
Timken Latrobe Steel Distribution 1551 Vienna Pkwy *TF:* 800-321-6446	Vienna	OH	44473	330-609-5137	609-2054
Tioga Pipe Supply Co Inc 2450 Wheatsheaf Ln *TF:* 800-523-3678 ■ *Web:* www.tiogapipe.com	Philadelphia	PA	19137	215-831-0700	533-1645
Titan Steel Corp 2500-B Broening Hwy *Web:* www.titansteel.com	Baltimore	MD	21224	410-631-5200	631-5212
Titanium Industries Inc 181 E Halsey Rd *TF:* 888-482-6486 ■ *Web:* www.titanium.com	Parsippany	NJ	07054	973-428-1900	428-7250
Toyota Tsusho America Inc 805 3rd Ave 16th Fl *TF:* 800-883-0100 ■ *Web:* www.taiamerica.com	New York	NY	10022	212-355-3600	355-3670
Transtar Metals 14400 S Figueroa St *Fax Area Code: 310 ■ *TF:* 800-344-4972 ■ *Web:* www.transtarmetals.com	Gardena	CA	90248	323-321-1700	679-0223*
Tubular Steel Inc 1031 Executive Pkwy Dr *TF:* 800-882-8527 ■ *Web:* www.tubularsteel.com	Saint Louis	MO	63141	314-851-9200	851-9336
TW Metals Inc PO Box 644 *Web:* www.twmetals.com	Exton	PA	19341	610-458-1300	458-1399
Universal Steel Co 6600 Grant Ave *TF:* 800-927-2659 ■ *Web:* www.univsteel.com	Cleveland	OH	44105	216-883-4972	341-0421
West Central Steel Inc 110 19th St NW *TF:* 800-992-8853 ■ *Web:* www.wcsteel.com	Willmar	MN	56201	320-235-4070	235-1816
Wrisco Industries Inc 355 Hiatt Dr Suite B *TF:* 800-627-2646 ■ *Web:* www.wrisco.com	Palm Beach Gardens	FL	33418	561-626-5700	627-3574

496 METALWORKING DEVICES & ACCESSORIES

SEE ALSO Machine Tools - Metal Cutting Types p. 1924; Machine Tools - Metal Forming Types p. 1925; Tool & Die Shops p. 2369

Company	City	State	ZIP	Phone	Fax
Acme Industrial Co 441 Maple Ave *TF:* 800-323-5582 ■ *Web:* www.acmeindustrial.com	Carpentersville	IL	60110	847-428-3911	428-1820
Advanced Machine & Engineering Co 2500 Latham St *TF:* 800-255-2331 ■ *Web:* www.ame.com	Rockford	IL	61103	815-962-6076	962-6483
Alcon Tool Co 587 Baird St *Web:* www.alcontool.com	Akron	OH	44311	330-773-9171	773-8042
Allied Machine & Engineering Corp 120 Deeds Dr *TF:* 800-321-5537 ■ *Web:* www.alliedmachine.com	Dover	OH	44622	330-343-4283	343-4781
American Broach & Machine Co 4600 Jackson Rd *Web:* www.americanbroach.com	Ann Arbor	MI	48103	734-761-5021	761-7626
American Cutting Edge Inc 480 Congress Park Dr *TF:* 888-252-3372 ■ *Web:* www.cbmfg.com	Dayton	OH	45459	937-438-2390	438-2398
American Drill Bushing Co 7141 Paramount Blvd *TF:* 800-423-4425 ■ *Web:* www.americandrillbushing.com	Pico Rivera	CA	90660	323-725-1515	725-8740
Apex Broach & Machine Co 22862 Hoover Rd *Web:* www.apexbroach.com	Warren	MI	48089	586-758-2626	758-2627
ASKO Inc 501 W 7th Ave *TF:* 800-321-1310 ■ *Web:* www.askoinc.com	Homestead	PA	15120	412-461-4110	461-5400
ATI Metal Working Products 1 Teledyne Pl *Fax Area Code: 800 ■ *Fax: Sales ■ *TF:* 800-521-2375 ■ *Web:* www.metalworkingproducts.com	La Vergne	TN	37086	615-641-4200	223-2219*
Balax Inc PO Box 96 *Web:* www.balax.com	North Lake	WI	53064	262-966-2355	966-1028
Besly Cutting Tools Inc 16200 Woodmint Ln *TF:* 800-435-2965 ■ *Web:* www.besly.com	South Beloit	IL	61080	815-389-2231	389-1339
Big Kaiser Precision Tooling Inc 641 Fargo Ave *TF:* 800-553-5113 ■ *Web:* www.bigkaiser.com	Elk Grove Village	IL	60007	847-228-7660	228-0881
Boley Tool & Machine Works Inc 1044 Spring Bay Rd *Web:* www.boleytool.com	East Peoria	IL	61611	309-694-2722	694-7879
Brubaker Tool Corp 200 Front St *TF:* 800-522-8665 ■ *Web:* www.brubakertool.com	Millersburg	PA	17061	717-692-2113	692-4995
Buck Chuck Co 2155 Traversefield Dr *TF:* 800-228-2825 ■ *Web:* www.buckchuckusa.com	Traverse City	MI	49686	231-947-5755	947-4953
Carbro Corp 15724 Condon Ave PO Box 278 *TF:* 888-738-4400	Lawndale	CA	90260	310-643-8400	643-9703
Carl Zeiss Inc Industrial Measuring Technology Div 6250 Sycamore Ln N *TF:* 800-752-6181 ■ *Web:* www.zeiss.com/imt	Maple Grove	MN	55369	763-744-2400	533-0218
CERATIZIT USA Inc 5369 Rt 982 N PO Box 272 *TF:* 800-245-6880 ■ *Web:* www.ceratizit.com	Latrobe	PA	15650	724-694-8100	694-8620
Cincinnati Gilbert Machine Tool Co LLC 3366 Beekman St *Web:* www.cincinnatigilbert.com	Cincinnati	OH	45223	513-541-4815	541-4885
CJT Koolcarb Inc 494 Mission St *TF:* 800-323-2299 ■ *Web:* www.cjtkoolcarb.com	Carol Stream	IL	60188	630-690-5933	690-6355
ClappDiCO Corp 6325 Industrial Pkwy *TF:* 800-537-6445 ■ *Web:* www.clappdico.com	Whitehouse	OH	43571	419-877-5358	877-5196
Climax Portable Machine Tools Inc 2712 E 2nd St *TF:* 800-333-8311 ■ *Web:* www.cpmt.com	Newberg	OR	97132	503-538-2185	537-5282
Cogsdill Tool Products Inc PO Box 7007	Camden	SC	29020	803-438-4000	438-5263
Cole Carbide Industries Inc 24703 Ryan Rd *Web:* www.colecarbide.com	Warren	MI	48091	586-757-8700	758-6930
Deltronic Corp 3900 W Segerstrom Ave *TF:* 800-451-6922 ■ *Web:* www.deltronic.com	Santa Ana	CA	92704	714-545-0401	641-0946
Detroit Edge Tool Co 6570 E Nevada St *TF:* 800-404-2038 ■ *Web:* www.detroitedge.com	Detroit	MI	48234	313-366-4120	366-1661
Dundick Corp 4616 W 20th St *TF:* 800-322-4243 ■ *Web:* www.dundick.com	Cicero	IL	60804	708-656-6363	656-2359
Duramet Corp 11350 Stephens Rd *TF:* 800-783-2280	Warren	MI	48089	586-759-2280	759-1657
Edmunds Gages 45 Spring Ln *Web:* www.edmundsgages.com	Farmington	CT	06032	860-677-2813	677-4243
Enmark Tool & Gage Co Inc 18100 Cross Ln *Web:* www.enmarktool.com	Fraser	MI	48026	586-293-2797	293-1037
Fastcut Tool Corp 200 Front St *TF:* 800-682-8832 ■ *Web:* www.fastcut.com	Millersburg	PA	17061	717-692-8232	692-2707
Fullerton Tool Co Inc 121 Perry St *TF:* 800-248-8315 ■ *Web:* www.fullertontool.com	Saginaw	MI	48602	989-799-4550	792-3335
Gaiser Tool Co 4544 McGrath St *Web:* gaisertool.com	Ventura	CA	93003	805-644-5583	644-2013
Garr Tool Co 7800 N Alger Rd *TF:* 800-248-9003 ■ *Web:* www.garrtool.com	Alma	MI	48801	989-463-6171	463-3609
General Broach Co 307 Salisbury St *Web:* www.generalbroach.com	Morenci	MI	49256	517-458-7555	458-6821
General Cutting Tool Inc 6440 N Ridgeway Ave *Web:* www.generalcuttingtools.com	Lincolnwood	IL	60712	847-677-8770	677-8786
General Industrial Diamond Inc (GIDCO) 140 Algonquin Pkwy *Web:* www.gidco.com	Whippany	NJ	07981	973-884-2500	884-0392
Giddings & Lewis Machine Tools 142 Doty St PO Box 590 *Web:* www.glmachinetools.com	Fond du Lac	WI	54936	920-921-9400	906-2522
Glastonbury Southern Gage 46 Industrial Park Rd *Fax Area Code: 800 ■ *TF:* 800-251-4243 ■ *Web:* www.gsgage.com	Erin	TN	37061	931-289-4243	242-7142*
Gleason Cutting Tools Corp 1351 Windsor Rd *Web:* www.gleason.com	Loves Park	IL	61111	815-877-8900	877-0264
Goss & DeLeeuw Machine Co 100 Harding St *Web:* www.goss-deleeuw.com	Kensington	CT	06037	860-828-4121	828-8132
Guhring Inc 1445 Commerce Ave *TF:* 800-776-6170 ■ *Web:* www.guhring.com	Brookfield	WI	53045	262-784-6730	784-1984
Hanlo Gages & Engineering Co 34403 Glendale St *Web:* www.hanlogages.com	Livonia	MI	48150	734-422-4224	422-2244
Hannibal Carbide Tool Inc 5000 Paris Gravel Rd *TF:* 800-451-9436 ■ *Web:* www.hannibalcarbide.com	Hannibal	MO	63401	573-221-2775	221-1147
Hardinge Inc 1 Hardinge Dr *NASDAQ: HDNG* ■ *TF:* 800-843-8801 ■ *Web:* www.hardinge.com	Elmira	NY	14905	607-734-2281	732-4925
Hayden Twist Drill & Tool Co Inc 22822 Globe St *TF:* 800-521-1780 ■ *Web:* www.haydendrills.com	Warren	MI	48089	586-754-7700	754-3312
Heidenhain Corp 333 State Pkwy *Web:* www.heidenhain.com	Schaumburg	IL	60173	847-490-1191	490-3931
High Tech Tool Inc 7803 South Loop E *Web:* www.hightechtool.com	Houston	TX	77012	713-641-2303	641-6664
Hoppe Tool Inc 107 1st Ave *TF Sales:* 800-742-6571 ■ *Web:* www.hoppetool.com	Chicopee	MA	01020	413-592-9213	592-4688
Hougen Mfg Inc 3001 Hougen Dr *TF Orders:* 800-462-7818 ■ *Web:* www.hougen.com	Swartz Creek	MI	48473	810-635-7111	635-8277
Huron Machine Products Inc 228 SW 21st Terr *Fax: Sales ■ *TF:* 800-327-8186 ■ *Web:* www.huronmachine.com	Fort Lauderdale	FL	33312	954-587-4541	583-2154*
Husqvarna Inc 17400 W 119th St *Web:* www.husqvarna.com	Olathe	KS	66061	800-421-2222	825-0028
Industrial Tools Inc 1111 S Rose Ave *TF:* 800-266-5561 ■ *Web:* www.indtools.com	Oxnard	CA	93033	805-483-1111	483-6302
Invo Spline Inc 2357 E Nine-Mile Rd *TF Cust Svc:* 800-959-0884	Warren	MI	48090	586-757-8840	757-8849
Iowa Precision Industries Inc 5480 6th St SW *Web:* www.iowaprecision.com	Cedar Rapids	IA	52404	319-364-9181	364-3436
ITW Workholding Group 2155 Traverse Field Dr *TF:* 800-228-2825	Traverse City	MI	49686	231-947-5755	947-4953
Jasco Cutting Tools 1390 Mt Read Blvd *TF:* 800-868-1074 ■ *Web:* www.jascotools.com	Rochester	NY	14606	585-546-1254	254-2655
Jasco Tools Inc 1390 Mt Read Blvd PO Box 60497 *TF:* 800-724-5497 ■ *Web:* www.jascotools.com	Rochester	NY	14606	585-254-7000	254-2655
Jergens Inc 15700 S Waterloo Rd *TF:* 800-537-4367 ■ *Web:* www.jergensinc.com	Cleveland	OH	44110	216-486-2100	481-6193
Kennametal Inc 1600 Technology Way PO Box 231 *NYSE: KMT* ■ *TF Cust Svc:* 800-446-7738 ■ *Web:* www.kennametal.com	Latrobe	PA	15650	724-539-5000	539-8787
KEO Cutters Inc 25040 Easy St *TF:* 888-390-2050 ■ *Web:* www.keocutters.com	Warren	MI	48089	586-771-2050	771-2062
Lancaster Knives Inc 165 Court St *TF:* 800-869-9666 ■ *Web:* www.lancasterknives.com	Lancaster	NY	14086	716-683-5050	683-5068
Liberty Special Tool Co 4815 Delemere Ave	Royal Oak	MI	48073	248-280-2600	
Lovejoy Tool Co Inc 133 Main St *TF:* 800-843-8376 ■ *Web:* www.lovejoytool.com	Springfield	VT	05156	802-885-2194	885-9511
Madison Cutting Tools Inc 485 Narragansett Park Dr *Web:* www.madisoncuttingtools.com	Pawtucket	RI	02861	401-333-0400	333-4011
Melin Tool Co 5565 Venture Dr Unit C *Fax Area Code: 800 ■ *TF:* 800-521-1078 ■ *Web:* www.endmill.com	Cleveland	OH	44130	216-362-4200	521-1558*
NED Corp 18 Grafton St 2nd Fl *TF:* 800-343-6086 ■ *Web:* www.nedcorp.com	Worcester	MA	01604	508-798-8546	799-2796
Niagara Cutter Inc 200 John James Audubon Pkwy *TF:* 888-689-8400 ■ *Web:* www.niagaracutter.com	Amherst	NY	14228	716-689-8400	689-8485
North American Tool Corp 215 Elmwood Ave *Fax Area Code: 800 ■ *TF:* 800-872-8277 ■ *Web:* www.natool.com	South Beloit	IL	61080	815-389-2300	872-3299*
Norton Co Diamond Tool Div 65 Beale Rd *TF Cust Svc:* 800-215-4614	Arden	NC	28704	828-684-2500	684-9167
Onsrud Cutter LP 800 Liberty Dr *TF:* 800-234-1560 ■ *Web:* www.onsrud.com	Libertyville	IL	60048	847-362-1560	362-5028
OSG Tap & Die Inc 676 E Fullerton Ave *TF:* 800-837-2223 ■ *Web:* www.osgtool.com	Glendale Heights	IL	60139	630-790-1400	653-2821
PCC Specialty Products Inc 809 Philip Dr	Waukesha	WI	53186	262-547-6886	547-8166
Powers Fasteners Inc 2 Powers Ln *TF:* 800-524-3244 ■ *Web:* www.powers.com	Brewster	NY	10509	914-235-6300	576-6483
Precitech Precision Inc 44 Blackbrook Rd *TF:* 800-295-2510 ■ *Web:* www.precitech.com	Keene	NH	03431	603-357-2511	358-6174
Products Engineering Corp 2645 Maricopa St *Web:* www.productsengineering.com	Torrance	CA	90503	310-787-4500	787-4501
Quinco Tool Products Co 21000 Hubbell Rd *Fax Area Code: 800 ■ *TF:* 800-521-1910 ■ *Web:* www.quinco.com	Oak Park	MI	48237	248-968-5000	468-4730*
Regal-Beloit Corp 200 State St *NYSE: RBC* ■ *Web:* www.regal-beloit.com	Beloit	WI	53511	608-364-8800	364-8818
Reiff & Nestor Co 50 Reiff St PO Box 147 *TF:* 800-521-3422 ■ *Web:* www.rntap.com	Lykens	PA	17048	717-453-7113	453-7555
RMT Technology 435 Eastern Ave *TF:* 800-228-9949 ■ *Web:* www.rmt.net	Bellwood	IL	60104	708-344-3280	544-7143
Royal Machine & Tool Corp 4 Willowbrook Dr *Web:* www.royalworkholding.com	Berlin	CT	06037	860-828-6555	828-1591
S-T Industries Inc 301 Armstrong Blvd N *TF:* 800-326-2039 ■ *Web:* www.stindustries.com	Saint James	MN	56081	507-375-3211	375-4503
Scotchman Industries Inc 180 E Hwy 14 *TF:* 800-843-8844 ■ *Web:* www.scotchman.com	Philip	SD	57567	605-859-2542	859-2499
Scully Jones Seibert Corp 1901 S Rockwell St *TF:* 800-752-8665 ■ *Web:* www.scullyjones.com	Chicago	IL	60608	773-247-5900	247-6088
Seco Tools 11177 E Eight-Mile Rd *Fax: Cust Svc ■ *Web:* www.secotools.com	Warren	MI	48089	586-497-5000	497-5627*
SKF Precision Technologies 1230 Cheyenne Ave *TF:* 800-445-6267 ■ *Web:* www.skfpt.com	Grafton	WI	53024	262-377-2434	377-9438
Smith TM Tool International Corp 360 Hubbard Ave PO Box 1065 *TF:* 800-521-4894 ■ *Web:* www.tmsmith-tool.com	Mount Clemens	MI	48046	586-468-1465	468-7190
Somma Tool Co Inc 109 Scott Rd *Web:* www.sommatool.com	Waterbury	CT	06705	203-753-2114	756-5489
Spiralock Corp 25235 Dequindre Rd *TF:* 800-521-2688 ■ *Web:* www.spiralock.com	Madison Heights	MI	48071	248-543-7800	543-1403
Star Cutter Co 23461 Industrial Park Dr *TF:* 800-968-2801 ■ *Web:* www.starcutter.com	Farmington	MI	48335	248-474-8200	474-9518
Starrett Webber Gage Div 24500 Detroit Rd *Web:* www.starrett-webber.com	Cleveland	OH	44145	440-835-0001	892-9555
Stilson Products 15935 Sturgeon St *TF:* 888-400-5978	Roseville	MI	48066	586-778-1100	778-4660
Strong Tool Co 1251 E 286th St *TF:* 800-362-0293 ■ *Web:* www.strongtool.com	Cleveland	OH	44132	216-289-2450	289-4562
Tapmatic Corp 802 Clearwater Loop *TF:* 800-854-6019 ■ *Web:* www.tapmatic.com	Post Falls	ID	83854	208-773-8048	773-3021
Thread Check Inc 390 Oser Ave *TF:* 800-767-7633 ■ *Web:* www.threadcheck.com	Hauppauge	NY	11788	631-231-1515	231-1625
TM Smith Tool International Corp 360 Hubbard Ave PO Box 1065 *TF:* 800-521-4894 ■ *Web:* www.tmsmith-tool.com	Mount Clemens	MI	48046	586-468-1465	468-7190

Phone Fax

Toolmasters LLC 1400 Railroad Ave .... Rockford IL 61104 815-968-0961 968-5559
Web: www.toolmastersllc.com

Tools for Bending Inc 194 W Dakota Ave .... Denver CO 80223 303-777-7170 777-4749
TF Cust Svc: 800-873-3305 ■ *Web:* www.toolsforbending.com

Union Butterfield Corp 301 Industrial Ave PO Box 9000 .... Crystal Lake IL 60039 815-459-2040 432-9482*
**Fax Area Code:* 800 ■ *TF:* 800-222-8665 ■ *Web:* www.unionbutterfield.com

United Drill Bushing Corp 12200 Woodruff Ave .... Downey CA 90241 562-803-1521 486-3465*
**Fax Area Code:* 800 ■ *TF:* 800-486-3466 ■ *Web:* www.ucc-udb.com

US Drill Head Co 5298 River Rd .... Cincinnati OH 45233 513-941-0300 941-9110
Web: www.usdrillhead.com

Utica Enterprises Co 13231 23-Mile Rd .... Shelby Township MI 48315 586-726-4300 726-4316

Valenite LLC 1675 Whitcomb Ave .... Madison Heights MI 48071 248-589-1000 488-0695*
**Fax Area Code:* 800 ■ *TF Cust Svc:* 800-488-9112 ■ *Web:* www.valenite.com

Viking Drill & Tool Inc 355 State St .... Saint Paul MN 55107 651-227-8911 227-1793
TF: 800-328-4655 ■ *Web:* www.vikingdrill.com

Vulcan Tool Co 730 Lorraine Ave .... Dayton OH 45401 937-253-6194 253-1062
Web: www.vulcancut.com

WA Whitney Co 650 Race St .... Rockford IL 61101 815-964-6771 964-3175
TF: 800-435-2823 ■ *Web:* www.wawhitney.com

Walker Magnetics Group Inc 20 Rockdale St .... Worcester MA 01606 508-853-3232 852-8649
TF: 800-962-4638 ■ *Web:* www.walkermagnet.com

Walter USA Inc N22 W23855 Ridgeview Pkwy W .... Waukesha WI 53188 262-347-2401 347-2500
TF: 800-945-5554 ■ *Web:* www.walter-tools.com

Wapakoneta Machine Co 300 North St PO Box 429 .... Wapakoneta OH 45895 419-738-2131 738-5828
TF: 800-837-2131 ■ *Web:* www.wapakonetamachine.com

Webber Gage Div Starrett 24500 Detroit Rd .... Cleveland OH 44145 440-835-0001 892-9555
Web: www.starrett-webber.com

Weldon Tool Co 200 Front St .... Millersburg PA 17061 717-692-2113 692-5270
TF: 800-622-7742 ■ *Web:* www.endmills.com

Westfield Gage Co Inc 34 Hudson Dr PO Box 1130 .... Southwick MA 01077 413-569-9444 569-9449
Web: www.westfieldgage.com

Wisconsin Machine Tool Corp 3225 Gateway Rd Suite 100 .... Brookfield WI 53045 262-317-3048 317-3049
TF: 800-243-3078 ■ *Web:* www.machine-tool.com

Zagar Inc 24000 Lakeland Blvd .... Cleveland OH 44132 216-731-0500 731-8591
Web: www.zagar.com

Zeiss Carl Inc Industrial Measuring Technology Div
6250 Sycamore Ln N .... Maple Grove MN 55369 763-744-2400 533-0218
TF: 800-752-6181 ■ *Web:* www.zeiss.com/imt

Zenith Cutter Co 5200 Zenith Pkwy .... Loves Park IL 61111 815-282-5200 282-5232
TF: 800-223-5202 ■ *Web:* www.zenithcutter.com

497 METALWORKING MACHINERY

SEE ALSO Rolling Mill Machinery p. 2300

Phone Fax

ADS Machinery Corp 1201 Vine Ave NE .... Warren OH 44483 330-399-3601 399-1190
Web: www.adsmachinery.com

Armstrong Mfg Co 2135 NW 21st Ave .... Portland OR 97209 503-228-8381 228-8384
Web: www.armstrongblue.com

Artos Engineering Co W 228 N 2792 Duplainville Rd .... Waukesha WI 53186 262-524-6600 524-0400
Web: www.artosnet.com

Bachi Co 1201 Ardmore Ave W .... Itasca IL 60143 630-773-5600 773-5610
Web: www.bachiwinder.com

Balance Technology Inc 7035 Jomar Dr .... Whitmore Lake MI 48189 734-769-2100 769-2542
Web: www.balancetechnology.com

Belvac Production Machinery Inc 237 Graves Mill Rd .... Lynchburg VA 24502 434-239-0358 239-1964
TF: 800-423-5822 ■ *Web:* www.belvac.com

Bodine Assembly & Test Systems 230 Long Hill Cross Rd .... Shelton CT 06484 203-712-1900 712-1907
Web: www.bodine-assembly.com

Diversified Machine Inc 5353 Wilcox St .... Montague MI 49437 231-894-9051 894-4706
Web: www.divmi.com

Eubanks Engineering Co 3022 Inland Empire Blvd .... Ontario CA 91764 909-483-2456 483-2498
Web: www.eubanks.com

FANTA Equipment Co 6521 Storer Ave .... Cleveland OH 44102 216-281-1515 281-7755
Web: www.fantaequip.com

Finishing Equipment Inc 3640 Kennebec Dr .... Saint Paul MN 55122 651-452-1860 452-9851

Hayes-Lemmerz Equipment & Engineering 533 N Court St .... Au Gres MI 48703 989-876-7161 876-7162
Web: www.hayes-lemmerz.com

Hogan Mfg Inc 1638 Main St PO Box 398 .... Escalon CA 95320 209-838-7323 838-8648
Web: www.hoganmfg.com

Jovil Mfg Co Inc 10 Precision Rd .... Danbury CT 06810 203-798-7255 790-8645
Web: www.jovil.com

Merrill Tool & Machine Co Inc 21659 W Gratiot Rd .... Merrill MI 48637 989-643-7981 643-7875
Web: www.merrilltool.com

Mitsubishi Materials USA Corp 17401 Eastman St .... Irvine CA 92614 949-862-5100 862-5169
TF: 800-523-0800

Muller-Ray Corp 805 Housatonic Ave .... Bridgeport CT 06604 203-367-6910 367-6975

Pannier Corp 207 Sandusky St .... Pittsburgh PA 15212 412-323-4900 323-4962
TF: 800-233-2009 ■ *Web:* www.pannier.com

PCC Specialty Products Inc 809 Philip Dr .... Waukesha WI 53186 262-547-6886 547-8166

Pines Mfg Inc 30505 Clemens Rd .... Westlake OH 44145 440-835-5553 835-5556
TF: 800-207-2840 ■ *Web:* www.pines-mfg.com

Red Bud Industries 200 B & E Industrial Dr .... Red Bud IL 62278 618-282-3801 282-6718
TF: 800-851-4612 ■ *Web:* www.redbudindustries.com

Rowe Machinery & Automation Inc 76 Hinckley Rd .... Clinton ME 04927 207-426-2351 426-7453
TF: 800-247-2645 ■ *Web:* www.runwithrowe.com

Superior Machine Co of South Carolina Inc 692 N Cashua Rd .... Florence SC 29502 843-664-3001 664-3007
TF: 800-736-9898

Sweed Machinery Inc 653 2nd Ave PO Box 228 .... Gold Hill OR 97525 541-855-1512 855-1165
TF Sales: 800-888-1352 ■ *Web:* www.sweed.com

TDS Automation Inc 1801 E Bremer Ave .... Waverly IA 50677 319-483-4700 483-4797
Web: www.tdsautomation.com

Tridan International Inc 130 N Jackson St .... Danville IL 61832 217-443-3592 443-3894
TF: 800-369-3544 ■ *Web:* www.tridan.com

US Baird Corp 1700 Stratford Ave PO Box 9706 .... Stratford CT 06615 203-375-3361 378-6006
Web: www.usbaird.com

Weldun International Ltd 9850 Red Arrow Hwy .... Bridgman MI 49106 269-465-6986 465-5126*
**Fax:* Hum Res ■ *Web:* www.weldun.com

West Bond Inc 1551 Gene Autry Way .... Anaheim CA 92805 714-978-1551 978-0431
Web: www.westbond.com

Wright-K Technology Inc 2025 E Genesee Ave .... Saginaw MI 48601 989-752-3103 752-0670
TF: 800-752-3103 ■ *Web:* www.wright-k.com

498 METERS & OTHER COUNTING DEVICES

Phone Fax

3D Instruments Inc 2900 Whitestar Ave .... Huntington Beach CA 92649 714-399-9200 399-9221
Web: www.3dinstruments.com

AMETEK Inc Dixson Div 287 27 Rd .... Grand Junction CO 81503 970-244-1241 245-6267
TF: 888-302-0639 ■ *Web:* www.ametekdixson.com

AMETEK Sensor Technology Drexelbrook Div
205 Keith Valley Rd .... Horsham PA 19044 215-674-1234 674-2731
TF Cust Svc: 800-553-9092 ■ *Web:* www.drexelbrook.com

Badger Meter Inc 4545 W Brown Deer Rd .... Milwaukee WI 53223 414-355-0400
AMEX: BMI ■ *TF:* 800-876-3837 ■ *Web:* www.badgermeter.com

Beede Electrical Instrument Co 88 Village St .... Penacook NH 03303 603-753-6362 753-6201
Web: www.beede.com

Clark-Reliance Corp 16633 Foltz Pkwy .... Strongsville OH 44149 440-572-1500 238-8828
Web: www.clark-reliance.com

Controlotron Corp 155 Plant Ave .... Hauppauge NY 11788 631-231-3600 231-3334
TF: 800-275-8479 ■ *Web:* www.controlotron.com

Danaher Controls 1675 Delany Rd .... Gurnee IL 60031 847-662-2666 662-4150
TF: 800-873-8731 ■ *Web:* www.dancon.com

Dixson Div AMETEK Inc 287 27 Rd .... Grand Junction CO 81503 970-244-1241 245-6267
TF: 888-302-0639 ■ *Web:* www.ametekdixson.com

Drexelbrook Div AMETEK Sensor Technology
205 Keith Valley Rd .... Horsham PA 19044 215-674-1234 674-2731
TF Cust Svc: 800-553-9092 ■ *Web:* www.drexelbrook.com

Duncan Parking Technologies Inc 340 Industrial Park Rd .... Harrison AR 72601 870-741-5481 741-6806
TF Cust Svc: 800-338-6226 ■ *Web:* www.duncanindustries.com

Electro-Sensors Inc 6111 Blue Circle Dr .... Minnetonka MN 55343 952-930-0100 930-0130
NASDAQ: ELSE ■ *TF:* 800-328-6170 ■ *Web:* www.electro-sensors.com

Elster American Meter Co 2221 Industrial Rd .... Nebraska City NE 68410 402-873-8200 873-7616
TF: 888-295-7928 ■ *Web:* www.americanmeter.com

EMCO (Engineering Measurements Co)
1831 Lefthand Cir Suite C .... Longmont CO 80501 303-651-0550 682-7069
TF: 800-356-9362 ■ *Web:* www.emcoflow.com

Engineering Measurements Co (EMCO)
1831 Lefthand Cir Suite C .... Longmont CO 80501 303-651-0550 682-7069
TF: 800-356-9362 ■ *Web:* www.emcoflow.com

FMC Measurement Solutions 1602 Wagner Ave .... Erie PA 16510 814-898-5000 899-8249*
**Fax:* Hum Res ■ *TF:* 800-867-6484 ■
Web: www.fmctechnologies.com/MeasurementSolutions.aspx

Greenwald Industries 212 Middlesex Ave .... Chester CT 06412 860-526-0800 526-4205
TF: 800-221-0982 ■ *Web:* www.greenwaldindustries.com

Isspro Inc 2515 NE Riverside Way PO Box 11177 .... Portland OR 97211 503-288-4488 249-2999
TF: 888-447-7776 ■ *Web:* www.issproinc.com

Laser Technology Inc 7070 S Tucson Way .... Englewood CO 80112 303-649-1000 649-9710
TF: 800-280-6113 ■ *Web:* www.lasertech.com

Max Machinery Inc 1420 Healdsburg Ave .... Healdsburg CA 95448 707-433-7281 433-0571
Web: www.maxmachinery.com

Maxima Technologies Stewart Warner 1811 Rohrerstown Rd .... Lancaster PA 17601 717-581-1000 569-6372
Web: www.stewartwarner.com

McKesson Automated Prescription Systems
2800 S MacArthur Dr .... Alexandria LA 71301 318-229-4010 845-7179*
**Fax Area Code:* 800 ■ *TF:* 800-551-6578 ■ *Web:* www.mckessonaps.com

Metretek Inc 305 East Dr Suite A .... Melbourne FL 32904 321-259-9700 259-2900
TF: 800-327-8559 ■ *Web:* www.metretekfl.com

Minarik Corp 905 E Thompson Ave .... Glendale CA 91201 818-637-7500 507-8821
Web: www.minarikcorp.com

Pierburg Instruments Inc 47519 Halyard Dr .... Plymouth MI 48170 734-446-8360 414-9685
TF: 800-222-5283 ■ *Web:* www.pierburginstruments.com

PMP Corp 25 Security Dr .... Avon CT 06001 860-677-9656 674-0196
TF Cust Svc: 800-243-6628 ■ *Web:* www.pmp-corp.com

POM Inc 200 S Elmira Ave PO Box 430 .... Russellville AR 72802 479-968-2880 968-2840
TF: 800-331-7275 ■ *Web:* www.pom.com

Racine Federated Inc Hedland Div 8635 Washington Ave .... Racine WI 53406 262-639-6770 245-3569*
**Fax Area Code:* 800 ■ **Fax:* Sales ■ *TF:* 800-433-5263 ■ *Web:* www.hedland.com

Schlumberger Ltd 5599 San Felipe .... Houston TX 77056 713-513-2000 350-8114*
NYSE: SLB ■ **Fax Area Code:* 212 ■ *Web:* www.slb.com

Sparling Instruments Co Inc 4097 N Temple City Blvd .... El Monte CA 91731 626-444-0571 444-2314
TF Sales: 800-800-3569 ■ *Web:* www.sparlinginstruments.com

Teleflex Electrical Systems 6980 Professional Pkwy E .... Sarasota FL 34240 941-907-1000 907-1020
Web: www.tflx.com

Teleflex Morse Marine Products 640 N Lewis Rd .... Limerick PA 19468 610-495-7011 495-7470
Web: www.tfxmarine.com

Thermo Polysonics 9303 W Sam Houston Pkwy S .... Houston TX 77099 713-272-0404 272-5388

Thomas G Faria Corp 385 Norwich-New London Tpke .... Uncasville CT 06382 860-848-9271 848-2704
TF: 800-473-2742 ■ *Web:* www.faria-instruments.com

Woodward FST 700 N Centennial St .... Zeeland MI 49464 616-772-9171 772-7322
TF: 800-253-3295

499 MICROGRAPHICS PRODUCTS & SERVICES

Phone Fax

Anacomp Inc 15378 Ave of Science .... San Diego CA 92128 858-716-3400 716-3775
Web: www.anacomp.com

BMI Imaging Systems 1115 E Arques Ave .... Sunnyvale CA 94085 408-736-7444 736-4397
TF Cust Svc: 800-359-3456 ■ *Web:* www.bmiimaging.com

Comgraphics Inc 329 W 18th St 10th Fl .... Chicago IL 60616 312-226-0900 226-9411
Web: www.cgichicago.com

Comstor Productivity Center Inc 2219 N Dickey Rd .... Spokane WA 99212 509-534-5080 536-0281
TF: 800-776-2451 ■ *Web:* www.comstorinc.com

DPF Data Services Group Inc 1990 Swarthmore Ave .... Lakewood NJ 08701 732-370-8840 370-1751
TF: 800-431-4416 ■ *Web:* www.dpfdata.com

DST Output 2534 Madison Ave .... Kansas City MO 64108 816-221-1234 843-6579
Web: www.dstoutput.com

Eye Communication Systems Inc 455 E Industrial Dr .... Hartland WI 53029 262-367-1360 367-1362
TF: 800-558-2153 ■ *Web:* www.eyecom.com

GID Inc 2635 Zanker Rd .... San Jose CA 95134 408-232-5500 232-5501*
**Fax:* Sales ■ *Web:* www.gid-it.com

HF Group Inc 203 W Artesia Blvd .... Compton CA 90220 310-605-0755 608-1556
Web: www.myhfi.com

Imaging Assoc 7297 P Lee Hwy .... Falls Church VA 22042 703-536-0101 536-0102
Web: www.scanfilm.com

Indus International Inc 340 S Oak St PO Box 890 .... West Salem WI 54669 608-786-0300 786-0786
TF: 800-843-9377 ■ *Web:* www.indususa.com

Information Imaging Corp
20 S Linden Ave Bldg 2-B .... South San Francisco CA 94080 650-244-9911 244-9689
TF: 800-373-1834

Lason Inc 1305 Stephenson Hwy .... Troy MI 48083 248-597-5800 837-7100
Web: www.lason.com

Micro Com Systems Ltd 27 E 7th Ave .... Vancouver BC V5T1M5 604-872-6771 872-2533
Web: www.microcomsys.com

MicroFilm Products Co 157 Avalon Gardens Dr .... Nanuet NY 10954 845-371-3780 371-3780
TF: 800-642-7668 ■ *Web:* www.microfilmproducts.com

microMEDIA Imaging Systems Inc 1979 Marcus Ave .... Lake Success NY 11042 516-355-0300 355-0316
Web: www.imagingservices.com

Mohr Microfilm Corp 20 S Linden Ave Bldg 2-B .... South San Francisco CA 94080 650-244-9911 244-9689
TF: 800-373-1834

Prestige Products 9440 Tangerine Pl Suite 107 .... Fort Lauderdale FL 33324 954-474-4183 370-8516

500 MILITARY BASES

SEE ALSO Coast Guard Installations p. 1457

500-1 Air Force Bases

				Phone	Fax
Altus Air Force Base 100 Inez Blvd	Altus AFB	OK	73523	580-482-8100	481-5966
Web: www.altus.af.mil					
Andrews Air Force Base	Andrews AFB	MD	20762	301-981-4825	981-9039
Web: public.andrews.amc.af.mil/					
Arnold Air Force Base	Arnold AFB	TN	37389	931-454-3000	454-6086
Barksdale Air Force Base	Barksdale AFB	LA	71110	318-456-3065	456-5986
Web: www.barksdale.af.mil					
Beale Air Force Base	Beale AFB	CA	95903	530-634-3000	634-8895
Web: www.beale.af.mil					
Bolling Air Force Base 110 Luke Ave	Washington	DC	20038	202-767-4011	404-6300
Web: www.bolling.af.mil					
Brooks City-Base	San Antonio	TX	78235	210-536-1110	536-4736
Web: www.brooks.af.mil					
Cannon Air Force Base 100 S DL Ingram Blvd Suite 1098	Cannon AFB	NM	88103	505-784-3311	784-2338
Web: www.cannon.af.mil					
Charleston Air Force Base 102 E Hill Blvd	Charleston AFB	SC	29404	843-963-5608	963-5604
Web: public.charleston.amc.af.mil					
Columbus Air Force Base 555 7th St	Columbus AFB	MS	39710	662-434-7068	434-7009
Web: www.columbus.af.mil					
Davis-Monthan Air Force Base 5275 E Granite St	Davis-Monthan AFB	AZ	85707	520-228-3204	228-3328
Web: www.dm.af.mil					
Dover Air Force Base	Dover AFB	DE	19902	302-677-3372	677-2901
Web: public.dover.amc.af.mil					
Dyess Air Force Base	Dyess AFB	TX	79607	325-696-3113	696-2866
Web: www.dyess.af.mil					
Edwards Air Force Base	Edwards AFB	CA	93523	661-277-1110	277-2732
Web: www.edwards.af.mil					
Eglin Air Force Base	Eglin AFB	FL	32542	850-882-3931	882-6156
Web: www.eglin.af.mil					
Eielson Air Force Base	Eielson AFB	AK	99702	907-377-1110	377-1215
Web: www.eielson.af.mil					
Ellsworth Air Force Base 1958 Scott Dr	Ellsworth AFB	SD	57706	605-385-5056	385-4668
Web: www.ellsworth.af.mil					
Elmendorf Air Force Base	Elmendorf AFB	AK	99506	907-552-8153	552-5111
Web: www.elmendorf.af.mil					
Fairchild Air Force Base	Fairchild AFB	WA	99011	509-247-1212	247-5640
Web: public.fairchild.amc.af.mil/					
Goodfellow Air Force Base 351 Kearney Blvd	Goodfellow AFB	TX	76908	325-654-3877	654-5414
Web: www.goodfellow.af.mil					
Grand Forks Air Force Base	Grand Forks AFB	ND	58205	701-747-3000	747-5022
Web: public.grandforks.amc.af.mil					
Hanscom Air Force Base	Hanscom AFB	MA	01731	781-377-4441	377-5077
Web: www.hanscom.af.mil					
Hickam Air Force Base 800 Scott Cir	Hickam AFB	HI	96853	808-449-2490	449-3017
Web: www2.hickam.af.mil					
Hill Air Force Base	Hill AFB	UT	84056	801-777-5201	777-4640
Web: www.hill.af.mil					
Holloman Air Force Base	Holloman AFB	NM	88330	505-572-5406	572-5908
Web: www.holloman.af.mil					
Keesler Air Force Base	Biloxi	MS	39534	228-377-1110	377-3940
Web: www.keesler.af.mil					
Kirtland Air Force Base	Kirtland AFB	NM	87117	505-846-5991	
Web: www.kirtland.af.mil					
Lackland Air Force Base	Lackland AFB	TX	78236	210-671-1110	671-4592
Web: www.lackland.af.mil					
Langley Air Force Base	Langley AFB	VA	23665	757-764-1110	764-3315*
**Fax:* Library ■ *Web:* www.langley.af.mil					
Laughlin Air Force Base 561 Liberty Dr Suite 3	Laughlin AFB	TX	78843	830-298-5988	298-5047
Web: www.laughlin.af.mil					
Little Rock Air Force Base 1250 Thomas Ave	Little Rock AFB	AR	72099	501-987-1110	987-6978
Web: www.littlerock.af.mil					
Los Angeles Air Force Base 483 N Aviation Blvd	El Segundo	CA	90245	310-653-1750	
Web: www.losangeles.af.mil					
Luke Air Force Base	Luke AFB	AZ	85309	623-856-5853	856-6013
Web: www.luke.af.mil					
MacDill Air Force Base	MacDill AFB	FL	33621	813-828-7895	828-3653
Web: public.macdill.amc.af.mil					
Malmstrom Air Force Base	Malmstrom AFB	MT	59402	406-731-1110	731-4048
Web: www.malmstrom.af.mil					
Maxwell Air Force Base 55 Le May Plaza S	Maxwell AFB	AL	36112	334-953-2014	953-3379
Web: www.maxwell.af.mil					
McChord Air Force Base	McChord AFB	WA	98438	253-982-2621	984-5825
Web: public.mcchord.amc.af.mil					
McConnell Air Force Base	McConnell AFB	KS	67221	316-759-6100	759-3148
McGuire Air Force Base	McGuire AFB	NJ	08641	609-754-2104	754-6999
Web: public.mcguire.amc.af.mil					
Minot Air Force Base 201 Summit Dr	Minot AFB	ND	58705	701-723-6212	723-6534
Web: www.minot.af.mil					
Moody Air Force Base	Moody AFB	GA	31699	229-257-3395	257-4804
Web: www.moody.af.mil					
Mountain Home Air Force Base	Mountain Home AFB	ID	83648	208-828-6800	828-4205
Web: www.mountainhome.af.mil					
Nellis Air Force Base 4430 Grissom Ave Suite 107	Nellis AFB	NV	89191	702-652-2750	652-9838
Web: www.nellis.af.mil					
Offutt Air Force Base	Offutt AFB	NE	68113	402-294-1110	294-7172
Web: www.offutt.af.mil					
Patrick Air Force Base	Patrick AFB	FL	32925	321-494-5933	494-7302
Peterson Air Force Base	Peterson AFB	CO	80914	719-556-4696	554-9779
Web: www.peterson.af.mil					
Pope Air Force Base	Pope AFB	NC	28308	910-394-1110	394-4266
Web: public.pope.amc.af.mil					
Randolph Air Force Base 1 Washington Cir	Randolph AFB	TX	78150	210-652-1110	652-5412
Web: www.randolph.af.mil					
Robins Air Force Base	Robins AFB	GA	31098	478-926-1113	926-9597
Web: www.robins.af.mil					
Scott Air Force Base	Scott AFB	IL	62225	618-256-1110	
Web: public.scott.amc.af.mil					
Seymour Johnson Air Force Base 1510 Wright Brothers Ave	Seymour Johnson AFB	NC	27531	919-722-0027	722-0007
Web: www.seymourjohnson.af.mil					
Shaw Air Force Base 517 Lance Ave Suite 106	Shaw AFB	SC	29152	803-895-2019	895-2028*
**Fax:* PR ■ *Web:* www.shaw.af.mil					
Sheppard Air Force Base	Sheppard AFB	TX	76311	940-676-2511	
Web: www.sheppard.af.mil					
Shriever Air Force Base	Shriever AFB	CO	80912	719-567-5040	567-5306
Web: www.schriever.af.mil					
Tinker Air Force Base 3001 Staff Dr	Tinker AFB	OK	73145	405-739-2026	739-2882
Web: www-ext.tinker.af.mil					
Travis Air Force Base	Travis AFB	CA	94535	707-424-2011	424-5936
Web: public.travis.amc.af.mil					
Tyndall Air Force Base	Tyndall AFB	FL	32403	850-283-1110	283-3225
Web: www.tyndall.af.mil					
Vance Air Force Base 246 Brown Pkwy	Vance AFB	OK	73705	580-213-5000	213-6376
Vandenberg Air Force Base	Vandenberg AFB	CA	93437	805-606-3595	606-8303
Web: www.vandenberg.af.mil					
Warren Francis E Air Force Base 5305 Randall Ave	Warren AFB	WY	82005	307-773-1110	773-2074
Web: www.warren.af.mil					
Whiteman Air Force Base	Whiteman AFB	MO	65305	660-687-6123	687-7948
Web: www.whiteman.af.mil					
Wright-Patterson Air Force Base	Wright-Patterson AFB	OH	45433	937-257-1110	255-3370
Web: www.wpafb.af.mil					

500-2 Army Bases

				Phone	Fax
Fort AP Hill	Fort AP Hill	VA	22427	804-633-8120	633-8459
Web: www.aphill.army.mil					
Fort Belvoir	Fort Belvoir	VA	22060	703-806-4891	805-3151
Web: www.belvoir.army.mil					
Fort Benning	Fort Benning	GA	31905	706-545-5111	545-3329
Web: www.infantry.army.mil/fbhome					
Fort Bliss	Fort Bliss	TX	79916	915-568-2121	568-2995
Web: www.bliss.army.mil					
Fort Bragg	Fort Bragg	NC	28310	910-396-3111	396-4568
Web: www.bragg.army.mil					
Fort Buchanan	Fort Buchanan	PR	00934	787-707-5776	707-3323
Web: www.buchanan.army.mil					
Fort Campbell	Fort Campbell	KY	42223	270-798-2151	798-6247
Web: www.campbell.army.mil					
Fort Carson	Fort Carson	CO	80913	719-526-4143	526-1021
Web: www.carson.army.mil					
Fort Detrick	Frederick	MD	21702	301-619-7613	619-3207
Web: www.detrick.army.mil					
Fort Dix	Fort Dix	NJ	08640	609-562-1011	562-3337
Web: www.dix.army.mil					
Fort Drum	Fort Drum	NY	13602	315-772-6011	772-5165
Web: www.drum.army.mil					
Fort Eustis	Fort Eustis	VA	23604	757-878-5251	878-1502
Web: www.eustis.army.mil					
Fort Gillem 4705 N Wheeler Dr	Forest Park	GA	30297	404-469-7326	464-3101
Web: www.mcpherson.army.mil/fort_gillem.htm					
Fort Gordon	Fort Gordon	GA	30905	706-791-0110	791-2061
Web: www.gordon.army.mil					
Fort Hamilton	Brooklyn	NY	11252	718-630-4101	630-4723
Web: www.hamilton.army.mil					
Fort Hood	Fort Hood	TX	76544	254-287-1110	288-2750
Web: www.hood.army.mil					
Fort Huachuca	Fort Huachuca	AZ	85613	520-538-7111	533-5008
Web: huachuca-www.army.mil					
Fort Irwin	Fort Irwin	CA	92310	760-380-3078	380-3075
Web: www.irwin.army.mil					
Fort Jackson	Fort Jackson	SC	29207	803-751-7511	751-3533
Fort Knox	Fort Knox	KY	40121	502-624-4704	624-6074
Web: www.knox.army.mil					
Fort Leavenworth	Fort Leavenworth	KS	66027	913-684-4021	684-3624
Web: www.leavenworth.army.mil					
Fort Lee 500 Lee Ave	Fort Lee	VA	23801	804-765-3000	734-4659
Web: www.lee.army.mil					
Fort Leonard Wood	Fort Leonard Wood	MO	65473	573-596-0131	563-4012
Web: www.wood.army.mil					
Fort Lewis	Fort Lewis	WA	98433	253-967-0146	967-0612
Web: www.lewis.army.mil					
Fort McPherson 1777 Hardee Ave SW	Fort McPherson	GA	30330	404-464-5668	464-5628
Web: www.mcpherson.army.mil					
Fort Meade 4550 Parade Field Ln Rm 102	Fort Meade	MD	20755	301-677-1361	677-1305
Web: www.ftmeade.army.mil					
Fort Monmouth	Fort Monmouth	NJ	07703	732-532-9000	532-6262
Web: www.monmouth.army.mil					
Fort Monroe	Fort Monroe	VA	23651	757-788-2000	788-3358
Web: www-tradoc.army.mil					
Fort Myer	Fort Myer	VA	22211	703-696-0584	696-2678
Web: www.fmmc.army.mil					
Fort Polk	Fort Polk	LA	71459	337-531-2911	531-6014
Web: www.jrtc-polk.army.mil					
Fort Richardson	Fort Richardson	AK	99505	907-384-1110	384-2060
Web: www.usarak.army.mil/main					
Fort Riley	Fort Riley	KS	66442	785-239-3032	239-2592
Web: www.riley.army.mil					
Fort Rucker	Fort Rucker	AL	36362	334-255-2252	255-1004
Web: www-rucker.army.mil					
Fort Sam Houston	Fort Sam Houston	TX	78234	210-221-1211	221-1198
Web: www.cs.amedd.army.mil					
Fort Shafter	Fort Shafter	HI	96858	808-438-9375	438-6354
Fort Sill	Fort Sill	OK	73503	580-442-8111	355-6756
Web: sill-www.army.mil					
Fort Stewart	Fort Stewart	GA	31314	912-767-1411	767-1542
Web: www.stewart.army.mil					
Fort Story	Fort Story	VA	23459	757-422-7755	422-7750
Web: www.eustis.army.mil/Fort_story					
Fort Wainwright	Fort Wainwright	AK	99703	907-353-6701	353-6711
Web: www.wainwright.army.mil					

500-3 Marine Corps Bases

				Phone	Fax
Marine Corps Air Station Beaufort PO Box 55001	Beaufort	SC	29904	843-228-7121	228-6005
Web: www.beaufort.usmc.mil					
Marine Corps Air Station Cherry Point	Cherry Point	NC	28533	252-466-2811	466-5201
Web: www.cherrypoint.usmc.mil					
Marine Corps Air Station Miramar PO Box 452001	San Diego	CA	92145	858-577-1245	577-4834
Web: www.miramar.usmc.mil					
Marine Corps Air Station New River PSC Box 21002	Jacksonville	NC	28545	910-449-5432	449-6478
Web: www.newriver.usmc.mil					
Marine Corps Air Station Yuma	Yuma	AZ	85369	928-269-2252	269-3282
Web: www.yuma.usmc.mil					
Marine Corps Base Camp Lejeune	Camp Lejeune	NC	28542	910-451-1113	451-5882
Web: www.lejeune.usmc.mil/mcb					
Marine Corps Base Camp Pendleton Box 555010	Camp Pendleton	CA	92055	760-725-5012	725-5776
Web: www.cpp.usmc.mil					
Marine Corps Base Hawaii PO Box 63002	Kaneohe Bay	HI	96863	808-257-8840	257-2511
Web: www.mcbh.usmc.mil					

Marine Corps Bases (Cont'd)

	City	State	ZIP	Phone	Fax
Marine Corps Base Quantico	Quantico	VA	22134	703-784-2741	784-0065
Web: www.quantico.usmc.mil					
Marine Corps Logistics Base Albany 814 Radford Blvd Code 70000	Albany	GA	31704	229-639-5215	639-5480
Web: www.ala.usmc.mil					
Marine Corps Logistics Base Barstow PO Box 110130	Barstow	CA	92311	760-577-6430	577-6350
Web: www.bam.usmc.mil					
Marine Corps Recruit Depot Parris Island PO Box 19660	Parris Island	SC	29905	843-228-2705	228-2122
Web: www.mcrdpi.usmc.mil					
Marine Corps Recruit Depot San Diego 1600 Henderson Ave	San Diego	CA	92145	619-524-8727	
Web: www.mcrdsd.usmc.mil					

500-4 Naval Installations

	City	State	ZIP	Phone	Fax
Naval Air Station Brunswick 1251 Orion St	Brunswick	ME	04011	207-921-2000	921-2001
Web: www.nasb.navy.mil					
Naval Air Station Corpus Christi 11101 D St	Corpus Christi	TX	78419	361-961-2811	961-3402
Web: nascc.cnatra.navy.mil					
Naval Air Station Fallon 4755 Pasture Rd	Fallon	NV	89496	775-426-2801	426-2848
Web: www.fallon.navy.mil					
Naval Air Station Jacksonville	Jacksonville	FL	32212	904-542-2415	542-2413
Web: www.nasjax.navy.mil					
Naval Air Station Joint Reserve Base Fort Worth	Fort Worth	TX	76127	817-782-5000	782-7601
Naval Air Station Joint Reserve Base New Orleans 400 Russell Ave	New Orleans	LA	70143	504-678-3254	678-3244
Web: www.airnav.com/airport/NBG					
Naval Air Station Joint Reserve Base Willow Grove	Willow Grove	PA	19090	215-443-1000	443-6017
Web: www.airnav.com/airport/NXX					
Naval Air Station Key West	Key West	FL	33040	305-293-4408	293-4415
Web: www02.clf.navy.mil/keywest					
Naval Air Station Kingsville	Kingsville	TX	78363	361-516-6333	516-6875
Web: www.nask.navy.mil					
Naval Air Station Lemoore	Lemoore	CA	93246	559-998-3300	998-3395
Web: www.lemoore.navy.mil					
Naval Air Station Meridian 255 Rosenbaum Ave	Meridian	MS	39309	601-679-2211	679-2447
Web: www.cnet.navy.mil/meridian/					
Naval Air Station North Island PO Box 357033	San Diego	CA	92135	619-545-8123	545-0182
Web: www.nasni.navy.mil					
Naval Air Station Oceana	Virginia Beach	VA	23460	757-433-3131	433-3156
Web: www.nasoceana.navy.mil					
Naval Air Station Patuxent River 2268 Cedar Point Rd Bldg 408 Suite 204	Patuxent River	MD	20670	301-342-7710	342-7509
Naval Air Station Pensacola 190 Radford Blvd	Pensacola	FL	32508	850-452-0111	452-3939
Web: www.naspensacola.navy.mil					
Naval Air Station Whidbey Island 3730 N Charles Porter Ave	Oak Harbor	WA	98278	360-257-2286	
Web: naswi.ahf.nmci.navy.mil					
Naval Air Station Whiting Field 7550 USS Essex St	Milton	FL	32570	850-623-7341	623-7601*
**Fax:* PR ■ *Web:* wwwcfs.cnet.navy.mil/naswf					
Naval Air Systems Command Lakehurst Rt 547	Lakehurst	NJ	08733	732-323-2811	323-7676
Web: www.lakehurst.navy.mil					
Naval Base Kitsap 120 S Dewey St	Bremerton	WA	98314	360-476-2574	
Web: www.nbk.navy.mil					
Naval Base San Diego 3455 Senn Rd	San Diego	CA	92136	619-556-7359	556-2423
Web: www.navbasesd.navy.mil					
Naval Station Everett 2000 W Marine View Dr	Everett	WA	98207	425-304-3000	304-3096
Web: www.everett.navy.mil					
Naval Station Mayport	Mayport	FL	32228	904-270-5401	
Web: www.nsmayport.navy.mil					
Naval Station Newport	Newport	RI	02841	401-841-3456	841-2265
Web: www.nsnpt.navy.mil					
Naval Station Norfolk 1530 Gilbert St Suite 2000	Norfolk	VA	23511	757-444-0000	444-0348
Web: www.navstanorva.navy.mil					
Naval Station Pearl Harbor 850 Ticonderoga St Suite 100	Pearl Harbor	HI	96860	808-473-2888	473-2876
Web: www.pearlharbor.navy.mil					
Naval Submarine Base Kings Bay	Kings Bay	GA	31547	912-573-4714	573-4717
Web: www.subasekb.navy.mil					
Naval Submarine Base New London PO Box 100	Groton	CT	06349	860-694-3011	694-4699
Web: www.subasenlon.navy.mil					
Naval Support Activity	Annapolis	MD	21402	410-293-2385	293-3133
Web: www.usna.edu/NavalStation					
Naval Training Center Great Lakes 2601 Paul Jones St	Great Lakes	IL	60088	847-688-3500	688-4235
Web: www.nsgreatlakes.navy.mil					

501 MILITARY SERVICE ACADEMIES

	City	State	ZIP	Phone	Fax
Royal Military College of Canada PO Box 17000 Stn Forces	Kingston	ON	K7K7B4	613-541-6000	541-6599
Web: www.rmc.ca					
US Air Force Academy Dept of the Air Force Headquarters USAFA	USAF Academy	CO	80840	719-333-1110	333-3012
TF: 800-443-9266 ■ *Web:* www.usafa.af.mil					
US Military Academy Admissions Bldg 606	West Point	NY	10996	845-938-5746	938-8121
TF: 800-822-8762 ■ *Web:* www.usma.edu					
US Naval Academy 121 Blake Rd	Annapolis	MD	21402	410-293-1000	293-4348*
**Fax:* Admissions ■ *TF Admissions:* 888-249-7707 ■ *Web:* www.usna.edu					

502 MILLWORK

SEE ALSO Construction Materials - Lumber & Building Supplies p. 1549; Doors & Windows - Wood p. 1591; Home Improvement Centers p. 1788; Shutters - Window (All Types) p. 2316

	City	State	ZIP	Phone	Fax
All-Wood Components Inc 3205 Bay St PO Box 3068	Union Gap	WA	98903	509-452-7494	452-7655
Web: www.allwoodcomp.com					
Allen Millwork Inc 6505 St Vincent Ave PO Box 6480	Shreveport	LA	71136	318-868-6541	865-6102
TF: 800-551-8737 ■ *Web:* www.allenmillwork.com					
American Millwork Corp 4840 Beck Dr	Elkhart	IN	46516	574-295-4158	293-5378
Web: www.americanmillwork.com					
Anderson Wood Products Co 1381 Beech St	Louisville	KY	40211	502-778-5591	778-5599
TF: 800-825-5591 ■ *Web:* www.andersonwood.com					
Appalachian Wood Products Inc 171 Appalachian Dr PO Box 1408	Clearfield	PA	16830	814-765-2003	762-8083
Web: www.appwood.com					
Associated Door Plywood Co Inc PO Box 10128	Terre Haute	IN	47801	812-232-1371	234-4364
Automated Building Components Inc 300 Morse Ave PO Box 40	Excelsior	MN	55331	952-474-4374	470-3610
Barber & Ross Co PO Box 1294	Leesburg	VA	20177	703-777-4200	771-1450
Web: www.barberandross.com					
Barnett Millworks Inc 4915 Hamilton Blvd PO Box 389	Theodore	AL	36590	251-443-7710	443-6123*
**Fax:* Sales					
Black Millwork Co Inc 230 W Crescent Ave	Allendale	NJ	07401	201-934-0100	934-8867
TF: 800-864-2356 ■ *Web:* www.blackmillwork.com					
Bright Wood Corp 335 NW Hess St PO Drawer 828	Madras	OR	97741	541-475-2243	475-7086
Web: www.brightwood.com					
Brockway-Smith Co (BWAY) 146 Dascomb Rd	Andover	MA	01810	978-475-7100	242-4533*
**Fax Area Code:* 800 ■ *TF:* 800-225-7912 ■ *Web:* www.brosco.com					
BWAY (Brockway-Smith Co) 146 Dascomb Rd	Andover	MA	01810	978-475-7100	242-4533*
**Fax Area Code:* 800 ■ *TF:* 800-225-7912 ■ *Web:* www.brosco.com					
Carter-Lee Lumber Co Inc 1717 W Washington St	Indianapolis	IN	46222	317-639-5431	639-6982*
**Fax:* Sales ■ *Web:* www.carterlee.com					
Causeway Lumber Co 2601 S Andrews Ave	Fort Lauderdale	FL	33316	954-763-1224	768-5921
TF: 800-375-5050 ■ *Web:* www.causewaylumber.com					
Central Woodwork Inc 870 Keough Rd	Collierville	TN	38017	901-363-4141	363-4171
TF: 800-788-3775 ■ *Web:* www.centralwoodwork.com					
Clopay Corp 8585 Duke Blvd	Mason	OH	45040	513-770-4800	770-3984
TF: 800-282-2260 ■ *Web:* www.clopay.com					
Colonial Stair & Woodwork Co 48 N Main St	Jeffersonville	OH	43128	740-426-6326	625-9295
TF: 800-625-6326 ■ *Web:* www.colonialstair.com					
Columbia Woodworking Inc 935 Brentwood Rd NE	Washington	DC	20018	202-526-2387	526-5163
Contact Lumber Co 9200 SE Sunnybrook Blvd Suite 200	Clackamas	OR	97015	503-228-7361	221-1340
TF: 800-547-1038 ■ *Web:* www.contactlumber.com					
Cox Interior Inc 1751 Old Columbia Rd	Campbellsville	KY	42718	270-789-3129	465-7977
TF: 800-733-1751 ■ *Web:* www.coxinterior.com					
CW Ohio Inc 1209 Maple Ave	Conneaut	OH	44030	440-593-5800	593-4545
TF: 800-677-5801 ■ *Web:* www.cwohio.com					
DeLeers Millwork Inc 1735 Sal St	Green Bay	WI	54302	920-465-6764	465-8835
Web: www.deleersmillwork.com					
Do+Able Products Inc 5150 Edison Ave	Chino	CA	91710	909-590-4444	591-9244
TF: 800-829-3648 ■ *Web:* www.doable.com					
Dubois Wood Products Inc 707 E 6th St PO Drawer 386	Huntingburg	IN	47542	812-683-3613	683-3847
Web: www.duboiswood.com					
Eastern Millwork Co PO Box 4128	Reading	PA	19606	610-779-3550	779-1241
TF: 800-422-8545 ■ *Web:* www.easternmillwork.com					
Eggers Industries Inc 1 Eggers Dr	Two Rivers	WI	54241	920-793-1351	793-2958
Web: www.eggersindustries.com					
FE Schumacher & Co Inc 200 Mill St SE	Hartville	OH	44632	330-877-9307	877-6012
Fetzers' Inc 6223 W Double Eagle Cir	Salt Lake City	UT	84118	801-484-6103	484-6122
Web: www.fetzersinc.com					
Georgia-Pacific Corp 133 Peachtree St NE	Atlanta	GA	30303	404-652-4000	230-5774
Web: www.gp.com					
Giffin Interior & Fixture Inc 500 Scotti Dr	Bridgeville	PA	15017	412-221-1166	221-3745
Glide Lumber Products Co PO Box 370	Glide	OR	97443	541-496-3571	496-0373
Graves Lumber Co 1315 S Cleveland-Massillon Rd	Copley	OH	44321	330-666-1115	666-1377
TF: 877-500-5515 ■ *Web:* www.graveslumber.com					
Hoff Cos Inc 1840 N Lakes Ave	Meridian	ID	83642	208-884-2002	884-1115
Homeshield Colonial Craft 2270 Woodale Dr	Mounds View	MN	55112	763-231-4000	783-7218
TF: 800-727-5187 ■ *Web:* www.home-shield.com					
Horner Millwork Corp 1255 Grand Army Hwy	Somerset	MA	02726	508-679-6479	
TF: 800-543-5403 ■ *Web:* www.hornermillwork.com					
Huttig Building Products Inc 555 Maryville University Dr	Saint Louis	MO	63141	314-216-2600	216-2769*
NYSE: HBP ■ **Fax:* Mktg ■ *TF:* 800-325-4466 ■ *Web:* www.huttig.com					
iLevel by Weyerhaeuser 200 E Mallard Dr	Boise	ID	83706	208-364-1200	364-1300
TF Cust Svc: 800-338-0515 ■ *Web:* www.ilevel.com					
Imperial Woodworking Co 310 N Woodwork Ln	Palatine	IL	60067	847-358-6920	358-0905
Web: www.imperialwoodworking.com					
Jeld-Wen Inc 401 Harbor Isles Blvd	Klamath Falls	OR	97601	541-882-3451	850-2621
TF: 800-535-3462 ■ *Web:* www.jeld-wen.com					
Lafayette Wood-Works Inc 3004 Cameron St	Lafayette	LA	70506	337-233-5250	233-1147
TF: 800-960-3311 ■ *Web:* www.lafwoodworks.com					
Liberty Wood & Construction Inc 3300 Benzing Rd	Orchard Park	NY	14127	716-824-6067	824-6075
TF: 800-448-2200 ■ *Web:* www.libertywood.com					
LJ Smith Co 35280 Scio-Bowerston Rd	Bowerston	OH	44695	740-269-2221	269-9047
Web: www.ljsmith.net					
Louisiana-Pacific Corp 414 Union St Suite 2000	Nashville	TN	37219	615-986-5600	986-5666
NYSE: LPX ■ *TF:* 877-744-5600 ■ *Web:* www.lpcorp.com					
Mann & Parker Lumber Co Inc 335 N Constitution Ave	New Freedom	PA	17349	717-235-4834	235-5547
TF: 800-632-9098 ■ *Web:* www.m-pgoldbrand.com					
Merrimack Valley Wood Products Co 1 B St Derry Industrial Park	Derry	NH	03038	603-432-2581	437-2646
TF: 800-955-0701 ■ *Web:* www.mvwp.com					
Milliken Millwork Inc 6361 Sterling Dr N	Sterling Heights	MI	48312	586-264-0950	264-5430
TF: 800-686-9218 ■ *Web:* www.millikenmillwork.com					
Monarch Industries Inc 99 Main St	Warren	RI	02885	401-247-5200	247-5601*
**Fax:* Sales ■ *TF:* 800-669-9663 ■ *Web:* www.monarchinc.com					
MW Manufacturers Inc 433 N Main St	Rocky Mount	VA	24151	540-483-0211	950-3220*
**Fax Area Code:* 800 ■ *TF:* 888-999-8400 ■ *Web:* www.mwwindows.com					
New England Door Corp 15 Campanelli Cir	Canton	MA	02021	781-821-2737	821-8050
TF: 800-969-5151 ■ *Web:* www.nedoor.com					
Nordic Interior Inc 56-01 Maspeth Ave	Maspeth	NY	11378	718-456-7000	456-9340
TF: 800-464-0066					
Northcutt Woodworks LP 101 S 4th St PO Box 820	Crockett	TX	75835	936-544-2028	544-9537
Norwood Sash & Door Mfg Co 4953 Section Ave	Norwood	OH	45212	513-531-5700	531-5706
Web: www.norwoodsd.com					
Ohline Corp 1930 W 139th St	Gardena	CA	90249	310-327-4630	538-5742
TF: 800-585-3197 ■ *Web:* www.ohline.com					
Parenti & Raffaelli Ltd 215 Prospect Ave E	Mount Prospect	IL	60056	847-253-5550	253-6055
Web: www.parentiwoodwork.com					
PGM Products LLC 1 Commerce Dr Barrington Business Center Bldg 4	Barrington	NJ	08007	856-546-0704	546-0539
Web: www.pgmproducts.com					
Randall Brothers Inc 665 Marietta St NW	Atlanta	GA	30313	404-892-6666	875-6102
TF Cust Svc: 800-476-4539 ■ *Web:* www.randallbrothers.com					
Raynor Garage Doors 1101 E River Rd	Dixon	IL	61021	815-288-1431	288-3720*
**Fax:* Cust Svc ■ *TF:* 800-472-9667 ■ *Web:* www.raynor.com					
Riverside Millwork Co Inc 77 Merrimack St	Penacook	NH	03303	603-753-6318	753-6076
TF: 800-852-3430 ■ *Web:* www.rivcoinc.com					
ROW Window Co 612 Moen Ave	Joliet	IL	60434	815-725-5491	725-6926
TF: 800-966-3769 ■ *Web:* www.rowwindowco.com					
Ruffin & Payne Inc 4200 E Vawter Ave	Richmond	VA	23222	804-329-2691	321-4940
Scherer Brothers Lumber Co 9 9th Ave NE	Minneapolis	MN	55413	612-379-9633	627-0679
Web: www.schererbros.com					
Schuck Component Systems Inc 8205 N 67th Ave	Glendale	AZ	85302	623-931-3661	937-3435
TF: 800-666-3661 ■ *Web:* www.schuckaz.com					
Schumacher FE & Co Inc 200 Mill St SE	Hartville	OH	44632	330-877-9307	877-6012
Shaw/Stewart Lumber Co 645 Johnson St NE	Minneapolis	MN	55413	651-488-2525	378-1484*
**Fax Area Code:* 612 ■ **Fax:* Sales					
Shelly Enterprises Inc PO Box 235	Perkasie	PA	18944	215-723-5108	723-7523
Web: www.shellyenterprises.cc					

Phone | Fax

Shuster's Building Components 2920 Clay Pike Irwin PA 15642 724-446-7000 676-0640*
*Fax Area Code: 800 ■ TF: 800-366-6733 ■ Web: www.shusters.com
Sierra Lumber Manufacturers Inc 375 W Hazelton Ave Stockton CA 95203 209-943-7777 943-7783
Sierra Pacific Industries 19794 Riverside Ave Anderson CA 96007 530-378-8000 378-8109
Web: www.sierrapacificind.com
Smith LJ Co 35280 Scio-Bowerston Rd Bowerston OH 44695 740-269-2221 269-9047
Web: www.ljsmith.net
Somerset Door & Column Co 174 Sagamore St Somerset PA 15501 814-444-9427 443-1658
TF: 800-242-7916 ■ Web: www.somersetdoor.com
Standard Lumber Co 1912 Lehigh Ave Glenview IL 60026 847-729-7800 729-8500
Stephenson Millwork Co Inc 210 Harper St Wilson NC 27893 252-237-1141 237-4377
Web: www.smcinc.com
Taney Corp 5130 Allendale Ln Taneytown MD 21787 410-756-6671 756-4103
Web: www.taneystair.com
Taylor Brothers Inc 905 Graves Mill Rd PO Box 11198 Lynchburg VA 24506 434-237-8100 237-4227
TF: 800-288-6767 ■ Web: www.taylorbrothers.com
Tucker Door & Trim Corp 650 Hwy 83 Monroe GA 30655 770-267-4622 267-5997
Washington Woodworking Co Inc 2010 Beaver Rd Landover MD 20785 301-341-2500 341-2512
Web: www.washingtonwoodworking.com
Wayne-Dalton Corp 1 Door Dr PO Box 67 Mount Hope OH 44660 330-674-7015 763-8047
TF: 800-827-3667 ■ Web: www.wayne-dalton.com
Werzalit of America Inc 40 Holly Ave PO Box 373 Bradford PA 16701 814-362-3881 362-4237
TF: 800-999-3730 ■ Web: www.werzalit-usa.com
Woodfold Mfg Inc 1811 18th Ave PO Box 346 Forest Grove OR 97116 503-357-7181 357-7185
Web: www.woodfold.com
Woodgrain Millworks Inc 300 NW 16th St PO Box 566 Fruitland ID 83619 208-452-3801 452-5474
TF: 800-452-3801 ■ Web: www.woodgrain.com
Woodharbor Doors & Cabinetry Inc 3277 9th St SW Mason City IA 50401 641-423-0444 423-0345
Web: www.woodharbor.com
Young Mfg Co Inc 521 S Main St PO Box 167 Beaver Dam KY 42320 270-274-3306 274-9522
TF: 800-545-6595

503 MINERAL PRODUCTS - NONMETALLIC

SEE ALSO Insulation & Acoustical Products p. 1857

Phone | Fax

3M Industrial Mineral Products Div
3M Center Bldg 220-3E-11 Saint Paul MN 55144 800-447-2914 424-7442
Web: www.3m.com/market/industrial/impd
Amsat Div Fluid Energy Processing & Equipment Co
153 Penn Ave Hatfield PA 19440 215-368-2510 368-6235
Web: www.fluidenergype.com
Asbury Graphite Mills Inc 405 Old Main St Asbury NJ 08802 908-537-2155 537-2908
Web: www.asburygraphite.com
Astro Met Inc 9974 Springfield Pike Cincinnati OH 45215 513-772-1242 772-9080
Web: www.astromet.com
Austin Productions Inc 835 Marconi Ave Unit A Ronkonkoma NY 11779 631-981-7300 467-8823
TF: 800-645-7303 ■ Web: www.austin-allaboutyourhome.com
Big River Industries Inc 12652 Airline Hwy Erwinville LA 70729 225-627-4242 627-5901
TF: 800-969-5634 ■ Web: www.bigriverind.com
Brubaker-Mann Inc 36011 Soap Mine Rd Barstow CA 92311 760-256-2520 256-0127
Buffalo Crushed Stone Co Inc 2544 Clinton St Buffalo NY 14224 716-826-7310 826-1342
Burgess Pigment Co Inc 187 Pierce Ave PO Box 4146 Macon GA 31208 478-746-5658 746-4882
TF: 800-841-8999 ■ Web: www.burgesspigment.com
Carpenter-Certech Inc 1 Park Pl W Wood Ridge NJ 07075 201-939-7400 939-1423
Ceradyne Inc 3169 Redhill Ave Costa Mesa CA 92626 714-549-0421 549-5787*
NASDAQ: CRDN ■ *Fax: Sales ■ TF: 800-839-2189 ■ Web: www.ceradyne.com
Ceramic Powders Inc 1806 S Terry Dr PO Box 2893 Joliet IL 60436 815-729-4315 729-0829
Chemrock Corp 225 City Ave Suite 14 Bala Cynwyd PA 19004 610-660-8803 660-8817
Christy Refractories Co 4641 McRee Ave Saint Louis MO 63110 314-773-7500 773-8371
Web: www.christyco.com/refract.html
Consolidated Ceramic Products Inc 838 Cherry St Blanchester OH 45107 937-783-2476 783-2539
Web: www.ccpi-inc.com
Continental Mineral Processing Corp
11817 Mosteller Rd PO Box 62005 Cincinnati OH 45262 513-771-7190 771-9153
Web: www.continentalmineral.com
Crystex Composites LLC 125 Clifton Blvd Clifton NJ 07011 973-779-8866 779-2013
Web: www.crystexllc.com
Dri-Rite Co Inc 13116 S Western Ave PO Box 389 Blue Island IL 60406 708-385-7556 385-0622
Web: www.dririte.com
Eagle-Picher Minerals Inc PO Box 12130 Reno NV 89510 775-824-7600 824-7601
TF Cust Svc: 800-228-3865
Ferro Corp Electronic Materials Div 4150 E 56th St Cleveland OH 44105 216-641-8580 750-7339
Fluid Energy Processing & Equipment Co Amsat Div
153 Penn Ave Hatfield PA 19440 215-368-2510 368-6235
Web: www.fluidenergype.com
GE Advanced Materials 1 Plastics Ave Pittsfield MA 01201 413-448-7110 448-5573
Web: www.geadvancedmaterials.com
GE Quartz 4901 Campbell Rd Willoughby OH 44094 216-266-4121 266-2360
TF: 800-438-2100 ■ Web: www.gequartz.com
Graphel Corp 6115 Centre Park Dr West Chester OH 45071 513-779-6166 777-8959
TF: 800-255-1104 ■ Web: www.graphelcorp.com
Graphite Metallizing Corp 1050 Nepperhan Ave Yonkers NY 10703 914-968-8400 968-8468
Web: www.graphalloy.com
Graphite Sales Inc 16710 W Park Circle Dr Chagrin Falls OH 44023 440-543-8221 543-5183
TF: 800-321-4147 ■ Web: www.graphitesales.com
Grefco Minerals Inc 225 City Ave Suite 14 Bala Cynwyd PA 19004 610-660-8820 822-9119
Web: www.grefco.com
Harborlite Corp 1950 E 'W' Ave PO Box 100 Vicksburg MI 49097 269-649-1352 649-3707
TF: 800-403-4869 ■ Web: www.worldminerals.com
Hill & Griffith Co 1085 Summer St Cincinnati OH 45204 513-921-1075 244-4199
TF: 800-543-0425 ■ Web: www.hillandgriffith.com
Hydraulic Press Brick Co 7225 Woodland Dr Suite 200 Indianapolis IN 46278 317-290-1140 290-1071
JS McCormick Co 503 Hegner Way Sewickley PA 15143 412-749-8222 749-2766
Keystone Filler & Mfg Co 214 Railroad St Muncy PA 17756 570-546-3148 546-7067
Kocour Co 4800 S St Louis Ave Chicago IL 60632 773-847-1111 847-3399
TF: 888-562-6871 ■ Web: www.kocournet.com
La Habra Products Inc 4125 E La Palma Ave Suite 250 Anaheim CA 92807 714-778-2266 774-2079
TF: 800-649-8933 ■ Web: www.lahabrastucco.com
Limestone Dust Corp
Saint Claires Crossing Bldg 230 PO Box 152 Bluefield VA 24605 276-326-1103 322-5656
TF: 800-204-0520
McCormick JS Co 503 Hegner Way Sewickley PA 15143 412-749-8222 749-2766
Merlex Stucco Co 2911 N Orange-Olive Rd Orange CA 92865 714-637-1700 637-4865
Web: www.merlex.com
Metaullics Systems 31935 Aurora Rd Solon OH 44139 440-349-8800 248-3432
TF: 800-638-2859 ■ Web: www.metaullics.com
Miller & Co LLC 9700 W Higgins Rd Suite 1000 Rosemont IL 60018 847-696-2400 696-2419
TF: 800-727-9847 ■ Web: www.millerandco.com
Miller Studios PO Box 997 New Philadelphia OH 44663 330-339-1100 339-4379
Web: www.miller-studios.com
Mission Stucco Co Inc 7751 E 70th St Paramount CA 90723 562-634-1400 634-4440

Phone | Fax

Multicoat Corp 23331 Antonio Pkwy Rancho Santa Margarita CA 92688 949-888-7100 888-2555
TF: 877-685-8426 ■ Web: www.multicoatproducts.com
New Jersey Pulverizing Co 250 Hickory Ln Bayville NJ 08721 732-269-1400 269-1414
NYCO Minerals Inc 803 Mountain View Dr Willsboro NY 12996 518-963-4262 963-1110
Web: www.nycominerals.com
Oil-Dri Corp of America 410 N Michigan Ave Suite 400 Chicago IL 60611 312-321-1515 321-1271
NYSE: ODC ■ TF: 800-233-9802 ■ Web: www.oildri.com
Sacramento Stucco Co 860 Riske Ln West Sacramento CA 95691 916-372-7442 372-4836
Web: www.sacstucco.com
Saint-Gobain Proppants 5300 Gerber Rd Fort Smith AR 72904 479-782-2001 782-9984
TF: 800-643-2149 ■ Web: www.saint-gobainproppants.com
San Jose Delta Assoc Inc 482 Sapena Ct Santa Clara CA 95054 408-727-1448 727-6019
Web: www.sanjosedelta.com
Schundler Co 150 Whitman Ave Edison NJ 08817 732-287-2244 287-4185
Web: www.schundler.com
Silbrico Corp 6300 River Rd Hodgkins IL 60525 708-354-3350 354-6698
TF: 800-323-4287 ■ Web: www.silbrico.com
Solite LLC 3900 Shannon St Chesapeake VA 23324 757-494-5200 545-3793
Squires-Belt Material Co 5467 Federal Blvd San Diego CA 92101 619-266-6100 266-6111
Web: www.squiresbelt.com
Tec Minerals Inc Hwy 787 Cleveland TX 77327 281-592-6428 592-7541
TF: 800-833-5442
US Diamond Wheel Co 101 Kendall Point Dr Oswego IL 60543 630-898-9000 898-1796
TF: 800-223-0457
USG Corp 125 S Franklin St Chicago IL 60606 312-606-4000 606-4093
NYSE: USG ■ TF: 800-621-9622 ■ Web: www.usg.com
Vesuvius USA 955 N 5th St Charleston IL 61920 217-345-7044 345-7124
Web: www.vesuvius.com
Von Roll Isola USA 1 W Campbell Rd Schenectady NY 12306 518-344-7100 344-7384*
*Fax: Cust Svc ■ TF: 800-654-7652 ■ Web: www.vonrollisola-usa.com
Winter Brothers Material Co 13098 Gravois Rd Saint Louis MO 63127 314-843-1400 843-1403
TF: 800-722-5424 ■ Web: www.winterbrothersmaterial.com
Ziegler Chemical & Mineral Corp 366 N Broadway Suite 210 Jericho NY 11753 516-681-9600 681-9604
Web: www.zieglerchemical.com
Zircar Products Inc 100 N Main St Florida NY 10921 845-651-6600 651-0441
Web: www.zircar.com

504 MINING - COAL

Phone | Fax

Alliance Resource Partners LP 1717 S Boulder Ave Suite 400 Tulsa OK 74119 918-295-7600 295-7358
NASDAQ: ARLP ■ Web: www.arlp.com
Alpha Natural Resources Inc 1 Alpha Pl Abingdon VA 24212 276-619-4410 623-2853
NYSE: ANR ■ TF: 866-322-5742 ■ Web: www.alphanr.com
AMVEST Corp 1 Boars Head Pt Charlottesville VA 22903 434-977-3350 295-3203
Web: www.amvestcorp.com
AMVEST West Virginia Coal Co PO Box 180 Fola Rd Bickmore WV 25019 304-872-6100 872-6771
Web: www.amvestcorp.com
Anker Energy Corp 2708 Cranberry Sq Morgantown WV 26508 304-594-1616 594-3695
Appalachian Fuels LLC 1500 N Big Run Rd Ashland KY 41102 606-928-3433 928-0450
Arch Coal Inc 1 City Place Suite 300 Saint Louis MO 63141 314-994-2700 994-2719*
NYSE: ACI ■ *Fax: Sales ■ TF: 800-238-7398 ■ Web: www.archcoal.com
Bennoc Inc 38722 National Rd PO Box 208 Morristown OH 43759 740-782-1330 782-1333
Black Beauty Coal Co 7100 Eagle Crest Blvd Evansville IN 47715 812-434-8500 428-0712
TF: 800-477-0514
Blattner DH & Sons Inc 400 CR 50 Avon MN 56310 320-356-7351 356-7392
TF: 800-877-2866 ■ Web: www.dhblattner.com
BNI Coal Ltd 1637 Burnt Boat Dr PO box 897 Bismarck ND 58502 701-222-8828 222-1547
Web: www.bnicoal.com
Bridger Coal Co 9 1/2 Mile SE Point of Rocks Point of Rocks WY 82942 307-382-9741 362-5330
C & K Coal Co 1062 E Main St PO Box 69 Clarion PA 16214 814-226-6911 226-9517
Cleveland-Cliffs Inc 1100 Superior Ave 18th Fl Cleveland OH 44114 216-694-5700 694-4880
NYSE: CLF ■ TF: 800-521-5701 ■ Web: www.cleveland-cliffs.com
Colowyo Coal Co 5731 Hwy 13 Meeker CO 81641 970-824-4451 824-4459
Cordero Rojo Complex PO Box 1449 Gillette WY 82717 307-682-8005 685-4558
Coteau Properties Co 204 County Rd 15 Beulah ND 58523 701-873-2281 873-7226
Cravat Coal Co 40580 Cadiz-Piedmont Rd Cadiz OH 43907 740-942-4656 942-8449
DH Blattner & Sons Inc 400 CR 50 Avon MN 56310 320-356-7351 356-7392
TF: 800-877-2866 ■ Web: www.dhblattner.com
Drummond Co Inc PO Box 10246 Birmingham AL 35202 205-945-6500 945-6557*
*Fax: Hum Res ■ Web: www.drummondco.com
East Fairfield Coal Co 10900 South Ave PO Box 217 North Lima OH 44452 330-549-2165 549-0618
Web: www.eastfairfield.com
Eastern Associated Coal Corp 202 Laidley Tower Charleston WV 25324 304-344-0300 340-1834
Fording Canadian Coal Trust 205 9th Ave SE Suite 1000 Calgary AB T2G0R3 403-260-9800 264-7339
NYSE: FDG ■ Web: www.fording.ca
Foundation Coal Holdings Inc
999 Corporate Blvd Suite 300 Linthicum Heights MD 21090 410-689-7500 689-7511
NYSE: FCL ■ Web: www.foundationcoal.com
Freeman Energy Corp PO Box 4630 Springfield IL 62708 217-698-3300 698-3381
Web: www.freemanenergy.com
Hepburnia Coal Co PO Box I Grampian PA 16838 814-236-0473 236-1624
Holmes Limestone Co 4255 SR 39 Berlin OH 44610 330-893-2721 893-2941
Huber JM Corp 333 Thornall St Edison NJ 08837 732-549-8600 549-2239*
*Fax: Hum Res ■ Web: www.huber.com
Humphreys Enterprises Inc SR 610 PO Box 668 Norton VA 24273 276-679-1400 679-4142
International Coal Group Inc 2000 Ashland Dr Ashland KY 41101 606-920-7400
NYSE: ICO ■ Web: www.intlcoal.com
James River Coal Co 901 E Byrd St Suite 1600 Richmond VA 23219 804-780-3000 780-0643
NASDAQ: JRCC ■ TF: 800-944-5190 ■ Web: www.jamesrivercoal.com
Jewell Smokeless Coal Corp Rt 460 W PO Box 70 Vansant VA 24656 276-935-8810 935-6019
Jim Walter Resources Inc 16243 Hwy 216 Box 133 Brookwood AL 35444 205-554-6150 481-6161
Web: www.jimwalterresources.com
JM Huber Corp 333 Thornall St Edison NJ 08837 732-549-8600 549-2239*
*Fax: Hum Res ■ Web: www.huber.com
Johnson RG Co Inc 25 S College St Washington PA 15301 724-222-6810 222-6815
Lee Ranch Coal Co PO Box 757 Grants NM 87020 505-285-4651 285-4650
Marrara Brothers Inc 200 Kingston Rd PO Box 1176 Kingwood WV 26537 304-329-1191 329-1953
Massey Energy Co 4 N 4th St Richmond VA 23219 804-788-1800 788-1870
NYSE: MEE ■ Web: www.masseycoal.com
McIntire William Coal Co PO Box 171 Shelocta PA 15774 724-354-2922 354-2102
Monterey Coal Co 14300 Brushy Mound Rd Carlinville IL 62626 217-854-3291 854-6807
Natural Resource Partners LP 601 Jefferson St Suite 3600 Houston TX 77002 713-751-7507 650-7580
NYSE: NRP ■ TF: 888-334-7102 ■ Web: www.nrplp.com
North American Coal Corp 14785 Preston Rd Suite 1100 Dallas TX 75254 972-239-2625 448-5437
Web: www.nacoal.com
Ohio River Collieries Co PO Box 128 Bannock OH 43972 740-968-3504 968-3071
Ohio Valley Coal Co 56854 Pleasant Ridge Rd Alledonia OH 43902 740-926-1351 926-9112
Paramont Coal Corp 5703 Crutchfield Dr Norton VA 24273 276-395-3316
Peabody Coal Co 701 Market St Saint Louis MO 63101 314-342-3400 827-6166*
*Fax Area Code: 270 ■ Web: www.peabodyenergy.com
Peabody Energy Corp 701 Market St Suite 700 Saint Louis MO 63101 314-342-3400 342-3499
NYSE: BTU ■ Web: www.peabodyenergy.com

Phone Fax

Pittsburg & Midway Coal Mining Co PO Box 6518 ... Englewood CO 80155 303-930-3600 930-4204
Powder River Coal Co 2298 Bishop Rd ... Gillette WY 82718 307-686-1991 682-2218
RG Johnson Co Inc 25 S College St ... Washington PA 15301 724-222-6810 222-6815
Rio Tinto Energy America 505 S Gillette Ave PO Box 3009 ... Gillette WY 82717 307-687-6000 687-6015
TF: 800-305-1142 ■ *Web:* www.rtea.com
Sigmon Coal 549 Londonderry Rd ... Cumberland Gap TN 37724 423-869-2000 869-8826
Sky Haven Coal Inc 5510 State Park Rd ... Penfield PA 15849 814-765-1665 765-6298
Sun Coal Co 1111 Northshore Dr Suite N 600 ... Knoxville TN 37919 865-558-0300 558-3280
Svonavec Inc 150 W Union St Suite 201 ... Somerset PA 15501 814-445-7324 443-4691
TECO Coal Corp 200 Allison Blvd ... Corbin KY 40701 606-523-4444 523-4490
Web: www.tecocoal.com
Thunder Basin Coal Co PO Box 406 ... Wright WY 82732 307-939-1300 464-2313
United Co 1005 Glenway Ave ... Bristol VA 24201 276-466-3322 645-1451
Usibelli Coal Mine Inc 100 River Rd PO Box 1000 ... Healy AK 99743 907-683-2226 683-2253
Web: www.usibelli.com
Walter Jim Resources Inc 16243 Hwy 216 Box 133 ... Brookwood AL 35444 205-554-6150 481-6161
Web: www.jimwalterresources.com
Western Energy Co 138 Rosebud Ln PO Box 99 ... Colstrip MT 59323 406-748-5100 748-5181
Westmoreland Coal Co 2 N Cascade Ave 14th Fl ... Colorado Springs CO 80903 719-442-2600 448-5825
AMEX: WLB ■ *TF:* 800-922-7279 ■ *Web:* www.westmorelandcoal.com
Westmoreland Resources Inc 100 Sarpy Creek Rd PO Box 449 ... Hardin MT 59034 406-342-5241 342-5401
Wilmore Coal Co 509 15th St ... Windber PA 15963 814-467-4519 467-4559
Wyodak Resources Development Corp 3338 Garner Lake Rd ... Gillette WY 82716 307-682-3410 682-0208

505 MINING - METALS

Phone Fax

Agnico-Eagle Mines Ltd 145 King St E Suite 500 ... Toronto ON M5C2Y7 416-947-1212 367-4681
NYSE: AEM ■ *Web:* www.agnico-eagle.com
Alloy & Metal Processors Inc 623 33rd Pl N ... Birmingham AL 35222 205-322-2344 328-3649
Anooraq Resources Corp 800 W Pender St Suite 1020 ... Vancouver BC V6C2V6 604-684-6365 684-8092
AMEX: ANO ■ *TF:* 800-667-2114 ■ *Web:* www.anooraqresources.com
Apollo Gold Corp 5655 S Yosemite St Suite 200 ... Greenwood Village CO 80111 720-886-9656
AMEX: AGT ■ *TF:* 877-465-3484 ■ *Web:* www.apollogold.com
Arizona Star Resource Corp 220 Bay St Suite 1405 ... Toronto ON M5J2W4 416-359-7800 359-7801
Web: www.arizonastar.com
Asarco Inc 1421 W Pima Mine Rd ... Sahuarita AZ 85629 520-625-7513 625-4756
Web: www.asarco.com
Asarco Inc Ray Complex PO Box 8 ... Hayden AZ 85235 520-356-7811 356-3804
Aurizon Mines Ltd 666 Burrard St Suite 3120 ... Vancouver BC V6C2X8 604-687-6600 687-3932
AMEX: AZK ■ *Web:* www.aurizon.com
B2 Gold Corp 595 Burrard St Suite 3100 PO Box 49143 ... Vancouver BC V7X1J1 604-681-8371 681-6209
TF: 800-316-8855 ■ *Web:* www.b2gold.com
Barrick Gold Corp 161 Bay St BCE Place Suite 3700 ... Toronto ON M5J2S1 416-861-9911 861-2492
NYSE: ABX ■ *TF:* 800-720-7415 ■ *Web:* www.barrick.com
Barrick Goldstrike Mines Inc Box 29 ... Elko NV 89803 775-738-8043 738-6543
Web: www.barrick.com
Black Hills Exploration & Production 350 Indiana St Suite 400 ... Golden CO 80401 720-210-1300 210-1301
Web: www.bhep.com
Brush Engineered Materials Inc 17876 St Clair Ave ... Cleveland OH 44110 216-486-4200 383-4091
NYSE: BW ■ *TF Cust Svc:* 800-321-2076 ■ *Web:* www.beminc.com
Cameco Corp 2121 11th St W ... Saskatoon SK S7M1J3 306-956-6200 956-6201
NYSE: CCJ ■ *Web:* www.cameco.com
Canyon Resources Corp 14142 Denver West Pkwy Suite 250 ... Golden CO 80401 303-278-8464 279-3772
AMEX: CAU ■ *Web:* www.canyonresources.com
Claude Resources Inc 224 4th Ave S Suite 200 ... Saskatoon SK S7K5M5 306-668-7505 668-7500
AMEX: CGR ■ *Web:* www.clauderesources.com
Cleveland-Cliffs Inc 1100 Superior Ave 18th Fl ... Cleveland OH 44114 216-694-5700 694-4880
NYSE: CLF ■ *TF:* 800-521-5701 ■ *Web:* www.cleveland-cliffs.com
Climax Molybdenum Co PO Box 220 ... Fort Madison IA 52627 319-463-7151 463-7640*
**Fax:* Hum Res
Coeur d'Alene Mines Corp PO Box 'I' ... Coeur d'Alene ID 83816 208-667-3511 667-2213
NYSE: CDE ■ *TF:* 800-624-2824 ■ *Web:* www.coeur.com
COGEMA Inc 4800 Hamden Ln Suite 1100 ... Bethesda MD 20814 301-986-8585 652-5690
Web: www.cogema-inc.com
COGEMA Resources Inc PO Box 730 ... Mills WY 82644 307-234-5019
Constellation Copper Corp 3900 S Wadsworth Blvd Suite 495 ... Denver CO 80235 720-288-0055 863-1736*
TSX: CCU ■ **Fax Area Code:* 303 ■ *TF:* 877-370-5400 ■
Web: www.constellationcopper.com
Corriente Resources Inc 800 W Pender St Suite 520 ... Vancouver BC V6C2V6 604-687-0449 687-0827
TSX: CTQ ■ *Web:* www.corriente.com
Crown Gold Inc PO Box 1168 ... Baltimore MD 21203 410-539-7400 659-4747
Crown Resources Corp 4251 Kipling St Suite 390 ... Wheat Ridge CO 80033 303-534-1030 534-1809
Web: www.crownresources.com
Crystallex International Corp 18 King St E Suite 1210 ... Toronto ON M5C1C4 416-203-2448 203-0099
TSX: KRY ■ *Web:* www.crystallex.com
Eldorado Gold Corp 550 Burrard St Suite 1188 ... Vanouver BC V6C2B5 604-687-4018 687-4026
AMEX: EGO ■ *TF:* 888-353-8166 ■ *Web:* www.eldoradogold.com
Falconbridge US 4955 Steubenville Pike Suite 245 ... Pittsburgh PA 15205 412-787-0220 787-0287
Web: www.falconbridge.com
First Quantum Minerals Ltd 543 Granville St Suite 800 ... Vancouver BC V6C1X8 604-688-6577 688-3818
TSX: FM ■ *TF:* 888-688-6577 ■ *Web:* www.first-quantum.com
FNX Mining Co Inc 55 University Ave Suite 700 ... Toronto ON M5J2H7 416-628-5929 360-0550
AMEX: FNX ■ *Web:* www.fnxmining.com
Freeport-McMoRan Copper & Gold Inc 1615 Poydras St ... New Orleans LA 70112 504-582-4000 582-1639*
NYSE: FCX ■ **Fax:* Hum Res ■ *TF:* 800-535-7094 ■ *Web:* www.fcx.com
Gammon Gold Inc 1701 Hollis St Suite 400 PO Box 2067 ... Halifax NS B3J3M8 902-468-0614 468-0631
AMEX: GRS ■ *Web:* www.gammongold.com
Glamis Gold Ltd 5190 Neil Rd Suite 310 ... Reno NV 89502 775-827-4600 827-5044
NYSE: GLG ■ *TF:* 800-452-6472 ■ *Web:* www.glamis.com
Gold Reserve Inc 926 W Sprague Ave Suite 200 ... Spokane WA 99201 509-623-1500 623-1634
AMEX: GRZ ■ *TF:* 800-625-9550 ■ *Web:* www.goldreserveinc.com
Goldcorp Inc 130 Adelaide St W Suite 3201 ... Toronto ON M5H3P5 416-865-0326 359-9787
NYSE: GG ■ *TF:* 800-813-1412 ■ *Web:* www.goldcorp.com
Golden Star Resources Ltd 10901 W Toller Dr Suite 300 ... Littleton CO 80127 303-830-9000 830-9094
AMEX: GSS ■ *TF:* 800-553-8436 ■ *Web:* www.gsr.com
Goldfield Corp 1684 W Hibiscus Blvd ... Melbourne FL 32901 321-724-1700 724-1703
AMEX: GV ■ *Web:* www.goldfieldcorp.com
Great Basin Gold Ltd 800 W Pender St Suite 1020 ... Vancouver BC V6C2V6 604-684-6365 684-8092
AMEX: GBN ■ *TF:* 800-667-2114 ■ *Web:* www.greatbasingold.com
Hecla Mining Co 6500 N Mineral Dr Suite 200 ... Coeur d'Alene ID 83815 208-769-4100 769-4107
NYSE: HL ■ *Web:* www.hecla-mining.com
Hibbing Taconite Co PO Box 589 ... Hibbing MN 55746 218-262-5950 262-6817
IAMGOLD Corp 401 Bay St Suite 3200 PO Box 153 ... Toronto ON M5H2Y4 416-360-4710 360-4750
AMEX: IAG ■ *TF:* 888-464-9999 ■ *Web:* www.iamgold.com
Imperial Metals Corp 580 Hornby St Suite 200 ... Vancouver BC V6C3B6 604-669-8959 687-4030
TSX: III ■ *Web:* www.imperialmetals.com
Inmet Mining Corp 330 Bay St Suite 1000 ... Toronto ON M5H2S8 416-361-6400 368-4692
Web: www.inmetmining.com
International Minerals Corp 7950 E Acoma Dr Suite 211 ... Scottsdale AZ 85260 480-483-9932 483-9926
TSX: IMZ ■ *Web:* www.intlminerals.com
International Uranium Corp 1050 17th St Suite 950 ... Denver CO 80265 303-628-7798 389-4125
TSX: IUC ■ *Web:* www.intluranium.com

Phone Fax

Iron Gold Quebec Inc
1111 Saint Charles St W East Tower Suite 750 ... Longueuil QC J4K5G4 450-677-0040 677-3382
Web: www.cambior.com
Ivanhoe Mines Ltd 999 Canada Pl Suite 654 ... Vancouver BC V6C3E1 604-688-5755 682-2060
NYSE: IVN ■ *TF:* 888-273-9999 ■ *Web:* www.ivanhoe-mines.com
Kennecott Uranium Co PO Box 1500 ... Rawlins WY 82301 307-328-1476 324-4925
Kennecott Utah Copper Corp PO Box 6001 ... Magna UT 84044 801-252-3000 569-6020
Kimber Resources Inc 800 W Pender St Suite 215 ... Vancouver BC V6C2V6 604-669-2251 669-8577
AMEX: KBX ■ *TF:* 866-824-1100 ■ *Web:* www.kimberresources.com
Kinross Gold Corp 40 King St W Suite 5200 ... Toronto ON M5H3Y2 416-365-5123 363-6622
NYSE: KGC ■ *Web:* www.kinross.com
Kinross Gold USA Inc 670 Sierra Rose Dr ... Reno NV 89511 775-829-1000
TF: 800-644-3547
Meridian Gold Co 9670 Gateway Dr Suite 200 ... Reno NV 89521 775-850-3777 850-3733
NYSE: MDG ■ *TF:* 800-557-4699 ■ *Web:* www.meridiangold.com
Metallic Ventures Gold Inc 5450 Riggins Ct Suite 2 ... Reno NV 89502 775-826-7567 826-4314
TSX: MVG ■ *Web:* www.metallicventuresgold.com
Metallurg Inc 1140 Ave of the Americas Suite 1800 ... New York NY 10017 212-835-0200 687-9621
Web: www.metallurg.com
Mine Management Inc 905 W Riverside Ave Suite 311 ... Spokane WA 99201 509-838-6050 838-0486
AMEX: MGN ■ *Web:* www.minesmanagement.com
MK Resources Co 60 E South Temple St Suite 1225 ... Salt Lake City UT 84111 801-297-6900 297-6950*
**Fax:* Hum Res ■ *TF:* 800-664-6528 ■ *Web:* www.mkgold.com
Molycorp Inc 67750 Bailey Rd ... Mountain Pass CA 92366 760-856-6680 856-2253
Web: www.molycorp.com
NA Degerstrom Inc 3303 N Sullivan Rd ... Spokane WA 99216 509-928-3333 927-2010
TF: 800-637-3773 ■ *Web:* www.nadinc.com
New Gold Inc 595 Howe St Suite 601 ... Vancouver BC V6C2T5 604-687-1629 687-2845
AMEX: NGD ■ *Web:* www.newgoldinc.com
Newmont Mining Corp 889 Harbourside Dr Suite 300 ... North Vancouver BC V7P3S1 604-985-2572 980-0731
TF: 800-663-8780 ■ *Web:* www.newmont.com
Newmont Mining Corp 1700 Lincoln St ... Denver CO 80203 303-863-7414 837-5837
NYSE: NEM ■ *Web:* www.newmont.com
NewWest Resources Group 1658 Cole Blvd Bldg 6 Suite 210 ... Lakewood CO 80401 303-425-7042 425-6634
Nord Resources Corp 1 W Wetmore Rd Suite 107 ... Tucson AZ 85705 520-292-0266 292-0268
TF: 800-543-2599 ■ *Web:* www.nordresources.com
North American Palladium Ltd 130 Adelaide St W Suite 2116 ... Toronto ON M5H3P5 416-360-7590 360-7709
AMEX: PAL ■ *Web:* www.napalladium.com
Northgate Minerals Corp 815 Hornby St Suite 406 ... Vancouver BC V6Z2E6 604-681-4004 681-4003
AMEX: NXG ■ *Web:* www.northgateminerals.com
Northshore Mining Corp 10 Outer Dr ... Silver Bay MN 55614 218-226-4125 226-6096
Web: www.nsmining.com
NovaGold Resources Inc
200 Grandville St Suite 2300 PO Box 24 ... Vancouver BC V6C1S4 604-669-6227 669-6272
AMEX: NG ■ *TF:* 866-699-6227 ■ *Web:* www.novagold.net
Pacific Rim Mining Co 625 Howe St Suite 410 ... Vancouver BC V6C2T6 604-689-1976 689-1978
AMEX: PMU ■ *TF:* 888-775-7097 ■ *Web:* www.pacrim-mining.com
Pan American Silver Corp 625 Howe St Suite 1500 ... Vancouver BC V6C2T6 604-684-1175 684-0147
NASDAQ: PAAS ■ *Web:* www.panamericansilver.com
Placer Dome Exploration Inc 240 S Rock Blvd Suite 117 ... Reno NV 89502 775-856-2552 856-3091
Web: www.placerdome.com
PT Freeport Indonesia Co 1615 Poydras St ... New Orleans LA 70112 504-582-4000 582-1639*
**Fax:* Hum Res ■ *TF:* 800-535-7094
QIT-Fer et Titane Inc 1625 Rt Marie-Victorin ... Tracy QC J3R1M6 450-746-3000 746-4438
Web: www.qit.com
Queenstake Resources Ltd 999 18th St Suite 2940 ... Denver CO 80202 303-297-1557 297-1587
AMEX: QEE ■ *TF:* 800-276-6070 ■ *Web:* www.queenstake.com
Republic Geothermal Inc PO Box 3388 ... Santa Fe Springs CA 90670 562-945-3661 945-5826
Royal Gold Inc 1660 Wynkoop St Suite 1000 ... Denver CO 80202 303-573-1660 595-9385
NASDAQ: RGLD ■ *Web:* www.royalgold.com
Rubicon Minerals Corp 800 W Pender St Suite 1540 ... Vancouver BC V6C2V6 604-623-3333
AMEX: RBY ■ *TF:* 866-365-4706 ■ *Web:* www.rubiconminerals.com
Saint Cloud Mining Co PO Box 1670 ... Truth or Consequences NM 87901 505-743-5215 743-3333
Web: www.stcloudmining.com
Seabridge Gold Inc 106 Front St Suite 400 ... Toronto ON M5A1E1 416-367-9292 367-2711
AMEX: SA ■ *Web:* www.seabridgegold.net
Sherritt International Corp 1133 Yonge St ... Toronto ON M4T2Y7 416-924-4551 924-5015
TSX: S ■ *Web:* www.sherritt.com
Silver Standard Resources Inc
999 W Hastings St Suite 1180 ... Vancouver BC V6C2W2 604-689-3846 689-3847
NASDAQ: SSRI ■ *Web:* www.silverstandard.com
Smith Bros Mining Co 1331 NW 99th Ave ... Plantation FL 33322 954-622-1115
Southern Peru Copper Corp 2575 E Camelback Rd Suite 500 ... Phoenix AZ 85106 602-977-6500
NYSE: PCU ■ *Web:* www.southernperu.com
Southwestern Resources Corp 701 W Georgia St Suite 1650 ... Vancouver BC V7Y1C6 604-669-2525 688-5175
TSX: SWG ■ *Web:* www.swgold.com
Stillwater Mining Co 536 E Pike Ave PO Box 1330 ... Columbus MT 59019 406-322-8700 322-9985
NYSE: SWC ■ *Web:* www.stillwatermining.com
Stratcor Inc 4955 Steubenville Pike Suite 305 ... Pittsburgh PA 15205 412-787-4500 787-5030
TF: 800-573-6052 ■ *Web:* www.stratcor.com
Strategic Minerals Corp 30 Main St Suite 300 ... Danbury CT 06810 203-790-1555 790-5750
Web: www.stratcor.com
Teck Cominco American Inc 15918 E Euclid Ave ... Spokane WA 99216 509-747-6111 922-8767
Web: www.teckcominco.com
Teck Cominco Ltd 200 Burrard St Suite 600 ... Vancouver BC V6C3L9 604-687-1117 687-6100
Web: www.teckcominco.com
Tenke Mining Corp 885 W Georgia St Suite 2101 ... Vancouver BC V6C3E8 604-689-7842 689-4250
TSX: TNK ■ *TF:* 888-689-7842 ■ *Web:* www.tenke.com
Tilden Mining Co PO Box 2000 ... Ishpeming MI 49849 906-475-3250 475-3592
Umetco Minerals Corp PO Box 1029 ... Grand Junction CO 81502 970-245-3700 245-7543
United Taconite LLC PO Box 180 ... Eveleth MN 55734 218-744-7800 744-5841
TF: 800-560-4532
Uranium Resources Inc 650 S Edmonds Ln Suite 108 ... Lewisville TX 75067 972-219-3330 219-3311
US Energy Corp 877 N 8th West ... Riverton WY 82501 307-856-9271 857-3050
NASDAQ: USEG ■ *Web:* www.usnrg.com
US Zinc PO Box 538 ... Hillsboro IL 62049 217-535-3931 532-2013
Vale Inco 200 Bay St Suite 1600 PO Box 70 ... Toronto ON M5J2K2 416-361-7511 361-7781
Web: www.valeinco.com
Vista Gold Corp 7961 Shaffer Pkwy Suite 5 ... Littleton CO 80127 720-981-1185 981-1186
AMEX: VGZ ■ *TF:* 866-981-1185 ■ *Web:* www.vistagold.com
Western Copper Corp 1111 W Georgia St Suite 2050 ... Vancouver BC V6E4M3 604-684-9497 688-4670
AMEX: WTZ
Western Nuclear Inc 2801 Youngfield St Suite 340 ... Golden CO 80401 303-274-1767 274-1762
Wharf Resources USA Inc 10928 Wharf Rd ... Lead SD 57754 605-584-1441 584-4188
Xstrata Canada Corp 100 King St W Suite 6900 PO Box 403 ... Toronto ON M5X1E3 416-775-1500 775-1744
Web: www.xstrata.com
Yamana Gold Inc 150 York St Suite 1102 ... Toronto ON M5H3S5 416-815-0220 815-0021
AMEX: AUY ■ *TF:* 888-809-0925 ■ *Web:* www.yamana.com
Zinifex Canada Inc 1113 Jade Ct Suite 401 ... Thunder Bay ON P7B6M7 807-346-1668 345-0284
Web: www.zinifex.com

506 MINING - MINERALS

506-1 Chemical & Fertilizer Minerals Mining

Phone / Fax

American Borate Corp 5700 Cleveland St Suite 420 ... Virginia Beach VA 23462 757-490-2242 490-1548
TF: 800-486-1072
General Chemical Soda Ash Partners PO Box 551 ... Green River WY 82935 307-875-3350 872-3406
Grace Pacific Corp PO Box 78 ... Honolulu HI 96810 808-674-8383 674-1040
Web: www.gracepacificcorp.com
Moab Salt LLC PO Box 1208 ... Moab UT 84532 435-259-7171 259-7100
New Riverside Ochre Co Inc PO Box 460 ... Cartersville GA 30120 770-382-4568 387-1658
TF Orders: 800-248-0176 ■ *Web:* www.nroonline.com
OCI Chemical Corp 1800 W Oak Commons Ct ... Marietta GA 30062 770-261-0400 261-0399*
**Fax:* Sales ■ *TF:* 800-865-1774 ■ *Web:* www.ocichemical.com
Potash Corp 1101 Skokie Blvd ... Northbrook IL 60062 847-849-4200 849-4695
TF: 800-645-2183 ■ *Web:* www.potashcorp.com
Potash Corp of Saskatchewan Inc 122 1st Ave S Suite 500 ... Saskatoon SK S7K7G3 306-933-8500 933-8844
NYSE: POT ■ *TF:* 800-667-3930 ■ *Web:* www.potashcorp.com
Solvay Minerals Inc 3333 Richmond Ave ... Houston TX 77098 713-525-6800 525-7805
TF: 800-443-2785 ■ *Web:* www.solvaychemicals.us
United Salt Corp 4800 San Felipe St ... Houston TX 77056 713-877-2600 877-2604
TF: 800-554-8658 ■ *Web:* www.unitedsalt.com
US Borax Inc 26877 Tourney Rd ... Valencia CA 91355 661-287-5400 287-5495
TF: 800-533-4872 ■ *Web:* www.borax.com

506-2 Clay, Ceramic, Refractory Minerals Mining

Phone / Fax

AMCOL International Corp 1500 W Shure Dr ... Arlington Heights IL 60004 847-392-4600 506-6199
NYSE: ACO ■ *TF:* 800-323-0629 ■ *Web:* www.amcol.com
American Colloid Co 1500 W Shure Dr ... Arlington Heights IL 60004 847-392-4600 506-6199
TF: 800-323-0629 ■ *Web:* www.colloid.com
Black Hills Bentonite Co 55 Saltcreek Hwy ... Casper WY 82601 307-265-3740 235-8511
TF Orders: 800-788-9443 ■ *Web:* www.bhbentonite.com
CT Harris Inc 9411 Deepstep Rd ... Sandersville GA 31082 478-552-5070 552-7699
TF: 800-547-6404
Dixie Clay Co 305 Dixie Clay Rd ... Bath SC 29816 803-593-2592 593-8761
Harris CT Inc 9411 Deepstep Rd ... Sandersville GA 31082 478-552-5070 552-7699
TF: 800-547-6404
HC Spinks Clay Co Inc 275 Carothers Loop PO Box 820 ... Paris TN 38242 731-642-5414 642-5493
Web: www.spinksclay.com
Hecla Mining Co 6500 N Mineral Dr Suite 200 ... Coeur d'Alene ID 83815 208-769-4100 769-4107
NYSE: HL ■ *Web:* www.hecla-mining.com
Holmes Limestone Co 4255 SR 39 ... Berlin OH 44610 330-893-2721 893-2941
IMERYS 100 Mansell Ct E Suite 300 ... Roswell GA 30076 770-594-0660 645-3384
TF: 800-374-3224
Kentucky-Tennessee Clay Co 1441 Donelson Pike ... Nashville TN 37217 615-365-0852 365-0842
TF: 800-814-4538 ■ *Web:* www.k-tclay.com
Kyanite Mining Corp US Rt 15 S ... Dillwyn VA 23936 434-983-2043 983-5178
Web: www.kyanite.com
Milwhite Inc 5487 South Padre Island Hwy ... Brownsville TX 78521 956-547-1970
TF: 800-442-0082 ■ *Web:* www.milwhite.com
Riverside Clay Co Inc 201 Truss Ferry Rd ... Pell City AL 35128 205-338-3366 338-7456
TF: 800-226-4542
Riverside Refractories Inc 201 Truss Ferry Rd ... Pell City AL 35128 205-338-3366 338-7456
TF: 800-226-4542 ■ *Web:* www.riversiderefractories.com
RT Vanderbilt Co Inc 30 Winfield St ... Norwalk CT 06855 203-853-1400 853-1452
TF Cust Svc: 800-243-6064 ■ *Web:* www.rtvanderbilt.com
Southern Clay Products Inc 1212 Church St ... Gonzales TX 78629 830-672-2891 672-1903*
**Fax:* Cust Svc ■ *TF:* 800-324-2891 ■ *Web:* www.scprod.com
Texas Industries Inc 1341 W Mockingbird Ln Suite 700W ... Dallas TX 75247 972-647-6700 647-3878
NYSE: TXI ■ *Web:* www.txi.com
Thiele Kaolin Co PO Box 1056 ... Sandersville GA 31082 478-552-3951 552-4105*
**Fax:* Mail Rm ■ *Web:* www.thielekaolin.com
US Silica Co 106 Sand Mine Rd PO Box 187 ... Berkeley Springs WV 25411 304-258-2500 258-8295
TF: 800-243-7500 ■ *Web:* www.u-s-silica.com
Wyo-Ben Inc 1345 Discovery Dr ... Billings MT 59102 406-652-6351 656-0748
TF Cust Svc: 800-548-7055 ■ *Web:* www.wyoben.com

506-3 Minerals Mining (Misc)

Phone / Fax

Anooraq Resources Corp 800 W Pender St Suite 1020 ... Vancouver BC V6C2V6 604-684-6365 684-8092
AMEX: ANO ■ *TF:* 800-667-2114 ■ *Web:* www.anooraqresources.com
Barretts Minerals Inc 8625 Hwy 91 S ... Dillon MT 59725 406-683-4231 683-3351
Gouverneur Talc Co Inc 1837 State Hwy 812 ... Gouverneur NY 13642 315-287-0100 287-0948
TF: 800-243-6064 ■ *Web:* www.rtvanderbilt.com/gouv.htm
Harborlite Corp 130 Castilian Dr ... Goleta CA 93117 805-562-9905
ILC Resources 500 New York Ave ... Des Moines IA 50313 515-243-8106 244-3200
TF: 800-247-2133 ■ *Web:* www.ilcresources.com
Luzenac America Inc 345 Inverness Dr S Suite 310 ... Centennial CO 80112 303-643-0400 643-0446
TF: 800-525-8252 ■ *Web:* www.luzenac.com
Milwhite Inc 5487 South Padre Island Hwy ... Brownsville TX 78521 956-547-1970
TF: 800-442-0082 ■ *Web:* www.milwhite.com
Mountain Province Diamonds Inc 401 Bay St Suite 2700 ... Toronto ON M5H2Y4 416-361-3562 603-8565
AMEX: MDM ■ *Web:* www.mountainprovince.com
RT Vanderbilt Co Inc 30 Winfield St ... Norwalk CT 06855 203-853-1400 853-1452
TF Cust Svc: 800-243-6064 ■ *Web:* www.rtvanderbilt.com
Standard Mineral Co 400 Talcmine Rd ... Robbins NC 27325 910-948-2267 948-4840
Stornoway Diamond Corp 625 Howe St Suite 800 ... Vancouver BC V6C2T6 604-331-2259 668-8366
TSX: SWY ■ *TF:* 888-338-2200 ■ *Web:* www.stornowaydiamonds.com
Tahera Diamond Corp
77 King St W PO Box 1020 TDC Postal Station ... Toronto ON M5K1P2 416-777-1998 777-1898
TSX: TAH ■ *TF:* 877-777-2004 ■ *Web:* www.tahera.com
Vanderbilt Minerals Corp 30 Winfield St ... Norwalk CT 06855 203-853-1400 853-1452
TF: 800-243-6064 ■ *Web:* www.rtvanderbilt.com
WGI Heavy Minerals Inc 810 E Sherman Ave ... Coeur d'Alene ID 83814 208-666-6000 666-4000
TSX: WG ■ *TF:* 888-542-7638 ■ *Web:* www.wgiheavyminerals.com

506-4 Sand & Gravel Pits

Phone / Fax

Best Sand Corp 11830 Ravenna Rd PO Box 87 ... Chardon OH 44024 440-285-3132 285-4109
TF: 800-237-4986 ■ *Web:* www.fairmountminerals.com
Brox Industries Inc 1471 Methuen St ... Dracut MA 01826 978-454-9105 805-9720
Web: www.broxindustries.com
Buckhart Sand & Gravel Inc PO Box 347 ... Mechanicsburg IL 62545 217-525-1752 498-7248
Cadman Inc 7554 185th Ave NE Suite 100 PO Box 97038 ... Redmond WA 98073 425-868-1234 961-7390
TF: 888-322-6847 ■ *Web:* www.cadman.com
Cemex Inc PO Box 3004 ... Florida City FL 33034 305-247-3011 248-9112
Web: www.cemexusa.com
Edward C Levy Co 9300 Dix St ... Dearborn MI 48120 313-843-7200 429-2448*
**Fax:* Sales ■ *Web:* www.edwclevy.com
Elmer Larson LLC 21218 Airport Rd ... Sycamore IL 60178 815-895-4837 895-4437
Web: www.elmerlarsonllc.com
ER Jahna Industries Inc 202 E Stuart Ave PO Drawer 840 ... Lake Wales FL 33859 863-676-9431 676-5137
Web: www.jahna.com
Everist LG Inc 300 S Phillips Ave Suite 200 ... Sioux Falls SD 57117 605-334-5000 334-3656
Web: www.lgeverist.com
Fairfax Sand & Crushed Stone Co 8490 Garrett Hwy ... Oakland MD 21550 301-334-8101 334-9836
TF: 800-325-8663
Fairmount Minerals Inc 18153 Northshore Dr PO Box 121 ... Grand Haven MI 49417 616-842-7900 846-1440
Fisher Sand & Gravel Co 3020 Energy Dr PO Box 1034 ... Dickinson ND 58602 701-456-9184 456-9168
TF: 800-932-8740
Florida Rock Industries Inc 155 E 21st St ... Jacksonville FL 32206 904-355-1781 791-1807
NYSE: FRK ■ *TF:* 800-874-8382 ■ *Web:* www.flarock.com
Frank W Whitcomb Construction Corp PO Box 1000 ... Walpole NH 03608 603-445-5555 445-5307
TF: 800-238-7283
Hills Materials Co 3975 Sturgis Rd PO Box 2320 ... Rapid City SD 57709 605-394-3300 341-3446
Web: www.hillsmaterials.com
Hilltop Basic Resources Inc 1 W 4th St Suite 1100 ... Cincinnati OH 45202 513-651-5000 684-8222
Web: www.hilltopbasicresources.com
Holland Corp 9131 Noland Rd Suite 86 ... Lenexa KS 66215 913-888-5277 888-0253
Jahna ER Industries Inc 202 E Stuart Ave PO Drawer 840 ... Lake Wales FL 33859 863-676-9431 676-5137
Web: www.jahna.com
Janesville Sand & Lycon Co 1110 Harding St ... Janesville WI 53547 608-754-7701 754-8555
TF: 800-955-7702 ■ *Web:* www.jsandg.com
Lafarge North America Inc 12950 Worldgate Dr Suite 600 ... Herndon VA 20170 703-480-3600 796-2214
NYSE: LAF ■ *Web:* www.lafargenorthamerica.com
Larson Elmer LLC 21218 Airport Rd ... Sycamore IL 60178 815-895-4837 895-4437
Web: www.elmerlarsonllc.com
Laurel Sand & Gravel Inc DBA SW Barrick & Sons
14504 Greenview Dr Suite 210 ... Laurel MD 20708 301-953-7650 470-4075
TF: 800-762-2294
Levy Edward C Co 9300 Dix St ... Dearborn MI 48120 313-843-7200 429-2448*
**Fax:* Sales ■ *Web:* www.edwclevy.com
LG Everist Inc 300 S Phillips Ave Suite 200 ... Sioux Falls SD 57117 605-334-5000 334-3656
Web: www.lgeverist.com
Lien Pete & Sons Inc 3401 Universal Dr ... Rapid City SD 57702 605-342-7224 342-6979
Web: www.petelien.com
Lorusso SM & Sons Inc 331 West St ... Walpole MA 02081 508-668-2600 660-3023
Mark Sand & Gravel Co 525 Kennedy Park Rd PO Box 458 ... Fergus Falls MN 56538 218-736-7523 736-2647
TF: 800-427-8316
Martin Marietta Materials Inc 2710 Wycliff Rd ... Raleigh NC 27607 919-781-4550
NYSE: MLM ■ *Web:* www.martinmarietta.com
Material Service Corp 181 W Madison ... Chicago IL 60602 312-372-3600 782-1916
TF: 800-642-8936 ■ *Web:* www.materialservice.com
McCabe Sand & Gravel Co 120 Berkley St ... Taunton MA 02780 508-823-0771 823-7305
Michels Corp 817 W Main St ... Brownsville WI 53006 920-583-3132 583-3429
Web: www.michels-usa.com
Miles Sand & Gravel Inc 1220 M St SE PO Box 130 ... Auburn WA 98071 253-833-3700 833-3746
New Enterprise Stone & Lime Co Inc
3912 Brumbaugh Rd PO Box 77 ... New Enterprise PA 16664 814-766-2211 766-4400
Web: www.nesl.com
O & G Industries Inc 112 Wall St ... Torrington CT 06790 860-489-9261 496-4286
Web: www.ogindustries.com
Oglebay Norton Co 1001 Lakeside Ave 15th Fl ... Cleveland OH 44114 216-861-3300 861-8709
TF: 800-321-4230 ■ *Web:* www.oglebaynorton.com
Pete Lien & Sons Inc 3401 Universal Dr ... Rapid City SD 57702 605-342-7224 342-6979
Web: www.petelien.com
Pike Industries Inc 3 Eastgate Park Rd ... Belmont NH 03220 603-527-5100 527-5101
TF: 800-283-7453 ■ *Web:* www.pikeindustries.com
Pounding Mill Quarry Corp 171 St Clair's Crossing ... Bluefield VA 24605 276-326-1145 322-1718
TF: 888-661-7625 ■ *Web:* www.pmqc.com
Rochester Sand & Gravel Inc 4105 E River Rd NE ... Rochester MN 55906 507-288-7447 252-3477
Rogers Group Inc 421 Great Circle Rd ... Nashville TN 37228 615-242-0585
Web: www.rogersgroupinc.com
SM Lorusso & Sons Inc 331 West St ... Walpole MA 02081 508-668-2600 660-3023
Standard Sand & Silica Co 1850 Hwy 17-92 PO Box 1059 ... Davenport FL 33836 863-422-7100 421-7349
TF: 877-444-7263 ■ *Web:* www.standardsand.com
SW Barrick & Sons 14504 Greenview Dr Suite 210 ... Laurel MD 20708 301-953-7650 470-4075
TF: 800-762-2294
Syar Industries Inc 2301 Napa Vallejo Hwy ... Napa CA 94558 707-252-8711 257-2630
Texas Industries Inc 1341 W Mockingbird Ln Suite 700W ... Dallas TX 75247 972-647-6700 647-3878
NYSE: TXI ■ *Web:* www.txi.com
Thelen Sand & Gravel Inc 28955 W SR-173 ... Antioch IL 60002 847-395-3313 395-3452
TF: 800-537-2324 ■ *Web:* www.thelensg.com
Tower Rock Stone Co
19829 Lower Frenchman Rd PO Box 111 ... Sainte Genevieve MO 63670 573-883-7415 883-3067
Unimin Corp 258 Elm St ... New Canaan CT 06840 203-966-8880 966-1557
TF: 800-223-2236 ■ *Web:* www.unimin.com
US Silica Co 106 Sand Mine Rd PO Box 187 ... Berkeley Springs WV 25411 304-258-2500 258-8295
TF: 800-243-7500 ■ *Web:* www.u-s-silica.com
Valco Inc 200 S 17th St PO Box 550 ... Rocky Ford CO 81067 719-254-7464 254-7468
Web: www.valco-inc.com
Wendling Quarries Inc 2647 225th St PO Box 230 ... De Witt IA 52742 563-659-9181 659-3393
Web: www.wendlingquarries.com
Westroc Inc 670 W 220 S ... Pleasant Grove UT 84062 801-785-5600 785-7408
Web: www.westrocinc.com
Whibco Inc 87 E Commerce St ... Bridgeton NJ 08302 856-455-9200 455-8884
TF: 800-631-8010
Whitcomb Frank W Construction Corp PO Box 1000 ... Walpole NH 03608 603-445-5555 445-5307
TF: 800-238-7283

506-5 Stone Quarries - Crushed & Broken Stone

Phone / Fax

Aggregate Industries Management Inc
7529 Standish Pl Suite 200 ... Rockville MD 20855 301-284-3600 284-3645
Web: www.aggregate-us.com
Anderson Columbia Co Inc 871 NW Guerdon St PO Box 1829 ... Lake City FL 32056 386-752-7585 755-5430
Web: www.andersoncolumbia.com
Ararat Rock Products Co 525 Quarry Rd ... Mount Airy NC 27030 336-786-4693 786-2189
Bellco Materials Inc 453 N Ash St PO Box 466 ... Nowata OK 74048 918-273-1416 273-1460
Berks Products Corp 965 Berkshire Blvd ... Reading PA 19610 610-374-5131 375-1469
TF: 800-282-2375 ■ *Web:* www.berksproducts.com
Brox Industries Inc 1471 Methuen St ... Dracut MA 01826 978-454-9105 805-9720
Web: www.broxindustries.com
Burroughs Materials Corp 51445 W 12-Mile Rd ... Wixom MI 48393 248-348-8511 349-9007
Cemex Inc PO Box 3004 ... Florida City FL 33034 305-247-3011 248-9112
Web: www.cemexusa.com
Cessford Construction Co 3808 Old Hwy 61 ... Burlington IA 52601 319-753-2297 753-0926
TF: 800-747-2297 ■ *Web:* www.cessfordconstruction.com
Charles W Barger & Sons Construction Co Inc
10 Bordens School Ln ... Lexington VA 24450 540-463-2106 463-2108

Stone Quarries - Crushed & Broken Stone (Cont'd)

Phone *Fax*

Columbia Quarry Co 200 Todd Center Dr ... Columbia IL 62236 618-281-7631 281-6120
Web: www.columbiaquarry.com

Eastern Industries Inc 4401 Camp Meeting Rd Suite 200 ... Center Valley PA 18034 610-866-0932 867-1886
Web: www.eastern-ind.com

Edward C Levy Co 9300 Dix St ... Dearborn MI 48120 313-843-7200 429-2448*
**Fax:* Sales ■ *Web:* www.edwclevy.com

Elmer Larson LLC 21218 Airport Rd ... Sycamore IL 60178 815-895-4837 895-4437
Web: www.elmerlarsonllc.com

ER Jahna Industries Inc 202 E Stuart Ave PO Drawer 840 ... Lake Wales FL 33859 863-676-9431 676-5137
Web: www.jahna.com

Erie Stone/Irving Materials Inc 500 Erie Stone Rd ... Huntington IN 46750 260-356-7214 356-6032
Web: www.irvmat.com

Everist LG Inc 300 S Phillips Ave Suite 200 ... Sioux Falls SD 57117 605-334-5000 334-3656
Web: www.lgeverist.com

Fairfax Sand & Crushed Stone Co 8490 Garrett Hwy ... Oakland MD 21550 301-334-8101 334-9836
TF: 800-325-8663

Florida Crushed Stone Co 1616 S 14th St PO Box 49180 ... Leesburg FL 34749 352-787-0608 787-7886
TF: 800-767-0608 ■ *Web:* www.fcsco.com

Florida Rock Industries Inc 155 E 21st St ... Jacksonville FL 32206 904-355-1781 791-1807
NYSE: FRK ■ *TF:* 800-874-8382 ■ *Web:* www.flarock.com

Frank W Whitcomb Construction Corp PO Box 1000 ... Walpole NH 03608 603-445-5555 445-5307
TF: 800-238-7283

Franklin Industrial Minerals 612 10th Ave N ... Nashville TN 37203 615-259-4222 726-2693
TF: 800-626-8147 ■ *Web:* www.frankmin.com

Grace Pacific Corp PO Box 78 ... Honolulu HI 96810 808-674-8383 674-1040
Web: www.gracepacificcorp.com

Hamm NR Quarry Inc 609 Perry Pl PO Box 17 ... Perry KS 66073 785-597-5111 597-5117

Hanson Aggregates North America 8505 Freeport Pkwy Suite 500 ... Irving TX 75063 972-621-0345 621-0506
TF: 800-687-6549 ■ *Web:* www.hanson-america.com

Hanson Building Products North America 3500 Maple Ave ... Dallas TX 75219 214-525-5500 525-5563
TF: 800-527-2362 ■ *Web:* www.hanson-america.com

HB Mellot Estate Inc 100 Mellott Dr Suite 100 ... Warfordsburg PA 17267 301-678-2000 678-2012

Hills Materials Co 3975 Sturgis Rd PO Box 2320 ... Rapid City SD 57709 605-394-3300 341-3446
Web: www.hillsmaterials.com

Holland Corp 9131 Noland Rd Suite 86 ... Lenexa KS 66215 913-888-5277 888-0253

Hunt Midwest Enterprises Inc 8300 NE Underground Dr ... Kansas City MO 64161 816-455-2500
TF: 800-551-6877 ■ *Web:* www.huntmidwest.com

Hunt Midwest Mining Inc 8300 NE Underground Dr ... Kansas City MO 64161 816-455-2500 455-4462
Web: www.huntmidwest.com

Jahna ER Industries Inc 202 E Stuart Ave PO Drawer 840 ... Lake Wales FL 33859 863-676-9431 676-5137
Web: www.jahna.com

JF Shea Co Inc Redding Div 17400 Clear Creek Rd ... Redding CA 96001 530-246-2200 246-0554
Web: www.jfshea.com

John S Lane & Son Inc 730 E Mountain Rd PO Box 125 ... Westfield MA 01086 413-568-8986 562-7651

Kerford Limestone Co Inc 1815 Y St PO Box 80268 ... Lincoln NE 68501 402-434-1700 434-1799
TF: 800-759-2526

Keystone Lime Co Inc PO Box 278 ... Springs PA 15562 814-662-2711 662-4421

Lafarge North America Inc 12950 Worldgate Dr Suite 600 ... Herndon VA 20170 703-480-3600 796-2214
NYSE: LAF ■ *Web:* www.lafargenorthamerica.com

Lane John S & Son Inc 730 E Mountain Rd PO Box 125 ... Westfield MA 01086 413-568-8986 562-7651

Larson Elmer LLC 21218 Airport Rd ... Sycamore IL 60178 815-895-4837 895-4437
Web: www.elmerlarsonllc.com

Levy Edward C Co 9300 Dix St ... Dearborn MI 48120 313-843-7200 429-2448*
**Fax:* Sales ■ *Web:* www.edwclevy.com

LG Everist Inc 300 S Phillips Ave Suite 200 ... Sioux Falls SD 57117 605-334-5000 334-3656
Web: www.lgeverist.com

Martin Marietta Materials Inc 2710 Wycliff Rd ... Raleigh NC 27607 919-781-4550
NYSE: MLM ■ *Web:* www.martinmarietta.com

Material Service Corp 181 W Madison ... Chicago IL 60602 312-372-3600 782-1916
TF: 800-642-8936 ■ *Web:* www.materialservice.com

Meckley's Limestone Products Inc RR 1 Box 1682 ... Herndon PA 17830 570-758-3001 758-2400
Web: www.meckleys.com

Mellott HB Estate Inc 100 Mellott Dr Suite 100 ... Warfordsburg PA 17267 301-678-2000 678-2012

Meshberger Brothers Stone Corp 6311 W SR 218 ... Bluffton IN 46714 260-334-5311 334-5353
Web: www.meshbergerbros.com

Michels Corp 817 W Main St ... Brownsville WI 53006 920-583-3132 583-3429
Web: www.michels-usa.com

Michigan Limestone Operations LP 1035 Calcite Rd ... Rogers City MI 49779 989-734-2131 734-4779
TF: 800-221-3803 ■ *Web:* www.mlo.net

Midwest Minerals Inc 709 N Locust St ... Pittsburg KS 66762 620-231-8120 235-0840
Web: www.midwestminerals.com

Mulzer Crushed Stone Inc 534 Mozart St PO Box 249 ... Tell City IN 47586 812-547-7921 547-6757
Web: www.mulzer.com

Nally & Gibson Georgetown LLC
100 Farmers Bank Dr Suite 400 ... Georgetown KY 40324 502-868-0231 868-0234

New Enterprise Stone & Lime Co Inc
3912 Brumbaugh Rd PO Box 77 ... New Enterprise PA 16664 814-766-2211 766-4400
Web: www.nesl.com

NR Hamm Quarry Inc 609 Perry Pl PO Box 17 ... Perry KS 66073 785-597-5111 597-5117

Pennsy Supply Inc 1001 Paxton St ... Harrisburg PA 17104 717-233-4511 238-7312
Web: www.pennsysupply.com

Pike Industries Inc 3 Eastgate Park Rd ... Belmont NH 03220 603-527-5100 527-5101
TF: 800-283-7453 ■ *Web:* www.pikeindustries.com

Piqua Materials Inc 1750 W Statler Rd ... Piqua OH 45356 937-773-4824 773-0791
TF: 800-338-2962

Pounding Mill Quarry Corp 171 St Clair's Crossing ... Bluefield VA 24605 276-326-1145 322-1718
TF: 888-661-7625 ■ *Web:* www.pmqc.com

Rochester Sand & Gravel Inc 4105 E River Rd NE ... Rochester MN 55906 507-288-7447 252-3477

Rockville Crushed Stone Inc
6401 Golden Triangle Dr Suite 400 ... Greenbelt MD 20770 301-982-1400

Rogers Group Inc 421 Great Circle Rd ... Nashville TN 37228 615-242-0585
Web: www.rogersgroupinc.com

Shea JF Co Inc Redding Div 17400 Clear Creek Rd ... Redding CA 96001 530-246-2200 246-0554
Web: www.jfshea.com

Stone Industries Inc 400 Central Ave PO Box 8310 ... Haledon NJ 07538 973-595-6250 595-6920
Web: www.braenstone.com

Stoneco Inc 7555 Whiteford Rd ... Ottawa Lake MI 49267 734-856-2257 854-2607

Syar Industries Inc 2301 Napa Vallejo Hwy ... Napa CA 94558 707-252-8711 257-2630

Texas Crushed Stone Co 5300 S IH-35 ... Georgetown TX 78628 512-863-5511 244-6055
TF: 800-772-8272

Texas Industries Inc 1341 W Mockingbird Ln Suite 700W ... Dallas TX 75247 972-647-6700 647-3878
NYSE: TXI ■ *Web:* www.txi.com

Tilcon NY Inc 162 Old Mill Rd ... West Nyack NY 10994 845-358-4500 480-3128
TF: 800-872-7762 ■ *Web:* www.tilconny.com

Tower Rock Stone Co
19829 Lower Frenchman Rd PO Box 111 ... Sainte Genevieve MO 63670 573-883-7415 883-3067

Trap Rock Industries Inc PO Box 419 ... Kingston NJ 08528 609-924-0300
Web: www.traprock.com

US Lime & Minerals Inc 5429 LBJ Fwy Suite 230 ... Dallas TX 75240 972-991-8400 385-1340
NASDAQ: USLM ■ *TF:* 800-991-5463 ■ *Web:* www.uslm.com

Valley Quarries Inc 297 Quarry Rd PO Box J ... Chambersburg PA 17201 717-267-2244 267-2521
Web: www.valleyquarries.com

Phone *Fax*

Vulcan Materials Co
1200 Urban Center Dr PO Box 385014 ... Birmingham AL 35238 205-298-3000 298-2942
NYSE: VMC ■ *Web:* www.vulcanmaterials.com

Vulcan Materials Co Western Div 3200 San Fernando Rd ... Los Angeles CA 90065 323-258-2777 258-1583
TF: 800-225-6280 ■ *Web:* www.vulcanmaterials.com

Wendling Quarries Inc 2647 225th St PO Box 230 ... De Witt IA 52742 563-659-9181 659-3393
Web: www.wendlingquarries.com

Whitcomb Frank W Construction Corp PO Box 1000 ... Walpole NH 03608 603-445-5555 445-5307
TF: 800-238-7283

Wyroc Inc 2142 Industrial Ct PO Box 1239 ... Vista CA 92085 760-727-0878 727-9238
Web: www.wyroc.com

506-6 Stone Quarries - Dimension Stone

Phone *Fax*

APAC Inc 900 Ashwood Pkwy Suite 700 ... Atlanta GA 30338 770-392-5300 392-5393
TF: 800-241-7074 ■ *Web:* www.apac.com

Cadman Inc 7554 185th Ave NE Suite 100 PO Box 97038 ... Redmond WA 98073 425-868-1234 961-7390
TF: 888-322-6847 ■ *Web:* www.cadman.com

Fletcher Granite Co Inc 534 Groton Rd ... Westford MA 01886 978-251-4031 251-8773
TF: 800-253-8168 ■ *Web:* www.fletchergranite.com

Liter's Quarry Inc 5918 Haunz Ln ... Louisville KY 40241 502-241-7637 241-9410
Web: www.litersquarry.com

LW Rozzo Inc 17200 Pines Blvd ... Pembroke Pines FL 33029 954-435-8501 436-6243

New Enterprise Stone & Lime Co Inc
3912 Brumbaugh Rd PO Box 77 ... New Enterprise PA 16664 814-766-2211 766-4400
Web: www.nesl.com

Pounding Mill Quarry Corp 171 St Clair's Crossing ... Bluefield VA 24605 276-326-1145 322-1718
TF: 888-661-7625 ■ *Web:* www.pmqc.com

Swenson Granite Co LLC 369 N State St ... Concord NH 03301 603-225-2783 227-9541
Web: www.swensongranite.com

Tower Rock Stone Co
19829 Lower Frenchman Rd PO Box 111 ... Sainte Genevieve MO 63670 573-883-7415 883-3067

Wendling Quarries Inc 2647 225th St PO Box 230 ... De Witt IA 52742 563-659-9181 659-3393
Web: www.wendlingquarries.com

507 MISSILES, SPACE VEHICLES, PARTS

SEE ALSO Weapons & Ordnance (Military) p. 2413

Phone *Fax*

AeroAstro Inc 20145 Ashbrook Pl ... Ashburn VA 20147 703-723-9800 723-9850
TF: 800-669-5437 ■ *Web:* www.aeroastro.com

Aerojet Hwy 50 Aerojet Rd ... Rancho Cordova CA 95742 916-355-1000 351-8667
Web: www.aerojet.com

Aerojet Redmond Rocket Center 11411 139th Pl NE ... Redmond WA 98052 425-885-5000 882-5804*
**Fax:* Mail Rm ■ *Web:* www.rocket.com

Alliant Techsystems Inc (ATK) 5050 Lincoln Dr ... Edina MN 55436 952-351-3000 351-3009
NYSE: ATK ■ *Web:* www.atk.com

Applied Aerospace Structures Corp 3437 S Airport Way ... Stockton CA 95206 209-982-0160 983-3375
Web: www.aascworld.com

ATK (Alliant Techsystems Inc) 5050 Lincoln Dr ... Edina MN 55436 952-351-3000 351-3009
NYSE: ATK ■ *Web:* www.atk.com

Boeing Co 100 N Riverside Plaza ... Chicago IL 60606 312-544-2000 544-2082*
NYSE: BA ■ **Fax:* PR ■ *Web:* www.boeing.com

Boeing Co Integrated Defense Systems PO Box 516 ... Saint Louis MO 63166 314-232-0232
Web: www.boeing.com/ids

Coleman Aerospace Corp 7675 Municipal Dr ... Orlando FL 32819 407-354-0047 354-1112
Web: www.crc.com

DRS Unmanned Technologies Inc 6300 Columbia St ... Mineral Wells TX 76067 817-850-3860 850-3880
Web: www.drs.com

EDO Defense Systems 1500 New Horizons Blvd ... North Amityville NY 11701 631-630-4000 630-0470
Web: www.edocorp.com

Esterline Mason 13955 Balboa Blvd ... Sylmar CA 91342 818-361-3366 365-6809*
**Fax:* Sales ■ *TF:* 800-232-7700 ■ *Web:* www.mason-electric.com

G & H Technology Inc 750 W Ventura Blvd ... Camarillo CA 93010 805-484-0543 987-5062
Web: www.ghtech.com

Hamilton Sundstrand Corp 1 Hamilton Rd ... Windsor Locks CT 06096 860-654-6000 654-4741
Web: www.hamiltonsundstrandcorp.com

Herley Lancaster 3061 Industry Dr ... Lancaster PA 17603 717-397-2777 397-7079*
**Fax:* Sales ■ *Web:* www.herley.com

Hi-Shear Technology Corp 24225 Garnier St ... Torrance CA 90505 310-784-2100 325-5354
AMEX: HSR ■ *Web:* www.hstc.com

HITCO Carbon Composites Inc 1600 W 135th St ... Gardena CA 90249 310-527-0700 516-5714*
**Fax:* Sales ■ *Web:* www.hitco.com

Honeywell Space Systems 13350 US Hwy 19 N ... Clearwater FL 33764 727-539-4000
Web: content.honeywell.com/dses/space/

International Launch Services 1660 International Dr Suite 800 ... McLean VA 22102 571-633-7400 633-7500
Web: www.ilslaunch.com

Keystone Engineering Co 4401 Donald Douglas Dr ... Long Beach CA 90808 562-420-1381 420-2355
Web: www.keystoneengineering.com

Kistler Aerospace Corp 4300 Amelia Earhart Ln ... Oklahoma City OK 73159 405-488-1200 488-1204
Web: www.kistleraerospace.com

L'Garde Inc 15181 Woodlawn Ave ... Tustin CA 92780 714-259-0771 259-7822
Web: www.lgarde.com

Lockheed Martin Corp 6801 Rockledge Dr ... Bethesda MD 20817 301-897-6000 897-6083
NYSE: LMT ■ *Web:* www.lockheedmartin.com

Lockheed Martin Missiles & Fire Control Dallas PO Box 650003 ... Dallas TX 75265 972-603-1000 603-1578*
**Fax:* Hum Res ■ *Web:* www.missilesandfirecontrol.com

Lockheed Martin Missiles & Fire Control Orlando
5600 Sand Lake Rd ... Orlando FL 32819 407-356-2000 356-2010
Web: www.missilesandfirecontrol.com

Lockheed Martin Space Systems Co Michoud Operations
13800 Old Gentilly Rd ... New Orleans LA 70129 504-257-3311 257-4431
Web: www.lockheedmartin.com/michoud

Lourdes Industries Inc 65 Hoffman Ave ... Hauppauge NY 11788 631-234-6600 234-7595
TF: 800-368-3728 ■ *Web:* www.lourdesinc.com

Mason Controls 13955 Balboa Blvd ... Sylmar CA 91342 818-361-3366 365-6809*
**Fax:* Sales ■ *TF:* 800-232-7700 ■ *Web:* www.mason-electric.com

Orbital Sciences Corp 21839 Atlantic Blvd ... Dulles VA 20166 703-406-5000
NYSE: ORB ■ *TF:* 877-672-4825 ■ *Web:* www.orbital.com

Pratt & Whitney Government Engines & Space Propulsion Div PO Box 109600 ... West Palm Beach FL 33410 561-796-2000 796-5876*
**Fax:* Sales ■ *TF:* 800-327-3246

Pratt & Whitney Space Propulsion & Chemical Systems Div
600 Metcalf Rd ... San Jose CA 95138 408-779-9121 776-4870

Raytheon Integrated Defense Systems 50 Apple Hill Dr ... Tewksbury MA 01876 978-858-5290 858-1170
Web: www.raytheon.com/businesses/rids

Raytheon Missile Systems PO Box 11337 Bldg 807 Suite A8 ... Tucson AZ 85734 520-794-3000

Reinhold Industries Inc 12827 E Imperial Hwy ... Santa Fe Springs CA 90670 562-944-3281 944-7238
NASDAQ: RNHDA ■ *Web:* www.reinhold-ind.com

	City	State	Zip	Phone	Fax
Rockwell Collins Electromechanical Systems 17000 S Red Hill Ave. *TF:* 800-866-5775 ■ *Web:* www.rockwellcollins.com/electromechanical	Irvine	CA	92614	949-250-1015	250-0497
Sea Launch Co LLC 2700 Nimitz Rd *Web:* www.sea-launch.com	Long Beach	CA	90802	562-951-7000	
Space Vector Corp 9223 Deering Ave. *Web:* www.spacevector.com	Chatsworth	CA	91311	818-734-2600	886-4362
SPACEHAB Inc 12130 Hwy 3 Bldg 1 *NASDAQ: SPAB* ■ *Web:* www.spacehab.com	Webster	TX	77598	713-558-5000	558-5960
Sparta Inc 25531 Conner Center Dr Suite 120 *Web:* www.sparta.com	Lake Forest	CA	92630	949-768-8161	583-9113
Universal Propulsion Co 25401 N Central Ave *Web:* www.upco.goodrich.com	Phoenix	AZ	85085	623-516-3340	516-3355
Westar Aerospace & Defense Group Inc 4 Research Park Dr *Web:* www.westar.com	Saint Louis	MO	63304	636-300-5000	300-5005

508 MOBILE HOMES & BUILDINGS

	City	State	Zip	Phone	Fax
American Family Homes Inc PO Box 438 *Web:* www.taylormadehomes.com	Anderson	MO	64831	417-845-3311	845-6044
American Homestar Corp 2450 S Shore Blvd Suite 300 **Fax: Acctg* ■ *TF:* 800-234-6269 ■ *Web:* www.americanhomestar.com	League City	TX	77573	281-334-9700	334-6193*
Bonnavilla Homes 111 Grant St PO Box 127 *Web:* www.bonnavillahomes.com	Aurora	NE	68818	402-694-5250	694-5873
Buccaneer Homes of Alabama Inc 330 Buccaneer St PO Box 1418 *TF:* 800-326-2822 ■ *Web:* www.buccaneerhomes.com	Hamilton	AL	35570	205-921-3135	921-7390
Burlington Homes of Maine Inc 620 Main St. *TF:* 800-255-5218 ■ *Web:* www.burlingtonhomes.com	Oxford	ME	04270	207-539-4406	539-2900
Cavalier Homes Inc 32 Wilson Blvd Suite 100 *AMEX: CAV* ■ **Fax: Sales* ■ *TF:* 877-747-9800 ■ *Web:* www.cavalierhomebuilders.com	Addison	AL	35540	256-747-9800	747-3044*
Cavco Industries Inc 1001 N Central Ave 8th Fl *NASDAQ: CVCO* ■ *TF:* 800-790-9111 ■ *Web:* www.cavco.com	Phoenix	AZ	85004	602-256-6263	256-6189
Champion Enterprises Inc 2701 Cambridge Dr Suite 300 *NYSE: CHB* ■ *Web:* www.championhomes.net	Auburn Hills	MI	48326	248-340-9090	340-0888
Champion Home Builders Co 2701 Cambridge Dr Suite 300 *NYSE: CHB* ■ *Web:* www.championhomes.net	Auburn Hills	MI	48326	248-340-9090	340-0888
Chariot Eagle Inc 931 NW 37th Ave. *Web:* www.charioteagle.com	Ocala	FL	34475	352-629-7007	629-6920
Chief Industries Inc 3942 W Old Hwy 30 PO Box 2078 *Web:* www.chiefind.com	Grand Island	NE	68802	308-389-7200	389-7221
Clayton Homes Inc PO Box 9780 *Web:* www.clayton.net	Maryville	TN	37802	865-380-3000	380-3788
Commodore Corp 1423 Lincolnway E *TF:* 800-554-4285 ■ *Web:* www.commodorehomes.com	Goshen	IN	46526	574-533-7100	534-2716
Elliott Manufactured Homes Inc PO Box 209	Waurika	OK	73573	580-228-3572	228-3110
Fairmont Homes Inc 502 S Oakland St. *TF:* 800-777-8787 ■ *Web:* www.fairmonthomes.com	Nappanee	IN	46550	574-773-7941	773-2185
Fleetwood Enterprises Inc 3125 Myers St. *NYSE: FLE* ■ *Web:* www.fleetwood.com	Riverside	CA	92503	951-351-3500	351-3690
Fleetwood Homes of Idaho Inc 2611 E Comstock Ave **Fax: Sales* ■ *TF:* 800-334-8958	Nampa	ID	83687	208-466-2438	467-1616*
Fleetwood Homes of North Carolina Inc 349 E Railroad St *TF:* 800-649-6713 ■ *Web:* www.fleetwood.com	Pembroke	NC	28372	910-521-9731	521-3403
Fleetwood Homes of Northern California Inc 18 N Pioneer Ave. *TF:* 800-666-1210 ■ *Web:* www.fleetwoodhomes-norcal.com	Woodland	CA	95776	530-662-3223	662-6425
Fleetwood Homes of Virginia Inc 90 Weaver St *TF:* 800-888-6811 ■ *Web:* www.fleetwood.com	Rocky Mount	VA	24151	540-483-5171	483-4948
Fleetwood Homes of Washington Inc 211 5th St *TF Sales:* 800-275-6869 ■ *Web:* www.fleetwood.com	Woodland	WA	98674	360-225-9461	225-5808
Franklin Homes Inc 10655 Hwy 43 *TF:* 800-332-4511 ■ *Web:* www.franklinhomesusa.com	Russellville	AL	35653	256-332-4510	331-2203
Fuqua Homes Inc 7100 S Cooper St. *TF:* 800-336-0874 ■ *Web:* www.fuquahomes.com	Arlington	TX	76001	817-465-3211	465-5125
Giles Industries Inc 405 S Broad St. *TF:* 800-844-4537 ■ *Web:* www.gilesindustries.com	New Tazewell	TN	37825	423-626-7243	626-6919
Homark Co Inc 100 3rd St PO Box 309 *Web:* www.detroiter.com	Red Lake Falls	MN	56750	218-253-2777	253-2116
Homes of Merit Inc PO Box 1606 *TF:* 800-589-8942 ■ *Web:* www.homesofmerit.net	Bartow	FL	33831	863-533-0593	533-0310
Horton Homes Inc 101 Industrial Blvd *TF:* 800-282-2680 ■ *Web:* www.hortonhomes.com	Eatonton	GA	31024	706-485-8506	485-4446
Jacobsen Homes 600 Packard Ct PO Box 368 *TF Sales:* 800-843-1559 ■ *Web:* www.jachomes.com	Safety Harbor	FL	34695	727-726-1138	726-7019
Liberty Homes Inc 1101 Eisenhower Dr N *TF:* 800-733-0431 ■ *Web:* www.libertyhomesinc.com	Goshen	IN	46526	574-533-0431	533-0438
Manufactured Housing Enterprises Inc 09302 US SR 6 *TF:* 800-821-0220 ■ *Web:* www.mheinc.com	Bryan	OH	43506	419-636-4511	636-9144
Mark Line Industries Inc 51687 County Rd 133 *TF:* 888-627-5563 ■ *Web:* www.marklineindustries.com	Bristol	IN	46507	574-825-5851	825-9139
Marquis Homes PO Box 190 *TF:* 800-222-7876	Shippenville	PA	16254	814-226-6822	226-6827
McGrath RentCorp DBA Mobile Modular Management Corp 5700 Las Positas Rd *NASDAQ: MGRC* ■ *TF:* 800-352-2900 ■ *Web:* www.mgrc.com	Livermore	CA	94551	925-606-9200	453-3200
Mobile Modular Management Corp 5700 Las Positas Rd *NASDAQ: MGRC* ■ *TF:* 800-352-2900 ■ *Web:* www.mgrc.com	Livermore	CA	94551	925-606-9200	453-3200
Mobile/Modular Express Inc 1301 Trimble Rd **Fax: Sales* ■ *Web:* www.mobilemodular.com	Edgewood	MD	21040	410-676-3700	676-7288*
Nobility Homes Inc 3741 SW 7th St. *NASDAQ: NOBH* ■ *TF:* 800-476-6624 ■ *Web:* www.nobilityhomes.com	Ocala	FL	34474	352-732-5157	732-4203
Norris Industries Inc 1160 Hwy 11 W PO Box 99 *TF:* 800-550-1096	Bean Station	TN	37708	865-993-3343	993-2832
Oxford Homes Inc 7 Oxford Homes Ln PO Box 679 *TF:* 800-341-0436 ■ *Web:* www.oxfordhomesinc.com	Oxford	ME	04270	207-539-4412	539-4259
Palm Harbor Homes Inc 15303 Dallas Pkwy Suite 800 *NASDAQ: PHHM* ■ *TF:* 800-456-8744 ■ *Web:* www.palmharbor.com	Addison	TX	75001	972-991-2422	991-5949
Patriot Homes Inc 57420 County Rd 3 S **Fax: Sales* ■ *Web:* www.patriothomes.com	Elkhart	IN	46517	574-293-6507	522-2339*
R-Anell Custom Homes Inc 3549 Hwy 16 N *TF:* 800-951-5511 ■ *Web:* www.r-anell.com	Denver	NC	28037	704-483-5511	483-5674
Resun Leasing Inc 22810 Quicksilver Dr *TF:* 800-554-6506 ■ *Web:* www.resuncorp.com	Dulles	VA	20166	703-661-6190	661-6196
Ritz-Craft Corp of Pennsylvania Inc 15 Industrial Park Rd *TF:* 800-326-9827 ■ *Web:* www.ritz-craft.com	Mifflinburg	PA	17844	570-966-1053	966-9248
Satellite Industries Inc 2530 Xenium Ln N *TF:* 800-328-3332 ■ *Web:* www.satelliteindustries.com	Minneapolis	MN	55441	763-553-1900	551-7246
Skyline Corp 2520 By-Pass Rd *NYSE: SKY* ■ *TF:* 800-348-7469 ■ *Web:* www.skylinecorp.com	Elkhart	IN	46514	574-294-6521	295-8601
Sunshine Homes Inc 100 Sunshine Ave *TF:* 800-462-7847 ■ *Web:* www.sunshinehomes-inc.com	Red Bay	AL	35582	256-356-4427	356-9694
Taylor Made Homes Inc DBA American Family Homes Inc PO Box 438 *Web:* www.taylormadehomes.com	Anderson	MO	64831	417-845-3311	845-6044
Titan Homes Inc 951 Rt 12 S PO Box 177 *TF:* 800-937-4146	Sangerfield	NY	13455	315-841-4122	841-4660
VFP Inc 2840 Electric Rd Suite A-201 *Web:* www.vfpinc.com	Roanoke	VA	24018	540-977-0500	977-5555
Virginia Homes Mfg Corp 142 Virginia Homes Ln PO Box 410 *Web:* www.virginiahomesmfg.com	Boydton	VA	23917	434-738-6107	738-6926
Wick Building Systems Inc 405 Walter Rd. **Fax: Sales* ■ *TF:* 800-356-9682 ■ *Web:* www.wickbuildings.com	Mazomanie	WI	53560	608-795-4281	795-2294*
Williams Scotsman Inc 8211 Town Center Dr *TF:* 800-782-1500 ■ *Web:* www.willscot.com	Baltimore	MD	21236	410-931-6000	931-6000

509 MODELING AGENCIES

SEE ALSO Modeling Schools p. 1975; Talent Agencies p. 2337

	City	State	Zip	Phone	Fax
Blitz Models & Talents 487 Adelaide St W Suite 305	Toronto	ON	M5V1T4	416-703-5799	703-6232
Boss Models USA 321 W 13th St *Web:* www.bossmodels.com	New York	NY	10011	212-242-2444	633-6127
Click Model Management 129 W 27th St 12th Fl *Web:* www.clickmodel.com	New York	NY	10001	212-206-1616	206-6228
Dallas Model Group 12700 Hillcrest Rd Suite 180	Dallas	TX	75230	972-980-7647	934-0941
DNA Model Management Inc 520 Broadway 11th Fl *Web:* www.dnamodels.com	New York	NY	10012	212-226-0080	226-7711
Elite Model Management Corp 404 Park Ave S 9th Fl *Web:* www.elitemodel.com	New York	NY	10016	212-529-9700	529-9592
Ford Models Inc 111 5th Ave 9th Fl *Web:* www.fordmodels.com	New York	NY	10003	212-219-6500	966-1531
IMG Models 304 Park Ave S PH-N *Web:* www.imgworld.com	New York	NY	10010	212-253-8882	253-8883
Irene Marie Inc 728 Ocean Dr *Web:* www.irenemarie.com	Miami Beach	FL	33139	305-672-2929	674-1342
LA Models 7700 Sunset Blvd *Web:* www.lamodels.com	Los Angeles	CA	90046	323-436-7700	436-7755
Marilyn Inc 32 Union Sq E PH *Web:* www.marilynagency.com	New York	NY	10003	212-260-6500	260-0821
Next Model Management 15 Watts St 6th Fl *Web:* www.nextmodels.com	New York	NY	10013	212-925-5100	925-5931
San Diego Model Management 438 Camino del Rio S Suite 116 *Web:* www.sdmodel.com	San Diego	CA	92108	619-296-1018	296-3422
Wilhelmina Models Inc 300 Park Ave S *Web:* www.wilhelmina.com	New York	NY	10010	212-473-0700	473-3223
Women Management 199 Lafayette St 7th Fl *Web:* www.womenmanagement.com	New York	NY	10012	212-334-7480	334-7492

510 MODELING SCHOOLS

	City	State	Zip	Phone	Fax
Ambiance Models & Talent Inc 1096 Dayton Blvd *Web:* www.ambiancemodels.com	Chattanooga	TN	37405	423-265-2121	265-2190
Barbizon International LLC 311 N University Dr Suite 1002 *Web:* www.barbizonmodeling.com	Coral Springs	FL	33065	954-345-4140	345-8055
John Robert Powers International 4311 Wilshire Blvd Suite 200 *Web:* www.jrpowers.net	Los Angeles	CA	90010	323-857-5300	857-5559
Mayo-Hill School of Modeling 7887 San Felipe St Suite 127 *Web:* www.mayohill.com	Houston	TX	77063	713-789-7340	789-6163
Premiere School of Self-Improvement & Professional Modeling Inc 3455 Dakota Ave S **Fax Area Code: 651* ■ *Web:* www.premiere-modeling.com	Minneapolis	MN	55416	952-920-0681	687-9096*

511 MOPS, SPONGES, WIPING CLOTHS

SEE ALSO Brushes & Brooms p. 1397; Cleaning Products p. 1446

	City	State	Zip	Phone	Fax
A & B Wiper Supply Inc 5601 Paschall Ave *TF:* 800-333-7247 ■ *Web:* www.bestrags.com	Philadelphia	PA	19143	215-482-6100	482-6190
ABCO Products Inc 6800 NW 36th Ave *TF:* 888-694-2226 ■ *Web:* www.abcoproducts.com	Miami	FL	33147	305-694-2226	694-0451
Acme Sponge & Chamois Co Inc 855 E Pine St *Web:* www.acmesponge.com	Tarpon Springs	FL	34689	727-937-3222	942-3064
Acme Wiping Materials Co 1327 Palmetto St	Los Angeles	CA	90013	213-624-8756	624-5185
Bro-Tex Inc 800 Hampden Ave *TF:* 800-328-2282 ■ *Web:* www.brotex.com	Saint Paul	MN	55114	651-645-5721	646-1876
Butler Home Products Inc 311 Hopping Brook Rd PO Box 8000 *TF:* 800-343-3368 ■ *Web:* www.thebutler.com	Holliston	MA	01746	508-429-8100	429-1289
Cadie Products Corp 151 E 11th St *Web:* www.cadie.com	Paterson	NJ	07524	973-278-8300	278-0303
Colman Wolf Sanitary Supply Co 15201 E 11-Mile Rd *Web:* www.colmansupply.com	Roseville	MI	48066	586-779-5500	779-5505
Continental Mfg Co 305 Rock Industrial Pk Dr *TF:* 800-325-1051 ■ *Web:* www.continental-mfg.com	Bridgeton	MO	63044	314-656-4301	770-9938
Disco Inc 1895 Brannan Rd *TF:* 800-548-5150 ■ *Web:* www.katyindustries.com	McDonough	GA	30253	770-474-7575	474-9464
Ettore Products Co 2100 N Loop Rd *TF:* 800-438-8673 ■ *Web:* www.ettore.com	Alameda	CA	94502	510-748-4130	748-4146
Golden Star Inc 400 E 10th Ave **Fax Area Code: 800* ■ *TF:* 800-821-2792 ■ *Web:* www.goldenstar.com	North Kansas City	MO	64116	816-842-0233	487-4079*
Greenwood Mop & Broom Inc 312 Palmer St PO Drawer 1426 *TF:* 800-635-6849 ■ *Web:* www.greenwoodmopandbroom.com	Greenwood	SC	29648	864-227-8411	227-3200
Houston Wiper & Mill Supply Co 1234 Kress St *TF:* 800-633-5968 ■ *Web:* www.houstonwiper.com	Houston	TX	77020	713-672-0571	673-7637
Intex Supply Co 670 Alpha Dr *TF Cust Svc:* 800-753-5822	Highland Heights	OH	44143	440-449-6550	449-9868
Kleen-Tex Industries Inc 1516 Orchard Hill Rd *TF:* 800-241-2323 ■ *Web:* www.kleen-tex.com	LaGrange	GA	30240	706-882-8134	882-0729

Phone Fax

Libman Co 220 N Sheldon St Arcola IL 61910 217-268-4200 268-3439
TF: 800-646-6262 ■ Web: www.mamalibman.com

Magla Products LLC 159 South St Morristown NJ 07960 973-984-7998 984-2382
TF: 800-247-5281 ■ Web: www.magla.com

Mednik Riverbend 6740 Romiss Ct Saint Louis MO 63134 314-535-9090 524-2230
TF: 800-325-7193

Milliken & Co KEX Div 201 Lukken Industrial Dr W MS 801 LaGrange GA 30240 800-342-5539 880-5358*
*Fax Area Code: 706 ■ Web: www.milliken-kex.com

Nylonge Corp 1301 Lowell St Elyria OH 44035 440-323-6161 323-6166
Web: www.nylonge.com

O-Cedar/Vileda Inc 505 N Railroad Ave North Lake IL 60164 708-452-4100 452-9967
TF: 800-543-8105 ■ Web: www.ocedar.com

Plezall Wipers Inc 2705 N Commerce Pkwy Miramar FL 33025 954-443-5700 443-0828
TF: 800-237-8724

Signature Works Inc 1 Signature Dr Hazlehurst MS 39083 601-894-1771 894-2993
TF: 800-647-2468

Southern Wipers 100 Fairview Rd Asheville NC 28803 828-274-2100 274-0000
TF: 800-544-9387 ■ Web: www.slosman.com

Spontex Inc 100 Spontex Dr Columbia TN 38401 931-388-5632 388-4481
TF: 800-251-4222 ■ Web: www.spontexusa.com

Stough Broom & Mop Co 163 N Wesson St Tallassee AL 36078 334-283-2170 283-2408

Tranzonic Cos 670 Alpha Dr Highland Heights OH 44143 440-449-6550 445-8366*
*Fax Area Code: 800 ■ TF: 800-553-7979 ■ Web: www.tranzonic.com

TxF Products 2702 Mortris Shephard Dr PO Box 1118 Brownwood TX 76804 325-646-1504 643-5943
TF: 800-441-7894 ■ Web: www.txfproducts.com

United Textile Co Inc 2225 Grant Ave San Lorenzo CA 94580 510-276-2288 278-1981
TF: 800-233-0077 ■ Web: www.uti-rags.com

Wilen Products Inc 3760 S Side Industrial Pkwy Atlanta GA 30354 404-366-2111 361-8832
Web: www.wilen.com

Wipe-Tex International Corp 110 E 153rd St Bronx NY 10451 718-665-0013 665-0787
TF: 800-643-9607 ■ Web: www.wipe-tex.com

512 MORTGAGE LENDERS & LOAN BROKERS

SEE ALSO Banks - Commercial & Savings p. 1368

Phone Fax

AAA Financial Corp 9600 W Sample Rd Coral Springs FL 33065 954-344-2530 344-0257
TF: 800-881-2530 ■ Web: www.aaafinancial.com

Aames Financial Corp 350 S Grand Ave 43rd Fl Los Angeles CA 90071 323-210-5000 210-5037
TF: 800-829-2929 ■ Web: www.aames.net

Accredited Home Lenders Inc 15333 Ave of Science San Diego CA 92128 858-676-2100 716-1629*
NASDAQ: LEND ■ *Fax: Cust Svc ■ TF: 800-690-6000 ■ Web: www.accredhome.com

Ace Mortgage Funding Inc 7820 Innovation Blvd Suite 350 Indianapolis IN 46278 317-246-5740 227-2864
TF: 888-223-9975 ■ Web: www.acerefi.com

American Home Mortgage Investment Corp
520 Broadhollow Rd Melville NY 11747 516-949-3900
NYSE: AHM ■ TF: 800-755-3100 ■ Web: www.americanhm.com

American Mortgage Acceptance Co 625 Madison Ave 5th Fl New York NY 10022 212-317-5700 751-3550
AMEX: AMC ■ Web: www.americanmortgageco.com

American Mortgage Express
10251 Vista Sorrento Pkwy Suite 300 San Diego CA 92121 619-521-3000 521-3000
TF: 800-700-0263 ■ Web: www.amefinancial.com

AmNet Mortgage Inc 10421 Wateridge Cir Suite 250 San Diego CA 92121 858-909-1200 909-1249
Web: www.amerreit.com

BRT Realty Trust 60 Cutter Mill Rd Suite 303 Great Neck NY 11021 516-466-3100 466-3132
NYSE: BRT ■ TF: 800-450-5816 ■ Web: www.brtrealty.com

Capital Alliance Income Trust Ltd
100 Pine St Suite 2450 San Francisco CA 94111 415-288-9575 288-9590
AMEX: CAA ■ Web: www.caitreit.com

CapitalSource Inc 4445 Willard Ave 12th Fl Chevy Chase MD 20815 301-841-2700 841-2340
NYSE: CSE ■ TF: 866-876-8723 ■ Web: www.capitalsource.com

Carteret Mortgage Corp 6211 Centreville Rd Suite 800 Centreville VA 20121 703-802-8000 802-8001
TF: 877-227-8373 ■ Web: www.carteretmortgage.com

CCO Mortgage Corp DBA Charter One Mortgage
10561 Telegraph Rd Glen Allen VA 23059 804-627-4000 627-4010
TF: 800-876-2434 ■ Web: www.ccomortgage.com

Centex Corp Financial Services Group 2728 N Harwood Dallas TX 75201 214-981-5000 758-7822
TF: 888-480-2432 ■ Web: www.centex.com

Centex Home Equity Corp 2728 N Harwood Dallas TX 75201 214-981-5000 756-2062*
*Fax: Cust Svc ■ TF: 888-480-2432 ■ Web: www.centex.com

Charter One Mortgage 10561 Telegraph Rd Glen Allen VA 23059 804-627-4000 627-4010
TF: 800-876-2434 ■ Web: www.ccomortgage.com

CharterMac 625 Madison Ave New York NY 10022 212-317-5700 751-3559
NYSE: CHC ■ TF: 800-600-6422 ■ Web: www.chartermac.com

Chase Manhattan Mortgage Corp 194 Wood Ave S Iselin NJ 08830 732-205-0600 205-8751*
*Fax: Cust Svc ■ TF: 800-848-9136 ■ Web: pre-qualify.com

CIBC Mortgage Inc 100 University Ave Toronto ON M5J2X4 416-785-3255 294-8393*
*Fax Area Code: 800 ■ TF: 800-465-2422 ■ Web: www.cibc.com

CitiFinancial Mortgage Co 8333 Ridgeport Dr Irving TX 75062 800-217-1000 984-2597*
*Fax Area Code: 813 ■ *Fax: Hum Res ■ TF: 800-217-1000 ■
Web: www.citifinancialmortgage.com

CitiMortgage Inc 15851 Clayton Rd Ballwin MO 63011 800-283-7918 256-4337*
*Fax Area Code: 636 ■ *Fax: Cust Svc ■ Web: www.citimortgage.com

Colony Mortgage Corp 22983 Lorraine Rd Fairview Park OH 44026 440-777-9999 716-8365
TF: 800-423-3085 ■ Web: www.colonymortgage.com

Consumer Portfolio Services Inc 16355 Laguna Canyon Rd Irvine CA 92618 949-753-6800 753-6805
NASDAQ: CPSS ■ Web: www.consumerportfolio.com

Continental Wingate Co Inc 63 Kendrick St Needham MA 02494 781-707-9000 707-9097
TF: 800-332-0372 ■ Web: www.cwcapital.com

Countrywide Financial Corp 4500 Park Granada Calabasas CA 91302 818-225-3000 225-4431*
NYSE: CFC ■ *Fax: Hum Res ■ TF: 800-669-6607 ■ Web: my.countrywide.com

CreditMax 625 N Flagler Dr Suite 625 West Palm Beach FL 33401 561-352-2200 352-2199
TF: 888-537-8123 ■ Web: www.creditmax.com

CRIIMI MAE Inc 701 13th St NW Suite 1000 Washington DC 20005 202-715-9500
TF: 800-266-0535 ■ Web: www.cwcapital.com

CTX Mortgage Co 3100 McKinnon St Dallas TX 75201 214-981-5000 468-4093*
*Fax: Cust Svc ■ TF: 800-666-5363 ■ Web: www.ctxmort.com

Delta Financial Corp 1000 Woodbury Rd Suite 200 Woodbury NY 11797 516-364-8500 364-9459
AMEX: DFC ■ TF: 800-225-5335 ■ Web: www.deltafinancial.com

ditech.com 3200 Park Center Dr Suite 150 Costa Mesa CA 92626 800-803-7656 800-5801*
*Fax Area Code: 714 ■ TF: 800-803-7656 ■ Web: www.ditech.com

Dominion Capital Inc 120 Tredegar St Richmond VA 23219 804-819-2000 819-2227

E-LOAN Inc 6230 Stone Ridge Mall Rd Pleasanton CA 94588 925-847-6900 847-0831
TF: 888-356-2622 ■ Web: www.eloan.com

Emigrant Mortgage Co Inc 5 E 42nd St New York NY 10017 212-850-4361 850-4870
TF: 888-364-4726 ■ Web: www.emigrant.com

EverHome Mortgage Co 8100 Nations Way Jacksonville FL 32256 904-281-6000 281-6380*
*Fax: Cust Svc ■ TF Cust Svc: 800-669-9721 ■ Web: www.everhomemortgage.com

Extraco Mortgage 7503 Bosque Blvd Waco TX 76712 254-772-0202 751-0702*
*Fax: Cust Svc ■ TF: 800-227-4894 ■ Web: www.extracomortgage.com

Family First Mortgage Corp 33 Old Kings Rd N Palm Coast FL 32137 386-246-6955 246-6953
Web: www.familyfirstmortgage.com

Phone Fax

Fannie Mae 3900 Wisconsin Ave NW Washington DC 20016 202-752-7000 752-5980
NYSE: FNM ■ TF: 800-732-6643 ■ Web: www.fanniemae.com

Farmer Mac (Federal Agricultural Mortgage Corp)
1133 21st St NW Suite 600 Washington DC 20036 202-872-7700 872-7713
NYSE: AGM ■ TF: 800-879-3276 ■ Web: www.farmermac.com

Federal Agricultural Mortgage Corp (Farmer Mac)
1133 21st St NW Suite 600 Washington DC 20036 202-872-7700 872-7713
NYSE: AGM ■ TF: 800-879-3276 ■ Web: www.farmermac.com

Federal Home Loan Mortgage Corp 8200 Jones Branch Dr McLean VA 22102 703-903-2000 903-2447
NYSE: FRE ■ TF: 800-373-3343 ■ Web: www.freddiemac.com

Finance America 16802 Aston St Irvine CA 92606 949-440-1000 440-1449*
*Fax: Mktg ■ TF: 800-690-8200 ■ Web: www.financeamerica.com

Financial Freedom Senior Funding Corp 1 Banting Irvine CA 92618 949-341-9200 341-9201
TF: 800-500-5150 ■ Web: www.ffsenior.com

First Connecticut Capital Corp 1000 Bridgeport Ave Shelton CT 06484 203-944-5400 944-5405
TF: 800-401-3222 ■ Web: www.firstctcapital.com

First Eastern Mortgage Corp 100 Brickstone Sq Andover MA 01810 978-749-3100 749-3148
TF: 800-777-2240 ■ Web: www.firsteastern.com

First Equity Mortgage Bankers Inc
9130 S Dadeland Blvd Suite 1901 Miami FL 33156 305-666-3333 666-3181
TF: 800-910-8499 ■ Web: www.fembi.com

First Fidelity Mortgage Corp 2 Ravinia Dr Suite 1600 Atlanta GA 30346 678-287-3000 287-3001
Web: www.firstfidelitycompanies.com

First NLC Financial Services Inc
700 W Hillsboro Blvd Bldg 1 Suite 204 Deerfield Beach FL 33441 954-420-0060 964-8209*
*Fax Area Code: 800 ■ TF: 800-950-3314 ■ Web: www.firstnlc.com

First Residential Mortgage Network Inc
9721 Ormsby Station Rd Suite 100 Louisville KY 40223 502-315-4700 736-1909
TF: 800-585-9005 ■ Web: www.1stresidential.net

Forest City Residential Management Inc
50 Public Sq Suite 1200 Cleveland OH 44113 216-621-6060 263-4800

Freddie Mac 8200 Jones Branch Dr McLean VA 22102 703-903-2000 903-2447
NYSE: FRE ■ TF: 800-373-3343 ■ Web: www.freddiemac.com
North Central Region 333 W Wacker Dr Suite 2500 Chicago IL 60606 312-407-7400 407-7398
TF: 800-373-3343 ■ Web: www.freddiemac.com
Northeast Region 8200 Jones Branch Dr McLean VA 22102 703-903-2000 903-2447
TF: 800-373-3343 ■ Web: www.freddiemac.com
Southeast/Southwest Region
2300 Windy Ridge Pkwy Suite 200N Atlanta GA 30339 770-857-8800 857-8805
TF: 800-373-3343 ■ Web: www.freddiemac.com
Western Region 21700 Oxnard St Suite 1900 Woodland Hills CA 91367 818-710-3000 710-3039
Web: www.freddiemac.com

Freedom Mortgage Corp 10500 Kincaid Dr Fishers IN 46038 317-594-8900
TF: 800-984-5363 ■ Web: www.freedommortgage.com

Gershman Investment Corp 7 N Bemiston Ave Clayton MO 63105 314-889-0600 862-1636
TF: 800-457-2357 ■ Web: www.gershman.com

Ginnie Mae 451 7th St SW Suite B-133 Washington DC 20410 202-708-1535 708-0490
Web: www.ginniemae.gov

GMAC Mortgage Corp 100 Witmer Rd Horsham PA 19044 215-682-1000 682-3318*
*Fax: Hum Res ■ TF: 800-627-0128 ■ Web: www.gmacmortgage.com

Government National Mortgage Assn DBA Ginnie Mae
451 7th St SW Suite B-133 Washington DC 20410 202-708-1535 708-0490
Web: www.ginniemae.gov

Green Tree Servicing LLC 345 Saint Peter St Suite 600 Saint Paul MN 55102 651-293-3400 293-3622*
*Fax: Hum Res ■ TF: 800-423-9527 ■ Web: www.gtservicing.com

H & R Block Mortgage Corp 3 Burlington Woods 2nd Fl Burlington MA 01803 781-852-5600 852-5799
TF: 800-974-1899

Hanover Capital Mortgage Holdings Inc
55 Broadway Suite 3002 New York NY 10006 212-227-0075 227-5434
AMEX: HCM ■ Web: www.hanovercapitalholdings.com

HomeAdvisor 1 Microsoft Way Redmond WA 98052 425-882-8080 936-7329
TF: 800-642-7676 ■ Web: houseandhome.msn.com

HomeBanc Corp 2002 Summit Blvd Suite 100 Atlanta GA 30319 404-303-4000 303-4069
NYSE: HMB ■ Web: www.homebanc.com

HomeBanc Mortgage Corp 2002 Summit Blvd Suite 100 Atlanta GA 30319 404-459-7400
TF: 866-926-8466 ■ Web: www.homebanc.com

HomePath c/o FannieMae 3900 Wisconsin Ave NW Washington DC 20016 202-752-7016
TF: 800-732-6643 ■ Web: www.fanniemae.com/homebuyers/homepath

HomeSteps 500 Plano Pkwy Carrollton TX 75010 800-972-7555 702-2098*
*Fax Area Code: 972 ■ Web: www.homesteps.com

HSBC Mortgage Corp (USA) 2929 Walden Ave Depew NY 14043 800-338-4626 651-6945*
*Fax Area Code: 716 ■ Web: www.us.hsbc.com

Huntington Mortgage Co 7575 Huntington Park Dr Columbus OH 43235 614-480-6505 480-6880*
*Fax: Cust Svc ■ TF: 800-323-4695

IMX Inc 1445 N Loop W Suite 865 Houston TX 77008 800-401-4639 673-7130*
*Fax Area Code: 832 ■ Web: www.imx.com

IndyMac Bank 1 Banting Irvine CA 92618 949-585-3301 788-4660
TF: 800-731-0383 ■ Web: www.indymacbank.com

Inland Mortgage Corp 2901 Butterfield Rd Oak Brook IL 60523 630-218-8000 218-4957
TF: 800-828-8999 ■ Web: www.inlandgroup.com/if/finance.htm#

Intuit Lender Services Inc 2632 Marine Way Bldg 10 Mountain View CA 94043 650-944-6000 944-2788*
*Fax: Hum Res ■ TF: 888-565-2488

JI Kislak Inc 7900 Miami Lakes Dr W Miami Lakes FL 33016 305-364-4100 820-7111*
*Fax: Cust Svc ■ TF: 800-233-7164 ■ Web: www.bankonus.com

Kislak JI Inc 7900 Miami Lakes Dr W Miami Lakes FL 33016 305-364-4100 820-7111*
*Fax: Cust Svc ■ TF: 800-233-7164 ■ Web: www.bankonus.com

Legg Mason Real Estate Investors Inc
10880 Wilshire Blvd Suite 1750 Los Angeles CA 90024 310-234-2100 234-2150
Web: www.lmrei.com

LendingTree Inc 11115 Rushmore Dr Charlotte NC 28277 704-541-5351 541-1824
TF: 877-510-2659 ■ Web: www.lendingtree.com

Lennar Financial Services Inc 700 NW 107th Ave 3rd Fl Miami FL 33172 305-223-9966 553-5022
TF: 800-741-8262

Lion Inc 2000 S Colorado Blvd Suite 350 Denver CO 80222 303-455-1800 455-4100
TF: 800-786-8083 ■ Web: www.lioninc.com

M & I Home Lending Solutions 4121 NW Urbandale Dr Urbandale IA 50322 515-281-2807 277-2569*
*Fax Area Code: 800 ■ TF: 800-827-2654 ■ Web: www.mihomelendingsolutions.com

M & I Mortgage Corp W 57 N 14280 Doerr Way Cedarburg WI 53012 262-376-8484 376-8498
TF: 800-236-1221 ■ Web: www.mibank.com/mortgageonline

M & T Mortgage Corp 1 Fountain Plaza Buffalo NY 14203 716-848-7600 848-3797
TF: 800-724-7575

Market Street Mortgage Corp PO Box 22128 Tampa FL 33622 727-724-7000 724-9191
TF: 800-669-3210 ■ Web: www.marketstreetmortgage.com

Mercantile Mortgage Corp 2 Hopkins Plaza Suite 900 Baltimore MD 21201 410-347-8940 244-0823
TF: 800-874-7880 ■ Web: www.mercmortgage.com

Midland Loan Services Inc 10851 Mastin Overland Park KS 66210 913-253-9000 253-9001
TF: 800-327-8083 ■ Web: www.midlandls.com

Midland Mortgage Co PO Box 26648 Oklahoma City OK 73126 800-654-4566 767-5500*
*Fax Area Code: 405 ■ Web: www.mymidlandmortgage.com

MortgageIT Holdings Inc 33 Maiden Ln New York NY 10038 212-651-7700 363-4646
NYSE: MHL ■ TF: 877-684-4826 ■ Web: www.mortgageit.com

MSN House & Home 1 Microsoft Way Redmond WA 98052 425-882-8080 936-7329
TF: 800-642-7676 ■ Web: houseandhome.msn.com

Municipal Mortgage & Equity LLC (MuniMae)
621 E Pratt St Suite 300 Baltimore MD 21202 888-788-3863 727-5387*
NYSE: MMA ■ *Fax Area Code: 410 ■ Web: www.munimae.com

Phone | Fax

MuniMae (Municipal Mortgage & Equity LLC)
621 E Pratt St Suite 300 — Baltimore MD 21202 888-788-3863 727-5387*
NYSE: MMA ■ **Fax Area Code:* 410 ■ *Web:* www.munimae.com
National City Mortgage Co 3232 Newmark Dr — Miamisburg OH 45342 937-297-3600 910-4103
TF Cust Svc: 800-253-7313 ■ *Web:* www.nationalcitymortgage.com
National Rural Utilities Cooperative Finance Corp
2201 Cooperative Way Woodland Pk — Herndon VA 20171 703-709-6700 709-6777
TF: 800-424-2954 ■ *Web:* www.nrucfc.org
New Century Financial Corp 18400 Von Karman Ave Suite 1000 — Irvine CA 92612 949-440-7030 440-7035
NYSE: NEW ■ *TF:* 800-967-7623 ■ *Web:* www.ncen.com
New South Federal Savings Bank 2000 Crestwood Blvd — Irondale AL 35210 205-951-4000 951-1027
TF: 800-366-1010 ■ *Web:* www.newsouthfederal.com
New York Mortgage Co LLC 1301 Ave of the Americas 7th Fl — New York NY 10019 212-634-9400 634-9428
TF: 800-491-6962 ■ *Web:* www.nymc.com
Nexstar Financial Corp 19 Research Pk Ct — Saint Charles MO 63304 636-685-9100
TF: 877-706-7382 ■ *Web:* www.nexstar.com
Option One Mortgage Corp 3 Ada — Irvine CA 92618 949-790-3600 790-8505*
**Fax:* Cust Svc ■ *TF:* 800-704-0800 ■ *Web:* www.oomc.com
Origen Financial Inc 27777 Franklin Rd Suite 1700 — Southfield MI 48034 248-746-7000 746-7091
NASDAQ: ORGN ■ *TF:* 866-467-4436 ■ *Web:* www.oflc.com
PHH Mortgage Corp 3000 Leadenhall Rd — Mount Laurel NJ 08054 856-917-6000 917-8291*
**Fax:* Cust Svc ■ *TF:* 800-210-8849 ■ *Web:* www.phhmortgage.com
Pulte Mortgage LLC 7475 S Joliet St — Englewood CO 80112 303-740-8800 694-2082
TF: 800-488-0053 ■ *Web:* www.pulte.com/finance
Quicken Loans 20555 Victor Pkwy — Livonia MI 48152 734-805-7285
TF: 888-565-2488 ■ *Web:* www.quickenloans.com
QuickenMortgage 2632 Marine Way Bldg 10 — Mountain View CA 94043 650-944-6000 944-2788*
**Fax:* Hum Res ■ *TF:* 888-565-2488
RAIT Investment Trust 2929 Arch St Suite 1703 — Philadelphia PA 19104 215-701-9555 701-8282
NYSE: RAS ■ *TF:* 800-826-6096 ■ *Web:* www.raitinvestmenttrust.com
Redwood Trust Inc 1 Belvedere Pl Suite 300 — Mill Valley CA 94941 415-389-7373 381-1773
NYSE: RWT ■ *Web:* www.redwoodtrust.com
Regions Mortgage Inc 215 Forrest St — Hattiesburg MS 39401 800-986-2462 223-3453*
**Fax Area Code:* 334 ■ *TF:* 800-392-5669 ■ *Web:* www.regionsmortgage.com
Resource Bancshares Mortgage Group Inc
9710 Two Notch Rd — Columbia SC 29223 803-462-8000 462-7628*
**Fax:* Cust Svc ■ *TF:* 800-627-1991 ■ *Web:* www.rbmg.com
Saxon Capital Inc 4860 Cox Rd Suite 300 — Glen Allen VA 23060 804-967-7400 217-7708
NYSE: SAX ■ *Web:* www.saxoncapitalinc.com
Saxon Mortgage Inc 4840 Cox Rd — Glen Allen VA 23060 804-967-7400 967-7408
TF: 800-538-8202 ■ *Web:* www.saxonmortgage.com
Security Savings Mortgage Corp 217 2nd St NW Suite 1000 — Canton OH 44702 330-455-5600 455-7726*
**Fax:* Cust Svc ■ *TF:* 800-421-8059
Sovereign Bank Wholesale Lending Div
1022 E Lancaster Ave — Rosemont PA 19010 610-525-1860 526-1943*
**Fax:* Mktg ■ *TF:* 888-696-8879 ■ *Web:* www.sovereignwholesale.com
SunTrust Mortgage Inc 1001 Semmes Ave — Richmond VA 23224 804-291-0740 291-0136*
**Fax:* Mktg ■ *TF:* 800-634-7928 ■ *Web:* www.suntrustmortgage.com
Transnational Financial Network Inc
401 Taraval St 2nd Fl — San Francisco CA 94116 415-242-7800 242-7830
AMEX: TFN ■ *TF:* 888-229-2344 ■ *Web:* www.transnational.com
Universal American Mortgage Co
311 Park Place Blvd Suite 500 — Clearwater FL 33759 727-791-2111 791-2118
TF: 800-696-4619 ■ *Web:* www.uamc.com
USA Lending Group 6925 Union Park Dr Suite 600 — Midvale UT 84047 801-676-1200 676-1201
TF: 877-434-8042 ■ *Web:* www.11loan.com
USA Mortgage Inc 12140 Woodcrest Executive Dr Suite 150 — Saint Louis MO 63141 314-628-2000 628-2035
TF: 877-434-4555 ■ *Web:* www.loansurfer.com
Vanderbilt Mortgage & Finance Inc 500 Alcoa Trail — Maryville TN 37804 865-380-3000 380-3750
TF: 800-970-7250 ■ *Web:* www.vmf.com
Vestin Group Inc 8379 W Sunset Rd — Las Vegas NV 89113 702-227-0965 227-5247
TF: 800-232-7613 ■ *Web:* www.vestinmortgage.com
Wachovia Mortgage Corp 1100 Corporate Ctr Dr — Raleigh NC 27607 866-642-9405 852-6075*
**Fax Area Code:* 919 ■ *Web:* www.wachovia.com
Washington Mutual Mortgage Loan Corp
4305 Harrison Blvd Suite 10 — Ogden UT 84403 801-626-2203 626-2270
TF: 800-756-8000 ■ *Web:* www.wamumortgage.com
Wells Fargo Home Mortgage 405 SW 5th St — Des Moines IA 50328 515-237-6000 221-4784*
**Fax:* Mktg ■ *TF:* 800-288-3212 ■ *Web:* wellsfargo.com/mortgage/

513 MORTUARY, CREMATORY, CEMETERY PRODUCTS & SERVICES

Phone | Fax

AJ Desmond & Sons Funeral Directors 2600 Crooks Rd — Troy MI 48084 248-362-2500 362-0190
TF: 800-210-7135 ■ *Web:* www.desmondfuneralhome.com
Baue Funeral Homes 620 Jefferson St — Saint Charles MO 63301 636-724-0073 946-3084
TF: 888-724-0073 ■ *Web:* www.baue.com
Bradford-O'Keefe Funeral Homes Inc 675 E Howard Ave — Biloxi MS 39530 228-374-5650 435-3638
Web: www.bradfordokeefe.com
Carriage Services Inc 1900 St James Pl 4th Fl — Houston TX 77056 713-332-8450 332-8401
NYSE: CSV ■ *TF:* 800-692-3092 ■ *Web:* www.carriageservices.com
Church & Chapel Metal Arts Inc 2616 W Grand Ave — Chicago IL 60612 773-489-3700 489-3434
Web: www.church-chapel.com
Cornerstone Family Services 155 Rittenhouse Cir — Bristol PA 19007 215-826-2800 826-2854
NASDAQ: STON ■ *TF:* 877-857-8890 ■ *Web:* www.cornerstonefs.com
Dignity Memorial 1929 Allen Pkwy — Houston TX 77019 713-522-5141 763-3801*
**Fax Area Code:* 818 ■ *TF:* 800-894-2024 ■ *Web:* www.dignitymemorial.com
Earthman Funeral Directors 2420 Fannin St — Houston TX 77002 713-659-3000 659-2507
TF: 800-654-2609 ■ *Web:* www.earthmanfunerals.com
Forest Lawn Memorial-Parks & Mortuaries
1712 S Glendale Ave — Glendale CA 91205 323-254-7251 551-5071*
**Fax:* Cust Svc ■ *TF:* 800-204-3131 ■ *Web:* www.forestlawn.com
Neptune Society 4312 Woodman Ave 3rd Fl — Sherman Oaks CA 91423 818-953-9995 953-9844
TF: 888-637-8863 ■ *Web:* www.neptunesociety.com
Palm Mortuary Inc 1325 N Main St — Las Vegas NV 89101 702-464-8300 464-8394
TF: 800-542-2902 ■ *Web:* www.palmmortuary.com
Parklawn Memorial Gardens 12800 Veirs Mill Rd — Rockville MD 20853 301-881-2151 881-2169
Restland Funeral Home & Cemetery 13005 Greenville Ave — Dallas TX 75243 972-238-7111 470-5745
TF: 800-749-7379 ■ *Web:* www.restlandfuneralhome.com
Rose Hills Co 3888 S Workman Mill Rd — Whittier CA 90601 562-699-0921 699-6372
TF: 800-328-7526 ■ *Web:* www.rosehills.com
Service Corp International 1929 Allen Pkwy — Houston TX 77019 713-522-5141 525-9056*
NYSE: SCI ■ **Fax:* Hum Res ■ *Web:* www.sci-corp.com
Spring Grove Cemetery 4521 Spring Grove Ave — Cincinnati OH 45232 513-681-6680 853-6802
TF: 888-853-2230 ■ *Web:* www.springgrove.org
Stewart Enterprises Inc 1333 S Clearview Pkwy — Jefferson LA 70121 504-729-1400 729-1984
NASDAQ: STEIE ■ *TF:* 800-257-1610 ■ *Web:* www.stewartenterprises.com
StoneMor Partners LP DBA Cornerstone Family Services
155 Rittenhouse Cir — Bristol PA 19007 215-826-2800 826-2854
NASDAQ: STON ■ *TF:* 877-857-8890 ■ *Web:* www.cornerstonefs.com
Wilson Financial Group Inc 15915 Katy Fwy Suite 500 — Houston TX 77094 281-579-2760 579-9089

514 MOTION PICTURE DISTRIBUTION & RELATED SERVICES

Phone | Fax

ABC News VideoSource 125 West End Ave 5th Fl — New York NY 10023 212-456-5421 456-5428
TF: 800-789-1250 ■ *Web:* www.abcnewsvsource.com
AIMS Multimedia 20765 Superior St — Chatsworth CA 91311 818-773-4300 341-6700
TF: 800-367-2467 ■ *Web:* www.aimsmultimedia.com
Alliance Entertainment Corp 4250 Coral Ridge Dr — Coral Springs FL 33065 954-255-4000 255-4825
TF: 800-329-7664 ■ *Web:* www.aent.com
AMC Film Marketing 21700 Oxnard St Suite 640 — Woodland Hills CA 91367 818-587-6400 587-6498
Anchor Bay Entertainment Inc 1699 Stutz Dr — Troy MI 48084 248-816-0909 816-3335
TF: 800-786-8777 ■ *Web:* www.anchorbayentertainment.com
Baker & Taylor Inc 2550 W Tyvola Rd Suite 300 — Charlotte NC 28217 704-998-3100 998-3316
TF: 800-775-1800 ■ *Web:* www.btol.com
Bridgestone Multimedia Group Inc 300 N McKemy Ave — Chandler AZ 85226 480-940-5777 438-2702*
**Fax Area Code:* 602 ■ *TF Cust Svc:* 800-622-3070
Buena Vista Home Entertainment Inc
500 S Buena Vista St MC 6570 — Burbank CA 91521 818-560-1000
TF Cust Svc: 800-723-4763 ■ *Web:* www.bvhe.com
Buena Vista International Inc 500 S Buena Vista St — Burbank CA 91521 818-560-1000 560-1930
Buena Vista Pictures Distribution Inc 500 S Buena Vista Dr — Burbank CA 91521 818-560-5665 972-3905
Carsey-Werner Distribution LLC 12001 Ventura Pl 6th Fl — Studio City CA 91604 818-299-9600 299-9650
Web: www.carseywerner.com
CBS Enterprises Inc 2401 Colorado Ave Suite 110 — Santa Monica CA 90404 310-264-3300 264-3301
CBS Paramount Television 5555 Melrose Ave — Los Angeles CA 90038 323-956-5000 862-0282
Web: www.cbsparamount.com/television
Central Park Media Corp 250 W 57th St Suite 317 — New York NY 10107 646-957-8301 977-8709*
**Fax Area Code:* 212 ■ *TF:* 800-833-7456 ■ *Web:* www.centralparkmedia.com
Clearvue & SVE 6465 N Avondale Ave — Chicago IL 60631 773-775-9433 444-9855*
**Fax Area Code:* 800 ■ *TF:* 800-253-2788 ■ *Web:* www.clearvue.com
Crown Media Holdings Inc
6430 S Fiddlers Green Cir Suite 225 — Greenwood Village CO 80111 303-220-7990 220-7660
NASDAQ: CRWN ■ *TF:* 800-820-7990 ■ *Web:* www.hallmarkchannel.com
Deluxe Media Services Inc 568 Atrium Dr — Vernon Hills IL 60061 847-990-4100 549-8354
TF: 800-745-7265 ■ *Web:* www.bydeluxe.com
Desert Island Films 11 Coggeshall Cir — Middletown RI 02842 401-846-3453 846-0919
TF: 800-766-8550 ■ *Web:* www.desertislandfilms.com
DG Fastchannel Inc 750 W John Carpenter Fwy Suite 700 — Irving TX 75039 972-581-2000 581-2001
NASDAQ: DGIT ■ *TF:* 800-324-5672 ■ *Web:* www.dgfastchannel.com
Distribution Video & Audio (DV&A) 133 Candy Ln — Palm Harbor FL 34683 727-447-4147 441-3069
TF: 800-683-4147 ■ *Web:* www.dva.com
Facets Multimedia Inc 1517 W Fullerton Ave — Chicago IL 60614 773-281-9075 929-5437
TF: 800-331-6197 ■ *Web:* www.facets.org
Films for the Humanities & Sciences PO Box 2053 — Princeton NJ 08543 609-671-1000 671-0266
TF: 800-257-5126 ■ *Web:* www.films.com
First Look Studios Inc 2000 Ave of the Stars Suite 410 — Century City CA 90067 424-202-5000
Web: www.firstlookstudios.com
First Run Features 630 9th Ave Suite 1213 — New York NY 10036 212-243-0600 989-7649
TF: 800-229-8575 ■ *Web:* www.firstrunfeatures.com
Fox Consumer Products PO Box 900 — Beverly Hills CA 90213 310-369-1000
Fujisankei Communications International Inc
150 E 52nd St 34th Fl — New York NY 10022 212-753-8100 688-0392
Web: www.fujisankei.com
GT Brands Holdings 100 Park Ave Suite 1102 — New York NY 10017 212-951-3000 213-9319
Web: www.goodtimes.com
Hip Interactive Corp 240 Superior Blvd — Mississauga ON L5T2L2 905-362-3760 362-1995
TSX: HP
Image Entertainment Inc 20525 Nordhoff St Suite 200 — Chatsworth CA 91311 818-407-9100 407-9151
NASDAQ: DISK ■ *TF:* 800-473-3475 ■ *Web:* www.image-entertainment.com
Ingram Entertainment Inc 2 Ingram Blvd — La Vergne TN 37089 615-287-4000 287-4982
TF: 800-759-5000 ■ *Web:* www.ingramentertainment.com
Insight Media 2162 Broadway — New York NY 10024 212-721-6316 799-5309
TF: 800-233-9910 ■ *Web:* www.insight-media.com
Inspired Corp 103 Eisenhower Pkwy — Roseland NJ 07068 973-226-1234 226-6696
TF: 800-738-3747 ■ *Web:* www.inspiredcorp.com
International Historic Films Inc 3533 S Archer Ave — Chicago IL 60609 773-927-9091 927-9211
Web: www.ihffilm.com
Kultur International Films Ltd 195 Hwy 36 — West Long Branch NJ 07764 732-229-2343 229-0066
TF: 800-458-5887 ■ *Web:* www.kultur.com
Lions Gate Films Inc 2700 Colorado Ave Suite 200 — Marina del Rey CA 90404 310-449-9200 255-3970
TF: 800-424-7070 ■ *Web:* www.lionsgatefilms.com
Metro-Goldwyn-Mayer Inc (MGM) 10250 Constellation Blvd — Los Angeles CA 90067 310-449-3000 449-3092*
**Fax:* Mktg ■ *Web:* www.mgm.com
MGM Domestic Television Distribution LLC
10250 Constellation Blvd — Los Angeles CA 90067 310-449-3000 449-3092
Web: www.mgm.com/television.do
MGM Pictures 10250 Constellation Blvd — Los Angeles CA 90067 310-449-3000 449-3092
Web: www.mgm.com
MGM/UA Distribution Co 10250 Constellation Blvd — Los Angeles CA 90067 310-449-3000 449-3100
Web: www.mgm.com
MGM/UA Home Entertainment 10250 Constellation Blvd — Century City CA 90067 310-449-3000 449-3100*
**Fax:* Mail Rm ■ *Web:* www.mgm.com
Miramax Films Corp 161 Ave of the Americas — New York NY 10013 917-606-5500
Web: www.miramax.com
MPI Media Group 16101 S 108th Ave — Orland Park IL 60467 708-460-0555 460-0175
TF: 800-777-2223 ■ *Web:* www.mpimedia.com
New Line Cinema Corp 888 7th Ave 19th Fl — New York NY 10106 212-649-4900 649-4966
Web: www.newline.com
Paramount Home Entertainment 5555 Melrose Ave — Los Angeles CA 90038 323-956-5000
Web: www.paramount.com/homevideo
Paramount Pictures Corp 5555 Melrose Ave — Los Angeles CA 90038 323-956-5000 862-4564
Web: www.paramount.com
Pyramid Media PO Box 1048 — Santa Monica CA 90406 310-828-7577 398-7869
TF: 800-421-2303 ■ *Web:* www.pyramidmedia.com
Questar Inc 680 N Lake Shore Dr Suite 900 — Chicago IL 60611 312-266-9400 266-9523
TF: 800-544-8422 ■ *Web:* www.questarhomevideo.com
Resolution Inc 19 Gregory Dr — South Burlington VT 05403 802-862-8881 865-2308
TF: 800-862-8900 ■ *Web:* www.resolut.com
Roadside Attractions LLC 421 S Beverly Dr 8th Fl — Beverly Hills CA 90212 310-789-4710 789-4711
Web: www.roadsideattractions.com
Scholastic Corp 557 Broadway — New York NY 10012 212-343-6100
NASDAQ: SCHL ■ *TF Cust Svc:* 800-724-6527 ■ *Web:* www.scholastic.com
Sony Pictures Classics 550 Madison Ave 8th Fl — New York NY 10022 212-833-8833 833-8844
Web: www.sonypictures.com/classics
Sony Pictures Entertainment Inc 10202 W Washington Blvd — Culver City CA 90232 310-244-4000 244-2626
TF: 800-326-9551 ■ *Web:* www.sonypictures.com
Sony Pictures Home Entertainment
10202 W Washington Blvd — Culver City CA 90232 310-244-4000 244-2626
Web: www.sonypictures.com/spe
Swank Motion Pictures Inc 201 S Jefferson Ave — Saint Louis MO 63103 314-534-6300 289-2192
TF: 800-876-5577 ■ *Web:* www.swank.com
Terra Entertainment 12335 Santa Monica Blvd Suite 336 — Los Angeles CA 90025 310-268-1210 268-1240
TF: 877-788-3772 ■ *Web:* www.terra-ent.com
Twentieth Century Fox Film Corp 10201 W Pico Blvd — Los Angeles CA 90035 310-369-1000
Web: www.foxmovies.com

				Phone	Fax
Twentieth Century Fox Home Entertainment Inc 10201 W Pico Blvd *Web:* www.foxhome.com	Los Angeles	CA	90035	310-369-1000	
Twentieth Century Fox Licensing & Merchandising 10201 W Pico Blvd	Los Angeles	CA	90035	310-369-1000	
TWI 420 W 45th St *Web:* www.imgworld.com	New York	NY	10036	212-541-5640	265-5483
Unicorn Video Inc 8374 Market St	Lakewood Ranch	FL	34202	941-753-4400	753-0600
Universal Music & Video Distribution 2220 Colorado Ave	Santa Monica	CA	90404	310-865-5000	235-4905
Universal Studios Home Video 10 Universal City Plaza 6th Fl *Web:* homevideo.universalstudios.com	Universal City	CA	91608	818-777-2100	933-2555
Universal Studios Inc 100 Universal City Plaza *Web:* www.universalstudios.com	Universal City	CA	91608	818-777-1000	866-9459
Video Data Bank 112 S Michigan Ave *Web:* www.vdb.org	Chicago	IL	60603	312-345-3550	541-8073
Video Products Distributors 150 Parkshore Dr *TF:* 800-366-2111 ■ *Web:* www.vpdinc.com	Folsom	CA	95630	916-605-1500	605-1760
Warner Bros Domestic Television Distribution 4000 Warner Blvd	Burbank	CA	91522	818-954-6000	
Warner Bros Entertainment 4000 Warner Blvd *Web:* www.warnerbros.com	Burbank	CA	91522	818-954-6000	
Warner Bros Television Production Inc 4000 Warner Blvd *Web:* www2.warnerbros.com	Burbank	CA	91522	818-954-6000	
WRS Motion Picture & Video Laboratory 213 Tech Rd *Web:* www.wrslabs.com	Pittsburgh	PA	15205	412-722-9011	937-1200

515 MOTION PICTURE PRE- & POST-PRODUCTION SERVICES

				Phone	Fax
Aardvark Post 13400 Riverside Dr Suite 210 *Web:* www.aardvarkpost.com	Sherman Oaks	CA	91423	818-461-1630	461-1640
Advanced Media Post 4001 W Magnolia Blvd *Web:* www.ampost.com	Burbank	CA	91505	818-973-1660	973-1669
Alpha Cine/Forde Labs 1001 Lenora St *Web:* www.alphacine.com	Seattle	WA	98121	206-682-8230	682-6649
Ascent Media Group Inc 520 Broadway 5th Fl *Web:* www.ascentmedia.com	Santa Monica	CA	90401	310-434-7000	434-7001
Avatar Studios Inc 2675 Scott Ave Suite G *TF:* 800-737-6065 ■ *Web:* www.avatar-studios.com	Saint Louis	MO	63103	314-533-2242	533-3349
Avenue Edit Inc 625 N Michigan Ave Suite 2300 *Web:* www.avenue-edit.com	Chicago	IL	60611	312-943-7100	943-9760
Beyond Pix 950 Battery St 3rd Fl *Web:* www.beyondpix.com	San Francisco	CA	94111	415-434-1027	434-1032
Broadway Video Inc 1619 Broadway *Web:* www.broadwayvideo.com	New York	NY	10019	212-265-7600	713-1535
CafeFX 3130 Skyway Dr *Web:* www.computercafe.com	Santa Maria	CA	93455	805-922-9479	922-3225
Center City Film & Video 1503 Walnut St *Web:* www.ccfv.com	Philadelphia	PA	19102	215-568-4134	568-6011
Cinema Libre Studio 8328 DeSoto Ave *Web:* www.cinemalibrestudio.com	Canoga Park	CA	91304	818-349-8822	349-9922
CIS Hollywood 1144 N Las Palmas Ave *Web:* www.cishollywood.com	Hollywood	CA	90038	323-463-8811	962-1859
Colossalvision HDTV 26 Broadway *Web:* www.colossalvision.com	New York	NY	10004	212-269-6333	269-4334
Company 3 535 5th Ave 5th Fl *Web:* www.company3.com	New York	NY	10017	212-687-4000	687-8023
Composite Image Systems 1144 N Las Palmas Ave *Web:* www.cishollywood.com	Hollywood	CA	90038	323-463-8811	962-1859
Crawford Communications Inc 3845 Pleasantdale Rd **Fax Area Code:* 678 ■ *TF:* 800-831-8027 ■ *Web:* www.crawford.com	Atlanta	GA	30340	404-876-7149	421-6717*
Crest National 1000 N Highland Ave *Web:* www.crestnational.com	Hollywood	CA	90038	323-860-1300	476-1282
Crew Cuts Film & Tape Inc 28 W 44th St 22nd Fl *Web:* www.crewcuts.com	New York	NY	10036	212-302-2828	302-9846
Crossman Post Production LLC DBA Crossman Digital Post 35 Lone Hollow *TF:* 888-553-1958 ■ *Web:* www.crossmanpost.com	Sandy	UT	84092	801-553-1958	553-0953
DeLuxe Laboratories Inc 1377 N Serrano Ave *TF:* 800-233-5893 ■ *Web:* www.bydeluxe.com	Hollywood	CA	90027	323-462-6171	461-0608
Digital Symphony 1011 W Alameda Ave Suite F *Web:* www.digitalsymphony.net	Burbank	CA	91506	818-973-7600	238-9600
Downstream 1650 NW Naito Pkwy Suite 301 *Web:* www.downstream.com	Portland	OR	97209	503-226-1944	226-1283
Edit Bay 571 N Poplar Suite 'I' *Web:* www.theeditbay.com	Orange	CA	92868	714-978-7878	978-7858
Elastic Creative 550 Bryant St *Web:* www.elasticcreative.com	San Francisco	CA	94107	415-495-5595	543-8370
Elevation 905 Bernina Ave *TF:* 800-813-2214 ■ *Web:* www.elevate.tv	Atlanta	GA	30307	404-221-1705	221-0037
Encore Hollywood 6344 Fountain Ave *Web:* www.encorehollywood.com/	Hollywood	CA	90028	323-466-7663	467-5539
Film Technology Co Inc 726 N Cole Ave *Web:* www.filmtech.com	Hollywood	CA	90038	323-464-3456	464-7439
FilmCore 1222 6th St *Web:* www.filmcore.com	Santa Monica	CA	90401	310-587-2400	587-2401
Filmworks/Astro Lab 61 W Erie St *Web:* www.filmworkersastro.com	Chicago	IL	60610	312-280-5500	280-5510
FOX Studios 10201 W Pico Blvd *Web:* www.foxstudios.com	Los Angeles	CA	90035	310-369-1000	969-0468
Go Edit Inc 940 N Orange Dr Suite 140 *Web:* www.goedit.tv	Hollywood	CA	90038	323-337-1174	337-1440
GTN Inc 13320 Northend Ave *TF:* 888-225-5486 ■ *Web:* www.gtninc.com	Oak Park	MI	48237	248-548-2500	548-8614
HDMG Corp 6573 City West Pkwy *Web:* www.hdmg.com	Eden Prairie	MN	55344	952-943-1711	943-1957
Industrial Light & Magic Div Lucasfilm Ltd PO Box 29909 *Web:* www.ilm.com	San Francisco	CA	94129	415-746-3000	746-3015
LA Digital Post 11311 Camarillo St *Web:* www.ladigital.com	West Toluca Lake	CA	91602	818-487-5000	487-5015
LaserPacific Media Corp 809 N Cahuenga Blvd *Web:* www.laserpacific.com	Hollywood	CA	90038	323-462-6266	464-3233
Level 3 Post 2901 W Alameda Ave *Web:* www.level3post.com	Burbank	CA	91505	818-840-7200	840-7801
Lucasfilm Ltd Industrial Light & Magic Div PO Box 29909 *Web:* www.ilm.com	San Francisco	CA	94129	415-746-3000	746-3015
Lucasfilm Ltd Skywalker Sound Div 5858 Lucas Valley Rd *Web:* www.skysound.com	Nicosia	CA	94946	415-662-1300	
Mad House 240 Madison Ave 14th Fl *Web:* www.madhousenyc.com	New York	NY	10016	212-867-1515	697-7168
Mad River Post Inc 2415 Main St *Web:* www.madriverpost.com	Santa Monica	CA	90405	310-392-1577	392-3261
Manhattan Transfer-Miami 2850 Tigertail Ave *TF:* 800-826-8864 ■ *Web:* www.mtmiami.com	Coconut Grove	FL	33133	305-857-0350	857-0175
Match Frame 8531 Fairhaven *TF:* 800-929-2790 ■ *Web:* www.matchframe.com	San Antonio	TX	78229	210-614-5678	616-0299
Method 1546 7th St *Web:* www.methodstudios.com	Santa Monica	CA	90401	310-899-6500	899-6501
Modern Videofilm Inc 4411 W Olive Ave *Web:* www.mvfinc.com	Burbank	CA	91505	818-840-1700	840-1745
Pacific Ocean Post DBA POP Sound 625 Arizona Ave *Web:* www.popstudios.com	Santa Monica	CA	90401	310-458-9192	587-1222
Pacific Title & Arts Studio Inc 6350 Santa Monica Blvd *Web:* www.pactitle.com	Hollywood	CA	90038	323-464-0121	461-8325
Point.360 2777 Ontario St *NASDAQ: PTSX* ■ *Web:* www.point360.com	Burbank	CA	90028	818-565-1400	847-2503
Post Group Inc 6335 Homewood Ave *Web:* www.postgroup.com	Hollywood	CA	90028	323-462-2300	462-0836
Post Modern Co 2734 Walnut St *Web:* www.postmodernco.com	Denver	CO	80205	303-539-7001	539-7002
Post Modern Group LLC 2941 Alton Pkwy *Web:* www.postmoderngroup.com	Irvine	CA	92606	949-608-8700	608-8729
Postique 23475 Northwestern Hwy *TF:* 800-923-3322 ■ *Web:* www.gracewild.com/postique	Southfield	MI	48075	248-352-2610	352-3708
Postworks New York 100 Ave of the Americas 10th Fl *Web:* www.pwny.com	New York	NY	10013	212-894-4050	941-0439
R!OT NY 545 5th Ave 2nd Fl *Web:* www.rioting.com	New York	NY	10017	212-907-1200	907-1201
Rainmaker LP 50 W 2nd Ave *TF:* 800-616-4433 ■ *Web:* www.rainmaker.com	Vancouver	BC	V5Y1B3	604-874-8700	872-2106
Raleigh Film & Television Studios 5300 Melrose Ave *Web:* www.raleighstudios.com	Hollywood	CA	90038	323-466-3111	871-5600
Resolution Inc 19 Gregory Dr *TF:* 800-862-8900 ■ *Web:* www.resolut.com	South Burlington	VT	05403	802-862-8881	865-2308
Rhythm & Hues Inc 5404 Jandy Pl *Web:* www.rhythm.com	Los Angeles	CA	90066	310-448-7500	448-7600
RPG Productions 632 S Glenwood Pl *Web:* www.rpgproductions.com	Burbank	CA	91506	818-848-0240	848-2257
Saul Zaentz Co 2600 10th St *TF:* 800-227-0466 ■ *Web:* www.zaentz.com	Berkeley	CA	94710	510-549-1528	486-2115
Saul Zaentz Film Center 2600 10th St *TF:* 800-227-0466 ■ *Web:* www.zaentz.com	Berkeley	CA	94710	510-549-1528	486-2115
Skywalker Sound Div Lucasfilm Ltd 5858 Lucas Valley Rd *Web:* www.skysound.com	Nicosia	CA	94946	415-662-1300	
Sound One Corp 1619 Broadway 8th Fl *Web:* www.soundone.com	New York	NY	10019	212-765-4757	603-4363
Soundelux Entertainment Group 7080 Hollywood Blvd Suite 1100 *Web:* www.soundelux.com	Hollywood	CA	90028	323-603-3200	603-3233
Syndicate The 1207 4th St Suite 200 *Web:* www.computercafe.com	Santa Monica	CA	90401	310-260-2320	260-2420
Table Rock Productions 269 S Beverly Dr Suite 486 *Web:* www.tablerockers.com	Beverly Hillsq	CA	90212	805-451-1057	969-3925
Technicolor Complete Post Inc 6087 Sunset Blvd *Web:* www.technicolor.com	Hollywood	CA	90028	323-467-1244	461-2561
Technicolor Inc 4050 Lankershim Blvd *Web:* www.technicolor.com	North Hollywood	CA	91604	818-769-8500	505-5159
Todd-AO 2901 Alameda Ave 2nd Fl *Web:* www.toddao.com	Burbank	CA	91505	818-840-7225	840-7871
Victory Studios 2247 15th Ave W *TF:* 888-282-1776 ■ *Web:* www.victorystudios.com	Seattle	WA	98119	206-282-1776	282-3535
Visiontext 2813 W Alameda Ave 2nd Fl Suite 210 *Web:* www.visiontext.co.uk	Burbank	CA	91505	818-840-7999	840-7997
White Hawk Pictures Inc 567 Bishopgate Ln *Web:* www.whitehawkpictures.com	Jacksonville	FL	32204	904-634-0500	359-9455
WRS Motion Picture & Video Laboratory 213 Tech Rd *Web:* www.wrslabs.com	Pittsburgh	PA	15205	412-722-9011	937-1200
Zaentz Saul Co 2600 10th St *TF:* 800-227-0466 ■ *Web:* www.zaentz.com	Berkeley	CA	94710	510-549-1528	486-2115

516 MOTION PICTURE PRODUCTION - SPECIAL INTEREST

SEE ALSO Animation Companies p. 1278; Motion Picture & Television Production p. 1979

				Phone	Fax
Active Parenting Publishers 1955 Vaughn Rd Suite 108 *TF:* 800-825-0060 ■ *Web:* www.activeparenting.com	Kennesaw	GA	30144	770-429-0565	429-0334
AIMS Multimedia 20765 Superior St *TF:* 800-367-2467 ■ *Web:* www.aimsmultimedia.com	Chatsworth	CA	91311	818-773-4300	341-6700
American Educational Products Inc 401 Hickory St PO Box 2121 *TF:* 800-446-8767 ■ *Web:* www.amep.com	Fort Collins	CO	80522	970-484-7445	484-1198
Atlantic Video Inc 650 Massachusetts Ave NW *Web:* www.atlanticvideo.com	Washington	DC	20001	202-408-0900	408-8496
Automotive Services Training Network 4101 International Pkwy *TF:* 800-223-2786 ■ *Web:* www.twlk.com/auto/	Carrollton	TX	75007	972-309-4000	309-5152
Baby Einstein Co LLC 500 S Buena Vista St **Fax Area Code:* 818 ■ *Web:* www.babyeinstein.com	Burbank	CA	91521	800-793-1454	549-2060*
Broadview Media Inc 4455 W 77th St *Web:* www.broadviewmedia.com	Edina	MN	55435	952-835-4455	835-0971
Channel One Network 261 Madison Ave 3rd Fl *Web:* www.primediatelevision.com	New York	NY	10016	212-915-4000	915-4134
Classic Worldwide Productions Inc 5001 E Royalton Rd *Web:* www.classicworldwide.com	Cleveland	OH	44147	440-838-5377	838-1240
Clearvue & SVE 6465 N Avondale Ave **Fax Area Code:* 800 ■ *TF:* 800-253-2788 ■ *Web:* www.clearvue.com	Chicago	IL	60631	773-775-9433	444-9855*
Clock Wise Productions Inc 79 W 119 St Suite 3 **Fax Area Code:* 801 ■ *Web:* www.clockwiseproductions.com	New York	NY	10026	212-343-3099	843-7088*
Coastal Training Technologies Corp 500 Studio Dr *TF:* 888-776-8268 ■ *Web:* www.coastal.com	Virginia Beach	VA	23452	757-498-9014	498-3657
Cookie Jar Group 266 King St W 2nd Fl *Web:* www.thecookiejarcompany.com	Toronto	ON	M5V1H8	416-977-3238	977-4526
CRM Learning 2218 Faraday Ave Suite 110 *TF:* 800-421-0833 ■ *Web:* www.crmlearning.com	Carlsbad	CA	92008	760-431-9800	931-5792
Disney Educational Productions 105 Terry Dr Suite 120 **Fax Area Code:* 215 ■ *Web:* dep.disney.go.com/educational/index	Newtown	PA	18940	800-295-5010	579-8589*
DSAT 30151 Tomas St *TF:* 800-729-7234 ■ *Web:* www.dsatproductions.com	Rancho Santa Margarita	CA	92688	949-858-1953	267-1254
EDR Media LLC 23330 Commerce Pk Rd *Web:* www.edr.com	Beachwood	OH	44122	216-292-7300	292-0545

Company / Address	City	State	Zip	Phone	Fax
Fire & Emergency Training Network 4101 International Pkwy; *TF:* 800-845-2443 ■ *Web:* www.trinityworkplacelearning.com/fire	Carrollton	TX	75007	972-309-4000	309-5452
Gail & Rice Productions Inc 21301 Civic Ctr Dr; *TF:* 800-860-1931 ■ *Web:* www.gail-rice.com	Southfield	MI	48076	248-799-5000	799-5001
Grace & Wild Inc 23689 Industrial Park Dr; *TF:* 800-451-6010 ■ *Web:* www.gracewild.com	Farmington Hills	MI	48335	248-471-6010	473-8330
Hammond Communications Group Inc 173 Trade St; *TF:* 888-424-1878 ■ *Web:* www.hammondcg.com	Lexington	KY	40511	859-254-1878	254-4290
IMAX Corp 2525 Speakman Dr Sheridan Science & Technology Pk; *NASDAQ: IMAX* ■ *Web:* www.imax.com	Mississauga	ON	L5K1B1	905-403-6500	403-6450
IMS Productions 4555 W 16th St; *Web:* www.imsproductions.tv	Indianapolis	IN	46222	317-244-7484	492-8746
Industrial Training Systems Corp 4101 International Pkwy; *TF:* 800-727-2487	Carrollton	TX	75007	972-309-4000	568-5432
Intaglio LLC 5809 Cross Roads Commerce Pkwy Suite 200; *TF:* 800-632-9153 ■ *Web:* www.intaglioav.com	Grand Rapids	MI	49519	616-243-3300	243-0923
Iris Films 2600 10th St Suite 413; *Web:* www.irisfilms.org	Berkeley	CA	94710	510-845-5414	841-3336
Jack Morton Worldwide 498 7th Ave 7th Fl; *Web:* www.jackmorton.com	New York	NY	10018	212-401-7270	401-7016
Keystone Learning Systems LLC 5300 Westview Dr Suite 405; **Fax Area Code:* 301 ■ *TF:* 800-949-5590 ■ *Web:* www.keystonelearning.com	Frederick	MD	21703	410-800-4000	624-1733*
Kultur International Films Ltd 195 Hwy 36; *TF:* 800-458-5887 ■ *Web:* www.kultur.com	West Long Branch	NJ	07764	732-229-2343	229-0066
Law Enforcement Training Network 4101 International Pkwy; **Fax:* News Rm ■ *TF:* 800-535-5386 ■ *Web:* www.twlk.com/law/	Carrollton	TX	75007	972-309-4000	309-4215*
Learning Communications LLC 38 Discovery Suite 250; *TF:* 800-622-3610 ■ *Web:* www.learncom.com	Irvine	CA	92618	949-788-9209	727-4323
Lingner Group Productions Inc 1435 N Meridian St Suite 100; *Web:* www.lgpinc.com	Indianapolis	IN	46202	317-631-2500	638-7184
Marcus Productions Inc 1 Oakwood Blvd Suite 120; *Web:* www.marcusproductions.com	Hollywood	FL	33020	954-922-9166	920-2780
Medcom Trainex 6060 Phyllis Dr; *TF Cust Svc:* 800-877-1443 ■ *Web:* www.medcomrn.com	Cypress	CA	90630	714-891-1443	898-4852
Medialink Worldwide Inc 708 3rd Ave 8th Fl; *NASDAQ: MDLK* ■ *TF:* 800-843-0677 ■ *Web:* www.medialink.com	New York	NY	10017	212-682-8300	682-2370
Morton Jack Worldwide 498 7th Ave 7th Fl; *Web:* www.jackmorton.com	New York	NY	10018	212-401-7270	401-7016
National Film Board of Canada PO Box 6100 Station Centre-Ville; *Web:* www.nfb.ca	Montreal	QC	H3C3H5	514-283-9000	283-7564
New Amsterdam Entertainment Inc 675 3rd Ave Suite 2521; *Web:* www.newamsterdamnyc.com	New York	NY	10017	212-922-1930	922-0674
Nightingale-Conant Corp 6245 W Howard St; *TF Cust Svc:* 800-323-3938 ■ *Web:* www.nightingale.com	Niles	IL	60714	847-647-0300	647-5552
NTN Buzztime Inc 5966 La Place Ct Suite 100; *AMEX: NTN* ■ *TF:* 888-752-9686 ■ *Web:* www.ntn.com	Carlsbad	CA	92008	760-438-7400	438-3505
Onstream Media Corp 1291 SW 29th Ave; *NASDAQ: ONSM* ■ *Web:* www.onstreammedia.com	Pompano Beach	FL	33069	954-917-6655	917-6660
PRIMEDIA Television 261 Madison Ave 3rd Fl; *Web:* www.primediatelevision.com	New York	NY	10016	212-915-4000	915-4134
PRN Corp 600 Harrison St 4th Fl; *Web:* www.prn.com	San Francisco	CA	94107	415-808-3500	808-3535
Questar Inc 680 N Lake Shore Dr Suite 900; *TF:* 800-544-8422 ■ *Web:* www.questarhomevideo.com	Chicago	IL	60611	312-266-9400	266-9523
THINKFilm Co 23 E 22nd St 5th Fl; *Web:* www.thinkfilmcompany.com	New York	NY	10010	212-444-7900	444-7901
TWL Knowledge Group Inc 4101 International Pkwy; **Fax:* Cust Svc ■ *TF:* 800-624-2272 ■ *Web:* www.twlk.com	Carrollton	TX	75007	972-309-4000	309-4706*
Veritech Corp 168 Denslow Rd; *TF:* 800-525-5912 ■ *Web:* www.veritechmedia.com	East Longmeadow	MA	01028	413-525-3368	525-7449
Wabash Valley Broadcasting DBA IMS Productions 4555 W 16th St; *Web:* www.imsproductions.tv	Indianapolis	IN	46222	317-244-7484	492-8746
Weston Woods Studios 143 Main St; *TF:* 800-243-5020 ■ *Web:* teacher.scholastic.com/products/westonwoods	Norwalk	CT	06851	203-845-0197	845-0498
Zelo Productions Inc 3 S Newton St; *Web:* www.zeloproductions.com	Denver	CO	80219	303-936-8995	936-8995

517 MOTION PICTURE & TELEVISION PRODUCTION

SEE ALSO Animation Companies p. 1278; Motion Picture Production - Special Interest p. 1978

Company / Address	City	State	Zip	Phone	Fax
@radical.media 435 Hudson St 6th Fl; *Web:* www.radicalmedia.com	New York	NY	10014	212-462-1500	462-1600
4Kids Productions Inc 53 W 23rd St 11th Fl; *Web:* www.4kidsentertainmentinc.com	New York	NY	10010	212-590-2100	727-8933
40 Acres & A Mule Filmworks Inc 124 DeKalb Ave	Brooklyn	NY	11217	718-624-3703	624-2008
ABC Family Worldwide Inc 500 S Buena Vista St	Burbank	CA	91521	818-560-1000	569-5939
American Zoetrope 916 Kearny St; *Web:* www.zoetrope.com	San Francisco	CA	94133	415-788-7500	989-7910
Apostle Pictures 568 Broadway Suite 301; *Web:* www.apostlenyc.com	New York	NY	10012	212-541-4323	541-4330
Associated Television International 4401 Wilshire Blvd; *Web:* www.associatedtelevision.com	Los Angeles	CA	90010	323-556-5600	556-5610
Atlantic Video Inc 650 Massachusetts Ave NW; *Web:* www.atlanticvideo.com	Washington	DC	20001	202-408-0900	408-8496
Avatar Studios Inc 2675 Scott Ave Suite G; *TF:* 800-737-6065 ■ *Web:* www.avatar-studios.com	Saint Louis	MO	63103	314-533-2242	533-3349
Big Deahl Productions Inc 1450 N Dayton St; *Web:* www.bigdeahl.com	Chicago	IL	60622	312-573-0733	573-6036
Big Foot Productions Inc 3709 36th Ave; *Web:* www.bigfootnyc.com	Long Island City	NY	11101	718-729-1900	729-8638
Big Idea Inc 230 Franklin Rd Bldg 2A; *Web:* www.bigidea.com	Franklin	TN	37064	615-224-2200	224-2250
Boxing Cat Films 11500 Hart St	North Hollywood	CA	91605	818-765-4870	765-4975
Brillstein Grey Entertainment 9150 Wilshire Blvd Suite 350	Beverly Hills	CA	90212	310-275-6135	275-6180
Brooksfilms Ltd 9336 W Washington Blvd	Culver City	CA	90232	310-202-3292	202-3225
Bruckheimer Jerry Films 1631 10th St; *Web:* www.jbfilms.com	Santa Monica	CA	90404	310-664-6260	664-6261
Bunim/Murray Productions 6007 Sepulveda Blvd; *Web:* www.bunim-murray.com	Van Nuys	CA	91411	818-756-5150	756-5140
Carlisle Kevin & Assoc 2337 Hercules Dr	Los Angeles	CA	90046	323-882-8288	882-8222
Carrie Productions 444 Riverside Dr Suite 110	Burbank	CA	91505	818-567-3292	
Castle Rock Entertainment 335 N Maple Dr Suite 350	Beverly Hills	CA	90210	310-285-2300	285-2345
CBS News 524 W 57th St; **Fax:* News Rm ■ *Web:* www.cbsnews.com	New York	NY	10019	212-975-4114	975-1893*
CBS Paramount Television 5555 Melrose Ave; *Web:* www.cbsparamount.com/television	Los Angeles	CA	90038	323-956-5000	862-0282
CBS Studio Center 4024 Radford Ave; **Fax:* Mail Rm ■ *Web:* www.cbssc.com	Studio City	CA	91604	818-655-5000	655-5409*
Center City Film & Video 1503 Walnut St; *Web:* www.ccfv.com	Philadelphia	PA	19102	215-568-4134	568-6011
Chambers Communications Corp 2975 Chad Dr; *Web:* www.cmc.net/~chambers	Eugene	OR	97408	541-485-5611	342-1568
Chelsea Pictures Inc 122 Hudson St 6th Fl; *Web:* www.chelsea.com	New York	NY	10013	212-431-3434	431-0199
Cheyenne Enterprises 406 Wilshire Blvd	Santa Monica	CA	90401	310-455-5000	688-8000
Chicago Story 401 W Superior St; *TF:* 800-642-3173 ■ *Web:* www.thestorycompanies.com	Chicago	IL	60610	312-642-3173	642-3149
Chuck Fries Productions 1880 Century Park E Suite 213	Los Angeles	CA	90067	310-203-9520	203-9519
Cinergi 2308 Broadway	Santa Monica	CA	90404	310-315-6000	828-0443
CKX Inc 650 Madison Ave; *NASDAQ: CKXE* ■ *Web:* ir.ckx.com	New York	NY	10022	212-838-3100	872-1473
Clean Break Productions 14046 Aubrey Rd	Beverly Hills	CA	90210	818-995-1221	995-0089
Columbia TriStar Motion Picture Group 10202 W Washington Blvd; **Fax:* Mail Rm ■ *Web:* www.sonypictures.com/movies	Culver City	CA	90232	310-244-4000	244-2626*
Crawford Communications Inc 3845 Pleasantdale Rd; **Fax Area Code:* 678 ■ *TF:* 800-831-8027 ■ *Web:* www.crawford.com	Atlanta	GA	30340	404-876-7149	421-6717*
Culver Studios 9336 W Washington Blvd; *Web:* www.theculverstudios.com	Culver City	CA	90232	310-202-1234	
David E Kelley Productions 1600 Rosecrans Ave Bldg 4B	Manhattan Beach	CA	90266	310-727-2200	727-2423
Dick Clark Productions Inc 9200 Sunset Blvd 10th Fl; *Web:* www.dickclarkproductions.com	Los Angeles	CA	90069	310-786-8900	777-2187
Dimension Films 375 Greenwich St; *Web:* www.weinsteinco.com	New York	NY	10013	212-941-3800	941-3949
Disney Walt Pictures 500 S Buena Vista St; *Web:* disney.go.com/disneypictures	Burbank	CA	91521	818-560-1000	843-5346
Dreamworks Animation LLC 1000 Flower St; *NYSE: DWA* ■ *Web:* www.dreamworks.com	Glendale	CA	91201	818-695-5000	695-7574
DreamWorks LLC 1000 Flower St; *Web:* www.dreamworks.com	Glendale	CA	91201	818-695-5000	
Eddie Murphy Productions ML Management Assoc 125 W 55 St 8th Fl	New York	NY	10019	212-333-5500	333-5358
Edmonds Entertainment 1635 N Cahuenga Blvd 5th Fl; *Web:* www.edmondsent.com	Los Angeles	CA	90028	323-860-1550	860-1554
Edward R Pressman Film Corp 1648 N Wilcox Ave; *Web:* www.pressman.com	Hollywood	CA	90028	323-871-8383	871-1870
El Dorado Pictures Inc 725 Arizona Ave Suite 404; *Web:* www.alecbaldwin.com/eldorado	Santa Monica	CA	90401	310-458-4800	458-4802
EUE/Screen Gems Ltd 222 E 44th St; *Web:* www.screengemsstudios.com	New York	NY	10017	212-867-4030	867-4503
F & F Productions LLC 14333 Myerlake Cir; *Web:* www.fandfproductions.com	Clearwater	FL	33760	727-535-6776	535-6547
Family Communications Inc 4802 5th Ave; *Web:* www.fci.org	Pittsburgh	PA	15213	412-687-2990	687-1226
Farrell/Minoff Productions 14011 Ventura Blvd Suite 401	Sherman Oaks	CA	91423	818-789-5766	789-7459
First Kiss Productions 468 N Camden Dr Suite 200	Beverly Hills	CA	90210	310-860-5611	860-5600
First Look Studios Inc 2000 Ave of the Stars Suite 410; *Web:* www.firstlookstudios.com	Century City	CA	90067	424-202-5000	
Flower Films Inc 4000 Warner Blvd Bungalow 3	Burbank	CA	91522	818-954-5840	954-5830
Focus Features 65 Bleeker St 3rd Fl; *Web:* www.focusfeatures.com	New York	NY	10012	212-539-4000	539-4099
Fortis Films 8581 Santa Monica Blvd Suite 1; *Web:* www.sandra.com/fortis.html	West Hollywood	CA	90069	310-659-4533	659-4373
Forward Entertainment 9255 Sunset Blvd Suite 805	Los Angeles	CA	90069	310-278-6700	278-6770
Fox Entertainment Group Inc 1211 Ave of the Americas; *Web:* www.fox.com	New York	NY	10036	212-852-7111	822-8634
Fox Filmed Entertainment 10201 W Pico Blvd; *Web:* www.foxmovies.com	Los Angeles	CA	90035	310-369-1000	
Fox Searchlight Pictures 10201 W Pico Blvd Bldg 38; *Web:* www.foxsearchlight.com	Los Angeles	CA	90035	310-369-1000	
Fox Television Studios 10201 W Pico Blvd; *Web:* www.fox.com	Los Angeles	CA	90035	310-369-1000	
FreMantle Media Ltd 4000 W Alameda Ave 3rd Fl; *Web:* www.fremantlemedia.com	Burbank	CA	91505	818-748-1110	563-6410
Fries Chuck Productions 1880 Century Park E Suite 213	Los Angeles	CA	90067	310-203-9520	203-9519
Fujisankei Communications International Inc 150 E 52nd St 34th Fl; *Web:* www.fujisankei.com	New York	NY	10022	212-753-8100	688-0392
Furthur Films 100 Universal City Plaza Bldg 1320 Suite 1-C	Universal City	CA	91608	818-777-6700	866-1278
Goatsingers 177 W Broadway 2nd Fl	New York	NY	10013	212-966-3045	966-4362
Gold Circle Films 9420 Wilshire Blvd Suite 250; *Web:* www.goldcirclefilms.com	Beverly Hills	CA	90212	310-278-4800	278-0885
Goldwyn Samuel Films LLC 9570 W Pico Blvd Suite 400; *Web:* www.samuelgoldwynfilms.com	Los Angeles	CA	90035	310-860-3100	860-3195
Gracie Films 10202 W Washington Blvd Sidney Poitier Bldg Suite 2221; *Web:* www.graciefilms.com	Culver City	CA	90232	310-244-4222	244-1681
Grammnet Productions 5555 Melrose Ave Lucy Bungalow Rm 206	Los Angeles	CA	90038	323-956-5547	862-1774
Griffin Merv Productions 130 S El Camino Dr; *Web:* www.merv.com	Beverly Hills	CA	90212	310-385-2727	385-2701
Guthy-Renker Corp 41550 Eclectic St Suite 200; *TF:* 800-321-4730 ■ *Web:* www.guthy-renker.com	Palm Desert	CA	92260	760-773-9022	773-9016
Hallmark Hall of Fame Productions Inc 12001 Ventura Pl Suite 300; *TF:* 800-425-5627	Studio City	CA	91604	818-505-9191	505-9842
Harpo Films Inc 345 N Maple Dr Suite 315	Beverly Hills	CA	90210	310-278-5559	278-6110
Harpo Productions Inc 110 N Carpenter; *Web:* www.oprah.com	Chicago	IL	60607	312-633-1000	633-1976
Havoc Films 16 W 19th St 12th Fl	New York	NY	10011	212-924-1629	924-3105
HBO (Home Box Office Inc) 1100 Ave of the Americas; *Web:* www.hbo.com	New York	NY	10036	212-512-1000	
HBO Films 1100 Ave of the Americas; *Web:* www.hbo.com/films	New York	NY	10036	212-512-1000	
HBO Independent Productions 2500 Broadway Suite 400	Santa Monica	CA	90404	310-382-3000	
Hearst Entertainment Productions Inc 20335 Ventura Blvd Suite 300	Woodland Hills	CA	91364	818-444-5010	444-5011
Hearst Entertainment & Syndication Group 300 W 57th St; *Web:* www.hearstcorp.com/entertainment	New York	NY	10019	212-649-2500	245-2306
Henson Jim Co Inc 1416 N La Brea Ave; *Web:* www.henson.com	Hollywood	CA	90028	323-802-1500	802-1825
Henson Jim Pictures 1416 N LaBrea Ave; *Web:* www.henson.com	Hollywood	CA	90028	323-802-1500	802-1825
HKM Productions Inc 1641 N Ivar Ave; *Web:* www.hkm.com	Hollywood	CA	90028	323-465-9494	465-4203
Home Box Office Inc (HBO) 1100 Ave of the Americas; *Web:* www.hbo.com	New York	NY	10036	212-512-1000	
Howard Stern Production Co 10 E 44th St	New York	NY	10017	212-867-1200	867-2434

Entry	City	State	ZIP	Phone	Fax
Icon Productions 808 Wilshire Blvd 4th Fl	Santa Monica	CA	90401	310-434-7300	434-7377
Web: www.iconmovies.us					
Imagine Entertainment Inc 9465 Wilshire Blvd 7th Fl	Beverly Hills	CA	90212	310-858-2000	858-2020
Web: www.imagine-entertainment.com					
Irish Dreamtime 310 Main St Suite 200	Santa Monica	CA	90405	310-449-3411	586-8138
Jerry Bruckheimer Films 1631 10th St	Santa Monica	CA	90404	310-664-6260	664-6261
Web: www.jbfilms.com					
Jerry Weintraub Productions 4000 Warner Blvd Bungalow 1	Burbank	CA	91522	818-954-2500	954-1399
Jim Henson Co 1416 N La Brea Ave	Hollywood	CA	90028	323-802-1500	802-1825
Web: www.henson.com					
Jim Henson Pictures 1416 N LaBrea Ave	Hollywood	CA	90028	323-802-1500	802-1825
Web: www.henson.com					
John Wells Productions 4000 Warner Blvd Bldg 1	Burbank	CA	91522	818-954-1687	954-3657
Jon Voight Entertainment 1901 Ave of the Stars Suite 605	Los Angeles	CA	90067	310-843-0223	553-9895
JTN Productions 13743 Ventura Blvd Suite 200	Sherman Oaks	CA	91423	818-789-5891	789-5892
Web: www.jtnproductions.com					
Kelley David E Productions					
1600 Rosecrans Ave Bldg 4B	Manhattan Beach	CA	90266	310-727-2200	727-2423
Kevin Carlisle & Assoc 2337 Hercules Dr	Los Angeles	CA	90046	323-882-8288	882-8222
King World Productions Inc 2401 Colorado Ave Suite 110	Santa Monica	CA	90404	310-264-3300	264-3301
Web: www.kingworld.com					
Kingsgate Films Inc 9229 Sunset Blvd Suite 720	Los Angeles	CA	90069	310-281-5880	281-2633
Web: kingsgatefilms.com					
KoMut Entertainment Corp 4024 Radford Ave	Studio City	CA	91604	818-655-5642	655-8690
Krofft Sid & Marty Pictures					
CBS Studio Ctr 4024 Radford Ave Bldg 5 Suite 102	Studio City	CA	91604	818-655-5314	655-8235
Levinson/Fontana Co 185 Broome St	New York	NY	10002	212-206-3585	206-3581
Web: www.levinson.com/index_lf.htm					
Lightstorm Entertainment 919 Santa Monica Blvd	Santa Monica	CA	90401	310-656-6100	656-6102
Lincoln Financial Sports 1 Julian Price Pl	Charlotte	NC	28208	704-374-3669	374-3852
Web: lincolnfinancialsports.com					
Lions Gate Entertainment Corp					
2700 Colorado Ave Suite 200	Santa Monica	CA	90404	310-255-3899	255-3870
NYSE: LGF ■ *TF:* 888-609-6120 ■ *Web:* www.lionsgate-ent.com					
Lions Gate Entertainment Corp Lions Gate Television Div					
2700 Colorado Ave Suite 200	Marina del Rey	CA	90404	310-449-9200	255-3970
TF: 800-424-7070 ■ *Web:* www.lionsgatefilms.com					
Lions Gate Films Inc 2700 Colorado Ave Suite 200	Marina del Rey	CA	90404	310-449-9200	255-3970
TF: 800-424-7070 ■ *Web:* www.lionsgatefilms.com					
LivePlanet Inc 2644 30th St	Santa Monica	CA	90405	310-664-2400	664-2401
Web: www.liveplanet.com					
Lucasfilm Ltd PO Box 29901	San Francisco	CA	94129	415-448-2000	
Web: www.lucasfilm.com					
Lucasfilm Ltd Animation 1110 Gorgas St PO Box 29901	San Francisco	CA	94129	415-662-1800	
Web: www.lucasfilm.com/divisions/animation					
M80 Films 1040 Las Palmas Ave Upper Bldg 5	Los Angeles	CA	90038	310-899-9100	860-5181*
**Fax Area Code:* 323					
Mandalay Pictures 4751 Wilshire Blvd 3rd Fl	Los Angeles	CA	90010	323-549-4300	549-9824
Web: www.mandalay.com					
Merv Griffin Productions 130 S El Camino Dr	Beverly Hills	CA	90212	310-385-2727	385-2701
Web: www.merv.com					
Metro-Goldwyn-Mayer Inc (MGM) 10250 Constellation Blvd	Los Angeles	CA	90067	310-449-3000	449-3092*
**Fax:* Mktg ■ *Web:* www.mgm.com					
Metro-Goldwyn-Mayer Pictures 10250 Constellation Blvd	Los Angeles	CA	90067	310-449-3000	449-3092*
**Fax:* Mktg ■ *Web:* www.mgm.com					
MGM Domestic Television Distribution LLC					
10250 Constellation Blvd	Los Angeles	CA	90067	310-449-3000	449-3092
Web: www.mgm.com/television.do					
MGM Pictures 10250 Constellation Blvd	Los Angeles	CA	90067	310-449-3000	449-3092
Web: www.mgm.com					
Midnight Entertainment 11846 Ventura Blvd Suite 208	Studio City	CA	91604	818-752-0197	752-1789
Mirage Enterprises 9220 Sunset Blvd Suite 106	West Hollywood	CA	90069	310-888-2830	888-2825
Web: www.mirageenterprises.com					
Miramax Films Corp 161 Ave of the Americas	New York	NY	10013	917-606-5500	
Web: www.miramax.com					
Montecito Picture Co 1482 E Valley Rd Suite 477	Montecito	CA	93108	805-565-8590	565-4539
Morgan Creek Productions					
10351 Santa Monica Blvd Suite 200	Los Angeles	CA	90025	310-432-4848	432-4844
Web: www.morgancreek.com					
MPCA 1333 2nd St	Santa Monica	CA	90401	310-319-9500	319-9501
Web: www.mpcafilm.com					
Mr Mudd 5225 Wilshire Blvd Suite 604	Los Angeles	CA	90036	323-932-5656	932-5666
Murphy Eddie Productions					
ML Management Assoc 125 W 55 St 8th Fl	New York	NY	10019	212-333-5500	333-5358
National Lampoon Inc 8228 Sunset Blvd	Los Angeles	CA	90046	310-474-5252	474-1219
AMEX: NLN ■ *Web:* www.nationallampoon.com					
NBA Entertainment 450 Harmon Meadow Blvd	Secaucus	NJ	07094	201-865-1500	865-2626*
**Fax:* Mail Rm					
New Crime Productions 555 Rose Ave	Venice	CA	90291	310-396-2199	396-4249
New Line Cinema Corp 888 7th Ave 19th Fl	New York	NY	10106	212-649-4900	649-4966
Web: www.newline.com					
Newmarket Films LLC 202 N Cannon Dr	Beverly Hills	CA	90210	310-858-7472	858-7473
Web: www.newmarketfilms.com					
News Corp Ltd 1211 Ave of the Americas 7th Fl	New York	NY	10036	212-852-7000	852-7145*
NYSE: NWS ■ **Fax:* Investor Rel ■ *Web:* www.newscorp.com					
NTV International Corp 645 5th Ave Suite 303	New York	NY	10022	212-489-8390	660-6998
Web: www.ntvic.com					
Olmos Productions Inc					
Walt Disney Co 500 S Buena Vista St MC 1675	Burbank	CA	91521	818-560-8651	560-8655
Overbrook Entertainment 450 N Roxbury Dr 4th Fl	Beverly Hills	CA	90210	310-432-2400	432-2401
Paramount Pictures Corp 5555 Melrose Ave	Los Angeles	CA	90038	323-956-5000	862-4564
Web: www.paramount.com					
Parkway Productions 7095 Hollywood Blvd Suite 1009	Hollywood	CA	90028	323-874-6207	
Peace Arch Entertainment Group Inc 1867 Young St Suite 650	Toronto	ON	M4S1Y5	416-783-8383	487-6141
AMEX: PAE ■ *Web:* www.peacearch.com					
Phoenix Pictures					
10202 W Washington Blvd Frankovich Bldg	Culver City	CA	90232	310-244-6100	839-8915
Web: www.phoenixpictures.com					
Picturehouse 597 5th Ave 4th Fl	New York	NY	10107	212-303-1700	421-2373
Web: www.picturehouse.com					
Pixar Animation Studios 1200 Park Ave	Emeryville	CA	94608	510-752-3000	752-3151
NASDAQ: PIXR ■ *TF:* 800-888-9856 ■ *Web:* www.pixar.com					
Playboy Entertainment Group Inc 2706 Media Center Dr	Los Angeles	CA	90065	323-276-4000	276-4500
Pressman Edward R Film Corp 1648 N Wilcox Ave	Hollywood	CA	90028	323-871-8383	871-1870
Web: www.pressman.com					
Procter & Gamble Productions Inc 1 Procter & Gamble Plaza	Cincinnati	OH	45202	513-983-1100	
Quince Productions Inc 12400 Ventura Blvd Suite 371	Studio City	CA	91604	818-623-8305	623-8308
Radical Media 435 Hudson St 6th Fl	New York	NY	10014	212-462-1500	462-1600
Web: www.radicalmedia.com					
Raleigh Film & Television Studios 5300 Melrose Ave	Hollywood	CA	90038	323-466-3111	871-5600
Web: www.raleighstudios.com					
Raleigh Studios 1600 Rosecrans Ave	Manhattan Beach	CA	90266	310-727-2700	727-2710
Web: www.raleighstudios.com					
Red Hour Films 629 N La Brea Ave	Los Angeles	CA	90036	323-602-5000	602-5001
Red Strokes Entertainment Inc					
9465 Wilshire Blvd Suite 319	Beverly Hills	CA	90212	310-786-7887	786-7827
Red Wagon Entertainment					
10202 W Washington Blvd Hepburn Bldg W	Culver City	CA	90232	310-244-4466	244-1480
Regency Enterprises 10201 W Pico Blvd Bldg 12	Los Angeles	CA	90035	310-369-8300	969-0470
Web: www.newregency.com					
Revelations Entertainment 1221 2nd St 4th Fl	Santa Monica	CA	90401	310-394-3131	394-3133
Web: www.revelationsent.com					
Revolution Studios 2900 W Olympic Blvd	Santa Monica	CA	90404	310-255-7000	255-7001
Web: www.revolutionstudios.com					
RHI Entertainment LLC 1325 Ave of the Americas 21st Fl	New York	NY	10019	212-977-9001	977-9049
Web: www.rhifilms.com					
Rudin Scott Productions 500 S Buena Vista	Burbank	CA	91521	818-560-4600	560-4608
Rush Communications Inc 512 7th Ave 43rd Fl	New York	NY	10018	212-840-9399	840-9390
Samuel Goldwyn Films LLC 9570 W Pico Blvd Suite 400	Los Angeles	CA	90035	310-860-3100	860-3195
Web: www.samuelgoldwynfilms.com					
Saturn Films 9000 Sunset Blvd Suite 911	West Hollywood	CA	90069	310-887-0900	248-2965
Web: www.saturnfilms.com					
Scott Rudin Productions 500 S Buena Vista	Burbank	CA	91521	818-560-4600	560-4608
Screen Gems 10202 W Washington Blvd	Culver City	CA	90232	310-244-4000	244-2626
Scripps Productions 9721 Sherrill Blvd	Knoxville	TN	37932	865-690-9950	690-3832*
**Fax:* Hum Res					
Sesame Workshop 1 Lincoln Plaza	New York	NY	10023	212-595-3456	875-7359
Web: www.sesameworkshop.org					
Sid & Marty Krofft Pictures					
CBS Studio Ctr 4024 Radford Ave Bldg 5 Suite 102	Studio City	CA	91604	818-655-5314	655-8235
Sikelia Productions 110 W 57th St 5th Fl	New York	NY	10019	212-906-8800	906-8891
Sony Pictures Entertainment Inc 10202 W Washington Blvd	Culver City	CA	90232	310-244-4000	244-2626
TF: 800-326-9551 ■ *Web:* www.sonypictures.com					
Sony Pictures Television 10202 W Washington Blvd	Culver City	CA	90232	310-244-4000	244-2626
Web: www.sonypictures.com					
Sony Wonder 550 Madison Ave	New York	NY	10022	212-833-8100	833-5414
Web: www.sonywonder.com					
Sony/BMG Music Entertainment Video 550 Madison Ave	New York	NY	10022	212-833-8000	833-4818
Web: www.sonymusicvideo.com					
South Fork Pictures 1101 Montana Ave Suite B	Santa Monica	CA	90403	310-395-5155	395-3975
Spirit Dance Entertainment 1023 N Orange Dr	Los Angeles	CA	90038	323-512-7988	512-7996
Spyglass Entertainment Group 10900 Wilshire Blvd 10th Fl	Los Angeles	CA	90024	310-443-5800	443-5912
Web: www.spyglassent.com					
Starz Media LLC 2950 N Hollywood Way 3rd Fl	Burbank	CA	91505	818-748-4000	748-4619
Web: www.starz.com					
Steamroller Productions Inc 417 1/2 Radford Ave	Studio City	CA	91604	818-505-6635	505-6636
Stern Howard Production Co 10 E 44th St	New York	NY	10017	212-867-1200	867-2434
Studio Canal US 301 N Canon Dr Suite 207	Beverly Hills	CA	90210	310-247-0994	247-0998
Tapestry Films 9328 Civic Center Dr	Beverly Hills	CA	90210	310-275-1191	275-1266
Telepictures Productions 3500 W Olive Ave Suite 1000	Burbank	CA	91505	818-972-0777	972-0864
Web: www.telepicturestv.com					
Touchstone Pictures 500 S Buena Vista St	Burbank	CA	91521	818-560-1000	
Web: touchstone.movies.go.com					
Touchstone Television Production LLC 500 S Buena Vista St	Burbank	CA	91521	818-560-1000	
Tribeca Productions 375 Greenwich St 8th Fl	New York	NY	10013	212-941-4040	941-3997
Web: www.tribecafilm.com					
Tribune Entertainment Co 5800 Sunset Blvd	Los Angeles	CA	90028	323-460-5800	460-5892
Web: www.tribtv.com					
True Blue Productions PO Box 27127	Los Angeles	CA	90027	323-661-9191	661-9190
Twentieth Century Fox Film Corp 10201 W Pico Blvd	Los Angeles	CA	90035	310-369-1000	
Web: www.foxmovies.com					
Twentieth Century Fox Television					
10201 W Pico Blvd Bldg 28 Rm 30	Los Angeles	CA	90035	310-369-5962	369-8726
Twentieth Television 2121 Ave of the Stars 21st Fl	Los Angeles	CA	90067	310-369-3293	
United Artists Corp 10250 Constellation Blvd	Los Angeles	CA	90067	310-449-3000	449-3092
Web: www.unitedartists.com					
United Artists Pictures Inc 10250 Constellation Blvd	Los Angeles	CA	90067	310-449-3000	449-3028
Web: www.unitedartists.com					
Universal Pictures 100 Universal City Plaza	Universal City	CA	91608	818-777-1000	
Web: www.universalpictures.com					
Universal Studios Inc 100 Universal City Plaza	Universal City	CA	91608	818-777-1000	866-9459
Web: www.universalstudios.com					
UniWorld Entertainment 100 Ave of the Americas 16th Fl	New York	NY	10013	212-219-1600	274-8565
Web: www.uniworldgroup.com					
Viacom Entertainment Group 4555 Melrose Ave	Hollywood	CA	90038	323-956-5000	
Web: www.viacom.com					
View Askew Productions Inc PO Box 400	Red Bank	NJ	07701	732-842-6933	842-3772
Web: www.viewaskew.com					
Voight Jon Entertainment 1901 Ave of the Stars Suite 605	Los Angeles	CA	90067	310-843-0223	553-9895
Voodoo Films Inc 728 E Hennepin Ave	Minneapolis	MN	55414	612-617-0000	617-9999
TF: 888-866-3666 ■ *Web:* www.voodoofilms.com					
Walt Disney Pictures 500 S Buena Vista St	Burbank	CA	91521	818-560-1000	843-5346
Web: disney.go.com/disneypictures					
Walt Disney Studio Entertainment 500 S Buena Vista St	Burbank	CA	91521	818-560-1000	560-1930
Web: disney.go.com/disneypictures					
Warner Bros Entertainment 4000 Warner Blvd	Burbank	CA	91522	818-954-6000	
Web: www.warnerbros.com					
Warner Bros Television Production Inc 4000 Warner Blvd	Burbank	CA	91522	818-954-6000	
Web: www2.warnerbros.com					
Warner Home Video 4000 Warner Blvd	Burbank	CA	91522	818-954-6000	
Web: www.warnervideo.com					
Warner Independent Pictures 4000 Warner Blvd	Burbank	CA	91522	818-954-6000	
Web: wip.warnerbros.com					
Weinstein Co 375 Greenwich St	New York	NY	10013	212-941-3800	941-3949
Web: www.weinsteinco.com					
Weintraub Jerry Productions 4000 Warner Blvd Bungalow 1	Burbank	CA	91522	818-954-2500	954-1399
Wells John Productions 4000 Warner Blvd Bldg 1	Burbank	CA	91522	818-954-1687	954-3657
White Hawk Pictures Inc 567 Bishopgate Ln	Jacksonville	FL	32204	904-634-0500	359-9455
Web: www.whitehawkpictures.com					
Wind Dancer Production Group 745 S Marengo Ave Suite 204	Pasadena	CA	91106	626-356-4618	
Winkler Films 211 S Beverly Dr Suite 200	Beverly Hills	CA	90212	310-858-5780	858-5799
Wolf Films 100 Universal City Plaza Bldg 2252	Universal City	CA	91608	818-777-1236	866-1446
Working Title Films 9720 Wilshire Blvd 4th Fl	Beverly Hills	CA	90212	310-777-3100	777-5243
Web: www.workingtitlefilms.com					
Worldwide Pants Inc 1697 Broadway	New York	NY	10019	212-975-5300	975-4780

MOTION PICTURE THEATERS

SEE Theaters - Motion Picture p. 2366

518 MOTOR SPEEDWAYS

Entry	City	State	ZIP	Phone	Fax
Ace Speedway 3401 Altamahaw Race Track Rd	Altamahaw	NC	27204	336-585-1200	585-1209
Web: www.acespeedway.com					

				Phone	Fax
Adams County Speedway 12th & John St	Corning	IA	50841	712-785-3271	785-3272
Web: www.acspeedway.com					
All Star Speedway 176 Exeter Rd Rt 27	Epping	NH	03042	978-815-2305	927-3182
Web: www.all-starspeedway.com					
Antioch Speedway PO Box 4575	Antioch	CA	94531	925-779-9220	779-9213
Web: www.antiochspeedway.com					
Atco Raceway 1000 Jackson Rd	Atco	NJ	08004	856-768-2167	753-9604
Web: www.atcorace.com					
Atlanta Dragway 500 E Ridgeway Rd	Commerce	GA	30529	706-335-2301	335-7135
Web: www.atlantadragway.com					
Atlanta Motor Speedway 1500 Hwy 19-41	Hampton	GA	30228	770-946-3920	946-3928
Web: www.atlantamotorspeedway.com					
Bandimere Speedway 3051 S Rooney Rd	Morrison	CO	80465	303-697-6001	697-0815
TF: 800-664-8946 ■ *Web:* www.bandimere.com					
Big Country Speedway 4820 S Greeley Hwy	Cheyenne	WY	82007	307-632-2107	
Web: www.bigcountryspeedway.com					
Bloomington Speedway 5185 S Fairfax Rd	Bloomington	IN	47401	812-824-8753	824-7400
Web: www.bloomingtonspeedway.com					
Bolivar Speedway USA PO Box 683	Bolivar	MO	65613	417-326-3966	
Web: www.bolivarspeedwayusa.com					
Brainerd International Raceway 5523 Birchdale Rd	Brainerd	MN	56401	218-824-7220	824-7240
Web: www.brainerdraceway.com					
Bristol Motor Speedway 151 Speedway Blvd PO Box 3966	Bristol	TN	37620	423-764-1161	764-1646
Web: www.bristolmotorspeedway.com					
California Speedway 9300 Cherry Ave	Fontana	CA	92335	909-429-5000	429-5500
TF: 800-944-7223 ■ *Web:* www.californiaspeedway.com					
Carolina Dragway 302 Dragstrip Rd	Jackson	SC	29803	803-471-2285	266-4651
Web: www.carolinadragway.com					
Chicagoland Speedway 500 Speedway Blvd	Joliet	IL	60433	815-727-7223	727-7895
Web: www.chicagolandspeedway.com					
Colorado National Speedway 4281 Weld County Rd 10	ErieDacono	CO	80514	303-828-0116	828-2403
Web: www.coloradospeedway.com					
Columbus Motor Speedway Inc 1841 Williams Rd	Columbus	OH	43207	614-491-1047	491-6010
Web: www.columbusspeedway.com					
Concord Motorsport Park 7940 US Hwy 601 S	Concord	NC	28025	704-782-4221	782-4420
Web: www.concordmotorsportpark.com					
Corpus Christi Speedway SR-358 & SR-44	Corpus Christi	TX	78405	361-289-8847	
Web: www.ccspeedway.biz					
Darlington Raceway 1301 Harry Bird Hwy	Darlington	SC	29532	866-459-7223	395-8920*
**Fax Area Code:* 843 ■ *Web:* www.darlingtonraceway.com					
Daytona International Speedway					
1801 W International Speedway Blvd	Daytona Beach	FL	32114	386-254-2700	257-0281
Web: www.daytonainternationalspeedway.com					
Daytona USA 1801 W International Speedway Blvd	Daytona Beach	FL	32114	386-947-6800	947-6802
Web: www.daytonausa.com					
Dover Downs International Speedway					
1131 N DuPont Hwy PO Box 843	Dover	DE	19903	302-674-4600	741-8971
Web: www.doverspeedway.com					
Dubuque Fairgrounds Speedway 14569 Old Highway Rd	Dubuque	IA	52002	563-588-1406	744-3598
Web: www.dbqfair.com					
Eagle Raceway 617 S 238th St	Eagle	NE	68347	402-238-2595	
Web: www.eagleraceway.com					
El Paso Speedway Park 1447 Marina Ave	El Paso	TX	79938	915-791-8749	541-6398*
**Fax Area Code:* 505 ■ *Web:* www.epspeedwaypark.com					
Elko Speedway 26350 France Ave	Elko	MN	55020	952-461-7223	461-3397
TF: 800-479-3630 ■ *Web:* www.goelkospeedway.com					
Evergreen Speedway 14405 179th Ave SE Bldg 305	Monroe	WA	98272	360-805-6100	805-6110
Web: www.evergreenspeedway.com					
Florence Motor Speedway 836 E Smith St	Timmonsville	SC	29161	843-346-7711	346-4637
Web: www.florencemotorspeedway.com					
Gainesville Raceway 11211 N County Rd 225	Gainesville	FL	32609	352-377-0046	371-4212
Web: www.gainesvilleraceway.com					
Gateway International Raceway					
700 Raceway Blvd PO Box 200	Madison	IL	62060	618-482-2400	482-3919
TF: 866-357-7333 ■ *Web:* www.gatewayraceway.com					
Grandview Speedway 43 Passmore Rd	Bechtelsville	PA	19505	610-754-7688	754-6303
Web: www.grandviewspeedway.com					
Greenville-Pickens Speedway 3800 Calhoun Memorial Hwy	Greenville	SC	29611	864-269-0852	269-7683
Web: www.greenvillepickens.com					
Hamilton County Speedway 1200 Bluff St	Webster City	IA	50595	515-832-1443	832-6972
Web: www.hamiltoncountyspeedway.com					
Heart O' Texas Speedway 203 Trailwood Ave	Waco	TX	76710	254-829-2294	776-1576
Web: www.heartotexspeedway.com					
Heartland Park Topeka 7530 S Topeka Blvd	Topeka	KS	66619	785-862-4781	862-2016
TF: 800-437-2237 ■ *Web:* www.hpt.com					
Hickory Motor Speedway 3130 Hwy 70 SE	Newton	NC	28658	828-464-3655	465-5017
Web: www.hickorymotorspeedway.com					
Holland International Speedway 2 N Main St	Holland	NY	14080	716-537-2272	537-9749
Web: www.hollandspeedway.com					
Homestead-Miami Speedway 1 Speedway Blvd	Homestead	FL	33035	305-230-5000	230-5140
Web: www.homesteadmiamispeedway.com					
Houston Motor Speedway 11620 N Lake Houston Pkwy	Houston	TX	77044	281-458-1972	458-2836
Web: www.houstonspeedway.com					
Houston Raceway Park 2525 FM 565 S	Baytown	TX	77520	281-383-2666	383-3777
Web: www.houstonraceway.com					
Huntsville Dragway 502 Quarter Mountain Rd	Harvest	AL	35749	256-859-0807	859-9261
Web: www.huntsvilledragway.com					
I-70 Speedway 12773 N Outer Rd	Odessa	MO	64076	816-230-0080	230-8222
Web: www.i70speedway.net					
Infineon Raceway Hwys 37 & 121	Sonoma	CA	95476	707-938-8448	938-8430
TF: 800-870-7223 ■ *Web:* www.infineonraceway.com					
International Speedway Corp					
1801 W International Speedway Blvd	Daytona Beach	FL	32114	386-254-2700	257-0281
NASDAQ: ISCA ■ *Web:* www.iscmotorsports.com					
Jennerstown Speedway					
Intersection of Rt 30 & Rt 985 PO Box 230	Jennerstown	PA	15547	814-629-6677	629-6171
Web: www.jennerstown.com					
Kalamazoo Speedway 7656 Ravine Rd	Kalamazoo	MI	49009	269-349-3978	692-2848
Web: www.kalamazoospeedway.com					
Kentucky Speedway 4760 Sparta Pike	Sparta	KY	41086	859-567-3400	567-3441
Web: www.kentuckyspeedway.com					
Kil-Kare Speedway 1166 Dayton-Xenia Rd	Xenia	OH	45385	937-429-2961	426-5049
Web: www.kilkare.com					
Lacrosse Fairgrounds Speedway					
N 4985 County Hwy M PO Box 853	West Salem	WI	54669	608-786-1525	786-1524
Web: www.lacrossespeedway.com					
Lake Ozark Speedway 3736 S Hwy 54	Lake Ozark	MO	65049	573-302-4499	302-0808
Web: www.capitalspeedway.com					
Langley Speedway 11 Dale Lemonds Dr	Hampton	VA	23666	757-865-7223	865-1147
Web: www.langley-speedway.com					
Lanier International Speedway 1 Raceway Dr	Braselton	GA	30517	770-967-8600	967-4411
Web: www.lanierspeedway.com					
Las Vegas Motor Speedway 7000 Las Vegas Blvd N	Las Vegas	NV	89115	702-644-4444	632-8021
TF: 800-644-4444 ■ *Web:* www.lvms.com					
Lime Rock Park 497 Lime Rock Rd	Lakeville	CT	06039	860-435-5000	435-5010
TF: 800-722-3577 ■ *Web:* www.limerock.com					

				Phone	Fax
Lonesome Pine Raceway					
10800 Norton-Coeburn Rd PO Box 180	Coeburn	VA	24230	276-395-3434	
Los Angeles County Fairplex 1101 W McKinley Ave	Pomona	CA	91768	909-623-3111	865-3602
Web: www.fairplex.com					
Lubbock Motor Speedway 114th St & ML King Blvd	Lubbock	TX	79404	806-748-0750	863-2188
Web: www.lubbockmotorspeedway.com					
Magic Valley Speedway 2144 Hillcrest Ln	Twin Falls	ID	83301	208-734-3700	732-5559
Web: www.magicvalleyspeedway.com					
Mansfield Motorsports Speedway 100 Crall Rd	Mansfield	OH	44903	419-525-7223	524-0187
Web: www.mansfield-speedway.com					
Maple Grove Raceway 30 Stauffer Park Ln	Mohnton	PA	19540	610-856-7812	856-1601
Web: www.maplegroveraceway.com					
Marion County International Raceway					
2303 Richwood-LaRue Rd	La Rue	OH	43332	740-499-3666	499-2185
TF: 800-422-6247 ■ *Web:* www.mcir.com					
Martinsville Speedway 340 Speedway Rd	Martinsville	VA	24112	276-956-3151	956-1298
Web: www.martinsvillespeedway.com					
Mazda Raceway Laguna Seca 1021 Monterey Salinas Hwy	Salinas	CA	93908	831-648-5111	373-0533
Web: www.laguna-seca.com					
Memphis Motorsports Park 5500 Victory Ln	Millington	TN	38053	901-358-7223	358-7274
TF: 866-407-7333 ■ *Web:* www.memphismotorsports.com					
Michigan International Speedway 12626 US 12	Brooklyn	MI	49230	517-592-6666	592-3848
TF: 800-354-1010 ■ *Web:* www.mispeedway.com					
Mid-Ohio Sports Car Course					
7721 Steam Corners Rd PO Box 3108	Lexington	OH	44904	419-884-4000	884-0042
TF: 800-643-6446 ■ *Web:* www.midohio.com					
Midway Speedway 20377 Silver Dr	Lebanon	MO	65536	417-532-2060	533-3203
Web: www.lebanonmidwayspeedway.com					
Milwaukee Mile 7722 W Greenfield Ave	West Allis	WI	53214	414-453-8277	453-9920
Web: www.milwaukeemile.com					
Monett Speedway 685 Chapel Dr	Monett	MO	65708	417-732-2766	732-5979
Web: www.monettspeedway.com					
Motordrome Speedway I-70 & Exit 49	Smithton	PA	15479	724-872-7555	
Web: www.motordrome.com					
Myrtle Beach Speedway 4300 Hwy 501	Myrtle Beach	SC	29579	843-236-0500	236-0525
Web: www.myrtlebeachspeedway.com					
New Hampshire International Speedway 1122 Rt 106N	Loudon	NH	03307	603-783-4744	783-9691
Web: www.nhis.com					
New River Valley Speedway 6749 Lee Hwy	Radford	VA	24141	540-639-1700	731-4756
New York International Raceway Park					
2011 New Rd PO Box 296	Leicester	NY	14481	585-382-3030	382-9061
Web: www.nyirp.com					
Ocean Speedway 4400 Auto Plaza Rd	Capitola	CA	95010	831-476-9466	464-2420
Web: www.oceanspeedway.com					
Oglethorpe Speedway Park 200 Jesup Rd PO Box 687	Pooler	GA	31322	912-964-8200	964-9501
Web: www.ospracing.net					
Old Bridge Township Raceway Park 230 Pension Rd	Englishtown	NJ	07726	732-446-6331	446-1373
Web: www.etownraceway.com					
Old Dominion Speedway 10611 Dumfries Rd	Manassas	VA	20112	703-361-7223	361-8796
Web: www.olddominionspeedway.com					
Orange Show Speedway 689 S 'E' St	San Bernardino	CA	92408	909-888-6788	889-7666
Web: www.orangeshowspeedway.net					
Oxford Plains Speedway 877 Main St PO Box 208	Oxford	ME	04270	207-539-8865	539-8860
Web: www.oxfordplains.com					
Park Jefferson Speedway Hwy 105	Jefferson	SD	57038	605-966-5517	494-1893*
**Fax Area Code:* 402 ■ *Web:* www.parkjeffersonspeedway.com					
Peoria Speedway 3520 W Farmington Rd	Peoria	IL	61604	309-673-3342	673-3342
Web: www.peoriaspeedway.com					
Pocono Raceway Long Pond Rd PO Box 500	Long Pond	PA	18334	570-646-2300	646-2010
TF: 800-722-3929 ■ *Web:* www.poconoraceway.com					
Proctor Speedway 800 N Boundary Ave	Proctor	MN	55810	218-624-0606	
Web: www.proctorspeedway.com					
Quincy Raceways 8000 Broadway St	Quincy	IL	62305	217-224-3843	224-3859
Web: www.quincyraceways.com					
Redwood Acres Raceway 3750 Harris St	Eureka	CA	95503	707-442-3232	443-9495
Riverhead Raceway PO Box 148	Lindenhurst	NY	11757	631-842-7223	789-1160
Web: www.riverheadraceway.com					
Road America N 7390 Hwy 67	Elkhart Lake	WI	53020	920-892-4576	892-4550
TF: 800-365-7223 ■ *Web:* www.roadamerica.com					
Road Atlanta Raceway 5300 Winder Hwy	Braselton	GA	30517	770-967-6143	967-2668
TF: 800-849-7223 ■ *Web:* www.roadatlanta.com					
Rockingham Dragway 2153 Hwy US 1 N	Rockingham	NC	28379	910-582-3400	582-8667
Web: www.rockinghamdragway.com					
San Antonio Speedway 14901 State Hwy 16 S	San Antonio	TX	78264	210-628-1499	628-6760
Web: www.sanantoniospeedway.com					
Sandusky Speedway 614 W Perkins Ave	Sandusky	OH	44870	419-625-4084	625-8110
Web: www.sanduskyspeedway.com					
Saugus Speedway 22500 Soledad Canyon Rd	Saugus	CA	91350	661-259-3886	259-8534
Web: www.saugusspeedway.com					
Sebring International Raceway 113 Midway Dr	Sebring	FL	33870	863-655-1442	655-1777
Web: www.sebringraceway.com					
South Boston Speedway					
1188 James D Hagood Hwy PO Box 1066	South Boston	VA	24592	434-572-4947	575-8992
TF: 877-440-1540 ■ *Web:* www.southbostonspeedway.com					
South Sound Speedway 3730 183rd Ave SW	Rochester	WA	98579	360-273-6420	273-8113
Web: www.southsoundspeedway.com					
Southen New Mexico Speedway Inc 3590 W Picacho Ave	Las Cruces	NM	88005	505-524-7913	541-6398
TF: 800-658-9650 ■ *Web:* www.snmspeedway.com					
Stafford Motor Speedway 55 West St PO Box 105	Stafford Springs	CT	06076	860-684-2783	684-6236
Web: www.staffordspeedway.com					
Summit Motorsports Park 1300 SR 18	Norwalk	OH	44857	419-668-5555	663-0502
Web: www.summitmotorsportspark.com					
Superior Speedway 4700 Tower Ave	Superior	WI	54880	715-394-7848	394-7025
Web: www.superiorspeedway.com					
Texas Motorplex 7500 W Hwy 287	Ennis	TX	75119	972-878-2641	878-1848
TF: 800-668-6775 ■ *Web:* www.texasmotorplex.com					
Thompson Speedway 205 E Thompson Rd PO Box 278	Thompson	CT	06277	860-923-2280	923-2398
Web: www.thompsonspeedway.com					
Tucson Raceway Park					
11955 S Harison Rd Pima County Fairgrounds	Tucson	AZ	85747	520-762-9200	762-5053
Web: www.tucsonracewaypark.com					
Viking Speedway Douglas County Fairgrounds 3rd Ave W	Alexandria	MN	56308	320-762-1559	
Web: vikingspeedway.net					
Volusia Speedway Park 1500 E Hwy 40	De Leon Springs	FL	32130	386-985-4402	985-6258
Web: www.volusiaspeedwaypark.com					
Watkins Glen International Inc 2790 CR 16	Watkins Glen	NY	14891	607-535-2481	535-8918
Web: www.theglen.com					
Wenatchee Valley Super Oval PO Box 2445	Wenatchee	WA	98807	509-886-5801	884-9712
Web: www.wvso.com					
West Liberty Raceway 101 N Clay St PO Box 261	West Liberty	IA	52776	319-627-2414	627-2299
Winchester Speedway SR 32 PO Box 31	Winchester	IN	47394	765-584-9701	584-8111
Web: www.winchesterspeedway.com					

519 MOTOR VEHICLES - COMMERCIAL & SPECIAL PURPOSE

SEE ALSO All-Terrain Vehicles p. 1277; Automobiles - Mfr p. 1360; Campers, Travel Trailers, Motor Homes p. 1405; Motorcycles & Motorcycle Parts & Accessories p. 1983; Snowmobiles p. 2318; Weapons & Ordnance (Military) p. 2413

Company	City	State	ZIP	Phone	Fax
Accubuilt Inc 2550 Central Point Pkwy *Web:* www.accubuilt.com	Lima	OH	45804	419-222-1501	222-4450
Allianz Sweeper Co 1690 Eiffel St *TF:* 800-862-3822 ■ *Web:* www.allianzsweeper.com	Boucherville	QC	J4B7W1	450-616-8100	616-8103
Allied Body Works Inc 625 S 96th St *TF:* 800-733-7450 ■ *Web:* www.alliedbody.com	Seattle	WA	98108	206-763-7811	763-8836
Altec Industries Inc 210 Inverness Center Dr *Web:* www.altec.com	Birmingham	AL	35242	205-991-7733	991-9993
American LaFrance Aerials Inc 64 Cocalico Creek Rd *Web:* www.americanlafrance.com/Products/Aerials	Ephrata	PA	17522	717-859-1176	859-2774
American LaFrance Corp 8500 Palmetto Commerce Pkwy *TF:* 888-253-8725 ■ *Web:* www.americanlafrance.com	Lodson	SC	29456	843-486-7400	486-7580
Arrow Truck Bodies & Equipment Inc 1639 S Campus St *Web:* www.arrowtruckbodies.com	Ontario	CA	91761	909-947-3991	947-4932
ASV Inc 840 Lilly Ln *NASDAQ: ASVI* ■ *TF:* 800-346-5954 ■ *Web:* www.asvi.com	Grand Rapids	MN	55744	218-327-3434	327-9122
Auto Truck Inc 1200 N Ellis St *TF:* 877-284-4440 ■ *Web:* www.autotruck.com	Bensenville	IL	60106	630-860-5600	860-5631
Benson International Inc Rt 14 S PO Box 970 *TF:* 877-489-9020 ■ *Web:* www.bensonintl.com	Mineral Wells	WV	26150	304-489-9020	489-2828
Berrien Buggy Inc 10644 US Hwy 31 *Web:* www.berrienbuggy.com	Berrien Springs	MI	49103	269-471-1411	
Blue Bird Corp 402 Blue Bird Blvd *TF:* 800-486-7122 ■ *Web:* www.blue-bird.com	Fort Valley	GA	31030	478-825-2021	822-2457
Bobcat Co 250 E Beaton Dr *Web:* www.bobcat.com	West Fargo	ND	58078	701-241-8700	241-8704
Brand FX Body Co 404 4th Ave W *Web:* www.brandfxbody.com	Swea City	IA	50590	515-272-4372	272-4218
Bristol-Donald Co Inc 50 Roanoke Ave *Web:* www.bristoldonald.com/	Newark	NJ	07105	973-589-2640	589-2610
Brumbaugh Body Co Inc RR 5 PO Box 579	Duncansville	PA	16635	814-696-9552	696-8640
Capacity of Texas Inc 401 Capacity Dr *TF:* 800-323-0135 ■ *Web:* www.capacitytexas.com	Longview	TX	75604	903-759-0610	759-3209
Carnegie Body Co 9500 Brookpark Rd *TF:* 800-362-1989 ■ *Web:* www.carnegiebody.com	Cleveland	OH	44129	216-749-5000	749-5740
Champion Bus Inc 331 Graham Rd **Fax:* Mktg ■ *TF:* 800-776-4943 ■ *Web:* www.championbus.com	Imlay City	MI	48444	810-724-6474	724-1844*
Chance Rides Mfg Inc 4219 Irving St *TF:* 800-242-6231 ■ *Web:* www.rides.com	Wichita	KS	67209	316-942-7411	942-7416
Club Car Inc PO Box 204658 *TF:* 800-227-0739 ■ *Web:* www.clubcar.com	Augusta	GA	30917	706-863-3000	860-7231
Coach & Equipment Mfg Corp 130 Horizon Pk Dr PO Box 36 *Web:* www.coach-equipment.com	Penn Yan	NY	14527	315-536-2321	
Collins Industries Inc 15 Compound Dr *Web:* www.collinsind.com	Hutchinson	KS	67502	620-663-5551	663-1630
Columbia ParCar Corp 1115 Commercial Ave *TF:* 800-222-4653 ■ *Web:* www.parcar.com	Reedsburg	WI	53959	608-524-8888	524-8380
Crane Carrier Co 1925 N Sheridan Rd *Web:* www.cranecarrier.com	Tulsa	OK	74115	918-836-1651	832-7348
Curtis Tractor Cab Inc 111 Higgins St *TF:* 800-343-7676 ■ *Web:* www.curtisintl.com	Worcester	MA	01606	508-853-2200	854-3190
Dealers Truck Equipment Co 2460 Midway St *TF:* 800-259-7569 ■ *Web:* www.dealerstruck.com	Shreveport	LA	71108	318-635-7567	635-3144
Delphi Body Works Inc 313 S Washington St *Web:* www.delphibodyworks.com	Delphi	IN	46923	765-564-2212	564-4255
Delta-Waseca Inc 5200 Willson Rd Suite 307 *Web:* www.deltawaseca.com	Minneapolis	MN	55424	952-922-5569	922-1195
Diamond Coach Corp 2300 W 4th St *TF:* 800-442-4645 ■ *Web:* www.diamondcoach.com	Oswego	KS	67356	620-795-2191	795-4816
Douglass Truck Bodies Inc 231 21st St *TF:* 800-635-7641 ■ *Web:* www.douglasstruckbodies.com	Bakersfield	CA	93301	661-327-0258	327-3894
DST Industries Inc 34364 Goddard Rd **Fax:* Hum Res ■ *TF:* 800-327-6174 ■ *Web:* www.dstindustries.com	Romulus	MI	48174	734-941-0300	941-0489*
E-ONE Inc 1601 SW 37th Ave *Web:* www.e-one.com	Ocala	FL	34474	352-237-1122	237-1151
E-Z-GO 1451 Marvin Griffin Rd *Web:* www.ezgo.com	Augusta	GA	30906	706-798-4311	771-4605
Ebus Inc 9250 Washburn Rd *Web:* www.ebus.com	Downey	CA	90242	562-904-3474	
Electric Golf Car Co 1022 Douglas Blvd *TF:* 800-700-8857 ■ *Web:* www.electricgolfcar.com	Roseville	CA	95678	916-773-2244	773-6829
Elgin Sweeper Co 1300 W Bartlett Rd *Web:* www.elginsweeper.com	Elgin	IL	60120	847-741-5370	742-3035
Elliott Machine Works Inc 146 Rensch Ave *TF:* 800-299-0412 ■ *Web:* www.elliottmachine.com	Galion	OH	44833	419-468-4709	468-4642
Erie Vehicle Co 60 E 51st St *TF:* 888-550-3743 ■ *Web:* www.erievehiclecompany.com	Chicago	IL	60615	773-536-6300	536-5779
Featherlite Luxury Coaches Inc 4441 Orange Blvd *TF:* 888-826-8273 ■ *Web:* www.featherlitecoaches.com	Sanford	FL	32771	407-323-1120	321-0676
Fisher Engineering 50 Gordon Dr PO Box 529 **Fax:* Hum Res ■ *Web:* www.fisherplows.com	Rockland	ME	04841	207-701-4200	701-4313*
Fleet Engineers Inc 1800 E Keating Ave *TF Cust Svc:* 800-333-7890 ■ *Web:* www.fleetengineers.com	Muskegon	MI	49442	231-777-2537	777-2720
Fleet Equipment Corp 567 Commerce St *Web:* www.fectrucks.com	Franklin Lakes	NJ	07417	201-337-7332	337-3294
Florig Equipment Inc 906 W Ridge Pike *Web:* www.florig.com	Conshohocken	PA	19428	610-825-0900	825-0909
Fontaine Modification Co 9827 Mt Holly Rd *TF:* 800-989-2113 ■ *Web:* www.fontainemod.com	Charlotte	NC	28214	704-391-1355	392-8460
Fontaine Truck Equipment Co 2490 Pinson Valley Pkwy *TF:* 800-824-3033 ■ *Web:* www.fontaine.com	Birmingham	AL	35217	205-841-8582	849-9615
Frank J Zamboni & Co Inc 15714 Colorado Ave *Web:* www.zamboni.com	Paramount	CA	90723	562-633-0751	633-9365
Freightliner Corp 4747 N Channel Ave **Fax:* Hum Res ■ *TF Cust Svc:* 800-385-4357 ■ *Web:* www.freightliner.com	Portland	OR	97217	503-745-8000	745-6657*
Gehl Co 143 Water St *NASDAQ: GEHL* ■ *Web:* www.gehl.com	West Bend	WI	53095	262-334-9461	338-7517
GEMTOP Mfg Inc 8811 SE Herbert Ct **Fax:* Sales ■ *Web:* www.gemtopmfg.com	Clackamas	OR	97015	503-659-3733	659-1449*
General Body Co 2415 E Higgins Rd	Elk Grove Village	IL	60007	847-640-8305	640-0251
General Motors Corp (GMC) 300 Renaissance Center *NYSE: GM* ■ **Fax Area Code:* 248 ■ *Web:* www.gm.com	Detroit	MI	48265	313-556-5000	696-7300*
General Safety Equipment Corp 5181 260th St	Wyoming	MN	55092	651-462-1000	462-1700
George Heiser Body Co Inc 11210 Tukwila International Blvd	Seattle	WA	98168	206-622-7985	622-7135
Gillig Corp 25800 Clawiter Rd *TF:* 800-735-1500 ■ *Web:* www.gillig.com	Hayward	CA	94545	510-785-1500	785-6819
Gowans-Knight Co Inc 49 Knight St *TF:* 800-352-4871 ■ *Web:* www.gowansknight.com	Watertown	CT	06795	860-274-8801	274-7937
Hackney & Sons Inc 911 W 5th St *TF:* 800-763-0700 ■ *Web:* www.hackneyandsons.com	Washington	NC	27889	252-946-6521	975-8340
Heil Environmental Industries Ltd 5751 Cornelison Rd Bldg B *TF:* 800-824-4345 ■ *Web:* www.heil.com	Chattanooga	TN	37411	423-899-9100	855-3478
Heiser George Body Co Inc 11210 Tukwila International Blvd	Seattle	WA	98168	206-622-7985	622-7135
Hercules Mfg Co 800 Bob Posey St *TF:* 800-633-3031 ■ *Web:* www.herculesvanbodies.com	Henderson	KY	42420	270-826-9501	826-0439
Hesse Inc 6700 St John Ave *TF:* 800-821-5562 ■ *Web:* www.grouphesse.com	Kansas City	MO	64123	816-483-7808	241-9010
HME Inc 1950 Byron Ctr Ave *TF:* 800-669-9192 ■ *Web:* www.hmetruck.com	Wyoming	MI	49519	616-534-1463	534-1967
IC Corp 751 S Harkrider St *Web:* www.ic-corp.com	Conway	AR	72032	501-327-7761	505-2568
International Truck & Engine Corp 4201 Winfield Rd *Web:* www.navistar.com	Warrenville	IL	60555	630-753-5000	753-6888
Jerr-Dan Corp 1080 Hykes Rd **Fax:* Sales ■ *TF Sales:* 800-926-9666 ■ *Web:* www.jerr-dan.com	Greencastle	PA	17225	717-597-7111	593-6183*
Johnson Truck Bodies LLC 215 E Allen St *TF Sales:* 800-922-8360 ■ *Web:* www.johnsontruckbodies.com	Rice Lake	WI	54868	715-234-7071	234-4628
Kenworth Truck Co 10630 NE 38th Pl *Web:* www.kenworth.com	Kirkland	WA	98033	425-828-5000	828-5088
Kidron Inc PO Box 17 *TF:* 800-321-5421 ■ *Web:* www.kidron.com	Kidron	OH	44636	330-857-3011	857-8451
KME Fire Apparatus 68 Sicker Rd *TF:* 800-394-5593 ■ *Web:* www.kovatch.com	Latham	NY	12110	518-785-0900	785-1794
Knapheide Mfg Co 1848 Westphalia Strasse PO Box 7140 *Web:* www.knapheide.com	Quincy	IL	62305	217-222-7131	222-5939
Labrie Environmental Group 175 du Pont *TF:* 800-463-6638 ■ *Web:* www.labriegroup.com	Saint-Nicolas	QC	G7A2T3	418-831-8250	831-5255
Les Entreprises Michel Corbeil Inc 830 12th Ave *TF:* 888-439-3577 ■ *Web:* www.corbeilbus.com	Saint-Lin-Laurentides	QC	J5M2V9	450-439-3577	439-6852
Lodal Inc 620 N Hooper St **Fax:* Orders ■ *TF:* 800-435-3500 ■ *Web:* www.lodal.com	Kingsford	MI	49802	906-779-1700	779-1160*
LZ Truck Equipment Co Inc 1881 Rice St *TF:* 800-247-1082 ■ *Web:* www.lztruckequipment.com	Roseville	MN	55113	651-488-2571	488-9857
Mack Trucks Inc 2100 Mack Blvd **Fax:* Mail Rm ■ *Web:* www.macktrucks.com	Allentown	PA	18105	610-709-3011	709-2405*
Marion Body Works Inc 211 W Ramsdell St *Web:* www.marionbody.com	Marion	WI	54950	715-754-5261	754-5776
Masterack-Crown Inc 7315 E Lincon Way *TF Cust Svc:* 800-321-4934 ■ *Web:* www.crown-na.com	Apple Creek	OH	44606	330-262-6010	262-4095
Mayflower Vehicle System 55 N Garfield St	Norwalk	OH	44857	419-668-8132	668-1096
McLaughlin Body Co 2430 River Dr *Web:* www.mclbody.com	Moline	IL	61265	309-762-7755	762-2823
McNeilus Cos PO Box 70 *Web:* www.mcneiluscompanies.com	Dodge Center	MN	55927	507-374-6321	374-6306
Medical Coaches Inc PO Box 129 *TF:* 800-432-1339 ■ *Web:* www.medcoach.com	Oneonta	NY	13820	607-432-1333	432-8190
Metro Truck Body Inc 1201 Jon St *Web:* www.metrotruckbody.com	Torrance	CA	90502	310-532-5570	532-0754
Meyer Truck Equipment Inc 196 W State Rd 56 *TF:* 800-456-3451 ■ *Web:* meyertruckeq.com	Jasper	IN	47546	812-695-3451	695-3397
Mickey Truck Bodies Inc 1305 Trinity Ave PO Box 2044 *TF:* 800-334-9061 ■ *Web:* www.mickeybody.com	High Point	NC	27261	336-882-6806	882-6856
Millennium Transit Services LLC 42 Earl Cummings Loop W *Web:* www.millenniumtransit.com	Roswell	NM	88201	505-347-7500	347-7504
Miller Industries Inc 8503 Hilltop Dr *NYSE: MLR* ■ *TF:* 800-292-0330 ■ *Web:* www.millerind.com	Ooltewah	TN	37363	423-238-4171	238-5371
Monroe Truck Equipment Inc 1051 W 7th St *TF:* 800-356-8134 ■ *Web:* www.monroetruck.com	Monroe	WI	53566	608-328-8127	328-4278
Morgan Corp 35 Thousand Oaks Blvd *TF:* 800-666-7426 ■ *Web:* www.morgancorp.com	Morgantown	PA	19543	610-286-5025	286-2226
Morgan Olson Corp 1801 S Nottawa Rd *TF:* 800-624-9005 ■ *Web:* www.morganolson.com	Sturgis	MI	49091	269-659-0200	651-4259
Motor Coach Industries International Co 1700 E Golf Rd Suite 300 *TF:* 800-743-3624 ■ *Web:* www.mcicoach.com	Schaumburg	IL	60173	847-285-2000	285-2066
Oshkosh Truck Corp 2307 Oregon St *NYSE: OSK* ■ *Web:* www.oshkoshtruck.com	Oshkosh	WI	54903	920-235-9151	233-9540
PACCAR Inc 777 106th Ave NE *NASDAQ: PCAR* ■ *Web:* www.paccar.com	Bellevue	WA	98004	425-455-7400	468-8216
PACCAR Inc International Div 777 106th Ave NE 12th Fl *Web:* www.paccar.com/PACCINT	Bellevue	WA	98004	425-468-7800	468-7850
Pak-Mor Ltd 2191 Rudeloff Rd *Web:* www.pakmor.com	Sequin	TX	78155	830-303-7256	303-3648
Parco-Hesse Corp 1060 Andre-Line Rd *TF:* 800-363-5975 ■ *Web:* www.grouphesse.com	Granby	QC	J2J1J9	450-378-4696	378-3614
Parkhurst Mfg Co 18997 Hwy Y *TF:* 800-821-7380 ■ *Web:* www.parkhurstmfg.com	Sedalia	MO	65301	660-826-8685	826-8688
Peterbilt Motors Co 1700 Woodbrook St **Fax:* Hum Res ■ *Web:* www.peterbilt.com	Denton	TX	76205	940-591-4000	591-4259*
Pierce Mfg Inc 2600 American Dr *TF Cust Svc:* 888-974-3723 ■ *Web:* www.piercemfg.com	Appleton	WI	54914	920-832-3000	832-3208
Prevost Car Inc 35 boul Gagnon *TF:* 800-463-8876 ■ *Web:* www.prevostcar.com	Sainte-Claire	QC	G0R2V0	418-883-2888	883-4157
R & S/Godwin Truck Body Co LLC 5168 S US Hwy 23 *TF:* 800-826-7413 ■ *Web:* www.rstruckbody.com	Ivel	KY	41642	606-874-2151	874-9136
Reading Truck Body Inc Hancock Blvd & Gerry St *TF:* 800-458-2226 ■ *Web:* www.readingbody.com	Reading	PA	19611	610-775-3301	775-8683
Riggs Industries Inc 2478 Lincoln Hwy *TF:* 800-229-5205	Stoystown	PA	15563	814-629-5621	629-6588
RKI Inc 2301 Central Pkwy *Web:* www.rki-us.com	Houston	TX	77092	713-688-4414	688-5776
Road Rescue Inc 2914 Spartan Pl *TF:* 800-328-3804 ■ *Web:* www.roadrescue.com	Marion	SC	29571	843-676-2900	676-2998
Rocket Supply Corp 404 N Hwy 115 *TF:* 800-252-6871 ■ *Web:* www.rocketsupply.com	Roberts	IL	60962	217-395-2278	395-2564
Saf-T-Cab Inc 3241 S Parkway Dr *TF:* 800-344-7491 ■ *Web:* www.saftcab.com	Fresno	CA	93725	559-268-5541	268-5822
Scania USA Inc 121 Interpark Blvd Suite 601 *TF:* 800-272-2642 ■ *Web:* www.scania.com	San Antonio	TX	78216	210-403-0007	403-0211
Scelzi Equipment Inc 1030 W Gladstone St *TF:* 866-972-3594 ■ *Web:* www.seinc.com	Azusa	CA	91702	626-334-0573	334-2753
Schetky Northwest Sales Inc 8430 NE Killingsworth St *TF:* 800-255-8341 ■ *Web:* www.schetkynw.com	Portland	OR	97220	503-287-4141	287-2931
Seagrave Fire Apparatus LLC 105 E 12th St *Web:* www.seagrave.com	Clintonville	WI	54929	715-823-2141	823-5768
Segway Inc 14 Technology Dr *TF:* 866-473-4929 ■ *Web:* www.segway.com	Bedford	NH	03110	603-222-6000	222-6001
Shealy's Truck Center Inc 1340 Bluff Rd *TF:* 800-951-8580 ■ *Web:* www.shealytruck.com	Columbia	SC	29201	803-771-0176	771-4879
Skaug Truck Body Works Inc 1404 1st St	San Fernando	CA	91340	818-365-9123	365-6634
Somerset Welding & Steel Inc 10558 Somerset Pike *TF Sales:* 800-598-8552 ■ *Web:* www.jjbodies.com	Somerset	PA	15501	814-444-3400	445-9303

Company	City	State	Zip	Phone	Fax
Spartan Motors Inc 1000 Reynolds Rd.	Charlotte	MI	48813	517-543-6400	543-9269
NASDAQ: SPAR ■ *Web:* www.spartanmotors.com					
Specialized Vehicles Corp 911 W 5th St.	Washington	NC	27889	252-946-6521	975-8340
TF: 800-763-0700 ■ *Web:* www.svcvehicles.com					
STAHL/A Scott Fetzer Co 3201 W Old Lincoln Way	Wooster	OH	44691	330-264-7441	264-3319
TF: 800-392-7251 ■ *Web:* www.stahl.cc					
Steelweld Equipment Co Inc 235 North Service Rd W	Saint Clair	MO	63077	636-629-3704	629-3734
Web: www.steelweld.net					
Sterling Truck Corp 12120 Telegraph Rd	Redford Township	MI	48239	313-592-4200	592-4246
TF Cust Svc: 888-785-4357 ■ *Web:* www.sterlingtrucks.com					
Supreme Corp 2581 E Kercher Rd PO Box 463	Goshen	IN	46528	574-642-4888	642-4540
TF: 800-642-4889 ■ *Web:* www.supremeind.com					
Supreme Industries Inc 2581 E Kerchen Rd.	Goshen	IN	46528	574-642-3070	642-3208
AMEX: STS ■ *TF:* 800-642-4889 ■ *Web:* www.supremeind.com					
Sutphen Corp PO Box 158	Amlin	OH	43002	614-889-1005	889-0874
TF: 800-726-7030 ■ *Web:* www.sutphen.com					
TABC Inc 6375 Paramont Blvd	Long Beach	CA	90805	562-984-3305	984-6825
Tafco Equipment Co Inc 1304 W 1st St.	Blue Earth	MN	56013	507-526-3247	526-7346
TF Sales: 800-328-3189 ■ *Web:* www.tafcoequip.com					
Tesco Williamsen Inc 1925 W Indiana Ave	Salt Lake City	UT	84104	801-973-9400	973-2838
TF: 800-828-9847 ■ *Web:* www.tescowilliamsen.com					
Thiele Manufacturing LLC 309 Spruce St	Windber	PA	15963	814-467-4504	467-4172
Web: www.thielebody.com					
Thomas Built Buses Inc 1408 Courtesy Rd	High Point	NC	27260	336-889-4871	881-6509
Web: www.thomasbus.com					
Thor Industries Inc 419 W Pike St.	Jackson Center	OH	45334	937-596-6849	596-7929
NYSE: THO ■ *Web:* www.thorindustries.com					
Trail King Industries Inc 147 Industrial Pk Rd.	Brookville	PA	15825	814-849-2342	849-5063
TF: 800-545-1549 ■ *Web:* www.trailking.com					
Truck Cab Manufacturers Inc PO Box 58400	Cincinnati	OH	45258	513-922-1300	922-8888
Web: www.truckcab.com					
Truck Utilities Inc 2370 English St.	Saint Paul	MN	55109	651-484-3305	484-0076
TF: 800-869-1075 ■ *Web:* www.truckutilities.com					
Trux Inc 1365 Lakeland Ave	Bohemia	NY	11716	631-563-1300	563-1397
Tymco Inc 225 E Industrial Blvd	Waco	TX	76705	800-258-9626	799-2722*
**Fax Area Code:* 254 ■ *TF:* 800-258-9626 ■ *Web:* www.tymco.com					
Unicell Body Co 571 Howard St	Buffalo	NY	14206	716-853-8628	854-7208
TF Cust Svc: 800-628-8914 ■ *Web:* www.unicell.com					
Viking-Cives USA 14331 Mill St	Harrisville	NY	13648	315-543-2321	543-2366
Web: www.vikingcives.com					
Volvo Construction Equipment of North America Inc					
1 Volvo Dr	Asheville	NC	28803	828-650-2000	650-2501
Web: www.volvo.com/constructionequipment					
Volvo Group North America Inc 570 Lexington Ave 20th Fl.	New York	NY	10022	212-418-7400	418-7436
Web: www.volvo.com					
Volvo Trucks North America Inc 7900 National Service Rd.	Greensboro	NC	27409	336-393-2000	393-2362
Web: www.volvo.com/trucks/na					
Weld-Built Body Co Inc 276 Long Island Ave	Wyandanch	NY	11798	631-643-9700	491-4728
Web: www.weldbuilt.com					
Wheeled Coach Industries Inc 2737 N Forsyth Rd	Winter Park	FL	32792	407-677-7777	679-1337
TF: 800-342-0720 ■ *Web:* www.wheeledcoach.com					
Wolf Coach Inc 7 B St Auburn Industrial Pk	Auburn	MA	01501	508-791-1950	799-2384
Web: www.wolfcoach.com					
Worldwide Equipment Inc					
1999 Kentucky Rt 1428 E PO Box 1370	Prestonsburg	KY	41653	606-874-2172	874-9079
TF: 800-307-4746 ■ *Web:* www.teamworldwide.com					
Yamaha Golf Cars of California Inc 5605 S Front Rd	Livermore	CA	94551	925-371-5350	371-5311
Web: www.yamahagolfcarsofca.com					
Zamboni Frank J & Co Inc 15714 Colorado Ave	Paramount	CA	90723	562-633-0751	633-9365
Web: www.zamboni.com					

520 MOTORCYCLES & MOTORCYCLE PARTS & ACCESSORIES

Company	City	State	Zip	Phone	Fax
American Honda Motor Co Inc 1919 Torrance Blvd.	Torrance	CA	90501	310-783-2000	783-2110*
**Fax:* Hum Res ■ *TF:* 800-999-1009 ■ *Web:* www.honda.com					
American Ironhorse Motorcycle Co 4600 Blue Mound Rd	Fort Worth	TX	76106	817-665-2000	
Web: www.americanironhorse.com					
American Suzuki Motor Corp 3251 E Imperial Hwy	Brea	CA	92821	714-996-7040	524-2512
Web: www.suzuki.com					
Andrews Products Inc 431 Kingston Ct	Mount Prospect	IL	60056	847-759-0190	759-0848
Web: www.andrews-products.com					
Answer Products Inc 28209 Ave Stanford	Valencia	CA	91355	661-257-4411	294-4180
TF Cust Svc: 800-423-0273 ■ *Web:* www.answerproducts.com					
Big Dog Motorcycles 1520 E Douglas Ave	Wichita	KS	67214	316-267-9121	267-2597
Web: www.bigdogmotorcycles.com					
Buell Motorcycle Co 2815 Buell Dr	East Troy	WI	53120	262-642-2020	642-2030
Web: www.buell.com					
Corbin 2360 Technology Pkwy	Hollister	CA	95023	831-634-1100	634-1059
TF: 800-538-7035 ■ *Web:* www.corbin.com					
Cycle Shack Inc 1104 San Mateo Ave	South San Francisco	CA	94080	650-583-7014	583-9154
Web: www.cycle-shack.com					
CycoActive Inc 701 34th Ave	Seattle	WA	98122	206-323-2349	325-6016
TF: 800-491-2926 ■ *Web:* www.cycoactive.com					
Edelbrock Corp 2700 California St	Torrance	CA	90503	310-781-2222	320-1187
TF: 800-739-3737 ■ *Web:* www.edelbrock.com					
Fulmer Co 122 Gayoso Ave	Memphis	TN	38103	901-525-5711	525-7993
TF: 800-467-2400 ■ *Web:* www.fulmerhelmets.com					
Gabilan Mfg Inc 590 Work St.	Salinas	CA	93901	831-422-7824	422-9583
Web: www.gabilanmanufacturing.com					
Harley-Davidson Inc 3700 W Juneau Ave.	Milwaukee	WI	53208	414-342-4680	343-4621*
NYSE: HDI ■ **Fax:* Hum Res ■ *TF:* 800-443-2153 ■ *Web:* www.harley-davidson.com					
Harley-Davidson Motor Co PO Box 653	Milwaukee	WI	53201	414-342-4680	343-4977
Web: www.harley-davidson.com					
Kawasaki Motors Corp USA PO Box 25252	Santa Ana	CA	92799	949-770-0400	460-5600
Web: www.kawasaki.com					
Mag-Knight 18121 117th St SE	Snohomish	WA	98290	360-805-0100	805-0811
Web: www.mag-knight.com					
Motovan Corp 1391 Guy Lussac	Boucherville	QC	J4B7K1	450-449-3903	449-7773
Web: www.motovan.com					
National Cycle Inc 2200 Maywood Dr	Maywood	IL	60153	708-343-0400	343-0625
TF: 877-972-7336 ■ *Web:* www.nationalcycle.com					
Polaris Industries Inc 2100 Hwy 55	Medina	MN	55340	763-542-0500	542-0599
NYSE: PII ■ *Web:* www.polarisindustries.com					
Powroll Inc 4115 SW 19th St PO Box 920	Redmond	OR	97756	541-923-1290	923-5637
Web: www.powroll.com					
Rivco Products Inc 440 S Pine St	Burlington	WI	53105	262-763-8222	763-8949
TF: 888-801-8222 ■ *Web:* www.rivcoproducts.com					
Yamaha Motor Corp USA 6555 Katella Ave.	Cypress	CA	90630	714-761-7300	761-7302
TF Cust Svc: 800-962-7926 ■ *Web:* www.yamaha-motor.com					

MOTORS - FLUID POWER

SEE Pumps & Motors - Fluid Power p. 1983

521 MOTORS (ELECTRIC) & GENERATORS

SEE ALSO Automotive Parts & Supplies - Mfr p. 1360

Company	City	State	Zip	Phone	Fax
ADS/Transicoil 9 Iron Bridge Dr	Collegeville	PA	19426	484-902-1100	902-1150
TF: 800-323-7115 ■ *Web:* www.adstcoil.com					
Advanced Power & Controls LLC 605 E Alton Ave Suite A	Santa Ana	CA	92705	714-540-9010	540-5313
Web: www.advancedpowercontrols.com					
Aerotech Inc 101 Zeta Dr	Pittsburgh	PA	15238	412-963-7470	963-7459
Web: www.aerotechinc.com					
Airflyte Electronics Co 56 New Hook Rd.	Bayonne	NJ	07002	201-436-2230	436-6024
Web: www.airflyteelectronics.com					
Alaska Diesel Electric Inc 4420 14th Ave NW	Seattle	WA	98107	206-789-3880	782-5455
TF: 800-762-0165 ■ *Web:* www.northern-lights.com					
Alliance Winding Equipment Inc 3939 Vanguard Dr	Fort Wayne	IN	46809	260-478-2200	
Web: www.alliance-winding.com					
AMETEK Lamb Electric 627 Lake St.	Kent	OH	44240	330-673-3451	673-8994
Web: www.ameteklamb.com					
AMETEK Prestolite Motors 627 Lake St.	Kent	OH	44240	330-673-3452	678-8227
AMETEK Specialty Motors 627 Lake St	Kent	OH	44240	330-673-3451	678-8231
Web: www.gselectric.com					
AMK Drives & Controls Inc 5631 S Laburnum Ave	Richmond	VA	23231	804-222-0323	222-0339
Web: www.amkdrives.com					
AO Smith Corp 11270 W Park Pl Suite 170	Milwaukee	WI	53224	414-359-4000	359-4180
NYSE: AOS ■ *TF:* 800-359-4065 ■ *Web:* www.aosmith.com					
Arco Electric Products Corp 2325 E Michigan Rd.	Shelbyville	IN	46176	317-398-9713	398-2655
TF: 800-428-4370 ■ *Web:* www.arco-electric.com					
Aura Systems Inc 2330 Utah Ave	El Segundo	CA	90245	310-643-5300	643-7457
TF Cust Svc: 800-909-2872 ■ *Web:* www.aurasystems.com					
Autotrol Corp 365 E Prairie St PO Box 557	Crystal Lake	IL	60039	815-459-3080	459-3227
TF: 800-228-6207 ■ *Web:* www.autotrol.com					
Axsys Technologies Motion Control Products					
7603 St Andrew Ave Suite H	San Diego	CA	92154	619-671-5400	671-9292
TF Cust Svc: 800-777-3393 ■ *Web:* www.axsys.com					
Baldor Electric Co PO Box 2400	Fort Smith	AR	72902	479-646-4711	648-5792*
NYSE: BEZ ■ **Fax:* Sales ■ *Web:* www.baldor.com					
Baldor Linear Motion Products 600 S Zero St.	Fort Smith	AR	72901	479-649-5151	649-5147
Web: www.baldor.com					
Berger Lahr Motion Technology Inc					
44191 Plymouth Oaks Blvd	Plymouth	MI	48170	734-459-8300	459-8622
Web: www.bergerlahrmotion.com					
Bodine Electric Co 2500 W Bradley Pl.	Chicago	IL	60618	773-478-3515	478-3232
TF: 800-726-3463 ■ *Web:* www.bodine-electric.com					
Bogue Systems Inc 100 Pennsylvania Ave	Paterson	NJ	07503	973-523-2200	278-8468
Bosch Rexroth Corp 5150 Prairie Stone Pkwy	Hoffman Estates	IL	60192	847-645-3600	645-6201
TF: 800-860-1055 ■ *Web:* www.boschrexroth-us.com					
Buehler Motor Inc 175 Southport Dr Suite 900	Morrisville	NC	27560	919-380-3333	380-3256
Web: www.buehlermotor.com					
CALEX Mfg Co 2401 Stanwell Dr.	Concord	CA	94520	925-687-4411	687-3333
TF: 800-542-3355 ■ *Web:* www.calex.com					
Cirrus Logic Inc 5980 N Shannon Rd.	Tucson	AZ	85741	520-690-8600	888-3329
TF: 800-421-1865 ■ *Web:* www.apexmicrotech.com					
Cleveland Motion Controls Inc Torque Systems Div					
6 Enterprise Rd	Billerica	MA	01821	978-667-5100	600-0280
TF: 800-669-5112 ■ *Web:* www.torquesystems.com					
Coleman Powermate Inc 3901 Liberty Street Rd	Aurora	IL	60504	630-585-7332	585-7534
Web: www.colemanpowermate.com					
Continental Electric Motors Inc 4 Timber Ln Bldg A	Marlboro	NJ	07746	732-863-0888	863-1886
Web: www.cecoinc.com					
Custom Sensors & Technologies 14501 Princeton Avew.	Moorpark	CA	93021	805-552-3599	552-3577
Web: www.cst.schneider-electric.com					
Danaher Motion 1500 Mittel Blvd	Wood Dale	IL	60191	630-860-7300	694-3305
TF: 866-993-2624 ■ *Web:* www.danahermotion.com					
DRS Power Technology Inc 2 Fox Rd.	Hudson	MA	01749	978-562-2933	562-6830
Web: www.drs.com					
Ducommun Technologies Inc 23301 Wilmington Ave	Carson	CA	90745	310-513-7200	513-7298
TF: 800-421-5032 ■ *Web:* www.ductech.com					
Dumore Corp 1030 Veterans St.	Mauston	WI	53948	608-847-6420	338-6673*
**Fax Area Code:* 800 ■ *TF:* 888-467-8288 ■ *Web:* www.dumorecorp.com					
EAD Motors Inc 1 Progress Dr	Dover	NH	03820	603-742-3330	742-9080
Web: www.eadmotors.com					
Electric Apparatus Co 409 N Roosevelt PO Box 227	Howell	MI	48844	517-546-0520	546-0547
Web: www.elecapp.net					
Electric Machinery Co Inc 800 Central Ave NE	Minneapolis	MN	55413	612-378-8000	378-8050
Web: www.electricmachinery.com					
Electric Motors & Specialties Inc 701 W King St PO Box 180	Garrett	IN	46738	260-357-4141	357-3888
Web: www.emsmotors.com					
Electrical Products Co 531 N 4th St	Tipp City	OH	45371	937-667-2431	669-5199
TF: 800-543-9450 ■ *Web:* www.aosmith.com/compinfo/tippcity.htm					
Electro Sales Inc 100 Fellsway W.	Somerville	MA	02145	617-666-0500	628-2800
TF: 888-789-0500 ■ *Web:* www.electrosales.com					
Elwood Corp Gettys Group 2701 N Green Bay Rd	Racine	WI	53404	262-637-6591	764-4298*
**Fax Area Code:* 414 ■ *TF:* 800-558-9489 ■ *Web:* www.elwoodcorp.com/gettys.html					
Emerson Electric Co 8000 W Florissant Ave	Saint Louis	MO	63136	314-553-2000	553-3527
NYSE: EMR ■ *Web:* www.gotoemerson.com					
Emerson Motor Co 8000 W Florissant Ave	Saint Louis	MO	63136	314-553-2000	553-3712
Web: www.gotoemerson.com					
Emoteq Corp 10002 E 43rd St S	Tulsa	OK	74146	918-627-1845	660-0207
TF Sales: 800-221-7572 ■ *Web:* www.emoteq.com					
Everson Tesla Inc 615 Daniel's Rd	Nazareth	PA	18064	610-746-1520	746-1530
Web: www.eversontesla.com					
Franklin Electric Co Inc 400 E Spring St.	Bluffton	IN	46714	260-824-2900	827-5800
NASDAQ: FELE ■ *TF:* 800-269-0063 ■ *Web:* www.fele.com					
GE Consumer Products Appliance Park Rm 129	Louisville	KY	40225	502-452-4311	452-0054*
**Fax:* Cust Svc ■ *TF:* 800-626-2000 ■ *Web:* www.geconsumerproducts.com					
Generac Power Systems Inc PO Box 8	Waukesha	WI	53187	262-544-4811	544-4851
Web: www.generac.com					
Glentek Inc 208 Standard St.	El Segundo	CA	90245	310-322-3026	322-7709
TF: 800-232-4485 ■ *Web:* www.glentek.com					
Hankscraft Inc 300 Wengel Dr	Reedsburg	WI	53959	608-524-4341	524-4342
Web: www.hankscraft-motors.com					
Hansen Corp 901 S 1st St.	Princeton	IN	47670	812-385-3415	385-3013*
**Fax:* Sales ■ *Web:* www.hansen-motor.com					
Hansome Energy Systems Inc 365 Dalziel Rd	Linden	NJ	07036	908-862-9044	862-8195
Howell Electric Motors 1503 Exeter Rd.	Akron	OH	44306	330-734-3600	734-3601
TF: 800-346-9350					

				Phone	Fax
Hurst Mfg 1551 E Broadway	Princeton	IN	47670	812-385-2564	386-7504*
*Fax: Sales ■ Web: www.hurstmfg.com					
Ideal Electric Co 330 E 1st St	Mansfield	OH	44902	419-522-3611	522-9386
Web: www.idealelectricco.com					
Imperial Electric Co 1503 Exeter Rd	Akron	OH	44306	330-734-3600	734-3601
Web: www.imperialelectric.com					
Johnson Electric North America Inc 10 Progress Dr	Shelton	CT	06484	203-447-5362	447-5383
Web: www.johnsonmotor.com					
Joliet Equipment Corp 1 Doris Ave PO Box 114	Joliet	IL	60434	815-727-6606	727-6626
TF: 800-435-9350 ■ Web: www.joliet-equipment.com					
Kato Engineering Inc PO Box 8447	Mankato	MN	56002	507-625-4011	345-2798
Web: www.kato-eng.com					
Katolight Corp 100 Power Dr	Mankato	MN	56001	507-625-7973	625-2968
TF: 800-325-5450 ■ Web: www.katolight.com					
Kinetek Inc 1751 Lake Cook Rd ArborLake Ctr Suite 550	Deerfield	IL	60015	847-267-4473	945-9645
Web: www.kinetekinc.com					
Kirkwood Industries Inc 4825 W 130th St	Cleveland	OH	44135	216-267-6200	362-3878
TF Cust Svc: 800-262-2266 ■ Web: www.kirkwood-ind.com					
Kohler Power Systems 444 Highland Dr	Kohler	WI	53044	920-565-3381	453-6302
TF: 800-544-2444 ■ Web: www.kohlerpowersystems.com					
Kollmorgen Corp 347 King St	Northampton	MA	01060	413-586-2330	586-1324
Web: www.kollmorgen.com					
Kraft Power Corp 199 Wildwood Ave	Woburn	MA	01801	781-938-9100	933-7812
TF: 800-969-6121 ■ Web: www.kraftpower.com					
Kurz Electric Solutions Inc 1325 McMahon Dr	Neenah	WI	54956	920-886-8200	886-8201
TF: 800-776-3629 ■ Web: www.kurz.com					
Leeson Electric Corp 2100 Washington St	Grafton	WI	53024	262-377-8810	
Web: www.leeson.com					
Letourneau Technologies Power System					
6401 W Sam Houston Pkwy North	Houston	TX	77041	713-983-4700	983-4730
Web: www.letourneau-inc.com					
Lexel Corp PO Box 508	Franksville	WI	53126	262-886-2002	886-4639
Lincoln Motors 28300 Euclid Ave Suite 200	Wickliffe	OH	44092	216-731-4790	731-5401
TF: 800-668-6748 ■ Web: www.lincolnmotors.com					
Louis Allis Large Motor Corp 645 Lester Doss Rd	Warrior	AL	35180	205-590-2986	590-1571
TF: 866-568-4700 ■ Web: www.louisallis.com					
Mabuchi Motor America Corp 3001 W Big Beaver Rd Suite 520	Troy	MI	48084	248-816-3100	816-3242
Web: www.mabuchi-motor.co.jp/english					
Mamco Corp 8630 Industrial Dr	Franksville	WI	53126	262-886-9069	886-4639
Web: www.mamcomotors.com					
Marathon Electric Inc 100 E Randolf St PO Box 8003	Wausau	WI	54402	715-675-3311	675-8051
Web: www.marathonelectric.com					
Martindale Electric Co 1375 Hird Ave	Lakewood	OH	44107	216-521-8567	521-9476
Web: www.martindaleco.com					
Merkle-Korff Industries Inc 1776 Winthrop Dr	Des Plaines	IL	60018	847-296-8800	699-0832
Web: www.merkle-korff.com					
Minarik Corp 905 E Thompson Ave	Glendale	CA	91201	818-637-7500	507-8821
Web: www.minarikcorp.com					
Molon Motor & Coil Corp 3737 Industrial Ave	Rolling Meadows	IL	60008	847-253-6000	259-5491
TF: 800-526-6867 ■ Web: www.molon.com					
Motor Appliance Corp 555 Spirit of St Louis Blvd	Chesterfield	MO	63005	636-532-3406	532-4609
TF: 800-622-3406 ■ Web: www.macmc.com					
Motor Products Owosso Corp 201 S Delaney Rd	Owosso	MI	48867	989-725-5151	723-6035
TF: 800-248-3841 ■ Web: www.motorproducts.net					
Motor Specialty Inc PO Box 081278	Racine	WI	53408	262-632-2794	632-8899
Web: www.motorspecialty.com					
National Electric Coil Inc 800 King Ave	Columbus	OH	43212	614-488-1151	488-3075
Web: www.national-electric-coil.com					
Nidec America Corp 100 River Ridge Dr Suite 300	Norwood	MA	02062	781-769-0619	551-6825
Web: www.nidec.com					
Northland Div Scott Fetzer Co 968 Bradley St	Watertown	NY	13601	315-782-2350	788-1180
Web: www.northlandmotor.com					
Ohio Electric Motors Inc 30 Paint Fork Rd PO Box 168	Barnardsville	NC	28709	828-626-2901	626-2155
Web: www.ohioelectricmotors.com					
PennEngineering & Mfg Corp 5190 Old Easton Rd	Danboro	PA	18916	215-766-8853	766-3680
TF: 800-237-4736 ■ Web: www.penn-eng.com					
Phytron Inc 600 Blair Park Rd Suite 220	Williston	VT	05495	802-872-1600	872-0311
Web: www.phytron.com					
Piller Inc 45 Turner Rd	Middletown	NY	10941	845-695-5300	692-0295
TF: 800-597-6937 ■ Web: www.piller.com					
Polyspede Electronics Co Inc 6770 Twin Hills Ave	Dallas	TX	75231	214-363-7245	363-6361
TF: 800-765-9744 ■ Web: www.polyspede.com					
ProVision Technologies Inc 69 Railroad Ave Suite A-7	Hilo	HI	96720	808-969-3281	934-7462
Web: www.provisiontechnologies.com					
RAE Corp 4615 W Prime Pkwy	McHenry	IL	60050	815-385-3500	344-1580
TF: 800-323-7049 ■ Web: www.raemotors.com					
Reagan Equipment Co Inc 2550 Belle Chasse Hwy	Gretna	LA	70053	504-368-9760	368-9768
TF: 800-494-6808 ■ Web: www.reaganpower.com					
Reuland Electric Co 17969 E Railroad St	City of Industry	CA	91748	626-964-6411	270-4469
Web: www.reulandelectric.com					
Rudox Engine & Equipment Co 765 Rt 17 PO Box 467	Carlstadt	NJ	07072	201-438-0111	438-3403
Web: www.rudox.com					
Scott Fetzer Co Northland Div 968 Bradley St	Watertown	NY	13601	315-782-2350	788-1180
Web: www.northlandmotor.com					
Shinano Kenshi Corp 5737 Mesmer Ave	Culver City	CA	90230	310-915-7300	915-7304
Web: www.shinano.com					
Siemens Energy & Automation Inc 3333 Old Milton Pkwy	Alpharetta	GA	30005	770-751-2000	740-2534
TF: 800-964-4114 ■ Web: automation.usa.siemens.com					
Siemens Power Generation 4400 Alafaya Trail	Orlando	FL	32826	407-736-2000	736-5009*
*Fax: Hum Res ■ Web: www.powergeneration.siemens.com					
SL-Montevideo Technology Inc 2002 Black Oak Ave	Montevideo	MN	56265	320-269-6562	269-7662
Web: www.slmti.com					
Smith AO Corp 11270 W Park Pl Suite 170	Milwaukee	WI	53224	414-359-4000	359-4180
NYSE: AOS ■ TF: 800-359-4065 ■ Web: www.aosmith.com					
Specialty Motors Inc 25060 Ave Tibbitts	Valencia	CA	91355	661-257-7388	257-7389
TF: 800-232-2612 ■ Web: www.specialtymotors.com					
Stature Electric Inc 22543 Fisher Rd PO Box 6660	Watertown	NY	13601	315-782-5910	782-1917
Web: www.statureelectric.com					
Sterling Electric Inc 7997 Allison Ave	Indianapolis	IN	46268	317-872-0471	872-0907
TF Cust Svc: 800-654-6220 ■ Web: www.sterlingelectric.com					
Stimple & Ward Co 3400 Babcock Blvd	Pittsburgh	PA	15237	412-364-5200	364-5299
TF: 800-792-6457 ■ Web: www.swcoils.com					
Swiger Coils Systems Inc 4677 Manufacturing Rd	Cleveland	OH	44135	216-362-7500	362-1496
TF: 800-321-3310 ■ Web: www.swigercoil.com					
Toledo Commutator 1101 S Chestnut St	Owosso	MI	48867	989-725-8192	725-5930
Toshiba International Corp 13131 W Little York Rd	Houston	TX	77041	713-466-0277	466-8773
TF: 800-231-1412 ■ Web: www.tic.toshiba.com					
Unico Inc 3725 Nicholson Rd	Franksville	WI	53126	262-886-5678	504-7396
TF: 800-245-1859 ■ Web: www.unicous.com					
Unitron LP 10925 Miller Rd PO Box 38902	Dallas	TX	75238	214-340-8600	341-2099
TF: 800-527-1279 ■ Web: www.unitronlp.com					
UQM Technologies Inc 7501 Miller Dr	Frederick	CO	80504	303-278-2002	278-7007
AMEX: UQM ■ Web: www.uqm.com					
US Electrical Motors 8100 W Florissant Ave Bldg K	Saint Louis	MO	63136	314-553-2000	553-1101
TF: 888-637-7333 ■ Web: www.usmotors.com					
Vicor Corp 25 Frontage Rd	Andover	MA	01810	978-470-2900	475-6715*
NASDAQ: VICR ■ *Fax: Sales ■ TF: 800-869-5300 ■ Web: www.vicr.com					
Wabtec Railway Electronics 21200 Dorsey Mill Rd	Germantown	MD	20876	301-515-2000	515-2100
TF: 800-447-8573					
Warfield Electric Co Inc 175 Industry Ave	Frankfort	IL	60423	815-469-4094	469-4168
TF: 800-435-9346 ■ Web: www.warfieldelectric.com					
Welco Technologies 805 Lindbergh Ct Suite 200	Hebron	KY	41048	859-334-5200	334-5201
TF: 800-715-6006 ■ Web: www.welco-tech.com					
Wenthe-Davidson Engineering Co					
16300 W Rogers Dr PO Box 510286	New Berlin	WI	53151	262-782-1550	782-2020
Web: www.wenthe-davidson.com					
Yamaha Motor Corp USA 6555 Katella Ave	Cypress	CA	90630	714-761-7300	761-7302
TF Cust Svc: 800-962-7926 ■ Web: www.yamaha-motor.com					
Yaskawa Electric America Inc 2121 Norman Dr S	Waukegan	IL	60085	847-887-7000	887-7310*
*Fax: Mktg ■ TF: 800-927-5292 ■ Web: www.yaskawa.com					

522 MOVING COMPANIES

SEE ALSO Trucking Companies p. 2386

Companies that have the moving of household belongings as their primary business.

				Phone	Fax
A Colonial Moving & Storage Co 17 Mercer St	Hackensack	NJ	07601	201-343-5777	343-1934
Web: www.colonialmoving.com					
Ace World Wide Moving 1900 E College Ave	Cudahy	WI	53110	414-764-1000	764-1650
TF: 800-223-6683 ■ Web: www.aceworldwide.com					
Air Van Moving Group 10510 NE Northup Way Suite 110	Kirkland	WA	98033	425-629-4101	629-4120
TF: 800-877-1442 ■ Web: www.airvanmoving.com					
Allied International NA Inc 700 Oakmont Ln	Westmont	IL	60559	630-570-3500	570-3496
TF: 800-323-1909 ■ Web: www.allied.com					
Allied Van Lines Inc 700 Oakmont Ln	Westmont	IL	60559	630-570-3000	570-3394*
*Fax: Sales ■ TF Cust Svc: 800-762-4689 ■ Web: www.alliedvan.com					
American Red Ball International 9750 3rd Ave NE Suite 200	Seattle	WA	98115	206-526-1730	526-2967
TF: 800-669-6424 ■ Web: www.americanredball.com					
American Red Ball Transit Co Inc 1335 Sadlier Circle E Dr	Indianapolis	IN	46239	317-353-8331	351-0652*
*Fax: Cust Svc ■ TF: 800-733-8077 ■ Web: www.americanredball.com					
Amodio Van & Storage 1 Hartford Sq	New Britain	CT	06052	860-223-2725	223-0370
TF: 800-927-6683 ■ Web: www.amodiovan.com/					
Andrews Van Lines Inc 310 S 7th St	Norfolk	NE	68701	402-371-5440	371-1349
TF Cust Svc: 800-228-8146 ■ Web: www.andrewsvanlines.com					
Arnoff Moving & Storage Inc 1282 Dutchess Tpke	Poughkeepsie	NY	12603	845-471-1504	452-3606
TF: 800-633-6683 ■ Web: www.arnoff.com					
Arpin Van Lines 99 James P Murphy Hwy	West Warwick	RI	02893	401-828-8111	821-5860
TF: 800-343-3500 ■ Web: www.arpin.com					
Atlantic Relocation Systems Inc 1314 Chattahoochee Ave NW	Atlanta	GA	30318	404-351-5311	350-6530
TF Cust Svc: 800-241-1140 ■ Web: www.atlanticrelocation.com					
Atlas Van Lines Inc 1212 St George Rd	Evansville	IN	47711	812-424-2222	421-7129*
*Fax: Cust Svc ■ TF: 800-638-9797 ■ Web: www.atlasvanlines.com					
B Von Paris & Sons Inc 8691 Larkin Rd	Savage	MD	20763	410-888-8500	888-9062*
*Fax: Cust Svc ■ TF: 800-866-6355 ■ Web: www.vonparis.com					
Barrett Moving & Storage Co 7100 Washington Ave S	Eden Prairie	MN	55344	952-944-6550	828-7110
TF: 800-879-1283 ■ Web: www.barrettmoving.com					
Bay State Moving Systems Inc 60 Haynes Cir	Chicopee	MA	01020	413-592-6381	594-3676
TF: 800-388-7411 ■ Web: www.baystatemoving.com					
Bekins Co 330 S Mannheim Rd	Hillside	IL	60162	708-547-2000	
Web: www.bekins.com					
Bekins Van Lines LLC 330 S Mannheim Rd	Hillside	IL	60162	708-547-2000	547-2107
TF: 800-723-5467 ■ Web: www.bekins.com					
Berger Transfer & Storage Inc 2950 Long Lake Rd	Saint Paul	MN	55113	651-639-2260	639-2277
TF: 800-328-2459 ■ Web: www.berger-transfer.com					
Beverly Hills Transfer & Storage Co 221 S Beverly Dr	Beverly Hills	CA	90212	310-276-1121	538-0416
TF: 800-999-7114 ■ Web: www.beverlyhillstransfer.com					
Bisson Moving & Storage 76 New Meadows Rd	West Bath	ME	04530	207-442-7991	386-0348
TF: 800-370-4011 ■ Web: www.movebisson.com					
Bohrens Moving & Storage Inc 3 Applegate Dr	Robbinsville	NJ	08691	609-208-1470	208-1471
TF: 800-326-4736 ■ Web: www.bohrensmoving.com					
Bolliger Inc 120 Viaduct Rd	Stamford	CT	06907	203-324-5999	324-2672
TF: 800-243-9517 ■ Web: www.bolliger.net					
Buehler Moving & Storage Co 3899 Jackson St	Denver	CO	80205	303-388-4000	388-0296
TF: 800-234-6683 ■ Web: www.movingservices.com/buehler					
Capital City Transfer Inc 1465 Johnson St NE	Salem	OR	97301	503-581-6683	581-6924
Cartwright Cos The 11901 Cartwright Ave	Grandview	MO	64030	816-763-2700	763-7863
TF: 877-455-5991 ■ Web: www.cartwrighttrans.com					
Castine Moving & Storage 1235 Chestnut St	Athol	MA	01331	978-249-9105	249-5337
TF: 800-225-8068 ■ Web: www.castinemovers.com					
Coast to Coast Moving & Storage Co 136 41st St	Brooklyn	NY	11232	718-443-5800	445-6435
TF: 800-872-6683 ■ Web: www.ctcvanlines.com					
Cook Moving Systems Inc 1845 Dale Rd	Buffalo	NY	14225	716-897-0700	893-0500
TF: 800-828-7144 ■ Web: www.movingsystems.com/cook					
Corrigan Moving Systems 23923 Research Dr	Farmington Hills	MI	48335	248-471-4000	471-3746
TF: 800-267-7442 ■ Web: www.corriganmoving.com					
Davidson Transfer & Storage Co 6600 Frankford Ave	Baltimore	MD	21206	410-488-9200	488-7415
TF: 800-285-4387 ■ Web: www.davidsontransfer.com					
DeVries Moving Packing & Storage					
3808 N Sullivan Rd Bldg 22	Spokane Valley	WA	99216	509-924-6000	924-0041
TF: 800-333-6352 ■ Web: www.devriesmoving.com					
East Side Moving & Storage PO Box 86216	Portland	OR	97286	503-777-4181	775-8443
TF: 800-547-4600 ■ Web: www.move-northwest.com					
Graebel Van Lines Inc 16346 E Airport Circle	Aurora	CO	80011	303-214-6683	214-2164
TF: 800-723-6683 ■ Web: www.graebel.com					
Hartford Despatch Moving & Storage Inc 225 Prospect St	East Hartford	CT	06108	860-528-9551	282-1224
TF: 800-678-9000 ■ Web: www.hartforddespatch.com					
Haviland-Callan Inc 900 Hwy 212	Michigan City	IN	46360	219-874-3274	872-0776
TF: 800-348-2235 ■ Web: www.haviland-callan.com					
Hilford Moving & Storage 1595 S Arundell Ave	Ventura	CA	93003	805-642-0221	654-8402
TF: 800-739-6683 ■ Web: www.hilford.com					
Hollister Moving & Storage PO Box 1987	Hollister	CA	95024	831-637-6250	636-5029
TF: 800-696-6250					
I-Go Van & Storage 9820 S 142nd St	Omaha	NE	68138	402-891-1222	891-6762
TF: 800-228-9276 ■ Web: www.igovanandstorage.com/					
Interconex Inc 383 Main Ave 7th Fl	Norwalk	CT	06851	203-295-2250	295-2251
TF: 800-952-7230 ■ Web: www.interconex.com					
Johnson Storage & Moving Co 221 Broadway	Denver	CO	80203	303-785-4310	698-0512
TF: 800-289-6683 ■ Web: www.johnsonstorage.com					
King Relocation Services 13535 Larwin Cir	Santa Fe Springs	CA	90670	562-921-0555	802-3060
TF: 800-854-3679 ■ Web: www.kingrelocation.com					
Lido Van & Storage Co Inc 2200 Alton Pkwy	Irvine	CA	92606	949-863-9000	474-7240
TF: 800-339-5436 ■ Web: www.lidomoving.com/					
Mayflower Transit LLC 1 Mayflower Dr	Fenton	MO	63026	636-305-4000	326-1106
TF: 800-428-1234 ■ Web: www.mayflower.com					
McCollister's Transportation Group Inc					
1800 Rt 130 N PO Box 9	Burlington	NJ	08016	609-386-0600	386-5608
TF: 800-257-9595 ■ Web: www.mccollisters.com					

Phone | Fax

Moving Express 9180 Kelvin Ave ... Chatsworth CA 91311 818-591-8579 775-1988
TF: 800-844-3977 ■ Web: www.movingexpress.com
Nassau World Wide Movers Inc 63 Lamar St ... West Babylon NY 11704 631-491-3600 491-3600
TF: 800-327-9343 ■ Web: www.nwwm.net
National Van Lines Inc 2800 W Roosevelt Rd ... Broadview IL 60155 708-450-2900 450-0069*
*Fax: Cust Svc ■ TF: 800-323-1962 ■ Web: www.nationalvanlines.com
Nationwide Van Lines Inc 5450 S State Rd 7 Suite 39 ... Hollywood FL 33314 954-585-3945 585-3970
TF: 800-310-0056 ■ Web: www.movingnationwide.com
Nelson Westerberg Inc 1500 Arthur Ave Suite 200 ... Elk Grove Village IL 60007 847-437-2080 437-2199
TF: 800-245-2080 ■ Web: www.nelsonwesterberg.com
North American Van Lines Inc PO Box 988 ... Fort Wayne IN 46801 260-429-2511 429-2374*
*Fax: Sales ■ TF: 800-348-2111 ■ Web: www.navl.com
NorthStar Moving Corp 9120 Mason Ave ... Chatsworth CA 91311 818-727-0128 727-7527
TF: 800-275-7767 ■ Web: www.northstarmoving.com
Palmer Moving & Storage 24660 Dequindre Rd ... Warren MI 48091 586-834-3400 834-3414
TF: 800-521-3954 ■ Web: www.palmermoving.com
Paxton Van Lines Inc 5300 Port Royal Rd ... Springfield VA 22151 703-321-7600 321-7729
TF: 800-336-4536 ■ Web: www.paxton.com
Pickens-Kane Moving Co 410 N Milwaukee Ave ... Chicago IL 60610 312-942-0330 942-0319
TF: 800-853-6462 ■ Web: www.pickenskane.com
S & M Moving Systems Inc 12128 Burke St ... Santa Fe Springs CA 90670 562-567-2100 693-5690
TF: 800-336-5556 ■ Web: www.smmoving.com
Security Storage Co 1701 Florida Ave NW ... Washington DC 20009 202-234-5600 234-3513
TF: 800-736-6825 ■ Web: www.sscw.com
Smith Dray Line 320 Frontage Rd ... Greenville SC 29611 864-269-3696 269-3023
TF: 800-327-5673 ■ Web: www.smithdray.com
Starving Students Moving & Storage Co
1850 Sawtelle Blvd Suite 300 ... Los Angeles CA 90025 800-254-0375 825-1145
TF: 800-441-6683 ■ Web: ssmovers.com
Stevens Worldwide Van Lines 527 Morley Dr ... Saginaw MI 48601 989-755-3000 755-0570
TF: 800-678-3836 ■ Web: www.stevensworldwide.com
Suddath Cos 815 S Main St ... Jacksonville FL 32207 904-390-7100 390-7135*
*Fax: Hum Res ■ TF: 800-395-7100 ■ Web: www.suddath.com
Truckin Movers Corp 1031 Harvest St ... Durham NC 27704 919-682-2300 688-2264
TF: 800-334-1651 ■ Web: www.truckinmovers.com
Two Guys Relocation Systems Inc 3571 Pacific Hwy ... San Diego CA 92101 619-296-7995 296-7704
Two Men & A Truck International Inc 3400 Belle Chase Way ... Lansing MI 48911 517-394-7210 394-7432
TF: 800-345-1070 ■ Web: www.twomen.com
UniGroup Inc 1 Premier Dr ... Fenton MO 63026 636-305-5000 326-1106
TF: 800-325-3924 ■ Web: www.unigroupinc.com
UniGroup Worldwide UTS 1 Worldwide Dr ... Saint Louis MO 63026 636-305-6000 305-6097
TF: 800-325-3924 ■ Web: www.unigroupworldwide.com
United Van Lines Inc 1 United Dr ... Fenton MO 63026 636-326-3100 326-1106
TF: 800-325-3924 ■ Web: www.unitedvanlines.com
Wald Relocation Services Ltd
8708 W Little York Rd Suite 190 ... Houston TX 77040 713-512-4800 512-4881
TF: 800-527-1408 ■ Web: www.waldrelocation.com
Werner-Donaldson Moving Services Inc 2901 E 10th Ave ... Tampa FL 33605 813-228-7481 880-9454
TF: 800-444-2839 ■ Web: www.wdmoving.com
Wheaton Van Lines Inc PO Box 50800 ... Indianapolis IN 46250 317-849-7900 849-3718
TF: 800-932-7799 ■ Web: www.wheatonworldwide.com

523 MUSEUMS

SEE ALSO Museums & Halls of Fame - Sports p. 2007; Museums - Children's p. 2006

Listings for museums are organized alphabetically within state and province groupings. (Canadian provinces are interfiled among the US states, in alphabetical order.)

Alabama

Phone | Fax

Alabama Constitution Village 109 Gates Ave ... Huntsville AL 35801 256-564-8100 564-8151
TF: 800-678-1819 ■ Web: www.earlyworks.com/village.html
Alabama Dept of Archives & History 624 Washington Ave ... Montgomery AL 36104 334-242-4363 240-3433
Web: www.archives.state.al.us
Alabama Jazz Hall of Fame 1631 4th Ave N ... Birmingham AL 35203 205-254-2731 254-2785
Web: www.jazzhall.com
Alabama Museum of Natural History
6th Ave Smith Hall University of Alabama ... Tuscaloosa AL 35487 205-348-7550 348-9292
Web: www.amnh.ua.edu
American Sport Art Museum & Archives 1 Academy Dr ... Daphne AL 36526 251-626-3303 621-2527
Web: www.asama.org
Anniston Museum of Natural History 800 Museum Dr ... Anniston AL 36202 256-237-6766 237-6776
Web: www.annistonmuseum.org
Arlington Antebellum Home & Gardens 331 Cotton Ave SW ... Birmingham AL 35211 205-780-5656 788-0585
Web: www.informationbirmingham.com/arlington/index.htm
Barber Vintage Motorsports Museum 6030 Barber Motorsports Pkwy ... Leeds AL 35094 205-699-7275 702-8700
Web: www.barbermuseum.org
Bessemer Hall of History 1905 Alabama Ave ... Bessemer AL 35020 205-426-1633
Web: www.bessemerhallofhistory.com
Birmingham Civil Rights Institute 520 16th St N ... Birmingham AL 35203 205-328-9696 323-5219
TF: 866-328-9696 ■ Web: www.bcri.org
Birmingham Museum of Art 2000 8th Ave N ... Birmingham AL 35203 205-254-2566 254-2714
Web: www.artsbma.org
Bragg-Mitchell Mansion 1906 Springhill Ave ... Mobile AL 36607 251-471-6364 478-3800
TF: 866-471-6364 ■ Web: www.braggmitchellmansion.com
Burritt on the Mountain 3101 Burritt Dr ... Huntsville AL 35801 256-536-2882 532-1784
Web: www.burrittmuseum.com
Civil Rights Memorial 400 Washington Ave ... Montgomery AL 36104 334-956-8200
F Scott & Zelda Fitzgerald Museum 919 Felder Ave ... Montgomery AL 36106 334-264-4222
Web: www.fitzgerald-museum.com
First White House of the Confederacy
644 Washington Ave ... Montgomery AL 36104 334-242-1861
Fitzgerald F Scott & Zelda Museum 919 Felder Ave ... Montgomery AL 36106 334-264-4222
Web: www.fitzgerald-museum.com
Fort Conde Museum 150 S Royal St ... Mobile AL 36602 251-208-7569 208-7659
Hank Williams Museum & Memorial 118 Commerce St ... Montgomery AL 36104 334-262-3600 262-3603
Web: www.thehankwilliamsmuseum.com
Historic Huntsville Depot 320 Church St ... Huntsville AL 35801 256-564-8100 535-6018
TF: 800-678-1819 ■ Web: www.earlyworks.com/depot.html
Huntsville Museum of Art 300 Church St S ... Huntsville AL 35801 256-535-4350 532-1743
TF: 800-786-9095 ■ Web: www.hsvmuseum.org
Jasmine Hill Gardens & Outdoor Museum 3001 Jasmine Hill Rd ... Wetumpka AL 36093 334-567-6463
Web: www.jasminehill.org
Kentuck Museum & Annex 503 Main Ave ... Northport AL 35476 205-758-1257 758-1258
Mann Wildlife Learning Museum
325 Vandiver Blvd Montgomery Zoo ... Montgomery AL 36110 334-240-4900 240-4916
Web: www.mannmuseum.com
McWane Center Science Museum 200 19th St N ... Birmingham AL 35203 205-714-8300 714-8400
TF: 877-462-9263 ■ Web: www.mcwane.org
Mobile Museum of Art 4850 Museum Dr ... Mobile AL 36608 251-208-5200 208-5201
Web: www.mobilemuseumofart.com
Montgomery Museum of Fine Arts 1 Museum Dr ... Montgomery AL 36117 334-244-5700 240-4384
Web: www.mmfa.org
National African-American Archives & Museum 564 ML King Ave ... Mobile AL 36603 251-433-8511 433-4265
North Alabama Railroad Museum 694 Chase Rd ... Huntsville AL 35815 256-851-6276
Web: www.northalabamarailroadmuseum.com
Old Tavern Museum 500 28th Ave ... Tuscaloosa AL 35401 205-758-2238 758-8163
Phoenix Fire Museum 203 S Claiborne St ... Mobile AL 36602 251-208-7554
Richards-DAR House Museum 256 N Joachim St ... Mobile AL 36603 251-208-7320
Web: www.richardsdarhouse.com
Rosa Parks Library & Museum
252 Montgomery St Troy University Montgomery ... Montgomery AL 36104 334-241-8661 241-9756
Web: montgomery.troy.edu/museum
Sloss Furnaces National Historic Landmark 20 32nd St N ... Birmingham AL 35222 205-324-1911 324-6758
Web: www.slossfurnaces.com
Southern Museum of Flight 4343 73rd St N ... Birmingham AL 35206 205-833-8226 836-2439
Web: www.southernmuseumofflight.org
US Space & Rocket Center 1 Tranquility Base ... Huntsville AL 35805 256-837-3400 837-6137
TF: 800-637-7223 ■ Web: www.spacecamp.com/museum/
Weeden House Museum 300 Gates Ave SE ... Huntsville AL 35801 256-536-7718
Web: www.weedenhousemuseum.com
Westervelt Warner Museum of American Art
8316 Mountbatten Rd NE North River Yacht Club ... Tuscaloosa AL 35406 205-343-4543 345-1493
Web: www.warnermuseum.org

Alaska

Phone | Fax

Alaska Aviation Heritage Museum 4721 Aircraft Dr ... Anchorage AK 99502 907-248-5325 248-6391
Web: www.alaskaairmuseum.com
Alaska Native Heritage Center 8800 Heritage Center Dr ... Anchorage AK 99504 907-330-8000 330-8030
TF: 800-315-6608 ■ Web: www.alaskanative.net
Alaska State Museum 395 Whittier St ... Juneau AK 99801 907-465-2901 465-2976
Web: www.museums.state.ak.us
Anchorage Museum of History & Art 121 W 7th Ave ... Anchorage AK 99501 907-343-4326 343-6149
Web: www.anchoragemuseum.org
Anderson Oscar House Museum 420 M St Elderberry Park ... Anchorage AK 99501 907-274-2336
Baranov Museum Kodiak Historical Society 101 Marine Way ... Kodiak AK 99615 907-486-5920 486-3166
Web: www.baranov.us
Elmendorf Air Force Base Wildlife Museum 8481 19th St ... Elmendorf AFB AK 99506 907-552-2282
Fraternal Order of Alaska State Troopers Museum
245 W 5th Ave ... Anchorage AK 99501 907-279-5050 279-5054
TF: 800-770-5050 ■ Web: www.alaskatroopermuseum.com
Heritage Library Museum 301 W Northern Lights Blvd ... Anchorage AK 99503 907-265-2834 265-2860
Imaginarium Science Discovery Center 737 W 5th Ave Suite G ... Anchorage AK 99501 907-276-3179 258-4306
Web: www.imaginarium.org
Jackson Sheldon Museum 104 College Dr ... Sitka AK 99835 907-747-8981 747-3004
Web: www.museums.state.ak.us
Juneau-Douglas City Museum 114 W 4th St ... Juneau AK 99801 907-586-3572 586-3203
Web: www.juneau.lib.ak.us/parksrec/museum/
Last Chance Mining Museum & Historic Park 1001 Basin Rd ... Juneau AK 99801 907-586-5338 586-5820
Oscar Anderson House Museum 420 M St Elderberry Park ... Anchorage AK 99501 907-274-2336
Pioneer Museum Airport Way & Peger Rd ... Fairbanks AK 99707 907-456-8579
Sheldon Jackson Museum 104 College Dr ... Sitka AK 99835 907-747-8981 747-3004
Web: www.museums.state.ak.us
Tongass Historical Museum 629 Dock St ... Ketchikan AK 99901 907-225-5600 225-5602
University of Alaska Museum of the North 907 Yukon Dr ... Fairbanks AK 99775 907-474-7505 474-5469
Web: www.uaf.edu/museum

Alberta

Phone | Fax

Aero Space Museum of Calgary 4629 McCall Way NE ... Calgary AB T2E8A5 403-250-3752 250-8399
Web: www.asmac.ab.ca
Alberta Aviation Museum 11410 Kingsway Ave ... Edmonton AB T5G0X4 780-451-1175 451-1607
Web: www.albertaaviationmuseum.com
Glenbow Museum 130 9th Ave SE ... Calgary AB T2G0P3 403-268-4100 262-4045
Web: www.glenbow.org
Grain Academy/Museum 1410 Olympic Way SE Stampede Park ... Calgary AB T2P2K8 403-263-4594 290-5528
Naval Museum of Alberta 1820 24th St SW ... Calgary AB T2T0G6 403-242-0002 240-1966
Web: www.navalmuseum.ab.ca
Reynolds-Alberta Museum PO Box 6360 ... Wetaskiwin AB T9A2G1 780-361-1351 361-1239
TF: 800-661-4726 ■ Web: www.cd.gov.ab.ca
Royal Alberta Museum 12845 102nd Ave ... Edmonton AB T5N0M6 780-453-9100 454-6629
Web: www.royalalbertamuseum.ca
Royal Tyrrell Museum of Palaeontology
Hwy 838 Midland Provincial Park ... Drumheller AB T0J0Y0 403-823-7707 823-7131
TF: 888-440-4240 ■ Web: www.tyrrellmuseum.com
TELUS World of Science 11211 142nd St ... Edmonton AB T5M4A1 780-451-3344 455-5882
Web: www.telusworldofscienceedmonton.com

Arizona

Phone | Fax

390th Memorial Museum 6000 E Valencia Rd ... Tucson AZ 85706 520-574-0287 574-3030
Web: www.390th.org
Arizona Doll & Toy Museum 7th & Monroe St ... Phoenix AZ 85004 602-253-9337
Arizona Historical Society Museum 1300 N College Ave ... Tempe AZ 85281 480-929-0292 967-5450
Web: www.arizonahistoricalsociety.org
Arizona Historical Society Pioneer Museum 2340 N Fort Valley Rd ... Flagstaff AZ 86001 928-774-6272 774-1596
Web: www.arizonahistoricalsociety.org/default.asp
Arizona Mining & Mineral Museum 1502 W Washington St ... Phoenix AZ 85007 602-255-3791 255-3777
Web: www.admmr.state.az.us
Arizona Museum of Natural History 53 N MacDonald St ... Mesa AZ 85201 480-644-2169 644-3424
Web: www.cityofmesa.org/swmuseum
Arizona Museum for Youth 35 N Robson St ... Mesa AZ 85201 480-644-2468 644-2466
Web: www.cityofmesa.org/amfy/
Arizona Science Center 600 E Washington St ... Phoenix AZ 85004 602-716-2000 716-2099
Web: www.azscience.org
Arizona-Sonora Desert Museum 2021 N Kinney Rd ... Tucson AZ 85743 520-883-1380 883-2500
Web: www.desertmuseum.org
Arizona State Capitol Museum 1700 W Washington St ... Phoenix AZ 85007 602-542-4675 542-4690
Web: www.dlapr.lib.az.us
Arizona State Museum
1013 E University Blvd University of Arizona ... Tucson AZ 85721 520-621-6302 626-6761
Web: www.statemuseum.arizona.edu

Arizona (Cont'd)

	City	State	ZIP	Phone	Fax
Arizona State University Art Museum 10th St & Mill Ave Nelson Fine Arts Center Arizona State University *Web:* asuartmuseum.asu.edu	Tempe	AZ	85287	480-965-2787	965-5254
Arizona State University Life Sciences Center 300 E University Dr Life Sciences Bldg A	Tempe	AZ	85287	480-965-9011	965-2519
Arizona State University Museum of Anthropology Anthropology Bldg PO Box 872402	Tempe	AZ	85287	480-965-6213	965-7671
Arizona Wing Commemorative Air Force Museum 2017 N Greenfield Rd Falcon Field *Web:* www.arizonawingcaf.org	Mesa	AZ	85215	480-924-1940	981-1954
Bead Museum 5754 W Glenn Dr *Web:* www.beadmuseumaz.org/	Glendale	AZ	85301	623-931-2737	930-8561
Center for Creative Photography 1030 N Olive Rd Bldg 103 University of Arizona *Web:* dizzy.library.arizona.edu/branches/ccp	Tucson	AZ	85721	520-621-7968	621-9444
Chicano Museum 147 E Adams St	Phoenix	AZ	85004	602-257-5536	257-5539
DeGrazia Gallery in the Sun 6300 N Swan Rd *TF:* 800-545-2185 ■ *Web:* www.degrazia.org	Tucson	AZ	85718	520-299-9191	299-1381
Flandrau Science Center & Planetarium University of Arizona 1601 E University Blvd *Web:* www.flandrau.org	Tucson	AZ	85721	520-621-4515	621-8451
Fort Huachuca Museum Fort Huachuca Army Post	Sierra Vista	AZ	85636	520-533-5736	533-5736
Fort Lowell Museum 2900 N Craycroft Rd	Tucson	AZ	85712	520-885-3832	
Grand Canyon National Park Museum Collection Grand Canyon National Park PO Box 129	Grand Canyon	AZ	86023	928-638-7769	638-7769
Hall of Flame Museum of Firefighting 6101 E Van Buren St *Web:* www.hallofflame.org	Phoenix	AZ	85008	602-275-3473	275-0896
Heard Museum 2301 N Central Ave *Web:* www.heard.org	Phoenix	AZ	85004	602-252-8840	252-9757
Hoo-hoogam Ki Museum 10005 E Osborn Rd Salt River Indian Reservation	Scottsdale	AZ	85256	480-850-8190	850-8961
International Wildlife Museum 4800 W Gates Pass Rd *Web:* www.thewildlifemuseum.org	Tucson	AZ	85745	520-629-0100	618-3561
Mesa Historical Museum 2345 N Horne St *Web:* www.mesaaz.org	Mesa	AZ	85203	480-835-7358	835-1442
Meteor Crater & Museum of Astrogeology Exit 233 off I-40 Meteor Crater Rd *TF:* 800-289-5898 ■ *Web:* www.meteorcrater.com	Winslow	AZ	86047	928-289-2362	289-2598
Museo Chicano 147 E Adams St	Phoenix	AZ	85004	602-257-5536	257-5539
Museum of Northern Arizona 3101 N Fort Valley Rd *TF:* 800-423-1069 ■ *Web:* www.musnaz.org	Flagstaff	AZ	86001	928-774-5211	779-1527
Northern Arizona University Art Museum Old Main Bldg 10 Rm 205 North Campus *Web:* www.nau.edu/artgallery	Flagstaff	AZ	86011	928-523-3471	523-1424
Old Pueblo Archaeology Center 5100 W Ina Rd *Web:* www.oldpueblo.org	Tucson	AZ	85743	520-798-1201	798-1966
Petersen House Museum 1414 W Southern Ave *Web:* www.tempe.gov/museum	Tempe	AZ	85282	480-350-5100	350-5150
Phoenix Art Museum 1625 N Central Ave *Web:* www.phxart.org	Phoenix	AZ	85004	602-257-1880	253-8662
Phoenix Museum of History 105 N 5th St *Web:* www.pmoh.org	Phoenix	AZ	85004	602-253-2734	253-2348
Phoenix Police Museum 101 S Central Ave Suite 100 *Web:* www.phoenixpolicemuseum.com	Phoenix	AZ	85004	602-534-7278	495-2491
Pima Air & Space Museum 6000 E Valencia Rd *Web:* www.pimaair.org	Tucson	AZ	85706	520-574-0462	574-9238
Pioneer Arizona Living History Museum 3901 W Pioneer Rd *Web:* www.pioneer-arizona.com	Phoenix	AZ	85086	623-465-1052	465-0683
Pueblo Grande Museum & Archaeological Park 4619 E Washington St *TF:* 877-706-4408 ■ *Web:* www.ci.phoenix.az.us/PARKS/pueblo.html	Phoenix	AZ	85034	602-495-0901	495-5645
Robert S Dietz Museum of Geology Arizona State University School of Earth & Space Elploration Physical Sciences Complex F-Wing Rm 686	Tempe	AZ	85287	480-965-5081	965-8102
Rosson House Historic Museum 7th & Washington Sts *Web:* www.rossonhousemuseum.org	Phoenix	AZ	85004	602-262-5029	
Scottsdale Historical Museum 7333 E Civic Center Mall *Web:* www.scottsdalemuseum.com	Scottsdale	AZ	85251	480-945-4499	970-3251
Scottsdale Museum of Contemporary Art 7380 E 2nd St *Web:* scottsdalearts.org	Scottsdale	AZ	85251	480-874-4666	874-4699
Shemer Arts Center & Museum 5005 E Camelback Rd *Web:* phoenix.gov/PARKS/shemer.html	Phoenix	AZ	85018	602-262-4727	262-1605
Sosa-Carrillo-Fremont House Museum 151 S Granada Ave	Tucson	AZ	85701	520-622-0956	
Tempe Historical Museum 809 E Southern Ave *Web:* www.tempe.gov/museum	Tempe	AZ	85282	480-350-5100	350-5150
Tucson Museum of Art & Historic Block 140 N Main Ave *Web:* www.tucsonarts.com	Tucson	AZ	85701	520-624-2333	624-7202
University of Arizona Museum of Art Park Ave & Speedway Blvd University of Arizona *Web:* artmuseum.arizona.edu	Tucson	AZ	85721	520-621-7567	621-8770

Arkansas

	City	State	ZIP	Phone	Fax
Aerospace Education Center 3301 E Roosevelt Rd *Web:* www.aerospaced.org	Little Rock	AR	72206	501-376-4232	372-4826
Arkansas Arts Center 501 E 9th St *TF:* 800-264-2787 ■ *Web:* www.arkarts.com	Little Rock	AR	72202	501-372-4000	375-8053
Arkansas Museum of Science & History Museum of Discovery 500 President Clinton Ave Suite 150 *TF:* 800-880-6475 ■ *Web:* www.amod.org	Little Rock	AR	72201	501-396-7050	396-7054
Arkansas State University Museum 110 Cooley Dr PO Box 490 *Web:* museum.astate.edu	State University	AR	72467	870-972-2074	972-2793
EMOBA -The Museum of Black Arkansans & Performing Arts Center 1208 Louisiana St *Web:* it1.ualr.edu/emoba	Little Rock	AR	72202	501-372-0018	661-1323
Fort Smith Art Center 423 N 6th St *Web:* www.ftsartcenter.com	Fort Smith	AR	72901	479-784-2787	784-9071
Fort Smith Museum of History 320 Rogers Ave	Fort Smith	AR	72901	479-783-7841	783-3244
Fort Smith Trolley Museum 100 S 4th St *Web:* www.fstm.org	Fort Smith	AR	72901	479-783-0205	782-0649
Historic Arkansas Museum 200 E 3rd St *Web:* www.arkansashistory.com	Little Rock	AR	72201	501-324-9351	324-9345
Josephine Tussaud Wax Museum 250 Central Ave	Hot Springs	AR	71901	501-623-5836	
MacArthur Museum of Arkansas Military History 503 E 9th St *Web:* www.arkmilitaryheritage.com	Little Rock	AR	72202	501-376-4602	376-4593
Mid-America Science Museum 500 Mid-America Blvd *TF:* 800-632-0583 ■ *Web:* www.direclynx.net/~masm	Hot Springs	AR	71913	501-767-3461	767-1170
Museum of Discovery 500 President Clinton Ave Suite 150 *Web:* www.amod.org	Little Rock	AR	72201	501-396-7050	396-7054
Old State House Museum 300 W Markham St *Web:* www.oldstatehouse.org	Little Rock	AR	72201	501-324-9685	324-9688
Terry House Community Gallery 7th & Rock St *Web:* www.arkarts.com	Little Rock	AR	72202	501-372-4000	375-8053
University of Arkansas Little Rock Gallery 2801 S University Ave *Web:* www.ualr.edu/artdept/gallery	Little Rock	AR	72204	501-569-3183	683-7022

British Columbia

	City	Prov.	Postal Code	Phone	Fax
Biblical Museum of Canada 3180 E 58th Ave Unit 70 *Web:* www.biblicalmuseum.com	Vancouver	BC	V5S3S8	604-432-6122	
Canadian Museum of Flight 5333 216th St Hangar 3 *Web:* www.canadianflight.org	Langley	BC	V2Y2N3	604-532-0035	532-0056
Canadian Museum of Rail Travel 5700 Van Horne St S Box 400 *Web:* www.crowsnest.bc.ca/cmrt	Cranbrook	BC	V1C4H9	250-489-3918	489-5744
Comox Air Force Museum 19 Wing Comox *Web:* www.comoxairforcemuseum.ca	Lazo	BC	V0R2K0	250-339-8162	339-8162
Granville Island Model Ships Museum 1502 Duranleau St Granville Island *Web:* www.modelshipsmuseum.com	Vancouver	BC	V6H3S4	604-683-1939	683-7533
Granville Island Model Trains Museum 1502 Duranleau St Granville Island *Web:* www.modeltrainsmuseum.com	Vancouver	BC	V6H3S4	604-683-1939	683-7533
North Vancouver Museum & Archives 3203 Institute Rd *Web:* www.district.north-van.bc.ca/nvma	North Vancouver	BC	V7K3E5	604-990-3700	987-5609
Royal British Columbia Museum 675 Belleville St *TF:* 888-447-7977 ■ *Web:* www.royalbcmuseum.bc.ca	Victoria	BC	V8W9W2	250-356-7226	356-8197
University of British Columbia Museum of Anthropology 6393 NW Marine Dr *Web:* www.moa.ubc.ca	Vancouver	BC	V6T1Z2	604-822-5087	822-2974
Vancouver Museum 1100 Chestnut St Vanier Park *Web:* www.vanmuseum.bc.ca	Vancouver	BC	V6J3J9	604-736-4431	736-5417

California

	City	State	ZIP	Phone	Fax
African American Historical & Cultural Museum of San Joaquin Valley 1857 Fulton St	Fresno	CA	93721	559-268-7102	268-7171
African American Museum & Library in Oakland 659 14th St *Web:* www.oaklandlibrary.org/AAMLO	Oakland	CA	94612	510-637-0200	637-0204
Agua Caliente Cultural Museum 219 S Palm Canyon Dr *Web:* www.accmuseum.org	Palm Springs	CA	92262	760-323-0151	320-0350
Ainsley House 300 Grant St	Campbell	CA	95008	408-866-2119	866-2795
Albinger Archaeological Museum 113 E Main St	Ventura	CA	93001	805-648-5823	
Alice Arts Center 1428 Alice St	Oakland	CA	94612	510-238-7219	238-7225
Anaheim Museum 241 S Anaheim Blvd *Web:* www.anaheimmuseum.com	Anaheim	CA	92805	714-778-3301	778-6740
Ardenwood Historic Farm 34600 Ardenwood Blvd *Web:* www.ebparks.org/parks/arden.htm	Fremont	CA	94555	510-796-0663	796-0231
Asian Art Museum 200 Larkin St Civic Center Plaza *Web:* www.asianart.org	San Francisco	CA	94102	415-581-3500	581-4700
Autry National Center Museum of the American West 4700 Western Heritage Way *Web:* www.autry-museum.org	Los Angeles	CA	90027	323-667-2000	660-5721
Bakersfield Museum of Art 1930 R St *Web:* www.bmoa.org/	Bakersfield	CA	93301	661-323-7219	323-7266
Berkeley Art Museum & Pacific Film Archive 2626 Bancroft Way *Web:* www.bampfa.berkeley.edu	Berkeley	CA	94720	510-642-0808	642-4889
Bonita Historical Museum 4035 Bonita Rd *Web:* www.bonitacalifornia.org	Bonita	CA	91902	619-267-5141	267-2143
Bowers Museum of Cultural Art 2002 N Main St *Web:* www.bowers.org	Santa Ana	CA	92706	714-567-3600	567-3603
Brand Library & Art Center 1601 W Mountain St *Web:* library.ci.glendale.ca.us	Glendale	CA	91201	818-548-2051	548-5079
Buena Vista Museum of Natural History 2018 Chester Ave *Web:* sharktoothhill.com	Bakersfield	CA	93301	661-324-6350	324-7522
Cabot's Pueblo Museum 67-616 E Desert View Ave *Web:* www.cabotsmuseum.org	Desert Hot Springs	CA	92240	760-329-7610	329-2738
California Academy of Sciences 875 Howard St *Web:* www.calacademy.org/	San Francisco	CA	94103	415-321-8000	321-8610
California African American Museum 600 State Dr Exposition Park *Web:* www.caamuseum.org	Los Angeles	CA	90037	213-744-7432	744-2050
California Living Museum (CALM) 10500 Alfred Harrell Hwy *Web:* www.calmzoo.org	Bakersfield	CA	93306	661-872-2256	872-2205
California Military Museum 1119 2nd St *Web:* www.militarymuseum.org	Sacramento	CA	95814	916-442-2883	442-7532
California Museum for History Women & the Arts 1020 'O' St *Web:* www.californiamuseum.org	Sacramento	CA	95814	916-653-7524	653-0314
California Museum of Photography 3824 Main St *Web:* www.cmp.ucr.edu	Riverside	CA	92501	951-784-3686	827-4797
California Science Center 700 State Dr *Web:* www.californiasciencecenter.org	Los Angeles	CA	90037	213-744-7400	744-2650
California State Archives 1020 'O' St *Web:* www.ss.ca.gov/archives/archives.htm	Sacramento	CA	95814	916-653-7715	653-7134
California State Capitol Museum 10th & L Sts *TF:* 866-240-4655 ■ *Web:* www.capitolmuseum.ca.gov	Sacramento	CA	95814	916-324-0333	445-3628
California State Indian Museum c/o Capital District Office 101 J St *Web:* www.parks.ca.gov/default.asp?page_id=486	Sacramento	CA	95816	916-324-0971	322-5231
California State Railroad Museum c/o Capital District Office 101 J St *Web:* www.csrmf.org	Sacramento	CA	95814	916-445-7387	327-5655
Campbell Historical Museum 51 N Central Ave	Campbell	CA	95008	408-866-2119	866-2795
Carnegie Art Museum 424 S 'C' St *Web:* www.vcnet.com/carnart	Oxnard	CA	93030	805-385-8157	483-3654
Cartoon Art Museum 655 Mission St *Web:* www.cartoonart.org	San Francisco	CA	94105	415-227-8666	243-8666
Centennial Heritage Museum 3101 W Harvard St *Web:* www.centennialmuseum.org	Santa Ana	CA	92704	714-540-0404	540-1932
Center for Beethoven Studies & Museum 150 E San Fernando St Dr MLK Jr Library 5th Fl *Web:* www2.sjsu.edu/depts/beethoven/	San Jose	CA	95112	408-808-2058	808-2060
Chabot Space & Science Center 10000 Skyline Blvd *Web:* www.chabotspace.org	Oakland	CA	94619	510-336-7300	336-7491
Chula Vista Heritage Museum 360 3rd Ave *Web:* www.chulavistalibrary.com/heritage_museum	Chula Vista	CA	91910	619-427-8092	
Clarke Historical Museum 240 E St *Web:* www.clarkemuseum.org	Eureka	CA	95501	707-443-1947	443-0290

Name / Address	City	State	ZIP	Phone	Fax
Coachella Valley Museum & Cultural Center 82616 Miles Ave PO Box 595	Indio	CA	92202	760-342-6651	863-5232
Web: www.coachellavalleymuseum.org					
Colton Hall Museum Pacific St Civic Center	Monterey	CA	93940	831-646-5640	646-3422
Web: www.monterey.org/museum					
Contemporary Jewish Museum 121 Steuart St	San Francisco	CA	94105	415-344-8800	344-8815
Web: www.jmsf.org					
Crocker Art Museum 216 'O' St	Sacramento	CA	95814	916-264-5423	264-7372
Web: www.crockerartmuseum.org					
Crown Point Press 20 Hawthorne St	San Francisco	CA	94105	415-974-6273	495-4220
Web: www.crownpoint.com					
de Saisset Museum at Santa Clara University 500 El Camino Real	Santa Clara	CA	95053	408-554-4528	554-7840
Web: www.scu.edu/deSaisset					
Death Valley Museum PO Box 579 Death Valley National Pk	Death Valley	CA	92328	760-786-2331	786-3283
Web: www.nps.gov/deva					
Discovery Science Center 2500 N Main St	Santa Ana	CA	92705	714-542-2823	542-2828
Web: www.discoverycube.org					
Dr Willella Howe-Waffle House & Medical Museum 120 Civic Center Dr	Santa Ana	CA	92701	714-547-9645	
Web: www.santaanahistory.com/house.html					
Euphrat Museum of Art 21250 Stevens Creek Blvd De Anza College	San Jose	CA	95014	408-864-8836	
Exploratorium 3601 Lyon St	San Francisco	CA	94123	415-563-7337	561-0370
Web: www.exploratorium.edu					
Firehouse Museum 1572 Columbia St	San Diego	CA	92101	619-232-3473	
Flying Leatherneck Aviation Museum Anderson Ave MCAS Miramar	San Diego	CA	94018	858-693-1723	693-0037
Web: www.flyingleathernecks.org					
Forest Lawn Museum 1712 S Glendale Ave	Glendale	CA	91205	800-204-3131	
Web: www.forestlawn.com					
Fort MacArthur Museum 3601 S Gaffey St	San Pedro	CA	90731	310-548-2631	241-0847
Web: www.ftmac.org					
Fresno Art Museum 2233 N 1st St	Fresno	CA	93703	559-441-4220	441-4227
Web: www.fresnoartmuseum.com					
Fresno Metropolitan Museum of Art History & Science 1555 Van Ness Ave	Fresno	CA	93721	559-441-1444	441-8607
Web: www.fresnomet.org					
General Phineas Banning Residence Museum 401 E 'M' St	Wilmington	CA	90744	310-548-7777	548-2644
Web: banningmuseum.org					
George C Page Museum at La Brea Tar Pits 5801 Wilshire Blvd	Los Angeles	CA	90036	323-857-6311	933-3974
Web: www.tarpits.org					
Getty J Paul Museum 1200 Getty Center Dr	Los Angeles	CA	90049	310-440-7300	440-7720*
**Fax:* Hum Res ■ *Web:* www.getty.edu/museum					
Great Valley Museum of Natural History 1100 Stoddard Ave	Modesto	CA	95350	209-575-6196	549-7039
Grier-Musser Museum 403 S Bonnie Brae St	Los Angeles	CA	90057	213-413-1814	
Haggin Museum 1201 N Pershing Ave	Stockton	CA	95203	209-462-4116	462-1404
Web: www.hagginmuseum.org					
Hart William S Museum 24151 San Fernando Rd	Newhall	CA	91321	661-254-4584	254-6499
Web: www.hartmuseum.org					
Hearst Phoebe Apperson Museum of Anthropology University of California 103 Kroeber Hall	Berkeley	CA	94720	510-642-3682	642-6271
Web: hearstmuseum.berkeley.edu					
Hellenic Heritage Museum 1650 Senter Rd	San Jose	CA	95112	408-247-4685	
Web: www.hellenicheritageinstitute.org					
Henry Wilson Coil Masonic Library & Museum 1111 California St	San Francisco	CA	94108	415-776-7000	776-7170
Heritage of the Americas Museum 12110 Cuyamaca College Dr W	El Cajon	CA	92019	619-670-5194	670-5198
Web: www.cuyamaca.net/museum					
Heritage Square Museum 3800 Homer St	Los Angeles	CA	90031	323-225-2700	
Web: www.heritagesquare.org					
Historical Glass Museum 1157 N Orange St	Redlands	CA	92373	909-798-0868	
History San Jose - San Jose Historical Museum 1650 Senter Rd	San Jose	CA	95112	408-287-2290	287-2291
Web: www.historysanjose.org					
Hobby City Doll & Toy Museum 1238 S Beach Blvd	Anaheim	CA	92804	714-527-2323	236-9762
Hollywood Entertainment Museum 7021 Hollywood Blvd	Hollywood	CA	90028	323-465-7900	469-9576
Web: www.hollywoodmuseum.com					
Hollywood Museum 1660 N Highland Ave	Hollywood	CA	90028	323-464-7776	464-3777
Web: www.thehollywoodmuseum.com					
Hollywood Wax Museum 6767 Hollywood Blvd	Hollywood	CA	90028	323-462-8860	462-3953
Web: www.hollywoodwax.com					
Intel Museum 2200 Mission College Blvd	Santa Clara	CA	95052	408-765-0503	765-1217
TF: 800-628-8686 ■ *Web:* www.intel.com/museum/index.htm					
International Surfing Museum 411 Olive Ave	Huntington Beach	CA	92648	714-960-3483	960-1434
Web: www.surfingmuseum.org					
J Paul Getty Museum 1200 Getty Center Dr	Los Angeles	CA	90049	310-440-7300	440-7720*
**Fax:* Hum Res ■ *Web:* www.getty.edu/museum					
Japanese-American Museum 535 N 5th St	San Jose	CA	95112	408-294-3138	294-1657
Web: www.jamsj.org					
Japanese American National Museum 369 E 1st St	Los Angeles	CA	90012	213-625-0414	625-0414
TF: 800-461-5266 ■ *Web:* www.janm.org					
Jensen-Alvarado Historic Ranch & Museum 4307 Briggs St	Riverside	CA	92509	951-369-6055	369-1153
Judah L Magnes Museum 2911 Russell St	Berkeley	CA	94705	510-549-6950	849-3673
Web: www.magnes.org					
Junipero Serra Museum 2727 Presidio Dr	San Diego	CA	92103	619-297-3258	297-3281
Web: www.sandiegohistory.org					
Kearney Mansion Museum 7160 W Kearney Blvd	Fresno	CA	93706	559-441-0862	441-1372
Web: www.valleyhistory.org					
Kern County Museum 3801 Chester Ave	Bakersfield	CA	93301	661-852-5000	322-6415
Web: www.kcmuseum.org					
Kern Valley Museum 49 Big Blue Rd PO Box 651	Kernville	CA	93238	760-376-6683	
Legion of Honor Museum 100 34th Ave Lincoln Park	San Francisco	CA	94121	415-750-3600	
Web: www.thinker.org/legion					
Legion of Valor Museum 2425 Fresno St Veterans Memorial Auditorium	Fresno	CA	93721	559-498-0510	498-3773
Web: www.legionofvalormuseum.org					
Long Beach Museum of Art 2300 E Ocean Blvd	Long Beach	CA	90803	562-439-2119	439-3587
Web: www.lbma.org					
Los Angeles County Museum of Art 5905 Wilshire Blvd	Los Angeles	CA	90036	323-857-6000	857-6212
Web: www.lacma.org					
Magnes Museum 2911 Russell St	Berkeley	CA	94705	510-549-6950	849-3673
Web: www.magnes.org					
March Field Air Museum 22550 Van Buren Blvd	Riverside	CA	92518	951-697-6600	697-6605
Web: www.marchfield.org					
Maritime Museum of San Diego 1492 N Harbor Dr	San Diego	CA	92101	619-234-9153	234-8345
Web: www.sdmaritime.org					
McClellan Aviation Museum 3200 Freedom Park Dr	McClellan	CA	95652	916-643-3192	643-0389
Web: www.mcclellanaviationmuseum.org					
McHenry Museum 1402 'I' St	Modesto	CA	95354	209-577-5366	491-4407
Web: www.mchenrymuseum.org					
Merritt Museum of Anthropology 12500 Campus Dr	Oakland	CA	94619	510-531-4911	436-2405
Meux Home Museum 1007 R St	Fresno	CA	93721	559-233-8007	233-2331
Web: www.meux.mus.ca.us					
Mexican Museum Fort Mason Center Bldg D	San Francisco	CA	94123	415-202-9700	441-7683
Web: www.mexicanmuseum.org					
Mills College Art Museum 5000 MacArthur Blvd	Oakland	CA	94613	510-430-2164	430-3168
Web: www.mills.edu/campus_life/art_museum/index.php					
Mingei International Museum of Folk Art 1439 El Prado Balboa Park	San Diego	CA	92101	619-239-0003	239-0605
Web: www.mingei.org					
Minter Field Air Museum 401 Vultee St PO Box 445	Shafter	CA	93263	661-393-0291	393-3296
Web: www.minterfieldairmuseum.com					
Mission Basilica San Diego de Alcala 10818 San Diego Mission Rd	San Diego	CA	92108	619-283-7319	283-7762
Web: www.missionsandiego.com					
Mission Inn Museum 3696 Mission Inn Ave	Riverside	CA	92501	951-788-9556	341-6574
Web: www.missioninnmuseum.com					
Monterey Maritime & History Museum 5 Custom House Plaza Stanton Center	Monterey	CA	93940	831-373-2469	655-3054
Web: www.montereyhistory.org					
Monterey Museum of Art 559 Pacific St	Monterey	CA	93940	831-372-5477	372-5680
Web: www.montereyart.org					
Museo Italo-Americano Fort Mason Center Bldg C	San Francisco	CA	94123	415-673-2200	673-2292
Web: www.museoitaloamericano.org					
Museum of Contemporary Art 250 S Grand Ave California Plaza	Los Angeles	CA	90012	213-621-2766	620-8674
Web: www.moca.org					
Museum of Contemporary Art 1001 Kettner Blvd	San Diego	CA	92101	619-234-1001	234-1070
Web: www.mcasandiego.org					
Museum of Craft & Folk Art 51 Yerba Buena Ln	San Francisco	CA	94103	415-227-4888	227-4351
Web: www.mocfa.org					
Museum of History & Art 1100 Orange Ave	Coronado	CA	92118	619-437-8788	435-8504
Web: www.coronadohistory.org					
Museum of Jurassic Technology 9341 Venice Blvd	Culver City	CA	90232	310-836-6131	287-2267
Web: www.mjt.org					
Museum of Latin American Art 628 Alamitos Ave	Long Beach	CA	90802	562-437-1689	437-7043
Web: www.molaa.com					
Museum of Local History 190 Anza St	Fremont	CA	94539	510-623-7907	
Web: www.museumoflocalhistory.org					
Museum of Making Music 5790 Armada Dr	Carlsbad	CA	92008	760-438-5996	438-8964
Web: www.museumofmakingmusic.org					
Museum of Neon Art 501 W Olympic Blvd Suite 101	Los Angeles	CA	90015	213-489-9918	489-9932
Web: neonmona.org					
Museum of Photographic Arts 1649 El Prado	San Diego	CA	92101	619-238-7559	238-8777
Web: www.mopa.org/					
Museum of San Diego History 1649 El Prado Balboa Park	San Diego	CA	92101	619-232-6203	232-6297
Web: www.sandiegohistory.org					
Museum of Tolerance 9786 W Pico Blvd	Los Angeles	CA	90035	310-553-8403	772-7655
TF: 800-900-9036 ■ *Web:* www.wiesenthal.com					
National Steinbeck Center 1 Main St	Salinas	CA	93901	831-796-3833	796-3828
Web: www.steinbeck.org					
Natural History Museum of Los Angeles County 900 Exposition Blvd	Los Angeles	CA	90007	213-763-3466	746-2999
Web: www.nhm.org					
Newland House Museum 19820 Beach Blvd	Huntington Beach	CA	92648	714-962-5777	
Web: www.hbsurfcity.com/history/newland.htm					
Niles Depot 36997 Mission Blvd	Fremont	CA	94536	510-797-4449	
Web: nilesdepot.railfan.net					
Nixon Richard M Library & Birthplace 18001 Yorba Linda Blvd	Yorba Linda	CA	92886	714-993-5075	528-0544
Web: www.nixonfoundation.org					
Norton Simon Museum 411 W Colorado Blvd	Pasadena	CA	91105	626-449-6840	796-4978
Web: www.nortonsimon.org					
Oakland Museum of California 1000 Oak St	Oakland	CA	94607	510-238-2200	238-2258
TF: 800-625-6873 ■ *Web:* www.museumca.org					
Oakland Museum Sculpture Court 1111 Broadway City Center	Oakland	CA	94607	510-238-3401	238-2258
TF: 888-625-6873					
Orange County Museum of Art Newport Beach 850 San Clemente Dr	Newport Beach	CA	92660	949-759-1122	759-5623
Web: www.ocma.net					
Orange County Museum of Art South Coast Plaza 3333 Bear St 3rd Fl	Costa Mesa	CA	92626	949-759-1122	759-5623
Web: www.ocma.net					
Pacific Asia Museum 46 N Los Robles Ave	Pasadena	CA	91101	626-449-2742	449-2754
Web: www.pacificasiamuseum.org					
Pacific Grove Museum of Natural History 165 Forest Ave	Pacific Grove	CA	93950	831-648-5716	372-3256
Web: www.pgmuseum.org					
Pacific Southwest Railway Museum 4695 Nebo Dr	La Mesa	CA	91941	619-465-7776	
Web: www.psrm.org					
Page George C Museum at La Brea Tar Pits 5801 Wilshire Blvd	Los Angeles	CA	90036	323-857-6311	933-3974
Web: www.tarpits.org					
Palm Springs Air Museum 745 N Gene Autry Trail	Palm Springs	CA	92262	760-778-6262	320-2548
Web: www.air-museum.org					
Palm Springs Art Museum 101 Museum Dr	Palm Springs	CA	92262	760-325-7186	327-5069
Web: www.psmuseum.org					
Pardee Home Museum 672 11th St	Oakland	CA	94607	510-444-2187	444-7120
Web: www.pardeehome.org					
Petersen Automotive Museum 6060 Wilshire Blvd	Los Angeles	CA	90036	323-930-2277	930-6642
Web: www.petersen.org					
Phoebe Apperson Hearst Museum of Anthropology University of California 103 Kroeber Hall	Berkeley	CA	94720	510-642-3682	642-6271
Web: hearstmuseum.berkeley.edu					
Planes of Fame Air Museum Chino Airport 7000 Merrill Ave Box 17	Chino	CA	91710	909-597-3722	597-4755
Web: www.planesoffame.org					
Port Hueneme Museum 220 N Market St	Port Hueneme	CA	93041	805-488-2023	488-6993
Queen Mary Seaport 1126 Queens Hwy	Long Beach	CA	90802	562-435-3511	437-4531
TF: 800-437-2934 ■ *Web:* www.queenmary.com					
Rancho Los Alamitos Historic Ranch & Gardens 6400 E Bixby Hill Rd	Long Beach	CA	90815	562-431-3541	430-9694
Web: www.rancholosalamitos.com					
Rancho Los Cerritos Historic Ranch 4600 Virginia Rd	Long Beach	CA	90807	562-570-1755	570-1893
Web: www.rancholoscerritos.org					
Randall Museum 199 Museum Way	San Francisco	CA	94114	415-554-9600	554-9609
Web: www.randallmuseum.org					
Reagan Ronald Presidential Library & Museum 40 Presidential Dr	Simi Valley	CA	93065	805-577-4000	577-4074
TF: 800-410-8354 ■ *Web:* www.reagan.utexas.edu					
Reuben H Fleet Science Center 1875 El Prado	San Diego	CA	92101	619-238-1233	685-5771
Web: www.rhfleet.org					
Richard M Nixon Library & Birthplace 18001 Yorba Linda Blvd	Yorba Linda	CA	92886	714-993-5075	528-0544
Web: www.nixonfoundation.org					
Ripley's Believe It or Not! Museum 7850 Beach Blvd	Buena Park	CA	90620	714-522-7045	
Web: www.ripleysbuenapark.com					
Ripley's Believe It or Not! Museum 6780 Hollywood Blvd	Hollywood	CA	90028	323-466-6335	466-6512
Ripley's Believe It or Not! Museum 175 Jefferson St	San Francisco	CA	94133	415-771-6188	771-1246
Web: www.ripleysf.com					

California (Cont'd)

Phone | Fax

Riverside Art Museum 3425 Mission Inn Ave . . . Riverside CA 92501 951-684-7111 684-7332
Web: www.riversideartmuseum.org

Riverside Metropolitan Museum 3580 Mission Inn Ave . . . Riverside CA 92501 951-826-5273 369-4970
Web: www.riversideca.gov/museum/

Robert V Fullerton Art Museum
5500 University Pkwy California State University
San Bernardino. . . . San Bernardino CA 92407 909-537-7373 537-7068
Web: museum.csusb.edu

Ronald Reagan Presidential Library & Museum
40 Presidential Dr . . . Simi Valley CA 93065 805-577-4000 577-4074
TF: 800-410-8354 ■ *Web:* www.reagan.utexas.edu

Rosicrucian Egyptian Museum & Planetarium
1342 Naglee Ave Rosicrucian Park . . . San Jose CA 95191 408-947-3636 947-3677
Web: www.rosicrucian.org

San Bernardino County Museum 2024 Orange Tree Ln. . . . Redlands CA 92374 909-307-2669 307-0539
Web: www.co.san-bernardino.ca.us/museum

San Diego Air & Space Museum
2001 Pan American Plaza Balboa Park . . . San Diego CA 92101 619-234-8291 233-4526
Web: www.aerospacemuseum.org

San Diego Aircraft Carrier Museum
910 N Harbor Dr Navy Pier . . . San Diego CA 92101 619-544-9600 544-9188
Web: www.midway.org

San Diego Archaeological Center
16666 San Pasqual Valley Rd . . . Escondido CA 92027 760-291-0370 291-0371
Web: www.sandiegoarchaeology.org

San Diego Automotive Museum
2080 Pan American Plaza Balboa Park . . . San Diego CA 92101 619-231-2886 231-9869
Web: www.sdautomuseum.org

San Diego Hall of Champions Sports Museum
2131 Pan American Plaza Balboa Park . . . San Diego CA 92101 619-234-2544 234-4543
Web: www.sdhoc.com

San Diego Model Railroad Museum
1649 El Prado Balboa Park . . . San Diego CA 92101 619-696-0199 696-0239
Web: www.sdmodelrailroadm.com

San Diego Museum of Art 1450 El Prado Balboa Park . . . San Diego CA 92101 619-232-7931 232-9367
Web: www.sdmart.com

San Diego Museum of Man 1350 El Prado Balboa Park . . . San Diego CA 92101 619-239-2001 239-2749
Web: www.museumofman.org

San Diego Natural History Museum 1788 El Prado . . . San Diego CA 92101 619-232-3821 232-0248
Web: www.sdnhm.org

San Francisco Fire Department Museum
655 Presidio Ave . . . San Francisco CA 94115 415-563-4630

San Francisco Museum of Modern Art 151 3rd St . . . San Francisco CA 94103 415-357-4000 357-4037
Web: www.sfmoma.org

San Joaquin County Historical Society & Museum
11793 N Micke Grove Rd. . . . Lodi CA 95240 209-331-2055 331-2057
Web: www.sanjoaquinhistory.org

San Jose Museum of Art 110 S Market St. . . . San Jose CA 95113 408-271-6840 294-2977
Web: www.sjmusart.org

San Jose Museum of Quilts & Textiles 520 S 1st St . . . San Jose CA 95113 408-971-0323 971-7226
Web: www.sjquiltmuseum.org

Santa Barbara Museum of Art 1130 State St. . . . Santa Barbara CA 93101 805-963-4364 966-6840
Web: www.sbmuseart.org

Santa Barbara Museum of Natural History
2559 Puesta Del Sol Rd. . . . Santa Barbara CA 93105 805-682-4711 569-3170
Web: www.sbnature.org

Santa Cruz Harley-Davidson Museum 1148 Soquel Ave . . . Santa Cruz CA 95062 831-421-9600 427-9309
Web: www.santacruzharley.com

Seabee Museum 1000 23rd Ave Bldg 99 . . . Port Hueneme CA 93043 805-982-5163 982-5595
Web: www.seabeehf.org

Seymour Pioneer Museum
Society of California Pioneers 300 4th St . . . San Francisco CA 94107 415-957-1849 957-9858
Web: www.californiapioneers.org

Sherman Indian Museum 9010 Magnolia Ave. . . . Riverside CA 92503 951-276-6719 276-6336
Web: www.shermanindianmuseum.org

Simon Norton Museum 411 W Colorado Blvd. . . . Pasadena CA 91105 626-449-6840 796-4978
Web: www.nortonsimon.org

Southwest Museum 234 Museum Dr . . . Los Angeles CA 90065 323-221-2164 224-8223
Web: www.southwestmuseum.org

Stanley Ranch Museum 12174 Euclid St PO Box 4297 . . . Garden Grove CA 92842 714-530-8871 534-2611

Steinbeck Spirit of Monterey Wax Museum
700 Cannery Row Suite 2 . . . Monterey CA 93940 831-375-3770 373-0341
Web: www.wax-museum.com

Tech Museum of Innovation 201 S Market St. . . . San Jose CA 95113 408-294-8324 279-7167
Web: www.thetech.org

The Paley Center for Media 465 N Beverly Dr . . . Beverly Hills CA 90210 310-786-1000 786-1086
Web: www.paleycenter.org

Timken Museum of Art 1500 El Prado Balboa Park. . . . San Diego CA 92101 619-239-5548 531-9640
Web: www.timkenmuseum.org

Towe Auto Museum 2200 Front St. . . . Sacramento CA 95818 916-442-6802 442-2646
Web: www.toweautomuseum.org

Triton Museum of Art 1505 Warburton Ave. . . . Santa Clara CA 95050 408-247-3754 247-3796
Web: www.tritonmuseum.org

Turtle Bay Exploration Park 840 Auditorium Dr . . . Redding CA 96001 530-243-8850 243-8929
Web: www.turtlebay.org

UCLA Fowler Museum of Cultural History
University of California 308 Charles E Young Dr. . . . Los Angeles CA 90095 310-825-4361 206-7007
Web: www.fmch.ucla.edu

UCLA Hammer Museum 10899 Wilshire Blvd . . . Los Angeles CA 90024 310-443-7000 443-7099
Web: www.hammer.ucla.edu

University Art Museum 1250 Bellflower Blvd CSULB. . . . Long Beach CA 90840 562-985-5761 985-7602
Web: www.csulb.edu/org/uam

USC Fisher Gallery 823 Exposition Blvd University Park . . . Los Angeles CA 90089 213-740-4561 740-7676
Web: www.usc.edu/org/fishergallery

USS Hornet Museum 707 W Hornet Ave Pier 3 . . . Alameda CA 94501 510-521-8448 749-3699
Web: www.uss-hornet.org

Ventura County Maritime Museum 2731 S Victoria Ave . . . Oxnard CA 93035 805-984-6260 984-5970

Ventura County Museum of History & Art 100 E Main St. . . . Ventura CA 93001 805-653-0323 653-5267
Web: www.venturamuseum.org

Veterans Museum & Memorial Center 2115 Park Blvd. . . . San Diego CA 92101 619-239-2300 239-7445
Web: www.veteranmuseum.org

Wax Museum at Fisherman's Wharf
145 Jefferson St Suite 500 . . . San Francisco CA 94133 415-202-0402 771-9248
TF: 800-439-4305 ■ *Web:* www.waxmuseum.com

Wells Fargo History Museum 333 S Grand Ave. . . . Los Angeles CA 90071 213-253-7166 680-2269
Web: www.wellsfargohistory.com

Wells Fargo History Museum
400 Capitol Mall 7th Fl Wells Fargo Center. . . . Sacramento CA 95814 916-440-4161 492-2931
Web: www.wellsfargohistory.com

Wells Fargo History Museum 2733 San Diego Ave . . . San Diego CA 92110 619-238-3929
Web: www.wellsfargohistory.com/

Wells Fargo History Museum 420 Montgomery St . . . San Francisco CA 94163 415-396-2619 975-7430
Web: www.wellsfargohistory.com

Phone | Fax

Western Aerospace Museum
Oakland International Airport North Field 8260 Boeing St
Bldg 621. . . . Oakland CA 94614 510-638-7100 638-6530
Web: www.westernaerospacemuseum.org

Whaley House Museum 2476 San Diego Ave. . . . San Diego CA 92110 619-297-7511 291-3576
Web: www.whaleyhouse.org

William S Hart Museum 24151 San Fernando Rd . . . Newhall CA 91321 661-254-4584 254-6499
Web: www.hartmuseum.org

Wings of History Air Museum
12777 Murphy Ave PO Box 495 . . . San Martin CA 95046 408-683-2290 683-2291
Web: www.wingsofhistory.org

Yerba Buena Center for the Arts 701 Mission St . . . San Francisco CA 94103 415-978-2700 978-9635
Web: www.yerbabuenaarts.org

Colorado

Phone | Fax

American Numismatic Assn Money Museum
818 N Cascade Ave . . . Colorado Springs CO 80903 719-632-2646 634-4085
TF: 800-367-9723 ■ *Web:* www.money.org/moneymus.html

Aspen Art Museum 590 N Mill St. . . . Aspen CO 81611 970-925-8050 925-8054
Web: www.aspenartmuseum.org

Aurora History Museum 15051 E Alameda Pkwy . . . Aurora CO 80012 303-739-6660 739-6657
Web: www.auroramuseum.org

Boulder History Museum 1206 Euclid Ave . . . Boulder CO 80302 303-449-3464 938-8322
Web: www.boulderhistorymuseum.org

Boulder Museum of Contemporary Art 1750 13th St . . . Boulder CO 80302 303-443-2122 447-1633
Web: www.bmoca.org

Brown Molly House 1340 Pennsylvania St . . . Denver CO 80203 303-832-4092 832-2340
Web: www.mollybrown.org

Buffalo Bill Memorial Museum 987 1/2 Lookout Mountain Rd. . . . Golden CO 80401 303-526-0744 526-0197
Web: www.buffalobill.org

Byers-Evans House Museum 1310 Bannock St . . . Denver CO 80204 303-620-4933 620-4795
Web: www.coloradohistory.org

Carriage House Museum 11 Lake Cir . . . Colorado Springs CO 80906 719-634-7711

Center of Southwest Studies 1000 Rim Dr . . . Durango CO 81301 970-247-7456 247-7422
Web: swcenter.fortlewis.edu

Colorado History Museum 1300 Broadway. . . . Denver CO 80203 303-866-3682 866-5739
Web: www.coloradohistory.org

Colorado Railroad Museum 17155 W 44th Ave . . . Golden CO 80402 303-279-4591 279-4229
TF: 800-365-6263 ■ *Web:* crrm.org

Colorado Springs Fine Arts Center 30 W Dale St . . . Colorado Springs CO 80903 719-634-5581 634-0570
Web: www.csfineartscenter.org

Colorado Springs Pioneers Museum 215 S Tejon St. . . . Colorado Springs CO 80903 719-385-5990 385-5645
Web: www.cspm.org

Comanche Crossing Museum 56060 Colfax Ave Suite E . . . Strasburg CO 80136 303-622-4322

Denver Art Museum 100 W 14th Avenue Pkwy . . . Denver CO 80204 720-865-5000 913-0001
Web: www.denverartmuseum.org

Denver Firefighters Museum 1326 Tremont Pl . . . Denver CO 80204 303-892-1436 892-1436
TF: 888-623-7085 ■ *Web:* www.denverfirefightersmuseum.org

Denver Museum of Miniatures Dolls & Toys 1880 Gaylord St . . . Denver CO 80206 303-322-1053 322-3704
Web: www.dmmdt.com

Denver Museum of Nature & Science 2001 Colorado Blvd. . . . Denver CO 80205 303-370-6357 331-6492
TF: 800-925-2250 ■ *Web:* www.dmnh.org

Discovery Science Center 703 E Prospect Rd . . . Fort Collins CO 80525 970-472-3990 472-3997
Web: www.dcsm.org

Forney Museum of Transportation 4303 Brighton Blvd. . . . Denver CO 80216 303-297-1113 297-3113
Web: www.forneymuseum.com

Fort Collins Museum 200 Matthews St. . . . Fort Collins CO 80524 970-221-6738 416-2236
Web: www.ci.fort-collins.co.us/museum/

Fort Collins Museum of Contemporary Art
201 S College Ave . . . Fort Collins CO 80524 970-482-2787 482-0804
Web: www.fcmoca.org

Ghost Town Museum 400 S 21st St . . . Colorado Springs CO 80904 719-634-0696 634-2435
Web: www.ghosttownmuseum.com

Golden Pioneer Museum 923 10th St. . . . Golden CO 80401 303-278-7151 278-2755
Web: www.goldenpioneermuseum.com

Leanin' Tree Museum of Western Art 6055 Longbow Dr . . . Boulder CO 80301 303-530-1442 530-7283
TF: 800-777-8716 ■ *Web:* www.leanintree.com

Manitou Cliff Dwellings Museum Hwy 24 W. . . . Manitou Springs CO 80829 719-685-5242 685-1562
TF: 800-354-9971 ■ *Web:* www.cliffdwellingsmuseum.com

May Natural History Museum & Museum of Space Exploration 710 Rock Creek Canyon Rd. . . . Colorado Springs CO 80926 719-576-0450 576-3644
TF: 800-666-3841 ■ *Web:* www.maymuseum-camp-rvpark.com

McAllister House Museum 423 N Cascade Ave . . . Colorado Springs CO 80903 719-635-7925

Miramont Castle Museum 9 Capitol Hill Ave . . . Manitou Springs CO 80829 719-685-1011 685-1985
TF: 888-685-1011

Mizel Museum of Judaica 400 S Kearney St . . . Denver CO 80224 303-394-9990 394-1119
Web: www.mizelmuseum.org

Molly Brown House 1340 Pennsylvania St . . . Denver CO 80203 303-832-4092 832-2340
Web: www.mollybrown.org

Museo de las Americas 861 Santa Fe Dr. . . . Denver CO 80204 303-571-4401 607-9761
Web: www.museo.org

Museum of Contemporary Art Denver 1485 Delgany . . . Denver CO 80202 303-298-7554 298-7553
Web: www.mcartdenver.org

Museum of Outdoor Arts 1000 Englewood Pkwy Suite 2-230 . . . Englewood CO 80110 303-806-0444 806-0504
Web: www.artcom.com/museums/nv/mr/80111.htm

Rocky Mountain Motorcycle Museum & Hall of Fame
5865 N Nevada Ave . . . Colorado Springs CO 80918 719-487-8005 487-8005

Rocky Mountain Quilt Museum 1111 Washington Ave . . . Golden CO 80401 303-277-0377 215-1636
Web: www.rmqm.org

State Historical Society of Colorado DBA Colorado Historical Society 1300 Broadway . . . Denver CO 80203 303-866-3682 866-5739
Web: www.coloradohistory.org

University of Colorado Museum of Natural History
Henderson Bldg Box 218 UCB University of Colorado . . . Boulder CO 80309 303-492-6892 492-4195
Web: cumuseum.colorado.edu

Vance Kirkland Museum 1311 Pearl St . . . Denver CO 80203 303-832-8576 832-8404
Web: www.vancekirkland.org

Western Museum of Mining & Industry
225 N Gate Blvd. . . . Colorado Springs CO 80921 719-488-0880 488-9261
TF: 800-752-6558 ■ *Web:* www.wmmi.org

Wings Over the Rockies Air & Space Museum
7711 E Academy Blvd . . . Denver CO 80230 303-360-5360 360-5328
Web: www.wingsmuseum.org

Connecticut

Phone | Fax

Allyn Lyman Art Museum 625 Williams St. . . . New London CT 06320 860-443-2545 442-1280
Web: www.lymanallyn.org

American Clock & Watch Museum 100 Maple St . . . Bristol CT 06010 860-583-6070 583-1862
Web: www.clockmuseum.org

Phone | Fax

Baldwin Raymond E Museum of Connecticut History
231 Capitol Ave ... Hartford CT 06106 860-757-6500 757-6533
Web: www.cslib.org/museum.htm
Barnum Museum 820 Main St ... Bridgeport CT 06604 203-331-1104 331-0079
Web: www.barnum-museum.org
Bruce Museum of Arts & Science 1 Museum Dr ... Greenwich CT 06830 203-869-0376 869-0963
Web: www.brucemuseum.org
Catherine Mitchell Museum 967 Academy Hill ... Stratford CT 06615 203-378-0630 378-2562
Connecticut Audubon Society Birdcraft Museum & Sanctuary
314 Unquowa Rd ... Fairfield CT 06824 203-259-0416 259-1344
Web: www.ctaudubon.org
Connecticut Historical Society Museum 1 Elizabeth St ... Hartford CT 06105 860-236-5621 236-2664
Web: www.chs.org
Connecticut State Museum of Natural History
University of Connecticut 2019 Hillside Rd Unit 1023 ... Storrs CT 06269 860-486-4460 486-0827
Web: www.mnh.uconn.edu
Discovery Museum & Planetarium 4450 Park Ave ... Bridgeport CT 06604 203-372-3521 374-1929
Web: www.discoverymuseum.org
Edward E King Museum 840 Main St ... East Hartford CT 06108 860-289-6429 291-9166
Eli Whitney Museum 915 Whitney Ave ... Hamden CT 06517 203-777-1833 777-1229
Web: www.eliwhitney.org
Ethnic Heritage Center
270 Fitch St Southern Connecticut State University ... New Haven CT 06515 203-392-6126 392-5140
Web: www.southernct.edu/departments/ehc
Fairfield Historical Society Museum 636 Old Post Rd ... Fairfield CT 06824 203-259-1598 255-2716
Web: www.fairfieldhistoricalsociety.org
Henry Whitfield State Museum 248 Old Whitfield St ... Guilford CT 06437 203-453-2457 453-7544
Web: www.chc.state.ct.us/whitfieldhouse.htm
Hill-Stead Museum 35 Mountain Rd ... Farmington CT 06032 860-677-4787 677-0174
Web: www.hillstead.org
Housatonic Museum of Art
Housatonic Community College 900 Lafayette Blvd ... Bridgeport CT 06604 203-332-5000 332-5123
Web: www.hcc.commnet.edu
Institute for American Indian Studies 38 Curtis Rd ... Washington Green CT 06793 860-868-0518 868-1649
Web: www.fieldtrip.com/ct
King Edward E Museum 840 Main St ... East Hartford CT 06108 860-289-6429 291-9166
Knights of Columbus Museum 1 State St ... New Haven CT 06511 203-772-2130 773-3000
TF: 800-524-3611 ■ *Web:* www.kofc.org/un/about/museum/index.cfm
Lock Museum of America 230 Main St Rt 6 PO Box 104 ... Terryville CT 06786 860-589-6359 589-6359
Web: www.lockmuseum.com
Lockwood-Mathews Mansion Museum 295 West Ave ... Norwalk CT 06850 203-838-9799 838-1434
Web: www.ohwy.com/ct/l/lomamamu.htm
Lyman Allyn Art Museum 625 Williams St ... New London CT 06320 860-443-2545 442-1280
Web: www.lymanallyn.org
Mark Twain House & Museum 351 Farmington Ave ... Hartford CT 06105 860-247-0998 278-8148
Web: www.marktwainhouse.org
Mattatuck Museum of the Mattatuck Historical Society
144 W Main St ... Waterbury CT 06702 203-753-0381 756-6283
Web: www.mattatuckmuseum.org
Menczer Museum of Medicine & Dentistry
230 Scarborough St ... Hartford CT 06105 860-236-5613 236-8401
Web: library.uchc.edu/hms
Mitchell Catherine Museum 967 Academy Hill ... Stratford CT 06615 203-378-0630 378-2562
Mystic Seaport -- The Museum of America & the Sea
75 Greenmanville Ave PO Box 6000 ... Mystic CT 06355 860-572-0711 572-5328
TF: 888-973-2767 ■ *Web:* www.mysticseaport.org
New Britain Museum of American Art 56 Lexington St ... New Britain CT 06052 860-229-0257 229-3445
Web: www.nbmaa.org
Noah Webster House 227 S Main St ... West Hartford CT 06107 860-521-5362 521-4036
Web: noahwebsterhouse.org
Peabody Museum of Natural History
170 Whitney Ave Yale University ... New Haven CT 06520 203-432-3750 432-9816
Web: www.peabody.yale.edu/
Raymond E Baldwin Museum of Connecticut History
231 Capitol Ave ... Hartford CT 06106 860-757-6500 757-6533
Web: www.cslib.org/museum.htm
Shore Line Trolley Museum 17 River St ... East Haven CT 06512 203-467-6927 467-7635
Web: www.bera.org
Slater Memorial Museum 108 Crescent St ... Norwich CT 06360 860-887-2506 885-0379
Stamford Historical Society Museum 1508 High Ridge Rd ... Stamford CT 06903 203-329-1183 322-1607
Web: www.stamfordhistory.org
Stamford Museum & Nature Center 39 Scofieldtown Rd ... Stamford CT 06903 203-322-1646 322-0408
Web: www.stamfordmuseum.org
Wadsworth Atheneum Museum of Art 600 Main St ... Hartford CT 06103 860-278-2670 527-0803
Web: www.wadsworthatheneum.org
Yale Center for British Art 1080 Chapel St ... New Haven CT 06520 203-432-2800 432-9695
Web: www.yale.edu/ycba
Yale University Art Gallery 1111 Chapel St ... New Haven CT 06520 203-432-0600 432-7159
Web: www.yale.edu/artgallery
Yale University Collection of Musical Instruments
15 Hillhouse Ave ... New Haven CT 06511 203-432-0822 432-8342
Web: www.yale.edu/musicalinstruments

Delaware

Phone | Fax

Anna Hazzard Museum 17 Christian St ... Rehoboth Beach DE 19971 302-226-1119
Barratt's Chapel & Museum 6362 Bay Rd ... Frederica DE 19946 302-335-5544
Web: hometown.aol.com/barratts/home.html
Biggs Sewell C Museum of American Art 406 Federal St ... Dover DE 19901 302-674-2111 674-5133
Web: www.biggsmuseum.org
Delaware Agricultural Museum & Village 866 N DuPont Hwy ... Dover DE 19901 302-734-1618 734-0457
Web: www.agriculturalmuseum.org
Delaware Archaeology Museum 316 S Governor's Ave ... Dover DE 19904 302-739-3260 739-3943
Web: www.destatemuseums.org
Delaware Art Museum 2301 Kentmere Pkwy ... Wilmington DE 19806 302-571-9590 571-0220
Web: www.delart.org
Delaware History Museum 504 N Market St ... Wilmington DE 19801 302-656-0637 655-7844
Web: www.hsd.org/dhm.htm
Delaware Museum of Natural History 4840 Kennett Pike ... Wilmington DE 19807 302-658-9111 658-2610
Web: www.delmnh.org
Dover Air Force Base Air Mobility Command Museum
1301 Heritage Rd ... Dover AFB DE 19902 302-677-5938 677-5940
Web: www.amcmuseum.org
Hagley Museum & Library 298 Buck Rd E ... Greenville DE 19807 302-658-2400 658-0568
Web: www.hagley.lib.de.us
Harrington Museum 108-110 Fleming St ... Harrington DE 19952 302-398-3698 398-9589
Indian River Lifesaving Museum
130 Costal Hwy Indian River Inlet ... Rehoboth Beach DE 19971 302-227-6991 227-6438
Web: indianriverstation.org
Johnson Victrola Museum Bank Ln ... Dover DE 19901 302-739-3262 739-3943
Web: www.destatemuseums.org
Kalmar Nyckel Shipyard & Museum 1124 E 7th St ... Wilmington DE 19801 302-429-7447 429-0350
Web: www.kalnyc.org
Lewes Historical Society 110 Shipcarpenter St ... Lewes DE 19958 302-645-7670 645-2375
Web: www.historiclewes.org

Phone | Fax

Messick Agricultural Museum 325 Walt Messick Rd ... Harrington DE 19952 302-398-3729 398-4732
Mike's Famous Harley-Davidson Museum
2160 New Castle Ave ... New Castle DE 19720 302-658-8800 656-9958
TF: 800-326-6874 ■ *Web:* www.mikesfamous.com
Museum of Small Town Life 316 S Governors Ave ... Dover DE 19901 302-739-4266
Web: www.destatemuseums.org/museums/stl/stl_main.shtml
Old Swedes Church & Hendrickson House Museum
606 Church St ... Wilmington DE 19801 302-652-5629 652-8615
Web: www.oldswedes.org
Rockwood Mansion Park 610 Shipley Rd ... Wilmington DE 19809 302-761-4340 761-4345
Web: www.co.new-castle.de.us
Sewell C Biggs Museum of American Art 406 Federal St ... Dover DE 19901 302-674-2111 674-5133
Web: www.biggsmuseum.org
Winterthur Museum & Country Estate 5105 Kennett Pike ... Winterthur DE 19735 302-888-4600 888-4880
TF: 800-448-3883 ■ *Web:* www.winterthur.org

District of Columbia

Phone | Fax

African-American Civil War Memorial & Museum
1200 U St NW ... Washington DC 20001 202-667-2667 667-6771
Web: www.afroamcivilwar.org
Anacostia Museum (Smithsonian Institution)
1901 Fort Pl SE ... Washington DC 20560 202-287-3306 287-3183
Web: anacostia.si.edu
Arthur M Sackler Gallery (Smithsonian Institution)
1050 Independence Ave SW ... Washington DC 20560 202-633-4880 357-4911
Web: www.asia.si.edu
B'nai B'rith Klutznick National Jewish Museum
2020 K St NW ... Washington DC 20006 202-857-6583 857-6601
Web: www.bnaibrith.org
Cathedral Church of Saint Peter & Saint Paul
3101 Wisconsin Ave NW ... Washington DC 20016 202-537-6200
TF: 800-622-6304 ■ *Web:* www.cathedral.org/cathedral
City Museum of Washington DC
801 K St NW Historical Society of Washington DC ... Washington DC 20001 202-383-1800 383-1872
Web: www.citymuseumdc.org
Corcoran Gallery of Art 500 17th St NW ... Washington DC 20006 202-639-1700 639-1768
Web: www.corcoran.org
DAR Museum 1776 D St NW ... Washington DC 20006 202-879-3241 628-0820
Web: www.dar.org/museum
Decatur House Museum 1610 H St NW ... Washington DC 20006 202-842-0920 842-0030
Web: www.decaturhouse.org
Dumbarton Oaks 1703 32nd St NW ... Washington DC 20007 202-339-6401 339-6419
Web: www.doaks.org
Frederick Douglass Museum & Hall of Fame for Caring Americans 320 A St NE ... Washington DC 20002 202-544-6130
Web: www.caringinstitute.org
Freer Gallery of Art (Smithsonian Institution)
1050 Independence Ave SW ... Washington DC 20560 202-633-4880 357-4911
Web: www.asia.si.edu
Hillwood Museum & Gardens 4155 Linnean Ave NW ... Washington DC 20008 202-686-8500 966-7846
TF: 877-445-5966 ■ *Web:* www.hillwoodmuseum.org
Hirshhorn Museum & Sculpture Garden (Smithsonian Institution) Independence Ave & 7th St SW ... Washington DC 20560 202-633-4674 786-2682
Web: hirshhorn.si.edu
International Spy Museum 800 F St NW ... Washington DC 20004 202-393-7798 393-7797
TF: 866-779-6873 ■ *Web:* www.spymuseum.org
Kreeger Museum 2401 Foxhall Rd NW ... Washington DC 20007 202-338-3552 337-3051
TF: 877-337-3050 ■ *Web:* www.kreegermuseum.com
Lillian & Albert Small Jewish Museum 701 3rd St NW ... Washington DC 20001 202-789-0900 789-0485
Web: www.loc.gov/rr/main/religion/jhw.html
Marian Koshland Science Museum 6th & 'E' Sts NW ... Washington DC 20001 202-334-1201 334-1548
TF: 888-567-4526 ■ *Web:* www.koshland-science-museum.org
National Air & Space Museum (Smithsonian Institution)
Independence Ave & 6th St SW ... Washington DC 20560 202-633-1000
Web: www.nasm.si.edu/museum/udvarhazy
National Building Museum 401 F St NW ... Washington DC 20001 202-272-2448 272-2564
Web: www.nbm.org
National Gallery of Art 6th St & Constitution Ave NW ... Washington DC 20565 202-737-4215 842-2356
Web: www.nga.gov
National Geographic Society Explorers Hall
1145 17th St NW ... Washington DC 20036 202-857-7589 857-5530
TF: 800-647-5463 ■ *Web:* www.nationalgeographic.com/explorer
National Museum of African Art (Smithsonian Institution)
950 Independence Ave SW MRC 708 ... Washington DC 20560 202-633-4600 357-4879
Web: www.nmafa.si.edu
National Museum of American History (Smithsonian Institution) 14th St & Constitution Ave NW ... Washington DC 20560 202-633-1000 633-8053*
**Fax:* PR ■ *Web:* americanhistory.si.edu
National Museum of the American Indian (Smithsonian Institution) 4th St & Independence Ave SW ... Washington DC 20004 202-633-1000
Web: www.nmai.si.edu
National Museum of American Jewish Military History (JWV-NMI) 1811 R St NW ... Washington DC 20009 202-265-6280 462-3192
Web: www.nmajmh.org
National Museum of Health & Medicine
6900 Georgia Ave NW ... Washington DC 20306 202-782-2200 782-3573
Web: www.nmhm.washingtondc.museum
National Museum of Natural History (Smithsonian Institution)
10th St & Constitution Ave NW ... Washington DC 20560 202-633-2664 357-4779
Web: www.mnh.si.edu/
National Museum of Women in the Arts
1250 New York Ave NW ... Washington DC 20005 202-783-5000 393-3234
TF: 800-222-7270 ■ *Web:* www.nmwa.org
National Postal Museum (Smithsonian Institution)
2 Massachusetts Ave NE ... Washington DC 20002 202-633-5555 633-9393
Web: www.postalmuseum.si.edu/
Navy Museum
805 Kidder Breese St SE Washington Navy Yard ... Washington DC 20374 202-433-4882 433-8200
Web: www.history.navy.mil
Octagon Museum 1799 New York Ave NW ... Washington DC 20006 202-638-3221 626-7420
Web: www.archfoundation.org/octagon/
Phillips Collection 1600 21st St NW ... Washington DC 20009 202-387-2151 387-2436
Web: www.phillipscollection.org
Pope John Paul II Cultural Center 3900 Harewood Rd NE ... Washington DC 20017 202-635-5400 635-5411
Web: www.jp2cc.org
Renwick Gallery of the Smithsonian American Art Museum
1661 Pennsylvania Ave NW ... Washington DC 20006 202-633-2850 786-2810
Web: americanart.si.edu/renwick
Sackler Arthur M Gallery (Smithsonian Institution)
1050 Independence Ave SW ... Washington DC 20560 202-633-4880 357-4911
Web: www.asia.si.edu
Small Lillian & Albert Jewish Museum 701 3rd St NW ... Washington DC 20001 202-789-0900 789-0485
Web: www.loc.gov/rr/main/religion/jhw.html

District of Columbia (Cont'd)

Phone Fax

Smithsonian Institution
SI Bldg Rm 153 MRC 010 PO Box 37012 ... Washington DC 20113 202-633-1000
Web: www.si.edu
Textile Museum 2320 'S' St NW ... Washington DC 20008 202-667-0441 483-0994
Web: www.textilemuseum.org
US Holocaust Memorial Museum
100 Raoul Wallenburg Pl SW ... Washington DC 20024 202-488-0400 488-2613
Web: www.ushmm.org
Woodrow Wilson House Museum 2340 'S' St NW ... Washington DC 20008 202-387-4062 483-1466
Web: www.woodrowwilsonhouse.org

Florida

Phone Fax

African American Museum of the Arts 325 S Clara Ave ... DeLand FL 32721 386-736-4004 736-4088
Web: www.africanmuseumdeland.org
Alexander Brest Museum
2800 University Blvd N Jacksonville University ... Jacksonville FL 32211 904-256-7371 256-7375
Amelia Island Museum of History 233 S 3rd St ... Fernandina Beach FL 32034 904-261-7378 261-9701
Web: www.ameliaislandmuseumofhistory.org
American Police Hall of Fame & Museum 6350 Horizon Dr ... Titusville FL 32780 321-264-0911 264-0033
Web: www.aphf.org
American Victory Mariners Memorial & Museum Ship
705 Channelside Dr ... Tampa FL 33602 813-228-8766 228-8769
Web: www.americanvictory.org
Audubon House & Tropical Garden 205 Whitehead St ... Key West FL 33040 305-294-2116 294-4513
Web: www.audubonhouse.com
Bailey Matthews Shell Museum
3075 Sanibel-Captiva Rd PO Box 1580 ... Sanibel FL 33957 239-395-2233 395-6706
TF: 888-679-6450 ■ *Web:* www.shellmuseum.org
Bass Museum of Art 2121 Park Ave ... Miami Beach FL 33139 305-673-7530 673-7062
Web: www.bassmuseum.org
Black Archives Research Center & Museum
Florida A & M University Carnegie Center ... Tallahassee FL 32307 850-599-3020 561-2604
Boca Raton Museum of Art 501 Plaza Real Mizner Park ... Boca Raton FL 33432 561-392-2500 391-6410
Web: www.bocamuseum.org
Bonnet House Museum & Garden 900 N Birch Rd ... Fort Lauderdale FL 33304 954-563-5393 561-4174
Web: www.bonnethouse.org
Brest Alexander Museum
2800 University Blvd N Jacksonville University ... Jacksonville FL 32211 904-256-7371 256-7375
Brogan Mary Museum of Art & Science 350 S Duval St ... Tallahassee FL 32301 850-513-0700 513-0143
Web: www.thebrogan.org
Broward County Historical Commission 151 SW 2nd St ... Fort Lauderdale FL 33301 954-765-4670 765-4437
Web: www.broward.org/history/
Casements The 25 Riverside Dr ... Ormond Beach FL 32176 386-676-3216 676-3363
Cason Cottage Museum 5 NE 1st St ... Delray Beach FL 33444 561-243-0223 243-6884
Charles Hosmer Morse Museum of American Art
445 N Park Ave ... Winter Park FL 32789 407-645-5311 647-1284
Web: www.morsemuseum.org
Collier County Museum 3301 Tamiami Trail E ... Naples FL 34112 239-774-8476 774-8580
Web: www.colliermuseum.com
Colonial Spanish Quarter 29 Saint George St ... Saint Augustine FL 32084 904-825-6830 825-6874
Web: www.historicstaugustine.com
Cornell Fine Arts Museum 1000 Holt Ave ... Winter Park FL 32789 407-646-2526 646-2524
Web: www.rollins.edu/cfam
Crowley Museum & Nature Center 16405 Myakka Rd ... Sarasota FL 34240 941-322-1000 322-1000
Web: www.CrowleyMuseumNatureCtr.org
Cummer Museum of Art & Gardens 829 Riverside Ave ... Jacksonville FL 32204 904-356-6857 353-4101
Web: www.cummer.org
Dali Salvador Museum 1000 3rd St S ... Saint Petersburg FL 33701 727-823-3767 894-6068
TF: 800-442-3254 ■ *Web:* www.salvadordalimuseum.org
East Martello Museum & Gallery 3501 S Roosevelt Blvd ... Key West FL 33040 305-296-3913
Web: www.kwahs.com/martello.htm
Flagler Museum 1 Whitehall Way ... Palm Beach FL 33480 561-655-2833 655-2826
Web: www.flaglermuseum.us
Florida Agricultural Museum 7900 Old Kings Rd ... Palm Coast FL 32137 386-446-7630 446-7631
Florida Heritage Museum 167 San Marco Ave ... Saint Augustine FL 32084 904-829-3800 829-6678
TF: 800-397-4071
Florida Holocaust Museum 55 5th St S ... Saint Petersburg FL 33701 727-820-0100 821-8435
TF: 800-960-7448 ■ *Web:* www.flholocaustmuseum.org
Florida International Museum
244 2nd Ave N Saint Petersburg College
Downtown Center ... Saint Petersburg FL 33701 727-341-7900 341-7908
Web: www.floridamuseum.org/
Florida Museum of Natural History
Museum Rd & Newell Dr PO Box 117800 ... Gainesville FL 32611 352-392-1721 392-8783
Web: www.flmnh.ufl.edu
Florida State University Museum of Fine Arts
W Tennessee & Copeland Sts Fine Arts Bldg ... Tallahassee FL 32306 850-644-6836 644-7229
Forest Capital State Museum 204 Forest Park Dr ... Perry FL 32348 850-584-3227 584-3488
Fort Lauderdale Antique Car Museum
1527 SW 1st Ave ... Fort Lauderdale FL 33315 954-779-7300 779-2501
Web: www.antiquecarmuseum.org
Fort Lauderdale Historical Society 219 SW 2nd Ave ... Fort Lauderdale FL 33301 954-463-4431 523-6228
Fort Lauderdale Museum of Art 1 E Las Olas Blvd ... Fort Lauderdale FL 33301 954-525-5500 524-6011
Web: www.museumofart.org
Fred Dana Marsh Museum
2099 N Beach St Tomoka State Park ... Ormond Beach FL 32174 386-676-4050 676-4060
Frost Art Museum at Florida International University
SW 8th St & 107th Ave University Park PC110 ... Miami FL 33199 305-348-2890 348-2762
Web: www.fiu.edu/~museum
Gillespie Museum of Minerals 234 E Michigan Ave Hewit Pl ... DeLand FL 32724 386-822-7330 822-7328
Web: www.gillespiemuseum.stetson.edu
Gold Coast Railroad Museum 12450 SW 152nd St ... Miami FL 33177 305-253-0063 233-4641
TF: 888-608-7246 ■ *Web:* www.goldcoast-railroad.org
Goodwood Museum & Gardens 1600 Miccosukee Rd ... Tallahassee FL 32308 850-877-4202 877-3090
Web: www.goodwoodmuseum.org
Government House Museum 48 King St ... Saint Augustine FL 32084 904-825-5033 825-5096
Gulf Beaches Historical Museum 115 10th Ave ... Saint Pete Beach FL 33706 727-552-1610 363-6704
Gulf Coast Museum of Art 12211 Walsingham Rd ... Largo FL 33778 727-518-6833 518-1852
Web: www.gulfcoastmuseum.org
Halifax Historical Museum 252 S Beach St ... Daytona Beach FL 32114 386-255-6976 255-7605
Web: www.halifaxhistorical.org
Harry S Truman's Little White House Museum
111 Front St Truman Annex ... Key West FL 33040 305-294-9911 294-9988
Web: www.trumanlittlewhitehouse.com
Henry B Plant Museum 401 W Kennedy Blvd ... Tampa FL 33606 813-254-1891 258-7272
Web: www.plantmuseum.com
Henry Morrison Flagler Museum 1 Whitehall Way ... Palm Beach FL 33480 561-655-2833 655-2826
Web: www.flaglermuseum.us
Heritage House Museum & Robert Frost Cottage
410 Caroline St ... Key West FL 33040 305-296-3573 292-5723
Web: www.heritagehousemuseum.org

Phone Fax

Historical Museum of Southern Florida 101 W Flagler St ... Miami FL 33130 305-375-1492 375-1609
Web: www.historical-museum.org
Indian Temple Mound Museum
139 Miracle Strip Pkwy SE ... Fort Walton Beach FL 32548 850-833-9595 833-9675
Web: www.fwb.org
Jacksonville Maritime Museum 1015 Museum Cir Unit 2 ... Jacksonville FL 32207 904-398-9011 398-7248
Web: www.jaxmarmus.com
Jacksonville Museum of Modern Art 333 N Laura St ... Jacksonville FL 32202 904-366-6911 366-6901
Web: www.jmoma.org
Jewish Museum of Florida 301 Washington Ave ... Miami Beach FL 33139 305-672-5044 672-5933
Web: www.jewishmuseum.com
John G Riley Center/Museum of African American History & Culture 419 E Jefferson St ... Tallahassee FL 32301 850-681-7881 681-7000
Web: www.rileymuseum.org
John & Mable Ringling Museum of Art 5401 Bay Shore Rd ... Sarasota FL 34243 941-359-5700 359-5745
Web: www.ringling.org
Karpeles Manuscript Library Museum 101 W 1st St ... Jacksonville FL 32206 904-356-2992 356-4338
Web: www.rain.org/~karpeles/jax.html
Key West Lighthouse & Keepers Quarters Museum
938 Whitehead St ... Key West FL 33040 305-294-0012 294-0012
Web: www.kwahs.com/lighthouse.htm
Key West Museum of Art & History at the Custom House
281 Front St ... Key West FL 33040 305-295-6616 295-6649
Web: www.kwahs.com
Key West Shipwreck Historeum Museum 1 Whitehead St ... Key West FL 33040 305-292-8990 292-1617
Web: www.shipwreckhistoreum.com
Kingsley Plantation 11676 Palmetto Ave ... Jacksonville FL 32226 904-251-3537 251-3577
Knott House Museum 301 E Park Ave ... Tallahassee FL 32301 850-922-2459 413-7261
Web: www.flheritage.com/museum/sites/knotthouse/
Lawrence E Will Museum 530 S Main St ... Belle Glade FL 33430 561-996-3453 996-2304
Lightner Museum 75 King St ... Saint Augustine FL 32084 904-824-2874 824-2712
Web: www.lightnermuseum.org
Lowe Art Museum University of Miami 1301 Stanford Dr ... Coral Gables FL 33124 305-284-3535 284-2024
Web: www.miami.edu/lowe/
Loxahatchee River Historical Museum
805 N US Hwy 1 Burt Reynolds Park ... Jupiter FL 33477 561-747-6639 575-3292
Web: www.lrhs.org
Marsh Fred Dana Museum
2099 N Beach St Tomoka State Park ... Ormond Beach FL 32174 386-676-4050 676-4060
Mary Brogan Museum of Art & Science 350 S Duval St ... Tallahassee FL 32301 850-513-0700 513-0143
Web: www.thebrogan.org
Mel Fisher Maritime Museum 200 Greene St ... Key West FL 33040 305-294-2633 294-5671
Web: www.melfisher.org
Mennello Museum of American Folk Art 900 E Princeton St ... Orlando FL 32803 407-246-4278 246-4329
Web: www.mennellomuseum.com
Miami Art Museum 101 W Flagler St ... Miami FL 33130 305-375-3000 375-1725
Web: www.miamiartmuseum.org
Miami Museum of Science & Planetarium 3280 S Miami Ave ... Miami FL 33129 305-646-4200 646-4300
Web: www.miamisci.org
Morikami Museum & Japanese Gardens
4000 Morikami Park Rd ... Delray Beach FL 33446 561-495-0233 499-2557
Web: www.morikami.org
Morse Charles Hosmer Museum of American Art
445 N Park Ave ... Winter Park FL 32789 407-645-5311 647-1284
Web: www.morsemuseum.org
Museum of the Americas 2500 NW 79th Ave Suite 104 ... Doral FL 33122 305-599-8089
Web: www.museumamericas.org
Museum of Arts & Sciences 352 S Nova Rd ... Daytona Beach FL 32114 386-255-0285 255-5040
Web: www.moas.org
Museum of Contemporary Art 770 NE 125th St ... North Miami FL 33161 305-893-6211 891-1472
Web: www.mocanomi.com
Museum of Discovery & Science 401 SW 2nd St ... Fort Lauderdale FL 33312 954-467-6637 467-0046
Web: www.mods.org
Museum of the Everglades 105 W Broadway PO Box 8 ... Everglades City FL 34139 239-695-0008 695-0036
Museum of Fine Arts 255 Beach Dr NE ... Saint Petersburg FL 33701 727-896-2667 894-4638
Web: www.fine-arts.org
Museum of Florida History
500 S Bronough St RA Gray Bldg ... Tallahassee FL 32399 850-488-1484 245-6433
Web: dhr.dos.state.fl.us/museum
Museum of Science & History of Jacksonville
1025 Museum Cir ... Jacksonville FL 32207 904-396-7062 396-5799
Web: www.themosh.org
Museum of Science & Industry 4801 E Fowler Ave ... Tampa FL 33617 813-987-6300 987-6310
TF: 800-995-6674 ■ *Web:* www.mosi.org
Museum of Southern History 4304 Herschel St ... Jacksonville FL 32210 904-388-3574
Web: www.scv-kirby-smith.org/museum_history.htm
My Jewish Discovery Place Children's Museum
6501 W Sunrise Blvd ... Fort Lauderdale FL 33313 954-792-6700 792-4839
Web: www.sorefjcc.org
Naples Museum of Art 5833 Pelican Bay Blvd ... Naples FL 34108 239-597-1111 597-8163
TF: 800-597-1900 ■ *Web:* www.thephil.org
National Museum of Naval Aviation
1750 Radford Blvd Suite C ... Pensacola FL 32508 850-452-3604 452-3296
TF: 800-327-5002 ■ *Web:* www.naval-air.org
Norton Museum of Art 1451 S Olive Ave ... West Palm Beach FL 33401 561-832-5194 659-4689
Web: www.norton.org
Old Dillard Museum 1009 NW 4th St ... Fort Lauderdale FL 33311 754-322-8828 322-8824
Web: www.flamuseums.org/fam/flamuseums
Old Florida Museum 254-D San Marco Ave ... Saint Augustine FL 32084 904-824-8874 824-6848
TF: 800-813-3208 ■ *Web:* www.oldfloridamuseum.com
Old Fort Lauderdale Village & Museum
231 SW 2nd Ave ... Fort Lauderdale FL 33301 954-463-4431 523-6228
Web: www.oldfortlauderdale.org
Old Jail Museum 167 San Marco Ave ... Saint Augustine FL 32084 904-829-3800 829-6678
TF: 800-397-4071
Orange County Regional History Center 65 E Central Blvd ... Orlando FL 32801 407-836-8500 836-8550
TF: 800-965-2030 ■ *Web:* www.thehistorycenter.org
Orlando Museum of Art 2416 N Mills Ave ... Orlando FL 32803 407-896-4231 896-9920
Web: omart.org
Orlando Science Center 777 E Princeton St ... Orlando FL 32803 407-514-2000 514-2277
TF: 888-672-4386 ■ *Web:* www.osc.org
Ormond Memorial Art Museum & Gardens
78 E Granada Blvd ... Ormond Beach FL 32176 386-676-3347 676-3244
Web: www.ormondartmuseum.org
Palm Beach Photographic Centre 55 NE 2nd Ave ... Delray Beach FL 33444 561-276-9797 276-1932
Web: www.workshop.org
Pena-Peck House Museum 143 Saint George St ... Saint Augustine FL 32084 904-829-5064 829-6210
Pensacola Museum of Art 407 S Jefferson St ... Pensacola FL 32502 850-432-6247 469-1532
Web: www.pensacolamuseumofart.org
Pinellas County Heritage Village 11909 125th St N ... Largo FL 33774 727-582-2123 582-2455
Web: www.pinellascounty.org/heritage
Plant Henry B Museum 401 W Kennedy Blvd ... Tampa FL 33606 813-254-1891 258-7272
Web: www.plantmuseum.com
Potter's Wax Museum 17 King St ... Saint Augustine FL 32084 904-829-9056 824-3434
TF: 800-584-4781 ■ *Web:* www.potterswax.com
Ringling John & Mable Museum of Art 5401 Bay Shore Rd ... Sarasota FL 34243 941-359-5700 359-5745
Web: www.ringling.org

				Phone	Fax
Ripley's Believe It or Not! Museum 19 San Marco Ave	Saint Augustine	FL	32084	904-824-1606	829-1790
Web: www.staugustine-ripleys.com					
Ripley's Believe It or Not! Orlando Odditorium 8201 International Dr	Orlando	FL	32819	407-363-4418	345-0803
Web: www.ripleysorlando.com					
Ritz Theatre & La Villa Museum 829 N Davis St	Jacksonville	FL	32202	904-632-5555	632-5553
Saint Augustine Lighthouse & Museum 81 Lighthouse Ave	Saint Augustine	FL	32080	904-829-0745	808-1248
Web: www.staugustinelighthouse.com					
Saint Petersburg Museum of History 335 2nd Ave NE	Saint Petersburg	FL	33701	727-894-1052	823-7276
Web: www.stpetemuseumofhistory.org					
Salvador Dali Museum 1000 3rd St S	Saint Petersburg	FL	33701	727-823-3767	894-6068
TF: 800-442-3254 ■ *Web:* www.salvadordalimuseum.org					
Science Center of Pinellas County 7701 22nd Ave N	Saint Petersburg	FL	33710	727-384-0027	343-5729
Web: www.sciencecenterofpinellas.com					
South Florida Museum 201 10th St W	Bradenton	FL	34205	941-746-4131	747-2556
Web: www.southfloridamuseum.org					
South Florida Science Museum 4801 Dreher Trail N	West Palm Beach	FL	33405	561-832-1988	833-0551
Web: www.sfsm.org					
Southeast Museum of Photography 1200 W International Speedway Blvd Daytona Beach Community College Bldg 100	Daytona Beach	FL	32114	386-506-4475	506-4487
Web: www.smponline.org					
Spanish Military Hospital Museum 3 Aviles St	Saint Augustine	FL	32084	904-827-0807	827-0590
TF: 800-597-7177 ■ *Web:* www.ancientcitytours.net/spanish_hospital.html					
Stranahan House 335 SE 6th Ave	Fort Lauderdale	FL	33301	954-524-4736	525-2838
Web: www.stranahanhouse.com					
Tallahassee Antique Car Museum 6800 Mahan Dr	Tallahassee	FL	32308	850-942-0137	576-8500
Web: www.tacm.com					
Tallahassee Museum of History & Natural Science 3945 Museum Dr	Tallahassee	FL	32310	850-576-1636	574-8243
Web: www.tallahasseemuseum.org					
Tampa Bay History Center 225 S Franklin St	Tampa	FL	33602	813-228-0097	223-7021
Web: www.tampabayhistorycenter.org					
Tampa Museum of Art 2306 N Howard Ave	Tampa	FL	33607	813-274-8130	274-8732
Web: www.tampagov.net/dept_Museum/					
University Gallery University of Florida 13th St & 4th Ave	Gainesville	FL	32611	352-392-0201	846-0266
Web: www.arts.ufl.edu/galleries					
University of South Florida Contemporary Art Museum 4202 E Fowler Ave Bldg CAM101	Tampa	FL	33620	813-974-2849	974-5130
Web: cam.arts.usf.edu					
Vizcaya Museum & Gardens 3251 S Miami Ave	Miami	FL	33129	305-250-9133	285-2004
Web: www.vizcayamuseum.org					
Will Lawrence E Museum 530 S Main St	Belle Glade	FL	33430	561-996-3453	996-2304
Wings Over Miami Aircraft Museum 14710 SW 128th St Tamiami Executive Airport	Miami	FL	33196	305-233-5197	232-4134
Web: www.wingsovermiami.com					
Wolfsonian Museum 1001 Washington Ave	Miami Beach	FL	33139	305-531-1001	531-2133
Web: www.wolfsonian.fiu.edu					
World Chess Hall of Fame & Museum 13755 SW 119th Ave	Miami	FL	33186	786-242-4255	477-9516*
**Fax Area Code:* 305 ■ *Web:* www.chessmuseum.org					
Wrecker's Museum 322 Duval St	Key West	FL	33040	305-294-9502	294-9501
Ximenez-Fatio House Museum 20 Aviles St	Saint Augustine	FL	32084	904-829-3575	829-3445
Web: www.ximenezfatiohouse.org					
Ybor City Museum State Park 1818 9th Ave	Tampa	FL	33605	813-247-6323	
Web: www.floridastateparks.org/Yborcity					

Georgia

				Phone	Fax
African-American Panoramic Experience Museum (APEX) 135 Auburn Ave NE	Atlanta	GA	30303	404-521-2739	523-3248
Web: www.apexmuseum.org					
APEX (African-American Panoramic Experience Museum) 135 Auburn Ave NE	Atlanta	GA	30303	404-521-2739	523-3248
Web: www.apexmuseum.org					
Atlanta History Center 130 W Paces Ferry Rd	Atlanta	GA	30305	404-814-4000	814-2041
Web: www.atlantahistorycenter.com					
Augusta Museum of History 560 Reynolds St	Augusta	GA	30901	706-722-8454	724-5192
Web: www.augustamuseum.org					
Beach Institute African American Cultural Center 502 E Harris St	Savannah	GA	31401	912-234-8000	234-8001
Web: www.kingtisdell.org/beachinst.html					
BellSouth Telephone Museum 675 W Peachtree St NE BellSouth Center	Atlanta	GA	30375	404-223-3661	
Web: www.bellsouthgapioneers.org					
Breman William Jewish Heritage Museum 1440 Spring St NW	Atlanta	GA	30309	678-222-3700	881-4009*
**Fax Area Code:* 404 ■ *Web:* www.thebreman.org					
Cannonball House & Confederate Museum 856 Mulberry St	Macon	GA	31201	478-745-5982	745-5944
Web: www.cannonballhouse.org					
Carlos Michael C Museum 571 S Kilgo St	Atlanta	GA	30322	404-727-4282	727-4292
Web: www.carlos.emory.edu					
Challenger Learning Center 701 Front Ave Coca-Cola Space Science Center	Columbus	GA	31901	706-649-1470	649-1478
Web: www.ccssc.org/clc.htm					
Coca-Cola Space Science Center 701 Front Ave	Columbus	GA	31901	706-649-1470	649-1478
Web: www.ccssc.org					
Columbus Museum 1251 Wynnton Rd	Columbus	GA	31906	706-748-2562	748-2570
Web: www.columbusmuseum.com					
Davenport House Museum 324 E State St	Savannah	GA	31401	912-236-8097	233-7938
Web: www.davenportsavga.com					
Fernbank Museum of Natural History 767 Clifton Rd NE	Atlanta	GA	30307	404-378-0127	370-8087
Web: www.fernbank.edu/museum/index.html					
Fernbank Science Center 156 Heaton Park Dr NE	Atlanta	GA	30307	678-874-7102	874-7110
Web: fsc.fernbank.edu					
Georgia Museum of Art 90 Carlton St University of Georgia	Athens	GA	30602	706-542-4662	542-1051
Web: www.uga.edu/gamuseum/					
Georgia Music Hall of Fame 200 ML King Jr Blvd	Macon	GA	31202	478-751-3334	751-3100
TF: 888-427-6257 ■ *Web:* www.gamusichall.com					
Gertrude Herbert Institute of Art 506 Telfair St	Augusta	GA	30901	706-722-5495	722-3670
Web: www.ghia.org					
Gilbert Ralph Mark Civil Rights Museum 460 ML King Jr Blvd	Savannah	GA	31401	912-231-8900	234-2577
Web: www.savannahcivilrightsmuseum.com					
Goethe Institut Atlanta/German Cultural Center 1197 Peachtree St NE	Atlanta	GA	30361	404-892-2388	892-3832
Web: www.goethe.de/uk/atl/					
High Museum of Art 1280 Peachtree St NE	Atlanta	GA	30309	404-733-4200	733-4502
Web: www.high.org					
Jimmy Carter Library & Museum 441 Freedom Pkwy	Atlanta	GA	30307	404-865-7100	865-7102
Web: www.jimmycarterlibrary.org					
King-Tisdell Cottage Black History Museum 514 E Huntingdon St	Savannah	GA	31401	912-234-8000	234-8001
Web: www.kingtisdell.org					
Lucy Craft Laney Museum 1116 Phillips St	Augusta	GA	30901	706-724-3576	724-3576
Web: www.lucycraftlaneymuseum.com					
Michael C Carlos Museum 571 S Kilgo St	Atlanta	GA	30322	404-727-4282	727-4292
Web: www.carlos.emory.edu					
Mighty Eighth Airforce Heritage Museum 175 Bourne Ave	Pooler	GA	31322	912-748-8888	748-0209
Web: www.mightyeighth.org					
Morris Museum of Art 1 10th St	Augusta	GA	30901	706-724-7501	724-7612
Web: www.themorris.org					
Museum of Arts & Sciences 4182 Forsyth Rd	Macon	GA	31210	478-477-3232	477-3251
Web: www.masmacon.com					
Museum of Design Atlanta 285 Peachtree Center Ave	Atlanta	GA	30303	404-688-2467	521-9311
Web: www.museumofdesign.org					
National Infantry Museum Baltzell Ave Bldg 396	Fort Benning	GA	31905	706-545-2958	545-5158
Web: www.benningmwr.com/museum.cfm					
National Museum of Patriotism 1405 Spring St NW	Atlanta	GA	30309	404-875-0691	875-0415
TF: 877-276-1692 ■ *Web:* www.museumofpatriotism.org					
National Science Center Fort Discovery 1 7th St	Augusta	GA	30901	706-821-0200	821-0269
TF: 800-325-5445 ■ *Web:* www.nscdiscovery.org					
Oak Hill & Martha Berry Museum PO Box 490189	Mount Berry	GA	30149	706-291-1883	802-0902
Web: www.berry.edu/oakhill/index.asp					
Oglethorpe University Museum of Art 4484 Peachtree Rd NE	Atlanta	GA	30319	404-364-8555	364-8556
Web: museum.oglethorpe.edu					
Port Columbus National Civil War Naval Museum 1002 Victory Dr	Port Columbus	GA	31901	706-327-9798	324-7225
Web: www.portcolumbus.org					
Ralph Mark Gilbert Civil Rights Museum 460 ML King Jr Blvd	Savannah	GA	31401	912-231-8900	234-2577
Web: www.savannahcivilrightsmuseum.com					
Robert C Williams American Museum of Papermaking 500 10th St NW	Atlanta	GA	30318	404-894-7840	894-4778
TF: 800-558-6611 ■ *Web:* ipst.gatech.edu/amp/					
Savannah History Museum 303 ML King Jr Blvd	Savannah	GA	31401	912-238-1779	651-6827
Web: www.chsgeorgia.org					
Ships of the Sea Maritime Museum 41 ML King Jr Blvd	Savannah	GA	31401	912-232-1511	234-7363
Web: www.shipsofthesea.org					
Telfair Museum of Art 121 Barnard St	Savannah	GA	31401	912-232-1177	790-8803
Web: www.telfair.org					
Tubman African American Museum 340 Walnut St	Macon	GA	31201	478-743-8544	743-9063
Web: www.tubmanmuseum.com					
Tybee Island Lighthouse & Museum 30 Meddin Dr	Tybee Island	GA	31328	912-786-5801	786-6538
Web: www.tybeelighthouse.org					
Westville 1850's Village 1 ML King Blvd	Lumpkin	GA	31815	229-838-6310	838-4000
TF: 888-733-1850 ■ *Web:* www.westville.org					
William Breman Jewish Heritage Museum 1440 Spring St NW	Atlanta	GA	30309	678-222-3700	881-4009*
**Fax Area Code:* 404 ■ *Web:* www.thebreman.org					
Williams Robert C American Museum of Papermaking 500 10th St NW	Atlanta	GA	30318	404-894-7840	894-4778
TF: 800-558-6611 ■ *Web:* ipst.gatech.edu/amp/					
World of Coca-Cola Atlanta 55 ML King Jr Dr	Atlanta	GA	30303	404-676-5151	676-5432
Web: www.woccatlanta.com					
Wren's Nest House Museum 1050 Ralph David Abernathy Blvd SW	Atlanta	GA	30310	404-753-7735	753-8535

Hawaii

				Phone	Fax
Arizona Memorial Museum Assn 1 Arizona Memorial Pl	Honolulu	HI	96818	808-422-5664	483-8608
TF: 888-485-1941 ■ *Web:* www.arizonamemorial.org					
Bishop Museum 1525 Bernice St	Honolulu	HI	96817	808-847-3511	848-4146*
**Fax:* Hum Res ■ *Web:* www.bishopmuseum.org					
Contemporary Museum 2411 Makiki Heights Dr	Honolulu	HI	96822	808-526-0232	536-5973
Web: www.tcmhi.org					
Hawaii's Plantation Village 94-695 Waipahu St	Waipahu	HI	96797	808-677-0110	676-6727
Web: www.hawaiiplantationvillage.org					
Honolulu Academy of Arts 900 S Beretania St	Honolulu	HI	96814	808-532-8700	532-8787
Web: www.honoluluacademy.org					
Iolani Palace King & Richards Sts	Honolulu	HI	96813	808-522-0832	532-1051
Web: www.iolanipalace.org					
Japanese Cultural Center of Hawaii 2454 S Beretania St	Honolulu	HI	96826	808-945-7633	944-1123
Web: www.jcch.com					
Judiciary History Center 417 S King St	Honolulu	HI	96813	808-539-4999	539-4996
Lyman House Memorial Museum 276 Haili St	Hilo	HI	96720	808-935-5021	969-7685
Web: www.lymanmuseum.org					
Mission Houses Museum 553 S King St	Honolulu	HI	96813	808-531-0481	545-2280
Web: www.missionhouses.org					
Polynesian Cultural Center 55-370 Kamehameha Hwy	Laie	HI	96762	808-293-3000	293-3027
TF: 800-367-7060 ■ *Web:* www.polynesia.com					
Tropic Lightning Museum Schofield Barracks Bldg 361 Waianae Ave	Honolulu	HI	96857	808-655-0438	655-8301
Web: www.25idl.army.mil					
US Army Museum of Hawaii Fort DeRussy Kalia Rd Bldg 32	Honolulu	HI	96830	808-438-2821	438-2819
Web: www.hiarmymuseumsoc.org					
USS Bowfin Submarine Museum & Park 11 Arizona Memorial Dr	Honolulu	HI	96818	808-423-1341	422-5201
Web: www.bowfin.org					

Idaho

				Phone	Fax
Bannock County Historical Museum 3000 Alvord Loop	Pocatello	ID	83201	208-233-0434	
Basque Museum & Cultural Center 611 Grove St	Boise	ID	83702	208-343-2671	336-4801
Web: www.basquemuseum.com					
Boise Art Museum 670 Julia Davis Dr	Boise	ID	83702	208-345-8330	345-2247
Web: www.boiseartmuseum.org					
Discovery Center of Idaho 131 Myrtle St	Boise	ID	83702	208-343-9895	343-0105
Web: www.dcidaho.com					
Idaho Black History Museum 508 Julia Davis Dr	Boise	ID	83702	208-433-0017	433-0048
Web: www.ibhm.org					
Idaho Historical Museum 610 N Julia Davis Dr	Boise	ID	83702	208-334-2120	334-4059
TF: 877-653-4367 ■ *Web:* www.idahohistory.net/museum.html					
Idaho Military History Museum 4748 Lindbergh St Bldg 924	Boise	ID	83705	208-422-4841	422-4837
Web: inghro.state.id.us/museum					
Idaho Museum of Natural History Idaho State University 921 S 8th Ave Stop 8096	Pocatello	ID	83209	208-282-2262	282-5893
Museum of North Idaho 115 NW Blvd PO Box 812	Coeur d'Alene	ID	83816	208-664-3448	664-3448
Web: www.museumni.org					
Nez Perce County Historical Society & Museum 0306 3rd St	Lewiston	ID	83501	208-743-2535	
Warhawk Air Museum 201 Municipal Dr	Nampa	ID	83687	208-465-6446	465-6232
Web: www.warhawkairmuseum.org					

Illinois

				Phone	Fax
ABA Museum of Law 321 N Clark St	Chicago	IL	60610	312-988-6222	988-5494
TF: 800-285-2221 ■ *Web:* www.abanet.org/museum					

Illinois (Cont'd)

Museum	City	State	Zip	Phone	Fax
Abraham Lincoln Presidential Library & Museum 112 N 6th St *TF:* 800-610-2094 ■ *Web:* www.alincoln-library.com	Springfield	IL	62701	217-524-7216	785-6250
African American Museum Hall of Fame 309 Du Sable St	Peoria	IL	61605	309-673-2206	495-0166
Art Institute of Chicago 111 S Michigan Ave *Web:* www.artic.edu/aic/	Chicago	IL	60603	312-443-3600	
Balzekas Museum of Lithuanian Culture 6500 S Pulaski Rd	Chicago	IL	60629	773-582-6500	582-5133
Burpee Museum of Natural History 737 N Main St *Web:* www.burpee.org	Rockford	IL	61103	815-965-3433	965-2703
Chicago History Museum 1601 N Clark St *Web:* www.chicagohs.org	Chicago	IL	60614	312-642-4600	266-2077
Clarke House Museum 1827 S Indiana Ave	Chicago	IL	60616	312-745-0040	745-0077
Daughters of Union Veterans of the Civil War 503 S Walnut St *Web:* www.duvcw.org	Springfield	IL	62704	217-544-0616	544-0606
David & Alfred Smart Museum of Art 5550 S Greenwood Ave	Chicago	IL	60637	773-702-0200	702-3121
Dickson Mounds State Museum 10956 N Dickson Mounds Rd *Web:* www.museum.state.il.us/ismsites/dickson/	Lewistown	IL	61542	309-547-3721	547-3189
DuSable Museum of African American History 740 E 56th Pl *Web:* www.dusablemuseum.org	Chicago	IL	60637	773-947-0600	947-0716
Early American Museum 600 N Lombard St *Web:* www.earlyamericanmuseum.org	Mahomet	IL	61853	217-586-2612	586-3491
Erlander Home Museum 404 S 3rd St *Web:* www.swedishhistorical.org	Rockford	IL	61104	815-963-5559	963-5559
Ernest Hemingway Museum 200 N Oak Park Ave *Web:* www.ehfop.org	Oak Park	IL	60302	708-848-2222	386-2952
Ethnic Heritage Museum 1129 S Main St	Rockford	IL	61101	815-962-7402	962-7402
Field Museum of Natural History 1400 S Lake Shore Dr *Web:* www.fieldmuseum.org	Chicago	IL	60605	312-922-9410	427-7269
Frank Lloyd Wright Home & Studio 951 Chicago Ave *Web:* www.wrightplus.org	Oak Park	IL	60302	708-848-1976	848-1248
Glessner House Museum 1800 S Prairie Ave *Web:* www.glessnerhouse.org	Chicago	IL	60616	312-326-1480	326-1397
Grand Army of the Republic Memorial Museum 629 S 7th St *Web:* gar-museum.com	Springfield	IL	62703	217-522-4373	
Hellenic Museum & Cultural Center 801 W Adams St *Web:* www.hellenicmuseum.org	Chicago	IL	60607	312-655-1234	655-1221
Hemingway Ernest Museum 200 N Oak Park Ave *Web:* www.ehfop.org	Oak Park	IL	60302	708-848-2222	386-2952
Illinois State Military Museum 1301 N MacArthur Blvd Bldg 30 *Web:* www.il.ngb.army.mil/museum	Springfield	IL	62702	217-761-3910	761-3709
Illinois State Museum 502 S Spring St *Web:* www.museum.state.il.us	Springfield	IL	62706	217-782-7386	782-1254
International Museum of Surgical Science 1524 N Lake Shore Dr *Web:* www.imss.org	Chicago	IL	60610	312-642-6502	642-9516
Krannert Art Museum 500 E Peabody Dr University of Illinois *Web:* www.art.uiuc.edu/kam	Champaign	IL	61820	217-333-1860	333-0883
Lakeview Museum of Arts & Sciences 1125 W Lake St *Web:* www.lakeview-museum.org	Peoria	IL	61614	309-686-7000	686-0280
Lincoln's New Salem State Historic Site 15588 History Ln *Web:* www.lincolnsnewsalem.com	Petersburg	IL	62675	217-632-4000	632-4010
Lizzadro Museum of Lapidary Art 220 Cottage Hill Ave Wilder Park *Web:* www.lizzadromuseum.org	Elmhurst	IL	60126	630-833-1616	833-1225
Midway Village & Museum Center 6799 Guilford Rd *Web:* www.midwayvillage.com	Rockford	IL	61107	815-397-9112	397-9156
Museum of Broadcast Communications 400 N State St *Web:* www.museum.tv	Chicago	IL	60610	312-245-8200	245-8207
Museum of Contemporary Art 220 E Chicago Ave *TF:* 800-622-7858 ■ *Web:* www.mcachicago.org	Chicago	IL	60611	312-280-2660	397-4095
Museum of Contemporary Photography 600 S Michigan Ave Columbia College *Web:* www.mocp.org	Chicago	IL	60605	312-663-5554	344-8067
Museum of Funeral Customs 1440 Monument Ave *Web:* www.funeralmuseum.org	Springfield	IL	62702	217-544-3480	544-3484
Museum of Holography 1134 W Washington Blvd	Chicago	IL	60607	312-226-1007	
Museum of Science & Industry 5700 S Lake Shore Dr *TF:* 800-468-6674 ■ *Web:* www.msichicago.org	Chicago	IL	60637	773-684-1414	684-7141
National Museum of Mexican Art 1852 W 19th St *Web:* www.mfacmchicago.org	Chicago	IL	60608	312-738-1503	738-1503
National Vietnam Veterans Art Museum 1801 S Indiana Ave *Web:* www.nvvam.org	Chicago	IL	60616	312-326-0270	326-9767
Notebaert Peggy Nature Museum 2430 N Cannon Dr *Web:* www.naturemuseum.org	Chicago	IL	60614	773-755-5100	755-5199
Octave Chanute Aerospace Museum 1011 Pacesetter Dr *TF:* 877-726-8685 ■ *Web:* www.aeromuseum.org	Rantoul	IL	61866	217-893-1613	892-5774
Oriental Institute Museum 1155 E 58th St University of Chicago *Web:* oi.uchicago.edu	Chicago	IL	60637	773-702-9514	702-9853
Peace Museum 100 N Central Park Ave 2nd Fl *Web:* www.peacemuseum.org	Chicago	IL	60624	773-638-6450	638-6452
Peggy Notebaert Nature Museum 2430 N Cannon Dr *Web:* www.naturemuseum.org	Chicago	IL	60614	773-755-5100	755-5199
PMA (Polish Museum of America) 984 N Milwaukee Ave *Web:* pma.prcua.org	Chicago	IL	60622	773-384-3352	384-3799
Polish Museum of America (PMA) 984 N Milwaukee Ave *Web:* pma.prcua.org	Chicago	IL	60622	773-384-3352	384-3799
Quincy Museum 1601 Maine St *Web:* www.thequincymuseum.com	Quincy	IL	62301	217-224-9323	224-9323
Rockford Art Museum 711 N Main St *Web:* www.rockfordartmuseum.org	Rockford	IL	61103	815-968-2787	316-2179
Ronald Reagan Museum 300 E College Ave *Web:* reagan.eureka.edu	Eureka	IL	61530	309-467-6407	467-6437
Sousa Archives & Center for American Music (SACAM) 1103 S 6th St 236 Harding Band Bldg *Web:* www.library.uiuc.edu/sousa	Champaign	IL	61820	217-244-9309	244-8695
Spertus Museum 618 S Michigan Ave *TF:* 888-322-1740 ■ *Web:* www.spertus.edu	Chicago	IL	60605	312-922-9012	922-6406
Spurlock Museum University of Illinois at Urbana 600 S Gregory St *Web:* www.spurlock.uiuc.edu	Urbana	IL	61801	217-333-2360	244-9419
Swedish American Museum 5211 N Clark St *Web:* www.samac.org	Chicago	IL	60640	773-728-8111	728-8870
Tinker Swiss Cottage Museum 411 Kent St *Web:* www.tinkercottage.com	Rockford	IL	61102	815-964-2424	964-2466
Ukrainian National Museum 2249 W Superior St *Web:* www.ukrainiannationalmuseum.org	Chicago	IL	60612	312-421-8020	
University Museum Southern Illinois University Faner Hall Rm 2469 *Web:* www.museum.siu.edu	Carbondale	IL	62901	618-453-5388	453-7409
Wright Frank Lloyd Home & Studio 951 Chicago Ave *Web:* www.wrightplus.org	Oak Park	IL	60302	708-848-1976	848-1248

Indiana

Museum	City	State	Zip	Phone	Fax
Auburn Cord Duesenberg Museum 1600 S Wayne St *Web:* www.acdmuseum.org	Auburn	IN	46706	260-925-1444	925-6266
Cathedral of the Immaculate Conception Museum 915 S Clinton St	Fort Wayne	IN	46802	260-424-1485	424-7625
Children's Museum of Indianapolis 3000 N Meridian St *TF:* 800-826-5431 ■ *Web:* www.childrensmuseum.org	Indianapolis	IN	46208	317-924-5431	920-2001
Colfax Cultural Center Galleries 914 Lincoln Way W	South Bend	IN	46616	574-968-0814	289-4550
Conner Prairie Living History Museum 13400 Allisonville Rd *TF:* 800-966-1836 ■ *Web:* www.connerprairie.org	Fishers	IN	46038	317-776-6000	776-6014
Dan Quayle Center PO Box 856 *Web:* www.quaylemuseum.org	Huntington	IN	46750	260-356-6356	356-1455
Diehm Jack D Museum of Natural History 600 Franke Park Dr	Fort Wayne	IN	46808	260-427-6708	
Eiteljorg Museum of American Indian & Western Art 500 W Washington St *Web:* www.eiteljorg.org	Indianapolis	IN	46204	317-636-9378	275-1400
Evansville Museum of Arts History & Science 411 SE Riverside Dr *Web:* www.emuseum.org	Evansville	IN	47713	812-425-2406	421-7509
Firefighters' Museum 226 W Washington Blvd	Fort Wayne	IN	46802	260-426-0051	
Fort Wayne Museum of Art 311 E Main St *Web:* www.fwmoa.org	Fort Wayne	IN	46802	260-422-6467	422-1374
Freetown Village Living History Museum PO Box 1041 *Web:* www.freetown.org	Indianapolis	IN	46206	317-631-1870	631-0224
History Center 302 E Berry St *Web:* www.fwhistorycenter.com	Fort Wayne	IN	46802	260-426-2882	424-4419
Indiana Medical History Museum 3045 W Vermont St *TF:* 866-910-7329 ■ *Web:* www.imhm.org	Indianapolis	IN	46222	317-635-7329	635-7349
Indiana State Museum 650 W Washington St *Web:* www.in.gov/ism/	Indianapolis	IN	46204	317-232-1637	232-7090
Indiana University Art Museum 1133 E 7th St *Web:* www.indiana.edu/~iuam	Bloomington	IN	47405	812-855-5445	855-1023
Indianapolis Motor Speedway & Hall of Fame Museum 4790 W 16th St *Web:* www.brickyard.com/museum/	Indianapolis	IN	46222	317-492-6747	492-6449
Indianapolis Museum of Art 4000 Michigan Rd *Web:* www.ima-art.org	Indianapolis	IN	46208	317-923-1331	931-1978
Indianapolis Museum of Contemporary Art 340 N Senate Ave *Web:* www.indymoca.org/public	Indianapolis	IN	46204	317-634-6622	634-1977
Jack D Diehm Museum of Natural History 600 Franke Park Dr	Fort Wayne	IN	46808	260-427-6708	
James Whitcomb Riley Museum Home 528 Lockerbie St *Web:* www.rileykids.org/museum	Indianapolis	IN	46202	317-631-5885	
Lincoln Museum 200 E Berry St *Web:* www.thelincolnmuseum.org	Fort Wayne	IN	46802	260-455-3864	455-6922
Macedonian Tribune Museum 124 W Wayne St Suite 204 *Web:* www.macedonian.org	Fort Wayne	IN	46802	260-422-5900	422-1348
Mathers Museum of World Cultures 416 N Indiana Ave *Web:* www.indiana.edu/mathers	Bloomington	IN	47408	812-855-6873	855-0205
Monroe County Historical Museum 202 E 6th St *Web:* www.kiva.net/~mchm/museum.htm	Bloomington	IN	47408	812-332-2517	355-5593
Northern Indiana Center for History 808 W Washington St *Web:* www.centerforhistory.org	South Bend	IN	46601	574-235-9664	235-9059
Reitz Home Museum 224 SE 1st St *Web:* reitzhome.evansville.net	Evansville	IN	47706	812-426-1871	426-2179
Riley James Whitcomb Museum Home 528 Lockerbie St *Web:* www.rileykids.org/museum	Indianapolis	IN	46202	317-631-5885	
Science Central 1950 N Clinton St *TF:* 800-442-6376 ■ *Web:* www.sciencecentral.org	Fort Wayne	IN	46805	260-424-2400	422-2899
Snite Museum of Art University of Notre Dame *Web:* www.nd.edu/~sniteart	Notre Dame	IN	46556	574-631-5466	631-8501
South Bend Regional Museum of Art 120 S Saint Joseph St *Web:* sbrma.org	South Bend	IN	46601	574-235-9102	235-5782
Studebaker National Museum 201 S Chapin St *TF:* 888-391-5600 ■ *Web:* www.studebakermuseum.org	South Bend	IN	46601	574-235-9714	235-5522
Swope Art Museum 25 S 7th St *Web:* www.swope.org	Terre Haute	IN	47807	812-238-1676	238-1677
Wylie House Museum 307 E 2nd St *Web:* www.indiana.edu/~libwylie	Bloomington	IN	47401	812-855-6224	

Iowa

Museum	City	State	Zip	Phone	Fax
African American Historical Museum & Cultural Center of Iowa 55 12th Ave SE *TF:* 877-526-1863 ■ *Web:* www.blackiowa.org	Cedar Rapids	IA	52406	319-862-2101	862-2105
Cedar Rapids Museum of Art 410 3rd Ave SE *Web:* www.crma.org	Cedar Rapids	IA	52401	319-366-7503	366-4111
Coe College Permanent Collection of Art 1220 1st Ave NE *Web:* www.public.coe.edu/departments/Art/title.html	Cedar Rapids	IA	52402	319-399-8217	399-8019
Des Moines Art Center 4700 Grand Ave *Web:* www.desmoinesartcenter.org	Des Moines	IA	50312	515-277-4405	271-0357
Dubuque Museum of Art 701 Locust St *Web:* www.dbqart.com	Dubuque	IA	52001	563-557-1851	557-7826
Duffy's Collectible Cars 250 Classic Car Ct SW *Web:* www.duffys.com/	Cedar Rapids	IA	52404	319-364-7000	364-4036
Figge Art Museum 225 W 2nd St *Web:* www.figgeartmuseum.org	Davenport	IA	52801	563-326-7804	326-7876
Granger House Museum 970 10th St *Web:* community.marion.ia.us/granger	Marion	IA	52302	319-377-6672	
Herbert Hoover Presidential Library & Museum 210 Parkside Dr *Web:* www.hoover.archives.gov	West Branch	IA	52358	319-643-5301	643-5825
Hoover Herbert Presidential Library & Museum 210 Parkside Dr *Web:* www.hoover.archives.gov	West Branch	IA	52358	319-643-5301	643-5825
Hoyt Sherman Place 1501 Woodland Ave *Web:* www.hoytsherman.org	Des Moines	IA	50309	515-243-0913	237-3582
Iowa Gold Star Museum 7105 NW 70th Ave Camp Dodge	Johnston	IA	50131	515-252-4531	727-3107
Iowa Masonic Library & Museum 813 1st Ave SE	Cedar Rapids	IA	52402	319-365-1438	365-1439
John Wayne Birthplace 216 S 2nd St *Web:* www.johnwaynebirthplace.org	Winterset	IA	50273	515-462-1044	462-3289

	City	State	ZIP	Phone	Fax
Living History Farms 2600 111th St	Urbandale	IA	50322	515-278-5286	278-9808
Web: www.lhf.org					
National Balloon Museum 1601 N Jefferson St PO Box 149	Indianola	IA	50125	515-961-3714	
Web: www.nationalballoonmuseum.com					
National Czech & Slovak Museum & Library 30 16th Ave SW	Cedar Rapids	IA	52404	319-362-8500	363-2209
Web: www.ncsml.org					
National Farm Toy Museum 1110 16th Ave SE	Dyersville	IA	52040	563-875-2727	875-8467
Web: www.nftmonline.com					
National Mississippi River Museum & Aquarium 350 E 3rd St Ice Harbor	Dubuque	IA	52001	563-557-9545	583-1241
TF: 800-226-3369 ■ *Web:* www.mississippirivermuseum.com					
Pella Historical Village 507 Franklin St	Pella	IA	50219	641-628-4311	628-9192
Web: www.pellatuliptime.com/historical-village/					
Science Center of Iowa 401 W ML King Jr Pkwy	Des Moines	IA	50309	515-274-6868	274-3404
Web: www.sciowa.org					
Science Station & McLeod/Busse IMAX Dome Theatre 427 1st St SE	Cedar Rapids	IA	52401	319-366-0968	366-4590
Web: www.sciencestation.org					
Sioux City Art Center 225 Nebraska St	Sioux City	IA	51101	712-279-6272	255-2921
Web: www.siouxcityartcenter.org					
Sioux City Public Museum 2901 Jackson St	Sioux City	IA	51104	712-279-6174	252-5615
Web: www.sioux-city.org/museum					
State Historical Society of Iowa 600 E Locust St	Des Moines	IA	50319	515-281-5111	242-6498
Web: www.iowahistory.org					
University of Iowa Museum of Art 150 N Riverside Dr	Iowa City	IA	52242	319-335-1727	335-3677
Web: www.uiowa.edu/uima/					
University Museum 3219 Hudson Rd University of Northern Iowa	Cedar Falls	IA	50614	319-273-2188	273-6924
Web: www.uni.edu/museum					
Wayne John Birthplace 216 S 2nd St	Winterset	IA	50273	515-462-1044	462-3289
Web: www.johnwaynebirthplace.org					

Kansas

	City	State	ZIP	Phone	Fax
Boot Hill Museum Front St	Dodge City	KS	67801	620-227-8188	227-7673
Web: www.boothill.org					
Coleman Factory Outlet Store & Museum 235 N Saint Francis St	Wichita	KS	67202	316-264-0836	219-5287
TF: 800-835-3278 ■ *Web:* www.coleman.com					
Combat Air Museum 602 J St Forbes Field	Topeka	KS	66619	785-862-3303	862-3304
Web: www.combatairmuseum.org					
Dwight D Eisenhower Presidential Library & Museum 200 SE 4th St	Abilene	KS	67410	785-263-6700	263-6715
TF: 877-746-4453 ■ *Web:* www.eisenhower.utexas.edu					
Edwin A Ulrich Museum of Art 1845 Fairmount St Wichita State University	Wichita	KS	67260	316-978-3664	978-3898
Web: ulrich.wichita.edu					
Eisenhower Dwight D Presidential Library & Museum 200 SE 4th St	Abilene	KS	67410	785-263-6700	263-6715
TF: 877-746-4453 ■ *Web:* www.eisenhower.utexas.edu					
Great Plains Transportation Museum 700 E Douglas St	Wichita	KS	67202	316-263-0944	
Web: www.gptm.us					
Holmes Lowell D Museum of Anthropology 114 Neff Hall Wichita State University	Wichita	KS	67260	316-978-3195	978-3351
Web: webs.wichita.edu/anthropology/					
Indian Center Museum 650 N Seneca St	Wichita	KS	67203	316-262-5221	262-4216
Web: www.theindiancenter.com					
Kansas African American Museum 601 N Water St	Wichita	KS	67203	316-262-7651	265-6953
Kansas Aviation Museum 3350 S George Washington Blvd	Wichita	KS	67210	316-683-9242	683-0573
Web: www.kansasaviationmuseum.org					
Kansas Museum of History 6425 SW 6th St	Topeka	KS	66615	785-272-8681	272-8682
Web: www.kshs.org/places/museum.htm					
Kansas National Guard Museum 6700 S Topeka Blvd Forbes Field Bldg 301	Topeka	KS	66619	785-862-1020	862-1066
Lowell D Holmes Museum of Anthropology 114 Neff Hall Wichita State University	Wichita	KS	67260	316-978-3195	978-3351
Web: webs.wichita.edu/anthropology/					
Mulvane Art Museum 1700 SW College Ave Washburn University	Topeka	KS	66621	785-231-1010	234-2703
Web: www.washburn.edu/mulvane					
Museum of World Treasures 835 E 1st St	Wichita	KS	67202	316-263-1311	263-1495
Web: www.worldtreasures.org					
National Agricultural Center & Hall of Fame 630 Hall of Fame Dr	Bonner Springs	KS	66012	913-721-1075	721-1202
Web: www.aghalloffame.com					
Old Cowtown Museum 1871 Sim Park Dr	Wichita	KS	67203	316-660-1871	264-2937
Web: www.oldcowtown.org					
Santa Fe Trail Center 1349 K-156 Hwy	Larned	KS	67550	620-285-2054	285-7491
Web: www.santafetrailcenter.org					
Society of Decorative Painters Museum 393 N McLean Blvd	Wichita	KS	67203	316-269-9300	269-9191
Spencer Museum of Art 1301 Mississippi St University of Kansas	Lawrence	KS	66045	785-864-4710	864-3112
Web: www.spencerart.ku.edu					
Strawberry Hill Museum & Cultural Center 720 N 4th St	Kansas City	KS	66101	913-371-3264	
Web: www.strawberryhillmuseum.org					
Ulrich Edwin A Museum of Art 1845 Fairmount St Wichita State University	Wichita	KS	67260	316-978-3664	978-3898
Web: ulrich.wichita.edu					
Wichita Art Museum 1400 W Museum Blvd	Wichita	KS	67203	316-268-4921	268-4980
Web: www.wichitaartmuseum.org					
Wichita-Sedgwick County Historical Museum 204 S Main St	Wichita	KS	67202	316-265-9314	265-9319
Web: www.wichitahistory.org					
Wyandotte County Historical Society & Museum 631 N 126th St	Bonner Springs	KS	66012	913-721-1078	721-1394

Kentucky

	City	State	ZIP	Phone	Fax
American Saddlebred Museum 4083 Iron Works Pkwy	Lexington	KY	40511	859-259-2746	255-4909
TF: 800-829-4438 ■ *Web:* www.american-saddlebred.com					
Audubon John James Museum 3100 Hwy 41 N	Henderson	KY	42419	270-827-1893	826-2286
Web: www.go-henderson.com/audubon					
Aviation Museum of Kentucky Hangar Dr Blue Grass Airport	Lexington	KY	40544	859-231-1219	381-8739
Web: www.aviationky.org					
Bluegrass Scenic Railroad & Museum 175 Beasley Rd Woodford County Park	Versailles	KY	40383	859-873-2476	873-0408
Web: www.bgrm.org					
Conrad/Caldwell House Museum 1402 St James Ct	Louisville	KY	40208	502-636-5023	636-1264
Web: www.conradcaldwell.org					
Edison Thomas House 729-31 E Washington St	Louisville	KY	40202	502-585-5247	585-5231
Web: www.edisonhouse.org					
Farmington Historic Home Museum 3033 Bardstown Rd	Louisville	KY	40205	502-452-9920	456-1976
Web: www.farmingtonhistorichome.org					
Filson Historical Society Museum 1310 S 3rd St	Louisville	KY	40208	502-635-5083	635-5086
Web: www.filsonhistorical.org					
Frazier Historical Arms Museum 829 W Main St	Louisville	KY	40202	502-412-2280	412-8148
TF: 866-886-7103 ■ *Web:* www.frazierarmsmuseum.org					
Headley-Whitney Museum 4435 Old Frankfort Pike	Lexington	KY	40510	859-255-6653	255-8375
TF: 800-310-5085 ■ *Web:* www.headley-whitney.org					
International Museum of the Horse 4089 Iron Works Pkwy	Lexington	KY	40511	859-259-4231	225-4613
TF: 800-678-8813 ■ *Web:* www.imh.org/imh/imhmain.html					
John James Audubon Museum 3100 Hwy 41 N	Henderson	KY	42419	270-827-1893	826-2286
Web: www.go-henderson.com/audubon					
Kentucky Derby Museum 704 Central Ave	Louisville	KY	40208	502-634-0676	636-5855
Web: www.derbymuseum.org					
Kentucky History Museum 100 W Broadway	Frankfort	KY	40601	502-564-3016	564-4701
Web: www.kyhistory.org					
Kentucky Military History Museum 125 E Main St	Frankfort	KY	40601	502-564-3265	564-4054
TF: 877-444-7867 ■ *Web:* www.kyhistory.org					
Kentucky Museum Western Kentucky University College Heights 1 Big Red Way	Bowling Green	KY	42101	270-745-2592	745-4878
Web: web2.wku.edu/library/kylm/					
Lexington History Museum 215 W Main St	Lexington	KY	40507	859-254-0530	254-8372
Web: www.lexingtonhistorymuseum.org					
Louisville Fire History & Learning Center 3228 River Park Dr	Louisville	KY	40211	502-574-3731	
Louisville Science Center 727 W Main St	Louisville	KY	40202	502-561-6100	561-6145
TF: 800-591-2203 ■ *Web:* www.louisvillescience.org					
Muhammad Ali Center 144 N 6th St	Louisville	KY	40202	502-584-9254	589-4905
Web: www.alicenter.org					
National Corvette Museum 350 Corvette Dr	Bowling Green	KY	42101	270-781-7973	781-5286
TF: 800-538-3883 ■ *Web:* www.corvettemuseum.com					
Old State Capitol Museum 100 W Broadway	Frankfort	KY	40601	502-564-3016	564-4701
TF: 877-444-7867 ■ *Web:* www.kyhistory.org					
Shaker Village of Pleasant Hill 3501 Lexington Rd	Harrodsburg	KY	40330	859-734-5411	734-5411
TF: 800-734-5611 ■ *Web:* www.shakervillageky.org					
Speed Art Museum 2035 S 3rd St	Louisville	KY	40208	502-634-2700	636-2899
Web: www.speedmuseum.org					
Thomas Edison House 729-31 E Washington St	Louisville	KY	40202	502-585-5247	585-5231
Web: www.edisonhouse.org					
University of Kentucky Art Museum Rose St & Euclid Ave	Lexington	KY	40506	859-257-5716	323-1994
Web: www.uky.edu/ArtMuseum/					
University of Kentucky Museum of Anthropology 211 Lafferty Hall	Lexington	KY	40506	859-257-1944	323-1968
Web: www.uky.edu/AS/Anthropology/Museum					
University of Louisville Photo Archives Ekstrom Library University of Louisville	Louisville	KY	40292	502-852-6752	852-8734

Louisiana

	City	State	ZIP	Phone	Fax
Alexandre Mouton House/Lafayette Museum 1122 Lafayette St	Lafayette	LA	70501	337-234-2208	234-2208
American Italian Renaissance Foundation Museum 537 S Peters St	New Orleans	LA	70130	504-522-7294	522-1657
Web: www.airf.org					
Ark-La-Tex Antique & Classic Vehicle Museum 601 Spring St	Shreveport	LA	71101	318-222-0227	222-5042
TF: 888-664-4854					
Cathedral of Saint John the Evangelist Museum 515 Cathedral St	Lafayette	LA	70501	337-232-1322	232-1379
Confederate Museum 929 Camp St	New Orleans	LA	70130	504-523-4522	523-8595
Web: www.confederatemuseum.com					
Eighth Air Force Museum Barksdale Air Force Base	Bossier City	LA	71110	318-456-3067	456-5558
Enchanted Mansion Doll Museum 190 Lee Dr	Baton Rouge	LA	70808	225-769-0005	766-6822
Web: www.enchantedmansion.org					
Freeport McMoRan Science Complex 409 Williams Blvd Rivertown	Kenner	LA	70062	504-468-7231	471-2159
Gallier House Museum 1132 Royal St	New Orleans	LA	70116	504-525-5661	568-9735
Web: www.hgghh.org					
Grandmother's Buttons Museum 9814 Royal St	Saint Francisville	LA	70775	225-635-4107	635-6067
TF: 800-580-6941 ■ *Web:* www.grandmothersbuttons.com					
Heritage Museum & Cultural Center 1606 Main St	Baker	LA	70714	225-774-1776	775-5635
Web: www.bakerheritagemuseum.org					
Historic New Orleans Collection 533 Royal St	New Orleans	LA	70130	504-523-4662	598-7108
Web: www.hnoc.org					
House of Broel's Historic Mansion & Dollhouse Museum 2220 St Charles Ave	New Orleans	LA	70130	504-522-2220	524-6775
TF: 800-827-4325 ■ *Web:* www.houseofbroel.com					
Imperial Calcasieu Museum 204 W Sallier St	Lake Charles	LA	70601	337-439-3797	439-6040
Lafayette Museum 1122 Lafayette St	Lafayette	LA	70501	337-234-2208	234-2208
Lafayette Natural History Museum & Planetarium 433 Jefferson St	Lafayette	LA	70501	337-291-5544	291-5464
Web: www.lnhm.org					
Longue Vue House & Gardens 7 Bamboo Rd	New Orleans	LA	70124	504-488-5488	486-7015
Web: www.longuevue.com					
Louisiana Art & Science Museum 100 S River Rd	Baton Rouge	LA	70802	225-344-5272	344-9477
Web: www.lasm.org					
Louisiana Naval War Memorial 305 S River Rd	Baton Rouge	LA	70802	225-342-1942	342-2039
Web: www.usskidd.com					
Louisiana State Exhibit Museum 3015 Greenwood Rd	Shreveport	LA	71109	318-632-2020	632-2056
Louisiana State Museum 751 Chartres St	New Orleans	LA	70116	504-568-6968	568-4995
TF: 800-568-6968 ■ *Web:* lsm.crt.state.la.us					
Louisiana State University Museum of Art 100 Lafayette St	Baton Rouge	LA	70801	225-389-7200	389-7219
Web: www.lsumoa.com					
Louisiana State University Museum of Natural Science 119 Foster Hall Louisiana State University	Baton Rouge	LA	70803	225-578-2855	578-3075
Web: www.museum.lsu.edu/LSUMNS/index.html					
Louisiana State University Rural Life Museum & Windrush Gardens 4560 Essen Ln	Baton Rouge	LA	70809	225-765-2437	765-2639
Web: rurallife.lsu.edu					
Louisiana Toy Train Museum 519 Williams Blvd Rivertown	Kenner	LA	70062	504-468-7231	471-2159
Web: www.rivertownkenner.com/toytrain.html					
Magnolia Mound Plantation 2161 Nicholson Dr	Baton Rouge	LA	70802	225-343-4955	343-6739
Web: www.magnoliamound.org					
Mardi Gras Museum 415 Williams Blvd Rivertown	Kenner	LA	70062	504-468-7231	471-2159
Meadows Museum of Art of Centenary College 2911 Centenary Blvd	Shreveport	LA	71104	318-869-5169	869-5730
Web: www.centenary.edu/meadows/					
Musee Conti-Wax Museum of Louisiana Legends 917 Rue Conti French Quarter	New Orleans	LA	70112	504-525-2605	566-7636
TF: 800-233-5405 ■ *Web:* www.historyofneworleans.com					
New Orleans Museum of Art 1 Collins Diboll Cir	New Orleans	LA	70124	504-488-2631	484-6662
Web: www.noma.org					
New Orleans Pharmacy Museum 514 Chartres St	New Orleans	LA	70130	504-565-8027	565-8028
Web: www.pharmacymuseum.org/main.htm					
Norton RW Art Gallery 4747 Creswell Ave	Shreveport	LA	71106	318-865-4201	869-0435
Web: www.softdisk.com/comp/norton					

Louisiana (Cont'd)

Museum	City	State	Zip	Phone	Fax
Nottoway Plantation 30970 Hwy 405	White Castle	LA	70788	225-545-2730	545-8632
TF: 866-428-4748 ■ *Web:* www.nottoway.com					
Ogden Museum of Southern Art 925 Camp St	New Orleans	LA	70130	504-539-9600	539-9602
Web: www.ogdenmuseum.org					
Old Arsenal Museum PO Box 94125	Baton Rouge	LA	70804	225-342-0401	
Pioneer Heritage Center					
1 University Pl Louisiana State University	Shreveport	LA	71115	318-797-5332	797-5237
Pitot House Museum 1440 Moss St	New Orleans	LA	70119	504-482-0312	482-0363
Web: www.pitothouse.org					
Plaquemine Lock Museum 57730 Main St	Plaquemine	LA	70764	225-687-7158	687-8933
TF: 877-987-7158					
Ripley's Believe It or Not! Museum 620 Decatur St	New Orleans	LA	70130	504-586-1233	
Web: www.ripleysneworleans.com					
RW Norton Art Gallery 4747 Creswell Ave	Shreveport	LA	71106	318-865-4201	869-0435
Web: www.softdisk.com/comp/norton					
Saints Hall of Fame Museum 415 Williams Blvd Rivertown	Kenner	LA	70062	504-468-7231	471-2159
Web: www.rivertownkenner.com/saints.html					
Sci-Port Discovery Center 820 Clyde Fant Pkwy	Shreveport	LA	71101	318-424-3466	222-5592
TF: 877-724-7678 ■ *Web:* www.sciport.org					
Southern University Museum of Art Martin L Harvey Hall	Baton Rouge	LA	70813	225-771-4513	771-4498
Web: www.sus.edu/suma/default.htm					
Southern University Museum of Art 610 Texas St Suite 110	Shreveport	LA	71101	318-678-4631	678-4607
TF: 800-458-1472					
Spring Street Historical Museum 525 Spring St	Shreveport	LA	71101	318-424-0964	424-0964
Web: www.springstreetmuseum.com					
Stages of the Stars Music Museum 705 Elvis Presley Blvd	Shreveport	LA	71101	318-220-9434	220-9434
Touchstone Wildlife & Art Museum 3386 Hwy 80 E	Haughton	LA	71037	318-949-2323	
University Art Museum 710 E St Mary Blvd	Lafayette	LA	70503	337-482-5326	262-1268
Web: museum.louisiana.edu					
West Baton Rouge Museum 845 N Jefferson Ave	Port Allen	LA	70767	225-336-2422	336-2448
Web: www.westbatonrougemuseum.com					
West Feliciana Historical Society Museum					
11757 Ferdinand St	Saint Francisville	LA	70775	225-635-6330	635-4626
TF: 800-789-4221					

Maine

Museum	City	State	Zip	Phone	Fax
Abbe Museum 26 Mount Desert St	Bar Harbor	ME	04609	207-288-3519	288-8979
Web: www.abbemuseum.org					
Bangor Museum & Center for History 25 Broad St	Bangor	ME	04401	207-942-5766	941-0266
Web: www.bangorhistorical.org					
Bowdoin College Museum of Art 9400 College Stn	Brunswick	ME	04011	207-725-3275	725-3762
Web: academic.bowdoin.edu/artmuseum					
Brick Store Museum 117 Main St	Kennebunk	ME	04043	207-985-4802	985-6887
Web: www.brickstoremuseum.org					
Colby College Museum of Art 5600 Mayflower Hill	Waterville	ME	04901	207-859-5600	859-5606
Web: www.colby.edu/museum					
Cole Land Transportation Museum 405 Perry Rd	Bangor	ME	04401	207-990-3600	990-2653
Web: www.colemuseum.org					
Farnsworth Art Museum 16 Museum St	Rockland	ME	04841	207-596-6457	596-0509
Web: farnsworthmuseum.org					
Hudson Museum 5746 Maine Center for the Arts	Orono	ME	04469	207-581-1901	581-1950
Web: www.umaine.edu/hudsonmuseum					
Institute of Contemporary Art					
522 Congress St Maine College of Art	Portland	ME	04101	207-879-5742	780-0816
Maine Forest & Logging Museum Rt 178 Leonard's Mills	Bradley	ME	04411	207-581-2871	581-9398
Web: www.leonardsmills.com					
Maine Historical Society					
489 Congress St Maine Historical Society	Portland	ME	04101	207-774-1822	775-4301
Web: www.mainehistory.com					
Maine Maritime Museum 243 Washington St	Bath	ME	04530	207-443-1316	443-1665
Web: www.bathmaine.com					
Maine Narrow Gauge Railroad Co & Museum 58 Fore St	Portland	ME	04101	207-828-0814	879-6132
Web: www.mngrr.org					
Maine State Museum					
83 State House Stn State House Complex	Augusta	ME	04333	207-287-2301	287-6633
Web: www.state.me.us/museum					
Museum at Portland Head Light 1000 Shore Rd	Cape Elizabeth	ME	04107	207-799-2661	799-2800
Web: www.portlandheadlight.com/park.html					
Old Fort Western 16 Cony St	Augusta	ME	04330	207-626-2385	626-2304
Web: www.oldfortwestern.org					
Old Town Museum 353 Main St	Old Town	ME	04468	207-827-7256	
Web: www.old-town.org/museum					
Penobscot Marine Museum 5 Church St	Searsport	ME	04974	207-548-2529	548-2520
Web: www.acadia.net/pmmuseum					
Portland Fire Museum 157 Spring St	Portland	ME	04101	207-772-2040	
Web: www.portlandfiremuseum.com					
Portland Harbor Museum Fort Rd - SMCC Campus	South Portland	ME	04106	207-799-6337	799-3862
Web: www.portlandharbormuseum.org					
Portland Museum of Art 7 Congress Sq	Portland	ME	04101	207-775-6148	773-7324
Web: www.portlandmuseum.org					
State House State & Capitol Sts	Augusta	ME	04333	207-287-2301	287-6633
Web: www.maine.gov					
Tate House Museum 1270 Westbrook St	Portland	ME	04102	207-774-6177	774-6198
Web: www.tatehouse.org					
University of Maine Museum of Art					
40 Harlow St Norumbega Hall	Bangor	ME	04401	207-561-3350	561-3351
Web: www.umma.umaine.edu					

Manitoba

Museum	City	Prov	Postal	Phone	Fax
Ivan Franko Museum 200 McGregor St	Winnipeg	MB	R2W5L6	204-589-4397	589-3404
Living Prairie Museum 2795 Ness Ave	Winnipeg	MB	R3J3S4	204-832-0167	986-4172
Web: www.winnipeg.ca/publicworks/naturalist/livingprairie					
Manitoba Museum 190 Rupert Ave	Winnipeg	MB	R3B0N2	204-956-2830	942-3679
Web: www.manitobamuseum.mb.ca					
Royal Canadian Artillery Museum Horsham Rd Bldg N-118	Shilo	MB	R0K2A0	204-765-3000	

Maryland

Museum	City	State	Zip	Phone	Fax
Accokeek Foundation 3400 Bryan Point Rd	Accokeek	MD	20607	301-283-2113	283-2049
Web: www.accokeek.org					
American Visionary Art Museum 800 Key Hwy	Baltimore	MD	21230	410-244-1900	244-5858
Web: www.avam.org					
Annapolis Maritime Museum 723 2nd St	Annapolis	MD	21403	410-295-0104	295-3022
Web: www.annapolismaritimemuseum.org					
B & O Railroad Museum 901 W Pratt St	Baltimore	MD	21223	410-752-2490	752-2499
Web: www.borail.org					
B Olive Cole Pharmacy Museum 650 W Lombard St	Baltimore	MD	21201	410-727-0746	727-2253
Baltimore Civil War Museum 601 President St	Baltimore	MD	21202	410-385-5188	385-1675
Web: www.mdhs.org					
Baltimore Maritime Museum Pratt St Pier 3	Baltimore	MD	21202	410-396-3453	396-3393
Web: www.baltomaritimemuseum.org					
Baltimore Museum of Art 10 Art Museum Dr	Baltimore	MD	21218	443-573-1700	573-1582
Web: www.artbma.org					
Baltimore Museum of Industry 1415 Key Hwy	Baltimore	MD	21230	410-727-4808	727-4869
Web: www.thebmi.org					
Baltimore Streetcar Museum 1901 Falls Rd	Baltimore	MD	21211	410-547-0264	547-0264
Web: www.baltimoremd.com/streetcar					
Banneker-Douglas Museum 84 Franklin St	Annapolis	MD	21401	410-216-6180	974-2553
TF: 866-521-6173 ■ *Web:* www.bdmuseum.com					
Calvert Marine Museum					
14150 Solomons Island Rd PO Box 97	Solomons	MD	20688	410-326-2042	326-6691
Web: www.calvertmarinemuseum.com					
Calvin B Taylor House Museum 208 N Main St	Berlin	MD	21811	410-641-1019	
Web: www.taylorhousemuseum.org					
Chesapeake Bay Maritime Museum PO Box 636	Saint Michaels	MD	21663	410-745-2916	745-6088
Web: www.cbmm.org					
Cole B Olive Pharmacy Museum 650 W Lombard St	Baltimore	MD	21201	410-727-0746	727-2253
Contemporary Museum The 100 W Centre St	Baltimore	MD	21201	410-783-5720	783-5722
Web: www.contemporary.org					
Edgar Allan Poe House 203 N Amity St	Baltimore	MD	21223	410-396-7932	
Web: www.eapoe.org					
Fire Museum of Maryland 1301 York Rd	Lutherville	MD	21093	410-321-7500	769-8433
Web: www.firemuseummd.org					
Fort McHenry National Monument & Historic Shrine					
2400 E Fort Ave	Baltimore	MD	21230	410-962-4290	962-2500
Web: www.nps.gov/fomc/					
Hammond-Harwood House 19 Maryland Ave	Annapolis	MD	21401	410-263-4683	267-6891
Web: www.hammondharwoodhouse.org					
Historic Annapolis Foundation Museum 77 Main St	Annapolis	MD	21401	410-268-5576	
TF: 800-639-9153 ■ *Web:* www.annapolis.org					
Homewood House Museum					
3400 N Charles St Johns Hopkins University	Baltimore	MD	21218	410-516-5589	516-7859
Web: www.jhu.edu/historichouses					
Jewish Museum of Maryland 15 Lloyd St	Baltimore	MD	21202	410-732-6400	732-6451
TF: 877-376-7190 ■ *Web:* www.jhsm.org					
Lacrosse Hall of Fame & Museum 113 W University Pkwy	Baltimore	MD	21210	410-235-6882	366-6735
Web: www.lacrosse.org/museum/index.phtml					
Lovely Lane United Methodist Church & Museum					
2200 Saint Paul St	Baltimore	MD	21218	410-889-4458	889-1501
Web: www.lovelylanemuseum.com					
Maryland Historical Society Museum & Library					
201 W Monument St	Baltimore	MD	21201	410-685-3750	385-2105
Web: www.mdhs.org					
Maryland Science Center 601 Light St	Baltimore	MD	21230	410-685-2370	545-5974
Web: www.mdsci.org					
Mount Clare Museum House					
1500 Washington Blvd Carroll Park	Baltimore	MD	21230	410-837-3262	837-0251
Web: www.mountclare.org					
National Great Blacks in Wax Museum 1601-03 E North Ave	Baltimore	MD	21213	410-563-3404	675-5040
Web: www.ngbiwm.com					
National Museum of Dentistry 31 S Greene St	Baltimore	MD	21201	410-706-8314	706-8313
Web: www.dentalmuseum.umaryland.edu					
Ocean City Life-Saving Station Museum 813 S Boardwalk	Ocean City	MD	21842	410-289-4991	289-4991
Web: www.ocmuseum.org					
Poe Edgar Allan House 203 N Amity St	Baltimore	MD	21223	410-396-7932	
Web: www.eapoe.org					
Reginald F Lewis Museum of Maryland African American					
History & Culture 830 E Pratt St	Baltimore	MD	21202	443-263-1800	333-1138*
*Fax Area Code: 410 ■ *Web:* www.africanamericanculture.org					
Star-Spangled Banner Flag House & 1812 Museum					
844 E Pratt St	Baltimore	MD	21202	410-837-1793	837-1812
Web: www.flaghouse.org					
Taylor Calvin B House Museum 208 N Main St	Berlin	MD	21811	410-641-1019	
Web: www.taylorhousemuseum.org					
Top of the World Observation Level & Museum					
401 E Pratt St World Trade Center 27th Fl	Baltimore	MD	21202	410-837-8439	837-0845
Web: www.bop.org/toptheworld/topoftheworld.aspx					
US Naval Academy Museum 118 Maryland Ave	Annapolis	MD	21402	410-293-2108	293-5220
Walters Art Museum 600 N Charles St	Baltimore	MD	21201	410-547-9000	783-7969
Web: www.thewalters.org					
Ward Museum of Wildfowl Art 909 S Schumaker Dr	Salisbury	MD	21804	410-742-4988	742-3107
Web: www.wardmuseum.org					
Washington County Museum of Fine Arts 91 Key St	Hagerstown	MD	21740	301-739-5727	745-3741
Web: www.washcomuseum.org					
Washington Monument & Museum at Mount Vernon Place					
699 N Charles St	Baltimore	MD	21202	410-396-7837	396-7945
Wheels Of Yesterday Antique & Classic Cars Museum					
12708 Ocean Gateway	Ocean City	MD	21842	410-213-7329	

Massachusetts

Museum	City	State	Zip	Phone	Fax
American Jewish Historical Society 160 Herrick Rd	Newton Centre	MA	02459	617-559-8880	559-8881
Web: www.ajhs.org					
American Textile History Museum 491 Dutton St	Lowell	MA	01854	978-441-0400	441-1412
Web: www.athm.org					
Berkshire County Historical Society 780 Holmes Rd	Pittsfield	MA	01201	413-442-1793	443-1449
Busch-Reisinger Museum					
32 Quincy St Harvard University Art Museums	Cambridge	MA	02138	617-495-9400	496-2359
Web: www.artmuseums.harvard.edu/busch					
Cape Cod Maritime Museum 135 South St	Hyannis	MA	02601	508-775-1723	775-1706
Web: www.capecodmaritimemuseum.org					
Cape Cod Museum of Natural History 869 Rte 6A	Brewster	MA	02631	508-896-3867	896-8844
Web: www.ccmnh.org					
Clark Sterling & Francine Art Institute 225 South St	Williamstown	MA	01267	413-458-9545	458-2324*
*Fax: PR ■ *Web:* www.clarkart.edu					
Connecticut Valley Historical Museum 220 State St	Springfield	MA	01103	413-263-6800	263-6875
TF: 800-625-7738 ■ *Web:* www.quadrangle.org/CVHM.htm					
Fogg Art Museum 32 Quincy St Harvard University	Cambridge	MA	02138	617-495-9400	495-9936
Web: www.artmuseums.harvard.edu/fogg					
Fuller Craft Museum 455 Oak St	Brockton	MA	02301	508-588-6000	587-6191
Web: www.fullermuseum.org					
Gardner Isabella Stewart Museum 280 The Fenway	Boston	MA	02115	617-566-1401	278-5175
Web: www.gardnermuseum.org					
George Walter Vincent Smith Art Museum 220 State St	Springfield	MA	01103	413-263-6800	263-6875
TF: 800-625-7738 ■ *Web:* www.quadrangle.org/GWVS.htm					
Gibson House Museum 137 Beacon St	Boston	MA	02116	617-267-6338	267-5121
Web: www.thegibsonhouse.org					
Harvard Museum of Natural History					
26 Oxford St Harvard University	Cambridge	MA	02138	617-495-3045	496-8308
Web: www.mcz.harvard.edu					

				Phone	Fax
Harvard University Art Museums 32 Quincy St *Web:* www.artmuseums.harvard.edu	Cambridge	MA	02138	617-495-9400	496-2359
Higgins Armory Museum 100 Barber Ave *Web:* www.higgins.org	Worcester	MA	01606	508-853-6015	852-7697
Hinchman House Natural Science Museum 7 Milk St *Web:* www.mmo.org/museums	Nantucket	MA	02554	508-228-0898	228-1031
Historic Deerfield PO Box 321 *Web:* www.historic-deerfield.org	Deerfield	MA	01342	413-774-5581	775-7220
Isabella Stewart Gardner Museum 280 The Fenway *Web:* www.gardnermuseum.org	Boston	MA	02115	617-566-1401	278-5175
Jasper Rand Art Museum 6 Elm St	Westfield	MA	01085	413-568-7833	568-0988
John F Kennedy Museum 397 Main St	Hyannis	MA	02601	508-790-3077	790-1970
Kennedy John F Library & Museum Columbia Point *TF:* 866-535-1960 ■ *Web:* www.jfklibrary.org	Boston	MA	02125	617-514-1600	514-1652
Martha's Vineyard Historical Society Museum Cook & School Sts PO Box 1310 *Web:* www.marthasvineyardhistory.org	Edgartown	MA	02539	508-627-4441	627-4436
MIT Museum 265 Massachusetts Ave *Web:* web.mit.edu/museum	Cambridge	MA	02139	617-253-4444	253-8994
Museum of Afro-American History 46 Joy St *Web:* www.afroammuseum.org	Boston	MA	02114	617-725-0022	720-5225
Museum of Art 465 Huntington Ave *Web:* www.mfa.org	Boston	MA	02115	617-267-9300	
Museum of Fine Arts 220 State St *TF:* 800-625-7738	Springfield	MA	01103	413-263-6800	263-6889
Museum of the National Center of Afro-American Artists 300 Walnut Ave *Web:* www.ncaaa.org/museum.html	Boston	MA	02119	617-442-8614	445-5525
Museum of Science Science Park *TF:* 866-770-4363 ■ *Web:* www.mos.org	Boston	MA	02114	617-589-0100	589-0454
National Heritage Museum 33 Marrett Rd *Web:* www.monh.org	Lexington	MA	02421	781-861-6559	861-9846
New Bedford Whaling Museum 18 Johnny Cake Hill *Web:* www.whalingmuseum.org	New Bedford	MA	02740	508-997-0046	994-4350
Nichols House Museum 55 Mt Vernon St *Web:* www.nicholshousemuseum.org	Boston	MA	02108	617-227-6993	723-8026
Old Sturbridge Village 1 Old Sturbridge Village Rd *Web:* www.osv.org	Sturbridge	MA	01566	508-347-3362	347-0375
Paul Revere House 19 North Sq *Web:* www.paulreverehouse.org	Boston	MA	02113	617-523-2338	523-1775
Peabody Essex Museum E India Sq *Web:* www.pem.org	Salem	MA	01970	978-745-1876	744-6776
Peabody Museum of Archaeology & Ethnology 11 Divinity Ave *Web:* www.peabody.harvard.edu	Cambridge	MA	02138	617-496-1027	495-7535
Pilgrim Hall Museum 75 Court St *Web:* www.pilgrimhall.org	Plymouth	MA	02360	508-746-1620	747-4228
Quadrangle The-Springfield Library & Museum Assn 220 State St *TF:* 800-625-7738 ■ *Web:* www.quadrangle.org	Springfield	MA	01103	413-263-6800	263-6875
Rand Jasper Art Museum 6 Elm St	Westfield	MA	01085	413-568-7833	568-0988
Revere Paul House 19 North Sq *Web:* www.paulreverehouse.org	Boston	MA	02113	617-523-2338	523-1775
Salem Witch Museum 19 1/2 Washington Sq N *TF:* 800-544-1692 ■ *Web:* www.salemwitchmuseum.com	Salem	MA	01970	978-744-1692	745-4414
Sandwich Glass Museum 129 Main St PO box 103 *Web:* www.sandwichglassmuseum.org	Sandwich	MA	02563	508-888-0251	888-4941
Smith George Walter Vincent Art Museum 220 State St *TF:* 800-625-7738 ■ *Web:* www.quadrangle.org/GWVS.htm	Springfield	MA	01103	413-263-6800	263-6875
Springfield Library & Museums 220 State St *TF:* 800-625-7738 ■ *Web:* www.spfldlibmus.org	Springfield	MA	01103	413-263-6800	263-6875
Sterling & Francine Clark Art Institute 225 South St **Fax:* PR ■ *Web:* www.clarkart.edu	Williamstown	MA	01267	413-458-9545	458-2324*
Storrowton Village Museum 1305 Memorial Ave Eastern States Exposition *Web:* www.thebige.com/village/storrowton_village.html	West Springfield	MA	01089	413-205-5051	205-5054
Titanic Museum 208 Main St *Web:* www.titanic1.org	Indian Orchard	MA	01151	413-543-4770	583-3633
USS Constitution Museum Charlestown Navy Yard Bldg 22 *Web:* www.ussconstitutionmuseum.org	Boston	MA	02129	617-426-1812	242-0496
Whaling Museum 13 Broad St	Nantucket	MA	02554	508-228-1894	228-5618
Willard House & Clock Museum 11 Willard St *Web:* www.willardhouse.org	North Grafton	MA	01536	508-839-3500	
Worcester Art Museum 55 Salisbury St *Web:* www.worcesterart.org	Worcester	MA	01609	508-799-4406	798-5646
Worcester Historical Museum 30 Elm St *Web:* www.worcesterhistory.org	Worcester	MA	01609	508-753-8278	753-9070

Michigan

				Phone	Fax
Alfred P Sloan Museum 1221 E Kearsley St *Web:* www.sloanmuseum.com	Flint	MI	48503	810-237-3450	237-3451
All Around the African World Museum & Resource Center 1136 Shepard	Lansing	MI	48912	517-484-7480	318-0908
Ann Arbor Hands-On Museum 220 E Ann St *Web:* www.aahom.org	Ann Arbor	MI	48104	734-995-5439	995-1188
Automotive Hall of Fame 21400 Oakwood Blvd *Web:* www.automotivehalloffame.org	Dearborn	MI	48124	313-240-4000	240-8641
Charles H Wright Museum of African American History 315 E Warren Ave *Web:* www.maah-detroit.org	Detroit	MI	48201	313-494-5800	494-5855
Chrysler Walter P Museum 1 Chrysler Dr *TF:* 888-456-1924 ■ *Web:* www.chryslerheritage.com	Auburn Hills	MI	48326	248-944-0001	944-0460
Cranbrook Art Museum 39221 Woodward Ave *TF:* 800-462-7262 ■ *Web:* www.cranbrookart.edu/museum	Bloomfield Hills	MI	48303	248-645-3319	645-3324
Cranbrook Art Museum 39221 Woodward Ave *TF:* 877-902-7262 ■ *Web:* www.cranbrookart.edu/museum	Bloomfield Hills	MI	48303	248-645-3323	645-3324
Cranbrook Institute of Science 39221 Woodward Ave *Web:* www.cranbrook.edu	Bloomfield Hills	MI	48304	248-645-3260	645-3050
Detroit Historical Museum 5401 Woodward Ave *Web:* www.detroithistorical.org	Detroit	MI	48202	313-833-1805	833-5342
Detroit Institute of Arts 5200 Woodward Ave *Web:* www.dia.org	Detroit	MI	48202	313-833-7900	
Detroit Science Center 5020 John R St *Web:* www.detroitsciencecenter.org	Detroit	MI	48202	313-577-8400	832-1623
Dossin Great Lakes Museum 100 Strand Dr Belle Isle *Web:* www.detroithistorical.org	Detroit	MI	48207	313-852-4051	822-4610
Exhibit Museum of Natural History 1109 Geddes Ave University of Michigan *Web:* www.exhibits.lsa.umich.edu	Ann Arbor	MI	48109	734-764-0478	647-2767
Flint Institute of Arts 1120 E Kearsley St *Web:* www.flintarts.org	Flint	MI	48503	810-234-1695	234-1692
Ford Gerald R Museum 303 Pearl St NW *Web:* www.ford.utexas.edu	Grand Rapids	MI	49504	616-254-0400	254-0386
Ford Henry Estate-University of Michigan 4901 Evergreen Rd *Web:* www.umd.umich.edu/fairlane	Dearborn	MI	48128	313-593-5590	593-5243
Ford Henry Museum 20900 Oakwood Blvd *TF:* 800-835-5237 ■ *Web:* www.hfmgv.org	Dearborn	MI	48124	313-271-1620	982-6225
Gallerie 454 15105 Kercheval Ave *Web:* www.gallerie454.com	Grosse Pointe Park	MI	48230	313-822-4454	822-3768
Gerald R Ford Museum 303 Pearl St NW *Web:* www.ford.utexas.edu	Grand Rapids	MI	49504	616-254-0400	254-0386
Grand Rapids Art Museum 155 Division Ave N *Web:* www.gramonline.org/	Grand Rapids	MI	49503	616-831-1000	559-0422
Greenfield Village 20900 Oakwood Blvd **Fax:* Cust Svc ■ *TF:* 800-835-5237 ■ *Web:* www.hfmgv.org/village	Dearborn	MI	48124	313-271-1620	982-6225*
Henry Ford Museum 20900 Oakwood Blvd *TF:* 800-835-5237 ■ *Web:* www.hfmgv.org	Dearborn	MI	48124	313-271-1620	982-6225
Historic Hack House Museum 775 County St	Milan	MI	48160	734-439-7522	
Holocaust Memorial Center 28123 Orchard Lake Rd *Web:* holocaustcenter.org	Farmington Hills	MI	48334	248-553-2400	553-2433
Impression 5 Science Center 200 Museum Dr *Web:* www.impression5.org	Lansing	MI	48933	517-485-8116	485-8125
International Gospel Music Hall of Fame & Museum 18301 W McNichols Rd *Web:* www.igmhf.org/	Detroit	MI	48219	313-592-0017	592-8762
International Institute of Metropolitan Detroit 111 E Kirby St *Web:* www.iimd.org	Detroit	MI	48202	313-871-8600	871-1651
Kelsey Museum of Archaeology 434 S State St University of Michigan *Web:* www.lsa.umich.edu/kelsey/	Ann Arbor	MI	48109	734-763-3559	763-8976
Kempf House Museum 312 S Division St *Web:* kempfhousemuseum.org	Ann Arbor	MI	48104	734-994-4898	
Kingman Museum 175 Limit St *Web:* www.kingmanmuseum.org	Battle Creek	MI	49017	269-965-5117	965-3330
Kresge Art Museum Michigan State University *Web:* www.msu.edu/unit/kamuseum	East Lansing	MI	48824	517-353-9834	355-6577
Leslie Science Center 1831 Traver Rd	Ann Arbor	MI	48105	734-997-1553	997-1072
Manistee County Historical Museum 425 River St	Manistee	MI	49660	231-723-5531	
Michigan Historical Museum 702 W Kalamazoo	Lansing	MI	48915	517-373-3559	241-3647
Michigan Library & Historical Center 702 W Kalamazoo St	Lansing	MI	48915	517-373-3559	373-0851
Michigan State University Museum W Circle Dr *Web:* museum.cl.msu.edu	East Lansing	MI	48824	517-355-2370	432-2846
Michigan Women's Historical Center & Hall of Fame 213 W Main St *Web:* www.michiganwomenshalloffame.org	Lansing	MI	48933	517-484-1880	372-0170
Midland Center for the Arts Inc 1801 W St Andrews Rd *Web:* www.mcfta.org	Midland	MI	48640	989-631-5930	631-7890
Minibeast Zooseum & Education Center 6907 W Grand River Ave	Lansing	MI	48906	517-886-0630	886-0630
Monroe County Historical Museum 126 S Monroe St	Monroe	MI	48161	734-240-7780	240-7788
Montrose Historical & Telephone Pioneer Museum 144 E Hickory St	Montrose	MI	48457	810-639-6644	
Motown Museum 2648 W Grand Blvd *Web:* motownmuseum.com	Detroit	MI	48208	313-875-2264	875-2267
Museum of Surveying 220 S Museum Dr *Web:* www.surveyhistory.org	Lansing	MI	48933	517-484-6605	484-3711
National Museum of the Tuskegee Airmen 6325 W Jefferson **Fax Area Code:* 800	Detroit	MI	48209	313-843-8849	595-6576*
Olds RE Transportation Museum 240 Museum Dr *Web:* www.reoldsmuseum.org	Lansing	MI	48933	517-372-0422	372-2901
Public Museum of Grand Rapids 272 Pearl St NW Van Andel Museum Center *TF:* 800-459-4253 ■ *Web:* www.grmuseum.org	Grand Rapids	MI	49504	616-456-3977	456-3873
RE Olds Transportation Museum 240 Museum Dr *Web:* www.reoldsmuseum.org	Lansing	MI	48933	517-372-0422	372-2901
Sloan Alfred P Museum 1221 E Kearsley St *Web:* www.sloanmuseum.com	Flint	MI	48503	810-237-3450	237-3451
University of Michigan Museum of Art 915 E Washington St Suite 0540 Rackham Bldg *Web:* www.umma.umich.edu	Ann Arbor	MI	48109	734-764-0395	764-3731
Voigt House Victorian Museum 115 College Ave SE *Web:* www.grmuseum.org	Grand Rapids	MI	49503	616-456-4600	456-4603
Walter P Chrysler Museum 1 Chrysler Dr *TF:* 888-456-1924 ■ *Web:* www.chryslerheritage.com	Auburn Hills	MI	48326	248-944-0001	944-0460
Wright Charles H Museum of African American History 315 E Warren Ave *Web:* www.maah-detroit.org	Detroit	MI	48201	313-494-5800	494-5855
Yankee Air Museum Willow Run Airport *Web:* www.yankeeairmuseum.org	Ypsilanti	MI	48197	734-483-4030	483-5076
Ypsilanti Historical Museum 220 N Huron St	Ypsilanti	MI	48197	734-482-4990	483-7481

Minnesota

				Phone	Fax
American Swedish Institute 2600 Park Ave *TF Sales:* 800-579-3336 ■ *Web:* www.americanswedishinst.org/	Minneapolis	MN	55407	612-871-4907	871-8682
Bakken The 3537 Zenith Ave S *Web:* www.thebakken.org	Minneapolis	MN	55416	612-927-6508	927-7265
Bell Museum of Natural History 10 Church St SE *Web:* www.bellmuseum.org	Minneapolis	MN	55455	612-624-7083	626-7704
Dakota County Historical Museum 130 3rd Ave N *Web:* www.dakotahistory.org	South Saint Paul	MN	55075	651-552-7548	552-7265
Depot The Saint Louis County Heritage & Arts Center 506 W Michigan St *Web:* www.duluthdepot.org	Duluth	MN	55802	218-727-8025	733-7506
Fitger's Brewery Complex Museum 600 E Superior St *TF:* 888-348-4377 ■ *Web:* www.fitgers.com	Duluth	MN	55802	218-722-0410	
Foshay Tower Observation Deck & Museum 821 Marquette Ave	Minneapolis	MN	55402	612-359-3030	359-3034
Gibbs Museum of Pioneer & Dakotah Life 2097 W Larpenteur Ave *Web:* www.rchs.com/gbbsfm2.htm	Saint Paul	MN	55113	651-646-8629	659-0345
Great Lakes Floating Maritime Museum 350 Harbor Dr *Web:* www.williamirvin.com	Duluth	MN	55802	218-722-7876	722-9206
Hennepin History Museum 2303 3rd Ave S *Web:* www.hhmuseum.org	Minneapolis	MN	55404	612-870-1329	870-1320
Ironworld Discovery Center 801 SW Hwy 169 Suite 1 *TF:* 800-372-6437 ■ *Web:* www.ironworld.com	Chisholm	MN	55719	218-254-7959	254-7971
Karpeles Manuscript Library Museum 902 E 1st St *Web:* www.rain.org/~karpeles/dulfrm.html	Duluth	MN	55805	218-728-0630	
Lake Superior Maritime Visitors Center 600 Lake Ave S *Web:* www.lsmma.com	Duluth	MN	55802	218-727-2497	720-5270
Lake Superior Railroad Museum 506 W Michigan St *Web:* www.duluth.com/lsrm	Duluth	MN	55802	218-733-7590	733-7596
Mill City Museum 704 S 2nd St *Web:* www.millcitymuseum.org	Minneapolis	MN	55401	612-341-7555	341-7506
Minneapolis Institute of Arts 2400 3rd Ave S *TF:* 888-642-2787 ■ *Web:* www.artsmia.org	Minneapolis	MN	55404	612-870-3000	870-3004

Minnesota (Cont'd)

	City	State	Zip	Phone	Fax
Minnesota Historical Society History Center Museum 345 Kellogg Blvd W *TF:* 800-657-3773 ■ *Web:* www.mnhs.org	Saint Paul	MN	55102	651-296-6126	296-1004
Minnesota Museum of American Art Kellogg Blvd & Market St *Web:* www.mmaa.org	Saint Paul	MN	55102	651-266-1030	291-2947
Minnesota State University Moorhead Regional Science Center Minnesota State University Moorhead 1104 7th Ave S *Web:* www.mnstate.edu/regsci/	Moorhead	MN	56563	218-477-2904	477-5864
Minnesota Transportation Museum 193 E Pennsylvania Ave *Web:* www.mtmuseum.org	Saint Paul	MN	55130	651-228-0263	293-0857
Minnesota Wing Commemorative Air Force Museum 310 Airport Rd *Web:* www.cafmn.org	South Saint Paul	MN	55075	651-455-6942	455-2160
Museum of Russian Art 5500 Stevens Ave S *Web:* www.tmora.org	Minneapolis	MN	55419	612-821-9045	821-4392
Pavek Museum of Broadcasting 3515 Raleigh Ave *Web:* www.pavekmuseum.org	Saint Louis Park	MN	55416	952-926-8198	929-6105
Schubert Club Museum of Musical Instruments Landmark Center 75 W 5th St *Web:* www.schubert.org/museum.html	Saint Paul	MN	55102	651-292-3267	
Science Museum of Minnesota 120 W Kellogg Blvd *Web:* www.smm.org	Saint Paul	MN	55102	651-221-9444	221-4777
Tweed Museum of Art 1201 Ordean Ct *Web:* www.d.umn.edu/tma	Duluth	MN	55812	218-726-8222	726-8503
Twin Cities Model Railroad Museum 1021 Bandana Blvd E Suite 222 *Web:* www.tcmrm.org	Saint Paul	MN	55108	651-647-9628	636-4140
Walker Art Center 1750 Hennepin Ave *Web:* www.walkerart.org	Minneapolis	MN	55403	612-375-7600	375-7618
Weisman Art Museum 333 E River Rd *Web:* www.weisman.umn.edu	Minneapolis	MN	55455	612-625-9494	625-9630

Mississippi

	City	State	Zip	Phone	Fax
African American Military History Museum 305 E 6th St *Web:* hattiesburg.org/aamhm	Hattiesburg	MS	39401	601-583-8624	
Amory Regional Museum 715 3rd St S *Web:* www.amoryms.us/museum2.htm	Amory	MS	38821	662-256-2761	256-2761
Armed Forces Museum *Web:* www.armedforcesmuseum.us	Camp Shelby	MS	39407	601-558-2757	558-2377
Elvis Presley Birthplace & Museum 306 Elvis Presley Dr *Web:* www.elvispresleybirthplace.com	Tupelo	MS	38802	662-841-1245	690-6623
International Checker Hall of Fame 220 Lynn Ray Rd	Petal	MS	39465	601-582-7090	582-7090
International Museum of Muslim Cultures 117 E Pascagoula St *Web:* www.muslimmuseum.org	Jackson	MS	39201	601-960-0440	960-0414
Landrum's Homestead & Village 1356 Hwy 15 S *Web:* www.landrums.com	Laurel	MS	39443	601-649-2546	428-1663
Lauren Rogers Museum of Art 565 N 5th Ave *Web:* www.lrma.org	Laurel	MS	39440	601-649-6374	649-6379
Manship House Museum 420 E Fortification St *Web:* www.mdah.state.ms.us/museum/manship.html	Jackson	MS	39202	601-961-4724	354-6043
Mississippi Agriculture & Forestry Museum/National Agricultural Aviation Museum 1150 Lakeland Dr *TF:* 800-844-8687 ■ *Web:* www.mdac.state.ms.us	Jackson	MS	39216	601-713-3365	982-4292
Mississippi Archives & History Library 200 North St *Web:* mdah.state.ms.us	Jackson	MS	39201	601-576-6876	576-6964
Mississippi Museum of Art 201 E Pascagoula St *Web:* www.msmuseumart.org	Jackson	MS	39201	601-960-1515	960-1505
Mississippi Museum of Natural Science 2148 Riverside Dr *Web:* www.mdwfp.state.ms.us/museum	Jackson	MS	39202	601-354-7303	354-7227
Mississippi State Historical Museum 100 S State St *Web:* www.mdah.state.ms.us/musetxt.html#capitol	Jackson	MS	39201	601-576-6920	576-6981
Museum of the Southern Jewish Experience Old Morrison Rd *Web:* www.msje.org	Utica	MS	39175	601-362-6357	366-6293
Oaks House Museum 823 N Jefferson St	Jackson	MS	39202	601-353-9339	
Ohr-O'Keefe Museum of Art 1596 Glenn Swetman St *Web:* www.georgeohr.org	Biloxi	MS	39530	228-374-5547	436-3641
Oren Dunn City Museum 689 Rutherford Rd PO Box 2674	Tupelo	MS	38803	662-841-6438	841-6458
Rogers Lauren Museum of Art 565 N 5th Ave *Web:* www.lrma.org	Laurel	MS	39440	601-649-6374	649-6379
Smith Robertson Museum & Cultural Center 528 Bloom St	Jackson	MS	39202	601-960-1457	960-2070

Missouri

	City	State	Zip	Phone	Fax
Air & Military Museum 2305 E Kearney St *Web:* www.ammomuseum.org	Springfield	MO	65803	417-864-7997	
Airline History Museum 201 Lou Holland Dr Hangar 9 *TF:* 800-513-9484 ■ *Web:* www.airlinehistorymuseum.com	Kansas City	MO	64116	816-421-3401	421-3421
Alexander Majors Historic House & Museum 8201 State Line Rd	Kansas City	MO	64114	816-333-5556	
American Jazz Museum 1616 E 18th St *Web:* www.americanjazzmuseum.com	Kansas City	MO	64108	816-474-8463	474-0074
American Kennel Club Museum of the Dog 1721 S Mason Rd *Web:* www.akc.org/affiliates/museum/aboutmuseum.cfm	Saint Louis	MO	63131	314-821-3647	821-7381
American Presidential Museum 2849 Gretner Rd *TF:* 866-334-8683 ■ *Web:* www.americanpresidentialmuseum.com	Branson	MO	65616	417-334-8683	334-4927
American Royal Museum & Visitors Center 1701 American Royal Ct *TF:* 800-821-5857 ■ *Web:* www.americanroyal.com	Kansas City	MO	64102	816-221-9800	221-8189
Arabia Steamboat Museum 400 Grand Blvd. *TF:* 800-471-1856 ■ *Web:* www.1856.com	Kansas City	MO	64106	816-471-1856	471-1616
Black World History Museum 2505 St Louis Ave	Saint Louis	MO	63106	314-241-7057	241-7058
Chatillon-DeMenil Mansion & Museum 3352 DeMenil Pl	Saint Louis	MO	63118	314-771-5828	771-3475
City Museum 701 N 15th St Box 29 *Web:* www.citymuseum.org	Saint Louis	MO	63103	314-231-2489	231-1009
Civilian Conservation Corps Museum 16 Hancock Ave *Web:* www.cccalumni.org/museum.html	Saint Louis	MO	63125	314-487-8666	487-9488
Cole County Historical Museum 109 Madison St	Jefferson City	MO	65101	573-635-1850	
Concordia Historical Institute 804 Seminary Pl *Web:* chi.lcms.org	Saint Louis	MO	63105	314-505-7900	505-7901
Contemporary Art Museum Saint Louis 3750 Washington Blvd *Web:* www.contemporarystl.org	Saint Louis	MO	63108	314-535-4660	535-1226
Dutton Family Theatre 3454 W Hwy 76 *TF:* 800-942-4626 ■ *Web:* www.theduttons.com	Branson	MO	65616	417-332-2772	334-2314
Eugene Field House & Saint Louis Toy Museum 634 S Broadway *Web:* www.eugenefieldhouse.org	Saint Louis	MO	63102	314-421-4689	588-9328
Excelsior Springs Historical Museum 101 E Broadway	Excelsior Springs	MO	64024	816-630-0101	
Field Eugene House & Saint Louis Toy Museum 634 S Broadway *Web:* www.eugenefieldhouse.org	Saint Louis	MO	63102	314-421-4689	588-9328
Foster Ralph Museum College of the Ozarks Box 17	Point Lookout	MO	65726	417-334-6411	335-2618
General Sweeny's Museum of Civil War History 5228 S State Hwy ZZ *Web:* www.civilwarmuseum.com	Republic	MO	65738	417-732-1224	
Harry S Truman Presidential Library & Museum 500 W Hwy 24 *TF:* 800-833-1225 ■ *Web:* www.trumanlibrary.org	Independence	MO	64050	816-833-1400	833-4368
Historic Aircraft Restoration Museum 3127 Creve Coeur Mill Rd *Web:* www.historicaircraftrestorationmuseum.org	Saint Louis	MO	63146	314-434-3368	878-9575
Historic Sappington House Museum 1015 S Sappington Rd	Crestwood	MO	63126	314-822-8171	
History Museum for Springfield/Greene County 830 Boonville Ave 3rd Fl *Web:* www.historymuseumsgc.org	Springfield	MO	65802	417-864-1976	864-2019
Hollywood Wax Museum 3030 W Hwy 76 *Web:* www.hollywoodwax.com	Branson	MO	65616	417-337-8277	334-8202
Holocaust Museum & Learning Center 12 Millstone Campus Dr *Web:* www.hmlc.org	Saint Louis	MO	63146	314-432-0020	432-1277
John Wornall House Museum 6115 Wornall Rd	Kansas City	MO	64113	816-444-1858	361-8165
Kansas City Museum 3218 Gladstone Blvd *Web:* www.unionstation.org/kcmuseum.cfm	Kansas City	MO	64123	816-483-8300	483-6050
Kemper Museum of Contemporary Art 4420 Warwick Blvd *Web:* www.kemperart.org	Kansas City	MO	64111	816-753-5784	753-5806
Laumeier Sculpture Park & Museum 12580 Rott Rd *Web:* www.laumeier.com	Saint Louis	MO	63127	314-821-1209	821-1248
Laura Ingalls Wilder Museum & Home 3068 Hwy A *TF:* 877-924-7126 ■ *Web:* www.lauraingallswilderhome.com	Mansfield	MO	65704	417-924-3626	924-8580
Liberty Memorial Museum 100 W 26th St *Web:* www.libertymemorialmuseum.org	Kansas City	MO	64108	816-784-1918	784-1929
Miniature Museum of Greater Saint Louis 4746 Gravois *Web:* miniaturemuseum.org/	Saint Louis	MO	63116	314-832-7790	
Missouri History Museum 5700 Lindell Blvd PO Box 11940 *Web:* www.mohistory.org	Saint Louis	MO	63112	314-746-4599	454-3162
Missouri State Museum Capitol Bldg Rm B2 *Web:* www.mostateparks.com/jeffersonland.htm	Jefferson City	MO	65101	573-751-2854	526-2927
Missouri Veterinary Medical Foundation Museum 2500 Country Club Dr	Jefferson City	MO	65109	573-636-8737	659-7175
Museum of Anthropology 104 Swallow Hall University of Missouri *Web:* coas.missouri.edu/anthromuseum	Columbia	MO	65211	573-882-3573	884-3627
Museum of Art & Archaeology Pickard Hall University of Missouri *Web:* museum.research.missouri.edu	Columbia	MO	65211	573-882-3591	884-4039
Museum of Contemporary Religious Art 221 N Grand Blvd Saint Louis University Campus *Web:* mocra.slu.edu/	Saint Louis	MO	63103	314-977-7170	977-2999
Museum of Missouri Military History 2007 Retention Dr *Web:* www.moguard.com	Jefferson City	MO	65101	573-638-9603	638-9848
Museum of Transportation 3015 Barrett Station Rd *Web:* www.thetrainmuseum.org	Saint Louis	MO	63122	314-965-7998	965-0242
Museums at 18th & Vine 1616 E 18th St *Web:* americanjazzmuseum.com	Kansas City	MO	64108	816-474-8463	474-0074
National World War I Museum 100 W 26th St *Web:* www.libertymemorialmuseum.org	Kansas City	MO	64108	816-784-1918	784-1929
Nelson-Atkins Museum of Art 4525 Oak St *Web:* www.nelson-atkins.org	Kansas City	MO	64111	816-561-4000	561-7154
Pony Express National Museum 914 Penn St *TF:* 800-530-5930 ■ *Web:* www.ponyexpress.org	Saint Joseph	MO	64503	816-279-5059	233-9370
Ralph Foster Museum College of the Ozarks Box 17	Point Lookout	MO	65726	417-334-6411	335-2618
Ripley's Believe It or Not! Museum 3326 W Hwy 76 *TF:* 800-998-4418 ■ *Web:* www.ripleysbranson.com	Branson	MO	65616	417-337-5300	337-5229
Roy Rogers-Dale Evans Museum 3950 Green Mountain Dr *Web:* www.royrogers.com	Branson	MO	65616	417-339-1900	
Saint Louis Art Museum 1 Fine Arts Dr *Web:* www.slam.org	Saint Louis	MO	63110	314-721-0072	721-6172
Saint Louis Science Center 5050 Oakland Ave *TF:* 800-456-7572 ■ *Web:* www.slsc.org	Saint Louis	MO	63110	314-289-4400	289-4420
Saint Louis University Museum of Art 3663 Lindell Blvd O'Donnell Hall *Web:* sluma.slu.edu	Saint Louis	MO	63103	314-977-3399	977-3581
Shoal Creek Living History Museum 7000 NE Barry Rd Hodge Park *Web:* www.kcmo.org/parks.nsf/web/shoal	Kansas City	MO	64156	816-792-2655	792-3469
Soldiers Memorial Military Museum 1315 Chestnut St	Saint Louis	MO	63103	314-622-4550	622-4237
Springfield Art Museum 1111 E Brookside Dr *Web:* www.ci.springfield.mo.us/egov/art	Springfield	MO	65807	417-837-5700	837-5704
State Historical Society of Missouri 1020 Lowry St *Web:* www.umsystem.edu/shs	Columbia	MO	65201	573-882-7083	884-4950
Toy & Miniature Museum 5235 Oak St *Web:* www.umkc.edu/tmm	Kansas City	MO	64112	816-333-2055	333-2055
Truman Harry S Presidential Library & Museum 500 W Hwy 24 *TF:* 800-833-1225 ■ *Web:* www.trumanlibrary.org	Independence	MO	64050	816-833-1400	833-4368
Walters-Boone County Historical Museum 3801 Ponderosa St *Web:* members.sockets.net/~bchs	Columbia	MO	65201	573-443-8936	875-5268
Wilder Laura Ingalls Museum & Home 3068 Hwy A *TF:* 877-924-7126 ■ *Web:* www.lauraingallswilderhome.com	Mansfield	MO	65704	417-924-3626	924-8580
Wornall John House Museum 6115 Wornall Rd	Kansas City	MO	64113	816-444-1858	361-8165

Montana

	City	State	Zip	Phone	Fax
Children's Museum of Montana 22 Railroad Sq *Web:* childrensmuseumofmt.org	Great Falls	MT	59401	406-452-6661	452-4462
CM Russell Museum 400 13th St N *Web:* www.cmrussell.org	Great Falls	MT	59401	406-727-8787	727-2402
Holter Museum of Art 12 E Lawrence St *Web:* www.holtermuseum.org	Helena	MT	59601	406-442-6400	442-2404
Malmstrom Air Force Base Museum & Air Park 21 77th St N Rm 144 341 Spacewing/MU	Malmstrom AFB	MT	59402	406-731-2705	731-2769
Montana Historical Society Museum 225 N Roberts St *TF:* 800-243-9900 ■ *Web:* www.montanahistoricalsociety.org	Helena	MT	59620	406-444-2694	444-2696
Museum of the Plains Indians PO Box 410	Browning	MT	59417	406-338-2230	338-7404
Museum of the Rockies 600 W Kagy Blvd Montana State University *Web:* www.montana.edu/wwwmor/	Bozeman	MT	59717	406-994-5283	994-2682
Paris Gibson Square Museum of Art 1400 1st Ave N *Web:* www.the-square.org	Great Falls	MT	59401	406-727-8255	727-8256

	City	State	Zip	Phone	Fax
Peter Yegen Jr Yellowstone County Museum 1950 Terminal Cir *Web:* www.pyjrycm.org	Billings	MT	59105	406-256-6811	254-6031
Russell CM Museum 400 13th St N *Web:* www.cmrussell.org	Great Falls	MT	59401	406-727-8787	727-2402
World Museum of Mining 155 Museum Way *Web:* www.miningmuseum.org	Butte	MT	59701	406-723-7211	723-7211
Yellowstone Art Museum 401 N 27th St *Web:* yellowstone.artmuseum.org	Billings	MT	59101	406-256-6804	256-6817
Yellowstone Western Heritage Center 2822 Montana Ave *Web:* www.ywhc.org	Billings	MT	59101	406-256-6809	256-6850

Nebraska

	City	State	Zip	Phone	Fax
Bank of Florence Museum 8502 N 30th St	Omaha	NE	68112	402-496-9923	455-1424
Durham Western Heritage Museum 801 S 10th St *Web:* www.dwhm.org	Omaha	NE	68108	402-444-5071	444-5397
El Museo Latino 4701 S 25th St *Web:* www.elmuseolatino.org	Omaha	NE	68107	402-731-1137	733-7012
Freedom Park US Naval Museum 2497 Freedom Park Rd	Omaha	NE	68110	402-345-1959	345-3835
Great Plains Art Collection 1155 Q St *Web:* www.unl.edu/plains/gallery/gallery.html	Lincoln	NE	68588	402-472-6220	
Hastings Museum 1350 N Burlington Ave *Web:* www.hastingsmuseum.org	Hastings	NE	68901	402-461-2399	461-2379
Joslyn Art Museum 2200 Dodge St *Web:* www.joslyn.org	Omaha	NE	68102	402-342-3300	342-2376
Kountze Mallory Planetarium 67th & Dodge Sts Durham Science Ctr Rm 129 **Fax Area Code: 800*	Omaha	NE	68182	402-554-3722	554-3100*
Lentz Center for Asian Culture 1155 Q St Hewit Pl *Web:* www.unl.edu/lentz	Lincoln	NE	68588	402-472-5841	
Mallory Kountze Planetarium 67th & Dodge Sts Durham Science Ctr Rm 129 **Fax Area Code: 800*	Omaha	NE	68182	402-554-3722	554-3100*
Museum of Nebraska History 131 Centennial Mall N *TF:* 800-833-6747 ■ *Web:* www.nebraskahistory.org/sites/mnh/	Lincoln	NE	68508	402-471-4754	471-3314
National Museum of Roller Skating 4730 South St *Web:* www.rollerskatingmuseum.com	Lincoln	NE	68506	402-483-7551	483-1465
Nebraska Jewish Historical Museum 333 S 132nd St	Omaha	NE	68154	402-334-6441	334-6507
Sheldon Memorial Art Gallery 12th & R Sts *Web:* www.sheldonartgallery.org	Lincoln	NE	68588	402-472-2461	472-4258
Strategic Air & Space Museum 28210 W Park Hwy *TF:* 800-358-5029 ■ *Web:* www.strategicairandspace.com	Ashland	NE	68003	402-944-3100	944-3160
Stuhr Museum of the Prairie Pioneer 3133 W Hwy 34 *Web:* www.stuhrmuseum.org	Grand Island	NE	68801	308-385-5316	385-5028
University of Nebraska State Museum University of Nebraska Morrill Hall 14th & Vine *Web:* www-museum.unl.edu	Lincoln	NE	68588	402-472-2642	472-8899

Nevada

	City	State	Zip	Phone	Fax
Atomic Testing Museum 755 E Flamingo Rd *Web:* www.atomictestingmuseum.org	Las Vegas	NV	89119	702-794-5151	794-5155
Boulder City/Hoover Dam Museum 1305 Arizona St *Web:* www.bcmha.org	Boulder City	NV	89005	702-294-1988	294-4380
Carson Valley Museum & Cultural Center 1477 Hwy 395 N	Gardnerville	NV	89410	775-782-2555	783-8802
Churchill County Museum & Archives 1050 S Maine St *Web:* www.ccmuseum.org	Fallon	NV	89406	775-423-3677	423-3662
Clark County Museum 1830 S Boulder Hwy	Henderson	NV	89015	702-455-7955	455-7948
Guggenheim Hermitage Museum 3355 Las Vegas Blvd S Venetian Resort Hotel & Casino *Web:* www.guggenheimlasvegas.org	Las Vegas	NV	89109	702-414-2440	414-2442
Las Vegas Art Museum 9600 W Sahara Ave *Web:* www.lasvegasartmuseum.org	Las Vegas	NV	89117	702-360-8000	360-8080
Las Vegas Natural History Museum 900 Las Vegas Blvd N *Web:* www.vegaswebworld.com/lvnathistory	Las Vegas	NV	89101	702-384-3466	
Liberace Museum 1775 E Tropicana Ave *Web:* www.flatwaremedia.com/liberace/museum.cfm	Las Vegas	NV	89119	702-798-5595	798-7386
Lost City Museum of Archeology 721 S Moapa Valley Blvd *Web:* www.comnett.net/~lostcity/	Overton	NV	89040	702-397-2193	397-8987
May Wilbur D Museum 1595 N Sierra St *Web:* www.maycenter.com	Reno	NV	89503	775-785-5961	785-4707
National Automobile Museum 10 S Lake St *Web:* www.automuseum.org	Reno	NV	89501	775-333-9300	333-9309
Nevada Gambling Museum 50 S 'C' St	Virginia City	NV	89440	775-847-9022	847-9613
Nevada Historical Society Museum 1650 N Virginia St *Web:* dmla.clan.lib.nv.us/docs/museums	Reno	NV	89503	775-688-1190	688-2917
Nevada Museum of Art 160 W Liberty St *Web:* www.nevadaart.org	Reno	NV	89501	775-329-3333	329-1541
Nevada State Museum 600 N Carson St *Web:* dmla.clan.lib.nv.us/docs/museums	Carson City	NV	89701	775-687-4810	687-4168
Nevada State Museum & Historical Society 700 Twin Lakes Dr *Web:* dmla.clan.lib.nv.us/docs/museums	Las Vegas	NV	89107	702-486-5205	486-5172
Nevada State Railroad Museum 2180 S Carson St *Web:* www.nsrm-friends.org	Carson City	NV	89701	775-687-6953	687-8294
Northeastern Nevada Museum 1515 Idaho St *Web:* www.museum-elko.us	Elko	NV	89801	775-738-3418	778-9318
Roberts House Museum 1207 N Carson St	Carson City	NV	89701	775-887-2174	882-3559
Sparks Heritage Museum 820 Victorian Ave *Web:* www.sparksheritagemuseum.org	Sparks	NV	89431	775-355-1144	355-6788
University of Nevada Las Vegas Barrick Museum of Natural History 4505 S Maryland Pkwy *Web:* hrcweb.lv-hrc.nevada.edu	Las Vegas	NV	89154	702-895-3381	895-5737
Warren Engine Co No 1 Fire Museum 777 S Stewart St	Carson City	NV	89701	775-887-2210	887-2209
Way It Was Museum 113 C St	Virginia City	NV	89440	775-847-0766	
Wilbur D May Museum 1595 N Sierra St *Web:* www.maycenter.com	Reno	NV	89503	775-785-5961	785-4707

New Brunswick

	City	State	Zip	Phone	Fax
Kings Landing Historical Settlement 20 Kings Landing Service Entrance Rd Unit 2 *TF:* 888-666-5547 ■ *Web:* www.kingslanding.nb.ca	Kings Lndg Hist Settlemnt	NB	E6K3W3	506-363-4999	363-4989
Musee Acadien Universite de Moncton *Web:* www.umoncton.ca/maum	Moncton	NB	E1A3E9	506-858-4088	858-4043
New Brunswick Museum 1 Market Sq *Web:* www.gnb.ca/0130	Saint John	NB	E2L4Z6	506-643-2300	643-6081

New Hampshire

	City	State	Zip	Phone	Fax
Canterbury Shaker Village 288 Shaker Rd *TF:* 866-783-9511 ■ *Web:* www.shakers.org	Canterbury	NH	03224	603-783-9511	783-9152
Currier Museum of Art 201 Myrtle Way *Web:* www.currier.org	Manchester	NH	03104	603-669-6144	669-7194
Hood Museum of Art Dartmouth College Wheelock St *Web:* hoodmuseum.dartmouth.edu	Hanover	NH	03755	603-646-2808	646-1400
Lawrence L Lee Scouting Museum 40 Bodwell Rd PO Box 1121 *Web:* www.scoutingmuseum.org	Manchester	NH	03105	603-669-8919	627-1492
Mount Kearsarge Indian Museum Kearsarge Mountain Rd *Web:* www.indianmuseum.com	Warner	NH	03278	603-456-2600	456-3092
Museum of New Hampshire History 6 Eagle Sq *Web:* www.nhhistory.org	Concord	NH	03301	603-226-3189	228-6308
New Hampshire Historical Society Museum 30 Park St *Web:* www.nhhistory.org	Concord	NH	03301	603-225-3381	224-0463
New Hampshire Institute of Art 148 Concord St *TF:* 866-241-4918 ■ *Web:* www.nhia.edu	Manchester	NH	03104	603-623-0313	647-0658
SEE Science Center 200 Bedford St *Web:* www.see-sciencecenter.org	Manchester	NH	03101	603-669-0400	669-0400
Strawbery Banke Museum 420 Court St *Web:* www.strawberybanke.org	Portsmouth	NH	03801	603-433-1100	433-1129

New Jersey

	City	State	Zip	Phone	Fax
Afro-American Historical Society Museum 1841 Kennedy Blvd	Jersey City	NJ	07305	201-547-5262	547-5392
Aljira Center for Contemporary Arts 591 Broad St *Web:* www.aljira.org	Newark	NJ	07102	973-622-1600	622-6526
American Labor Museum/Botto House National Landmark 83 Norwood St *Web:* www.geocities.com/labormuseum	Haledon	NJ	07508	973-595-7953	595-7291
Atlantic City Historical Museum Garden Pier Boardwalk New Jersey Ave *Web:* www.acmuseum.org	Atlantic City	NJ	08401	609-347-5839	347-5284
Atlantic County Historical Society Museum 907 Shore Rd *Web:* www.aclink.org/achs	Somers Point	NJ	08244	609-927-5218	927-5218
Havens Meredith Fire Museum 244 Perry St	Trenton	NJ	08618	609-989-4038	989-4280
Jersey City Museum 350 Montgomery St *Web:* www.jerseycitymuseum.org	Jersey City	NJ	07302	201-413-0303	413-9922
Liberty Science Center Liberty State Park Historic Central Railroad of New Jersey Bldg *Web:* www.lsc.org	Jersey City	NJ	07305	201-200-1000	
Marine Mammal Stranding Center 3625 Brigantine Blvd *Web:* www.mmsc.org	Brigantine	NJ	08203	609-266-0538	266-6300
Meredith Havens Fire Museum 244 Perry St	Trenton	NJ	08618	609-989-4038	989-4280
Montclair Art Museum 3 S Mountain Ave *Web:* www.montclair-art.com	Montclair	NJ	07042	973-746-5555	746-0536
Morris Museum 6 Normandy Heights Rd *Web:* www.morrismuseum.org	Morristown	NJ	07960	973-971-3700	538-0154
New Jersey Historical Society Museum 52 Park Pl *Web:* www.jerseyhistory.org	Newark	NJ	07102	973-596-8500	596-6957
New Jersey State Museum 205 W State St *Web:* www.state.nj.us/state/museum	Trenton	NJ	08625	609-292-6300	599-4098
Newark Museum 49 Washington St *Web:* www.newarkmuseum.org	Newark	NJ	07102	973-596-6550	642-0459
Noyes Museum Lily Lake Rd *Web:* www.noyesmuseum.org	Oceanville	NJ	08231	609-652-8848	652-6166
Old Barracks Museum 101 Barrack St *TF:* 888-227-7225 ■ *Web:* www.barracks.org	Trenton	NJ	08608	609-396-1776	777-4000
Paterson Museum 2 Market St Thomas Rogers Bldg *Web:* www.thepatersonmuseum.com	Paterson	NJ	07501	973-321-1260	881-3435
Ripley's Believe It or Not! Museum New York Ave & Boardwalk *Web:* www.ripleys.com/bion/atlantic.html	Atlantic City	NJ	08401	609-347-2001	347-2009
Trenton City Museum at Ellarslie Mansion Cadawalader Park *Web:* www.ellarslie.org	Trenton	NJ	08608	609-989-3632	989-3624

New Mexico

	City	State	Zip	Phone	Fax
Albuquerque Museum 2000 Mountain Rd NW *Web:* www.cabq.gov/museum	Albuquerque	NM	87104	505-243-7255	764-6546
American International Rattlesnake Museum 202 San Felipe NW Suite A *Web:* www.rattlesnakes.com	Albuquerque	NM	87104	505-242-6569	242-6569
Archaeology & Material Culture Museum 22 Calvary Rd *Web:* www.museumarch.org	Cedar Crest	NM	87008	505-281-2005	
Archdiocese of Santa Fe Museum 223 Cathedral Pl	Santa Fe	NM	87501	505-983-3811	992-0341
Bataan Memorial Museum 1050 Old Pecos Trail	Santa Fe	NM	87505	505-474-1670	474-1670
Bradbury Science Museum 15th & Central PO Box 1663 *Web:* www.lanl.gov/worldview/museum	Los Alamos	NM	87545	505-667-4444	665-6932
El Rancho de las Golondrinas Museum 334 Los Pinos Rd *Web:* www.golondrinas.org	Santa Fe	NM	87507	505-471-2261	471-5623
Explora 1701 Mountain Rd NW *Web:* www.explora.mus.nm.us	Albuquerque	NM	87104	505-224-8300	224-8325
Georgia O'Keeffe Museum 217 Johnson St *Web:* www.okeeffemuseum.org	Santa Fe	NM	87501	505-995-0785	946-1091
Historical Lawmen Museum 845 Motel Blvd *TF:* 800-332-2121	Las Cruces	NM	88007	505-525-1911	647-7800
Hubbard Museum of the American West 841 Hwy 70 W PO Box 40 *Web:* www.hubbardmuseum.com	Ruidoso Downs	NM	88346	505-378-4142	378-4166
Indian Pueblo Cultural Center 2401 12th St NW *TF:* 800-766-4405 ■ *Web:* www.indianpueblo.org	Albuquerque	NM	87104	505-843-7270	842-6959
Institute of American Indian Arts Museum 108 Cathedral Pl *TF:* 800-804-6423 ■ *Web:* www.iaiancad.org	Santa Fe	NM	87501	505-983-8900	983-1222
Las Cruces Museum of Art 490 N Water St *Web:* www.las-cruces.org/public-services/museums/mfa.shtm	Las Cruces	NM	88001	505-541-2137	541-2173
Las Cruces Museum of Natural History 700 Telshor Blvd	Las Cruces	NM	88001	505-541-2155	525-3645
Log Cabin Museum 671 N Main St *Web:* www.las-cruces.org/public-services/museums/logcabin.shtm	Las Cruces	NM	88001	505-541-2155	525-3645
Los Alamos Historical Museum PO Box 43 *Web:* www.losalamos.com/Historicalsociety	Los Alamos	NM	87544	505-662-6272	662-6312
Maxwell Museum of Anthropology University of New Mexico *Web:* www.unm.edu/~maxwell/	Albuquerque	NM	87131	505-277-4405	277-1547
Museum of Archaeology & Biblical History 10110 Constitution NE *Web:* www.mabh.org	Albuquerque	NM	87112	505-217-1330	217-1333

New Mexico (Cont'd)

				Phone	Fax
Museum of Fine Arts 107 W Palace Ave *Web:* www.museumofnewmexico.org	Santa Fe	NM	87501	505-476-5072	476-5076
Museum of Indian Arts & Culture 710 Camino Lejo *Web:* www.miaclab.org	Santa Fe	NM	87501	505-476-1250	476-1330
Museum of International Folk Art 706 Camino Lejo *Web:* www.moifa.org	Santa Fe	NM	87505	505-476-1200	476-1300
Museum of Spanish Colonial Arts 750 Camino Lejo *Web:* www.spanishcolonial.org	Santa Fe	NM	87505	505-982-2226	982-4585
National Atomic Museum 1905 Mountain Rd NW *Web:* www.atomicmuseum.com	Albuquerque	NM	87107	505-245-2137	242-4537
New Mexico Farm & Ranch Heritage Museum 4100 Dripping Springs Rd	Las Cruces	NM	88011	505-522-4100	522-3085
New Mexico Holocaust & Intolerance Museum & Study Center 415 Central Ave NW *Web:* www.nmholocaustmuseum.org	Albuquerque	NM	87102	505-247-0606	323-3946
New Mexico Museum of Natural History & Science 1801 Mountain Rd NW *Web:* www.museums.state.nm.us/nmmnh	Albuquerque	NM	87104	505-841-2800	841-2866
New Mexico Museum of Space History PO Box 5430 *TF:* 877-333-6589 ■ *Web:* www.spacefame.org	Alamogordo	NM	88311	505-437-2840	434-2245
New Mexico State University Museum University Ave & Solano St Kent Hall PO Box 30001 MSC 3564 *Web:* www.nmsu.edu/~museum/	Las Cruces	NM	88003	505-646-3739	646-1419
O'Keeffe Georgia Museum 217 Johnson St *Web:* www.okeeffemuseum.org	Santa Fe	NM	87501	505-995-0785	946-1091
Roswell Museum & Art Center 100 W 11th St *Web:* www.roswellmuseum.org	Roswell	NM	88201	505-624-6744	624-6765
Space Murals Museum 12450 Hwy 70 E	Las Cruces	NM	88012	505-382-0977	382-7623
Telephone Pioneer Museum of New Mexico 110 4th St NW *Web:* www.nmculture.org	Albuquerque	NM	87102	505-842-2937	
Tinkertown Museum 121 Sandia Crest Rd *Web:* www.tinkertown.com	Sandia Park	NM	87047	505-281-5233	286-9335
University of New Mexico Art Museum University of New Mexico Center for the Arts Rm 1017 *TF:* 800-225-5866 ■ *Web:* unmartmuseum.unm.edu	Albuquerque	NM	87131	505-277-4001	277-7315
University of New Mexico Museums 200 Yale Blvd NE Institute of Meteoritics University of New Mexico	Albuquerque	NM	87131	505-277-2747	277-3577
Wheelwright Museum of the American Indian 704 Camino Lejo *TF:* 800-607-4636 ■ *Web:* www.wheelwright.org	Santa Fe	NM	87505	505-982-4636	989-7386
White Sands Missile Range Museum & Missile Park US Hwy 70 *Web:* www.wsmr-history.org	White Sands	NM	88002	505-678-8824	678-2199

New York

				Phone	Fax
Albany Institute of History & Art 125 Washington Ave *Web:* www.albanyinstitute.org	Albany	NY	12210	518-463-4478	462-1522
Albright-Knox Art Gallery 1285 Elmwood Ave *Web:* www.albrightknox.org	Buffalo	NY	14222	716-882-8700	882-1958
Alice Austen House Museum & Garden 2 Hylan Blvd *Web:* www.aliceausten.8m.com/museum	Staten Island	NY	10305	718-816-4506	815-3959
American Folk Art Museum 45 W 53rd St *Web:* www.folkartmuseum.org	New York	NY	10019	212-265-1040	265-2350
American Museum of Natural History 175-208 Central Park W *Web:* www.amnh.org	New York	NY	10024	212-769-5000	496-3500
American Numismatic Society 96 Fulton St *Web:* www.amnumsoc.org	New York	NY	10028	212-571-4470	571-4479
Amherst Museum 3755 Tonawanda Creek Rd *Web:* www.amherstmuseum.org	Amherst	NY	14228	716-689-1440	689-1409
Austen Alice House Museum & Garden 2 Hylan Blvd *Web:* www.aliceausten.8m.com/museum	Staten Island	NY	10305	718-816-4506	815-3959
Bartow-Pell Mansion Museum 895 Shore Rd Pelham Bay Park *Web:* www.bartowpellmansionmuseum.org	Bronx	NY	10464	718-885-1461	885-9164
Bear Mountain Trailside Museums & Zoo Bear Mountain State Pk Rt 9 W	Bear Mountain	NY	10911	845-786-2701	786-7157
Benjamin & Dr Edgar R Cofeld Judaic Museum of Temple Beth Zion 805 Delaware Ave	Buffalo	NY	14209	716-836-6565	831-1126
Bronx County Historical Society 3309 Bainbridge Ave *Web:* www.bronxhistoricalsociety.org	Bronx	NY	10467	718-881-8900	881-4827
Bronx Museum of the Arts 1040 Grand Concourse *Web:* www.bronxmuseum.org	Bronx	NY	10456	718-681-6000	681-6181
Brooklyn Museum of Art 200 Eastern Pkwy *Web:* www.brooklynmuseum.org	Brooklyn	NY	11238	718-638-5000	501-6136
Buffalo & Erie County Historical Society 25 Nottingham Ct *Web:* intotem.buffnet.net/bechs	Buffalo	NY	14216	716-873-9644	873-8754
Buffalo Fire Historical Museum 1850 William St	Buffalo	NY	14206	716-892-8400	
Buffalo Museum of Science 1020 Humboldt Pkwy *Web:* www.sciencebuff.org	Buffalo	NY	14211	716-896-5200	897-6723
Children's Museum of Science & Technology 250 Jordan Rd *Web:* www.cmost.org	Troy	NY	12180	518-235-2120	235-6836
Cloisters Museum Fort Tryon Park *Web:* www.metmuseum.org	New York	NY	10040	212-923-3700	795-3640
Cooper-Hewitt National Design Museum (Smithsonian Institution) 2 E 91st St *Web:* ndm.si.edu	New York	NY	10128	212-849-8300	849-8401
Corning Museum of Glass 1 Museum Way *TF Cust Svc:* 800-732-6845 ■ *Web:* www.cmog.org	Corning	NY	14830	607-937-5371	974-8470
Dahesh Museum of Art 580 Madison Ave *Web:* www.daheshmuseum.org	New York	NY	10022	212-759-0606	759-1235
Doyle New York 175 E 87th St *TF:* 800-808-0902 ■ *Web:* www.doylenewyork.com	New York	NY	10128	212-427-2730	369-0892
Dyckman Farmhouse Museum 4881 Broadway at 204th St *Web:* www.dyckmanfarmhouse.org	New York	NY	10034	212-304-9422	304-0635
Ellis Island Immigration Museum Ellis Island *Web:* www.ellisisland.com	New York	NY	10004	212-344-0996	344-0219
Empire State Aerosciences Museum 250 Rudy Chase Dr *Web:* www.esam.org	Glenville	NY	12302	518-377-2191	377-1959
Empire State Plaza Art Collection Empire State Plaza Curatorial & Services Rm 2978	Albany	NY	12242	518-473-7521	474-0984
Erie Canal Museum 318 Erie Blvd E *Web:* www.eriecanalmuseum.org	Syracuse	NY	13202	315-471-0593	471-7220
Everson Museum of Art 401 Harrison St *Web:* www.everson.org	Syracuse	NY	13202	315-474-6064	474-6943
Fillmore Millard House 24 Shearer Ave	East Aurora	NY	14052	716-652-8875	
Franklin D Roosevelt Presidential Library & Museum 4079 Albany Post Rd *TF:* 800-337-8474 ■ *Web:* www.fdrlibrary.marist.edu	Hyde Park	NY	12538	845-229-8114	486-1147
Frick Collection 1 E 70th St *Web:* www.frick.org	New York	NY	10021	212-288-0700	628-4417
Genesee Country Village & Museum 1410 Flint Hill Rd *Web:* www.gcv.org	Mumford	NY	14511	585-538-6822	538-6927
Guggenheim Solomon R Museum 1071 5th Ave *TF:* 800-329-6109 ■ *Web:* www.guggenheim.org	New York	NY	10128	212-423-3500	423-3640
Harbor Defense Museum Fort Hamilton Bldg 230 US Army Garrison	Brooklyn	NY	11252	718-630-4349	630-4888
Herbert F Johnson Museum of Art Cornell University *Web:* www.museum.cornell.edu	Ithaca	NY	14853	607-255-6464	255-9940
Hudson River Museum of Westchester 511 Warburton Ave *Web:* www.hrm.org	Yonkers	NY	10701	914-963-4550	963-8558
Hyde Collection 161 Warren St *Web:* www.hydecollection.org	Glens Falls	NY	12801	518-792-1761	792-9197
International Center of Photography 1133 Ave of the Americas *Web:* www.icp.org	New York	NY	10036	212-857-9700	768-4688
International Museum of Photography & Film at George Eastman House 900 East Ave *Web:* www.eastmanhouse.org	Rochester	NY	14607	585-271-3361	271-3970
Intrepid Sea-Air-Space Museum W 46th St & 12th Ave Pier 86 *TF:* 877-957-7447 ■ *Web:* www.intrepidmuseum.org	New York	NY	10036	212-245-0072	
Irish American Heritage Museum 2267 Rt 145 *Web:* www.irishamericanheritagemuseum.org	East Durham	NY	12423	518-634-7497	634-7497
Iron Island Museum 998 Lovejoy St	Buffalo	NY	14206	716-892-3084	
Iroquois Indian Museum 324 Caverns Rd PO Box 7 *Web:* www.iroquoismuseum.org	Howes Cave	NY	12092	518-296-8949	296-8955
Jacques Marchais Museum of Tibetan Art 338 Lighthouse Ave *Web:* www.tibetanmuseum.com	Staten Island	NY	10306	718-987-3500	351-0402
Jefferson County Historical Society 228 Washington St	Watertown	NY	13601	315-782-3491	782-2913
Jewish Museum 1109 5th Ave *Web:* www.thejewishmuseum.org	New York	NY	10128	212-423-3200	423-3232
Johnson Herbert F Museum of Art Cornell University *Web:* www.museum.cornell.edu	Ithaca	NY	14853	607-255-6464	255-9940
Karpeles Manuscript Library 453 Porter Ave *Web:* www.rain.org/~karpeles/	Buffalo	NY	14201	716-885-4139	885-4139
Long Island Museum of American Art History & Carriages 1200 Rt 25A *Web:* www.longislandmuseum.org	Stony Brook	NY	11790	631-751-0066	751-0353
Louis Armstrong House & Archives 65-30 Kissena Blvd *Web:* www.satchmo.net	Flushing	NY	11367	718-997-3670	997-3677
Lower East Side Tenement Museum National Historic Site 108 Orchard St *Web:* www.tenement.org	New York	NY	10002	212-431-0233	431-0402
Marchais Jacques Museum of Tibetan Art 338 Lighthouse Ave *Web:* www.tibetanmuseum.com	Staten Island	NY	10306	718-987-3500	351-0402
Memorial Art Gallery of the University of Rochester 500 University Ave *Web:* mag.rochester.edu/index_flash.html	Rochester	NY	14607	585-473-7720	473-6266
Metropolitan Museum of Art 1000 5th Ave *TF:* 800-468-7386 ■ *Web:* www.metmuseum.org	New York	NY	10028	212-879-5500	570-3825
Millard Fillmore House 24 Shearer Ave	East Aurora	NY	14052	716-652-8875	
Morris-Jumel Mansion 65 Jumel Terr at 160th St *Web:* www.morrisjumel.org	New York	NY	10032	212-923-8008	923-8947
Mount Vernon Hotel Museum & Garden 421 E 61st St *Web:* www.mvhm.org	New York	NY	10021	212-838-6878	838-7390
Munson-Williams-Proctor Arts Institute 310 Genesee St *Web:* www.mwpai.org	Utica	NY	13502	315-797-0000	797-5608
Museo del Barrio 1230 5th Ave *Web:* www.elmuseo.org	New York	NY	10029	212-831-7272	831-7927
Museum for African Art 36-01 43rd Ave *Web:* www.africanart.org	Long Island City	NY	11101	718-784-7700	784-7718
Museum of American Financial History 28 Broadway *TF:* 877-983-4626 ■ *Web:* www.mafh.org	New York	NY	10004	212-908-4110	908-4601
Museum of American Illustration 128 E 63rd St *TF:* 800-746-8738 ■ *Web:* www.societyillustrators.org	New York	NY	10021	212-838-2560	838-2561
Museum of Arts & Design 40 W 53rd St *Web:* www.americancraftmuseum.org	New York	NY	10019	212-956-3535	459-0926
Museum of the City of New York 1220 5th Ave *Web:* www.mcny.org	New York	NY	10029	212-534-1672	423-0758
Museum of Jewish Heritage 36 Battery Pl Battery Park City *Web:* www.mjhnyc.org	New York	NY	10280	212-968-1800	437-4311
Museum of Modern Art 11 W 53rd St *Web:* www.moma.org	New York	NY	10019	212-708-9400	708-9889
Museum of the Moving Image 3601 35th Ave *Web:* www.ammi.org	Astoria	NY	11106	718-784-4520	784-4681
Museum of Science & Technology (MOST) 500 S Franklin St *Web:* www.most.org	Syracuse	NY	13202	315-425-9068	425-9072
Museum of Television & Radio 25 W 52nd St *Web:* www.mtr.org	New York	NY	10019	212-621-6600	621-6700
National Academy Museum of Art 1083 5th Ave *Web:* www.nationalacademy.org	New York	NY	10128	212-369-4880	360-6795
National Museum of the American Indian (Smithsonian Institution) 1 Bowling Green *TF:* 800-242-6624 ■ *Web:* www.nmai.si.edu	New York	NY	10004	212-514-3700	
National Women's Hall of Fame 76 Fall St PO Box 335 *Web:* www.greatwomen.org	Seneca Falls	NY	13148	315-568-8060	568-2976
Neuberger Museum of Art 735 Anderson Hill Rd Purchase College SUNY *Web:* www.neuberger.org	Purchase	NY	10577	914-251-6100	251-6101
New Museum of Contemporary Art 235 Bowery *Web:* www.newmuseum.org	New York	NY	10002	212-219-1222	431-5328
New York City Fire Museum 278 Spring St *Web:* www.nycfiremuseum.org	New York	NY	10013	212-691-1303	924-0430
New York City Police Museum 100 Old Slip *Web:* www.nycpolicemuseum.org	New York	NY	10004	212-480-3100	480-9757
New York Hall of Science 47-01 111th St Flushing Meadows *Web:* www.nyhallsci.org	Queens	NY	11368	718-699-0005	699-1341
New York Historical Society 170 Central Park W *TF:* 888-860-6947 ■ *Web:* www.nyhistory.org	New York	NY	10024	212-873-3400	874-8706
New York State Museum Madison Ave Cultural Education Center Empire State Plaza *Web:* www.nysm.nysed.gov	Albany	NY	12230	518-474-5877	486-3696
New York Transit Museum Boerum Pl & Schermerhorn St Subway Stn *Web:* mta.info/mta/museum	Brooklyn	NY	11201	718-694-1600	
Niagara Gorge Discovery Center PO Box 1132	Niagara Falls	NY	14303	716-278-1070	282-5179
Pedaling History Bicycle Museum 3943 N Buffalo Rd *Web:* www.pedalinghistory.com	Orchard Park	NY	14127	716-662-3853	662-4594
Pierpont Morgan Library 225 Madison Ave *TF Orders:* 800-861-0001 ■ *Web:* www.morganlibrary.org	New York	NY	10016	212-685-0008	685-4740
Queens County Farm Museum 7350 Little Neck Pkwy Floral Pk *Web:* www.queensfarm.org	Queens	NY	11004	718-347-3276	347-3243

				Phone	Fax
Queens Museum of Art					
New York City Bldg Flushing Meadows Corona Park	Queens	NY	11368	718-592-9700	592-5778
Web: www.queensmuseum.org					
Roberson Museum & Science Center 30 Front St	Binghamton	NY	13905	607-772-0660	771-8905
TF: 888-269-5325 ■ *Web:* www.roberson.org					
Rochester Museum & Science Center 657 East Ave	Rochester	NY	14607	585-271-4320	271-5935
Web: www.rmsc.org					
Roosevelt Franklin D Library & Museum					
4079 Albany Post Rd	Hyde Park	NY	12538	845-229-8114	486-1147
TF: 800-337-8474 ■ *Web:* www.fdrlibrary.marist.edu					
Sainte Marie among the Iroquois Living History Museum					
106 Lake Dr	Liverpool	NY	13088	315-453-6767	453-6772
Schenectady Museum & Suits-Bueche Planetarium					
15 Nott Terrace Heights	Schenectady	NY	12308	518-382-7890	382-7893
Web: www.schenectadymuseum.org					
Shaker Museum & Library 88 Shaker Museum Rd	Old Chatham	NY	12136	518-794-9100	794-8621
Web: www.smandl.org					
Solomon R Guggenheim Museum 1071 5th Ave	New York	NY	10128	212-423-3500	423-3640
TF: 800-329-6109 ■ *Web:* www.guggenheim.org					
South Street Seaport Museum 12 Fulton St	New York	NY	10038	212-748-8600	748-8610
Web: www.southstseaport.org					
Staten Island Institute of Arts & Sciences					
75 Stuyvesant Pl	Staten Island	NY	10301	718-727-1135	273-5683
Web: www.siiasmuseum.org					
Steel Plant Museum					
560 Ridge Rd Lackawanna Public Library	Lackawanna	NY	14218	716-823-0630	827-1997
Web: www.steelplantmuseum.org					
Strong - National Museum of Play 1 Manhattan Sq	Rochester	NY	14607	585-263-2700	263-2493
Web: www.strongmuseum.org					
Studio Museum in Harlem 144 W 125th St	New York	NY	10027	212-864-4500	864-4800
Web: www.studiomuseuminharlem.org					
Suffolk County Historical Society 300 W Main St	Riverhead	NY	11901	631-727-2881	727-3467
Susan B Anthony House 17 Madison St	Rochester	NY	14608	585-235-6124	235-6212
Web: www.susanbanthonyhouse.org					
Ten Broeck Mansion 9 Ten Broeck Pl	Albany	NY	12210	518-436-9826	436-1489
Web: www.tenbroeck.org					
Theodore Roosevelt Inaugural National Historic Site					
641 Delaware Ave	Buffalo	NY	14202	716-884-0095	884-0330
Web: www.nps.gov/thri/					
Tinker Homestead & Farm Museum 1585 Calkins Rd	Henrietta	NY	14467	585-359-7042	
Toy Town Museum 636 Girard Ave	East Aurora	NY	14052	716-687-5151	687-5098
Web: www.toytownusa.com					
Ukrainian Museum 222 E 6th St	New York	NY	10003	212-228-0110	228-1947
Web: www.ukrainianmuseum.org					
University Art Museum 1400 Washington Ave SUNY Albany	Albany	NY	12222	518-442-4035	442-5075
Web: www.albany.edu/museum					
Victorian Doll Museum 4332 Buffalo Rd	North Chili	NY	14514	585-247-0130	
Whitney Museum of American Art 945 Madison Ave	New York	NY	10021	212-570-3600	570-7729*
**Fax:* Library ■ *TF:* 800-944-8639 ■ *Web:* www.whitney.org					
Yager Museum Hartwick College West St	Oneonta	NY	13820	607-431-4480	431-4468
Web: info.hartwick.edu/museum					
Yeshiva University Museum 15 W 16th St	New York	NY	10011	212-294-8330	294-8335
Web: www.yu.edu/museum					

North Carolina

				Phone	Fax
Antique Car Museum/Grovewood Gallery 111 Grovewood Rd	Asheville	NC	28804	828-253-7651	254-2489
TF: 877-622-7238 ■ *Web:* www.grovewood.com					
Asheville Art Museum 2 S Pack Sq at Pack Pl	Asheville	NC	28801	828-253-3227	257-4503
Web: www.ashevilleart.org					
Backing Up Classics Auto Museum 4545 Concord Pkwy S	Concord	NC	28027	704-788-9500	788-9495
Web: www.backingupclassics.com					
Biltmore House One N Pack Sq	Asheville	NC	28801	828-225-6300	255-1744
TF: 800-543-1895 ■ *Web:* www.biltmore.com					
Charlotte Hawkins Brown Museum 6136 Burlington Rd	Sedalia	NC	27342	336-449-4846	449-0176
Web: www.chbrownmuseum.nchistoricsites.org					
Charlotte Historic Trolley Museum 2104 South Blvd	Charlotte	NC	28203	704-375-0850	
Charlotte Museum of History & Hezekiah Alexander Homesite					
3500 Shamrock Dr	Charlotte	NC	28215	704-568-1774	566-1817
Web: www.charlottemuseum.org					
Charlotte Nature Museum 1658 Sterling Rd	Charlotte	NC	28209	704-372-6261	333-8948
TF: 800-935-0553 ■ *Web:* www.discoveryplace.org/naturemuseum.asp					
Colburn Earth Science Museum 2 S Pack Sq	Asheville	NC	28801	828-254-7162	257-4505
Web: www.colburnmuseum.org					
Contemporary Art Museum 409 W Martin St 4th Fl	Raleigh	NC	27603	919-836-0088	836-2239
Web: www.camnc.org					
Duke Homestead State Historic Site & Tobacco Museum					
2828 Duke Homestead Rd	Durham	NC	27705	919-477-5498	479-7092
Web: www.ibiblio.org/dukehome					
EnergyExplorium 13339 Hagers Ferry Rd MG03E	Huntersville	NC	28078	704-875-5600	875-5602
TF: 800-777-0003 ■ *Web:* www.dukepower.com/ee					
Estes-Winn Memorial Automobile Museum					
111 Grovewood Rd	Asheville	NC	28804	828-253-7651	254-2489
Web: www.grovewood.com/automuseum.htm					
Exploris 201 E Hargett St	Raleigh	NC	27601	919-834-4040	
Web: www.exploris.org					
Fieldcrest Cannon Textile Museum Cannon Village Visitor					
Center 200 West Ave	Kannapolis	NC	28081	704-938-3200	932-4188
Web: www.cannonvillage.com/textilemuseum.htm					
Folk Art Center PO Box 9545	Asheville	NC	28815	828-298-7928	298-7962
Web: www.southernhighlandguild.org					
Greensboro Historical Museum 130 Summit Ave	Greensboro	NC	27401	336-373-2043	373-2204
Web: www.greensborohistory.org					
Greenville Museum of Art 802 S Evans St	Greenville	NC	27834	252-758-1946	758-1946
Web: www.gmoa.org					
International Civil Rights Center & Museum 134 S Elm St	Greensboro	NC	27401	336-274-9199	274-6244
TF: 800-748-7116 ■ *Web:* www.sitinmovement.org					
Joel Lane House Museum & Gardens 728 W Hargett St	Raleigh	NC	27603	919-833-3431	
Web: www.joellane.org					
Legends of Harley Drag Racing Museum 1126 S Saunders St	Raleigh	NC	27603	919-832-2261	833-6846
TF: 800-394-2758 ■ *Web:* www.rayprice.com					
Levine Museum of the New South 200 E 7th St	Charlotte	NC	28202	704-333-1887	333-1896
Web: www.museumofthenewsouth.org					
Mattye Reed African Heritage Museum					
Dudley Bldg NC & A&T State University	Greensboro	NC	27411	336-334-3209	334-4378
Mint Museum of Art 2730 Randolph Rd	Charlotte	NC	28207	704-337-2000	337-2101
Web: www.mintmuseum.org					
Mint Museum of Craft & Design 220 N Tryon St	Charlotte	NC	28202	704-337-2000	337-2101
Web: www.mintmuseum.org					
Museum of Anthropology					
Wingate Rd Wake Forest University PO Box 7267	Winston-Salem	NC	27109	336-758-5282	758-5116
Web: www.wfu.edu/MOA					
Museum of the Cherokee Indian PO Box 1599	Cherokee	NC	28719	828-497-3481	497-4985
TF: 888-665-7249 ■ *Web:* cherokeemuseum.org					
Museum of Early Southern Decorative Arts					
924 S Main St	Winston-Salem	NC	27101	336-721-7360	721-7367
TF: 800-441-5305 ■ *Web:* www.mesda.org					
Nasher Museum of Art at Duke University					
2001 Campus Dr Duke University	Durham	NC	27701	919-684-5135	681-8624
Web: www.duke.edu/duma					
Natural Science Center of Greensboro 4301 Lawndale Dr	Greensboro	NC	27455	336-288-3769	288-2531
Web: www.natsci.org					
North Carolina Central University Art Museum					
1801 Fayetteville St	Durham	NC	27707	919-530-6211	560-5649
Web: ariel.acc.nccu.edu/artmuseum					
North Carolina Museum of Art 2110 Blue Ridge Rd	Raleigh	NC	27607	919-839-6262	733-8034
Web: ncartmuseum.org					
North Carolina Museum of History 5 E Edenton St	Raleigh	NC	27601	919-807-7900	733-8655
Web: ncmuseumofhistory.org/					
North Carolina Museum of Life & Science 433 Murray Ave	Durham	NC	27704	919-220-5429	220-5575
Web: www.ncmls.org					
North Carolina Museum of Natural Sciences 11 W Jones St	Raleigh	NC	27601	919-733-7450	733-1573
Web: www.naturalsciences.org					
North Carolina Railroad Museum SR 1011 PO Box 40	New Hill	NC	27562	919-362-5416	
Web: www.nhvry.org					
Old Salem 600 S Main St	Winston-Salem	NC	27101	336-721-7300	721-7335
TF: 800-441-5305 ■ *Web:* www.oldsalem.org					
Petty Richard Museum 142 W Academy St	Randleman	NC	27317	336-495-1143	495-1543
Web: www.pettyracing.com					
Raleigh City Museum 220 Fayetteville St Mall Suite 100	Raleigh	NC	27601	919-832-3775	832-3085
Web: www.raleighcitymuseum.org					
Reed Mattye African Heritage Museum					
Dudley Bldg NC & A&T State University	Greensboro	NC	27411	336-334-3209	334-4378
Reynolda House Museum of American Art					
2250 Reynolda Rd	Winston-Salem	NC	27106	336-758-5150	758-5704
TF: 888-663-1149 ■ *Web:* www.reynoldahouse.org					
Richard Petty Museum 142 W Academy St	Randleman	NC	27317	336-495-1143	495-1543
Web: www.pettyracing.com					
Schiele Museum of Natural History & Lynn Planetarium					
1500 E Garrison Blvd	Gastonia	NC	28054	704-866-6908	866-6041
Web: www.schielemuseum.org					
SciWorks Science Center & Environmental Park of					
Forsyth County 400 Hanes-Mill Rd	Winston-Salem	NC	27105	336-767-6730	661-1777
Web: www.sciworks.org					
Smith McDowell House Museum 283 Victoria Rd	Asheville	NC	28803	828-253-9231	253-5518
Web: www.wnchistory.org/smhmwebpage.htm					
Weatherspoon Art Museum Spring Garden & Tate Sts	Greensboro	NC	27402	336-334-5770	334-5907
Web: www.uncg.edu/wag					

North Dakota

				Phone	Fax
Bonanzaville USA					
Cass County Historical Society 1351 W Main Ave	West Fargo	ND	58078	701-282-2822	282-7606
TF: 800-700-5317 ■ *Web:* www.bonanzaville.com					
Fargo Air Museum 1609 19th Ave N	Fargo	ND	58102	701-293-8043	293-8103
Web: www.fargoairmuseum.org					
Game & Fish Lobby Wildlife Museum 100 N Bismarck Expy	Bismarck	ND	58501	701-328-6300	328-6352
Myra Museum 2405 Belmont Rd	Grand Forks	ND	58201	701-775-2216	
Web: grandforkshistory.com					
North Dakota Museum of Art					
Centennial Dr University of North Dakota	Grand Forks	ND	58202	701-777-4195	777-4425
Web: www.ndmoa.com					

Nova Scotia

				Phone	Fax
Anne Murray Centre 36 Main St PO Box 610	Springhill	NS	B0M1X0	902-597-8614	597-2001
Web: www.annemurray.com/amc					
Black Cultural Centre for Nova Scotia 1149 Main St	Dartmouth	NS	B2Z1A8	902-434-6223	434-2306
TF: 800-465-0767 ■ *Web:* www.bccns.com					
Fisheries Museum of the Atlantic					
68 Bluenose Dr PO Box 1363	Lunenburg	NS	B0J2C0	902-634-4794	634-8990
Web: museum.gov.ns.ca/fma/					
Maritime Museum of the Atlantic 1675 Lower Water St	Halifax	NS	B3J1S3	902-424-7490	424-0612
Web: museum.gov.ns.ca/mma					
Murray Anne Centre 36 Main St PO Box 610	Springhill	NS	B0M1X0	902-597-8614	597-2001
Web: www.annemurray.com/amc					
Nova Scotia Museum of Industry 147 N Foord St	Stellarton	NS	B0K1S0	902-755-5425	755-7045
Web: museum.gov.ns.ca/moi					
Nova Scotia Museum of Natural History 1747 Summer St	Halifax	NS	B3H3A6	902-424-7353	424-0560
Web: museum.gov.ns.ca/mnh/					

Ohio

				Phone	Fax
Akron Art Museum 1 S High St	Akron	OH	44308	330-376-9185	376-1180
Web: www.akronartmuseum.org					
American Classical Music Hall of Fame 1225 Elm St	Cincinnati	OH	45202	513-621-3263	621-9333
Web: www.americanclassicalmusic.org					
Arms Family Museum of Local History 648 Wick Ave	Youngstown	OH	44502	330-743-2589	743-7210
Web: www.mahoninghistory.org/armhome.stm					
Blair Museum of Lithopanes					
Toledo Botanical Garden 5403 Elmer Dr	Toledo	OH	43615	419-245-1356	
Web: www.lithophanemuseum.org					
Boonshoft Museum of Discovery 2600 DeWeese Pkwy	Dayton	OH	45414	937-275-7431	275-5811
Web: www.boonshoftmuseum.org					
Butler Institute of American Art 524 Wick Ave	Youngstown	OH	44502	330-743-1711	743-9567
Web: www.butlerart.com					
Carillon Historical Park 100 Carillon Blvd	Dayton	OH	45409	937-293-2841	293-5798
Web: www.carillonpark.org					
Carriage Hills Farm Museum 7800 E Shull Rd	Dayton	OH	45424	937-879-0461	879-8904
Web: www.metroparks.org					
Century Village 14653 E Park St	Burton	OH	44021	440-834-1492	834-4012
Web: www.geaugahistorical.org					
Cincinnati Art Museum 953 Eden Park Dr	Cincinnati	OH	45202	513-721-5204	721-0129
TF: 877-472-4226 ■ *Web:* www.cincinnatiartmuseum.com					
Cincinnati History Museum					
1301 Western Ave Cincinnati Museum Center	Cincinnati	OH	45203	513-287-7000	287-7029
TF: 800-733-2077 ■ *Web:* www.cincymuseum.org					
Citizens Motorcar Co America's Packard Museum					
420 S Ludlow St	Dayton	OH	45402	937-226-1917	224-1918
Web: www.americaspackardmuseum.org					
Cleveland Museum of Art 11150 East Blvd	Cleveland	OH	44106	216-421-7340	229-5095*
**Fax:* Mktg ■ *TF Sales:* 888-262-7175 ■ *Web:* www.clemusart.com					

Ohio (Cont'd)

Museum	City	State	Zip	Phone	Fax
Cleveland Museum of Natural History 1 Wade Oval Dr University Cir *TF:* 800-317-9155 ■ *Web:* www.cmnh.org	Cleveland	OH	44106	216-231-4600	231-5919
Columbus Museum of Art 480 E Broad St *Web:* www.columbusmuseum.org	Columbus	OH	43215	614-221-6801	221-0226
COSI Columbus 333 W Broad St *TF:* 888-819-2674 ■ *Web:* www.cosicolumbus.org	Columbus	OH	43215	614-228-2674	228-6363
COSI Toledo 1 Discovery Way *Web:* www.cositoledo.org	Toledo	OH	43604	419-244-2674	255-2674
Crawford Auto-Aviation Museum 10825 East Blvd *Web:* www.wrhs.org/crawford	Cleveland	OH	44106	216-721-5722	721-0645
Dayton Art Institute 456 Belmonte Park N *TF:* 800-296-4426 ■ *Web:* www.daytonartinstitute.org	Dayton	OH	45405	937-223-5277	223-3140
Dittrick Museum of Medical History 11000 Euclid Ave *Web:* www.cwru.edu/artsci/dittrick/home.htm	Cleveland	OH	44106	216-368-3648	368-0165
Dunham Tavern Museum 6709 Euclid Ave *Web:* www.dunhamtavern.org	Cleveland	OH	44103	216-431-1060	
Goodyear World of Rubber Museum 1144 E Market St	Akron	OH	44316	330-796-2121	796-2222
Great Lakes Science Center 601 Erieside Ave *Web:* www.greatscience.com	Cleveland	OH	44114	216-694-2000	696-2140
Hale Farm & Village 2686 Oakhill Rd PO Box 296 *TF:* 800-589-9703 ■ *Web:* www.wrhs.org/halefarm	Bath	OH	44210	330-666-3711	666-9497
Harriet Beecher Stowe House 2950 Gilbert Ave *Web:* www.ohiohistory.org/places/stowe	Cincinnati	OH	45206	513-751-0651	
HealthSpace Cleveland 8911 Euclid Ave *Web:* www.healthspacecleveland.org	Cleveland	OH	44106	216-231-5010	231-5129
Heritage Museum 530 E Town St	Columbus	OH	43215	614-228-6515	228-7809
Heritage Village Museum 11450 Lebanon Pike *Web:* www.heritagevillagecincinnati.org	Cincinnati	OH	45241	513-563-9484	563-0914
Hower House 60 Fir Hill University of Akron *Web:* www3.uakron.edu/howerhse	Akron	OH	44325	330-972-6909	384-2635
Hywet Stan Hall & Gardens 714 N Portage Path *TF:* 888-836-5533 ■ *Web:* www.stanhywet.org	Akron	OH	44403	330-836-5533	836-2680
International Women's Air & Space Museum 1501 N Marginal Rd Burke Lakefront Airport Rm 165 *Web:* www.iwasm.org	Cleveland	OH	44114	216-623-1111	623-1113
Inventure Place 221 S Broadway *TF:* 800-968-4332 ■ *Web:* www.invent.org	Akron	OH	44308	330-762-4463	762-6313
Kelton House Museum 586 E Town St	Columbus	OH	43215	614-464-2022	464-3346
Kent State University Museum E Main & S Lincoln Sts Rockwell Hall *Web:* dept.kent.edu/museum/	Kent	OH	44242	330-672-3450	672-3218
Kettering-Moraine Museum & Historical Society 35 Moraine Cir S	Dayton	OH	45439	937-299-2722	
Krohn Conservatory 1501 Eden Park Dr	Cincinnati	OH	45202	513-421-5707	421-6007
Lake View Cemetery 12316 Euclid Ave	Cleveland	OH	44106	216-421-2665	421-2415
McDonough Museum of Art 1 University Plaza Youngstown State University Campus *Web:* www.fpa.ysu.edu	Youngstown	OH	44555	330-941-1400	941-1492
Museum of Contemporary Art Cleveland 8501 Carnegie Ave *Web:* www.mocacleveland.org	Cleveland	OH	44106	216-421-8671	421-0737
Museum of Natural History & Science 1301 Western Ave Cincinnati Museum Center *TF:* 800-733-2077 ■ *Web:* www.cincymuseum.org	Cincinnati	OH	45203	513-287-7000	287-7029
National Afro-American Museum & Cultural Center 1350 Brush Row Rd PO Box 578 *TF:* 800-752-2603 ■ *Web:* www.ohiohistory.org/places/afroam	Wilberforce	OH	45384	937-376-4944	376-2007
National Cleveland-Style Polka Hall of Fame 605 E 22nd St *TF:* 866-667-6552 ■ *Web:* www.polkafame.com	Euclid	OH	44123	216-261-3263	261-4131
National Inventors Hall of Fame 221 S Broadway St Inventure Place *TF:* 800-968-4332 ■ *Web:* www.invent.org	Akron	OH	44308	330-762-4463	762-6313
National Museum of the United States Air Force 1100 Spaatz St Wright-Patterson Air Force Base *Web:* www.wpafb.af.mil/museum	Dayton	OH	45433	937-255-3284	255-3286
National Underground Railroad Freedom Center 50 E Freedom Way *TF:* 877-648-4838 ■ *Web:* www.undergroundrailroad.com	Cincinnati	OH	45202	513-333-7500	333-7716
Ohio Craft Museum 1665 W 5th Ave *Web:* www.ohiocraft.org/museum.html	Columbus	OH	43212	614-486-4402	486-7110
Ohio Historical Center 1982 Velma Ave *TF:* 800-686-6124 ■ *Web:* www.ohiohistory.org	Columbus	OH	43211	614-297-2300	
Patterson Homestead Museum & Rental Facility 1815 Brown St *Web:* www.daytonhistory.org/patt_rent.htm	Dayton	OH	45409	937-222-9724	222-0345
Police Museum 217 S High St Rm 402	Akron	OH	44308	330-375-2390	375-2412
Rock & Roll Hall of Fame & Museum 1 Key Plaza *TF:* 800-349-7625 ■ *Web:* www.rockhall.com	Cleveland	OH	44114	216-781-7625	515-1283
Roscoe Village 381 Hill St *TF:* 800-877-1830 ■ *Web:* www.roscoevillage.com	Coshocton	OH	43812	740-622-9310	623-6555
Sauder Village 22611 SR 2 *TF:* 800-590-9755 ■ *Web:* www.saudervillage.org	Archbold	OH	43502	419-446-2541	445-5251
Slate Run Living Historical Farm 1375 SR 674 N	Canal Winchester	OH	43110	614-833-1880	
SS Willis B Boyer Maritime Museum 26 Main St International Park *Web:* www.internationalpark.org	Toledo	OH	43605	419-936-3070	
Stan Hywet Hall & Gardens 714 N Portage Path *TF:* 888-836-5533 ■ *Web:* www.stanhywet.org	Akron	OH	44403	330-836-5533	836-2680
Steamship William G Mather Museum 305 Mather Way *Web:* wgmather.nhlink.net/	Cleveland	OH	44114	216-574-9053	574-2536
Stowe House 2950 Gilbert Ave *Web:* www.ohiohistory.org/places/stowe	Cincinnati	OH	45206	513-751-0651	
Taft Museum of Art 316 Pike St *Web:* www.taftmuseum.org	Cincinnati	OH	45202	513-241-0343	241-7762
Thurber House 77 Jefferson Ave *Web:* www.thurberhouse.org	Columbus	OH	43215	614-464-1032	280-3645
Toledo Firefighters Museum 918 W Sylvania Ave *Web:* www.toledofiremuseum.com	Toledo	OH	43612	419-478-3473	936-3293
Toledo Lake Erie & Western Railway & Museum 49 N 6th St *Web:* www.tlew.org	Waterville	OH	43566	419-878-2177	
Toledo Museum of Art 2445 Monroe St *TF:* 800-644-6862 ■ *Web:* www.toledomuseum.org	Toledo	OH	43620	419-255-8000	255-5638
War Vet Museum 23 E Main St	Canfield	OH	44406	330-533-6311	533-6311
Western Reserve Historical Society Museum 10825 East Blvd **Fax:* Library ■ *Web:* www.wrhs.org	Cleveland	OH	44106	216-721-5722	721-5702*
Wexner Center for the Arts 1871 N High St Ohio State University *Web:* www.wexarts.org	Columbus	OH	43210	614-292-0330	292-3369
Wolcott House Museum 1031 River Rd *Web:* www.maumee.org/recreation/wolcott.htm	Maumee	OH	43537	419-893-9602	893-3108
Youngstown Historical Center 151 W Wood St *TF:* 800-262-6137 ■ *Web:* www.ohiohistory.org/places/youngst	Youngstown	OH	44503	330-743-5934	743-2999

Oklahoma

Museum	City	State	Zip	Phone	Fax
45th Infantry Division Museum 2145 NE 36th St *Web:* www.45thdivisionmuseum.com	Oklahoma City	OK	73111	405-424-5313	424-3748
Arkansas River Historical Society Museum 5350 Cimarron Rd *TF:* 888-512-7678 ■ *Web:* www.tulsaweb.com/port/museum.htm	Catoosa	OK	74015	918-266-2291	266-7678
Cherokee Heritage Center & National Museum 21992 S Keeler Rd *TF:* 888-999-6007 ■ *Web:* www.cherokeeheritage.org	Park Hill	OK	74451	918-456-6007	456-6165
Elsing Museum 777 S Lewis Ave Oral Roberts University *Web:* elsing.oru.edu	Tulsa	OK	74104	918-495-6262	
Five Civilized Tribes Museum 1101 Honor Heights Dr	Muskogee	OK	74401	918-683-1701	683-3070
Fred Jones Jr Museum of Art 555 Elm Ave University of Oklahoma *Web:* www.ou.edu/fjjma	Norman	OK	73019	405-325-3272	325-7696
Gilcrease Museum 1400 N Gilcrease Museum Rd *TF:* 888-655-2278 ■ *Web:* www.gilcrease.org	Tulsa	OK	74127	918-596-2700	596-2770
Harn Homestead & 1889er Museum 313 NE 16th St *Web:* www.harnhomestead.com	Oklahoma City	OK	73104	405-235-4058	235-4041
International Photography Hall of Fame & Museum 2100 NE 52nd St *Web:* iphf.org	Oklahoma City	OK	73111	405-424-4055	424-4058
JM Davis Arms & Historical Museum 333 N Lynn Riggs Blvd *Web:* www.thegunmuseum.com	Claremore	OK	74017	918-341-5707	341-5771
Jones Fred Jr Museum of Art 555 Elm Ave University of Oklahoma *Web:* www.ou.edu/fjjma	Norman	OK	73019	405-325-3272	325-7696
Lincoln County Historical Society Museum of Pioneer History 717 Manvel Ave *TF:* 888-258-2809	Chandler	OK	74834	405-258-2425	258-2809
National Cowboy & Western Heritage Museum 1700 NE 63rd St *Web:* www.nationalcowboymuseum.org	Oklahoma City	OK	73111	405-478-2250	478-4714
Oklahoma City Museum of Art 415 Couch Dr *TF:* 800-579-9278 ■ *Web:* www.okcmoa.com	Oklahoma City	OK	73102	405-236-3100	236-3122
Oklahoma City National Memorial & Memorial Center Museum 620 N Harvey Ave *Web:* www.oklahomacitynationalmemorial.org	Oklahoma City	OK	73102	405-235-3313	235-3315
Oklahoma Jazz Hall of Fame 322 N Greenwood Ave *TF:* 800-348-9336 ■ *Web:* www.okjazz.org	Tulsa	OK	74120	918-596-1001	596-1005
Oklahoma Museum of History 2401 N Laird Ave *Web:* www.ok-history.mus.ok.us	Oklahoma City	OK	73105	405-521-2491	522-5402
Oklahoma Museum of Natural History 2401 Chautaugua Ave *Web:* www.omnh.ou.edu	Norman	OK	73072	405-325-4712	325-7699
Oklahoma State Firefighters Museum 2716 NE 50th St	Oklahoma City	OK	73111	405-424-3440	424-1032
Oklahoma Territorial Museum 406 E Oklahoma Ave	Guthrie	OK	73044	405-282-1889	282-7286
Omniplex Science Museum 2100 NE 52nd St *TF:* 800-532-7652 ■ *Web:* www.omniplex.org	Oklahoma City	OK	73111	405-602-6664	602-3768
Philbrook Museum of Art & Gardens 2727 S Rockford Rd *TF:* 800-324-7941 ■ *Web:* www.philbrook.org	Tulsa	OK	74114	918-749-7941	743-4230
Sherwin Miller Museum of Jewish Art 2021 E 71st St *Web:* www.jewishmuseum.net	Tulsa	OK	74136	918-492-1818	492-1888
Tulsa Air & Space Museum 3624 N 74 East Ave *Web:* www.tulsaairandspacemuseum.com	Tulsa	OK	74115	918-834-9900	834-6723
Will Rogers Memorial Museum 1720 W Will Rogers Blvd *TF:* 800-324-9455 ■ *Web:* www.willrogers.org/memorial.html	Claremore	OK	74017	918-341-0719	343-8119
Woolaroc Ranch Museum & Wildlife Preserve Hwy 123 S *TF:* 888-966-5276 ■ *Web:* www.woolaroc.org	Bartlesville	OK	74003	918-336-0307	336-0084
World Organization of China Painters Museum 2641 NW 10th St *Web:* www.theshop.net/wocporg	Oklahoma City	OK	73107	405-521-1234	521-1265

Ontario

Museum	City	Province	Postal Code	Phone	Fax
Bytown Museum 540 Wellingtron St PO Box 523 Station B *Web:* www.bytownmuseum.com	Ottawa	ON	K1P5P6	613-234-4570	234-4846
Canada Agriculture Museum Prince of Wales Dr *Web:* www.agriculture.technomuses.ca	Ottawa	ON	K1A0C6	613-991-3044	947-2374
Canada Aviation Museum 11 Aviation Pkwy Rockcliffe Airport *Web:* www.aviation.technomuses.ca	Ottawa	ON	K1K4R3	613-993-2010	
Canada Science & Technology Museum 1867 St Laurent Blvd *Web:* www.sciencetech.technomuses.ca/	Ottawa	ON	K1G5A3	613-991-3044	990-3654
Canadian Museum of Contemporary Photography 1 Rideau Canal *TF:* 877-541-8888 ■ *Web:* cmcp.gallery.ca	Ottawa	ON	K1N9N6	613-990-8257	990-6542
Canadian Museum of Nature 240 McLeod St **Fax:* Mktg ■ *TF:* 800-263-4433 ■ *Web:* www.nature.ca	Ottawa	ON	K1P6P4	613-566-4700	364-4021*
Currency Museum of the Bank of Canada 245 Sparks St *Web:* www.bank-banque-canada.ca/museum	Ottawa	ON	K1A0G9	613-782-8914	782-7761
Fort Henry National Historic Site PO Box 213 *TF Cust Svc:* 800-437-2233 ■ *Web:* www.forthenry.com	Kingston	ON	K7L4V8	613-542-7388	542-3054
Gardiner Museum of Ceramic Art 111 Queen's Park *Web:* www.gardinermuseum.on.ca	Toronto	ON	M5S2C7	416-586-8080	586-8085
George R Gardiner Museum of Ceramic Art 111 Queen's Park *Web:* www.gardinermuseum.on.ca	Toronto	ON	M5S2C7	416-586-8080	586-8085
Guinness World Records Museum 4943 Clifton Hill *Web:* www.guinnessniagarafalls.com	Niagara Falls	ON	L2G3N5	905-356-2299	356-8614
Lithuanian Museum/Archives of Canada 2185 Stavebank Rd	Mississauga	ON	L5C1T3	905-566-8755	275-1336
Mackenzie House Museum 82 Bond St *Web:* www.toronto.ca/culture/mackenzie_house.htm	Toronto	ON	M5B1X2	416-392-6915	392-0114
Movieland Wax Museum of the Stars 4950 Clifton Hill *Web:* www.cliftonhill.com/niagara_falls_attractions/movieland_wax_museum/	Niagara Falls	ON	L2G3N4	905-358-3061	358-5738
Ontario Science Centre 770 Don Mills Rd *Web:* www.ontariosciencecentre.ca	Toronto	ON	M3C1T3	416-429-4100	696-3166
Presqu'ile Provincial Park Museum 328 Presqu'ile Pkwy	Brighton	ON	K0K1H0	613-475-4324	475-2209
Ripley's Believe It or Not! Museum 4983 Clifton Hill *Web:* www.ripleys.com	Niagara Falls	ON	L2G3N5	905-356-2238	374-7345
Royal Canadian Military Institute 426 University Ave *TF:* 800-585-1072 ■ *Web:* www.rcmi.org	Toronto	ON	M5G1S9	416-597-0286	597-6919
Royal Ontario Museum 100 Queen's Park *Web:* www.rom.on.ca	Toronto	ON	M5S2C6	416-586-8000	586-5863
Scarborough Historical Museum 1007 Brimley Rd	Toronto	ON	M1P3E8	416-338-8807	338-8805
Toronto Aerospace Museum 65 Carl Hall Rd *Web:* www.torontoaerospacemuseum.com	Toronto	ON	M3K2B6	416-638-6078	
Toronto's First Post Office 260 Adelaide St E *Web:* www.townofyork.com	Toronto	ON	M5A1N1	416-865-1833	865-9414
York Museum 2694 Eglinton Ave W	Toronto	ON	M5M1V1	416-394-2759	394-2803

Oregon

Museum	City	State	Zip	Phone	Fax
Antique Powerland Museum 3995 Brooklake Rd NE *Web:* www.antiquepowerland.com	Brooks	OR	97303	503-393-2424	

				Phone	Fax
Bush House Museum 600 Mission St SE *Web:* www.oregonlink.com/bush_house	Salem	OR	97302	503-363-4714	
Columbia River Maritime Museum 1792 Marine Dr *Web:* www.crmm.org	Astoria	OR	97103	503-325-2323	325-2331
Hallie Ford Museum of Art 700 State St *Web:* www.willamette.edu/museum_of_art	Salem	OR	97301	503-370-6855	375-5458
High Desert Museum 59800 S Hwy 97 *Web:* www.highdesertmuseum.org	Bend	OR	97702	541-382-4754	382-5256
Jensen Arctic Museum 590 W Church St *Web:* www.wou.edu/jensenmuseum	Monmouth	OR	97361	503-838-8468	838-8289
Jordan Schnitzer Museum of Art 1430 Johnson Ln *Web:* uoma.uoregon.edu/	Eugene	OR	97403	541-346-3027	346-0976
Keizer Heritage Museum 980 Chemawa Rd NE *Web:* www.keizerheritage.org	Keizer	OR	97307	503-393-9660	393-0209
Klamath County Museum 1451 Main St	Klamath Falls	OR	97601	541-883-4208	883-5170
Lane County Historical Museum 740 W 13th Ave *Web:* www.lchmuseum.org	Eugene	OR	97402	541-682-4242	682-7361
Marion County Historical Society Museum 260 12th St SE *Web:* www.open.org/~mchs	Salem	OR	97301	503-364-2128	391-5356
Oregon Air & Space Museum 90377 Boeing Dr	Eugene	OR	97402	541-461-1101	461-1101
Oregon Electric Railway Museum 3995 Brooklake Rd *Web:* www.trainweb.org/oerhs/oerm.htm	Brooks	OR	97303	503-888-4014	399-8051
Oregon Historical Society 1200 SW Park Ave *Web:* www.ohs.org	Portland	OR	97205	503-222-1741	221-2035
Oregon Maritime Center & Museum 115 SW Ash St Suite 400-C *Web:* www.oregonmaritimemuseum.org	Portland	OR	97204	503-224-7724	224-7767
Oregon Museum of Science & Industry 1945 SE Water Ave *TF:* 800-955-6674 ■ *Web:* www.omsi.edu	Portland	OR	97214	503-797-4000	797-4500
Pittock Mansion 3229 NW Pittock Dr *Web:* www.pittockmansion.com	Portland	OR	97210	503-823-3623	823-3619
Portland Art Museum 1219 SW Park Ave *Web:* www.portlandartmuseum.org	Portland	OR	97205	503-226-2811	226-4842
Springfield Museum 590 Main St *Web:* www.springfieldmuseum.com	Springfield	OR	97477	541-726-2300	726-3688
Tillamook County Pioneer Museum 2106 2nd St *Web:* www.tcpm.org	Tillamook	OR	97141	503-842-4553	842-4553
University of Oregon Museum of Natural & Cultural History 1680 E 15th Ave *Web:* natural-history.uoregon.edu	Eugene	OR	97403	541-346-3024	346-5334

Pennsylvania

				Phone	Fax
Academy of Natural Sciences Museum 1900 Benjamin Franklin Pkwy *Web:* www.acnatsci.org	Philadelphia	PA	19103	215-299-1000	299-1028
African-American Museum in Philadelphia 701 Arch St *Web:* www.aampmuseum.org	Philadelphia	PA	19106	215-574-0380	574-3110
Allentown Art Museum 31 N 5th St *Web:* www.allentownartmuseum.org	Allentown	PA	18101	610-432-4333	434-7409
American Civil War Museum 297 Steinwehr Ave *TF:* 800-877-7775 ■ *Web:* www.e-gettysburg.cc	Gettysburg	PA	17325	717-334-6245	334-9686
American Helicopter Museum & Education Center 1220 American Blvd W *Web:* www.helicoptermuseum.org	West Chester	PA	19380	610-436-9600	436-8642
American Swedish Historical Museum 1900 Pattison Ave *Web:* www.americanswedish.org	Philadelphia	PA	19145	215-389-1776	389-7701
Andy Warhol Museum 117 Sandusky St *Web:* www.warhol.org	Pittsburgh	PA	15212	412-237-8300	237-8340
Atwater Kent Museum 15 S 7th St *Web:* www.philadelphiahistory.org	Philadelphia	PA	19106	215-685-4830	685-4837
Barnes Foundation 300 N Latch's Ln *Web:* www.barnesfoundation.org	Merion	PA	19066	610-667-0290	664-4026
Brandywine River Museum 200 S Creek Rd *Web:* www.brandywinemuseum.org	Chadds Ford	PA	19317	610-388-2700	388-1197
Carnegie Museum of Art 4400 Forbes Ave *Web:* www.cmoa.org	Pittsburgh	PA	15213	412-622-3131	622-3112
Carnegie Museum of Natural History 4400 Forbes Ave *Web:* www.carnegiemnh.org	Pittsburgh	PA	15213	412-622-3131	622-6258
Carnegie Science Center 1 Allegheny Ave *TF:* 077-975-C707 ■ *Web:* www.carnegiesciencecenter.org	Pittsburgh	PA	15212	412-237-3400	237-3375
Civil War & Underground Railroad Museum of Philadelphia 1805 Pine St *Web:* www.civilwarmuseumphiladelphia.org	Philadelphia	PA	19103	215-735-8196	735-3812
Da Vinci Discovery Center of Science & Technology 3145 Hamilton Blvd Bypass *Web:* www.davinci-center.org	Allentown	PA	18103	484-664-1002	
Electric City Trolley Station & Museum 300 Cliff St *Web:* www.ectma.org/museum.html	Scranton	PA	18503	570-963-6590	963-6447
Elfreth's Alley Museum 126 Elfreth's Alley *Web:* www.elfrethsalley.org	Philadelphia	PA	19106	215-574-0560	922-7869
Erie Art Museum 411 State St *Web:* www.erieartmuseum.org	Erie	PA	16501	814-459-5477	452-1744
Erie County History Center 419 State St Erie County Historical Society *Web:* www.eriecountyhistory.org	Erie	PA	16501	814-454-1813	454-6890
Everhart Museum 1901 Mulberry St *Web:* everhart-museum.org	Scranton	PA	18510	570-346-7186	346-0652
Fabric Workshop & Museum 1315 Cherry St 5th Fl *Web:* www.fabricworkshopandmuseum.org	Philadelphia	PA	19107	215-568-1111	568-8211
Firefighters Historical Museum 428 Chestnut St Old Station House 4	Erie	PA	16507	814-456-5969	
Fort Pitt Museum 101 Commonwealth Pl *Web:* www.fortpittmuseum.com	Pittsburgh	PA	15222	412-281-9284	281-1417
Foster Stephen Memorial Museum University of Pittsburgh 4301 Forbes Ave *Web:* www.pitt.edu/~amerimus/museum.htm	Pittsburgh	PA	15260	412-624-4100	624-7447
Franklin Institute Science Museum 222 N 20th St *TF:* 800-285-0684 ■ *Web:* www.fi.edu	Philadelphia	PA	19103	215-448-1200	448-1235
Frick Art & Historical Center 7227 Reynolds St *Web:* www.frickart.org	Pittsburgh	PA	15208	412-371-0600	371-6140
Gettysburg Battle Theatre 571 Steinwehr Ave	Gettysburg	PA	17325	717-334-6100	334-6110
Holocaust Museum & Resource Center 601 Jefferson Ave *Web:* www.jfednepa.org	Scranton	PA	18510	570-961-2300	346-6147
Houdini Museum 1433 N Main Ave *Web:* www.houdini.org	Scranton	PA	18508	570-342-5555	
Hugh Moore Historical Park & National Canal Museum 30 Centre Sq *Web:* canals.org	Easton	PA	18042	610-559-6613	250-6686
Independence Seaport Museum 211 S Columbus Blvd *Web:* www.phillyseaport.org	Philadelphia	PA	19106	215-925-5439	925-6713
Institute of Contemporary Art 118 S 36th St University of Pennsylvania *Web:* www.icaphila.org	Philadelphia	PA	19104	215-898-7108	898-5050
Kemerer Museum of Decorative Arts 427 N New St	Bethlehem	PA	18018	610-868-6868	866-0460
Lake Shore Railway Museum 31 Wall St Lake Shore Historical Society	North East	PA	16428	814-725-1911	725-1911
Lancaster Cultural History Museum 7 W King St *Web:* www.lancasterheritage.com	Lancaster	PA	17603	717-299-6440	299-6916
Lehigh County Museum 432 W Walnut St *Web:* lchs.museum/	Allentown	PA	18102	610-435-4664	435-9812
Lincoln Train Museum 425 Steinwehr Ave *Web:* www.gettysburgbattlefieldtours.com	Gettysburg	PA	17325	717-334-5678	334-6110
Mario Lanza Museum 712 Montrose St Columbia House *Web:* www.mario-lanza-institute.org	Philadelphia	PA	19147	215-238-9691	238-9694
Moore Hugh Historical Park & National Canal Museum 30 Centre Sq *Web:* canals.org	Easton	PA	18042	610-559-6613	250-6686
Mummers Museum 1100 S 2nd St *Web:* riverfrontmummers.com	Philadelphia	PA	19147	215-336-3050	389-5630
Museum of Indian Culture 2825 Fish Hatchery Rd *Web:* www.museumofindianculture.org	Allentown	PA	18103	610-797-2121	797-2801
National Constitution Center 525 Arch St Independence Mall *TF:* 866-917-1787 ■ *Web:* www.constitutioncenter.org	Philadelphia	PA	19106	215-409-6600	409-6650
National Liberty Museum 321 Chestnut St *Web:* www.libertymuseum.org	Philadelphia	PA	19106	215-925-2800	925-3800
National Museum of American Jewish History 55 N 5th St *Web:* www.nmajh.org	Philadelphia	PA	19106	215-923-3811	923-0763
National Toy Train Museum 300 Paradise Ln *Web:* www.traincollectors.org	Strasburg	PA	17579	717-687-8976	687-0742
National Watch & Clock Museum 514 Poplar St *Web:* www.nawcc.org/museum	Columbia	PA	17512	717-684-8261	684-0878
North Museum of Natural History & Science 400 College Ave *Web:* www.northmuseum.org	Lancaster	PA	17603	717-291-3941	358-4504
Old Economy Village 14th & Church Sts *Web:* www.oldeconomyvillage.org	Ambridge	PA	15003	724-266-4500	266-7506
Pennsylvania Academy of the Fine Arts Museum 118 N Broad St *Web:* www.pafa.org/splashFlash.jsp	Philadelphia	PA	19102	215-972-7600	567-2429
Pennsylvania Anthracite Heritage Museum RR1 Bald Mountain Rd	Scranton	PA	18504	570-963-4804	963-4194
Pennsylvania National Fire Museum 1820 N 4th St	Harrisburg	PA	17102	717-232-8915	232-8916
Philadelphia Museum of Art 26th & Benjamin Franklin Pkwy *Web:* www.philamuseum.org	Philadelphia	PA	19130	215-763-8100	236-4465
Photo Antiquities - Museum of Photographic History 531 E Ohio St *Web:* www.photoantiquities.com	Pittsburgh	PA	15212	412-231-7881	231-1217
Polish American Cultural Center Museum 308 Walnut St *Web:* www.polishamericancenter.org	Philadelphia	PA	19106	215-922-1700	922-1518
Reading Public Museum & Art Gallery 500 Museum Rd *Web:* readingpublicmuseum.org	Reading	PA	19611	610-371-5850	371-5632
Rodin Museum 22nd & Benjamin Franklin Pkwy *Web:* www.rodinmuseum.org	Philadelphia	PA	19130	215-568-6026	236-4465
Rosenbach Museum & Library 2008 DeLancey Pl *Web:* www.rosenbach.org	Philadelphia	PA	19103	215-732-1600	545-7529
Senator John Heinz Pittsburgh Regional History Center 1212 Smallman St *Web:* www.pghhistory.org	Pittsburgh	PA	15222	412-454-6000	454-6039
Shriver House Museum 309 Baltimore St *Web:* www.schriverhouse.com	Gettysburg	PA	17325	717-337-2800	
Soldier's National Museum 777 Baltimore St	Gettysburg	PA	17325	717-334-4890	
Soldiers & Sailors National Military Museum & Memorial 4141 5th Ave *Web:* www.soldiersandsailorshall.org	Pittsburgh	PA	15213	412-621-4253	683-9339
State Museum of Pennsylvania 300 North St *Web:* www.statemuseumpa.org	Harrisburg	PA	17120	717-787-4980	783-4558
Stenton Museum 4601 N 18th St *Web:* www.stenton.org	Philadelphia	PA	19140	215-329-7312	329-7312
Stephen Foster Memorial Museum University of Pittsburgh 4301 Forbes Ave *Web:* www.pitt.edu/~amerimus/museum.htm	Pittsburgh	PA	15260	412-624-4100	624-7447
University of Pennsylvania Museum of Archaeology & Anthropology 33rd & Spruce Sts *Web:* www.upenn.edu/museum	Philadelphia	PA	19104	215-898-4000	898-0657
Wagner Free Institute of Science 1700 W Montgomery Ave *Web:* www.pacsci.org/wagner/	Philadelphia	PA	19121	215-763-6529	763-1299
Warhol Andy Museum 117 Sandusky St *Web:* www.warhol.org	Pittsburgh	PA	15212	412-237-8300	237-8340
Woodmere Art Museum 9201 Germantown Ave *Web:* www.woodmereartmuseum.org	Philadelphia	PA	19118	215-247-0476	247-2387

Prince Edward Island

				Phone	Fax
Green Gables House Parks Canada 2 Palmers Ln	Charlottetown	PE	C1A5V6	902-672-6350	963-7869
International Fox Hall of Fame Museum 286 Fitzroy St	Summerside	PE	C1N1J2	902-436-2400	
Prince Edward Island Museum & Heritage Foundation 2 Kent St	Charlottetown	PE	C1A1M6	902-368-6600	368-6608

Quebec

				Phone	Fax
Canadian Centre for Architecture 1920 Baile St *Web:* cca.qc.ca	Montreal	QC	H3H2S6	514-939-7000	939-7020
Canadian Museum of Civilization 100 Laurier St *TF:* 800-555-5621 ■ *Web:* www.civilization.ca	Gatineau	QC	J8X4H2	819-776-7000	776-8300
Canadian Postal Museum 100 Laurier St *Web:* www.civilization.ca/cpm/cpme.asp	Gatineau	QC	J8X4H2	819-776-8200	776-7062
Choco-Musee Erico 634 Saint-Jean St *Web:* www.chocomusee.com	Quebec	QC	G1R1P8	418-524-2122	524-4558
Economusee Les Brodeuses 5364 Saint-Laurent Blvd	Montreal	QC	H2T1S1	514-276-4181	
Jules Saint-Michel Luthier - Economuseum of Violin-Making 57 Ontario St W *Web:* www.luthiersaintmichel.com	Montreal	QC	H2X1Y8	514-288-4343	288-9296
McCord Museum of Canadian History 690 Sherbrooke St W *Web:* www.musee-mccord.qc.ca	Montreal	QC	H3A1E9	514-398-7100	398-5045
Montreal Holocaust Memorial Centre 5151 cote Sainte-Catherine *Web:* www.mhmc.ca	Montreal	QC	H3W1M6	514-345-2605	344-2651
Montreal Science Centre Saint-Laurent Blvd & de la Commune St King-Edward Pier *TF:* 877-496-4724 ■ *Web:* www.montrealsciencecentre.com	Montreal	QC	H2Y2E2	514-496-4724	496-0067
Musee de la Civilisation 85 Dalhousie St *Web:* www.mcq.org/mcq/index.html	Quebec	QC	G1K8R2	418-643-2158	646-9705
Musee de l'Amerique Francaise 2 cote de la Fabrique *TF:* 866-710-8031 ■ *Web:* www.mcq.org	Quebec	QC	G1R4R7	418-692-2843	692-5206

Quebec (Cont'd)

Phone Fax

Musee de la Moto (Harley-Davidson Museum)
2495 Hamel Blvd W ..... Quebec QC G1P2H9 418-683-1340 683-7597
Web: www.premont-harley.com
Musee du Quebec Parc des Champs-de-Bataille ..... Quebec QC G1R5H3 418-643-2150 646-3330
TF: 866-220-2150 ■ *Web:* www.mdq.org/english
Pointe-a-Calliere - The Montreal Museum of Archaeology & History 350 Royale Pl ..... Montreal QC H2Y3Y5 514-872-9150 872-8585
Web: www.pacmuseum.qc.ca
Richard Robitaille Fourrures - Economusee de la Fourrure
329 Saint-Paul St ..... Quebec QC G1K3W8 418-692-9699 692-3646
Saint-Laurent Art Museum 615 ave Sainte-Croix ..... Saint-Laurent QC H4L3X6 514-747-7367 747-8892

Rhode Island

Phone Fax

Artillery Co of Newport Military Museum 23 Clark St ..... Newport RI 02840 401-846-8488
Web: www.newportartillery.org/museum.html
Culinary Archives & Museum at Johnson & Wales University
315 Harborside Blvd ..... Providence RI 02905 401-598-2805 598-2807
Web: www.culinary.org
Governor Henry Lippitt House Museum 199 Hope St ..... Providence RI 02906 401-453-0688 453-8221
Haffenreffer Museum of Anthropology 300 Tower St ..... Bristol RI 02809 401-253-8388 253-1198
Web: www.brown.edu/Facilities/Haffenreffer
Heritage Harbor Museum 222 Richmond St Suite 206 ..... Providence RI 02903 401-751-7979 751-8822
Web: www.heritageharbor.org
Museum of Newport History at the Brick Market
127 Thames St ..... Newport RI 02840 401-841-8770 846-1853
Web: newporthistorical.org
Museum of Yachting Fort Adams State Park ..... Newport RI 02840 401-847-1018 847-8320
Web: www.moy.org
National Museum of American Illustration
Vernon Ct 492 Bellevue Ave ..... Newport RI 02840 401-851-8949 851-8974
Web: www.americanillustration.org
Naval War College Museum Coasters Harbor Island ..... Newport RI 02841 401-841-4052 841-7074
Web: www.nwc.navy.mil/museum/
Newport Art Museum 76 Bellevue Ave ..... Newport RI 02840 401-848-8200 848-8205
Web: www.newportartmuseum.com
Newport Historical Society 82 Touro St ..... Newport RI 02840 401-846-0813 846-1853
Web: www.newporthistorical.org
Providence Athenaeum 251 Benefit St ..... Providence RI 02903 401-421-6970 421-2860
Web: www.providenceathenaeum.org
Providence Jewelry Museum 1 Spectacle St ..... Providence RI 02910 401-274-0999 861-2170
Web: www.providencejewelrymuseum.com
Rhode Island Historical Society 110 Benevolent St ..... Providence RI 02906 401-331-8575 351-0127
Web: www.rihs.org
Rhode Island School of Design Museum 224 Benefit St ..... Providence RI 02903 401-454-6502 454-6556
Web: www.risd.edu
Roger Williams Park Museum of Natural History
Roger Williams Park ..... Providence RI 02905 401-785-9450 461-5146
Web: www.osfn.org/museum
Warwick Museum of Art 3259 Post Rd ..... Warwick RI 02886 401-737-0010 737-1796
Web: www.warwickmuseum.org

Saskatchewan

Phone Fax

Moose Jaw Museum & Art Gallery 461 Langdon Crescent ..... Moose Jaw SK S6H0X6 306-692-4471 694-8016
Web: www.mjmag.ca
Prince Albert Historical Museum 10 River St E ..... Prince Albert SK S6V8A9 306-764-2992
Royal Canadian Mounted Police Centennial Museum
5907 Dewdney St W ..... Regina SK S4P3J7 306-780-5838 780-6349
TF: 877-526-0585 ■ *Web:* rbcm1.rbcm.gov.bc.ca
Royal Saskatchewan Museum 2445 Albert St ..... Regina SK S4P4W7 306-787-2815 787-2820
Web: www.royalsaskmuseum.ca/
Western Development Museum 2935 Melville St ..... Saskatoon SK S7J5A6 306-934-1400 934-4467
Web: www.wdm.ca

South Carolina

Phone Fax

Avery Research Center for African-American History & Culture
125 Bull St ..... Charleston SC 29424 843-953-7609 953-7607
Web: www.cofc.edu/avery
Bob Jones University Museum & Gallery
Bob Jones University 1700 Wade Hampton Blvd ..... Greenville SC 29614 864-242-5100 770-1306
Web: www.bjumg.org
Cayce Historical Museum 1800 12th St Ext ..... Cayce SC 29033 803-796-9020 796-9072
Web: www.caycesc.net/museum.aspx
Challenger Learning Center 2600-A Barhamville Rd ..... Columbia SC 29204 803-929-3951 929-3959
Web: www.richlandone.org/departments/challenger/index.htm
Charleston Museum 360 Meeting St ..... Charleston SC 29403 843-722-2996 722-1784
Web: www.charlestonmuseum.com
Citadel Archives & Museum 171 Moultrie St The Citadel ..... Charleston SC 29409 843-953-6846 953-6956
Web: www.citadel.edu/museum/
Coastal Discovery Museum 100 William Hilton Pkwy ..... Hilton Head Island SC 29926 843-689-6767 689-6769
Web: www.coastaldiscovery.org
Columbia Museum of Art 1515 Main St ..... Columbia SC 29201 803-799-2810 343-2150
Web: www.colmusart.org
Fort Jackson Museum 2179 Sumter St ..... Fort Jackson SC 29207 803-751-7419 751-4434
Franklin G Burroughs-Simeon B Chapin Art Museum
3100 S Ocean Blvd ..... Myrtle Beach SC 29577 843-238-2510 238-2910
Web: www.myrtlebeachartmuseum.org
Gibbes Museum of Art 135 Meeting St ..... Charleston SC 29401 843-722-2706 720-1682
Web: www.gibbesmuseum.org
Greenville County Museum of Art 420 College St ..... Greenville SC 29601 864-271-7570 271-7579
Web: www.greenvillemuseum.org
Horry County Museum 428 Main St ..... Conway SC 29526 843-915-5320 248-1854
Web: www.horrycountymuseum.org
IP Stanback Museum & Planetarium
South Carolina State University 300 College St NE ..... Orangeburg SC 29117 803-536-7174 536-8309
Karpeles Manuscript Library Museum 68 Spring St ..... Charleston SC 29403 843-853-4651 853-4651
Web: www.rain.org/~karpeles/
Patriots Point Naval & Maritime Museum
Charleston Harbor 40 Patriots Point Rd ..... Mount Pleasant SC 29464 843-884-2727 881-4232
TF: 800-248-3508 ■ *Web:* www.state.sc.us/patpt/
Ripley's Believe It or Not! Museum 901 N Ocean Blvd ..... Myrtle Beach SC 29577 843-448-2331 626-2168
Web: www.ripleys.com
Roper Mountain Science Center 402 Roper Mountain Rd ..... Greenville SC 29615 864-355-8900
Web: www.ropermountain.org
South Carolina Civil War Museum 4857 Hwy 17 Bypass S ..... Myrtle Beach SC 29577 843-293-4344
South Carolina Confederate Relic Room & Museum
301 Gervais St ..... Columbia SC 29201 803-737-8095 737-8099
Web: www.state.sc.us/crr
South Carolina Museum & Library of Confederate History
15 Boyce Ave ..... Greenville SC 29601 864-421-9039
Web: www.confederatemuseum.org
South Carolina State Museum 301 Gervais St ..... Columbia SC 29202 803-898-4921 898-4977
Web: www.museum.state.sc.us
Stanback IP Museum & Planetarium
South Carolina State University 300 College St NE ..... Orangeburg SC 29117 803-536-7174 536-8309
University of South Carolina McKissick Museum
University of South Carolina 816 Bull St ..... Columbia SC 29208 803-777-7251 777-2829
Web: www.cas.sc.edu/mcks/

South Dakota

Phone Fax

Adams Museum 54 Sherman St ..... Deadwood SD 57732 605-578-1714
Web: adamsmuseumandhouse.org
Center for Western Studies
2101 S Summit Ave Augustana College ..... Sioux Falls SD 57197 605-274-4007 274-4999
TF: 800-727-2844 ■ *Web:* www.augie.edu/CWS/
Custer County 1881 Courthouse Museum 411 Mt Rushmore Rd ..... Custer SD 57730 605-673-2443 673-2443
Web: www.1881courthousemuseum.com
Delbridge Museum of Natural History 805 S Kiwanis Ave ..... Sioux Falls SD 57104 605-367-7003 367-8340
Web: www.gpzoo.org
Fort Meade Museum Sheridan St Bldg 55 ..... Fort Meade SD 57741 605-347-9822
Ghosts of Deadwood Gulch Wax Museum 12 Lee St ..... Deadwood SD 57732 605-578-2510 578-3250
Journey Museum 222 New York St ..... Rapid City SD 57701 605-394-6923 394-6940
Web: www.journeymuseum.org
Minnilusa Pioneer Museum 222 New York St ..... Rapid City SD 57701 605-394-6923 394-6940
Museum of Geology
501 E Saint Joseph St South Dakota School of Mines & Technology ..... Rapid City SD 57701 605-394-2467 394-6131
TF: 800-544-8162 ■ *Web:* www.sdsmt.edu/services/museum
Museum of South Dakota State Historical Society
900 Governors Dr Cultural Heritage Center ..... Pierre SD 57501 605-773-3458 773-6041
Web: www.sdhistory.org
National Museum of Woodcarving Hwy 16 W PO Box 747 ..... Custer SD 57730 605-673-4404 673-3843
Web: www.blackhills.com/woodcarving
National Music Museum 414 E Clark St ..... Vermillion SD 57069 605-677-5306 677-6995
Web: www.usd.edu/smm
National Presidential Wax Museum 609 Hwy 16A ..... Keystone SD 57751 605-666-4455 666-4276
Web: www.presidentialwaxmuseum.com
Old Courthouse Museum 200 W 6th St ..... Sioux Falls SD 57104 605-367-4210 367-6004
Over WH Museum 414 E Clark St ..... Vermillion SD 57069 605-677-5228
Pettigrew Home & Museum 131 N Duluth Ave ..... Sioux Falls SD 57104 605-367-7097 331-0467
Sioux Empire Medical Museum 1305 W 18th St ..... Sioux Falls SD 57117 605-333-6397 333-1577
South Dakota Air & Space Museum 2890 Davis Dr ..... Ellsworth AFB SD 57706 605-385-5188 385-6295
South Dakota Discovery Center & Aquarium 805 W Sioux Ave ..... Pierre SD 57501 605-224-8295 224-2865
Web: www.sd-discovery.com
South Dakota National Guard Museum 301 E Dakota St ..... Pierre SD 57501 605-224-9991 773-5380
Washington Pavilion of Arts & Science 301 S Main Ave ..... Sioux Falls SD 57104 605-367-7397 367-7399
TF: 877-927-4728 ■ *Web:* www.washingtonpavilion.org
WH Over Museum 414 E Clark St ..... Vermillion SD 57069 605-677-5228

Tennessee

Phone Fax

Adventure Science Center 800 Fort Negley Blvd ..... Nashville TN 37203 615-862-5160 862-5178
Web: www.adventuresci.com
Alex Haley House Museum 200 S Church St ..... Henning TN 38041 731-738-2240
American Museum of Science & Energy 300 S Tulane Ave ..... Oak Ridge TN 37830 865-576-3200 576-6024
Web: www.amse.org
Art Museum of the University of Memphis
142 Communication & Fine Arts Bldgs ..... Memphis TN 38152 901-678-2224 678-5118
Web: www.people.memphis.edu/~artmuseum/amhome.html
B Carroll Reece Museum Gilbreath Dr ..... Johnson City TN 37614 423-439-4392 439-4283
Web: cass.etsu.edu/museum
Battles for Chattanooga Museum 1110 E Brow Rd ..... Lookout Mountain TN 37350 423-821-2812
TF: 800-854-0675 ■ *Web:* www.battlesforchattanooga.com
Belle Meade Plantation 5025 Harding Rd ..... Nashville TN 37205 615-356-0501 356-2336
TF Info: 800-270-3991 ■ *Web:* www.bellemeadeplantation.com
Center for Southern Folklore 119 S Main St PO Box 226 ..... Memphis TN 38101 901-525-3655 544-9965
Web: www.southernfolklore.com
Chattanooga African-American Museum
200 E ML King Blvd ..... Chattanooga TN 37403 423-266-8658 267-1076
Web: www.caamhistory.com
Chattanooga Regional History Museum 400 Chestnut St ..... Chattanooga TN 37402 423-265-3247 266-9280
Web: www.chattanoogahistory.com
Country Music Hall of Fame & Museum 222 5th Ave S ..... Nashville TN 37203 615-416-2001 255-2245
TF: 800-852-6437 ■ *Web:* www.countrymusichalloffame.com
Dixon Gallery & Gardens 4339 Park Ave ..... Memphis TN 38117 901-761-5250 682-0943
Web: www.dixon.org/
Doak House Museum 690 Erwin Hwy ..... Greeneville TN 37743 423-636-8554 638-7166
TF: 800-729-0256 ■ *Web:* doakhouse.tusculum.edu
East Tennessee History Center 601 Gay St ..... Knoxville TN 37902 865-215-8830 215-8819
Web: www.east-tennessee-history.org
Farragut Folklife Museum 11408 Municipal Center Dr ..... Farragut TN 37922 865-966-7057 675-2096
Web: www.townoffarragut.org/arts.html
Fire Museum of Memphis 118 Adams Ave ..... Memphis TN 38103 901-320-5650 529-8422
Web: www.firemuseum.com
Frank H McClung Museum
1327 Circle Park Dr University of Tennessee ..... Knoxville TN 37996 865-974-2144 974-3827
Web: mcclungmuseum.utk.edu
Graceland (Elvis Presley Mansion) 3734 Elvis Presley Blvd ..... Memphis TN 38186 901-332-3322 344-3131
TF: 800-238-2000 ■ *Web:* www.elvis.com/graceland
Grand Ole Opry Museum 2802 Opryland Dr ..... Nashville TN 37214 615-889-6611 871-5772
Haley Alex House Museum 200 S Church St ..... Henning TN 38041 731-738-2240
Handy WC Museum 352 Beale St ..... Memphis TN 38103 901-522-1556 527-8784
Harry V Steadman Mountain Heritage Farmstead Museum
853 Bays Mountain Park Rd ..... Kingsport TN 37660 423-229-9361 224-2589
Web: www.baysmountain.com/exhibitdept/farm.html
Hartzler-Towner Multicultural Museum 1008 19th Ave S ..... Nashville TN 37212 615-340-7500 340-7551
Web: www.scarrittbennett.org/museum
Hermitage The (Home of Andrew Jackson) 4580 Rachel's Ln ..... Hermitage TN 37076 615-889-2941 889-9289
Web: www.thehermitage.com
Historic Jonesborough Visitors Center & Museum
117 Boone St ..... Jonesborough TN 37659 423-753-1010 753-1020
Web: www.historicjonesborough.com
Houston Museum of Decorative Arts 201 High St ..... Chattanooga TN 37403 423-267-7176 756-2156
Web: www.thehoustonmuseum.com
Hunter Museum of American Art 10 Bluff View St ..... Chattanooga TN 37403 423-267-0968 267-9844
Web: www.huntermuseum.org

	City	State	ZIP	Phone	Fax
International Towing & Recovery Hall of Fame & Museum					
3315 Broad St	Chattanooga	TN	37408	423-267-3132	267-0867
Web: www.internationaltowingmuseum.org					
James White's Fort 205 E Hill Ave	Knoxville	TN	37915	865-525-6514	525-6514
Web: www.discoveret.org/jwf/					
Jonesborough-Washington County History Museum					
117 Boone St	Jonesborough	TN	37659	423-753-1015	753-1020
Knoxville Museum of Art 1050 World Fair Park Dr	Knoxville	TN	37916	865-525-6101	546-3635
Web: www.knoxart.org					
McClung Frank H Museum					
1327 Circle Park Dr University of Tennessee	Knoxville	TN	37996	865-974-2144	974-3827
Web: mcclungmuseum.utk.edu					
Memphis Brooks Museum of Art					
1934 Poplar Ave Overton Park	Memphis	TN	38104	901-544-6200	276-2344
Web: www.brooksmuseum.org					
Memphis Pink Palace Museum 3050 Central Ave	Memphis	TN	38111	901-320-6320	320-6391
Web: www.memphismuseums.org					
Memphis Rock 'n' Soul Museum 191 Beale St	Memphis	TN	38103	901-205-2533	205-2534
Web: www.memphisrocknsoul.org					
Memphis Transportation Museum 125 N Rowlett St	Collierville	TN	38017	901-683-2266	683-2266
Messianic Museum 1928 Hamill Rd	Hixson	TN	37343	423-876-8150	876-8156
TF: 888-876-8150					
Mississippi River Museum 101 Mud Island Dr	Memphis	TN	38103	901-576-7241	576-6666
TF: 800-507-6507 ■ *Web:* www.mudisland.com					
Museum of Appalachia 2819 Andersonville Hwy	Clinton	TN	37716	865-494-7680	494-8957
Web: www.museumofappalachia.com					
National Civil Rights Museum 450 Mulberry St	Memphis	TN	38103	901-521-9699	521-9740
Web: www.civilrightsmuseum.org					
National Medal of Honor Museum of Military History					
PO Box 11467	Chattanooga	TN	37401	423-394-0710	
Web: www.mohm.org					
National Ornamental Metal Museum 374 Metal Museum Dr	Memphis	TN	38106	901-774-6380	774-6382
Web: www.metalmuseum.org					
Nelson Willie & Friends Showcase Museum					
2613A McGavock Pike	Nashville	TN	37214	615-885-1515	885-0733
Parthenon The West End & N 25th Aves Centennial Park	Nashville	TN	37201	615-862-8431	880-2265
Web: www.nashville.gov/parthenon					
Reece B Carroll Museum Gilbreath Dr	Johnson City	TN	37614	423-439-4392	439-4283
Web: cass.etsu.edu/museum					
Rocky Mount Museum 200 Hyder Hill Rd	Piney Flats	TN	37686	423-538-7396	538-1086
TF: 888-538-1791 ■ *Web:* pages.preferred.com/~rmm					
Slave Haven Underground Railroad Museum 826 N 2nd St	Memphis	TN	38107	901-527-3427	527-8784
Soulsville USA - Stax Museum of American Soul Music					
926 E McLemore Ave	Memphis	TN	38106	901-946-2535	507-1463
Web: www.soulsvilleusa.com					
Steadman Harry V Mountain Heritage Farmstead Museum					
853 Bays Mountain Park Rd	Kingsport	TN	37660	423-229-9361	224-2589
Web: www.baysmountain.com/exhibitdept/farm.html					
Tennessee Agricultural Museum 440 Hogan Rd	Nashville	TN	37204	615-837-5197	837-5224
Web: picktnproducts.org/agmuseum					
Tennessee Sports Hall of Fame Museum 501 Broadway	Nashville	TN	37203	615-242-4750	242-4752
Web: tshf.net					
Tennessee State Museum 505 Deaderick St	Nashville	TN	37243	615-741-2692	741-7231
TF: 800-407-4324 ■ *Web:* www.tnmuseum.org					
Tennessee Valley Railroad Museum 4119 Cromwell Rd	Chattanooga	TN	37421	423-894-8028	894-8029
Web: www.tvrail.com					
Upper Room Chapel & Museum 1908 Grand Ave	Nashville	TN	37212	615-340-7207	340-7293
TF: 800-972-0433 ■ *Web:* www.upperroom.org					
WC Handy Museum 352 Beale St	Memphis	TN	38103	901-522-1556	527-8784
Willie Nelson & Friends Showcase Museum					
2613A McGavock Pike	Nashville	TN	37214	615-885-1515	885-0733

Texas

	City	State	ZIP	Phone	Fax
12th Armored Division Memorial Museum 1289 N 2nd St	Abilene	TX	79601	325-677-6515	677-6515
Web: www.12tharmoreddivision.com/museum.html					
African American Museum 3536 Grand Ave Fair Park	Dallas	TX	75210	214-565-9026	421-8204
Web: www.aamdallas.org					
Alamo The 300 Alamo Plaza	San Antonio	TX	78205	210-225-1391	229-1343
Web: www.thealamo.org					
Amarillo Museum of Art 2200 S Van Buren St	Amarillo	TX	79109	806-371-5050	373-9235
Web: www.amarilloart.org					
American Airlines CR Smith Museum					
4601 Hwy 360 at FAA Rd	Fort Worth	TX	76155	817-967-1560	967-5737
Web: www.crsmithmuseum.org					
American Cowboy Museum 11822 Almeda St	Houston	TX	77045	713-433-4441	433-4441
American Quarter Horse Heritage Center & Museum					
2601 I-40 E	Amarillo	TX	79104	806-376-5181	376-1005
TF: 888-209-8322					
American Wind Power Center 1701 Canyon Lake Dr	Lubbock	TX	79403	806-747-8734	740-0668
Web: www.windmill.com					
Amon Carter Museum 3501 Camp Bowie Blvd	Fort Worth	TX	76107	817-738-1933	989-5099
TF: 800-573-1933 ■ *Web:* www.cartermuseum.org					
Arlington Museum of Art 201 W Main St	Arlington	TX	76010	817-275-4600	860-4800
Web: www.arlingtonmuseum.org					
Asian Cultures Museum 1809 N Chaparral St	Corpus Christi	TX	78401	361-882-2641	882-5718
Web: www.geocities.com/asiancm					
Austin Museum of Art Downtown 823 Congress Ave Suite 100	Austin	TX	78701	512-495-9224	495-9029
Web: www.amoa.org					
Austin Museum of Art Laguna Gloria 3809 W 35th St	Austin	TX	78703	512-458-8191	458-1571
Web: www.amoa.org					
Ball-Edelman-McFarland House Museum 1110 Penn St	Fort Worth	TX	76102	817-332-5875	336-2346
Web: www.historicfortworth.org					
Battleship Texas SHS					
San Jacinto Battleground State Historic Site 3523 Battleground Rd	La Porte	TX	77571	281-479-2411	479-5618
Web: www.tpwd.state.tx.us/park/battlesh					
Bayou Bend Collection & Gardens 1 Westcott St	Houston	TX	77007	713-639-7750	639-7770
Web: www.mfah.org/bayoubend					
Blanton Jack S Museum of Art					
23rd & San Jacinto Sts University of Texas at Austin Rm 1308	Austin	TX	78712	512-471-7324	471-7023
Web: www.blantonmuseum.org					
Bob Bullock Texas State History Museum 1800 N Congress Ave	Austin	TX	78701	512-936-8746	936-4699
TF: 866-369-7108 ■ *Web:* www.thestoryoftexas.com					
Buckhorn Saloon & Museum 318 E Houston St	San Antonio	TX	78205	210-247-4000	247-4020
Web: www.buckhornmuseum.com					
Buddy Holly Center 1801 Crickets Ave	Lubbock	TX	79401	806-767-2686	767-0732
Web: www.buddyhollycenter.org					
Buffalo Gap Historic Village 133 William St	Buffalo Gap	TX	79508	325-572-3365	572-5449
Web: www.mcwhiney.org/buffalogap.html					
Bush George Library & Museum					
1000 George Bush Dr W	College Station	TX	77845	979-691-4000	691-4050
Web: bushlibrary.tamu.edu					
Carter Amon Museum 3501 Camp Bowie Blvd	Fort Worth	TX	76107	817-738-1933	989-5099
TF: 800-573-1933 ■ *Web:* www.cartermuseum.org					
Carver George Washington Museum & Cultural Art Center					
1165 Angelina St	Austin	TX	78702	512-974-4926	974-3699
Cattle Raisers Museum 1301 W 7th St	Fort Worth	TX	76102	817-332-8551	332-8749
TF: 800-242-7420 ■ *Web:* www.cattleraisersmuseum.org					
Cavanaugh Flight Museum					
4572 Claire Chennault Addison Airport	Addison	TX	75001	972-380-8800	248-0907
Web: www.cavanaughflightmuseum.com					
Center for Women & Their Work 1710 Lavaca St	Austin	TX	78701	512-477-1064	477-1090
Web: www.womenandtheirwork.org					
Charles D Tandy Archaeological Museum					
2001 W Seminary Dr	Fort Worth	TX	76115	817-923-1921	921-8765
Confederate Air Force Museum Rio Grande Valley Wing					
955 S Minnesota St Brownsville Airport	Brownsville	TX	78521	956-541-8585	
Web: www.rgvwingcaf.com					
Conspiracy Museum 110 S Market St	Dallas	TX	75202	214-741-3040	
Web: www.guidelive.com/profile/103268/					
Contemporary Arts Museum 5216 Montrose Blvd	Houston	TX	77006	713-284-8250	284-8275
Web: www.camh.org					
Corpus Christi Museum of Science & History					
1900 N Chaparral St	Corpus Christi	TX	78401	361-883-2862	884-7392
Web: www.ccmuseum.com					
Dallas Firefighters Museum 3801 Parry Ave	Dallas	TX	75226	214-821-1500	821-1500
Dallas Heritage Village 1515 S Harwood	Dallas	TX	75215	214-421-5141	428-6351
Web: www.oldcitypark.org					
Dallas Holocaust Museum 211 N Record St Suite 100	Dallas	TX	75202	214-741-7500	747-2270
TF: 888-620-9933 ■ *Web:* www.dallasholocaustmuseum.org					
Dallas Museum of Art 1717 N Harwood St	Dallas	TX	75201	214-922-1200	954-0174
TF: 800-585-5770 ■ *Web:* www.dm-art.org					
El Paso Centennial Museum					
University & Wiggins University of Texas	El Paso	TX	79968	915-747-5565	747-5411
Web: www.utep.edu/museum					
El Paso Museum of Archaeology at Wilderness Park					
4301 Transmountain Rd	El Paso	TX	79924	915-755-4332	759-6824
Web: www.epas.com/museum.htm					
El Paso Museum of Art 1 Art Festival Plaza	El Paso	TX	79901	915-532-1707	532-1010
Web: www.elpasoartmuseum.org					
El Paso Museum of History 510 Santa Fe St	El Paso	TX	79901	915-351-3588	
Elisabet Ney Museum 304 E 44th St	Austin	TX	78751	512-458-2255	453-0638
Web: www.ci.austin.tx.us/elisabetney					
English Field Air & Space Museum 2014 English Rd	Amarillo	TX	79108	806-335-1812	335-1993
Fielder House Museum 1616 W Abram St	Arlington	TX	76013	817-460-4001	460-1315
Web: www.fielderhouse.org					
Forbidden Gardens 23500 Franz Rd	Katy	TX	77493	281-347-8000	347-8080
Web: www.forbidden-gardens.com					
Fort Bend Museum 500 Houston St	Richmond	TX	77469	281-342-6478	342-2439
Web: www.fortbendmuseum.org					
Fort Bliss Air Defense/Artillery Museum					
Marshall Rd Bldg 1735	El Paso	TX	79916	915-568-5412	568-6941
Fort Sam Houston Museum & National Historic Landmark 1210 Stanley Rd Bldg 123	Fort Sam Houston	TX	78234	210-221-1886	221-1311
Fort Worth Museum of Science & History					
1501 Montgomery St	Fort Worth	TX	76107	817-255-9300	732-7635
TF: 888-255-9300 ■ *Web:* www.fortworthmuseum.org					
French Legation Museum 802 San Marcos St	Austin	TX	78702	512-472-8180	472-9457
Web: www.frenchlegationmuseum.org					
Frontiers of Flight Museum 6911 Lemon Ave	Dallas	TX	75209	214-350-1651	351-0101
Web: www.flightmuseum.com					
Garland Landmark Museum 200 Museum Plaza Dr	Garland	TX	75040	972-205-2749	205-3634
TF: 888-879-0264					
George Bush Library & Museum					
1000 George Bush Dr W	College Station	TX	77845	979-691-4000	691-4050
Web: bushlibrary.tamu.edu					
George Ranch Historical Park 10215 FM 762	Richmond	TX	77469	281-545-9212	343-9316
Web: www.georgeranch.org					
George Washington Carver Museum & Cultural Art Center					
1165 Angelina St	Austin	TX	78702	512-974-4926	974-3699
Grace Museum 102 Cypress St	Abilene	TX	79601	325-673-4587	675-5993
Web: www.thegracemuseum.org					
Guiness World Records Museum 329 Alamo Plaza	San Antonio	TX	78205	210-226-2828	226-7462
Web: www.sa-guinness-haunted.com					
Heard Natural Science Museum & Wildlife Sanctuary					
1 Nature Pl	McKinney	TX	75069	972-562-5566	548-9119
Web: www.heardmuseum.org					
Heritage Farmstead Museum 1900 W 15th St	Plano	TX	75075	972-881-0140	422-6481
Web: www.heritagefarmstead.org					
Historic Brownsville Museum 641 E Madison St	Brownsville	TX	78520	956-548-1313	548-1391
Web: www.brownsvillemuseum.org					
Holocaust Museum Houston 5401 Caroline St	Houston	TX	77004	713-942-8000	942-7953
Web: www.hmh.org					
Houston Fire Museum 2403 Milam St	Houston	TX	77006	713-524-2526	520-7566
Web: www.houstonfiremuseum.org					
Houston Museum of Natural Science					
1 Hermann Circle Dr Hermann Park	Houston	TX	77030	713-639-4600	639-4761
Web: www.hmns.org					
Insights Science Museum 505 N Santa Fe St	El Paso	TX	79901	915-542-2990	532-7416
Web: www.insightsmuseum.org					
Institute of Texan Cultures 801 S Bowie St HemisFair Park	San Antonio	TX	78205	210-458-2300	458-2205
TF: 800-776-7651 ■ *Web:* www.texancultures.utsa.edu					
International Museum of Cultures 7500 W Camp Wisdom Rd	Dallas	TX	75236	972-708-7406	708-7341
Web: www.internationalmuseumofcultures.org					
Interurban Railway Station Museum 901 E 15th St	Plano	TX	75074	972-941-2117	
Jack S Blanton Museum of Art					
23rd & San Jacinto Sts University of Texas at Austin Rm 1308	Austin	TX	78712	512-471-7324	471-7023
Web: www.blantonmuseum.org					
John E Conner Museum 905 W Santa Gertrudis Ave	Kingsville	TX	78363	361-593-2810	593-2112
Web: www.tamuk.edu/museum					
Johnson Lyndon B Library & Museum 2313 Red River St	Austin	TX	78705	512-721-0200	721-0170
Web: www.lbjlib.utexas.edu					
Johnson Space Center 1601 Nasa Rd 1	Houston	TX	77058	281-244-2100	283-7724
Web: www.spacecenter.org					
Kimbell Art Museum 3333 Camp Bowie Blvd	Fort Worth	TX	76107	817-332-8451	877-1264
Web: www.kimbellart.org					
Lawndale Art & Performance Center 4912 Main St	Houston	TX	77002	713-528-5858	528-4140
Web: www.tsha.utexas.edu					
Log Cabin Village 2100 Log Cabin Village Ln	Fort Worth	TX	76109	817-926-5881	922-0246
Web: www.logcabinvillage.org					
Lone Star Flight Museum 2002 Terminal Dr	Galveston	TX	77554	409-740-7722	740-7612
Web: www.lsfm.org					
Louis Tussaud's Plaza Wax Museum & Ripley's Believe It or Not! Museum 301 Alamo Plaza	San Antonio	TX	78205	210-224-9299	224-1516
Web: www.plazawaxmuseum.com					
Lyndon B Johnson Library & Museum 2313 Red River St	Austin	TX	78705	512-721-0200	721-0170
Web: www.lbjlib.utexas.edu					

Texas (Cont'd)

				Phone	Fax
Marion Koogler McNay Art Museum					
6000 N New Braunfels Ave	San Antonio	TX	78209	210-824-5368	824-0218
Web: www.mcnayart.org					
McNay Marion Koogler Art Museum					
6000 N New Braunfels Ave	San Antonio	TX	78209	210-824-5368	824-0218
Web: www.mcnayart.org					
Meadows Museum					
5900 Bishop Blvd Southern Methodist University	Dallas	TX	75205	214-768-2516	768-1688
Web: www.smu.edu/meadowsmuseum					
Menil Collection 1515 Sul Ross St	Houston	TX	77006	713-525-9400	525-9444
Web: www.menil.org					
Mexic-Arte Museum 419 Congress Ave	Austin	TX	78701	512-480-9373	480-8626
Web: www.main.org/mexic-arte					
Modern Art Museum of Fort Worth 1320 Darnell St	Fort Worth	TX	76107	817-738-9215	735-1161
Web: www.mamfw.org					
Museum of the American Railroad 1105 Washington St Fair Park	Dallas	TX	75315	214-428-0101	426-1937
Web: www.dallasrailwaymuseum.com					
Museum of the Art 1717 N Harwood St	Dallas	TX	75201	214-922-1200	954-0174
TF: 800-585-5770 ■ *Web:* www.dallasmuseumofart.org					
Museum of Fine Arts 1001 Bissonnet St	Houston	TX	77005	713-639-7300	639-7784
TF: 888-733-6324 ■ *Web:* www.mfah.org					
Museum of Health & Medical Science 1515 Hermann Dr	Houston	TX	77004	713-521-1515	526-1434
Web: www.mhms.org					
Museum of Nature & Science 1318 S 2nd Ave	Dallas	TX	75210	214-421-3466	428-4356
Web: www.natureandscience.org/					
Museum of Texas Tech University 3301 4th St	Lubbock	TX	79409	806-742-2442	742-1136
Web: www.depts.ttu.edu/museumttu/					
National Border Patrol Museum 4315 Transmountain Rd	El Paso	TX	79924	915-759-6060	759-0992
TF: 877-276-8738 ■ *Web:* www.borderpatrolmuseum.com					
National Center for Children's Illustrated Literature Museum					
102 Cedar St	Abilene	TX	79601	325-673-4586	673-0085
Web: www.nccil.org					
National Cowgirl Museum & Hall of Fame 1720 Gendy St	Fort Worth	TX	76107	817-336-4475	336-2470
TF: 800-476-3263 ■ *Web:* www.cowgirl.net					
National Museum of Funeral History 415 Barren Springs Dr	Houston	TX	77090	281-876-3063	876-4403
Web: www.nmfh.org					
National Ranching Heritage Center					
3121 4th St PO Box 43200	Lubbock	TX	79409	806-742-0498	742-0616
Web: www.nrhc.ttu.edu					
National Scouting Museum 1329 W Walnut Hill Ln	Irving	TX	75038	972-580-2100	
TF: 800-303-3047 ■ *Web:* www.bsamuseum.org					
Nelson A Rockefeller Center for Latin American Art					
San Antonio Museum of Art 200 W Jones Ave	San Antonio	TX	78215	210-978-8100	978-8134
Web: www.samuseum.org					
Ney Elisabet Museum 304 E 44th St	Austin	TX	78751	512-458-2255	453-0638
Web: www.ci.austin.tx.us/elisabetney					
O Henry Home & Museum 409 E 5th St	Austin	TX	78701	512-472-1903	472-7102
Web: www.ci.austin.tx.us/parks/ohenry.htm					
Palace of Wax & Ripley's Believe It or Not!					
601 E Palace Pkwy	Grand Prairie	TX	75050	972-263-2391	263-5954
Web: www.palaceofwax.com					
Panhandle-Plains Historical Museum 2503 4th Ave	Canyon	TX	79015	806-651-2244	651-2250
Web: www.panhandleplains.org					
Pate Museum of Transportation 18501 Hwy 377 S	Cresson	TX	76035	817-396-4305	827-0711*
**Fax Area Code:* 800					
Pioneer Old Trail Drivers & Former Texas Rangers Museum					
3805 Broadway	San Antonio	TX	78209	210-822-9011	
Plaza Wax Museum 301 Alamo Plaza	San Antonio	TX	78205	210-224-9299	224-1516
Web: www.plazawaxmuseum.com					
Republic of Texas Museum 510 E Anderson Ln	Austin	TX	78752	512-339-1997	339-1998
River Legacy Living Science Center 703 NW Green Oaks Blvd	Arlington	TX	76006	817-860-6752	860-1595
Web: www.riverlegacy.org					
Rockefeller Nelson A Center for Latin American Art					
San Antonio Museum of Art 200 W Jones Ave	San Antonio	TX	78215	210-978-8100	978-8134
Web: www.samuseum.org					
San Antonio Museum of Art 200 W Jones Ave	San Antonio	TX	78215	210-978-8100	978-8134
Web: www.samuseum.org					
San Jacinto Museum of History 1 Monument Cir	La Porte	TX	77571	281-479-2421	479-2428
Web: www.sanjacinto-museum.org					
Science Spectrum Museum 2579 S Loop 289	Lubbock	TX	79423	806-745-2525	745-1115
Web: www.sciencespectrum.com					
Sixth Floor Museum 411 Elm St Suite 120 Dealey Plaza	Dallas	TX	75202	214-747-6660	747-6662
TF: 888-485-4854 ■ *Web:* www.jfk.org					
South Texas Institute for the Arts					
1902 N Shoreline Blvd	Corpus Christi	TX	78401	361-825-3500	825-3520
Web: www.stia.org					
Space Center Houston 1601 Nasa Rd 1	Houston	TX	77058	281-244-2100	283-7724
Web: www.spacecenter.org					
Spanish Governor's Palace 105 Plaza de Armas	San Antonio	TX	78205	210-224-0601	223-5562
Steves Homestead Museum 509 King William St	San Antonio	TX	78204	210-225-5924	223-9014
Web: www.saconservation.org/tours/steves.htm					
Stillman House & Museum 1305 E Washington St	Brownsville	TX	78520	956-542-3929	541-5524
Stockyards Museum 131 E Exchange Ave	Fort Worth	TX	76106	817-625-5087	625-5083
Tandy Charles D Archaeological Museum					
2001 W Seminary Dr	Fort Worth	TX	76115	817-923-1921	921-8765
Texas Maritime Museum 1202 Navigation Cir	Rockport	TX	78382	361-729-1271	729-9938
TF: 866-729-2469 ■ *Web:* www.texasmaritimemuseum.org					
Texas Memorial Museum 2400 Trinity St	Austin	TX	78705	512-471-1604	471-4794
Web: www.utexas.edu/depts/tmm/					
Texas Military Forces Museum 2200 W 35th St Camp Mabry	Austin	TX	78703	512-782-5659	782-6750
Web: www.texasmilitaryforcesmuseum.org					
Texas Transportation Museum 11731 Wetmore Rd	San Antonio	TX	78247	210-490-3554	
Web: www.txtransportationmuseum.org					
Umlauf Sculpture Garden & Museum 605 Robert E Lee Rd	Austin	TX	78704	512-445-5582	445-5583
Web: www.umlaufsculpture.org					
USS Lexington Museum on the Bay					
2914 N Shoreline Blvd	Corpus Christi	TX	78403	361-888-4873	883-8361
TF: 800-523-9539 ■ *Web:* www.usslexington.com					
Vintage Flying Museum					
505 NW 38th St Hanger 33 S Meacham Field	Fort Worth	TX	76106	817-624-1935	485-4454
Web: www.vintageflyingmuseum.org					
Witte Museum 3801 Broadway St	San Antonio	TX	78209	210-357-1900	357-1882
Web: www.wittemuseum.org					
Women's Museum 3800 Parry Ave	Dallas	TX	75226	214-915-0860	915-0860
Web: www.thewomensmuseum.org					

Utah

				Phone	Fax
Beehive House 67 E South Temple St	Salt Lake City	UT	84150	801-240-2671	240-2033
Brigham Young University Earth Science Museum					
1683 N Canyon Rd	Provo	UT	84602	801-422-3680	
Brigham Young University Museum of Art North Campus Dr	Provo	UT	84602	801-422-8287	422-0527
Web: cfac.byu.edu/moa/					
Brigham Young University Museum of Peoples & Cultures					
700 N 100 East 105 Allen Hall	Provo	UT	84602	801-422-0020	422-0026
Web: fhss.byu.edu/anthro/mopc/main.htm					
Browning Firearms Museum 2501 Wall Ave Union Stn	Ogden	UT	84401	801-393-9886	621-0230
Web: www.theunionstation.org/browning.htm					
Browning-Kimball Car Museum 25th St & Wall Ave Union Stn	Ogden	UT	84401	801-393-9886	621-0230
Chase Home Museum of Utah Folk Art					
617 E South Temple	Salt Lake City	UT	84102	801-533-5760	533-4202
Crandall Historical Printing Museum 275 E Center St	Provo	UT	84606	801-377-7777	374-3333
Daughters of Utah Pioneers Museum 2148 Grant Ave	Ogden	UT	84401	801-393-4460	
Dinosaur Museum & Park 1544 E Park Blvd	Ogden	UT	84401	801-393-3466	399-0895
Web: www.dinosaurpark.org					
Fort Douglas Military Museum 32 Potter St Fort Douglas	Salt Lake City	UT	84113	801-581-1710	581-1710
Web: www.fortdouglas.org					
Hill Aerospace Museum 7961 Wardleigh Rd Bldg 1955	Hill AFB	UT	84056	801-777-6818	775-3034
Web: www.hill.af.mil/museum					
John Hutchings Museum of Natural History 55 N Center St	Lehi	UT	84043	801-768-7180	
Web: www.hutchingsmuseum.org					
Millstream Car Museum 1450 Washington Blvd	Ogden	UT	84404	801-394-9425	392-9145
Monte L Bean Life Science Museum					
Brigham Young University 645 E 1430 North	Provo	UT	84602	801-422-5051	378-3733
Web: mlbean.byu.edu					
Museum of Church History & Art 45 N West Temple St	Salt Lake City	UT	84150	801-240-3310	240-5342
Museum of Natural History					
Weber State University Lind Lecture Hall	Ogden	UT	84408	801-626-6653	
Museum of Utah Art & History 125 S Main St	Salt Lake City	UT	84111	801-355-5554	355-5222
Web: www.muahnet.org					
Natural History Museum 2501 Wall Ave Union Stn	Ogden	UT	84401	801-393-9886	621-0230
Pioneer Memorial Museum 300 N Main St	Salt Lake City	UT	84103	801-532-6479	538-1119
Roy Historical Museum 5550 S 1700 West	Roy	UT	84067	801-776-3626	
Salt Lake Art Center 20 S West Temple	Salt Lake City	UT	84101	801-328-4201	322-4323
Web: www.slartcenter.org					
Social Hall Heritage Museum 55 S State St	Salt Lake City	UT	84103	801-321-8745	321-8776
Springville Museum of Art 126 E 400 South	Springville	UT	84663	801-489-2727	489-2739
Web: sma.nebo.edu					
Union Station 2501 Wall Ave	Ogden	UT	84401	801-393-9886	621-0230
Web: www.ogden-ut.com/UnionStation.html					
Utah Museum of Fine Arts					
410 Campus Center Dr University of Utah	Salt Lake City	UT	84112	801-581-7332	585-5198
Web: www.umfa.utah.edu					
Utah Museum of Natural History					
1390 E Presidents Cir University of Utah	Salt Lake City	UT	84112	801-581-6928	585-3684
Web: www.umnh.utah.edu					
Utah State Railroad Museum 2501 Wall Ave Union Stn	Ogden	UT	84401	801-393-9886	621-0230
Web: www.theunionstation.org					
Wattis-Dumke Model Railroad Museum					
2501 Wall Ave Union Stn	Ogden	UT	84401	801-393-9886	621-0230
Web: www.theunionstation.org/model.htm					
Wheeler Historic Farm 6351 S 900 East	Salt Lake City	UT	84121	801-264-2241	264-2213
Web: www.wheelerfarm.com					

Vermont

				Phone	Fax
Bennington Museum 75 Main St	Bennington	VT	05201	802-447-1571	442-8305
Web: www.bennington.com/museum					
ECHO at the Leahy Center 1 College St	Burlington	VT	05401	802-864-1848	864-6832
Web: www.echovermont.org					
Fairbanks Museum & Planetarium 1302 Main St	Saint Johnsbury	VT	05819	802-748-2372	748-1893
Web: www.fairbanksmuseum.org					
Fleming Robert Hull Museum					
61 Colchester Ave University of Vermont	Burlington	VT	05405	802-656-0750	656-8059
Web: www.uvm.edu/~fleming					
Lake Champlain Maritime Museum 4472 Basin Harbor Rd	Vergennes	VT	05491	802-475-2022	475-2953
Web: www.lcmm.org					
National Museum of the Morgan Horse					
122 Bostwick Rd PO Box 700	Shelburne	VT	05482	802-985-8665	985-5242
Web: www.morganmuseum.org					
Robert Hull Fleming Museum					
61 Colchester Ave University of Vermont	Burlington	VT	05405	802-656-0750	656-8059
Web: www.uvm.edu/~fleming					
Rokeby Museum 4334 Rt 7	Ferrisburg	VT	05456	802-877-3406	877-3406
Web: www.rokeby.org					
Shelburne Museum 5555 Shelburne Rd	Shelburne	VT	05482	802-985-3346	985-2331
Web: www.shelburnemuseum.org					

Virginia

				Phone	Fax
Agecroft Hall 4305 Sulgrave Rd	Richmond	VA	23221	804-353-4241	353-2151
Web: www.agecrofthall.com					
Alexandria Archaeology Museum 105 N Union St Rm 327	Alexandria	VA	22314	703-838-4399	838-6491
Web: oha.ci.alexandria.va.us/archaeology/					
Alexandria Black History Museum 902 Wythe St	Alexandria	VA	22314	703-838-4356	706-3999
Web: oha.alexandriava.gov/bhrc					
Anderson Gallery					
Virginia Commonwealth University 907 1/2 W Franklin St	Richmond	VA	23284	804-828-1522	828-8585
Web: www.vcu.edu/artweb/gallery					
Arlington Historical Museum 1805 S Arlington Ridge Rd	Arlington	VA	22202	703-892-4204	
Web: www.arlingtonhistoricalsociety.org					
Art Museum of Western Virginia 1 Market Sq	Roanoke	VA	24011	540-342-5760	342-5798
Web: www.artmuseumroanoke.org					
Atlantic Wildfowl Heritage Museum 1113 Atlantic Ave	Virginia Beach	VA	23451	757-437-8432	437-9055
Web: www.awhm.org					
Beth Ahabah Museum & Archives 1109 W Franklin St	Richmond	VA	23220	804-353-2668	358-3451
Web: www.bethahabah.org					
Black History Museum & Cultural Center of Virginia					
00 Clay St	Richmond	VA	23219	804-780-9093	780-9107
Web: www.blackhistorymuseum.org					
Carlyle House Historic Park 121 N Fairfax St	Alexandria	VA	22314	703-549-2997	549-5738
Web: www.carlylehouse.org					
Chimborazo Medical Museum 3216 E Broad St	Richmond	VA	23223	804-226-1981	
Chrysler Museum of Art 245 W Olney Rd	Norfolk	VA	23510	757-664-6200	664-6201
Web: www.chrysler.org					
DeWitt Wallace Decorative Arts Museum 325 Francis St	Williamsburg	VA	23185	757-220-7724	
TF: 800-447-8679 ■ *Web:* www.colonialwilliamsburg.com					
Drug Enforcement Administration Museum & Visitors Center					
700 Army Navy Dr	Arlington	VA	22202	202-307-3463	307-8956
Web: www.deamuseum.org					
Edgar Allan Poe Museum 1914-16 E Main St	Richmond	VA	23223	804-648-5523	648-8729
TF: 888-213-2763 ■ *Web:* www.poemuseum.org/					
Endview Plantation 362 Yorktown Rd	Newport News	VA	23603	757-887-1862	888-3369
Web: www.endview.org					

Name / Address	City	State	ZIP	Phone	Fax
Federal Reserve Money Museum 701 E Byrd St	Richmond	VA	23219	804-697-8135	
Flowerdew Hundred Museum 1617 Flowerdew Hundred Rd	Hopewell	VA	23860	804-541-8897	
Web: www.flowerdew.org					
Fort Ward Museum & Historic Site 4301 W Braddock Rd	Alexandria	VA	22304	703-838-4848	671-7350
Web: oha.ci.alexandria.va.us/fortward/					
Gadsby's Tavern Museum 134 N Royal St	Alexandria	VA	22314	703-838-4242	838-4270
Web: oha.ci.alexandria.va.us/gadsby/					
General Douglas MacArthur Memorial MacArthur Sq	Norfolk	VA	23510	757-441-2965	441-5389
Web: sites.communitylink.org/mac/					
Hampton Roads Naval Museum 1 Waterside Dr Suite 248	Norfolk	VA	23510	757-322-2987	445-1867
Web: www.hrnm.navy.mil					
Harrison Museum of African-American Culture 523 Harrison Ave NW	Roanoke	VA	24016	540-345-4818	345-4831
Web: www.harrisonmuseum.com					
Henricus Historical Park Henricus Park Rd	Richmond	VA	23832	804-706-1340	
Web: www.henricus.org					
Hermitage Foundation Museum 7637 N Shore Rd	Norfolk	VA	23505	757-423-2052	423-1604
Web: www.hermitagefoundation.org					
History Museum & Historical Society of Western Virginia 1 Market Sq Square Bldg Suite 3	Roanoke	VA	24011	540-342-5770	224-1256
Web: www.history-museum.org					
Hostetter D Ralph Museum of Natural History Eastern Mennonite University	Harrisonburg	VA	22802	540-432-4400	432-4488
Hunter House Victorian Museum 240 W Freemason St	Norfolk	VA	23510	757-623-9814	
Lee-Fendall House Museum 614 Oronoco St	Alexandria	VA	22314	703-548-1789	548-0931
Web: www.leefendallhouse.org					
Lightship Museum Water St & London Slip	Portsmouth	VA	23704	757-393-8741	
Web: www.portsnavalmuseums.com					
Lyceum History Museum 201 S Washington St	Alexandria	VA	22314	703-838-4994	838-4997
Web: oha.ci.alexandria.va.us/lyceum/					
Magnolia Grange & Museum 10201 Iron Bridge Rd	Chesterfield	VA	23832	804-777-9663	777-9643
Web: www.co.chesterfield.va.us/tourism					
Mariners' Museum 100 Museum Dr	Newport News	VA	23606	757-596-2222	591-7311
TF: 800-581-7245 ■ *Web:* www.mariner.org					
Maymont 1700 Hampton St	Richmond	VA	23220	804-358-7166	358-9994
Web: www.maymont.org					
Meadow Farm Museum 3400 Mountain Rd General Sheppard Crump Memorial Park	Glen Allen	VA	23060	804-501-5520	501-5284
Moses Myers House 331 Bank St	Norfolk	VA	23510	757-333-1086	333-1089
Muscarelle Museum of Art PO Box 8795	Williamsburg	VA	23187	757-221-2700	221-2711
Web: www.wm.edu/muscarelle					
Museum of the Confederacy 1201 E Clay St	Richmond	VA	23219	804-649-1861	644-7150
Web: www.moc.org					
National Firearms Museum 11250 Waples Mill Rd	Fairfax	VA	22030	703-267-1600	267-3913
Web: www.nrahq.org/shooting/museum					
National Museum of the Marine Corps 18900 Jefferson Davis Hwy	Triangle	VA	22172	703-221-1581	221-2988
TF: 877-635-1775 ■ *Web:* www.usmcmuseum.org					
NAUTICUS The National Maritime Center 1 Waterside Dr	Norfolk	VA	23510	757-664-1000	623-1287
Web: www.thenmc.org					
Newsome House Museum & Cultural Center 2803 Oak Ave	Newport News	VA	23607	757-247-2380	928-6754
Web: www.newsomehouse.org					
Old City Cemetery Museums & Arboretum 401 Taylor St	Lynchburg	VA	24501	434-847-1465	856-2004
Web: www.gravegarden.org					
Old Coast Guard Station 24th St & Oceanfront	Virginia Beach	VA	23451	757-422-1587	491-8609
Web: www.oldcoastguardstation.com					
Old Dominion Railway Museum 102 Hull St	Richmond	VA	23224	800-451-6358	
Old Guard Museum Sheridan Ave Fort Myer Bldg 249	Arlington	VA	22211	703-696-6670	696-4256
Poe Edgar Allan Museum 1914-16 E Main St	Richmond	VA	23223	804-648-5523	648-8729
TF: 888-213-2763 ■ *Web:* www.poemuseum.org/					
Portlock Galleries at SoNo 3815 Bainbridge Blvd	Chesapeake	VA	23324	757-502-4901	
Portsmouth Naval Shipyard Museum 2 High St	Portsmouth	VA	23704	757-393-8591	393-5244
Richmond National Battlefield Park 3215 E Broad St	Richmond	VA	23223	804-226-1981	771-8522
Web: www.nps.gov/rich/					
Saint Dennis Chapel Museum 609 Brown Ave	Hopewell	VA	23860	804-458-4682	
Salem Museum 801 E Main St	Salem	VA	24153	540-389-6760	389-6760
Web: www.salemmuseum.org					
Science Museum of Virginia 2500 W Broad St	Richmond	VA	23220	804-864-1400	864-1488
TF: 800-659-1727 ■ *Web:* www.smv.org					
Science Museum of Western Virginia & Hopkins Planetarium 1 Market Sq	Roanoke	VA	24011	540-342-5710	224-1240
Web: www.smwv.org					
Sherwood Forest Plantation 14501 John Tyler Memorial Hwy	Charles City	VA	23030	804-829-5377	829-2947
Web: www.sherwoodforest.org					
Stabler-Leadbeater Apothecary Museum 105 S Fairfax St	Alexandria	VA	22314	703-838-3852	836-3713
Web: www.apothecarymuseum.org					
US Army Transportation Museum Bldg 300 Besson Hall	Fort Eustis	VA	23604	757-878-1182	878-5656
Web: www.transchool.eustis.army.mil/Museum/Museum.html					
US Patent & Trademark Museum 600 Dulany St Suite IC65	Alexandria	VA	22314	571-272-0095	706-0484*
**Fax Area Code:* 703					
Valentine Richmond History Center 1015 E Clay St	Richmond	VA	23219	804-649-0711	643-3510
Web: www.richmondhistorycenter.com					
Virginia Aquarium & Marine Science Center 717 General Booth Blvd	Virginia Beach	VA	23451	757-437-4949	437-4976
Web: www.vmsm.com					
Virginia Aviation Museum 5701 Huntsman Rd	Richmond	VA	23250	804-236-3622	236-3623
Web: www.vam.smv.org					
Virginia Historical Society Museum of Virginia History 428 N Boulevard	Richmond	VA	23220	804-358-4901	355-2399
Web: www.vahistorical.org					
Virginia Holocaust Museum 2000 E Cary St	Richmond	VA	23223	804-257-5400	257-4314
Web: www.va-holocaust.com/					
Virginia Living Museum 524 J Clyde Morris Blvd	Newport News	VA	23601	757-595-1900	599-4897
Web: www.valivingmuseum.org					
Virginia Museum of Fine Arts 200 North Blvd	Richmond	VA	23220	804-340-1400	340-1548
Web: www.vmfa.state.va.us					
Virginia Museum of Transportation 303 Norfolk Ave	Roanoke	VA	24016	540-342-5670	342-6898
Web: www.vmt.org					
Virginia War Museum 9285 Warwick Blvd	Newport News	VA	23607	757-247-8523	247-8627
Web: www.warmuseum.org					
Watermen's Museum 309 Water St	Yorktown	VA	23690	757-887-2641	888-2089
Web: www.watermens.org					
Wilton House Museum 215 S Wilton Rd	Richmond	VA	23226	804-282-5936	288-9805
TF: 877-994-5866 ■ *Web:* wiltonhousemuseum.org					

Washington

Name / Address	City	State	ZIP	Phone	Fax
Bellevue Arts Museum 510 Bellevue Way NE	Bellevue	WA	98004	425-519-0770	637-1799
Web: www.bellevuearts.org					
Bigelow House Museum 918 Glass Ave NE	Olympia	WA	98506	360-753-1215	
Burke Museum of Natural History & Culture University of Washington 17th Ave NE & NE 45th St	Seattle	WA	98195	206-543-5590	685-3039
Web: www.washington.edu/burkemuseum					
Camp 6 Logging Museum 5400 N Pearl St Point Defiance Park	Tacoma	WA	98407	253-752-0047	
Web: www.camp-6-museum.org/c6.html					
Carr's One of a Kind in the World Museum 5225 N Freya St	Spokane	WA	99207	509-489-8859	489-8859
Center for Wooden Boats 1010 Valley St	Seattle	WA	98109	206-382-2628	382-2699
Web: www.cwb.org					
Clark County Historical Museum 1511 Main St	Vancouver	WA	98660	360-993-5679	993-5683
DuPont Historical Museum 207 Barksdale Ave	Dupont	WA	98327	253-964-2399	964-3554
Web: www.dupontmuseum.com					
Fireworks Fine Crafts Gallery 3307 Utah Ave S	Seattle	WA	98134	206-682-8707	467-6366
TF: 800-505-8882 ■ *Web:* www.fireworksgallery.net					
Fort Lewis Military Museum Fort Lewis Bldg 4320	Fort Lewis	WA	98433	253-967-7207	966-3029
Web: www.lewis.army.mil/DPTMS/POMFI/museum.htm					
Frye Art Museum 704 Terry Ave	Seattle	WA	98104	206-622-9250	223-1707
Web: www.fryeart.org					
Henderson House Museum 602 Deschutes Way SW	Tumwater	WA	98501	360-754-4217	
Henry Art Gallery University of Washington 15th Ave NE & NE 41st St	Seattle	WA	98195	206-543-2281	685-3123
Web: www.henryart.org					
Jundt Art Museum 202 E Cataldo Ave Gonzaga University	Spokane	WA	99258	509-328-4220	323-5525
Web: www.gonzaga.edu/campus+resources					
Karpeles Manuscript Library Museum 407 S 'G' St	Tacoma	WA	98405	253-383-2575	572-6044
Web: www.rain.org/~karpeles/taqfrm.html					
Lacey Museum 829 1/2 Lacey St SE	Lacey	WA	98503	360-438-0209	
Meeker Mansion 312 Spring St	Puyallup	WA	98371	253-848-1770	
Web: www.meekermansion.org					
Museum of Flight 9404 East Marginal Way S	Seattle	WA	98108	206-764-5700	764-5707
Web: www.museumofflight.org					
Museum of Glass 1801 Dock St	Tacoma	WA	98402	253-284-4750	369-1769
TF: 866-468-7386 ■ *Web:* www.museumofglass.org					
Museum of History & Industry 2700 24th Ave E	Seattle	WA	98112	206-324-1125	324-1346
Web: www.seattlehistory.org					
Nordic Heritage Museum 3014 NW 67th St	Seattle	WA	98117	206-789-5707	789-3271
Web: www.nordicmuseum.com					
Northwest Museum of Arts & Culture 2316 W 1st Ave	Spokane	WA	99204	509-456-3931	363-5303
Web: www.northwestmuseum.org					
Northwest Railway Museum 38625 SE King St PO Box 459	Snoqualmie	WA	98065	425-888-0373	888-9311
Web: www.trainmuseum.org					
Odyssey Maritime Discovery Center 2205 Alaskan Way Pier 66	Seattle	WA	98121	206-374-4000	374-4002
Web: www.ody.org					
Olympic Flight Museum 7637A Old Hwy 99 SE	Olympia	WA	98501	360-705-3925	
Web: www.olympicflightmuseum.com					
Pacific Science Center 200 2nd Ave N	Seattle	WA	98109	206-443-2001	443-3631
Web: www.pacsci.org					
Pearson Air Museum 1115 E 5th St	Vancouver	WA	98661	360-694-7026	694-0824
Web: www.pearsonairmuseum.org					
Port Townsend Marine Science Center 532 Battery Way	Port Townsend	WA	98368	360-385-5582	385-7248
TF: 800-566-3932 ■ *Web:* www.ptmsc.org					
Seattle Art Museum 100 University St	Seattle	WA	98101	206-625-8900	654-3135
Web: www.seattleartmuseum.org					
Seattle Asian Art Museum 1400 E Prospect St Volunteer Park	Seattle	WA	98112	206-654-3206	654-3191
Web: www.seattleartmuseum.org					
Tacoma Art Museum 1701 Pacific Ave	Tacoma	WA	98402	253-272-4258	627-1898
Web: www.tacomaartmuseum.org					
Tenino Depot Museum 339 West Park PO Box 339	Tenino	WA	98589	360-264-4321	
Two Rivers Heritage Museum 1 16th St	Washougal	WA	98671	360-835-8742	
Washington State Capital Museum 211 21st Ave SW	Olympia	WA	98501	360-753-2580	586-8322
Web: www.wshs.org/wscm					
Washington State History Museum 1911 Pacific Ave	Tacoma	WA	98402	253-272-3500	272-9518
TF: 888-238-4373 ■ *Web:* www.wshs.org/wshm					
Wing Luke Asian Museum 407 7th Ave S	Seattle	WA	98104	206-623-5124	623-4559
Web: www.wingluke.org					
Working Waterfront Maritime Museum 705 Dock St	Tacoma	WA	98402	253-272-2750	
Web: www.wwfrontmuseum.org					
World Kite Museum & Hall of Fame 303 W Sid Snyder Dr	Long Beach	WA	98631	360-642-4020	642-4020
Web: www.worldkitemuseum.com					

West Virginia

Name / Address	City	State	ZIP	Phone	Fax
Avampato Discovery Museum 300 Leon Sullivan Way 1 Clay Sq	Charleston	WV	25301	304-561-3575	
Web: www.avampatodiscoverymuseum.org					
Challenger Learning Center 316 Washington Ave Wheeling Jesuit University	Wheeling	WV	26003	304-243-4325	243-2497
TF: 800-624-6992 ■ *Web:* www.wju.edu/clc					
Comer Museum West Virginia University PO Box 6070 Mineral Resource Bldg	Morgantown	WV	26506	304-293-4211	293-5708
Cook-Hayman Pharmacy Museum Health Sciences Center N Rm 1132	Morgantown	WV	26506	304-293-7806	293-5483
Huntington Museum of Art Inc 2033 McCoy Rd	Huntington	WV	25701	304-529-2701	529-7447
Web: www.hmoa.org					
Kruger Street Toy & Train Museum 144 Kruger St	Wheeling	WV	26003	304-242-8133	242-1925
TF: 877-242-8133 ■ *Web:* www.toyandtrain.com					
Marks Toy Museum 915 2nd St	Moundsville	WV	26041	304-845-6022	
Web: www.marxtoymuseum.com					
Morgantown Glass Museum 1628 Mileground Rd	Morgantown	WV	26505	304-291-2957	
Web: morgantownglassmuseum.com					
Museums of Oglebay Institute The Burton Center Oglebay Park	Wheeling	WV	26003	304-242-7272	242-7289
TF: 800-624-6988 ■ *Web:* www.oionline.com					
West Virginia State Museum 1900 Kanawha Blvd E The Cultural Center	Charleston	WV	25305	304-558-0220	558-2779
Web: www.wvculture.org/museum					

Wisconsin

Name / Address	City	State	ZIP	Phone	Fax
Allis Charles Art Museum 1801 N Prospect Ave	Milwaukee	WI	53202	414-278-8295	278-0335
Web: www.cavtmuseums.org/ca/home.html					
America's Black Holocaust Museum 2233 N 4th St	Milwaukee	WI	53212	414-264-2500	264-0112
Web: www.blackholocaustmuseum.org					
Charles Allis Art Museum 1801 N Prospect Ave	Milwaukee	WI	53202	414-278-8295	278-0335
Web: www.cavtmuseums.org/ca/home.html					
Chazen Museum of Art 800 University Ave University of Wisconsin	Madison	WI	53706	608-263-2246	263-8188
Web: www.lvm.wisc.edu					
Circus World Museum 550 Water St	Baraboo	WI	53913	608-356-8341	356-1800
TF: 866-693-1500 ■ *Web:* www.circusworldmuseum.com					
Discovery World 500 N Harbor Dr	Milwaukee	WI	53202	414-765-9966	765-0311
Web: www.pierwisconsin.org					
EAA AirVenture Museum 300 Poberezny Rd	Oshkosh	WI	54902	920-426-4800	426-6560
Web: www.airventuremuseum.org					
Fairlawn Museum 906 E 2nd St	Superior	WI	54880	715-394-5712	394-2043
Web: www.superiorpublicmuseums.org					

Wisconsin (Cont'd)

Name / Address	City	State	Zip	Phone	Fax
Greene Memorial Museum 3209 N Maryland Ave Lapham Hall UWM Campus	Milwaukee	WI	53211	414-229-4561	229-5452
Haggerty Patrick & Beatrice Museum of Art 13th & Clybourn Sts Marquette University *Web:* www.marquette.edu/haggerty	Milwaukee	WI	53223	414-288-7290	288-5415
Hazelwood Historic Home Museum 1008 S Monroe Ave *Web:* www.browncohistoricalsoc.org/hazelwood	Green Bay	WI	54301	920-437-1840	455-4518
International Clown Hall of Fame Inc 640 S 84th St Suite 526 *Web:* www.theclownmuseum.org	West Allis	WI	53203	414-290-0105	290-0106
Kenosha Public Museum 5500 1st Ave *Web:* www.kenosha.org/museum//	Kenosha	WI	53140	262-653-4140	653-4437
Madison Geology Museum 1215 W Dayton St University of Wisconsin Weeks Hall	Madison	WI	53706	608-262-2399	262-0693
Milwaukee Art Museum 700 N Art Museum Dr *Web:* www.mam.org	Milwaukee	WI	53202	414-224-3200	
Milwaukee Public Museum 800 W Wells St *Web:* www.mpm.edu	Milwaukee	WI	53233	414-278-2700	319-4656
Mitchell Gallery of Flight 5300 S Howell Ave General Mitchell International Airport *Web:* www.mitchellgallery.org	Milwaukee	WI	53207	414-747-5300	747-4525
National Railroad Museum 2285 S Broadway St *Web:* www.nationalrrmuseum.org	Green Bay	WI	54304	920-437-7623	437-1291
Neville Public Museum of Brown County 210 Museum Pl *Web:* www.co.brown.wi.us/museum/index/	Green Bay	WI	54303	920-448-4460	448-4458
Old World Wisconsin S 103 West 37890 Hwy 67 *Web:* www.wisconsinhistory.org/oww	Eagle	WI	53119	262-594-6300	594-6342
Oneida Nation Museum W892 County Rd EE PO Box 365 *TF:* 800-236-2214	De Pere	WI	54155	920-869-2768	869-2959
Oshkosh Public Museum 1331 Algoma Blvd *Web:* www.publicmuseum.oshkosh.net	Oshkosh	WI	54901	920-424-4731	424-4738
Patrick & Beatrice Haggerty Museum of Art 13th & Clybourn Sts Marquette University *Web:* www.marquette.edu/haggerty	Milwaukee	WI	53223	414-288-7290	288-5415
Villa Terrace Decorative Arts Museum & Gardens 2220 N Terrace Ave *Web:* www.villaterracemuseum.org	Milwaukee	WI	53202	414-271-3656	271-3986
William F Eisner Museum of Advertising & Design 208 N Water St *Web:* www.eisnermuseum.org	Milwaukee	WI	53202	414-847-3290	847-3299
Wisconsin Black Historical Society Museum 2620 W Center St *Web:* www.wbhsm.org	Milwaukee	WI	53206	414-372-7677	372-4888
Wisconsin Historical Museum 30 N Carroll St *Web:* www.wisconsinhistory.org/museum	Madison	WI	53703	608-264-6555	264-6575
Wisconsin Maritime Museum 75 Maritime Dr *TF:* 866-724-2356 ■ *Web:* www.wisconsinmaritime.org	Manitowoc	WI	54220	920-684-0218	684-0219
Wisconsin Veterans Museum 30 W Mifflin St *Web:* museum.dva.state.wi.us	Madison	WI	53703	608-264-6086	264-7615

Wyoming

Name / Address	City	State	Zip	Phone	Fax
Buffalo Bill Historical Center 720 Sheridan Ave *Web:* www.bbhc.org	Cody	WY	82414	307-587-4771	587-5714
Cheyenne Depot Museum 121 W 15th St 1 Depot Sq *Web:* www.cheyennedepotmuseum.org	Cheyenne	WY	82001	307-632-3905	632-0614
Cheyenne Frontier Days Old West Museum 4610 N Carey Ave *Web:* www.oldwestmuseum.org	Cheyenne	WY	82001	307-778-7290	778-7288
FE Warren Heritage Museum 7405 Marne Loop Warren AFB Bldg 210 *Web:* www.pawnee.com/fewmuseum	Fort Warren AFB	WY	82005	307-773-2980	773-2791
Fort Caspar Museum 4001 Fort Caspar Rd *Web:* www.fortcasparwyoming.com	Casper	WY	82604	307-235-8462	235-8464
Geological Museum 1000 E University Ave	Laramie	WY	82071	307-766-4227	766-6679
Jackson Hole Historical Society & Museum 105 Mercill *Web:* www.jacksonholehistory.org	Jackson	WY	83001	307-733-9605	739-9019
Laramie Plains Museum 603 Ivinson Ave	Laramie	WY	82070	307-742-4448	
Museum of the Mountain Man 700 E Hennick St *TF:* 877-686-6266 ■ *Web:* www.pinedaleonline.com/MMMuseum	Pinedale	WY	82941	307-367-4101	367-6768
National Museum of Wildlife Art 2820 Rungius Rd PO Box 6825 *TF:* 800-313-9553 ■ *Web:* www.wildlifeart.org	Jackson	WY	83002	307-733-5771	733-5787
Nelson Museum of the West 1714 Carey Ave *Web:* www.nelsonmuseum.com	Cheyenne	WY	82001	307-635-7670	778-3926
Nicolaysen Art Museum 400 E Collins Dr *Web:* www.thenic.org	Casper	WY	82601	307-235-5247	235-0923
Ripley's Believe It or Not! Museum 140 N Cache St *Web:* www.ripleys.com/bion/jackson.html	Jackson Hole	WY	83001	307-734-0000	734-0078
Sweetwater County Historical Museum 3 E Flaming Gorge Way *Web:* www.sweetwatermuseum.org	Green River	WY	82935	307-872-6435	872-3234
Warren FE Heritage Museum 7405 Marne Loop Warren AFB Bldg 210 *Web:* www.pawnee.com/fewmuseum	Fort Warren AFB	WY	82005	307-773-2980	773-2791
Werner Wildlife Museum 405 E 15th St	Casper	WY	82601	307-235-2108	
Wyoming Dinosaur Center 110 Carter Ranch Rd *Web:* server1.wyodino.org	Thermopolis	WY	82443	307-864-2997	864-5762
Wyoming State Museum 2301 Central Ave *Web:* wyomuseum.state.wy.us	Cheyenne	WY	82002	307-777-7022	777-5375

Yukon Territory

Name / Address	City	State	Zip	Phone	Fax
MacBride Museum 1124 1st Ave *Web:* www.macbridemuseum.com	Whitehorse	YT	Y1A1A4	867-667-2709	633-6607

524 MUSEUMS - CHILDREN'S

Children's museums are organized alphabetically by states.

Name / Address	City	State	Zip	Phone	Fax
Children's Hands-On Museum 2213 University Blvd *TF:* 877-349-4235 ■ *Web:* www.chomonline.org	Tuscaloosa	AL	35401	205-349-4235	349-4276
EarlyWorks Children's Museum 404 Madison St *Web:* www.earlyworks.com/earlyworks.html	Huntsville	AL	35801	256-564-8100	564-8151
Gulf Coast Exploreum Science Center 65 Government St *TF:* 877-625-4386 ■ *Web:* www.exploreum.net	Mobile	AL	36602	251-208-6883	208-6889
Sci-Quest Hands on Science Center 102-D Wynn Dr *Web:* www.sci-quest.org	Huntsville	AL	35805	256-837-0606	837-4536
Tucson Children's Museum 200 S 6th Ave *Web:* www.tucsonchildrensmuseum.org	Tucson	AZ	85702	520-884-7511	792-0639
Bay Area Discovery Museum 557 McReynolds Rd *Web:* www.baykidsmuseum.org	Sausalito	CA	94965	415-339-3900	339-3905
Bowers Kidseum 1802 N Main St *Web:* www.bowers.org/kidseum/kidseum.asp	Santa Ana	CA	92706	714-480-1520	480-0053
Brock Lori Children's Museum 3801 Chester Ave	Bakersfield	CA	93301	661-852-5000	322-6415
Children's Discovery Museum of the Desert 71-701 Gerald Ford Dr *Web:* www.cdmod.org	Rancho Mirage	CA	92270	760-321-0602	321-1605
Children's Discovery Museum of San Jose 180 Woz Way *Web:* www.cdm.org	San Jose	CA	95110	408-298-5437	298-6826
Children's Museum of Stockton 402 W Weber Ave *Web:* www.stocktongov.com/childrensmuseum	Stockton	CA	95203	209-465-4386	465-4394
Discovery Center 1937 N Winery Ave *Web:* www.thediscoverycenter.net	Fresno	CA	93703	559-251-5533	251-5531
Discovery Museum History Center 101 'I' St *Web:* www.thediscovery.org	Sacramento	CA	95814	916-264-7057	264-5100
Discovery Museum Science & Space Center 3615 Auburn Blvd *Web:* www.thediscovery.org	Sacramento	CA	95821	916-485-8836	575-3925
Gull Wings Children's Museum 418 W 4th St *Web:* www.gullwings.org	Oxnard	CA	93030	805-483-3005	483-3226
Lori Brock Children's Museum 3801 Chester Ave	Bakersfield	CA	93301	661-852-5000	322-6415
Museum of Children's Art 538 9th St Suite 210 *Web:* www.mocha.org	Oakland	CA	94607	510-465-8770	465-0772
My Museum 601 Wave St Suite 100 *Web:* www.mymuseum.org	Monterey	CA	93940	831-649-6444	649-1304
Youth Science Institute 296 Garden Hill Dr *Web:* www.ysi-ca.org	Los Gatos	CA	95032	408-356-4945	358-3683
Zeum 221 4th St *Web:* www.zeum.org	San Francisco	CA	94103	415-820-3320	820-3330
Children's Museum of Denver 2121 Children's Museum Dr *Web:* www.mychildsmuseum.org	Denver	CO	80211	303-433-7444	433-9520
Children's Museum of Durango 802 E 2nd Ave *Web:* www.childsmuseum.org	Durango	CO	81301	970-259-9234	259-6320
Connecticut Children's Museum 22 Wall St *Web:* www.childrensbuilding.org	New Haven	CT	06511	203-562-5437	787-9414
Discovery Creek Children's Museum of Washington 2233 Wisconsin Ave NW Suite 410 *Web:* www.discoverycreek.org	Washington	DC	20007	202-337-5111	337-5344
Children's Museum 498 Crawford Blvd *Web:* www.cmboca.org	Boca Raton	FL	33432	561-368-6875	395-7764
Children's Science Explorium 300 S Military Trail	Boca Raton	FL	33486	561-347-3913	
G Wiz Hands on Science Museum 1001 Blvd of the Arts *Web:* www.gwiz.org	Sarasota	FL	34236	941-309-4949	906-7292
Great Explorations - The Childrens Museum 1925 4th St N *Web:* www.greatexplorations.org	Saint Petersburg	FL	33704	727-826-5454	823-7287
Kid City Children's Museum of Tampa 7550 North Blvd *Web:* www.flachildrensmuseum.com	Tampa	FL	33604	813-935-8441	915-0063
Miami Children's Museum 980 MacArthur Cswy *Web:* www.miamichildrensmuseum.org	Miami	FL	33132	305-373-5437	373-5431
Young at Art Children's Museum 11584 W SR-84 *Web:* www.youngatartmuseum.org	Davie	FL	33325	954-424-0085	370-5057
Imagine It! Children's Museum of Atlanta 275 Centennial Olympic Park Dr NW *Web:* www.imagineit-cma.org	Atlanta	GA	30313	404-659-5437	223-3675
Hawaii Children's Discovery Center 111 Ohe St *Web:* www.discoverycenterhawaii.org	Honolulu	HI	96813	808-524-5437	524-5400
Chicago Children's Museum 700 E Grand Ave Suite 127 *Web:* www.chichildrensmuseum.org	Chicago	IL	60611	312-527-1000	527-9082
Discovery Center Museum 711 N Main St *Web:* www.discoverycentermuseum.org	Rockford	IL	61103	815-963-6769	968-0164
Exploration Station-A Children's Museum 1095 W Perry St *Web:* www.btpd.org/exploration_station.htm	Bourbonnais	IL	60914	815-935-5665	928-6054
Hands on Children's Art Museum of Chicago 1800 W 103rd St *Web:* www.handsonart.org	Chicago	IL	60643	773-233-9933	233-9955
Orpheum Children's Science Museum 346 N Neil St *Web:* www.m-crossroads.org/orpheum	Champaign	IL	61820	217-352-5895	352-9512
Hannah Lindahl Children's Museum 1402 S Main St *Web:* www.hlcm.org	Mishawaka	IN	46544	574-254-4540	254-4585
HealthWorks! Kids' Museum 111 W Jefferson St Suite 200 *Web:* www.qualityoflife.org/healthworks	South Bend	IN	46601	574-287-5437	239-6459
Koch Family Children's Museum of Evansville 22 SE 5th St *Web:* www.cmoekids.org	Evansville	IN	47708	812-477-4929	477-4339
Muncie Children's Museum 515 S High St *Web:* www.munciechildrensmuseum.com	Muncie	IN	47305	765-286-1660	286-1662
Children's Museum of Kansas City 4601 State Ave *Web:* www.kidmuzm.org	Kansas City	KS	66102	913-287-8888	287-8332
Exploration Place 300 N McLean Blvd *TF:* 877-904-1444 ■ *Web:* www.exploration.org	Wichita	KS	67203	316-263-3373	263-4545
Kansas Cosmosphere & Space Center 1100 N Plum St *TF:* 800-397-0330 ■ *Web:* www.cosmo.org	Hutchinson	KS	67501	620-662-2305	662-3693
Explorium of Lexington 440 W Short St *Web:* www.explorium.com	Lexington	KY	40507	859-258-3253	258-3255
Children's Museum of Acadiana 201 E Congress St *Web:* www.childrensmuseumofacadiana.com	Lafayette	LA	70501	337-232-8500	232-8167
Children's Museum of Lake Charles 327 Broad St *Web:* www.child-museum.org	Lake Charles	LA	70601	337-433-9420	433-0144
Louisiana Children's Museum 420 Julia St *Web:* www.lcm.org	New Orleans	LA	70130	504-523-1357	529-3666
Children's Discovery Museum 265 Water St *Web:* www.childrensdiscoverymuseum.org	Augusta	ME	04330	207-622-2209	623-8389
Children's Museum of Maine 142 Free St *Web:* www.childrensmuseumofme.org	Portland	ME	04101	207-828-1234	828-5726
Chesapeake Children's Museum 25 Silopanna Rd *Web:* www.theccm.org	Annapolis	MD	21403	410-990-1993	990-1007
Port Discovery Children's Museum in Baltimore 35 Market Pl *Web:* www.portdiscovery.org	Baltimore	MD	21202	410-727-8120	727-3042
Boston Children's Museum 300 Congress St *Web:* www.bostonkids.org	Boston	MA	02210	617-426-6500	426-1944
Cape Cod Children's Museum 577 Great Neck Rd S *Web:* www.capecodchildrensmuseum.pair.com/	Mashpee	MA	02649	508-539-8788	539-3285
Cape Cod Discovery Museum 444 Main St	Dennisport	MA	02639	508-398-1600	
Children's Museum at Holyoke 444 Dwight St *Web:* www.childrensmuseumholyoke.org	Holyoke	MA	01040	413-536-7048	533-2999
EcoTarium 222 Harrington Way *Web:* www.ecotarium.org	Worcester	MA	01604	508-929-2700	929-2701

	City	State	Zip	Phone	Fax
Detroit Public Schools Children's Museum 6134 2nd Ave *Web:* www.detroitchildrensmuseum.org	Detroit	MI	48202	313-873-8100	873-3384
Flint Children's Museum 1602 W 3rd Ave *Web:* www.flintchildrensmuseum.org	Flint	MI	48504	810-767-5437	767-4936
Grand Rapids Children's Museum 11 Sheldon Ave NE *Web:* www.grcm.org	Grand Rapids	MI	49503	616-235-4726	235-4728
Duluth Children's Museum 506 W Michigan St *Web:* www.duluthchildrensmuseum.org	Duluth	MN	55802	218-733-7543	733-7547
Minnesota Children's Museum 10 W 7th St *Web:* www.mcm.org	Saint Paul	MN	55102	651-225-6001	225-6006
Lynn Meadows Discovery Center 246 Dolan Ave *Web:* www.lmdc.org	Gulfport	MS	39507	228-897-6039	248-0071
Discovery Center of Springfield 438 E Saint Louis St *Web:* www.discoverycenter.org	Springfield	MO	65806	417-862-9910	862-6898
Kaleidoscope 2501 McGee St *Web:* www.hallmarkkaleidoscope.com	Kansas City	MO	64108	816-274-8301	274-3148
Magic House Saint Louis Children's Museum 516 S Kirkwood Rd *Web:* www.magichouse.org	Saint Louis	MO	63122	314-822-8900	822-8930
Worldways Children's Museum 15479 Clayton Rd *Web:* www.worldways.org	Ballwin	MO	63011	636-207-7405	207-7407
Lincoln Children's Museum 1420 P St *Web:* www.lincolnchildrensmuseum.org	Lincoln	NE	68508	402-477-0128	477-2004
Omaha Children's Museum 500 S 20th St *Web:* www.ocm.org	Omaha	NE	68102	402-342-6164	342-6165
Children's Museum of Northern Nevada 813 N Carson St *Web:* www.cmnn.org	Carson City	NV	89701	775-884-2226	884-2179
Lied Discovery Children's Museum 833 Las Vegas Blvd N *Web:* www.ldcm.org	Las Vegas	NV	89101	702-382-3445	382-0592
Children's Metamorphosis 6 W Broadway *Web:* www.childrensmet.org	Derry	NH	03038	603-425-2560	425-2829
Children's Museum of Portsmouth 280 Marcy St *Web:* www.childrens-museum.org	Portsmouth	NH	03801	603-436-3853	436-7706
Santa Fe Children's Museum 1050 Old Pecos Trail *Web:* www.santafechildrensmuseum.org	Santa Fe	NM	87505	505-989-8359	989-7506
Brooklyn Children's Museum 145 Brooklyn Ave *Web:* www.bchildmus.org	Brooklyn	NY	11213	718-735-4400	604-7442
Children's Museum of the Arts 182 Lafayette St *Web:* www.cmany.org	New York	NY	10013	212-274-0986	274-1776
Children's Museum of History, Natural History, Science & Technology 311 Main St *Web:* museum4kids.net	Utica	NY	13501	315-724-6129	724-6120
Children's Museum of Manhattan 212 W 83rd St *Web:* www.cmom.org	New York	NY	10024	212-721-1223	721-1127
Discovery Center of the Southern Tier 60 Morgan Rd *Web:* www.thediscoverycenter.org	Binghamton	NY	13903	607-773-8661	773-8019
Explore & More-A Children's Museum 300 Gleed Ave *Web:* www.exploreandmore.org	East Aurora	NY	14052	716-655-5131	655-5466
Long Island Children's Museum 11 Davis Avenue *Web:* www.licm.org	Garden City	NY	11530	516-224-5800	302-8188
Staten Island Children's Museum 1000 Richmond Terr at Snug Harbor	Staten Island	NY	10301	718-273-2060	273-2836
Discovery Place 301 N Tryon St *TF:* 800-935-0553 ■ *Web:* www.discoveryplace.org	Charlotte	NC	28202	704-372-6261	337-2670
Greensboro Children's Museum 220 N Church St *Web:* www.gcmuseum.com	Greensboro	NC	27401	336-574-2898	574-3810
Rocky Mount Children's Museum 270 Gay St *Web:* www.ci.rocky-mount.nc.us/museum	Rocky Mount	NC	27804	252-972-1167	972-1535
Yunker Farm Children's Museum 1201 28th Ave N *Web:* www.childrensmuseum-yunker.org	Fargo	ND	58102	701-232-6102	232-4605
Children's Museum of Cleveland 10730 Euclid Ave *Web:* www.clevelandchildrensmuseum.org	Cleveland	OH	44106	216-791-7114	791-8838
Cincinnati Fire Museum 315 W Court St *Web:* www.cincyfiremuseum.com	Cincinnati	OH	45202	513-621-5553	621-1456
Cinergy Children's Museum 1301 Western Ave Cincinnati Museum Center *TF:* 800-733-2077 ■ *Web:* www.cincymuseum.org	Cincinnati	OH	45203	513-287-7000	287-7079
AC Gilbert's Discovery Village 116 Marion St NE *Web:* www.acgilbert.org	Salem	OR	97301	503-371-3631	316-3485
Portland Children's Museum 4015 SW Canyon Rd *Web:* www.portlandcm2.org	Portland	OR	97221	503-223-6500	223-6600
Science Factory Children's Museum & Planetarium 2300 Leo Harris Pkwy *Web:* www.sciencefactory.org	Eugene	OR	97401	541-682-7888	484-9027
Children's Museum of Pittsburgh 10 Children's Way *Web:* www.pittsburghkids.org	Pittsburgh	PA	15212	412-322-5059	322-4932
ExpERIEnce Children's Museum 420 French St *Web:* www.eriechildrensmuseum.org	Erie	PA	16507	814-453-3743	459-9735
Explore & More Hands-On Children's Museum 20 E High St *Web:* www.exploreandmore.com/index1.html	Gettysburg	PA	17325	717-337-9151	334-8799
Hands-On House Children's Museum of Lancaster 721 Landis Valley Rd *Web:* www.handsonhouse.org	Lancaster	PA	17601	717-569-5437	581-9283
Please Touch Museum 210 N 21st St *Web:* www.pleasetouchmuseum.org	Philadelphia	PA	19103	215-963-0666	963-0424
Providence Children's Museum 100 South St *Web:* www.childrenmuseum.org	Providence	RI	02903	401-273-5437	273-1004
Children's Museum of the Lowcountry 25 Ann St *Web:* www.explorecml.org	Charleston	SC	29403	843-853-8962	853-1042
Children's Museum of South Carolina 2501 N Kings Hwy *Web:* www.cmsckids.org	Myrtle Beach	SC	29578	843-946-9469	946-7011
EdVenture Children's Museum 211 Gervais St *Web:* www.edventure.org	Columbia	SC	29201	803-779-3100	779-3144
Children's Museum of Memphis 2525 Central Ave *Web:* www.cmom.com	Memphis	TN	38104	901-458-2678	458-4033
Children's Museum of Oak Ridge 461 W Outer Dr *Web:* www.childrensmuseumofoakridge.org	Oak Ridge	TN	37830	865-482-1074	481-4889
Creative Discovery Museum 321 Chestnut St *Web:* www.cdmfun.org	Chattanooga	TN	37402	423-756-2738	267-9344
East Tennessee Discovery Center 516 N Beaman St Chilhowee Park *Web:* www.etdiscovery.org	Knoxville	TN	37914	865-594-1494	594-1469
Hands On! Regional Museum 315 E Main St *Web:* www.handsonmuseum.org	Johnson City	TN	37601	423-434-4263	928-6915
Austin Children's Museum 201 Colorado St *Web:* www.austinkids.org	Austin	TX	78701	512-472-2499	472-2495
Children's Museum of Houston 1500 Binz St *Web:* www.cmhouston.org	Houston	TX	77004	713-522-1138	522-5747
Dallas Children's Museum 3535 Grand Ave Suite 308 *Web:* www.dallaschildrens.org	Dallas	TX	75210	214-428-5555	428-2003
Don Harrington Discovery Center 1200 Streit Dr *TF:* 800-784-9548 ■ *Web:* www.dhdc.org	Amarillo	TX	79106	806-355-9547	355-5703
Grace Museum 102 Cypress St *Web:* www.thegracemuseum.org	Abilene	TX	79601	325-673-4587	675-5993
Harrington Don Discovery Center 1200 Streit Dr *TF:* 800-784-9548 ■ *Web:* www.dhdc.org	Amarillo	TX	79106	806-355-9547	355-5703
Imaginarium of South Texas 5300 San Dario Ave Suite 505 *Web:* imaginariumstx.org	Laredo	TX	78040	956-728-0404	725-7776
San Antonio Children's Museum 305 E Houston St *Web:* www.sakids.org	San Antonio	TX	78205	210-212-4453	242-1313
Science Place The 1318 2nd Ave *Web:* www.scienceplace.org	Dallas	TX	75210	214-428-5555	428-4356
Discovery Gateway 444 W 100 South *Web:* www.discoverygateway.org	Salt Lake City	UT	84101	801-456-5437	456-5440
Treehouse Museum 455 23rd St *Web:* www.treehousemuseum.org	Ogden	UT	84401	801-394-9663	393-6820
Children's Museum of Richmond 2626 W Broad St *TF:* 877-295-2667 ■ *Web:* www.c-mor.org	Richmond	VA	23220	804-474-7000	474-7099
Children's Museum of Virginia 221 High St *Web:* www.childrensmuseumva.com	Portsmouth	VA	23704	757-393-8393	393-8083
Virginia Discovery Museum 524 E Main St *Web:* www.vadm.org	Charlottesville	VA	22902	434-977-1025	977-9681
Children's Museum Seattle 305 Harrison St *Web:* www.thechildrensmuseum.org	Seattle	WA	98109	206-441-1768	448-0910
Children's Museum of Tacoma 936 Broadway *Web:* www.childrensmuseumoftacoma.org	Tacoma	WA	98402	253-627-6031	627-2436
Hands On Children's Museum 106 11th Ave SW *Web:* www.hocm.org	Olympia	WA	98501	360-956-0818	754-8626
Betty Brinn Children's Museum 929 E Wisconsin Ave *Web:* www.bbcmkids.org	Milwaukee	WI	53202	414-291-0888	291-0906
Madison Children's Museum 100 State St *Web:* www.madisonchildrensmuseum.com	Madison	WI	53703	608-256-6445	256-3226

525 MUSEUMS & HALLS OF FAME - SPORTS

	City	State	Zip	Phone	Fax
1932 & 1980 Lake Placid Winter Olympic Museum Olympic Center 2634 Main St *TF:* 800-462-6236 ■ *Web:* www.orda.org	Lake Placid	NY	12946	518-523-1655	523-9275
Alabama Sports Hall of Fame 2150 Richard Arrington Jr Blvd N *Web:* www.ashof.org	Birmingham	AL	35203	205-323-6665	252-2212
Alberta Sports Hall of Fame & Museum 30 Riverview Park *Web:* www.albertasportshalloffame.com	Red Deer	AB	T4N1E3	403-341-8614	341-8619
American Indian Athletic Hall of Fame 155 Indian Ave	Lawrence	KS	66046	785-749-8481	
American Museum of Fly Fishing PO Box 42 *Web:* www.amff.com	Manchester	VT	05254	802-362-3300	362-3308
American Water Ski Hall of Fame & Museum 1251 Holy Cow Rd *TF:* 800-533-2972 ■ *Web:* www.waterskihalloffame.com	Polk City	FL	33868	863-324-2472	324-3996
Babe Ruth Birthplace Museum 216 Emory St *Web:* www.baberuthmuseum.com	Baltimore	MD	21230	410-727-1539	727-1652
Baseball Hall of Fame 910 S 3rd St *TF:* 888-375-9707	Minneapolis	MN	55415	612-375-9707	
Baseball Reliquary PO Box 1850 *Web:* www.baseballreliquary.org	Monrovia	CA	91017	626-791-7647	
Bob Feller Museum 310 Mill St PO Box 95 *TF:* 866-996-2806 ■ *Web:* www.bobfellermuseum.org	Van Meter	IA	50261	515-996-2806	996-2952
Bobby Riggs Tennis Museum 875 Santa Fe Dr *Web:* www.bobbyriggstennis.com	Encinitas	CA	92024	760-753-4705	944-8474
Braves Museum & Hall of Fame 755 Hank Aaron Dr *Web:* www.bravesmuseum.com	Atlanta	GA	30315	404-614-2310	614-1423
British Columbia Sports Hall of Fame & Museum 777 Pacific Blvd S *Web:* www.bcsportshalloffame.com	Vancouver	BC	V6B4Y8	604-687-5520	687-5510
Canada Olympic Hall of Fame & Museum 88 Canada Olympic Rd SW *Web:* www.coda.ca	Calgary	AB	T3B5R5	403-247-5486	286-7213
Canada's Sports Hall of Fame 115 Princes' Blvd Exhibition Place *Web:* www.cshof.ca	Toronto	ON	M6K3C3	416-260-6789	260-9347
Canadian Baseball Hall of Fame & Museum 386 Church St PO Box 1838 *TF:* 877-250-2255 ■ *Web:* www.baseballhalloffame.ca	Saint Marys	ON	N4X1C2	519-284-1838	284-1234
Canadian Football Hall of Fame & Museum 58 Jackson St W *Web:* www.footballhof.com	Hamilton	ON	L8P1L4	905-528-7566	528-9781
Canadian Golf Hall of Fame & Museum Glen Abbey Golf Course 1333 Dorval Dr Suite 1 *TF:* 800-263-0009 ■ *Web:* www.cghf.org	Oakville	ON	L6M4X7	905-849-9700	845-7040
Catskill Fly Fishing Center & Museum 1031 Old Rt 17 PO Box 1295 *Web:* www.cffcm.org	Livingston Manor	NY	12758	845-439-4810	
Chicagoland Sports Hall of Fame 1150 N River Rd	Des Plaines	IL	60016	847-294-1700	294-2861
College Football Hall of Fame 111 Saint Joseph St *TF:* 800-440-3263 ■ *Web:* collegefootball.org	South Bend	IN	44601	574-235-9999	235-5720
Colorado Sports Hall of Fame 1701 Bryant St Suite 500 INVESCO Field at Mile High *Fax Area Code: 303 ■ *Web:* www.coloradosports.org	Denver	CO	80204	720-258-3888	244-1003*
Delaware Sports Museum & Hall of Fame 801 S Madison St *Web:* www.desports.org	Wilmington	DE	19801	302-425-3263	425-3713
Don Garlits Museums 13700 SW 16th Ave *TF:* 877-271-3278 ■ *Web:* www.garlits.com	Ocala	FL	34473	352-245-8661	245-6895
Eastern Museum of Motor Racing PO Box 688 *Web:* www.emmr.org	Mechanics	PA	17055	717-528-8279	
Florida Air Museum at Sun 'n Fun 4175 Medulla Rd *Web:* www.sun-n-fun.org	Lakeland	FL	33811	863-644-0741	648-9264
Georgia Golf Hall of Fame 1 11th St *TF:* 888-874-4443 ■ *Web:* www.gghf.org	Augusta	GA	30901	706-724-4443	724-4428
Georgia Sports Hall of Fame 301 Cherry St *Web:* www.gshf.org	Macon	GA	31201	478-752-1585	752-1587
Green Bay Packers Hall of Fame 1265 Lombardi Ave *TF:* 888-442-7225 ■ *Web:* www.packers.com/hall_of_fame	Green Bay	WI	54304	920-569-7512	569-7122
Greyhound Hall of Fame 407 S Buckeye Ave *TF:* 800-932-7881 ■ *Web:* www.greyhoundhalloffame.com	Abilene	KS	67410	785-263-3000	263-2604
Harness Racing Museum & Hall of Fame 240 Main St PO Box 590 *Web:* www.harnessmuseum.com	Goshen	NY	10924	845-294-6330	294-3463
Hendrick Motorsports Museum 4411 Papa Joe Hendrick Blvd *TF:* 877-467-4890 ■ *Web:* www.hendrickmotorsports.com	Charlotte	NC	28262	704-455-3400	455-0346
Himes Museum of Motor Racing Nostalgia 15 O'Neil Ave	Bay Shore	NY	11706	631-666-4912	
Hockey Hall of Fame 30 Yonge St BCE Pl *Web:* www.hhof.com	Toronto	ON	M5E1X8	416-360-7735	360-1316
IGFA Fishing Hall of Fame & Museum 300 Gulf Stream Way *Web:* igfa.org	Dania Beach	FL	33004	954-922-4212	924-4220
Indiana Basketball Hall of Fame 1 Hall of Fame Ct *Web:* www.hoopshall.com	New Castle	IN	47362	765-529-1891	529-0273
Indiana Football Hall of Fame PO Box 1035	Richmond	IN	47375	765-966-2235	966-2235

Phone Fax

International Bowling Museum & Hall of Fame
111 Stadium Plaza .... Saint Louis MO 63102 314-231-6340 231-4054
TF: 800-966-2695 ■ *Web:* www.bowlingmuseum.com

International Boxing Hall of Fame Museum
1 Hall of Fame Dr. .... Canastota NY 13032 315-697-7095 697-5356
Web: www.ibhof.com

International Gymnastics Hall of Fame & Museum
120 N Robinson Ave East Concourse .... Oklahoma City OK 73102 405-235-5600 235-5678
Web: www.ighof.com

International Hockey Hall of Fame & Museum
277 York St Box 82 .... Kingston ON K7L4V6 613-544-2355 544-2844
Web: www.ihhof.com

International Jewish Sports Hall of Fame 7922 Turncrest Dr. .... Potomac MD 20854 301-299-3300 765-9865
Web: www.jewishsports.net

International Motorsports Hall of Fame & Museum
3198 Speedway Blvd .... Talladega AL 35161 256-362-5002
Web: www.motorsportshalloffame.com

International Snowmobile Hall of Fame 25929 County Rd 59 .... Bovey MN 55709 218-245-1725
Web: www.ishof.com

International Sports Hall of Fame & Olympic Museum
PO Box 166 .... Depoe Bay OR 97341 541-765-2923

International Swimming Hall of Fame
1 Hall of Fame Dr. .... Fort Lauderdale FL 33316 954-462-6536 525-4031
Web: www.ishof.org

International Tennis Hall of Fame & Museum
194 Bellevue Ave .... Newport RI 02840 401-849-3990 849-8780
TF: 800-457-1144 ■ *Web:* www.tennisfame.org

International Women's Sports Hall of Fame
Eisenhower Park .... East Meadow NY 11554 516-542-4700 542-4716
TF: 800-227-3988

International Wrestling Institute & Museum 1690 W 19th St S .... Newton IA 50208 641-791-1517 791-0461
Web: www.wrestlingmuseum.org

Ivan Allen Jr Braves Museum & Hall of Fame
755 Hank Aaron Dr .... Atlanta GA 30315 404-614-2310 614-1423
Web: www.bravesmuseum.com

Jack Nicklaus Museum 2355 Olentangy River Rd .... Columbus OH 43210 614-247-5959 247-5906
Web: www.nicklausmuseum.org

Kansas Sports Hall of Fame 238 N Mead St .... Wichita KS 67202 316-262-2038 263-2539
Web: www.kshof.org

Legends of the Game Baseball Museum 1000 Ballpark Way .... Arlington TX 76011 817-273-5023 273-5093
Web: museum.texasrangers.com

Louisiana Sports Hall of Fame
Prather Coliseum Rm 112 Northwestern State University .... Natchitoches LA 71497 318-357-6467 357-4515

Louisville Slugger Museum 800 W Main St .... Louisville KY 40202 502-588-7228 585-1179
TF: 877-775-8443 ■ *Web:* www.sluggermuseum.org

Lovelace Athletic Museum & Hall of Honor
Auburn Univ Athletic Dept PO Box 351 .... Auburn AL 36831 334-844-0764 844-0847
Web: www.lovelacemuseum.com

Manitoba Sports Hall of Fame & Museum
450 Portage Ave 5th Fl .... Winnipeg MB R3C0E7 204-774-0002 925-5792
Web: www.halloffame.mb.ca

Mississippi Sports Hall of Fame & Museum 1152 Lakeland Dr .... Jackson MS 39216 601-982-8264 982-4702
TF: 800-280-3263 ■ *Web:* www.msfame.com

Missouri Sports Hall of Fame 3861 E Stan Musial Dr .... Springfield MO 65809 417-889-3100 889-2761
TF: 800-498-5678 ■ *Web:* mosportshalloffame.com

Motorcycle Hall of Fame Museum 13515 Yarmouth Dr .... Pickerington OH 43147 614-856-2222 856-2221
TF: 800-262-5646 ■ *Web:* www.ama-cycle.org/museum

Motorsports Hall of Fame of America 43700 Expo Center Dr. .... Novi MI 48375 248-349-7223 349-2113
TF: 800-250-7223 ■ *Web:* www.mshf.com

Muskegon Area Sports Hall of Fame
LC Walker Arena 955 4th St .... Muskegon MI 49440 231-726-2939 726-4620

Naismith Memorial Basketball Hall of Fame
1000 W Columbus Ave .... Springfield MA 01105 413-781-6500 781-1939
TF: 877-446-6752 ■ *Web:* www.hoophall.com

National Art Museum of Sport
University Pl at IUPUI 850 W Michigan St .... Indianapolis IN 46202 317-274-3627 274-3878
Web: namos.iupui.edu

National Baseball Hall of Fame & Museum 25 Main St .... Cooperstown NY 13326 607-547-7200 547-2044
TF: 888-425-5633 ■ *Web:* www.baseballhalloffame.org

National Football Foundation & College Hall of Fame
111 S Saint Joseph St .... South Bend IN 46601 574-235-9999 235-5720
Web: www.collegefootball.org

National Fresh Water Fishing Hall of Fame
10360 Hall of Fame Dr PO Box 690 .... Hayward WI 54843 715-634-4440 634-4440
TF: 866-268-4333 ■ *Web:* freshwater-fishing.org

National Italian American Sports Hall of Fame
1431 W Taylor St .... Chicago IL 60607 312-226-5566 226-5678
Web: www.niashf.org

National Jousting Hall of Fame 94 Natural Chimneys Ln .... Mount Solon VA 22843 540-350-2510 350-2140
TF: 888-430-2267 ■ *Web:* www.nationaljousting.com/fame.htm

National Museum of Polo & Hall of Fame
9011 Lake Worth Rd .... Lake Worth FL 33467 561-969-3210 964-8299
Web: www.polomuseum.com

National Museum of Racing & Hall of Fame
191 Union Ave .... Saratoga Springs NY 12866 518-584-0400 584-4574
TF: 800-562-5394 ■ *Web:* www.racingmuseum.org

National Pastime: Museum of Minor League Baseball
175 Toyota Plaza Suite 300 .... Memphis TN 38103 901-722-0207 726-5502
Web: www.memphisredbirds.com/Ballpark/museum.asp

National Polish-American Sports Hall of Fame
11727 Gallagher St .... Hamtramck MI 48212 313-407-3300 876-7724
Web: www.polishsportshof.com

National Soaring Museum 51 Soaring Hill Dr. .... Elmira NY 14903 607-734-3128 732-6745
Web: www.soaringmuseum.org

National Soccer Hall of Fame 18 Stadium Cir .... Oneonta NY 13820 607-432-3351 432-8429
Web: www.soccerhall.org

National Softball Hall of Fame & Museum
2801 NE 50th St .... Oklahoma City OK 73111 405-424-5266 424-3855
TF: 800-654-8337 ■ *Web:* www.softball.org/hall_of_fame

National Sports Foundation PO Box 888886 .... Atlanta GA 30356 678-417-0041 417-0043
Web: www.natlsportsfoundation.com

National Sports Museum 80 Broad St 5th Fl .... New York NY 10004 212-837-7950 837-7949
Web: www.thesportsmuseum.com

National Sportscasters & Sportswriters Hall of Fame
322 E Innes St .... Salisbury NC 28144 704-633-4275 633-2027
Web: www.nssahalloffame.com

National Sprint Car Hall of Fame & Museum
1 Sprint Capital Pl .... Knoxville IA 50138 641-842-6176 842-6177
TF: 800-874-4488 ■ *Web:* www.sprintcarhof.com

National Wrestling Hall of Fame 405 W Hall of Fame Ave .... Stillwater OK 74075 405-377-5243 377-5244
Web: www.wrestlinghalloffame.com

NCAA Hall of Champions
1 NCAA Plaza 700 W Washington St .... Indianapolis IN 46204 317-916-4265 917-6596
TF: 800-735-6222 ■ *Web:* www.ncaahallofchampions.org

Negro Leagues Baseball Museum 1616 E 18th St .... Kansas City MO 64108 816-221-1920 221-8424
TF: 888-221-6526 ■ *Web:* www.nlbm.com

Phone Fax

New Brunswick Sports Hall of Fame 503 Queen St .... Fredericton NB E3B1B8 506-453-3747 459-0481
Web: www.nbsportshalloffame.nb.ca

New England Sports Museum 100 Legends Way .... Boston MA 02114 617-624-1235 624-1818
Web: www.sportsmuseum.org

New Jersey Sports Hall of Fame
New Jersey Sports & Exposition Authority 50 SR 120 .... East Rutherford NJ 07073 201-507-8134 460-4035

Nolan Ryan Exhibit Center 2925 S Hwy 35 .... Alvin TX 77511 281-388-1134 388-1135
TF: 800-350-7926 ■ *Web:* www.nolanryanfoundation.org

North Carolina Auto Racing Hall of Fame
119 Knob Hill Rd Lakeside Park .... Mooresville NC 28117 704-663-5331 663-6949
Web: www.ncarhof.com

North Carolina Sports Hall of Fame
5 E Edenton St North Carolina Museum of History .... Raleigh NC 27601 919-807-7900 733-8655

North Carolina Tennis Hall of Fame 3802 Jaycee Park Dr .... Greensboro NC 27455 336-852-8577
Web: www.nctennis.com

Northwestern Ontario Sports Hall of Fame 219 May St S .... Thunder Bay ON P7E1B5 807-622-2852 622-2736

Oklahoma Sports Hall of Fame & Jim Thorpe Museum
4040 N Lincoln Blvd .... Oklahoma City OK 73105 405-427-1400 495-7602
Web: www.jimthorpeassoc.org

Oregon Sports Hall of Fame & Museum 321 SW Salmon St .... Portland OR 97204 503-227-7466 227-6925
Web: www.oregonsportshall.com

Paul W Bryant Museum 300 Paul W Bryant Dr .... Tuscaloosa AL 35487 205-348-4668 348-8883
TF: 866-772-2327 ■ *Web:* bryantmuseum.ua.edu

Peter J McGovern Little League Baseball Museum
PO Box 3485 .... South Williamsport PA 17701 570-326-3607 326-2267
Web: www.littleleague.org/museum

Philadelphia Jewish Sports Hall of Fame & Adolph & Rose Levis Museum 401 S Broad St .... Philadelphia PA 19147 215-446-3045 790-1042
Web: www.phillyjewishsports.com

Philadelphia Sports Hall of Fame Foundation 410 Waverly Rd .... Wyncote PA 19095 215-886-6657
Web: www.phillyhof.org

Pro Football Hall of Fame 2121 George Halas Dr NW .... Canton OH 44708 330-456-8207 456-8175
Web: www.profootballhof.com

ProRodeo Hall of Fame & Museum of the American Cowboy 101 ProRodeo Dr .... Colorado Springs CO 80919 719-528-4764 548-4874
Web: prorodeo.org/hof

Roger Maris Museum 3902 13th Ave S Box 9978 .... Fargo ND 58106 701-282-2222 282-2229
Web: www.rogermarismuseum.com

Rose Bowl Hall of Fame 391 S Orange Grove Blvd .... Pasadena CA 91184 626-449-4100 449-9066
Web: www.tournamentofroses.com

Saint John Sports Hall of Fame 171 Adelaide St .... Saint John NB E2K1W9 506-658-4731 658-2902

Saint Louis Cardinals Hall of Fame 111 Stadium Plaza Dr .... Saint Louis MO 63102 314-231-6340 231-4054
TF: 800-966-2695 ■ *Web:* stlouis.cardinals.mlb.com

Saskatchewan Baseball Hall of Fame & Museum
PO Box 1388 .... Battleford SK S0M0E0 306-446-1983 446-0509
Web: www.saskbaseball.ca

Saskatchewan Sports Hall of Fame & Museum
2205 Victoria Ave .... Regina SK S4P0S4 306-780-9232 780-9427
Web: www.sshfm.com

Shanaman Sports Museum of Tacoma
2727 E 'D' St Tacoma Dome .... Tacoma WA 98421 253-272-3663 593-7620
Web: www.tacomasportsmuseum.com

Skate Canada Hall of Fame 865 Shefford Rd .... Ottowa ON K1J1H9 613-747-1007 748-5718
Web: www.skatecanada.ca

Snowmobile Hall of Fame & Museum
8481 W Hwy 70 PO Box 720 .... Saint Germain WI 54558 715-542-4488 542-4477
Web: www.snowmobilehalloffame.com

Sports Immortals Museum 6830 N Federal Hwy .... Boca Raton FL 33487 561-997-2575 997-6949
Web: www.sportsimmortals.com

Sports Legends at Camden Yards 301 W Camden St .... Baltimore MD 21201 410-727-1539 727-1652
Web: www.sportslegendsatcamdenyards.com

Ted Williams Museum & Hitters Hall of Fame
2455 N Citrus Hills Blvd .... Hernando FL 34442 352-527-6566 527-4163
Web: www.twmuseum.com

Texas Sports Hall of Fame 1108 S University Parks Dr .... Waco TX 76706 254-756-1633 756-2384
TF: 800-567-9561 ■ *Web:* www.tshof.org

Trapshooting Hall of Fame & Museum 601 W National Rd .... Vandalia OH 45377 937-898-1945 898-5472
Web: www.traphof.org

University of Iowa Athletics Hall of Fame KHF Bldg 446 .... Iowa City IA 52242 319-384-1031 384-1032
TF: 866-469-2326 ■ *Web:* www.hawkeyesports.com

US Golf Assn Museum 77 Liberty Corner Rd .... Far Hills NJ 07931 908-234-2300 234-9687
TF: 800-222-8742 ■ *Web:* www.usga.org

US Hockey Hall of Fame PO Box 657 .... Eveleth MN 55734 218-744-5167 744-2590
TF: 800-443-7825 ■ *Web:* www.ushockeyhall.com

US National Ski Hall of Fame & Museum 610 Palms Ave .... Ishpeming MI 49849 906-485-6323 486-4570
Web: skihall.com

US Olympic Hall of Fame 1750 E Boulder St .... Colorado Springs CO 80909 719-866-4500 866-4728
TF: 888-659-8687 ■ *Web:* www.usoc.org

Virginia Sports Hall of Fame 206 High St .... Portsmouth VA 23704 757-393-8031 393-8288
Web: www.virginiasportshalloffame.com

Volleyball Hall of Fame Heritage State Park 444 Dwight St .... Holyoke MA 01040 413-536-0926 539-6673
Web: www.volleyhall.org

Women's Basketball Hall of Fame 700 Hall of Fame Dr .... Knoxville TN 37915 865-633-9000 633-9294
Web: www.wbhof.com

World Figure Skating Museum & Hall of Fame
20 1st St .... Colorado Springs CO 80906 719-635-5200 635-9548
Web: www.worldskatingmuseum.org

World Golf Hall of Fame 1 World Golf Pl .... Saint Augustine FL 32092 904-940-4000
Web: www.wgv.com

World Sports Humanitarian Hall of Fame
855 Broad St Lower Level .... Boise ID 83702 208-343-7224 343-0831
Web: www.sportshumanitarian.com

526 MUSIC DISTRIBUTORS

Phone Fax

Allegro Corp 14134 NE Airport Way .... Portland OR 97230 503-257-8480 257-9061*
**Fax:* Orders ■ *TF:* 800-288-2007 ■ *Web:* www.allegro-music.com

Alliance Entertainment Corp 4250 Coral Ridge Dr .... Coral Springs FL 33065 954-255-4000 255-4825
TF: 800-329-7664 ■ *Web:* www.aent.com

Alternative Distribution Alliance 72 Spring St 12th Fl .... New York NY 10012 212-343-2485 343-2504
TF: 800-239-3232 ■ *Web:* www.ada-music.com

Baker & Taylor Inc 2550 W Tyvola Rd Suite 300 .... Charlotte NC 28217 704-998-3100 998-3316
TF: 800-775-1800 ■ *Web:* www.btol.com

BMG Distribution Co 1540 Broadway .... New York NY 10036 212-833-8000
Web: www.bmg.com

Caroline Distribution 104 W 29th St 4th Fl .... New York NY 10001 212-886-7500 643-5563
TF: 800-275-2250

Digital Music Group Inc 2151 River Plaza Dr Suite 200 .... Sacramento CA 95833 916-239-6010 239-6018
NASDAQ: DMGI ■ *Web:* www.digitalmusicgroupinc.com

EMI Christian Music Group 101 Winners Cir .... Brentwood TN 37024 615-371-6800 371-6980
TF: 800-669-8586 ■ *Web:* www.emicmg.com

Phone | Fax

EMI Music Distribution 501 Flynn Rd. Camarillo CA 93012 805-384-1192 384-5607
Gotham Distributing Corp 60 Portland Rd Conshohocken PA 19428 610-649-7650 649-0315
TF: 800-446-8426
GT Brands Holdings 100 Park Ave Suite 1102 New York NY 10017 212-951-3000 213-9319
Web: www.goodtimes.com
Handleman Co 500 Kirts Blvd Troy MI 48084 248-362-4400 362-3615
NYSE: HDL ■ *Web:* www.handleman.com
Inspired Corp 103 Eisenhower Pkwy Roseland NJ 07068 973-226-1234 226-6696
TF: 800-738-3747 ■ *Web:* www.inspiredcorp.com
K-Tel International Inc 2655 Cheshire Ln N Suite 100 Plymouth MN 55447 763-559-5566 559-5505
TF: 800-328-6640 ■ *Web:* www.k-tel.com
Koch Entertainment Distribution 22 Harbor Pk Dr Port Washington NY 11050 516-484-1000 484-4746
TF: 800-332-7553 ■ *Web:* www.kochdistribution.com
Loud Music Inc 101 W Yale St Orlando FL 32804 407-843-6909
Malaco Music Group Inc 3023 W Northside Dr Jackson MS 39213 601-982-4522 982-4528
TF Cust Svc: 800-272-7936 ■ *Web:* www.malaco.com
Music City Record Distributors Inc 25 Lincoln St Nashville TN 37210 615-255-7315 255-7329
TF: 800-467-1050 ■ *Web:* www.mcrd.com
Navarre Corp 7400 49th Ave N New Hope MN 55428 763-535-8333 533-2156
NASDAQ: NAVR ■ *TF:* 800-728-4000 ■ *Web:* www.navarre.com
Provident-Integrity Distribution 741 Cool Springs Blvd Franklin TN 37067 615-261-6500 261-5909*
**Fax:* Hum Res ■ *TF Sales:* 800-333-9000 ■ *Web:* www.providentmusic.com
RED Distribution 79 5th Ave 15th Fl New York NY 10003 212-404-0600 404-0619
TF: 800-733-1966 ■ *Web:* www.redmusic.com
Select-O-Hits Inc 1981 Fletcher Creek Dr Memphis TN 38133 901-388-1190 388-3002
TF: 800-346-0723 ■ *Web:* www.selectohits.com
Sony-BMG Entertainment 1540 Broadway New York NY 10036 212-833-8000 930-4511*
**Fax:* Sales ■ *Web:* www.sonybmg.com
Sony Music Distribution 550 Madison Ave New York NY 10022 212-833-8000
Universal Music & Video Distribution 2220 Colorado Ave Santa Monica CA 90404 310-865-5000 235-4905
Walt Disney Records 500 S Buena Vista St Burbank CA 91521 818-560-1000
Web: disney.go.com/DisneyRecords

527 MUSIC PROGRAMMING SERVICES

Phone | Fax

DMX Music Inc 600 Congress Ave Suite 1400 Austin TX 78701 512-380-8500 380-8501
TF: 800-345-5000 ■ *Web:* www.dmxmusic.com
Jones Radio Network Inc 8200 S Akron St Suite 103 Centennial CO 80112 303-784-8700 784-8217
TF: 800-609-5663 ■ *Web:* www.jonesradio.com
Music Choice 110 Gibraltar Rd Suite 200 Horsham PA 19044 215-784-5840 784-5869
Web: www.musicchoice.com
Muzak LLC 3318 Lakemont Blvd Fort Mill SC 29708 803-396-3000 396-3136
TF: 800-331-3340 ■ *Web:* www.muzak.com
PlayNetwork Inc 8727 148th Ave NE Redmond WA 98052 425-497-8100 497-8181
TF Sales: 888-567-7529 ■ *Web:* www.playnetwork.com

528 MUSIC STORES

SEE ALSO Book, Music, Video Clubs p. 1388

Phone | Fax

a & b sound Ltd 3434 Cornett Rd Vancouver BC V5M2H1 604-430-2999 430-5488
Web: www.absound.ca
Amazon.com Inc 1200 12th Ave S Suite 1200 Seattle WA 98144 206-266-1000 266-7601*
NASDAQ: AMZN ■ **Fax:* Hum Res ■ *TF Cust Svc:* 800-201-7575 ■
Web: www.amazon.com
Archambault Group Inc 500 rue Sainte-Catherine E Montreal QC H2L2C6 514-849-6206 849-0764
TF: 877-849-8589 ■ *Web:* www.archambault.ca
Best Buy Co Inc 7601 Penn Ave S Richfield MN 55423 612-291-1000 238-3160*
NYSE: BBY ■ **Fax Area Code:* 952 ■ **Fax:* Cust Svc ■ *TF:* 800-369-5050 ■
Web: www.bestbuy.com
Borders Inc 100 Phoenix Dr Ann Arbor MI 48108 734-477-1100 477-1313
TF Cust Svc: 800-566-6616 ■ *Web:* www.bordersstores.com
CD Connection.com 1176 Aster Ave Suite A Sunnyvale CA 94086 408-985-7905 985-0464
Web: www.cdconnection.com
CD Plus 70 Driver Rd Brampton ON L6T5V2 905-624-7339 624-7310
Web: www.cdplus.com
CD Universe 101 N Plains Industrial Rd Wallingford CT 06492 203-294-1648 294-0391
TF: 800-231-7937 ■ *Web:* www.cduniverse.com
CD Warehouse 900 N Broadway Oklahoma City OK 73102 405-236-8742 949-2566
TF: 800-641-9394 ■ *Web:* www.cdwarehouse.com
Circuit City Group 9950 Mayland Dr Richmond VA 23233 804-527-4000 527-4171*
**Fax:* Acctg ■ *TF:* 800-251-2665 ■ *Web:* www.circuitcity.com
Coconuts Music & Movies 38 Corporate Cir Albany NY 12203 518-452-1242 869-4819
TF: 800-540-1242 ■ *Web:* www.coconuts.com
Djangos 2344 NW 21st Place Portland OR 97210 503-241-6584 241-6436
Web: www.djangomusic.com
eMusic.com Inc 100 Park Ave 17th Fl New York NY 10017 212-201-9240 201-9204
Web: www.emusic.com
FirstCom Music 1325 Capital Pkwy Suite 109 Carrollton TX 75006 972-446-8742
TF: 800-858-8880 ■ *Web:* www.firstcom.com
For Your Entertainment 38 Corporate Cir Albany NY 12203 518-452-1242 869-4819
TF: 800-540-1242 ■ *Web:* www.fye.com
Global Electronic Music Marketplace PO Box 4062 Palm Springs CA 92262 760-318-6250 318-6251
TF: 800-207-4366 ■ *Web:* gemm.com
Half.com Inc PO Box 1469 Draper UT 84020 800-545-9857 349-5782*
**Fax Area Code:* 877 ■ *TF:* 800-545-9857 ■ *Web:* www.half.ebay.com
Hastings Entertainment Inc 3601 Plains Blvd Amarillo TX 79102 806-351-2300 351-2211
NASDAQ: HAST ■ *TF Cust Svc:* 877-427-8464 ■ *Web:* www.gohastings.com
HMV Canada 5401 Eglinton Ave W Suite 110 Etobicoke ON M9C5K6 416-620-4470 620-5064
Web: www.hmv.com
IndiSonic Inc 126 N 3rd St Suite 512 Minneapolis MN 55401 612-349-9013 305-9160
TF: 877-492-7916 ■ *Web:* www.indisonic.com
Inspired Distribution LLC 103 Eisenhower Pkwy Roseland NJ 07068 973-226-1234 226-6696
TF: 800-272-4214 ■ *Web:* www.peterpan.com
J & R Music World 23 Park Row New York NY 10038 212-732-8600 238-9191
TF: 800-221-8180 ■ *Web:* www.jr.com
Mississippi Music Inc 222 S Main St Hattiesburg MS 39401 601-544-5821 544-5841
TF: 800-844-5821 ■ *Web:* www.mississippimusic.com
Musicland Group Inc 10400 Yellow Circle Dr Minnetonka MN 55343 952-931-8000 931-8300
TF Cust Svc: 800-538-3465 ■ *Web:* www.musicland.com
Musicnotes Inc 8020 Excelsior Dr Suite 201 Madison WI 53717 608-662-1680 662-1688
TF: 800-944-4667 ■ *Web:* www.musicnotes.com
Newbury Comics Inc 5 Guest St Brighton MA 02135 617-254-1666 254-2540
Web: www.newbury.com
Sam Goody 10400 Yellow Circle Dr Minnetonka MN 55343 952-931-8000 931-8300
TF Cust Svc: 800-371-4225 ■ *Web:* www.samgoody.com

Phone | Fax

SightSound Technologies Inc 311 S Craig St Suite 205 Pittsburgh PA 15213 412-621-6100 341-2442
Web: www.sightsound.com
Spec's Music Inc 501 Collins Ave Miami Beach FL 33139 305-534-3667 532-3329
TF: 800-540-1242 ■ *Web:* www.twec.com/corpsite/stores
Strawberries Music & Video 38 Corporate Cir Albany NY 12203 518-452-1242 869-4819
TF: 800-540-1242 ■ *Web:* www.twec.com/corpsite/stores
The Record Exchange 1105 W Idaho St Boise ID 83702 208-344-8010 336-2660
Web: www.therecordexchange.com
Tower Records 2500 Del Monte St Bldg C West Sacramento CA 95691 916-373-2500 373-3012
TF: 800-225-0880 ■ *Web:* www.towerrecords.com
Trans World Entertainment Corp 38 Corporate Cir Albany NY 12203 518-452-1242 869-4819
NASDAQ: TWMC ■ *TF:* 800-540-1242 ■ *Web:* www.twec.com
Transcontinent Record Sales Inc DBA Record Theatre
1762 Main St Buffalo NY 14208 716-883-9520 884-1432
TF: 800-836-0751 ■ *Web:* www.recordtheatre.com
Ultimate Band List 10900 Wilshire Blvd Suite 1400 Los Angeles CA 90024 323-634-4000 634-4299
Web: ubl.artistdirect.com
Value Music Concepts Inc 825-C Franklin Ct Marietta GA 30067 770-919-2115 919-2219
Web: www.musicforasong.com
Virgin Megastores USA
c/o SJ Communications 17012 Enadia Way Lake Balboa CA 91406 818-881-3889 332-4212
TF: 877-484-7446 ■ *Web:* www.virginmega.com
Wherehouse Music 2330 Carson St Carson CA 90810 518-452-1242 516-9057*
**Fax Area Code:* 310 ■ *Web:* www.wherehouse.com
Winmark Corp 4200 Dahlberg Dr Suite 100 Minneapolis MN 55422 763-520-8500 520-8410
NASDAQ: WINA ■ *TF:* 800-433-2540 ■ *Web:* www.winmarkcorporation.com

529 MUSICAL INSTRUMENT STORES

Phone | Fax

Alamo Music Center 425 N Main Ave San Antonio TX 78205 210-224-1010 226-8742
TF: 800-822-5010 ■ *Web:* www.alamomusic.com
American Musical Supply PO Box 152 Spicer MN 56288 320-796-2088 796-6036
TF: 800-458-4076 ■ *Web:* www.americanmusical.com
Amro Music Stores 2918 Poplar Ave Memphis TN 38111 901-323-8888 325-6407
TF: 800-661-2676 ■ *Web:* www.amromusic.com
Apollo's Axes LLC 15603 Cassandra Pl Tampa FL 33624 813-908-8647 227-4767*
**Fax Area Code:* 570 ■ *TF:* 800-827-9196 ■ *Web:* www.apollosaxes.com
Ardsley Musical Instrument Service Ltd 219 Sprain Rd Scarsdale NY 10583 914-693-6639 693-6974
Web: www.ardsleymusic.com
Ash Sam Music Corp PO Box 9047 Hicksville NY 11802 516-932-6400 931-3881
TF: 888-615-5904 ■ *Web:* www.samashmusic.com
Bananas at Large 1504 4th St San Rafael CA 94901 415-457-7600 457-9148
Web: www.bananas.com
Bodine's Inc 6436 Penn Ave S Richfield MN 55423 612-866-2025 866-0463
TF: 800-535-6424 ■ *Web:* www.bodinespiano.com
Brook Mays Music Co 8605 John Carpenter Fwy Dallas TX 75247 214-631-0928 637-9399*
**Fax Area Code:* 800 ■ *TF Cust Svc:* 800-637-8966 ■ *Web:* www.brookmays.com
Buddy Rogers Music Inc 6891 Simpson Ave Cincinnati OH 45239 513-729-1950 728-6010
TF: 888-276-8742 ■ *Web:* www.buddyrogers.com
Elderly Instruments 1100 N Washington Ave Lansing MI 48906 517-372-7890 372-5155
TF: 888-473-5810 ■ *Web:* www.elderly.com
Fletcher Music Centers Inc 3966 Airway Cir Clearwater FL 33762 727-571-1088 572-4405
TF: 800-258-1088 ■ *Web:* www.fletchermusic.com
Foxes Music Co 416 S Washington St Falls Church VA 22046 703-533-7393 536-2171
TF: 800-446-4414 ■ *Web:* www.foxesmusic.com
Giardinelli PO Box 4370 Medford OR 97501 541-772-5173 652-4534*
**Fax Area Code:* 800 ■ *TF:* 800-249-8361 ■ *Web:* www.giardinelli.com
Graves Piano & Organ Co Inc 5798 Karl Rd Columbus OH 43229 614-847-4322 847-0808
TF: 800-686-4322 ■ *Web:* www.gravespiano.com
Gruhn Guitars 400 Broadway Nashville TN 37203 615-256-2033 255-2021
Web: www.gruhn.com
Guitar Center Inc 5795 Lindero Canyon Rd Westlake Village CA 91362 818-735-8800 735-8822
NASDAQ: GTRC ■ *TF:* 800-905-0585 ■ *Web:* www.guitarcenter.com
Guitar Imports 334 N Marshall Way Suite 3 Layton UT 84041 801-544-4060 340-0107
TF: 877-544-4060 ■ *Web:* www.guitarimports.com
H & H Music Co 10303 Katy Fwy Houston TX 77024 281-531-9222 467-6840*
**Fax Area Code:* 713 ■ *TF:* 800-446-8742
House of Guitars Corp 645 Titus Ave Rochester NY 14617 585-544-3500 544-8860
Hume Music Inc 5331 SW 22nd Suite 2 Topeka KS 66614 785-266-6366 266-6393
TF: 800-657-5748 ■ *Web:* www.humemusic.com
International Violin Co Ltd 1421 Clarkview Rd Baltimore MD 21209 410-832-2525 832-2528
TF: 800-542-3538 ■ *Web:* www.internationalviolin.com
JW Pepper & Son Inc 2480 Industrial Blvd Paoli PA 19301 610-648-0500 993-9716
TF: 800-345-6296 ■ *Web:* www.jwpepper.com
Ken Stanton Music Inc 119 Cobb Pkwy N Suite A Marietta GA 30062 770-427-2491 422-8455
TF: 800-282-9011 ■ *Web:* www.kenstantonmusic.com
Keyboard World Inc 23-25 E Main St Frostburg MD 21532 301-729-1817 689-2628
TF: 800-947-4266 ■ *Web:* www.keyboardworld.com
Long & McQuade Musical Instruments 722 Rosebank Rd Pickering ON L1W4B2 905-837-9785 837-9786
Web: www.long-mcquade.com
Ludwig Music House Inc 3600 Rider Trail S Earth City MO 63045 314-298-9696 739-3203
TF: 800-783-7007
M Steinert & Sons Co 162 Boylston St Boston MA 02116 617-426-1900 426-1905
Web: www.msteinert.com
Music & Arts Centers Inc 4626 Wedgewood Blvd Frederick MD 21703 301-620-4040 620-2567
TF: 800-237-7760 ■ *Web:* www.musicarts.com
Music Go Round Inc 4200 Dahlberg Dr Suite 100 Minneapolis MN 55422 763-520-8419 520-8489
Web: www.musicgoround.com
Music123 1 Cherry Hill Suite 800 Cherry Hill NJ 08002 856-779-6300 779-0231
TF: 888-590-9700 ■ *Web:* www.music123.com
Musician's Friend Inc PO Box 4370 Medford OR 97501 541-772-5173 776-1370
TF: 800-391-8762 ■ *Web:* www.musiciansfriend.com
Musiciansbuy.com Inc 11-7830 Byron Dr West Palm Beach FL 33404 561-842-7451 840-9032
TF: 877-778-7845 ■ *Web:* www.musiciansbuy.com
Paragon Music Center Inc 2119 W Hillsborough Ave Tampa FL 33603 813-876-3459 876-0972
Web: www.paragon-music.com
Sam Ash Music Corp PO Box 9047 Hicksville NY 11802 516-932-6400 931-3881
TF: 888-615-5904 ■ *Web:* www.samashmusic.com
SameDayMusic 65 Greenwood Ave Midland Park NJ 07432 866-744-7736 276-0186*
**Fax Area Code:* 312 ■ *Web:* www.samedaymusic.com
Schmitt Music Co 100 N 6th St Suite 850B Minneapolis MN 55403 612-339-4811
TF: 800-767-3434 ■ *Web:* www.schmittmusic.com
Stanton's Sheet Music 330 S 4th St Columbus OH 43215 614-224-4257 224-5929
TF: 800-426-8742 ■ *Web:* www.stantons.com
Strait Music Co 2428 W Ben White Blvd Austin TX 78704 512-476-6927 476-6968
TF: 800-725-8877 ■ *Web:* www.straitmusic.com
US Music Corp 444 E Courtland St Mundelein IL 60060 847-949-0444 949-8444
TF: 800-877-6863 ■ *Web:* www.usmusiccorp.com
Washington Music Center 11151 Veirs Mill Rd Wheaton MD 20902 301-946-8808 946-0487
Web: www.wmcworld.com
West Music Inc 1212 5th St PO Box 5521 Coralville IA 52241 319-351-2000 351-0479
TF: 800-373-2000 ■ *Web:* www.westmusic.com

Phone Fax

Woodwind & Brasswind 4004 Technology Dr. South Bend IN 46628 574-251-3500 251-3501
TF: 800-348-5003 ■ *Web:* www.wwbw.com

zZounds Music 65 Greenwood Ave Midland Park NJ 07432 800-996-8637 276-0186*
*Fax Area Code: 312 ■ *Web:* www.zzounds.com

530 MUSICAL INSTRUMENTS

Phone Fax

Alembic Inc 3005 Wiljan Ct. Santa Rosa CA 95407 707-523-2611 523-2935
Web: www.alembic.com

Alesis Corp 300 Corporate Pointe Suite 300 Culver City CA 90230 310-693-7005 693-7040
Web: www.alesis.com

Allen Organ Co 150 Locust St PO Box 36 Macungie PA 18062 610-966-2200 965-3098
Web: www.allenorgan.com

Austin Organs Inc 156 Woodland St. Hartford CT 06105 860-522-8293 524-9828
Web: www.austinorgans.com

Avedis Zildjian Co 22 Longwater Dr Norwell MA 02061 781-871-2200 871-3984
TF: 800-229-8672 ■ *Web:* www.zildjian.com

Baldwin Piano Co 309 Plus Park Blvd Nashville TN 37217 615-871-4500 889-5509
TF: 800-444-2766 ■ *Web:* www.gibson.com

Bevin Brothers 10 Bevin Rd PO Box 60 East Hampton CT 06424 860-267-4431 267-8557
Web: www.bevinbells.com

Burkart-Phelan Inc 2 Shaker Rd Suite D-107 Shirley MA 01464 978-425-4500 425-9800
Web: www.burkart.com

Carvin Guitars 12340 World Trade Dr. San Diego CA 92128 858-487-1600 487-7620
TF: 800-854-2235 ■ *Web:* www.carvin.com

Casio Inc 570 Mt Pleasant Ave Dover NJ 07801 973-361-5400 537-8910*
*Fax: Hum Res ■ *TF Cust Svc:* 800-634-1895 ■ *Web:* www.casio.com

CF Martin & Co Inc DBA Martin Guitar Co 510 Sycamore St Nazareth PA 18064 610-759-2837 759-5757
TF: 800-345-3103 ■ *Web:* www.mguitar.com

Chesbro Music Co Inc PO Box 2009 Idaho Falls ID 83403 208-522-8691 522-8712
TF Cust Svc: 800-243-7276 ■ *Web:* www.chesbromusic.com

Chime Master Systems PO Box 936 Lancaster OH 43130 740-746-8500 746-9566
TF: 800-344-7464 ■ *Web:* www.chimemaster.com

Commercial Music Co Inc 1550 Edison St. Dallas TX 75207 214-741-6381 748-4088
TF: 800-442-7281 ■ *Web:* www.commercialmusic.com

Conn-Selmer Inc 600 Industrial Pkwy Elkhart IN 46516 574-522-1675 295-5405
TF: 800-759-9124 ■ *Web:* www.conn-selmer.com

Davitt & Hanser Music Co 2395 Arbor Tech Dr. Hebron KY 41048 859-817-7100 451-4944*
*Fax Area Code: 800 ■ *TF:* 800-999-5558 ■ *Web:* www.hansermusicgroup.com

Deering Banjo Co 3733 Kenora Dr Spring Valley CA 91977 619-464-8252 464-0833
TF: 800-845-7791 ■ *Web:* www.deeringbanjos.com

E & O Mari Inc 256 Broadway Newburgh NY 12550 845-562-4400 562-4491
TF: 800-750-3034 ■ *Web:* www.labella.com

Edwards Instrument Co 530 S Hwy H Elkhorn WI 53121 262-723-4221 723-4245
TF: 800-562-6838 ■ *Web:* www.edwards-instruments.com

Emerson Flutes USA 600 Industrial Pkwy Elkhart IN 46515 574-522-1675 522-1750
TF: 800-759-9124 ■ *Web:* www.emersonflutes.com

Ernie Ball 151 Suburban Rd San Luis Obispo CA 93401 805-544-7726 544-3826
TF: 866-823-2255 ■ *Web:* www.ernieball.com

Fender Musical Instruments Corp
8860 E Chaparral Rd Suite 100 Scottsdale AZ 85250 480-596-9690 596-1384
TF: 800-488-1818 ■ *Web:* www.fender.com

Fernandez Guitars International Inc
11044 Weddington St Suite 13 North Hollywood CA 91601 818-487-1940 760-0937
Web: www.fernandesguitars.com

Frank Holton & Co 320 N Church St Elkhorn WI 53121 262-723-2220 723-6959

Fred Gretsch Enterprises PO Box 2468 Savannah GA 31402 912-748-7070 748-6005
Web: www.gretsch.com

General Music Corp 1164 Tower Ln Bensenville IL 60106 630-766-8230 766-8281
TF: 800-323-0280 ■ *Web:* www.generalmusic.com

Getzen Co Inc 530 S Hwy H PO Box 440 Elkhorn WI 53121 262-723-4221 723-4245
TF: 800-366-5584 ■ *Web:* www.getzen.com

GHS Corp 2813 Wilber Ave Battle Creek MI 49015 269-968-3351 968-6913
TF: 800-388-4447 ■ *Web:* www.ghsstrings.com

Gibson Guitar Corp DBA Gibson Musical Instruments
309 Plus Park Blvd Nashville TN 37217 615-871-4500 884-7256
TF: 800-444-2766 ■ *Web:* www.gibson.com

Gibson Musical Instruments 309 Plus Park Blvd Nashville TN 37217 615-871-4500 884-7256
TF: 800-444-2766 ■ *Web:* www.gibson.com

Gibson Piano Ventures Inc DBA Baldwin Piano Co
309 Plus Park Blvd Nashville TN 37217 615-871-4500 889-5509
TF: 800-444-2766 ■ *Web:* www.gibson.com

Hammond Suzuki USA 733 Annoreno Dr Addison IL 60101 630-543-0277 543-0279
TF: 888-674-2623 ■ *Web:* www.hammondorganco.com

Hohner Inc 1000 Technology Pk Dr Glen Allen VA 23059 804-515-1900 515-0347
TF: 800-446-6010 ■ *Web:* www.hohnerusa.com

Hoshino USA Inc 1726 Winchester Rd Bensalem PA 19020 215-638-8670 245-8583
Web: www.ibanez.com

J D'Addario & Co Inc 595 Smith St Farmingdale NY 11735 631-439-3300 439-3333
TF: 800-323-2746 ■ *Web:* www.daddario.com

JD Calato Mfg Co Inc 4501 Hyde Park Blvd. Niagara Falls NY 14305 716-285-3546 285-2710
TF Cust Svc: 800-358-4590 ■ *Web:* www.regaltip.com

Kaman Music Corp 20 Old Windsor Rd Bloomfield CT 06002 860-509-8888 509-8890
TF: 800-647-2244 ■ *Web:* www.kamanmusic.com

Kawai America Corp 2055 E University Dr. Compton CA 90220 310-631-1771 604-6913
TF: 800-421-2177 ■ *Web:* www.kawaius.com

Korg USA Inc 316 S Service Rd Melville NY 11747 631-390-6500 390-8737
Web: www.korg.com

La Bella Strings 256 Broadway Newburgh NY 12550 845-562-4400 562-4491
TF: 800-750-3034 ■ *Web:* www.labella.com

Latin Percussion Inc 160 Belmont Ave. Garfield NJ 07026 973-478-6903 772-3568
Web: www.lpmusic.com

Leblanc Inc 7001 Leblanc Blvd Kenosha WI 53141 262-658-1644 658-2824
TF: 800-558-9421 ■ *Web:* www.gleblanc.com

Lowrey Organ Co 825 E 26th St La Grange Park IL 60526 708-352-3388 352-3464
TF: 800-451-5939 ■ *Web:* www.lowrey.com

Ludwig Industries 2806 Mason St Monroe NC 28110 704-289-6459 289-8133
Web: www.ludwig-drums.com

Lyon & Healy Harps Inc 168 N Ogden Ave. Chicago IL 60607 312-786-1881 226-1502
TF: 800-621-3881 ■ *Web:* www.lyonhealy.com

Maas-Rowe Carillons Inc 2255 Meyers Ave Escondido CA 92029 760-743-1311 747-2677
TF: 800-854-2023 ■ *Web:* www.maasrowe.com

Manhasset Specialty Co 3505 Fruitvale Blvd Yakima WA 98902 509-248-3810 248-3834
TF: 800-795-0965 ■ *Web:* www.manhasset-specialty.com

Martin Guitar Co 510 Sycamore St. Nazareth PA 18064 610-759-2837 759-5757
TF: 800-345-3103 ■ *Web:* www.mguitar.com

Mason & Hamlin Piano Co 35 Duncan St Haverhill MA 01830 978-374-8888 374-8080
Web: www.masonhamlin.com

Meisel Music Inc PO Box 90 Springfield NJ 07081 973-379-5000 379-5020
Web: www.meiselmusic.com

Musicorp PO Box 63366 North Charleston SC 29419 843-745-8501 745-8502
TF: 800-845-1922 ■ *Web:* www.musicorp.com

Phone Fax

Noble & Cooley Co 42 Water St Granville MA 01034 413-357-6321 357-6314
Web: www.noblecooley.com

Organ Supply Industries Inc 2320 W 50th St. Erie PA 16506 814-835-2244 838-0349
TF: 800-458-0289 ■ *Web:* www.organsupply.com

OS Kelly Co 318 E North St. Springfield OH 45503 937-322-4921 322-1322

Ovation Guitars 37 Greenwoods Rd New Hartford CT 06057 860-379-7575 379-8972
TF Cust Svc: 800-552-4681 ■ *Web:* www.ovationguitars.com

Paul Reed Smith Guitars 380 Log Canoe Cir Stevensville MD 21666 410-643-9970 643-9980
Web: www.prsguitars.com

Peavey Electronics Corp 5022 Hartley Peavey Dr Meridian MS 39305 601-483-5365 486-1278
TF: 877-732-8391 ■ *Web:* www.peavey.com

PianoDisc 1101 N Market Blvd Suite 3 Sacramento CA 95834 916-567-9999 567-1941
TF: 800-566-3472 ■ *Web:* www.pianodisc.com

Prestini Musical Instruments Inc 2020 N Aurora Dr Nogales AZ 85621 520-287-4931 287-7049
TF: 800-528-6569 ■ *Web:* www.prestiniusa.com

Remo Inc 28101 Industry Dr Valencia CA 91355 661-294-5600 294-5700
TF: 800-525-5134 ■ *Web:* www.remo.com

Reuter Organ Co 1220 Timberedge Rd Lawrence KS 66049 785-843-2622 843-3302
Web: www.reuterorgan.com

Roland Corp US 5100 S Eastern Ave Los Angeles CA 90040 323-890-3700 890-3701
Web: www.rolandus.com

Saint Louis Music Inc 1400 Ferguson Ave Saint Louis MO 63133 314-727-4512 727-8929
TF: 800-727-4512 ■ *Web:* www.stlouismusic.com

Schaff Piano Supply Co 451 Oakwood Rd Lake Zurich IL 60047 847-438-4556 438-4615
TF: 800-747-4266 ■ *Web:* www.schaffpiano.com

Schulmerich Carillons Inc 1 Carillon Hill Sellersville PA 18960 215-257-2771 257-1910
TF: 800-772-3557 ■ *Web:* www.schulmerichbells.com

Selmer Co Inc 600 Industrial Pkwy Elkhart IN 46515 574-522-1675 522-0334
TF: 800-348-7426 ■ *Web:* www.selmer.com

Sound Enhancement Products Inc 325 Cary Point Dr Cary IL 60013 847-639-4646 639-4723
TF: 800-284-5172 ■ *Web:* www.morleypedals.com

Steinway Musical Instruments Inc 800 South St Suite 305 Waltham MA 02453 781-894-9770 894-9803
NYSE: LVB ■ *Web:* www.steinwaymusical.com

Steinway & Sons 1 Steinway Pl Long Island City NY 11105 718-721-2600 932-4332
TF: 800-366-1853 ■ *Web:* www.steinway.com

Suzuki Musical Instrument Corp PO Box 261030 San Diego CA 92196 619-873-2000 873-1997
TF Cust Svc: 800-854-1594 ■ *Web:* www.suzukimusic.com

Taylor-Listug Inc 1980 Gillespie Way El Cajon CA 92020 619-258-1207 258-1623
Web: www.taylorguitars.com

Ultimate Support Systems Inc 5836 Wright Dr Loveland CO 80538 970-776-1920 776-1941
TF: 800-525-5628 ■ *Web:* www.ultimatesupport.com

US Music Corp 444 E Courtland St. Mundelein IL 60060 847-949-0444 949-8444
TF: 800-877-6863 ■ *Web:* www.usmusiccorp.com

Verne Q Powell Flutes Inc 1 Clock Tower Pl Suite 300 Maynard MA 01754 978-461-6111 461-6155
Web: www.powellflutes.com

Wenger Corp 555 Park Dr PO Box 448 Owatonna MN 55060 507-455-4100 455-4258
TF: 800-733-0393 ■ *Web:* www.wengercorp.com

Wicks Pipe Organ Co 1100 5th St Highland IL 62249 618-654-2191 654-3770
TF Cust Svc: 800-444-9425 ■ *Web:* www.wicks.com

Wm S Haynes Co Inc 12 Piedmont St. Boston MA 02116 617-482-7456 482-1870
Web: www.wmshaynes.com

Yamaha Corp of America 6600 Orangethorpe Ave Buena Park CA 90620 714-522-9011 522-9235*
*Fax: Hum Res ■ *Web:* www.yamaha.com

Yamaha Musical Products 3445 E Paris Ave SE Grand Rapids MI 49512 616-940-4900 575-1380
Web: www.yamaha.com/band

531 MUTUAL FUNDS

Phone Fax

AARP Investment Funds PO Box 219735 Kansas City MO 64121 800-253-2277 821-6234
Web: aarp.scudder.com

AIM Investments 11 Greenway Plaza Suite 100 Houston TX 77046 713-626-1919 214-4109*
*Fax: Mail Rm ■ *TF:* 800-347-1919 ■ *Web:* www.aimfunds.com

Alger Fund PO Box 8480 Boston MA 02266 800-992-3863
Web: www.algerfund.com

Allegiant Funds
c/o Professional Funds Distributor LLC 760
Moore Rd King of Prussia PA 19406 800-622-3863
Web: www.allegiantfunds.com

American AAdvantage Funds
4151 Amon Carter Blvd MD 2450 Fort Worth TX 76155 817-967-3509 967-0768
TF: 800-388-3344 ■ *Web:* www.aafunds.com

American Century Mutual Funds PO Box 419200 Kansas City MO 64141 816-531-5575 340-7962*
*Fax: Cust Svc ■ *TF:* 800-345-2021 ■ *Web:* www.americancentury.com

American Funds Group 135 S State College Blvd Brea CA 92821 714-671-7000 671-7133
TF: 800-421-0180 ■ *Web:* www.americanfunds.com

American Skandia PO Box 8012 Boston MA 02266 800-752-6342
Web: www.americanskandia.prudential.com

AMF Funds 230 W Monroe St Suite 2810 Chicago IL 60606 800-527-3713 214-1424*
*Fax Area Code: 312 ■ *Web:* www.shayassets.com

AmSouth Investment Services Inc (AIS)
250 Riverchase Pkwy E RCS 4th Fl Birmingham AL 35244 205-560-7998 560-7089
TF: 800-316-4009 ■ *Web:* www.amsouth.com/ais

Aquila Group of Funds 380 Madison Ave Suite 2300 New York NY 10017 212-697-6666 687-5373
TF: 800-762-5955 ■ *Web:* www.aquilafunds.com

Artisan Funds PO Box 8412 Boston MA 02266 800-344-1770
Web: www.artisanfunds.com

Asset Management Fund 230 W Monroe St Suite 2810 Chicago IL 60606 800-527-3713 214-1424*
*Fax Area Code: 312 ■ *Web:* www.shayassets.com

Aston Funds PO Box 9765 Providence RI 02940 312-268-1400
Web: www.astonfunds.com

Barclays Global Investors Funds 45 Fremont St 5th Fl San Francisco CA 94105 415-597-2000 597-2012*
*Fax: Mktg ■ *TF:* 888-204-3956

Baron Funds 767 5th Ave 49th Fl New York NY 10153 212-583-2000 583-2150
TF: 800-992-2766 ■ *Web:* www.baronfunds.com

Bear Stearns Inc 383 Madison Ave New York NY 10179 212-272-2000
Web: www.bearstearns.com

Bernstein Funds 1345 Ave of the Americas 36th Fl New York NY 10105 212-756-4097 407-5850
Web: www.bernstein.com

BlackRock Funds 40 E 52nd St New York NY 10022 212-754-5300 754-8775
TF: 888-825-2257 ■ *Web:* www.blackrock.com/funds/brfunds

BNY Hamilton Funds PO Box 182785 Columbus OH 43218 800-426-9363 470-8720*
*Fax Area Code: 614 ■ *Web:* www.bnyhamiltonfunds.com

Brandywine Funds PO Box 701 Milwaukee WI 53201 800-656-3017 773-6933*
*Fax Area Code: 414 ■ *Web:* www.brandywinefunds.com

Brazos Mutual Funds 5949 Sherry Ln Suite 1600 Dallas TX 75225 866-521-5642 706-5114*
*Fax Area Code: 214 ■ *TF:* 800-426-9157 ■ *Web:* www.brazosfund.com

Calvert Group Mutual Funds
4550 Montgomery Ave Suite 1000N Bethesda MD 20814 301-951-4800 657-1982
TF: 800-727-5578 ■ *Web:* www.calvertgroup.com

CDC Nvest Funds PO Box 219579 Kansas City MO 64121 800-225-5478
Web: www.cdcnvestfunds.com

CGM Funds 222 Berkeley St Suite 1013 Boston MA 02116 617-859-7714 859-7295
TF: 800-345-4048 ■ *Web:* www.cgmfunds.com

	City	State	Zip	Phone	Fax
Citifunds PO Box 9083	Boston	MA	02266	800-331-1792	483-2577*
**Fax Area Code:* 617					
Citizens Funds 1 Harbor Pl Suite 400	Portsmouth	NH	03801	603-436-5152	433-4209
TF: 800-223-7010 ■ *Web:* www.efund.com					
Clipper Fund 9601 Wilshire Blvd Suite 800	Beverly Hills	CA	90210	310-247-3940	273-0514
TF: 800-776-5033 ■ *Web:* www.clipperfund.com					
Columbia Funds Services Inc PO Box 8081	Boston	MA	02266	800-345-6611	
Web: www.columbiafunds.com					
Davis Funds PO Box 8406	Boston	MA	02266	800-279-0279	806-7601*
**Fax Area Code:* 520 ■ *Web:* www.davisfunds.com					
Delaware Investments Funds 2005 Market St	Philadelphia	PA	19103	215-255-1200	255-1362*
**Fax:* Cust Svc ■ *TF:* 800-523-1918 ■ *Web:* www.delawarefunds.com					
Delaware Pooled Trust Funds					
Delaware Investments 2005 Market St 1 Commerce Sq	Philadelphia	PA	19103	800-231-8002	255-1162*
**Fax Area Code:* 215					
Diversified Funds 4 Manhattanville Rd	Purchase	NY	10577	914-697-8000	697-8050
TF: 800-926-0044					
Dodge & Cox Funds 555 California St 40th Fl	San Francisco	CA	94104	415-981-1710	986-2924
TF: 800-621-3979 ■ *Web:* www.dodgeandcox.com					
Domini Social Investments PO Box 9785	Providence	RI	02940	800-582-6757	
Web: www.domini.com					
Dreyfus Family of Funds 200 Park Ave	New York	NY	10166	212-922-6000	922-7533
TF: 800-645-6561					
DWS Funds PO Box 219669	Kansas City	MO	64121	800-728-3337	821-6234
Web: www.scudder.com					
DWS Scudder 222 S Riverside Plaza	Chicago	IL	60606	312-537-7000	
Web: www.scudder.com					
Eaton Vance Mutual Funds 255 State St	Boston	MA	02109	617-482-8260	482-4720*
**Fax:* Mktg ■ *TF:* 800-225-6265 ■ *Web:* www.eatonvance.com					
Enterprise Group of Funds					
3343 Peachtree Rd NE East Tower Suite 450	Atlanta	GA	30326	404-261-1116	261-1118
TF: 800-432-4320 ■ *Web:* www.enterprisefunds.com					
Evergreen Investments PO Box 8400	Boston	MA	02266	800-343-2898	446-7991*
**Fax Area Code:* 888 ■ **Fax:* Cust Svc ■ *Web:* www1.evergreeninvestments.com					
Excelsior Funds PO Box 8529	Boston	MA	02266	800-446-1012	
Web: www.excelsiorfunds.com					
Federated Funds PO Box 8606	Boston	MA	02266	800-245-4770	681-3824*
**Fax Area Code:* 781 ■ *Web:* www.federatedinvestors.com					
Fidelity Advisor Funds PO Box 770002	Cincinnati	OH	45277	800-522-7297	476-5857*
**Fax Area Code:* 617 ■ **Fax:* Mktg ■ *Web:* www.fidelity.com					
Fidelity Freedom Funds PO Box 770001	Cincinnati	OH	45277	800-343-3548	
Fidelity Investment Funds PO Box 770001	Cincinnati	OH	45277	800-343-3548	
Web: www.fidelity.com					
Fidelity Select Funds PO Box 770002	Cincinnati	OH	45277	800-544-8888	
Web: www.fidelity.com					
Fidelity Spartan Funds PO Box 770002	Cincinnati	OH	45277	800-544-8888	
Web: www.fidelity.com					
Fifth Third Funds PO Box 182706	Columbus	OH	43218	800-282-5706	428-3391*
**Fax Area Code:* 614 ■ *Web:* www.53.com					
First American Funds PO Box 3011	Milwaukee	WI	53201	800-677-3863	
Web: www.firstamericanfunds.com					
First Eagle Funds PO Box 219324	Kansas City	MO	64121	800-334-2143	843-4039*
**Fax Area Code:* 816 ■ *Web:* www.firsteaglefunds.com					
First Eagle SoGen Funds PO Box 219324	Kansas City	MO	64121	800-334-2143	843-4039*
**Fax Area Code:* 816 ■ *Web:* www.firsteaglesogen.com					
First Funds PO Box 8050	Boston	MA	02266	800-442-1941	796-2928*
**Fax Area Code:* 781 ■ *Web:* www.firstfunds.com					
First Investors Funds 110 Wall St	New York	NY	10005	212-858-8000	858-8099
TF: 800-423-4026 ■ *Web:* www.firstinvestors.com					
Firsthand Funds PO Box 8356	Boston	MA	02266	888-883-3863	
Web: www.firsthandfunds.com					
Franklin Templeton Mutual Funds PO Box 33030	Saint Petersburg	FL	33733	800-632-2301	
Web: www.franklintempleton.com					
Gabelli Funds 1 Corporate Ctr	Rye	NY	10580	914-921-5100	921-5118
TF: 800-422-3554 ■ *Web:* www.gabelli.com/funds					
Gartmore Funds PO Box 182205	Columbus	OH	43218	800-848-0920	428-3278*
**Fax Area Code:* 614 ■ *Web:* www.gartmorefunds.com					
Gateway Funds 3805 Edwards Rd Suite 600	Cincinnati	OH	45209	513-719-1100	719-1199
TF: 800-354-6339 ■ *Web:* www.gatewayfund.com					
GE Elfun Funds 101 Savings St	Pawtucket	RI	02860	800-242-0134	
TF: 800-242-0134 ■ *Web:* www.gefunds.com/elfun					
GE Mutual Funds 101 Savings St	Pawtucket	RI	02860	800-242-0134	
Web: www.gefinancialpro.com/products/mf.html					
Glenmede Funds 1650 Market St Suite 1200	Philadelphia	PA	19103	215-419-6000	419-6199
TF: 800-966-3200 ■ *Web:* www.glenmede.com					
GMO Trust Funds 100 Summer St	Boston	MA	02110	617-330-7500	261-0134
Web: www.gmo.com					
Goldman Sachs Funds PO Box 219711	Kansas City	MO	64121	312-655-4435	655-4489
TF: 800-526-7384 ■ *Web:* www.gs.com/funds					
Guardian Group of Funds PO Box 219611	Kansas City	MO	64121	800-343-0817	843-8595*
**Fax Area Code:* 816 ■ *Web:* www.ggof.com					
Hartford Mutual Funds PO Box 9140	Minneapolis	MN	55480	888-843-7824	738-5534*
**Fax Area Code:* 651 ■ *Web:* www.thehartfordmutualfunds.com					
Heartland Funds 789 N Water St Suite 500	Milwaukee	WI	53202	414-347-7777	347-1339
TF: 800-432-7856 ■ *Web:* www.heartlandfunds.com/individuals/funds					
HighMark Funds PO Box 8416	Boston	MA	02266	800-433-6884	
Web: www.highmarkfunds.com					
Horace Mann Growth Fund 1 Horace Mann Plaza	Springfield	IL	62715	217-789-2500	788-5161
TF: 800-999-1030 ■ *Web:* www.horacemann.com					
ICAP Funds 803 W Michigan Suite A	Milwaukee	WI	53233	888-221-4227	221-6178*
**Fax Area Code:* 414 ■ *Web:* www.icapfunds.com					
ING Funds 7337 E Doubletree Ranch Rd	Scottsdale	AZ	85258	480-477-3000	477-2700
TF: 800-334-3444 ■ *Web:* www.ingfunds.com					
Ivy Funds 6300 Lamar Ave	Overland Park	KS	66202	913-236-2000	236-2017
TF: 888-923-3355 ■ *Web:* www.ivyfunds.com					
Janus Funds 151 Detroit St	Denver	CO	80206	303-333-3863	394-7797*
**Fax:* Mktg ■ *TF:* 800-525-3713 ■ *Web:* ww3.janus.com					
Japan Fund PO Box 446	Portland	ME	04112	800-535-2726	821-6234
Web: www.thejapanfund.com					
John Hancock Funds 101 Huntington Ave 10th Fl	Boston	MA	02199	617-375-1500	375-6250
TF: 800-338-8080 ■ *Web:* www.jhfunds.com					
Kaufmann Fund 140 E 45th St 43rd Fl	New York	NY	10017	212-922-0123	661-2266
Kopp Funds 7701 France Ave S Suite 500	Edina	MN	55435	952-841-0400	841-0411
TF: 888-533-5677 ■ *Web:* www.koppfunds.com					
Lazard Funds 30 Rockefeller Plaza 57th Fl	New York	NY	10112	800-823-6300	332-5613*
**Fax Area Code:* 212 ■ *Web:* www.lazardnet.com/lam/us/lazardfunds.shtml					
Legg Mason Family of Funds 100 Light St	Baltimore	MD	21202	410-539-0000	454-4174*
**Fax:* Mktg ■ *TF:* 800-368-2558 ■ *Web:* www.leggmason.com/funds					
Loomis Sayles Funds 1 Financial Ctr	Boston	MA	02111	617-482-2450	
TF: 800-633-3330 ■ *Web:* www.loomissayles.com/mutual_funds/index.asp					
MainStay Funds 169 Lackawanna Ave	Parsippany	NJ	07054	800-695-9950	334-4653*
**Fax Area Code:* 973 ■ *Web:* www.mainstayfunds.com					
Mairs & Power Funds 332 Minnesota St Suite W-1520	Saint Paul	MN	55101	651-222-8478	222-8470
TF: 800-304-7404 ■ *Web:* www.mairsandpower.com					
Marshall Funds PO Box 1348	Milwaukee	WI	53201	800-236-3863	287-8511*
**Fax Area Code:* 414 ■ *Web:* www.marshallfunds.com					

	City	State	Zip	Phone	Fax
Marsico Funds PO Box 3210	Milwaukee	WI	53201	888-860-8686	221-6178*
**Fax Area Code:* 414 ■ *Web:* www.marsicofunds.com					
MAS Funds 100 Front St Suite 1100	West Conshohocken	PA	19428	610-940-5000	940-5284
TF: 800-354-8185					
Merger Fund PO Box 701	Milwaukee	WI	53201	414-765-4124	287-3781
TF: 800-343-8959					
Merrill Lynch Family of Funds PO Box 45289	Jacksonville	FL	32232	800-637-3863	
Web: www.mlim.ml.com/USA					
Morgan Stanley Family of Funds 1585 Broadway	New York	NY	10036	212-761-4000	761-0086
TF: 800-223-2440 ■ *Web:* www.morganstanleyindividual.com					
Morgan Stanley Institutional Funds 73 Tremont St	Boston	MA	02108	617-557-8000	557-8697
TF: 800-548-7786 ■ *Web:* www.morganstanley.com/institutional					
Munder Funds 480 Pierce St	Birmingham	MI	48009	248-647-9200	647-5931
TF: 800-468-6337 ■ *Web:* www.munderfunds.com					
Nations Funds PO Box 34602	Charlotte	NC	28254	800-321-7854	388-9980*
**Fax Area Code:* 704 ■ *Web:* www.nationsfunds.com					
Neuberger Berman Funds PO Box 8403	Boston	MA	02266	212-476-8800	476-8848
TF: 800-877-9700 ■ *Web:* www.nb.com					
Nicholas Family of Funds 700 N Water St Suite 1010	Milwaukee	WI	53202	414-272-6133	
TF: 800-227-5987 ■ *Web:* www.nicholasfunds.com					
Northeast Investors Funds 150 Federal St	Boston	MA	02110	617-523-3588	523-5412
TF: 800-225-6704 ■ *Web:* www.northeastinvestors.com					
Northern Funds PO Box 75986	Chicago	IL	60675	312-557-2790	557-0411
TF: 800-595-9111 ■ *Web:* www.northernfunds.com					
Northern Institutional Funds 801 S Canal St C5S	Chicago	IL	60607	800-637-1380	557-0411*
**Fax Area Code:* 312 ■ *Web:* www.northerninstitutionalfunds.com					
Nuveen Mutual Funds PO Box 463	East Syracuse	NY	13057	800-257-8787	
Web: www.nuveen.com					
Oak Assoc Funds PO Box 219441	Kansas City	MO	64121	888-462-5386	843-7275*
**Fax Area Code:* 816 ■ *Web:* www.oakfunds.com					
Oakmark Family of Funds 2 N La Salle St Suite 500	Chicago	IL	60602	312-621-0600	621-0372
TF: 800-625-6275 ■ *Web:* www.oakmark.com					
OppenheimerFunds Inc					
2 World Financial Center 225 Liberty St	New York	NY	10281	212-323-0200	323-4070
TF: 800-525-7048 ■ *Web:* www.oppenheimerfunds.com					
Pax World Fund Family 222 State St	Portsmouth	NH	03801	603-431-8022	
TF: 800-767-1729 ■ *Web:* www.paxworld.com					
PBHG Funds Inc 1400 Liberty Ridge Dr	Wayne	PA	19087	610-647-4100	722-5843
TF: 800-433-0051 ■ *Web:* www.pbhgfunds.com					
Phoenix Mutual Funds PO Box 8301	Boston	MA	02266	800-243-1574	796-3245*
**Fax Area Code:* 781 ■ *Web:* www.phoenixinvestments.com					
PIMCO Funds 2187 Atlantic St	Stamford	CT	06902	800-628-1237	352-4962*
**Fax Area Code:* 203 ■ *Web:* www.allianzinvestors.com					
PIMCO Institutional Funds PO Box 219024	Kansas City	MO	64121	800-927-4648	
Web: www.allianzinvestors.com					
Pioneer Funds 60 State St	Boston	MA	02109	617-742-7825	422-4265*
**Fax:* Mail Rm ■ *TF:* 800-225-6292 ■ *Web:* www.pioneerfunds.com					
Preferred Group of Mutual Funds PO Box 8320	Boston	MA	02266	800-662-4769	
Web: www.preferredgroup.com					
Price T Rowe Mutual Funds 100 E Pratt St	Baltimore	MD	21202	410-345-2000	539-4425
TF: 800-638-5660 ■ *Web:* www.troweprice.com					
Putnam Family of Funds PO Box 41203	Providence	RI	02940	800-225-1581	250-8411
Web: www.putnam.com					
Rainier Investment Management Mutual Funds					
601 Union St Suite 2801	Seattle	WA	98101	206-464-0400	464-0616
TF: 800-248-6314 ■ *Web:* www.rainierfunds.com					
Royce Funds 1414 Ave of the Americas	New York	NY	10019	800-337-6923	
Web: www.roycefunds.com					
RS Investments PO Box 219717	Kansas City	MO	64121	800-766-3863	
Web: www.rsinvestments.com					
Rydex Funds 9601 Blackwell Rd Suite 500	Rockville	MD	20850	301-296-5100	296-5107
TF: 800-820-0888 ■ *Web:* www.rydexfunds.com					
Salomon Brothers Investment Series 300 First Stamford Pl	Stamford	CT	06902	866-811-7256	
Schwab Mutual Funds 101 Montgomery St	San Francisco	CA	94104	415-627-7000	
TF: 800-435-4000					
Security Funds 1 Security Benefit Pl	Topeka	KS	66636	785-438-3000	438-5177
TF: 800-888-2461 ■ *Web:* www.securitybenefit.com					
SEI Global Funds Services 1 Freedom Valley Dr PO Box 1098	Oaks	PA	19456	610-676-3185	
TF: 800-342-5734 ■ *Web:* www.seiglobalfundservices.com					
Selected Funds PO Box 8243	Boston	MA	02266	800-243-1575	796-2955*
**Fax Area Code:* 781 ■ *Web:* www.selectedfunds.com					
Seligman Group of Funds 100 Park Avenue	New York	NY	10017	212-850-1864	922-5726
TF: 800 221 7844 ■ *Web:* www.seligman.com/individual/overview.htm					
Sentinel Funds PO Box 1499	Montpelier	VT	05601	802-229-7355	229-7428
TF: 800-282-3863 ■ *Web:* www.sentinelfunds.com					
Sequoia Fund Inc 767 5th Ave Suite 4701	New York	NY	10153	212-832-5280	832-5298
TF: 800-686-6884 ■ *Web:* www.sequoiafund.com					
Smith Barney Mutual Funds PO Box 9699	Providence	RI	02940	800-451-2010	
Web: www.citigroupam.com/pub/pageserv/aboutsbmf					
Sound Shore Fund 3435 Stelzer Rd	Columbus	OH	43219	800-754-8758	343-5884*
**Fax Area Code:* 866 ■ *TF:* 800-551-1980 ■ *Web:* www.soundshorefund.com					
Spectra Fund Alger Shareholder Services 30 Montgomery St	Jersey City	NJ	07302	800-711-6141	547-3628*
**Fax Area Code:* 201 ■ *Web:* public.alger.com/Algerpub/content/showHome					
SSgA funds 1 Lincoln St	Boston	MA	02111	617-664-6089	664-6011
TF: 800-997-7327 ■ *Web:* www.ssgafunds.com					
State Farm Mutual Funds PO Box 219548	Kansas City	MO	64121	800-447-4930	471-4832*
**Fax Area Code:* 816 ■ *Web:* www.statefarm.com/mutual/mutual.htm					
STI Classic Funds PO Box 4418 MC 712	Atlanta	GA	30302	800-428-6970	813-7205*
**Fax Area Code:* 404 ■ *Web:* www.sticlassicfunds.com					
SunAmerica Mutual Funds 1 World Financial Center 14th Fl	New York	NY	10281	212-551-5100	551-5620
TF: 800-858-8850 ■ *Web:* www.sunamericafunds.com					
T Rowe Price Mutual Funds 100 E Pratt St	Baltimore	MD	21202	410-345-2000	539-4425
TF: 800-638-5660 ■ *Web:* www.troweprice.com					
Tamarack Funds PO Box 219757	Kansas City	MO	64121	800-422-2766	
Web: www.tamarackfunds.com					
TARGET Funds PO Box 8098	Philadelphia	PA	19101	800-840-8339	
TCW Galileo Funds PO Box 9821	Providence	RI	02940	800-386-3829	
Web: www.tcwgroup.com					
Third Avenue Funds 622 3rd Ave 32nd Fl	New York	NY	10017	212-888-5222	
TF: 800-880-8442 ■ *Web:* www.thirdavenuefunds.com					
Thornburg Investment Management Funds					
119 E Marcy St Suite 202	Santa Fe	NM	87501	505-984-0200	984-8973
TF: 800-533-9337 ■ *Web:* www.thornburginvestments.com					
TIAA-CREF Mutual Funds PO Box 8009	Boston	MA	02266	800-223-1200	
Web: www.tiaa-cref.org/mfs					
Torray Fund 7501 Wisconsin Ave Suite 1100	Bethesda	MD	20814	301-493-4600	530-0642
TF: 800-443-3036 ■ *Web:* www.torray.com					
Transamerica IDEX Mutual Funds PO Box 9015	Clearwater	FL	33758	727-299-1800	329-4339*
**Fax Area Code:* 888 ■ **Fax:* Mail Rm ■ *TF Cust Svc:* 800-233-4339 ■ *Web:* www.idexfunds.com					
TRUST for Credit Unions (TCU) 4900 Sears Tower 51st Fl	Chicago	IL	60606	312-655-4400	655-4458
TF: 800-621-2550 ■ *Web:* www.trustcu.com					
Turner Funds 1205 Westlakes Dr Suite 100	Berwyn	PA	19312	610-251-0268	251-0731
TF: 800-424-4865 ■ *Web:* www.turnerinvestments.com					
Tweedy Browne Funds 350 Park Ave 9th Fl	New York	NY	10022	212-916-0600	916-0649
TF: 800-432-4789 ■ *Web:* www.tweedy.com					

				Phone	Fax
UBS Global Asset Management Mutual Funds PO Box 9786 *Web:* us.ubs-globalam.com	Providence	RI	02940	800-647-1568	
USAA Funds 9800 Fredericksburg Rd USAA Bldg *TF:* 800-531-8448 ■ *Web:* ww3.usaa.com/lcs_corp/Logon	San Antonio	TX	78288	210-498-7290	498-3999
Value Line Funds PO Box 219729	Kansas City	MO	64121	800-223-0818	
Van Kampen Funds 1 Parkview Plaza PO Box 5555 *TF:* 800-341-2911 ■ *Web:* www.vankampen.com	Oakbrook Terrace	IL	60181	800-341-2911	
Van Wagoner Funds 101 Sabin St *Web:* www.vanwagoner.com	Pawtucket	RI	02860	800-228-2121	
Vanguard Funds PO Box 1110 *Web:* www.vanguard.com	Valley Forge	PA	19482	800-871-3879	
VantagePoint Funds 777 N Capitol St NW *TF:* 800-669-7400 ■ *Web:* www2.icmarc.org/xp/vl/funds/	Washington	DC	20002	202-962-4600	962-4601
Victory Funds 127 Public Sq *Web:* www.victoryconnect.com/vcn/home_victoryFunds.jsp	Cleveland	OH	44114	800-539-3863	
W & R Funds 6300 Lamar Ave *TF:* 800-366-5465 ■ *Web:* www1.waddell.com	Shawnee Mission	KS	66202	913-236-2000	236-5044
Waddell & Reed Advisors Funds 6300 Lamar Ave **Fax Area Code:* 800 ■ **Fax:* Cust Svc ■ *TF:* 800-366-5465 ■ *Web:* www1.waddell.com	Shawnee Mission	KS	66202	913-236-2000	532-2749*
Weitz Funds 1125 S 103rd St Suite 600 *TF:* 800-304-9745 ■ *Web:* www.weitzfunds.com	Omaha	NE	68124	402-391-1980	391-2125
Wells Fargo Funds PO Box 8266 **Fax Area Code:* 781 ■ *Web:* www.wellsfargo.com/funds/	Boston	MA	02266	800-222-8222	796-7704*
Wilshire Target Funds Inc PO Box 9807 *Web:* www.wilfunds.com	Providence	RI	02940	888-200-6796	
WM Group of Funds PO Box 9757 *Web:* www.wmgroupoffunds.com	Providence	RI	02940	800-222-5852	

532 NAVIGATION & GUIDANCE INSTRUMENTS & SYSTEMS

				Phone	Fax
AAI Corp 124 Industry Ln PO Box 126 *Web:* www.aaicorp.com	Hunt Valley	MD	21030	410-666-1400	628-3215
Aerosonic Corp 1212 N Hercules Ave *AMEX: AIM* ■ *Web:* www.aerosonic.com	Clearwater	FL	33765	727-461-3000	447-5926
Alpine Electronics of America 19145 Gramercy Pl **Fax:* Hum Res ■ *TF:* 800-257-4631 ■ *Web:* www.alpine-usa.com	Torrance	CA	90501	310-326-8000	212-0884*
Applied Signal Technology Inc 400 W California Ave *NASDAQ: APSG* ■ **Fax:* Mail Rm ■ *Web:* www.appsig.com	Sunnyvale	CA	94086	408-749-1888	738-1928*
Astronautics Corp of America 4115 N Teutonia Ave PO Box 523 *TF:* 800-366-0666 ■ *Web:* www.astronautics.com	Milwaukee	WI	53201	414-449-4000	447-8231
BAE Systems Inc 1601 Research Blvd *Web:* www.baesystems.com/WorldwideLocations/UnitedStates	Rockville	MD	20850	301-838-6000	
Ball Aerospace & Technologies Corp 1600 Commerce St **Fax:* Mail Rm ■ *Web:* www.ballaerospace.com	Boulder	CO	80301	303-939-4000	460-2315*
Ball Aerospace & Technology Corp Aerospace Systems Div 1600 Commerce St **Fax:* Mail Rm	Boulder	CO	80301	303-939-4000	460-2315*
Boeing Co Integrated Defense Systems PO Box 516 *Web:* www.boeing.com/ids	Saint Louis	MO	63166	314-232-0232	
Boeing Phantom Works 2201 Seal Beach Blvd PO Box 2515 *Web:* www.boeing.com/phantom	Seal Beach	CA	90740	562-797-2020	
Butler National Corp 19920 W 161st St *Web:* www.butlernational.com	Olathe	KS	66062	913-780-9595	780-5088
CMC Electronics Inc 600 Dr Frederik Philips Blvd *Web:* www.cmcelectronics.ca	Saint-Laurent	QC	H4M2S9	514-748-3148	748-3100
CMI Inc 316 E 9th St *TF:* 866-835-0690 ■ *Web:* www.alcoholtest.com	Owensboro	KY	42303	270-685-6545	685-6678
Computer Sciences Raytheon 1201 Edward H White II St PO Box 4127 CSR 1500 *Web:* www.computersciencesraytheon.com	Patrick AFB	FL	32925	321-494-5272	494-6540
Cubic Corp PO Box 85587 *AMEX: CUB* ■ *Web:* www.cubic.com	San Diego	CA	92186	858-277-6780	505-1532
Cubic Defense Systems Inc PO Box 85587 *Web:* www.cubic.com/cda1/	San Diego	CA	92186	858-277-6780	505-1524
Del Mar Avionics 1601-C Alton Pkwy *TF:* 800-854-0481 ■ *Web:* www.dma.com	Irvine	CA	92606	949-250-3200	261-0529
DRS C3 Systems LLC 400 Professional Dr *TF:* 800-252-4734 ■ *Web:* www.drs.com	Gaithersburg	MD	20879	301-921-8100	921-8010
DRS Sensors & Targeting Systems - Infrared Technologies Div 13544 N Central Expy PO Box 740188 *TF:* 877-377-4783 ■ *Web:* www.drs.com	Dallas	TX	75243	972-560-6000	560-6049
DRS Surveillance Support Systems Inc 6200 118th Ave N *Web:* www.drs.com	Largo	FL	33773	727-541-6681	544-4944
DRS Technologies Canada Co 115 Emily St *Web:* www.drs.com	Carlton Place	ON	K7C4J5	613-253-3020	253-3033
DRS Technologies Inc 5 Sylvan Way *NYSE: DRS* ■ *TF:* 866-898-1500 ■ *Web:* www.drs.com	Parsippany	NJ	07054	973-898-1500	898-4730
DRS Training & Control Systems 645 Anchors St NW **Fax:* Hum Res ■ *TF:* 800-326-6724 ■ *Web:* www.drs.com	Fort Walton Beach	FL	32548	850-302-3000	302-3371*
Dukane Communication Systems 2900 Dukane Dr *Web:* www.dukcorp.com	Saint Charles	IL	60174	630-584-2300	584-2370
Dynalec Corp 87 W Main St *Web:* www.dynalec.com	Sodus	NY	14551	315-483-6923	483-6656
Eaton Corp 1111 Superior Ave Eaton Center *NYSE: ETN* ■ *Web:* www.eaton.com	Cleveland	OH	44114	216-523-5000	523-4787
EDO Combat Systems 1801 Sara Dr Suite E *TF:* 800-296-4336 ■ *Web:* www.edocombat.com	Chesapeake	VA	23320	757-424-1004	424-1602
EDO Corp 60 E 42nd St 42nd Fl *NYSE: EDO* ■ *Web:* www.edocorp.com	New York	NY	10165	212-716-2000	716-2050
EDO Defense Systems 1500 New Horizons Blvd *Web:* www.edocorp.com	North Amityville	NY	11701	631-630-4000	630-0470
Epsilon Systems Solutions Inc 1565 Hotel Cir S Suite 200 *Web:* www.epsilonsystems.com	San Diego	CA	92108	619-702-1700	702-1711
Esterline Technologies Corp 500 108th Ave NE Suite 1500 *NYSE: ESL* ■ *Web:* www.esterline.com	Bellevue	WA	98004	425-453-9400	453-2916
FLIR Systems Inc 27700-A SW Pkwy Ave *NASDAQ: FLIR* ■ **Fax:* Sales ■ *TF:* 800-322-3731 ■ *Web:* www.flir.com	Wilsonville	OR	97070	503-498-3547	498-3904*
Frontier Electronic Systems Corp 4500 W 6th Ave **Fax:* Hum Res ■ *TF:* 800-677-1769 ■ *Web:* www.fescorp.com	Stillwater	OK	74074	405-624-1769	624-7866*
Gables Engineering Inc 247 Greco Ave *Web:* www.gableseng.com	Coral Gables	FL	33146	305-442-2578	774-4465
Garmin Ltd 1200 E 151st St *NASDAQ: GRMN* ■ *TF:* 888-442-7646 ■ *Web:* www.garmin.com	Olathe	KS	66062	913-397-8200	397-8282
GE Aviation Systems Div 3290 Patterson Ave SE *Web:* www.geaviationsystems.com	Grand Rapids	MI	49512	616-241-7000	241-7533
General Dynamics Advanced Information Systems 1421 Jefferson Davis Hwy Suite 600 *Web:* www.gd-ais.com	Arlington	VA	22202	703-271-7300	271-7302
General Dynamics C4 Systems 400 John Quincy Adams Rd Bldg 80 *TF:* 888-483-2472 ■ *Web:* www.gdc4s.com	Taunton	MA	02780	508-880-4000	880-4800
Gilfillan Div ITT Industries Inc 7821 Orion Ave *TF:* 800-264-9234 ■ *Web:* www.ittgil.com	Van Nuys	CA	91406	818-988-2600	901-2435
Goodrich Corp 2730 W Tyvola Rd 4 Coliseum Ctr *NYSE: GR* ■ *TF:* 800-784-7009 ■ *Web:* www.goodrich.com	Charlotte	NC	28217	704-423-7000	423-7002
Honeywell Aerospace 1944 E Sky Harbor Cir **Fax Area Code:* 602 ■ *Web:* www.honeywellaerospace.com	Phoenix	AZ	85034	800-601-3099	365-3343*
Honeywell Aerospace Electronic Systems 1944 E Sky Harbor Cir	Phoenix	AZ	85034	800-601-3099	
Honeywell Defense Avionics Systems 9201 San Mateo Blvd NE *TF:* 800-376-5311 ■ *Web:* content.honeywell.com/das	Albuquerque	NM	87113	505-828-5000	828-5500
Honeywell Inc Commercial Aviation Systems 21111 N 19th Ave *TF:* 800-601-3099 ■ *Web:* www.honeywell.com	Phoenix	AZ	85027	602-436-2311	822-7000
Honeywell Space & Aviation Control 21111 N 19th Ave *TF:* 800-601-3099 ■ *Web:* www.sac.honeywell.com	Phoenix	AZ	85027	602-436-2311	436-7000
Honeywell Space Systems 13350 US Hwy 19 N *Web:* content.honeywell.com/dses/space/	Clearwater	FL	33764	727-539-4000	
Infrared Technologies Div - DRS Sensors & Targeting Systems 13544 N Central Expy PO Box 740188 *TF:* 877-377-4783 ■ *Web:* www.drs.com	Dallas	TX	75243	972-560-6000	560-6049
Innovative Solutions & Support Inc 720 Pennsylvania Dr *NASDAQ: ISSC* ■ *Web:* www.innovative-ss.com	Exton	PA	19341	610-646-9800	646-0149
Interstate Electronics Corp 602 E Vermont Ave *TF:* 800-854-6979 ■ *Web:* www.iechome.com	Anaheim	CA	92805	714-758-0500	758-4148
ITT Defense 1650 Tysons Blvd Suite 1700 *Web:* defense.itt.com	McLean	VA	22102	703-790-6300	790-6360
ITT Industries Inc 4 W Red Oak Ln *NYSE: ITT* ■ *Web:* www.itt.com	White Plains	NY	10604	914-641-2000	696-2950
ITT Industries Inc Gilfillan Div 7821 Orion Ave *TF:* 800-264-9234 ■ *Web:* www.ittgil.com	Van Nuys	CA	91406	818-988-2600	901-2435
Jewell Instruments LLC 850 Perimeter Rd *TF:* 800-227-5955 ■ *Web:* www.jewellinstruments.com	Manchester	NH	03103	603-669-6400	669-5962
Kearfott Guidance & Navigation Corp 1150 McBride Ave *Web:* www.kearfott.com	Little Falls	NJ	07424	973-785-6000	785-6025
Kollsman Inc 220 Daniel Webster Hwy *TF:* 800-258-1350 ■ *Web:* www.kollsman.com	Merrimack	NH	03054	603-889-2500	889-7966
KVH Industries Inc 50 Enterprise Center *NASDAQ: KVHI* ■ *TF:* 888-584-4773 ■ *Web:* www.kvh.com	Middletown	RI	02842	401-847-3327	849-0045
L-3 Avionics Systems 5353 52nd St SE **Fax:* Hum Res ■ *TF:* 800-253-9525 ■ *Web:* www.as.l-3com.com	Grand Rapids	MI	49512	616-949-6600	285-4457*
L-3 Communications Corp Aviation Recorders Div 6000 Fruitville Rd *Web:* www.l-3ar.com	Sarasota	FL	34232	941-371-0811	377-5598
L-3 Communications Corp Communication Systems East Div 1 Federal St *Web:* www.l-3com.com/CS-East	Camden	NJ	08103	856-338-3000	338-6014
L-3 Communications Corp Communication Systems West Div 640 N 2200 West *Web:* www.l-3com.com/csw	Salt Lake City	UT	84116	801-594-2000	594-2127
L-3 Communications Corp Ocean Systems Div 15825 Roxford St *TF:* 800-654-8184	Sylmar	CA	91342	818-367-0111	
L-3 Communications Corp Randtron Antenna Systems Div 130 Constitution Dr *Web:* www.l-3com.com/randtron	Menlo Park	CA	94025	650-326-9500	326-1033
Laitram LLC 220 Laitram Ln *TF:* 800-533-8253 ■ *Web:* www.laitram.com	Harahan	LA	70123	504-733-6000	733-2143
Lockheed Martin Advanced Technology Laboratories 3 Executive Campus 6th Fl S *Web:* www.atl.external.lmco.com	Cherry Hill	NJ	08002	856-792-9815	792-9915
Lockheed Martin Canada 3001 Solandt Rd *Web:* www.lockheedmartin.com/canada	Kanata	ON	K2K2M8	613-599-3270	599-3282
Lockheed Martin Corp 6801 Rockledge Dr *NYSE: LMT* ■ *Web:* www.lockheedmartin.com	Bethesda	MD	20817	301-897-6000	897-6083
Lockheed Martin MS2 199 Borton Landing Rd *TF:* 800-325-4019 ■ *Web:* www.lockheedmartin.com/manassas	Moorestown	NJ	08057	856-722-4100	
Lockheed Martin Sippican 7 Barnabas Rd *Web:* www.sippican.com	Marion	MA	02738	508-748-1160	748-3626
Lockheed Martin Systems Integration - Owego 1801 SR-17C **Fax:* Mktg	Owego	NY	13827	607-751-2000	751-3259*
Loral Space & Communications Ltd 600 3rd Ave *NASDAQ: LORL* ■ *Web:* www.loral.com	New York	NY	10016	212-697-1105	338-5660
Lowrance Electronics Inc 12000 E Skelly Dr *NASDAQ: LEIX* ■ **Fax:* Hum Res ■ *Web:* www.lowrance.com	Tulsa	OK	74128	918-437-6881	234-1705*
Mackay Communications Inc 3691 Trust Dr *Web:* www.mackaycomm.com	Raleigh	NC	27616	919-850-3000	954-1707
Micro Systems Inc 35 Hill Ave *Web:* www.gomicrosystems.com	Fort Walton Beach	FL	32548	850-244-2332	243-1378
Motorola Inc 1301 E Algonquin Rd *NYSE: MOT* ■ **Fax:* Hum Res ■ *TF:* 800-331-6456 ■ *Web:* www.motorola.com	Schaumburg	IL	60196	847-576-5000	538-3617*
MPD Inc 316 E 9th St *TF:* 866-225-5673 ■ *Web:* www.mpdinc.com	Owensboro	KY	42303	270-685-6200	685-6494
Narco Avionics 270 Commerce Dr *TF Sales:* 800-223-3636 ■ *Web:* www.narco-avionics.com	Fort Washington	PA	19034	215-643-2900	643-0197
NavCom Defense Electronics Inc 4323 Arden Dr *TF:* 800-729-8191 ■ *Web:* www.navcom.com	El Monte	CA	91731	626-442-0123	350-3191
Northrop Grumman Corp 1840 Century Park E *NYSE: NOC* ■ *Web:* www.northropgrumman.com	Los Angeles	CA	90067	310-553-6262	201-3023
Northrop Grumman Electronic Systems 1580-A W Nursery Rd *Web:* www.es.northropgrumman.com/index.html	Linthicum	MD	21090	410-765-4441	
Northrop Grumman Information Technology 2101 Gaither Rd Suite 600 *Web:* www.it.northropgrumman.com/index.asp	Rockville	MD	20850	301-527-6400	527-6401
Orbit International Corp 80 Cabot Ct *NASDAQ: ORBT* ■ *TF:* 800-663-5366 ■ *Web:* www.orbitintl.com	Hauppauge	NY	11788	631-435-8300	435-8458
Orbital Sciences Corp 21839 Atlantic Blvd *NYSE: ORB* ■ *TF:* 877-672-4825 ■ *Web:* www.orbital.com	Dulles	VA	20166	703-406-5000	
Parker Electronic Systems 300 Marcus Blvd *Web:* www.parker.com	Smithtown	NY	11787	631-231-3737	434-8152
Radio Holland USA Inc 8943 Gulf Fwy *Web:* www.radiohollandusa.com	Houston	TX	77017	713-943-3325	378-2101
Randtron Antenna Systems Div L-3 Communications Corp 130 Constitution Dr *Web:* www.l-3com.com/randtron	Menlo Park	CA	94025	650-326-9500	326-1033
Raymarine Inc 21 Manchester St *TF:* 800-539-5539 ■ *Web:* www.raymarine.com	Merrimack	NH	03054	603-881-5200	864-4756
Raytheon Air Traffic Management Systems 870 Winter St *Web:* www.raytheon.com/products/cnsatm	Waltham	MA	02451	781-522-3000	522-5200
Raytheon Canada Ltd 360 Albert St Suite 1640 *Web:* www.raytheon.ca/	Ottawa	ON	K1R7X7	613-233-4121	233-1099
Raytheon Co Space & Airborne Systems 2000 East El Segundo Blvd *Web:* www.raytheon.com/businesses/rsas/index.html	El Segundo	CA	90245	310-647-1000	647-0785
Raytheon Integrated Defense Systems 50 Apple Hill Dr *Web:* www.raytheon.com/businesses/rids	Tewksbury	MA	01876	978-858-5290	858-1170

Phone Fax

Raytheon Intelligence & Information Systems
1200 S Jupiter Rd .... Garland TX 75042 972-205-5409 205-8988
TF: 800-752-6163 ■ Web: www.raytheon.com/businesses/riis
Raytheon Missile Systems PO Box 11337 Bldg 807 Suite A8 .... Tucson AZ 85734 520-794-3000
Raytheon Network Centric Systems 2501 W University .... McKinney TX 75071 972-952-2000
Rockwell Collins Inc 400 Collins Rd NE .... Cedar Rapids IA 52498 319-295-1000 295-9347*
NYSE: COL ■ *Fax: PR ■ Web: www.rockwellcollins.com
Rodale Electronics Inc 20 Oser Ave .... Hauppauge NY 11788 631-231-0044 231-1345
Web: www.rodaleelectronics.com
Rostra Precision Controls Inc 2519 Dana Dr .... Laurinburg NC 28352 910-276-4853 276-1354
TF Cust Svc: 800-782-3379 ■ Web: www.rostra.com
S-TEC Corp 1 S-Tec Way .... Mineral Wells TX 76067 940-325-9406 325-3904
TF: 800-872-7832 ■ Web: www.s-tec.com
Safe Flight Instrument Corp 20 New King St .... White Plains NY 10604 914-946-9500 946-7882
Web: www.safeflight.com
SEA/Datamarine Inc 7030 220th St SW .... Mountlake Terrace WA 98043 425-771-2182 771-2650
TF: 800-426-1330 ■ Web: www.sea-dmi.com
SELEX Inc 11300 W 89th St .... Overland Park KS 66214 913-495-2600 492-0870
TF: 800-765-0861 ■ Web: www.selex-si-us.com
Sensis Corp 85 Collamer Crossing .... East Syracuse NY 13057 315-445-0550 445-9401
Web: www.sensis.com
Sparton Corp 2400 E Ganson St .... Jackson MI 49202 517-787-8600 787-8046
NYSE: SPA ■ TF: 800-248-9579 ■ Web: www.sparton.com
Sperry Marine Northrop Grumman 1070 Seminole Trail .... Charlottesville VA 22901 434-974-2000 974-2259
TF Cust Svc: 800-368-2010 ■ Web: www.sperrymarine.northropgrumman.com
Systron Donner Inertial 355 Lennon Ln .... Walnut Creek CA 94598 925-979-4400 979-9827
TF: 800-227-1625 ■ Web: www.systron.com
Techsonic Industries Inc 678 Hummingbird Ln .... Eufaula AL 36027 334-687-6613 687-1163
TF: 800-633-1468 ■ Web: www.techsonic.com
Telair International 4175 Guardian St .... Simi Valley CA 93063 805-306-8066 306-8091
TF: 800-989-4827 ■ Web: www.telair.com
Teledyne Benthos Inc 49 Edgerton Dr .... North Falmouth MA 02556 508-563-1000 563-6444
Web: www.benthos.com
Telephonics Corp 815 Broad Hollow Rd .... Farmingdale NY 11735 631-755-7000 755-7046
TF: 877-755-7700 ■ Web: www.telephonics.com
Textron Systems Corp 201 Lowell St .... Wilmington MA 01887 978-657-5111 657-1843
Web: www.systems.textron.com
Thales ATM 23501 W 84th St .... Shawnee KS 66227 913-422-2600 422-2989*
*Fax: Hum Res ■ TF: 800-526-3433 ■ Web: www.thalesatm.com
Thales North America Inc 675 N Washington St Suite 400 .... Alexandria VA 22314 703-838-9685 838-1688
Web: www.thalesgroup.com
Transbotics Corp 3400 Latrobe Dr .... Charlotte NC 28211 704-362-1115 364-4039
Web: www.transbotics.com
Trimble Navigation Ltd 935 Stewart Dr .... Sunnyvale CA 94085 408-481-8000 481-8585
NASDAQ: TRMB ■ TF: 800-827-8000 ■ Web: www.trimble.com
Whistler Group Inc 13016 N Walton Blvd .... Bentonville AR 72712 479-273-6012 273-3188
TF Cust Svc: 800-531-0004 ■ Web: www.whistlergroup.com
XATA Corp 151 E Cliff Rd Suite 10 .... Burnsville MN 55337 952-894-3680 894-2463
NASDAQ: XATA ■ TF Tech Supp: 800-262-9282 ■ Web: www.xata.com

533 NEWS SYNDICATES, SERVICES, BUREAUS

Phone Fax

AccuWeather Inc 385 Science Park Rd .... State College PA 16803 814-235-8650 238-1339
TF Sales: 800-566-6606 ■ Web: www.accuweather.com/
Agence France-Presse (AFP) 1500 K St NW Suite 600 .... Washington DC 20005 202-289-0700 414-0525
Web: www.afp.com
AlterNet 77 Federal St 2nd Fl .... San Francisco CA 94107 415-284-1420 284-1414
Web: www.alternet.org
American Baptist News Service PO Box 851 .... Valley Forge PA 19482 610-768-2000 768-2320
TF: 800-222-3872 ■ Web: www.abc-usa.org/news
American Stock Exchange Broadcast Services 86 Trinity Pl .... New York NY 10006 212-306-1000 306-1024
TF: 866-422-2639
Andrews McMeel Universal 4520 Main St Suite 700 .... Kansas City MO 64111 816-932-6700 932-6684
TF: 800-851-8923 ■ Web: www.amuniversal.com
Artists & Writers Syndicate 582 Brummel Ct NW .... Washington DC 20012 202-882-8882
Associated Press (AP) 450 W 33rd St .... New York NY 10001 212-621-1500 621-1679
Web: www.ap.org
Associated Press Information Services 450 W 33rd St .... New York NY 10001 212-621-1585 621-5488
TF: 800-272-2551 ■ Web: www.apnews.com
Atlantic Syndication 4520 Main St Suite 700 .... Kansas City MO 64111 816-932-6600 359-2752*
*Fax Area Code: 941 ■ Web: www.atlanticsyndication.com
Bankrate Inc 1 N Wacker Dr Suite 4343 .... Villa Park IL 60181 630-834-7555 834-7283
TF: 800-509-4636 ■ Web: www.bankrate.com
Baptist Press 901 Commerce St .... Nashville TN 37203 615-244-2355 782-8736
Web: www.sbc.net
Black Press Service Inc (BPS) 166 Madison Ave 4th Fl .... New York NY 10016 212-686-6850 686-7308
Bloomberg LP 731 Lexington Ave .... New York NY 10022 212-318-2000 893-5000
Web: www.bloomberg.com
Bloomberg News 731 Lexington Ave .... New York NY 10022 212-318-2000 369-5000*
*Fax Area Code: 917 ■ Web: about.bloomberg.com/index.html
Business Wire 44 Montgomery St 39th Fl .... San Francisco CA 94104 415-986-4422 788-5335
TF: 800-227-0845 ■ Web: www.businesswire.com
California Newspaper Service Bureau 915 E 1st St .... Los Angeles CA 90012 213-229-5300 229-5481
TF: 800-788-7840
Century News Service 450 W Broad St Suite 321 .... Falls Church VA 22046 703-532-3267 532-3396
Comics.com 200 Madison Ave 4th Fl .... New York NY 10016 212-293-8500 293-8616
TF: 800-221-4816 ■ Web: www.comics.com
Copley News Service 123 Camino de la Reina Suite 202-S .... San Diego CA 92108 619-293-1818
TF: 800-238-6196 ■ Web: www.copleynews.com
Creators Syndicate Inc 5777 W Century Blvd Suite 700 .... Los Angeles CA 90045 310-337-7003 337-7625
Web: www.creators.com
CSTV Networks Inc 2035 Corte Del Nogal Suite 250 .... Carlsbad CA 92011 760-431-8221 431-8108
Web: www.cstv.com
Disaster News Network 9195-C Red Branch Rd .... Columbia MD 21045 410-884-7350 884-7353
TF: 888-384-3028 ■ Web: www.disasternews.net
Dow Jones Newswires 800 Plaza 2 Harborside Financial Ctr .... Jersey City NJ 07311 201-938-5400 938-5600
Web: www.djnewswires.com
Dow Jones & Wall Street Journal News Service Washington Bureau 1025 Connecticut Ave NW Suite 800 .... Washington DC 20036 202-862-9200 223-8039
Elias Sports Bureau Inc 500 5th Ave Suite 2140 .... New York NY 10110 212-869-1530 354-0980
Web: www.esb.com
Federal Network Inc (FedNet) 50 'F' St NW Suite 1C .... Washington DC 20001 202-393-7300 393-5965
Web: www.fednet.net
Federal News Services 1000 Vermont Ave NW 5th Fl .... Washington DC 20005 202-347-1400 393-4733
Web: www.fednews.com
FedNet (Federal Network Inc) 50 'F' St NW Suite 1C .... Washington DC 20001 202-393-7300 393-5965
Web: www.fednet.net
Hearst News Service 1850 K St NW Suite 1000 .... Washington DC 20006 202-263-6400 263-6441
Web: www.hearst.com
Hispanic Link Inc 1420 'N' St NW .... Washington DC 20005 202-234-0280 234-4090
Web: www.hispaniclink.org
ITAR-TASS Agency 780 3rd Ave 19th Fl .... New York NY 10017 212-245-4250 245-4258
Web: www.itar-tass.com

Phone Fax

Jewish Telegraphic Agency Inc 330 7th Ave 17th Fl .... New York NY 10001 212-643-1890 643-8498
Web: www.jta.org
Kansas Press Assn Inc 5423 SW 7th St .... Topeka KS 66606 785-271-5304 271-7341
Web: www.kspress.com
King Features Syndicate Inc 300 W 57th St 15th Fl .... New York NY 10019 212-969-7550 280-1550*
*Fax Area Code: 646 ■ TF: 800-526-5464 ■ Web: www.kingfeatures.com
Knight Ridder/Tribune Information Services
700 12th St NW Suite 1000 .... Washington DC 20005 202-383-6080 393-2460
TF: 800-383-6181 ■ Web: www.mctdirect.com
KRT Direct 700 12th St NW Suite 1000 .... Washington DC 20005 202-383-6080 393-2460
TF: 800-383-6181 ■ Web: www.mctdirect.com
Los Angeles Times-Washington Post News Service Inc
1150 15th St NW .... Washington DC 20071 202-334-6173 334-5096
Web: www.newsservice.com
Market Wire Inc 200 N Sepulveda Blvd Suite 1050 .... El Segundo CA 90245 310-765-3200 765-3297
TF: 800-774-9473 ■ Web: www.marketwire.com
Metro Networks Inc 2800 Post Oak Blvd Suite 4000 .... Houston TX 77056 713-407-6000 407-6849
Web: www.metronetworks.com
New York Times News Service Div 620 8th Ave 9th Fl .... New York NY 10018 212-556-1927 556-3535
TF: 888-346-9867 ■ Web: www.nytsyn.com
New York Times Syndicate Div 500 7th Ave .... New York NY 10018 212-499-3300
Web: yourhealthdaily.com
New Yorker Magazine Cartoon Bank Div
28 Wells Ave Bldg 3 4th Fl .... Yonkers NY 10701 914-478-5527 478-5604
TF: 800-897-8666 ■ Web: www.cartoonbank.com
Newhouse News Service
1101 Connecticut Ave NW Suite 300 .... Washington DC 20036 202-383-7800 296-9537
Web: www.newhousenews.com
Newspaper Enterprise Assn 200 Madison Ave 4th Fl .... New York NY 10016 212-293-8500 293-8760
TF: 800-221-4816
Pacific News Service 275 9th St 3rd Fl .... San Francisco CA 94103 415-503-4170 503-0970
Web: news.newamericamedia.org/news/
PR Newswire 810 7th Ave 35th Fl32nd Fl .... New York NY 10019 201-360-6000 596-1537*
*Fax Area Code: 212 ■ TF: 800-832-5522 ■ Web: www.prnewswire.com
Religion News Service 1101 Connecticut Ave NW Suite 350 .... Washington DC 20036 202-463-8777 463-0033
TF: 800-767-6781 ■ Web: www.religionnews.com
Reuters America Inc 3 Times Square .... New York NY 10036 646-223-4000 223-6001
Web: www.reuters.com
Scripps Howard News Service
1090 Vermont Ave NW 10th Fl .... Washington DC 20005 202-408-1484 408-5950
Web: www.shns.com
Sports Network 2200 Byberry Rd Suite 200 .... Hatboro PA 19040 215-441-8444 441-9019
TF: 800-583-5499 ■ Web: www.sportsnetwork.com
SportsTicker Enterprises 55 Realty Dr Suite 200 .... Cheshire CT 06410 203-272-2072 336-0383*
*Fax Area Code: 800 ■ TF: 800-367-8935 ■ Web: www.pa-sportsticker.com
Stats Inc 8130 Lehigh Ave .... Morton Grove IL 60053 847-677-3322 967-8029
Web: www.stats.com
Stephens Media Group Washington News Bureau
666 11th St NW Rm 535 .... Washington DC 20001 202-783-1760 783-1955
TF: 800-366-7390 ■ Web: www.stephensdc.com
Talk Radio News Service 209 Pennsylvania Ave SE .... Washington DC 20003 202-337-8715 337-1174
Web: www.talkradionews.com
Tribune Media Services Inc 435 N Michigan Ave Suite 1500 .... Chicago IL 60611 312-222-4444 222-3459*
*Fax: Edit ■ TF: 800-245-6536 ■ Web: www.tms.tribune.com
United Feature Syndicate Inc 200 Madison Ave 4th Fl .... New York NY 10016 212-293-8500 293-8717
TF: 800-888-3000 ■ Web: www.unitedfeatures.com
United Media 200 Madison Ave 4th Fl .... New York NY 10016 212-293-8500 293-8717
TF: 800-221-4816 ■ Web: www.unitedmedia.com
United Methodist News Service 810 12th Ave S .... Nashville TN 37203 615-742-5470 742-5125
TF: 800-251-8140 ■ Web: www.umcom.org
United Press International (UPI) 1133 19th St NW .... Washington DC 20036 202-898-8000 898-8057
TF: 800-783-4874 ■ Web: www.upi.com
Universal Press Syndicate 4520 Main St Suite 700 .... Kansas City MO 64111 816-932-6600 931-5018
TF: 800-255-6734 ■ Web: www.amuniversal.com/ups
Washington Bureau News Service
5900 Princess Garden Pkwy Suite 230 .... Lanham MD 20706 301-429-5944 429-2752
Web: www.find-inc.com
Washington Post Writers Group 1150 15th St NW .... Washington DC 20071 202-334-6375 334-5669
TF: 800-879-9794 ■ Web: www.postwritersgroup.com
Wireless Flash News Service 827 Washington St .... San Diego CA 92103 619-220-7191 220-8590
Web: www.flashnews.com

534 NEWSLETTERS

534-1 Banking & Finance Newsletters

Phone Fax

Asset Sales Report 1 State St Plaza .... New York NY 10004 212-803-8200 292-5296
TF: 888-280-4820 ■ Web: www.sourcemedia.com
Bank Asset/Liability Management
807 Las Cimas Pkwy Suite 300 .... Austin TX 78746 800-572-2797 305-6575*
*Fax Area Code: 512 ■ Web: www.sheshunoff.com/store/805.html
Bank Network News 1 State St Plaza 27th Fl .... New York NY 10004 212-803-8200 843-9600
TF: 800-535-8403 ■ Web: www.sourcemedia.com
Banking Daily 1231 25th St NW .... Washington DC 20037 202-452-4200 452-7504
TF: 800-372-1033 ■ Web: www.bna.com
Bankruptcy Court Decisions 360 Hiatt Dr .... Palm Beach Gardens FL 33418 561-622-6520 622-2423
TF: 800-621-5463 ■ Web: www.lrp.com
Best's Underwriting Newsletter Ambest Rd .... Oldwick NJ 08858 908-439-2200 439-3363
Bestweek Life/Health Ambest Rd .... Oldwick NJ 08858 908-439-2200 439-3363
Web: www.ambest.com
Bestweek Property/Casualty Ambest Rd .... Oldwick NJ 08858 908-439-2200 439-3363
Commercial Lending Litigation News 360 Hiatt Dr .... Palm Beach Gardens FL 33418 561-622-6520 622-2423
TF: 800-621-5463 ■ Web: www.lrp.com
Consumer Bankruptcy News 360 Hiatt Dr .... Palm Beach Gardens FL 33418 561-622-6520 622-2423
TF: 800-621-5463 ■ Web: www.lrp.com
Consumer Credit & Truth-In-Lending Compliance Report
807 Las Cimas Pkwy Suite 300 .... Austin TX 78756 800-753-7577 305-6575*
*Fax Area Code: 512 ■ TF: 800-572-2797 ■ Web: www.sheshunoff.com/store/864.html
Controller's Report 3 Park Ave 30th Fl .... New York NY 10016 212-244-0360 564-0465
TF: 800-401-5937 ■ Web: www.ioma.com
Corporate Financing Week PO Box 5018 .... Brentwood TN 37024 800-715-9195 377-0525*
*Fax Area Code: 615 ■ Web: www.corporatefinancingweek.com
Credit Card News 1 State St Plaza 27th Fl .... New York NY 10004 212-803-8200 843-9600
TF: 800-535-8403 ■ Web: www.sourcemedia.com
Credit Investment News 225 Park Ave S 7th Fl .... New York NY 10003 212-224-3800 224-3491
Credit Union Directors Newsletter 5710 Mineral Point Rd .... Madison WI 53705 608-231-4000 231-1869*
*Fax: Cust Svc ■ TF: 800-356-8010 ■ Web: www.cuna.org
Credit Union Information Service
11300 Rockville Pike Suite 1100 .... Rockville MD 20852 301-816-8950 816-8945
TF Cust Svc: 800-929-4824 ■ Web: www.cuceo.com

Banking & Finance Newsletters (Cont'd)

Name / Address	City	State	ZIP	Phone	Fax
Debit Card News 1 State St Plaza 27th Fl	New York	NY	10004	212-803-8200	843-9600*
*Fax: Mktg ■ TF: 800-535-8403 ■ Web: www.sourcemedia.com					
Defined Contribution News 225 Park Ave S 7th Fl	New York	NY	10003	212-224-3800	224-3491
TF: 800-543-4444 ■ Web: www.definedsavingsalert.com					
Electronic Commerce & Law Report 1231 25th St NW	Washington	DC	20037	202-452-4200	452-7504
TF: 800-372-1033 ■ Web: www.bna.com					
Equipment Leasing Newsletter 1617 JFK Blvd Suite 1750	Philadelphia	PA	19103	215-557-2310	557-2301
TF: 800-999-1916 ■ Web: www.lawjournalnewsletters.com					
Executive 5710 Mineral Point Rd	Madison	WI	53705	608-231-4000	231-4370
TF Circ: 800-356-8010 ■ Web: www.cuna.org					
First Friday PO Box 5488	Madison	WI	53705	608-238-2646	238-2646
Forecaster 19623 Ventura Blvd	Tarzana	CA	91356	818-345-4421	345-0468
Global Money Management 225 Park Ave S 7th Fl	New York	NY	10003	212-224-3800	224-3491
TF: 800-715-9195 ■ Web: www.globalmoneymanagement.com					
Insurance Accountant 1 State St Plaza	New York	NY	10004	212-803-8200	292-5296
TF: 800-221-1809 ■ Web: www.sourcemedia.com					
Internal Auditing Alert 395 Hudson St 4th Fl	New York	NY	10014	212-367-6300	367-6305
TF: 800-950-1205					
International Business & Finance Daily 1231 25th St NW	Washington	DC	20037	202-452-4200	452-7504
TF: 800-372-1033 ■ Web: www.bna.com					
International Tax Monitor 1231 25th St NW	Washington	DC	20037	202-452-4200	452-7504
TF: 800-372-1033 ■ Web: www.bna.com					
Lender Liability Law Report 1901 Fort Myer Dr Suite 501	Arlington	VA	22209	703-528-0145	528-1736
TF Cust Svc: 800-572-2797 ■ Web: www.sheshunoff.com/store/884.html					
Louisiana Banker PO Box 2871	Baton Rouge	LA	70821	225-387-3282	343-3159
Web: www.lba.org					
Managing 401K Plans 30 Park Ave 30th Fl	New York	NY	10016	212-244-0360	564-0465
TF: 800-401-5937 ■ Web: www.ioma.com					
Managing Accounts Payable 3 Park Ave 30th Fl	New York	NY	10016	212-244-0360	564-0465
TF: 800-401-5937 ■ Web: www.ioma.com					
Managing Benefits Plans 3 Park Ave 30th Fl	New York	NY	10016	212-244-0360	564-0465
TF: 800-401-5937 ■ Web: www.ioma.com					
Managing Credit Receivables & Collections 3 Park Ave 30th Fl	New York	NY	10016	212-244-0360	564-0465
TF: 800-401-5937 ■ Web: www.ioma.com					
Money Management Letter 225 Park Ave S 7th Fl	New York	NY	10003	212-224-3300	224-3171
Web: www.moneymanagementletter.com					
New York Banker 99 Park Ave 4th Fl	New York	NY	10016	212-297-1600	297-1683*
*Fax: PR ■ Web: www.nyba.com					
Price Perceptions 3030 NW Expy Suite 725	Oklahoma City	OK	73112	405-604-8726	604-9696
TF: 800-231-0477 ■ Web: www.cis-okc.com/priceperceptions.asp					
Regulatory Risk Monitor 11300 Rockville Pike Suite 1100	Rockville	MD	20852	301-816-8950	816-8945
TF: 800-929-4824 ■ Web: www.rrmonitor.com/frcjsp/					
SEC Accounting Report 395 Hudson St 4th Fl	New York	NY	10014	212-367-6300	367-6305
TF: 800-431-9025					
Security Letter 166 E 96th St	New York	NY	10128	212-348-1553	534-2957
Smart Card Alert 550 Van Buren St	Chicago	IL	60607	312-913-1334	913-1365
TF: 800-535-8403 ■ Web: www.cardtechnology.com					
Specialty Lender 1 SNL Plaza PO Box 2124	Charlottesville	VA	22902	434-977-1600	977-4466
Web: www.snl.com					
VentureWire 800 Plaza 2 Harborside Financial Ctr	Jersey City	NJ	07311	866-291-1800	291-1300
TF: 800-326-3613 ■ Web: www.venturewire.com					

534-2 Business & Professional Newsletters

Name / Address	City	State	ZIP	Phone	Fax
Accounting Dept Management & Administration Report 3 Park Ave 30th Fl	New York	NY	10016	212-244-0360	564-0465
TF: 800-401-5937 ■ Web: www.ioma.com					
Accounting for Law Firms 1617 JFK Blvd Suite 1750	Philadelphia	PA	19103	215-557-2300	557-2301
TF: 800-999-1916 ■ Web: www.lawcatalog.com					
Accounting Office Management & Administration Report 3 Park Ave 30th Fl	New York	NY	10016	212-244-0360	564-0465
TF: 800-401-5937 ■ Web: www.ioma.com					
AIArchitect 1735 New York Ave NW	Washington	DC	20006	202-626-7465	626-7365
American Nurse 8515 Georgia Ave Suite 400	Silver Spring	MD	20910	301-628-5000	628-5001
TF: 800-274-4262 ■ Web: www.nursingworld.org					
American Speaker 2807 N Parham Rd Suite 200	Richmond	VA	23294	804-762-9600	320-2079*
*Fax Area Code: 570 ■ TF: 800-722-9221 ■ Web: www.briefings.com					
Antitrust & Trade Regulation Daily 1231 25th St NW	Washington	DC	20037	202-452-4200	452-7504
TF: 800-372-1033 ■ Web: www.bna.com					
Authors Guild Bulletin 31 E 28th St 7th Fl	New York	NY	10016	212-563-5904	564-5363
Web: www.authorsguild.org					
Business Crimes Bulletin 1617 JFK Blvd Suite 1750	Philadelphia	PA	19103	800-999-1916	696-1848*
*Fax Area Code: 212 ■ TF: 800-888-8300 ■ Web: www.lawcatalog.com					
Communication at Work 360 Hiatt Dr	Palm Beach Gardens	FL	33418	561-622-9914	622-2423
TF: 800-621-5463 ■ Web: www.lrp.com					
Consultants News 1 Phoenix Mill Ln 3rd Fl	Peterborough	NH	03458	603-924-0900	924-4034
TF: 800-531-0007 ■ Web: www.kennedyinfo.com/mc/cn.html					
Corporate Counsellor 1617 JFK Blvd Suite 1750	Philadelphia	PA	19103	215-557-2310	557-2301
TF: 800-999-1916 ■ Web: www.lawjournalnewsletters.com					
Corporate Writer & Editor 316 N Michigan Ave Suite 300	Chicago	IL	60601	312-960-4140	960-4106
TF: 800-878-5331 ■ Web: www.ragan.com/ME2/Sites/Default.asp					
Corrections Professional 360 Hiatt Dr	Palm Beach Gardens	FL	33418	561-622-6520	622-2423
TF: 800-621-5463 ■ Web: www.lrp.com					
Cross Border Monitor 111 W 57th St 9th Fl	New York	NY	10019	212-554-0600	586-1181
TF: 800-938-4685					
Customer Communicator 28 W 25th St 8th Fl	New York	NY	10010	212-228-0246	228-0376
TF: 800-232-4317 ■ Web: www.customerservicegroup.com/tcc.php					
Customer Service Newsletter 28 W 25th St 8th Fl	New York	NY	10010	212-228-0246	228-0376
Web: www.customerservicegroup.com/csn.php					
Customers First 360 Hiatt Dr	Palm Beach Gardens	FL	33418	561-622-9914	622-2423
TF: 800-621-5463 ■ Web: www.lrp.com					
Daily Report for Executives 1231 25th St NW	Washington	DC	20037	202-452-4200	452-7504
TF: 800-372-1033 ■ Web: www.bna.com					
Daily Tax Report 1231 25th St NW	Washington	DC	20037	202-452-4200	452-7504
TF: 800-372-1033 ■ Web: www.bna.com					
Design Firm Management & Administration Report 3 Park Ave 30th Fl	New York	NY	10016	212-244-0360	564-0465
Web: www.ioma.com					
Distribution Center Management 28 W 25th St 8th Fl	New York	NY	10010	212-228-0246	228-0376
TF: 800-232-4317 ■ Web: www.distributiongroup.com/dcm.html					
Downtown Idea Exchange 28 W 25th St 8th Fl	New York	NY	10003	212-228-0246	228-0376
TF: 800-232-4317 ■ Web: www.downtowndevelopment.com/dix.php					
Economic Opportunity Report 8737 Colesville Rd Suite 1100	Silver Spring	MD	20910	301-587-6300	587-1081
TF: 800-274-6737 ■ Web: www.bpinews.com/hr/pages/eor.cfm					
Effective Telephone Techniques 360 Hiatt Dr	Palm Beach Gardens	FL	33418	561-622-9914	622-2423
TF: 800-621-5463 ■ Web: www.lrp.com					
Executive Excellence 1860 N 1120 West	Provo	UT	84604	801-375-4060	377-5960
TF: 800-304-9782 ■ Web: www.eep.com					
Executive Recruiter News 1 Phoenix Mill Ln 5th Fl	Peterborough	NH	03458	603-924-0900	924-4034
TF: 800-531-0007 ■ Web: www.kennedyinfo.com/er/ern.html					
Executive Strategies PO Box 9070	McLean	VA	22102	703-905-8000	905-8040
TF: 800-543-2053 ■ Web: www.nibm.net					
Federal EEO Advisor 360 Hiatt Dr	Palm Beach Gardens	FL	33418	561-622-6520	622-2423
TF: 800-621-5462 ■ Web: www.lrp.com					
Federal Human Resources Week 360 Hiatt Dr	Palm Beach Gardens	FL	33418	561-622-6520	622-2423
TF: 800-621-5463 ■ Web: www.lrp.com					
First Line Supervisor 360 Hiatt Dr	Palm Beach Gardens	FL	33418	561-622-9914	622-9060
TF: 800-621-5463 ■ Web: www.lrp.com					
First-Rate Customer Service 2807 N Parhan Rd Suite 200	Richmond	VA	23294	804-762-9600	320-2079*
*Fax Area Code: 570 ■ TF: 800-722-9221 ■ Web: www.briefings.com					
From 9 To 5 360 Hiatt Dr	Palm Beach Gardens	FL	33418	561-622-9914	622-9060
TF: 800-621-5463 ■ Web: www.lrp.com					
Getting Along 360 Hiatt Dr	Palm Beach Gardens	FL	33418	561-622-9914	622-9060
TF: 800-621-5463 ■ Web: www.lrp.com					
Government Communicators Insider 316 N Michigan Ave Suite 300	Chicago	IL	60601	312-960-4140	960-4106
TF: 800-878-5331 ■ Web: www.ragan.com					
Government Employee Relations Report 1231 25th St NW	Washington	DC	20037	202-452-4200	452-7504
TF: 800-372-1033 ■ Web: www.bna.com					
Human Resources Dept Management Report 3 Park Ave 30th Fl	New York	NY	10016	212-244-0360	564-0465
TF: 800-401-5937 ■ Web: www.ioma.com					
Human Resources Report 1231 25th St NW	Washington	DC	20037	202-452-4200	452-7504
TF: 800-372-1033 ■ Web: www.bna.com					
International Trade Reporter 1231 25th St NW	Washington	DC	20037	202-452-4200	452-7504
TF: 800-372-1033 ■ Web: www.bna.com					
Journal of Employee Communication Management 316 N Michigan Ave Suite 300	Chicago	IL	60601	312-960-4100	960-4106
Web: www.ragan.com					
Laboratory Industry Report 3 Park Ave 30th Fl	New York	NY	10016	212-244-0360	564-0465
TF: 800-401-5937 ■ Web: www.ioma.com/issues/LIR					
Law Firm Partnership & Benefits Report 1617 JFK Blvd Suite 1750	Philadelphia	PA	19103	215-557-2310	557-2301
TF: 800-999-1916 ■ Web: www.lawjournalnewsletters.com					
Law Office Management & Administration Report 3 Park Ave 30th Fl	New York	NY	10016	212-244-0360	564-0465
TF: 800-401-5937 ■ Web: www.ioma.com					
Law Officer's Bulletin 610 Opperman Dr	Eagan	MN	55123	651-687-7000	562-1521*
*Fax Area Code: 301 ■ TF: 800-344-5008 ■ Web: west.thomson.com					
Leadership For The Front Lines 7201 McKinney Cir	Frederick	MD	21704	301-698-7100	901-9075*
*Fax Area Code: 800 ■ *Fax: Cust Svc ■ TF: 800-243-0876					
Leadership Strategies 2807 N Parham Rd Suite 200	Richmond	VA	23294	804-762-9600	320-2079*
*Fax Area Code: 590 ■ TF: 800-722-9221 ■ Web: www.briefings.com					
Legislative Network for Nurses 8737 Colesville Rd Suite 1100	Silver Spring	MD	20910	301-587-6300	587-1081
TF: 800-274-6737 ■ Web: www.bpinews.com					
Mail Center Management Report 3 Park Ave 30th Fl	New York	NY	10016	212-244-0360	564-0465
TF: 800-401-5937 ■ Web: www.ioma.com					
Maintenance Management 7201 McKinney Cir	Frederick	MD	21704	301-698-7100	901-9075*
*Fax Area Code: 800 ■ *Fax: Cust Svc ■ TF: 800-243-0876					
Manager's Edge 2807 N Parhan Rd Suite 200	Richmond	VA	23294	804-762-9600	320-2079*
*Fax Area Code: 570 ■ TF: 800-722-9221 ■ Web: www.briefings.com					
Manager's Intelligence Report 316 N Michigan Ave Suite 300	Chicago	IL	60601	312-960-4100	960-4106
TF: 800-878-5331 ■ Web: www.ragan.com					
Managing Customer Service 3 Park Ave 30th Fl	New York	NY	10016	212-244-0360	564-0465
TF: 800-401-5937 ■ Web: www.ioma.com					
Managing International Credit & Collections 3 Park Ave 30th Fl	New York	NY	10016	212-244-0360	564-0465
TF: 800-401-5937 ■ Web: www.ioma.com					
Managing Logistics 3 Park Ave 30th Fl	New York	NY	10016	212-244-0360	564-0465
TF: 800-401-5937 ■ Web: www.ioma.com					
Minorities in Business Insider 8204 Fenton St	Silver Spring	MD	20910	301-588-6380	588-6385
TF: 800-666-6380 ■ Web: www.cdpublications.com/pubs					
Motivational Manager 316 N Michigan Ave Suite 300	Chicago	IL	60601	312-960-4100	960-4106
TF: 800-878-5331 ■ Web: www.motivateandinspire.com					
Organized Executive 2807 N Parham Rd Suite 200	Richmond	VA	23294	804-762-9600	320-2079*
*Fax Area Code: 570 ■ TF: 800-722-9221 ■ Web: www.briefings.com					
Partner's Report for CPA Firm Owners 3 Park Ave 30th Fl	New York	NY	10016	212-244-0360	564-0465
Partner's Report for Law Firm Owners 3 Park Ave 30th Fl	New York	NY	10016	212-244-0360	564-0465
TF: 800-401-5937 ■ Web: www.ioma.com					
Pay for Performance 3 Park Ave 30th Fl	New York	NY	10016	212-244-0360	564-0465
TF: 800-401-5937 ■ Web: www.ioma.com					
Payroll Manager's Report 3 Park Ave 30th Fl	New York	NY	10016	212-244-0360	564-0465
TF: 800-401-5937 ■ Web: www.ioma.com					
Payroll Practitioner's Monthly 3 Park Ave 30th Fl	New York	NY	10016	212-244-0360	564-0465
TF: 800-401-5937 ■ Web: www.ioma.com					
Positive Leadership 316 N Michigan Ave Suite 300	Chicago	IL	60601	312-960-4140	960-4106
TF: 800-878-5331					
Preventing Business Fraud 3 Park Ave 30th Fl	New York	NY	10016	212-244-0360	564-0465
TF: 800-401-5937 ■ Web: www.ioma.com					
Principal's Report 3 Park Ave 30th Fl	New York	NY	10016	212-244-0360	564-0465
TF: 800-401-5937 ■ Web: www.ioma.com					
Professional Apartment Management 149 5th Ave 16th Fl	New York	NY	10010	800-519-3692	473-8786*
*Fax Area Code: 212 ■ TF: 800-643-8095 ■ Web: www.brownstone.com/html/home.htm					
Quality First 360 Hiatt Dr	Palm Beach Gardens	FL	33418	561-622-6520	622-2423
TF: 800-621-5463					
Ragan Report 316 N Michigan Ave Suite 300	Chicago	IL	60601	312-960-4100	960-4106
TF Cust Svc: 800-878-5331 ■ Web: www.ragan.com					
Recruiting Trends 1 Phoenix Mill Ln 3rd Fl	Peterborough	NH	03458	603-924-0900	924-0434
TF: 800-531-0007 ■ Web: www.kennedyinfo.com/rt/rectrends.html					
Report on Salary Surveys 3 Park Ave 30th Fl	New York	NY	10016	212-244-0360	564-0465
TF: 800-401-5937 ■ Web: www.ioma.com					
Security Director's Report 3 Park Ave 30th Fl	New York	NY	10016	212-244-0360	564-0465
TF: 800-401-5937 ■ Web: www.ioma.com/issues/SDR					
Small Tax Control 7910 Woodmont Ave Suite 1000	Bethesda	MD	20814	301-951-1240	656-1709
Web: www.imfpubs.com					
Successful Supervisor 360 Hiatt Dr	Palm Beach Gardens	FL	33418	561-622-9914	622-2423
TF: 800-621-5463 ■ Web: www.lrp.com					
Supplier Selection & Management Report 3 Park Ave 30th Fl	New York	NY	10016	212-244-0360	564-0465
TF: 800-401-5937 ■ Web: www.ioma.com					
Team Leader 360 Hiatt Dr	Palm Beach Gardens	FL	33418	561-622-9914	622-2423
TF: 800-621-5463 ■ Web: www.lrp.com					
Team Management Briefings 2807 N Parhan Rd Suite 200	Richmond	VA	23294	804-762-9600	684-2136*
*Fax Area Code: 703 ■ TF: 800-722-9221 ■ Web: www.briefings.com					
Teamwork 360 Hiatt Dr	Palm Beach Gardens	FL	33418	561-622-6520	622-2423
TF: 800-621-5463 ■ Web: www.dartnellcorp.com					
Tradeshow Week 5700 Wilshire Blvd Suite 120	Los Angeles	CA	90036	323-965-5300	965-5304
TF: 800-375-4212 ■ Web: www.tradeshowweek.com					
Trend Letter 2807 N Prhan Rd Suite 200	Richmond	VA	23294	804-762-9600	684-2136*
*Fax Area Code: 703 ■ TF: 800-722-9221 ■ Web: www.briefings.com					
Working Together 360 Hiatt Dr	Palm Beach Gardens	FL	33418	561-622-6520	622-2423
TF: 800-621-5463 ■ Web: www.lrp.com					
Your New Pryor Report: Managers Edge 2807 N Parham Rd Suite 200	Richmond	VA	23294	804-762-9600	217-8996
TF Cust Svc: 800-722-9221 ■ Web: www.briefings.com					

534-3 Computer & Internet Newsletters

Phone | Fax

American Programmer 37 Broadway Suite 1 ... Arlington MA 02474 781-648-8700 648-1950
Web: www.cutter.com/itjournal

Biotechnology Software 140 Huguenot St 3rd Fl ... New Rochelle NY 10801 914-740-2100 740-2109
TF: 800-654-3237 ■ *Web:* www.liebertpub.com

CADCAMNet 8220 Stone Trail Dr ... Bethesda MD 20817 301-365-9085 365-4586
Web: www.cadcamnet.com

Computer Economics Report 2082 Business Ctr Dr Suite 240 ... Irvine CA 92612 949-831-8700 442-7688
TF: 800-326-8100 ■ *Web:* www.computereconomics.com

Computer Publishing & Advertising Report 60 Longridge Rd ... Stamford CT 06902 203-325-8193 325-8915

Convergence 118 Turnpike Rd ... Southborough MA 01772 508-460-3333 460-1192
TF: 800-622-1108 ■ *Web:* www.networkworld.com/newsletters/converg/index.html

Data Management Strategies 37 Broadway Suite 1 ... Arlington MA 02474 781-648-8700 648-1950
TF: 800-964-8702 ■ *Web:* www.cutter.com/bia

DemoLetter 177 Bovet Rd Suite 400 ... San Mateo CA 94402 650-577-2700 577-7840
TF: 800-633-4312 ■ *Web:* www.demo.com/demoletter

Electronic Information Report 60 Longridge Rd Suite 300 ... Stamford CT 06902 203-325-8193 325-8915
Web: www.simbanet.com

eMarketer 75 Broad St 32nd Fl ... New York NY 10004 212-763-6010 763-6020
TF: 800-405-0844 ■ *Web:* www.emarketer.com

Identity Management 118 Turnpike Rd ... Southborough MA 01772 508-460-3333 460-1192
TF: 800-622-1108 ■ *Web:* www.networkworld.com/newsletters/dir/index.html

Infoperceptives 123 7th Ave ... Brooklyn NY 11215 718-369-7682 965-3039
Web: www.tech-news.com/infoperspectives

Insider Weekly for AS/400 Managers
990 Washington St Suite 308 ... Dedham MA 02026 781-320-9460 320-9466
TF: 888-400-4768 ■ *Web:* www.the400group.com/aiw/index.jsp

Internet Newsletter 1617 JFK Blvd Suite 1750 ... Philadelphia PA 19103 215-557-2300 557-2301
TF: 800-999-1916

Intranet Report 316 N Michigan Ave Suite 300 ... Chicago IL 60601 312-960-4100 960-4106*
**Fax:* Cust Svc ■ *TF:* 800-878-5331

IT Metrics 37 Broadway Suite 1 ... Arlington MA 02474 781-648-8702 648-1950
TF: 800-964-8702 ■ *Web:* www.cutter.com/benchmark

Legal Tech Newsletter 1617 JFK Blvd Suite 1750 ... Philadelphia PA 19103 215-557-2310 557-2301
TF: 800-999-1916 ■ *Web:* www.lawjournalnewsletters.com

Linux Today 23 Old Kings Hwy S ... Darien CT 06820 203-662-2800 655-4686
Web: linuxtoday.com

Microprocessor Report 298 S Sunnyvale Ave Suite 101 ... Sunnyvale CA 94086 408-243-8838 737-2242
TF: 800-527-0288 ■ *Web:* www.mdronline.com/mpr

Object-Oriented Strategies 37 Broadway Suite 1 ... Arlington MA 02474 781-648-8700 648-1950
TF: 800-964-8702 ■ *Web:* www.cutter.com/webservices

Software Success 990 Washington St Suite 308 ... Dedham MA 02026 781-320-9460 320-9466
TF: 888-479-6663 ■ *Web:* www.softwaresuccess.com

Technology Executive 118 Turnpike Rd ... Southborough MA 01772 508-460-3333 460-1192
TF: 800-622-1108 ■ *Web:* www.networkworld.com/newsletters/techexec/index.html

Washington Internet Daily 2115 Ward Ct NW ... Washington DC 20037 202-872-9200 293-3435
TF: 800-771-9202 ■ *Web:* www.warren-news.com

Web Content Report 316 N Michigan Ave Suite 400 ... Chicago IL 60601 312-960-4100 960-4106*
**Fax:* Cust Svc ■ *TF:* 800-878-5331 ■ *Web:* www.ragan.com

Webreference 23 Old Kings Hwy S ... Darien CT 06820 203-662-2800 655-4686
Web: www.webreference.com

534-4 Education Newsletters

Phone | Fax

Aid for Education Report 8204 Fenton St ... Silver Spring MD 20910 301-588-6380 588-6385*
**Fax:* Edit ■ *TF:* 800-666-6380 ■ *Web:* cdpublications.com/pubs

California School Law Digest 747 Dresher Rd Suite 500 ... Horsham PA 19044 215-784-0860 784-9639*
**Fax:* Mktg ■ *TF:* 800-341-7874 ■ *Web:* www.shoplrp.com/product/p-300049.html

California Special Education Alert (CASEA)
360 Hiatt Dr ... Palm Beach Gardens FL 33418 561-622-6520 622-2423
TF: 800-621-5463 ■ *Web:* www.lrp.com

Campus Crime 8737 Colesville Rd Suite 1100 ... Silver Spring MD 20910 301-587-6300 587-1081*
**Fax:* Edit ■ *TF:* 800-274-6737 ■ *Web:* www.bpinews.com/edu/pages/cc.cfm

CASEA (California Special Education Alert)
360 Hiatt Dr ... Palm Beach Gardens FL 33418 561-622-6520 622-2423
TF: 800-621-5463 ■ *Web:* www.lrp.com

Corporate Training & Development Advisor 60 Longridge Rd ... Stamford CT 06902 203-325-8193 325-8915*
**Fax:* Sales ■ *Web:* www.simbanet.com/products/pr_ctrsr.html#nl1

Early Childhood Report 360 Hiatt Dr ... Palm Beach Gardens FL 33418 561-622-6520 622-2423
TF: 800-621-5463 ■ *Web:* www.lrp.com

Education Grants Alert 360 Hiatt Dr ... Palm Beach Gardens FL 33418 561-622-6520 622-2423
TF: 800-621-5463 ■ *Web:* www.lrp.com

Education Technology News
8737 Colesville Rd Suite 1100 ... Silver Spring MD 20910 301-587-6300 587-1081*
**Fax:* Edit ■ *TF:* 800-274-6737 ■ *Web:* www.bpinews.com/edu/pages/etn.cfm

Education USA 747 Dresher Rd Suite 500 ... Horsham PA 19044 215-784-0860 784-9639
TF Cust Svc: 800-341-7874 ■ *Web:* www.lrp.com

Educational Research Network Inc PO Box 789 ... West Barnstable MA 02668 781-646-1814 646-1814
Web: www.ernweb.com

Electronic Education Report 60 Longridge Rd Suite 300 ... Stamford CT 06902 203-325-8193 325-8915*
**Fax:* Sales ■ *Web:* www.simbanet.com/publications/news_eer.htm

Federal Research Report 8737 Colesville Rd Suite 1100 ... Silver Spring MD 20910 301-587-6300 587-1081*
**Fax:* Edit ■ *TF:* 800-274-6737

Library of Congress Information Bulletin
101 Independence Ave SE ... Washington DC 20540 202-707-2905 707-9199
Web: www.loc.gov/loc/lcib

Library Hotline 360 Park Ave S ... New York NY 10010 646-746-7059 746-6536*
**Fax:* Mktg ■ *Web:* www.reedbusiness.com

New Jersey Education Law Report PO Box 241 ... Burtonsville MD 20866 301-384-1573 879-8803

New York Education Law Report 360 Hiatt Dr ... Palm Beach FL 33418 561-622-6520 622-1375*
**Fax:* Edit ■ *TF:* 800-341-7874 ■ *Web:* www.lrp.com

Report on Literacy Programs
8737 Colesville Rd Suite 1100 ... Silver Spring MD 20910 301-587-6300 589-8493
TF: 800-274-6737 ■ *Web:* www.bpinews.com/edu/pages/rlp.cfm

Report on Preschool Programs
8737 Colesville Rd Suite 1100 ... Silver Spring MD 20910 301-587-6300 589-8493
TF: 800-274-6737 ■ *Web:* www.bpinews.com/edu/pages/rpp.cfm

Research Libraries Group News 1200 Villa St ... Mountain View CA 94041 650-962-9951 964-0943
TF: 800-537-7546 ■ *Web:* www.rlg.org

School Law News 360 Hiatt Dr ... Palm Beach Gardens FL 33418 800-341-7874 622-2423*
**Fax Area Code:* 561 ■ *TF:* 800-638-8437 ■ *Web:* www.lrp.com

School Superintendent's Insider 360 Hiatt Dr ... Palm Beach Gardens FL 33418 561-622-6520 622-0757
TF: 800-341-7874 ■ *Web:* www.shoplrp.com

School-to-Work Report 8737 Colesville Rd Suite 1100 ... Silver Spring MD 20910 301-587-6300 589-8493
TF: 800-274-6737

Special Education Report 360 Hiatt Dr ... Palm Beach Gardens FL 33418 561-622-6520 622-2423
TF Sales: 800-621-5463 ■ *Web:* www.lrp.com

Student Aid News 360 Hiatt Dr ... Palm Beach Gardens FL 33418 800-341-7874 622-2423*
**Fax Area Code:* 561 ■ *TF:* 800-638-8437 ■ *Web:* www.lrp.com

Teacher Education Reports
4401A Connecticut Ave NW PMB 212 ... Washington DC 20008 202-822-8280 822-8284
Web: www.teach-now.org

Vocational Training News 360 Hiatt Dr ... Palm Beach Gardens FL 33418 800-341-7874 622-2423*
**Fax Area Code:* 561 ■ *TF:* 800-638-8437 ■ *Web:* www.lrp.com

What Works in Teaching & Learning 360 Hiatt Dr ... Palm Beach Gardens FL 33418 561-622-6520 622-2423
TF Sales: 800-621-5463 ■ *Web:* www.lrp.com

534-5 Energy & Environmental Newsletters

Phone | Fax

AltFuels Advisor 40 Washington St Suite 110 ... Wellesley MA 02481 866-285-7215 489-7308*
**Fax Area Code:* 781 ■ *Web:* www.altfuels.com/afa.php

Asbestos & Lead Abatement Report
8737 Colesville Rd Suite 1100 ... Silver Spring MD 20910 301-589-5103 587-4530
TF: 800-274-6737

Chemical Regulation Daily 1231 25th St NW ... Washington DC 20037 202-452-4200 452-7504
TF: 800-372-1033 ■ *Web:* www.bna.com

Chemical Regulation Reporter 1231 25th St NW ... Washington DC 20037 202-452-4200 452-7504
TF: 800-372-1033 ■ *Web:* www.bna.com

Clean Air Report 1225 S Clark St Suite 1400 ... Arlington VA 22202 703-416-8516 416-8543
Web: www.insideepa.com

Coal Outlook 1200 G St NW Suite 1100 ... Washington DC 20005 202-383-2160 904-4209*
**Fax Area Code:* 212 ■ *Web:* www.platts.com

Congressional Quarterly Green Sheets
1255 22nd St NW Suite 700 ... Washington DC 20037 202-419-8500 380-3810*
**Fax Area Code:* 800 ■ *TF:* 800-432-2250 ■ *Web:* www.cq.com

Daily Environment Report 1231 25th St NW ... Washington DC 20037 202-452-4200 452-7504
TF: 800-372-1033 ■ *Web:* www.bna.com

Electric Utility Week 2 Penn Plaza 25th Fl ... New York NY 10121 212-904-3070 904-3738
TF: 800-752-8878 ■ *Web:* www.platts.com

Energy Compass 5 E 37th St 5th Fl ... New York NY 10016 212-532-1112 532-4838
TF: 888-427-7496 ■ *Web:* www.energyintel.com

Energy Insight 1200 G St NW Suite 1100 ... Washington DC 20005 202-383-2000 904-4209*
**Fax Area Code:* 212 ■ *Web:* www.platts.com

Environment Reporter 1231 25th St NW ... Washington DC 20037 202-452-4200 452-7504
TF: 800-372-1033 ■ *Web:* www.bna.com

Environmental Compliance Bulletin 1231 25th St NW ... Washington DC 20037 202-452-4200 452-4610
TF: 800-372-1033 ■ *Web:* www.bna.com

Environmental Compliance & Litigation Strategy
1617 JFK Blvd Suite 1750 ... Philadelphia PA 19103 877-256-2472 557-2301*
**Fax Area Code:* 215 ■ *TF:* 800-999-1916 ■ *Web:* www.lawjournalnewsletters.com

Environmental Laboratory Washington Report
360 Hiatt Dr ... Palm Beach Gardens FL 33418 561-622-6520 622-2423
TF: 800-621-5463 ■ *Web:* www.lrp.com

Gas Daily 1200 G St NW Suite 1100 ... Washington DC 20005 202-383-2000 904-4209*
**Fax Area Code:* 212 ■ *Web:* www.platts.com

Global Power Report 2 Penn Plaza 25th Fl ... New York NY 10121 800-752-8878 904-3738*
**Fax Area Code:* 212 ■ *TF:* 800-223-6180 ■ *Web:* www.platts.com

Ground Water Monitor 8737 Colesville Rd Suite 1100 ... Silver Spring MD 20910 301-587-6300 587-1081
TF: 800-274-6737 ■ *Web:* www.bpinews.com/enviro/pages/cwr.cfm

Hazardous Waste News 8737 Colesville Rd Suite 1100 ... Silver Spring MD 20910 301-587-6300 587-1081
TF: 800-274-6737

HazMat Transportation News
8737 Colesville Rd Suite 1100 ... Silver Spring MD 20910 301-587-6300 587-1081
TF: 800-274-6737 ■ *Web:* www.bpinews.com

Inside Energy 2 Penn Plaza 25th Fl ... New York NY 10121 800-752-8878 904-2723*
**Fax Area Code:* 212 ■ *TF:* 800-223-6180 ■ *Web:* www.platts.com

Inside FERC 2 Penn Plaza 25th Fl ... New York NY 10121 800-752-8878 904-2723*
**Fax Area Code:* 212 ■ *Web:* www.platts.com

Inside FERC's Gas Market Report 2 Penn Plaza 25th Fl ... New York NY 10121 212-904-3070 904-3738
TF: 800-223-6180 ■ *Web:* www.platts.com

Inside NRC 2 Penn Plaza 25th Fl ... New York NY 10121 800-752-8878 904-3738*
**Fax Area Code:* 212 ■ *TF:* 800-223-6180 ■ *Web:* www.platts.com

International Environment Daily 1231 25th St NW ... Washington DC 20037 202-452-4200 452-7504
TF: 800-372-1033 ■ *Web:* www.bna.com

Land Use Law Report 8737 Colesville Rd Suite 1100 ... Silver Spring MD 20910 301-587-6300 587-1081
TF: 800-274-6767

Megawatt Daily 1200 G St NW Suite 1100 ... Washington DC 20005 202-383-2000 904-4209*
**Fax Area Code:* 212 ■ *Web:* www.platts.com

Natural Gas Week 5 E 37th St 5th Fl ... New York NY 10013 212-532-1112 532-4838
TF: 888-427-7496 ■ *Web:* www.energyintel.com

Noise Regulation Report 8737 Colesville Rd Suite 1100 ... Silver Spring MD 20910 301-587-6300 587-1081
TF: 800-274-6737

Northeast Power Report 2 Penn Plaza 25th Fl ... New York NY 10121 800-752-8878 904-2723*
**Fax Area Code:* 212 ■ *Web:* www.platts.com

Nuclear News PO Box 97781 ... Chicago IL 60678 708-352-6611 352-0499
TF: 800-323-3044 ■ *Web:* www.ans.org/pubs/magazines/nn

Nuclear Waste News 8737 Colesville Rd Suite 1100 ... Silver Spring MD 20910 301-589-5103 587-4530
TF: 800-274-6737 ■ *Web:* www.bpinews.com

Nuclearfuel 1200 G St NW Suite 1000 ... Washington DC 20005 202-383-2100 904-4209*
**Fax Area Code:* 212 ■ *TF:* 800-223-6180 ■ *Web:* www.platts.com

Nucleonics Week 1200 G St NW Suite 1100 ... Washington DC 20005 202-383-2100 904-4209*
**Fax Area Code:* 212 ■ *TF:* 800-223-6180 ■ *Web:* www.platts.com

Oil Daily 5 E 37th St 5th Fl ... New York NY 10016 212-532-1112 532-4938
TF: 888-427-7496 ■ *Web:* www.energyintel.com

Oil Express 11300 Rockville Pike Suite 1100 ... Rockville MD 20852 301-816-8950 816-8945
TF: 800-929-4824 ■ *Web:* www.opisnet.com/news/index.asp

Oil Price Information Service 3349 Hwy 138 Bldg D Suite D ... Wall NJ 07719 732-901-8800 901-5993
TF Cust Svc: 888-301-2645 ■ *Web:* www.opisnet.com

Pesticide & Toxic Chemical News
1725 K St NW Suite 506 ... Washington DC 20006 202-887-6320 887-6337
TF: 888-732-7070 ■ *Web:* www.foodchemicalnews.com/products.asp

Petro-Chemical News 709 Turmeric Ln ... Durham NC 27713 919-544-1717 544-1999
Web: www.petrochemical-news.com

Sludge 8737 Colesville Rd Suite 1100 ... Silver Spring MD 20910 301-587-6300 587-1081
TF: 800-274-6737

Solid Waste Report 8737 Colesville Rd Suite 1100 ... Silver Spring MD 20910 301-587-6300 587-1081
TF: 800-274-6737 ■ *Web:* www.bpinews.com/enviro/pages/swr.cfm

State Environment Daily 1231 25th St NW ... Washington DC 20037 202-452-4200 452-7504
TF: 800-372-1033 ■ *Web:* www.bna.com

SWANA-Solid Waste Assn of North America
1100 Wayne Ave Suite 700 ... Silver Spring MD 20910 301-585-2898 589-7068
TF: 800-467-9262 ■ *Web:* www.swana.org

Toxics Law Daily 1231 25th St NW ... Washington DC 20037 202-452-4200 452-7504
TF: 800-372-1033 ■ *Web:* www.bna.com

Toxics Law Reporter 1251 25th St NW ... Washington DC 20037 202-452-4200 452-7504
TF: 800-372-1033 ■ *Web:* www.bna.com

Utility Environment Report 2 Penn Plaza 25th Fl ... New York NY 10121 800-752-8878 904-3738*
**Fax Area Code:* 212 ■ *Web:* www.platts.com

Water Tech Online
c/o National Trade Publications Inc 13 Century Hill Dr ... Latham NY 12110 518-783-1281
Web: waternet.com

World Gas Intelligence 5 E 37th St 5th Fl ... New York NY 10016 212-532-1112 532-4479
Web: www.energyintel.com

534-6 General Interest Newsletters

Phone | Fax

ARTnewsletter 48 W 38th St 9th Fl ... New York NY 10018 212-398-1690 819-0394
TF Cust Svc: 800-284-4625 ■ *Web:* artnews.com/artnewsletter

General Interest Newsletters (Cont'd)

Name / Address	City	State	ZIP	Phone	Fax
Aviso 1575 'I' St NW Suite 400	Washington	DC	20005	202-289-1818	289-6578
Bottom Line/Personal 281 Tresser Blvd 8th Fl	Stamford	CT	06901	203-973-5900	967-3621*
*Fax: Edit ■ TF Cust Svc: 800-274-5611 ■ Web: www.boardroom.com					
Bottom Line/Tomorrow 281 Tresser Blvd	Stamford	CT	06901	203-973-5900	967-3621*
*Fax: Edit ■ TF Cust Svc: 800-274-5611 ■ Web: www.boardroom.com					
CatWatch 800 Connecticut Ave 4-West	Norwalk	CT	06854	203-857-3100	857-3103
TF: 800-424-7887 ■ Web: www.belvoir.com					
DogWatch 800 Connecticut Ave 4-West	Norwalk	CT	06854	203-857-3100	857-3103
TF: 800-424-7887 ■ Web: www.belvoir.com					
Frm Weekly 224 7th St	Garden City	NY	11530	516-746-6700	294-8141
Kiplinger California Letter 1729 H St NW	Washington	DC	20006	202-887-6400	778-8976
TF: 800-544-0155 ■ Web: www.kiplinger.com					
Kiplinger Retirement Report 1729 H St NW	Washington	DC	20006	202-887-6400	778-8976
TF: 800-544-0155 ■ Web: www.kiplinger.com/retirementreport					
NRTA/AARP Bulletin 601 'E' St NW	Washington	DC	20049	202-434-2277	434-2809*
*Fax: Hum Res ■ TF: 888-867-2277 ■ Web: www.aarp.org/nrta					
Older Americans Report 8737 Colesville Rd Suite 1100	Silver Spring	MD	20910	301-587-6300	587-1081*
*Fax: Edit ■ TF: 800-274-6737 ■ Web: www.bpinews.com/hr/pages/oar.cfm					
Passport 5315 N Clark St PMB 501	Chicago	IL	60640	773-769-6760	
TF: 800-542-6670 ■ Web: www.passportnewsletter.com					
Preferred Traveler 4501 Forbes Blvd	Lanham	MD	20706	301-459-8020	731-0525*
*Fax: Edit ■ Web: www.preferredtraveller.com					
Sotheby's Newsletter 1334 York Ave	New York	NY	10021	212-606-7000	606-7028*
*Fax: Hum Res ■ Web: www.sothebys.com/					
Tax Hotline 281 Tresser Blvd	Stamford	CT	06901	203-973-5900	967-3621*
*Fax: Edit ■ TF Cust Svc: 800-274-5611 ■ Web: www.boardroom.com					

534-7 Government & Law Newsletters

Name / Address	City	State	ZIP	Phone	Fax
Alcoholic Beverage Control PO Box 7376	Alexandria	VA	22307	703-768-9600	768-9690
TF: 800-876-2545 ■ Web: statecapitals.com/alcoholbev.html					
ATLA Law Reporter 1050 31st St NW	Washington	DC	20007	202-965-3500	625-7084
TF: 800-424-2727 ■ Web: www.atla.org					
Bankruptcy Law Letter 610 Opperman Dr	Eagan	MN	55123	651-687-7000	687-8722
TF: 800-937-8529 ■ Web: west.thomson.com					
Bankruptcy Strategist 1617 JFK Blvd Suite 1750	Philadelphia	PA	19103	215-557-2300	557-2301
TF: 800-722-7670 ■ Web: www.lawcatalog.com					
BD Week 11300 Rockville Pike Suite 1100	Rockville	MD	20852	301-816-8950	816-8945
TF: 800-929-4824 ■ Web: www.bdweek.com/bdwjsp/index.jsp					
Bioethics Legal Review 1617 JFK Blvd Suite 1750	Philadelphia	PA	19103	215-557-2300	557-2301
TF: 800-999-1916 ■ Web: www.lawjournalnewsletters.com					
Civil Rights PO Box 7376	Alexandria	VA	22307	703-768-9600	768-9690
TF: 800-876-2545 ■ Web: statecapitals.com/civilrights.html					
Class Action Litigation Report 1231 25th St NW	Washington	DC	20037	202-452-4200	452-7504
TF: 800-372-1033 ■ Web: www.bna.com					
Commercial Leasing Law & Strategy 1617 JFK Blvd Suite 1750	Philadelphia	PA	19103	215-557-2300	557-2301
TF: 800-999-1916 ■ Web: www.lawcatalog.com					
Community Development Digest 8204 Fenton St	Silver Spring	MD	20910	301-588-6380	588-6385
TF: 800-666-6380 ■ Web: www.cdpublications.com					
Community Health Funding Week 8204 Fenton St	Silver Spring	MD	20910	301-588-6380	588-0519
TF: 800-666-6380 ■ Web: www.cdpublications.com					
Computer Technology Law Report 1231 25th St NW	Washington	DC	20037	202-452-4200	452-7504
TF: 800-372-1033 ■ Web: www.bna.com					
Congress Daily 600 New Hampshire Ave The Watergate	Washington	DC	20037	202-266-7000	296-6110
TF: 800-424-2921 ■ Web: nationaljournal.com					
Congressional Quarterly Budget Tracker 1255 22nd St NW	Washington	DC	20037	202-419-8500	380-3810*
*Fax Area Code: 800 ■ TF: 800-432-2250 ■ Web: www.cq.com					
Congressional Quarterly Green Sheets 1255 22nd St NW Suite 700	Washington	DC	20037	202-419-8500	380-3810*
*Fax Area Code: 800 ■ TF: 800-432-2250 ■ Web: www.cq.com					
Congressional Quarterly HealthBeat 1255 22nd St NW	Washington	DC	20037	202-419-8500	380-3810*
*Fax Area Code: 800 ■ TF: 800-432-2250 ■ Web: www.cq.com					
Congressional Quarterly Homeland Security 1255 22nd St NW	Washington	DC	20037	202-419-8500	380-3810*
*Fax Area Code: 800 ■ TF: 800-432-2250 ■ Web: www.cq.com					
Congressional Quarterly House Action Reports 1255 22nd St NW	Washington	DC	20037	202-419-8500	380-3810*
*Fax Area Code: 800 ■ TF: 800-432-2250 ■ Web: www.cq.com					
Congressional Quarterly Monitor 1255 22nd St NW	Washington	DC	20037	202-419-8500	380-3810*
*Fax Area Code: 800 ■ TF Cust Svc: 800-432-2250 ■ Web: www.cq.com					
Congressional Quarterly Weekly Report 1255 22nd St NW	Washington	DC	20037	202-887-8500	785-8784
Web: www.cq.com					
Consumer Financial Services Law Report 360 Hiatt Dr	Palm Beach Gardens	FL	33418	561-622-6520	622-2423
TF: 800-621-5463 ■ Web: www.lrp.com					
Corporate Compliance & Regulatory 1617 JFK Blvd Suite 1750	Philadelphia	PA	19103	215-557-2300	557-2301
TF: 800-999-1916 ■ Web: www.lawjournalnewsletters.com					
Corporate Law Daily 1231 25th St NW	Washington	DC	20037	202-452-4200	452-7504
TF: 800-372-1033 ■ Web: www.bna.com					
Criminal Law Reporter 1231 25th St NW	Washington	DC	20037	202-452-4200	452-7504
TF: 800-372-1033 ■ Web: www.bna.com					
Daily Labor Report 1231 25th St NW	Washington	DC	20037	202-452-4200	452-7504
TF: 800-372-1033 ■ Web: www.bna.com					
Defense Today 1325 G St NW Suite 1003	Washington	DC	20005	202-638-4260	662-9744
TF: 800-926-5464 ■ Web: www.kingpublishing.com/publications/dw					
Development Director's Letter 8204 Fenton St	Silver Spring	MD	20910	301-588-6380	588-6385
TF: 800-666-6380 ■ Web: www.cdpublications.com/pubs					
Disability Law Compliance Report 610 Opperman Dr	Eagan	MN	55123	651-687-7000	687-8722
TF Cust Svc: 800-328-4880 ■ Web: west.thomson.com/store/product.asp?product_id=14939085					
DWI Journal PO Box 241	Burtonsville	MD	20886	301-384-1573	879-8803
TF: 800-359-6049					
e-Commerce Law & Strategy 1617 JFK Blvd Suite 1750	Philadelphia	PA	19103	215-557-2300	557-2301
TF: 800-999-1916 ■ Web: www.lawjournalnewsletters.com					
e-Discovery Law & Strategy 1617 JFK Blvd Suite 1750	Philadelphia	PA	19103	215-557-2300	557-2301
TF: 800-999-1916 ■ Web: www.lawjournalnewsletters.com					
Economic Development PO Box 7376	Alexandria	VA	22307	703-768-9600	768-9690
Web: statecapitals.com/ecodev.html					
Emergency Preparedness News 8737 Colesville Rd Suite 1000	Silver Spring	MD	20910	301-587-6300	589-8493*
*Fax: Mktg ■ TF: 800-274-6737 ■ Web: www.bpinews.com/hs/pages/epn.cfm					
Employment Discrimination Report 1231 25th St NW	Washington	DC	20037	202-452-4200	452-7504
TF: 800-372-1033 ■ Web: www.bna.com					
Employment Law Strategist 1617 JFK Blvd Suite 1750	Philadelphia	PA	19103	215-557-2300	557-2301
TF: 800-722-7670 ■ Web: www.americanlawyer.com					
Expert Evidence Report 1231 25th St NW	Washington	DC	20037	202-452-4200	452-7504
TF: 800-372-1033 ■ Web: www.bna.com					
Family Law Reporter 1231 25th St NW	Washington	DC	20037	202-452-4200	452-7504
TF: 800-372-1033 ■ Web: www.bna.com					
FBO Weekly Release 11300 Rockville Pike Suite 1100	Rockville	MD	20852	301-287-2700	816-8945
TF Cust Svc: 800-824-1195					
Federal Action Affecting the States PO Box 7376	Alexandria	VA	22307	703-768-9600	768-9600
Web: statecapitals.com/fedaction.html					
Federal Assistance Monitor 8204 Fenton St	Silver Spring	MD	20910	301-588-6380	588-6385
TF: 800-666-6380 ■ Web: www.cdpublications.com					
Federal Contracts Report 1231 25th St NW	Washington	DC	20037	202-452-4200	452-7504
TF: 800-372-1033 ■ Web: www.bna.com					
Federal Discovery News 360 Hiatt Dr	Palm Beach Gardens	FL	33418	561-622-6520	622-2423
TF: 800-621-5463 ■ Web: www.lrp.com					
Franchising Business & Law Alert 1617 JFK Blvd Suite 1750	Philadelphia	PA	19103	215-557-2300	557-2301
TF: 800-999-1916 ■ Web: www.lawjournalnewsletters.com					
Government Accounting & Auditing Update 395 Hudson St	New York	NY	10014	212-367-6300	367-6305
TF: 800-431-9025					
Government Contracts Update 11300 Rockville Pike Suite 1100	Rockville	MD	20852	301-287-2700	816-8945
TF Cust Svc: 888-287-2223 ■ Web: www.ucg.com					
Health Care Fraud Report 1231 25th St NW	Washington	DC	20037	202-452-4200	452-7504
TF: 800-372-1033 ■ Web: www.bna.com					
Health Law Reporter 1231 25th St NW	Washington	DC	20037	202-452-4200	452-7504
TF: 800-372-1033 ■ Web: www.bna.com					
Homeland Security Funding Week 8204 Fenton St	Silver Spring	MD	20910	301-588-6380	588-6385
TF: 800-666-6380 ■ Web: www.cdpublications.com					
Hospital Litigation Reporter 590 Dutch Valley Rd NE	Atlanta	GA	30324	404-881-1141	881-0074
TF: 800-926-7926 ■ Web: www.straffordpub.com/products/hlr					
Hospitality Law 360 Hiatt Dr	Palm Beach Gardens	FL	33418	561-622-6520	622-2423
TF: 800-621-5463 ■ Web: www.lrp.com					
Housing & Development Reporter 610 Opperman Dr	Eagan	MN	55123	651-687-7000	741-1414*
*Fax Area Code: 800 ■ TF: 800-937-8529					
Insurance Coverage Law Bulletin 1617 JFK Blvd Suite 1750	Philadelphia	PA	19103	215-557-2300	557-2301
TF: 800-999-1916 ■ Web: www.lawjournalnewsletters.com					
Insurance Regulation PO Box 7376	Alexandria	VA	22307	703-768-9600	768-9690
Web: statecapitals.com					
Intellectual Property Strategist 1617 JFK Blvd Suite 1750	Philadelphia	PA	19103	215-557-2300	557-2301
TF: 800-722-7670 ■ Web: www.americanlawyer.com					
International Drug Report 112 State St Suite 1200	Albany	NY	12207	518-463-6232	432-3378
Web: www.ineoa.org					
Internet Law & Strategy 1617 JFK Blvd Suite 1750	Philadelphia	PA	19103	215-557-2300	557-2301
TF: 800-999-1916 ■ Web: www.lawjournalnewsletters.com					
IRS Practice & Policy Bulletin 1231 25th St NW	Washington	DC	20037	202-452-4200	253-0322*
*Fax Area Code: 800 ■ *Fax: Cust Svc ■ TF Cust Svc: 800-372-1033 ■ Web: www.bna.com					
Kiplinger Tax Letter 1729 H St NW	Washington	DC	20006	202-887-6400	778-8976
TF: 800-544-0155 ■ Web: www.kiplinger.com					
Kiplinger Washington Letter 1729 H St NW	Washington	DC	20006	202-887-6400	778-8976
TF: 800-544-0155					
Landlord Law Report 8204 Fenton St	Silver Spring	MD	20910	301-588-6380	588-6385
TF: 800-666-6380 ■ Web: www.cdpublications.com/pubs/landlordlaw.php					
Matrimonial Strategist 1617 JFK Blvd Suite 1750	Philadelphia	PA	19103	215-557-2300	557-2301
TF: 800-722-7670 ■ Web: www.lawcatalog.com					
Medical Malpractice Law & Strategy 1617 JFK Blvd Suite 1750	Philadelphia	PA	19103	215-557-2300	557-2301
TF: 800-722-7670 ■ Web: www.lawcatalog.com					
Medical Research Law & Policy Report 1231 25th St NW	Washington	DC	20037	202-452-4200	452-7504
TF: 800-372-1033 ■ Web: www.bna.com					
Medicare Compliance Alert 11300 Rockville Pike Suite 1100	Rockville	MD	20852	301-287-2700	816-8945
TF: 800-929-4824 ■ Web: www.compliancealert.net					
Mergers & Acquisitions Law Report 1231 25th St NW	Washington	DC	20037	202-452-4200	452-7504
TF: 800-372-1033 ■ Web: www.bna.com					
Money & Politics Report 1231 25th St NW	Washington	DC	20037	202-452-4200	452-7504
TF: 800-372-1033 ■ Web: www.bna.com					
Motor Vehicle Regulation PO Box 7376	Alexandria	VA	22307	703-768-9600	768-9690
Web: statecapitals.com/motorreg.html					
Municipal Litigation Reporter 590 Dutch Valley Rd NE	Atlanta	GA	30324	404-881-1141	881-0074
TF: 800-926-7926 ■ Web: www.straffordpub.com					
National Intelligence Report 3 Park Ave 30th Fl	New York	NY	10016	212-244-0360	564-0465
TF: 800-401-5937 ■ Web: www.ioma.com/issues/NIR					
Native American Report 8737 Colesville Rd Suite 1100	Silver Spring	MD	20910	301-587-6300	
TF: 800-274-6737 ■ Web: www.bpinews.com					
New York Real Estate Law Reporter 1617 JFK Blvd Suite 1750	Philadelphia	PA	19103	215-557-2311	
TF: 800-999-1916 ■ Web: www.lawcatalog.com					
Non-Profit Legal & Tax Letter PO Box 368	Lovettsville	VA	20180	540-822-3928	822-3945
Web: www.taxexemptresources.com					
Outlook from the State Capitals PO Box 7376	Alexandria	VA	22307	703-768-9600	768-9690
Web: statecapitals.com/theoutlook.html					
Patent Strategy & Management 1617 JFK Blvd Suite 1750	Philadelphia	PA	19103	215-557-2300	557-2301
TF: 800-999-1916 ■ Web: www.lawjournalnewsletters.com					
Patent Trademark & Copyright Law Daily 1231 25th St NW	Washington	DC	20037	202-452-4200	452-7504
TF: 800-372-1033 ■ Web: www.bna.com					
Pharmaceutical Law & Industry Report 1231 25th St NW	Washington	DC	20037	202-452-4200	452-7504
TF: 800-372-1033 ■ Web: www.bna.com					
Postal World 11300 Rockville Pike Suite 1100	Rockville	MD	20852	301-287-2700	816-8945
TF: 800-929-4824 ■ Web: www.ucg.com					
Privacy & Security Law Report 1231 25th St NW	Washington	DC	20037	202-452-4200	452-7504
TF: 800-372-1033 ■ Web: www.bna.com					
Private Security Case Law Reporter 590 Dutch Valley Rd NE	Atlanta	GA	30324	404-881-1141	881-0074
TF: 800-926-7926 ■ Web: www.straffordpub.com/products/psc					
Product Liability Law & Strategy 1617 JFK Blvd Suite 1750	Philadelphia	PA	19103	215-557-2300	557-2301
TF: 800-722-7670 ■ Web: www.lawcatalog.com					
Product Safety & Liability Report 1231 25th St W	Washington	DC	20037	202-452-4200	452-7504
TF: 800-372-1033 ■ Web: www.bna.com					
Public Safety & Justice Policies PO Box 7376	Alexandria	VA	22307	703-768-9600	768-9690
TF: 800-876-2545 ■ Web: www.statecapitals.com/publicsafety.html					
Real Estate Law Report 610 Opperman Dr	Eagan	MN	55123	651-687-7000	741-1414*
*Fax Area Code: 800 ■ *Fax: Sales ■ TF Cust Svc: 800-328-4880 ■ Web: west.thomson.com/product/14939166/product.asp					
Roll Call 50 F St NW Suite 700	Washington	DC	20001	202-824-6800	824-0475
Web: www.rollcall.com					
Same Sex Partnership Law Report 1617 JFK Blvd Suite 1750	Philadelphia	PA	19103	215-557-2300	557-2304
TF: 800-999-1916 ■ Web: www.lawjournalnewsletters.com					
Securities Law Daily 1231 25th St NW	Washington	DC	20037	202-452-4200	452-7504
TF: 800-372-1033 ■ Web: www.bna.com					
Securities Regulation & Law Report 1231 25th St NW	Washington	DC	20037	202-452-4200	452-7504
TF: 800-372-1033 ■ Web: www.bna.com					
Silica Legal News Report 1617 JFK Blvd Suite 1750	Philadelphia	PA	19103	215-557-2300	557-2301
TF: 800-999-1916 ■ Web: www.lawjournalnewsletters.com					
Taxation & Revenue Policies PO Box 7376	Alexandria	VA	22307	703-768-9600	768-9690
TF: 800-876-2545 ■ Web: www.statecapitals.com/taxandrev.html					
Taxes-Property PO Box 7376	Alexandria	VA	22307	703-768-9600	768-9690
Web: www.statecapitals.com/taxprop.html					

				Phone	Fax
Washington International Business Report 818 Connecticut Ave NW 12th Fl	Washington	DC	20006	202-872-8181	872-8696
Web: www.ibgc.com					
Workplace Law Report 1231 25th St NW	Washington	DC	20037	202-452-4200	452-7504
TF: 800-372-1033 ■ Web: www.bna.com					
World Securities Law Report 1231 25th St NW	Washington	DC	20037	202-452-4200	452-7504
TF: 800-372-1033 ■ Web: www.bna.com					

534-8 Health & Social Issues Newsletters

				Phone	Fax
Affordable Housing Update 8204 Fenton St	Silver Spring	MD	20910	301-558-6385	588-6385
TF: 800-666-6380 ■ Web: www.cdpublications.com					
Aging News Alert 8204 Fenton St	Silver Spring	MD	20910	301-588-6385	588-6385
TF: 800-666-6380 ■ Web: www.cdpublications.com/pubs/					
AICR Newsletter 1759 R St NW	Washington	DC	20009	202-328-7744	328-7226
TF: 800-843-8114 ■ Web: www.aicr.org					
AIDS Policy & Law 360 Hiatt Dr	Palm Beach Gardens	FL	33418	561-622-6520	622-2423
TF: 800-621-5463 ■ Web: www.lrp.com					
Alcoholism & Drug Abuse Weekly 1105 N Market St	Wilmington	DE	19801	302-427-3924	
Web: www3.interscience.wiley.com					
Alternatives 7811 Montrose Rd	Potomac	MD	20854	301-340-2100	424-5059
TF: 800-861-5967 ■ Web: www.drdavidwilliams.com					
American Parkinson's Disease Assn 135 Parkinson Ave	Staten Island	NY	10305	718-981-8001	981-4399
TF: 800-223-2732 ■ Web: www.apdaparkinson.org					
Americans with Disabilities Newsletter 610 Opperman Dr	Eagan	MN	55123	651-687-7000	687-7849*
*Fax: Mktg					
Amnesty Action 510 Plaza 16th Fl	New York	NY	10001	212-807-8400	627-1451
TF: 800-266-3789 ■ Web: www.amnestyusa.org					
APCO Bulletin 351 N Williamson Blvd	Daytona Beach	FL	32114	386-322-2500	322-2501
TF: 888-272-6911 ■ Web: www.apcointl.org/services/bulletin/					
Arthritis Advisor 800 Connecticut Ave 4 West	Norwalk	CT	06854	203-857-3100	857-3103
TF: 800-424-7887 ■ Web: www.arthritis-advisor.com					
Bottom Line/Health 281 Tresser Blvd	Stamford	CT	06901	203-973-5900	967-3621
TF Cust Svc: 800-289-0409 ■ Web: www.boardroom.com					
Cancer Economics PO Box 9905	Washington	DC	20016	202-362-1809	318-4030
TF: 800-513-7042 ■ Web: www.cancerletter.com					
Cancer Letter PO Box 9905	Washington	DC	20016	202-362-1809	318-4030
TF: 800-513-7042 ■ Web: www.cancerletter.com					
Child Protection Law Report 8737 Colesville Rd Suite 1000	Silver Spring	MD	20910	301-587-6300	589-8493*
*Fax: Mktg ■ TF: 800-274-6737 ■ Web: www.bpinews.com/hr/pages/cpr.cfm					
Children & Youth Funding Report 8204 Fenton St	Silver Spring	MD	20910	301-588-6385	588-6385
TF: 800-666-6380 ■ Web: www.cdpublications.com/pubs					
Clinical Cancer Letter PO Box 9905	Washington	DC	20016	202-362-1809	318-4030
TF: 800-513-7042					
Congressional Quarterly HealthBeat 1255 22nd St NW	Washington	DC	20037	202-419-8500	380-3810*
*Fax Area Code: 800 ■ TF: 800-432-2250 ■ Web: www.cq.com					
Consumer Reports On Health 101 Truman Ave	Yonkers	NY	10703	914-378-2000	378-2900
TF: 800-234-1645 ■ Web: www.consumerreports.org/main/crh/home.jsp					
CTD News 747 Dresher Rd Suite 500	Horsham	PA	19044	215-784-0860	784-9639
TF: 800-341-7874 ■ Web: www.ctdnews.com					
Dairy Council Digest 10255 W Higgins Rd Suite 900	Rosemont	IL	60018	847-803-2000	803-2077
TF Cust Svc: 800-426-8271 ■ Web: www.nationaldairycouncil.org/NationalDairyCouncil/Health/Digest					
Disability Funding Week 8204 Fenton St	Silver Spring	MD	20910	301-588-6385	588-6385
TF: 800-666-6380 ■ Web: www.cdpublications.com/pubs					
Drug Detection Report 8737 Colesville Rd Suite 1000	Silver Spring	MD	20910	301-587-6300	589-8493*
*Fax: Mktg ■ TF: 800-274-6737 ■ Web: www.bpinews.com/hr/pages/ddr.cfm					
Environment of Care Leader 11300 Rockville Pike Suite 1100	Rockville	MD	20852	301-287-2700	816-8945
TF: 800-929-4824					
Family Relations PO Box 7376	Alexandria	VA	22307	703-768-9600	768-9690
Web: statecapitals.com/familyrelations.html					
Focus on Healthy Aging 800 Connecticut Ave 4 West	Norwalk	CT	06854	203-857-3100	857-3103
TF: 800-424-7887 ■ Web: www.focusonhealthyaging.com					
Food & Fitness Advisor 800 Connecticut Ave	Norwalk	CT	06854	203-857-3100	857-3103
TF: 800-424-7887 ■ Web: www.foodandfitnessadvisor.com/weill.html					
Harvard Health Letter 1 Atlantic St Suite 604	Stamford	CT	06901	203-975-8854	975-9901
Web: www.health.harvard.edu/About_Harvard_Health_Publications.htm					
Harvard Heart Letter 1 Atlantic St Suite 604	Stamford	CT	06901	203-975-8854	975-9901
Web: www.health.harvard.edu					
Harvard Men's Health Watch 1 Atlantic St Suite 604	Stamford	CT	06901	203-975-8854	975-9901
Web: www.health.harvard.edu					
Harvard Mental Health Letter 1 Atlantic St Suite 604	Stamford	CT	06901	203-975-8854	975-9901
Web: www.health.harvard.edu					
Harvard Women's Health Watch 1 Atlantic St Suite 604	Stamford	CT	06901	203-975-8854	975-9901
Web: www.health.harvard.edu					
Health Care Daily Report 1231 25th St NW	Washington	DC	20037	202-452-4200	452-7504
TF: 800-372-1033 ■ Web: www.bna.com					
Health Care Policy Report 1231 25th St NW	Washington	DC	20037	202-452-4200	452-7504
TF: 800-372-1033 ■ Web: www.bna.com					
Health & Healing 7811 Montrose Rd	Potomac	MD	20854	301-340-2100	424-5059
TF: 800-861-5967 ■ Web: www.drwhitaker.com					
Health Law Week 590 Dutch Valley Rd NE	Atlanta	GA	30324	404-881-1141	881-0074
TF: 800-926-7926 ■ Web: www.straffordpub.com					
Health News 800 Connecticut Ave	Norwalk	CT	06854	203-857-3100	857-3103
TF: 800-424-7887 ■ Web: www.belvoir.com					
Health Plan & Provider Report 1231 25th St NW	Washington	DC	20037	202-452-4200	452-7504
TF: 800-372-1033 ■ Web: www.bna.com					
Healthcare Disparities Report 8204 Fenton St	Silver Spring	MD	20910	301-588-6385	588-6380
TF: 800-666-6380 ■ Web: www.cdpublications.com					
HealthFacts 239 Thompson St	New York	NY	10012	212-674-7105	674-7100
Web: www.medicalconsumers.org					
Healthy Years 800 Connecticut Ave 4 West	Norwalk	CT	06854	203-857-3100	857-3103
TF: 800-424-7887 ■ Web: www.belvoir.com					
Heart Advisor 800 Connecticut Ave 4-West	Norwalk	CT	06854	203-857-3100	857-3103
TF: 800-424-7887 ■ Web: www.heart-advisor.com					
Heartsense 7811 Montrose Rd	Potomac	MD	20854	301-340-2100	340-2561
TF: 800-861-5970 ■ Web: www.drsinatra.com					
Home Care Accreditation Alert 11300 Rockville Pike Suite 1100	Rockville	MD	20852	301-287-2700	816-8945
TF: 800-929-4824					
Home Health Line 11300 Rockville Pike Suite 1100	Rockville	MD	20852	301-287-2700	816-8945
TF: 800-929-4824 ■ Web: www.ucg.com					
International Medical Device Regulatory Monitor 9700 Philadelphia Ct	Lanham	MD	20706	301-731-5200	731-5203
TF: 800-774-6809 ■ Web: www.omniprint.net					
Johns Hopkins Medical Letter Health After 50 632 Broadway 11th Fl	New York	NY	10012	212-651-8500	505-5462
Web: www.johnshopkinshealthalerts.com/health_after_50					
Lark Letter 7811 Montrose Rd	Potomac	MD	20854	301-340-2100	424-5059
TF: 800-861-5967 ■ Web: www.drlark.com					
Mayo Clinic Health Letter 200 1st St NW	Rochester	MN	55905	507-284-2094	284-0252
TF: 800-707-7040 ■ Web: bookstore.mayoclinic.com					
Mayo Clinic Women's Healthsource 200 1st St SW	Rochester	MN	55905	507-284-2094	284-0252
TF: 800-707-7040 ■ Web: bookstore.mayoclinic.com					
Medicare Compliance Alert 11300 Rockville Pike Suite 1100	Rockville	MD	20852	301-287-2700	816-8945
TF: 800-929-4824 ■ Web: www.compliancealert.net					
Men's Health Advisor 800 Connecticut Ave 4 West	Norwalk	CT	06854	203-857-3100	857-3103
TF: 800-424-7887 ■ Web: www.menshealthadvisor.com					
Mental Health Law Reporter 8737 Colesville Rd Suite 1000	Silver Spring	MD	20910	301-587-6300	589-8493*
*Fax: Mktg ■ TF: 800-274-6737 ■ Web: www.bpinews.com/hs/pages/mhl.cfm					
Mental Health Report 8737 Colesville Rd Suite 1000	Silver Spring	MD	20910	301-587-6300	589-8493*
*Fax: Mktg ■ TF: 800-274-6737 ■ Web: www.bpinews.com/hs/pages/mhr.cfm					
Mental Health Weekly 208 Governor St	Providence	RI	02906	401-764-0658	934-1344
Web: www.wiley.com/WileyCDA/WileyTitle/productCd-MHW.html					
Mind Mood & Memory 800 Connecticut Ave 4 West	Norwalk	CT	06854	203-857-3100	857-3103
TF: 800-424-7887 ■ Web: www.belvoir.com					
Naturally Well Today 7811 Montrose Rd	Potomac	MD	20854	301-340-2100	424-5059
TF: 800-861-5967 ■ Web: www.drmarcuslaux.com					
Nutrition Action 1875 Connecticut Way NW Suite 300	Washington	DC	20009	202-332-9110	265-4954
Web: www.cspinet.org/nah					
Nutrition Research 111 River St	Hoboken	NJ	07030	201-748-6000	
TF: 800-825-7550					
OSHA Up-to-Date 1121 Spring Lake Dr	Itasca	IL	60143	630-285-1121	285-1315
TF Cust Svc: 800-621-7619 ■ Web: www.nsc.org					
Physician Office Lab News 11300 Rockville Pike Suite 1100	Rockville	MD	20852	301-287-2700	816-8945
TF: 800-929-4824 ■ Web: www.ucg.com					
Physician Practice Coder 11300 Rockville Pike Suite 1100	Rockville	MD	20852	301-287-2700	816-8945
TF: 800-929-4824					
Public Assistance & Welfare Trends PO Box 7376	Alexandria	VA	22307	703-768-9600	768-9690
Web: statecapitals.com/publicassist.html					
Public Health PO Box 7376	Alexandria	VA	22307	703-768-9600	768-9690
Web: statecapitals.com/publichealth.html					
Report on Disability Programs 8737 Colesville Rd Suite 1000	Silver Spring	MD	20910	301-587-6300	589-8493*
*Fax: Mktg ■ TF: 800-274-6737 ■ Web: www.bpinews.com/hr/pages/rdp.cfm					
Simple Living 7811 Montrose Rd	Potomac	MD	20854	301-340-2100	424-5059
TF: 800-861-5967 ■ Web: www.simpleliving.com					
Substance Abuse Funding Week 8204 Fenton St	Silver Spring	MD	20910	301-588-6385	588-6385
TF: 800-666-6380 ■ Web: www.cdpublications.com/pubs					
The Bell 2001 N. Beauregard St 12th Fl	Alexandria	VA	22311	703-684-7722	684-5968
TF: 800-969-6642 ■ Web: www.nmha.org/newsroom/bell/index.cfm					
Tufts Health & Nutrition Letter 196 Boston Ave Suite 2100	Medford	MA	02155	617-627-5632	627-3081
Web: www.healthletter.tufts.edu					
UC Berkeley Wellness Letter 632 Broadway 11th Fl	New York	NY	10012	212-505-2255	505-5462
Web: www.berkeleywellness.com					
Wellness Advisor 7811 Montrose Rd	Potomac	MD	20854	301-340-2100	424-5059
TF: 800-861-5967 ■ Web: www.holfordhealth.com					
Women's Health Advisor 800 Connecticut Ave 4 West	Norwalk	CT	06854	203-857-3100	857-3103
TF: 800-424-7887 ■ Web: www.womens-health-advisor.com					

534-9 Investment Newsletters

				Phone	Fax
All-Star Fund Trader 60 5th Ave	New York	NY	10011	212-620-2200	206-5126
TF: 800-888-9896 ■ Web: www.newsletters.forbes.com					
Bert Dohmen's Wellington Letter 1100 Glendon Ave Suite 1130	Los Angeles	CA	90024	310-476-6933	440-2919
Web: dohmencapital.com					
Blue Chip Economic Indicators 3663 Madison Ave	Kansas City	MO	64111	816-931-0131	
TF Cust Svc: 800-234-1660 ■ Web: www.aspenpublishers.com					
Blue Chip Financial Forecasts 3663 Madison Ave	Kansas City	MO	64111	816-931-0131	
TF Cust Svc: 800-234-1660 ■ Web: www.aspenpublishers.com					
Broadcast Investor 1 Lower Ragsdale Dr Bldg 1 Suite 130	Monterey	CA	93940	831-624-1536	625-3225
Web: www.kagan.com					
Cable TV Investor 1 Lower Ragsdale Dr Bldg 1 Suite 130	Monterey	CA	93940	831-624-1536	625-3225
Web: www.kagan.com					
Cabot Market Letter 176 North St PO Box 2049	Salem	MA	01970	978-745-5532	745-1283
TF Orders: 800-777-2658 ■ Web: www.cabot.net					
Chartist 5122 Katella Ave Suite 200	Los Alamitos	CA	90720	562-596-2385	596-1280
TF: 800-942-4278 ■ Web: www.thechartist.com					
Credit Investment News 225 Park Ave S 7th Fl	New York	NY	10003	212-224-3800	224-3491
Dag Peter Portfolio Strategy & Management 65 Lake Front Dr	Akron	OH	44319	330-644-2782	
Web: www.peterdag.com					
Derivatives Week 225 Park Ave S 8th Fl	New York	NY	10003	212-224-3800	224-3491
Web: www.derivativesweek.com					
Dow Theory Forecasts 7412 Calumet Ave	Hammond	IN	46324	219-931-6480	931-6487
Web: www.dowtheory.com					
Dow Theory Letters PO Box 1759	La Jolla	CA	92038	858-454-0481	454-1265
Web: www.dowtheoryletters.com					
Drip Investor 7412 Calumet Ave	Hammond	IN	46324	219-931-6480	931-6487
Web: www.dripinvestor.com					
Elliott Wave Theorist PO Box 1618	Gainesville	GA	30503	770-536-0309	536-2514
TF: 800-336-1618 ■ Web: www.elliottwave.com					
Emerging Markets Week 225 Park Ave S 7th Fl	New York	NY	10003	212-224-3800	224-3491
Web: www.emergingmarketsweek.com					
Fabian's Investment Resources 2100 Main St Suite 300	Huntington Beach	CA	92648	800-950-8765	536-7066*
*Fax Area Code: 714 ■ TF: 800-950-8765 ■ Web: www.fabian.com					
Future Market Service 330 S Wells St Suite 612	Chicago	IL	60606	312-554-8456	939-4135
TF: 800-621-5271 ■ Web: www.crbtrader.com					
Global Market Perspective PO Box 1618	Gainesville	GA	30503	770-536-0309	536-2514
TF: 800-336-1618 ■ Web: www.elliottwave.com/products/gmp					
Gold Mining Stock Report PO Box 1217	Lafayette	CA	94549	925-284-1165	284-1294
Web: www.goldminingstockreport.com					
Gold Newsletter 2400 Jefferson Hwy Suite 600	Jefferson	LA	70121	504-837-3033	837-4885
TF: 800-877-8847 ■ Web: www.goldnewsletter.com					
Granville Market Letter PO Box 413006	Kansas City	MO	64141	816-474-5353	421-3897
TF: 800-876-5388 ■ Web: www.granvilleletter.com					
Growth Fund Guide PO Box 6600	Rapid City	SD	57709	605-341-1971	341-7260
TF: 800-621-8322					
Growth Stock Outlook 4405 East-West Hwy Suite 305	Bethesda	MD	20814	301-654-5205	986-0722
TF: 800-742-5476					
IA Week 11300 Rockville Pike Suite 1100	Rockville	MD	20852	301-287-2700	816-8945
Web: www.iaweek.com/iajsp/index.jsp					
Investment Quality Trends 7440 Girard Ave Suite 4	La Jolla	CA	92037	858-459-3818	459-3819
Web: www.iqtrends.com					
Investor Relations 1 Phoenix Mill Ln	Peterborough	NH	03458	603-924-0900	924-4034
TF: 800-531-0007 ■ Web: www.irzone.com/irn					
Investors Intelligence 30 Church St	New Rochelle	NY	10801	914-632-0422	632-0335
Web: www.investorsintelligence.com					
John Dessauer's Investor's World 9420 Key West Ave	Rockville	MD	20850	301-279-4200	
TF: 800-219-8592 ■ Web: www.dessauerinvestorsworld.com					
Louis Rukeyser's Mutual Funds 1750 Old Meadow Rd Suite 300	McLean	VA	22102	703-905-8000	905-8130
TF: 800-892-9702 ■ Web: www.rukeyser.com					
Motion Picture Investor 1 Lower Ragsdale Dr Bldg 1 Suite 130	Monterey	CA	93940	831-624-1536	625-3225
Web: www.kagan.com					

Investment Newsletters (Cont'd)

Phone Fax

Mutual Fund Letter 5122 Katella Ave Suite 200 ... Los Alamitos CA 90720 562-596-2385 596-1280
TF: 800-942-4278 ■ *Web:* www.thechartist.com

Option Advisor 5151 Pfeiffer Rd Suite 250 ... Cincinnati OH 45242 513-589-3800 589-3810
TF: 800-448-2080 ■ *Web:* www.schaeffersresearch.com

Personal Finance 1750 Old Meadow Rd Suite 300 ... McLean VA 22102 703-905-8000 905-8100
TF: 800-832-2330 ■ *Web:* www.pfnewsletter.com

Private Asset Management 225 Park Ave S 7th Fl ... New York NY 10003 212-224-3800 224-3491
Web: www.iiwealthmanagement.com

Profitable Investing 9420 Key West Ave ... Rockville MD 20850 301-279-4200
TF: 800-219-8592 ■ *Web:* www.richardband.com

Prudent Speculator 32392 Coast Hwy Suite 260 ... Laguna Beach CA 92651 949-499-3215 499-3218
TF: 800-258-7786 ■ *Web:* www.theprudentspeculator.com

Richard Band's Profitable Investing 9420 Key West Ave ... Rockville MD 20850 301-279-4200
TF: 800-219-8592 ■ *Web:* www.richardband.com

Richard Young's Intelligence Report 7811 Montrose Rd ... Potomac MD 20854 301-340-2100 424-5059
TF: 800-301-8969 ■ *Web:* www.intelligencereport.com

Systems & Forecasts 150 Great Neck Rd Suite 301 ... Great Neck NY 11021 516-829-6444 466-4676
Web: www.systemsandforecasts.com

Timer Digest PO Box 1688 ... Greenwich CT 06836 203-629-3503 629-2175
TF: 800-356-2527 ■ *Web:* www.timerdigest.com

Utility Forecaster 1750 Old Meadow Rd Suite 300 ... McLean VA 22102 703-905-8000 905-8100
TF: 800-832-2330 ■ *Web:* www.utilityforecaster.com

Value Line 600 220 E 42nd St 6th Fl ... New York NY 10017 212-907-1500 818-9670
Web: www.valueline.com

Value Line Convertibles Survey 220 E 42nd St 6th Fl ... New York NY 10017 212-907-1500 818-9670
Web: www.valueline.com

Value Line Investment Survey 220 E 42nd St 6th Fl ... New York NY 10017 212-907-1500 818-9670
Web: www.valueline.com

Value Line Mutual Funds Survey 220 E 42nd St 6th Fl ... New York NY 10017 212-907-1500 818-9670
Web: www.valueline.com

Value Line Options Survey 200 E 42nd St 6th Fl ... New York NY 10017 212-907-1500 818-9670
Web: www.valueline.com

Wall Street Digest 8830 S Tamiami Tr Suite 110 ... Sarasota FL 34238 941-954-5500 364-8447
TF: 800-785-5050 ■ *Web:* www.wallstreetdigest.com

Wall Street Letter 225 Park Ave S 7th Fl ... New York NY 10003 212-224-3300 224-3491
Web: www.wallstreetletter.com

Wireless Telecom Investor
1 Lower Ragsdale Dr Bldg 1 Suite 130 ... Monterey CA 93940 831-624-1536 625-3225
TF: 800-307-2529 ■ *Web:* www.kagan.com

Young's Richard Intelligence Report 7811 Montrose Rd ... Potomac MD 20854 301-340-2100 424-5059
TF: 800-301-8969 ■ *Web:* www.intelligencereport.com

534-10 Marketing & Sales Newsletters

Phone Fax

Book Marketing Update 135 E Plumstead Ave ... Lansdowne PA 19050 610-259-1070 284-3704
TF: 800-989-1400 ■ *Web:* www.bookmarket.com/newsletters.html

Competitive Advantage 1101 King St Suite 110 ... Alexandria VA 22314 703-518-2343 684-2136
TF: 800-722-9221 ■ *Web:* www.briefings.com

Downtown Promotion Reporter 28 W 25th St 8th Fl ... New York NY 10010 212-228-0246 228-0376
TF: 800-232-4317 ■ *Web:* www.downtowndevelopment.com/dpr.php

Educational Marketer 11 Riverbend Dr S PO Box 4234 ... Stamford CT 06907 203-358-9900 358-5824
Web: www.simbanet.com/publications/news_em.htm

eMarketer 75 Broad St 32nd Fl ... New York NY 10004 212-763-6010 763-6020
TF: 800-405-0844 ■ *Web:* www.emarketer.com

Friday Report 224 7th St ... Garden City NY 11530 516-746-6700 294-8141
TF: 800-229-6700

Marketing for Lawyers 345 Park Ave S ... New York NY 10010 212-779-9200 696-1848
TF: 800-888-8300

Marketing Library Services 143 Old Marlton Pike ... Medford NJ 08055 609-654-6266 654-4309
TF: 800-300-9868 ■ *Web:* www.infotoday.com/mls

Overcoming Objections 360 Hiatt Dr ... Palm Beach Gardens FL 33418 561-622-9914 622-2423
TF: 800-621-5463

Sales Management Report 316 N Michigan Ave Suite 300 ... Chicago IL 60601 312-960-4100 960-4105
TF: 800-878-5331

Salesmanship 360 Hiatt Dr ... Palm Beach Gardens FL 33418 561-622-9914 622-2423
TF: 800-621-5463 ■ *Web:* www.dartnellcorp.com

Selling to Seniors 8204 Fenton St ... Silver Spring MD 20910 301-588-6380 588-6385
TF: 800-666-6380 ■ *Web:* www.cdpublications.com/products.php

Successful Closing Techniques 360 Hiatt Dr ... Palm Beach Gardens FL 33418 561-622-9914 622-2423
TF: 800-621-5463

534-11 Media & Communications Newsletters

Phone Fax

Accuracy in Media Report
4455 Connecticut Ave NW Suite 330 ... Washington DC 20008 202-364-4401 364-4098
TF: 800-787-4567 ■ *Web:* www.aim.org

Book Publishing Report 60 Long Ridge Rd Suite 300 ... Stamford CT 06902 203-325-8193 325-8915
Web: www.simbanet.com

Broadband Advertising 1 Lower Ragsdale Dr Bldg 1 Suite 130 ... Monterey CA 93940 831-624-1536 625-3225
TF: 800-307-2529 ■ *Web:* www.kagan.com

Broadband Technology 1 Lower Ragsdale Dr Bldg 1 Suite 130 ... Monterey CA 93940 831-624-1536 625-3225
TF: 800-307-2529 ■ *Web:* www.kagan.com

Broadcast Stats 1 Lower Ragsdale Dr Bldg 1 Suite 130 ... Monterey CA 93940 831-624-1536 625-3225
TF: 800-307-2529

Broadcasters Letter
1400 Independence Ave SW Office of Communications
Whitten Bldg Rm 402-A ... Washington DC 20250 202-720-4623 720-5773
Web: www.usda.gov/agency/oc/bmtc/broad.htm

Capell's Circulation Report 104 W 40th St Suite 1700 ... New York NY 10018 212-370-9700 370-9780
Web: www.djgmarketing.com

Children's Book Insider 901 Columbia Rd ... Fort Collins CO 80525 970-495-0056 493-1810
TF: 800-807-1916 ■ *Web:* www.write4kids.com/aboutcbi.html

Communication Briefings 1101 King St Suite 110 ... Alexandria VA 22314 703-548-3800 684-2136
TF: 800-888-2084 ■ *Web:* www.briefings.com/newsletter.asp?nl=cb

Communication & Technology Insider
316 N Michigan Ave Suite 300 ... Chicago IL 60601 312-960-4140 960-4106
TF: 800-878-5331 ■ *Web:* www.ragan.com

Communications Business Daily 2115 Ward Ct NW ... Washington DC 20037 202-872-9200 293-3435
TF: 800-771-9202 ■ *Web:* www.warren-news.com

Communications Daily 2115 Ward Ct NW ... Washington DC 20037 202-872-9200 293-3435
TF: 800-771-9202 ■ *Web:* www.warren-news.com/cdtrial.htm

Computer Publishing & Advertising Report 60 Longridge Rd ... Stamford CT 06902 203-325-8193 325-8915

DBS Report 1 Lower Ragsdale Dr Bldg 1 Suite 130 ... Monterey CA 93940 831-624-1536 625-3225
TF: 800-307-2529 ■ *Web:* www.kagan.com

Digital Television 1 Lower Ragsdale Dr Bldg 1 Suite 130 ... Monterey CA 93940 831-624-1536 625-3225
TF: 800-307-2529 ■ *Web:* www.kagan.com

Editorial Eye 66 Canal Center Plaza Suite 200 ... Alexandria VA 22314 703-683-0683 683-4915
TF: 800-683-8380 ■ *Web:* www.eeicommunications.com/eye

Phone Fax

Entertainment Law & Finance 1617 JFK Blvd Suite 1750 ... Philadelphia PA 19103 215-557-2300 557-2301
TF: 800-999-1916 ■ *Web:* www.lawcatalog.com

First Draft 316 N Michigan Ave Suite 300 ... Chicago IL 60601 312-960-4100 960-4106
TF: 800-878-5331 ■ *Web:* www.ragan.com

Ideas Unlimited for Editors 9700 Philadelphia Ct ... Lanham MD 20706 301-731-5200 731-5203
TF: 800-774-6809

Intellectual Property Strategist 1617 JFK Blvd Suite 1750 ... Philadelphia PA 19103 215-557-2300 557-2301
TF: 800-722-7670 ■ *Web:* www.americanlawyer.com

Jack O'Dwyer's PR Newsletter 271 Madison Ave Suite 600 ... New York NY 10016 212-679-2471 683-2750
Web: www.odwyerpr.com

Kagan Media Money 1 Lower Ragsdale Dr Bldg 1 Suite 130 ... Monterey CA 93940 831-624-1536 625-3225
TF: 800-307-2529 ■ *Web:* www.kagan.com

Media Industry Newsletter 110 William St 11th Fl ... New York NY 10038 212-621-4900 621-4800
Web: www.minonline.com

Media Law Reporter 1231 25th St NW ... Washington DC 20037 202-452-4200 452-7504
TF: 800-372-1033 ■ *Web:* www.bna.com

Media Relations 316 N Michigan Ave Suite 300 ... Chicago IL 60601 312-960-4100 960-4106
TF: 800-878-5331 ■ *Web:* www.ragan.com

Media Sports Business 126 Clock Tower Pl ... Carmel CA 93923 831-624-1536 625-3225
Web: www.kagan.com

O'Dwyer's Jack PR Newsletter 271 Madison Ave Suite 600 ... New York NY 10016 212-679-2471 683-2750
Web: www.odwyerpr.com

Professional Publishing Report 60 Long Ridge Rd Suite 300 ... Stamford CT 06902 203-325-8193 325-8915
Web: www.simbanet.com

Public Broadcasting Report 2115 Ward Ct NW ... Washington DC 20037 202-872-9200 293-3435
Web: www.warren-news.com

Satellite Week 2115 Ward Ct NW ... Washington DC 20037 202-872-9200 293-3435
TF: 800-771-9202 ■ *Web:* www.warren-news.com

Speechwriter's Newsletter 316 N Michigan Ave Suite 300 ... Chicago IL 60601 312-960-4100 960-4106
TF: 800-878-5331 ■ *Web:* www.ragan.com

State Telephone Regulation Report 2115 Ward Ct NW ... Washington DC 20037 202-872-9200 293-3435
TF: 800-771-9202 ■ *Web:* www.warren-news.com

Telecom AM 2115 Ward Ct NW ... Washington DC 20037 202-872-9200 293-3435
TF: 800-771-9202 ■ *Web:* www.warren-news.com

Telecom Manager's Voice Report
11300 Rockville Pike Suite 1100 ... Rockville MD 20852 301-816-8950 816-8945
TF: 800-929-4824 ■ *Web:* www.thevoicereport.com

Telecommunications Report 7201 McKinney Cir ... Frederick MD 21704 301-698-7100 901-9075*
**Fax Area Code:* 800 ■ *TF Cust Svc:* 800-822-6338 ■ *Web:* www.tr.com/newsletters/tri

TR's Last-Mile Telecom Report 7201 McKinney Cir ... Frederick MD 21704 301-698-7100 901-9075*
**Fax Area Code:* 800 ■ *TF:* 800-822-6338 ■ *Web:* www.tr.com/newsletters/lmtr

TV Program Investor 126 Clock Tower Pl ... Carmel CA 93923 831-624-1536 625-3225
Web: www.kagan.com

Wireless Broadband 1 Lower Ragsdale Dr Bldg 1 Suite 130 ... Monterey CA 93940 831-624-1536 625-3225
TF: 800-307-2529 ■ *Web:* www.kagan.com

Wireless Market Stats 1 Lower Ragsdale Dr Bldg 1 Suite 130 ... Monterey CA 93940 831-624-1536 625-3225
TF: 800-307-2529 ■ *Web:* www.kagan.com

Yellow Pages & Directory Report
60 Long Ridge Rd Suite 300 ... Stamford CT 06902 203-325-8193 325-8915
Web: www.simbanet.com

534-12 Science & Technology Newsletters

Phone Fax

Advanced Coatings & Surface Technology
7550 W I-10 Suite 400 ... San Antonio TX 78229 210-348-1000 690-3329*
**Fax Area Code:* 888 ■ *TF:* 877-463-7678 ■
Web: www.mindbranch.com/products/N152-0001.html

Advanced Mfg Technology 7550 W I-10 Suite 400 ... San Antonio TX 78229 210-348-1000 690-3329*
**Fax Area Code:* 888 ■ *TF:* 877-463-7678 ■
Web: www.mindbranch.com/products/N152-0002.html

Defense Daily 1011 Arlington Blvd Suite 131 ... Arlington VA 22209 703-522-5655 522-6448
Web: www.defensedaily.com

Diagnostic Testing & Technology Report 3 Park Ave 30th Fl ... New York NY 10016 212-244-0360 564-0465
TF: 800-401-5937 ■ *Web:* www.ioma.com

Flame Retardancy News 70 NW Canaan Ave ... Norwalk CT 06850 203-853-4266 229-0087
Web: www.bccresearch.com

Food Ingredient News 70 New Canaan Ave ... Norwalk CT 06850 203-853-4266 229-0087
Web: www.bccresearch.com/letters

Fuel Cell Technology News 70 New Canaan Ave ... Norwalk CT 06850 203-853-4266 229-0087
Web: www.bccresearch.com

Futuretech: Emerging Technologies
7550 W I-10 Suite 400 ... San Antonio TX 77229 210-348-1000 690-3329*
**Fax Area Code:* 888 ■ *TF:* 877-463-7678

Genetic Engineering News 140 Huguenot St 3rd Fl ... New Rochelle NY 10801 914-740-2100 740-2101
TF: 800-799-9436 ■ *Web:* www.genengnews.com

Genetic Technology News 7550 W I-10 Suite 400 ... San Antonio TX 78229 210-348-1000 690-3329*
**Fax Area Code:* 888 ■ *TF:* 877-463-7678 ■
Web: www.mindbranch.com/products/N152-0004.html

Geophysical Research Letter 2000 Florida Ave NW ... Washington DC 20009 202-462-6900 328-0566
TF: 800-966-2481 ■ *Web:* www.agu.org/journals/gl/

High Tech Ceramics News 70 New Canaan Ave ... Norwalk CT 06850 203-853-4266 229-0087
Web: www.bccresearch.com

High-Tech Materials 7550 W I-10 Suite 400 ... San Antonio TX 77229 210-348-1000 690-3329*
**Fax Area Code:* 888 ■ *TF:* 877-463-7678 ■
Web: www.mindbranch.com/products/N152-0005.html

In Vivo 10 Hoyt St ... Norwalk CT 06851 203-838-4401 838-3214
Web: www.windhoverinfo.com

Industrial Bioprocessing 7550 W I-10 Suite 400 ... San Antonio TX 78229 210-348-1000 690-3329*
**Fax Area Code:* 888 ■ *TF:* 877-463-7678 ■
Web: www.mindbranch.com/products/N152-0006.html

International Pharmaceutical Regulatory Monitor
9700 Philadelphia Ct ... Lanham MD 20706 301-731-5200 731-5203
TF: 800-345-2611 ■ *Web:* www.pharmaceuticalmonitor.com/index.htm

Medical Materials Update 70 New Canaan Ave ... Norwalk CT 06850 203-853-4266 229-0087
Web: www.bccresearch.com

Membrane & Separation Technology News
70 New Canaan Ave ... Norwalk CT 06850 203-853-4266 229-0087
Web: www.bccresearch.com

Microelectronics Technology Alert 7550 W 1-10 Suite 400 ... San Antonio TX 78229 210-348-1000 610-3329*
**Fax Area Code:* 888 ■ *TF:* 877-463-7678 ■
Web: www.mindbranch.com/products/N152-0015.html

Nanoparticle News 70 New Canaan Ave ... Norwalk CT 06850 203-853-4266 229-0087
Web: www.bccresearch.com

Nanotech Alert 7550 W I-10 Suite 400 ... San Antonio TX 78229 210-348-1000 690-3329*
**Fax Area Code:* 888 ■ *TF:* 877-463-7678 ■
Web: www.mindbranch.com/products/N152-0016.html

Physical Review Letters 1 Research Rd ... Ridge NY 11961 631-591-4000 591-4141
Web: prl.aps.org

Sensor Technology 7550 W I-10 Suite 400 ... San Antonio TX 77229 210-348-1000 690-3329*
**Fax Area Code:* 888 ■ *TF:* 877-463-7678 ■
Web: www.mindbranch.com/products/N152-0012.html

World Food Chemical News 1725 K St NW Suite 506 ... Washington DC 20006 202-887-6320 887-6339
TF: 800-272-7737

534-13 Trade & Industry Newsletters

				Phone	*Fax*
Aviation Daily 1200 G St NW Suite 900	Washington	DC	20005	202-383-2350	383-2438
TF: 800-752-4959 ■ *Web:* www.aviationnow.com/avnow/news/channel_aviationdaily.jsp					
Car Dealer Insider 11300 Rockville Pike Suite 1100	Rockville	MD	20852	301-816-8950	816-8945
TF Cust Svc: 800-929-4824 ■ *Web:* www.dealersedge.com					
Construction Claims Monthly 2272 Airport Rd S	Naples	FL	34112	800-274-6737	508-2592
TF: 800-274-6737 ■ *Web:* www.codinginstitute.com					
Construction Labor Report 1231 25th St NW	Washington	DC	20037	202-452-4200	452-7504
TF: 800-372-1033 ■ *Web:* www.bna.com					
Contractor's Business Management Report 3 Park Ave 30th Fl	New York	NY	10016	212-244-0360	564-0465
Web: www.ioma.com/issues/CBMR					
Cotton's Week 1918 North Pkwy	Memphis	TN	38112	901-274-9030	725-0510
TF: 800-377-9030 ■ *Web:* www.cotton.org/news/cweek/index.cfm					
Cremation Report 11300 Rockville Pike Suite 1100	Rockville	MD	20852	301-816-8950	816-8945
TF: 800-929-4824 ■ *Web:* www.fcsworldwide.com					
Cruise Industry News 441 Lexington Ave Suite 1209	New York	NY	10017	212-986-1025	986-1033
Web: www.cruiseindustrynews.com					
Death Care Business Advisor 360 Hiatt Dr	Palm Beach Gardens	FL	33418	561-622-6520	622-2423
TF: 800-621-5463 ■ *Web:* www.lrp.com					
Diagnostic Imaging Intelligence Report 3 Park Ave 30th Fl	New York	NY	10016	212-244-0360	564-0465
TF: 800-401-5937 ■ *Web:* www.ioma.com					
Doane's Agricultural Report 77 Westport Plaza Suite 250	Saint Louis	MO	63146	314-569-2700	569-1083
TF: 800-535-2342 ■ *Web:* www.doane.com					
Engineering Outlook 1308 W Green St 303 Engineering Hall	Urbana	IL	61801	217-333-1510	244-7705
Web: www.engr.uiuc.edu/communications/outlook					
Food Chemical News 1725 K St NW Suite 506	Washington	DC	20006	202-887-6320	887-6335
TF: 888-272-7737 ■ *Web:* www.foodchemicalnews.com					
Food & Drink Weekly 6862 Elm St Suite 350	McLean	VA	22101	703-734-8787	556-7865
Web: www.sparksco.com					
Funeral Service Insider 11300 Rockville Pike Suite 1100	Rockville	MD	20852	301-287-2700	816-8945
TF: 800-929-4824 ■ *Web:* www.fcsworldwide.com/fsi.html					
Inventory Management Report 3 Park Ave 30th Fl	New York	NY	10016	212-244-0360	564-0465
Kane's Beverage Week 14305 Shoreham Dr	Silver Spring	MD	20905	301-384-1573	879-8803
TF: 800-359-6049					
Kiplinger Agriculture Letter 1729 H St NW	Washington	DC	20006	202-887-6400	778-8976
TF Circ: 800-544-0155 ■ *Web:* www.kiplinger.com					
Managing Exports & Imports 3 Park Ave 30th Fl	New York	NY	10016	212-244-0360	564-0465
TF: 800-401-5937 ■ *Web:* www.ioma.com					
Metals Week 55 Water St	New York	NY	10041	212-438-2000	438-3079*
**Fax:* Edit ■ *TF:* 800-223-6180 ■ *Web:* www.platts.com					
National Farmers Union News 11900 E Cornell Ave	Aurora	CO	80014	303-337-5500	368-1390
TF: 800-347-1961 ■ *Web:* www.nfu.org					
Office World News 301 N Fairfax St	Alexandria	VA	22314	703-549-9040	683-7552
TF: 800-542-6672					
PhotoLetter 1910 35th Ave Pine Lake Farm	Osceola	WI	54020	715-248-3800	248-7394
TF: 800-624-0266 ■ *Web:* www.photosource.com/cart/pl.php					
Pro Farmer 6612 Chancellor Dr Suite 300	Cedar Falls	IA	50613	319-277-1278	277-7982
TF Cust Svc: 800-772-0023 ■ *Web:* www.agweb.com/profarmer.asp					
Service Dealers PO Box 241	Burtonsville	MD	20886	301-384-1573	879-8803
TF: 800-359-6049					
Shopping Centers Today 1221 Ave of the Americas	New York	NY	10020	646-728-3800	589-5555*
**Fax Area Code:* 212 ■ *Web:* www.icsc.org					
Uniform Commercial Code Law Letter PO Box 64526	Saint Paul	MN	55164	651-687-7000	340-9378*
**Fax Area Code:* 800 ■ *TF Cust Svc:* 800-328-4880 ■ *Web:* west.thomson.com					
Union Labor Report 1231 25th St NW	Washington	DC	20037	202-452-4200	452-7504
TF: 800-372-1033 ■ *Web:* www.bna.com					
Urban Transport News 65 E Wacker Pl Suite 400	Chicago	IL	60601	312-782-3900	782-3901
Web: www.highbeam.com					
US Rail News 65 E Wacker Pl Suite 400	Chicago	IL	60601	312-782-3900	782-3901
Web: www.highbeam.com					
Weekly of Business Aviation 1200 G St NW Suite 900	Washington	DC	20005	202-383-2350	383-2438
TF: 800-752-4959 ■ *Web:* www.aviationnow.com/avnow/news/channel_businessweekly.jsp					

535 NEWSPAPERS

SEE ALSO Publishing Companies - Newspaper Publishers p. 2152

535-1 Daily Newspapers - Canada

				Phone	*Fax*
24 Heures 465 McGill St 3rd Fl	Montreal	QC	H2Y4B4	514-373-2424	373-2400
Web: www.montreal.24heures.ca					
24 Hours Vancouver 1070 SE Marine Dr	Vancouver	BC	V5X2V4	604-321-2231	322-3206
Web: www.24hrs.ca					
Brandon Sun 501 Rosser Ave	Brandon	MB	R7A0K4	204-727-2451	727-0385
Web: www.brandonsun.com					
Calgary Herald PO Box 2400 Stn M	Calgary	AB	T2P0W8	403-235-7100	235-7379
Web: www.canada.com/calgary					
Calgary Sun 2615 12th St NE	Calgary	AB	T2E7W9	403-250-4200	250-4180*
**Fax:* Edit ■ *Web:* www.calgarysun.com					
Cape Breton Post 255 George St	Sydney	NS	B1P6K6	902-564-5451	562-7077
Web: www.capebretonpost.com					
Chatham Daily News 45 4th St	Chatham	ON	N7M2G4	519-354-2000	354-9489
Web: www.chathamdailynews.ca					
Chronicle-Herald & Mail-Star 1650 Argyle St PO Box 610	Halifax	NS	B3J2T2	902-426-2811	426-1158
Web: www.herald.ns.ca					
Chronicle-Journal 75 S Cumberland St	Thunder Bay	ON	P7B1A3	807-343-6200	343-9409
Web: www.chroniclejournal.com					
Daily Courier 550 Doyle Ave	Kelowna	BC	V1Y7V1	250-762-4445	762-3866
Daily Gleaner 984 Prospect St W	Fredericton	NB	E3B5A2	506-452-6671	457-6606
Web: www.canadaeast.com					
Daily Miner & News 33 Main St S	Kenora	ON	P9N3X7	807-468-5555	468-4318
Web: www.kenoradailyminerandnews.com					
Daily News 393 Seymour St	Kamloops	BC	V2C6P6	250-372-2331	372-0823
Web: www.kamloopsnews.ca					
Edmonton Journal PO Box 2421	Edmonton	AB	T5J2S6	780-429-5100	429-5500
TF: 800-663-7810 ■ *Web:* www.canada.com/edmontonjournal/					
Edmonton Sun 4990 92nd Ave Suite 250	Edmonton	AB	T6B3A1	780-468-0100	468-0139
Web: www.edmontonsun.com					
Expositor The 53 Dalhousie St	Brantford	ON	N3T5S8	519-756-2020	756-4911
Web: www.brantfordexpositor.ca					
Gazette The 1010 Sainte-Catherine St W Suite 200	Montreal	QC	H3B5L1	514-987-2222	987-2399
TF: 800-361-8478 ■ *Web:* www.canada.com/montrealgazette					
Globe & Mail 444 Front St W	Toronto	ON	M5V2S9	416-585-5000	585-5085
Web: www.theglobeandmail.com					
Guardian The 165 Prince St	Charlottetown	PE	C1A4R7	902-629-6000	566-3808
Web: www.theguardian.pe.ca					
Halifax Daily News 1601 Lower Water St	Halifax	NS	B3J3P6	902-444-4444	422-5667
Web: www.hfxnews.ca					
Intelligencer The 45 Bridge St E	Belleville	ON	K8N1L5	613-962-9171	962-9652
Web: www.intelligencer.ca					
Journal Le Droit PO Box 8860 Stn T 47 rue Clarence Suite 222	Ottawa	ON	K1G3J9	613-562-0111	562-7553
TF: 800-267-6961 ■ *Web:* www.cyberpresse.ca/droit					
Kingston Whig-Standard 6 Cataraqui St	Kingston	ON	K7L4Z7	613-544-5000	530-4118
Web: www.thewhig.com/webapp/sitepages					
La Presse 7 Saint-Jacques St	Montreal	QC	H2Y1K9	514-285-7272	285-4816
Web: www.cyberpresse.ca					
La Tribune 1950 rue Roy	Sherbrooke	QC	J1K2X8	819-564-5450	564-5480
Web: www.cyberpresse.ca/tribune					
La Voix de l'Est 76 rue Dufferin	Granby	QC	J2G9L4	450-375-4555	777-7221
Web: www.cyberpresse.ca/vde					
L'Acadie-Nouvelle 476 St Peter Blvd CP 5536	Caraquet	NB	E1W1B7	506-727-4444	727-7620
Web: www.acadienouvelle.com					
Le Devoir 2050 Bleury St 9th Fl	Montreal	QC	H3A3M9	514-985-3333	985-3360
TF: 800-463-7559 ■ *Web:* www.ledevoir.com					
Le Journal de Montreal 4545 Frontenac St	Montreal	QC	H2H2R7	514-521-4545	521-4416
TF: 800-521-4545 ■ *Web:* www.journalmtl.com/jmtl/jdm_fr/index.htm					
Le Journal de Quebec 450 Bechard St	Quebec	QC	G1M2E9	418-683-1573	688-8181
Le nouvelliste 1920 rue Bellefeuille	Trois-Rivieres	QC	G9A3Y2	819-376-2501	376-0946
Le Quotidien du Saguenay-Lac-Saint-Jean 1051 boul Talbot	Chicoutimi	QC	G7H5C1	418-690-8800	690-8805
Web: www.cyberpresse.ca/quotidien					
Le Soleil 410 Charest Blvd E PO Box 1547	Quebec	QC	G1K7J6	418-686-3233	686-3374
Web: www.cyberpresse.ca					
Lethbridge Herald 504 7th St S	Lethbridge	AB	T1J2H1	403-328-4411	328-4536
Web: www.lethbridgeherald.com					
London Free Press 369 York St	London	ON	N6A4G1	519-679-1111	667-4528
Web: www.lfpress.com					
National Post 1450 Don Mills Rd Suite 300	Toronto	ON	M3B3R5	416-383-2300	442-2212
Web: www.nationalpost.com					
Northern News 8 Duncan Ave PO Box 1030	Kirkland Lake	ON	P2N3L4	705-567-5321	567-5377
Web: www.northernnews.ca					
Nugget The 259 Worthington St W	North Bay	ON	P1B3B5	705-472-3200	472-5128
Web: www.nugget.ca					
Observer The 140 S Front St	Sarnia	ON	N7T7M8	519-344-3641	332-2951
Web: www.theobserver.ca					
Ottawa Citizen 1101 Baxter Rd PO Box 5020	Ottawa	ON	K2C3M4	613-829-9100	726-1198*
**Fax:* News Rm ■ *TF:* 800-267-6100 ■ *Web:* www.canada.com/ottawa/ottawacitizen/					
Ottawa Sun 6 Antares Dr Phase 3	Ottawa	ON	K1G5H7	613-739-7000	739-8041
Web: www.mvmagazine.com					
Peterborough Examiner The 730 The King's Way	Peterborough	ON	K9J8L4	705-745-4641	743-4581
Prince George Citizen 150 Brunswick St	Prince George	BC	V2L2B3	250-562-2441	562-7453
Web: www.princegeorgecitizen.com					
Record The 160 King St E	Kitchener	ON	N2G4E5	519-894-2231	894-3829
Web: www.therecord.com					
Record The 1195 Galt St E	Sherbrooke	QC	J1G1Y7	819-569-6345	569-3945
Web: www.sherbrookerecord.com					
Red Deer Advocate 2950 Bremner Ave	Red Deer	AB	T4R1M9	403-343-2400	341-6560
Web: www.reddeeradvocate.com					
Regina Leader Post 1964 Park St	Regina	SK	S4P3G4	306-781-5211	565-2588
Web: www.leaderpost.com					
Review 4801 Valley Way	Niagara Falls	ON	L2E6T6	905-358-5711	356-0785
Web: www.niagarafallsreview.ca					
Sault Star 145 Old Garden River Rd	Sault Sainte Marie	ON	P6A5M5	705-759-3030	942-8690
Web: www.saultstar.com					
Spectator The 44 Frid St	Hamilton	ON	L8N3G3	905-526-3333	526-1395
TF: 800-263-6902 ■ *Web:* www.thespec.com					
Standard The 17 Queen St	Saint Catharines	ON	L2R5G5	905-684-7251	684-6032
Web: www.stcatharinesstandard.ca					
Standard-Freeholder 44 Pitt St	Cornwall	ON	K6J3P3	613-933-3160	933-7521
Web: www.standard-freeholder.com					
Star Phoenix 204 5th Ave N	Saskatoon	SK	S7K2P1	306-657-6397	657-6437
Web: www.thesp.com					
StarPhoenix 204 5th Ave N	Saskatoon	SK	S7K2P1	306-657-6231	657-6437
Web: www.canada.com/saskatoon/starphoenix					
Sudbury Star 33 MacKenzie St	Sudbury	ON	P3C4Y1	705-674-5271	674-0624
Web: www.thesudburystar.com					
Sun Times 290 9th St E	Owen Sound	ON	N4K1N7	519-376-2250	376-7190
Web: www.owensoundsuntimes.com					
Telegram The PO Box 5970	Saint John's	NL	A1C5X7	709-364-6300	364-3939
Web: www.thetelegram.com					
Telegraph-Journal 210 Crown St PO Box 50	Saint John	NB	E2L3V8	506-632-8888	645-3295
Web: www.canadaeast.com					
Thompson Citizen 141 Commercial Pl	Thompson	MB	R8N1T1	204-677-4534	677-3681
Times Colonist 2621 Douglas St	Victoria	BC	V8T4M2	250-380-5211	380-5353
Web: www.timescolonist.com					
Times-Transcript 939 Main St PO Box 1001	Moncton	NB	E1C8P3	506-859-4900	859-4993
Web: www.canadaeast.com					
Toronto Star 1 Yonge St	Toronto	ON	M5E1E6	416-869-4000	869-4328*
**Fax:* News Rm ■ *Web:* www.thestar.com					
Toronto Sun 333 King St E	Toronto	ON	M5A3X5	416-947-2222	947-2043
Web: www.torontosun.com					
Tribune The 228 E Main St	Welland	ON	L3B5P5	905-732-2411	732-4883
Web: www.wellandtribune.ca					
Vancouver Province 200 Granville St Suite 1	Vancouver	BC	V6C3N3	604-605-2000	605-2720
Web: www.vancouverprovince.com					
Vancouver Sun 200 Granville St Suite 1	Vancouver	BC	V6C3N3	604-605-2000	605-2323*
**Fax:* News Rm ■ *Web:* www.canada.com/vancouver/vancouversun					
Windsor Star 167 Ferry St	Windsor	ON	N9A4M5	519-255-5711	255-5515
Web: www.canada.com/windsor					
Winnipeg Free Press 1355 Mountain Ave	Winnipeg	MB	R2X3B6	204-697-7000	697-7412*
**Fax:* News Rm ■ *Web:* www.winnipegfreepress.com					
Winnipeg Sun 1700 Church Ave	Winnipeg	MB	R2X3A2	204-694-2022	697-0759*
**Fax:* News Rm ■ *Web:* www.winnipegsun.com					
World Journal 2288 Clark Dr	Vancouver	BC	V5N3G8	604-876-1338	876-9191

535-2 Daily Newspapers - US

Listings here are organized by city names within state groupings. Most of the fax numbers given connect directly to the newsroom.

Alabama

				Phone	*Fax*
Anniston Star 4305 McClellan Blvd PO Box 189	Anniston	AL	36202	256-236-1551	241-1991
TF: 888-649-1551 ■ *Web:* www.annistonstar.com					
Birmingham News 2201 4th Ave N	Birmingham	AL	35203	205-325-2222	325-3282
TF: 800-283-4015 ■ *Web:* www.bhamnews.com					
Decatur Daily 201 1st Ave SE	Decatur	AL	35601	256-353-4612	340-2392
TF: 888-353-4612 ■ *Web:* www.decaturdaily.com					
Dothan Eagle PO Box 1968	Dothan	AL	36302	334-792-3141	712-7979
TF: 800-811-1771 ■ *Web:* www.dothaneagle.com					
Times Daily PO Box 797	Florence	AL	35631	256-766-3434	740-4717
Web: www.timesdaily.com					

Daily Newspapers - US (Cont'd)

Alabama (Cont'd)

Phone Fax

Gadsden Times 401 Locust St .... Gadsden AL 35901 256-549-2000 549-2105
TF: 800-762-2464 ■ *Web:* www.gadsdentimes.com
Huntsville Times 2317 S Memorial Pkwy .... Huntsville AL 35801 256-532-4000 532-4420
TF: 800-239-5271 ■ *Web:* www.htimes.com
Mobile Register 401 N Water St .... Mobile AL 36602 251-219-5400 219-5799
TF: 800-239-1340 ■ *Web:* www.mobileregister.com
Montgomery Advertiser 425 Molton St .... Montgomery AL 36104 334-262-1611 261-1521
TF: 800-488-3579 ■ *Web:* www.montgomeryadvertiser.com
Daily Sentinel 701 Veterans Dr .... Scottsboro AL 35768 256-259-1020 259-2709
Web: www.thedailysentinel.com
Messenger The PO Box 727 .... Troy AL 36081 334-566-4270 566-4281
Web: www.troymessenger.com
Tuscaloosa News 315 28th Ave .... Tuscaloosa AL 35401 205-345-0505 722-0187
TF: 800-888-8639 ■ *Web:* www.tuscaloosanews.com

Alaska

Phone Fax

Anchorage Daily News 1001 Northway Dr .... Anchorage AK 99508 907-257-4200 258-2157*
**Fax:* Edit ■ *Web:* www.adn.com
Fairbanks Daily News Miner 200 N Cushman St .... Fairbanks AK 99707 907-456-6661 452-7917
Web: www.news-miner.com
Juneau Empire 3100 Channel Dr .... Juneau AK 99801 907-586-3740 586-9097
Web: www.juneauempire.com

Arizona

Phone Fax

Bisbee Daily Review 12 Main St PO Box 127 .... Bisbee AZ 85603 520-432-2231 432-2356
Arizona Daily Sun 1751 Thompson St .... Flagstaff AZ 86001 928-774-4545 774-4790
Web: www.azdailysun.com
East Valley Tribune 120 W 1st Ave .... Mesa AZ 85210 480-898-6500 898-6362
TF: 888-887-4286 ■ *Web:* www.eastvalleytribune.com
Arizona Republic 200 E Van Buren St .... Phoenix AZ 85004 602-444-8000 444-8044*
**Fax:* News Rm ■ *TF:* 800-331-9303 ■ *Web:* www.azcentral.com/arizonarepublic
Daily Courier 1958 Commerce Ctr Cir .... Prescott AZ 86301 928-445-3333 445-2062
TF: 888-349-3436 ■ *Web:* www.communitypapers.com/dailycourier
Scottsdale Tribune 6991 Camelback Rd Suite A110 .... Scottsdale AZ 85251 480-970-2330 970-2360
Web: www.eastvalleytribune.com
Daily News-Sun 10102 Santa Fe Dr .... Sun City AZ 85351 623-977-8351 876-3698
Web: www.dailynews-sun.com
Arizona Daily Star 4850 S Park Ave .... Tucson AZ 85714 520-573-4220 573-4107
TF: 800-695-4111 ■ *Web:* www.azstarnet.com
Tucson Citizen 4850 S Park Ave .... Tucson AZ 85714 520-573-4561 573-4569
TF: 800-695-4492 ■ *Web:* www.tucsoncitizen.com
Yuma Daily Sun 2055 Arizona Ave .... Yuma AZ 85364 928-783-3333 539-6807
TF: 800-995-9862 ■ *Web:* www.yumasun.com

Arkansas

Phone Fax

Jacksonville Patriot 903 S Pine St PO Box 1058 .... Cabot AR 72023 501-982-6506 843-6447
Web: www.jacksonvillepatriot.com
Times Record 3600 Wheeler Ave .... Fort Smith AR 72901 479-785-7700 784-0413
TF: 888-274-4051 ■ *Web:* www.swtimes.com
Sentinel-Record 300 Spring St .... Hot Springs National Park AR 71901 501-623-7711 623-8465
Web: www.hotsr.com
Jonesboro Sun 518 Carson St .... Jonesboro AR 72401 870-935-5525 935-5823
TF: 800-237-5341 ■ *Web:* www.jonesborosun.com
Arkansas Democrat-Gazette 121 E Capital St .... Little Rock AR 72203 501-378-3400 372-4765
TF Cust Svc: 800-482-1121 ■ *Web:* www.arkansasonline.com
Newport Daily Independent PO Box 1750 .... Newport AR 72112 870-523-5855 523-6540
Web: www.newportindependent.com
Pine Bluff Commercial 300 S Beech St .... Pine Bluff AR 71601 870-534-3400 534-0113
Web: www.pbcommercial.com
Morning News of Northwest Arkansas 2560 N Lowell Rd .... Springdale AR 72764 479-751-6200 872-5055
TF: 888-692-1222 ■ *Web:* www.nwaonline.com

California

Phone Fax

China Daily Press 2121 W Mission Rd .... Alhambra CA 91803 626-281-8500 281-7900
Bakersfield Californian 1707 Eye St .... Bakersfield CA 93302 661-395-7500 395-7519*
**Fax:* Edit ■ *Web:* www.bakersfield.com
Record-Gazette 218 N Murray St .... Banning CA 92220 951-849-4586 849-2437
Web: www.recordgazette.net
El Mexicano 4045 Bonita Rd Suite 209 .... Bonita CA 91902 619-267-6010 267-5965
Ventura County Star 550 Camarillo Center Dr .... Camarillo CA 93010 805-437-0000 482-6167
TF: 800-221-7827 ■ *Web:* www.venturacountystar.com
Chico Enterprise Record 400 E Park Ave PO Box 9 .... Chico CA 95927 530-891-1234 342-3617
TF: 800-827-1421 ■ *Web:* www.chicoer.com
Diario San Diego 236 F St Suite A1 .... Chula Vista CA 91910 619-409-1777 409-1771*
**Fax:* News Rm
Daily Pilot 1375 Sunflower Ave .... Costa Mesa CA 92626 714-966-4600 966-4679
Web: www.dailypilot.com
Los Angeles Times Orange County 1375 Sunflower Ave .... Costa Mesa CA 92626 714-966-5600 966-7711
TF: 800-528-4637
Sam Ramon Valley Times 524 Hartz Ave .... Danville CA 94526 925-743-2202 837-4334
Web: www.contracostatimes
Davis Enterprise 315 G St .... Davis CA 95616 530-756-0800 756-6707
Web: www.davisenterprise.com
Imperial Valley Press 205 N 8th St .... El Centro CA 92243 760-337-3400 353-3003
Web: www.ivpressonline.com
North County Times 207 E Pennsylvania Ave .... Escondido CA 92025 760-745-6611 745-3769
TF News Rm: 800-200-0704 ■ *Web:* www.nctimes.com
Times-Standard PO Box 3580 .... Eureka CA 95502 707-442-1711 441-0501
Web: www.times-standard.com
Daily Republic 1250 Texas St .... Fairfield CA 94533 707-425-4646 425-5924
Web: local.dailyrepublic.net
Argus The 39797 Paseo Padre Pkwy .... Fremont CA 94538 510-661-2600 353-7029
TF: 800-595-9595 ■ *Web:* www.insidebayarea.com/argus
Fresno Bee 1626 'E' St .... Fresno CA 93786 559-441-6111 441-6436
TF: 800-877-7300 ■ *Web:* www.fresnobee.com
Asbarez Armenian Daily 419 W Colorado St .... Glendale CA 91204 818-500-9363 956-3230
Web: www.asbarez.com
Union The 464 Sutton Way .... Grass Valley CA 95945 530-273-9561 477-4292
Web: www.theunion.com

Phone Fax

Sentinel The 300 W 6th St .... Hanford CA 93230 559-582-0471 587-1876
TF: 800-582-0471 ■ *Web:* www.hanfordsentinel.com
Daily Review 22533 Foothill Blvd .... Hayward CA 94541 510-783-6111 293-2490
TF: 800-595-9595 ■ *Web:* www.insidebayarea.com/review
Lodi News-Sentinel 125 N Church St .... Lodi CA 95240 209-369-2761 369-6706
Web: www.lodinews.com
Press-Telegram 604 Pine Ave .... Long Beach CA 90844 562-435-1161 437-7892
Web: www.presstelegram.com
Daily Commerce 915 E 1st St .... Los Angeles CA 90012 213-229-5300 229-5481
TF: 800-788-7840
Hoy 207 S Broadway 6th Fl .... Los Angeles CA 90012 213-237-3001 237-4406
Web: www.hoyinternet.com
Investor's Business Daily 12655 Beatrice St .... Los Angeles CA 90066 310-448-6000 577-7303*
**Fax:* Cust Svc ■ *TF:* 800-831-2525 ■ *Web:* www.investors.com
La Opinion 700 S Flower St Suite 3000 .... Los Angeles CA 90017 213-622-8332 896-2171
Web: www.laopinion.com
Los Angeles Times 202 W 1st St .... Los Angeles CA 90012 213-237-5000 237-4712
TF: 800-528-4637 ■ *Web:* www.latimes.com
Appeal-Democrat 1530 Ellis Lake Dr PO Box 431 .... Marysville CA 95901 530-741-2345 741-0140*
**Fax:* News Rm ■ *TF:* 800-831-2345 ■ *Web:* www.appeal-democrat.com
Merced Sun-Star PO Box 739 .... Merced CA 95341 209-722-1511 388-2460
Web: www.mercedsun-star.com
Modesto Bee 1325 H St .... Modesto CA 95354 209-578-2000 578-2207
TF: 800-776-4233 ■ *Web:* www.modbee.com
Monterey County Herald 8 Upper Ragsdale Dr .... Monterey CA 93940 831-372-3311 372-8401
TF: 888-646-4422 ■ *Web:* www.montereyherald.com
Napa Valley Register PO Box 150 .... Napa CA 94559 707-226-3711 224-3963
TF: 800-504-6397 ■ *Web:* www.napanews.com
Marin Independent Journal 150 Alameda Del Prado .... Novato CA 94948 415-883-8600 883-5458
TF: 800-782-5277 ■ *Web:* www.marinij.com
Alameda Times-Star 401 13th St .... Oakland CA 94612 510-208-6333 208-6477
Web: www.timesstar.com
Oakland Tribune 401 13th St .... Oakland CA 94612 510-208-6300 208-6477
Web: www.insidebayarea.com/oaklandtribune
Inland Valley Daily Bulletin 2041 E 4th St .... Ontario CA 91764 909-987-6397 948-9038
Web: www.dailybulletin.com
Desert Sun 750 N Gene Autry Trail .... Palm Springs CA 92263 760-322-8889 778-4654
TF: 800-233-3741 ■ *Web:* www.thedesertsun.com
Antelope Valley Press PO Box 4050 .... Palmdale CA 93590 661-273-2700 947-4870*
**Fax:* Edit ■ *TF:* 888-874-2527 ■ *Web:* www.avpress.com
Palo Alto Daily News 324 High St .... Palo Alto CA 94301 650-327-6397 853-0904
Web: www.paloaltodailynews.com
Pasadena Star-News 911 E Colorado Blvd .... Pasadena CA 91106 626-578-6300 432-5248
TF: 800-788-1200 ■ *Web:* www.pasadenastarnews.com
Tri-Valley Herald 4770 Willow Rd .... Pleasanton CA 94588 925-734-8600 416-4850
Web: www.insidebayarea.com/trivalleyherald
Valley Times PO Box 607 .... Pleasanton CA 94566 925-462-4160 847-2189
Record Searchlight PO Box 492397 .... Redding CA 96049 530-243-2424 225-8236
TF: 800-666-1331 ■ *Web:* www.redding.com
Journal The 4301 Lakeside Dr .... Richmond CA 94806 510-262-2724 262-2776
Press-Enterprise 3512 14th St .... Riverside CA 92501 951-684-1200 368-9023
TF: 800-933-1400 ■ *Web:* www.pe.com
Sacramento Bee 2100 Q St .... Sacramento CA 95816 916-321-1000 321-1109
TF Cust Svc: 800-284-3233 ■ *Web:* www.sacbee.com
Californian The 123 W Alisal St .... Salinas CA 93901 831-424-2221 754-4293
Web: www.californianonline.com
Sun The 2239 Gannett Pkwy .... San Bernardino CA 92407 909-889-9666 885-8741
TF: 800-922-0922 ■ *Web:* www.sbsun.com
San Diego Daily Transcript 2131 3rd Ave .... San Diego CA 92101 619-232-4381 236-8126*
**Fax:* Edit ■ *TF:* 800-697-6397 ■ *Web:* www.sddt.com
San Diego Union-Tribune 350 Camino De La Reina .... San Diego CA 92108 619-299-3131 293-1896
TF: 800-244-6397 ■ *Web:* www.signonsandiego.com
Hokubei Mainichi 1710 Octavia St .... San Francisco CA 94109 415-567-7330 567-1110
Web: www.hokubei.com
Ming Pao Daily News 2585 Third St Suite 100 .... San Francisco CA 94107 415-358-3615 358-3610
Web: www.mingpaosf.com
San Francisco Chronicle 901 Mission St .... San Francisco CA 94103 415-777-1111 896-1107
TF: 866-732-4766 ■ *Web:* www.sfgate.com/chronicle
San Francisco Examiner 450 Mission St .... San Francisco CA 94105 415-359-2600 359-2766
Web: www.examiner.com
Hemet News 474 W Esplanade Ave .... San Jacinto CA 92583 951-763-3400 763-3450
Web: www.pe.com
San Jose Mercury News 750 Ridder Park Dr .... San Jose CA 95190 408-920-5000 288-8060
Web: www.mercurynews.com
Tribune The PO Box 112 .... San Luis Obispo CA 93406 805-781-7800 781-7905
TF: 800-477-8799 ■ *Web:* www.sanluisobispo.com
San Mateo County Times 1080 S Amphlett Blvd .... San Mateo CA 94402 650-348-4321 348-4446
TF: 800-595-9595 ■ *Web:* www.insidebayarea.com/sanmateocountytimes
Orange County Register 625 N Grand Ave .... Santa Ana CA 92701 714-796-7000 796-5052
TF: 877-469-7344 ■ *Web:* www.ocregister.com
Santa Barbara News-Press 715 Anacapa St .... Santa Barbara CA 93101 805-564-5200 966-6258
TF: 800-654-3292 ■ *Web:* www.newspress.com
Santa Cruz Sentinel PO Box 638 .... Santa Cruz CA 95061 831-423-4242 429-9620
Web: www.santacruzsentinel.com
Santa Maria Times PO Box 400 .... Santa Maria CA 93456 805-925-2691 928-5657
Web: www.santamariatimes.com
Press Democrat 427 Mendocino Ave .... Santa Rosa CA 95401 707-546-2020 521-5330
TF: 800-675-5056 ■ *Web:* www.pressdemo.com
Tahoe Daily Tribune 3079 Harrison Ave .... South Lake Tahoe CA 96150 530-541-3880 541-0373
Web: www.tahoedailytribune.com
Record The 530 E Market St .... Stockton CA 95201 209-943-6397 547-8186
TF: 800-606-9741 ■ *Web:* www.recordnet.com
Daily Breeze 5215 Torrance Blvd .... Torrance CA 90503 310-540-5511 540-6272*
**Fax:* Edit ■ *Web:* www.dailybreeze.com
Turlock Journal PO Box 800 .... Turlock CA 95381 209-634-9141 632-8813
Web: www.turlockjournal.com
Reporter 916 Cotting Ln .... Vacaville CA 95688 707-448-6401 447-8411
Web: www.thereporter.com
Vallejo Times Herald 440 Curtola Pkwy .... Vallejo CA 94590 707-644-1141 643-0128
TF: 800-600-1141 ■ *Web:* www.timesheraldonline.com
Daily Press 13891 Park Ave PO Box 1389 .... Victorville CA 92393 760-241-7744 241-1860
TF: 800-553-2006 ■ *Web:* www.vvdailypress.com
Visalia Times-Delta PO Box 31 .... Visalia CA 93279 559-735-3200 735-3399
Web: www.visaliatimesdelta.com
Contra Costa Times 2640 Shadelands Dr .... Walnut Creek CA 94598 925-935-2525 943-8362
Web: www.contracostatimes.com/mld/cctimes
San Gabriel Valley Tribune 1210 N Azusa Canyon Rd .... West Covina CA 91790 626-962-8811 338-9157
TF: 800-788-1200 ■ *Web:* www.sgvtribune.com
Nguoi Viet News 14771 Moran St .... Westminster CA 92683 714-892-9414 894-1381
Web: www.nguoi-viet.com
Whittier Daily News 7612 Green Leaf Ave .... Whittier CA 90602 562-698-0955 698-0450
TF: 800-788-1200 ■ *Web:* www.whittierdailynews.com
Daily News of Los Angeles 21221 Oxnard St .... Woodland Hills CA 91367 818-713-3000 713-0058
TF: 800-346-6397 ■ *Web:* www.dailynews.com

Colorado

	City	State	Zip	Phone	Fax
Aspen Daily News 517 E Hopkins Ave *TF:* 800-889-9020 ■ *Web:* www.aspendailynews.com	Aspen	CO	81611	970-925-2220	920-2118
Aspen Times 310 E Main St *Web:* www.aspentimes.com	Aspen	CO	81611	970-925-3414	925-6240
Boulder Daily Camera 1048 Pearl St *TF:* 800-783-1202 ■ *Web:* www.dailycamera.com	Boulder	CO	80302	303-442-1202	449-9358
Colorado Daily 2610 Pearl St *Web:* www.coloradodaily.com	Boulder	CO	80302	303-443-6272	443-9357
Dirt 1048 Pearl St *Web:* www.boulderdirt.com	Boulder	CO	80302	303-473-1170	473-1155
Gazette The 30 S Prospect St *TF News Rm:* 800-800-4899 ■ *Web:* www.gazette.com	Colorado Springs	CO	80903	719-632-5511	636-0266
Denver Post 1560 Broadway *TF:* 800-336-7678 ■ *Web:* www.denverpost.com	Denver	CO	80202	303-820-1010	820-1369
Rocky Mountain News 101 W Colfax Ave *TF:* 800-933-1990 ■ *Web:* www.rockymountainnews.com	Denver	CO	80202	303-892-5000	892-2841
Durango Herald 1275 Main Ave *TF:* 800-530-8318 ■ *Web:* www.durangoherald.com	Durango	CO	81301	970-247-3504	259-5011
Coloradoan The 1300 Riverside Ave *TF:* 800-872-0001 ■ *Web:* www.coloradoan.com	Fort Collins	CO	80524	970-493-6397	224-7899
Daily Sentinel PO Box 668 *TF:* 800-332-5832 ■ *Web:* www.gjsentinel.com	Grand Junction	CO	81502	970-242-5050	244-8578
Greeley Tribune 501 8th Ave *TF:* 800-275-0321 ■ *Web:* www.greeleytrib.com	Greeley	CO	80631	970-352-0211	356-5780
Gunnison Country Times 218 N Wisconsin St *Web:* www.gunnisontimes.com	Gunnison	CO	81230	970-641-1414	641-6515
Lamar Daily News 310 S 5th St PO Box 1217 *Web:* www.lamardaily.com	Lamar	CO	81052	719-336-2266	336-2526
Daily Times-Call 350 Terry St *TF:* 800-796-8201 ■ *Web:* www.longmontfyi.com	Longmont	CO	80501	303-776-2244	678-8615
Loveland Daily Reporter-Herald 201 E 5th St *TF:* 800-216-0680 ■ *Web:* www.lovelandfyi.com	Loveland	CO	80537	970-669-5050	667-1111
Pueblo Chieftain 825 W 6th St PO Box 440 *TF:* 800-279-6397 ■ *Web:* www.chieftain.com	Pueblo	CO	81003	719-544-3520	

Connecticut

	City	State	Zip	Phone	Fax
Connecticut Post 410 State St *TF Edit:* 800-542-5620 ■ *Web:* www.connpost.com	Bridgeport	CT	06604	203-333-0161	367-8158
News-Times 333 Main St *Web:* www.newstimes.com	Danbury	CT	06810	203-744-5100	792-8730
Hartford Courant 285 Broad St *TF:* 800-524-4242 ■ *Web:* www.courant.com	Hartford	CT	06115	860-241-6200	520-6941
Journal Inquirer 306 Progress Dr PO Box 510 *TF:* 800-237-3606 ■ *Web:* www.journalinquirer.com	Manchester	CT	06045	860-646-0500	646-9867
Record-Journal 11 Crown St *Web:* www.record-journal.com	Meriden	CT	06450	203-235-1661	639-0210
Citizens News 71 Weid Dr	Naugatuck	CT	06770	203-729-2228	729-9099
Herald The 1 Herald Sq	New Britain	CT	06050	860-225-4601	223-8171
New Haven Register 40 Sargent Dr *TF:* 800-925-2509 ■ *Web:* www.nhregister.com	New Haven	CT	06511	203-789-5200	865-7894
Day The 47 Eugene O'Neil Dr PO Box 1231 *TF:* 800-542-3354 ■ *Web:* www.theday.com	New London	CT	06320	860-442-2200	442-5599
Hour The 346 Main Ave *Web:* www.thehour.com	Norwalk	CT	06851	203-846-3281	840-1802
Norwich Bulletin 66 Franklin St *Web:* www.norwichbulletin.com	Norwich	CT	06360	860-887-9211	887-9666
Advocate The 75 Tresser Blvd **Fax:* Edit ■ *Web:* www.stamfordadvocate.com	Stamford	CT	06901	203-964-2200	964-2345*
Republican-American 389 Meadow St *TF:* 800-992-3232 ■ *Web:* www.rep-am.com	Waterbury	CT	06702	203-574-3636	596-9277

Delaware

	City	State	Zip	Phone	Fax
Delaware State News PO Box 737 *TF:* 800-282-8586 ■ *Web:* www.newszap.com	Dover	DE	19903	302-674-3600	741-8252
News Journal 950 W Basin Rd *TF:* 800-235-9100 ■ *Web:* www.delawareonline.com/newsjournal	New Castle	DE	19720	302-324-2500	324-5509

District of Columbia

	City	State	Zip	Phone	Fax
Washington Examiner 1015 15th St NW Suite 500 **Fax:* Edit ■ *TF:* 800-531-1223 ■ *Web:* www.examiner.com/Washington_DC-Top_News.html	Washington	DC	20005	202-903-2000	459-4999*
Washington Post 1150 15th St NW *TF:* 800-627-1150 ■ *Web:* www.washingtonpost.com	Washington	DC	20071	202-334-6000	
Washington Times 3600 New York Ave NE *Web:* www.washingtontimes.com	Washington	DC	20002	202-636-3000	636-8906

Florida

	City	State	Zip	Phone	Fax
Herald The 102 Manatee Ave W *Web:* www.bradenton.com	Bradenton	FL	34205	941-748-0411	745-7097
Citrus County Chronicle 1624 N Meadowcrest Blvd *TF:* 888-852-2340 ■ *Web:* www.chronicleonline.com	Crystal River	FL	34429	352-563-6363	563-3280
Daytona Beach News-Journal 901 6th St *Web:* www.news-journalonline.com	Daytona Beach	FL	32117	386-252-1511	258-8465
Miami Herald Broward Edition 1520 E Sunrise Blvd *TF:* 800-441-0444 ■ *Web:* www.miami.com	Fort Lauderdale	FL	33304	954-462-3000	538-7000
South Florida Sun-Sentinel 200 E Las Olas Blvd *TF Cust Svc:* 800-548-6397 ■ *Web:* www.sun-sentinel.com	Fort Lauderdale	FL	33301	954-356-4000	356-4559
News-Press 2442 Dr ML King Jr Blvd *TF News Rm:* 800-468-0350 ■ *Web:* www.news-press.com	Fort Myers	FL	33901	239-335-0200	334-0708
Tribune 600 Edwards Rd **Fax Area Code:* 866 ■ *TF:* 800-444-8742 ■ *Web:* www.fptribune.com	Fort Pierce	FL	34982	772-461-2050	894-9851*
Northwest Florida Daily News PO Box 2949 *TF:* 800-755-1185 ■ *Web:* www.nwfdailynews.com	Fort Walton Beach	FL	32549	850-863-1111	863-7834
Gainesville Sun 2700 SW 13th St *TF Circ:* 800-443-9493 ■ *Web:* www.sunone.com	Gainesville	FL	32614	352-378-1411	338-3128
Florida Times-Union 1 Riverside Ave *TF:* 800-472-6397 ■ *Web:* www.jacksonville.com	Jacksonville	FL	32202	904-359-4111	359-4478
Key West Citizen 3420 Northside Dr *Web:* www.keysnews.com/	Key West	FL	33040	305-294-6641	292-3008
Ledger The 300 W Lime St *TF:* 888-431-7323 ■ *Web:* www.theledger.com	Lakeland	FL	33815	863-802-7000	802-7809
Daily Commercial 212 E Main St *TF:* 877-702-0600 ■ *Web:* www.dailycommercial.com	Leesburg	FL	34748	352-365-8200	365-1951
Diario Las Americas 2900 NW 39th St *Web:* www.diariolasamericas.com	Miami	FL	33142	305-633-3341	635-7668
El Nuevo Herald 1 Herald Plaza *TF:* 800-441-0444 ■ *Web:* www.elnuevoherald.com	Miami	FL	33132	305-376-3535	376-2378
Miami Herald 1 Herald Plaza *TF:* 800-437-2535 ■ *Web:* www.miamiherald.com	Miami	FL	33132	305-350-2111	376-5287
Naples Daily News 1075 Central Ave *TF:* 888-262-3161 ■ *Web:* www.naplesnews.com	Naples	FL	34102	239-262-3161	263-4816
Ocala Star-Banner PO Box 490 *TF:* 800-541-2172 ■ *Web:* www.starbanner.com	Ocala	FL	34478	352-867-4010	867-4018
El Nuevo Dia 4780 N Orange Blossom Trail *Web:* www.endiorlando.com	Orlando	FL	32810	321-206-3000	206-3001
Orlando Sentinel 633 N Orange Ave *TF:* 800-347-6868 ■ *Web:* www.orlandosentinel.com	Orlando	FL	32801	407-420-5000	420-5350
News-Herald 501 W 11th St *TF:* 800-345-8688 ■ *Web:* www.newsherald.com	Panama City	FL	32401	850-747-5000	747-5097
Pensacola News Journal 101 E Romana St *TF:* 800-288-2021 ■ *Web:* www.gulfcoastgateway.com	Pensacola	FL	32508	850-435-8500	435-8633
Sun Herald 23170 Harborview Rd *TF:* 877-818-6204 ■ *Web:* www.sun-herald.com	Port Charlotte	FL	33980	941-206-1000	629-2085
Port Saint Lucie News 695 NW Enterprise Dr *Web:* www.tcpalm.com/tcp/stuart_news	Port Saint Lucie	FL	34995	772-408-5300	408-5369
Florida Today 6650 US Hwy 1 *TF:* 800-633-8449 ■ *Web:* www.flatoday.com	Rockledge	FL	32955	321-242-3500	242-6620
Saint Augustine Record 1 News Pl *Web:* www.staugustine.com	Saint Augustine	FL	32086	904-829-6562	819-3558
Saint Petersburg Times 490 1st Ave S *TF:* 800-333-7505 ■ *Web:* www.sptimes.com	Saint Petersburg	FL	33701	727-893-8111	893-8675
Seminole Herald PO Box 1667 *Web:* www.mysanfordherald.com	Sanford	FL	32772	407-322-2611	323-9408
Sarasota Herald-Tribune 1741 Main St *TF:* 866-284-7102 ■ *Web:* www.heraldtribune.com	Sarasota	FL	34236	941-953-7755	361-4800
Highlands Today 315 US Hwy 27 N *TF:* 800-645-3423 ■ *Web:* www.highlandstoday.com	Sebring	FL	33870	863-386-5800	382-2509
Stuart News PO Box 9009 *TF:* 800-381-6397 ■ *Web:* www.tcpalm.com/tcp/stuart_news	Stuart	FL	34995	772-287-1550	221-4246
Tallahassee Democrat 277 N Magnolia Dr *TF:* 800-777-2154 ■ *Web:* www.tallahassee.com	Tallahassee	FL	32302	850-599-2100	599-2295
Tampa Tribune 202 S Parker St *TF:* 800-282-5588 ■ *Web:* www.tampatrib.com	Tampa	FL	33606	813-259-7600	259-7676
Vero Beach Press-Journal PO Box 1268 *TF:* 866-894-9851 ■ *Web:* www.tcpalm.com/tcp/press_journal	Vero Beach	FL	32961	772-562-2315	978-2364
Palm Beach Post 2751 S Dixie Hwy **Fax:* News Rm ■ *TF:* 800-432-7595 ■ *Web:* www.palmbeachpost.com	West Palm Beach	FL	33405	561-820-4100	820-4407*

Georgia

	City	State	Zip	Phone	Fax
Albany Herald 126 N Washington St **Fax:* Edit ■ *TF:* 800-685-4639 ■ *Web:* www.albanyherald.com	Albany	GA	31701	229-888-9300	888-9357*
Athens Banner-Herald 1 Press Pl *TF:* 800-533-4252 ■ *Web:* www.onlineathens.com	Athens	GA	30601	706-549-0123	208-2246
Atlanta Journal-Constitution 72 Marietta St **Fax:* News Rm ■ *TF:* 800-846-6672 ■ *Web:* www.ajc.com	Atlanta	GA	30303	404-526-5151	526-5746*
Augusta Chronicle 725 Broad St **Fax:* News Rm ■ *TF:* 800-822-4077 ■ *Web:* chronicle.augusta.com	Augusta	GA	30901	706-724-0851	722-7403*
Brunswick News PO Box 1557 *Web:* www.thebrunswicknews.com	Brunswick	GA	31521	912-265-8320	280-0926
Columbus Ledger-Enquirer 17 W 12th St *TF:* 800-282-7859 ■ *Web:* www.ledger-enquirer.com	Columbus	GA	31902	706-324-5526	576-6290
Rockdale Citizen PO Box 136 *Web:* www.rockdalecitizen.com	Conyers	GA	30012	770-483-7108	483-5797
Newton Citizen 6225 Highway 278 NW Suite 35 *Web:* www.newtoncitizen.com	Covington	GA	30014	770-787-7303	787-8603
Gainesville Times 345 Green St NW *TF:* 800-395-5005 ■ *Web:* www.gainesvilletimes.com	Gainesville	GA	30501	770-532-1234	532-0457
Gwinnett Daily Post 725 Old Norcross Rd *Web:* www.gwinnettdailypost.com	Lawrenceville	GA	30045	770-963-9205	339-8081
Macon Telegraph 120 Broadway *TF:* 800-679-6397 ■ *Web:* www.macon.com	Macon	GA	31201	478-744-4200	744-4385
Marietta Daily Journal PO Box 449 *Web:* www.mdjonline.com	Marietta	GA	30061	770-428-9411	422-9533
La Vision 2200 Norcross Pkwy Suite 210 *Web:* www.lavisionnewspaper.com	Norcross	GA	30071	770-963-7521	963-7218
Rome News-Tribune PO Box 1633 *Web:* www.romenews-tribune.com	Rome	GA	30162	706-291-6397	234-6478
Savannah Morning News 1375 Chatham Pkwy *Web:* www.savannahnow.com	Savannah	GA	31405	912-236-9511	525-0795
Valdosta Daily Times PO Box 968 *TF:* 800-600-4838 ■ *Web:* www.valdostadailytimes.com	Valdosta	GA	31603	229-244-1880	244-2560
Telegraph The 1553 Watson Blvd **Fax:* News Rm ■ *TF:* 800-679-6397	Warner Robins	GA	31093	478-923-6432	328-7682*

Hawaii

	City	State	Zip	Phone	Fax
Hawaii Tribune-Herald 355 Kinoole St *Web:* www.hawaiitribune-herald.com	Hilo	HI	96720	808-935-6621	961-3680
Honolulu Advertiser PO Box 3110 *TF:* 877-233-1133 ■ *Web:* www.honoluluadvertiser.com	Honolulu	HI	96801	808-525-8000	525-8037
Honolulu Star-Bulletin 500 Ala Moana Blvd 7 Waterfront Plaza Suite 500 *TF:* 800-417-3484 ■ *Web:* www.starbulletin.com	Honolulu	HI	96813	808-529-4700	529-4750
Maui News PO Box 550 **Fax:* Edit ■ *TF:* 800-827-0347 ■ *Web:* www.mauinews.com	Wailuku	HI	96793	808-244-3981	242-9087*

Idaho

	City	State	Zip	Phone	Fax
Idaho Statesman 1200 N Curtis Rd *TF:* 800-635-8934 ■ *Web:* www.idahostatesman.com	Boise	ID	83706	208-377-6400	377-6449
Coeur d'Alene Press 201 N 2nd St *Web:* www.cdapress.com	Coeur d'Alene	ID	83814	208-664-8176	664-0212
Post-Register PO Box 1800 *TF:* 800-574-6397 ■ *Web:* www.postregister.com	Idaho Falls	ID	83403	208-522-1800	529-9683
Lewiston Morning Tribune PO Box 957 *Web:* www.lmtribune.com	Lewiston	ID	83501	208-743-9411	746-1185
Idaho Press-Tribune 1618 N Midland Blvd *Web:* www.idahopress.com	Nampa	ID	83651	208-467-9251	467-9562
Idaho State Journal 305 S Arthur Ave *TF:* 800-275-0774 ■ *Web:* www.idahostatejournal.com	Pocatello	ID	83204	208-232-4161	233-8007

Daily Newspapers - US (Cont'd)

Idaho (Cont'd)

Newspaper	City	State	ZIP	Phone	Fax
Times-News PO Box 548 TF: 800-658-3883 ■ Web: www.magicvalley.com	Twin Falls	ID	83303	208-733-0931	734-5538

Illinois

Newspaper	City	State	ZIP	Phone	Fax
Telegraph The PO Box 278 *Fax: Edit ■ TF: 800-477-1447 ■ Web: www.thetelegraph.com	Alton	IL	62002	618-463-2500	463-2578*
Daily Herald 155 E Algonquin Rd Web: www.dailyherald.com	Arlington Heights	IL	60005	847-427-4300	427-1301
Beacon News 101 S River St TF: 800-244-5844 ■ Web: www.suburbanchicagonews.com/beaconnews	Aurora	IL	60506	630-844-5800	844-1043
Belleville News-Democrat 120 S Illinois St TF: 877-338-7416 ■ Web: www.belleville.com	Belleville	IL	62220	618-234-1000	234-9597
Pantagraph PO Box 2907 TF: 800-747-7323 ■ Web: www.pantagraph.com	Bloomington	IL	61702	309-829-9000	829-7000
Southern Illinoisan 710 N Illinois Ave PO Box 2108 TF: 800-228-0429 ■ Web: www.thesouthern.com	Carbondale	IL	62902	618-529-5454	457-2935
Centralia Sentinel 232 E Broadway TF: 800-371-9892 ■ Web: www.morningsentinel.com	Centralia	IL	62801	618-532-5604	532-1212
News Gazette 15 Main St Web: www.news-gazette.com	Champaign	IL	61824	217-351-5252	351-5374
Chicago Defender 200 S Michigan Ave Suite 1700 Web: www.chicagodefender.com	Chicago	IL	60604	312-225-2400	225-6954
Chicago Sun-Times 350 N Orleans St Web: www.suntimes.com	Chicago	IL	60654	312-321-3000	321-3084
Chicago Tribune 435 N Michigan Ave TF: 800-874-2863 ■ Web: www.chicagotribune.com	Chicago	IL	60611	312-222-3232	222-4760
Northwest Herald PO Box 250 *Fax: News Rm ■ TF: 800-589-8910 ■ Web: www.nwherald.com	Crystal Lake	IL	60039	815-459-4122	459-5640*
Commercial-News 17 W North St *Fax: News Rm ■ TF: 800-729-2922 ■ Web: www.commercial-news.com	Danville	IL	61832	217-446-1000	446-6648*
Herald & Review 601 E Williams St PO Box 311 Web: www.herald-review.com	Decatur	IL	62525	217-429-5151	421-7965
Telegraph 113 S Peoria Ave Web: www.saukvalley.com	Dixon	IL	61021	815-284-2224	284-2078
Courier-News 300 Lake St PO Box 531 TF: 800-445-3538 ■ Web: www.suburbanchicagonews.com/couriernews	Elgin	IL	60121	847-888-7800	888-7836
Journal-Standard 27 S State Ave TF: 800-325-6397 ■ Web: www.journalstandard.com	Freeport	IL	61032	815-232-1171	232-0105
Register-Mail 140 S Prairie St PO Box 310 TF: 800-747-7181 ■ Web: www.register-mail.com	Galesburg	IL	61401	309-343-7181	343-2382
Jacksonville Journal-Courier 235 W State St TF: 800-682-9132 ■ Web: www.journal-courier.net	Jacksonville	IL	62650	217-245-6121	245-1226
Herald-News 300 Caterpillar Dr TF: 800-397-9397 ■ Web: www.suburbanchicagonews.com/heraldnews	Joliet	IL	60436	815-729-6161	729-6059
Daily Journal 8 Dearborn Sq Web: www.daily-journal.com	Kankakee	IL	60901	815-937-3300	937-3876
News-Tribune 426 2nd St TF: 800-892-6452 ■ Web: www.newstrib.com	La Salle	IL	61301	815-223-3200	224-6443
Macomb Journal 203 N Randolph St TF: 800-237-6858 ■ Web: www.macombjournal.com	Macomb	IL	61455	309-833-2114	833-2346
Dispatch The 1720 5th Ave Web: qconline.com	Moline	IL	61265	309-764-4344	797-0317
Daily Times 110 W Jefferson St Web: www.mywebtimes.com	Ottawa	IL	61350	815-433-2000	433-1639
Reporter 12247 S Harlem Ave Web: www.thereporteronline.net	Palos Heights	IL	60463	708-448-6161	448-4012
Pekin Daily Times PO Box 430 Web: www.pekintimes.com	Pekin	IL	61555	309-346-1111	346-9815
Peoria Journal Star 1 News Plaza *Fax: News Rm ■ TF: 800-225-5757 ■ Web: pjstar.com	Peoria	IL	61643	309-686-3000	686-3296*
Peoria Times-Observer 1616 W Pioneer Pkwy Web: www.peoriatimesobserver.com	Peoria	IL	61615	309-692-4910	691-7857
Quincy Herald-Whig PO Box 1049 TF: 800-373-9444 ■ Web: www.whig.com	Quincy	IL	62306	217-223-5100	221-3395
Rock Island Argus 1724 4th Ave Web: qconline.com	Rock Island	IL	61201	309-786-6441	786-7639
Rockford Register Star 99 E State St *Fax: News Rm ■ TF: 800-383-7827 ■ Web: www.rrstar.com	Rockford	IL	61104	815-987-1200	987-1365*
Shelbyville Daily Union 100 W Main St Web: www.shelbyvilledailyunion.com	Shelbyville	IL	62565	217-774-2161	774-5732
State Journal-Register 1 Copley Plaza TF: 800-397-6397 ■ Web: www.sj-r.com	Springfield	IL	62701	217-788-1300	788-1551
Daily Southtown 6901 W 159th St Web: www.dailysouthtown.com	Tinley Park	IL	60477	708-633-6700	633-5999
News Sun 2383 N Delany Rd Web: www.suburbanchicagonews.com/NewsSun	Waukegan	IL	60087	847-336-7000	249-7202

Indiana

Newspaper	City	State	ZIP	Phone	Fax
Herald Bulletin 1133 Jackson St TF: 800-750-5049 ■ Web: www.heraldbulletin.com	Anderson	IN	46015	765-622-1212	640-4815
Herald-Republican 45 S Public Sq Web: www.kpcnews.com	Angola	IN	46703	260-665-3117	665-2322
Times-Mail PO Box 849 *Fax: News Rm ■ Web: www.tmnews.com	Bedford	IN	47421	812-275-3355	277-3472*
Herald-Times 1900 S Walnut St Web: www.heraldtimesonline.com	Bloomington	IN	47401	812-332-4401	331-4383
Republic The 333 2nd St TF: 800-876-7811 ■ Web: www.therepublic.com	Columbus	IN	47201	812-372-7811	379-5711
Truth The PO Box 487 TF: 800-585-5416 ■ Web: www.etruth.com	Elkhart	IN	46515	574-294-1661	294-3895
Evansville Courier & Press 300 E Walnut St TF: 800-288-3200 ■ Web: www.courierpress.com	Evansville	IN	47713	812-424-7711	422-8196
Journal Gazette 600 W Main St TF: 800-444-3303 ■ Web: www.fortwayne.com/mld/journalgazette	Fort Wayne	IN	46802	260-461-8222	461-8648
News-Sentinel 600 W Main St TF: 800-444-3303 ■ Web: www.fortwayne.com/mld/newssentinel	Fort Wayne	IN	46802	260-461-8439	461-8817
Daily Journal 2575 N Morton St TF: 888-736-7101 ■ Web: www.thejournalnet.com	Franklin	IN	46131	317-736-7101	736-2766
Goshen News 114 S Main St PO Box 569 TF: 800-487-2151 ■ Web: www.goshennews.com	Goshen	IN	46527	574-533-2151	534-8830
Indianapolis Star 307 N Pennsylvania St TF: 800-669-7827 ■ Web: www.indystar.com	Indianapolis	IN	46204	317-444-4000	444-6600
Kokomo Tribune 300 N Union St TF: 800-382-0696 ■ Web: www.kokomotribune.com	Kokomo	IN	46901	765-459-3121	854-6733
Journal & Courier 217 N 6th St TF News Rm: 800-407-5813 ■ Web: www.jconline.com	Lafayette	IN	47901	765-423-5511	420-5246
Chronicle-Tribune 610 S Adams St TF: 800-955-7888 ■ Web: www.chronicle-tribune.com	Marion	IN	46953	765-664-5111	668-4256
Post-Tribune 1433 E 83rd Ave TF: 800-876-8974 ■ Web: www.post-trib.com	Merrillville	IN	46410	219-648-3055	648-3232
Muncie Star-Press 345 S High St TF: 800-783-7827 ■ Web: www.thestarpress.com	Muncie	IN	47305	765-747-5700	213-5858
Times The 601 W 45th Ave TF: 800-837-3232 ■ Web: www.nwitimes.com	Munster	IN	46321	219-933-3200	933-3249
Palladium-Item PO Box 308 Web: www.pal-item.com	Richmond	IN	47375	765-962-1575	973-4570
South Bend Tribune 225 W Colfax Ave TF: 800-220-7378 ■ Web: www.southbendtribune.com	South Bend	IN	46626	574-235-6464	239-2642
Tribune-Star PO Box 149 TF: 800-783-8742 ■ Web: www.tribstar.com	Terre Haute	IN	47808	812-231-4200	231-4321

Iowa

Newspaper	City	State	ZIP	Phone	Fax
Hawk Eye 800 S Main St TF: 800-397-1708 ■ Web: www.thehawkeye.com	Burlington	IA	52601	319-754-8461	754-6824
Gazette The 500 3rd Ave SE TF: 800-397-8212 ■ Web: www.gazetteonline.com	Cedar Rapids	IA	52401	319-398-8313	398-5846
Daily Nonpareil 535 W Broadway Suite 300 TF: 800-283-1882 ■ Web: www.nonpareilonline.com	Council Bluffs	IA	51503	712-328-1811	325-5776
Quad-City Times 500 E 3rd St TF: 800-437-4641 ■ Web: www.qctimes.com	Davenport	IA	52801	563-383-2200	383-2370
Des Moines Register 715 Locust St TF: 800-247-5346 ■ Web: www.desmoinesregister.com	Des Moines	IA	50309	515-284-8000	286-2504
Telegraph Herald 801 Bluff St *Fax: Edit ■ TF: 800-553-4801 ■ Web: www.thonline.com	Dubuque	IA	52001	563-588-5611	588-5745*
Messenger The 713 Central Ave TF: 800-622-6613 ■ Web: messengernews.net	Fort Dodge	IA	50501	515-573-2141	574-4529
Globe-Gazette 300 N Washington St PO Box 271 TF: 800-421-0546 ■ Web: www.globegazette.com	Mason City	IA	50402	641-421-0500	421-7108
Ottumwa Courier 213 E 2nd St *Fax: News Rm ■ TF: 800-532-1504 ■ Web: www.ottumwacourier.com	Ottumwa	IA	52501	641-684-4611	684-7326*
Sioux City Journal 515 Pavonia St TF: 800-397-3530 ■ Web: www.siouxcityjournal.com	Sioux City	IA	51101	712-293-4300	279-5059
Pilot Tribune PO Box 1187 TF: 800-798-6397 ■ Web: www.stormlakepilottribune.com	Storm Lake	IA	50588	712-732-3130	732-3152
Waterloo Cedar Falls Courier PO Box 540 TF: 800-798-1730 ■ Web: www.wcfcourier.com	Waterloo	IA	50701	319-291-1400	291-2069

Kansas

Newspaper	City	State	ZIP	Phone	Fax
Beloit Call 119 E Main St PO Box 366	Beloit	KS	67420	785-738-3537	738-6442
Goodland Star-News 1205 Main St Web: www.nwkansas.com	Goodland	KS	67735	785-899-2338	899-6186
Hiawatha World 607 Utah St TF: 800-803-3321	Hiawatha	KS	66434	785-742-2111	742-2276
Hutchinson News 300 W 2nd St TF: 800-766-3311 ■ Web: www.hutchnews.com	Hutchinson	KS	67504	620-694-5700	662-4186
Kansas City Kansan 8200 State Ave Web: www.kansascitykansan.com	Kansas City	KS	66112	913-371-4300	342-8620
Lawrence Journal-World 609 New Hampshire St *Fax: Edit ■ TF: 800-578-8748 ■ Web: www.ljworld.com	Lawrence	KS	66044	785-843-1000	843-4512*
Norton Telegram 215 S Kansas St Web: www.nwkansas.com	Norton	KS	67654	785-877-3361	877-3732
Russell County News 958 Wichita Ave *Fax: News Rm	Russell	KS	67665	785-483-2116	483-4012*
Salina Journal PO Box 740 Web: www.saljournal.com	Salina	KS	67402	785-823-6363	827-6363
Topeka Capital-Journal 616 SE Jefferson St TF: 800-777-7171 ■ Web: www.cjonline.com	Topeka	KS	66607	785-295-1111	295-1230
Wellington Daily News PO Box 368 Web: www.wgtndailynews.com	Wellington	KS	67152	620-326-3326	326-3290
Wichita Eagle 825 E Douglas Ave Web: www.kansas.com/mld/eagle/	Wichita	KS	67202	316-268-6000	268-6627
Winfield Daily Courier PO Box 543 Web: www.winfieldcourier.com	Winfield	KS	67156	620-221-1100	221-1101

Kentucky

Newspaper	City	State	ZIP	Phone	Fax
Daily Independent 226 17th St TF: 800-955-5860 ■ Web: www.dailyindependent.com	Ashland	KY	41101	606-326-2600	326-2678
Daily News 813 College St PO Box 90012 TF: 800-599-6397 ■ Web: www.bgdailynews.com	Bowling Green	KY	42102	270-781-1700	783-3237
Times-Tribune PO Box 516 *Fax: News Rm ■ Web: www.corbintimes.com	Corbin	KY	40702	606-528-2464	528-9850*
News-Enterprise 408 W Dixie Ave TF: 800-653-6344 ■ Web: www.thenewsenterprise.com	Elizabethtown	KY	42701	270-769-1200	769-6965
Kentucky Enquirer 226 Grandview Dr Web: www.enquirer.com	Fort Mitchell	KY	41017	859-578-5555	578-5565
State Journal 1216 Wilkinson Blvd Web: www.state-journal.com	Frankfort	KY	40601	502-227-4556	607-0123
Lexington Herald-Leader 100 Midland Ave TF: 800-274-7355 ■ Web: www.kentucky.com/mld/kentucky	Lexington	KY	40508	859-231-3100	231-3224
Courier-Journal 525 W Broadway PO Box 740031 TF: 800-765-4011 ■ Web: www.courier-journal.com	Louisville	KY	40201	502-582-4011	582-4200
Messenger-Inquirer 1480 Fredrica St Web: www.messenger-inquirer.com	Owensboro	KY	42302	270-926-0123	686-7868
Paducah Sun PO Box 2300 *Fax: News Rm ■ TF: 800-959-1771 ■ Web: www.paducahsun.com	Paducah	KY	42002	270-575-8600	442-7859*

Louisiana

Newspaper	City	State	ZIP	Phone	Fax
Alexandria Daily Town Talk PO Box 7558 TF: 800-523-8391 ■ Web: www.thetowntalk.com	Alexandria	LA	71306	318-487-6397	487-6488
Advocate The 7290 Blue Bonnet Blvd TF: 800-960-6397 ■ Web: www.2theadvocate.com	Baton Rouge	LA	70810	225-383-1111	388-0371
Courier The 3030 Barrow St Web: www.houmatoday.com	Houma	LA	70360	985-879-1557	857-2244
Daily Advertiser The 1100 Bertrand Dr *Fax: Edit ■ Web: www.theadvertiser.com	Lafayette	LA	70506	337-289-6300	289-6443*
American Press 4900 Hwy 90 E TF News Rm: 800-531-4080 ■ Web: www.americanpress.com	Lake Charles	LA	70615	337-494-4080	494-4070
News-Star 411 N 4th St TF: 800-259-7788 ■ Web: www.thenewsstar.com	Monroe	LA	71201	318-322-5161	362-0273
Times-Picayune 3800 Howard Ave *Fax: News Rm ■ TF: 800-925-0000 ■ Web: www.nola.com	New Orleans	LA	70125	504-826-3279	826-3007*

	City	State	Zip	Phone	Fax
Times 222 Lake St	Shreveport	LA	71101	318-459-3200	459-3301
TF: 800-551-8892 ■ *Web:* www.shreveporttimes.com					

Maine

	City	State	Zip	Phone	Fax
Kennebec Journal 274 Western Ave	Augusta	ME	04330	207-623-3811	623-2220
TF: 800-537-5508 ■ *Web:* kennebecjournal.mainetoday.com					
Bangor Daily News 491 Main St	Bangor	ME	04401	207-990-8000	941-9476*
**Fax:* Edit ■ *TF:* 800-432-7964 ■ *Web:* www.bangornews.com					
Sun-Journal PO Box 4400	Lewiston	ME	04243	207-784-5411	777-3436
TF: 800-482-0759 ■ *Web:* www.sunjournal.com					
Portland Press Herald 390 Congress St	Portland	ME	04104	207-791-6650	791-6920
Web: pressherald.mainetoday.com					
Morning Sentinel 31 Front St	Waterville	ME	04901	207-873-3341	861-9191
TF: 800-452-4666 ■ *Web:* morningsentinel.mainetoday.com					

Maryland

	City	State	Zip	Phone	Fax
Capital The 2000 Capital Dr	Annapolis	MD	21401	410-268-5000	268-4643
Web: www.capitalonline.com					
Baltimore Sun 501 N Calvert St	Baltimore	MD	21278	410-332-6000	332-6455
TF: 800-829-8000 ■ *Web:* www.baltimoresun.com					
Cumberland Times-News 19 Baltimore St	Cumberland	MD	21502	301-722-4600	722-5270
TF: 800-742-8149 ■ *Web:* www.times-news.com					
Star Democrat 29088 Airpark Dr PO Box 600	Easton	MD	21601	410-822-1500	770-4019
Web: www.stardem.com					
Frederick News Post 200 E Patrick St	Frederick	MD	21701	301-662-1177	662-1615
TF: 800-486-1177 ■ *Web:* www.fredericknewspost.com					
Daily Times 115 E Carroll St	Salisbury	MD	21801	410-749-7171	749-7290
TF: 877-335-6278 ■ *Web:* www.delmarvanow.com/news					
Carroll County Times 201 Railroad Ave	Westminster	MD	21157	410-848-4400	857-8749*
**Fax:* Edit ■ *Web:* www.carrollcountytimes.com					

Massachusetts

	City	State	Zip	Phone	Fax
Sun Chronicle PO Box 600	Attleboro	MA	02703	508-222-7000	236-0462
Web: www.thesunchronicle.com					
Salem Evening News 32 Dunham Rd	Beverly	MA	01915	978-745-6969	927-4524
TF: 800-745-5440 ■ *Web:* www.salemnews.com					
Boston Globe 135 Morrissey Blvd	Boston	MA	02125	617-929-2000	929-3192
Web: www.boston.com/news/globe					
Boston Herald 300 Harrison Ave	Boston	MA	02118	617-426-3000	619-6450
TF: 800-225-2040 ■ *Web:* www.bostonherald.com					
Enterprise The 60 Main St	Brockton	MA	02303	508-586-6200	586-6506
Web: www.enterprise.southofboston.com					
Herald-News 207 Pocasset St	Fall River	MA	02722	508-676-8211	676-2566
Web: www.heraldnews.com					
Sentinel & Enterprise PO Box 730	Fitchburg	MA	01420	978-343-6911	342-1158
Web: www.sentinelandenterprise.com					
MetroWest Daily News 33 New York Ave	Framingham	MA	01701	508-626-4412	626-4400*
**Fax:* News Rm ■ *Web:* www.metrowestdailynews.com					
Haverhill Gazette 181 Merrimack St	Haverhill	MA	01831	978-374-0321	521-6790
TF: 800-370-0321 ■ *Web:* www.hgazette.com					
Cape Cod Times 319 Main St	Hyannis	MA	02601	508-775-1200	771-3292*
**Fax:* Edit ■ *TF:* 800-451-7887 ■ *Web:* www.capecodonline.com					
Lowell Sun PO Box 1477	Lowell	MA	01853	978-458-7100	970-4600
TF: 800-694-7100 ■ *Web:* www.lowellsun.com					
Daily Item The 38 Exchange St PO Box 951	Lynn	MA	01903	781-593-7700	598-2891
Web: www.thedailyitemoflynn.com					
Malden Evening News 277 Commercial St	Malden	MA	02148	781-321-8000	321-8008
Standard-Times 25 Elm St	New Bedford	MA	02740	508-997-7411	997-7491*
**Fax:* News Rm ■ *TF:* 800-286-9876 ■ *Web:* www.s-t.com					
Eagle-Tribune 100 Turnpike St	North Andover	MA	01845	978-946-2000	687-6045
Web: www.eagletribune.com					
Daily Hampshire Gazette 115 Conz St	Northampton	MA	01060	413-584-5000	585-5299
Web: www.gazettenet.com					
Berkshire Eagle 75 S Church St PO Box 1171	Pittsfield	MA	01202	413-447-7311	499-3419
TF: 800-234-7404 ■ *Web:* www.berkshireeagle.com					
Patriot Ledger 400 Crown Colony Dr	Quincy	MA	02169	617-786-7000	786-7025
Web: ledger.southofboston.com					
Republican The 1860 Main St	Springfield	MA	01101	413-788-1000	788-1301*
**Fax:* Edit ■ *TF:* 800-458-5877 ■ *Web:* www.masslive.com					
Telegram & Gazette 20 Franklin St PO Box 15012	Worcester	MA	01615	508-793-9100	793-9281*
**Fax:* News Rm ■ *TF:* 800-678-6680 ■ *Web:* www.telegram.com					

Michigan

	City	State	Zip	Phone	Fax
Daily Telegram 133 N Winter St	Adrian	MI	49221	517-265-5111	263-4152
TF: 800-968-5111 ■ *Web:* www.lenconnect.com					
Ann Arbor News 340 E Huron St	Ann Arbor	MI	48104	734-994-6989	994-6879*
**Fax:* Edit ■ *TF:* 800-466-6989 ■ *Web:* www.mlive.com/aanews					
Huron Daily Tribune 211 N Heisterman St	Bad Axe	MI	48413	989-269-6461	269-9435
Web: www.michiganthumb.com					
Battle Creek Enquirer 155 W Van Buren St	Battle Creek	MI	49017	269-964-7161	964-8242
TF: 800-333-4139 ■ *Web:* www.battlecreekenquirer.com					
Bay City Times 311 5th St	Bay City	MI	48708	989-895-8551	893-0649*
**Fax:* Edit ■ *Web:* www.mlive.com/bctimes					
Detroit Free Press 600 W Fort St	Detroit	MI	48226	313-222-6400	222-5981*
**Fax:* News Rm ■ *TF:* 800-678-6400 ■ *Web:* www.freep.com					
Detroit News 615 W Lafayette Blvd	Detroit	MI	48226	313-222-6400	222-2335*
**Fax:* News Rm ■ *TF:* 800-678-6400 ■ *Web:* www.detnews.com					
Flint Journal 200 E 1st St	Flint	MI	48502	810-766-6100	767-7518*
**Fax:* Edit ■ *TF Circulation:* 800-875-6200 ■ *Web:* www.flintjournal.com					
Grand Rapids Press 155 Michigan St NW	Grand Rapids	MI	49503	616-222-5400	222-5409
TF: 800-878-1400 ■ *Web:* www.mlive.com/grpress					
Holland Sentinel 54 W 8th St	Holland	MI	49423	616-392-2311	393-6710
TF: 800-968-3495 ■ *Web:* www.hollandsentinel.com					
Jackson Citizen Patriot 214 S Jackson St	Jackson	MI	49201	517-787-2300	787-9711
TF: 800-878-6397					
Kalamazoo Gazette 401 S Burdick St	Kalamazoo	MI	49007	269-345-3511	388-8447*
**Fax:* Edit ■ *TF:* 800-466-6397 ■ *Web:* www.mlive.com/kzgazette					
Lansing State Journal 120 E Lenawee St	Lansing	MI	48919	517-377-1000	377-1298
TF: 800-234-1719 ■ *Web:* www.lsj.com					
Mining Journal PO Box 430	Marquette	MI	49855	906-228-2500	228-2617
Web: www.miningjournal.net					
Midland Daily News 124 S McDonald St	Midland	MI	48640	989-835-7171	835-6991
TF: 800-835-6679 ■ *Web:* www.ourmidland.com					
Monroe Evening News PO Box 1176	Monroe	MI	48161	734-242-1100	242-0937*
**Fax:* Edit ■ *Web:* www.monroenews.com					
Macomb Daily 100 Macomb Daily Dr	Mount Clemens	MI	48043	586-469-4510	469-2892*
**Fax:* Edit ■ *Web:* www.macombdaily.com					
Muskegon Chronicle PO Box 59	Muskegon	MI	49443	231-722-3161	722-2552
TF: 800-783-3161 ■ *Web:* www.mlive.com/muchronicle					
Oakland Press PO Box 436009	Pontiac	MI	48343	248-332-8181	332-8885*
**Fax:* News Rm ■ *Web:* www.theoaklandpress.com					
Times Herald 911 Military St	Port Huron	MI	48060	810-985-7171	989-6294*
**Fax:* Edit ■ *TF:* 800-462-4057 ■ *Web:* www.thetimesherald.com					
Daily Tribune 210 E 3rd St	Royal Oak	MI	48067	248-541-3000	541-7041
TF: 877-373-2387 ■ *Web:* www.dailytribune.com					
Saginaw News 203 S Washington Ave	Saginaw	MI	48607	989-752-7171	752-3115
TF: 800-875-6397 ■ *Web:* www.mlive.com/sanews					
Herald-Palladium 3450 Hollywood Rd PO Box 128	Saint Joseph	MI	49085	269-429-2400	429-4398
TF: 800-356-4262 ■ *Web:* www.heraldpalladium.com					
South Haven Daily Tribune 225 Center St	South Haven	MI	49090	269-637-1104	637-8415
Traverse City Record-Eagle PO Box 632	Traverse City	MI	49685	231-946-2000	946-8632
Web: www.record-eagle.com					

Minnesota

	City	State	Zip	Phone	Fax
Duluth News-Tribune 424 W 1st St	Duluth	MN	55802	218-723-5281	720-4120
TF Circ: 800-456-8080 ■ *Web:* www.duluthsuperior.com/mld/duluthtribune					
Free Press 418 S 2nd St	Mankato	MN	56001	507-625-4451	388-4355
TF: 800-657-4662 ■ *Web:* www.mankatofreepress.com					
Star Tribune 425 Portland Ave	Minneapolis	MN	55488	612-673-4000	673-4359
TF: 800-827-8742 ■ *Web:* www.startribune.com					
Post-Bulletin 18 1st Ave SE	Rochester	MN	55904	507-285-7600	285-7772
TF: 800-562-1758 ■ *Web:* www.postbulletin.com					
Saint Cloud Times PO Box 768	Saint Cloud	MN	56302	320-255-8700	255-8773
Web: www.sctimes.com					
Saint Paul Pioneer Press 345 Cedar St	Saint Paul	MN	55101	651-228-5490	228-5500
TF: 800-950-9080 ■ *Web:* www.twincities.com/mld/pioneerpress					
West Central Tribune PO Box 839	Willmar	MN	56201	320-235-1150	235-6769
TF: 800-450-1150 ■ *Web:* www.wctrib.com					

Mississippi

	City	State	Zip	Phone	Fax
Delta Democrat Times 988 N Broadway St	Greenville	MS	38701	662-335-1155	335-2860
Web: www.ddtonline.com					
Sun Herald 205 DeBuys Rd	Gulfport	MS	39507	228-896-2100	896-2104*
**Fax:* News Rm ■ *TF:* 800-346-5022 ■ *Web:* www.sunherald.com					
Hattiesburg American 825 N Main St	Hattiesburg	MS	39401	601-582-4321	584-3130*
**Fax:* News Rm ■ *TF:* 800-844-2637 ■ *Web:* www.hattiesburgamerican.com					
Clarion-Ledger 201 S Congress St	Jackson	MS	39201	601-961-7000	961-7211
TF: 800-367-3384 ■ *Web:* www.clarionledger.com					
Meridian Star PO Box 1591	Meridian	MS	39302	601-693-1551	485-1275
TF: 800-232-2525 ■ *Web:* www.meridianstar.com					
Mississippi Press PO Box 849	Pascagoula	MS	39568	228-762-0033	934-1474*
**Fax:* News Rm ■ *Web:* www.gulflive.com					
Northeast Mississippi Daily Journal 1242 S Green St	Tupelo	MS	38804	662-842-2611	842-2233
TF: 800-264-6397 ■ *Web:* www.djournal.com					
Vicksburg Post PO Box 821668	Vicksburg	MS	39182	601-636-4545	634-0897
Web: www.vicksburgpost.com					

Missouri

	City	State	Zip	Phone	Fax
Examiner The 500 NW RD Mize Rd	Blue Springs	MO	64014	816-229-9161	229-6785
Web: www.examiner.net					
Branson Daily Independent 590 W Pacific St	Branson	MO	65616	417-334-2285	334-4789
Linn County Leader PO Box 40	Brookfield	MO	64628	660-258-7237	258-7238
Web: www.linncountyleader.com					
Southeast Missourian PO Box 699	Cape Girardeau	MO	63702	573-335-6611	334-7288*
**Fax:* News Rm ■ *TF:* 800-879-1210 ■ *Web:* www.semissourian.com					
Columbia Daily Tribune 101 N 4th St	Columbia	MO	65201	573-815-1700	815-1701
TF: 800-333-6799 ■ *Web:* www.columbiatribune.com					
Columbia Missourian 221 S 8th St	Columbia	MO	65201	573-882-5700	882-5702*
**Fax:* News Rm ■ *Web:* columbiamissourian.com					
Excelsior Springs Standard 417 Thompson Ave	Excelsior Springs	MO	64024	816-637-6155	637-8411
Web: www.excelsiorspringsstandard.com					
Branson Daily News 200 Industrial Park Dr	Hollister	MO	65672	417-334-3161	335-3933
TF: 800-490-8020 ■ *Web:* www.bransondailynews.com					
Examiner The 410 S Liberty St	Independence	MO	64050	816-254-8600	254-0211
Web: examiner.net					
Daily Capital News 210 Monroe St	Jefferson City	MO	65101	573-636-3131	761-0235
TF: 866-865-1690 ■ *Web:* www.newstribune.com					
Jefferson City Post-Tribune 210 Monroe St	Jefferson City	MO	65101	573-636-3131	761-0235
TF: 866-896-8088 ■ *Web:* www.newstribune.com					
Joplin Globe 117 E 4th St	Joplin	MO	64801	417-623-3480	623-8598
TF: 800-444-8514 ■ *Web:* www.joplinglobe.com					
Kansas City Star 1729 Grand Ave	Kansas City	MO	64108	816-234-4141	234-4926
TF: 877-962-7827 ■ *Web:* www.kansascity.com/mld/kansascity					
Daily Journal 1513 Saint Joe Dr PO Box A	Park Hills	MO	63601	573-431-2010	431-7640
Web: www.mydjconnection.com					
Daily American Republic 208 Poplar St	Poplar Bluff	MO	63901	573-785-1414	785-2706
TF: 800-276-2242 ■ *Web:* www.darnews.com					
Saint Joseph News-Press PO Box 29	Saint Joseph	MO	64502	816-271-8500	271-8692
TF: 800-779-6397 ■ *Web:* www.stjoenews-press.com					
Saint Louis Post-Dispatch 900 N Tucker Blvd	Saint Louis	MO	63101	314-340-8000	340-3050
TF: 800-365-0820 ■ *Web:* www.stltoday.com					
Springfield News Leader 651 Boonville Ave	Springfield	MO	65806	417-836-1100	837-1381
TF Circ: 800-695-2005 ■ *Web:* www.news-leader.com					

Montana

	City	State	Zip	Phone	Fax
Billings Gazette 401 N Broadway	Billings	MT	59101	406-657-1200	657-1208*
**Fax:* Edit ■ *TF:* 800-543-2505 ■ *Web:* www.billingsgazette.com					
Montana Standard 25 W Granite St	Butte	MT	59701	406-496-5500	496-5551
TF: 800-877-1074 ■ *Web:* www.mtstandard.com					
Great Falls Tribune 205 River Dr S	Great Falls	MT	59405	406-791-1444	791-1431*
**Fax:* News Rm ■ *TF:* 800-438-6600 ■ *Web:* www.greatfallstribune.com					
Helena Independent Record 317 Cruse Ave PO Box 4249	Helena	MT	59604	406-447-4000	447-4052
TF: 800-523-2272 ■ *Web:* www.helenair.com					
Independent-Record 317 Cruse Ave	Helena	MT	59601	406-447-4000	447-4052
TF: 800-523-2272 ■ *Web:* www.helenair.com					
Daily Inter Lake 727 E Idaho St	Kalispell	MT	59901	406-755-7000	752-6114
Web: www.dailyinterlake.com					
Missoulian PO Box 8029	Missoula	MT	59807	406-523-5200	523-5294
TF: 800-366-7102 ■ *Web:* www.missoulian.com					

Daily Newspapers - US (Cont'd)

Nebraska

Newspaper	City	State	Zip	Phone	Fax
Grand Island Independent 422 W 1st St *TF:* 800-658-3160 ■ *Web:* www.theindependent.com	Grand Island	NE	68801	308-382-1000	382-8129
Holdrege Daily Citizen 418 Garfield St PO Box 344	Holdrege	NE	68949	308-995-4441	995-5992
Lincoln Journal-Star 926 P St *Fax: News Rm ■ *TF:* 800-742-7315 ■ *Web:* www.journalstar.com	Lincoln	NE	68508	402-475-4200	473-7291*
Norfolk Daily News PO Box 977 *TF:* 877-371-1020 ■ *Web:* www.norfolkdailynews.com	Norfolk	NE	68702	402-371-1020	371-5802
Omaha World-Herald 1314 Douglas St *TF:* 800-284-6397 ■ *Web:* www.omaha.com	Omaha	NE	68102	402-444-1000	345-0183
Star-Herald PO Box 1709 *Fax: News Rm ■ *TF:* 800-846-6102 ■ *Web:* www.starherald.com	Scottsbluff	NE	69363	308-632-9000	632-9001*

Nevada

Newspaper	City	State	Zip	Phone	Fax
Nevada Appeal 580 Mallory Way *TF:* 800-221-8013 ■ *Web:* www.nevadaappeal.com	Carson City	NV	89701	775-882-2111	887-2420
Reno Gazette-Journal Carson City Edition 5055 Metric Way Suite 101	Carson City	NV	89706	775-885-5560	885-5565
Las Vegas Sun 2275 Corporate Cir Dr Suite 300 *Web:* www.lasvegassun.com	Henderson	NV	89074	702-385-3111	383-7264
Las Vegas Review-Journal 1111 W Bonanza Rd *Web:* www.reviewjournal.com	Las Vegas	NV	89106	702-383-0211	383-4676
Reno Gazette-Journal 955 Kuenzoi St *TF:* 800-648-5048 ■ *Web:* www.rgj.com	Reno	NV	89501	775-788-6200	788-6458

New Hampshire

Newspaper	City	State	Zip	Phone	Fax
Berlin Reporter 151 Main St PO Box 38 *Web:* www.breporter.com	Berlin	NH	03570	603-752-1200	752-2339
Concord Monitor 1 Monitor Dr PO Box 1177 *Web:* www.concordmonitor.com	Concord	NH	03302	603-224-5301	224-8120
Foster's Daily Democrat 150 Venture Dr *TF:* 800-660-8310 ■ *Web:* www.fosters.com	Dover	NH	03820	603-742-4455	749-7079
Union Leader 100 William Loeb Dr *Fax: Edit ■ *TF:* 800-562-8218 ■ *Web:* www.theunionleader.com	Manchester	NH	03109	603-668-4321	668-0382*
Telegraph The PO Box 1008 *Fax: News Rm ■ *Web:* www.nashuatelegraph.com	Nashua	NH	03061	603-882-2741	882-2681*
Portsmouth Herald 111 New Hampshire Ave *TF:* 800-439-0303 ■ *Web:* www.seacoastonline.com	Portsmouth	NH	03801	603-436-1800	433-5760
Valley News 24 Interchange Dr *TF:* 800-874-2226 ■ *Web:* www.vnews.com	West Lebanon	NH	03784	603-298-8711	298-0212

New Jersey

Newspaper	City	State	Zip	Phone	Fax
Millville/Bridgeton News 100 E Commerce St *Web:* www.nj.com/bridgeton	Bridgeton	NJ	08302	856-451-1000	455-3098
Courier-News 1201 Rt 22 W *Web:* www.c-n.com	Bridgewater	NJ	08807	908-722-8800	707-3252
Courier-Post PO Box 5300 *TF:* 800-677-6289 ■ *Web:* www.courierpostonline.com	Cherry Hill	NJ	08034	856-663-6000	663-2831
Home News Tribune 35 Kennedy Blvd *Fax: News Rm ■ *TF:* 800-627-4663 ■ *Web:* www.thnt.com	East Brunswick	NJ	08816	732-246-5500	565-7208*
Record The 150 River St *TF:* 888-473-2673	Hackensack	NJ	07601	201-646-4000	646-4135
Jersey Journal 30 Journal Sq *Fax: News Rm ■ *Web:* www.thejerseyjournal.com	Jersey City	NJ	07306	201-653-1000	653-1414*
Asbury Park Press 3601 Hwy 66 PO Box 1550 *Fax: News Rm ■ *Web:* www.app.com	Neptune	NJ	07754	732-922-6000	643-4014*
Star-Ledger The 1 Star Ledger Plaza *TF:* 800-501-2100 ■ *Web:* www.nj.com/starledger	Newark	NJ	07102	973-877-4141	392-5845
New Jersey Herald 2 Spring St *Web:* www.njherald.com	Newton	NJ	07860	973-383-1500	383-8477
Daily Record 800 Jefferson Rd PO Box 217 *Fax: Edit ■ *TF:* 800-398-8991 ■ *Web:* www.dailyrecord.com	Parsippany	NJ	07054	973-428-6200	428-6666*
Press of Atlantic City 11 Devins Ln *Web:* www.pressofatlanticcity.com	Pleasantville	NJ	08232	609-272-1100	272-7224
Times The 500 Perry St *Web:* www.nj.com/times	Trenton	NJ	08618	609-989-5454	394-2819
Times of Trenton 500 Perry St *Web:* www.nj.com	Trenton	NJ	08618	609-396-3232	394-2819
Trentonian 600 Perry St *Web:* www.trentonian.com	Trenton	NJ	08602	609-989-7800	393-6072
Daily Journal 891 E Oak Rd *TF:* 800-222-0104 ■ *Web:* www.thedailyjournal.com	Vineland	NJ	08360	856-691-5000	563-5308
Herald News 1 Garret Mountain Plaza Suite 8 *Fax: Edit ■ *Web:* www.northjersey.com	West Paterson	NJ	07424	973-569-7000	569-7129*
Burlington County Times 4284 Rt 130 *Web:* www.phillyburbs.com	Willingboro	NJ	08046	609-871-8000	871-0490
Gloucester County Times 309 S Broad St *Web:* www.nj.com/gloucester	Woodbury	NJ	08096	856-845-3300	845-5480

New Mexico

Newspaper	City	State	Zip	Phone	Fax
Albuquerque Journal 7777 Jefferson St NE *TF:* 800-990-5765 ■ *Web:* www.abqjournal.com	Albuquerque	NM	87109	505-823-7777	823-3994
Albuquerque Tribune 7777 Jefferson St NE *TF:* 800-665-8742 ■ *Web:* www.abqtrib.com	Albuquerque	NM	87109	505-823-3653	823-3689
Carlsbad Current-Argus 620 S Main St PO Box 1629 *Web:* www.currentargus.com	Carlsbad	NM	88221	505-887-5501	885-1066
Daily Times 201 N Allen Ave *TF:* 800-395-6397 ■ *Web:* www.daily-times.com	Farmington	NM	87401	505-325-4545	564-4630
Gallup Independent 500 N 9th St *TF:* 800-545-3817 ■ *Web:* www.gallupindependent.com	Gallup	NM	87305	505-863-6811	722-5750
Las Cruces Sun-News 256 W Las Cruces Ave *TF:* 800-745-5851 ■ *Web:* www.lcsun-news.com	Las Cruces	NM	88005	505-541-5400	541-5498
Observer The PO Box 15878 *Web:* www.observer-online.com	Rio Rancho	NM	87174	505-892-8080	892-5719
Santa Fe New Mexican PO Box 2048 *Fax: News Rm ■ *Web:* www.santafenewmexican.com	Santa Fe	NM	87504	505-983-3303	986-9147*

New York

Newspaper	City	State	Zip	Phone	Fax
Times Union 645 Albany Shaker Rd PO Box 15000 *TF:* 800-955-4388 ■ *Web:* www.timesunion.com	Albany	NY	12212	518-454-5420	454-5628
Daily News 2 Apollo Dr PO Box 870 *TF:* 888-217-6397	Batavia	NY	14021	585-343-8000	343-2623
Press & Sun Bulletin PO box 1270 *TF:* 800-365-0077 ■ *Web:* www.binghamtonpress.com	Binghamton	NY	13902	607-798-1234	798-1113
Daily Challenge 1195 Atlantic Ave *Web:* www.challenge-group.com	Brooklyn	NY	11216	718-636-9500	857-9115
Buffalo News 1 News Plaza PO Box 100 *TF:* 800-777-8680 ■ *Web:* www.buffnews.com	Buffalo	NY	14240	716-849-4444	856-5150
Evening Observer 8-10 E 2nd St PO Box 391 *TF:* 800-836-0931 ■ *Web:* observertoday.com	Dunkirk	NY	14048	716-366-3000	366-3005
Star-Gazette 201 Baldwin St *TF:* 800-836-8970 ■ *Web:* www.star-gazette.com	Elmira	NY	14902	607-734-5151	733-4408
Finger Lakes Times 218 Genesee St *TF:* 800-388-6652 ■ *Web:* www.fltimes.com	Geneva	NY	14456	315-789-3333	789-4077
Post-Star Lawrence & Cooper Sts PO Box 2157 *TF:* 800-724-2543 ■ *Web:* www.poststar.com	Glens Falls	NY	12801	518-792-3131	761-1255
Register-Star 364 Warren St *Web:* www.registerstar.com	Hudson	NY	12534	518-828-1616	828-9437
Ithaca Journal 123 W State St *Web:* www.theithacajournal.com	Ithaca	NY	14850	607-272-2321	272-4248
Post-Journal PO Box 190 *TF:* 866-756-9600 ■ *Web:* post-journal.com	Jamestown	NY	14702	716-487-1111	664-5305
Daily Freeman 79 Hurley Ave *Web:* www.dailyfreeman.com	Kingston	NY	12401	845-331-5000	331-3557
Newsday Inc 235 Pinelawn Rd *Fax: News Rm ■ *TF:* 800-639-7329 ■ *Web:* www.newsday.com	Melville	NY	11747	631-843-2020	843-2953*
Times Herald-Record 40 Mulberry St PO Box 2046 *TF:* 800-295-2181 ■ *Web:* www.recordonline.com	Middletown	NY	10940	845-341-1100	343-2170
AM New York 330 W 34th St 17th Fl *Web:* www.am-ny.com	New York	NY	10001	212-239-5555	239-2828
Financial Times 1330 Ave of the Americas *TF:* 800-628-8088 ■ *Web:* www.ft.com	New York	NY	10019	212-641-6500	641-6479
Hoy 330 W 34th St 17th Fl *Fax Area Code: 212 ■ *Fax: Edit ■ *TF:* 866-836-3256 ■ *Web:* www.hoyinternet.com	New York	NY	10001	917-339-0800	971-4414*
International Herald Tribune 229 W 43rd St 2nd Fl *Web:* www.iht.com	New York	NY	10036	212-556-7714	556-7706
New York Daily News 450 W 33rd St 3rd Fl *TF:* 800-692-6397 ■ *Web:* www.nydailynews.com	New York	NY	10001	212-210-2100	643-7831
New York Post 1211 Ave of the Americas *TF:* 800-552-7678 ■ *Web:* www.nypost.com	New York	NY	10036	212-930-8000	930-8540
New York Sun 105 Chambers St 2nd Fl *TF:* 866-692-7861 ■ *Web:* www.nysun.com	New York	NY	10007	212-406-2000	571-9836
New York Times 229 W 43rd St *Web:* www.nytimes.com	New York	NY	10036	212-556-1234	556-8828
Niagara Gazette PO Box 549 *Web:* www.niagara-gazette.com	Niagara Falls	NY	14302	716-282-2311	286-3895
Olean Times-Herald 639 Norton Dr *Fax: News Rm ■ *TF:* 800-722-8812 ■ *Web:* www.oleantimesherald.com	Olean	NY	14760	716-372-3121	373-6397*
Daily Star 102 Chestnut St PO Box 250 *TF:* 800-721-1000 ■ *Web:* www.thedailystar.com	Oneonta	NY	13820	607-432-1000	432-5707
Press-Republican 170 Margaret St PO Box 459 *TF:* 800-288-7323 ■ *Web:* www.pressrepublican.com	Plattsburgh	NY	12901	518-561-2300	561-3362
Poughkeepsie Journal 85 Civic Ctr Plaza *TF:* 800-765-1120 ■ *Web:* www.poughkeepsiejournal.com	Poughkeepsie	NY	12601	845-437-4800	437-4921
Daily Record 11 Centre Park *Web:* www.nydailyrecord.com	Rochester	NY	14614	585-232-6920	232-2740
Democrat & Chronicle 55 Exchange Blvd *Fax: News Rm ■ *TF:* 800-473-5274 ■ *Web:* www.democratandchronicle.com	Rochester	NY	14614	585-232-7100	258-2237*
Rome Sentinel PO Box 471 *Web:* romesentinel.com	Rome	NY	13442	315-337-4000	339-6281
Daily Gazette 2345 Maxon Rd Ext *TF:* 800-262-2211 ■ *Web:* www.dailygazette.com	Schenectady	NY	12301	518-374-4141	395-3089
Staten Island Advance 950 Fingerboard Rd *Web:* www.silive.com	Staten Island	NY	10305	718-981-1234	981-5679
Post-Standard PO Box 4915 *TF:* 800-765-4569 ■ *Web:* www.syracuse.com/poststandard	Syracuse	NY	13221	315-470-0011	470-3081
Record The 501 Broadway *Web:* www.troyrecord.com	Troy	NY	12180	518-270-1200	270-1202
Observer-Dispatch 221 Oriskany Plaza *Web:* www.uticaod.com	Utica	NY	13501	315-792-5000	792-5033
Watertown Daily Times 260 Washington St *TF:* 800-642-6222 ■ *Web:* www.watertowndailytimes.com	Watertown	NY	13601	315-782-1000	661-2523
Rockland Journal-News 1 Crossfield Ave *Web:* www.thejournalnews.com	West Nyack	NY	10994	845-358-2200	578-2477
Journal News 1 Gannett Dr *TF:* 800-942-1010 ■ *Web:* www.thejournalnews.com	White Plains	NY	10604	914-694-9300	694-5018

North Carolina

Newspaper	City	State	Zip	Phone	Fax
Courier-Tribune 500 Sunset Ave *TF:* 800-967-1838 ■ *Web:* www.courier-tribune.com	Asheboro	NC	27203	336-625-2101	626-7074
Asheville Citizen Times 14 O'Henry Ave *TF:* 800-800-4204 ■ *Web:* www.citizen-times.com	Asheville	NC	28801	828-252-5622	251-0585
Times-News PO Box 481 *TF:* 800-488-0085 ■ *Web:* www.thetimesnews.com	Burlington	NC	27216	336-227-0131	229-2463
Charlotte Observer 600 S Tryon St *TF:* 800-332-0686 ■ *Web:* www.charlotte.com/mld/observer	Charlotte	NC	28202	704-358-5000	358-5036
Herald-Sun 2828 Pickett Rd *TF:* 800-672-0061 ■ *Web:* www.herald-sun.com	Durham	NC	27705	919-419-6500	419-6837
Bladen Daily Journal 228 W Broad St PO Box 70 *Web:* www.bladenjournal.com	Elizabethtown	NC	28337	910-862-4163	862-6602
Fayetteville Observer 458 Whitfield St *TF:* 800-345-9895 ■ *Web:* www.fayettevillenc.com	Fayetteville	NC	28306	910-323-4848	486-3545
Gaston Gazette 1893 Remount Rd *TF:* 800-273-3315 ■ *Web:* www.gastongazette.com	Gastonia	NC	28054	704-869-1700	867-5751
Goldsboro News-Argus PO Box 10629 *Fax: News Rm ■ *Web:* www.newsargus.com	Goldsboro	NC	27532	919-778-2211	778-5408*
News & Record 200 E Market St *TF:* 800-553-6880 ■ *Web:* www.news-record.com	Greensboro	NC	27401	336-373-7000	373-7382
Daily Reflector PO Box 1967 *TF:* 800-849-6166 ■ *Web:* www.reflector.com	Greenville	NC	27835	252-329-9500	754-8140
Times-News PO Box 490 *TF:* 800-849-8050 ■ *Web:* www.hendersonvillenews.com	Hendersonville	NC	28793	828-692-0505	693-5581
Hickory Daily Record 1100 Park Pl *TF:* 800-849-8586 ■ *Web:* www.hickoryrecord.com	Hickory	NC	28603	828-322-4510	324-8179
High Point Enterprise 210 Church Ave *TF:* 800-933-5760 ■ *Web:* www.hpe.com	High Point	NC	27262	336-888-3500	841-5582
Daily News 724 Bell Fork Rd PO Box 196 *TF:* 800-659-2873 ■ *Web:* www.jdnews.com	Jacksonville	NC	28541	910-353-1171	353-7316
Independent Tribune 924 Cloverleaf Plaza *Fax: News Rm ■ *Web:* www.independenttribune.com	Kannapolis	NC	28083	704-782-3155	786-0645*
Mount Airy News PO Box 808 *TF:* 800-826-6397 ■ *Web:* www.mtairynews.com	Mount Airy	NC	27030	336-786-4141	789-2816
Sun Journal 3200 Wellons Blvd *Web:* www.newbernsunjournal.com	New Bern	NC	28563	252-638-8101	638-4664

				Phone	Fax
News & Observer 215 S McDowell St.	Raleigh	NC	27602	919-829-4500	829-4529
TF: 800-365-3115 ■ *Web:* www.newsobserver.com					
Salisbury Post 131 W Innes St.	Salisbury	NC	28144	704-633-8950	639-0003
TF: 800-633-8957 ■ *Web:* www.salisburypost.com					
Statesville Record & Landmark PO Box 1071	Statesville	NC	28687	704-873-1451	872-3150
Web: www.statesville.com					
Star-News PO Box 840	Wilmington	NC	28402	910-343-2000	343-2227
TF: 800-272-1277 ■ *Web:* www.starnewsonline.com					
Wilson Daily Times PO Box 2447	Wilson	NC	27894	252-243-5151	243-7501*
**Fax:* News Rm ■ *TF:* 800-849-8811 ■ *Web:* www.wilsondaily.com					
Winston-Salem Journal 418 N Marshall St.	Winston-Salem	NC	27101	336-727-7211	727-7315
TF: 800-642-0925 ■ *Web:* www.journalnow.com					

North Dakota

				Phone	Fax
Bismarck Tribune 707 E Front Ave	Bismarck	ND	58506	701-223-2500	223-2063*
**Fax:* Edit ■ *TF:* 866-476-5348 ■ *Web:* www.bismarcktribune.com					
Forum The 101 N 5th St	Fargo	ND	58102	701-235-7311	241-5487
TF: 800-747-7311 ■ *Web:* www.in-forum.com					
Grand Forks Herald 375 2nd Ave N	Grand Forks	ND	58203	701-780-1100	780-1123
Web: www.grandforks.com					
Minot Daily News 301 4th St SE	Minot	ND	58761	701-857-1900	857-1907
TF: 800-735-3119 ■ *Web:* www.minotdailynews.com					

Ohio

				Phone	Fax
Akron Beacon Journal 44 E Exchange St.	Akron	OH	44309	330-996-3000	376-9235
TF: 800-777-2442 ■ *Web:* www.ohio.com/mld/beaconjournal					
Star Beacon PO Box 2100	Ashtabula	OH	44005	440-998-2323	998-7938
TF: 800-554-6768 ■ *Web:* www.starbeacon.com					
Repository 500 Market Ave S	Canton	OH	44702	330-580-8300	454-5745*
**Fax:* News Rm ■ *TF:* 877-580-8300 ■ *Web:* www.cantonrep.com					
Chillicothe Gazette 50 W Main St PO Box 4400	Chillicothe	OH	45601	740-773-2111	772-9505
Web: www.chillicothegazette.com					
Cincinnati Enquirer 312 Elm St	Cincinnati	OH	45202	513-721-2700	768-8340
TF: 800-876-4500 ■ *Web:* news.enquirer.com					
Cincinnati Post 125 E Court St.	Cincinnati	OH	45202	513-352-2000	621-3962
Web: www.cincypost.com					
Kentucky Post 125 E Court St Suite 500	Cincinnati	OH	45202	859-292-2600	621-3962*
**Fax Area Code:* 513 ■ *TF:* 800-937-4954 ■ *Web:* www.kypost.com					
Plain Dealer 1801 Superior Ave	Cleveland	OH	44114	216-999-5000	999-6366
TF: 800-688-4802 ■ *Web:* www.cleveland.com					
Columbus Dispatch 34 S 3rd St	Columbus	OH	43215	614-461-5000	461-7580*
**Fax:* News Rm ■ *TF:* 800-848-1110 ■ *Web:* www.dispatch.com					
Dayton Daily News 1611 S Main St	Dayton	OH	45409	937-225-2000	225-2489
Web: www.daytondailynews.com					
Crescent-News 624 W 2nd St PO Box 249	Defiance	OH	43512	419-784-5441	784-1492
TF: 800-589-5441 ■ *Web:* www.crescent-news.com					
Chronicle-Telegram 225 East Ave.	Elyria	OH	44035	440-329-7000	329-7282
TF: 800-848-6397 ■ *Web:* www.chroniclet.com					
Courier The PO Box 609	Findlay	OH	45839	419-422-5151	422-2937
Web: www.thecourier.com					
Journal News 228 Court St.	Hamilton	OH	45011	513-863-8200	896-9489
Web: www.journal-news.com					
Lancaster Eagle-Gazette 138 W Chestnut St	Lancaster	OH	43130	740-681-4500	681-4505
TF: 888-420-3883 ■ *Web:* www.lancastereaglegazette.com					
Lima News 3515 Elida Rd	Lima	OH	45807	419-223-1010	229-2926
TF: 800-686-9924 ■ *Web:* www.limanews.com					
Morning Journal 1657 Broadway Ave	Lorain	OH	44052	440-245-6901	245-6912
Web: www.morningjournal.com					
News Journal 70 W 4th St	Mansfield	OH	44902	419-522-3311	521-7415
TF: 800-472-5547 ■ *Web:* www.mansfieldnewsjournal.com					
Star The Marion 150 Court St.	Marion	OH	43302	740-387-0400	375-5188
TF: 800-626-1331 ■ *Web:* www.marionstar.com					
Times Leader 200 S 4th St	Martins Ferry	OH	43935	740-633-1131	633-1122
TF: 800-244-5671 ■ *Web:* www.timesleaderonline.com					
Medina Gazette 885 W Liberty St.	Medina	OH	44256	330-725-4166	721-4016
TF: 800-633-4623 ■ *Web:* www.medina-gazette.com					
Middletown Journal PO Box 490	Middletown	OH	45042	513-422-3611	423-6940
Web: www.middletown.com					
Times Reporter 629 Wabash Ave NW	New Philadelphia	OH	44663	330-364-5577	364-8416
TF: 800-837-8666 ■ *Web:* www.timesreporter.com					
Advocate The 22 N 1st St	Newark	OH	43055	740-345-4053	328-8581
TF: 800-555-8350 ■ *Web:* www.newarkadvocate.com					
Daily Sentinel 111 Court St PO Box 729	Pomeroy	OH	45769	740-992-2155	992-2157
Web: www.mydailysentinel.com					
Portsmouth Daily Times PO Box 581	Portsmouth	OH	45662	740-353-3101	353-4676
TF: 800-298-5232 ■ *Web:* www.portsmouth-dailytimes.com					
Record-Courier 126 N Chestnut St PO Box 1201	Ravenna	OH	44266	330-296-9657	296-2698
TF: 800-560-9657 ■ *Web:* www.recordpub.com					
Sandusky Register 314 W Market St	Sandusky	OH	44870	419-625-5500	625-3007
TF: 800-466-1243 ■ *Web:* www.sanduskyregister.com					
Daily Globe 37 W Main St.	Shelby	OH	44875	419-342-3261	342-4246
Web: sdgnewsgroup.com					
Springfield News-Sun 202 N Limestone St.	Springfield	OH	45503	937-328-0300	328-0328
TF: 888-890-7323 ■ *Web:* www.springfieldnewssun.com					
Blade 541 N Superior St	Toledo	OH	43660	419-724-6000	724-6439
TF: 888-252-3301 ■ *Web:* www.toledoblade.com					
Tribune Chronicle 240 Franklin St SE	Warren	OH	44482	330-841-1600	841-1717
TF: 888-550-8742 ■ *Web:* www.tribune-chronicle.com					
News-Herald 7085 Mentor Ave	Willoughby	OH	44094	440-951-0000	975-2293*
**Fax:* News Rm ■ *TF:* 800-947-2737 ■ *Web:* www.news-herald.com					
Daily Record 212 E Liberty St PO Box 918	Wooster	OH	44691	330-264-1125	264-3756
TF: 888-323-1662 ■ *Web:* www.the-daily-record.com					
Vindicator The 107 Vindicator Sq PO Box 780	Youngstown	OH	44501	330-747-1471	747-6712
TF: 800-686-5199 ■ *Web:* www.vindy.com					
Times Recorder 34 S 4th St	Zanesville	OH	43701	740-452-4561	450-6759*
**Fax:* News Rm ■ *TF:* 800-886-7326 ■ *Web:* www.zanesvilletimesrecorder.com					

Oklahoma

				Phone	Fax
Edmond Sun PO Box 2470	Edmond	OK	73083	405-341-2121	340-7363
Web: www.edmondsun.com					
Enid News & Eagle 227 W Broadway	Enid	OK	73701	580-233-6600	233-7645
Web: www.enidnews.com					
Frederick Leader 304 W Grand Ave PO Box 488	Frederick	OK	73542	580-335-2188	335-2047
Henryetta Free-Lance 812 W Main St	Henryetta	OK	74437	918-652-3311	652-7347
Lawton Constitution 102 SW 3rd St Po Box 2069	Lawton	OK	73502	580-353-0620	585-5140
TF: 800-364-3636 ■ *Web:* www.lawton-constitution.com					
Muskogee Daily Phoenix PO Box 1968	Muskogee	OK	74402	918-684-2828	684-2865
TF: 800-730-3649 ■ *Web:* www.muskogeephoenix.com					
Norman Transcript 215 E Comanche St	Norman	OK	73069	405-321-1800	366-3516
Web: www.normantranscript.com					
Journal Record Oklahoma City 101 N Robinson St Suite 101	Oklahoma City	OK	73102	405-235-3100	278-2890
Web: www.journalrecord.com					
Oklahoman The 9000 N Broadway	Oklahoma City	OK	73114	405-475-3311	475-3970
TF: 800-375-6397 ■ *Web:* www.newsok.com					
Tulsa World 315 S Boulder Ave	Tulsa	OK	74102	918-583-2161	581-8353
TF: 800-897-3557 ■ *Web:* www.tulsaworld.com					
Wewoka Times PO Box 61	Wewoka	OK	74884	405-257-3341	257-3342
Web: www.wewokatimes.com					

Oregon

				Phone	Fax
Albany Democrat-Herald 600 Lyons St SW	Albany	OR	97321	541-926-2211	926-4799
TF: 800-677-3993 ■ *Web:* www.democratherald.com					
Bulletin The 1777 SW Chandler Ave.	Bend	OR	97702	541-382-1811	385-5804
TF: 800-503-3933 ■ *Web:* www.bendbulletin.com					
Register-Guard 3500 Chad Dr	Eugene	OR	97408	541-485-1234	683-7631
Web: www.registerguard.com					
Daily Courier 409 SE 7th St	Grants Pass	OR	97526	541-474-3700	474-3824
TF: 800-228-0457 ■ *Web:* www.thedailycourier.com					
Herald & News PO Box 788	Klamath Falls	OR	97601	541-885-4410	885-4456
TF: 800-275-0982 ■ *Web:* www.heraldandnews.com					
Medford Mail Tribune PO Box 1108	Medford	OR	97501	541-776-4411	776-4390
TF: 800-366-2527 ■ *Web:* www.mailtribune.com					
Daily Journal of Commerce 921 SW Washington St Suite 210	Portland	OR	97205	503-226-1311	802-7239*
**Fax:* News Rm ■ *Web:* www.djc-or.com					
Oregonian 1320 SW Broadway	Portland	OR	97201	503-221-8100	227-5306
TF News Rm: 800-238-8195 ■ *Web:* www.oregonlive.com					
News-Review 345 NE Winchester St.	Roseburg	OR	97470	541-672-3321	957-4270*
**Fax:* Edit ■ *TF:* 800-683-3321 ■ *Web:* www.newsreview.info					
Statesman Journal 280 Church St NE	Salem	OR	97301	503-399-6611	399-6706*
**Fax:* News Rm ■ *Web:* www.statesmanjournal.com					
Dalles Chronicle 315 Federal St	The Dalles	OR	97058	541-296-2141	298-1365
TF: 800-375-7832 ■ *Web:* www.thedalleschronicle.com					

Pennsylvania

				Phone	Fax
Morning Call 101 N 6th St	Allentown	PA	18101	610-820-6500	820-6693
TF: 800-666-5492 ■ *Web:* www.mcall.com					
Altoona Mirror 301 Cayuga Ave	Altoona	PA	16602	814-946-7411	946-7540
TF: 800-222-1962 ■ *Web:* www.altoonamirror.com					
Beaver County Times 400 Fair Ave.	Beaver	PA	15009	724-775-3200	775-4180*
**Fax:* Edit ■ *Web:* www.timesonline.com					
Dispatch The 116 E Market St	Blairsville	PA	15717	724-459-6100	459-7366
TF: 888-636-1116 ■ *Web:* www.pittsburghlive.com					
Press-Enterprise 3185 Lackawanna Ave	Bloomsburg	PA	17815	570-784-2121	784-9226
TF: 800-228-3483 ■ *Web:* www.pressenterprise.net					
Butler Eagle PO Box 271	Butler	PA	16003	724-282-8000	282-4180
Web: www.butlereagle.com					
Sentinel The 457 E North St.	Carlisle	PA	17013	717-243-2611	243-3121
TF: 800-829-5570 ■ *Web:* www.cumberlink.com					
Public Opinion 77 N 3rd St.	Chambersburg	PA	17201	717-264-6161	264-0377*
**Fax:* News Rm ■ *Web:* www.publicopiniononline.com					
Intelligencer The 333 N Broad St.	Doylestown	PA	18901	215-345-3000	345-3150
Web: www.phillyburbs.com					
Express-Times 30 N 4th St	Easton	PA	18042	610-258-7171	258-7130
TF: 800-360-3601 ■ *Web:* penn.nj.com					
Erie Times-News 205 W 12th St.	Erie	PA	16534	814-870-1600	870-1808
TF: 800-352-0043 ■ *Web:* www.goerie.com					
Gettysburg Times 1570 Fairfield Rd	Gettysburg	PA	17325	717-334-1131	334-7408
Web: www.gettysburgtimes.com					
Tribune-Review 622 Cabin Hill Dr.	Greensburg	PA	15601	724-834-1151	838-5171
Web: www.triblive.com					
Evening Sun 135 Baltimore St PO Box 514	Hanover	PA	17331	717-637-3736	637-0900
TF: 800-877-3786 ■ *Web:* www.eveningsun.com					
Patriot-News 812 Market St	Harrisburg	PA	17101	717-255-8100	255-8456
TF: 800-692-7207 ■ *Web:* www.pennlive.com					
Hazleton Standard Speaker 21 N Wyoming St.	Hazleton	PA	18201	570-455-3636	455-4244
TF: 800-843-6680 ■ *Web:* www.standardspeaker.com					
Wayne Independent 220 8th St	Honesdale	PA	18431	570-253-3055	253-5387
Web: www.wayneindependent.com					
Indiana Gazette 899 Water St.	Indiana	PA	15701	724-465-5555	465-8267
Web: online.indianagazette.com					
Tribune-Democrat 425 Locust St	Johnstown	PA	15907	814-532-5050	539-1409
TF: 800-473-0998 ■ *Web:* www.tribune-democrat.com					
Intelligencer Journal 8 W King St	Lancaster	PA	17603	717-291-8622	399-6507
TF: 800-809-4666 ■ *Web:* www.lancasteronline.com/news.shtm					
Lancaster New Era 8 W King St	Lancaster	PA	17603	717-291-8733	399-6506
TF: 800-809-4666 ■ *Web:* lancasteronline.com/pages/paper/newera/					
Reporter The 307 Derstine Ave.	Lansdale	PA	19446	215-855-8440	855-3432
Web: www.thereporteronline.com					
Lebanon Daily News 718 Poplar St.	Lebanon	PA	17042	717-272-5611	274-1608
Web: www.ldnews.com					
Bucks County Courier Times 8400 Rt 13	Levittown	PA	19057	215-949-4000	949-4177*
**Fax:* Edit ■ *Web:* www.phillyburbs.com/couriertimes					
Daily News 409 Walnut St	McKeesport	PA	15132	412-664-9161	664-3974
Meadville Tribune 947 Federal Ct.	Meadville	PA	16335	814-724-6370	724-8755
TF: 800-879-0006 ■ *Web:* www.meadvilletribune.com					
Valley Independent Eastgate 19	Monessen	PA	15062	724-684-5200	684-2603
Web: www.pittsburghlive.com/x/valleyindependent					
Valley Mirror 3910 Main St.	Munhall	PA	15120	412-462-0626	462-1847
Web: www.valleymirror.com					
New Castle News PO Box 60	New Castle	PA	16103	724-654-6651	654-5976
Web: www.ncnewsonline.com					
Times Herald PO Box 591	Norristown	PA	19404	610-272-2500	272-0660
Web: www.timesherald.com					
Derrick The 1510 W 1st St PO Box 928	Oil City	PA	16301	814-676-7444	677-8347
TF: 800-352-1002 ■ *Web:* www.thederrick.com					
Evening Bulletin 1518 Walnut St Suite 1010	Philadelphia	PA	19102	215-735-3012	735-3019
TF: 866-261-8650 ■ *Web:* www.theeveningbulletin.com					
Philadelphia Daily News 400 N Broad St.	Philadelphia	PA	19130	215-854-2000	854-5910
Web: www.philly.com/mld/dailynews					
Philadelphia Inquirer 400 N Broad St	Philadelphia	PA	19130	215-854-2000	854-5099
Web: www.philly.com/mld/inquirer					
Pittsburgh Post-Gazette 34 Blvd of the Allies	Pittsburgh	PA	15222	412-263-1100	391-8452
Web: www.post-gazette.com					
Pittsburgh Tribune-Review 503 Martindale St 3rd Fl	Pittsburgh	PA	15212	412-321-6460	320-7963
TF: 800-433-3045 ■ *Web:* www.pittsburghlive.com/x/tribune-review					
Mercury The 24 N Hanover St	Pottstown	PA	19464	610-323-3000	323-0682
Web: www.pottsmerc.com					

Daily Newspapers - US (Cont'd)

Pennsylvania (Cont'd)

	City	State	ZIP	Phone	Fax
Pottsville Republican 111 Mahantongo St *TF:* 800-622-1737 ■ *Web:* www.pottsville.com	Pottsville	PA	17901	570-622-3456	628-6068
Delaware County Daily Times 500 Mildred Ave *Web:* www.delcotimes.com	Primos	PA	19017	610-622-8800	622-8889
Reading Eagle 345 Penn St *TF:* 800-633-7222 ■ *Web:* www.readingeagle.com	Reading	PA	19601	610-371-5000	371-5098
Scranton Times-Tribune 149 Penn Ave *TF:* 800-228-4637 ■ *Web:* www.scrantontimes.com	Scranton	PA	18503	570-348-9100	348-9135
Herald The 52 S Dock St *Web:* www.sharonherald.com	Sharon	PA	16146	724-981-6100	981-5116
Centre Daily Times 3400 E College Ave **Fax:* News Rm ■ *TF:* 800-327-5500 ■ *Web:* www.centredaily.com	State College	PA	16804	814-238-5000	238-1811*
Pocono Record 511 Lenox St **Fax:* News Rm ■ *TF:* 800-756-4237 ■ *Web:* www.poconorecord.com	Stroudsburg	PA	18360	570-421-3000	421-6284*
Daily Item 200 Market St PO Box 607 *TF:* 800-792-2303 ■ *Web:* www.dailyitem.com	Sunbury	PA	17801	570-286-5671	286-7695
Valley News Dispatch 210 4th Ave *TF:* 877-698-2553 ■ *Web:* www.pittsburghlive.com/x/valleynewsdispatch	Tarentum	PA	15084	724-226-1006	226-4677
Herald-Standard 8 E Church St Suite 18 *TF:* 800-342-8254 ■ *Web:* www.heraldstandard.com	Uniontown	PA	15401	724-439-7500	439-7559
Observer-Reporter 122 S Main St **Fax:* News Rm ■ *TF:* 800-222-6397 ■ *Web:* www.observer-reporter.com	Washington	PA	15301	724-222-2200	225-2077*
Daily Local News 250 N Bradford Ave *TF:* 800-456-6397 ■ *Web:* www.dailylocal.com	West Chester	PA	19382	610-696-1775	430-1194
Citizens' Voice 75 N Washington St **Fax:* News Rm ■ *Web:* www.citizensvoice.com	Wilkes-Barre	PA	18711	570-821-2000	821-2247*
Times Leader 15 N Main St **Fax:* News Rm ■ *Web:* www.timesleader.com	Wilkes-Barre	PA	18711	570-829-7100	829-5537*
Williamsport Sun-Gazette 252 W 4th St *TF:* 800-339-0289 ■ *Web:* www.sungazette.com	Williamsport	PA	17701	570-326-1551	326-0314
York Daily Record 1891 Loucks Rd *Web:* www.ydr.com	York	PA	17408	717-771-2000	771-2009
York Dispatch 205 N George St *TF:* 800-483-5517 ■ *Web:* www.yorkdispatch.com	York	PA	17401	717-854-1575	843-2814

Rhode Island

	City	State	ZIP	Phone	Fax
Newport Daily News 101 Malbone Rd *Web:* www.newportdailynews.com	Newport	RI	02840	401-849-3300	849-3306
Times The 23 Exchange St *Web:* www.pawtuckettimes.com	Pawtucket	RI	02860	401-722-4000	727-9280
Providence Journal 75 Fountain St *TF:* 888-697-7656 ■ *Web:* www.projo.com	Providence	RI	02902	401-277-7000	277-7346
Evening Call Publishing Co 75 Main St *Web:* www.woonsocketcall.com	Woonsocket	RI	02895	401-762-3000	765-2834

South Carolina

	City	State	ZIP	Phone	Fax
Anderson Independent-Mail PO Box 2507 *TF:* 800-859-6397 ■ *Web:* www.independentmail.com	Anderson	SC	29622	864-224-4321	260-1276
Island Packet 10 Buck Island Rd *TF:* 877-706-8100 ■ *Web:* www.islandpacket.com	Bluffton	SC	29910	843-706-8100	706-3070
Post & Courier 134 Columbus St **Fax:* News Rm ■ *Web:* www.charleston.net	Charleston	SC	29403	843-577-7111	937-5579*
State The 1401 Shop Rd *TF:* 800-888-5353 ■ *Web:* www.thestate.com	Columbia	SC	29201	803-771-6161	771-8430
Morning News 310 S Dargan St *Web:* www.morningnewsonline.com	Florence	SC	29501	843-317-6397	317-7292
Greenville News 305 S Main St *TF:* 800-800-5116 ■ *Web:* greenvilleonline.com	Greenville	SC	29601	864-298-4100	298-4395
Index Journal 610 Phoenix St *Web:* www.indexjournal.com	Greenwood	SC	29648	864-223-1411	223-7331
Sun News 914 Frontage Rd E *TF:* 800-568-1800 ■ *Web:* www.myrtlebeachonline.com/mld/sunnews/	Myrtle Beach	SC	29578	843-626-8555	626-0356
Times & Democrat PO Box 1766 *TF:* 877-534-1060 ■ *Web:* www.thetandd.com	Orangeburg	SC	29115	803-533-5500	533-5595
Herald The 132 W Main St *TF:* 800-697-4111 ■ *Web:* www.heraldonline.com	Rock Hill	SC	29730	803-329-4000	329-4021
Spartanburg Herald-Journal 189 W Main St *TF:* 800-922-4158 ■ *Web:* www.goupstate.com	Spartanburg	SC	29306	864-582-4511	594-6350
Item The 20 N Magnolia St PO Box 1677 *Web:* www.theitem.com	Sumter	SC	29151	803-774-1200	774-1210

South Dakota

	City	State	ZIP	Phone	Fax
Aberdeen American News 124 S 2nd St *TF:* 800-925-4100 ■ *Web:* www.aberdeennews.com/mld/americannews	Aberdeen	SD	57402	605-225-4100	225-0421
Capital Journal 333 W Dakota Ave *TF:* 800-658-3063 ■ *Web:* www.capjournal.com	Pierre	SD	57501	605-224-7301	224-9210
Rapid City Journal 507 Main St *TF:* 800-843-2300 ■ *Web:* www.rapidcityjournal.com	Rapid City	SD	57701	605-394-8300	394-8463
Argus Leader 200 S Minnesota Ave **Fax:* Edit ■ *TF:* 800-530-6897 ■ *Web:* www.argusleader.com	Sioux Falls	SD	57104	605-331-2200	331-2294*
Black Hills Pioneer 315 Seaton Cir *TF:* 800-676-2761 ■ *Web:* www.zwire.com/site/news.cfm?brd=1300	Spearfish	SD	57783	605-642-2761	642-9060

Tennessee

	City	State	ZIP	Phone	Fax
Chattanooga Times Free Press 400 E 11th St *Web:* www.timesfreepress.com	Chattanooga	TN	37403	423-757-6497	757-6383
Leaf-Chronicle PO Box 31029 *Web:* www.theleafchronicle.com	Clarksville	TN	37040	931-552-1808	552-5859
Greeneville Sun 121 W Summer St *Web:* www.greene.xtn.net	Greeneville	TN	37743	423-638-4181	638-7348
Jackson Sun 245 W LaFayette St *TF:* 800-372-3922 ■ *Web:* www.jacksonsun.com	Jackson	TN	38301	731-427-3333	425-9639
Johnson City Press 204 W Main St *Web:* www.johnsoncitypress.com	Johnson City	TN	37604	423-929-3111	929-7484
Kingsport Times-News 701 Lynn Garden Dr *TF:* 800-251-0328 ■ *Web:* www.timesnews.net	Kingsport	TN	37660	423-246-8121	392-1385
Knoxville News-Sentinel 2332 News Sentinel Dr **Fax:* Edit ■ *TF:* 800-237-5821 ■ *Web:* www.knoxnews.com	Knoxville	TN	37921	865-521-8181	342-8635*
Daily Times 307 E Harper St *Web:* www.thedailytimes.com	Maryville	TN	37804	865-981-1100	981-1175
Commercial Appeal 495 Union Ave *TF:* 800-444-6397 ■ *Web:* www.commercialappeal.com	Memphis	TN	38103	901-529-2345	529-2522
Citizen Tribune 1609 W 1st North St PO Box 625 *TF:* 800-624-0281 ■ *Web:* www.citizentribune.com	Morristown	TN	37815	423-581-5630	581-8863
Daily News Journal 224 N Walnut St *Web:* www.dnj.com	Murfreesboro	TN	37130	615-893-5860	893-4186
City Paper The 3322 W End Ave *Web:* www.nashvillecitypaper.com	Nashville	TN	37203	615-298-9833	298-2780
Tennessean 1100 Broadway *TF:* 800-342-8237 ■ *Web:* www.tennessean.com	Nashville	TN	37203	615-259-8800	259-8093

Texas

	City	State	ZIP	Phone	Fax
Abilene Reporter-News 101 Cypress St **Fax:* Edit ■ *TF:* 800-588-6397 ■ *Web:* www.reporternews.com	Abilene	TX	79601	325-673-4271	670-5242*
Amarillo Globe News 900 S Harrison St *Web:* amarillo.com	Amarillo	TX	79101	806-376-4488	373-0810
Austin American-Statesman 305 S Congress Ave *TF:* 800-627-2121 ■ *Web:* www.statesman.com	Austin	TX	78704	512-445-3500	445-3679
Bay City Tribune 2901 Carey Smith Blvd *Web:* www.baycitytribune.com	Bay City	TX	77414	979-245-5555	244-5908
Beaumont Enterprise 380 Main St *Web:* www.beaumontenterprise.com	Beaumont	TX	77701	409-833-3311	880-0757
Banner-Press PO Box 585 *Web:* www.brenhambanner.com	Brenham	TX	77834	979-836-7956	830-8577
Brownsville Herald The 1135 E Van Buren St *TF:* 800-488-4301 ■ *Web:* www.brownsvilleherald.com	Brownsville	TX	78520	956-542-4301	542-0840
El Bravo 1144 Lincoln St	Brownsville	TX	78521	956-542-5800	542-6023
Bryan-College Station Eagle 1729 Briarcrest Dr *Web:* www.bcseagle.com	Bryan	TX	77802	979-776-4444	776-8923
Brazosport Facts 720 S Main St *TF:* 800-864-8340 ■ *Web:* www.thefacts.com	Clute	TX	77531	979-265-7411	265-9052
Caller-Times 820 N Lower Broadway **Fax:* Edit ■ *TF:* 800-827-2011 ■ *Web:* www.caller.com	Corpus Christi	TX	78401	361-884-2011	886-3732*
Dallas Morning News 508 Young St *TF:* 800-431-0010 ■ *Web:* www.dallasnews.com	Dallas	TX	75202	214-977-8222	977-8319
Focus Daily News 1337 Marilyn Ave *Web:* www.focus-news.com	De Soto	TX	75115	972-223-9175	223-9202
Herald Democrat PO Box 329 *Web:* www.heralddemocrat.com	Denison	TX	75021	903-465-7171	465-7188
Denton Record-Chronicle 314 E Hickory St *TF:* 800-275-1722 ■ *Web:* www.dentonrc.com	Denton	TX	76201	940-387-3811	566-6888
El Paso Times 300 N Campbell St Times Plaza **Fax:* News Rm ■ *TF:* 800-351-6007 ■ *Web:* www.elpasotimes.com	El Paso	TX	79901	915-546-6100	546-6415*
Fort Worth Star-Telegram 685 John B Sias Memorial Pkwy *TF:* 800-776-7827 ■ *Web:* www.dfw.com/mld/startelegram	Fort Worth	TX	76134	817-390-7400	390-7789
Galveston County Daily News PO Box 628 *TF:* 800-561-3611 ■ *Web:* galvestondailynews.com	Galveston	TX	77553	409-683-5200	740-3421
Valley Morning Star PO Box 511 *TF:* 866-578-7827 ■ *Web:* www.valleystar.com	Harlingen	TX	78551	956-430-6200	430-6233
Houston Chronicle 801 Texas Ave *TF:* 800-735-3800 ■ *Web:* www.chron.com	Houston	TX	77002	713-362-7171	362-6806
Killeen Daily Herald 1809 Florence Rd *Web:* www.kdhnews.com	Killeen	TX	76541	254-634-2125	200-7640
Laredo Morning Times 111 Esperanza Dr **Fax:* Edit ■ *TF:* 800-728-3118 ■ *Web:* lmtonline.com	Laredo	TX	78041	956-728-2500	724-3036*
Longview News-Journal 320 E Methvin St **Fax:* News Rm ■ *TF:* 800-825-9799 ■ *Web:* www.news-journal.com	Longview	TX	75601	903-757-3311	757-3742*
Lubbock Avalanche-Journal 710 Ave J *TF:* 800-692-4021 ■ *Web:* www.lubbockonline.com	Lubbock	TX	79401	806-762-8844	744-9603
Lufkin Daily News PO Box 1089 *Web:* www.lufkindailynews.com	Lufkin	TX	75902	936-632-6631	632-6655
Monitor The 1400 E Nolana Loop *TF:* 800-366-4343 ■ *Web:* www.themonitor.com	McAllen	TX	78504	956-683-4000	683-4401
Midland Reporter-Telegram PO Box 1650 *TF:* 800-542-3952 ■ *Web:* www.mywesttexas.com	Midland	TX	79702	432-682-5311	570-7650
Odessa American PO Box 2952 *TF:* 888-375-6262 ■ *Web:* www.oaoa.com	Odessa	TX	79760	432-337-4661	333-7742
Pecos Enterprise PO Box 2057 *Web:* www.pecos.net	Pecos	TX	79772	432-445-5475	445-4321
Plano Star Courier 624 Crona Dr Suite 170 *Web:* www.planostar.com	Plano	TX	75074	972-398-4200	398-4270
Port Arthur News PO Box 789 **Fax:* Edit ■ *Web:* www.panews.com	Port Arthur	TX	77641	409-729-6397	724-6854*
Herald-Coaster The 1902 S 4th St *Web:* www.herald-coaster.com	Rosenberg	TX	77471	281-232-3737	342-3219
San Angelo Standard-Times 34 W Harris Ave *TF:* 800-588-1884 ■ *Web:* www.sanangelostandardtimes.com	San Angelo	TX	76903	325-653-1221	659-8173
Metrocom Herald 17400 Judson Rd *Web:* www.primetimenewspapers.com	San Antonio	TX	78247	210-453-3300	828-3787
San Antonio Express-News Ave 'E' & 3rd St *TF:* 800-555-1551 ■ *Web:* www.mysanantonio.com	San Antonio	TX	78205	210-250-3000	250-3105
Herald Democrat 603 S Sam Rayburn Fwy *TF:* 800-827-7183 ■ *Web:* www.heralddemocrat.com	Sherman	TX	75090	903-893-8181	868-2106
Temple Daily Telegram PO Box 6114 *TF:* 800-460-6397 ■ *Web:* www.temple-telegram.com	Temple	TX	76503	254-778-4444	778-4444
Texarkana Gazette PO Box 621 *TF:* 800-955-8518 ■ *Web:* www.texarkanagazette.com	Texarkana	TX	75504	903-794-3311	794-3315
Tyler Morning Telegraph PO Box 2030 **Fax:* News Rm ■ *TF:* 800-333-8411 ■ *Web:* www.tylerpaper.com	Tyler	TX	75710	903-597-8111	595-0335*
Victoria Advocate PO Box 1518 **Fax:* News Rm ■ *TF:* 800-234-8108 ■ *Web:* www.thevictoriaadvocate.com	Victoria	TX	77902	361-575-1451	574-1220*
Waco Tribune-Herald PO Box 2588 *TF:* 800-678-8742 ■ *Web:* www.wacotrib.com	Waco	TX	76702	254-757-5757	757-0302
Times Record News PO Box 120 *TF:* 800-627-1646 ■ *Web:* www.timesrecordnews.com	Wichita Falls	TX	76307	940-767-8341	767-1741

Utah

	City	State	ZIP	Phone	Fax
Herald Journal 75 W 300 North PO Box 487 *TF:* 800-275-0423 ■ *Web:* www.hjnews.com	Logan	UT	84323	435-752-2121	753-6642
Standard-Examiner 332 Standard Way *TF:* 800-234-5505 ■ *Web:* www.standard.net	Ogden	UT	84404	801-625-4200	625-4299
Daily Herald 1555 N Freedom Blvd *TF:* 800-880-8075 ■ *Web:* www.harktheherald.com	Provo	UT	84604	801-373-5050	373-5489
Spectrum The 275 E Saint George Blvd *Web:* www.thespectrum.com	Saint George	UT	84770	435-674-6200	674-6265
Deseret News PO Box 1257 *TF:* 888-337-6397 ■ *Web:* deseretnews.com	Salt Lake City	UT	84110	801-236-6000	237-2121
Salt Lake Tribune 90 S 400 West Suite 700 *Web:* www.sltrib.com	Salt Lake City	UT	84101	801-257-8742	257-8525

Vermont

	City	State	ZIP	Phone	Fax
Burlington Free Press 191 College St.	Burlington	VT	05401	802-863-3441	660-1802
TF: 800-427-3124 ■ *Web:* www.burlingtonfreepress.com					
Rutland Herald PO Box 668	Rutland	VT	05702	802-775-5511	747-6133
TF: 800-776-5512 ■ *Web:* www.rutlandherald.com					

Virginia

	City	State	ZIP	Phone	Fax
Express 1515 N Court House Rd.	Arlington	VA	22201	703-469-2800	469-2831
Web: www.readexpress.com					
Bristol Herald-Courier 320 Bob Morrison Blvd.	Bristol	VA	24201	276-669-2181	669-3696
TF: 888-228-2098 ■ *Web:* www.bristolnews.com					
Danville Register & Bee PO Box 331	Danville	VA	24543	434-793-2311	797-2299
TF: 800-323-2951 ■ *Web:* www.registerbee.com					
Free Lance Star 616 Amelia St.	Fredericksburg	VA	22401	540-374-5000	373-8455*
**Fax:* News Rm ■ *TF:* 800-877-0500 ■ *Web:* www.fredericksburg.com					
Daily News-Record 231 S Liberty St PO Box 193	Harrisonburg	VA	22803	540-574-6200	433-9112
Web: www.dnronline.com					
News & Advance PO Box 10129	Lynchburg	VA	24506	434-385-5555	385-5538
TF: 800-275-8831 ■ *Web:* www.newsadvance.com					
Daily Journal 9275 Corporate Cir	Manassas	VA	20110	703-257-4600	257-4960
Martinsville Bulletin PO Box 3711	Martinsville	VA	24115	276-638-8801	638-7409
TF: 800-234-6575 ■ *Web:* www.martinsvillebulletin.com					
Daily Press 7505 Warwick Blvd	Newport News	VA	23607	757-247-4600	245-8618
Web: www.dailypress.com					
Virginian-Pilot 150 W Brambleton Ave.	Norfolk	VA	23510	757-446-2000	446-2414
TF: 800-446-2004 ■ *Web:* www.hamptonroads.com/pilotonline					
Progress-Index 15 Franklin St.	Petersburg	VA	23803	804-732-3456	732-8417
Web: www.progress-index.com/site/news.asp?brd=2271					
Richmond Times-Dispatch 300 E Franklin St	Richmond	VA	23219	804-649-6000	775-8059
TF: 800-468-3382 ■ *Web:* www.timesdispatch.com					
Roanoke Times 201 W Campbell Ave SW	Roanoke	VA	24011	540-981-3340	981-3346
TF: 800-346-1234 ■ *Web:* www.roanoke.com					
News Leader 11 N Central Ave	Staunton	VA	24401	540-885-7281	885-1904
TF: 800-793-2459 ■ *Web:* www.newsleader.com					
Winchester Star 2 N Kent St.	Winchester	VA	22601	540-667-3200	667-1649
TF: 800-296-8639 ■ *Web:* www.winchesterstar.com					
Potomac News 14010 Smoke Town Rd	Woodbridge	VA	22192	703-878-8000	878-8099
Web: www.potomacnews.com					

Washington

	City	State	ZIP	Phone	Fax
Daily World 315 S Michigan St.	Aberdeen	WA	98520	360-532-4000	533-6039
TF: 800-829-7880 ■ *Web:* www.thedailyworld.com					
Bellingham Herald 1155 N State St	Bellingham	WA	98225	360-676-2600	756-2826*
**Fax:* News Rm ■ *Web:* www.bellinghamherald.com					
Kitsap Sun PO Box 259	Bremerton	WA	98337	360-377-3711	415-2681
TF: 888-377-3711 ■ *Web:* www.kitsapsun.com					
Daily Herald 1213 California Ave.	Everett	WA	98201	425-339-3000	339-3049
Web: www.heraldnet.com					
Daily News 770 11th Ave PO Box 189	Longview	WA	98632	360-577-2500	577-2538*
**Fax:* News Rm ■ *TF:* 800-341-4745 ■ *Web:* www.tdn.com					
Skagit Valley Herald 1000 E College Way PO Box 578	Mount Vernon	WA	98273	360-424-3251	424-5300*
**Fax:* News Rm ■ *TF:* 800-683-3300 ■ *Web:* www.goskagit.com					
Olympian The PO Box 407	Olympia	WA	98507	360-754-5400	357-0202*
**Fax:* News Rm ■ *Web:* www.theolympian.com					
Peninsula Daily News 305 W 1st St PO Box 1330	Port Angeles	WA	98362	360-452-2345	417-3521
TF: 800-826-7714 ■ *Web:* www.peninsuladailynews.com					
Seattle Daily Journal of Commerce PO Box 11050	Seattle	WA	98111	206-622-8272	622-8416
Web: www.djc.com					
Seattle Post-Intelligencer 101 Elliott Ave W 2nd Fl	Seattle	WA	98119	206-448-8000	448-8166
TF: 800-542-0820 ■ *Web:* seattlepi.nwsource.com					
Seattle Times 1120 John St	Seattle	WA	98109	206-464-2111	464-2261
Web: seattletimes.nwsource.com					
Spokesman Review 999 W Riverside Ave.	Spokane	WA	99201	509-459-5000	459-5482
TF: 800-338-8801 ■ *Web:* www.spokesmanreview.com					
News Tribune 1950 S State St	Tacoma	WA	98405	253-597-8686	597-8274
TF: 800-388-8742 ■ *Web:* www.thenewstribune.com					
Tri-City Herald PO Box 2608	Tri-Cities	WA	99302	509-582-1500	582-1510
TF: 800-411-5085 ■ *Web:* www.tri-cityherald.com					
Columbian 701 W 8th St PO Box 180	Vancouver	WA	98660	360-694-3391	699-6033
TF: 800-743-3391 ■ *Web:* www.columbian.com					
Wenatchee World 14 N Mission St.	Wenatchee	WA	98801	509-663-5161	665-1183
TF: 800-572-4433 ■ *Web:* www.wenworld.com					
Yakima Herald-Republic PO Box 9668	Yakima	WA	98909	509-248-1251	577-7767
TF: 800-343-2799 ■ *Web:* www.yakima-herald.com					

West Virginia

	City	State	ZIP	Phone	Fax
Register-Herald 801 N Kanawha St.	Beckley	WV	25801	304-255-4400	255-4427
TF: 800-950-0250 ■ *Web:* www.register-herald.com					
Bluefield Daily Telegraph 928 Bluefield Ave	Bluefield	WV	24701	304-327-2800	327-6179
TF: 800-763-2459 ■ *Web:* www.bdtonline.com					
Charleston Daily Mail 1001 Virginia St E.	Charleston	WV	25301	304-348-5140	348-4847
TF: 800-982-6397 ■ *Web:* www.dailymail.com					
Charleston Gazette 1001 Virginia St E	Charleston	WV	25301	304-348-5140	348-1233
TF: 800-982-6397 ■ *Web:* www.wvgazette.com					
Clarksburg Exponent Telegram 324 Hewes Ave.	Clarksburg	WV	26301	304-626-1400	624-4188
TF: 800-982-6034 ■ *Web:* www.cpubco.com					
Exponent Telegram 324 Hewes Ave	Clarksburg	WV	26301	304-624-6411	624-4188
TF: 800-982-6034 ■ *Web:* www.cpubco.com					
Herald-Dispatch 946 5th Ave	Huntington	WV	25720	304-526-4000	526-2857
TF: 800-444-2446 ■ *Web:* www.herald-dispatch.com					
West Virginia Daily News PO Box 471	Lewisburg	WV	24901	304-645-1206	645-7104
Journal The 207 W King St.	Martinsburg	WV	25401	304-263-8931	267-2903*
**Fax:* PR ■ *TF:* 800-448-1895 ■ *Web:* journal-news.net					
Daily Athenaeum 284 Prospect St PO Box 6427	Morgantown	WV	26506	304-293-2540	293-6857
Web: www.da.wvu.edu					
Dominion Post 1251 Earl L Core Rd	Morgantown	WV	26505	304-292-6301	291-2326
TF: 800-654-4676 ■ *Web:* olive.dominionpost.com					
Parkersburg News 519 Juliana St.	Parkersburg	WV	26101	304-485-1891	485-5122
Web: www.newsandsentinel.com					
Welch Daily News PO Box 569	Welch	WV	24801	304-436-3144	436-3146
Intelligencer The 1500 Main St	Wheeling	WV	26003	304-233-0100	232-1399
Web: theintelligencer.net					
Wheeling News-Register 1500 Main St	Wheeling	WV	26003	304-233-0100	232-1399*
**Fax:* Edit ■ *Web:* www.news-register.net					

Wisconsin

	City	State	ZIP	Phone	Fax
Post-Crescent 306 W Washington St PO Box 59	Appleton	WI	54911	920-993-1000	733-1945
TF: 800-236-6397 ■ *Web:* www.postcrescent.com					
Beloit Daily News 149 State St.	Beloit	WI	53511	608-365-8811	365-1420
TF: 800-356-3411 ■ *Web:* www.beloitdailynews.com					
Leader-Telegram 701 S Farwell St	Eau Claire	WI	54701	715-833-9200	858-7308*
**Fax:* Edit ■ *TF:* 800-236-8808 ■ *Web:* www.leadertelegram.com					
Reporter The PO Box 630	Fond du Lac	WI	54936	920-922-4600	922-5388
TF: 800-261-7323 ■ *Web:* www.fdlreporter.com					
Green Bay Press-Gazette PO Box 23430	Green Bay	WI	54305	920-431-8400	431-8379
TF: 800-289-8221 ■ *Web:* www.greenbaypressgazette.com					
Janesville Gazette 1 S Parker Dr PO Box 5001	Janesville	WI	53547	608-754-3311	755-8349*
**Fax:* Edit ■ *TF:* 800-362-6712 ■ *Web:* www.gazetteextra.com					
Kenosha News 5800 7th Ave.	Kenosha	WI	53140	262-657-1000	657-8455
TF: 800-292-2700 ■ *Web:* www.kenoshanews.com					
La Crosse Tribune 401 N 3rd St	La Crosse	WI	54601	608-782-9710	782-9723*
**Fax:* Edit ■ *TF:* 800-262-0420 ■ *Web:* www.lacrossetribune.com					
Capital Times 1901 Fish Hatchery Rd.	Madison	WI	53713	608-252-6400	252-6445
TF: 800-362-8333 ■ *Web:* www.madison.com/index.php?redir=TCT					
Wisconsin State Journal 1901 Fish Hatchery Rd	Madison	WI	53713	608-252-6100	252-6119
TF: 800-362-8333 ■ *Web:* www.madison.com/wisconsinstatejournal/					
Herald Times Reporter 902 Franklin St.	Manitowoc	WI	54221	920-684-4433	686-2103
TF: 800-783-7323 ■ *Web:* www.htrnews.com					
Milwaukee Journal Sentinel 333 W State St	Milwaukee	WI	53203	414-224-2000	224-2047
TF: 800-456-5943 ■ *Web:* www.jsonline.com					
Oshkosh Northwestern PO Box 2926	Oshkosh	WI	54903	920-235-7700	426-6600
TF: 800-924-6168 ■ *Web:* www.thenorthwestern.com					
Journal Times 212 4th St	Racine	WI	53403	262-634-3322	631-1780
Web: www.journaltimes.com					
Sheboygan Press PO Box 358	Sheboygan	WI	53082	920-457-7711	457-3573
TF: 800-686-3900 ■ *Web:* www.sheboygan-press.com					
Waukesha County Freeman PO Box 7	Waukesha	WI	53187	262-542-2501	542-8259*
**Fax:* News Rm					
Wausau Daily Herald PO Box 1286	Wausau	WI	54402	715-842-2101	848-9361
TF: 800-477-4838 ■ *Web:* www.wausaudailyherald.com					

Wyoming

	City	State	ZIP	Phone	Fax
Star-Tribune 170 Star Ln.	Casper	WY	82604	307-266-0500	266-0568
Web: www.trib.com					
Wyoming Tribune-Eagle 702 W Lincolnway	Cheyenne	WY	82001	307-634-3361	633-3189
TF: 800-561-6268 ■ *Web:* www.wyomingnews.com					

535-3 National Newspapers

	City	State	ZIP	Phone	Fax
Christian Science Monitor 210 Massachusetts Ave.	Boston	MA	02115	617-450-2000	450-7575
TF: 800-288-7090 ■ *Web:* www.csmonitor.com					
USA Today 7950 Jones Branch Dr	McLean	VA	22108	703-854-3400	854-3053*
**Fax:* News Rm ■ *TF Cust Svc:* 800-872-0001 ■ *Web:* www.usatoday.com					
Wall Street Journal PO Box 300	Princeton	NJ	08543	609-520-7023	520-7810
Web: online.wsj.com					
Wall Street Journal (Eastern Edition) 200 Liberty St.	New York	NY	10281	212-416-2000	416-4155*
**Fax:* News Rm ■ *TF:* 800-568-7625					
Wall Street Journal (Midwestern Edition)					
1 S Wacker Dr Suite 2100	Chicago	IL	60606	312-750-4000	750-4153
Wall Street Journal (Western Edition)					
6500 Wilshire Blvd Suite 1400	Los Angeles	CA	90048	323-658-7505	658-3828

535-4 Weekly Newspapers

Listings here are organized by city names within state groupings.

Alabama

	City	State	ZIP	Phone	Fax
Corner News PO Box 3240	Auburn	AL	36831	334-821-7150	887-0037
Web: www.thecornernews.com					
Birmingham Times 115 3rd Ave W	Birmingham	AL	35204	205-251-5158	323-2294
Web: www.thebirminghamtimes.com					
Over The Mountain Journal 2016 Columbiana Rd	Birmingham	AL	35216	205-823-9646	824-1246
Web: www.otmj.com					
Shelby County Reporter PO Box 947	Columbiana	AL	35051	205-669-3131	669-4217
Web: www.shelbycountyreporter.com					
Courier Journal 1828 Darby Dr.	Florence	AL	35630	256-764-4268	760-9618
Web: www.courierjournal.net					
Greenville Advocate PO Box 507	Greenville	AL	36037	334-382-3111	382-7104
Web: www.greenvilleadvocate.com					
Hartselle Enquirer PO Box 929	Hartselle	AL	35640	256-773-6566	773-1953
Web: www.hartselleenquirer.com					
Montgomery Independent 141 Market Pl	Montgomery	AL	36117	334-265-7323	265-7320
Web: www.al.com/montgomery					

Alaska

	City	State	ZIP	Phone	Fax
Anchorage Press 540 E 5th Ave	Anchorage	AK	99501	907-561-7737	561-7777
Web: www.anchoragepress.com					
Capital City Weekly 134 S Franklin St	Juneau	AK	99801	907-789-4144	789-0987
Web: www.capitalcityweekly.com					

Arizona

	City	State	ZIP	Phone	Fax
Apache Junction Independent					
850 S Ironwood Dr Suite 112	Apache Junction	AZ	85220	480-982-7799	671-0016*
**Fax:* News Rm ■ *Web:* www.newszap.com/apache/					
East Mesa Independent 850 S Ironwood Dr Suite 112	Apache Junction	AZ	85220	480-982-7799	671-0016*
**Fax:* News Rm ■ *Web:* www.newszap.com/eastmesa/					
Chandler Independent 325 E Elliott Rd Suite 21	Chandler	AZ	85225	480-497-0048	926-1019
Web: www.newszap.com/chandler/					
West Valley View 200 W Wigwam Blvd	Litchfield Park	AZ	85340	623-535-8439	935-2103
Web: www.westvalleyview.com					
Ahwatukee Foothills News 10631 S 51st St	Phoenix	AZ	85044	480-898-7900	893-1684*
**Fax:* News Rm ■ *Web:* www.ahwatukee.com					

Weekly Newspapers (Cont'd)

Arizona (Cont'd)

Name / Address	City	State	ZIP	Phone	Fax
Paradise Valley Independent 11000 N Scottsdale Rd Suite 210 *Fax: News Rm ■ *Web:* www.newszap.com/paradise/	Scottsdale	AZ	85254	480-483-0977	948-0496*
Sun Cities Independent 10220 W Bell Rd Suite 116 *Web:* www.newszap.com/suncity/	Sun City	AZ	85351	623-972-6101	974-6004

Arkansas

Name / Address	City	State	ZIP	Phone	Fax
Brinkley Argus PO Box 711	Brinkley	AR	72021	870-734-1056	
East Arkansas News Leader PO Box 308	Wynne	AR	72396	870-238-2375	238-4655

California

Name / Address	City	State	ZIP	Phone	Fax
Alameda Journal 1516 Oak St	Alameda	CA	94501	510-748-1666	748-1665
Montclarion The 1516 Oak St	Alameda	CA	94501	510-339-3939	748-1680
Anaheim Bulletin 1771 S Lewis St	Anaheim	CA	92805	714-634-1567	704-3714
Fullerton News-Tribune 1771 S Lewis St	Anaheim	CA	92805	714-634-1567	704-3714
Orange City News 1771 S Lewis St	Anaheim	CA	92805	714-634-1567	704-3714
Yorba Linda Star 1771 S Lewis St *TF:* 877-469-7344	Anaheim	CA	92805	714-796-7000	704-3714
Bakersfield News Observer 1219 20th St	Bakersfield	CA	93301	661-324-9466	324-9472
Beverly Hills Courier 8840 W Olympic Blvd *Web:* www.thebeverlyhillscourier.com	Beverly Hills	CA	90211	310-278-1322	271-5118
Ceres Courier PO Box 7 *Web:* www.mantecabulletin.com/ceres	Ceres	CA	95307	209-537-5032	537-0543
Chino Champion PO Box 607 *Web:* www.championnewspapers.com	Chino	CA	91708	909-628-5501	590-1217
Chino Hills Champion PO Box 607 *Web:* www.championnewspapers.com	Chino	CA	91708	909-628-5501	590-1217
Star-News The 321 'E' St *Web:* www.thestarnews.com	Chula Vista	CA	91910	619-427-3000	426-6346
Hawthorne Community News 312 E Imperial Ave	El Segundo	CA	90245	310-322-1830	322-2787
Elk Grove Citizen PO Box 1777 *Web:* www.egcitizen.com	Elk Grove	CA	95759	916-685-3945	686-6675
Humboldt Beacon The 936 Main St *Web:* www.humboldtbeacon.com	Fortuna	CA	95540	707-725-6166	725-6837
Garden Grove Journal 12866 Main St Suite 203 *Web:* www.ggjournal.com	Garden Grove	CA	92840	714-539-6018	892-7052
Gardena Valley News 15005 S Vermont Ave *TF:* 800-329-6351	Gardena	CA	90247	310-329-6351	329-7501
Burbank Leader 111 W Wilson Ave *Web:* www.burbankleader.com	Glendale	CA	91203	818-637-3200	241-1975
Hesperia Resorter PO Box 400937	Hesperia	CA	92340	760-244-0021	244-6609
Pinnacle The 380 San Benito St *Web:* www.pinnaclenews.com	Hollister	CA	95023	831-637-6300	637-8174
Huntington Beach Independent 19895 Beach Blvd Suite 107 *Web:* www.hbindependent.com	Huntington Beach	CA	92648	714-536-7313	536-7279
Tustin News 2006 McGaw *Fax: News Rm	Irvine	CA	92614	949-553-2900	553-2925*
Kingsburg Recorder PO Box 128 *Web:* www.kingsburgrecorder.com	Kingsburg	CA	93631	559-897-2993	897-4868
Independent The PO Box 1198 *Web:* www.independentnews.com	Livermore	CA	94551	925-447-8700	447-0212
Los Altos Town Crier 138 Main St *Web:* www.latc.com	Los Altos	CA	94022	650-948-9000	948-6647
East Los Angeles/Brooklyn Belvedere Comet 111 S Ave 59 *Web:* www.egpnews.com	Los Angeles	CA	90042	323-341-7970	341-7976
Los Angeles Downtown News 1264 W 1st St *Web:* www.ladowntownnews.com	Los Angeles	CA	90026	213-481-1448	250-4617
Los Gatos Weekly-Times 634 N Santa Cruz Ave Suite 206 *Web:* www.lgwt.com	Los Gatos	CA	95030	408-354-3110	354-3917
Mammoth Times The PO Box 3929 *Web:* www.mammothtimes.com	Mammoth Lakes	CA	93546	760-934-3929	934-3951
Argonaut The PO Box 11209 *Web:* www.argonautnewspaper.com	Marina del Rey	CA	90295	310-822-1629	821-8029
Almanac The 3525 Alameda De Las Pulgas *Web:* www.almanacnews.com	Menlo Park	CA	94025	650-854-2626	854-0677
Milpitas Post 59 Maryland Dr *Web:* www.themilpitaspost.com	Milpitas	CA	95035	408-262-2454	263-9710
Bay Area Press 1520 Broadway *Web:* www.bayarearapidpress.com	Oakland	CA	94612	510-835-2731	839-0164
Paradise Post PO Drawer 70 *TF:* 800-924-0908 ■ *Web:* www.paradisepost.com	Paradise	CA	95967	530-877-4413	877-1326
Paso Robles Press PO Box 427 *Web:* www.pasoroblespress.com	Paso Robles	CA	93447	805-237-6060	237-6066
Palos Verdes Peninsula News 500 Silver Spur Rd Suite 300 *Fax: Edit ■ *Web:* pvnews.nminews.com	Rancho Palos Verdes	CA	90275	310-377-6877	544-4322*
Riverside County Record PO Box 3187 *Web:* www.riversidecountyrecord.com	Riverside	CA	92519	951-685-6191	685-2961
Community Voice PO Box 2038 *Web:* www.thecommunityvoice.com	Rohnert Park	CA	94927	707-285-3220	285-3226
Rialto Record PO Box 6247 *Web:* www.iecn.com	San Bernardino	CA	92412	909-381-9898	384-0406
Cupertino Courier 1095 The Alameda *Web:* www.cupertinocourier.com	San Jose	CA	95126	408-200-1000	200-1013
Sunnyvale Sun 1095 The Alameda *Web:* www.sunnyvalesun.com	San Jose	CA	95126	408-200-1000	200-1013
Willow Glen Resident 1095 The Alameda *Web:* www.wgresident.com	San Jose	CA	95126	408-200-1000	200-1013
Carlsbad Sun PO Box 789	San Marcos	CA	92079	760-729-7698	
Sun The 216 Main St	Seal Beach	CA	90740	562-430-7555	430-3469
Sonoma Index-Tribune PO Box C *Web:* www.sonomanews.com	Sonoma	CA	95476	707-938-2111	938-1600
Covina Highlander Press Courier 1210 N Azusa Canyon Rd *TF:* 800-788-1200	West Covina	CA	91790	626-962-8811	854-8719
Glendora Press 1210 N Azusa Canyon Rd	West Covina	CA	91790	626-962-8811	854-8719
San Dimas/La Verne Highlander 1210 N Azusa Canyon Rd	West Covina	CA	91790	626-854-8700	338-9157

Colorado

Name / Address	City	State	ZIP	Phone	Fax
Aurora Sentinel 10730 E Bethany Dr Suite 304 *Web:* www.aurorasentinel.com	Aurora	CO	80014	303-750-7555	750-7699
Eagle Valley Enterprise PO Box 450 *Web:* www.eaglevalleyenterprise.com	Eagle	CO	81631	970-328-6656	328-6393
Columbine Courier 9719 W Coal Mine Ave Unit N *Web:* www.columbinecourier.com	Littleton	CO	80123	303-933-2233	933-4449
Vail Trail PO Drawer 6200 *Web:* www.vailtrail.com	Vail	CO	81658	970-748-0049	748-6427

Connecticut

Name / Address	City	State	ZIP	Phone	Fax
East Hartford Gazette 1406 Main St *Web:* www.easthartfordgazette.com	East Hartford	CT	06108	860-289-6468	289-6469
Fairfield Minuteman 1492 Post Rd *Web:* www.zwire.com/site/news.cfm?brd=1653	Fairfield	CT	06824	203-255-8877	259-6414
Rivereast News Bulletin PO Box 373 *Web:* www.glcitizen.com	Glastonbury	CT	06033	860-633-4691	657-3258
Hartford News 563 Franklin Ave	Hartford	CT	06114	860-296-6128	296-3350
Milford Weekly PO Box 5339 *Web:* www.milfordweekly.com	Milford	CT	06460	203-876-6800	877-4772
Stratford Bard PO Box 5339 *Web:* www.zwire.com/site/news.cfm?brd=1637	Milford	CT	06460	203-876-6800	877-4772
Bridgeport News 1000 Bridgeport Ave *TF:* 800-843-6791	Shelton	CT	06484	203-926-2080	926-2091
Milford Mirror 1000 Bridgeport Ave *TF:* 800-843-6791 ■ *Web:* www.milfordmirror.com	Shelton	CT	06484	203-926-2080	926-2091
Stratford Star 1000 Bridgeport Ave *TF:* 800-843-6791	Shelton	CT	06484	203-926-2080	926-2091
Sunday Voices-The Weekly Star PO Box 383	Southbury	CT	06488	203-263-2116	266-0199
Voices PO Box 383 *Web:* www.voicesnews.com	Southbury	CT	06488	203-263-2116	266-0199
Reminder The PO Box 210 *TF:* 888-456-2211 ■ *Web:* www.remindernet.com	Vernon	CT	06066	860-875-3366	872-4614
Westport Minuteman 1775 Post Rd E *Web:* www.westportminuteman.com	Westport	CT	06880	203-226-8877	221-7540

Delaware

Name / Address	City	State	ZIP	Phone	Fax
Dover Post PO Box 664 *TF:* 800-942-1616 ■ *Web:* www.doverpost.com	Dover	DE	19903	302-678-3616	678-8291
Sussex Post PO Box 737 *TF:* 800-282-8586 ■ *Web:* www.newszap.com/dover/	Dover	DE	19903	302-934-9261	645-2267
Cape Gazette PO Box 213 *Web:* capegazette.com	Lewes	DE	19958	302-645-7700	645-1664
Delaware Beachcomber PO Box 309 *Web:* www.delmarvanow.com/debeachcomber	Rehoboth Beach	DE	19971	302-227-9466	227-9469
Delaware Coast Press PO Box 309 *Web:* www.delmarvanow.com/deweybeach	Rehoboth Beach	DE	19971	302-227-9466	227-9469
Dialog The 1925 Delaware Ave *Web:* www.cdow.org	Wilmington	DE	19806	302-573-3109	573-6948

Florida

Name / Address	City	State	ZIP	Phone	Fax
Bonita Banner PO Box 40 *Web:* www.bonitanews.com	Bonita Springs	FL	34133	239-765-0110	213-6088
Brandon News 505 W Robertson St	Brandon	FL	33511	813-657-4501	689-9545
Hernando Today 15299 Cortez Blvd *Web:* www.hernandotoday.com	Brooksville	FL	34613	352-544-5200	799-5246
Coral Springs/Parkland Forum 4611 Johnson Rd Suite 4 *TF:* 800-275-8820	Coconut Creek	FL	33073	954-420-0955	420-0415
Margate/Coconut Creek Forum 4611 Johnson Rd Suite 4	Coconut Creek	FL	33073	954-420-0955	752-0415
Forum Gazette 4801 S University Dr Suite 101 *TF:* 800-275-8820	Davie	FL	33328	954-680-4460	680-6695
Boca Times 1701 Green Rd Suite B *TF:* 800-275-8820	Deerfield Beach	FL	33064	954-698-6397	429-1207
Boynton Beach Times 1701 Green Rd Suite B *Fax: Edit ■ *TF:* 800-275-8820	Deerfield Beach	FL	33064	954-698-6397	429-1207*
Deerfield Times 1701 Green Rd Suite B *TF Sales:* 800-275-8820	Deerfield Beach	FL	33064	954-698-6397	429-1207
Delray Beach Times 1701 Green Rd Suite B *TF:* 800-275-8820	Deerfield Beach	FL	33064	954-698-6397	429-1207
Observer The 43 NE 2nd St	Deerfield Beach	FL	33441	954-428-9045	428-9096
Sunrise Times 1701 Green Rd	Deerfield Beach	FL	33064	954-698-6397	698-6719
Tamarac/North Lauderdale Forum 1701 Green Rd *Web:* www.sun-sentinel.com/services/newspaper/fpg/	Deerfield Beach	FL	33064	954-698-6397	698-6719
Eastsider 3115 NW 10th Terr Suite 102 *TF:* 800-684-4870	Fort Lauderdale	FL	33309	954-563-3311	563-4230
Fort Myers Observer 19260 San Carlos Blvd	Fort Myers Beach	FL	33931	239-765-0400	765-0846
La Voz de La Calle 4696 E 10th Ct *Web:* www.lavozdelacalle.net	Hialeah	FL	33013	305-687-5555	681-0500
Osceola News-Gazette PO Box 422068 *TF:* 800-327-2166 ■ *Web:* www.oscnewsgazette.com	Kissimmee	FL	34742	407-846-7600	846-8516
Lake Worth Herald/Coastal Observer PO Box 191 *TF:* 888-544-0047	Lake Worth	FL	33460	561-585-9387	585-5434
Lehigh Acres News-Star PO Box 908 *Web:* www.lehighnewsstar.com	Lehigh Acres	FL	33970	239-369-2191	369-1396
Longboat Observer 5570 Gulf of Mexico Dr PO Box 8100 *Web:* www.longboatobserver.com	Longboat Key	FL	34228	941-383-5509	383-7193
Broward News & Senior News 767 S State Rd 7 Suite 1 *Web:* www.flabrowardseniornews.com	Margate	FL	33068	954-977-7770	977-7779
Tribune PO Box 419000 *TF:* 800-633-8449	Melbourne	FL	32941	321-242-3801	242-0760
Miami Today PO Box 1368 *Web:* www.miamitodaynews.com	Miami	FL	33101	305-358-2663	358-4811
Suncoast News 6214 US Hwy 19 *TF:* 800-376-4786	New Port Richey	FL	34652	727-815-1000	847-2902
Clay Today 1560 Kingsley Ave Suite 1 *TF:* 888-424-6220 ■ *Web:* www.claytoday.biz	Orange Park	FL	32073	904-264-3200	269-6958
West Boca Times 1701 Green Rd Suite B *Fax: Edit ■ *TF:* 800-275-8820	Pompano Beach	FL	33064	954-698-6397	429-1207*
Pelican Press 5011 Ocean Blvd Suite 206 *Web:* www.pelicanpress.org	Sarasota	FL	34242	941-349-4949	346-7118
News-Sun 2227 US 27 S *Web:* www.newssun.com	Sebring	FL	33870	863-385-6155	385-1954
Seminole Beacon 9911 Seminole Blvd *TF:* 866-224-9233 ■ *Web:* www.tbnweekly.com	Seminole	FL	33772	727-397-5563	397-5900
Kendall News Gazette 6796 SW 62nd Ave *Web:* www.communitynewspapers.com	South Miami	FL	33143	305-669-7355	661-0954
Carrollwood News 5625 W Waters Ave *Web:* carrollwood.tbo.com	Tampa	FL	33634	813-865-1500	249-5316
Temple Terrace News 15310 Amberly Dr Suite 102	Tampa	FL	33647	813-977-2854	975-9488

				Phone	Fax
Town 'n Country News 5625 W Waters Ave *Web:* carrollwood.tbo.com	Tampa	FL	33634	813-865-1500	249-5316
Daily Sun 1100 Main St. *TF:* 800-726-6592 ■ *Web:* www.thevillagesdailysun.com	The Villages	FL	32159	352-753-1119	753-2380
Star Advocate 1100 S Hopkins Ave	Titusville	FL	32780	321-360-1030	630-1055
Venice Gondolier Sun 200 E Venice Ave *TF:* 866-357-6204 ■ *Web:* www.venicegondolier.com	Venice	FL	34285	941-207-1000	485-3036
Forum The 11576 Pierson Rd Suite K-5	Wellington	FL	33414	561-791-7790	791-7593
Town-Crier 12794 W Forest Hill Blvd Suite 31 *Web:* www.thecrier.com	Wellington	FL	33414	561-793-7606	793-6090

Georgia

				Phone	Fax
Revue & News The 319 N Main St *Web:* www.northfulton.com	Alpharetta	GA	30004	770-442-3278	475-1216
Suburban Review PO Box 912 *TF:* 800-533-4252	Athens	GA	30603	706-549-0123	559-7148
DeKalb Neighbor 3060 Mercer University Dr Suite 210 *Web:* www.neighbornewspapers.com	Atlanta	GA	30341	770-454-9388	454-9131
Northside Neighbor & Sandy Springs Neighbor 5290 Roswell Rd NW Suite M *Web:* www.neighbornewspapers.com	Atlanta	GA	30342	404-256-3100	256-3292
Metropolitan Spirit 700 Broad St *Web:* www.metspirit.com	Augusta	GA	30901	706-738-1142	733-6663
Paulding Neighbor 31 Courthouse Sq *Web:* www.neighbornewspapers.com	Dallas	GA	30132	770-445-9401	445-0565
Douglas Neighbor 8434 Price Ave *Web:* www.neighbornewspapers.com	Douglasville	GA	30134	770-942-1611	942-4348
Crier Newspapers LLC 5064 Nandina Ln *Web:* www.thecrier.net	Dunwoody	GA	30338	770-451-4147	451-4223
Columbia News Times 4272 Washington Rd Suite 3B *TF:* 888-464-9988 ■ *Web:* newstimes.augusta.com	Evans	GA	30809	706-863-6165	868-9824
Fayette Neighbor 635 N Glynn St Suite 1 *Web:* www.neighbornewspapers.com	Fayetteville	GA	30214	770-461-1136	461-1385
Clayton Neighbor 5300 Frontage Rd Suite B *Web:* www.neighbornewspapers.com/clayton/	Forest Park	GA	30297	404-363-8484	363-0212
Henry Neighbor 5300 Frontage Rd Suite B *Web:* www.neighbornewspapers.com/henry/	Forest Park	GA	30297	404-363-8484	363-0212
South Fulton Neighbor 5300 Frontage Rd Suite B *Web:* www.neighbornewspapers.com	Forest Park	GA	30297	404-363-8484	363-0212
Leader-Tribune The PO Box 1060	Fort Valley	GA	31030	478-825-2432	825-4130
Austell-Mableton-Powder Springs Neighbor PO Box 449 *Web:* www.neighbornewspapers.com	Marietta	GA	30061	770-428-9411	422-9533
East Cobb Neighbor PO Box 449	Marietta	GA	30061	770-428-9411	422-9533
Kennesaw-Acworth Neighbor PO Box 449 *Web:* www.neighbornewspapers.com	Marietta	GA	30061	770-428-9411	422-9533
Alpharetta-Roswell Neighbor 10930 Crabapple Rd Suite 9	Roswell	GA	30075	770-993-7400	518-6062
Barrow County News PO Drawer C *Web:* www.barrowcountynews.com	Winder	GA	30680	770-867-7557	867-1034

Hawaii

				Phone	Fax
Midweek 45-525 Luluku Rd *Web:* www.midweek.com	Kaneohe	HI	96744	808-235-5881	247-7246

Illinois

				Phone	Fax
Times Record 219 S College Ave *TF:* 800-582-4373 ■ *Web:* www.aledotimesrecord.com	Aledo	IL	61231	309-582-5112	582-5319
Herald/Country Market 500 Brown Blvd *Web:* www.bbherald.com	Bourbonnais	IL	60914	815-933-1131	933-3785
Bridgeport News 3252 S Halstead St *Web:* www.bridgeportnews.net	Chicago	IL	60608	312-842-5883	842-5097
Chicago's Northwest Side Press 4937 N Milwaukee Ave	Chicago	IL	60630	773-286-6100	286-8151
Inside Publications 4159 Northwestern Ave 2nd Fl *Web:* www.insideonline.com	Chicago	IL	60618	773-313-2000	313-2006
Collinsville Journal 2 Executive Dr **Fax:* News Rm ■ *TF:* 800-766-3278	Collinsville	IL	62234	618-344-0264	344-3831*
Granite City Journal 2 Executive Dr *TF:* 800-766-3278	Collinsville	IL	62234	618-877-7700	344-3831
Des Plaines Journal 622 Graceland Ave *Web:* www.journal-topics.com	Des Plaines	IL	60016	847-299-5511	298-8549
Suburban Life 1101 W 31st St Suite 100 **Fax:* Edit	Downers Grove	IL	60515	630-368-1100	368-1199*
Galena Gazette PO Box 319 *TF:* 800-373-6397 ■ *Web:* www.galenagazette.com	Galena	IL	61036	815-777-0019	777-3809
Great Lakes Bulletin PO Box 268	Grayslake	IL	60030	847-223-8161	223-8810
Lombardian 116 S Main St	Lombard	IL	60148	630-627-7010	627-7027
Rockford Journal 11512 N 2nd St	Machesney Park	IL	61115	815-877-4044	654-4857
Naperville Sun 1500 W Ogden Ave *Web:* www.suburbanchicagonews.com/sunpub/naper	Naperville	IL	60540	630-355-0063	416-5163
Cicero-Berwyn-Stickney Forest View Life 7222 W Cermak Rd *Web:* www.chicagosuburbannews.com	North Riverside	IL	60546	708-447-9810	447-9871
Suburban Life Citizen 709 Enterprise Dr **Fax:* Edit	Oak Brook	IL	60523	630-368-1100	368-1199*
Skyline 1140 Lake St	Oak Park	IL	60301	708-383-3200	383-3678
Regional News 12247 S Harlem Ave *Web:* www.theregionalnews.com	Palos Heights	IL	60463	708-448-4000	448-4012
Chicago Heights Star 6901 W 159th St *Web:* www.starnewspapers.com/index/s-ch-nws.html	Tinley Park	IL	60477	708-802-8800	802-8088
Chicago Ridge/Worth Star 6901 W 159th St *Web:* www.starnewspapers.com/index/s-wornws.html	Tinley Park	IL	60477	708-802-8800	802-8088
Homer Township Star 6901 W 159th St *Web:* www.starnewspapers.com/index/s-ho-nws.html	Tinley Park	IL	60477	708-802-8800	802-8088
Matteson-Richton Park Star 6901 W 159th St	Tinley Park	IL	60477	708-802-8800	802-8088
Washington Courier 100 Ford Ln	Washington	IL	61571	309-444-3139	444-8505
Fox Valley Shopping News PO Box 609	Yorkville	IL	60560	630-553-7431	553-0310

Indiana

				Phone	Fax
Hendricks County Flyer 8109 Kingston St Suite 500 *TF:* 800-359-3747 ■ *Web:* www.flyergroup.com	Avon	IN	46123	317-272-5800	272-5887
Clarion News 301 N Capitol Ave	Corydon	IN	47112	812-738-4552	738-1909
Noblesville Ledger 13095 Publishers Dr *Web:* www.thenoblesvilleledger.com	Fishers	IN	46038	317-598-6300	598-6340
Topics 13095 Publishers Dr **Fax:* News Rm ■ *Web:* www.topics.com	Fishers	IN	46038	317-444-5500	444-5550*
Westside Community News 608 S Vine St **Fax:* News Rm	Indianapolis	IN	46241	317-241-7363	240-6397*
Papers The PO Box 188 *TF:* 800-733-4111	Milford	IN	46542	574-658-4111	658-4701
Banner-Gazette PO Box 38 *Web:* www.gbpnews.com	Pekin	IN	47165	812-967-3176	967-3194
Giveaway The PO Box 38 *Web:* www.gbpnews.com	Pekin	IN	47165	812-967-3176	967-3194

Kentucky

				Phone	Fax
Citizen Voice & Times PO Box 660	Irvine	KY	40336	606-723-5161	723-5509
West Kentucky News PO Box 1135 *Web:* www.ky-news.com	Paducah	KY	42002	270-442-7380	442-5220
Madison County Advertiser PO Box 99	Richmond	KY	40475	859-623-1669	623-2337

Louisiana

				Phone	Fax
Bossier Press Tribune 4250 Viking Dr *Web:* www.bossierpress.com	Bossier City	LA	71111	318-747-7900	747-5298
News-Banner PO Drawer 90	Covington	LA	70434	985-892-7980	893-1527
Times of Acadiana 1100 Bertrand Dr *TF:* 877-289-2216 ■ *Web:* www.timesofacadiana.com	Lafayette	LA	70506	337-289-6300	289-6496
Avoyelles Journal PO Box 36	Marksville	LA	71351	318-253-5413	253-7223
Ouachita Citizen PO Box 758 *Web:* www.ouachitacitizen.com	West Monroe	LA	71294	318-322-3161	325-2285

Maine

				Phone	Fax
Bar Harbor Times PO Box 68	Bar Harbor	ME	04609	207-288-3311	288-5813
Coastal Journal PO Box 705 *TF:* 800-649-6241 ■ *Web:* www.coastaljournal.com	Bath	ME	04530	207-443-6241	443-5605
Biddeford-Saco-OOB Courier PO Box 1894 *TF:* 800-617-3984 ■ *Web:* www.biddefordsacooobcourier.com	Biddeford	ME	04005	207-282-4337	282-4339
Forecaster The PO Box 66797 *Web:* www.theforecaster.net	Falmouth	ME	04105	207-781-3661	781-2060

Maryland

				Phone	Fax
Baltimore Times 2513 N Charles St *Web:* www.btimes.com	Baltimore	MD	21218	410-366-3900	243-1627
Aegis The PO Box 189 *TF:* 888-879-1710 ■ *Web:* www.theaegis.com	Bel Air	MD	21014	410-838-4400	838-7867
Weekender The PO Box 189 *TF:* 888-879-1710	Bel Air	MD	21014	410-838-4400	838-7867
Columbia Flier 10750 Little Patuxent Pkwy	Columbia	MD	21044	410-730-3620	997-4564
Howard County Times 10750 Little Patuxent Pkwy *Web:* news.mywebpal.com/index.cfm?pnpid=573	Columbia	MD	21044	410-730-3620	997-4564
Dundalk Eagle PO Box 8936 *Web:* www.dundalkeagle.com	Dundalk	MD	21222	410-288-6060	288-6963
Gaithersburg Gazette 1200 Quince Orchard Blvd **Fax:* Edit ■ *Web:* www.gazette.net/gaithersburg/news/	Gaithersburg	MD	20878	301-948-3120	670-7183*
Maryland Gazette 306 Crain Hwy SW *Web:* www.hometownglenburnie.com	Glen Burnie	MD	21061	410-766-3700	766-7031
Laurel Leader 555 Main St	Laurel	MD	20707	301-725-2000	317-8736
Enterprise The PO Box 700	Lexington Park	MD	20653	301-862-2111	737-1665
Garrett County Weekender 685 Mosser Rd Suite 20	McHenry	MD	21541	301-387-8926	359-0377
Maryland Beachcomber 12417 Ocean Gateway Suite A-7 *Web:* www.delmarvanow.com/mdbeachcomber	Ocean City	MD	21842	410-213-9442	213-9458
Northeast Times Booster 409 Washington Ave *TF:* 877-696-0660	Towson	MD	21204	410-337-2400	337-2490
Northeast Times Reporter 409 Washington Ave *TF:* 877-696-0660	Towson	MD	21204	410-337-2400	337-2490

Massachusetts

				Phone	Fax
Sunday Republican 1860 Main St *Web:* www.masslive.com	Springfield	MA	01101	413-788-1000	788-1301

Michigan

				Phone	Fax
Camden Publications 331 E Bell St *TF:* 800-222-6336 ■ *Web:* www.farmersadvance.com	Camden	MI	49232	517-368-0365	368-5131
Cedar Springs Post PO Box 370 *Web:* www.cedarspringspost.com	Cedar Springs	MI	49319	616-696-3655	696-9010
Dearborn Times-Herald 13730 Michigan Ave	Dearborn	MI	48126	313-584-4000	584-1357
Deckerville Recorder PO Box 519	Deckerville	MI	48427	810-376-3805	376-4058
Detroit Monitor 33490 Groesbeck Hwy	Fraser	MI	48026	586-296-6007	296-6072
Grosse Pointe News 96 Kercheval Ave *Web:* www.grossepointenews.com	Grosse Pointe Farms	MI	48236	313-882-6900	882-1585
Ada/Cascade/Forest Hills Advance PO Box 9 *Web:* www.advancenewspapers.com	Jenison	MI	49429	616-669-2700	669-4848
Grand Valley Advance PO Box 9 *Web:* www.advancenewspapers.com	Jenison	MI	49428	616-669-2700	669-4848
Kentwood Advance PO Box 9 *Web:* www.advancenewspapers.com	Jenison	MI	49429	616-669-2700	669-4848
Northfield Advance PO Box 9	Jenison	MI	49429	616-669-2700	669-4848
Walker/Westside Advance PO Box 9 *Web:* www.advancenewspapers.com	Jenison	MI	49429	616-669-2700	669-4848
Wyoming Advance PO Box 9 *Web:* www.advancenewspapers.com	Jenison	MI	49429	616-669-2700	669-4848
County Press PO Box 220 *Web:* www.countypress.com	Lapeer	MI	48446	810-664-0811	664-5852
Observer & Eccentric The 36251 Schoolcraft Rd *Web:* www.observer-eccentric.com	Livonia	MI	48150	734-591-2300	591-7279
Manistee News Advocate PO Box 317	Manistee	MI	49660	231-723-3592	723-4733
Bay Voice PO Box 760 *Web:* www.voicenews.com	New Baltimore	MI	48047	586-716-8100	716-8918
County Line Reminder PO Box 560	Ortonville	MI	48462	248-627-2843	627-3473
Independent Advisor 1907 W M-21 *TF:* 877-723-1119	Owosso	MI	48867	989-723-1118	725-1834
Sanilac County News PO Box 72	Sandusky	MI	48471	810-648-4000	648-4002
News-Herald 1 Heritage Pl Suite 100 *Web:* www.thenewsherald.com	Southgate	MI	48195	734-246-0800	246-2727

Weekly Newspapers (Cont'd)

Michigan (Cont'd)

				Phone	Fax
Spinal Column Newsweekly PO Box 14	Union Lake	MI	48387	248-360-6397	360-1220
Web: www.spinalcolumnonline.com					
Clinton-Fraser-Mount Clemens-Macomb-Harrison Advisor 48075 Van Dyke Ave	Utica	MI	48317	586-731-1000	731-8172
Web: www.sourcenewspapers.com					
Sterling Heights/Utica/Shelby Source Newspaper 48075 Van Dyke Ave	Utica	MI	48317	586-731-1000	731-8172
Web: www.sourcenewspapers.com					
Penasee Globe 133 E Superior St	Wayland	MI	49348	269-792-2271	792-2030

Minnesota

				Phone	Fax
Focus News 3989 Central Ave NE Suite 200	Columbia Heights	MN	55421	763-706-0890	706-0891
Budgeteer News 222 W Superior St Suite 100	Duluth	MN	55802	218-723-1207	727-7348
Web: www.duluth.com/placed					
Morrison County Record 216 SE 1st St	Little Falls	MN	56345	320-632-2345	632-2348
TF: 888-637-2345 ■ *Web:* www.mcrecord.com					
Downtown Journal 1115 Hennepin Ave S	Minneapolis	MN	55403	612-825-9205	825-0929
Web: www.skywaynews.net/					
Shoreview/Arden Hills Bulletin PO Box 120608	New Brighton	MN	55112	651-633-2777	633-3846
Web: bulletin-news.com					
Roseville Review 2515 E 7th Ave	North Saint Paul	MN	55109	651-777-8800	777-8288
Web: www.rosevillereview.com					
South-West Review 2515 E 7th Ave	North Saint Paul	MN	55109	651-777-8800	777-8288
Web: www.southwestreviewnews.com					
Plainview News 409 W Broadway	Plainview	MN	55964	507-534-3121	534-3920
Proctor Journal 215 5th St	Proctor	MN	55810	218-624-3344	624-7037
Web: www.proctormn.com					
Brooklyn Park Sun Post 4080 W Broadway Ave Suite 113	Robbinsdale	MN	55422	763-536-7500	536-7519
Northern Watch PO Box 100	Thief River Falls	MN	56701	218-681-4450	681-4455
Web: www.nwatch.com					

Mississippi

				Phone	Fax
Times The 4 Willow Pointe Box 15	Hattiesburg	MS	39402	601-268-2331	268-2965*
**Fax:* News Rm ■ *Web:* www.thetimeswire.com					

Missouri

				Phone	Fax
Bethany Republican-Clipper 202 N 16 St PO Box 351	Bethany	MO	64424	660-425-6325	425-3441
Web: www.bethanyclipper.com					
Chesterfield Journal 14522 S Outer 40 Dr	Chesterfield	MO	63017	314-821-1110	821-0843
Citizen Journal 14522 S Outer 40 Dr	Chesterfield	MO	63017	314-821-1110	821-0843
TF: 800-766-3278					
Press Journal 14522 S Outer 40 Dr	Chesterfield	MO	63017	314-821-1110	821-0843
TF: 866-440-4500					
Webster-Kirkwood Journal 14522 S Outer 40 Dr	Chesterfield	MO	63017	314-821-1110	821-0843
Farmington Press PO Box 70	Farmington	MO	63640	573-756-8927	756-9160
Web: www.mydjconnection.com					
Jefferson County Journal 1405 N Truman Blvd	Festus	MO	63028	636-931-6636	931-2638
News Democrat Journal 1405 N Truman Blvd	Festus	MO	63028	636-296-1800	931-2638
North County Journal 7751 N Lindbergh Blvd	Hazelwood	MO	63042	314-972-1111	831-7643
TF: 866-440-4500					
North Side Journal 7751 N Lindbergh Blvd	Hazelwood	MO	63042	314-972-1111	831-7643
TF: 866-440-4500					
Liberty Tribune 104 N Main St	Liberty	MO	64068	816-781-4941	781-0909
Web: www.libertytribune.com/					
Big Nickel Advertiser 127 W Main St	Malden	MO	63863	573-276-5148	276-3687
Raytown Post PO Box 18477	Raytown	MO	64133	816-353-5545	353-5589
Raytown Tribune 10227 E 61st St	Raytown	MO	64133	816-358-6398	358-5141
Web: www.raytowntribune.com					
Oakville/Mehlville Journal 4210 Chippewa St	Saint Louis	MO	63116	314-664-2700	664-8533
Saint Louis American 4242 Lindell Blvd	Saint Louis	MO	63108	314-533-8000	533-0038
Web: www.stlamerican.com					
South City Journal 4210 Chippewa St	Saint Louis	MO	63116	314-664-2700	664-8533
South County Journal 4210 Chippewa St	Saint Louis	MO	63116	314-664-2700	664-8533
South Side Journal 4210 Chippewa St	Saint Louis	MO	63116	314-664-2700	664-8533
South West City Journal 4210 Chippewa St	Saint Louis	MO	63116	314-664-2700	664-8533
Southwest County Journal 4210 Chippewa St	Saint Louis	MO	63116	314-664-2700	664-8533
Saint Charles Journal 4212 N Service Rd	Saint Peters	MO	63376	636-946-6111	946-0086
Saint Peters Journal 4212 N Service Rd	Saint Peters	MO	63376	636-724-1111	946-0086
West County Journal 14522 S Outer 40 Dr	Town & Country	MO	63017	314-821-1110	821-0843
Washington Missourian 14 W Main St PO Box 336	Washington	MO	63090	636-239-7701	239-0915
TF: 888-239-7701 ■ *Web:* www.emissourian.com					

Montana

				Phone	Fax
Billings Times 2919 Montana Ave	Billings	MT	59101	406-245-4994	245-5115

Nebraska

				Phone	Fax
Bellevue Leader 604 Fort Crook Rd N PO Box 1219	Bellevue	NE	68005	402-733-7300	733-9116
Web: www.bellevueleader.com					
West Nebraska Register PO Box 608	Grand Island	NE	68802	308-382-4660	382-6569
Web: www.gidiocese.org/wnr/					

Nevada

				Phone	Fax
Ely Times 297 11th St E PO Box 150820	Ely	NV	89315	775-289-4491	289-4566
Web: www.elynews.com					

New Hampshire

				Phone	Fax
Messenger The PO Box 1190	Hillsboro	NH	03244	603-464-3388	464-4106
TF: 800-281-2859 ■ *Web:* www.themessengernh.com					
Broadcaster The 255 Main St	Nashua	NH	03063	603-886-6075	886-8180
Web: www.nhbroadcaster.com					

New Jersey

				Phone	Fax
Suburban News/Elizabeth City News 301 Central Ave	Clark	NJ	07066	732-396-4404	396-4770*
**Fax:* Edit ■ *TF:* 800-472-0102					
Suburbanite 210 Knickerbocker Rd 2nd Fl	Cresskill	NJ	07626	201-894-6700	568-4360
Twin-Boro News 210 Knickerbocker Rd	Cresskill	NJ	07626	201-894-6715	568-6209
Current The 3129 Fire Rd	Egg Harbor Township	NJ	08234	609-383-8994	383-9072
Hunterdon County Democrat PO Box 32	Flemington	NJ	08822	908-782-4747	782-4706
Web: www.nj.com/hunterdon					
Hunterdon Observer PO Box 32	Flemington	NJ	08822	908-782-4747	782-4706
Sentinel The PO Box 5001	Freehold	NJ	07728	732-358-5200	780-4192
Web: www.gmnews.com					
Hoboken Reporter 1400 Washington St	Hoboken	NJ	07030	201-798-7800	798-0018
Web: www.zwire.com/site/news.cfm?brd=1292					
Hudson Reporter 1400 Washington St PO Box 3069	Hoboken	NJ	07030	201-798-7800	798-0018
Web: www.hudsonreporter.com					
Suburban Trends 300 Kakeout Rd	Kinnelon	NJ	07405	973-283-5600	283-5623
Times-Beacon 345 E Bay Ave	Manahawkin	NJ	08050	609-597-3211	978-4592
Web: www.timesbeacon.com					
Central Record PO Box 1027	Medford	NJ	08055	609-654-5000	654-8237
Web: www.zwire.com/site/news.cfm?brd=2244					
Reminder Newspaper PO Box 1600	Millville	NJ	08332	856-825-8811	825-0011
Web: www.nreminder.com					
Independent Press 80 South St	New Providence	NJ	07974	908-464-1025	464-9085
Web: www.nj.com/independentpress/					
Bergen News Palisades 111 Grand Ave	Palisades Park	NJ	07650	201-947-5000	947-5055*
**Fax:* Edit ■ *Web:* www.bergennews.com					
Town Topics 4 Mercer St	Princeton	NJ	08540	609-924-2200	924-8818
Web: www.towntopics.com					
Atom Tabloid PO Box 1061	Rahway	NJ	07065	732-574-1200	388-4143
Two River Times 46 Newman Springs Rd E Suite C	Red Bank	NJ	07701	732-219-5788	747-7213
Web: www.tworivertimes.net					
Cape May County Herald 1508 Rt 47	Rio Grande	NJ	08242	609-886-8600	886-1879
Web: www.capemaycountyherald.com					
Cape May County Gazette Leader 2087 S Shore Rd	Seaville	NJ	08230	609-624-8900	624-3470
Community Life 372 Kinderkamack Rd	Westwood	NJ	07675	201-664-2501	664-1332

New Mexico

				Phone	Fax
Las Cruces Bulletin PO Box 637	Las Cruces	NM	88004	505-524-8061	526-4621*
**Fax:* News Rm ■ *Web:* www.lascrucesbulletin.com					

New York

				Phone	Fax
Queens Courier 38-15 Bell Blvd	Bayside	NY	11361	718-224-5863	224-5441
Web: www.queenscourier.com					
Bay News 1733 Sheepshead Bay Rd	Brooklyn	NY	11235	718-615-2500	615-3835
TF: 800-564-5433					
Brooklyn Heights Press & Cobble Hill News 30 Henry St	Brooklyn	NY	11201	718-858-2300	858-3291
Web: www.brooklyneagle.com					
Kings Courier 1733 Sheepshead Bay Rd	Brooklyn	NY	11235	718-615-2500	615-3835
TF: 800-564-5433					
New York Harbor Watch 1733 Sheepshead Bay Rd	Brooklyn	NY	11235	718-615-2500	615-3830
TF: 800-564-5433					
Plattsburgh Free Trader PO Box 338	Elizabethtown	NY	12932	518-873-6368	873-6360
TF: 800-277-6567					
Queens Tribune 174-15 Horace Harding Expy	Fresh Meadows	NY	11365	718-357-7400	357-9417
Web: www.queenstribune.com					
Chronicle The PO Box 153	Glens Falls	NY	12801	518-792-1126	793-1587
Web: www.readthechronicle.com					
North Country Free Press PO Box 330	Granville	NY	12832	518-642-1234	642-1344
TF: 800-354-4232					
Forum South 102-05 159th Ave	Howard Beach	NY	11414	718-845-3221	738-7645
New York Observer 915 Broadway 9th Fl	New York	NY	10010	212-755-2400	688-4889*
**Fax:* Edit ■ *Web:* www.observer.com					
People's Weekly World 235 W 23rd St	New York	NY	10011	212-924-2523	229-1713
Web: pww.org					
Villager The 145 6th Ave 1st Fl	New York	NY	10013	212-229-1890	229-2790
Web: www.thevillager.com					
Our Town 36 Ridge St	Pearl River	NY	10965	845-735-1342	620-9533
Times Newsweekly PO Box 860299	Ridgewood	NY	11386	718-821-7500	456-0120
Web: www.timesnewsweekly.com					
Suffolk Life Newspaper PO Box 9167	Riverhead	NY	11901	631-369-0800	591-5190
Web: www.suffolklife.com					
Traveler Watchman PO Box 725	Southold	NY	11971	631-765-3425	765-1756
Suburban News PO Box 106	Spencerport	NY	14559	585-352-3411	352-4811
Web: www.westsidenewsonline.com					
Southern Duchess News 84 E Main St	Wappingers Falls	NY	12590	845-297-3723	297-6810

North Carolina

				Phone	Fax
Mountain Times PO Box 1815	Boone	NC	28607	828-264-6397	262-0282
Web: www.mountaintimes.com					
Chapel Hill News 505 W Franklin St	Chapel Hill	NC	27516	919-932-2000	968-4953
TF: 800-365-6115 ■ *Web:* www.chapelhillnews.com					
Journal-Patriot PO Box 70	North Wilkesboro	NC	28659	336-838-4117	838-9864
Pilot The PO Box 58	Southern Pines	NC	28388	910-692-7271	692-9382
Web: www.thepilot.com					

North Dakota

				Phone	Fax
West Fargo Pioneer PO Box 457	West Fargo	ND	58078	701-282-2443	282-9248
Web: www.westfargopioneer.com					
Plains Reporter PO Box 1447	Williston	ND	58802	701-572-2165	572-9563
TF: 800-950-2165					

Ohio

				Phone	Fax
Sun Messenger 3355 Richmond Rd Suite 171	Beachwood	OH	44122	216-464-6397	464-8816
Web: www.sunnews.com					

Phone | Fax

Sun Press 3355 Richmond Rd Suite 171 .... Beachwood OH 44122 216-464-6397 464-8816
Web: www.sunnews.com
Sun Scoop Journal 3355 Richmond Rd Suite 171 .... Beachwood OH 44122 216-464-6397 464-8816
Web: www.sunnews.com
News Sun 32 Park St .... Berea OH 44017 216-986-7550 986-7551
TF: 800-362-8008 ■ *Web:* www.sunnews.com
Parma Sun Post 32 Park St .... Berea OH 44017 216-986-7550 986-7551
Web: www.sunnews.com
Boardman Town Crier 100 DeBartolo Pl Suite 210 .... Boardman OH 44512 330-629-6200 629-6210
Cincinnati Downtowner 600 Vine St Suite 106 .... Cincinnati OH 45202 513-241-9906 241-7235
Hilltop News Press 5556 Cheviot Rd .... Cincinnati OH 45247 513-923-3111 923-1806
Web: news.communitypress.com
Northwest Press 5556 Cheviot Rd .... Cincinnati OH 45247 513-923-3111 923-1806
Web: www.communitypress.com
Western Hills Press 5556 Cheviot Rd .... Cincinnati OH 45247 513-923-3111 923-1806
Web: www.communitypress.com
Rural-Urban Record PO Box 966 .... Columbia Station OH 44028 440-236-8982 236-9198
Web: www.rural-urbanrecord.com
Dublin News 5257 Sinclair Rd PO Box 29912 .... Columbus OH 43229 614-785-1212 842-4760*
**Fax:* Edit ■ *Web:* www.snponline.com
Eastside Messenger 3500 Sullivant Ave .... Columbus OH 43204 614-272-5422 272-0684
Web: www.columbusmessenger.com
Northland News 5257 Sinclair Rd PO Box 29912 .... Columbus OH 43229 614-785-1212 842-4760
Web: www.snponline.com
Southeast Messenger 3500 Sullivant Ave .... Columbus OH 43204 614-272-5422 272-0684
Web: www.columbusmessenger.com
Southwest Messenger 3500 Sullivant Ave .... Columbus OH 43204 614-272-5422 272-0684
Web: www.columbusmessenger.com
Upper Arlington News 5257 Sinclair Rd PO Box 29912 .... Columbus OH 43229 614-785-1212 842-4760*
**Fax:* Edit ■ *Web:* www.snponline.com
Westerville News 5257 Sinclair Rd PO Box 29912 .... Columbus OH 43229 614-785-1212 842-4760
Web: www.snponline.com
Westland News 5257 Sinclair Rd PO Box 29912 .... Columbus OH 43229 614-785-1212 842-4760
Web: www.snponline.com
Westside Messenger 3500 Sullivant Ave .... Columbus OH 43204 614-272-5422 272-0684
Web: www.columbusmessenger.com
Enon Messenger PO Box 335 .... Enon OH 45323 937-864-1136 845-3577
Web: www.tcnewsnet.com
Early Bird The 5312 Sebring Warner Rd .... Greenville OH 45331 937-548-3330 548-3376
TF: 800-548-5312 ■ *Web:* www.earlybirdpaper.com
Centerville-Bellbrook Times 3085 Woodman Dr Suite 170 .... Kettering OH 45420 937-294-7000 294-2981
Web: www.tcnewsnet.com
Sunday Western Star 200 Harmon Ave .... Lebanon OH 45036 513-932-3010 932-6056
Web: www.western-star.com
Delaware This Week 7801 N Central Dr .... Lewis Center OH 43035 740-888-6100 888-6006
Web: www.thisweeknews.com
Dublin Villager 7801 N Central Dr .... Lewis Center OH 43035 740-888-6100 888-6006
Web: www.thisweeknews.com
Hilliard This Week 7801 N Central Dr .... Lewis Center OH 43035 740-888-6100 888-6006
Web: www.thisweeknews.com
Reynoldsburg This Week 7801 N Central Dr .... Lewis Center OH 43035 740-888-6100 888-6006
Web: www.thisweeknews.com
Southside This Week 7801 N Central Dr .... Lewis Center OH 43035 740-888-6100 888-6006
Web: www.thisweeknews.com
This Week in Upper Arlington 7801 N Central Dr .... Lewis Center OH 43035 740-888-6100 888-6006
Web: www.thisweeknews.com
Westerville This Week 7801 N Central Dr .... Lewis Center OH 43035 740-888-6100 888-6006
Web: www.thisweeknews.com
Worthington This Week 7801 N Central Dr .... Lewis Center OH 43035 740-888-6100 888-6006
Web: www.thisweeknews.com
Fairfield Echo 7378 Liberty One Dr .... Liberty Township OH 45044 513-755-5060 777-3237
Web: www.fairfield-echo.com
Pulse-Journal 7378 Liberty One Dr .... Liberty Township OH 45044 513-755-5060 755-5077
Web: www.pulsejournal.com
Forest Hills Journal 394 Wards Corner Rd Suite 170 .... Loveland OH 45140 513-248-8600 248-1938
Web: news.communitypress.com
Loveland Herald 394 Wards Corner Rd Suite 170 .... Loveland OH 45140 513-248-8600 248-1938
Web: news.communitypress.com
Suburban Press & Metro Press PO Box 169 .... Millbury OH 43447 419-836-2221 836-1319
TF: 800-300-6158 ■ *Web:* www.presspublications.com
Sun Herald 28895 Lorain Rd .... North Olmsted OH 44070 216-986-6070 986-6071
TF: 800-466-7861 ■ *Web:* www.sunnews.com
West Side Sun News 28895 Lorain Rd .... North Olmsted OH 44070 216-986-6070 986-6071
TF: 800-466-7861 ■ *Web:* www.sunnews.com
Beacon The 205 SE Catawba Rd Suite G .... Port Clinton OH 43452 419-732-2154 734-5382
Web: www.thebeacon.net
Cuyahoga Falls News-Press PO Box 1549 .... Stow OH 44224 330-688-0088 688-1588
TF: 800-966-6565 ■ *Web:* www.recordpub.com
Gateway News 1619 Commerce Dr .... Stow OH 44224 330-688-0088 688-1588
TF: 800-560-9657 ■ *Web:* www.recordpub.com
Budget The PO Box 249 .... Sugarcreek OH 44681 330-852-4634 852-4421
West Toledo Herald 5739 N Main St .... Sylvania OH 43560 419-885-9222 885-0764
Web: www.heraldpapers.org
West Life PO Box 45014 .... Westlake OH 44145 440-871-5797 871-3824
Web: www.westlifenews.com
Star-Republican 47 South St .... Wilmington OH 45177 937-382-7796 382-4392
Boardman News 6221 Market St .... Youngstown OH 44512 330-758-6397 758-2658

Oklahoma

Phone | Fax

El Reno Tribune PO Box 9 .... El Reno OK 73036 405-262-5180 262-3541
Web: www.elrenotribune.com
Holdenville News PO Box 751 .... Holdenville OK 74848 405-379-5411 379-5413

Oregon

Phone | Fax

Hillsboro Argus PO Box 588 .... Hillsboro OR 97123 503-648-1131 648-9191
Web: www.hillsboroargus.com
Woodburn Independent PO Box 96 .... Woodburn OR 97071 503-981-3441 981-1253
Web: www.woodburnindependent.com

Pennsylvania

Phone | Fax

Lancaster Farming PO Box 609 .... Ephrata PA 17522 717-626-1164 733-6058
Web: www.lancasterfarming.com
Shoppers Guide PO Box 328 .... Everett PA 15537 814-652-5191 652-9544
TF: 800-596-5428
North Penn Life 290 Commerce Dr PO Box 1628 .... Fort Washington PA 19034 215-542-0200 643-9475
Bucks County Tribune 390 Easton Rd .... Horsham PA 19044 215-675-8250 675-8251
Progress of Montgomery County 390 Easton Rd .... Horsham PA 19044 215-675-8250 675-8251
Web: www.progresnews.com

Phone | Fax

Almanac The 395 Valley Brook Rd .... McMurray PA 15317 724-941-7725 941-8685*
**Fax:* Edit ■ *Web:* www.thealmanac.net
Germantown Courier 335 E Price St .... Philadelphia PA 19144 215-848-8792 848-0475
Leader The 2385 W Cheltenham Ave Suite 182 .... Philadelphia PA 19150 215-885-4111 885-0226
Web: www.zwire.com/site/news.cfm?brd=1682
Mount Airy Times Express 335 E Price St .... Philadelphia PA 19144 215-848-8792 848-0475
Northeast Breeze 9999 Gantry Rd .... Philadelphia PA 19115 215-969-5100 969-5400
Review The 6220 Ridge Ave .... Philadelphia PA 19128 215-483-7300 483-2073
Web: www.zwire.com/site/news.cfm?brd=1680
Northeast Times 2512 Metropolitan Dr .... Trevose PA 19053 215-355-9009 355-4812
Web: www.northeasttimes.com
Suburban Advertiser PO Box 409 .... Wayne PA 19087 610-688-3000 964-1346
Web: www.suburbanadvertiser.com
Main Line Life 311 E Lancaster Ave .... Wynnewood PA 19096 610-896-9555 896-9560
Web: www.mainlinelife.com
York Sunday News 1891 Loucks Rd PO Box 15122 .... York PA 17408 717-767-6397 771-2009
TF: 800-483-5517 ■ *Web:* www.ydr.com

Rhode Island

Phone | Fax

Newport Mercury 101 Malbone Rd .... Newport RI 02840 401-849-3300 849-3335
TF: 800-320-2378 ■ *Web:* www.newportmercury.com
Newport This Week 33 Marlborough St .... Newport RI 02840 401-847-7766 846-4974
Web: www.eastbayri.com/newport/newport.php

South Carolina

Phone | Fax

Bluffton Today 52 Persimmon St .... Bluffton SC 29910 843-815-0800 815-0898
Web: www.blufftontoday.com
Chronicle Independent PO Box 1137 .... Camden SC 29021 803-432-6157 432-7609
TF: 800-698-3514 ■ *Web:* www.chronicle-independent.com
Georgetown Times PO Box 2778 .... Georgetown SC 29442 843-546-4148 546-2395
Myrtle Beach Herald 3364 Huger St .... Myrtle Beach SC 29577 843-626-3131 448-4860
Web: www.myrtlebeachherald.com
Star The 106 E Buena Vista Ave .... North Augusta SC 29841 803-279-2793 278-4070
Web: www.northaugustastar.com
Moultrie News PO Box 279 .... Sullivans Island SC 29482 843-849-1778 849-0214
Web: www.islandpapers.com
Press & Standard 228 Washington St .... Walterboro SC 29488 843-549-2586 549-2446

South Dakota

Phone | Fax

Meade County Times-Tribune PO Box 69 .... Sturgis SD 57785 605-347-2503 347-2321
Web: www.bhcn.com

Tennessee

Phone | Fax

Dickson Herald PO Box 587 .... Dickson TN 37056 615-446-2811 446-5560
Web: www.dicksonherald.com
Farragutpress 11863 Kingston Pike .... Knoxville TN 37934 865-675-6397 675-1675
Web: www.farragutpress.com
South Pittsburg Hustler PO Box 765 .... South Pittsburg TN 37380 423-837-6312 837-8715
Monroe County Advocate & Democrat PO Box 389 .... Sweetwater TN 37874 423-337-7101 337-5932
Web: www.monroe.xtn.net

Texas

Phone | Fax

Preston Hollow People 4311 Oaklawn Ave Suite 350 .... Dallas TX 75219 214-739-2244 363-6948
Web: www.peoplenewspapers.com
Edinburg Review 215 E University Dr .... Edinburg TX 78540 956-383-2705 383-3172
Grapevine Sun PO Box 400 .... Grapevine TX 76099 817-488-8561 488-5339
Houston Forward Times PO Box 8346 .... Houston TX 77288 713-526-4727 526-3170
Web: www.forwardtimes.com
Leader The PO Box 924487 .... Houston TX 77292 713-686-8494 686-0970
Humble Observer 907 E Main St Suite B .... Humble TX 77338 281-446-4438 964-4423
Web: www.thehumbleobserver.com
Hardin County News PO Box 8240 .... Lumberton TX 77657 409-755-4912 755-7731
Web: www.thehardincountynews.com
Valley Town Crier 1811 N 23rd St .... McAllen TX 78501 956-682-2423 630-6371
TF: 800-285-5667 ■ *Web:* www.valleytowncrier.com
Mid County Chronicle PO Box 2140 .... Nederland TX 77627 409-722-0479 729-7626
Pearland Journal 2206 E Broadway Suite A .... Pearland TX 77581 281-485-2785 485-4464
Web: www.pearlandjournal.com
North San Antonio Times 17400 Judson Rd .... San Antonio TX 78247 210-453-3300 828-3787
Web: www.clickitsa.com

Utah

Phone | Fax

Millard County Chronicle Progress PO Box 249 .... Delta UT 84624 435-864-2400 514-2931*
**Fax Area Code:* 775
Standard Examiner 2072 Layton Hills Mall .... Layton UT 84041 801-629-5220 629-5238
TF: 800-651-2105 ■ *Web:* standard-examiner.standard.net

Vermont

Phone | Fax

World The 403 US Rte 302-Berlin .... Barre VT 05641 802-479-2582 479-7916
TF: 800-639-9753 ■ *Web:* www.vt-world.com

Virginia

Phone | Fax

Eastern Loudoun Times 9 E Market St PO Box 359 .... Leesburg VA 20178 703-777-1111 771-0036
Loudoun Times-Mirror PO Box 359 .... Leesburg VA 20178 703-777-1111 771-0036
Web: www.timescommunity.com
Alexandria Gazette Packet 7913 W Park Dr .... McLean VA 22102 703-821-5050 917-0991
Web: www.connectionnewspapers.com
Arlington Connection 7913 W Park Dr .... McLean VA 22102 703-917-6444 917-0991
Web: www.connectionnewspapers.com
Mechanicsville Local PO Box 1118 .... Mechanicsville VA 23111 804-746-1235 730-0476
TF: 800-476-0197 ■ *Web:* www.mechlocal.com

Weekly Newspapers (Cont'd)

Virginia (Cont'd)

				Phone	Fax
Fairfax County Times 1760 Reston Pkwy Suite 411	Reston	VA	20190	703-437-5400	437-6019
Web: www.timescommunity.com					
Springfield Times Courier 1760 Reston Pkwy Suite 411	Reston	VA	20190	703-437-5400	437-6019
Fauquier Times-Democrat PO Box 631	Warrenton	VA	20188	540-347-4222	349-8676
Web: www.fauquier.com					
Virginia Gazette 216 Ironbound Rd	Williamsburg	VA	23188	757-220-1736	220-1665
TF: 800-944-6908 ■ Web: www.vagazette.com					

Washington

				Phone	Fax
Reflector The PO Box 2020	Battle Ground	WA	98604	360-687-5151	687-5162
Web: www.thereflector.com					
Bothell/Kenmore Reporter PO Box 90130	Bellevue	WA	98009	425-453-4221	453-4215
Web: reporternewspapers.com					
Dispatch The PO Box 248	Eatonville	WA	98328	360-832-4411	832-4972
Web: www.dispatchnews.com					
Journal of the San Juan Islands PO Box 519	Friday Harbor	WA	98250	360-378-4191	378-5128
Web: www.sanjuanjournal.com					
Issaquah Press PO Box 1328	Issaquah	WA	98027	425-392-6434	391-1541
Web: www.issaquahpress.com					
Kirkland Courier 733 7th Ave Suite 204	Kirkland	WA	98033	425-822-9166	
Enterprise The 4303 198th St SW	Lynnwood	WA	98036	425-673-6500	774-8622
TF: 800-944-3630 ■ Web: www.enterprisenewspapers.com					
Globe The PO Box 145	Marysville	WA	98270	360-659-1300	658-0350
Web: www.marysvilleglobe.com					
Port Orchard Independent PO Box 27	Port Orchard	WA	98366	360-876-4414	876-4458
Web: www.portorchardindependent.com					
Puyallup Herald PO Box 517	Puyallup	WA	98371	253-841-2481	840-8249
Web: www.puyallup-herald.com					
Beacon Hill News/South District Journal 4000 Aurora Ave N Suite 100	Seattle	WA	98103	206-461-1300	
Capitol Hill Times 4000 Aurora Ave N Suite 100	Seattle	WA	98103	206-461-1300	
West Seattle Herald 2604 California Ave SW	Seattle	WA	98116	206-932-0300	937-1223
Web: www.westseattleherald.com					
Central Kitsap Reporter 9989 Silverdale Way NW Suite 109	Silverdale	WA	98383	360-698-9605	308-9363
Web: www.centralkitsapreporter.com					
Everett News Tribune PO Box 499	Snohomish	WA	98291	360-568-4121	568-1484
Snohomish County Tribune PO Box 499	Snohomish	WA	98291	360-568-4121	568-1484
Web: www.snoho.com					
Lewis County News PO Box 10	Winlock	WA	98596	360-785-3151	785-0863

West Virginia

				Phone	Fax
Coal Valley News 475 Main St	Madison	WV	25130	304-369-1165	369-1166
Web: www.coalvalleynews.com					

Wisconsin

				Phone	Fax
Burlington Standard Press 700 N Pine St	Burlington	WI	53105	262-763-3511	763-2238
Web: standardpress.com					
Country Today 701 S Farwell St	Eau Claire	WI	54701	715-833-9270	858-7307
TF: 800-236-4004 ■ Web: www.thecountrytoday.com					
Sawyer County Record PO Box 919	Hayward	WI	54843	715-634-4881	634-8191
Foto News 807 E 1st St	Merrill	WI	54452	715-536-7121	539-3686
Web: www.zwire.com/site/news.cfm?brd=2172					
Milwaukee Courier 2003 W Capitol Dr PO Box 06279	Milwaukee	WI	53206	414-449-4860	449-4872
Web: www.milwaukeecourier.org					
Bulletin The 24417 75th St	Paddock Lake	WI	53168	262-843-1535	843-1539
TF: 800-846-1101					
Wisconsin State Farmer PO Box 152	Waupaca	WI	54981	715-258-5546	258-8162
TF: 800-236-3313 ■ Web: www.wisfarmer.com					

Wyoming

				Phone	Fax
Jackson Hole News & Guide PO Box 7445	Jackson	WY	83002	307-733-2047	733-2138
Web: www.jhnewsandguide.com					

535-5 Weekly Newspapers - Alternative

				Phone	Fax
Ace Weekly 486 W 2nd St	Lexington	KY	40507	859-225-4889	226-0569
Web: www.aceweekly.com					
Arkansas Times PO Box 34010	Little Rock	AR	72203	501-375-2985	375-3623
Web: www.arktimes.com					
ArtVoice 810 Main St	Buffalo	NY	14202	716-881-6604	881-6682
Web: www.artvoice.com					
Athens NEWS 14 N Court St	Athens	OH	45701	740-594-8219	592-5695
Web: www.athensnews.com					
Austin Chronicle PO Box 49066	Austin	TX	78765	512-454-5766	458-6910
Web: www.austinchronicle.com					
Baltimore City Paper 812 Park Ave	Baltimore	MD	21201	410-523-2300	523-0138
Web: www.citypaper.com					
Birmingham Weekly 2014 6th Ave N	Birmingham	AL	35203	205-939-4030	212-1005
Web: www.bhamweekly.com					
Black & White 2210 2nd Ave N 2nd Fl	Birmingham	AL	35203	205-933-0460	933-0467
Web: www.bwcitypaper.com					
Boise Weekly 523 Broad St	Boise	ID	83702	208-344-2055	342-4733
Web: www.boiseweekly.com					
Boston Phoenix 126 Brookline Ave	Boston	MA	02215	617-536-5390	859-8201
Web: thephoenix.com/					
Bostons Weekly Dig 242 E Berkeley St 5th Fl	Boston	MA	02118	617-426-8942	426-8942
Web: www.weeklydig.com					
Boulder Weekly 690 S Lashley Ln	Boulder	CO	80305	303-494-5511	494-2585
Web: www.boulderweekly.com					
C-Ville Weekly 106 E Main St	Charlottesville	VA	22902	434-817-2749	817-2758
Web: www.c-ville.com					
Charleston City Paper 1049 B Morrison Dr	Charleston	SC	29403	843-577-5304	576-0380
Web: www.charlestoncitypaper.com					
Chicago Reader 11 E Illinois St	Chicago	IL	60611	312-828-0350	828-9926
Web: www.chicagoreader.com					
Chico News & Review 353 E 2nd St	Chico	CA	95928	530-894-2300	894-0143
TF: 800-225-3369 ■ Web: www.newsreview.com					
Cincinnati CityBeat 811 Race St	Cincinnati	OH	45202	513-665-4700	665-4368
Web: www.citybeat.com					
City Link 4611 Johnson Rd Suite 4	Coconut Creek	FL	33073	954-356-4943	356-4949
Web: southflorida.metromix.com/					
City Newspaper 250 N Goodman St	Rochester	NY	14607	585-244-3329	244-1126
Web: www.rochester-citynews.com					
City Pages 300 3rd St	Wausau	WI	54403	715-845-5171	848-5887
Web: www.thecitypages.com					
Cityview 414-61st St	Des Moines	IA	50312	515-953-4822	953-1394
Web: www.dmcityview.com					
Cleveland Free Times 800 W St Clair Ave 2nd Fl	Cleveland	OH	44113	216-479-2033	861-6504*
*Fax: Edit ■ Web: www.freetimes.com					
Coast The 5435 Portland Pl	Halifax	NS	B3K6R7	902-422-6278	425-0013
Web: www.thecoast.ca					
Colorado Springs Independent 235 S Nevada Ave	Colorado Springs	CO	80903	719-577-4545	577-4107
Web: www.csindy.com					
Columbus Alive 62 E Broad St	Columbus	OH	43215	614-221-2449	461-8746
Web: www.columbusalive.com					
Creative Loafing Atlanta 384 Northyards Blvd Suite 600	Atlanta	GA	30313	404-688-5623	522-1532
TF: 800-950-5623 ■ Web: atlanta.creativeloafing.com					
Creative Loafing Charlotte 820 Hamilton St Suite C-2	Charlotte	NC	28206	704-522-8334	522-8088
Web: charlotte.creativeloafing.com					
Creative Loafing Tampa 810 N Howard Ave	Tampa	FL	33606	813-739-4800	739-4801
Web: tampa.creativeloafing.com					
Dallas Observer 2501 Oak Lawn Ave Suite 700	Dallas	TX	75219	214-757-9000	757-8590
Web: www.dallasobserver.com					
Dayton City Paper 322 S Patterson Blvd	Dayton	OH	45402	937-222-8855	222-6113
Web: www.daytoncitypaper.com					
East Bay Express 1335 Stanford Ave Suite 100	Emeryville	CA	94608	510-879-3700	879-3794
Web: www.eastbayexpress.com					
Easy Reader 832 Hermosa Ave PO Box 427	Hermosa Beach	CA	90254	310-372-4611	318-6292
Web: www.easyreader.info					
Eugene Weekly 1251 Lincoln St	Eugene	OR	97401	541-484-0519	484-4044
Web: www.eugeneweekly.com					
Fairfield County Weekly 350 Fairfield Ave Suite 605	Bridgeport	CT	06604	203-382-9666	382-9657
Web: fairfieldweekly.com					
Flagpole PO Box 1027	Athens	GA	30603	706-549-9523	548-8981
Web: www.flagpole.com					
Folio Weekly 9456 Philips Hwy Suite 11	Jacksonville	FL	32256	904-260-9770	260-9773
TF: 800-940-9770 ■ Web: www.folioweekly.com					
Fort Worth Weekly 3311 Hamilton Ave	Fort Worth	TX	76107	817-321-9700	335-9575
Web: www.fwweekly.com					
Gambit Weekly 3923 Bienville St	New Orleans	LA	70119	504-486-5900	483-3116
Web: www.bestofneworleans.com					
Georgia Straight 1701 W Broadway	Vancouver	BC	V6J1Y3	604-730-7000	730-7010
Web: www.straight.com					
Hartford Advocate 121 Wawarme Ave 1st Fl	Hartford	CT	06114	860-548-9300	548-9335
Web: hartfordadvocate.com					
Honolulu Weekly 1111 Ford Street Mall Suite 214	Honolulu	HI	96813	808-528-1475	528-3144
Web: www.honoluluweekly.com					
Hour Magazine 355 Saint Catherine St W 7th Fl	Montreal	QC	H3B1A5	514-848-0777	848-9004
TF: 877-631-8647 ■ Web: www.hour.ca					
Houston Press 1621 Milam St Suite 100	Houston	TX	77002	713-280-2400	280-2496
Web: www.houstonpress.com					
Illinois Times PO Box 5256	Springfield	IL	62705	217-753-2226	753-2281
Web: www.illinoistimes.com					
Independent Weekly PO Box 2690	Durham	NC	27715	919-286-1972	286-4274
TF: 800-948-8699 ■ Web: indyweek.com/durham/current					
Isthmus 101 King St	Madison	WI	53703	608-251-5627	251-2165
Web: www.thedailypage.com					
Ithaca Times 109 N Cayuga St	Ithaca	NY	14851	607-277-7000	277-1012
Web: www.ithacatimes.com					
Jackson Free Press PO Box 2047	Jackson	MS	39225	601-362-6121	510-9019
Web: www.jacksonfreepress.com					
LA Weekly 6715 Sunset Blvd	Los Angeles	CA	90028	323-465-4414	465-3220
Web: www.laweekly.com					
Las Vegas Weekly 2290 Corporate Circle Suite 250	Henderson	NV	89074	702-990-2550	990-2424
Web: www.lasvegasweekly.com					
Long Island Press 575 Underhill Blvd Suite 210	Syosset	NY	11791	516-284-3300	284-3311
Web: www.longislandpress.com					
Louisville Eccentric Observer 640 S 4th St Suite 100	Louisville	KY	40202	502-895-9770	895-9779
Web: www.leoweekly.com					
Maui Time Weekly 33 N Market St Suite 201	Wailuku	HI	96793	808-244-0777	244-0446
Web: www.mauitime.com					
Memphis Flyer 460 Tennessee St	Memphis	TN	38103	901-521-9000	521-0129
Web: www.memphisflyer.com					
Metro Pulse 602 S Gay St Mezzanine Suite	Knoxville	TN	37902	865-522-5399	522-2955
Web: www.metropulse.com					
Metro Santa Cruz 115 Cooper St	Santa Cruz	CA	95060	831-457-9000	457-5828
Web: metroactive.com/cruz					
Metro Silicon Valley 550 S 1st St	San Jose	CA	95113	408-298-8000	298-0602
Web: metroactive.com					
Metro Times 733 Saint Antoine St	Detroit	MI	48226	313-961-4060	961-6598
Web: www.metrotimes.com					
Metroland 419 Madison Ave	Albany	NY	12210	518-463-2500	463-3712
Web: www.metroland.net					
Miami New Times 2800 Biscayne Blvd	Miami	FL	33137	305-576-8000	571-7677
Web: www.miaminewtimes.com					
Minneapolis/St. Paul City Pages 401 N 3rd St Suite 550	Minneapolis	MN	55401	612-375-1015	372-3737
Web: www.citypages.com					
Missoula Independent 317 S Orange St	Missoula	MT	59801	406-543-6609	543-4367
Web: www.missoulanews.com					
Monday Magazine 818 Broughton St	Victoria	BC	V8W1E4	250-382-6188	381-2662
TF: 800-661-6335 ■ Web: www.mondaymag.com/monday					
Monterey County Weekly 668 Williams Ave	Seaside	CA	93955	831-394-5656	394-2909
Web: www.montereycountyweekly.com					
Montreal Mirror 465 McGill St 3rd Floor	Montreal	QC	H2Y4B4	514-393-1010	393-3173
Web: www.montrealmirror.com					
Mountain Xpress PO Box 144	Asheville	NC	28802	828-251-1333	251-1311
Web: www.mountainx.com					
Nashville Scene 2120 8th Ave S	Nashville	TN	37204	615-244-7989	254-4743
Web: www.nashscene.com					
New Haven Advocate 900 Chapel St Suite 1100	New Haven	CT	06510	203-789-0010	787-1418
Web: newhavenadvocate.com					
New Times Broward Palm Beach PO Box 14128	Fort Lauderdale	FL	33302	954-233-1600	233-1571
Web: www.newtimesbpb.com					
New York Press 333 7th Ave 14th Fl	New York	NY	10001	212-244-2282	244-9864
Web: www.nypress.com					
Newcity 770 N Halsted St Suite 306	Chicago	IL	60622	312-243-8786	243-8802
Web: www.newcitychicago.com					
North Bay Bohemian 847 5th St	Santa Rosa	CA	95404	707-527-1200	527-1288
Web: www.bohemian.com					

	City	State	Zip	Phone	Fax
NOW Magazine 189 Church St *Web:* www.nowtoronto.com	Toronto	ON	M5B1Y7	416-364-1300	364-1166
NUVO 3951 N Meridian St Suite 200 *Web:* www.nuvo.net	Indianapolis	IN	46208	317-254-2400	254-2405
OC Weekly 1666 N Main St Suite 500 *Web:* www.ocweekly.com	Santa Ana	CA	92701	714-550-5950	550-5903
Oklahoma Gazette 3701 N Shartel Ave *Web:* www.okgazette.com	Oklahoma City	OK	73118	405-528-6000	528-4600
Orlando Weekly 100 W Livingston St *Web:* www.orlandoweekly.com	Orlando	FL	32801	407-377-0400	377-0420
Other Paper The PO Box 29913 *Web:* www.theotherpaper.com	Columbus	OH	43229	614-847-3800	848-3838
Pacific Northwest Inlander 1020 W Riverside Ave *Web:* www.inlander.com	Spokane	WA	99201	509-325-0634	325-0638
Pacific Sun PO Box 8507 *Web:* www.pacificsun.com	San Rafael	CA	94915	415-485-6700	485-6226
Palo Alto Weekly 703 High St *Web:* www.paloaltoonline.com	Palo Alto	CA	94301	650-326-8210	326-3928
Pasadena Weekly 50 S Delacey Ave Suite 200 *Web:* www.pasadenaweekly.com	Pasadena	CA	91105	626-584-1500	795-0149
Philadelphia City Paper 123 Chestnut St 3rd Fl *Web:* www.citypaper.net	Philadelphia	PA	19106	215-735-8444	
Phoenix New Times PO Box 2510 *Web:* www.phoenixnewtimes.com	Phoenix	AZ	85002	602-271-0040	340-8806
Pitch The 1701 Main St *Web:* www.pitch.com	Kansas City	MO	64108	816-561-6061	756-0502
Pittsburgh City Paper 650 Smithfield St Suite 2200 *Web:* www.pittsburghcitypaper.ws	Pittsburgh	PA	15222	412-316-3342	316-3388
Portland Phoenix 16 York St Suite 102 *Web:* www.portlandphoenix.com	Portland	ME	04101	207-773-8900	773-8905
Providence Phoenix 150 Chestnut St	Providence	RI	02903	401-273-6397	273-0920
PW-Philadelphia Weekly 1500 Sansom St 3rd Fl *Web:* www.philadelphiaweekly.com	Philadelphia	PA	19102	215-563-7400	563-0620
Random Lengths News 1300 S Pacific Ave *Web:* www.randomlengthsnews.com	San Pedro	CA	90731	310-519-1442	832-1000
Reader The 5015 Underwood Ave Suite 101 *Web:* www.thereader.com	Omaha	NE	68132	402-341-7323	341-6967
Reno News & Review 708 N Center St *Web:* www.newsreview.com	Reno	NV	89501	775-324-4440	324-4572
Riverfront Times 6358 Delmar Blvd Suite 200 *Web:* www.riverfronttimes.com	Saint Louis	MO	63130	314-754-5966	754-5955
Sacramento News & Review 1015 20th St *Web:* www.newsreview.com	Sacramento	CA	95814	916-498-1234	498-7920
Salt Lake City Weekly 248 S Main St *Web:* www.slweekly.com	Salt Lake City	UT	84101	801-575-7003	575-6106
San Antonio Current 1500 N Saint Mary's St *Web:* www.sacurrent.com	San Antonio	TX	78215	210-227-0044	227-6611
San Diego CityBeat 3550 Camino Del Rio N Suite 207 *Web:* www.sdcitybeat.com	San Diego	CA	92108	619-281-7526	281-5273
San Diego Reader PO Box 85803 *Web:* www.sdreader.com	San Diego	CA	92186	619-235-3000	231-0489
San Francisco Bay Guardian 135 Mississippi St *Web:* www.sfbg.com	San Francisco	CA	94107	415-255-3100	255-8959
San Luis Obispo New Times 505 Higuera St *TF:* 800-215-0300 ■ *Web:* newtimesslo.com	San Luis Obispo	CA	93401	805-546-8208	546-8641
Santa Barbara Independent 122 W Figueroa St *Web:* www.independent.com	Santa Barbara	CA	93101	805-965-5205	965-5518
Santa Fe Reporter 132 E Marcy St *Web:* www.sfreporter.com	Santa Fe	NM	87501	505-988-5541	988-5348
Scene 1468 W 9th St Suite 805 *Web:* www.clevescene.com	Cleveland	OH	44113	216-241-7550	802-7212
Seattle Weekly 1008 Western Ave Suite 300 *Web:* www.seattleweekly.com	Seattle	WA	98104	206-623-0500	467-4377
Seven Days 255 S Champlain St PO Box 1164 *Web:* www.sevendaysvt.com	Burlington	VT	05402	802-864-5684	865-1015
SF Weekly 185 Berry St Lobby 4 Suite 3800 *Web:* www.sfweekly.com	San Francisco	CA	94107	415-536-8100	777-1839
Shepherd Express 207 E Buffalo St Suite 410 *Web:* www.shepherd-express.com	Milwaukee	WI	53202	414-276-2222	276-3312
Stranger The 1535 11th Ave 3rd Fl *Web:* www.thestranger.com	Seattle	WA	98122	206-323-7101	323-7203
Style Weekly 1707 Summit Ave Suite 201 *Web:* www.styleweekly.com	Richmond	VA	23230	804-358-0825	358-9089
Syracuse New Times 1415 W Genesee St *Web:* www.syracusenewtimes.com	Syracuse	NY	13204	315-422-7011	422-1721
Tucson Weekly PO Box 27087 *Web:* www.tucsonweekly.com	Tucson	AZ	85726	520-792-3630	792-2096
Urban Tulsa PO Box 50499 *Web:* www.urbantulsa.com	Tulsa	OK	74150	918-592-5550	592-5970
Valley Advocate 116 Pleasant St Suite 3350 *Web:* www.valleyadvocate.com	Easthampton	MA	01027	413-529-2840	529-2844
Ventura County Reporter 700 E Main St *Web:* www.vcreporter.com	Ventura	CA	93001	805-648-2244	648-7801
Village Voice 36 Cooper Sq *TF Cust Svc:* 800-875-2997 ■ *Web:* www.villagevoice.com	New York	NY	10003	212-475-3300	475-8944
Washington City Paper 2390 Champlain St NW *Web:* www.washingtoncitypaper.com	Washington	DC	20009	202-332-2100	332-8500
Weekly Alibi 2118 Central Ave SE Suite 151 *Web:* alibi.com	Albuquerque	NM	87106	505-346-0660	256-9651
Westword PO Box 5970 *Web:* www.westword.com	Denver	CO	80217	303-296-7744	296-5416
Willamette Week 2220 NW Quimby St *Web:* www.wweek.com	Portland	OR	97210	503-243-2122	243-1115
Worcester Magazine 172 Shrewsbury St *Web:* www.worcestermag.com	Worcester	MA	01604	508-749-3166	749-3165

536 NURSES ASSOCIATIONS - STATE

SEE ALSO Associations & Organizations - Professional & Trade - Health & Medical Professionals Associations p. 1326

	City	State	Zip	Phone	Fax
Alabama State Nurses Assn (ASNA) 360 N Hull St *TF:* 800-270-2762 ■ *Web:* www.alabamanurses.org	Montgomery	AL	36104	334-262-8321	262-8578
Alaska Nurses Assn (AaNA) 3701 E Tudor Rd Suite 208 *Web:* www.aknurse.org	Anchorage	AK	99507	907-274-0827	272-0292
Arizona Nurses Assn (AzNA) 1850 E Southern Ave Suite 1 *Web:* www.aznurse.org	Tempe	AZ	85282	480-831-0404	839-4780
Arkansas Nurses Assn (ARNA) 1123 S University Suite 1015 *Web:* www.arna.org	Little Rock	AR	72204	501-244-2363	244-9903
American Nurses Assn California (ANA\C) 1121 L St Suite 409 *Web:* www.anacalifornia.org	Sacramento	CA	95814	916-447-0225	442-4394
California Nurses Assn (CNA) 2000 Franklin St *Web:* www.calnurses.org	Oakland	CA	94612	510-273-2200	663-1625
Colorado Nurses Assn (CNA) 1221 S Clarkson St Suite 205 *Web:* www.nurses-co.org	Denver	CO	80210	303-757-7483	757-8833
Connecticut Nurses Assn (CNA) 377 Research Pkwy Suite 2D *Web:* www.ctnurses.org	Meriden	CT	06450	203-238-1207	238-3437
Delaware Nurses Assn (DNA) 2644 Capitol Trail Suite 330 *TF:* 800-381-0939 ■ *Web:* www.nursingworld.org/snas/de	Newark	DE	19711	302-368-2333	366-1775
District of Columbia Nurses Assn (DCNA) 5100 Wisconsin Ave NW Suite 306 *TF:* 800-783-2705 ■ *Web:* www.dcna.org	Washington	DC	20016	202-244-2705	362-8285
Florida Nurses Assn (FNA) 1325 E Concord St PO Box 536985 *Web:* www.floridanurse.org	Orlando	FL	32853	407-896-3261	896-9042
Georgia Nurses Assn (GNA) 3032 Briarcliff Rd NE *TF:* 800-324-0462 ■ *Web:* www.georgianurses.org	Atlanta	GA	30329	404-325-5536	325-0407
Hawaii Nurses Assn (HNA) 677 Ala Moana Blvd Suite 301 *TF:* 800-486-8550 ■ *Web:* www.hawaiinurses.org	Honolulu	HI	96813	808-531-1628	524-2760
Idaho Nurses Assn (INA) 2417 Bank Dr Suite 111 *Web:* www.nursingworld.org/snas/id	Boise	ID	83709	208-345-0500	345-1163
Illinois Nurses Assn (INA) 105 W Adams St Suite 2101 *Web:* www.illinoisnurses.com	Chicago	IL	60603	312-419-2900	419-2920
Indiana State Nurses Assn (ISNA) 2915 N High School Rd *Web:* www.indiananurses.org	Indianapolis	IN	46224	317-299-4575	297-3525
Iowa Nurses Assn (INA) 1501 42nd St Suite 471 *Web:* www.iowanurses.org	West Des Moines	IA	50266	515-225-0495	225-2201
Kansas State Nurses Assn (KSNA) 1208 SW Tyler St *Web:* www.nursingworld.org/snas/ks	Topeka	KS	66612	785-233-8638	233-5222
Kentucky Nurses Assn (KNA) 1400 S 1st St PO Box 2616 *TF:* 800-348-5411 ■ *Web:* www.kentucky-nurses.org	Louisville	KY	40201	502-637-2546	637-8236
Louisiana State Nurses Assn (LSNA) 5800 One Perkins Pl Suite 2B *TF:* 800-457-6378 ■ *Web:* www.lsna.org	Baton Rouge	LA	70808	225-201-0993	201-0971
Maine State Nurses Assn (MSNA) 160 Capitol St Suite 1 *Web:* www.mainenurse.org	Augusta	ME	04330	207-622-1057	623-4072
Maryland Nurses Assn (MNA) 21 Governor's Ct Suite 195 *Web:* www.nursingworld.org/snas/md	Baltimore	MD	21244	410-944-5800	944-5802
Massachusetts Assn of Registered Nurses (MARN) PO Box 70668 *TF:* 866-627-6262 ■ *Web:* www.marnonline.org	Worcester	MA	01607	508-881-8812	
Massachusetts Nurses Assn (MNA) 340 Turnpike St *TF:* 800-882-2056 ■ *Web:* www.massnurses.org	Canton	MA	02021	781-821-4625	821-4445
Michigan Nurses Assn (MNA) 2310 Jolly Oak Rd *TF:* 800-646-8773 ■ *Web:* www.minurses.org	Okemos	MI	48864	517-349-5640	349-5818
Minnesota Nurses Assn (MNA) 1625 Energy Park Dr *TF:* 800-536-4662 ■ *Web:* www.mnnurses.org	Saint Paul	MN	55108	651-646-4807	647-5301
Mississippi Nurses Assn (MNA) 31 Woodgreen Pl *Web:* www.msnurses.org	Madison	MS	39110	601-898-0670	898-0190
Missouri Nurses Assn (MONA) 1904 Bubba Ln PO Box 105228 *TF:* 888-662-6662 ■ *Web:* www.missourinurses.org	Jefferson City	MO	65110	573-636-4623	636-9576
Montana Nurses Assn (MNA) 104 Broadway Suite G-2 *Web:* www.mtnurses.org	Helena	MT	59601	406-442-6710	442-1841
Nebraska Nurses Assn (NNA) 1320 Lincoln Mall Suite 9 *TF:* 800-201-3625 ■ *Web:* www.nursingworld.org/snas/ne	Lincoln	NE	68508	402-475-3859	475-3961
Nevada Nurses Assn (NNA) 1155 W 4th St Suite 224 PO Box 34660 *Web:* www.nvnurses.org	Reno	NV	89533	775-747-2333	329-3334
New Hampshire Nurses Assn (NHNA) 48 West St *Web:* www.nhnurses.org	Concord	NH	03301	603-225-3783	228-6672
New Jersey State Nurses Assn (NJSNA) 1479 Pennington Rd *TF:* 888-876-5762 ■ *Web:* www.njsna.org	Trenton	NJ	08618	609-883-5335	883-5343
New Mexico Nurses Assn (NMNA) PO Box 29568 *Web:* www.nmna.org	Santa Fe	NM	87592	505-471-3324	471-3314
New York Professional Nurses Union (NYPNU) 1104 Lexington Ave Suite 2D *Web:* www.nypnu.org	New York	NY	10021	212-988-5565	
New York State Nurses Assn (NYSNA) 11 Cornell Rd *TF:* 800-724-6976 ■ *Web:* www.nysna.org	Latham	NY	12110	518-782-9400	782-9530
North Carolina Nurses Assn (NCNA) 103 Enterprise St PO Box 12025 *TF:* 800-626-2153 ■ *Web:* www.ncnurses.org	Raleigh	NC	27605	919-821-4250	829-5807
North Dakota Nurses Assn (NDNA) 531 Airport Rd Suite D *Web:* www.ndna.org	Bismarck	ND	58504	701-223-1385	223-0575
Ohio Nurses Assn (ONA) 4000 E Main St *Web:* www.ohnurses.org	Columbus	OH	43213	614-237-5414	237-6074
Oklahoma Nurses Assn (ONA) 6414 N Santa Fe Ave Suite A *Web:* www.oknurses.com	Oklahoma City	OK	73116	405-840-3476	840-3013
Oregon Nurses Assn (ONA) 18765 SW Boones Ferry Rd *TF:* 800-634-3552 ■ *Web:* www.oregonrn.org	Tualatin	OR	97062	503-293-0011	293-0013
Pennsylvania Assn of Staff Nurses & Allied Professionals (PASNAP) 1100 E Hector St Suite 332 *TF:* 800-500-7850 ■ *Web:* www.pennanurses.org	Conshohocken	PA	19428	610-567-2907	567-2915
Pennsylvania State Nurses Assn (PSNA) 2578 Interstate Dr Suite 101 *TF:* 888-707-7762 ■ *Web:* www.psna.org	Harrisburg	PA	17110	717-657-1222	657-3796
Rhode Island State Nurses Assn (RISNA) 550 S Water St Suite 540B *Web:* www.risnarn.org	Providence	RI	02903	401-421-9703	421-6793
South Carolina Nurses Assn (SCNA) 1821 Gadsden St *Web:* www.scnurses.org	Columbia	SC	29201	803-252-4781	779-3870
South Dakota Nurses Assn (SDNA) PO Box 1015 *Web:* www.nursingworld.org/snas/sd	Pierre	SD	57501	605-945-4265	945-4266
Tennessee Nurses Assn (TNA) 545 Mainstream Dr Suite 405 *Web:* www.tnaonline.org	Nashville	TN	37228	615-254-0350	254-0303
Texas Nurses Assn (TNA) 7600 Burnet Rd Suite 440 *TF:* 800-862-2022 ■ *Web:* www.texasnurses.org	Austin	TX	78757	512-452-0645	452-0648
Utah Nurses Assn (UTA) 4505 S Wastch Blvd Suite 290 *TF:* 800-236-1617 ■ *Web:* www.utahnurses.org	Salt Lake City	UT	84124	801-272-4510	272-4322
Vermont State Nurses Assn (VSNA) 100 Dorset St Suite 13 *TF:* 800-540-9390 ■ *Web:* www.vsna-inc.org	South Burlington	VT	05403	802-651-8886	651-8998
Virginia Nurses Assn (VNA) 7113 Three Chopt Rd Suite 204 *TF:* 800-868-6877 ■ *Web:* www.virginianurses.com	Richmond	VA	23226	804-282-1808	282-4916
Washington State Nurses Assn (WSNA) 575 Andover Pk W Suite 101 *TF:* 800-231-8482 ■ *Web:* www.wsna.org	Seattle	WA	98188	206-575-7979	575-1908
West Virginia Nurses Assn (WVNA) 405 Capitol St Suite 600 *TF:* 800-400-1226 ■ *Web:* www.wvnurses.org	Charleston	WV	25301	304-342-1169	346-1861
Wisconsin Nurses Assn (WNA) 6117 Monona Dr *Web:* www.wisconsinnurses.org	Madison	WI	53716	608-221-0383	221-2788
Wyoming Nurses Assn (WNA) 1603 Capitol Ave Rm 305	Cheyenne	WY	82001	307-635-3955	635-2173

537 OFFICE & SCHOOL SUPPLIES

SEE ALSO Office Supply Stores p. 2034; Paper - Mfr - Writing Paper p. 2046; Pens, Pencils, Parts p. 2090; Printing & Photocopying Supplies p. 2141

Company	City	State	Zip	Phone	Fax
3M Consumer & Office Div 3M Ctr *TF:* 800-364-3577	Saint Paul	MN	55144	651-733-1110	736-2133
A & W Products Co Inc 14 Gardner St *TF:* 800-223-5156 ■ *Web:* www.awproducts.com	Port Jervis	NY	12771	845-856-5156	856-9772
Aakron Rule Corp 8 Indianola Ave *TF:* 800-828-1570 ■ *Web:* www.aakronrule.com	Akron	NY	14001	716-542-5483	542-1537
American Product Distributors Inc 8350 Arrowridge Blvd *TF:* 877-769-0752 ■ *Web:* www.americanproduct.com	Charlotte	NC	28273	704-522-9411	522-9413
American Solutions for Business 31 E Minnesota Ave *TF:* 800-862-3690 ■ *Web:* www.americanbus.com	Glenwood	MN	56334	320-634-5471	634-5265
Ames Supply Co 1936 University Ln *TF:* 800-323-3856 ■ *Web:* www.amessupply.com	Lisle	IL	60532	630-964-2440	964-0497
Apex Office Products Inc 5209 N Howard Ave *TF:* 800-227-1563 ■ *Web:* www.apexofficeproducts.com	Tampa	FL	33603	813-871-2010	875-9059
Arlington Industries Inc 1616 Lakeside Dr *TF:* 800-323-4147 ■ *Web:* www.arli.com	Waukegan	IL	60085	847-689-2754	689-1616
Arthur Brown & Brother Inc 2 W 46th St *TF:* 800-772-7367 ■ *Web:* www.artbrown.com	New York	NY	10036	212-575-5555	575-5825
Avery Dennison Corp 150 N Orange Grove Blvd *NYSE:* AVY ■ *TF Cust Svc:* 800-252-8379 ■ *Web:* www.averydennison.com	Pasadena	CA	91103	626-304-2000	304-2192
Avery Dennison Worldwide Office Products Div 50 Pointe Dr *TF:* 800-462-8379 ■ *Web:* www.avery.com	Brea	CA	92821	714-674-8500	674-6929
Bartizan Corp 217 Riverdale Ave *TF:* 800-431-2682 ■ *Web:* www.bartizan.com	Yonkers	NY	10705	914-965-7977	965-7746
Baumgarten's 144 Ottley Dr *TF:* 800-247-5547 ■ *Web:* www.b3.net	Atlanta	GA	30324	404-874-7675	881-1442
Best Computer Supplies 895 E Patriot Blvd Suite 110 *TF:* 800-544-3472 ■ *Web:* www.theschoolsupplier.com	Reno	NV	89511	775-850-2600	850-2610
Brodart Co Contract Library Furniture Div 280 North Rd Clinton County Industrial Park *TF:* 888-521-1884 ■ *Web:* www.shopbrodart.com	McElhattan	PA	17748	570-769-7412	769-7641
C-Line Products Inc 1100 Business Ctr Dr *TF:* 800-323-6084 ■ *Web:* www.c-lineproducts.com	Mount Prospect	IL	60056	847-827-6661	827-3329
Cardinal Brands Inc 643 Massachusetts St Suite 200 *TF:* 800-364-8713 ■ *Web:* www.cardinalbrands.com	Lawrence	KS	66044	785-344-1400	344-1200
Cardinal Office Systems Inc 576 E Main St *TF:* 800-589-5886 ■ *Web:* www.cardinalos.com	Frankfort	KY	40601	502-875-3300	875-3737
Case Logic Inc 6303 Dry Creek Pkwy *TF:* 800-447-4848 ■ *Web:* www.caselogic.com	Longmont	CO	80503	303-652-1000	652-1094
Champion Industries Inc 2450-90 1st Ave *NASDAQ:* CHMP ■ **Fax:* Cust Svc ■ *TF:* 800-624-3431 ■ *Web:* www.champion-industries.com	Huntington	WV	25703	304-528-2791	528-2746*
Costas Custom Office Supply 575 San Mateo Ave	San Bruno	CA	94066	650-871-9410	588-7545
CPP International LLC PO Box 7525 *TF:* 800-888-3190 ■ *Web:* www.carolinapad.com	Charlotte	NC	28241	704-588-3190	588-1123
Dahle North America Inc 375 Jaffrey Rd *TF:* 800-243-8145 ■ *Web:* www.dahle.com	Peterborough	NH	03458	603-924-0003	924-1616
Dart Mfg Co Inc 4012 Bronze Way **Fax Area Code:* 800 ■ *TF:* 800-345-3278 ■ *Web:* www.dartpromo.com	Dallas	TX	75237	214-333-4221	833-3278*
Datavision & Devices 2709 Brookmere Rd *TF:* 800-237-5658 ■ *Web:* www.datavisionergonomics.com	Charlottesville	VA	22901	800-237-5658	808-9254
Deflect-O Corp PO Box 50057 **Fax:* Sales ■ *TF:* 800-428-4328 ■ *Web:* www.deflecto.com	Indianapolis	IN	46250	317-849-9555	915-4456*
Douglas Stewart Co 2402 Advance Rd *TF:* 800-279-2795 ■ *Web:* www.dstewart.com	Madison	WI	53718	608-221-1155	221-5217
Eaton Office Supply Co Inc 180 John Glenn Dr *TF:* 800-365-3237 ■ *Web:* www.eatonofficesupply.com	Amherst	NY	14228	716-691-6100	691-0074
Fellowes Inc 1789 Norwood Ave **Fax:* Cust Svc ■ *TF:* 800-945-4545 ■ *Web:* www.fellowes.com	Itasca	IL	60143	630-893-1600	893-1718*
GBS Corp 7233 Freedom Ave NW *TF:* 800-552-2427 ■ *Web:* www.gbscorp.com	North Canton	OH	44720	330-494-5330	494-8316
Great North American Cos 2828 Forest Ln Suite 2000 *TF:* 800-527-2782 ■ *Web:* www.gnamerican.com	Dallas	TX	75234	972-481-6100	481-6200
Hopaco-Boise Office Solutions 94-1489 Moaniani St *TF:* 888-372-6473	Waipahu	HI	96797	808-676-3100	676-3198
IIMAK 310 Commerce Dr *TF:* 888-464-4625 ■ *Web:* www.iimak.com	Amherst	NY	14228	716-691-6333	691-3395
International Imaging Materials Inc 310 Commerce Dr *TF:* 888-464-4625 ■ *Web:* www.iimak.com	Amherst	NY	14228	716-691-6333	691-3395
Kensington Technology Group 333 Twin Dolphin Dr 6th Fl *TF:* 800-243-2972 ■ *Web:* www.kensington.com	Redwood Shores	CA	94065	650-572-2700	267-2800
Lee Products Co 800 E 80th St *TF:* 800-989-3544 ■ *Web:* www.leeproducts.com	Bloomington	MN	55420	952-854-3544	854-7177
Magna Visual Inc 9400 Watson Rd *TF:* 800-843-3399 ■ *Web:* www.magnavisual.com	Saint Louis	MO	63126	314-843-9000	843-0000
McGill Inc 131 E Prairie St *TF:* 800-982-9884 ■ *Web:* www.mcgillinc.com	Marengo	IL	60152	815-568-7244	568-6860
MeadWestvaco Corp 5 High Ridge Pk *NYSE:* MWV ■ *TF:* 800-958-4785 ■ *Web:* www.meadwestvaco.com	Stamford	CT	06905	203-461-7400	
Mod-Systems Inc 2172-B River Rd PO Box 585 *TF:* 800-637-2937 ■ *Web:* www.modsystems.net	Greer	SC	29652	864-879-3850	879-3158
New Century Direct 205 S Puente St **Fax Area Code:* 800 ■ *TF:* 800-767-0777	Brea	CA	92820	714-441-4500	786-7939*
New England Newspaper Supply Co 9 Railroad Ave *TF:* 800-347-7377 ■ *Web:* www.nensco.com	Millbury	MA	01527	508-865-0800	865-0811
Nina Enterprises 1350 S Leavitt St *TF:* 800-886-8688	Chicago	IL	60608	312-733-6400	733-8356
PBS Supply Co Inc 7013 S 216th St *TF:* 877-727-7515 ■ *Web:* www.pbssupply.com	Kent	WA	98032	253-395-5550	395-5575
PerfectData Corp 1323 Conshohocken Rd *TF:* 800-973-7332 ■ *Web:* www.perfectdata.com	Plymouth Meeting	PA	19462	610-277-1010	277-4390
PerkCom LLC 924 Chevy Way *Web:* www.perkcom.com	Medford	OR	97504	541-772-4224	734-9893
Promedia Computer Supplies Ltd Co 12806 Schabarum Ave Unit C-D *TF:* 800-583-5833 ■ *Web:* www.promedia-usa.com	Irwindale	CA	91706	626-960-5778	960-5770
Quill Corp 100 Shelter Rd **Fax Area Code:* 800 ■ *TF Orders:* 800-789-1331 ■ *Web:* www2.quillcorp.com	Lincolnshire	IL	60069	847-634-4800	789-8955*
Reliable Corp 263 Shuman Blvd *TF Cust Svc:* 800-359-5000 ■ *Web:* www.reliable.com	Naperville	IL	60563	800-735-4000	326-3233
Richards SP Co 6300 Highlands Pkwy **Fax:* Hum Res ■ *TF:* 888-436-6881 ■ *Web:* www.sprichards.com	Smyrna	GA	30082	770-436-6881	433-3586*
Sanford Brands Div Newell Rubbermaid Inc 2707 Butterfield Rd **Fax:* Cust Svc ■ *TF:* 800-323-0749 ■ *Web:* www.sanford.com	Oak Brook	IL	60523	630-481-2200	481-2099*
Sierra Office Supply & Printing 4007 Transport St *TF:* 800-433-0282 ■ *Web:* www.sierrabg.com	Palo Alto	CA	94303	650-845-2091	845-2099
SP Richards Co 6300 Highlands Pkwy **Fax:* Hum Res ■ *TF:* 888-436-6881 ■ *Web:* www.sprichards.com	Smyrna	GA	30082	770-436-6881	433-3586*
Stanley Fastening Systems LP Rt 2 *Web:* www.stanleybostitch.com	East Greenwich	RI	02818	401-884-2500	884-3122
Staples Business Advantage 45 Cedar Ln **Fax:* Cust Svc ■ *TF Orders:* 888-333-6494 ■ *Web:* www.stapleslink.com	Englewood	NJ	07631	800-999-9077	999-9081*
Staples National Advantage 45 Cedar Ln *TF:* 800-999-9077 ■ *Web:* www.staples.com	Englewood	NJ	07631	800-999-9077	999-9081
Stewart Douglas Co 2402 Advance Rd *TF:* 800-279-2795 ■ *Web:* www.dstewart.com	Madison	WI	53718	608-221-1155	221-5217
TAB Products Co 605 4th St *TF:* 888-822-9777 ■ *Web:* www.tab.com	Mayville	WI	53050	920-387-3131	387-1805
United Stationers Inc 1 Parkway N Blvd Suite 100 *NASDAQ:* USTR ■ *TF:* 800-424-4003 ■ *Web:* www.unitedstationers.com	Deerfield	IL	60015	847-627-7000	627-7001
US Gerslyn Ltd 147 E 2nd St	Mineola	NY	11501	516-282-2077	
Van Ausdall & Farrar Inc 6430 E 75th St *TF:* 800-467-7474 ■ *Web:* www.vanausdall.com	Indianapolis	IN	46250	317-634-2913	638-1843
Weeks-Lerman Group 58-38 Page Pl *TF:* 800-544-5959 ■ *Web:* www.weekslerman.com	Maspeth	NY	11378	718-803-5000	821-1515

538 OFFICE SUPPLY STORES

Company	City	State	Zip	Phone	Fax
Airline Stationery Co 284 Madison Ave *Web:* www.airlineinc.com	New York	NY	10017	212-532-6525	779-7257
AJ Stationers Inc 7601 Brandon Woods Blvd *Web:* www.ajstationers.com/	Baltimore	MD	21226	410-360-4900	360-4291
Allied Office Products Inc 100 Delawanna Ave *TF:* 800-275-2554 ■ *Web:* www.askallied.com	Clifton	NJ	07014	973-594-3000	594-3600
Arctic Office Products 100 W Fireweed Ln *Web:* arctic.officeretailer.com	Anchorage	AK	99503	907-276-2322	279-4359
Ashland Office Supply Co Inc 2100 29th St *TF:* 800-926-1267 ■ *Web:* www.ashlandoffice.com	Ashland	KY	41101	606-329-1400	329-2452
Church & Stagg Office Supply Co Inc 3421 6th Ave *TF:* 800-239-5336 ■ *Web:* www.churchandstagg.com	Birmingham	AL	35222	205-251-2951	324-6874
Corporate Express Inc 1 Environmental Way *TF:* 888-664-3945 ■ *Web:* www.corporate-express.com	Broomfield	CO	80021	303-664-2000	664-3474
D & D Office Supplies 1751 Lincoln Hwy Rt 30 *Web:* www.ddoffice.com	North Versailles	PA	15137	412-829-1200	829-1201
DBI Inc 912 E Michigan Ave *Web:* www.dbiyes.com	Lansing	MI	48912	517-485-3200	485-3202
Eakes Office Plus 617 W 3rd St *TF:* 800-652-9396 ■ *Web:* www.eakes.com	Grand Island	NE	68801	308-382-8026	382-7401
Egyptian Stationers Inc 107 W Main St *TF:* 800-642-3949 ■ *Web:* www.egyptian-stationers.com	Belleville	IL	62220	618-234-2323	234-0693
Farr's Stationers Inc PO Box 3349	Costa Mesa	CA	92628	714-549-3277	549-3350
Fisher Hawaii 450 Cooke St *Web:* www.fisherhawaii.biz	Honolulu	HI	96813	808-524-8770	524-8785
Friend HA & Co Inc 1535 Lewis Ave *TF:* 800-323-4394 ■ *Web:* www.friendsstationery.com	Zion	IL	60099	847-746-1248	746-4962
Gobin's Inc 615 N Santa Fe Ave *TF:* 800-425-2324 ■ *Web:* www.gobins.com	Pueblo	CO	81003	719-544-2324	544-2378
Great American Office LLC 513 Donald St *Web:* www.gaos.com	Bedford	NH	03110	603-472-5199	296-0791
HA Friend & Co Inc 1535 Lewis Ave *TF:* 800-323-4394 ■ *Web:* www.friendsstationery.com	Zion	IL	60099	847-746-1248	746-4962
Halsey & Griffith Inc 313 Datura St **Fax:* Cust Svc ■ *TF:* 800-466-1921 ■ *Web:* www.halsey-griffith.com/	West Palm Beach	FL	33401	561-820-8000	820-8026*
Hurst Office Suppliers Inc 257 E Short St *TF:* 800-926-4423 ■ *Web:* www.hurstgroup.net	Lexington	KY	40507	859-255-4422	255-4471
Iowa Office Supply Inc DBA IOS Office Solutions 731 Lake Ave *TF:* 800-373-9182 ■ *Web:* www.iowaofficesupply.com	Storm Lake	IA	50588	712-732-4801	732-4426
Kennedy Office Supply 4211-A Atlantic Ave *TF:* 800-733-9401 ■ *Web:* www.kennedyofficesupply.com	Raleigh	NC	27604	919-878-5400	790-9649
Koch Brothers 325 Grand Ave *TF:* 800-944-5624 ■ *Web:* www.kochbros.com	Des Moines	IA	50309	515-283-2451	243-3147
Laser Tek Industries 4909 US Hwy 12 *TF:* 800-322-8137 ■ *Web:* www.laser-tek.com	Richmond	IL	60071	815-675-1199	675-6149
Latta Inc 1502 4th Ave *Web:* www.lattas.com	Huntington	WV	25701	304-523-8400	525-5038
Louisiana Office Supply Co 5550 Florida Blvd *TF:* 866-342-0286 ■ *Web:* www.losco.com	Baton Rouge	LA	70806	225-927-1110	927-3085
Newport Stationers Inc 17681 Mitchell N *Web:* www.newportstationers.com	Irvine	CA	92614	949-863-1200	852-8970
Office Depot Inc 2200 Old Germantown Rd *NYSE:* ODP ■ **Fax:* Hum Res ■ *TF:* 800-937-3600 ■ *Web:* www.officedepot.com	Delray Beach	FL	33445	561-438-4800	438-4406*
Office Resources Inc 374 Congress St *TF:* 866-423-9100 ■ *Web:* www.ori.com	Boston	MA	02210	617-423-9100	423-5590
Office Suppliers Inc 13716 Crayton Blvd *TF:* 800-225-2723 ■ *Web:* www.osimd.com	Hagerstown	MD	21742	301-797-3120	797-1504
OfficeMax Inc 150 E Pierce Rd *NYSE:* OMX ■ **Fax:* Sales ■ *TF:* 800-472-6473 ■ *Web:* www.officemax.com	Itasca	IL	60143	630-438-7800	773-6708*
Patrick & Co 611 Mission St 2nd Fl *TF:* 800-792-0755 ■ *Web:* www.patco.net	San Francisco	CA	94105	415-392-2640	546-4952
Phillips Group 501 Fulling Mill Rd *TF:* 800-538-7500 ■ *Web:* www.buyphillips.com	Middletown	PA	17057	717-944-0400	948-5248
Printers & Stationers Inc 113 N Court St *TF:* 800-624-5334 ■ *Web:* www.psi-online.net	Florence	AL	35630	256-764-8061	764-5024
Sav-On Office Supplies 6601 Will Rogers Blvd Suite B *TF:* 866-571-8177 ■ *Web:* www.sav-onofficesupplies.com	Fort Worth	TX	76140	817-568-5200	568-5204
Smith & Butterfield Co Inc 2800 Lynch Rd *TF:* 800-321-6543 ■ *Web:* www.smithbutterfield.com	Evansville	IN	47733	812-422-3261	429-0532
Staples Inc 500 Staples Dr *NASDAQ:* SPLS ■ *TF:* 800-378-2753 ■ *Web:* www.staples.com	Framingham	MA	01702	508-253-5000	253-8989
Stationers Inc 1945 5th Ave *TF:* 800-862-7200 ■ *Web:* www.stationers-wv.com	Huntington	WV	25703	304-528-2780	528-2795
Supply Room Cos Inc 14140 N Washington Hwy *TF:* 800-849-7239 ■ *Web:* www.thesupplyroom.com	Ashland	VA	23005	804-412-1200	412-1313
Triplett Office Essentials Corp 3553 109th St *TF:* 800-437-5034 ■ *Web:* www.tripletts.com	Des Moines	IA	50322	515-270-9150	270-9683
Wist Office Products Co 107 W Julie Dr *TF:* 800-999-9478 ■ *Web:* www.wist.com	Tempe	AZ	85283	480-921-2900	921-2121
Xpedx Paper & Graphics 1376 Rankin Rd *Web:* www.xpedxstores.com/about.html	Troy	MI	48083	248-585-3980	585-0945
Xpedx Paper Store 3351 W Addison St *TF:* 800-866-6332	Chicago	IL	60618	773-463-6423	442-6415

539 OIL & GAS EXTRACTION

Company / Address	City	State	Zip	Phone	Fax
Abraxas Petroleum Corp 500 NE Loop 1604 E Suite 100	San Antonio	TX	78232	210-490-4788	490-8816
AMEX: ABP ■ *Web:* www.abraxaspetroleum.com					
Adams Resources & Energy Inc 4400 Post Oak Pkwy	Houston	TX	77027	713-881-3600	881-3491
AMEX: AE ■ *Web:* www.adamsresources.com					
Adkins RL Corp 301 Oak St	Sweetwater	TX	79556	325-235-4316	235-3460
Web: www.adkinssupply.com					
Aeropres Corp 1324 N Hearne Ave Suite 200	Shreveport	LA	71107	318-221-6282	213-1270
Web: www.aeropres.com					
American Trading & Production Corp					
10 E Baltimore St Suite 1600	Baltimore	MD	21202	410-347-7150	347-7151
Web: www.atapco.com					
Anadarko Petroleum Corp 1201 Lake Robbins Dr	The Woodlands	TX	77380	832-636-1000	636-8022
NYSE: APC ■ *TF:* 800-800-1101 ■ *Web:* www.anadarko.com					
Anadarko Petroleum Corp Alaska Div 3201 C St Suite 603	Anchorage	AK	99503	907-273-6300	563-9479
Web: www.anadarko.com					
Apache Corp 2000 Post Oak Blvd Suite 100	Houston	TX	77056	713-296-6000	296-6488*
NYSE: APA ■ **Fax:* Mail Rm ■ *TF:* 800-272-2434 ■ *Web:* www.apachecorp.com					
Apco Argentina Inc 1 William Center Suite 26-4	Tulsa	OK	74172	918-573-2164	573-0576
NASDAQ: APAGF					
Aramco Services Co 9009 West Loop S	Houston	TX	77096	713-432-4000	432-8566
TF: 800-343-4272 ■ *Web:* www.aramcoservices.com					
ATP Oil & Gas Corp 4600 Post Oak Pl Suite 200	Houston	TX	77027	713-622-3311	622-5101
NASDAQ: ATPG ■ *Web:* www.atpog.com					
Aviva Petroleum Inc 8235 Douglas Ave Suite 400	Dallas	TX	75225	214-691-3464	691-6151
Barnwell Industries Inc 1100 Alakea St Suite 2900	Honolulu	HI	96813	808-531-8400	531-7181
AMEX: BRN ■ *Web:* www.brninc.com					
Bayou State Oil Corp 1115 Hawn Ave	Shreveport	LA	71107	318-222-0737	222-0730
Belden & Blake Corp 5200 Stoneham Rd	North Canton	OH	44720	330-497-5471	497-5463
TF: 800-837-4344					
Berry Petroleum Co 5201 Truxtun Ave Suite 300	Bakersfield	CA	93309	661-616-3900	616-3883
NYSE: BRY ■ *Web:* www.bry.com					
Bettis Boyle & Stovall Inc 505 5th St PO Box 1240	Graham	TX	76450	940-549-2060	549-7405
BHP Billiton Petroleum (Americas) Inc					
1360 Post Oak Blvd Suite 150	Houston	TX	77056	713-961-8500	961-8400
Web: www.bhpbilliton.com					
Blue Dolphin Energy Co 801 Travis St Suite 2100	Houston	TX	77002	713-227-7660	227-7626
NASDAQ: BDCO ■ *Web:* www.blue-dolphin.com					
BP America Production Co 6900 W Interstate 40 Suite 300	Amarillo	TX	79106	806-371-4400	371-4468
BP Canada Energy Co 240 4th Ave SW	Calgary	AB	T2P4H4	403-233-1313	233-5610*
**Fax:* Mail Rm ■ *Web:* www.bp.com					
BP Plc 28100 Torch Pkwy	Warrenville	IL	60555	630-420-5111	298-0738*
NYSE: BP ■ **Fax Area Code:* 281 ■ *TF:* 866-427-6947 ■ *Web:* www.bp.com					
BPI Energy Holdings Inc 30775 Bainbridge Rd Suite 280	Solon	OH	44139	440-248-4200	
AMEX: BPG ■ *Web:* www.bpi-energy.com					
Bridwell Oil Co 810 8th St	Wichita Falls	TX	76301	940-723-4351	397-0161
Brigham Exploration Co					
6300 Bridge Point Pkwy Bldg 2 Suite 500	Austin	TX	78730	512-427-3300	427-3400
NASDAQ: BEXP ■ *Web:* www.bexp3d.com					
Cabot Oil & Gas Corp 1200 Enclave Pkwy	Houston	TX	77077	281-589-4600	589-4910*
NYSE: COG ■ **Fax:* Hum Res ■ *TF:* 800-434-3985 ■ *Web:* www.cabotog.com					
Callon Petroleum Co 200 N Canal St	Natchez	MS	39120	601-442-1601	446-1410
NYSE: CPE ■ *TF:* 800-541-1294 ■ *Web:* www.callon.com					
Calpine Energy Inc 717 Texas Ave Suite 1000	Houston	TX	77002	713-830-2000	830-2001
TF: 800-251-6165 ■ *Web:* www.calpine.com					
Canada Southern Petroleum Ltd 706 7th Ave SW Suite 250	Calgary	AB	T2P0Z1	403-269-7741	261-5667
NASDAQ: CSPLF ■ *Web:* www.cansopet.com					
Canadian Natural Resources Ltd 2500-855 2nd St SW	Calgary	AB	T2P4J8	403-517-6700	517-7350
NYSE: CNQ ■ *Web:* www.cnrl.com					
Canadian Superior Energy Inc 400 3rd Ave SW Suite 3300	Calgary	AB	T2P4H2	403-294-1411	216-2374
TSX: SNG ■ *TF:* 877-294-1411 ■ *Web:* www.cansup.com					
Cano Petroleum Inc 309 W 7th St Suite 1600	Fort Worth	TX	76102	817-698-0900	698-0796
AMEX: CFW ■ *Web:* www.canopetro.com					
Carrizo Oil & Gas Inc 1000 Louisiana Suite 1500	Houston	TX	77002	713-328-1000	328-1035
NASDAQ: CRZO ■ *Web:* www.carrizo.cc					
Castle Energy Corp 357 S Gulph Rd Suite 260	King of Prussia	PA	19406	610-992-9900	992-9922
NASDAQ: CECX					
Celtic Exploration Ltd 505 3rd St SW Suite 500	Calgary	AB	T2P3E6	403-201-9153	201-9163
TSX: CLT ■ *Web:* www.celticex.com					
Centurion Energy International Inc 205 5th Ave SW Suite 1700	Calgary	AB	T2P2V7	403 263 6002	263 6008
TSX: CUX ■ *Web:* www.centurionenergy.com					
CGAS Exploration Inc 300 Capitol St Suite 700	Charleston	WV	25301	304-343-5505	343-5525
TF: 800-686-2427					
Challenger Minerals Inc 15375 Memorial Dr Suite G-200	Houston	TX	77079	281-925-7200	925-7280
Web: www.gsfdrill.com					
Chesapeake Energy Corp 6100 N Western Ave	Oklahoma City	OK	73118	405-848-8000	767-4800
NYSE: CHK ■ *Web:* www.chkenergy.com					
Chevron Corp 6001 Bollinger Canyon Rd	San Ramon	CA	94583	925-842-1000	420-0335*
NYSE: CVX ■ **Fax Area Code:* 866 ■ *TF Cust Svc:* 800-243-8766 ■					
Web: www.chevron.com					
Cimarex Energy Co 1700 Lincoln St Suite 1800	Denver	CO	80203	303-295-3995	295-3494
NYSE: XEC ■ *Web:* www.cimarex.com					
Citation Oil & Gas Corp 8223 Willow Place S	Houston	TX	77070	281-469-9664	517-7594
Clayton Williams Energy Inc 6 Desta Dr Suite 3000	Midland	TX	79705	432-682-6324	682-1452
NASDAQ: CWEI ■ *Web:* www.claytonwilliams.com					
Cobra Oil & Gas Corp 2201 Kell Blvd	Wichita Falls	TX	76308	940-723-4331	716-5170
Web: www.cobraogc.com					
Compton Petroleum Corp 425 1st St SW Suite 3300	Calgary	AB	T2P3L8	403-237-9400	237-9410
TSX: CMT ■ *Web:* www.comptonpetroleum.com					
Comstock Resources Inc 5300 Town & Country Blvd Suite 500	Frisco	TX	75034	972-668-8800	668-8812
NYSE: CRK ■ *TF:* 800-877-1322 ■ *Web:* www.comstockresources.com					
ConocoPhillips 600 N Dairy Ashford Rd	Houston	TX	77079	281-293-1000	
NYSE: COP ■ *TF:* 800-527-5476 ■ *Web:* www.conocophillips.com					
ConocoPhillips Canada 401 9th Ave SW PO Box 130 Stn M	Calgary	AB	T2P2H7	403-233-4000	233-5143
Web: www.conocophillips.ca					
Contango Oil & Gas Co 3700 Buffalo Speedway Suite 960	Houston	TX	77098	713-960-1901	960-1065
AMEX: MCF ■ *Web:* contango.com					
Continental Resources of Illinois 830 IL Hwy 15 E	Mount Vernon	IL	62864	618-242-1717	242-7056
Coral Oil & Gas Inc 5600 San Felipe Suite 4	Houston	TX	77056	713-222-7304	224-8101
Credo Petroleum Corp 1801 Broadway Suite 900	Denver	CO	80202	303-297-2200	297-2204
NASDAQ: CRED ■ *TF:* 800-297-2366 ■ *Web:* www.credopetroleum.com					
Crosstex Energy Inc 2501 Cedar Springs Rd Suite 600	Dallas	TX	75201	214-953-9500	953-9501
NASDAQ: XTXI ■ *Web:* www.crosstexenergy.com					
Crown Central Petroleum Corp 1 N Charles St	Baltimore	MD	21201	410-539-7400	659-4875*
**Fax:* Hum Res ■ *Web:* www.crowncentral.com					
Dallas Production Inc 4600 Greenville Ave Suite 300	Dallas	TX	75206	214-369-9266	692-1536
DCP Midstream Partners LP 370 17th St Suite 2775	Denver	CO	80202	303-633-2900	605-2225
NYSE: DPM					
Denbury Resources Inc 5100 Tennyson Pkwy Suite 3000	Plano	TX	75024	972-673-2000	673-2001
NYSE: DNR ■ *TF:* 800-364-5482 ■ *Web:* www.denbury.com					
Devon Energy Corp 20 N Broadway	Oklahoma City	OK	73102	405-235-3611	552-4667
NYSE: DVN ■ *TF:* 800-361-3377 ■ *Web:* www.devonenergy.com					
Dominion Exploration & Production Inc 1450 Poydras St	New Orleans	LA	70112	504-593-7000	593-7465*
**Fax:* Mail Rm ■ *Web:* www.dom.com					
Dorchester Minerals LP 3838 Oak Lawn Ave Suite 300	Garland	TX	75219	214-559-0330	559-0301
NASDAQ: DMLP					
Dugan Production Corp 709 E Murray Dr	Farmington	NM	87499	505-325-1821	327-4613
TF: 800-618-1821					
Duke Energy Field Services 370 17th St Suite 2500	Denver	CO	80202	303-595-3331	605-2227
Web: www.duke-energy.com					
Duke Energy Inc 3050 Post Oak Blvd Suite 695	Houston	TX	77056	713-888-0895	888-0899
AMEX: DNE ■ *Web:* www.duneenergy.com					
Duncan Oil Inc 1777 S Harrison St Suite P1	Denver	CO	80210	303-759-3303	757-0252
TF: 800-359-3303					
EnCana Corp 855 2nd St SW Suite 1800	Calgary	AB	T2P2S5	403-645-2000	645-3400
NYSE: ECA ■ *Web:* www.encana.com					
Encore Acquisition Co 777 Main St Suite 1400	Fort Worth	TX	76102	817-877-9955	877-1655
NYSE: EAC ■ *Web:* www.encoreacq.com					
Eni Petroleum Co Inc 1201 Louisiana St Suite 3500	Houston	TX	77002	713-393-6100	393-6205
Web: www.enipetroleum.com					
Equitable Resources Inc 225 N Shore Dr	Pittsburgh	PA	15212	412-395-3200	553-5757
NYSE: EQT ■ *Web:* www.eqt.com					
Exxon Mobil Corp 5959 Las Colinas Blvd	Irving	TX	75039	972-444-1000	444-1198
NYSE: XOM ■ *TF:* 800-252-1800 ■ *Web:* www.exxon.mobil.com/corporate/					
ExxonMobil Canada 237 4th Ave SW	Calgary	AB	T2P0H6	403-260-7910	237-2197
Web: www.mobil.ca					
ExxonMobil Production Co 800 Bell St	Houston	TX	77002	713-656-3636	680-6322
Fairborne Energy Ltd 3400-450 1st St SW	Calgary	AB	T2P5H1	403-290-7750	290-7724
TSX: FEL ■ *Web:* www.fairborne-energy.com					
FieldPoint Petroleum Corp 1703 Edelweiss Dr Suite 301	Cedar Park	TX	78613	512-250-8692	335-1294
AMEX: FPP ■ *Web:* www.fppcorp.com					
Flying J Inc 1104 Country Hill Dr	Ogden	UT	84403	801-624-1000	395-8005
TF: 800-842-6428 ■ *Web:* www.flyingj.com					
Forest Oil Corp 707 17th St Suite 3600	Denver	CO	80202	303-812-1400	812-1602
NYSE: FST ■ *Web:* www.forestoil.com					
Frontier Oil Co 125 N Market St Suite 1720	Wichita	KS	67202	316-263-1201	
Frontier Oil Corp 10000 Memorial Dr Suite 600	Houston	TX	77024	713-688-9600	688-0616
NYSE: FTO ■ *Web:* www.frontieroil.com					
Galaxy Energy Corp 1331 17th St Suite 1050	Denver	CO	80202	303-293-2300	293-2417
AMEX: GAX ■ *Web:* www.galaxyenergy.com					
Gary-Williams Energy Corp 370 17th St Suite 5300	Denver	CO	80202	303-628-3800	628-3834
Web: www.gwec.com					
Gasco Energy Inc 8 Inverness Dr E Suite 100	Englewood	CO	80112	303-483-0044	483-0011
AMEX: GSX ■ *Web:* www.gascoenergy.com					
Gastar Exploration Ltd 1331 Lamar St Suite 1080	Houston	TX	77010	713-739-1800	739-0458
AMEX: GST ■ *Web:* www.gastar.com					
GeoResources Inc 1407 W Dakota Pkwy Suite 1-B	Williston	ND	58802	701-572-2020	572-0277
NASDAQ: GEOI ■ *TF:* 800-735-5984 ■ *Web:* www.geoi.net					
Giant Industries Inc 23733 N Scottsdale Rd	Scottsdale	AZ	85255	480-585-8888	585-8948
NYSE: GI ■ *TF:* 800-937-4937 ■ *Web:* www.giant.com					
GMX Resources Inc					
9400 N Broadway 1 Benham Pl Suite 600	Oklahoma City	OK	73114	405-600-0711	600-0600
NASDAQ: GMXR ■ *Web:* www.gmxresources.com					
Great Western Drilling Co Inc 700 W Louisiana St	Midland	TX	79701	432-682-5241	684-3702
Web: www.gwdc.com					
Grey Wolf Inc 10370 Richmond Ave Suite 600	Houston	TX	77042	713-435-6100	435-6170
AMEX: GW ■ *TF:* 800-553-7563 ■ *Web:* www.greywolfdrilling.com					
Gunnison Energy Corp 1801 Broadway Suite 1200	Denver	CO	80202	303-296-4222	296-4555
Web: www.oxbow.com					
Harken Energy Corp 180 State St Suite 200	Southlake	TX	76092	817-424-2424	488-4307
AMEX: HEC ■ *Web:* www.harkenenergy.com					
Harvest Natural Resources Inc 1177 Enclave Pkwy Suite 300	Houston	TX	77077	281-899-5700	899-5702
NYSE: HNR ■ *Web:* www.harvestnr.com					
Headington Oil Co 7557 Rambler Rd Suite 1100	Dallas	TX	75231	214-696-0606	696-7728
TF: 800-245-5773 ■ *Web:* www.headington.com					
Hess Corp 1185 Ave of the Americas	New York	NY	10036	212-997-8500	536-8390
NYSE: AHC ■ *TF:* 800-437-7645 ■ *Web:* www.hess.com					
Houston Exploration Co 1100 Louisiana St Suite 2000	Houston	TX	77002	713-830-6800	830-6885
NYSE: THX ■ *TF:* 800-261-3283 ■ *Web:* www.houstonexploration.com					
Huber JM Corp 333 Thornall St	Edison	NJ	08837	732-549-8600	549-2239*
**Fax:* Hum Res ■ *Web:* www.huber.com					
Hunt Oil Co 1900 N Akard St	Dallas	TX	75201	214-978-8000	978-8888
TF: 800-435-7794 ■ *Web:* www.huntoil.com					
Husky Energy Inc 707 8th Ave SW	Calgary	AB	T2P3G7	403-298-6111	298-7464
TSX: HSE ■ *Web:* www.huskyenergy.ca					
Hyperdynamics Corp 4800 Sugar Grove Suite 510	Stafford	TX	77477	713-353-9400	353-9421
AMEX: HDY ■ *Web:* www.hypd.com					
Interline Resources Inc 160 W Canyon Crest Rd	Alpine	UT	84004	801-756-3031	756-8843
Web: www.interlineresources.com					
Ivanhoe Energy Inc 999 Canada Pl Suite 654	Vancouver	BC	V6C3E1	604-688-8323	682-2060
NASDAQ: IVAN ■ *TF:* 888-273-9999 ■ *Web:* www.ivanhoe-energy.com					
Jack Lawton LLC 1409 Kirkman St	Lake Charles	LA	70601	337-497-0137	497-9461
Jerry Scott Drilling Co Inc 11977 N Hwy 99 PO Box 1488	Seminole	OK	74818	405-382-2202	382-8334
JM Huber Corp 333 Thornall St	Edison	NJ	08837	732-549-8600	549-2239*
**Fax:* Hum Res ■ *Web:* www.huber.com					
King Ranch Inc 2 Miles West of Hwy 141 PO Box 1090	Kingsville	TX	78364	361-592-6411	592-6885
TF: 800-375-6411 ■ *Web:* www.king-ranch.com					
Lario Oil & Gas Co 301 S Market St	Wichita	KS	67202	316-265-5611	265-5610
TF: 800-865-5611					
Lawton Jack LLC 1409 Kirkman St	Lake Charles	LA	70601	337-497-0137	497-9461
Lenape Resources Inc 9489 Alexander Rd	Alexander	NY	14005	585-344-1200	344-3283
Web: www.lenaperesources.com					
Mack Energy Co 1202 N 10th St	Duncan	OK	73533	580-252-5580	255-1471
TF: 800-299-5580 ■ *Web:* www.mackenergy.com					
Magellan Petroleum Corp 10 Columbus Blvd 10th Fl	Hartford	CT	06106	860-293-2006	293-2349
NASDAQ: MPET ■ *Web:* www.magpet.com					
Maguire Oil Co 1201 Elm St Suite 4000	Dallas	TX	75270	214-741-5137	658-8005
TF: 800-969-6248					
Marathon Oil Co 5555 San Felipe St	Houston	TX	77056	713-629-6600	296-2952
Web: www.marathon.com/Our_Business/Marathon_Oil_Company/					
Marathon Oil Corp 5555 San Felipe Rd	Houston	TX	77056	713-629-6600	296-2952
NYSE: MRO ■ *Web:* www.marathon.com					
McGoldrick Oil Co 8808 McGoldrick Dr	Shreveport	LA	71129	318-687-6490	687-3710
TF: 800-844-6490					
McMoRan Oil & Gas Co 1615 Poydras St	New Orleans	LA	70112	504-582-4000	582-1639
TF: 800-535-7094					
Meridian Resource Corp 1401 Enclave Pkwy Suite 300	Houston	TX	77077	281-558-8080	558-5595
NYSE: TMR ■ *Web:* www.tmrc.com					
Mexco Energy Corp 214 W Texas Ave Suite 1101	Midland	TX	79701	432-682-1119	682-1123
AMEX: MXC					
Mosbacher Energy Co 712 Main St Suite 2200	Houston	TX	77002	713-546-2500	546-2509
Mull Drilling Co Inc 221 N Main St Suite 300	Wichita	KS	67202	316-264-6366	264-6440
Web: www.mulldrlg.com					
Murphy Oil Corp 200 Peach St	El Dorado	AR	71730	870-862-6411	864-6373
NYSE: MUR ■ *TF:* 800-643-2364 ■ *Web:* www.murphyoilcorp.com					
National Energy Group Inc 4925 Greenville Ave Suite 1352	Dallas	TX	75206	214-692-9211	692-9310
TF: 800-733-9211 ■ *Web:* www.negx.com					
National Helium Corp Rt 2 Box 234	Liberal	KS	67901	620-624-7231	626-1209
National Onshore LP 1300 N Sam Houston Pkwy E	Houston	TX	77032	281-987-8600	986-8809

	City	State	Zip	Phone	Fax
Newfield Exploration Co 363 N Sam Houston Pkwy E Suite 2020 — *NYSE: NFX* ■ *TF:* 800-419-4789 ■ *Web:* www.newfld.com	Houston	TX	77060	281-847-6000	405-4242
Nexen Inc 801 7th Ave SW — *NYSE: NXY* ■ *Web:* www.nexeninc.com	Calgary	AB	T2P3P7	403-699-4000	699-5800
Nexen Petroleum USA Inc 12790 Merit Dr Suite 800	Dallas	TX	75251	972-450-4600	450-4729
NGAS Resources Inc 120 Prosperous Pl Suite 201 — *NASDAQ: NGAS* ■ *TF:* 800-977-2363 ■ *Web:* ngas.com	Lexington	KY	40509	859-263-3948	263-4228
Niko Resources Ltd 400 3rd Ave SW Suite 4600 — *TSX: NKO* ■ *Web:* www.nikoresources.com	Calgary	AB	T2P4H2	403-262-1020	263-2686
Noble Energy Inc 100 Glenborough Dr Suite 100 — *NYSE: NBL* ■ *Web:* www.nobleenergyinc.com	Houston	TX	77067	281-872-3100	872-3111
North Coast Energy Inc 1 GOJO Plaza Suite 325 — *TF:* 800-645-6427 ■ *Web:* www.northcoastenergy.com	Akron	OH	44311	330-572-8500	252-0199
Northwest Natural Gas Development Corp 220 NW 2nd Ave — **Fax:* Cust Svc ■ *TF:* 800-422-4012 ■ *Web:* www.nwnatural.com	Portland	OR	97209	503-226-4211	721-2517*
Occidental International Corp 1717 Pennsylvania Ave NW Suite 400 — *Web:* www.oxy.com	Washington	DC	20006	202-857-3000	857-3030
Occidental Oil & Gas Corp 5 Greenway Plaza Suite 110 — *Web:* www.oxy.com	Houston	TX	77046	713-215-7000	215-7201
Occidental Petroleum Corp 10889 Wilshire Blvd — *NYSE: OXY* ■ *Web:* www.oxy.com	Los Angeles	CA	90024	310-208-8800	443-6690
ONEOK Inc 100 W 5th St — *NYSE: OKE* ■ *Web:* www.oneok.com	Tulsa	OK	74103	918-588-7000	588-7145
Oxbow Carbon & Minerals Inc 1601 Forum Pl Suite 1400 — *Web:* www.oxbow.com	West Palm Beach	FL	33401	561-697-4300	640-8727
Parallel Petroleum Corp 1004 N Big Spring St Suite 400 — *NASDAQ: PLLL* ■ *TF:* 800-299-3727 ■ *Web:* www.parallel-petro.com	Midland	TX	79701	432-684-3727	684-3905
Patina Oil & Gas Corp 1625 Broadway Suite 2000 — *NYSE: POG* ■ *Web:* www.patinaoil.com	Denver	CO	80202	303-389-3600	389-3680
Penn Virginia Corp 100 Matsonford Rd Bldg 3 Suite 300 — *NYSE: PVA* ■ *Web:* www.pennvirginia.com	Radnor	PA	19087	610-687-8900	687-3688
Penn West Petroleum Ltd PO Box 1450 Stn M — *TSX: PWT* ■ *TF:* 866-693-2707 ■ *Web:* www.pennwest.com	Calgary	AB	T2P2L8	403-777-2500	777-2699
Petrobras America Inc 10777 Westheimer Rd Suite 1200 — *Web:* www.petrobras.com.br	Houston	TX	77042	713-781-9798	917-3790
Petrohawk Energy Corp 1100 Louisiana Suite 4400 — *NASDAQ: HAWK* ■ *Web:* www.petrohawk.com	Houston	TX	77002	832-204-2700	204-2800
PetroKazakhstan Inc 140 4th Ave SW Suite 1460 — *NYSE: PKZ* ■ *Web:* www.petrokazakhstan.com	Calgary	AB	T2P3N3	403-221-8435	221-8425
Petroleum Development Corp 103 E Main St — *NASDAQ: PETD* ■ *TF:* 800-624-3821 ■ *Web:* www.petd.com	Bridgeport	WV	26330	304-842-6256	842-0913
Petrominerals Corp 1221 Puerta Del Sol	San Clemente	CA	92673	949-366-3888	366-3889
Pioneer Natural Resources Co 303 W Wall St Suite 101 — *NYSE: PXD* ■ *TF:* 800-532-5291	Midland	TX	79701	432-683-4768	571-5063
Plains Exploration & Production Co 700 Milam St Suite 3100 — *NYSE: PXP* ■ **Fax Area Code:* 832 ■ *TF:* 800-934-6083 ■ *Web:* www.plainsxp.com	Houston	TX	77002	713-579-6000	239-6500*
Pogo Producing Co 5 Greenway Plaza Suite 2700 — *NYSE: PPP* ■ *TF:* 800-626-4611 ■ *Web:* www.pogoproducing.com	Houston	TX	77046	713-297-5000	297-5100
PrimeEnergy Corp 1 Landmark Sq Suite 1100 — *NASDAQ: PNRG*	Stamford	CT	06901	203-358-5700	358-5786
PYR Energy Corp 1675 Broadway Suite 2450 — *AMEX: PYR* ■ *Web:* www.pyrenergy.com	Denver	CO	80202	303-825-3748	825-3768
Questar Exploration & Production Co 180 E 100 South — *Web:* www.denbury.com	Salt Lake City	UT	84145	801-324-2600	324-2066
Range Resources Corp 777 Main St Suite 800 — *NYSE: RRC* ■ *Web:* www.rangeresources.com	Fort Worth	TX	76102	817-870-2601	870-2316
Read & Stevens Inc 400 N Pennsylvania St Suite 1000	Roswell	NM	88201	505-622-3770	622-8643
Remington Oil & Gas Corp 8201 Preston Rd Suite 750 — *NYSE: REM* ■ *TF:* 800-521-5481 ■ *Web:* www.remoil.net	Dallas	TX	75225	214-210-2650	210-2643
RL Adkins Corp 301 Oak St — *Web:* www.adkinssupply.com	Sweetwater	TX	79556	325-235-4316	235-3460
Royal Oil & Gas Corp 1 Indian Spring Rd — *TF:* 800-346-0246	Indiana	PA	15701	724-463-0246	465-0202
Sage Energy Co 100 NE Loop 410 Suite 1300	San Antonio	TX	78216	210-404-2828	404-1300
Saint Mary Land & Exploration Co 1776 Lincoln St Suite 700 — *NYSE: SM* ■ *Web:* www.stmaryland.com	Denver	CO	80203	303-861-8140	861-0934
Samson Energy Co LP 2 W 2nd St Samson Plaza — **Fax:* Hum Res ■ *TF:* 800-283-1791	Tulsa	OK	74103	918-583-1791	591-1704*
Samson Investment Co 2 W 2nd St — *TF:* 800-283-1791 ■ *Web:* www.samson.com	Tulsa	OK	74103	918-583-1791	591-1796
Scott Jerry Drilling Co Inc 11977 N Hwy 99 PO Box 1488	Seminole	OK	74818	405-382-2202	382-8334
Seaboard Oil Co 3100 N A St Bldg B Suite 200	Midland	TX	79705	432-684-7005	684-7060
Seneca Resources Corp 1201 Louisiana St Suite 400 — *TF:* 800-622-6695 ■ *Web:* www.nationalfuelgas.com/seneca/	Houston	TX	77002	713-654-2600	654-2654
Shell Canada Ltd 400 4th Ave SW — *TSX: SHC* ■ **Fax:* PR ■ *Web:* www.shell.ca	Calgary	AB	T2P0J4	403-691-3111	269-8031*
Shell Oil Co 910 Louisanna St — *TF:* 888-467-4355 ■ *Web:* www.shellus.com	Houston	TX	77002	713-241-6161	241-4044
Shell Western Exploration & Production Inc 200 N Dairy Ashford Rd — **Fax Area Code:* 713 ■ *Web:* www.shellus.com/sepco	Houston	TX	77079	281-544-2121	241-4044*
Slawson Cos Inc 727 N Waco St Suite 400 — *Web:* www.slawsoncompanies.com	Wichita	KS	67203	316-263-3201	268-0702
Southern Bay Energy LLC 110 Cypress Station Dr Suite 220 — *TF:* 800-249-8178	Houston	TX	77090	281-537-9920	537-8324
Southwestern Energy Co 2350 N Sam Houston Pkwy E Suite 300 — *NYSE: SWN* ■ *Web:* www.swn.com	Houston	TX	77032	281-618-4700	618-4757
Spirit Energy 76 14141 Southwest Fwy — **Fax:* Hum Res	Sugar Land	TX	77478	281-491-7600	287-7339*
Statex Petroleum Inc 1801 Royal Ln Suite 606 — *TF:* 800-989-3427	Dallas	TX	75229	972-869-2800	869-2900
Stelbar Oil Corp Inc 155 N Market St Suite 500	Wichita	KS	67202	316-264-8378	264-0592
Stone Energy Corp 625 E Kaliste Saloom Rd — *NYSE: SGY* ■ *TF:* 800-551-3340 ■ *Web:* www.stoneenergy.com	Lafayette	LA	70508	337-237-0410	232-8061
Storm Cat Energy Corp 1125 17th St Suite 2310 — *AMEX: SCU* ■ *Web:* www.stormcatenergy.com	Denver	CO	80202	303-991-5070	991-5075
SulphCo Inc 850 Spice Islands Dr — *AMEX: SUF* ■ *Web:* www.sulphco.com	Sparks	NV	89431	775-829-1310	829-1351
Suncor Energy Inc 112 4th Ave SW PO Box 38 — *NYSE: SU* ■ *TF:* 866-786-2671 ■ *Web:* www.suncor.com	Calgary	AB	T2P2V5	403-269-8100	269-6200
Sunoco Inc 1735 Market St Suite LL — *NYSE: SUN* ■ *TF:* 800-786-6261 ■ *Web:* www.sunocoinc.com	Philadelphia	PA	19103	215-977-3000	977-3409
Superior Well Services Inc Rt 286 E Airport Professional Bldg 1 Suite 121 — *NASDAQ: SWSI* ■ *TF:* 888-465-8904 ■ *Web:* www.superiorwells.com	Indiana	PA	15701	724-465-8904	465-8907
Swift Energy Co 16825 Northchase Dr Suite 400 — *NYSE: SFY* ■ **Fax:* Hum Res ■ *TF:* 800-777-2412 ■ *Web:* www.swiftenergy.com	Houston	TX	77060	281-874-2700	874-2162*
Syntroleum Corp 4322 S 49th West Ave — *NASDAQ: SYNM* ■ *Web:* www.syntroleum.com	Tulsa	OK	74107	918-592-7900	592-7979
Talisman Energy Inc 888 3rd St SW Suite 3400 — *NYSE: TLM* ■ *Web:* www.talisman-energy.com	Calgary	AB	T2P5C5	403-237-1234	237-1902
Tanganyika Oil Co Ltd 885 W Georgia St Suite 2101 — *TSX: TYK* ■ *TF:* 888-689-7842 ■ *Web:* www.tanganyikaoil.com	Vancouver	BC	V6C3E8	604-689-7842	689-4250
Tengasco Inc 10215 Technology Dr Suite 301 — *AMEX: TGC* ■ *Web:* www.tengasco.com	Knoxville	TN	37902	865-675-1554	675-1621
Tesoro Corp 300 Concord Plaza Dr — *NYSE: TSO* ■ *TF:* 800-837-6762 ■ *Web:* www.tesoropetroleum.com	San Antonio	TX	78216	210-828-8484	745-4474
Teton Energy Corp 410 17th St Suite 1850 — *AMEX: TEC* ■ *Web:* www.teton-energy.com	Denver	CO	80202	303-565-4600	565-4606
Texcal Energy LLC 1021 Main St Suite 2500 — *Web:* www.texcalenergy.com	Houston	TX	77002	713-533-4000	520-7098
THUMS Long Beach Co 111 W Ocean Blvd Suite 800 — *Web:* www.oxy.com	Long Beach	CA	90802	562-624-3400	624-3295
Tidelands Oil Production Co 301 E Ocean Blvd Suite 300 — *Web:* www.tidelandsoil.com	Long Beach	CA	90802	562-436-9918	495-1950
Toreador Resources Corp 4809 Cole Ave Suite 108 — *NASDAQ: TRGL* ■ *TF:* 800-966-2141 ■ *Web:* www.toreador.net	Dallas	TX	75205	214-559-3933	559-3945
Transmeridian Exploration Inc 397 N Sam Houston Pkwy E Suite 300 — *AMEX: TMY* ■ *Web:* www.tmei.com	Houston	TX	77060	281-999-9091	999-9094
Tri-Valley Corp 4550 California Ave Suite 600 — *AMEX: TIV* ■ *TF:* 800-579-9314 ■ *Web:* www.tri-valleycorp.com	Bakersfield	CA	93309	661-864-0500	864-0600
True Cos 455 N Poplar St PO Drawer 2360 — *Web:* www.truecos.com	Casper	WY	82602	307-237-9301	266-0252
Ultra Petroleum Corp 363 N Sam Houston Pkwy E Suite 1200 — *AMEX: UPL* ■ *Web:* www.ultrapetroleum.com	Houston	TX	77060	281-876-0120	876-2831
Unit Corp 7130 S Lewis Ave Suite 1000 — *NYSE: UNT* ■ *TF:* 800-722-3612 ■ *Web:* www.unitcorp.com	Tulsa	OK	74136	918-493-7700	493-7711
UNO Inc 301 W Main Suite 600	Ardmore	OK	73401	580-226-3960	226-3560
Vintage Petroleum Inc 110 W 7th St Suite 2300 — *Web:* www.vintagepetroleum.com	Tulsa	OK	74119	918-592-0101	878-5282
W & T Offshore Inc 8 Greenway Plaza Suite 1330 — *NYSE: WTI*	Houston	TX	77046	713-626-8525	626-8527
Wagner & Brown Ltd 300 N Marienfeld St Suite 1100 — *TF:* 800-777-7936	Midland	TX	79702	432-682-7936	686-5928
Wagner Oil Co 500 Commerce St Suite 600 — *TF:* 800-457-5332 ■ *Web:* www.wagneroil.com	Fort Worth	TX	76102	817-335-2222	332-3876
Ward Petroleum Corp 502 S Fillmore St — *Web:* www.wardpetroleum.com	Enid	OK	73703	580-234-3229	242-6850
Warren Resources Inc 489 5th Ave 32nd Fl — *NASDAQ: WRES* ■ *Web:* www.warrenresources.com	New York	NY	10017	212-697-9660	697-9466
Wexpro Co 180 E 100 South — *Web:* www.questar.com	Salt Lake City	UT	84145	801-324-2600	324-2637
Wheeler Oil Co 6320 Southwest Blvd Suite 100	Fort Worth	TX	76109	817-332-6145	332-6148
Whiting Petroleum Corp 1700 Broadway Suite 2300 — *NYSE: WLL* ■ *Web:* www.whiting.com	Denver	CO	80290	303-837-1661	861-4023
Williams Clayton Energy Inc 6 Desta Dr Suite 3000 — *NASDAQ: CWEI* ■ *Web:* www.claytonwilliams.com	Midland	TX	79705	432-682-6324	682-1452
Wilshire Enterprises Inc 1 Gateway Center Suite 1030 — *AMEX: WOC* ■ *TF:* 888-697-3962 ■ *Web:* www.wilshireenterprisesinc.com	Newark	NJ	07102	201-420-2796	420-6012
XTO Energy Inc 810 Houston St — *NYSE: XTO* ■ *Web:* www.xtoenergy.com	Fort Worth	TX	76102	817-870-2800	870-1671
Yates Petroleum Corp 105 S 4th St — **Fax:* Hum Res	Artesia	NM	88210	505-748-1471	748-4571*

540 OIL & GAS FIELD EQUIPMENT

	City	State	Zip	Phone	Fax
Alberta Oil Tool 9530 60th Ave — *Web:* www.albertaoiltool.com	Edmonton	AB	T6E0C1	780-434-8566	436-4329
Baker Hughes Inc 3900 Essex Ln Suite 1200 — *NYSE: BHI* ■ *TF:* 800-229-7447 ■ *Web:* www.bakerhughes.com	Houston	TX	77027	713-439-8600	439-8699
Bolt Technology Corp 4 Duke Pl — *AMEX: BTJ* ■ *Web:* www.bolt-technology.com	Norwalk	CT	06854	203-853-0700	854-9601
Brandt Co 2800 N Frazier St — **Fax:* Hum Res	Conroe	TX	77303	936-756-4800	756-4925*
Carbo Ceramics Inc 6565 N MacArthur Blvd Suite 1050 — *NYSE: CRR* ■ *TF:* 800-551-3247 ■ *Web:* www.carboceramics.com	Irving	TX	75039	972-401-0090	401-0705
Cooper Cameron Corp 1333 West Loop S Suite 1700 — *NYSE: CAM* ■ *Web:* www.coopercameron.com	Houston	TX	77027	713-513-3300	513-3355
Dril-Quip Inc 13550 Hempstead Hwy — *NYSE: DRQ* ■ *Web:* www.dril-quip.com	Houston	TX	77040	713-939-7711	939-8063
Drillers Service Inc 1792 Highland Ave NE PO Box 1407 — *TF:* 800-334-2308 ■ *Web:* www.dsidsi.com	Hickory	NC	28603	828-322-1100	322-7857
Driltech Mission LLC 13500 NW CR 235 — *Web:* www.driltechmission.com	Alachua	FL	32615	386-462-4100	462-3247
Flotek Industries Inc 7030 Empire Central Dr — *AMEX: FTK* ■ *Web:* www.flotekind.com	Houston	TX	77040	713-849-9911	896-4511
FMC Technologies Inc 1803 Gears Rd — *NYSE: FTI* ■ *TF:* 800-869-6999 ■ *Web:* www.fmctechnologies.com	Houston	TX	77067	281-591-4000	591-4102
Gearench Inc 4450 S Hwy 6 PO Box 192 — *TF:* 800-221-1848 ■ *Web:* www.gearench.com	Clifton	TX	76634	254-675-8651	675-6100
George E Failing Co (GEFCO) 2215 S Van Buren St — *TF:* 800-759-7441 ■ *Web:* www.gefco.com	Enid	OK	73701	580-234-4141	233-6807
Gulf Island Fabrication Inc 583 Thompson Rd — *NASDAQ: GIFI* ■ **Fax:* Mktg ■ *TF:* 888-465-2100 ■ *Web:* www.gulfisland.com	Houma	LA	70363	985-872-2100	876-4870*
Halliburton Energy Services 10200 Bellaire Blvd — *Web:* www.halliburton.com/	Houston	TX	77072	281-575-4400	575-5939
Harbison-Fischer Mfg PO Box 2477 — *TF:* 800-364-7867 ■ *Web:* www.hfpumps.com	Fort Worth	TX	76113	817-297-2211	297-4248
Hughes Christensen Co PO Box 2539 — **Fax:* Hum Res ■ *Web:* www.bakerhughes.com/hcc/	Houston	TX	77252	281-363-6000	363-6025*
Hydra-Rig Inc 6000 E Berry St — *Web:* www.hydrarig.com	Fort Worth	TX	76119	817-457-3825	457-3897
Hydril Co 3300 N Sam Houston Pkwy E — *NASDAQ: HYDL* ■ **Fax:* Hum Res ■ *TF:* 800-231-0023 ■ *Web:* www.hydril.com	Houston	TX	77032	281-449-2000	985-3295*
IDM Equipment Ltd 11616 N Galayda St — *Web:* www.idmequipment.com	Houston	TX	77086	281-447-2731	477-9077
Kimray Inc 52 NW 42nd St — *Web:* www.kimray.com	Oklahoma City	OK	73118	405-525-6601	525-7520
Lufkin Industries Inc 601 S Raguet St — *NASDAQ: LUFK* ■ *Web:* www.lufkin.com	Lufkin	TX	75902	936-634-2211	637-5474
M & M Supply Co 901 W Peach Ave PO Box 548 — *TF:* 800-404-7879 ■ *Web:* www.mmsupply.com	Duncan	OK	73534	580-252-7879	252-7708
Martin/Decker Totco Instrumentation Inc 1200 Cypress Creek Rd — *TF:* 800-423-3319	Cedar Park	TX	78613	512-340-5000	340-5223
Morris Industries Inc 777 Rt 23 PO Box 278 — *TF:* 800-835-0777 ■ *Web:* www.morrispipe.com	Pompton Plains	NJ	07444	973-835-6600	835-7414
Morrison Brothers Co PO Box 238 — *TF Cust Svc:* 800-553-4840 ■ *Web:* www.morbros.com	Dubuque	IA	52004	563-583-5701	583-5028
NATCO Group Inc 2950 N Loop W Suite 700 — *NYSE: NTG* ■ *TF:* 877-288-6270 ■ *Web:* www.natcogroup.com	Houston	TX	77092	713-683-9292	683-6768
National Oilwell Varco Inc 10000 Richmond Ave — *NYSE: NOV* ■ *TF:* 888-262-8645 ■ *Web:* www.natoil.com	Houston	TX	77042	713-346-7500	935-8233

Phone Fax

Natural Gas Services Group Inc 2911 S CR 1260 .... Midland TX 79706 432-563-3974 563-4139
AMEX: NGS ■ *TF:* 888-891-6275 ■ *Web:* www.ngsgi.com
Norriseal 11122 W Little York Rd .... Houston TX 77041 713-466-3552 896-7386*
**Fax: Sales* ■ *Web:* www.norriseal.com
Omsco ShawCor 6418 Esperson St .... Houston TX 77011 713-844-3700 926-7103*
**Fax: Sales* ■ *TF:* 800-426-6726 ■ *Web:* www.omscoind.com
Orbix Corp 4550 S Hwy 6 .... Clifton TX 76634 254-675-8371 675-2747
Pacific Energy Management LLC 5900 Cherry Ave .... Long Beach CA 90805 562-728-2800 728-2801
NYSE: PPX ■ *Web:* www.pacpipe.com
Perry Equipment Corp
118 Washington Walters Industrial Pk .... Mineral Wells TX 76067 940-325-2575 325-4622
TF: 800-877-7326 ■ *Web:* www.pecousa.com
Petrotherm 4122 E Chapman Ave Suite 10 .... Orange CA 92869 714-744-9234 744-1705
TF: 888-468-8645 ■ *Web:* www.petrothermheaters.com
Plant Process Equipment Inc 280 Reynolds Ave .... League City TX 77573 281-332-2589 332-6280
Web: www.plant-process.com
Reed Hycalog 6501 Navigation Blvd .... Houston TX 77011 713-924-5200 924-5327*
**Fax: Hum Res* ■ *Web:* www.reedhycalog.com
Schramm Inc 800 E Virginia Ave .... West Chester PA 19380 610-696-2500 696-6950
Web: www.schramminc.com
ShawCor Ltd 25 Bethridge Rd .... Toronto ON M9W1M7 416-743-7111 743-7199
TSX: SCL.A ■ *Web:* www.shawcor.com
Smeal Mfg Co 610 W 4th St .... Snyder NE 68664 402-568-2221 568-2223
Web: www.smealderricks.com
Smith International Inc 411 N Sam Houston Pkwy Suite 600 .... Houston TX 77060 281-443-3370 233-5199
NYSE: SII ■ *TF:* 800-877-6484 ■ *Web:* www.smith.com
Southern Co Inc 3101 Carrier St .... Memphis TN 38116 901-345-2531 345-3555
TF: 800-264-7626 ■ *Web:* www.socomemphis.com
Southwest Oilfield Products 10340 Wallisville Rd .... Houston TX 77013 713-675-7541 675-5200
TF: 800-392-4600 ■ *Web:* www.swoil.com
Standco Industries Inc Oilfield Products Div 2701 Clinton Dr .... Houston TX 77020 713-224-6311 229-9312
TF: 800-231-6018
Stewart & Stevenson LLC 1000 Louisiana St .... Houston TX 77002 713-751-2600 751-2601
Web: www.ssss.com
Stratco Inc 14821 N 73rd St .... Scottsdale AZ 85260 480-991-0450 991-0314
Web: www.stratco.com
TD Williamson Inc 5727 S Lewis St Suite 300 .... Tulsa OK 74105 918-447-5001 447-5050
TF: 888-839-6766 ■ *Web:* www.tdwilliamson.com
Titan Specialties Inc 11785 Hwy 152 PO Box 2316 .... Pampa TX 79066 806-665-3781 665-8882
TF Sales: 800-692-4486 ■ *Web:* www.titanspecialties.com
TIW Corp 12300 S Main St .... Houston TX 77035 713-729-2110 728-4767
Web: www.tiwtools.com
Total Energy Services Ltd 300 5th Ave SW Suite 2550 .... Calgary AB T2P3C4 403-216-3939 234-8731
TSX: TOT ■ *TF:* 877-818-6825 ■ *Web:* www.totalenergy.to
Trican Well Service Ltd 645 7th Ave SW Suite 2900 .... Calgary AB T2P4G8 403-266-0202 237-7716
TSX: TCW ■ *Web:* www.trican.ca
Tuboscope Brandt 2835 Holmes Rd .... Houston TX 77051 713-799-5100 799-5406
Varco Shaffer PO Box 1473 .... Houston TX 77251 713-937-5000 937-5779*
**Fax: Hum Res*
Vetco Gray Inc 3010 Briarpark Dr Suite 300 .... Houston TX 77042 713-683-2400 683-2413
Web: www.vetcogray.com
Weatherford Artificial Lift Systems 918 Hodgkins St .... Houston TX 77032 281-449-1383 449-6235
Web: www.weatherford.com
Weatherford International Inc 515 Post Oak Blvd Suite 200 .... Houston TX 77027 713-693-4000 693-4313*
NYSE: WFT ■ **Fax: Hum Res* ■ *TF:* 800-257-3826 ■ *Web:* www.weatherford.com
Williamson TD Inc 5727 S Lewis St Suite 300 .... Tulsa OK 74105 918-447-5001 447-5050
TF: 888-839-6766 ■ *Web:* www.tdwilliamson.com
Winston F2S Corp 1604 Cherokee Trace .... White Oak TX 75693 903-757-7341 759-6986
TF: 800-527-8465 ■ *Web:* www.winstonf2s.com
Wood Group Pressure Control 3250 Briar Pk Suite 100 .... Houston TX 77042 281-398-8901 398-8086
Web: portal.woodgroup.com

541 OIL & GAS FIELD EXPLORATION SERVICES

Phone Fax

Adams Resources Exploration Co
4400 Post Oak Pkwy Suite 2700 .... Houston TX 77027 713-881-3600 881-3491
American Oil & Gas Inc 1050 17th St Suite 1850 .... Denver CO 80265 303-991-0173 595-0709
AMEX: AEZ ■ *Web:* www.americanoilandgasinc.com
Anadarko Petroleum Corp Alaska Div 3201 C St Suite 603 .... Anchorage AK 99503 907-273-6300 563-9479
Web: www.anadarko.com
Anchor Gasoline 114 E 5th St .... Tulsa OK 74103 918-584-5291 583-6373
TF: 800-321-4086
Arctic Slope Regional Corp 1230 Agvik St PO Box 129 .... Barrow AK 99723 907-852-8633 852-5733
TF: 800-770-2772 ■ *Web:* www.asrc.com
Arena Resources Inc 4920 S Lewis Ave Suite 107 .... Tulsa OK 74105 918-747-6060 747-7620
AMEX: ARD ■ *Web:* www.arenaresourcesinc.com
Atlas America Inc 311 Rouser Rd PO Box 611 .... Moon Township PA 15108 412-262-2830 262-2820
NASDAQ: ATLS ■ *Web:* www.atlasamerica.com
Baker Atlas Div Baker Hughes Inc 2001 Rankin Rd .... Houston TX 77073 713-625-4200 625-4525
Web: www.bakerhughes.com/bakeratlas
Baker Hughes Inc Baker Atlas Div 2001 Rankin Rd .... Houston TX 77073 713-625-4200 625-4525
Web: www.bakerhughes.com/bakeratlas
Baker Hughes INTEQ 1999 Rankin Rd .... Houston TX 77073 713-625-4200 625-5200
Web: www.bakerhughes.com/inteq/
Bill Barrett Corp 1099 18th St Suite 2300 .... Denver CO 80202 303-293-9100 291-0420
NYSE: BBG ■ *Web:* www.billbarrettcorp.com
Bois d'Arc Energy Inc 600 Travis St Suite 5200 .... Houston TX 77002 713-228-0438 228-1767
NYSE: BDE ■ *Web:* www.boisdarcenergy.com
BP Prudhoe Bay Royalty Trust 101 Barclay St .... New York NY 10286 212-815-6908 815-2293
NYSE: BPT
CAMAC Holdings Inc 1330 Post Oak Blvd Suite 2200 .... Houston TX 77056 713-965-5100 965-5128
Web: www.camacholdings.com
Canada Southern Petroleum Ltd 706 7th Ave SW Suite 250 .... Calgary AB T2P0Z1 403-269-7741 261-5667
NASDAQ: CSPLF ■ *Web:* www.cansopet.com
Central Resources Inc 1775 Sherman St Suite 2600 .... Denver CO 80203 303-830-0100 830-9297
Web: www.centralresources.com
CGG Americas Inc 16430 Park Ten Pl .... Houston TX 77084 281-646-2400 646-2660
Web: www.cgg.com
Cheniere Energy Inc 717 Texas Ave Suite 3100 .... Houston TX 77002 713-659-1361 659-5459
AMEX: LNG ■ *TF:* 888-948-2036 ■ *Web:* www.cheniere.com
Chevron Overseas Petroleum Co
6001 Bollinger Canyon Rd PO Box 6046 .... San Ramon CA 94583 925-842-1000 842-1509
Chevron Petroleum Co 3901 Briar Pk St .... Houston TX 77042 713-954-6000
CNX Gas Corp 4000 Brownsville Rd .... South Park PA 15129 412-854-6719
NYSE: CXG ■ *Web:* www.cnxgas.com
ConocoPhillips 600 N Dairy Ashford Rd .... Houston TX 77079 281-293-1000
NYSE: COP ■ *TF:* 800-527-5476 ■ *Web:* www.conocophillips.com
Dawson Geophysical Co 508 W Wall St Suite 800 .... Midland TX 79701 432-684-3000 684-3030
NASDAQ: DWSN ■ *TF:* 800-332-9766 ■ *Web:* www.dawson3d.com
Delta Petroleum Corp 370 17th St Suite 4300 .... Denver CO 80202 303-293-9133 298-8251
NASDAQ: DPTR ■ *Web:* www.deltapetro.com

Phone Fax

Dominion Exploration & Production Inc 1450 Poydras St .... New Orleans LA 70112 504-593-7000 593-7465*
**Fax: Mail Rm* ■ *Web:* www.dom.com
Edge Petroleum Corp 1301 Travis St Suite 2000 .... Houston TX 77002 713-654-8960 650-6494
NASDAQ: EPEX ■ *Web:* www.edgepet.com
Energy Partners Ltd 201 St Charles Ave Suite 3400 .... New Orleans LA 70170 504-569-1875 569-1874
NYSE: EPL ■ *Web:* www.eplweb.com
Enterra Energy Trust 500 4th Ave SW Suite 2700 .... Calgary AB T2P2V6 403-263-0262 294-1197
NYSE: ENT ■ *Web:* www.enterraenergy.com
EOG Resources Inc 333 Clay St Suite 4200 .... Houston TX 77002 713-651-7000 651-6479
NYSE: EOG ■ *TF:* 877-363-3647 ■ *Web:* www.eogresources.com
EXCO Resources Inc 12377 Merit Dr Suite 1700 .... Dallas TX 75251 214-368-2084 368-2087
NYSE: XCO ■ *Web:* www.excoresources.com
Exploration Co The 777 E Sonterra Blvd Suite 350 .... San Antonio TX 78232 210-496-5300 496-3232
NASDAQ: TXCO ■ *TF:* 877-912-8926 ■ *Web:* www.txco.com
Exploration Consultants Ltd Inc
9801 Westheimer Blvd Suite 1060 .... Houston TX 77042 713-784-5800
Web: www.ecqc.com
ExxonMobil Exploration Co 233 Benmar Dr Suite 10 .... Houston TX 77060 713-656-3000 680-7436
Fidelity Exploration & Production Co
1700 Lincoln St Suite 2800 .... Denver CO 80203 303-893-3133 893-1964
TF: 800-986-3133 ■ *Web:* www.fidelityoil.com
First Calgary Petroleums Ltd 1414 8th St SW Suite 500 .... Calgary AB T2R1J6 403-264-6697 264-3955
TSX: FCP ■ *Web:* www.fcpl.ca
GeoGlobal Resources Inc 605 1st St SW Suite 310 .... Calgary AB T2P3F9 403-777-9250 777-9199
AMEX: GGR ■ *Web:* www.geoglobal.com
GlobalSantaFe Corp 15375 Memorial Dr .... Houston TX 77079 281-925-6000 925-6010
NYSE: GSF ■ *TF:* 800-231-5754 ■ *Web:* www.globalsantafe.com
Goodrich Petroleum Corp 333 Texas St Suite 1375 .... Shreveport LA 71101 318-429-1375 429-2296
Web: www.goodrichpetroleum.com
GulfMark Energy Inc 4400 Post Oak Pkwy Suite 2700 .... Houston TX 77027 713-881-3600 881-3491
Halliburton Energy Services 10200 Bellaire Blvd .... Houston TX 77072 281-575-4400 575-5939
Web: www.halliburton.com/
Highpine Oil & Gas Ltd 150 6th Ave SW Suite 4000 .... Calgary AB T2P3Y7 403-265-3333 265-3362
Web: www.highpineog.com
JED Oil Inc 1601 15th Ave .... Didsbury AB T0M0W0 403-335-2101 335-9391
AMEX: JDO ■ *Web:* www.jedoil.com
Kennecott Exploration Co 224 N 2200 West .... Salt Lake City UT 84116 801-238-2400 238-2430
Web: www.kennecottexploration.com
Linn Energy LLC 650 Washington Rd 8th Fl .... Pittsburgh PA 15228 412-440-1400
NASDAQ: LINE ■ *Web:* www.linnenergy.com
Mariner Energy Inc
2000 W Sam Houston Pkwy S 1 Briar Lake Plaza
Suite 2000 .... Houston TX 77042 713-954-5500 954-5555
NYSE: ME ■ *Web:* www.mariner-energy.com
MarkWest Hydrocarbon Inc 155 Inverness Dr W Suite 200 .... Englewood CO 80112 303-290-8700 290-8769
AMEX: MWP ■ *TF:* 800-730-8388 ■ *Web:* www.markwest.com
McMoRan Exploration Co 1615 Poydras St .... New Orleans LA 70112 504-582-4000 582-1847
NYSE: MMR ■ *TF:* 800-535-7094 ■ *Web:* www.mcmoran.com
New Jersey Natural Gas Co 1415 Wyckoff Rd .... Wall NJ 07719 732-938-1480 938-3154
TF: 800-221-0051 ■ *Web:* www.njliving.com
Norsk Hydro E & P Americas Inc
15990 N Bakers Landing Rd Suite 150 .... Houston TX 77079 281-504-1100 504-1101
Web: www.hydro.com
Occidental International Corp
1717 Pennsylvania Ave NW Suite 400 .... Washington DC 20006 202-857-3000 857-3030
Web: www.oxy.com
Occidental Petroleum Corp 10889 Wilshire Blvd .... Los Angeles CA 90024 310-208-8800 443-6690
NYSE: OXY ■ *Web:* www.oxy.com
Panhandle Royalty Co 5400 N Grand Blvd Suite 305 .... Oklahoma City OK 73112 405-948-1560 948-2038
AMEX: PHX ■ *Web:* www.panra.com
Patterson-UTI Energy Inc 4510 Lamesa Hwy .... Snyder TX 79549 325-573-1104 574-6390
NASDAQ: PTEN ■ *TF:* 800-245-0167 ■ *Web:* www.patenergy.com
Petrohawk Energy Corp 1100 Louisiana Suite 4400 .... Houston TX 77002 832-204-2700 204-2800
NASDAQ: HAWK ■ *Web:* www.petrohawk.com
Petroleum Geo-Services Inc 738 Hwy 6 South Suite 500 .... Houston TX 77079 281-589-8818 589-1482
Web: www.pgs.com
PetroQuest Energy Inc 400 E Kaliste Saloom Rd Suite 6000 .... Lafayette LA 70508 337-232-7028 232-0044
NYSE: PQ ■ *TF:* 800-755-8381 ■ *Web:* www.petroquest.com
Quicksilver Resources Inc 777 W Rosedale St Suite 300 .... Fort Worth TX 76104 817-665-5000 665-5014
NYSE: KWK ■ *Web:* www.qrinc.com
Sanchez Oil & Gas Corp 1920 Sandman St .... Laredo TX 78041 956-722-8092 718-1057
TF: 800-292-7699
Schlumberger Ltd 5599 San Felipe .... Houston TX 77056 713-513-2000 350-8114*
NYSE: SLB ■ **Fax Area Code: 212* ■ *Web:* www.slb.com
SEACOR Holdings Inc 460 Park Ave 12th Fl .... New York NY 10022 212-307-6633 582-8522
NYSE: CKH ■ *Web:* www.seacorsmit.com
Seitel Inc 10811 S Westview Cir Dr Bldg C Suite 100 .... Houston TX 77043 713-881-8900 881-8901
Web: www.seitel-inc.com
Sherritt International Corp 1133 Yonge St .... Toronto ON M4T2Y7 416-924-4551 924-5015
TSX: S ■ *Web:* www.sherritt.com
Slawson Cos Inc 727 N Waco St Suite 400 .... Wichita KS 67203 316-263-3201 268-0702
Web: www.slawsoncompanies.com
Spirit Energy 76 14141 Southwest Fwy .... Sugar Land TX 77478 281-491-7600 287-7339*
**Fax: Hum Res*
Superior Energy Services Inc 1105 Peters Rd .... Harvey LA 70058 504-362-4321 362-1430
NYSE: SPN ■ *TF:* 800-259-7774 ■ *Web:* www.superiorenergy.com
Tana Exploration Co LLC 1600 Smith St Suite 5000 .... Houston TX 77002 832-325-6000 325-6001
Taylor Energy Co 1 Lee Cir .... New Orleans LA 70130 504-581-5491 589-0591
Web: www.taylorenergy.com
TGC Industries Inc 1304 Summit Ave Suite 2 .... Plano TX 75074 972-881-1099 424-3943
AMEX: TGE ■ *TF:* 800-223-7470 ■ *Web:* www.tgcseismic.com
Total E & P USA Inc
1 Memorial City Plaza 800 Gessner Rd Suite 700 .... Houston TX 77024 713-647-3000 647-3003
Web: www.total.com
TransGlobe Energy Corp 605 5th Ave Suite 2500 .... Calgary AB T2P3H5 403-264-9888 264-9898
AMEX: TGA ■ *Web:* www.trans-globe.com
United Co 1005 Glenway Ave .... Bristol VA 24201 276-466-3322 645-1451
VAALCO Energy Inc 4600 Post Oak Pl Suite 309 .... Houston TX 77027 713-623-0801 623-0982
AMEX: EGY ■ *Web:* www.vaalco.com
Veritas DGC Inc 10300 Townpark Dr .... Houston TX 77072 832-351-8300 351-8788
NYSE: VTS ■ *TF:* 800-344-4266 ■ *Web:* www.veritasdgc.com
W-H Energy Services Inc 10370 Richmond Ave Suite 990 .... Houston TX 77042 713-974-9071 974-7029
NYSE: WHQ ■ *Web:* www.whes.com
Walter Oil & Gas Corp 1100 Louisiana St Suite 200 .... Houston TX 77002 713-659-1221 756-1155
TF: 888-756-7880 ■ *Web:* www.walteroil.com
WesternGeco 10001 Richmond Ave .... Houston TX 77042 713-789-9600 789-0172
Web: www.westerngeco.com
Williams Energy Services 1 Williams Center PO Box 2400 .... Tulsa OK 74102 918-573-2000 573-2296
TF: 800-945-5426 ■ *Web:* www.williams.com
Zion Oil & Gas Inc 6510 Abrams Rd Suite 300 .... Dallas TX 75231 214-221-4610 221-6510
Web: www.zionoil.com

542 OIL & GAS FIELD SERVICES

SEE ALSO Oil & Gas Field Exploration Services p. 2037

Phone Fax

Badger Daylighting Inc 6740 65th Ave. Red Deer AB T4P1A5 403-343-0303 343-0401
TF: 800-465-4273 ■ *Web:* www.badgerinc.com

Baker Atlas Div Baker Hughes Inc 2001 Rankin Rd Houston TX 77073 713-625-4200 625-4525
Web: www.bakerhughes.com/bakeratlas

Baker Hughes Inc 3900 Essex Ln Suite 1200 Houston TX 77027 713-439-8600 439-8699
NYSE: BHI ■ *TF:* 800-229-7447 ■ *Web:* www.bakerhughes.com

Baker Hughes Inc Baker Atlas Div 2001 Rankin Rd Houston TX 77073 713-625-4200 625-4525
Web: www.bakerhughes.com/bakeratlas

Basic Energy Services Inc 400 W Illinois Suite 800 Midland TX 79701 432-620-5500 570-0437
NYSE: BAS ■ *Web:* www.basicenergyservices.com

BJ Services Co 4601 West Way Park Blvd Houston TX 77041 713-462-4239 895-5897*
NYSE: BJS ■ **Fax:* Hum Res ■ *TF:* 800-234-6487 ■ *Web:* www.bjservices.com

Boots & Coots International Well Control Inc
11615 N Houston-Rosslyn Rd Houston TX 77086 713-621-7911 931-8392*
AMEX: WEL ■ **Fax Area Code:* 281 ■ *TF:* 800-256-9688 ■
Web: www.bootsandcoots.com

Central Industries Inc PO Box 1380 Scott LA 70583 337-233-3171 234-4008
TF: 800-326-3171 ■ *Web:* www.centralindinc.com

Colloid Environmental Technologies Co (CETCO)
1500 W Shure Dr Arlington Heights IL 60004 847-392-5800 577-6150
TF: 800-527-9948 ■ *Web:* www.cetco.com

Core Laboratories 6316 Windfern Rd Houston TX 77040 713-328-2673 328-2150
NYSE: CLB ■ *Web:* www.corelab.com

Crain Brothers Inc 2717 Grand Chenier Ave Grand Chenier LA 70643 337-538-2411 538-2700
TF: 800-737-2767 ■ *Web:* www.crainbrothers.com

Danos & Curole Marine Contractors Inc PO Box 1460 Larose LA 70373 985-693-3313 693-4698
TF: 800-487-5971 ■ *Web:* www.danos.com

Diamond Services Inc 503 S DeGravelle Rd Amelia LA 70340 985-631-2187 631-2442
TF: 800-879-1162 ■ *Web:* www.dscgom.com

Dowell Schlumberger Inc 300 Schlumberger Dr Sugar Land TX 77478 281-285-8400 285-8548*
**Fax:* Hum Res ■ *Web:* www.slb.com

Dynatec Corp 9555 Yonge St Suite 200 Richmond Hill ON L4C9M5 905-780-1980 780-1990
TSX: DY ■ *Web:* www.dynatec.ca

Evertson Well Service Inc PO Box 397 Kimball NE 69145 308-235-4871 235-2800
Web: www.evertson.com

FESCO Ltd 1000 Fesco Ave Alice TX 78332 361-661-7000 664-3157
Web: www.fescoinc.com

Fidelity Exploration & Production Co
1700 Lincoln St Suite 2800 Denver CO 80203 303-893-3133 893-1964
TF: 800-986-3133 ■ *Web:* www.fidelityoil.com

Global Industries Ltd PO Box 442 Sulphur LA 70664 337-583-5000 583-5100
NASDAQ: GLBL ■ *TF:* 800-525-3483 ■ *Web:* www.globalind.com

Goodrich Petroleum Corp 808 Travis St Suite 1320 Houston TX 77002 713-780-9494 780-9254
NYSE: GDP ■ *TF:* 800-256-2380 ■ *Web:* www.goodrichpetroleum.com

Gulfmark Offshore Inc 10111 Richmond Ave Suite 340 Houston TX 77042 713-963-9522 963-9796
NASDAQ: GMRK ■ *Web:* www.gulfmark.com

Halliburton Energy Services 10200 Bellaire Blvd Houston TX 77072 281-575-4400 575-5939
Web: www.halliburton.com/

Hanover Inc 11000 Corporate Ctr Dr Suite 200 Houston TX 77041 281-854-3000 854-3195
TF: 800-366-0980 ■ *Web:* www.hanover-co.com

Helix Energy Solutions Inc
400 N Sam Houston Pkwy E Suite 400 Houston TX 77060 281-618-0400 618-0500
NASDAQ: HELX ■ *TF:* 888-345-2347 ■ *Web:* www.caldive.com

Houma Industries PO Box 685 Harvey LA 70059 504-347-4585 348-4230
TF: 800-348-5340

ICO Inc 1811 Bering Dr Houston TX 77057 713-351-4100 335-2201
NASDAQ: ICOC ■ *TF:* 877-777-0877 ■ *Web:* www.icopolymers.com

Indel-Davis Inc 4401 S Jackson Ave Tulsa OK 74107 918-587-2151 446-1583
TF: 800-331-6300 ■ *Web:* www.indel-davis.com

Key Energy Services Inc 6 Desta Dr Suite 4400 Midland TX 79705 432-620-0300 620-0307
Web: www.keyenergy.com

Koch Specialty Plant Services 12221 E Sam Houston Pkwy N Houston TX 77044 713-427-7700 427-7748
TF: 800-497-1789 ■ *Web:* www.kochservices.com

M-I Swaco 5950 N Course Dr Houston TX 77072 713-739-0222 308-9555
Web: www.miswaco.com

Matrix Service Co 10701 E Ute St Tulsa OK 74116 918-838-8822 838-8810
NASDAQ: MTRX ■ *TF:* 800-866-8822 ■ *Web:* www.matrixservice.com

Milbar Hydro-Test Inc 651 Aero Dr Shreveport LA 71107 318-227-8210 222-2558
TF: 800-259-8210 ■ *Web:* www.milbarhydro-test.com

Nabors Industries Ltd 515 W Greens Rd Suite 1200 Houston TX 77067 281-874-0035 872-5205
NYSE: NBR ■ *TF:* 888-622-6777 ■ *Web:* www.nabors.com

Nabors Offshore Corp 515 W Greens Rd Suite 500 Houston TX 77067 281-874-0406 775-8462
Web: www.nabors.com

Newpark Resources Inc 3850 N Causeway Blvd Suite 1770 Metairie LA 70002 504-838-8222 833-9506
NYSE: NR ■ *Web:* www.newpark.com

Oceaneering International Inc 11911 FM 529 Houston TX 77041 713-329-4500 329-4951
NYSE: OII ■ *TF:* 800-527-1865 ■ *Web:* www.oceaneering.com

Oil States International Inc 7701-A S Cooper St Arlington TX 76001 817-548-4200 548-4250
NYSE: OIS ■ *Web:* www.oilstates.com

Oil Well Service Co 1241 E Burnett St Signal Hill CA 90755 562-595-4501 424-8026

Pool Co Texas Ltd PO Box 2545 Hobbs NM 88241 505-392-6591 392-3100
TF: 800-299-1388

Pride International Inc 5847 San Felipe Suite 3300 Houston TX 77057 713-789-1400 789-1430
NYSE: PDE ■ *TF:* 800-645-2067 ■ *Web:* www.prde.com

Production Management Industries LLC 9761 Hwy 90 E Morgan City LA 70380 985-631-3837 631-0729
TF: 800-229-3837 ■ *Web:* www.pmi.net

Reliable Production Service Inc 1090 Cinclare Dr Port Allen LA 70767 225-343-3900 343-3200

RPC Inc 2170 Piedmont Rd NE Atlanta GA 30324 404-321-2140 321-5483
NYSE: RES ■ *Web:* www.rpc.net

Schlumberger Wireline & Testing 210 Schlumberger Dr Sugar Land TX 77478 281-285-8500 285-8970*
**Fax:* Hum Res

Sperry Sun Drilling Services Inc
3000 North Sam Houston Pkwy E Houston TX 77032 281-871-4000 871-5565*
**Fax:* Hum Res

Stanley TK Inc PO Box 31 Waynesboro MS 39367 601-735-2855 735-2857
TF: 800-477-2855 ■ *Web:* www.tkstanley.com

Stewart & Stevenson LLC 1000 Louisiana St Houston TX 77002 713-751-2600 751-2601
Web: www.ssss.com

Stolt Offshore Inc 10787 Clay Rd Houston TX 77041 713-430-1100 461-0039
NASDAQ: SOSA ■ *TF:* 800-299-3483 ■ *Web:* www.stoltoffshore.com

T-3 Energy Services Inc 7135 Ardmore St Houston TX 77054 713-996-4110 996-4123
NASDAQ: TTES ■ *Web:* www.t3energyservices.com

Team Industrial Services Inc 200 Hermann Dr Alvin TX 77511 281-331-6154 331-4107
AMEX: TMI ■ *TF:* 800-662-8326 ■ *Web:* www.teamindustrialservices.com

Team Inc DBA Team Industrial Services Inc 200 Hermann Dr Alvin TX 77511 281-331-6154 331-4107
AMEX: TMI ■ *TF:* 800-662-8326 ■ *Web:* www.teamindustrialservices.com

TK Stanley Inc PO Box 31 Waynesboro MS 39367 601-735-2855 735-2857
TF: 800-477-2855 ■ *Web:* www.tkstanley.com

Trican Well Service Ltd 645 7th Ave SW Suite 2900 Calgary AB T2P4G8 403-266-0202 237-7716
TSX: TCW ■ *Web:* www.trican.ca

Phone Fax

Universal Compression Holdings Inc 4444 Brittmoore Rd Houston TX 77041 713-335-7000 466-0323
NYSE: UCO ■ *TF:* 800-234-4650 ■ *Web:* www.universalcompression.com

US Casing Div Weatherford International Inc PO Box 337 Lindsay OK 73052 405-756-4374 756-8350

Veco Corp 3601 C St Suite 1000 Anchorage AK 99503 907-264-8100 264-8130
TF: 800-284-2812 ■ *Web:* www.veco.com

Weatherford Completion Systems 11420 W Hwy 80 E Midland TX 79711 432-563-7957 563-7956
TF: 800-777-7957 ■ *Web:* www.weatherford.com

Weatherford International Inc US Casing Div PO Box 337 Lindsay OK 73052 405-756-4374 756-8350

Williams Energy Services 1 Williams Center PO Box 2400 Tulsa OK 74102 918-573-2000 573-2296
TF: 800-945-5426 ■ *Web:* www.williams.com

Wood Group Pressure Control 3250 Briar Pk Suite 100 Houston TX 77042 281-398-8901 398-8086
Web: portal.woodgroup.com

543 OIL & GAS WELL DRILLING

Phone Fax

Allis-Chalmers Energy Inc 5075 Westheimer St Suite 890 Houston TX 77056 713-369-0550 369-0555
AMEX: ALY ■ *Web:* www.alchenergy.com

Applied Drilling Technology Inc
15375 Memorial Dr Suite A-200 Houston TX 77079 281-925-7100 925-7167
TF: 800-990-2384

Atlantic Maritime Services Inc 2800 Post Oak Blvd Suite 5450 Houston TX 77056 713-621-7800 960-7560

Atwood Oceanics Inc 15835 Park Ten Place Dr Suite 200 Houston TX 77084 281-749-7800 492-0345
NYSE: ATW ■ *TF:* 800-231-5924 ■ *Web:* www.atwd.com

Berenergy Corp PO Box 5850 Denver CO 80217 303-295-2323 297-3752

BP Exploration (Alaska) Inc (BPXA) PO Box 196612 Anchorage AK 95519 907-561-5111

Bronco Drilling Co Inc 16217 N May St Edmond OK 73013 405-242-4444 285-9234
NASDAQ: BRNC ■ *Web:* broncodrill.com

Callon Petroleum Co 200 N Canal St Natchez MS 39120 601-442-1601 446-1410
NYSE: CPE ■ *TF:* 800-541-1294 ■ *Web:* www.callon.com

Chesley Pruet 315 E Oak St Rm 100 El Dorado AR 71730 870-863-7196 863-0077

Cyclone Drilling Inc PO Box 908 Gillette WY 82717 307-682-4161 682-3158
TF: 800-318-3724 ■ *Web:* www.cyclonedrilling.com

Diamond Offshore Drilling Inc 15415 Katy Fwy Houston TX 77094 281-492-5300 492-5316
NYSE: DO ■ *TF:* 800-848-1980 ■ *Web:* www.diamondoffshore.com

Drilex A Baker Hughes Co 2001 Rankin Rd Houston TX 77073 713-625-4200 625-5672

Ensco International Inc 500 N Akard St Suite 4300 Dallas TX 75201 214-397-3000 397-3376
NYSE: ESV ■ *TF:* 800-423-8006 ■ *Web:* www.enscous.com

Ensign Energy Services Inc 400 5th Ave SW Suite 1000 Calgary AB T2P0L6 403-262-1361 262-8215
Web: www.ensignenergy.com

Exploration Co The 777 E Sonterra Blvd Suite 350 San Antonio TX 78232 210-496-5300 496-3232
NASDAQ: TXCO ■ *TF:* 877-912-8926 ■ *Web:* www.txco.com

Fairman Drilling Co PO Box 288 Du Bois PA 15801 814-371-8410 371-8705
TF: 800-225-6540 ■ *Web:* www.fairmandrilling.com

GlobalSantaFe Corp 15375 Memorial Dr Houston TX 77079 281-925-6000 925-6010
NYSE: GSF ■ *TF:* 800-231-5754 ■ *Web:* www.globalsantafe.com

Grey Wolf Inc 10370 Richmond Ave Suite 600 Houston TX 77042 713-435-6100 435-6170
AMEX: GW ■ *TF:* 800-553-7563 ■ *Web:* www.greywolfdrilling.com

Halliburton Energy Services 10200 Bellaire Blvd Houston TX 77072 281-575-4400 575-5939
Web: www.halliburton.com/

Helmerich & Payne Inc 1437 S Boulder Ave Tulsa OK 74119 918-742-5531 588-5470
NYSE: HP ■ *TF:* 800-331-7250 ■ *Web:* www.hpinc.com

Hercules Offshore Inc 11 Greenway Plaza Suite 2950 Houston TX 77046 713-979-9300 979-9301
NASDAQ: HERO ■ *Web:* www.herculesoffshore.com

Justiss Oil Co Inc PO Box 2990 Jena LA 71342 318-992-4111 992-7201
TF: 800-256-2501 ■ *Web:* www.justissoil.com

Leonard Hudson Drilling Co 601 N Price Rd Pampa TX 79065 806-665-1816 665-0243
TF: 800-826-9587

Nabors Alaska Drilling Inc 2525 C St Suite 200 Anchorage AK 99503 907-263-6000 563-3734
Web: www.nabors.com/alaska

Nabors Drilling International Ltd 515 W Greens Rd Suite 1000 Houston TX 77067 281-874-0035 872-5205
TF: 877-622-6777 ■ *Web:* www.nabors.com/international

Nabors Drilling USA Inc 515 W Greens Rd Suite 1000 Houston TX 77067 281-874-0035 872-5205
TF: 888-622-6777 ■ *Web:* www.nabors.com/us

Nabors Industries Ltd 515 W Greens Rd Suite 1200 Houston TX 77067 281-874-0035 872-5205
NYSE: NBR ■ *TF:* 888-622-6777 ■ *Web:* www.nabors.com

Noble Corp 13135 S Dairy Ashford Rd Suite 800 Sugar Land TX 77478 281-276-6100 491-2092
NYSE: NE ■ *TF:* 800-231-6326 ■ *Web:* www.noblecorp.com

ONEOK Resources Co 100 W 5th St Tulsa OK 74103 918-588-7700 588-7331*
**Fax:* Hum Res ■ *Web:* www.oneok.com

Parker Drilling Co 1401 Enclave Pkwy Suite 600 Houston TX 77077 281-406-2000 406-2001
NYSE: PKD ■ *TF:* 800-545-3645 ■ *Web:* www.parkerdrilling.com

Patterson Drilling Co PO Box 1416 Snyder TX 79550 325-574-6300 574-6390
TF: 800-245-0167

Patterson-UTI Energy Inc 4510 Lamesa Hwy Snyder TX 79549 325-573-1104 574-6390
NASDAQ: PTEN ■ *TF:* 800-245-0167 ■ *Web:* www.patenergy.com

Pioneer Drilling Co 1250 NE Loop 410 Suite 1000 San Antonio TX 78209 210-828-7689 447-6080
AMEX: PDC ■ *Web:* www.pioneerdrlg.com

Precision Drilling Corp 150 6th Ave SW Suite 4200 Calgary AB T2P3Y7 403-716-4500 716-4869
NYSE: PDS ■ *Web:* www.precisiondrilling.com

Pride Offshore Inc 410 S Van Ave Houma LA 70363 985-872-4700 857-4759
TF: 800-624-1106

Questar Exploration & Production Co 180 E 100 South Salt Lake City UT 84145 801-324-2600 324-2066
Web: www.denbury.com

Range Resources Corp 777 Main St Suite 800 Fort Worth TX 76102 817-870-2601 870-2316
NYSE: RRC ■ *Web:* www.rangeresources.com

Reliance Well Service PO Box 787 Magnolia AR 71754 870-234-2700 234-4776
TF: 800-458-6451

Rowan Drilling Co Inc 2800 Post Oak Blvd Suite 5450 Houston TX 77056 713-621-7800 960-7560

Rowan International Inc 2800 Post Oak Blvd Suite 5450 Houston TX 77056 713-621-7800 960-7560

Rowan Marine Services Inc 2800 Post Oak Blvd Suite 5450 Houston TX 77056 713-621-7800 960-7560

Rowandrill Inc 2800 Post Oak Blvd Suite 5450 Houston TX 77056 713-621-7800 960-7560

Shell Oil Co 910 Louisanna St Houston TX 77002 713-241-6161 241-4044
TF: 888-467-4355 ■ *Web:* www.shellus.com

Sperry Sun Drilling Services Inc
3000 North Sam Houston Pkwy E Houston TX 77032 281-871-4000 871-5565*
**Fax:* Hum Res

TODCO 2000 W Sam Houston Pkwy S Suite 800 Houston TX 77042 713-278-6000 278-6100
NYSE: THE ■ *TF:* 800-328-7447 ■ *Web:* www.theoffshoredrillingcompany.com

Total Energy Services Ltd 300 5th Ave SW Suite 2550 Calgary AB T2P3C4 403-216-3939 234-8731
TSX: TOT ■ *TF:* 877-818-6825 ■ *Web:* www.totalenergy.to

Transocean Inc 4 Greenway Plaza Houston TX 77046 713-232-7500 232-7027
NYSE: RIG ■ *TF:* 888-748-6334 ■ *Web:* www.deepwater.com

Tri-Valley Corp 4550 California Ave Suite 600 Bakersfield CA 93309 661-864-0500 864-0600
AMEX: TIV ■ *TF:* 800-579-9314 ■ *Web:* www.tri-valleycorp.com

True Drilling LLC 455 N Poplar PO Drawer 2360 Casper WY 82602 307-237-9301 266-0373
Web: www.truecos.com/Drilling/

Union Drilling Inc 4055 International Plaza Suite 160 Fort Worth TX 76109 817-735-8793 546-4391
NASDAQ: UDRL ■ *TF:* 800-352-3839 ■ *Web:* www.uniond.com

Unit Corp 7130 S Lewis Ave Suite 1000 Tulsa OK 74136 918-493-7700 493-7711
NYSE: UNT ■ *TF:* 800-722-3612 ■ *Web:* www.unitcorp.com

Unit Drilling Co PO Box 702500 Tulsa OK 74170 918-493-7700 493-7711
TF: 800-722-3612 ■ *Web:* www.unitdrilling.com

Phone | Fax

Vermilion Energy Trust 2800 400 4th Ave SW....................Calgary AB T2P0J4 403-269-4884 269-6767
TSX: VET.un ■ *TF:* 866-895-8101 ■ *Web:* www.vermilionenergy.com

Westside Energy Corp 3131 Turtle Creek Blvd Suite 1300............Dallas TX 75219 214-522-8990 916-1401*
AMEX: WHT ■ **Fax Area Code:* 469 ■ *Web:* www.westsideenergy.com

544 OILS & GREASES - LUBRICATING

SEE ALSO Chemicals - Specialty p. 1442; Petroleum Refineries p. 2108

Phone | Fax

Acheson Colloids Co 1600 Washington Ave....................Port Huron MI 48060 810-984-5581 984-1446
TF: 800-255-1908 ■ *Web:* www.achesonindustries.com

American Grease Stick Co 2651 Hoyt St...............Muskegon Heights MI 49444 231-733-2101 733-1784
TF: 800-253-0403 ■ *Web:* www.agscompany.com

American Lubricants Co 1227 Deeds Ave PO Box 696.............Dayton OH 45401 937-222-2851 461-7729

Amsoil Inc 925 Tower Ave....................Superior WI 54880 715-392-7101 392-5225
TF Sales: 800-777-7094 ■ *Web:* www.amsoil.com

Anderol Inc 215 Merry Ln PO Box 518..............East Hanover NJ 07936 973-887-7410 887-8404
TF: 888-263-3765 ■ *Web:* www.anderol.com

Battenfeld Grease & Oil Corp of New York
1174 Erie Ave....................North Tonawanda NY 14120 716-695-2100 695-0367
Web: www.battenfeld-grease.com

Bel Ray Co Inc PO Box 526....................Farmingdale NJ 07727 732-938-2421 938-4232
Web: www.belray.com

Benz Oil Inc 2724 W Hampton Ave....................Milwaukee WI 53209 414-442-2900 442-8388
TF: 800-991-2369 ■ *Web:* www.benzoil.com

BG Products Inc 740 S Wichita St PO Box 1282..................Wichita KS 67201 316-265-2686 265-1082
TF: 800-961-6228 ■ *Web:* www.bgprod.com

Blachford Corp 401 Center Rd....................Frankfort IL 60423 815-464-2100 464-2112
TF: 800-435-5942 ■ *Web:* blachford.com

BP Lubricants USA Inc 1500 Valley Rd....................Wayne NJ 07470 973-633-2200 633-9867
TF: 800-633-6163 ■ *Web:* www.bp.com/lubricanthome.do

Break-Free Inc 13386 International Pkwy....................Jacksonville FL 32218 904-741-5400 741-5406
Web: www.break-free.com

Castrol Industrial North America Inc 150 W Warrenville Rd.......Naperville IL 60563 877-641-1600 648-9801
Web: www.castrol.com

Cenex 5500 Cenex Dr....................Inver Grove Heights MN 55077 651-355-6000
TF: 800-232-3639 ■ *Web:* www.cenex.com

Chem-Trend LP 1445 W McPherson Park Rd PO Box 860..........Howell MI 48844 517-546-4520
TF: 800-727-7730 ■ *Web:* www.chemtrend.com

Colorado Petroleum Products Co 4080 Globeville Rd.............Denver CO 80216 303-294-0302 294-9128
TF: 800-580-4080 ■ *Web:* www.colopetro.com

Condat Corp 250 S Industrial Dr....................Saline MI 48176 734-944-4994 944-4995
TF: 800-883-7876 ■ *Web:* www.condatcorp.com

CRC Industries Inc 885 Louis Dr....................Warminster PA 18974 215-674-4300 674-2196
TF Cust Svc: 800-556-5074 ■ *Web:* www.crcindustries.com

D-A Lubricant Co 1340 W 29th St....................Indianapolis IN 46208 317-923-5321 923-3884*
**Fax:* Cust Svc ■ *TF:* 800-645-5823 ■ *Web:* www.dalube.com

DA Stuart Co 4580 Weaver Pkwy....................Warrenville IL 60555 630-393-0833 393-0834
TF: 800-323-1438 ■ *Web:* www.dastuart.com

Delta Petroleum Co 10352 River Rd....................Saint Rose LA 70087 504-467-1399 467-1398
Web: www.deltacompanies.net

Dylon Industries 7700 Clinton Rd....................Cleveland OH 44144 216-651-1300 651-1777
TF: 800-237-8246 ■ *Web:* www.dylon.com

Elco Corp 1000 Belt Line St....................Cleveland OH 44109 216-749-2605 749-7462
TF: 800-321-0467 ■ *Web:* www.elcocorp.com

Ergon Inc Petroleum Specialties Marketing Div
2829 Jakeland Rd PO Box 1639....................Jackson MS 39215 601-933-3000 933-3373*
**Fax:* Hum Res ■ *TF:* 800-824-2626

Fiske Brothers Refining Co 129 Lockwood St....................Newark NJ 07105 973-589-9150 589-4432
TF: 800-733-4755 ■ *Web:* www.lubriplate.com

Fuchs Lubricants Canada Ltd Eastern Canada Div
405 Dobbie Dr....................Cambridge ON N1R5X9 519-622-2040 622-2220
Web: www.fuchs.ca

Fuchs Lubricants Canada Ltd Western Canada Div
19829-99A Ave....................Langley BC V1M3G4 604-888-1552 888-1145
Web: www.fuchs.ca

Fuchs Lubricants Co 17050 Lathrop Ave....................Harvey IL 60426 708-333-8900 333-9180
TF: 800-323-7755 ■ *Web:* www.fuchs.com

Hangsterfer's Laboratories Inc 175 Ogden Rd....................Mantua NJ 08051 856-468-0216 468-0200
TF: 800-433-5823 ■ *Web:* www.hangsterfers.com

Hercules Chemical Co Inc 111 South St....................Passaic NJ 07055 973-778-5000 777-4115
TF: 800-221-9330 ■ *Web:* www.herchem.com

Houghton International Inc 945 Madison Ave PO Box 930......Valley Forge PA 19482 610-666-4000 666-1376
TF: 888-459-9844 ■ *Web:* www.houghtonintl.com

Hydrotex Inc 1825 Monetary Ln Suite 100....................Carrollton TX 75006 972-389-8500 389-8526
TF: 800-527-9439 ■ *Web:* www.hydrotexlube.com

JD Streett & Co Inc 144 Weldon Pkwy....................Maryland Heights MO 63043 314-432-6600 432-4248
TF: 800-678-6600 ■ *Web:* www.jdstreett.com

Jesco Resources Inc PO Box 12337....................North Kansas City MO 64116 816-471-4590 471-2240
TF: 800-421-4590 ■ *Web:* www.jescolube.com

Jet-Lube Inc 4849 Homestead Rd Suite 232 PO Box 21258........Houston TX 77226 713-674-7617 678-4604
TF: 800-538-5823 ■ *Web:* www.jetlube.com

Kluber Lubrication North America LP 32 Industrial Dr.......Londonderry NH 03053 603-647-4104 647-4106
TF: 888-455-8237 ■ *Web:* www.kluberna.com

LPS Laboratories 4647 Hugh Howell Rd....................Tucker GA 30084 770-934-7800 543-1563*
**Fax Area Code:* 800 ■ *TF:* 800-241-8334 ■ *Web:* www.lpslabs.com

Lubricating Specialties Co 8015 Paramount Blvd.............Pico Rivera CA 90660 562-776-4000 776-4004
Web: www.lsc-online.com

Lubrication Engineers Inc 300 Bailey Ave....................Fort Worth TX 76107 817-834-6321 228-1142*
**Fax Area Code:* 800 ■ **Fax:* Sales ■ *TF:* 800-537-7683 ■ *Web:* www.le-inc.com

Lubrication Technologies Inc 900 Mendelssohn Ave N........Golden Valley MN 55427 763-545-0707 545-9256
TF: 800-328-5573 ■ *Web:* www.lube-tech.com

Lubrizol Corp 29400 Lakeland Blvd....................Wickliffe OH 44092 440-943-4200 347-3583
NYSE: LZ ■ *TF:* 800-522-4125 ■ *Web:* www.lubrizol.com

Master Chemical Corp 501 W Boundry St PO Box 10001........Perrysburg OH 43552 419-874-7902 874-0684
TF Sales: 800-874-6329 ■ *Web:* www.masterchemical.com

Metalworking Lubricants Co 25 W Silverdome Industrial Park.......Pontiac MI 48342 248-332-3500 332-4959
TF: 800-394-5494 ■ *Web:* www.metalworkinglubricants.com

Northland Products Co PO Box 418....................Waterloo IA 50704 319-234-5585 234-5580
TF: 800-772-1724

Oil Center Research LLC 106 Montrose Ave....................Lafayette LA 70503 337-993-3559 993-3149
TF: 800-256-8977 ■ *Web:* www.oilcenter.com

Oil Chem Inc 711 W 12th St....................Flint MI 48503 810-235-3040 238-5260
Web: www.oilcheminc.com

Orelube Corp 20 Sawgrass Dr....................Bellport NY 11713 631-205-9700 205-9797
TF: 800-645-9124 ■ *Web:* www.orelube.com

Penreco-Magie Bros Oil Co 9101 Fullerton Ave.............Franklin Park IL 60131 847-455-4500 455-0383
TF: 800-624-4347 ■ *Web:* www.penreco.com/about/magiebrosinfo.asp

Phoenix Oil Co 625 5th St....................Augusta GA 30903 706-722-5321 722-5973

Primrose Oil Co Inc 11444 Benton Dr PO Box 29665.............Dallas TX 75229 972-241-1100 241-4188
TF: 800-275-2772 ■ *Web:* www.primrose.com

Phone | Fax

Richards-Apex Inc 4202-24 Main St....................Philadelphia PA 19127 215-487-1100 487-3090
Web: www.richardsapex.com

Schaeffer Mfg Co Inc 102 Barton St....................Saint Louis MO 63104 314-865-4100 865-4107
TF Cust Svc: 800-325-9962 ■ *Web:* www.schaefferoil.com

Sentinel Lubricants Corp 15755 NW 15th Ave PO Box 694240.......Miami FL 33269 305-625-6400 625-6565
TF: 800-842-6400 ■ *Web:* www.sentinelsynthetic.com

Shell Lubricants 5700 S Lee Rd....................Cleveland OH 44137 216-332-4200 332-4343
TF: 800-321-8577

Southwestern Petroleum Corp 534 N Main St....................Fort Worth TX 76106 817-332-2336 877-4047
TF: 800-877-9372 ■ *Web:* www.swepcousa.com

STP Products Mfg Co 1221 Broadway....................Oakland CA 94612 510-271-7000 832-1463
TF: 888-464-7871 ■ *Web:* www.stp.com

Streett JD & Co Inc 144 Weldon Pkwy....................Maryland Heights MO 63043 314-432-6600 432-4248
TF: 800-678-6600 ■ *Web:* www.jdstreett.com

Stuart DA Co 4580 Weaver Pkwy....................Warrenville IL 60555 630-393-0833 393-0834
TF: 800-323-1438 ■ *Web:* www.dastuart.com

Sun Drilling Products Corp 503 Main St PO Box 129.........Belle Chasse LA 70037 504-393-2778 391-1383
TF: 800-962-6490 ■ *Web:* www.sundrilling.com

Texas Refinery Corp 840 N Main St....................Fort Worth TX 76106 817-332-1161 336-8441
TF: 800-827-0711 ■ *Web:* www.texasrefinery.com

Total Lubricants USA 5 N Stiles St....................Linden NJ 07036 908-862-9300 862-1647
TF: 800-344-2241

Valvoline Co 3499 Blazer Pkwy....................Lexington KY 40509 859-357-7777 357-7918
TF: 800-354-9061 ■ *Web:* www.valvoline.com

Wallover Oil Co Inc 1032 Pennsylvania Ave................East Liverpool OH 43920 330-385-9336 385-9975
TF Sales: 800-662-9626 ■ *Web:* www.walloveroil.com

WD-40 Co 1061 Cudahy Pl....................San Diego CA 92110 619-275-1400 275-5823
NASDAQ: WDFC ■ *TF:* 800-448-9340 ■ *Web:* www.wd40.com

Wynn's Oil Co 1050 W 5th St....................Azusa CA 91702 626-334-0231
TF: 800-989-8363 ■ *Web:* www.wynnsusa.com

545 OPHTHALMIC GOODS

SEE ALSO Personal Protective Equipment & Clothing p. 2105

Phone | Fax

AAi Foster Grant 500 George Washington Hwy................Smithfield RI 02917 401-231-3800 231-4625
TF: 800-388-0258 ■ *Web:* www.fostergrant.com

Advanced Medical Optics Inc (AMO) 1700 E Saint Andrew Pl....Santa Ana CA 92705 714-247-8200 247-8672
NYSE: EYE ■ *TF:* 866-427-8477 ■ *Web:* www.amo-inc.com

Aearo Co 5457 W 79th St....................Indianapolis IN 46268 317-692-6666 692-6772
TF Cust Svc: 800-327-3431 ■ *Web:* www.aearo.com

American Contact Lens Inc 15970 Bernardo Ctr...............San Diego CA 92127 858-487-8684 487-3046
TF: 800-959-4448 ■ *Web:* www.americancontactlens.com

AMO (Advanced Medical Optics Inc) 1700 E Saint Andrew Pl....Santa Ana CA 92705 714-247-8200 247-8672
NYSE: EYE ■ *TF:* 866-427-8477 ■ *Web:* www.amo-inc.com

Art-Craft Optical Co Inc 57 Goodway Dr S....................Rochester NY 14623 585-546-6640 546-5133
TF: 800-828-8288 ■ *Web:* www.artcraftoptical.com

Bausch & Lomb Inc 1400 N Goodman St....................Rochester NY 14609 585-338-6000 338-6007
NYSE: BOL ■ *TF:* 800-344-8815 ■ *Web:* www.bausch.com

Bausch & Lomb Inc Vision Care Div 1400 N Goodman St........Rochester NY 14609 585-338-6000 338-6896
TF: 800-344-8815

Bell Optical Laboratory Inc 2510 Lance Dr....................Dayton OH 45409 937-294-8022 294-5488
TF: 800-543-4864 ■ *Web:* www.bell-optical.com

Bolle Inc 9200 Cody St....................Overland Park KS 66214 913-752-3400 752-3550
TF: 800-222-6553 ■ *Web:* www.bolle.com

Bouton HL Co Inc 11 Kendrick Rd....................Wareham MA 02571 508-295-3300 295-3521
TF Cust Svc: 800-426-1881 ■ *Web:* www.hlbouton.com

Carl Zeiss Optical Inc 13017 N Kingston Ave....................Chester VA 23836 804-530-8300 561-2016*
**Fax Area Code:* 800 ■ *TF Cust Svc:* 800-338-2984 ■ *Web:* www.zeiss.com/optical

Carskadden Optical Co 1525 Highpoint Ct....................Zanesville OH 43701 740-452-9306 452-6119

Charmant USA 400 American Rd....................Morris Plains NJ 07950 973-538-1511 248-1524*
**Fax Area Code:* 800 ■ *TF:* 800-645-2121 ■ *Web:* www.charmant.com

CIBA Vision Corp 11460 Johns Creek Pkwy....................Duluth GA 30097 770-476-3937 242-5214
TF: 800-227-1524 ■ *Web:* www.cibavision.com

Conforma Laboratories Inc 4705 Colley Ave....................Norfolk VA 23508 757-423-5807 423-8706
TF: 800-426-1700 ■ *Web:* www.conforma.com

Cooper Cos Inc 21062 Bake Pkwy Suite 100...............Lake Forest CA 92630 949-597-4700 597-0662
NYSE: COO ■ *TF:* 888-822-2660 ■ *Web:* www.coopercos.com

CooperVision Inc 21062 Bake Pkwy Suite 200...............Lake Forest CA 92630 949-597-8130 597-0663
TF: 800-341-2030 ■ *Web:* www.coopercos.com

Costa Del Mar 123 N Orchard St Bldg 6...............Ormond Beach FL 32174 386-677-3700 677-3737
TF: 800-447-3700 ■ *Web:* www.costadelmar.com

Cumberland Optical Laboratory 806 Olympic St...............Nashville TN 37203 615-254-5868 254-5530
TF: 800-888-8316 ■ *Web:* www.cumberlandoptical.net

DAC Vision 3630 W Miller Suite 350....................Garland TX 75041 972-677-2700 677-2800
TF: 800-800-1550 ■ *Web:* www.dacvision.com

Dakota Smith Signature Eyewear 498 N Oak St...............Inglewood CA 90302 310-330-2700 245-3680*
**Fax Area Code:* 877 ■ *TF:* 800-765-3937 ■ *Web:* www.dakotasmith.com

De'Vons Optics Inc 10823 Bell Ct...............Rancho Cucamonga CA 91730 909-466-4700 466-4703
TF: 888-333-8667 ■ *Web:* www.devonsoptics.com

Dispensers Optical Service Corp 1815 Plantside Dr.............Louisville KY 40299 502-491-3440 499-8445
TF Cust Svc: 800-626-4545 ■ *Web:* www.dosc.com

Duffens Langley Optical Co 8140 Marshall Dr....................Lenexa KS 66214 913-492-5379 888-5375*
**Fax Area Code:* 800 ■ *TF:* 800-888-5379

Essilor of America Inc 13515 N Stemmons Fwy....................Dallas TX 75234 214-496-4000
TF: 800-366-6342 ■ *Web:* www.essilor.com

Eye-Kraft Optical Inc PO Box 400....................Saint Cloud MN 56302 320-251-0141 950-7070*
**Fax Area Code:* 800 ■ *TF:* 888-455-2022 ■ *Web:* www.eyekraft.com

Eyeglass Services Industries 469 Sunrise Hwy.................Lynbrook NY 11563 516-599-1135 599-4825

Eyetech 7016 6th St N....................Oakdale MN 55128 651-501-8114 501-8853
TF: 800-328-9060

Fosta-Tek Optics Inc 320 Hamilton St....................Leominster MA 01453 978-534-6511 537-2168
Web: www.fosta-tek.com

Gargoyles Inc 500 George Washington Hwy....................Smithfield RI 02917 401-231-3800 232-7235
TF: 800-388-0258

Gentex Optics Inc 324 Main St....................Simpson PA 18407 570-282-3550 282-8555
TF: 800-343-6062 ■ *Web:* www.gentexcorp.com

Hilsinger Co 33 W Bacon St....................Plainville MA 02762 508-699-4406 995-2154*
**Fax Area Code:* 800 ■ *TF:* 800-955-6544 ■ *Web:* www.hilco.com

HL Bouton Co Inc 11 Kendrick Rd....................Wareham MA 02571 508-295-3300 295-3521
TF Cust Svc: 800-426-1881 ■ *Web:* www.hlbouton.com

Homer Optical Co Inc 2401 Linden Ln....................Silver Spring MD 20910 301-585-9060 585-5934
TF: 800-627-2710 ■ *Web:* www.homeroptical.com

Hoya Holdings Inc 101 Metro Dr Suite 500....................San Jose CA 95110 408-441-0400 441-9400
Web: www.hoya.co.jp

Icare Industries Inc 4399 35th St N....................Saint Petersburg FL 33714 727-812-3000 522-1408
TF: 800-648-7463 ■ *Web:* www.icarelabs.com

IcareLabs 4399 35th St N....................Saint Petersburg FL 33714 727-812-3000 522-1408
TF: 800-648-7463 ■ *Web:* www.icarelabs.com

Johnson & Johnson Vision Care Inc 7500 Centurion Pkwy......Jacksonville FL 32256 904-443-1000 443-1083
TF: 800-874-5278 ■ *Web:* www.jnjvision.com

	Phone	Fax
LBI Eyewear 20801 Nordhoff St Chatsworth CA 91311 *TF:* 800-423-5175 ■ *Web:* lbieyewear.com	818-407-1890	407-1895
Luxottica Group 44 Harbor Park Dr Port Washington NY 11050 *TF:* 800-451-4839 ■ *Web:* www.luxotticagroup.com	516-484-3800	484-2876
Magnivision 3700 Commerce Pkwy Miramar FL 33025 **Fax:* Cust Svc ■ *TF:* 800-237-4231 ■ *Web:* www.magnivision.com	954-986-9000	986-0539*
Marchon Eyewear Inc 35 Hub Dr Melville NY 11747 *TF:* 800-645-1300 ■ *Web:* www.marchon.com	631-755-2020	755-2045
Maui Jim Inc 721 Wainee St Lahaina HI 96761 *TF:* 800-848-3644 ■ *Web:* www.mauijim.com	808-661-8841	661-0351
Neostyle Eyewear Corp 2605 State St San Diego CA 92103 *TF:* 800-854-2782 ■ *Web:* www.neostyle.com	619-299-0755	296-2281
Oakley Inc 1 Icon Foothill Ranch CA 92610 *NYSE:* OO ■ **Fax:* Cust Svc ■ *TF Cust Svc:* 800-403-7449 ■ *Web:* oakley.com	949-951-0991	699-3519*
Ocular Sciences Inc 475 Eccles Ave South San Francisco CA 94080 **Fax Area Code:* 888 ■ *TF:* 800-628-5367 ■ *Web:* www.ocularsciences.com	650-583-1400	301-0264*
Oliver Peoples Inc 8447 Wilshire Blvd 4th Fl Beverly Hills CA 90211 *TF:* 888-568-1655 ■ *Web:* www.oliverpeoples.com	323-951-0010	951-0030
Omega Optical Co Inc 13515 N Stemmons Fwy Dallas TX 75234 *TF:* 800-366-6342	972-241-4141	241-1162
Orange 21 Inc 2070 Las Palmas Dr Carlsbad CA 92009 *NASDAQ:* ORNG ■ *TF:* 800-779-3937 ■ *Web:* www.spyoptic.com	760-804-8420	804-8421
Rite-Style Optical Co 12240 Emmet St Omaha NE 68164 *TF:* 800-373-3200	402-492-8822	492-9414
Rosin Eyecare Center 6233 W Cermak Rd Berwyn IL 60402 *Web:* www.rosineyecare.com	708-749-2020	749-7944
Sax North Atlantic Services Inc 432 Fairfield Ave Stamford CT 06902 **Fax Area Code:* 800 ■ *TF:* 800-223-5127	203-348-3645	626-6933*
Serengeti Eyewear Inc 9200 Cody St Overland Park KS 66214 *TF Cust Svc:* 888-838-1449 ■ *Web:* www.serengeti-eyewear.com	913-752-3400	752-3550
Signature Eyewear Inc 498 N Oak St Inglewood CA 90302 **Fax Area Code:* 877 ■ *Web:* www.signatureeyewear.com	310-330-2700	245-3680*
Signet Armorlite Inc 130 N Bingham Dr San Marcos CA 92069 *TF:* 800-759-0075 ■ *Web:* www.signetarmorlite.com	760-744-4000	471-6255
Soderberg Inc 230 Eva St Saint Paul MN 55107 *TF:* 800-755-5655 ■ *Web:* www.soseyes.com	651-291-1400	291-7764
SOLA International Inc 10590 W Ocean Air Dr Suite 300 San Diego CA 92130 *Web:* www.sola.com	858-509-9899	509-9898
SOLA Optical USA Inc 2277 Pine View Way Petaluma CA 94954 *Web:* www.sola.com	707-763-9911	765-1378
Southern Optical Co Inc 1909 N Church St Greensboro NC 27405 *TF:* 800-888-8842	336-272-8146	273-6625
STAAR Surgical Co 1911 Walker Ave Monrovia CA 91016 *NASDAQ:* STAA ■ **Fax:* Mktg ■ *TF:* 800-292-7902 ■ *Web:* www.staar.com	626-303-7902	303-2962*
Standard Optical Co 1901 W Parkway Blvd West Valley City UT 84119 *TF:* 800-393-2273 ■ *Web:* www.standardoptical.net	801-972-0203	954-0054
Sun Rams Products Inc 8736 Lion St Rancho Cucamonga CA 91730 *TF:* 800-866-7267 ■ *Web:* www.sunrams.com	909-980-1160	941-0321
Titmus Optical Inc 3811 Corporate Dr Petersburg VA 23805 *TF Cust Svc:* 800-446-1802 ■ *Web:* www.titmus.com	804-732-6121	862-3734
Transitions Optical Inc 9251 Belcher Rd Pinellas Park FL 33782 *TF:* 800-848-1506 ■ *Web:* www.transitions.com	727-545-0400	546-3394
Universal/Univis Inc 23 W Bacon St Plainville MA 02762 *TF:* 800-899-5432	508-695-3584	695-6221
US Vision Inc 1 Harmon Dr Glen Oaks Industrial Pk Glendora NJ 08012 *TF:* 800-524-0789 ■ *Web:* www.usvision.com	856-228-1000	232-1848
Vision-Ease Lens Inc 6975 Saukview Dr Saint Cloud MN 56303 *TF Cust Svc:* 800-367-2544 ■ *Web:* www.vision-ease.com	320-251-8782	251-4312
Viva International Group 3140 Rt 22 W Branchburg NJ 08876 **Fax Area Code:* 800 ■ *TF:* 800-345-8482 ■ *Web:* www.vivagroup.com	908-595-6200	884-2329*
Walman Optical Co Inc 801 12th Ave N Minneapolis MN 55411 *TF:* 800-873-9256 ■ *Web:* www.walman.com	612-520-6000	520-6069
X-Cel Optical Co Inc 806 S Benton Dr Sauk Rapids MN 56379 *TF:* 800-747-9235 ■ *Web:* www.x-celoptical.com	320-251-8404	251-0511
Younger Optics 2925 California St Torrance CA 90503 *TF:* 800-366-5367 ■ *Web:* www.youngeroptics.com	310-783-1533	783-6477
Zeiss Optical Inc 13017 N Kingston Ave Chester VA 23836 **Fax Area Code:* 800 ■ *TF Cust Svc:* 800-338-2984 ■ *Web:* www.zeiss.com/optical	804-530-8300	561-2016*

546 OPTICAL GOODS STORES

	Phone	Fax
America's Best Contacts & Eyeglasses 7255 N Crescent Blvd Pennsauken NJ 08110 *TF:* 800-896-7247 ■ *Web:* www.twopair.com	856-486-4300	486-9615
Bard Optical 7722 N Crestline Dr Peoria IL 61615 *TF:* 800-752-3295 ■ *Web:* www.bardoptical.com	309-693-9540	693-9542
Cliff Weil Inc 8043 Industrial Pk Rd Mechanicsville VA 23116 *TF:* 800-446-9345 ■ *Web:* www.cliffweil.com	804-746-1321	746-2595
Colonial Opticians 4942 St Elmo Ave Bethesda MD 20814	301-657-3332	657-4092
Consolidated Vision Group Inc DBA America's Best Contacts & Eyeglasses 7255 N Crescent Blvd Pennsauken NJ 08110 *TF:* 800-896-7247 ■ *Web:* www.twopair.com	856-486-4300	486-9615
Cooperative Optical 2424 E Eight-Mile Rd Detroit MI 48234 *TF:* 800-368-5160 ■ *Web:* www.coopoptical.com	313-366-5100	366-2246
Crown Vision Center 211 E Broadway Alton IL 62002 *Web:* www.crownvisioncenter.com	314-741-8183	
DOC Optics Corp 19800 W Eight-Mile Rd Southfield MI 48075 *TF:* 800-289-3937 ■ *Web:* www.docoptics.com	248-354-7100	353-1603
Doctors Vision Center 413 Mill St Rocky Mount NC 27804 *Web:* www.doctorsvisioncenter.com	252-985-1371	985-2303
Dr Bizer's Vision World 516 E Lewis & Clark Pkwy Clarksville IN 47129	812-282-2020	288-2807
Dr Tavel Optical Group 2839 Lafayette Rd Indianapolis IN 46222 *Web:* www.taveloptical.com	317-924-1300	924-3741
Emerging Vision Inc 100 Quentin Roosevelt Blvd Suite 508 Garden City NY 11530 *TF:* 800-332-6302	516-390-2100	390-2110
Empire Vision Centers 2921 Erie Blvd E Syracuse NY 13224 *TF:* 877-446-3145 ■ *Web:* www.empirevision.com	315-446-5120	
Europtics Inc 2960 E 2nd Ave Suite C Denver CO 80206 *Web:* www.eoptics.com	303-322-7507	322-7591
Exact Eye Care 431 Pierce St Sioux City IA 51101 *Web:* www.exacteyecare.com	712-252-4691	252-5339
Eye Care Centers of America Inc 11103 West Ave San Antonio TX 78213 *TF:* 800-669-1183 ■ *Web:* www.ecca.com	210-340-3531	524-6784
Eye To Eye Vision Center 2100 Roswell Rd Suite 100D Marietta GA 30062 *Web:* www.eyetoeyevisioncenter.com	770-578-1900	578-6623
Eye Glass World Inc 3801 S Congress Ave Lake Worth FL 33461 **Fax:* Hum Res ■ *TF:* 800-529-4345 ■ *Web:* www.eyeglassworld.com	561-965-9110	969-7840*
Eye-Mart Express Inc 2110 Hutton Dr Suite 100 Carrollton TX 75006 *TF:* 800-755-3936 ■ *Web:* www.eyemartexpress.com	972-488-2002	488-8563
Eye-Mate Inc 77 N Centre Ave Rockville Centre NY 11570 *TF:* 800-393-6283 ■ *Web:* www.eyemate.com	516-678-9613	678-0626
Eyemasters 11103 West Ave San Antonio TX 78213 *Web:* www.eyemasters.com	210-340-3531	
Folline Vision Centers Inc 1670 Springdale Dr Suite 6 Camden SC 29020	803-432-2573	432-4618
For Eyes/Insight Optical 285 W 74th Pl Hialeah FL 33014 *TF:* 800-367-3937 ■ *Web:* www.foreyes.com	305-557-9004	556-2575
General Vision Services LLC 520 8th Ave 9th Fl New York NY 10018 *TF:* 800-847-4661 ■ *Web:* www.generalvision.com	212-594-2580	967-4781
H Rubin Vision Centers 7539 Garners Sperry Rd Columbia SC 29209 **Fax:* Cust Svc ■ *Web:* www.hrubinvision.com	803-779-9313	779-9551*
Henry Ford OptimEyes 655 W 13-Mile Rd Madison Heights MI 48071 *TF:* 800-393-2273 ■ *Web:* www.optimeyes.com	248-588-9300	588-3355
Horner-Rausch Optical 968 Main St Nashville TN 37206	615-226-0251	226-8527
JC Penney Optical Co 6501 Legacy Dr Plano TX 75024 *Web:* www.jcpeyes.com	972-431-1000	
LensCrafters Inc 4000 Luxottica Pl Mason OH 45040 *TF:* 800-283-5367 ■ *Web:* www.lenscrafters.com	513-765-6000	
Lockport Optical 36 East Ave Lockport NY 14094	716-434-6900	434-8461
Magnifying Center 10086 W McNab Rd Tamarac FL 33321 *TF:* 800-364-1612 ■ *Web:* www.magnifyingcenter.com	954-722-1580	726-1757
Malbar Vision Center 409 N 78th St Omaha NE 68114 *TF:* 800-701-3937 ■ *Web:* www.malbar.com	402-393-4500	393-7457
National Vision Inc 296 Grayson Hwy Lawrenceville GA 30045 *TF:* 800-571-5202 ■ *Web:* www.nationalvision.com	770-822-3600	822-3601
Optical Shop of Aspen International 25 Brookline Dr Aliso Viejo CA 92656 *TF:* 800-647-2345 ■ *Web:* www.osainternational.com	949-360-1010	425-4785
OptiCare Health Systems Inc 87 Grandview Ave Waterbury CT 06708 *TF:* 800-225-5393 ■ *Web:* www.opticare.com	203-574-2020	596-2230
Opticare Vision Center 700 S Main St Suite 105 Lapeer MI 48446	810-664-1329	664-1307
Palmetto Optical 5115 Forest Dr Suite B-160 Columbia SC 29206 *TF:* 800-845-2231	803-799-8168	799-0854
Pearle Vision Inc 4000 Luxottica Pl Mason OH 45040 **Fax Area Code:* 330 ■ *TF:* 800-282-3931 ■ *Web:* www.pearlevision.com	877-486-6486	486-3596*
Penney JC Optical Co 6501 Legacy Dr Plano TX 75024 *Web:* www.jcpeyes.com	972-431-1000	
ProCare Vision Centers Inc 1949 Newark-Granville Rd Granville OH 43023 *TF:* 800-837-5569	740-587-3937	587-3589
Raymond Opticians Inc 359 Main St Mount Kisco NY 10549	914-666-4202	244-1542
Refac Optical Group 5 Harmon Dr Bldg D Blackwood NJ 08012 *AMEX:* REF ■ *Web:* www.refacopticalgroup.com	856-228-0077	228-5577
Rite-Style Optical Co 12240 Emmet St Omaha NE 68164 *TF:* 800-373-3200	402-492-8822	492-9414
Rosin Eyecare Center 6233 W Cermak Rd Berwyn IL 60402 *Web:* www.rosineyecare.com	708-749-2020	749-7944
Rubin H Vision Centers 7539 Garners Sperry Rd Columbia SC 29209 **Fax:* Cust Svc ■ *Web:* www.hrubinvision.com	803-779-9313	779-9551*
Rubold Management Co 3102 Millwood Ave Columbia SC 29205 **Fax:* Cust Svc ■ *Web:* www.primecarevision.com	803-251-3308	251-3303*
Rx Optical 1700 S Park St Kalamazoo MI 49001 *TF:* 800-792-2737 ■ *Web:* www.rxoptical.com	269-342-0003	342-4284
Saint Charles Vision 840 St Charles Ave New Orleans LA 70118 *Web:* www.stcharlesvision.com	504-522-0826	866-8217
ShopKo Optical Centers 1450 W Main Ave De Pere WI 54115 *Web:* www.shopko.com	920-429-7200	429-7889
Singer Specs 211 W Lincoln Hwy Exton PA 19341	610-524-8886	524-7333
Southern Optical 501 Merritt Ave Nashville TN 37203 *TF:* 800-333-8498	615-256-6631	259-2303
Standard Optical Co 1901 W Parkway Blvd West Valley City UT 84119 *TF:* 800-393-2273 ■ *Web:* www.standardoptical.net	801-972-0203	954-0054
Stein Optical Express 825 W Mooreland Blvd Waukesha WI 53188 *TF:* 800-349-5120 ■ *Web:* www.ecca.com	262-542-9885	542-4740
Sterling Optical 100 Quentin Roosevelt Blvd Garden City NY 11530 *TF:* 800-332-6302 ■ *Web:* www.sterlingoptical.com	516-390-2100	390-2110
Sunglass Hut International Inc 4000 Luxottica Pl Mason OH 45040 *TF:* 800-767-0990 ■ *Web:* www.sunglasshut.com	513-765-6000	
SVS Vision 140 Macomb Pl Mount Clemens MI 48043 *TF:* 800-225-3095 ■ *Web:* www.svsvision.com	586-468-7370	468-7682
Today's Vision 6970 FM 1960 W Suite A Houston TX 77069 *Web:* www.todaysvision.com	281-469-2020	469-7531
Total Vision Care 854 Plaza Blvd Lancaster PA 17601	717-295-3111	295-7320
Union Eyecare Centers 4750 Beidler Rd Willoughby OH 44094 *TF:* 800-443-9699 ■ *Web:* www.unioneyecare.com	216-986-9700	986-1996
United Optical 2811 Lord Baltimore Dr Baltimore MD 21244 **Fax Area Code:* 410 ■ *Web:* www.united-optical.com	888-267-8422	265-6068*
US Vision Inc 1 Harmon Dr Glen Oaks Industrial Pk Glendora NJ 08012 *TF:* 800-524-0789 ■ *Web:* www.usvision.com	856-228-1000	232-1848
Vision World 469 Sunrise Hwy Lynbrook NY 11563	516-599-1135	599-4825
Visionworks 11103 West Ave San Antonio TX 78213 *Web:* www.visionworkseyewear.com	210-340-3531	
Weil Cliff Inc 8043 Industrial Pk Rd Mechanicsville VA 23116 *TF:* 800-446-9345 ■ *Web:* www.cliffweil.com	804-746-1321	746-2595

547 OPTICAL INSTRUMENTS & LENSES

SEE ALSO Laboratory Analytical Instruments p. 1884

	Phone	Fax
3M Precision Optics Inc 4000 McMann Rd Cincinnati OH 45245 *TF:* 800-877-0787 ■ *Web:* www.3mprecisionoptics.com	513-752-7000	752-2841
ABB Optical Inc 5360 NW 35th Ave Fort Lauderdale FL 33309 *TF:* 800-852-8089 ■ *Web:* www.abboptical.com	954-733-2300	735-4386
Allergan Inc PO Box 19534 Irvine CA 92623 *NYSE:* AGN ■ **Fax:* Mail Rm ■ *TF:* 800-347-4500 ■ *Web:* www.allergan.com	714-246-4500	246-4971*
Applied Fiber Inc 1300 W Oakridge Dr Albany GA 31707 *TF:* 800-226-5394 ■ *Web:* www.appliedfiber.com	229-888-3212	888-3119
Axsys Technologies Inc 175 Capital Blvd Suite 103 Rocky Hill CT 06067 *NASDAQ:* AXYS ■ *Web:* www.axsys.com	860-257-0200	594-5750
Burris Co Inc 331 E 8th St Greeley CO 80631 *TF:* 888-228-7747 ■ *Web:* www.burrisoptics.com	970-356-1670	356-8702
Bushnell Corp DBA Bushnell Performance Optics 9200 Cody St Overland Park KS 66214 *TF:* 800-423-3537 ■ *Web:* www.bushnell.com	913-752-3400	752-3550
Bushnell Performance Optics 9200 Cody St Overland Park KS 66214 *TF:* 800-423-3537 ■ *Web:* www.bushnell.com	913-752-3400	752-3550
Carl Zeiss Inc 1 Zeiss Dr Thornwood NY 10594 *Web:* www.zeiss.com	914-747-1800	682-8296
Carl Zeiss Optical Inc 13017 N Kingston Ave Chester VA 23836 **Fax Area Code:* 800 ■ *TF Cust Svc:* 800-338-2984 ■ *Web:* www.zeiss.com/optical	804-530-8300	561-2016*
Coherent Auburn Group 2303 Lindbergh St Auburn CA 95602 **Fax:* Hum Res ■ *TF Sales:* 800-343-4912 ■ *Web:* www.coherentinc.com	530-823-9550	889-5363*
CST/Berger Corp 255 W Fleming St Watseka IL 60970 *TF:* 800-435-1859 ■ *Web:* www.cstsurvey.com	815-432-5237	432-5390
Daedal Div Parker Hannifin Corp 1140 Sandy Hill Rd Irwin PA 15642 *TF:* 800-245-6903 ■ *Web:* www.parker.com/daedal	724-861-8200	861-3300
Deltronic Corp 3900 W Segerstrom Ave Santa Ana CA 92704 *TF:* 800-451-6922 ■ *Web:* www.deltronic.com	714-545-0401	641-0946

Phone | Fax

Diversified Optical Products Inc 282 Main St .... Salem NH 03079 603-898-1880 893-4359
TF: 800-230-1600 ■ *Web:* www.diop.com

DRS Sensors & Targeting Systems - Optronics Div
2330 Commerce Park Dr NE Suite 2 .... Palm Bay FL 32905 321-984-9030 984-8746
Web: www.drs.com

Edmund Optics Inc 101 E Gloucester Pike .... Barrington NJ 08007 856-547-3488 573-6295
TF: 800-363-1992 ■ *Web:* www.edmundoptics.com

ELCAN Optical Technologies 450 Leitz Rd .... Midland ON L4R5B8 705-526-5401 526-5831
Web: www.elcan.com

EXFO Burleigh Products Group Inc 7647 Main St Fishers .... Victor NY 14564 585-924-9355 924-9072
TF: 800-663-3936 ■ *Web:* www.exfo.com

Exotic Electro-Optics 36570 Briggs Rd .... Murrieta CA 92563 951-926-2994 926-1984
Web: www.exotic-eo.com

Exotic Materials Inc DBA Exotic Electro-Optics
36570 Briggs Rd .... Murrieta CA 92563 951-926-2994 926-1984
Web: www.exotic-eo.com

Fosta-Tek Optics Inc 320 Hamilton St .... Leominster MA 01453 978-534-6511 537-2168
Web: www.fosta-tek.com

Fraser-Volpe Corp
Warminster Industrial Park 1025 Thomas Dr .... Warminster PA 18974 215-443-5240 443-0966
Web: www.fraser-volpe.com

Fujinon Inc 10 High Point Dr .... Wayne NJ 07470 973-633-5600 633-5216
TF: 800-872-0196 ■ *Web:* www.fujinon.co.jp/

G-S Supplies 408 Saint Paul St .... Rochester NY 14605 585-295-0250 232-3866
TF: 800-295-3050 ■ *Web:* www.gssupplies.com

General Scientific Corp 1201 M St SE Suite 120 .... Washington DC 20003 202-547-4299 547-7550
Web: www.genscicorp.com

Hitachi High Technologies America Inc
10 N Martingale Rd Suite 500 .... Schaumburg IL 60173 847-273-4141 273-4407
Web: www.hii-hitachi.com

II-VI Inc 375 Saxonburg Blvd .... Saxonburg PA 16056 724-352-4455 360-5848
NASDAQ: IIVI ■ *Web:* www.ii-vi.com

Intevac Inc 3560 Bassett St .... Santa Clara CA 95054 408-986-9888 986-8636*
NASDAQ: IVAC ■ **Fax:* Hum Res ■ *TF:* 800-468-3822 ■ *Web:* www.intevac.com

ITT Night Vision 7635 Plantation Rd .... Roanoke VA 24019 540-563-0371 362-7370
TF: 800-533-5502 ■ *Web:* www.ittnv.com

JML Optical Industries Inc 820 Linden Ave .... Rochester NY 14625 585-342-8900 342-6125
TF Sales: 800-456-5462 ■ *Web:* www.jmloptical.com

Kollmorgen Corp Electro-Optical Div 347 King St .... Northampton MA 01060 413-586-2330 586-1324*
**Fax:* Sales

LightPath Technologies Inc 2603 Challenger Tech Ct Suite 100 .... Orlando FL 32826 407-382-4003 382-4007
NASDAQ: LPTH ■ *Web:* www.lightpath.com

Lincoln Laser Co 234 E Mohave St .... Phoenix AZ 85004 602-257-0407 257-0728
Web: www.lincolnlaser.com

Meade Instruments Corp 6001 Oak Canyon .... Irvine CA 92618 949-451-1450 451-1460
NASDAQ: MEAD ■ *TF:* 800-626-3233 ■ *Web:* www.meade.com

Melles Griot Inc 2051 Talomar Airport Rd Suite 200 .... Carlsbad CA 92009 760-438-5131 804-0049
TF Cust Svc: 800-645-2737 ■ *Web:* www.mellesgriot.com

Microvision Inc 6222 185th Ave NE .... Redmond CA 98052 425-415-6847 415-6600
NASDAQ: MVIS ■ *TF:* 888-822-6847 ■ *Web:* www.microvision.com

New Focus Inc 2584 Junction Ave .... San Jose CA 95134 408-919-1500 919-1501
TF Sales: 866-683-6287 ■ *Web:* www.newfocus.com

Newport Corp 1791 Deere Ave .... Irvine CA 92606 949-863-3144 253-1680*
NASDAQ: NEWP ■ **Fax:* Sales ■ *TF Sales:* 800-222-6440 ■ *Web:* www.newport.com

Olympus America Inc 2 Corporate Center Dr .... Melville NY 11747 631-844-5000 844-5110*
**Fax:* Sales ■ *TF:* 800-446-5967 ■ *Web:* www.olympusamerica.com

Optronics Div - DRS Sensors & Targeting Systems
2330 Commerce Park Dr NE Suite 2 .... Palm Bay FL 32905 321-984-9030 984-8746
Web: www.drs.com

Parker Hannifin Corp Daedal Div 1140 Sandy Hill Rd .... Irwin PA 15642 724-861-8200 861-3300
TF: 800-245-6903 ■ *Web:* www.parker.com/daedal

PerkinElmer Inc 45 William St .... Wellesley MA 02481 781-237-5100 237-9386
NYSE: PKI ■ *Web:* www.perkinelmer.com

Raytheon Canada Ltd 360 Albert St Suite 1640 .... Ottawa ON K1R7X7 613-233-4121 233-1099
Web: www.raytheon.ca/

Raytheon Network Centric Systems 2501 W University .... McKinney TX 75071 972-952-2000

Recon/Optical Inc 550 W Northwest Hwy .... Barrington IL 60010 847-381-2400 381-4987
Web: www.roi.bourns.com

Ross Optical Industries Inc 1410 Gail Borden Pl Suite A-3 .... El Paso TX 79935 915-595-5417 595-5466
TF: 800-880-5417 ■ *Web:* www.rossoptical.com

SCHOTT North America Inc 555 Taxter Rd .... Elmsford NY 10523 914-831-2200 831-2201
Web: www.us.schott.com

Seiler Instrument & Mfg Co Inc 170 E Kirkham Ave .... Saint Louis MO 63119 314-968-2282 968-2637
TF: 800-489-2282 ■ *Web:* www.seilerinst.com

Servo Corp of America 123 Frost St .... Westbury NY 11590 516-938-9700 938-9644
Web: www.servo.com

Stevens Water Monitoring Systems
12067 NE Glenn Widing Dr Suite 106 .... Portland OR 97220 503-469-8000 469-8100
TF: 800-452-5272 ■ *Web:* www.stevenswater.com

StockerYale Inc 32 Hampshire Rd .... Salem NH 03079 603-893-8778 893-5604
NASDAQ: STKR ■ *TF:* 800-843-8011 ■ *Web:* www.stockeryale.com

Swift Instruments Inc 2055 Gateway Pl Suite 500 .... San Jose CA 95110 408-200-7500 292-7967
TF: 800-523-4544 ■ *Web:* www.swift-optics.com

Telesensory Inc 38083 Cherry St .... Newark CA 94560 510-793-3075 793-2017
Web: www.telesensory.com

Tinsley Laboratories Inc 4040 Lakeside Dr .... Richmond CA 94806 510-222-8110 223-4534
Web: www.asphere.com

Veeco Instruments Inc 1 Terminal Dr .... Plainview NY 11803 516-349-8300 349-8321
NASDAQ: VECO ■ *TF:* 800-645-7566 ■ *Web:* www.veeco.com

Western Ophthalmics Corp 19019 36th Ave W Suite G .... Lynnwood WA 98036 425-672-9332 423-4284*
**Fax Area Code:* 800 ■ *TF:* 800-426-9938 ■ *Web:* west-op.com

Xenonics Holdings Inc 2236 Rutherford Rd Suite 123 .... Carlsbad CA 92008 760-438-4004 438-1184
AMEX: XNN ■ *Web:* www.xenonics.com

Zeiss Carl Inc 1 Zeiss Dr .... Thornwood NY 10594 914-747-1800 682-8296
Web: www.zeiss.com

Zeiss Optical Inc 13017 N Kingston Ave .... Chester VA 23836 804-530-8300 561-2016*
**Fax Area Code:* 800 ■ *TF Cust Svc:* 800-338-2984 ■ *Web:* www.zeiss.com/optical

Zygo Corp 21 Laurel Brook Rd .... Middlefield CT 06455 860-347-8506 347-8372
NASDAQ: ZIGO ■ *TF:* 800-994-6669 ■ *Web:* www.zygo.com

548 ORGAN & TISSUE BANKS

SEE ALSO Eye Banks p. 1629

Phone | Fax

Alabama Tissue Center 201 London Pkwy Suite 300 .... Birmingham AL 35211 205-949-1681 949-1718
TF: 800-227-2907

Alamo Tissue Service Ltd 4414 Centerview St Suite 167 .... San Antonio TX 78228 210-738-2663 732-4263
TF: 800-226-9091

AlloSource 6278 S Troy Cir .... Centennial CO 80111 720-873-0213 873-0212
TF: 888-873-8330 ■ *Web:* www.allosource.org

AppTec Laboratory Services 2540 Executive Dr .... Saint Paul MN 55120 651-675-2000 675-2005
TF: 888-794-0077 ■ *Web:* www.apptec-usa.com

Bio-Tissue 7000 SW 97th Ave Suite 211 .... Miami FL 33173 305-412-4430 412-4429
TF: 888-296-8858 ■ *Web:* www.biotissue.com

Blood & Tissue Center of Central Texas 4300 N Lamar Blvd .... Austin TX 78756 512-206-1266 458-3859
Web: www.bloodandtissue.org

Bone Bank Allografts 4808 Research Dr .... San Antonio TX 78240 210-696-7616 696-7609
TF: 800-397-0088 ■ *Web:* www.bonebank.com

Caitlin Raymond International Registry
University of Massachusetts Medical Center 55 Lake Ave N .... Worcester MA 01655 508-334-8969 334-8969
TF: 800-726-2824 ■ *Web:* www.crir.org

California Cryobank Inc 11915 Jake Range Ave .... Los Angeles CA 90025 310-443-5244 208-8477
TF: 800-231-3373 ■ *Web:* www.cryobank.com

California Cryobank Inc 700 Welch Rd Suite 103 .... Palo Alto CA 94304 650-324-1900 324-1946
Web: www.cryobank.com

California Cryobank Inc 950 Massachusetts Ave .... Cambridge MA 02139 617-497-8646 497-6531
TF: 800-231-3373 ■ *Web:* www.cryobank.com

Central Florida Tissue & Eye Bank Inc 8663 Commodity Cir .... Orlando FL 32819 407-226-3888
TF: 800-753-9109 ■ *Web:* www.tissuebank.org

Cleveland Clinic Andrology Laboratory & Reproductive Tissue Bank 9500 Euclid Ave Cleveland Clinic Foundation
Desk A19.1 .... Cleveland OH 44195 216-444-3019 445-6049
TF: 800-223-2273

Community Tissue Services 3425 N 1st St Suite 103 .... Fresno CA 93726 559-224-1168 229-7217
TF: 800-201-8477 ■ *Web:* www.communitytissue.org

Community Tissue Services 7770 E 88th St .... Indianapolis IN 46256 317-842-0009 842-0243
TF: 800-984-7783 ■ *Web:* www.communitytissue.org

Community Tissue Services 349 S Main St .... Dayton OH 45402 937-222-0228 461-9217
TF: 800-684-7783 ■ *Web:* www.communitytissue.org

Community Tissue Services 2736 N Holland-Sylvania Rd .... Toledo OH 43615 419-536-4924 536-4973
TF: 866-684-7783 ■ *Web:* www.communitytissue.org

Community Tissue Services 16361 NE Cameron Blvd .... Portland OR 97230 503-408-9394 408-9395
TF: 800-545-8668 ■ *Web:* www.communitytissue.org

Community Tissue Services 7821 Bartram Ave Suite E .... Philadelphia PA 19153 215-937-9662 937-9858
TF: 800-456-5445 ■ *Web:* www.communitytissue.org

Community Tissue Services 328 S Adams St .... Fort Worth TX 76104 817-332-1898 332-1958
TF: 800-905-2556 ■ *Web:* www.communitytissue.org

Comprehensive Tissue Center
11402 University Ave Rm 7415 .... Edmonton AB T6G2J3 780-407-7510 407-7509

Cryobiology Inc 4830D Knightsbridge Blvd .... Columbus OH 43214 614-451-4375 451-5284
TF: 800-359-4375 ■ *Web:* www.cryobio.com

Cryogenic Laboratories Inc 1944 Lexington Ave N .... Roseville MN 55113 651-489-8000 489-8989
TF: 800-466-2796 ■ *Web:* www.cryolab.com

Doheny Eye & Tissue Transplant Bank
1127 Wilshire Blvd Suite 602 .... Los Angeles CA 90017 213-482-9355 482-9343
Web: www.dettb.org

Donor Alliance Inc 720 S Colorado Blvd Suite 800-N .... Denver CO 80246 303-329-4747 321-1183
TF: 888-868-4747 ■ *Web:* www.donoralliance.org

Gift of Hope Organ & Tissue Donor Network
660 N Industrial Dr .... Elmhurst IL 60126 630-758-2600
TF: 800-545-4438 ■ *Web:* www.giftofhope.org

Gift of Life Donor Program 401 N 3rd St .... Philadelphia PA 19123 215-557-8090
TF: 800-543-6391 ■ *Web:* www.donors1.org

Idant Laboratories 350 5th Ave Suite 7120 .... New York NY 10118 212-330-8500 330-8536
Web: www.idant.com

Indiana Organ Procurement Organization
429 N Pennsylvania St Suite 201 .... Indianapolis IN 46204 317-685-0389 685-1687
TF: 888-275-4676 ■ *Web:* www.iopo.org

Interpore Cross International 181 Technology Dr .... Irvine CA 92618 949-453-3200 453-3225
TF: 800-722-4489 ■ *Web:* www.interpore.com/home.html

IsoTis OrthoBiologics US 2 Goodyear .... Irvine CA 92618 949-595-8710 595-8711
TF: 800-550-7155 ■ *Web:* www.isotis.com

Kentucky Organ Donor Affiliates 106 E Broadway .... Louisville KY 40202 502-581-9511 589-5157
TF: 800-525-3456 ■ *Web:* www.kyorgandonor.org

Legacy of Life 4804 Research Dr .... San Antonio TX 78240 210-696-7677 691-1472
TF: 800-397-3077 ■ *Web:* www.legacyoflife.net

LifeBanc 20600 Chagrin Blvd Suite 350 .... Cleveland OH 44122 216-752-5433 751-4204
TF: 888-552-5433 ■ *Web:* www.lifebanc.org

LifeCell Corp 1 Millennium Way .... Branchburg NJ 08876 908-947-1100 947-1200
NASDAQ: LIFC ■ *TF:* 800-367-5737 ■ *Web:* www.lifecell.com

Lifeline of Ohio 770 Kinnear Rd Suite 200 .... Columbus OH 43212 614-291-5667 291-0660
TF: 800-525-5667 ■ *Web:* www.lifelineofohio.org

LifeLink Tissue Bank 8510 Sunstate St .... Tampa FL 33634 813-886-8111 888-9419
TF: 800-683-2400 ■ *Web:* www.lifelinkfound.org/bank.asp

LifeNet 1864 Concert Dr .... Virginia Beach VA 23453 757-464-4761 464-5721
TF: 800-847-7831 ■ *Web:* www.lifenet.org

LifeShare of the Carolinas 5000 D Airport Center Pkwy .... Charlotte NC 28208 704-697-3303 512-3056
TF: 800-932-4483 ■ *Web:* www.lifesharecarolinas.org

LifeShare Transplant Donor Services of Oklahoma
7200 N Broadway .... Oklahoma City OK 73116 405-840-5551 840-9748
TF: 888-580-5680 ■ *Web:* www.lifeshareoklahoma.org

Lifesharing Community Organ & Tissue Donation
3465 Camino del Rio S Suite 410 .... San Diego CA 92108 619-521-1983 521-2833
Web: www.lifesharing.org

Lost Mountain Tissue Bank 3175 Cherokee St NW .... Kennesaw GA 30144 770-428-1070 428-2164
TF: 800-243-1070

Louisiana Organ Procurement Agency 4441 N I-10 Service Rd .... Metairie LA 70006 504-837-3355 837-3587
TF: 800-521-4483 ■ *Web:* www.yourlegacy.org

Mercy Medical Center Surgical Bone Bank
701 10th St SE .... Cedar Rapids IA 52403 319-398-6756 398-6229

Mid-America Transplant Services
1139 Olivette Executive Pkwy .... Saint Louis MO 63132 314-991-1661 993-5179
TF: 888-376-4854 ■ *Web:* www.mts-stl.org

Mid-South Tissue Bank 5600 Pleasant View Rd Suite 107 .... Memphis TN 38134 901-683-6566 683-9910
TF: 888-366-6775 ■ *Web:* www.midsouthtissue.org

Musculoskeletal Transplant Foundation 125 May St Suite 300 .... Edison NJ 08837 732-661-0202
Web: www.mtf.org

Nevada Donor Network Inc 2085 E Sahara Ave .... Las Vegas NV 89104 702-796-9600 796-4225
Web: www.nvdonor.org

New England Organ Bank 1 Gateway Center Suite 202 .... Newton MA 02458 617-244-8000 244-8755
TF: 800-446-6362 ■ *Web:* www.neob.org

New York Cryo 900 Northern Blvd Suite 230 .... Great Neck NY 11021 516-487-2700 487-2007
Web: www.nycryo.com

Northern California Transplant Bank
7700 Edgewater Dr Suite 526 .... Oakland CA 94621 510-957-9595 957-9594

Northwest Tissue Center 921 Terry Ave .... Seattle WA 98104 206-292-1879 292-1873
TF: 800-858-2282 ■ *Web:* www.nwtc.org

NuMed Technologies Inc 7225 S 85th E Ave Suite 200 .... Tulsa OK 74133 918-249-2697 461-0682
TF: 800-640-3131

OneLegacy Transplant Donor Network
221 S Figueroa St Suite 500 .... Los Angeles CA 90012 213-229-5600 229-5601
TF: 800-786-4077 ■ *Web:* www.onelegacy.org

Regional Tissue Bank QEII Health Sciences Centre
5788 University Ave Rm 431 McKenzie Bldg Ctr .... Halifax NS B3H1V7 902-473-4171 473-2170
TF: 800-314-6515 ■ *Web:* www.cdha.nshealth.ca/tissuebank/tissueBank.html

ReproTech Ltd 1944 Lexington Ave N .... Roseville MN 55113 651-489-0827 489-0442
TF: 888-489-8944 ■ *Web:* www.reprot.com

Rocky Mountain Tissue Bank 2993 S Peoria St Suite 390 .... Aurora CO 80014 303-337-3330 337-9383
TF: 800-424-5169 ■ *Web:* www.rmtb.org

				Phone	Fax
RTI Donor Services Northeast Div 1 Edgewater Plaza Suite 704 *Web:* rtidonorservices.com	Staten Island	NY	10305	718-273-5913	226-1035
Rubinoff Bone & Tissue Bank 600 University Ave Mt Sinai Hospital Rm 539	Toronto	ON	M5G1X5	416-586-8870	586-4458
ScienceCare Anatomical Inc 21410 N 19th Ave Suite 126 *TF:* 800-417-3747 ■ *Web:* www.sciencecare.com	Phoenix	AZ	85027	602-331-3641	331-4344
Sierra Eye & Tissue Donor Services 1760 Creekside Oak Dr Suite 160 *TF:* 800-762-8819 ■ *Web:* www.dcids.org/sierra.htm	Sacramento	CA	95833	916-456-1450	569-0300
South Texas Blood & Tissue Center 6211 IH-10 W *TF:* 800-292-5534 ■ *Web:* www.bloodntissue.org	San Antonio	TX	78201	210-731-5555	731-5501
Southeast Tissue Alliance 6241 NW 23rd St Suite 400 *TF:* 866-432-1164 ■ *Web:* www.donorcare.org	Gainesville	FL	32653	352-248-2114	384-9722
Tennessee/DCI Donor Services 1714 Hayes St *TF:* 888-234-4440 ■ *Web:* www.dcids.org	Nashville	TN	37203	615-234-5200	234-5270
Tissue Banks International (TBI) 815 Park Ave *TF:* 800-756-4824 ■ *Web:* www.tbionline.org	Baltimore	MD	21201	410-752-3800	783-0183
Transplant Services Center University of Texas 5323 Harry Hines Blvd MC 9074 *TF:* 800-433-6667	Dallas	TX	75390	214-648-2609	648-2086
Tutogen Medical Inc 13709 Progress Blvd Box 19 *AMEX:* TTG ■ *TF:* 800-698-4996 ■ *Web:* www.tutogen.com	Alachua	FL	32615	386-462-0402	462-1421
University of California San Francisco Tissue Bank 3924 Williams Rd Suite 201 *TF:* 800-553-5536	San Jose	CA	95117	408-345-3515	345-3520
University of Miami Dept of Orthopedic Rehabilitation Tissue Bank 1600 NW 10th Ave Rm 8080 *TF:* 888-684-7783	Miami	FL	33136	305-243-6465	326-8321
Wright Medical Technology Inc 5677 Airline Rd **Fax:* Cust Svc ■ *TF:* 800-238-7188 ■ *Web:* www.wmt.com	Arlington	TN	38002	901-867-9971	867-9534*

549 PACKAGE DELIVERY SERVICES

				Phone	Fax
Air Courier Dispatch 1395 S Marietta Pkwy Bldg 200 Suite 222 *TF:* 800-257-7162 ■ *Web:* www.acdair.com	Marietta	GA	30067	770-933-9496	933-9598
Air T Inc 3524 Airport Rd *NASDAQ:* AIRT ■ *Web:* www.airt.net/mac	Maiden	NC	28650	828-464-8741	465-5281
AirNet Systems Inc 7250 Star Check Dr *AMEX:* ANS ■ **Fax Area Code:* 800 ■ **Fax:* Hum Res ■ *TF:* 888-888-8463 ■ *Web:* www.airnet.com	Columbus	OH	43217	614-409-4900	432-1580*
Careful Courier Service Inc 1117 Independence Ave *Web:* www.carefulcourier.com	Mountain View	CA	94043	650-903-9393	903-9397
Caribbean Transportation Services 7304 W Market St *TF:* 800-767-2494 ■ *Web:* www.caribbeantrans.com	Greensboro	NC	27409	336-668-7500	668-7517
Central Delivery Service 6501 Virginia Manor Rd *TF:* 800-938-4151 ■ *Web:* www.centraldelivery.com	Beltsville	MD	20705	301-210-0100	210-1223
Corporate Express Inc 1 Environmental Way *TF:* 888-664-3945 ■ *Web:* www.corporate-express.com	Broomfield	CO	80021	303-664-2000	664-3474
Deutsche Post Global Mail Ltd 196 Van Buren St 2nd Fl *TF:* 800-426-7478 ■ *Web:* www.deutschepost-globalmail.com	Herndon	VA	20170	703-450-5777	450-7638
DHL Airways DBA DHL Worldwide Express 1200 S Pine Island Rd *Web:* www.dhl.com	Plantation	FL	33324	800-225-5345	
DHL Worldwide Express 1200 S Pine Island Rd *Web:* www.dhl.com	Plantation	FL	33324	800-225-5345	
Dynamex Inc 5429 LBJ Fwy Suite 100 *NASDAQ:* DDMX ■ **Fax Area Code:* 972 ■ *Web:* www.dynamex.com	Dallas	TX	75240	214-560-9000	560-9349*
Dynamics Inc 1455 Estes *TF:* 800-323-6850	Elk Grove Village	IL	60007	847-264-2525	981-6526
Federal Express Corp DBA FedEx Express PO Box 727 *TF:* 800-463-3339 ■ *Web:* www.fedex.com	Memphis	TN	38194	901-369-3600	
FedEx Custom Critical Inc 1475 Boettler Rd *TF Cust Svc:* 800-762-3787 ■ *Web:* customcritical.fedex.com	Uniontown	OH	44685	234-310-4090	
FedEx Express PO Box 727 *TF:* 800-463-3339 ■ *Web:* www.fedex.com	Memphis	TN	38194	901-369-3600	
FedEx Ground 1000 FedEx Dr **Fax:* Hum Res	Moon Township	PA	15108	412-269-1000	262-6668*
Financial Courier Service Inc 6099 Mt Moriah Ext Suite 13	Memphis	TN	38115	901-761-4555	366-6165
Hot Shot Messenger Inc 747 N Shepherd Dr Suite 100 *Web:* www.hotshot.to	Houston	TX	77007	713-869-5525	862-6354
International Bonded Couriers Inc 3333 New Hyde Park Rd Suite 300 *TF:* 800-422-4124 ■ *Web:* www.ibcinc.com	New Hyde Park	NY	11042	516-627-8200	627-8262
Jersey Shore Courier Service Inc PO Box 2025	Red Bank	NJ	07701	732-747-0644	
Network Courier Service Corp 9010 Bellanca Ave **Fax:* Cust Svc ■ *TF:* 800-938-1801 ■ *Web:* www.netcour.com	Los Angeles	CA	90045	310-410-7700	410-7716*
Priority Express Courier Service 5 Chelsea Pkwy *TF:* 800-526-4646	Boothwyn	PA	19061	610-364-3300	364-3310
Purolator Courier Ltd 5995 Avebury Rd *TF:* 888-744-7123 ■ *Web:* www.purolator.com	Mississauga	ON	L5R3T8	905-712-1084	712-6696
Sterling Courier Systems Inc 570 Herndon Pkwy Suite 300 *TF:* 800-633-6666 ■ *Web:* www.sterlingcourier.com	Herndon	VA	20170	703-471-4488	471-4557
TNT Express Worldwide Corp 3 Huntington Quadrangle Suite 201S *TF Cust Svc:* 800-558-5555 ■ *Web:* www.tnt.com	Melville	NY	11747	631-760-0700	760-0985
Tricor America Inc 717 Airport Blvd *TF:* 800-669-7631 ■ *Web:* www.tricor.com	South San Francisco	CA	94080	650-877-3650	583-3197
Unishippers Assn Inc 746 E Winchester Suite 200 *TF:* 800-999-8721 ■ *Web:* www.unishippers.com	Salt Lake City	UT	84107	801-487-0600	487-7468
United Parcel Service Inc (UPS) 55 Glenlake Pkwy NE *NYSE:* UPS ■ *TF Cust Svc:* 800-742-5877 ■ *Web:* www.ups.com	Atlanta	GA	30328	404-828-6000	828-6440
United Shipping Solutions 6985 Union Park Center Suite 565 *TF:* 866-744-7486 ■ *Web:* www.usshipit.com	Midvale	UT	84047	801-352-0012	352-0339
Universal Express Inc 5295 Town Center Rd Suite 101 *Web:* www.usxp.com	Boca Raton	FL	33486	561-367-6177	367-6124
US Airways Inc Air Cargo Service Air Cargo Dr Bldg D Door 9 BWI Airport	Baltimore	MD	21240	410-993-4682	859-5316
Velocity Express Corp 1 Morningside Dr N Suite B300 *NASDAQ:* VEXP ■ *TF:* 888-839-7669 ■ *Web:* www.velocityexp.com	Westport	CT	06880	888-839-7669	
Washington Express Service LLC 12240 Indian Creek Ct Suite 100 *TF:* 800-939-5463 ■ *Web:* www.washingtonexpress.net	Beltsville	MD	20705	301-210-0899	419-7075
World Courier Inc 1313 4th Ave *TF:* 800-223-4461 ■ *Web:* www.worldcourier.com	New Hyde Park	NY	11040	516-354-2600	354-2637
Worldwide Express 2828 Routh St Suite 400 *TF:* 800-758-7447 ■ *Web:* www.wwex.com	Dallas	TX	75201	214-720-2400	720-2446
WPX Delivery Solutions 3320 W Valley Hwy N Suite 110 *TF:* 800-562-1091 ■ *Web:* www.wpx.com	Auburn	WA	98001	253-876-2760	876-2799
Yamato Transport USA Inc 80 Seaview Dr *TF:* 800-492-6286 ■ *Web:* www.ytc-usa.com	Secaucus	NJ	07094	201-583-9696	583-9699

550 PACKAGING MACHINERY & EQUIPMENT

				Phone	Fax
A-B-C Packaging Machine Corp 811 Live Oak St *TF:* 800-237-5975 ■ *Web:* www.abcpackaging.com	Tarpon Springs	FL	34689	727-937-5144	938-1239
Accraply Div Barry-Wehmiller Cos Inc 3580 Holly Ln N *TF:* 800-328-3997 ■ *Web:* www.accraply.com	Plymouth	MN	55447	763-557-1313	519-9656
ACMA USA Inc 501 Southlake Blvd *TF:* 800-525-2735 ■ *Web:* www.acmagd.com	Richmond	VA	23236	804-794-9777	794-6187
Acraloc Corp 113 Flint Rd PO Box 4129 *Web:* www.acraloc.com	Oak Ridge	TN	37831	865-483-1368	483-3500
Adolph Gottscho Inc 835 Lehigh Ave *Web:* www.gottscho.com	Union	NJ	07083	908-688-2400	687-9250
Angelus Sanitary Can Machine Co 4900 Pacific Blvd *Web:* www.angelusmachine.com	Los Angeles	CA	90058	323-583-2171	587-5607
ARPAC Group 9511 W River St *Web:* www.arpacgroup.com	Schiller Park	IL	60176	847-678-3668	
Automated Packaging Systems Inc 10175 Phillip Pkwy *TF Sales:* 800-824-5282 ■ *Web:* www.autobag.com	Streetsboro	OH	44241	330-528-2000	342-2400
B & H Mfg Co 3461 Roeding Rd *TF:* 888-643-0444 ■ *Web:* www.bhlabeling.com	Ceres	CA	95307	209-537-5785	537-6854
Barry-Wehmiller Cos Inc 8020 Forsyth Blvd **Fax:* Sales ■ *TF:* 800-862-8200 ■ *Web:* www.barry-wehmiller.com	Clayton	MO	63105	314-862-8000	862-2744*
Barry-Wehmiller Cos Inc Accraply Div 3580 Holly Ln N *TF:* 800-328-3997 ■ *Web:* www.accraply.com	Plymouth	MN	55447	763-557-1313	519-9656
Belco Packaging Systems Inc 910 S Mountain Ave *TF:* 800-833-1833 ■ *Web:* www.belcopackaging.com	Monrovia	CA	91016	626-357-9566	359-3440
Bell-Mark Corp 331 Changebridge Rd *Web:* www.bell-mark.com	Pine Brook	NJ	07058	973-882-0202	808-4616
Bosch Robert Corp Packaging Technology Div 2440 Summer Blvd *TF:* 800-292-6724 ■ *Web:* www.boschpackaging.com	Raleigh	NC	27616	919-877-2016	877-0976
Butler Automatic Inc 41 Leona Dr *TF:* 800-544-0070 ■ *Web:* www.butlerautomatic.com	Middleborough	MA	02346	508-923-0544	923-0886
Campbell Wrapper Corp 1415 Fortune Ave **Fax:* Sales ■ *TF:* 800-727-4210 ■ *Web:* www.campbellwrapper.com	De Pere	WI	54115	920-983-7100	983-7300*
Cloud Packaging Solutions 1938 Wolf Rd *Web:* www.cloudps.com	Des Plaines	IL	60018	847-390-9410	390-6170
Corrugated Gear & Services Inc 100 Anderson Rd *Web:* www.corrugatedgear.com	Alpharetta	GA	30004	770-475-8929	442-3371
Data Technology Inc 260-J Fordham Rd *TF:* 800-331-5797 ■ *Web:* www.data-technology.com	Wilmington	MA	01887	978-694-0055	657-7977
Doboy Inc 869 S Knowles Ave *Web:* www.doboy.com	New Richmond	WI	54017	715-246-6511	246-6539
Dynaric Inc 5740 Bayside Rd *TF:* 800-526-0827 ■ *Web:* www.dynaric.com	Virginia Beach	VA	23455	757-363-5850	
Elliott Mfg Co Inc 2664 Cherry Ave PO Box 11277 *Web:* www.elliott-mfg.com	Fresno	CA	93772	559-233-6235	233-9833
Elmar Worldwide Inc 200 Gould Ave PO Box 245 *TF Cust Svc:* 800-433-3562 ■ *Web:* www.elmarworldwide.com	Depew	NY	14043	716-681-5650	681-4660
Evergreen Packaging Equipment 2400 6th St SW *Web:* www.evergreenpackaging.com	Cedar Rapids	IA	52406	319-399-3200	399-3543
Fischbein Co 151 Walker Rd *Web:* www.fischbein.com	Statesville	NC	28625	704-871-1159	872-3303
Fowler Products Co 150 Collins Industrial Blvd *Web:* www.fowlerproducts.com	Athens	GA	30601	706-549-3300	548-1278
Gottscho Adolph Inc 835 Lehigh Ave *Web:* www.gottscho.com	Union	NJ	07083	908-688-2400	687-9250
Hartness International Inc 1200 Garlington Rd PO Box 26509 *TF:* 800-845-8791 ■ *Web:* www.hartness.com	Greenville	SC	29616	864-297-1200	288-5390
Heisler Industries Inc 224 Passaic Ave *Web:* www.heislerind.com	Fairfield	NJ	07004	973-227-6300	227-7627
ITW Angleboard 595 Telser Rd Suite 100 **Fax Area Code:* 847 ■ *TF:* 800-252-4777 ■ *Web:* www.itwangleboard.com	Lake Zurich	IL	60047	800-457-5777	719-9221*
Kirk Rudy Inc 125 Lorraine Pkwy *Web:* www.kirkrudy.com	Woodstock	GA	30188	770-427-4203	427-4036
Kliklok-Woodman USA 5224 Snapfinger Woods Dr *Web:* www.kliklok.com	Decatur	GA	30035	770-981-5200	987-7160
Kortec Inc 29 Old Right Rd *Web:* www.kortec.com	Ipswich	MA	01938	978-238-7100	238-7171
Krones Inc 9600 S 58th St PO Box 321801 **Fax:* Cust Svc ■ *TF:* 800-752-3787 ■ *Web:* www.krones.de	Franklin	WI	53132	414-409-4000	409-4100*
Label-Aire Inc 550 Burning Tree Rd *Web:* www.label-aire-inc.com	Fullerton	CA	92833	714-441-0700	526-0300
Lantech Inc 11000 Bluegrass Pkwy *TF:* 800-866-0322 ■ *Web:* www.lantech.com	Louisville	KY	40299	502-267-4200	266-5031
Liberty Industries Inc 840 McClurg Rd *TF:* 800-860-4744 ■ *Web:* www.libertyindustries.com	Youngstown	OH	44512	330-539-5460	729-2111
Loveshaw Corp 2206 Easton Tpke PO Box 83 *TF Cust Svc:* 800-747-1586 ■ *Web:* www.loveshaw.com	South Canaan	PA	18459	570-937-4921	937-3229
Matthews International Corp Graphics Systems Div 252 Park West Dr *TF:* 800-245-1129 ■ *Web:* www.matthewsgsd.com	Pittsburgh	PA	15275	412-788-2111	788-2297
Metro Machine & Engineering Corp 8001 Wallace Rd *Web:* www.metromachine.com	Eden Prairie	MN	55344	952-937-2800	937-2374
Mid-States Packaging Inc 119 S Boggs St *Web:* www.midstatespackaging.com	DeGraff	OH	43318	937-585-5361	585-6819
Moen Industries 12333 E Los Nietos Rd *TF:* 800-423-4747 ■ *Web:* www.moenindustries.com	Santa Fe Springs	CA	90670	562-946-6381	946-3200
MTS Medication Technologies Inc 2003 Gandy Blvd N Suite 800 *AMEX:* MPP ■ *TF:* 800-334-6663 ■ *Web:* www.mtsp.com	Saint Petersburg	FL	33702	727-571-1616	579-8067
Muller Martini Mailroom Systems Inc 444 Innovation Way *TF:* 800-331-5674 ■ *Web:* www.mullermartini.com/ms	Allentown	PA	18109	610-266-7000	231-3990
Nalbach Engineering Co Inc 621 E Plainfield Rd *Web:* www.nalbach.com	Countryside	IL	60525	708-579-9100	579-0122
National Instrument Co Inc 4119 Fordleigh Rd *TF:* 800-526-1301 ■ *Web:* www.filamatic.com	Baltimore	MD	21215	410-764-0900	764-7719
New England Machinery Inc 6204 29th St E *Web:* www.neminc.com	Bradenton	FL	34203	941-755-5550	751-6281
New Jersey Machine Inc 56 Etna Rd **Fax:* Sales ■ *TF Sales:* 800-432-2990 ■ *Web:* www.njmcli.com	Lebanon	NH	03766	603-448-0300	448-4810*
New Way Packaging Machinery Inc 210 Blettner Ave PO Box 467 *Web:* www.labeler.com	Hanover	PA	17331	717-637-2133	637-2966
Ossid Corp PO Drawer 1968 4000 College Rd *TF:* 800-334-8369 ■ *Web:* www.ossid.com	Rocky Mount	NC	27802	252-446-6177	442-7694
Package Machinery Co 380 Union St Suite 58 *Web:* www.packagemachinery.com	West Springfield	MA	01089	413-732-4000	732-1163
Packaging Systems International Inc 4990 Acoma St *Web:* www.pkgsys.com	Denver	CO	80216	303-296-4445	298-1016
Packaging Technologies 807 W Kimberly Rd *TF Sales:* 800-257-5622 ■ *Web:* www.packt.com	Davenport	IA	52806	563-391-1100	391-4951
Pearson RA Co 8120 W Sunset Hwy *TF:* 800-732-7766 ■ *Web:* www.pearsonpkg.com	Spokane	WA	99224	509-838-6226	747-8532

Phone Fax

PMC Industries 275 Hudson St. Hackensack NJ 07601 201-342-3684 342-3568
Web: www.pmc-industries.com

Prodo-Pak Corp 77 Commerce St. Garfield NJ 07026 973-777-7770 772-0471
Web: www.prodo-pak.com

RA Pearson Co 8120 W Sunset Hwy Spokane WA 99224 509-838-6226 747-8532
TF: 800-732-7766 ■ *Web:* www.pearsonpkg.com

Renco Machine Co 1421 Eastman Ave. Green Bay WI 54302 920-448-8000 448-8008
TF: 888-320-8552 ■ *Web:* www.rencomachine.com

Ro-An Industries Corp 64-20 Admiral Ave Middle Village NY 11379 718-821-1115 821-3838
TF: 800-255-7626 ■ *Web:* www.roan.com

Robert Bosch Corp Packaging Technology Div
2440 Summer Blvd Raleigh NC 27616 919-877-2016 877-0976
TF: 800-292-6724 ■ *Web:* www.boschpackaging.com

Rutherford Engineering Inc 5469 Pine Ln PO Box 560 Roscoe IL 61073 815-623-2141 623-7170

Sabel Engineering Corp 20366 E 8th St PO Box 1223 Sonoma CA 95476 707-938-4771 938-4772
Web: www.sabelengr.com

SCA Consumer Packaging 1401 Pleasant St DeKalb IL 60115 815-756-8451 756-5187
TF: 800-756-7638 ■ *Web:* www.scapackaging.alloyd.com

Scandia Packaging Machinery Co 15 Industrial Rd Clifton NJ 07004 973-473-6100 473-7226
Web: www.scandiapack.com

Schneider Packaging Equipment Co Inc 5370 Guy Young Rd Brewerton NY 13029 315-676-3035 676-2875
Web: www.schneiderequip.com

Shibuya Hoppmann Corp 13129 Airpark Dr Suite 120 Elkwood VA 22718 540-829-2654 829-1724
TF Cust Svc: 800-368-3582 ■ *Web:* www.hoppmann.com

Sidel Inc 5600 Sun Ct. Norcross GA 30092 770-449-8058 447-0084
TF: 800-453-7439 ■ *Web:* www.usa.sidel.com

Standard Knapp Inc 63 Pickering St. Portland CT 06480 860-342-1100 342-0782
TF Cust Svc: 800-628-9565 ■ *Web:* www.standard-knapp.com

Stolle Machinery Co LLC 6949 S Potomac St Centennial CO 80112 303-708-9044 708-9045
TF: 800-228-4593 ■ *Web:* www.stollemachinery.com

Summit Packaging Systems Inc 4000 Gay St PO Box 5304 Manchester NH 03108 603-669-5410 644-2594

SWF Cos 1949 E Manning Ave Reedley CA 93654 559-638-8484 638-7478
TF: 800-344-8951 ■ *Web:* www.swfcompanies.com

Thiele Technologies Inc 315 27th Ave NE Minneapolis MN 55418 612-782-1200 782-1203
TF: 800-932-3647 ■ *Web:* www.thieletech.com

Tri-Pak Machinery Inc 1102 N Commerce St Harlingen TX 78550 956-423-5140 423-9362
TF: 800-531-7343 ■ *Web:* www.tri-pakmachinery.com

Triangle Package Machinery Co 6655 W Diversey Ave. Chicago IL 60707 773-889-0200 889-4221
TF: 800-621-4170 ■ *Web:* www.trianglepackage.com

Waste Technology Corp 5400 Rio Grande Ave. Jacksonville FL 32254 904-355-5558 358-7013
TF: 800-231-9286

Weiler Engineering Inc 1395 Gateway Dr. Elgin IL 60124 847-697-4900 697-4944
Web: www.weilerengineering.com

551 PACKAGING MATERIALS & PRODUCTS - PAPER OR PLASTICS

SEE ALSO Bags - Paper p. 1366; Bags - Plastics p. 1367; Blister Packaging p. 1384; Paper - Mfr - Coated & Laminated Paper p. 2045; Paper Converters p. 2046; Plastics Foam Products p. 2119

Phone Fax

Admiral Packaging inc 10 Admiral St Providence RI 02908 401-274-7000 331-1910
TF: 800-556-6454 ■ *Web:* www.admiralpkg.com

Advanced Paper Forming 541 W Rincon St. Carona CA 92880 951-738-1800 738-1234
Web: www.advancedpaper.com

Aldelano Packaging Corp 2010 S Lynx Ave. Ontario CA 91761 909-861-3970 861-6039
TF: 800-972-2599 ■ *Web:* www.aldelano.com

Alliance Rubber Co 210 Carpenter Dam Rd. Hot Springs AR 71901 501-262-2700 262-8192
TF: 800-626-5940 ■ *Web:* www.rubberband.com

American Packaging Corp 777 Driving Park Ave. Rochester NY 14613 585-254-9500 254-5801
TF: 800-551-8801 ■ *Web:* www.ampkcorp.com

American Packaging Corp Extrusion Div
777 Driving Park Ave. Rochester NY 14613 585-254-9500 254-5801
TF: 800-551-8801 ■ *Web:* www.ampkcorp.com

American Transparent Plastics Corp 180 National Rd Edison NJ 08817 732-287-3000 287-1421
TF Orders: 800-942-8725

Automated Packaging Systems Inc 10175 Phillip Pkwy Streetsboro OH 44241 330-528-2000 342-2400
TF Sales: 800-824-5282 ■ *Web:* www.autobag.com

BagcraftPapercon 3900 W 43rd St. Chicago IL 60632 773-254-8000 254-8204
TF: 800-621-8468 ■ *Web:* www.bagcraft.com

Beaverite Corp 9394 Bridge St128 Main St Beaver Falls NY 13305 315-346-6011 346-1575
TF Cust Svc: 800-424-6337 ■ *Web:* www.beaverite.com

Bedford Industries Inc 1659 Rowe Ave Worthington MN 56187 507-376-4136 376-6742
TF Cust Svc: 800-533-5314 ■ *Web:* www.bedfordind.com

Bemis Co Inc 1 Neenah Center 4th Fl PO Box 669 Neenah WI 54957 920-727-4100
NYSE: BMS ■ *Web:* www.bemis.com

Bemis Co Inc Bemis Clysar Div
2200 Badger Ave PO Box 2968 Oshkosh WI 54903 920-303-7800 303-7820*
**Fax: Cust Svc* ■ *TF:* 800-425-9727 ■ *Web:* www.clysar.com

Bemis Co Inc Milprint Div 3550 Moser St PO Box 2968 Oshkosh WI 54903 920-527-2300 527-2310
Web: www.milprint.com

Bemis Co Inc Paper Packaging Div 2445 Deer Park Blvd Omaha NE 68105 402-938-2500 938-2609
TF: 800-541-4303 ■ *Web:* www.bemispaper.com

Berry Covalence Coated Products 918 8th Ave PO Box 1158 Columbus GA 31902 706-323-7316 322-5970
Web: www.covalencecoatedproducts.com

Bomarko Inc 1955 N Oak Rd PO Box 1510 Plymouth IN 46563 574-936-9901 936-5314
Web: www.bomarko.com

BPM Inc 200 W Front St. Peshtigo WI 54157 715-582-4551 582-4853
TF: 800-826-0494 ■ *Web:* www.bpmpaper.com

Bryce Corp 4505 Old Lamar Ave PO Box 18338 Memphis TN 38118 901-369-4400 369-4419*
**Fax: Sales* ■ *TF:* 800-238-7277 ■ *Web:* www.brycecorp.com

Burrows Paper Corp Packaging Group 1722 53rd St Fort Madison IA 52627 319-372-4241 372-2537
TF: 800-779-7779 ■ *Web:* www.burrowspaper.com

Carton Service - Packaging Insights First Quality Dr Shelby OH 44875 419-342-5010 342-4804
TF: 800-533-7744 ■ *Web:* www.cartonservice.com

Cascades Inc 404 Marie-Victorin Blvd Kingsey Falls QC J0A1B0 819-363-5100 363-5155
TSX: CAS ■ *Web:* www.cascades.com

Catty Corp 6111 White Oaks Rd Harvard IL 60033 815-943-2288 943-4473
TF: 800-572-2766 ■ *Web:* www.cattycorp.com

CCL Industries Inc 105 Gordon Baker Rd Suite 800 Willowdale ON M2H3P8 416-756-8500 756-8555
TSX: CCLa ■ *Web:* www.cclind.com

Cello-Foil Products Inc 155 Brook St. Battle Creek MI 49017 269-964-7137 964-2565
Web: www.cello-foil.com

Cello-Pack Corp 55 Innsbruck Dr. Cheektowaga NY 14227 716-668-3111 668-3816
TF: 800-778-3111 ■ *Web:* www.cello-pack.com

Clear Lam Packaging Inc 1950 Pratt Blvd Elk Grove Village IL 60007 847-439-8570 439-8589
TF: 800-305-4409 ■ *Web:* www.clearlam.com

Cleo Inc 4025 Viscount Ave Memphis TN 38118 901-369-6300 362-1099
TF: 800-289-2536 ■ *Web:* www.cleowrap.com

Command Plastic Corp 124 West Ave Tallmadge OH 44278 330-434-3497 434-8316
TF: 800-321-8001 ■ *Web:* www.commandplastic.com

Consolidated Container Co 3101 Towercreek Pkwy SE Suite 300 Atlanta GA 30339 678-742-4600 742-4750
Web: www.ccclc.com

Crowell Corp 1 Coral Rd PO Box 3227 Newport DE 19804 302-998-0557 998-0626
TF: 800-441-7525 ■ *Web:* www.crowellcorp.com

Cryovac Div Sealed Air Corp 100 Rogers Bridge Rd Bldg A Duncan SC 29334 864-433-2000 433-2689
TF: 800-845-7551

Curwood Inc 2200 Badger Ave PO Box 2968 Oshkosh WI 54903 920-303-7300 303-7309
TF: 800-544-4672 ■ *Web:* www.curwood.com

DuPont Packaging & Industrial Polymers
Barley Mill Plaza 26-2122 PO Box 80026 Wilmington DE 19880 302-774-1161
TF: 800-628-6208 ■ *Web:* www.dupont.com/packaging

Exopack LLC 3070 Southport Rd PO Box 5687 Spartanburg SC 29304 864-596-7140 596-7222
TF: 877-447-3539 ■ *Web:* www.exopack.com

Fibercel Packaging LLC 46 Brooklyn St PO Box 610 Portville NY 14770 716-933-8703 933-6948
TF: 800-545-8546 ■ *Web:* www.fibercel.com

Fisher Container Corp 1111 Busch Pkwy. Buffalo Grove IL 60089 847-541-0000 541-0075
TF: 800-837-2247 ■ *Web:* www.fishercontainer.com

Flextron Industries Inc 720 Mount Rd. Aston PA 19014 610-459-4600 459-5379
TF: 800-633-2181 ■ *Web:* www.flextronindustries.com

Flower City Tissue Mills Inc PO Box 13497 Rochester NY 14613 585-458-9200 458-3812
TF: 800-595-2030 ■ *Web:* www.flowercitytissue.com

Fortifiber Corp 1001 Tahoe Blvd. Incline Village NV 89451 775-833-6161 833-6151
TF: 800-443-4079 ■ *Web:* www.fortifiber.com

FP International 1090 Mills Way Redwood City CA 94063 650-261-5300 361-1713
TF: 800-866-9946 ■ *Web:* www.fpintl.com

FPC Flexible Packaging Corp 1891 Eglinton Ave E. Toronto ON M1L2L7 416-288-3060 288-0808
TF: 888-288-7386 ■ *Web:* www.fpcflexible.com

Free-Flow Packaging Corp DBA FP International
1090 Mills Way Redwood City CA 94063 650-261-5300 361-1713
TF: 800-866-9946 ■ *Web:* www.fpintl.com

Gateway Packaging Co
20 Central Industrial Dr Northgate Industrial Park Granite City IL 62040 618-451-0010 876-4856
Web: www.gatewaypackaging.com

General Plastic Extrusions Inc 1238 Kasson Dr Prescott WI 54021 715-262-3806 262-3836
TF: 800-532-3888 ■ *Web:* www.generalplastic.com

Genpak Corp 68 Warren St. Glens Falls NY 12801 518-798-9511 798-3302
TF: 800-626-6695 ■ *Web:* www.genpak.com

Gift Wrap Co 338 Industrial Blvd Midway GA 31320 912-884-9727 884-9702
TF: 800-443-4429 ■ *Web:* www.giftwrapcompany.com

Gordon L Packaging Inc 22 W Padonia Rd Suite 304A Timonium MD 21093 410-308-2202 308-2207
Web: www.lgordonpackaging.com

Green Bay Packaging Inc 1700 N Webster Ct Green Bay WI 54302 920-433-5111
TF: 800-558-4008 ■ *Web:* www.gbp.com

Group360 Inc 10818 Midwest Industrial Blvd Saint Louis MO 63132 314-423-9300 423-6104
TF: 800-666-8243 ■ *Web:* www.group360.com

Gujarat Glass International Inc
401 Rt 73 N Bldg 10 Suite 202 Lake Center Executive Park Marlton NJ 08053 856-293-6400 293-6401
Web: www.theglassgroup.com

HCP Packaging USA Inc 370 Monument Rd. Hinsdale NH 03451 603-256-3141 256-6979
Web: www.hcpackaging.com

Highland Supply Corp 1111 6th St Highland IL 62249 618-654-2161 654-3411
TF: 800-472-3645 ■ *Web:* www.highlandsupply.com

Honeywell Specialty Films 98 Westwood Rd. Pottsville PA 17901 570-621-6000 621-6109
TF Cust Svc: 800-934-5679

Huhtamaki Americas 9201 Packaging Dr DeSoto KS 66018 913-583-3025 583-8781*
**Fax: Hum Res* ■ *TF:* 800-255-4243 ■ *Web:* www.huhtamaki.com

Indiana Ribbon Inc 106 N 2nd St. Wolcott IN 47995 219-279-2112 279-4747*
**Fax Area Code: 800* ■ *TF:* 800-531-3100 ■ *Web:* www.giftwrapgifts.com

Innovative Enterprises Inc 25 Town & Country Dr Washington MO 63090 636-390-0300 390-4004
TF: 800-280-0300 ■ *Web:* www.innovative-1.com

International Converter Inc 721 Farson St. Belpre OH 45714 740-423-7525 423-5799
TF: 800-962-8572 ■ *Web:* www.ici-laminating.com

International Paper Co 6400 Poplar Ave Memphis TN 38297 901-419-7000
NYSE: IP ■ *TF Prod Info:* 800-223-1268 ■ *Web:* www.internationalpaper.com

International Paper Co Kraft Packaging Div 6400 Poplar Ave Memphis TN 38197 901-419-9000
TF: 800-238-6399 ■ *Web:* www.internationalpaper.com

International Paper Co Kraft Paper Div 6400 Poplar Ave. Memphis TN 38197 901-419-9000
Web: www.internationalpaper.com

ITW Hi-Cone 1140 W Bryn Mawr Ave Itasca IL 60143 630-438-5300 438-5315
Web: www.itwhicone.com

Jim Pattison Packaging Group
1067 W Cordova St Suite 1800 Vancouver BC V6C1C7 604-688-6764 687-2601
Web: www.jimpattison.com

Kimberly-Clark Corp Technical Paper Div
1400 Holcomb Bridge Rd. Roswell GA 30076 920-721-2000 721-4219
TF: 800-544-1847 ■ *Web:* www.kimberly-clark.com

Komplete Packaging Inc (KPAK) 2020 Singleton Blvd Dallas TX 75212 214-252-8100 646-9922
TF: 800-811-6374 ■ *Web:* www.kpak.com

KPAK (Komplete Packaging Inc) 2020 Singleton Blvd. Dallas TX 75212 214-252-8100 646-9922
TF: 800-811-6374 ■ *Web:* www.kpak.com

Kraft Packaging Div International Paper Co 6400 Poplar Ave Memphis TN 38197 901-419-9000
TF: 800-238-6399 ■ *Web:* www.internationalpaper.com

Kraft Paper Div International Paper Co 6400 Poplar Ave. Memphis TN 38197 901-419-9000
Web: www.internationalpaper.com

L Gordon Packaging Inc 22 W Padonia Rd Suite 304A Timonium MD 21093 410-308-2202 308-2207
Web: www.lgordonpackaging.com

LallyPak Inc 1209 Central Ave Hillside NJ 07205 908-351-4141 351-4411
TF: 800-523-8484 ■ *Web:* www.lallypak.com

Laminations 3010 E Venture Dr Appleton WI 54911 920-831-0596 831-0612
TF: 800-925-2626 ■ *Web:* www.laminations-net.com

Lauterbach Group 1450 S West Ave. Waukesha WI 53189 262-549-1730 549-3614
TF: 800-558-2126 ■ *Web:* www.lauterbachgroup.com

Lerman Container Co 10 Great Hill Rd Naugatuck CT 06770 203-723-6681 723-6687
TF: 800-453-7626 ■ *Web:* www.lermancontainer.com

Letica Corp 52585 Dequindre Rd PO Box 5005 Rochester MI 48307 248-652-0557
TF: 866-538-4221 ■ *Web:* www.letica.com

LPS Industries Inc 10 Caesar Pl Moonachie NJ 07074 201-438-3515 438-0040
TF Sales: 800-275-4577 ■ *Web:* www.lpsind.com

Menominee Paper Co 144 1st St Menominee MI 49858 906-863-5595 864-3320

Milprint Div Bemis Co Inc 3550 Moser St PO Box 2968 Oshkosh WI 54903 920-527-2300 527-2310
Web: www.milprint.com

Multifilm Packaging Corp 1040 N McLean Blvd Elgin IL 60123 847-695-7600 695-7645
TF: 800-837-9727 ■ *Web:* www.multifilm.com

Novacel 21 3rd St Palmer MA 01069 617-527-4980 964-4669
TF: 800-561-7906 ■ *Web:* www.novacelonline.com

Oracle Packaging 220 E Polo Rd Winston-Salem NC 27105 336-777-5000 777-5440
Web: www.oraclepackaging.com

Overwraps Packaging LP 3950 La Reunion Pkwy Dallas TX 75212 214-634-0427 634-9531
Web: www.overwraps.com

Pactiv Corp 1900 W Field Ct. Lake Forest IL 60045 847-482-2000 482-4738
NYSE: PTV ■ *TF:* 888-828-2850 ■ *Web:* www.pactiv.com

Paper-Pak Products Inc 1029 Old Creek Rd Greenville NC 27834 252-752-1100 933-8433*
**Fax Area Code: 800* ■ *TF:* 800-428-8363 ■ *Web:* www.paperpak.com

Perfecseal Inc 3500 N Main st PO Box 2968 Oshkosh WI 54903 920-303-7000 303-7002
TF: 800-568-7626 ■ *Web:* www.perfecseal.com

Pliant Corp 1475 Woodfield Rd Suite 700 Schaumburg IL 60173 847-969-3300 969-3338
Web: www.pliantcorp.com

Plus Mark Inc PO Box 549 Greeneville TN 37744 423-639-7878 636-2065

Company	City	State	Zip	Phone	Fax
Polyair Inter Pack Inc 330 Humberline Dr *AMEX: PPK* ■ *TF:* 888-456-4348 ■ *Web:* www.polyair.com	Toronto	ON	M9W1R2	416-679-6600	679-6610
Power Packaging - An Exel Co 525 Dunham Rd *Web:* www.powerpackaging.com	Saint Charles	IL	60174	630-377-3838	377-4603
Pratt Industries USA 1800C Sarasota Pkwy *Web:* www.prattindustries.com	Conyers	GA	30013	770-918-5678	918-5679
Prescotech Industries 2000 N New York Ave	Evansville	IN	47711	812-424-3392	465-4775
Printpack Inc 4335 Wendell Dr **Fax:* Sales ■ *TF:* 800-241-9984 ■ *Web:* www.printpack.com	Atlanta	GA	30336	404-691-5830	505-7407*
Printpack Inc Film Products Div PO Box 110 *TF:* 800-572-4345	New Castle	DE	19720	302-323-0900	323-1698
Rexam Inc 4201 Congress St Suite 340 *TF:* 800-289-2800 ■ *Web:* www.rexam.com	Charlotte	NC	28209	704-551-1500	551-1571
Robinson Industries Inc 3051 Curtis Rd *TF:* 800-525-0391 ■ *Web:* www.robinsonind.com	Coleman	MI	48618	989-465-6111	465-1217
Rock-Tenn Co 504 Thrasher St PO Box 4098 *NYSE: RKT* ■ *TF:* 800-762-5836 ■ *Web:* www.rocktenn.com	Norcross	GA	30091	770-448-2193	263-4483
Rollprint Packaging Products Inc 320 S Stewart Ave *TF:* 800-276-7629 ■ *Web:* www.rollprint.com	Addison	IL	60101	630-628-1700	628-8510
Scholle Custom Packaging Inc 200 W North Ave *Web:* www.scholle.com	Northlake	IL	60164	708-562-7290	562-6569
Scott Fetzer Co Western Plastics Div 105 Western Dr *Web:* www.wplastics.com	Portland	TN	37148	615-325-7331	325-4924
Sealed Air Corp 200 Riverfront Blvd *NYSE: SEE* ■ *Web:* www.sealedaircorp.com	Elmwood Park	NJ	07407	201-791-7600	
Sealed Air Corp Cryovac Div 100 Rogers Bridge Rd Bldg A *TF:* 800-845-7551	Duncan	SC	29334	864-433-2000	433-2689
Sealed Air Corp Packaging Products Div 301 Mayhill St *TF:* 800-346-5855	Saddle Brook	NJ	07663	201-712-7000	712-7070
Shields Bag & Printing Co 1009 Rock Ave *TF:* 800-541-8630 ■ *Web:* www.shieldsbag.com	Yakima	WA	98902	509-248-7500	248-6304
SI Jacobson Mfg Co 1414 Jacobson Dr *TF:* 800-621-5492 ■ *Web:* www.sij.com	Waukegan	IL	60085	847-623-1414	623-2556
Silgan Holdings Inc 4 Landmark Sq Suite 400 *NASDAQ: SLGN* ■ *Web:* www.silganholdings.com	Stamford	CT	06901	203-975-7110	975-7902
Sonoco 1 N 2nd St *NYSE: SON* ■ **Fax:* PR ■ *TF:* 800-377-2692 ■ *Web:* www.sonoco.com	Hartsville	SC	29550	843-383-7000	383-7008*
Southern Container Corp 115 Engineers Rd *Web:* www.southern-container.com	Hauppauge	NY	11788	631-231-0400	231-0174
Southern Container Ltd 10410 Papalote St Suite 130 *Web:* www.southerncontainer.com	Houston	TX	77041	713-466-5661	466-4223
Specialized Packaging International Inc 3190 Whitney Ave Bldg 7 *Web:* www.spgroup-inc.com	Hamden	CT	06518	203-248-3370	230-8906
Technipaq Inc 975 Lutter Dr *Web:* www.technipaq.com	Crystal Lake	IL	60014	815-477-1800	477-0777
Tegrant Corp 800 5th Ave *TF:* 800-289-9966 ■ *Web:* www.tegrant.com	New Brighton	PA	15066	724-843-8200	843-4845
UFP Technologies Inc 172 E Main St *NASDAQ: UFPT* ■ *Web:* www.ufpt.com	Georgetown	MA	01833	978-352-2200	352-7169
Unger Co 12401 Berea Rd *TF:* 800-321-1418 ■ *Web:* www.ungerco.com	Cleveland	OH	44111	216-252-1400	252-1427
Unicorr 455 Sackett Point Rd *TF:* 800-229-4269 ■ *Web:* www.unicorr.com	North Haven	CT	06473	203-248-2161	248-0241
Viskase Cos Inc 8205 S Cass Suite 115 *TF:* 800-323-8562 ■ *Web:* www.viskase.com	Darien	IL	60561	630-874-0700	874-0178
Warp Bros Flex-O-Glass Inc 4647 W Augusta Blvd *TF:* 800-621-3345 ■ *Web:* www.warpbros.com	Chicago	IL	60651	773-261-5200	261-5204
Wausau Paper Corp 100 Paper Place *NYSE: WPP* ■ *Web:* www.wausaupaper.com	Mosinee	WI	54455	715-693-4470	692-2083
Wausau Paper Corp Printing & Writing Paper Div 1 Clark's Island *Web:* www.wpprintingandwriting.com/default.aspx	Wausau	WI	54403	715-675-3361	675-8355
Wausau Paper Corp Specialty Paper Div 100 Paper Pl *Web:* www.wpspecialtyproducts.com	Mosinee	WI	54455	715-692-2062	692-2094
Western Plastics Div Scott Fetzer Co 105 Western Dr *Web:* www.wplastics.com	Portland	TN	37148	615-325-7331	325-4924
Weyerhaeuser Co 33663 Weyerhaeuser Way S *NYSE: WY* ■ *TF:* 800-525-5440 ■ *Web:* www.weyerhaeuser.com	Federal Way	WA	98003	253-924-2345	924-2685
Winpak Ltd 100 Salteaux Crescent *TSX: WPK* ■ *Web:* www.winpak.com	Winnipeg	MB	R3J3T3	204-889-1015	832-7781
WS Packaging Group Inc 1102 Jefferson St *TF:* 800-236-3424 ■ *Web:* www.wspackaging.com	Algoma	WI	54201	920-487-3424	487-5644
Zimmer Custom-Made Packaging Inc 1450 E 20th St **Fax:* Hum Res ■ *TF:* 888-692-4299 ■ *Web:* www.zcmp.com	Indianapolis	IN	46218	317-636-3333	263-3427*

552 PACKING & CRATING

Company	City	State	Zip	Phone	Fax
Bentley World Packaging Ltd 4080 N Port Washington Rd *Web:* www.bentleywp.com	Milwaukee	WI	53212	414-967-8000	967-8001
Craters & Freighters 331 Corporate Cir Suite J **Fax Area Code:* 303 ■ *Web:* www.cratersandfreighters.com	Golden	CO	80401	800-736-3335	399-9964*
Export Packaging Co 525 E 10th Ave	Moline	IL	61264	309-787-0440	787-0448
Fapco Inc 216 Post Rd *TF:* 800-782-0167 ■ *Web:* www.fapcoinc.com	Buchanan	MI	49107	269-695-6889	695-5145
Handle With Care Packaging Stores 5675 DTC Blvd Suite 280 *TF:* 800-525-6309 ■ *Web:* www.gopackagingstore.com	Greenwood Village	CO	80111	303-741-6626	741-6653
Hydrosol Inc 8407 S 77th Ave *Web:* www.hydrosol.com	Bridgeview	IL	60455	708-598-7100	598-6572
Navis Logistics Network 5675 DTC Blvd Suite 280 *TF:* 800-525-6309 ■ *Web:* www.gonavis.com	Greenwood Village	CO	80111	303-741-6626	741-6653
Navis Pack & Ship Centers 5675 DTC Blvd Suite 280 *TF:* 800-525-6309 ■ *Web:* www.gonavis.com	Greenwood Village	CO	80111	303-741-6626	741-6653
Neff Packaging Solutions 2001 Kuntz Rd *TF:* 800-445-4383 ■ *Web:* www.neffpackaging.com	Dayton	OH	45404	937-233-3333	233-0238
Tech Packaging Inc 11902 Central Pkwy *Web:* www.techpackaging.net	Jacksonville	FL	32224	904-564-9838	564-9839
Trans-Pak Inc 520 Marburg Way *Web:* www.transpak.com	San Jose	CA	95133	408-254-0500	254-0551
Venchurs Packaging 800 Liberty St *Web:* www.venchurs.com	Adrian	MI	49221	517-263-8937	265-7468
Warren Industries Inc 3100 Mt Pleasant St *Web:* www.wrnind.com	Racine	WI	53404	262-639-7800	639-0920

553 PAINTS, VARNISHES, RELATED PRODUCTS

Company	City	State	Zip	Phone	Fax
3M Transportation Div 3M Center *TF:* 888-364-3577	Saint Paul	MN	55144	651-733-1110	
Aexcel Corp 7373 Production Dr *Web:* www.aexcelcorp.com	Mentor	OH	44060	440-974-3800	974-3808
Akron Paint & Varnish Inc 1390 Firestone Pkwy *TF:* 800-772-3452 ■ *Web:* www.apv-eng-coatings.com	Akron	OH	44301	330-773-8911	773-1028
Akzo Nobel Coatings Inc 2031 Nelson Miller Pkwy *Web:* www.akzonobelusa.com	Louisville	KY	40223	502-254-0470	253-0573
Akzo Nobel Inc 525 W Van Buren St *TF Cust Svc:* 800-227-7070 ■ *Web:* www.akzonobelusa.com	Chicago	IL	60607	312-544-7000	544-7198
American Safety Technologies Inc 565 Eagle Rock Ave *TF:* 800-631-7841 ■ *Web:* www.astantislip.com	Roseland	NJ	07068	973-403-2600	403-0046
AP Nonweiler Co 3321 County Rd A PO Box 1007	Oshkosh	WI	54903	920-231-0850	231-8085
Barr WM & Co Inc PO Box 1879 **Fax Area Code:* 800 ■ *TF:* 800-782-9928 ■ *Web:* www.wmbarr.com	Memphis	TN	38101	901-775-0100	621-9508*
Behr Process Corp 3400 W Segerstrom Ave *TF:* 800-854-0133 ■ *Web:* www.behrpaint.com	Santa Ana	CA	92704	714-545-7101	241-1002
Benjamin Moore & Co 101 Paragon Dr *TF:* 800-344-0400 ■ *Web:* www.benjaminmoore.com	Montvale	NJ	07645	201-573-9600	949-6645
Bondo Corp 3700 Atlanta Industrial Pkwy NW *TF:* 800-622-8754 ■ *Web:* www.bondo-online.com	Atlanta	GA	30331	404-696-2730	696-6814
California Products Corp 150 Dascomb Rd **Fax Area Code:* 800 ■ *TF:* 800-225-1141 ■ *Web:* www.californiapaints.com	Andover	MA	01810	978-623-9980	533-6788*
Carboline Co 350 Hanley Industrial Ct *TF:* 800-848-4645 ■ *Web:* www.carboline.com	Saint Louis	MO	63144	314-644-1000	644-4617
Chemical Coatings Inc 22 S Center St *TF:* 800-522-8266	Hickory	NC	28601	828-728-8266	
Cintech Industrial Coatings 2217 Langdon Farm Rd *Web:* www.cintechindustrial.com	Cincinnati	OH	45237	513-631-4270	366-4444
Columbia Paint & Coatings 112 N Haven St *TF:* 800-537-8530 ■ *Web:* www.columbiapaint.com	Spokane	WA	99202	509-535-9741	535-3421
Coronado Paint Co Inc 308 S Old County Rd **Fax Area Code:* 800 ■ *TF:* 800-883-4193 ■ *Web:* www.coronadopaint.com	Edgewater	FL	32132	386-428-6461	394-9022*
DAP Inc 2400 Boston St Suite 200 **Fax:* Cust Svc ■ *TF Cust Svc:* 800-584-3840 ■ *Web:* www.dap.com	Baltimore	MD	21224	410-675-2100	558-1068*
Davis Paint Co Inc 1311 Iron St *TF:* 800-821-2029 ■ *Web:* www.davispaint.com	North Kansas City	MO	64116	816-471-4447	471-1460
Day-Glo Color Corp 4515 St Clair Ave *TF:* 800-289-3294 ■ *Web:* www.dayglo.com	Cleveland	OH	44103	216-391-7070	391-7751
Diamond Vogel Paint & Wax Co 1020 Albany Pl SE *TF:* 800-728-6435 ■ *Web:* www.vogelpaint.com	Orange City	IA	51041	712-737-4116	737-4997
Duckback Products 2644 Hegan Ln *TF:* 800-825-5382 ■ *Web:* www.superdeck.com	Chico	CA	95928	530-343-3261	343-3283
Dunn-Edwards Corp 4885 E 52nd Pl *TF:* 800-537-4098 ■ *Web:* www.dunnedwards.com	Los Angeles	CA	90040	323-771-3330	771-4440
DuPont Automotive 950 Stephenson Hwy **Fax:* Sales ■ *TF:* 800-441-0575 ■ *Web:* automotive.dupont.com/en/index.html	Troy	MI	48083	248-583-8000	583-8157*
DuPont Performance Coatings 1007 Market St *TF:* 800-441-7515 ■ *Web:* www.performance-coatings.org	Wilmington	DE	19898	302-774-1000	999-4399
Duron Inc 10406 Tucker St *TF:* 800-723-8766 ■ *Web:* www.duron.com	Beltsville	MD	20705	301-937-4700	
Ferro Corp 1000 Lakeside Ave *NYSE: FOE* ■ *Web:* www.ferro.com	Cleveland	OH	44114	216-641-8580	875-6195
Ferro Corp Liquid Coatings & Dispersions Div 1301 N Flora St *TF:* 800-882-1456	Plymouth	IN	46563	574-935-5131	935-4261
Ferro Corp Plastics Colorants Div 103 Railroad Ave *TF:* 800-521-9094 ■ *Web:* www.ferro.com	Stryker	OH	43557	419-682-3311	682-4924
FinishMaster Inc 54 Monument Cir Suite 600 *TF:* 888-311-3678 ■ *Web:* www.finishmaster.com	Indianapolis	IN	46204	317-237-3678	237-2150
Finnaren & Haley Inc 901 Washington St *TF:* 800-843-9800 ■ *Web:* www.fhpaint.com	Conshohocken	PA	19428	610-825-1900	825-1184
Flex Bon Paints 2131 Andrea Ln *TF:* 800-353-9266 ■ *Web:* www.flexbon.com	Fort Myers	FL	33912	239-489-2332	433-0203
Frazee Industries Inc 6625 Miramar Rd *TF:* 800-477-9991 ■ *Web:* www.frazeepaint.com	San Diego	CA	92121	858-626-3600	452-3568
Gallagher-Kaiser Corp 13710 Mt Elliott St *Web:* www.gkcorp.com	Detroit	MI	48212	313-368-3100	368-3109
General Coatings Technology Inc 24 Woodward Ave *TF:* 800-522-3664	Ridgewood	NY	11385	718-821-1232	381-6935
Harrison Paint Co 1329 Harrison Ave SW *TF:* 800-321-0680 ■ *Web:* www.harrisonpaint.com	Canton	OH	44706	330-455-5125	454-1750
HB Fuller Co 1200 Willow Lake Blvd PO Box 64683 *NYSE: FUL* ■ *TF:* 800-828-2981 ■ *Web:* www.hbfuller.com	Saint Paul	MN	55164	651-236-5900	236-5898
Hentzen Coatings Inc 6937 W Mill Rd *Web:* www.hentzen.com	Milwaukee	WI	53218	414-353-4200	353-0286
ICI Americas Inc 10 Finderne Ave *TF:* 800-998-9986 ■ *Web:* www.ici.com/UnitedStatesofAmerica	Bridgewater	NJ	08807	908-203-5000	685-5005
ICI Paints North America 15885 Sprague Rd *TF Cust Svc:* 800-221-4100 ■ *Web:* www.icipaints.com	Strongsville	OH	44136	440-297-8000	
Insl-X Products Corp 50 Holt Dr *TF:* 800-225-5554 ■ *Web:* www.insl-x.com	Stony Point	NY	10980	845-786-5000	786-5831
JONES-BLAIR Co NEOGARD Div 2728 Empire Central St **Fax:* Cust Svc ■ *TF:* 800-492-9400 ■ *Web:* www.jones-blair.com	Dallas	TX	75235	214-353-1600	325-6321*
Kelly-Moore Paint Co Inc 987 Commercial St **Fax:* Hum Res ■ *TF:* 800-874-4436 ■ *Web:* www.kellymoore.com	San Carlos	CA	94070	650-592-8337	508-8563*
KJ Quinn & Co Inc 34 Folly Mill Rd *Web:* www.quretech.com	Seabrook	NH	03874	603-474-5753	474-7122
Kop-Coat Inc 436 7th Ave Koppers Bldg Suite 1850 *Web:* www.kop-coat.com	Pittsburgh	PA	15219	412-227-2700	227-2618
Kwal Paint 3900 Joliet St *TF Cust Svc:* 800-383-8406 ■ *Web:* www.kwalhowells.com	Denver	CO	80239	303-371-5600	373-5688
Lancaster Distributing Co 1310 Union St *TF:* 800-845-8287 ■ *Web:* www.lancasterco.com	Spartanburg	SC	29302	864-583-3011	542-1315
Landers Segal Color Co 305 W Grand Ave *TF:* 800-526-2783 ■ *Web:* www.pigments.com	Montvale	NJ	07645	201-307-5995	307-5855
Lansco Colors 305 W Grand Ave *TF:* 800-526-2783 ■ *Web:* www.pigments.com	Montvale	NJ	07645	201-307-5995	307-5855
LaPolla Industries Inc 15402 Vantage Pkwy E Suite 322 *AMEX: LPA* ■ *TF:* 800-382-4931 ■ *Web:* www.lapollaindustries.com	Houston	TX	77032	281-219-4100	219-4102
MAB Paints 600 Reed Rd *TF:* 800-622-1899 ■ *Web:* www.mabpaints.com	Broomall	PA	19008	610-353-5100	353-8189
Mantros-Haeuser & Co Inc 1175 Post Rd E *TF:* 800-344-4229 ■ *Web:* www.mbzgroup.com	Westport	CT	06880	203-454-1800	227-0558
Martin-Senour Paints 101 Prospect Ave NW *TF:* 800-677-5270 ■ *Web:* www.martinsenour.com	Cleveland	OH	44115	216-566-2000	566-3114
Masterchem Industries LLC 3135 Old Hwy M *TF:* 800-325-3552 ■ *Web:* www.masterchem.com	Imperial	MO	63052	636-942-2510	942-3663
Mautz Paint Co 6314 Odana Rd *Web:* www.mautzpaint.com	Madison	WI	53719	608-273-4927	273-4969
Michelman Inc 9080 Shell Rd *TF:* 800-477-0498 ■ *Web:* www.michem.com	Cincinnati	OH	45236	513-793-7766	793-2504

Phone Fax

Minwax Co 10 Mountainview Rd .... Upper Saddle River NJ 07458 201-818-7500 818-7605
TF: 800-526-0495 ■ Web: www.minwax.com

Mobile Paint Mfg Co 4775 Hamilton Blvd .... Theodore AL 36582 251-443-6110 408-0410
TF: 800-621-6952 ■ Web: www.blpmobilepaint.com

Mohawk Finishing Products 22 S Center St .... Hickory NC 28601 828-261-0325 721-1545*
*Fax Area Code: 800 ■ TF: 800-545-0047 ■ Web: www.mohawk-finishing.com

Moore Benjamin & Co 101 Paragon Dr .... Montvale NJ 07645 201-573-9600 949-6645
TF: 800-344-0400 ■ Web: www.benjaminmoore.com

Muralo Co Inc 148 E 5th St .... Bayonne NJ 07002 201-437-0770 437-0664
TF: 800-631-3440 ■ Web: www.muralo.com

NEOGARD Div JONES-BLAIR Co 2728 Empire Central St .... Dallas TX 75235 214-353-1600 325-6321*
*Fax: Cust Svc ■ TF: 800-492-9400 ■ Web: www.jones-blair.com

Norton & Son Inc 148 E 5th St .... Bayonne NJ 07002 201-437-0770 437-2316
TF: 800-631-3440 ■ Web: www.muralo.com

O'Leary Paint 300 E Oakland Ave .... Lansing MI 48906 517-487-2066 487-1680
TF: 800-477-2066 ■ Web: www.olearypaint.com

Parker Paint Mfg Co Inc 3003 S Tacoma Way .... Tacoma WA 98409 253-473-1122 473-0448
TF: 800-826-4308 ■ Web: www.parkerpaint.com

Penn Color Inc 400 Old Dublin Pike .... Doylestown PA 18901 215-345-6550 345-0270
TF: 800-523-6032 ■ Web: www.penncolor.com

Pioneer Mfg 4529 Industrial Pkwy .... Cleveland OH 44135 216-671-5500 671-5502
TF: 800-877-1500 ■ Web: www.pioneer-mfg.com

Plasti-Kote Co Inc 1000 Lake Rd .... Medina OH 44256 330-725-4511 723-3674
TF: 800-431-5928 ■ Web: www.plasti-kote.com

Porter Paints Inc 400 S 13th St .... Louisville KY 40203 502-588-9200 588-9242*
*Fax: Mktg ■ TF: 800-332-6270 ■ Web: www.porterpaints.com

PPG Industries Inc 1 PPG Pl .... Pittsburgh PA 15272 412-434-3131 434-2011*
NYSE: PPG ■ *Fax: Hum Res ■ Web: www.ppg.com

Progress Paint Co Inc 201 E Market St .... Louisville KY 40202 502-584-0151 587-2440
TF: 800-626-6407 ■ Web: www.progresspaint.com

Quinn KJ & Co Inc 34 Folly Mill Rd .... Seabrook NH 03874 603-474-5753 474-7122
Web: www.quretech.com

Red Spot Paint & Varnish Co Inc 1107 E Louisiana St .... Evansville IN 47711 812-428-9100
TF: 800-457-3544 ■ Web: www.redspot.com

Republic Powdered Metals Inc 2628 Pearl Rd .... Medina OH 44256 330-225-3192 273-5061
TF: 800-551-7081 ■ Web: www.rpmrepublic.com

Rodda Paint Co 6107 N Marine Dr .... Portland OR 97203 503-521-4300 521-4400
Web: www.roddapaint.com

Roymal Inc 475 Sunapee St .... Newport NH 03773 603-863-2410 863-9065
Web: www.roymalinc.com

RPM International Inc 2628 Pearl Rd .... Medina OH 44256 330-273-5090 225-8743
NYSE: RPM ■ TF: 800-776-4488 ■ Web: www.rpminc.com

Rust-Oleum Corp 11 Hawthorn Pkwy .... Vernon Hills IL 60061 847-367-7700 816-2300
TF: 800-323-3584 ■ Web: www.rustoleum.com

Samuel Cabot Inc 100 Hale St .... Newburyport MA 01950 978-465-1900
TF: 800-877-8246 ■ Web: www.cabotstain.com

Sermatech International Inc 1566 Medical Dr Suite 300 .... Pottstown PA 19464 610-819-1270 819-1271
Web: www.sermatech.com

Sherwin-Williams Co 101 Prospect Ave NW .... Cleveland OH 44115 216-566-2000 566-3670
NYSE: SHW ■ TF: 800-996-7566 ■ Web: www.sherwin.com

Sherwin-Williams Co Automotive Div
4440 Warrensville Ctr Rd .... Warrensville Heights OH 44128 216-332-8330

Sherwin-Williams Co Coatings Div 101 Prospect Ave NW .... Cleveland OH 44115 216-566-2000

Sherwin-Williams Co Consumer Group
26300 Fargo Ave .... Bedford Heights OH 44146 216-292-7400 591-1310*
*Fax: Sales

Sterling-Clark-Lurton Corp PO Box 130 .... Norwood MA 02062 781-762-5400 762-1095
TF: 800-225-9872 ■ Web: www.sclsterling.com

Supro Corp 2650 Pomona Blvd .... Pomona CA 91768 909-595-2208 595-5619

Talbot Industries Inc 5725 Howard Bush Dr .... Neosho MO 64850 417-451-7440 451-6244
TF: 800-749-6894

TCI Powder Coatings Inc 734 Dixon Dr .... Ellaville GA 31806 229-937-5411 937-2064
TF: 800-533-9067 ■ Web: www.tcipowder.com

Tnemec Co Inc 6800 Corporate Dr .... Kansas City MO 64120 816-483-3400 483-3969
TF: 800-483-3969 ■ Web: www.tnemec.com

United Gilsonite Laboratories 1369 Jefferson Ave PO Box 70 .... Scranton PA 18501 570-344-1202 969-7634
TF: 800-845-5227 ■ Web: www.ugl.com

Valspar Corp 1101 S 3rd St .... Minneapolis MN 55415 612-332-7371 375-7723
NYSE: VAL ■ TF: 800-328-8044 ■ Web: www.valspar.com

Valspar Refinish Inc 210 Crosby St .... Picayune MS 39466 601-798-4731 798-6147
TF Cust Svc: 800-556-1347 ■ Web: www.valsparrefinish.com

Vista Paint Corp 2020 E Orangethorpe Ave .... Fullerton CA 92831 714-680-3800 680-3809
TF: 800-698-4782 ■ Web: www.vistapaint.com

Willamette Valley Co 1075 Arrowsmith St .... Eugene OR 97402 541-484-9621 345-7480
TF: 800-333-9826 ■ Web: www.wilvaco.com

WM Barr & Co Inc PO Box 1879 .... Memphis TN 38101 901-775-0100 621-9508*
*Fax Area Code: 800 ■ TF: 800-782-9928 ■ Web: www.wmbarr.com

Wolf Gordon Inc 33-00 47th Ave .... Long Island City NY 11101 718-361-6611 361-1090
TF: 800-347-0550 ■ Web: www.wolf-gordon.com

Yenkin-Majestic Paint Corp 1920 Leonard Ave .... Columbus OH 43219 614-253-8511 253-6327
TF: 800-848-1898 ■ Web: www.yenkin-majestic.com

Zinsser Co Inc 173 Belmont Dr .... Somerset NJ 08875 732-469-8100 652-2498
Web: www.zinsser.com

554 PALLETS & SKIDS

Phone Fax

Allied Container Corp 435 E Hedding St .... San Jose CA 95112 408-293-3628 293-2014

American Pallet Inc 1001 Knox Rd .... Oakdale CA 95361 209-847-6122 847-6154
Web: www.americanpallet.com

Anderson Forest Products Inc
1267 Old Edmonton Rd PO Box 520 .... Tompkinsville KY 42167 270-487-6778 487-8953
TF: 800-489-6778 ■ Web: www.afp-reelsandpallets.com

Ball Brothers Forest Products Inc
Old Hwy 63 PO Box 548 .... Koshkonong MO 65692 417-867-5664 867-5662

Brunswick Box Co Inc 852 Planters Rd PO Box 7 .... Lawrenceville VA 23868 434-848-2222 848-3647
TF: 800-343-9913 ■ Web: www.brunswickbox.com

Clinch-Tite Corp 5264 Lake St PO Box 456 .... Sandy Lake PA 16145 724-376-7315 376-2785
TF: 800-241-0900 ■ Web: www.clinchtite.com

Cutter Lumber Products 10 Rickenbacker Cir .... Livermore CA 94551 925-443-5959 443-0648
Web: www.cutterlumber.com

Daniel Lumber Co Inc 309 Pierce St PO Box 340 .... LaGrange GA 30241 706-884-5686 883-8010
TF: 800-251-0398

Day Lumber Corp 34 S Broad St PO Box 9 .... Westfield MA 01086 413-568-3511 568-6668

Delisa Pallet Corp 91-97 Blanchard St .... Newark NJ 07105 973-344-8600 344-0689
Web: www.delisapallet.com

Eastern Wood Products Inc 2020 Mill Ln PO Box 1056 .... Williamsport PA 17703 570-326-1946 327-1390
TF: 800-445-5428

Edwards Wood Products Inc
2215 Old Lawyers Rd PO Box 219 .... Marshville NC 28103 704-624-5098 624-6812
Web: www.ewpi.com

Girard Wood Products Co Inc 820 E Main PO Box 830 .... Puyallup WA 98371 253-845-0505 845-5463
TF: 800-532-0505 ■ Web: www.girardwoodproducts.com

Hill Wood Products Inc 948 Ashawa Rd PO Box 398 .... Cook MN 55723 218-666-5933 666-5726
Web: www.hillwoodproducts.com

Hinchcliff Products Co 13477 Prospect Rd .... Strongsville OH 44149 440-238-5200 238-5202
Web: www.hinchcliffproducts.com

Hunter Woodworks Inc 21038 S Wilmington Ave PO Box 4937 .... Carson CA 90749 323-775-2544 775-2540
TF: 800-966-4751 ■ Web: www.hunterpallets.com

Ifco Systems 6829 Flintlock Rd .... Houston TX 77040 713-332-6145 332-6146
TF: 800-771-1148 ■ Web: www.ifcosystems.de

Indiana Wood Products Inc
58228 County Rd 43 PO Box 1168 .... Middlebury IN 46540 574-825-2129 825-7519

Litco International Inc 1 Litco Dr .... Vienna OH 44473 330-539-5433 539-5388
Web: www.litco.com

Morgan Wood Products PO Box 177 .... Powell OH 43065 614-336-4000 336-7970

Mountain Valley Farms & Lumber Inc 1240 Nawakwa Rd .... Biglerville PA 17307 717-677-6166 677-9283
Web: www.mtvalleyfarms.com

Nelson Co 2116 Sparrows Point Rd .... Baltimore MD 21219 410-477-3000 388-0246
Web: www.nelsoncompany.com

Nepa Pallet & Container Co Inc
12027 Three Lakes Rd PO Box 399 .... Snohomish WA 98291 360-568-3185 568-9135
TF: 800-562-3932

Packing Material Co 27280 Haggerty Rd Suite C-16 .... Farmington Hills MI 48331 248-489-7000 489-7009
TF: 888-927-4797 ■ Web: www.packingmaterial.com

Pallet Masters Inc 655 E Florence Ave .... Los Angeles CA 90001 323-758-6559 758-9600
TF: 800-675-2571 ■ Web: www.palletmasters.com

PalletOne Inc 1470 US Hwy 17 S .... Bartow FL 33830 863-533-1147 533-3065
TF: 800-771-1148 ■ Web: www.palletone.com

Potomac Supply Corp 1398 Kinsale Rd .... Kinsale VA 22488 804-472-2527 472-4300
TF Sales: 800-365-3900 ■ Web: www.potomacsupply.com

Precision Pallet Co 721 Parkwood Ave .... Romeoville IL 60446 815-886-1061 886-0829
TF: 800-255-8532

Precision Wood Products Inc
16363 NE Sandy Blvd PO Box 529 .... Vancouver WA 98660 503-285-0393 252-6046
TF: 877-743-9663

Remmey the Pallet Co 317 Davisville Rd PO Box 558 .... Willow Grove PA 19090 267-913-0002 913-0510
TF: 800-725-5385 ■ Web: www.remmey.com

Savanna Pallets Co 106 E 1st Ave PO Box 308 .... McGregor MN 55760 218-768-2077 768-3112
TF: 800-348-5708 ■ Web: www.savannapallets.com

Seaman Timber Co Inc PO Box 372 1051 Hwy 25 S .... South Montevallo AL 35115 205-665-2536 665-2545
TF: 800-782-8155 ■ Web: www.seamantimber.com

United Wholesale Lumber Co 8009 Doe Ave .... Visalia CA 93291 559-651-2037 651-0742
TF: 800-651-2037 ■ Web: www.uwlco.com

Walczak Lumber Inc Rt 106 PO Box 340 .... Clifford PA 18413 570-222-9651 222-9650
TF: 800-445-1215

Walters Brothers Lumber Mfg Co Inc 10489 W Hwy 27/70 .... Radisson WI 54867 715-945-2217 945-2878

Williamsburg Millwork Corp PO Box 427 .... Bowling Green VA 22427 804-994-2151 994-5371
TF: 888-699-8900

WNC Pallet & Forest Products Co Inc
1414 Smokey Park Hwy PO Box 38 .... Candler NC 28715 828-667-5426 665-4759
Web: www.wncpallet.com

Yoder Lumber Co Inc 3799 County Rd 70 .... Sugarcreek OH 44681 330-893-3131 893-3032
Web: www.yoderlumber.com

555 PAPER - MFR

SEE ALSO Packaging Materials & Products - Paper or Plastics p. 2043

555-1 Coated & Laminated Paper

Phone Fax

Appleton Papers Inc PO Box 359 .... Appleton WI 54912 920-734-9841
TF: 800-558-8390 ■ Web: www.appletonpapers.com

Arkwright Inc 538 Main St .... Fiskeville RI 02823 401-821-1000 826-3926
TF Cust Svc: 800-942-5900 ■ Web: www.arkwright-ri.com

Avery Dennison Retail Ticketing 7 Bishop St .... Framingham MA 01702 508-383-4373 383-5006
Web: www.averydennison.com

Avery Dennison Worldwide Graphics Div
250 Chester St Bldg 6 .... Painesville OH 44077 440-358-3700 358-3665
TF: 800-443-9380 ■ Web: www.averygraphics.com

Bowater Inc 55 E Camper Down Way .... Greenville SC 29601 864-271-7733 282-9591*
NYSE: BOW ■ *Fax: Hum Res ■ TF: 800-845-6002 ■ Web: www.bowater.com

Bowater Inc Coated Paper Div 5300 Cureton Ferry Rd .... Catawba SC 29704 803-981-8161
Web: www.bowater.com/en/divisionsCoatedSpecialty.shtml

BPM Inc 200 W Front St .... Peshtigo WI 54157 715-582-4551 582-4853
TF: 800-826-0494 ■ Web: www.bpmpaper.com

Cardinal Industries Inc 37 W 750 Rt 64 .... Saint Charles IL 60175 630-513-5400 513-5609
TF: 800-323-5018 ■ Web: www.cardind.com

Cascades Fine Papers Group Thunder Bay Inc
PO Box 10640 550 Shipyard Rd .... Thunder Bay ON P7B6V1 807-683-2110 683-2372

Deerfield Specialty Papers Inc 4302 Mike Padgett Hwy .... Augusta GA 30906 706-798-1861 798-2270

Dietzgen 250 S Northwest Hwy Suite 203 .... Park Ridge IL 60068 800-473-1200 473-9070
TF Cust Svc: 800-473-1270 ■ Web: www.dietzgen.com

Fortifiber Corp 1001 Tahoe Blvd .... Incline Village NV 89451 775-833-6161 833-6151
TF: 800-443-4079 ■ Web: www.fortifiber.com

Fraser Papers Inc 2273 Congress St .... Portland ME 04102 207-523-2350 523-2392
TF: 800-920-9988 ■ Web: www.fraserpapers.com

French Paper Co 100 French St .... Niles MI 49120 269-683-1100 683-3025
TF: 800-253-5952 ■ Web: www.mrfrench.com

Horizon Paper Co Inc 100 First Stamford Pl Suite 350 .... Stamford CT 06902 203-358-0855 358-0828
TF: 866-358-0855 ■ Web: www.horizonpaper.com

InteliCoat Technologies 28 Gaylord St .... South Hadley MA 01075 413-536-7800 861-4128*
*Fax Area Code: 800 ■ *Fax: Cust Svc ■ TF: 800-628-9285 ■ Web: www.intelicoat.com

Kimberly-Clark Corp Technical Paper Div
1400 Holcomb Bridge Rd .... Roswell GA 30076 920-721-2000 721-4219
TF: 800-544-1847 ■ Web: www.kimberly-clark.com

Knowlton Specialty Papers Inc 213 Factory St .... Watertown NY 13601 315-782-0600 782-7517
Web: www.knowlton-co.com

MeadWestvaco Specialty Paper 40 Willow St .... South Lee MA 01260 413-243-1231 243-4602*
*Fax: Mktg ■ Web: www.meadwestvaco.com/specialtypapers.nsf

Mepco Label Systems PO Box 932 .... Stockton CA 95201 209-946-0201 946-0164
TF: 800-975-2235 ■ Web: www.mepcolabel.com

Nashua Corp 11 Trafalgar Sq 2nd Fl .... Nashua NH 03063 603-880-2323 880-5671
NASDAQ: NSHA ■ TF: 800-258-1370 ■ Web: www.nashua.com

National/AZON 1148 Rochester Rd .... Troy MI 48083 248-307-9308 318-7323*
*Fax Area Code: 866 ■ TF: 800-325-5939 ■ Web: www.azon.com

NewPage Corp 10 W 2nd St .... Dayton OH 45402 877-855-7243 242-9327*
*Fax Area Code: 937 ■ Web: www.newpagecorp.com

Permalin Products Corp 205 W 39th St 16th Fl .... New York NY 10018 212-768-7400 768-8520
TF: 800-417-3762 ■ Web: www.permalin.com

Sappi Fine Paper North America 225 Franklin St 28th Fl .... Boston MA 02110 617-423-7300 423-5494*
NYSE: SPP ■ *Fax: Mail Rm ■ Web: www.sappi.com

Stora Enso North America Corp 2 Landmark Sq 3rd Fl .... Stamford CT 06901 203-356-2300 356-2340
NYSE: SEO ■ TF: 888-807-8672 ■ Web: www.storaenso.com/na

Coated & Laminated Paper (Cont'd)

Phone Fax

TST/Impreso Inc 652 Southwestern Blvd ....Coppell TX 75019 972-462-0100 845-3759*
Fax Area Code: 800 ■ *Fax:* Cust Svc ■ *TF:* 800-527-2878 ■ *Web:* www.tstimpreso.com
Universal Blueprint Paper Co 327 Bryan Ave..................Fort Worth TX 76104 817-332-9634 332-5406
Web: www.universalblue.com
Wausau Paper Corp 100 Paper Place..........................Mosinee WI 54455 715-693-4470 692-2083
NYSE: WPP ■ *Web:* www.wausaupaper.com
Wausau Paper Corp Specialty Paper Div 100 Paper Pl............Mosinee WI 54455 715-692-2062 692-2094
Web: www.wpspecialtyproducts.com

555-2 Writing Paper

Phone Fax

3M Consumer & Office Div 3M Ctr..........................Saint Paul MN 55144 651-733-1110 736-2133
TF: 800-364-3577
American Pad & Paper Co LLC
3101 E George Bush Hwy Suite 200.......................Richardson TX 75082 800-426-1368 558-0436
Web: www.ampad.com
American Scholar Inc 335 Crooked Hill Rd ....Brentwood NY 11717 631-273-6550 273-6019
Web: www.americanscholar.com
Anna Griffin Inc 2270 Marietta Blvd.........................Atlanta GA 30318 404-817-8170 817-0590
TF: 888-817-8170 ■ *Web:* www.annagriffin.com
Cascades Fine Papers Group Inc 2 Rolland Ave............Saint-Jerome QC J7Z5S1 450-569-3910 569-3947*
Fax: Mktg ■ *Web:* www.cascades.com
Cascades Inc 404 Marie-Victorin Blvd ....Kingsey Falls QC J0A1B0 819-363-5100 363-5155
TSX: CAS ■ *Web:* www.cascades.com
Case Stationery Co Inc 179 Saw Mill River Rd..................Yonkers NY 10701 914-965-5100 965-2362
TF: 800-431-2422 ■ *Web:* www.casestationery.com
CR Gibson Inc 404 BNA Dr Bldg 100 Suite 600................Nashville TN 37217 615-724-2900 871-0501
TF: 800-243-6004 ■ *Web:* www.crgibson.com
Crane & Co Inc 30 South St..................................Dalton MA 01226 413-684-2600 684-0726*
Fax: Orders ■ *TF Cust Svc:* 800-572-0024 ■ *Web:* www.crane.com
DiversaFile LLC 721 111th St...............................Arlington TX 76011 817-640-0800 640-0849
Web: www.diversafile.com
Domtar Inc 395 boul de Maisonneuve O........................Montreal QC H3A1L6 514-848-5400 848-6609*
NYSE: DTC ■ *Fax:* Mktg ■ *TF:* 800-267-2040 ■ *Web:* www.domtar.com
Fay Paper Products Inc PO Box 38..........................Norwood MA 02062 781-769-4620 769-8522
TF: 800-765-4620 ■ *Web:* www.faypaper.com
Geographics LLC 93 North Ave..............................Garwood NJ 07027 800-526-4280 789-9461*
Fax Area Code: 908 ■ *Web:* www.geographics.com
Gordon Paper Co Inc PO Box 1806..........................Norfolk VA 23501 757-464-3581 363-9355
TF: 800-457-7366 ■ *Web:* www.gordonpaper.com
Griffin Anna Inc 2270 Marietta Blvd.........................Atlanta GA 30318 404-817-8170 817-0590
TF: 888-817-8170 ■ *Web:* www.annagriffin.com
Mafcote Industries Inc 108 Main St..........................Norwalk CT 06851 203-847-8500 849-9177
TF Cust Svc: 800-221-3056 ■ *Web:* www.mafcote.com
MeadWestvaco Consumer & Office Products
4751 Hempstead Station Dr..............................Kettering OH 45429 937-495-6323 495-3168
TF: 800-648-6323 ■ *Web:* www.meadwestvaco.com/cop.nsf
Mohawk Fine Papers Inc 465 Saratoga St......................Cohoes NY 12047 518-237-1740 237-7394
TF: 800-843-6455 ■ *Web:* www.mohawkpaper.com
Neenah Paper Inc 3460 Preston Ridge Rd Suite 600 ....Alpharetta GA 30005 678-566-6500
NYSE: NP ■ *Web:* www.neenah.com
Paper Conversions Inc 6761 Thompson Rd N.................Syracuse NY 13211 315-437-1641 437-3634
TF: 800-729-2823 ■ *Web:* www.padmaker.com
Performance Office Papers 21673 Cedar Ave....................Lakeville MN 55044 952-469-1400 488-5058*
Fax Area Code: 800 ■ *TF:* 800-458-7189 ■ *Web:* www.perfpapers.com
Roaring Spring Blank Book Co 740 Spang St PO Box 35 .... Roaring Spring PA 16673 814-224-5141 224-5429
TF Cust Svc: 800-441-1653 ■ *Web:* www.rspaperproducts.com
Rytex Co 100 N Park Ave.....................................Peru IN 46970 800-277-5458 329-1669
Web: www.rytex.com
Schurman Fine Papers 500 Chadbourne Rd Box 6030 ....Fairfield CA 94533 707-428-0200 428-0641
TF Sales: 800-333-6724 ■ *Web:* www.papyrusonline.com
Southworth Co 265 Main St....................................Agawam MA 01001 413-789-1200 786-1529
TF: 800-225-1839 ■ *Web:* www.southworth.com
Specialty Loose Leaf Inc 1 Cabot St...........................Holyoke MA 01040 413-532-0106 887-0195
TF: 800-848-8020 ■ *Web:* www.specialtyll.com
Top Flight Inc 1300 Central Ave.........................Chattanooga TN 37408 423-266-8171 266-6857
TF: 800-777-3740 ■ *Web:* www.topflightpaper.com
Wausau Paper Corp 100 Paper Place..........................Mosinee WI 54455 715-693-4470 692-2083
NYSE: WPP ■ *Web:* www.wausaupaper.com
Wausau Paper Corp Printing & Writing Paper Div
1 Clark's Island ....Wausau WI 54403 715-675-3361 675-8355
Web: www.wpprintingandwriting.com/default.aspx
William Arthur Inc 7 Alewive Park Rd PO Box 460........ West Kennebunk ME 04094 207-985-6581 985-0407
TF: 800-985-6581 ■ *Web:* www.williamarthur.com

556 PAPER - WHOL

Phone Fax

Abitibi-Consolidated Sales Corp 4 Gannett Dr................White Plains NY 10604 914-640-8600 640-8900
TF: 800-848-7213 ■ *Web:* www.abitibiconsolidated.com
Anchor Paper Co Inc 480 Broadway St ....Saint Paul MN 55101 651-298-1311 298-0060
TF: 800-652-9755 ■ *Web:* www.anchorpaper.com
AT Clayton & Co Inc 300 Atlantic St ....Stamford CT 06901 203-658-1200 658-1326
TF: 800-282-5298 ■ *Web:* www.atclayton.com
Atlantic Packaging Co 806 N 23rd St ....Wilmington NC 28405 910-343-0624 763-5421
TF: 800-722-5841 ■ *Web:* www.atlanticpkg.com
Bradner Smith & Co 2300 Arthur Ave...................Elk Grove Village IL 60007 847-290-8485 290-8486
TF: 800-678-1852 ■ *Web:* www.bradnersmith.com
Cascades Fine Papers Group Inc 2 Rolland Ave............Saint-Jerome QC J7Z5S1 450-569-3910 569-3947*
Fax: Mktg ■ *Web:* www.cascades.com
Central Lewmar Paper Co 60 McClellan St.......................Newark NJ 07114 973-622-6377 623-4323
Web: www.centrallewmar.com
Central National-Gottesman Inc 3 Manhattanville Rd ....Purchase NY 10577 914-696-9000 696-1066
Web: www.lindenmeyr.com
CJ Duffey Paper Co Inc 528 Washington Ave N ....Minneapolis MN 55401 612-338-8701 338-1320
TF: 800-752-8190 ■ *Web:* www.duffeypaper.com
Clampitt Paper Co of Dallas 9207 Ambassador Row ....Dallas TX 75247 214-638-3300 634-7837
TF: 800-856-0138 ■ *Web:* www.clampitt.com
Clayton AT & Co Inc 300 Atlantic St ....Stamford CT 06901 203-658-1200 658-1326
TF: 800-282-5298 ■ *Web:* www.atclayton.com
Clifford Paper Inc
600 E Crescent Ave 3rd Fl Sherbrooke
Office Centre...Upper Saddle River NJ 07458 201-934-5115 934-5188
Web: www.cliffordpaper.com
Cole Papers Inc 1300 N 38th St...................................Fargo ND 58102 701-282-5311 282-5513
TF: 800-800-8090 ■ *Web:* www.colepapers.com
Donco Paper Supply Co 737 N Michigan Ave Suite 1450 ....Chicago IL 60611 312-337-7822 337-7891
Web: www.doncopaper.com

Phone Fax

Eastern Data Paper Inc PO Box 202 ....Little Falls NJ 07424 973-472-5252 472-5333
TF: 800-524-2528
Elof Hansson Inc 565 Taxter Rd...............................Elmsford NY 10523 914-345-8380 345-8112
Web: www.elof-hansson.com
Frank Parsons Paper Co Inc 2270 Beaver Rd ....Landover MD 20785 301-386-4700 386-0949*
Fax: Cust Svc ■ *TF:* 800-944-9940 ■ *Web:* www.frankparsons.com
Gould Paper Corp 11 Madison Ave 14th Fl.....................New York NY 10010 212-301-0000 481-0067
TF: 800-275-4685 ■ *Web:* www.gouldpaper.com
GPA 1151 W 40th St ....Chicago IL 60609 312-243-6860 395-3581*
Fax Area Code: 800 ■ *TF:* 800-395-9000 ■ *Web:* www.gpalabels.com
GreenLine Paper Co 631 S Pine St................................York PA 17403 717-845-8697 846-3806
TF: 800-641-1117 ■ *Web:* www.greenlinepaper.com
Hansson Elof Inc 565 Taxter Rd ....Elmsford NY 10523 914-345-8380 345-8112
Web: www.elof-hansson.com
Hearn Paper Co 556 N Meridian Rd ....Youngstown OH 44509 330-792-6533 792-4762
TF: 800-225-2989 ■ *Web:* www.hearnpaper.com
Heinzel Imports-Exports Inc 220 E 42nd St Suite 3010............New York NY 10017 212-953-3210 953-3211
Web: www.heinzelsales.com
Hudson Valley Paper Co 981 Broadway ....Albany NY 12207 518-471-5111 455-8803
TF: 800-473-5525
Kelly Paper Co 288 Brea Canyon Rd ....City of Industry CA 91789 909-859-8200 859-8903
TF: 800-675-3559 ■ *Web:* www.kellypaper.com
Lindenmeyr Book Publishing Papers 521 5th Ave 6th Fl..........New York NY 10175 212-551-3900 213-1457
Web: www.lindenmeyr.com/bookpub_frameset.htm
Lindenmeyr Central 3 Manhattanville Rd ....Purchase NY 10577 914-696-9300 696-9333
TF: 800-221-3042 ■ *Web:* www.lindenmeyr.com/central_frameset.htm
Lindenmeyr Munroe Paper Corp 115 Moonachie Ave ....Moonachie NJ 07074 201-440-6491 440-6492
TF: 800-631-0193 ■ *Web:* www.lindenmeyr.com/munroe_frameset.htm
Mac Papers Inc 3300 Phillips Hwy.........................Jacksonville FL 32207 904-348-3300 348-3388
TF: 800-622-2968 ■ *Web:* www.macpapers.com
Marquardt & Co 161 6th Ave 2nd Fl..........................New York NY 10013 212-645-7200 536-0282
TF: 800-813-7788 ■ *Web:* www.marquardtpaper.com
Midland Paper 101 E Palatine Rd.............................Wheeling IL 60090 847-777-2700 777-2555
TF: 800-323-8522 ■ *Web:* www.midlandpaper.com
Millcraft Paper Co 6800 Grant Ave ....Cleveland OH 44105 216-441-5500 441-4128
TF: 800-826-4444 ■ *Web:* www.millcraft.com
Murnane Paper Corp 345 Fischer Farm Rd ....Elmhurst IL 60126 630-530-8222 530-8325
Web: www.murnanepaper.com
Newell Paper Co 1212 Grand Ave PO Box 631 ....Meridian MS 39301 601-693-1783 483-4900
TF: 800-844-8894 ■ *Web:* www.newellpaper.com
Paper Corp of the US 161 Ave of the Americas 3rd Fl............New York NY 10013 212-645-5900 337-5552
TF: 800-462-0182
PaperDirect Inc 1005 E Woodmen Rd..................Colorado Springs CO 80920 719-594-4100 531-2820
TF: 800-272-7377 ■ *Web:* www.paperdirect.com
Parsons Frank Paper Co Inc 2270 Beaver Rd ....Landover MD 20785 301-386-4700 386-0949*
Fax: Cust Svc ■ *TF:* 800-944-9940 ■ *Web:* www.frankparsons.com
Perez Trading Co Inc 3490 NW 125th St..............................Miami FL 33167 305-769-0761 681-7963
TF: 800-999-7599 ■ *Web:* www.pereztrading.com
Perkins-Goodwin Co Inc 300 Atlantic St 5th Fl ....Stamford CT 06901 203-363-7800 363-7809
Quimby-Walstrom Paper Co 2944 Walkent Dr NW............Grand Rapids MI 49544 616-784-4700 784-7813
TF: 800-632-5930 ■ *Web:* www.quimby.com
Roosevelt Paper Co 1 Roosevelt Dr ....Mount Laurel NJ 08054 856-303-4100 642-1949*
Fax: Sales ■ *TF:* 800-523-3470 ■ *Web:* www.rooseveltpaper.com
Spicers Paper Inc 12310 E Slauson Ave ....Santa Fe Springs CA 90670 562-698-1199 945-2597
TF: 800-774-2377 ■ *Web:* www.spicers.com
Streco Fibres Inc 168 Business Park Dr Suite 200 ....Virginia Beach VA 23462 757-473-3720 473-3721
Web: www.streco.com/index.html
Tayloe Paper Co Inc 6717 E 13th St ....Tulsa OK 74112 918-835-6911 835-7255
TF: 800-825-6911 ■ *Web:* www.tayloepaper.com
Unisource Worldwide Inc 6600 Governors Lake Pkwy.............Norcross GA 30071 770-447-9000 209-6550
TF: 800-282-7958 ■ *Web:* www.unisourcelink.com
Websource 161 Ave of the Americas 3rd Fl ....New York NY 10013 212-255-1600 337-8292
TF: 800-221-3213 ■ *Web:* www.websource-paper.com
White Paper Co 9990 River Way ....Delta BC V4G1M9 604-951-3900 951-3944
TF: 888-840-7300 ■ *Web:* www.whitepaper.com
Wilcox Paper Co Inc 2301 Traffic St NE....................Minneapolis MN 55413 612-378-2400 378-2815
TF: 800-394-5261 ■ *Web:* www.wilcoxpaper.com
Wisconsin Paper 3000 N 112th St...........................Wauwatosa WI 53222 414-771-3771 771-3918
TF: 800-242-0790 ■ *Web:* www.wipaper.com

557 PAPER CONVERTERS

Phone Fax

Ameri-Fax Corp 7709 W 20th Ave ....Hialeah FL 33014 305-828-1701 824-1606
TF: 800-969-1601 ■ *Web:* www.faxpaper.com
Artistry in Motion Inc 15101 Keswick St.......................Van Nuys CA 91405 818-994-7388 994-7688
Web: www.artistryinmotion.com
B & B Paper Converters Inc 12500 Elmwood Ave...............Cleveland OH 44111 216-941-8100 941-8174
BagcraftPapercon 3900 W 43rd St...............................Chicago IL 60632 773-254-8000 254-8204
TF: 800-621-8468 ■ *Web:* www.bagcraft.com
C-P Converters Inc DBA C-P Flexible Packaging
15 Grumbacher Rd..York PA 17406 717-764-1193 764-2039
Web: www.cpconverters.com
Caraustar Industries Inc
5000 Austell-Powder Sprngs Rd Suite 300...........................Austell GA 30106 770-948-3100
NASDAQ: CSAR ■ *Web:* www.caraustar.com
Case Paper Co Inc 500 Mamaroneck Ave 2nd Fl..................Harrison NY 10528 914-899-3500 777-1028
TF: 800-222-2922 ■ *Web:* www.casepaper.com
Chargeurs Inc 421 S Union St ....Troy OH 45373 937-335-5611 339-9223
TF: 800-561-7981
Cindus Corp 515 Station Ave.....................................Cincinnati OH 45215 513-948-9951 948-8805
TF: 800-543-4691 ■ *Web:* www.cindus.com
Crocker Technical Papers 431 Westminster St.................Fitchburg MA 01420 978-345-7771 342-4052
Crusader Paper Co Inc 350 Holt Rd.........................North Andover MA 01845 978-794-4900 794-1625
Web: www.crusaderpaper.com
Damsky Paper Co 3501 1st Ave N............................Birmingham AL 35222 205-521-9840 521-9853
Web: www.damskypaper.com
Delta Craft Paper Co 99 Bud-Mill Dr ....Buffalo NY 14206 716-856-5135 856-5130
TF: 800-735-5735 ■ *Web:* www.deltacraft.com
Extra Packaging Corp 631 Golden Harbour Dr...............Boca Raton FL 33432 561-416-2060 416-9545
TF: 800-872-7548 ■ *Web:* www.extrapackaging.com
Fabricon Products 1721 W Pleasant Ave ....River Rouge MI 48218 313-841-8200 841-4819
TF: 800-676-9727 ■ *Web:* www.fabriconproducts.com
Fay Paper Products Inc PO Box 38 ....Norwood MA 02062 781-769-4620 769-8522
TF: 800-765-4620 ■ *Web:* www.faypaper.com
Graphic Converting Inc 877 N Larch Ave.......................Elmhurst IL 60126 630-758-4100 833-1058
TF: 800-447-1935 ■ *Web:* www.graphicconverting.com
Hampden Papers Inc PO Box 149.................................Holyoke MA 01041 413-536-1000 532-9161
TF: 800-456-0200 ■ *Web:* www.hampdenpapers.com
Hazen Paper Co 240 S Water St PO Box 189......................Holyoke MA 01041 413-538-8204 533-1420
Web: www.hazen.com
Insulair Inc 35275 Welty Rd.....................................Vernalis CA 95385 209-839-0911 839-1353
TF: 800-343-3402 ■ *Web:* www.insulair.com

				Phone	Fax
International Converter Inc 721 Farson St	Belpre	OH	45714	740-423-7525	423-5799
TF: 800-962-8572 ■ *Web:* www.ici-laminating.com					
Interstate Paper Supply Co Inc 103 Good St	Roscoe	PA	15477	724-938-2218	938-3415
Web: www.ipscoinc.com					
Kanzaki Specialty Papers Inc 20 Cummings St	Ware	MA	01082	413-967-6204	967-5723
Web: www.kanzakiusa.com/					
Label Art Southeast Div 100 Clover Green	Peachtree City	GA	30269	770-631-7324	522-3581*
**Fax Area Code:* 888 ■ *TF:* 800-232-7833 ■ *Web:* www.labelart.com					
Lauterbach Group 1450 S West Ave	Waukesha	WI	53189	262-549-1730	549-3614
TF: 800-558-2126 ■ *Web:* www.lauterbachgroup.com					
Loyola Paper Co 951 W Lunt Ave	Elk Grove Village	IL	60007	847-956-7770	956-6897
Mac Paper Converters PO Box 5369	Jacksonville	FL	32247	904-733-9660	733-9622
TF: 800-334-7026					
Mafcote Industries Inc 108 Main St	Norwalk	CT	06851	203-847-8500	849-9177
TF Cust Svc: 800-221-3056 ■ *Web:* www.mafcote.com					
Marvel Products Inc PO Box 763	Fairfield	CT	06824	203-255-3511	255-3199
Newark Paperboard Products Inc 20 Jackson Dr	Cranford	NJ	07016	908-276-4000	276-2888
TF: 800-777-7890 ■ *Web:* www.newarkgroup.com					
North Hill Paper Converters 278 19th St NE	Calgary	AB	T2E8P7	403-248-9993	248-1001
Web: www.northhill.net/converting/home.htm					
Northeastern PA Carton & Finishing Co Inc					
4820 Birney Ave US Rt 11	Moosic	PA	18507	570-457-7711	457-3801
Web: www.nepacartons.com					
PAC Paper Inc 6416 NW Whitney Rd	Vancouver	WA	98665	360-695-7771	694-0943
TF: 800-223-4981 ■ *Web:* www.pacpaperinc.com					
Pacon Corp 2525 N Casaloma Dr	Appleton	WI	54912	920-830-5050	830-5099
TF: 800-333-2545 ■ *Web:* www.pacon.com					
Paper Systems Inc 185 S Pioneer Blvd	Springboro	OH	45066	937-746-6841	746-1089
TF: 888-564-6774 ■ *Web:* www.papersystems.com					
PM Co 1500 Kemper Meadow Dr	Cincinnati	OH	45240	513-825-7626	626-2140*
**Fax Area Code:* 800 ■ *TF:* 800-327-4359 ■ *Web:* www.pmcompany.com					
Pride-Made Products Inc 740 Lloyd Rd	Matawan	NJ	07747	732-583-3030	583-7855
Web: www.pridemadeproducts.com					
Putney Paper Co Inc 67 Kathan Meadow Rd	Putney	VT	05346	802-387-5571	387-5297
RiteMade Paper Converters 1015 Tyler St	Fredericksburg	VA	22401	540-371-8626	371-4154
TF Cust Svc: 800-368-3485 ■ *Web:* www.ritemade.com					
Riverside Paper Co 110 N Kensington Dr	Appleton	WI	54915	920-991-2200	991-2326
TF Cust Svc: 800-443-6326 ■ *Web:* www.riversidepaper.com					
Rollsource Papers 2392 S Wolf Rd	Des Plaines	IL	60018	847-699-3100	699-9690
TF: 800-525-7785					
Smith-Lee Co Inc 537 Fitch St	Oneida	NY	13421	315-363-2500	363-9573
TF: 800-448-3363 ■ *Web:* www.smith-lee.com					
Solo Cup Co 1505 E Main St	Urbana	IL	61802	217-384-1800	365-2318*
**Fax:* Hum Res ■ *TF Cust Svc:* 800-367-2877 ■ *Web:* www.solocup.com					
Spinnaker Coating Inc 518 E Water St	Troy	OH	45373	937-332-6500	335-2843
TF: 800-543-9452 ■ *Web:* www.spinnakercoating.com					
Texpack USA Inc 1001 Brickell Bay Dr Suite 2402	Miami	FL	33131	305-358-9696	358-9797
Web: www.texpack.com					
TimeMed Labeling Systems Inc 144 Tower Dr	Burr Ridge	IL	60527	630-986-1800	986-0016
TF Cust Svc: 800-323-4840 ■ *Web:* www.timemed.com					
Tufco Technologies Inc PO Box 23500	Green Bay	WI	54305	920-336-0054	336-9041
NASDAQ: TFCO ■ *TF:* 800-558-8145 ■ *Web:* www.tufco.com					
Wedlock Paper Converters Ltd 2327 Stanfield Rd	Mississauga	ON	L4Y1R6	905-277-9461	272-1108
Web: www.wedlockpaper.com					
West Carrollton Parchment Co 1 S Elm St	West Carrollton	OH	45449	937-859-3621	859-7610
Web: www.wcparchment.com					

558 PAPER FINISHERS (EMBOSSING, COATING, GILDING, STAMPING)

				Phone	Fax
Colad Group 801 Exchange St	Buffalo	NY	14210	716-961-1776	961-1753
TF: 800-950-1755 ■ *Web:* www.colad.com					
Complemar Partners 500 Lee Rd Suite 200	Rochester	NY	14606	585-647-5800	647-5800
TF: 866-742-5274 ■ *Web:* www.complemar.com					
Diecrafters Inc 1349 S 55th Ct	Cicero	IL	60804	708-656-3336	656-3386
Web: www.diecrafters.com					
East Coast Finishing LLC PO Box 39	Fairview	NJ	07022	201-943-3236	943-3093
Graphic Arts Finishers Inc 32 Cambridge St	Charlestown	MA	02129	617-241-9292	241-7326
Jen-Coat Inc 132 N Elm St	Westfield	MA	01086	413-562-2315	568-6944*
**Fax:* Sales ■ *Web:* www.jencoat.com					
Loroco Industries Inc 5000 Creek Rd	Cincinnati	OH	45242	513-891-9544	891-9549
Web: www.loroco-industries.com					
Madison Cutting Die Inc 2547 Progress Rd	Madison	WI	53716	608-221-3422	223-6850
TF: 800-395-9405 ■ *Web:* www.mcd.net					
Malahide Design & Mfg Inc 209 Griffith Rd	Stratford	ON	N5A6S4	519-273-0603	273-1773
TF: 800-867-5077 ■ *Web:* www.hotstamping.com					
Markal Finishing Corp 400 Bostwick Ave	Bridgeport	CT	06605	203-384-8219	336-1231
McGraphics Inc 601 Hagan St	Nashville	TN	37203	615-242-8779	254-3031*
**Fax:* Orders ■ *TF:* 888-280-8200 ■ *Web:* www.mcgraphicsinc.com					
Paper Coating Co 3536 Medford St	Los Angeles	CA	90063	323-264-2222	266-1703
Unifoil Corp 12 Daniel Rd E	Fairfield	NJ	07004	973-244-9900	244-5555
Web: www.unifoil.com					
Walton Press 402 Mayfield Dr	Monroe	GA	30655	770-267-2596	267-9463
TF: 800-354-0235 ■ *Web:* www.waltonpress.com					

559 PAPER INDUSTRIES MACHINERY

				Phone	Fax
Arthur J Evers Corp 1009 Broad St	Riverton	NJ	08077	856-829-4900	829-4298
Baumfolder Corp 1660 Campbell Rd	Sidney	OH	45365	937-492-1281	492-7280
TF: 800-543-6107 ■ *Web:* www.baumfolder.com					
Black Clawson Converting Machinery Inc 46 N 1st St	Fulton	NY	13069	315-598-7121	593-0396
Web: bcconverting.com					
Bolton-Emerson Americas Inc PO Box 569	Lawrence	MA	01842	978-686-3961	688-8225
Cranston Machinery Co Inc 2251 SE Oak Grove Blvd	Oak Grove	OR	97267	503-654-7751	654-6172
TF: 800-547-1012 ■ *Web:* www.cranston-machinery.com					
Curt G Joa Inc 100 Crocker Ave PO Box 903	Sheboygan Falls	WI	53085	920-467-6136	467-2924
Web: www.joa.com					
Dietzco Div Entwistle Co Bigelow St	Hudson	MA	01749	508-481-4000	481-4004
Web: www.entwistleco.com					
Double E Co 319 Manley St	West Bridgewater	MA	02379	508-588-8099	580-2915
Web: www.doubleeusa.com					
Entwistle Co Dietzco Div Bigelow St	Hudson	MA	01749	508-481-4000	481-4004
Web: www.entwistleco.com					
Evers Arthur J Corp 1009 Broad St	Riverton	NJ	08077	856-829-4900	829-4298
Faustel Inc W 194 N 11301 McCormick Dr PO Box 1000	Germantown	WI	53022	262-253-3333	253-3334
Web: www.faustel.com					
HG Weber & Co Inc 725 Fremont St	Kiel	WI	53042	920-894-2221	894-3786
Web: www.hgweber.com					
Holyoke Machine Co 514 Main St	Holyoke	MA	01040	413-534-5612	532-9244
Web: www.holyokemachine.com					
Kadant Black Clawson 7312 Central Park Blvd	Mason	OH	45040	513-229-8100	424-1168
Web: www.blackclawson.com					
Kadant Inc 1 Acton Pl Suite 202	Acton	MA	01720	978-776-2000	635-1593
NYSE: KAI ■ *Web:* www.kadant.com					
Kempsmith Machine Co 1820 S 73rd St PO Box 14336	Milwaukee	WI	53214	414-256-8160	476-0564
Web: www.kempsmith-dl.com					
Maxson Automatic Machinery Co 70 Airport Rd PO Box 1517	Westerly	RI	02891	401-596-0162	596-1050
Web: www.maxsonautomatic.com					
Metso Corp Paper Div 516 Alfred St PO Box 502	Biddeford	ME	04005	207-282-1521	283-0926
Web: www.metsopaper.com					
Mokry-Tesmer Inc 707 Maryetta St	Middletown	OH	45042	513-424-5135	424-7346
TF: 800-383-5135					
Montague Machine Co 15 Rastallis St	Turners Falls	MA	01376	413-863-4301	863-8206
TF: 800-555-6891					
Pacific Hoe Co 2700 SE Tacoma St PO Box 82155	Portland	OR	97202	503-234-9501	234-3506
TF: 800-547-5537 ■ *Web:* www.pacific-hoe.com					
Paco Winders Mfg Inc 2040 Bennett Rd	Philadelphia	PA	19116	215-673-6265	673-2027
Web: www.pacowinders.com					
Paper Converting Machine Co PO Box 19005	Green Bay	WI	54307	920-494-5601	494-8865
Web: www.pcmc.com					
Paper Machinery Corp 8900 W Bradley Rd PO Box 240100	Milwaukee	WI	53224	414-354-8050	354-8614
Web: www.papermc.com					
Pemco Inc 3333 Crocker Ave	Sheboygan	WI	53082	920-458-2500	458-1265
Renard Machine 1367 Reber St	Green Bay	WI	54302	920-432-8412	432-8430
Rice Barton Corp 25 Southgate St	Worcester	MA	01610	508-752-2821	752-2820
TF: 800-225-9415					
Sandusky International Inc 615 W Market St	Sandusky	OH	44870	419-626-5340	626-8674
Web: www.sanduskyintl.com					
Sherwood Tool Inc 10 Main St	Kensington	CT	06037	860-828-4161	828-5387
TF: 888-313-0954 ■ *Web:* www.sherwoodtool.com					
Shreiner Co 1 Taylor Dr PO Box 347	Killbuck	OH	44637	330-276-6135	276-1605
TF: 800-722-9915 ■ *Web:* www.shreinerco.com					
Standard Paper Box Machine Co Inc 347 Coster St	Bronx	NY	10474	718-328-3300	842-7772
TF: 800-367-8755					
Stowe Woodward Co 1 Technology Dr	Westborough	MA	01581	508-616-9458	616-9479
Web: www.stowewoodward.com					
Voith Paper Inc 2200 N Roemer Rd PO Box 2337	Appleton	WI	54912	920-731-7724	739-8081
Web: www.voithpaper.com					
Ward Machinery Co 10615 Beaver Dam Rd	Hunt Valley	MD	21030	410-584-7700	771-8406
TF: 800-847-9273 ■ *Web:* www.wardmachinery.com					
Weber HG & Co Inc 725 Fremont St	Kiel	WI	53042	920-894-2221	894-3786
Web: www.hgweber.com					
Xerium Technologies Inc 1 Technology Dr	Westborough	MA	01581	508-616-9468	616-9487
NYSE: XRM ■ *Web:* www.xerium.com					
Zerand Corp 15800 W Overland Dr	New Berlin	WI	53151	262-827-3800	827-3913
TF: 800-889-9984 ■ *Web:* www.zerand.com					
Zink Mfg 15 Burt St PO Box 550	Fulton	NY	13069	315-592-4254	592-4257

560 PAPER MILLS

SEE ALSO Paperboard Mills p. 2049; Pulp Mills p. 2159

				Phone	Fax
AbitibiBowater 1155 Metcalfe St Suite 800	Montreal	QC	H3B5H2	514-875-2160	875-6284
TF: 800-361-2888 ■ *Web:* www.abitibibowater.com					
Augusta News Print Co 2434 Doug Bernard Pkwy PO Box 1647	Augusta	GA	30913	706-798-3440	312-6473
Blandin Paper Co 115 SW 1st St	Grand Rapids	MN	55744	218-327-6200	327-6212
Blue Heron Paper Co 427 Main St	Oregon City	OR	97045	503-650-4211	650-4595*
**Fax:* Sales ■ *TF:* 800-331-9991 ■ *Web:* www.blueheronpaper.com					
Boise Cascade LLC 1111 W Jefferson St	Boise	ID	83702	208-384-6161	384-7189
Web: www.bc.com					
Boise Paper Solutions Corp 222 NE Park Plaza Dr Suite 105	Vancouver	WA	98684	360-891-8787	
Web: www.bc.com/paper					
Bowater Inc 55 E Camper Down Way	Greenville	SC	29601	864-271-7733	282-9591*
NYSE: BOW ■ **Fax:* Hum Res ■ *TF:* 800-845-6002 ■ *Web:* www.bowater.com					
Bowater Inc Newsprint & Directory Div					
55 E Camper Down Way PO Box 1028	Greenville	SC	29602	864-271-7733	282-9496
TF: 800-845-6002 ■ *Web:* www.bowater.com/en/divisionsNewsprint.shtml					
BPM Inc 200 W Front St	Peshtigo	WI	54157	715-582-4551	582-4853
TF: 800-826-0494 ■ *Web:* www.bpmpaper.com					
Brant Allen Industries 80 Field Point Rd 3rd Fl	Greenwich	CT	06830	203-661-3344	661-3349
Burrows Paper Corp 501 W Main St	Little Falls	NY	13365	315-823-2300	823-0867
TF: 800-272-7122 ■ *Web:* www.burrowspaper.com					
Canfor Corp 1700 W 75th Ave Suite 100	Vancouver	BC	V6P6G2	604-661-5241	661-5226
TSX: CFP ■ *Web:* www.canfor.com					
Cascades Fine Papers Group Inc 2 Rolland Ave	Saint-Jerome	QC	J7Z5S1	450-569-3910	569-3947*
**Fax:* Mktg ■ *Web:* www.cascades.com					
Cascades Inc 404 Marie-Victorin Blvd	Kingsey Falls	QC	J0A1B0	819-363-5100	363-5155
TSX: CAS ■ *Web:* www.cascades.com					
Cascades Tissue Group Inc 77 rue Marie-Victorin	Candiac	QC	J5R1C3	450-444-6400	444-6477
TF: 800-361-4070 ■ *Web:* www.cascades.com					
Catalyst Paper Corp 3600 Lysander Ln	Richmond	BC	V7B1C3	604-247-4400	247-0512
TSX: CTL ■ *Web:* www.catalystpaper.com					
Cauthorne Paper Co 205 Hull St	Richmond	VA	23224	804-232-6736	231-4779
TF: 800-552-3011 ■ *Web:* www.cauthornepaper.com					
Climax Mfg Co 7840 SR 26	Lowville	NY	13367	315-376-8000	376-2034
TF: 800-225-4629 ■ *Web:* www.climaxpkg.com					
Ecological Fibers Inc 40 Pioneer Dr	Lunenburg	MA	01462	978-537-0003	537-2238
Web: ecofibers.com					
FiberMark Inc Technical Specialities Div					
161 Wellington Rd	Brattleboro	VT	05031	802-257-0365	257-5900
TF Cust Svc: 800-784-8558 ■ *Web:* www.fibermark.com					
Finch Pruyn & Co Inc 1 Glen St	Glens Falls	NY	12801	518-793-2541	793-7364
TF: 800-833-9981 ■ *Web:* www.finchpaper.com					
Fox River Paper Co 100 W Lawrence St	Appleton	WI	54911	920-733-7341	733-2975
TF: 800-993-7300 ■ *Web:* www.foxriverpaper.com					
Fox Valley Corp 100 W Lawrence St PO Box 727	Appleton	WI	54912	920-739-8982	739-0369
TF: 800-993-7300					
Georgia-Pacific Corp 133 Peachtree St NE	Atlanta	GA	30303	404-652-4000	230-5774
Web: www.gp.com					
Glatfelter 96 S George St Suite 500	York	PA	17401	717-225-4711	846-7208
NYSE: GLT ■ *Web:* www.glatfelter.com					
Grays Harbor Paper LP 801 23rd St	Hoquiam	WA	98550	360-532-9600	538-5636
Web: www.ghplp.com					
Hollingsworth & Vose Co 112 Washington St	East Walpole	MA	02032	508-668-0295	668-6526
Web: www.hollingsworth-vose.com					
Inland Empire Paper Co 3320 N Argonne Rd	Spokane	WA	99212	509-924-1911	927-8461
Web: www.iepco.com					
International Paper Co 6400 Poplar Ave	Memphis	TN	38297	901-419-7000	
NYSE: IP ■ *TF Prod Info:* 800-223-1268 ■ *Web:* www.internationalpaper.com					

Phone | Fax

Interstate Resources Inc 1800 N Kent St Suite 1200 ... Arlington VA 22209 703-243-3355 243-4681
Web: www.iripaper.com
Katahdin Paper Co 50 Main St ... East Millinocket ME 04430 207-723-5131 723-2200
Kimberly-Clark Corp 351 Phelps Dr ... Irving TX 75038 972-281-1200 281-1435
NYSE: KMB ■ TF: 800-544-1847 ■ Web: www.kimberly-clark.com
Kruger Inc 3285 Bedford Rd ... Montreal QC H3S1G5 514-737-1131 343-3124
Web: www.kruger.com
Longview Fibre Paper & Packaging Co
300 Fibre Way PO Box 639 ... Longview WA 98632 360-425-1550 575-5934
Web: www.longviewfibre.com
Madison Paper Co 13101 S Pulaski Rd ... Alsip IL 60803 708-389-8520 389-8237
Madison Paper Industries Main St PO Box 129 ... Madison ME 04950 207-696-3307 696-1155*
*Fax: Cust Svc ■ TF: 800-323-3443 ■ Web: www.madisonpaper.com
Manistique Papers Inc 453 S Mackinac Ave ... Manistique MI 49854 906-341-2175 341-5635
TF: 800-743-2389 ■ Web: www.manistiquepapers.com
Marcal Paper Mills Inc 1 Market St ... Elmwood Park NJ 07407 201-796-4000 796-0470
TF: 800-631-8451 ■ Web: www.marcalpaper.com
Mead Specialty Paper 547A Sissonville Rd ... Potsdam NY 13676 315-265-4000 265-4004
MeadWestvaco Corp 5 High Ridge Pk ... Stamford CT 06905 203-461-7400
NYSE: MWV ■ TF: 800-958-4785 ■ Web: www.meadwestvaco.com
MeadWestvaco Corp Kraft Div
5600 Virginia Ave PO Box 118005 ... Charleston SC 29423 843-745-3000 745-3641
Monadnock Paper Mills Inc 117 Antrim Rd ... Bennington NH 03442 603-588-3311 588-3158*
*Fax: Sales ■ TF Orders: 800-221-2159 ■ Web: www.mpm.com
New York Times Co Forest Products Group
229 W 43rd St 12th Fl ... New York NY 10036 212-556-5955 556-1736
Newbrook Paper Corp 215 14th St ... Jersey City NJ 07310 201-659-6700 659-6707
NewPage Corp 10 W 2nd St ... Dayton OH 45402 877-855-7243 242-9327*
*Fax Area Code: 937 ■ Web: www.newpagecorp.com
Norbord Inc 1 Toronto St 6th Fl ... Toronto ON M5C2W4 416-643-8820 365-3292
TSX: NBD ■ TF: 877-263-9367 ■ Web: www.norbord.com
Potlatch Corp 601 W 1st Ave Suite 1600 ... Spokane WA 99201 509-835-1500 835-1555
NYSE: PCH ■ Web: www.potlatchcorp.com
Pratt Industries USA 1800C Sarasota Pkwy ... Conyers GA 30013 770-918-5678 918-5679
Web: www.prattindustries.com
Riverside Paper Corp 800 S Lawe St ... Appleton WI 54915 920-991-2200 991-2326
TF Cust Svc: 800-443-6326 ■ Web: www.riversidepaper.com
Robbins Sabin Paper Co 497 Circle Freeway Dr Suite 490 ... Cincinnati OH 45246 513-874-5270 874-5785
TF: 800-424-5574 ■ Web: www.sabinrobbins.com
Sabin Robbins Paper Co 497 Circle Freeway Dr Suite 490 ... Cincinnati OH 45246 513-874-5270 874-5785
TF: 800-424-5574 ■ Web: www.sabinrobbins.com
Schweitzer-Mauduit International Inc
100 North Point Center E Suite 600 ... Alpharetta GA 30022 770-569-4272 569-4275
NYSE: SWM ■ TF: 800-514-0186 ■ Web: www.schweitzer-mauduit.com
Seaman Paper Co of Massachusetts Inc 51 Main St ... Otter River MA 01436 978-939-5356 939-2359
Web: www.satinwrap.com
SP Newsprint Co 709 Papermill Rd ... Dublin GA 31027 478-272-1600 275-6301
Web: www.spnewsprinteast.com
Stora Enso North America Corp 2 Landmark Sq 3rd Fl ... Stamford CT 06901 203-356-2300 356-2340
NYSE: SEO ■ TF: 888-807-8672 ■ Web: www.storaenso.com/na
UPM-Kymmene Inc 999 Oakmont Plaza Dr Suite 200 ... Westmont IL 60559 630-850-3310 850-3322
Web: www.upm-kymmene.com
Valentine Paper Co 139 Joe Brown Rd ... Lockport LA 70374 985-532-3313 532-2969
Web: www.valentinepaper.com
Wausau Papers Otis Mill Inc 1 Mill St ... Jay ME 04239 207-897-7200 897-7207
TF: 800-876-5772
West Carrollton Parchment Co 1 S Elm St ... West Carrollton OH 45449 937-859-3621 859-7610
Web: www.wcparchment.com
White Birch Paper Co Bear Island Div 10026 Old Ridge Rd ... Ashland VA 23005 804-227-3394 227-4014
Web: www.whitebirchpaper.com

561 PAPER PRODUCTS - SANITARY

Phone | Fax

Arquest Inc 101 Interchange Plaza ... Cranbury NJ 08512 609-395-9500 395-9778
Web: www.arquest.com
Associated Hygienic Products LLC
3400 River Green Ct Suite 600 ... Duluth GA 30096 770-497-9800
TF: 888-639-5863 ■ Web: www.ahp-dsg.com
Atlas Paper Mills Ltd 3725 E 10th Ct ... Hialeah FL 33013 305-835-8046 691-6018
Web: www.atlaspapermills.com
Bright of America Inc 300 Greenbrier Rd ... Summersville WV 26651 304-872-3000 872-3033
TF: 800-877-1925
Cascades Tissue Group Inc 77 rue Marie-Victorin ... Candiac QC J5R1C3 450-444-6400 444-6477
TF: 800-361-4070 ■ Web: www.cascades.com
EMJA Co Inc PO Box 767189 ... Roswell GA 30076 770-992-9464 594-8446
TF: 800-992-3652 ■ Web: www.emja.com
Erving Paper Mills 97 E Main St ... Erving MA 01344 413-422-2700 422-2710
TF: 800-225-8014
Georgia-Pacific Corp 133 Peachtree St NE ... Atlanta GA 30303 404-652-4000 230-5774
Web: www.gp.com
Hoffmaster PO Box 2038 ... Oshkosh WI 54903 920-235-9330 235-1642
TF: 800-558-9300 ■ Web: www.hoffmaster.com
Hospital Specialty Co 670 Alpha Dr ... Cleveland OH 44143 440-720-1800 362-0073*
*Fax Area Code: 800 ■ TF: 800-321-9832 ■ Web: www.hospeco.com
International Absorbents Inc 1569 Dempsey Rd ... North Vancouver BC V7K1S8 604-681-6181 904-4105
AMEX: IAX ■ TF: 866-514-6559 ■ Web: www.absorbent.com
Kimberly-Clark Corp 351 Phelps Dr ... Irving TX 75038 972-281-1200 281-1435
NYSE: KMB ■ TF: 800-544-1847 ■ Web: www.kimberly-clark.com
Kleen Test Products Inc 1611 Sunset Rd ... Port Washington WI 53074 414-357-7444 357-6355
TF: 800-558-6842 ■ Web: www.kleentest.com
Marcal Paper Mills Inc 1 Market St ... Elmwood Park NJ 07407 201-796-4000 796-0470
TF: 800-631-8451 ■ Web: www.marcalpaper.com
Nice-Pak Products Inc 2 Nice-Pak Pk ... Orangeburg NY 10962 845-365-1700 365-1717
TF: 800-999-6423 ■ Web: www.nicepak.com
Orchids Paper Products Co 4826 Hunt St ... Pryor OK 74361 918-825-0616 825-0060
AMEX: TIS ■ TF: 800-832-4908 ■ Web: www.orchidspaper.com
Paper-Pak Products Inc 1029 Old Creek Rd ... Greenville NC 27834 252-752-1100 933-8433*
*Fax Area Code: 800 ■ TF: 800-428-8363 ■ Web: www.paperpak.com
Personal Products Co 199 Grandview Rd ... Skillman NJ 08558 908-874-1000
Web: www.jnj.com/our_company/family_of_companies
Playtex Products Inc 300 Nyala Farms Rd ... Westport CT 06880 203-341-4000 341-4027*
NYSE: PYX ■ *Fax: Hum Res ■ TF: 800-999-9700 ■ Web: www.playtexproductsinc.com
Potlatch Corp 601 W 1st Ave Suite 1600 ... Spokane WA 99201 509-835-1500 835-1555
NYSE: PCH ■ Web: www.potlatchcorp.com
Potlatch Corp Consumer Products Div
1600 Riviera Ave Suite 305 ... Walnut Creek CA 94596 925-947-5500 947-4702
Principle Business Enterprises Inc PO Box 129 ... Dunbridge OH 43414 419-352-1551 352-8340
TF Cust Svc: 800-467-3224
Procter & Gamble Paper Products Co
1 Procter & Gamble Plaza ... Cincinnati OH 45202 513-983-1100
Web: www.pg.com
Proctor & Gamble Co - Tambrands 2879 Hotel Rd ... Auburn ME 04210 207-753-4000 753-5227
Web: www.tampax.com

Phone | Fax

Roses Southwest Papers Inc 1701 2nd St SW ... Albuquerque NM 87102 505-842-0134 242-0342
Web: www.rosessouthwest.com
SCA Americas 1510 Chester Pike Baldwin Tower ... Eddystone PA 19022 610-499-3700 499-3391
TF Cust Svc: 800-992-9939 ■ Web: www.scanorthamerica.com
SCA Tissue North America 1451 McMahon Dr PO Box 2400 ... Neenah WI 54957 920-725-7031 720-4597
TF: 866-722-6659 ■ Web: www.scatissue.com
Tranzonic Cos 670 Alpha Dr ... Highland Heights OH 44143 440-449-6550 445-8366*
*Fax Area Code: 800 ■ TF: 800-553-7979 ■ Web: www.tranzonic.com
Wausau Paper Corp 100 Paper Place ... Mosinee WI 54455 715-693-4470 692-2083
NYSE: WPP ■ Web: www.wausaupaper.com
Whitestone Acquisition Corp 4265 W Vernal Pike ... Bloomington IN 47404 812-332-3703 333-3270
Web: www.whitestonecorp.com

562 PAPER PRODUCTS - WHOL

Phone | Fax

A & M Tape & Packaging 5201 Nob Hill Rd ... Sunrise FL 33351 954-572-2500 572-8902
TF: 800-231-8806 ■ Web: www.mrboxonline.com
AD Schinner Co Inc 8133 N Grandville Woods Rd ... Milwaukee WI 53223 414-434-0277 434-0291
TF: 800-776-4709
American Hotel Register Co 100 S Milwaukee Ave ... Vernon Hills IL 60061 847-743-3000 743-2091
TF: 800-323-5686 ■ Web: www.americanhotel.com
American Paper & Twine Co 7400 Cockrill Bend Blvd ... Nashville TN 37209 615-350-9000 350-8999
TF: 800-251-2437 ■ Web: www.aptcommerce.com
Andrews Paper & Chemical Co
1 Channel Dr PO Box 509 ... Port Washington NY 11050 516-767-2800 767-1632
Barkoff Container & Supply Co 26599 Corporate Ave ... Hayward CA 94545 510-887-3000 784-0295
Web: www.barkoffcontainer.com
Brame Specialty Co Inc 2021 S Briggs Ave ... Durham NC 27703 919-598-1500 596-9264
TF: 800-672-0011 ■ Web: www.brameco.com
Bunzl USA Inc 701 Emerson Rd Suite 500 ... Saint Louis MO 63141 314-997-5959 997-0247
NYSE: BNL ■ TF: 888-997-4515 ■ Web: www.bunzldistribution.com
Bunzl/Grossman Paper Co Inc 1305 Jersey Ave ... North Brunswick NJ 08902 732-846-6500 846-3776
TF: 800-234-0169
Cascades Fine Papers Group Inc 2 Rolland Ave ... Saint-Jerome QC J7Z5S1 450-569-3910 569-3947*
*Fax: Mktg ■ Web: www.cascades.com
Conley Paper & Packaging 1312 4th St SE ... Canton OH 44707 330-456-8243 588-2572*
*Fax: Cust Svc ■ TF: 800-362-6001 ■ Web: www.conleypackaging.com
Dacotah Paper Co 3940 15th Ave NW ... Fargo ND 58102 701-277-3300 281-0446
TF: 800-726-1767 ■ Web: www.dacotahpaper.com
Ernest Paper Products 5777 Smithway St ... Commerce CA 90040 323-583-6561 589-2794
TF: 800-233-7788 ■ Web: www.ernestpaper.com
First Choice Distribution 1770 NE 58th Ave ... Des Moines IA 50313 515-262-9776 261-3453
TF: 800-369-8733
Fleetwood-Signode 2222 Windsor Ct ... Addison IL 60101 630-268-9999 268-9919
TF: 800-862-7997 ■ Web: www.fleetsig.com
Garland C Norris Co 1101 Terry Rd ... Apex NC 27502 919-387-1059 387-1325
TF: 800-331-8920 ■ Web: www.gcnorris.com
George H Swatek Inc 1095 Edgewater Ave PO Box 356 ... Ridgefield NJ 07657 201-941-2400 941-8681
GreenLine Paper Co 631 S Pine St ... York PA 17403 717-845-8697 846-3806
TF: 800-641-1117 ■ Web: www.greenlinepaper.com
Harder Paper & Packaging 5301 Verona Rd ... Madison WI 53711 608-271-5127 271-4677
TF: 800-261-3400
Heartland Paper Co 808 W Cherokee St ... Sioux Falls SD 57104 605-336-1190 332-8378
TF Cust Svc: 800-843-7922 ■ Web: www.heartland-paper.com
Houston Paper & Janitorial Supply Inc 600 Monument St ... Dothan AL 36303 334-794-7561 671-3738
TF: 800-239-7561 ■ Web: www.houstonpaper.com
Hy-Grade Distributors Inc 574 Main St ... Tonawanda NY 14150 716-695-3960 693-0953
Web: www.hy-gradedist.com
International Absorbents Inc 1569 Dempsey Rd ... North Vancouver BC V7K1S8 604-681-6181 904-4105
AMEX: IAX ■ TF: 866-514-6559 ■ Web: www.absorbent.com
Johnston Paper Co 2 Eagle Dr ... Auburn NY 13021 315-253-8435 253-8744
TF: 800-800-7123 ■ Web: www.johnstonpaper.com
Joseph Weil & Sons Inc 825 E 26th St ... La Grange Park IL 60526 708-579-9595 579-9897
TF: 800-621-5955 ■ Web: www.josephweil.com
Kent H Landsberg Co 1640 S Greenwood Ave ... Montebello CA 90640 323-726-7776 721-0190*
*Fax: Cust Svc ■ Web: www.landsberg.com
Lagasse Inc 1122 Longford Rd ... Oaks PA 19456 610-933-9015 355-1219*
*Fax Area Code: 800 ■ TF: 800-345-6020 ■ Web: www.lagassenet.com
Landsberg Kent H Co 1640 S Greenwood Ave ... Montebello CA 90640 323-726-7776 721-0190*
*Fax: Cust Svc ■ Web: www.landsberg.com
Leonard Paper Co 725 N Haven St ... Baltimore MD 21205 410-563-0800 563-0249
TF Cust Svc: 800-327-5547 ■ Web: www.leonardpaper.com
M Conley Co 1312 4th St SE ... Canton OH 44707 330-456-8243 588-2572*
*Fax: Cust Svc ■ TF: 800-362-6001 ■ Web: www.conleypackaging.com
Main Paper & Party Inc 615 E Main St ... League City TX 77573 281-332-1119 332-7298
Web: www.mainpaperparty.com
Mayfield Paper Co 1115 S Hill St ... San Angelo TX 76903 325-653-1444 653-7031
TF: 800-725-1441 ■ Web: www.mayfieldpaper.com
National Paper & Sanitary Supply 2511 S 156th Cir ... Omaha NE 68130 402-330-5507 330-4109
TF: 800-647-2737 ■ Web: www.npaper.com
Norris Garland C Co 1101 Terry Rd ... Apex NC 27502 919-387-1059 387-1325
TF: 800-331-8920 ■ Web: www.gcnorris.com
Northwest Arkansas Paper Co 2400 Cantrell Rd Suite 116 ... Little Rock AR 72202 501-374-5884 374-5129
TF: 800-643-3068
Pacific Packaging Products Inc 24 Industrial Way ... Wilmington MA 01887 978-657-9100 658-4933
TF: 800-777-0300 ■ Web: www.pacificpkg.com
Packaging Distribution Services Inc (PDS) 2308 Sunset Rd ... Des Moines IA 50321 515-243-3156 243-1741
TF: 800-747-2699 ■ Web: www.pdspack.com
Paper Products Co Inc 36 Terminal Way ... Pittsburgh PA 15219 412-481-6200 481-4787
TF: 800-837-2702 ■ Web: www.paperproducts-pgh.com
Paterson Pacific Parchment Co 625 Greg St ... Sparks NV 89431 775-353-3000 353-3017
TF: 800-678-8104 ■ Web: www.patersonpaper.com
PDS (Packaging Distribution Services Inc) 2308 Sunset Rd ... Des Moines IA 50321 515-243-3156 243-1741
TF: 800-747-2699 ■ Web: www.pdspack.com
Perez Trading Co Inc 3490 NW 125th St ... Miami FL 33167 305-769-0761 681-7963
TF: 800-999-7599 ■ Web: www.pereztrading.com
Phillips Distribution Inc
3000 E Houston St PO Box 200067 ... San Antonio TX 78220 210-227-2397 222-0790
TF: 800-580-2397 ■ Web: www.phillipsdistribution.com
Pollock Paper & Packaging 1 Pollock Pl ... Grand Prairie TX 75050 972-263-2126 262-4737
TF: 800-843-7320 ■ Web: www.pollockpaper.com
Saint Louis Paper & Box Co 3843 Garfield Ave ... Saint Louis MO 63113 314-531-7900 531-0968
TF: 800-779-7901 ■ Web: www.stlpaper.com
Schinner AD Co Inc 8133 N Grandville Woods Rd ... Milwaukee WI 53223 414-434-0277 434-0291
TF: 800-776-4709
Schwarz 8338 Austin Ave ... Morton Grove IL 60053 847-966-2550 966-1271
TF: 800-323-4903 ■ Web: www.schwarz.com
Shorr Packaging Inc 800 N Commerce St ... Aurora IL 60504 630-978-1000 978-1300
TF: 888-978-1122 ■ Web: www.shorr.com
Snyder Paper Corp 250 26th St Dr SE ... Hickory NC 28602 828-328-2501 328-6972
TF: 800-222-8562 ■ Web: www.snyderpaper.com
Swatek George H Inc 1095 Edgewater Ave PO Box 356 ... Ridgefield NJ 07657 201-941-2400 941-8681

Company	City	State	Zip	Phone	Fax
Tayloe Paper Co Inc 6717 E 13th St	Tulsa	OK	74112	918-835-6911	835-7255
TF: 800-825-6911 ■ *Web:* www.tayloepaper.com					
TEC Products Co Inc 100 Middlesex Ave PO Box 309	Carteret	NJ	07008	732-969-8700	969-8770
TF: 800-922-1998 ■ *Web:* www.tecprod.com/tec.htm					
Tricorbraun Inc 10330 Old Olive St Rd	Saint Louis	MO	63141	314-569-3633	569-5087
TF: 800-325-7782 ■ *Web:* www.tricorbraun.com					
TSN Inc 4001 Salazar Way PO Box 679	Frederick	CO	80530	303-530-0600	530-1919
TF: 800-800-4131 ■ *Web:* www.tsndist.com					
Unisource Worldwide Inc 6600 Governors Lake Pkwy	Norcross	GA	30071	770-447-9000	209-6550
TF: 800-282-7958 ■ *Web:* www.unisourcelink.com					
Weil Joseph & Sons Inc 825 E 26th St	La Grange Park	IL	60526	708-579-9595	579-9897
TF: 800-621-5955 ■ *Web:* www.josephweil.com					
White River Paper Co 1118 Rt 14	Hartford	VT	05047	802-295-3188	295-5494
TF: 800-639-7226 ■ *Web:* www.wrpaper.com					
Wurzburg Inc 710 S 4th St PO Box 710	Memphis	TN	38101	901-525-1441	578-2610
TF: 800-274-4885 ■ *Web:* www.wurzburg.com					
xpedx 5285 Tri-Ridge Blvd	Loveland	OH	45140	513-965-2900	965-2849
Web: www.xpedx.com					

563 PAPERBOARD & CARDBOARD - DIE-CUT

Company	City	State	Zip	Phone	Fax
Alvah Bushnell Co 519 E Chelten Ave	Philadelphia	PA	19144	215-842-9520	843-7725
TF: 800-255-7434 ■ *Web:* www.bushnellco.com					
Blanks/USA Inc 8625 Xylon Ct	Minneapolis	MN	55445	763-391-8001	328-7312*
**Fax Area Code:* 800 ■ *TF:* 800-328-7311 ■ *Web:* www.laserblanks.com					
Book Covers Inc 4501 W 16th St	Chicago	IL	60623	773-521-7800	521-2125*
**Fax:* Cust Svc					
Cardinal Brands Inc 643 Massachusetts St Suite 200	Lawrence	KS	66044	785-344-1400	344-1200
TF: 800-364-8713 ■ *Web:* www.cardinalbrands.com					
Chilcote Co 2140-60 Superior Ave	Cleveland	OH	44114	216-781-6000	771-2572
TF Sales: 800-827-5679					
Chilcote Co Taprell Loomis Div 2160 Superior Ave	Cleveland	OH	44114	216-781-6000	771-2572
TF: 800-827-5679 ■ *Web:* www.tap-usa.com					
Crescent Cardboard Co LLC 100 W Willow Rd	Wheeling	IL	60090	847-537-3400	537-7153
TF: 800-323-1055 ■ *Web:* www.crescentcardboard.com					
Demco Inc 4810 Forest Run Rd	Madison	WI	53704	608-241-1201	241-1799
TF Orders: 800-356-1200 ■ *Web:* www.demco.com					
Esselte Corp 48 S Service Rd Suite 400	Melville	NY	11747	631-675-5700	675-3456
TF Cust Svc: 800-645-6051 ■ *Web:* www.esselte.com					
GBS Filing Solutions 224 Morges Rd	Malvern	OH	44644	330-863-1828	444-9427*
**Fax Area Code:* 800 ■ *TF:* 800-873-4427 ■ *Web:* www.gbscorp.com					
Gussco Mfg Inc 5112 2nd Ave	Brooklyn	NY	11232	718-492-7900	492-0886
TF: 800-248-7726 ■ *Web:* www.gussco.com					
Jackson Co Inc 767 Airport Rd	Fall River	MA	02720	508-679-5256	673-6588
Kruysman 32-00 Skillman Ave	Long Island City	NY	11101	718-433-3800	433-3050
TF: 800-221-3218 ■ *Web:* www.kruysman.com					
MeadWestvaco Consumer Packaging Group 299 Park Ave	New York	NY	10171	212-318-5400	
Web: www.meadwestvaco.com/packaging.nsf					
Smead Mfg Co 600 Smead Blvd	Hastings	MN	55033	651-437-4111	437-9134
TF Cust Svc: 888-737-6323 ■ *Web:* www.smead.com					
Tabbies Div Xertrex International Inc 1530 W Glenlake Ave	Itasca	IL	60143	630-773-4020	773-4696
TF: 800-822-2437 ■ *Web:* www.tabbies.com					
Topps Co Inc 1 Whitehall St	New York	NY	10004	212-376-0300	376-0573
NASDAQ: TOPP ■ *Web:* www.topps.com					
University Products Inc PO Box 101	Holyoke	MA	01041	413-532-3372	532-9281*
**Fax Area Code:* 800 ■ *TF Cust Svc:* 800-628-1912 ■ *Web:* www.universityproducts.com					
Upper Deck Co LLC 5909 Sea Otter Pl	Carlsbad	CA	92008	760-929-6500	929-6548
TF Cust Svc: 800-873-7332 ■ *Web:* www.upperdeck.com					
Warren Industries Inc 3100 Mt Pleasant St	Racine	WI	53404	262-639-7800	639-0920
Web: www.wrnind.com					
Westcott Displays Inc 450 Amsterdam St	Detroit	MI	48202	313-872-1200	875-3275
Web: www.westcottdisplays.com					
Xertrex International Inc 1530 W Glenlake Ave	Itasca	IL	60143	630-773-4020	773-4696
TF: 800-822-2437					
Xertrex International Inc Tabbies Div 1530 W Glenlake Ave	Itasca	IL	60143	630-773-4020	773-4696
TF: 800-822-2437 ■ *Web:* www.tabbies.com					

564 PAPERBOARD MILLS

SEE ALSO Paper Mills p. 2047; Pulp Mills p. 2159

Company	City	State	Zip	Phone	Fax
Brownville Specialty Paper Products Inc 1 Bridge St	Brownville	NY	13615	315-782-4500	782-3964
TF: 800-724-0299 ■ *Web:* www.bspp.com					
Cascades Boxboard Group Inc 772 Sherbrooke St W Suite 300	Montreal	QC	H3A1G1	514-284-9800	289-1773
TF: 800-465-9917 ■ *Web:* www.cascades.com					
Cascades Inc 404 Marie-Victorin Blvd	Kingsey Falls	QC	J0A1B0	819-363-5100	363-5155
TSX: CAS ■ *Web:* www.cascades.com					
Domtar Inc 395 boul de Maisonneuve O	Montreal	QC	H3A1L6	514-848-5400	848-6609*
NYSE: DTC ■ **Fax:* Mktg ■ *TF:* 800-267-2040 ■ *Web:* www.domtar.com					
Evanite Fiber Corp PO Box E	Corvallis	OR	97339	541-753-1211	753-0388
TF Cust Svc: 800-441-5567 ■ *Web:* www.evanite.com					
FiberMark Inc 161 Wellington Rd	Brattleboro	VT	05301	802-257-0365	257-5907*
**Fax:* Sales ■ *Web:* www.fibermark.com					
FiberMark Inc Technical Specialities Div 161 Wellington Rd	Brattleboro	VT	05031	802-257-0365	257-5900
TF Cust Svc: 800-784-8558 ■ *Web:* www.fibermark.com					
Georgia-Pacific Corp 133 Peachtree St NE	Atlanta	GA	30303	404-652-4000	230-5774
Web: www.gp.com					
Green Bay Packaging Inc Mill Div 1601 N Quincy St	Green Bay	WI	54302	920-433-5111	433-5105
TF: 800-558-4008 ■ *Web:* www.gbp.com					
International Paper Co 6400 Poplar Ave	Memphis	TN	38297	901-419-7000	
NYSE: IP ■ *TF Prod Info:* 800-223-1268 ■ *Web:* www.internationalpaper.com					
Interstate Paper LLC 2366 Interstate Paper Rd	Riceboro	GA	31323	912-884-3371	884-7448*
**Fax:* Sales					
Longview Fibre Paper & Packaging Co 300 Fibre Way PO Box 639	Longview	WA	98632	360-425-1550	575-5934
Web: www.longviewfibre.com					
Lydall Inc 1 Colonial Rd	Manchester	CT	06042	860-646-1233	646-4917
NYSE: LDL ■ *TF:* 800-365-9325 ■ *Web:* www.lydall.com					
MeadWestvaco Corp 5 High Ridge Pk	Stamford	CT	06905	203-461-7400	
NYSE: MWV ■ *TF:* 800-958-4785 ■ *Web:* www.meadwestvaco.com					
Menominee Paper Co 144 1st St	Menominee	MI	49858	906-863-5595	864-3320
Michigan Paperboard Co 79 Fountain St E	Battle Creek	MI	49017	269-963-4004	963-1306
Newark Group 20 Jackson Dr	Cranford	NJ	07016	908-276-4000	276-2888
TF: 800-777-7890 ■ *Web:* www.newarkgroup.com					
Newman & Co Inc 6101 Tacony St	Philadelphia	PA	19135	215-333-8700	332-8586
TF: 800-523-3256					
Packaging Corp of America 1900 W Field Ct	Lake Forest	IL	60045	847-482-2000	615-6379
NYSE: PKG ■ *TF:* 888-828-2850 ■ *Web:* www.packagingcorp.com					
Pactiv Corp 1900 W Field Ct	Lake Forest	IL	60045	847-482-2000	482-4738
NYSE: PTV ■ *TF:* 888-828-2850 ■ *Web:* www.pactiv.com					
Potlatch Corp 601 W 1st Ave Suite 1600	Spokane	WA	99201	509-835-1500	835-1555
NYSE: PCH ■ *Web:* www.potlatchcorp.com					
Potlatch Corp Pulp & Paperboard Div 805 Mill Rd	Lewiston	ID	83501	208-799-1429	750-7809*
**Fax:* Hum Res ■ *Web:* www.potlatchcorp.com					
Simkins Industries Inc 260 East St	New Haven	CT	06511	203-787-7171	787-7402
Web: www.simkinsindustries.com					
Smurfit-Stone Container Corp 6 City Pl	Saint Louis	MO	63141	314-656-5300	
NASDAQ: SSCC ■ *TF:* 877-772-2999 ■ *Web:* www.smurfit-stone.com					
Sonoco 1 N 2nd St	Hartsville	SC	29550	843-383-7000	383-7008*
NYSE: SON ■ **Fax:* PR ■ *TF:* 800-377-2692 ■ *Web:* www.sonoco.com					
Tembec Inc 800 boul Rene Levesque O Bureau 1050	Montreal	QC	H3B1X1	514-871-0137	397-0896
TSX: TBC ■ *Web:* www.tembec.ca					

565 PARKING SERVICE

Company	City	State	Zip	Phone	Fax
Ace Parking Management Inc 645 Ash St	San Diego	CA	92101	619-233-6624	233-0741
TF: 800-925-7275 ■ *Web:* www.aceparking.com					
Airport Fast Park 250 W Court St Suite 200E	Cincinnati	OH	45202	513-241-0415	241-0497
Web: www.airportfastpark.com					
Allright Corp 2401 21st Ave S Suite 200	Nashville	TN	37212	615-297-4255	297-6240
AMPCO System Parking 808 S Olive St	Los Angeles	CA	90014	213-624-6065	623-4298
Web: www.abm.com					
Central Parking Corp 2401 21st Ave S Suite 200	Nashville	TN	37212	615-297-4255	297-6240
NYSE: CPC ■ *TF:* 800-423-6613 ■ *Web:* www.parking.com					
Colonial Parking Inc 1050 Thomas Jefferson St NW Suite 100	Washington	DC	20007	202-295-8100	295-8111
Web: www.ecolonial.com					
Denison Parking 36 S Pennsylvania St Suite 200	Indianapolis	IN	46204	317-655-3100	655-3101
Web: www.denisonparking.com					
Diamond Parking Inc 605 1st Ave Suite 6000	Seattle	WA	98104	206-284-3100	285-5598
TF: 800-340-7275 ■ *Web:* diamondparking.com					
Edison Properties LLC 100 Washington St	Newark	NJ	07102	973-643-7700	643-2272
TF: 800-248-7275 ■ *Web:* www.parkfast.com					
Imperial Parking Corp 601 W Cordova St Suite 300	Vancouver	BC	V6B1G1	604-681-7311	681-4098
Web: www.impark.com					
InterPark 200 N LaSalle St Suite 1400	Chicago	IL	60601	312-935-2900	935-2999
Web: www.interparkholdings.com					
Lanier Parking Systems 730 Peachtree St Midtown Exchange Suite 1050	Atlanta	GA	30308	404-881-6076	881-1815
Web: www.lanierparking.com					
Park To Fly Inc 7855 N Frontage Rd	Orlando	FL	32812	407-851-8044	851-8011
TF: 888-851-8875 ■ *Web:* www.parktofly.com					
Park 'N Fly 2060 Mt Paran Rd Suite 207	Atlanta	GA	30327	404-264-1000	264-1114*
**Fax:* Hum Res ■ *TF:* 800-325-4863 ■ *Web:* www.pnf.com					
Parking Co of America 11101 Lakewood Blvd	Downey	CA	90241	562-862-2118	862-4409
TF: 866-727-5728 ■ *Web:* www.digitalsign.com/pca					
Parking Management Inc 1725 Desales St NW Suite 300	Washington	DC	20036	202-785-9191	303-3672
Web: www.pmi-parking.com					
Republic Parking System 633 Chestnut St Republic Ctr Suite 2000	Chattanooga	TN	37450	423-756-2771	265-5728
Web: www.republicparking.com					
Robbins Parking Service Ltd 1102 Fort St	Victoria	BC	V8V3K8	250-382-4411	380-7275
Web: www.robbinsparking.com					
Standard Parking Corp 900 N Michigan Ave Suite 1600	Chicago	IL	60611	312-274-2000	640-6169*
NASDAQ: STAN ■ **Fax:* Hum Res ■ *TF:* 888-700-7275 ■ *Web:* www.standardparking.com					
SunPark Inc 6 Fountain Plaza	Buffalo	NY	14202	716-332-4200	332-4202
TF: 866-400-7275 ■ *Web:* www.sunpark.com					
System Parking Inc 111 E Wacker Dr Suite 1407	Chicago	IL	60601	312-819-5050	819-5056
Web: www.systemparking.com					

PARKS - AMUSEMENT

SEE Amusement Park Companies p. 1277; Amusement Parks p. 1277

566 PARKS - NATIONAL - CANADA

Park	City	Prov	Postal Code	Phone	Fax
Parks Canada 25 Eddy St MC 25-7 N 7th Fl	Gatineau	QC	K1A0M5	819-997-0055	953-9745
TF: 888-773-8888 ■ *Web:* www.pc.gc.ca					
Aulavik National Park PO Box 29	Sachs Harbour	NT	X0E0Z0	867-690-3904	690-4808
Web: www.pc.gc.ca/pn-np/nt/aulavik					
Auyuittuq National Park PO Box 353	Pangnirtung	NU	X0A0R0	867-473-2500	473-8612
Web: www.pc.gc.ca/pn-np/ab/auyuittuq					
Banff National Park Box 900	Banff	AB	T1L1K2	403-762-1550	762-3380
TF: 877-737-3783 ■ *Web:* www.pc.gc.ca/pn-np/ab/banff					
Bruce Peninsula National Park 7374 Hwy 6 PO Box 189	Tobermory	ON	N0H2R0	519-596-2233	596-2298
TF: 877-737-3783 ■ *Web:* www.pc.gc.ca/pn-np/on/bruce					
Cape Breton Highlands National Park	Ingonish Beach	NS	B0C1L0	902-224-2306	285-2866
Web: www.pc.gc.ca/pn-np/ns/cbreton					
Elk Island National Park Site 4 RR 1	Fort Saskatchewan	AB	T8L2N7	780-992-2950	992-2951
Web: www.pc.gc.ca/pn-np/ab/elkisland					
Ellesmere Island National Park PO Box 278	Iqaluit	NU	X0A0H0	867-975-4673	975-4674
Web: www.pc.gc.ca/pn-np/nu/quttinirpaaq					
Fathom Five National Marine Park Box 189	Tobermory	ON	N0H2R0	519-596-2233	596-2298
Web: www.pc.gc.ca/amnc-nmca/on/fathomfive					
Forillon National Park 122 Gaspe Blvd	Gaspe	QC	G4X1A9	418-368-5505	368-6837
TF: 888-773-8888 ■ *Web:* www.pc.gc.ca/pn-np/qc/forillon					
Fundy National Park PO Box 1001	Alma	NB	E4H1B4	506-887-6000	887-6008
TF Campground R: 877-737-3783 ■ *Web:* www.pc.gc.ca/pn-np/nb/fundy					
Georgian Bay Islands National Park 901 Wye Valley Rd Box 9	Midland	ON	L4R4K6	705-526-9804	526-5939
Web: www.pc.gc.ca/pn-np/on/georg					
Glacier National Park PO Box 350	Revelstoke	BC	V0E2S0	250-837-7500	837-7536
Web: www.pc.gc.ca/pn-np/bc/glacier/index_E.asp					
Grasslands National Park PO Box 150	Val Marie	SK	S0N2T0	306-298-2257	298-2042
Web: www.pc.gc.ca/pn-np/sk/grasslands					
Gros Morne National Park PO Box 130	Rocky Harbour	NL	A0K4N0	709-458-2417	458-2059
TF Campground R: 877-737-3783 ■ *Web:* www.pc.gc.ca/pn-np/nl/grosmorne					

Listing	City	Prov/State	Postal	Phone	Fax
Gwaii Haanas National Park Reserve/Haida Heritage Site PO Box 37 *Web:* www.pc.gc.ca/pn-np/bc/gwaiihaanas	Queen Charlotte	BC	V0T1S0	250-559-8818	559-8366
Ivvavik National Park Western Arctic Field Unit PO Box 1840 *Web:* www.pc.gc.ca/pn-np/yt/ivvavik	Inuvik	NT	X0E0T0	867-777-8800	777-8820
Jasper National Park PO Box 10 *TF Campground R:* 877-737-3783 ■ *Web:* www.pc.gc.ca/pn-np/ab/jasper	Jasper	AB	T0E1E0	780-852-6176	852-5601
Kejimkujik National Park PO Box 236 *TF Campground R:* 877-737-3783 ■ *Web:* www.pc.gc.ca/pn-np/ns/kejimkujik	Maitland Bridge	NS	B0T1B0	902-682-2772	682-3367
Kluane National Park and Reserve PO Box 5495 *Web:* www.pc.gc.ca/pn-np/yt/kluane	Haines Junction	YT	Y0B1L0	867-634-7250	634-7208
Kootenay National Park PO Box 220 *TF Campground R:* 877-737-3783 ■ *Web:* www.pc.gc.ca/pn-np/bc/kootenay	Radium Hot Springs	BC	V0A1M0	250-347-9505	347-6307
Kouchibouguac National Park 186 Rt 117 *TF Campground R:* 877-737-3783 ■ *Web:* www.pc.gc.ca/pn-np/nb/kouchibouguac	Kouchibouguac	NB	E4X2P1	506-876-2443	876-4802
La Mauricie National Park 702 5th St PO Box 160 *TF Campground R:* 877-737-3783 ■ *Web:* www.pc.gc.ca/pn-np/qc/mauricie	Shawinigan	QC	G9N6T9	819-538-3232	536-3661
Mingan Archipelago National Park Reserve 1340 de la Digue St *TF:* 888-773-8888 ■ *Web:* www.pc.gc.ca/pn-np/qc/mingan	Havre-Saint-Pierre	QC	G0G1P0	418-538-3331	538-3595
Mount Revelstoke National Park PO Box 350 *Web:* www.pc.gc.ca/pn-np/bc/revelstoke	Revelstoke	BC	V0E2S0	250-837-7500	837-7536
Nahanni National Park Reserve PO Box 348 *Web:* www.pc.gc.ca/pn-np/nt/nahanni	Fort Simpson	NT	X0E0N0	867-695-3151	695-2446
Pacific Rim National Park Reserve 2185 Ocean Terrace Rd Box 280 *TF Campground R:* 877-737-3783 ■ *Web:* www.pc.gc.ca/pn-np/bc/pacificrim	Ucluelet	BC	V0R3A0	250-726-7721	726-3520
Point Pelee National Park 407 Monarch Ln RR 1 *TF:* 888-773-8888 ■ *Web:* www.pc.gc.ca/pn-np/on/pelee	Leamington	ON	N8H3V4	519-322-2365	322-1277
Prince Albert National Park PO Box 100 *TF Campground R:* 877-737-3783 ■ *Web:* www.pc.gc.ca/pn-np/sk/princealbert	Waskesiu Lake	SK	S0J2Y0	306-663-4522	663-5424
Prince Edward Island National Park 2 Palmers Lane *TF Campground R:* 888-733-8888 ■ *Web:* www.pc.gc.ca/pn-np/pe/pei-ipe	Charlottetown	PE	C1A5V6	902-672-6350	672-6370
Pukaskwa National Park Hwy 627 PO Box 212 *Web:* www.pc.gc.ca/pn-np/on/pukaskwa	Heron Bay	ON	P0T1R0	807-229-0801	229-2097
Quttinirpaaq National Park PO Box 278 *Web:* www.pc.gc.ca/pn-np/nu/quttinirpaaq	Iqaluit	NU	X0A0H0	867-975-4673	975-4674
Riding Mountain National Park General Delivery *TF Campground R:* 877-737-3783 ■ *Web:* www.pc.gc.ca/pn-np/mb/riding	Wasagaming	MB	R0J2H0	204-848-7275	848-2596
Saguenay-Saint Lawrence Marine Park 182 rue de l'Eglise PO Box 220 *Web:* www.pc.gc.ca/amnc-nmca/qc/saguenay	Tadoussac	QC	G0T2A0	418-235-4703	235-4686
Saint Lawrence Islands National Park 2 County Rd 5 RR 3 *Web:* www.pc.gc.ca/pn-np/on/lawren	Mallorytown	ON	K0E1R0	613-923-5261	923-1021
Sirmilik National Park PO Box 300 *Web:* www.pc.gc.ca/pn-np/nu/sirmilik	Pond Inlet	NU	X0A0S0	867-899-8092	899-8104
Terra Nova National Park General Delivery *TF Campground R:* 877-737-3783 ■ *Web:* www.pc.gc.ca/pn-np/nl/terranova	Glovertown	NL	A0G2L0	709-533-2801	533-2706
Tuktut Nogait National Park PO Box 91 *Web:* www.pc.gc.ca/pn-np/nt/tuktutnogait	Paulatuk	NT	X0E1N0	867-580-3233	580-3234
Vuntut National Park General Delivery *Web:* www.pc.gc.ca/pn-np/yt/vuntut	Old Crow	YT	Y0B1N0	867-667-3910	966-3432
Wapusk National Park PO Box 127 *TF:* 888-748-2928 ■ *Web:* www.pc.gc.ca/pn-np/mb/wapusk	Churchill	MB	R0B0E0	204-675-8863	675-2026
Waterton Lakes National Park Box 200 *Web:* www.watertonpark.com	Waterton Park	AB	T0K2M0	403-859-2224	859-5152
Wood Buffalo National Park PO Box 750 *Web:* www.pc.gc.ca/pn-np/nt/woodbuffalo	Fort Smith	NT	X0E0P0	867-872-7900	872-3910
Yoho National Park PO Box 99 *Web:* www.pc.gc.ca/pn-np/bc/yoho	Field	BC	V0A1G0	250-343-6783	343-6012

567 PARKS - NATIONAL - US

SEE ALSO Attractions - Nature Centers, Parks, Other Natural Areas p. 1352; Cemeteries - National p. 1412; Parks - State p. 2055

Listing	City	State	Zip	Phone	Fax
National Park Service (NPS) 1849 C St NW Rm 1013 *Web:* www.nps.gov	Washington	DC	20240	202-208-6843	219-0910
National Park Service Regional Offices					
Alaska Region 240 W 5th Ave Suite 114	Anchorage	AK	99501	907-644-3510	644-3816
Intermountain Region 12795 W Alameda Pkwy	Denver	CO	80225	303-969-2500	
National Capital Region 1100 Ohio Dr SW *Web:* www.nps.gov/ncro	Washington	DC	20242	202-619-7000	619-7220
Midwest Region 601 Riverfront Dr	Omaha	NE	68102	402-661-1524	661-1984
Northeast Region US Custom House 200 Chestnut St *Web:* www.nps.gov/nero	Philadelphia	PA	19106	215-597-7013	597-0815
Pacific West Region 1111 Jackson St Suite 700	Oakland	CA	94607	510-817-1304	817-1485
Southeast Region 100 Alabama St SW 1924 Building	Atlanta	GA	30303	404-562-3100	

Alabama

Listing	City	State	Zip	Phone	Fax
Horseshoe Bend National Military Park 11288 Horseshoe Bend Rd *Web:* www.nps.gov/hobe/	Daviston	AL	36256	256-234-7111	329-9905
Little River Canyon National Preserve 2141 Gault Ave N *Web:* www.nps.gov/liri/	Fort Payne	AL	35967	256-845-9605	997-9129
Russell Cave National Monument 3729 County Rd 98 *Web:* www.nps.gov/ruca/	Bridgeport	AL	35740	256-495-2672	495-9220
Tuskegee Airmen National Historic Site 1616 Chappie James Ave *Web:* www.nps.gov/tuai/	Tuskegee	AL	36083	334-724-0922	724-0952
Tuskegee Institute National Historic Site 1212 W Montgomery Rd *Web:* www.nps.gov/tuin/	Tuskegee Institute	AL	36088	334-727-3200	727-1448

Alaska

Listing	City	State	Zip	Phone	Fax
Alagnak Wild River PO Box 245 *Web:* www.nps.gov/alag/	King Salmon	AK	99613	907-246-3305	246-2116
Aniakchak National Monument & Preserve PO Box 245 *Web:* www.nps.gov/ania/	King Salmon	AK	99613	907-246-3305	246-2116
Bering Land Bridge National Preserve PO Box 220 *Web:* www.nps.gov/bela/	Nome	AK	99762	907-443-2522	443-6139
Cape Krusenstern National Monument PO Box 1029 *Web:* www.nps.gov/cakr/	Kotzebue	AK	99752	907-442-3890	442-8316
Denali National Park & Preserve PO Box 9 *Web:* www.nps.gov/dena/	Denali Park	AK	99755	907-683-2294	683-9617
Gates of the Arctic National Park & Preserve 4175 Geist Rd *TF:* 866-869-6887 ■ *Web:* www.nps.gov/gaar/	Fairbanks	AK	99709	907-457-5752	455-0601
Glacier Bay National Park & Preserve 1 Park Rd PO Box 140 *Web:* www.nps.gov/glba/	Gustavus	AK	99826	907-697-2230	697-2654
Katmai National Park & Preserve #1 King Salmon Mall PO Box 7 *Web:* www.nps.gov/katm/	King Salmon	AK	99613	907-246-3305	246-2116
Kenai Fjords National Park PO Box 1727 *Web:* www.nps.gov/kefj/	Seward	AK	99664	907-224-7500	224-7505
Klondike Gold Rush National Historical Park 2nd St & Broadway PO Box 517 *Web:* www.nps.gov/klgo/	Skagway	AK	99840	907-983-2921	983-9249
Kobuk Valley National Park PO Box 1029 *TF:* 800-478-7252 ■ *Web:* www.nps.gov/kova/	Kotzebue	AK	99752	907-442-3890	442-8316
Lake Clark National Park & Preserve 240 West 5th Ave Suite 236 *Web:* www.nps.gov/lacl/	Anchorage	AK	99501	907-644-3626	644-3810
Noatak National Preserve PO Box 1029 *Web:* www.nps.gov/noat/	Kotzebue	AK	99752	907-442-3890	442-8316
Sitka National Historical Park 103 Monastery St *Web:* www.nps.gov/sitk/	Sitka	AK	99835	907-747-6281	747-5938
Wrangell-Saint Elias National Park & Preserve Mile 106.8 Richardson Hwy *Web:* www.nps.gov/wrst/	Copper Center	AK	99573	907-822-5234	822-7216
Yukon-Charley Rivers National Preserve 4175 Geist Rd *Web:* www.nps.gov/yuch/	Fairbanks	AK	99709	907-457-5752	455-0601

American Samoa

Listing	City	State	Zip	Phone	Fax
National Park of American Samoa *Web:* www.nps.gov/npsa/	Pago Pago	AS	96799	684-633-7082	633-7085

Arizona

Listing	City	State	Zip	Phone	Fax
Canyon de Chelly National Monument PO Box 588 *Web:* www.nps.gov/cach/	Chinle	AZ	86503	928-674-5500	674-5507
Casa Grande Ruins National Monument 1100 Ruins Dr *Web:* www.nps.gov/cagr/	Coolidge	AZ	85228	520-723-3172	723-7209
Chiricahua National Monument 13063 East Bonita Canyon Rd *Web:* www.nps.gov/chir/	Wilcox	AZ	85643	520-824-3560	824-3421
Coronado National Memorial 4101 E Montezuma Canyon Rd *Web:* www.nps.gov/coro/	Hereford	AZ	85615	520-366-5515	366-5705
Fort Bowie National Historic Site 3203 S Old Ft Bowie Rd *Web:* www.nps.gov/fobo/	Bowie	AZ	85605	520-847-2500	847-2221
Glen Canyon National Recreation Area PO Box 1507 691 Scenic View Dr *Web:* www.nps.gov/glca/	Page	AZ	86040	928-608-6200	608-6259
Grand Canyon National Park PO Box 129 **Fax:* Mail Rm ■ *Web:* www.nps.gov/grca/	Grand Canyon	AZ	86023	928-638-7888	638-7797*
Hohokam Pima National Monument c/o Casa Grande Ruins National Monument PO Box 518 *Web:* www.nps.gov/pima/	Coolidge	AZ	85228	520-723-3172	723-7209
Hubbell Trading Post National Historic Site PO Box 150 1/2 Mile W. Hwy 191 on Hwy 264 *Web:* www.nps.gov/hutr/	Ganado	AZ	86505	928-755-3475	755-3405
Montezuma Castle National Monument 527 South Main St *Web:* www.nps.gov/moca/	Camp Verde	AZ	86322	928-567-5276	567-3597
Navajo National Monument HC 71 Box 3 *Web:* www.nps.gov/nava/	Tonalea	AZ	86044	928-672-2700	672-2703
Organ Pipe Cactus National Monument 10 Organ Pipe Dr *Web:* www.nps.gov/orpi/	Ajo	AZ	85321	520-387-6849	
Petrified Forest National Park PO Box 2217 *Web:* www.nps.gov/pefo/	Petrified Forest	AZ	86028	928-524-6228	524-3567
Pipe Spring National Monument HC 65 Box 5 406 North Pipe Spring Rd *Web:* www.nps.gov/pisp/	Fredonia	AZ	86022	928-643-7105	643-7583
Rainbow Bridge National Monument c/o Glen Canyon National Recreation Area PO Box 1507 *Web:* www.nps.gov/rabr/	Page	AZ	86040	928-608-6200	608-6259
Saguaro National Park 3693 S Old Spanish Trail *Web:* www.nps.gov/sagu/	Tucson	AZ	85730	520-733-5100	733-5183
Sunset Crater Volcano National Monument c/o Flagstaff Area National Monuments 6400 N Hwy 89 *Web:* www.nps.gov/sucr/	Flagstaff	AZ	86004	928-526-0502	714-0565
Tonto National Monument HC02 Box 4602 *Web:* www.nps.gov/tont/	Roosevelt	AZ	85545	928-467-2241	467-2225
Tumacacori National Historical Park 1891 E Frontage Rd PO Box 67 *Web:* www.nps.gov/tuma/	Tumacacori	AZ	85640	520-398-2341	
Tuzigoot National Monument 527 S Main St *Web:* www.nps.gov/tuzi/	Camp Verde	AZ	86322	928-634-5564	567-3597
Walnut Canyon National Monument c/o Flagstaff Area National Monuments 6400 N Hwy 89 *Web:* www.nps.gov/waca/	Flagstaff	AZ	86004	928-526-3367	527-0246
Wupatki National Monument Flagstaff Area National Monuments 6400 N Hwy 89 *Web:* www.nps.gov/wupa/	Flagstaff	AZ	86004	928-679-2365	679-2349

Arkansas

Listing	City	State	Zip	Phone	Fax
Arkansas Post National Memorial 1741 Old Post Rd *Web:* www.nps.gov/arpo/	Gillett	AR	72055	870-548-2207	548-2431
Buffalo National River 402 N Walnut St Suite 136 *Web:* www.nps.gov/buff/	Harrison	AR	72601	870-741-5443	741-7286
Fort Smith National Historic Site 301 Parker Ave *Web:* www.nps.gov/fosm/	Fort Smith	AR	72901	479-783-3961	783-5307
Hot Springs National Park 101 Reserve St *Web:* www.nps.gov/hosp/	Hot Springs	AR	71901	501-620-6715	620-6778
Little Rock Central High School National Historic Site 2120 Daisy L Gatson Bates Dr *Web:* www.nps.gov/chsc/	Little Rock	AR	72202	501-374-1957	376-4728
Pea Ridge National Military Park 15930 Hwy 62 E *Web:* www.nps.gov/peri/	Garfield	AR	72732	479-451-8122	451-0219

California

Listing	City	State	Zip	Phone	Fax
Cabrillo National Monument 1800 Cabrillo Memorial Dr *Web:* www.nps.gov/cabr/	San Diego	CA	92106	619-557-5450	226-6311

Phone Fax

Channel Islands National Park 1901 Spinnaker Dr .... Ventura CA 93001 805-658-5730 658-5799
Web: www.nps.gov/chis/
Death Valley National Park PO Box 579 .... Death Valley CA 92328 760-786-3200 786-3283
Web: www.nps.gov/deva/
Devils Postpile National Monument PO Box 3999 .... Mammoth Lakes CA 93545 760-934-2289 934-2289
Web: www.nps.gov/depo/
Eugene O'Neill National Historic Site PO Box 280 .... Danville CA 94526 925-838-0249 838-9471
Web: www.nps.gov/euon/
Fort Point National Historic Site Fort Mason Bldg 201....... San Francisco CA 94123 415-556-1693 561-4390
Web: www.nps.gov/fopo/
Golden Gate National Recreation Area
Fort Mason Bldg 201 .... San Francisco CA 94123 415-561-4700 561-4750*
**Fax:* Hum Res ■ *Web:* www.nps.gov/goga/
John Muir National Historic Site 4202 Alhambra Ave............ Martinez CA 94553 925-228-8860 228-8192
Web: www.nps.gov/jomu/
Joshua Tree National Park 74485 National Park Dr ...... Twentynine Palms CA 92277 760-367-5500 367-6392
Web: www.nps.gov/jotr/
Kings Canyon & Sequoia National Parks
47050 Generals Hwy .... Three Rivers CA 93271 559-565-3341 565-3730
Web: www.nps.gov/seki/
Lassen Volcanic National Park 38050 Hwy 36 E .... Mineral CA 96063 530-595-4444 595-3262
Web: www.nps.gov/lavo/
Lava Beds National Monument 1 Indian Well Headquarters .... Tulelake CA 96134 530-667-8100
Web: www.nps.gov/labe/
Manzanar National Historic Site 5001 Hwy 395 .... Independence CA 93526 760-878-2932 878-2949
Web: www.nps.gov/manz/
Mojave National Preserve 2701 Barstow Rd .... Barstow CA 92311 760-252-6100 252-6174
Web: www.nps.gov/moja/
Muir Woods National Monument .... Mill Valley CA 94941 415-388-2596 389-6957
Web: www.nps.gov/muwo/
Pinnacles National Monument 5000 Hwy 146.................... Paicines CA 95043 831-389-4485
Web: www.nps.gov/pinn/
Point Reyes National Seashore 1 Bear Valley Rd .... Point Reyes Station CA 94956 415-663-8522 663-8132
Web: www.nps.gov/pore/
Redwood National and State Parks 1111 2nd St .... Crescent City CA 95531 707-465-7306 464-1812
Web: www.nps.gov/redw/
Rosie the Riveter/World War II Home Front National Historical Park 1401 Marina Way S Suite C .... Richmond CA 94804 510-232-5050
Web: www.nps.gov/rori/
San Francisco Maritime National Historical Park
Lower Fort Mason Bldg E Rm 265 .... San Francisco CA 94123 415-561-7000 556-1624
Web: www.nps.gov/safr/
Santa Monica Mountains National Recreation Area
401 W Hillcrest Dr .... Thousand Oaks CA 91360 805-370-2300 370-1850
Web: www.nps.gov/samo/
Sequoia & Kings Canyon National Parks
47050 Generals Hwy .... Three Rivers CA 93271 559-565-3341 565-3730
Web: www.nps.gov/seki/
Whiskeytown-Shasta-Trinity National Recreation Area
PO Box 188 .... Whiskeytown CA 96095 530-242-3400 246-5154
Web: www.nps.gov/whis/
Yosemite National Park 9039 Village Dr PO Box 577 .... Yosemite CA 95389 209-372-0200 379-1800
Web: www.nps.gov/yose/

Colorado

Phone Fax

Bent's Old Fort National Historic Site 35110 Hwy 194 E.......... La Junta CO 81050 719-383-5010 383-2129
Web: www.nps.gov/beol/
Black Canyon of the Gunnison National Park 102 Elk Creek ...... Gunnison CO 81230 970-641-2337 641-3127
Web: www.nps.gov/blca/
Colorado National Monument .... Fruita CO 81521 970-858-3617 858-0372
Web: www.nps.gov/colm/
Curecanti National Recreation Area 102 Elk Creek............. Gunnison CO 81230 970-641-2337 641-3127
Web: www.nps.gov/cure/
Dinosaur National Monument 4545 E Hwy 40.................... Dinosaur CO 81610 970-374-3000 374-3003
Web: www.nps.gov/dino/
Florissant Fossil Beds National Monument PO Box 185.......... Florissant CO 80816 719-748-3253 748-3164
Web: www.nps.gov/flfo/
Great Sand Dunes National Park & Preserve 11500 Hwy 150 .... Mosca CO 81146 719-378-6300 378-6310
Web: www.nps.gov/grsa/
Hovenweep National Monument McElmo Rt .... Cortez CO 81321 970-562-4282 562-4283
Web: www.nps.gov/hove/
Mesa Verde National Park PO Box 8 .... Mesa Verde CO 81330 970-529-4465 529-4637
Web: www.nps.gov/meve/
Rocky Mountain National Park 1000 Hwy 36 .... Estes Park CO 80517 970-586-1206 586-1256
Web: www.nps.gov/romo/
Yucca House National Monument
c/o Mesa Verde National Park PO Box 8..................... Mesa Verde CO 81330 970-529-4465 529-4637
Web: www.nps.gov/yuho/

Connecticut

Phone Fax

Weir Farm National Historic Site 735 Nod Hill Rd .... Wilton CT 06897 203-834-1896 834-2421
Web: www.nps.gov/wefa/

District of Columbia

Phone Fax

Constitution Gardens 900 Ohio Drive SW .... Washington DC 20024 202-426-6841 724-0764
Web: www.nps.gov/coga/
Ford's Theatre National Historic Site 900 Ohio Drive SW ...... Washington DC 20024 202-426-6924 426-1845
Web: www.nps.gov/foth/
Franklin Delano Roosevelt Memorial
c/o National Capital Parks Central 900 Ohio Dr SW .... Washington DC 20024 202-426-6841
Web: www.nps.gov/frde/
Frederick Douglass National Historic Site
1900 Anacostia Dr SE .... Washington DC 20020 202-426-5961 426-0880
Web: www.nps.gov/frdo/
Jefferson Memorial
c/o National Capital Parks - Central 900 Ohio Dr SW......... Washington DC 20024 202-426-6841 426-1835
Web: www.nps.gov/thje/
Korean War Veterans Memorial
c/o National Capital Parks - Central 900 Ohio Dr SW......... Washington DC 20004 202-426-6841
Web: www.nps.gov/kowa/
Lincoln Memorial
c/o National Capital Parks - Central 900 Ohio Dr SW......... Washington DC 20024 202-426-6841 724-0764
Web: www.nps.gov/linc/
Mary McLeod Bethune Council House National Historic Site
1318 Vermont Ave NW .... Washington DC 20005 202-673-2402 673-2414
Web: www.nps.gov/mamc/
National Mall
c/o National Capitol Parks - Central 900 Ohio Dr SW......... Washington DC 20024 202-426-6841 724-0764
Web: www.nps.gov/nama/
Pennsylvania Avenue National Historic Site
c/o National Capitol Parks - Central 900 Ohio Dr SW......... Washington DC 20024 202-606-9686
Web: www.nps.gov/paav/
President's Park (White House)
c/o White House Visitor Center 1450 Pennsylvania Ave NW .... Washington DC 20230 202-208-1631 208-1643
Web: www.nps.gov/whho/
Rock Creek Park 3545 Williamsburg Ln NW .... Washington DC 20008 202-895-6000 895-6015
Web: www.nps.gov/rocr
Vietnam Veterans Memorial
c/o National Capitol Park - Central 900 Ohio Drive SW .... Washington DC 20024 202-426-6841 426-1844
Web: www.thewall-usa.com
Washington Monument
c/o National Capitol Parks - Central 900 Ohio Dr SW.......... Washington DC 20024 202-426-6841
Web: www.nps.gov/wamo/

Florida

Phone Fax

Big Cypress National Preserve 33100 Tamiami Trail E .... Ochopee FL 34141 239-695-2000 695-3901
Web: www.nps.gov/bicy/
Biscayne National Park 9700 SW 328th St.................. Homestead FL 33033 305-230-1144 230-1190
Web: www.nps.gov/bisc/
Canaveral National Seashore 212 S Washington Ave .... Titusville FL 32796 321-267-1110 264-2906
Web: www.nps.gov/cana/
Castillo de San Marcos National Monument
1 S Castillo Dr .... Saint Augustine FL 32084 904-829-6506 823-9388
Web: www.nps.gov/casa/
De Soto National Memorial 3000 75th St NW................. Bradenton FL 34209 941-792-0458 792-5094
Web: www.nps.gov/deso/
Dry Tortugas National Park PO Box 6208 .... Key West FL 33041 305-242-7700 242-7711
Web: www.nps.gov/drto/
Everglades National Park 40001 SR-9336................... Homestead FL 33034 305-242-7700 242-7728
Web: www.nps.gov/ever/
Fort Caroline National Memorial 12713 Fort Caroline Rd....... Jacksonville FL 32225 904-641-7155 641-3798
Web: www.nps.gov/foca/
Fort Matanzas National Monument 8635 A1A S .... Saint Augustine FL 32080 904-471-0116 471-7605
Web: www.nps.gov/foma/
Gulf Islands National Seashore (Florida)
1801 Gulf Breeze Pkwy .... Gulf Breeze FL 32563 850-934-2600 932-9654
Web: www.nps.gov/guis/
Timucuan Ecological & Historic Preserve
c/o Fort Caroline National Memorial 12713 Fort Caroline Rd.. Jacksonville FL 32225 904-641-7155 641-3798
Web: www.nps.gov/timu/

Georgia

Phone Fax

Andersonville National Historic Site 496 Cemetery Rd........ Andersonville GA 31711 229-924-0343 928-9640
Web: www.nps.gov/ande/
Chattahoochee River National Recreation Area
1978 Island Ford Pkwy .... Atlanta GA 30350 678-538-1200 399-8087*
**Fax Area Code:* 770 ■ *Web:* www.nps.gov/chat/
Chickamauga & Chattanooga National Military Park
3370 Lafayette Rd .... Fort Oglethorpe GA 30742 706-866-9241 752-5215*
**Fax Area Code:* 423 ■ *Web:* www.nps.gov/chch/
Cumberland Island National Seashore
117 W Saint Mary's St PO Box 806 .... Saint Marys GA 31558 912-882-4335 673-7747
TF: 877-860-6787 ■ *Web:* www.nps.gov/cuis/
Fort Frederica National Monument
6515 Frederica Rd .... Saint Simons Island GA 31522 912-638-3639 634-5357
Web: www.nps.gov/fofr/
Fort Pulaski National Monument US Hwy 80 E................. Savannah GA 31410 912-786-5787 786-6023
Web: www.nps.gov/fopu/
Jimmy Carter National Historic Site 300 N Bond St................ Plains GA 31780 229-824-4104 824-3441
Web: www.nps.gov/jica/
Kennesaw Mountain National Battlefield Park
900 Kennesaw Mountain Dr............................... Kennesaw GA 30152 770-427-4686 528-8398
Web: www.nps.gov/kemo/
Martin Luther King Jr National Historic Site
450 Auburn Ave NE .... Atlanta GA 30312 404-331-5190 730-3112
Web: www.nps.gov/malu/
Ocmulgee National Monument 1207 Emery Hwy.................. Macon GA 31217 478-752-8257 752-8259
Web: www.nps.gov/ocmu/

Hawaii

Phone Fax

Haleakala National Park PO Box 369......................... Makawao HI 96768 808-572-4400 572-1304
Web: www.nps.gov/hale/
Hawaii Volcanoes National Park PO Box 52.......... Hawaii National Park HI 96718 808-985-6000 985-6004
Web: www.nps.gov/havo/
Kalaupapa National Historical Park PO Box 2222 .... Kalaupapa HI 96742 808-567-6802 567-6729
Web: www.nps.gov/kala/
Kaloko-Honokohau National Historical Park
73-4786 Kanalani St Suite 14 .... Kailua-Kona HI 96740 808-329-6881
Web: www.nps.gov/kaho/
Pu'uhonua O Honaunau National Historical Park PO Box 129..... Honaunau HI 96726 808-328-2326 328-8251
Web: www.nps.gov/puho/
Puukohola Heiau National Historic Site 62-3601 Kawaihae Rd .... Kawaihae HI 96743 808-882-7218 882-1215
Web: www.nps.gov/puhe/
USS Arizona Memorial 1 Arizona Memorial Pl .... Honolulu HI 96818 808-422-0561 483-8608
Web: www.nps.gov/usar/

Idaho

Phone Fax

City of Rocks National Reserve PO Box 169........................ Almo ID 83312 208-824-5519 824-5563
Web: www.nps.gov/ciro/
Craters of the Moon National Monument & Preserve PO Box 29 ...... Arco ID 83213 208-527-3257 527-3073
Web: www.nps.gov/crmo/
Hagerman Fossil Beds National Monument 221 N State St ...... Hagerman ID 83332 208-837-4793 837-4857
Web: www.nps.gov/hafo/
Minidoka Internment National Monument PO Box 570............ Hagerman ID 83332 208-837-4793 837-4857
Web: www.nps.gov/miin/
Nez Perce National Historical Park 39063 US Hwy 95............ Spalding ID 83540 208-843-2261 843-2817
Web: www.nps.gov/nepe/

Illinois

				Phone	Fax
Lincoln Home National Historic Site 413 S 8th St *Web:* www.nps.gov/liho/	Springfield	IL	62701	217-492-4241	492-4673

Indiana

				Phone	Fax
George Rogers Clark National Historical Park 401 S 2nd St *Web:* www.nps.gov/gero/	Vincennes	IN	47591	812-882-1776	882-7270
Indiana Dunes National Lakeshore 1100 N Mineral Springs Rd *Web:* www.nps.gov/indu/	Porter	IN	46304	219-926-7561	926-7561
Lincoln Boyhood National Memorial 2916 E. South St PO Box 1816 *Web:* www.nps.gov/libo/	Lincoln City	IN	47552	812-937-4541	937-9929

Iowa

				Phone	Fax
Effigy Mounds National Monument 151 Hwy 76 *Web:* www.nps.gov/efmo/	Harpers Ferry	IA	52146	563-873-3491	873-3743
Herbert Hoover National Historic Site 110 Parkside Dr *Web:* www.nps.gov/heho/	West Branch	IA	52358	319-643-2541	643-5367

Kansas

				Phone	Fax
Brown vs Board of Education National Historic Site 1515 SE Monroe St *Web:* www.nps.gov/brvb/	Topeka	KS	66612	785-354-4273	354-7213
Fort Larned National Historic Site Rt 3 Box 69 *Web:* www.nps.gov/fols/	Larned	KS	67550	620-285-6911	285-3571
Fort Scott National Historic Site PO Box 918 *Web:* www.nps.gov/fosc/	Fort Scott	KS	66701	620-223-0310	223-0188
Nicodemus National Historic Site 304 Washington Ave *Web:* www.nps.gov/nico/	Nicodemus	KS	67625	785-839-4233	839-4325
Tallgrass Prairie National Preserve PO Box 585 226 Broadway *Web:* www.nps.gov/tapr/	Cottonwood Falls	KS	66845	620-273-6034	273-6099

Kentucky

				Phone	Fax
Abraham Lincoln Birthplace National Historic Site 2995 Lincoln Farm Rd *Web:* www.nps.gov/abli/	Hodgenville	KY	42748	270-358-3137	358-3874
Cumberland Gap National Historical Park US Hwy 25E S PO Box 1848 *Web:* www.nps.gov/cuga/	Middlesboro	KY	40965	606-248-2817	248-7276
Mammoth Cave National Park 1 Mammoth Cave Pkwy PO Box 7 *Web:* www.nps.gov/maca/	Mammoth Cave	KY	42259	270-758-2180	758-2349

Louisiana

				Phone	Fax
Cane River Creole National Historical Park 400 Rapids Dr *Web:* www.nps.gov/cari/	Natchitoches	LA	71457	318-352-0383	352-4549
Jean Lafitte National Historical Park & Preserve 419 Rue Decatur *Web:* www.nps.gov/jela/	New Orleans	LA	70130	504-589-3882	589-3851
New Orleans Jazz National Historical Park 419 Rue Decatur *TF:* 877-520-0677 ■ *Web:* www.nps.gov/jazz/	New Orleans	LA	70130	504-589-4806	589-3865
Poverty Point National Monument c/o Poverty Point State Historic Site PO Box 276 *TF:* 888-926-5492 ■ *Web:* www.nps.gov/popo/	Epps	LA	71237	318-926-5492	926-5366

Maine

				Phone	Fax
Acadia National Park PO Box 177 *Web:* www.nps.gov/acad/	Bar Harbor	ME	04609	207-288-3338	288-8813
Saint Croix Island International Historic Site c/o Acadia National Park PO Box 177 *Web:* www.nps.gov/sacr/	Bar Harbor	ME	04609	207-288-3338	288-8813

Maryland

				Phone	Fax
Antietam National Battlefield 5831 Dunker Church Rd *Web:* www.nps.gov/anti/	Sharpsburg	MD	21782	301-432-5124	432-4590
Assateague Island National Seashore 7206 National Seashore Ln *Web:* www.nps.gov/asis/	Berlin	MD	21811	410-641-1441	
Catoctin Mountain Park 6602 Foxville Rd *Web:* www.nps.gov/cato/	Thurmont	MD	21788	301-663-9330	
Chesapeake & Ohio Canal National Historical Park 1850 Dual Hwy Suite 100 *Web:* www.nps.gov/choh/	Hagerstown	MD	21740	301-739-4200	739-5275
Clara Barton National Historic Site 5801 Oxford Rd *Web:* www.nps.gov/clba/	Glen Echo	MD	20812	301-320-1410	
Fort McHenry National Monument & Historic Shrine 2400 E Fort Ave *Web:* www.nps.gov/fomc/	Baltimore	MD	21230	410-962-4290	962-2500
Fort Washington Park 13551 Fort Washington Rd *Web:* www.nps.gov/fowa/	Fort Washington	MD	20744	301-763-4600	763-1389
Greenbelt Park 6565 Greenbelt Rd *Web:* www.nps.gov/gree/	Greenbelt	MD	20770	301-344-3948	344-1012
Hampton National Historic Site 535 Hampton Ln *Web:* www.nps.gov/hamp/	Towson	MD	21286	410-823-1309	823-8394
Monocacy National Battlefield 4801 Urbana Pike *Web:* www.nps.gov/mono/	Frederick	MD	21704	301-662-3515	662-3420
Piscataway Park 13551 Fort Washington Rd *Web:* www.nps.gov/pisc/	Fort Washington	MD	20744	301-763-4600	763-1389
Thomas Stone National Historic Site 6655 Rose Hill Rd *Web:* www.nps.gov/thst/	Port Tobacco	MD	20677	301-392-1776	934-8793

Massachusetts

				Phone	Fax
Adams National Historical Park 135 Adams St *Web:* www.nps.gov/adam/	Quincy	MA	02169	617-773-1177	472-7562
Boston African-American National Historic Site 14 Beacon St Suite 401 *Web:* www.nps.gov/boaf/	Boston	MA	02108	617-742-5415	720-0848
Boston Harbor Islands National Recreation Area 408 Atlantic Ave Suite 228 *Web:* www.nps.gov/boha/	Boston	MA	02110	617-223-8666	223-8671
Boston National Historical Park Charlestown Navy Yard *Web:* www.nps.gov/bost/	Boston	MA	02129	617-242-5601	242-6006
Cape Cod National Seashore 99 Marconi Site Rd *Web:* www.nps.gov/caco/	Wellfleet	MA	02667	508-349-3785	349-9052
Frederick Law Olmsted National Historic Site 99 Warren St *Web:* www.nps.gov/frla/	Brookline	MA	02445	617-566-1689	232-4073
John F Kennedy National Historic Site 83 Beals St *Web:* www.nps.gov/jofi/	Brookline	MA	02446	617-566-7937	730-9884
Longfellow National Historic Site 105 Brattle St *Web:* www.nps.gov/long/	Cambridge	MA	02138	617-876-4491	497-8718
Lowell National Historical Park 67 Kirk St *Web:* www.nps.gov/lowe/	Lowell	MA	01852	978-970-5000	275-1762
Minute Man National Historical Park 174 Liberty St *Web:* www.nps.gov/mima/	Concord	MA	01742	978-369-6993	318-7800
New Bedford Whaling National Historical Park 33 William St *Web:* www.nps.gov/nebe/	New Bedford	MA	02740	508-996-4095	984-1250
Salem Maritime National Historic Site 174 Derby St *Web:* www.nps.gov/sama/	Salem	MA	01970	978-740-1660	740-1685
Saugus Iron Works National Historic Site 244 Central St *Web:* www.nps.gov/sair/	Saugus	MA	01906	781-233-0050	231-7345
Springfield Armory National Historic Site 1 Armory Sq Suite 2 Bldg 13 *Web:* www.nps.gov/spar/	Springfield	MA	01105	413-734-8551	747-8062

Michigan

				Phone	Fax
Isle Royale National Park 800 East Lakeshore Dr *Web:* www.nps.gov/isro/	Houghton	MI	49931	906-482-0984	482-8753
Keweenaw National Historical Park 25970 Red Jacket Rd PO Box 471 *Web:* www.nps.gov/kewe/	Calumet	MI	49913	906-337-3168	337-3169
Pictured Rocks National Lakeshore PO Box 40 N8391 Sandpoint Rd *Web:* www.nps.gov/piro/	Munising	MI	49862	906-387-2607	387-4025
Sleeping Bear Dunes National Lakeshore 9922 Front St *Web:* www.nps.gov/slbe/	Empire	MI	49630	231-326-5134	326-5382

Minnesota

				Phone	Fax
Grand Portage National Monument PO Box 668 *Web:* www.nps.gov/grpo/	Grand Marais	MN	55604	218-387-2788	387-2790
Mississippi National River & Recreation Area 111 E Kellogg Blvd Suite 105 *Web:* www.nps.gov/miss/	Saint Paul	MN	55101	651-290-4160	290-3214
Pipestone National Monument 36 Reservation Ave *Web:* www.nps.gov/pipe/	Pipestone	MN	56164	507-825-5464	825-5466
Voyageurs National Park 3131 Hwy 53 S *Web:* www.nps.gov/voya/	International Falls	MN	56649	218-283-9821	285-7407

Mississippi

				Phone	Fax
Brice's Crossroads National Battlefield Site 2680 Natchez Trace Pkwy *TF:* 800-305-7417 ■ *Web:* www.nps.gov/brcr/	Tupelo	MS	38804	662-680-4025	680-4033
Gulf Islands National Seashore (Mississippi) 3500 Park Rd *Web:* www.nps.gov/guis/	Ocean Springs	MS	39564	228-875-0823	875-2358
Natchez National Historical Park 1 Melrose Montebello Pkwy *Web:* www.nps.gov/natc/	Natchez	MS	39120	601-446-5790	442-9516
Natchez Trace National Scenic Trail 2680 Natchez Trace Pkwy *Web:* www.nps.gov/natt/	Tupelo	MS	38804	662-680-4025	680-4036
Natchez Trace Parkway 2680 Natchez Trace Pkwy *TF:* 800-305-7417 ■ *Web:* www.nps.gov/natr/	Tupelo	MS	38804	662-680-4025	680-4036
Tupelo National Battlefield c/o Natchez Trace Pkwy 2680 Natchez Trace Pkwy *TF:* 800-305-7417 ■ *Web:* www.nps.gov/tupe/	Tupelo	MS	38804	662-680-4025	680-4033
Vicksburg National Military Park 3201 Clay St *Web:* www.nps.gov/vick/	Vicksburg	MS	39183	601-636-0583	636-9497

Missouri

				Phone	Fax
George Washington Carver National Monument 5646 Carver Rd *Web:* www.nps.gov/gwca/	Diamond	MO	64840	417-325-4151	325-4231
Harry S Truman National Historic Site 223 N Main St *Web:* www.nps.gov/hstr/	Independence	MO	64050	816-254-9929	254-4491
Jefferson National Expansion Memorial 11 N 4th St *Web:* www.nps.gov/jeff/	Saint Louis	MO	63102	314-655-1700	655-1641
Ozark National Scenic Riverways 404 Watercress Dr PO Box 490 *Web:* www.nps.gov/ozar/	Van Buren	MO	63965	573-323-4236	323-4140
Ulysses S Grant National Historic Site 7400 Grant Rd *Web:* www.nps.gov/ulsg/	Saint Louis	MO	63123	314-842-3298	842-1659
Wilson's Creek National Battlefield 6424 W Farm Rd 182 *Web:* www.nps.gov/wicr/	Republic	MO	65738	417-732-2662	732-1167

Montana

				Phone	Fax
Big Hole National Battlefield PO Box 237 *Web:* www.nps.gov/biho/	Wisdom	MT	59761	406-689-3155	689-3151

	City	State	Zip	Phone	Fax
Bighorn Canyon National Recreation Area 5 Ave B PO Box 7458 *Web:* www.nps.gov/bica/	Fort Smith	MT	59035	406-666-2412	666-2415
Glacier National Park PO Box 128 *Web:* www.nps.gov/glac/	West Glacier	MT	59936	406-888-7800	888-7808
Grant-Kohrs Ranch National Historic Site 266 Warren Ln *Web:* www.nps.gov/grko/	Deer Lodge	MT	59722	406-846-2070	846-3962
Little Bighorn Battlefield National Monument PO Box 39 *Web:* www.nps.gov/libi/	Crow Agency	MT	59022	406-638-3204	638-2623

Nebraska

	City	State	Zip	Phone	Fax
Agate Fossil Beds National Monument 301 River Rd *Web:* www.nps.gov/agfo/	Harrison	NE	69346	308-668-2211	668-2318
Homestead National Monument of America 8523 W State Hwy 4 *Web:* www.nps.gov/home/	Beatrice	NE	68310	402-223-3514	228-4231
Missouri National Recreational River PO Box 591 *Web:* www.nps.gov/mnrr/	O'Neill	NE	68763	402-336-3970	667-2552
Niobrara National Scenic River PO Box 591 *Web:* www.nps.gov/niob/	O'Neill	NE	68763	402-336-3970	
Scotts Bluff National Monument PO Box 27 *Web:* www.nps.gov/scbl/	Gering	NE	69341	308-436-4340	436-7611

Nevada

	City	State	Zip	Phone	Fax
Great Basin National Park 100 Great Basin National Park *Web:* www.nps.gov/grba/	Baker	NV	89311	775-234-7331	234-7269
Lake Mead National Recreation Area 601 Nevada Hwy *Web:* www.nps.gov/lame/	Boulder City	NV	89005	702-293-8990	293-8936

New Hampshire

	City	State	Zip	Phone	Fax
Saint-Gaudens National Historic Site 139 St Gaudens Rd *Web:* www.sgnhs.org	Cornish	NH	03745	603-675-2175	675-2701

New Jersey

	City	State	Zip	Phone	Fax
Edison National Historic Site Main St & Lakeside Ave *Web:* www.nps.gov/edis/	West Orange	NJ	07052	973-324-9973	736-8496
Morristown National Historical Park 30 Washington Pl *Web:* www.nps.gov/morr/	Morristown	NJ	07960	973-543-4030	

New Mexico

	City	State	Zip	Phone	Fax
Aztec Ruins National Monument 84 County Rd 2900 *Web:* www.nps.gov/azru/	Aztec	NM	87410	505-334-6174	334-6372
Bandelier National Monument 15 Entrance Rd *Web:* www.nps.gov/band/	Los Alamos	NM	87544	505-672-0343	672-9607
Capulin Volcano National Monument PO Box 40 *Web:* www.nps.gov/cavo/	Capulin	NM	88414	505-278-2201	278-2211
Carlsbad Caverns National Park 3225 National Parks Hwy *Web:* www.nps.gov/cave/	Carlsbad	NM	88220	505-785-2232	785-2133
Chaco Culture National Historical Park PO Box 280 *Web:* www.nps.gov/chcu/	Nageezi	NM	87037	505-786-7014	786-7061
El Malpais National Monument 123 E Roosevelt Ave *Web:* www.nps.gov/elma/	Grants	NM	87020	505-285-4641	285-5661
El Morro National Monument HC 61 Box 43 *Web:* www.nps.gov/elmo/	Ramah	NM	87321	505-783-4226	783-4689
Fort Union National Monument PO Box 127 *Web:* www.nps.gov/foun/	Watrous	NM	87753	505-425-8025	454-1155
Gila Cliff Dwellings National Monument HC 68 Box 100 *Web:* www.nps.gov/gicl/	Silver City	NM	88061	505-536-9461	536-9344
Pecos National Historical Park PO Box 418 *Web:* www.nps.gov/peco/	Pecos	NM	87552	505-757-6414	757-8460
Petroglyph National Monument 6001 Unser Blvd NW *Web:* www.nps.gov/petr/	Albuquerque	NM	87120	505-899-0205	899-0207
Salinas Pueblo Missions National Monument PO Box 517 *Web:* www.nps.gov/sapu/	Mountainair	NM	87036	505-847-2585	847-2441
White Sands National Monument PO Box 1086 *Web:* www.nps.gov/whsa/	Holloman AFB	NM	88330	505-679-2599	

New York

	City	State	Zip	Phone	Fax
African Burial Ground National Monument Office of Public Education and Interpretation 290 Broadway *Web:* www.africanburialground.gov	New York	NY	19106	212-637-2039	
Castle Clinton National Monument Battery Park *Web:* www.nps.gov/cacl/	New York	NY	10004	212-344-7220	825-6874
Eleanor Roosevelt National Historic Site 4097 Albany Post Rd *Web:* www.nps.gov/elro/	Hyde Park	NY	12538	845-229-9115	229-0739
Federal Hall National Memorial 26 Wall St *Web:* www.nps.gov/feha/	New York	NY	10005	212-825-6888	825-6874
Fire Island National Seashore 120 Laurel St *Web:* www.nps.gov/fiis/	Patchogue	NY	11772	631-289-4810	289-4898
Fort Stanwix National Monument 112 E Park St *Web:* www.nps.gov/fost/	Rome	NY	13440	315-338-7730	334-5051
Gateway National Recreation Area 210 New York Ave *Web:* www.nps.gov/gate/	Staten Island	NY	10305	718-354-4606	354-4605
General Grant National Memorial Riverside Dr & W 122nd St *Web:* www.nps.gov/gegr/	New York	NY	10027	212-666-1640	932-9631
Governors Island National Monument 10 South St Slip #7 *Web:* www.governorsislandnationalmonument.org	New York	NY	10004	212-825-3045	825-3055
Hamilton Grange National Memorial 122 St @ Riverside Dr *Web:* www.nps.gov/hagr/	New York	NY	10027	212-666-1640	
Home of Franklin D Roosevelt National Historic Site 4097 Albany Post Rd *Web:* www.nps.gov/hofr/	Hyde Park	NY	12538	845-229-9115	229-0739
Martin Van Buren National Historic Site 1013 Old Post Rd *Web:* www.nps.gov/mava/	Kinderhook	NY	12106	518-758-9689	758-6986
Sagamore Hill National Historic Site 20 Sagamore Hill Rd *Web:* www.nps.gov/sahi/	Oyster Bay	NY	11771	516-922-4788	922-4792
Saint Paul's Church National Historic Site 897 S Columbus Ave *Web:* www.nps.gov/sapa/	Mount Vernon	NY	10550	914-667-4116	667-3024
Saratoga National Historical Park 648 Route 32 *Web:* www.nps.gov/sara/	Stillwater	NY	12170	518-664-9821	664-3349
Statue of Liberty National Monument & Ellis Island Liberty Island *Web:* www.nps.gov/stli/	New York	NY	10004	212-363-3200	
Theodore Roosevelt Birthplace National Historic Site 28 E 20th St *Web:* www.nps.gov/thrb/	New York	NY	10003	212-283-5154	677-3587
Theodore Roosevelt Inaugural National Historic Site 641 Delaware Ave *Web:* www.nps.gov/thri/	Buffalo	NY	14202	716-884-0095	884-0330
Vanderbilt Mansion National Historic Site 4097 Albany Post Rd *Web:* www.nps.gov/vama/	Hyde Park	NY	12538	845-229-9115	229-0739
Women's Rights National Historical Park 136 Fall St *Web:* www.nps.gov/wori/	Seneca Falls	NY	13148	315-568-2991	568-2141

North Carolina

	City	State	Zip	Phone	Fax
Blue Ridge Parkway 199 Hemphill Knob Rd *Web:* www.nps.gov/blri/	Asheville	NC	28803	828-271-4779	271-4313
Cape Hatteras National Seashore 1401 National Park Dr *Web:* www.nps.gov/caha/	Manteo	NC	27954	252-473-2111	473-2595
Cape Lookout National Seashore 131 Charles St *Web:* www.nps.gov/calo/	Harkers Island	NC	28531	252-728-2250	728-2160
Carl Sandburg Home National Historic Site 81 Carl Sadburg Ln *Web:* www.nps.gov/carl/	Flat Rock	NC	28731	828-693-4178	693-4179
Fort Raleigh National Historic Site 1401 National Park Dr *Web:* www.nps.gov/fora/	Manteo	NC	27954	252-473-5772	473-2595
Guilford Courthouse National Military Park 2332 New Garden Rd *Web:* www.nps.gov/guco/	Greensboro	NC	27410	336-288-1776	282-2296
Moores Creek National Battlefield 40 Patriots Hall Dr *Web:* www.nps.gov/mocr/	Currie	NC	28435	910-283-5591	283-5351
Wright Brothers National Memorial 1401 National Park Dr *Web:* www.nps.gov/wrbr/	Manteo	NC	27954	252-473-2111	473-2595

North Dakota

	City	State	Zip	Phone	Fax
Fort Union Trading Post National Historic Site 15550 Hwy 1804 *Web:* www.nps.gov/fous/	Williston	ND	58801	701-572-9083	572-7321
Knife River Indian Villages National Historic Site 564 County Rd 37 PO Box 9 *Web:* www.nps.gov/knri/	Stanton	ND	58571	701-745-3300	745-3708
Theodore Roosevelt National Park 315 2nd Ave Box 7 *Web:* www.nps.gov/thro/	Medora	ND	58645	701-623-4466	623-4840

Ohio

	City	State	Zip	Phone	Fax
Cuyahoga Valley National Park 15610 Vaughn Rd **Fax Area Code:* 440 ■ *TF:* 800-445-9667 ■ *Web:* www.nps.gov/cuva/	Brecksville	OH	44141	216-524-1497	546-5989*
Dayton Aviation Heritage National Historical Park 16 S Williams St *Web:* www.nps.gov/daav/	Dayton	OH	45402	937-225-7705	222-4512
First Ladies National Historic Site 205 Market Ave S *Web:* www.nps.gov/fila/	Canton	OH	44702	330-452-0876	456-3414
Hopewell Culture National Historical Park 16062 SR-104 *Web:* www.nps.gov/hocu/	Chillicothe	OH	45601	740-774-1125	774-1140
James A Garfield National Historic Site 8095 Mentor Ave *Web:* www.nps.gov/jaga/	Mentor	OH	44060	440-255-8722	974-2045
Perry's Victory & International Peace Memorial 93 Delaware Ave PO Box 549 *Web:* www.nps.gov/pevi/	Put-in-Bay	OH	43456	419-285-2184	285-2516
William Howard Taft National Historic Site 2038 Auburn Ave *Web:* www.nps.gov/wiho/	Cincinnati	OH	45219	513-684-3262	684-3627

Oklahoma

	City	State	Zip	Phone	Fax
Chickasaw National Recreation Area 1008 W 2nd St *Web:* www.nps.gov/chic/	Sulphur	OK	73086	580-622-3165	622-6931
Washita Battlefield National Historic Site 426 E Broadway *Web:* www.nps.gov/waba/	Cheyenne	OK	73628	580-497-2742	497-2712

Oregon

	City	State	Zip	Phone	Fax
Crater Lake National Park PO Box 7 *Web:* www.nps.gov/crla/	Crater Lake	OR	97604	541-594-3000	594-3010
John Day Fossil Beds National Monument 32651 Hwy 19 *Web:* www.nps.gov/joda/	Kimberly	OR	97848	541-987-2333	987-2336
Oregon Caves National Monument 19000 Caves Hwy *Web:* www.nps.gov/orca/	Cave Junction	OR	97523	541-592-2100	592-3981

Pennsylvania

	City	State	Zip	Phone	Fax
Allegheny Portage Railroad National Historic Site 110 Federal Park Rd *Web:* www.nps.gov/alpo/	Gallitzin	PA	16641	814-886-6150	884-0206
Delaware National Scenic River Delaware Water Gap National Recreation Area 1 River Rd *Web:* www.nps.gov/dela/	Bushkill	PA	18324	570-426-2435	588-2780
Delaware Water Gap National Recreation Area 1 River Rd *Web:* www.nps.gov/dewa/	Bushkill	PA	18324	570-426-2435	426-2402
Edgar Allan Poe National Historic Site 532 N 7th St *Web:* www.nps.gov/edal/	Philadelphia	PA	19123	215-597-8780	597-1901

Pennsylvania (Cont'd)

	City	State	Zip	Phone	Fax
Eisenhower National Historic Site 250 Eisenhower Farm Ln *Web:* www.nps.gov/eise/	Gettysburg	PA	17325	717-338-9114	338-0821
Flight 93 National Memorial National Park Service 109 W Main St - Suite 104 *Web:* www.flight93memorialproject.org	Somerset	PA	15501	814-443-4557	443-2180
Fort Necessity National Battlefield 1 Washington Pkwy. *Web:* www.nps.gov/fone/	Farmington	PA	15437	724-329-5512	329-8682
Friendship Hill National Historic Site 223 New Geneva Rd *Web:* www.nps.gov/frhi/	Point Marion	PA	15474	724-725-9190	725-1999
Gettysburg National Military Park 97 Taneytown Rd *Web:* www.nps.gov/gett/	Gettysburg	PA	17325	717-334-1124	334-1891
Great Egg Harbor National Scenic & Recreational River c/o National Park Service 200 Chestnut St *Web:* www.nps.gov/greg/	Philadelphia	PA	19106	215-597-5823	597-5747
Hopewell Furnace National Historic Site 2 Mark Bird Ln *Web:* www.nps.gov/hofu/	Elverson	PA	19520	610-582-8773	582-2768
Independence National Historical Park 143 S 3rd St *Web:* www.nps.gov/inde/	Philadelphia	PA	19106	215-597-8787	597-1548
Johnstown Flood National Memorial 733 Lake Rd *Web:* www.nps.gov/jofl/	South Fork	PA	15956	814-495-4643	495-7463
Steamtown National Historic Site 150 S Washington Ave *TF:* 888-693-9391 ■ *Web:* www.nps.gov/stea/	Scranton	PA	18503	570-340-5200	340-5328
Thaddeus Kosciuszko National Memorial c/o Independence National Historical Park 143 S 3rd St *Web:* www.nps.gov/thko/	Philadelphia	PA	19106	215-597-9618	861-4950
Upper Delaware Scenic & Recreational River 274 River Rd *Web:* www.nps.gov/upde	Beach Lake	PA	18405	570-685-4871	729-8565
Valley Forge National Historical Park 1400 N Outer Line Dr *Web:* www.nps.gov/vafo/	King of Prussia	PA	19406	610-783-1077	783-1060

Puerto Rico

	City	State	Zip	Phone	Fax
San Juan National Historic Site 501 Norzagaray St *Web:* www.nps.gov/saju/	San Juan	PR	00901	787-729-6960	289-7972

Rhode Island

	City	State	Zip	Phone	Fax
Roger Williams National Memorial 282 N Main St *Web:* www.nps.gov/rowi/	Providence	RI	02903	401-521-7266	521-7239

South Carolina

	City	State	Zip	Phone	Fax
Charles Pinckney National Historic Site 1214 Middle St. *Web:* www.nps.gov/chpi/	Sullivans Island	SC	29482	843-881-5516	881-7070
Congaree National Park 100 National Park Rd *Web:* www.nps.gov/cosw/	Hopkins	SC	29061	803-776-4396	783-4241
Cowpens National Battlefield 4001 Chesnee Hwy. *Web:* www.nps.gov/cowp/	Gaffney	SC	29341	864-461-2828	461-7795
Fort Sumter National Monument 1214 Middle St *Web:* www.nps.gov/fosu/	Sullivans Island	SC	29482	843-883-3123	883-3910
Kings Mountain National Military Park 2625 Park Rd *Web:* www.nps.gov/kimo/	Blacksburg	SC	29702	864-936-7921	936-9897
Ninety Six National Historic Site 1103 Hwy 248 *Web:* www.nps.gov/nisi/	Ninety Six	SC	29666	864-543-4068	543-2058

South Dakota

	City	State	Zip	Phone	Fax
Badlands National Park 25216 Ben Reifel Rd PO Box 6 *Web:* www.nps.gov/badl/	Interior	SD	57750	605-433-5361	433-5404
Jewel Cave National Monument 11149 US Hwy 16 Bldg B-12 *Web:* www.nps.gov/jeca/	Custer	SD	57730	605-673-2288	673-3294
Minuteman Missile National Historic Site 21280 SD Hwy 240 *Web:* www.nps.gov/mimi/	Philip	SD	57567	605-433-5552	433-5558
Mount Rushmore National Memorial 13000 Hwy 244 Bldg 31 Suite 1 *Web:* www.nps.gov/moru/	Keystone	SD	57751	605-574-2523	574-2307
Wind Cave National Park 26611 US Hwy 385 *Web:* www.nps.gov/wica/	Hot Springs	SD	57747	605-745-4600	745-4207

Tennessee

	City	State	Zip	Phone	Fax
Andrew Johnson National Historic Site 121 Monument Ave. *Web:* www.nps.gov/anjo/	Greeneville	TN	37743	423-638-3551	638-9194
Big South Fork National River & Recreation Area 4564 Leatherwood Rd *Web:* www.nps.gov/biso/	Oneida	TN	37841	423-569-9778	569-5505
Fort Donelson National Battlefield PO Box 434 *Web:* www.nps.gov/fodo/	Dover	TN	37058	931-232-5706	232-4085
Great Smoky Mountains National Park 107 Park Headquarters Rd. *Web:* www.nps.gov/grsm/	Gatlinburg	TN	37738	865-436-1200	436-1220
Obed Wild & Scenic River 208 N Maiden St *Web:* www.nps.gov/obed/	Wartburg	TN	37887	423-346-6294	346-3362
Shiloh National Military Park 1055 Pittsburg Landing Rd. *Web:* www.nps.gov/shil/	Shiloh	TN	38376	731-689-5696	689-5450
Stones River National Battlefield 3501 Old Nashville Hwy *Web:* www.nps.gov/stri/	Murfreesboro	TN	37129	615-893-9501	893-9508

Texas

	City	State	Zip	Phone	Fax
Alibates Flint Quarries National Monument PO Box 1460 *Web:* www.nps.gov/alfl/	Fritch	TX	79036	806-857-3151	857-2319
Amistad National Recreation Area 4121 Hwy 90 West *Web:* www.nps.gov/amis/	Del Rio	TX	78840	830-775-7491	778-9248
Big Bend National Park PO Box 129 *Web:* www.nps.gov/bibe/	Big Bend National Park	TX	79834	432-477-2251	477-1175
Big Thicket National Preserve 6044 FM420 *Web:* www.nps.gov/bith/	Kountze	TX	77625	409-951-6700	951-6868
Chamizal National Memorial 800 S San Marcial St. *Web:* www.nps.gov/cham/	El Paso	TX	79905	915-532-7273	532-7240
Fort Davis National Historic Site PO Box 1379 *Web:* www.nps.gov/foda/	Fort Davis	TX	79734	432-426-3224	426-3122
Guadalupe Mountains National Park 400 Pine Canyon Rd *Web:* www.nps.gov/gumo/	Salt Flat	TX	79847	915-828-3251	828-3269
Lake Meredith National Recreation Area 419 E Broadway *Web:* www.nps.gov/lamr/	Fritch	TX	79036	806-857-3151	857-2319
Lyndon B Johnson National Historical Park 100 Lady Bird Ln *Web:* www.nps.gov/lyjo/	Johnson City	TX	78636	830-868-7128	868-7863
Padre Island National Seashore PO Box 181300 *Web:* www.nps.gov/pais/	Corpus Christi	TX	78480	361-949-8173	949-8023
Palo Alto Battlefield National Historic Site 1623 Central Blvd Suite 213 *Web:* www.nps.gov/paal/	Brownsville	TX	78520	956-541-2785	541-6356
Rio Grande Wild & Scenic River PO Box 129 *Web:* www.nps.gov/rigr/	Big Bend National Park	TX	79834	432-477-2251	477-1175
San Antonio Missions National Historical Park 2202 Roosevelt Ave *Web:* www.nps.gov/saan/	San Antonio	TX	78210	210-534-8833	534-1106

Utah

	City	State	Zip	Phone	Fax
Arches National Park PO Box 907 *Web:* www.nps.gov/arch/	Moab	UT	84532	435-719-2100	719-2305
Bryce Canyon National Park PO Box 640201 *Web:* www.nps.gov/brca/	Bryce Canyon	UT	84764	435-834-5322	834-4102
Canyonlands National Park 2282 S West Resource Blvd *Web:* www.nps.gov/cany/	Moab	UT	84532	435-719-2313	719-2300
Capitol Reef National Park HC 70 Box 15 *Web:* www.nps.gov/care/	Torrey	UT	84775	435-425-3791	425-3026
Cedar Breaks National Monument 2390 W Hwy 56 Suite 11 *Web:* www.nps.gov/cebr/	Cedar City	UT	84720	435-586-9451	586-3813
Golden Spike National Historic Site PO Box 897 *Web:* www.nps.gov/gosp/	Brigham City	UT	84302	435-471-2209	471-2341
Natural Bridges National Monument HC 60 Box 1 *Web:* www.nps.gov/nabr/	Lake Powell	UT	84533	435-692-1234	692-1111
Timpanogos Cave National Monument RR 3 Box 200 *Web:* www.nps.gov/tica/	American Fork	UT	84003	801-756-5239	756-5661
Zion National Park SR 9 *Web:* www.nps.gov/zion/	Springdale	UT	84767	435-772-3256	772-3426

Vermont

	City	State	Zip	Phone	Fax
Marsh-Billings-Rockefeller National Historical Park 54 Elm St *Web:* www.nps.gov/mabi/	Woodstock	VT	05091	802-457-3368	457-3405

Virgin Islands

	City	State	Zip	Phone	Fax
Buck Island Reef National Monument 2100 Church St #100 Christiansted *Web:* www.nps.gov/buis/	Saint Croix	VI	00820	340-773-1460	773-5995
Christiansted National Historic Site 2100 Church St #100 Christiansted *Web:* www.nps.gov/chri/	Saint Croix	VI	00820	340-773-1460	773-4995
Salt River Bay National Historical Park & Ecological Preserve c/o Christiansted National Historic Site 2100 Church St #100 *Web:* www.nps.gov/sari/	Saint Croix	VI	00820	340-773-1460	773-5995
Virgin Islands Coral Reef National Monument c/o Virgin Islands National Park 1300 Cruz Bay Creek *Web:* www.nps.gov/vicr/	Saint John	VI	00830	340-776-6201	
Virgin Islands National Park 1300 Cruz Bay Creek *Web:* www.nps.gov/viis/	Saint John	VI	00830	340-776-6201	775-9592

Virginia

	City	State	Zip	Phone	Fax
Appomattox Court House National Historical Park Hwy 24 PO Box 218 *Web:* www.nps.gov/apco/	Appomattox	VA	24522	434-352-8987	352-8330
Arlington House-Robert E Lee Memorial George Washington Memorial Pkwy Turkey Run Park *Web:* www.nps.gov/arho/	McLean	VA	22101	703-235-1530	
Booker T Washington National Monument 12130 Booker T Washington Hwy. *Web:* www.nps.gov/bowa/	Hardy	VA	24101	540-721-2094	721-8311
Cedar Creek & Belle Grove National Historical Park PO Box 700 *Web:* www.nps.gov/cebe/	Middletown	VA	22645	540-868-9176	869-4527
Colonial National Historical Park Rt 238 & Colonial Pkwy. *Web:* www.nps.gov/colo/	Yorktown	VA	23690	757-898-3400	898-6346
Fredericksburg & Spotsylvania National Military Park 120 Chatham Ln. *Web:* www.nps.gov/frsp/	Fredericksburg	VA	22405	540-371-0802	371-1907
George Washington Birthplace National Monument 1732 Popes Creek Rd *Web:* www.nps.gov/gewa/	Washington's Birthplace	VA	22443	804-224-1732	224-2142
George Washington Memorial Parkway Turkey Run Park *Web:* www.nps.gov/gwmp/	McLean	VA	22101	703-289-2500	289-2598
Lyndon Baines Johnson Memorial Grove on the Potomac Turkey Run Park George Washington Memorial Pkwy *Web:* www.nps.gov/lyba/	McLean	VA	22101	703-289-2500	289-2598
Maggie L Walker National Historic Site 3215 East Broad St *Web:* www.nps.gov/malw/	Richmond	VA	23223	804-771-2017	771-2226
Manassas National Battlefield Park 12521 Lee Hwy *Web:* www.nps.gov/mana/	Manassas	VA	20109	703-361-1339	361-7106
Petersburg National Battlefield 1539 Hickory Hill Rd. *Web:* www.nps.gov/pete/	Petersburg	VA	23803	804-732-3531	732-0835
Prince William Forest Park 18100 Park Headquarters Rd. *Web:* www.nps.gov/prwi/	Triangle	VA	22172	703-221-7181	221-3258
Richmond National Battlefield Park 3215 E Broad St. *Web:* www.nps.gov/rich/	Richmond	VA	23223	804-226-1981	771-8522

				Phone	Fax
Shenandoah National Park 3655 US Hwy 211E	Luray	VA	22835	540-999-3500	999-3601
Web: www.nps.gov/shen/					
Theodore Roosevelt Island Park c/o Turkey Run Park George Washington Memorial Pkwy	McLean	VA	22101	703-289-2500	289-2598
Web: www.nps.gov/this/					
Wolf Trap National Park for the Performing Arts 1551 Trap Rd	Vienna	VA	22182	703-255-1800	255-1971
Web: www.nps.gov/wotr/					

Washington

				Phone	Fax
Ebey's Landing National Historical Reserve PO Box 774 162 Cemetery Rd	Coupeville	WA	98239	360-678-6084	678-2246
Web: www.nps.gov/ebla/					
Fort Vancouver National Historic Site 612 E Reserve St	Vancouver	WA	98661	360-816-6230	
TF: 800-832-3599 ■ *Web:* www.nps.gov/fova/					
Klondike Gold Rush National Historical Park - Seattle Unit 319 2nd Ave S	Seattle	WA	98104	206-220-4240	
Web: www.nps.gov/klse/					
Lake Chelan National Recreation Area c/o North Cascades National Park PO Box 7	Stehekin	WA	98852	509-682-2549	856-1934*
**Fax Area Code:* 360 ■ *Web:* www.nps.gov/lach/					
Lake Roosevelt National Recreation Area 1008 Crest Dr	Coulee Dam	WA	99116	509-633-9441	633-9332
Web: www.nps.gov/laro/					
Mount Rainier National Park 55210 238th Ave E	Ashford	WA	98304	360-569-2211	569-2170
Web: www.nps.gov/mora/					
North Cascades National Park 810 SR 20	Sedro Woolley	WA	98284	360-856-5700	856-1934
Web: www.nps.gov/noca/					
Olympic National Park 600 E Park Ave	Port Angeles	WA	98362	360-565-3130	565-3015
Web: www.nps.gov/olym/					
Ross Lake National Recreation Area c/o North Cascades National Park 810 SR 20	Sedro Woolley	WA	98284	360-854-7200	856-1934
Web: www.nps.gov/rola/					
San Juan Island National Historical Park PO Box 429	Friday Harbor	WA	98250	360-378-2240	378-2615
Web: www.nps.gov/sajh/					
Whitman Mission National Historic Site 328 Whitman Mission Rd	Walla Walla	WA	99362	509-522-6360	522-6355
Web: www.nps.gov/whmi/					

West Virginia

				Phone	Fax
Appalachian National Scenic Trail PO Box 807	Harpers Ferry	WV	25425	304-535-6331	535-2667
Web: www.nps.gov/appa/					
Bluestone National Scenic River 104 Main St PO Box 246	Glen Jean	WV	25846	304-465-0508	465-0591
Web: www.nps.gov/blue/					
Gauley River National Recreation Area 104 Main St PO Box 246	Glen Jean	WV	25846	304-465-0508	465-0591
Web: www.nps.gov/gari/					
Harpers Ferry National Historic Park PO Box 65	Harpers Ferry	WV	25425	304-535-6029	535-6244
Web: www.nps.gov/hafe/					
New River Gorge National River 104 Main St PO Box 246	Glen Jean	WV	25846	304-465-0508	465-0591
Web: www.nps.gov/neri/					
Potomac Heritage National Scenic Trail PO Box B	Harpers Ferry	WV	25425	304-535-4014	
Web: www.nps.gov/pohe/					

Wisconsin

				Phone	Fax
Apostle Islands National Lakeshore 415 Washington Ave	Bayfield	WI	54814	715-779-3397	779-3049
Web: www.nps.gov/apis/					
Saint Croix National Scenic Riverway 401 Hamilton St PO Box 708	Saint Croix Falls	WI	54024	715-483-3284	483-3288
Web: www.nps.gov/sacn/					

Wyoming

				Phone	Fax
Devils Tower National Monument Hwy 110 Bldg 170	Devils Tower	WY	82714	307-467-5283	467-5350
Web: www.nps.gov/deto/					
Fort Laramie National Historic Site 965 Grey Rocks Rd	Fort Laramie	WY	82212	307-837-2221	837-2120
Web: www.nps.gov/fola/					
Fossil Butte National Monument PO Box 592	Kemmerer	WY	83101	307-877-4455	877-4457
Web: www.nps.gov/fobu/					
Grand Teton National Park Teton Park Rd PO Drawer 170	Moose	WY	83012	307-739-3300	739-3438
Web: www.nps.gov/grte/					
John D Rockefeller Jr Memorial Parkway PO Box 170	Moose	WY	83012	307-739-3300	739-3438
Web: www.nps.gov/jodr/					
Yellowstone National Park PO Box 168	Yellowstone National Park	WY	82190	307-344-7381	344-2323*
**Fax:* Mail Rm ■ *Web:* www.nps.gov/yell/					

568 PARKS - STATE

SEE ALSO Attractions - Nature Centers, Parks, Other Natural Areas p. 1352; Parks - National - Canada p. 2049; Parks - National - US p. 2050

Alabama

				Phone	Fax
Bladon Springs State Park 3921 Bladon Rd	Bladon Springs	AL	36919	334-754-9207	754-9207
Web: www.alapark.com/parks					
Blue Springs State Park 2595 Hwy 10	Clio	AL	36017	334-397-4875	397-4875
Web: www.alapark.com/parks					
Buck's Pocket State Park 393 County Rd 174	Grove Oak	AL	35975	256-659-2000	659-2000
Web: www.alapark.com/parks					
Cathedral Caverns State Park 637 Cave Rd	Woodville	AL	35776	256-728-8193	728-8193
Web: www.alapark.com/parks					
Cheaha Resort State Park 19644 Hwy 281	Delta	AL	36258	256-488-5111	488-5885
TF: 800-610-5801 ■ *Web:* www.alapark.com/parks					
Chewacla State Park 124 Shell Toomer Pkwy	Auburn	AL	36830	334-887-5621	821-2439
Web: www.alapark.com/parks					
Chickasaw State Park 26955 US Hwy 43	Gallion	AL	36742	334-295-8230	295-8230
Web: www.alapark.com/parks					
DeSoto Resort State Park 13883 County Rd 89	Fort Payne	AL	35967	256-845-0051	845-8286
Web: www.alapark.com/parks					
Florala State Park 22738 Azalea Dr	Florala	AL	36442	334-858-6425	858-6425
Web: www.alapark.com/parks					
Frank Jackson State Park 100 Jerry Adams Dr	Opp	AL	36467	334-493-6988	493-2478
Web: www.alapark.com/parks					
Gulf State Park 20115 State Hwy 135	Gulf Shores	AL	36542	251-948-7275	948-7726
Web: www.alapark.com/parks					
Joe Wheeler Resort State Park 201 McLean Dr	Rogersville	AL	35652	256-247-5466	247-1449
Web: www.alapark.com/parks					
Lake Guntersville Resort State Park 7966 Alabama Hwy 227	Guntersville	AL	35976	256-571-5444	
Web: www.dcnr.state.al.us/parks/lake_guntersville_1a.html					
Lake Lurleen State Park 13226 Lake Lurleen Rd	Coker	AL	35452	205-339-1558	339-8885
Web: www.alapark.com/parks					
Lakepoint Resort State Park 104 Lakepoint Dr	Eufaula	AL	36027	334-687-8011	687-3273
TF: 800-544-5253 ■ *Web:* www.alapark.com/parks					
Meaher State Park 5200 Battleship Pkwy E	Spanish Fort	AL	36577	251-626-5529	626-5529
Web: www.alapark.com/parks					
Monte Sano State Park 5105 Nolen Ave	Huntsville	AL	35801	256-534-3757	539-7069
TF: 800-252-7275 ■ *Web:* www.alapark.com/parks					
Oak Mountain State Park 200 Terrace Dr PO Box 278	Pelham	AL	35124	205-620-2520	620-2531
Web: www.alapark.com/parks					
Paul M. Grist State Park 1546 Grist Rd	Selma	AL	36701	334-872-5846	872-5846
Web: www.alapark.com/parks					
Rickwood Caverns State Park 370 Rickwood Park Rd	Warrior	AL	35180	205-647-9692	647-9692
Web: www.alapark.com/parks					
Roland Cooper State Park 285 Deer Run Dr	Camden	AL	36726	334-682-4838	682-4050
Web: www.alapark.com/parks					
Wind Creek State Park 4325 Alabama Hwy 128	Alexander City	AL	35010	256-329-0845	234-4870
Web: www.alapark.com/parks					

Alaska

				Phone	Fax
Afognak Island State Park c/o Kodiak Area Office 1400 Abercrombie Dr	Kodiak	AK	99615	907-486-6339	
Web: www.dnr.state.ak.us/parks/units/kodiak/afognak.htm					
Alaska Chilkat Bald Eagle Preserve c/o Southeast Area Office 400 Willoughby Ave, 4th Fl	Juneau	AK	99801	907-465-4563	
Web: www.dnr.state.ak.us/parks/units/eagleprv.htm					
Anchor River State Recreation Area c/o Kenai/PWS Area Office PO Box 1247	Soldotna	AK	99669	907-262-5581	
Web: www.dnr.state.ak.us/parks/units/anchoriv.htm					
Baranof Castle Hill State Historic Site c/o Southeast Area Office 400 Willoughby Ave, 4th Fl	Juneau	AK	99801	907-465-4563	
Web: www.dnr.state.ak.us/parks/units/sitka.htm					
Beecher Pass State Marine Park c/o Southeast Area Office 400 Willoughby Ave, 4th Fl	Juneau	AK	99801	907-465-4563	
Bettles Bay State Marine Park c/o Kenai/PWS Area Office PO Box 1247	Soldotna	AK	99669	907-262-5581	
Web: www.dnr.state.ak.us/parks/units/pwssmp/smpwhit2.htm					
Big Bear/Baby Bear State Marine Park c/o Southeast Area Office 400 Willoughby Ave, 4th Fl	Juneau	AK	99801	907-465-4563	
Web: www.dnr.state.ak.us/parks/units/sitka.htm					
Big Delta State Historical Park c/o Northern Area Office 3700 Airport Way	Fairbanks	AK	99709	907-451-2695	
Web: www.dnr.state.ak.us/parks/units/deltajct/bigdelta.htm					
Big Lake North State Recreation Site c/o Mat-Su/CB Area Office HC 32 Box 6706	Wasilla	AK	99654	907-745-3975	
Big Lake South State Recreation Site c/o Mat-Su/CB Area Office HC 32 Box 6706	Wasilla	AK	99654	907-745-3975	
Birch Lake State Recreation Area c/o Northern Area Office 3700 Airport Way	Fairbanks	AK	99709	907-451-2695	
Web: www.dnr.state.ak.us/parks/units/birch.htm					
Black Sands Beach State Marine Park c/o Southeast Area Office 400 WIlloughby Ave, 4th Fl	Juneau	AK	99801	907-465-4563	
Blair Lake State Recreation Site c/o Mat-Su/CB Area Office HC 32 Box 6706	Wasilla	AK	99654	907-745-3975	
Blueberry Lake State Recreation Site c/o Kenai/PWS Area Office PO Box 1247	Soldotna	AK	99669	907-262-5581	
Boswell Bay State Marine Park c/o Kenai/PWS Area Office PO Box 1247	Soldotna	AK	99669	907-262-5581	
Web: www.dnr.state.ak.us/parks/units/pwssmp/smpcord.htm					
Buskin River State Recreation Site c/o Kodiak Area Office 1400 Abercrombie Dr	Kodiak	AK	99615	907-486-6339	
Web: www.dnr.state.ak.us/parks/units/kodiak/buskin.htm					
Caines Head State Recreation Area c/o Kenai/PWS Area Office PO Box 1247	Soldotna	AK	99669	907-262-5581	
Web: www.dnr.state.ak.us/parks/units/caineshd.htm					
Canoe Passage State Marine Park c/o Kenai/PWS Area Office PO Box 1247	Soldotna	AK	99669	907-262-5581	
Web: www.dnr.state.ak.us/parks/units/pwssmp/smpcord.htm					
Captain Cook State Recreation Area c/o Kenai/PWS Area Office PO Box 1247	Soldotna	AK	99669	907-262-5581	
Web: www.dnr.state.ak.us/parks/units/captcook.htm					
Chena River State Recreation Area c/o Northern Area Office 3700 Airport Way	Fairbanks	AK	99709	907-451-2695	
Web: www.dnr.state.ak.us/parks/units/chena					
Chena River State Recreation Site c/o Northern Area Office 3700 Airport Way	Fairbanks	AK	99709	907-451-2695	
Web: www.dnr.state.ak.us/parks/units/chenasrs.htm					
Chilkat Islands State Marine Park c/o Southeast Area Office 400 Willoughby Ave, 4th Fl	Juneau	AK	99801	907-465-4563	
Web: www.dnr.state.ak.us/parks/units/haines.htm					
Chilkat State Park c/o Southeast Area Office 400 Willoughby Ave, 4th Fl	Juneau	AK	99801	907-465-4563	
Web: www.dnr.state.ak.us/parks/units/haines.htm					
Chilkoot Lake State Recreation Site c/o Southeast Area Office 400 Willoughby Ave, 4th Fl	Juneau	AK	99801	907-465-4563	
Web: www.dnr.state.ak.us/parks/units/haines.htm					
Chugach State Park c/o Chugach Area Office HC 52 Box 8999	Indian	AK	99540	907-345-5014	345-6982
Web: www.dnr.state.ak.us/parks/units/chugach					
Clam Gulch State Recreation Area c/o Kenai/PWS Area Office PO Box 1247	Soldotna	AK	99669	907-262-5581	
Web: www.dnr.state.ak.us/parks/units/clamglch.htm					
Clearwater State Recreation Site c/o Northern Area Office 3700 Airport Way	Fairbanks	AK	99709	907-451-2695	
Web: www.dnr.state.ak.us/parks/units/deltajct/clearwtr.htm					
Crooked Creek State Recreation Site c/o Kenai/PWS Area Office PO Box 1247	Soldotna	AK	99669	907-262-5581	
Web: www.dnr.state.ak.us/parks/units/kasilof.htm					
Dall Bay State Marine Park c/o Southeast Area Office 400 Willoughby Ave, 4th Fl	Juneau	AK	99801	907-465-4563	
Decision Point State Marine Park c/o Kenai/PWS Area Office PO Box 1247	Soldotna	AK	99669	907-262-5581	
Web: www.dnr.state.ak.us/parks/units/pwssmp/smpwhit1.htm					

Alaska (Cont'd)

Phone Fax

Deep Creek State Recreation Area
c/o Kenai/PWS Area Office PO Box 1247 .... Soldotna AK 99669 907-262-5581
Web: www.dnr.state.ak.us/parks/units/deepck.htm
Delta State Recreation Site
c/o Northern Area Office 3700 Airport Way.................. Fairbanks AK 99709 907-451-2695
Web: www.dnr.state.ak.us/parks/units/deltajct/deltasrs.htm
Denali State Park c/o Mat-Su/CB Area Office HC 32 Box 6706....... Wasilla AK 99654 907-745-3975
Web: www.dnr.state.ak.us/parks/units/denali1.htm
Donnelly Creek State Recreation Site
c/o Northern Area Office 3700 Airport Way.................. Fairbanks AK 99709 907-451-2695
Web: www.dnr.state.ak.us/parks/units/deltajct/donnelly.htm
Driftwood Bay State Marine Park
c/o Kenai/PWS Area Office PO Box 1247 .... Soldotna AK 99669 907-262-5581
Web: www.dnr.state.ak.us/parks/units/pwssmp/smpsewd.htm
Dry Creek State Recreation Site
c/o Mat-Su/CB Area Office HC 32 Box 6706 .... Wasilla AK 99654 907-745-3975
Eagle Beach State Recreation Area
c/o Southeast Area Office 400 Willoughby Ave, 4th Fl .... Juneau AK 99801 907-465-4563
Eagle Trail State Recreation Site
c/o Northern Area Office 3700 Airport Way.................. Fairbanks AK 99709 907-451-2695
Web: www.dnr.state.ak.us/parks/units/tok.htm
Entry Cove State Marine Park
c/o Kenai/PWS Area Office PO Box 1247 .... Soldotna AK 99669 907-262-5581
Web: www.dnr.state.ak.us/parks/units/pwssmp/smpwhit1.htm
Ernest Gruening State Historical Park
c/o Southeast Area Office 400 Willoughby Ave, 4th Fl .... Juneau AK 99801 907-465-4563
Fielding Lake State Recreation Site
c/o Northern Area Office 3700 Airport Way.................. Fairbanks AK 99709 907-451-2695
Web: www.dnr.state.ak.us/parks/units/deltajct/fielding.htm
Finger Lake State Recreation Area
c/o Mat-Su/CB Area Office HC 32 Box 6706 .... Wasilla AK 99654 907-745-3975
Fort Abercrombie State Historical Park
c/o Kodiak Area Office 1400 Abercrombie Dr .... Kodiak AK 99615 907-486-6339
Web: www.dnr.state.ak.us/parks/units/kodiak/ftaber.htm
Funter Bay State Marine Park
c/o Southeast Area Office 400 Willoughby Ave, 4th Fl .... Juneau AK 99801 907-465-4563
Granite Bay State Marine Park
c/o Kenai/PWS Area Office PO Box 1247 .... Soldotna AK 99669 907-262-5581
Web: www.dnr.state.ak.us/parks/units/pwssmp/smpwhit2.htm
Grindall Island State Marine Park
c/o Southeast Area Office 400 Willoughby Ave, 4th Fl .... Juneau AK 99801 907-465-4563
Halibut Point State Recreation Site
c/o Southeast Area Office 400 Willoughby Ave, 4th Fl .... Juneau AK 99801 907-465-4563
Web: www.dnr.state.ak.us/parks/units/sitka.htm
Harding Lake State Recreation Area
c/o Northern Area Office 3700 Airport Way.................. Fairbanks AK 99709 907-451-2695
Web: www.dnr.state.ak.us/parks/units/harding.htm
Horseshoe Bay State Marine Park
c/o Kenai/PWS Area Office PO Box 1247 .... Soldotna AK 99669 907-262-5581
Web: www.dnr.state.ak.us/parks/units/pwssmp/smpwhit2.htm
Independence Mine State Historical Park
c/o Mat-Su/CB Area Office HC 32 Box 6706 .... Wasilla AK 99654 907-745-3975
Web: www.dnr.state.ak.us/parks/units/indmine.htm
Jack Bay State Marine Park
c/o Kenai/PWS Area Office PO Box 1247 .... Soldotna AK 99669 907-262-5581
Web: www.dnr.state.ak.us/parks/units/pwssmp/smpvald.htm
Joe Mace Island State Marine Park
c/o Southeast Area Office 400 Willoughby Ave, 4th Fl .... Juneau AK 99801 907-465-4563
Johnson Creek State Recreation Site
c/o Southeast Area Office 400 Willoughby Ave, 4th Fl .... Juneau AK 99801 907-465-4563
Johnson Lake State Recreation Area
c/o Kenai/PWS Area Office PO Box 1247 .... Soldotna AK 99669 907-262-5581
Web: www.dnr.state.ak.us/parks/units/kasilof.htm
Juneau Trail System
c/o Southeast Area Office 400 Willoughby Ave, 4th Fl .... Juneau AK 99801 907-465-4563
Kachemak Bay State Park & State Wilderness Park
c/o Kenai/PWS Area Office PO Box 1247 .... Soldotna AK 99669 907-262-5581
Web: www.dnr.state.ak.us/parks/units/kbay/kbay.htm
Kasilof River State Recreation Site
c/o Kenai/PWS Area Office PO Box 1247 .... Soldotna AK 99669 907-262-5581
Web: www.dnr.state.ak.us/parks/units/kasilof.htm
Kayak Island State Marine Park
c/o Kenai/PWS Area Office PO Box 1247 .... Soldotna AK 99669 907-262-5581
Web: www.dnr.state.ak.us/parks/units/pwssmp/smpcord.htm
Kenai River Special Management Area
c/o Kenai/PWS Area Office PO Box 1247 .... Soldotna AK 99669 907-262-5581
Web: www.dnr.state.ak.us/parks/units/kenairiv.htm
Kepler-Bradley Lakes State Recreation Area
c/o Mat-Su/CB Area Office HC 32 Box 6706 .... Wasilla AK 99654 907-745-3975
King Mountain State Recreation Site
c/o Mat-Su/CB Area Office HC 32 Box 6706 .... Wasilla AK 99654 907-745-3975
Lake Aleknagik State Recreation Site
550 W 7th Ave, Suite 1380 .... Anchorage AK 99510 907-269-8698 269-8698
Lake Louise State Recreation Area
c/o Mat-Su/CB Area Office HC 32 Box 6706 .... Wasilla AK 99654 907-745-3975
Liberty Falls State Recreation Site
c/o Mat-Su/CB Area Office HC 32 Box 6706 .... Wasilla AK 99654 907-745-3975
Lowell Point State Recreation Site
c/o Kenai/PWS Area Office PO Box 1247 .... Soldotna AK 99669 907-262-5581
Lower Chatanika River State Recreation Area
c/o Northern Area Office 3700 Airport Way.................. Fairbanks AK 99709 907-451-2695
Web: www.dnr.state.ak.us/parks/units/chatanik.htm
Magoun Islands State Marine Park
c/o Southeast Area Office 400 Willoughby Ave, 4th Fl .... Juneau AK 99801 907-465-4563
Web: www.dnr.state.ak.us/parks/units/sitka.htm
Matanuska Glacier State Recreation Site
c/o Mat-Su/Copper Basin Area Office HC 32 Box 6706........... Wasilla AK 99654 907-745-3975
Moon Lake State Recreation Site
c/o Northern Area Office 3700 Airport Way.................. Fairbanks AK 99709 907-451-2695
Web: www.dnr.state.ak.us/parks/units/tok.htm
Mosquito Lake State Recreation Site
c/o Southeast Area Office 400 Willoughby Ave, 4th Fl .... Juneau AK 99801 907-465-4563
Web: www.dnr.state.ak.us/parks/units/haines.htm
Nancy Lake State Recreation Area
c/o Mat-Su/CB Area Office HC 32 Box 6706 .... Wasilla AK 99654 907-745-3975
Web: www.dnr.state.ak.us/parks/units/nancylk/nancylk.htm
Nancy Lake State Recreation Site
c/o Mat-Su/CB Area Office HC 32 Box 6706 .... Wasilla AK 99654 907-745-3975
Ninilchik State Recreation Area
c/o Kenai/PWS Area Office PO Box 1247 .... Soldotna AK 99669 907-262-5581
Web: www.dnr.state.ak.us/parks/units/nilchik.htm
Old Sitka State Historic Site
c/o Southeast Area Office 400 Willoughby Ave, 4th Fl .... Juneau AK 99801 907-465-4563
Web: www.dnr.state.ak.us/parks/units/sitka.htm
Oliver Inlet State Marine Park
c/o Southeast Area Office 400 Willoughby Ave, 4th Fl .... Juneau AK 99801 907-465-4563
Pasagshak River State Recreation Site
c/o Kodiak Area Office 1400 Abercrombie Dr .... Kodiak AK 99615 907-486-6339
Web: www.dnr.state.ak.us/parks/units/kodiak/pasagshak.htm
Petroglyph Beach State Historic Site
c/o Southeast Area Office 400 Willoughby Ave, 4th Fl .... Juneau AK 99801 907-465-4563
Point Bridget State Park
c/o Southeast Area Office 400 Willoughby Ave, 4th Fl .... Juneau AK 99801 907-465-4563
Web: www.dnr.state.ak.us/parks/units/ptbridg1.htm
Porcupine Creek State Recreation Site
c/o Mat-Su/Copper Basin Area Office HC 32 Box 6706........... Wasilla AK 99654 907-745-3975
Portage Cove State Recreation Site
c/o Southeast Area Office 400 Willoughby Ave, 4th Fl .... Juneau AK 99801 907-465-4563
Web: www.dnr.state.ak.us/parks/units/haines.htm
Potter Section House State Historic Site
c/o Chugach Area Office HC 52 Box 8999...................... Indian AK 99540 907-345-5014
Quartz Lake State Recreation Area
c/o Northern Area Office 3700 Airport Way.................. Fairbanks AK 99709 907-451-2695
Web: www.dnr.state.ak.us/parks/units/deltajct/quartz.htm
Refuge Cove State Recreation Site
c/o Southeast Area Office 400 Willoughby Ave, 4th Fl .... Juneau AK 99801 907-465-4563
Rocky Lake State Recreation Site
c/o Mat-Su/CB Area Office HC 32 Box 6706 .... Wasilla AK 99654 907-745-3975
Safety Cove State Marine Park
c/o Kenai/PWS Area Office PO Box 1247 .... Soldotna AK 99669 907-262-5581
Web: www.dnr.state.ak.us/parks/units/pwssmp/smpsewd.htm
Saint James Bay State Marine Park
c/o Southeast Area Office 400 Willoughby Ave, 4th Fl .... Juneau AK 99801 907-465-4563
Salcha River State Recreation Site
c/o Northern Area Office 3700 Airport Way.................. Fairbanks AK 99709 907-451-2695
Web: www.dnr.state.ak.us/parks/units/salcha.htm
Sandspit Point State Marine Park
c/o Kenai/PWS Area Office PO Box 1247 .... Soldotna AK 99669 907-262-5581
Web: www.dnr.state.ak.us/parks/units/pwssmp/smpsewd.htm
Sawmill Bay State Marine Park
c/o Kenai/PWS Area Office PO Box 1247 .... Soldotna AK 99669 907-262-5581
Web: www.dnr.state.ak.us/parks/units/pwssmp/smpvald.htm
Sea Lion Cove State Marine Park
c/o Southeast Area Office 400 Willoughby Ave, 4th Fl .... Juneau AK 99801 907-465-4563
Web: www.dnr.state.ak.us/parks/units/sitka.htm
Security Bay State Marine Park
c/o Southeast Area Office 400 Willoughby Ave, 4th Fl .... Juneau AK 99801 907-465-4563
Web: www.dnr.state.ak.us/parks/units/sitka.htm
Settlers Cove State Recreation Site
c/o Southeast Area Office 400 Willoughby Ave, 4th Fl .... Juneau AK 99801 907-465-4563
Shelter Island State Marine Park
c/o Southeast Area Office 400 Willoughby Ave, 4th Fl .... Juneau AK 99801 907-465-4563
Shoup Bay State Marine Park
c/o Kenai/PWS Area Office PO Box 1247 .... Soldotna AK 99669 907-262-5581
Web: www.dnr.state.ak.us/parks/units/pwssmp/smpvald.htm
Shuyak Island State Park
c/o Kodiak Area Office 1400 Abercrombie Dr .... Kodiak AK 99615 907-486-6339
Web: www.dnr.state.ak.us/parks/units/kodiak/shuyak.htm
South Esther Island State Marine Park
c/o Kenai/PWS Area Office PO Box 1247 .... Soldotna AK 99669 907-262-5581
Web: www.dnr.state.ak.us/parks/units/pwssmp/smpwhit2.htm
Squirrel Creek State Recreation Site
c/o Mat-Su/CB Area Office HC 32 Box 6706 .... Wasilla AK 99654 907-745-3975
Stariski State Recreation Site
c/o Kenai/PWS Area Office PO Box 1247 .... Soldotna AK 99669 907-262-5581
Sullivan Island State Marine Park
c/o Southeast Area Office 400 Willoughby Ave, 4th Fl .... Juneau AK 99801 907-465-4563
Web: www.dnr.state.ak.us/parks/units/haines.htm
Summit Lake State Recreation Site
c/o Mat-Su/CB Area Office HC 32 Box 6706 .... Wasilla AK 99654 907-745-3975
Web: www.dnr.state.ak.us/parks/units/summit.htm
Sunny Cove State Marine Park
c/o Kenai/PWS Area Office PO Box 1247 .... Soldotna AK 99669 907-262-5581
Web: www.dnr.state.ak.us/parks/units/pwssmp/smpsewd.htm
Surprise Cove State Marine Park
c/o Kenai/PWS Area Office PO Box 1247 .... Soldotna AK 99669 907-262-5581
Web: www.dnr.state.ak.us/parks/units/pwssmp/smpwhit1.htm
Taku Harbor State Marine Park
c/o Southeast Area Office 400 Willoughby Ave, 4th Fl .... Juneau AK 99801 907-465-4563
Thom's Place State Marine Park
c/o Southeast Area Office 400 Willoughby Ave, 4th Fl .... Juneau AK 99801 907-465-4563
Thumb Cove State Marine Park
c/o Kenai/PWS Area Office PO Box 1247 .... Soldotna AK 99669 907-262-5581
Web: www.dnr.state.ak.us/parks/units/pwssmp/smpsewd.htm
Tok River State Recreation Site
c/o Northern Area Office 3700 Airport Way.................. Fairbanks AK 99709 907-451-2695
Web: www.dnr.state.ak.us/parks/units/tok.htm
Tokositna River State Recreation Site
c/o Mat-Su/CB Area Office HC 32 Box 6706 .... Wasilla AK 99654 907-745-3975
Totem Bight State Historical Park
c/o Southeast Area Office 400 Willoughby Ave, 4th Fl .... Juneau AK 99801 907-465-4563
Web: www.dnr.state.ak.us/parks/units/totembgh.htm
Upper Chatanika River State Recreation Site
c/o Northern Area Office 3700 Airport Way.................. Fairbanks AK 99709 907-451-2695
Web: www.dnr.state.ak.us/parks/units/chatanik.htm
Wickersham State Historic Site
c/o Southeast Area Office 400 Willoughby Ave, 4th Fl .... Juneau AK 99801 907-465-4563
Web: www.dnr.state.ak.us/parks/units/wickrshm.htm
Willow Creek State Recreation Area
c/o Mat-Su/CB Area Office HC 32 Box 6706 .... Wasilla AK 99654 907-745-3975
Wood-Tikchik State Park 550 W 7th Ave, Suite 1390........... Anchorage AK 99510 907-269-8698
Web: www.dnr.state.ak.us/parks/units/woodtik.htm
Woody Island State Recreation Site
c/o Kodiak Area Office 1400 Abercrombie Dr .... Kodiak AK 99615 907-486-6339
Worthington Glacier State Recreation Site
c/o Kenai/PWS Area Office PO Box 1247 .... Soldotna AK 99669 907-262-5581
Ziegler Cove State Marine Park
c/o Kenai/PWS Area Office PO Box 1247 .... Soldotna AK 99669 907-262-5581
Web: www.dnr.state.ak.us/parks/units/pwssmp/smpwhit1.htm

Arizona

Phone Fax

Alamo Lake State Park PO Box 38........................... Wenden AZ 85357 928-669-2088
Web: www.pr.state.az.us/Parks/parkhtml/alamo.html
Boyce Thompson Arboretum State Park 37615 US Hwy 60 .... Superior AZ 85273 520-689-2811 689-5858
Web: www.pr.state.az.us/Parks/parkhtml/boyce.html
Buckskin Mountain State Park 5476 Hwy 95 .... Parker AZ 85344 928-667-3231
Web: www.pr.state.az.us/Parks/parkhtml/buckskin.html

Name / Address	City	State	Zip	Phone	Fax
Catalina State Park PO Box 36986 *Web:* www.pr.state.az.us/Parks/parkhtml/catalina.html	Tucson	AZ	85740	520-628-5798	628-5797
Cattail Cove State Park PO Box 1990 *Web:* www.pr.state.az.us/Parks/parkhtml/cattail.html	Lake Havasu City	AZ	86405	928-855-1223	855-1730
Dead Horse Ranch State Park 675 Dead Horse Ranch Rd *Web:* www.pr.state.az.us/Parks/parkhtml/deadhorse.html	Cottonwood	AZ	86326	928-634-5283	
Fool Hollow Lake Recreation Area 1500 N Fool Hollow Lake Rd *Web:* www.pr.state.az.us/Parks/parkhtml/foolhollow.html	Show Low	AZ	85901	928-537-3680	
Fort Verde State Historic Park PO Box 397 *Web:* www.pr.state.az.us/Parks/parkhtml/fortverde.html	Camp Verde	AZ	86322	928-567-3275	567-4036
Homolovi Ruins State Park HCR 63 Box 5 *Web:* www.pr.state.az.us/Parks/parkhtml/homolovi.html	Winslow	AZ	86047	928-289-4106	289-2021
Jerome State Historic Park PO Box D *Web:* www.pr.state.az.us/Parks/parkhtml/jerome.html	Jerome	AZ	86331	928-634-5381	
Kartchner Caverns State Park PO Box 1849 *Web:* www.pr.state.az.us/Parks/parkhtml/kartchner.html	Benson	AZ	85602	520-586-4100	
Lake Havasu State Park 699 London Bridge Rd *Web:* www.pr.state.az.us/Parks/parkhtml/havasu.html	Lake Havasu City	AZ	86403	928-855-2784	453-9358
Lost Dutchman State Park 6109 N Apache Tr *Web:* www.pr.state.az.us/Parks/parkhtml/dutchman.html	Apache Junction	AZ	85219	480-982-4485	
Lyman Lake State Park PO Box 1428 *Web:* www.pr.state.az.us/Parks/parkhtml/lyman.html	Saint Johns	AZ	85936	928-337-4441	
McFarland State Historic Park PO Box 109 *Web:* www.pr.state.az.us/Parks/parkhtml/mcfarland.html	Florence	AZ	85232	520-868-5216	
Oracle State Park 3820 Wildlife Dr *Web:* www.pr.state.az.us/Parks/parkhtml/oracle.html	Oracle	AZ	85623	520-896-2425	
Patagonia Lake State Park 400 Patagonia Lake Rd *Web:* www.pr.state.az.us/Parks/parkhtml/patagonia.html	Patagonia	AZ	85624	520-287-6965	
Picacho Peak State Park PO Box 275 *Web:* www.pr.state.az.us/Parks/parkhtml/picacho.html	Picacho	AZ	85241	520-466-3183	
Red Rock State Park 4050 Red Rock Loop Rd *Web:* www.pr.state.az.us/Parks/parkhtml/redrock.html	Sedona	AZ	86336	928-282-6907	282-5972
Riordan Mansion State Historic Park 409 W Riordan Rd *Web:* www.pr.state.az.us/Parks/parkhtml/riordan.html	Flagstaff	AZ	86001	928-779-4395	556-0253
Roper Lake State Park 101 E Roper Lake Rd *Web:* www.pr.state.az.us/Parks/parkhtml/roper.html	Safford	AZ	85546	928-428-6760	428-7879
San Rafael Ranch State Park HC 2 Box 200 *Web:* www.pr.state.az.us/Parks/parkhtml/sanrafael.html	Patagonia	AZ	85624	520-394-2447	
Slide Rock State Park PO Box 10358 *Web:* www.pr.state.az.us/Parks/parkhtml/sliderock.html	Sedona	AZ	86339	928-282-3034	
Tombstone Courthouse State Historic Park PO Box 216 *Web:* www.pr.state.az.us/Parks/parkhtml/tombstone.html	Tombstone	AZ	85638	520-457-3311	
Tonto Natural Bridge State Park PO Box 1245 *Web:* www.pr.state.az.us/Parks/parkhtml/tonto.html	Payson	AZ	85547	928-476-4202	476-2264
Tubac Presidio State Historic Park PO Box 1296 *Web:* www.pr.state.az.us/Parks/parkhtml/tubac.html	Tubac	AZ	85646	520-398-2252	
Yuma Crossing State Historic Park 201 N 4th Ave *Web:* www.pr.state.az.us/Parks/parkhtml/yumacross.html	Yuma	AZ	85364	928-329-0471	
Yuma Territorial Prison State Historic Park PO Box 10792 *Web:* www.pr.state.az.us/Parks/parkhtml/yuma.html	Yuma	AZ	85366	928-783-4771	

Arkansas

Name / Address	City	State	Zip	Phone	Fax
Arkansas Museum of Natural Resources PO Box 7 *Web:* www.arkansasstateparks.com/parks/park.asp?id=42	Smackover	AR	71762	870-725-2877	725-2161
Arkansas Post Museum 5530 Hwy 165 S *Web:* www.arkansasstateparks.com/parks/park.asp?id=45	Gillett	AR	72055	870-548-2634	
Bull Shoals-White River State Park 129 Bull Shoals Park *Web:* www.arkansasstateparks.com/parks/park.asp?id=8	Bull Shoals	AR	72642	870-431-5521	
Cane Creek State Park 50 State Park Rd *Web:* www.arkansasstateparks.com/parks/park.asp?id=34	Star City	AR	71667	870-628-4714	628-3611
Conway Cemetery State Park c/o Arkansas State Parks 1 Capitol Mall *Web:* www.arkansasstateparks.com/parks/park.asp?id=54	Little Rock	AR	72201	888-287-2757	
Cossatot River State Park-Natural Area 1980 Hwy 278 W *Web:* www.arkansasstateparks.com/parks/park.asp?id=39	Wickes	AR	71973	870-385-2201	385-7858
Crater of Diamonds State Park 209 State Park Rd *Web:* www.craterofdiamondsstatepark.com	Murfreesboro	AR	71958	870-285-3113	285-4169
Crowley's Ridge State Park 2092 Hwy 168 N *Web:* www.arkansasstateparks.com/parks/park.asp?id=7	Paragould	AR	72450	870-573-6751	
Daisy State Park 103 E Park *Web:* www.arkansasstateparks.com/parks/park.asp?id=12	Kirby	AR	71950	870-398-4487	
DeGray Lake Resort State Park 2027 State Park Entrance Rd *Web:* www.degray.com	Bismarck	AR	71929	501-865-2801	
Delta Heritage Trail State Park PO Box 193 *Web:* www.arkansasstateparks.com/parks/park.asp?id=55	Watson	AR	71674	870-644-3474	
Devil's Den State Park 11333 W Arkansas Hwy 74 *Web:* www.arkansasstateparks.com/parks/park.asp?id=4	West Fork	AR	72774	479-761-3325	761-3676
Hampson Archeological Museum State Park PO Box 156 *Web:* www.arkansasstateparks.com/parks/park.asp?id=31	Wilson	AR	72395	870-655-8622	655-8061
Herman Davis State Park c/o Arkansas State Parks 1 Capitol Mall *Web:* www.arkansasstateparks.com/parks/park.asp?id=56	Little Rock	AR	72201	888-287-2757	
Hobbs State Park-Conservation Area 21392 E Hwy 12 *Web:* www.arkansasstateparks.com/parks/park.asp?id=38	Rogers	AR	72756	479-789-2380	
Jacksonport State Park 205 Avenue St *Web:* www.arkansasstateparks.com/parks/park.asp?id=17	Newport	AR	72112	870-523-2143	523-4620
Lake Catherine State Park 1200 Catherine Park Rd *Web:* www.arkansasstateparks.com/parks/park.asp?id=2	Hot Springs	AR	71913	501-844-4176	844-4244
Lake Charles State Park 3705 Hwy 25 *Web:* www.arkansasstateparks.com/parks/park.asp?id=14	Powhatan	AR	72458	870-878-6595	
Lake Chicot State Park 2542 Hwy 257 *Web:* www.arkansasstateparks.com/parks/park.asp?id=10	Lake Village	AR	71653	870-265-5480	
Lake Dardanelle State Park 100 State Park Dr *Web:* www.arkansasstateparks.com/parks/park.asp?id=6	Russellville	AR	72802	479-967-5516	
Lake Fort Smith State Park PO Box 4 *Web:* www.arkansasstateparks.com/parks/park.asp?id=18	Mountainburg	AR	72946	479-369-2469	
Lake Frierson State Park 7904 Hwy 141 *Web:* www.arkansasstateparks.com/parks/park.asp?id=33	Jonesboro	AR	72401	870-932-2615	
Lake Ouachita State Park 5451 Mountain Pine Rd *Web:* www.arkansasstateparks.com/parks/park.asp?id=9	Mountain Pine	AR	71956	501-767-9366	
Lake Poinsett State Park 5752 State Park Ln *Web:* www.arkansasstateparks.com/parks/park.asp?id=13	Harrisburg	AR	72432	870-578-2064	
Logoly State Park PO Box 245 *Web:* www.arkansasstateparks.com/parks/park.asp?id=27	McNeil	AR	71752	870-695-3561	
Louisiana Purchase State Park c/o Arkansas State Parks 1 Capitol Mall *Web:* www.arkansasstateparks.com/parks/park.asp?id=37	Little Rock	AR	72201	888-287-2757	
Lower White River Museum State Park 2009 Main St *Web:* www.arkansasstateparks.com/parks/park.asp?id=43	Des Arc	AR	72040	870-256-3711	256-9202
Mammoth Spring State Park PO Box 36 *Web:* www.arkansasstateparks.com/parks/park.asp?id=25	Mammoth Spring	AR	72554	870-625-7364	625-3255
Millwood State Park 1564 Hwy 32 E *Web:* www.arkansasstateparks.com/parks/park.asp?id=26	Ashdown	AR	71822	870-898-2800	898-2632
Moro Bay State Park 6071 Hwy 600 *Web:* www.arkansasstateparks.com/parks/park.asp?id=20	Jersey	AR	71651	870-463-8555	
Mount Magazine State Park 16878 Hwy 309 S *Web:* www.arkansasstateparks.com/parks/park.asp?id=41	Paris	AR	72855	479-963-8502	963-1031
Mount Nebo State Park 16728 W State Hwy 155 *Web:* www.arkansasstateparks.com/parks/park.asp?id=5	Dardanelle	AR	72834	479-229-3655	
Old Davidsonville State Park 7953 Hwy 166 S *Web:* www.arkansasstateparks.com/parks/park.asp?id=23	Pocahontas	AR	72455	870-892-4708	
Old Washington Historic State Park PO Box 98 *Web:* www.oldwashingtonstatepark.com	Washington	AR	71862	870-983-2684	
Ozark Folk Center State Park PO Box 500 *Web:* www.ozarkfolkcenter.com	Mountain View	AR	72560	870-269-3851	269-2909
Parkin Archeological State Park PO Box 1110 *Web:* www.arkansasstateparks.com/parks/park.asp?id=40	Parkin	AR	72373	870-755-2500	755-2676
Petit Jean State Park 1285 Petit Jean Mountain Rd *Web:* www.petitjeanstatepark.com	Morrilton	AR	72110	501-727-5441	
Pinnacle Mountain State Park 11901 Pinnacle Valley Rd *Web:* www.arkansasstateparks.com/parks/park.asp?id=3	Little Rock	AR	72223	501-868-5806	868-5018
Plantation Agriculture Museum PO Box 87 *Web:* www.arkansasstateparks.com/parks/park.asp?id=44	Scott	AR	72142	501-961-1409	
Powhatan Historic State Park PO Box 93 *Web:* www.arkansasstateparks.com/parks/park.asp?id=46	Powhatan	AR	72458	870-878-6765	
Prairie Grove Battlefield State Park 506 E Douglas St *Web:* www.arkansasstateparks.com/parks/park.asp?id=30	Prairie Grove	AR	72753	479-846-2990	
Queen Wilhelmina State Park 3877 Hwy 88 W *Web:* www.arkansasstateparks.com/parks/park.asp?id=11	Mena	AR	71953	479-394-2863	
South Arkansas Arboretum c/o South Arkansas Community College PO Box 7010 *Web:* www.arkansasstateparks.com/parks/park.asp?id=52	El Dorado	AR	71731	870-862-8131	
Toltec Mounds Archeological State Park 490 Toltec Mounds Rd *Web:* www.arkansasstateparks.com/toltecmounds/	Scott	AR	72142	501-961-9442	961-9221
Village Creek State Park 201 County Rd 754 *Web:* www.arkansasstateparks.com/parks/park.asp?id=21	Wynne	AR	72396	870-238-9406	238-9415
White Oak Lake State Park 563 Hwy 387 *Web:* www.arkansasstateparks.com/parks/park.asp?id=16	Bluff City	AR	71722	870-685-2748	
Withrow Springs State Park 33424 Spur 23 *Web:* www.arkansasstateparks.com/parks/park.asp?id=15	Huntsville	AR	72740	479-559-2593	
Woolly Hollow State Park 82 Woolly Hollow Rd *Web:* www.arkansasstateparks.com/parks/park.asp?id=35	Greenbrier	AR	72058	501-679-2098	

California

Name / Address	City	State	Zip	Phone	Fax
Admiral William Standley State Recreation Area c/o North Coast Redwoods District Office PO Box 2006 *Web:* www.parks.ca.gov/default.asp?page_id=424	Eureka	CA	95502	707-247-3318	
Ahjumawi Lava Springs State Park c/o Northern Buttes District Office 400 Glen Dr *Web:* www.parks.ca.gov/default.asp?page_id=464	Oroville	CA	95966	530-335-2777	
Anderson Marsh State Historic Park c/o Northern Buttes District Office 400 Glen Dr *Web:* www.parks.ca.gov/default.asp?page_id=483	Oroville	CA	95966	707-994-0688	
Andrew Molera State Park c/o Monterey District Office 2211 Garden Rd *Web:* www.parks.ca.gov/default.asp?page_id=582	Monterey	CA	93940	831-667-2315	
Angel Island State Park 98 Main St Suite 236 *Web:* www.angelisland.com	Tiburon	CA	94920	415-897-0715	
Annadel State Park c/o Diablo Vista District Office 845 Casa Grande Rd *Web:* www.parks.ca.gov/default.asp?page_id=480	Petaluma	CA	94954	707-938-1519	
Año Nuevo State Reserve c/o Santa Cruz District Office 303 Big Trees Park Rd *Web:* www.parks.ca.gov/default.asp?page_id=523	Felton	CA	95018	650-879-2025	
Antelope Valley California Poppy Reserve c/o Inland Empire District Office 17801 Lake Perris Dr *Web:* www.parks.ca.gov/default.asp?page_id=627	Perris	CA	92571	661-724-1180	
Antelope Valley Indian Museum State Historic Park c/o Inland Empire District Office 17801 Lake Perris Dr *Web:* www.avim.parks.ca.gov	Perris	CA	92571	661-946-3055	
Anza-Borrego Desert State Park c/o Colorado Desert District Office 200 Palm Canyon Dr *Web:* www.anzaborrego.statepark.org	Borrego Springs	CA	92004	760-767-4205	767-3427
Armstrong Redwoods State Reserve c/o North Bay District Office PO Box 123 *Web:* www.parks.ca.gov/default.asp?page_id=450	Duncan Mills	CA	95430	707-869-2015	869-5629
Arthur B. Ripley Desert Woodland State Park c/o Inland Empire District Office 17801 Lake Perris Dr *Web:* www.parks.ca.gov/default.asp?page_id=634	Perris	CA	92571	661-942-0662	
Asilomar State Beach & Conference Grounds c/o Monterey District Office 2211 Garden Rd *Web:* www.parks.ca.gov/default.asp?page_id=566	Monterey	CA	93940	831-646-6440	
Auburn State Recreation Area c/o Gold Fields District Office 7806 Folsom-Auburn Rd *Web:* www.parks.ca.gov/default.asp?page_id=502	Folsom	CA	95630	530-885-4527	
Austin Creek State Recreation Area c/o North Bay District Office PO Box 123 *Web:* www.parks.ca.gov/default.asp?page_id=452	Duncan Mills	CA	95430	707-865-2391	
Azalea State Reserve c/o North Coast Redwoods District Office PO Box 2006 *Web:* www.parks.ca.gov/default.asp?page_id=420	Eureka	CA	95502	707-677-3132	
Bale Grist Mill State Historic Park c/o Diablo Vista District Office 845 Casa Grande Rd *Web:* www.parks.ca.gov/default.asp?page_id=482	Petaluma	CA	94954	707-942-4575	
Bean Hollow State Beach c/o Santa Cruz District Office 303 Big Trees Park Rd *Web:* www.parks.ca.gov/default.asp?page_id=527	Felton	CA	95018	650-879-2170	
Benbow Lake State Recreation Area c/o North Coast Redwoods District Office PO Box 2006 *Web:* www.parks.ca.gov/default.asp?page_id=426	Eureka	CA	95502	707-923-3238	
Benicia Capitol State Historic Park c/o Diablo Vista District Office 845 Casa Grande Rd *Web:* www.parks.ca.gov/default.asp?page_id=475	Petaluma	CA	94954	707-745-3385	
Benicia State Recreation Area c/o Diablo Vista District Office 845 Casa Grande Rd *Web:* www.parks.ca.gov/default.asp?page_id=476	Petaluma	CA	94954	707-648-1911	
Bethany Reservoir State Recreation Area c/o Central Valley District Office 22708 Broadway St *Web:* www.parks.ca.gov/default.asp?page_id=562	Columbia	CA	95310	209-874-2056	
Bidwell Mansion State Historic Park c/o Northern Buttes District Office 400 Glen Dr *Web:* www.parks.ca.gov/default.asp?page_id=460	Oroville	CA	95966	530-895-6144	
Bidwell-Sacramento River State Park c/o Northern Buttes District Office 400 Glen Dr *Web:* www.parks.ca.gov/default.asp?page_id=463	Oroville	CA	95966	530-342-5185	

California (Cont'd)

Phone | Fax

Big Basin Redwoods State Park 21600 Big Basin Way .... Boulder Creek CA 95006 831-338-8860
Web: www.parks.ca.gov/default.asp?page_id=540

Bodie State Historic Park PO Box 515 .... Bridgeport CA 93517 760-647-6445
Web: www.parks.ca.gov/default.asp?page_id=509

Bolsa Chica State Beach
c/o Orange Coast District Office 3030 Avenida del Presidente .... San Clemente CA 92672 714-846-3460
Web: www.parks.ca.gov/default.asp?page_id=642

Border Field State Park
c/o San Diego Coast District Office 4477 Pacific Hwy .... San Diego CA 92110 619-575-3613
Web: www.parks.ca.gov/default.asp?page_id=664

Bothe-Napa Valley State Park
c/o Diablo Vista District Office 845 Casa Grande Rd .... Petaluma CA 94954 707-942-4575
Web: www.parks.ca.gov/default.asp?page_id=477

Brannan Island State Recreation Area
c/o Gold Fields District Office 7806 Folsom-Auburn Rd .... Folsom CA 95630 916-777-7701
Web: www.parks.ca.gov/default.asp?page_id=487

Burleigh H. Murray Ranch
c/o Santa Cruz District Office 303 Big Trees Park Rd .... Felton CA 95018 650-726-8819
Web: www.parks.ca.gov/default.asp?page_id=535

Burton Creek State Park c/o Sierra District Office PO Box 266 .... Tahoma CA 96142 530-583-5475
Web: www.parks.ca.gov/default.asp?page_id=512

Butano State Park
c/o Santa Cruz District Office 303 Big Trees Park Rd .... Felton CA 95018 650-879-2040
Web: www.parks.ca.gov/default.asp?page_id=536

Calaveras Big Trees State Park
c/o Central Valley District Office 22708 Broadway St .... Columbia CA 95310 209-795-2334
Web: www.parks.ca.gov/default.asp?page_id=551

California Citrus State Historic Park
c/o Inland Empire District Office 17801 Lake Perris Dr .... Perris CA 92571 951-780-6222
Web: www.parks.ca.gov/default.asp?page_id=649

California State Capitol Museum
c/o Capital District Office 101 J St .... Sacramento CA 95814 916-324-0333
Web: www.parks.ca.gov/parkindex/results.asp?ckAlpha3=on&searchtype=14

California State Indian Museum
c/o Capital District Office 101 J St .... Sacramento CA 95816 916-324-0971 322-5231
Web: www.parks.ca.gov/default.asp?page_id=486

California State Mining & Mineral Museum
c/o Central Valley District Office 22708 Broadway St .... Columbia CA 95310 209-742-7625
Web: www.parks.ca.gov/default.asp?page_id=588

California State Railroad Museum
c/o Capital District Office 101 J St .... Sacramento CA 95814 916-445-7387 327-5655
Web: www.csrmf.org

Candlestick Point State Recreation Area
c/o Diablo Vista District Office 845 Casa Grande Rd .... Petaluma CA 94954 415-671-0145
Web: www.parks.ca.gov/default.asp?page_id=519

Cardiff State Beach
c/o San Diego Coast District Office 4477 Pacific Hwy .... San Diego CA 92110 760-753-5091
Web: www.parks.ca.gov/default.asp?page_id=656

Carlsbad State Beach
c/o San Diego Coast District Office 4477 Pacific Hwy .... San Diego CA 92110 760-438-3143
Web: www.parks.ca.gov/default.asp?page_id=653

Carmel River State Beach
c/o Monterey District Office 2211 Garden Rd .... Monterey CA 93940 831-624-4909
Web: www.parks.ca.gov/default.asp?page_id=567

Carnegie State Vehicular Recreation Area
c/o Twin Cities District Office 13300 White Rock Rd .... Rancho Cordova CA 95742 925-447-9027
Web: www.parks.ca.gov/default.asp?page_id=410

Carpinteria State Beach
c/o Channel Coast District Office 911 San Pedro St .... Ventura CA 93001 805-684-2811
Web: www.parks.ca.gov/default.asp?page_id=599

Caspar Headlands State Beach & State Reserve
c/o Mendocino District Office PO Box 440 .... Mendocino CA 95460 707-937-5804
Web: www.parks.ca.gov/parkindex

Castaic Lake State Recreation Area
c/o Angeles District Office 1925 Las Virgenes .... Calabasas CA 91302 213-798-2961
Web: www.parks.ca.gov/default.asp?page_id=628

Castle Crags State Park
c/o Northern Buttes District Office 400 Glen Dr .... Oroville CA 95966 530-235-2684
Web: www.parks.ca.gov/default.asp?page_id=454

Castle Rock State Park
c/o Santa Cruz District Office 303 Big Trees Park Rd .... Felton CA 95018 408-867-2952
Web: www.parks.ca.gov/default.asp?page_id=538

Caswell Memorial State Park
c/o Central Valley District Office 22708 Broadway St .... Columbia CA 95310 209-599-3810
Web: www.parks.ca.gov/default.asp?page_id=557

Cayucos State Beach
c/o San Luis Obispo Coast District Office 750 Hearst Castle Rd .... San Simeon CA 93452 805-549-3312
Web: www.parks.ca.gov/default.asp?page_id=596

China Camp State Park
c/o North Bay District Office PO Box 123 .... Duncan Mills CA 95430 415-456-0766
Web: www.parks.ca.gov/default.asp?page_id=466

Chino Hills State Park
c/o Inland Empire District Office 17801 Lake Perris Dr .... Perris CA 92571 951-780-6222
Web: www.parks.ca.gov/default.asp?page_id=648

Chumash Painted Cave State Historic Park
c/o Channel Coast District Office 911 San Pedro St .... Ventura CA 93001 805-968-1033
Web: www.parks.ca.gov/default.asp?page_id=602

Clay Pit State Vehicular Recreation Area
c/o Northern Buttes District Office 400 Glen Dr .... Oroville CA 95966 530-538-2200
Web: www.parks.ca.gov/default.asp?page_id=409

Clear Lake State Park
c/o Northern Buttes District Office 400 Glen Dr .... Oroville CA 95966 707-279-4293
Web: www.parks.ca.gov/default.asp?page_id=473

Colonel Allensworth State Historic Park
c/o Central Valley District Office 22708 Broadway St .... Columbia CA 95310 661-849-3433
Web: www.parks.ca.gov/default.asp?page_id=583

Columbia State Historic Park
c/o Central Valley District Office 22708 Broadway St .... Columbia CA 95310 209-588-9128
Web: www.parks.ca.gov/default.asp?page_id=552

Colusa-Sacramento River State Recreation Area
c/o Northern Buttes District Office 400 Glen Dr .... Oroville CA 95966 530-458-4927
Web: www.parks.ca.gov/default.asp?page_id=461

Corona del Mar State Beach
c/o Orange Coast District Office 3030 Avenida del Presidente .... San Clemente CA 92672 949-492-0802
Web: www.parks.ca.gov/default.asp?page_id=652

Crystal Cove State Park
c/o Orange Coast District Office 3030 Avenida del Presidente .... San Clemente CA 92672 949-494-3539
Web: www.parks.ca.gov/default.asp?page_id=644

Cuyamaca Rancho State Park
c/o Colorado Desert District Office 200 Palm Canyon Dr .... Borrego Springs CA 92004 760-765-0755 765-3021
TF: 800-444-7275 ■ *Web:* www.parks.ca.gov/default.asp?page_id=667

D L Bliss State Park c/o Sierra District Office PO Box 266 .... Tahoma CA 96142 530-525-3345
Web: www.parks.ca.gov/default.asp?page_id=505

Del Norte Coast Redwoods State Park
c/o North Coast Redwoods District Office PO Box 2006 .... Eureka CA 95502 707-464-6101
Web: www.parks.ca.gov/default.asp?page_id=414

Delta Meadows
c/o Gold Fields District Office 7806 Folsom-Auburn Rd .... Folsom CA 95630 916-777-7701
Web: www.parks.ca.gov/default.asp?page_id=492

Dockweiler State Beach
c/o Los Angeles County Dept of Beaches & Harbors 13837 Fiji Way .... Marina del Rey CA 90292 310-305-9503
Web: www.parks.ca.gov/default.asp?page_id=617

Doheny State Beach 25300 Dana Point Harbor Dr .... Dana Point CA 92629 949-496-6172
Web: www.parks.ca.gov/default.asp?page_id=645

Donner Memorial State Park
c/o Sierra District Office PO Box 266 .... Tahoma CA 96142 530-582-7892
Web: www.parks.ca.gov/default.asp?page_id=503

Edward Z'Berg Sugar Pine Point State Park
c/o Sierra District Office PO Box 266 .... Tahoma CA 96142 530-525-7232
Web: www.parks.ca.gov/default.asp?page_id=510

El Capitan State Beach
c/o Channel Coast District Office 911 San Pedro St .... Ventura CA 93001 805-968-1033
Web: www.parks.ca.gov/default.asp?page_id=601

El Presidio de Santa Barbara State Historic Park
c/o Channel Coast District Office 911 San Pedro St .... Ventura CA 93001 805-965-0093
Web: www.parks.ca.gov/default.asp?page_id=608

Emerald Bay State Park c/o Sierra District Office PO Box 266 .... Tahoma CA 96142 530-525-7277
Web: www.parks.ca.gov/default.asp?page_id=506

Emma Wood State Beach
c/o Channel Coast District Office 911 San Pedro St .... Ventura CA 93001 805-968-1033
Web: www.parks.ca.gov/default.asp?page_id=604

Empire Mine State Historic Park
c/o Sierra District Office PO Box 266 .... Tahoma CA 96142 530-273-8522
Web: www.parks.ca.gov/default.asp?page_id=499

Folsom Lake State Recreation Area
c/o Gold Fields District Office 7806 Folsom-Auburn Rd .... Folsom CA 95630 916-988-0205
Web: www.parks.ca.gov/default.asp?page_id=500

Folsom Powerhouse State Historic Park
c/o Folsom Lake State Recreation Area 7806 Folsom-Auburn Rd .... Folsom CA 95630 916-985-4843
Web: www.parks.ca.gov/default.asp?page_id=501

Forest of Nisene Marks State Park
c/o Santa Cruz District Office 303 Big Trees Park Rd .... Felton CA 95018 831-763-7062
Web: www.parks.ca.gov/default.asp?page_id=666

Fort Humboldt State Historic Park
c/o North Coast Redwoods District Office PO Box 2006 .... Eureka CA 95502 707-445-6567
Web: www.parks.ca.gov/default.asp?page_id=665

Fort Ross State Historic Park
c/o North Bay District Office PO Box 123 .... Duncan Mills CA 95430 707-847-3286
Web: www.parks.ca.gov/default.asp?page_id=449

Fort Tejon State Historic Park
c/o Central Valley District Office 22708 Broadway St .... Columbia CA 95310 661-248-6692 248-8373
Web: www.parks.ca.gov/default.asp?page_id=585

Franks Tract State Recreation Area
c/o Gold Fields District Office 7806 Folsom-Auburn Rd .... Folsom CA 95630 916-777-7701
Web: www.parks.ca.gov/default.asp?page_id=490

Fremont Peak State Park
c/o Monterey District Office 2211 Garden Rd .... Monterey CA 93940 831-623-4255
Web: www.parks.ca.gov/default.asp?page_id=564

Garrapata State Park
c/o Monterey District Office 2211 Garden Rd .... Monterey CA 93940 831-624-4909
Web: www.parks.ca.gov/default.asp?page_id=579

Gaviota State Park
c/o Channel Coast District Office 911 San Pedro St .... Ventura CA 93001 805-968-1033
Web: www.parks.ca.gov/default.asp?page_id=606

George J. Hatfield State Recreation Area
c/o Central Valley District Office 22708 Broadway St .... Columbia CA 95310 209-632-1852
Web: www.parks.ca.gov/default.asp?page_id=556

Governor's Mansion State Historic Park
c/o Capital District Office 101 J St .... Sacramento CA 95814 916-323-3047
Web: www.parks.ca.gov/default.asp?page_id=498

Gray Whale Cove State Beach
c/o Santa Cruz District Office 303 Big Trees Park Rd .... Felton CA 95018 650-726-8819
Web: www.parks.ca.gov/default.asp?page_id=528

Great Valley Grasslands State Park
c/o Central Valley District Office 22708 Broadway St .... Columbia CA 95310 209-826-1197
Web: www.parks.ca.gov/default.asp?page_id=559

Greenwood State Beach
c/o Mendocino District Office PO Box 440 .... Mendocino CA 95460 707-937-5804
Web: www.parks.ca.gov/default.asp?page_id=447

Grizzly Creek Redwoods State Park
c/o North Coast Redwoods District Office PO Box 2006 .... Eureka CA 95502 707-777-3683
Web: www.parks.ca.gov/default.asp?page_id=421

Grover Hot Springs State Park
c/o Sierra District Office PO Box 266 .... Tahoma CA 96142 530-694-2248
Web: www.parks.ca.gov/default.asp?page_id=508

Half Moon Bay State Beach
c/o San Mateo Coast Sector Office 95 Kelly Ave .... Half Moon Bay CA 94019 650-726-8819 726-8816
Web: www.parks.ca.gov/default.asp?page_id=531

Harry A. Merlo State Recreation Area
c/o North Coast Redwoods District Office PO Box 2006 .... Eureka CA 95502 707-677-3132
Web: www.parks.ca.gov/default.asp?page_id=431

Hearst San Simeon State Historical Monument
750 Hearst Castle Rd .... San Simeon CA 93452 805-927-2020
TF: 800-444-4445 ■ *Web:* www.parks.ca.gov/default.asp?page_id=591

Heber Dunes State Vehicular Recreation Area
c/o Ocotillo Wells District Office PO Box 356 .... Borrego Springs CA 92004 760-768-9379
Web: www.parks.ca.gov/default.asp?page_id=408

Hendy Woods State Park
c/o Mendocino District Office PO Box 440 .... Mendocino CA 95460 707-895-3141
Web: www.parks.ca.gov/default.asp?page_id=438

Henry Cowell Redwoods State Park
c/o Santa Cruz District Office 303 Big Trees Park Rd .... Felton CA 95018 831-335-4598
Web: www.parks.ca.gov/default.asp?page_id=546

Henry W. Coe State Park
c/o Monterey District Office 2211 Garden Rd .... Monterey CA 93940 408-779-2728
Web: www.parks.ca.gov/default.asp?page_id=561

Hollister Hills State Vehicular Recreation Area
c/o Hollister Hills District Office 7800 Cienega Rd .... Hollister CA 95023 831-637-3874
Web: www.parks.ca.gov/default.asp?page_id=404

Humboldt Lagoons State Park
c/o North Coast Redwoods District Office PO Box 2006 .... Eureka CA 95502 707-677-3132
Web: www.parks.ca.gov/default.asp?page_id=416

Phone | Fax

Humboldt Redwoods State Park
c/o North Coast Redwoods District Office PO Box 2006 Eureka CA 95502 707-946-2409
Web: www.parks.ca.gov/default.asp?page_id=425

Hungry Valley State Vehicular Recreation Area
c/o Hungry Valley District Office PO Box 1360 46001 Orwin Way Gorman CA 93534 661-248-7007
Web: www.parks.ca.gov/default.asp?page_id=405

Huntington State Beach
c/o Orange Coast District Office 3030 Avenida del Presidente San Clemente CA 92672 714-846-3460
Web: www.parks.ca.gov/default.asp?page_id=643

Indian Grinding Rock State Historic Park
c/o Central Valley District Office 22708 Broadway St Columbia CA 95310 209-296-7488
Web: www.parks.ca.gov/default.asp?page_id=553

Indio Hills Palms
c/o Colorado Desert District Office 200 Palm Canyon Dr Borrego Springs CA 92004 619-393-3059
Web: www.parks.ca.gov/default.asp?page_id=640

Jack London State Historic Park
c/o Diablo Vista District Office 845 Casa Grande Rd Petaluma CA 94954 707-938-5216
Web: www.parks.ca.gov/default.asp?page_id=478

Jedediah Smith Redwoods State Park
c/o North Coast Redwoods District Office PO Box 2006 Eureka CA 95502 707-464-6101
Web: www.parks.ca.gov/default.asp?page_id=413

John Little State Reserve
c/o Monterey District Office 2211 Garden Rd Monterey CA 93940 831-667-2315
Web: www.parks.ca.gov/default.asp?page_id=568

John Marsh Home
c/o Diablo Vista District Office 845 Casa Grande Rd Petaluma CA 94954 707-989-9548
Web: www.parks.ca.gov/default.asp?page_id=525

Jug Handle State Reserve
c/o Mendocino District Office PO Box 440 Mendocino CA 95460 707-937-5804
Web: www.parks.ca.gov/default.asp?page_id=441

Julia Pfeiffer Burns State Park
c/o Monterey District Office 2211 Garden Rd Monterey CA 93940 831-667-2315
Web: www.parks.ca.gov/default.asp?page_id=578

Kenneth Hahn State Recreation Area
c/o Angeles District Office 1925 Las Virgenes Calabasas CA 91302 323-298-3660
Web: www.parks.ca.gov/default.asp?page_id=612

Kings Beach State Recreation Area
c/o Sierra District Office PO Box 266 Tahoma CA 96142 530-546-4212
Web: www.parks.ca.gov/default.asp?page_id=511

Kruse Rhododendron State Reserve
c/o North Bay District Office PO Box 123 Duncan Mills CA 95430 707-847-2391
Web: www.parks.ca.gov/default.asp?page_id=448

La Purisima Mission State Historic Park
c/o Channel Coast District Office 911 San Pedro St Ventura CA 93001 805-733-3713
Web: www.parks.ca.gov/default.asp?page_id=598

Lake Del Valle State Recreation Area
c/o Diablo Vista District Office 845 Casa Grande Rd Petaluma CA 94954 510-635-0135
Web: www.parks.ca.gov/default.asp?page_id=537

Lake Oroville State Recreation Area
c/o Northern Buttes District Office 400 Glen Dr Oroville CA 95966 530-538-2200
Web: www.parks.ca.gov/default.asp?page_id=462

Lake Perris State Recreation Area
c/o Inland Empire District Office 17801 Lake Perris Dr Perris CA 92571 951-657-0676
Web: www.parks.ca.gov/default.asp?page_id=651

Lake Valley State Recreation Area
c/o Sierra District Office PO Box 266 Tahoma CA 96142 530-577-0802
Web: www.parks.ca.gov/default.asp?page_id=515

Leland Stanford Mansion State Historic Park
c/o Capital District Office 101 J St Sacramento CA 95814 916-324-0575 324-5885
Web: www.stanfordmansion.org

Leo Carillo State Park
c/o Angeles District Office 1925 Las Virgenes Calabasas CA 91302 818-880-0350
Web: www.parks.ca.gov/default.asp?page_id=616

Leucadia State Beach
c/o San Diego Coast District Office 4477 Pacific Hwy San Diego CA 92110 760-633-2740
Web: www.parks.ca.gov/default.asp?page_id=661

Lighthouse Field State Beach
c/o Santa Cruz District Office 303 Big Trees Park Rd Felton CA 95018 831-420-5270
Web: www.parks.ca.gov/default.asp?page_id=550

Limekiln State Park
c/o San Luis Obispo Coast District Office 750 Hearst Castle Rd San Simeon CA 93452 831-667-2403
Web: www.parks.ca.gov/default.asp?page_id=577

Little River State Beach
c/o North Coast Redwoods District Office PO Box 2006 Eureka CA 95502 707-677-3132
Web: www.parks.ca.gov/default.asp?page_id=419

Los Encinos State Historic Park
c/o Angeles District Office 1925 Las Virgenes Calabasas CA 91302 818-784-4849
Web: www.parks.ca.gov/default.asp?page_id=619

Los Osos Oaks State Reserve
c/o San Luis Obispo Coast District 750 Hearst Castle Rd San Simeon CA 93452 805-772-7434
Web: www.parks.ca.gov/default.asp?page_id=597

MacKerricher State Park
c/o Mendocino District Office PO Box 440 Mendocino CA 95460 707-964-9112
Web: www.parks.ca.gov/default.asp?page_id=436

Maillard Redwoods State Reserve
c/o Mendocino District Office PO Box 440 Mendocino CA 95460 707-937-5804
Web: www.parks.ca.gov/default.asp?page_id=439

Malakoff Diggins State Historic Park
c/o Sierra District Office PO Box 266 Tahoma CA 96142 530-265-2740
Web: www.parks.ca.gov/default.asp?page_id=494

Malibu Creek State Park
c/o Angeles District Office 1925 Las Virgenes Calabasas CA 91302 818-880-0367
Web: www.parks.ca.gov/default.asp?page_id=614

Malibu Lagoon State Beach
c/o Angeles District Office 1925 Las Virgenes Calabasas CA 91302 818-880-0350
Web: www.parks.ca.gov/default.asp?page_id=835

Manchester State Park
c/o Mendocino District Office PO Box 440 Mendocino CA 95460 707-937-5804
Web: www.parks.ca.gov/default.asp?page_id=437

Mandalay State Beach
c/o Channel Coast District Office 911 San Pedro St Ventura CA 93001 805-968-1033
Web: www.parks.ca.gov/default.asp?page_id=609

Manresa State Beach
c/o Santa Cruz District Office 303 Big Trees Park Rd Felton CA 95018 831-761-1795
Web: www.parks.ca.gov/default.asp?page_id=545

Marconi Conference Center State Historic Park PO Box 789 Marshall CA 94940 415-663-9020
Web: www.parks.ca.gov/default.asp?page_id=467

Marina State Beach c/o Monterey District Office 2211 Garden Rd Monterey CA 93940 831-384-7695
Web: www.parks.ca.gov/default.asp?page_id=581

Marshall Gold Discovery State Historic Park
c/o Gold Fields District Office 7806 Folsom-Auburn Rd Folsom CA 95630 530-622-3470
Web: www.parks.ca.gov/default.asp?page_id=484

Phone | Fax

McArthur-Burney Falls Memorial State Park
c/o Northern Buttes District Office 400 Glen Dr Oroville CA 95966 530-335-2777
Web: www.parks.ca.gov/default.asp?page_id=455

McConnell State Recreation Area
c/o Central Valley District Office 22708 Broadway St Columbia CA 95310 209-394-7755
Web: www.parks.ca.gov/default.asp?page_id=554

McGrath State Beach
c/o Channel Coast District Office 911 San Pedro St Ventura CA 93001 805-654-4744
Web: www.parks.ca.gov/default.asp?page_id=607

Mendocino Headlands State Park
c/o Mendocino District Office PO Box 440 Mendocino CA 95460 707-937-5804
Web: www.parks.ca.gov/default.asp?page_id=442

Mendocino Woodlands State Park
c/o Mendocino District Office PO Box 440 Mendocino CA 94560 707-937-5755
Web: www.parks.ca.gov/default.asp?page_id=443

Millerton Lake State Recreation Area
c/o San Joaquin District PO Box 205 Friant CA 93626 559-822-2225
Web: www.parks.ca.gov/default.asp?page_id=587

Mono Lake Tufa State Reserve PO Box 99 Lee Vining CA 93541 760-647-6331
Web: www.parks.ca.gov/default.asp?page_id=514

Montaña de Oro State Park
c/o San Luis Obispo Coast District Office 750 Hearst Castle Rd San Simeon CA 93452 805-528-0513
Web: www.parks.ca.gov/default.asp?page_id=592

Montara State Beach
c/o Santa Cruz District Office 303 Big Trees Park Rd Felton CA 94018 650-726-8819
Web: www.parks.ca.gov/default.asp?page_id=532

Monterey State Beach
c/o Monterey District Office 2211 Garden Rd Monterey CA 93940 831-384-7695
Web: www.parks.ca.gov/default.asp?page_id=576

Monterey State Historic Park
c/o Monterey District Office 2211 Garden Rd Monterey CA 93940 831-649-7118
Web: www.parks.ca.gov/default.asp?page_id=575

Montgomery Woods State Reserve
c/o Mendocino District Office PO Box 440 Mendocino CA 95460 707-937-5804
Web: www.parks.ca.gov/default.asp?page_id=434

Moonlight State Beach
c/o San Diego Coast District Office 4477 Pacific Hwy San Diego CA 92110 858-642-4200
Web: www.parks.ca.gov/default.asp?page_id=659

Morro Bay State Park
c/o San Luis Obispo Coast District Office 750 Hearst Castle Rd San Simeon CA 93452 805-772-7434
Web: www.parks.ca.gov/default.asp?page_id=594

Morro Strand State Beach
c/o San Luis Obispo Coast District Office 750 Hearst Castle Rd San Simeon CA 93452 805-772-7434
Web: www.parks.ca.gov/default.asp?page_id=593

Moss Landing State Beach
c/o Monterey District Office 2211 Garden Rd Monterey CA 93940 831-384-7695
Web: www.parks.ca.gov/default.asp?page_id=574

Mount Diablo State Park
c/o Diablo Vista District Office 845 Casa Grande Rd Petaluma CA 94954 925-837-2525
Web: www.parks.ca.gov/default.asp?page_id=517

Mount San Jacinto State Park
c/o Inland Empire District Office 17801 Lake Perris Dr Perris CA 92571 951-659-2607
Web: www.parks.ca.gov/default.asp?page_id=636

Mount Tamalpais State Park
c/o North Bay District Office PO Box 123 Duncan Mills CA 95430 415-388-2070
Web: www.parks.ca.gov/default.asp?page_id=471

Natural Bridges State Beach
c/o Santa Cruz District Office 303 Big Trees Park Rd Felton CA 95018 831-423-4609
Web: www.parks.ca.gov/default.asp?page_id=541

Navarro River Redwoods State Park
c/o Mendocino District Office PO Box 440 Mendocino CA 95460 707-937-5804
Web: www.parks.ca.gov/default.asp?page_id=435

New Brighton State Beach
c/o Santa Cruz District Office 303 Big Trees Park Rd Felton CA 95018 831-464-6330
Web: www.parks.ca.gov/default.asp?page_id=542

Oceano Dunes State Vehicular Recreation Area
c/o Oceano Dunes District Office 575 Camino Mercado Arroyo Grande CA 93420 805-473-7230
Web: www.parks.ca.gov/default.asp?page_id=406

Ocotillo Wells State Vehicular Recreation Area
c/o Ocotillo Wells District Office PO Box 356 Borrego Springs CA 92004 760-767-5391
Web: www.parks.ca.gov/default.asp?page_id=407

Old Sacramento State Historic Park
c/o Capital District Office 101 J St Sacramento CA 95814 916-442-7644
Web: www.parks.ca.gov/default.asp?page_id=497

Old Town San Diego State Historic Park
c/o San Diego Coast District Office 4477 Pacific Hwy San Diego CA 92110 619-220-5422 688-3229
TF: 800-777-0369 ■ *Web:* www.parks.ca.gov/default.asp?page_id=663

Olompali State Historic Park PO Box 1016 Novato CA 94948 415-892-3383
Web: www.parks.ca.gov/default.asp?page_id=465

Pacheco State Park
c/o Central Valley District Office 22708 Broadway St Columbia CA 95310 209-826-6283
Web: www.parks.ca.gov/default.asp?page_id=560

Pacifica State Beach
c/o Santa Cruz District Office 303 Big Trees Park Rd Felton CA 95018 650-738-7381
Web: www.parks.ca.gov/default.asp?page_id=524

Palomar Mountain State Park
c/o Colorado Desert District Office 200 Palm Canyon Dr Borrego Springs CA 92004 760-742-3462
Web: www.parks.ca.gov/default.asp?page_id=637

Patrick's Point State Park 4150 Patrick's Point Dr Trinidad CA 95570 707-677-3570
Web: www.parks.ca.gov/default.asp?page_id=417

Pelican State Beach
c/o North Coast Redwoods District Office PO Box 2006 Eureka CA 95502 707-464-6101
Web: www.parks.ca.gov/default.asp?page_id=412

Pescadero State Beach
c/o Santa Cruz District Office 303 Big Trees Park Rd Felton CA 95018 650-726-8819
Web: www.parks.ca.gov/default.asp?page_id=522

Petaluma Adobe State Historic Park
c/o Diablo Vista District Office 845 Casa Grande Rd Petaluma CA 94954 707-762-4871
Web: www.parks.ca.gov/default.asp?page_id=474

Pfeiffer Big Sur State Park
c/o Monterey District Office 2211 Garden Rd Monterey CA 93940 831-667-2315
Web: www.parks.ca.gov/default.asp?page_id=570

Picacho State Recreation Area
c/o Colorado Desert District Office 200 Palm Canyon Dr Borrego Springs CA 92004 760-393-3052
Web: www.picacho.statepark.org

Pigeon Point Light Station State Historic Park
210 Pigeon Point Rd Pescadero CA 94060 650-879-0633
Web: www.parks.ca.gov/default.asp?page_id=533

Pio Pico State Historic Park
c/o Angeles District Office 1925 Las Virgenes Calabasas CA 91302 562-695-1217
Web: www.parks.ca.gov/default.asp?page_id=621

California (Cont'd)

				Phone	Fax
Pismo State Beach c/o Oceano Dunes District Office 575 Camino Mercado *Web:* www.parks.ca.gov/default.asp?page_id=595	Arroyo Grande	CA	93420	805-489-2684	
Plumas-Eureka State Park 310 Johnsville Rd *Web:* www.parks.ca.gov/default.asp?page_id=507	Blairsden	CA	96103	530-836-2380	
Point Dume State Beach c/o Angeles District Office 1925 Las Virgenes *Web:* www.parks.ca.gov/default.asp?page_id=623	Calabasas	CA	91302	310-457-8143	
Point Lobos State Reserve c/o Monterey District Office 2211 Garden Rd *Web:* www.parks.ca.gov/default.asp?page_id=571	Monterey	CA	93940	831-624-4909	
Point Montara Light Station c/o Santa Cruz District Office 303 Big Trees Park Rd *Web:* www.parks.ca.gov/default.asp?page_id=534	Felton	CA	95018	650-728-7177	
Point Mugu State Park c/o Angeles District Office 1925 Las Virgenes *Web:* www.parks.ca.gov/default.asp?page_id=630	Calabasas	CA	91302	805-488-5223	
Point Sur State Historic Park c/o Monterey District Office 2211 Garden Rd *Web:* www.parks.ca.gov/default.asp?page_id=565	Monterey	CA	93940	831-625-4419	
Pomponio State Beach c/o Santa Cruz District Office 303 Big Trees Park Rd *Web:* www.parks.ca.gov/default.asp?page_id=521	Felton	CA	95018	831-335-6318	
Portola Redwoods State Park c/o Santa Cruz District Office 303 Big Trees Park Rd *Web:* www.parks.ca.gov/default.asp?page_id=539	Felton	CA	95018	650-948-9098	
Prairie City State Vehicular Recreation Area c/o Twin Cities District Office 13300 White Rock Rd *Web:* www.parks.ca.gov/default.asp?page_id=411	Rancho Cordova	CA	95742	916-985-7378	
Prairie Creek Redwoods State Park c/o North Coast Redwoods District Office PO Box 2006 *Web:* www.parks.ca.gov/default.asp?page_id=415	Eureka	CA	95502	707-464-6101	
Providence Mountains State Recreation Area c/o Inland Empire District Office 17801 Lake Perris Dr *Web:* www.parks.ca.gov/default.asp?page_id=615	Perris	CA	92571	760-928-2586	
Railtown 1897 State Historic Park c/o Capital District Office 101 J St *Web:* www.railtown1897.org	Sacramento	CA	95814	209-984-3953	
Red Rock Canyon State Park c/o Inland Empire District Office 17801 Lake Perris Dr *Web:* www.parks.ca.gov/default.asp?page_id=631	Perris	CA	92571	661-942-0662	
Refugio State Beach c/o Channel Coast District Office 911 San Pedro St *Web:* www.parks.ca.gov/default.asp?page_id=603	Ventura	CA	93001	805-968-1033	
Richardson Grove State Park c/o North Coast Redwoods District Office PO Box 2006 *Web:* www.parks.ca.gov/default.asp?page_id=422	Eureka	CA	95502	707-247-3318	
Robert H. Meyer Memorial State Beach c/o Angeles District Office 1925 Las Virgenes *Web:* www.parks.ca.gov/default.asp?page_id=633	Calabasas	CA	91302	310-457-8143	
Robert Louis Stevenson State Park c/o Diablo Vista District Office 845 Casa Grande Rd *Web:* www.parks.ca.gov/default.asp?page_id=472	Petaluma	CA	94954	707-942-4575	
Robert W. Crown Memorial State Beach c/o Diablo Vista District Office 845 Casa Grande Rd *Web:* www.parks.ca.gov/default.asp?page_id=526	Petaluma	CA	94954	510-562-7275	
Russian Gulch State Park c/o Mendocino District Office PO Box 440 *Web:* www.parks.ca.gov/default.asp?page_id=432	Mendocino	CA	95460	707-937-4296	
Saddleback Butte State Park c/o Inland Empire District Office 17801 Lake Perris Dr *Web:* www.parks.ca.gov/default.asp?page_id=618	Perris	CA	92571	661-942-0662	
Salinas River State Beach c/o Monterey District Office 2211 Garden Rd *Web:* www.parks.ca.gov/default.asp?page_id=573	Monterey	CA	93940	831-384-7695	
Salt Point State Park c/o North Bay District Office PO Box 123 *Web:* www.parks.ca.gov/default.asp?page_id=453	Duncan Mills	CA	95430	707-847-3221	
Salton Sea State Recreation Area c/o Colorado Desert District Office 200 Palm Canyon Dr *Web:* www.saltonsea.statepark.org	Borrego Springs	CA	92004	760-393-3052	
Samuel P. Taylor State Park PO Box 251 *Web:* www.parks.ca.gov/default.asp?page_id=469	Lagunitas	CA	94938	415-488-9897	
San Bruno Mountain State Park c/o Diablo Vista District Office 845 Casa Grande Rd *Web:* www.parks.ca.gov/default.asp?page_id=518	Petaluma	CA	94954	707-989-9548	
San Buenaventura State Beach c/o Channel Coast District Office 911 San Pedro St *Web:* www.parks.ca.gov/default.asp?page_id=600	Ventura	CA	93001	805-648-3918	
San Clemente State Beach c/o Orange Coast District Office 3030 Avenida del Presidente *Web:* www.parks.ca.gov/default.asp?page_id=646	San Clemente	CA	92672	949-492-3156	
San Elijo State Beach c/o San Diego Coast District Office 4477 Pacific Hwy *Web:* www.parks.ca.gov/default.asp?page_id=662	San Diego	CA	92110	760-753-5091	
San Gregorio State Beach c/o Santa Cruz District Office 303 Big Trees Park Rd *Web:* www.parks.ca.gov/default.asp?page_id=529	Felton	CA	95018	650-726-8819	
San Juan Bautista State Historic Park c/o Monterey District Office 2211 Garden Rd *Web:* www.parks.ca.gov/default.asp?page_id=563	Monterey	CA	93940	831-623-4881	
San Luis Reservoir State Recreation Area c/o Central Valley District Office 22708 Broadway St *Web:* www.parks.ca.gov/default.asp?page_id=558	Columbia	CA	95310	209-826-1196	
San Onofre State Beach c/o Orange Coast District Office 3030 Avenida del Presidente *Web:* www.parks.ca.gov/default.asp?page_id=647	San Clemente	CA	92672	714-492-4872	
San Pasqual Battlefield State Historic Park 15808 San Pasqual Valley Rd *Web:* www.parks.ca.gov/default.asp?page_id=655	Escondido	CA	92027	760-737-2201	
San Simeon State Park c/o San Luis Obispo Coast District Office 750 Hearst Castle Rd *Web:* www.parks.ca.gov/default.asp?page_id=590	San Simeon	CA	93452	805-927-2020	
Santa Cruz Mission State Historic Park c/o Santa Cruz District Office 303 Big Trees Park Rd *Web:* www.parks.ca.gov/default.asp?page_id=548	Felton	CA	95018	831-335-6318	
Santa Monica State Beach c/o Angeles District Office 1925 Las Virgenes *Web:* www.parks.ca.gov/default.asp?page_id=624	Calabasas	CA	91302	310-458-8974	
Santa Susana Pass State Historic Park c/o Angeles District Office 1925 Las Virgenes *Web:* www.parks.ca.gov/default.asp?page_id=611	Calabasas	CA	91302	213-620-6152	
Schooner Gulch State Beach c/o Mendocino District Office PO Box 440 *Web:* www.parks.ca.gov/default.asp?page_id=446	Mendocino	CA	95460	707-937-5804	
Seacliff State Beach c/o Santa Cruz District Office 303 Big Trees Park Rd *Web:* www.parks.ca.gov/default.asp?page_id=543	Felton	CA	95018	831-685-6500	
Shasta State Historic Park c/o Northern Buttes District Office 400 Glen Dr *Web:* www.parks.ca.gov/default.asp?page_id=456	Oroville	CA	95966	530-243-8194	
Silver Strand State Beach c/o San Diego Coast District Office 4477 Pacific Hwy *Web:* www.parks.ca.gov/default.asp?page_id=654	San Diego	CA	92110	619-435-5184	
Silverwood Lake State Recreation Area c/o Inland Empire District Office 17801 Lake Perris Dr *Web:* www.parks.ca.gov/default.asp?page_id=650	Perris	CA	92571	760-389-2281	
Sinkyone Wilderness State Park PO Box 245 *Web:* www.parks.ca.gov/default.asp?page_id=429	Whitethorn	CA	95489	707-986-7711	
Smithe Redwoods State Reserve c/o North Coast Redwoods District Office PO Box 2006 *Web:* www.parks.ca.gov/default.asp?page_id=427	Eureka	CA	95502	707-247-3318	
Sonoma Coast State Beach c/o North Bay District Office PO Box 123 *Web:* www.parks.ca.gov/default.asp?page_id=451	Duncan Mills	CA	95430	707-875-3483	
Sonoma State Historic Park c/o Diablo Vista District Office 845 Casa Grande Rd *Web:* www.parks.ca.gov/default.asp?page_id=479	Petaluma	CA	94954	707-938-9560	
South Carlsbad State Beach c/o San Diego Coast District 9609 Waples St, Suite 200 *Web:* www.parks.ca.gov/default.asp?page_id=660	San Diego	CA	92121	760-438-3143	
South Yuba River State Park 17660 Pleasant Valley Rd *Web:* www.parks.ca.gov/default.asp?page_id=496	Penn Valley	CA	95946	530-432-2546	
Standish-Hickey State Recreation Area c/o North Coast Redwoods District Office PO Box 206 *Web:* www.parks.ca.gov/default.asp?page_id=423	Eureka	CA	95502	707-925-6482	
Sugarloaf Ridge State Park c/o Diablo Vista District Office 845 Casa Grande Rd *Web:* www.parks.ca.gov/default.asp?page_id=481	Petaluma	CA	94954	707-833-5712	
Sunset State Beach c/o Santa Cruz District Office 303 Big Trees Park Rd *Web:* www.parks.ca.gov/default.asp?page_id=544	Felton	CA	95018	831-763-7062	
Sutter's Fort State Historic Park c/o Capital District, Historic Sites Sector 101 J St *Web:* www.parks.ca.gov/default.asp?page_id=485	Sacramento	CA	95814	916-445-4422	447-9318
Tahoe State Recreation Area c/o Sierra District Office PO Box 266 *Web:* www.parks.ca.gov/default.asp?page_id=504	Tahoma	CA	96142	530-583-3074	
Tolowa Dunes State Park 1375 Elk Valley Rd *Web:* www.parks.ca.gov/default.asp?page_id=430	Crescent City	CA	95531	707-465-2145	
Tomales Bay State Park c/o North Bay District Office PO Box 123 *Web:* www.parks.ca.gov/default.asp?page_id=470	Duncan Mills	CA	95430	415-669-1140	
Tomo-Kahni State Historic Park c/o Inland Empire District Office 17801 Lake Perris Dr *Web:* www.parks.ca.gov/default.asp?page_id=610	Perris	CA	92571	661-942-0662	
Topanga State Park c/o Angeles District Office 1925 Las Virgenes *Web:* www.parks.ca.gov/default.asp?page_id=629	Calabasas	CA	91302	310-455-2465	
Torrey Pines State Beach c/o San Diego Coast District 9609 Waples St, Suite 200 *Web:* www.parks.ca.gov/default.asp?page_id=658	San Diego	CA	92121	858-755-2063	
Torrey Pines State Reserve c/o San Diego Coast District 12600 N Torrey Pines Rd *Web:* www.parks.ca.gov/default.asp?page_id=657	San Diego	CA	92037	858-755-2063	
Trinidad State Beach c/o North Coast Redwoods District Office PO Box 2006 *Web:* www.parks.ca.gov/default.asp?page_id=418	Eureka	CA	95502	707-677-3132	
Tule Elk State Reserve c/o Central Valley District Office 22708 Broadway St *Web:* www.parks.ca.gov/default.asp?page_id=584	Columbia	CA	95310	661-764-6881	
Turlock Lake State Recreation Area c/o Central Valley District Office 22708 Broadway St *Web:* www.parks.ca.gov/default.asp?page_id=555	Columbia	CA	95310	209-874-2056	
Twin Lakes State Beach c/o Santa Cruz District Office 303 Big Trees Park Rd *Web:* www.parks.ca.gov/default.asp?page_id=547	Felton	CA	95018	831-427-4868	
Van Damme State Park c/o Mendocino District Office PO Box 440 *Web:* www.parks.ca.gov/default.asp?page_id=433	Mendocino	CA	95460	707-937-5804	
Verdugo Mountains c/o Angeles District Office 1925 Las Virgenes *Web:* www.parks.ca.gov/default.asp?page_id=635	Calabasas	CA	91302	213-620-6152	
Washoe Meadows State Park c/o Sierra District Office PO Box 266 *Web:* www.parks.ca.gov/default.asp?page_id=516	Tahoma	CA	96142	530-525-3345	
Wassama Round House State Historic Park c/o Central Valley District Office 22708 Broadway St *Web:* www.parks.ca.gov/default.asp?page_id=586	Columbia	CA	95310	559-822-2332	
Watts Towers of Simon Rodia State Historic Park c/o Angeles District Office 1925 Las Virgenes *Web:* www.parks.ca.gov/default.asp?page_id=613	Calabasas	CA	91302	213-847-4646	
Weaverville Joss House State Historic Park c/o Northern Buttes District Office 400 Glen Dr *Web:* www.parks.ca.gov/default.asp?page_id=457	Oroville	CA	95966	530-623-5282	
Westport-Union Landing State Beach c/o Mendocino District Office PO Box 440 *Web:* www.parks.ca.gov/default.asp?page_id=440	Mendocino	CA	95460	707-937-5804	
Wilder Ranch State Park c/o Santa Cruz District Office 303 Big Trees Park Rd *Web:* www.parks.ca.gov/default.asp?page_id=549	Felton	CA	95018	831-426-0505	
Will Rogers State Beach c/o Angeles District Office 1925 Las Virgenes *Web:* www.parks.ca.gov/default.asp?page_id=625	Calabasas	CA	91302	310-305-9503	
Will Rogers State Historic Park c/o Angeles District Office 1925 Las Virgenes *Web:* www.parks.ca.gov/default.asp?page_id=626	Calabasas	CA	91302	310-454-8212	
William B. Ide Adobe State Historic Park c/o Northern Buttes District Office 400 Glen Dr *Web:* www.parks.ca.gov/default.asp?page_id=458	Oroville	CA	95966	530-529-8599	
William Randolph Hearst Memorial State Beach c/o San Luis Obispo Coast District Office 750 Hearst Castle Rd *Web:* www.parks.ca.gov/default.asp?page_id=589	San Simeon	CA	93452	805-927-2020	

Park	City	State	Zip	Phone	Fax
Woodland Opera House State Historic Park c/o Capital District Office 101 J Street *Web:* www.parks.ca.gov/default.asp?page_id=488	Sacramento	CA	95814	530-666-9617	
Woodson Bridge State Recreation Area c/o Northern Buttes District Office 400 Glen Dr *Web:* www.parks.ca.gov/default.asp?page_id=459	Oroville	CA	95966	530-839-2112	
Zmudowski State Beach c/o Monterey District Office 2211 Garden Rd *Web:* www.parks.ca.gov/default.asp?page_id=572	Monterey	CA	93940	831-384-7695	

Colorado

Park	City	State	Zip	Phone	Fax
Arkansas Headwaters Recreation Area 307 W Sackett Ave *Web:* parks.state.co.us	Salida	CO	81201	719-539-7289	
Barr Lake State Park 13401 Picadilly Rd *Web:* parks.state.co.us	Brighton	CO	80603	303-659-6005	
Bonny Lake State Park 30010 County Rd 3 *Web:* parks.state.co.us	Idalia	CO	80735	970-354-7306	
Boyd Lake State Park 3720 N County Rd 11-C *Web:* parks.state.co.us	Loveland	CO	80539	970-669-1739	
Castlewood Canyon State Park 2989 S Hwy 83 *Web:* parks.state.co.us	Franktown	CO	80116	303-688-5242	
Chatfield State Park 11500 N Roxborough Park Rd *Web:* parks.state.co.us	Littleton	CO	80125	303-791-7275	
Cherry Creek State Park 4201 S Parker Rd *Web:* parks.state.co.us	Aurora	CO	80014	303-699-3860	699-3864
Cheyenne Mountain State Park 4255 Sinton Rd *Web:* parks.state.co.us	Colorado Springs	CO	80907	719-227-5256	
Crawford State Park PO Box 147 *Web:* parks.state.co.us	Crawford	CO	81415	970-921-5721	
Eldorado Canyon State Park 9 Kneale Rd PO Box B *Web:* parks.state.co.us	Eldorado Springs	CO	80025	303-494-3943	499-2729
Eleven Mile State Park 4229 County Rd 92 *Web:* parks.state.co.us	Lake George	CO	80827	719-748-3401	
Golden Gate Canyon State Park 92 Crawford Gulch Rd	Golden	CO	80403	303-582-3707	582-3712
Harvey Gap State Park c/o Rifle Gap State Park 5775 Hwy 325 *Web:* parks.state.co.us	Rifle	CO	81650	970-625-1607	
Highline Lake State Park 1800 11.8 Rd *Web:* parks.state.co.us	Loma	CO	81524	970-858-7208	
Jackson Lake State Park 26363 County Rd 3 *Web:* parks.state.co.us	Orchard	CO	80649	970-645-2551	
James M. Robb - Colorado River State Park PO Box 700 *Web:* parks.state.co.us	Clifton	CO	81520	970-434-3388	
Lake Pueblo State Park 640 Pueblo Reservoir Rd *Web:* parks.state.co.us	Pueblo	CO	81005	719-561-9320	
Lathrop State Park 70 County Rd 502 *Web:* parks.state.co.us	Walsenburg	CO	81089	719-738-2376	
Lory State Park 708 Lodgepole Dr *Web:* parks.state.co.us	Bellvue	CO	80512	970-493-1623	
Mancos State Park 42545 County Rd N *Web:* parks.state.co.us	Mancos	CO	81328	970-533-7065	
Mueller State Park PO Box 39 *Web:* parks.state.co.us	Divide	CO	80814	719-687-2366	
Navajo State Park 1526 County Road 982 Box 1697	Arboles	CO	81121	970-883-2208	
North Sterling State Park 24005 County Rd 330 *Web:* parks.state.co.us	Sterling	CO	80751	970-522-3657	
Paonia State Park PO Box 147 *Web:* parks.state.co.us	Crawford	CO	81415	970-921-5721	
Pearl Lake State Park PO Box 750 *Web:* parks.state.co.us	Clark	CO	80428	970-879-3922	
Ridgway State Park 28555 Hwy 550 *Web:* parks.state.co.us	Ridgway	CO	81432	970-626-5822	
Rifle Falls State Park 5775 Hwy 325 *Web:* parks.state.co.us	Rifle	CO	81650	970-625-1607	
Rifle Gap State Park 5775 Hwy 325 *Web:* parks.state.co.us	Rifle	CO	81650	970-625-1607	
Roxborough State Park 4751 N Roxborough Dr *Web:* parks.state.co.us	Littleton	CO	80125	303-973-3959	
Saint Vrain State Park 3525 State Hwy 119 *Web:* parks.state.co.us	Longmont	CO	80504	303-678-9402	
San Luis State Park & Wildlife Area County Ln 6 N PO Box 175 *Web:* parks.state.co.us	Mosca	CO	81146	719-378-2020	
Spinney Mountain State Park c/o Eleven Mile State Park 4229 County Rd 92 *Web:* parks.state.co.us	Lake George	CO	80827	719-748-3401	
Stagecoach State Park PO Box 98 *Web:* parks.state.co.us	Oak Creek	CO	80467	970-736-2436	
State Forest State Park 56750 Hwy 14 *Web:* parks.state.co.us	Walden	CO	80480	970-723-8366	723-8325
Steamboat Lake State Park PO Box 750 *Web:* parks.state.co.us	Clark	CO	80428	970-879-3922	
Sweitzer Lake State Park 1735 E Rd PO Box 173 *Web:* parks.state.co.us	Delta	CO	81416	970-874-4258	
Sylvan Lake State Park 10200 Brush Creek Rd PO Box 1475 *Web:* parks.state.co.us	Eagle	CO	81631	970-328-2021	
Trinidad Lake State Park 32610 State Hwy 12 *Web:* parks.state.co.us	Trinidad	CO	81082	719-846-6951	
Vega State Park PO Box 186 *Web:* parks.state.co.us	Collbran	CO	81624	970-487-3407	
Yampa River State Park PO Box 759 *Web:* parks.state.co.us	Hayden	CO	81639	970-276-2061	

Connecticut

Park	City	State	Zip	Phone	Fax
American Legion & Peoples State Forests PO Box 161 *Web:* www.dep.state.ct.us/stateparks/forests/amerlegion.htm	Pleasant Valley	CT	06063	860-379-2469	
Bigelow Hollow State Park & Nipmuck State Forest c/o Shenipsit State Forest 166 Chestnut Hill Rd *Web:* www.dep.state.ct.us/stateparks/parks/bigelow.htm	Stafford Springs	CT	06076	860-684-3430	
Black Rock State Park c/o Topsmead State Forest PO Box 1081 *Web:* www.dep.state.ct.us/stateparks/parks/blackrock.htm	Litchfield	CT	06759	860-567-5694	
Bluff Point State Park c/o Fort Trumbull State Park 90 Walbach St *Web:* www.dep.state.ct.us/stateparks/parks/bluffpoint.htm	New London	CT	06320	860-444-7591	
Burr Pond State Park 384 Burr Mountain Rd *Web:* www.dep.state.ct.us/stateparks/parks/burrpond.htm	Torrington	CT	06790	860-482-1817	
Chatfield Hollow State Park 381 Rt 80 *Web:* www.dep.state.ct.us/stateparks/parks/chatfield.htm	Killingworth	CT	06419	860-663-2030	
Cockaponset State Forest c/o Chatfield Hollow State Park 381 Route 80 *Web:* www.dep.state.ct.us/stateparks/forests/cockaponset.htm	Killingworth	CT	06419	860-663-2030	
Collis P. Huntington State Park c/o Putnam Memorial State Park 492 Black Road Tpke *Web:* www.dep.state.ct.us/stateparks/parks/huntington.htm	Redding	CT	06896	203-938-2285	
Connecticut Valley Railroad State Park 1 Railroad Ave PO Box 452 *Web:* www.essexsteamtrain.com	Essex	CT	06426	860-767-0103	767-0104
Day Pond State Park c/o Eastern District HQ 209 Hebron Rd *Web:* www.dep.state.ct.us/stateparks/parks/daypond.htm	Marlborough	CT	06447	860-295-9523	
Dennis Hill State Park c/o Burr Pond State Park 385 Burr Mountain Rd *Web:* www.dep.state.ct.us/stateparks/parks/dennishill.htm	Torrington	CT	06790	860-482-1817	
Devil's Hopyard State Park 366 Hopyard Rd *Web:* www.dep.state.ct.us/stateparks/parks/devilshopyard.htm	East Haddam	CT	06423	860-873-8566	
Dinosaur State Park 400 West St *Web:* www.dep.state.ct.us/stateparks/parks/dinosaur.htm	Rocky Hill	CT	06067	860-529-5816	257-1405
Fort Griswold Battlefield State Park c/o Fort Trumbull State Park 90 Walbach St *Web:* www.dep.state.ct.us/stateparks/parks/fort_griswold.htm	New London	CT	06320	860-444-7591	
Fort Trumbull State Park 90 Walbach St *Web:* www.dep.state.ct.us/stateparks/parks/fort_trumbull.htm	New London	CT	06320	860-444-7591	
Gay City State Park c/o Eastern District HQ 209 Hebron Rd *Web:* www.dep.state.ct.us/stateparks/parks/gaycity.htm	Marlborough	CT	06447	203-295-9523	
Gillette Castle State Park 67 River Rd *Web:* www.dep.state.ct.us/stateparks/parks/gillettecastle.htm	East Haddam	CT	06423	860-526-2336	
Haddam Meadows State Park c/o Chatfield Hollow State Park 381 Rt 80 *Web:* www.dep.state.ct.us/stateparks/parks/haddammeadows.htm	Killingworth	CT	06419	203-663-2030	
Haley Farm State Park c/o Fort Trumbull State Park 90 Walbach St *Web:* dep.state.ct.us/stateparks/parks/haleyfarm.htm	New London	CT	06320	860-444-7591	
Hammonasset Beach State Park 1288 Boston Post Rd PO Box 271 *Web:* www.dep.state.ct.us/stateparks/parks/hammonasset.htm	Madison	CT	06443	203-245-2785	245-9201
Harkness Memorial State Park 275 Great Neck Rd *Web:* www.dep.state.ct.us/stateparks/parks/harkness.htm	Waterford	CT	06385	203-443-5725	
Haystack Mountain State Park c/o Burr Pond State Park 385 Burr Mountain Rd *Web:* www.dep.state.ct.us/stateparks/parks/haystack.htm	Torrington	CT	06790	860-482-1817	
Hopeville Pond State Park 193 Roode Rd *Web:* www.dep.state.ct.us/stateparks/parks/hopeville.htm	Jewett City	CT	06351	860-376-2920	
Housatonic Meadows State Park c/o Macedonia Brook State Park 159 Macedonia Brook Rd *Web:* www.dep.state.ct.us/stateparks/parks/housatonic.htm	Kent	CT	06757	860-927-3238	
Hurd State Park c/o Gillette Castle State Park 67 River Rd *Web:* dep.state.ct.us/stateparks/parks/hurd.htm	East Haddam	CT	06423	860-526-2336	
Indian Well State Park c/o Osbornedale State Park PO Box 113 *Web:* www.dep.state.ct.us/stateparks/parks/indianwell.htm	Derby	CT	06418	203-735-4311	
James L. Goodwin State Forest Goodwin Forest Conservation Education Center 23 Potter Rd *Web:* dep.state.ct.us/educ/goodwin/goodwinforest.htm	Hampton	CT	06226	860-455-9534	455-9857
John A. Minetto State Park c/o Burr Pond State Park 385 Burr Mountain Rd *Web:* www.dep.state.ct.us/stateparks/parks/minetto.htm	Torrington	CT	06790	860-482-1817	
Kent Falls State Park c/o Macedonia Brook State Park 159 Macedonia Brook Rd *Web:* www.dep.state.ct.us/stateparks/parks/kentfalls.htm	Kent	CT	06757	860-927-3238	
Kettletown State Park 1400 Georges Hill Rd *Web:* www.dep.state.ct.us/stateparks/parks/kettletown.htm	Southbury	CT	06488	203-264-5678	
Lake Waramaug State Park 30 Lake Waramaug Rd *Web:* www.dep.state.ct.us/stateparks/parks/lakewaramaug.htm	New Preston	CT	06777	860-868-2592	
Macedonia Brook State Park 159 Macedonia Brook Rd *Web:* www.dep.state.ct.us/stateparks/parks/macedonia.htm	Kent	CT	06757	860-927-3238	
Mansfield Hollow State Park c/o Mashamoquet Brook State Park RFD 1 147 Wolf Den Rd *Web:* dep.state.ct.us/stateparks/parks/mansfield.htm	Pomfret Center	CT	06259	860-928-6121	
Mashamoquet Brook State Park 147 Wolf Den Dr *Web:* www.dep.state.ct.us/stateparks/parks/mashamoquet.htm	Pomfret Center	CT	06259	860-928-6121	
Mohawk State Forest 20 Mohawk Mountain Rd *Web:* www.dep.state.ct.us/stateparks/forests/mohawk.htm	Goshen	CT	06756	860-491-3620	
Mount Tom State Park c/o Lake Waramaug State Park 30 Lake Waramaug Rd *Web:* www.dep.state.ct.us/stateparks/parks/mounttom.htm	New Preston	CT	06777	860-868-2592	
Natchaug State Forest c/o Mashamoquet Brook State Park RFD #1 Wolf Den Rd *Web:* www.dep.state.ct.us/stateparks/forests/natchaug.htm	Pomfret Center	CT	06259	860-928-6121	
Nipmuck State Forest & Bigelow Hollow State Park c/o Shenipsit State Forest 166 Chestnut Hill Rd *Web:* www.dep.state.ct.us/stateparks/parks/bigelow.htm	Stafford Springs	CT	06076	860-684-3430	
Osbornedale State Park 555 Roosevelt Dr *Web:* www.dep.state.ct.us/stateparks/parks/osbornedale.htm	Derby	CT	06418	203-735-4311	
Pachaug State Forest Route 49 PO Box 5 *Web:* www.dep.state.ct.us/stateparks/forests/pachaug.htm	Voluntown	CT	06384	860-376-4075	
Penwood State Park 57 Gunn Mill Rd *Web:* www.dep.state.ct.us/stateparks/parks/penwood.htm	Bloomfield	CT	06002	860-242-1158	
Putnam Memorial State Park 429 Black Rock Tpke *Web:* www.dep.state.ct.us/stateparks/parks/putnam.htm	Redding	CT	06896	203-938-2285	
Quaddick State Park c/o Mashamoquet Brook State Park 147 Wolf Den Dr *Web:* dep.state.ct.us/stateparks/parks/quaddick.htm	Pomfret Center	CT	06259	860-928-6121	
Rocky Neck State Park PO Box 676 *Web:* www.dep.state.ct.us/stateparks/parks/rockyneck.htm	Niantic	CT	06357	860-739-5471	
Salmon River State Forest c/o Eastern District HQ 209 Hebron Rd *Web:* www.dep.state.ct.us/stateparks/forests/salmon.htm	Marlborough	CT	06447	860-295-9523	
Selden Neck State Park c/o Gillette Castle State Park 67 River Rd *Web:* dep.state.ct.us/stateparks/camping/rvrcmp.htm	East Haddam	CT	06423	860-526-2336	
Shenipsit State Forest 166 Chestnut Hill Rd *Web:* www.dep.state.ct.us/stateparks/forests/ctforests.htm	Stafford Springs	CT	06076	860-684-3430	684-4130
Sherwood Island State Park PO Box 188 *Web:* www.dep.state.ct.us/stateparks/parks/sherwood.htm	Greens Farms	CT	06436	203-226-6983	
Silver Sands State Park c/o Osbornedale State Park PO Box 113 *Web:* www.dep.state.ct.us/stateparks/parks/silversands.htm	Derby	CT	06418	203-735-4311	
Sleeping Giant State Park 200 Mount Carmel Ave *Web:* www.dep.state.ct.us/stateparks/parks/sleepinggiant.htm	Hamden	CT	06518	203-789-7498	
Southford Falls State Park Quaker Farms Rd Rt 188 *Web:* www.dep.state.ct.us/stateparks/parks/southford.htm	Southbury	CT	06488	203-264-5169	
Squantz Pond State Park 178 Shortwoods Rd *Web:* www.dep.state.ct.us/stateparks/parks/squantz.htm	New Fairfield	CT	06810	203-797-4165	

Connecticut (Cont'd)

Phone | Fax

Stratton Brook State Park 57 Gun Mill Rd. Bloomfield CT 06002 860-658-1388
Web: www.dep.state.ct.us/stateparks/parks/stratton.htm
Talcott Mountain State Park
c/o Penwood State Park 57 Gunn Mill Rd Bloomfield CT 06002 860-242-1158
Web: www.dep.state.ct.us/stateparks/parks/talcott.htm
Topsmead State Forest PO Box 1081 Litchfield CT 06759 860-567-5694
Web: www.dep.state.ct.us/stateparks/forests/topsmead.htm
Wadsworth Falls State Park
c/o Chatfield Hollow State Park 381 Rt 80 Killingworth CT 06419 860-663-2030
Web: www.dep.state.ct.us/stateparks/parks/wadsworth.htm
West Rock Ridge State Park
c/o Sleeping Giant State Park 200 Mount Carmel Ave Hamden CT 06518 203-789-7498
Web: www.dep.state.ct.us/stateparks/parks/westrock.htm
Wharton Brook State Park
c/o Sleeping Giant State Park 200 Mount Carmel Ave Hamden CT 06518 203-789-7498
Web: dep.state.ct.us/stateparks/parks/wharton.htm

Delaware

Phone | Fax

Bellevue State Park 800 Carr Rd Wilmington DE 19809 302-761-6963 761-6951
Web: www.destateparks.com/bvsp/bvsp.htm
Brandywine Creek State Park PO Box 3782 Greenville DE 19807 302-577-3534
Web: www.destateparks.com/bcsp/bcsp.asp
Cape Henlopen State Park 42 Cape Henlopen Dr Lewes DE 19958 302-645-8983
Web: www.destateparks.com/chsp/chsp.htm
Delaware Seashore State Park 130 Coastal Hwy Rehoboth Beach DE 19971 302-227-2800
Web: www.destateparks.com/dssp/dssp.asp
Fenwick Island State Park
c/o Delaware Seashore State Park Inlet 850 Rehoboth Beach DE 19971 302-227-2800
Web: www.destateparks.com/fenwick/fisp.asp
Fort Delaware State Park PO Box 170 Delaware City DE 19706 302-834-7941 836-2539
Web: www.destateparks.com/fdsp
Fort DuPont State Park
c/o Fort Delaware State Park PO Box 170 Delaware City DE 19706 302-834-7941
Web: www.destateparks.com/fdsp/fdpp.htm
Fox Point State Park c/o Bellevue State Park 800 Carr Rd Wilmington DE 19809 302-761-6963
Web: www.destateparks.com/foxpt/foxpt.htm
Holts Landing State Park PO Box 76 Millville DE 19970 302-539-9060
Web: www.destateparks.com/holts/hlsp.htm
Killens Pond State Park 5025 Killens Pond Rd Felton DE 19943 302-284-4526 284-4694
Web: www.destateparks.com/kpsp/kpsp.htm
Lums Pond State Park 1068 Howell School Rd Bear DE 19701 302-368-6989
Web: www.destateparks.com/lpsp/lpsp.asp
Trap Pond State Park 33587 Baldcypress Ln Laurel DE 19956 302-875-5153
Web: www.destateparks.com/tpsp/tpsp.htm
White Clay Creek State Park 425 Wedgewood Rd Newark DE 19711 302-368-6900
Web: www.destateparks.com/wccsp
Wilmington State Parks 1021 W 18th St Wilmington DE 19802 302-577-7020 577-7084
Web: www.destateparks.com/wilmsp/wilmsp.htm

Florida

Phone | Fax

Alafia River State Park 14326 S County Rd 39 Lithia FL 33547 813-672-5320
Web: www.floridastateparks.org/alafiariver
Alfred B. Maclay Gardens State Park 14326 S County Rd 39 Lithia FL 33547 813-672-5320
Web: www.floridastateparks.org/alafiariver
Amelia Island State Park 12157 Heckscher Dr Jacksonville FL 32226 904-251-2320
Web: www.floridastateparks.org/ameliaisland
Anastasia State Park 1340-A A1A S Saint Augustine FL 32080 904-461-2033 461-2006
TF: 800-326-3521 ■ *Web:* www.floridastateparks.org/anastasia
Anclote Key Preserve State Park
c/o Honeymoon Island State Park 1 Causeway Blvd Dunedin FL 34698 727-469-5942
Web: www.floridastateparks.org/anclotekey
Bahia Honda State Park 36850 Overseas Hwy Big Pine Key FL 33043 305-872-2353
Web: www.floridastateparks.org/bahiahonda
Bald Point State Park 146 Box Cut Alligator Point FL 32346 850-349-9146
Web: www.floridastateparks.org/baldpoint
Big Lagoon State Park 12301 Gulf Beach Hwy Pensacola FL 32507 850-492-1595 492-4380
Web: www.floridastateparks.org/biglagoon
Big Shoals State Park PO Drawer G White Springs FL 32096 386-397-4331
Web: www.floridastateparks.org/bigshoals
Big Talbot Island State Park 12157 Heckscher Dr Jacksonville FL 32226 904-251-2320
Web: www.floridastateparks.org/bigtalbotisland
Bill Baggs Cape Florida State Park 1200 S Crandon Blvd Key Biscayne FL 33149 305-361-5811 365-0003
Web: www.floridastateparks.org/capeflorida
Blackwater River State Park 7720 Deaton Bridge Rd Holt FL 32564 850-983-5363 983-5364
Web: www.floridastateparks.org/blackwaterriver
Blue Spring State Park 2100 W French Ave Orange City FL 32763 386-775-3663
Web: www.floridastateparks.org/bluespring
Bulow Creek State Park 2099 N Beach St Ormond Beach FL 32174 386-676-4050 676-4060
Web: www.floridastateparks.org/bulowcreek
Bulow Plantation Ruins Historic State Park PO Box 655 Bunnell FL 32110 386-517-2084
Web: www.floridastateparks.org/bulowplantation
Caladesi Island State Park 1 Causeway Blvd Dunedin FL 34698 727-469-5918 298-2320
Web: www.floridastateparks.org/caladesiisland
Camp Helen State Park
23937 Panama City Beach Pkwy Panama City Beach FL 32413 850-233-5059 236-3204
Web: www.floridastateparks.org/camphelen
Cayo Costa State Park PO Box 1150 Boca Grande FL 33921 941-964-0375 964-1154
Web: www.floridastateparks.org/cayocosta
Cedar Key Museum State Park 12231 SW 166 Ct Cedar Key FL 32625 352-543-5350
Web: www.floridastateparks.org/cedarkeymuseum
Cedar Key Scrub State Reserve PO Box 187 Cedar Key FL 32625 352-543-5567
Web: www.floridastateparks.org/cedarkeyscrub
Collier-Seminole State Park 20200 E Tamiami Trail Naples FL 34114 239-394-3397 394-5113
Web: www.floridastateparks.org/collier-seminole
Constitution Convention Museum State Park
200 Allen Memorial Way Port Saint Joe FL 32456 850-229-8029
Web: www.floridastateparks.org/constitutionconvention
Crystal River Archaeological State Park
3400 N Museum Pointe Crystal River FL 34428 352-795-3817
Web: www.floridastateparks.org/crystalriver
Dade Battlefield Historic State Park
7200 County Rd 603 S Battlefield Dr Bushnell FL 33513 352-793-4781
Web: www.floridastateparks.org/dadebattlefield
Dagny Johnson Key Largo Hammock Botanical State Park
PO Box 487 Key Largo FL 33037 305-451-1202
Web: www.floridastateparks.org/keylargohammock

Phone | Fax

De Leon Springs State Park 601 Ponce De Leon Blvd De Leon Springs FL 32130 386-985-4212 985-2014
Web: www.floridastateparks.org/deleonsprings
Deer Lake State Park 357 Main Park Rd Santa Rosa Beach FL 32459 850-231-0337 231-1879
Web: www.floridastateparks.org/deerlake
Delnor-Wiggins Pass State Park 11100 Gulf Shore Dr Naples FL 34108 239-597-6196 597-8223
Web: www.floridastateparks.org/delnor-wiggins
Devil's Millhopper Geological State Park
4732 Millhopper Rd Gainesville FL 32653 352-955-2008
Web: www.floridastateparks.org/devilsmillhopper
Don Pedro Island State Park PO Box 1150 Boca Grande FL 33921 941-964-0375 964-1154
Web: www.floridastateparks.org/donpedroisland
Dr. Julian G. Bruce Saint George Island State Park
1900 E Gulf Beach Dr Saint George Island FL 32328 850-927-2111
Web: www.floridastateparks.org/stgeorgeisland
Dudley Farm Historic State Park 18730 W Newberry Rd Newberry FL 32669 352-472-1142
Web: www.floridastateparks.org/dudleyfarm
Dunn's Creek 320 Cisco Rd Pomona Park FL 32181 386-329-3721 329-3718
Web: www.floridastateparks.org/dunnscreek
Econfina River State Park 4384 Econfina Rd Lamont FL 32336 850-922-6007
Web: www.floridastateparks.org/econfinariver
Eden Gardens State Park PO Box 26 Point Washington FL 32454 850-231-4214
Web: www.floridastateparks.org/edengardens
Edward Ball Wakulla Springs State Park
550 Wakulla Park Dr Wakulla Springs FL 32327 850-224-5950 561-7251
Web: www.floridastateparks.org/wakullasprings
Egmont Key State Park 4905 34th St S #5000 Saint Petersburg FL 33711 727-893-2627 893-2627
Web: www.floridastateparks.org/egmontkey
Fakahatchee Strand Preserve State Park PO Box 548 Copeland FL 34137 239-695-4593
Web: www.floridastateparks.org/fakahatcheestrand
Falling Waters State Park 1130 State Park Rd Chipley FL 32428 850-638-6130
Web: www.floridastateparks.org/fallingwaters
Fanning Springs State Park 18020 NW Hwy 19 Fanning Springs FL 32693 352-463-3420 463-3420
Web: www.floridastateparks.org/fanningsprings
Faver-Dykes State Park 1000 Faver Dykes Rd Saint Augustine FL 32086 904-794-0997 446-6781*
*Fax Area Code: 386 ■ *Web:* www.floridastateparks.org/faver-dykes
Florida Caverns State Park 3345 Caverns Rd Marianna FL 32446 850-482-9598
Web: www.floridastateparks.org/floridacaverns
Forest Capital Museum State Park 204 Forest Park Dr Perry FL 32348 850-584-3227
Web: www.floridastateparks.org/forestcapital
Fort Clinch State Park 2601 Atlantic Ave Fernandina Beach FL 32034 904-277-7274 277-7225
Web: www.floridastateparks.org/fortclinch
Fort Cooper State Park 3100 S Old Floral City Rd Inverness FL 34450 352-726-0315
Web: www.floridastateparks.org/fortcooper
Fort George Island Cultural State Park
12157 Heckscher Dr Jacksonville FL 32226 904-251-2320
Web: www.floridastateparks.org/fortgeorgeisland
Fort Mose Historic State Park
c/o Anastasia State Park 1340-A A1A S Saint Augustine FL 32080 904-461-2033
Web: www.floridastateparks.org/fortmose
Fort Pierce Inlet State Park 905 Shorewinds Dr Fort Pierce FL 34949 772-468-3985
Web: www.floridastateparks.org/fortpierceinlet
Fort Zachary Taylor Historic State Park PO Box 6560 Key West FL 33041 305-292-6713 292-6881
Web: www.floridastateparks.org/forttaylor
Fred Gannon Rocky Bayou State Park 4281 Hwy 20 Niceville FL 32578 850-833-9144
Web: www.floridastateparks.org/rockybayou
Gainesville-Hawthorne State Trail 3400 SE 15th St Gainesville FL 32641 352-466-3397
Web: www.floridastateparks.org/gainesville-hawthorne
Gamble Plantation Historic State Park 3708 Patten Ave Ellenton FL 34222 941-723-4536
Web: www.floridastateparks.org/gambleplantation
Gamble Rogers Memorial State Recreation Area at Flagler Beach 3100 S A1A Flagler Beach FL 32136 386-517-2086 517-2089
Web: www.floridastateparks.org/gamblerogers
Gasparilla Island State Park PO Box 1150 Boca Grande FL 33921 941-964-0375 964-1154
Web: www.floridastateparks.org/gasparillaisland
Grayton Beach State Park
c/o Deer Lake State Park 357 Main Park Rd Santa Rosa Beach FL 32459 850-231-4210
Web: www.floridastateparks.org/graytonbeach
Henderson Beach State Park 17000 Emerald Coast Pkwy Destin FL 32541 850-837-7550
Web: www.floridastateparks.org/hendersonbeach
Highlands Hammock State Park 5931 Hammock Rd Sebring FL 33872 863-386-6094 386-6095
Web: www.floridastateparks.org/highlandshammock
Hillsborough River State Park 15402 US 301 N Thonotosassa FL 33592 813-987-6771
Web: www.floridastateparks.org/hillsboroughriver
Homosassa Springs Wildlife State Park
4150 S Suncoast Blvd Homosassa FL 34446 352-628-5343 628-4243
Web: www.floridastateparks.org/homosassasprings
Honeymoon Island State Park 1 Causeway Blvd Dunedin FL 34698 727-469-5942
Web: www.floridastateparks.org/honeymoonisland
Hontoon Island State Park 2309 River Ridge Rd DeLand FL 32720 386-736-5309
Web: www.floridastateparks.org/hontoonisland
Hugh Taylor Birch State Park 3109 E Sunrise Blvd Fort Lauderdale FL 33304 954-564-4521 762-3737
Web: www.floridastateparks.org/hughtaylorbirch
Ichetucknee Springs State Park 12087 SW US Hwy 27 Fort White FL 32038 386-497-2511
Web: www.floridastateparks.org/ichetuckneesprings
Indian Key Historic State Park
c/o Lignumvitae Key Botanical State Park PO Box 1052 Islamorada FL 33036 305-664-2540
Web: www.floridastateparks.org/indiankey
John D. MacArthur Beach State Park
10900 SR 703 (A1A) North Palm Beach FL 33408 561-624-6950
Web: www.floridastateparks.org/macarthurbeach
John Gorrie Museum State Park PO Box 267 Apalachicola FL 32329 850-653-9347
Web: www.floridastateparks.org/johngorriemuseum
John Pennekamp Coral Reef State Park PO Box 487 Key Largo FL 33037 305-451-1202 853-3555
Web: www.floridastateparks.org/pennekamp
John U. Lloyd Beach State Park 6503 N Ocean Dr Dania FL 33004 954-923-2833
Web: www.floridastateparks.org/lloydbeach
Jonathan Dickinson State Park 16450 SE Federal Hwy Hobe Sound FL 33455 772-546-2771
Web: www.floridastateparks.org/jonathandickinson
Kissimmee Prairie Preserve State Park
33104 NW 192 Ave Okeechobee FL 34972 239-462-5360
Web: www.floridastateparks.org/kissimmeeprairie
Koreshan State Historic Site PO Box 7 Estero FL 33928 239-992-0311 992-1607
Web: www.floridastateparks.org/koreshan
Lake Griffin State Park 3089 US 441-27 Fruitland Park FL 34731 352-360-6760
Web: www.floridastateparks.org/lakegriffin
Lake Jackson Mounds Archaeological State Park
3600 Indian Mounds Rd Tallahassee FL 32303 850-922-6007 488-0366
Web: www.floridastateparks.org/lakejacksonmounds
Lake June-in-Winter Scrub State Park
c/o Highlands Hammock State Park 5931 Hammock Rd Sebring FL 33872 863-386-6099
Web: www.floridastateparks.org/lakejuneinwinter
Lake Kissimmee State Park 14248 Camp Mack Rd Lake Wales FL 33853 863-696-1112
Web: www.floridastateparks.org/lakekissimmee
Lake Louisa State Park 7305 US Hwy 27 Clermont FL 34714 352-394-3969
Web: www.floridastateparks.org/lakelouisa
Lake Manatee State Park 20007 Hwy 64 E Bradenton FL 34202 941-741-3028
Web: www.floridastateparks.org/lakemanatee

				Phone	Fax
Lake Talquin State Park 1022 DeSoto Park Dr *Web:* www.floridastateparks.org/laketalquin	Tallahassee	FL	32301	850-922-6007	
Lignumvitae Key Botanical State Park PO Box 1052 *Web:* www.floridastateparks.org/lignumvitaekey	Islamorada	FL	33036	305-664-2540	
Little Manatee River State Park 215 Lightfoot Rd *Web:* www.floridastateparks.org/littlemanateeriver	Wimauma	FL	33598	813-671-5005	
Little Talbot Island State Park 12157 Heckscher Dr *Web:* www.floridastateparks.org/littletalbotisland	Jacksonville	FL	32226	904-251-2320	251-2325
Long Key State Park PO Box 776 *Web:* www.floridastateparks.org/longkey	Long Key	FL	33001	305-664-4815	
Lovers Key State Park 8700 Estero Blvd *Web:* www.floridastateparks.org/loverskey	Fort Myers Beach	FL	33931	239-463-4588	463-8851
Lower Wekiva River Preserve State Park 1800 Wekiwa Cir *Web:* www.floridastateparks.org/lowerwekivariver	Apopka	FL	32712	407-884-2008	884-2039
Manatee Springs State Park 11650 NW 115th St *Web:* www.floridastateparks.org/manateesprings	Chiefland	FL	32626	352-493-6072	
Marjorie Kinnan Rawlings Historic State Park 18700 S County Road 325 *Web:* www.floridastateparks.org/marjoriekinnanrawlings	Cross Creek	FL	32640	352-466-3672	
Mike Roess Gold Head Branch State Park 6239 SR 21 *Web:* www.floridastateparks.org/goldhead	Keystone Heights	FL	32656	352-473-4701	
Myakka River State Park 13208 SR 72 *TF:* 800-326-3521 ■ *Web:* www.floridastateparks.org/myakkariver	Sarasota	FL	34241	941-361-6511	361-6501
Natural Bridge Battlefield Historic State Park 7502 Natural Bridge Rd *Web:* www.floridastateparks.org/naturalbridge	Tallahassee	FL	32305	850-922-6007	488-0366
Ochlockonee River State Park PO Box 5 *Web:* www.floridastateparks.org/ochlockoneeriver	Sopchoppy	FL	32358	850-962-2771	
O'Leno State Park 410 SE Oleno Park Rd *Web:* www.floridastateparks.org/oleno	High Springs	FL	32643	386-454-1853	
Oleta River State Park 3400 NE 163rd St *Web:* www.floridastateparks.org/oletariver	North Miami Beach	FL	33160	305-919-1846	919-1845
Olustee Battlefield Historic State Park PO Box 40 *Web:* www.floridastateparks.org/olustee	Olustee	FL	32072	386-758-0400	
Oscar Scherer State Park 1843 S Tamiami Trail *Web:* www.floridastateparks.org/oscarscherer	Osprey	FL	34229	941-483-5956	480-3007
Paynes Creek Historic State Park 888 Lake Branch Rd *Web:* www.floridastateparks.org/paynescreek	Bowling Green	FL	33834	863-375-4717	375-4510
Paynes Prairie Preserve State Park 100 Savannah Blvd *Web:* www.floridastateparks.org/paynesprairie	Micanopy	FL	32667	352-466-3397	
Peacock Springs State Park Administration Office 18081 185th Rd *Web:* www.floridastateparks.org/peacocksprings	Live Oak	FL	32060	386-776-2194	
Perdido Key State Park 12301 Gulf Beach Hwy *Web:* www.floridastateparks.org/perdidokey	Pensacola	FL	32507	850-492-1595	492-4380
Ponce de Leon Springs State Park 2860 Ponce de Leon Springs Rd *Web:* www.floridastateparks.org/poncedeleonsprings	Ponce de Leon	FL	32455	850-836-4281	
Rainbow Springs State Park 19158 SW 81st Place Rd *Web:* www.floridastateparks.org/rainbowsprings	Dunnellon	FL	34432	352-465-8555	
Ravine Gardens State Park 1600 Twigg St *Web:* www.floridastateparks.org/ravinegardens	Palatka	FL	32177	386-329-3721	329-3718
Rock Springs Run State Reserve c/o Wekiwa Springs State Park 1800 Wekiwa Cir *Web:* www.floridastateparks.org/rockspringsrun	Apopka	FL	32712	407-884-2008	884-2039
Saint Andrews State Park 4607 State Park Ln *Web:* www.floridastateparks.org/standrews	Panama City	FL	32408	850-233-5140	
Saint Lucie Inlet Preserve State Park 4810 SE Cove Rd *Web:* www.floridastateparks.org/stlucieinlet	Stuart	FL	34997	772-219-1880	
San Felasco Hammock Preserve State Park 12720 NW 109 Ln *Web:* www.floridastateparks.org/sanfelascohammock	Alachua	FL	32615	386-462-7905	
San Marcos de Apalache Historic State Park 148 Old Fort Rd *Web:* www.floridastateparks.org/sanmarcos	Saint Marks	FL	31355	850-925-6216	
San Pedro Underwater Archaeological Preserve State Park PO Box 1052 *Web:* www.floridastateparks.org/sanpedro	Islamorada	FL	33036	305-664-2540	
Savannas Preserve State Park 9551 Gumbo Limbo Ln *Web:* www.floridastateparks.org/savannas	Jensen Beach	FL	34957	772-398-2779	
Sebastian Inlet State Park 9700 S A1A *Web:* www.floridastateparks.org/sebastianinlet	Melbourne Beach	FL	32951	321-984-4852	984-4854
Silver River State Park 1425 NE 58th Ave *Web:* www.floridastateparks.org/silverriver	Ocala	FL	34470	352-236-7148	236-7150
Stephen Foster Folk Culture Center State Park PO Drawer G *Web:* www.floridastateparks.org/stephenfoster	White Springs	FL	32096	386-397-2733	
Stump Pass Beach State Park Barrier Islands State Parks PO Box 1150 *Web:* www.floridastateparks.org/stumppass	Boca Grande	FL	33921	941-964-0375	964-1154
Suwannee River State Park 20185 County Rd 132 *Web:* www.floridastateparks.org/suwanneeriver	Live Oak	FL	32060	386-362-2746	
Tarkiln Bayou Preserve State Park c/o Big Lagoon State Park *Web:* www.floridastateparks.org/tarkilnbayou	Pensacola	FL	32507	850-492-1595	
TH Stone Memorial Saint Joseph Peninsula State Park 8899 Cape San Blas Rd *Web:* www.floridastateparks.org/stjoseph	Port Saint Joe	FL	32456	850-227-1327	227-1488
The Barnacle Historic State Park 3485 Main Hwy *Web:* www.floridastateparks.org/thebarnacle	Coconut Grove	FL	33133	305-442-6866	442-6872
Three Rivers State Park 7908 Three Rivers Park Rd *Web:* www.floridastateparks.org/threerivers	Sneads	FL	32460	850-482-9006	
Tomoka State Park 2099 N Beach St *Web:* www.floridastateparks.org/tomoka	Ormond Beach	FL	32174	386-676-4050	676-4050
Topsail Hill Preserve State Park 7525 W Scenic Hwy 30A *Web:* www.floridastateparks.org/topsailhill	Santa Rosa Beach	FL	32459	850-267-0299	
Torreya State Park 2576 NW Torreya Park Rd *Web:* www.floridastateparks.org/torreya	Bristol	FL	32321	850-643-2674	
Waccasassa Bay Preserve State Park PO Box 187 *Web:* www.floridastateparks.org/waccasassabay	Cedar Key	FL	32625	352-543-5567	
Washington Oaks Gardens State Park 6400 N Oceanshore Blvd *Web:* www.floridastateparks.org/washingtonoaks	Palm Coast	FL	32173	386-446-6780	446-6781
Wekiwa Springs State Park 1800 Wekiwa Cir *Web:* www.floridastateparks.org/wekiwasprings	Apopka	FL	32712	407-884-2008	884-2039
Werner-Boyce Salt Springs State Park PO Box 490 *Web:* www.floridastateparks.org/werner-boyce	Port Richey	FL	34673	727-816-1890	816-1888
William Beardall Tosohatchee State Reserve 3365 Taylor Creek Rd	Christmas	FL	32709	407-568-5893	568-1704
Windley Key Fossil Reef Geological State Park c/o Lignumvitae Key Botanical State Park PO Box 1052 *Web:* www.floridastateparks.org/windleykey	Islamorada	FL	33036	305-664-2540	
Ybor City Museum State Park 1818 9th Ave *Web:* www.floridastateparks.org/Yborcity	Tampa	FL	33605	813-247-6323	
Yulee Sugar Mill Ruins Historic State Park c/o Crystal River Archaeological State Park 3400 N Museum Pointe *Web:* www.floridastateparks.org/yuleesugarmill	Crystal River	FL	34428	352-795-3817	

Georgia

				Phone	Fax
A H Stephens State Historic Park 456 Alexander St N *Web:* gastateparks.org/info/ahsteph	Crawfordville	GA	30631	706-456-2602	
Amicalola Falls State Park & Lodge 418 Amicalola Falls State Park Rd *Web:* gastateparks.org/info/amicalola	Dawsonville	GA	30534	706-265-4703	
Black Rock Mountain State Park 3085 Black Rock Mountain Pkwy *Web:* gastateparks.org/info/blackrock	Mountain City	GA	30562	706-746-2141	
Bobby Brown State Park 2509 Bobby Brown State Park Rd *Web:* gastateparks.org/info/bobbybrown	Elberton	GA	30635	706-213-2046	
Chief Vann House State Historic Site 82 GA Hwy 225 N *Web:* gastateparks.org/info/chiefvann	Chatsworth	GA	30705	706-695-2598	
Cloudland Canyon State Park 122 Cloudland Canyon Park *Web:* gastateparks.org/info/cloudland	Rising Fawn	GA	30738	706-657-4050	
Crooked River State Park 6222 Charlie Smith Sr Hwy *Web:* gastateparks.org/info/crookriv	Saint Mary's	GA	31558	912-882-5256	
Dahlonega Gold Museum State Historic Site 1 Public Sq *Web:* gastateparks.org/info/dahlonega	Dahlonega	GA	30533	706-864-2257	
Elijah Clark State Park 2959 McCormick Hwy *Web:* gastateparks.org/info/elijah	Lincolnton	GA	30817	706-359-3458	
Etowah Indian Mounds State Historic Site 813 Indian Mounds Rd SW *Web:* gastateparks.org/info/etowah	Cartersville	GA	30120	770-387-3747	
F D Roosevelt State Park 2970 GA Hwy 190 *TF:* 800-864-7275 ■ *Web:* gastateparks.org/info/fdr	Pine Mountain	GA	31822	706-663-4858	663-8906
Florence Marina State Park Rt 1 Box 36 *Web:* gastateparks.org/info/flormarin	Omaha	GA	31821	229-838-4244	
Fort King George State Historic Site 1600 Wayne St *Web:* gastateparks.org/info/ftkinggeorge	Darien	GA	31305	912-437-4770	
Fort McAllister State Historic Park 3894 Fort McAllister Rd *TF:* 800-864-7275 ■ *Web:* gastateparks.org/info/ftmcallister	Richmond Hill	GA	31324	912-727-2339	727-3614
Fort Morris State Historic Site 2559 Fort Morris Rd *Web:* gastateparks.org/info/ftmorris	Midway	GA	31320	912-884-5999	
Fort Mountain State Park 181 Fort Mountain Park Rd *Web:* gastateparks.org/info/fortmt	Chatsworth	GA	30705	706-695-2621	
Fort Yargo State Park 210 S Broad St *Web:* gastateparks.org/info/ftyargo	Winder	GA	30680	770-867-3489	
General Coffee State Park 46 John Coffee Rd *Web:* gastateparks.org/info/gencoffee	Nicholls	GA	31554	912-384-7082	
George L. Smith State Park 371 George L Smith State Park Rd *Web:* gastateparks.org/info/georgels	Twin City	GA	30471	478-763-2759	
George T. Bagby State Park 330 Bagby Pkwy *Web:* gastateparks.org/info/georgetb	Fort Gaines	GA	31751	229-768-2571	
Georgia Veterans State Park 2459 US 280 W *Web:* gastateparks.org/info/georgiavet	Cordele	GA	31015	229-276-2371	
Gordonia-Alatamaha State Park 322 Park Ln US 280 W *Web:* gastateparks.org/info/gordonalt	Reidsville	GA	30453	912-557-7744	
Hamburg State Park 6071 Hamburg State Park Rd *Web:* gastateparks.org/info/hamburg	Mitchell	GA	30820	478-552-2393	
Hard Labor Creek State Park Knox Chapel Rd *Web:* gastateparks.org/info/hardlabor	Rutledge	GA	30663	706-557-3001	
Hart State Park 330 Hart Park Rd *Web:* gastateparks.org/info/hart	Hartwell	GA	30643	706-376-8756	
High Falls State Park 76 High Falls Park Dr *Web:* gastateparks.org/info/highfall	Jackson	GA	30233	478-993-3053	
Hofwyl-Broadfield Plantation State Historic Site 5556 US Hwy 17 N *Web:* gastateparks.org/info/hofwyl	Brunswick	GA	31525	912-264-7333	
Indian Springs State Park 678 Lake Clark Rd *Web:* gastateparks.org/info/indspr	Flovilla	GA	30216	770-504-2277	
James H. "Sloppy" Floyd State Park 2800 Sloppy Floyd Lake Rd *Web:* gastateparks.org/info/sloppy	Summerville	GA	30747	706-857-0826	
Jarrell Plantation State Historic Site 711 Jarrell Plantation Rd *Web:* gastateparks.org/info/jarrell	Juliette	GA	31046	478-986-5172	
Jefferson Davis Memorial State Historic Site 338 Jeff Davis Park Rd *Web:* gastateparks.org/info/jeffd	Fitzgerald	GA	31750	229-831-2335	
John Tanner State Park 354 Tanner's Beach Rd *Web:* gastateparks.org/info/jtanner	Carrollton	GA	30117	770-830-2222	
Kolomoki Mounds State Historic Park 205 Indian Mounds Rd *Web:* gastateparks.org/info/kolomoki	Blakely	GA	39823	229-724-2150	
Lapham-Patterson House State Historic Site 626 N Dawson St *Web:* gastateparks.org/info/lapham	Thomasville	GA	31792	229-225-4004	
Laura S. Walker State Park 5653 Laura Walker Rd *Web:* gastateparks.org/info/lwalker	Waycross	GA	31503	912-287-4900	
Little Ocmulgee State Park & Lodge PO Drawer 149 *Web:* gastateparks.org/info/liocmulgee	McRae	GA	31055	229-868-7474	
Little White House State Historic Site 401 Little White House Rd *Web:* gastateparks.org/info/littlewhite	Warm Springs	GA	31830	706-655-5870	655-5872
Magnolia Springs State Park 1053 Magnolia Springs Dr *Web:* gastateparks.org/info/magspr	Millen	GA	30442	478-982-1660	
Mistletoe State Park 3723 Mistletoe Rd *Web:* gastateparks.org/info/mistletoe	Appling	GA	30802	706-541-0321	
Moccasin Creek State Park 3655 Hwy 197 *Web:* gastateparks.org/info/moccasin	Clarkesville	GA	30523	706-947-3194	
New Echota State Historic Site 1211 Chatsworth Hwy NE *Web:* gastateparks.org/info/echota	Calhoun	GA	30701	706-624-1321	
Panola Mountain State Park 2600 Hwy 155 SW *Web:* gastateparks.org/info/panolamt	Stockbridge	GA	30281	770-389-7801	
Pickett's Mill Battlefield State Historic Site 4432 Mt Tabor Church Rd *Web:* gastateparks.org/info/picketts	Dallas	GA	30157	770-443-7850	
Providence Canyon State Park Rt 1 Box 158 *Web:* gastateparks.org/info/providence	Lumpkin	GA	31815	229-838-6202	838-6735
Red Top Mountain State Park & Lodge 50 Lodge Rd SE *Web:* gastateparks.org/info/redtop	Cartersville	GA	30121	770-975-0055	
Reed Bingham State Park 542 Reed Bingham Rd *Web:* gastateparks.org/info/reedbing	Adel	GA	31620	229-896-3551	
Richard B. Russell State Park 2650 Russell State Park Rd *Web:* gastateparks.org/info/richbruss	Elberton	GA	30635	706-213-2045	
Robert Toombs House State Historic Site 216 E Robert Toombs Ave *Web:* gastateparks.org/info/rtoombs	Washington	GA	30673	706-678-2226	

Georgia (Cont'd)

Phone Fax

Seminole State Park 7870 State Park Dr ... Donalsonville GA 39845 229-861-3137
Web: gastateparks.org/info/seminole

Skidaway Island State Park 52 Diamond Cswy ... Savannah GA 31411 912-598-2300 598-2365
Web: gastateparks.org/info/skidaway

Smithgall Woods Conservation Area & Lodge 61 Tsalaki Trail ... Helen GA 30545 706-878-3087
Web: gastateparks.org/info/smithgall

Sprewell Bluff State Park 740 Sprewell Bluff Rd ... Thomaston GA 30286 706-646-6026
Web: gastateparks.org/info/sprewell

Stephen C. Foster State Park 17515 Hwy 177 ... Fargo GA 31631 912-637-5274
Web: gastateparks.org/info/scfoster

Sweetwater Creek State Park ... Lithia Springs GA 30122 770-732-5871
Web: gastateparks.org/info/sweetwater

Tallulah Gorge State Park 338 Jane Hurt Yarn Dr ... Tallulah Falls GA 30573 706-754-7970
Web: gastateparks.org/info/tallulah

Traveler's Rest State Historic Site 11 Stage Coach Private Dr ... Toccoa GA 30577 706-886-2256
Web: gastateparks.org/info/travelers

Tugaloo State Park 1763 Tugaloo State Park Rd ... Lavonia GA 30553 706-356-4362
Web: gastateparks.org/info/tugaloo

Unicoi State Park & Lodge 1788 Highway 356 Rd ... Helen GA 30545 800-573-9659
Web: gastateparks.org/info/unicoi

Victoria Bryant State Park 1105 Bryant Park Rd ... Royston GA 30662 706-245-6270
Web: gastateparks.org/info/vicbryant

Vogel State Park 7485 Vogel State Park Rd ... Blairsville GA 30512 706-745-2628
Web: gastateparks.org/info/vogel

Watson Mill Bridge State Park 650 Watson Mill Rd ... Comer GA 30629 706-783-5349
Web: gastateparks.org/info/watson

Wormsloe State Historic Site 7601 Skidaway Rd ... Savannah GA 31406 912-353-3023 692-4530
Web: gastateparks.org/info/wormsloe

Hawaii

Phone Fax

Ahukini State Recreation Pier
c/o Kauai District Office 3060 Eiwa St, Rm 306 ... Lihue HI 96766 808-274-3444
Web: www.hawaii.gov/dlnr/dsp/kauai.html

Aiea Bay State Recreation Area
c/o Oahu District Office PO Box 621 ... Honolulu HI 96809 808-587-0300
Web: www.hawaii.gov/dlnr/dsp/oahu.html

Akaka Falls State Park c/o Hawaii District Office PO Box 936 ... Hilo HI 96721 808-974-6200
Web: www.hawaii.gov/dlnr/dsp/hawaii.html

Diamond Head State Monument
c/o Oahu District Office PO Box 621 ... Honolulu HI 96809 808-587-0300
Web: www.hawaii.gov/dlnr/dsp/oahu.html

Haena State Park c/o Kauai District Office 3060 Eiwa St, Rm 306 ... Lihue HI 96766 808-274-3444
Web: www.hawaii.gov/dlnr/dsp/kauai.html

Halekii-Pihana Heiau State Monument
c/o Maui District Office 54 S High St, Rm 101 ... Wailuku HI 96793 808-984-8109
Web: www.hawaii.gov/dlnr/dsp/maui.html

Hanauma Bay State Underwater Park
c/o Oahu District Office PO Box 621 ... Honolulu HI 96809 808-587-0300
Web: www.hawaii.gov/dlnr/dsp/oahu.html

Hapuna Beach State Recreation Area
c/o Hawaii District Office PO Box 936 ... Hilo HI 96721 808-974-6200
Web: www.hawaii.gov/dlnr/dsp/hawaii.html

Heeia State Park c/o Oahu District Office PO Box 621 ... Honolulu HI 96809 808-587-0300
Web: www.hawaii.gov/dlnr/dsp/oahu.html

Iao Valley State Monument
c/o Maui District Office 54 S High St, Rm 101 ... Wailuku HI 96793 808-984-8109
Web: www.hawaii.gov/dlnr/dsp/maui.html

Iolani Palace State Monument
c/o Oahu District Office PO Box 621 ... Honolulu HI 96809 808-587-0300
Web: www.hawaii.gov/dlnr/dsp/oahu.html

Kaena Point State Park c/o Oahu District Office PO Box 621 ... Honolulu HI 96809 808-587-0300
Web: www.hawaii.gov/dlnr/dsp/oahu.html

Kahana Valley State Park c/o Oahu District Office PO Box 621 ... Honolulu HI 96809 808-587-0300
Web: www.hawaii.gov/dlnr/dsp/oahu.html

Kakaako Waterfront Park c/o Oahu District Office PO Box 621 ... Honolulu HI 96809 808-587-0300
Web: www.hawaii.gov/dlnr/dsp/oahu.html

Kalopa State Recreation Area
c/o Hawaii District Office PO Box 936 ... Hilo HI 96721 808-974-6200
Web: www.hawaii.gov/dlnr/dsp/hawaii.html

Kaumahina State Wayside
c/o Maui District Office 54 S High St, Rm 101 ... Wailuku HI 96793 808-984-8109
Web: www.hawaii.gov/dlnr/dsp/maui.html

Keaiwa Heiau State Recreation Area
c/o Oahu District Office PO Box 621 ... Honolulu HI 96809 808-587-0300
Web: www.hawaii.gov/dlnr/dsp/oahu.html

Kealakekua Bay State Historical Park
c/o Hawaii District Office PO Box 936 ... Hilo HI 96721 808-974-6200
Web: www.hawaii.gov/dlnr/dsp/hawaii.html

Kekaha Kai (Kona Coast) State Park
c/o Hawaii District Office PO Box 936 ... Hilo HI 96721 808-974-6200
Web: www.hawaii.gov/dlnr/dsp/hawaii.html

Kohala Historical Sites State Monument
c/o Hawaii District Office PO Box 936 ... Hilo HI 96721 808-974-6200
Web: www.hawaii.gov/dlnr/dsp/hawaii.html

Kokee State Park c/o Kauai District Office 3060 Eiwa St, Rm 306 ... Lihue HI 96766 808-274-3444
Web: www.hawaii.gov/dlnr/dsp/kauai.html

Kukaniloko Birthstones State Monument
c/o Oahu District Office PO Box 621 ... Honolulu HI 96809 808-587-0300
Web: www.hawaii.gov/dlnr/dsp/oahu.html

Laie Point State Wayside c/o Oahu District Office PO Box 621 ... Honolulu HI 96809 808-587-0300
Web: www.hawaii.gov/dlnr/dsp/oahu.html

Lapakahi State Historical Park
c/o Hawaii District Office PO Box 936 ... Hilo HI 96721 808-974-6200
Web: www.hawaii.gov/dlnr/dsp/hawaii.html

Lava Tree State Monument c/o Hawaii District Office PO Box 936 ... Hilo HI 96721 808-974-6200
Web: www.hawaii.gov/dlnr/dsp/hawaii.html

MacKenzie State Recreation Area
c/o Hawaii District Office PO Box 936 ... Hilo HI 96721 808-974-6200
Web: www.hawaii.gov/dlnr/dsp/hawaii.html

Makapuu Point State Wayside
c/o Oahu District Office PO Box 621 ... Honolulu HI 96809 808-587-0300
Web: www.hawaii.gov/dlnr/dsp/oahu.html

Makena State Park
c/o Maui District Office 54 S High St, Rm 101 ... Wailuku HI 96793 808-984-8109
Web: www.hawaii.gov/dlnr/dsp/maui.html

Malaekahana State Recreation Area
c/o Oahu District Office PO Box 621 ... Honolulu HI 96809 808-587-0300
Web: www.hawaii.gov/dlnr/dsp/oahu.html

Manuka State Wayside c/o Hawaii District Office PO Box 936 ... Hilo HI 96721 808-974-6200
Web: www.hawaii.gov/dlnr/dsp/hawaii.html

Phone Fax

Mauna Kea State Recreation Area
c/o Hawaii District Office PO Box 936 ... Hilo HI 96721 808-974-6200
Web: www.hawaii.gov/dlnr/dsp/hawaii.html

Na Pali Coast State Park
c/o Kauai District Office 3060 Eiwa St, Rm 306 ... Lihue HI 96766 808-274-3444
Web: www.state.hi.us/dlnr/dsp/NaPali/na_pali.htm

Nuuanu Pali State Wayside
c/o Oahu District Office PO Box 621 ... Honolulu HI 96809 808-587-0300
Web: www.hawaii.gov/dlnr/dsp/oahu.html

Old Kona Airport State Recreation Area
c/o Hawaii District Office PO Box 936 ... Hilo HI 96721 808-974-6200
Web: www.hawaii.gov/dlnr/dsp/hawaii.html

Palaau State Park c/o Oahu District Office PO Box 621 ... Honolulu HI 96809 808-587-0300
Web: www.hawaii.gov/dlnr/dsp/molokai.html

Polihale State Park
c/o Kauai District Office 3060 Eiwa St, Rm 306 ... Lihue HI 96766 808-274-3444
Web: www.hawaii.gov/dlnr/dsp/kauai.html

Polipoli Spring State Recreation Area
c/o Maui District Office 54 S High St, Rm 101 ... Wailuku HI 96793 808-984-8109
Web: www.hawaii.gov/dlnr/dsp/maui.html

Puaa Kaa State Wayside
c/o Maui District Office 54 S High St, Rm 101 ... Wailuku HI 96793 808-984-8109
Web: www.hawaii.gov/dlnr/dsp/maui.html

Puu o Mahuka Heiau State Monument
c/o Oahu District Office PO Box 621 ... Honolulu HI 96809 808-587-0300
Web: www.hawaii.gov/dlnr/dsp/oahu.html

Puu Ualakaa State Wayside
c/o Oahu District Office PO Box 621 ... Honolulu HI 96809 808-587-0300
Web: www.hawaii.gov/dlnr/dsp/oahu.html

Royal Mausoleum State Monument
c/o Oahu District Office PO Box 621 ... Honolulu HI 96809 808-587-0300
Web: www.hawaii.gov/dlnr/dsp/oahu.html

Russian Fort Elizabeth State Historical Park
c/o Kauai District Office 3060 Eiwa St, Rm 306 ... Honolulu HI 96766 808-274-3444
Web: www.hawaii.gov/dlnr/dsp/kauai.html

Sand Island State Recreation Area
c/o Oahu District Office PO Box 621 ... Honolulu HI 96809 808-587-0300
Web: www.hawaii.gov/dlnr/dsp/oahu.html

Ulupo Heiau State Monument
c/o Oahu District Office PO Box 621 ... Honolulu HI 96809 808-587-0300
Web: www.hawaii.gov/dlnr/dsp/oahu.html

Waahila Ridge State Recreation Area
c/o Oahu District Office PO Box 621 ... Honolulu HI 96809 808-587-0300
Web: www.hawaii.gov/dlnr/dsp/oahu.html

Wahiawa Freshwater State Recreation Area
c/o Oahu District Office PO Box 621 ... Honolulu HI 96809 808-587-0300
Web: www.hawaii.gov/dlnr/dsp/oahu.html

Waianapanapa State Park
c/o Maui District Office 54 S High St, Rm 101 ... Wailuku HI 96793 808-984-8109
Web: www.hawaii.gov/dlnr/dsp/maui.html

Wailoa River State Recreation Area
c/o Hawaii District Office PO Box 936 ... Hilo HI 96721 808-964-6200
Web: www.hawaii.gov/dlnr/dsp/hawaii.html

Wailua River State Park
c/o Kauai District Office 3060 Eiwa St, Rm 306 ... Lihue HI 96766 808-274-3444
Web: www.hawaii.gov/dlnr/dsp/kauai.html

Wailua Valley State Wayside
c/o Maui District Office 54 S High St, Rm 101 ... Wailuku HI 96793 808-984-8109
Web: www.hawaii.gov/dlnr/dsp/maui.html

Wailuku River State Park c/o Hawaii District Office PO Box 936 ... Hilo HI 96721 808-974-6200
Web: www.hawaii.gov/dlnr/dsp/hawaii.html

Waimea Canyon State Park
c/o Kauai District Office 3060 Eiwa St, Rm 306 ... Lihue HI 96766 808-274-3444
Web: www.hawaii.gov/dlnr/dsp/kauai.html

Waimea State Recreation Pier
c/o Kauai District Office 3060 Eiwa St, Rm 306 ... Lihue HI 96766 808-274-3444

Idaho

Phone Fax

Bear Lake State Park PO Box 297 ... Paris ID 83261 208-847-1045 847-1056
TF: 866-634-3246 ■ *Web:* www.idahoparks.org/parks/bearlake.aspx

Bruneau Dunes State Park 27608 Sand Dunes Rd ... Mountain Home ID 83647 208-366-7919 366-2844
Web: www.parksandrecreation.idaho.gov/parks/bruneaudunesstatepark.aspx

Coeur d'Alene Parkway State Park
2750 Kathleen Ave Suite 1 ... Coeur d'Alene ID 83815 208-699-2224
Web: www.idahoparks.org/parks/coeurdaleneparkway.aspx

Dworshak State Park PO Box 2028 ... Orofino ID 83544 208-476-5994 476-7225
TF: 866-634-3246 ■ *Web:* www.idahoparks.org/parks/dworshak.aspx

Eagle Island State Park 4000 W Hatchery Rd ... Eagle ID 83616 208-939-0696 939-9708
Web: www.idahoparks.org/parks/eagleisland.aspx

Farragut State Park 13550 E Hwy 54 ... Athol ID 83801 208-683-2425 683-7416
Web: www.idahoparks.org/parks/farragut.aspx

Harriman State Park 3489 Green Canyon Rd ... Island Park ID 83429 208-558-7368 558-7045
TF: 866-634-3246 ■ *Web:* www.idahoparks.org/parks/harriman.aspx

Hells Gate State Park 5100 Hells Gate Rd ... Lewiston ID 83501 208-799-5015 799-5187
TF: 866-634-3246 ■ *Web:* www.idahoparks.org/parks/hellsgate.aspx

Henrys Lake State Park 3917 E 5100 North ... Island Park ID 83429 208-558-7532
TF: 866-634-3246 ■ *Web:* www.idahoparks.org/parks/henryslake.aspx

Heyburn State Park 1291 Chatcolet Rd ... Plummer ID 83851 208-686-1308 686-3003
TF: 866-634-3246 ■ *Web:* www.idahoparks.org/parks/heyburn.aspx

Lake Cascade State Park PO Box 709 ... Cascade ID 83616 208-382-6544 382-4071
TF: 866-634-3246 ■ *Web:* www.idahoparks.org/parks/lakecascade.aspx

Lake Walcott State Park 959 E Minidoka Dam ... Rupert ID 83350 208-436-1258 436-1268
Web: www.idahoparks.org/parks/lakewalcott.aspx

Land of the Yankee Fork State Park PO Box 1086 ... Challis ID 83226 208-879-5244 879-5243
Web: www.idahoparks.org/parks/yankeefork.aspx

Lucky Peak State Park 9725 E Hwy 21 ... Boise ID 83716 208-334-2432
Web: www.idahoparks.org/parks/luckypeak.aspx

Massacre Rocks State Park 3592 N Park Ln ... American Falls ID 83211 208-548-2672 548-2671
Web: www.idahoparks.org/parks/massacrerocks.aspx

McCroskey State Park 2750 Kathleen Ave ... Coeur d'Alene ID 83815 208-666-6711
Web: www.idahoparks.org/parks/maryminervamccroskey.aspx

Old Mission State Park Box 30 ... Cataldo ID 83810 208-682-3814 682-4032
Web: www.idahoparks.org/parks/oldmission.aspx

Ponderosa State Park Box 89 ... McCall ID 83638 208-634-2164 634-5370
Web: www.idahoparks.org/parks/ponderosa.aspx

Priest Lake State Park 314 Indian Creek Park Rd ... Coolin ID 83821 208-443-2200 443-3893
TF: 866-634-3246 ■ *Web:* www.idahoparks.org/parks/priestlake.aspx

Round Lake State Park PO Box 170 ... Sagle ID 83860 208-263-3489
TF: 866-634-3246 ■ *Web:* www.idahoparks.org/parks/roundlake.aspx

Three Island Crossing State Park Box 609 ... Glenns Ferry ID 83623 208-366-2394 366-7913
TF: 866-634-3246 ■ *Web:* www.idahoparks.org/parks/threeislandcrossing.aspx

Winchester Lake State Park PO Box 186 ... Winchester ID 83555 208-924-7563 924-5941
TF: 866-634-3246 ■ *Web:* www.idahoparks.org/parks/winchesterlake.aspx

Illinois

Name / Address	City	State	Zip	Phone	Fax
Anderson Lake Conservation Area 647 N IL Hwy 100	Astoria	IL	61501	309-759-4484	
Web: dnr.state.il.us/Lands/Landmgt/PARKS/R1/ANDERSON.HTM					
Apple River Canyon State Park 8763 E Canyon Rd	Apple River	IL	61001	815-745-3302	
Web: dnr.state.il.us/Lands/Landmgt/PARKS/R1/APPLE.HTM					
Argyle Lake State Park 640 Argyle Park Rd	Colchester	IL	62326	309-776-3422	
Web: dnr.state.il.us/Lands/Landmgt/PARKS/R1/ARGYLE.HTM					
Banner Marsh State Fish & Wildlife Area 19721 N US 24	Canton	IL	61520	309-647-9184	
Web: dnr.state.il.us/Lands/Landmgt/PARKS/R1/banner.htm					
Beall Woods State Park 9285 Beall Woods Ave	Mount Carmel	IL	62863	618-298-2442	
Web: dnr.state.il.us/Lands/Landmgt/PARKS/R5/BEALL.HTM					
Beaver Dam State Park 14548 Beaver Dam Ln	Plainview	IL	62685	217-854-8020	
Web: dnr.state.il.us/Lands/Landmgt/PARKS/R4/beaver.htm					
Big Bend State Fish & Wildlife Area PO Box 181	Prophetstown	IL	61277	815-537-2270	
Web: dnr.state.il.us/lands/Landmgt/PARKS/R1/BIGBEND.HTM					
Big River State Forest RR 1 Box 118	Keithsburg	IL	61442	309-374-2496	
Web: dnr.state.il.us/Lands/Landmgt/PARKS/R1/BIGRIVER.HTM					
Buffalo Rock State Park & Effigy Tumuli PO Box 2034 1300 N 27th Rd	Ottawa	IL	61350	815-433-2220	
Web: dnr.state.il.us/Lands/Landmgt/PARKS/I&M/EAST/BUFFALO/Home.htm					
Cache River State Natural Area 930 Sunflower Ln	Belknap	IL	62908	618-634-9678	
Web: dnr.state.il.us/lands/landmgt/PARKS/R5/CACHERVR.HTM					
Cahokia Mounds State Historic Site 30 Ramey St	Collinsville	IL	62234	618-346-5160	346-5162
Web: www.cahokiamounds.com					
Carlyle Lake State Fish & Wildlife Area RR 2	Vandalia	IL	62471	618-425-3533	
Web: dnr.state.il.us/Lands/Landmgt/PARKS/R4/CARLYLE.HTM					
Castle Rock State Park 1365 W Castle Rd	Oregon	IL	61061	815-732-7329	
Web: dnr.state.il.us/Lands/Landmgt/PARKS/R1/CASTLE.HTM					
Cave-In-Rock State Park 1 New State Park Rd Box 338	Cave-In-Rock	IL	62919	618-289-4325	
Web: dnr.state.il.us/Lands/Landmgt/PARKS/R5/CAVEROCK.HTM					
Chain O'Lakes State Park 8916 Wilmot Rd	Spring Grove	IL	60081	847-587-5512	
Web: dnr.state.il.us/Lands/Landmgt/PARKS/R2/CHAINO.HTM					
Channahon State Park PO Box 54	Channahon	IL	60410	815-467-4271	
Web: dnr.state.il.us/Lands/Landmgt/PARKS/I&M/EAST/CHANNAHO/Park.htm					
Clinton Lake State Recreation Area RR 1 Box 4	DeWitt	IL	61735	217-935-8722	
Web: dnr.state.il.us/Lands/Landmgt/PARKS/R3/CLINTON.HTM					
Coffeen Lake State Fish & Wildlife Area 15084 N 4th Ave	Coffeen	IL	62017	217-537-3351	
Web: dnr.state.il.us/Lands/Landmgt/PARKS/R4/Coffeen.htm					
Crawford County State Fish & Wildlife Area 12609 E 1700th Ave	Hutsonville	IL	62433	618-563-4405	
Web: dnr.state.il.us/Lands/Landmgt/PARKS/R5/Crawford.htm					
Delabar State Park RR 2 Box 27	Oquawka	IL	61469	309-374-2496	
Web: dnr.state.il.us/Lands/Landmgt/PARKS/R1/DELABAR.HTM					
Des Plaines State Fish & Wildlife Area 24621 N River Rd	Wilmington	IL	60481	815-423-5326	
Web: dnr.state.il.us/Lands/Landmgt/PARKS/I&M/EAST/DESPLAIN/PARK.HTM					
Dixon Springs State Park RR 2 Box 178	Golconda	IL	62938	618-949-3394	
Web: dnr.state.il.us/Lands/Landmgt/PARKS/R5/DIXON.HTM					
Donnelley/DePue State Fish & Wildlife Areas 1001 W 4th St PO Box 52	DePue	IL	61322	815-447-2353	
Web: dnr.state.il.us/Lands/Landmgt/PARKS/R1/Don.htm					
Eagle Creek State Recreation Area PO Box 16	Findlay	IL	62534	217-756-8260	
Web: dnr.state.il.us/Lands/Landmgt/PARKS/R3/EAGLECRK.HTM					
Edgar (Jim) Panther Creek State Fish & Wildlife Area 10149 County Hwy 11	Chandlerville	IL	62627	217-452-7741	
Web: dnr.state.il.us/Lands/Landmgt/PARKS/R4/jepc.htm					
Edward R. Madigan State Fish & Wildlife Area 1366 1010th Ave	Lincoln	IL	62656	217-735-2424	
Web: dnr.state.il.us/Lands/Landmgt/PARKS/R4/Edmad.htm					
Eldon Hazlet State Recreation Area 20100 Hazlet Park Rd	Carlyle	IL	62231	618-594-3015	
Web: dnr.state.il.us/Lands/Landmgt/PARKS/R4/ELDON.HTM					
Ferne Clyffe State Park PO Box 10	Goreville	IL	62939	618-995-2411	
Web: dnr.state.il.us/Lands/Landmgt/PARKS/R5/FERNE.HTM					
Fort Massac State Park 1308 E 5th St	Metropolis	IL	62960	618-524-4712	
Web: dnr.state.il.us/Lands/Landmgt/PARKS/R5/frmindex.htm					
Fox Ridge State Park 18175 State Park Rd	Charleston	IL	61920	217-345-6416	
Web: dnr.state.il.us/Lands/Landmgt/PARKS/R3/FOX/FOX.HTM					
Frank Holten State Recreation Area 4500 Pocket Rd	East Saint Louis	IL	62205	618-874-7920	
Web: dnr.state.il.us/Lands/Landmgt/PARKS/R4/frank.htm					
Franklin Creek State Natural Area 1872 Twist Rd	Franklin Grove	IL	61031	815-456-2878	
Web: dnr.state.il.us/Lands/Landmgt/PARKS/R1/FRANKLIN.HTM					
Fults Hill Prairie & Kidd Lake State Natural Areas c/o Randolph County State Recreation Area 4301 S Lake Dr	Chester	IL	62233	618-826-2706	
Web: dnr.state.il.us/Lands/Landmgt/PARKS/R4/fhp.htm					
Gebhard Woods State Park 401 Ottawa St PO Box 272	Morris	IL	60450	815-942-0796	
Web: dnr.state.il.us/Lands/Landmgt/PARKS/I&M/EAST/GEBHARD/Park.htm					
Giant City State Park 235 Giant City Rd	Makanda	IL	62958	618-457-4836	
Web: dnr.state.il.us/Lands/Landmgt/PARKS/R5/GC.HTM					
Goose Lake Prairie State Natural Area 5010 N Jugtown Rd	Morris	IL	60450	815-942-2899	
Web: dnr.state.il.us/Lands/Landmgt/PARKS/I&M/EAST/GOOSE/HOME.HTM					
Green River State Wildlife Area 375 Game Rd	Harmon	IL	61042	815-379-2324	
Web: dnr.state.il.us/Lands/Landmgt/PARKS/R1/green.htm					
Hamilton County State Fish & Wildlife Area RR 4 Box 242	McLeansboro	IL	62859	618-773-4340	
Web: dnr.state.il.us/Lands/Landmgt/PARKS/R5/HAMILTON.HTM					
Harry "Babe" Woodyard State Natural Area 19284 E 670 North	Georgetown	IL	61846	217-442-4915	
Web: dnr.state.il.us/Lands/Landmgt/PARKS/R3/hbw.htm					
Hazel & Bill Rutherford Wildlife Prairie State Park 3826 N Taylor Rd	Hanna City	IL	61536	309-676-0998	676-7783
Web: www.wildlifeprairiestatepark.org					
Heidecke Lake State Fish & Wildlife Area 5010 N Jugtown Rd	Morris	IL	60450	815-942-6352	
Web: dnr.state.il.us/Lands/Landmgt/PARKS/R2/Heidecke.htm					
Henderson County Conservation Area RR 1, Box 118	Keithsburg	IL	61442	309-374-2496	
Web: dnr.state.il.us/lands/Landmgt/PARKS/R1/HENDERSO.HTM					
Hennepin Canal Parkway State Park 16006 875 E St	Sheffield	IL	61361	815-454-2328	
Web: dnr.state.il.us/Lands/Landmgt/PARKS/R1/HENNPIN.HTM					
Hidden Springs State Forest RR 1 Box 200	Strasburg	IL	62465	217-644-3091	
Web: dnr.state.il.us/Lands/Landmgt/PARKS/R3/HSFOREST.HTM					
Horseshoe Lake State Fish & Wildlife Area (Alexander County) PO Box 85	Miller City	IL	62962	618-776-5689	
Web: dnr.state.il.us/Lands/Landmgt/PARKS/R5/HORSHU.HTM					
Horseshoe Lake State Park (Madison County) 3321 Hwy 111	Granite City	IL	62040	618-931-0270	
Web: dnr.state.il.us/Lands/Landmgt/PARKS/R4/HORSESP.HTM					
Illini State Park 2660 E 2350th Rd	Marseilles	IL	61341	815-795-2448	
Web: dnr.state.il.us/Lands/Landmgt/PARKS/I&M/EAST/ILLINI/PARK.HTM					
Illinois Beach State Park Lake Front	Zion	IL	60099	847-662-4811	662-6433
Web: dnr.state.il.us/Lands/Landmgt/PARKS/R2/ILBEACH.HTM					
Illinois Caverns State Natural Area 10981 Conservation Rd	Baldwin	IL	62217	618-458-6699	
Web: dnr.state.il.us/Lands/Landmgt/PARKS/R4/ILC.HTM					
Illinois & Michigan Canal State Trail PO Box 272	Morris	IL	60450	815-942-0796	942-9690
Web: dnr.state.il.us/Lands/Landmgt/PARKS/I&M/Main.htm					
Iroquois County State Wildlife Area RR 1 2803 East 3300 North Rd	Beaverville	IL	60912	815-435-2218	
Web: dnr.state.il.us/Lands/Landmgt/PARKS/R3/IROQUOIS.HTM					
JEPC (Jim Edgar Panther Creek State Fish & Wildlife Area) 10149 County Hwy 11	Chandlerville	IL	62627	217-452-7741	
Web: dnr.state.il.us/Lands/Landmgt/PARKS/R4/jepc.htm					
Jim Edgar Panther Creek State Fish & Wildlife Area (JEPC) 10149 County Hwy 11	Chandlerville	IL	62627	217-452-7741	
Web: dnr.state.il.us/Lands/Landmgt/PARKS/R4/jepc.htm					
Johnson-Sauk Trail State Park 28616 Sauk Trail Rd	Kewanee	IL	61443	309-853-5589	
Web: dnr.state.il.us/Lands/Landmgt/PARKS/R1/JOHNSON.HTM					
Jubilee College State Park 13921 W Rt 150	Brimfield	IL	61517	309-446-3758	446-3183
Web: dnr.state.il.us/Lands/Landmgt/PARKS/R1/JUBILEE.HTM					
Kankakee River State Park 5314 W Rt 102 PO Box 37	Bourbonnais	IL	60914	815-933-1383	
Web: dnr.state.il.us/Lands/Landmgt/PARKS/R2/KANKAKEE.HTM					
Kaskaskia River State Fish & Wildlife Area 10981 Conservation Rd	Baldwin	IL	62217	618-785-2555	
Web: dnr.state.il.us/Lands/Landmgt/PARKS/R4/kaskas.htm					
Kickapoo State Recreation Area 10906 Kickapoo Park Rd	Oakwood	IL	61858	217-442-4915	
Web: dnr.state.il.us/Lands/Landmgt/PARKS/R3/KICKAPOO.HTM					
Kinkaid Lake State Fish & Wildlife Area 52 Cinder Hill Dr	Murphysboro	IL	62966	618-684-2867	
Web: dnr.state.il.us/lands/landmgt/PARKS/R5/Kinkaid.htm					
Lake Le-Aqua-Na State Recreation Area 8542 N Lake Rd	Lena	IL	61048	815-369-4282	
Web: dnr.state.il.us/Lands/Landmgt/PARKS/R1/LEAQUANA.HTM					
Lake Murphysboro State Park 52 Cinder Hill Dr	Murphysboro	IL	62966	618-684-2867	
Web: dnr.state.il.us/Lands/Landmgt/PARKS/R5/MURPHYSB.HTM					
LaSalle Lake State Fish & Wildlife Area 2660 E 2350th Rd	Marseilles	IL	61341	815-357-1608	
Web: dnr.state.il.us/Lands/Landmgt/PARKS/R1/LASALLE.HTM					
Lincoln Trail Homestead State Memorial c/o Spitler Woods State Natural Area 705 Spitler Park Dr	Mount Zion	IL	62549	217-864-3121	
Web: dnr.state.il.us/lands/Landmgt/PARKS/R3/LINCTRL.HTM					
Lincoln Trail State Park 16985 E 1350th Rd	Marshall	IL	62441	217-826-2222	
Web: dnr.state.il.us/lands/landmgt/PARKS/R3/LINCOLN.HTM					
Lowden-Miller State Forest 1365 W Castle Rock Rd	Oregon	IL	61061	815-732-7329	
Web: dnr.state.il.us/Lands/Landmgt/PARKS/R1/LOWDENMI.HTM					
Lowden State Park 1411 N River Rd	Oregon	IL	61061	815-732-6828	
Web: dnr.state.il.us/Lands/Landmgt/PARKS/R1/LOWDENSP.HTM					
Mackinaw River State Fish & Wildlife Area 15470 Nelson Rd	Mackinaw	IL	61755	309-963-4969	
Web: dnr.state.il.us/Lands/Landmgt/PARKS/R1/MACKINA.HTM					
Marseilles State Fish & Wildlife Area 2660 E 2350th Rd	Marseilles	IL	61341	815-795-2448	
Marshall State Fish & Wildlife Area 236 State Rt 26	Lacon	IL	61540	309-246-8351	
Web: dnr.state.il.us/Lands/Landmgt/PARKS/R1/MARSHALL.HTM					
Matthiessen State Park PO Box 509	Utica	IL	61373	815-667-4868	
Web: dnr.state.il.us/Lands/Landmgt/PARKS/R1/mttindex.htm					
Mautino State Fish & Wildlife Area 16006-875 E St	Sheffield	IL	61361	815-454-2328	
Web: dnr.state.il.us/Lands/Landmgt/PARKS/R1/MAUTINO.HTM					
Mazonia-Braidwood State Fish & Wildlife Areas PO Box 126	Braceville	IL	60407	815-237-0063	
Web: dnr.state.il.us/lands/Landmgt/PARKS/R2/MAZONIA.HTM					
Mermet Lake State Fish & Wildlife Area 1812 Grinnell Rd	Belknap	IL	62908	618-524-5577	
Web: dnr.state.il.us/Lands/Landmgt/PARKS/R5/MERMET.HTM					
Middle Fork State Fish & Wildlife Area 10906 Kickapoo Park Rd	Oakwood	IL	61858	217-442-4915	
Web: dnr.state.il.us/Lands/Landmgt/PARKS/R3/Middle.htm					
Mississippi Palisades State Park 16327A IL Rt 84	Savanna	IL	61074	815-273-2731	
Web: dnr.state.il.us/Lands/Landmgt/PARKS/R1/PALISADE.HTM					
Mississippi River State Fish & Wildlife Area 17836 State Highway 100 N	Grafton	IL	62037	618-376-3303	
Web: dnr.state.il.us/Lands/Landmgt/PARKS/R4/MISS.HTM					
Moraine Hills State Park 914 S River Rd	McHenry	IL	60051	815-385-1624	
Web: dnr.state.il.us/Lands/Landmgt/PARKS/R2/MORHILLS.HTM					
Moraine View State Recreation Area 27374 Moraine View Park Rd	LeRoy	IL	61752	309-724-8032	
Web: dnr.state.il.us/lands/Landmgt/PARKS/R3/MORAINE.HTM					
Morrison-Rockwood State Park 18750 Lake Rd	Morrison	IL	61270	815-772-4708	
Web: dnr.state.il.us/Lands/Landmgt/PARKS/R1/MORRISON.HTM					
Nauvoo State Park PO Box 426	Nauvoo	IL	62354	217-453-2512	
Web: dnr.state.il.us/Lands/Landmgt/PARKS/R4/NAUVOO.HTM					
Newton Lake State Fish & Wildlife Area 3490 E 500th Ave	Newton	IL	62448	618-783-3478	
Web: dnr.state.il.us/Lands/Landmgt/PARKS/R5/NEWTON.HTM					
Peabody River King State Fish & Wildlife Area 10981 Conservation Rd	Baldwin	IL	62217	618-785-2555	
Web: dnr.state.il.us/Lands/Landmgt/PARKS/R4/PEABODY.HTM					
Pere Marquette State Park Rt 100 PO Box 158	Grafton	IL	62037	618-786-3323	
Web: dnr.state.il.us/Lands/Landmgt/PARKS/R4/Peremarq.htm					
Piney Creek Ravine State Natural Area c/o Randolph SFWA 4301 S Lake Dr	Chester	IL	62233	618-826-2706	
Web: dnr.state.il.us/lands/landmgt/PARKS/R4/pcr.htm					
Powerton Lake State Fish & Wildlife Area 7982 S Park Rd	Manito	IL	61546	309-968-7135	
Web: dnr.state.il.us/lands/Landmgt/PARKS/R1/POWERTON.HTM					
Prophetstown State Recreation Area Riverside Dr PO Box 181	Prophetstown	IL	61277	815-537-2926	
Web: dnr.state.il.us/Lands/Landmgt/PARKS/R1/PROPHET.HTM					
Pyramid State Recreation Area 1562 Pyramid Park Rd	Pinckneyville	IL	62274	618-357-2574	
Web: dnr.state.il.us/Lands/Landmgt/PARKS/R5/PYRAMID.HTM					
Ramsey Lake State Recreation Area Ramsey Lake Rd PO Box 97	Ramsey	IL	62080	618-423-2215	
Web: dnr.state.il.us/Lands/Landmgt/PARKS/R5/RAMSEY.HTM					
Randolph County State Recreation Area 4301 S Lake Dr	Chester	IL	62233	618-826-2706	
Web: dnr.state.il.us/Lands/Landmgt/PARKS/R4/RAND.HTM					
Ray Norbut State Fish & Wildlife Area RR 1 Box 55C	Griggsville	IL	62340	217-833-2811	
Web: dnr.state.il.us/Lands/Landmgt/PARKS/R4/ray.htm					
Red Hills State Park 1100 N and 400 E RR 2 Box 252A	Sumner	IL	62466	618-936-2469	
Web: dnr.state.il.us/Lands/Landmgt/PARKS/R5/REDHLS.HTM					
Rend Lake State Fish & Wildlife Area 10885 E Jefferson Rd	Bonnie	IL	62816	618-279-3110	
Web: dnr.state.il.us/Lands/Landmgt/PARKS/R5/RENDLAKE/REND.HTM					
Rice Lake State Fish & Wildlife Area 19721 N US Hwy 24	Canton	IL	61520	309-647-9184	
Web: dnr.state.il.us/Lands/Landmgt/PARKS/R1/Rice.htm					
Rock Cut State Park 7318 Harlem Rd	Loves Park	IL	61111	815-885-3311	
Web: dnr.state.il.us/Lands/Landmgt/PARKS/R1/ROCKCUT.HTM					
Rock Island Trail State Park 311 E Williams St PO Box 64	Wyoming	IL	61491	309-695-2228	
Web: dnr.state.il.us/Lands/Landmgt/PARKS/R1/ROCKISLE.HTM					
Saline County State Fish & Wildlife Area 85 Glen O Jones Rd	Equality	IL	62934	618-276-4405	
Web: dnr.state.il.us/Lands/Landmgt/PARKS/R5/SALINE.HTM					
Sam Dale Lake State Conservation Area RR 1	Johnsonville	IL	62850	618-835-2292	
Web: dnr.state.il.us/Lands/Landmgt/PARKS/R5/SAMDALE.HTM					
Sam Parr State Fish & Wildlife Area 13225 E State Hwy 33	Newton	IL	62448	618-783-2661	
Web: dnr.state.il.us/Lands/Landmgt/PARKS/R5/SAMPARR.HTM					
Sand Ridge State Forest PO Box 111	Forest City	IL	61532	309-597-2212	
Web: dnr.state.il.us/Lands/Landmgt/PARKS/R4/SAND.HTM					
Sanganois State Fish & Wildlife Area 3594 County Road 200 N	Chandlerville	IL	62627	309-546-2628	
Web: dnr.state.il.us/Lands/Landmgt/PARKS/R4/SANGILL.HTM					
Sangchris Lake State Park 9898 Cascade Rd	Rochester	IL	62563	217-498-9208	
Web: dnr.state.il.us/Lands/Landmgt/PARKS/R4/SANGCH.HTM					
Shabbona Lake State Park 4201 Shabbona Grove Rd	Shabbona	IL	60550	815-824-2106	
Web: dnr.state.il.us/Lands/Landmgt/PARKS/R1/SHABBONA.HTM					
Shelbyville State Fish & Wildlife Area RR 1 Box 42A	Bethany	IL	61914	217-665-3112	
Web: dnr.state.il.us/Lands/Landmgt/PARKS/R3/SHELBY.HTM					

Illinois (Cont'd)

Name / Address	City	State	Zip	Phone	Fax
Siloam Springs State Park 938 E 3003rd Ln *Web:* dnr.state.il.us/Lands/Landmgt/PARKS/R4/SILOAMSP.HTM	Clayton	IL	62324	217-894-6205	
Silver Springs State Fish & Wildlife Area 13608 Fox Rd *Web:* dnr.state.il.us/Lands/Landmgt/PARKS/R2/SILVERSP.HTM	Yorkville	IL	60560	630-553-6297	
Snakeden Hollow State Fish & Wildlife Area 1936 State Hwy 167 *Web:* dnr.state.il.us/Lands/Landmgt/PARKS/R1/SNAKE.HTM	Victoria	IL	61485	309-879-2607	
South Shore State Park c/o Eldon Hazlet State Recreation Area 20100 Hazlet Park Rd *Web:* dnr.state.il.us/Lands/Landmgt/PARKS/R4/sts.htm	Carlyle	IL	62231	618-594-3015	
Spitler Woods State Natural Area 705 Spitler Park Dr *Web:* dnr.state.il.us/Lands/Landmgt/PARKS/R3/SPITLER.HTM	Mount Zion	IL	62549	217-864-3121	
Spring Lake State Fish & Wildlife Area 7982 S Park Rd *Web:* dnr.state.il.us/Lands/Landmgt/PARKS/R1/SPL.HTM	Manito	IL	61546	309-968-7135	
Starved Rock State Park PO Box 509 *Web:* dnr.state.il.us/Lands/Landmgt/PARKS/I&M/EAST/STARVE/PARK.HTM	Utica	IL	61373	815-667-4726	
Stephen A. Forbes State Park 6924 Omega Rd *Web:* dnr.state.il.us/Lands/Landmgt/PARKS/R5/STEPHEN.HTM	Kinmundy	IL	62854	618-547-3381	
Ten Mile Creek State Fish & Wildlife Area RR 1 Box 179 *Web:* dnr.state.il.us/Lands/Landmgt/PARKS/R5/TEN.HTM	McLeansboro	IL	62859	618-643-2862	
Trail of Tears State Forest 3240 State Forest Rd *Web:* dnr.state.il.us/Lands/Landmgt/PARKS/R5/TRLTEARS.HTM	Jonesboro	IL	62952	618-833-4910	
Tunnel Hill State Trail Highway 146 E PO Box 671 *Web:* dnr.state.il.us/Lands/Landmgt/PARKS/R5/tunnel.htm	Vienna	IL	62995	618-658-2168	
Turkey Bluffs State Fish & Wildlife Area 4301 S Lakeside Dr	Chester	IL	62233	618-826-2706	
Union County State Fish & Wildlife Area 2755 Refuge Rd *Web:* dnr.state.il.us/Lands/Landmgt/PARKS/R5/UNIONCO.HTM	Jonesboro	IL	62952	618-833-5175	
Volo Bog State Natural Area 28478 W Brandenburg Rd *Web:* dnr.state.il.us/Lands/Landmgt/PARKS/R2/VOLOBOG.HTM	Ingleside	IL	60041	815-344-1294	
Walnut Point State Park 2331 E County Rd 370 N *Web:* dnr.state.il.us/lands/Landmgt/PARKS/R3/WALNUTPT.HTM	Oakland	IL	61943	217-346-3336	
Washington County State Recreation Area 18500 Conservation Dr *Web:* dnr.state.il.us/Lands/Landmgt/PARKS/R4/WASHCO.HTM	Nashville	IL	62263	618-327-3137	
Wayne Fitzgerrell State Recreation Area 11094 Ranger Rd *Web:* dnr.state.il.us/Lands/Landmgt/PARKS/R5/WAYNE.HTM	Whittington	IL	62897	618-629-2320	
Weinberg-King State Park PO Box 203 *Web:* dnr.state.il.us/Lands/Landmgt/PARKS/R4/WEINBERG.HTM	Augusta	IL	62311	217-392-2345	
Weldon Springs State Park 1159 500 N RR 2 Box 87 *Web:* dnr.state.il.us/Lands/Landmgt/PARKS/R3/WELDONRA.HTM	Clinton	IL	61727	217-935-2644	
White Pines Forest State Park 6712 W Pines Rd *Web:* dnr.state.il.us/Lands/Landmgt/PARKS/R1/WHITEPNS.HTM	Mount Morris	IL	61054	815-946-3717	
William G. Stratton State Park 401 Ottawa St	Morris	IL	60450	815-942-0796	
William W. Powers State Recreation Area 12949 Avenue O *Web:* dnr.state.il.us/Lands/Landmgt/PARKS/R2/Wmpow.htm	Chicago	IL	60633	773-646-3270	
Wolf Creek State Park RR 1 Box 99 *Web:* dnr.state.il.us/Lands/Landmgt/PARKS/R3/WOLFCREK.HTM	Windsor	IL	61957	217-459-2831	
Woodford State Fish & Wildlife Area RR 1 *Web:* dnr.state.il.us/lands/Landmgt/PARKS/R1/WOODFORD.HTM	Low Point	IL	61545	309-822-8861	

Indiana

Name / Address	City	State	Zip	Phone	Fax
Brookville Lake PO Box 100 *Web:* www.in.gov/dnr/parklake/properties/res_brookville.html	Brookville	IN	47012	765-647-2657	
Brown County State Park 1405 State Road 46 W PO Box 608 *Web:* www.in.gov/dnr/parklake/properties/park_browncounty.html	Nashville	IN	47448	812-988-6406	
Cagles Mill Lake 1317 W Lieber Rd, Suite 1 *Web:* www.in.gov/dnr/parklake/properties/res_caglesmill.html	Cloverdale	IN	46120	765-795-4576	
Cecil M. Harden Lake 1588 S Raccoon Pkwy *Web:* www.in.gov/dnr/parklake/properties/res_cecil.html	Rockville	IN	47872	765-344-1412	
Chain O'Lakes State Park 2355 E 75 South *Web:* www.in.gov/dnr/parklake/properties/park_chainolakes.html	Albion	IN	46701	260-636-2654	
Charlestown State Park PO Box 38 *Web:* www.in.gov/dnr/parklake/properties/park_charlestown.html	Charlestown	IN	47111	812-256-5600	
Clifty Falls State Park 1501 Green Rd *Web:* www.in.gov/dnr/parklake/properties/park_cliftyfalls.html	Madison	IN	47250	812-273-8885	
Deam Lake State Recreation Area 1217 Deam Lake Rd *Web:* www.in.gov/dnr/forestry/stateforests/deamlake.htm	Borden	IN	47106	812-246-5421	
Falls of the Ohio State Park 201 W Riverside Dr *Web:* www.in.gov/dnr/parklake/properties/park_fallsoftheohio.html	Clarksville	IN	47129	812-280-9970	280-7110
Fort Harrison State Park 5753 Glenn Rd *Web:* www.in.gov/dnr/parklake/properties/park_fortharrison.html	Indianapolis	IN	46216	317-591-0904	
Hardy Lake 4171 E Harrod Rd *Web:* www.in.gov/dnr/parklake/properties/res_hardy.html	Scottsburg	IN	47170	812-794-3800	
Harmonie State Park 3451 Harmonie State Park Rd *Web:* www.in.gov/dnr/parklake/properties/park_harmonie.html	New Harmony	IN	47631	812-682-4821	
Indiana Dunes State Park 1600 North 25 East *Web:* www.in.gov/dnr/parklake/properties/park_dunes.html	Chesterton	IN	46304	219-926-1952	
J. Edward Roush Lake 517 N Warren Rd *Web:* www.in.gov/dnr/parklake/reservoirs/huntington.html	Huntington	IN	46750	260-468-2165	
Lincoln State Park Highway 162 Box 216 *Web:* www.in.gov/dnr/parklake/properties/park_lincoln.html	Lincoln City	IN	47552	812-937-4710	
McCormick's Creek State Park 250 McCormick's Creek Rd *Web:* www.in.gov/dnr/parklake/properties/park_mccormick.html	Spencer	IN	47460	812-829-2235	
Mississinewa Lake 4673 S 625 East *Web:* www.in.gov/dnr/parklake/properties/res_mississinewa.html	Peru	IN	46970	765-473-6528	
Monroe Lake 4850 S State Rd 446 *Web:* www.in.gov/dnr/parklake/properties/res_monroe.html	Bloomington	IN	47401	812-837-9546	
Mounds State Park 4306 Mounds Rd *Web:* www.in.gov/dnr/parklake/properties/park_mounds.html	Anderson	IN	46017	765-642-6627	
O'Bannon Woods State Park 7240 Old Forest Rd *Web:* www.in.gov/dnr/forestry/stateforests/harcraw.htm	Corydon	IN	47112	812-738-8232	
Ouabache State Park 4930 E State Rd 201 *Web:* www.in.gov/dnr/parklake/properties/park_ouabache.html	Bluffton	IN	46714	260-824-0926	
Patoka Lake 3084 N Dillard Rd *Web:* www.in.gov/dnr/parklake/properties/res_patoka.html	Birdseye	IN	47513	812-685-2464	
Pokagon State Park 450 Ln 100 Lake James *Web:* www.in.gov/dnr/parklake/properties/park_pokagon.html	Angola	IN	46703	260-833-2012	
Potato Creek State Park 25601 State Rd 4 PO Box 908 *Web:* www.in.gov/dnr/parklake/properties/park_potatocreek.html	North Liberty	IN	46554	574-656-8186	
Salamonie Lake 9214 West-Lost Bridge W *Web:* www.in.gov/dnr/parklake/properties/res_salamonie.html	Andrews	IN	46702	260-468-2125	
Shades State Park Rt 1 Box 72 *Web:* www.in.gov/dnr/parklake/properties/park_shades.html	Waveland	IN	47989	765-435-2810	
Shakamak State Park 6265 W State Rd 48 *Web:* www.in.gov/dnr/parklake/properties/park_shakamak.html	Jasonville	IN	47438	812-665-2158	
Spring Mill State Park Box 376 *Web:* www.in.gov/dnr/parklake/properties/park_springmill.html	Mitchell	IN	47446	812-849-4129	
Starve Hollow State Recreation Area 4345 S County Rd 275 W *Web:* www.in.gov/dnr/forestry/stateforests/starvhlw.htm	Vallonia	IN	47281	812-358-3464	
Summit Lake State Park 5993 N Messick Rd *Web:* www.in.gov/dnr/parklake/properties/park_summitlake.html	New Castle	IN	47362	765-766-5873	
Tippecanoe River State Park 4200 N US Hwy 35 *Web:* www.in.gov/dnr/parklake/properties/park_tippecanoeriver.html	Winamac	IN	46996	574-946-3213	
Turkey Run State Park 8121 E Park Rd *Web:* www.in.gov/dnr/parklake/properties/park_turkeyrun.html	Marshall	IN	47859	765-597-2635	
Versailles State Park Box 205 US Hwy 50 *Web:* www.in.gov/dnr/parklake/properties/park_versailles.html	Versailles	IN	47042	812-689-6424	
White River State Park 801 W Washington St *TF:* 800-665-9056 ■ *Web:* www.in.gov/whiteriver	Indianapolis	IN	46204	317-233-2434	233-2367
Whitewater Memorial State Park 1418 S State Rd 101 *Web:* www.in.gov/dnr/parklake/properties/park_whitewater.html	Liberty	IN	47353	765-458-5565	
Wyandotte Caves State Recreation Area 7315 S Wyandotte Cave Rd *Web:* www.in.gov/dnr/forestry/stateforests/wyandtcv.htm	Leavenworth	IN	47137	812-738-2782	

Iowa

Name / Address	City	State	Zip	Phone	Fax
Ambrose A. Call State Park Rt 1 Box 264 *Web:* www.iowadnr.com/parks/state_park_list/ambrose.html	Algona	IA	50511	515-295-3669	
Backbone State Park 1347 129th St *Web:* www.iowadnr.com/parks/state_park_list/backbone.html	Dundee	IA	52038	563-924-2527	924-2827
Badger Creek State Recreation Area c/o Walnut Woods State Park 8951 SW 52nd Ave	North Des Moines	IA	50265	515-285-4502	
Beed's Lake State Park 1422 165th St *Web:* www.iowadnr.com/parks/state_park_list/beeds.html	Hampton	IA	50441	641-456-2047	
Bellevue State Park 24668 Hwy 52 *Web:* www.iowadnr.com/parks/state_park_list/bellevue.html	Bellevue	IA	52031	563-872-4019	872-4773
Big Creek State Park 12397 NW 89th Ct *Web:* www.iowadnr.com/parks/state_park_list/big_creek.html	Polk City	IA	50226	515-984-6473	984-9320
Black Hawk State Park 228 S Blossom *Web:* www.iowadnr.com/parks/state_park_list/black_hawk.html	Lake View	IA	51450	712-657-8712	657-0999
Brushy Creek State Recreation Area 3175 290th St *Web:* www.iowadnr.com/parks/state_park_list/brushy_creek.html	Lehigh	IA	50557	515-543-8298	843-8395
Cedar Rock PO Box 250 *Web:* www.iowadnr.com/parks/state_park_list/cedar_rock.html	Quasqueton	IA	52326	319-934-3572	
Clear Lake State Park 2730 S Lakeview Dr *Web:* www.iowadnr.com/parks/state_park_list/clear_lake.html	Clear Lake	IA	50428	641-357-4212	357-4242
Dolliver Memorial State Park 2757 Dolliver Park Ave *Web:* www.iowadnr.com/parks/state_park_list/dolliver.html	Lehigh	IA	50557	515-359-2539	359-2542
Elinor Bedell State Park c/o Gull Point State Park 1500 Harpen St *Web:* www.iowadnr.com/parks/state_park_list/elinor_bedell.html	Milford	IA	51351	712-337-3211	
Elk Rock State Park 811 146th Ave *Web:* www.iowadnr.com/parks/state_park_list/elk_rock.html	Knoxville	IA	50138	641-842-6008	
Fairport State Recreation Area c/o Wildcat Den State Park 1884 Wildcat Den Rd *Web:* www.iowadnr.com/parks/state_park_list/fairport.html	Muscatine	IA	52761	563-263-4337	264-8329
Fort Atkinson State Preserve c/o Volga River State Recreation Area 10225 Ivy Rd *Web:* www.iowadnr.com/parks/state_park_list/fort_atkinson.html	Fayette	IA	52142	563-425-4161	
Fort Defiance State Park c/o Gull Point State Park 1500 Harpen St *Web:* www.iowadnr.com/parks/state_park_list/fort_defiance.html	Milford	IA	51351	712-337-3211	
Geode State Park 3249 Racine Ave *Web:* www.iowadnr.com/parks/state_park_list/geode.html	Danville	IA	52623	319-392-4601	
George Wyth Memorial State Park 3659 Wyth Rd *Web:* www.iowadnr.com/parks/state_park_list/george_wyth.html	Waterloo	IA	50703	319-232-5505	232-1508
Green Valley State Park 1480 130th St *Web:* www.iowadnr.com/parks/state_park_list/green_valley.html	Creston	IA	50801	641-782-5131	782-8330
Gull Point State Park 1500 Harpen St *Web:* www.iowadnr.com/parks/state_park_list/gull_point.html	Milford	IA	51351	712-337-3211	
Honey Creek State Park 12194 Honey Creek Pl *Web:* www.iowadnr.com/parks/state_park_list/honey_creek.html	Moravia	IA	52571	641-724-3739	724-9846
Lacey-Keosauqua State Park PO Box 398 *Web:* www.iowadnr.com/parks/state_park_list/lacey_keo.html	Keosauqua	IA	52565	319-293-3502	293-3329
Lake Ahquabi State Park 1650 118th Ave *Web:* www.iowadnr.com/parks/state_park_list/lake_ahquabi.html	Indianola	IA	50125	515-961-7101	962-9424
Lake Anita State Park 55111 750th St *Web:* www.iowadnr.com/parks/state_park_list/lake_anita.html	Anita	IA	50020	712-762-3564	762-4352
Lake Darling State Park 111 Lake Darling Rd *Web:* www.iowadnr.com/parks/state_park_list/lake_darling.html	Brighton	IA	52540	319-694-2323	
Lake Keomah State Park 2720 Keomah Ln *Web:* www.iowadnr.com/parks/state_park_list/lake_keomah.html	Oskaloosa	IA	52577	641-673-6975	673-0647
Lake Macbride State Park 3525 Hwy 382 NE *Web:* www.iowadnr.com/parks/state_park_list/lake_macbride.html	Solon	IA	52333	319-624-2200	624-2188
Lake Manawa State Park 1100 South Shore Dr *Web:* www.iowadnr.com/parks/state_park_list/lake_manawa.html	Council Bluffs	IA	51501	712-366-0220	366-0474
Lake of Three Fires State Park 2303 Lake Rd *Web:* www.iowadnr.com/parks/state_park_list/lake_three_fires.html	Bedford	IA	50833	712-523-2700	523-3104
Lake Wapello State Park 15248 Campground Rd *Web:* www.iowadnr.com/parks/state_park_list/lake_wapello.html	Drakesville	IA	52552	641-722-3371	722-3384
Ledges State Park 1519 250th St *Web:* www.iowadnr.com/parks/state_park_list/ledges.html	Madrid	IA	50156	515-432-1852	432-0757
Lewis & Clark State Park 21914 Park Loop *Web:* www.iowadnr.com/parks/state_park_list/lewis_clark.html	Onawa	IA	51040	712-423-2829	
Maquoketa Caves State Park 10970 98th St *Web:* www.iowadnr.com/parks/state_park_list/maquoketa_caves.html	Maquoketa	IA	52060	563-652-5833	652-0061
McIntosh Woods State Park 1200 E Lake St *Web:* www.iowadnr.com/parks/state_park_list/mcintosh_woods.html	Ventura	IA	50482	641-829-3847	829-3841
Mines of Spain State Recreation Area 8991 Bellevue Heights *Web:* www.iowadnr.com/parks/state_park_list/mines_spain.html	Dubuque	IA	52003	563-556-0620	556-8474
Nine Eagles State Park RR 1 *Web:* www.iowadnr.com/parks/state_park_list/nine_eagles.html	Davis City	IA	50065	641-442-2855	442-2856
Palisades-Kepler State Park 700 Kepler Dr *Web:* www.iowadnr.com/parks/state_park_list/palisades.html	Mount Vernon	IA	52314	319-895-6039	895-9660
Pikes Peak State Park 15316 Great River Rd *Web:* www.iowadnr.com/parks/state_park_list/pikes_peak.html	McGregor	IA	52157	563-873-2341	873-3167
Pilot Knob State Park 2148 340th St *Web:* www.iowadnr.com/parks/state_park_list/pilot_knob.html	Forest City	IA	50436	641-581-4835	
Pine Lake State Park 22620 County Hwy S56 *Web:* www.iowadnr.com/parks/state_park_list/pine_lake.html	Eldora	IA	50627	641-858-5832	858-5641
Pleasant Creek State Recreation Area 4530 McClintock Rd *Web:* www.iowadnr.com/parks/state_park_list/pleasant_creek.html	Palo	IA	52324	319-436-7716	436-7715
Prairie Rose State Park 680 Rd M47 *Web:* www.iowadnr.com/parks/state_park_list/prairie_rose.html	Harlan	IA	51537	712-773-2701	773-2702
Preparation Canyon State Park c/o Lewis and Clark State Park 21914 Park Loop *Web:* www.iowadnr.com/parks/state_park_list/preparation_canyon.html	Onawa	IA	51040	712-423-2829	
Red Haw State Park 24550 US Hwy 34 *Web:* www.iowadnr.com/parks/state_park_list/red_haw.html	Chariton	IA	50049	641-774-5632	774-8821
Rice Lake State Park c/o Ambrose A. Call State Park Rt 1, Box 264	Algona	IA	50511	641-581-4835	
Rock Creek State Park 5627 Rock Creek E *Web:* www.iowadnr.com/parks/state_park_list/rock_creek.html	Kellogg	IA	50135	641-236-3722	236-5599

	City	State	Zip	Phone	Fax
Shimek State Forest 33653 Route J56 *Web:* www.iowadnr.com/forestry/shimek.html	Farmington	IA	52626	319-878-3811	
Springbrook State Park 2437 160th Rd *Web:* www.iowadnr.com/parks/state_park_list/springbrook.html	Guthrie Center	IA	50115	641-747-3591	747-8401
Stephens State Forest 1111 N 8th St *Web:* www.iowadnr.com/forestry/stephens.html	Chariton	IA	50049	641-774-4559	
Stone State Park 5001 Talbot Rd *Web:* www.iowadnr.com/parks/state_park_list/stone.html	Sioux City	IA	51103	712-255-4698	
Twin Lakes State Park c/o Black Hawk Lake State Park 228 S Blossom St *Web:* www.iowadnr.gov/parks/	Lake View	IA	51450	712-657-8712	657-2289
Union Grove State Park 1215 220th St *Web:* www.iowadnr.com/parks/state_park_list/union_grove.html	Gladbrook	IA	50635	641-473-2556	473-3059
Viking Lake State Park 2780 Viking Lake Rd *Web:* www.iowadnr.com/parks/state_park_list/viking_lake.html	Stanton	IA	51573	712-829-2235	829-2842
Volga River State Recreation Area 10225 Ivy Rd *Web:* www.iowadnr.com/parks/state_park_list/volga_river.html	Fayette	IA	52142	563-425-4161	425-3004
Walnut Woods State Park 3155 Walnut Woods Dr *Web:* www.iowadnr.com/parks/state_park_list/walnut_woods.html	West Des Moines	IA	50265	515-285-4502	285-7476
Wapsipinicon State Park 21301 County Rd E34 *Web:* www.iowadnr.com/parks/state_park_list/wapsipinicon.html	Anamosa	IA	52205	319-462-2761	462-4878
Waubonsie State Park 2585 Waubonsie Park Rd *Web:* www.iowadnr.com/parks/state_park_list/waubonsie.html	Hamburg	IA	51640	712-382-2786	382-9860
Wildcat Den State Park 1884 Wildcat Den Rd *Web:* www.iowadnr.com/parks/state_park_list/wildcat_den.html	Muscatine	IA	52761	563-263-4337	264-8329
Wilson Island State Recreation Area 32801 Campground Ln *Web:* www.iowadnr.com/parks/state_park_list/wilson_island.html	Missouri Valley	IA	51555	712-642-2069	642-4390
Yellow River State Forest 729 State Forest Rd *Web:* www.iowadnr.com/forestry/yellowriver.html	Harpers Ferry	IA	52146	563-586-2254	

Kansas

	City	State	Zip	Phone	Fax
Cedar Bluff State Park Rt 2 Box 76A *Web:* www.kdwp.state.ks.us/news/state_parks/locations/cedar_bluff	Ellis	KS	67637	785-726-3212	
Cheney State Park 16000 NE 50th St *Web:* www.kdwp.state.ks.us/news/state_parks/locations/cheney	Cheney	KS	67025	316-542-3664	542-9979
Clinton State Park 798 N 1415 Rd *Web:* www.kdwp.state.ks.us/news/state_parks/locations/clinton	Lawrence	KS	66049	785-842-8562	
Crawford State Park 1 Lake Rd *Web:* www.kdwp.state.ks.us/news/state_parks/locations/crawford	Farlington	KS	66734	620-362-3671	
Cross Timbers State Park 144 Hwy 105 *Web:* www.kdwp.state.ks.us/news/state_parks/locations/cross_timbers	Toronto	KS	66777	620-637-2213	
Eisenhower State Park 29810 S Fairlawn Rd *Web:* www.kdwp.state.ks.us/news/state_parks/locations/eisenhower	Lyndon	KS	66523	785-528-4102	
El Dorado State Park 618 NE Bluestem Rd *Web:* www.kdwp.state.ks.us/news/state_parks/locations/el_dorado	El Dorado	KS	67042	316-321-7180	
Elk City State Park 4825 Squaw Creek Rd *Web:* www.kdwp.state.ks.us/news/state_parks/locations/elk_city	Independence	KS	67301	620-331-6295	
Fall River State Park 144 Hwy 105 *Web:* www.kdwp.state.ks.us/news/state_parks/locations/fall_river	Toronto	KS	66777	620-637-2213	
Glen Elder State Park 2131 180 Rd *Web:* www.kdwp.state.ks.us/news/state_parks/locations/glen_elder	Glen Elder	KS	67446	785-545-3345	
Hillsdale State Park 26001 W 255th St *Web:* www.kdwp.state.ks.us/news/state_parks/locations/hillsdale	Paola	KS	66071	913-783-4507	
Kanopolis State Park 200 Horsethief Rd *Web:* www.kdwp.state.ks.us/news/state_parks/locations/kanopolis	Marquette	KS	67464	785-546-2565	
Lovewell State Park 2446 250 Rd *Web:* www.kdwp.state.ks.us/news/state_parks/locations/lovewell	Webber	KS	66970	785-753-4971	
Meade State Park 13051 V Rd *Web:* www.kdwp.state.ks.us/news/state_parks/locations/meade	Meade	KS	67864	620-873-2572	
Milford State Park 8811 State Park Rd *Web:* www.kdwp.state.ks.us/news/state_parks/locations/milford	Milford	KS	66514	785-238-3014	
Mushroom Rock State Park 200 Horsethief Rd *Web:* www.kdwp.state.ks.us/news/state_parks/locations/mushroom_rock	Marquette	KS	67464	785-546-2565	
Perry State Park 5441 Westlake Rd *Web:* www.kdwp.state.ks.us/news/state_parks/locations/perry	Ozawkie	KS	66070	785-246-3449	246-0224
Pomona State Park 22900 S Hwy 368 *Web:* www.kdwp.state.ks.us/news/state_parks/locations/pomona	Vassar	KS	66543	785-828-4933	
Prairie Dog State Park PO Box 431 *Web:* www.kdwp.state.ks.us/news/state_parks/locations/prairie_dog	Norton	KS	67654	785-877-2953	
Prairie Spirit Trail State Park 419 S Oak St *Web:* www.kdwp.state.ks.us/news/state_parks/locations/prairie_spirit_trail	Garnett	KS	66032	785-448-6767	
Sand Hills State Park 4207 E 56th *Web:* www.kdwp.state.ks.us/news/state_parks/locations/sand_hills	Hutchinson	KS	67502	316-542-3664	
Scott State Park 520 W Scott Lake Dr *Web:* www.kdwp.state.ks.us/news/state_parks/locations/scott	Scott City	KS	67871	620-872-2061	
Tuttle Creek State Park 5800-A River Pond Rd *Web:* www.kdwp.state.ks.us/news/state_parks/locations/tuttle_creek	Manhattan	KS	66502	785-539-7941	
Webster State Park 1210 Nine Rd *Web:* www.kdwp.state.ks.us/news/state_parks/locations/webster	Stockton	KS	67669	785-425-6775	
Wilson State Park Rt 1 Box 181 *Web:* www.kdwp.state.ks.us/news/state_parks/locations/wilson	Sylvan Grove	KS	67481	785-658-2465	

Kentucky

	City	State	Zip	Phone	Fax
Barren River Lake State Resort Park 1149 State Park Rd *Fax Area Code: 270 ■ *TF:* 800-325-0057 ■ *Web:* www.parks.ky.gov/resortparks/br	Lucas	KY	42156	800-325-0057	646-3645*
Ben Hawes State Park 400 Boothfield Rd *Web:* www.parks.ky.gov/stateparks/bh	Owensboro	KY	42301	270-684-9808	
Big Bone Lick State Park 3380 Beaver Rd *Web:* www.parks.ky.gov/stateparks/bb	Union	KY	41091	859-384-3522	
Blue Licks Battlefield State Resort Park Highway 68 *Web:* www.parks.ky.gov/resortparks/bl	Mount Olivet	KY	41064	800-443-7008	
Boone Station State Historic Site 240 Gentry Rd *Web:* parks.ky.gov/statehistoricsites/bs	Lexington	KY	40502	859-263-1073	
Buckhorn Lake State Resort Park 4441 Kentucky Hwy 1833 *Web:* www.parks.ky.gov/resortparks/bk	Buckhorn	KY	41721	800-325-0058	
Carr Creek State Park Highway 15 *Web:* www.parks.ky.gov/stateparks/ck	Sassafras	KY	41759	606-642-4050	
Carter Caves State Resort Park 344 Caveland Dr *Web:* www.parks.ky.gov/resortparks/cc	Olive Hill	KY	41164	800-325-0059	
Columbus-Belmont State Park 350 Park Rd *Web:* www.parks.ky.gov/stateparks/cb	Columbus	KY	42032	270-677-2327	
Constitution Square State Historic Site 134 S 2nd St *Web:* parks.ky.gov/statehistoricsites/cs	Danville	KY	40422	859-239-7089	
Cumberland Falls State Resort Park 7351 Hwy 90 *Web:* www.parks.ky.gov/resortparks/cf	Corbin	KY	40701	800-325-0063	
Dale Hollow Lake State Resort Park 6371 State Park Rd *Web:* www.parks.ky.gov/resortparks/dh	Burkesville	KY	42717	800-325-2282	
Dr. Thomas Walker State Historic Site 4929 KY 459 *Web:* parks.ky.gov/statehistoricsites/dt	Barbourville	KY	40906	606-546-4400	
E P "Tom" Sawyer State Park 3000 Freys Hill Rd *Web:* www.parks.ky.gov/stateparks/ep	Louisville	KY	40241	502-426-8950	429-7273
Fort Boonesborough State Park 4375 Boonesborough Rd *Web:* parks.ky.gov/stateparks/fb	Richmond	KY	40475	859-527-3131	
General Burnside Island State Park 8801 S Highway 27 *Web:* parks.ky.gov/stateparks/ge	Burnside	KY	42519	606-561-4104	
General Butler State Resort Park 1608 Highway 227 *Web:* www.parks.ky.gov/resortparks/gb	Carrollton	KY	41008	866-462-8853	
Grayson Lake State Park 314 Grayson Lake Park Rd *Web:* parks.ky.gov/stateparks/gl	Olive Hill	KY	41164	606-474-9727	
Green River Lake State Park 179 Park Office Rd *Web:* parks.ky.gov/stateparks/gr	Campbellsville	KY	42718	270-465-8255	
Greenbo Lake State Resort Park HC 60 Box 562 *Web:* www.parks.ky.gov/resortparks/go	Greenup	KY	41144	800-325-0083	
Isaac Shelby Cemetery State Historic Site 6725 Kentucky Hwy 300 *Web:* parks.ky.gov/statehistoricsites/is	Stanford	KY	40484	859-239-7089	
Jefferson Davis Monument State Historic Site Highway 68 E *Web:* parks.ky.gov/statehistoricsites/jd	Fairview	KY	42221	270-886-1765	
Jenny Wiley State Resort Park 75 Theatre Ct *Web:* www.parks.ky.gov/resortparks/jw	Prestonsburg	KY	41653	800-325-0142	
John James Audubon State Park 3100 US Hwy 41 N *Web:* www.parks.ky.gov/stateparks/au	Henderson	KY	42419	270-826-2247	
Kenlake State Resort Park 542 Kenlake Rd *Web:* www.parks.ky.gov/resortparks/kl	Hardin	KY	42048	800-325-1043	
Kentucky Dam Village State Resort Park 166 Upper Village Dr *Web:* www.parks.ky.gov/resortparks/kd	Gilbertsville	KY	42044	800-325-0146	
Kincaid Lake State Park 565 Kincaid Park Rd *Web:* parks.ky.gov/stateparks/kn	Falmouth	KY	41040	859-654-3531	
Kingdom Come State Park 502 Park Rd *Web:* parks.ky.gov/stateparks/kc	Cumberland	KY	40823	606-589-2479	
Lake Barkley State Resort Park 3500 State Park Rd *Web:* www.parks.ky.gov/resortparks/lb	Cadiz	KY	42211	800-325-1708	
Lake Cumberland State Resort Park 5465 State Park Rd *Web:* www.parks.ky.gov/resortparks/lc	Jamestown	KY	42629	800-325-1709	
Lake Malone State Park 331 State Rd 8001 *Web:* parks.ky.gov/stateparks/lm	Dunmor	KY	42339	270-657-2111	
Levi Jackson State Park 998 Levi Jackson Mill Rd *Web:* parks.ky.gov/stateparks/lj	London	KY	40744	606-878-8000	
Lincoln Homestead State Park 5079 Lincoln Park Rd *Web:* parks.ky.gov/stateparks/lh	Springfield	KY	40069	859-336-7461	
Mineral Mound State Park 48 Finch Ln *Web:* parks.ky.gov/stateparks/mm	Eddyville	KY	42038	270-388-3673	
My Old Kentucky Home State Park 501 E Stephen Foster Ave *Web:* parks.ky.gov/stateparks/mk	Bardstown	KY	40004	502-348-3502	
Natural Bridge State Resort Park 2135 Natural Bridge Rd *Web:* www.parks.ky.gov/resortparks/nb	Slade	KY	40376	800-325-1710	
Nolin Lake State Park PO Box 340 *Web:* parks.ky.gov/stateparks/nl	Bee Spring	KY	42207	270-286-4240	
Old Fort Harrod State Park 100 S College St *Web:* parks.ky.gov/stateparks/fh	Harrodsburg	KY	40330	859-734-3314	
Old Mulkey Meetinghouse State Historic Site 1819 Old Mulkey Park Rd *Web:* parks.ky.gov/statehistoricsites/om	Tompkinsville	KY	42167	270-487-8481	
Paintsville Lake State Park PO Box 920 *Web:* parks.ky.gov/stateparks/pl	Staffordsville	KY	41256	606-297-8486	
Pennyrile Forest State Resort Park 20781 Pennyrile Lodge Rd *Web:* www.parks.ky.gov/resortparks/pf	Dawson Springs	KY	42408	800-325-1711	
Perryville Battlefield State Historic Site 1825 Battlefield Rd *Web:* parks.ky.gov/statehistoricsites/pb	Perryville	KY	40468	606-332-8631	
Pine Mountain State Resort Park 1050 State Park Rd *Web:* www.parks.ky.gov/resortparks/pm	Pineville	KY	40977	800-325-1712	
Rough River Dam State Resort Park 450 Lodge Rd *Web:* www.parks.ky.gov/resortparks/rr	Falls of Rough	KY	40119	800-325-1713	
Taylorsville Lake State Park 1320 Park Rd *Web:* parks.ky.gov/stateparks/tl	Taylorsville	KY	40071	502-477-8713	
Waveland Museum State Historic Site 225 Waveland Museum Ln *Web:* parks.ky.gov/statehistoricsites/wv	Lexington	KY	40514	859-272-3611	
White Hall State Historic Site 500 White Hall Shrine Rd *Web:* parks.ky.gov/statehistoricsites/wh	Richmond	KY	40475	859-623-9178	
William Whitley House State Historic Site 625 William Whitley Rd *Web:* parks.ky.gov/statehistoricsites/ww	Stanford	KY	40484	606-355-2881	
Yatesville Lake State Park PO Box 767 *Web:* parks.ky.gov/stateparks/yl	Louisa	KY	41230	606-673-1492	

Louisiana

	City	State	Zip	Phone	Fax
Audubon State Historic Site 11788 Louisiana Hwy 965 *TF:* 888-677-2838 ■ *Web:* www.crt.state.la.us/parks/iaudubon.aspx	Saint Francisville	LA	70775	225-635-3739	784-0578
Bayou Segnette State Park 7777 Westbank Expy *TF:* 888-677-2296 ■ *Web:* www.crt.state.la.us/parks/ibyusegne.aspx	Westwego	LA	70094	504-736-7140	436-4788
Centenary State Historic Site 3522 College St *TF:* 888-677-2364 ■ *Web:* www.crt.state.la.us/parks/icentenary.aspx	Jackson	LA	70748	225-634-7925	
Chemin-A-Haut State Park 14656 State Park Rd *TF:* 888-677-2436 ■ *Web:* www.crt.state.la.us/parks/icheminah.aspx	Bastrop	LA	71220	318-283-0812	
Chicot State Park 3469 Chicot Park Rd *TF:* 888-677-2442 ■ *Web:* www.crt.state.la.us/parks/ichicot.aspx	Ville Platte	LA	70586	337-363-2403	
Cypremort Point State Park 306 Beach Ln *TF:* 888-867-4510 ■ *Web:* www.crt.state.la.us/parks/iCyprempt.aspx	Cypremort Point	LA	70538	337-867-4510	
Fairview-Riverside State Park 119 Fairview Dr *TF:* 888-677-3247 ■ *Web:* www.crt.state.la.us/parks/iFairview.aspx	Madisonville	LA	70447	985-845-3318	
Fontainebleau State Park 67825 US Hwy 190 *TF:* 888-677-3668 ■ *Web:* www.crt.state.la.us/parks/iFontaine.aspx	Mandeville	LA	70448	985-624-4443	
Fort Jesup State Historic Site 32 Geoghagan Rd *TF:* 888-677-5378 ■ *Web:* www.crt.state.la.us/parks/iFtjesup.aspx	Many	LA	71449	318-256-4117	
Fort Pike State Historic Site 27100 Chef Menteur Hwy *TF:* 888-662-5703 ■ *Web:* www.crt.state.la.us/parks/iFortpike.aspx	New Orleans	LA	70129	504-662-5703	
Fort Saint Jean Baptiste State Historic Site 155 Rue Jefferson *TF:* 888-677-7853 ■ *Web:* www.crt.state.la.us/parks/iftstjean.aspx	Natchitoches	LA	71457	318-357-3101	
Grand Isle State Park Admiral Craig Dr *TF:* 888-787-2559 ■ *Web:* www.crt.state.la.us/parks/igrdisle.aspx	Grand Isle	LA	70358	985-787-2559	
Jimmie Davis State Park 1209 State Park Rd *TF:* 888-677-2263 ■ *Web:* www.crt.state.la.us/parks/ijimmiedavis.aspx	Chatham	LA	71226	318-249-2595	
Lake Bistineau State Park 103 State Park Rd *TF:* 888-677-2478 ■ *Web:* www.crt.state.la.us/parks/ibistino.aspx	Doyline	LA	71023	318-745-3503	
Lake Bruin State Park 201 State Park Rd *TF:* 888-677-2784 ■ *Web:* www.crt.state.la.us/parks/iLkbruin.aspx	Saint Joseph	LA	71366	318-766-3530	
Lake Claiborne State Park 225 State Park Rd *TF:* 888-677-2524 ■ *Web:* www.crt.state.la.us/parks/iClaiborn.aspx	Homer	LA	71040	318-927-2976	

Louisiana (Cont'd)

Phone Fax

Lake D'Arbonne State Park 3628 Evergreen Rd............Farmerville LA 71241 318-368-2086
TF: 888-677-5200 ■ *Web:* www.crt.state.la.us/parks/iDarbonne.aspx
Lake Fausse Pointe State Park 5400 Levee Rd............Saint Martinville LA 70582 318-229-4764
TF: 888-677-7200 ■ *Web:* www.crt.state.la.us/parks/ilakefaus.aspx
Locust Grove State Historic Site
c/o Audubon State Historic Site PO Box 546............Saint Francisville LA 70775 225-635-3739
TF: 888-677-2838 ■ *Web:* www.crt.state.la.us/parks/ilocust.aspx
Longfellow-Evangeline State Historic Site
1200 N Main St............Saint Martinville LA 70582 337-394-3754
TF: 888-677-2900 ■ *Web:* www.crt.state.la.us/parks/ilongfell.aspx
Los Adaes State Historic Site 6354 Hwy 485............Robeline LA 71469 318-472-9449
TF: 888-677-5378 ■ *Web:* www.crt.state.la.us/parks/iLosadaes.aspx
Louisiana State Arboretum 4213 Chicot Park Rd............Ville Platte LA 70586 337-363-6289
TF: 888-677-6100 ■ *Web:* www.crt.state.la.us/parks/iarbor.aspx
Mansfield State Historic Site 15149 Hwy 175............Mansfield LA 71052 318-872-1474
TF: 888-677-6267 ■ *Web:* www.crt.state.la.us/parks/iMansfld.aspx
Marksville State Historic Site 837 ML King Dr............Marksville LA 71351 318-253-8954
TF: 888-253-8954 ■ *Web:* www.crt.state.la.us/parks/iMarksvle.aspx
North Toledo Bend State Park 2907 N Toledo Park Rd............Zwolle LA 71486 318-645-4715
TF: 888-677-6400 ■ *Web:* www.crt.state.la.us/parks/intoledo.aspx
Palmetto Island State Park
c/o Louisiana Office of State Parks PO Box 44426............Baton Rouge LA 70804 225-342-8111
TF: 888-677-1400 ■ *Web:* www.crt.state.la.us/parks/iconstruction.aspx
Plaquemine Lock State Historic Site 57730 Main St............Plaquemine LA 70764 225-687-7158
TF: 877-987-7158 ■ *Web:* www.crt.state.la.us/parks/iPlaqlock.aspx
Port Hudson State Historic Site 236 Hwy 61............Jackson LA 70748 225-654-3775 654-4413
TF: 888-677-3400 ■ *Web:* www.crt.state.la.us/parks/ipthudson.aspx
Poverty Point Reservoir State Park 1500 Poverty Point Pkwy............Delhi LA 71232 318-878-7536
TF: 800-474-0392 ■ *Web:* www.crt.state.la.us/parks/ireservoir.aspx
Poverty Point State Historic Site 6859 Hwy 577............Pioneer LA 71266 318-926-5492
TF: 888-926-5492 ■ *Web:* www.crt.state.la.us/parks/ipvertypt.aspx
Rebel State Historic Site 1260 Hwy 1221............Marthaville LA 71450 318-472-6255
TF: 888-677-3600 ■ *Web:* www.crt.state.la.us/parks/irebel.aspx
Rosedown Plantation State Historic Site
12501 LA Hwy 10............Saint Francisville LA 70775 225-635-3322
TF: 888-376-1867 ■ *Web:* www.crt.state.la.us/parks/irosedown.aspx
Saint Bernard State Park 501 St Bernard Pkwy............Braithwaite LA 70040 504-682-2101
TF: 888-677-7823 ■ *Web:* www.crt.state.la.us/parks/iStbernrd.aspx
Sam Houston Jones State Park 107 Sutherland Rd............Lake Charles LA 70611 337-855-2665
TF: 888-677-7264 ■ *Web:* www.crt.state.la.us/parks/iShjones.aspx
South Toledo Bend State Park 120 Bald Eaglel Rd............Anacoco LA 71403 337-286-9075
TF: 888-398-4770 ■ *Web:* www.crt.state.la.us/parks/istb.aspx
Tickfaw State Park 27225 Patterson Rd............Springfield LA 70462 225-294-5020
TF: 888-981-2020 ■ *Web:* www.crt.state.la.us/parks/itickfaw.aspx
Winter Quarters State Historic Site 4929 Hwy 608............Newellton LA 71357 318-467-9750
TF: 888-677-9468 ■ *Web:* www.crt.state.la.us/parks/iwinter.aspx

Maine

Phone Fax

Allagash Wilderness Waterway
c/o Bureau of Parks & Lands Northern Region 106 Hogan Rd............Bangor ME 04401 207-941-4014
Web: www.maine.gov/doc/parks/programs/db_search
Aroostook State Park 87 State Park Rd............Presque Isle ME 04769 207-768-8341
Web: www.maine.gov/doc/parks/programs/db_search
Baxter State Park 64 Balsam Dr............Millinocket ME 04462 207-723-5140
Web: www.baxterstateparkauthority.com
Birch Point State Park
c/o Bureau of Parks & Lands 106 Hogan Rd............Bangor ME 04401 207-941-4014
Web: www.maine.gov/doc/parks/programs/db_search
Bradbury Mountain State Park 528 Hallowell Rd............Pownal ME 04069 207-688-4712
Web: www.maine.gov/doc/parks/programs/db_search
Camden Hills State Park 280 Belfast Rd............Camden ME 04843 207-236-3109
Web: www.maine.gov/doc/parks/programs/db_search
Cobscook Bay State Park RR 1 Box 127............Dennysville ME 04628 207-726-4412
Web: www.maine.gov/doc/parks/programs/db_search
Colonial Pemaquid State Historic Site PO Box 117............New Harbor ME 04554 207-677-2423
Web: www.maine.gov/doc/parks/programs/db_search
Crescent Beach State Park 66 Two Lights Rd............Cape Elizabeth ME 04107 207-799-5871
Web: www.maine.gov/doc/parks/programs/db_search
Damariscotta Lake State Park 8 State Park Rd............Jefferson ME 04348 207-549-7600
Web: www.maine.gov/doc/parks/programs/db_search
Eagle Island State Historic Site PO Box 161............South Harpswell ME 04079 207-624-6075
Web: www.maine.gov/doc/parks/programs/db_search
Ferry Beach State Park 95 Bayview Rd............Saco ME 04072 207-283-0067
Web: www.maine.gov/doc/parks/programs/db_search
Fort Edgecomb State Historic Site 66 Fort Rd............Edgecomb ME 04556 207-882-7777
Web: www.maine.gov/doc/parks/programs/db_search
Fort Halifax State Historic Site
c/o Bureau of Parks & Lands 106 Hogan Rd............Bangor ME 04401 207-941-4014
Web: www.maine.gov/doc/parks/programs/db_search
Fort Kent State Historic Site
c/o Bureau of Parks & Lands 106 Hogan Rd............Bangor ME 04401 207-941-4014
Web: www.maine.gov/doc/parks/programs/db_search
Fort Knox State Historic Site 711 Fort Knox Rd............Prospect ME 04981 207-469-7719
Web: www.maine.gov/doc/parks/programs/db_search
Fort McClary State Historic Site 28 Oldfields Rd............South Berwick ME 03908 207-384-5160
Web: www.maine.gov/doc/parks/programs/db_search
Fort O'Brien State Historic Site
c/o Bureau of Parks & Lands 106 Hogan Rd............Bangor ME 04401 207-941-4014
Web: www.maine.gov/doc/parks/programs/db_search
Fort Point State Park
c/o Bureau of Parks & Lands 106 Hogan Rd............Bangor ME 04401 207-941-4014
Web: www.maine.gov/doc/parks/programs/db_search
Fort Popham State Historic Site 10 Perkins Farm Ln............Phippsburg ME 04562 207-389-1335
Web: www.maine.gov/doc/parks/programs/db_search
Grafton Notch State Park 1941 Bear River Rd............Newry ME 04261 207-824-2912
Web: www.maine.gov/doc/parks/programs/db_search
Holbrook Island Sanctuary PO Box 35............Brooksville ME 04617 207-326-4012
Web: www.maine.gov/doc/parks/programs/db_search
John Paul Jones State Historic Site
c/o Bureau of Parks & Lands 107 State House Stn............Augusta ME 04333 207-384-5160
Web: www.maine.gov/doc/parks/programs/db_search
Katahdin Iron Works State Historic Site
c/o Bureau of Parks & Lands 106 Hogan Rd............Bangor ME 04401 207-941-4014
Web: www.maine.gov/doc/parks/programs/db_search
Lake Saint George State Park 278 Belfast Augusta Rd............Liberty ME 04949 207-589-4255
Web: www.maine.gov/doc/parks/programs/db_search
Lamoine State Park 23 State Park Rd............Ellsworth ME 04605 207-667-4778
Web: www.maine.gov/doc/parks/programs/db_search
Lily Bay State Park 13 Myrle's Way............Greenville ME 04441 207-695-2700
Web: www.maine.gov/doc/parks/programs/db_search
Moose Point State Park 310 W Main St............Searsport ME 04974 207-548-2882
Web: www.maine.gov/doc/parks/programs/db_search
Mount Blue State Park 299 Center Hill Rd............Weld ME 04285 207-585-2347
Web: www.maine.gov/doc/parks/programs/db_search
Peacock Beach State Park RR 1, Box 2305............Richmond ME 04357 207-582-2813
Web: www.maine.gov/doc/parks/programs/db_search
Peaks-Kenny State Park 401 State Park Rd............Dover-Foxcroft ME 04426 207-564-2003
Web: www.maine.gov/doc/parks/programs/db_search
Popham Beach State Park 10 Perkins Farm Ln............Phippsburg ME 04562 207-389-1335
Web: www.maine.gov/doc/parks/programs/db_search
Quoddy Head State Park 973 S Lubec Rd............Lubec ME 04652 207-733-0911
Web: www.maine.gov/doc/parks/programs/db_search
Range Ponds State Park PO Box 475............Poland Spring ME 04274 207-998-4104
Web: www.maine.gov/doc/parks/programs/db_search
Rangeley Lake State Park HC 32 Box 5000............Rangeley ME 04970 207-864-3858
Web: www.maine.gov/doc/parks/programs/db_search
Reid State Park 375 Seguinland Rd............Georgetown ME 04548 207-371-2303
Web: www.maine.gov/doc/parks/programs/db_search
Roque Bluffs State Park 145 Schoppee Point Rd............Roque Bluffs ME 04654 207-255-3475
Web: www.maine.gov/doc/parks/programs/db_search
Sebago Lake State Park 11 Park Access Rd............Casco ME 04055 207-693-6613
Web: www.maine.gov/doc/parks/programs/db_search
Shackford Head State Park
c/o Bureau of Parks & Lands 106 Hogan Ave............Bangor ME 04401 207-941-4014
Web: www.maine.gov/doc/parks/programs/db_search
Swan Lake State Park 100 W Park Ln............Swanville ME 04915 207-525-4404
Web: www.maine.gov/doc/parks/programs/db_search
Two Lights State Park 7 tower Dr............Cape Elizabeth ME 04107 207-799-5871
Web: www.maine.gov/doc/parks/programs/db_search
Vaughan Woods State Park 28 Oldfields Rd............South Berwick ME 03908 207-384-5160
Web: www.maine.gov/doc/parks/programs/db_search
Warren Island State Park PO Box 105............Lincolnville ME 04849 207-941-4014
Web: www.maine.gov/doc/parks/programs/db_search
Whaleback Shell Midden State Historic Site
c/o Damariscotta River Assn PO Box 333............Damariscotta ME 04543 207-563-1393
Web: www.maine.gov/doc/parks/programs/db_search
Wolfe's Neck Woods State Park 426 Wolfe's Neck Rd............Freeport ME 04032 207-865-4465
Web: www.maine.gov/doc/parks/programs/db_search

Maryland

Phone Fax

Assateague State Park 7307 Stephen Decatur Hwy............Berlin MD 21811 410-641-2120 641-3615
TF: 888-432-2267 ■ *Web:* www.dnr.state.md.us/publiclands/eastern/assateague.html
Big Run State Park
c/o New Germany State Park 349 Headquarters Ln............Grantsville MD 21536 301-895-5453
Web: www.dnr.state.md.us/publiclands/western/bigrun.html
Calvert Cliffs State Park
c/o Smallwood State Park 2750 Sweden Point Rd............Marbury MD 20658 301-743-7613
Web: www.dnr.state.md.us/publiclands/southern/calvertcliffs.html
Casselman River Bridge State Park
c/o New Germany State Park 349 Headquarters Ln............Grantsville MD 21536 301-895-5453
Web: www.dnr.state.md.us/publiclands/western/casselman.html
Cedarville State Forest 10201 Bee Oak Rd............Brandywine MD 20613 301-888-1410
Web: www.dnr.state.md.us/publiclands/southern/cedarville.html
Choptank River Fishing Piers 29761 Bolingbroke Point Dr............Trappe MD 21673 410-820-1668
Web: www.dnr.state.md.us/publiclands/eastern/choptankpier.html
Cunningham Falls State Park 14039 Catoctin Hollow Rd............Thurmont MD 21788 301-271-7574
Web: www.dnr.state.md.us/publiclands/western/cunninghamfalls.html
Dans Mountain State Park
c/o Rocky Gap State Park 12500 Pleasant Valley Rd............Flintstone MD 21530 301-722-1480
Web: www.dnr.state.md.us/publiclands/western/dansmountain.html
Deep Creek Lake State Park & Natural Resources Management Area 898 State Park Rd............Swanton MD 21561 301-387-5563 387-4462
Web: www.dnr.state.md.us/publiclands/western/deepcreeklake.html
Elk Neck State Park 4395 Turkey Point Rd............North East MD 21901 410-287-5333
Web: www.dnr.state.md.us/publiclands/central/elkneck.html
Fair Hill Natural Resources Management Area 300 Tawes Dr............Elkton MD 21921 410-398-1246
Web: www.dnr.state.md.us/publiclands/central/fairhill.html
Fort Frederick State Park 11100 Fort Frederick Rd............Big Pool MD 21711 301-842-2155
Web: www.dnr.state.md.us/publiclands/western/fortfrederick.html
Gambrill State Park
c/o Cunningham Falls State Park 14039 Catoctin Hollow Rd............Thurmont MD 21702 301-271-7574
Web: www.dnr.state.md.us/publiclands/western/gambrill.html
Garrett State Forest 1431 Potomac Camp Rd............Oakland MD 21550 301-334-2038
Web: www.dnr.state.md.us/publiclands/western/garrett.html
Gathland State Park
c/o Greenbrier State Park 21843 National Pike............Boonsboro MD 21713 301-791-4767
Web: www.dnr.state.md.us/publiclands/western/gathland.html
Green Ridge State Forest 28700 Headquarters Dr NE............Flintstone MD 21530 301-478-3124
Web: www.dnr.state.md.us/publiclands/western/greenridge.html
Greenbrier State Park 21843 National Pike............Boonsboro MD 21713 301-791-4767
Web: www.dnr.state.md.us/publiclands/western/greenbrier.html
Greenwell State Park 25420 Rosedale Manor Ln............Hollywood MD 20636 301-373-9775
Web: www.dnr.state.md.us/publiclands/southern/greenwell.html
Gunpowder Falls State Park 2813 Jerusalem Rd PO Box 480............Kingsville MD 21087 410-592-2897
Web: www.dnr.state.md.us/publiclands/central/gunpowder.html
Hart-Miller Island State Park
c/o Gunpowder Falls State Park 2813 Jerusalem Rd PO Box 480............Kingsville MD 21087 410-592-2897
Web: www.dnr.state.md.us/publiclands/central/hartmiller.html
Herrington Manor State Park 222 Herrington Ln............Oakland MD 21550 301-334-9180
Web: www.dnr.state.md.us/publiclands/western/herringtonmanor.html
Janes Island State Park 26280 Alfred Lawson Dr............Crisfield MD 21817 410-968-1565 968-2515
Web: www.dnr.state.md.us/publiclands/eastern/janesisland.html
Martinak State Park 137 Deep Shore Rd............Denton MD 21629 410-820-1668
Web: www.dnr.state.md.us/publiclands/eastern/martinak.html
Merkle Wildlife Sanctuary 11704 Fenno Rd............Upper Marlboro MD 20772 301-888-1410
Web: www.dnr.state.md.us/publiclands/southern/merkle.html
Monocacy River Natural Resources Management Area
c/o Seneca Creek State Park 11950 Clopper Rd............Gaithersburg MD 20878 301-924-2127
Web: www.dnr.state.md.us/publiclands/central/monocacy.html
Morgan Run Natural Environment Area
c/o Patapsco Valley State Park 8020 Baltimore National Pike............Ellicott City MD 21043 410-461-5005
Web: www.dnr.state.md.us/publiclands/central/morganrun.html
New Germany State Park 349 Headquarters Ln............Grantsville MD 21536 301-895-5453
Web: www.dnr.state.md.us/publiclands/western/newgermany.html
North Point State Park
c/o Gunpowder Falls State Park 2813 Jerusalem Rd PO Box 480............Kingsville MD 21087 410-592-2897
Web: www.dnr.state.md.us/publiclands/central/northpoint.html
Patapsco Valley State Park 8020 Baltimore National Pike............Ellicott City MD 21043 410-461-5005
Web: www.dnr.state.md.us/publiclands/central/patapscovalley.html

Phone *Fax*

Patuxent River State Park
c/o Seneca Creek State Park 11950 Clopper Rd .... Gaithersburg MD 20878 301-924-2127
Web: www.dnr.state.md.us/publiclands/central/patuxentriver.html
Pocomoke River State Park 3461 Worcester Hwy .... Snow Hill MD 21863 410-632-2566 632-2914
Web: www.dnr.state.md.us/publiclands/eastern/pocomokeriver.html
Pocomoke State Forest 6572 Snow Hill Rd .... Snow Hill MD 21863 410-632-3732
Web: www.dnr.state.md.us/publiclands/eastern/pocomokeforest.html
Point Lookout State Park 11175 Point Lookout Rd .... Scotland MD 20687 301-872-5688 872-5084
Web: www.dnr.state.md.us/publiclands/southern/pointlookout.html
Potomac State Forest 1431 Potomac Camp Rd .... Oakland MD 21550 301-334-2038
Web: www.dnr.state.md.us/publiclands/western/potomacforest.html
Rocks State Park 3318 Rocks Chrome Hill Rd .... Jarrettsville MD 21084 410-557-7994
Web: www.dnr.state.md.us/publiclands/central/rocks.html
Rocky Gap State Park 12500 Pleasant Valley Rd .... Flintstone MD 21530 301-722-1480
Web: www.dnr.state.md.us/publiclands/western/rockygap.html
Rosaryville State Park 8714 Rosaryville Rd .... Upper Marlboro MD 20772 301-856-9656
Web: www.dnr.state.md.us/publiclands/southern/rosaryville.html
Saint Clement's Island State Park
c/o Point Lookout State Park 11175 Point Lookout Rd .... Scotland MD 20687 301-872-5688
Web: www.dnr.state.md.us/publiclands/southern/stclements.html
Saint Mary's River State Park
c/o Point Lookout State Park 11175 Point Lookout Rd .... Scotland MD 20687 301-872-5688
Web: www.dnr.state.md.us/publiclands/southern/stmarysriver.html
Sandy Point State Park 1100 E College Pkwy .... Annapolis MD 21409 410-974-2149 974-2647
Web: www.dnr.state.md.us/publiclands/southern/sandypoint.html
Sassafras Natural Resources Management Area
c/o Tuckahoe State Park 13070 Crouse Mill Rd .... Queen Anne MD 21657 410-820-1668
Web: www.dnr.state.md.us/publiclands/sassafrasplan.html
Savage River State Forest 127 Headquarters Ln .... Grantsville MD 21536 301-895-5759
Web: www.dnr.state.md.us/publiclands/western/savageriver.html
Seneca Creek State Park 11950 Clopper Rd .... Gaithersburg MD 20878 301-924-2127
Web: www.dnr.state.md.us/publiclands/central/seneca.html
Sideling Hill Exhibit Center
c/o Fort Frederick State Park 11100 Fort Frederick Rd .... Big Pool MD 21711 301-842-2155
Web: www.dnr.state.md.us/publiclands/western/sidelinghill.html
Smallwood State Park 2750 Sweden Point Rd .... Marbury MD 20658 301-743-7613
Web: www.dnr.state.md.us/publiclands/southern/smallwood.html
Soldiers Delight Natural Environment Area
c/o Patapsco Valley State Park 8020 Baltimore
National Pike .... Ellicott City MD 21043 410-461-5005
Web: www.dnr.state.md.us/publiclands/central/soldiers.html
Somers Cove Marina 715 Broadway PO Box 67 .... Crisfield MD 21817 410-968-0925 968-1408
TF: 800-967-3474 ■ *Web:* www.dnr.state.md.us/publiclands/eastern/somerscove.html
South Mountain State Park
c/o Greenbrier State Park 21843 National Pike .... Boonsboro MD 21713 301-791-4767
Web: www.dnr.state.md.us/publiclands/western/southmountain.html
Susquehanna State Park
c/o Rocks State Park 3318 Rocks Chrome Hill Rd .... Jarrettsville MD 21084 410-557-7994
Web: www.dnr.state.md.us/publiclands/central/susquehanna.html
Swallow Falls State Park
c/o Herrington Manor State Park 222 Herrington Ln .... Oakland MD 21550 301-387-6938
Web: www.dnr.state.md.us/publiclands/western/swallowfalls.html
Tuckahoe State Park 13070 Crouse Mill Rd .... Queen Anne MD 21657 410-820-1668
Web: www.dnr.state.md.us/publiclands/eastern/tuckahoe.html
Washington Monument State Park
c/o Greenbrier State Park 21843 National Pike .... Boonsboro MD 21713 301-791-4767
Web: www.dnr.state.md.us/publiclands/western/washington.html
Wye Island Natural Resources Management Area
632 Wye Island Rd .... Queenstown MD 21658 410-827-7577
Web: www.dnr.state.md.us/publiclands/eastern/wyeisland.html
Wye Oak State Park
c/o Tuckahoe State Park 13070 Crouse Mill Rd .... Queen Anne MD 21657 410-820-1668
Web: www.dnr.state.md.us/publiclands/eastern/wyeoak.html
Youghiogheny River Natural Resources Management Area
c/o Deep Creek Lake State Park 898 State Park Rd .... Swanton MD 21561 301-387-5563 387-4462
Web: www.dnr.state.md.us/publiclands/western/youghiogheny.html

Massachusetts

Phone *Fax*

Ames Nowell State Park Linwood St .... Abington MA 02351 781-857-1336
Web: www.mass.gov/dcr/parks/southeast/ames.htm
Ashland State Park c/o Hopkinton State Park 71 Cedar St .... Hopkinton MA 01748 508-435-4303
Web: www.mass.gov/dcr/parks/northeast/ashl.htm
Bash Bish Falls State Park
c/o Mount Washington State Forest RD 3 East St ..... Mount Washington MA 01258 413-528-0330
Web: www.mass.gov/dcr/parks/western/bash.htm
Beartown State Forest 69 Blue Hill Rd PO Box 97 .... Monterey MA 01245 413-528-0904
Web: www.mass.gov/dcr/parks/western/bear.htm
Blackstone River & Canal Heritage State Park 287 Oak St .... Uxbridge MA 01569 508-278-7604
Web: www.mass.gov/dcr/parks/central/blst.htm
Borderland State Park Massapoag Ave .... North Easton MA 02356 508-238-6566
Web: www.mass.gov/dcr/parks/southeast/bord.htm
Bradley Palmer State Park 40 Asbury St .... Topsfield MA 01983 978-887-5931
Web: www.mass.gov/dcr/parks/northeast/brad.htm
Brimfield State Forest 100 Dearth Hill Rd .... Brimfield MA 01010 413-267-9687
Web: www.mass.gov/dcr/parks/central/brim.htm
C M Gardner State Park PO Box 105 .... Chester MA 01011 413-354-6347
Web: www.mass.gov/dcr/parks/western/gdsp.htm
Callahan State Park 93 Commonwealth Rd .... Wayland MA 01778 508-653-9641
Web: www.mass.gov/dcr/parks/northeast/call.htm
Cape Cod Rail Trail c/o Nickerson State Park 3488 Main St .... Brewster MA 02631 508-896-3491
Web: www.mass.gov/dcr/parks/southeast/ccrt.htm
Carroll A Holmes Recreation Area (Lake Wyola)
94 Lake View Rd .... Shutesbury MA 01072 413-367-0317
Web: www.mass.gov/dcr/parks/central/lwsp.htm
Chester-Blandford State Forest PO Box 105 .... Chester MA 01011 413-354-6347
Web: www.mass.gov/dcr/parks/western/chbl.htm
Chicopee Memorial State Park 570 Burnett Rd .... Chicopee Falls MA 01020 413-594-9416
Web: www.mass.gov/dcr/parks/central/chip.htm
Clarksburg State Park 1199 Middle Rd .... Clarksburg MA 01247 413-664-8345
Web: www.mass.gov/dcr/parks/western/clsp.htm
Cochituate State Park 93 Commonwealth Rd .... Wayland MA 01778 508-653-9641
Web: www.mass.gov/dcr/parks/northeast/coch.htm
Connecticut River Greenway State Park 136 Damon Rd ...... Northampton MA 01060 413-586-8706
Web: www.mass.gov/dcr/parks/central/crgw.htm
DAR State Forest c/o 555 East St .... Williamsburg MA 01096 413-268-7098
Web: www.mass.gov/dcr/parks/western/darf.htm
Demarest Lloyd State Park Barney's Joy Rd .... Dartmouth MA 02748 508-636-8816
Web: www.mass.gov/dcr/parks/southeast/deml.htm
Dighton Rock State Park
c/o Freetown State Forest PO Box 171 .... Assonet MA 02702 508-822-7537
Web: www.mass.gov/dcr/parks/southeast/digr.htm
Douglas State Forest 107 Wallum Lake Rd .... Douglas MA 01516 508-476-7872
Web: www.mass.gov/dcr/parks/central/doug.htm

Dunn State Park Route 101 .... Gardner MA 01440 978-632-7897
Web: www.mass.gov/dcr/parks/central/dunn.htm
Ellisville Harbor State Park Rt 3A .... Plymouth MA 02360 508-866-2580
Web: www.mass.gov/dcr/parks/southeast/ells.htm
Erving State Forest 200 E Main St Rt 2A .... Erving MA 01344 978-544-3939
Web: www.mass.gov/dcr/parks/central/ervf.htm
F. Gilbert Hills State Forest 45 Mill St .... Foxboro MA 02035 508-543-5850
Web: www.mass.gov/dcr/parks/southeast/fgil.htm
Fall River Heritage State Park 200 Davol St .... Fall River MA 02720 508-675-5759
Web: www.mass.gov/dcr/parks/southeast/frhp.htm
Federated Women's Club State Forest Rt 122 .... Baldwinville MA 01436 978-939-8962
Web: www.mass.gov/dcr/parks/central/fwsf.htm
Fort Phoenix State Reservation Green St .... Fairhaven MA 02719 508-992-4524
Web: www.mass.gov/dcr/parks/southeast/ftph.htm
Freetown-Fall River State Forest Slab Bridge Rd .... Assonet MA 02702 508-644-5522
Web: www.mass.gov/dcr/parks/southeast/free.htm
Gardner Heritage State Park 265 Center St .... Gardner MA 01440 978-632-7897
Web: www.mass.gov/dcr/parks/central/ghsp.htm
Georgetown-Rowley State Forest 40 Asbury St .... Topsfield MA 01983 978-887-5931 887-7292
Web: www.mass.gov/dcr/parks/northeast/grow.htm
Granville State Forest 323 W Hartland Rd .... Granville MA 01034 413-357-6611
Web: www.mass.gov/dcr/parks/western/gran.htm
Great Brook Farm State Park 984 Lowell Rd PO Box 0829 .... Carlisle MA 01741 978-369-6312
Web: www.mass.gov/dcr/parks/northeast/gbfm.htm
Halibut Point State Park 16 Gaffield Ave .... Rockport MA 01966 978-546-2997
Web: www.mass.gov/dcr/parks/northeast/halb.htm
Hampton Ponds State Park 1048 North Rd .... Westfield MA 01085 413-532-3985 533-1837
Web: www.mass.gov/dcr/parks/central/hamp.htm
Harold Parker State Forest 1951 Turnpike St .... North Andover MA 01845 978-686-3391
Web: www.mass.gov/dcr/parks/northeast/harp.htm
Holyoke Heritage State Park 221 Appleton St .... Holyoke MA 01040 413-534-1723 534-0909
Web: www.mass.gov/dcr/parks/central/hhsp.htm
Hopkinton State Park 71 Cedar St .... Hopkinton MA 01748 508-435-4303
Web: www.mass.gov/dcr/parks/northeast/hpsp.htm
Horseneck Beach State Reservation PO Box 328 .... Westport MA 02791 508-636-8816
Web: www.mass.gov/dcr/parks/southeast/hbch.htm
JA Skinner State Park PO Box 91 .... Hadley MA 01035 413-586-0350
Web: www.mass.gov/dcr/parks/central/skin.htm
Jug End State Reservation & Wildlife Management Area c/o Mount Washington State Forest RD 3
East St .... Mount Washington MA 01258 413-528-0330
Web: www.mass.gov/dcr/parks/western/juge.htm
Kenneth Dubuque Memorial State Forest
c/o Mohawk State Forest PO Box 7 .... Charlemont MA 01339 413-339-5504
Web: www.mass.gov/dcr/parks/western/dubq.htm
Lake Dennison Recreation Area Rt 202 .... Winchendon MA 01475 978-939-8962
Web: www.mass.gov/dcr/parks/central/lden.htm
Lake Lorraine State Park 44 Lake Dr .... Springfield MA 01118 413-543-6628
Lawrence Heritage State Park 1 Jackson St .... Lawrence MA 01840 978-794-1655
Web: www.mass.gov/dcr/parks/northeast/lwhp.htm
Leominster State Forest 90 Fitchburg Rd Rt 31 .... Westminster MA 01473 978-874-2303
Web: www.mass.gov/dcr/parks/central/lmsf.htm
Lowell-Dracut-Tyngsboro State Forest PO Box 0829 .... Carlisle MA 01741 978-369-6312
Web: www.mass.gov/dcr/parks/northeast/ldtf.htm
Lowell Heritage State Park PO Box 0829 .... Carlisle MA 01741 978-369-6312
Web: www.mass.gov/dcr/parks/northeast/llhp.htm
Manuel F. Correllus State Forest PO Box 1612 .... Vineyard Haven MA 02568 508-693-2540
Web: www.mass.gov/dcr/parks/southeast/corr.htm
Massasoit State Park 1361 Middleboro Ave .... East Taunton MA 02718 508-822-7405
Web: www.mass.gov/dcr/parks/southeast/mass.htm
Maudslay State Park Curzon Mill Rd .... Newburyport MA 01950 978-465-7223
Web: www.mass.gov/dcr/parks/northeast/maud.htm
Mohawk Trail State Forest
175 Mohawk Trail/ Rt 2 PO Box 7 .... Charlemont MA 01339 413-339-5504
Web: www.mass.gov/dcr/parks/western/mhwk.htm
Monroe State Forest
c/o Mohawk Trail State Forest PO Box 7 .... Charlemont MA 01339 413-339-5504
Web: www.mass.gov/dcr/parks/western/mnro.htm
Moore State Park Mill St .... Paxton MA 01612 508-792-3969
Web: www.mass.gov/dcr/parks/central/more.htm
Mount Everett State Reservation c/o RD 3 East St ...... Mount Washington MA 01258 413-528-0330
Web: www.mass.gov/dcr/parks/western/meve.htm
Mount Grace State Forest Winchester Rd .... Warwick MA 01378 978-544-3939
Web: www.mass.gov/dcr/parks/central/mgrc.htm
Mount Greylock State Reservation
Rockwell Rd PO Box 138 .... Lanesborough MA 01237 413-499-4262
Web: www.mass.gov/dcr/parks/western/mgry.htm
Mount Holyoke Range State Park Rt 116 .... Amherst MA 01059 413-586-0350
Web: www.mass.gov/dcr/parks/central/hksp.htm
Mount Sugarloaf State Reservation Rt 116 .... South Deerfield MA 01373 413-545-5993
Web: www.mass.gov/dcr/parks/central/msug.htm
Mount Tom State Reservation 125 Reservation Rd .... Holyoke MA 01027 413-534-1186
Web: www.mass.gov/dcr/parks/central/mtom.htm
Mount Washington State Forest RD 3 East St .... Mount Washington MA 01258 413-528-0330
Web: www.mass.gov/dcr/parks/western/mwas.htm
Myles Standish Monument State Reservation .... Plymouth MA 02360 508-866-2580
Web: www.mass.gov/dcr/parks/southeast/mssm.htm
Myles Standish State Forest PO Box 66 .... South Carver MA 02366 508-866-2526
Web: www.mass.gov/dcr/parks/southeast/mssf.htm
Nasketucket Bay State Reservation
c/o Fort Phoenix State Reservation Green St .... Fairhaven MA 02719 508-992-4524
Web: www.mass.gov/dcr/parks/southeast/nbsr.htm
Natural Bridge State Park PO Box 1757 .... North Adams MA 01247 413-663-6392
Web: www.mass.gov/dcr/parks/western/nbdg.htm
Nickerson State Park 3488 Main St .... Brewster MA 02631 508-896-3491
TF: 877-422-6762 ■ *Web:* www.mass.gov/dcr/parks/southeast/nick.htm
Norwottuck Rail Trail
c/o Connecticut River Greenway State Park 136
Damon Rd .... Northampton MA 01060 413-586-8706
Web: www.mass.gov/dcr/parks/central/nwrt.htm
October Mountain State Forest 317 Woodland Rd .... Lee MA 01238 413-243-1778
Web: www.mass.gov/dcr/parks/western/octm.htm
Otter River State Forest New Winchendon Rd .... Baldwinville MA 01436 978-939-8962
Web: www.mass.gov/dcr/parks/central/ottr.htm
Pearl Hill State Park 595 Main St .... Townsend MA 01474 508-597-8802
Web: www.mass.gov/dcr/parks/central/phil.htm
Pilgrim Memorial (Plymouth Rock) State Park Water St .... Plymouth MA 02360 508-866-2580
Web: www.mass.gov/dcr/parks/southeast/plgm.htm
Pittsfield State Forest 1041 Cascade St .... Pittsfield MA 01201 413-442-8992
Web: www.mass.gov/dcr/parks/western/pitt.htm
Purgatory Chasm State Reservation Purgatory Rd .... Sutton MA 01590 508-234-3733
Web: www.mass.gov/dcr/parks/central/purg.htm
Quinsigamond State Park 10 N Lake Ave .... Worcester MA 01605 508-755-6880 755-5347
Web: www.mass.gov/dcr/parks/central/quin.htm
Robinson State Park 428 North St .... Agawam MA 01001 413-786-2877
Web: www.mass.gov/dcr/parks/central/robn.htm

Massachusetts (Cont'd)

Phone Fax

Rutland State Park Rt 122A .... Rutland MA 01543 508-886-6333
Web: www.mass.gov/dcr/parks/central/rtld.htm
Salisbury Beach State Reservation PO Box 5303 .... Salisbury MA 01952 978-462-4481
Web: www.mass.gov/dcr/parks/northeast/salb.htm
Sandisfield State Forest PO Box 97......................... Monterey MA 01245 413-229-8212
Web: www.mass.gov/dcr/parks/western/sand.htm
Sandy Point State Reservation PO Box 5303 .... Salisbury MA 01952 978-462-4481
Web: www.mass.gov/dcr/parks/northeast/sndp.htm
Savoy Mountain State Forest 260 Central Shaft Rd .... Florida MA 01247 413-663-8469
Web: www.mass.gov/dcr/parks/western/svym.htm
Scusset Beach State Reservation
140 Scusset Beach Rd.............................. Sagamore Beach MA 02562 508-888-0859
Web: www.mass.gov/dcr/parks/southeast/scus.htm
Shawme-Crowell State Forest PO Box 621 .... Sandwich MA 02563 508-888-0351
Web: www.mass.gov/dcr/parks/southeast/schr.htm
South Cape Beach State Park Great Neck Rd .... Mashpee MA 02649 508-457-0495
Web: www.mass.gov/dcr/parks/southeast/socp.htm
Spencer State Forest Howe Pond Rd.......................... Spencer MA 01562 508-886-6333
Web: www.mass.gov/dcr/parks/central/spen.htm
Streeter Point Recreation Area Rt 20 .... Sturbridge MA 01566 508-347-9257
Web: www.mass.gov/dcr/parks/central/stpt.htm
Tolland State Forest 410 Tolland Rd PO Box 342.............. East Otis MA 01029 413-269-6002
Web: www.mass.gov/dcr/parks/western/toll.htm
Upton State Forest 205 Westboro Rd.......................... Upton MA 01568 508-278-6486
Web: www.mass.gov/dcr/parks/northeast/uptn.htm
Wachusett Mountain State Reservation
Mountain Rd PO Box 248 .... Princeton MA 01541 978-464-2987
Web: www.mass.gov/dcr/parks/central/wach.htm
Wahconah Falls State Park
c/o Pittsfield State Forest 1041 Cascade St.................Pittsfield MA 01201 413-442-8992
Web: www.mass.gov/dcr/parks/western/wahf.htm
Walden Pond State Reservation 915 Walden St .... Concord MA 01742 978-369-3254
Web: www.mass.gov/dcr/parks/northeast/wldn.htm
Watson Pond State Park Bay Rd .... Taunton MA 02783 508-884-8280
Web: www.mass.gov/dcr/parks/southeast/wpsp.htm
Wells State Park PO Box 602.............................. Sturbridge MA 01566 508-347-9257
Web: www.mass.gov/dcr/parks/central/well.htm
Wendell State Forest Montague Rd .... Wendell MA 01379 413-659-3797
Web: www.mass.gov/dcr/parks/central/wndl.htm
Western Gateway Heritage State Park
9 Furnace St Bypass Bldg 4.......................... North Adams MA 01247 413-663-6312
Web: www.mass.gov/dcr/parks/western/wghp.htm
Whitehall State Park 71 Cedar St .... Hopkinton MA 01748 508-435-4303
Web: www.mass.gov/dcr/parks/northeast/whit.htm
Willard Brook State Forest 595 Main St .... Townsend MA 01474 978-597-8802
Web: www.mass.gov/dcr/parks/central/wilb.htm
Willowdale State Forest 40 Asbury St......................... Topsfield MA 01983 978-887-5931
Web: www.mass.gov/dcr/parks/northeast/wild.htm
Windsor State Forest East St .... Williamsburg MA 01096 413-684-0948
Web: www.mass.gov/dcr/parks/western/wnds.htm
Wompatuck State Park Union St .... Hingham MA 02536 781-749-7160
Web: www.mass.gov/dcr/parks/southeast/womp.htm

Michigan

Phone Fax

Albert E. Sleeper State Park 6573 State Park Rd ....Caseville MI 48725 989-856-4411
Web: www.michigandnr.com/parksandtrails/ParksandTrailsInfo.aspx?id=494
Algonac State Park 8732 River Rd......................... Marine City MI 48039 810-765-5605
Web: www.michigandnr.com/parksandtrails/ParksandTrailsInfo.aspx?id=433
Aloha State Park 4347 3rd St..............................Cheboygan MI 49721 231-625-2522
Web: www.michigandnr.com/parksandtrails/ParksandTrailsInfo.aspx?id=434
Bald Mountain Recreation Area 1330 E Greenshield Rd.........Lake Orion MI 48360 248-693-6767
Web: www.michigandnr.com/parksandtrails/ParksandTrailsInfo.aspx?id=435
Baraga State Park 1300 US 41 S.................................. Baraga MI 49908 906-353-6558
Web: www.michigandnr.com/parksandtrails/ParksandTrailsInfo.aspx?id=408
Bass River Recreation Area
c/o P. J. Hoffmaster State Park 6585 Lake Harbor Rd......... Muskegon MI 49441 231-798-3711
Web: www.michigandnr.com/ParksandTrails/ParksandTrailsInfo.aspx?id=436
Bay City Recreation Area 3582 State Park Dr..................... Bay City MI 48706 989-684-3020
Web: www.michigandnr.com/parksandtrails/ParksandTrailsInfo.aspx?id=437
Bewabic State Park 720 Idlewild Rd ....Crystal Falls MI 49920 906-875-3324
Web: www.michigandnr.com/parksandtrails/ParksandTrailsInfo.aspx?id=411
Brighton Recreation Area 6360 Chilson Rd......................... Howell MI 48843 810-229-6566
Web: www.michigandnr.com/parksandtrails/ParksandTrailsInfo.aspx?id=438
Brimley State Park 9200 W 6-Mile Rd..............................Brimley MI 49715 906-248-3422
Web: www.michigandnr.com/parksandtrails/ParksandTrailsInfo.aspx?id=414
Burt Lake State Park 6635 State Park Dr.................... Indian River MI 49749 231-238-9392
Web: www.michigandnr.com/parksandtrails/ParksandTrailsInfo.aspx?id=439
Cambridge Junction Historic State Park 13220 M-50.............Brooklyn MI 49230 517-467-4414
Web: www.michigandnr.com/parksandtrails/ParksandTrailsInfo.aspx?id=440
Charles Mears State Park W Lowell St PO Box 370.............Pentwater MI 49449 231-869-2051
Web: www.michigandnr.com/parksandtrails/ParksandTrailsInfo.aspx?id=470
Cheboygan State Park 4490 Beach Rd.........................Cheboygan MI 49721 231-627-2811
Web: www.michigandnr.com/parksandtrails/ParksandTrailsInfo.aspx?id=441
Clear Lake State Park 20500 M-33 North .... Atlanta MI 49709 989-785-4388
Web: www.michigandnr.com/parksandtrails/ParksandTrailsInfo.aspx?id=442
Coldwater Lake State Park Copeland Rd........................Coldwater MI 49036 517-780-7866
Web: www.michigandnr.com/parksandtrails/ParksandTrailsInfo.aspx?id=443
Colonial Michilimackinac State Park & Old Mackinac Point Lighthouse c/o Mackinac State Historic Parks
PO Box 370 ....Mackinac Island MI 49757 231-436-4100
Web: www.mackinacparks.com
Craig Lake State Park 851 County Rd AKE PO Box 88...........Champion MI 49814 906-339-4461
Web: www.michigandnr.com/parksandtrails/ParksandTrailsInfo.aspx?id=415
Dodge #4 State Park 4250 Parkway Dr .... Waterford MI 48327 248-682-7323 682-5587
Web: www.michigandnr.com/parksandtrails/ParksandTrailsInfo.aspx?id=445
Duck Lake State Park 3560 Memorial Dr................ North Muskegon MI 49445 231-744-3480
Web: www.michigandnr.com/parksandtrails/ParksandTrailsInfo.aspx?id=446
F J McLain State Park 18350 Hwy M-203........................ Hancock MI 49930 906-482-0278
Web: www.michigandnr.com/parksandtrails/ParksandTrailsInfo.aspx?id=423
Fayette Historic State Park 13700 13.25 Ln........................ Garden MI 49835 906-644-2603
Web: www.michigandnr.com/parksandtrails/ParksandTrailsInfo.aspx?id=417
Fisherman's Island State Park PO Box 456 Bells Bay Rd........ Charlevoix MI 49720 231-547-6641
Web: www.michigandnr.com/parksandtrails/ParksandTrailsInfo.aspx?id=447
Fort Custer Recreation Area 5163 Fort Custer Dr................ Augusta MI 49012 269-731-4200
Web: www.michigandnr.com/parksandtrails/ParksandTrailsInfo.aspx?id=448
Fort Wilkins State Park 15223 US Hwy 41 ....Copper Harbor MI 49918 906-289-4215
Web: www.michigandnr.com/parksandtrails/ParksandTrailsInfo.aspx?id=419
Fred Meijer White Pine Trail State Park 6093 M-115 .... Cadillac MI 49601 231-775-7911
Web: www.michigandnr.com/parksandtrails/ParksandTrailsInfo.aspx?id=508
Grand Haven State Park 1001 Harbor Ave.................... Grand Haven MI 49417 616-847-1309
Web: www.michigandnr.com/ParksandTrails/ParksandTrailsInfo.aspx?id=449

Phone Fax

Grand Mere State Park
c/o Warren Dunes State Park 12032 Red Arrow Hwy.............Sawyer MI 49125 269-426-4013
Web: www.michigandnr.com/parksandtrails/ParksandTrailsInfo.aspx?id=450
Harrisville State Park 248 State Park Rd PO Box 326 ....Harrisville MI 48740 989-724-5126
Web: www.michigandnr.com/parksandtrails/ParksandTrailsInfo.aspx?id=451
Hart-Montague Trail State Park
c/o Silver Lake State Park 9679 W State Park Dr.................Mears MI 49436 231-873-3083
Web: www.michigandnr.com/parksandtrails/ParksandTrailsInfo.aspx?id=452
Hartwick Pines State Park 4216 Ranger Rd ....Grayling MI 49738 989-348-7068
Web: www.michigandnr.com/parksandtrails/ParksandTrailsInfo.aspx?id=453
Highland Recreation Area 5200 E Highland Rd...............White Lake MI 48383 248-889-3750
Web: www.michigandnr.com/parksandtrails/ParksandTrailsInfo.aspx?id=455
Historic Mill Creek State Park
c/o Mackinac State Historic Parks PO Box 370...........Mackinac Island MI 49757 231-436-4100
Web: www.mackinacparks.com
Holland State Park 2215 Ottawa Beach Rd ....Holland MI 49424 616-399-9390
Web: www.michigandnr.com/ParksandTrails/ParksandTrailsInfo.aspx?id=458
Holly Recreation Area 8100 Grange Hall Rd ....Holly MI 48442 248-634-8811
Web: www.michigandnr.com/parksandtrails/ParksandTrailsInfo.aspx?id=459
Indian Lake State Park 8970W County Rd 442................Manistique MI 49854 906-341-2355
Web: www.michigandnr.com/parksandtrails/ParksandTrailsInfo.aspx?id=420
Interlochen State Park M-137 ....Interlochen MI 49643 231-276-9511
Web: www.michigandnr.com/parksandtrails/ParksandTrailsInfo.aspx?id=460
Ionia Recreation Area 2880 W David Hwy..............................Ionia MI 48846 616-527-3750
Web: www.michigandnr.com/parksandtrails/ParksandTrailsInfo.aspx?id=461
Island Lake Recreation Area 12950 E Grand River Rd ....Brighton MI 48116 810-229-7067
Web: www.michigandnr.com/parksandtrails/ParksandTrailsInfo.aspx?id=462
J W Wells State Park N7670 Hwy M-35 .... Cedar River MI 49887 906-863-9747
Web: www.michigandnr.com/parksandtrails/ParksandTrailsInfo.aspx?id=432
Kal-Haven Trail State Park
c/o Van Buren State Park 23960 Ruggles Rd .... South Haven MI 49090 269-637-2788
Web: www.michigandnr.com/parksandtrails/ParksandTrailsInfo.aspx?id=463
Lake Gogebic State Park N9995 State Hwy M-64............. Marenisco MI 49947 906-842-3341
Web: www.michigandnr.com/parksandtrails/ParksandTrailsInfo.aspx?id=421
Lake Hudson Recreation Area 5505 Morey Hwy ....Clayton MI 49235 517-445-2265
Web: www.michigandnr.com/parksandtrails/ParksandTrailsInfo.aspx?id=464
Lakelands Trail State Park
8555 Silver Hill Rd 8555 Silver Hill Rt 1...................... Pinckney MI 48169 734-426-4913
Web: www.michigandnr.com/parksandtrails/ParksandTrailsInfo.aspx?id=465
Lakeport State Park 7605 Lakeshore Rd ....Lakeport MI 48059 810-327-6224
Web: www.michigandnr.com/parksandtrails/ParksandTrailsInfo.aspx?id=466
Laughing Whitefish Falls Scenic Site
c/o Indian Lake State Park 8970W County Rd 442............Manistique MI 49854 906-341-2355
Web: www.michigandnr.com/parksandtrails/ParksandTrailsInfo.aspx?id=422
Leelanau State Park 15310 N Lighthouse Point Rd..............Northport MI 49670 231-386-5422
Web: www.michigandnr.com/parksandtrails/ParksandTrailsInfo.aspx?id=467
Ludington State Park PO Box 709 ....Ludington MI 49431 231-843-2423
Web: www.michigandnr.com/parksandtrails/ParksandTrailsInfo.aspx?id=468
Mackinac Island State Park & Fort Mackinac
c/o Mackinac State Historic Parks PO Box 370...........Mackinac Island MI 49757 231-436-4100 436-4210
Web: www.michigandnr.com/parksandtrails/ParksandTrailsInfo.aspx?id=418
Maybury State Park 20145 Beck Rd.............................Northville MI 48167 248-349-8390
Web: www.michigandnr.com/parksandtrails/ParksandTrailsInfo.aspx?id=469
Meridian-Baseline State Park
c/o Waterloo Recreation Area 16345 McClure Rd................ Chelsea MI 48118 734-475-8307
Web: www.michigandnr.com/parksandtrails/ParksandTrailsInfo.aspx?id=471
Metamora-Hadley Recreation Area 3871 Hurd Rd ....Metamora MI 48455 810-797-4439
Web: www.michigandnr.com/parksandtrails/ParksandTrailsInfo.aspx?id=472
Muskallonge Lake State Park 30042 County Rd 407 .... Newberry MI 49868 906-658-3338
Web: www.michigandnr.com/parksandtrails/ParksandTrailsInfo.aspx?id=424
Muskegon State Park 3560 Memorial Dr............... North Muskegon MI 49445 231-744-3480
Web: www.michigandnr.com/parksandtrails/ParksandTrailsInfo.aspx?id=475
Negwegon State Park c/o Harrisville State Park PO Box 326 ......Harrisville MI 48740 989-724-5126
Web: www.michigandnr.com/parksandtrails/ParksandTrailsInfo.aspx?id=476
Newaygo State Park 2793 Beech St............................. Newaygo MI 49337 231-856-4452
Web: www.michigandnr.com/parksandtrails/ParksandTrailsInfo.aspx?id=477
North Higgins Lake State Park 11747 N Higgins Lake Dr...... Roscommon MI 48653 989-821-6125
Web: www.michigandnr.com/parksandtrails/ParksandTrailsInfo.aspx?id=478
Onaway State Park 3622 N M-211............................... Onaway MI 49765 989-733-8279
Web: www.michigandnr.com/parksandtrails/ParksandTrailsInfo.aspx?id=479
Orchard Beach State Park 2064 N Lakeshore Rd .... Manistee MI 49660 231-723-7422
Web: www.michigandnr.com/parksandtrails/ParksandTrailsInfo.aspx?id=480
Ortonville Recreation Area 5779 Hadley Rd ....Ortonville MI 48462 810-797-4439
Web: www.michigandnr.com/parksandtrails/ParksandTrailsInfo.aspx?id=481
Otsego Lake State Park 7136 Old 27 S............................ Gaylord MI 49735 989-732-5485
P H Hoeft State Park 5001 US 23 N .... Rogers City MI 49779 989-734-2543
Web: www.michigandnr.com/parksandtrails/ParksandTrailsInfo.aspx?id=456
P J Hoffmaster State Park 6585 Lake Harbor Rd .... Muskegon MI 49441 231-798-3711
Web: www.michigandnr.com/parksandtrails/ParksandTrailsInfo.aspx?id=457
Palms Book State Park
c/o Indian Lake State Park 8970W County Rd 442............Manistique MI 49854 906-341-2355
Web: www.michigandnr.com/parksandtrails/ParksandTrailsInfo.aspx?id=425
Petoskey State Park 2475 M-119 Hwy .... Petoskey MI 49712 231-347-2311
Web: www.michigandnr.com/parksandtrails/ParksandTrailsInfo.aspx?id=483
Pinckney Recreation Area 8555 Silver Hill .... Pinckney MI 48169 734-426-4913
Web: www.michigandnr.com/parksandtrails/ParksandTrailsInfo.aspx?id=484
Pontiac Lake Recreation Area 7800 Gale Rd ....Waterford MI 48327 248-666-1020
Web: www.michigandnr.com/parksandtrails/ParksandTrailsInfo.aspx?id=485
Porcupine Mountains Wilderness State Park
33303 Headquarters Rd..Ontonagon MI 49953 906-885-5275
Web: www.michigandnr.com/parksandtrails/ParksandTrailsInfo.aspx?id=426
Port Crescent State Park 1775 Port Austin Rd ....Port Austin MI 48467 989-738-8663
Web: www.michigandnr.com/parksandtrails/ParksandTrailsInfo.aspx?id=486
Proud Lake Recreation Area 3540 Wixom Rd.........Commerce Township MI 48382 248-685-2433
Web: www.michigandnr.com/parksandtrails/ParksandTrailsInfo.aspx?id=487
Rifle River Recreation Area 2550 E Rose City Rd PO Box 98 .... Lupton MI 48635 989-473-2258
Web: www.michigandnr.com/parksandtrails/ParksandTrailsInfo.aspx?id=489
Sanilac Petroglyphs Historic State Park
c/o Sleeper State Park 6573 State Park Rd....................Caseville MI 48725 989-856-4411
Web: www.michigandnr.com/parksandtrails/ParksandTrailsInfo.aspx?id=490
Saugatuck Dunes State Park 6575 138th Ave................. Saugatuck MI 49453 269-637-2788
Web: www.michigandnr.com/parksandtrails/ParksandTrailsInfo.aspx?id=491
Seven Lakes State Park 14390 Fish Lake Rd.........................Holly MI 48442 248-634-7271
Web: www.michigandnr.com/parksandtrails/ParksandTrailsInfo.aspx?id=492
Silver Lake State Park 9679 W State Park Rd......................Mears MI 49436 231-873-3083
Web: www.michigandnr.com/parksandtrails/ParksandTrailsInfo.aspx?id=493
Sleepy Hollow State Park 7835 E Price Rd ....Laingsburg MI 48848 517-651-6217
Web: www.michigandnr.com/parksandtrails/ParksandTrailsInfo.aspx?id=495
South Higgins Lake State Park 106 State Park Dr............ Roscommon MI 48653 989-821-6374
Web: www.michigandnr.com/parksandtrails/ParksandTrailsInfo.aspx?id=496
Sterling State Park 2800 State Park Rd.......................... Monroe MI 48162 734-289-2715
Web: www.michigandnr.com/parksandtrails/ParksandTrailsInfo.aspx?id=497
Straits State Park 720 Church St..........................Saint Ignace MI 49781 906-643-8620
Web: www.michigandnr.com/parksandtrails/ParksandTrailsInfo.aspx?id=427
Tahquamenon Falls State Park 41382 W M-123..................Paradise MI 49768 906-492-3415
Web: www.michigandnr.com/parksandtrails/ParksandTrailsInfo.aspx?id=428

Phone Fax

Tawas Point State Park 686 Tawas Beach Rd East Tawas MI 48730 989-362-5041
Web: www.michigandnr.com/parksandtrails/ParksandTrailsInfo.aspx?id=499
Thompson's Harbor State Park
c/o Cheboygan Field Office 120 A St PO Box 117 Cheboygan MI 49721 231-627-9011
Web: www.michigandnr.com/parksandtrails/ParksandTrailsInfo.aspx?id=500
Traverse City State Park 1132 US-31 N Traverse City MI 49686 231-922-5270
Web: www.michigandnr.com/parksandtrails/ParksandTrailsInfo.aspx?id=501
Tri-Centennial State Park & Harbor 1900 Atwater St Detroit MI 48207 313-396-0217
Web: www.michigandnr.com/parksandtrails/ParksandTrailsInfo.aspx?id=697
Twin Lakes State Park 6204 E Poyhonen Rd Toivola MI 49965 906-288-3321
Web: www.michigandnr.com/parksandtrails/ParksandTrailsInfo.aspx?id=429
Van Buren State Park 23960 Ruggles Rd South Haven MI 49090 269-637-2788
Web: www.michigandnr.com/parksandtrails/ParksandTrailsInfo.aspx?id=502
Van Buren Trail State Park
c/o Van Buren State Park 23960 Ruggles Rd South Haven MI 49090 269-637-2788
Web: www.michigandnr.com/parksandtrails/ParksandTrailsInfo.aspx?id=503
Van Riper State Park 851 County Rd AKE PO Box 88 Champion MI 49814 906-339-4461
Web: www.michigandnr.com/parksandtrails/ParksandTrailsInfo.aspx?id=430
W C Wetzel State Park 28681 Old North River Rd Harrison Township MI 48045 810-765-5605
Web: www.michigandnr.com/parksandtrails/ParksandTrailsInfo.aspx?id=507
W J Hayes State Park 1220 Wampler's Lake Rd Onsted MI 49265 517-467-7401
Web: www.michigandnr.com/parksandtrails/ParksandTrailsInfo.aspx?id=454
Wagner Falls Scenic Site
c/o Indian Lake State Park 8970W County Rd 442 Manistique MI 49854 906-341-2355
Web: www.michigandnr.com/parksandtrails/ParksandTrailsInfo.aspx?id=431
Warren Dunes State Park 12032 Red Arrow Hwy Sawyer MI 49125 269-426-4013
Web: www.michigandnr.com/parksandtrails/ParksandTrailsInfo.aspx?id=504
Warren Woods State Park
c/o Warren Dunes State Park 12032 Red Arrow Hwy Sawyer MI 49125 269-426-4013
Web: www.michigandnr.com/parksandtrails/ParksandTrailsInfo.aspx?id=505
Waterloo Recreation Area 16345 McClure Rd Chelsea MI 48118 734-475-8307
Web: www.michigandnr.com/parksandtrails/ParksandTrailsInfo.aspx?id=506
Wilderness State Park 903 Wilderness Park Dr Carp Lake MI 49718 231-436-5381
Web: www.michigandnr.com/parksandtrails/ParksandTrailsInfo.aspx?id=509
William Mitchell State Park 6093 E M-115 Cadillac MI 49601 231-775-7911
Web: www.michigandnr.com/parksandtrails/ParksandTrailsInfo.aspx?id=474
Wilson State Park 910 N 1st St PO Box 333 Harrison MI 48625 989-539-3021
Web: www.michigandnr.com/parksandtrails/ParksandTrailsInfo.aspx?id=510
Yankee Springs Recreation Area 2104 S Briggs Rd Middleville MI 49333 269-795-9081
Web: www.michigandnr.com/parksandtrails/ParksandTrailsInfo.aspx?id=511
Young State Park 02280 Boyne City Rd Boyne City MI 49712 231-582-7523
Web: www.michigandnr.com/parksandtrails/ParksandTrailsInfo.aspx?id=512

Minnesota

Phone Fax

Afton State Park 6959 Peller Ave S Hastings MN 55033 651-436-5391 436-6912
Web: www.dnr.state.mn.us/state_parks/afton
Banning State Park 61101 Banning Park Rd PO Box 643 Sandstone MN 55072 320-245-2668 245-0251
Web: www.dnr.state.mn.us/state_parks/banning
Bear Head Lake State Park 9301 Bear Head State Park Rd Ely MN 55731 218-365-7229 365-7204
Web: www.dnr.state.mn.us/state_parks/bear_head_lake
Beaver Creek Valley State Park 15954 County Rd 1 Caledonia MN 55921 507-724-2107 724-2107
Web: www.dnr.state.mn.us/state_parks/beaver_creek_valley
Big Bog State Recreation Area 55716 Hwy 72 NE Waskish MN 56685 218-647-8592 647-8730
Web: www.dnr.state.mn.us/state_parks/big_bog
Big Stone Lake State Park
35889 Meadowbrook State Park Rd Ortonville MN 56278 320-839-3663 839-3676
Web: www.dnr.state.mn.us/state_parks/big_stone_lake
Blue Mounds State Park 1410 161st St Luverne MN 56156 507-283-1307 283-1306
Web: www.dnr.state.mn.us/state_parks/blue_mounds
Buffalo River State Park 155 South St Hwy 10 PO Box 352 Glyndon MN 56547 218-498-2124 498-2583
Web: www.dnr.state.mn.us/state_parks/buffalo_river
Camden State Park 1897 County Rd Lynd MN 56157 507-865-4530 865-4608
Web: www.dnr.state.mn.us/state_parks/camden
Carley State Park c/o Whitewater State Park 19041 Hwy 74 Altura MN 55910 507-932-3007 932-5938
Web: www.dnr.state.mn.us/state_parks/carley
Cascade River State Park 3481 W Hwy 61 Lutsen MN 55612 218-387-3053 387-3054
Web: www.dnr.state.mn.us/state_parks/cascade_river
Charles A. Lindbergh State Park
1615 Lindbergh Dr S PO Box 364 Little Falls MN 56345 320-616-2525 616-2526
Web: www.dnr.state.mn.us/state_parks/charles_a_lindbergh
Crow Wing State Park 3124 State Park Rd Brainerd MN 56401 218-825-3075 825-3077
Web: www.dnr.state.mn.us/state_parks/crow_wing
Cuyuna Country State Recreation Area 307 3rd St PO Box 404 Ironton MN 56455 218-546-5926 546-7369
Web: www.dnr.state.mn.us/state_parks/cuyuna_country
Father Hennepin State Park
41294 Father Hennepin Park Rd PO Box 397 Isle MN 56342 320-676-8763 676-3748
Web: www.dnr.state.mn.us/state_parks/father_hennepin
Flandrau State Park 1300 Summit Ave New Ulm MN 56073 507-233-9800 359-1544
Web: www.dnr.state.mn.us/state_parks/flandrau
Forestville/Mystery Cave State Park 21071 County 118 Preston MN 55965 507-352-5111 352-5113
Web: www.dnr.state.mn.us/state_parks/forestville_mystery_cave
Fort Ridgely State Park 72158 County Rd 30 Fairfax MN 55332 507-426-7840 426-7112
Web: www.dnr.state.mn.us/state_parks/fort_ridgely
Fort Snelling State Park 101 Snelling Lake Rd Saint Paul MN 55111 612-725-2389 725-2391
Web: www.dnr.state.mn.us/state_parks/fort_snelling
Franz Jevne State Park
c/o Zippel State Park 3684 54th Ave NW Williams MN 56686 218-783-6252 783-6253
Web: www.dnr.state.mn.us/state_parks/franz_jevne
Frontenac State Park 29223 County 28 Blvd Frontenac MN 55026 651-345-3401 345-3694
Web: www.dnr.state.mn.us/state_parks/frontenac
Garden Island State Recreation Area
c/o Zippel Bay State Park 3684 54th Ave NW Williams MN 56686 218-783-6252 783-6253
Web: www.dnr.state.mn.us/state_parks/garden_island
George H. Crosby Manitou State Park
c/o Tettegouche State Park 5702 Hwy 61 Silver Bay MN 55614 218-226-6365 226-6366
Web: www.dnr.state.mn.us/state_parks/george_crosby_manitou
Glacial Lakes State Park 25022 County Rd 41 Starbuck MN 56381 320-239-2860 239-4605
Web: www.dnr.state.mn.us/state_parks/glacial_lakes
Glendalough State Park 25287 Whitetail Ln Battle Lake MN 56515 218-644-0110 864-0587
Web: www.dnr.state.mn.us/state_parks/glendalough
Gooseberry Falls State Park 3206 Hwy 61 Two Harbors MN 55616 218-834-3855 834-3787
Web: www.dnr.state.mn.us/state_parks/gooseberry_falls
Grand Portage State Park 9393 E Hwy 61 Grand Portage MN 55605 218-475-2360 475-2365
Web: www.dnr.state.mn.us/state_parks/grand_portage
Great River Bluffs State Park 43605 Kipp Dr Winona MN 55987 507-643-6849 643-6849
Web: www.dnr.state.mn.us/state_parks/great_river_bluffs
Hayes Lake State Park 48990 County Rd 4 Roseau MN 56751 218-425-7504 425-7971
Web: www.dnr.state.mn.us/state_parks/hayes_lake
Hill Annex Mine State Park PO Box 376 Calumet MN 55716 218-247-7215 247-7449
Web: www.dnr.state.mn.us/state_parks/hill_annex_mine
Interstate State Park 307 Milltown Rd PO Box 254 Taylors Falls MN 55084 651-465-5711 465-0517
Web: www.dnr.state.mn.us/state_parks/interstate
Itasca State Park 36750 Main Park Dr Park Rapids MN 56470 218-266-2100 266-3942
Web: www.dnr.state.mn.us/state_parks/itasca

Phone Fax

Jay Cooke State Park 780 Hwy 210 Carlton MN 55718 218-384-4610 384-4851
Web: www.dnr.state.mn.us/state_parks/jay_cooke
John A. Latsch State Park
c/o Whitewater State Park 19041 Hwy 74 Altura MN 55910 507-932-3007 932-5938
Web: www.dnr.state.mn.us/state_parks/john_latsch
Judge C R Magney State Park 4051 E Hwy 61 Grand Marais MN 55604 218-387-3039 387-3051
Web: www.dnr.state.mn.us/state_parks/judge_cr_magney
Kilen Woods State Park 50200 860th St Rt 1 Box 122 Lakefield MN 56150 507-662-6258 662-5501
Web: www.dnr.state.mn.us/state_parks/kilen_woods
Lac Qui Parle State Park 14047 20th St NW Watson MN 56295 320-752-4450 734-4452
Web: www.dnr.state.mn.us/state_parks/lac_qui_parle
Lake Bemidji State Park 3401 State Park Rd NE Bemidji MN 56601 218-755-3843 755-4073
Web: www.dnr.state.mn.us/state_parks/lake_bemidji
Lake Bronson State Park Box 9 Lake Bronson MN 56734 218-754-2200 754-6141
Web: www.dnr.state.mn.us/state_parks/lake_bronson
Lake Carlos State Park 2601 County Rd 38 NE Carlos MN 56319 320-852-7200 852-7349
Web: www.dnr.state.mn.us/state_parks/lake_carlos
Lake Louise State Park
c/o Forestville/Mystery Cave State Park 21071 County Road 118 Preston MN 55965 507-352-5111 352-5113
Web: www.dnr.state.mn.us/state_parks/lake_louise
Lake Maria State Park 11411 Clementa Ave NW Monticello MN 55362 763-878-2325 878-2620
Web: www.dnr.state.mn.us/state_parks/lake_maria
Lake Shetek State Park 163 State Park Rd Currie MN 56123 507-763-3256 763-3330
Web: www.dnr.state.mn.us/state_parks/lake_shetek
Maplewood State Park 39721 Park Entrance Rd Pelican Rapids MN 56572 218-863-8383 863-8384
Web: www.dnr.state.mn.us/state_parks/maplewood
McCarthy Beach State Park 7622 McCarthy Beach Rd Side Lake MN 55781 218-254-7979 254-7980
Web: www.dnr.state.mn.us/state_parks/mccarthy_beach
Mille Lacs Kathio State Park 15066 Kathio State Park Rd Onamia MN 56359 320-532-3523 532-3529
Web: www.dnr.state.mn.us/state_parks/mille_lacs_kathio
Minneopa State Park 54497 Gadwall Rd Mankato MN 56001 507-389-5464 389-5174
Web: www.dnr.state.mn.us/state_parks/minneopa
Minnesota Valley State Recreation Area
c/o Fort Snelling State Park 101 Snelling Lake Rd Saint Paul MN 55111 612-725-2389
Web: www.dnr.state.mn.us/state_parks/minnesota_valley
Monson Lake State Park 1690 15th St NE Sunburg MN 56289 320-366-3797 366-3882
Web: www.dnr.state.mn.us/state_parks/monson_lake
Moose Lake State Park 4252 County Rd 137 Moose Lake MN 55767 218-485-5420 485-5422
Web: www.dnr.state.mn.us/state_parks/moose_lake
Myre-Big Island State Park 19499 780th Ave Albert Lea MN 56007 507-379-3403 379-3405
Web: www.dnr.state.mn.us/state_parks/myre_big_island
Nerstrand-Big Woods State Park 9700 170th St E Nerstrand MN 55053 507-333-4840 333-4852
Web: www.dnr.state.mn.us/state_parks/nerstrand_big_woods
Old Mill State Park 33489 240th ave NW Rt 1 Box 43 Argyle MN 56713 218-437-8174 437-8104
Web: www.dnr.state.mn.us/state_parks/old_mill
Red River State Recreation Area 515 2nd St NW East Grand Forks MN 56721 218-773-4950 773-4951
Web: www.dnr.state.mn.us/state_parks/red_river
Rice Lake State Park 8485 Rose St Owatonna MN 55060 507-455-5871 446-2326
Web: www.dnr.state.mn.us/state_parks/rice_lake
Saint Croix State Park 30065 St Croix Park Rd Hinckley MN 55037 320-384-6591 384-7070
Web: www.dnr.state.mn.us/state_parks/st_croix
Sakatah Lake State Park 50499 Sakatah Lake State Park Rd Waterville MN 56096 507-362-4438 362-4558
Web: www.dnr.state.mn.us/state_parks/sakatah_lake
Savanna Portage State Park 55626 Lake Pl McGregor MN 55760 218-426-3271 426-4437
Web: www.dnr.state.mn.us/state_parks/savanna_portage
Scenic State Park 56956 Scenic Hwy 7 Bigfork MN 56628 218-743-3362 743-1362
Web: www.dnr.state.mn.us/state_parks/scenic
Schoolcraft State Park
c/o Hill Annex Mine State Park PO Box 376 Calumet MN 55716 218-247-7215 247-7449
Web: www.dnr.state.mn.us/state_parks/schoolcraft
Sibley State Park 800 Sibley Park Rd NE New London MN 56273 320-354-2055 354-2372
Web: www.dnr.state.mn.us/state_parks/sibley
Soudan Underground Mine State Park PO Box 335 Soudan MN 55782 218-753-2245 753-2246
Web: www.dnr.state.mn.us/state_parks/soudan_underground_mine
Split Rock Creek State Park 336 50th Ave Jasper MN 56144 507-348-7908 348-8940
Web: www.dnr.state.mn.us/state_parks/split_rock_creek
Split Rock Lighthouse State Park
3755 Split Rock Lighthouse Rd Two Harbors MN 55616 218-226-6377 226-6378
Web: www.dnr.state.mn.us/state_parks/split_rock_lighthouse
Temperance River State Park 7620 W Hwy 61 Box 33 Schroeder MN 55613 218-663-7476 663-7374
Web: www.dnr.state.mn.us/state_parks/temperance_river
Tettegouche State Park 5702 Hwy 61 Silver Bay MN 55614 218-226-6365 226-6366
Web: www.dnr.state.mn.us/state_parks/tettegouche
Upper Sioux Agency State Park 5908 Hwy 67 Granite Falls MN 56241 320-564-4777 564-4838
Web: www.dnr.state.mn.us/state_parks/upper_sioux_agency
Whitewater State Park 19041 Hwy 74 Altura MN 55910 507-932-3007 932-5938
Web: www.dnr.state.mn.us/state_parks/whitewater
Wild River State Park 39797 Park Trail Center City MN 55012 651-583-2125 583-3101
Web: www.dnr.state.mn.us/state_parks/wild_river
William O'Brien State Park 16821 O'Brien Trail N Marine-on-Saint Croix MN 55047 651-433-0500 433-0504
Web: www.dnr.state.mn.us/state_parks/william_obrien
Zippel Bay State Park 3684 54th Ave NW Williams MN 56686 218-783-6252 783-6253
Web: www.dnr.state.mn.us/state_parks/zippel_bay

Mississippi

Phone Fax

Buccaneer State Park 1150 S Beach Blvd Waveland MS 39576 228-467-3822
Web: www.mdwfp.com/parkView/parks.asp?ID=6841
Clark Creek Natural Area 366 Fort Adams Pond Rd Jackson MS 39669 601-888-6040
Web: www.mdwfp.com/parkView/parks.asp?ID=5852
Clarkco State Park 386 Clarkco Rd Quitman MS 39355 601-776-6651
Web: www.mdwfp.com/parkView/parks.asp?ID=4842
Florewood State Park 1999 County Rd 145 Greenwood MS 38930 662-455-3821
Web: www.mdwfp.com/parkView/parks.asp?ID=3822
George Payne Cossar State Park 165 County Rd 170 Oakland MS 38948 662-623-7356
Web: www.mdwfp.com/parkView/parks.asp?ID=2811
Golden Memorial State Park 2104 Damascus Rd Walnut Grove MS 39189 601-253-2237
Web: www.mdwfp.com/parkView/parks.asp?ID=4843
Great River Road State Park PO Box 292 Rosedale MS 38769 662-759-6762
Web: www.mdwfp.com/parkView/parks.asp?ID=3823
Holmes County State Park 5369 State Park Rd Durant MS 39063 662-653-3351
Web: www.mdwfp.com/parkView/parks.asp?ID=3824
Hugh White State Park PO Box 725 Grenada MS 38902 662-226-4934
Web: www.mdwfp.com/parkView/parks.asp?ID=2812
J P Coleman State Park 613 County Rd 321 Iuka MS 38852 662-423-6515
Web: www.mdwfp.com/parkView/parks.asp?ID=1814
John W. Kyle State Park 4235 State Park Rd Sardis MS 38666 662-487-1345
Web: www.mdwfp.com/parkView/parks.asp?ID=2813
Lake Lincoln State Park 2573 Sunset Dr Wesson MS 39191 601-643-9044
Web: www.mdwfp.com/parkView/parks.asp?ID=5853
Lake Lowndes State Park 3319 Lake Lowndes Rd Columbus MS 39702 662-328-2110
Web: www.mdwfp.com/parkView/parks.asp?ID=1815
LeFleur's Bluff State Park 2140 Riverside Dr Jackson MS 39202 601-987-3923 354-6930

Mississippi (Cont'd)

				Phone	Fax
Legion State Park 635 Legion State Park Rd *Web:* www.mdwfp.com/parkView/parks.asp?ID=1831	Louisville	MS	39339	662-773-8323	
Leroy Percy State Park PO Box 176 *Web:* www.mdwfp.com/parkView/parks.asp?ID=3825	Hollandale	MS	38748	662-827-5436	
Natchez State Park 230-B Wickcliff Rd *Web:* www.mdwfp.com/parkView/parks.asp?ID=5845	Natchez	MS	39120	601-442-2658	
Paul B. Johnson State Park 319 Geiger Lake Rd *TF:* 800-467-2757 ■ *Web:* www.ohwy.com/ms/p/paulbjoh.htm	Hattiesburg	MS	39401	601-582-7721	545-5611
Percy Quin State Park 2036 Percy Quin Dr *Web:* www.mdwfp.com/parkView/parks.asp?ID=5847	McComb	MS	39648	601-684-3938	
Roosevelt State Park 2149 Hwy 13 S *Web:* www.mdwfp.com/parkView/parks.asp?ID=4848	Morton	MS	39117	601-732-6316	
Shepard State Park 1034 Graveline Rd *Web:* www.mdwfp.com/parkView/parks.asp?ID=6849	Gautier	MS	39553	228-497-2244	
Tishomingo State Park PO Box 880 *Web:* www.mdwfp.com/parkView/parks.asp?ID=1816	Tishomingo	MS	38873	662-438-6914	
Tombigbee State Park 264 Cabin Dr *TF:* 800-467-2757 ■ *Web:* www.mdwfp.com/parkView/parks.asp?ID=1817	Tupelo	MS	38804	662-842-7669	840-5594
Trace State Park 2139 Faulkner Rd *Web:* www.mdwfp.com/parkView/parks.asp?ID=1818	Belden	MS	38826	662-489-2958	
Wall Doxey State Park 3946 Hwy 7 S *Web:* www.mdwfp.com/parkView/parks.asp?ID=2819	Holly Springs	MS	38635	662-252-4231	

Missouri

				Phone	Fax
Arrow Rock State Historic Site PO Box 1 *Web:* www.mostateparks.com/arrowrock.htm	Arrow Rock	MO	65320	660-837-3330	
Battle of Athens State Historic Site Rt 1 Box 26 *Web:* www.mostateparks.com/athens.htm	Revere	MO	63465	660-877-3871	
Battle of Carthage State Park c/o Harry S Truman Birthplace State Historic Site 1009 Truman *Web:* www.mostateparks.com/carthage.htm	Lamar	MO	64759	417-682-2279	
Battle of Lexington State Historic Site 1300 N John Shea Dr *Web:* www.mostateparks.com/lexington	Lexington	MO	64067	660-259-4654	
Bennett Spring State Park 26250 Hwy 64A *Web:* www.mostateparks.com/bennett.htm	Lebanon	MO	65536	417-532-4338	
Big Lake State Park 204 Lake Shore Dr *Web:* www.mostateparks.com/biglake.htm	Craig	MO	64437	660-442-3770	
Big Oak Tree State Park 13640 S Hwy 102 *Web:* www.mostateparks.com/bigoak.htm	East Prairie	MO	63845	573-649-3149	
Big Sugar Creek State Park c/o Roaring River State Park Rt 4 Box 4100 *Web:* www.mostateparks.com/bigsugar.htm	Cassville	MO	65625	417-847-2539	
Bollinger Mill State Historic Site 113 Bollinger Mill Rd *Web:* www.mostateparks.com/bollinger.htm	Burfordville	MO	63739	573-243-4591	
Boone's Lick State Historic Site c/o Arrow Rock State Historic Site PO Box 1 *Web:* www.mostateparks.com/booneslick.htm	Arrow Rock	MO	65320	660-837-3330	
Bothwell Lodge State Historic Site 19349 Bothwell State Park Rd *Web:* www.mostateparks.com/bothwell.htm	Sedalia	MO	65301	660-827-0510	
Castlewood State Park 1401 Kiefer Creek Rd *Web:* www.mostateparks.com/castlewood.htm	Ballwin	MO	63021	636-227-4433	
Confederate Memorial State Historic Site 211 W 1st St *Web:* www.mostateparks.com/confedmem.htm	Higginsville	MO	64037	660-584-2853	
Crowder State Park 76 Hwy 128 *Web:* www.mostateparks.com/crowder.htm	Trenton	MO	64683	660-359-6473	
Cuivre River State Park 678 State Rt 147 *Web:* www.mostateparks.com/cuivre.htm	Troy	MO	63379	636-528-7247	
Deutschheim State Historic Site 109 W 2nd St *Web:* www.mostateparks.com/deutschheim.htm	Hermann	MO	65041	573-486-2200	
Dillard Mill State Historic Site 142 Dillard Mill Rd *Web:* www.mostateparks.com/dillardmill.htm	Davisville	MO	65456	573-244-3120	
Dr. Edmund A Babler Memorial State Park 800 Guy Park Dr *Web:* www.mostateparks.com/babler.htm	Chesterfield	MO	63005	636-458-3813	
Elephant Rocks State Park c/o Fort Davidson State Historic Site PO Box 509 *Web:* www.mostateparks.com/elephantrock.htm	Pilot Knob	MO	63663	573-546-3454	
Felix Valle House State Historic Site 198 Merchant St *Web:* www.mostateparks.com/felixvalle.htm	Sainte Genevieve	MO	63670	573-883-7102	
Finger Lakes State Park 1505 E Peabody Rd *Web:* www.mostateparks.com/fingerlakes.htm	Columbia	MO	65202	573-443-5315	443-4999
First Missouri State Capitol State Historic Site 200-216 S Main St **Fax Area Code:* 636 ■ *TF:* 800-334-6946 ■ *Web:* www.mostateparks.com/firstcapitol.htm	Saint Charles	MO	63301	800-334-6946	940-3324*
Fort Davidson State Historic Site PO Box 509 *Web:* www.mostateparks.com/ftdavidson.htm	Pilot Knob	MO	63663	573-546-3454	
General John J. Pershing Boyhood Home State Historic Site 1100 Pershing Dr *Web:* www.mostateparks.com/pershingsite.htm	Laclede	MO	64651	660-963-2525	
Governor Daniel Dunklin's Grave State Historic Site c/o Southern Missouri Historic District 2901 Hwy 61 *Web:* www.mostateparks.com/dunklinsgrave.htm	Festus	MO	63028	636-937-3697	
Graham Cave State Park 217 Hwy TT *TF:* 800-334-6946 ■ *Web:* www.mostateparks.com/grahamcave.htm	Montgomery City	MO	63361	573-564-3476	564-2534
Grand Gulf State Park Rt 3 Box 3554 *Web:* www.mostateparks.com/grandgulf.htm	Thayer	MO	65791	417-264-7600	
Ha Ha Tonka State Park 1491 State Rd D *Web:* www.mostateparks.com/hahatonka.htm	Camdenton	MO	65020	573-346-2986	
Harry S Truman Birthplace State Historic Site 1009 Truman St *Web:* www.mostateparks.com/trumansite.htm	Lamar	MO	64759	417-682-2279	
Harry S Truman State Park 28761 State Park Rd *Web:* www.mostateparks.com/trumanpark.htm	Warsaw	MO	65355	660-438-7711	
Hawn State Park 12096 Park Dr *Web:* www.mostateparks.com/hawn.htm	Sainte Genevieve	MO	63670	573-883-3603	
Hunter-Dawson State Historic Site PO Box 308 *Web:* www.mostateparks.com/hunterdawson.htm	New Madrid	MO	63869	573-748-5340	
Iliniwek Village State Historic Site c/o Battle of Athens State Historic Site Rt 1 Box 26 *Web:* www.mostateparks.com/iliniwek.htm	Revere	MO	63465	660-877-3871	
Jefferson Landing State Historic Site & Missouri State Museum Jefferson St & Capitol Ave *Web:* www.mostateparks.com/jeffersonland.htm	Jefferson City	MO	65101	573-751-2854	
Jewell Cemetery State Historic Site c/o Rock Bridge Memorial State Park 5901 S Hwy 163 *Web:* www.mostateparks.com/jewellcem.htm	Columbia	MO	65203	573-449-7402	
Johnson's Shut-Ins State Park HCR 1 Box 126 *Web:* www.mostateparks.com/jshutins.htm	Middlebrook	MO	63656	573-546-2450	
Katy Trail State Park Missouri Dept of Natural Resources PO Box 196 **Fax Area Code:* 573 ■ *TF:* 800-334-6946 ■ *Web:* www.mostateparks.com/katytrail	Jefferson City	MO	65102	800-334-6946	751-8656*
Knob Noster State Park 873 SE 10th *Web:* www.mostateparks.com/knobnoster.htm	Knob Noster	MO	65336	660-563-2463	
Lake of the Ozarks State Park PO Box 170 *Web:* www.mostateparks.com/lakeozark.htm	Kaiser	MO	65047	573-348-2694	
Lake Wappapello State Park HC 2 Box 102 *Web:* www.mostateparks.com/lakewappapello.htm	Williamsville	MO	63967	573-297-3232	
Lewis & Clark State Park 801 Lake Crest Blvd *Web:* www.mostateparks.com/lewisandclark.htm	Rushville	MO	64484	816-579-5564	
Locust Creek Covered Bridge State Historic Site c/o Gen. John J Pershing Boyhood Home State Historic Site 1100 Pershing Dr *Web:* www.mostateparks.com/locustbridge.htm	Laclede	MO	64651	660-963-2525	
Long Branch State Park 28615 Visitor Center Rd *Web:* www.mostateparks.com/longbranch.htm	Macon	MO	63552	660-773-5229	
Mark Twain Birthplace State Historic Site 37352 Shrine Rd *Web:* www.mostateparks.com/twainsite.htm	Florida	MO	65283	573-565-3449	
Mark Twain State Park 20057 State Park Rd *Web:* www.mostateparks.com/twainpark.htm	Stoutsville	MO	65283	573-565-3440	
Mastodon State Historic Site 1050 Museum Dr *TF:* 800-334-6946 ■ *Web:* www.mostateparks.com/mastodon.htm	Imperial	MO	63052	636-464-2976	
Meramec State Park 115 Meramec Park Dr *Web:* www.mostateparks.com/meramec.htm	Sullivan	MO	63080	573-468-6072	
Missouri Mines State Historic Site PO Box 492 *Web:* www.mostateparks.com/momines.htm	Park Hills	MO	63601	573-431-6226	
Montauk State Park RR 5 Box 279 *Web:* www.mostateparks.com/montauk.htm	Salem	MO	65560	573-548-2201	
Morris State Park c/o Hunter-Dawson State Historic Site PO Box 308 *Web:* www.mostateparks.com/morris.htm	New Madrid	MO	63869	573-748-5340	
Nathan Boone Homestead State Historic Site 7850 N State Hwy V *Web:* www.mostateparks.com/boonehome.htm	Ash Grove	MO	65604	417-751-3266	
Onondaga Cave State Park 7556 Hwy H *Web:* www.mostateparks.com/onondaga.htm	Leasburg	MO	65535	573-245-6576	
Osage Village State Historic Site c/o Harry S Truman Birthplace State Historic Site 1009 Truman *Web:* www.mostateparks.com/osagevillage.htm	Lamar	MO	64759	417-682-2279	
Pershing State Park 29277 Hwy 130 *Web:* www.mostateparks.com/pershingpark.htm	Laclede	MO	64651	660-963-2299	
Pomme de Terre State Park HC 77 Box 890 *Web:* www.mostateparks.com/pommedeterre.htm	Pittsburg	MO	65724	417-852-4291	
Prairie State Park 128 NW 150th Ln *Web:* www.mostateparks.com/prairie.htm	Liberal	MO	64769	417-843-6711	
Roaring River State Park Rt 4 Box 4100 *Web:* www.mostateparks.com/roaringriver.htm	Cassville	MO	65625	417-847-2539	
Robertsville State Park PO Box 186 *Web:* www.mostateparks.com/robertsville.htm	Robertsville	MO	63072	636-257-3788	
Rock Bridge Memorial State Park 5901 S Hwy 163 *TF:* 800-334-6946 ■ *Web:* www.mostateparks.com/rockbridge.htm	Columbia	MO	65203	573-449-7402	442-2249
Route 66 State Park 97 N Outer Rd Suite 1 *Web:* www.mostateparks.com/route66.htm	Eureka	MO	63025	636-938-7198	938-7804
Saint Francois State Park 8920 US Hwy 67 N *Web:* www.mostateparks.com/stfrancois.htm	Bonne Terre	MO	63628	573-358-2173	
Saint Joe State Park 2800 Pimville Rd *Web:* www.mostateparks.com/stjoe.htm	Park Hills	MO	63601	573-431-1069	
Sam A. Baker State Park Rt 1 Box 113 *Web:* www.mostateparks.com/baker.htm	Patterson	MO	63956	573-856-4411	
Sandy Creek Covered Bridge State Historic Site c/o Mastodon State Historic Site 1050 Museum Dr *Web:* www.mostateparks.com/sandybridge.htm	Imperial	MO	63052	636-464-2976	
Sappington Cemetery State Historic Site c/o Arrow Rock State Historic Site PO Box 1 *Web:* www.mostateparks.com/sappingtoncem.htm	Arrow Rock	MO	65320	660-837-3330	
Scott Joplin House State Historic Site 2658 Delmar Blvd *Web:* www.mostateparks.com/scottjoplin.htm	Saint Louis	MO	63103	314-340-5790	340-5793
Stockton State Park 19100 S Hwy 215 *Web:* www.mostateparks.com/stockton.htm	Dadeville	MO	63635	417-276-4259	
Table Rock State Park 5272 State Hwy 165 *Web:* www.mostateparks.com/tablerock.htm	Branson	MO	65616	417-334-4704	334-4782
Taum Sauk Mountain State Park c/o Johnson's Shut-Ins State Park HC Route 1 Box 126 *Web:* www.mostateparks.com/taumsauk.htm	Middlebrook	MO	63656	573-546-2450	
Thomas Hart Benton Home & Studio State Historic Site 3616 Belleview *Web:* www.mostateparks.com/benton.htm	Kansas City	MO	64111	816-931-5722	
Thousand Hills State Park 20431 State Hwy 157 *Web:* www.mostateparks.com/thousandhills.htm	Kirksville	MO	63501	660-665-6995	
Towosahgy State Historic Site c/o Hunter-Dawson State Historic Site 312 Dawson Rd *Web:* www.mostateparks.com/towosahgy.htm	New Madrid	MO	63869	573-748-5340	
Trail of Tears State Park 429 Moccasin Springs *Web:* www.mostateparks.com/trailoftears.htm	Jackson	MO	63755	573-334-1711	
Union Covered Bridge State Historic Site c/o Mark Twain Birthplace State Historic Site 37352 Shrine Rd *Web:* www.mostateparks.com/unionbridge.htm	Florida	MO	65283	573-565-3449	
Van Meter State Park Rt 1 Box 47 *Web:* www.mostateparks.com/vanmeter.htm	Miami	MO	65344	660-886-7537	
Wakonda State Park 32836 State Park Rd *Web:* www.mostateparks.com/wakonda.htm	LaGrange	MO	63448	573-655-2280	
Wallace State Park 10621 NE Hwy 121 *Web:* www.mostateparks.com/wallace.htm	Cameron	MO	64429	816-632-3745	
Washington State Park 13041 State Hwy 104 *Web:* www.mostateparks.com/washington.htm	DeSoto	MO	63020	636-586-2995	
Watkins Woolen Mill State Park & State Historic Site 26600 Park Rd N *Web:* www.mostateparks.com/wwmill	Lawson	MO	64062	816-580-3387	
Weston Bend State Park 16600 Hwy 45 N *Web:* www.mostateparks.com/westonbend.htm	Weston Bend	MO	64098	816-640-5443	

Montana

				Phone	Fax
Ackley Lake State Park 4600 Giant Springs Rd *Web:* fwp.mt.gov/lands/site_282450.aspx	Great Falls	MT	59405	406-454-5840	
Anaconda Smoke Stack State Park 3201 Spurgin Rd *Web:* fwp.mt.gov/lands/site_280918.aspx	Missoula	MT	59804	406-542-5500	
Bannack State Park 4200 Bannack Rd *Web:* fwp.mt.gov/lands/site_281798.aspx	Dillon	MT	59725	406-834-3413	
Beaverhead Rock State Park c/o Bannack State Park 4200 Bannack Rd *Web:* fwp.mt.gov/lands/site_281875.aspx	Dillon	MT	59725	406-834-3413	

	City	State	ZIP	Phone	Fax
Beavertail Hill State Park 3201 Spurgin Rd *Web:* fwp.mt.gov/lands/site_280871.aspx	Missoula	MT	59804	406-542-5500	
Big Arm State Park 490 N Meridian Rd *Web:* fwp.mt.gov/lands/site_280041.aspx	Kalispell	MT	59901	406-752-5501	
Black Sandy State Park 930 Custer Ave W *Web:* fwp.mt.gov/lands/site_281944.aspx	Helena	MT	59601	406-495-3270	
Chief Plenty Coups State Park PO Box 100 *Web:* fwp.mt.gov/lands/site_283264.aspx	Pryor	MT	59066	406-252-1289	
Clark's Lookout State Park c/o Bannack State Park 4200 Bannack Rd *Web:* fwp.mt.gov/lands/site_281963.aspx	Dillon	MT	59725	406-834-3413	
Cooney State Park PO Box 254 *Web:* fwp.mt.gov/lands/site_283293.aspx	Joliet	MT	59041	406-445-2326	
Council Grove State Park 3201 Spurgin Rd *Web:* fwp.mt.gov/lands/site_280907.aspx	Missoula	MT	59804	406-542-5500	
Elkhorn State Park 930 Custer Ave W *Web:* fwp.mt.gov/lands/site_281892.aspx	Helena	MT	59601	406-495-3270	
Finley Point State Park 490 N Meridian Rd *Web:* fwp.mt.gov/lands/site_280032.aspx	Kalispell	MT	59901	406-887-2715	
First Peoples Buffalo Jump State Park PO Box 109 *Web:* fwp.mt.gov/lands/site_282807.aspx	Ulm	MT	59485	406-866-2217	
Fort Owen State Park 3201 Spurgin Rd *Web:* fwp.mt.gov/lands/site_280846.aspx	Missoula	MT	59804	406-542-5500	
Frenchtown Pond State Park 3201 Spurgin Rd *Web:* fwp.mt.gov/lands/site_280880.aspx	Missoula	MT	59804	406-542-5500	
Giant Springs State Park 4600 Giant Springs Rd *Web:* fwp.mt.gov/lands/site_282690.aspx	Great Falls	MT	59405	406-454-5840	761-8477
Granite Ghost Town State Park 3201 Spurgin Rd *Web:* fwp.mt.gov/lands/site_280883.aspx	Missoula	MT	59804	406-542-5500	
Greycliff Prairie Dog Town State Park 2300 Lake Elmo Dr *Web:* fwp.mt.gov/lands/site_283312.aspx	Billings	MT	59105	406-247-2940	
Hell Creek State Park PO Box 1630 *Web:* fwp.mt.gov/lands/site_283992.aspx	Miles City	MT	59301	406-234-0900	
Lake Elmo State Park 2300 Lake Elmo Dr *Web:* fwp.mt.gov/lands/site_283333.aspx	Billings	MT	59105	406-247-2955	
Lake Mary Ronan State Park 490 N Meridian Rd *Web:* fwp.mt.gov/lands/site_280125.aspx	Kalispell	MT	59901	406-849-5082	
Lewis & Clark Caverns State Park PO Box 489 *Web:* fwp.mt.gov/lands/site_281895.aspx	Whitehall	MT	59759	406-287-3541	
Logan State Park 490 N Meridian Rd *Web:* fwp.mt.gov/lands/site_280148.aspx	Kalispell	MT	59901	406-293-7190	
Lone Pine State Park 490 N Meridian *Web:* fwp.mt.gov/lands/site_280065.aspx	Kalispell	MT	59901	406-752-5501	
Lost Creek State Park 3201 Spurgin Rd *Web:* fwp.mt.gov/lands/site_280851.aspx	Missoula	MT	59804	406-542-5500	
Madison Buffalo Jump State Park 1400 S 19th St *Web:* fwp.mt.gov/lands/site_281935.aspx	Bozeman	MT	59715	406-994-4042	
Makoshika State Park PO Box 1242 *Web:* fwp.mt.gov/lands/site_283890.aspx	Glendive	MT	59330	406-377-6256	
Medicine Rocks State Park PO Box 1630 *Web:* fwp.mt.gov/lands/site_283951.aspx	Miles City	MT	59301	406-234-0900	
Missouri Headwaters State Park c/o Region 3 Office 1400 S 19th St *Web:* fwp.mt.gov/lands/site_281910.aspx	Bozeman	MT	59715	406-994-4042	
Painted Rocks State Park 3201 Spurgin Rd *Web:* fwp.mt.gov/lands/site_280864.aspx	Missoula	MT	59804	406-542-5500	
Parker Homestead State Park c/o Lewis & Clark Caverns State Park PO Box 489 *Web:* fwp.mt.gov/lands/site_281960.aspx	Whitehall	MT	59759	406-287-3541	
Pictograph Cave State Park c/o Region 5 Office 2300 Lake Elmo Dr *Web:* fwp.mt.gov/lands/site_283286.aspx	Billings	MT	59105	406-247-2955	248-5026
Pirogue Island State Park PO Box 1630 *Web:* fwp.mt.gov/lands/site_283962.aspx	Miles City	MT	59301	406-234-0900	
Placid Lake State Park 3201 Spurgin Rd *Web:* fwp.mt.gov/lands/site_280895.aspx	Missoula	MT	59804	406-677-6804	
Rosebud Battlefield State Park PO Box 1630 *Web:* fwp.mt.gov/lands/site_283981.aspx	Miles City	MT	59301	406-234-0900	
Salmon Lake State Park 3201 Spurgin Rd *Web:* fwp.mt.gov/lands/site_280904.aspx	Missoula	MT	59804	406-677-6804	
Sluice Boxes State Park 4600 Giant Springs Rd *Web:* fwp.mt.gov/lands/site_282818.aspx	Great Falls	MT	59406	406-454-5840	
Smith River State Park 4600 Giant Springs Rd *Web:* fwp.mt.gov/lands/site_-1.aspx	Great Falls	MT	59405	406-454-5840	
Spring Meadow Lake State Park 930 Custer Ave W *Web:* fwp.mt.gov/lands/site_281949.aspx	Helena	MT	59620	406-495-3270	
Thompson Falls State Park 490 N Meridian Rd *Web:* fwp.mt.gov/lands/site_280084.aspx	Kalispell	MT	59901	406-752-5501	
Tongue River Reservoir State Park PO Box 1630 *Web:* fwp.mt.gov/lands/site_283967.aspx	Miles City	MT	59301	406-234-0900	
Travelers Rest State Park PO Box 995 *Web:* fwp.mt.gov/lands/site_2233810.aspx	Lolo	MT	59847	406-273-4253	
Wayfarers State Park 490 N Meridian Rd *Web:* fwp.mt.gov/lands/site_280159.aspx	Kalispell	MT	59901	406-752-5501	
West Shore State Park 490 N Meridian Rd *Web:* fwp.mt.gov/lands/site_280091.aspx	Kalispell	MT	59901	406-752-5501	
Whitefish Lake State Park 490 N Meridian Rd *Web:* fwp.mt.gov/lands/site_280100.aspx	Kalispell	MT	59901	406-862-3991	
Wild Horse Island State Park 490 N Meridian Rd *Web:* fwp.mt.gov/lands/site_280179.aspx	Kalispell	MT	59901	406-752-5501	
Yellow Bay State Park 490 N Meridian Rd *Web:* fwp.mt.gov/lands/site_280115.aspx	Kalispell	MT	59901	406-752-5501	

Nebraska

	City	State	ZIP	Phone	Fax
Alexandria State Recreation Area 57426 710th Rd *Web:* www.ngpc.state.ne.us/parks/guides/parksearch/findpark.asp	Fairbury	NE	68352	402-729-5777	
Arbor Lodge State Historical Park PO Box 15 *Web:* www.ngpc.state.ne.us/parks/guides/parksearch/findpark.asp	Nebraska City	NE	68410	402-873-7222	
Arnold State Recreation Area HC 69 Box 117 *Web:* www.ngpc.state.ne.us/parks/guides/parksearch/findpark.asp	Anselmo	NE	68813	308-749-2235	
Ash Hollow State Historical Park PO Box 70 *Web:* www.ngpc.state.ne.us/parks/guides/parksearch/findpark.asp	Lewellen	NE	69147	308-778-5651	
Ashfall Fossil Beds State Historical Park 86930 517th Ave *Web:* www.ngpc.state.ne.us/parks/guides/parksearch/findpark.asp	Royal	NE	68773	402-893-2000	
Atkinson Lake State Recreation Area PO Box 508 *Web:* www.ngpc.state.ne.us/parks/guides/parksearch/findpark.asp	Bassett	NE	68714	402-684-2921	
Blue River State Recreation Area 3019 Apple St *Web:* www.ngpc.state.ne.us/parks/guides/parksearch/findpark.asp	Lincoln	NE	68503	402-471-0641	
Bluestem State Recreation Area 3019 Apple St *Web:* www.ngpc.state.ne.us/parks/guides/parksearch/findpark.asp	Lincoln	NE	68503	402-471-5545	
Bowman Lake State Recreation Area RR 2, Box 117 *Web:* www.ngpc.state.ne.us/parks/guides/parksearch/findpark.asp	Loup City	NE	68853	308-745-0230	
Bowring Ranch State Historical Park PO Box 38 *Web:* www.ngpc.state.ne.us/parks/guides/parksearch/findpark.asp	Merriman	NE	69218	308-684-3428	
Box Butte Reservoir State Recreation Area PO Box 392 *Web:* www.ngpc.state.ne.us/parks/guides/parksearch/findpark.asp	Crawford	NE	69339	308-665-2903	
Branched Oak State Recreation Area 12000 W Branched Oak Rd *Web:* www.ngpc.state.ne.us/parks/guides/parksearch/findpark.asp	Raymond	NE	68428	402-783-3400	
Bridgeport State Recreation Area PO Box 65 *Web:* www.ngpc.state.ne.us/parks/guides/parksearch/findpark.asp	Gering	NE	69341	308-436-2383	
Brownville State Recreation Area c/o Indian Cave State Park RR 1, Box 30 *Web:* www.ngpc.state.ne.us/parks/guides/parksearch/findpark.asp	Shubert	NE	68437	402-883-2575	
Buffalo Bill Ranch State Historical Park 2921 Scouts Rest Ranch Rd *Web:* www.ngpc.state.ne.us/parks/guides/parksearch/findpark.asp	North Platte	NE	69101	308-535-8035	
Calamus State Recreation Area HC 79 Box 20L *Web:* www.ngpc.state.ne.us/parks/guides/parksearch/findpark.asp	Burwell	NE	68823	308-346-5666	
Chadron State Park 15951 Hwy 385 *Web:* www.ngpc.state.ne.us/parks/guides/parksearch/findpark.asp	Chadron	NE	69337	308-432-6167	
Champion Lake State Recreation Area 73122 338 Ave *Web:* www.ngpc.state.ne.us/parks/guides/parksearch/findpark.asp	Enders	NE	69027	308-394-5118	
Champion Mill State Historical Park 73122 338 Ave *Web:* www.ngpc.state.ne.us/parks/guides/parksearch/findpark.asp	Enders	NE	69027	308-394-5118	
Cheyenne State Recreation Area PO Box 944 *Web:* www.ngpc.state.ne.us/parks/guides/parksearch/findpark.asp	Grand Island	NE	68832	308-385-6210	
Conestoga State Recreation Area RR 4 Box 41B *Web:* www.ngpc.state.ne.us/parks/guides/parksearch/findpark.asp	Lincoln	NE	68524	402-796-2362	
Cottonwood Lake State Recreation Area PO Box 38 *Web:* www.ngpc.state.ne.us/parks/guides/parksearch/findpark.asp	Merriman	NE	69218	308-684-3428	
Cowboy State Recreation Trail c/o District III Office 2201 N 13th St	Norfolk	NE	68701	402-370-3374	370-3256
Crystal Lake State Recreation Area 7425 S US Hwy 281 *Web:* www.ngpc.state.ne.us/parks/guides/parksearch/findpark.asp	Doniphan	NE	68832	308-385-6210	
Dead Timber State Recreation Area 227 County Rd & 12 Blvd *Web:* www.ngpc.state.ne.us/parks/guides/parksearch/findpark.asp	Scribner	NE	68057	402-664-3597	
DLD State Recreation Area 7425 S US Hwy 281 *Web:* www.ngpc.state.ne.us/parks/guides/parksearch/findpark.asp	Doniphan	NE	68832	308-385-6211	
Enders Reservoir State Recreation Area 73122 338th Ave *Web:* www.ngpc.state.ne.us/parks/guides/parksearch/findpark.asp	Enders	NE	69027	308-394-5118	
Eugene T. Mahoney State Park 28500 W Park Hwy *Web:* www.ngpc.state.ne.us/parks/guides/parksearch/findpark.asp	Ashland	NE	68003	402-944-2523	
Fort Atkinson State Historical Park PO Box 240 *Web:* www.ngpc.state.ne.us/parks/guides/parksearch/findpark.asp	Fort Calhoun	NE	68023	402-468-5611	468-5066
Fort Hartsuff State Historical Park RR 1 Box 37 *Web:* www.ngpc.state.ne.us/parks/guides/parksearch/findpark.asp	Burwell	NE	68823	308-346-4715	
Fort Kearny State Historical Park 1020 'V' Rd *Web:* www.ngpc.state.ne.us/parks/guides/parksearch/findpark.asp	Kearney	NE	68847	308-865-5305	
Fort Kearny State Recreation Area c/o Fort Kearny State Historical Park 1020 'V' Rd *Web:* www.ngpc.state.ne.us/parks/guides/parksearch/findpark.asp	Kearney	NE	68847	308-865-5305	
Fort Robinson State Park PO Box 392 *Web:* www.ngpc.state.ne.us/parks/guides/parksearch/findpark.asp	Crawford	NE	69339	308-665-2900	
Fremont Lakes State Recreation Area 2351 County Rd 18 *Web:* www.ngpc.state.ne.us/parks/guides/parksearch/findpark.asp	Ames	NE	68621	402-727-3290	
Gallagher Canyon State Recreation Area 1 East Park Dr 25A *Web:* www.ngpc.state.ne.us/parks/guides/parksearch/findpark.asp	Elwood	NE	68937	308-785-2685	
Indian Cave State Park 65296 720 Rd *Web:* www.ngpc.state.ne.us/parks/guides/parksearch/findpark.asp	Shubert	NE	68437	402-883-2575	
Johnson Lake State Recreation Area 1 East Park Dr 25A *Web:* www.ngpc.state.ne.us/parks/guides/parksearch/findpark.asp	Elwood	NE	68937	308-785-2685	
Keller Park State Recreation Area PO Box 508 *Web:* www.ngpc.state.ne.us/parks/guides/parksearch/findpark.asp	Bassett	NE	68714	402-684-2921	
Lake Maloney State Recreation Area 301 E State Farm Rd *Web:* www.ngpc.state.ne.us/parks/guides/parksearch/findpark.asp	North Platte	NE	69101	308-535-8025	
Lake McConaughy State Recreation Area 1450 Hwy 61N *Web:* www.ngpc.state.ne.us/parks/guides/parksearch/findpark.asp	Ogallala	NE	69153	308-284-8800	
Lake Minatare State Recreation Area PO Box 188 *Web:* www.ngpc.state.ne.us/parks/guides/parksearch/findpark.asp	Minatare	NE	69356	308-783-2911	
Lake Ogallala State Recreation Area 1450 Hwy 61N *Web:* www.ngpc.state.ne.us/parks/guides/parksearch/findpark.asp	Ogallala	NE	69153	308-284-8800	
Lewis & Clark State Recreation Area 54731 897 Rd *Web:* www.ngpc.state.ne.us/parks/guides/parksearch/findpark.asp	Crofton	NE	68730	402-388-4169	
Long Lake State Recreation Area 524 Panzer St PO Box 508 *Web:* www.ngpc.state.ne.us/parks/guides/parksearch/findpark.asp	Bassett	NE	68714	402-684-2921	
Long Pine State Recreation Area 524 Panzer St PO Box 508 *Web:* www.ngpc.state.ne.us/parks/guides/parksearch/findpark.asp	Bassett	NE	68714	402-684-2921	
Louisville State Recreation Area 15810 Hwy 50 *Web:* www.ngpc.state.ne.us/parks/guides/parksearch/findpark.asp	Louisville	NE	68037	402-234-6855	
Medicine Creek State Recreation Area 40611 Rd 728 *Web:* www.ngpc.state.ne.us/parks/guides/parksearch/findpark.asp	Cambridge	NE	69022	308-697-4667	
Memphis State Recreation Area 3019 Apple St *Web:* www.ngpc.state.ne.us/parks/guides/parksearch/findpark.asp	Lincoln	NE	68503	402-471-5566	
Merritt Reservoir State Recreation Area 420 E 1st St *Web:* www.ngpc.state.ne.us/parks/guides/parksearch/findpark.asp	Valentine	NE	69201	402-376-3320	
Mormon Island State Recreation Area 7425 S Hwy 281 *Web:* www.ngpc.state.ne.us/parks/guides/parksearch/findpark.asp	Doniphan	NE	68832	308-385-6211	
Niobrara State Park 89261 522 Ave *Web:* www.ngpc.state.ne.us/parks/guides/parksearch/findpark.asp	Niobrara	NE	68760	402-857-3373	
North Loup State Recreation Area 7425 S US Hwy 281 *Web:* www.ngpc.state.ne.us/parks/guides/parksearch/findpark.asp	Doniphan	NE	68832	308-385-6211	
Olive Creek State Recreation Area 3019 Apple St *Web:* www.ngpc.state.ne.us/parks/guides/parksearch/findpark.asp	Lincoln	NE	68503	402-471-5566	
Oliver Reservoir State Recreation Area 210615 Hwy 71 *Web:* www.ngpc.state.ne.us/parks/guides/parksearch/findpark.asp	Gering	NE	69341	308-436-3777	
Pawnee State Recreation Area RR 4 Box 41B *Web:* www.ngpc.state.ne.us/parks/guides/parksearch/findpark.asp	Lincoln	NE	68524	402-796-2362	
Pelican Point State Recreation Area 640 County Rd 19 *Web:* www.ngpc.state.ne.us/parks/guides/parksearch/findpark.asp	Craig	NE	68019	402-374-1727	
Pibel Lake State Recreation Area HC 79 Box 20L *Web:* www.ngpc.state.ne.us/parks/guides/parksearch/findpark.asp	Burwell	NE	68823	308-346-5666	
Pioneer State Recreation Area 3019 Apple St *Web:* www.ngpc.state.ne.us/parks/guides/parksearch/findpark.asp	Lincoln	NE	68503	402-471-5566	
Platte River State Park 14421 346th St *Web:* www.ngpc.state.ne.us/parks/guides/parksearch/findpark.asp	Louisville	NE	68037	402-234-2217	
Ponca State Park PO Box 688 *Web:* www.ngpc.state.ne.us/parks/guides/parksearch/findpark.asp	Ponca	NE	68770	402-755-2284	
Red Willow Reservoir State Recreation Area RR 1 Box 145 *Web:* www.ngpc.state.ne.us/parks/guides/parksearch/findpark.asp	McCook	NE	69001	308-345-5899	
Riverview Marina State Recreation Area PO Box 15 *Web:* www.ngpc.state.ne.us/parks/guides/parksearch/findpark.asp	Nebraska City	NE	68410	402-873-7222	
Rock Creek Lake State Recreation Area 73122 338 Ave *Web:* www.ngpc.state.ne.us/parks/guides/parksearch/findpark.asp	Enders	NE	69027	308-394-5118	
Rock Creek Station State Historical Park 57426 710th Rd *Web:* www.ngpc.state.ne.us/parks/guides/parksearch/findpark.asp	Fairbury	NE	68352	402-729-5777	
Rock Creek Station State Recreation Area 57426 710th Rd *Web:* www.ngpc.state.ne.us/parks/guides/parksearch/findpark.asp	Fairbury	NE	68352	402-729-5777	
Rockford State Recreation Area 3019 Apple St *Web:* www.ngpc.state.ne.us/parks/guides/parksearch/findpark.asp	Lincoln	NE	68503	402-471-5566	

Nebraska (Cont'd)

Phone | Fax

Sandy Channel State Recreation Area 1020 'V' Rd. .... Kearney NE 68847 308-865-5305
Web: www.ngpc.state.ne.us/parks/guides/parksearch/findpark.asp
Schramm Park State Recreation Area 15810 Hwy 50............ Louisville NE 68037 402-234-6855
Web: www.ngpc.state.ne.us/parks/schramm.html
Sherman Reservoir State Recreation Area RR 2 Box 117 .... Loup City NE 68853 308-745-0230
Web: www.ngpc.state.ne.us/parks/guides/parksearch/findpark.asp
Smith Falls State Park HC 13 Box 25 .... Valentine NE 69201 402-376-1306
Web: www.ngpc.state.ne.us/parks/guides/parksearch/findpark.asp
Stagecoach State Recreation Area 3019 Apple St .... Lincoln NE 68503 402-471-5566
Web: www.ngpc.state.ne.us/parks/guides/parksearch/findpark.asp
Summit Lake State Recreation Area 640 County Rd 19 .... Craig NE 69019 402-374-1727
Web: www.ngpc.state.ne.us/parks/guides/parksearch/findpark.asp
Sutherland Reservoir State Recreation Area
301 E State Farm Rd .... North Platte NE 69101 308-535-8025
Web: www.ngpc.state.ne.us/parks/guides/parksearch/findpark.asp
Swanson Reservoir State Recreation Area RR 2 Box 20 .... Stratton NE 69043 308-276-2671
Web: www.ngpc.state.ne.us/parks/guides/parksearch/findpark.asp
Two Rivers State Recreation Area 27702 'F' St .... Waterloo NE 68069 402-359-5165
Web: www.ngpc.state.ne.us/parks/guides/parksearch/findpark.asp
Union Pacific State Recreation Area 1020 'V' Rd. .... Kearney NE 68847 308-865-5305
Web: www.ngpc.state.ne.us/parks/guides/parksearch/findpark.asp
Verdon State Recreation Area
c/o Indian Cave State Park RR 1, Box 30 .... Shubert NE 68437 402-883-2575
Web: www.ngpc.state.ne.us/parks/guides/parksearch/findpark.asp
Victoria Springs State Recreation Area HC 69 Box 117.......... Anselmo NE 68813 308-749-2235
Web: www.ngpc.state.ne.us/parks/guides/parksearch/findpark.asp
Wagon Train State Recreation Area 3019 Apple St .... Lincoln NE 68503 402-471-5566
Web: www.ngpc.state.ne.us/parks/guides/parksearch/findpark.asp
Walgren Lake State Recreation Area 15951 Hwy 385 .... Chadron NE 69337 308-432-6167
Web: www.ngpc.state.ne.us/parks/guides/parksearch/findpark.asp
War Axe State Recreation Area PO Box 427..................... Gibbon NE 68840 308-468-5700
Web: www.ngpc.state.ne.us/parks/guides/parksearch/findpark.asp
Wildcat Hills State Recreation Area 210615 Hwy 71 .... Gering NE 69341 308-436-3777
Web: www.ngpc.state.ne.us/parks/guides/parksearch/findpark.asp
Willow Creek State Recreation Area 54876 852 Rd................ Pierce NE 68767 402-329-4053
Web: www.ngpc.state.ne.us/parks/guides/parksearch/findpark.asp
Windmill State Recreation Area PO Box 427 .... Gibbon NE 68840 308-468-5700
Web: www.ngpc.state.ne.us/parks/guides/parksearch/findpark.asp

Nevada

Phone | Fax

Beaver Dam State Park PO Box 985 .... Caliente NV 89008 775-728-4460
Web: www.parks.nv.gov/bd.htm
Belmont Courthouse State Historic Site
c/o Fallon Region Headquarters 16799 Lahontan Dam............ Fallon NV 89406 775-867-3001
Web: www.parks.nv.gov/bc.htm
Berlin-Ichthyosaur State Park HC 61 Box 61200 .... Austin NV 89310 775-964-2440 964-2012
Web: www.parks.nv.gov/bi.htm
Big Bend of the Colorado State Recreation Area
PO Box 32850 .... Laughlin NV 89028 702-298-1859
Web: parks.nv.gov/bb.htm
Cathedral Gorge State Park PO Box 176 .... Panaca NV 89042 775-728-4460
Web: www.parks.nv.gov/cg.htm
Cave Lake State Park PO Box 151761.............................. Ely NV 89315 775-728-4460
Web: www.parks.nv.gov/cl.htm
Dayton State Park PO Box 1478.............................. Dayton NV 89403 775-687-5678
Web: parks.nv.gov/dsp.htm
Echo Canyon State Park HC 74 Box 295 .... Pioche NV 89043 775-962-5103
Web: www.parks.nv.gov/ec.htm
Fort Churchill State Historic Park 1000 Hwy 95A........... Silver Springs NV 89429 775-577-2345
Web: www.parks.nv.gov/fc.htm
Kershaw-Ryan State Park PO Box 985......................... Caliente NV 89008 775-726-3564 726-3557
Web: www.parks.nv.gov/kr.htm
Lahontan State Recreation Area 16799 Lahontan Dam............ Fallon NV 89406 775-577-2235
Web: www.parks.nv.gov/lah.htm
Lake Tahoe Nevada State Park PO Box 8867 .... Incline Village NV 89452 775-831-0494 831-2514
Web: www.parks.nv.gov/lt.htm
Mormon Station State Historic Park .... Genoa NV 89411 775-782-2590
Web: www.parks.nv.gov/ms.htm
Old Las Vegas Mormon Fort State Historic Park
500 E Washington Ave.................................. Las Vegas NV 89101 702-486-3511 486-3734
Web: www.parks.nv.gov/olvmf.htm
Rye Patch State Recreation Area
2505 Rye Patch Reservoir Rd .... Lovelock NV 89419 775-538-7321
Web: www.parks.nv.gov/rp.htm
South Fork State Recreation Area
353 Lower South Fork Unit 8 .... Spring Creek NV 89815 775-744-4346
Web: www.parks.nv.gov/sf.htm
Spring Mountain Ranch State Park PO Box 124............ Blue Diamond NV 89004 702-875-4141
Web: www.parks.nv.gov/smr.htm
Spring Valley State Park HC 74 Box 201....................... Pioche NV 89043 775-962-5102
Web: www.parks.nv.gov/sv.htm
Valley of Fire State Park Valley Fire Rd PO Box 515 .... Overton NV 89040 702-397-2088 397-2621
Web: www.parks.nv.gov/vf.htm
Walker Lake State Recreation Area
c/o Fallon Region Headquarters 16799 Lahontan Dam .... Fallon NV 89406 775-867-3001
Web: www.parks.nv.gov/walk.htm
Ward Charcoal Ovens State Historic Park PO Box 151761............ Ely NV 89315 775-728-4460
Web: www.parks.nv.gov/ww.htm
Washoe Lake State Park 4855 East Lake Blvd................ Carson City NV 89704 775-687-4319
Web: www.parks.nv.gov/wl.htm
Wild Horse State Recreation Area HC 31 Box 265 .... Elko NV 89801 775-758-6493
Web: www.parks.nv.gov/wh.htm

New Hampshire

Phone | Fax

Ahern State Park Rt 106.................................... Laconia NH 03246 603-823-7722
Web: www.nhstateparks.org/ParksPages/Ahern/Ahern.html
Androscoggin Wayside Park Rt 16............................... Errol NH 03579 603-538-6707
Web: www.nhstateparks.org/ParksPages/Androscoggin/Androscoggin.html
Annett Wayside Park Cathedral Rd............................ Rindge NH 03461 603-485-2034
Web: www.nhstateparks.org/ParksPages/Annett/Annett.html
Bear Brook State Park 157 Deerfield Rd .... Allenstown NH 03275 603-271-3556 271-3553
Web: www.nhstateparks.org/ParksPages/BearBrook/BearBrk.html
Beaver Brook Falls Wayside Park .... Colebrook NH 03576 603-538-6707
Web: www.nhstateparks.org/ParksPages/BeaverBrook/BeaverBrook.html
Bedell Bridge State Park .... Haverhill NH 03765 603-823-7722
Web: www.nhstateparks.org/ParksPages/BedellBridge/BedellBridge.html
Cardigan State Park .... Orange NH 03741 603-823-7722
Web: www.nhstateparks.org/ParksPages/Cardigan/Cardigan.html
Chesterfield Gorge Natural Area Rt 9 .... Chesterfield NH 03443 603-363-8373
Web: www.nhstateparks.org/ParksPages/ChesterfieldGorge/Chesterfield.html
Clough State Park .... Weare NH 03281 603-529-7112
Web: www.nhstateparks.org/ParksPages/Clough/Clough.html
Coleman State Park Rt 26 Little Diamond Pond Rd .... Stewartstown NH 03597 603-237-5382
Web: www.nhstateparks.org/ParksPages/Coleman/Coleman.html
Crawford Notch State Park Rt 302....................... Harts Location NH 03812 603-374-2272
Web: www.nhstateparks.org/ParksPages/CrawfordNotch/CrawfordNotch.html
Daniel Webster Birthplace .... Franklin NH 03235 603-934-5057
Web: www.nhstateparks.org/ParksPages/DanWebster/DanielWebster.html
Deer Mountain Campground 5309 N Main St.................. Pittsburg NH 03592 603-538-6965
Web: www.nhstateparks.org/ParksPages/DeerMountain/DeerMountainCmp.html
Dixville Notch State Park Rt 26.............................. Dixville NH 03576 603-538-6707
Web: www.nhstateparks.org/ParksPages/DixvilleNotch/Dixville.html
Echo Lake State Park .... Conway NH 03818 603-356-2672
Web: www.nhstateparks.org/ParksPages/EchoLake/EchoLake.html
Eisenhower Memorial Wayside Park Rt 302 .... Carroll NH 03598 603-323-2087
Web: www.nhstateparks.org/ParksPages/Eisenhower/Eisenhower.html
Ellacoya State Park 280 Scenic Dr. .... Gilford NH 03246 603-293-7821
Web: www.nhstateparks.org/ParksPages/Ellacoya/Ellacoya.html
Endicott Rock Rt 3 .... Laconia NH 03246 603-823-7722
Web: www.nhstateparks.org/ParksPages/Endicott/Endicott.html
Forest Lake State Park .... Dalton NH 03598 603-837-9150
Web: www.nhstateparks.org/ParksPages/ForestLake/ForestLake.html
Fort Constitution Historic Site 25 Wentworth Rd .... New Castle NH 03854 603-436-1552
Web: www.nhstateparks.org/ParksPages/FortConstitution/FortConstitution.html
Fort Stark Historic Site Wildrose Ln .... New Castle NH 03854 603-436-1552
Web: www.nhstateparks.org/ParksPages/FortStark/FortStark.html
Franconia Notch State Park .... Franconia NH 03580 603-745-8391
Web: www.franconianotchstatepark.com
Franklin Pierce Homestead Historic Site
c/o Hillsborough Historical Society PO Box 896.............. Hillsboro NH 03244 603-478-3165
Web: www.nhstateparks.org/ParksPages/FranklinPierce/FranklinPierce.html
Gardner Memorial Wayside Park Rt 4A........................ Wilmot NH 03287 603-485-2034
Web: www.nhstateparks.org/ParksPages/Gardner/Gardner.html
Governor Wentworth Historic Site Rt 109 .... Wolfeboro NH 03894 603-823-7722
Web: www.nhstateparks.org/ParksPages/GovWentworth/GovWentworth.html
Greenfield State Park Rt 136................................ Greenfield NH 03047 603-547-3497
Web: www.nhstateparks.org/ParksPages/Greenfield/Grnfld.html
Hampton Beach State Park Rt 1A .... Hampton NH 03842 603-926-3784
Web: www.nhstateparks.org/ParksPages/Hampton/Hampton.html
Hannah Duston Memorial .... Boscawen NH 03303 603-485-2034
Web: www.nhstateparks.org/ParksPages/HannahDuston/HannahDuston.html
Jenness State Beach Rt 1A .... Rye NH 03870 603-436-1552
Web: www.nhstateparks.org/ParksPages/Jenness/Jenness.html
John Wingate Weeks Historic Site .... Lancaster NH 03584 603-788-4004
Web: www.nhstateparks.org/ParksPages/Weeks/Weeks.html
Kingston State Park 124 Main St............................. Kingston NH 03848 603-642-5471
Web: www.nhstateparks.org/ParksPages/Kingston/Kingston.html
Lake Francis State Park 439 River Rd........................ Pittsburg NH 03592 603-538-6965
Web: www.nhstateparks.org/ParksPages/LakeFrancis/LakeFrancis.html
Lake Tarleton State Park Route 25C .... Piermont NH 03779 603-823-7722
Web: www.nhstateparks.org/ParksPages/LakeTarleton/LakeTarleton.html
Madison Boulder Natural Area .... Madison NH 03849 603-823-7722
Web: www.nhstateparks.org/ParksPages/MadisonBoulder/MadisonBoulder.html
Milan Hill State Park Rt 16 .... Milan NH 03588 603-466-3860
Web: www.nhstateparks.org/ParksPages/MilanHill/MilanHill.html
Miller State Park Rt 101E................................ Peterborough NH 03458 603-924-3672
Web: www.nhstateparks.org/ParksPages/Miller/Miller.html
Mollidgewock State Park Rt 16 .... Errol NH 03579 603-482-3373
Web: www.nhstateparks.org/ParksPages/Mollidgewock/Mollidgewock.html
Monadnock State Park Rt 124.................................. Jaffrey NH 03452 603-532-8862
Web: www.nhstateparks.org/ParksPages/Monadnock/Monadnock.html
Moose Brook State Park RFD 1 30 Jimtown Rd .... Gorham NH 03581 603-466-3860
Web: www.nhparks.state.nh.us/ParksPages/MooseBrook/MooseBrook.html
Mount Sunapee State Park .... Newbury NH 03255 603-763-5561
Web: www.nhstateparks.org/ParksPages/Sunapee/Sunapee.html
Mount Washington State Park Rt 302 .... Sargent's Purchase NH 03581 603-466-3347
Web: www.nhstateparks.org/ParksPages/MtWash/MtWash.html
Nansen Wayside Park Rt 16 .... Milan NH 03588 603-823-7722
Web: www.nhstateparks.org/ParksPages/Nansen/Nansen.html
North Beach Rt 1A.. Hampton NH 03842 603-436-1552
Web: www.nhparks.state.nh.us/ParksPages/NorthBeach/NorthBeach.html
North Hampton State Beach Rt 1A.............................. Hampton NH 03862 603-436-1552
Web: www.nhstateparks.org/ParksPages/NHampton/NHampton.html
Northwood Meadows State Park .... Northwood NH 03261 603-485-2034
Web: www.nhstateparks.org/ParksPages/NorthwoodMeadows/NorthwoodMdws.html
Odiorne Point State Park Rt 1A .... Rye NH 03870 603-436-7406
Web: www.nhstateparks.org/ParksPages/Odiorne/Odiorne.html
Pawtuckaway State Park 128 Mountain Rd.................. Nottingham NH 03290 603-895-3031
Web: www.nhstateparks.org/ParksPages/Pawtuckaway/Pawtuckaway.html
Pillsbury State Park .... Washington NH 03280 603-863-2860
Web: www.nhstateparks.org/ParksPages/Pillsbury/Pillsbury.html
Pisgah State Park PO Box 242.............................. Winchester NH 03470 603-239-8153
Web: www.nhstateparks.org/ParksPages/Pisgah/Pisgah.html
Rhododendron State Park Rt 119W .... Fitzwilliam NH 03447 603-532-8862
Web: www.nhstateparks.org/ParksPages/Rhododendron/Rhododendron.html
Robert Frost Farm Historic Site Route 28 .... Derry NH 03038 603-432-3091
Web: www.nhstateparks.org/ParksPages/FrostFarm/Frost.html
Rollins State Park .... Warner NH 03278 603-456-3808
Web: www.nhstateparks.org/ParksPages/Rollins/Rollins.html
Rye Harbor State Park .... Rye NH 03870 603-436-1552
Web: www.nhstateparks.org/ParksPages/RyeHarbor/RyeHarbor.html
Sculptured Rocks Natural Area .... Groton NH 03241 603-823-7722
Web: www.nhstateparks.org/ParksPages/SculpturedRocks/SculpturedRocks.html
Silver Lake State Park Rt 122 .... Hollis NH 03049 603-465-2342
Web: www.nhstateparks.org/ParksPages/SilverLake/SilverLake.html
Taylor Mill Historic Site Island Pond Rd......................... Derry NH 03038 603-431-6774
Umbagog Lake State Park Rt 26 .... Cambridge NH 03579 603-482-7795
Web: www.nhstateparks.org/ParksPages/Umbagog/Umbagog.html
Wadleigh State Park Rt 114..................................... Sutton NH 03260 603-927-4724
Web: www.nhstateparks.org/ParksPages/Wadleigh/Wadleigh.html
Wallis Sands State Beach Rt 1A .... Rye NH 03870 603-436-9404
Web: www.nhstateparks.org/ParksPages/Wallis/Wallis.html
Wellington State Park .... Bristol NH 03222 603-744-2197
Web: www.nhstateparks.org/ParksPages/Wellington/Wellington.html
Wentworth-Coolidge Mansion Historic Site
375 Little Harbor Rd .... Portsmouth NH 03801 603-436-6607
Web: www.nhparks.state.nh.us/ParksPages/WentworthCoolidge/WentCoolHom.html
Wentworth State Park .... Wolfeboro NH 03894 603-569-3699
Web: www.nhstateparks.org/ParksPages/Wentworth/Wentworth.html
White Lake State Park Rt 16 .... Tamworth NH 03886 603-323-7350
Web: www.nhstateparks.org/ParksPages/WhiteLake/WhiteLake.html
Winslow State Park Kearsarge Mountain Rd .... Wilmot NH 03287 603-526-6168
Web: www.nhstateparks.org/ParksPages/Winslow/Winslow.html

New Jersey

	City	State	Zip	Phone	Fax
Abram S. Hewitt State Forest c/o Wawayanda State Park 885 Warwick Tpke	Hewitt	NJ	07421	973-853-4462	
Web: www.njparksandforests.org/parks/abram.html					
Allaire State Park PO Box 220	Farmingdale	NJ	07727	732-938-2371	
Web: www.njparksandforests.org/parks/allaire.html					
Allamuchy Mountain State Park c/o Stephens State Park 800 Willow Grove St	Hackettstown	NJ	07840	908-852-3790	
Web: www.njparksandforests.org/parks/allamuch.html					
Atsion Recreation Area c/o Wharton State Forest 4110 Nesco Rd	Hammonton	NJ	08037	609-268-0444	
Web: www.njparksandforests.org/parks/wharton.html					
Barnegat Lighthouse State Park PO Box 167	Barnegat Light	NJ	08006	609-494-2016	
Web: www.njparksandforests.org/parks/barnlig.html					
Bass River State Forest 762 Stage Rd	Tuckerton	NJ	08087	609-296-1114	
Web: www.njparksandforests.org/parks/bass.html					
Batsto Village State Historic Site RD 9	Hammonton	NJ	08037	609-561-0024	
Web: www.njparksandforests.org/historic/index.html					
Belleplain State Forest County Rt 50 PO Box 450	Woodbine	NJ	08270	609-861-2404	
Web: www.njparksandforests.org/parks/belle.html					
Boxwood Hall State Historic Site 1073 E Jersey St	Elizabeth	NJ	07201	908-282-7167	
Web: www.njparksandforests.org/historic/index.html					
Brendan T. Byrne State Forest PO Box 215	New Lisbon	NJ	08064	609-726-1191	
Web: www.njparksandforests.org/parks/byrne.html					
Bull's Island Recreation Area 2185 Daniel Bray Hwy	Stockton	NJ	08559	609-397-2949	
Web: www.njparksandforests.org/parks/bull.html					
Cape May Point State Park PO Box 107	Cape May Point	NJ	08212	609-884-2159	
Web: www.njparksandforests.org/parks/capemay.html					
Cheesequake State Park 300 Gordon Rd	Matawan	NJ	07747	732-566-2161	
Web: www.njparksandforests.org/parks/cheesequake.html					
Corson's Inlet State Park c/o Belleplain State Forest County Rt 550, PO Box 450	Woodbine	NJ	08270	609-861-2404	
Web: www.njparksandforests.org/parks/corsons.html					
Craig House State Historic Site 347 Freehold-Englishtown Rd	Manalapan	NJ	07726	732-462-9616	
Web: www.njparksandforests.org/historic/index.html					
Delaware & Raritan Canal State Park 145 Mapleton Rd	Princeton	NJ	08540	609-924-5705	
Web: www.njparksandforests.org/parks/drcanal.html					
Double Trouble State Park PO Box 175	Bayville	NJ	08721	732-341-6662	
Web: www.njparksandforests.org/parks/double.html					
Farny State Park c/o Ringwood State Park 1304 Sloatsburg Rd	Ringwood	NJ	07456	973-962-7031	
Web: www.njparksandforests.org/parks/farny.html					
Fort Mott State Park 454 Fort Mott Rd	Pennsville	NJ	08070	856-935-3218	
Web: www.njparksandforests.org/parks/fortmott.html					
Grover Cleveland Birthplace State Historic Site 207 Bloomfield Ave	Caldwell	NJ	07006	973-226-0001	
Web: www.njparksandforests.org/historic/grover_cleveland/gc_home.htm					
Hacklebarney State Park c/o Voorhees State Park 119 Hacklebarney Rd	Long Valley	NJ	07853	908-638-6969	
Web: www.njparksandforests.org/parks/hackle.html					
Hancock House State Historic Site 3 Front St	Hancock's Bridge	NJ	08038	856-935-4373	
Web: www.njparksandforests.org/historic/hancockhouse/hancockhouse-index.htm					
High Point State Park 1480 Rt 23	Sussex	NJ	07461	973-875-4800	
Web: www.njparksandforests.org/parks/highpoint.html					
Hopatcong State Park PO Box 8519	Landing	NJ	07850	973-398-7010	
Web: www.njparksandforests.org/parks/hopatcong.html					
Indian King Tavern State Historic Site 233 Kings Hwy	Haddonfield	NJ	08033	856-429-6792	
Web: www.njparksandforests.org/historic/indianking/index.html					
Island Beach State Park PO Box 37	Seaside Park	NJ	08752	732-793-0506	
Web: www.njparksandforests.org/parks/island.html					
Jenny Jump State Forest PO Box 150	Hope	NJ	07844	908-459-4366	
Web: www.njparksandforests.org/parks/jennyjump.html					
Kittatinny Valley State Park PO Box 621	Andover	NJ	07821	973-786-6445	
Web: www.njparksandforests.org/parks/kittval.html					
Liberty State Park 200Morris Pesin Dr	Jersey City	NJ	07305	201-915-3440	915-3408
Web: www.njparksandforests.org/parks/liberty.html					
Long Pond Ironworks State Park c/o Ringwood State Park 1304 Sloatsburg Rd	Ringwood	NJ	07456	973-962-7031	
Web: www.njparksandforests.org/parks/longpond.html					
Monmouth Battlefield State Park 347 Freehold-Englishtown Rd	Manalapan	NJ	07726	732-462-9616	
Web: www.njparksandforests.org/parks/monbat.html					
Norvin Green State Forest c/o Ringwood State Park 1304 Sloatsburg Rd	Ringwood	NJ	07456	973-962-7031	
Web: www.njparksandforests.org/parks/norvin.html					
Old Dutch Parsonage State Historic Site 71 Somerset St	Somerville	NJ	08876	908-725-1015	
Parvin State Park 701 Almond Rd	Pittsgrove	NJ	08318	856-358-8616	
Web: www.njparksandforests.org/parks/parvin.html					
Penn State Forest c/o Bass River State Forest 762 Stage Rd	Tuckerton	NJ	08087	609-296-1114	
Web: www.njparksandforests.org/parks/penn.html					
Princeton Battlefield State Park 500 Mercer Rd	Princeton	NJ	08540	609-921-0074	
Web: www.njparksandforests.org/parks/princeton.html					
Ramapo Mountain State Forest c/o Ringwood State Park 1304 Sloatsburg Rd	Ringwood	NJ	07456	973-962-7031	
Web: www.njparksandforests.org/parks/ramapo.html					
Rancocas State Park c/o Brendan T. Byrne State Forest PO Box 215	New Lisbon	NJ	08064	609-726-1191	
Web: www.njparksandforests.org/parks/rancocas.html					
Ringwood State Park 1304 Sloatsburg Rd	Ringwood	NJ	07456	973-962-7031	
Web: www.njparksandforests.org/parks/ringwood.html					
Rockingham State Historic Site PO Box 496	Kingston	NJ	08528	609-683-7132	
Web: www.rockingham.net					
Round Valley Recreation Area 1220 Lebanon-Stanton Rd	Lebanon	NJ	08833	908-236-6355	
Web: www.njparksandforests.org/parks/round.html					
Somers Mansion State Historic Site 1000 Shore Rd	Somers Point	NJ	08244	609-927-2212	
Web: www.njparksandforests.org/historic/index.html					
Spruce Run Recreation Area 68 Van Syckel's Rd	Clinton	NJ	08809	908-638-8572	
Web: www.njparksandforests.org/parks/spruce.html					
Stephens State Park 800 Willow Grove St	Hackettstown	NJ	07840	908-852-3790	
Web: www.njparksandforests.org/parks/stephens.html					
Steuben House State Historic Site 1209 Main St	River Edge	NJ	07661	201-487-1739	
Web: www.njparksandforests.org/historic/index.html					
Stokes State Forest 1 Coursen Rd	Branchville	NJ	07826	973-948-3820	
Web: www.njparksandforests.org/parks/stokes.html					
Swartswood State Park PO Box 123	Swartswood	NJ	07877	973-383-5230	
Web: www.njparksandforests.org/parks/swartswood.html					
The Hermitage State Historic Site 335 N Franklin Tpke	Ho-Ho-Kus	NJ	07423	201-445-8311	445-0437
Web: www.thehermitage.org					
Trenton Battle Monument State Historic Site 348 N Warren St	Trenton	NJ	08638	609-737-0623	
Web: www.njparksandforests.org/historic/Trentonbattlemonument/index.htm					
Twin Lights State Historic Site Lighthouse Rd	Highlands	NJ	07732	732-872-1886	
Web: twin-lights.org					
Voorhees State Park 251 County Rd 513	Glen Gardner	NJ	08826	908-638-6969	
Web: www.njparksandforests.org/parks/voorhees.html					
Wallace House State Historic Site 71 Somerset St	Somerville	NJ	08876	908-725-1015	
Web: www.njparksandforests.org/historic/olddutch-wallace/odwh-wallacehouse.htm					
Walt Whitman House State Historic Site 330 Mickle Blvd	Camden	NJ	08103	609-964-5383	
Web: www.njparksandforests.org/historic/whitman/index.html					
Washington Crossing State Park 355 Washington Crossing-Pennington Rd	Titusville	NJ	08560	609-737-0623	
Web: www.njparksandforests.org/parks/washcros.html					
Washington Rock State Park c/o Liberty State Park Morris Pesin Dr	Jersey City	NJ	07305	201-915-3401	
Web: www.njparksandforests.org/parks/washrock.html					
Wawayanda State Park 885 Warwick Tpke	Hewitt	NJ	07421	973-853-4462	
Web: www.njparksandforests.org/parks/wawayanda.html					
Wharton State Forest 4110 Nesco Rd	Hammonton	NJ	08037	609-561-0024	
Web: www.njparksandforests.org/parks/wharton.html					
Worthington State Forest HC 62 Box 2	Columbia	NJ	07832	908-841-9575	
Web: www.njparksandforests.org/parks/worthington.html					

New Mexico

	City	State	Zip	Phone	Fax
Bluewater Lake State Park PO Box 3419	Prewitt	NM	87045	505-876-2391	
Web: www.emnrd.state.nm.us/PRD/Bluewater.htm					
Bottomless Lakes State Park HC 12 Box 1200	Roswell	NM	88201	505-624-6058	624-6029
Web: www.emnrd.state.nm.us/PRD/bottomless.htm					
Brantley Lake State Park PO Box 2288	Carlsbad	NM	88221	505-457-2384	457-2385
Web: www.emnrd.state.nm.us/PRD/ParksPages/Brantley.htm					
Caballo Lake State Park PO Box 32	Caballo	NM	87931	505-743-3942	
Web: www.emnrd.state.nm.us/PRD/caballo.htm					
Cimarron Canyon State Park PO Box 185	Eagle Nest	NM	87718	505-377-6271	
Web: www.emnrd.state.nm.us/PRD/CimarronCanyon.htm					
City of Rocks State Park PO Box 50	Faywood	NM	88034	505-536-2800	
Web: www.emnrd.state.nm.us/PRD/cityrocks.htm					
Clayton Lake State Park 141 Clayton Lake Rd	Clayton	NM	88415	505-374-8808	
Web: www.emnrd.state.nm.us/PRD/Clayton.htm					
Conchas Lake State Park PO Box 976	Conchas Dam	NM	88416	505-868-2270	
Web: www.emnrd.state.nm.us/PRD/Conchas.htm					
Coyote Creek State Park PO Box 477	Guadalupita	NM	87722	505-387-2328	
Web: www.emnrd.state.nm.us/PRD/CoyoteCreek.htm					
El Vado Lake State Park PO Box 367	Tierra Amarilla	NM	87575	505-588-7247	
Web: www.emnrd.state.nm.us/PRD/elvado.htm					
Elephant Butte Lake State Park PO Box 13	Elephant Butte	NM	87935	505-744-5923	
Web: www.emnrd.state.nm.us/PRD/elephant.htm					
Fenton Lake State Park 455 Fenton Lake	Jemez Springs	NM	87025	505-829-3630	
Web: www.emnrd.state.nm.us/PRD/Fenton.htm					
Heron Lake State Park PO Box 159	Los Ojos	NM	87551	505-588-7470	
Web: www.emnrd.state.nm.us/PRD/heron.htm					
Hyde Memorial State Park 740 Hyde Park Rd	Santa Fe	NM	87501	505-983-7175	
Web: www.emnrd.state.nm.us/PRD/Hyde.htm					
Leasburg Dam State Park PO Box 6	Radium Springs	NM	88054	505-524-4068	526-5420
Web: www.emnrd.state.nm.us/PRD/leasburg.htm					
Living Desert Zoo & Gardens State Park PO Box 100	Carsbad	NM	88221	505-887-5516	885-4478
Web: www.emnrd.state.nm.us/PRD/LivingDesert.htm					
Manzano Mountains State Park HC 66 Box 202	Mountainair	NM	87036	505-847-2820	
Web: www.emnrd.state.nm.us/PRD/Manzano.htm					
Morphy Lake State Park PO Box 477	Guadalupita	NM	87722	505-387-2328	
Web: www.emnrd.state.nm.us/PRD/MorphyLake.htm					
Navajo Lake State Park 1448 NM 511 #1	Najavo Dam	NM	87419	505-632-2278	
Web: www.emnrd.state.nm.us/PRD/navajo.htm					
Oasis State Park 1891 Oasis Rd	Portales	NM	88130	505-356-5331	356-5331
Web: www.emnrd.state.nm.us/PRD/Oasis.htm					
Oliver Lee Memorial State Park 409 Dog Canyon Rd	Alamogordo	NM	88310	505-437-8284	439-1290
Web: www.emnrd.state.nm.us/PRD/oliverlee.htm					
Pancho Villa State Park PO Box 450	Columbus	NM	88029	505-531-2711	
Web: www.emnrd.state.nm.us/PRD/PanchoVilla.htm					
Percha Dam State Park PO Box 32	Caballo	NM	87931	505-743-3942	
Web: www.emnrd.state.nm.us/PRD/Percha.htm					
Rio Grande Nature Center State Park 2901 Candelaria Rd NW	Albuquerque	NM	87107	505-344-7240	344-4505
Web: www.emnrd.state.nm.us/PRD/RGNC.htm					
Rockhound State Park PO Box 1064	Deming	NM	88030	505-546-6182	
Web: www.emnrd.state.nm.us/PRD/Rockhound.htm					
Santa Rosa Lake State Park PO Box 384	Santa Rosa	NM	88433	505-472-3110	472-5956
Web: www.emnrd.state.nm.us/PRD/santarosa.htm					
Smokey Bear Historical State Park PO Box 591	Capitan	NM	88316	505-354-2748	
Web: www.SmokeyBearPark.com					
Storrie Lake State Park HC 33 Box 109 #2	Las Vegas	NM	87701	505-425-7278	
Web: www.emnrd.state.nm.us/PRD/StorrieLake.htm					
Sugarite Canyon State Park HC 63 Box 386	Raton	NM	87740	505-445-5607	
Web: www.emnrd.state.nm.us/PRD/Sugarite.htm					
Sumner Lake State Park HC 64 Box 125	Fort Sumner	NM	88119	505-355-2541	355-2542
Web: www.emnrd.state.nm.us/PRD/SumnerLake.htm					
Ute Lake State Park PO Box 52	Logan	NM	88426	505-487-2284	
Web: www.emnrd.state.nm.us/PRD/UteLake.htm					
Villanueva State Park PO Box 40	Villanueva	NM	87583	505-421-2957	421-3231
Web: www.emnrd.state.nm.us/PRD/Villanueva.htm					

New York

	City	State	Zip	Phone	Fax
Allan H. Treman State Marine Park c/o Robert H. Treman State Park 105 Enfield Falls Rd	Ithaca	NY	14850	607-273-3440	
Web: nysparks.state.ny.us/parks/info.asp?parkId=103					
Allegany State Park 2373 ASP, Rt 1, Suite 3	Salamanca	NY	14779	716-354-9121	
Web: nysparks.state.ny.us/parks/info.asp?parkId=91					
Battle Island State Park 2150 State Rt 48	Fulton	NY	13069	315-593-3408	
Web: nysparks.state.ny.us/parks/info.asp?parkId=15					
Bayard Cutting Arboretum State Park PO Box 466	Oakdale	NY	11769	631-581-1002	
Web: nysparks.state.ny.us/parks/info.asp?parkId=43					
Bayswater Point State Park c/o Gantry Plaza State Park 50-50 2nd St	Long Island City	NY	11101	718-471-2212	
Web: nysparks.state.ny.us/parks/info.asp?parkId=27					
Bear Mountain State Park c/o Palisades Interstate Park Commission	Bear Mountain	NY	10911	845-786-2701	
Web: nysparks.state.ny.us/parks/info.asp?parkId=55					
Beaver Island State Park 2136 W Oakfield Rd	Grand Island	NY	14072	716-773-3271	
Web: nysparks.state.ny.us/parks/info.asp?parkId=94					
Belmont Lake State Park PO Box 247	Babylon	NY	11702	631-667-5055	
Web: nysparks.state.ny.us/parks/info.asp?parkId=159					
Bennington Battlefield State Historic Site c/o Grafton Lakes State Park PO Box 163	Grafton	NY	12082	518-686-7109	279-1902
Web: www.nysparks.com/sites/info.asp?siteID=3					
Bethpage State Park Bethpage Pkwy	Farmingdale	NY	11735	516-249-0701	
Web: nysparks.state.ny.us/parks/info.asp?parkId=67					

New York (Cont'd)

Name / Address	City	State	ZIP	Phone	Fax
Big Six Mile Creek Marina State Park					
c/o Beaver Island State Park 2136 W Oakfield Rd	Grand Island	NY	14072	716-773-3271	
Web: nysparks.state.ny.us/parks/info.asp?parkId=40					
Blauvelt State Park					
c/o Palisades Interstate Park Commission	Bear Mountain	NY	10911	845-359-0544	
Web: nysparks.state.ny.us/parks/info.asp?parkId=53					
Bonavista State Park Golf Course 7194 County Rd 132	Ovid	NY	14521	607-869-5482	
Web: nysparks.state.ny.us/parks/info.asp?parkId=30					
Bowman Lake State Park 745 Bliven Sherman Rd	Oxford	NY	13830	607-334-2718	
Web: nysparks.state.ny.us/parks/info.asp?parkId=16					
Buckhorn Island State Park					
c/o Beaver Island State Park 2136 W Oakfield Rd	Grand Island	NY	14072	716-773-3271	
Web: nysparks.state.ny.us/parks/info.asp?parkId=21					
Burnham Point State Park 340765 NYS Rt 12E	Cape Vincent	NY	13618	315-654-2522	
Web: nysparks.state.ny.us/parks/info.asp?parkId=140					
Buttermilk Falls State Park					
c/o Robert H. Tremin State Park 105 Enfield Falls Rd	Ithaca	NY	14850	607-273-3440	
Web: nysparks.state.ny.us/parks/info.asp?parkId=25					
Caleb Smith State Park Preserve PO Box 963	Smithtown	NY	11787	631-265-1054	
Web: nysparks.state.ny.us/parks/info.asp?parkId=160					
Camp Hero State Park 50 S Fairview Ave	Montauk	NY	11954	631-668-3781	
Web: nysparks.state.ny.us/parks/info.asp?parkId=82					
Canandaigua Lake State Marine Park 620 S Main St	Canandaigua	NY	14424	315-789-2331	
Web: nysparks.state.ny.us/parks/info.asp?parkId=4					
Canoe-Picnic Point State Park					
c/o Cedar Point State Park 36661 Cedar Point State Park Dr	Clayton	NY	13624	315-654-2522	
Web: nysparks.state.ny.us/parks/info.asp?parkId=118					
Captree State Park					
c/o Long Island Regional Office PO Box 247	Babylon	NY	11702	631-669-0449	
Web: nysparks.state.ny.us/parks/info.asp?parkId=151					
Caumsett State Historic Park 25 Lloyd Harbor Rd	Huntington	NY	11743	631-423-1770	423-8645
Web: www.nysparks.com/sites/info.asp?siteID=4					
Cayuga Lake State Park 2678 Lower Lake Rd	Seneca Falls	NY	13148	315-568-5163	
Web: nysparks.state.ny.us/parks/info.asp?parkId=9					
Cedar Island State Park					
c/o Keewaydin State Park PO Box 247	Alexandria Bay	NY	13607	315-482-3331	
Web: nysparks.state.ny.us/parks/info.asp?parkId=141					
Cedar Point State Park 36661 Cedar Point State Park Dr	Clayton	NY	13624	315-654-2522	
Web: nysparks.state.ny.us/parks/info.asp?parkId=126					
Chenango Valley State Park 153 State Park Rd	Chenango Forks	NY	13746	607-648-5251	
Web: nysparks.state.ny.us/parks/info.asp?parkId=5					
Cherry Plain State Park 26 State Park Rd PO Box 11	Cherry Plain	NY	12040	518-733-5400	
Web: nysparks.state.ny.us/parks/info.asp?parkId=115					
Chittenango Falls State Park 2300 Rathbun Rd	Cazenovia	NY	13035	315-655-9620	
Web: nysparks.state.ny.us/parks/info.asp?parkId=11					
Clarence Fahnestock State Park 1498 Rt 301	Carmel	NY	10512	845-225-7207	
Web: nysparks.state.ny.us/parks/info.asp?parkId=129					
Clark Reservation State Park 6105 E Seneca Tpke	Jamesville	NY	13078	315-492-1590	
Web: nysparks.state.ny.us/parks/info.asp?parkId=17					
Clay Pit Ponds State Park Preserve 83 Nielsen Ave	Staten Island	NY	10309	718-967-1976	
Web: nysparks.state.ny.us/parks/info.asp?parkId=32					
Clermont State Historic Site 1 Clermont Ave	Germantown	NY	12526	518-537-4240	537-6240
Web: www.nysparks.com/sites/info.asp?siteID=5					
Clinton House State Historic Site					
PO Box 88 549 Main St	Poughkeepsie	NY	12602	845-471-1630	471-8777
Web: nysparks.state.ny.us/sites/info.asp?siteID=1					
Cold Spring Harbor State Park					
c/o Caumsett State Historic Park 25 Lloyd Harbor Rd	Huntington	NY	11743	631-423-1770	
Web: nysparks.state.ny.us/parks/info.asp?parkId=85					
Coles Creek State Park PO Box 442	Waddington	NY	13694	315-388-5636	
Web: nysparks.state.ny.us/parks/info.asp?parkId=156					
Connetquot River State Park Preserve PO Box 505	Oakdale	NY	11769	631-581-1005	
Web: nysparks.state.ny.us/parks/info.asp?parkId=69					
Crailo State Historic Site 9 1/2 Riverside Ave	Rensselaer	NY	12144	518-463-8738	
Web: www.nysparks.com/sites/info.asp?siteID=7					
Crown Point State Historic Site 739 Bridge Rd	Crown Point	NY	12928	518-597-4666	597-3666
Web: www.nysparks.com/sites/info.asp?siteID=8					
Cumberland Bay State Park 152 Cumberland Head Rd	Plattsburg	NY	12901	518-563-5240	
Web: nysparks.state.ny.us/parks/info.asp?parkId=127					
Darien Lakes State Park 10289 Harlow Rd	Darien Center	NY	14040	585-547-9242	
Web: nysparks.state.ny.us/parks/info.asp?parkId=63					
Darwin Martin House State Historic Site 125 Jewett Pkwy	Buffalo	NY	14214	716-856-3858	856-4009
Web: nysparks.state.ny.us/sites/info.asp?siteID=35					
Delta Lake State Park 8797 State Rt 46	Rome	NY	13440	315-337-4670	
Web: nysparks.state.ny.us/parks/info.asp?parkId=18					
Devil's Hole State Park					
c/o Niagara Frontier Region PO Box 1132	Niagara Falls	NY	14303	716-284-4691	
Web: nysparks.state.ny.us/parks/info.asp?parkId=28					
Dewolf Point State Park 45920 County Rt 191	Fineview	NY	13640	315-482-2012	
Web: nysparks.state.ny.us/parks/info.asp?parkId=142					
Earl W. Brydges Artpark State Park 450 S 4th St	Lewiston	NY	14092	716-754-9000	
Web: nysparks.state.ny.us/parks/info.asp?parkId=106					
Eel Weir State Park RD 3	Ogdensburg	NY	13669	315-393-1138	
Web: nysparks.state.ny.us/parks/info.asp?parkId=122					
Empire-Fulton Ferry State Park 26 New Dock St	Brooklyn	NY	11201	718-858-4708	
Web: nysparks.state.ny.us/parks/info.asp?parkId=70					
Evangola State Park 10191 Old Lake Shore Rd	Irving	NY	14081	716-549-1802	
Web: nysparks.state.ny.us/parks/info.asp?parkId=101					
Fair Haven Beach State Park Rt 104A, PO Box 16	Fair Haven	NY	13064	315-947-5205	
Web: nysparks.state.ny.us/parks/info.asp?parkId=34					
Fillmore Glen State Park 1686 State Rt 38	Moravia	NY	13118	315-497-0130	
Web: nysparks.state.ny.us/parks/info.asp?parkId=35					
Fort Montgomery State Historic Site					
c/o Bear Mountain State Park	Bear Mountain	NY	10911	845-786-2701	786-5367
Web: www.nysparks.com/sites/info.asp?siteID=36					
Fort Niagara State Park Rt 18F	Youngstown	NY	14174	716-745-7273	
Web: www.nysparks.com/parks/info.asp?parkId=109					
Fort Ontario State Historic Site 1 E 4th St	Oswego	NY	13126	315-343-4711	343-1430
Web: www.nysparks.com/sites/info.asp?siteID=9					
Four Mile Creek State Park Lake Rd	Youngstown	NY	14174	716-745-3802	
Web: www.nysparks.com/parks/info.asp?parkId=110					
Franklin D. Roosevelt State Park 2957 Crompond Rd	Yorktown Heights	NY	10598	914-245-4434	
Web: www.nysparks.com/parks/info.asp?parkId=139					
Ganondagan State Historic Site 1488 Victor-Bloomfield Rd	Victor	NY	14564	585-924-5848	
Web: www.nysparks.com/sites/info.asp?siteID=10					
Gantry Plaza State Park 50-50 2nd St	Long Island City	NY	11101	718-786-6385	
Web: www.nysparks.com/parks/info.asp?parkId=86					
Gilbert Lake State Park 18 CCC Rd	Laurens	NY	13796	607-432-2114	
Web: www.nysparks.com/parks/info.asp?parkId=19					
Glimmerglass State Park 1527 County Hwy 31	Cooperstown	NY	13326	607-547-8662	
Web: www.nysparks.com/parks/info.asp?parkId=22					
Golden Hill State Park 9691 Lower Lake Rd	Barker	NY	14102	716-795-3885	
Web: www.nysparks.com/parks/info.asp?parkId=111					
Goosepond Mountain State Park					
c/o Palisades Interstate Park Commission	Bear Mountain	NY	10911	845-786-2701	
Web: www.nysparks.com/parks/info.asp?parkId=56					
Governor Alfred E. Smith/Sunken Meadow State Park					
PO Box 716	Kings Park	NY	11754	631-269-4333	
Web: www.nysparks.com/parks/info.asp?parkId=44					
Grafton Lakes State Park 61 N Long Pond Rd	Grafton	NY	12082	518-279-1155	
Web: www.nysparks.com/parks/info.asp?parkId=116					
Grant Cottage State Historic Site PO Box 2294	Wilton	NY	12831	518-587-8277	
Web: www.nysparks.com/sites/info.asp?siteID=11					
Grass Point State Park 42247 Grassy Point Rd	Alexandria Bay	NY	13607	315-686-4472	
Web: nysparks.state.ny.us/parks/info.asp?parkId=123					
Green Lakes State Park 7900 Green Lakes Rd	Fayetteville	NY	13066	315-637-6111	
Web: www.nysparks.com/parks/info.asp?parkId=23					
Hamlin Beach State Park 1 Camp Rd	Hamlin	NY	14464	585-964-2462	964-7821
TF: 800-456-2267 ■ *Web:* www.nysparks.com/parks/info.asp?parkId=6					
Harriet Hollister Spencer State Recreation Area					
10820 Rt 36 S	Dansville	NY	14437	585-335-8111	
Web: www.nysparks.com/parks/info.asp?parkId=98					
Harriman State Park					
c/o Palisades Interstate Park Commission	Bear Mountain	NY	10911	845-786-2701	
Web: nysparks.state.ny.us/parks/info.asp?parkId=143					
Heckscher State Park PO Box 160	East Islip	NY	11730	631-581-2100	
Web: www.nysparks.com/parks/info.asp?parkId=153					
Hempstead Lake State Park	West Hempstead	NY	11552	516-766-1029	
Web: www.nysparks.com/parks/info.asp?parkId=155					
Herkimer Home State Historic Site 200 State Rt 169	Little Falls	NY	13365	315-823-0398	823-0587
Web: www.nysparks.com/sites/info.asp?siteID=12					
High Tor State Park					
c/o Palisades Interstate Park Commission	Bear Mountain	NY	10911	845-634-8074	
Web: www.nysparks.com/parks/info.asp?parkId=58					
Highland Lakes State Park					
c/o Palisades Interstate Park Commission	Bear Mountain	NY	10911	845-786-2701	
Web: www.nysparks.com/parks/info.asp?parkId=76					
Higley Flow State Park 442 Cold Brook Dr	Colton	NY	13625	315-262-2880	
Web: www.nysparks.com/parks/info.asp?parkId=144					
Hither Hills State Park 50 S Fairview Ave	Montauk	NY	11754	631-668-2554	
Web: www.nysparks.com/parks/info.asp?parkId=48					
Hudson Highlands State Park Rt 9D	Beacon	NY	10512	845-225-7207	
Web: www.nysparks.com/parks/info.asp?parkId=130					
Hudson River Islands State Park					
Schodack Island State Park	Schodack Landing	NY	12156	518-732-0187	732-0263
Web: www.nysparks.com/parks/info.asp?parkId=107					
Hunt's Pond State Park					
c/o Bowman Lake State Park 745 Bliven Sherman Rd	Oxford	NY	13830	607-859-2249	
Web: www.nysparks.com/parks/info.asp?parkId=1					
Hyde Hall State Historic Site PO Box 721	Cooperstown	NY	13326	607-547-5098	547-8462
Web: www.nysparks.com/sites/info.asp?siteID=13					
Irondequoit Bay State Marine Park					
c/o Hamlin Beach State Park 1 Camp Rd	Hamlin	NY	14464	585-964-2462	
Web: www.nysparks.com/parks/info.asp?parkId=7					
Jacques Cartier State Park PO Box 380	Morristown	NY	13664	315-375-6371	
Web: www.nysparks.com/parks/info.asp?parkId=145					
James Baird State Park 14 Maintenance Ln	Pleasant Valley	NY	12569	845-452-1489	
Web: www.nysparks.com/parks/info.asp?parkId=59					
John Boyd Thacher State Park 1 Hailes Cave Rd	Voorheesville	NY	12186	518-872-1237	872-9133
Web: www.nysparks.com/parks/info.asp?parkId=125					
John Brown Farm State Historic Site 2 John Brown Rd	Lake Placid	NY	12946	518-523-3900	
Web: www.nysparks.com/sites/info.asp?siteID=14					
John Burroughs Memorial State Historic Site					
c/o Mine Kill State Park PO Box 923, Rte 30	North Blenheim	NY	12131	518-827-6111	827-6782
Web: www.nysparks.com/sites/info.asp?siteID=15					
John Jay Homestead State Historic Site PO Box 832	Katonah	NY	10536	914-232-5651	232-8085
Web: www.nysparks.com/sites/info.asp?siteID=16					
Johnson Hall State Historic Site Hall Ave	Johnstown	NY	12095	518-762-8712	762-2330
Web: www.nysparks.com/sites/info.asp?siteID=17					
Jones Beach State Park PO Box 1000	Wantagh	NY	11793	516-785-1600	
Web: www.nysparks.com/parks/info.asp?parkId=46					
Joseph Davis State Park 4143 Lower River Rd	Lewiston	NY	14092	716-754-4596	
Web: www.nysparks.com/parks/info.asp?parkId=108					
Keewaydin State Park PO Box 247 46165 NYS Rt 12	Alexandria Bay	NY	13607	315-482-3331	
Web: www.nysparks.com/parks/info.asp?parkId=146					
Keuka Lake State Park 3370 Pepper Rd	Bluff Point	NY	14478	315-536-3666	
Web: www.nysparks.com/parks/info.asp?parkId=37					
Knox's Headquarters State Historic Site PO Box 207	Vails Gate	NY	12584	845-561-5498	
Web: www.nysparks.com/sites/info.asp?siteID=18					
Kring Point State Park 25950 Kring Point Rd	Redwood	NY	13679	315-482-2444	
Web: www.nysparks.com/parks/info.asp?parkId=149					
Lake Erie State Park 5905 Lake Rd	Brockton	NY	14716	716-792-9214	
Web: www.nysparks.com/parks/info.asp?parkId=96					
Lake Superior State Park					
c/o Sullivan County Dept of Public Works Box 5012	Monticello	NY	12701	845-794-3000	
Web: www.nysparks.com/parks/info.asp?parkId=77					
Lake Taghkanic State Park 1528 Rt 82	Ancram	NY	12502	518-851-3631	851-3633
Web: www.nysparks.com/parks/info.asp?parkId=131					
Lakeside Beach State Park Rt 18	Waterport	NY	14571	585-682-4888	
Web: www.nysparks.com/parks/info.asp?parkId=8					
Letchworth State Park 1 Letchworth State Park	Castile	NY	14427	585-493-3600	
Web: www.nysparks.com/parks/info.asp?parkId=12					
Lodi Point State Marine Park					
c/o Sampson State Park 6096 Rt 96A	Romulus	NY	14541	315-585-6392	
Web: www.nysparks.com/parks/info.asp?parkId=38					
Long Point State Park - Finger Lakes 2063 Lake Rd	Aurora	NY	13026	315-497-0130	
Web: www.nysparks.com/parks/info.asp?parkId=39					
Long Point State Park on Lake Chautauqua 4459 Rt 430	Bemus Point	NY	14712	716-386-2722	
Web: www.nysparks.com/parks/info.asp?parkId=3					
Long Point State Park - Thousand Islands					
7495 State Park Rd	Three Mile Bay	NY	13693	315-649-5258	
Web: www.nysparks.com/parks/info.asp?parkId=152					
Lorenzo State Historic Site 17 Rippleton Rd	Cazenovia	NY	13035	315-655-3200	655-4304
Web: www.nysparks.com/sites/info.asp?siteID=19					
Macomb Reservation State Park 201 Campsite Rd	Schuyler Falls	NY	12985	518-643-9952	
Web: www.nysparks.com/parks/info.asp?parkId=148					
Margaret Lewis Norrie State Park Old Post Rd PO Box 893	Staatsburg	NY	12580	845-889-4646	889-8321
Web: nysparks.state.ny.us/parks/info.asp?parkId=134					
Mark Twain State Park & Soaring Eagles Golf Course					
201 Middle Rd	Horseheads	NY	14845	607-739-0034	
Web: www.nysparks.com/parks/info.asp?parkId=41					
Mary Island State Park					
c/o Cedar Point State Park 36661 Cedar Point State Park Dr	Clayton	NY	13624	315-654-2522	
Web: www.nysparks.com/parks/info.asp?parkId=150					
Max V. Shaul State Park Rt 30 Box 23	Fultonham	NY	12071	518-827-4711	
Web: www.nysparks.com/parks/info.asp?parkId=135					
Mine Kill State Park PO Box 923 Rt 30	North Blenheim	NY	12131	518-827-6111	827-6782
Web: www.nysparks.com/parks/info.asp?parkId=117					
Minnewaska State Park Preserve PO Box 893	New Paltz	NY	12561	845-256-0579	
Web: www.nysparks.com/parks/info.asp?parkId=78					

Phone Fax

Montauk Downs State Park 50 S Fairview Ave — Montauk NY 11954 631-668-3781
Web: www.nysparks.com/parks/info.asp?parkId=165
Montauk Point State Park
c/o Montauk Downs State Park 50 S Fairview Ave — Montauk NY 11954 631-668-3781
Web: www.nysparks.com/parks/info.asp?parkId=136
Moreau Lake State Park 605 Old Saratoga Rd — Gansevoort NY 12831 518-793-0511 761-6843
Web: www.nysparks.com/parks/info.asp?parkId=119
New Windsor Cantonment State Historic Site PO Box 207 — Vails Gate NY 12584 845-561-1765
Web: www.nysparks.com/sites/info.asp?siteID=20
Niagara Falls State Park PO Box 1132 — Niagara Falls NY 14303 716-278-1796
Web: www.nysparks.com/parks/info.asp?parkId=113
Nissequogue River State Park St Johnland Rd PO Box 639 — Kings Park NY 11754 631-269-4927
Web: www.nysparks.com/parks/info.asp?parkId=79
Nyack Beach State Park PO Box 217 — Congers NY 10920 845-268-3020
Web: www.nysparks.com/parks/info.asp?parkId=62
Oak Orchard State Marine Park
c/o Lakeside Beach State Park Rt 18 — Waterport NY 14571 585-682-4888
Web: www.nysparks.com/parks/info.asp?parkId=13
Ogden Mills & Ruth Livingston Mills State Park
Old Post Rd PO Box 893 — Staatsburg NY 12580 845-889-4646
Web: www.nysparks.com/parks/info.asp?parkId=133
Olana State Historic Site 5720 Rt 9G — Hudson NY 12534 518-828-0135 828-6742
Web: www.nysparks.com/sites/info.asp?siteID=21
Old Croton Aqueduct State Historic Park 15 Walnut St — Dobbs Ferry NY 10522 914-693-5259 674-8529
Web: www.nysparks.com/sites/info.asp?siteID=34
Old Erie Canal State Historic Park RD 2 Andrus Rd — Kirkville NY 13082 315-687-7821
Web: nysparks.state.ny.us/sites/info.asp?siteID=31
Old Fort Niagara State Historic Site PO Box 169 — Youngstown NY 14174 716-745-7611 745-9141
Web: www.nysparks.com/sites/info.asp?siteID=22
Oquaga Creek State Park 5995 County Rte 20 — Bainbridge NY 13733 607-467-4160
Web: www.nysparks.com/parks/info.asp?parkId=2
Orient Beach State Park PO Box 117 — Orient NY 11957 631-323-2440
Web: www.nysparks.com/parks/info.asp?parkId=50
Oriskany Battlefield State Historic Site 7801 State Rt 69 — Oriskany NY 13424 315-768-7224 377-3081
Web: www.nysparks.com/sites/info.asp?siteID=23
Peebles Island State Park PO Box 219 — Waterford NY 12188 518-237-8643
Web: nysparks.state.ny.us/parks/info.asp?parkId=120
Philipse Manor Hall State Historic Site PO Box 496 — Yonkers NY 10702 914-965-4027 965-6485
Web: www.nysparks.com/sites/info.asp?siteID=24
Pinnacle State Park & Golf Course 1904 Pinnacle Rd — Addison NY 14801 607-359-2767
Web: nysparks.state.ny.us/parks/info.asp?parkId=99
Pixley Falls State Park 11430 State Rt 46 — Boonville NY 13309 315-942-4713
Web: www.nysparks.com/parks/info.asp?parkId=20
Planting Fields Arboretum State Historic Park/Coe Hall Historic House Museum PO Box 58 — Oyster Bay NY 11771 516-922-9200 922-8610
Web: www.nysparks.com/sites/info.asp?siteID=33
Point Au Roche State Park 19 Camp Red Cloud Rd — Plattsburg NY 12901 518-563-0369
Web: www.nysparks.com/parks/info.asp?parkId=162
Reservoir State Park
c/o Niagara Frontier Region PO Box 1132 — Niagara Falls NY 14303 716-284-4691
Web: www.nysparks.com/parks/info.asp?parkId=112
Riverbank State Park 679 Riverside Dr — New York NY 10031 212-694-3600
Web: www.nysparks.com/parks/info.asp?parkId=75
Robert H Treman State Park 105 Enfield Falls Rd — Ithaca NY 14850 607-273-3440
Web: www.nysparks.com/parks/info.asp?parkId=104
Robert Moses State Park - Long Island
c/o Long Island Regional Office PO Box 247 — Babylon NY 11702 631-669-0449
Web: www.nysparks.com/parks/info.asp?parkId=45
Robert Moses State Park - Thousand Islands PO Box 548 — Massena NY 13662 315-769-8663
Web: www.nysparks.com/parks/info.asp?parkId=157
Roberto Clemente State Park W Tremont Ave & Mattewson Rd — Bronx NY 10453 718-299-8750
Web: nysparks.state.ny.us/parks/info.asp?parkId=33
Rockefeller State Park Preserve PO Box 338 — Tarrytown NY 10591 914-631-1470
Web: www.nysparks.com/parks/info.asp?parkId=60
Rockland Lake State Park PO Box 217 — Congers NY 10920 845-268-3020
Web: nysparks.state.ny.us/parks/info.asp?parkId=64
Sackets Harbor Battlefield State Historic Site
PO Box 27 505 W Washington St — Sackets Harbor NY 13685 315-646-3634 646-1203
Web: nysparks.state.ny.us/sites/info.asp?siteID=25
Saint Lawrence State Park Golf Course
4955 State Hwy 37 — Ogdensburg NY 13669 315-393-2286
Web: www.nysparks.com/parks/info.asp?parkId=163
Sampson State Park 6096 Rt 96A — Romulus NY 14541 315-585-6392
Web: www.nysparks.com/parks/info.asp?parkId=100
Saratoga Spa State Park 19 Roosevelt Dr — Saratoga Springs NY 12866 518-584-2535
Web: www.nysparks.com/parks/info.asp?parkId=124
Schodack Island State Park
1 Schodack Way PO Box 7 — Schodack Landing NY 12156 518-732-0187
Web: www.nysparks.com/parks/info.asp?parkId=87
Schoharie Crossing State Historic Site
PO Box 140 129 Schoharie St — Fort Hunter NY 12069 518-829-7516 829-7491
Web: www.nysparks.com/sites/info.asp?siteID=33
Schuyler Mansion State Historic Site 32 Catherine St — Albany NY 12202 518-434-0834 434-3821
Web: nysparks.state.ny.us/sites/info.asp?siteID=27
Selkirk Shores State Park 7101 State Rt 3 — Pulaski NY 13142 315-298-5737
Web: www.nysparks.com/parks/info.asp?parkId=24
Senate House State Historic Site 296 Fair St — Kingston NY 12401 845-338-2786 334-8173
Web: www.nysparks.com/sites/info.asp?siteID=28
Seneca Lake State Park 1 Lakefront Dr — Geneva NY 14456 315-789-2331
Web: www.nysparks.com/parks/info.asp?parkId=97
Shadmoor State Park
c/o Montauk Downs State Park 50 S Fairview Ave — Montauk NY 11954 631-668-3781
Web: www.nysparks.com/parks/info.asp?parkId=83
Silver Lake State Park c/o Letchworth State Park — Castile NY 14427 585-493-3600
Web: www.nysparks.com/parks/info.asp?parkId=14
Southwick Beach State Park 8119 Southwicks Pl — Woodville NY 13650 315-846-5338
Web: www.nysparks.com/parks/info.asp?parkId=154
Staatsburgh State Historic Site Old Post Rd PO Box 308 — Staatsburg NY 12580 845-889-8851 889-8321
Web: www.nysparks.com/sites/info.asp?siteID=2
Sterling Forest State Park 116 Old Forge Rd — Tuxedo NY 10987 845-351-5907
Web: www.nysparks.com/parks/info.asp?parkId=81
Steuben Memorial State Historic Site
c/o Oriskany Battlefield SHS 7801 State Rt 69 — Oriskany NY 13424 315-831-3737 337-3081
Web: www.nysparks.com/sites/info.asp?siteID=6
Stony Brook State Park 10820 Rt 36 S — Dansville NY 14437 585-335-8111
Web: www.nysparks.com/parks/info.asp?parkId=102
Stony Point Battlefield State Historic Site PO Box 182 — Stony Point NY 10980 845-786-2521
Web: nysparks.state.ny.us/sites/info.asp?siteID=29
Storm King State Park
c/o Palisades Interstate Park Commission — Bear Mountain NY 10911 845-786-2701
Web: www.nysparks.com/parks/info.asp?parkId=65
Taconic State Park - Copake Falls Area
Rte 344 PO Box 100 — Copake Falls NY 12517 518-329-3993
Web: www.nysparks.com/parks/info.asp?parkId=137
Taconic State Park - Rudd Pond Area 59 Rudd Pond Dr — Millerton NY 12546 518-789-3059
Web: www.nysparks.com/parks/info.asp?parkId=132
Tallman Mountain State Park
c/o Palisades Interstate Park Commission — Bear Mountain NY 10911 845-359-0544
Web: www.nysparks.com/parks/info.asp?parkId=66
Taughannock Falls State Park 2221 Taughannock Rd — Trumansburg NY 14886 607-387-6739
Web: www.nysparks.com/parks/info.asp?parkId=93
Thompson's Lake State Park 68 Thompson's Lake Rd — East Berne NY 12059 518-872-1674 872-9133
Web: www.nysparks.com/parks/info.asp?parkId=128
Valley Stream State Park PO Box 670 — Valley Stream NY 11580 516-825-4128
Web: www.nysparks.com/parks/info.asp?parkId=51
Verona Beach State Park PO Box 245 — Verona Beach NY 13162 315-762-4463
Web: www.nysparks.com/parks/info.asp?parkId=26
Walt Whitman Birthplace State Historic Site
246 Old Walt Whitman Rd — Huntington Station NY 11746 631-427-5240 427-5247
Web: www.nysparks.com/sites/info.asp?siteID=30
Washington's Headquarters State Historic Site PO Box 1783 — Newburgh NY 12551 845-562-1195
Web: nysparks.state.ny.us/sites/info.asp?siteID=32
Waterson Point State Park
c/o Wellesley Island State Park 44927 Cross Island Rd — Fineview NY 13640 315-482-2722
Web: nysparks.state.ny.us/parks/info.asp?parkID=147
Watkins Glen State Park PO Box 304 — Watkins Glen NY 14891 607-535-4511
Web: www.nysparks.com/parks/info.asp?parkId=105
Wellesley Island State Park 44927 Cross Island Rd — Fineview NY 13640 315-482-2722
Web: www.nysparks.com/parks/info.asp?parkId=164
Westcott Beach State Park PO Box 339 — Sackets Harbor NY 13685 315-646-2239
Web: www.nysparks.com/parks/info.asp?parkId=161
Whetstone Gulf State Park RD 2 Box 69 — Lowville NY 13367 315-376-6630
Web: www.nysparks.com/parks/info.asp?parkId=42
Whirlpool State Park
c/o Niagara Frontier Region PO Box 1132 — Niagara Falls NY 14303 716-284-4691
Web: www.nysparks.com/parks/info.asp?parkId=29
Wildwood State Park PO Box 518 N Wading River Rd — Wading River NY 11792 631-929-4314
Web: www.nysparks.com/parks/info.asp?parkId=52
Wilson-Tuscarora State Park PO Box 324 3371 Lake Rd — Wilson NY 14172 716-751-6361
Web: www.nysparks.com/parks/info.asp?parkId=31
Woodlawn Beach State Park S 3585 Lake Shore Rd — Blasdell NY 14219 716-826-1930 827-0293
Web: www.nysparks.com/parks/info.asp?parkId=47

North Carolina

Phone Fax

Carolina Beach State Park PO Box 475 — Carolina Beach NC 28428 910-458-8206 458-6350
Web: ils.unc.edu/parkproject/visit/cabe/home.html
Cliffs of the Neuse State Park 345-A Park Entrance Rd — Seven Springs NC 28578 919-778-6234 778-7447
Web: ils.unc.edu/parkproject/visit/clne/home.html
Crowders Mountain State Park 522 Park Office Ln — Kings Mountain NC 28086 704-853-5375 853-5391
Web: www.crowdersmountain.com
Eno River State Park 6101 Cole Mill Rd — Durham NC 27705 919-383-1686 382-7378
Web: ils.unc.edu/parkproject/visit/enri/home.html
Falls Lake State Recreation Area 13304 Creedmoor Rd — Wake Forest NC 27587 919-676-1027 676-2954
Web: ils.unc.edu/parkproject/visit/fala/home.html
Fort Fisher State Recreation Area 1000 Loggerhead Rd — Kure Beach NC 28449 910-458-5798 458-5799
Web: ils.unc.edu/parkproject/visit/fofi/home.html
Fort Macon State Park PO Box 127 — Atlantic Beach NC 28512 252-726-3775 726-2497
Web: ils.unc.edu/parkproject/visit/foma/home.html
Goose Creek State Park 2190 Camp Leach Rd — Washington NC 27889 252-923-2191 923-0052
Web: ils.unc.edu/parkproject/visit/gocr/home.html
Gorges State Park PO Box 100 — Sapphire NC 28774 828-966-9009
Web: ils.unc.edu/parkproject/visit/gorg/home.html
Hammocks Beach State Park 1572 Hammock Beach Rd — Swansboro NC 28584 910-326-4881 326-2060
Web: ils.unc.edu/parkproject/visit/habe/home.html
Hanging Rock State Park PO Box 278 — Danbury NC 27016 336-593-8480 593-9166
Web: ils.unc.edu/parkproject/visit/haro/home.html
Jockey's Ridge State Park PO Box 592 — Nags Head NC 27959 252-441-7132 441-8416
Web: ils.unc.edu/parkproject/visit/jori/home.html
Jones Lake State Park 4117 NC 242 Hwy — Elizabethtown NC 28337 910-588-4550
Web: ils.unc.edu/parkproject/visit/jone/home.html
Jordan Lake State Recreation Area 280 State Park Rd — Apex NC 27523 919-362-0586 362-1621
Web: ils.unc.edu/parkproject/visit/jord/home.html
Kerr Lake State Recreation Area 6254 Satterwhite Point Rd — Henderson NC 27537 252-438-7791 438-7582
Web: www.ils.unc.edu/parkproject/visit/kela/home.html
Lake James State Park PO Box 340 — Nebo NC 28761 828-652-5047 659-8911
Web: ils.unc.edu/parkproject/visit/laja/home.html
Lake Norman State Park 159 Inland Sea Ln — Troutman NC 28166 704-528-6350 528-5623
Web: ils.unc.edu/parkproject/visit/lano/home.html
Lake Waccamaw State Park 1866 State Park Dr — Lake Waccamaw NC 28450 910-646-4748 646-4915
Web: ils.unc.edu/parkproject/visit/lawa/home.html
Lumber River State Park 2819 Princess Ann Rd — Orrum NC 28369 910-628-9844 628-8172
Web: ils.unc.edu/parkproject/visit/luri/home.html
Medoc Mountain State Park 1541 Medoc State Park Rd — Hollister NC 27844 252-586-6588
Web: ils.unc.edu/parkproject/visit/memo/home.html
Merchants Millpond State Park 71 US Hwy 158E — Gatesville NC 27938 252-357-1191 357-0149
Web: ils.unc.edu/parkproject/visit/memi/home.html
Morrow Mountain State Park 49104 Morrow Mountain Rd — Albemarle NC 28001 704-982-4402 982-5323
Web: ils.unc.edu/parkproject/visit/momo/home.html
Mount Jefferson State Natural Area PO Box 48 — Jefferson NC 28640 336-246-9653 246-3386
Web: ils.unc.edu/parkproject/visit/moje/home.html
Mount Mitchell State Park 2388 State Hwy 128 — Burnsville NC 28714 828-675-4611 675-9655
Web: ils.unc.edu/parkproject/visit/momi/home.html
New River State Park PO Box 48 — Jefferson NC 28640 336-982-2587 982-3943
Web: ils.unc.edu/parkproject/visit/neri/home.html
Occoneechee Mountain State Natural Area
c/o Eno River State Park 6101 Cole Mill Rd — Durham NC 27705 919-383-1686
Web: ils.unc.edu/parkproject/visit/ocmo/home.html
Pettigrew State Park 2252 Lake Shore Rd — Creswell NC 27928 252-797-4475 797-7405
Web: ils.unc.edu/parkproject/visit/pett/home.html
Pilot Mountain State Park 1792 Pilot Knob Park Rd — Pinnacle NC 27043 336-325-2355 325-2751
Web: ils.unc.edu/parkproject/visit/pimo/home.html
Raven Rock State Park 3009 Raven Rock Rd — Lillington NC 27546 910-893-4888 814-2200
Web: ils.unc.edu/parkproject/visit/raro/home.html
Singletary Lake State Park 6707 NC 53 Hwy E — Kelly NC 28448 910-669-2928 669-2034
Web: ils.unc.edu/parkproject/visit/sila/home.html
South Mountains State Park
3001 South Mountains State Park Ave — Connelly Springs NC 28612 828-433-4772 433-4778
Web: ils.unc.edu/parkproject/visit/somo/home.html
Stone Mountain State Park 3042 Frank Pkwy — Roaring Gap NC 28668 336-957-8185 957-3985
Web: ils.unc.edu/parkproject/visit/stmo/home.html
Weymouth Woods Sandhills Nature Preserve
1024 Fort Bragg Rd — Southern Pines NC 28387 910-692-2167 692-8042
Web: ils.unc.edu/parkproject/visit/wewo/home.html
William B. Umstead State Park 8801 Glenwood Ave — Raleigh NC 27612 919-571-4170 571-4161
Web: ils.unc.edu/parkproject/visit/wium/home.html

North Dakota

Phone | Fax

Beaver Lake State Park 3850 70th St SE ... Wishek ND 58495 701-452-2752
Web: www.ndparks.com/Parks/blsp.htm

Black Tiger Bay State Recreation Area 152 S Duncan Dr ... Devils Lake ND 58301 701-766-4015
Web: www.ndparks.com/Parks/DLSP.htm

Cross Ranch State Nature Preserve
c/o North Dakota Parks & Recreation Dept 1600 E Century Ave Suite 3 ... Bismarck ND 58503 701-328-5357
Web: www.ndparks.com/Nature/Preserves.htm

Cross Ranch State Park 1403 River Rd ... Center ND 58530 701-794-3731 794-3262
Web: www.ndparks.com/Parks/CRSP.htm

De Mores State Historic Site PO Box 106 ... Medora ND 58645 701-623-4355
Web: www.state.nd.us/hist/chateau/chateau.htm

Double Ditch State Historic Site
c/o State Historical Society of North Dakota 612 E Boulevard Ave ... Bismarck ND 58505 701-328-2666 328-3710
Web: www.state.nd.us/hist/doubleditch/doubleditch.htm

Doyle Memorial State Park ... Wishek ND 58495 701-452-2351
Web: www.ndparks.com/Parks/DMSP.htm

Former Governors' Mansion State Historic Site
612 E Boulevard Ave ... Bismarck ND 58505 701-328-2666 328-3710
Web: www.state.nd.us/hist/fgm/fgm.htm

Fort Abercrombie State Historic Site PO Box 148 ... Abercrombie ND 58001 701-553-8513
Web: www.state.nd.us/HIST/abercrombie/abercrombie.html

Fort Abraham Lincoln State Park 4480 Fort Lincoln Rd ... Mandan ND 58554 701-667-6340 667-6349
Web: www.ndparks.com/Parks/FLSP.htm

Fort Buford State Historic Site 15349 39th Ln NW ... Williston ND 58801 701-572-9034
Web: www.state.nd.us/hist/buford/buford.htm

Fort Clark Trading Post State Historic Site HC 2 Box 26 ... Center ND 58530 701-794-8832
Web: www.state.nd.us/HIST/ftClark/index.html

Fort Ransom State Park 5981 Walt Hjelle Pkwy ... Fort Ransom ND 58033 701-973-4331 973-4151
Web: www.ndparks.com/Parks/FRSP.htm

Fort Stevenson State Park 1252A 41st St NW ... Garrison ND 58540 701-337-5576 337-5313
Web: www.ndparks.com/Parks/fssp.htm

Fort Totten State Historic Site PO Box 224 ... Fort Totten ND 58335 701-766-4441
Web: www.state.nd.us/hist/totten/totten.htm

Gingras Trading Post State Historic Site RR 1 Box 55 ... Walhalla ND 58202 701-549-2775
Web: www.state.nd.us/HIST/gingras/index.html

Graham's Island State Park 152 S Duncan Dr ... Devils Lake ND 58301 701-766-4015
Web: www.ndparks.com/parks/DLSP.htm

Gunlogson State Nature Preserve
c/o North Dakota Parks & Recreation Dept 1600 E Century Ave Suite 3 ... Bismarck ND 58503 701-328-5357
Web: www.ndparks.com/Nature/Preserves.htm

H R Morgan State Nature Preserve
c/o North Dakota Parks & Recreation Dept 1600 E Century Ave Suite 3 ... Bismarck ND 58503 701-328-5357
Web: www.ndparks.com/Nature/Preserves.htm

Head of the Mountain State Nature Preserve
c/o North Dakota Parks & Recreation Dept 1600 E Century Ave Suite 3 ... Bismarck ND 58503 701-328-5357
Web: www.ndparks.com/Nature/Preserves.htm

Homen State Forest
c/o North Dakota Forest Service 307 1st St E ... Bottineau ND 58318 701-228-5422 228-5448
Web: www.ndsu.nodak.edu/forestservice/stateforest/homen.htm

Icelandic State Park 13571 Hwy 5 ... Cavalier ND 58220 701-265-4561 265-4443
Web: www.ndparks.com/Parks/ISP.htm

Indian Hills State Recreation Area & Resort 7302 14th St NW ... Garrison ND 58540 701-743-4122
Web: www.ndparks.com/parks/Stevenson/IndianHills.htm

Lake Metigoshe State Park 2 Lake Metigoshe State Park ... Bottineau ND 58318 701-263-4651 263-4648
Web: www.ndparks.com/Parks/LMSP.htm

Lake Sakakawea State Park PO Box 732 ... Riverdale ND 58565 701-487-3315 487-3305
Web: www.ndparks.com/Parks/LSSP.htm

Lewis & Clark State Park 4904 119th Rd NW ... Epping ND 58843 701-859-3071 859-3001
Web: www.ndparks.com/Parks/LCSP.htm

Little Missouri State Park
c/o Cross Ranch State Park 1403 River Rd ... Center ND 58530 701-974-3731
Web: www.ndparks.com/Parks/Little_Mo/Home.htm

Mouse River State Forest
c/o North Dakota Forest Service 307 1st St E ... Bottineau ND 58318 701-228-5422 228-5448
Web: www.ndsu.nodak.edu/ndsu/lbakken/forest/stateforest/mouse_river.htm

Sentinel Butte State Nature Preserve
c/o North Dakota Parks & Recreation Dept 1600 E Century Ave Suite 3 ... Bismarck ND 58503 701-328-5357
Web: www.ndparks.com/Nature/Preserves.htm

Sheyenne River State Forest
c/o North Dakota Forest Service 307 1st St E ... Bottineau ND 58318 701-228-5422 228-5448
Web: www.ndsu.nodak.edu/forestservice/stateforest/sheyenne_river.htm

Sully Creek State Recreation Area
c/o Fort Abraham Lincoln State Park 4480 Fort Lincoln Rd ... Mandan ND 58554 701-667-6340 667-6349
Web: www.ndparks.com/Parks/Little_Mo/Home.htm

Tetrault Woods State Forest
c/o North Dakota Forest Service 307 1st St E ... Bottineau ND 58318 701-228-5422 228-5448
Web: www.ndsu.nodak.edu/forestservice/stateforest/tetrault_woods.htm

Turtle Mountain State Forest
c/o North Dakota Forest Service 307 1st St E ... Bottineau ND 58318 701-228-5422 228-5448
Web: www.ndsu.nodak.edu/forestservice/stateforest/turtle_mtn.htm

Turtle River State Park 3084 Park Ave ... Arvilla ND 58214 701-594-4445 594-2556
Web: www.ndparks.com/Parks/TRSP.htm

Whitestone Hill Battlefield State Historic Site RR 1 Box 125 ... Kulm ND 58456 701-396-7731
Web: www.state.nd.us/HIST/whitestone/index.html

Ohio

Phone | Fax

A. W. Marion State Park
c/o Deer Creek State Park 20635 Waterloo Rd ... Mount Sterling OH 43143 740-869-3124
Web: www.ohiodnr.com/parks/parks/awmarion.htm

Adams Lake State Park
c/o Shawnee State Park 4404 State Rt 125 ... Portsmouth OH 45663 740-858-6652
Web: www.ohiodnr.com/parks/parks/adams.htm

Alum Creek State Park 3615 S Old State Rd ... Delaware OH 43015 740-548-4631
Web: www.ohiodnr.com/parks/parks/alum.htm

Barkcamp State Park 65330 Barkcamp Rd ... Belmont OH 43718 740-484-4064
Web: www.ohiodnr.com/parks/parks/barkcamp.htm

Beaver Creek State Park 12021 Echo Dell Rd ... East Liverpool OH 43920 330-385-3091
Web: www.ohiodnr.com/parks/parks/beaverck.htm

Blue Rock State Park
c/o Dillon State Park 5265 Dillon Hills Dr ... Nashport OH 43830 740-453-4377
Web: www.ohiodnr.com/parks/parks/bluerock.htm

Buck Creek State Park 1901 Buck Creek Ln ... Springfield OH 45502 937-322-5284
Web: www.ohiodnr.com/parks/parks/buckck.htm

Buckeye Lake State Park 2905 Liebs Island Rd ... Millersport OH 43046 740-467-2690
Web: www.ohiodnr.com/parks/parks/buckeye.htm

Phone | Fax

Burr Oak State Park 5250 Beach Rd ... Glouster OH 45732 740-767-3570
Web: www.ohiodnr.com/parks/parks/burroak.htm

Caesar Creek State Park 8570 E State Rt 73 ... Waynesville OH 45068 513-897-3055
Web: www.ohiodnr.com/parks/parks/caesarck.htm

Catawba Island State Park 4049 E Moores Dock Rd ... Port Clinton OH 43452 419-797-4530
Web: www.ohiodnr.com/parks/parks/lakeerie.htm

Cleveland Lakefront State Park 8701 Lakeshore Blvd NE ... Cleveland OH 44108 216-881-8141
Web: www.ohiodnr.com/parks/parks/clevelkf.htm

Cowan Lake State Park 1750 Osborn Rd ... Wilmington OH 45177 937-382-1096
Web: www.ohiodnr.com/parks/parks/cowanlk.htm

Crane Creek State Park 13531 W State Rt 2 ... Oak Harbor OH 43449 419-836-7758
Web: www.ohiodnr.com/parks/parks/cranecrk.htm

Deer Creek State Park 20635 Waterloo Rd ... Mount Sterling OH 43143 740-869-3124
Web: www.ohiodnr.com/parks/parks/deercrk.htm

Delaware State Park 5202 US Hwy 23 N ... Delaware OH 43015 740-369-2761
Web: www.ohiodnr.com/parks/parks/delaware.htm

Dillon State Park 5265 Dillon Hills Dr ... Nashport OH 43830 740-453-4377
Web: www.ohiodnr.com/parks/parks/dillon.htm

East Fork State Park 3294 Elklick Rd ... Bethel OH 45106 513-734-4323
Web: www.ohiodnr.com/parks/parks/eastfork.htm

East Harbor State Park 1169 N Buck Rd ... Lakeside-Marblehead OH 43440 419-734-4424
Web: www.ohiodnr.com/parks/parks/eastharbor.htm

Findley State Park 25381 State Rt 58 ... Wellington OH 44090 440-647-4490
Web: www.ohiodnr.com/parks/parks/findley.htm

Forked Run State Park 63300 State Rt 124 PO Box 127 ... Reedsville OH 45772 740-378-6206
Web: www.ohiodnr.com/parks/parks/forkedrn.htm

Geneva State Park PO Box 429 4499 Pandanarum Rd ... Geneva OH 44041 440-466-8400
Web: www.ohiodnr.com/parks/parks/geneva.htm

Grand Lake Saint Marys State Park 834 Edgewater Dr ... Saint Marys OH 45885 419-394-3611
Web: www.ohiodnr.com/parks/parks/grndlake.htm

Great Seal State Park 635 Rocky Rd ... Chillicothe OH 45601 740-663-2125
Web: www.ohiodnr.com/parks/parks/grtseal.htm

Guilford Lake State Park 6835 E Lake Rd ... Lisbon OH 44432 330-222-1712
Web: www.ohiodnr.com/parks/parks/guilford.htm

Harrison Lake State Park 26246 Harrison Lake Rd ... Fayette OH 43521 419-237-2593
Web: www.ohiodnr.com/parks/parks/harrison.htm

Headlands Beach State Park
c/o Cleveland Lakefront State Park 8701 Lakeshore Blvd NE ... Cleveland OH 44108 216-881-8141
Web: www.ohiodnr.com/parks/parks/headlnds.htm

Hocking Hills State Park 19852 State Rt 664 S ... Logan OH 43138 740-385-6842
Web: www.ohiodnr.com/parks/parks/hocking.htm

Hueston Woods State Park 6301 Park Office Rd ... College Corner OH 45003 513-523-6347
Web: www.ohiodnr.com/parks/parks/huestonw.htm

Independence Dam State Park 27722 State Rt 424 ... Defiance OH 43512 419-237-1503
Web: www.ohiodnr.com/parks/parks/indpndam.htm

Indian Lake State Park 12774 State Rt 235 N ... Lakeview OH 43331 937-843-2717
Web: www.ohiodnr.com/parks/parks/indianlk.htm

Jackson Lake State Park 35 Tommy Been Rd PO Box 174 ... Oak Hill OH 45656 740-596-5253
Web: www.ohiodnr.com/parks/parks/jacksonl.htm

Jefferson Lake State Park 501 Township Rd 261A ... Richmond OH 43944 740-765-4459
Web: www.ohiodnr.com/parks/parks/jefferso.htm

John Bryan State Park 3790 State Rt 370 ... Yellow Springs OH 45387 937-767-1274
Web: www.ohiodnr.com/parks/parks/jhnbryan.htm

Kelleys Island State Park
c/o Catawba Island State Park 4049 E Moores Dock Rd ... Port Clinton OH 43452 419-797-4530
Web: www.ohiodnr.com/parks/parks/lakeerie.htm

Kiser Lake State Park 4889 N State Rt 235 ... Saint Paris OH 43072 937-362-3822
Web: www.ohiodnr.com/parks/parks/kisrlake.htm

Lake Alma State Park
c/o Lake Hope State Park 27331 State Rt 278 ... McArthur OH 45651 740-384-4474
Web: www.ohiodnr.com/parks/parks/lakealma.htm

Lake Hope State Park 27331 State Rt 278 ... McArthur OH 45651 740-596-5253
Web: www.ohiodnr.com/parks/parks/lakehope.htm

Lake Logan State Park 20160 State Rd 664 ... Logan OH 43138 740-385-6842
Web: www.ohiodnr.com/parks/parks/lklogan.htm

Lake Loramie State Park 4401 Fort Loramie Swanders Rd ... Minster OH 45865 937-295-2011
Web: www.ohiodnr.com/parks/parks/lkloramie.htm

Lake Milton State Park 16801 Mahoning Ave ... Lake Milton OH 44429 330-654-4989
Web: www.ohiodnr.com/parks/parks/lkmilton.htm

Lake White State Park 2767 State Rt 551 ... Waverly OH 45690 740-947-4059
Web: www.ohiodnr.com/parks/parks/lkwhitew.htm

Little Miami Scenic State Park
c/o Caesar Creek State Park 8570 E State Rt 73 ... Waynesville OH 45068 513-897-3055
Web: www.ohiodnr.com/parks/parks/lilmiami.htm

Madison Lake State Park
c/o Deer Creek State Park 20635 Waterloo Rd ... Mount Sterling OH 43143 740-869-3124
Web: www.ohiodnr.com/parks/parks/madison.htm

Malabar Farm State Park 4050 Bromfield Rd ... Lucas OH 44843 419-892-2784 892-3988
Web: www.ohiodnr.com/parks/parks/malabar.htm

Marblehead Lighthouse State Park
c/o East Harbor State Park 1169 N Buck Rd ... Lakeside-Marblehead OH 43440 419-734-4424
Web: www.ohiodnr.com/parks/parks/marblehead.htm

Mary Jane Thurston State Park 1-466 State Rt 65 ... McClure OH 43534 419-832-7662
Web: www.ohiodnr.com/parks/parks/mjthrstn.htm

Maumee Bay State Park 1400 State Park Rd ... Oregon OH 43618 419-836-7758 836-8711
Web: www.ohiodnr.com/parks/parks/maumeebay.htm

Middle Bass Island State Park
c/o Catawba Island State Park 4049 E Moores Dock Rd ... Port Clinton OH 43452 419-797-4530
Web: www.ohiodnr.com/parks/parks/middlebass.htm

Mohican State Park 3116 State Rt 3 ... Loudonville OH 44842 419-994-5125
Web: www.ohiodnr.com/parks/parks/mohican.htm

Mosquito Lake State Park 1439 State Rt 305 ... Cortland OH 44410 330-637-2856
Web: www.ohiodnr.com/parks/parks/mosquito.htm

Mount Gilead State Park 4119 State Rt 95 ... Mount Gilead OH 43338 419-946-1961
Web: www.ohiodnr.com/parks/parks/mtgilead.htm

Muskingum River State Park 1390 Ellis Dam Rd ... Zanesville OH 43701 740-453-4377
Web: www.ohiodnr.com/parks/parks/muskngmr.htm

Nelson-Kennedy Ledges State Park
c/o Punderson State Park PO Box 338 ... Newberry OH 44065 440-564-2279
Web: www.ohiodnr.com/parks/parks/nelsonk.htm

Oak Point State Park
c/o Catawba Island State Park 4049 E Moores Dock Rd ... Port Clinton OH 43452 419-797-4530
Web: www.ohiodnr.com/parks/parks/lakeerie.htm

Paint Creek State Park 14265 US Hwy 50 ... Bainbridge OH 45612 937-365-1401
Web: www.ohiodnr.com/parks/parks/paintcrk.htm

Pike Lake State Park 1847 Pike Lake Rd ... Bainbridge OH 45612 740-493-2212
Web: www.ohiodnr.com/parks/parks/pikelake.htm

Portage Lakes State Park 5031 Manchester Rd ... Akron OH 44319 330-644-2220 644-7550
Web: www.ohiodnr.com/parks/parks/portage.htm

Punderson State Park PO Box 338 11755 Kinsman Rd ... Newbury OH 44065 440-564-2279
TF: 800-282-5393 ■ *Web:* www.ohiodnr.com/parks/parks/punderson.htm

Pymatuning State Park PO Box 1000 ... Andover OH 44003 440-293-6030
Web: www.ohiodnr.com/parks/parks/pymatuning.htm

Quail Hollow State Park 13340 Congress Lake Ave ... Hartville OH 44632 330-877-1528
Web: www.ohiodnr.com/parks/parks/quailhlw.htm

Phone | Fax

Rocky Fork State Park 9800 N Shore Dr ... Hillsboro OH 45133 937-393-4284
Web: www.ohiodnr.com/parks/parks/rockyfrk.htm
Salt Fork State Park 14755 Cadiz Rd ... Lore City OH 43755 740-439-3521 432-1515
Web: www.ohiodnr.com/parks/parks/saltfork.htm
Scioto Trail State Park 144 Lake Rd ... Chillicothe OH 45601 740-663-2125
Web: www.ohiodnr.com/parks/parks/sciototr.htm
Shawnee State Park 4404 State Rt 125 ... West Portsmouth OH 45663 740-858-6652
Web: www.ohiodnr.com/parks/parks/shawnee.htm
South Bass Island State Park
c/o Catawba Island State Park 4049 E Moores Dock Rd ... Port Clinton OH 43452 419-797-4530
Web: www.ohiodnr.com/parks/parks/lakeerie.htm
Stonelick State Park 2895 Lake Dr ... Pleasant Plain OH 45162 513-734-4323
Web: www.ohiodnr.com/parks/parks/stonelck.htm
Strouds Run State Park
c/o Burr Oak State Park 1022 Burr Oak Lodge Rd ... Glouster OH 45732 740-592-2302
Web: www.ohiodnr.com/parks/parks/strouds.htm
Sycamore State Park
c/o Hueston Woods State Park 6301 Park Office Rd ... College Corner OH 45003 513-523-6347
Web: www.ohiodnr.com/parks/parks/sycamore.htm
Tar Hollow State Park 16396 Tar Hollow Rd ... Laurelville OH 43135 740-887-4818
Web: www.ohiodnr.com/parks/parks/tarhollw.htm
Tinkers Creek State Park
c/o Punderson State Park 11755 Kinsman Rd ... Newbury OH 44065 440-564-2279
Web: www.ohiodnr.com/parks/parks/tinkers.htm
Van Buren State Park
c/o Mary Jane Thurston State Park 1-466 State Rt 65 ... McClure OH 43534 419-832-7662
Web: www.ohiodnr.com/parks/parks/vanburen.htm
West Branch State Park 5708 Esworthy Rd ... Ravenna OH 44266 330-296-3239
Web: www.ohiodnr.com/parks/parks/westbrnc.htm
Wolf Run State Park 16170 Wolf Run Rd ... Caldwell OH 43724 740-732-5035
Web: www.ohiodnr.com/parks/parks/wolfrun.htm

Oklahoma

Phone | Fax

Adair State Park Hwy 51 & Hwy 59 ... Stilwell OK 74960 918-696-6613 696-2908
Web: www.oklahomaparks.com
Alabaster Caverns State Park Hwy 50 & Hwy 50-A ... Freedom OK 73842 580-621-3381 621-3572
Web: www.oklahomaparks.com
Arrowhead State Park HC 67 Box 57 ... Canadian OK 74425 918-339-2204 339-7236
Web: www.oklahomaparks.com
Beaver Dunes State Park PO Box 1190 ... Beaver OK 73932 580-625-3373 625-3525
Web: www.oklahomaparks.com
Beavers Bend Resort Park PO Box 10 ... Broken Bow OK 74728 580-494-6300 494-6689
Web: www.oklahomaparks.com
Bernice State Park 901 State Park Rd ... Grove OK 74344 918-786-9447 787-5634
Web: www.oklahomaparks.com
Black Mesa State Park & Nature Preserve County Rd 325 ... Kenton OK 73946 580-426-2222 426-2405
Web: www.oklahomaparks.com
Boggy Depot State Park Hwy 7 & Park Access Ln ... Atoka OK 74525 580-889-5625 889-8816
Web: www.oklahomaparks.com
Boiling Springs State Park Rt 2 Box 299 ... Woodward OK 73802 580-256-7664 256-4338
Web: www.oklahomaparks.com
Brushy Lake State Park Rt 3 Box 36 ... Sallisaw OK 74955 918-775-6507 775-0970
Web: www.oklahomaparks.com
Cherokee Landing State Park Hwy 82 S ... Park Hill OK 74451 918-457-5716 457-4871
Web: www.oklahomaparks.com
Cherokee State Park PO Box 220 ... Disney OK 74340 918-435-8066 435-4067
Web: www.oklahomaparks.com
Clayton Lake State Park HC 60 Box 33-10 ... Clayton OK 74536 918-569-7981 569-7981
Web: www.oklahomaparks.com
Crowder Lake University Park RR 1 Box 186 ... Colony OK 73031 580-343-2443 774-7059
Web: www.swosu.edu/academics/crowderlake/
Disney/Little Blue State Park
c/o Cherokee State Park PO Box 220 ... Disney OK 74340 918-435-8066
Web: www.oklahomaparks.com
Dripping Springs State Park 16830 Dripping Springs Rd ... Okmulgee OK 74447 918-756-5971 759-9933
Web: www.oklahomaparks.com
Fort Cobb Lake State Park 1269 Copperhead Rd ... Fort Cobb OK 73038 405-643-2249 643-5167
Web: www.oklahomaparks.com
Foss State Park HC 66 Box 111 ... Foss OK 73647 580-592-4433 592-4701
Web: www.oklahomaparks.com
Great Plains State Park Hwy 183 & County Rd ... Mountain Park OK 73552 580-569-2032 569-2375
Web: www.oklahomaparks.com
Great Salt Plains State Park Rt 1 Box 28 ... Jet OK 73749 580-626-4731 626-4730
Web: www.oklahomaparks.com
Greenleaf State Park Rt 1 Box 119 ... Braggs OK 74423 918-487-5196 487-5406
Web: www.oklahomaparks.com
Heavener Runestone State Park 18365 Runestone Rd ... Heavener OK 74937 918-653-2241 653-3435
Web: www.oklahomaparks.com
Hochatown State Park
c/o Beavers Bend State Park PO Box 10 ... Broken Bow OK 94728 580-494-6452 494-6453
Honey Creek State Park 901 State Park Rd ... Grove OK 74344 918-786-9447 787-5634
Web: www.oklahomaparks.com
Hugo Lake State Park PO Box 907 ... Hugo OK 74743 580-326-0303 326-0505
Keystone State Park 1926 S Hwy 151 ... Sand Springs OK 74063 918-865-4477 865-2050
Web: www.oklahomaparks.com
Lake Eucha State Park PO Box 349 Hwy 59 S ... Jay OK 74346 918-253-8790
Web: www.oklahomaparks.com
Lake Eufaula State Park HC 60 Box 1340 ... Checotah OK 74426 918-689-5311 689-5039
Web: www.touroklahoma.com/detail.asp?id=1+5U+7777
Lake Murray State Park 18407 Scenic State Hwy 77 ... Ardmore OK 73401 580-223-4044 223-4052
Web: www.oklahomaparks.com
Lake Texoma State Park PO Box 248 ... Kingston OK 73439 580-564-2566 564-2262
Web: www.oklahomaparks.com
Lake Thunderbird State Park 13101 Alameda Dr ... Norman OK 73026 405-360-3572 366-8150
Web: www.oklahomaparks.com
Lake Wister State Park 25567 US Hwy 270 ... Wister OK 74966 918-655-7212 655-7274
Web: www.oklahomaparks.com
Little Sahara State Park 101 Main St ... Waynoka OK 73860 580-824-1471 824-1472
Web: www.oklahomaparks.com
McGee Creek State Park 576-A S McGee Creek Dam Rd ... Atoka OK 74525 580-889-5822 889-7868
Web: www.oklahomaparks.com
Natural Falls State Park Rt 4 Box 32 ... West Siloam Springs OK 74338 918-422-5802 422-0026
Web: www.oklahomaparks.com
Okmulgee State Park 16830 Dripping Springs Rd ... Okmulgee OK 74447 918-756-5971 759-9933
Web: www.oklahomaparks.com/parks.asp
Osage Hills State Park Hwy 60 W ... Bartlesville OK 74006 918-336-4141 337-2176
Web: www.oklahomaparks.com
Quartz Mountain Resort 22469 Lodge Rd ... Lone Wolf OK 73655 580-563-2424 563-2422
Web: www.quartzmountainresort.com
Raymond Gary State Park HC 63 Box 1450 ... Fort Towson OK 74735 580-873-2307 326-2305
Web: www.oklahomaparks.com
Red Rock Canyon State Park PO Box 502 ... Hinton OK 73047 405-542-6344 542-6342
Web: www.oklahomaparks.com
Robbers Cave State Park PO Box 9 ... Wilburton OK 74578 918-465-2565 465-5763
Web: www.oklahomaparks.com
Roman Nose Resort Park Rt 1 Box 2-2 ... Watonga OK 73772 580-623-4215 623-2190
Web: www.oklahomaparks.com
Sequoyah Bay State Park 6237 E 100th St N ... Wagoner OK 74467 918-683-0878 687-6797
Web: www.oklahomaparks.com
Sequoyah State Park & Western Hills Guest Ranch
17131 Park 10 ... Hulbert OK 74441 918-772-2545 772-2030
TF: 800-368-1486 ■ *Web:* www.oklahomaparks.com
Snowdale State Park PO Box 6 ... Salina OK 74365 918-434-2651 435-4067
Web: www.oklahomaparks.com
Spavinaw State Park Hwy 82 S ... Spavinaw OK 74366 918-589-2651 435-4067
Web: www.oklahomaparks.com
Talimena State Park PO Box 318 ... Talihina OK 74571 918-567-2052 567-2052
Web: www.oklahomaparks.com
Tenkiller State Park HCR 68 Box 1095 ... Vian OK 74962 918-489-5643 489-2111
Web: www.oklahomaparks.com
Twin Bridges State Park 14801 Hwy 137 S ... Fairland OK 74343 918-540-2545 540-2545
Web: www.oklahomaparks.com
Wah-Sha-She State Park Hwy 10 W ... Copan OK 74022 918-336-4141 337-2176
Web: www.oklahomaparks.com
Walnut Creek State Park 1926 State Hwy 151 ... Sand Springs OK 74063 918-865-4991
Web: www.oklahomaparks.com

Oregon

Phone | Fax

Agate Beach State Recreation Site
c/o Beverly Beach Management Unit 198 NE 123rd St ... Newport OR 97365 800-551-6949
Web: www.oregonstateparks.org/park_212.php
Ainsworth State Park
c/o Columbia River Gorge Management Unit PO Box 100 ... Corbett OR 97019 800-551-6949
Web: www.oregonstateparks.org/park_146.php
Alderwood State Wayside
c/o Southern Willamette Management Unit PO Box 511 ... Lowell OR 97452 800-551-6949
Web: www.oregonstateparks.org/park_80.php
Alfred A. Loeb State Park
c/o Harris Beach Management Unit 1655 Hwy 101 N ... Brookings OR 97415 800-551-6949
Web: www.oregonstateparks.org/park_72.php
Alsea Bay Historic Interpretive Center
c/o South Beach Management Unit 5580 S Coast Hwy ... Newport OR 97366 800-551-6949
Web: www.oregonstateparks.org/park_202.php
Arcadia Beach State Recreation Site
c/o Nehalem Bay Management Unit 9500 Sandpiper Lane -
PO Box 366 ... Nehalem OR 97131 800-551-6949
Web: www.oregonstateparks.org/park_187.php
Bald Peak State Scenic Viewpoint
c/o Champoeg Management Unit 7679 Champoeg Rd NE ... Saint Paul OR 97137 800-551-6949
Web: www.oregonstateparks.org/park_110.php
Bandon State Natural Area
c/o Bullards Beach Management Unit PO Box 569 ... Bandon OR 97411 800-551-6949
Web: www.oregonstateparks.org/park_64.php
Banks-Vernonia State Trail 24600 NW Bachona Rd ... Buxton OR 97109 800-551-6949
Web: www.oregonstateparks.org/park_145.php
Battle Mountain Forest State Scenic Corridor
c/o Blue Mountain Management Unit PO Box 85 ... Meacham OR 97859 800-551-6949
Web: www.oregonstateparks.org/park_238.php
Beachside State Recreation Site
c/o South Beach Management Unit 5580 S Coast Hwy ... Newport OR 97366 800-551-6949
Web: www.oregonstateparks.org/park_122.php
Benson State Recreation Area
c/o Columbia River Gorge Management Unit PO Box 100 ... Corbett OR 97019 800-551-6949
Web: www.oregonstateparks.org/park_147.php
Beverly Beach State Park 198 NE 123rd St ... Newport OR 97365 541-265-9278
Web: www.oregonstateparks.org/park_227.php
Blue Mountain Forest State Scenic Corridor
c/o Blue Mountain Management Unit PO Box 85 ... Meecham OR 97859 800-551-6949
Web: www.oregonstateparks.org/park_237.php
Bob Straub State Park
c/o Cape Lookout Management Unit 13000 Whiskey Creek
Rd W ... Tillamook OR 97141 800-551-6949
Web: www.oregonstateparks.org/park_183.php
Boiler Bay State Scenic Viewpoint
c/o Beverly Beach Management Unit 198 NE 123rd St ... Newport OR 97365 800-551-6949
Web: www.oregonstateparks.org/park_213.php
Bolon Island Tideways State Scenic Corridor
c/o Honeyman Management Unit 84505 Hwy 101 S ... Florence OR 97439 800-551-6949
Web: www.oregonstateparks.org/park_114.php
Bonnie Lure State Recreation Area
c/o Tryon Creek Management Unit 11321 SW
Terwilliger Blvd ... Portland OR 97219 800-551-6949
Web: www.oregonstateparks.org/park_140.php
Booth State Scenic Corridor
c/o LaPine Management Unit 15800 State Recreation Rd ... La Pine OR 97739 800-551-6949
Web: www.oregonstateparks.org/park_52.php
Bradley State Scenic Viewpoint
c/o Fort Stevens Management Unit 100 Peter Iredale Rd ... Hammond OR 97121 800-551-6949
Web: www.oregonstateparks.org/park_176.php
Bridal Veil Falls State Scenic Viewpoint
c/o Columbia River Gorge Management Unit PO Box 100 ... Corbett OR 97019 800-551-6949
Web: www.oregonstateparks.org/park_149.php
Bullards Beach State Park PO Box 569 ... Bandon OR 97411 541-347-2209
Web: www.oregonstateparks.org/park_71.php
Cape Arago State Park
c/o Sunset Bay Management Unit 89814 Cape Arago Hwy ... Coos Bay OR 97420 541-888-3778
Web: www.oregonstateparks.org/park_94.php
Cape Blanco State Park 39745 S Hwy 101 ... Port Orford OR 97465 541-332-6774
Web: www.oregonstateparks.org/park_62.php
Cape Kiwanda State Natural Area
c/o Cape Lookout Management Unit 13000 Whiskey Creek
Rd W ... Tillamook OR 97141 800-551-6949
Web: www.oregonstateparks.org/park_180.php
Cape Lookout State Park 13000 Whiskey Creek Rd W ... Tillamook OR 97141 503-842-4981
Web: www.oregonstateparks.org/park_186.php
Cape Meares State Scenic Viewpoint
c/o Cape Lookout Management Unit 13000 Whiskey Creek
Rd W ... Tillamook OR 97141 800-551-6949
Web: www.oregonstateparks.org/park_181.php
Cape Sebastian State Scenic Corridor
c/o Harris Beach Management Unit 1655 Hwy 101 N ... Brookings OR 97415 800-551-6949
Web: www.oregonstateparks.org/park_73.php
Carl G. Washburne Memorial State Park 9311 Hwy 101 N ... Florence OR 97439 541-547-3416
Web: www.oregonstateparks.org/park_123.php
Cascadia State Park PO Box 736 ... Cascadia OR 97329 541-367-6021
Web: www.oregonstateparks.org/park_210.php

Oregon (Cont'd)

Phone Fax

Casey State Recreation Site
c/o Joseph Stewart Management Unit 35251 Hwy 62 Trail OR 97541 541-560-3334 560-3855
Web: www.oregonstateparks.org/park_28.php

Catherine Creek State Park
c/o Blue Mountain Management Unit PO Box 85 Meacham OR 97859 800-551-6949
Web: www.oregonstateparks.org/park_17.php

Champoeg State Heritage Area 7679 Champoeg Rd NE Saint Paul OR 97137 503-678-1251
Web: www.oregonstateparks.org/park_113.php

Chandler State Wayside
c/o LaPine Management Unit 15800 State Recreation Rd La Pine OR 97739 800-551-6949
Web: www.oregonstateparks.org/park_53.php

Cline Falls State Scenic Viewpoint
c/o Tumalo Management Unit 62976 OB Riley Rd Bend OR 97701 800-551-6949
Web: www.oregonstateparks.org/park_38.php

Clyde Holliday State Recreation Site PO Box 10 Mount Vernon OR 97865 541-932-4453
Web: www.oregonstateparks.org/park_11.php

Collier Memorial State Park 46000 Hwy 97 N Chiloquin OR 97624 541-783-2471
Web: www.oregonstateparks.org/park_228.php

Coquille Myrtle Grove State Natural Site
c/o Bullards Beach Management Unit PO Box 569 Bandon OR 97411 800-551-6949
Web: www.oregonstateparks.org/park_65.php

Cove Palisades State Park 7300 Jordan Rd Culver OR 97734 541-546-3412
Web: www.oregonstateparks.org/park_32.php

Crissey Field State Recreation Site
c/o Harris Beach Management Unit 1655 Hwy 101 N Brookings OR 97415 800-551-6949
TF: 800-551-6949 ■ *Web:* www.oregonstateparks.org/park_74.php

Crown Point State Scenic Corridor
c/o Columbia River Gorge Management Unit PO Box 100 Corbett OR 97019 800-551-6949
Web: www.oregonstateparks.org/park_150.php

D River State Recreation Site
c/o Beverly Beach Management Unit 198 NE 123rd St Newport OR 97365 800-551-6949
Web: www.oregonstateparks.org/park_214.php

Dabney State Recreation Area
c/o Columbia River Gorge Management Unit PO Box 100 Corbett OR 97019 800-551-6949
Web: www.oregonstateparks.org/park_151.php

Darlingtonia State Natural Site
c/o Honeyman Management Unit 84505 Hwy 101 S Florence OR 97439 800-551-6949
Web: www.oregonstateparks.org/park_115.php

Del Rey Beach State Recreation Site
c/o Fort Stevens Management Unit 100 Peter Iredale Rd Hammond OR 97121 800-551-6949
Web: www.oregonstateparks.org/park_177.php

Deschutes River State Recreation Area 89600 Biggs-Rufus Hwy Wasco OR 97065 541-739-2322
Web: www.oregonstateparks.org/park_37.php

Detroit Lake State Recreation Area PO Box 549 Detroit OR 97342 503-854-3346
Web: www.oregonstateparks.org/park_93.php

Devil's Lake State Recreation Area
c/o Beverly Beach Management Unit 198 NE 123rd St Newport OR 97365 800-551-6949
Web: www.oregonstateparks.org/park_216.php

Devil's Punchbowl State Natural Area
c/o Beverly Beach Management Unit 198 NE 123rd St Newport OR 97365 800-551-6949
Web: www.oregonstateparks.org/park_217.php

Dexter State Recreation Site
c/o Southern Willamette Management Unit PO Box 511 Lowell OR 97452 541-937-1173
Web: www.oregonstateparks.org/park_244.php

Driftwood Beach State Recreation Site
c/o South Beach Management Unit 5580 S Coast Hwy Newport OR 97366 800-551-6949
Web: www.oregonstateparks.org/park_203.php

Ecola State Park c/o Nehalem State Park PO Box 366 Nehalem OR 97131 503-436-2844
Web: www.oregonstateparks.org/park_188.php

Elijah Bristow State Park
c/o Southern Willamette Management Unit PO Box 511 Lowell OR 97452 800-551-6949
Web: www.oregonstateparks.org/park_83.php

Ellmaker State Wayside
c/o Beverly Beach Management Unit 198 NE 123rd St Newport OR 97365 800-551-6949
Web: www.oregonstateparks.org/park_218.php

Emigrant Springs State Heritage Area
c/o Blue Mountain Management Unit PO Box 85 Meacham OR 97859 800-551-6959
Web: www.oregonstateparks.org/park_23.php

Erratic Rock State Natural Site
c/o Willamette Mission Management Unit 10991 Wheatland Rd NE Gervais OR 97026 800-551-6949
Web: www.oregonstateparks.org/park_135.php

Face Rock State Scenic Viewpoint
c/o Bullards Beach Management Unit PO Box 569 Bandon OR 97411 800-551-6949
Web: www.oregonstateparks.org/park_66.php

Fall Creek State Recreation Area
c/o Southern Willamette Management Unit PO Box 511 Lowell OR 97452 541-937-1173
Web: www.oregonstateparks.org/park_241.php

Farewell Bend State Recreation Area 23751 Old Hwy 30 Huntington OR 97907 541-869-2365
Web: www.oregonstateparks.org/park_7.php

Fogarty Creek State Recreation Area
c/o Beverly Beach Management Unit 198 NE 123rd St Newport OR 97365 800-551-6949
Web: www.oregonstateparks.org/park_220.php

Fort Rock State Natural Area
c/o LaPine Management Unit 15800 State Recreation Rd La Pine OR 97739 800-551-6949
Web: www.oregonstateparks.org/park_40.php

Fort Stevens State Park 100 Peter Iredale Rd Hammond OR 97121 503-861-1671
Web: www.oregonstateparks.org/park_179.php

Frenchglen Hotel State Heritage Site
c/o Clyde Holliday Management Unit PO Box 10 Mount Vernon OR 97865 800-551-6949
Web: www.oregonstateparks.org/park_3.php

Geisel Monument State Heritage Site
c/o Cape Blanco Management Unit PO Box 1345 Port Orford OR 97465 800-551-6949
Web: www.oregonstateparks.org/park_55.php

George W. Joseph State Natural Area
c/o Columbia River Gorge Management Unit PO Box 100 Corbett OR 97019 800-551-6949
Web: www.oregonstateparks.org/park_153.php

Gleneden Beach State Recreation Site
c/o Beverly Beach Management Unit 198 NE 123rd St Newport OR 97365 800-551-6949
Web: www.oregonstateparks.org/park_221.php

Golden & Silver Falls State Natural Area
c/o Sunset Bay Management Unit 89814 Cape Arago Hwy Coos Bay OR 97420 541-888-3778
Web: www.oregonstateparks.org/park_96.php

Goose Lake State Recreation Area
c/o LaPine Management Unit 15800 State Recreation Rd La Pine OR 97739 800-551-6949
Web: www.oregonstateparks.org/park_1.php

Government Island State Recreation Area
c/o Columbia River Gorge Management Unit PO Box 100 Corbett OR 97019 800-551-6949
Web: www.oregonstateparks.org/park_250.php

Governor Patterson Memorial State Recreation Site
c/o South Beach Management Unit 5580 S Coast Hwy Newport OR 97439 800-551-6949
Web: www.oregonstateparks.org/park_117.php

Guy W. Talbot State Park
c/o Columbia River Gorge Management Unit PO Box 100 Corbett OR 97019 800-551-6949
Web: www.oregonstateparks.org/park_154.php

H. B. Van Duzer Forest State Scenic Corridor
c/o Beverly Beach Management Unit 198 NE 123rd St Newport OR 97365 800-551-6949
Web: www.oregonstateparks.org/park_222.php

Harris Beach State Park 1655 Hwy 101 N Brookings OR 97415 541-469-2021
Web: www.oregonstateparks.org/park_79.php

Hat Rock State Park
c/o Blue Mountain Management Unit PO Box 85 Meacham OR 97859 800-551-6959
Web: www.oregonstateparks.org/park_19.php

Heceta Head Lighthouse State Scenic Viewpoint
c/o Washburne Management Unit 93111 Hwy 101 N Florence OR 97439 800-551-6949
Web: www.oregonstateparks.org/park_124.php

Hilgard Junction State Park
c/o Blue Mountain Management Unit PO Box 85 Meacham OR 97859 800-551-6949
Web: www.oregonstateparks.org/park_20.php

Historic Columbia River Highway State Trail
c/o Columbia River Gorge Management Unit PO Box 100 Corbett OR 97019 800-551-6949
Web: www.oregonstateparks.org/park_155.php

Hoffman Memorial State Wayside
c/o Bullards Beach Management Unit PO Box 569 Bandon OR 97411 800-551-6949
Web: www.oregonstateparks.org/park_67.php

Holman State Wayside
c/o Willamette Mission Management Unit 10991 Wheatland Rd NE Gervais OR 97026 800-551-6949
Web: www.oregonstateparks.org/park_136.php

Hug Point State Recreation Site
c/o Nehalem Bay Management Unit 9500 Sandpiper Lane - PO Box 366 Nehalem OR 97131 800-551-6949
Web: www.oregonstateparks.org/park_191.php

Humbug Mountain State Park
c/o Cape Blanco Management Unit PO Box 1345 Port Orford OR 97465 541-332-6774
Web: www.oregonstateparks.org/park_56.php

Jackson F. Kimball State Recreation Site
c/o Collier Memorial Management Unit 46000 Hwy 97 N Chiloquin OR 97624 800-551-6949
Web: www.oregonstateparks.org/park_229.php

Jasper State Recreation Site
c/o Southern Willamette Management Unit PO Box 511 Lowell OR 97452 541-937-1173
Web: www.oregonstateparks.org/park_243.php

Jessie M. Honeyman Memorial State Park
c/o Honeyman Management Unit 84505 Hwy 101 S Florence OR 97439 800-551-6949
Web: www.oregonstateparks.org/park_134.php

John B. Yeon State Scenic Corridor
c/o Columbia River Gorge Management Unit PO Box 100 Corbett OR 97019 800-551-6949
Web: www.oregonstateparks.org/park_156.php

Joseph H. Stewart State Recreation Area 35251 Hwy 62 Trail OR 97541 541-560-3334
Web: www.oregonstateparks.org/park_30.php

Kam Wah Chung State Heritage Site
c/o Clyde Holliday Management Unit PO Box 10 Mount Vernon OR 97865 800-551-6949
Web: www.oregonstateparks.org/park_8.php

Koberg Beach State Recreation Site
c/o Columbia River Gorge Management Unit PO Box 100 Corbett OR 97019 800-551-6949
Web: www.oregonstateparks.org/park_157.php

Lake Owyhee State Park
c/o Farewell Bend Management Unit 23751 Old Hwy 30 Huntington OR 97907 800-551-6949
Web: www.oregonstateparks.org/park_14.php

LaPine State Park 15800 State Recreation Rd La Pine OR 97739 800-551-6949
Web: www.oregonstateparks.org/park_41.php

Lewis & Clark State Recreation Site
c/o Columbia River Gorge Management Unit PO Box 100 Corbett OR 97019 800-551-6949
Web: www.oregonstateparks.org/park_159.php

Lost Creek State Recreation Site
c/o South Beach Management Unit 5580 S Coast Hwy Newport OR 97366 800-551-6949
Web: www.oregonstateparks.org/park_205.php

Lowell State Recreation Site
c/o Southern Willamette Management Unit PO Box 511 Lowell OR 97452 541-937-1173
Web: www.oregonstateparks.org/park_242.php

Manhattan Beach State Recreation Site
c/o Nehalem Bay Management Unit 9500 Sandpiper Lane - PO Box 366 Nehalem OR 97131 800-551-6949
Web: www.oregonstateparks.org/park_193.php

Maud Williamson State Recreation Site
c/o Willamette Mission Management Unit 10991 Wheatland Rd NE Gervais OR 97026 800-551-6949
Web: www.oregonstateparks.org/park_137.php

Mayer State Park
c/o Columbia River Gorge Management Unit PO Box 100 Corbett OR 97019 800-551-6949
Web: www.oregonstateparks.org/park_161.php

McVay Rock State Recreation Site
c/o Harris Beach Management Unit 1655 Hwy 101 N Brookings OR 97415 800-551-6949
Web: www.oregonstateparks.org/park_75.php

Memaloose State Park PO Box 472 Mosier OR 97040 541-478-3008
Web: www.oregonstateparks.org/park_163.php

Milo McIver State Park 24101 SE Entrance Rd Estacada OR 97023 503-630-7150
Web: www.oregonstateparks.org/park_142.php

Minam State Recreation Area
c/o Wallowa Lake Management Unit 72214 Marina Lane Joseph OR 97846 800-551-6949
Web: www.oregonstateparks.org/park_26.php

Molalla River State Park
c/o Willamette Mission Management Unit 7679 Champoeg Rd NE Saint Paul OR 97137 800-551-6949
Web: www.oregonstateparks.org/park_111.php

Munson Creek Falls State Natural Site
c/o Cape Lookout Management Unit 13000 Whiskey Creek Rd W Tillamook OR 97141 800-551-6949
Web: www.oregonstateparks.org/park_245.php

Muriel O. Ponsler Memorial State Scenic Viewpoint
c/o Washburne Management Unit 93111 Hwy 101 N Florence OR 97439 800-551-6949
Web: www.oregonstateparks.org/park_125.php

Nehalem Bay State Park 9500 Sandpiper Lane PO Box 366 Nehalem OR 97131 503-368-5154
Web: www.oregonstateparks.org/park_201.php

Neptune State Scenic Viewpoint
c/o Washburne Management Unit 93111 Hwy 101 N Florence OR 97439 800-551-6949
Web: www.oregonstateparks.org/park_126.php

Neskowin Beach State Recreation Site
c/o Beverly Beach Management Unit 198 NE 123rd St Newport OR 97365 800-551-6949
Web: www.oregonstateparks.org/park_223.php

North Santiam State Recreation Area
c/o Detroit Management Unit PO Box 549 Detroit OR 97342 800-551-6949
Web: www.oregonstateparks.org/park_92.php

OC&E Woods Line State Trail
c/o Collier Memorial Management Unit 46000 Hwy 97 N Chiloquin OR 97624 800-551-6949
Web: www.oregonstateparks.org/park_230.php

Phone Fax

Oceanside Beach State Recreation Site
c/o Cape Lookout Management Unit 13000 Whiskey Creek Rd W ... Tillamook OR 97141 800-551-6949
Web: www.oregonstateparks.org/park_182.php

Ona Beach State Park
c/o South Beach Management Unit 5580 S Coast Hwy ... Newport OR 97366 800-551-6949
Web: www.oregonstateparks.org/park_206.php

Ontario State Recreation Site
c/o Farewell Bend Management Unit 23751 Old Hwy 30 ... Huntington OR 97907 800-551-6949
Web: www.oregonstateparks.org/park_4.php

Oswald West State Park
c/o Nehalem Bay State Park PO Box 366 ... Nehalem OR 97131 503-368-5154
Web: www.oregonstateparks.org/park_195.php

Otter Crest State Scenic Viewpoint
c/o Beverly Beach Management Unit 198 NE 123rd St ... Newport OR 97365 800-551-6949
Web: www.oregonstateparks.org/park_224.php

Otter Point State Recreation Site
c/o Cape Blanco Management Unit PO Box 1345 ... Port Orford OR 97465 800-551-6949
Web: www.oregonstateparks.org/park_58.php

Paradise Point State Recreation Site
c/o Cape Blanco Management Unit PO Box 1345 ... Port Orford OR 97465 800-551-6949
Web: www.oregonstateparks.org/park_59.php

Peter Skene Ogden State Scenic Viewpoint
c/o Cove Palisades Management Unit 7300 Jordan Rd ... Culver OR 97734 800-551-6949
Web: www.oregonstateparks.org/park_50.php

Pilot Butte State Scenic Viewpoint
c/o Tumalo Management Unit 62976 OB Riley Rd ... Bend OR 97701 800-551-6949
Web: www.oregonstateparks.org/park_42.php

Pistol River State Scenic Viewpoint
c/o Harris Beach Management Unit 1655 Hwy 101 N ... Brookings OR 97415 800-551-6949
Web: www.oregonstateparks.org/park_76.php

Port Orford Heads State Park
c/o Cape Blanco Management Unit PO Box 1345 ... Port Orford OR 97465 800-551-6949
Web: www.oregonstateparks.org/park_61.php

Portland Women's Forum State Scenic Viewpoint
c/o Columbia River Gorge Management Unit PO Box 100 ... Corbett OR 97019 800-551-6949
Web: www.oregonstateparks.org/park_164.php

Prineville Reservoir State Park 19020 SE Parkland Dr ... Prineville OR 97754 541-447-4363
Web: www.oregonstateparks.org/park_34.php

Prospect State Scenic Viewpoint
c/o Joseph Stewart Management Unit 35251 Hwy 62 ... Trail OR 97541 800-551-6949
Web: www.oregonstateparks.org/park_29.php

Red Bridge State Wayside
c/o Blue Mountain Management Unit PO Box 85 ... Meacham OR 97859 800-551-6949
Web: www.oregonstateparks.org/park_21.php

Roads End State Recreation Site
c/o Beverly Beach Management Unit 198 NE 123rd St ... Newport OR 97365 800-551-6949
Web: www.oregonstateparks.org/park_225.php

Rooster Rock State Park PO Box 100 ... Corbett OR 97019 503-695-2261
Web: www.oregonstateparks.org/park_175.php

Saddle Mountain State Natural Area
c/o Nehalem Bay Management Unit 9500 Sandpiper Lane - PO Box 366 ... Nehalem OR 97131 800-551-6949
Web: www.oregonstateparks.org/park_197.php

Samuel H. Boardman State Scenic Corridor
c/o Harris Beach Management Unit 1655 Hwy 101 N ... Brookings OR 97415 800-551-6949
Web: www.oregonstateparks.org/park_77.php

Sarah Helmick State Recreation Site
c/o Willamette Mission Management Unit 10991 Wheatland Rd NE ... Gervais OR 97026 800-551-6949
Web: www.oregonstateparks.org/park_138.php

Seal Rock State Recreation Site
c/o South Beach Management Unit 5580 S Coast Hwy ... Newport OR 97366 800-551-6949
Web: www.oregonstateparks.org/park_207.php

Seneca Fouts Memorial State Natural Area
c/o Columbia River Gorge Management Unit PO Box 100 ... Corbett OR 97019 800-551-6949
Web: www.oregonstateparks.org/park_167.php

Seven Devils State Recreation Site
c/o Bullards Beach Management Unit PO Box 569 ... Bandon OR 97411 800-551-6949
Web: www.oregonstateparks.org/park_69.php

Shepperd's Dell State Natural Area
c/o Columbia River Gorge Management Unit PO Box 100 ... Corbett OR 97019 800-551-6949
Web: www.oregonstateparks.org/park_168.php

Shore Acres State Park
c/o Sunset Bay Management Unit 89814 Cape Arago Hwy ... Coos Bay OR 97420 541-888-3778
Web: www.oregonstateparks.org/park_97.php

Silver Falls State Park 20024 Silver Falls Hwy SE ... Sublimity OR 97385 503-873-8681 873-8925
Web: www.oregonstateparks.org/park_211.php

Smelt Sands State Recreation Site
c/o South Beach Management Unit 5580 S Coast Hwy ... Newport OR 97366 800-551-6949
Web: www.oregonstateparks.org/park_128.php

Smith Rock State Park 9241 NE Crooked River Dr ... Terrebonne OR 97760 541-548-7501
Web: www.oregonstateparks.org/park_51.php

South Beach State Park 5580 S Coast Hwy ... South Beach OR 97366 541-867-4715
Web: www.oregonstateparks.org/park_209.php

Starvation Creek State Park
c/o Columbia River Gorge Management Unit PO Box 100 ... Corbett OR 97019 503-695-2261
Web: www.oregonstateparks.org/park_170.php

Stonefield Beach State Recreation Site
c/o Area 3 Field Office 84505 Hwy 101 S ... Florence OR 97439 541-997-5755
Web: www.oregonstateparks.org/park_130.php

Succor Creek State Natural Area
c/o Farewell Bend Management Unit 23751 Old Hwy 30 ... Huntington OR 97907 800-551-6949
Web: www.oregonstateparks.org/park_13.php

Sumpter Valley Dredge State Heritage Area
c/o Clyde Holliday Management Unit PO Box 10 ... Mount Vernon OR 97865 800-551-6949
Web: www.oregonstateparks.org/park_239.php

Sunset Bay State Park
c/o Sunset Bay Management Unit 89814 Cape Arago Hwy ... Coos Bay OR 97420 541-888-4902
Web: www.oregonstateparks.org/park_100.php

Tokatee Klootchman State Natural Site
c/o Washburne Management Unit 93111 Hwy 101 N ... Florence OR 97439 800-551-6949
Web: www.oregonstateparks.org/park_129.php

Tolovana Beach State Recreation Site
c/o Nehalem Bay Management Unit 9500 Sandpiper Lane - PO Box 366 ... Nehalem OR 97131 800-551-6949
Web: www.oregonstateparks.org/park_199.php

Touvelle State Recreation Site
c/o Valley of the Rogue Management Unit 3792 N River Rd ... Gold Hill OR 97525 800-551-6949
Web: www.oregonstateparks.org/park_106.php

Tryon Creek State Natural Area 11321 SW Terwilliger Blvd ... Portland OR 97219 503-636-9886
Web: www.oregonstateparks.org/park_144.php

Tub Springs State Wayside
c/o Valley of the Rogue Management Unit 3792 N River Rd ... Gold Hill OR 97525 800-551-6949
Web: www.oregonstateparks.org/park_107.php

Tumalo State Park 62976 OB Riley Rd ... Bend OR 97701 541-382-3586
Web: www.oregonstateparks.org/park_45.php

Ukiah-Dale Forest State Scenic Corridor
c/o Blue Mountain Management Unit PO Box 85 ... Meacham OR 97859 800-551-6949
Web: www.oregonstateparks.org/park_22.php

Umpqua Lighthouse State Park
c/o Honeyman Management Unit 84505 Hwy 101 S ... Florence OR 97439 800-551-6949
Web: www.oregonstateparks.org/park_121.php

Unity Forest State Scenic Corridor
c/o Farewell Bend Management Unit 23751 Old Hwy 30 ... Huntington OR 97907 800-551-6949
Web: www.oregonstateparks.org/park_9.php

Unity Lake State Recreation Site
c/o Clyde Holliday Management Unit PO Box 10 ... Mount Vernon OR 97865 800-551-6949
Web: www.oregonstateparks.org/park_10.php

Valley of the Rogue State Park 3792 N River Rd ... Gold Hill OR 97525 541-582-1118
Web: www.oregonstateparks.org/park_109.php

Viento State Park PO Box 472 ... Mosier OR 97040 541-374-8811
Web: www.oregonstateparks.org/park_171.php

Vinzenz Lausmann Memorial State Natural Area
c/o Columbia River Gorge Management Unit PO Box 100 ... Corbett OR 97019 800-551-6949
Web: www.oregonstateparks.org/park_172.php

W.B. Nelson State Recreation Site
c/o South Beach Management Unit 5580 S Coast Hwy ... Newport OR 97366 800-551-6949
Web: www.oregonstateparks.org/park_131.php

Wallowa Lake Highway Forest State Scenic Corridor
c/o Wallowa Lake Management Unit 72214 Marina Ln ... Joseph OR 97846 541-432-4185
Web: www.oregonstateparks.org/park_24.php

Wallowa Lake State Park 72214 Marina Lane ... Joseph OR 97846 541-432-4185
Web: www.oregonstateparks.org/park_27.php

Washburne State Wayside
c/o Southern Willamette Management Unit PO Box 511 ... Lowell OR 97452 800-551-6949
Web: www.oregonstateparks.org/park_87.php

White River Falls State Park
c/o Deschutes River Management Unit PO Box 2330 ... Wasco OR 97065 800-551-6949
Web: www.oregonstateparks.org/park_36.php

Willamette Mission State Park 10991 Wheatland Rd NE ... Gervais OR 97026 503-393-1172 393-8863
Web: www.oregonstateparks.org/park_139.php

Willamette Stone State Heritage Site
c/o Tryon Creek Management Unit 11321 SW Terwilliger Blvd ... Portland OR 97219 800-551-6949
Web: www.oregonstateparks.org/park_246.php

William M. Tugman State Park 72549 Hwy 101 ... Lakeside OR 97449 800-551-6949
Web: www.oregonstateparks.org/park_98.php

Winchuck State Recreation Site
c/o Harris Beach Management Unit 1655 Hwy 101 N ... Brookings OR 97415 800-551-6949
Web: www.oregonstateparks.org/park_78.php

Wolf Creek Inn State Heritage Site PO Box 6 ... Wolf Creek OR 97497 541-866-2474
Web: www.oregonstateparks.org/park_108.php

Wygant State Natural Area
c/o Columbia River Gorge Management Unit PO Box 100 ... Corbett OR 97019 800-551-6949
Web: www.oregonstateparks.org/park_174.php

Yachats Ocean Road State Natural Site
c/o South Beach Management Unit 5580 S Coast Hwy ... Newport OR 97366 800-551-6949
Web: www.oregonstateparks.org/park_132.php

Yachats State Recreation Area
c/o South Beach Management Unit 5580 S Coast Hwy ... Newport OR 97366 800-551-6949
Web: www.oregonstateparks.org/park_133.php

Yaquina Bay State Recreation Site
c/o South Beach Management Unit 5580 S Coast Hwy ... Newport OR 97366 800-551-6949
Web: www.oregonstateparks.org/park_208.php

Pennsylvania

Phone Fax

Allegheny Islands State Park c/o Region 2 Office ... Prospect PA 15834 724-865-2131
Web: www.dcnr.state.pa.us/stateparks/parks/alleghenyislands.aspx

Archbald Pothole State Park c/o Lackawanna State Park ... Dalton PA 18414 570-945-3239
Web: www.dcnr.state.pa.us/stateparks/parks/archbaldpothole.asp

Bald Eagle State Park 149 Main Park Rd ... Howard PA 16841 814-625-2775
Web: www.dcnr.state.pa.us/stateparks/parks/baldeagle.aspx

Beltzville State Park 2950 Pohopoco Dr ... Lehighton PA 18235 610-377-0045
Web: www.dcnr.state.pa.us/stateparks/parks/beltzville.aspx

Bendigo State Park 533 State Park Rd ... Johnsonburg PA 15845 814-965-2646
Web: www.dcnr.state.pa.us/stateparks/parks/bendigo.aspx

Benjamin Rush State Park
c/o Fort Washington State Park ... Fort Washington PA 19034 215-591-5250
Web: www.dcnr.state.pa.us/stateparks/parks/benjaminrush.aspx

Big Pocono State Park c/o Tobyhanna State Park ... Tobyhanna PA 18466 570-894-8336
Web: www.dcnr.state.pa.us/stateparks/parks/bigpocono.aspx

Big Spring State Park
c/o Colonel Denning State Park 1599 Doubling Gap Rd ... Newville PA 17241 717-776-5272
Web: www.dcnr.state.pa.us/stateparks/parks/bigspring.aspx

Black Moshannon State Park 4216 Beaver Rd ... Philipsburg PA 16866 814-342-5960
Web: www.dcnr.state.pa.us/stateparks/parks/blackmoshannon.aspx

Blue Knob State Park 124 Park Rd ... Imler PA 16655 814-276-3576
Web: www.dcnr.state.pa.us/stateparks/parks/blueknob.aspx

Boyd Big Tree Conservation Area
c/o Little Buffalo State Park RR 2 Box 256A ... Newport PA 17074 717-567-9255
Web: www.dcnr.state.pa.us/stateparks/parks/boydbigtree.aspx

Buchanan's Birthplace State Park
c/o Cowans Gap State Park 6235 Aughwick Rd ... Fort Loudon PA 17224 717-485-3948
Web: www.dcnr.state.pa.us/stateparks/parks/buchanansbirthplace.aspx

Bucktail State Park c/o Region 1 Office ... Emporium PA 15834 814-486-3365
Web: www.dcnr.state.pa.us/stateparks/parks/bucktail.aspx

Caledonia State Park 101 Pine Grove Rd ... Fayetteville PA 17222 717-352-2161 352-7026
Web: www.dcnr.state.pa.us/stateparks/parks/caledonia.aspx

Canoe Creek State Park RR 2, Box 560 ... Hollidaysburg PA 16648 814-695-6807
Web: www.dcnr.state.pa.us/stateparks/parks/canoecreek.aspx

Chapman State Park RR 2, Box 1610 ... Clarendon PA 16313 814-723-0250
Web: www.dcnr.state.pa.us/stateparks/parks/chapman.aspx

Cherry Springs State Park
c/o Lyman Run State Park 454 Lyman Run Rd ... Galeton PA 16922 814-435-5010
Web: www.dcnr.state.pa.us/stateparks/parks/cherrysprings.aspx

Clear Creek State Park 38 Clear Creek State Park Rd ... Sigel PA 15860 814-752-2368
Web: www.dcnr.state.pa.us/stateparks/parks/clearcreek.aspx

Codorus State Park 2600 Smith Station Rd ... Hanover PA 17331 717-637-2816 637-4720
Web: www.dcnr.state.pa.us/stateparks/parks/codorus.aspx

Colonel Denning State Park 1599 Doubling Gap Rd ... Newville PA 17241 717-776-5272
Web: www.dcnr.state.pa.us/stateparks/parks/coloneldenning.aspx

Colton Point State Park
c/o Leonard Harrison State Park 4797 Route 660 ... Wellsboro PA 16901 570-724-3061
Web: www.dcnr.state.pa.us/stateparks/parks/coltonpoint.aspx

Cook Forest State Park PO Box 120 ... Cooksburg PA 16217 814-744-8407
Web: www.dcnr.state.pa.us/stateparks/parks/cookforest.aspx

Cowans Gap State Park 6235 Aughwick Rd ... Fort Loudon PA 17224 717-485-3948
Web: www.dcnr.state.pa.us/stateparks/parks/cowansgap.aspx

Delaware Canal State Park 11 Lodi Hill Rd ... Upper Black Eddy PA 18972 610-982-5560
Web: www.dcnr.state.pa.us/stateparks/parks/delawarecanal.aspx

Pennsylvania (Cont'd)

				Phone	Fax
Denton Hill State Park c/o Lyman Run 454 Lyman Run Rd *Web:* www.dcnr.state.pa.us/stateparks/parks/dentonhill.aspx	Galeton	PA	16922	814-435-2115	
Elk State Park c/o Bendigo State Park 533 State Park Rd. *Web:* www.dcnr.state.pa.us/stateparks/parks/elk.aspx	Johnsonburg	PA	15845	814-965-2646	
Evansburg State Park 851 May Hall Rd *Web:* www.dcnr.state.pa.us/stateparks/parks/evansburg.aspx	Collegeville	PA	19426	610-409-1150	
Fort Washington State Park 500 Bethlehem Pike *Web:* www.dcnr.state.pa.us/stateparks/parks/fortwashington.aspx	Fort Washington	PA	19034	215-591-5250	
Fowlers Hollow State Park c/o Colonel Denning State Park 1599 Doubling Gap Rd *Web:* www.dcnr.state.pa.us/stateparks/parks/fowlershollow.aspx	Newville	PA	17241	717-776-5272	
Frances Slocum State Park 565 Mount Olivet Rd *Web:* www.dcnr.state.pa.us/stateparks/parks/francesslocum.aspx	Wyoming	PA	18644	570-696-3525	
French Creek State Park 843 Park Rd *Web:* www.dcnr.state.pa.us/stateparks/parks/frenchcreek.aspx	Elverson	PA	19520	610-582-9680	
Gifford Pinchot State Park 2200 Rosstown Rd *Web:* www.dcnr.state.pa.us/stateparks/parks/giffordpinchot.aspx	Lewisberry	PA	17339	717-432-5011	
Gouldsboro State Park c/o Tobyhanna State Park PO Box 387 *Web:* www.dcnr.state.pa.us/stateparks/parks/gouldsboro.aspx	Tobyhanna	PA	18466	570-894-8336	
Greenwood Furnace State Park 15795 Greenwood Rd *Web:* www.dcnr.state.pa.us/stateparks/parks/greenwoodfurnace.aspx	Huntingdon	PA	16652	814-667-1800	
Hickory Run State Park RR 1, Box 81 *Web:* www.dcnr.state.pa.us/stateparks/parks/hickoryrun.aspx	White Haven	PA	18661	570-443-0400	
Hillman State Park c/o Raccoon Creek State Park 3000 State Rt 18 *Web:* www.dcnr.state.pa.us/stateparks/parks/hillman.aspx	Hookstown	PA	15050	724-899-2200	
Hills Creek State Park 111 Spillway Rd *Web:* www.dcnr.state.pa.us/stateparks/parks/hillscreek.aspx	Wellsboro	PA	16901	570-724-4246	
Hyner Run State Park 56 Hyner Park Rd *Web:* www.dcnr.state.pa.us/stateparks/parks/hynerrun.aspx	Hyner	PA	17738	570-923-6000	
Hyner View State Park c/o Hyner Run State Park 56 Hyner Park Rd *Web:* www.dcnr.state.pa.us/stateparks/parks/hynerview.aspx	Hyner	PA	17738	570-923-6000	
Jacobsburg Environmental Education Center 835 Jacobsburg Rd *Web:* www.dcnr.state.pa.us/stateparks/parks/jacobsburg.aspx	Wind Gap	PA	18091	610-746-2801	
Jennings Environmental Education Center 2951 Prospect Rd *Web:* www.dcnr.state.pa.us/stateparks/parks/jennings.aspx	Slippery Rock	PA	16057	724-794-6011	
Joseph E. Ibberson Conservation Area c/o Little Buffalo State Park 1579 State Park Rd. *Web:* www.dcnr.state.pa.us/stateparks/parks/josepheibberson.aspx	Newport	PA	17074	717-567-9255	
Kettle Creek State Park 97 Kettle Creek Park Ln *Web:* www.dcnr.state.pa.us/stateparks/parks/kettlecreek.aspx	Renovo	PA	17764	570-923-6004	
Keystone State Park 1150 Keystone Park Rd *Web:* www.dcnr.state.pa.us/stateparks/parks/keystone.aspx	Derry	PA	15627	724-668-2939	
Kings Gap Environmental Education & Training Center 500 Kings Gap Rd *Web:* www.dcnr.state.pa.us/stateparks/parks/kingsgap.aspx	Carlisle	PA	17015	717-486-5031	
Kinzua Bridge State Park c/o Bendigo State Park 533 State Park Rd *Web:* www.dcnr.state.pa.us/stateparks/parks/kinzuabridge.aspx	Johnsonburg	PA	15845	814-965-2646	
Kooser State Park 943 Glades Pike *Web:* www.dcnr.state.pa.us/stateparks/parks/kooser.aspx	Somerset	PA	15501	814-445-8673	
Lackawanna State Park RR 1, Box 230 *Web:* www.dcnr.state.pa.us/stateparks/parks/lackawanna.aspx	Dalton	PA	18414	570-945-3239	
Laurel Hill State Park 1454 Laurel Hill Park Rd. *Web:* www.dcnr.state.pa.us/stateparks/parks/laurelhill.aspx	Somerset	PA	15501	814-445-7725	
Laurel Mountain State Park c/o Linn Run State Park PO Box 50 *Web:* www.dcnr.state.pa.us/stateparks/parks/laurelmountain.aspx	Rector	PA	15677	724-238-6623	
Laurel Ridge State Park 1117 Jim Mountain Rd *Web:* www.dcnr.state.pa.us/stateparks/parks/laurelridge.aspx	Rockwood	PA	15557	724-455-3744	
Laurel Summit State Park c/o Linn Run State Park PO Box 50. *Web:* www.dcnr.state.pa.us/stateparks/parks/laurelsummit.aspx	Rector	PA	15677	724-238-6623	
Lehigh Gorge State Park RR 1 Box 81 *Web:* www.dcnr.state.pa.us/stateparks/parks/lehighgorge.aspx	White Haven	PA	18661	570-443-0400	
Leonard Harrison State Park 4797 Route 660 *Web:* www.dcnr.state.pa.us/stateparks/parks/leonardharrison.aspx	Wellsboro	PA	16901	570-724-3061	
Linn Run State Park PO Box 50 *Web:* www.dcnr.state.pa.us/stateparks/parks/linnrun.aspx	Rector	PA	15677	724-238-6623	
Little Buffalo State Park 1579 State Park Rd *Web:* www.dcnr.state.pa.us/stateparks/parks/littlebuffalo.aspx	Newport	PA	17074	717-567-9255	
Little Pine State Park 4205 Little Pine Creek Rd *Web:* www.dcnr.state.pa.us/stateparks/parks/littlepine.aspx	Waterville	PA	17776	570-753-6000	
Locust Lake State Park c/o Tuscarora State Park 687 Tuscarora Park Rd *Web:* www.dcnr.state.pa.us/stateparks/parks/locustlake.aspx	Barnesville	PA	18214	570-467-2404	
Lyman Run State Park 454 Lyman Run Rd *Web:* www.dcnr.state.pa.us/stateparks/parks/lymanrun.aspx	Galeton	PA	16922	814-435-5010	
Marsh Creek State Park 675 Park Rd *Web:* www.dcnr.state.pa.us/stateparks/parks/marshcreek.aspx	Downingtown	PA	19335	610-458-5119	
Maurice K. Goddard State Park 684 Lake Wilhelm Rd *Web:* www.dcnr.state.pa.us/stateparks/parks/mauricekgoddard.aspx	Sandy Lake	PA	16145	724-253-4833	
McCalls Dam State Park c/o R.B. Winter State Park 17215 Buffalo Rd *Web:* www.dcnr.state.pa.us/stateparks/parks/mccallsdam.aspx	Mifflinburg	PA	17844	570-966-1455	
McConnells Mill State Park RR 2, Box 16 *Web:* www.dcnr.state.pa.us/stateparks/parks/mcconnellsmill.aspx	Portersville	PA	16051	724-368-8091	
Memorial Lake State Park RR 1, Box 7045 *Web:* www.dcnr.state.pa.us/stateparks/parks/memoriallake.aspx	Grantville	PA	17028	717-865-6470	
Milton State Park c/o Shikellamy State Park Bridge Ave *Web:* www.dcnr.state.pa.us/stateparks/parks/milton.aspx	Sunbury	PA	17801	570-988-5557	
Mont Alto State Park c/o Caledonia State Park 101 Pine Grove Rd *Web:* www.dcnr.state.pa.us/stateparks/parks/montalto.aspx	Fayetteville	PA	17222	717-352-2161	352-7026
Moraine State Park 225 Pleasant Valley Rd *Web:* www.dcnr.state.pa.us/stateparks/parks/moraine.aspx	Portersville	PA	16051	724-368-8811	
Mount Pisgah State Park RR 3, Box 362A *Web:* www.dcnr.state.pa.us/stateparks/parks/mtpisgah.aspx	Troy	PA	16947	570-297-2734	
Nescopeck State Park c/o Hickory Run State Park RR 1, Box 81 *Web:* www.dcnr.state.pa.us/stateparks/parks/nescopeck.aspx	White Haven	PA	18661	570-443-0400	
Neshaminy State Park 3401 State Rd. *Web:* www.dcnr.state.pa.us/stateparks/parks/neshaminy.aspx	Bensalem	PA	19020	215-639-4538	
Nockamixon State Park 1542 Mountain View Dr *Web:* www.dcnr.state.pa.us/stateparks/parks/nockamixon.aspx	Quakertown	PA	18951	215-529-7300	
Nolde Forest Environmental Education Center 2910 New Holland Rd *Web:* www.dcnr.state.pa.us/stateparks/parks/noldeforest.aspx	Reading	PA	19607	610-796-3699	
Norristown Farm Park 2500 Upper Farm Rd *Web:* www.dcnr.state.pa.us/stateparks/parks/norristownfarmpark.aspx	Norristown	PA	19403	610-270-0215	
Ohiopyle State Park PO Box 105 *Web:* www.dcnr.state.pa.us/stateparks/parks/ohiopyle.aspx	Ohiopyle	PA	15470	724-329-8591	
Oil Creek State Park 305 State Park Rd. *Web:* www.dcnr.state.pa.us/stateparks/parks/oilcreek.aspx	Oil City	PA	16301	814-676-5915	
Ole Bull State Park HCR 62, Box 9 *Web:* www.dcnr.state.pa.us/stateparks/parks/olebull.aspx	Cross Fork	PA	17729	814-435-5000	
Parker Dam State Park 28 Fairview Rd *Web:* www.dcnr.state.pa.us/stateparks/parks/parkerdam.aspx	Penfield	PA	15849	814-765-0630	
Patterson State Park c/o Lyman Run State Park 454 Lyman Run Rd *Web:* www.dcnr.state.pa.us/stateparks/parks/patterson.aspx	Galeton	PA	16922	814-435-5010	
Penn-Roosevelt State Park c/o Greenwood Furnace State Park RR 2, Box 118 *Web:* www.dcnr.state.pa.us/stateparks/parks/pennroosevelt.aspx	Huntingdon	PA	16652	814-667-1800	
Pine Grove Furnace State Park 1100 Pine Grove Rd *TF:* 888-727-2757 ■ *Web:* www.dcnr.state.pa.us/stateparks/parks/pinegrovefurnace.aspx	Gardners	PA	17324	717-486-7174	486-4961
Poe Paddy State Park c/o Reeds Gap State Park 1405 New Lancaster Valley Rd *Web:* www.dcnr.state.pa.us/stateparks/parks/poepaddy.aspx	Milroy	PA	17063	717-667-3622	
Poe Valley State Park c/o Reeds Gap State Park 1405 New Lancaster Valley Rd *Web:* www.dcnr.state.pa.us/stateparks/parks/poevalley.aspx	Milroy	PA	17063	814-349-2460	
Point State Park 101 Commonwealth Pl *Web:* www.dcnr.state.pa.us/stateparks/parks/point.aspx	Pittsburgh	PA	15222	412-471-0235	
Presque Isle State Park 301 Peninsula Dr Suite 1 *Web:* www.dcnr.state.pa.us/stateparks/parks/presqueisle.aspx	Erie	PA	16505	814-833-7424	833-0266
Prince Gallitzin State Park 966 Marina Rd *Web:* www.dcnr.state.pa.us/stateparks/parks/princegallitzin.aspx	Patton	PA	16668	814-674-1000	
Promised Land State Park RR 1, Box 96 *Web:* www.dcnr.state.pa.us/stateparks/parks/promisedland.aspx	Greentown	PA	18426	570-676-3428	
Prompton State Park c/o Lackawanna State Park RR 1, Box 230 *Web:* www.dcnr.state.pa.us/stateparks/parks/prompton.aspx	Dalton	PA	18414	570-945-3239	
Prouty Place State Park c/o Lyman Run State Park 454 Lyman Run Rd *Web:* www.dcnr.state.pa.us/stateparks/parks/proutyplace.aspx	Galeton	PA	16922	814-435-5010	
Pymatuning State Park 2660 Williamsfield Rd *Web:* www.dcnr.state.pa.us/stateparks/parks/pymatuning.aspx	Jamestown	PA	16134	724-932-3141	
R. B. Winter State Park 17215 Buffalo Rd *Web:* www.dcnr.state.pa.us/stateparks/parks/rbwinter.aspx	Mifflinburg	PA	17844	570-966-1455	
Raccoon Creek State Park 3000 State Rt 18 *Web:* www.dcnr.state.pa.us/stateparks/parks/raccooncreek.aspx	Hookstown	PA	15050	724-899-2200	
Ralph Stover State Park c/o Delaware Canal State Park 11 Lodi Hill Rd *Web:* www.dcnr.state.pa.us/stateparks/parks/ralphstover.aspx	Upper Black Eddy	PA	18972	610-982-5560	
Ravensburg State Park c/o R. B. Winter State Park 17215 Buffalo Rd *Web:* www.dcnr.state.pa.us/stateparks/parks/ravensburg.aspx	Mifflinburg	PA	17844	570-966-1455	
Reeds Gap State Park 1405 New Lancaster Valley Rd. *Web:* www.dcnr.state.pa.us/stateparks/parks/reedsgap.aspx	Milroy	PA	17063	717-667-3622	
Ricketts Glen State Park 695 State Rt 487 *Web:* www.dcnr.state.pa.us/stateparks/parks/rickettsglen.aspx	Benton	PA	17814	570-477-5675	
Ridley Creek State Park 1023 Sycamore Mills Rd. *Web:* www.dcnr.state.pa.us/stateparks/parks/ridleycreek.aspx	Media	PA	19063	610-892-3900	
Ryerson Station State Park 361 Bristoria Rd *Web:* www.dcnr.state.pa.us/stateparks/parks/ryersonstation.aspx	Wind Ridge	PA	15380	724-428-4254	
S. B. Elliott State Park c/o Parker Dam State Park 28 Fairview Rd *Web:* www.dcnr.state.pa.us/stateparks/parks/sbelliott.aspx	Penfield	PA	15849	814-765-0630	
Salt Springs State Park c/o Lackawanna State Park RR 1, Box 230 *Web:* www.dcnr.state.pa.us/stateparks/parks/saltsprings.aspx	Dalton	PA	18414	570-945-3239	
Samuel S. Lewis State Park c/o Gifford Pinchot State Park 2200 Rosstown Rd *Web:* www.dcnr.state.pa.us/stateparks/parks/samuelslewis.aspx	Lewisberry	PA	17339	717-432-5011	
Sand Bridge State Park c/o R. B. Winter State Park RR 2, Box 314 *Web:* www.dcnr.state.pa.us/stateparks/parks/sandbridge.aspx	Mifflinburg	PA	17844	570-966-1455	
Shawnee State Park 132 State Park Rd *Web:* www.dcnr.state.pa.us/stateparks/parks/shawnee.aspx	Schellsburg	PA	15559	814-733-4218	
Shikellamy State Park Bridge Ave *Web:* www.dcnr.state.pa.us/stateparks/parks/shikellamy.aspx	Sunbury	PA	17801	570-988-5557	
Sinnemahoning State Park 8288 First Fork Rd *Web:* www.dcnr.state.pa.us/stateparks/parks/sinnemahoning.aspx	Austin	PA	16720	814-647-8401	
Sizerville State Park 199 E Cowley Run Rd *Web:* www.dcnr.state.pa.us/stateparks/parks/sizerville.aspx	Emporium	PA	15834	814-486-5605	
Susquehanna State Park c/o Shikellamy State Park Bridge Ave *Web:* www.dcnr.state.pa.us/stateparks/parks/susquehanna.aspx	Sunbury	PA	17801	570-988-5557	
Susquehannock State Park 1880 Park Dr *Web:* www.dcnr.state.pa.us/stateparks/parks/susquehannock.aspx	Drumore	PA	17518	717-432-5011	
Swatara State Park c/o Memorial Lake State Park RR 1, Box 7045 *Web:* www.dcnr.state.pa.us/stateparks/parks/swatara.aspx	Grantville	PA	17028	717-865-6470	
Tobyhanna State Park PO Box 387 *Web:* www.dcnr.state.pa.us/stateparks/parks/tobyhanna.aspx	Tobyhanna	PA	18466	570-894-8336	
Trough Creek State Park RR 1, Box 211 *Web:* www.dcnr.state.pa.us/stateparks/parks/troughcreek.aspx	James Creek	PA	16657	814-658-3847	
Tuscarora State Park 687 Tuscarora Park Rd *Web:* www.dcnr.state.pa.us/stateparks/parks/tuscarora.aspx	Barnesville	PA	18214	570-467-2404	
Tyler State Park 101 Swamp Rd *Web:* www.dcnr.state.pa.us/stateparks/parks/tyler.aspx	Newtown	PA	18940	215-968-2021	
Upper Pine Bottom State Park c/o Little Pine State Park 4205 Little Pine Creek Rd *Web:* www.dcnr.state.pa.us/stateparks/parks/upperpinebottom.aspx	Waterville	PA	17776	570-753-6000	
Warriors Path State Park c/o Trough Creek State Park RR 1, Box 211 *Web:* www.dcnr.state.pa.us/stateparks/parks/warriorspath.aspx	James Creek	PA	16657	814-658-3847	
Whipple Dam State Park c/o Greenwood Furnace State Park RR 2, Box 118 *Web:* www.dcnr.state.pa.us/stateparks/parks/whippledam.aspx	Huntingdon	PA	16652	814-667-1800	
White Clay Creek Preserve PO Box 172 *Web:* www.dcnr.state.pa.us/stateparks/parks/whiteclaycreek.aspx	Landenberg	PA	19350	610-274-2900	
Worlds End State Park PO Box 62 *Web:* www.dcnr.state.pa.us/stateparks/parks/worldsend.aspx	Forksville	PA	18616	570-924-3287	
Yellow Creek State Park 170 Rt 259 Hwy *Web:* www.dcnr.state.pa.us/stateparks/parks/yellowcreek.aspx	Penn Run	PA	15765	724-357-7913	

Rhode Island

				Phone	Fax
Arcadia Management Area 1037 Hartford Pike *Web:* www.riparks.com/arcadia.htm	North Scituate	RI	02857	401-789-3094	
Beavertail State Park c/o Goddard Memorial State Park Beavertail Rd *Web:* www.riparks.com/beaverta1.htm	Jamestown	RI	02835	401-423-9941	885-7720
Blackstone River Bikeway c/o Lincoln Woods State Park 2 Manchester Print Works Rd *Web:* www.riparks.com/blacksto.htm	Lincoln	RI	02865	401-723-7892	

				Phone	Fax
Brenton Point State Park c/o Fort Adams State Park 84 Adams Dr *Web:* www.riparks.com/BRENTON.HTM	Newport	RI	02840	401-847-2400	841-9821
Burlingame State Park Santuary Rd *Web:* www.riparks.com/burlingastatepark.htm	Charlestown	RI	02813	401-322-8910	
Charlestown Breachway Charlestown Beach Rd *Web:* www.riparks.com/charlesbreach.htm	Charlestown	RI	02813	401-364-7000	322-3083
Colt State Park Hope St *Web:* www.riparks.com/colt.htm	Bristol	RI	02809	401-253-7482	253-6766
East Bay Bike Path c/o Colt State Park Hope St *Web:* www.riparks.com/eastbay.htm	Bristol	RI	02809	401-253-7482	
East Beach c/o Burlingame State Park 1 Burlingame State Park Rd *Web:* www.riparks.com/eastbeach.htm	Charlestown	RI	02813	401-322-0450	322-3083
East Matunuck State Beach 950 Succotash Rd *Web:* www.riparks.com/eastmatunuck.htm	South Kingstown	RI	02881	401-789-8585	
Fishermen's Memorial State Park 1011 Point Judith Rd *Web:* www.riparks.com/fisherma.htm	Narragansett	RI	02882	401-789-8374	
Fort Adams State Park 84 Adams Dr *Web:* www.riparks.com/fortadams.htm	Newport	RI	02840	401-847-2400	841-9821
Fort Wetherill State Park c/o Goddard Memorial State Park Ives Rd *Web:* www.riparks.com/fortweth.htm	Warwick	RI	02818	401-423-1771	
George Washington Management Area 2185 Putnam Pike	Gloucester	RI	02814	401-568-2013	
Goddard Memorial State Park 1095 Ives Rd *Web:* www.riparks.com/goddard.htm	Warwick	RI	02818	401-884-2010	885-7720
Haines Memorial State Park c/o Colt State Park Hope St *Web:* www.riparks.com/haines.htm	Bristol	RI	02809	401-433-3001	253-6766
Lincoln Woods State Park 2 Manchester Print Works Rd *Web:* www.riparks.com/lincoln.htm	Lincoln	RI	02865	401-723-7892	724-7951
Misquamicut State Beach c/o Burlingame State Park 1 Burlingame State Park Rd *Web:* www.riparks.com/misquamicut.htm	Charlestown	RI	02813	401-596-9097	
Roger W. Wheeler State Beach 100 Sand Hill Cove Rd *Web:* www.riparks.com/wheeler.htm	Narragansett	RI	02882	401-789-3563	
Salty Brine State Beach c/o Fishermen's Memorial State Park 1011 Point Judith Rd *Web:* www.riparks.com/saltybrine.htm	Narragansett	RI	02882	401-789-3563	
Scarborough State Beach c/o Fishermen's Memorial State Park 1011 Point Judith Rd *Web:* www.riparks.com/scarborough.htm	Narragansett	RI	02882	401-789-2324	
Snake Den State Park 2321 Hartford Ave *Web:* www.riparks.com/snakeden.htm	Johnston	RI	02919	401-222-2632	
World War II Memorial State Park c/o Lincoln Woods State Park 2 Manchester Print Works Rd *Web:* www.riparks.com/worldwar.htm	Lincoln	RI	02865	401-762-9717	

South Carolina

				Phone	Fax
Aiken State Natural Area 1145 State Park Rd *Web:* www.southcarolinaparks.com/park-finder/state-park/1831.aspx	Windsor	SC	29856	803-649-2857	
Andrew Jackson State Park 196 Andrew Jackson Park Rd *Web:* www.southcarolinaparks.com/park-finder/state-park/1797.aspx	Lancaster	SC	29720	803-285-3344	
Baker Creek State Park Rt 1 Box 50 *Web:* www.southcarolinaparks.com/park-finder/state-park/1764.aspx	McCormick	SC	29835	864-443-2457	
Barnwell State Park 223 State Park Rd *Web:* www.southcarolinaparks.com/park-finder/state-park/1773.aspx	Blackville	SC	29817	803-284-2212	
Caesars Head State Park 8155 Geer Hwy *Web:* www.southcarolinaparks.com/park-finder/state-park/1648.aspx	Cleveland	SC	29635	864-836-6115	836-3081
Calhoun Falls State Recreation Area 46 Maintenance Shop Rd *Web:* www.southcarolinaparks.com/park-finder/state-park/1652.aspx	Calhoun Falls	SC	29628	864-447-8267	447-8638
Charles Towne Landing State Historic Site 1500 Old Towne Rd *Web:* www.southcarolinaparks.com/park-finder/state-park/1575.aspx	Charleston	SC	29407	843-852-4200	852-4205
Cheraw State Park 100 State Park Rd *Web:* www.southcarolinaparks.com/park-finder/state-park/1554.aspx	Cheraw	SC	29520	843-537-9656	
Chester State Park 759 State Park Dr *Web:* www.southcarolinaparks.com/park-finder/state-park/1564.aspx	Chester	SC	29706	803-385-2680	
Colleton State Park 147 Wayside Ln *Web:* www.southcarolinaparks.com/park-finder/state-park/1876.aspx	Canadys	SC	29433	843-538-8206	
Colonial Dorchester State Historic Site 300 State Park Rd *Web:* www.southcarolinaparks.com/park-finder/state-park/725.aspx	Summerville	SC	29485	843-873-1740	
Croft State Natural Area 450 Croft State Park Rd *Web:* www.southcarolinaparks.com/park-finder/state-park/1443.aspx	Spartanburg	SC	29302	864-585-1283	
Devils Fork State Park 161 Holcombe Cir *Web:* www.southcarolinaparks.com/park-finder/state-park/1355.aspx	Salem	SC	29676	864-944-2639	944-8777
Dreher Island State Recreation Area 3677 State Park Rd *TF:* 866-345-7275 ■ *Web:* www.southcarolinaparks.com/park-finder/state-park/1371.aspx	Prosperity	SC	29127	803-364-4152	364-0756
Edisto Beach State Park 8377 State Cabin Rd *Web:* www.southcarolinaparks.com/park-finder/state-park/1298.aspx	Edisto Island	SC	29438	843-869-2756	869-4428
Givhans Ferry State Park 746 Givhans Ferry Rd *Web:* www.southcarolinaparks.com/park-finder/state-park/1219.aspx	Ridgeville	SC	29472	843-873-0692	
Goodale State Park 650 Park Rd *Web:* www.southcarolinaparks.com/park-finder/state-park/1199.aspx	Camden	SC	29020	803-432-2772	
Hamilton Branch State Recreation Area 111 Campground Rd *Web:* www.southcarolinaparks.com/park-finder/state-park/1188.aspx	Plum Branch	SC	29845	864-333-2223	
Hampton Plantation State Historic Site 1950 Rutledge Rd *Web:* www.southcarolinaparks.com/park-finder/state-park/1142.aspx	McClellanville	SC	29458	843-546-9361	527-4995
Hickory Knob State Resort Park Rt 4 Box 199-B *Web:* www.southcarolinaparks.com/park-finder/state-park/1109.aspx	McCormick	SC	29835	864-391-2450	391-5390
Hunting Island State Park 2555 Sea Island Pkwy *Web:* www.southcarolinaparks.com/park-finder/state-park/1019.aspx	Hunting Island	SC	29920	843-838-2011	838-4263
Huntington Beach State Park 16148 Ocean Hwy *Web:* www.southcarolinaparks.com/park-finder/state-park/1020.aspx	Murrells Inlet	SC	29576	843-237-4440	237-3387
Jones Gap State Park 303 Jones Gap Rd *Web:* www.southcarolinaparks.com/park-finder/state-park/962.aspx	Marietta	SC	29661	864-836-3647	
Keowee-Toxaway State Natural Area 108 Residence Dr *Web:* www.southcarolinaparks.com/park-finder/state-park/972.aspx	Sunset	SC	29685	864-868-2605	
Kings Mountain State Park 1277 Park Rd *Web:* www.southcarolinaparks.com/park-finder/state-park/945.aspx	Blacksburg	SC	29702	803-222-3209	222-6948
Lake Greenwood State Recreation Area 302 State Park Rd *Web:* www.southcarolinaparks.com/park-finder/state-park/926.aspx	Ninety Six	SC	29666	864-543-3535	
Lake Hartwell State Recreation Area 19138-A S Hwy 11 *Web:* www.southcarolinaparks.com/park-finder/state-park/927.aspx	Fair Play	SC	29643	864-972-3352	
Lake Warren State Park 1079 Lake Warren Rd *Web:* www.southcarolinaparks.com/park-finder/state-park/935.aspx	Hampton	SC	29924	803-943-5051	943-4736
Lake Wateree State Recreation Area 881 State Park Rd *Web:* www.southcarolinaparks.com/park-finder/state-park/936.aspx	Winnsboro	SC	29180	803-482-6401	482-6126
Landsford Canal State Park 2051 Park Dr *Web:* www.southcarolinaparks.com/park-finder/state-park/916.aspx	Catawba	SC	29704	803-789-5800	
Lee State Natural Area 487 Loop Rd *Web:* www.southcarolinaparks.com/park-finder/state-park/891.aspx	Bishopville	SC	29010	803-428-5307	
Little Pee Dee State Park 1298 State Park Rd *Web:* www.southcarolinaparks.com/park-finder/state-park/881.aspx	Dillon	SC	29536	843-774-8872	
Musgrove Mill State Historic Site 398 State Park Rd *Web:* www.southcarolinaparks.com/park-finder/state-park/3888.aspx	Clinton	SC	29325	864-938-0100	
Myrtle Beach State Park 4401 S Kings Hwy *Web:* www.southcarolinaparks.com/park-finder/state-park/795.aspx	Myrtle Beach	SC	29575	843-238-5325	
Oconee State Park 624 State Park Rd *Web:* www.southcarolinaparks.com/park-finder/state-park/750.aspx	Mountain Rest	SC	29664	864-638-5353	638-8776
Oconee Station State Historic Site 500 Oconee Station Rd *Web:* www.southcarolinaparks.com/park-finder/state-park/1887.aspx	Walhalla	SC	29691	864-638-0079	
Paris Mountain State Park 2401 State Park Rd *TF:* 866-345-7275 ■ *Web:* www.southcarolinaparks.com/park-finder/state-park/722.aspx	Greenville	SC	29609	864-244-5565	
Poinsett State Park 6660 Poinsett Park Rd *Web:* www.southcarolinaparks.com/park-finder/state-park/662.aspx	Wedgefield	SC	29168	803-494-8177	
Redcliffe Plantation State Historic Site 181 Redcliffe Rd *Web:* www.southcarolinaparks.com/park-finder/state-park/2015.aspx	Beech Island	SC	29842	803-827-1473	
Rivers Bridge State Historic Site 325 State Park Rd *Web:* www.southcarolinaparks.com/park-finder/state-park/566.aspx	Ehrhardt	SC	29801	803-267-3675	
Rose Hill Plantation State Historic Site 2677 Sardis Rd *Web:* www.southcarolinaparks.com/park-finder/state-park/540.aspx	Union	SC	29379	864-427-5966	
Sadlers Creek State Recreation Area 940 Sadlers Creek Rd *Web:* www.southcarolinaparks.com/park-finder/state-park/1888.aspx	Anderson	SC	29626	864-226-8950	
Santee State Park 251 State Park Rd *Web:* www.southcarolinaparks.com/park-finder/state-park/535.aspx	Santee	SC	29142	803-854-2408	854-4834
Sesquicentennial State Park 9564 Two Notch Rd *Web:* www.southcarolinaparks.com/park-finder/state-park/469.aspx	Columbia	SC	29223	803-788-2706	788-4414
Table Rock State Park 158 E Ellison Ln *Web:* www.southcarolinaparks.com/park-finder/state-park/350.aspx	Pickens	SC	29671	864-878-9813	878-9077
Woods Bay State Natural Area 11020 Woods Bay Rd *Web:* www.southcarolinaparks.com/park-finder/state-park/216.aspx	Olanta	SC	29114	843-659-4445	

South Dakota

				Phone	Fax
Adams Homestead & Nature Preserve 272 Westshore Dr *Web:* www.sdgfp.info/parks/regions/heartland/adamshomestead.htm	McCook Lake	SD	57049	605-232-0873	
Angostura Recreation Area 13157 N Angostura Rd *Web:* www.sdgfp.info/parks/regions/SouthernHills/Angostura.htm	Hot Springs	SD	57747	605-745-6996	
Bear Butte State Park Box 688 E Hwy 79 *Web:* www.sdgfp.info/parks/regions/northernhills/bearbutte.htm	Sturgis	SD	57785	605-347-5240	
Beaver Creek Nature Area c/o Palisades State Park 25495 485th Ave *Web:* www.sdgfp.info/Parks/Regions/Heartland/BeaverCreek.htm	Garretson	SD	57030	605-594-3824	
Big Sioux Recreation Area c/o Palisades State Park 25495 485th Ave *Web:* www.sdgfp.info/parks/regions/heartland/bigsioux.htm	Garretson	SD	57030	605-594-3824	
Big Stone Island Nature Area c/o Hartford Beach State Park RR 1 Box 50 *Web:* www.sdgfp.info/parks/regions/GlacialLakes/BigStone.htm	Corona	SD	57227	605-432-6374	
Burke Lake Recreation Area c/o Snake Creek Recreation Area 35316 SD Hwy 44 *Web:* www.sdgfp.info/Parks/Regions/Heartland/BurkeLake.htm	Platte	SD	57369	605-337-2587	
Buryanek Recreation Area c/o Snake Creek Recreation Area 35316 SD Hwy 44 *Web:* www.sdgfp.info/Parks/Regions/Heartland/Buryanek.htm	Platte	SD	57369	605-337-2587	
Chief White Crane Recreation Area c/o Lewis & Clark Recreation Area 43349 SD Hwy 52 *Web:* www.sdgfp.info/Parks/Regions/LewisClark/ChiefWhiteCrane.htm	Yankton	SD	57442	605-668-2985	
Cow Creek Recreation Area 20439 Marina Loop Rd *Web:* www.sdgfp.info/Parks/Regions/OaheSharpe/CowCreek.htm	Ft Pierre	SD	57532	605-223-7722	
Custer State Park 13329 US Hwy 16A *Web:* www.sdgfp.info/parks/Regions/Custer	Custer	SD	57730	605-255-4515	255-4460
Farm Island Recreation Area 1301 Farm Island Rd *Web:* www.sdgfp.info/Parks/Regions/OaheSharpe/FarmIsland.htm	Pierre	SD	57501	605-773-2885	
Fisher Grove State Park c/o Lake Louise Recreation Area 35250 191st St *Web:* www.sdgfp.info/Parks/Regions/GlacialLakes/fishergrove.htm	Miller	SD	57362	605-853-2533	
Fort Sisseton State Historical Park c/o Roy Lake State Park 11545 434th Ave *Web:* www.sdgfp.info/Parks/Regions/GlacialLakes/fortsisseton.htm	Lake City	SD	57247	605-448-5474	
George S. Mickelson Trail c/o Black Hills Trails Office HC 37 Box 604 *Web:* www.sdgfp.info/parks/regions/northernhills/mickelsontrail	Lead	SD	57754	605-584-3896	
Hartford Beach State Park RR 1, Box 50 *Web:* www.sdgfp.info/parks/regions/glaciallakes/hartfordbeach.htm	Corona	SD	57227	605-432-6374	
Indian Creek Recreation Area 12905 288th Ave *Web:* www.sdgfp.info/parks/regions/oahesharpe/indiancreek.htm	Mobridge	SD	57601	605-845-7112	
LaFramboise Island Nature Area c/o Farm Island Recreation Area 1301 Farm Island Rd *Web:* www.sdgfp.info/parks/regions/oahesharpe/laframboiseisland.htm	Pierre	SD	57501	605-773-2885	
Lake Alvin Recreation Area c/o Newton Hills State Park 28771 482nd Ave *Web:* www.sdgfp.info/parks/regions/heartland/lakealvin.htm	Canton	SD	57013	605-987-2263	
Lake Cochrane Recreation Area c/o Pelican Lake Recreation Area 400 W Kemp *Web:* www.sdgfp.info/parks/regions/glaciallakes/lakecochrane.htm	Watertown	SD	57201	605-882-5200	
Lake Herman State Park 23409 State Park Dr *Web:* www.sdgfp.info/parks/regions/heartland/lakeherman.htm	Madison	SD	57042	605-256-5003	
Lake Hiddenwood Recreation Area c/o West Whitlock Recreation Area 16157A W Whitlock Rd *Web:* www.sdgfp.info/parks/regions/oahesharpe/lakehiddenwood.htm	Gettysburg	SD	57442	605-765-9410	
Lake Louise Recreation Area 35250 191st St *Web:* www.sdgfp.info/parks/regions/glaciallakes/lakelouise.htm	Miller	SD	57362	605-853-2533	
Lake Poinsett Recreation Area 46109 202nd St *Web:* www.state.sd.us/gfp/sdparks/poinsett/poinsett.htm	Bruce	SD	57220	605-627-5441	
Lake Thompson Recreation Area 21176 Flood Club Rd *Web:* www.sdgfp.info/Parks/Regions/GlacialLakes/lakethompson.htm	Lake Preston	SD	57249	605-847-4893	
Lake Vermillion Recreation Area 26140 451st Ave *Web:* www.sdgfp.info/parks/regions/heartland/lakevermillion.htm	Canistota	SD	57012	605-296-3643	
Lewis & Clark Recreation Area 43349 SD Hwy 52 *Web:* www.sdgfp.info/Parks/Regions/LewisClark/LewisClark.htm	Yankton	SD	57078	605-668-2985	
Little Moreau Recreation Area c/o Shadehill Recreation Area 19150 Summerville Box 63 *Web:* www.sdgfp.info/Parks/Regions/OaheSharpe/LittleMoreau.htm	Shadehill	SD	57653	605-374-5114	
Llewellyn Johns Recreation Area c/o Shadehill Recreation Area 19150 Summerville Box 63 *Web:* www.sdgfp.info/Parks/Regions/northernhills/llewellynjohns.htm	Shadehill	SD	57653	605-374-5114	
Mina Lake Recreation Area c/o Richmond Lake Recreation Area 37908 Youth Camp Rd *Web:* www.sdgfp.info/parks/regions/glaciallakes/minalake.htm	Aberdeen	SD	57401	605-626-3488	
Newton Hills State Park 28767 482nd Ave *Web:* www.sdgfp.info/Parks/Regions/heartland/newtonhills.htm	Canton	SD	57013	605-987-2263	

South Dakota (Cont'd)

Name / Address	City	State	Zip	Phone	Fax
North Point Recreation Area 38180 297th St *Web:* www.sdgfp.info/Parks/Regions/LewisClark/NorthPoint.htm	Lake Andes	SD	57356	605-487-7046	
North Wheeler Recreation Area c/o North Point Recreation Area 38180 297th St *Web:* www.sdgfp.info/Parks/Regions/LewisClark/northwheeler.htm	Lake Andes	SD	57356	605-487-7046	
Oahe Downstream Recreation Area 20439 Marina Loop Rd *Web:* www.sdgfp.info/Parks/Regions/oahesharpe/oahedownstream.htm	Fort Pierre	SD	57532	605-223-7722	
Oakwood Lakes State Park 46109 202nd St *Web:* www.state.sd.us/gfp/sdparks/oakwood/oakwood.htm	Bruce	SD	57220	605-627-5441	
Okobojo Point Recreation Area c/o Oahe Downstream Rd 20439 Marina Loop Rd *Web:* www.sdgfp.info/Parks/Regions/oahesharpe/okobojopoint.htm	Fort Pierre	SD	57532	605-223-7722	
Palisades State Park 25495 485th Ave *TF:* 800-710-2267 ■ *Web:* www.sdgfp.info/parks/regions/heartland/palisades.htm	Garretson	SD	57030	605-594-3824	594-2369
Pease Creek Recreation Area c/o Snake Creek Recreation Area 35316 SD Hwy 44 *Web:* www.sdgfp.info/parks/regions/lewisclark/peasecreek.htm	Platte	SD	57369	605-337-2587	
Pelican Lake Recreation Area 400 W Kemp *Web:* www.sdgfp.info/Parks/Regions/GlacialLakes/PelicanLake.htm	Watertown	SD	57201	605-882-5200	
Pickerel Lake Recreation Area 12980 446th Ave *Web:* www.sdgfp.info/Parks/Regions/GlacialLakes/pickerellake.htm	Grenville	SD	57239	605-882-5200	
Pierson Ranch Recreation Area c/o Lewis & Clark Recreation Area 43349 SD Hwy 52 *Web:* www.sdgfp.info/Parks/Regions/LewisClark/PiersonRanch.htm	Yankton	SD	57442	605-668-2985	
Platte Creek Recreation Area c/o Snake Creek Recreation Area 35316 SD Hwy 44 *Web:* www.sdgfp.info/Parks/Regions/heartland/plattecreek.htm	Platte	SD	57369	605-337-2587	
Randall Creek Recreation Area 38180 297th St *Web:* www.sdgfp.info/parks/regions/lewisclark/randallcreek.htm	Lake Andes	SD	57356	605-487-7046	
Richmond Lake Recreation Area 37908 Youth Camp Rd *Web:* www.sdgfp.info/parks/regions/glaciallakes/richmondlake.htm	Aberdeen	SD	57401	605-626-3488	
Roy Lake State Park 11545 Northside Dr *Web:* www.sdgfp.info/parks/regions/glaciallakes/roylake.htm	Lake City	SD	57247	605-448-5701	
Sandy Shore Recreation Area c/o South Dakota Dept of Game Fish & Parks 400 W Kemp Ave *Web:* www.sdgfp.info/Parks/Regions/GlacialLakes/SandyShore.htm	Watertown	SD	57201	605-882-5200	
Shadehill Recreation Area 19150 Summerville Rd Box 63 *Web:* www.sdgfp.info/parks/Regions/northernhills/shadehill.htm	Shadehill	SD	57653	605-374-5114	
Sica Hollow State Park c/o Roy Lake State Park 11545 Northside Dr *Web:* www.sdgfp.info/parks/regions/glaciallakes/sicahollow.htm	Lake City	SD	57247	605-448-5701	
Snake Creek Recreation Area 35316 SD Hwy 44 *Web:* www.sdgfp.info/Parks/Regions/heartland/snakecreek.htm	Platte	SD	57369	605-337-2587	
Spirit Mound Historic Prairie c/o Newton Hills State Park 28771 482nd Ave *Web:* www.sdgfp.info/Parks/Regions/Heartland/SpiritMound.htm	Canton	SD	57013	605-987-2263	
Spring Creek Recreation Area c/o Oahe Downstream Recreation Area 20439 Marina Loop Rd *Web:* www.sdgfp.info/parks/Regions/oahesharpe/springcreek.htm	Fort Pierre	SD	57532	605-223-7722	
Springfield Recreation Area c/o Lewis & Clark Recreation Area 43349 SD Hwy 52 *Web:* www.sdgfp.info/parks/Regions/LewisClark/Springfield.htm	Yankton	SD	57078	605-668-2985	
Swan Creek Recreation Area c/o West Whitlock Recreation Area 16157A West Whitlock Rd *Web:* www.sdgfp.info/parks/Regions/oahesharpe/swancreek.htm	Gettysburg	SD	57442	605-765-9410	
Union Grove State Park c/o Newton Hills State Park 28771 482nd Ave *Web:* www.sdgfp.info/parks/Regions/heartland/uniongrove.htm	Canton	SD	57013	605-987-2263	
Walkers Point Recreation Area 23409 State Park Dr *Web:* www.sdgfp.info/parks/Regions/heartland/walkerspoint.htm	Madison	SD	57042	605-256-5003	
West Bend Recreation Area c/o Farm Island Recreation Area 1301 Farm Island Rd *Web:* www.sdgfp.info/parks/Regions/oahesharpe/westbend.htm	Pierre	SD	57501	605-773-2885	
West Pollock Recreation Area c/o Indian Creek Recreation Area 12905 288th Ave *Web:* www.sdgfp.info/parks/Regions/oahesharpe/westpollock.htm	Mobridge	SD	57601	605-845-7112	
West Whitlock Recreation Area 16157A West Whitlock Rd *Web:* www.sdgfp.info/parks/Regions/oahesharpe/westwhitlock.htm	Gettysburg	SD	57442	605-765-9410	

Tennessee

Name / Address	City	State	Zip	Phone	Fax
Bicentennial Capitol Mall State Park 600 James Robertson Pkwy *Web:* www.state.tn.us/environment/parks/bicenmal	Nashville	TN	37243	615-741-5280	
Big Cypress Tree State Park 295 Big Cypress Rd *Web:* state.tn.us/environment/parks/BigCypress	Greenfield	TN	38230	731-235-2700	
Big Hill Pond State Park 984 John Howell Rd *Web:* state.tn.us/environment/parks/BigHillPond	Pocahontas	TN	38061	731-645-7967	
Big Ridge State Park 1015 Big Ridge Rd *Web:* www.state.tn.us/environment/parks/bigridge	Maynardville	TN	37807	865-992-5523	
Bledsoe Creek State Park 400 Zeiglers Fort Rd *Web:* state.tn.us/environment/parks/bledsoecreek	Gallatin	TN	37066	615-452-3706	
Booker T. Washington State Park 5801 Champion Rd *Web:* www.state.tn.us/environment/parks/bookertwashington	Chattanooga	TN	37416	423-894-4955	855-7879
Burgess Falls State Natural Area 4000 Burgess Falls Dr *Web:* www.state.tn.us/environment/parks/burgessfalls	Sparta	TN	38583	931-432-5312	
Cedars of Lebanon State Park 328 Cedar Forest Rd *Web:* state.tn.us/environment/parks/cedars	Lebanon	TN	37087	615-443-2769	443-2793
Chickasaw State Park 20 Cabin Ln *Web:* www.state.tn.us/environment/parks/chickasaw	Henderson	TN	38340	731-989-5141	
Cordell Hull Birthplace State Park 1300 Cordell Hull Memorial Dr *Web:* www.state.tn.us/environment/parks/cordellhull	Byrdstown	TN	38549	931-864-3247	864-6389
Cove Lake State Park 110 Cove Lake Ln *Web:* www.state.tn.us/environment/parks/covelake	Caryville	TN	37714	423-566-9701	566-9717
Cumberland Mountain State Park 24 Office Dr *Web:* www.state.tn.us/environment/parks/CumberlandMtn	Crossville	TN	38555	931-484-6138	
David Crockett State Park PO Box 398 1400 W Gaines *Web:* state.tn.us/environment/parks/davidcrockettsp	Lawrenceburg	TN	38464	931-762-9408	766-0047
Davy Crockett Birthplace State Park 1245 Davy Crockett Park Rd *Web:* state.tn.us/environment/parks/davycrockettshp	Limestone	TN	37681	423-257-2167	257-2430
Dunbar Cave State Natural Area 401 Old Dunbar Cave Rd *Web:* www.state.tn.us/environment/parks/dunbarcave	Clarksville	TN	37043	931-648-5526	
Edgar Evins State Park 1630 Edgar Evins State Park Rd *Web:* www.state.tn.us/environment/parks/edgarevins	Silver Point	TN	38582	931-858-2446	
Fall Creek Falls State Resort Park 2009 Village Camp Rd Rt 3 Box 300 *Web:* www.state.tn.us/environment/parks/fallcreekfalls	Pikeville	TN	37367	423-881-5298	
Fort Loudoun State Historic Park 338 Fort Loudoun Rd *Web:* www.state.tn.us/environment/parks/fortloudoun	Vonore	TN	37885	423-884-6217	
Fort Pillow State Historic Park 3122 Park Rd *Web:* www.state.tn.us/environment/parks/fortpillow	Henning	TN	38041	731-738-5581	738-9117
Frozen Head State Natural Area 964 Flat Fork Rd *Web:* www.state.tn.us/environment/parks/frozenhead	Wartburg	TN	37887	423-346-3318	346-6629
Harpeth River State Park Hwy 70 *Web:* www.state.tn.us/environment/parks/harpethriver	Kingston Springs	TN	37887	615-797-6096	
Harrison Bay State Park 8411 Harrison Bay Rd *Web:* www.state.tn.us/environment/parks/harrisonbay	Harrison	TN	37341	423-344-6214	
Henry Horton State Resort Park 4358 Nashville Hwy *Web:* www.state.tn.us/environment/parks/henryhorton	Chapel Hill	TN	37034	931-364-2222	
Hiwassee/Ocoee Scenic River State Park PO Box 5 *Web:* state.tn.us/environment/parks/Hiwassee	Delano	TN	37325	615-263-4133	
Indian Mountain State Park 143 State Park Cir *Web:* www.state.tn.us/environment/parks/indianmountain	Jellico	TN	37762	423-784-7958	
Johnsonville State Historic Park Rt 1 Box 374 *Web:* www.state.tn.us/environment/parks/johnsonville	New Johnsonville	TN	37134	931-535-2789	535-3776
Justin P. Wilson Cumberland Trail State Park 220 Park Rd *Web:* www.state.tn.us/environment/parks/cumberlandtrail	Caryville	TN	38555	423-566-2229	566-2290
Long Hunter State Park 2910 Hobson Pike *Web:* www.state.tn.us/environment/parks/longhunter	Hermitage	TN	37076	615-855-2422	
Meeman-Shelby Forest State Park 910 Riddick Rd *TF:* 800-471-5293 ■ *Web:* www.state.tn.us/environment/parks/meemanshelby	Millington	TN	38053	901-876-5215	876-3217
Montgomery Bell State Resort Park 1020 Jackson Hill Rd *Web:* www.state.tn.us/environment/parks/montgomerybell	Burns	TN	37029	615-797-9052	
Mousetail Landing State Park Rt 3 Box 280B *Web:* www.state.tn.us/environment/parks/mousetaillanding	Linden	TN	37096	731-847-0841	
Natchez Trace State Park 24845 Natchez Trace Rd *Web:* www.state.tn.us/environment/parks/natcheztrace	Wildersville	TN	38388	731-968-3742	
Nathan Bedford Forrest State Park 1825 Pilot Knob Rd *Web:* www.state.tn.us/environment/parks/nbforrest	Eva	TN	38333	731-584-6356	584-1841
Norris Dam State Resort Park 125 Village Green Cir *Web:* www.state.tn.us/environment/parks/norrisdam	Lake City	TN	37769	865-426-7461	
Old Stone Fort State Archaeological Park 732 Stone Fort Dr *Web:* www.state.tn.us/environment/parks/oldstonefort	Manchester	TN	37355	931-723-5073	
Panther Creek State Park 2010 Panther Creek Park Rd *Web:* www.state.tn.us/environment/parks/panthercreek	Morristown	TN	37814	423-587-7046	587-7047
Paris Landing State Park 16055 Hwy 79N *Web:* www.state.tn.us/environment/parks/parislanding	Buchanan	TN	38222	731-641-4465	
Pickett State Park 4605 Pickett Park Hwy *Web:* www.state.tn.us/environment/parks/pickett	Jamestown	TN	38556	931-879-5821	
Pickwick Landing State Resort Park PO Box 15 *Web:* www.state.tn.us/environment/parks/pickwicklanding	Pickwick Dam	TN	38365	731-689-3129	
Pinson Mounds State Archaeological Park 460 Ozier Rd *Web:* www.state.tn.us/environment/parks/pinsonmounds	Pinson	TN	38366	731-988-5614	
Port Royal State Historic Park 3300 Old Clarksville Hwy *Web:* www.state.tn.us/environment/parks/portroyal	Adams	TN	37010	931-648-5526	
Radnor Lake State Park 1160 Otter Creek Rd *Web:* www.state.tn.us/environment/parks/RadnorLake	Nashville	TN	37220	615-373-3467	
Red Clay State Historic Park 1140 Red Clay Park Rd *Web:* www.state.tn.us/environment/parks/redclay	Cleveland	TN	37311	423-478-0339	
Reelfoot Lake State Park 3120 SR 213 *Web:* www.state.tn.us/environment/parks/reelfootlake	Tiptonville	TN	38079	731-253-7756	
Roan Mountain State Park 1015 Hwy 143 *Web:* www.state.tn.us/environment/parks/roanmtn	Roan Mountain	TN	37687	423-772-0190	
Rock Island State Park 82 Beach Rd *Web:* www.state.tn.us/environment/parks/rockisland	Rock Island	TN	38581	931-686-2471	
Sergeant Alvin C. York State Historic Park General Delivery Hwy 127 *Web:* www.state.tn.us/environment/parks/sgtyork	Pall Mall	TN	38577	931-879-9406	
South Cumberland Recreation Area Rt 1 Box 2196 *Web:* state.tn.us/environment/parks/southcumberland	Monteagle	TN	37356	931-692-3887	
Standing Stone State Park 1674 Standing Stone Park Hwy *Web:* www.state.tn.us/environment/parks/standstn	Hilham	TN	38568	931-823-6347	
Sycamore Shoals State Historic Park 1651 W Elk Ave *Web:* www.state.tn.us/environment/parks/sycamoreshoals	Elizabethton	TN	37643	423-543-5808	543-0078
T. O. Fuller State Park 1500 Mitchell Rd *Web:* www.state.tn.us/environment/parks/tofuller	Memphis	TN	38109	901-543-7581	785-8485
Tims Ford State Park 570 Tims Ford Dr *Web:* www.state.tn.us/environment/parks/timsford	Winchester	TN	37398	931-962-1183	
Warriors' Path State Park PO Box 5026 *Web:* www.state.tn.us/environment/parks/warriorspath	Kingsport	TN	37663	423-239-8531	239-4982

Texas

Name / Address	City	State	Zip	Phone	Fax
Abilene State Park 150 Park Rd 32 *Web:* www.tpwd.state.tx.us/spdest/findadest/parks/abilene	Tuscola	TX	79562	325-572-3204	572-3008
Acton State Historic Site c/o Cleburne State Park 5800 Park Rd 21 *Web:* www.tpwd.state.tx.us/spdest/findadest/parks/acton/	Cleburne	TX	76031	817-645-4215	
Admiral Nimitz State Historic Site 328 E Main St *Web:* www.thc.state.tx.us/museums/musnimitz.html	Fredericksburg	TX	78624	830-997-4379	
Atlanta State Park 927 Park Rd 42 *Web:* www.tpwd.state.tx.us/spdest/findadest/parks/atlanta	Atlanta	TX	75551	903-796-6476	
Balmorhea State Park PO Box 15 *Web:* www.tpwd.state.tx.us/spdest/findadest/parks/balmorhea	Toyahvale	TX	79786	432-375-2370	
Barton Warnock Environmental Education Center HC 70 Box 375 *Web:* www.tpwd.state.tx.us/spdest/findadest/parks/barton_warnock	Terlingua	TX	79852	432-424-3327	
Bastrop State Park PO Box 518 *Web:* www.tpwd.state.tx.us/spdest/findadest/parks/bastrop	Bastrop	TX	78602	512-321-2101	
Bentsen-Rio Grande Valley State Park 2800 S Bensen Palm Dr *Web:* www.worldbirdingcenter.org/sites/mission	Mission	TX	78572	956-585-1107	584-9126
Big Bend Ranch State Park PO Box 2319 *Web:* www.tpwd.state.tx.us/spdest/findadest/parks/big_bend_ranch/	Presidio	TX	79845	432-229-3416	
Big Spring State Park 1 Scenic Dr *Web:* www.tpwd.state.tx.us/spdest/findadest/parks/big_spring/	Big Spring	TX	79720	432-263-4931	
Blanco State Park PO Box 493 *Web:* www.tpwd.state.tx.us/spdest/findadest/parks/blanco/	Blanco	TX	78606	830-833-4333	
Bonham State Park 1363 State Park 24 *Web:* www.tpwd.state.tx.us/spdest/findadest/parks/bonham	Bonham	TX	75418	903-583-5022	
Brazos Bend State Park 21901 FM 762 *Web:* www.tpwd.state.tx.us/spdest/findadest/parks/brazos_bend/	Needville	TX	77461	409-553-5101	
Buescher State Park PO Box 75 *Web:* www.tpwd.state.tx.us/spdest/findadest/parks/buescher	Smithville	TX	78957	512-237-2241	
Caddo Lake State Park 245 Park Rd 2 *Web:* www.tpwd.state.tx.us/spdest/findadest/parks/caddo_lake/	Karnack	TX	75661	903-679-3351	
Caddoan Mounds State Historic Site 1649 S Hwy 21 W *Web:* www.tpwd.state.tx.us/spdest/findadest/parks/caddoan_mounds	Alto	TX	75925	936-858-3218	
Caprock Canyons State Park & Trailway PO Box 204 *Web:* www.tpwd.state.tx.us/spdest/findadest/parks/caprock_canyons/	Quitaque	TX	79255	806-455-1492	
Casa Navarro State Historic Site 228 S Laredo St *Web:* www.tpwd.state.tx.us/spdest/findadest/parks/casa_navarro/	San Antonio	TX	78207	210-226-4801	226-4801

Phone Fax

Cedar Hill State Park 1570 FM 1382 Cedar Hill TX 75104 972-291-3900
Web: www.tpwd.state.tx.us/spdest/findadest/parks/cedar_hill/

Choke Canyon State Park PO Box 2 Calliham TX 78007 361-786-3868
Web: www.tpwd.state.tx.us/spdest/findadest/parks/choke_canyon/

Cleburne State Park 5800 Park Rd 21 Cleburne TX 76031 817-645-4215
Web: www.tpwd.state.tx.us/spdest/findadest/parks/cleburne

Colorado Bend State Park Box 118 Bend TX 76824 325-628-3240
Web: www.tpwd.state.tx.us/spdest/findadest/parks/colorado_bend

Confederate Reunion Grounds State Historic Site
c/o Fort Parker State Park 194 Park Rd 28 Mexia TX 76667 254-562-5751
Web: www.tpwd.state.tx.us/spdest/findadest/parks/confederate_reunion_grounds

Cooper Lake State Park 1664 Farm Rd 1529 S Cooper TX 75432 903-395-3100
Web: www.tpwd.state.tx.us/spdest/findadest/parks/cooper_lake

Copper Breaks State Park 777 Park Rd 62 Quanah TX 79252 940-839-4331
Web: www.tpwd.state.tx.us/spdest/findadest/parks/copper_breaks

Daingerfield State Park 455 Park Rd 17 Daingerfield TX 75638 903-645-2921
Web: www.tpwd.state.tx.us/spdest/findadest/parks/daingerfield

Davis Mountains State Park PO Box 1458 Fort Davis TX 79734 432-426-3337
Web: www.tpwd.state.tx.us/spdest/findadest/parks/davis_mountains

Devils River State Natural Area HC 01 Box 513 Del Rio TX 78840 830-395-2133
Web: www.tpwd.state.tx.us/spdest/findadest/parks/devils_river

Devil's Sinkhole State Natural Area PO Box 678 Rocksprings TX 78880 830-683-3762
Web: www.tpwd.state.tx.us/spdest/findadest/parks/devils_sinkhole

Dinosaur Valley State Park PO Box 396 Glen Rose TX 76043 254-897-4588
Web: www.tpwd.state.tx.us/spdest/findadest/parks/dinosaur_valley

Eisenhower Birthplace State Historic Site 609 S Lamar Ave Denison TX 75021 903-465-8908
Web: www.tpwd.state.tx.us/spdest/findadest/parks/eisenhower_birthplace

Eisenhower State Park 50 Park Rd 20 Denison TX 75020 903-465-1956
Web: www.tpwd.state.tx.us/spdest/findadest/parks/eisenhower

Enchanted Rock State Natural Area
16710 Ranch Rd 965 Fredericksburg TX 78624 325-247-3903
Web: www.tpwd.state.tx.us/spdest/findadest/parks/enchanted_rock

Fairfield Lake State Park 123 State Park Rd 64 Fairfield TX 75840 214-389-4514
Web: www.tpwd.state.tx.us/spdest/findadest/parks/fairfield_lake

Falcon State Park PO Box 2 Falcon Heights TX 78545 956-848-5327
Web: www.tpwd.state.tx.us/spdest/findadest/parks/falcon

Fannin Battleground State Historic Site
c/o Goliad State Park 108 Park Rd 6 Goliad TX 77963 361-645-3405
Web: www.tpwd.state.tx.us/spdest/findadest/parks/fannin

Fanthorp Inn State Historic Site PO Box 296 Anderson TX 77830 936-873-2633
Web: www.tpwd.state.tx.us/spdest/findadest/parks/fanthorp_inn

Fort Griffin State Park & Historic Site 1701 N US Hwy 283 Albany TX 76430 325-762-3592
Web: www.tpwd.state.tx.us/spdest/findadest/parks/fort_griffin

Fort Lancaster State Historic Site PO Box 306 Sheffield TX 79781 432-836-4391
Web: www.tpwd.state.tx.us/spdest/findadest/parks/fort_lancaster

Fort Leaton State Historic Site PO Box 2319 Presidio TX 79845 432-229-3413
Web: www.tpwd.state.tx.us/spdest/findadest/parks/fort_leaton

Fort McKavett State Historic Site PO Box 68 Fort McKavett TX 76841 325-396-2358
Web: www.tpwd.state.tx.us/spdest/findadest/parks/fort_mckavett

Fort Parker State Park 194 Park Rd 28 Mexia TX 76667 254-562-5751
Web: www.tpwd.state.tx.us/spdest/findadest/parks/fort_parker

Fort Richardson State Park Historic Site & Lost Creek Reservoir State Trailway 228 State Park Rd 61 Jacksboro TX 76458 817-567-3506
Web: www.tpwd.state.tx.us/spdest/findadest/parks/fort_richardson

Franklin Mountains State Park 1331 McKelligon Canyon Rd El Paso TX 79930 915-566-6441
Web: www.tpwd.state.tx.us/spdest/findadest/parks/franklin

Fulton Mansion State Historic Site PO Box 1859 Fulton TX 78358 361-729-0386
Web: www.tpwd.state.tx.us/spdest/findadest/parks/fulton_mansion

Galveston Island State Park 14901 FM 3005 Galveston TX 77554 409-737-1222
Web: www.tpwd.state.tx.us/spdest/findadest/parks/galveston

Garner State Park HCR 70 Box 599 Concan TX 78838 830-232-6132
Web: www.tpwd.state.tx.us/spdest/findadest/parks/garner

Goliad State Park 108 Park Rd 6 Goliad TX 77963 361-645-3405
Web: www.tpwd.state.tx.us/spdest/findadest/parks/goliad_and_mission_espiritu_santo

Goose Island State Park 202 S Palmetto St Rockport TX 78382 361-729-2858
Web: www.tpwd.state.tx.us/spdest/findadest/parks/goose_island

Government Canyon State Natural Area 12861 Galm Rd San Antonio TX 78254 210-688-9055
Web: www.tpwd.state.tx.us/spdest/findadest/parks/government_canyon

Guadalupe River State Park 3350 Park Rd 31 Spring Branch TX 78070 830-438-2656
Web: www.tpwd.state.tx.us/spdest/findadest/parks/guadalupe_river

Hill Country State Natural Area 10600 Bandera Creek Rd Bandera TX 78003 830-796-4413
Web: www.tpwd.state.tx.us/spdest/findadest/parks/hill_country

Honey Creek State Natural Area
c/o Guadalupe River State Park 3350 Park Rd 31 Spring Branch TX 78070 210-438-2656
Web: www.tpwd.state.tx.us/spdest/findadest/parks/honey_creek

Hueco Tanks State Historic Site 6900 Hueco Tanks Rd No 1 El Paso TX 79938 915-857-1135 857-3628
Web: www.tpwd.state.tx.us/spdest/findadest/parks/hueco_tanks

Huntsville State Park PO Box 508 Huntsville TX 77342 936-295-5644
Web: www.tpwd.state.tx.us/spdest/findadest/parks/huntsville

Inks Lake State Park 3630 Park Rd 4 W Burnet TX 78611 512-793-2223
Web: www.tpwd.state.tx.us/spdest/findadest/parks/inks

Kickapoo Cavern State Park PO Box 705 Brackettville TX 78832 830-563-2342
Web: www.tpwd.state.tx.us/spdest/findadest/parks/kickapoo_cavern

Lake Arrowhead State Park 229 Park Rd 63 Wichita Falls TX 76310 940-528-2211
Web: www.tpwd.state.tx.us/spdest/findadest/parks/lake_arrowhead

Lake Bob Sandlin State Park 341 State Park Rd 2117 Pittsburg TX 75686 903-572-5531
Web: www.tpwd.state.tx.us/spdest/findadest/parks/lake_bob_sandlin

Lake Brownwood State Park 200 Highway Park Rd 15 Lake Brownwood TX 76801 325-784-5223
Web: www.tpwd.state.tx.us/spdest/findadest/parks/lake_brownwood

Lake Casa Blanca International State Park
5102 Bob Bullock Loop Laredo TX 78044 956-725-3826
Web: www.tpwd.state.tx.us/spdest/findadest/parks/lake_casa_blanca

Lake Colorado City State Park 4582 FM 2836 Colorado City TX 79512 325-728-3931
Web: www.tpwd.state.tx.us/spdest/findadest/parks/lake_colorado_city

Lake Corpus Christi State Park Box 1167 Mathis TX 78368 361-547-2635
Web: www.tpwd.state.tx.us/spdest/findadest/parks/lake_corpus_christi

Lake Livingston State Park 300 Park Rd 65 Livingston TX 77351 936-365-2201
Web: www.tpwd.state.tx.us/spdest/findadest/parks/lake_livingston

Lake Mineral Wells State Park & Trailway
100 Park Rd 71 Mineral Wells TX 76067 940-328-1171
Web: www.tpwd.state.tx.us/spdest/findadest/parks/lake_mineral_wells

Lake Somerville State Park 14222 Park Rd 57 Somerville TX 77879 979-535-7763
Web: www.tpwd.state.tx.us/spdest/findadest/parks/lake_somerville

Lake Tawakoni State Park
c/o Purtis Creek State Park 10822 FM 2475 Wills Point TX 75169 903-560-7123
Web: www.tpwd.state.tx.us/spdest/findadest/parks/lake_tawakoni

Lake Texana State Park 46 Park Rd 1 Edna TX 77957 361-782-5718
Web: www.tpwd.state.tx.us/spdest/findadest/parks/lake_texana

Lake Whitney State Park PO Box 1175 Whitney TX 76692 254-694-3793
Web: www.tpwd.state.tx.us/spdest/findadest/parks/lake_whitney

Landmark Inn State Historic Site 402 E Florence St Castroville TX 78009 830-931-2133
Web: www.tpwd.state.tx.us/spdest/findadest/parks/landmark_inn

Lipantitlan State Historic Site
c/o Lake Corpus Christi State Park PO Box 1167 Mathis TX 78368 361-547-2635
Web: www.tpwd.state.tx.us/spdest/findadest/parks/lipantitlan

Lockhart State Park 4179 State Park Rd Lockhart TX 78644 512-398-3479
Web: www.tpwd.state.tx.us/spdest/findadest/parks/lockhart

Phone Fax

Longhorn Cavern State Park PO Box 732 Burnet TX 78611 830-598-2283
Web: www.tpwd.state.tx.us/spdest/findadest/parks/longhorn_cavern

Lost Maples State Natural Area 37221 FM 187 Vanderpool TX 78885 830-966-3413
Web: www.tpwd.state.tx.us/spdest/findadest/parks/lost_maples

Lyndon B. Johnson State Park & Historic Site PO Box 238 Stonewall TX 78671 830-644-2252
Web: www.tpwd.state.tx.us/spdest/findadest/parks/lyndon_b_johnson

Magoffin Home State Historic Site 1120 Magoffin Ave El Paso TX 79901 915-533-5147
Web: www.tpwd.state.tx.us/spdest/findadest/parks/magoffin_home/

Martin Creek Lake State Park 9515 CR 2181D Tatum TX 75691 903-836-4336
Web: www.tpwd.state.tx.us/spdest/findadest/parks/martin_creek

Martin Dies Jr State Park RR 4 Box 274 Jasper TX 75951 409-384-5231
Web: www.tpwd.state.tx.us/spdest/findadest/parks/martin_dies_jr

Matagorda Island Wildlife Management Area 1700 7th St Bay City TX 77414 979-244-6824
Web: www.tpwd.state.tx.us/huntwild/hunt/wma/find_a_wma/list/?id=48

McKinney Falls State Park 5808 McKinney Falls Pkwy Austin TX 78744 512-243-1643 243-0536
Web: www.tpwd.state.tx.us/spdest/findadest/parks/mckinney_falls

Meridian State Park 173 Park Rd 7 Meridian TX 76665 254-435-2536
Web: www.tpwd.state.tx.us/spdest/findadest/parks/meridian

Mission Tejas State Park RR 2 Box 108 Grapeland TX 75844 936-687-2394
Web: www.tpwd.state.tx.us/spdest/findadest/parks/mission_tejas

Monahans Sandhills State Park PO Box 1738 Monahans TX 79756 432-943-2092
Web: www.tpwd.state.tx.us/spdest/findadest/parks/monahans_sandhills

Monument Hill & Kreische Brewery State Historic Sites
414 State Loop 92 La Grange TX 78945 979-968-5658
Web: www.tpwd.state.tx.us/spdest/findadest/parks/monument_hill_and_kreische_brewery

Mother Neff State Park 1680 Texas 236 Hwy Moody TX 76557 254-853-2389
Web: www.tpwd.state.tx.us/spdest/findadest/parks/mother_neff

Mustang Island State Park 17047 State Hwy 361 Port Aransas TX 78373 361-749-5246 749-6455
Web: www.tpwd.state.tx.us/spdest/findadest/parks/mustang_island

Palmetto State Park 78 Park Rd 11 S Gonzales TX 78629 830-672-3266
Web: www.tpwd.state.tx.us/spdest/findadest/parks/palmetto

Palo Duro Canyon State Park 11450 Park Rd 5 Canyon TX 79015 806-488-2227 488-2729
Web: www.tpwd.state.tx.us/spdest/findadest/parks/palo_duro

Pedernales Falls State Park 2585 Park Rd 6026 Johnson City TX 78636 830-868-7304
Web: www.tpwd.state.tx.us/spdest/findadest/parks/pedernales_falls

Port Isabel Lighthouse State Historic Site
421 E Queen Isabella Blvd Port Isabel TX 78578 956-943-2262
Web: www.tpwd.state.tx.us/spdest/findadest/parks/port_isabel_lighthouse

Possum Kingdom State Park PO Box 70 Caddo TX 76429 940-549-1803
Web: www.tpwd.state.tx.us/spdest/findadest/parks/possum_kingdom

Purtis Creek State Park 14225 FM 316 Eustace TX 75124 903-425-2332
Web: www.tpwd.state.tx.us/spdest/findadest/parks/purtis_creek

Ray Roberts Lake State Park 100 PW 4137 Pilot Point TX 76258 940-686-2148
Web: www.tpwd.state.tx.us/spdest/findadest/parks/ray_roberts_lake

Rusk/Palestine State Park RR 4 Box 431 Rusk TX 75785 903-683-5126
Web: www.tpwd.state.tx.us/spdest/findadest/parks/rusk_and_palestine

Sabine Pass Battleground State Park & Historic Site
c/o Sea Rim State Park PO Box 1066 Sabine Pass TX 77655 409-971-2559
Web: www.tpwd.state.tx.us/spdest/findadest/parks/sabine_pass_battleground

Sam Bell Maxey House State Historic Site 812 S Church St Paris TX 75460 903-785-5716
Web: www.tpwd.state.tx.us/spdest/findadest/parks/sam_bell_maxey_house

San Angelo State Park 3900 - 2 Mercedes San Angelo TX 76901 325-949-4757
Web: www.tpwd.state.tx.us/spdest/findadest/parks/san_angelo

San Jacinto Battleground State Historic Site
3527 Battleground Rd La Porte TX 77571 281-479-2431 479-5618
Web: www.tpwd.state.tx.us/spdest/findadest/parks/san_jacinto_battleground

Sea Rim State Park PO Box 356 Sabine Pass TX 77655 409-971-2559
Web: www.tpwd.state.tx.us/spdest/findadest/parks/sea_rim

Sebastopol State Historic Site PO Box 900 Seguin TX 78156 830-379-4833
Web: www.tpwd.state.tx.us/spdest/findadest/parks/sebastopol

Seminole Canyon State Park & Historic Site PO Box 820 Comstock TX 78837 432-292-4464
Web: www.tpwd.state.tx.us/spdest/findadest/parks/seminole_canyon

Sheldon Lake State Park & Environmental Learning Center
15315 Beaumont Hwy at Park Rd 138 Houston TX 77049 281-456-2800
Web: www.tpwd.state.tx.us/spdest/findadest/parks/sheldon_lake

South Llano River State Park HC 15 Box 224 Junction TX 76849 325-446-3994
Web: www.tpwd.state.tx.us/spdest/findadest/parks/south_llano_river

Starr Family State Historic Site 407 W Travis St Marshall TX 75670 903-935-3044
Web: www.tpwd.state.tx.us/spdest/findadest/parks/starr_family

Stephen F Austin State Park PO Box 125 San Felipe TX 77473 979-885-3613
Web: www.tpwd.state.tx.us/spdest/findadest/parks/stephen_f_austin_and_san_felipe

Texas State Railroad State Park PO Box 39 Rusk TX 75785 903-683-2561
Web: www.tpwd.state.tx.us/spdest/findadest/parks/texas_state_railroad

Tyler State Park 789 Park Rd 16 Tyler TX 75706 903-597-5338
Web: www.tpwd.state.tx.us/spdest/findadest/parks/tyler

Varner-Hogg Plantation State Historic Site PO Box 696 West Columbia TX 77486 979-345-4656
Web: www.tpwd.state.tx.us/spdest/findadest/parks/varner_hogg_plantation

Village Creek State Park PO Box 8565 Lumberton TX 77657 409-755-7322
Web: www.tpwd.state.tx.us/spdest/findadest/parks/village_creek

Washington-on-the-Brazos State Historic Site PO Box 305 Washington TX 77880 936-878-2214
Web: www.tpwd.state.tx.us/spdest/findadest/parks/washington_on_the_brazos

Utah

Phone Fax

Anasazi State Park Museum 460 N Hwy 12 Boulder UT 84716 435-335-7308
Web: www.stateparks.utah.gov/park/index.php?id=ANSP

Antelope Island State Park 4528 West 1700 South Syracuse UT 84075 801-652-2043
Web: www.stateparks.utah.gov/park/index.php?id=AISP

Bear Lake State Park PO Box 184 Garden City UT 84028 435-946-3343
Web: www.stateparks.utah.gov/park/index.php?id=BLSP

Camp Floyd/Stagecoach Inn State Park & Museum
18035 W 1540 North Fairfield UT 84013 801-768-8932
Web: www.stateparks.utah.gov/park/index.php?id=CFSP

Coral Pink Sand Dunes State Park PO Box 95 Kanab UT 84741 435-648-2800
Web: www.stateparks.utah.gov/park/index.php?id=CPSP

Dead Horse Point State Park PO Box 609 Moab UT 84532 435-259-2614
Web: www.stateparks.utah.gov/park/index.php?id=DHSP

Deer Creek State Park PO Box 257 Midway UT 84049 435-654-0171
Web: www.stateparks.utah.gov/park/index.php?id=DCSP

East Canyon State Park 5535 S Hwy 66 Morgan UT 84050 801-829-6866
Web: www.stateparks.utah.gov/park/index.php?id=ECSP

Edge of the Cedars State Park Museum 660 West 400 North Blanding UT 84511 435-678-2238
Web: www.stateparks.utah.gov/park_pages/edge.htm

Escalante State Park 710 N Reservoir Rd Escalante UT 84726 435-826-4466
Web: www.stateparks.utah.gov/park/about.php?id=ESSP

Fremont Indian State Park & Museum
11550 W Clear Creek Canyon Rd Sevier UT 84766 435-527-4631
Web: www.stateparks.utah.gov/park/index.php?id=FISP

Goblin Valley State Park PO Box 637 Green River UT 84525 435-564-3633 564-3223
Web: www.stateparks.utah.gov/park/index.php?id=GVSP

Goosenecks State Park
c/o Edge of Cedars State Park 660 West 400 North Blanding UT 84511 435-678-2238
Web: www.stateparks.utah.gov/park/index.php?id=GNSP

Great Salt Lake State Marina PO Box 16658 Salt Lake City UT 84116 801-250-1898
Web: www.stateparks.utah.gov/park/index.php?id=GSSP

Utah (Cont'd)

				Phone	Fax
Green River State Park PO Box 637 *Web:* www.stateparks.utah.gov/park/index.php?id=GRSP	Green River	UT	84525	435-564-3633	
Gunlock State Park 4405 W 3600 S *Web:* www.stateparks.utah.gov/park/index.php?id=GLSP	Hurricane	UT	84737	435-680-0715	
Historic Union Pacific Rail Trail State Park PO Box 754 *Web:* www.stateparks.utah.gov/park/index.php?id=RTSP	Park City	UT	84060	435-649-6839	
Huntington State Park PO Box 1343 *Web:* www.stateparks.utah.gov/park/index.php?id=HNSP	Huntington	UT	84528	435-687-2491	
Hyrum State Park 405 West 300 South *Web:* www.stateparks.utah.gov/park/index.php?id=HLSP	Hyrum	UT	84319	435-245-6866	
Iron Mission State Park 635 N Main St *Web:* www.stateparks.utah.gov/park/index.php?id=IMSP	Cedar City	UT	84720	435-586-9290	
Jordanelle State Park SR 319 515 Box 4 *Web:* www.stateparks.utah.gov/park/index.php?id=JDSP	Heber City	UT	84032	435-649-9540	
Kodachrome Basin State Park PO Box 238 *Web:* www.stateparks.utah.gov/park/index.php?id=KDSP	Cannonville	UT	84718	435-679-8562	
Millsite State Park c/o Huntington State Park PO Box 1343 *Web:* www.stateparks.utah.gov/park/index.php?id=MSSP	Huntington	UT	84528	435-687-2491	
Otter Creek State Park PO Box 43 *Web:* www.stateparks.utah.gov/park/index.php?id=OCSP	Antimony	UT	84712	435-624-3268	
Palisade State Park 2200 E Palisade Rd *Web:* www.stateparks.utah.gov/park/index.php?id=PSSP	Sterling	UT	84665	435-835-7275	
Piute State Park c/o Otter Creek State Park PO Box 43 *Web:* www.stateparks.utah.gov/park/index.php?id=PISP	Antimony	UT	84712	435-624-3268	
Quail Creek State Park PO Box 1943 *Web:* www.stateparks.utah.gov/park/about.php?id=QCSP	Saint George	UT	84771	435-879-2378	
Red Fleet State Park 8750 N Hwy 191 *Web:* www.stateparks.utah.gov/park/index.php?id=RFSP	Vernal	UT	84078	435-789-4432	
Rockport State Park 9040 N State Hwy 302 *Web:* www.stateparks.utah.gov/park/index.php?id=RPSP	Peoa	UT	84061	801-336-2241	
Sand Hollow State Park 4405 W 3600 S *Web:* www.stateparks.utah.gov/park/index.php?id=SHSP	Hurricane	UT	84737	435-680-0715	
Scofield State Park 1343 Huntington *Web:* www.stateparks.utah.gov/park/index.php?id=SFSP	Price	UT	84528	435-448-9449	
Snow Canyon State Park 1002 Snow Canyon Dr *Web:* www.stateparks.utah.gov/park/index.php?id=SNSP	Ivins	UT	84738	435-628-2255	
Starvation State Park PO Box 584 *Web:* www.stateparks.utah.gov/park/index.php?id=SVSP	Duchesne	UT	84021	435-738-2326	
Steinaker State Park 4335 N Hwy 191 *Web:* www.stateparks.utah.gov/park/index.php?id=STSP	Vernal	UT	84078	435-789-4432	
Territorial Statehouse State Park 50 W Capitol Ave *Web:* www.stateparks.utah.gov/park/index.php?id=TESP	Fillmore	UT	84631	435-743-5316	
Utah Field House of Natural History State Park 496 E Main St *Web:* www.stateparks.utah.gov/park/index.php?id=UFSP	Vernal	UT	84078	435-789-3799	
Utah Lake State Park 4400 W Center St *Web:* www.stateparks.utah.gov/park/index.php?id=ULSP	Provo	UT	84601	801-375-0731	373-4215
Wasatch Mountain State Park PO Box 10 *Web:* www.stateparks.utah.gov/park/index.php?id=WMSP	Midway	UT	84049	435-654-1791	
Willard Bay State Park 900 West 650 North #A *TF:* 800-322-3770 ■ *Web:* www.stateparks.utah.gov/park/index.php?id=WBSP	Willard	UT	84340	435-734-9494	734-2659
Yuba State Park PO Box 159 *Web:* www.stateparks.utah.gov/park/index.php?id=YLSP	Levan	UT	84639	435-758-2611	

Vermont

				Phone	Fax
Alburg Dunes State Park 151 Coon Point Rd *Web:* www.vtstateparks.com/htm/alburg.cfm	Alburg	VT	05440	802-796-4170	
Allis State Park 284 Allis State Park Rd *Web:* www.vtstateparks.com/htm/allis.cfm	Randolph	VT	05060	802-276-3175	
Ascutney State Park 1826 Black Mountain Rd *Web:* www.vtstateparks.com/htm/ascutney.cfm	Windsor	VT	05089	802-674-2060	
Big Deer State Park 1467 Boulder Beach Rd *Web:* www.vtstateparks.com/htm/bigdeer.cfm	Groton	VT	05046	802-584-3822	
Bomoseen State Park 22 Cedar Mountain Rd *Web:* www.vtstateparks.com/htm/bomoseen.cfm	Fair Haven	VT	05743	802-265-4242	
Boulder Beach State Park 2278 Boulder Beach Rd *Web:* www.vtstateparks.com/htm/boulder.cfm	Groton	VT	05046	802-584-3823	
Branbury State Park 3570 Lake Dunmore Rd Rt 53 *Web:* www.vtstateparks.com/htm/branbury.cfm	Brandon	VT	05733	802-247-5925	
Brighton State Park 102 State Park Rd *Web:* www.vtstateparks.com/htm/brighton.cfm	Island Pond	VT	05846	802-723-4360	
Burton Island State Park Box 123 *Web:* www.vtstateparks.com/htm/burton.cfm	Saint Albans Bay	VT	05481	802-524-6353	
Button Bay State Park 5 Button Bay State Park Rd *Web:* www.vtstateparks.com/htm/buttonbay.cfm	Vergennes	VT	05491	802-475-2377	
Camp Plymouth State Park 2008 Scout Camp Rd *Web:* www.vtstateparks.com/htm/plymouth.cfm	Ludlow	VT	05149	802-228-2025	
Coolidge State Park 855 Coolidge State Park Rd *Web:* www.vtstateparks.com/htm/coolidge.cfm	Plymouth	VT	05056	802-672-3612	
Crystal Lake State Park 96 Bellwater Ave *Web:* www.vtstateparks.com/htm/crystal.cfm	Barton	VT	05822	802-525-6205	
D.A.R. State Park 6750 VT Rt 17 W *Web:* www.vtstateparks.com/htm/dar.cfm	Addison	VT	05491	802-759-2354	
Elmore State Park 856 VT Rt 12 *Web:* www.vtstateparks.com/htm/elmore.cfm	Lake Elmore	VT	05657	802-888-2982	
Emerald Lake State Park 65 Emerald Lake Ln *Web:* www.vtstateparks.com/htm/emerald.cfm	East Dorset	VT	05253	802-362-1655	
Fort Dummer State Park 517 Old Guilford Rd *Web:* www.vtstateparks.com/htm/fortdummer.cfm	Brattleboro	VT	05301	802-254-2610	
Gifford Woods State Park 34 Gifford Woods *Web:* www.vtstateparks.com/htm/gifford.cfm	Killington	VT	05751	802-775-5354	
Grand Isle State Park 36 East Shore S *Web:* www.vtstateparks.com/htm/grandisle.cfm	Grand Isle	VT	05458	802-372-4300	
Green River Reservoir State Park 29 Sunset Drive Suite 1 *Web:* www.vtstateparks.com/htm/grriver.cfm	Morrisville	VT	05661	802-888-1349	
Half Moon Pond State Park 1621 Black Pond Rd *Web:* www.vtstateparks.com/htm/halfmoon.cfm	Fair Haven	VT	05743	802-273-2848	
Jamaica State Park 285 Salmon Hole Ln *Web:* www.vtstateparks.com/htm/jamaica.cfm	Jamaica	VT	05343	802-874-4600	
Kettle Pond State Park 4239 VT Rd 232 *Web:* www.vtstateparks.com/htm/kettlepond.cfm	Marshfield	VT	05658	802-426-3042	
Kill Kare State Park c/o Burton Island State Park Box 123 *Web:* www.vtstateparks.com/htm/killkare.cfm	Saint Albans Bay	VT	05481	802-524-6021	
Kingsland Bay State Park 787 Kingsland Bay State Park Rd *Web:* www.vtstateparks.com/htm/kingsland.cfm	Ferrisburgh	VT	05456	802-877-3445	
Knight Island State Park c/o Burton Island State Park Box 123 *Web:* www.vtstateparks.com/htm/knightisland.cfm	Saint Albans Bay	VT	05481	802-524-6353	
Knight Point State Park 44 Knight Point Rd *Web:* www.vtstateparks.com/htm/knightpoint.cfm	North Hero	VT	05474	802-372-8389	
Lake Carmi State Park 460 Marsh Farm Rd *Web:* www.vtstateparks.com/htm/carmi.cfm	Enosburg Falls	VT	05450	802-933-8383	
Lake Saint Catherine State Park 3034 VT Rt 30 S *Web:* www.vtstateparks.com/htm/catherine.cfm	Poultney	VT	05764	802-287-9158	
Lake Shaftsbury State Park 262 Shaftsbury State Park Rd *Web:* www.vtstateparks.com/htm/shaftsbury.cfm	Shaftsbury	VT	05262	802-375-9978	
Little River State Park 3444 Little River Rd *Web:* www.vtstateparks.com/htm/littleriver.cfm	Waterbury	VT	05676	802-244-7103	
Lowell Lake State Park 1756 Little Pond Rd *Web:* www.vtstateparks.com/htm/lowell.cfm	Londonderry	VT	05148	802-824-4035	
Maidstone State Park Rt 1 Box 388 *Web:* www.vtstateparks.com/htm/maidstone.cfm	Guildhall	VT	05905	802-676-3930	
Molly Stark State Park 705 Rt 9 E *Web:* www.vtstateparks.com/htm/mollystark.cfm	Wilmington	VT	05363	802-464-5460	
Mount Philo State Park 5425 Mt Philo Rd *Web:* www.vtstateparks.com/htm/philo.cfm	Charlotte	VT	05445	802-425-2390	
New Discovery State Park 4239 VT Rt 232 *Web:* www.vtstateparks.com/htm/newdiscovery.cfm	Marshfield	VT	05658	802-426-3042	
North Hero State Park 3803 Lakeview Dr *Web:* www.vtstateparks.com/htm/northhero.cfm	North Hero	VT	05474	802-372-8727	
Quechee State Park 764 Dewey Mills Rd *Web:* www.vtstateparks.com/htm/quechee.cfm	White River Junction	VT	05001	802-295-2990	
Ricker Pond State Park 18 Ricker Pond Camp Ground Rd *Web:* www.vtstateparks.com/htm/ricker.cfm	Groton	VT	05046	802-584-3821	
Sand Bar State Park 1215 US Rt 2 *Web:* www.vtstateparks.com/htm/sandbar.cfm	Milton	VT	05468	802-893-2825	
Seyon Lodge State Park 400 Seyon Park Rd *Web:* www.vtstateparks.com/htm/seyon.cfm	Groton	VT	05046	802-584-3829	
Silver Lake State Park 214 North Rd *Web:* www.vtstateparks.com/htm/silver.cfm	Bethel	VT	05032	802-234-9451	
Smugglers Notch State Park 6443 Mountain Rd *Web:* www.vtstateparks.com/htm/smugglers.cfm	Stowe	VT	05672	802-253-4014	
Stillwater State Park 445 Stillwater Rd *Web:* www.vtstateparks.com/htm/stillwater.cfm	Groton	VT	05046	802-584-3822	
Thetford Hill State Park 622 Academy Rd *Web:* www.vtstateparks.com/htm/thetford.cfm	Thetford	VT	05074	802-785-2266	
Townshend State Park 2755 State Forest Rd *Web:* www.vtstateparks.com/htm/townshend.cfm	Townshend	VT	05353	802-365-7500	
Underhill State Park PO Box 249 *Web:* www.vtstateparks.com/htm/underhill.cfm	Underhill Center	VT	05490	802-899-3022	
Waterbury Center State Park 177 Reservoir Rd *Web:* www.vtstateparks.com/htm/waterbury.cfm	Waterbury Center	VT	05677	802-244-1226	
Wilgus State Park Box 196 *Web:* www.vtstateparks.com/htm/wilgus.cfm	Ascutney	VT	05030	802-674-5422	
Woodford State Park 142 State Park Rd *Web:* www.vtstateparks.com/htm/woodford.cfm	Bennington	VT	05201	802-447-7169	
Woods Island State Park c/o Burton Island State Park Box 123 *Web:* www.vtstateparks.com/htm/woodsisland.cfm	Saint Albans Bay	VT	05481	802-524-6353	

Virginia

				Phone	Fax
Bear Creek Lake State Park 22 Bear Creek Lake Rd *Web:* www.dcr.state.va.us/parks/bearcreek.htm	Cumberland	VA	23040	804-492-4410	
Belle Isle State Park 1632 Belle Isle Rd *Web:* www.dcr.state.va.us/parks/bellisle.htm	Lancaster	VA	22503	804-462-5030	
Breaks Interstate Park PO Box 100 *Web:* www.parks.ky.gov/stateparks/bi	Breaks	VA	24607	800-982-5122	
Caledon Natural Area 11617 Caledon Rd *Web:* www.dcr.state.va.us/parks/caledon.htm	King George	VA	22485	540-663-3861	
Chippokes Plantation State Park 695 Chippokes Park Rd *Web:* www.dcr.state.va.us/parks/chippoke.htm	Surry	VA	23883	757-294-3625	
Claytor Lake State Park 6620 Ben H Boden Dr *Web:* www.dcr.state.va.us/parks/claytor.htm	Dublin	VA	24084	540-643-2500	
Clinch Mountain Wildlife Management Area 2387 Tumbling Creek Rd *Web:* www.dgif.state.va.us/hunting/wma/clinch_mountain.html	Saltville	VA	24370	276-783-3422	
Douthat State Park Rt 1 Box 212 *Web:* www.dcr.state.va.us/parks/douthat.htm	Millboro	VA	24460	540-862-8100	
Fairy Stone State Park 967 Fairystone Lake Dr *Web:* www.dcr.state.va.us/parks/fairyst.htm	Stuart	VA	24171	276-930-2424	
False Cape State Park 4001 Sandpiper Rd *TF:* 800-933-7275 ■ *Web:* www.dcr.state.va.us/parks/falscape.htm	Virginia Beach	VA	23456	757-426-7128	426-0055
First Landing State Park 2500 Shore Dr *Web:* www.dcr.state.va.us/parks/1stland.htm	Virginia Beach	VA	23451	757-412-2300	
George Washington's Grist Mill Historical State Park PO Box 110 *Web:* www.dcr.state.va.us/parks/georgewa.htm	Mount Vernon	VA	22121	703-780-2000	
Grayson Highlands State Park 829 Grayson Highland Ln *Web:* www.dcr.state.va.us/parks/graysonh.htm	Mouth of Wilson	VA	24363	276-579-7092	
Holliday Lake State Park Rt 2 Box 622 *Web:* www.dcr.state.va.us/parks/holliday.htm	Appomattox	VA	24522	434-248-6308	
Hungry Mother State Park 2854 Park Blvd *Web:* www.dcr.state.va.us/parks/hungrymo.htm	Marion	VA	24354	276-781-7400	
James River State Park Rt 1 Box 787 *Web:* www.dcr.state.va.us/parks/jamesriv.htm	Gladstone	VA	24553	434-933-4355	
Kiptopeke State Park 3540 Kiptopeke Dr *Web:* www.dcr.state.va.us/parks/kiptopek.htm	Cape Charles	VA	23310	757-331-2267	
Lake Anna State Park 6800 Lawyers Rd *Web:* www.dcr.state.va.us/parks/lakeanna.htm	Spotsylvania	VA	22553	540-854-5503	
Leesylvania State Park 2001 Daniel K Ludwig Dr *Web:* www.dcr.state.va.us/parks/leesylva.htm	Woodbridge	VA	22191	703-730-8205	
Mason Neck State Park 7301 High Point Rd *Web:* www.dcr.state.va.us/parks/masonnec.htm	Lorton	VA	22079	703-550-0960	
Natural Tunnel State Park Rt 3 Box 250 *Web:* www.dcr.state.va.us/parks/naturalt.htm	Duffield	VA	24244	276-940-2674	
New River Trail State Park 176 Orphanage Dr *Web:* www.dcr.state.va.us/parks/newriver.htm	Foster Falls	VA	24360	276-699-6778	
Occoneechee State Park 1192 Occoneechee Park Rd *Web:* www.dcr.state.va.us/parks/occoneec.htm	Clarksville	VA	23927	434-374-2210	
Pocahontas State Park 10301 State Park Rd *TF:* 800-933-7275 ■ *Web:* www.dcr.state.va.us/parks/pocahont.htm	Chesterfield	VA	23832	804-796-4255	796-4004
Raymond R. "Andy" Guest Jr. Shenandoah River State Park PO Box 235 Daughter of Stars Dr *Web:* www.dcr.state.va.us/parks/andygues.htm	Bentonville	VA	22610	540-622-6840	622-6841
Sailor's Creek Battlefield State Park 788 Twin Lakes Rd *Web:* www.dcr.state.va.us/parks/sailorcr.htm	Green Bay	VA	23942	434-392-3435	
Shot Tower Historical State Park Rt 1 Box 81X *Web:* www.dcr.state.va.us/parks/shottowr.htm	Austinville	VA	24312	276-699-6778	
Sky Meadows State Park 11012 Edmonds Ln *Web:* www.dcr.state.va.us/parks/skymeado.htm	Delaplane	VA	20144	540-592-3556	
Smith Mountain Lake State Park 1235 State Park Rd *Web:* www.dcr.state.va.us/parks/smithmtn.htm	Huddleston	VA	24104	540-297-6066	

	City	State	Zip	Phone	Fax
Southwest Virginia Museum Historical State Park 10 W 1st St *Web:* www.dcr.state.va.us/parks/swvamus.htm	Big Stone Gap	VA	24219	276-523-1322	
Staunton River Battlefield State Park 1035 Fort Hill Tr *Web:* www.dcr.state.va.us/parks/srbbsp.htm	Randolph	VA	23962	434-454-4312	
Staunton River State Park 1170 Staunton Tr *Web:* www.dcr.state.va.us/parks/staunton.htm	Scottsburg	VA	24589	434-572-4623	
Twin Lakes State Park 788 Twin Lakes Rd *Web:* www.dcr.state.va.us/parks/twinlake.htm	Green Bay	VA	23942	434-392-3435	
Westmoreland State Park 1650 State Park Rd *Web:* www.dcr.state.va.us/parks/westmore.htm	Montross	VA	22520	804-493-8821	
Wilderness Road State Park Rt 2 Box 115 *Web:* www.dcr.state.va.us/parks/wildroad.htm	Ewing	VA	24248	276-445-3065	
York River State Park 5526 Riverview Rd *Web:* www.dcr.state.va.us/parks/yorkrive.htm	Williamsburg	VA	23188	757-566-3036	

Washington

	City	State	Zip	Phone	Fax
Alta Lake State Park 40 Star Rt *Web:* www.parks.wa.gov/parkpage.asp?selectedpark=Alta%20Lake	Pateros	WA	98846	509-923-2473	
Anderson Lake State Park PO Box 42650 *Web:* www.parks.wa.gov/parkpage.asp?selectedpark=Anderson%20Lake	Olympia	WA	98504	360-385-1259	
Battle Ground Lake State Park 18002 NE 249th St *TF:* 888-226-7688 ■ *Web:* www.parks.wa.gov/parkpage.asp?selectedpark=Battle%20Ground%20Lake	Battle Ground	WA	98604	360-687-4621	
Bay View State Park 1093 Bayview Edison Rd *Web:* www.parks.wa.gov/parkpage.asp?selectedpark=Bay%20View	Mount Vernon	WA	98273	360-757-0227	757-1029
Beacon Rock State Park 34841 State Rd 14 *Web:* www.parks.wa.gov/parkpage.asp?selectedpark=Beacon%20Rock	Skamania	WA	98648	509-427-8265	427-3242
Belfair State Park 410 NE Beck Rd *Web:* www.parks.wa.gov/parkpage.asp?selectedpark=Belfair	Belfair	WA	98528	360-275-0668	275-8734
Birch Bay State Park 5105 Helwig Rd *Web:* www.parks.wa.gov/parkpage.asp?selectedpark=Birch%20Bay	Blaine	WA	98230	360-371-2800	371-0455
Blake Island State Park PO Box 277 *Web:* www.parks.wa.gov/parkpage.asp?selectedpark=Blake%20Island	Manchester	WA	98353	360-731-8330	
Bogachiel State Park 185983 Hwy 101 *Web:* www.parks.wa.gov/parkpage.asp?selectedpark=Bogachiel	Forks	WA	98331	360-374-6356	
Bridgeport State Park c/o Alta Lake State Park 40 Star Rt *Web:* www.parks.wa.gov/parkpage.asp?selectedpark=Bridgeport	Pateros	WA	98846	509-923-2473	
Bridle Trails State Park c/o Lake Sammamish State Park 20606 SE 56th St *Web:* www.parks.wa.gov/parkpage.asp?selectedpark=Bridle%20Trails	Issaquah	WA	98027	425-455-7010	
Brooks Memorial State Park 2465 Hwy 97 *Web:* www.parks.wa.gov/parkpage.asp?selectedpark=Brooks%20Memorial	Goldendale	WA	98620	509-773-4611	
Camano Island State Park 2269 S Lowell Point Rd *Web:* www.parks.wa.gov/parkpage.asp?selectedpark=Camano%20Island	Stanwood	WA	98292	360-387-3031	
Cape Disappointment State Park PO Box 488 *Web:* www.parks.wa.gov/parkpage.asp?selectedpark=Cape%20Disappointment	Ilwaco	WA	98624	360-642-3078	
Centennial Trail State Park c/o Riverside State Park 9711 W Charles Rd *Web:* www.parks.wa.gov/parkpage.asp?selectedpark=Centennial%20Trail	Nine Mile Falls	WA	99206	509-456-5065	
Columbia Hills State Park PO Box 426 *Web:* www.parks.wa.gov/parkpage.asp?selectedpark=Columbia%20Hills	Dallesport	WA	98617	509-767-1159	
Columbia Plateau Trail State Park 100 SW Main St *Web:* www.parks.wa.gov/parkpage.asp?selectedpark=Columbia+Plateau+Trail	Washtucna	WA	99371	509-235-4696	
Conconully State Park PO Box 95 *Web:* www.parks.wa.gov/parkpage.asp?selectedpark=Conconully	Conconully	WA	98819	509-826-7408	
Crawford State Park c/o Mount Spokane State Park N 26107 Mt Spokane Park Dr *Web:* www.parks.wa.gov/parkpage.asp?selectedpark=Crawford	Mead	WA	99021	509-446-4065	
Curlew Lake State Park 974 Curlew Lake State Park Rd *Web:* www.parks.wa.gov/parkpage.asp?selectedpark=Curlew%20Lake	Republic	WA	99166	509-775-3592	
Damon Point State Park c/o Ocean City State Park 148 State Rt 115 *Web:* www.parks.wa.gov/parkpage.asp?selectedpark=Damon%20Point	Hoquiam	WA	98550	360-289-3553	
Daroga State Park 1 S Daroga Park Rd *Web:* www.parks.wa.gov/parkpage.asp?selectedpark=Daroga	Orondo	WA	98843	509-664-6380	
Dash Point State Park 5700 SW Dash Point Rd *TF:* 888-226-7688 ■ *Web:* www.parks.wa.gov/parkpage.asp?selectedpark=Dash%20Point	Federal Way	WA	98023	253-661-4955	661-4995
Deception Pass State Park 41229 State Rt 20 *Web:* www.parks.wa.gov/parkpage.asp?selectedpark=Deception%20Pass	Oak Harbor	WA	98277	360-675-2417	675-8991
Dosewallips State Park PO Drawer K *Web:* www.parks.wa.gov/parkpage.asp?selectedpark=Dosewallips	Brinnon	WA	98320	360-796-4415	
Doug's Beach State Park c/o Maryhill State Park 50 Hwy 97 *Web:* www.parks.wa.gov/parkpage.asp?selectedpark=Doug%27s%20Beach	Goldendale	WA	98620	509-773-5007	
Fay Bainbridge State Park 15446 Sunrise Dr NE *Web:* www.parks.wa.gov/parkpage.asp?selectedpark=Fay%20Bainbridge	Bainbridge Island	WA	98110	206-842-3931	
Federation Forest State Park 49201 Enumclaw-Chinook Pass Rd *Web:* www.parks.wa.gov/parkpage.asp?selectedpark=Federation%20Forest	Enumclaw	WA	98022	360-663-2207	
Fields Spring State Park PO Box 37 *Web:* www.parks.wa.gov/parkpage.asp?selectedpark=Fields%20Spring	Anatone	WA	99401	509-256-3332	
Flaming Geyser State Park 23700 SE Flaming Geyser Rd *Web:* www.parks.wa.gov/parkpage.asp?selectedpark=Flaming%20Geyser	Auburn	WA	98092	253-931-3930	
Fort Casey State Park 1280 S Fort Casey Rd *Web:* www.parks.wa.gov/parkpage.asp?selectedpark=Fort%20Casey	Coupeville	WA	98239	360-678-4519	
Fort Columbia State Park PO Box 488 *Web:* www.parks.wa.gov/parkpage.asp?selectedpark=Fort%20Columbia	Chinook	WA	98614	360-642-3078	
Fort Ebey State Park 395 N Fort Ebey Rd *Web:* www.parks.wa.gov/parkpage.asp?selectedpark=Fort%20Ebey	Coupeville	WA	98239	360-678-4636	
Fort Flagler State Park 10541 Flagler Rd *Web:* www.parks.wa.gov/parkpage.asp?selectedpark=Fort%20Flagler	Nordland	WA	98358	360-385-1259	
Fort Okanogan State Park c/o Alta Lake State Park 40 Star Rt *Web:* www.parks.wa.gov/parkpage.asp?selectedpark=Fort%20Okanogan	Pateros	WA	98846	509-923-2473	
Fort Simcoe State Park 5150 Fort Simcoe Rd *Web:* www.parks.wa.gov/parkpage.asp?selectedpark=Fort%20Simcoe	White Swan	WA	98952	509-874-2372	
Fort Ward State Park c/o Fay Bainbridge State Park 15446 Sunrise Dr NE *Web:* www.parks.wa.gov/parkpage.asp?selectedpark=Fort%20Ward	Bainbridge Island	WA	98118	206-842-3931	
Fort Worden State Park 200 Battery Way *Web:* www.parks.wa.gov/parkpage.asp?selectedpark=Fort%20Worden	Port Townsend	WA	98368	360-385-4730	
Ginkgo Petrified Forest State Park PO Box 1203 *Web:* www.parks.wa.gov/alpha.asp	Vantage	WA	98950	509-856-2700	
Goldendale Observatory State Park 1602 Observatory Dr *Web:* www.parks.wa.gov/parkpage.asp?selectedpark=Goldendale%20Observatory	Goldendale	WA	98620	509-773-3141	
Grayland Beach State Park c/o Twin Harbors State Park Hwy 105 *Web:* www.parks.wa.gov/parkpage.asp?selectedpark=Grayland%20Beach	Westport	WA	98595	360-268-9717	
Griffiths-Priday Ocean State Park PO Box 42650 *Web:* www.parks.wa.gov/parkpage.asp?selectedpark=Griffiths%2DPriday	Olympia	WA	98504	360-902-8500	
Hope Island State Park c/o Jarrell Cove State Park E 391 Wingert Rd *Web:* www.parks.wa.gov/parkpage.asp?selectedpark=Hope+Island+%28Mason%29	Shelton	WA	98584	360-426-9226	
Ike Kinswa State Park 873 SR 122 *Web:* www.parks.wa.gov/parkpage.asp?selectedpark=Ike%20Kinswa	Silver Creek	WA	98585	360-983-3402	
Illahee State Park 3540 Bahia Vista *Web:* www.parks.wa.gov/parkpage.asp?selectedpark=Illahee	Bremerton	WA	98310	360-478-6460	
Iron Horse State Park c/o Ginkgo Petrified Forest State Park PO Box 1203 *Web:* www.parks.wa.gov/parkpage.asp?selectedpark=Iron%20Horse	Vantage	WA	98950	509-856-2700	
Jarrell Cove State Park E 391 Wingert Rd *Web:* www.parks.wa.gov/parkpage.asp?selectedpark=Jarrell%20Cove	Shelton	WA	98584	360-426-9226	
Joemma Beach State Park PO Box 898 *Web:* www.parks.wa.gov/parkpage.asp?selectedpark=Joemma%20Beach	Lakebay	WA	98349	253-884-1944	
Joseph Whidbey State Park PO Box 42650 *Web:* www.parks.wa.gov/parkpage.asp?selectedpark=Joseph%20Whidbey	Olympia	WA	89504	360-902-8500	
Kanaskat-Palmer State Park 32101 Kanaskat-Cumberland Rd *Web:* www.parks.wa.gov/parkpage.asp?selectedpark=Kanaskat%2DPalmer	Ravensdale	WA	98051	360-886-0148	
Kitsap Memorial State Park 202 NE Park St *Web:* www.parks.wa.gov/parkpage.asp?selectedpark=Kitsap%20Memorial	Poulsbo	WA	98370	360-779-3205	
Kopachuck State Park 11101 56th St NW *Web:* www.parks.wa.gov/parkpage.asp?selectedpark=Kopachuck	Gig Harbor	WA	98335	253-265-3606	
Lake Chelan State Park 7544 S Lakeshore Dr *Web:* www.parks.wa.gov/parkpage.asp?selectedpark=Lake%20Chelan	Chelan	WA	98816	509-687-3710	
Lake Easton State Park PO Box 26 *Web:* www.parks.wa.gov/parkpage.asp?selectedpark=Lake%20Easton	Easton	WA	98925	509-656-2230	
Lake Sammamish State Park 20606 SE 56th St *Web:* www.parks.wa.gov/parkpage.asp?selectedpark=Lake%20Sammamish	Issaquah	WA	98027	425-455-7010	
Lake Sylvia State Park PO Box 701 *Web:* www.parks.wa.gov/parkpage.asp?selectedpark=Lake%20Sylvia	Montesano	WA	98563	360-249-3621	
Lake Wenatchee State Park 21588 A Hwy 207 *Web:* www.parks.wa.gov/parkpage.asp?selectedpark=Lake%20Wenatchee	Leavenworth	WA	98826	509-763-3101	
Larrabee State Park 245 Chuckanut Dr *Web:* www.parks.wa.gov/parkpage.asp?selectedpark=Larrabee	Bellingham	WA	98226	360-676-2093	
Lewis & Clark State Park 4583 Jackson Hwy *Web:* www.parks.wa.gov/parkpage.asp?selectedpark=Lewis%20%26%20Clark	Winlock	WA	98596	360-864-2643	
Lewis & Clark Trail State Park 36149 Hwy 12 *Web:* www.parks.wa.gov/alpha.asp	Dayton	WA	99328	509-337-6457	
Lime Kiln Point State Park 1567 Westside Rd *Web:* www.parks.wa.gov/parkpage.asp?selectedpark=Lime%20Kiln%20Point	Friday Harbor	WA	98250	360-378-2044	
Lincoln Rock State Park 13253 State Rt 2 *Web:* www.parks.wa.gov/parkpage.asp?selectedpark=Lincoln%20Rock	East Wenatchee	WA	98802	509-884-8702	
Manchester State Park PO Box 338 *Web:* www.parks.wa.gov/parkpage.asp?selectedpark=Manchester	Manchester	WA	98353	360-871-4065	
Maryhill State Park 50 Hwy 97 *Web:* www.parks.wa.gov/parkpage.asp?selectedpark=Maryhill	Goldendale	WA	98620	509-773-5007	
Millersylvania State Park 12245 Tilley Rd S *Web:* www.parks.wa.gov/parkpage.asp?selectedpark=Millersylvania	Olympia	WA	98512	360-753-1519	664-2180
Moran State Park 3572 Olga Rd *Web:* www.parks.wa.gov/parkpage.asp?selectedpark=Moran	Eastsound	WA	98245	360-376-2326	
Mount Pilchuck State Park c/o Wenburg State Park 15430 E Lake Goodwin Rd *Web:* www.parks.wa.gov/mtpilchuck.asp	Stanwood	WA	98292	360-652-7417	
Mount Spokane State Park N 26107 Mt Spokane Park Dr *Web:* www.parks.wa.gov/parkpage.asp?selectedpark=Mount%20Spokane	Mead	WA	90021	509-238-4258	238-4078
Mystery Bay State Park PO Box 42650 *Web:* www.parks.wa.gov/parkpage.asp?selectedpark=Mystery%20Bay	Olympia	WA	98504	360-902-8500	
Nolte State Park 36921 Veazie Cumberland Rd *Web:* www.parks.wa.gov/parkpage.asp?selectedpark=Nolte	Enumclaw	WA	98022	360-825-4646	
Ocean City State Park 148 State Rt 115 *Web:* www.parks.wa.gov/parkpage.asp?selectedpark=Ocean%20City	Hoquiam	WA	98550	360-289-3553	
Olallie State Park c/o Lake Sammamish State Park 20606 SE 56th St *Web:* www.parks.wa.gov/parkpage.asp?selectedpark=Olallie	Issaquah	WA	98027	360-455-7010	
Old Fort Townsend State Park 1370 Old Fort Townsend Rd *Web:* www.parks.wa.gov/parkpage.asp?selectedpark=Old%20Fort%20Townsend	Port Townsend	WA	98368	360-385-3595	
Olmstead Place State Park 921 N Ferguson Rd *Web:* www.parks.wa.gov/parkpage.asp?selectedpark=Olmstead%20Place	Ellensburg	WA	98926	509-925-1943	
Osoyoos Lake State Park 2207 Juniper *Web:* www.parks.wa.gov/parkpage.asp?selectedpark=Osoyoos%20Lake	Oroville	WA	98844	509-476-3321	
Pacific Beach State Park c/o Ocean City State Park 148 State Rt 115 *Web:* www.parks.wa.gov/parkpage.asp?selectedpark=Pacific%20Beach	Hoquiam	WA	98550	360-289-3553	
Pacific Pines State Park c/o Fort Canby State Park PO Box 488 *Web:* www.parks.wa.gov/parkpage.asp?selectedpark=Pacific%20Pines	Ilwaco	WA	98624	360-642-3078	
Palouse Falls State Park 10152 SR 127 *Web:* www.parks.wa.gov/parkpage.asp?selectedpark=Palouse%20Falls	Pomeroy	WA	99347	509-549-3551	
Paradise Point State Park Rt 1 Box 33914 *Web:* www.parks.wa.gov/parkpage.asp?selectedpark=Paradise%20Point	Ridgefield	WA	98642	360-263-2350	
Peace Arch State Park PO Box 87 *Web:* www.parks.wa.gov/parkpage.asp?selectedpark=Peace%20Arch	Blaine	WA	98230	360-332-8221	
Pearrygin Lake State Park 861 Bear Creek Rd *Web:* www.parks.wa.gov/parkpage.asp?selectedpark=Pearrygin%20Lake	Winthrop	WA	98862	509-996-2370	
Penrose Point State Park 321 158th KPS *Web:* www.parks.wa.gov/parkpage.asp?selectedpark=Penrose%20Point	Lakebay	WA	98349	253-884-2514	
Peshastin Pinnacles State Park c/o Wenatchee Confluence State Park 333 Olds Station Rd *Web:* www.parks.wa.gov/parkpage.asp?selectedpark=Peshastin%20Pinnacles	Wenatchee	WA	98801	509-664-6373	
Potholes State Park 6762 Hwy 262 E *Web:* www.parks.wa.gov/parkpage.asp?selectedpark=Potholes	Othello	WA	99344	509-346-2759	
Potlatch State Park PO Box 1051 *Web:* www.parks.wa.gov/parkpage.asp?selectedpark=Potlatch	Hoodsport	WA	98548	360-877-5361	
Rainbow Falls State Park 4008 State Hwy 6 *Web:* www.parks.wa.gov/parkpage.asp?selectedpark=Rainbow%20Falls	Chehalis	WA	98532	360-291-3767	291-3377
Rasar State Park 38730 Cape Horn Rd *Web:* www.parks.wa.gov/parkpage.asp?selectedpark=Rasar	Concrete	WA	98237	360-826-3942	
Riverside State Park 9711 W Charles Rd *Web:* www.parks.wa.gov/parkpage.asp?selectedpark=Riverside	Nine Mile Falls	WA	99206	509-456-5064	
Rockport State Park 51905 State Rt 20 *Web:* www.parks.wa.gov/parkpage.asp?selectedpark=Rockport	Rockport	WA	98283	360-853-8461	
Sacajawea State Park 2503 Sacajawea Park Rd *Web:* www.parks.wa.gov/parkpage.asp?selectedpark=Sacajawea	Pasco	WA	99301	509-545-2361	
Saint Edward State Park 14445 Juanita Dr NE *Web:* www.parks.wa.gov/parkpage.asp?selectedpark=Saint%20Edward	Kenmore	WA	98028	425-823-2992	
Saltwater State Park 25205 8th Pl S *Web:* www.parks.wa.gov/parkpage.asp?selectedpark=Saltwater	Des Moines	WA	98198	253-661-4956	
Scenic Beach State Park PO Box 7 *Web:* www.parks.wa.gov/parkpage.asp?selectedpark=Scenic%20Beach	Seabeck	WA	98380	360-830-5079	
Schafer State Park W 1365 Schafer Park Rd *Web:* www.parks.wa.gov/parkpage.asp?selectedpark=Schafer	Elma	WA	98541	360-482-3852	
Seaquest State Park Box 3030 Spirit Lake Hwy *Web:* www.parks.wa.gov/parkpage.asp?selectedpark=Seaquest	Castle Rock	WA	98611	360-274-8633	
Sequim Bay State Park 269035 Hwy 101 *Web:* www.parks.wa.gov/parkpage.asp?selectedpark=Sequim%20Bay	Sequim	WA	98382	360-683-4235	
Shine Tidelands State Park 202 NE Park St *Web:* www.parks.wa.gov/parkpage.asp?selectedpark=Shine%20Tidelands	Poulsbo	WA	98370	360-779-3205	
South Whidbey Island State Park 4128 S Smugglers Cove Rd *Web:* www.parks.wa.gov/parkpage.asp?selectedpark=South%20Whidbey	Freeland	WA	98249	360-331-4559	

Washington (Cont'd)

Phone | Fax

Spencer Spit State Park 521-A Bakerview Rd — Lopez Island WA 98261 360-468-3176
Web: www.parks.wa.gov/parkpage.asp?selectedpark=Spencer%20Spit
Squilchuck State Park
c/o Wenatchee Confluence State Park 333 Olds Station Rd — Wenatchee WA 98801 509-664-6373
Web: www.parks.wa.gov/parkpage.asp?selectedpark=Squilchuck
Steamboat Rock State Park PO Box 370 — Electric City WA 99123 509-633-1304
Web: www.parks.wa.gov/parkpage.asp?selectedpark=Steamboat%20Rock
Steptoe Battlefield State Park
c/o Central Ferry State Park 10152 State Hwy 127 — Pomeroy WA 99347 509-549-3551
Web: www.parks.wa.gov/parkpage.asp?selectedpark=Steptoe+Battlefield
Steptoe Butte State Park
c/o Central Ferry State Park 10152 State Hwy 127 — Pomeroy WA 99347 509-549-3551
Web: www.parks.wa.gov/parkpage.asp?selectedpark=Steptoe%20Butte
Sun Lakes State Park 34875 Park Lane Rd NE — Coulee City WA 99115 509-632-5583
Web: www.parks.wa.gov/parkpage.asp?selectedpark=Sun%20Lakes
Tolmie State Park 7730 61st Ave NE — Olympia WA 98506 360-456-6464 459-0104
Web: www.parks.wa.gov/parkpage.asp?selectedpark=Tolmie
Triton Cove State Park
c/o Dosewallips State Park PO Drawer K — Brinnon WA 98320 360-796-4415
Web: www.parks.wa.gov/parkpage.asp?selectedpark=Triton%20Cove
Twanoh State Park 12190 E Hwy 106 — Union WA 98592 360-275-2222
Web: www.parks.wa.gov/parkpage.asp?selectedpark=Twanoh
Twenty-Five Mile Creek State Park 20530 S Lakeshore Rd — Chelan WA 98816 509-687-3710 687-0350
Web: www.parks.wa.gov/parkpage.asp?selectedpark=Twenty%2DFive%20Mile%20Creek
Twin Harbors Beach State Park Hwy 105 — Westport WA 98595 360-268-9717
Web: www.parks.wa.gov/parkpage.asp?selectedpark=Twin%20Harbors
Wallace Falls State Park PO Box 106 — Gold Bar WA 98251 360-793-0420
Web: www.parks.wa.gov/parkpage.asp?selectedpark=Wallace%20Falls
Wenatchee Confluence State Park 333 Olds Station Rd — Wenatchee WA 98801 509-664-6373
Web: www.parks.wa.gov/parkpage.asp?selectedpark=Wenatchee%20Confluence
Wenberg State Park 15430 E Lake Goodwin Rd — Stanwood WA 98292 360-652-7417
Web: www.parks.wa.gov/parkpage.asp?selectedpark=Wenberg
Westport Light State Park PO Box 42650 — Olympia WA 98504 360-268-9717
Web: www.parks.wa.gov/parkpage.asp?selectedpark=Westport%20Light
Yakima Sportsman State Park 904 Keys Rd — Yakima WA 98901 509-575-2774
Web: www.parks.wa.gov/parkpage.asp?selectedpark=Yakima%20Sportsman

West Virginia

Phone | Fax

Audra State Park Rt 4 Box 564 — Buckhannon WV 26201 304-457-1162
Web: www.audrastatepark.com
Babcock State Park HC 35 Box 150 — Clifftop WV 25831 304-438-3004
Web: www.babcocksp.com
Beartown State Park HC 64 Box 189 — Hillsboro WV 24946 304-653-4254
Web: www.beartownstatepark.com
Beech Fork State Park 5601 Long Branch Rd — Barboursville WV 25504 304-528-5794
Web: www.beechforksp.com
Berkeley Springs State Park 121 S Washington St — Berkeley Springs WV 25411 304-258-2711
Web: www.berkeleyspringssp.com
Blackwater Falls State Park PO Drawer 490 — Davis WV 26260 304-259-5216
Web: www.blackwaterfalls.com
Blennerhassett Island Historical State Park 137 Juliana St — Parkersburg WV 26101 304-420-4800
Web: www.blennerhassettislandstatepark.com
Bluestone State Park HC 78 Box 3 — Hinton WV 25951 304-466-2805
Web: www.bluestonesp.com
Cabwaylingo State Forest Rt 1 Box 85 — Dunlow WV 25511 304-385-4255
Web: www.cabwaylingo.com
Cacapon Resort State Park Rt 1 Box 230 — Berkeley Springs WV 25411 304-258-1022
Web: www.cacaponresort.com
Calvin Price State Forest
c/o Watoga State Park HC 82 Box 252 — Marlinton WV 24954 304-799-4087
Web: www.wvforestry.com/calvinpricestateforest.cfm
Camp Creek State Forest
c/o Camp Creek State Park PO Box 119 — Camp Creek WV 25820 304-425-9481
Web: www.wvforestry.com/campcreekstateforest.cfm
Camp Creek State Park PO Box 119 — Camp Creek WV 25820 304-425-9481
Web: www.campcreekstatepark.com
Canaan Valley Resort State Park HC 70 Box 330 — Davis WV 26260 304-866-4121
Web: www.canaanresort.com
Carnifex Ferry Battlefield State Park Rt 2 Box 435 — Summersville WV 26651 304-872-0825
Web: www.carnifexferrybattlefieldstatepark.com
Cass Scenic Railroad State Park PO Box 107 — Cass WV 24927 304-456-4300
Web: www.cassrailroad.com
Cathedral State Park Rt 1 Box 370 — Aurora WV 26705 304-735-3771
Web: www.cathedralstatepark.com
Cedar Creek State Park 2947 Cedar Creek Rd — Glenville WV 26351 304-462-7158
Web: www.cedarcreeksp.com
Chief Logan State Park General Delivery — Logan WV 25601 304-792-7125
Web: www.chieflоganstatepark.com
Coopers Rock State Forest Rt 1 Box 270 — Bruceton Mills WV 26525 304-594-1561 594-9024
Web: www.coopersrockstateforest.com
Droop Mountain Battlefield State Park HC 64 Box 189 — Hillsboro WV 24946 304-653-4254
Web: www.droopmountainbattlefield.com
Greenbrier River Trail c/o Watoga State Park HC 82 Box 252 — Marlinton WV 24954 304-799-4087
Web: www.greenbrierrivertrail.com
Greenbrier State Forest HC 30 Box 154 — Caldwell WV 24925 304-536-1944
Web: www.greenbriersf.com
Hawks Nest State Park PO Box 857 — Ansted WV 25812 304-658-5212 658-4549
TF: 800-225-5982 ■ *Web:* www.hawksnestsp.com
Holly River State Park PO Box 70 — Hacker Valley WV 26222 304-493-6353
Web: www.hollyriver.com
Kanawha State Forest Rt 2 Box 285 — Charleston WV 25314 304-558-3500 558-3508
Web: www.kanawhastateforest.com
Kumbrabow State Forest PO Box 65 — Huttonsville WV 26273 304-335-2219
Web: www.kumbrabow.com
Little Beaver State Park 1402 Grandview Rd — Beaver WV 25813 304-763-2494
Web: www.littlebeaverstatepark.com
Lost River State Park 321 Park Dr — Mathias WV 26812 304-897-5372
Web: www.lostriversp.com
Moncove Lake State Park Rt 4 Box 73-A — Gap Mills WV 24941 304-772-3450
Web: www.moncovelakestatepark.com
North Bend Rail Trail c/o North Bend State Park Rt 1 Box 221 — Cairo WV 26337 304-643-2931
Web: www.wvparks.com/northbendrailtrail
North Bend State Park Rt 1 Box 221 — Cairo WV 26337 304-643-2931
Web: www.northbendsp.com
Panther State Forest Box 287 — Panther WV 24872 304-938-2252
Web: www.pantherstateforest.com
Pinnacle Rock State Park PO Box 1 — Bramwell WV 24715 304-248-8565
Web: www.pinnaclerockstatepark.com
Pipestem Resort State Park PO Box 150 — Pipestem WV 25979 304-466-1800 466-2803
Web: www.pipestemresort.com

Phone | Fax

Pricketts Fort State Park Rt 3 Box 403 — Fairmont WV 26554 304-367-2731 363-3857
Web: www.prickettsfortstatepark.com
Seneca State Forest Rt 1 Box 140 — Dunmore WV 24934 304-799-6213
Web: www.senecastateforest.com
Stonewall Jackson Lake State Park 149 State Park Trail — Roanoke WV 26447 304-269-0523
Tomlinson Run State Park PO Box 97 — New Manchester WV 26056 304-564-3651
Web: www.tomlinsonrunsp.com
Tu-Endie-Wei State Park PO Box 486 — Point Pleasant WV 25550 304-675-0869
Web: www.tu-endie-weistatepark.com
Twin Falls Resort State Park PO Box 1023 — Mullens WV 25882 304-294-4000
Web: www.twinfallsresort.com
Tygart Lake State Park Rt 1 Box 260 — Grafton WV 26354 304-265-6144
Web: www.tygartlake.com
Valley Falls State Park Rt 6 Box 244 — Fairmont WV 26554 304-367-2719 367-2763
Web: www.valleyfallsstatepark.com
Watoga State Park HC 82 Box 252 — Marlinton WV 24954 304-799-4087 653-4620
TF: 800-225-5982 ■ *Web:* www.watoga.com
Watters Smith Memorial State Park PO Box 296 — Lost Creek WV 26385 304-745-3081
Web: www.watterssmithstatepark.com

Wisconsin

Phone | Fax

Amnicon Falls State Park 6294 S State Rd 35 — Superior WI 54880 715-398-3000
Web: www.dnr.state.wi.us/ORG/land/parks/specific/amnicon
Aztalan State Park 1213 S Main St — Lake Mills WI 53551 920-648-8774 648-5166
Web: www.dnr.state.wi.us/ORG/land/parks/specific/aztalan
Belmont Mound State Park
c/o Yellowstone Lake State Park 7896 Lake Rd — Blanchardville WI 53516 608-523-4427
Big Bay State Park Box 589 — Bayfield WI 54814 715-747-6425
Web: www.dnr.state.wi.us/ORG/land/parks/specific/bigbay
Big Foot Beach State Park 1452 Hwy H — Lake Geneva WI 53147 262-248-2528
Web: www.dnr.state.wi.us/org/land/parks/specific/bigfoot
Black River State Forest 910 Hwy 54 E — Black River Falls WI 54615 715-284-4103
Web: www.dnr.state.wi.us/org/land/Forestry/StateForests/SF-BlackRiver
Blue Mound State Park Box 98 — Blue Mounds WI 53517 608-437-5711
Web: www.dnr.state.wi.us/org/land/parks/specific/bluemound
Browntown-Cadiz Springs State Recreation Area
PO Box 805 — New Glarus WI 53574 608-966-3777
Web: www.dnr.state.wi.us/org/land/parks/specific/browntown
Brule River State Forest 6250 S Ranger Rd — Brule WI 54820 715-372-5678 372-4836
Web: www.dnr.state.wi.us/org/land/Forestry/StateForests/SF-Brule
Brunet Island State Park Rt 2 Box 158 — Cornell WI 54732 715-239-6888
Web: www.dnr.state.wi.us/org/land/parks/specific/brunetisland
Buckhorn State Park W8450 Buckhorn Park Ave — Necedah WI 54646 608-565-2789
Web: www.dnr.state.wi.us/org/land/parks/specific/buckhorn
Capital Springs Centennial State Recreation Area
3101 Lake Farm Rd — Madison WI 53711 608-224-3606
Web: www.dnr.state.wi.us/org/land/parks/specific/capsprings
Chippewa Moraine Ice Age State Recreation Area
13394 County Hwy M — New Auburn WI 54757 715-967-2800 967-2801
Web: www.dnr.state.wi.us/org/land/parks/specific/chipmoraine
Copper Culture State Park N10008 Paust Ln — Crivitz WI 54114 715-757-3979
Copper Falls State Park 36764 Copper Falls Rd — Mellen WI 54546 715-274-5123
Web: www.dnr.state.wi.us/org/land/parks/specific/copperfalls
Council Grounds State Park N1895 Council Grounds Dr — Merrill WI 54452 715-536-8773
Devil's Lake State Park S5975 Park Rd — Baraboo WI 53913 608-356-8301 356-4281
Web: www.dnr.state.wi.us/org/land/parks/specific/devilslake
Fischer Creek State Recreation Area 4319 Expo Dr — Manitowoc WI 54220 920-683-4185
Flambeau River State Forest W1613 County Rd — Winter WI 54896 715-332-5271
Web: www.dnr.state.wi.us/org/land/Forestry/StateForests/SF-Flambeau
Governor Dodge State Park 4175 Hwy 23 — Dodgeville WI 53533 608-935-2315
Web: www.dnr.state.wi.us/org/land/parks/specific/govdodge
Governor Knowles State Forest 325 SR 70 — Grantsburg WI 54840 715-463-2897
Web: www.dnr.state.wi.us/org/land/Forestry/stateforests/SF-Knowles
Governor Nelson State Park 5140 County Hwy M — Waunakee WI 53597 608-831-3005 831-4071
Web: www.dnr.state.wi.us/org/land/parks
Governor Thompson State Park N 10008 Paust Ln — Crivitz WI 54115 715-757-3979 757-3779
Web: www.dnr.state.wi.us/ORG/land/parks/specific/govthompson
Harrington Beach State Park 531 Hwy D — Belgium WI 53004 262-285-3015
Web: www.dnr.state.wi.us/org/land/parks/specific/harrington
Hartman Creek State Park N2480 Hartman Creek Rd — Waupaca WI 54981 715-258-2372
Web: www.dnr.state.wi.us/org/land/parks/specific/hartman
Havenwoods State Forest 6141 N Hopkins St — Milwaukee WI 53209 414-527-0232 527-0761
Web: www.dnr.state.wi.us/org/land/parks/specific/havenwoods
Heritage Hill State Historical Park 2640 S Webster Ave — Green Bay WI 54301 920-448-5150
Web: www.heritagehillgb.org
High Cliff State Park N7630 State Park Rd — Sherwood WI 54169 920-989-1106
Web: www.dnr.state.wi.us/org/land/parks/specific/highcliff
Hoffman Hills Recreation Area 921 Brickyard Rd — Menomonie WI 54751 715-232-1242
Web: www.dnr.state.wi.us/org/land/parks/specific/hoffmanhills
Interstate State Park PO Box 703 — Saint Croix Falls WI 54024 715-483-3747
Web: www.dnr.state.wi.us/org/land/parks/specific/interstate
Kettle Moraine State Forest - Lapham Peak Unit
W329 N846 County Hwy C — Delafield WI 53018 262-646-3025
Web: www.dnr.state.wi.us/org/land/parks/specific/lapham
Kettle Moraine State Forest - Loew Lake Unit
c/o Pike Lake Unit 3544 Kettle Moraine Rd — Hartland WI 53027 262-670-3400
Kettle Moraine State Forest - Northern Unit
N1765 Hwy G — Campbellsport WI 53010 262-626-2116
Web: www.dnr.state.wi.us/org/land/parks/specific/kmn
Kettle Moraine State Forest - Pike Lake Unit
3344 Kettle Moraine Rd — Hartford WI 53027 262-670-3400
Web: www.dnr.state.wi.us/org/land/parks/specific/pikelake
Kettle Moraine State Forest - Southern Unit
S91 W39091 Hwy 59 — Eagle WI 53119 262-594-6201
Web: www.dnr.state.wi.us/org/land/parks/specific/kms
Kinnickinnic State Park W11983 820th Ave — River Falls WI 54022 715-425-1129
Kohler-Andrae State Park 1020 Beach Park Ln — Sheboygan WI 53081 920-451-4080
Web: www.dnr.state.wi.us/org/land/parks/specific/ka
Lake Kegonsa State Park 2405 Door Creek Rd — Stoughton WI 53589 608-873-9695 873-0674
TF: 888-947-2757 ■ *Web:* www.dnr.state.wi.us/org/land/parks/
Lake Wissota State Park 18127 County Hwy 'O' — Chippewa Falls WI 54729 715-382-4574 382-5187
Web: www.dnr.state.wi.us/org/land/parks/specific/lakewissota
Lakeshore State Park 2300 N Martin Luther King Jr Dr — Milwaukee WI 53212 414-263-8570
Web: www.dnr.state.wi.us/org/land/parks/specific/lakeshore
Merrick State Park PO Box 127 — Fountain City WI 54629 608-687-4936
Mill Bluff State Park PO Box 99 — Ontario WI 54651 608-427-6692
Mirror Lake State Park E10320 Fern Dell Rd — Baraboo WI 53913 608-254-2333
Natural Bridge State Park
c/o Devil's Lake State Park S5975 Park Rd — Baraboo WI 53913 608-356-8301
Nelson Dewey State Park Box 658 — Cassville WI 53806 608-725-5374
New Glarus Woods State Park W5446 County Hwy NN — New Glarus WI 53574 608-527-2335
Web: www.dnr.state.wi.us/org/land/parks/specific/ngwoods
Newport State Park 475 County Rd NP — Ellison Bay WI 54210 920-854-2500 854-1914
Web: www.dnr.state.wi.us/org/land/parks/specific/newport

				Phone	Fax
Northern Highland - American Legion State Forest					
4125 County Hwy M	Boulder Junction	WI	54512	715-385-2727	
Web: www.dnr.state.wi.us/org/land/Forestry/StateForests/sf-nh-al					
Pattison State Park 6294 S State Rd 35	Superior	WI	54880	715-399-3111	
Web: www.dnr.state.wi.us/org/land/parks/specific/pattison					
Peninsula State Park PO Box 218	Fish Creek	WI	54212	920-868-3258	
Web: www.dnr.state.wi.us/org/land/parks/specific/peninsula					
Perrot State Park Rt 1 Box 407	Trempealeau	WI	54661	608-534-6409	
Peshtigo River State Forest N 10008 Paust Ln	Crivitz	WI	54114	715-757-3965	
Web: www.dnr.state.wi.us/org/land/Forestry/StateForests/meet.htm#Peshtigo					
Point Beach State Forest 9400 County Hwy 'O'	Two Rivers	WI	54241	920-794-7480	
Web: www.dnr.state.wi.us/org/land/parks/specific/pointbeach					
Potawatomi State Park 3740 County PD	Sturgeon Bay	WI	54235	920-746-2890	
Web: www.dnr.state.wi.us/org/land/parks/specific/Potawatomi					
Rib Mountain State Park 5301 Rib Mountain Dr	Wausau	WI	54401	715-842-2522	
Richard Bong State Recreation Area 26313 Burlington Rd	Kansasville	WI	53139	262-878-5600	878-5615
Web: www.dnr.state.wi.us/org/land/parks/specific/bong					
Roche-A-Cri State Park 1767 Hwy 13	Friendship	WI	53934	608-339-6881	
Web: www.dnr.state.wi.us/org/land/parks/specific/roche-a-cri					
Rock Island State Park Rt 1 Box 118A	Washington Island	WI	54246	920-847-2235	
Web: www.dnr.state.wi.us/org/land/parks/specific/rockisland					
Rocky Arbor State Park					
c/o Mirror Lake State Park E10320 Fern Dell Rd	Baraboo	WI	53913	608-254-8001	
Tower Hill State Park 5808 County Rd C	Spring Green	WI	53588	608-588-2116	
Whitefish Dunes State Park 3275 County Hwy WD	Sturgeon Bay	WI	54235	920-823-2400	
Web: www.dnr.state.wi.us/org/land/parks/specific/whitefish					
Wildcat Mountain State Park E13660 SR 33, Box 99	Ontario	WI	54651	608-337-4775	
Web: www.dnr.state.wi.us/org/land/parks/specific/wildcat					
Willow River State Park 1034 County Hwy A	Hudson	WI	54016	715-386-5931	386-0431
Web: www.dnr.state.wi.us/org/land/parks/specific/willowriver					
Wyalusing State Park 13081 State Park Ln	Bagley	WI	53801	608-996-2261	996-2410
Web: www.dnr.state.wi.us/org/land/parks/specific/wyalusing					
Yellowstone Lake State Park 8495 Lake Rd	Blanchardville	WI	53516	608-523-4427	
Web: www.dnr.state.wi.us/org/land/parks/specific/yellowstone/index.html					

Wyoming

				Phone	Fax
Bear River State Park 601 Bear River Dr	Evanston	WY	82930	307-789-6547	
Web: wyoparks.state.wy.us/brslide.htm					
Boysen State Park 15 Ash Boysen Rt	Shoshoni	WY	82649	307-876-2796	
Web: wyoparks.state.wy.us/boslide.htm					
Buffalo Bill State Park 47 Lakeside Rd	Cody	WY	82414	307-587-9227	
Web: wyoparks.state.wy.us/buffalo.htm					
Connor Battlefield State Historic Site					
c/o Fort Kearny State Historic Site PO Box 520	Story	WY	82842	307-684-7629	
Web: wyoparks.state.wy.us/coslide.htm					
Curt Gowdy State Park 1319 Hynds Lodge Rd	Cheyenne	WY	82009	307-632-7946	635-1056
Web: wyoparks.state.wy.us/curt.htm					
Edness K. Wilkins State Park PO Box 1596	Evansville	WY	82636	307-577-5150	
Web: wyoparks.state.wy.us/ewslide.htm					
Fort Bridger State Historic Site PO Box 35	Fort Bridger	WY	82933	307-782-3842	
Web: wyoparks.state.wy.us/fbslide.htm					
Fort Fetterman State Historic Site 752 Hwy 93	Douglas	WY	82633	307-684-7629	
Web: wyoparks.state.wy.us/ffslide.htm					
Fort Fred Steele State Historic Site					
c/o Seminoe State Park Box 30 HCR 67	Sinclair	WY	82334	307-320-3013	
Web: wyoparks.state.wy.us/fsslide.htm					
Fort Phil Kearny State Historic Site PO Box 520	Story	WY	82842	307-684-7629	
Web: wyoparks.state.wy.us/fkslide.htm					
Glendo State Park PO Box 398	Glendo	WY	82213	307-735-4433	
Web: wyoparks.state.wy.us/glslide.htm					
Guernsey State Park PO Box 429	Guernsey	WY	82214	307-836-2334	
Web: wyoparks.state.wy.us/guslide.htm					
Hawk Springs State Recreation Area					
c/o Guernsey State Park PO Box 429	Guernsey	WY	82214	307-836-2334	
Web: wyoparks.state.wy.us/hwslide.htm					
Historic Governors' Mansion 300 E 21st St	Cheyenne	WY	82009	307-777-7878	
Web: wyoparks.state.wy.us/hgmslide.htm					
Hot Springs State Park 220 Park St	Thermopolis	WY	82443	307-864-2176	
Web: wyoparks.state.wy.us/hsslide.htm					
Independence Rock State Historic Site PO Box 1596	Evansville	WY	82636	307-577-5150	
Web: wyoparks.state.wy.us/irslide.htm					
Keyhole State Park 353 McKean Rd	Moorcroft	WY	82721	307-756-3596	
Web: wyoparks.state.wy.us/keslide.htm					
Medicine Lodge State Archaeological Site PO Box 62	Hyattville	WY	82428	307-469-2234	
Web: wyoparks.state.wy.us/mlslide.htm					
Seminoe State Park Box 30 HCR 67	Sinclair	WY	82334	307-320-3013	
Web: wyoparks.state.wy.us/seslide.htm					
Sinks Canyon State Park 3079 Sinks Canyon Rd	Lander	WY	82520	307-332-3077	
Web: wyoparks.state.wy.us/scslide.htm					
South Pass City State Historic Site					
125 South Pass Main	South Pass City	WY	82520	307-332-3684	
Web: wyoparks.state.wy.us/spcslide.htm					
Trail End State Historic Site 400 Clarendon Ave	Sheridan	WY	82801	307-674-4589	672-1720
Web: www.trailend.org					
Wyoming Territorial Prison State Historic Site					
975 Snowy Range Rd	Laramie	WY	82070	307-746-6161	
Web: www.wyoprisonpark.org					

569 PARTY GOODS

				Phone	Fax
Alin Party Supplies Co 14150 Artesia Blvd	Cerritos	CA	90703	562-282-0422	282-0432
Web: www.alinpartysupply.com					
Amscan Inc 80 Grasslands Rd	Elmsford	NY	10523	914-345-2020	345-3884
TF: 800-284-4333 ■ *Web:* www.amscan.com					
Balloons Everywhere Inc 16474 Greeno Rd	Fairhope	AL	36532	251-210-2100	210-2105
TF: 800-239-2000 ■ *Web:* www.balloons.com					
Beistle Co 1 Beistle Plaza	Shippensburg	PA	17257	717-532-2131	532-7789
Web: www.beistle.com					
Birthday Express 11220 120th Ave NE	Kirkland	WA	98033	425-250-1064	641-2028
NASDAQ: BDAY ■ *TF:* 800-424-7843 ■ *Web:* www.birthdayexpress.com					
Celebrate Express Inc DBA Birthday Express					
11220 120th Ave NE	Kirkland	WA	98033	425-250-1064	641-2028
NASDAQ: BDAY ■ *TF:* 800-424-7843 ■ *Web:* www.birthdayexpress.com					
Designware Inc 1 American Rd	Cleveland	OH	44144	216-252-7300	252-6778
TF: 800-321-3040 ■ *Web:* www.agdesignware.com					
Discount Party Warehouse Inc 538 Larkfield Rd	East Northport	NY	11731	631-368-5200	368-5213
iParty Corp 270 Bridge St Suite 301	Dedham	MA	02026	781-329-3952	326-7143
AMEX: IPT ■ *TF:* 888-727-8970 ■ *Web:* www.iparty.com					
Paper Shack & Party Store Inc 2430 E Texas St	Bossier City	LA	71111	318-746-8636	747-6091
Web: www.papershackpartystore.com					
Paper Store Inc 20 Main St	Acton	MA	01720	978-263-2198	263-2466
Web: www.thepaperstore.com					
Party America 980 Atlantic Ave Suite 103	Alameda	CA	94501	510-747-1800	747-1810
Web: www.partyamerica.com					
Party City Corp 400 Commons Way	Rockaway	NJ	07866	973-983-0888	983-1313
TF: 800-883-2100 ■ *Web:* www.partycity.com					
Party Fair Inc Pond Road Shopping Ctr 4345 Rt 9 N	Freehold	NJ	07728	732-780-1110	780-5174
Web: www.partyfair.com					
Party Land Inc 5215 Militia Hill Rd	Plymouth Meeting	PA	19462	484-342-6213	941-6301*
*Fax Area Code: 610 ■ *TF:* 800-778-9563 ■ *Web:* www.partyland.com					
Stumps Inc 1 Party Pl PO Box 305	South Whitley	IN	46787	260-723-5171	723-6979
TF: 800-348-5084 ■ *Web:* www.stumpsparty.com					

570 PATTERNS - INDUSTRIAL

				Phone	Fax
Allen Pattern of Michigan 202 McGrath Pl	Battle Creek	MI	49014	269-963-4131	963-4327
American Model & Pattern Co 22926 Industrial Dr W	Saint Clair Shores	MI	48080	586-778-5450	776-7111
Web: www.theamericanteam.com					
Anderson Global Inc 500 W Sherman Blvd	Muskegon Heights	MI	49444	231-733-2164	733-1288
Central Pattern Co 8830 Pershall Rd	Hazelwood	MO	63042	314-524-3626	522-8399
Web: www.centralpattern.com					
Cunningham Pattern & Engineering Inc 4399 US 31 N	Columbus	IN	47201	812-379-9571	379-9574
Web: www.cpepattern.com					
D & F Corp 42455 Merrill Rd	Sterling Heights	MI	48314	586-254-5300	254-5610
TF: 800-959-3456 ■ *Web:* www.d-f.com					
Foley Pattern Co Inc 500 W 11th St PO Box 150	Auburn	IN	46706	260-925-4113	925-4115
Freeman Mfg & Supply Co 1101 Moore Rd	Avon	OH	44011	440-934-1902	934-7200
TF: 800-321-8511 ■ *Web:* www.freemansupply.com					
General Pattern Co Inc 3075 84th Ln NE	Blaine	MN	55449	763-780-3518	780-3770
Web: www.generalpattern.com					
Gopher Pattern Works Inc 422 Roosevelt St NE	Minneapolis	MN	55413	612-331-5512	331-6513
Hub Pattern Corp 2113 Salem Ave	Roanoke	VA	24016	540-342-3505	343-5337
TF: 800-482-3505 ■ *Web:* www.hubcorp.net					
Jacob Pattern Works Inc 449 Old Reading Pike	Pottstown	PA	19464	610-326-1100	326-7981
Paragon Pattern & Mfg Co 2620 Park St	Muskegon Heights	MI	49444	231-733-1582	739-1276
Web: www.paragonpattern.com					
Production Pattern Co 560 Solon Rd	Bedford	OH	44146	440-439-3243	439-0918
Web: www.fsigroup.com/ppc.htm					
Progress Pattern Corp 32235 Industrial Rd	Livonia	MI	48150	734-422-0200	422-0201
United Industries Inc 1901 Revere Beach Pkwy	Everett	MA	02149	617-387-9500	387-6331
Web: www.united-ind.com					

571 PATTERNS - SEWING

				Phone	Fax
Bonfit America Inc 8460 Higuera St	Culver City	CA	90232	310-204-7880	204-7893
TF: 800-526-6348 ■ *Web:* www.bonfit.com					
Folkwear Patterns 2000 Riverside Dr Suite 3	Asheville	NC	28804	828-252-4778	252-8809
Web: www.folkwear.com					
Kwik-Sew Pattern Co Inc 3000 Washington Ave N	Minneapolis	MN	55411	612-521-7651	521-1662
TF: 888-594-5739 ■ *Web:* www.kwiksew.com					
McCall Pattern Co DBA Butterick McCall Vogue & Wallies					
Wallpaper Covering Inc 615 McCall Rd	Manhattan	KS	66502	785-776-4041	776-1567
TF: 800-255-2762 ■ *Web:* www.mccall.com					
Simplicity Pattern Co Inc 2 Park Ave 12th Fl	New York	NY	10016	212-372-0500	372-0628
TF: 888-588-2700 ■ *Web:* www.simplicity.com					
Stretch & Sew Inc PO Box 25306	Tempe	AZ	85285	480-966-1462	966-1914
TF: 800-547-7717 ■ *Web:* www.stretch-and-sew.com					

572 PAWN SHOPS

				Phone	Fax
Camco Inc DBA SuperPawn 3021 Business Ln	Las Vegas	NV	89103	702-735-4444	739-7888
TF: 800-511-2568 ■ *Web:* www.superpawn.com					
Cash America International Inc 1600 W 7th St	Fort Worth	TX	76102	817-335-1100	570-1721*
NYSE: CSH ■ *Fax: Mktg ■ *TF:* 800-223-8738 ■ *Web:* www.cashamericaonline.com					
EZCORP Inc 1901 Capital Pkwy	Austin	TX	78746	512-314-3400	314-3404
NASDAQ: EZPW ■ *TF:* 800-873-7296 ■ *Web:* www.ezcorp.com					
EZPAWN 1901 Capital Pkwy	Austin	TX	78746	512-314-3400	314-3404
TF: 800-873-7296 ■ *Web:* www.ezpawn.com					
First Cash Financial Services Inc					
690 E Lamar Blvd Suite 400	Arlington	TX	76011	817-460-3947	461-7019
NASDAQ: FCFS ■ *Web:* www.firstcash.com					
PawnMart Inc 6400 Atlantic Blvd Suite 190	Norcross	GA	30071	678-720-0660	720-0671
TF: 800-729-6261 ■ *Web:* www.pawnmart.com					
SuperPawn 3021 Business Ln	Las Vegas	NV	89103	702-735-4444	739-7888
TF: 800-511-2568 ■ *Web:* www.superpawn.com					

573 PAYROLL SERVICES

SEE ALSO Data Processing & Related Services p. 1585; Professional Employer Organizations (PEOs) p. 2142

				Phone	Fax
ADP ProBusiness Div 4125 Hopyard Rd	Pleasanton	CA	94588	925-737-3500	225-9077
Web: www.probusiness.com					
Advantage Payroll Services Inc 126 Merrow Rd PO Box 1330	Auburn	ME	04211	207-784-0178	786-0490
TF Cust Svc: 800-876-0178 ■ *Web:* www.advantagepayroll.com					
Automatic Data Processing Inc (ADP) 1 ADP Blvd	Roseland	NJ	07068	973-994-5000	974-3378
NYSE: ADP ■ *TF:* 800-225-5237 ■ *Web:* www.adp.com					
Ceridian Canada Ltd 125 Garry St	Winnipeg	MB	R3C3P2	204-946-0770	956-4026
TF: 866-975-1808 ■ *Web:* www.ceridian.ca					
Ceridian Corp 3311 E Old Shakopee Rd	Minneapolis	MN	55425	952-853-8100	
NYSE: CEN ■ *TF:* 800-767-4969 ■ *Web:* www.ceridian.com					
CheckPoint HR 2035 Lincoln Hwy Suite 1080	Edison	NJ	08817	732-287-8270	287-2297
TF: 800-385-0331 ■ *Web:* www.checkpointhr.com					
DSI Payroll Services 300 Atrium Dr	Somerset	NJ	08873	732-748-1700	
TF: 800-254-0780 ■ *Web:* www.dsipayrollservices.com					

Phone Fax

Media Services 500 S Sepulveda Blvd 4th Fl................Los Angeles CA 90049 310-440-9600 472-9979
TF: 800-333-7518 ■ *Web:* www.media-services.com
Paychex Inc 911 Panorama Trail S.........................Rochester NY 14625 585-385-6666 383-3449*
NASDAQ: PAYX ■ **Fax:* Hum Res ■ *TF:* 800-828-4411 ■ *Web:* www.paychex.com
Paychex Major Market Services
2527 Camino Ramon Suite 185.......................... San Ramon CA 94583 925-242-0700 790-0223
Web: www.paychex.com/products/mms.html?link=payxhome
PayMaxx Inc 302 S Royal Oaks Blvd .... Franklin TN 37064 615-791-4000 236-5460
TF: 877-729-6299 ■ *Web:* www.paymaxx.com
Payroll 1 Inc 333 W 7th St.............................. Royal Oak MI 48067 248-548-7020 548-3879
TF: 888-999-7291 ■ *Web:* www.payroll1.com
Paywise Inc 122 E 42nd St Suite 520 ....New York NY 10168 212-953-1287 953-9690
TF: 800-975-8607 ■ *Web:* www.paywise.com
SurePayroll 4709 Golf Rd Suite 900............................ Skokie IL 60076 847-676-8420 676-5136
TF: 877-954-7873 ■ *Web:* www.surepayroll.com
TeamStaff Inc 300 Atrium Dr ....Somerset NJ 08873 732-748-1700 748-3253
NASDAQ: TSTF ■ *TF:* 800-374-1001 ■ *Web:* www.teamstaff.com
TTS Payrolls Inc 21 Penn Plaza Suite 1008 ....New York NY 10001 866-887-4749 473-1799
Web: www.ttspayrolls.com

574 PENS, PENCILS, PARTS

SEE ALSO Art Materials & Supplies - Mfr p. 1285; Office & School Supplies p. 2034

Phone Fax

Accutec Inc 168 Main Ave .... Wallington NJ 07057 973-471-3131 471-3494
TF: 800-222-8832
Alvin & Co Inc 1335 Blue Hills Ave .... Bloomfield CT 06002 860-243-8991 777-2896*
**Fax Area Code:* 800 ■ *TF:* 800-444-2584 ■ *Web:* www.alvinco.com
AT Cross Co 1 Albion Rd.......................................Lincoln RI 02865 401-333-1200 722-1729*
AMEX: ATX ■ **Fax Area Code:* 800 ■ **Fax:* Cust Svc ■ *TF:* 800-722-1719 ■
Web: www.cross.com
Avery Dennison Corp 150 N Orange Grove Blvd................. Pasadena CA 91103 626-304-2000 304-2192
NYSE: AVY ■ *TF Cust Svc:* 800-252-8379 ■ *Web:* www.averydennison.com
BIC Corp 1 BIC Way Suite 1 ....Shelton CT 06484 203-783-2000 783-2660*
**Fax:* Hum Res ■ *TF:* 800-546-1111 ■ *Web:* www.bicworld.com
California Cedar Products Co 1340 N Washingtron St ....Stockton CA 95203 209-944-5800 944-9072
Web: www.calcedar.com
Cross AT Co 1 Albion Rd.......................................Lincoln RI 02865 401-333-1200 722-1729*
AMEX: ATX ■ **Fax Area Code:* 800 ■ **Fax:* Cust Svc ■ *TF:* 800-722-1719 ■
Web: www.cross.com
Dixon Ticonderoga Co 195 International Pkwy................. Heathrow FL 32746 407-829-9000 829-2572*
AMEX: DXT ■ **Fax:* Cust Svc ■ *TF:* 800-824-9430 ■ *Web:* www.dixonticonderoga.com
Dri Mark Products Inc 15 Harbor Pk Dr................. Port Washington NY 11050 516-484-6200 484-6279
TF: 800-645-9118 ■ *Web:* www.drimark.com
Fisher Space Pen Co 711 Yucca St ....Boulder City NV 89005 702-293-3011 293-6616
TF: 800-634-3494 ■ *Web:* www.spacepen.com
Garland Industries Inc 1 S Main St ....Coventry RI 02816 401-828-9582 823-7460
Web: www.garlandpen.com
General Pencil Co Inc PO Box 5311 .... Redwood City CA 94063 650-369-4889 369-7169
Web: www.generalpencil.com
Harcourt Pencil Co 7765 S 175 W..............................Milroy IN 46156 765-629-2244 629-2218
TF: 800-215-4024 ■ *Web:* www.harcourtoutlines.com
Hartley-Racon 280 N Midland Ave Bldg C-1................Saddle Brook NJ 07663 201-703-0663 703-0733
HPC Global 14 Industrial Dr .... Hanover PA 17331 717-637-6681 637-9190
TF: 800-233-4463 ■ *Web:* www.hpc-online.com
Hub Pen Co Inc 230 Quincy Ave.............................. Quincy MA 02169 617-471-9900 471-2990
TF: 800-388-2323 ■ *Web:* www.hubpen.com
Jensen's Inc 715 W Jackson St ....Shelbyville TN 37160 931-684-5021 685-9229
Listo Pencil Corp 1925 Union St ....Alameda CA 94501 510-522-2910 522-3798
TF: 800-547-8648 ■ *Web:* www.listo.com
Montblanc North America 430 Mountain Ave ....Murray Hill NJ 07974 908-508-2300
TF: 800-995-4810
Moon Products Inc 1150 5th Ave N PO Box 1309............. Lewisburg TN 37091 931-359-1501 359-8381
TF: 800-541-3758 ■ *Web:* www.moonproducts.com
Musgrave Pencil Co Inc PO Box 290........................Shelbyville TN 37162 931-684-3611 685-1049
TF: 800-736-2450 ■ *Web:* www.musgravepencil.com
National Pen Corp 16885 Via Del Compo Ct Suite 100.......... San Diego CA 92127 858-675-3000 675-0890
TF: 800-854-1000 ■ *Web:* www.pens.com
Newell Rubbermaid Inc Office Products Group
10B Glenlake Pkwy Suite 600 .... Atlanta GA 30328 770-407-3800 407-3970
Pencoa Mfg Corp 117 State St.............................. Westbury NY 11590 516-997-2330 989-7704*
**Fax Area Code:* 800 ■ *TF Cust Svc:* 800-989-7527 ■ *Web:* www.pencoa.com
Pentel of America Ltd 2805 Columbia St........................Torrance CA 90503 310-320-3831 533-0697
TF: 800-262-1127 ■ *Web:* www.pentel-usa.com
Pilot Corp of America 60 Commerce Dr....................... Trumbull CT 06611 203-377-8800 377-4024
Web: www.pilotpen.com
Rotary Pen Corp 746 Colfax Ave.............................. Kenilworth NJ 07033 908-245-2437 245-1557
Sanford Brands Div Newell Rubbermaid Inc
2707 Butterfield Rd .... Oak Brook IL 60523 630-481-2200 481-2099*
**Fax:* Cust Svc ■ *TF:* 800-323-0749 ■ *Web:* www.sanford.com
Sargent Art Inc 100 E Diamond Ave..............................Hazleton PA 18201 570-454-3596 459-1752
TF: 800-424-3596 ■ *Web:* www.sargentart.com
Scripto Tokai Corp PO Box 5555 ....Rancho Cucamonga CA 91729 909-476-4600 476-0810
Web: www.scripto21.com
Sheaffer Pen Corp 301 Ave H........................... Fort Madison IA 52627 319-372-3300 372-1263
TF: 800-346-3736 ■ *Web:* www.sheaffer.com
Staedtler Inc 21900 Plummer St ....Chatsworth CA 91311 818-882-6000 882-3767
TF: 800-800-3691 ■ *Web:* www.staedtler-usa.com
Union Pen Co PO Box 220 .... Hagaman NY 12086 800-846-6600 770-7018*
**Fax Area Code:* 518 ■ *Web:* www.unionpen.com

575 PERFORMING ARTS FACILITIES

SEE ALSO Convention Centers p. 1559; Stadiums & Arenas p. 2329; Theaters - Broadway p. 2365; Theaters - Resident p. 2366

Most of the fax numbers provided for these facilities are for the box office.

Alabama

Phone Fax

Alabama Theatre 1817 3rd Ave N ....Birmingham AL 35203 205-252-2262 251-3155
Web: www.alabamatheatre.com
Bama Theatre 600 Greensboro Ave ....Tuscaloosa AL 35401 205-758-5195 345-2787
Web: www.tuscarts.org
Birmingham Festival Theater PO Box 55321.................Birmingham AL 35255 205-933-2383
Web: www.bftonline.org
Birmingham-Jefferson Convention Complex
2100 Richard Arrington Jr Blvd N........................Birmingham AL 35203 205-458-8400 458-8437
TF: 877-843-2522 ■ *Web:* www.bjcc.org
Boutwell Municipal Auditorium 1930 8th Ave N..............Birmingham AL 35203 205-254-2820 254-2921
Davis Theatre for the Performing Arts
251 Montgomery St.. Montgomery AL 36104 334-241-9567 241-9756
Library Theatre 200 Municipal Dr..............................Hoover AL 35216 205-444-7888 444-7894
Web: www.thelibrarytheatre.com
Playhouse in the Park 4851 Museum Dr Mobile Municipal Park ..... Mobile AL 36608 251-344-1537
Web: www.mobilepip.org
Renaissance Theatre Inc 1216B Meridian St Lincoln Center.......Huntsville AL 35801 256-536-3117
Web: www.renaissancetheatre.net
Riverfront Amphitheatre 200 Coosa St Suite A.............. Montgomery AL 36104 334-240-4090 240-4094
Saenger Theatre 6 S Joachim St ....Mobile AL 36602 251-208-5600 208-5609
Web: www.mobilesaenger.com
Tuscaloosa Fine Arts Centre 9500 Old Greensboro Rd..........Tuscaloosa AL 35405 205-391-2400 391-2329
Von Braun Center 700 Monroe St..........................Huntsville AL 35801 256-533-1953 551-2203
Web: www.vonbrauncenter.com
Wynton M Blount Cultural Park 6000 Vaughn Rd............ Montgomery AL 36116 334-244-5700 273-9666
Web: www.blountculturalpark.org

Alaska

Phone Fax

Alaska Center for the Performing Arts 621 W 6th Ave.......... Anchorage AK 99501 907-263-2900 263-2927
Web: www.alaskapac.org
Charles W Davis Concert Hall
University of Alaska Fairbanks Music Dept PO Box 755660...... Fairbanks AK 99775 907-474-7555 474-6420
Palace Theatre & Saloon Airport Way & Peger Rd............. Fairbanks AK 99709 907-452-7274 456-6997
TF: 800-354-7274

Arizona

Phone Fax

Arizona State University's Kerr Cultural Center
6110 N Scottsdale Rd .... Scottsdale AZ 85253 480-596-2660 483-9646
Web: www.asukerr.com
Celebrity Theatre 440 N 32nd St .... Phoenix AZ 85008 602-267-1600 267-4882
Web: www.celebritytheatre.com
Chandler Center for the Arts 250 N Arizona Ave.................Chandler AZ 85225 480-782-2680 782-2684
Web: www.chandlercenter.org
Cricket Pavilion 2121 N 83rd Ave .... Phoenix AZ 85035 602-254-7200 254-6060
Web: www.cricket-pavilion.com
Dodge Theatre 400 W Washington St.......................... Phoenix AZ 85003 602-379-2800 379-2002
Web: www.dodgetheatre.com
Grady Gammage Memorial Auditorium 1200 S Forest Ave .... Tempe AZ 85188 480-965-3434 965-3583
Web: www.asugammage.com
Herberger Theater Center 222 E Monroe St .... Phoenix AZ 85004 602-254-7399 258-9521
Web: www.herbergertheater.org
Maricopa County Events Center 19403 RH Johnson Blvd..... Sun City West AZ 85375 623-544-2888 544-4050
Web: www.maricopacountyeventscenter.com
Marquee Theatre 730 N Mill Ave .... Tempe AZ 85281 480-829-0607 829-1552
Orpheum Theatre 203 W Adams St .... Phoenix AZ 85003 602-534-5600 534-5622
Web: www.ci.phoenix.az.us/STAGES/orpheum.html
Rialto The 318 E Congress St................................Tucson AZ 85701 520-740-0126
Web: www.rialtotheatre.com
Scottsdale Center for the Performing Arts 7380 E 2nd St.......Scottsdale AZ 85251 480-994-2787 874-4699
Web: www.scottsdaleperformingarts.org
Tempe Performing Arts Center 132 E 6th St..................... Tempe AZ 85281 480-350-8108
Tucson Convention Center 260 S Church Ave....................Tucson AZ 85701 520-791-4101 791-5572
Web: www.tucsonaz.gov/tcc

Arkansas

Phone Fax

Fort Smith Convention Center 55 S 7th St .... Fort Smith AR 72901 479-788-8932 788-8930
Web: www.fortsmith.org
Robinson Center 426 W Markham St 7 Statehouse Plaza .... Little Rock AR 72201 501-376-4781 374-2255
TF: 800-844-4781 ■ *Web:* www.littlerockmeetings.com

British Columbia

Phone Fax

Orpheum Theatre 865 Seymour St .... Vancouver BC V6B3L4 604-665-3050 665-3001
Web: www.city.vancouver.bc.ca/theatres

California

Phone Fax

Ahmanson Theatre
135 N Grand Ave Music Center of Los Angeles County ....Los Angeles CA 90012 213-628-2772 972-7224
Web: www.taperahmanson.com
Alex Theatre 216 N Brand Blvd ....Glendale CA 91203 818-243-2611 241-2089
Web: www.alextheatre.org
Annenberg Theater
101 Museum Dr Palm Springs Art Museum...............Palm Springs CA 92262 760-325-4490 322-3246
Web: psmuseum.org/performances
B Street Theatre 2711 B St .... Sacramento CA 95816 916-443-5300 443-0874
Web: www.bstreettheatre.org
Bayview Opera House 4705 3rd St....................... San Francisco CA 94124 415-824-0386 824-7124
Web: www.bayviewoperahouse.org
Bill Graham Civic Auditorium 99 Grove St................ San Francisco CA 94102 415-974-4000 974-4084
Web: www.billgrahamcivic.com
Bren Events Center 100 Bren Events Ctr .... Irvine CA 92697 949-824-5050 824-5097
Web: www.bren.uci.edu
Bruce Ariss Wharf Theatre Fisherman's Wharf Wharf 1 .... Monterey CA 93940 831-649-2332 373-7944
California Center for the Arts 340 N Escondido Blvd .... Escondido CA 92025 760-839-4138
TF: 800-988-4253 ■ *Web:* www.artcenter.org
California Theatre of Performing Arts 562 W 4th St .... San Bernardino CA 92401 909-885-5152 885-8672
TF: 800-511-6449 ■ *Web:* www.theatricalarts.com/defaultcai.htm
Center for the Performing Arts 255 Almaden Blvd .... San Jose CA 95113 408-295-9600 277-3535
TF: 800-726-5673 ■ *Web:* www.sjcc.com/cftpa
Cerritos Center for the Performing Arts 12700 Center Court Dr .... Cerritos CA 90703 562-916-8533 916-8514
Web: www.cerritoscenter.com
Coors Amphitheatre 2050 Entertainment Cir ....Chula Vista CA 91911 619-671-3600
Web: www.hob.com/venues/concerts/coors

Phone Fax

EXIT Theatre 156 Eddy St ... San Francisco CA 94102 415-931-1094 931-2699
Web: www.sffringe.org
Ford Amphitheatre 2580 Cahuenga Blvd E ... Hollywood CA 90068 323-461-3673 871-5904
Web: www.fordamphitheatre.org
Fox Theater 2001 H St ... Bakersfield CA 93301 661-324-1369 324-1854
Web: www.foxtheateronline.com
Fox Theatre 2215 Broadway ... Redwood City CA 94063 650-369-4119 369-4129
Web: www.foxdream.com
Fresno Convention Center 848 M St ... Fresno CA 93721 559-445-8100 445-8110
Web: www.fresnoconventioncenter.com
Galaxy Concert Theatre 3503 S Harbor Blvd ... Santa Ana CA 92704 714-957-0600 957-6605
Web: www.galaxytheatre.com
Garden Grove Playhouse
12001 Saint Mark St PO Box 5991 ... Garden Grove CA 92846 714-897-5122
Web: www.gardengroveplayhouse.com
Gary Soren Smith Center for the Fine & Performing Arts
43600 Mission Blvd Ohlone College ... Fremont CA 94539 510-659-6031 659-6188
Web: www2.ohlone.cc.ca.us/org/smith_ctr
Glendale Centre Theatre 324 N Orange St ... Glendale CA 91203 818-244-8481 244-5042
Web: www.glendalecentretheatre.com
Granger Music Hall 1615 E 4th St ... National City CA 91950 619-477-3451
Greek Theatre 2700 N Vermont Ave ... Los Angeles CA 90027 323-665-5857 666-8202
Web: www.greektheatrela.com
Grove Theater Center 111-B W Olive Ave ... Burbank CA 91502 818-238-9988 495-1218*
**Fax Area Code:* 866 ■ *Web:* www.gtc.org
Hollywood Bowl 2301 N Highland Ave ... Hollywood CA 90078 323-850-2000 850-2155
Web: www.hollywoodbowl.org
Hyundai Pavilion at Glen Helen 2575 Glen Helen Pkwy ... San Bernardino CA 92407 909-880-6500 885-6563
Web: www.hyundaipavilion.com
Irvine Barclay Theatre 4242 Campus Dr ... Irvine CA 92612 949-854-4646 854-8490
Web: www.thebarclay.org
Kodak Theatre 6801 Hollywood Blvd Suite 180 ... Hollywood CA 90028 323-308-6300 308-6381
Web: www.kodaktheatre.com
Loews Theatre at the Metreon 101 4th St ... San Francisco CA 94103 415-369-6201 369-6220
Long Beach Playhouse 5021 E Anaheim St ... Long Beach CA 90804 562-494-1014 961-8616
Web: www.lbph.com
Luckman Fine Arts Complex 5151 State University Dr ... Los Angeles CA 90032 323-343-6611 343-6423
Web: www.luckmanarts.org
Marines Memorial Theatre 609 Sutter St Suite 200 ... San Francisco CA 94102 415-441-7444 776-9674
Web: www.marinesmemorialtheatre.com
McCallum Theatre 73000 Fred Waring Dr ... Palm Desert CA 92260 760-346-6505 341-9508
Web: www.mccallumtheatre.com
Monterey Peninsula College Theatre 980 Fremont St ... Monterey CA 93940 831-646-4213
Montgomery Theater 271 S Market St ... San Jose CA 95113 408-295-9600 277-3535
TF: 800-726-5673 ■ *Web:* www.sjcc.com/montgomery_theater
Music Center of Los Angeles County 135 N Grand Ave ... Los Angeles CA 90012 213-972-7211 972-7323
Web: www.musiccenter.org
New Conservatory Theatre Centre 25 Van Ness Ave ... San Francisco CA 94102 415-861-4914 861-6988
Web: www.nctcsf.org
Old Globe 1363 Old Globe Way ... San Diego CA 92102 619-231-1941 231-5879
Web: www.oldglobe.org
Orange County Performing Arts Center
600 Town Center Dr ... Costa Mesa CA 92626 714-556-2121 549-1352
Web: www.ocpac.org
Oxnard Performing Arts & Convention Center 800 Hobson Way ... Oxnard CA 93030 805-486-2424 483-7303
Web: www.oxnardpacc.com
Palace of Fine Arts Theatre 3301 Lyon St ... San Francisco CA 94123 415-567-6642 567-4062
Web: www.palaceoffinearts.org
Palm Canyon Theatre 538 N Palm Canyon Dr ... Palm Springs CA 92262 760-323-5123 323-7365
Web: www.palmcanyontheatre.org
Paramount Theatre 2025 Broadway ... Oakland CA 94612 510-465-6400 893-5098
Web: www.paramounttheatre.com
Pasadena Center 300 E Green St ... Pasadena CA 91101 626-793-2122 793-8014
Web: www.pasadenacal.com/faciliti.htm
Pentages Theatre 6233 Hollywood Blvd ... Hollywood CA 90028 323-468-1770
Web: www.nederlander.com/wc/info/venue.htm?ID=2
Plaza Theater 128 S Palm Canyon Dr ... Palm Springs CA 92262 760-327-0225 322-3196
Web: www.psfollies.com/plaza.html
Redding Civic Auditorium 777 Auditorium Dr ... Redding CA 96001 530-225-4130 225-4118
TF: 888-225-4130
Redlands Bowl PO Box 466 ... Redlands CA 92373 909-793-7316 793-5086
Web: www.redlandsbowl.org
Richard & Karen Carpenter Performing Arts Center
6200 Atherton St ... Long Beach CA 90815 562-985-7000 985-7023
Web: www.carpenterarts.org
Richmond Memorial Convention Center
403 Civic Center Plaza ... Richmond CA 94804 510-620-6950 620-6583
Riverside Municipal Auditorium 3485 Mission Inn Ave ... Riverside CA 92501 951-787-7678 682-8464
Web: www.riversidemunicipalauditorium.com
Robert and Margrit Mondavi Center for the Performing Arts
1 Shields Ave ... Davis CA 95616 530-754-2787 754-5383
TF: 866-754-2787 ■ *Web:* www.mondaviarts.org
San Francisco War Memorial & Performing Arts Center
401 Van Ness Ave Suite 110 ... San Francisco CA 94102 415-621-6600 621-5091
Web: www.sfwmpac.org
San Jose Center for the Performing Arts 255 Almaden Blvd ... San Jose CA 95110 408-277-5277 277-3535
Web: www.sjcc.com/cftpa
San Jose Convention & Cultural Facilities 408 Almaden Blvd ... San Jose CA 95110 408-277-5277 277-3535
TF: 800-533-2345 ■ *Web:* www.sjcc.com
Santa Cruz Civic Auditorium 307 Church St ... Santa Cruz CA 95060 831-420-5260 420-5261
Web: www.ci.santa-cruz.ca.us/pr/civic
Santa Monica Civic Auditorium 1855 Main St ... Santa Monica CA 90401 310-458-8551 394-3411
Web: www.santamonicacivic.org
Second Space Theater 928 E Olive Ave ... Fresno CA 93728 559-266-0211 266-1342
Shoreline Amphitheatre 1 Amphitheatre Pkwy ... Mountain View CA 94043 650-967-3000 967-4994
Web: www.shorelineamp.com
Shrine Auditorium & Exposition Center
665 W Jefferson Blvd ... Los Angeles CA 90007 213-748-5116 742-9922
Web: www.shrineauditorium.com
Sleep Train Amphitheatre 2677 Forty Mile Rd ... Marysville CA 95901 530-743-5200 634-0157
Web: www.sleeptrainamphitheatre.com
Sleep Train Pavilion at Concord 2000 Kirker Pass Rd ... Concord CA 94521 925-676-8742 676-7262
Web: www.livenation.com/venue/getVenue/venueId/1503
State Theatre PO Box 1492 ... Modesto CA 95354 209-527-4697
Web: www.thestate.org
Sturges Center for the Fine Arts 780 N 'E' St ... San Bernardino CA 92410 909-384-5415 384-5449
Web: www.sturgescenter.org
Terrace Theater 300 E Ocean Blvd ... Long Beach CA 90802 562-436-3661 499-7552
Web: www.longbeachcc.com/terrace.htm
Theatre in Old Town 4040 Twiggs St ... San Diego CA 92110 619-688-2494 688-0960
Web: www.theatreinoldtown.com
Thousand Oaks Civic Arts Plaza
2100 Thousand Oaks Blvd ... Thousand Oaks CA 91362 805-449-2700
Web: www.toaks.org/theatre
Tower Theatre for the Performing Arts 815 E Olive Ave ... Fresno CA 93728 559-485-9050
Web: www.towertheatrefresno.org
Walt Disney Concert Hall 111 S Grand Ave ... Los Angeles CA 90012 323-850-2000
Web: wdch.laphil.com
Warnors Theatre 1400 Fulton St ... Fresno CA 93721 559-264-6863 264-5643
Web: tickets.warnors.com
Western Stage Theatre 156 Homestead Ave ... Salinas CA 93901 831-755-6816 770-6105
Web: www.westernstage.org
Wiltern Theatre 3790 Wilshire Blvd ... Los Angeles CA 90010 213-388-1400 388-0242
Web: www.thewiltern.com
Yerba Buena Center for the Arts 701 Mission St ... San Francisco CA 94103 415-978-2700 978-9635
Web: www.yerbabuenaarts.org

Colorado

Phone Fax

Arvada Center for the Arts & Humanities 6901 Wadsworth Blvd ... Arvada CO 80003 720-898-7200 898-7204
Web: www.arvadacenter.org
Aurora Fox Arts Center 9900 E Colfax Ave ... Aurora CO 80010 303-739-1970 739-1975
Web: www.aurorafox.org
Denver Center for the Performing Arts 1101 13th St ... Denver CO 80204 303-893-4000 595-9634
TF: 800-641-1222 ■ *Web:* www.denvercenter.org
Denver Performing Arts Complex 1245 Champa St ... Denver CO 80204 720-865-4220 865-4247
Web: artscomplex.com
Historic Paramount Theatre 1621 Glenarm St ... Denver CO 80202 303-825-4904 741-1831
Macky Auditorium Concert Hall
17th St & University Ave 285 UCB ... Boulder CO 80309 303-492-8423 492-1651
Web: www.colorado.edu/Macky
Newman Center for the Performing Arts 2344 E Iliff Ave ... Denver CO 80208 303-871-6200 871-6507
Web: www.du.edu/newmancenter
Paramount Theatre 1631 Glenarm Pl ... Denver CO 80202 303-405-1100 575-1920
Web: www.paramountdenver.com
Pikes Peak Center 190 S Cascade Ave ... Colorado Springs CO 80903 719-477-2100 520-7462
Web: www.pikespeakcenter.org
Red Rocks Amphitheater 18300 W Alameda Pkwy ... Morrison CO 80465 720-865-2474 295-4467*
**Fax Area Code:* 303 ■ *Web:* www.redrocksonline.com
Sangre de Cristo Arts & Conference Center 210 N Santa Fe Ave ... Pueblo CO 81003 719-295-7200 295-7230
Web: www.sdc-arts.org
Wheeler Opera House 320 E Hyman St ... Aspen CO 81611 970-920-5770 920-5780
Web: www.wheeleroperahouse.com

Connecticut

Phone Fax

ADVO SummerWind Performing Arts Center 40 Griffin Rd ... Windsor CT 06095 860-687-9836 688-5449
Web: www.swind.org
Alliance Theatre at University of New Haven
300 Orange Ave Dodds Hall ... West Haven CT 06516 203-932-7085 931-6097
Austin Arts Center 300 Summit St ... Hartford CT 06106 860-297-2199 297-5380
Web: www.austinarts.org
Bushnell Center for the Performing Arts 166 Capitol Ave ... Hartford CT 06106 860-987-6000 987-6070
TF: 888-824-2874 ■ *Web:* www.bushnell.org
Fairmount Theatre 33 Main St Annex ... New Haven CT 06512 203-467-3832 467-3832
Garde Arts Center 325 State St ... New London CT 06320 860-444-7373 701-0189
Web: www.gardearts.org
John Lyman Center for the Performing Arts
501 Crescent St ... New Haven CT 06515 203-392-6154 392-6158
Web: tickets.southernct.edu
Lincoln Theater
200 Bloomfield Ave University of Hartford Campus ... West Hartford CT 06117 860-768-4228 768-4229
TF: 800-274-8587
Long Wharf Theatre 222 Sargent Dr ... New Haven CT 06511 203-787-4284 776-2287
TF: 800-782-8497 ■ *Web:* www.longwharf.org
Meadows Music Theatre 61 Savitt Way ... Hartford CT 06120 860-548-7370 548-7386
Web: www.meadowsmusic.com
Norwalk Concert Hall 125 East Ave ... Norwalk CT 06851 203-854-7900 854-7939
Oakdale Theatre 95 S Turnpike Rd ... Wallingford CT 06492 203-269-8721 284-1816
Web: www.oakdale.com
Palace Theater of the Arts 61 Atlantic St ... Stamford CT 06901 203-325-4466 358-2313
Playhouse on the Green 177 State St ... Bridgeport CT 06604 203-333-3666 696-0045
Web: www.playhouseonthegreen.org
Quick Center for the Arts Fairfield University 1073 Benson Rd ... Fairfield CT 06824 203-254-4010 254-4113
TF: 877-278-7396 ■ *Web:* www.quickcenter.com
Sacred Heart University Edgerton Center for Performing Arts
5151 Park Ave ... Fairfield CT 06825 203-371-7908 365-4858
Web: www.edgertoncenter.org
Shubert Theater 247 College St ... New Haven CT 06510 203-624-1825 789-2286
Web: www.shubert.com
Stamford Center for the Arts 307 Atlantic St ... Stamford CT 06901 203-358-2305 358-2313
Web: www.stamfordcenterforthearts.org
Sterling Farms Theatre Complex 1349 Newfield Ave ... Stamford CT 06905 203-329-8207 322-3656
Web: www.curtaincallinc.com
TheaterWorks 233 Pearl St ... Hartford CT 06103 860-527-7838 525-0758
Web: www.theaterworkshartford.org
Westport Country Playhouse 25 Powers Ct ... Westport CT 06880 203-227-4177 454-3238
TF: 888-927-7529 ■ *Web:* www.westportplayhouse.org
Woolsey Hall College & Grove Sts Yale University ... New Haven CT 06520 203-432-8620
Yale University Theatre 222 York St ... New Haven CT 06520 203-432-1234 432-6423

Delaware

Phone Fax

Christina Cultural Arts Center 705 Market St ... Wilmington DE 19801 302-652-0101 652-7480
Web: www.ccac-de.org
DuPont Theatre 10th & Market Sts DuPont Bldg ... Wilmington DE 19801 302-656-4401 594-1437
TF: 800-338-0881 ■ *Web:* www.duponttheatre.com
Grand Opera House 818 N Market St ... Wilmington DE 19801 302-652-5577 657-5692
TF: 800-374-7263 ■ *Web:* www.grandopera.org
Schwartz Center for the Arts 226 S State St ... Dover DE 19901 302-678-5152 678-1267
Web: www.schwartzcenter.com

District of Columbia

Phone Fax

African Heritage Dance Center 4018 Minnesota Ave NE ... Washington DC 20019 202-399-5252
Arena Stage 1101 6th St SW ... Washington DC 20024 202-554-9066 488-4056
Web: www.arenastage.org
Carter Barron Amphitheatre 4850 Colorado Ave NW ... Washington DC 20008 202-426-0486
Web: www.nps.gov/rocr/cbarron
DAR Constitution Hall 18th & D Sts ... Washington DC 20006 202-628-4780 628-2570
Web: www.dar.org/conthall
Discovery Theater 1100 Jefferson Dr SW ... Washington DC 20560 202-357-1500 357-2588
Web: www.discoverytheater.org

District of Columbia (Cont'd)

	City	State	ZIP	Phone	Fax
John F Kennedy Center for the Performing Arts					
2700 F St NW	Washington	DC	20566	202-416-8000	416-8205
TF: 800-444-1324 ■ *Web:* kennedy-center.org					
Kennedy Center for the Performing Arts 2700 F St NW	Washington	DC	20566	202-416-8000	416-8205
TF: 800-444-1324 ■ *Web:* kennedy-center.org					
National Theatre 1321 Pennsylvania Ave NW	Washington	DC	20004	202-628-6161	628-5487
TF: 800-447-7400 ■ *Web:* www.nationaltheatre.org					
Warner Theatre 1299 Pennsylvania Ave NW Suite 111	Washington	DC	20004	202-783-4000	783-0204
Web: www.warnertheatre.com					

Florida

	City	State	ZIP	Phone	Fax
American Stage 211 3rd St S	Saint Petersburg	FL	33701	727-823-1600	821-2444
Web: www.americanstage.org					
Bailey Hall 3501 SW Davie Rd	Davie	FL	33314	954-201-6884	201-6316
Barbara B Mann Performing Arts Hall					
8099 College Pkwy SW	Fort Myers	FL	33919	239-489-3033	481-4620
TF: 800-440-7469 ■ *Web:* www.bbmannpah.com					
Bob Carr Performing Arts Centre 401 W Livingston St	Orlando	FL	32801	407-849-2000	843-0758
Web: www.orlandocentroplex.com					
Broward Center for the Performing Arts					
201 SW 5th Ave	Fort Lauderdale	FL	33312	954-462-0222	462-3541
TF: 800-564-9539 ■ *Web:* www.browardcenter.org					
Carnival Center for the Performing Arts 1300 Biscayne Blvd	Miami	FL	33132	786-468-2000	468-2001
Web: www.carnivalcenter.org					
Centre for the Arts at Mizner Park					
433 Plaza Real Suite 339	Boca Raton	FL	33432	561-368-8445	368-4008
Web: www.centre4artsboca.com					
Charlotte County Memorial Auditorium 75 Taylor St	Punta Gorda	FL	33950	941-639-5833	639-3814
TF: 800-329-9988					
Coral Springs Center for the Arts 2855 Coral Springs Dr	Coral Springs	FL	33065	954-344-5990	344-5980
Web: www.coralspringscenterforthearts.com					
Curtis M Phillips Center for the Performing Arts					
315 Hull Rd	Gainesville	FL	32611	352-392-1900	392-3775
Web: www.cpa.ufl.edu					
Eckerd Ruth Hall 1111 McMullen Booth Rd	Clearwater	FL	33759	727-791-7060	791-6020
TF: 800-875-8682 ■ *Web:* www.rutheckerdhall.com					
Florida Theatre 128 E Forsyth St Suite 300	Jacksonville	FL	32202	904-355-5661	358-1874
Web: www.floridatheatre.com					
GableStage 1200 Anastasia Ave Biltmore Hotel	Coral Gables	FL	33134	305-446-1116	445-8645
Web: www.gablestage.org					
Gleason Jackie Theater of the Performing Arts					
1700 Washington Ave	Miami Beach	FL	33139	305-673-7300	538-6810
Web: www.gleasontheater.com					
Gusman Center for the Performing Arts 174 E Flagler St	Miami	FL	33131	305-374-2444	374-0303
Web: www.gusmancenter.org					
Jackie Gleason Theater of the Performing Arts					
1700 Washington Ave	Miami Beach	FL	33139	305-673-7300	538-6810
Web: www.gleasontheater.com					
James L Knight International Center 400 SE Second Ave	Miami	FL	33131	305-372-4634	350-7910
Web: jlkc.com					
Knight James L International Center 400 SE Second Ave	Miami	FL	33131	305-372-4634	350-7910
Web: jlkc.com					
Kravis Raymond F Center for the Performing Arts					
701 Okeechobee Blvd	West Palm Beach	FL	33401	561-832-7469	833-0691*
**Fax:* Mktg ■ *TF:* 800-572-8471 ■ *Web:* www.kravis.org					
Lakeland Center 701 W Lime St	Lakeland	FL	33815	863-834-8100	834-8101
Web: www.thelakelandcenter.com					
Limelight Theatre 11 Old Mission Ave	Saint Augustine	FL	32084	904-825-1164	825-4662
Web: www.limelight-theatre.org					
Lincoln Theatre 541 Lincoln Rd	Miami Beach	FL	33139	305-673-3330	673-6749
Lyric Theater 819 NW 2nd Ave	Miami	FL	33136	305-358-1146	
Mahaffey Theater for the Performing Arts					
400 1st St S	Saint Petersburg	FL	33701	727-892-5798	892-5858
TF: 800-874-9015 ■ *Web:* www.mahaffeytheater.com					
Mann Barbara B Performing Arts Hall					
8099 College Pkwy SW	Fort Myers	FL	33919	239-489-3033	481-4620
TF: 800-440-7469 ■ *Web:* www.bbmannpah.com					
Marina Civic Center 8 Harrison Ave	Panama City	FL	32401	850-769-1217	785-5165
Web: www.marinaciviccenter.com					
Mary McLeod Bethune Performing Arts Center					
698 W International Speedway Blvd	Daytona Beach	FL	32114	386-481-2778	481-2927
Web: www.mmbcenter.com					
Miami-Dade County Auditorium 2901 W Flagler St	Miami	FL	33135	305-547-5414	541-7782
North Miami Beach/Julius Littman Performing Arts					
Theater 17011 NE 19th Ave	North Miami Beach	FL	33162	305-787-6005	787-6037
Ocean Center 101 N Atlantic Ave	Daytona Beach	FL	32118	386-254-4500	254-4512
TF: 800-858-6444 ■ *Web:* www.oceancenter.com					
Old School Square Cultural Arts Center 51 N Swinton Ave	Delray Beach	FL	33444	561-243-7922	243-7018
Web: www.oldschool.org					
Orlando Repertory Theatre 1001 E Princeton St	Orlando	FL	32803	407-896-7365	897-3284
Web: www.orlandorep.com					
Parker Playhouse 707 NE 8th St	Fort Lauderdale	FL	33304	954-764-1441	779-1160
Web: www.parkerplayhouse.com					
Peabody Auditorium 600 Auditorium Blvd	Daytona Beach	FL	32118	386-671-3460	671-3465
TF: 866-605-4276 ■ *Web:* www.peabodyauditorium.org					
Pensacola Civic Center 201 E Gregory St	Pensacola	FL	32502	850-432-0800	432-1707
Web: www.pensacolaciviccenter.com					
Pensacola Cultural Center 400 S Jefferson St	Pensacola	FL	32502	850-434-0257	438-2787
Web: www.pensacolalittletheatre.com					
Philharmonic Center for the Arts 5833 Pelican Bay Blvd	Naples	FL	34108	239-597-1111	597-8163
TF: 800-597-1900 ■ *Web:* www.thephil.org					
Phillips Curtis M Center for the Perofrming Arts					
315 Hull Rd	Gainesville	FL	32611	352-392-1900	392-3775
Web: www.cpa.ufl.edu					
Plaza Theatre 425 N Bumby Ave	Orlando	FL	32803	407-228-1220	228-4428
TF: 888-243-8849 ■ *Web:* www.theplazatheatre.com					
Pompano Beach Amphitheater NE 6th St & 18th Ave	Pompano Beach	FL	33060	954-946-2402	
Web: www.fantasma.com					
Raymond F Kravis Center for the Performing Arts					
701 Okeechobee Blvd	West Palm Beach	FL	33401	561-832-7469	833-0691*
**Fax:* Mktg ■ *TF:* 800-572-8471 ■ *Web:* www.kravis.org					
Red Barn Theatre 319 Duval St	Key West	FL	33040	305-296-9911	293-3035
Web: redbarntheater.com					
Ritz Theatre & La Villa Museum 829 N Davis St	Jacksonville	FL	32202	904-632-5555	632-5553
Ruth Eckerd Hall 1111 McMullen Booth Rd	Clearwater	FL	33759	727-791-7060	791-6020
TF: 800-875-8682 ■ *Web:* www.rutheckerdhall.com					
Saenger Theatre 118 S Palafox Pl	Pensacola	FL	32501	850-595-3880	595-3886
Web: www.pensacolasaenger.com					
Seaside Music Theater 221 Northbeach St	Daytona Beach	FL	32114	386-252-6200	252-1149
TF: 800-854-5592 ■ *Web:* www.seasidemusictheater.org					
Sound Advice Amphitheatre 601-7 Sansbury's Way	West Palm Beach	FL	33411	561-795-8883	795-6608
Web: www.soundadviceamp.com/index.php					
Sugden Community Theatre 701 5th Ave S	Naples	FL	34102	239-263-7990	434-7772
Web: www.naplesplayers.org					
Tallahassee-Leon County Civic Center 505 W Pensacola St	Tallahassee	FL	32301	850-487-1691	222-6947
TF: 800-322-3602 ■ *Web:* www.tlccc.org					
Tallahassee Little Theatre 1861 Thomasville Rd	Tallahassee	FL	32303	850-224-4597	224-4464
Web: www.tallahasseelittletheatre.org					
Tampa Bay Performing Arts Center 1010 N WC MacInnes Pl	Tampa	FL	33602	813-222-1000	222-1057
TF: 800-955-1045 ■ *Web:* www.tbpac.org					
Tampa Theater 711 N Franklin St	Tampa	FL	33602	813-274-8286	274-8978
Web: www.tampatheatre.org					
Tennessee Williams Theatre 5901 W College Rd	Key West	FL	33040	305-296-1520	292-3725
Web: www.tennesseewilliamstheatre.com					
University of West Florida Center for Fine & Performing Arts					
11000 University Pkwy Bldg 82	Pensacola	FL	32514	850-474-2541	857-6176
Web: uwf.edu/cfpa					
Van Wezel Performing Arts Center 777 N Tamiami Trail	Sarasota	FL	34236	941-953-3368	951-1449
TF: 800-826-9303 ■ *Web:* www.vanwezel.org					
Waterfront Playhouse Mallory Sq 310 Wall St	Key West	FL	33041	305-294-5015	294-0398
Web: www.waterfrontplayhouse.com					

Georgia

	City	State	ZIP	Phone	Fax
14th Street Playhouse 173 14th St	Atlanta	GA	30309	404-733-4750	733-4756
Academy Theatre 119 Center St	Avondale Estates	GA	30002	404-474-8332	
Web: www.academytheatre.org					
Boisfeuillet Jones Atlanta Civic Center 395 Piedmont Ave	Atlanta	GA	30308	404-523-6275	525-4634
Web: www.atlantaciviccenter.com					
Bradley Theater 1241 Broadway	Columbus	GA	31901	706-321-8425	321-9092
Douglass Theatre 355 ML King Jr Blvd	Macon	GA	31201	478-742-2000	742-0270
Web: www.douglasstheatre.org					
Fox Theatre 660 Peachtree St NE	Atlanta	GA	30308	404-881-2100	872-2972
Web: www.foxtheatre.org					
Georgia Mountains Center 301 Main St SW	Gainesville	GA	30501	770-534-8420	534-8425
Web: www.gainesville.org					
Grand Opera House 651 Mulberry St	Macon	GA	31201	478-301-5460	301-5469
Web: www2.mercer.edu/theGrand					
Gwinnett Center 6400 Sugarloaf Pkwy Bldg 100	Duluth	GA	30097	770-813-7500	813-7501
TF: 800-224-6422 ■ *Web:* www.gwinnettcenter.com					
Imperial Theatre 749 Broad St	Augusta	GA	30901	706-722-8293	312-1202
Web: www.imperialtheatre.com					
Macon City Auditorium 415 1st St	Macon	GA	31201	478-751-9152	751-9154
TF: 877-532-6144 ■ *Web:* www.maconcentreplex.com/auditorium					
Macon Little Theater 4220 Forsyth Rd	Macon	GA	31210	478-477-3342	471-8711
Web: www.maconlittletheatre.org					
Rialto Center for the Performing Arts 80 Forsyth St	Atlanta	GA	30303	404-413-9800	413-9801
Web: www.rialtocenter.org					
Robert W Woodruff Arts Center 1280 Peachtree St NE	Atlanta	GA	30309	404-733-4200	733-4281
Web: www.woodruff-arts.org					
Savannah Civic Center 301 W Oglethorp Ave	Savannah	GA	31401	912-651-6550	651-6552
TF: 800-351-7469 ■ *Web:* www.savannahcivic.com					
Spivey Hall					
Clayton College & State University 2000 Clayton State Blvd	Morrow	GA	30260	770-960-4200	
Web: www.spiveyhall.org					
Springer Opera House 103 10th St	Columbus	GA	31901	706-327-3688	324-4461
Web: www.springeroperahouse.org					
Townsend Center for the Performing Arts 1601 Maple St	Carrollton	GA	30118	678-839-4722	839-4804
Web: www.westga.edu/tcpa					
Woodruff Robert W Arts Center 1280 Peachtree St NE	Atlanta	GA	30309	404-733-4200	733-4281
Web: www.woodruff-arts.org					

Hawaii

	City	State	ZIP	Phone	Fax
Blaisdell Neal S Center 777 Ward Ave	Honolulu	HI	96814	808-527-5400	527-5433
Web: www.blaisdellcenter.com					
Neal S Blaisdell Center 777 Ward Ave	Honolulu	HI	96814	808-527-5400	527-5433
Web: www.blaisdellcenter.com					

Idaho

	City	State	ZIP	Phone	Fax
Idaho Falls Civic Auditorium 501 S Holmes Ave	Idaho Falls	ID	83401	208-612-8396	542-0476
Morrison Center for the Performing Arts					
2201 Campus Ln Boise State University	Boise	ID	83725	208-426-1609	426-3021
Web: mc.boisestate.edu					

Illinois

	City	State	ZIP	Phone	Fax
Apollo Fine Arts & Entertainment Centre 311 Main St	Peoria	IL	61602	309-673-4343	673-6052
Apollo Theater 2540 N Lincoln Ave	Chicago	IL	60614	773-935-6100	935-6214
Web: www.apollochicago.com					
Auditorium Theatre 50 E Congress Pkwy	Chicago	IL	60605	312-922-4046	431-2360
Web: www.auditoriumtheatre.org					
Bailiwick Arts Center 1229 W Belmont Ave	Chicago	IL	60657	773-883-1090	883-2017
Web: www.bailiwick.org					
Chicago Shakespeare Theater 800 E Grand Ave Navy Pier	Chicago	IL	60611	312-595-5600	595-5644
Web: www.chicagoshakes.com					
Civic Opera House 20 N Wacker Dr	Chicago	IL	60606	312-332-2244	332-8120
Web: www.lyricopera.org					
Coronado Theatre 314 N Main St	Rockford	IL	61101	815-968-2722	968-1318
Web: www.coronadopac.org					
Ford Center for the Performing Arts/Oriental Theatre					
24 W Randolph St	Chicago	IL	60601	312-977-1700	977-0517
Web: www.broadwayinchicago.com					
Goodman Theatre 170 N Dearborn St	Chicago	IL	60601	312-443-3811	443-3821
Web: www.goodman-theatre.org					
Krannert Center for the Performing Arts 500 S Goodwin Ave	Urbana	IL	61801	217-333-6700	244-0810
TF: 800-527-2849 ■ *Web:* www.krannertcenter.com					
Lifeline Theatre 6912 N Glenwood Ave	Chicago	IL	60626	773-761-1772	761-4582
Web: www.lifelinetheatre.com					
Marriott Theatre in Lincolnshire 10 Marriott Dr	Lincolnshire	IL	60069	847-634-0200	634-7022
Web: www.marriotttheatre.com					
Muni The 815 E Lake Dr	Springfield	IL	62707	217-793-6864	
Web: www.themini.org					
North Shore Center for the Performing Arts in Skokie					
9501 Skokie Blvd	Skokie	IL	60077	847-673-6300	679-1879
Web: www.northshorecenter.org					

				Phone	Fax
Paramount Theatre 23 E Galena Blvd	Aurora	IL	60506	630-896-7676	892-1084
Web: www.paramountarts.com					
Parkland College Theatre 2400 W Bradley Ave	Champaign	IL	61821	217-351-2528	373-3899
TF: 800-346-8089 ■ *Web:* www.parkland.edu/theatre					
Peoria Civic Center 201 SW Jefferson St	Peoria	IL	61602	309-673-8900	673-9223
Web: www.peoriaciviccenter.com					
Rosemont Theatre 5400 N River Rd	Rosemont	IL	60018	847-671-5100	671-6405
Web: www.rosemont.com/visiting/theatre.shtml					
Royal George Theatre Center 1641 N Halsted St	Chicago	IL	60614	312-988-9105	988-4027
Web: www.theroyalgeorgetheatre.com					
Springfield Theatre Centre 420 S 6th St	Springfield	IL	62701	217-523-0878	523-4895
Station Theatre 223 N Broadway Ave	Urbana	IL	61801	217-384-4000	
Web: www.stationtheatre.com					
Steppenwolf Theatre 1650 N Halsted St	Chicago	IL	60614	312-335-1888	335-0808
Web: www.steppenwolf.org					
Symphony Center 220 S Michigan Ave	Chicago	IL	60604	312-294-3000	294-3035*
*Fax: Mktg ■ *TF:* 800-223-7114					
Virginia Theatre 203 W Park Ave	Champaign	IL	61820	217-356-9053	356-5729
Web: www.thevirginia.org					

Indiana

				Phone	Fax
American Cabaret Theatre 401 E Michigan St	Indianapolis	IN	46204	317-631-0334	686-5443
Web: www.actindy.org					
Christel DeHaan Fine Arts Center 1400 E Hanna Ave University of Indianapolis	Indianapolis	IN	46227	317-788-3566	788-3383
TF: 800-232-8634 ■ *Web:* arts.uindy.edu					
DeHaan Christel Fine Arts Center 1400 E Hanna Ave University of Indianapolis	Indianapolis	IN	46227	317-788-3566	788-3383
TF: 800-232-8634 ■ *Web:* arts.uindy.edu					
Embassy Theatre 125 W Jefferson Blvd	Fort Wayne	IN	46802	260-424-6287	424-4806
Web: www.embassycentre.org					
Evansville Auditorium & Convention Center 715 Locust St	Evansville	IN	47708	812-435-5770	435-5500
Web: www.smgevansville.com/centre/centre.html					
Evansville Civic Theatre 717 N Fulton St	Evansville	IN	47710	812-423-2616	423-2616
Web: www.civic.evansville.net					
Hilbert Circle Theatre 45 Monument Cir	Indianapolis	IN	46204	317-262-1110	262-1159
Web: indianapolissymphony.org/hilbert					
Indiana Repertory Theatre 140 W Washington St	Indianapolis	IN	46204	317-635-5277	236-0767
Web: www.indianarep.com					
Indiana University Auditorium 1211 E 7th St	Bloomington	IN	47405	812-855-1103	855-4244
Web: www.iuauditorium.com					
Indianapolis Artsgarden Above the intersection of Washington & Illinois St	Indianapolis	IN	46204	317-624-2563	624-2564
Web: www.indyarts.org					
Madame Walker Theatre Center 617 Indiana Ave	Indianapolis	IN	46202	317-236-2099	236-2097
Web: www.walkertheatre.com					
Moreau Center for the Arts St Mary's College	Notre Dame	IN	46556	574-284-4625	284-4784
Morris Performing Arts Center 211 N Michigan St	South Bend	IN	46601	574-235-9190	235-5945
TF: 800-537-6415 ■ *Web:* www.morriscenter.org					
Murat Centre 502 N New Jersey St	Indianapolis	IN	46204	317-231-0000	231-9410
Web: www.murat.com					
South Bend Civic Theatre 211 W Madison PO Box 1146	South Bend	IN	46624	574-234-1112	288-3412
Web: www.sbct.org					
Victory Theatre 600 Main St	Evansville	IN	47708	812-435-6287	435-6299
Warren Performing Arts Center 9500 E 16th St	Indianapolis	IN	46229	317-532-6280	532-6440
Web: wchs.warren.k12.in.us/performingarts					

Iowa

				Phone	Fax
Civic Center of Greater Des Moines 221 Walnut St	Des Moines	IA	50309	515-243-0766	246-2305
Web: www.civiccenter.org					
Grand Opera House 135 W 8th St	Dubuque	IA	52001	563-588-1305	588-3497
Web: www.thegrandoperahouse.com					
Paramount Theatre 123 3rd Ave SE	Cedar Rapids	IA	52401	319-398-5211	362-2102
Web: www.uscellularcenter.com/theatre_info					
RiverCenter Adler Theatre 136 E 3rd St	Davenport	IA	52801	563-326-8500	326-8505
Web: www.rivorotr.com					

Kansas

				Phone	Fax
Century II Convention Center 225 W Douglas Ave	Wichita	KS	67202	316-264-9121	303-8688
Web: www.century2.org					
Helen Hocker Theater Center for the Performing Arts 700 SW Zoo Pkwy Gage Park	Topeka	KS	66606	785-368-0191	
Orpheum Performing Arts Centre 200 N Broadway Suite 102	Wichita	KS	67202	316-263-0884	263-8641
Web: www.wichitaorpheum.com					
Sandstone Amphitheater 633 N 130th St	Bonner Springs	KS	66012	913-721-3400	
Topeka Performing Arts Center 214 SE 8th Ave	Topeka	KS	66603	785-234-2787	234-2307
Web: www.tpactix.org					
Wichita Center for the Arts 9112 E Central Ave	Wichita	KS	67206	316-634-2787	634-0593
Web: www.wcfta.com					
Wichita Community Theatre 258 N Fountain St	Wichita	KS	67208	316-686-1282	652-0531
Web: www.wichitacommunitytheatre.com					

Kentucky

				Phone	Fax
Kentucky Center for the Arts 501 W Main St	Louisville	KY	40202	502-562-0100	562-0150
Web: www.kentuckycenter.org					
Kentucky Theater 214 E Main St	Lexington	KY	40507	859-231-7924	231-7924
Web: www.kentuckytheater.com					
Lexington Opera House 401 W Short St	Lexington	KY	40507	859-233-4567	253-2718
Web: www.lexingtonoperahouse.com					
Louisville Palace 625 S 4th St	Louisville	KY	40202	502-583-4555	583-9955
Web: www.louisvillepalace.com					

Louisiana

				Phone	Fax
Baton Rouge Little Theater 7155 Florida Blvd	Baton Rouge	LA	70806	225-924-6496	924-9972
Web: www.brlt.org					
Baton Rouge River Center 275 S River Rd	Baton Rouge	LA	70802	225-389-3030	389-4954
Web: www.brrivercenter.com					
Contemporary Arts Center 900 Camp St	New Orleans	LA	70130	504-528-3805	528-3828
Web: www.cacno.org					
East Bank Theatre 630 Barksdale Blvd	Bossier City	LA	71111	318-741-8310	741-8312
Web: bossierarts.org/ebt.asp					
Heymann Performing Arts Center 1373 S College Rd	Lafayette	LA	70503	337-291-5540	291-5580
Web: www.heymann-center.com					
Lake Charles Civic Center 900 Lakeshore Dr	Lake Charles	LA	70601	337-491-1256	491-1534
Web: www.lakecharlesciviccenter.bigstep.com					
Monroe Civic Center 401 Lea Joyner Expy	Monroe	LA	71201	318-329-2225	329-2548
Preservation Hall 726 Saint Peter St	New Orleans	LA	70116	504-522-2841	558-9192
TF: 888-946-5299 ■ *Web:* www.preservationhall.com					
Shaver Theater Louisiana State Univ Music & Dramatic Arts Bldg	Baton Rouge	LA	70803	225-578-4174	578-4135
Web: www.theatre.lsu.edu/prod_venues/shaver.htm					
Shreveport Civic Theatre 600 Clyde Fant Pkwy	Shreveport	LA	71101	318-673-5100	673-5105
Shreveport Little Theatre 812 Margaret Pl	Shreveport	LA	71101	318-424-4439	424-4440
Web: www.shreveportlittletheatre.org					
Strand Theatre 619 Louisiana Ave	Shreveport	LA	71101	318-226-1481	424-5434
TF: 800-313-6373 ■ *Web:* www.thestrandtheatre.com					
Theatre of Performing Arts 4005 Lakeshore Dr	Shreveport	LA	71109	318-525-0740	525-0720

Maine

				Phone	Fax
Criterion Theatre 35 Cottage St	Bar Harbor	ME	04609	207-288-9441	
Web: www.criteriontheater.com					
Cumberland County Civic Center 1 Civic Center Sq	Portland	ME	04101	207-775-3481	828-8344
Web: www.theciviccenter.com					
Maine Center for the Arts 5746 Maine Center for the Arts University of Maine	Orono	ME	04469	207-581-1804	581-1837
Web: www.ume.maine.edu/~mca					
Merrill Auditorium 20 Myrtle St	Portland	ME	04101	207-874-8200	874-8130
Web: www.portlandevents.com/Merrill.htm					

Manitoba

				Phone	Fax
Burton Cummings Theatre 364 Smith St	Winnipeg	MB	R3B2H2	204-956-5656	956-2581
Web: www.burtoncummingstheatre.com					
Lyric Theatre 55 Pavilion Crescent	Winnipeg	MB	R3P2N6	204-888-5466	889-8136
Web: www.partnersinthepark.org					

Maryland

				Phone	Fax
Annapolis Summer Garden Theatre 143 Compromise St	Annapolis	MD	21401	410-268-9212	
Web: www.summergarden.com					
Chesapeake Arts Center 194 Hammonds Ln	Brooklyn Park	MD	21225	410-636-6597	636-9653
Web: www.chesapeakearts.org					
Everyman Theatre 1727 N Charles St	Baltimore	MD	21201	410-752-2208	752-5891
Web: www.everymantheatre.org					
France-Merrick Performing Arts Center 12 N Eutaw St	Baltimore	MD	21201	410-837-7400	837-7410
Web: www.france-merrickpac.com					
Gordon Center for Performing Arts 3506 Gwynnbrook Ave	Owings Mills	MD	21117	410-356-7469	356-7605
Web: www.gordoncenter.com					
Joseph Meyerhoff Symphony Hall 1212 Cathedral St	Baltimore	MD	21201	410-783-8100	783-8077
TF: 800-442-1198					
Lyric Opera House 140 W Mt Royal Ave	Baltimore	MD	21201	410-685-5086	332-8234
Web: www.lyricoperahouse.com					
Maryland Hall for the Creative Arts 801 Chase St	Annapolis	MD	21401	410-263-5544	263-5114
TF: 866-438-3808 ■ *Web:* www.mdhallarts.org					
Maryland Theatre 21-27 S Potomac St	Hagerstown	MD	21740	301-790-3500	791-6114
Web: www.mdtheatre.org					
Merriweather Post Pavilion 10475 Little Patuxent Parkway	Columbia	MD	21044	410-715-5550	715-5560
Web: www.merriweathermusic.com					
Meyerhoff Joseph Symphony Hall 1212 Cathedral St	Baltimore	MD	21201	410-783-8100	783-8077
TF: 800-442-1198					
Pumpkin Theatre 8415 Bellona Lane Ruxton Towers Suite 115	Baltimore	MD	21204	410-828-1645	828-1954
Web: www.pumpkintheatre.com					
Recher Theatre 512 York Rd	Towson	MD	21204	410-337-7178	321-8175
Web: www.rechertheatre.com					

Massachusetts

				Phone	Fax
Bank of America Pavilion 290 Northern Ave	Boston	MA	02210	617-728-1600	737-2292
Web: www.bankofamericapavilion.com					
Berklee Performance Center 136 Massachusetts Ave	Boston	MA	02115	617-747-2261	375-9228
Web: www.berkleebpc.com					
Boston Center for the Arts 539 Tremont St	Boston	MA	02116	617-426-5000	426-5336
Web: www.bcaonline.org					
Boston Symphony Hall 301 Massachusetts Ave	Boston	MA	02115	617-266-1492	638-9367
Web: www.bso.org/symphonyhallhome.jhtml					
Charles Playhouse 74 Warrenton St	Boston	MA	02116	617-426-6912	695-1230
Web: broadwayacrossamerica.com					
Colonial Theatre 106 Boylston St	Boston	MA	02116	617-426-9366	880-2449
Web: broadwayacrossamerica.com					
Cutler Majestic Theatre at Emerson College 219 Tremont St	Boston	MA	02116	617-824-8000	824-8725
Web: www.maj.org					
Mechanics Hall 321 Main St	Worcester	MA	01608	508-752-5608	754-8442
Web: www.mechanicshall.org					
Shubert Theatre 265 Tremont St	Boston	MA	02116	617-482-9393	451-1436
South Shore Music Circus 130 Sohier St	Cohasset	MA	02025	781-383-9850	383-9804
Web: www.musiccircus.com					
Stuart Street Playhouse 200 Stuart St	Boston	MA	02116	617-457-2618	
Web: www.stuartstreetplayhouse.com					
Tweeter Center 885 S Main St	Mansfield	MA	02048	508-339-2331	339-0550
Web: www.tweetercenter.com/boston					
Wang Center for the Performing Arts Inc 270 Tremont St	Boston	MA	02116	617-482-9393	451-1436
Web: www.wangcenter.org					
Wilbur Theatre 246 Tremont St	Boston	MA	02116	617-423-4008	423-3054
Web: broadwayacrossamerica.com					

Michigan

				Phone	Fax
Ann Arbor Civic Theatre 322 W Ann St	Ann Arbor	MI	48104	734-971-2228	971-2769
Web: www.a2ct.org					
Buckham Alley Theatre 512 Buckham Alley	Flint	MI	48502	810-964-0791	
Web: www.buckhamtheatre.com					
Chenery Auditorium 714 S Westnedge Ave	Kalamazoo	MI	49007	269-337-0424	337-0490

Michigan (Cont'd)

				Phone	Fax
Circle Theatre 1607 Robinson Rd SE Brink Hall *Web:* www.circletheatre.org	Grand Rapids	MI	49506	616-632-1980	456-8540
Detroit Opera House 1526 Broadway *Web:* www.michiganopera.org	Detroit	MI	48226	313-961-3500	237-3412
Detroit Symphony Orchestra Hall 3711 Woodward Ave *Web:* www.detroitsymphony.com	Detroit	MI	48201	313-576-5100	576-5101
Dow Event Center 303 Johnson St *Web:* www.doweventcenter.com	Saginaw	MI	48607	989-759-1320	759-1322
Fisher Theatre 3011 W Grand Blvd *Web:* www.nederlanderdetroit.com/fisher	Detroit	MI	48202	313-872-1000	872-0632
Fox Theatre 2211 Woodward Ave *Web:* www.olympiaentertainment.com	Detroit	MI	48201	313-983-6611	
Gem Theatre 333 Madison Ave *Web:* www.gemtheatre.com	Detroit	MI	48226	313-963-9800	963-0873
Grand Rapids Civic Theatre 30 N Division Ave *TF:* 866-455-4728 ■ *Web:* www.grct.org	Grand Rapids	MI	49503	616-222-6650	222-6660
Interlochen Center for the Arts PO Box 199 *Web:* www.interlochen.org	Interlochen	MI	49643	231-276-7200	276-7444
Kellogg WK Auditorium 60 W Van Buren St	Battle Creek	MI	49017	269-965-9670	965-9672
Kerrytown Concert House 415 N 4th Ave *Web:* kerrytownconcerthouse.com	Ann Arbor	MI	48104	734-769-2999	769-7791
Majestic Theatre 4140 Woodward Ave *Web:* www.majesticdetroit.com	Detroit	MI	48201	313-833-9700	833-1213
Masonic Temple Theatre 500 Temple St *Web:* www.themasonic.com	Detroit	MI	48201	313-832-5900	832-1047
Michigan Theater 603 E Liberty St *Web:* michtheater.org	Ann Arbor	MI	48104	734-668-8397	668-7136
Midland Center for the Arts Inc 1801 W St Andrews Rd *Web:* www.mcfta.org	Midland	MI	48640	989-631-5930	631-7890
Millennium Centre 15600 JL Hudson Dr *Web:* www.millenniumcentre.net	Southfield	MI	48075	248-796-5191	796-5199
Music Hall Center for the Performing Arts 350 Madison Ave *Web:* www.musichall.org	Detroit	MI	48226	313-963-7622	887-8502
Power Center for the Performing Arts 121 Fletcher Ct	Ann Arbor	MI	48109	734-763-3333	
Riverside Arts Center 76 N Huron St *Web:* www.riversidearts.org	Ypsilanti	MI	48197	734-480-2787	
Riverwalk Theatre 228 Museum Dr *Web:* riverwalktheatre.com	Lansing	MI	48933	517-482-5700	482-9812
Second City Detroit 42705 Grand River Ave *Web:* www.secondcity.com	Novi	MI	48375	248-348-4448	348-3622
State Theatre 2115 Woodward Ave *Web:* www.statetheatredetroit.com	Detroit	MI	48201	313-961-5451	965-2808
University of Michigan - Flint Theater 303 E Kearsley St	Flint	MI	48502	810-762-3230	766-6630
Wharton Center for the Performing Arts Michigan State University *TF:* 800-942-7866 ■ *Web:* www.whartoncenter.com	East Lansing	MI	48824	517-432-2000	353-5329
Whiting Auditorium 1241 E Kearsley St *TF:* 888-823-6837 ■ *Web:* thewhiting.com	Flint	MI	48503	810-237-7333	237-7335
WK Kellogg Auditorium 60 W Van Buren St	Battle Creek	MI	49017	269-965-9670	965-9672

Minnesota

				Phone	Fax
Duluth Playhouse 506 W Michigan St *Web:* www.duluthplayhouse.org	Duluth	MN	55802	218-733-7555	733-7554
Fitzgerald Theater 10 E Exchange St *Web:* fitzgeraldtheater.publicradio.org	Saint Paul	MN	55101	651-290-1200	290-1195
Great American History Theatre 30 E 10th St *Web:* www.historytheatre.com	Saint Paul	MN	55101	651-292-4323	292-4322
Guthrie Theater 818 S 2nd St *TF:* 877-447-8243 ■ *Web:* www.guthrietheater.org	Minneapolis	MN	55415	612-225-6000	225-6004
Historic Orpheum Theatre 910 Hennepin Ave	Minneapolis	MN	55403	612-339-0075	339-4146
Historic Pantages Theatre 710 Hennepin Ave *Web:* www.hennepintheatredistrict.org	Minneapolis	MN	55403	612-339-0075	339-4146
Historic State Theatre 805 Hennepin Ave	Minneapolis	MN	55403	612-339-0075	339-4146
Jungle Theater 2951 Lindale Ave S *Web:* www.jungletheater.com	Minneapolis	MN	55408	612-822-7063	822-9408
MacPhail Center for the Arts 501 S 2nd St *Web:* www.macphail.org	Minneapolis	MN	55401	612-321-0100	321-9740
Mayo Civic Center 30 Civic Center Dr SE *TF:* 800-422-2199 ■ *Web:* www.mayociviccenter.com	Rochester	MN	55904	507-281-6184	281-6277
Midwest Wireless Civic Center 1 Civic Ctr Plaza *Web:* www.midwestwirelesscenter.com	Mankato	MN	56001	507-389-3000	345-1627
Music Box Theatre 1407 Nicollet Ave	Minneapolis	MN	55403	612-871-1414	874-8987
Northrop Memorial Auditorium 84 Church St SE 105 Northrop Auditorium *Web:* www.northrop.umn.edu	Minneapolis	MN	55455	612-625-6600	626-1750
Orchestra Hall 1111 Nicollet Mall *Web:* www.minnesotaorchestra.org/orchestra_hall	Minneapolis	MN	55403	612-371-5600	371-0838
Ordway Center for the Performing Arts 345 Washington St *Web:* www.ordway.org	Saint Paul	MN	55102	651-224-4222	282-3160
Penumbra Theatre 270 N Kent St *Web:* www.penumbratheatre.org	Saint Paul	MN	55102	651-224-3180	288-6789
Reif Center 720 Conifer Dr *Web:* www.reifcenter.org	Grand Rapids	MN	55744	218-327-5780	327-5798
Renegade Comedy Theatre 222 E Superior St *TF:* 888-722-6627 ■ *Web:* www.renegadecomedy.org	Duluth	MN	55802	218-722-6775	
Rochester Civic Theatre 20 Civic Center Dr SE *Web:* www.rochestercivictheatre.org	Rochester	MN	55904	507-282-8481	282-0608

Mississippi

				Phone	Fax
Alamo Theater 333 N Farish St	Jackson	MS	39202	601-352-3365	
Lyric Theatre 200 N Broadway *Web:* www.tctwebstage.com/lyric.htm	Tupelo	MS	38804	662-844-1935	844-0221
Mara Thalia Hall 255 E Pascagoula St *Web:* www.thaliamara.org	Jackson	MS	39201	601-960-1537	960-1583
Saenger Theatre for the Performing Arts 170 Reynoir St	Biloxi	MS	39530	228-435-6290	435-6211
Thalia Mara Hall 255 E Pascagoula St *Web:* www.thaliamara.org	Jackson	MS	39201	601-960-1537	960-1583

Missouri

				Phone	Fax
American Heartland Theatre 2450 Grand Blvd Suite 314 *Web:* ahtkc.com	Kansas City	MO	64108	816-842-0202	842-1881
Andy Williams Moon River Theatre 2500 W Hwy 76 *TF:* 800-666-6094 ■ *Web:* www.andywilliams.com	Branson	MO	65616	417-334-4500	337-9627
Branson Mall Music Theatre 2206 W Hwy 76	Branson	MO	65616	417-339-3939	334-5421
Champagne Theatre 1984 State Hwy 165 Welk Resort Center *TF:* 800-734-5515	Branson	MO	65616	417-337-7469	334-7744
Coterie Theatre 2450 Grand Blvd Suite 144 *Web:* www.thecoterie.com	Kansas City	MO	64108	816-474-6552	474-7112
Folly Theater 300 W 12th St *Web:* www.follytheater.com	Kansas City	MO	64105	816-474-4444	842-8709
Fox Theatre 539 N Grand Blvd Suite 300 *TF:* 800-293-5949 ■ *Web:* www.fabulousfox.com	Saint Louis	MO	63103	314-534-1678	534-1678
Gem Theater Cultural & Performing Arts Center 1615 E 18th St	Kansas City	MO	64108	816-474-6262	474-0074
Hammons Juanita K Hall for the Performing Arts 525 S John Q Hammons Pkwy *TF:* 888-476-7849 ■ *Web:* www.hammonshall.com	Springfield	MO	65806	417-836-6776	836-6891
Jim Stafford Theatre 3440 W Hwy 76 *TF:* 800-677-8533 ■ *Web:* www.jimstafford.com	Branson	MO	65616	417-335-8080	335-2643
Juanita K Hammons Hall for the Performing Arts 525 S John Q Hammons Pkwy *TF:* 888-476-7849 ■ *Web:* www.hammonshall.com	Springfield	MO	65806	417-836-6776	836-6891
Kansas City Music Hall 201 W 13th St *TF:* 800-821-7060	Kansas City	MO	64105	816-513-5000	513-5001
Legends Theater 3216 W Hwy 76 *TF:* 800-374-7469 ■ *Web:* www.legendsbranson.com	Branson	MO	65616	417-339-3003	332-2305
Lyric Theatre 1029 Central St *Web:* www.kc-opera.org	Kansas City	MO	64105	816-471-4933	471-0619
Macklanburg Playhouse 100 Willis Ave Stephens College Campus	Columbia	MO	65215	573-876-7199	876-7248
Maplewood Barn Community Theatre Nifong Blvd Nifong Park *Web:* www.maplewoodbarn.com	Columbia	MO	65201	573-449-7517	
Midland Theatre 1228 Main St	Kansas City	MO	64105	816-471-9703	221-1127
Missouri Theatre Center for the Arts 203 S 9th St *Web:* www.missouritheatre.com	Columbia	MO	65201	573-875-0600	449-4214
Muny Musical Theater Forest Park *Web:* www.muny.com	Saint Louis	MO	63112	314-361-1900	361-0009
Powell Symphony Hall 718 N Grand Blvd *TF:* 800-232-1880 ■ *Web:* www.saintlouissymphony.org	Saint Louis	MO	63103	314-533-2500	286-4142
Quality Hill Playhouse 303 W 10th St *Web:* www.qualityhillplayhouse.com	Kansas City	MO	64105	816-421-1700	221-6556
Remington Theatre 3701 W Hwy 76 *TF:* 800-884-4536 ■ *Web:* www.thegrandpalace.com/remington.asp	Branson	MO	65616	417-336-1220	339-3787
Rhynsburger Theatre 129 Fine Arts Building University of Missouri-Columbia Campus	Columbia	MO	65211	573-882-7529	884-4034
Roberts Orpheum Theater 416 N 9th St *Web:* www.robertsorpheum.com	Saint Louis	MO	63101	314-588-0388	588-9828
Shepherd of the Hills Homestead & Outdoor Theatre 5586 W Hwy 76 *TF:* 800-653-6288 ■ *Web:* www.branson.com/branson/shepherd/shepherd.htm	Branson	MO	65616	417-334-4191	334-4617
Stafford Jim Theatre 3440 W Hwy 76 *TF:* 800-677-8533 ■ *Web:* www.jimstafford.com	Branson	MO	65616	417-335-8080	335-2643
Stained Glass Theatre 1996 W Evangel *Web:* www.sgtheatre.com	Ozark	MO	65721	417-581-9192	485-2282
Starlight Entertainment 3115 W Hwy 76 *TF:* 800-468-6648	Branson	MO	65616	417-337-9333	337-5766
Starlight Theatre 4600 Starlight Rd Swope Park *Web:* www.kcstarlight.com	Kansas City	MO	64132	816-363-7827	361-6398
UMB Bank Pavilion 14141 Riverport Dr *Web:* www.riverport.com	Maryland Heights	MO	63043	314-298-9944	291-4719
Unicorn Theatre 3828 Main St *Web:* www.unicorntheatre.org	Kansas City	MO	64111	816-531-7529	531-0421

Montana

				Phone	Fax
Alberta Bair Theater for the Performing Arts 2722 3rd Ave N Suite 200 *TF:* 877-321-2074 ■ *Web:* albertabairtheater.org	Billings	MT	59101	406-256-8915	256-5060
Billings Studio Theatre 1500 Rimrock Rd *Web:* www.billingsstudiotheatre.org	Billings	MT	59102	406-248-1141	248-1576
Grand Street Theater 325 N Park Ave *Web:* www.grandstreet.net	Helena	MT	59601	406-442-4270	447-1573
Helena Civic Center 340 Neill Ave *Web:* www.ci.helena.mt.us/index.php?id=279	Helena	MT	59601	406-447-8492	447-8480
Mansfield Theater 2 Park Dr S	Great Falls	MT	59401	406-455-8510	455-8518

Nebraska

				Phone	Fax
Blue Barn Theatre 614 S 11th St *Web:* www.bluebarn.org	Omaha	NE	68102	402-345-1576	
Creighton University Mainstage & Studio Theatre 2500 California Plaza *Fax: Hum Res	Omaha	NE	68178	402-280-2700	280-2320*
Lied Center for Performing Arts 301 N 12th St *TF:* 800-432-3231 ■ *Web:* www.unl.edu/lied	Lincoln	NE	68588	402-472-4700	472-2725
Lincoln Community Playhouse 2500 S 56th St *Web:* www.lincolnplayhouse.com	Lincoln	NE	68506	402-489-7529	489-1035
Omaha Community Playhouse 6915 Cass St *TF:* 888-782-4338 ■ *Web:* www.omahaplayhouse.com	Omaha	NE	68132	402-553-0800	553-6288
Orpheum Theatre 409 S 16th St *Web:* www.omahaperformingarts.org	Omaha	NE	68102	402-345-0202	345-0222
Pershing Center 226 Centennial Mall S *Web:* www.pershingcenter.com	Lincoln	NE	68508	402-441-8744	441-7913

Nevada

				Phone	Fax
Artemus W Ham Concert Hall 4505 Maryland Pkwy *Web:* pac.nevada.edu	Las Vegas	NV	89154	702-895-3535	895-4714
Brewery Arts Center 449 W King St *Web:* www.breweryarts.org	Carson City	NV	89703	775-883-1976	883-1922
Ham Artemus W Concert Hall 4505 Maryland Pkwy *Web:* pac.nevada.edu	Las Vegas	NV	89154	702-895-3535	895-4714
Reed Whipple Cultural Arts Center 821 Las Vegas Blvd N	Las Vegas	NV	89101	702-229-6211	382-5199
University of Nevada Las Vegas Performing Arts Center 4505 Maryland Pkwy Box 455005 *Web:* pac.nevada.edu	Las Vegas	NV	89154	702-895-2787	895-4714
Whipple Reed Cultural Arts Center 821 Las Vegas Blvd N	Las Vegas	NV	89101	702-229-6211	382-5199

New Hampshire

				Phone	Fax
Capitol Center for the Arts 44 S Main St *Web:* www.ccanh.com	Concord	NH	03301	603-225-1111	224-3408

				Phone	Fax
Hopkins Center for the Arts 4 E Wheelock St	Hanover	NH	03755	603-646-2422	646-1375
Web: www.hop.dartmouth.edu					
Palace Theatre 80 Hanover St	Manchester	NH	03101	603-668-5588	668-5804
Web: palacetheatre.org					

New Jersey

				Phone	Fax
Count Basie Theatre 99 Monmouth St	Red Bank	NJ	07701	732-842-9000	842-9323
Web: www.countbasietheatre.org					
Dante Hall Theater of the Arts 14 N Mississippi Ave	Atlantic City	NJ	08401	609-344-8877	344-8878
Web: www.dantehall.org					
McCarter Theatre 91 University Pl	Princeton	NJ	08540	609-258-6500	497-0369
Web: www.mccarter.org					
Mill Hill Playhouse 205 E Front St	Trenton	NJ	08608	609-989-3038	989-4290
New Jersey Performing Arts Center 1 Center St	Newark	NJ	07102	973-642-8989	648-6724
TF: 888-466-5722 ■ *Web:* njpac.org					
Newark Symphony Hall 1020 Broad St	Newark	NJ	07102	973-643-8009	
Web: www.newarksymphonyhall.org					
Patriots Theater Memorial Dr	Trenton	NJ	08608	609-984-8484	777-0581
Web: www.thewarmemorial.com					
PNC Bank Art Center PO Box 144	Holmdel	NJ	07733	732-203-2500	335-8637
Web: www.artscenter.com					
State Theatre 15 Livingston Ave	New Brunswick	NJ	08901	732-247-7200	247-4005
TF: 877-782-8311 ■ *Web:* www.statetheatrenj.org					
Stockton Performing Arts Center					
Jimmie Leeds Rd PO Box 195 Richard Stockton College	Pomona	NJ	08240	609-652-9000	626-5523
Web: loki.stockton.edu/pac					

New Mexico

				Phone	Fax
Adobe Theater 9813 4th St NW	Albuquerque	NM	87107	505-898-9222	
Web: www.adobetheater.com					
Albuquerque Little Theatre 224 San Pasquale SW	Albuquerque	NM	87104	505-242-4750	843-9489
Web: www.albuquerquelittletheatre.org					
Armory of the Arts Theatre 1050 Old Pecos Trail	Santa Fe	NM	87505	505-982-7992	982-7993
Web: www.sfperformingarts.org					
Flickinger Center for Performing Arts 1110 New York Ave	Alamogordo	NM	88310	505-437-2202	434-0067
Web: www.zianet.com/flickinger					
Greer Garson Theatre Center					
1600 St Michael's Dr College of Santa Fe	Santa Fe	NM	87505	505-473-6511	473-6016
Web: www.garsontheatrecompany.org					
KiMo Theater 423 Central Ave NW	Albuquerque	NM	87102	505-768-3522	768-3542
Web: www.cabq.gov/kimo					
Las Cruces Community Theater PO Box 1281	Las Cruces	NM	88004	505-523-1200	525-0015
Web: www.lcctnm.org					
Lensic Performing Arts Center 211 W San Francisco St	Santa Fe	NM	87501	505-988-7050	988-4370
Web: www.lensic.com					
Popejoy Hall					
UNM Public Events 1 Univ of New Mexico MSC 04 2580	Albuquerque	NM	87131	505-277-3824	277-7353
Web: www.popejoyhall.com					
Santa Fe Playhouse 142 E DeVargas St	Santa Fe	NM	87501	505-988-4262	820-1922
Web: www.santafeplayhouse.org					

New York

				Phone	Fax
Alleyway Theatre 1 Curtain Up Alley	Buffalo	NY	14202	716-852-2600	852-2266
Web: alleyway.com/alleyway/					
Apollo Theatre 253 W 125th St	New York	NY	10027	212-531-5300	749-2743
Web: www.apollotheatre.com					
Artpark 450 S 4th St	Lewiston	NY	14092	716-754-9000	754-2741
TF: 800-659-7275 ■ *Web:* www.artpark.net					
Avery Fisher Hall W 65th St & Broadway	New York	NY	10023	212-875-5030	875-5027
Brooklyn Academy of Music 30 Lafayette Ave	Brooklyn	NY	11217	718-636-4111	636-4179
Web: www.bam.org					
Brooklyn Center for the Performing Arts 2900 Campus Rd	Brooklyn	NY	11210	718-951-4600	951-4343
Web: www.brooklyncenter.com					
Capitol Theatre 149 Westchester Ave	Port Chester	NY	10573	914-934-9362	
Web: www.thecapitoltheatre.net					
Carnegie Hall 881 7th Ave	New York	NY	10019	212-247-7800	581-6539
Web: www.carnegiehall.org					
Center for the Arts					
103 Center for the Arts North Campus University at Buffalo	Buffalo	NY	14260	716-645-2787	645-6973
Web: www.arts.buffalo.edu					
City Center 130 W 56th St	New York	NY	10019	212-247-0430	246-9778
Web: www.nycitycenter.org					
Eastman Theatre 26 Gibbs St	Rochester	NY	14604	585-274-1110	274-1067
Web: www.rochester.edu/eastman					
Egg The					
Empire State Plaza Concourse Level Performing Arts Center	Albany	NY	12220	518-473-1845	473-1848
Web: www.theegg.org					
Emelin Theater 153 Library Ln	Mamaroneck	NY	10543	914-698-0098	698-1404
Web: www.emelin.org					
Geva Theatre Center 75 Woodbury Blvd	Rochester	NY	14607	585-232-1366	232-4031
Web: www.gevatheatre.org					
Kavinoky Theatre 320 Porter Ave	Buffalo	NY	14201	716-881-7668	829-7790
Web: www.kavinokytheatre.com					
Kleinhans Music Hall 3 Symphony Cir	Buffalo	NY	14201	716-883-3560	883-7430
Web: www.kleinhansmusichall.org					
Landmark Theatre 362 S Salina St	Syracuse	NY	13202	315-475-7980	475-7993
Web: www.landmarktheatre.org					
Lehman Center for the Performing Arts Inc					
250 Bedford Park Blvd W	Bronx	NY	10468	718-960-8232	960-8233
Web: www.lehmancenter.org					
Lincoln Center for the Performing Arts					
70 Lincoln Center Plaza	New York	NY	10023	212-875-5223	875-5242
Web: www.lincolncenter.org					
Lucille Lortel Theatre 121 Christopher St	New York	NY	10014	212-924-2817	989-0036
Web: www.lortel.org/llt_theater					
Manhattan Center Studios 311 W 34th St	New York	NY	10001	212-695-6600	564-1092
Web: www.mcstudios.com					
Mid-Hudson Civic Center 14 Civic Center Plaza	Poughkeepsie	NY	12601	845-454-9800	454-5877
Web: www.midhudsonciviccenter.com					
New Phoenix Theatre 95 Johnson Park	Buffalo	NY	14201	716-853-1334	
New York State Theater 63rd St & Columbus Ave	New York	NY	10023	212-870-5570	870-5693
Web: www.nycballet.com/about/aboutnyst.html					
Palace Theatre 19 Clinton Ave	Albany	NY	12207	518-465-3334	427-0151
Web: www.palacealbany.com					
Paul Robeson Theatre 350 Masten Ave	Buffalo	NY	14209	716-884-2013	885-2590
Web: www.paulrobesontheatre.com					
Performing Arts Center 735 Anderson Hill Rd	Purchase	NY	10577	914-251-6200	251-6171
Web: www.artscenter.org					
Performing Arts Center at Rockwell Hall					
1300 Elmwood Ave Rockwell Hall Room 210	Buffalo	NY	14222	716-878-3005	878-4234
Web: www.buffalostate.edu/pac					
Proctor's Theatre 432 State St	Schenectady	NY	12305	518-382-3884	346-2468
Web: www.proctors.org					
Public Theater The 425 Lafayette St	New York	NY	10003	212-539-8500	539-8505
Web: www.publictheater.org					
Radio City Music Hall 1260 Ave of the Americas	New York	NY	10020	212-247-4777	
Web: www.radiocity.com					
Robeson Paul Theatre 350 Masten Ave	Buffalo	NY	14209	716-884-2013	885-2590
Web: www.paulrobesontheatre.com					
Rochester Auditorium Center 875 E Main St Suite 200	Rochester	NY	14605	585-423-0295	
Rockefeller Center 45 Rockefeller Plaza	New York	NY	10111	212-332-6500	319-1745
Web: www.rockefellercenter.com					
Saratoga Performing Arts Center					
108 Ave of the Pines	Saratoga Springs	NY	12866	518-584-9330	584-0809
Web: www.spac.org					
Shea's Performing Arts Center 650 Main St	Buffalo	NY	14202	716-847-1410	847-1644
TF: 800-217-4327 ■ *Web:* www.sheas.org					
Snug Harbor Cultural Center 1000 Richmond Terr	Staten Island	NY	10301	718-448-2500	442-8534
Web: www.snug-harbor.org					
Stanley Theatre 259 Genesee St	Utica	NY	13501	315-724-5919	724-1227
Web: www.cnyarts.com					
Tarrytown Music Hall 13 Main St	Tarrytown	NY	10591	914-631-3390	
Web: www.tarrytownmusichall.org/					
TRIBECA Performing Arts Center 199 Chambers St	New York	NY	10007	212-220-1459	732-2482
Web: www.tribecapac.org					

North Carolina

				Phone	Fax
Actor's Theatre of Charlotte 650 E Stonewall St	Charlotte	NC	28202	704-342-2251	342-1229
Web: www.actorstheatrecharlotte.org					
Alltel Pavilion at Walnut Creek 3801 Rock Quarry Rd	Raleigh	NC	27610	919-831-6400	831-6415
Web: www.alltelpavilion.com					
Asheville Civic Center 87 Haywood St	Asheville	NC	28801	828-259-5736	259-5777
Web: www.ashevilleciviccenter.com					
Asheville Community Theatre 35 E Walnut St	Asheville	NC	28801	828-254-1320	252-4723
Web: www.ashevilletheatre.org					
Broach Theatre 520 S Elm St	Greensboro	NC	27406	336-378-9300	378-9301
Web: www.broachtheatre.org					
Carolina Theatre 310 S Greene St	Greensboro	NC	27401	336-333-2600	333-2604
Web: www.carolinatheatre.com					
Carolina Theatre of Durham 309 W Morgan St	Durham	NC	27701	919-560-3040	560-3065
Web: www.carolinatheatre.org					
Diana Wortham Theatre at Pack Place 2 S Pack Sq	Asheville	NC	28801	828-257-4530	251-5652
Web: www.dwtheatre.com					
Flat Rock Playhouse 2661 Greenville Hwy	Flat Rock	NC	28731	828-693-0731	693-6795
Web: www.flatrockplayhouse.org					
Greensboro Coliseum Complex 1921 W Lee St	Greensboro	NC	27403	336-373-7400	373-2170
Web: www.greensborocoliseum.com					
Neighborhood Theatre 511 E 36th St	Charlotte	NC	28205	704-358-9298	373-0170
Web: www.neighborhoodtheatre.com					
North Carolina Blumenthal Performing Arts Center					
130 N Tryon St Suite 300	Charlotte	NC	28202	704-372-1000	444-2127
Web: www.performingartsctr.org					
Theatre in the Park 107 Pullen Rd	Raleigh	NC	27607	919-831-6058	831-9475
Web: www.theatreinthepark.com					
Wortham Diana Theatre at Pack Place 2 S Pack Sq	Asheville	NC	28801	828-257-4530	251-5652
Web: www.dwtheatre.com					

North Dakota

				Phone	Fax
Chester Fritz Auditorium					
3475 University Ave PO Box 9028 University of North Dakota	Grand Forks	ND	58202	701-777-3076	777-4710
TF: 800-375-4068 ■ *Web:* www.cfa.und.edu					
Empire Arts Center 415 DeMers Ave	Grand Forks	ND	58201	701-746-5500	746-0500
Web: www.empireartscenter.com					
Fargo Theatre 314 Broadway	Fargo	ND	58102	701-239-8385	235-0893
Web: www.fargotheatre.org					
Festival Concert Hall North Dakota State University	Fargo	ND	58105	701-231-9564	231-2085
Web: www.ndsu.nodak.edu/finearts					
Fire Hall Theatre 412 2nd Ave N	Grand Forks	ND	58203	701-746-0847	

Ohio

				Phone	Fax
Akron Civic Theatre 182 S Main St	Akron	OH	44308	330-535-3179	535-9828
Web: www.akroncivic.com					
Aronoff Center for the Arts 650 Walnut St	Cincinnati	OH	45202	513-721-3344	977-4150
Web: www.cincinnatiarts.org					
Benjamin & Marian Schuster Performing Arts Center					
109 Main St	Dayton	OH	45402	937-228-3630	449-5068
TF: 888-228-3630 ■ *Web:* www.schustercenter.org					
Blossom Music Center 1145 W Steels Corners Rd	Cuyahoga Falls	OH	44223	330-920-8040	920-0968
Web: www.hob.com/venues/concerts/blossom					
Cain Park Theatre Superior & Lee Rds Cain Park	Cleveland Heights	OH	44118	216-371-3000	
Web: www.cainpark.com					
Canton Palace Theatre 605 N Market Ave	Canton	OH	44702	330-454-8172	454-8171
Web: www.cantonpalacetheatre.org					
Cincinnati Music Hall 1241 Elm St	Cincinnati	OH	45202	513-621-1919	744-3345
Web: www.cincinnatiarts.org					
Cincinnati Playhouse in the Park 962 Mt Adams Cir	Cincinnati	OH	45202	513-345-2242	345-2250
TF: 800-582-3208 ■ *Web:* www.cincyplay.com					
Cleveland Play House 8500 Euclid Ave	Cleveland	OH	44106	216-795-7010	795-7005
Web: www.clevelandplayhouse.com					
Coach House Theatre 732 W Exchange St	Akron	OH	44302	330-434-7741	
Web: www.coachhousetheatre.org					
Dobama Theater 2490 Lee Blvd Suite 325	Cleveland Heights	OH	44118	216-932-6838	932-3259
Web: www.dobama.org					
Edward W Powers Auditorium 260 Federal Plaza W	Youngstown	OH	44503	330-744-4269	744-1441
Web: www.youngstownsymphony.com/symphony_center.html					
EJ Thomas Performing Arts Hall 198 Hill St University of Akron	Akron	OH	44325	330-972-7570	972-2700
Web: destinationdowntownakron.com/ej					
Fraze Pavilion 695 Lincoln Park Blvd	Kettering	OH	45429	937-296-3300	296-3302
Web: www.fraze.com					
Henry H Stambaugh Auditorium 1000 5th Ave	Youngstown	OH	44504	330-747-5175	747-1981
TF: 866-582-8963 ■ *Web:* www.stambaughauditorium.com					
Historic Ohio Theatre 3114 Lagrange St	Toledo	OH	43608	419-241-6785	241-2151

Ohio (Cont'd)

Name / Address	City	State	ZIP	Phone	Fax
Ohio Theatre 55 E State St *Web:* www.capa.com/columbus/venues/ohio_about.php	Columbus	OH	43215	614-469-1045	461-0429
Packard WD Music Hall 1703 Mahoning Ave NW *Web:* www.packardmusichall.com	Warren	OH	44483	330-841-2619	393-5348
Palace Theatre 34 W Broad St	Columbus	OH	43215	614-469-1332	460-2272
Playhouse Square Center 1501 Euclid Ave Suite 200 *TF:* 800-888-9941 ■ *Web:* www.playhousesquare.com	Cleveland	OH	44115	216-771-4444	771-0217
Powers Edward W Auditorium 260 Federal Plaza W *Web:* www.youngstownsymphony.com/symphony_center.html	Youngstown	OH	44503	330-744-4269	744-1441
Riverbend Music Center 6295 Kellogg Ave *Web:* www.riverbend-music.com	Cincinnati	OH	45230	513-232-5882	232-7577
Severance Hall 11001 Euclid Ave *TF:* 800-686-1411 ■ *Web:* www.clevelandorchestra.com	Cleveland	OH	44106	216-231-7300	231-0202
Stambaugh Henry H Auditorium 1000 5th Ave *TF:* 866-582-8963 ■ *Web:* www.stambaughauditorium.com	Youngstown	OH	44504	330-747-5175	747-1981
Stranahan Theater 4645 Heatherdowns Blvd *Web:* www.stranahantheater.org	Toledo	OH	43614	419-381-8851	381-9525
Taft Theatre 317 E 5th St *Web:* www.taftevents.com	Cincinnati	OH	45202	513-721-8883	721-2864
Thomas EJ Performing Arts Hall 198 Hill St University of Akron *Web:* destinationdowntownakron.com/ej	Akron	OH	44325	330-972-7570	972-2700
Valentine Theater 400 N Superior St *Web:* www.valentinetheatre.com	Toledo	OH	43604	419-242-2787	242-2791
Veterans Memorial Civic & Convention Center 7 Town Sq *TF:* 877-377-0674 ■ *Web:* www.limaciviccenter.com	Lima	OH	45801	419-224-5222	224-6964
Victoria Theatre 138 N Main St *TF:* 888-228-3630 ■ *Web:* www.victoriatheatre.com	Dayton	OH	45402	937-228-3630	449-5068
WD Packard Music Hall 1703 Mahoning Ave NW *Web:* www.packardmusichall.com	Warren	OH	44483	330-841-2619	393-5348
Weathervane Community Playhouse 1301 Weathervane Ln *Web:* www.weathervaneplayhouse.com	Akron	OH	44313	330-836-2626	873-2150
Youngstown Playhouse 600 Playhouse Ln *Web:* www.youngstownplayhouse.com	Youngstown	OH	44511	330-788-8739	788-1208

Oklahoma

Name / Address	City	State	ZIP	Phone	Fax
Civic Center Music Hall 201 N Walker St *Web:* www.okcciviccenter.org	Oklahoma City	OK	73102	405-297-2584	297-3890
Jewel Box Theatre 3700 N Walker Ave *Web:* www.jewelboxtheatre.org	Oklahoma City	OK	73118	405-521-1786	525-6562
Lyric Theatre of Oklahoma 1727 NW 16th St *Web:* www.lyrictheatreokc.com	Oklahoma City	OK	73106	405-524-9312	524-9316
Mabee Center 7777 S Lewis Ave *TF:* 800-678-1353 ■ *Web:* www.mabeecenter.com	Tulsa	OK	74171	918-495-6000	495-7438
Stage Center 400 W Sheridan Ave *Web:* www.stagecenter.com	Oklahoma City	OK	73102	405-270-4801	270-4806
Tulsa Performing Arts Center 110 E 2nd St *TF:* 800-364-7122 ■ *Web:* www.tulsapac.com	Tulsa	OK	74103	918-596-7122	596-7144

Ontario

Name / Address	City	State	ZIP	Phone	Fax
Centre in the Square 101 Queen St N *Web:* www.centre-square.com	Kitchener	ON	N2H6P7	519-578-5660	578-9230
Massey Hall 178 Victoria St *Web:* www.masseyhall.com	Toronto	ON	M5B1T7	416-593-4822	593-4224

Oregon

Name / Address	City	State	ZIP	Phone	Fax
Florence Events Center 715 Quince St *TF:* 888-968-4086 ■ *Web:* www.eventcenter.org	Florence	OR	97439	541-997-1994	902-0991
Historic Elsinore Theatre 170 High St SE *Web:* www.elsinoretheatre.com	Salem	OR	97301	503-375-3574	375-0284
Hult Center for the Performing Arts 1 Eugene Center *Web:* www.hultcenter.org	Eugene	OR	97401	541-682-5087	682-5426
McDonald Theatre 1010 Willamette St *Web:* www.mcdonaldtheatre.com	Eugene	OR	97401	541-345-4442	762-8093
Pentacle Theater 324 52nd Ave NW *Web:* www.oregonlink.com/pentacle_theater/index.html	Salem	OR	97304	503-364-7121	362-6393
Portland Center for the Performing Arts 1111 SW Broadway *Web:* www.pcpa.com	Portland	OR	97205	503-248-4335	274-7490
Woodmen of the World Hall 291 W 8th Ave *Web:* www.wowhall.org	Eugene	OR	97401	541-687-2746	687-1664

Pennsylvania

Name / Address	City	State	ZIP	Phone	Fax
19th Street Theatre 527 N 19th St *Web:* www.civictheatre.com	Allentown	PA	18104	610-432-8943	432-7381
Academy of Music Broad & Locust Sts *Web:* www.academyofmusic.org	Philadelphia	PA	19102	215-893-1999	
Annenberg Center for the Performing Arts 3680 Walnut St *Web:* www.annenbergcenter.org	Philadelphia	PA	19104	215-898-3900	898-7240
Benedum Center for the Performing Arts 719 Liberty Ave	Pittsburgh	PA	15222	412-456-6666	391-7219
Carnegie Music Hall 4400 Forbes Ave	Pittsburgh	PA	15213	412-622-3360	688-8664
Eichelberger Performing Arts Center 195 Stock St Suite 203 *Web:* www.goepac.com	Hanover	PA	17331	717-632-9356	637-4504
Erie Playhouse 13 W 10th St *Web:* www.erieplayhouse.org	Erie	PA	16501	814-454-2851	454-0601
Fulton Opera House 12 N Prince St *TF:* 888-480-1265 ■ *Web:* www.fultontheatre.org	Lancaster	PA	17608	717-397-7425	397-3780
Heinz Hall for the Performing Arts 600 Penn Ave *TF:* 800-743-8560 ■ *Web:* www.pittsburghsymphony.org	Pittsburgh	PA	15222	412-392-4800	392-4910
Kimmel Center for the Performing Arts 300 S Broad St Suite 901 *Web:* www.kimmelcenter.org	Philadelphia	PA	19102	215-790-5800	790-5801
Liacouras Center 1776 N Broad St *Web:* www.liacourascenter.com	Philadelphia	PA	19121	215-204-2400	204-2405
Mann Center for the Performing Arts 123 S Broad St Suite 1930 *Web:* www.manncenter.org	Philadelphia	PA	19109	215-546-7900	546-9524
Music Box Dinner Playhouse 196 Hughes St *Web:* www.musicbox.org	Swoyersville	PA	18704	570-283-2195	283-0751
Perelman Theater 260 S Broad St Suite 901	Philadelphia	PA	19102	215-790-5800	790-5801
Providence Playhouse 1256 Providence Rd	Scranton	PA	18508	570-342-9707	
Scranton Cultural Center 420 N Washington Ave *Web:* www.scrantonculturalcenter.org	Scranton	PA	18503	570-346-7369	346-7365
Society Hill Playhouse 507 S 8th St *Web:* www.societyhillplayhouse.com	Philadelphia	PA	19147	215-923-0210	923-1789
Sovereign Performing Arts Center 136 N 6th St *Web:* www.sovereigncenter.com	Reading	PA	19601	610-898-7299	898-7297
Verizon Hall 260 S Broad St Suite 901	Philadelphia	PA	19102	215-790-5800	790-5801
Wachovia Arena at Casey Plaza 255 Highland Park Blvd *Web:* www.wachoviaarena.com	Wilkes-Barre	PA	18702	570-970-7600	970-7601
Walnut Street Theatre 825 Walnut St *Web:* www.wstonline.org	Philadelphia	PA	19107	215-574-3550	574-3598
Warner Theatre 811 State St *Web:* www.erieevents.com/warner.html	Erie	PA	16501	814-452-4857	455-9931
Wilma Theater 265 S Broad St *Web:* www.wilmatheater.org	Philadelphia	PA	19107	215-893-9456	893-0895

Rhode Island

Name / Address	City	State	ZIP	Phone	Fax
AS220 Center for Arts 115 Empire St *Web:* www.as220.org	Providence	RI	02903	401-831-9327	454-7445
Perishable Theatre Arts Center 95 Empire St *Web:* www.perishable.org	Providence	RI	02903	401-331-2695	331-7811
Providence Performing Arts Center 220 Weybosset St *Web:* www.ppacri.org	Providence	RI	02903	401-421-2787	351-7827
Veterans Memorial Auditorium Ave of the Arts	Providence	RI	02903	401-222-1467	222-1466

South Carolina

Name / Address	City	State	ZIP	Phone	Fax
Alabama Theatre 4750 Hwy 17 S *TF:* 800-342-2262 ■ *Web:* www.alabama-theatre.com	North Myrtle Beach	SC	29582	843-272-1111	272-7748
Arts Center of Coastal Carolina 14 Shelter Cove Ln *Web:* www.artscenter-hhi.org	Hilton Head Island	SC	29928	843-686-3945	842-7877
Carolina Opry 8901 Hwy 17 N Suite A *TF:* 800-843-6779 ■ *Web:* www.cgp.net	Myrtle Beach	SC	29577	843-238-8888	913-1442
Charleston Area Convention Center Complex 5001 Coliseum Dr *Web:* www.charlestonconvention.com	Charleston	SC	29418	843-529-5011	529-5040
Dock Street Theatre 135 Church St *TF:* 800-454-7093	Charleston	SC	29401	843-577-5967	577-5422
Gaillard Municipal Auditorium 77 Calhoun St	Charleston	SC	29403	843-577-7400	724-7389
Greenville Little Theatre 444 College St *Web:* www.greenvillelittletheatre.com	Greenville	SC	29601	864-233-6238	233-6237
Ira & Nancy Koger Center for the Arts 1051 Greene St *Web:* www.koger.sc.edu	Columbia	SC	29201	803-777-7500	777-9774
Longstreet Theatre Greene & Sumter Sts	Columbia	SC	29208	803-777-4288	777-6669
Palace Theater 1420 Celebrity Cir Broadway at the Beach *TF:* 800-905-4228 ■ *Web:* www.palacetheatermyrtlebeach.com	Myrtle Beach	SC	29577	843-448-9224	626-9659
Peace Center for the Performing Arts 101 W Broad St *Web:* www.peacecenter.org	Greenville	SC	29601	864-467-3030	467-3040
Town Theatre 1012 Sumter St *Web:* www.towntheatre.com	Columbia	SC	29201	803-799-4764	799-6463
Township The 1703 Taylor St *Web:* www.thetownship.org	Columbia	SC	29201	803-576-2350	576-2359
Trustus Theatre 520 Lady St PO Box 11721 *Web:* www.trustus.org	Columbia	SC	29201	803-254-9732	771-9153
Warehouse Theatre 37 Augusta St *Web:* www.warehousetheatre.com	Greenville	SC	29601	864-235-6948	
Workshop Theatre 1136 Bull St *Web:* www.workshoptheatre.com	Columbia	SC	29201	803-799-4876	799-0227

South Dakota

Name / Address	City	State	ZIP	Phone	Fax
Black Hills Community Theatre 1202 E Saint Francis St *Web:* www.bhct.org	Rapid City	SD	57701	605-394-1787	394-2679
Matthews Opera House 614 Main St *Web:* www.moh-scah.com	Spearfish	SD	57783	605-642-7973	642-3477
Rushmore Plaza Civic Center 444 Mt Rushmore Rd N *TF:* 800-468-6463 ■ *Web:* www.gotmine.com	Rapid City	SD	57701	605-394-4115	394-4119
Washington Pavilion of Arts & Science 301 S Main Ave *TF:* 877-927-4728 ■ *Web:* www.washingtonpavilion.org	Sioux Falls	SD	57104	605-367-7397	367-7399

Tennessee

Name / Address	City	State	ZIP	Phone	Fax
Bessie Smith Performance Hall 200 E ML King Blvd	Chattanooga	TN	37401	423-266-8658	267-1076
Brown Clarence Theatre 206 McClung Tower *Web:* www.clarencebrowntheatre.com	Knoxville	TN	37996	865-974-6011	974-4867
Carl Perkins Civic Center 400 S Highland Ave *Web:* www.jacksoncentre.com/CivicCenterMain.htm	Jackson	TN	38301	731-425-8580	425-8589
Chattanooga Theatre Centre PO Box 4023 *Web:* www.theatrecentre.com	Chattanooga	TN	37405	423-267-8534	664-1211
Circuit Playhouse 1705 Poplar Ave *Web:* www.playhouseonthesquare.org	Memphis	TN	38104	901-726-4656	272-7530
Clarence Brown Theatre 206 McClung Tower *Web:* www.clarencebrowntheatre.com	Knoxville	TN	37996	865-974-6011	974-4867
Darkhorse Theater 4610 Charlotte Ave *Web:* www.darkhorsetheater.com	Nashville	TN	37209	615-297-7113	665-3336
Germantown Performing Arts Centre 1801 Exeter Rd *Web:* www.gpacweb.com	Germantown	TN	38138	901-751-7500	751-7514
Grand Ole Opry 2804 Opryland Dr *Web:* www.opry.com	Nashville	TN	37214	615-871-6779	871-6166
Knoxville Civic Auditorium/Coliseum 500 Howard Baker Jr Ave *Web:* www.knoxvillecoliseum.com	Knoxville	TN	37915	865-544-5399	215-8989
Laurel Theatre 1538 Laurel Ave *Web:* www.discoveret.org/jca/	Knoxville	TN	37916	865-522-5851	522-5386
Memphis Cook Convention Center 255 N Main St *TF:* 800-726-0915 ■ *Web:* www.memphisconvention.com	Memphis	TN	38103	901-576-1200	576-1212
Nashville Municipal Auditorium 417 4th Ave N *Web:* www.nashville.gov/ma	Nashville	TN	37201	615-862-6390	862-6394
Orpheum Theatre 203 S Main St *Web:* www.orpheum-memphis.com	Memphis	TN	38103	901-525-7800	526-0829
Playhouse on the Square 51 S Cooper St *Web:* www.playhouseonthesquare.org	Memphis	TN	38104	901-726-4656	272-7530
Ryman Auditorium 116 5th Ave N *Web:* www.ryman.com	Nashville	TN	37219	615-458-8700	251-1026
Soldiers & Sailors Memorial Auditorium 399 McCallie Ave *Web:* www.chattanoogaonstage.com	Chattanooga	TN	37402	423-757-5156	757-5326

Facility	City	State	Zip	Phone	Fax
Starwood Amphitheatre 3839 Murfreesboro Rd	Antioch	TN	37013	615-641-5800	641-7619
Web: www.starwoodamphitheatre.com					
Tennessee Performing Arts Center 505 Deaderick St	Nashville	TN	37243	615-782-4000	782-4001
Web: www.tpac.org					
Texas Troubadour Theatre 2416 Music Valley Dr Suite 108	Nashville	TN	37214	615-889-2474	885-6949
Theatre Memphis 630 Perkins Ext	Memphis	TN	38117	901-682-8601	763-4096
Web: www.theatrememphis.org					
Tivoli Theatre 709 Broad St	Chattanooga	TN	37402	423-757-5050	757-5326
University of Tennessee Music Hall 1741 Volunteer Blvd	Knoxville	TN	37996	865-974-3241	974-1941
Web: www.music.utk.edu					
University of Tennessee Opera Theatre 1741 Volunteer Blvd 211 Music Bldg	Knoxville	TN	37996	865-974-3241	974-1941

Texas

Facility	City	State	Zip	Phone	Fax
Abilene Civic Center 1100 N 6th St	Abilene	TX	79601	325-676-6211	676-6343
Web: www.abilenetx.com/CivicCenter					
Abilene Community Theatre 801 S Mockingbird Ln	Abilene	TX	79605	325-673-6271	
Alley Theatre 615 Texas Ave	Houston	TX	77002	713-228-9341	222-6542
Web: www.alleytheatre.org					
Amarillo Civic Center 401 S Buchanan St	Amarillo	TX	79101	806-378-4297	378-4234
Web: www.civicamarillo.com					
American Bank Center 1901 N Shoreline Blvd	Corpus Christi	TX	78401	361-826-4100	826-4905
Web: www.americanbankcenter.com					
Arneson River Theatre 418 Villita St La Villita	San Antonio	TX	78205	210-207-8610	207-4390
Web: lavillita.com/arneson/index.htm					
Austin Music Hall 208 Nueces St	Austin	TX	78701	512-263-4146	263-4194
Web: www.austinmusichall.com					
Bass Performance Hall 525 Commerce St	Fort Worth	TX	76102	817-212-4200	810-9294
Web: www.basshall.com					
Camille Lightner Playhouse 1 Dean Porter Park	Brownsville	TX	78520	956-542-8900	986-0639
Carpenter Performance Hall 3333 N MacArthur Blvd	Irving	TX	75062	972-252-2787	570-4962
Casa Manana Theatre 3101 W Lancaster Ave	Fort Worth	TX	76107	817-332-2272	332-5711
Web: www.casamanana.org					
Circle Theatre 230 W 4th St	Fort Worth	TX	76102	817-877-3848	877-3536
Web: www.circletheatre.com					
Cockrell Lila Theatre 200 E Market St	San Antonio	TX	78205	210-207-8500	223-1495
Creative Arts Theatre & School 1100 W Randol Mill Rd	Arlington	TX	76012	817-861-2287	274-0793
Web: www.creativearts.org					
Cynthia Woods Mitchell Pavilion 2005 Lake Robbins Dr	The Woodlands	TX	77380	281-363-3300	364-3011
Web: pavilion.woodlandscenter.org					
Dupree Theater 3333 N MacArthur Blvd	Irving	TX	75062	972-252-2787	570-4962
El Paso Convention & Performing Arts Center 1 Civic Center Plaza	El Paso	TX	79901	915-534-0600	534-0687
TF: 800-351-6024 ■ *Web:* www.visitelpaso.com/cpac_index.sstg					
Ensemble Theatre 3535 Main St	Houston	TX	77002	713-520-0055	520-1269
Web: www.ensemblehouston.com					
Grand 1894 Opera House 2020 Postoffice St	Galveston	TX	77550	409-765-1894	763-1068
TF: 800-821-1894 ■ *Web:* www.thegrand.com					
Harbor Playhouse 1 Bayfront Park	Corpus Christi	TX	78401	361-882-5500	888-4779
Web: www.harborplayhouse.com					
Hobby Center for the Performing Arts 800 Bagby St Suite 300	Houston	TX	77002	713-315-2400	315-2402
Web: www.thehobbycenter.org					
Irving Arts Center 3333 N MacArthur Blvd Suite 300	Irving	TX	75062	972-252-7558	570-4962
Web: www.irvingartscenter.com					
Jesse H Jones Hall for the Performing Arts 615 Louisiana St Suite 101	Houston	TX	77002	713-227-3974	315-4830
Web: www.houstontx.gov/joneshall/					
Jones Jesse H Hall for the Performing Arts 615 Louisiana St Suite 101	Houston	TX	77002	713-227-3974	315-4830
Web: www.houstontx.gov/joneshall/					
Jubilee Theatre 506 Main St	Fort Worth	TX	76102	817-338-4411	338-4206
Web: www.jubileetheatre.org					
Julie Rogers Theatre 765 Pearl St	Beaumont	TX	77701	409-838-3435	838-3715
TF: 800-782-3081					
Lightner Camille Playhouse 1 Dean Porter Park	Brownsville	TX	78520	956-542-8900	986-0639
Lila Cockrell Theatre 200 E Market St	San Antonio	TX	78205	210-207-8500	223-1495
Majestic Theatre 1925 Elm St	Dallas	TX	75201	214-880-0137	880-0097
Web: www.liveatthemajestic.com					
Majestic Theatre 224 E Houston St	San Antonio	TX	78205	210-226-5700	226-3377
Web: www.themajestic.com/theatre.htm					
Meyerson Morton H Symphony Center 2301 Flora St Suite 100	Dallas	TX	75201	214-670-3600	670-4334
Web: www.meyersonsymphonycenter.com					
Miller Outdoor Theatre 100 Concert Dr	Houston	TX	77030	713-533-3285	
Web: www.milleroutdoortheatre.com					
Mitchell Cynthia Woods Pavilion 2005 Lake Robbins Dr	The Woodlands	TX	77380	281-363-3300	364-3011
Web: pavilion.woodlandscenter.org					
Morton H Meyerson Symphony Center 2301 Flora St Suite 100	Dallas	TX	75201	214-670-3600	670-4334
Web: www.meyersonsymphonycenter.com					
Music Hall at Fair Park 909 1st Ave	Dallas	TX	75210	214-565-1116	565-0071
Web: www.liveatthemusichall.com					
One World Theatre 7701 Bee Caves Rd	Austin	TX	78746	512-330-9500	330-9600
Web: www.oneworldtheatre.org					
Palace Arts Center 300 S Main St	Grapevine	TX	76099	817-410-3550	410-3543
Web: www.palace-theatre.com					
Paramount Theatre 352 Cypress St	Abilene	TX	79601	325-676-9620	676-0642
Web: www.paramount-abilene.org					
Paramount Theatre 713 Congress Ave	Austin	TX	78701	512-472-2901	472-5824
Web: www.austintheatrealliance.org					
Patty Granville Performing Arts Center 300 N 5th St	Garland	TX	75040	972-205-2780	205-2775
Perot Theatre 219 Main St	Texarkana	TX	75504	903-792-4992	793-8511
Reliant Arena 1 Reliant Pk	Houston	TX	77054	832-667-1400	
Web: www.reliantpark.com					
Rockport Center for the Arts 902 Navigation Cir	Rockport	TX	78382	361-729-5519	729-3551
Web: www.rockportartcenter.org					
Rogers Julie Theatre 765 Pearl St	Beaumont	TX	77701	409-838-3435	838-3715
TF: 800-782-3081					
Ryan Little Theatre 1642 Sayles Blvd McMurry University Ryan Fine Arts Bldg	Abilene	TX	79697	325-793-3889	793-4662
Sammons Center for the Arts 3630 Harry Hines Blvd	Dallas	TX	75219	214-520-7789	522-9174
Web: www.sammonsartcenter.org					
San Antonio Municipal Auditorium 100 Auditorium Cir	San Antonio	TX	78205	210-207-8511	207-4263
TF: 877-504-8895 ■ *Web:* www.sanantonio.gov/convfac					
San Pedro Playhouse 800 W Ashby Pl San Pedro Park	San Antonio	TX	78212	210-733-7258	734-2651
Web: www.members.tripod.com/san_pedro_playhouse					
Scott Zachary Theatre Center 1510 Toomey Rd	Austin	TX	78704	512-476-0594	476-0314
Web: www.zachscott.com					
Theatre Three 2800 Routh St Suite 168	Dallas	TX	75201	214-871-3300	871-3139
Web: www.theatre3dallas.com					
University of Texas at Austin Performing Arts Center E 23rd St & E Robert Dedman Dr	Austin	TX	78705	512-471-1444	471-3636
TF: 800-687-6010 ■ *Web:* www.utpac.org					
Verizon Wireless Amphitheater 16765 Lookout Road	Selma	TX	78154	210-657-8300	657-8400
Web: www.vwatx.com/main.html					
Verizon Wireless Theater 520 Texas Ave	Houston	TX	77002	713-230-1666	230-1669
Web: www.verizonwirelesstheater.com					
Vortex Theatre 2307 Manor Rd	Austin	TX	78722	512-478-5282	472-8644
Web: www.vortexrep.org					
Wichita Falls Memorial Auditorium 1300 7th St	Wichita Falls	TX	76301	940-716-5506	716-5509
Williams Performing Arts Center 1625 Campus Ct Box 27843 Abilene Christian University	Abilene	TX	79699	325-674-2739	674-6887
Web: www.acu.edu/aboutacu/map_acu/pac.html					
Wortham Theater Center 501 Texas Ave	Houston	TX	77002	713-237-1439	237-9313
Web: www.worthamtheaterhouston.com					
Zachary Scott Theatre Center 1510 Toomey Rd	Austin	TX	78704	512-476-0594	476-0314
Web: www.zachscott.com					

Utah

Facility	City	State	Zip	Phone	Fax
Abravanel Maurice Hall 123 W South Temple	Salt Lake City	UT	84101	801-533-5626	869-9026
TF: 888-451-2787 ■ *Web:* www.utahsymphony.org					
Capitol Theatre 50 W 200 South	Salt Lake City	UT	84101	801-323-6800	538-2272
TF: 888-451-2787 ■ *Web:* www.arttix.org					
Hale Center Theater Orem 225 W 400 North	Orem	UT	84057	801-226-8600	852-3189
Web: www.haletheater.com					
Hale Centre Theater 3333 S Decker Lake Dr	West Valley City	UT	84119	801-984-9000	984-9009
Web: www.halecentretheatre.org					
Maurice Abravanel Hall 123 W South Temple	Salt Lake City	UT	84101	801-533-5626	869-9026
TF: 888-451-2787 ■ *Web:* www.utahsymphony.org					
Off Broadway Theatre 272 S Main St	Salt Lake City	UT	84101	801-355-4628	355-4641
Web: www.theobt.com					
Salt Lake Community College Grand Theatre 1575 S State St	Salt Lake City	UT	84115	801-957-3322	957-3059
Web: www.slcc.edu/the-grand					
Salt Lake County Center for the Arts 50 W 200 South	Salt Lake City	UT	84101	801-323-6800	538-2272
TF: 888-451-2787 ■ *Web:* www.arttix.org					
Terrace Plaza Playhouse 99 E 4700 South	Ogden	UT	84405	801-393-0070	
Web: www.terraceplayhouse.com					
Tuacahn Amphitheatre & Center for the Arts 1100 Tuacahn Dr	Ivins	UT	84738	435-652-3200	652-3227
Web: www.tuacahn.org					
Valley Center Playhouse 780 N 200 East	Lindon	UT	84042	801-785-1186	
Web: www.vcpnews.com					

Vermont

Facility	City	State	Zip	Phone	Fax
Barre Opera House 6 N Main St	Barre	VT	05641	802-476-8188	476-5648
Web: www.barreoperahouse.org					
Flynn Center for the Performing Arts 153 Main St	Burlington	VT	05401	802-863-5966	863-8776
Web: www.flynncenter.org					

Virginia

Facility	City	State	Zip	Phone	Fax
Chrysler Hall 215 St Pauls Blvd	Norfolk	VA	23510	757-664-6464	664-6990
Clark Street Playhouse 601 S Clark St	Arlington	VA	22202	703-418-4808	
TF: 800-494-7499					
Generic Theater 912 W 21st St	Norfolk	VA	23517	757-441-2160	441-2729
Web: www.generictheater.org					
George Mason Center for the Arts George Mason University	Fairfax	VA	22030	703-993-8888	993-8650
Web: www.gmu.edu/cfa					
Harrison Opera House 160 E Virginia Beach Blvd	Norfolk	VA	23510	757-623-1223	622-0058
Web: www.vaopera.org					
Jefferson Center 541 Luck Ave Suite 221	Roanoke	VA	24016	540-343-2624	343-3744
Web: www.jeffcenter.org					
Landmark Theater 6 N Laurel St	Richmond	VA	23220	804-646-4213	646-6101
TF: 877-297-5729					
Little Theatre of Alexandria 600 Wolfe St	Alexandria	VA	22314	703-683-5778	683-1378
Web: www.thelittletheatre.com					
Little Theatre of Norfolk 801 Claremont Ave	Norfolk	VA	23507	757-627-8551	
Web: www.ltnonline.org					
MetroStage 1201 N Royal St	Alexandria	VA	22314	703-548-9044	548-9089
Web: www.metrostage.org					
Mill Mountain Theatre 1 Market Sq 2nd Fl	Roanoke	VA	24011	540-342-5740	857-4391
TF: 800-317-6455 ■ *Web:* www.millmountain.org					
Peninsula Community Theatre 10251 Warwick Blvd	Newport News	VA	23601	757-595-5728	596-7436
Web: www.peninsulacommunitytheatre.org					
Roper Performing Arts Center 340 Granby St	Norfolk	VA	23510	757-822-1450	822-1451
Web: www.tcc.edu/roper					
Thomas Jefferson Theatre 125 S Old Glebe Rd	Arlington	VA	22204	703-228-5900	
Web: www.potomacstages.com/Jefferson.htm					
Virginia Beach Pavilion Convention Center 1000 19th St	Virginia Beach	VA	23451	757-385-2000	437-2077
Web: vbfun.com/conventioncenter/conventioncenter					
Willett Hall 3701 Willett Dr	Portsmouth	VA	23707	757-393-5144	
Web: www.willetthall.com					
Wolf Trap Foundation for the Performing Arts 1645 Trap Rd	Vienna	VA	22182	703-255-1900	255-4077
Web: www.wolf-trap.org					
Wolf Trap National Park for the Performing Arts 1551 Trap Rd	Vienna	VA	22182	703-255-1800	255-1971
Web: www.nps.gov/wotr/					

Washington

Facility	City	State	Zip	Phone	Fax
ACT Theatre 700 Union St Kreielsheimer Pl	Seattle	WA	98101	206-292-7660	292-7670
Web: www.acttheatre.org					
Behnke Center for Contemporary Performance 100 W Roy St	Seattle	WA	98119	206-217-9886	217-9887
Web: www.ontheboards.org					
Broadway Center for the Performing Arts 901 Broadway	Tacoma	WA	98402	253-591-5890	591-2013
TF: 800-291-7593 ■ *Web:* www.broadwaycenter.org					
Metropolitan Performing Arts Center 901 W Sprague Ave	Spokane	WA	99204	509-227-7638	227-7778
Web: www.mettheater.com					
Olympia Little Theatre 1925 Miller Ave NE	Olympia	WA	98506	360-786-9484	
Web: www.olympialittletheater.org					
Pantages Theater 901 Broadway	Tacoma	WA	98402	253-591-5890	591-2013
TF: 800-291-7593 ■ *Web:* www.broadwaycenter.org					
Paramount Theatre 911 Pine St	Seattle	WA	98101	206-467-5510	682-4837
Web: www.theparamount.com					
Rialto Theater 310 S 9th St	Tacoma	WA	98402	253-591-5890	591-2013
TF: 800-291-7593 ■ *Web:* www.broadwaycenter.org					
Seattle Center 305 Harrison St	Seattle	WA	98109	206-684-7200	684-7342
Web: www.seattlecenter.com					

Washington (Cont'd)

	City	State	ZIP	Phone	Fax
Spokane Center 334 W Spokane Falls Blvd *Web:* www.spokanecenter.com	Spokane	WA	99201	509-353-6500	353-6511
Spokane Civic Theatre 1020 N Howard St *TF:* 800-446-9576 ■ *Web:* www.spokanecivictheatre.com	Spokane	WA	99201	509-325-1413	325-9287
Tacoma Little Theatre 210 N 'I' St *Web:* www.tacomalittletheatre.com	Tacoma	WA	98403	253-272-2281	272-3972
Washington Center for the Performing Arts 512 Washington St SE *Web:* www.washingtoncenter.org	Olympia	WA	98501	360-753-8586	754-1177

West Virginia

	City	State	ZIP	Phone	Fax
Capitol Music Hall 1015 Main St *TF:* 800-624-5456 ■ *Web:* www.jamboreeusa.com/capitol.htm	Wheeling	WV	26003	304-234-0050	233-0058
Charleston Civic Center & Coliseum 200 Civic Center Dr *Web:* www.charlestonwvciviccenter.com	Charleston	WV	25301	304-345-1500	345-3492
Clay Center for the Arts & Sciences 1 Clay Sq *Web:* www.theclaycenter.org	Charleston	WV	25301	304-561-3500	561-3598
Oglebay Institute's Towngate Theatre 2118 Market St *Web:* www.oionline.com	Wheeling	WV	26003	304-233-4257	
Victoria Vaudeville Theater 1228 Market St *TF:* 800-505-7464 ■ *Web:* www.victoria-theater.com	Wheeling	WV	26003	304-233-7464	

Wisconsin

	City	State	ZIP	Phone	Fax
American Players Theater 5950 Golf Course Rd *Web:* www.americanplayers.org	Spring Green	WI	53588	608-588-7401	588-7085
Barrymore Theatre 2090 Atwood Ave *Web:* www.barrymorelive.com	Madison	WI	53704	608-241-8633	241-8861
Broom Street Theatre 1119 Williamson St *Web:* www.broomstreet.org	Madison	WI	53703	608-244-8338	
Marcus Center for the Performing Arts 929 N Water St *Web:* www.marcuscenter.org	Milwaukee	WI	53202	414-273-7206	273-0649
Milwaukee Chamber Theatre 158 N Broadway Broadway Theatre Center *Web:* www.chamber-theatre.com	Milwaukee	WI	53202	414-276-8842	277-4477
Mitby Theatre 3550 Anderson St *Web:* matcmadison.edu/mitbytheater/HTM	Madison	WI	53704	608-243-4000	243-4011
Overture Center for the Arts 201 State St *Web:* www.overturecenter.com	Madison	WI	53703	608-258-4177	258-4971
Pabst Theater 144 E Wells St *Web:* www.pabsttheater.org	Milwaukee	WI	53202	414-286-3665	286-2154
Rave The 2401 W Wisconsin Ave *Web:* www.therave.com	Milwaukee	WI	53233	414-342-7283	342-0359
Riverside Theatre 116 W Wisconsin Ave *Web:* www.riversidetheater.org	Milwaukee	WI	53203	414-765-9254	
Weidner Center for the Performing Arts 2420 Nicolet Dr University of Wisconsin at Green Bay *TF:* 800-328-8587 ■ *Web:* www.uwgb.edu/weidner	Green Bay	WI	54311	920-465-2726	465-2921
Wisconsin Union Theater 800 Langdon St *Web:* www.union.wisc.edu/theater	Madison	WI	53706	608-262-2201	265-5084

Wyoming

	City	State	ZIP	Phone	Fax
Atlas Theatre 211 W 16th St *Web:* www.cheyennelittletheatre.org	Cheyenne	WY	82001	307-638-6543	638-6430
Casper Events Center 1 Events Dr *TF:* 800-442-2256 ■ *Web:* www.caspereventscenter.com	Casper	WY	82601	307-235-8441	235-8445
Cheyenne Civic Center 510 W 20th St *TF:* 877-691-2787 ■ *Web:* www.cheyennecity.org/civic.htm	Cheyenne	WY	82001	307-637-6364	637-6365
Jackson Hole Playhouse 145 W Deloney Ave PO Box 2788 *Web:* www.jhplayhouse.com	Jackson	WY	83001	307-733-6994	739-0414
Stage III Community Theatre 900 N Center St	Casper	WY	82601	307-234-0946	

576 PERFORMING ARTS ORGANIZATIONS

SEE ALSO Associations & Organizations - General - Arts & Artists Organizations p. 1292

576-1 Dance Companies

	City	State	ZIP	Phone	Fax
Abilene Ballet Theatre 1265 N 2nd St *Web:* www.abileneballettheatre.org	Abilene	TX	79601	325-675-0303	
Ailey Alvin American Dance Theater 405 W 55th St *Web:* www.alvinailey.org	New York	NY	10019	212-405-9000	405-9001
Alabama Ballet 2726 1st Ave S *Web:* www.alabamaballet.org	Birmingham	AL	35233	205-322-4300	322-4444
Alabama Dance Theatre 1018 Madison Ave *Web:* www.alabamadancetheatre.com	Montgomery	AL	36104	334-241-2590	241-2504
Albany Berkshire Ballet 25 Monroe St *Web:* www.berkshireballet.org	Albany	NY	12210	518-426-0660	426-0671
Alonzo King's LINES Contemporary Ballet 26 7th St *Web:* www.linesballet.org	San Francisco	CA	94102	415-863-3040	863-1180
Alvin Ailey American Dance Theater 405 W 55th St *Web:* www.alvinailey.org	New York	NY	10019	212-405-9000	405-9001
American Ballet Theatre (ABT) 890 Broadway 3rd Fl *Web:* www.abt.org	New York	NY	10003	212-477-3030	254-5938
American Indian Dance Theatre 223 E 61st St	New York	NY	10021	212-308-9555	826-0724
American Repertory Ballet 80 Albany St 2nd Fl *Web:* www.arballet.org	New Brunswick	NJ	08901	732-249-1254	249-8475
Ann Arbor Civic Ballet 525 E Liberty St	Ann Arbor	MI	48104	734-668-8066	428-7782
Aspen Santa Fe Ballet 0245 Sage Way *Web:* www.aspensantafeballet.com	Aspen	CO	81611	970-925-7175	
Atlanta Ballet 1400 W Peachtree St NW *Web:* www.atlantaballet.com	Atlanta	GA	30309	404-873-5811	874-7905
Augusta Ballet 1301 Greene St Suite 200 *Web:* www.augustaballet.org	Augusta	GA	30901	706-261-0555	261-0551
Axis Dance Co 1428 Alice St Suite 200 *Web:* www.axisdance.org	Oakland	CA	94612	510-625-0110	625-0321
Ballet Arizona 3645 E Indian School Rd *TF:* 888-322-5538 ■ *Web:* www.balletaz.org	Phoenix	AZ	85018	602-381-0184	381-0189
Ballet Arkansas PO Box 26203 *Web:* www.balletarkansas.org	Little Rock	AR	72221	501-223-5150	
Ballet Austin 501 W 3rd St *Web:* www.balletaustin.org	Austin	TX	78705	512-476-9051	472-3073
Ballet British Columbia 677 Davie St 6th Fl *Web:* www.balletbc.com	Vancouver	BC	V6B2G6	604-732-5003	732-4417
Ballet Chicago 218 S Wabash Ave Suite 300 *Web:* www.balletchicago.org	Chicago	IL	60604	312-251-8838	251-8840
Ballet Florida 500 Fern St *TF:* 800-540-0172 ■ *Web:* www.balletflorida.com	West Palm Beach	FL	33401	561-659-1212	659-2222
Ballet Guild of the Lehigh Valley 556 Main St *Web:* www.bglv.org	Bethlehem	PA	18018	610-865-0353	865-2698
Ballet Hispanico of New York 167 W 89th St *Web:* www.ballethispanico.org	New York	NY	10024	212-362-6710	362-7809
Ballet Idaho 501 S 8th St Suite A *Web:* www.balletidaho.org	Boise	ID	83702	208-343-0556	424-3129
Ballet Lubbock 5702 Genoa Ave Suite A9 *Web:* www.balletlubbock.org	Lubbock	TX	79424	806-785-3090	785-3309
Ballet Magnificat 5406 I-55 N *Web:* www.balletmagnificat.com	Jackson	MS	39211	601-977-1001	977-8948
Ballet Memphis PO Box 3675 *Web:* www.balletmemphis.org	Cordova	TN	38088	901-737-7322	737-7037
Ballet Mississippi 201 E Pascagoula St Suite 106 PO Box 1787 *Web:* www.balletms.com	Jackson	MS	39215	601-960-1560	960-2135
Ballet Oklahoma 7421 N Classen Blvd *Web:* www.balletoklahoma.com	Oklahoma City	OK	73116	405-843-9898	843-9894
Ballet Pacifica 1824 Kaiser Ave *Web:* www.balletpacifica.com	Irvine	CA	92614	949-851-9130	851-9974
Ballet Quad Cities 613 17th St *Web:* www.balletquadcities.com	Rock Island	IL	61201	309-786-3779	786-2677
Ballet Tech 890 Broadway 8th Fl *Web:* www.ballettech.org	New York	NY	10003	212-777-7710	353-0936
Ballet Tennessee 3202 Kelly's Ferry Rd *Web:* www.ballettennessee.org	Chattanooga	TN	37419	423-821-2055	821-2156
Ballet Theatre of Maryland 801 Chase St Maryland Hall for the Creative Arts *Web:* www.balletmaryland.org	Annapolis	MD	21401	410-263-8289	626-1835
Ballet Theatre of New Mexico 6913 Natalie NE *Web:* www.btnm.org	Albuquerque	NM	87110	505-888-1054	888-1054
Ballet Theatre of Scranton 310 Penn Ave *Web:* www.ballettheatre.com	Scranton	PA	18503	570-347-0208	347-8774
Ballet West 50 W 200 South *Web:* www.balletwest.org	Salt Lake City	UT	84101	801-323-6900	359-3504
Ballet Western Reserve 218 W Boardman St Morley Center for the Arts *Web:* www.balletwesternreserve.org	Youngstown	OH	44503	330-744-1934	744-2631
BalletMet Columbus 322 Mt Vernon Ave *Web:* www.balletmet.org	Columbus	OH	43215	614-229-4860	229-4858
Baton Rouge Ballet Theatre 275 S River Rd River Center Theatre *Web:* www.batonrougeballet.org	Baton Rouge	LA	70802	225-766-8379	
Bill T Jones/Arnie Zane Dance Co 27 W 120th St Suite 1 *Web:* www.billtjones.org	New York	NY	10027	212-426-6655	426-5883
Boston Ballet 19 Clarendon St *Web:* www.bostonballet.org	Boston	MA	02116	617-695-6950	695-6995
Boulder Ballet 2590 Walnut St Suite 10 *Web:* www.boulderballet.org	Boulder	CO	80302	303-443-0028	441-5266
Brown Trisha Dance Co 625 W 55th St 2nd Fl *Web:* www.trishabrowncompany.org	New York	NY	10019	212-977-5365	977-5347
Buglisi/Foreman Dance 229 West 42nd St Suite 502 *Web:* www.buglisi-foreman.org	New York	NY	10036	212-719-3301	719-3302
California Ballet Co 4819 Ronson Ct *Web:* www.californiaballet.org	San Diego	CA	92111	858-560-5676	560-0072
Canyon Concert Ballet 1031 Conifer St Suite 3 *Web:* www.ccballet.org	Fort Collins	CO	80524	970-472-4156	472-4158
Carolina Ballet Inc 3401-131 Atlantic Ave *Web:* www.carolinaballet.com	Raleigh	NC	27604	919-719-0800	719-0910
Carolyn Dorfman Dance Co 2780 Morris Ave Suite 1-A *Web:* www.carolyndorfmandanceco.org	Union	NJ	07083	908-687-8855	686-5245
Cassandra Ballet of Toledo 3157 Sylvania Ave	Toledo	OH	43613	419-475-0458	
Central West Ballet Co 3125 McHenry Ave Suite D *Web:* www.centralwestballet.com	Modesto	CA	95350	209-576-8957	576-1308
Charleston Ballet 822 Virginia St E *Web:* www.thecharlestonballet.com	Charleston	WV	25301	304-342-6541	345-1134
Charleston Ballet Theatre 477 King St *Web:* www.charlestonballet.com	Charleston	SC	29403	843-723-7334	723-9099
Chitresh Das Dance Co 32 St Charles Ave *Web:* www.kathak.org	San Francisco	CA	94132	415-333-9000	333-9029
Cincinnati Ballet 1555 Central Pkwy *Web:* www.cincinnatiballet.com	Cincinnati	OH	45214	513-621-5219	621-4844
City Ballet Theatre Inc 527 N 27th St	Milwaukee	WI	53208	414-933-9746	933-9748
Cleo Parker Robinson Dance 119 Park Ave W *Web:* www.cleoparkerdance.org	Denver	CO	80205	303-295-1759	295-1328
Collage Dance Theatre 2934 1/2 Beverly Glen Cir Suite 25 *Web:* www.collagedancetheatre.org	Los Angeles	CA	90077	818-784-8669	981-4116
Colorado Ballet 1278 Lincoln St *Web:* www.coloradoballet.org	Denver	CO	80203	303-837-8888	861-7174
Columbia City Ballet 1545 Main St *TF:* 800-899-7408 ■ *Web:* www.columbiacityballet.com	Columbia	SC	29201	803-799-7605	799-7928
Configuration PO Box 48 *Web:* www.configurationdance.org	West Chatham	MA	02633	508-945-4096	945-4096
Connecticut Ballet 20 Acosta St *Web:* www.connecticutballet.com	Stamford	CT	06902	203-964-1211	961-1928
Contemporary Dance Theatre 1805 Larch Ave *Web:* www.cdt-dance.org	Cincinnati	OH	45224	513-591-1222	
Corpus Christi Ballet 1621 N Mesquite St *Web:* www.corpuschristiballet.com	Corpus Christi	TX	78401	361-882-4588	881-9291
Dallas Black Dance Theatre 4301 S Fitzhugh Ave *Web:* www.dbdt.com	Dallas	TX	75210	214-871-2376	871-2842
Dance Alloy 5530 Penn Ave *Web:* www.dancealloy.org	Pittsburgh	PA	15206	412-363-4321	363-4320
Dance Connecticut 224 Farmington Ave	Hartford	CT	06105	860-525-9396	249-8116
Dance Theatre of Harlem Inc 466 W 152nd St *Web:* www.dancetheatreofharlem.org	New York	NY	10031	212-690-2800	690-8736
David Taylor Dance Theatre 1760 Glen Moor Dr *Web:* www.dtdt.org	Lakewood	CO	80215	303-789-2030	789-2165
Dayton Ballet 140 N Main St *Web:* www.daytonballet.org	Dayton	OH	45402	937-449-5060	461-8353
Dayton Contemporary Dance Co 126 N Main St Suite 240 *TF:* 800-788-3310 ■ *Web:* www.dcdc.org	Dayton	OH	45402	937-228-3232	223-6156
Doug Varone & Dancers 37 W 32nd St Suite 4A *Web:* www.dougvaroneanddancers.org	New York	NY	10001	212-279-3344	279-3344
Ethnic Dance Theatre 4000 Winnetka Ave N *Web:* www.ethnicdancetheatre.com	New Hope	MN	55427	763-545-1333	559-0840

Organization	City	State	ZIP	Phone	Fax
Evansville Dance Theatre 333 N Plaza East Blvd Suite E *Web:* www.edtdance.org	Evansville	IN	47715	812-473-8937	473-0393
Fagan Garth Dance 50 Chestnut St *Web:* www.garthfagandance.org	Rochester	NY	14604	585-454-3260	454-6191
Festival Ballet of Providence 825 Hope St *Web:* www.festivalballet.com	Providence	RI	02906	401-353-1129	353-8853
First State Ballet Theatre 818 N Market St *Web:* www.firststateballet.com	Wilmington	DE	19801	302-658-7897	
Flamenco Vivo Carlota Santana 481 8th Ave Suite 744 *Web:* flamenco-vivo.org	New York	NY	10001	212-736-4499	736-1326
Fort Wayne Ballet Inc 324 Penn Ave *Web:* www.fortwayneballet.org	Fort Wayne	IN	46805	260-484-9646	484-9647
Fort Wayne Dance Collective 437 E Berry St *Web:* www.fwdc.org	Fort Wayne	IN	46802	260-424-6574	424-2789
Fresno Ballet 1401 N Wishon Ave	Fresno	CA	93728	559-233-2623	
Garth Fagan Dance 50 Chestnut St *Web:* www.garthfagandance.org	Rochester	NY	14604	585-454-3260	454-6191
Georgia Ballet 1255 Field Pkwy *Web:* www.georgiaballet.org	Marietta	GA	30066	770-528-0881	528-0891
Graham Martha Dance Center 344 E 59th St	New York	NY	10022	212-521-3611	826-6186
Grand Rapids Ballet Co 341 Ellsworth Ave SW *Web:* www.grballet.com	Grand Rapids	MI	49503	616-454-4771	454-0672
Greater Lansing Ballet Co 2224 E Michigan Ave *Web:* www.greaterlansingballet.org	Lansing	MI	48912	517-372-9887	372-9887
Hawaii State Ballet 1418 Kapiolani Blvd *Web:* www.hawaiistateballet.com	Honolulu	HI	96814	808-947-2755	
Honolulu Dance Theatre 3041 Manoa Rd *Web:* www.honoluludancetheatre.com	Honolulu	HI	96822	808-988-3202	988-5199
Houston Ballet 1921 W Bell St *Web:* www.houstonballet.org	Houston	TX	77019	713-523-6300	523-4038
HT Chen & Dancers 70 Mulberry St 2nd Fl *Web:* www.htchendance.org	New York	NY	10013	212-349-0126	349-0494
Hubbard Street Dance Chicago 1147 W Jackson Blvd *Web:* www.hubbardstreetdance.org	Chicago	IL	60607	312-850-9744	455-8240
Huntsville Ballet PO Box 373 *Web:* www.huntsvilleballet.org	Huntsville	AL	35804	256-539-0961	539-1837
Idaho Dance Theatre PO Box 6635 *Web:* theatre.boisestate.edu/idahodance	Boise	ID	83707	208-331-9592	331-8205
Inland Pacific Ballet 5050 Arrow Hwy *Web:* www.ipballet.org	Montclair	CA	91763	909-482-1590	482-1589
Interweave Dance Theatre 2224 Bruce St Suite C **Fax:* Sales ■ *Web:* bcn.boulder.co.us/arts/idt/idt.html	Boulder	CO	80202	303-449-0399	492-7722*
James Sewell Ballet 528 Hennepin Ave Suite 205 *Web:* www.jsballet.org	Minneapolis	MN	55403	612-672-0480	
Jenkins Margaret Dance Co 3973-A 25th St *Web:* www.mjdc.org	San Francisco	CA	94114	415-826-8399	826-8392
Joe Goode Performance Group 1007 General Kennedy Ave Suite 209 *Web:* www.joegoode.org	San Francisco	CA	94129	415-561-6565	561-6562
Joffrey Ballet of Chicago 70 E Lake St Suite 1300 *Web:* www.joffrey.com	Chicago	IL	60601	312-739-0120	739-0119
John Jasperse Co 140 2nd Ave Suite 501 *Web:* www.johnjasperse.org	New York	NY	10003	212-375-0187	375-8283
Jose Matteo's Ballet Theatre 400 Harvard St *Web:* www.ballettheatre.org	Cambridge	MA	02138	617-354-7467	354-7856
Kansas City Ballet 1616 Broadway *Web:* www.kcballet.org	Kansas City	MO	64108	816-931-2232	931-1172
Lar Lubovitch Dance Co 229 W 42nd St 8th Fl *Web:* www.lubovitch.org	New York	NY	10036	212-221-7909	221-7938
Lexington Ballet Co 161 N Mill St *Web:* www.lexingtonballet.org	Lexington	KY	40507	859-233-3925	
Limon Dance Co 307 W 38th St Suite 1105 *Web:* www.limon.org	New York	NY	10018	212-777-3353	777-4764
Liz Lerman Dance Exchange 7117 Maple Ave *Web:* www.danceexchange.org	Takoma Park	MD	20912	301-270-6700	270-2626
Louisville Ballet 315 E Main St *Web:* www.louisvilleballet.org	Louisville	KY	40202	502-583-3150	583-0006
Madison Ballet 2822 Index Rd *Web:* www.madisonballet.org	Madison	WI	53713	608-278-7990	278-7992
Maine State Ballet 348 US Route 1 *Web:* www.mainestateballet.org	Falmouth	ME	04105	207-781-7672	781-3663
Margaret Jenkins Dance Co 3973-A 25th St *Web:* www.mjdc.org	San Francisco	CA	94114	415-826-8399	826-8392
Mark Morris Dance Group 3 Lafayette Ave *Web:* www.mmdg.org	Brooklyn	NY	11217	718-624-8400	624-8900
Martha Graham Dance Center 344 E 59th St	New York	NY	10022	212-521-3611	826-6186
Maximum Dance Co 9220 SW 158th Ln *Web:* www.maximumdancecompany.com	Miami	FL	33157	305-259-9775	259-3160
Merce Cunningham Dance Co 55 Bethune St *Web:* www.merce.org	New York	NY	10014	212-255-8240	633-2453
Miami City Ballet 2200 Liberty Ave *TF:* 877-929-7010 ■ *Web:* www.miamicityballet.org	Miami Beach	FL	33139	305-929-7000	929-7012
Milwaukee Ballet 504 W National Ave *Web:* www.milwaukeeballet.org	Milwaukee	WI	53204	414-643-7677	649-4066
Minnesota Ballet 301 W 1st St Suite 800 *Web:* www.minnesotaballet.org	Duluth	MN	55802	218-529-3742	529-3744
Minnesota Dance Theatre 528 Hennepin Ave 6th Fl *Web:* www.mndance.org	Minneapolis	MN	55403	612-338-0627	338-5160
Montgomery Ballet 6009 E Shirley Ln *Web:* www.montgomeryballet.com	Montgomery	AL	36117	334-409-0522	409-2311
Mordine & Co Dance Theatre 1016 N Dearborn Pkwy *Web:* www.mordine.org	Chicago	IL	60610	312-654-9540	654-9542
Nai-Ni Chen Dance Co PO Box 1121 **Fax Area Code:* 201 ■ *Web:* www.nainichen.org	Fort Lee	NJ	07024	800-650-0246	242-9807*
Nashville Ballet 3630 Redmon St *Web:* www.nashvilleballet.com	Nashville	TN	37209	615-297-2966	297-9972
National Ballet 15701 Alameda Dr *Web:* www.nationalballet.com	Bowie	MD	20716	301-218-9822	249-9296
National Ballet of Canada Walter Carsen Centre for the National Ballet of Canada 470 Queens Quay W *Web:* www.national.ballet.ca	Toronto	ON	M5V3K4	416-345-9686	345-8323
Nevada Ballet Theatre 1651 Inner Cir *Web:* www.nevadaballet.com	Las Vegas	NV	89134	702-243-2623	804-0365
New Haven Ballet 70 Audubon St *Web:* www.newhavenballet.org	New Haven	CT	06510	203-782-9038	
New Jersey Ballet Co 15 Microlab Rd *Web:* www.njballet.org	Livingston	NJ	07039	973-597-9600	597-9442
New York City Ballet Inc 20 Lincoln Center New York State Theatre *TF:* 800-580-8730 ■ *Web:* www.nycballet.com	New York	NY	10023	212-870-5656	870-7791
New York Theatre Ballet 30 E 31st St *Web:* www.nytb.org	New York	NY	10016	212-679-0401	679-8171
North Carolina Dance Theatre 800 N College St *Web:* www.ncdance.org	Charlotte	NC	28206	704-372-0101	375-0260
Northern Ballet Theatre 36 Arlington St *Web:* nbti.org	Nashua	NH	03060	603-889-8406	889-6621
Northwest Florida Ballet 310 Perry Ave SE *Web:* www.nfballet.org	Fort Walton Beach	FL	32548	850-664-7787	664-0130
Oakland Ballet 130 Linden St *Web:* www.oaklandballet.org	Oakland	CA	94607	510-452-9288	452-9557
Ocheami Afrikan Dance Co PO Box 31635 *Web:* www.home.earthlink.net/~ocheami/	Seattle	WA	98103	206-329-8876	
ODC/San Francisco 3153 17th St *Web:* www.odcdance.org	San Francisco	CA	94110	415-863-6606	863-9833
Ohio Ballet 354 E Market St *Web:* www.ohioballet.org	Akron	OH	44325	330-972-7900	972-7902
Oregon Ballet Theatre 818 SE 6th Ave *Web:* www.obt.org	Portland	OR	97214	503-227-0977	227-4186
Orlando Ballet 1111 N Orange Ave *Web:* www.orlandoballet.org	Orlando	FL	32804	407-426-1733	426-1734
Pacific Northwest Ballet 301 Mercer St *Web:* www.pnb.org	Seattle	WA	98109	206-441-9411	441-2440
Parsons Dance Co 229 W 42nd St Suite 800 *Web:* www.parsonsdance.org	New York	NY	10036	212-869-9275	944-7417
Paul Taylor Dance Co 552 Broadway 2nd Fl *Web:* www.ptdc.org	New York	NY	10012	212-431-5562	966-5673
Peninsula Ballet Theatre 126 2nd Ave Suite 206 *Web:* www.peninsulaballet.org	San Mateo	CA	94401	650-340-9444	340-9495
Pennsylvania Ballet 1101 S Broad St *Web:* www.paballet.org	Philadelphia	PA	19147	215-551-7000	551-7224
Peoria Ballet 8800 N Industrial Rd *Web:* www.peoriaballet.com	Peoria	IL	61615	309-690-7990	690-7991
Philadelphia Dance Co 9 N Preston St *Web:* www.philadanco.org	Philadelphia	PA	19104	215-387-8200	387-8203
Pittsburgh Ballet Theatre 2900 Liberty Ave *Web:* www.pbt.org	Pittsburgh	PA	15201	412-281-0360	281-9901
Randy James Dance Works PO Box 4452 *Web:* www.rjdw.org	Highland Park	NJ	08904	732-247-2653	247-5353
Repertory Dance Theatre 1402 Linden St *Web:* repertorydance.org	Allentown	PA	18102	610-965-6216	967-2826
Repertory Dance Theatre 138 W 300 South *Web:* www.xmission.com/~rdt	Salt Lake City	UT	84101	801-534-1000	534-1110
Richmond Ballet 407 E Canal St 1st Fl *Web:* www.richmondballet.com	Richmond	VA	23219	804-344-0906	344-0901
Ririe-Woodbury Dance Co 138 W Broadway *Web:* www.ririewoodbury.com	Salt Lake City	UT	84101	801-297-4241	297-4235
Robinson Ballet Co 107 Union St *Web:* www.robinsonballet.org	Bangor	ME	04401	207-942-1990	
Rochester City Ballet 1326 University Ave *Web:* www.rochestercityballet.org	Rochester	NY	14607	585-461-5850	473-8847
Sacramento Ballet 1631 K St *Web:* www.sacballet.org	Sacramento	CA	95814	916-552-5800	552-5815
San Diego Ballet 5304 Metro St Suite B *Web:* www.sandiegoballet.org	San Diego	CA	92110	619-294-7378	294-7315
San Francisco Ballet 455 Franklin St *Web:* www.sfballet.org	San Francisco	CA	94102	415-861-5600	861-2684
Sarasota Ballet of Florida 5555 N Tamiami Trail *Web:* www.sarasotaballet.org	Sarasota	FL	34243	941-359-0099	358-1504
State Ballet of Rhode Island 52 Sherman Ave PO Box 155 *Web:* www.stateballet.com	Lincoln	RI	02865	401-334-2560	334-0412
State Street Ballet 322 State St *Web:* www.statestreetballet.com	Santa Barbara	CA	93101	805-965-6066	965-3590
Stuart Pimsler Dance & Theater 3000 E Main St *Web:* innerart.com/SPDT/dance.html	Columbus	OH	43209	614-461-0132	461-0132
Tallahassee Ballet Co 218 E 3rd Ave *Web:* www.tallaballet.com	Tallahassee	FL	32303	850-224-6917	224-7681
Texas Ballet Theater 6845 Green Oaks Rd *Web:* www.texasballettheater.org	Fort Worth	TX	76116	817-763-0207	763-0624
Texas International Theatrical Arts Society (TITAS) 3101 N Fitzhugh Suite 301 *Web:* www.titas.org	Dallas	TX	75204	214-528-6112	528-2617
Trisha Brown Dance Co 625 W 55th St 2nd Fl *Web:* www.trishabrowncompany.org	New York	NY	10019	212-977-5365	977-5347
Tulsa Ballet 4512 S Peoria Ave *Web:* www.tulsaballet.org	Tulsa	OK	74105	918-749-6030	749-0532
Tupelo Ballet Co 775 Poplarville Dr *Web:* www.tupeloballet.com	Tupelo	MS	38801	662-844-1928	844-1951
Urban Bush Women 138 S Oxford St Suite 4B *Web:* www.urbanbushwomen.org	Brooklyn	NY	11217	718-398-4537	398-4783
Virginia Ballet Theatre 134 W Olney Rd *Web:* www.virginiaballettheatre.com	Norfolk	VA	23510	757-622-4822	622-7904
Washington Ballet 3515 Wisconsin Ave NW *Web:* www.washingtonballet.org	Washington	DC	20016	202-362-3606	362-1311
Zenon Dance Co & School 528 Hennepin Ave Suite 400 *Web:* www.zenondance.org	Minneapolis	MN	55403	612-338-1101	338-2479

576-2 Opera Companies

Organization	City	State	ZIP	Phone	Fax
Academy of Vocal Arts Opera Theatre (AVA) 1920 Spruce St *Web:* www.avaopera.com	Philadelphia	PA	19103	215-735-1685	732-2189
Amarillo Opera PO Box 447 *Web:* www.amarilloopera.org	Amarillo	TX	79178	806-372-7464	372-7465
Anchorage Opera 1507 Spar Ave *Web:* www.anchorageopera.org	Anchorage	AK	99501	907-279-2557	279-7798
Annapolis Opera Inc 801 Chase St Maryland Hall for the Creative Arts Suite 304 *Web:* www.annapolisopera.org	Annapolis	MD	21401	410-267-8135	267-6440
Arizona Opera Co 4600 N 12th St *TF:* 877-473-1497 ■ *Web:* www.azopera.org	Phoenix	AZ	85014	602-266-7464	266-5806
Arizona Opera Co 3501 N Mountain Ave *Web:* www.azopera.org	Tucson	AZ	85719	520-293-4336	293-5097
Aspen Opera Theater 2 Music School Rd	Aspen	CO	81611	970-925-3254	920-1643
Atlanta Opera 728 West Peachtree St NW *TF:* 800-356-7372 ■ *Web:* www.atlantaopera.org	Atlanta	GA	30308	404-881-8801	881-1711
Augusta Opera 1301 Greene St Suite 100 *Web:* www.augustaopera.com	Augusta	GA	30901	706-826-4710	826-4732
Austin Lyric Opera 901 Barton Springs Rd *Web:* www.austinlyricopera.org	Austin	TX	78704	512-472-5927	472-4143
Baltimore Opera Co 110 W Mt Royal Ave Suite 306 *Web:* www.baltimoreopera.com	Baltimore	MD	21201	410-625-1600	625-6474
Boston Lyric Opera 45 Franklin St 4th Fl *Web:* www.blo.org	Boston	MA	02110	617-542-4912	542-4913
Central City Opera 400 S Colorado Blvd Suite 530 *TF:* 800-851-8175 ■ *Web:* www.centralcityopera.org	Denver	CO	80246	303-292-6500	292-4958
Charleston Light Opera Guild PO Box 1762 *Web:* www.charlestonlightoperaguild.org	Charleston	WV	25326	304-343-2287	
Chicago Opera Theater 70 E Lake St Suite 815 *Web:* www.chicagooperatheater.org	Chicago	IL	60601	312-704-8420	704-8421
Cincinnati Opera 1243 Elm St *Web:* www.cincinnatiopera.org	Cincinnati	OH	45202	513-768-5500	768-5556

Opera Companies (Cont'd)

Organization	City	State	ZIP	Phone	Fax
Civic Light Opera 7400 Sand Point Way NE Suite 101-N *Web:* www.clo-musicaltheatre.org	Seattle	WA	98133	206-363-4807	363-0702
Civic Opera Theater of Kansas City PO Box 413251 *Web:* www.kc-civicopera.org	Kansas City	MO	64141	913-262-6688	381-9366
Connecticut Grand Opera & Orchestra 307 Atlantic St *Web:* www.ctgrandopera.org	Stamford	CT	06901	203-359-0009	327-1417
Connecticut Opera 226 Farmington Ave *Web:* www.connecticutopera.org	Hartford	CT	06105	860-527-0713	293-1715
Dallas Opera 8350 N Central Expy Suite 210 *Web:* www.dallasopera.org	Dallas	TX	75206	214-443-1043	443-1060
Dayton Opera 138 N Main St *Web:* www.daytonopera.org	Dayton	OH	45402	937-228-7591	228-9612
Des Moines Metro Opera 106 W Boston Ave *Web:* www.dmmo.org	Indianola	IA	50125	515-961-6221	961-8175
Eugene Opera PO Box 11200 *Web:* www.eugeneopera.com	Eugene	OR	97440	541-221-2934	683-3783
Fargo-Moorhead Opera 114 Broadway Suite S-1 *Web:* www.fmopera.org	Fargo	ND	58102	701-239-4558	476-1991
Florentine Opera Co 700 N Water St Suite 950 *TF:* 800-326-7372 ■ *Web:* www.florentineopera.org	Milwaukee	WI	53202	414-291-5700	291-5706
Florida Grand Opera 8390 NW 25th St *TF:* 800-741-1010 ■ *Web:* www.fgo.org	Miami	FL	33122	305-854-1643	856-1042
Fort Worth Opera 1300 Gendy St *TF:* 877-396-7372 ■ *Web:* www.fwopera.org	Fort Worth	TX	76107	817-731-0833	731-0835
Fresno Grand Opera 2405 Capitol St Suite 103 *Web:* www.fresnograndopera.org	Fresno	CA	93721	559-442-5699	442-5649
Fullerton Civic Light Opera 201 E Chapman Ave *Web:* www.fclo.com	Fullerton	CA	92832	714-526-3832	992-1193
Glimmerglass Opera 7300 State Hwy 80 PO Box 191 *Web:* www.glimmerglass.org	Cooperstown	NY	13326	607-547-5704	547-6030
Hawaii Opera Theatre 987 Waimanu St *Web:* www.hawaiiopera.org	Honolulu	HI	96814	808-596-7372	596-0379
Houston Grand Opera 510 Preston St Suite 500 *TF:* 800-626-7372 ■ *Web:* www.houstongrandopera.org	Houston	TX	77002	713-546-0200	236-8121
Indianapolis Opera 250 E 38th St *Web:* www.indyopera.org	Indianapolis	IN	46205	317-283-3531	923-5611
Kentucky Opera Assn 101 S 8th St *TF:* 800-690-9236 ■ *Web:* www.kyopera.org	Louisville	KY	40202	502-584-4500	584-7484
Knoxville Opera Co 612 E Depot Ave *Web:* www.knoxvilleopera.com	Knoxville	TN	37917	865-524-0795	524-7384
Long Beach Opera 100 W Broadway Suite 110 *Web:* www.longbeachopera.org	Long Beach	CA	90802	562-439-2580	683-2109
Los Angeles Opera 135 N Grand Ave Suite 327 *Web:* www.losangelesopera.com	Los Angeles	CA	90012	213-972-7219	687-3490
Lyric Opera of Chicago 20 N Wacker Dr Civic Opera House Suite 860 *Web:* www.lyricopera.org	Chicago	IL	60606	312-332-2244	332-8120
Lyric Opera of Kansas City 1029 Central St *Web:* kc-opera.org	Kansas City	MO	64105	816-471-4933	471-0602
Metropolitan Opera 64th St & Broadway Lincoln Center *Web:* www.metopera.org	New York	NY	10023	212-799-3100	870-7410
Michigan Opera Theatre 1526 Broadway *Web:* www.motopera.org	Detroit	MI	48226	313-961-3500	237-3412
Minnesota Opera 620 N 1st St *TF:* 800-676-6737 ■ *Web:* www.mnopera.org	Minneapolis	MN	55401	612-333-2700	333-0869
Mississippi Opera PO Box 1551 *TF:* 877-676-7372 ■ *Web:* www.msopera.org	Jackson	MS	39215	601-960-1528	960-1526
Mobile Opera Inc 257 Dauphin St *Web:* www.mobileopera.org	Mobile	AL	36602	251-432-6772	431-7613
Musical Theatre Southwest 2401 Ross Ave SE *Web:* www.musicaltheatresw.com	Albuquerque	NM	87106	505-265-9119	262-9319
Nevada Opera Assn PO Box 3256 *Web:* www.nevadaopera.com	Reno	NV	89505	775-786-4046	786-4063
New Jersey State Opera 50 Park Pl 9th Fl *Web:* www.njstateopera.org	Newark	NJ	07102	973-623-5757	623-5761
New Orleans Opera Assn 1010 Common St Suite 1820 *TF:* 800-881-4459 ■ *Web:* www.neworleansopera.org	New Orleans	LA	70112	504-529-3000	529-7668
New York City Opera 20 Lincoln Center Plaza New York State Theater *Web:* www.nycopera.com	New York	NY	10023	212-870-5600	724-1120
Ohio Light Opera 329 E University St Freelander Theater *Web:* olo.wooster.edu	Wooster	OH	44691	330-263-2345	263-2272
Opera Birmingham 1807 3rd Ave N *Web:* www.operabirmingham.org	Birmingham	AL	35203	205-322-6737	322-6206
Opera Carolina 345 N College St Suite 409 *Web:* www.operacarolina.org	Charlotte	NC	28202	704-332-7177	332-6448
Opera Cleveland 1422 Euclid Ave Suite 1052 *Web:* www.clevelandopera.org	Cleveland	OH	44115	216-575-0903	575-1918
Opera Co of North Carolina 3600 Glenwood Ave Suite 101 *Web:* www.operanc.com	Raleigh	NC	27612	919-783-0098	783-5638
Opera Co of Philadelphia 1420 Locust St Suite 210 *Web:* www.operaphilly.com	Philadelphia	PA	19102	215-893-3600	893-7801
Opera Colorado 695 S Colorado Blvd Suite 20 *Web:* www.operacolorado.org	Denver	CO	80246	303-778-1500	778-6533
Opera Columbus 177 E Naghten St *Web:* www.operacolumbus.org	Columbus	OH	43215	614-461-8101	
Opera Company of Brooklyn 33 Indian Road Suite 1G *Web:* www.operabrooklyn.com	New York	NY	10034	212-567-3283	
Opera Idaho 501 S 8th St Suite B *Web:* www.operaidaho.org	Boise	ID	83702	208-345-3531	342-7566
Opera Illinois 416 Hamilton Blvd *Web:* www.operaillinois.com	Peoria	IL	61602	309-673-7253	673-7211
Opera Memphis 6745 Wolf River Pkwy *Web:* www.operamemphis.org	Memphis	TN	38120	901-257-3100	257-3109
Opera Omaha 1625 Farnam St Suite 100 *TF:* 877-346-7372 ■ *Web:* www.operaomaha.org	Omaha	NE	68102	402-346-4398	346-7323
Opera Pacific 600 W Warner Ave *TF Sales:* 800-346-7372 ■ *Web:* www.operapacific.org	Santa Ana	CA	92707	714-546-6000	546-6077
Opera Roanoke 541 Luck Ave Suite 209 *Web:* www.operaroanoke.org	Roanoke	VA	24016	540-982-2742	982-3601
Opera San Jose 2149 Paragon Dr *Web:* www.operasj.org	San Jose	CA	95131	408-437-4450	437-4455
Opera Santa Barbara 123 W Padre St Suite A *Web:* www.operasb.com	Santa Barbara	CA	93105	805-898-3890	898-3892
Opera Theatre of Northern Virginia PO Box 7027 *Web:* www.novaopera.org	Arlington	VA	22207	703-528-1433	812-5039
Opera Theatre of Saint Louis PO Box 191910 *Web:* www.opera-stl.org	Saint Louis	MO	63119	314-961-0171	961-7463
Opera Theatre at Wildwood 20919 Denny Rd *TF:* 888-278-7727 ■ *Web:* www.wildwoodpark.org	Little Rock	AR	72223	501-821-7275	821-7280
OperaDelaware PO Box 432 *Web:* www.operade.org	Wilmington	DE	19899	302-658-8063	658-4991
Orlando Opera 1111 N Orange Ave *TF:* 800-336-7372 ■ *Web:* www.orlandoopera.org	Orlando	FL	32804	407-426-1717	426-1705
Palm Beach Opera 415 S Olive Ave *TF:* 877-444-3030 ■ *Web:* www.pbopera.org	West Palm Beach	FL	33401	561-833-7888	833-8294
Pensacola Opera 75 S Tarragona St *Web:* www.pensacolaopera.com	Pensacola	FL	32502	850-433-6737	433-1082
Pittsburgh Civic Light Opera 719 Liberty Ave *Web:* www.pittsburghclo.org	Pittsburgh	PA	15222	412-281-3973	281-5339
Pittsburgh Opera 801 Penn Ave *Web:* www.pittsburghopera.org	Pittsburgh	PA	15222	412-281-0912	281-4324
Pocket Opera 469 Bryant St *Web:* www.pocketopera.org	San Francisco	CA	94107	415-972-8930	348-0931
Portland Opera 211 SE Caruthers St *Web:* www.portlandopera.org	Portland	OR	97214	503-241-1407	241-4212
Sacramento Opera Assn 3811 J St *Web:* www.sacopera.org	Sacramento	CA	95816	916-737-1000	737-1032
San Diego Civic Light Opera 2005 Pan American Plaza Starlight Bowl *Web:* www.starlighttheatre.org	San Diego	CA	92101	619-544-7827	544-7832
San Diego Opera 1200 3rd Ave Civic Center Plaza 18th Fl *Web:* www.sdopera.com	San Diego	CA	92101	619-232-7636	231-6915
San Francisco Opera 301 Van Ness Ave *Web:* www.sfopera.com	San Francisco	CA	94102	415-861-4008	
Santa Fe Opera PO Box 2408 *TF:* 800-280-4654 ■ *Web:* www.santafeopera.org	Santa Fe	NM	87504	505-986-5900	986-5999
Sarasota Opera 61 N Pineapple Ave *TF:* 888-673-7212 ■ *Web:* www.sarasotaopera.org	Sarasota	FL	34236	941-366-8450	955-5571
Seattle Opera PO Box 9248 *TF Sales:* 800-426-1619 ■ *Web:* www.seattleopera.org	Seattle	WA	98109	206-389-7600	389-7651
Shreveport Opera 212 Texas St Suite 101 *Web:* www.shreveopera.org	Shreveport	LA	71101	318-227-9503	227-9518
Skylight Opera Theatre 158 N Broadway *Web:* www.skylightopera.com	Milwaukee	WI	53202	414-291-7811	291-7815
Southeastern Regional Opera 914 Pulaski St	Columbia	SC	29201	803-771-6303	771-2625
Syracuse Opera 411 Montgomery St Suite 60 *Web:* www.syracuseopera.com	Syracuse	NY	13202	315-475-5915	475-6319
Tacoma Opera 917 Pacific Ave Suite 407 *Web:* www.tacomaopera.com	Tacoma	WA	98402	253-627-7789	627-1620
Toledo Opera 425 Jefferson Ave Suite 601 *TF:* 866-860-9048 ■ *Web:* www.toledoopera.org	Toledo	OH	43604	419-255-7464	255-6344
Tri-Cities Opera 315 Clinton St *Web:* www.tricitiesopera.com	Binghamton	NY	13905	607-729-3444	797-6344
Tulsa Opera 1610 S Boulder Ave *TF:* 866-298-2530 ■ *Web:* www.tulsaopera.com	Tulsa	OK	74119	918-582-4035	592-0380
Utah Opera Co 123 W South Temple *Web:* www.utahopera.org	Salt Lake City	UT	84101	801-533-5626	869-9026
Virginia Opera 160 E Virginia Beach Blvd *Web:* www.vaopera.org	Norfolk	VA	23510	757-627-9545	622-0058
Virginia Opera 6 N Laurel St Landmark Theater *Web:* www.vaopera.org	Richmond	VA	23220	804-644-8168	644-0415
Washington National Opera 2600 Virginia Ave NW Suite 301 *TF:* 800-876-7372 ■ *Web:* www.dc-opera.org	Washington	DC	20037	202-295-2420	295-2479
Wichita Grand Opera 225 W Douglas Ave Century II Performing Arts Center *Web:* www.wichitagrandopera.org	Wichita	KS	67202	316-683-3444	263-2126
Wolf Trap Opera Co 1645 Trap Rd *Web:* www.wolftrap.org/opera/opera.html	Vienna	VA	22182	703-255-1935	255-1896

576-3 Orchestras

Organization	City	State	ZIP	Phone	Fax
Abilene Philharmonic Orchestra 402 Cypress St Suite 130 *TF:* 800-460-0610 ■ *Web:* www.abilenephilharmonic.org	Abilene	TX	79601	325-677-6710	677-1299
Acadiana Symphony Orchestra 412 Travis St *Web:* www.acadianasymphony.org	Lafayette	LA	70503	337-232-4277	237-4712
Akron Symphony Orchestra 17 N Broadway *Web:* www.akronsymphony.org	Akron	OH	44308	330-535-8131	535-7302
Alabama Symphony Orchestra 3621 6th Ave S *Web:* www.alabamasymphony.org	Birmingham	AL	35222	205-251-6929	251-6840
Albany Symphony Orchestra PO Box 70065 *Web:* www.albanysymphony.org	Albany	GA	31708	229-317-6799	430-6798
Albany Symphony Orchestra 19 Clinton Ave *Web:* www.albanysymphony.com	Albany	NY	12207	518-465-4755	465-3711
Alexandria Symphony Orchestra 2121 Eisenhower Ave Suite 608 *Web:* www.alexsym.org	Alexandria	VA	22314	703-548-0885	548-0985
Allentown Symphony Orchestra 23 N 6th St *Web:* www.allentownsymphony.org	Allentown	PA	18101	610-432-6715	351-3890
Amarillo Symphony 1000 S Polk St *Web:* www.amarillosymphony.org	Amarillo	TX	79101	806-376-8782	376-7127
American Composers Orchestra 240 W 35th St Suite 405 *Web:* www.americancomposers.org	New York	NY	10001	212-977-8495	977-8995
American Symphony Orchestra 333 W 39th St Suite 1101 *Web:* www.americansymphony.org	New York	NY	10018	212-868-9276	868-9277
Anchorage Symphony Orchestra 400 D St Suite 230 *TF:* 866-364-8668 ■ *Web:* www.anchoragesymphony.org	Anchorage	AK	99501	907-274-8668	272-7916
Anderson Symphony Orchestra PO Box 741 *TF:* 888-644-9490 ■ *Web:* www.andersonsymphony.org	Anderson	IN	46015	765-644-2111	644-7703
Ann Arbor Symphony Orchestra 220 E Huron St Suite 470 *Web:* www.a2so.com	Ann Arbor	MI	48104	734-994-4801	994-3949
Annapolis Symphony Orchestra 801 Chase St Maryland Hall *Web:* www.annapolissymphony.org	Annapolis	MD	21401	410-269-1132	263-0616
Arapahoe Philharmonic 2100 W Littleton Blvd Suite 250 *Web:* www.arapahoe-phil.org	Littleton	CO	80120	303-781-1892	781-4918
Arkansas Symphony Orchestra 2417 N Tyler St PO Box 7328 *Web:* www.arkansassymphony.org	Little Rock	AR	72217	501-666-1761	666-3193
Asheville Symphony Orchestra 87 Haywood St PO Box 2852 *TF:* 888-860-7378 ■ *Web:* www.ashevillesymphony.org	Asheville	NC	28802	828-254-7046	254-1761
Aspen Chamber Symphony 2 Music School Rd	Aspen	CO	81611	970-925-3254	
Atlanta Pops 1830-A Briarcliff Cir PO Box 15037 *Web:* www.altieriandassociates.com/pops	Atlanta	GA	30333	404-636-0020	636-0020
Atlanta Symphony Orchestra 1280 Peachtree St NE Suite 4074 *Web:* www.atlantasymphony.org	Atlanta	GA	30309	404-733-4900	733-4901
Augusta Symphony 1301 Greene St Suite 200 *Web:* www.augustasymphony.org	Augusta	GA	30901	706-826-4705	826-4735
Aurora Symphony Orchestra PO Box 441481 *Web:* www.aurorasymphony.org	Aurora	CO	80044	303-873-6622	
Austin Chamber Music Center 3814 Medical Pkwy *Web:* www.austinchambermusic.org	Austin	TX	78756	512-454-7562	454-0029
Austin Civic Orchestra PO Box 27132 *Web:* www.austincivicorchestra.org	Austin	TX	78755	512-301-7370	301-3373
Austin Symphony Orchestra 1101 Red River St *TF:* 888-462-3787 ■ *Web:* www.austinsymphony.org	Austin	TX	78701	512-476-6064	476-6242
Bakersfield Symphony Orchestra 1328 34th St Suite A *Web:* www.bakersfieldsymphony.org	Bakersfield	CA	93301	661-323-7928	323-7331

Organization	City	State	Zip	Phone	Fax
Baltimore Symphony Orchestra 1212 Cathedral St. *Web:* www.baltimoresymphony.org	Baltimore	MD	21201	410-783-8100	783-8004
Bangor Symphony Orchestra 51-A Main St PO Box 1441 *TF:* 800-639-3221 ■ *Web:* www.bangorsymphony.com	Bangor	ME	04402	207-942-5555	990-1272
Baton Rouge Symphony PO Box 14209 *TF:* 877-800-4099 ■ *Web:* www.brso.org	Baton Rouge	LA	70898	225-383-0500	346-1191
Berkeley Symphony Orchestra 1942 University Ave Suite 207 *Web:* www.berkeleysymphony.org	Berkeley	CA	94704	510-841-2800	841-5422
Billings Symphony 2721 2nd Ave N *Web:* www.billingssymphony.org	Billings	MT	59101	406-252-3610	252-3353
Bismarck-Mandan Symphony Orchestra 215 N 6th St. *Web:* www.bismarckmandansymphony.org	Bismarck	ND	58501	701-258-8345	258-8345
Boise Philharmonic Assn Inc 516 S 9th St *Web:* www.boisephilharmonic.org	Boise	ID	83702	208-344-7849	336-9078
Boston Chamber Ensemble 6 Summer St.	Hyde Park	MA	02136	617-361-5975	
Boston Modern Orchestra Project 9 Birch St *Web:* www.bmop.org	Roslindale	MA	02131	617-363-0396	363-0395
Boston Philharmonic 295 Huntington Ave Suite 210 *Web:* www.bostonphil.org	Boston	MA	02115	617-236-0999	236-8613
Boston Pops 301 Massachusetts Ave Symphony Hall *TF:* 888-266-1200 ■ *Web:* www.bso.org	Boston	MA	02115	617-266-1492	638-9493
Boston Symphony Orchestra 301 Massachusetts Ave Symphony Hall *TF:* 888-266-1200 ■ *Web:* www.bso.org	Boston	MA	02115	617-266-1492	638-9367
Boulder Philharmonic Orchestra 2995 Wilderness Pl Suite 100 *Web:* www.boulderphil.org	Boulder	CO	80301	303-449-1343	443-9203
Bozeman Symphony 1822 W Lincoln St Suite 3 *Web:* www.bozemansymphony.org	Bozeman	MT	59715	406-585-9774	585-0285
Bridgeport (Greater) Symphony 446 University Ave *Web:* bridgeportsymphony.org	Bridgeport	CT	06604	203-576-0263	367-0064
Brockton Symphony Orchestra 156 W Elm St *Web:* www.brocktonsymphony.org	Brockton	MA	02301	508-588-3841	588-3818
Brooklyn Philharmonic 138-A Court St. *Web:* www.brooklynphilharmonic.org	Brooklyn	NY	11201	718-488-5700	488-5901
Buffalo Philharmonic Orchestra 499 Franklin St *Web:* www.bpo.org	Buffalo	NY	14202	716-885-0331	885-9372
Calgary Philharmonic Orchestra 205 8th Ave SE 2nd Fl *Web:* www.cpo-live.com	Calgary	AB	T2G0K9	403-571-0270	294-7424
California Philharmonic Orchestra 1120 Huntington Dr *Web:* www.calphil.org	San Marino	CA	91108	626-300-8200	300-8010
Camellia Symphony Orchestra PO Box 19786 *Web:* www.camelliasymphony.org	Sacramento	CA	95819	916-929-6655	929-4292
Canton Symphony Orchestra 1001 Market Ave N. *Web:* www.cantonsymphony.org	Canton	OH	44702	330-452-3434	452-4429
Cape Symphony Orchestra 712A Main St. *Web:* www.capesymphony.org	Yarmouth Port	MA	02675	508-362-1111	362-7916
Carson City Symphony 191 Heidi Cir PO Box 2001 *Web:* ccsymphony.com	Carson City	NV	89702	775-883-4154	883-4371
Cedar Rapids Symphony Orchestra 119 3rd Ave SE *TF:* 800-369-8863 ■ *Web:* www.crsymphony.org	Cedar Rapids	IA	52401	319-366-8206	366-5206
Chamber Orchestra of Philadelphia 1520 Locust St 5th Fl *Web:* www.chamberorchestra.org	Philadelphia	PA	19102	215-545-5451	545-3868
Champaign-Urbana Symphony Orchestra 701 Devonshire Dr Suite C-24 *Web:* www.cusymphony.org	Champaign	IL	61820	217-351-9139	398-0413
Charleston Symphony Orchestra 145 King St Suite 311 *Web:* www.charlestonsymphony.com	Charleston	SC	29401	843-723-7528	722-3463
Charlotte Philharmonic Orchestra 8008 Corporate Center Dr Suite 206 PO Box 470987 *Web:* www.charlottephilharmonic.org	Charlotte	NC	28247	704-543-5551	543-5542
Charlotte Symphony Orchestra 1300 Baxter St Suite 300 *Web:* www.charlottesymphony.org	Charlotte	NC	28204	704-972-2003	972-2012
Chattanooga Symphony & Opera 630 Chestnut St. *Web:* www.chattanoogasymphony.org	Chattanooga	TN	37402	423-267-8583	265-6520
Cheyenne Symphony Orchestra 1904 Thomes Ave *Web:* www.cheyennesymphony.org	Cheyenne	WY	82001	307-778-8561	634-7512
Chicago Chamber Orchestra 333 N Michigan Ave Suite 932 *Web:* www.chicagochamberorchestra.org	Chicago	IL	60601	312-357-1551	
Chicago Sinfonietta 70 E Lake St Suite 226 *Web:* www.chicagosinfonietta.org	Chicago	IL	60601	312-236-3681	236-5429
Chicago Symphony Orchestra 220 S Michigan Ave *TF:* 800-223-7114 ■ *Web:* www.cso.org	Chicago	IL	60604	312-294-3000	294-3035
Cincinnati Chamber Orchestra 105 W 4th St Suite 810 *Web:* www.ccocincinnati.com	Cincinnati	OH	45202	513-723-1182	723-1057
Cincinnati Symphony Orchestra 1241 Elm St Music Hall *Web:* www.cincinnatisymphony.org	Cincinnati	OH	45202	513-621-1919	744-3535
Civic Orchestra of Tucson PO Box 42764 *Web:* www.cotmusic.org	Tucson	AZ	85733	520-730-3371	
Cleveland Chamber Symphony 2001 Euclid Ave Cleveland State University *Web:* www.clevelandchambersymphony.org	Cleveland	OH	44115	216-687-9243	687-9279
Cleveland Orchestra 11001 Euclid Ave Severance Hall *TF:* 800-686-1141 ■ *Web:* www.clevelandorchestra.com	Cleveland	OH	44106	216-231-7300	231-0202
Cleveland Pops Orchestra 24000 Mercantile Rd Suite 11 *Web:* www.clevelandpops.com	Cleveland	OH	44122	216-765-7677	765-1931
Colorado Springs Philharmonic PO Box 60730 *Web:* www.csphilharmonic.org	Colorado Springs	CO	80960	719-884-2110	884-2111
Colorado Symphony Orchestra 1000 14th St Unit 15 *TF:* 877-292-7979 ■ *Web:* www.coloradosymphony.org	Denver	CO	80202	303-623-7876	293-2649
Columbus Symphony Orchestra 900 Broadway *Web:* www.csoga.org	Columbus	GA	31904	706-323-5059	323-7051
Columbus Symphony Orchestra 55 E State St *Web:* www.columbussymphony.com	Columbus	OH	43215	614-228-9600	224-7273
Corpus Christi Symphony Orchestra 555 N Carancahua St Suite 410 *TF:* 877-286-6683 ■ *Web:* www.ccsymphony.org	Corpus Christi	TX	78478	361-882-2717	882-4132
Da Camera of Houston 1427 Branard St. *TF:* 800-233-2226 ■ *Web:* www.dacamera.com	Houston	TX	77006	713-524-7601	524-4148
Dallas Symphony Orchestra 2301 Flora St Suite 300 *Web:* dallassymphony.com	Dallas	TX	75201	214-692-0203	871-4049
Dayton Philharmonic Orchestra 109 N Main St Suite 200 *Web:* www.daytonphilharmonic.com	Dayton	OH	45402	937-224-3521	223-9189
Daytona Beach Symphony Society 140 S Beach St Cress Bldg Suite 107 *Web:* www.dbss.org	Daytona Beach	FL	32114	386-253-2901	253-5774
Dearborn Symphony Orchestra 23400 Michigan Ave PO Box 2063 *Web:* www.dearbornsymphony.org	Dearborn	MI	48123	313-565-2424	565-2411
DeKalb Symphony Orchestra PO Box 1313 *Fax Area Code: 404 ■ *Web:* www.dekalbsymphony.com	Tucker	GA	30085	678-891-3565	299-4271*
Delaware Symphony Orchestra 818 N Market St. *Web:* www.desymphony.org	Wilmington	DE	19801	302-656-7442	656-7754
Des Moines Symphony 221 Walnut St *Web:* www.dmsymphony.org	Des Moines	IA	50309	515-280-4000	280-4005
Detroit Symphony Orchestra 3711 Woodward Ave. *Web:* www.detroitsymphony.com	Detroit	MI	48201	313-576-5111	576-5109
Dubuque Symphony Orchestra 2728 Asbury Rd Suite 900 *TF:* 866-803-9280 ■ *Web:* dubuquesymphony.org	Dubuque	IA	52001	563-557-1677	557-9841
Duluth-Superior Symphony Orchestra 506 W Michigan St. *Web:* www.dsso.com	Duluth	MN	55802	218-733-7575	733-7537
Durham Symphony Orchestra 120 Morris St *Web:* www.durhamsymphony.org	Durham	NC	27701	919-560-2736	560-2752
Eastern Connecticut Symphony Orchestra 289 State St *Web:* www.ectsymphony.org	New London	CT	06320	860-443-2876	444-7601
Edmonton Symphony Orchestra 9720 102nd Ave. *TF:* 800-563-5081 ■ *Web:* www.edmontonsymphony.com	Edmonton	AB	T5J4B2	780-428-1108	425-0167
El Paso Symphony Orchestra 1 Civic Center Plaza *Web:* www.epso.org	El Paso	TX	79901	915-532-3776	533-8162
Erie Philharmonic 1006 State St. *Web:* www.eriephil.org	Erie	PA	16501	814-455-1375	455-1377
Eugene Symphony 115 W 8th Ave Suite 115 *Web:* www.eugenesymphony.org	Eugene	OR	97401	541-687-9487	687-0527
Evansville Philharmonic Orchestra 530 Main St *Web:* www.evansvillephilharmonic.org	Evansville	IN	47708	812-425-5050	426-7008
Fairbanks Symphony Orchestra PO Box 82104 *Web:* www.fairbankssymphony.org	Fairbanks	AK	99708	907-474-5733	474-5147
Fairfax Symphony Orchestra 3905 Railroad Ave Suite 202-N *Web:* www.fairfaxsymphony.org	Fairfax	VA	22030	703-563-1990	293-9349
Fargo-Moorhead Symphony 810 4th Ave S Suite 250 *Web:* www.fmsymphony.org	Moorhead	MN	56560	218-233-8397	236-1845
Flagstaff Symphony Orchestra 113-A E Aspen Ave PO Box 122 *TF:* 888-520-7214 ■ *Web:* www.flagstaffsymphony.org	Flagstaff	AZ	86002	928-774-5107	774-5109
Florida Orchestra 101 S Hoover Blvd Suite 100 *TF:* 800-662-7286 ■ *Web:* www.floridaorchestra.org	Tampa	FL	33609	813-286-1170	286-8227
Florida Symphony Youth Orchestra 812 E Rollins St Suite 300 *Web:* www.fsyo.org	Orlando	FL	32803	407-999-7800	896-5250
Florida West Coast Symphony 709 N Tamiami Trail *TF:* 866-508-0611 ■ *Web:* www.fwcs.org	Sarasota	FL	34236	941-953-4252	953-3059
Fort Collins Symphony 214 S College Ave *Web:* www.fcsymphony.org	Fort Collins	CO	80524	970-482-4823	482-4858
Fort Smith Symphony Orchestra 511 Central Mall Suite 617 PO Box 3151 *Web:* www.fortsmithsymphony.org	Fort Smith	AR	72913	479-452-7575	452-8985
Fort Wayne Philharmonic 2340 Fairfield Ave *TF:* 888-402-2224 ■ *Web:* www.fortwaynephilharmonic.com	Fort Wayne	IN	46807	260-456-2224	456-8555
Fort Worth Symphony Orchestra Assn 330 E 4th St Suite 200 *Web:* www.fwsymphony.org	Fort Worth	TX	76102	817-665-6500	665-6600
Fresno Philharmonic 2377 W Shaw Ave Suite 101 *Web:* www.fresnophil.org	Fresno	CA	93711	559-261-0600	261-0700
Glendale Symphony Orchestra PO Box 1986 *Web:* www.glendalesymphony.org	Glendale	CA	91209	818-500-8720	500-8721
Grand Rapids Symphony 300 Ottawa Ave NW Suite 100 *Web:* www.grsymphony.org	Grand Rapids	MI	49503	616-454-9451	454-7477
Grant Park Orchestra 205 E Randolph Dr *Web:* www.grantparkmusicfestival.com	Chicago	IL	60601	312-742-7638	742-7662
Green Bay Symphony Orchestra 1240 Main St Suite 2 *Web:* www.gbsymphony.org	Green Bay	WI	54302	920-435-3465	435-1427
Greensboro Symphony Orchestra 200 N Davie St Suite 301 *Web:* www.greensborosymphony.org	Greensboro	NC	27401	336-335-5456	335-5580
Greenville Symphony Orchestra 200 S Main St *Web:* www.greenvillesymphony.org	Greenville	SC	29601	864-232-0344	467-3113
Greenwich Symphony Orchestra PO Box 35 *Web:* www.greenwichsym.org	Greenwich	CT	06836	203-869-2664	
Handel & Haydn Society 300 Massachusetts Ave *Web:* www.handelandhaydn.org	Boston	MA	02115	617-262-1815	266-4217
Harrisburg Symphony Orchestra 800 Corporate Circle Suite 101 *Web:* www.harrisburgsymphony.org	Harrisburg	PA	17110	717-545-5527	545-6501
Hartford Symphony Orchestra 99 Pratt Ave Suite 500 *Web:* www.hartfordsymphony.org	Hartford	CT	06103	860-246-8742	247-5430
Honolulu Symphony 650 Iwilei Rd Suite 202 *Web:* www.honolulusymphony.com	Honolulu	HI	96817	808-524-0815	524-1507
Houston Symphony Orchestra 615 Louisiana St Suite 102 *Web:* www.houstonsymphony.org	Houston	TX	77002	713-224-4240	222-7024
Huntsville Symphony Orchestra 700 Monroe St. *Web:* www.hso.org	Huntsville	AL	35801	256-539-4818	539-4819
Idaho State Civic Symphony 921 S 8th Ave Stop 8099 Idaho State University Fine Arts Dept *Web:* www.thesymphony.us	Pocatello	ID	83209	208-282-3636	282-4884
Illinois Symphony Orchestera 524 1/2 Capitol Ave *TF:* 800-401-7222 ■ *Web:* www.ilsymphony.org	Springfield	IL	62705	217-522-2838	522-7374
Indianapolis Symphony Orchestra 32 E Washington St Suite 600 *TF:* 800-366-8457 ■ *Web:* www.indianapolissymphony.org	Indianapolis	IN	46204	317-262-1100	262-1159
Jacksonville Symphony Orchestra 300 W Water St Suite 200 *TF:* 877-662-6731 ■ *Web:* www.jaxsymphony.org	Jacksonville	FL	32202	904-354-5479	354-9238
Johnson City Symphony Orchestra 3201 Bristol Hwy PO Box 533 *Web:* www.jcsymphony.com	Johnson City	TN	37605	423-926-8742	926-8979
Juneau Symphony Orchestra 522 W 10th St PO Box 21236 *Web:* www.juneausymphony.org	Juneau	AK	99802	907-586-4676	463-2555
Kalamazoo Symphony Orchestra 359 S Kalamazoo Mall Suite 100 *Web:* www.kalamazoosymphony.com	Kalamazoo	MI	49007	269-349-7759	349-9229
Kansas City Symphony 1020 Central St Suite 300 *Web:* www.kcsymphony.org	Kansas City	MO	64105	816-471-1100	471-0976
Kennedy Center Opera House Orchestra John F Kennedy Center for the Performing Arts 2700 F St NW *TF:* 800-444-1324 ■ *Web:* www.kennedy-center.org	Washington	DC	20566	202-416-8200	416-8205
Kentucky Symphony Orchestra 540 Linden Ave PO Box 72810 *Web:* www.kyso.org	Newport	KY	41072	859-431-6216	431-3097
Key West Symphony Orchestra PO Box 774 *Web:* www.keywestsymphony.com	Key West	FL	33041	305-292-1774	292-5623
Knoxville Symphony Orchestra 100 S Gay St Suite 302 *Web:* www.knoxvillesymphony.com	Knoxville	TN	37902	865-523-1178	546-3766
Lansing (Greater) Symphony Orchestra 230 N Washington Sq Suite 100 *Web:* www.lansingsymphony.org	Lansing	MI	48933	517-487-5001	487-0210
Las Cruces Symphony Orchestra 1075 N Horseshoe Cir *Web:* www.lascrucessymphony.com	Las Cruces	NM	88003	505-646-3709	646-1086
Lexington Philharmonic 161 N Mill St *TF:* 888-494-4226 ■ *Web:* www.lexphil.org	Lexington	KY	40507	859-233-4226	233-7896
Lincoln Symphony Orchestra 233 S 13th St Suite B-102 *Web:* www.lincolnsymphony.com	Lincoln	NE	68508	402-476-2211	476-2236
Long Beach Symphony Orchestra 110 W Ocean Blvd Suite 22 *Web:* www.lbso.org	Long Beach	CA	90802	562-436-3203	491-3599
Long Island Baroque Ensemble PO Box 7 *Web:* www.longislandbaroqueensemble.com	Locust Valley	NY	11560	631-724-7386	864-4426

Orchestras (Cont'd)

Organization	City	State	Zip	Phone	Fax
Long Island Philharmonic 1 Huntington Quadrangle Suite 2C21 *Web:* www.liphilharmonic.com	Melville	NY	11747	631-293-2223	293-2655
Los Angeles Chamber Orchestra 707 Wilshire Blvd Suite 1850 *Web:* www.laco.org	Los Angeles	CA	90017	213-622-7001	955-2071
Los Angeles Philharmonic Assn 111 S Grand Ave **Fax Area Code:* 213 ■ *Web:* www.laphil.org	Los Angeles	CA	90012	323-850-2000	972-7560*
Louisiana Philharmonic Orchestra 1010 Common St Suite 2120 *Web:* www.lpomusic.com	New Orleans	LA	70112	504-523-6530	595-8468
Louisville Orchestra 323 W Broadway Suite 700 *Web:* www.louisvilleorchestra.org	Louisville	KY	40202	502-587-8681	589-7870
Macon Symphony Orchestra 400 Poplar St *Web:* www.maconsymphony.com	Macon	GA	31201	478-301-5300	301-5505
Madison Symphony Orchestra 222 W Washington St Suite 460 *Web:* www.madisonsymphony.org	Madison	WI	53703	608-257-3734	280-6192
Manitoba Chamber Orchestra 393 Portage Ave Portage Pl Suite Y300 *Web:* www.manitobachamberorchestra.org	Winnipeg	MB	R3B3H6	204-783-7377	783-7383
Marin Symphony 4340 Redwood Hwy Suite 409C *Web:* www.marinsymphony.org	San Rafael	CA	94903	415-479-8100	479-8110
Maryland Symphony Orchestra 30 W Washington St *Web:* www.marylandsymphony.org	Hagerstown	MD	21740	301-797-4000	797-2314
Massachusetts Symphony Orchestra 10 Tuckerman St Tuckerman Hall *Web:* www.tuckermanhall.org/pops.html	Worcester	MA	01609	508-754-1234	752-3671
Memphis Symphony Orchestra 585 S Mendenhall Rd *Web:* www.memphissymphony.org	Memphis	TN	38117	901-537-2525	537-2550
Mesa Symphony Orchestra 56 S Center St *Web:* www.mesasymphony.org	Mesa	AZ	85210	480-827-2143	827-2070
Miami Symphony Orchestra 10300 SW 72nd St Sunset Center Suite 499 *Web:* www.miamisymphony.org	Miami	FL	33173	305-275-5666	275-4363
Milwaukee Symphony Orchestra 700 N Water St Suite 700 *TF:* 800-291-7605 ■ *Web:* www.milwaukeesymphony.org	Milwaukee	WI	53202	414-291-6010	291-7610
Minnesota Orchestra 1111 Nicollet Mall Orchestra Hall *Web:* www.minnesotaorchestra.org	Minneapolis	MN	55403	612-371-5600	371-0838
Mississippi Symphony Orchestra 201 E Pascagoula St *Web:* www.msorchestra.com	Jackson	MS	39201	601-960-1565	960-1564
Mobile Symphony PO Box 3127 *Web:* www.mobilesymphony.org	Mobile	AL	36652	251-432-2010	432-6618
Modesto Symphony Orchestra 911 13th St *Web:* www.modestosymphony.org	Modesto	CA	95354	209-523-4156	523-0201
Monterey Symphony 10th & Mission PO Box 3965 *Web:* www.montereysymphony.org	Carmel	CA	93921	831-624-8511	624-3837
Montreal Symphony Orchestra 260 de Maisonneuve Blvd W 2nd Fl *Web:* www.osm.ca	Montreal	QC	H2X1Y9	514-842-9951	842-0728
Muncie Symphony Orchestra 2000 University Ave c/o Ball State University *Web:* www.munciesymphony.org	Muncie	IN	47306	765-285-5531	285-9128
Music of the Baroque 111 Wabash Ave Suite 810 *Web:* www.baroque.org	Chicago	IL	60602	312-551-1415	551-1444
Napa Valley Symphony 1100 Lincoln Ave Suite 108 *Web:* www.napavalleysymphony.org	Napa	CA	94558	707-226-6872	226-3046
Naples Philharmonic Orchestra 5833 Pelican Bay Blvd Philharmonic Center for the Arts *TF:* 800-597-1900 ■ *Web:* www.thephil.org	Naples	FL	34108	239-597-1900	597-8163
Nashville Chamber Orchestra 1114 17th Ave S Suite 202 *Web:* www.nco.org	Nashville	TN	37212	615-256-6546	322-1228
Nashville Symphony 1 Symphony Pl *Web:* www.nashvillesymphony.org	Nashville	TN	37201	615-687-6500	687-6505
National Philharmonic 5301 Tuckerman Lane Music Center at Strathmore *Web:* www.nationalphilharmonic.org	North Bethesda	MD	20852	301-493-9283	493-9284
National Symphony Orchestra JFK Center for the Performing Arts 2700 F St NW *TF:* 800-444-1324 ■ *Web:* kennedy-center.org/nso	Washington	DC	20566	202-416-8000	416-8105
New Hampshire Music Festival Orchestra 52 Symphony Ln *Web:* www.nhmf.org	Center Harbor	NH	03226	603-279-3300	279-3484
New Haven Symphony Orchestra PO Box 9718 *Web:* www.newhavensymphony.com	New Haven	CT	06536	203-865-0831	789-8907
New Jersey Symphony Orchestra 60 Park Pl *Web:* www.njsymphony.org	Newark	NJ	07102	973-624-3713	624-2115
New Mexico Symphony Orchestra 4407 Menaul Blvd NE *TF:* 800-251-6676 ■ *Web:* www.nmso.org	Albuquerque	NM	87110	505-881-9590	881-9456
New West Symphony 2100 E Thousand Oaks Blvd Suite D *Web:* www.newwestsymphony.org	Thousand Oaks	CA	91362	805-497-5800	497-5839
New World Symphony 541 Lincoln Rd *TF:* 800-597-3331 ■ *Web:* www.nws.org	Miami Beach	FL	33139	305-673-3330	673-6749
New York Philharmonic 10 Lincoln Center Plaza Avery Fisher Hall **Fax:* Mktg ■ *Web:* www.newyorkphilharmonic.org	New York	NY	10023	212-875-5900	875-5717*
New York Pops 333 W 52nd St Suite 600 *Web:* www.newyorkpops.org	New York	NY	10019	212-765-7677	315-3199
North Arkansas Symphony 605 W Dixon St PO Box 1243 *Web:* www.nasymphony.org	Fayetteville	AR	72702	479-521-4166	695-1229
North Carolina Symphony 2 E South St Memorial Auditorium *Web:* www.ncsymphony.org	Raleigh	NC	27601	919-733-2750	733-9920
Northeastern Pennsylvania Philharmonic 4101 Birney Ave *TF:* 800-836-3413 ■ *Web:* www.nepaphil.org	Moosic	PA	18507	570-341-1568	941-0318
Oklahoma City Philharmonic 428 W California Ave Suite 210 *Web:* www.okcphilharmonic.org	Oklahoma City	OK	73102	405-232-7575	232-4353
Omaha Symphony 1605 Howard St *Web:* www.omahasymphony.org	Omaha	NE	68102	402-342-3836	342-3819
Opera Orchestra of New York 239 W 72nd St Suite 2R *Web:* www.oony.org	New York	NY	10023	212-799-1982	721-9170
Orange County's Pacific Symphony 3631 S Harbor Blvd Suite 100 *Web:* pacificsymphony.entericorp.com	Santa Ana	CA	92704	714-755-5788	755-5789
Orchestra New England PO Box 200123 *Web:* www.orchestranewengland.org	New Haven	CT	06520	203-777-4690	772-0578
Orchestra of Saint Luke's 330 W 42nd St 9th Fl *Web:* www.oslmusic.org	New York	NY	10036	212-594-6100	594-3291
Orchestre Metropolitain du Grand Montreal 486 Saint Catherine St W Suite 401 *Web:* www.orchestremetropolitain.com	Montreal	QC	H3B1A6	514-598-0870	840-9195
Oregon Symphony Orchestra 921 SW Washington St Suite 200 *TF:* 800-228-7343 ■ *Web:* www.orsymphony.org	Portland	OR	97205	503-228-4294	228-4150
Orlando Philharmonic Orchestra 812 E Rollins St Suite 300 *TF:* 888-262-8122 ■ *Web:* www.orlandophil.org	Orlando	FL	32803	407-896-6700	896-5512
Orpheus Chamber Orchestra 490 Riverside Dr 11th Fl *Web:* www.orpheusnyc.com	New York	NY	10027	212-896-1700	896-1717
Ottawa Symphony Orchestra 2 Daly Ave Suite 250 *Web:* www.ottawasymphony.com	Ottawa	ON	K1N6E2	613-231-7802	231-3610
Owensboro Symphony Orchestra 211 E 2nd St *Web:* www.owensborosymphony.org	Owensboro	KY	42303	270-684-0661	683-0740
Paducah Symphony Orchestra 2101 Broadway *TF:* 800-738-3727 ■ *Web:* www.paducahsymphony.com	Paducah	KY	42001	270-444-0065	444-0456
Pasadena Symphony 2500 E Colorado Blvd Suite 260 *Web:* www.pasadenasymphony.org	Pasadena	CA	91107	626-793-7172	793-7180
Pensacola Symphony Orchestra 205 E Zaragossa St *Web:* www.pensacolasymphony.com	Pensacola	FL	32502	850-435-2533	444-9910
Peoria Symphony Orchestra 203 Harrison St *Web:* www.peoriasymphony.org	Peoria	IL	61602	309-637-2787	637-7388
Peter Nero & the Philly Pops 260 S Broad St 16th Fl *Web:* www.phillypops.com	Philadelphia	PA	19102	215-893-1900	893-1948
Philadelphia Orchestra 260 S Broad St Suite 1600 *TF:* 800-457-8354 ■ *Web:* www.philorch.org	Philadelphia	PA	19102	215-893-1900	893-1948
Philharmonia Baroque Orchestra 180 Redwood St Suite 200 *Web:* www.philharmonia.org	San Francisco	CA	94102	415-252-1288	252-1488
Philharmonic Orchestra of New Jersey PO Box 4064 *Web:* www.ponj.org	Warren	NJ	07059	908-226-7300	226-7337
Phoenix Symphony 455 N 3rd St Suite 390 *TF:* 800-776-9080 ■ *Web:* www.phoenixsymphony.org	Phoenix	AZ	85004	602-495-1117	253-1772
Pittsburgh Symphony Orchestra 600 Penn Ave Heinz Hall for the Performing Arts *TF:* 800-743-8560 ■ *Web:* www.pittsburghsymphony.org	Pittsburgh	PA	15222	412-392-4800	392-3311
Plano Symphony Orchestra 2701-C W 15th St Suite 187 *Web:* www.planosymphony.org	Plano	TX	75075	972-473-7262	473-4639
Plymouth Philharmonic Orchestra 16 Court St PO Box 3174 *Web:* www.plymouthphilharmonic.com	Plymouth	MA	02361	508-746-8008	746-0115
Portland Baroque Orchestra 1020 SW Taylor St Suite 275 *TF:* 800-494-8497 ■ *Web:* www.pbo.org	Portland	OR	97205	503-222-6000	226-6635
Portland Symphony Orchestra 477 Congress St PO Box 3573 *Web:* www.portlandsymphony.com	Portland	ME	04104	207-773-6128	773-6089
ProMusica Chamber Orchestra 243 N 5th St Suite 202 *Web:* www.promusicacolumbus.org	Columbus	OH	43215	614-464-0066	464-4141
Raleigh Symphony Orchestra 2414 White Cliff Rd PO Box 25878 *Web:* www.raleighsymphony.com	Raleigh	NC	27611	919-546-9755	546-0251
Redlands Symphony 1200 E Colton Ave *Web:* www.redlandssymphony.com	Redlands	CA	92373	909-335-5202	335-5213
Reno Chamber Orchestra 925 Riverside Dr Suite 5 *Web:* www.renochamberorchestra.org	Reno	NV	89503	775-348-9413	348-0643
Reno Philharmonic Orchestra 925 Riverside Dr Suite 3 *Web:* www.renophilharmonic.com	Reno	NV	89503	775-323-6393	323-6711
Rhode Island Philharmonic Orchestra 667 Waterman Ave *Web:* www.ri-philharmonic.org	East Providence	RI	02914	401-831-3123	248-7071
Richmond Symphony 300 W Franklin St Suite 103E *Web:* www.richmondsymphony.com	Richmond	VA	23220	804-788-4717	788-1541
Richmond Symphony Orchestra 380 Hubelchison Pkwy PO Box 982 *Web:* www.richmondsymphony.org	Richmond	IN	47375	765-966-5181	962-8447
Ridgefield Symphony Orchestra 90 E Ridge PO Box 289 *Web:* www.ridgefieldsymphony.org	Ridgefield	CT	06877	203-438-3889	438-0222
River City Brass Band 500 Grant St Suite 2720 One Mellon Center *TF:* 800-292-7222 ■ *Web:* www.rcbb.com	Pittsburgh	PA	15219	412-434-7222	434-6436
Roanoke Symphony Orchestra 541 Luck Ave Suite 200 *TF:* 866-277-9127 ■ *Web:* rso.com	Roanoke	VA	24016	540-343-6221	343-0065
Rochester Orchestra & Chorale 400 S Broadway *TF:* 877-286-8742 ■ *Web:* rochestersymphony.org	Rochester	MN	55904	507-286-8742	280-4136
Rochester Philharmonic Orchestra 108 East Ave *Web:* www.rpo.org	Rochester	NY	14604	585-454-7311	325-4905
Rockford Symphony Orchestra 711 N Main St *Web:* www.rockfordsymphony.com	Rockford	IL	61103	815-965-0049	965-0642
Saint Louis Symphony Orchestra 718 N Grand Blvd *TF:* 800-232-1880 ■ *Web:* www.slso.org	Saint Louis	MO	63103	314-533-2500	286-4111
Saint Paul Chamber Orchestra 408 Saint Peter St 3rd Fl *Web:* www.thespco.org	Saint Paul	MN	55102	651-292-3248	292-3281
San Antonio Symphony 222 E Houston Suite 200 PO Box 658 *Web:* www.sasymphony.org	San Antonio	TX	78293	210-554-1000	554-1008
San Diego Symphony Orchestra 1245 7th Ave *Web:* www.sandiegosymphony.com	San Diego	CA	92101	619-235-0804	231-8178
San Francisco Symphony 201 Van Ness Ave *Web:* www.sfsymphony.org	San Francisco	CA	94102	415-552-8000	431-6857
Santa Barbara Symphony 1900 State St Suite G *Web:* www.thesymphony.org	Santa Barbara	CA	93101	805-898-9626	898-9326
Santa Cruz Symphony 307 Church St *Web:* www.santacruzsymphony.com	Santa Cruz	CA	95060	831-462-0553	426-1193
Santa Fe Symphony 551 W Cordova Rd Suite D PO Box 9692 *TF:* 800-480-1319 ■ *Web:* www.sf-symphony.org	Santa Fe	NM	87504	505-983-3530	982-3888
Santa Rosa Symphony 50 Santa Rosa Ave Suite 410 *Web:* www.santarosasymphony.com	Santa Rosa	CA	95404	707-546-8742	546-0460
Scottsdale Symphony Orchestra 8524 E Thomas Rd Grace Chapel *Web:* www.scotsymph.org	Scottsdale	AZ	85251	480-945-8071	946-8770
Seattle Symphony 200 University St *Web:* www.seattlesymphony.org	Seattle	WA	98101	206-215-4700	215-4701
Shreveport Symphony Orchestra 619 Louisiana Ave Suite 400 *Web:* www.shreveportsymphony.com	Shreveport	LA	71101	318-222-7496	222-7490
Sioux City Symphony Orchestra PO Box 754 *Web:* www.siouxcitysymphony.org	Sioux City	IA	51102	712-277-2111	252-0224
South Bend Symphony Orchestra 127 N Michigan St *TF:* 888-316-4674 ■ *Web:* www.southbendsymphony.com	South Bend	IN	46601	574-232-6343	232-6627
South Carolina Philharmonic 1237 Gadsden St Suite 102 *Web:* www.scphilharmonic.com	Columbia	SC	29201	803-771-7937	771-0268
South Dakota Symphony Orchestra 315 N Main Ave Suite 204 *TF:* 866-681-7376 ■ *Web:* www.sdsymphony.org	Sioux Falls	SD	57104	605-335-7933	335-1958
Spokane Symphony 818 W Riverside Ave Suite 100 *Web:* www.spokanesymphony.org	Spokane	WA	99201	509-326-3136	326-3921
Springfield Symphony Orchestra 1350 Main St *Web:* www.springfieldsymphony.org	Springfield	MA	01103	413-733-0636	781-4129
Springfield Symphony Orchestra 411 N Sherman Pkwy *Web:* www.springfieldmosymphony.org	Springfield	MO	65802	417-864-6683	864-8967
Symphony of the Mountains 1200 E Center St *Web:* www.symphonyofthemountains.org	Kingsport	TN	37660	423-392-8423	392-8428
Symphony Nova Scotia 6101 University Ave Dalhousie Arts Center *TF:* 800-874-1669 ■ *Web:* www.symphonynovascotia.ca	Halifax	NS	B3H3J5	902-494-3820	494-2883
Symphony Silicon Valley 345 S 1st St *Web:* www.symphonysiliconvalley.org	San Jose	CA	95113	408-286-2600	286-2600

	City	State	Zip	Phone	Fax
Syracuse Symphony Orchestra 411 Montgomery St Suite 40 *TF:* 800-724-3810 ■ *Web:* www.syracusesymphony.org	Syracuse	NY	13202	315-424-8222	424-1131
Tacoma Symphony 738 Broadway Suite 100 *Web:* www.tacomasymphony.org	Tacoma	WA	98402	253-272-7264	274-8187
Tallahassee Symphony Orchestra 1345 Thomasville Rd *Web:* www.tsolive.org	Tallahassee	FL	32303	850-224-0461	222-9092
Thayer Symphony Orchestra 14 Munument Sq 4th Fl *Web:* www.thayersymphony.org	Leominster	MA	01453	978-466-1800	840-1000
Toledo Symphony 1838 Parkwood Ave Suite 310 *TF:* 800-348-1253 ■ *Web:* www.toledosymphony.com	Toledo	OH	43604	419-246-8000	321-6890
Topeka Symphony 2100 SE 29th St PO Box 2206 *Web:* www.topekasymphony.org	Topeka	KS	66601	785-232-2032	232-6204
Traverse Symphony Orchestra 121 E Front St Suite 301 *TF:* 866-947-7120 ■ *Web:* www.tso-online.org	Traverse City	MI	49684	231-947-7120	947-8118
Trenton (Greater) Symphony Orchestra 28 W State St Suite 202 *Web:* www.trentonsymphony.org	Trenton	NJ	08608	609-394-1338	394-1394
Tucson Symphony Orchestra 2175 N 6th Ave *Web:* www.tucsonsymphony.org	Tucson	AZ	85705	520-792-9155	792-9314
Tupelo Symphony Orchestra 1800 W Main St PO Box 474 *Web:* www.tupelosymphony.com	Tupelo	MS	38801	662-842-8433	842-9565
Tuscaloosa Symphony Orchestra 614 Greensboro Ave PO Box 20001 *Web:* www.tsoonline.org	Tuscaloosa	AL	35402	205-752-5515	345-2787
US Air Force Strings 201 McChord St Bolling Air Force Base *Web:* www.usafband.af.mil	Washington	DC	20032	202-767-4225	767-0686
Utah Symphony & Opera 123 W South Temple *Web:* www.utahsymphonyopera.org	Salt Lake City	UT	84101	801-533-5626	869-9026
Vermont Symphony Orchestra 2 Church St Suite 19 *TF:* 800-876-9293 ■ *Web:* www.vso.org	Burlington	VT	05401	802-864-5741	864-5109
Virginia Symphony Orchestra 861 Glenrock Rd Suite 200 *Web:* www.virginiasymphony.org	Norfolk	VA	23502	757-466-3060	466-3046
Wallingford Symphony Orchestra PO Box 6023 *Web:* www.wallingfordsymphony.org	Wallingford	CT	06492	203-697-2261	
Washington Metropolitan Philharmonic PO Box 120 *Web:* www.washingtonmetrophilharmonic.org	Mount Vernon	VA	22121	703-799-8229	360-7391
Washington Symphony Orchestra 1225 'I' St NW Suite 110 *Web:* www.washingtonsymphony.org	Washington	DC	20005	202-546-9797	289-5981
Waterbury Symphony Orchestra PO Box 1762 *Web:* www.waterburysymphony.org	Waterbury	CT	06721	203-574-4283	756-3507
Waterloo-Cedar Falls Symphony Orchestra Gallagher-Bluedorn Performing Arts Center Suite 17 *Web:* www.wcfsymphony.org	Cedar Falls	IA	50614	319-273-3373	
Westchester Philharmonic 123 Main St Lobby Level *Web:* www.westchesterphil.org	White Plains	NY	10601	914-682-3707	682-3716
Western Piedmont Symphony 243 3rd Ave NE Suite 1-N *Web:* www.wpsymphony.org	Hickory	NC	28601	828-324-8603	324-1301
Wheeling Symphony Orchestra 1025 Main St Suite 811 *TF:* 800-395-9241 ■ *Web:* www.wheelingsymphony.org	Wheeling	WV	26003	304-232-6191	232-6192
Wichita Symphony Orchestra 225 W Douglas St Suite 207 *Web:* www.wso.org	Wichita	KS	67202	316-267-5259	267-1937
Windsor Symphony Orchestra 487 Oullette Ave *Web:* www.windsorsymphony.com	Windsor	ON	N9A4J2	519-973-1238	973-0764
Winnipeg Symphony Orchestra 555 Main St Centenial Concert Center *Web:* www.wso.mb.ca	Winnipeg	MB	R3B1C3	204-949-3950	956-4271
Winston-Salem Symphony 680 W 4th St *Web:* www.wssymphony.org	Winston-Salem	NC	27101	336-725-1035	725-3924
Wyoming Symphony Orchestra 130 W 2nd St *Web:* www.wyomingsymphony.org	Casper	WY	82601	307-266-1478	266-4522
Youngstown Symphony Orchestra 260 Federal Plaza W *Web:* www.youngstownsymphony.com	Youngstown	OH	44503	330-744-4269	744-1441

576-4 Theater Companies

	City	State	Zip	Phone	Fax
Academy Theatre 119 Center St *Web:* www.academytheatre.org	Avondale Estates	GA	30002	404-474-8332	
ACT Theatre 700 Union St Kreielsheimer Pl *Web:* www.acttheatre.org	Seattle	WA	98101	206-292-7660	292-7670
Actors Theatre of Louisville 316 W Main St *TF:* 800-428-5849 ■ *Web:* www.actorstheatre.org	Louisville	KY	40202	502-584-1265	561-3300
Alabama Shakespeare Festival 1 Festival Dr *TF:* 800-841-4273 ■ *Web:* www.asf.net	Montgomery	AL	36117	334-271-5300	271-5348
Alaska Junior Theater 329 F St Suite 204 *Web:* www.akjt.org	Anchorage	AK	99501	907-272-7546	272-3035
Alley Theatre 615 Texas Ave *Web:* www.alleytheatre.org	Houston	TX	77002	713-228-9341	222-6542
Alliance Theatre Co 1280 Peachtree St NE Woodruff Arts Center *Web:* www.alliancetheatre.org	Atlanta	GA	30309	404-733-4650	733-4625
American Conservatory Theater 30 Grant Ave 6th Fl *Web:* www.act-sfbay.org	San Francisco	CA	94108	415-834-3200	834-3360
American Musical Theatre of San Jose 1717 Technology Dr *TF:* 888-455-7469 ■ *Web:* www.amtsj.org	San Jose	CA	95110	408-453-7108	453-7123
American Repertory Theatre 64 Brattle St *Web:* www.amrep.org	Cambridge	MA	02138	617-495-2668	495-1705
American Stage 211 3rd St S *Web:* www.americanstage.org	Saint Petersburg	FL	33701	727-823-1600	821-2444
Arden Theatre Co 40 N 2nd St *Web:* www.ardentheatre.org	Philadelphia	PA	19106	215-922-8900	922-7011
Arena Stage 1101 6th St SW *Web:* www.arenastage.org	Washington	DC	20024	202-554-9066	488-4056
Arizona Theatre Co 343 S Scott Ave *TF:* 888-772-9449 ■ *Web:* www.aztheatreco.org	Tucson	AZ	85701	520-884-8210	628-9129
Arkansas Repertory Theatre 601 Main St *TF:* 866-684-3737 ■ *Web:* www.therep.org	Little Rock	AR	72201	501-378-0445	378-0012
Artists Repertory Theatre 1516 SW Alder St *Web:* www.artistsrep.org	Portland	OR	97205	503-241-9807	241-8268
Asolo Theatre Co 5555 N Tamiami Tr *TF:* 800-361-8388 ■ *Web:* www.asolo.org	Sarasota	FL	34243	941-351-9010	351-5796
Augusta Players 1301 Greene St Suite 304 *Web:* www.augustaplayers.com	Augusta	GA	30901	706-826-4707	
Bailiwick Repertory Theater 1229 W Belmont Ave *Web:* www.bailiwick.org	Chicago	IL	60657	773-883-1090	883-2017
Bakersfield Community Theater 2400 S Chester Ave	Bakersfield	CA	93304	661-831-8114	
Barter Theatre 133 W Main St *Web:* www.bartertheatre.com	Abingdon	VA	24210	276-628-2281	619-3335
Baton Rouge Little Theater 7155 Florida Blvd *Web:* www.brlt.org	Baton Rouge	LA	70806	225-924-6496	924-9972
Berkeley Repertory Theatre 2025 Addison St *TF:* 888-427-8849 ■ *Web:* www.berkeleyrep.org	Berkeley	CA	94704	510-647-2900	647-2976
Berkshire Theatre Festival PO Box 797 *TF:* 866-811-4111 ■ *Web:* www.berkshiretheatre.org	Stockbridge	MA	01262	413-298-5536	298-3368
Biloxi Little Theatre 220 Lee St *Web:* www.4blt.org/	Biloxi	MS	39530	228-432-8543	392-7639
Birmingham Festival Theater PO Box 55321 *Web:* www.bftonline.org	Birmingham	AL	35255	205-933-2383	
BoarsHead Michigan Public Theater 425 S Grand Ave Center for the Arts *Web:* www.boarshead.org	Lansing	MI	48933	517-484-7805	484-2564
Brown Clarence Theatre 206 McClung Tower *Web:* www.clarencebrowntheatre.com	Knoxville	TN	37996	865-974-6011	974-4867
Caldwell Theatre Co 7873 N Federal Hwy *TF:* 877-245-7432 ■ *Web:* www.caldwelltheatre.com	Boca Raton	FL	33487	561-241-7380	997-6917
Capital Repertory Theatre 111 N Pearl St Market Street Theater *Web:* www.capitalrep.org	Albany	NY	12207	518-462-4531	465-0213
Carpenter Square Theatre 400 W Sheridan Ave *Web:* www.carpentersquare.com	Oklahoma City	OK	73102	405-232-6500	270-4806
Casa Manana Theatre 3101 W Lancaster Ave *Web:* www.casamanana.org	Fort Worth	TX	76107	817-332-2272	332-5711
Center Stage 700 N Calvert St *Web:* www.centerstage.org	Baltimore	MD	21202	410-986-4000	539-3912
Center Theatre Group 601 W Temple St *Web:* www.taperahmanson.com	Los Angeles	CA	90012	213-628-2772	972-7402
Charleston Stage Co 629 Johnny Dodds Blvd *TF:* 800-454-7093 ■ *Web:* www.charlestonstage.com	Mount Pleasant	SC	29404	843-577-5967	577-5422
Children's Musical Theater San Jose 1401 Parkmoor Ave *Web:* www.cmtsj.org	San Jose	CA	95126	408-288-5437	288-6241
Cincinnati Playhouse in the Park 962 Mt Adams Cir *TF:* 800-582-3208 ■ *Web:* www.cincyplay.com	Cincinnati	OH	45202	513-345-2242	345-2250
Circle Theatre 1607 Robinson Rd SE Brink Hall *Web:* www.circletheatre.org	Grand Rapids	MI	49506	616-632-1980	456-8540
City Lights Theatre 529 S 2nd St *Web:* www.cltc.org	San Jose	CA	95112	408-295-4200	295-8318
City Theatre Co 1300 Bingham St *Web:* www.citytheatrecompany.org	Pittsburgh	PA	15203	412-431-4400	431-5535
Clarence Brown Theatre 206 McClung Tower *Web:* www.clarencebrowntheatre.com	Knoxville	TN	37996	865-974-6011	974-4867
Cleveland Play House 8500 Euclid Ave *Web:* www.clevelandplayhouse.com	Cleveland	OH	44106	216-795-7010	795-7005
Cleveland Public Theatre 6415 Detroit Ave *Web:* www.cptonline.org	Cleveland	OH	44102	216-631-2727	631-2575
Community Theater of Little Rock 2600 W Markham St School for the Blind	Little Rock	AR	72205	501-663-9494	
Community Theatre of Greensboro 200 N Davie St *Web:* www.ctgso.com	Greensboro	NC	27401	336-333-7470	333-2607
Corn Stock Theatre 1700 Park Rd *TF:* 800-220-1185 ■ *Web:* www.cornstocktheatre.com	Peoria	IL	61604	309-676-2196	676-9036
Court Theatre 5535 S Ellis Ave *Web:* www.courttheatre.org	Chicago	IL	60637	773-702-7005	834-1897
Dallas Theater Center 3636 Turtle Creek Blvd *Web:* www.dallastheatercenter.org	Dallas	TX	75219	214-526-8210	521-7666
Delaware Theatre Co 200 Water St *Web:* www.delawaretheatre.com	Wilmington	DE	19801	302-594-1104	594-1107
Denver Center Theatre Co 1101 13th St *TF:* 800-641-1222 ■ *Web:* www.denvercenter.org	Denver	CO	80204	303-893-4000	595-9634
Downtown Cabaret Theatre 263 Golden Hill St *Web:* www.dtcab.com	Bridgeport	CT	06604	203-576-1636	576-1444
Ensemble Theatre of Cincinnati 1127 Vine St *Web:* www.cincyetc.com	Cincinnati	OH	45202	513-421-3555	562-4104
Erie Playhouse 13 W 10th St *Web:* www.erieplayhouse.org	Erie	PA	16501	814-454-2851	454-0601
Evansville Civic Theatre 717 N Fulton St *Web:* www.civic.evansville.net	Evansville	IN	47710	812-423-2616	423-2616
Fairbanks Shakespeare Theatre PO Box 73447 *Web:* www.fairbanks-shakespeare.org	Fairbanks	AK	99707	907-457-7638	457-4511
Fargo-Moorhead Community Theatre 333 4th St S *TF:* 877-687-7469 ■ *Web:* www.fmct.org	Fargo	ND	58103	701-235-6778	235-2685
Florida Stage 262 S Ocean Blvd *TF:* 800-514-3837 ■ *Web:* www.floridastage.org	Manalapan	FL	33462	561-585-3404	588-4708
Foothills Theatre Co 100 Front St Suite 137 *Web:* www.foothillstheatre.com	Worcester	MA	01608	508-754-3314	767-0676
Ford's Theatre 511 10th St NW *TF:* 800-899-2367 ■ *Web:* www.fordstheatre.org	Washington	DC	20004	202-638-2941	347-6269
Fort Smith Little Theatre 401 N 6th St *Web:* www.fslt.org	Fort Smith	AR	72913	479-783-2966	
Fort Wayne Civic Theater 303 E Main St Performing Arts Ctr *Web:* www.fwcivic.org	Fort Wayne	IN	46802	260-422-8641	422-6699
GableStage 1200 Anastasia Ave Biltmore Hotel *Web:* www.gablestage.org	Coral Gables	FL	33134	305-446-1116	445-8645
Garden Grove Playhouse 12001 Saint Mark St PO Box 5991 *Web:* www.gardengroveplayhouse.com	Garden Grove	CA	92846	714-897-5122	
Garland Civic Theatre 108 N 6th St *Web:* www.garlandcivictheatre.org	Garland	TX	75040	972-485-8884	487-2159
Geffen Playhouse 10886 Le Conte Ave *Web:* www.geffenplayhouse.com	Los Angeles	CA	90024	310-208-6500	208-0341
Generic Theater 912 W 21st St *Web:* www.generictheater.org	Norfolk	VA	23517	757-441-2160	441-2729
George Street Playhouse 9 Livingston Ave *Web:* www.georgestplayhouse.org	New Brunswick	NJ	08901	732-246-7717	247-9151
Georgia Shakespeare 4484 Peachtree Rd NE *Web:* www.gashakespeare.org	Atlanta	GA	30319	404-504-3400	504-3414
Geva Theatre Center 75 Woodbury Blvd *Web:* www.gevatheatre.org	Rochester	NY	14607	585-232-1366	232-4031
Goodman Theatre 170 N Dearborn St *Web:* www.goodman-theatre.org	Chicago	IL	60601	312-443-3811	443-3821
Goodspeed Musicals PO Box A *Web:* www.goodspeed.org	East Haddam	CT	06423	860-873-8664	873-2329
Great Lakes Theater Festival 1501 Euclid Ave Suite 300 *TF:* 800-766-6048 ■ *Web:* www.greatlakestheater.org	Cleveland	OH	44115	216-241-5490	241-6315
Grove Theater Center 111-B W Olive Ave **Fax Area Code:* 866 ■ *Web:* www.gtc.org	Burbank	CA	91502	818-238-9988	495-1218*
Guthrie Theater 818 S 2nd St *TF:* 877-447-8243 ■ *Web:* www.guthrietheater.org	Minneapolis	MN	55415	612-225-6000	225-6004
Hartford Stage Co 50 Church St *Web:* www.hartfordstage.org	Hartford	CT	06103	860-525-5601	525-4420
Huntington Beach Playhouse 7111 Talbert Ave *Web:* www.hbph.com	Huntington Beach	CA	92648	714-375-0696	847-0457
Huntington Theatre Co 264 Huntington Ave Boston University Theatre *Web:* www.huntingtontheatre.org	Boston	MA	02115	617-266-7900	353-8300
Indiana Repertory Theatre 140 W Washington St *Web:* www.indianarep.com	Indianapolis	IN	46204	317-635-5277	236-0767
Indianapolis Civic Theatre Inc 3200 Cold Spring Rd *Web:* www.civictheatre.org	Indianapolis	IN	46222	317-923-4597	923-3548
International City Theatre 1 World Trade Ctr Suite 300 PO Box 32069 *Web:* www.ictlongbeach.com	Long Beach	CA	90832	562-495-4595	436-7895
Intiman Theatre 201 Mercer St Seattle Ctr *Web:* www.intiman.org	Seattle	WA	98109	206-269-1901	269-1928

Theater Companies (Cont'd)

	City	State	Zip	Phone	Fax
Invisible Theatre 1400 N 1st Ave	Tucson	AZ	85719	520-882-9721	884-5410
Web: www.invisibletheatre.com					
Irish Classical Theatre 625 Main St	Buffalo	NY	14203	716-853-4282	853-0592
Web: www.irishclassicaltheatre.com					
Jubilee Theatre 506 Main St	Fort Worth	TX	76102	817-338-4411	338-4206
Web: www.jubileetheatre.org					
Jungle Theater 2951 Lindale Ave S	Minneapolis	MN	55408	612-822-7063	822-9408
Web: www.jungletheater.com					
Kansas City Repertory Theatre 4949 Cherry St	Kansas City	MO	64110	816-235-2727	235-2704
TF: 888-502-2700 ■ *Web:* www.kcrep.org					
La Jolla Playhouse PO Box 12039	La Jolla	CA	92039	858-550-1070	550-1075
Web: www.lajollaplayhouse.com					
Laguna Playhouse 606 Laguna Canyon Rd	Laguna Beach	CA	92651	949-497-2787	497-6948
Web: www.lagunaplayhouse.com					
Lincoln Center Theater 150 W 65th St	New York	NY	10023	212-362-7600	873-0761
Web: www.lct.org					
Little Theatre of Alexandria 600 Wolfe St	Alexandria	VA	22314	703-683-5778	683-1378
Web: www.thelittletheatre.com					
Long Wharf Theatre 222 Sargent Dr	New Haven	CT	06511	203-787-4284	776-2287
TF: 800-782-8497 ■ *Web:* www.longwharf.org					
Lost Nation Theater 39 Main St	Montpelier	VT	05602	802-229-0492	223-9608
Web: www.lostnationtheater.org					
Lyric Theatre of Oklahoma 1727 NW 16th St	Oklahoma City	OK	73106	405-524-9312	524-9316
Web: www.lyrictheatreokc.com					
Madison Repertory Theatre 1 S Pinckney St Suite 340	Madison	WI	53703	608-256-0029	256-7433
Web: www.madisonrep.org					
Maltz Jupiter Theatre 1001 E Indiantown Rd	Jupiter	FL	33477	561-743-2666	743-0107
TF: 800-445-1666 ■ *Web:* www.jupitertheatre.org					
Manhattan Theatre Club Inc 311 W 43rd St 8th Fl	New York	NY	10036	212-399-3000	399-4329
Web: www.manhattantheatreclub.com					
McCarter Theatre 91 University Pl	Princeton	NJ	08540	609-258-6500	497-0369
Web: www.mccarter.org					
Merrimack Repertory Theatre 50 E Merrimack St	Lowell	MA	01852	978-454-6324	
Web: www.merrimackrep.org					
Milwaukee Repertory Theater 108 E Wells St	Milwaukee	WI	53202	414-224-1761	224-9097
Web: www.milwaukeerep.com					
Minnesota Repertory Theatre					
1215 Ordean Ct Marshall Performing Arts Ctr	Duluth	MN	55812	218-726-8564	726-6798
Music Theatre Louisville 624 W Main St Suite 402	Louisville	KY	40202	502-589-4060	589-0741
Web: www.musictheatrelouisville.com					
Music Theatre of Wichita					
225 W Douglas St Suite 202 Century II Concert Hall	Wichita	KS	67202	316-265-3107	265-8708
Web: www.musictheatreofwichita.org					
National Theatre of the Deaf (NTD) 139 N Main St	West Hartford	CT	06107	860-236-4193	236-4163
Web: ntd.org					
Nebraska Repertory Theatre 12th & R Sts 215 Temple Bldg	Lincoln	NE	68588	402-472-2072	472-9055
TF: 800-432-3231 ■ *Web:* www.unl.edu/rep					
New Stage Theatre 1100 Carlisle St	Jackson	MS	39202	601-948-3531	948-3538
Web: www.newstagetheatre.com					
North Carolina Theatre 1 E South St Memorial Auditorium	Raleigh	NC	27601	919-831-6941	831-6951
Web: www.nctheatre.com					
Northlight Theatre 9501 Skokie Blvd	Skokie	IL	60077	847-679-9501	679-1879
Web: www.northlight.org					
Old Globe Theatre 1363 Old Globe Way	San Diego	CA	92101	619-231-1941	231-5879
Web: www.oldglobe.org					
Omaha Community Playhouse 6915 Cass St	Omaha	NE	68132	402-553-0800	553-6288
TF: 888-782-4338 ■ *Web:* www.omahaplayhouse.com					
Pacific Repertory Theater Monte Verde & 8th St	Carmel	CA	93921	831-622-0700	622-0703
Web: www.pacrep.org					
Paper Bag Players 225 W 99th St	New York	NY	10025	212-663-0390	663-1076
TF: 800-777-2247 ■ *Web:* www.paperbagplayers.org					
Park Playhouse Inc 1 Steuben Pl	Albany	NY	12207	518-434-2035	424-5081
Web: www.parkplayhouse.com					
Pasadena Playhouse 39 S El Molino Ave	Pasadena	CA	91101	626-792-8672	792-6142
Web: www.pasadenaplayhouse.org					
Penobscot Theatre Co 131 Main St	Bangor	ME	04401	207-942-3333	947-6678
TF: 877-782-8499 ■ *Web:* ptc.maineguide.com					
Pensacola Little Theatre					
400 S Jefferson St Pensacola Cultural Ctr	Pensacola	FL	32502	850-432-2042	438-2787
Web: www.pensacolalittletheatre.com					
People's Light & Theatre Co 39 Conestoga Rd	Malvern	PA	19355	610-647-1900	640-9521
Web: www.peopleslight.org					
Performing Arts Chicago 410 S Michigan Ave Suite 911	Chicago	IL	60605	312-242-6237	
Perseverance Theatre 914 3rd St	Douglas	AK	99824	907-364-2421	364-2603
Web: www.perseverancetheatre.org					
Philadelphia Theatre Co 230 S 15th St 4th Fl	Philadelphia	PA	19102	215-985-1400	985-5800
Web: www.phillytheatreco.com					
Pittsburgh Public Theater 621 Penn Ave	Pittsburgh	PA	15222	412-316-8200	316-8219
Web: www.ppt.org					
Playhouse on the Square 51 S Cooper St	Memphis	TN	38104	901-726-4656	272-7530
Web: www.playhouseonthesquare.org					
PlayMakers Repertory Co					
University of North Carolina Center for Dramatic Art					
CB #3235	Chapel Hill	NC	27599	919-962-7529	904-8396*
**Fax Area Code:* 866 ■ *Web:* www.playmakersrep.org					
Portland Center Stage 1111 SW Broadway Ave	Portland	OR	97205	503-248-6309	228-7058
Web: www.pcs.org					
Portland Stage Co PO Box 1458	Portland	ME	04104	207-774-1043	774-0576
Web: www.portlandstage.com					
Prince Music Theater 1412 Chestnut St	Philadelphia	PA	19102	215-972-1000	972-1020
Web: www.princemusictheater.org					
Public Theater The 425 Lafayette St	New York	NY	10003	212-539-8500	539-8505
Web: www.publictheater.org					
Repertory Theatre of Saint Louis					
130 Edgar Rd PO Box 191730	Saint Louis	MO	63119	314-968-7340	968-9638
Web: www.repstl.org					
Rochester Repertory Theatre Co 314 1/2 S Broadway	Rochester	MN	55904	507-289-1737	
Web: www.rochesterrep.org					
Roundabout Theatre Co 231 W 39th St Suite 1200	New York	NY	10018	212-719-9393	869-8817
Web: www.roundabouttheatre.org					
Sacramento Theatre Co 1419 H St	Sacramento	CA	95814	916-443-6722	446-4066
Web: www.sactheatre.org					
San Diego Repertory Theatre 79 Horton Plaza	San Diego	CA	92101	619-231-3586	231-4304
Web: www.sandiegorep.com					
San Jose Repertory Theatre 101 Paseo de San Antonio	San Jose	CA	95113	408-367-7266	367-7237
Web: www.sjrep.com					
San Jose Stage Co 490 S 1st St	San Jose	CA	95113	408-283-7142	283-7146
Web: www.sanjose-stage.com					
San Pedro Playhouse 800 W Ashby Pl San Pedro Park	San Antonio	TX	78212	210-733-7258	734-2651
Web: www.members.tripod.com/san_pedro_playhouse					
Sandra Feinstein-Gamm Theatre 172 Exchange St	Pawtucket	RI	02860	401-723-4266	723-0440
Web: www.gammtheatre.org					
Seaside Music Theater 221 Northbeach St	Daytona Beach	FL	32114	386-252-6200	252-1149
TF: 800-854-5592 ■ *Web:* www.seasidemusictheater.org					
Seattle Repertory Theatre 155 Mercer St PO Box 900923	Seattle	WA	98109	206-443-2210	443-2379
TF: 877-900-9285 ■ *Web:* www.seattlerep.org					
Second City Chicago 1616 N Wells St	Chicago	IL	60614	312-664-4032	664-9837
TF: 877-778-4707 ■ *Web:* www.secondcity.com					
Second City Detroit 42705 Grand River Ave	Novi	MI	48375	248-348-4448	348-3622
Web: www.secondcity.com					
Shakespeare Theatre 516 8th St SE	Washington	DC	20003	202-547-3230	547-0226
TF: 877-487-8849 ■ *Web:* www.shakespearetheatre.org					
Shattered Globe Theatre 2936 N Southport Suite 210	Chicago	IL	60657	773-770-0330	296-0968
Web: www.shatteredglobe.org					
Shreveport Little Theatre 812 Margaret Pl	Shreveport	LA	71101	318-424-4439	424-4440
Web: www.shreveportlittletheatre.org					
Signature Theatre 3806 S Four Mile Run Dr	Arlington	VA	22206	703-820-9771	820-7790
Web: sig-online.org					
South Carolina Children's Theatre 153 Augusta Rd	Greenville	SC	29601	864-235-2885	235-0208
Web: www.scchildrenstheatre.org					
South Coast Repertory 655 Town Ctr Dr	Costa Mesa	CA	92626	714-708-5500	708-5576
Web: www.scr.org					
Springfield Little Theatre 311 E Walnut St	Springfield	MO	65806	417-869-1334	869-4047
Web: www.landerstheatre.org					
Stage Coach Theatre 5296 Overland Rd	Boise	ID	83705	208-342-2000	
Web: www.stagecoachtheatre.com					
Stages Repertory Theatre 3201 Allen Pkwy Suite 101	Houston	TX	77019	713-527-0220	527-8669
Web: www.stagestheatre.com					
Stockton Civic Theatre 2312 Rose Marie Ln	Stockton	CA	95207	209-473-2400	473-1502
Web: www.sctlivetheatre.com					
Studio Arena Theatre 710 Main St	Buffalo	NY	14202	716-856-8025	856-3415
TF: 800-777-8243 ■ *Web:* www.studioarena.org					
Swine Palace Productions					
Tower Dr Louisiana State University	Baton Rouge	LA	70803	225-578-3527	578-4135
Web: www.swinepalace.com					
Syracuse Stage 820 E Genesee St	Syracuse	NY	13210	315-443-4008	443-9846
Web: www.syracusestage.org					
Tacoma Musical Playhouse 7116 6th Ave	Tacoma	WA	98406	253-565-6867	564-7863
Web: www.tmp.org					
Tempe Little Theatre 132 E 6th St	Tempe	AZ	85281	480-350-8388	
Web: www.tempelittletheatre.org					
Tennessee Repertory Theatre 427 Chestnut St	Nashville	TN	37203	615-244-4878	
Web: www.tnrep.org					
Theater of the Stars PO Box 11748	Atlanta	GA	30355	404-252-8960	252-1460
Web: www.theaterofthestars.com					
THEATERWORK 1336 Ruffina Cir	Santa Fe	NM	87507	505-471-1799	
Web: theaterwork.org					
Theatre For A New Audience 154 Christopher St #3D	New York	NY	10014	212-229-2819	229-2911
Web: www.tfana.org					
Theatre Arlington 305 W Main St	Arlington	TX	76010	817-275-7661	275-3370
Web: www.theatrearlington.org					
Theatre Cedar Rapids 102 3rd St SE	Cedar Rapids	IA	52401	319-366-8592	366-8593
Web: theatrecr.org					
Theatre Charlotte 501 Queens Rd	Charlotte	NC	28207	704-334-9128	347-5216
Web: theatrecharlotte.org					
Theatre Harrisburg 513 Hurlock St	Harrisburg	PA	17110	717-232-5501	232-5912
Web: www.theatreharrisburg.com					
Theatre IV 114 W Broad St	Richmond	VA	23220	804-344-8040	643-2671
Web: www.theatreiv.org					
Theatre Tulsa 207 N Main St	Tulsa	OK	74103	918-587-8402	587-8403
Web: www.theatretulsa.org					
Theatre Tuscaloosa 9500 Old Greensboro Rd Suite 135	Tuscaloosa	AL	35405	205-391-2277	391-2329
Web: www.theatretusc.com					
Theatre Under the Stars 800 Bagby St Suite 200	Houston	TX	77002	713-558-2600	558-2650
Web: www.tuts.com					
Theatre of Youth (TOY) 203 Allen St	Buffalo	NY	14201	716-884-4400	819-9653
Web: www.theatreofyouth.org					
TheatreWorks PO Box 50458	Palo Alto	CA	94303	650-463-1950	463-1963
Web: theatreworks.org					
Toledo Repertoire Theatre 16 10th St	Toledo	OH	43604	419-243-9277	324-1930
Web: www.toledorep.org					
Trinity Repertory Co 201 Washington St	Providence	RI	02903	401-521-1100	751-5577
Web: www.trinityrep.com					
Tuscaloosa Children's Theatre 10889 Magnolia Ln	Coaling	AL	35453	205-462-0100	
Web: www.tuscaloosachildrenstheatre.com					
Unicorn Theatre 3828 Main St	Kansas City	MO	64111	816-531-7529	531-0421
Web: www.unicorntheatre.org					
Utah Musical Theatre 3402 University Cir Weber State University	Ogden	UT	84408	801-626-8500	626-6811
Web: community.weber.edu/umt					
Virginia Stage Co Monticello & Tazewell Sts	Norfolk	VA	23514	757-627-6988	628-5958
Web: www.vastage.com					
Warehouse Theatre 37 Augusta St	Greenville	SC	29601	864-235-6948	
Web: www.warehousetheatre.com					
West Virginia Public Theatre 2 Waterfront Pl Suite 2700	Morgantown	WV	26501	304-291-4122	291-4125
TF: 877-999-9878 ■ *Web:* www.wvpublictheatre.org					
Western Nevada Musical Theater Co					
2201 W College Pkwy Western Nevada					
Community College	Carson City	NV	89703	775-445-4249	445-3154
Web: www.wncc.edu/performing_arts					
Westport Community Theatre 110 Myrtle Ave	Westport	CT	06880	203-226-1983	
Web: www.westportcommunitytheatre.com					
Wild Swan Theater 416 W Huron St	Ann Arbor	MI	48103	734-995-0530	668-7292
Web: www.wildswantheater.org					
Wilma Theater 265 S Broad St	Philadelphia	PA	19107	215-893-9456	893-0895
Web: www.wilmatheater.org					
Wilmington Drama League 10 W Lea Blvd	Wilmington	DE	19802	302-764-1172	764-7904
Web: www.wdl.org					
Yale Repertory Theatre 1120 Chapel St PO Box 1257	New Haven	CT	06505	203-432-1234	432-6423
Web: www.yale.edu/yalerep					

577 PERFUMES

SEE ALSO Cosmetics, Skin Care, and Other Personal Care Products p. 1578

	City	State	Zip	Phone	Fax
Alpine Aromatics International Inc 51 Ethel Rd W	Piscataway	NJ	08854	732-572-5600	572-0944
TF: 800-631-5389 ■ *Web:* www.alpinearomatics.com					
Aramis Inc 5 Thornton Rd	Oakland	NJ	07436	973-492-3600	492-3690
Web: www.elcompanies.com					
Avon Products Inc 1251 Ave of the Americas	New York	NY	10020	212-282-5000	282-6825
NYSE: AVP ■ *TF Cust Svc:* 800-367-2866 ■ *Web:* www.avon.com					
Bijan Boutique 420 N Rodeo Dr	Beverly Hills	CA	90210	310-273-6544	273-6535
Web: www.bijan.com					
Body Shop The 5036 One World Way	Wake Forest	NC	27587	919-554-4900	554-4361
TF Cust Svc: 800-747-4827 ■ *Web:* www.thebodyshop.com					
Calvin Klein Cosmetics 725 5th Ave Trump Tower	New York	NY	10022	212-759-8888	
TF: 800-715-4023					

				Phone	Fax
Chanel Inc 9 W 57th St 44th Fl *TF:* 800-550-0005 ■ *Web:* www.chanel.com	New York	NY	10019	212-688-5055	752-1851
Coty & Lancaster Inc 1 Park Ave 4th Fl *Web:* www.coty.com	New York	NY	10016	212-389-7000	532-7003
Crabtree & Evelyn Ltd 102 Peake Brook Rd *TF:* 800-624-5211 ■ *Web:* www.crabtree-evelyn.com	Woodstock	CT	06281	860-928-2761	928-0462
E Com Ventures Inc 251 International Pkwy *NASDAQ: ECMV* ■ *TF:* 866-600-3600 ■ *Web:* www.perfumania.com	Sunrise	FL	33325	954-335-9100	335-9166
Eagle Marketing Inc Perfume Originals Products Div 2412 Sequoia Pk *TF:* 800-233-7424 ■ *Web:* www.eimi.com/perfume.html	Yukon	OK	73099	405-354-1027	354-7882
Elizabeth Arden Inc 2400 SW 145th Ave *NASDAQ: RDEN* ■ *TF:* 800-227-2445 ■ *Web:* www.elizabetharden.com	Miramar	FL	33327	954-364-6900	364-6910
Estee Lauder International Inc 767 5th Ave *Web:* www.esteelauder.com	New York	NY	10153	212-572-4200	
Estee Lauder USA 767 5th Ave *Web:* www.esteelauder.com	New York	NY	10153	212-572-4200	572-3941
FragranceNet.com Inc 104 Parkway Dr S *TF:* 800-727-3867 ■ *Web:* www.fragrancenet.com	Hauppauge	NY	11788	631-582-5204	582-8433
Guerlain Inc 19 E 57th St *Web:* www.guerlain.com	New York	NY	10022	212-931-2400	931-2445
H2O Plus Inc 845 W Madison St *TF Cust Svc:* 800-690-2284 ■ *Web:* www.h20plus.com	Chicago	IL	60607	312-850-9283	633-1470
Inter Parfums Inc 551 5th Ave Suite 1500 *NASDAQ: IPAR* ■ *TF:* 800-533-6010 ■ *Web:* www.interparfumsinc.com	New York	NY	10176	212-983-2640	983-4197
Intercontinental Fragrances Inc 10422 W Gulf Bank Rd *TF:* 800-443-9198 ■ *Web:* www.infrin.com	Houston	TX	77040	713-896-9991	896-9500
Key West Fragrance & Cosmetics Factory Inc 540 Greene St *TF Orders:* 800-445-2563 ■ *Web:* www.keywestaloe.com	Key West	FL	33040	305-293-1885	
Klein Calvin Cosmetics 725 5th Ave Trump Tower *TF:* 800-715-4023	New York	NY	10022	212-759-8888	
New Dana Perfumes Corp 6601 Lyons Rd Suite B-4	Coconut Creek	FL	33073	954-725-6810	725-6811
Noville Inc 124 Case Dr *TF:* 888-668-4553 ■ *Web:* www.noville.com	South Plainfield	NJ	07080	908-754-2222	754-0167
Parfums Boucheron 3 E 57th St	New York	NY	10022	212-715-7333	715-7377
Parfums Christian Dior 19 E 57th St **Fax:* Mktg ■ *Web:* www.dior.com	New York	NY	10022	212-931-2200	751-7445*
Parfums de Coeur Ltd 85 Old Kings Hwy N *TF:* 800-887-2738 ■ *Web:* www.parfumsdecoeur.com	Darien	CT	06820	203-655-8807	656-2121
Parfums Givenchy Inc 19 E 57th St *TF:* 800-479-6427 ■ *Web:* www.parfumsgivenchy.com	New York	NY	10022	212-931-2600	931-2630
Parlux Fragrances Inc 3725 SW 30th Ave *NASDAQ: PARL* ■ *Web:* www.parlux.com	Fort Lauderdale	FL	33312	954-316-9008	316-8155
Perfumania Inc 251 International Pkwy *TF:* 866-600-3600 ■ *Web:* www.perfumania.com	Sunrise	FL	33325	954-335-9100	335-9166
Perfume Originals Products Div Eagle Marketing Inc 2412 Sequoia Pk *TF:* 800-233-7424 ■ *Web:* www.eimi.com/perfume.html	Yukon	OK	73099	405-354-1027	354-7882
Quest International Fragrances USA Inc 400 International Dr *TF:* 800-598-5986 ■ *Web:* www.questinternational.com	Mount Olive	NJ	07828	973-691-7100	691-6871
Shaw Mudge & Co 828 Bridgeport Ave PO Box 2279 *Web:* www.shawmudge.com	Shelton	CT	06484	203-925-5000	925-5098
Ulta3 Inc 1135 Arbor Dr *TF:* 866-304-3704 ■ *Web:* www.ulta.com	Romeoville	IL	60446	630-226-0020	226-8210

578 PERSONAL EMERGENCY RESPONSE SYSTEMS

				Phone	Fax
AlertOne Services Inc 24 W 4th St *TF:* 800-693-5433 ■ *Web:* www.alert-1.com	Williamsport	PA	17701	570-321-5433	321-9882
American Medical Alert Corp 3265 Lawson Blvd *NASDAQ: AMAC* ■ *TF:* 800-645-3244 ■ *Web:* www.amacalert.com	Oceanside	NY	11572	516-536-5850	536-5276
Applied Digital Solutions Inc 1690 S Congress Ave Suite 200 *NASDAQ: ADSX* ■ *Web:* www.adsx.com	Delray Beach	FL	33445	561-805-8000	805-8001
Health Watch Inc 6400 Park of Commerce Blvd Suite 1-A *TF:* 888-994-1835 ■ *Web:* www.health-watch.com	Boca Raton	FL	33487	561-994-6699	
Life Alert 16027 Ventura Blvd Suite 400 *TF:* 800-700-7000 ■ *Web:* www.lifealert.com	Encino	CA	91436	818-700-7000	922-3367
LifeFone 16 Yellowstone Ave *TF:* 800-882-2280 ■ *Web:* www.lifefone.com	White Plains	NY	10607	914-948-0282	686-0669
Lifeline Systems Inc 111 Lawrence St *NASDAQ: LIFE* ■ *TF:* 800-451-0525 ■ *Web:* www.lifelinesys.com	Framingham	MA	01702	508-988-1000	988-1384
Medic Aid Response Systems Ltd 167 Village Rd *TF:* 800-565-9135 ■ *Web:* www.medicaid-canada.com	Herring Cove	NS	B3V1H2	902-477-6125	477-0749
Pioneer Medical Systems 37 Washington St *TF:* 800-338-2303 ■ *Web:* www.pioneermed.com	Melrose	MA	02176	781-662-2222	662-6628

579 PERSONAL PROTECTIVE EQUIPMENT & CLOTHING

SEE ALSO Medical Supplies - Mfr p. 1955; Safety Equipment - Mfr p. 2302; Safety Equipment - Whol p. 2302; Sporting Goods p. 2323

				Phone	Fax
3M Occupational Health & Environmental Safety Products Div 3M Ctr Bldg 235-2W-75 **Fax Area Code:* 800 ■ **Fax:* Cust Svc ■ *TF:* 800-328-1667 ■ *Web:* www.3m.com/occsafety	Saint Paul	MN	55144	651-733-8029	542-9373*
3M Safety Security & Protection Services Div 3M Center *TF:* 800-364-3577 ■ *Web:* www.3m.com	Saint Paul	MN	55144	651-733-1110	
Aearo Co 5457 W 79th St *TF Cust Svc:* 800-327-3431 ■ *Web:* www.aearo.com	Indianapolis	IN	46268	317-692-6666	692-6772
Aerial Machine & Tool Corp 4298 Jeb Stuart Hwy *Web:* www.aerialmachineandtool.com	Vesta	VA	24177	276-952-2006	952-2231
AGO Industries Inc PO Box 7132 *Web:* www.ago1.com	London	ON	N5Y4J9	519-452-3780	452-3053
AHPC Holdings Inc 500 Park Blvd Suite 1260 *NASDAQ: GLOV* ■ *TF:* 800-828-2964	Itasca	IL	60143	630-285-9191	285-9289
Allen-Vanguard Corp 2400 St Laurent Blvd *TF:* 800-644-9078 ■ *Web:* www.allenvanguard.com	Ottawa	ON	K1G6C4	613-739-9646	739-4536
American Body Armor & Equipment Inc 13386 International Pkwy *TF:* 800-654-9943 ■ *Web:* www.americanbodyarmor.com	Jacksonville	FL	32218	904-741-5400	741-5407
American Health Products Corp 80 International Blvd Unit A *TF:* 800-828-2964 ■ *Web:* www.ahpc.com	Glendale Heights	IL	60139	630-407-0242	407-0238
Ansell Healthcare Inc 200 Schulz Dr *TF:* 800-232-1309 ■ *Web:* www.ansell.com	Red Bank	NJ	07701	732-345-5400	219-5114
Ansell Occupational Healthcare 1300 Walnut St *TF Cust Svc:* 800-800-0444 ■ *Web:* www.ansellpro.com	Coshocton	OH	43812	740-622-4311	623-3556
Athletic Supporter Ltd 24601 Hallwood Ct *TF:* 800-521-6500	Farmington Hills	MI	48335	248-474-6000	474-4615
Bacou-Dalloz 900 Douglas Pike *TF:* 800-343-3411 ■ *Web:* www.bacou-dalloz.com	Smithfield	RI	02917	401-233-0333	232-1830
Bell Sports Corp 6225 N State Hwy 161 Suite 300 **Fax Area Code:* 214 ■ *TF:* 866-525-2355 ■ *Web:* www.bellsports.com	Irving	TX	75038	469-417-6600	492-1639*
Best Mfg Co 579 Edison St *TF Cust Svc:* 800-241-0323 ■ *Web:* www.bestglove.com	Menlo	GA	30731	706-862-2302	862-6000
Bike Athletic Co 3303 Cumberland Blvd *Web:* www.bikeathletic.com	Atlanta	GA	30339	678-742-8255	742-3182
Biomarine Inc 456 Creamery Way *TF:* 800-378-2287 ■ *Web:* www.neutronicsinc.com	Exton	PA	19341	610-524-8800	524-8807
Bouton HL Co Inc 11 Kendrick Rd *TF Cust Svc:* 800-426-1881 ■ *Web:* www.hlbouton.com	Wareham	MA	02571	508-295-3300	295-3521
Bullard Co 1898 Safety Way *TF:* 800-827-0423 ■ *Web:* www.bullard.com	Cynthiana	KY	41031	859-234-6611	234-8987
Carleton Technologies Inc 10 Cobham Dr *TF:* 800-395-4074 ■ *Web:* www.carltech.com	Orchard Park	NY	14127	716-662-0006	662-0747
Choctaw-Kaul Distribution Co 3540 Vinewood Ave *Web:* www.choctawkaul.com	Detroit	MI	48208	313-894-9494	894-7977
David Clark Co Inc 360 Franklin St **Fax:* Sales ■ *TF Cust Svc:* 800-298-6235 ■ *Web:* www.davidclark.com	Worcester	MA	01615	508-751-5800	753-5827*
Desco Industries Inc 3651 Walnut Ave *Web:* www.desco.com	Chino	CA	91710	909-627-8178	627-7449
DHB Industries Inc 2102 SW 2nd St *AMEX: DHB* ■ *Web:* www.dhbt.com	Pompano Beach	FL	33069	954-630-0900	630-9225
Dispensers Optical Service Corp 1815 Plantside Dr *TF Cust Svc:* 800-626-4545 ■ *Web:* www.dosc.com	Louisville	KY	40299	502-491-3440	499-8445
Diversified Optical Products Inc Cairns Advanced Technologies Div 282 Main St *TF:* 800-230-1600 ■ *Web:* www.cairnsat.com	Salem	NH	03079	603-898-1880	893-4359
Encon Safety Products Co 6825 W Sam Houston Pkwy N *TF:* 800-283-6266 ■ *Web:* www.enconsafety.com	Houston	TX	77041	713-466-1449	466-1819
Essex PB& R Corp 8007 Chivvis Dr *Web:* www.essexind.com/propellex_frame.htm	Saint Louis	MO	63123	314-351-6116	351-7181
Fibre-Metal Products Co Rt 1 at S Brinton Wake Rd PO Box 248 *TF:* 800-523-7048 ■ *Web:* www.fibre-metal.com	Concordville	PA	19331	610-459-5300	358-9138
Fire-End & Croker Corp 7 Westchester Plaza *TF:* 800-759-3473 ■ *Web:* www.fire-end.com	Elmsford	NY	10523	914-592-3640	592-3892
Fisher Scientific International Inc Safety Div 2000 Park Ln **Fax:* Mktg ■ *TF Cust Svc:* 800-766-7000 ■ *Web:* www1.fishersci.com/safety/safe_index.jsp	Pittsburgh	PA	15275	412-490-8300	490-8635*
Galls Inc 2680 Palumbo Dr *TF:* 800-477-7766 ■ *Web:* www.galls.com	Lexington	KY	40509	859-266-7227	269-4360
Gateway Safety Inc 4722 Spring Rd *TF:* 800-822-5347 ■ *Web:* www.gatewaysafety.com	Cleveland	OH	44131	216-749-1100	749-0526
General Econopak Inc 1725 N 6th St *TF:* 888-871-8568 ■ *Web:* www.generaleconopak.com	Philadelphia	PA	19122	215-763-8200	763-8118
Gerson Louis M Co Inc 15 Sproat St *TF:* 800-225-8623 ■ *Web:* www.gersonco.com	Middleboro	MA	02346	508-947-4000	947-5442
Gexco 3460 Vine St PO Box 6514 *TF:* 800-829-8222	Norco	CA	92860	951-735-4951	479-5154
Gibson & Barnes 1675 Pioneer Way **Fax Area Code:* 800 ■ *TF:* 800-748-6693 ■ *Web:* www.gibson-barnes.com	El Cajon	CA	92020	619-440-6976	748-6694*
Globe Mfg Co PO Box 128 37 Loudon Rd **Fax Area Code:* 800 ■ *TF:* 800-232-8323 ■ *Web:* www.globefiresuits.com	Pittsfield	NH	03263	603-435-8323	442-6388*
GRABBER Performance Group 4600 Danvers Dr SE *TF:* 800-423-1233 ■ *Web:* www.grabberwarmers.com	Grand Rapids	MI	49512	616-940-1914	977-7718
Graham Professional Div Little Rapids Corp 2273 Larsen Rd PO Box 19100 **Fax Area Code:* 800 ■ **Fax:* Cust Svc ■ *TF Cust Svc:* 800-558-6765 ■ *Web:* www.littlerapids.com/graham/	Green Bay	WI	54304	920-494-8701	494-7877*
Hamilton Sundstrand Corp 1 Hamilton Rd *Web:* www.hamiltonsundstrandcorp.com	Windsor Locks	CT	06096	860-654-6000	654-4741
Handgards Inc 901 Hawkins Blvd *TF:* 800-351-8161 ■ *Web:* www.handgards.com	El Paso	TX	79915	915-779-6606	779-1312
HeatMax Inc 505 Hill Rd *TF:* 800-432-8629 ■ *Web:* www.heatmax.com	Dalton	GA	30721	706-226-1800	226-2195
Helmet House Inc 26855 Malibu Hill Rd *TF:* 800-421-7247 ■ *Web:* www.helmethouse.com	Calabasas Hills	CA	91301	818-880-0000	880-4550
HL Bouton Co Inc 11 Kendrick Rd *TF Cust Svc:* 800-426-1881 ■ *Web:* www.hlbouton.com	Wareham	MA	02571	508-295-3300	295-3521
Hoover Industries Inc 7260 NW 68th St *Web:* www.hooverindustries.com	Miami	FL	33166	305-888-9791	887-4632
ILC Dover Inc 1 Moonwalker Rd *TF:* 800-631-9567 ■ *Web:* www.ilcdover.com	Frederica	DE	19946	302-335-3911	335-0762
IMMI 18881 US 31 N *Web:* www.imminet.com	Westfield	IN	46074	317-896-9531	896-2142
Indiana Mills & Mfg Inc DBA IMMI 18881 US 31 N *Web:* www.imminet.com	Westfield	IN	46074	317-896-9531	896-2142
International Sew-Right Co 6190 Don Murie St *Web:* www.safetyclothing.com	Niagara Falls	ON	L2E6X8	905-374-3600	374-6121
Jackson Products Inc 801 Corporate Ctr Dr Suite 300 *TF:* 800-253-7281 ■ *Web:* www.jpisafety.com	Saint Charles	MO	63304	636-300-2700	207-2805
Kappler Inc 115 Grimes Dr *TF:* 800-600-4019 ■ *Web:* www.kappler.com	Guntersville	AL	35976	256-505-4000	505-4151
Kimberly-Clark PO Box 619100 **Fax Area Code:* 817 ■ *TF:* 800-321-1435 ■ *Web:* www.kimberly-clark.com	Dallas	TX	75261	972-281-1200	577-7777*
Kimberly-Clark Corp Professional Health Care Business 1400 Holcomb Bridge Rd *Web:* www.kchealthcare.com	Roswell	GA	30076	770-587-8000	587-7718
Lakeland Industries Inc 701-7 Koehler Ave *NASDAQ: LAKE* ■ *TF:* 800-645-9291 ■ *Web:* www.lakeland.com	Ronkonkoma	NY	11779	631-981-9700	981-9751
Landauer Inc 2 Science Rd *NYSE: LDR* ■ *TF:* 800-323-8830 ■ *Web:* www.landauerinc.com	Glenwood	IL	60425	708-755-7000	755-7016
Lion Apparel Inc 6450 Poe Ave **Fax:* Hum Res ■ *TF:* 800-548-6614 ■ *Web:* www.lionapparel.com	Dayton	OH	45414	937-898-1949	898-2848*
Little Rapids Corp 2273 Larsen Rd *TF:* 800-496-3040 ■ *Web:* www.littlerapids.com	Green Bay	WI	54303	920-496-3040	494-5340
Little Rapids Corp Graham Professional Div 2273 Larsen Rd PO Box 19100 **Fax Area Code:* 800 ■ **Fax:* Cust Svc ■ *TF Cust Svc:* 800-558-6765 ■ *Web:* www.littlerapids.com/graham/	Green Bay	WI	54304	920-494-8701	494-7877*
Louis M Gerson Co Inc 15 Sproat St *TF:* 800-225-8623 ■ *Web:* www.gersonco.com	Middleboro	MA	02346	508-947-4000	947-5442
Magla Products LLC 159 South St *TF:* 800-247-5281 ■ *Web:* www.magla.com	Morristown	NJ	07960	973-984-7998	984-2382
MAPA Spontex Inc 100 Spontex Dr *TF Cust Svc:* 800-537-2897 ■ *Web:* www.mapaglove.com	Columbia	TN	38401	931-388-5632	388-8924
MCR Safety 5321 E Shelby Dr **Fax Area Code:* 800 ■ **Fax:* Sales ■ *TF:* 800-955-6887 ■ *Web:* www.mcrsafety.com	Memphis	TN	38118	901-795-5810	999-3908*
Medline Industries Inc 1 Medline Pl *TF Cust Svc:* 800-633-5463 ■ *Web:* www.medline.com	Mundelein	IL	60060	847-949-5500	643-3126

Company	City	State	Zip	Phone	Fax
Miller Products Co Inc 2511 S Tricenter Blvd *TF:* 800-782-7437 ■ *Web:* www.millerproducts.com	Durham	NC	27713	919-313-2100	313-2101
Mine Safety Appliances Co (MSA) 121 Gamma Dr *NYSE: MSA* ■ *TF:* 800-672-2222 ■ *Web:* www.msanet.com	Pittsburgh	PA	15238	412-967-3000	967-3326
Moldex Metric Inc 10111 W Jefferson Blvd **Fax:* Sales ■ *TF:* 800-421-0668 ■ *Web:* www.moldex.com	Culver City	CA	90232	310-837-6500	837-9563*
MTS Safety Products Inc 150 2nd St *TF:* 800-647-8168 ■ *Web:* www.mts-safety.com	Belmont	MS	38827	662-454-9245	454-9385
National Safety Apparel Inc 3865 W 150th St *TF:* 800-553-0672 ■ *Web:* www.nsamfg.com	Cleveland	OH	44111	216-941-1111	941-1130
Newtex Industries Inc 8050 Victor Mendon Rd *TF:* 800-836-1001 ■ *Web:* www.newtex.com	Victor	NY	14564	585-924-9135	924-4645
Niedner Ltd 675 Merrill St *TF:* 800-567-2703 ■ *Web:* www.wildfire-equipment.com	Coaticook	QC	J1A2S2	819-849-2751	849-7539
Norcross Safety Products LLC 1136 2nd St *TF Cust Svc:* 800-777-9021 ■ *Web:* www.nspusa.com	Rock Island	IL	61201	309-786-7741	786-8670
North Safety Products 2000 Plainfield Pike **Fax Area Code:* 800 ■ *TF Cust Svc:* 800-430-4110 ■ *Web:* www.northsafety.com	Cranston	RI	02921	401-943-4400	572-6346*
Para-Flite Inc 5800 Magnolia Ave *Web:* www.paraflite.com	Pennsauken	NJ	08109	856-663-1275	663-3028
Parmelee Industries Inc 8101 Lenexa Dr *TF:* 800-821-5218 ■ *Web:* www.ussafety.com	Lenexa	KS	66214	913-599-5555	599-1703
Parmelee Industries Inc US Safety Div 8101 Lenexa Dr *TF:* 800-821-5218 ■ *Web:* www.ussafety.com	Lenexa	KS	66214	913-599-5555	599-1703
Performance Designs Inc 1300 E International Speedway Blvd *Web:* www.performancedesigns.com	DeLand	FL	32724	386-738-2224	734-8297
Plastic Safety Systems Inc 2444 Baldwin Rd *TF:* 800-662-6338 ■ *Web:* www.plasticsafety.com	Cleveland	OH	44104	216-231-8590	231-2702
PolyConversions Inc 505 Condit Dr *TF:* 888-893-3330 ■ *Web:* www.polyconversions.com	Rantoul	IL	61866	217-893-3330	893-3003
Precept Medical Products Inc 370 Airport Rd *TF:* 800-851-4431 ■ *Web:* www.preceptmed.com	Arden	NC	28704	828-681-0209	687-3605
Protech Armored Products 13386 International Pkwy *TF:* 800-428-0588	Jacksonville	FL	32218	904-741-5400	741-5407
Right-Gard Corp 531 N 4th St PO Box 286 **Fax Area Code:* 717 ■ *Web:* www.right-gard.com	Denver	PA	17517	800-535-1122	484-2180*
Sabee Products Inc 1843 W Reeve St *Web:* www.sabeeproducts.com	Appleton	WI	54914	920-830-2814	830-2878
Saf-T-Gard International Inc 205 Huehl Rd *TF:* 800-548-4273 ■ *Web:* www.saftgard.com	Northbrook	IL	60062	847-291-1600	291-1610
Safariland Ltd Inc 3120 E Mission Blvd *TF:* 800-347-1200 ■ *Web:* www.safariland.com	Ontario	CA	91761	909-923-7300	923-7400
Safe-T-Gard Corp 12105 W Cedar Dr *TF Cust Svc:* 800-356-9026 ■ *Web:* www.safetgard.com	Lakewood	CO	80228	303-763-8900	763-8071
Salisbury WH & Co 7520 N Long Ave **Fax Area Code:* 866 ■ *TF:* 877-406-4501 ■ *Web:* www.whsalisbury.com	Skokie	IL	60077	847-679-6700	824-4922*
Schutt Sports 1200 E Union Ave PO Box 426 *TF:* 800-637-2047 ■ *Web:* www.schuttsports.com	Litchfield	IL	62056	217-324-2712	324-2732
Scott Health & Safety PO Box 569 *TF:* 800-247-7257 ■ *Web:* www.scotthealthsafety.com	Monroe	NC	28111	704-291-8300	291-8340
Scott USA Inc PO Box 2030 *TF:* 800-292-5874 ■ *Web:* www.scottusa.com	Sun Valley	ID	83353	208-622-1000	622-1005
Seattle Mfg Corp 6930 Salashan Pkwy *TF:* 800-426-6251 ■ *Web:* www.smcgear.net	Ferndale	WA	98248	360-366-5534	366-5723
Sellstrom Mfg Co 1 Sellstrom Dr *TF:* 800-323-7402 ■ *Web:* www.sellstrom.com	Palatine	IL	60067	847-358-2000	358-2036
Sola Communications Inc 113 N Patch St *TF:* 800-458-8301 ■ *Web:* www.solacomm.com	Scott	LA	70583	337-235-1515	235-5119
SSL Americas Inc 3585 Engineering Dr Suite 200 *TF:* 888-387-3927 ■ *Web:* www.ssl-international.com	Norcross	GA	30092	770-582-2222	582-2233
Standard Textile Co Inc 1 Knollcrest Dr *TF:* 800-888-5000 ■ *Web:* www.standardtextile.com	Cincinnati	OH	45237	513-761-9255	761-0467
Stearns Inc 1100 Stearns Dr *TF:* 800-328-3208 ■ *Web:* www.stearnsinc.com	Sauk Rapids	MN	56379	320-252-1642	252-4425
Steel Grip Inc 700 Garfield St *TF:* 800-223-1595 ■ *Web:* www.steelgripinc.com	Danville	IL	61832	217-442-6240	442-9370
Steele Inc 26122 Iowa Ave NE *TF:* 888-783-3538 ■ *Web:* www.steelevest.com	Kingston	WA	98346	360-297-4555	297-2816
Steiner Industries 5801 N Tripp Ave *TF:* 800-621-4515 ■ *Web:* www.steinerindustries.com	Chicago	IL	60646	773-588-3444	588-3450
Stemaco Products Inc 2211 Ogden Rd	Rock Hill	SC	29730	803-328-2191	328-2808
Strong Enterprises Inc 11236 Satellite Blvd *TF:* 800-344-6319 ■ *Web:* www.strongparachutes.com	Orlando	FL	32837	407-859-9317	850-6978
TASER International Inc 17800 N 85th St *NASDAQ: TASR* ■ *TF:* 800-978-2737 ■ *Web:* www.etaser.com	Scottsdale	AZ	85255	480-905-2000	991-0791
Tillotson Corp 1 Cranberry Hill Suite 105	Lexington	MA	02421	781-402-1731	402-1737
Tillotson Healthcare Corp 8-10 Glenshaw St *TF:* 800-445-6830 ■ *Web:* www.thcnet.com	Orangeburg	NY	10962	845-365-8200	365-8201
Tingley Rubber Corp 1 Cragwood Rd *TF Cust Svc:* 800-631-5498 ■ *Web:* www.tingleyrubber.com	South Plainfield	NJ	07080	908-757-7474	757-9239
Titmus Optical Inc 3811 Corporate Dr *TF Cust Svc:* 800-446-1802 ■ *Web:* www.titmus.com	Petersburg	VA	23805	804-732-6121	862-3734
TVI Corp 7100 Holladay Tyler Rd Suite 200 *NASDAQ: TVIN* ■ *TF:* 800-598-9711 ■ *Web:* www.tvicorp.com	Glenn Dale	MD	20769	301-352-8800	352-8818
United Pioneer Co 2777 Summer St Suite 206 *TF:* 800-466-9823 ■ *Web:* www.upcjackets.com	Stamford	CT	06905	203-504-6260	504-6259
US Safety Div Parmelee Industries Inc 8101 Lenexa Dr *TF:* 800-821-5218 ■ *Web:* www.ussafety.com	Lenexa	KS	66214	913-599-5555	599-1703
Uvex Safety Inc 10 Thurber Blvd *TF:* 800-343-3411 ■ *Web:* www.uvex.com	Smithfield	RI	02917	401-232-1200	231-4903
VF Imagewear Inc 3375 Joseph Martin Hwy **Fax:* Sales ■ *TF:* 800-832-6469 ■ *Web:* www.vfc.com	Martinsville	VA	24115	276-632-7200	956-7826*
WH Salisbury & Co 7520 N Long Ave **Fax Area Code:* 866 ■ *TF:* 877-406-4501 ■ *Web:* www.whsalisbury.com	Skokie	IL	60077	847-679-6700	824-4922*
White Knight Engineered Products 10 National Ave *TF:* 800-743-4700 ■ *Web:* www.wkep.com	Fletcher	NC	28732	828-687-0940	687-6275
White Rubber Corp 837 Cleveland Rd *Web:* www.whitesafetyline.com	Ravenna	OH	44266	330-296-6497	296-2254
Wolf X-Ray Corp 100 W Industry Ct *TF Cust Svc:* 800-356-9729 ■ *Web:* www.wolfxray.com	Deer Park	NY	11729	631-242-9729	925-5003

580 PEST CONTROL SERVICES

Company	City	State	Zip	Phone	Fax
Antimite Assoc Inc 7365 Hellman Ave *TF:* 800-675-6483 ■ *Web:* www.antimite.net	Rancho Cucamonga	CA	91730	909-483-5300	483-9843
Arrow Exterminators Inc 8613 Roswell Rd *TF:* 800-281-8978 ■ *Web:* www.arrowexterminators.com	Atlanta	GA	30350	770-993-8705	640-0073
Cats USA Pest Control PO Box 151 *TF:* 800-924-3626	North Hollywood	CA	91603	818-506-1000	506-4973
Copesan Services Inc 3490 N 127th St *TF:* 800-267-3726 ■ *Web:* www.copesan.com	Brookfield	WI	53005	262-783-6261	783-6267
Dodson Brothers Exterminating Co Inc PO Box 10249 *TF:* 800-446-0977 ■ *Web:* www.dodsonbros.com	Lynchburg	VA	24506	434-847-9051	847-2034
Ecolab Inc 370 N Wabasha St *NYSE: ECL* ■ *TF:* 800-392-3392 ■ *Web:* www.ecolab.com	Saint Paul	MN	55102	651-293-2233	293-2069
Ecolab Pest Elimination Services 370 N Wabasha St *TF:* 800-352-5326 ■ *Web:* www.ecolab.com	Saint Paul	MN	55102	651-293-2233	293-2092
Ehrlich JC Co Inc PO Box 13848 *TF:* 800-488-9495 ■ *Web:* www.jcehrlich.com	Reading	PA	19612	610-372-9700	378-9525
Fischer Environmental Service Inc PO Box 1319 *TF:* 800-391-2565 ■ *Web:* www.fischerenv.com	Mandeville	LA	70471	985-626-7378	626-7490
Florida Pest Control & Chemical Co Inc 116 NW 16th Ave *Web:* www.flapest.com	Gainesville	FL	32601	352-376-2661	376-2791
Home Paramount Pest Control Companies Inc 2011 Rock Spring Rd PO Box 850 *TF:* 800-492-5544 ■ *Web:* www.home-paramount.com	Forest Hill	MD	21050	410-510-0700	638-4291
Horizon Termite & Pest Control Corp 45 Cross Ave *TF:* 888-612-2847 ■ *Web:* www.horizonpestcontrol.com	Midland Park	NJ	07432	201-447-2530	447-9541
JC Ehrlich Co Inc PO Box 13848 *TF:* 800-488-9495 ■ *Web:* www.jcehrlich.com	Reading	PA	19612	610-372-9700	378-9525
Knockout Pest Control Inc 1009 Front St *TF:* 800-244-7378 ■ *Web:* www.knockoutpest.com	Uniondale	NY	11553	516-489-7817	489-4348
Lawn Doctor Inc 142 SR 34 *TF:* 800-631-5660 ■ *Web:* www.lawndoctor.com	Holmdel	NJ	07733	732-946-0029	946-9089
Massey Services Inc 610 N Wymore Rd **Fax:* Cust Svc ■ *TF:* 800-432-1820 ■ *Web:* www.masseyservices.com	Maitland	FL	32751	407-645-2500	645-0098*
MasterCare Termite & Pest Control 20722 S Main St	Carson	CA	90745	310-523-3638	523-4849
McCall Service Inc 2861 College St *TF:* 800-342-6948 ■ *Web:* www.mccallservice.com	Jacksonville	FL	32205	904-389-5561	389-3212
McCloud WB & Co 2500 W Higgins Rd Suite 850 *TF Cust Svc:* 800-332-7805 ■ *Web:* www.mccloudservices.com	Hoffman Estates	IL	60169	847-585-0650	585-0655
NaturaLawn of America Inc 1 E Church St *TF:* 800-989-5444 ■ *Web:* www.nl-amer.com	Frederick	MD	21701	301-694-5440	846-0320
Nutrilawn Inc 185 The West Mall Suite 115 *TF:* 800-396-6096 ■ *Web:* www.nutri-lawn.com	Toronto	ON	M9C5K8	416-620-7100	620-7771
Orkin Exterminating Co Inc 2170 Piedmont Rd NE **Fax:* Cust Svc ■ *TF:* 800-346-7546 ■ *Web:* www.orkin.com	Atlanta	GA	30324	404-888-2000	633-2323*
PermaTreat Pest Control Inc 10745 Courthouse Rd *TF:* 800-944-8592 ■ *Web:* www.permatreat.com	Fredericksburg	VA	22408	540-891-7811	891-7813
Presto-X Co PO Box 2578 *TF:* 800-759-1942 ■ *Web:* www.prestox.com	Omaha	NE	68103	402-554-1942	554-1544
Rentokil Initial 4067 Industrial Pk Dr Bldg 3 *Web:* www.rentokil-initial.com	Norcross	GA	30071	770-476-2590	497-3350
Rollins Inc 2170 Piedmont Rd NE *NYSE: ROL* ■ **Fax:* Hum Res ■ *Web:* www.rollins.com	Atlanta	GA	30324	404-888-2000	888-2672*
Schendel Pest Services 1824 S Kansas Ave *TF:* 800-233-3956 ■ *Web:* www.schendelpest.com	Topeka	KS	66612	785-232-9357	232-4165
Scotts Lawn Service 14111 Scottslawn Rd *TF:* 888-872-6887 ■ *Web:* www.scottslawnservice.com	Marysville	OH	43040	937-644-0011	578-5444
Smithereen Exterminators Inc 7400 N Melvina Ave *TF:* 800-336-3500 ■ *Web:* www.smithereen.com	Niles	IL	60714	847-647-0010	647-0606
Spencer Pest Control 205 Norcross St *Web:* www.spencerpest.com	Roswell	GA	30075	770-998-0998	998-3311
Spring-Green Lawn Care Corp 11909 Spaulding School Dr *TF:* 800-435-4051 ■ *Web:* www.spring-green.com	Plainfield	IL	60544	815-436-8777	436-9056
Terminix International Co LP 860 Ridge Lake Blvd **Fax:* Mktg ■ *TF:* 800-654-7848 ■ *Web:* www.terminix.com	Memphis	TN	38120	901-766-1333	766-1491*
TruGreen ChemLawn 860 Ridge Lake Blvd *TF:* 800-878-4733 ■ *Web:* www.trugreen.com	Memphis	TN	38120	901-681-1800	681-1900
Truly Nolen of America Inc 3636 E Speedway Blvd *TF:* 800-528-3442 ■ *Web:* www.trulynolen.com	Tucson	AZ	85716	520-327-3447	322-4011
Turf Management Systems Inc 2399 Royal Windsor *Web:* www.weed-man.com	Mississauga	ON	L5J1K9	905-823-8550	823-4594
Waltham Services Inc 817 Moody St *TF:* 800-562-9287 ■ *Web:* www.walthamservices.com	Waltham	MA	02453	781-893-1810	893-4659
WB McCloud & Co 2500 W Higgins Rd Suite 850 *TF Cust Svc:* 800-332-7805 ■ *Web:* www.mccloudservices.com	Hoffman Estates	IL	60169	847-585-0650	585-0655
Weed Man 2399 Royal Windsor *Web:* www.weedmanusa.com	Mississauga	ON	L5J1K9	905-823-8550	823-4594
Western Exterminator Co 305 N Crescent Way *TF:* 800-698-2440 ■ *Web:* www.west-ext.com	Anaheim	CA	92801	714-517-9000	533-1199
Young Pest Control Inc 2011 W Platt St *TF:* 800-330-6996	Tampa	FL	33606	813-251-1025	254-2686

PESTICIDES

SEE Fertilizers & Pesticides p. 1635

581 PET PRODUCTS

SEE ALSO Leather Goods - Personal p. 1889; Livestock & Poultry Feeds - Prepared p. 1917

Company	City	State	Zip	Phone	Fax
American Leather Specialties Corp 87 34th St	Brooklyn	NY	11232	718-965-3900	499-2481
American Nutrition Inc 2890 Reeves Ave *TF:* 800-257-4530 ■ *Web:* www.anibrands.com	Ogden	UT	84402	801-394-3477	394-3674
Applica Consumer Products Inc 3633 Flamingo Rd *TF Cust Svc:* 800-231-9786 ■ *Web:* www.applicainc.com	Miramar	FL	33027	954-883-1000	883-1070
Applica Inc 3633 Flamingo Rd *NYSE: APN* ■ *TF:* 800-557-9463 ■ *Web:* www.applicainc.com	Miramar	FL	33027	954-883-1000	883-1070
Aquatrol Inc 237-H N Euclid Way *TF:* 800-237-7735	Anaheim	CA	92801	714-533-3381	533-9254
Bailey Farms LLC 549 Karem Dr *TF:* 800-655-1705	Marshall	WI	53559	608-655-3439	655-4767
Barr Enterprises Inc 7276 W Chickadee Rd *TF:* 800-826-2341	Greenwood	WI	54437	715-267-6335	267-7214
Benco Pet Foods Inc 22 S 1st St	Zanesville	OH	43701	740-454-8575	455-6230
BioZyme Inc 6010 Stockyards Expy *TF:* 800-821-3070 ■ *Web:* www.biozymeinc.com	Saint Joseph	MO	64504	816-238-3326	238-7549
Blitz USA Inc 404 26th Ave NW *TF Cust Svc:* 800-331-3795 ■ *Web:* www.blitzusa.com	Miami	OK	74354	918-540-1515	542-1380
Central Pet 301 Island Rd *TF:* 800-631-7724 ■ *Web:* www.centralpet.com	Mahwah	NJ	07430	201-529-5050	529-1285
Church & Dwight Co Inc 469 N Harrison St *NYSE: CHD* ■ *Web:* www.churchdwight.com	Princeton	NJ	08543	609-683-5900	
Clorox Co 1221 Broadway *NYSE: CLX* ■ *TF Cust Svc:* 800-292-2808 ■ *Web:* www.thecloroxcompany.com	Oakland	CA	94612	510-271-7000	832-1463
Clorox Pet Products Co 1221 Broadway PO Box 24305 *Web:* www.scoopaway.com	Oakland	CA	94623	510-271-7000	832-1463
Colgate-Palmolive Co 300 Park Ave *NYSE: CL* ■ *Web:* www.colgate.com	New York	NY	10022	212-310-2000	310-2595

	Phone	Fax

Dad's Pet Care Inc 18746 Mill St ... Meadville PA 16335 814-724-7710 337-2743
TF: 800-458-1801 ■ *Web:* www.dadspetcare.com
Delight Products Co 1200 Industrial Dr ... Springfield TN 37172 615-384-7546 384-7929
Doctors Foster & Smith Inc 2253 Air Park Rd ... Rhinelander WI 54501 715-369-3305 562-7169*
**Fax Area Code:* 800 ■ **Fax:* Cust Svc ■ *TF:* 800-826-7206 ■ *Web:* www.drsfostersmith.com
Doskocil Mfg Co Inc 4209 Barnett Blvd ... Arlington TX 76017 817-467-5116 419-6886*
**Fax:* Sales ■ *TF:* 800-433-5185 ■ *Web:* www.petmate.com
Eagle Pack Pet Foods Inc 1011 W 11th St ... Mishawaka IN 46544 574-259-7834 259-0730
TF: 800-255-5959 ■ *Web:* www.eaglepack.com
Edstrom Industries Inc 819 Bakke Ave ... Waterford WI 53185 262-534-5181 534-5184
TF: 800-558-5913 ■ *Web:* www.edstrom.com
Ethical Products Inc 27 Federal Plaza ... Bloomfield NJ 07003 973-748-8282 707-0701
TF: 800-223-7768 ■ *Web:* www.ethicalpet.com
FL Emmert Co Inc 2007 Dunlap St ... Cincinnati OH 45214 513-721-5808 721-6087
TF: 800-441-3343 ■ *Web:* www.emmert.com
Golden Products 901 Chouteau Ave ... Saint Louis MO 63102 314-982-2400 982-3338
Got Pet Food 1840 14th St ... Santa Monica CA 90404 310-393-9393
Web: gotpetfood.com
Great Western Pet Supply 2001 N Black Canyon Hwy ... Phoenix AZ 85009 602-255-0166 255-0841
TF: 800-646-3611 ■ *Web:* www.greatwesternpetsupply.com
Hartz Mountain Corp 400 Plaza Dr ... Secaucus NJ 07094 201-271-4800 271-0164
TF: 800-929-6700 ■ *Web:* www.hartz.com
Heath Mfg Co 140 Mill St ... Coopersville MI 49404 616-997-8181 997-9491
TF: 800-678-8183 ■ *Web:* www.heathmfg.com
Heinz HJ Co of Canada Ltd 90 Shepherd Ave E Suite 400 ... North York ON M2N7K5 416-226-5757 226-5064
Hill's Pet Nutrition Inc 400 SW 8th St PO Box 148 ... Topeka KS 66601 785-354-8523 368-5509
TF: 800-255-0449 ■ *Web:* www.hillspet.com
HJ Heinz Co of Canada Ltd 90 Shepherd Ave E Suite 400 ... North York ON M2N7K5 416-226-5757 226-5064
Iams Co 7250 Poe Ave ... Dayton OH 45414 937-898-7387
TF Cust Svc: 800-675-3849 ■ *Web:* www.iams.com
John A Van Den Bosch Co 4511 Holland Ave ... Holland MI 49424 616-848-2000 848-2100
TF Cust Svc: 800-968-6477 ■ *Web:* www.vbosch.com
Kaytee Products Inc 521 Clay St ... Chilton WI 53014 920-849-2321 849-4734
TF: 800-669-9580 ■ *Web:* www.kaytee.com
Kennel-Aire LLC 801 E North St ... Ottawa KS 66067 785-242-8484 242-8383
TF: 800-346-0134 ■ *Web:* www.kennel-aire.com
Manna Pro Corp 707 Spirit 40 Park Dr Suite 150 ... Chesterfield MO 63005 636-681-1700 681-1799
TF: 800-690-9908 ■ *Web:* www.mannapro.com
Mark Hershey Farms Inc 479 Horseshoe Pike ... Lebanon PA 17042 717-867-4624 867-4313
TF: 888-801-3301 ■ *Web:* www.markhersheyfarms.com
Mars Pet Care 315 Cool Springs Blvd ... Franklin TN 37067 615-807-4626 468-2686
TF: 800-789-4639 ■ *Web:* www.marspetcare.com
Mars Snack Food 800 High St ... Hackettstown NJ 07840 908-852-1000 850-2734
TF: 800-432-1093 ■ *Web:* www.mars.com
Menu Foods Inc 9130 Griffith Morgan Ln ... Pennsauken NJ 08110 856-662-7412 662-4673
Merrick Pet Foods 101 SE 11th Ave Suite 200 ... Amarillo TX 79101 806-322-2800 322-2854
TF: 800-664-7387 ■ *Web:* www.merrickpetcare.com
MFM Industries Inc 2800 E Silver Springs Blvd Suite 204 ... Ocala FL 34471 352-854-0070 854-1576
TF Cust Svc: 800-922-6369 ■ *Web:* www.cedarfreshscoop.com
MIDWEST Homes for Pets 4211 E Jackson St ... Muncie IN 47303 765-289-3355 289-6524
TF: 800-428-8560 ■ *Web:* www.midwesthomes4pets.com
Moyer & Son Inc 113 E Reliance Rd ... Souderton PA 18964 215-723-6000 721-2814
TF: 800-345-0419 ■ *Web:* www.emoyer.com
Multipet International Inc 265 W Commercial Ave ... Moonachie NJ 07074 201-438-6600 438-2990
TF: 800-900-6738 ■ *Web:* www.multipet.com
Natural Life Pet Products Inc 112 N Elon St Suite A ... Pittsburg KS 66762 620-230-0888 230-0403
TF: 800-367-2391 ■ *Web:* www.nlpp.com
Nature House Inc 3100 N Grant Ave Purple Martin Junction ... Griggsville IL 62340 217-833-2393 533-7826*
**Fax Area Code:* 773 ■ *TF:* 800-255-2692 ■ *Web:* www.naturesociety.org
Nestle Purina PetCare Co 901 Chouteau Ave ... Saint Louis MO 63102 314-982-1000 982-3327
TF: 800-778-7462 ■ *Web:* www.purina.com
North States Industries Inc 1507 92nd Ln NE ... Blaine MN 55449 763-486-1754 486-1763
TF: 800-848-8421 ■ *Web:* www.northstatesind.com
Novalek Inc 2242 Davis Ct ... Hayward CA 94545 510-782-4058 784-0945
TF: 800-877-7387 ■ *Web:* www.novalek.com
Nutro Products Inc 445 Wilson Way ... City of Industry CA 91744 626-968-0532 968-3962
TF: 800-833-5330 ■ *Web:* www.nutroproducts.com
Oil-Dri Corp of America 410 N Michigan Ave Suite 400 ... Chicago IL 60611 312-321-1515 321-1271
NYSE: ODC ■ *TF:* 800-233-9802 ■ *Web:* www.oildri.com
Orrco Inc 515 Collins Blvd ... Orrville OH 44667 330-683-5015 683-0738
TF: 800-321-3085 ■ *Web:* www.orrvillepet.com
Penn-Plax Inc 35 Marcus Blvd ... Hauppauge NY 11788 631-273-3787 879-6075*
**Fax Area Code:* 888 ■ *TF:* 800-645-6055 ■ *Web:* www.pennplax.com
Pet Food Express 2131 Williams St ... San Leandro CA 94577 510-346-7777 346-7788
TF: 877-472-7777 ■ *Web:* petfoodexpress.com
Pet Supermarket Inc 1100 International Pkwy ... Sunrise FL 33323 954-351-0834 351-0897
TF: 800-361-0049 ■ *Web:* www.petsupermarket.com
Pet Supplies "Plus" Inc 22710 Haggerty Rd Suite 100 ... Farmington Hills MI 48335 248-374-1900 374-7900
TF: 866-477-7747 ■ *Web:* www.petsuppliesplus.com
Pet Valu Canada Inc 121 McPherson St ... Markham ON L3R3L3 905-946-1200 305-6166
TSX: PVC ■ *TF:* 800-738-8258 ■ *Web:* www.petvalu.com
PETCO Animal Supplies Inc 9125 Rehco Rd ... San Diego CA 92121 858-453-7845 638-2164
NASDAQ: PETC ■ *TF:* 877-738-6742 ■ *Web:* www.petco.com
PetFoodDirect.com 189 Main St ... Harleysville PA 19438 215-513-1999 513-7286
TF Cust Svc: 800-865-1333 ■ *Web:* www.petfooddirect.com
Petland Discounts 355 Crooked Hill Rd ... Brentwood NY 11717 631-273-6363 273-6513
Web: www.petlanddiscounts.com
Petland Inc 250 Riverside St ... Chillicothe OH 45601 740-775-2464 775-2574
TF: 800-221-5935 ■ *Web:* www.petland.com
PetMed Express Inc 1441 SW 29th Ave ... Pompano Beach FL 33069 954-979-5995 971-0544
NASDAQ: PETS ■ *TF:* 800-738-6337 ■ *Web:* www.1800petmeds.com
PETsMART Inc 19601 N 27th Ave ... Phoenix AZ 85027 623-580-6100 580-6502
NASDAQ: PETM ■ *TF Cust Svc:* 800-738-1385 ■ *Web:* www.petsmart.com
Pied Piper Mills Inc 423 E Lake Dr ... Hamlin TX 79520 325-576-3684 576-3460
TF: 800-338-4610 ■ *Web:* www.piedpiperpetfood.net
Prevue Pet Products Inc 224 N Maplewood Ave ... Chicago IL 60612 312-243-3624 243-4224
TF: 800-243-3624 ■ *Web:* www.prevuepet.com
Prince Corp 8351 County Rd H ... Marshfield WI 54449 715-384-3105 387-6924
TF: 800-777-2486 ■ *Web:* www.prince-corp.com
Pro-Pet LLC 1400 McKinley Rd ... Saint Marys OH 45885 419-394-3374 394-8024
TF: 800-245-4125 ■ *Web:* www.joypetfood.com
Radio Systems Corp 10427 Electric Ave ... Knoxville TN 37932 865-777-5404 777-5419
TF Cust Svc: 800-732-2677 ■ *Web:* www.petsafe.net
Ralco Nutrition Inc 1600 Hahn Rd ... Marshall MN 56258 507-532-5748 532-5740
TF: 800-533-5306 ■ *Web:* www.ralconutrition.com
RMC Inc 1040 S High St ... Harrisonburg VA 22801 540-434-5333 434-7090
Royal Canin USA Inc 500 Fountain Lakes Blvd Suite 100 ... Saint Charles MO 63301 636-926-0003 552-7920*
**Fax Area Code:* 800 ■ *TF:* 800-592-6687 ■ *Web:* www.royalcanin.us
Sergeant's Pet Care Products 2625 S 158th Plaza ... Omaha NE 68130 402-938-7000 938-7091
TF: 800-224-7387 ■ *Web:* www.sergeants.com
Silverstone Pet Inc DBA Pass Pets
65 Centre Pointe Suite 106 ... Saint Charles MO 63304 636-447-7900 447-8880
Simmons Allied Pet Foods Inc 101 N Broadway ... Siloan Springs AR 72761 479-524-8151 524-6179
TF: 800-241-8504 ■ *Web:* www.simmonspetfood.com
Star Milling Co 24067 Water St ... Perris CA 92570 951-657-3143 657-3114
TF: 800-733-6455 ■ *Web:* www.starmilling.com
Sunshine Mills Inc 500 6th St SW ... Red Bay AL 35582 256-356-9541 356-8287*
**Fax:* Sales ■ *TF:* 800-633-3349 ■ *Web:* www.sunshinemills.com
Tetra Holdings US Inc 3001 Commerce St ... Blacksburg VA 24060 540-951-5400 951-5491
TF: 800-526-0650 ■ *Web:* www.tetra-fish.com
Texas Farm Products Co 915 S Fredonia St ... Nacogdoches TX 75964 936-564-3711 560-8200
TF: 800-392-3110 ■ *Web:* www.texasfarm.com
Triumph Pet Industries Inc 500 6th St SW ... Red Bay AL 35582 256-356-9541 331-5140*
**Fax Area Code:* 800 ■ *TF:* 800-331-5144 ■ *Web:* www.triumphpet.com
Van Den Bosch John A Co 4511 Holland Ave ... Holland MI 49424 616-848-2000 848-2100
TF Cust Svc: 800-968-6477 ■ *Web:* www.vbosch.com
Virbac Corp 3200 Meacham Blvd ... Fort Worth TX 76137 817-831-5030 831-8327
TF: 800-338-3659 ■ *Web:* www.virbac.com
Wells Pet Food Corp 617 S 'D' St ... Monmouth IL 61462 309-734-3121 734-7420
TF: 800-447-8435
Wild Birds Unlimited Inc 11711 N College Ave Suite 146 ... Carmel IN 46032 317-571-7100 571-7110
TF: 800-326-4928 ■ *Web:* www.wbu.com

582 PETROLEUM & PETROLEUM PRODUCTS - WHOL

	Phone	Fax

Ada Resources Inc 6603 Kirbyville St ... Houston TX 77033 713-644-2111 640-0121
TF: 800-945-6113 ■ *Web:* www.adaresources.com
Allied Oil & Supply Inc 2209 S 24th St ... Omaha NE 68103 402-344-4343 344-4360
TF: 800-333-3717 ■ *Web:* www.allied-oil.com
AmeriGas Propane Inc PO Box 965 ... Valley Forge PA 19482 610-337-7000 992-3242*
**Fax:* Mktg ■ *Web:* www.amerigas.com
Apex Oil Co Inc 8235 Forsyth Blvd Suite 400 ... Clayton MO 63105 314-889-9600 854-8539
Web: www.apexoil.com
Arkansas Valley Petroleum Inc 8336 E 73rd St Suite 100 ... Tulsa OK 74133 918-252-0508 250-4921
TF: 800-888-1389
Bell Gas Inc PO Box 490 ... Roswell NM 88202 505-622-4800 622-4710
Blue Rhino Corp 104 Cambridge Plaza Dr ... Winston-Salem NC 27104 336-659-6900 659-6750
TF: 800-258-7466 ■ *Web:* www.bluerhino.com
Bluewave Energy 30 Oland Ct ... Dartmouth NS B3B1V2 902-481-0515 481-6236
Web: www.bluewaveenergy.ca
BP Lubricants USA Inc 1500 Valley Rd ... Wayne NJ 07470 973-633-2200 633-9867
TF: 800-633-6163 ■ *Web:* www.bp.com/lubricanthome.do
Brewer Oil Co 1301 W Main St ... Artesia NM 88210 505-748-1248 746-3866
Web: www.breweroil.com
Campbell Oil Co Inc 611 Erie St S ... Massillon OH 44646 330-833-8555 833-1083
TF: 800-589-8555
Cargill Energy PO Box 9300 ... Minneapolis MN 55440 952-742-7575
TF: 800-227-4455 ■ *Web:* www.cargill.com
Carson Oil Co Inc 3125 NW 35th Ave ... Portland OR 97210 503-224-8500 222-0186
TF: 800-998-7767 ■ *Web:* www.carsonoil.com
Castle Oil Corp 500 Mamaroneck Ave ... Harrison NY 10528 914-381-6600 381-6601
Web: www.castleoil.com
Castrol Canada Inc 3660 Lake Shore Blvd W ... Toronto ON M8W1P2 416-252-5511 252-1774
Web: www.castrolcanada.com
Chemoil Corp 4 Embarcadero Ctr Suite 1100 ... San Francisco CA 94111 415-268-2700 268-2701
Web: www.chemoil.com
Colonial Group Inc 101 N Lathrop Ave ... Savannah GA 31415 912-236-1331 235-2938
Colonial Oil Industries Inc PO Box 576 ... Savannah GA 31402 912-236-1331 235-3868
TF: 800-944-3835
Condon Oil Co Inc PO Box 184 ... Ripon WI 54971 920-748-3186 748-3201
TF: 800-452-1212 ■ *Web:* www.condoncompanies.com
Crown Oil & Gas Co 1 N Charles St ... Baltimore MD 21201 410-539-7400 659-4747
Web: www.crowncentral.com
Dead River Co PO Box 1427 ... Bangor ME 04402 207-947-8641 990-0828
Web: www.deadriver.com
District Petroleum Products Inc 1814 River Rd Suite 100 ... Huron OH 44839 419-433-8373 433-9646
Dixie Oil Co Inc PO Box 1007 ... Tifton GA 31793 229-382-2700 387-6905
Drake Petroleum Co Inc 221 Quinebaug Rd ... North Grosvenordale CT 06255 860-935-5200 935-9396
Web: www.drakepetro.com
Duke Energy Field Services 370 17th St Suite 2500 ... Denver CO 80202 303-595-3331 605-2227
Web: www.duke-energy.com
Englefield Oil Co 447 James Pkwy ... Heath OH 43056 740-928-8215 928-3844
TF: 800-282-1675 ■ *Web:* www.englefieldoil.com
Ever-Ready Oil Co PO Box 25845 ... Albuquerque NM 87125 505-842-6120 247-3918
TF: 800-259-6120 ■ *Web:* www.ever-ready.com
Farm & Home Oil Co 3115 State Rd PO Box 389 ... Telford PA 18969 215-257-0131 257-2088
TF: 800-473-1562 ■ *Web:* www.fhoil.com
Flint Hills Resources LP 4111 E 37th St N ... Wichita KS 67220 316-828-5500 828-4228
Web: www.fhr.com
Flying J Inc 1104 Country Hill Dr ... Ogden UT 84403 801-624-1000 395-8005
TF: 800-842-6428 ■ *Web:* www.flyingj.com
Gate Petroleum Co 9540 San Jose Blvd ... Jacksonville FL 32257 904-737-7220 732-7660
Web: www.gatepetro.com
George E Warren Corp 3001 Ocean Dr Suite 203 ... Vero Beach FL 32963 772-778-7100 778-7171
Getty Petroleum Marketing Inc 1500 Hempstead Tpke ... East Meadow NY 11554 516-542-4900 832-8632
Global Partners LP 800 South St Suite 200 ... Waltham MA 02454 781-894-8800 398-4160
NYSE: GLP ■ *TF:* 800-685-7222 ■ *Web:* www.globalp.com
Gulf Oil LP 90 Everett Ave ... Chelsea MA 02150 617-889-9000 884-3325*
**Fax:* Mktg ■ *TF:* 800-256-4853 ■ *Web:* www.gulfoil.com
Gull Industries 3404 4th Ave S ... Seattle WA 98134 206-624-5900 624-5412
TF: 800-866-4855
H & W Petroleum Co Inc 9617 Wallisville Rd ... Houston TX 77013 713-896-4300 673-5412
TF: 800-406-3835 ■ *Web:* www.hwpetro.com
Harold E Dickey Co PO Box 809 ... Packwood IA 52580 319-695-3601 695-3051
Herdrich Petroleum 210 E US 52 ... Rushville IN 46173 765-932-3224 932-4622
Hicks Oil & Hicks Gas Inc 204 N Rt 54 ... Roberts IL 60962 217-395-2281 395-2572
TF: 800-252-6871
Humboldt Petroleum Inc PO Box 131 ... Eureka CA 95502 707-443-3069 445-4433
Inergy LP 2 Brush Creek Blvd Suite 200 ... Kansas City MO 64112 816-842-8181 842-1904
NASDAQ: NRGY ■ *TF:* 877-446-3749 ■ *Web:* www.inergypropane.com
Inter City Oil Co Inc PO Box 3048 ... Duluth MN 55803 218-728-3641 728-5140
TF: 800-642-5542
Interior Fuels Co PO Box 70199 ... Fairbanks AK 99707 907-456-1312 456-1659
Jardine Petroleum Co 1117 N 400 East ... North Salt Lake UT 84054 801-298-3252 531-2280
TF: 800-777-9251 ■ *Web:* www.jpetro.com
Jefferson City Oil Co Inc PO Box 576 ... Jefferson City MO 65102 573-634-2025 634-5246
JH Williams Oil Co Inc 1237 E Twiggs St ... Tampa FL 33602 813-228-7776 224-9413
TF: 800-683-0536 ■ *Web:* www.jhwoil.com
Keystops LLC PO Box 2809 ... Franklin KY 42135 270-586-8283 586-3112
TF: 800-346-6456
Lakeside Oil Co Inc 555 W Brown Deer Rd Suite 200 ... Milwaukee WI 53217 414-540-4000 540-4100
TF: 800-289-3835
Leffler Energy Inc PO Box 302 ... Mount Joy PA 17552 717-653-1411 653-2728
TF: 800-984-1411 ■ *Web:* www.lefflerenergy.com
Lucky Lady Oil Co 107 NW 28th St ... Fort Worth TX 76106 817-740-7400 740-0245
TF: 800-303-1412
Lyden Oil Co Inc 3711 Lee Harps Rd ... Youngstown OH 44515 330-792-1100 792-1462
TF: 800-362-9410 ■ *Web:* www.lydenoilcompany.com

Company	City	State	Zip	Phone	Fax
Martin Midstream Partners LP 4200 Stone Rd NASDAQ: MMLP	Kilgore	TX	75662	903-983-6200	988-6403
Mid-Atlantic Petroleum Properties LLC 12311 Middlebrook Rd. Web: www.mappllc.com	Germantown	MD	20874	301-972-4116	972-3137
Miller Oil Co PO Box 1858 TF: 800-333-4645 ■ Web: www.milleroil.com	Norfolk	VA	23501	757-623-6600	640-2175
Mitsubishi International Corp 655 3rd Ave Web: www.micusa.com	New York	NY	10017	212-605-2000	
Montour Oil Service Co 112 Broad St PO Box 128 TF: 800-332-8915	Montoursville	PA	17754	570-368-8611	368-8618
National Oil & Gas Inc PO Box 476 TF: 800-322-8454	Bluffton	IN	46714	260-824-2220	824-2223
NOCO Energy Corp 2440 Sheridan Dr TF: 800-500-6626 ■ Web: www.noco.com	Tonawanda	NY	14150	716-614-1000	832-6461
North East Oil PO Box 1386	Ahoskie	NC	27910	252-332-5021	332-5173
O2Diesel Corp 100 Commerce Dr Suite 301 AMEX: OTD ■ Web: www.o2diesel.net	Newark	DE	19713	302-266-6000	266-7076
Parker Oil Co Inc PO Box 120 Web: www.parkeroilcompany.com	South Hill	VA	23970	434-447-3146	447-2646
Peerless Distributing Co 21700 Northwestern Hwy Suite 1160	Southfield	MI	48075	248-559-1800	559-1861
Petroleum Products Corp 900 S Eisenhower Blvd	Middletown	PA	17057	717-939-0466	939-0294
PetroLiance LLC 739 N State St TF: 800-628-7231 ■ Web: www.petroliance.com	Elgin	IL	60123	847-741-2577	741-2590
Phoenix Fuel Co Inc 2502 N Black Canyon Hwy TF: 800-444-5823 ■ Web: www.phoenixfuel.com	Phoenix	AZ	85009	602-278-6271	278-7196
Piasa Motor Fuels Inc PO Box 484	Alton	IL	62002	618-254-7341	254-8281
Ramos Oil Co Inc 1515 S River Rd TF: 800-477-7266 ■ Web: www.ramosoil.com	West Sacramento	CA	95691	916-371-2570	371-0635
Rentech Inc 1331 17th St Suite 720 AMEX: RTK ■ Web: www.rentechinc.com	Denver	CO	80202	303-298-8008	298-8010
Rhodes 101 Stop 1620 N Kings Hwy	Cape Girardeau	MO	63701	573-334-7733	334-2578
Risser Oil Corp 2865 Executive Dr TF: 800-572-0075 ■ Web: www.therissercompanies.com	Clearwater	FL	33762	727-573-4000	572-9075
Rite Way Oil & Gas Co Inc PO Box 27049 TF: 800-279-6401	Omaha	NE	68127	402-331-6400	331-7408
River City Petroleum Inc PO Box 235 TF: 800-441-2108 ■ Web: www.rcpfuel.com	West Sacramento	CA	95691	916-371-4960	371-7983
Russell Petroleum Corp 3378 Tankview Ct.	Montgomery	AL	36108	334-834-3750	834-3755
Sapp Brothers Petroleum Inc 660 S Main St. TF: 800-922-0382	West Point	NE	68788	402-372-5485	372-3878
Sasol Wax Americas Inc 2 Corporate Dr Suite 434 TF: 800-423-7071 ■ Web: www.sasolwax.com	Shelton	CT	06484	203-925-4300	926-9844
Shell Oil Co 910 Louisanna St TF: 888-467-4355 ■ Web: www.shellus.com	Houston	TX	77002	713-241-6161	241-4044
Sierra Energy 1020 Winding Creek Rd Suite 100 TF: 800-576-2264 ■ Web: www.sierraenergy.net	Roseville	CA	95678	916-218-1600	218-1680
Silco Oil Co Inc 181 E 56th Ave Suite 600 TF: 800-707-4526	Denver	CO	80216	303-292-0500	293-8069
Sinclair Marketing 550 E South Temple TF: 800-325-3265 ■ Web: www.sinclairoil.com	Salt Lake City	UT	84102	801-524-2700	524-2721
Sinclair Oil Corp 550 E South Temple TF: 800-552-8695 ■ Web: www.sinclairoil.com	Salt Lake City	UT	84102	801-524-2700	524-2720
Southern Maryland Oil Co Inc (SMO) 6355 Crain Hwy *Fax: Cust Svc ■ TF: 800-492-3420 ■ Web: www.southernmdoil.com	La Plata	MD	20646	301-932-3600	934-4890*
Spencer Cos Inc 120 Woodson St NW TF: 800-633-2910 ■ Web: www.spencercos.com	Huntsville	AL	35801	256-533-1150	535-2910
Sprague Energy 2 International Dr Suite 200 *Fax: Hum Res ■ TF: 800-225-1560 ■ Web: www.spragueenergy.com	Portsmouth	NH	03801	603-431-1000	430-7299*
SulphCo Inc 850 Spice Islands Dr AMEX: SUF ■ Web: www.sulphco.com	Sparks	NV	89431	775-829-1310	829-1351
Sun Coast Resources Inc 6922 Cavalcade St TF: 800-677-3835 ■ Web: www.suncoastresources.com	Houston	TX	77028	713-844-9600	844-9696
Tauber Oil Co PO Box 4645 Web: www.tauberoil.com	Houston	TX	77210	713-869-8700	869-8069
Tesoro Refining & Marketing Co 3450 S 344th Way Suite 201 TF: 800-473-1123 ■ Web: www.tsocorp.com	Auburn	WA	98001	253-896-8700	896-8887
Time Oil Co 2737 W Commodore Way TF: 800-552-0748 ■ Web: www.timeoil.com	Seattle	WA	98199	206-285-2400	286-4394
Transammonia Inc 320 Park Ave Web: www.transammonia.com	New York	NY	10022	212-223-3200	759-1410
Truman Arnold Cos 701 S Robison Rd TF: 800-235-5343 ■ Web: www.tacair.com	Texarkana	TX	75504	903-794-3835	832-7226
US Oil Co Inc 425 S Washington St TF: 800-444-0202 ■ Web: www.usoil.com	Combined Locks	WI	54113	920-739-6101	788-5910
Vesco Oil Corp 16055 W 12-Mile Rd TF: 800-527-5358 ■ Web: www.vesco-oil.com	Southfield	MI	48076	248-557-1600	557-2236
Warren George E Corp 3001 Ocean Dr Suite 203	Vero Beach	FL	32963	772-778-7100	778-7171
Webber Energy Fuels 700 Main St TF: 800-932-2371 ■ Web: www.wenergy.com	Bangor	ME	04401	207-942-5501	941-9597
Western Petroleum Co 9531 W 78th St Suite 102 TF: 800-972-3835 ■ Web: www.westernpetro.com	Eden Prairie	MN	55344	952-941-9090	941-7470
Williams JH Oil Co Inc 1237 E Twiggs St TF: 800-683-0536 ■ Web: www.jhwoil.com	Tampa	FL	33602	813-228-7776	224-9413
Wooten Oil Co Inc PO Box 858	Goldsboro	NC	27533	919-734-1357	735-4677
World Fuel Services Corp 9800 NW 41st St Suite 400 NYSE: INT ■ TF: 800-345-3818 ■ Web: www.wfscorp.com	Miami	FL	33178	305-428-8000	392-5600
World Fuel Services Inc 9800 NW 41st St Suite 400 TF: 800-345-3818 ■ Web: www.wfscorp.com	Miami	FL	33178	305-428-8000	392-5600

583 PETROLEUM REFINERIES

Company	City	State	Zip	Phone	Fax
Alon USA Energy Inc 7616 LBJ Fwy Suite 300 NYSE: ALJ ■ Web: www.alonusa.com	Dallas	TX	75251	972-367-3600	367-3728
Arabian American Development Co 10830 N Central Expy Suite 175	Dallas	TX	75231	214-692-7872	692-7874
BP Plc 28100 Torch Pkwy NYSE: BP ■ *Fax Area Code: 281 ■ TF: 866-427-6947 ■ Web: www.bp.com	Warrenville	IL	60555	630-420-5111	298-0738*
Calumet Lubricants Co 2780 Waterfront Pkwy Dr E Suite 200 TF: 800-437-3188 ■ Web: www.calumetlub.com	Indianapolis	IN	46214	317-328-5660	328-5668
Calumet Specialty Products Partners LP 2780 Waterfront Pkwy E Dr Suite 200 NASDAQ: CLMT ■ Web: www.calumetlubricants.com	Indianapolis	IN	46214	317-328-5660	328-5668
Caribbean Petroleum Corp RR 28 KM 2 Industrial Luchetti Pk	Bayamon	PR	00961	787-785-0520	787-1245
Chevron Canada Ltd 1050 W Pender St Suite 1500 TF: 800-663-1650 ■ Web: www.chevron.ca	Vancouver	BC	V6E3T4	604-668-5300	668-5559
Chevron Corp 6001 Bollinger Canyon Rd NYSE: CVX ■ *Fax Area Code: 866 ■ TF Cust Svc: 800-243-8766 ■ Web: www.chevron.com	San Ramon	CA	94583	925-842-1000	420-0335*
Chevron Phillips Chemical Puerto Rico Core Inc PO Box 10003	Guayama	PR	00785	787-864-1515	864-2302
CITGO Asphalt Refining Co 204 Grove Rd Suite B TF: 800-443-4232	Thorofare	NJ	08086	856-224-7200	224-7201
CITGO Petroleum Corp 1293 Eldridge Pkwy Web: www.spsecurities.com	Houston	TX	77077	832-486-4000	
Coffeyville Resources LLC 10 E Cambridge Circle Dr Web: www.coffeyvillegroup.com	Kansas City	KS	66103	913-982-0500	981-0001
ConocoPhillips 600 N Dairy Ashford Rd NYSE: COP ■ TF: 800-527-5476 ■ Web: www.conocophillips.com	Houston	TX	77079	281-293-1000	
Cross Oil Refining & Marketing Inc 484 E 6th St TF: 800-725-3066 ■ Web: www.crossoil.com	Smackover	AR	71762	870-881-8700	864-8656
Crown Central Petroleum Corp 1 N Charles St *Fax: Hum Res ■ Web: www.crowncentral.com	Baltimore	MD	21201	410-539-7400	659-4875*
Demenno/Kerdoon 2000 N Alameda St	Compton	CA	90222	310-537-7100	639-2946
Duke Energy Corp 5400 Westheimer Ct *Fax: Hum Res ■ Web: www.duke-energy.com	Houston	TX	77056	713-627-5400	989-1503*
Eddy Refining Co 3355 W Alabama St Suite 630	Houston	TX	77098	713-355-6766	222-2419
Ergon Refining 2611 Haining Rd TF: 877-888-9758 ■ Web: www.ergon.com	Vicksburg	MS	39183	601-933-3000	630-8311
Ergon-West Virginia Inc 9995 Ohio River Blvd PO Box 356	Newell	WV	26050	304-387-4343	387-7032
Exxon Mobil Corp 5959 Las Colinas Blvd NYSE: XOM ■ TF: 800-252-1800 ■ Web: www.exxon.mobil.com/corporate/	Irving	TX	75039	972-444-1000	444-1198
Flint Hills Resources LP 4111 E 37th St N Web: www.fhr.com	Wichita	KS	67220	316-828-5500	828-4228
Flying J Inc 1104 Country Hill Dr TF: 800-842-6428 ■ Web: www.flyingj.com	Ogden	UT	84403	801-624-1000	395-8005
Frontier Refining Inc 2700 E 5th St	Cheyenne	WY	82007	307-634-3551	771-8794
Galaxie Corp 5170 Galaxie Dr	Jackson	MS	39206	601-366-8465	366-8466
Gary-Williams Energy Corp 370 17th St Suite 5300 Web: www.gwec.com	Denver	CO	80202	303-628-3800	628-3834
Giant Industries Inc 23733 N Scottsdale Rd NYSE: GI ■ TF: 800-937-4937 ■ Web: www.giant.com	Scottsdale	AZ	85255	480-585-8888	585-8948
Great Lakes Carbon LLC 16945 Northchase Dr Suite 2200 TF: 800-395-7054 ■ Web: www.glcarbon.com	Houston	TX	77060	281-775-4700	775-4744
Hermes Consolidated Inc DBA Wyoming Refining Co 1600 Broadway Suite 2300	Denver	CO	80202	303-894-9966	837-9089
Hess Corp 1185 Ave of the Americas NYSE: AHC ■ TF: 800-437-7645 ■ Web: www.hess.com	New York	NY	10036	212-997-8500	536-8390
Holly Corp 100 Crescent Ct Suite 1600 NYSE: HOC ■ Web: www.hollycorp.com	Dallas	TX	75201	214-871-3555	871-3560
Hunt Oil Co 1900 N Akard St TF: 800-435-7794 ■ Web: www.huntoil.com	Dallas	TX	75201	214-978-8000	978-8888
Hunt Refining Co 100 Towncenter Blvd Suite 300 Web: www.huntrefining.com	Tuscaloosa	AL	35406	205-391-3300	752-6480
Imperial Oil Resources Ltd 237 4th Ave SW PO Box 2480 Stn M	Calgary	AB	T2P3M9	403-237-3737	237-2072
International Group Inc 85 Old Eagle School Rd TF: 800-852-6537 ■ Web: www.igiwax.com	Wayne	PA	19087	610-687-9030	687-2792
La Gloria Oil & Gas Co 425 McMurrey Dr	Tyler	TX	75710	903-579-3400	596-0103
Laketon Refining Corp 2784 W Lukens Lake Rd PO Box 231	Laketon	IN	46943	260-982-2171	982-2091
Lion Oil Co PO Box 1639 *Fax: Hum Res ■ TF: 800-993-7466	Jackson	MS	39215	601-933-3000	933-3373*
Lyondell-Citgo Refining Co 12000 Lyondell St	Houston	TX	77017	713-321-4111	
Marathon Oil Corp 5555 San Felipe Rd NYSE: MRO ■ Web: www.marathon.com	Houston	TX	77056	713-629-6600	296-2952
Montana Refining Co 1900 10th St NE	Great Falls	MT	59404	406-761-4100	761-0174
Murphy Oil Corp 200 Peach St NYSE: MUR ■ TF: 800-643-2364 ■ Web: www.murphyoilcorp.com	El Dorado	AR	71730	870-862-6411	864-6373
Murphy Oil USA Inc 200 Peach St TF: 800-643-2364 ■ Web: www.murphyoilcorp.com	El Dorado	AR	71730	870-862-6411	864-6373
National Co-op Refinery Assn 1391 Iron Horse Rd Web: www.ncrarefinery.com	McPherson	KS	67460	620-241-2340	241-5531
Navajo Refining Co 501 E Main St	Artesia	NM	88210	505-748-3311	746-5458
Neste Petroleum Inc 1800 West Loop S Suite 1700	Houston	TX	77027	713-407-4400	407-4480
Paramount Petroleum Corp 14700 Downey Ave *Fax: Hum Res ■ Web: www.ppcla.com	Paramount	CA	90723	562-531-2060	630-3276*
Petro-Canada 150 6th Ave SW NYSE: PCZ ■ TF: 800-668-0220 ■ Web: www.petro-canada.ca	Calgary	AB	T2P3E3	403-296-8000	296-3030
Petro-Hunt LLC 1601 Elm St Thanksgiving Tower Suite 3400 Web: www.petro-hunt.com	Dallas	TX	75201	214-880-8400	880-7101
Placid Refining Co LLC 1940 Louisiana Hwy 1 N Web: www.placidrefining.com	Port Allen	LA	70767	225-387-0278	346-7403
Red Apple Group Inc 823 11th Ave	New York	NY	10019	212-956-5803	247-4509
San Joaquin Refining Co Inc 3129 Standard St Web: www.sjr.com	Bakersfield	CA	93308	661-327-4257	327-3236
Shell Canada Ltd 400 4th Ave SW TSX: SHC ■ *Fax: PR ■ Web: www.shell.ca	Calgary	AB	T2P0J4	403-691-3111	269-8031*
Shell Chemical Puerto Rico PO Box 186 *Fax: Acctg	Yabucoa	PR	00767	787-893-2424	893-3020*
Shell Oil Co 910 Louisanna St TF: 888-467-4355 ■ Web: www.shellus.com	Houston	TX	77002	713-241-6161	241-4044
Silver Eagle Refining 2355 S 1100 W TF: 800-927-9736	Woods Cross	UT	84087	801-298-3211	298-1112
Sinclair Casper Refining 5700 E Hwy 20-26	Casper	WY	82609	307-265-2800	232-2461
Sinclair Oil Corp 550 E South Temple TF: 800-552-8695 ■ Web: www.sinclairoil.com	Salt Lake City	UT	84102	801-524-2700	524-2720
Somerset Oil Inc 600 Monticello St Web: www.somersetoil.com	Somerset	KY	42501	606-679-6301	677-2710
Southland Oil Co 5170 Galaxie Dr TF: 800-222-7630 ■ Web: www.southlandoilco.com	Jackson	MS	39206	601-981-4151	362-1967
Sunoco Inc 1735 Market St Suite LL NYSE: SUN ■ TF: 800-786-6261 ■ Web: www.sunocoinc.com	Philadelphia	PA	19103	215-977-3000	977-3409
Tesoro Alaska Petroleum Co 471 W 36th Ave Suite 100 TF: 800-478-4447	Anchorage	AK	99503	907-561-5521	561-5047
Tesoro Corp 300 Concord Plaza Dr NYSE: TSO ■ TF: 800-837-6762 ■ Web: www.tesoropetroleum.com	San Antonio	TX	78216	210-828-8484	745-4474
Texas Oil & Chemical Co 7752 FM 418 TF: 800-324-1123	Silsbee	TX	77656	409-385-1400	385-2453
Ultramar Ltd 2200 ave McGill College TF Cust Svc: 800-363-6949 ■ Web: www.ultramar.ca	Montreal	QC	H3A3L3	514-499-6111	499-6320
United Refining Co Inc 15 Bradley St TF: 800-458-6097 ■ Web: www.urc.com	Warren	PA	16365	814-723-1500	726-4709
US Oil & Refining Co 3001 Marshall Ave TF: 800-424-2012 ■ Web: www.usor.com	Tacoma	WA	98421	253-383-1651	383-9970
Valero Energy Corp 1 Valero Way NYSE: VLO ■ TF: 800-531-7911 ■ Web: www.valero.com	San Antonio	TX	78249	210-370-2000	345-2646
Western Refining Inc 6500 Trowbridge Dr NYSE: WNR ■ Web: www.westernrefining.com	El Paso	TX	79905	915-775-3300	881-0002
World Oil Co 9302 Garfield Ave TF: 800-266-6551	South Gate	CA	90280	562-928-0100	928-0391
Wyoming Refining Co 1600 Broadway Suite 2300	Denver	CO	80202	303-894-9966	837-9089
Young Refining Corp 7982 Huey Rd	Douglasville	GA	30134	770-942-2343	942-3850

584 PETROLEUM STORAGE TERMINALS

Phone *Fax*

Capital Properties Inc 100 Dexter Rd ... East Providence RI 02914 401-435-7171 435-7179
AMEX: CPI

Gottry Corp 175 Ensminger Rd ... Tonawanda NY 14150 716-876-3800 876-0218
TF: 800-836-6720

Houston Fuel Oil Terminal Co 16642 Jacintoport Blvd ... Houston TX 77015 281-452-3390 452-6306
Web: www.hfotco.com

Intercontinental Terminal Co 17 S Briar Hollow Ln Suite 402 ... Houston TX 77027 713-623-9100 623-9191
Web: www.iterm.com

LBC Houston LP 11666 Port Rd ... Seabrook TX 77586 281-474-4433 291-3428
TF: 888-922-4433 ■ *Web:* www.lbchouston.com

Magellan Midstream Partners LP 1 Williams Ctr ... Tulsa OK 74172 918-574-7000 573-6714*
NYSE: MMP ■ **Fax:* Mail Rm ■ *TF:* 800-574-6671 ■ *Web:* www.magellanlp.com

NuStar Terminal Canada Partnership
4090 Port Malcolm Rd ... Point Tupper NS B9A1Z5 902-625-1711 625-3098

Oiltanking Houston LP 15602 Jacinto Port Blvd ... Houston TX 77015 281-457-7900 457-7917
Web: www.oiltanking.com

Petroleum Fuel & Terminal Co 4084 Hwy 44 ... Garyville LA 70051 985-535-6256 535-6123

RKA Petroleum 28340 Wick Rd ... Romulus MI 48174 734-946-2199 946-4772
TF: 800-875-3835 ■ *Web:* www.rkapetroleum.com

TransMontaigne Partners LP 1670 Broadway Suite 3100 ... Denver CO 80202 303-626-8200 626-8228
NYSE: TLP ■ *Web:* www.transmontaigne.com

Unocal Beaumont Terminal Hwy 366 PO Box 237 ... Nederland TX 77627 409-722-3441 724-3289
Web: www.unocal.com/umt/pipe_beau.html

585 PHARMACEUTICAL COMPANIES

SEE ALSO Biotechnology Companies p. 1380; Diagnostic Products p. 1587; Medicinal Chemicals & Botanical Products p. 1957; Pharmaceutical & Diagnostic Products - Veterinary p. 2111; Pharmaceutical Companies - Generic Drugs p. 2111; Vitamins & Nutritional Supplements p. 2405

Phone *Fax*

A & S Pharmaceutical Corp 480 Barnum Ave ... Bridgeport CT 06608 203-368-2538 368-6541
TF: 866-368-2539

aaiPharma Inc 2320 Scientific Pk Dr ... Wilmington NC 28405 910-254-7000 815-2300
TF: 800-575-4224 ■ *Web:* www.aaipharma.com

Abbott Laboratories 100 Abbott Park Rd ... Abbott Park IL 60064 847-937-6100
NYSE: ABT ■ *TF:* 800-323-9100 ■ *Web:* www.abbott.com

Abbott Laboratories Pharmaceutical Products Div
100 Abbott Park Rd ... Abbott Park IL 60064 847-937-6100 935-1422*
**Fax:* Mktg ■ *TF:* 800-255-5162 ■ *Web:* www.abbott.com

Accentia BioPharmaceuticals Inc
324 S Hyde Park Ave Suite 350 ... Tampa FL 33606 813-864-2554 258-6912
NASDAQ: ABPI ■ *TF:* 888-423-1046 ■ *Web:* www.accentia.net

Accucaps Industries Ltd 2125 Ambassador Dr ... Windsor ON N9C3R5 519-969-5404 969-0768
TF: 800-665-7210 ■ *Web:* www.accucaps.com

Advanced Life Sciences Inc 1440 Davey Rd ... Woodridge IL 60517 630-739-6744 739-6754
NASDAQ: ADLS ■ *Web:* www.advancedlifesciences.com

Advancis Pharmaceutical Corp
20425 Seneca Meadows Pkwy ... Germantown MD 20876 301-944-6600 944-6700
NASDAQ: AVNC ■ *Web:* www.advancispharm.com

Akorn Inc 2500 Millbrook Dr ... Buffalo Grove IL 60089 847-279-6100 279-6123
AMEX: AKN ■ *TF:* 800-932-5676 ■ *Web:* www.akorn.com

AkPharma Inc PO Box 111 ... Pleasantville NJ 08232 609-645-5100 645-0767
TF: 800-994-4711 ■ *Web:* www.akpharma.com

Alcon Laboratories Inc 6201 South Fwy ... Fort Worth TX 76134 817-293-0450 551-4629
NYSE: ACL ■ *TF:* 800-757-9195 ■ *Web:* www.alconlabs.com

Alfacell Corp 300 Atrium Dr ... Somerset NJ 08873 732-652-4525 652-4575
NASDAQ: ACEL ■ *Web:* www.alfacell.com

Allergan Canada Inc 110 Cochrane Dr ... Markham ON L3R9S1 905-940-1660 940-1902
TF: 800-668-6424 ■ *Web:* www.allergan.com

Allergan Inc PO Box 19534 ... Irvine CA 92623 714-246-4500 246-4971*
NYSE: AGN ■ **Fax:* Mail Rm ■ *TF:* 800-347-4500 ■ *Web:* www.allergan.com

Allergan Inc North America Region PO Box 19534 ... Irvine CA 92623 714-246-4500 246-4971*
**Fax:* Mail Rm ■ *TF:* 800-347-4500 ■ *Web:* www.allergan.com

Allergan Inc Worldwide Operations PO Box 19534 ... Irvine CA 92623 714-246-4500 246-4971*
**Fax:* Mail Rm ■ *TF:* 800-347-4500

Allion Healthcare Inc 1660 Walt Whitman Rd Suite 105 ... Melville NY 11747 631-547-6520 249-5863
NASDAQ: ALLI ■ *Web:* www.allionhealthcare.com

Alpharma Inc 1 Executive Dr ... Fort Lee NJ 07024 201-947-7774 947-3275*
NYSE: ALO ■ **Fax:* Cust Svc ■ *TF:* 800-645-4216 ■ *Web:* www.alpharma.com

Altana Inc Savage Laboratories Div 60 Baylis Rd ... Melville NY 11747 631-454-7677 454-0732
TF: 800-231-0206 ■ *Web:* www.savagelabs.com

Alteon Inc 6 Campus Dr ... Parsippany NJ 07054 201-934-5000 934-8880
AMEX: ALT ■ *Web:* www.alteon.com

Altus Pharmaceuticals Inc 125 Sidney St ... Cambridge MA 02139 617-299-2900 299-2999
NASDAQ: ALTU ■ *TF:* 888-258-2532 ■ *Web:* www.altus.com

Alva-Amco Pharmacal Cos Inc 7711 N Merrimac Ave ... Niles IL 60714 847-663-0700 663-1400
TF: 800-792-2582 ■ *Web:* www.alva-amco.com

Alza Corp 1900 Charleston Rd ... Mountain View CA 94043 650-564-5000 564-7070*
**Fax:* Hum Res ■ *Web:* www.alza.com

Amphastar Pharmaceuticals Inc 11570 6th St ... Rancho Cucamonga CA 91730 909-980-9484 980-8296
TF: 800-423-4136 ■ *Web:* www.amphastar.com

Amylin Pharmaceuticals Inc 9360 Towne Ctr Dr ... San Diego CA 92121 858-552-2200 552-2212
NASDAQ: AMLN ■ *Web:* www.amylin.com

Anadys Pharmaceuticals Inc 3115 Merryfield Row ... San Diego CA 92121 858-530-3600 527-1540
NASDAQ: ANDS ■ *Web:* www.anadyspharma.com

Angiotech Pharmaceuticals Inc 1618 Station St ... Vancouver BC V6A1B6 604-221-7676 221-2330
NASDAQ: ANPI ■ *Web:* www.angiotech.com

AP Pharma Inc 123 Saginaw Dr ... Redwood City CA 94063 650-366-2626 365-6490
NASDAQ: APPA ■ *Web:* www.appharma.com

Apotex Inc 150 Signet Dr ... Weston ON M9L1T9 416-749-9300 401-3849
TF: 800-268-4623 ■ *Web:* www.apotex.com

Apothecus Pharmaceutical Corp 220 Townsend Sq ... Oyster Bay NY 11771 516-624-8200 624-8201
TF: 800-227-2393 ■ *Web:* www.apothecus.com

Astellas Pharma US Inc 3 Parkway N ... Deerfield IL 60015 847-317-8800 317-7296
TF: 800-888-7704 ■ *Web:* www.astellas.us

AstraZeneca Canada Inc 1004 Middlegate Rd ... Mississauga ON L4Y1M4 905-277-7111 270-3248
TF: 800-565-5877 ■ *Web:* www.astrazeneca.ca

AstraZeneca LP 1800 Concord Pike PO Box 15437 ... Wilmington DE 19850 302-886-3000
NYSE: AZN ■ *TF:* 800-456-3669 ■ *Web:* www.astrazeneca-us.com

AutoImmune Inc 1199 Madia St ... Pasadena CA 91103 626-792-1235 792-1236
Web: www.autoimmuneinc.com

Auxilium Pharmaceuticals Inc 40 Valley Stream Pkwy ... Malvern PA 19355 484-321-5900 321-5999
NASDAQ: AUXL ■ *Web:* www.auxilium.com

Phone *Fax*

Avalon Pharmaceuticals Inc
20358 Seneca Meadows Pkwy ... Germantown MD 20876 301-556-9900 556-9910
NASDAQ: AVRX ■ *Web:* www.avalonrx.com

Aventis Pharma Inc 2150 St Elzear Blvd W ... Laval QC H7L4A8 514-331-9220 334-8016
TF: 800-363-6364 ■ *Web:* www.aventis-pharma.ca

Axcan Pharma Inc 597 Laurier Blvd ... Mont-Saint-Hilaire QC J3H6C4 450-467-5138 464-9979
NASDAQ: AXCA ■ *TF:* 800-565-3255 ■ *Web:* www.axcan.com

Axm Pharma Inc 20955 Pathfinder Rd Suite 100 ... Diamond Bar CA 91765 909-843-6338 843-6350
AMEX: AXJ ■ *Web:* www.axmpharma.com

Banner Pharmacaps Inc 4125 Premier Dr ... High Point NC 27265 336-812-4729 812-8777
TF: 800-447-1140 ■ *Web:* www.banpharm.com

Banner Pharmacaps Ltd 5807 47th Ave ... Olds AB T4H1S7 403-556-2531 556-7079*
**Fax Area Code:* 866 ■ *TF Cust Svc:* 866-507-3484

Barrier Therapeutics Inc 600 College Rd E Suite 3200 ... Princeton NJ 08540 609-945-1200 945-1212
NASDAQ: BTRX ■ *Web:* www.barriertherapeutics.com

Bausch & Lomb Inc 1400 N Goodman St ... Rochester NY 14609 585-338-6000 338-6007
NYSE: BOL ■ *TF:* 800-344-8815 ■ *Web:* www.bausch.com

Bausch & Lomb Pharmaceuticals Inc 8500 Hidden River Pkwy ... Tampa FL 33637 813-975-7700 975-7770
TF: 800-323-0000 ■ *Web:* www.bausch.com/us/resource/pharma

Baxter International Inc 1 Baxter Pkwy ... Deerfield IL 60015 847-948-2000 948-3948
NYSE: BAX ■ *Web:* www.baxter.com

Bayer Corp 100 Bayer Rd ... Pittsburgh PA 15205 412-777-2000 778-4430
NYSE: BAY ■ *TF:* 800-662-2927 ■ *Web:* www.bayerus.com

Bayer Corp Consumer Care Div
36 Columbia Rd PO Box 1910 ... Morristown NJ 07962 973-254-5000 408-8113
Web: www.bayerus.com/consumer

Bayer Inc 77 Belfield Rd ... Toronto ON M9W1G6 416-248-0771 248-1297*
**Fax:* Hum Res ■ *TF:* 800-622-2937 ■ *Web:* bayer.ca

Bentley Pharmaceuticals Inc 2 Holland Way ... Exeter NH 03833 603-658-6100 658-6101
NYSE: BNT ■ *Web:* www.bentleypharm.com

Berlex Canada Inc 334 rue Avro ... Pointe-Claire QC H9R5W5 514-631-7400 782-2242
Web: www.berlex.ca

Berlex Laboratories Inc 6 W Belt ... Wayne NJ 07470 973-694-4100 305-5475
TF: 888-237-2394 ■ *Web:* www.berlex.com

Bioenvision Inc 345 Park Ave 41st Fl ... New York NY 10154 212-750-6700 750-6777
NASDAQ: BIVN ■ *Web:* www.bioenvision.com

BioSante Pharmaceuticals Inc 111 Barclay Blvd Suite 280 ... Lincolnshire IL 60069 847-478-0500 478-9152
AMEX: BPA ■ *Web:* www.biosantepharma.com

BioSpecifics Technologies Corp 35 Wilbur St ... Lynbrook NY 11563 516-593-7000 593-7039
Web: www.biospecifics.com

Biosyn Inc 2085 B Quaker Pointe Dr ... Quakerstown PA 18951 215-914-0900 914-0914
Web: www.biosyn-inc.com

Biovail Corp 7150 Mississauga Rd ... Mississauga ON L5N8M5 905-286-3000 286-3050
NYSE: BVF ■ *Web:* www.biovail.com

Blistex Inc 1800 Swift Dr ... Oak Brook IL 60523 630-571-2870 571-3437
TF Cust Svc: 800-837-1800 ■ *Web:* www.blistex.com

Boehringer Ingelheim Ltd 5180 S Service Rd ... Burlington ON L7L5H4 905-639-0333 639-3769
TF: 800-263-9107 ■ *Web:* www.boehringer-ingelheim.com

Boehringer Ingelheim Pharmaceuticals Inc
900 Ridgebury Rd ... Ridgefield CT 06877 203-798-9988 798-4735*
**Fax:* Cust Svc ■ *TF:* 800-243-0127 ■ *Web:* www.boehringer-ingelheim.com

Bradley Pharmaceuticals Inc 383 Rt 46 W ... Fairfield NJ 07004 973-882-1505 575-5366
NYSE: BDY ■ *TF:* 800-929-9300 ■ *Web:* www.bradpharm.com

Brioschi Inc 19-01 Pollitt Dr ... Fair Lawn NJ 07410 201-796-4226 796-0391
TF: 800-274-6724 ■ *Web:* www.brioschi-usa.com

Bristol-Myers Squibb Canada Inc 2365 Cote de Liesse Rd ... Montreal QC H4N2M7 514-333-3200 335-4102
TF: 800-267-1088 ■ *Web:* www.bmscanada.ca

Bristol-Myers Squibb Co 345 Park Ave ... New York NY 10154 212-546-4000 546-4020
NYSE: BMY ■ *Web:* www.bms.com

Bristol-Myers Squibb Co Worldwide Medicines Group
Rt 206 & Provinceline Rd ... Princeton NJ 08540 609-252-4000

Bristol-Myers Squibb Co Worldwide Medicines Group Intercontinental Div Rt 206 & Provinceline Rd ... Princeton NJ 08540 609-252-4000 818-3145

Caraco Pharmaceutical Laboratories Ltd 1150 Elijah McCoy Dr ... Detroit MI 48202 313-871-8400 871-8314
AMEX: CPD ■ *Web:* www.caraco.com

Care-Tech Laboratories Inc 3224 S Kingshighway Blvd ... Saint Louis MO 63139 314-772-4610 772-4613
TF: 800-325-9681 ■ *Web:* www.caretechlabs.com

Carrington Laboratories Inc 2001 Walnut Hill Ln ... Irving TX 75038 972-518-1300 518-1020
NASDAQ: CARN ■ *TF Cust Svc:* 800-527-5216 ■ *Web:* www.carringtonlabs.com

Carter-Horner Inc 6600 Kitimat Rd ... Mississauga ON L5N1L9 905-826-6200 826-0389
TF: 800-387-2130 ■ *Web:* www.carterhorner.com

CB Fleet Inc 4615 Murray Pl PO Box 11349 ... Lynchburg VA 24502 434-528-4000 528-4235*
**Fax:* Cust Svc ■ *TF:* 800-999-9711 ■ *Web:* www.cbfleet.com

Cellegy Pharmaceuticals Inc 2085 B Quaker Pointe Dr ... Quakertown PA 18951 215-529-6084 529-6086
Web: www.cellegy.com

Centocor Inc 200 Great Valley Pkwy ... Malvern PA 19355 610-651-6000 651-6100
TF: 800-972-9063 ■ *Web:* www.centocor.com

Chattem Inc 1715 W 38th St ... Chattanooga TN 37409 423-821-4571 821-0395
NASDAQ: CHTT ■ *TF:* 800-366-6077 ■ *Web:* www.chattem.com

ChemGenex Pharmaceuticals Ltd 3475 Edison Way Suite M ... Menlo Park CA 94025 650-474-9800 474-9808
NASDAQ: CXSP ■ *Web:* www.chemgenex.com

Chugai Pharma USA Inc 1 Crossroads Dr Bldg A 2nd Fl ... Bedminster NJ 07921 908-947-2700 947-2662
TF: 888-887-9062

Cirrus Healthcare Products LLC
60 Main St PO Box 220 ... Cold Spring Harbor NY 11724 631-692-7600 692-9844
TF: 800-327-6151 ■ *Web:* www.cirrushealthcare.com

Coley Pharmaceuticals Group 93 Worcester St Suite 101 ... Wellesley MA 02481 781-431-9000 431-6403
NASDAQ: COLY ■ *Web:* www.coleypharma.com

Columbia Laboratories Inc
354 Eisenhower Pkwy 2nd Fl Plaza 1 ... Livingston NJ 07039 973-994-3999 994-3001
NASDAQ: CBRX ■ *TF:* 866-566-5636 ■ *Web:* www.columbialabs.com

Combe Inc 1101 Westchester Ave ... White Plains NY 10604 914-694-5454 694-6233
TF: 800-873-7400 ■ *Web:* www.combe.com

CombinatoRx Inc 245 1st St 16th Fl ... Cambridge MA 02412 617-425-7000 425-7010
NASDAQ: CRXX ■ *Web:* www.combinatorx.com

Cortex Pharmaceuticals Inc 15231 Barranca Pkwy ... Irvine CA 92618 949-727-3157 727-3657
AMEX: COR ■ *Web:* www.cortexpharm.com

CoTherix Inc 2000 Sierra Point Pkwy Suite 600 ... Brisbane CA 94005 650-808-6500 808-6899
NASDAQ: CTRX ■ *Web:* www.cotherix.com

Covidien Ltd 15 Hampshire St ... Mansfield MA 02048 508-261-8000 261-8062
NYSE: COV ■ *Web:* www.covidien.com

Critical Therapeutics Inc 60 Westview St ... Lexington MA 02421 781-402-5700 402-5729
NASDAQ: CRTX ■ *Web:* www.criticaltherapeutics.com

Daiichi Sankyo Inc 2 Hilton Ct ... Parsippany NJ 07054 973-359-2600 359-2645
TF: 800-374-5589 ■ *Web:* www.daiichius.com

Darby Group Cos Inc 300 Jericho Quad ... Jericho NY 11753 516-683-1800 957-7362*
**Fax Area Code:* 800 ■ *TF:* 800-468-1001 ■ *Web:* www.darbygroup.com

Del Laboratories Inc 726 Reckson Plaza PO Box 9357 ... Uniondale NY 11553 516-844-2020
TF: 800-952-5080 ■ *Web:* www.dellabs.com

Dermik Laboratories Inc 55 Corporate Blvd ... Bridgewater NJ 08807 908-243-6000
TF: 800-666-6030 ■ *Web:* www.dermik.com

Dey LP 2751 Napa Valley Corporate Dr ... Napa CA 94558 707-224-3200 224-9264
TF: 800-869-9005 ■ *Web:* www.dey.com

Dickinson Brands Inc 31 E High St ... East Hampton CT 06424 860-267-2279 267-1111
TF: 888-860-2279 ■ *Web:* www.witchhazel.com

Doak Dermatologics 383 Rt 46 W ... Fairfield NJ 07004 973-882-1505 575-5366
TF: 800-929-9300 ■ *Web:* www.doakderm.com

				Phone	Fax
Dr Reddy's Laboratories Inc 200 Summerset Corporate Blvd 7th Fl	Bridgewater	NJ	08807	908-203-4900	203-4970
NYSE: RDY ■ *Web:* www.drreddys.com					
Eco-Med Pharmaceuticals Inc 7050B Bramalea Rd Unit 58	Mississauga	ON	L5S1S9	905-405-1050	405-0775
Web: www.eco-med.com					
Edwards Lifesciences Corp 1 Edwards Way	Irvine	CA	92614	949-250-2500	250-2525*
NYSE: EW ■ **Fax:* Cust Svc ■ *TF:* 800-424-3278 ■ *Web:* www.edwards.com					
Eisai Inc 500 Frank W Burr Blvd Glenpointe Ctr W 5th Fl	Teaneck	NJ	07666	201-692-1100	692-1804
TF: 888-793-4724 ■ *Web:* www.eisai.com					
Eli Lilly Canada Inc 3650 Danforth Ave	Toronto	ON	M1N2E8	416-694-3221	699-7241*
**Fax:* Hum Res ■ *TF:* 800-268-4446 ■ *Web:* www.lilly.ca					
Eli Lilly & Co Lilly Corporate Ctr	Indianapolis	IN	46285	317-276-2000	535-4615*
NYSE: LLY ■ **Fax Area Code:* 800 ■ **Fax:* Cust Svc ■ *TF Prod Info:* 800-545-5979 ■ *Web:* www.lilly.com					
Endo Pharmaceuticals Holdings Inc 100 Endo Blvd	Chadds Ford	PA	19317	610-558-9800	558-8979
NASDAQ: ENDP ■ *TF Cust Svc:* 800-462-3636 ■ *Web:* www.endo.com					
F & F Foods Inc 3501 W 48th Pl	Chicago	IL	60632	773-927-3737	927-3906
TF: 800-621-0225 ■ *Web:* www.fffoods.com					
Ferndale Laboratories Inc 780 W Eight-Mile Rd	Ferndale	MI	48220	248-548-0900	548-8427
TF: 800-621-6003 ■ *Web:* www.ferndalelabs.com					
Fleet CB Inc 4615 Murray Pl PO Box 11349	Lynchburg	VA	24502	434-528-4000	528-4235*
**Fax:* Cust Svc ■ *TF:* 800-999-9711 ■ *Web:* www.cbfleet.com					
Forest Laboratories Inc 909 3rd Ave 23rd Fl	New York	NY	10022	212-421-7850	750-9152
NYSE: FRX ■ *TF:* 800-947-5227 ■ *Web:* www.frx.com					
Forest Pharmaceutical Inc 13600 Shoreline Dr	Saint Louis	MO	63045	314-493-7000	493-7450
TF: 800-678-1605 ■ *Web:* www.frx.com					
G & W Laboratories Inc 111 Coolidge St	South Plainfield	NJ	07080	908-753-2000	753-5174*
**Fax:* Sales ■ *TF:* 800-922-1038 ■ *Web:* www.gwlabs.com					
Galderma Laboratories Inc 14501 N Fwy	Fort Worth	TX	76177	817-961-5000	
TF: 800-582-8225 ■ *Web:* www.galderma.com					
Germiphene Corp PO Box 1748	Brantford	ON	N3T5V7	519-759-7100	759-1625
TF: 800-265-9931 ■ *Web:* www.germiphene.com					
GlaxoSmithKline PO Box 13398	Research Triangle Park	NC	27709	919-483-2100	315-1053*
NYSE: GSK ■ **Fax:* Hum Res ■ *TF:* 888-825-5249 ■ *Web:* us.gsk.com					
GlaxoSmithKline 7333 Mississauga Rd N	Mississauga	ON	L5N6L4	905-819-3000	819-3099
Web: www.gsk.ca/en					
Halozyme Therapeutics Inc 11588 Sorrento Valley Rd Suite 17	San Diego	CA	92121	858-794-8889	259-2539
AMEX: HTI ■ *Web:* www.halozyme.com					
Hana Biosciences Inc 400 Oyster Point Blvd Suite 215	South San Francisco	CA	94080	650-588-6404	588-2787
AMEX: HBX ■ *Web:* www.hanabiosciences.com					
Hi-Tech Pharmacal Co Inc 369 Bayview Ave	Amityville	NY	11701	631-789-8228	789-3143
NASDAQ: HITK ■ *TF:* 800-262-9010 ■ *Web:* www.diabeticproducts.com					
Hoffmann-LaRoche Inc 340 Kingsland St	Nutley	NJ	07110	973-235-5000	235-7605
TF: 800-526-6367 ■ *Web:* www.roche.com					
Hoffmann-La Roche Ltd 2455 Meadowpine Blvd	Mississauga	ON	L5N6L7	905-542-5555	542-7130
TF: 800-561-1759 ■ *Web:* www.rochecanada.com					
Hope Pharmaceuticals Inc 8260 E Gelding Dr Suite 104	Scottsdale	AZ	85260	480-607-1970	607-1971
TF: 800-755-9595 ■ *Web:* www.hopepharm.com					
Hospira Inc 275 N Field Dr	Lake Forest	IL	60045	224-212-2000	
NYSE: HSP ■ *TF:* 877-946-7747 ■ *Web:* www.hospira.com					
Human Genome Sciences Inc 9410 Key West Ave	Rockville	MD	20850	301-309-8504	309-8512
NASDAQ: HGSI ■ *Web:* www.hgsi.com					
Humco Holding Group Inc 7400 Alumax Dr	Texarkana	TX	75501	903-831-7808	831-7736
TF: 800-662-3435 ■ *Web:* www.humco.com					
Hythiam Inc 11150 Santa Monica Blvd Suite 1500	Los Angeles	CA	90025	310-268-0011	444-5300
NASDAQ: HYTM ■ *Web:* www.hythiam.com					
Immtech International Inc 150 Fairway Dr Suite 150	Vernon Hills	IL	60061	847-573-0033	573-8288
AMEX: IMM ■ *TF:* 877-898-8038 ■ *Web:* www.immtech-international.com					
Infinity Pharmaceuticals Inc 780 Memorial Dr	Cambridge	MA	02139	617-453-1000	453-1001
NASDAQ: INFI ■ *Web:* www.ipi.com					
Innovative Health Products Inc 6950 Bryan Dairy Rd	Largo	FL	33777	727-544-8866	544-4386
TF: 800-654-2347 ■ *Web:* www.onlineihp.com					
Integrated BioPharma Inc 225 Long Ave	Hillside	NJ	07205	973-926-0816	926-1735
AMEX: INB ■ *TF:* 888-319-6962 ■ *Web:* www.ibiopharma.com					
InterMune Inc 3280 Bayshore Blvd	Brisbane	CA	94005	415-466-2200	466-2300
NASDAQ: ITMN ■ *TF:* 877-862-2292 ■ *Web:* www.intermune.com					
Interpharm Holdings Inc 75 Adams Ave	Hauppauge	NY	11788	631-952-0214	952-9587
AMEX: IPA ■ *Web:* www.interpharminc.com					
IVAX Corp 4400 Biscayne Blvd	Miami	FL	33137	305-575-6000	575-6465*
**Fax:* Hum Res ■ *Web:* www.ivax.com					
Jaapharm Canada Inc 510 Rowntree Dairy Rd Unit 4	Woodbridge	ON	L4L8H2	905-851-7885	856-5838
Web: www.jaapharm.com					
Janssen-Ortho Inc 19 Green Belt Dr	North York	ON	M3C1L9	416-382-5000	449-2658
TF: 800-387-8781 ■ *Web:* www.janssen-ortho.com					
Janssen Pharmaceutica Inc 1125 Trenton-Harbourton Rd	Titusville	NJ	08560	609-730-2000	730-2323
TF: 800-526-7736 ■ *Web:* www.janssen.com					
Jazz Pharmaceuticals Inc 3180 Porter Dr	Palo Alto	CA	94304	650-496-3777	496-3781
NASDAQ: JAZZ ■ *TF Sales:* 888-867-7426 ■ *Web:* www.jazzpharma.com					
Johnson & Johnson-Merck Consumer Pharmaceuticals Co 7050 Camp Hill Rd	Fort Washington	PA	19034	215-273-7700	273-4070
Kenwood Therapeutics 383 Rt 46 W	Fairfield	NJ	07004	973-882-1505	575-5366
TF: 800-929-9300 ■ *Web:* www.bradpharm.com/products/kenwood/prescription/index.html					
King Bio Pharmaceuticals Inc 3 Westside Dr	Asheville	NC	28806	828-255-0201	255-0940
TF: 888-827-6414 ■ *Web:* www.kingbio.com					
King Pharmaceuticals Inc 501 5th St	Bristol	TN	37620	423-989-8000	989-8741
NYSE: KG ■ *TF:* 800-776-3637 ■ *Web:* www.kingpharm.com					
Konsyl Pharmaceuticals Inc 8050 Industrial Park Rd	Easton	MD	21601	410-822-5192	820-7032
TF: 800-356-6795 ■ *Web:* www.konsyl.com					
Kos Pharmaceuticals Inc 2100 N Commerce Pkwy	Weston	FL	33326	954-331-3400	331-3889
NASDAQ: KOSP ■ *TF:* 800-998-3464 ■ *Web:* www.kospharm.com					
Kramer Laboratories Inc 8778 SW 8th St	Miami	FL	33174	305-223-1287	223-5510
TF: 800-824-4894 ■ *Web:* www.kramerlabs.com					
Kyowa Hakko USA Inc 212 Carnegie Center Suite 101	Princeton	NJ	08540	609-919-1100	919-1111
TF: 888-464-6574 ■ *Web:* www.kyowa-usa.com					
Leiner Health Products Inc 901 E 233rd St	Carson	CA	90745	310-835-8400	952-7760
TF: 800-421-1168 ■ *Web:* leiner.com					
Ligand Pharmaceuticals Inc 10275 Science Ctr Dr	San Diego	CA	92121	858-550-7500	550-7506
NASDAQ: LGND ■ *TF:* 800-964-5793 ■ *Web:* www.ligand.com					
Lilly Eli Canada Inc 3650 Danforth Ave	Toronto	ON	M1N2E8	416-694-3221	699-7241*
**Fax:* Hum Res ■ *TF:* 800-268-4446 ■ *Web:* www.lilly.ca					
Lilly Eli & Co Lilly Corporate Ctr	Indianapolis	IN	46285	317-276-2000	535-4615*
NYSE: LLY ■ **Fax Area Code:* 800 ■ **Fax:* Cust Svc ■ *TF Prod Info:* 800-545-5979 ■ *Web:* www.lilly.com					
Major Pharmaceutical Co 31778 Enterprise Dr	Livonia	MI	48150	734-525-8700	525-8393
TF: 800-521-5098					
Manhattan Pharmaceuticals Inc 810 7th Ave 4th Fl	New York	NY	10019	212-582-3950	582-3957
AMEX: MHA ■ *Web:* www.manhattanpharma.com					
McNeil Consumer & Specialty Pharmaceuticals 7050 Camp Hill Rd	Fort Washington	PA	19034	215-273-7000	273-4070*
**Fax:* Cust Svc ■ *TF:* 800-962-5357					
Medicis Pharmaceutical Corp 8125 N Hayden Rd	Scottsdale	AZ	85258	602-808-8800	808-0822
NYSE: MRX ■ *TF Cust Svc:* 800-550-5115 ■ *Web:* www.medicis.com					
MedPointe Pharmaceuticals 265 Davidson Ave Suite 300	Somerset	NJ	08873	732-564-2200	564-2434
Web: www.medpointeinc.com					
Melaleuca Inc 3910 S Yellowstone Hwy	Idaho Falls	ID	83402	208-522-0700	528-2090*
**Fax Area Code:* 888 ■ *TF Sales:* 800-282-3000 ■ *Web:* www.melaleuca.com					
Mentholatum Co Inc 707 Sterling Dr	Orchard Park	NY	14127	716-677-2500	677-9528
TF: 800-688-7660 ■ *Web:* www.mentholatum.com					
Merck & Co Inc 1 Merck Dr PO Box 100	Whitehouse Station	NJ	08889	908-423-1000	
NYSE: MRK ■ *TF Cust Svc:* 800-672-6372 ■ *Web:* www.merck.com					
Merck & Co Inc Human Health Div 770 Sumneytown Pike PO Box 4	West Point	PA	19486	215-652-5000	652-3777*
**Fax:* Mail Rm ■ *TF:* 800-672-6372 ■ *Web:* www.merck.com					
Merck Frosst Canada & Co 16711 Transcanada Hwy	Kirkland	QC	H9H3L1	514-428-8600	428-2670
TF: 800-361-7031 ■ *Web:* www.merckfrosst.ca					
Merz Pharmaceuticals Inc 4215 Tudor Ln	Greensboro	NC	27410	336-856-2003	856-0107
TF: 800-334-0514 ■ *Web:* www.merzusa.com					
MGI Pharma Inc 5775 W Old Shakopee Rd Suite 100	Bloomington	MN	55437	952-346-4700	346-4800
NASDAQ: MOGN ■ *TF Orders:* 800-562-4531 ■ *Web:* www.mgipharma.com					
Mikart Inc 1750 Chattahoochee Ave NW	Atlanta	GA	30318	404-351-4510	350-0432
TF: 888-464-5278 ■ *Web:* www.mikart.com					
Mission Pharmacal PO Box 786099	San Antonio	TX	78278	210-696-8400	696-6010
TF: 800-531-3333 ■ *Web:* www.missionpharmacal.com					
Monarch Pharmaceuticals Inc 501 5th St	Bristol	TN	37620	423-989-8000	274-8634
TF: 800-776-3637					
Noramco Inc 1440 Olympic Dr	Athens	GA	30601	706-353-4490	353-3205
Web: www.noramco.com					
NovaDel Pharma Inc 25 Minneakoning Rd	Flemington	NJ	08822	908-782-3431	782-2445
AMEX: NVD ■ *Web:* www.novadel.com					
Novartis Consumer Health PO Box 83288	Lincoln	NE	68501	402-464-6311	467-8889*
**Fax:* Hum Res ■ *TF:* 800-452-0051 ■ *Web:* www.novartis.com/consumerhealth					
Novartis Pharmaceuticals Canada Inc 385 boul Bouchard	Dorval	QC	H9S1A9	514-631-6775	435-4423*
**Fax Area Code:* 800 ■ **Fax:* Cust Svc ■ *TF:* 800-465-2244 ■ *Web:* www.novartis.ca					
Novartis Pharmaceuticals Corp 1 Health Plaza	East Hanover	NJ	07936	862-778-8300	781-8265*
**Fax Area Code:* 973 ■ *TF Cust Svc:* 888-669-6682 ■ *Web:* www.pharma.us.novartis.com					
Noven Pharmaceuticals Inc 11960 SW 144th St	Miami	FL	33186	305-253-5099	251-1887
NASDAQ: NOVN ■ *TF:* 800-253-5099 ■ *Web:* www.noven.com					
Novo Nordisk of North America Inc 100 College Rd W	Princeton	NJ	08540	609-987-5800	987-5394
TF: 800-727-6500 ■ *Web:* www.novonordisk-us.com					
Novo Nordisk Pharmaceuticals Inc 100 College Rd W	Princeton	NJ	08540	609-987-5800	987-5394
TF Cust Svc: 800-727-6500 ■ *Web:* www.novonordisk-us.com					
NUCRYST Pharmaceuticals Corp 50 Audubon Rd Suite B	Wakefield	MA	01880	781-224-1444	246-6002
NASDAQ: NCST ■ *TF:* 877-630-1234 ■ *Web:* www.nucryst.com					
Numark Laboratories Inc 164 Northfield Ave	Edison	NJ	08837	732-417-1870	225-0066
TF: 800-338-8079 ■ *Web:* www.numarklabs.com					
Nutramax Products Inc Cough & Cold Div 170 Oak Hill Way	Brockton	MA	02301	508-584-8100	584-8704
Web: www.nutramax.com/cough_cold.html					
Ono Pharma USA Inc 2000 Lenox Dr	Lawrenceville	NJ	08648	609-219-1010	219-9229
Web: www.ono.co.jp					
Organon Inc 56 Livingston Ave	Roseland	NJ	07068	973-325-4500	325-4589
TF: 800-631-1253 ■ *Web:* www.organon.com					
Ortho BioTech Products LP 430 Rt 22 E PO Box 6914	Bridgewater	NJ	08807	908-541-4000	
TF Cust Svc: 800-325-7504 ■ *Web:* www.orthobiotech.com/us.html					
Ortho-McNeil Pharmaceutical Inc PO Box 300	Raritan	NJ	08869	908-218-6000	732-0425*
**Fax:* Cust Svc ■ *Web:* www.ortho-mcneil.com					
Pain Therapeutics Inc 416 Browning Way	South San Francisco	CA	94080	650-624-8200	624-8222
NASDAQ: PTIE ■ *Web:* www.paintherapeutics.com					
Parkedale Pharmaceuticals Inc 870 Parkdale Rd	Rochester	MI	48307	248-651-9081	656-5508
TF Sales: 800-615-5464					
PDK Labs Inc 145 Ricefield Ln	Hauppauge	NY	11788	631-273-2630	273-1582
TF: 800-221-0855 ■ *Web:* www.pdklabs.com					
Pfizer Canada Inc 17300 TransCanada Hwy	Kirkland	QC	H9J2M5	514-695-0500	426-6831
TF: 800-463-6001 ■ *Web:* www.pfizer.ca					
Pfizer Canada Inc Consumer Healthcare 88 McNabb St	Markham	ON	L3R5L2	905-968-2321	563-2013*
**Fax Area Code:* 800 ■ *TF:* 800-387-6577 ■ *Web:* www.pfizer.ca					
Pfizer Inc 235 E 42nd St	New York	NY	10017	212-573-2323	573-7851
NYSE: PFE ■ *TF Prod Info:* 800-733-4717 ■ *Web:* www.pfizer.com					
Pfizer Inc Pharmaceuticals Group 235 E 42nd St	New York	NY	10017	212-573-2323	
Web: www.pfizer.com					
Pharmion Corp 2525 28th St Suite 200	Boulder	CO	80301	720-564-9100	564-9191
NASDAQ: PHRM ■ *TF:* 866-742-7646 ■ *Web:* www.pharmion.com					
Pharmos Corp 99 Wood Ave S Suite 311	Iselin	NJ	08830	732-452-9556	452-9557
NASDAQ: PARS ■ *TF:* 888-308-5520 ■ *Web:* www.pharmoscorp.com					
Procter & Gamble Pharmaceuticals Canada Inc PO Box 355 Station A	Toronto	ON	M5W1C5	416-730-4711	730-4771
TF: 800-668-0150 ■ *Web:* www.pgpharma.com/canada_welcome.shtml					
Procter & Gamble Pharmaceuticals Inc One Proctor & Gamble Plaza	Cincinnati	OH	45202	513-983-1100	
TF: 800-331-3774 ■ *Web:* www.pgpharma.com					
ProCyte Corp PO Box 808	Redmond	WA	98073	425-869-1239	869-1229
TF Cust Svc: 888-966-1010 ■ *Web:* www.procyte.com					
Prometheus Laboratories Inc 9410 Carroll Park Dr	San Diego	CA	92121	858-824-0895	824-0896
TF: 888-423-5227 ■ *Web:* www.prometheus-labs.com					
Protide Pharmaceuticals Inc 505 Oakwood Rd Suite 200	Lake Zurich	IL	60047	847-726-3100	726-3110
TF: 800-552-3569 ■ *Web:* www.protidepharma.com					
Purdue Pharma LP 1 Stamford Forum	Stamford	CT	06901	203-588-8000	588-8850
TF Cust Svc: 800-877-5666 ■ *Web:* www.purduepharma.com					
QLT USA Inc 2579 Midpoint Dr	Fort Collins	CO	80525	970-482-5868	482-9735
Web: www.qltinc.com					
Qualicaps Inc 6505 Franz Warner Pkwy	Whitsett	NC	27377	336-449-3900	449-3333
TF: 800-227-7853 ■ *Web:* www.qualicaps.com					
Quigley Corp 621 Shady Retreat Rd	Doylestown	PA	18091	215-345-0919	345-5920
NASDAQ: QGLY ■ *TF:* 877-265-3339 ■ *Web:* www.quigleyco.com					
Quintiles Canada Inc 100 Alexis-Nihon Suite 800	Saint Laurent	QC	H4M2P4	514-855-0888	855-0880
TF: 800-799-6166 ■ *Web:* www.quintiles.com					
Quintiles Transnational Corp PO Box 13979	Research Triangle Park	NC	27709	919-998-2000	998-9113
TF: 800-875-2888 ■ *Web:* www.quintiles.com					
Ratiopharm 6975 Credit View Rd Unit 5	Mississauga	ON	L5N8E9	905-858-9612	858-9610
Web: www.ratiopharm.ca					
RegeneRx Biopharmaceuticals Inc 3 Bethesda Metro Ctr Suite 630	Bethesda	MD	20814	301-280-1992	280-1996
AMEX: RGN ■ *Web:* www.regenerx.com					
Reliant Pharmaceuticals Inc 110 Allen Rd	Liberty Corner	NJ	07938	908-580-1200	542-9405
Web: www.reliantrx.com					
Roxane Laboratories Inc 1809 Wilson Rd	Columbus	OH	43228	614-276-4000	274-0974
TF Cust Svc: 800-520-1631 ■ *Web:* www.roxane.com					
SAFC 3050 Spruce St	Saint Louis	MO	63103	314-534-4900	652-0000
TF: 800-244-1173 ■ *Web:* www.safcglobal.com					
Salix Pharmaceuticals Inc 1700 Perimeter Park Dr	Morrisville	NC	27560	919-862-1000	862-1095
NASDAQ: SLXP ■ *TF:* 800-508-0024 ■ *Web:* www.salix.com					
Sanofi-Aventis US LLC 55 Corp Dr	Bridgewater	NJ	08807	908-231-4000	231-3614
TF: 800-981-2491 ■ *Web:* www.sanofi-aventis.us					
Savage Laboratories Div Altana Inc 60 Baylis Rd	Melville	NY	11747	631-454-7677	454-0732
TF: 800-231-0206 ■ *Web:* www.savagelabs.com					
Scherer Labs Inc 2333 Waukegan Rd Suite 300	Bannockburn	IL	60015	770-514-1333	284-7169*
**Fax Area Code:* 800 ■ *TF:* 800-310-5357					
Schering Canada Inc 3535 TransCanada Hwy	Pointe-Claire	QC	H9R1B4	514-426-7300	695-7641
Web: www.schering.ca					
Schering Corp 2000 Galloping Hill Rd	Kenilworth	NJ	07033	908-298-4000	595-3699
TF: 800-222-7579 ■ *Web:* www.schering-plough.com					

Phone Fax

Schering-Plough Corp 2000 Galloping Hill Rd .... Kenilworth NJ 07033 908-298-4000 595-3699*
NYSE: SGP ■ **Fax:* Mktg ■ *TF Mktg:* 888-793-7253 ■ *Web:* www.schering-plough.com
Schering-Plough HealthCare Products Corp PO Box 377 .... Memphis TN 38151 901-320-2011 320-2080
TF Cust Svc: 800-842-4090
Schering-Plough Pharmaceuticals 2000 Galloping Hill Rd .... Kenilworth NJ 07033 908-298-4000
TF: 888-793-7253 ■ *Web:* www.schering-plough.com
Schwarz Pharma Inc PO Box 2038 .... Milwaukee WI 53201 262-238-5400 238-0311
TF: 800-558-5114 ■ *Web:* www.schwarzusa.com
SciClone Pharmaceuticals Inc
901 Mariners Island Blvd Suite 205 .... San Mateo CA 94404 650-358-3456 358-3469
NASDAQ: SCLN ■ *TF:* 800-724-2566 ■ *Web:* www.sciclone.com
Sciele Pharma Inc 5 Concourse Pkwy Suite 1800 .... Atlanta GA 30328 770-442-9707 442-9594
NASDAQ: SCRX ■ *TF:* 800-849-9707 ■ *Web:* www.sciele.com
Shire Pharmaceuticals Inc 725 Chesterbrook Blvd .... Wayne PA 19087 484-595-8248 595-8200
Web: www.shire.com
Shire US Inc 725 Chesterbrook Blvd .... Wayne PA 19087 484-595-8800 595-8200
Web: www.shire.com
Solvay America Inc 3333 Richmond Ave .... Houston TX 77098 713-525-6000 525-7887
TF: 800-231-6313 ■ *Web:* www.solvay.com
Solvay Pharma Inc 60 Columbia Way Suite 102 .... Markham ON L3R0C9 905-944-2480 944-2481
TF: 800-268-4276 ■ *Web:* www.solvaypharma.ca
Solvay Pharmaceuticals Inc 901 Sawyer Rd .... Marietta GA 30062 770-578-9000 578-5597
TF: 800-241-1643 ■ *Web:* www.solvaypharmaceuticals-us.com
Somaxon Pharmaceuticals Inc
3721 Valley Centre Dr Suite 500 .... San Diego CA 92130 858-480-0400 509-1761
NASDAQ: SOMX ■ *Web:* www.somaxon.com
Somerset Pharmaceuticals Inc
3030 N Rocky Point Dr Suite 250 .... Tampa FL 33607 813-288-0040 282-3804
TF: 800-892-8889 ■ *Web:* www.somersetpharm.com
Stiefel Laboratories Inc 255 Alhambra Cir Suite 1000 .... Coral Gables FL 33134 305-443-3807 443-3467
TF: 888-784-3335 ■ *Web:* www.stiefel.com
Summa Laboratories Inc 2940 FM 3028 .... Mineral Wells TX 76067 940-325-0771 325-0807
Web: www.summalabs.com
Taisho Pharmaceutical California Inc
3878 Carson St Suite 216 .... Torrance CA 90503 310-543-2035 543-9636
TF: 877-531-4559
Targacept Inc 200 E 1st St Suite 300 .... Winston-Salem NC 27101 336-480-2100 480-2107
NASDAQ: TRGT ■ *Web:* www.targacept.com
Taro Pharmaceuticals Inc 130 East Dr .... Brampton ON L6T1C1 905-791-8276 791-4473
TF: 800-268-1975 ■ *Web:* www.taro.ca
UCB Pharma Inc 1950 Lake Park Dr .... Smyrna GA 30080 770-970-7500 970-8482*
**Fax:* Hum Res ■ *TF:* 800-477-7877 ■ *Web:* www.ucb-group.com
United Therapeutics Corp 1110 Spring St .... Silver Spring MD 20910 301-608-9292 608-9291
NASDAQ: UTHR ■ *Web:* www.unither.com
Upsher-Smith Laboratories Inc 6701 Evenstad Dr .... Maple Grove MN 55369 763-473-4412 476-4026
TF: 800-328-3344 ■ *Web:* www.upsher-smith.com
Valeant Pharmaceuticals International 3300 Hyland Ave .... Costa Mesa CA 92626 714-545-0100 334-6999*
NYSE: VRX ■ **Fax Area Code:* 800 ■ *TF:* 800-548-5100 ■ *Web:* www.valeant.com
Valera Pharmaceuticals Inc 7 Clarke Dr .... Cranbury NJ 08512 609-409-9010 409-1650
NASDAQ: VLRX ■ *TF:* 888-262-8855 ■ *Web:* www.valerapharma.com
Vanda Pharmaceuticals Inc 9605 Medical Center Dr Suite 300 .... Rockville MD 20850 240-599-4500 294-1900*
NASDAQ: VNDA ■ **Fax Area Code:* 301 ■ *Web:* www.vandapharmaceuticals.com
Vivus Inc 1172 Castro St .... Mountain View CA 94040 650-934-5200 934-5389
NASDAQ: VVUS ■ *TF:* 888-367-6873 ■ *Web:* www.vivus.com
Voyager Pharmaceutical Corp
8540 Colonnade Center Dr Suite 501 .... Raleigh NC 27615 919-846-4880 846-4881
Web: www.voyagerpharma.com
Watson Pharmaceuticals Inc 311 Bonnie Cir .... Corona CA 92880 951-493-5300 493-5842
NYSE: WPI ■ *TF:* 800-272-5525 ■ *Web:* www.watsonpharm.com
WF Young Inc 302 Benton Dr PO Box 1990 .... East Longmeadow MA 01028 413-526-9999 526-8990
TF: 800-628-9653 ■ *Web:* www.absorbine.com
Wyeth BioPharm 1 Burtt Rd .... Andover MA 01810 978-475-9214 247-2324
TF: 888-577-1500 ■ *Web:* www.wyeth.com/divisions/wyt_biopharma.asp
Wyeth Consumer Health Care International Inc
5 Giralda Farms .... Madison NJ 07940 973-660-5500 660-6487
TF Cust Svc: 800-322-3129 ■ *Web:* www.wyeth.com/divisions/wyt_consumer.asp
Wyeth Global Pharmaceuticals 500 Arcola Rd .... Collegeville PA 19426 610-902-1200
Web: www.wyeth.com
Wyeth Pharmaceuticals Inc 500 Arcola Rd .... Collegeville PA 19426 610-902-1200 995-4668
Web: www.wyeth.com/divisions/wty_pharma.asp
Xechem International Inc
100 Jersey Ave Bldg B Suite 310 .... New Brunswick NJ 08901 732-247-3300 247-4090
TF: 800-858-5854 ■ *Web:* www.xechem.com
Zila Inc 5227 N 7th St .... Phoenix AZ 85014 602-266-6700 234-2264
NASDAQ: ZILA ■ *Web:* www.zila.com
ZLB Behring LLC 1020 1st Ave PO Box 61501 .... King of Prussia PA 19406 610-878-4000 878-4009
TF: 800-683-1288 ■ *Web:* www.zlbbehring.com

586 PHARMACEUTICAL COMPANIES - GENERIC DRUGS

SEE ALSO Biotechnology Companies p. 1380; Diagnostic Products p. 1587; Medicinal Chemicals & Botanical Products p. 1957; Pharmaceutical & Diagnostic Products - Veterinary p. 2111; Pharmaceutical Companies p. 2109; Vitamins & Nutritional Supplements p. 2405

Phone Fax

Actavis North America 200 Elmora Ave .... Elizabeth NJ 07207 908-527-9100 527-0649
Web: www.actavis.us
Allerderm Laboratories Inc 3400 E McDowell Rd .... Phoenix AZ 85008 602-225-9090 225-0599
TF: 800-365-6868 ■ *Web:* www.allerderm.com
American Pharmaceutical Partners Inc 2020 Ruby St .... Melrose Park IL 60160 708-345-6170 450-7563
NASDAQ: APPX ■ *Web:* www.appdrugs.com
Andrx Corp 4955 Orange Dr .... Davie FL 33314 954-585-1400 585-1888*
NASDAQ: ADRX ■ **Fax:* Hum Res ■ *TF:* 800-595-1883 ■ *Web:* www.andrx.com
Apotex Corp 2400 N Commerce Pkwy Suite 400 .... Weston FL 33326 954-384-8007 706-5576*
**Fax Area Code:* 800 ■ *TF:* 800-706-5575 ■ *Web:* www.apotexcorp.com
Barr Pharmaceuticals Inc 223 Quaker Rd PO Box 2900 .... Pomona NY 10970 845-362-1100 930-3316*
NYSE: BRL ■ **Fax Area Code:* 201 ■ *TF:* 800-222-4043 ■ *Web:* www.barrlabs.com
Capricorn Pharma Inc 6900 English Muffin Way Unit A .... Frederick MD 21703 301-696-8520 696-1424
Web: www.capricornpharma.com
E Fougera & Co 60 Baylis Rd .... Melville NY 11747 631-454-6996 454-6996
TF: 800-645-9833 ■ *Web:* www.fougera.com
Ethex Corp 10888 Metro Ct .... Saint Louis MO 63043 314-646-3750 646-3751
TF: 800-321-1705 ■ *Web:* www.ethex.com
Fougera E & Co 60 Baylis Rd .... Melville NY 11747 631-454-6996 454-6996
TF: 800-645-9833 ■ *Web:* www.fougera.com
Genpharm Inc 85 Advance Rd .... Etobicoke ON M8Z2S6 416-236-2631 236-8766
TF: 800-668-3174 ■ *Web:* www.genpharm.ca
Glades Pharmaceuticals Inc 6340 Sugarloaf Pkwy Suite 400 .... Duluth GA 30097 770-945-0708 945-5424
TF: 866-867-7858 ■ *Web:* www.glades.com
Glenwood, LLC 111 Cedar Ln .... Englewood NJ 07631 201-569-0050 569-0250
TF: 800-542-0772 ■ *Web:* www.glenwood-llc.com

Phone Fax

Healthpoint Ltd 3909 Hulen St .... Fort Worth TX 76107 817-900-4000 900-4100*
**Fax:* Cust Svc ■ *TF:* 800-441-8227 ■ *Web:* www.healthpoint.com
Impax Laboratories Inc 3735 Castor Ave .... Philadelphia PA 19124 215-289-2220 289-2223
TF: 800-296-5227 ■ *Web:* www.impaxlabs.com
IVAX Pharmaceuticals Inc 4400 Biscayne Blvd .... Miami FL 33137 305-575-4100
TF: 800-327-4114 ■ *Web:* www.ivaxpharmaceuticals.com
Martec USA LLC 9229 Dart Pkwy .... Kansas City MO 64114 816-241-4144 483-5432
TF: 800-822-6782 ■ *Web:* www.martec-kc.com
Mayne Pharma USA Inc 650 From Rd Mack-Cali Centre II .... Paramus NJ 07652 201-225-5500 225-5515
Web: www.maynepharma.com/US
Mericon Industries Inc 8819 N Pioneer Rd .... Peoria IL 61615 309-693-2150 693-2158
TF: 800-242-6464 ■ *Web:* www.mericon-industries.com
Morton Grove Pharmaceuticals Inc 6451 Main St .... Morton Grove IL 60053 847-967-5600 967-2211
TF: 800-346-6854 ■ *Web:* www.mgp-online.com
Mylan Laboratories Inc 1500 Corporate Dr Suite 400 .... Canonsburg PA 15317 724-514-1800 514-1870
NYSE: MYL ■ *Web:* www.mylan.com
Nephron Pharmaceuticals Corp 4121 SW 34th St .... Orlando FL 32811 407-246-1389 872-0001
TF: 800-443-4313 ■ *Web:* www.nephronpharm.com
Par Pharmaceutical Cos Inc 1 Ram Ridge Rd .... Spring Valley NY 10977 845-425-7100 425-7907
NYSE: PRX ■ *Web:* www.parpharm.com
Par Pharmaceutical Inc 1 Ram Ridge Rd .... Spring Valley NY 10977 201-802-4000 802-4600
TF: 800-828-9393 ■ *Web:* www.parpharm.com
Pedinol Pharmacal Inc 30 Banfi Plaza N .... Farmingdale NY 11735 631-293-9500 293-7359
TF: 800-733-4665 ■ *Web:* www.pedinol.com
Perrigo Co 515 Eastern Ave .... Allegan MI 49010 269-673-8451 673-9128
NASDAQ: PRGO ■ *TF:* 800-253-3606 ■ *Web:* www.perrigo.com
Pharmics Inc 2702 S 3600 West Suite H .... Salt Lake City UT 84119 801-966-4138 966-4177
TF: 800-456-4138 ■ *Web:* www.pharmics.com
Pliva Inc 72 Eagle Rock Ave .... East Hanover NJ 07936 973-386-5566 386-9280
TF: 800-922-0547 ■ *Web:* www.plivainc.com
Ranbaxy Pharmaceuticals Inc 600 College Rd E Suite 2100 .... Princeton NJ 08540 609-720-9200 720-1155
Web: www.ranbaxyusa.com
Sandoz Inc 506 Carnegie Center Suite 400 .... Princeton NJ 08540 609-627-8500 627-8659
Web: www.us.sandoz.com
Seneca Pharmaceutical Inc 8621 Barefoot Industrial Rd .... Raleigh NC 27617 919-783-6936 782-8234
TF: 800-334-5528
Sepracor Inc 84 Waterford Dr .... Marlborough MA 01752 508-481-6700 357-7490
NASDAQ: SEPR ■ *Web:* www.sepracor.com
Stratus Pharmaceuticals Inc 14377 SW 142nd St .... Miami FL 33186 305-254-6793 254-6875
TF: 800-442-7882 ■ *Web:* www.stratuspharmaceuticals.com
Taro Pharmaceuticals USA Inc 3 Skyline Dr .... Hawthorne NY 10532 914-345-9001 345-8728
NASDAQ: TARO ■ *TF:* 800-544-1449 ■ *Web:* www.tarousa.com
Teva Pharmaceutical USA 1090 Horsham Rd .... North Wales PA 19454 215-591-3000 591-8600
NASDAQ: TEVA ■ *TF:* 800-545-8800 ■ *Web:* www.tevapharmusa.com
UDL Laboratories Inc 1718 Northrock Ct .... Rockford IL 61103 815-282-1201 282-9391
TF: 800-435-5272 ■ *Web:* www.udllabs.com
USL Pharma 301 S Cherokee St .... Denver CO 80223 303-607-4500 607-4503
TF: 800-445-8091 ■ *Web:* www.upsher-smith.com
Warner Chilcott
100 Enterprise Dr Suite 280 Rockaway 80
Corporate Center .... Rockaway NJ 07866 973-442-3200 442-3283
TF: 800-521-8813 ■ *Web:* www.wcrx.com
Watson Laboratories Inc 311 Bonnie Cir .... Corona CA 92880 951-270-1400 493-4229
TF: 800-272-5525 ■ *Web:* www.watsonpharm.com
West-Ward Pharmaceutical Corp 465 Industrial Way W .... Eatontown NJ 07724 732-542-1191 542-0940
TF Cust Svc: 800-631-2174
X-Gen Pharmaceuticals Inc
300 Daniels Anchor Dr PO Box 445 .... Big Flats NY 14814 607-732-4411 562-2760
TF: 866-390-4411 ■ *Web:* www.x-gen.us
Xanodyne Pharmaceuticals Inc 1 Riverfront Pl .... Newport KY 41071 859-371-6383 371-6391
TF: 877-926-6396 ■ *Web:* www.xanodyne.com

587 PHARMACEUTICAL & DIAGNOSTIC PRODUCTS - VETERINARY

Phone Fax

Abbott Laboratories Animal Health Div
1401 Sheridan Rd .... North Chicago IL 60064 847-937-6100 938-0659
TF: 888-299-7416 ■ *Web:* www.abbottanimalhealth.com
ABS Corp 7031 N 16th St .... Omaha NE 68112 402-453-6970 453-1052
Web: www.abs-corporation.com
Addison Biological Laboratory Inc 507 N Cleveland Ave .... Fayette MO 65248 660-248-2215 248-2554
TF: 800-331-2530 ■ *Web:* www.addisonlabs.com
ADM Animal Health & Nutrition Div 1877 NE 58th Ave .... Des Moines IA 50313 515-262-9763 266-1925
TF: 800-247-5450
Alltech Inc 3031 Catnip Hill Pike .... Nicholasville KY 40356 859-885-9613 885-6736
TF: 800-289-8324 ■ *Web:* www.alltech-bio.com
Alpharma Inc Animal Health Div 1 Executive Dr 3rd Fl .... Fort Lee NJ 07024 201-947-7774 947-0912
TF: 800-834-6470 ■ *Web:* www.alpharma.com/ahd
BASF Corp 100 Campus Dr .... Florham Park NJ 07932 973-245-6000 895-8002
NYSE: BF ■ *TF:* 800-526-1072 ■ *Web:* www.basf.com
Bell Pharmaceuticals PO Box 128 .... Belle Plaine MN 56011 952-873-2288 873-2289
TF: 800-328-5890
Bimeda Inc Oakbrook Terrace Tower Suite 2250 .... Oakbrook IL 60181 630-928-0361 928-0362
Web: www.bimeda.com
Bimeda Animal Health Oakbrook Terrace Tower Suite 2250 .... Oakbrook IL 60181 630-928-0361 928-0362
Web: www.bimeda.com
Bimeda-MTC Animal Health Inc 420 Beaverdale Rd .... Cambridge ON N3C2W4 519-654-8000 654-8001
Web: www.bimeda.com/dotcom/canadaabout.htm
Bio-Serv 1 8th St Suite 1 .... Frenchtown NJ 08825 908-996-2155 996-4123
TF: 800-996-9908 ■ *Web:* www.bio-serv.com
Biomune Co 8906 Rosehill Rd .... Lenexa KS 66215 913-894-0230 894-0236
TF: 800-846-0230 ■ *Web:* www.biomunecompany.com
Bioniche Animal Health Canada Inc 231 Dundas St E .... Belleville ON K8N1E2 613-966-8058 966-4177
TF: 800-265-5464 ■ *Web:* www.bionicheanimalhealth.com
Biovet Inc 4375 ave Beaudry .... Saint-Hyacinthe QC J2S8W2 450-771-7291 771-4158
TF: 888-824-6838 ■ *Web:* www.biovet-inc.com
Biovet USA Inc 3055 Old Hwy 8 Suite 100 .... Saint Anthony MN 55418 612-781-2952 781-2941
TF: 877-824-6838 ■ *Web:* www.biovet-inc.com
Boehringer Ingelheim Vetmedica Inc 2621 N Belt Hwy .... Saint Joseph MO 64506 816-233-2571 390-0605*
**Fax:* Hum Res ■ *TF:* 800-821-7467 ■ *Web:* www.bi-vetmedica.com
Cut-Heal Animal Care Products Inc 923 S Cedar Hill Rd .... Cedar Hill TX 75104 972-293-9700 293-8335
TF: 800-288-4325
Dairy Assn Co Inc 91 Williams St .... Lyndonville VT 05851 802-626-3610 626-3433
TF: 800-232-3610 ■ *Web:* www.bagbalm.com
Darby Group Cos Inc 300 Jericho Quad .... Jericho NY 11753 516-683-1800 957-7362*
**Fax Area Code:* 800 ■ *TF:* 800-468-1001 ■ *Web:* www.darbygroup.com
Dawe's LLC 3355 N Arlington Heights Rd .... Arlington Heights IL 60004 847-577-2020 577-1898
TF: 800-323-4317
Delmont Laboratories Inc 715 Harvard Ave PO Box 269 .... Swarthmore PA 19081 610-543-3365 543-6298
TF: 800-562-5541 ■ *Web:* www.delmont.com
DiagXotics Inc 3371 Rt 1 Suite 200 .... Lawrenceville NJ 08648 405-809-1314 809-1944
TF: 866-358-9282 ■ *Web:* www.diagxotics.com
Diamond Animal Health Inc 2538 SE 43rd St .... Des Moines IA 50327 515-263-8600 263-8661
TF Cust Svc: 800-924-8600

	City	State	ZIP	Phone	Fax
DMS Laboratories Inc 2 Darts Mill Rd	Flemington	NJ	08822	908-782-3353	782-0832
TF: 800-567-4367 ■ *Web:* www.rapidvet.com					
Dominion Veterinary Laboratories Inc 1199 Sanford St	Winnipeg	MB	R3E3A1	204-589-7361	943-9612
TF: 800-465-7122 ■ *Web:* www.domvet.com					
DVM Pharmaceuticals Inc 3915 S 48th St Terr	Saint Joseph	MO	64503	816-364-3777	676-6871
TF: 800-367-4902 ■ *Web:* www.dvmpharmaceuticals.com					
Elanco Animal Health 2001 W Main St	Greenfield	IN	46140	317-276-2000	276-9434
Web: www.elanco.com					
EVSCO Pharmaceuticals Div IGI Inc 101 Lincoln Ave	Buena	NJ	08310	856-697-5115	697-7465
TF: 800-267-5707					
Farnam Cos Inc 301 W Osborn Rd	Phoenix	AZ	85013	602-285-1660	285-1803
TF: 800-234-2269 ■ *Web:* www.farnam.com					
Fort Dodge Animal Health					
9225 Indian Creek Pkwy Bldg 32 Suite 400	Overland Park	KS	66210	913-664-7000	664-7120
TF: 800-477-1365 ■ *Web:* www.wyeth.com/divisions/fort_dodge.asp					
Heska Corp 3760 Rocky Mountain Ave	Loveland	CO	80538	970-493-7272	619-3005
NASDAQ: HSKA ■ *TF:* 800-464-3752 ■ *Web:* www.heska.com					
IGI Inc 105 Lincoln Ave PO Box 687	Buena	NJ	08310	856-697-1441	697-2259
AMEX: IG ■ *Web:* www.askigi.com					
IMMVAC Inc 6080 Bass Ln	Columbia	MO	65201	573-443-5363	874-7108
TF: 800-944-7563 ■ *Web:* www.immvac.com					
Ivy Animal Health Inc 8857 Bond St	Overland Park	KS	66214	913-888-2192	888-3007
TF: 800-828-2192 ■ *Web:* www.ivyanimalhealth.com					
King Bio Pharmaceuticals Inc 3 Westside Dr	Asheville	NC	28806	828-255-0201	255-0940
TF: 888-827-6414 ■ *Web:* www.kingbio.com					
Lake Immunogenics Inc 348 Berg Rd	Ontario	NY	14519	585-265-1973	265-2306
TF: 800-648-9990 ■ *Web:* www.lakeimmunogenics.com					
Lextron Inc 620 'O' St PO Box 1240	Greeley	CO	80632	970-353-2600	356-4623
Web: www.lextron-inc.com					
Lloyd Inc 604 W Thomas Ave	Shenandoah	IA	51601	712-246-4000	246-5245
TF: 800-831-0004 ■ *Web:* www.lloydinc.com					
Luitpold Pharmaceuticals Inc 1 Luitpold Dr PO Box 9001	Shirley	NY	11967	631-924-4000	924-1731
TF: 800-645-1706 ■ *Web:* www.luitpold.com					
Merial Ltd 3239 Satellite Blvd Bldg 500	Duluth	GA	30096	678-638-3000	
TF: 888-637-4251 ■ *Web:* www.merial.com					
MetaMorphix Inc 8000 Virginia Manor Rd Suite 140	Beltsville	MD	20705	301-617-9080	617-9075
Web: www.metamorphixinc.com					
MVP Laboratories Inc 4805 G St	Omaha	NE	68117	402-331-5106	331-8776
TF: 800-856-4648 ■ *Web:* www.mvplabs.com					
Nelson Laboratories Ltd 4001 N Lewis Ave	Sioux Falls	SD	57104	605-336-2451	336-2322
TF: 800-843-3322 ■ *Web:* www.nelsonlab.com					
Novartis Animal Health US Inc 1447 140th St	Larchwood	IA	51241	712-477-2811	628-4673*
**Fax Area Code:* 866 ■ *TF:* 800-454-3424 ■ *Web:* www.livestock.novartis.com					
Nutra-Blend Inc 3200 E 2nd St	Neosho	MO	64850	417-451-6111	451-4515
TF: 800-657-5657 ■ *Web:* www.nutrablend.net					
Pfizer Inc Animal Health Group 235 E 42nd St	New York	NY	10017	212-573-2323	
TF: 800-733-5500 ■ *Web:* www.pfizer.com/ah					
PM Resources Inc 13001 St Charles Rock Rd	Bridgeton	MO	63044	314-291-6720	291-2657
TF Cust Svc: 800-447-5463					
Polydex Pharmaceuticals Ltd 421 Comstock Rd	Toronto	ON	M1L2H5	416-755-2231	755-0334
NASDAQ: POLXF ■ *Web:* www.polydex.com					
ProtaTek International Inc 2635 University Ave W Suite 140	Saint Paul	MN	55114	651-644-5391	644-6831
Web: www.protatek.com					
Qualis Inc 4600 Park Ave	Des Moines	IA	50321	515-243-3000	282-1417
TF: 800-334-4514					
Schering-Plough Corp Animal Health Div 556 Morris Ave	Summit	NJ	07901	908-298-4000	
TF Cust Svc: 800-521-5767 ■ *Web:* www.spah.com					
Synbiotics Corp 11011 Via Frontera	San Diego	CA	92127	858-451-3771	613-1273
TF: 800-228-4305 ■ *Web:* www.synbiotics.com					
Texas Vet Lab Inc 1702 N Bell St	San Angelo	TX	76903	325-653-4505	653-4501
TF: 800-284-8403 ■ *Web:* www.texasvetlab.com					
Thomas Veterinary Drug 9165 W VanBuren St	Tolleson	AZ	85353	623-936-3363	936-4499
TF: 800-359-8387 ■ *Web:* www.thomasveterinarydrug.com					
TW Medical Veterinary Supply 3610 Lohman Ford Rd	Lago Vista	TX	78645	512-267-8800	267-8860
TF: 888-787-4483 ■ *Web:* www.twmedical.com					
Veterinary Pharmacies of America 2854 Antoine Dr	Houston	TX	77092	713-688-3321	329-7979*
**Fax Area Code:* 877 ■ *TF:* 877-838-7979 ■ *Web:* www.vetrxrx.com					
VetLife 1001 Office Park Rd Suite 201	West Des Moines	IA	50265	515-224-0788	224-0804
TF: 888-462-3493 ■ *Web:* www.vetlife.com					
Vetoquinol Canada Inc 2000 ch Georges	Lavaltrie	QC	G5T3S5	450-586-2252	586-4649
TF: 800-363-1700 ■ *Web:* www.vetoquinol.ca					
Vetoquinol EVSCO Pharmaceuticals 101 Lincoln Ave	Buena	NJ	08310	856-697-5115	697-7465
TF: 800-267-5707					
VetriCare 590 Main St Suite B	Templeton	CA	93465	805-434-5999	434-5967
TF: 800-238-5999 ■ *Web:* www.vetricare.net					
Wildlife Pharmaceuticals Inc					
1635 Blue Spruce Dr Suite 202	Fort Collins	CO	80524	970-484-6267	484-4941
TF: 877-883-9283 ■ *Web:* www.wildpharm.com					
Wyeth Corp Fort Dodge Animal Health Div					
9225 Indian Creek Pkwy Bldg 32 Suite 400	Overland Park	KS	66210	913-664-7000	664-7120
TF: 800-477-1365 ■ *Web:* www.wyeth.com/divisions/fort_dodge.asp					
XF Enterprises Inc DBA Xtra Factors Inc 211 Pedigo Dr	Pratt	KS	67124	620-672-5616	672-5564
TF: 800-783-5616					
Xtra Factors Inc 211 Pedigo Dr	Pratt	KS	67124	620-672-5616	672-5564
TF: 800-783-5616					

588 PHARMACY ASSOCIATIONS - STATE

SEE ALSO Associations & Organizations - Professional & Trade - Health & Medical Professionals Associations p. 1326

	City	State	ZIP	Phone	Fax
Alabama Pharmacy Assn 1211 Carmichael Way	Montgomery	AL	36106	334-271-4222	271-5423
TF: 800-529-7533 ■ *Web:* www.aparx.org					
Alaska Pharmacist's Assn 4107 Laurel St Suite 101	Anchorage	AK	99508	907-563-8880	563-7880
Web: www.alaskapharmacy.org					
Arizona Pharmacy Assn 1845 E Southern Ave	Tempe	AZ	85282	480-838-3385	838-3557
Web: www.azpharmacy.org					
Arkansas Pharmacists Assn 417 S Victory St	Little Rock	AR	72201	501-372-5250	372-0546
Web: www.arpharmacists.org					
California Pharmacists Assn (CPhA) 4030 Lennane Dr	Sacramento	CA	95834	916-779-1400	779-1401
TF: 800-444-3851 ■ *Web:* www.cpha.com					
Colorado Pharmacists Society 6825 E Tennessee Ave Suite 440	Denver	CO	80224	303-756-3069	756-3649
Web: www.copharm.org					
Connecticut Pharmacists Assn 35 Cold Spring Rd Suite 121	Rocky Hill	CT	06067	860-563-4619	257-8241
Web: www.ctpharmacists.org					
Delaware Pharmacists Society PO Box 454	Smyrna	DE	19977	302-659-3088	659-3089
Web: www.depharmacy.net					
Florida Pharmacy Assn 610 N Adams St	Tallahassee	FL	32301	850-222-2400	561-6758
Web: www.pharmview.com					
Georgia Pharmacy Assn (GPhA) 50 Lenox Pointe NE	Atlanta	GA	30324	404-231-5074	237-8435
Web: www.gpha.org					
Idaho State Pharmacy Assn 702 W Idaho St Suite 1000	Boise	ID	83702	208-947-7272	947-5910
Web: www.idahopharmacy.org					
Illinois Pharmacists Assn (IPhA) 204 W Cook St	Springfield	IL	62704	217-522-7300	522-7349
Web: www.ipha.org					
Indiana Pharmacists Alliance 729 N Pennsylvania St	Indianapolis	IN	46204	317-634-4968	632-1219
Web: www.indianapharmacists.org					
Iowa Pharmacy Assn 8515 Douglas Ave Suite 16	Des Moines	IA	50322	515-270-0713	270-2979
Web: www.iarx.org					
Kansas Pharmacists Assn 1020 SW Fairlawn Rd	Topeka	KS	66604	785-228-2327	228-9147
Web: www.kansaspharmacy.org					
Kentucky Pharmacists Assn 1228 US 127 S	Frankfort	KY	40601	502-227-2303	227-2258
Louisiana Pharmacists Assn 450 Laurel St Suite 1400	Baton Rouge	LA	70801	225-346-6883	344-1132
TF: 800-611-8307 ■ *Web:* www.louisianapharmacists.com					
Maine Pharmacy Assn 127 Pleasant Hill Rd	Scarborough	ME	04074	800-639-1609	396-5341*
**Fax Area Code:* 207 ■ *Web:* www.mparx.com					
Maryland Pharmacists Assn 650 W Lombard St	Baltimore	MD	21201	410-727-0746	727-2253
Web: www.marylandpharmacist.org					
Massachusetts Pharmacists Assn					
500 W Cummings Park Suite 3475	Woburn	MA	01801	781-933-1107	933-1109
Web: www.masspharmacists.org					
Michigan Pharmacists Assn 815 N Washington Ave	Lansing	MI	48906	517-484-1466	484-4893
Web: www.michiganpharmacists.org					
Minnesota Pharmacists Assn (MPhA) 1935 W County Rd B2	Roseville	MN	55113	651-697-1771	697-1776
Web: www.mpha.org					
Mississippi Pharmacists Assn 341 Edgewood Terrace Dr	Jackson	MS	39206	601-981-0416	981-0451
Web: www.mspharm.org					
Missouri Pharmacy Assn 211 E Capitol Ave	Jefferson City	MO	65101	573-636-7522	636-7485
Web: www.morx.com					
Montana Pharmacy Assn 34 W 6th Ave Suite 2E	Helena	MT	59601	406-449-3843	443-1592
Web: www.rxmt.org					
Nebraska Pharmacists Assn 6221 S 58th St Suite A	Lincoln	NE	68516	402-420-1500	420-1406
Web: www.npharm.org					
New Hampshire Pharmacists Assn 2 Eagle Sq Suite 400	Concord	NH	03301	603-229-0292	224-7769
Web: www.nhpharmacists.org					
New Jersey Pharmacists Assn 760 Alexander Rd CN1	Princeton	NJ	08543	609-275-4246	275-4066
Web: www.njpharma.org					
New Mexico Pharmacists Assn (NMPhA) 4800 Zuni SE	Albuquerque	NM	87108	505-265-8729	255-8476
Web: www.nm-pharmacy.com					
Pharmacists Society of the State of New York					
210 Washington Ave Ext	Albany	NY	12203	518-869-6595	464-0618
Web: www.pssny.org					
North Carolina Assn of Pharmacists 109 Church St	Chapel Hill	NC	27516	919-967-2237	968-9430
Web: www.ncpharmacists.org					
North Dakota Pharmacists Assn (NDPhA)					
1661 Capitol Way Suite 102	Bismarck	ND	58501	701-258-4968	258-9312
Web: www.nodakpharmacy.net					
Ohio Pharmacists Assn 2155 Riverside Dr	Columbus	OH	43221	614-586-1497	586-1545
Web: www.ohiopharmacists.org					
Oklahoma Pharmacists Assn 45 NE 52nd St	Oklahoma City	OK	73105	405-528-3338	528-1417
Web: www.opha.com					
Oregon State Pharmacy Assn					
29702-B SW Town Center Loop West	Wilsonville	OR	97070	503-582-9055	582-9046
Web: www.oregonpharmacy.org					
Pennsylvania Pharmacists Assn 508 N 3rd St	Harrisburg	PA	17101	717-234-6151	236-1618
Web: www.papharmacists.com					
Rhode Island Pharmacists Assn 1643 Warwick Ave PMB 113	Warwick	RI	02889	401-737-2600	737-0959
Web: www.ripharmacists.org					
South Carolina Pharmacy Assn 1350 Browning Rd	Columbia	SC	29210	803-354-9977	354-9207
Web: www.scrx.org					
South Dakota Pharmacists Assn PO Box 518	Pierre	SD	57501	605-224-2338	224-1280
Web: www.sdpha.org					
Tennessee Pharmacists Assn 500 Church St Suite 650	Nashville	TN	37219	615-256-3023	255-3528
Web: www.tnpharm.org					
Texas Pharmacy Assn 1624 E Anderson Ln PO Box 14709	Austin	TX	78761	512-836-8350	836-0308
Web: www.txpharmacy.com					
Utah Pharmacists Assn (UPhA) 1850 S Columbia Ln	Orem	UT	84097	801-762-0452	762-0454
Web: www.upha.com					
Virginia Pharmacists Assn 5501 Patterson Ave Suite 200	Richmond	VA	23226	804-285-4145	285-4227
Web: www.vapharmacy.org					
Washington State Pharmacy Assn 1501 Taylor Ave SW	Renton	WA	98055	425-228-7171	277-3897
Web: www.wsparx.org					
West Virginia Pharmacists Assn 2016 1/2 Kanawha Blvd E	Charleston	WV	25311	304-344-5302	344-5316
Pharmacy Society of Wisconsin 701 Heartland Trail	Madison	WI	53717	608-827-9200	827-9292
Web: www.pswi.org					
Wyoming Pharmacists Assn PO Box 366	Cheyenne	WY	82003	307-772-8044	
Web: www.wpha.net					

589 PHARMACY BENEFITS MANAGEMENT SERVICES

A pharmacy benefits management service (PBM) is a company that manages various pharmacy-related aspects of a health insurance plan, such as the assignment of pharmacy cards, claims filing and processing, formulary management, etc. For the most part, PBM clients are insurance companies, HMOs, or PPOs rather than individuals or pharmacies.

	City	State	ZIP	Phone	Fax
AmeriScript Inc 4301 Darrow Rd	Stow	OH	44224	330-686-7010	686-7010*
**Fax:* Mktg ■ *TF:* 800-681-6912 ■ *Web:* www.ameriscript.com					
BeneScript Services Inc 3720 DaVinci Ct Suite 200	Norcross	GA	30092	770-448-4344	448-4516
TF: 800-345-3189 ■ *Web:* www.benescript.com					
BioScrip Inc 100 Clearbrook Rd	Elmsford	NY	10523	914-460-1600	460-1660
NASDAQ: BIOS ■ *TF:* 888-818-3939 ■ *Web:* www.bioscrip.com					
Caremark Rx Inc 211 Commerce St Suite 800	Nashville	TN	37201	615-743-6600	743-6599
NYSE: CMX ■ *TF:* 800-633-9509 ■ *Web:* www.caremark.com					
CuraScript Inc 6272 Lee Vista Blvd	Orlando	FL	32822	407-852-4903	773-7386*
**Fax Area Code:* 888 ■ *TF:* 800-950-2840 ■ *Web:* www.curascript.com					
Express Scripts Inc 13900 Riverport Dr	Maryland Heights	MO	63043	314-770-1666	919-4649*
NASDAQ: ESRX ■ **Fax:* Hum Res ■ *TF:* 800-332-5455 ■ *Web:* www.express-scripts.com					
Maxor National Pharmacy Services Corp					
320 S Polk St Suite 100	Amarillo	TX	79101	806-324-5400	324-5495
TF: 800-658-6146 ■ *Web:* www.maxor.com					
Medco Health Solutions Inc 100 Parsons Pond Dr	Franklin Lakes	NJ	07417	201-269-3400	269-1222
NYSE: MHS ■ *TF Cust Svc:* 800-248-2268 ■ *Web:* www.medcohealth.com					
MedImpact Healthcare Systems Inc					
10680 Treena St Suite 500	San Diego	CA	92131	858-566-2727	790-6454
TF: 800-788-2949 ■ *Web:* www.medimpact.com					
National Medical Health Card Systems Inc DBA NMHCrx					
Pharmacy Benefits Manager 26 Harbor Park Dr	Port Washington	NY	11050	516-626-0007	605-6980
NASDAQ: NMHC ■ *TF:* 800-645-3332 ■ *Web:* www.nmhcrx.com					
National Prescription Administrators Inc					
711 Ridgedale Ave	East Hanover	NJ	07936	973-503-1000	503-1085*
**Fax:* Cust Svc ■ *Web:* www.npanet.com					

	Phone	Fax

NMHCrx Pharmacy Benefits Manager
26 Harbor Park Dr ... Port Washington NY 11050 516-626-0007 605-6980
NASDAQ: NMHC ■ *TF:* 800-645-3332 ■ *Web:* www.nmhcrx.com
PharmaCare Management Services Inc
695 George Washington Hwy ... Lincoln RI 02865 401-334-0069 334-4995
TF: 888-862-2699 ■ *Web:* www.pharmacare.com
Prescription Solutions 3515 Harbor Blvd ... Costa Mesa CA 92626 714-825-3600 483-7093*
**Fax Area Code:* 800 ■ *TF:* 800-562-6223 ■ *Web:* www.rxsolutions.com
Prime Therapeutics Inc 1020 Discovery Rd Suite 100 ... Eagan MN 55121 651-286-4000 286-4404
TF: 800-858-0723 ■ *Web:* www.primetherapeutics.com
RESTAT 724 Elm St ... West Bend WI 53095 262-338-5760 338-5767
TF Cust Svc: 800-248-1062 ■ *Web:* www.restat.com
RxAmerica LLC 221 N Charles Lindbergh Dr ... Salt Lake City UT 84116 801-961-6000 961-6330
TF: 800-770-8014 ■ *Web:* www.rxamerica.com
ScripNet 10050 Banburry Cross Dr Suite 290 ... Las Vegas NV 89144 702-248-2692 245-1745*
**Fax Area Code:* 888 ■ *TF:* 888-880-8562 ■ *Web:* www.scripnet.com
Script Care Inc 6380 Folsom Dr ... Beaumont TX 77706 409-833-9061 832-3109
TF: 800-880-9902 ■ *Web:* www.scriptcare.com
ScriptSave 333 E Wetmore Rd 4th Fl ... Tucson AZ 85705 520-888-8070 888-8069
TF: 800-347-5985 ■ *Web:* www.scriptsave.com
Serve You Custom Prescription Management
9051 W Heather Ave ... Milwaukee WI 53224 414-410-8100 410-8181
TF: 888-243-6890 ■ *Web:* www.serve-you-rx.com
Walgreens Health Services 1411 Lake Cook Rd ... Deerfield IL 60015 847-374-2640 374-2645
Web: www.walgreenshealth.com
WellPoint Pharmacy Management 8407 Fallbrook Ave ... West Hills CA 91304 800-700-2533 313-5580*
**Fax Area Code:* 818 ■ *Web:* www.wellpointrx.com

590 PHARMACY MANAGEMENT SERVICES

Companies that provide long-term care pharmacy services to individuals with special needs (e.g., chronic disease or advanced age); and those that provide pharmacy management services to hospitals or other institutions.

	Phone	Fax

Accredo Health Inc 1640 Century Center Pkwy Suite 101 ... Memphis TN 38134 901-385-3688 385-3689
TF: 877-222-7336 ■ *Web:* www.accredohealth.net/ahi
Compscript Inc 1225 Broken Sound Pkwy NW Suite A ... Boca Raton FL 33487 561-994-8585 590-6105*
**Fax Area Code:* 800 ■ *TF:* 800-832-8585
McKesson Medication Management
7115 Northland Terr Suite 500 ... Brooklyn Park MN 55428 763-354-1200 354-1175*
**Fax:* Hum Res ■ *TF:* 877-806-7888 ■ *Web:* www.medmanagement.com
McKesson Pharmaceutical 1 Post St ... San Francisco CA 94104 415-983-8300 983-7160
TF: 800-571-2889 ■ *Web:* healthsystems.mckesson.com
MedExpress Pharmacy Ltd 1431 W Innes St ... Salisbury NC 28144 704-633-3113 633-3353
TF: 800-808-8060
NeighborCare Inc 7 E Lee St ... Baltimore MD 21202 410-752-2600 576-0698
Web: www.neighborcare.com
Omnicare Inc 100 E RiverCenter Blvd Suite 1600 ... Covington KY 41011 859-392-3300 392-3333
NYSE: OCR ■ *TF:* 800-342-5627 ■ *Web:* www.omnicare.com
Pharmacy Systems Inc 5050 Bradenton Ave PO Box 130 ... Dublin OH 43017 614-766-0101 766-4448
Web: www.pharmacysystems.com
PharMerica Inc 3625 Queen Palm Dr ... Tampa FL 33619 813-318-6000 318-6167
TF: 877-975-2273 ■ *Web:* www.pharmerica.com

591 PHOTO PROCESSING & STORAGE

	Phone	Fax

ABC Photo & Imaging Services Inc 9016 Prince William St ... Manassas VA 20110 703-369-2566 631-8064
TF: 800-368-4044 ■ *Web:* www.imageabc.com
Advanced Photographic Solutions LLC 1525 Hardeman Ln NE ... Cleveland TN 37312 423-479-5481 479-8077
TF: 800-241-9234 ■ *Web:* www.advancedphoto.com
Burrell Professional Labs 1311 Merrillville Rd ... Crown Point IN 46307 219-663-3210 662-0915
TF: 800-348-8732 ■ *Web:* www.burrellprolabs.com
Candid Color Systems Inc 1300 Metropolitan Ave ... Oklahoma City OK 73108 405-947-8747 951-7353
TF: 800-336-4550 ■ *Web:* www.candid.com
Club Photo Inc 5311 Fleming Ct ... Austin TX 78744 512-444-1208 444-6336
Web: www.clubphoto.com
Dale Laboratories 2960 Simms St ... Hollywood FL 33020 954-925-0103 922-3008
TF: 800-327-1776 ■ *Web:* www.dalelabs.com
District Photo Inc 10501 Rhode Island Ave ... Beltsville MD 20705 301-937-5300 937-5627
Web: www.districtphoto.com
dotPhoto Inc
111 Silvia St American Enterprise Park at Ewing ... West Trenton NJ 08628 609-434-0340 434-0344
Web: www.dotphoto.com
Express Digital Graphics Inc DBA PhotoReflect
9200 Panorama Cir Suite 150 ... Englewood CO 80112 303-790-1004 790-1443
TF: 888-584-0089 ■ *Web:* www.photoreflect.com
FLM Graphics 123 Lehigh Dr ... Fairfield NJ 07004 973-575-9450 575-6424
TF: 800-257-9757 ■ *Web:* www.flmgraphics.com
FotoTime Inc 6711 Atlanta Dr ... Colleyville TX 76034 469-361-3441
TF: 888-705-0389 ■ *Web:* www.fototime.com
H & H Color Lab Inc 8906 E 67th St ... Raytown MO 64133 816-358-6677 313-1480
TF: 800-821-1305 ■ *Web:* www.hhcolorlab.com
iMemories 9181 E Bell Rd Suite 101 ... Scottsdale AZ 85260 480-767-2510 767-2511
Web: www.imemories.com
Kodak Imaging Network Inc 1480 64th St Suite 300 ... Emeryville CA 94608 510-229-1200 229-2700
TF: 800-360-9098 ■ *Web:* www.ofoto.com
McKenna Pro Imaging 2815 Falls Ave PO Box 5600 ... Waterloo IA 50704 319-235-6265 235-1121
TF: 800-238-3456 ■ *Web:* www.mckennapro.com
Meisel Visual Imaging 2019 McKenzie Dr ... Carrollton TX 75006 214-688-4900 688-4950
TF: 800-527-5186 ■ *Web:* www.meisel.com
Mystic Color Lab Inc PO Box 144 ... Mystic CT 06355 800-367-6061 289-2182*
**Fax Area Code:* 301 ■ *Web:* www.mysticcolorlab.com
National Graphx & Imaging LLC 9240 W Belmont Ave ... Franklin Park IL 60131 847-671-1122 671-1144
TF: 800-211-7978 ■ *Web:* www.nationalgraphx.com
Photo USA 3736 Franklin Rd ... Roanoke VA 24014 540-344-0961 344-3509
TF: 888-234-6320 ■ *Web:* www.photousa.com
PhotoChannel Networks Inc 425 Carrall St Suite 590 ... Vancouver BC V6B6E3 604-893-8955 893-8966
Web: www.photochannel.com
PhotoWorks Inc 71 Columbia St Suite 200 ... Seattle WA 98104 206-281-1390 284-5357
TF: 800-345-6967 ■ *Web:* www.photoworks.com
Prolab Visual Imaging Services Inc 123 NW 36th St ... Seattle WA 98107 206-547-5447 547-5448
TF: 800-426-6770 ■ *Web:* www.digitalimaging.com
Qualex Inc 3414 N Duke St ... Durham NC 27704 919-383-8535 382-2257
Quantity Photo Co 119 W Hubbard St ... Chicago IL 60610 312-644-8288 644-8299
Web: www.quantityphoto.com

	Phone	Fax

Reliance Color Labs Inc PO Box 3640 ... Hampton Park MD 20791 800-332-6567 289-2182*
**Fax Area Code:* 301 ■ *Web:* www.reliancecolor.com
Shutterfly.com 2800 Bridge Pkwy Suite 101 ... Redwood City CA 94065 650-610-5200 654-1299
Web: www.shutterfly.com
Snapfish 303 2nd St South Tower Suite 500 ... San Francisco CA 94107 301-595-5308 975-3708*
**Fax Area Code:* 415 ■ *Web:* www.snapfish.com
Yahoo! Photos 701 1st Ave ... Sunnyvale CA 94089 408-349-3300 349-3301
TF: 888-267-7574 ■ *Web:* photos.yahoo.com

592 PHOTOCOPYING EQUIPMENT & SUPPLIES

SEE ALSO Business Machines - Whol p. 1402

	Phone	Fax

Brother International Corp 100 Somerset Corporate Blvd ... Bridgewater NJ 08807 908-704-1700 704-8235
TF Cust Svc: 800-276-7746 ■ *Web:* www.brother-usa.com
Canon USA Inc 1 Canon Plaza ... Lake Success NY 11042 516-488-6700 328-4669*
NYSE: CAJ ■ **Fax:* Hum Res ■ *TF:* 800-828-4040 ■ *Web:* www.usa.canon.com
Eastman Kodak Co 343 State St ... Rochester NY 14650 800-698-3324
NYSE: EK ■ *Web:* www.kodak.com
Kodak Co 343 State St ... Rochester NY 14650 800-698-3324
NYSE: EK ■ *Web:* www.kodak.com
Konica Minolta Business Solutions USA Inc 100 Williams Dr ... Ramsey NJ 07446 201-825-4000
Web: www.kmbs.konicaminolta.us
Kyocera Mita America Inc 225 Sand Rd PO Box 40008 ... Fairfield NJ 07004 973-808-8444 882-4418
Web: www.kyoceramita.com
Oce-USA Inc 5450 N Cumberland Ave 6th Fl ... Chicago IL 60656 773-714-8500 693-7634
TF: 800-877-6232 ■ *Web:* www.oceusa.com
Ricoh Corp 5 Dedrick Pl ... West Caldwell NJ 07006 973-882-2000 244-2605*
**Fax:* Mail Rm ■ *TF:* 800-637-4264 ■ *Web:* www.ricoh-usa.com
Sharp Electronics Corp 1 Sharp Plaza ... Mahwah NJ 07430 201-529-8200 529-8413
TF: 800-237-4277 ■ *Web:* www.sharpusa.com
Toshiba America Inc 1251 Ave of the Americas Suite 4100 ... New York NY 10020 212-596-0600 593-3875
TF: 800-457-7777 ■ *Web:* www.toshiba.com
Xerox Canada Inc 5650 Yonge St ... North York ON M2M4G7 416-229-3769 733-6811
TF: 800-275-9376 ■ *Web:* www.xerox.ca
Xerox Corp 800 Long Ridge Rd ... Stamford CT 06904 203-968-3000 968-3508*
NYSE: XRX ■ **Fax:* Mail Rm ■ *TF:* 800-842-0024 ■ *Web:* www.xerox.com

593 PHOTOGRAPH STUDIOS - PORTRAIT

	Phone	Fax

Alderman Studios 325 Model Farm Rd ... High Point NC 27263 336-889-6121 889-7717
Bryn-Alan Studios Inc 606 W Kennedy Blvd ... Tampa FL 33606 813-253-2891 251-6548
TF: 800-749-2796 ■ *Web:* www.bryn-alan.com
CPI Corp 1706 Washington Ave ... Saint Louis MO 63103 314-231-1575 231-2398*
NYSE: CPY ■ **Fax:* Hum Res ■ *TF:* 800-669-9699 ■ *Web:* www.cpicorp.com
Jostens Inc 3601 Minnesota Ave Suite 400 ... Minneapolis MN 55435 952-830-3300 830-3309*
**Fax:* Hum Res ■ *TF:* 800-235-4774 ■ *Web:* www.jostens.com
Lifetouch Inc 11000 Viking Dr ... Eden Prairie MN 55344 952-826-4000 826-5982*
**Fax:* Cust Svc ■ *Web:* www.lifetouch.com
Lil' Angels LLC 4041 Hatcher Cir ... Memphis TN 38118 901-682-4470 682-2018
TF: 800-358-9101 ■ *Web:* www.angelsus.com
Olan Mills Inc Box 23456 ... Chattanooga TN 37422 423-622-5141 629-8106
TF: 800-251-6320 ■ *Web:* www.olanmills.com
PCA International Inc 815 Mathews Mint Hill Rd ... Matthews NC 28105 704-847-8011 847-8010
TF Cust Svc: 877-763-4456 ■ *Web:* www.pcaintl.com
Picture People 1157 Triton Dr Suite B ... Foster City CA 94404 650-578-9291 578-9881
TF: 800-827-4686 ■ *Web:* www.picturepeople.com
Root Studios Inc 1131 W Sheridan Rd ... Chicago IL 60660 773-761-5500 761-7039
TF: 800-962-8089
Shugart Studios Inc 812 College Ave ... Levelland TX 79336 806-894-4322 894-7388
TF: 800-888-4322 ■ *Web:* www.shugartstudios.com

594 PHOTOGRAPHIC EQUIPMENT & SUPPLIES

SEE ALSO Cameras & Related Supplies - Retail p. 1404

	Phone	Fax

3M Electro Solutions Div
6801 River Place Blvd 3M Austin Center ... Austin TX 78726 800-328-1371 984-6550*
**Fax Area Code:* 512 ■ *Web:* www.3m.com/meetings
Agfa Corp 100 Challenger Rd ... Ridgefield Park NJ 07660 201-440-2500 342-4742
TF: 800-581-2432 ■ *Web:* www.agfa.com/usa
AIPTEK Inc 51 Discovery Suite 100 ... Irvine CA 92618 949-585-9600 585-9345
Web: www.aiptek.com
Alan Gordon Enterprises Inc 5625 Melrose Ave ... Hollywood CA 90038 323-466-3561 871-2193
TF: 800-825-6684 ■ *Web:* www.alangordon.com
Apollo Presentation Products 300 Tower Pkwy ... Lincolnshire IL 60069 800-777-3750 247-1317
Web: www.apollopresentations.com
Avant Inc 238 Bemis Rd ... Fitchburg MA 01420 978-345-8200 345-8282
TF: 800-433-6843 ■ *Web:* www.photo-id.com
Ballantyne of Omaha Inc 4350 McKinley St ... Omaha NE 68112 402-453-4444 453-7238
AMEX: BTN ■ *TF:* 800-262-5016 ■ *Web:* www.ballantyne-omaha.com
BenQ America Corp 53 Discovery ... Irvine CA 92618 949-255-9500 255-9600
TF: 866-600-2367 ■ *Web:* www.benq.com
Beseler Charles Co 1560 NW Blvd ... Vineland NJ 08360 856-696-5700 966-4515*
**Fax Area Code:* 800 ■ *TF:* 800-237-3537 ■ *Web:* www.beselerphoto.com
Beta Screen Corp 707 Commercial Ave ... Carlstadt NJ 07072 201-939-2400 939-7656
TF: 800-272-7336 ■ *Web:* www.betascreen.com
Boxlight Corp 19302 Powder Hill Pl NE Suite 101 ... Poulsbo WA 98370 360-779-7901 779-3299
TF: 800-762-5757 ■ *Web:* www.boxlight.com
Canon USA Inc 1 Canon Plaza ... Lake Success NY 11042 516-488-6700 328-4669*
NYSE: CAJ ■ **Fax:* Hum Res ■ *TF:* 800-828-4040 ■ *Web:* www.usa.canon.com
Carr Corp 1547 11th St ... Santa Monica CA 90401 310-587-1113 395-9751
TF: 800-952-2398 ■ *Web:* www.carrcorporation.com
Casio Inc 570 Mt Pleasant Ave ... Dover NJ 07801 973-361-5400 537-8910*
**Fax:* Hum Res ■ *TF Cust Svc:* 800-634-1895 ■ *Web:* www.casio.com
Ceiva Logic Inc 214 E Magnolia Blvd ... Burbank CA 91502 818-562-1495 562-1491
TF Tech Supp: 877-693-7263 ■ *Web:* www.ceiva.com
Century Div Schneider Optics 7701 Haskell Ave ... Van Nuys CA 91406 818-766-3715 505-9865
TF: 800-228-1254 ■ *Web:* www.centuryoptics.com
Champion Photochemistry 1760 Meyerside Dr ... Mississauga ON L5T1A3 905-670-7900 670-2581
Web: www.championphotochemistry.com

	City	State	Zip	Phone	Fax
Charles Beseler Co 1560 NW Blvd *Fax Area Code: 800 ■ TF: 800-237-3537 ■ Web: www.beselerphoto.com	Vineland	NJ	08360	856-696-5700	966-4515*
Chicony America Inc 53 Parker Web: www.chicony.com.tw	Irvine	CA	92618	949-380-0928	380-9204
Concord Camera Corp 4000 Hollywood Blvd Suite 650N NASDAQ: LENS ■ TF: 800-339-4215 ■ Web: www.concord-camera.com	Hollywood	FL	33021	954-331-4200	981-3055
Da-Lite Screen Co Inc 3100 N Detroit St TF: 800-622-3737 ■ Web: www.da-lite.com	Warsaw	IN	46581	574-267-8101	267-7804
Dietzgen 250 S Northwest Hwy Suite 203 TF Cust Svc: 800-473-1270 ■ Web: www.dietzgen.com	Park Ridge	IL	60068	800-473-1200	473-9070
Draper Shade & Screen Co 411 S Pearl St TF: 800-238-7999 ■ Web: www.draperinc.com	Spiceland	IN	47385	765-987-7999	987-7142
DRS Data & Imaging Systems Inc 138 Bauer Dr Web: www.drs.com	Oakland	NJ	07436	201-337-3800	337-2704
Dukane Communication Systems 2900 Dukane Dr Web: www.dukcorp.com	Saint Charles	IL	60174	630-584-2300	584-2370
Eastman Kodak Co 343 State St NYSE: EK ■ Web: www.kodak.com	Rochester	NY	14650	800-698-3324	
Egoltronics Corp Inc PO Box 10 Web: www.egoltronics.com	Baker	WV	26801	304-897-6359	897-6556
Epson America Inc 3840 Kilroy Airport Way TF Cust Svc: 800-533-3731 ■ Web: www.epson.com	Long Beach	CA	90806	562-981-3840	290-5220
Faroudja 180 Baytech Dr Suite 110 Web: www.faroudja.com	San Jose	CA	95134	408-635-4241	957-0364
Fuji Photo Film USA Inc 200 Summit Lake Dr TF: 800-755-3854 ■ Web: www.fujifilm.com	Valhalla	NY	10595	914-789-8100	789-8295
Gordon Alan Enterprises Inc 5625 Melrose Ave TF: 800-825-6684 ■ Web: www.alangordon.com	Hollywood	CA	90038	323-466-3561	871-2193
Identatronics Inc 165 N Lively Blvd TF Cust Svc: 800-323-5403 ■ Web: www.identatronics.com	Elk Grove Village	IL	60007	847-437-2654	437-2660
InFocus Corp 27700-B SW Parkway Ave NASDAQ: INFS ■ TF: 800-294-6400 ■ Web: www.infocus.com	Wilsonville	OR	97070	503-685-8888	685-8887
I/O Magic Corp 4 Marconi Web: www.iomagic.com	Irvine	CA	92618	949-707-4800	855-3550
Kodak Co 343 State St NYSE: EK ■ Web: www.kodak.com	Rochester	NY	14650	800-698-3324	
Konica Minolta Sensing Americas Inc 101 Williams Dr TF: 888-473-2656 ■ Web: se.konicaminolta.us	Ramsey	NJ	07446	201-825-4000	
Mustek Inc 15271 Barranca Pkwy TF: 800-308-7226 ■ Web: www.mustek.com	Irvine	CA	92618	949-790-3800	788-3670
Nature Vision Inc 1480 Northern Pacific Rd NASDAQ: NRVN ■ TF: 866-777-0733 ■ Web: www.naturevisioninc.com	Brainerd	MN	56401	218-825-0733	825-0721
Navitar Inc 200 Commerce Dr TF Cust Svc: 800-828-6778 ■ Web: www.navitar.com	Rochester	NY	14623	585-359-4000	359-4999
Neumade Products Corp 30-40 Pecks Ln TF: 800-645-6687 ■ Web: www.neumade.com	Newtown	CT	06470	203-270-1100	270-7778
Neumade Products Corp Xetron Theatre Products Div 30-40 Pecks Ln TF: 800-526-0722	Newtown	CT	06470	203-270-1100	270-7778
Nikon Inc 1300 Walt Whitman Rd TF Cust Svc: 800-645-6687 ■ Web: www.nikonusa.com	Melville	NY	11747	631-547-4200	547-0299
O'Connor Engineering 100 Kalmus Dr Web: www.ocon.com	Costa Mesa	CA	92626	714-979-3993	957-8138
Oji ILFORD USA 1350 Main St TF: 888-453-6731 ■ Web: www.ilford.com	Springfield	MA	01103	413-732-8269	732-8033
Olympus America Inc 2 Corporate Center Dr *Fax: Sales ■ TF: 800-446-5967 ■ Web: www.olympusamerica.com	Melville	NY	11747	631-844-5000	844-5110*
Panasonic Communications & Systems Co 1 Panasonic Way *Fax: Hum Res ■ TF Cust Svc: 800-211-7262 ■ Web: www.panasonic.com	Secaucus	NJ	07094	201-348-7000	392-6007*
Panavision Inc 6219 DeSoto Ave TF: 800-367-7262 ■ Web: www.panavision.com	Woodland Hills	CA	91367	818-316-1000	316-1111
Pentax Imaging Co 600 12th St Suite 300 TF: 800-877-0155 ■ Web: www.pentaximaging.com	Golden	CO	80401	303-799-8000	728-0217
Phase One Inc 200 Broadhollow Rd Suite 312 TF: 888-742-7366 ■ Web: www.phaseone.com	Melville	NY	11747	631-757-0400	547-9898
Pic-Mount Imaging Corp 2300 Arrowhead Dr TF: 800-458-6875 ■ Web: www.pic-mount.com	Carson City	NV	89706	775-887-5100	887-5138
Pictorvision 7701 Haskel Ave Suite B TF: 800-876-5583 ■ Web: www.pictorvision.com	Van Nuys	CA	91406	818-785-9282	785-9787
Polaroid Corp 1265 Main St Suite W-3 *Fax: Hum Res ■ TF Cust Svc: 800-343-5000 ■ Web: www.polaroid.com	Waltham	MA	02451	781-386-2000	386-9698*
QuickSet International Inc 3650 Woodhead Dr TF Orders: 800-247-6563 ■ Web: www.tripods.com	Northbrook	IL	60062	847-498-0700	498-1258
Redlake MASD LLC 3440 E Britannia Dr TF: 800-453-1223 ■ Web: www.redlake.com	Tucson	AZ	85706	520-547-2772	547-2697
Reprographics One Inc 36060 Industrial Rd TF: 800-968-7788 ■ Web: www.reprographicsone.com	Livonia	MI	48150	734-542-8800	542-8480
Research Technology International Inc 4700 W Chase Ave TF Sales: 800-323-7520 ■ Web: www.rti-us.com	Lincolnwood	IL	60712	847-677-3000	677-1311
Ricoh Corp 5 Dedrick Pl *Fax: Mail Rm ■ TF: 800-637-4264 ■ Web: www.ricoh-usa.com	West Caldwell	NJ	07006	973-882-2000	244-2605*
RTI Group 4700 W Chase Ave TF Sales: 800-323-7520 ■ Web: www.rti-us.com	Lincolnwood	IL	60712	847-677-3000	677-1311
Sanyo Fisher Co 21605 Plummer St Web: us.sanyo.com	Chatsworth	CA	91311	818-998-7322	701-4194
Schneider Optics Century Div 7701 Haskell Ave TF: 800-228-1254 ■ Web: www.centuryoptics.com	Van Nuys	CA	91406	818-766-3715	505-9865
Sharp Electronics Corp 1 Sharp Plaza TF: 800-237-4277 ■ Web: www.sharpusa.com	Mahwah	NJ	07430	201-529-8200	529-8413
Sony Corp of America 550 Madison Ave TF: 800-282-2848 ■ Web: www.sony.com	New York	NY	10022	212-833-6800	
Stewart Filmscreen Corp 1161 W Sepulveda Blvd TF: 800-762-4999 ■ Web: www.stewartfilm.com	Torrance	CA	90502	310-326-1422	326-6870
Tiffen Co LLC 90 Oser Ave TF: 800-645-2522 ■ Web: www.tiffen.com	Hauppauge	NY	11788	631-273-2500	273-2557
Toshiba America Inc 1251 Ave of the Americas Suite 4100 TF: 800-457-7777 ■ Web: www.toshiba.com	New York	NY	10020	212-596-0600	593-3875
Toshiba America Information Systems Inc 9740 Irvine Blvd TF Cust Svc: 800-457-7777 ■ Web: www.tais.com	Irvine	CA	92618	949-583-3000	
Universal Blueprint Paper Co 327 Bryan Ave Web: www.universalblue.com	Fort Worth	TX	76104	817-332-9634	332-5406
Visual Departures Ltd PO Box 427 TF: 800-628-2003 ■ Web: www.visualdepartures.com	Riverside	CT	06878	203-487-0789	487-0791
Vivitar Corp 520 Graves Ave Web: www.vivitar.com	Oxnard	CA	93030	805-988-0463	981-2421
Vutec Corp 2741 NE 4th Ave TF: 800-770-4700 ■ Web: www.vutec.com	Pompano Beach	FL	33064	954-545-9000	545-9011
Waterhouse Inc 670 Queen St Suite 200 Web: www.waterhouseinc.net	Honolulu	HI	96813	808-592-4800	592-4820
Wein Products Inc 115 W 25th St Web: www.weinproducts.com	Los Angeles	CA	90007	213-749-6049	749-6250
Xetron Theatre Products Div Neumade Products Corp 30-40 Pecks Ln TF: 800-526-0722	Newtown	CT	06470	203-270-1100	270-7778

595 PHOTOGRAPHY - COMMERCIAL

	City	State	Zip	Phone	Fax
Herrington-Olson Photography Inc 769 22nd St Web: www.herrington-olson.com	Oakland	CA	94612	510-452-0501	452-8388
Image Inc 1100 S Lynndale Dr Web: www.imagestudios.com	Appleton	WI	54914	920-738-4080	738-4089
Kinetic Corp 200 Distillery Commons Suite 200 Web: www.kinetic.distillery.com	Louisville	KY	40206	502-719-9500	719-9509
Kreber Enterprises 221 Swathmore Ave TF: 800-775-3801 ■ Web: www.kreber.com	High Point	NC	27263	336-861-2700	861-2802
Universal Image 7121 Grand National Dr Suite 104 TF: 800-553-5499 ■ Web: www.universalphoto.com	Orlando	FL	32819	407-352-5302	351-5163

596 PHOTOGRAPHY - STOCK

	City	State	Zip	Phone	Fax
911 Pictures 60 Accabonac Rd Web: www.911pictures.com	East Hampton	NY	11937	631-324-2061	329-9264
Alaska Stock Images 2505 Fairbanks St TF: 800-487-4285 ■ Web: www.alaskastock.com	Anchorage	AK	99503	907-276-1343	258-7848
Bruce Coleman Inc 111 Brook St TF: 800-942-7917 ■ Web: www.brucecoleman.com	Scarsdale	NY	10583	914-713-4821	722-8347
Bygone Designs PO Box 229 Web: www.bygones.com	Newport	MN	55055	651-451-6737	
Coleman Bruce Inc 111 Brook St TF: 800-942-7917 ■ Web: www.brucecoleman.com	Scarsdale	NY	10583	914-713-4821	722-8347
Comstock Images 244 Sheffield St *Fax Area Code: 800 ■ TF: 800-225-2722 ■ Web: www.comstock.com	Mountainside	NJ	07092	908-518-6200	331-3033*
Corbis Corp 710 2nd Ave Suite 200 TF: 800-260-0444 ■ Web: pro.corbis.com	Seattle	WA	98104	206-373-6000	373-6100
Custom Medical Stock Photo Inc 3660 W Irving Park Rd TF: 800-373-2677 ■ Web: www.cmsp.com	Chicago	IL	60618	773-267-3100	267-6071
EarthWater Stock Photography 1728 Virginia Beach Blvd Suite 106 Web: www.earthwater.com	Virginia Beach	VA	23454	757-491-3060	422-2798
Film & Video Stock Shots 10442 Burbank Blvd TF: 888-436-6824 ■ Web: www.stockshots.com	North Hollywood	CA	91601	818-760-2098	760-3294
George Hall Check Six 426 Greenwood Beach Rd Web: www.check-6.com	Tiburon	CA	94920	415-381-6363	383-4935
George Hall Code Red 426 Greenwood Beach Rd Web: www.code-red.com	Tiburon	CA	94920	415-381-6363	383-4935
Getty Images Inc 601 N 34th St NYSE: GYI ■ TF: 800-462-4379 ■ Web: www.gettyimages.com	Seattle	WA	98103	206-925-5000	925-5001
Great American Stock 1375 N Barker Rd *Fax Area Code: 800 ■ TF: 800-624-5834 ■ Web: www.greatamericanstock.com	Brookfield	WI	53045	262-782-6000	782-6222*
Highway Images PO Box 72249 Web: www.highwayimages.com	Thorndale	PA	19372	610-380-0342	380-0315
Image Works 1679 Rt 212 TF: 800-475-8801 ■ Web: www.theimageworks.com	Woodstock	NY	12498	845-679-8500	679-0606
ImageState New York 29 E 19th St 4th Fl TF: 800-821-9600 ■ Web: www.imagestate.com	New York	NY	10003	212-505-2500	358-9101
ImagiGraphics Inc 20 Mills St	Kalamazoo	MI	49048	269-383-9195	345-6999
Index Stock Imagery Inc 23 W 18th St 3rd Fl TF: 800-729-7466 ■ Web: www.indexstock.com	New York	NY	10011	212-929-4644	633-1914
Ink Jet Art Solutions Inc 346 S 500 East Suite 200 TF: 800-777-2076 ■ Web: www.inkjetart.com	Salt Lake City	UT	84102	801-363-9700	363-9707
Jupiterimages Corp 8280 Greensboro Dr Suite 520 TF: 800-764-7427 ■ Web: www.jupiterimages.com	McLean	VA	22102	703-770-5350	770-5349
Midwestock 9218 Metcalf Ave Suite 145 *Fax Area Code: 888 ■ TF: 800-474-9974 ■ Web: www.midwestock.com	Overland Park	KS	66212	816-474-0229	474-0229*
Mountain Light Photography Inc 106 S Main St Web: www.mountainlight.com	Bishop	CA	93514	760-873-7700	873-3980
Photo Researchers Inc 60 E 56th St TF: 800-833-9033 ■ Web: www.photoresearchers.com	New York	NY	10022	212-758-3420	355-0731
Photo Resource Hawaii 111 Hekili St Suite 241 TF: 888-599-7773 ■ Web: www.photoresourcehawaii.com	Kailua	HI	96734	808-599-7773	235-5477
Photri 3701 S George Mason Dr Suite C-2N TF: 800-544-0385 ■ Web: www.microstock.com	Falls Church	VA	22041	703-931-8600	998-8407
PictureQuest 8280 Greensboro Dr Suite 520 TF: 800-764-7427 ■ Web: www.picturequest.com	McLean	VA	22102	703-770-5350	770-5349
Picturesque Stock Photo Agency 1520-3 Brookside Dr TF: 800-450-3377 ■ Web: www.picturesque.com	Raleigh	NC	27604	919-828-0023	
PunchStock 8517 Excelsior Dr Suite 200 TF: 800-390-0461 ■ Web: www.punchstock.com	Madison	WI	53717	608-828-2700	828-9669
Rainbow 61 Entrada TF: 800-810-3686 ■ Web: www.rainbowimages.com	Santa Fe	NM	87507	505-820-3434	
Silver Image Photo Agency 4104 NW 70th Terr Web: www.silver-image.com	Gainesville	FL	32606	352-373-5771	374-4074
Stockyard Photos 1410 Hutchins St Web: www.stockyard.com	Houston	TX	77003	713-520-0898	227-0399

597 PIECE GOODS & NOTIONS

SEE ALSO Fabric Stores p. 1630

	City	State	Zip	Phone	Fax
A Meyers & Sons Corp 325 W 38th St TF: 800-666-5577 ■ Web: www.safetypins.com	New York	NY	10018	212-279-6632	594-4093
Allen Robert Fabrics Inc 55 Cabot Blvd *Fax: Sales ■ TF: 800-333-3777 ■ Web: www.robertallendesign.com	Mansfield	MA	02048	508-339-9151	339-4106*
American Tape Measures Inc 4001 N Ravenswood Ave Suite 604 Web: www.americantapemeasures.com	Chicago	IL	60613	773-327-6667	327-6318
Aplix Inc PO Box 7505 TF: 800-438-0424 ■ Web: www.aplix.com	Charlotte	NC	28241	704-588-1920	588-1941
Associated Fabrics Corp 104 E 25th St *Fax Area Code: 800 ■ Web: www.afcnewyork.com	New York	NY	10010	212-689-7186	232-4077*
B & B Button & Trim 263 W 38th St 15th Fl	New York	NY	10018	212-921-2020	631-0075
B Berger Co 1380 Highland Rd TF Cust Svc: 800-288-8400	Macedonia	OH	44056	330-425-3838	425-9797
Barrow Industries 3 Edgewater Dr TF: 800-332-2776 ■ Web: www.barrowindustries.com	Norwood	MA	02062	781-828-6750	440-2683
Baum Textile Mills Inc 812 Jersey Ave TF: 866-842-7631 ■ Web: www.baumtextile.com	Jersey City	NJ	07310	201-659-0444	659-9719
Blank Textiles Inc 2 Bridge St Suite 220 TF: 800-237-3717	Irvington	NY	10533	914-478-3100	478-4456

Company	City	State	Zip	Phone	Fax
Blumenthal Lansing Co 1 Palmer Terr	Carlstadt	NJ	07072	201-935-6220	935-0055
TF: 800-448-9749 ■ *Web:* www.buttonsplus.com					
Boody Irving R & Co Inc 11 Penn Plaza Suite 310	New York	NY	10001	212-947-8300	947-8302
Brittany Fabrics Inc 57 W 38th St 4th Fl	New York	NY	10018	212-391-1250	391-5691
Brookwood Cos Inc 232 Madison Ave 10th Fl	New York	NY	10016	212-551-0100	686-5626
TF: 800-426-5468 ■ *Web:* www.brookwoodcos.net					
Brunschwig & Fils 75 Virginia Rd	North White Plains	NY	10603	914-684-5800	684-5842
TF: 800-538-8280 ■ *Web:* www.brunschwig.com					
Burch Fabrics Group 4200 Brockton Dr SE	Grand Rapids	MI	49512	616-698-2800	698-0011
TF: 800-841-8111 ■ *Web:* www.burchfabrics.com					
Carolyn Fabrics Inc 1948 W Green Dr	High Point	NC	27261	336-887-3101	887-2895
TF: 800-333-8400 ■ *Web:* www.carolynfabrics.com					
Charter Fabrics Inc 1430 Broadway 4th Fl	New York	NY	10018	212-391-8110	944-9095
Coats & Clark Inc 3430 Toringdon Way Suite 301	Charlotte	NC	28227	704-329-5800	329-5025
Cresthill Industries Inc 196 Ashburton Ave	Yonkers	NY	10701	914-965-9510	965-9534
Custom Metal Crafters Inc 815 N Mountain Rd	Newington	CT	06111	860-953-4210	953-1746
TF: 800-262-3140 ■ *Web:* www.custom-metal.com					
Delta Mills Marketing Co 1071 Ave of the Americas 12th Fl	New York	NY	10018	212-642-9700	
Design/Craft Fabrics Corp 2230 Ridge Dr	Glenview	IL	60025	847-904-7000	904-7102
Web: www.design-craft.com					
Dunlap Industries Inc PO Box 459	Dunlap	TN	37327	423-949-4021	949-3648
TF: 800-251-7214 ■ *Web:* www.dunlapworld.com					
Duralee Fabrics Ltd Inc 1775 5th Ave	Bay Shore	NY	11706	631-273-8800	275-3297*
**Fax Area Code:* 800 ■ **Fax:* Cust Svc ■ *TF Cust Svc:* 800-275-3872 ■ *Web:* www.duralee.com					
Eagle Button Co Inc PO Box 97	Carlstadt	NJ	07072	201-935-3990	935-7188
Web: www.eaglebutton.com					
Edgar Fabrics Inc 50 Commerce Dr	Hauppauge	NY	11788	631-435-8989	435-9151
EE Schenck Co PO Box 5200	Portland	OR	97208	503-284-4124	288-4475
TF: 800-433-0722 ■ *Web:* www.eeschenck.com					
Glick Textiles 2327 SW Fwy	Houston	TX	77098	713-942-9191	942-9292
TF: 800-231-7246 ■ *Web:* www.glicktextiles.com					
Grove Textiles Inc 150 E Grove St	Scranton	PA	18510	570-344-1174	344-1177
Haber Fabrics Corp 1745 Hayden Dr	Carrollton	TX	75006	972-416-8479	416-1679
TF: 800-527-1980 ■ *Web:* www.haberfabrics.com					
Hanes Industries 500 N McLin Creek Rd	Conover	NC	28613	828-464-4673	464-0459
TF: 800-438-9124 ■ *Web:* www.hanesindustries.com					
Hoffman California Fabrics Inc 25792 Obrero Dr	Mission Viejo	CA	92691	949-770-2922	770-4022
TF: 800-547-0100 ■ *Web:* www.hoffmanfabrics.com					
Ideal Fastener Corp PO Box 548	Oxford	NC	27565	919-693-3115	693-3118
TF: 800-334-6653 ■ *Web:* www.idealfastener.com					
Integrity Textiles Inc 909 Louis Dr PO Box 2457	Warminster	PA	18974	215-957-3339	957-5897
Irving R Boody & Co Inc 11 Penn Plaza Suite 310	New York	NY	10001	212-947-8300	947-8302
Jaftex Corp 49 W 37th St	New York	NY	10018	212-686-5194	545-0058
Janlynn Corp 2070 Westover Rd	Chicopee	MA	01022	413-206-0002	206-0060
TF: 800-445-5565 ■ *Web:* www.janlynn.com					
JHB International Inc 1955 S Quince St	Denver	CO	80231	303-751-8100	751-3131
TF: 800-525-9007 ■ *Web:* www.buttons.com					
John K Burch Co 4200 Brockton Dr SE	Grand Rapids	MI	49512	616-698-2800	698-0011
TF: 800-841-8111 ■ *Web:* www.burchfabrics.com					
Kabat Textile Corp 247 W 37th St 10th Fl	New York	NY	10018	212-398-0011	719-9706
Kaplan-Simon Co Inc 115 Messina Dr	Braintree	MA	02184	781-848-6500	848-6506
Keyston Bros 2801 Academy Way	Sacramento	CA	95815	916-646-1834	
Web: www.keystonbros.com					
Komar Apparel Supply Co LLC 6900 Washington Blvd	Montebello	CA	90640	323-890-3000	890-3003
TF: 800-872-7397 ■ *Web:* www.komar.com					
Kravet Fabrics Inc 225 Central Ave S	Bethpage	NY	11714	516-293-2000	293-2158
TF Cust Svc: 800-648-5728 ■ *Web:* www.kravet.com					
Line Mfg Inc PO Box 6505	Wolcott	CT	06716	203-879-1481	
Logantex Inc 70 W 36th St Suite 1001	New York	NY	10018	212-221-3900	398-9817
TF: 800-223-2004					
Lora Piana Co 8 Furance Ave	Stafford Springs	CT	06076	860-684-2766	684-7500
Maharam 45 Rasons Ct	Hauppauge	NY	11788	631-582-3434	582-1026
TF: 800-645-3943 ■ *Web:* www.maharam.com					
Majilite Corp 1530 Broadway Rd	Dracut	MA	01826	978-441-6800	441-0826
Web: www.majilite.com					
Marcus Brothers Textiles Inc 980 Ave of the Americas	New York	NY	10018	212-354-8700	768-0799
TF: 800-548-8295 ■ *Web:* www.marcusbrothers.com					
Mayar Silk Inc 15 W 36th St	New York	NY	10018	212-564-1380	564-2329
McKee Button Co Inc PO Box 230	Muscatine	IA	52761	563-263-2421	264-5365
TF Cust Svc: 800-553-9662 ■ *Web:* www.mckeebutton.com					
Merrimac Textile 3 Edgewater Dr	Norwood	MA	02062	781-440-2666	440-2683
Web: www.barrowindustries.com					
Meyers A & Sons Corp 325 W 38th St	New York	NY	10018	212-279-6632	594-4093
TF: 800-666-5577 ■ *Web:* www.safetypins.com					
Miroglio Textiles USA Inc 1430 Broadway 6th Fl	New York	NY	10018	212-382-2020	382-2609
Web: www.miroglio.com					
Modern Button Co 3957 S Hill St	Los Angeles	CA	90037	213-749-1215	747-6162
Web: www.zabin.com					
Peachtree Fabrics Inc 1400 English St	Atlanta	GA	30318	404-351-5400	351-5270
TF: 800-732-2437 ■ *Web:* www.peachtreefabrics.com					
Prym-Dritz Corp 950 Brisack Rd	Spartanburg	SC	29303	864-576-5050	587-3352*
**Fax:* Cust Svc ■ *TF Cust Svc:* 800-255-7796 ■ *Web:* www.dritz.com					
Raylon Corp 1430 Broadway	New York	NY	10018	212-221-3633	921-2947
Raytex Fabrics Inc 130 Crossways Park Dr	Woodbury	NY	11797	516-584-1111	584-1035
Richloom Fabrics Group 261 5th Ave	New York	NY	10016	212-685-5400	696-4407
Robert Allen Fabrics Inc 55 Cabot Blvd	Mansfield	MA	02048	508-339-9151	339-4106*
**Fax:* Sales ■ *TF:* 800-333-3777 ■ *Web:* www.robertallendesign.com					
Rockville Fabrics Corp 99 W Hawthorne Ave	Valley Stream	NY	10580	516-561-9810	
Web: www.rockvillefabrics.com					
Rome Fastener Corp PO Box 3013	Milford	CT	06460	203-874-6719	877-0201
Web: www.romefast.com					
Saint Louis Trimming Div Trimtex 400 Park Ave	Williamsport	PA	17701	570-326-9135	326-4250
TF: 800-326-9135 ■ *Web:* www.trimtex.com					
Schenck EE Co PO Box 5200	Portland	OR	97208	503-284-4124	288-4475
TF: 800-433-0722 ■ *Web:* www.eeschenck.com					
Scher Fabrics Inc 450 7th Ave Suite 1008	New York	NY	10123	212-382-2266	869-0920
TF: 800-289-0025					
Schott International Inc 2850 Gilchrist Rd	Akron	OH	44305	330-773-7851	773-7856
TF: 800-321-2178 ■ *Web:* www.schottint.com					
Scovill Fasteners Inc 1802 Scovill Dr	Clarkesville	GA	30523	706-754-1000	754-4000*
**Fax:* Cust Svc ■ *TF Cust Svc:* 800-756-4734 ■ *Web:* www.scovill.com					
Spradling International Inc 200 Cahaba Valley Pkwy PO Box 1668	Pelham	AL	35124	205-985-4206	985-9176
TF: 800-333-0955 ■ *Web:* www.spradlingvinyl.com					
Stroheim & Romann Inc 31-11 Thomson Ave	Long Island City	NY	11101	718-706-7000	361-0159
TF: 800-974-8444 ■ *Web:* www.stroheim.com					
Symphony Fabrics Corp 229 W 36th St 2nd Fl	New York	NY	10018	212-244-6700	736-0123
Web: www.symphonyfabrics.com					
Tag-It Pacific Inc 21900 Burbank Blvd Suite 270	Woodland Hills	CA	91367	818-444-4100	444-4105
AMEX: TAG ■ *TF:* 800-335-4443 ■ *Web:* www.tagitpacific.com					
Threadtex Inc 1350 Ave of the Americas 10th Fl	New York	NY	10019	212-713-1800	977-4480
Tiger Button Co Inc 307 W 38th St 4th Fl	New York	NY	10018	212-594-0570	695-0265
TF: 800-223-2754 ■ *Web:* www.tigerbutton.com					
Tingue Brown & Co 535 N Midland Ave	Saddle Brook	NJ	07663	201-796-4490	796-5820
TF Sales: 800-829-4536 ■ *Web:* www.tingue.com					
Titan Textile Co Inc 53 E 34th St	Paterson	NJ	07514	973-684-1600	684-2610*
**Fax:* Hum Res ■ *Web:* www.titantextile.com					
Trimtex Saint Louis Trimming Div 400 Park Ave	Williamsport	PA	17701	570-326-9135	326-4250
TF: 800-326-9135 ■ *Web:* www.trimtex.com					
United Notions Inc 13800 Hutton St	Dallas	TX	75234	972-484-8901	468-4209*
**Fax Area Code:* 800 ■ *TF:* 800-527-9447 ■ *Web:* www.unitednotions.com					
US Button Corp 328 Kennedy Dr	Putnam	CT	06260	860-928-2707	928-2847
TF: 800-243-1842 ■ *Web:* www.usbutton.com					
Velcro USA Inc 406 Brown Ave	Manchester	NH	03108	603-669-4880	669-3086
TF: 800-225-0180 ■ *Web:* www.velcro.com					
Warren of Stafford Corp 8 Furance Ave	Stafford Springs	CT	06076	860-684-2766	684-7500
Waterbury Button Co 1855 Peck Ln	Cheshire	CT	06410	203-271-9055	271-9852
TF: 800-431-4433 ■ *Web:* www.waterburybutton.com					
Weber & Sons Button Co Inc PO Box 96	Muscatine	IA	52761	563-263-9451	264-3953
Westgate Payne Fabrics Inc 1517 W North Carrier Pkwy Suite 116	Grand Prairie	TX	75050	972-647-2323	660-7096
TF: 800-527-2517 ■ *Web:* www.westgatefabrics.com					
Wonalancet Co 1130 Senoia Rd Suite A-2	Tyrone	GA	30290	770-774-2820	774-2824
YKK Snap Fasteners America Inc PO Box 240	Lawrenceburg	KY	40342	502-839-6971	839-6525*
**Fax:* Sales ■ *TF:* 800-786-2561 ■ *Web:* www.ykksnap-america.com					
YKK USA Inc 1251 Valley Brook Ave	Lyndhurst	NJ	07071	201-935-4200	935-4745
Web: www.ykkfastening.com					
Zabin Industries Inc 3957 S Hill St	Los Angeles	CA	90037	213-749-1215	747-6162
Web: www.zabin.com					
Zoffany/Sanderson 285 Grand Ave 3 Patriot Ctr	Englewood	NJ	07631	201-894-8400	894-6098*
**Fax Area Code:* 800 ■ *TF:* 800-894-6185					

598 PIPE & PIPE FITTINGS - METAL (FABRICATED)

SEE ALSO Metal Tube & Pipe p. 1964

Company	City	State	Zip	Phone	Fax
Acme Mfg Co 7601 State Rd	Philadelphia	PA	19136	215-338-2850	335-1905
TF: 800-899-2850					
Airdrome Precision Components 3251 E Airport Way	Long Beach	CA	90806	562-426-9411	492-6909
Web: www.airdrome.com					
Allegan Tubular Products Inc 1276 Lincoln Rd	Allegan	MI	49010	269-673-6636	673-2477
Web: www.allegantube.com					
Allied Chucker & Engineering Co 3529 Scheele Dr	Jackson	MI	49202	517-787-1370	787-2878
Alloy Stainless Products Co 611 Union Blvd	Totowa	NJ	07512	973-256-1616	256-5256
TF: 800-631-8372 ■ *Web:* www.alloystainless.com					
AY McDonald Mfg Co 4800 Chavenelle Rd	Dubuque	IA	52002	563-583-7311	588-0720
TF Cust Svc: 800-292-2737 ■ *Web:* www.aymcdonald.com					
Beck Mfg 330 E 9th St	Waynesboro	PA	17268	717-762-9141	762-9153
TF: 800-742-6621 ■ *Web:* www.beckmfg.com					
Bent Tube Inc 9649 W Van Buren Rd	Fowlerville	MI	48836	517-521-4330	521-4850
TF: 888-797-1931 ■ *Web:* benttube.com					
Betts Industries Inc 1800 Pennsylvania Ave W	Warren	PA	16365	814-723-1250	723-7030
Web: www.bettsind.com					
Burner Systems International Inc 3600 Cummings Rd	Chattanooga	TN	37419	423-822-3600	825-3710
TF: 800-251-6318 ■ *Web:* www.burnersystems.com					
Campbell Mfg Inc 127 E Spring St	Bechtelsville	PA	19505	610-367-2107	369-3580
TF: 800-523-0224 ■ *Web:* www.campbellmfg.com					
Carpenter & Paterson Inc 225 Merrimac St	Woburn	MA	01801	781-935-2950	935-7664
TF: 800-342-6437 ■ *Web:* www.carpenterpaterson.com					
Carpenter Powder Products 600 Mayer St	Bridgeville	PA	15017	412-257-5102	257-5154
TF: 866-790-9092 ■ *Web:* www.cartech.com					
Champion Manufacturing Industries Inc. 6021 N Galena Rd	Peoria	IL	61614	309-685-1031	685-1088
TF: 800-452-7473 ■ *Web:* www.championmfg.com					
Cobra Pipe Supply Inc 13 Homomick Rd	Colchester	CT	06415	860-537-5489	537-6159
TF: 877-474-7332 ■ *Web:* www.cobrapipesupply.com					
Colonial Engineering Inc 6400 Corporate Ave	Portage	MI	49002	269-323-2495	323-0630
TF: 800-374-0234 ■ *Web:* www.colonialengineering.com					
Connecticut Stamping & Bending Co 206 Newington Ave	New Britain	CT	06051	860-225-4637	229-4328
TF: 800-966-6964					
Continental Industries Inc 4102 S 74th East Ave	Tulsa	OK	74145	918-627-5210	788-1668*
**Fax Area Code:* 800 ■ *TF:* 800-558-1373 ■ *Web:* www.conind.com					
Douglas Brothers 423 Riverside Industrial Pkwy	Portland	ME	04103	207-797-6771	797-8385
TF: 800-341-0927 ■ *Web:* www.douglasbrothers.com					
Elkhart Products Corp 1255 Oak St	Elkhart	IN	46514	574-264-3181	264-4835
TF: 800-284-4851 ■ *Web:* www.elkhartproducts.com					
Empire Industries Inc 180 Olcott St	Manchester	CT	06040	860-647-1431	647-1160
TF: 800-243-4844 ■ *Web:* www.empireindustries.com					
Excelsior Mfg & Supply Corp 1465 E Industrial Dr	Itasca	IL	60143	630-773-5500	773-1612*
**Fax:* Cust Svc ■ *TF:* 800-548-8135 ■ *Web:* excelsiorhvac.com					
Fort Wayne Foundry Corp 4912 Lima Rd	Fort Wayne	IN	46808	260-483-0382	484-5719
Web: www.fortwaynefoundry.com					
General Plug & Mfg Co Inc 455 N Main St PO Box 26	Grafton	OH	44044	440-926-2411	926-3305
TF: 800-289-7584 ■ *Web:* www.generalplug.com					
Gerlin Inc 170 Tubeway Dr	Carol Stream	IL	60188	630-690-7000	690-9701
Web: www.gerlin.com					
Grant Prideco Inc 400 N Sam Houston Pkwy E Suite 900	Houston	TX	77060	281-878-8000	878-5736
NYSE: GRP ■ *TF:* 866-472-6861 ■ *Web:* www.grantprideco.com					
Griffin Pipe Products Co 1400 Opus Pl Suite 700	Downers Grove	IL	60515	630-719-6500	719-2252
Web: www.griffinpipe.com					
H-P Products Inc 512 W Gorgas St	Louisville	OH	44641	330-875-5556	875-7155
TF: 800-860-8823 ■ *Web:* www.hpproducts.net					
Hackney Ladish Inc 5945 Belt Line Rd Suite 290	Dallas	TX	75254	214-269-5600	269-5601
TF: 800-527-4500 ■ *Web:* www.hackneyladish.com					
Highfield Mfg Co 380 Mountain Grove St	Bridgeport	CT	06605	203-384-2281	368-3906
Web: www.highfield-mfg.com					
Hydro Tube Enterprises Inc 137 Artino St	Oberlin	OH	44074	440-774-1022	774-1482
Web: www.hydrotube.com					
JB Smith Mfg Co 6618 Navigation Blvd	Houston	TX	77011	713-928-5711	928-5219
Web: www.jbsmith.com					
Kelly Pipe Co LLC 11680 Bloomfield Ave	Santa Fe Springs	CA	90670	562-868-0456	863-4695
TF: 800-305-3559 ■ *Web:* www.kellypipe.com					
McDonald AY Mfg Co 4800 Chavenelle Rd	Dubuque	IA	52002	563-583-7311	588-0720
TF Cust Svc: 800-292-2737 ■ *Web:* www.aymcdonald.com					
McWane Inc 2900 Hwy 280 Suite 300	Birmingham	AL	35223	205-414-3100	414-3170
Web: www.mcwane.com					
MicroGroup Inc 7 Industrial Park Rd	Medway	MA	02053	508-533-4925	533-5691
TF: 800-255-8823 ■ *Web:* www.microgroup.com					
Mid States Pipe Fabricating Inc 205 Louis Hurley Rd	El Dorado	AR	71730	870-862-5167	862-4234
Web: www.m-p-f.com					
Mills Iron Works Inc 14834 Maple Ave	Gardena	CA	90247	323-321-6520	532-0476*
**Fax Area Code:* 310 ■ *TF:* 800-421-2281 ■ *Web:* www.millsiron.com					
Milwaukee Valve Co Inc 16550 W Stratton Dr	New Berlin	WI	53151	262-432-2800	432-2801
TF: 800-348-6544 ■ *Web:* www.milwaukeevalve.com					
Morton Welding Co Inc 70 Commerce Dr	Morton	IL	61550	309-263-2590	263-0862
Web: www.mortonwelding.com					
National Tube Form Inc 3405 Engle Rd	Fort Wayne	IN	46809	260-478-2363	478-1043
TF: 800-752-1458 ■ *Web:* www.nationaltubeform.com/-					

Phone Fax

NIBCO Inc 1516 Middlebury St .... Elkhart IN 46515 574-295-3000 295-3307
TF: 800-234-0227 ■ *Web:* www.nibco.com

Nor-Cal Products Inc 1967 S Oregon St .... Yreka CA 96097 530-842-4458 841-9189*
**Fax:* Sales ■ *TF:* 800-824-4166 ■ *Web:* www.n-c.com

Norca Corp 185 Great Neck Rd .... Great Neck NY 11022 516-466-9500 482-3367
Web: www.norca.com

NPC Inc 250 Elm St .... Milford NH 03055 603-673-8680 673-7271
TF: 800-626-2180 ■ *Web:* www.npc.com

Parker Hannifin Corp Brass Products Div 300 Parker Dr .... Otsego MI 49078 269-694-9411 694-4614
TF: 800-272-7537 ■ *Web:* www.parker.com/brassprod

Parker Hannifin Corp Instrumentation Connectors Div
1005 A Cleaner Way .... Huntsville AL 35805 256-881-2040 881-5072
Web: www.parker.com/icd

Penn Machine Co 106 Station St .... Johnstown PA 15905 814-288-1547 288-2260
TF: 800-763-0406 ■ *Web:* www.pennusa.com

Perma-Pipe Inc 7720 N Lehigh Ave .... Niles IL 60714 847-966-2235 470-1204
Web: www.permapipe.com

Propipe Technologies Inc 1800 Clayton Ave .... Middletown OH 45042 513-424-5311 424-5095

Pure-Flo Solutions Group 110-B W Cochran St .... Simi Valley CA 93065 805-520-7200 520-7205
TF: 800-926-8884 ■ *Web:* www.engvalves.com/pureflomain.htm

Richards Industries Inc 3170 Wasson Rd .... Cincinnati OH 45209 513-533-5600 871-0105*
**Fax:* Sales ■ *TF Cust Svc:* 800-543-7311 ■ *Web:* www.richardsind.com

Robert Mfg Co Inc 10667 Jersey Blvd .... Rancho Cucamonga CA 91730 909-987-4654 989-6911
TF: 800-877-6237 ■ *Web:* www.robertmfg.com

Romac Industries Inc 21919 20th Ave SE Suite 100 .... Bothell WA 98021 425-951-6200 951-6201
TF: 800-426-9341 ■ *Web:* www.romacindustries.com

Roscoe Moss Co 4360 Worth St .... Los Angeles CA 90063 323-261-4185 263-4497
TF: 800-767-2634 ■ *Web:* www.roscoemoss.com

Rovanco Piping Systems Inc 20535 SE Frontage Rd .... Joliet IL 60431 815-741-6700 741-4229
Web: www.rovanco.com

Shaw Group Inc 4171 Essen Ln .... Baton Rouge LA 70809 225-932-2500 932-2661
NYSE: SGR ■ *TF:* 800-747-3322 ■ *Web:* www.shawgrp.com

Smith JB Mfg Co 6618 Navigation Blvd .... Houston TX 77011 713-928-5711 928-5219
Web: www.jbsmith.com

Snap-Tite Inc 8325 Hessinger Dr .... Erie PA 16509 814-838-5700 833-0145
Web: www.snap-tite.com

Snoke Special Products Inc 2050 N Jackson St .... Jacksonville TX 75766 903-586-3618 586-0131

Steel Forgings Inc 1810 Barton Dr .... Shreveport LA 71107 318-222-3295 222-6185
Web: www.steelforgings.com

Swagelok Co 29500 Solon Rd .... Solon OH 44139 440-248-4600 519-1089
Web: www.swagelok.com

Synalloy Corp 2155 W Croft Cir .... Spartanburg SC 29302 864-585-3605 596-1501
NASDAQ: SYNL ■ *TF Orders:* 800-763-1001 ■ *Web:* www.synalloy.com

Tate Andale Inc 1941 Lansdowne Rd .... Baltimore MD 21227 410-247-8700 247-9672
TF: 800-296-8283 ■ *Web:* www.tateandale.com

Thermacor Process LP 1670 Hicks Field Rd E .... Fort Worth TX 76179 817-847-7300 847-7222
Web: www.thermacor.com

Tolco Inc 1375 Sampson Ave .... Corona CA 92879 951-737-5599 737-0330
TF: 888-233-1887 ■ *Web:* www.nibco.com/tolco

Tri-Clover Inc 9560 58th Pl Suite 300 .... Kenosha WI 53144 262-605-2600 605-2664

Tru-Flex Metal Hose Corp
2391 S State Rd 263 PO Box 247 .... West Lebanon IN 47991 765-893-4403 893-4114
TF: 800-255-6291 ■ *Web:* www.tru-flex.com

Tube Forming Inc 2101 W Belt Line Rd .... Carrollton TX 75006 972-512-2400 512-2401
TF: 800-513-0022

Tube Processing Corp 604 E Le Grande Ave .... Indianapolis IN 46203 317-787-1321 787-5384
TF: 800-776-4119 ■ *Web:* www.tubeproc.com

US Pipe & Foundry Co 3300 1st Ave N .... Birmingham AL 35222 205-254-7000 254-7149
Web: www.uspipe.com

Vacco Industries Inc 10350 Vacco St .... South El Monte CA 91733 626-443-7121 442-6943
Web: www.vacco.com

Victaulic Co 4901 Kesslersville Rd .... Easton PA 18040 610-559-3300 250-8817
TF Sales: 800-523-9864 ■ *Web:* www.victaulic.com

Watson McDaniel Co 428 Jones Blvd .... Pottstown PA 19464 610-495-5131 495-5134
Web: www.watsonmcdaniel.com

Watts Regulator Co 815 Chestnut St .... North Andover MA 01845 978-688-1811 689-2457*
**Fax:* Cust Svc ■ *Web:* www.wattsreg.com

Watts Water Technologies Inc 815 Chestnut St .... North Andover MA 01845 978-688-1811 689-2457*
NYSE: WTS ■ **Fax:* Cust Svc ■ *Web:* www.wattsind.com

Webster Valve Co 583 S Main St .... Franklin NH 03235 603-934-5110 934-1390

Weir Valves & Controls USA 285 Canal St .... Salem MA 01970 978-744-5690 740-9668
Web: www.weirvalves.com

Wellstream International Ltd 520 Skyview Dr .... Panama City Beach FL 32408 850-636-4800 234-6874
Web: www.wellstream.com

Wolverine Tube Inc 200 Clinton Ave W Suite 1000 .... Huntsville AL 35801 256-890-0460 890-0470
NYSE: WLV ■ *TF:* 800-633-3972 ■ *Web:* www.wlv.com

Woolf Aircraft Products Inc 6401 Cogswell Rd .... Romulus MI 48174 734-721-5330 721-3490
TF: 800-367-5475 ■ *Web:* www.woolfaircraft.com

World Wide Fittings Co Inc 7501 N Natchez Ave .... Niles IL 60714 847-588-2200 588-2212
Web: www.worldwidefittings.com

599 PIPE & PIPE FITTINGS - PLASTICS

Phone Fax

Advanced Drainage Systems Inc 4640 Trueman Blvd .... Hilliard OH 43026 614-658-0050 658-0204
TF: 800-821-6710 ■ *Web:* www.ads-pipe.com

Ameron International Corp 245 S Los Robles Ave .... Pasadena CA 91101 626-683-4000 683-4060
NYSE: AMN ■ *Web:* www.ameron.com

Ameron International Fiberglass-Composite Pipe Group
9720 Cypress Wood Dr Suite 325 .... Houston TX 77070 832-912-8282 912-9393
TF: 800-542-4070 ■ *Web:* www.ameronfpd.com

CANTEX Inc 202 Progress Rd .... Auburndale FL 33823 863-967-4161 967-4541
TF: 800-765-8704

Centron International Inc 600 FM 1195 S PO Box 490 .... Mineral Wells TX 76068 940-325-1341 325-9681
Web: www.centrongre.com

CertainTeed Corp 750 E Swedesford Rd .... Valley Forge PA 19482 610-341-7000 341-7797
TF Prod Info: 800-782-8777 ■ *Web:* www.certainteed.com

CertainTeed Corp Pipe & Plastics Div
750 E Swedesford Rd PO Box 860 .... Valley Forge PA 19482 610-341-7000 341-7413
TF: 800-274-8530 ■ *Web:* www.certainteed.com

Charlotte Pipe & Foundry Co Plastics Div
4210 Old Charlotte Hwy PO Box 1339 .... Monroe NC 28111 704-289-2531 348-6406
TF Sales: 800-438-6091

Chemtrol Div NIBCO Inc 1516 Middlebury St .... Elkhart IN 46516 574-295-3316 234-0557*
**Fax Area Code:* 800 ■ *TF:* 800-234-0227 ■ *Web:* www.nibco.com/cms.do?id=2&pld=1

Chevron Phillips Chemical Co Performance Pipe Div
5085 W Park Blvd Suite 500 .... Plano TX 75093 972-599-6600 599-7348
TF: 800-527-0662 ■ *Web:* www.cpchem.com/enu/performance_pipe.asp

Corrosion Controllers Inc 3444 SE 2nd Ave PO Box 1199 .... Washougal WA 98671 360-835-2171 835-2173
Web: www.ccifrp.com

Cresline-West Inc 600 Crosspointe Blvd .... Evansville IN 47715 812-428-9300 428-9353
TF: 800-528-5687 ■ *Web:* www.cresline.com

Diamond Plastics Corp 1212 Johnstown Rd PO Box 1608 .... Grand Island NE 68802 308-384-4400 384-9345
TF: 800-782-7473 ■ *Web:* www.dpcpipe.com

Phone Fax

Dura-Line Corp 835 Innovation Dr .... Knoxville TN 37932 865-218-3460 218-3462
TF: 800-847-7661 ■ *Web:* www.duraline.com

Dura Plastics Products Inc 533 E 3rd St .... Beaumont CA 92223 951-845-3161 845-7644
TF: 800-854-2323 ■ *Web:* www.duraplastics.com

EDO Specialty Plastics 15915 Perkins Rd .... Baton Rouge LA 70810 225-752-2705 752-2757
TF: 800-752-7473 ■ *Web:* www.fiberbond.com

Excalibur Extrusions Inc 110 E Crowther Ave .... Placentia CA 92870 714-528-8834 524-7453
TF: 800-648-6804 ■ *Web:* www.excaliburextrusions.com

Fernco PlumbQwik Inc 300 S Dayton St .... Davison MI 48423 810-653-9626 653-8714
TF: 800-521-1283 ■ *Web:* www.fernco.com

Fiber Glass Systems LP 2700 W 65th St .... Little Rock AR 72209 501-568-4010 568-3029
Web: www.smithfiberglass.com

Fiber Glass Systems LP Smith Fibercast Div
25 S Main St .... Sand Springs OK 74063 918-245-6651 245-7566
TF: 800-331-4406 ■ *Web:* www.smithfibercast.com

Freedom Plastics Inc 3206 Enterprise Rd .... Fort Pierce FL 34982 772-465-1222 489-3655
TF: 800-432-6143 ■ *Web:* www.freedomplastics.com

Fusibond Piping Systems Inc 2615 Curtiss St .... Downers Grove IL 60515 630-969-4488 969-2355
Web: www.fusibond.com

Genova-Minnesota Inc 500 12th St NW .... Faribault MN 55021 507-332-7421 332-2344
TF: 800-744-4500 ■ *Web:* www.genovaproducts.com

Genova Products Inc 7034 E Court St .... Davison MI 48423 810-744-4500 744-1653
TF: 800-521-7488 ■ *Web:* www.genovaproducts.com

George Fischer Sloane Mfg Co Inc 7777 Sloane Dr .... Little Rock AR 72206 501-490-7777 423-2689*
**Fax Area Code:* 877 ■ *TF:* 800-423-2686

Hancor Inc 401 Olive St .... Findlay OH 45840 419-422-6521 424-8300
Web: www.hancor.com

Isco Industries 926 Baxter Ave .... Louisville KY 40204 502-583-6591 584-9713
TF: 800-345-4726 ■ *Web:* www.isco-pipe.com

J-M Mfg Co Inc 9 Peach Tree Hill Rd .... Livingston NJ 07039 973-535-1633 533-4105*
**Fax:* Acctg ■ *TF:* 800-621-4404 ■ *Web:* www.jmm.com

Lasco Fittings Inc 514 Morgan St .... Brownsville TN 38012 731-772-3180 772-0835
TF: 800-776-2756 ■ *Web:* www.lascofittings.com

Maloney Technical Products 1300 E Berry St .... Fort Worth TX 76119 817-923-3344 923-1339
TF: 800-231-7236 ■ *Web:* www.maloneytech.com

Mueller Plastics Corp 625 W Johnson St .... Upper Sandusky OH 43351 419-294-3858 294-1799
TF: 800-348-8464 ■ *Web:* www.muellerindustries.com

National Pipe & Plastics Inc 3421 Old Vestal Rd .... Vestal NY 13850 607-729-9381 729-6130
TF: 800-836-4350 ■ *Web:* www.nationalpipe.com

Nebraska Plastics Inc 700 W Hwy 30 .... Cozad NE 69130 308-784-2500 784-3216
TF: 800-445-2887 ■ *Web:* www.countryestate.com

Normandy Industries Inc 1150 Freeport Rd PO Box 38805 .... Pittsburgh PA 15238 412-826-1825 826-1731
TF: 800-322-9463 ■ *Web:* www.normandyproducts.com

North American Pipe Corp 2801 Post Oak Blvd Suite 600 .... Houston TX 77056 713-840-7473 552-0087
Web: www.northamericanpipe.com

Oil Creek Plastics Inc 45619 State Hwy 27 PO Box 385 .... Titusville PA 16354 814-827-3661 827-9599
TF: 800-537-3661 ■ *Web:* www.oilcreek.com

PW Eagle Inc 1550 Valley River Dr .... Eugene OR 97401 541-343-0200 686-9248
NASDAQ: PWEI ■ *TF:* 800-347-0200 ■ *Web:* www.pweagleinc.com

Pyramid Industries 1422 Irwin Dr .... Erie PA 16505 814-455-7587 459-8094
Web: www.pyramidind.com

Rehau Inc 1501 Edwards Ferry Rd NE .... Leesburg VA 20176 703-777-5255 777-3053
TF: 800-247-9445 ■ *Web:* www.rehau-na.com

Resistoflex Co 1 Quality Way .... Marion NC 28752 828-724-4000 724-9469
Web: www.resistoflex.com

Silver-Line Plastics 900 Riverside Dr .... Asheville NC 28804 828-252-8755 285-8901
Web: www.slpipe.com

Smith Fibercast Div Fiber Glass Systems LP
25 S Main St .... Sand Springs OK 74063 918-245-6651 245-7566
TF: 800-331-4406 ■ *Web:* www.smithfibercast.com

Special Plastics Systems Inc 385 W Valley St .... San Bernardino CA 92401 909-888-2531 888-8931
TF: 800-423-4422 ■ *Web:* www.spscompany.com

Teel Plastics Inc 426 Hitchcock St .... Baraboo WI 53913 608-355-3080 355-3088
Web: www.teel.com

Texas United Pipe Inc 11627 N Houston Rosslyn Rd .... Houston TX 77086 281-448-3276 448-6983
TF Sales: 800-448-9463 ■ *Web:* www.texasunitedpipe.com

USPoly Co 4501 W 49th St .... Tulsa OK 74107 918-446-4471 446-9369
TF: 800-962-1514 ■ *Web:* www.uspolycompany.com

Vinylplex Inc 1800 Atkinson Ave .... Pittsburg KS 66762 620-231-8290 232-8547

Vinyltech Corp 201 S 61st Ave .... Phoenix AZ 85043 602-233-0071 233-9152
Web: www.vtpipe.com

Weiler Welding Co Inc 324 E 2nd St .... Dayton OH 45402 937-222-8312 222-2729
TF: 800-526-9353 ■ *Web:* www.weilerwelding.com

Wellstream International Ltd 520 Skyview Dr .... Panama City Beach FL 32408 850-636-4800 234-6874
Web: www.wellstream.com

Winrock Enterprises 2222 Cottondale Ln Suite 300 .... Little Rock AR 72201 501-663-5340 663-4456

600 PIPELINES (EXCEPT NATURAL GAS)

Phone Fax

Alyeska Pipeline Service Co PO Box 196660 .... Anchorage AK 99519 907-787-8700 787-8611
Web: www.alyeska-pipe.com

Belle Fourche Pipeline 455 N Poplar St .... Casper WY 82601 307-237-9301 266-0252
Web: www.truecos.com/bfpl

BP Exploration (Alaska) Inc (BPXA) PO Box 196612 .... Anchorage AK 95519 907-561-5111

BP Plc 28100 Torch Pkwy .... Warrenville IL 60555 630-420-5111 298-0738*
NYSE: BP ■ **Fax Area Code:* 281 ■ *TF:* 866-427-6947 ■ *Web:* www.bp.com

Buckeye Partners LP
5 Radnor Corporate Ctr 100 Matsonford Rd Suite 500 .... Radnor PA 19087 484-232-4000 254-4625*
NYSE: BPL ■ **Fax Area Code:* 610 ■ **Fax:* Mktg ■ *Web:* www.buckeye.com

Buckeye Pipe Line Co LP PO Box 368 .... Emmaus PA 18049 484-232-4000 254-4625*
**Fax Area Code:* 610 ■ **Fax:* Mktg ■ *Web:* www.buckeye.com

Chevron Pipe Line Co 2811 Hayes Rd .... Houston TX 77082 281-596-2828 596-2213
Web: www.chevron.com/prodserv/cpl

Chicap Pipeline Co 18401 S Wolf Rd .... Mokena IL 60448 708-479-9260 479-9208

CITGO Petroleum Corp 1293 Eldridge Pkwy .... Houston TX 77077 832-486-4000
Web: www.spsecurities.com

CITGO Pipeline Co 1293 Eldridge Pkwy .... Houston TX 77077 832-486-4000
Web: www.citgo.com

Collins Pipeline Co Hwy 588 E PO Box 1027 .... Collins MS 39428 601-765-6593 765-8648

Colonial Pipeline Co PO Box 1624 .... Alpharetta GA 30009 678-762-2200 762-2883*
**Fax:* Hum Res ■ *TF:* 800-275-3004 ■ *Web:* www.colpipe.com

Cook Inlet Pipe Line Co PO Box 91159 .... Anchorage AK 99509 907-263-7990 243-4231

Country Mark Co-op 1200 Refinery Rd .... Mount Vernon IN 47620 812-838-4341 838-8196
TF: 800-832-5490 ■ *Web:* www.countrymark.com

Dixie Pipeline Co 1117 Perimeter Ctr W Suite 301 W .... Atlanta GA 30338 770-396-2994 396-4276
Web: www.dixiepipeline.com

Dome Pipeline Corp 2959 Sierra Ct SW .... Iowa City IA 52240 319-354-7722 337-6147

Enbridge Energy Co Inc 119 N 25th St E .... Superior WI 54880 715-394-1400 394-1475

Enbridge Energy Partners LP 1100 Louisiana Suite 3300 .... Houston TX 77002 713-821-2000 650-3232
NYSE: EEP ■ *TF:* 888-650-8900 ■ *Web:* enbridgepartners.com

Enbridge Inc 425 1st St SW Suite 3000 .... Calgary AB T2P3L8 403-231-3900 231-3920
NYSE: ENB ■ *Web:* www.enbridge.com

				Phone	Fax
Express Pipeline 800 Werner Ct Suite 352	Casper	WY	82601	307-577-6002	237-5770
Web: www.expresspipeline.com					
ExxonMobil Pipeline Co 800 Bell St	Houston	TX	77002	713-656-1658	656-9586
Web: www.exxonmobilpipeline.com					
Genesis Energy LP 500 Dallas St Suite 2500	Houston	TX	77002	713-860-2500	860-2640
AMEX: GEL ■ *TF:* 800-284-3365 ■ *Web:* www.genesiscrudeoil.com					
Giant Industries Inc 23733 N Scottsdale Rd	Scottsdale	AZ	85255	480-585-8888	585-8948
NYSE: GI ■ *TF:* 800-937-4937 ■ *Web:* www.giant.com					
Gulf Central Pipeline Co Inc PO Box 2256	Wichita	KS	67201	316-828-5500	828-5327
Hess Pipeline Co Inc 420 Hook Rd	Bayonne	NJ	07002	201-437-1017	437-8845*
**Fax:* Hum Res					
Imperial Oil Resources Ltd					
237 4th Ave SW PO Box 2480 Stn M	Calgary	AB	T2P3M9	403-237-3737	237-2072
Jayhawk Pipeline LLC 2000 S Main St	McPherson	KS	67460	620-241-9270	241-9215
Web: www.jayhawkpl.com					
Kaneb Pipe Line Partners LP					
2435 N Central Expy Suite 700	Richardson	TX	75080	972-699-4000	699-4025
TF: 866-769-2987 ■ *Web:* www.kaneb.com					
Kaneb Services LLC 2435 N Central Expy Suite 700	Richardson	TX	75080	972-699-4000	699-4025
Web: www.kaneb.com					
Kiantone Pipeline Corp PO Box 129	West Seneca	NY	14224	716-675-2767	675-2741
Kinder Morgan Energy Partners LP 500 Dallas St Suite 1000	Houston	TX	77002	713-369-9000	369-9411*
NYSE: KMP ■ **Fax:* Hum Res ■ *TF:* 888-844-5657 ■ *Web:* www.kindermorgan.com					
Kinder Morgan Management LLC					
500 Dallas St 1 Allen Ctr Suite 1000	Houston	TX	77002	713-369-9000	369-9100
NYSE: KMR ■ *TF:* 800-324-2900 ■ *Web:* www.kindermorgan.com					
Koch Pipeline Co Inc 4111 E 37th St N	Wichita	KS	67220	316-828-5500	
Web: www.kochpipeline.com					
Locap Inc 6695 Locap Rd	Saint James	LA	70086	225-265-8355	632-1368*
**Fax Area Code:* 985					
Magellan Midstream Partners LP 1 Williams Ctr	Tulsa	OK	74172	918-574-7000	573-6714*
NYSE: MMP ■ **Fax:* Mail Rm ■ *TF:* 800-574-6671 ■ *Web:* www.magellanlp.com					
Marathon Ashland Pipe Line LLC 539 S Main St	Findlay	OH	45840	419-422-2121	425-7040
Web: www.marathon.com					
MarkWest Energy Partners LP					
155 Inverness Dr W Suite 200	Englewood	CO	80112	303-290-8700	290-8769
AMEX: MWE ■ *TF:* 800-730-8388 ■ *Web:* www.markwest.com					
Mid-Valley Pipeline Co 1820 US Hwy 80 W	Longview	TX	75604	903-295-0546	295-0132
Navajo Pipeline Co 311 W Quay	Artesia	NM	88210	505-748-8940	746-5480
Newpark Drilling Fluids LLC 5560B NW 72nd St	Oklahoma City	OK	73132	405-721-0207	721-0174
TF: 800-444-0682 ■ *Web:* www.newparkdf.com					
Olympic Pipeline Co 2319 Lind Ave SW	Renton	WA	98057	425-235-7736	271-5320
TF: 877-659-7473 ■ *Web:* www.olympicpipeline.com					
Pacific Energy Management LLC 5900 Cherry Ave	Long Beach	CA	90805	562-728-2800	728-2801
NYSE: PPX ■ *Web:* www.pacpipe.com					
Pioneer Pipe Line Co Inc 245 E 1100 North	North Salt Lake	UT	84054	801-299-3610	299-3630
Plains All American Pipeline LP 333 Clay St Suite 1600	Houston	TX	77002	713-646-4100	646-4305
NYSE: PAA ■ *TF Mktg:* 800-564-3036 ■ *Web:* www.plainsallamerican.com					
Plantation Pipe Line Co 1435 Windward Concourse	Alpharetta	GA	30005	770-751-4000	751-4050
Web: www.plantation-ppl.com					
Platte Pipe Line Co Inc 800 Werner Ct Suite 352	Casper	WY	82601	307-577-6002	237-5770
Portland Pipe Line Corp 30 Hill St	South Portland	ME	04106	207-767-0421	767-0442
SemGroup LP 6120 S Yale Ave Suite 700	Tulsa	OK	74136	918-388-8100	388-8290
Web: www.semgrouplp.com					
Shell Pipeline Co 910 Louisiana St	Houston	TX	77002	713-241-6161	241-4044
Web: www.shell.com					
Sunoco Inc 1735 Market St Suite LL	Philadelphia	PA	19103	215-977-3000	977-3409
NYSE: SUN ■ *TF:* 800-786-6261 ■ *Web:* www.sunocoinc.com					
Sunoco Logistics Partners LP 1818 Market St	Philadelphia	PA	19103	215-977-3000	977-3409
NYSE: SXL ■ *Web:* www.sunocoinc.com					
Teppco Crude Oil LP 210 Park Ave Suite 1600	Oklahoma City	OK	73102	405-239-7191	605-2051*
**Fax:* Mktg ■ *Web:* www.teppco.com					
Terasen Pipeline 1009 E Smith Rd	Bellingham	WA	98226	360-398-1541	398-7432
Tesoro Corp 300 Concord Plaza Dr	San Antonio	TX	78216	210-828-8484	745-4474
NYSE: TSO ■ *TF:* 800-837-6762 ■ *Web:* www.tesoropetroleum.com					
Texas Eastern Products Pipeline Co (TEPPCO)					
2929 Allen Pkwy	Houston	TX	77019	713-759-3636	759-3902
TF: 800-877-3636 ■ *Web:* www.teppco.com					
Ultramar Ltd 2200 ave McGill College	Montreal	QC	H3A3L3	514-499-6111	499-6320
TF Cust Svc: 800-363-6949 ■ *Web:* www.ultramar.ca					
United Brine Pipeline Corp 4800 San Felipe	Houston	TX	77056	713-877-1778	877-2605
Valero LP 1 Valero Way	San Antonio	TX	78249	210-592-2000	370-2646
NYSE: VLI ■ *TF:* 800-333-3377 ■ *Web:* www.valerolp.com					
West Texas Gulf Pipeline Co 3250 CR 4156	Hermleigh	TX	79526	325-728-3162	728-2945

601 PLANETARIUMS

				Phone	Fax
Abrams Planetarium Michigan State University	East Lansing	MI	48824	517-355-4676	432-3838
Web: www.pa.msu.edu/abrams					
Adler Planetarium & Astronomy Museum					
1300 S Lake Shore Dr	Chicago	IL	60605	312-922-7827	322-2257
Web: www.adlerplanetarium.org					
Albert Einstein Planetarium					
Independence Ave & 6th St SW	Washington	DC	20560	202-633-1000	
Aldrin Planetarium 4801 Dreher Trail N	West Palm Beach	FL	33405	561-832-1988	833-0551
Web: www.sfsm.org					
Andrus Planetarium 511 Warburton Ave Hudson River Museum	Yonkers	NY	10701	914-963-4550	963-8558
Web: www.hrm.org/planetarium.html					
Arizona State University Planetarium					
ASU Bateman Physical Science Center B Wing Rm 350	Tempe	AZ	85287	480-965-6891	965-7331
Web: phyastweb.la.asu.edu/planetarium/					
Arnim D Hummel Planetarium Eastern Kentucky University	Richmond	KY	40475	859-622-1547	622-6666
Web: www.planetarium.eku.edu					
Astronaut Memorial Planetarium & Observatory					
1519 Clearlake Rd Brevard Community College	Cocoa	FL	32922	321-632-1111	
Web: www.brevard.cc.fl.us/planet					
Bays Mountain Planetarium & Observatory					
853 Bays Mountain Park Rd	Kingsport	TN	37660	423-229-9447	224-2589
Web: www.baysmountain.com/planetdept/astronomy.html					
Beecher Ward Planetarium					
Youngstown State University 1 University Plaza	Youngstown	OH	44555	330-941-3616	941-3121
Web: cc.ysu.edu/physics-astro/planet.htm					
Berea College Weatherford Planetarium CPO 2191	Berea	KY	40404	859-985-3000	985-3351
Brackbill MT Planetarium					
1200 Park Rd Eastern Mennonite University	Harrisonburg	VA	22802	540-432-4400	432-4488
Buehler Planetarium & Observatory 3501 SW Davie Rd	Davie	FL	33314	954-201-6681	475-2858
Web: www.broward.edu/locations/central/buehler.jsp					
Buhl Planetarium & Observatory 1 Allegheny Ave	Pittsburgh	PA	15212	412-237-3400	237-3375
TF: 877-975-6787 ■ *Web:* www.buhlplanetarium.org					
Burke Baker Planetarium					
Houston Museum of Natural Science 1 Hermann Circle Dr	Houston	TX	77030	713-639-4600	523-4125
Casper Planetarium 904 N Poplar St	Casper	WY	82601	307-577-0310	
Cernan Earth & Space Center					
2000 N 5th Ave Triton College	River Grove	IL	60171	708-456-0300	583-3153
Charles Hayden Planetarium 1 Science Park	Boston	MA	02114	617-723-2500	589-0362
Web: www.mos.org					
Chemeketa Community College Planetarium					
4000 Lancaster Dr NE	Salem	OR	97305	503-399-5161	399-2519
Chesapeake Planetarium 312 Cedar Rd	Chesapeake	VA	23322	757-547-0153	547-0252
Christa McAuliffe Planetarium 2 Institute Dr	Concord	NH	03301	603-271-7827	271-7832
Web: www.starhop.com					
Clark Planetarium 110 S 400 West	Salt Lake City	UT	84101	801-456-7827	
Web: www.clarkplanetarium.net					
Community College of Southern Nevada Planetarium & Observatory 3200 E Cheyenne Ave	North Las Vegas	NV	89030	702-651-4759	651-4825
Web: www.ccsn.edu/planetarium					
Cormack Planetarium					
Roger Williams Park 1000 Elmwood Ave	Providence	RI	02907	401-785-9457	461-5146
Web: www.osfn.org/museum/planet.html					
Davis Russell C Planetarium 201 E Pascagoula St	Jackson	MS	39201	601-960-1550	960-1555
Discovery Museum & Planetarium 4450 Park Ave	Bridgeport	CT	06604	203-372-3521	374-1929
Web: www.discoverymuseum.org					
Downing Planetarium					
5320 N Maple Ave MS DP132 California State University Fresno	Fresno	CA	93740	559-278-4121	278-4070
Web: www.downing-planetarium.org					
Dreyfuss Planetarium 49 Washington St	Newark	NJ	07102	973-596-6529	642-0459
Web: www.newarkmuseum.org/planetarium					
Einstein Albert Planetarium					
Independence Ave & 6th St SW	Washington	DC	20560	202-633-1000	
Erie Planetarium 356 W 6th St	Erie	PA	16507	814-871-5790	879-0988
Ethyl IMAX Dome & Planetarium 2500 W Broad St	Richmond	VA	23220	804-864-1400	864-1488
TF: 800-659-1727 ■ *Web:* www.smv.org/ethyl					
Exhibit Museum of Natural History					
1109 Geddes Ave University of Michigan	Ann Arbor	MI	48109	734-764-0478	647-2767
Web: www.exhibits.lsa.umich.edu					
Faulkner Planetarium					
College of Southern Idaho 315 Falls Ave	Twin Falls	ID	83303	208-736-3059	736-4712
Fiske Planetarium					
Regent Dr CB 408 University of Colorado Campus	Boulder	CO	80309	303-492-5002	492-1725
Web: www.colorado.edu/fiske					
Flandrau Science Center & Planetarium					
University of Arizona 1601 E University Blvd	Tucson	AZ	85721	520-621-4515	621-8451
Web: www.flandrau.org					
Fleischmann Planetarium & Science Center University of Nevada	Reno	NV	89557	775-784-4811	784-4822
Web: planetarium.unr.nevada.edu/					
Gayle WA Planetarium 1010 Forest Ave	Montgomery	AL	36106	334-241-4799	241-2301
Web: montgomery.troy.edu/planet/					
George F Beattie Planetarium 701 S Mt Vernon Ave	San Bernardino	CA	92410	909-888-6511	384-9725
Gheens Science Hall & Rauch Planetarium					
Rauch Planetarium University of Louisville	Louisville	KY	40292	502-852-6664	852-0831
Web: www.louisville.edu/planetarium					
Hardin Planetarium					
1906 College Heights Blvd Western Kentucky University	Bowling Green	KY	42101	270-745-4044	745-4255*
**Fax:* Hum Res					
Hayden Charles Planetarium 1 Science Park	Boston	MA	02114	617-723-2500	589-0362
Web: www.mos.org					
Hayden Planetarium 81st St & Central Park W	New York	NY	10024	212-769-5900	496-3500
Henry Buhl Jr Planetarium & Observatory 1 Allegheny Ave	Pittsburgh	PA	15212	412-237-3400	237-3375
TF: 877-975-6787 ■ *Web:* www.buhlplanetarium.org					
Henry Hudson Planetarium 25 Quackenbush Sq	Albany	NY	12207	518-434-0405	434-0087
Holcomb JI Observatory & Planetarium					
702 W Lake Rd Butler University	Indianapolis	IN	46208	317-940-9333	940-9951
Web: www.butler.edu/holcomb					
Hopkins Planetarium 1 Market Sq	Roanoke	VA	24011	540-342-5710	224-1240
Web: www.smwv.org					
Hudson Henry Planetarium 25 Quackenbush Sq	Albany	NY	12207	518-434-0405	434-0087
Hummel Arnim D Planetarium Eastern Kentucky University	Richmond	KY	40475	859-622-1547	622-6666
Web: www.planetarium.eku.edu					
Hyde Memorial Observatory					
Holmes Park 70th St & Normal Blvd	Lincoln	NE	68506	402-441-8708	441-6468
Web: www.hydeobservatory.info/					
JI Holcomb Observatory & Planetarium					
702 W Lake Rd Butler University	Indianapolis	IN	46208	317-940-9333	940-9951
Web: www.butler.edu/holcomb					
John Deere Planetarium 820 38th St Augustana College	Rock Island	IL	61201	309-794-7327	794-7564
Jordan Maynard F Planetarium & Observatory					
University of Maine 5781 Wingate Hall	Orono	ME	04469	207-581-1341	581-1314
Web: umainesky.com					
Kenner Planetarium & MegaDome Cinema 2020 4th St	Kenner	LA	70062	504-468-7231	471-2159
Web: www.rivertownkenner.com/planetarium.html					
Kitt Peak National Observatory 950 N Cherry Ave	Tucson	AZ	85719	520-318-8600	318-8724
Web: www.noao.edu/kpno					
Lafayette Natural History Museum & Planetarium					
433 Jefferson St	Lafayette	LA	70501	337-291-5544	291-5464
Web: www.lnhm.org					
Lake Afton Public Observatory 1845 Fairmount	Wichita	KS	67260	316-794-8995	978-3350
Web: webs.wichita.edu/lapo					
Lick Observatory Mt Hamilton Rd	San Jose	CA	95140	408-274-5061	
Web: www.ucolick.org					
Lodestar Astronomy Center 1801 Mountain Rd NW	Albuquerque	NM	87104	505-841-5955	841-5999
Web: www.lodestar.unm.edu					
Longway Robert T Planetarium 1310 E Kearsley St	Flint	MI	48503	810-237-3400	237-3417
Web: www.longwayplanetarium.com					
Lowell Observatory 1400 W Mars Hill Rd	Flagstaff	AZ	86001	928-774-3358	774-6296
Web: www.lowell.edu					
Maria Mitchell Observatory 3 Vestal St	Nantucket	MA	02554	508-228-9273	228-1031
Web: www.mmo.org/museums					
Maynard F Jordan Planetarium & Observatory					
University of Maine 5781 Wingate Hall	Orono	ME	04469	207-581-1341	581-1314
Web: umainesky.com					
McAuliffe Christa Planetarium 2 Institute Dr	Concord	NH	03301	603-271-7827	271-7832
Web: www.starhop.com					
Meyer Robert R Planetarium					
900 Arkadelphia Rd Birmingham Southern College PO Box 549036	Birmingham	AL	35254	205-226-4770	226-7022
TF: 800-523-5793					
Moody Planetarium					
3301 4th St Museum of Texas Tech University	Lubbock	TX	79409	806-742-2432	742-1136
Web: www.depts.ttu.edu/museumttu/					
Morehead Planetarium					
250 E Franklin St UNC Chapel Hill Campus Box 3480	Chapel Hill	NC	27599	919-962-1236	962-1238
Web: www.unc.edu/depts/mhplanet					
MT Brackbill Planetarium					
1200 Park Rd Eastern Mennonite University	Harrisonburg	VA	22802	540-432-4400	432-4488
Mueller Planetarium University of Nebraska Morrill Hall	Lincoln	NE	68588	402-472-2641	472-8899
Web: www.spacelaser.com					

Phone Fax

Noble Planetarium
1501 Montgomery St Museum of Science & History .... Fort Worth TX 76107 817-732-1631 732-7635
TF: 888-255-9300 ■ *Web:* www.fwmuseum.org/noble.html
Ott Planetarium & Observatory
Weber State University Lind Lecture Hall 2nd Fl................. Ogden UT 84408 801-626-6855 626-7257
Web: departments.weber.edu/physics/palen/planet
Perkins Observatory PO Box 449 .... Delaware OH 43015 740-363-1257 363-1258
Web: www.perkins-observatory.org
Planetarium de Montreal 1000 Saint-Jacques St W ....Montreal QC H3C1G7 514-872-4530 872-8102
Web: www.planetarium.montreal.qc.ca
Pontchartrain Astronomy Society Observatory
409 Williams Blvd Rivertown................................ Kenner LA 70062 504-468-7231 471-2159
Web: www.pasnola.org
Portland Observatory 138 Congress St......................... Portland ME 04101 207-774-5561 774-2509
Web: www.portlandlandmarks.org/observatory.htm
Ritter Planetarium & Brooks Observatory
University of Toledo MS 113................................ Toledo OH 43606 419-530-2650 530-5167
Web: www.rpbo.utoledo.edu
Robert R Meyer Planetarium
900 Arkadelphia Rd Birmingham Southern College PO Box 549036 .... Birmingham AL 35254 205-226-4770 226-7022
TF: 800-523-5793
Robert T Longway Planetarium 1310 E Kearsley St.................. Flint MI 48503 810-237-3400 237-3417
Web: www.longwayplanetarium.com
Roger B Chaffee Planetarium 272 Pearl St NW.............Grand Rapids MI 49504 616-456-3977 456-3873
Rosicrucian Egyptian Museum & Planetarium
1342 Naglee Ave Rosicrucian Park .... San Jose CA 95191 408-947-3636 947-3677
Web: www.rosicrucian.org
Russell C Davis Planetarium 201 E Pascagoula St .... Jackson MS 39201 601-960-1550 960-1555
Saint Petersburg Junior College Planetarium
6605 5th Ave N Science Bldg .... Saint Petersburg FL 33703 727-341-4320
Sanford Museum & Planetarium 117 E Willow St.............. Cherokee IA 51012 712-225-3922 225-0446
Science Factory Children's Museum & Planetarium
2300 Leo Harris Pkwy .... Eugene OR 97401 541-682-7888 484-9027
Web: www.sciencefactory.org
Science Place The 1318 2nd Ave.............................. Dallas TX 75210 214-428-5555 428-4356
Web: www.scienceplace.org
Sharpe Planetarium 3050 Central Ave .... Memphis TN 38111 901-320-6320 320-6391
Web: www.memphismuseums.org
Southworth Planetarium 96 Falmouth St .... Portland ME 04104 207-780-4249 780-4051
Web: www.usm.maine.edu/planet
Space Transit Planetarium 3280 S Miami Ave .... Miami FL 33129 305-646-4400 646-4200
Web: www.miamisci.org
Staerkel William M Planetarium
2400 W Bradley Ave Parkland College...................... Champaign IL 61821 217-351-2568
Web: www.parkland.edu/coned/pla
Strasenburgh Planetarium
663 East Ave Rochester Museum & Science Center............ Rochester NY 14607 585-271-4320 271-5935
Web: www.rmsc.org/planetarium/planetframeset.htm
Tomchin Planetarium & Observatory
West Virginia University 425 Hodges Hall PO Box 6315....... Morgantown WV 26506 304-293-3422 293-5732
Web: www.as.wvu.edu/~planet
University of Arkansas Little Rock Planetarium
2801 S University Ave .... Little Rock AR 72204 501-569-3275 569-3314
Web: planetarium.ualr.edu
WA Gayle Planetarium 1010 Forest Ave.................... Montgomery AL 36106 334-241-4799 241-2301
Web: montgomery.troy.edu/planet/
Ward Beecher Planetarium
Youngstown State University 1 University Plaza .... Youngstown OH 44555 330-941-3616 941-3121
Web: cc.ysu.edu/physics-astro/planet.htm
William M Staerkel Planetarium
2400 W Bradley Ave Parkland College..................... Champaign IL 61821 217-351-2568
Web: www.parkland.edu/coned/pla

602 PLASTICS - LAMINATED - PLATE, SHEET, PROFILE SHAPES

Phone Fax

Abutco Plastics Industries Inc 270 S Pine St.................. Hazleton PA 18201 570-455-7527 455-4591
American Renolit Corp 1207 E Lincolnway .... LaPorte IN 46350 219-324-6886 324-5332
Web: www.americanrenolit.com
American Thermoplastic Extrusion Co
4851 NW 128th Street Rd .... Opa Locka FL 33054 305-769-9566 769-1998
TF: 800-426-9605
AMETEK Inc Westchester Plastics Div 42 Mountain Ave ..... Nesquehoning PA 18240 570-645-2191 645-6959
Web: www.ametek-westchesterplas.com
Applied Plastics Co Inc 7320 S 6th St.......................... Oak Creek WI 53154 414-764-2900 764-8606
TF: 800-959-0445 ■ *Web:* www.appliedplasticsinc.com
Atlantis Plastics Inc Linear Films Div 6940 W 76th St S............ Tulsa OK 74131 918-446-1651 227-2454
TF Cust Svc: 800-332-4437 ■ *Web:* www.atlantisplastics.com
Bourne Industries Inc 491 S Comstock St......................... Corunna MI 48817 989-743-3461 743-5481
Web: www.bourneindustries.com
Brockton Plastics Inc 230 Elliot St............................ Brockton MA 02302 508-587-2290 580-0524
Web: www.brocktonplastics.com
C-K Composites Inc 361 Bridgeport RD .... Mount Pleasant PA 15666 724-547-4581 547-2890
Web: www.ckcomposites.com
California Combining Corp 5607 S Santa Fe Ave............. Los Angeles CA 90058 323-589-5727 585-8078
Web: www.calcombining.com
CCL Plastic Packaging 2501 W Rosecrans Ave............... Los Angeles CA 90059 310-635-4444 635-6839
Web: www.ccltube.com
Columbus Cello-Poly Corp 4041 Roberts Rd .... Columbus OH 43228 614-876-1204 876-1072
TF: 800-837-1204 ■ *Web:* www.cello-poly.com
Composite Technologies of America Inc 1331 S Chillicothe Rd...... Aurora OH 44202 330-562-5201 562-7452
TF: 800-692-5201 ■ *Web:* www.omegapultrusions.com
Conimar Corp 1724 NE 22nd Ave .... Ocala FL 34470 352-732-7235 732-6888
TF: 800-874-9735 ■ *Web:* www.conimar.com
Connecticut Laminating Co Inc 162 James St.................. New Haven CT 06513 203-787-2184 787-4073
TF: 800-753-9119 ■ *Web:* www.ctlaminating.com
Current Inc 30 Tyler St PO Box 120183 .... East Haven CT 06512 203-469-1337 467-8435
TF: 877-436-6542 ■ *Web:* www.currentcomposites.com
DuPont Surfaces
4417 Lancaster Pike Chestnut Run Plaza Maple Run 721 ..... Wilmington DE 19805 302-774-1000 635-9486*
**Fax Area Code:* 800 ■ *TF:* 800-426-7426 ■ *Web:* www.corian.com
Dynea Overlays Inc 2144 Milwaukee Way .... Tacoma WA 98421 253-572-5600 627-2896
Web: www.dyneaoverlays.com
Edlon Inc 150 Pomeroy Ave .... Avondale PA 19311 610-268-3101 268-8898
TF Sales: 800-753-3566 ■ *Web:* www.edlon.com
Fiberesin Industries Inc 37031 E Wisconsin Ave............. Oconomowoc WI 53066 262-567-4427 567-4814
Web: www.fiberesin.com
Formica Corp 10155 Reading Rd .... Cincinnati OH 45241 513-786-3400
TF: 800-367-6422 ■ *Web:* www.formica.com
Franklin Fibre-Lamitex Corp 903 E 13th St.................... Wilmington DE 19802 302-652-3621 571-9754
TF: 800-233-9739 ■ *Web:* www.franklinfibre.com
Glassmaster Co 126 Glassmaster Rd .... Lexington SC 29072 803-359-2594 359-0897
Web: www.glassmaster.com

Phone Fax

Insulfab Plastics Inc 834 Hayne St .... Spartanburg SC 29301 864-582-7506 582-5215
TF: 800-845-7599 ■ *Web:* www.insulfab.com
Insultab Inc 45 Industrial Pkwy .... Woburn MA 01801 781-935-0800 935-0879
TF Cust Svc: 800-468-4822 ■ *Web:* www.insultab.com
Iten Industries 4602 Benefit Ave.............................. Ashtabula OH 44004 440-997-6134 992-3614
TF Orders: 800-227-4836 ■ *Web:* www.itenindustries.com
Klockner Pentaplast of America Inc
3585 Klockner Rd PO Box 500 .... Gordonsville VA 22942 540-832-3600 832-5656
TF: 800-446-3007 ■ *Web:* www.kpafilms.com
Lakeland Plastics Inc 1550 McCormick Blvd................... Mundelein IL 60060 847-680-1550 680-1595
TF: 800-225-2508 ■ *Web:* www.lakelandplastics.com
Lamart Corp 16 Richmond St .... Clifton NJ 07015 973-772-6262 772-3673
TF: 800-526-2789 ■ *Web:* www.lamartcorp.com
Laminating Co of America 20322 Windrow Dr .... Lake Forest CA 92630 949-587-3371 454-0066
Web: www.lcoa.com
Linear Films Div Atlantis Plastics Inc 6940 W 76th St S............ Tulsa OK 74131 918-446-1651 227-2454
TF Cust Svc: 800-332-4437 ■ *Web:* www.atlantisplastics.com
LSI Corp of America Inc 2100 Xenium Ln N .... Plymouth MN 55441 763-559-4664 559-4395
Web: www.lsi-casework.com
Madico Inc 45 Industrial Pkwy .... Woburn MA 01801 781-935-7850 935-6841
TF Cust Svc: 800-456-4331 ■ *Web:* www.madico.com
Mar-Bal Inc 16930 Munn Rd .... Chagrin Falls OH 44023 440-543-7526 543-4374
Web: www.mar-bal.com
Miniature Precision Components Inc 100 Wisconsin St.......... Walworth WI 53184 262-275-5791 275-6346
Web: www.mpc-inc.com
Olon Industries Inc 42 Armstrong Ave .... Georgetown ON L7G4R9 905-877-7300 877-7383
TF: 800-387-2319 ■ *Web:* www.olon.com
Petro Plastics Co Inc 450 South Ave.......................... Garwood NJ 07027 908-789-1200 789-1381
TF: 800-486-4738 ■ *Web:* www.petroplastics.com
Rochling Engineered Plastics 120 Rochling St PO Box 2729....... Gastonia NC 28053 704-922-7814 922-7651
TF Cust Svc: 800-541-4419 ■ *Web:* www.roechling.com
Rotuba Extruders Inc 1401 S Park Ave .... Linden NJ 07036 908-486-1000 486-0874
Web: www.rotuba.com/divisions_extrusion.htm
Rowmark Inc 2040 Industrial Dr.................................. Findlay OH 45840 419-425-2407 425-2927
TF: 800-243-3339 ■ *Web:* www.rowmark.com
Sabin Corp 3800 Constitution Ave......................... Bloomington IN 47403 812-323-4500 339-3395
TF: 800-264-4510 ■ *Web:* www.sabincorp.com
Schneller Inc 6200 49th St N .... Pinellas Park FL 33781 727-521-2393 525-7384
Web: www.schneller.com
Schneller Inc 6019 Powdermille Rd .... Kent OH 44240 330-673-1400 676-7122
Web: www.schneller.com
Spaulding Composites Co 55 Nadeau Dr .... Rochester NH 03867 603-332-0555 332-5357
TF: 800-801-0560 ■ *Web:* www.spauldingcom.com
United Lamination Inc 1311 Lackawanna Ave .... Mayfield PA 18433 570-876-1360 282-0420
Universal Laminates 14753 Aetna St .... Van Nuys CA 91411 818-782-3424 782-5134
Web: www.universallaminates.net
V-T Industries Inc 1000 Industrial Park .... Holstein IA 51025 712-368-4381 368-4111
TF: 800-827-1615 ■ *Web:* www.vtindustries.com
Vytech Industries Inc 5201 Old Pearman Dairy Rd .... Anderson SC 29625 864-224-8771 224-8410
TF: 800-225-8531 ■ *Web:* www.vytech.com
Westchester Plastics Chemical Products Div AMETEK Inc
42 Mountain Ave .... Nesquehoning PA 18240 570-645-2191 645-6959
Web: www.ametek-westchesterplas.com
Wilmington Fibre Specialty Co 700 Washington St............. New Castle DE 19720 302-328-7525 328-6630
TF: 800-220-5132 ■ *Web:* www.wilmfibre.com
Wilsonart International Inc 2400 Wilson Pl...................... Temple TX 76504 254-207-7000 207-2384
TF Cust Svc: 800-433-3222 ■ *Web:* www.wilsonart.com

603 PLASTICS - UNSUPPORTED - FILM, SHEET, PROFILE SHAPES

SEE ALSO Blister Packaging p. 1384

Phone Fax

3M Commercial Graphics Div
3M General Offices Bldg 220-6W-06....................... Saint Paul MN 55144 800-328-3908 737-9682*
**Fax Area Code:* 651 ■ **Fax:* Sales
3M Display & Graphics Div 3M Ctr .... Saint Paul MN 55144 651-733-1110 733-9973
TF: 800-364-3577
3M Safety Security & Protection Services Div 3M Center .... Saint Paul MN 55144 651-733-1110
TF: 800-364-3577 ■ *Web:* www.3m.com
3M Traffic Control Materials Div 3M Center Bldg 225-5S-08..... Saint Paul MN 55144 800-553-1380 591-9293
Web: www.3m.com/us/safety/tcm
Achilles USA Inc 1407 80th St SW................................ Everett WA 98203 425-353-7000 347-5785
Web: www.achillesusa.com
AEP Industries Inc 125 Phillips Ave .... South Hackensack NJ 07606 201-641-6600 807-2443
NASDAQ: AEPI ■ *TF:* 800-999-2374 ■ *Web:* www.aepinc.com
Allen Extruders Inc 1305 Lincoln Ave............................ Holland MI 49423 616-392-9004 394-0100
TF: 800-833-1305 ■ *Web:* www.allenx.com
Anaheim Custom Extruders 4640 E La Palma Ave................ Anaheim CA 92807 714-693-8508 693-9531
TF Cust Svc: 800-229-2760
Applied Extrusion Technologies Inc 15 Reads Way .... New Castle DE 19720 302-326-5500 326-5501
TF: 800-688-2044 ■ *Web:* www.aetfilms.com
Argent Automotive Systems 41016 Concept Dr .... Plymouth MI 48170 734-582-9800 582-9999
TF: 800-223-9890 ■ *Web:* www.argent-automotive.com
Arlon Adhesives & Films 2811 S Harbor Blvd .... Santa Ana CA 92704 714-540-2811 431-4305
TF: 800-854-0361 ■ *Web:* www.arlon.com
Atlantis Plastics Inc 1870 The Exchange Suite 200 .... Atlanta GA 30339 770-953-4567 618-7080
NASDAQ: ATPL ■ *TF:* 800-497-7659 ■ *Web:* www.atlantisplastics.com
Atlas Roofing Falcon Foam Div
8240 Byron Center Rd SW.............................. Byron Center MI 49315 616-878-1568 878-9942
TF: 800-917-9138 ■ *Web:* www.falconfoam.com
Avery Dennison Automotive Products Div
15939 Industrial Pkwy .... Cleveland OH 44135 216-267-8700
Web: www.iapna.averydennison.com
Avery Dennison Engineered Films Div
7600 Auburn Rd Bldg 18.................................... Concord OH 44077 440-358-4600 358-4684
Web: www.efd.averydennison.com
Avery Dennison Industrial Products Div
17700 Foltz Industrial Pkwy.............................. Strongsville OH 44149 440-878-7000 878-7318
Web: www.iapna.averydennison.com
Avery Dennison Performance Films Div 650 W 67th Ave .... Schererville IN 46375 219-322-5030 322-3236
Web: www.pfd.averydennison.com
Avery Dennison Worldwide Graphics Div
250 Chester St Bldg 6 .... Painesville OH 44077 440-358-3700 358-3665
TF: 800-443-9380 ■ *Web:* www.averygraphics.com
Banner Packaging Inc 3550 Moser St .... Oshkosh WI 54901 920-303-2300 233-1899
Bemis Co Inc 1 Neenah Center 4th Fl PO Box 669............... Neenah WI 54957 920-727-4100
NYSE: BMS ■ *Web:* www.bemis.com
Bemis Co Inc Bemis Polyethylene Packaging Div
1350 N Fruitridge Ave PO Box 905 .... Terre Haute IN 47808 812-460-6200 460-6370
TF: 800-457-0861 ■ *Web:* www.bemisppd.com
BER Plastic Corp 5 Curtis St PO Box 2 .... Riverdale NJ 07457 973-839-2100 839-7929
TF: 877-237-3456

	City	State	ZIP	Phone	Fax
Bixby International Corp 1 Preble Rd *TF:* 800-466-4102 ■ *Web:* www.bixbyintl.com	Newburyport	MA	01950	978-462-4100	465-5184
Brandywine Investment Group Homalite Div 11 Brookside Dr *TF:* 800-346-7802 ■ *Web:* www.homalite.com	Wilmington	DE	19804	302-652-3686	652-4578
Bunzl Extrusion Inc 1625 Ashton Park Dr *TF:* 800-755-7528 ■ *Web:* www.bunzlextrusion.com	Colonial Heights	VA	23834	804-518-1124	
Catalina Graphic Films Inc 27001 Agoura Rd Suite 100 *TF:* 800-333-3136 ■ *Web:* www.catalinagraphicfilms.com	Calabasas Hills	CA	91301	818-880-8060	880-1144
Chase Facile Holdings Inc 4 - 22 Erie St *Web:* www.chasecorp.com	Paterson	NJ	07524	973-684-1000	684-2749
Clopay Corp 8585 Duke Blvd *TF:* 800-282-2260 ■ *Web:* www.clopay.com	Mason	OH	45040	513-770-4800	770-3984
Clopay Plastic Products Co 8585 Duke Blvd *TF:* 800-282-2260 ■ *Web:* www.clopayplastics.com	Mason	OH	45040	513-770-4800	770-3863
Coburn Corp 1650 Corporate Rd W *Web:* www.coburn.com	Lakewood	NJ	08701	732-367-5511	367-2908
Conwed Corp 2810 Weeks Ave SE *TF:* 800-426-0149 ■ *Web:* www.conwedplastics.com	Minneapolis	MN	55414	612-623-1700	623-2501
Covalence Plastics 1401 W 94th St *Web:* www.covalenceplastics.com	Minneapolis	MN	55431	800-873-3941	
CUE Inc 11 Leonberg Rd *TF:* 800-283-4621 ■ *Web:* www.cue-inc.com	Cranberry Township	PA	16066	724-772-5225	772-5280
CYRO Industries 100 Enterprise Dr **Fax:* Hum Res ■ *Web:* www.cyro.com	Rockaway	NJ	07866	973-442-6000	442-6114*
D & B Plastics Inc 706 Highland Ct Dr PO Box 26 *TF:* 800-405-2247 ■ *Web:* www.dandbplastics.com	Fairmont	MN	56031	507-235-5950	235-6048
Danafilms Inc 5 Otis St PO Box 624 *TF:* 800-634-8289 ■ *Web:* www.danafilms.com	Westborough	MA	01581	508-366-8884	898-0106
Dielectrics Industries Inc 300 Burnett Rd *TF:* 800-472-7286 ■ *Web:* www.dielectrics.com	Chicopee	MA	01020	413-594-8111	594-2343
Dunmore Corp 145 Wharton Rd *TF:* 800-444-0242 ■ *Web:* www.dunmore.com	Bristol	PA	19007	215-781-8895	781-9293
Enbee Plastics Inc 35 E Main St **Fax Area Code:* 888 ■ *TF:* 800-255-9170 ■ *Web:* www.enbee.com	Middleboro	MA	02346	718-721-3700	431-1890*
Enflo Corp 315 Lake Ave *TF:* 888-887-4093 ■ *Web:* www.enflo.com	Bristol	CT	06010	860-589-0014	589-7179
Falcon Foam Div Atlas Roofing 8240 Byron Center Rd SW *TF:* 800-917-9138 ■ *Web:* www.falconfoam.com	Byron Center	MI	49315	616-878-1568	878-9942
Farber Plastics Inc 162 Hanse Ave *TF:* 800-338-6315	Freeport	NY	11520	516-378-4860	378-4312
Favorite Plastic Corp 1465 Utica Ave *TF Cust Svc:* 800-221-8077 ■ *Web:* www.favoriteplastics.com	Brooklyn	NY	11234	718-253-7000	377-1918
Film Technologies International Inc 2630 Fairfield Ave S *TF:* 800-777-1770 ■ *Web:* www.filmtechnologies.com	Saint Petersburg	FL	33712	727-327-2544	327-7132
FLEXcon Co Inc 1 Flexcon Industrial Pk *Web:* www.flexcon.com	Spencer	MA	01562	508-885-8200	885-8400
Fluoro Plastics Inc 3601 G St *TF Cust Svc:* 800-262-1910 ■ *Web:* www.fluoro-plastics.com	Philadelphia	PA	19134	215-425-5500	425-5521
Francesville Drain Tile Corp 4385 S County Rd 1450 W PO Box 368 *Web:* www.fratco.com	Francesville	IN	47946	219-567-9133	567-9296
Gary Plastic Packaging Corp 1340 Viele Ave *TF:* 800-221-8150 ■ *Web:* www.plasticboxes.com	Bronx	NY	10474	718-893-2200	378-2141
GE Specialty Film & Sheet 1 Plastics Ave *TF:* 800-451-3147 ■ *Web:* www.geplastics.com	Pittsfield	MA	01201	413-448-5400	
General Formulations Inc 309 S Union St *TF:* 800-253-3664 ■ *Web:* www.generalformulations.com	Sparta	MI	49345	616-887-7387	887-0537
Glasforms Inc 271 Barnard Ave *TF:* 888-297-3800 ■ *Web:* www.glassforms.com	San Jose	CA	95125	408-297-9300	297-0601
GSE Lining Technology Inc 19103 Gundle Rd *TF:* 800-435-2008 ■ *Web:* www.gseworld.com	Houston	TX	77073	281-443-8564	875-6010
Holm Industries Inc Saint Charles Div 315 N 9th St *TF:* 800-221-2209	Saint Charles	IL	60174	630-584-1880	584-8972
Homalite Div Brandywine Investment Group 11 Brookside Dr *TF:* 800-346-7802 ■ *Web:* www.homalite.com	Wilmington	DE	19804	302-652-3686	652-4578
Impact Plastics Inc 154 West St Bldg 3 Unit C *TF:* 800-625-7224	Cromwell	CT	06416	860-632-3550	632-3552
Interfilm Holdings Inc 223 Pine Rd *TF:* 800-648-4828 ■ *Web:* www.interfilm-usa.com	Easley	SC	29642	864-269-4690	269-5048
Intermex Inc 9330 LBJ Fwy Suite 260 *TF:* 800-527-2303	Dallas	TX	75243	214-575-0572	575-7306
JPS Elastomerics Corp 9 Sullivan Rd *TF:* 800-621-7663 ■ *Web:* www.jpselastomerics.com	Holyoke	MA	01040	413-533-8100	552-1199
Kama Corp 600 Dietrich Ave *TF:* 800-628-7598 ■ *Web:* www.alcoa.com/kama	Hazleton	PA	18201	570-455-2022	
Karolina Polymers Inc 1508 S Center St *TF:* 800-280-2247	Hickory	NC	28602	828-328-2247	322-3674
Kayline Processing Inc 31 Coates St *TF Sales:* 800-367-5546 ■ *Web:* www.kayline.com	Trenton	NJ	08611	609-695-1449	989-1094
Kendall Packaging Corp 10200 N Port Washington Rd *TF:* 800-237-0951 ■ *Web:* www.kendallpkg.com	Mequon	WI	53092	262-404-1200	404-1221
Kepner Plastics Fabricators Inc 3131 Lomita Blvd *Web:* www.kepnerplastics.com	Torrance	CA	90505	310-325-3162	326-8560
Lavanture Products Co PO Box 2088 *TF:* 800-348-7625 ■ *Web:* www.lavanture.com	Elkhart	IN	46515	574-264-0658	264-6601
Louisiana Plastic Industries 501 Downing Pines Rd	West Monroe	LA	71292	318-388-4562	387-5642
McNeel International Corp 5401 W Kennedy Blvd Suite 751	Tampa	FL	33609	813-286-8680	286-1535
Mitsubishi Polyester Film LLC 2001 Hood Rd **Fax:* Mktg ■ *TF:* 800-845-2009 ■ *Web:* www.m-petfilm.com	Greer	SC	29650	864-879-5000	879-5006*
MPI Technologies 37 East St *TF:* 888-674-8088 ■ *Web:* www.mpirelease.com	Winchester	MA	01890	781-729-8300	729-9093
Natvar 8720 US 70 W *TF:* 800-395-6288 ■ *Web:* www.natvar.com	Clayton	NC	27520	919-553-4151	553-4156
New Hampshire Plastics Inc 1 Bouchard St *TF:* 800-258-3036	Manchester	NH	03103	603-669-8523	622-4888
Northland Plastics Inc 1420 S 16th St PO Box 290 *TF:* 800-776-7163 ■ *Web:* www.northlandplastics.com	Sheboygan	WI	53082	920-458-0732	458-4881
Orcon Corp 1570 Atlantic St *TF:* 800-227-0505 ■ *Web:* www.orcon.com	Union City	CA	94587	510-489-8100	489-6436
Penn Fibre Plastics 2434 Bristol Rd *TF Cust Svc:* 800-662-7366 ■ *Web:* www.pennfibre.com	Bensalem	PA	19020	215-702-9551	702-9552
Performance Coating International 10 Henderson Dr *Web:* pcoatingsintl.com	West Caldwell	NJ	07006	973-227-1500	227-5402
Performance Materials Corp 1150 Calle Suerte *Web:* www.performancematerials.com	Camarillo	CA	93012	805-482-1722	482-8776
Plaskolite Inc 1770 Joyce Ave *TF:* 800-848-9124 ■ *Web:* www.plaskolite.com	Columbus	OH	43219	614-294-3281	297-7287
Primex Plastics Corp 1235 N 'F' St *TF:* 800-222-5116 ■ *Web:* www.primexplastics.com	Richmond	IN	47374	765-966-7774	935-1083
Prinsco Inc 108 W Hwy 7 PO Box 265 *TF:* 800-992-1725 ■ *Web:* www.prinsco.com	Prinsburg	MN	56281	320-978-4116	978-8602
Quality Films Inc 321 Duncan St PO Box 459 *TF:* 800-306-5263 ■ *Web:* www.qualityfilmsinc.com	Schoolcraft	MI	49087	269-679-5263	679-4261
Raven Industries Inc 205 E 6th St *NASDAQ:* RAVN ■ *TF:* 800-227-2836 ■ *Web:* www.ravenind.com	Sioux Falls	SD	57104	605-336-2750	335-0268
Ross & Roberts Inc 1299 W Broad St *TF:* 800-822-4220	Stratford	CT	06615	203-378-9363	377-8841
Ryko Plastics Products Inc 12903 Jurupa Ave *Web:* www.ryko-products.com	Fontana	CA	92337	951-749-2411	749-2414
Sheffield Plastics Inc 119 Salisbury Rd *TF Cust Svc:* 800-254-1707 ■ *Web:* www.sheffieldplasticsinc.com	Sheffield	MA	01257	413-229-8711	229-8717
Shepherd CE Co Inc 2221 Canada Dry St *TF:* 800-324-6733 ■ *Web:* www.ceshepherd.com	Houston	TX	77023	713-928-3763	928-2324
Sigma Plastics Group Page & Schuyler Aves Bldg 8 *Web:* www.sigmaplastics.com	Lyndhurst	NJ	07071	201-933-6000	933-6429
Sinclair & Rush Inc 123 Manufacturers Dr *TF:* 800-408-7125 ■ *Web:* www.sinclair-rush.com	Arnold	MO	63010	636-282-6800	282-6888
SLM Mfg Corp 215 Davidson Ave *TF:* 800-526-3708 ■ *Web:* www.slmcorp.com	Somerset	NJ	08873	732-469-7500	469-5546
Soliant LLC 1872 Hwy 9 Bypass *TF:* 800-288-9401 ■ *Web:* www.paintfilm.com	Lancaster	SC	29720	803-285-9401	313-8331
Southern Film Extruders Inc 2319 English Rd *TF:* 800-334-6101 ■ *Web:* www.southernfilm.com	High Point	NC	27262	336-885-8091	885-1221
Southwall Technologies Inc 3975 E Bayshore Rd *Web:* www.southwall.com	Palo Alto	CA	94303	650-962-9111	967-8713
Sto-Cote Products Inc 218 South Rd *TF:* 800-435-2621	Genoa City	WI	53128	262-279-6000	279-6744
Summit Plastics Inc 107 Laurel St *TF:* 800-790-7117 ■ *Web:* www.summitplastics.us	Summit	MS	39666	601-276-7500	276-2400
Sunlite Plastics Inc W 194 N 11340 McCormick Dr *Web:* www.sunliteplastics.com	Germantown	WI	53022	262-253-0600	253-0601
Tee Group Films 605 N Main St *Web:* www.tee-group.com	Ladd	IL	61329	815-894-2331	894-3387
Thatcher Tubes LLC 1005 Courtaulds Dr *TF:* 888-842-8243 ■ *Web:* www.thatchertubes.com	Woodstock	IL	60098	815-334-1200	334-1230
Thermoplastic Processes Inc 1268 Valley Rd *TF:* 888-554-6400 ■ *Web:* www.thermoplasticprocesses.com	Stirling	NJ	07980	908-561-3000	753-6749
Transilwrap Co Inc 9201 W Belmont Ave *TF:* 800-745-5802 ■ *Web:* www.transilwrap.com	Franklin Park	IL	60131	847-678-1800	233-0199
Tredegar Corp Film Products Div 1100 Boulders Pkwy *TF:* 800-411-7441 ■ *Web:* www.tredegarfilm.com	Richmond	VA	23225	804-330-1222	330-1201
Tri-Seal International Inc 900 Bradley Hill Rd *Web:* www.tekni-plex.com/companies/triseal.html	Blauvelt	NY	10913	845-353-3300	353-3376
Tulox Plastics Corp 401 S Miller Ave *TF Cust Svc:* 800-234-1118 ■ *Web:* www.tulox.com	Marion	IN	46953	765-664-5155	664-0257
Valley Decorating Co 2829 E Hamilton Ave *TF:* 800-245-2817 ■ *Web:* www.pomponcentral.com	Fresno	CA	93721	559-495-1100	495-1195
VCF Films Inc 1100 Sutton Ave *TF:* 888-823-4141 ■ *Web:* www.vcffilm.com	Howell	MI	48843	517-546-2300	546-2984
Victory Plastics International 25 Shelley Rd *Web:* www.victoryplastics.com	Haverhill	MA	01835	978-373-1551	373-6562
Vinylex Corp 2636 Byington Rd **Fax:* Cust Svc ■ *TF:* 800-624-4435 ■ *Web:* www.vinylex.com	Knoxville	TN	37931	865-690-2211	691-6273*
VPI Corp 3123 S 9th St *TF Orders:* 800-874-4240 ■ *Web:* www.vpicorp.com	Sheboygan	WI	53081	920-458-4664	458-1368
Watersaver Co Inc 5870 E 56th Ave *TF:* 800-525-2424 ■ *Web:* www.watersaver.com	Commerce City	CO	80022	303-289-1818	287-3136
Winzen Engineering 23350 Southport PO Box 692108	San Antonio	TX	78269	210-415-5041	698-2341
Winzen Film Inc 1212 Elm St *TF:* 800-779-7595 ■ *Web:* www.winzen.com	Sulphur Springs	TX	75482	903-885-7595	885-4702
Zippertubing Co 13000 S Broadway *TF:* 800-321-8178 ■ *Web:* www.zippertubing.com	Los Angeles	CA	90061	310-527-0488	767-1714

604 PLASTICS FOAM PRODUCTS

	City	State	ZIP	Phone	Fax
AASR Inc 2219 McKinney St *TF Cust Svc:* 800-621-0685	Houston	TX	77003	713-223-4474	229-0091
Action Products Co Inc 1 Action Rd *Web:* www.actionp.com	Odessa	MO	64076	816-633-5514	230-8122
Adams RL Plastics Inc 5955 Crossroads Commerce Pkwy *TF:* 800-968-2241 ■ *Web:* www.adamsplasticsinc.com	Wyoming	MI	49517	616-261-4400	249-8955
Advanced Materials Group Inc 20211 S Susana Rd *TF Cust Svc:* 800-395-3626 ■ *Web:* www.advmatl.com	Rancho Dominguez	CA	90221	310-537-5444	537-4557
American Converters Inc 5360 Main St NE *TF:* 888-360-8050 ■ *Web:* www.amconvas.com	Fridley	MN	55421	763-574-1044	574-1015
American Excelsior Co PO Box 5067 *TF:* 800-777-7645 ■ *Web:* www.amerexcel.com	Arlington	TX	76005	817-640-1555	649-7816
Astrofoam Molding Co Inc 4117 Calle Tesoro *TF:* 800-339-0967 ■ *Web:* www.astrofoam.com	Camarillo	CA	93012	805-482-7276	482-6599
Blue Ridge Products Inc PO Box 2028 *TF:* 800-345-1367	Hickory	NC	28603	828-322-7990	322-4732
Bontex Inc 1 Bontex Dr *TF:* 800-733-4234 ■ *Web:* www.bontex.com	Buena Vista	VA	24416	540-261-2181	261-3784
Burnett Process Inc 5928 Court Street Rd	Syracuse	NY	13206	315-437-1131	437-1136
Burnett WT & Co Inc 1500 Bush St **Fax:* Sales ■ *TF:* 800-638-0606	Baltimore	MD	21230	410-837-3000	799-2620*
Carlon Products Co PO Box 377 *TF Cust Svc:* 800-243-6682 ■ *Web:* www.carlonproducts.com	Derby	CT	06418	203-735-7474	732-5384
Carpenter Co 5016 Monument Ave *TF:* 800-288-3830 ■ *Web:* www.carpenter.com	Richmond	VA	23230	804-359-0800	353-0694
Cashiers Plastic Div Consolidated Metco Inc PO Box 37	Cashiers	NC	28717	828-743-3461	743-6465
Cellect LLC 12 New St *Web:* www.sentinelfoam.com	Saint Johnsville	NY	13452	518-568-7036	568-2614
Cellofoam North America Inc PO Box 406 *TF:* 800-241-3634 ■ *Web:* www.cellofoam.com	Conyers	GA	30012	770-929-3688	929-3608
Cellox Corp 1200 Industrial St *TF:* 888-217-6631 ■ *Web:* www.cellox.com	Reedsburg	WI	53959	608-524-2316	524-2362
Chestnut Ridge Foam Inc PO Box 781 *TF:* 800-234-2734	Latrobe	PA	15650	724-537-9000	537-9003
Clark Foam Products Corp 655 Remington Blvd *Web:* www.clarkfoam.net	Bolingbrook	IL	60440	630-226-5900	226-5959
Clayton Corp 866 Horan Dr *TF Cust Svc:* 800-325-6180 ■ *Web:* www.claytoncorp.com	Fenton	MO	63026	636-349-5333	349-5335
Consolidated Metco Inc Cashiers Plastic Div PO Box 37	Cashiers	NC	28717	828-743-3461	743-6465
Createc Corp 888 Keystone Crossing Suite 1600 *Web:* www.createccorp.com	Indianapolis	IN	46240	317-566-0022	566-9910
Creative Foam Corp 300 N Alloy Dr *TF:* 800-837-0630 ■ *Web:* www.creativefoam.com	Fenton	MI	48430	810-629-4149	629-7368
Crest Foam Industries Inc 100 Carol Pl *Web:* www.crestfoam.com	Moonachie	NJ	07074	201-807-0809	807-1113
Custom Pack Inc 443 Creamery Way *TF:* 800-722-7005 ■ *Web:* www.custompackinc.com	Exton	PA	19341	610-524-4222	524-4777
Dart Container Corp 500 Hogsback Rd *TF:* 800-248-5960 ■ *Web:* www.dart.biz	Mason	MI	48854	517-676-3800	676-3883
DIAB Group 315 Seahawk Dr *Web:* www.diabgroup.com	DeSoto	TX	75115	972-228-7600	228-2667

				Phone	Fax
Diversifoam Products 9091 County Rd 50	Rockford	MN	55373	763-477-5854	477-5863
TF: 800-669-0100					
Dow Thermoset Systems 1881 W Oak Pkwy	Marietta	GA	30062	770-428-2684	428-9431
TF: 800-735-3129 ■ *Web:* www.dow.com/polyurethane					
Duraco Inc 7400 W Industrial Dr	Forest Park	IL	60130	708-488-1025	488-1215
TF: 800-852-1025 ■ *Web:* www.duracoinc.com					
E-A-R Specialty Composites 7911 Zions Rd	Indianapolis	IN	46268	317-692-6666	692-6624
TF: 800-544-5180 ■ *Web:* www.earsc.com					
Edge-Sweets Co 2887 Three-Mile Rd NW	Grand Rapids	MI	49544	616-453-5458	453-6227
Web: www.edge-sweets.com					
Elliott Co of Indianapolis Inc 9200 Zionsville Rd	Indianapolis	IN	46268	317-291-1213	291-1219
TF Orders: 800-545-1213 ■ *Web:* www.elliottfoam.com					
Elm Packaging Co 1261 Brukner Dr	Troy	OH	45373	937-339-2655	339-2532
TF Cust Svc: 800-962-0635					
Fairmont Corp 2245 W Pershing Rd	Chicago	IL	60609	773-376-1300	376-3037
TF: 800-621-6907					
Federal Foam Technologies Inc 600 Wisconsin Dr	New Richmond	WI	54017	715-246-9500	246-9599
TF: 800-898-9559 ■ *Web:* www.federalfoam.com					
Flextron Industries Inc 720 Mount Rd	Aston	PA	19014	610-459-4600	459-5379
TF: 800-633-2181 ■ *Web:* www.flextronindustries.com					
FloraCraft Corp PO Box 400	Ludington	MI	49431	231-845-5127	845-0240
TF: 800-253-0409 ■ *Web:* www.floracraft.com					
FM Corp PO Box 1720	Rogers	AR	72757	479-636-3540	631-2392
Web: www.fmplastics.com					
Foam Fabricators Inc 950 Progress Blvd	New Albany	IN	47150	812-948-1696	948-2450
Web: www.foamfabricatorsinc.com					
Foam Molders & Specialty Corp 20004 State Rd	Cerritos	CA	90703	562-924-7757	402-9515
Web: www.foammolders.com					
Foam Rubber Products Inc 2000 Troy Ave	New Castle	IN	47362	765-521-2000	521-2759
TF: 800-878-3774					
Foamade Industries Inc 2550 Auburn Ct	Auburn Hills	MI	48326	248-852-6010	853-3442
TF: 800-221-7388 ■ *Web:* www.foamade.com					
Foamex International Inc 1000 Columbia Ave	Linwood	PA	19061	610-859-3000	859-3035
TF: 800-355-3626 ■ *Web:* www.foamex.com					
Fomo Products Inc 2775 Barber Rd	Norton	OH	44203	330-753-4585	753-9566*
*Fax: Cust Svc ■ *TF:* 800-321-5585 ■ *Web:* www.fomo.com					
FP International 1090 Mills Way	Redwood City	CA	94063	650-261-5300	361-1713
TF: 800-866-9946 ■ *Web:* www.fpintl.com					
Free-Flow Packaging Corp DBA FP International 1090 Mills Way	Redwood City	CA	94063	650-261-5300	361-1713
TF: 800-866-9946 ■ *Web:* www.fpintl.com					
Future Foam Inc 400 N 10th St	Council Bluffs	IA	51503	712-323-6718	323-7163
TF: 800-733-8067					
Fypon Ltd 960 W Barre Rd	Archbold	OH	43502	800-446-3040	446-9373
TF: 800-955-5748 ■ *Web:* www.fypon.com					
G & T Industries Inc 3413 Eastern Ave SE	Grand Rapids	MI	49508	616-452-8611	452-3619
TF: 800-686-2659 ■ *Web:* www.gtindustries.com					
G & T Industries of Indiana Inc 2741 Cathy Ln	Jasper	IN	47546	812-634-2252	634-2875
Gaco Western Inc PO Box 88698	Seattle	WA	98138	206-575-0450	575-0587
TF Cust Svc: 800-456-4226 ■ *Web:* www.gaco.com					
General Plastics Mfg Co 4910 Burlington Way	Tacoma	WA	98409	253-473-5000	473-5104
TF: 800-806-6051 ■ *Web:* www.generalplastics.com					
Gilman Brothers Co PO Box 38	Gilman	CT	06336	860-889-8444	889-5226
TF: 800-852-4220					
Guardian Packaging Inc 3615 Security St	Garland	TX	75042	214-349-1500	349-1584
TF: 800-259-1502 ■ *Web:* www.guardianpackaging.com					
Hibco Plastics Inc PO Box 157	Yadkinville	NC	27055	336-463-2391	463-5591
TF: 800-849-8683					
Innovative Plastics Corp 400 Rt 303	Orangeburg	NY	10962	845-359-7500	359-0237
Intertrade Industries Ltd 15632 Commerce Ln	Huntington Beach	CA	92649	714-894-5566	894-3927
Web: www.intertradeindustries.com					
Kelly Co Inc 179 Brook St	Clinton	MA	01510	978-368-8991	365-9679
Kerr Group Inc 1706 Hempstead Rd	Lancaster	PA	17601	717-299-6511	299-5844
TF: 800-367-1876 ■ *Web:* www.kerrgroup.com					
King & Co Inc PO Box 10	Clarksville	AR	72830	479-754-6090	754-8445
TF Cust Svc: 800-643-9530 ■ *Web:* www.thermo-tile.com					
Life-Like Products Inc 1600 Union Ave	Baltimore	MD	21211	410-889-1023	889-7619
TF Cust Svc: 800-638-1470 ■ *Web:* www.lifelikeproducts.com					
Liqui-Box Corp 6950 Worthington-Galena Rd	Worthington	OH	43085	614-888-9280	888-0982
Web: www.liquibox.com					
M & H Industries Inc 32500 Capitol St	Livonia	MI	48150	734-261-7560	261-9210
Minnesota Diversified Products Inc DBA Diversifoam Products 9091 County Rd 50	Rockford	MN	55373	763-477-5854	477-5863
TF: 800-669-0100					
Mossberg Industries Inc 204 N 2nd St	Garrett	IN	46738	260-357-5141	357-5144
Web: www.mossbergindustries.com					
Munot Plastics Inc 2935 W 17th St	Erie	PA	16505	814-838-7721	833-2095
Web: www.munotplastics.com					
North Carolina Foam Industries Inc 1515 Carter St	Mount Airy	NC	27030	336-789-9161	789-9586
TF: 800-346-8229 ■ *Web:* www.ncfi.com					
Nu-Foam Products Inc 220 S Elizabeth St PO Box 126	Spencerville	OH	45887	419-647-4191	647-4202
OPCO Inc PO Box 101	Latrobe	PA	15650	724-537-9300	537-9349
TF: 800-229-6726					
Pacific Packaging Products Inc 24 Industrial Way	Wilmington	MA	01887	978-657-9100	658-4933
TF: 800-777-0300 ■ *Web:* www.pacificpkg.com					
Perry Chemical & Mfg Co Inc PO Box 6419	Lafayette	IN	47903	765-474-3404	474-3423
TF: 800-592-6614 ■ *Web:* www.perrychemical.com					
Plastics Mfg Inc 7301 Caldwell Rd	Harrisburg	NC	28075	704-455-5191	455-1364
TF: 800-446-5191					
Plastomer Corp 37819 Schoolcraft Rd	Livonia	MI	48150	734-464-0700	464-4792
Web: www.plastomer.com					
PMC Global Inc 12243 Branford St	Sun Valley	CA	91352	818-896-1101	686-2531
TF: 800-423-5632 ■ *Web:* www.pmcglobalinc.com					
Poly Foam Inc 116 Pine St S	Lester Prairie	MN	55354	320-395-2551	395-2702
Web: www.polyfoaminc.com					
Poly Molding Corp 96 4th Ave	Haskell	NJ	07420	973-835-7161	835-2438
TF: 800-229-7161					
Polycel Structural Foam Inc 68 County Line Rd	Somerville	NJ	08876	908-722-5254	722-7457
Web: www.polycel.com					
Premier Industries Inc DBA Western Insulfoam Corp 1019 Pacific Ave Suite 1501	Tacoma	WA	98402	253-572-5111	383-7100
Web: www.premier-industries.com					
Radnor Holdings Corp 150 Radnor Chester Rd Radnor Financial Ctr	Radnor	PA	19087	610-341-9600	995-2697
Web: www.radnorholdings.com					
Radva Corp PO Box 2900	Radford	VA	24143	540-639-2458	731-3731
Web: www.radva.com					
Republic Packaging Corp 9160 S Green St	Chicago	IL	60620	773-233-6530	233-6005
Web: www.repco.com					
RL Adams Plastics Inc 5955 Crossroads Commerce Pkwy	Wyoming	MI	49517	616-261-4400	249-8955
TF: 800-968-2241 ■ *Web:* www.adamsplasticsinc.com					
Robbie Mfg Inc 10810 Mid America Ave	Lenexa	KS	66219	913-492-3400	492-1543
TF: 800-255-6328 ■ *Web:* www.robbiemfg.com					
Rogers Foam Corp 20 Vernon St	Somerville	MA	02145	617-623-3010	629-2585
Rogers Foam Corp Tainer Tech Div 20 Vernon St	Somerville	MA	02145	617-623-3010	629-2585
Sekisui America Corp Voltek Div 100 Shepard St	Lawrence	MA	01843	978-685-2557	685-9861
TF Cust Svc: 800-225-0668 ■ *Web:* www.voltek.com					
Shamrock Plastics Inc PO Box 3530	Peoria	IL	61612	309-243-7723	243-5852
Spongex Corp 6 Bridge St	Shelton	CT	06484	203-924-9335	924-0412
TF: 800-782-7749 ■ *Web:* www.spongexcorp.com					
Stephenson & Lawyer Inc 3831 Patterson Ave SE	Grand Rapids	MI	49512	616-949-8100	949-5171
TF: 800-968-5535 ■ *Web:* www.steplaw.com					
Storopack Inc 12007 S Woodruff Ave	Downey	CA	90241	562-803-1584	803-4462
TF: 800-829-1491 ■ *Web:* www.storopackinc.com/					
StyroChem International 3607 N Sylvania Ave	Fort Worth	TX	76111	817-759-4400	831-2269
TF: 800-448-6232 ■ *Web:* www.styrochem.com					
Styrotek Inc PO Box 1180	Delano	CA	93216	661-725-4957	725-7064
TF: 800-936-2611 ■ *Web:* www.styrotek.com					
Tainer Tech Div Rogers Foam Corp 20 Vernon St	Somerville	MA	02145	617-623-3010	629-2585
Tekni-Plex Inc 112 Church St Ext	Flemington	NJ	08822	908-782-4000	782-0990
Texas Fiber-Poly Foam Inc 1200 Rink St	Brenham	TX	77833	979-836-6625	830-0368
TF: 800-798-6729					
Thermo-Serv Inc 3901 Pipestone Rd	Dallas	TX	75212	214-631-0307	631-0566
TF: 800-527-2648 ■ *Web:* www.thermoserv.com					
ThermoSafe Brands 3930 N Ventura Dr Suite 450	Arlington Heights	IL	60004	847-398-0110	398-0653
TF: 800-323-7442 ■ *Web:* www.thermosafe.com					
TMP Technologies Inc 1200 Northland Ave	Buffalo	NY	14215	716-895-6100	895-6396
Web: www.tmptech.com					
TO Plastics Inc 1325 American Blvd Suite 6	Minneapolis	MN	55425	952-854-2131	854-2154
Web: www.toplastics.com					
UFP Technologies Inc 172 E Main St	Georgetown	MA	01833	978-352-2200	352-7169
NASDAQ: UFPT ■ *Web:* www.ufpt.com					
Unique Fabricating Inc 800 Standard Pkwy	Auburn Hills	MI	48326	248-853-2333	853-7720
Web: www.uniquefab.com					
Vita Foam Inc 1900 Stuart St	Chattanooga	TN	37406	423-698-3408	698-0706
TF Cust Svc: 800-627-3972					
Vita Olympic Inc 2222 Surrett Dr	High Point	NC	27263	336-431-1171	431-7747
TF: 800-431-1171 ■ *Web:* www.vitausa.com					
Voltek Div Sekisui America Corp 100 Shepard St	Lawrence	MA	01843	978-685-2557	685-9861
TF Cust Svc: 800-225-0668 ■ *Web:* www.voltek.com					
Western Insulfoam Corp 1019 Pacific Ave Suite 1501	Tacoma	WA	98402	253-572-5111	383-7100
Web: www.premier-industries.com					
WinCup 7980 W Buckeye Rd	Phoenix	AZ	85043	623-936-1791	936-6433*
*Fax: Hum Res ■ *TF:* 800-292-2877 ■ *Web:* www.wincup.com					
Woodbridge Foam Corp 4240 Sherwoodtowne Blvd	Mississauga	ON	L4Z2G6	905-896-3626	896-9262
Web: www.woodbridgegroup.com					
WT Burnett & Co Inc 1500 Bush St	Baltimore	MD	21230	410-837-3000	799-2620*
*Fax: Sales ■ *TF:* 800-638-0606					

605 PLASTICS MACHINING & FORMING

SEE ALSO Plastics Molding - Custom p. 2121

				Phone	Fax
Akra Plastic Products Inc 1504 E Cedar St	Ontario	CA	91761	909-930-1999	930-1948
Bardes Plastics Inc 5225 W Clinton Ave	Milwaukee	WI	53223	414-354-5300	354-6331
TF Cust Svc: 800-558-5161 ■ *Web:* www.bardesplastics.com					
Bo-Mer Mfg Co 13 Pulaski St	Auburn	NY	13021	315-252-7216	252-7450
TF: 800-221-6563 ■ *Web:* www.bo-mer.com					
Cal Plastics 2050 E 48th St	Los Angeles	CA	90058	323-581-6194	581-1805
Comco Plastics Inc 98-34 Jamaica Ave	Woodhaven	NY	11421	718-849-9000	441-5361
TF: 800-849-0731 ■ *Web:* www.comcoplastics.com					
Conroy & Knowlton Inc 2000 S Hoefner Ave	Commerce	CA	90040	323-665-5288	722-4670
TF: 888-295-9500 ■ *Web:* www.conroyknowlton.com					
East Jordan Plastics Inc PO Box 575	East Jordan	MI	49727	231-536-2243	536-7090
EGC Corp 11718 McGallion Rd	Houston	TX	77076	281-774-6100	774-6219
TF: 800-342-7677 ■ *Web:* www.egccorp.com					
Elixir Industries Inc Custom Aluminum Div 5600 NE 121st Ave	Vancouver	WA	98682	360-254-5077	254-4577
TF: 800-426-1782					
Empire West Inc 9270 Graton Rd PO Box 511	Graton	CA	95444	707-823-1190	823-8531
TF: 800-521-4261 ■ *Web:* www.empirewest.com					
Engineered Plastics Inc 211 Chase St PO Box 227	Gibsonville	NC	27249	336-449-4121	449-6352
TF: 800-711-1740 ■ *Web:* www.engplas.com					
Engineered Sinterings & Plastics Inc 140 Commercial St	Watertown	CT	06795	860-274-7546	274-4406
Web: www.engsint.com					
Ensinger Hyde Co 1 Main St	Grenloch	NJ	08032	856-227-0500	232-1754
TF: 800-234-4933 ■ *Web:* www.alhyde.com					
Fabri-Form Co 200 S Friendship Dr	New Concord	OH	43762	740-826-5000	826-5001
TF: 800-837-2574 ■ *Web:* www.fabri-form.com					
Fabri-Kal Corp Plastics Pl	Kalamazoo	MI	49001	269-385-5050	385-0197
TF: 800-888-5054 ■ *Web:* www.fabri-kal.com					
Filtrona Richmond Inc 1625-A Ashton Park Dr	Colonial Heights	VA	23834	804-275-2631	743-0321
FNW Industrial Plastics Inc 740 S 28th St	Washougal	WA	98671	360-835-2129	835-3521
TF: 800-634-5082 ■ *Web:* www.hdpeproducts.com					
Formall Inc 3908 Fountain Valley Dr	Knoxville	TN	37918	865-922-7514	922-3941
TF: 800-643-3676 ■ *Web:* www.formall.com					
Gage Industries Inc PO Box 1318	Lake Oswego	OR	97035	503-639-2177	624-1070
TF: 800-443-4243 ■ *Web:* www.gageindustries.com					
GML Inc 500 Oak Grove Pkwy	Saint Paul	MN	55127	651-490-0000	490-1651
TF: 800-344-8899 ■ *Web:* www.gmlmanufacturing.com					
Graham Machinery Group 1203 Eden Rd	York	PA	17402	717-848-3755	846-1931
Web: www.grahammachinerygroup.com					
Gregstrom Corp 64 Holton St	Woburn	MA	01801	781-935-6600	935-4905
Web: www.gregstrom.com					
Harvel Plastics Inc 300 Kuebler Rd	Easton	PA	18040	610-252-7355	253-4436
Web: www.harvel.com					
Inline Plastics Corp 42 Canal St	Shelton	CT	06484	203-924-5933	924-0370
TF: 800-826-5567 ■ *Web:* www.inlineplastics.com					
Jamestown Plastics Inc PO Box U	Brocton	NY	14716	716-792-4144	792-4154
Web: www.jamestownplastics.com					
Lamar Plastic Packaging Ltd 216 N Main St	Freeport	NY	11520	516-378-2500	378-6192
Mantex Corp 611 Industrial Pkwy	Imlay City	MI	48444	810-721-2100	721-9911
TF: 800-666-2689 ■ *Web:* www.mantex.net					
McNeal Enterprises Inc 2031 Ringwood Ave	San Jose	CA	95131	408-922-7290	922-7299
TF: 800-562-6325 ■ *Web:* www.mcneal.com					
Meyer Plastics Inc 5167 E 65th St	Indianapolis	IN	46220	317-259-4131	252-4687
TF: 800-968-4131 ■ *Web:* www.meyerplastics.com					
Morgan Hill Plastics Inc 640 E Dunne Ave	Morgan Hill	CA	95037	408-779-2118	779-0322
TF: 800-449-0322 ■ *Web:* www.morganhillplastics.com					
Multi-Form Plastics Inc 700 Kent Rd	Batavia	OH	45103	513-732-0961	732-0906
Panterra Engineered Plastics 68 Southfield Ave 2 Stamford Landing Suite 100	Stamford	CT	06902	203-921-0345	921-0344
Web: www.pepcore.com					
Paradise Plastics PO Drawer Y	Plant City	FL	33563	813-752-1155	754-3168
Web: www.paradiseplastics.com					
Parkway Products Inc 10293 Burlington Rd	Cincinnati	OH	45231	513-851-5550	851-1926
Web: www.parkwayproducts.com					
Parsons Mfg Corp 1055 O'Brien Dr	Menlo Park	CA	94025	650-324-4726	324-3051
TF: 800-221-0823 ■ *Web:* www.parsonscases.com					

	City	State	Zip	Phone	Fax
Parsons Precision Products Inc 3333 Main St	Parsons	KS	67357	620-421-3400	421-2301
Web: www.parsonsprecision.com					
Perkasie Industries Corp PO Box 179	Perkasie	PA	18944	215-257-6581	453-1703
TF Sales: 800-523-6747					
Placon Corp 6096 McKee Rd	Madison	WI	53719	608-271-5634	271-3162
TF: 800-541-1535 ■ *Web:* www.placon.com					
Plastic Products Mfg Corp 1724 Junction Ave	San Jose	CA	95112	408-436-8780	436-1918
Polygon Co 103 Industrial Park Dr PO Box 176	Walkerton	IN	46574	574-586-3145	586-7336
TF: 800-918-9261 ■ *Web:* www.polygoncompany.com					
Prent Corp 2225 Kennedy Rd	Janesville	WI	53545	608-754-0276	754-2410
Web: www.prent.com					
PSC Mfg Inc 3424 De La Cruz Blvd	Santa Clara	CA	95054	408-988-5115	988-4044
Web: www.pscinc.cc					
Quadrant Engineering Plastic Products USA					
2120 Fairmont Ave PO Box 14235	Reading	PA	19612	610-320-6600	320-6868*
**Fax:* Sales ■ *TF:* 800-366-0300 ■ *Web:* www.quadrantepp.com					
Ray Products Co Inc 1700 Chablis Ave	Ontario	CA	91761	909-390-9906	390-9984
TF: 800-423-7859 ■ *Web:* www.rayplastics.com					
Roncelli Plastics Inc 330 W Duarte Rd	Monrovia	CA	91016	626-358-2536	358-4329
Web: www.roncelli.com					
Ronningen Research & Development Co 6700 E 'YZ' Ave	Vicksburg	MI	49097	269-649-0520	649-0526
Web: www.ronningenresearch.com					
Soroc Products Inc Plastics Div 4349 S Dort Hwy	Burton	MI	48529	810-743-2660	743-5922
Web: www.sorocproducts.com					
Spaulding Composites Co Fab Div 55 Nadeau Dr	Rochester	NH	03867	603-332-0555	332-5357
TF: 800-964-0555 ■ *Web:* www.spauldingcom.com					
Speck Plastics Inc PO Box 421	Nazareth	PA	18064	610-759-1807	759-3916
TF: 800-755-2922 ■ *Web:* www.speckplastics.com					
Stewart Industries Inc 16 S Idaho St	Seattle	WA	98134	206-652-9110	652-9123
Total Plastics Inc 3316 Pagosa Ct	Indianapolis	IN	46226	317-543-3540	543-3553
TF: 800-382-4635 ■ *Web:* www.totalplastics.com					
Vinyl Source Inc 427 Thatcher Ln	Youngstown	OH	44515	330-792-6511	792-5870
TF: 800-824-4067					
Western Fibre Products Inc 10924 Vulcan St	South Gate	CA	90280	562-861-6665	862-9692

606 PLASTICS MATERIALS - WHOL

	City	State	Zip	Phone	Fax
A Daigger & Co Inc 620 Lakeview Pkwy	Vernon Hills	IL	60061	847-816-5060	320-7200*
**Fax Area Code:* 800 ■ *TF:* 800-621-7193 ■ *Web:* www.daigger.com					
Aetna Plastics Corp 1702 Saint Clair Ave	Cleveland	OH	44114	216-781-4421	781-4474
TF: 800-634-3074 ■ *Web:* www.aetnaplastics.com					
AIN Plastics Inc 1750 E Heights Dr	Madison Heights	MI	48071	248-356-4000	356-4745
TF Cust Svc: 800-521-1757 ■ *Web:* www.ainplastics.com					
All American Containers Inc 9330 NW 110th Ave	Miami	FL	33178	305-887-0797	888-4133
Web: www.americancontainers.com					
Allpak Co 1010 Lake St	Oak Park	IL	60301	708-383-7200	383-7206
Aztec Supply Co 954 N Batavia St	Orange	CA	92867	714-771-6580	771-3013
Web: www.aztecblaze.com					
Bamberger Polymers Inc 2 Jericho Plaza Suite 109	Jericho	NY	11753	516-622-3600	622-3610
TF: 800-888-8959 ■ *Web:* www.bambergerpolymers.com					
Buckley Industries Inc 1850 E 53rd St N	Wichita	KS	67219	316-744-7587	744-8463
TF: 800-835-2779 ■ *Web:* www.buckleyind.com					
Calsak Corp 1225 W 190th St Suite 375	Gardena	CA	90248	310-719-9500	719-1300
TF: 800-743-2595 ■ *Web:* www.calsak.com					
Cope Plastics Inc 4441 Industrial Dr	Godfrey	IL	62035	618-466-0221	466-7975
TF: 800-851-5510 ■ *Web:* www.copeplastics.com					
El Mar Plastics Inc 303 W Artesia Blvd	Compton	CA	90220	310-928-0205	928-0207
TF: 800-255-5210 ■ *Web:* www.elmarplastics.com					
GE Polymerland 9930 Kincey Ave	Huntersville	NC	28078	704-992-5100	752-7842*
**Fax Area Code:* 888 ■ *TF:* 800-752-7842 ■ *Web:* www.gepolymerland.com					
Gildenhorn Nate & Co Inc Rosenstein & Co Div					
413 N Cedar St	Mishawaka	IN	46545	574-255-9639	255-9727
GLS Corp 833 Ridgeview Dr	McHenry	IL	60050	815-385-8500	385-8533
TF: 800-457-8777 ■ *Web:* www.glscorp.com					
H Muehlstein & Co Inc 800 Connecticut Ave	Norwalk	CT	06854	203-855-6000	855-6221
TF: 800-257-3746 ■ *Web:* www.muehlstein.com					
H Sattler Plastics Co Inc 5410 W Roosevelt Rd	Chicago	IL	60644	312-733-2900	733-5290
Web: www.sattlerplastics.com					
Laird Plastics Inc 6800 Broken Sound Pkwy Suite 150	Boca Raton	FL	33487	561-443-9100	443-9108
TF: 800-610-1016 ■ *Web:* www.lairdplastics.com					
Louisiana Utilities Supply PO Box 3531	Baton Rouge	LA	70821	225-383-8916	387-5256
TF: 800-743-8916					
M Holland Co 400 Skokie Blvd Suite 600	Northbrook	IL	60062	847-272-7370	272-0525
TF: 800-872-7370 ■ *Web:* www.m-holland.com					
Momentum Technologies Inc 1507 Boettler Rd	Uniontown	OH	44685	330-896-5900	896-9943
TF: 800-720-0261 ■ *Web:* www.momentumtech.net					
Pacific Nursery Pots Inc PO Box 580	Morgan Hill	CA	95038	408-778-3426	778-6294
TF: 800-468-8686					
Pilcher Hamilton Corp 6845 Kingery Hwy	Willowbrook	IL	60527	630-655-8100	655-9948
Web: www.pilcherhamilton.com					
Plastic Sales Southern Inc 6490 Fleet St	Los Angeles	CA	90040	323-728-8309	722-4221
TF: 800-257-7747 ■ *Web:* www.plastic-sales.com					
PlastiFab Inc 1425 Palomares Ave	La Verne	CA	91750	909-596-1927	596-3020
TF: 800-421-9880 ■ *Web:* www.plastifabonline.com					
Polymer Plastics Corp 300 Edison Way	Reno	NV	89502	775-856-7000	856-7010
TF: 800-369-2213 ■ *Web:* www.polymerplastics.com					
Port Plastics Inc 15325 Fairfield Ranch Rd Suite 150	Chino Hills	CA	91709	909-393-5894	597-0116
TF: 800-800-0039 ■ *Web:* www.portplastics.com					
Regal Plastic Supply Co 111 E 10th Ave	North Kansas City	MO	64116	816-421-6290	421-8206
TF: 800-627-2102 ■ *Web:* www.regalplastic.com					
Regal Plastic Supply Co Southern Div 2356 Merrell Rd	Dallas	TX	75229	972-484-0741	484-0746
TF: 800-441-1553 ■ *Web:* www.regal-plastics.com					
Ryan Herco Products Corp 3010 N San Fernando Blvd	Burbank	CA	91504	818-841-1141	973-2600
TF: 800-848-1141 ■ *Web:* www.ryanherco.com					
Seelye Plastics Inc 9700 Newton Ave S	Bloomington	MN	55431	952-881-2658	881-3503*
**Fax:* Sales ■ *TF:* 800-328-2728 ■ *Web:* www.seelye-plastics.com					
Sekisui America Corp 100 Gaither Dr Suite A	Mount Laurel	NJ	08054	856-235-5115	235-0097
TF: 800-866-4005 ■ *Web:* www.sekisui-corp.com					
Superior Oil Co Inc 400 W Regent St	Indianapolis	IN	46225	317-781-4400	781-4401
TF: 800-553-5480 ■ *Web:* www.superioroil.com					
Targun Plastics Co 899 Skokie Blvd	Northbrook	IL	60062	847-509-9355	509-9359
Tech Products Inc 1264-D La Quinta Dr	Orlando	FL	32809	407-447-6108	447-6115
Web: www.techprod.com					
Tekra Corp 16700 W Lincoln Ave	New Berlin	WI	53151	262-784-5533	797-3276
TF: 800-448-3572 ■ *Web:* www.tekra.com					

607 PLASTICS MOLDING - CUSTOM

	City	State	Zip	Phone	Fax
AJ Plastic Products 19919 Shawnee Mission Pkwy	Shawnee	KS	66218	913-422-2027	422-2077
TF: 800-999-5518					
Akron Porcelain & Plastics Co PO Box 15157	Akron	OH	44314	330-745-2159	745-6688
Web: www.akronporcelain.com					
Aline Components Inc 1830 Tomlinson Rd	Kulpsville	PA	19443	215-368-0300	361-1400
Web: www.alinecomponents.com					
Alladin Plastics Inc 140 Industrial Dr	Surgoinsville	TN	37873	423-345-2351	345-3772
TF: 800-960-2351 ■ *Web:* www.alladinplastics.com					
American Metal & Plastics Inc 450 32nd St SW	Grand Rapids	MI	49548	616-452-6061	452-3835
Web: www.ampi-gr.com					
American Plastic Molding Corp 965 S Elm St	Scottsburg	IN	47170	812-752-7000	752-5155
TF: 877-527-8427 ■ *Web:* www.apmc.com					
American Plastics Group Inc 715 W Park Rd	Union	MO	63084	636-583-2583	583-4357
TF: 800-325-9927 ■ *Web:* www.chriskayeplastics.com					
American Urethane Inc 1905 Betson Ct	Odenton	MD	21113	410-672-2100	672-2191
Web: www.americanurethane.com					
Apollo Plastics Corp 5333 N Elston Ave	Chicago	IL	60630	773-282-9222	282-2763
Applied Composites Corp 333 N 6th St	Saint Charles	IL	60174	877-653-9577	653-9576
Web: appliedcompositescorp.birkey.com					
Applied Tech Products 565 Swedesford Rd Suite 315	Wayne	PA	19087	610-688-2200	688-1534
Web: www.appliedtechproducts.com					
Arkay Industries Inc 220 American Way	Monroe	OH	45050	513-360-0390	
Web: www.arkayindustries.com					
Arrowhead Plastic Engineering Inc 2909 S Hoyt Ave	Muncie	IN	47302	765-286-0533	286-1681
Web: www.arrowheadinc.com					
ASK Plastics Inc 9750 Ashton Rd	Philadelphia	PA	19114	215-969-0800	969-2164
Web: www.askplastics.com					
Bain Mfg Co Inc 2 Main St	Grenada	MS	38901	662-226-7921	226-7701
Web: www.bainsoftplastics.com					
Berry Plastics Corp 101 Oakley St	Evansville	IN	47710	812-424-2904	424-0128
TF: 800-234-1930 ■ *Web:* www.berryplastics.com					
BMJ Mold & Engineering Co Inc 1104 N Touby Pike	Kokomo	IN	46901	765-457-1166	459-3664
TF: 800-238-7785 ■ *Web:* www.bmjmold.com					
C Brewer Co 3630 Miraloma Ave	Anaheim	CA	92806	714-630-6810	630-5527
Web: www.cbrewer.com					
C & J Industries 760 Water St	Meadville	PA	16335	814-724-4950	724-4959
Web: www.cjindustries.com					
Canton Mfg 120 E 2nd St	Canton	PA	17724	570-673-5145	673-6819
Capsonic Group 460 S 2nd St	Elgin	IL	60123	847-888-7300	888-7543
Web: www.capsonic.com					
Chilton Products Div Western Industries Inc 300 E Breed St	Chilton	WI	53014	920-849-2381	849-4947
TF: 877-671-7063					
Commercial Plastics Co 800 E Allanson Rd	Mundelein	IL	60060	847-566-1700	566-4737
Web: www.ecommercialplastics.com					
Confer Plastics Inc 97 Witmer Rd	North Tonawanda	NY	14120	716-693-2056	694-3102
TF: 800-635-3213 ■ *Web:* www.conferplastics.com					
Connor Corp 2701 Dwenger Ave	Fort Wayne	IN	46803	260-424-1601	422-7202
Web: www.connorcorp.com					
Continental Structural Plastics PO Box 367	Petoskey	MI	49770	231-347-8791	347-9783
Web: www.cspplastics.com					
Core Molding Technologies Inc 800 Manor Park Dr	Columbus	OH	43228	614-870-5000	870-5051
AMEX: CMT ■ *Web:* www.coremt.com					
Cosmo Corp 30201 Aurora Rd	Cleveland	OH	44139	440-498-7500	498-7515
Web: www.cosmocorp.com					
Cuyahoga Molded Plastics Corp 1265 Babbitt Rd	Cleveland	OH	44132	216-261-2744	261-3537
TF: 800-805-9549 ■ *Web:* www.cuyahogaplastics.com					
D-M-E Co 29111 Stephenson Hwy	Madison Heights	MI	48071	248-398-6000	544-5705
TF: 800-626-6653 ■ *Web:* www.dme.net					
D & M Plastic Corp 150 French Rd	Burlington	IL	60109	847-683-2054	683-2731
Web: www.dmplastics.com					
Design & Molding Services Inc 25 Howard St	Piscataway	NJ	08854	732-752-0300	752-9672
Dickten & Masch LLC N 44 W 33341 Watertown Plank Rd	Nashotah	WI	53058	262-367-5200	367-5630
Web: www.dicktenplastics.com					
Diemolding Corp 125 Rasbach St	Canastota	NY	13032	315-697-2221	697-8083
Web: www.diemolding.com					
Double H Plastics Inc 50 W Street Rd	Warminster	PA	18974	215-674-4100	674-4109
TF: 800-523-3932 ■ *Web:* www.doublehplastics.com					
EFP Corp 223 Middleton Run Rd	Elkhart	IN	46516	574-295-4690	295-6512
TF: 800-205-8537 ■ *Web:* www.efpcorp.com					
Eifel Mold & Engineering 31071 Fraser Dr	Fraser	MI	48026	586-296-9640	296-7280
Web: www.eifel-inc.com					
Elgin Molded Plastics 909 Grace St	Elgin	IL	60120	847-931-2455	524-0087*
**Fax Area Code:* 800 ■ *TF:* 800-548-5483 ■ *Web:* www.elginmolded.com					
Engineered Plastic Components 53150 N Main St	Mattawan	MI	49071	269-668-3397	668-3276
Web: www.alcoa.com/epcmat					
Erie Plastics 844 Rt 6	Corry	PA	16407	814-664-4661	664-9323
Web: www.erieplastics.com					
Evans Industries Inc 200 Renaissance Ctr Suite 3150	Detroit	MI	48243	313-259-2266	259-4687
Evco Plastics Inc 100 W North St	DeForest	WI	53532	608-846-6000	846-6050
TF: 800-507-6000 ■ *Web:* www.evcoplastics.com					
Falcon Plastics Inc 250 W Wylie Ave	Washington	PA	15301	724-222-2620	222-4585
TF: 800-899-7856 ■ *Web:* www.falconplastics.com					
Fast Trak 330 Fairbanks St	Addison	IL	60101	630-543-0369	543-1062
Fawn Industries Inc 1920 Greenspring Dr Suite 140	Timonium	MD	21093	410-308-9200	308-9201
Web: www.fawn-ind.com					
Filtertek Inc 11411 Price Rd	Hebron	IL	60034	815-648-2416	648-2929
TF: 800-248-2461 ■ *Web:* www.filtertek.com					
Flambeau Inc 15981 Valplast Rd	Middlefield	OH	44062	440-632-1631	632-1581
TF: 800-457-5252 ■ *Web:* www.flambeau.com					
FPI Thermoplastic Technologies PO Box 1907	Morristown	NJ	07962	973-539-4200	539-1317
TF: 800-932-0715 ■ *Web:* www.fpiplastics.com					
Gruber Systems Inc 25636 Ave Stanford	Valencia	CA	91355	661-257-4060	257-4791
TF: 800-257-4070 ■ *Web:* www.gruber-systems.com					
Guardian Automotive Trim Inc 601 N Congress Ave	Evansville	IN	47715	812-473-6200	473-6320
GW Plastics Inc 239 Pleasant St	Bethel	VT	05032	802-234-9941	234-9940
Web: www.gwplastics.com					
Hoffer Plastics Corp 500 N Collins St	South Elgin	IL	60177	847-741-5740	741-3086
Web: www.hofferplastics.com					
Industrial Components Inc 2250 NW 102nd Ave	Miami	FL	33172	305-477-0387	594-7332
Web: www.icassemblies.com					
Industrial Molding Corp 616 E Slaton Rd	Lubbock	TX	79404	806-474-1000	474-1168
Web: www.indmolding.com					
Injectech Industries Inc 501 Welham Rd	Barrie	ON	L4N8Z6	705-737-2242	737-4523
Web: www.injectech.com					
Injectronics Inc 1 Union St	Clinton	MA	01510	978-368-8701	368-7941
TF: 888-368-8701 ■ *Web:* www.injectronics.com					
Innovative Injection Technologies Inc					
2360 Grand Ave	West Des Moines	IA	50265	515-225-6707	225-9673
Web: www.i2-tech.com					
Intec Group Inc 666 S Vermont St	Palatine	IL	60067	847-358-0088	358-4391
Web: www.intecgrp.com					
Ironwood Industries Inc 115 S Bradley Rd	Libertyville	IL	60048	847-362-8681	362-9190
Web: www.ironind.com					

Company	City	State	ZIP	Phone	Fax
Jarden Plastic Solutions PO Box 2750 *Web:* www.jardenplasticsolutions.com	Greenville	SC	29602	864-879-7600	877-4976
Jones Plastic & Engineering Co LLC 2410 S Plantside Dr *Web:* www.jonesplastic.com	Louisville	KY	40299	502-491-3785	499-2185
Jones & Vining Inc 1115 W Chestnut St 3rd Fl *Web:* www.jvmaine.com	Brockton	MA	02301	508-894-0018	894-0056
Jordan Specialty Plastics Inc 1751 Lake Cook Rd ArborLake Ctr Suite 550 *Web:* www.jordanindustries.com	Deerfield	IL	60015	847-945-5591	945-9645
Juno Inc 1100 McKinley St *Web:* www.junoinc.com	Anoka	MN	55303	763-553-1312	553-1360
Kamco Plastics Inc 851 E State Pkwy *Web:* www.kamcoplastics.com	Schaumburg	IL	60173	847-882-3550	882-6512
Kennerley Spratling Inc 2116 Farallon Dr	San Leandro	CA	94577	510-351-8230	352-9240
Kenro Inc 200 Industrial Dr *Web:* www.kenro.com	Fredonia	WI	53021	262-692-2411	692-9141
Key Plastics Inc 21700 Haggerty Rd Suite 100-N *Web:* www.keyplastics.com	Northville	MI	48167	248-449-6100	449-4105
KI Industries Inc 5540 McDermott Dr *Web:* www.kiindustries.com	Berkeley	IL	60163	708-449-1990	449-1997
Kurz-Kasch Inc 2271 Arbor Blvd *Web:* www.kurz-kasch.com	Dayton	OH	45439	937-299-0990	299-9292
Lacks Enterprises 5460 Cascade Rd SE *Web:* www.lacksenterprises.com	Grand Rapids	MI	49546	616-949-6570	285-2367
Lehigh Valley Plastics Inc 187 N Commerce Way *TF:* 800-354-5344 ■ *Web:* www.lehighvalleyplastics.com	Bethlehem	PA	18017	484-893-5500	893-5513
Leon Plastics Inc PO Box 350 *TF:* 800-285-5366 ■ *Web:* www.leonplastics.com	Grand Rapids	MI	49501	616-531-7970	531-3393
LMC Industries Inc 100 Manufacturers Dr *Web:* www.lmcindustries.com	Arnold	MO	63010	636-282-8080	282-7114
M & Q Plastic Products 1120 Welsh Rd Suite 170 *TF:* 877-726-7287 ■ *Web:* www.mqplasticproducts.com	North Wales	PA	19454	267-498-4000	498-0030
Mack Molding Co Inc 608 Warm Brook Rd **Fax:* Hum Res ■ *Web:* www.mack.com	Arlington	VT	05250	802-375-2511	375-0792*
MacLean Molded Products Inc 410 Mercantile Ct	Wheeling	IL	60090	847-541-1616	541-5849
Makray Mfg Co 4400 N Harlem Ave *Web:* www.makray.com	Norridge	IL	60706	708-456-7100	456-7178
Mar-Lee Companies 55 Marshall St *Web:* www.mar-leecompanies.com	Leominster	MA	01453	978-534-8305	534-0472
Marland Mold Inc 12 Betnr Industrial Dr *Web:* www2.marlandmold.com	Pittsfield	MA	01201	413-443-4481	443-4963
Master Molded Products Corp 1000 Davis Rd *Web:* www.mastermolded.com	Elgin	IL	60123	847-695-9700	695-9707
Meridian Automotive Systems Inc 999 Republic Dr	Allen Park	MI	48101	313-336-4182	336-4184
Midwest Plastic Components 7309 W 27th St *Web:* www.mpc-mn.com	Minneapolis	MN	55426	952-929-3312	929-1557
Miner Elastomer Products Corp 1200 E State St PO Box 471 *Web:* www.minerelastomer.com	Geneva	IL	60134	630-232-3000	232-3172
Molded Fiber Glass Cos 2925 MFG Pl *TF:* 800-456-5263 ■ *Web:* www.moldedfiberglass.com	Ashtabula	OH	44004	440-997-5851	994-5111
Molding Corp of America 10349 Norris Ave *TF:* 800-423-2747 ■ *Web:* www.moldingcorp.com	Pacoima	CA	91331	818-890-7877	890-7885
Moll Industries Inc 13455 Noel Rd Suite 2250 *Web:* www.mollindustries.com	Dallas	TX	75240	972-633-6900	
Mullinix Packages Inc 3511 Engle Rd *Web:* www.mullinixpackages.com	Fort Wayne	IN	46809	260-747-3149	747-1598
MXL Industries Inc 1764 Rohrerstown Rd *TF:* 800-233-0159 ■ *Web:* www.mxl-industries.com	Lancaster	PA	17601	717-569-8711	569-8716
National Molding Corp 5 Dubon Ct *TF:* 800-544-7162 ■ *Web:* www.nationalmolding.com	Farmingdale	NY	11735	631-293-8696	293-0988
National Molding Corp Security Plastics Div 14427 NW 60th Ave *TF:* 800-327-3787 ■ *Web:* www.securityplastics.com	Miami Lakes	FL	33014	305-823-5440	557-1431
New England Plastics Corp 126 Duchaine Blvd *TF Cust Svc:* 800-292-3500	New Bedford	MA	02745	508-998-3111	995-8895
Norland Plastics Co 117 Baughman Ave	Haysville	KS	67060	316-522-4887	522-1603
Nyloncraft Inc 616 W McKinley Ave *Web:* www.nyloncraft.com	Mishawaka	IN	46545	574-256-1521	255-3278
Nypro Inc 101 Union St *Web:* www.nypro.com	Clinton	MA	01510	978-365-9721	365-4352
NYX Inc 36800 Plymouth Rd *Web:* www.natplastics.com	Livonia	MI	48150	734-462-2385	
PECO Mfg Co Inc PO Box 82189 *Web:* www.peco-sunne.com	Portland	OR	97282	503-233-6401	233-6407
Pelham Products Inc 46 Payne Rd *Web:* www.pelhamproducts.com	Bethel	CT	06801	203-792-1515	798-1892
Phillips Plastics Corp 7 Long Lake Dr *Web:* www.phillipsplastics.com	Phillips	WI	54555	715-339-3005	339-3092
Pixley Richards Inc 9 Collins Ave Plymouth Industrial Pk *Web:* www.pixley.com	Plymouth	MA	02360	508-746-6082	746-9317
Plainfield Cos 1351 N Division St *Web:* www.plainfieldcompanies.com	Plainfield	IL	60544	815-436-5671	439-2970
Plas-Tec Corp 601 W Indiana St	Edon	OH	43518	419-272-2731	272-2733
Plaspros Inc 1143 Ridgeview Dr *Web:* www.plaspros.com	McHenry	IL	60050	815-430-2300	430-2260
Plastech Corp 56 E Broadway Ave Suite 210 *TF:* 800-223-0462 ■ *Web:* www.plastechcorporation.com	Forest Lake	MN	55025	651-407-5700	407-5650
Plastech Engineered Products Inc 835 Mason St *Web:* www.plastecheng.com	Dearborn	MI	48124	313-791-3001	791-8154
Plastek Group 2425 W 23rd St *Web:* www.plastekgroup.com	Erie	PA	16506	814-878-4400	878-4529
Plastic Components Inc N 116 W 18271 Morse Dr *Web:* www.plasticcomponents.com	Germantown	WI	53022	877-253-1496	
Plastic Design International Inc 111 Industrial Park Rd *Web:* www.plasticdesign.com	Middletown	CT	06457	860-632-2001	632-1776
Plastic Fabricating Co Inc 1650 S McComas St *Web:* www.pfabks.com	Wichita	KS	67213	316-942-1241	942-0687
Plastic Moldings Co LLC 2181 Grand Ave *TF:* 800-927-5040 ■ *Web:* www.plasticmoldings.com	Cincinnati	OH	45214	513-921-5040	921-5883
Plastic-Plate Inc 5460 Cascade Rd SE *Web:* www.lacksenterprises.com/consumer_electronics/CE_services.asp	Grand Rapids	MI	49546	616-949-6570	285-2367
Plastic Products Co Inc 30355 Akerson St *Web:* www.plasticproductsco.com	Lindstrom	MN	55045	651-257-5980	257-9774
Plastics Group Inc 7409 S Quincy St *Web:* www.theplasticsgroup.net	Willowbrook	IL	60527	630-325-1210	325-1393
Plastics Molding Co Inc 4211 N Broadway	Saint Louis	MO	63147	314-241-2479	241-3757
Port Erie Plastics Inc 909 Troupe Rd *Web:* www.porterie.com	Harborcreek	PA	16421	814-899-7602	899-7854
Precision Plastics Inc 900 W Connexion Way *Web:* www.pplastic.com	Columbia City	IN	46725	260-244-6114	244-5995
Premix Inc US Rt 20 PO Box 281 *Web:* www.premix.com	North Kingsville	OH	44068	440-224-2181	224-2766
Pro Corp-PMC 296 Nonotuck St	Florence	MA	01062	413-584-1780	586-5762
Product Miniature Co 627 Capitol Dr *Web:* www.pmplastic.com	Pewaukee	WI	53072	262-691-1700	691-4405
Proper Mold & Engineering Inc 13870 E 11-Mile Rd *Web:* www.pmecompanies.com	Warren	MI	48089	586-779-8787	779-4530
PTA Corp 148 Christian St *Web:* www.ptacorp.com	Oxford	CT	06478	203-888-0585	888-1757
Putnam Precision Molding Inc 11 Danco Rd *TF:* 800-752-7865 ■ *Web:* www.putnamprecisionmolding.com	Putnam	CT	06260	860-928-7911	928-2229
QMR Plastics 434 Highland Dr *Web:* www.mnrubber.com/qmrplastics	River Falls	WI	54022	715-426-4700	426-5115
R & R Technologies LLC 7560 E County Line Rd *Web:* www.rrtech.com	Edinburgh	IN	46124	812-526-2655	526-9294
REO Plastics Inc 11850 93rd Ave N *Web:* www.reoplastics.com	Maple Grove	MN	55369	763-425-4171	425-0735
Rodgard 92 Msgr Valente Dr *Web:* www.rodgard.com	Buffalo	NY	14206	716-823-1411	852-7690
Royal Plastics Inc 9410 Pineneedle Dr *TF:* 800-533-2163 ■ *Web:* www.royalplastics.com	Mentor	OH	44060	440-352-1357	352-6681
Sabin Corp 3800 Constitution Ave *TF:* 800-264-4510 ■ *Web:* www.sabincorp.com	Bloomington	IN	47403	812-323-4500	339-3395
Saint Clair Plastics Co 30855 Teton Pl *Web:* www.scplastics.com	Chesterfield Township	MI	48047	586-598-9930	598-7057
Sajar Plastics Inc 15285 S State Ave PO Box 37 *Web:* www.sajarplastics.com	Middlefield	OH	44062	440-632-5203	632-1848
Schiffmayer Plastics Corp 1201 Armstrong St *TF:* 800-621-1092 ■ *Web:* www.schiffmayerplastics.com	Algonquin	IL	60102	847-658-8140	658-0863
Seitz Corp PO Box 1398 *TF:* 800-243-5115 ■ *Web:* www.seitzcorp.com	Torrington	CT	06790	860-489-0476	482-6616
Shape Global Technology Inc 90 Community Dr *TF Sales:* 800-627-5836 ■ *Web:* www.shapenet.com	Sanford	ME	04073	207-324-5200	324-0875
Steere Enterprises Inc 285 Commerce St *TF:* 800-875-4926 ■ *Web:* www.steere.com	Tallmadge	OH	44278	330-633-4926	633-3921
Stelrema Corp 4055 E 250 North *Web:* www.gettig.com/Stelrema.html	Knox	IN	46534	574-772-2103	772-5628
Stoesser-Gordon Plastics 3250 Brickway Blvd *Web:* www.sgplastics.com	Santa Rosa	CA	95403	707-303-3000	303-3050
Sturgis Molded Products Co 1950 Clark St *Web:* www.smpco.com	Sturgis	MI	49091	269-651-9381	651-9224
Summa Industries 21250 Hawthorne Blvd Suite 500 *NASDAQ: SUMX* ■ *Web:* www.summaindustries.com	Torrance	CA	90503	310-792-7024	792-7079
Tech Group Inc 14677 N 74th St *Web:* www.techgrp.com	Scottsdale	AZ	85260	480-281-4544	281-4501
Tech II Inc PO Box 1468 *Web:* www.techii.com	Springfield	OH	45501	937-969-8352	969-8156
Texstars Inc PO Box 534036 *Web:* www.texstars.com	Grand Prairie	TX	75053	972-647-1366	606-0232
Thermotech Co 1302 S 5th St *Web:* www.thermotech.com	Hopkins	MN	55343	952-933-9400	933-9483
Titan Plastics Group 4295 N Roosevelt Rd *Web:* www.titanplasticsgroup.com	Stevensville	MI	49127	269-429-3201	429-6060
Toledo Molding & Die Inc 4 E Laskey Rd *TF:* 800-437-5116 ■ *Web:* www.tmdinc.com	Toledo	OH	43612	419-476-0581	476-6053
Tri-Star Plastics Inc 1915 E Via Burton *Web:* www.tri-starplastics.com	Anaheim	CA	92806	714-533-7360	533-4383
Tricon Industries Inc 2325 Wisconsin Ave *Web:* www.triconinc.com	Downers Grove	IL	60515	630-964-2330	964-5179
Tricon Industries Inc Electromechanical Div 2325 Wisconsin Ave *Web:* www.triconinc.com	Downers Grove	IL	60515	630-964-2330	964-5179
Trimold LLC 200 Pittsburgh Rd	Circleville	OH	43113	740-474-7591	474-1053
Tubed Products LLC 44 O'Neill St *Web:* www.ksplastic.com	Easthampton	MA	01027	413-527-1250	529-1275
Tuthill Corp Plastics Group 2050 Sunnydale Blvd *TF:* 800-447-5278 ■ *Web:* plastics.tuthill.com	Clearwater	FL	33765	727-446-8593	446-8595
United Plastics Group Inc 1420 Kensington Rd Suite 209 *Web:* www.unitedplasticsgroup.com	Oakbrook	IL	60523	630-706-5500	706-5510
Universal Plastic Mold Inc 13245 Los Angeles St *Web:* www.upminc.com	Baldwin Park	CA	91706	626-962-4001	960-7166
ValTech LLC 85 Pixley Industrial Pkwy *Web:* www.foster-grp.com	Rochester	NY	14624	585-295-8951	295-8956
Vaupell Industrial Plastics Inc 1144 NW 53rd St *TF:* 800-426-7738 ■ *Web:* www.vaupell.com	Seattle	WA	98107	206-784-9050	784-9708
Venture Plastics Inc 4000 Warren Rd *Web:* www.ventureplastics.com	Newton Falls	OH	44444	330-872-5774	872-3597
W-L Molding Co 8212 Shaver Rd *Web:* www.wlmolding.com	Portage	MI	49024	269-327-3075	323-8416
Wescon Products Co 2533 S West St *TF:* 800-835-0160 ■ *Web:* www.wesconproducts.com	Wichita	KS	67217	316-942-7266	942-5114
Western Industries Inc W 156 N 9073 Pilgrim Rd *Web:* www.westernind.com	Menomonee Falls	WI	53051	262-251-1915	251-6727
Western Industries Inc Chilton Products Div 300 E Breed St *TF:* 877-671-7063	Chilton	WI	53014	920-849-2381	849-4947
Westlake Plastics Co PO Box 127 *TF:* 800-999-1700 ■ *Web:* www.westlakeplastics.com	Lenni	PA	19052	610-459-1000	459-1084
Williams Industries Inc 2201 E Michigan Rd *TF:* 800-383-4701 ■ *Web:* www.williamsindustries.com	Shelbyville	IN	46176	317-392-4701	398-3561
Winfield Industries Inc 852 Kensington Ave *Web:* www.winfield-inds.com	Buffalo	NY	14215	716-833-6900	833-9405
Winzeler Gear Inc 7355 W Wilson Ave *Web:* www.winzelergear.com	Harwood Heights	IL	60706	708-867-7971	867-7974
WM Plastics Inc 5151 Bolger Ct *Web:* www.wmplastics.com	McHenry	IL	60050	815-578-8888	578-8818
Zappa Plastics Inc 165 Howard St *Web:* www.zappaplastics.com	Phillipsburg	NJ	08865	908-454-4500	454-4507

608 PLASTICS & OTHER SYNTHETIC MATERIALS

608-1 Synthetic Fibers & Filaments

Company	City	State	ZIP	Phone	Fax
Barnet William & Son Inc 1300 Hayne St *TF:* 800-922-7638 ■ *Web:* www.barnet.com	Arcadia	SC	29320	864-576-7154	574-7261
Buckeye Technologies Inc 1001 Tillman St *NYSE: BKI* ■ *Web:* www.bkitech.com	Memphis	TN	38112	901-320-8100	320-8204
Carlee Corp 28 Piermont Rd *TF:* 800-822-7533 ■ *Web:* www.carlee.com	Rockleigh	NJ	07647	201-768-6800	768-7614
Color-Fi Inc 320 Neeley St *TF:* 800-843-6382 ■ *Web:* www.colorfi.com	Sumter	SC	29150	803-436-4200	436-4220
Consolidated Fibers 8100 South Blvd PO Box 240416 *TF:* 800-243-8621 ■ *Web:* www.consolidatedfibers.com	Charlotte	NC	28224	704-554-8621	554-7782
Deltech Corp 11911 Scenic Hwy *Web:* www.deltechcorp.com	Baton Rouge	LA	70807	225-775-0150	358-3149
DuPont Advanced Fibers Systems 5401 Jefferson Davis Hwy *TF:* 800-441-7515 ■ *Web:* www2.dupont.com	Richmond	VA	23234	804-383-2000	383-4077
DuPont Canada Inc 7070 Mississauga Rd *Web:* ca.dupont.com	Mississauga	ON	L5N5M8	905-821-3300	821-5110

				Phone	Fax
DuPont Personal Protection 884 S 7th St *TF:* 800-931-3456 ■ *Web:* www.personalprotection.dupont.com	McBee	SC	29101	843-335-8211	335-8599
EDO Fiber Science 506 N Billy Mitchell Rd *Web:* www.edocorp.com/EDOFiberScience.htm	Salt Lake City	UT	84116	801-537-1800	363-9554
Fairfield Processing Corp 88 Rosa Hill Ave PO Box 1157 *TF:* 800-980-8000 ■ *Web:* www.poly-fil.com	Danbury	CT	06813	203-744-2090	792-9710
Hexcel Corp 281 Tresser Blvd 2 Stamford Plaza 16th Fl *NYSE: HXL* ■ *TF:* 800-444-3923 ■ *Web:* www.hexcel.com	Stamford	CT	06901	203-969-0666	
Honeywell Specialty Materials 101 Columbia Rd *TF:* 800-222-0094	Morristown	NJ	07962	973-455-2145	455-6154
International Fiber Corp 50 Bridge St *TF:* 888-698-1936 ■ *Web:* www.ifcfiber.com	North Tonawanda	NY	14120	716-693-4040	693-3528
InterTech Group Inc 4838 Jenkins Ave *Web:* www.theintertechgroup.com	North Charleston	SC	29405	843-744-5174	747-4092
INVISTA 4123 E 37th St North *TF:* 877-446-8478 ■ *Web:* www.invista.com	Wichita	KS	67220	316-828-1000	
Noble Fiber Technologies 300 Palm St *TF:* 877-978-2842 ■ *Web:* www.noblefiber.com	Scranton	PA	18505	570-558-5309	558-5351
Nylon Corp of America 333 Sundial Ave *TF:* 800-851-2001 ■ *Web:* www.nycoa.net	Manchester	NH	03103	603-627-5150	627-5154
Performance Fibers 15801 Woods Edge Rd **Fax Area Code:* 804 ■ *Web:* www.performancefibers.com	Colonial Heights	VA	23834	800-486-0148	520-3404*
RadiciSpandex Corp 3145 Northwest Blvd *Web:* www.radicispandex.com	Gastonia	NC	28052	704-864-5495	836-3143
Specialty Filaments Inc 125 College St 4th Fl *TF:* 800-451-3448 ■ *Web:* www.specialtyfilaments.com	Burlington	VT	05401	802-660-0021	863-2988
Stein Fibers Ltd 4 Computer Dr W Suite 200 *TF:* 888-489-2790 ■ *Web:* www.steinfibers.com	Albany	NY	12205	518-489-5700	489-5713
TenCate Grass North America 1131 Broadway St *TF:* 800-251-1033 ■ *Web:* www.tencate.com	Dayton	TN	37321	423-775-0792	775-4460
Toray Industries America Inc 461 5th Ave 9th Fl *Web:* www.toray.com	New York	NY	10017	212-697-8150	972-4279
Waltrich Plastic Corp 3005 Airport Rd PO Box D *Web:* www.waltrich.com	Walthourville	GA	31333	912-368-9341	369-3544
William Barnet & Son Inc 1300 Hayne St *TF:* 800-922-7638 ■ *Web:* www.barnet.com	Arcadia	SC	29320	864-576-7154	574-7261

608-2 Synthetic Resins & Plastics Materials

				Phone	Fax
A Schulman Inc 3550 W Market St *NASDAQ: SHLM* ■ *TF:* 800-662-3751 ■ *Web:* www.aschulman.com	Akron	OH	44333	330-666-3751	668-7204
Akcros Chemicals America 500 Jersey Ave *TF Cust Svc:* 800-500-7890 ■ *Web:* www.akcros.com	New Brunswick	NJ	08903	732-247-2202	247-2287
Albis Plastics Corp 19901 Southwest Fwy *Web:* www.albisna.com	Sugar Land	TX	77479	281-207-5467	207-5471
Alloy Polymers Inc 3310 Deepwater Terminal Rd *Web:* www.alloypolymers.com	Richmond	VA	23234	804-232-8000	230-0386
Alpha Corp 950 Hwy 57 E *Web:* www.aoc-resins.com	Collierville	TN	38017	901-854-2800	854-1183
AlphaGary Corp 170 Pioneer Dr *TF:* 800-232-9741 ■ *Web:* www.alphagary.com	Leominster	MA	01453	978-537-8071	840-5005
AOC LLC 950 Hwy 57 E *Web:* www.aoc-resins.com	Collierville	TN	38017	901-854-2800	854-1183
Arkema Inc 2000 Market St *TF:* 800-533-5552	Philadelphia	PA	19103	215-419-7000	419-7591
Asahi Kasei America Inc 535 Madison Ave 33rd Fl *Web:* www.ak-america.com	New York	NY	10022	212-371-9900	371-9050
Asahi Kasei Plastics North America Inc 1 Thermofil Way *TF:* 800-444-4408 ■ *Web:* www.asahikaseiplastics.com	Fowlerville	MI	48836	517-223-2000	223-2002
Basell North America Inc 912 Appleton Rd *TF:* 800-458-1416 ■ *Web:* www.basell.com	Elkton	MD	21921	410-996-1600	996-1660
Bayer Corp 100 Bayer Rd *NYSE: BAY* ■ *TF:* 800-662-2927 ■ *Web:* www.bayerus.com	Pittsburgh	PA	15205	412-777-2000	778-4430
Bayer Inc 77 Belfield Rd **Fax:* Hum Res ■ *TF:* 800-622-2937 ■ *Web:* bayer.ca	Toronto	ON	M9W1G6	416-248-0771	248-1297*
Bayer MaterialScience 100 Bayer Rd *TF:* 800-662-2927 ■ *Web:* polymers-usa.bayer.com	Pittsburgh	PA	15205	412-777-2000	
Capital Resin Corp 324 Dering Ave *Web:* www.capitalresin.com	Columbus	OH	43207	614-445-7177	445-7290
Chevron Phillips Chemical Co LP 10001 Six Pines Dr *TF:* 800-231-1212 ■ *Web:* www.cpchem.com	The Woodlands	TX	77380	832-813-4100	
Chomerics Div Parker Hannifin Corp 77 Dragon Ct *Web:* www.parker.com/chomerics	Woburn	MA	01801	781-935-4850	933-4318
CL Hauthaway & Sons Corp 638 Summer St *Web:* www.hauthaway.com	Lynn	MA	01905	781-592-6444	599-9565
Colorite Specialty Resins PO Box 116 *TF:* 800-215-1497 ■ *Web:* www.coloritepolymers.com	Burlington	NJ	08016	609-386-9200	386-3415
Cook Composites & Polymers Co 820 E 14th Ave *TF:* 800-821-3590 ■ *Web:* www.ccponline.com	North Kansas City	MO	64116	816-391-6000	391-6337
Crossfield Products Corp 3000 E Harcourt St *Web:* www.crossfieldproducts.com	Rancho Dominguez	CA	90221	310-886-9100	886-9119
Cytec Engineered Materials 2085 E Technology Cir Suite 300 *Web:* www.cytec.com	Tempe	AZ	85284	480-730-2000	730-2088
Daikin America Inc 20 Olympic Dr *TF Cust Svc:* 800-365-9570 ■ *Web:* www.daikin-america.com	Orangeburg	NY	10962	845-365-9500	365-9515
Day Michael Enterprise Inc PO Box 179 PO Box Seville Rd *TF:* 800-758-0960 ■ *Web:* www.mdayinc.com	Wadsworth	OH	44282	330-336-7611	336-2143
Dow Chemical Canada Inc 450 1st St SW Suite 2100 *TF:* 800-433-4398 ■ *Web:* www.dowcanada.com	Calgary	AB	T2P5H1	403-267-3500	267-3597
Dow Chemical Co 2030 Dow Ctr *NYSE: DOW* ■ *TF Cust Svc:* 800-331-6451 ■ *Web:* www.dow.com	Midland	MI	48674	989-636-1000	636-3518
DSM Engineering Plastics Inc 2267 W Mill Rd **Fax:* Cust Svc ■ *TF:* 800-333-4237 ■ *Web:* www.dsm.com	Evansville	IN	47720	812-435-7500	435-7706*
DuPont Canada Inc 7070 Mississauga Rd *Web:* ca.dupont.com	Mississauga	ON	L5N5M8	905-821-3300	821-5110
DuPont Engineering Polymers Lancaster Pike Rt 141 Barley Mill Plaza Bldg 22 *TF:* 800-441-7515 ■ *Web:* www2.dupont.com	Wilmington	DE	19805	302-999-4592	
DuPont Packaging & Industrial Polymers Barley Mill Plaza 26-2122 PO Box 80026 *TF:* 800-628-6208 ■ *Web:* www.dupont.com/packaging	Wilmington	DE	19880	302-774-1161	
Dyneon LLC 6744 33rd St N **Fax Area Code:* 800 ■ *TF:* 800-810-8499	Oakdale	MN	55128	651-737-1436	635-8061*
Eastman Chemical Co 200 S Wilcox Dr *NYSE: EMN* ■ **Fax:* Mktg ■ *TF Cust Svc:* 800-327-8626 ■ *Web:* www.eastman.com	Kingsport	TN	37660	423-229-2000	229-1194*
Engineered Polymer Solutions Inc 1400 N State St *TF:* 800-654-4242 ■ *Web:* www.epscca.com	Marengo	IL	60152	815-568-3020	568-4155
Esterline Technologies Corp 500 108th Ave NE Suite 1500 *NYSE: ESL* ■ *Web:* www.esterline.com	Bellevue	WA	98004	425-453-9400	453-2916
ExxonMobil Chemical Co 13501 Katy Fwy *Web:* www.exxonmobilchemical.com	Houston	TX	77079	281-870-6000	870-6661
Ferro Corp Filled & Reinforced Plastics Div 5001 O'Hara Dr *Web:* www.ferroevv.com	Evansville	IN	47711	812-423-5218	435-2113
Formosa Plastics Corp USA 9 Peach Tree Hill Rd **Fax:* Hum Res ■ *Web:* www.fpcusa.com	Livingston	NJ	07039	973-992-2090	716-7456*
Gallagher Corp 3908 Morrison Dr *TF:* 800-524-8597 ■ *Web:* www.gallaghercorp.com	Gurnee	IL	60031	847-249-3440	249-3473
GE Advanced Materials 1 Plastics Ave *Web:* www.geadvancedmaterials.com	Pittsfield	MA	01201	413-448-7110	448-5573
GE Plastics 1 Plastics Ave *TF:* 800-451-3147 ■ *Web:* www.geplastics.com	Pittsfield	MA	01201	413-448-7484	448-5573
Goldsmith & Eggleton Inc 300 1st St *TF:* 800-321-0954 ■ *Web:* www.goldsmith-eggleton.com	Wadsworth	OH	44281	330-336-6616	334-4709
Hauthaway CL & Sons Corp 638 Summer St *Web:* www.hauthaway.com	Lynn	MA	01905	781-592-6444	599-9565
Hercules Inc 1313 N Market St Hercules Plaza *NYSE: HPC* ■ *TF:* 800-441-7600 ■ *Web:* www.herc.com	Wilmington	DE	19894	302-594-5000	594-5400
Heritage Plastics Inc 1002 Hunt St *TF:* 800-245-4623 ■ *Web:* www.heritage-plastics.com	Picayune	MS	39466	601-798-8663	798-1946
Hexion Specialty Chemicals Inc 180 E Broad St **Fax:* Hum Res ■ *Web:* www.hexionchem.com	Columbus	OH	43215	614-225-4000	220-6693*
Huntsman Corp 500 Huntsman Way *NYSE: HUN* ■ *TF:* 800-421-2411 ■ *Web:* www.huntsman.com	Salt Lake City	UT	84108	801-584-5700	584-5781
Industrial Dielectrics Inc 407 S 7th St PO Box 357 *Web:* www.idiplastic.com	Noblesville	IN	46061	317-773-1766	773-3877
Innovene 2600 S Shore Blvd *TF:* 800-527-5419 ■ *Web:* www.innovene.com	League City	TX	77573	281-535-6600	535-4417
Interplastic Corp 1225 Willow Lake Blvd *TF:* 800-736-5497 ■ *Web:* www.interplastic.com	Saint Paul	MN	55110	651-481-6860	481-9834
Landec Corp 3603 Haven Ave *NASDAQ: LNDC* ■ *Web:* www.landec.com	Menlo Park	CA	94025	650-306-1650	368-9818
Lewcott Corp 86 Providence Rd *TF Sales:* 800-225-7725 ■ *Web:* www.lewcott.com	Millbury	MA	01527	508-865-1791	865-0302
Lord Corp 111 Lord Dr *TF:* 800-524-2885 ■ *Web:* www.lord.com	Cary	NC	27511	919-468-5979	
Lumera Corp 19910 N Creek Pkwy Suite 100 *NASDAQ: LMRA* ■ *Web:* www.lumera.com	Bothell	WA	98011	425-415-6900	398-6599
Markel Corp 435 School Ln **Fax:* Sales ■ *Web:* www.markelcorporation.com	Plymouth Meeting	PA	19462	610-272-8960	270-3138*
Marval Industries Inc 315 Hoyt Ave *Web:* www.marvalindustries.com	Mamaroneck	NY	10543	914-381-2400	381-2259
Mer-Kote Products Inc 501 S Van Ness Ave **Fax Area Code:* 310 ■ *TF:* 800-851-6303 ■ *Web:* www.merkote.com	Torrance	CA	90501	323-775-2461	320-4938*
Michael Day Enterprises Inc PO Box 179 PO Box Seville Rd *TF:* 800-758-0960 ■ *Web:* www.mdayinc.com	Wadsworth	OH	44282	330-336-7611	336-2143
Minova USA Inc 150 Carley Ct *TF:* 800-626-2948 ■ *Web:* www.minovausa.com	Georgetown	KY	40324	502-863-6800	863-6805
Mitsui Chemicals America Inc 800 Westchester Ave **Fax:* PR ■ *TF:* 800-682-2377 ■ *Web:* mitsuichemicals.com	Rye Brook	NY	10573	914-253-0777	253-0790*
Modern Dispersions Inc 78 Marguerite Ave *TF:* 800-633-6434 ■ *Web:* www.moderndispersions.com	Leominster	MA	01453	978-534-3370	537-6065
MRC Polymers Inc 3535 W 31st St *Web:* www.mrcpolymers.com	Chicago	IL	60623	773-890-9000	890-9007
NeoResins 730 Main St *TF:* 800-225-0947 ■ *Web:* www.neoresins.com	Wilmington	MA	01887	978-658-6600	657-7978
Neville Chemical Co 2800 Neville Rd *TF Cust Svc:* 877-704-4200 ■ *Web:* www.nevchem.com	Pittsburgh	PA	15225	412-331-4200	771-0226
NOVA Chemicals Corp 1000 7th Ave SW *NYSE: NCX* ■ *TF:* 866-289-6682 ■ *Web:* www.novachem.com	Calgary	AB	T2P5L5	403-750-3600	269-7410
Occidental Chemical Corp 5005 LBJ Fwy *TF:* 800-570-8880 ■ *Web:* www.oxychem.com	Dallas	TX	75244	972-404-3300	404-3669
Ouimet Corp 2967 Sidco Dr *TF:* 800-326-5152 ■ *Web:* www.ouimetcorp.com	Nashville	TN	37204	615-242-5478	244-6823
Parker Hannifin Corp Chomerics Div 77 Dragon Ct *Web:* www.parker.com/chomerics	Woburn	MA	01801	781-935-4850	933-4318
Perstorp Compounds Inc 238 Nonotuck St *Web:* www.thermosets.com	Florence	MA	01062	413-584-2472	586-4089
Perstorp Polyols Inc 600 Matzinger Rd *TF Cust Svc:* 800-537-0280 ■ *Web:* www.perstorppolyols.com	Toledo	OH	43612	419-729-5448	729-3291
Plastics Color & Compounding Inc 349 Lake Rd *TF:* 888-549-7820 ■ *Web:* www.plasticscolor.com	Dayville	CT	06241	860-774-3770	779-7320
Plastics Engineering Co Inc 3518 Lake Shore Rd *Web:* www.plenco.com	Sheboygan	WI	53083	920-458-2121	458-1923
Plastomer Technologies 23 Friends Ln *TF:* 800-798-1288 ■ *Web:* www.plastomertech.com	Newtown	PA	18940	215-968-5011	968-7640
Polymeric Resources Corp 55 Haul Rd	Wayne	NJ	07470	973-694-4141	694-3549
PolyOne Corp 33587 Walker Rd *NYSE: POL* ■ *TF:* 866-765-9663 ■ *Web:* www.polyone.com	Avon Lake	OH	44012	440-930-1000	930-3064
PSC Fabricating Co 1100 W Market St *Web:* www.pscofky.com	Louisville	KY	40203	502-625-7700	625-7837
Reichhold Inc 2400 Ellis Rd *TF:* 800-448-3482 ■ *Web:* www.reichhold.com	Durham	NC	27703	919-990-7500	990-7711
Resinall Corp 3065 High Ridge Rd *TF Cust Svc:* 800-421-0561 ■ *Web:* www.resinall.com	Stamford	CT	06905	203-329-7100	329-0167
Rhe Tech Inc 1500 E North Territorial Rd *TF:* 800-837-4921 ■ *Web:* www.rhetech.com	Whitmore Lake	MI	48189	734-769-0585	769-3565
Rogers Corp 1 Technology Dr *NYSE: ROG* ■ **Fax:* Hum Res ■ *TF:* 800-227-6437 ■ *Web:* www.rogers-corp.com	Rogers	CT	06263	860-774-9605	779-5777*
Rohm & Haas Co 100 Independence Mall W *NYSE: ROH* ■ **Fax:* Hum Res ■ *Web:* www.rohmhaas.com	Philadelphia	PA	19106	215-592-3000	592-3377*
Rondy & Co Inc 255 Wooster Rd N *Web:* www.rondy.net	Barberton	OH	44203	330-745-9016	745-4886
RTP Co 580 E Front St **Fax:* Hum Res ■ *TF:* 800-433-4787 ■ *Web:* www.rtpcompany.com	Winona	MN	55987	507-454-6900	452-6286*
Rubicon Inc 9156 Hwy 75 PO Box 517 *Web:* www.huntsman.com	Geismar	LA	70734	225-673-6141	673-6442
Rutland Plastic Technologies 10021 Rodney St *TF:* 800-438-5134 ■ *Web:* www.rutlandinc.com	Pineville	NC	28134	704-553-0046	552-6589
S & E Specialty Polymers LLC 140 Leominster-Shirley Rd *Web:* www.sespoly.com	Lunenburg	MA	01462	978-537-8261	537-5310
Saint-Gobain Performance Plastics Corp 150 Dey Rd *Web:* www.plastics.saint-gobain.com	Wayne	NJ	07470	973-696-4700	696-4056
Sartomer Co 502 Thomas Jones Way *TF:* 800-345-8247 ■ *Web:* www.sartomer.com	Exton	PA	19341	610-363-4100	363-4140
Schulman A Inc 3550 W Market St *NASDAQ: SHLM* ■ *TF:* 800-662-3751 ■ *Web:* www.aschulman.com	Akron	OH	44333	330-666-3751	668-7204
Scientific Polymer Products Inc 6265 Dean Pkwy *Web:* www.scientificpolymer.com	Ontario	NY	14519	585-265-0413	265-1390
Shintech Inc 3 Greenway Plaza Suite 1150 *Web:* www.shintechinc.com	Houston	TX	77046	713-965-0713	965-0629
Shuman Plastics Inc 35 Neoga St *Web:* www.shuman-plastics.com	Depew	NY	14043	716-685-2121	685-3236
SI Group Inc PO Box 1046 2750 Balltown Rd *Web:* www.siigroup.com	Schenectady	NY	12301	518-370-4200	346-6908
Soluol Chemical Co Inc PO Box 112 *Web:* www.soluol.com	West Warwick	RI	02893	401-821-8100	823-6673
Solutia Inc 575 Maryville Centre Dr **Fax:* Hum Res ■ *TF:* 800-325-4330 ■ *Web:* www.solutia.com	Saint Louis	MO	63141	314-674-1000	674-1585*
Spartech Corp 120 S Central Ave Suite 1700 *NYSE: SEH* ■ *TF:* 888-721-4242 ■ *Web:* www.spartech.com	Clayton	MO	63105	314-721-4242	721-1543
Spraylat Corp 143 Sparks Ave *TF:* 800-642-3595 ■ *Web:* www.spraylat.com	Pelham	NY	10803	914-738-1600	712-2838

Synthetic Resins & Plastics Materials (Cont'd)

	City	State	Zip	Phone	Fax
Sterling Fibers Inc 5005 Sterling Way	Pace	FL	32571	850-994-5311	994-2579
TF Cust Svc: 800-342-3779 ■ *Web:* www.sterlingfibers.com					
Texas Polymer Services Inc 6522 IH-10 W	Orange	TX	77632	409-883-4331	883-3013
Thermoclad Co 361 W 11th St	Erie	PA	16501	814-456-1243	459-2853
Web: www.thermoclad.com					
Ticona LLC 8040 Dixie Hwy	Florence	KY	41042	859-525-4740	372-3125*
**Fax:* Sales ■ *TF:* 800-833-4882 ■ *Web:* www.ticona-us.com					
Vi-Chem Corp 55 Cottage Grove St SW	Grand Rapids	MI	49507	616-247-8501	247-8703
TF: 800-477-8501 ■ *Web:* www.vichem.com					
Washington Penn Plastic Co Inc 2080 N Main St	Washington	PA	15301	724-228-1260	228-7344
Web: www.washpenn.com					
Wellman Inc 595 Shrewsbury Ave	Shrewsbury	NJ	07702	732-212-3300	212-3344
NYSE: WLM ■ *Web:* www.wellmaninc.com					
Westlake Chemical Corp 2801 Post Oak Blvd Suite 600	Houston	TX	77056	713-960-9111	963-1562
NYSE: WLK ■ *Web:* www.westlakechemical.com					
wTe Corp 7 Alfred Cir	Bedford	MA	01730	781-275-6400	275-8612
Web: www.wte.com					

608-3 Synthetic Rubber

	City	State	Zip	Phone	Fax
AirBoss of America Corp Rubber Compounding					
101 Glasgow St	Kitchener	ON	N2G4X8	519-576-5565	576-1315
TF: 800-294-5723 ■ *Web:* www.airbossrubbercompounding.com					
Akrochem Corp 255 Fountain St	Akron	OH	44304	330-535-2108	535-8947
TF: 800-321-2260 ■ *Web:* www.akrochem.com					
American Synthetic Rubber Corp					
4500 Campground Rd PO Box 32960	Louisville	KY	40232	502-449-8300	449-8468
TF Cust Svc: 800-262-9253					
Bryant Rubber Corp 1112 Lomita Blvd	Harbor City	CA	90710	310-530-2530	530-9143
Web: www.bryantrubber.com					
Elementis Specialities Inc					
329 Wyckoffs Mill Rd PO Box 700	Hightstown	NJ	08520	609-443-2500	443-2323
TF: 800-418-5196 ■ *Web:* www.elementisspecialities.com					
Firestone Polymers 381 W Wilbeth Rd	Akron	OH	44319	330-379-7000	379-7727
TF Cust Svc: 800-282-0222 ■ *Web:* www.firesyn.com					
Goodyear Tire & Rubber Co 1144 E Market St	Akron	OH	44316	330-796-2121	796-3753*
NYSE: GT ■ **Fax:* Cust Svc ■ *TF Cust Svc:* 800-321-2136 ■ *Web:* www.goodyear.com					
Lanxess Corp 111 RIDC Park West Dr	Pittsburgh	PA	15275	412-809-1000	
TF: 800-526-9377 ■ *Web:* www.lanxess.com					
Lyondell Chemical Co 1221 McKinney St	Houston	TX	77010	713-652-7200	652-4686
NYSE: LYO ■ *Web:* www.lyondell.com					
Midwest Elastomers Inc 700 Industrial Dr PO Box 412	Wapakoneta	OH	45895	419-738-8844	738-4411
TF: 800-786-3539 ■ *Web:* www.midwestelastomers.com					
Preferred Rubber Compounding Corp 1020 Lambert St	Barberton	OH	44203	330-798-4790	798-4795
Web: www.preferredrubber.com					
R & S Processing Co Inc 15712 Illinois Ave PO Box 2037	Paramount	CA	90723	562-531-1403	531-4318
Web: www.rsprocessing.com					
Teknor Apex Co 505 Central Ave	Pawtucket	RI	02861	401-725-8000	725-8095
TF: 800-556-3864 ■ *Web:* www.teknorapex.com					
Textile Rubber & Chemical Co Inc 1300 Tiarco Dr SW	Dalton	GA	30721	706-277-1300	277-3738
TF: 800-727-8453 ■ *Web:* www.trcc.com					
US Elastomer 161 Marble Mill Rd	Marietta	GA	30060	770-424-4850	425-6345
TF: 800-394-8735 ■ *Web:* www.uselastomer.com					

609 PLASTICS PRODUCTS - FIBERGLASS REINFORCED

	City	State	Zip	Phone	Fax
Ershigs Inc PO Box 1707	Bellingham	WA	98227	360-733-2620	733-2628
TF: 888-377-4447 ■ *Web:* www.ershigs.com					
Fibergrate Composite Structures Inc 5151 Beltline Rd Suite 700	Dallas	TX	75254	972-250-1633	250-1530
TF: 800-527-4043 ■ *Web:* www.fibergrate.com					
Glastic Corp 4321 Glenridge Rd	Cleveland	OH	44121	216-486-0100	486-1091
TF: 800-360-1319 ■ *Web:* www.glastic.com					
GMI Composites Inc 1355 W Sherman Blvd	Muskegon	MI	49441	231-755-1611	755-1613
TF: 800-330-4045					
Haysite Reinforced Plastics 5599 New Perry Hwy	Erie	PA	16509	814-868-3691	864-7803
Web: www.haysite.com					
Kemlite Co 23525 W Eames St	Channahon	IL	60410	815-467-8600	467-8664*
**Fax:* Hum Res ■ *TF:* 800-435-0080 ■ *Web:* www.kemlite.com					
McClarin Plastics Inc 15 Industrial Dr PO Box 486	Hanover	PA	17331	717-637-2241	637-2091
TF: 800-233-3189 ■ *Web:* www.mcclarinplastics.com					
Peterson Products Inc 1325 Old County Rd	Belmont	CA	94002	650-591-7311	591-7498
Web: www.petersonproducts.com					
Red Ewald Inc PO Box 519	Karnes City	TX	78118	830-780-3304	780-4272
TF: 800-242-3524 ■ *Web:* www.redewald.com					
Strongwell 400 Commonwealth Ave	Bristol	VA	24201	276-645-8000	645-8132
Web: www.strongwell.com					

610 PLASTICS PRODUCTS - HOUSEHOLD

	City	State	Zip	Phone	Fax
A & E Products/Mainetti 104 Carnegie Center Dr	Princeton	NJ	08540	609-806-2500	806-2502
Web: www.aehangers.com					
Aero Plastics Inc 163 Pioneer Dr	Leominster	MA	01453	978-537-4363	537-9927
TF: 800-458-0116 ■ *Web:* www.aeroplastics.com					
Contico International LLC 305 Rock Industrial Park Dr	Bridgeton	MO	63044	314-656-4349	327-5492*
**Fax Area Code:* 800 ■ *TF:* 800-831-7077 ■ *Web:* www.contico.com					
Creative Bath Products 250 Creative Dr	Central Islip	NY	11722	631-582-8000	582-2020
Web: www.creativebath.com					
Dial Industries Inc 3616 Noakes St	Los Angeles	CA	90023	323-263-6878	263-3147
TF: 800-624-8682					
Diamond Brands Div Jarden Home Brands					
345 S High St Suite 201	Muncie	IN	47305	765-281-5000	281-5450
TF Cust Svc: 800-392-2575 ■ *Web:* www.diamondbrands.com					
Duraco Products Inc 1109 E Lake St	Streamwood	IL	60107	630-837-6615	837-7136
TF: 800-888-7687 ■ *Web:* www.duraco.com					
Eagle Affiliates Inc 1000 S 2nd St	Plainfield	NJ	07063	908-757-4464	769-7599
TF: 800-221-0434 ■ *Web:* www.eagleaffiliates.com					
GT Water Products Inc 5239 N Commerce Ave	Moorpark	CA	93021	805-529-2900	529-4558
TF: 800-862-5647 ■ *Web:* www.gtwaterproducts.com					
Home Products International Inc 4501 W 47th St	Chicago	IL	60632	773-890-1010	890-0523
TF: 800-327-3534 ■ *Web:* www.hpii.com					
Igloo Products Corp 777 Igloo Rd	Katy	TX	77494	713-465-2571	935-7702
TF Cust Svc: 800-324-2653 ■ *Web:* www.igloocoolers.com					
Jarden Home Brands Diamond Brands Div					
345 S High St Suite 201	Muncie	IN	47305	765-281-5000	281-5450
TF Cust Svc: 800-392-2575 ■ *Web:* www.diamondbrands.com					
Jet Plastica Inc 1100 Schwab Rd	Hatfield	PA	19440	215-362-1501	362-5018
TF: 800-220-5381 ■ *Web:* www.jetplastica.com					
King Plastics Inc 840 N Elm St	Orange	CA	92867	714-997-7540	997-0491
TF: 800-997-7540 ■ *Web:* www.kingplastics.com					
Kraftware Corp 270 Cox St	Roselle	NJ	07203	908-259-8883	259-8885
TF: 800-221-1728 ■ *Web:* kraftwareonline.com					
Maryland Plastics Inc 251 E Central Ave	Federalsburg	MD	21632	410-754-5566	754-8882
TF Cust Svc: 800-544-5582 ■ *Web:* www.marylandplastics.com					
Newell Rubbermaid Inc Cleaning & Organization Group					
3124 Valley Ave	Winchester	VA	22601	540-667-8700	542-8583
TF: 800-347-9800 ■ *Web:* www.newellrubbermaid.com					
Prolon Inc PO Box 568	Port Gibson	MS	39150	601-437-4211	480-9828*
**Fax Area Code:* 888 ■ *TF:* 800-628-7749 ■ *Web:* www.prolon.biz					
Sterilite Corp PO Box 524	Townsend	MA	01469	978-597-8702	597-1195
TF: 800-225-1046 ■ *Web:* www.sterilite.com					
TAP Plastics Inc 6475 Sierra Ln	Dublin	CA	94568	925-829-4889	829-6921
TF: 800-894-0827 ■ *Web:* www.tapplastics.com					
Thermos Co 2550 W Golf Rd Suite 800	Rolling Meadows	IL	60008	847-439-7821	593-5570
TF Cust Svc: 800-243-0745 ■ *Web:* www.thermos.com					
Tupperware Corp 14901 S Orange Blossom Trail	Orlando	FL	32837	407-847-3111	826-8489
NYSE: TUP ■ *TF Cust Svc:* 800-772-4001 ■ *Web:* www.tupperware.com					
Union Products Inc 511 Lancaster St	Leominster	MA	01453	978-537-1631	537-0050
Web: www.unionproducts.com					
US Acrylic Inc 1320 Harris Rd	Libertyville	IL	60048	847-837-4800	837-1955
Web: www.usacrylic.com					
US Can Co 98 Amlajack Blvd	Newnan	GA	30265	770-253-7176	250-0302
TF: 800-929-4274					
Venturi Inc PO Box 6348	Traverse City	MI	49696	231-929-7732	929-7735
TF Cust Svc: 800-968-0104 ■ *Web:* www.venturi-inc.com					
WNA Comet East Inc 6 Stuart Rd	Chelmsford	MA	01824	978-256-6551	256-1614
TF: 800-225-0939 ■ *Web:* www.wna-inc.com					
Zyliss USA Corp 1 Post Suite 100	Irvine	CA	92618	949-699-1884	699-1788
TF: 888-794-7623 ■ *Web:* www.zylissusa.com					

611 PLASTICS PRODUCTS (MISC)

	City	State	Zip	Phone	Fax
Aigner Index Inc 218 MacArthur Ave	New Windsor	NY	12553	845-562-4510	562-2638
TF: 800-242-3919 ■ *Web:* www.holdex.com					
Alexander Plastics Inc DBA Creations at Dallas					
11937 Denton Dr	Dallas	TX	75234	972-241-4171	243-3447
TF: 800-421-4171 ■ *Web:* www.creationsatdallas.com					
All States Inc 1801 W Foster Ave	Chicago	IL	60640	773-728-0525	728-6410
TF Cust Svc: 800-621-5837					
Allied Plastics Inc 9445 E River Rd	Coon Rapids	MN	55433	763-862-4500	862-4556
TF: 800-328-3113 ■ *Web:* www.alliedplastics.com					
Armstrong Systems & Consulting 5101 Tremont Ave Suite A	Davenport	IA	52807	563-386-9090	391-2237
Ashland Hardware Systems 790 W Commercial Ave	Lowell	IN	46356	219-696-5950	626-1758*
**Fax Area Code:* 800 ■ *Web:* www.ashlandhardware.com					
Avery Dennison Fastener Div 224 Industrial Rd	Fitchburg	MA	01420	978-353-2100	848-2169*
**Fax Area Code:* 800 ■ *TF:* 800-805-6132 ■ *Web:* www.fastener.averydennison.com					
Beemak Plastics Inc 13921 Bettencourt St	Cerritos	CA	90703	310-886-5880	764-0330*
**Fax:* Orders ■ *TF:* 800-421-4393 ■ *Web:* www.beemak.com					
Bemis Mfg Co PO Box 901	Sheboygan Falls	WI	53085	920-467-4621	467-8573
TF: 800-558-7651 ■ *Web:* www.bemismfg.com					
Bowie Mfg Inc 313 S Hancock	Lake City	IA	51449	712-464-3191	464-8601
TF: 800-831-0960 ■ *Web:* www.bowiemfg.com					
Bruce Plastics Inc PO Box 4547	Pittsburgh	PA	15205	412-922-9888	922-2380
Web: www.bruceplastics.com					
Bunzl USA Inc 701 Emerson Rd Suite 500	Saint Louis	MO	63141	314-997-5959	997-0247
NYSE: BNL ■ *TF:* 888-997-4515 ■ *Web:* www.bunzldistribution.com					
Concept Plastics Inc 1210 Hickory Chapel Rd	High Point	NC	27260	336-889-2001	889-5752
TF: 800-225-9553 ■ *Web:* www.cpico.com					
Croan Engineering Co 5401 Business Dr	Huntington Beach	CA	92649	714-893-0561	895-5122
Crystal-Like Plastics 2547 N Ontario St	Burbank	CA	91504	818-846-1818	846-0877
TF: 800-554-6091 ■ *Web:* www.crystal-likeplastics.com					
Daramic Inc 5525 US Hwy 60 E	Owensboro	KY	42303	270-683-1561	686-9226
Web: www.daramic.com					
DelStar Technologies Inc 220 E St Elmo Rd	Austin	TX	78745	512-447-7000	447-7444
TF: 800-531-5112 ■ *Web:* www.delstarinc.com					
Dreco Inc 7887 Root Rd	North Ridgeville	OH	44039	440-327-6021	327-6865
Web: www.drecoinc.com					
Elk Composite Building Products Inc 9806 Lackman Rd	Lenexa	KS	66219	913-599-5300	495-4323
TF: 866-322-7452 ■ *Web:* www.elkcorp.com					
Elk Premium Building Products Inc 14911 Quorum Dr Suite 600	Dallas	TX	75254	972-851-0500	851-0550
Web: www.elkcorp.com					
Fiberglass Specialties Inc PO Box 1340	Henderson	TX	75653	903-657-6522	657-2318
TF: 800-527-1459 ■ *Web:* www.fsiweb.com					
Gabriel Mfg Co Inc 125 S Liberty Dr	Stony Point	NY	10980	845-942-0100	942-0159
TF: 800-454-3387 ■ *Web:* www.4gabriel.com					
General Polymeric Corp PO Box 380	Reading	PA	19607	610-374-5171	374-4990
TF: 800-654-4391					
Goodrich Corp Engineered Polymer Products Div					
6061 Goodrich Blvd	Jacksonville	FL	32226	904-757-3660	757-7116
TF: 800-366-8945 ■ *Web:* www.epp.goodrich.com					
Hanscom Inc 331 Market St	Warren	RI	02885	401-247-1999	247-4575
TF: 866-941-1455 ■ *Web:* www.hanscominc.com					
Hygolet Inc 349 SE 2nd Ave	Deerfield Beach	FL	33441	954-481-8601	481-8669
TF: 800-494-6538 ■ *Web:* www.hygolet.com					
Kalwall Corp 1111 Candia Rd	Manchester	NH	03109	603-627-3861	627-7905
TF: 800-258-9777 ■ *Web:* www.kalwall.com					
London Industries Inc 350 E High St	London	OH	43140	740-852-3200	852-4547
Web: www.londonind.com					
M & D Industries International Inc 7700 Anagram Dr	Eden Prairie	MN	55344	952-949-5600	576-5353*
**Fax Area Code:* 800 ■ *TF:* 888-469-5277 ■ *Web:* www.mdballoons.com					
Micro Plastics Inc 11 Industry Ln Hwy 178 N PO Box 149	Flippin	AR	72634	870-453-2261	453-8676
Web: www.microplastics.com					
MOCAP Inc 13100 Manchester Rd	Saint Louis	MO	63131	314-543-4000	543-4111
TF: 800-633-6775 ■ *Web:* www.mocap.com					
Newell Rubbermaid Inc Cleaning & Organization Group					
3124 Valley Ave	Winchester	VA	22601	540-667-8700	542-8583
TF: 800-347-9800 ■ *Web:* www.newellrubbermaid.com					
NEXPAK Corp 3475 Forest Lake Dr Suite 200	Uniontown	OH	44685	330-896-3050	896-3225
TF: 800-442-5742 ■ *Web:* www.nexpak.com					
OEM/Erie Inc 1810 W 20th St	Erie	PA	16502	814-459-8024	456-5108
Web: www.oemerie.com					
PI Inc PO Box 669	Athens	TN	37371	423-745-6213	746-1310
TF Cust Svc: 800-951-3542 ■ *Web:* www.pi-inc.com					

				Phone	Fax
Plastomer Technologies 23 Friends Ln *TF:* 800-798-1288 ■ *Web:* www.plastomertech.com	Newtown	PA	18940	215-968-5011	968-7640
Plastpro Inc 9 Peach Tree Hill Rd *TF:* 800-779-0561	Livingston	NJ	07039	973-758-4000	758-4001
Porex Technologies Corp 500 Bohannon Rd *TF Cust Svc:* 800-241-0195 ■ *Web:* www.porex.com	Fairburn	GA	30213	770-964-1421	969-0954
PSI Inc 10630 Marina Dr *TF:* 866-638-7926 ■ *Web:* www.psilighting.com	Olive Branch	MS	38654	662-895-8777	895-8796
Richco Inc 8145 River Dr *TF:* 800-466-8301 ■ *Web:* www.richco-inc.com	Morton Grove	IL	60053	773-539-4060	539-6770
Rogan Corp 3455 Woodhead Dr *TF:* 800-423-1543 ■ *Web:* www.rogancorp.com	Northbrook	IL	60062	847-498-2300	498-2334
Rubbermaid Commercial Products 3124 Valley Ave *TF:* 800-347-9800 ■ *Web:* www.rcpworksmarter.com	Winchester	VA	22601	540-667-8700	542-8583
Shakespeare Electronic Products Group 6111 Shakespeare Rd *TF:* 800-845-7750 ■ *Web:* www.shakespeare-ce.com	Columbia	SC	29223	803-754-7011	419-3099
Shakespeare Monofilaments & Specialty Polymers PO Box 4060 *TF:* 800-845-2110 ■ *Web:* www.skpplastics.com	Columbia	SC	29240	803-754-7011	754-7991
Smith McDonald Corp 304 Sonwil Dr *TF:* 800-753-8548 ■ *Web:* www.smithmcdonald.com	Buffalo	NY	14225	716-684-7200	684-2053
Spir-It Inc 200 Brickstone Sq Suite G-05 *TF:* 800-343-0996 ■ *Web:* www.spir-it.com	Andover	MA	01810	978-964-1551	964-1552
Supreme Corq LLC 5901 S 226th St *TF:* 800-794-4160 ■ *Web:* www.supremecorq.com	Kent	WA	98032	253-395-8712	395-8713
Thombert Inc 316 E 7th St N *TF:* 800-433-3572 ■ *Web:* www.thombert.com	Newton	IA	50208	641-792-4449	792-2390
Triad Products Co 1801 W 'B' St *TF:* 800-241-3704 ■ *Web:* www.triadproducts.com	Hastings	NE	68901	402-462-2181	462-2246
Value Plastics Inc 3325 S Timberline Rd *TF:* 888-404-5837 ■ *Web:* www.valueplastics.com	Fort Collins	CO	80525	970-267-5200	223-0953

612 PLUMBING FIXTURES & FITTINGS - METAL

				Phone	Fax
Accurate Partitions Corp 8000 Joliet Rd *Web:* www.accuratepartitions.com	McCook	IL	60525	708-442-6801	442-7439
Acorn Engineering Co PO Box 3527 *TF:* 800-488-8999 ■ *Web:* www.acorneng.com	City of Industry	CA	91744	626-336-4561	961-2200
Alsons Corp PO Box 282 *TF:* 800-421-0001 ■ *Web:* www.alsons.com	Hillsdale	MI	49242	517-439-1411	439-9644
American Brass Mfg Co 5000 Superior Ave *TF:* 800-431-6440 ■ *Web:* www.americanbrass.com	Cleveland	OH	44103	216-431-6565	431-9420
American Specialties Inc (ASI) 441 Saw Mill River Rd *Web:* www.americanspecialties.com	Yonkers	NY	10701	914-476-9000	476-0688
American Standard Inc 1 Centennial Ave PO Box 6820 *TF:* 800-223-0068	Piscataway	NJ	08855	732-980-6000	980-6122
Ames Co 1485 Tanforan Ave *Web:* www.ames-co.com	Woodland	CA	95776	530-666-2493	666-5320
Anderson Copper & Brass Co 4325 Frontage Rd *TF:* 800-323-5284	Oak Forest	IL	60452	708-535-9030	535-9038
Bootz Industries Box 18010 *Web:* www.bootz.com	Evansville	IN	47719	812-423-5401	429-2254
Bradley Corp W 142 N 9101 Fountain Blvd *TF:* 800-272-3539 ■ *Web:* www.bradleycorp.com	Menomonee Falls	WI	53051	262-251-6000	251-5817
Brass-Craft Mfg Co 39600 Orchard Hill Pl **Fax:* Sales ■ *Web:* www.brasscraft.com	Novi	MI	48375	248-305-6000	305-6012*
Brasstech Inc 2001 E Carnegie Ave *TF:* 888-436-0805 ■ *Web:* www.brasstech.com	Santa Ana	CA	92705	949-417-5207	417-5209
Central Brass Mfg Co Inc 2950 E 55th St *TF:* 800-321-8630 ■ *Web:* www.centralbrass.com	Cleveland	OH	44127	216-883-0220	883-0875
Champion-Arrowhead LLC 5147 Alhambra Ave *Web:* www.arrowheadbrass.com	Los Angeles	CA	90032	323-221-9137	221-2579
Chicago Faucets A Geberit Co 2100 S Clearwater Dr **Fax:* Sales ■ *TF:* 800-323-5060 ■ *Web:* www.chicagofaucets.com	Des Plaines	IL	60018	847-803-5000	298-3101*
Crane Plumbing 1235 Hartrey Ave *Web:* www.craneplumbing.com	Evanston	IL	60202	847-864-7600	864-7652
CSI Bath Accessories Div Moen Inc 25300 Al Moen Dr *TF:* 800-321-8809 ■ *Web:* www.moen.com	North Olmsted	OH	44070	440-962-2000	962-2145
Delta Faucet Co 55 E 111th St *Web:* deltacom.deltafaucet.com/wps/portal	Indianapolis	IN	46280	317-848-1812	
Elias Industries Inc 605 Epsilon Dr **Fax Area Code:* 800	Pittsburgh	PA	15238	412-782-4300	223-1067*
Eljer Plumbingware Inc 14801 Quorum Dr 3rd Fl *TF:* 800-423-5537 ■ *Web:* www.eljer.com	Dallas	TX	75254	972-560-2000	560-2268
Elkay Mfg Co 2222 Camden Ct *Web:* www.elkay.com	Oak Brook	IL	60523	630-574-8484	574-5012
Fisher Mfg Co PO Box 60 *TF:* 800-421-6162 ■ *Web:* www.fisher-mfg.com	Tulare	CA	93275	559-685-5200	685-5222
Fluidmaster Inc 30800 Rancho Viejo Rd **Fax:* Sales ■ *TF:* 800-631-2011 ■ *Web:* www.fluidmaster.com	San Juan Capistrano	CA	92675	949-728-2000	728-2205*
Fortune Brands Home & Hardware Inc 520 Lake Cook Rd *Web:* www.fortunebrands.com	Deerfield	IL	60015	847-484-4400	
Gerber Plumbing Fixtures Co 2500 International Pkwy *TF:* 877-530-3344 ■ *Web:* www.gerberonline.com	Woodridge	IL	60517	630-679-1420	679-1430
Global Partitions 2171 Liberty Hill Rd *Web:* www.globalpartitions.com	Eastanollee	GA	30538	706-827-2700	827-2710
Grohe America Inc 241 Covington Dr *TF:* 800-444-7643 ■ *Web:* www.groheamerica.com	Bloomingdale	IL	60108	630-582-7711	582-7722
Hansgrohe Inc 1121 Alderman Dr *TF:* 800-334-0455 ■ *Web:* www.hansgrohe-usa.com	Alpharetta	GA	30005	770-360-9880	360-9885
In-Sink-Erator 4700 21st St *TF:* 800-558-5712 ■ *Web:* www.insinkerator.com	Racine	WI	53406	262-554-5432	554-3546
Josam Co PO Box T **Fax Area Code:* 800 ■ *TF:* 800-365-6726 ■ *Web:* www.josam.com	Michigan City	IN	46361	219-872-5531	627-0008*
Keeney Mfg Co 1170 Main St **Fax:* Cust Svc ■ *TF Cust Svc:* 800-243-0526 ■ *Web:* www.upt.com	Newington	CT	06111	860-666-3342	665-0374*
Keystone Maax PO Box 544 *TF:* 800-355-5397 ■ *Web:* www.keystonebath.com	Southampton	PA	18966	215-825-5250	355-6881
Kohler Canada Co 180 Creditview Rd *TF:* 800-456-4537 ■ *Web:* www.ca.kohler.com	Vaughan	ON	L4L9N4	905-762-6599	850-2356
Kohler Plumbing North America 444 Highland Dr **Fax:* Sales ■ *TF:* 800-456-4537 ■ *Web:* www.us.kohler.com	Kohler	WI	53044	920-457-4441	459-1658*
Leggitt SH Co 1000 Civic Center Loop *TF:* 800-877-2495 ■ *Web:* www.marshallgas.com	San Marcos	TX	78666	512-396-0707	396-2619
Macristy Industries 206 Newington Ave *TF:* 800-966-6964 ■ *Web:* www.macristyindustries.com	New Britain	CT	06051	860-225-4637	229-4328
Masco Corp 21001 Van Born Rd *NYSE:* MAS ■ *Web:* www.masco.com	Taylor	MI	48180	313-274-7400	792-6135
Microphor Inc 452 E Hill Rd *TF Orders:* 800-358-8280 ■ *Web:* www.microphor.com	Willits	CA	95490	707-459-5563	459-6617
Moen Inc 25300 Al Moen Dr **Fax:* Hum Res ■ *TF Cust Svc:* 800-289-6636 ■ *Web:* www.moen.com	North Olmsted	OH	44070	440-962-2000	962-2089*
Moen Inc CSI Bath Accessories Div 25300 Al Moen Dr *TF:* 800-321-8809 ■ *Web:* www.moen.com	North Olmsted	OH	44070	440-962-2000	962-2145
Norman Supply Co 825 SW 5th St *TF:* 800-375-3457 ■ *Web:* www.normansupply.com	Oklahoma City	OK	73109	405-235-9511	232-2645
Oatey Co 4700 W 160th St **Fax Area Code:* 800 ■ *TF Cust Svc:* 800-321-9532 ■ *Web:* www.oatey.com	Cleveland	OH	44135	216-267-7100	321-9535*
Price Pfister Inc 19701 Da Vinci St *TF:* 800-732-8238 ■ *Web:* www.pricepfister.com	Lake Forest	CA	92610	949-672-4000	672-4610
Quality Metal Finishing Co Inc 421 N Walnut St *Web:* www.qmfco.com	Byron	IL	61010	815-234-2711	234-2243
SH Leggitt Co 1000 Civic Center Loop *TF:* 800-877-2495 ■ *Web:* www.marshallgas.com	San Marcos	TX	78666	512-396-0707	396-2619
Sloan Valve Co 10500 Seymour Ave *TF:* 800-982-5839 ■ *Web:* www.sloanvalve.com	Franklin Park	IL	60131	847-671-4300	671-6944
Speakman Co 400 Anchor Mill Rd **Fax Area Code:* 800 ■ *TF:* 800-537-2107 ■ *Web:* www.speakmancompany.com	New Castle	DE	19720	302-764-9100	977-2747*
Steinen William Mfg Co 29 E Halsey Rd *TF:* 800-724-3343 ■ *Web:* www.steinen.com	Parsippany	NJ	07054	973-887-6400	887-4632
Sterling Plumbing 444 Highland Dr *TF Cust Svc:* 888-783-7546 ■ *Web:* www.sterlingplumbing.com	Kohler	WI	53044	920-457-4441	453-5851
Symmons Industries Inc 31 Brooks Dr *TF:* 800-796-6667 ■ *Web:* www.symmons.com	Braintree	MA	02184	781-848-2250	843-3849
T & S Brass & Bronze Works Inc PO Box 1088 *TF Cust Svc:* 800-476-4103 ■ *Web:* www.tsbrass.com	Travelers Rest	SC	29690	864-834-4102	834-3518
Vance Industries Inc 230 Silvert Ct *Web:* www.vanceind.com	Bensenville	IL	60106	630-694-8500	694-8501
Water Saver Faucet Co 701 W Erie St 2nd Fl *TF Parts:* 800-973-7278 ■ *Web:* www.wsflab.com	Chicago	IL	60610	312-666-5500	666-8597
Waterpik Technologies Inc/Jandy Pool Products 6000 Condor Dr *NYSE:* PIK ■ **Fax:* Mktg ■ *Web:* www.waterpik.com	Moorpark	CA	93021	805-529-2000	529-5934*
William Steinen Mfg Co 29 E Halsey Rd *TF:* 800-724-3343 ■ *Web:* www.steinen.com	Parsippany	NJ	07054	973-887-6400	887-4632
Woodford Mfg Co 2121 Waynoka Rd *TF Sales:* 800-621-6032 ■ *Web:* www.woodfordmfg.com	Colorado Springs	CO	80915	719-574-0600	574-7699

613 PLUMBING FIXTURES & FITTINGS - PLASTICS

				Phone	Fax
AmBath Corp 1055 S Country Club Dr *TF:* 888-826-2284 ■ *Web:* www.ambath.com	Mesa	AZ	85210	480-844-2596	844-7544
American Shower & Bath Corp 540 Glen Ave *Web:* www.asbcorp.com	Moorestown	NJ	08057	856-235-7700	222-1637
Belding Tank Technologies Inc 200 N Gooding St *TF:* 800-253-4252 ■ *Web:* www.beldingtank.com	Belding	MI	48809	616-794-1130	794-3666
Florestone Products Co Inc 2851 Falcon Dr *TF:* 800-446-8827 ■ *Web:* www.florestone.com	Madera	CA	93637	559-661-4171	661-2070
Hytec Plumbing Products Div Kohler Canada Co 4150 Spallumcheen Dr *TF:* 800-871-8311 ■ *Web:* www.hytec.net	Armstrong	BC	V0E1B6	250-546-3067	546-8677
Kohler Canada Co Hytec Plumbing Products Div 4150 Spallumcheen Dr *TF:* 800-871-8311 ■ *Web:* www.hytec.net	Armstrong	BC	V0E1B6	250-546-3067	546-8677
Lasco Bathware 8101 E Kaiser Blvd Suite 200 **Fax:* Sales ■ *TF:* 800-877-2005 ■ *Web:* www.lascobathware.com	Anaheim	CA	92808	714-993-1220	998-3062*
Maax Corp 160 Saint Joseph Blvd *TSX:* MXA ■ *TF:* 800-463-6229 ■ *Web:* www.maax.com	Lachine	QC	H8S2L3	514-844-4155	985-4155
Olsonite Corp 25 Dart Rd **Fax Area Code:* 800 ■ *TF:* 800-521-8266 ■ *Web:* www.olsonite.com	Newnan	GA	30265	770-253-3930	342-1276*
Perrin Mfg Co 1020 Bixby Dr *TF:* 800-345-1875 ■ *Web:* www.perrin.com	City of Industry	CA	91745	626-961-3691	330-5266
Sanderson Plumbing Products Inc 1 Tuffy Ln PO Box 1367 *TF:* 800-647-1042	Columbus	MS	39705	662-328-4000	329-4399
Softub Inc 27615 Ave Hopkins *TF Sales:* 800-554-1120 ■ *Web:* www.softub.com	Valencia	CA	91355	661-702-1401	702-0732
Swan Corp 1 City Center Suite 2300 *TF:* 800-325-7008 ■ *Web:* www.theswancorp.com	Saint Louis	MO	63101	314-231-8148	231-8165
Thetford Corp 7101 Jackson Ave PO Box 1285 *TF:* 800-521-3032 ■ *Web:* www.thetford.com	Ann Arbor	MI	48106	734-769-6000	769-2023
Thetford Corp Recreational Vehicle Group PO Box 1285	Ann Arbor	MI	48106	734-769-6000	769-2023
Tomkins Industries Inc LASCO Products Group 151 Industrial St *TF:* 800-876-3044	Lancaster	TX	75134	972-227-6692	227-9242

614 PLUMBING FIXTURES & FITTINGS - VITREOUS CHINA & EARTHENWARE

				Phone	Fax
American Standard Cos Inc Bath & Kitchen Products Div 1 Centennial Ave PO Box 6820 *TF:* 800-223-0068 ■ *Web:* www.americanstandard-us.com	Piscataway	NJ	08855	732-980-3000	
American Standard Inc 1 Centennial Ave PO Box 6820 *TF:* 800-223-0068	Piscataway	NJ	08855	732-980-6000	980-6122
Briggs Plumbing Products 300 Eagle Rd **Fax Area Code:* 800 ■ *TF:* 800-888-4458 ■ *Web:* www.briggsplumbing.com	Goose Creek	SC	29445	843-569-7887	627-4449*
Crane Plumbing 1235 Hartrey Ave *Web:* www.craneplumbing.com	Evanston	IL	60202	847-864-7600	864-7652
Eljer Plumbingware Inc 14801 Quorum Dr 3rd Fl *TF:* 800-423-5537 ■ *Web:* www.eljer.com	Dallas	TX	75254	972-560-2000	560-2268
Gerber Plumbing Fixtures Co 2500 International Pkwy *TF:* 877-530-3344 ■ *Web:* www.gerberonline.com	Woodridge	IL	60517	630-679-1420	679-1430
ITT Industries Jabsco 666 E Dyer Rd *TF:* 800-845-7000 ■ *Web:* www.jabsco.com	Santa Ana	CA	92705	714-557-4700	628-8478
Kohler Canada Co 180 Creditview Rd *TF:* 800-456-4537 ■ *Web:* www.ca.kohler.com	Vaughan	ON	L4L9N4	905-762-6599	850-2356
Kohler Plumbing North America 444 Highland Dr **Fax:* Sales ■ *TF:* 800-456-4537 ■ *Web:* www.us.kohler.com	Kohler	WI	53044	920-457-4441	459-1658*
Mansfield Plumbing Products Inc 150 E 1st St PO Box 620 *TF:* 800-984-7802 ■ *Web:* www.mansfieldplumbing.com	Perrysville	OH	44864	419-938-5211	938-1427
Microphor Inc 452 E Hill Rd *TF Orders:* 800-358-8280 ■ *Web:* www.microphor.com	Willits	CA	95490	707-459-5563	459-6617
New Jersey Porcelain Lenape Products 600 Plum St *Web:* www.lenapebath.com	Trenton	NJ	08638	609-394-5376	394-0929
Norman Supply Co 825 SW 5th St *TF:* 800-375-3457 ■ *Web:* www.normansupply.com	Oklahoma City	OK	73109	405-235-9511	232-2645
Peerless Pottery Inc PO Box 145 *TF:* 800-457-5785 ■ *Web:* www.peerlesspottery.com	Rockport	IN	47635	812-649-6430	649-6429
Sterling Plumbing 444 Highland Dr *TF Cust Svc:* 888-783-7546 ■ *Web:* www.sterlingplumbing.com	Kohler	WI	53044	920-457-4441	453-5851

Phone | Fax

Sunrise Specialty Co 930 98th Ave .... Oakland CA 94603 510-729-7277 729-7270
TF: 800-646-9117 ■ *Web:* www.sunrisespecialty.com

TOTO USA Inc 1155 Southern Rd .... Morrow GA 30260 770-282-8686 282-8701*
**Fax:* Cust Svc ■ *TF:* 888-295-8134 ■ *Web:* www.totousa.com

Vance Industries Inc 230 Silvert Ct .... Bensenville IL 60106 630-694-8500 694-8501
Web: www.vanceind.com

615 PLUMBING, HEATING, AIR CONDITIONING EQUIPMENT & SUPPLIES - WHOL

SEE ALSO Refrigeration Equipment - Whol p. 2209

Phone | Fax

AB Young Cos Inc 15305 Stony Creek Way .... Noblesville IN 46060 317-565-5000 565-5010
TF: 800-886-7001 ■ *Web:* www.abyoung.com

ACR Group Inc 3200 Wilcrest Dr Suite 440 .... Houston TX 77042 713-780-8532 780-4067
Web: www.acrgroup.com

Air Monitor Corp 1050 Hopper Ave .... Santa Rosa CA 95403 707-544-2706 526-9970
TF: 800-247-3569 ■ *Web:* www.airmonitor.com

American Granby Inc 7652 Morgan Rd .... Liverpool NY 13090 315-451-1100 451-1876*
**Fax:* Acctg ■ *TF:* 800-776-2266 ■ *Web:* www.americangranby.com

Arizona Wholesale Supply Co 2020 E University Dr .... Phoenix AZ 85034 602-258-7901 258-8335
TF: 800-877-4954 ■ *Web:* www.arizonawholesalesupply.com

Atlas Heating & Vent Co Ltd 340 Roebling Rd .... South San Francisco CA 94080 650-873-7000 266-8079
Web: www.atlasheat.com

Baker Distributing Co 14610 Breakers Dr .... Jacksonville FL 32258 904-733-9633 407-4511
TF: 800-217-4698 ■ *Web:* www.bakerdist.com

Barnett Inc 801 W Bay St .... Jacksonville FL 32204 904-384-6530 388-2723*
**Fax:* Mktg ■ *TF:* 800-288-2000 ■ *Web:* www.e-barnett.com

Bayonne Plumbing 250 Ave E .... Bayonne NJ 07002 201-339-8000 339-2770
TF: 800-713-7473 ■ *Web:* www.bayonneplumbingsupply.com

Behler-Young Co 4900 Clyde Park SW .... Grand Rapids MI 49509 616-531-3400 531-1453
Web: www.behler-young.com

Berkheimer GW Co Inc 6000 Southport Rd .... Portage IN 46368 219-764-5200 764-5203
Web: www.gwberkheimer.com

Brauer Supply Co 4260 Forest Park Ave .... Saint Louis MO 63108 314-534-7150 534-1816
TF: 800-392-8776 ■ *Web:* www.brauersupply.com

Butcher Distributors Inc 101 Boyce Rd .... Broussard LA 70518 337-837-2088 837-2069
TF: 800-960-0008 ■ *Web:* www.butcherdistributors.com

Capitol Plumbing & Heating Supply Co Inc 3125 Cocker Ln .... Springfield IL 62711 217-793-4300 793-7637

Chicago Furnace Supply Co 4929 S Lincoln Ave .... Lisle IL 60532 630-971-0400 971-0255
Web: www.chicagofurnace.com

Coburn Supply Co Inc 390 Park St Suite 950 .... Beaumont TX 77701 409-838-6363 838-1920
TF: 800-832-8492 ■ *Web:* www.coburns.com

Comfort Supply Inc 407 Garden Oaks Blvd .... Houston TX 77018 713-845-4705 491-5080
TF: 800-281-7511 ■ *Web:* www.comfortsupply.com

Consolidated Supply Co 7337 SW Kable Ln .... Tigard OR 97224 503-620-7050 684-3254
TF: 800-929-5810 ■ *Web:* www.consolidatedsupply.com

Cooper Harry Supply Co Inc 605 N Sherman Pkwy .... Springfield MO 65802 417-865-8392 873-9146
TF: 800-426-6737 ■ *Web:* www.harrycooper.com

Dana Kepner Co Inc 700 Alcott St .... Denver CO 80204 303-623-6161 623-1667
TF: 800-332-3079 ■ *Web:* www.danakepner.com

Duncan Supply Co Inc 910 N Illinois St .... Indianapolis IN 46204 317-634-1335 264-6689
TF: 800-382-5528 ■ *Web:* www.duncansupply.com

Eastern Pennsylvania Supply Co
700 Scott St PO Box 1126 .... Wilkes-Barre PA 18773 570-823-1181 824-2514
TF: 800-432-8075 ■ *Web:* www.easternpenn.com

Emco Corp 1108 Dundas St E .... London ON N5W3A7 519-645-3900 453-9432
TF: 800-265-1065 ■ *Web:* www.emcoltd.com

Emerson-Swan Inc 300 Pond St .... Randolph MA 02368 781-986-2000 986-2028
TF: 800-346-9219 ■ *Web:* www.emersonswan.com

Engineering & Equipment Co Inc 910 N Washington St .... Albany GA 31701 229-435-5601 435-1502
TF: 800-688-8816

Everett J Prescott Inc 32 Prescott St .... Gardiner ME 04345 207-582-1851 582-5637
TF: 800-876-1357 ■ *Web:* www.ejprescott.com

Ferguson Enterprises Inc 12500 Jefferson Ave .... Newport News VA 23602 757-874-7795 989-2501
Web: www.ferguson.com

First Supply LLC 6800 Gisholt Dr .... Madison WI 53713 608-222-7799 223-6621
TF: 800-236-9795 ■ *Web:* www.1supply.com

Four Seasons Inc 1801 Waters Ridge Dr .... Lewisville TX 75057 972-316-8100 316-8220
TF: 800-433-7508 ■ *Web:* www.4s.com

Fresno Distributing Co Inc 2055 E McKinley Ave .... Fresno CA 93703 559-442-8800 264-3809
TF: 800-655-2542 ■ *Web:* www.fresnod.com

Gateway Supply Co Inc 1312 Hamrick St .... Columbia SC 29202 803-771-7160 376-5600
TF: 800-922-5312 ■ *Web:* www.gatewaysupply.net

Gensco Inc 4402 20th St E .... Tacoma WA 98424 253-620-8203 926-2073
TF: 800-729-3003 ■ *Web:* www.gensco.com

Goodin Co 2700 N 2nd St .... Minneapolis MN 55411 612-588-7811 588-7820*
**Fax Area Code:* 763 ■ *TF:* 800-328-8433 ■ *Web:* www.goodinco.com

Granite Group Wholesalers LLC 6 Storrs St .... Concord NH 03301 603-224-1901 224-6821*
**Fax Area Code:* 602 ■ *TF:* 800-258-3690 ■ *Web:* www.thegranitegroup.com

GW Berkheimer Co Inc 6000 Southport Rd .... Portage IN 46368 219-764-5200 764-5203
Web: www.gwberkheimer.com

Habegger Corp 4995 Winton Rd .... Cincinnati OH 45232 513-681-6313 681-9892
Web: www.habeggercorp.com

Hajoca Corp 127 Coulter Ave .... Ardmore PA 19003 610-649-1430 649-7258
TF: 800-284-3164 ■ *Web:* www.hajoca.com/

Hajoca Corp Keenan Supply Div 1341 Philadelphia St .... Pomona CA 91766 909-613-1363 613-1173
TF: 800-437-6593 ■ *Web:* www.hajoca.com/keenanpomona/

Handy NB Co 65 10th St .... Lynchburg VA 24504 434-847-4495 847-2404
TF: 800-284-6242 ■ *Web:* www.nbhandy.com

Harrison Piping Supply Co Inc 38777 Schoolcraft Rd .... Livonia MI 48150 734-464-4400 464-6488
TF: 800-482-3929 ■ *Web:* www.harrisonco.com

Harry Cooper Supply Co Inc 605 N Sherman Pkwy .... Springfield MO 65802 417-865-8392 873-9146
TF: 800-426-6737 ■ *Web:* www.harrycooper.com

Harvey Sid Industries Inc 605 Locust St .... Garden City NY 11530 516-745-9200 268-6542*
**Fax Area Code:* 800 ■ *Web:* www.sidharvey.com

Hercules Industries Inc 1310 W Evans Ave .... Denver CO 80223 303-937-1000 937-0903
TF: 800-356-5350 ■ *Web:* www.herculesindustries.com

ILLCO Inc DBA Illinois Supply Co 535 S River St .... Aurora IL 60506 630-892-7904 892-0318
Web: www.illco.com

Illinois Supply Co 535 S River St .... Aurora IL 60506 630-892-7904 892-0318
Web: www.illco.com

Indiana Supply Corp 3835 E 21st St .... Indianapolis IN 46218 317-359-5451 351-2135
TF: 800-686-0195 ■ *Web:* www.indianasupply.com

Interline Brands Inc 801 W Bay St .... Jacksonville FL 32204 904-421-1400 288-2828*
NYSE: IBI ■ **Fax Area Code:* 800 ■ *TF:* 800-288-2000 ■ *Web:* www.interlinebrands.com

Irr Supply Centers Inc 908 Niagara Falls Blvd .... North Tonawanda NY 14120 716-692-1600 692-1611
Web: www.irrsupply.com

J & B Supply Inc 4915 S Zero St .... Fort Smith AR 72903 479-649-4915 649-4911
TF: 800-345-5752 ■ *Web:* www.jandbsupply.com

JH Larson Co 10200 51st Ave N .... Plymouth MN 55442 763-545-1717 545-1144
TF: 800-292-7970 ■ *Web:* www.jhlarson.com

John M Frey Co Inc 2735 62nd St Ct .... Bettendorf IA 52722 563-332-9200 332-9880
TF: 800-397-3739 ■ *Web:* www.jmfcompany.com

Johnson Supply & Equipment Inc 10151 Stella Link Rd .... Houston TX 77025 713-661-6666 661-3684
TF: 800-833-5455 ■ *Web:* www.johnsonsupply.com

Keenan Supply Div Hajoca Corp 1341 Philadelphia St .... Pomona CA 91766 909-613-1363 613-1173
TF: 800-437-6593 ■ *Web:* www.hajoca.com/keenanpomona/

Keller Supply Co Inc 3209 17th Ave W .... Seattle WA 98119 206-285-3300 283-8668*
**Fax:* Acctg ■ *TF:* 800-285-3302 ■ *Web:* www.kellersupply.com

Kelly's Pipe & Supply Co Inc 2124 Industrial Rd .... Las Vegas NV 89102 702-382-4957 382-4879
TF: 888-382-4957 ■ *Web:* www.kellyspipe.com

Keystone Plumbing Sales Co 225 W 7th Ave .... Homestead PA 15120 412-462-8600 462-4705

Koch Air LLC 1900 W Lloyd Expy PO Box 1167 .... Evansville IN 47706 812-962-5200 962-5310
TF: 877-456-2422 ■ *Web:* www.kochair.com

Larson JH Co 10200 51st Ave N .... Plymouth MN 55442 763-545-1717 545-1144
TF: 800-292-7970 ■ *Web:* www.jhlarson.com

Lee Supply Corp 6610 Guion Rd .... Indianapolis IN 46268 317-290-2500 290-2512
TF: 800-873-1103 ■ *Web:* www.leesupply.net

Longley Supply Co Inc 2018 Oleander Dr .... Wilmington NC 28403 910-762-7793 762-9178

Michel RE Co Inc 1 RE Michel Dr .... Glen Burnie MD 21060 410-760-4000 761-3703
TF: 800-283-7362 ■ *Web:* www.remichel.com

Mid-Lakes Distributing Inc 1029 W Adams St .... Chicago IL 60607 312-733-1033 733-1721
TF: 888-733-2700 ■ *Web:* www.mid-lakes.com

Mid-States Supply Co 1716 Guinotte Ave .... Kansas City MO 64120 816-842-4290 842-3630
TF: 800-825-1410 ■ *Web:* www.midcoonline.com

Milwaukee Stove & Furnace Supply Co 5070 W State St .... Milwaukee WI 53208 414-258-0300 258-8552
Web: www.mstove.com

Mingledorffs Inc 6675 Jones Mill Ct .... Norcross GA 30092 770-446-6311 239-2200
TF: 800-282-4911 ■ *Web:* www.mingledorffs.com

Moore Supply Co 200 W Loop 336 N .... Conroe TX 77301 936-756-4445 441-8468
Web: www.mooresupply.com

Morley-Murphy Co 200 S Washington St Suite 305 .... Green Bay WI 54301 920-499-3171 499-9409
TF: 877-499-3171 ■ *Web:* www.morley-murphycompany.com

Morrison Supply Co Inc 311 E Vickery Blvd .... Fort Worth TX 76104 817-336-0451 338-1612
Web: www.morsco.com

Mountainland Supply Co 1505 W 130 South .... Orem UT 84058 801-224-6050 224-6058
TF: 800-666-5434 ■ *Web:* www.mtncom.net

NB Handy Co 65 10th St .... Lynchburg VA 24504 434-847-4495 847-2404
TF: 800-284-6242 ■ *Web:* www.nbhandy.com

Northeastern Supply Co Inc 8323 Pulaski Hwy .... Baltimore MD 21237 410-574-0010 574-3315*
**Fax:* Sales ■ *TF:* 800-999-5664 ■ *Web:* www.northeastern.com

Northwest Pipe Fittings Inc 33 S 8th St W .... Billings MT 59103 406-252-0142 248-8072
TF: 800-937-4737 ■ *Web:* www.northwestpipe.net

Parnell-Martin Cos LLC 1315 N Graham St .... Charlotte NC 28206 704-375-8651 335-7156
TF: 800-849-2443 ■ *Web:* www.parnellmartin.com

Plumb Supply Co 1622 NE 51st Ave .... Des Moines IA 50313 515-262-9511 262-9790
TF: 800-483-9511 ■ *Web:* www.plumbsupply.com

Plumbers Supply Co 1000 E Main St .... Louisville KY 40206 502-582-2261 585-5521
TF: 800-626-5133 ■ *Web:* www.plumbers-supply-co.com

Plumbing Distributors Inc 1025 Old Norcross Rd .... Lawrenceville GA 30045 770-963-9231 822-9509
TF: 800-262-9231 ■ *Web:* www.pdiplumbing.com

Prescott Everett J Inc 32 Prescott St .... Gardiner ME 04345 207-582-1851 582-5637
TF: 800-876-1357 ■ *Web:* www.ejprescott.com

RE Michel Co Inc 1 RE Michel Dr .... Glen Burnie MD 21060 410-760-4000 761-3703
TF: 800-283-7362 ■ *Web:* www.remichel.com

Redlon & Johnson 172-174 Saint John St .... Portland ME 04102 207-773-4755 772-2957
TF: 800-905-5250 ■ *Web:* www.redlon-johnson.com

Reeves-Wiedeman Co Inc 14861 W 100th St .... Lenexa KS 66215 913-492-7100 492-6962
Web: www.rwco.com

Refrigeration Sales Corp 9450 Allen Dr Suite A .... Valley View OH 44125 216-881-7800 525-8196
TF: 866-525-8196 ■ *Web:* www.refrigerationsales.net

Rexel Canada Inc 5600 Keaton Crescent .... Mississauga ON L5R3G3 905-712-4004 712-4024
Web: www.rexel.ca

Ridgewood Corp 270 Rt 17 S .... Mahwah NJ 07430 201-529-5500 529-5302
TF Cust Svc: 800-562-0214 ■ *Web:* www.ridgewoodcorp.com

Roberts-Hamilton Co Inc 7300 Northland Dr .... Brooklyn Park MN 55428 763-315-0100 315-0199
TF: 800-888-2222 ■ *Web:* www.robertshamilton.com

Robertson Heating Supply Co 2155 W Main St .... Alliance OH 44601 330-821-9180 821-8251
TF: 800-433-9532 ■ *Web:* www.robertsonheatingsupply.com

Roosevelt WA Co 2727 Commerce St .... La Crosse WI 54603 608-781-2000 781-8360
TF: 800-279-2726 ■ *Web:* www.waroosevelt.com

Samon's Tiger Stores Inc 2511 Monroe St NE .... Albuquerque NM 87110 505-884-4615 884-1725

Sauna Warehouse Inc 6 Orchard St Suite 201 .... Lake Forest CA 92630 949-609-2202 699-0830
TF: 800-906-2242 ■ *Web:* www.saunawarehouse.com

Security Supply Corp 196 Maple Ave .... Selkirk NY 12158 518-767-2226 767-2065
TF: 800-333-2226 ■ *Web:* www.secsupply.com

SG Supply Co 12900 S Throop St .... Calumet Park IL 60827 708-371-8800 371-2752
TF: 800-626-9130 ■ *Web:* www.sgsupply.com

Sid Harvey Industries Inc 605 Locust St .... Garden City NY 11530 516-745-9200 268-6542*
**Fax Area Code:* 800 ■ *Web:* www.sidharvey.com

SPS Cos Inc 6363 Hwy 7 .... Saint Louis Park MN 55416 952-929-1377 929-1862
Web: www.spscompanies.com

Standard Air & Lite Corp 2406 Woodmere Dr .... Pittsburgh PA 15205 412-920-6505 733-0010
TF: 800-472-2458 ■ *Web:* www.stdair.com

Temperature Equipment Corp 17725 Volbrecht Rd .... Lansing IL 60438 708-418-0900 418-5100
Web: www.tecmungo.com

Temperature Systems Inc 5001 Voges Rd .... Madison WI 53718 608-271-7500 274-1609
TF: 800-366-0930 ■ *Web:* www.tsihvac.com

Thomas Somerville Co 16155 Trade Zone Ave .... Upper Marlboro MD 20774 301-390-9575 390-1108
Web: www.tsomerville.com

Three States Supply Co LLC 666 EH Crump Blvd .... Memphis TN 38126 901-948-8651 948-2454
TF: 800-666-1565 ■ *Web:* www.threestates.com

Torrington Supply Co Inc 100 N Elm St .... Waterbury CT 06723 203-756-3641 753-4317
TF: 800-445-9936 ■ *Web:* www.torringtonsupply.com

United Pipe & Supply Co Inc 90099 Prairie Rd .... Eugene OR 97402 541-688-6511 688-8994
TF: 800-288-6511 ■ *Web:* www.unitedpipe.com

UP Electric/Wittock Supply Co 2650 Trautner Dr .... Saginaw MI 48603 989-497-2100 497-2101
TF: 800-562-7102 ■ *Web:* www.wittock.com

US Airconditioning Distributors 16900 Chestnut St .... City of Industry CA 91748 626-854-4500 854-4690*
**Fax:* Sales ■ *TF:* 800-937-7222 ■ *Web:* www.us-ac.com

Vamac Inc 4201 Jacque St .... Richmond VA 23230 804-353-7811 358-7855
TF: 800-768-2622 ■ *Web:* www.vamac.com

WA Roosevelt Co 2727 Commerce St .... La Crosse WI 54603 608-781-2000 781-8360
TF: 800-279-2726 ■ *Web:* www.waroosevelt.com

Waxman Industries Inc 24460 Aurora Rd .... Bedford Heights OH 44146 440-439-1830 439-8494*
**Fax:* Cust Svc ■ *TF:* 800-531-3342 ■ *Web:* www.waxmanind.com

Western Nevada Supply Co 950 S Rock Blvd .... Sparks NV 89431 775-359-5800 359-4649
TF: 800-648-1230 ■ *Web:* www.wns1.com

Wholesale Supply Group Inc 885 Keith St NW .... Cleveland TN 37320 423-478-1191 478-5120
Web: www.wsginc.com

Wilmar Industries Inc 200 E Park Dr Suite 200 .... Mount Laurel NJ 08054 856-439-1222 439-1333
TF: 800-345-3000 ■ *Web:* www.wilmar.com

Company	City	State	Zip	Phone	Fax
Winnelson 3110 Kettering Blvd	Dayton	OH	45439	937-294-7242	294-6921
Web: www.winholesale.com					
WinWholesale Inc 3110 Kettering Blvd	Dayton	OH	45439	937-294-6878	293-9591
Web: www.winholesale.com					
Woodhill Supply Inc 4665 Beidler Rd	Willoughby	OH	44094	440-269-1100	269-1027
TF: 800-362-6111 ■ *Web:* www.woodhillsupply.com					
Young AB Cos Inc 15305 Stony Creek Way	Noblesville	IN	46060	317-565-5000	565-5010
TF: 800-886-7001 ■ *Web:* www.abyoung.com					
Young Supply Co 888 W Baltimore St	Detroit	MI	48202	313-875-3280	875-3051
TF: 800-872-3280 ■ *Web:* www.youngsupply.com					

616 PLYWOOD & VENEERS

SEE ALSO Construction Materials - Lumber & Building Supplies p. 1549; Home Improvement Centers p. 1788

Company	City	State	Zip	Phone	Fax
Aetna Plywood Inc 1401 Saint Charles Rd	Maywood	IL	60153	708-343-1515	343-1616
Web: www.aetnaplywood.com					
Amos-Hill Assoc Inc 112 Shelby Ave PO Box 7	Edinburgh	IN	46124	812-526-2671	526-5865
Web: www.amoshill.com					
Anderson Hardwood Floors PO Box 1155	Clinton	SC	29325	864-833-6250	833-6664
Web: www.andersonfloors.com					
Arkansas Face Veneer Inc PO Box 706	Benton	AR	72018	501-778-7412	778-7414
Web: www.arkansasface.com					
Atlantic Veneer Corp 2457 Lennoxville Rd PO Box 660	Beaufort	NC	28516	252-728-3169	728-4203
TF: 800-334-7723					
Bald Knob Veneer Co PO Box 1029	Creswell	OR	97426	541-895-2151	895-2155
Barmon Door & Plywood Inc PO Box 98	Lake Stevens	WA	98258	425-334-1222	335-0404
Bradford Veneer & Panel Co 1143 Clark Pond Rd	North Haverhill	NH	03774	802-222-5241	222-5134
Web: www.bvpc.com					
Buffalo Veneer & Plywood Co Inc 501 6th Ave NE PO Box 95	Buffalo	MN	55313	763-682-1822	682-9769
California Panel & Veneer Co PO Box 3250	Cerritos	CA	90703	562-926-5834	926-3139
TF: 800-451-1745 ■ *Web:* www.calpanel.com					
Capital Veneer Works Inc PO Box 240785	Montgomery	AL	36124	334-264-1401	264-6923
Capitol Plywood Inc 160 Commerce Cir	Sacramento	CA	95815	916-922-8861	922-0775
TF: 800-326-1505 ■ *Web:* www.capitolplywood.com					
Chesapeake Hardwood Products Inc 201 Dexter St W	Chesapeake	VA	23324	757-543-1601	543-4335
TF: 800-446-8162 ■ *Web:* www.chpi.com					
Cleveland Plywood Co Inc 5900 Harvard Ave	Cleveland	OH	44105	216-641-6600	641-5241
TF: 800-727-2759 ■ *Web:* www.clevelandplywood.com					
Coastal Wood Products Inc 13285 Temple Ave	City of Industry	CA	91746	626-333-1104	333-3806
TF: 800-852-9663					
Columbia Forest Products Inc 222 SW Columbia St Suite 1575	Portland	OR	97201	503-224-5300	224-5294
TF: 800-547-4261 ■ *Web:* www.columbiaforestproducts.com					
Columbia Forest Products Inc Columbia Plywood Div PO Box 1780	Klamath Falls	OR	97601	541-882-7281	882-7295
TF: 800-547-1791 ■ *Web:* www.cfpwood.com					
Columbia Panel Mfg Co PO Box 7447	High Point	NC	27264	336-861-4100	861-4700
Constantine's Wood Center 1040 E Oakland Pk Blvd	Fort Lauderdale	FL	33334	954-561-1716	565-8149
TF: 800-443-9667 ■ *Web:* www.constantines.com					
Cummings Veneers Inc 601 E 4th St	New Albany	IN	47150	812-944-2269	944-0212
Darlington Veneer Co Inc PO Box 1087	Darlington	SC	29540	843-393-3861	393-8243
TF: 800-845-2388 ■ *Web:* www.darlingtonveneer.com					
David R Webb Co Inc 206 S Holland St PO Box 8	Edinburgh	IN	46124	812-526-2601	526-5842
Web: www.davidrwebb.com					
Davis Wood Products Inc PO Box 604	Hudson	NC	28638	828-728-8444	728-4601
Web: www.daviswoodproducts.com					
Eggers Industries Inc 1 Eggers Dr	Two Rivers	WI	54241	920-793-1351	793-2958
Web: www.eggersindustries.com					
Ellstrom Mfg Inc 1540 NW Ballard Way	Seattle	WA	98107	206-789-3000	782-2814
Erath Veneer Corp of Virginia Industrial Dr PO Box 507	Rocky Mount	VA	24151	540-483-5223	483-1580
Web: www.erathveneer.com					
Fiber-Tech Industries Inc 2000 Kenskill Ave	Washington Court House	OH	43160	740-335-9400	335-4843
TF: 800-879-4377 ■ *Web:* www.fiber-tech.net					
Flexible Materials Inc 1202 Port Rd	Jeffersonville	IN	47130	812-280-7000	280-7001
TF: 800-359-9663 ■ *Web:* www.flexwood.com					
Freeman Corp 415 Magnolia St	Winchester	KY	40392	859-744-4311	744-4363
Web: www.freemancorp.com					
Freres Lumber Co Inc PO Box 276	Lyons	OR	97358	503-859-2121	859-2112
G-L Veneer Co Inc 2224 E Slauson Ave	Huntington Park	CA	90255	323-582-5203	582-9681
TF: 800-588-5003 ■ *Web:* www.glveneer.com					
Georgia-Pacific Corp 133 Peachtree St NE	Atlanta	GA	30303	404-652-4000	230-5774
Web: www.gp.com					
Harbor Sales Co Inc 1000 Harbor Ct	Sudlersville	MD	21668	800-345-1712	868-9257
Web: www.harborsales.net					
Hardel Mutual Plywood Corp PO Box 566	Chehalis	WA	98532	360-740-0232	740-9570
TF: 800-562-6344 ■ *Web:* www.hardel.com					
Hasty Plywood Co PO Box 417	Maxton	NC	28364	910-844-5267	844-9483
Web: www.hasply.com					
Hood Industries Inc PO Box 17317	Hattiesburg	MS	39404	601-264-2559	296-4755
Web: www.hoodindustries.com					
Hoquiam Plywood Co Inc 1000 Woodlawn Rd	Hoquiam	WA	98550	360-533-3060	532-6980
Inland Plywood Co 375 N Cass Ave	Pontiac	MI	48342	248-334-4706	338-7407
TF: 800-521-4355 ■ *Web:* www.inlandplywood.com					
International Wood Industries Inc 250 D St	Turlock	CA	95380	209-632-3300	632-0160
Web: www.intlwoodind.com					
Louisiana-Pacific Corp 414 Union St Suite 2000	Nashville	TN	37219	615-986-5600	986-5666
NYSE: LPX ■ *TF:* 877-744-5600 ■ *Web:* www.lpcorp.com					
MacBeath Hardwood Co 2150 Oakdale Ave	San Francisco	CA	94124	415-401-7046	401-8961
TF: 800-233-0782 ■ *Web:* www.macbeath.com					
Marion Plywood Corp PO Box 497	Marion	WI	54950	715-754-5231	754-2582
Web: www.marionplywood.com					
McKnight Plywood Inc 201 N 1st St	West Helena	AR	72390	870-572-2501	572-2511
TF: 800-566-2145					
Murphy Co 2350 Prairie Rd	Eugene	OR	97402	541-688-9033	461-4546
Murphy Plywood Co 2350 Prairie Rd	Eugene	OR	97408	541-461-4545	461-4546
Norbord Inc 1 Toronto St 6th Fl	Toronto	ON	M5C2W4	416-643-8820	365-3292
TSX: NBD ■ *TF:* 877-263-9367 ■ *Web:* www.norbord.com					
Norbord Industries Inc 1 Toronto St Suite 600	Toronto	ON	M5C2W4	416-365-0710	365-3292
TF: 800-387-1740 ■ *Web:* www.norbord.com					
North American Plywood Corp 12343 Hawkins St	Santa Fe Springs	CA	90670	562-941-7575	944-8368
TF Sales: 800-421-1372 ■ *Web:* www.northamply.com					
Pacific Lumber Co 125 Main St PO Box 37	Scotia	CA	95565	707-764-2222	764-4171
Web: www.palco.com					
Panel Products LLC 8250 Agate Rd	White City	OR	97503	541-826-3142	826-8022
Pasquier Panel Products Inc 1510 Puyallup St PO Box 1170	Sumner	WA	98390	253-863-6323	891-7993
Web: www.pasquierpanel.com					
Pavco Industries Inc PO Box 612	Pascagoula	MS	39568	228-762-3172	762-3959
TF: 800-346-7206 ■ *Web:* www.pavcoind.com					
Phillips Plywood Co Inc 13599 Desmond St	Pacoima	CA	91331	818-897-7736	897-6571
TF: 800-649-6410 ■ *Web:* www.phillipsplywood.com					
Plywood Supply Inc 7036 NE 175th St	Kenmore	WA	98028	425-485-8585	485-6195
TF: 800-683-9663 ■ *Web:* www.plywoodsupply.com					
Pope & Talbot Inc 1500 SW 1st Ave Suite 200	Portland	OR	97201	503-228-9161	220-2755
NYSE: POP ■ *Web:* www.poptal.com					
Potlatch Corp 601 W 1st Ave Suite 1600	Spokane	WA	99201	509-835-1500	835-1555
NYSE: PCH ■ *Web:* www.potlatchcorp.com					
Potlatch Corp Wood Products Div 805 Mill Rd PO Box 1388	Lewiston	ID	83501	208-799-0123	799-1918
Web: www.potlatchcorp.com					
Robert Weed Plywood Corp 705 Maple St PO Box 487	Bristol	IN	46507	574-848-4408	848-5679
Web: www.robertweedplywood.com					
Roseburg Forest Products Co PO Box 1088	Roseburg	OR	97470	541-679-3311	
TF: 800-548-5275 ■ *Web:* www.rfpco.com					
RS Bacon Veneer Co 6951 High Grove Blvd	Burr Ridge	IL	60527	630-323-1414	323-1499
TF: 800-443-7995 ■ *Web:* www.baconveneer.com					
Scotch Lumber Co 119 W Main St PO Box 38	Fulton	AL	36446	334-636-4424	636-7107
TF: 800-936-4424					
SDS Lumber Co PO Box 266	Bingen	WA	98605	509-493-2155	493-2535
Web: www.sdslumber.com					
South Coast Lumber Co 885 Railroad Ave PO Box 670	Brookings	OR	97415	541-469-2136	469-9105
Web: www.socomi.com					
Standard Plywoods Inc DBA Anderson Hardwood Floors PO Box 1155	Clinton	SC	29325	864-833-6250	833-6664
Web: www.andersonfloors.com					
States Industries Inc PO Box 7037	Eugene	OR	97401	541-688-7871	
TF: 800-626-1981 ■ *Web:* www.statesind.com					
StemWood Corp 2710 Grant Line Rd	New Albany	IN	47150	812-945-6646	945-7549
Stimson Lumber Co 520 SW Yamhill St Suite 700	Portland	OR	97204	503-222-1676	295-1849
TF: 800-445-9758 ■ *Web:* www.stimsonlumber.com					
Stoll Brothers Lumber Inc PO Box 367	Odon	IN	47562	812-636-4053	636-8025
Texas Plywood & Lumber Co Inc 1001 E Ave K	Grand Prairie	TX	75050	972-262-1331	624-2225
Web: www.texasplywood.com					
Trimac Panel Products PO Box 25277	Portland	OR	97298	503-297-1826	297-9049
Web: www.trimacpanel.com					
United Plywood & Lumber Inc 1640 Mims Ave SW	Birmingham	AL	35211	205-925-7601	923-9511
TF: 800-272-6486 ■ *Web:* www.unitedplywoods.com					
Wavell-Huber Wood Products Inc 180 N 170 West	North Salt Lake	UT	84054	562-431-6528	936-6078*
**Fax Area Code:* 801 ■ *Web:* www.wavell-huber.com					
Webb David R Co Inc 206 S Holland St PO Box 8	Edinburgh	IN	46124	812-526-2601	526-5842
Web: www.davidrwebb.com					
Weed Robert Plywood Corp 705 Maple St PO Box 487	Bristol	IN	46507	574-848-4408	848-5679
Web: www.robertweedplywood.com					
West Fraser Timber Co Ltd 858 Beatty St Suite 501	Vancouver	BC	V6B1C1	604-895-2700	681-6061
TSX: WFT ■ *Web:* www.westfraser.com					
Westcoast Forest Products 19406 68th Dr NE	Arlington	WA	98223	360-435-2175	435-3232
Weyerhaeuser Canada Ltd 925 W Georgia St	Vancouver	BC	V6C3L2	604-661-8000	
Winnsboro Plywood Co PO Box 449	Winnsboro	SC	29180	803-635-4696	635-3023
Wisconsin Veneer & Plywood Inc PO Box 140	Mattoon	WI	54450	715-489-3611	489-3268

617 POINT-OF-SALE (POS) & POINT-OF-INFORMATION (POI) SYSTEMS

Company	City	State	Zip	Phone	Fax
@pos Transaction Systems 3051 N 1st St	San Jose	CA	95134	408-468-5400	433-0774
3M Digital Signage 600 Ericksen Ave NE Suite 200	Bainbridge Island	WA	98110	206-855-2000	855-4930
TF: 888-460-8866 ■ *Web:* www.3mdigitalsignage.com					
3M Electro & Communications Div 3M Center	Saint Paul	MN	55144	651-733-1110	737-7117
TF: 800-364-3577					
Casio Inc 570 Mt Pleasant Ave	Dover	NJ	07801	973-361-5400	537-8910*
**Fax:* Hum Res ■ *TF Cust Svc:* 800-634-1895 ■ *Web:* www.casio.com					
Catuity Inc 300 Preston Ave Suite 302	Charlottesville	VA	22902	434-979-0724	943-6850*
NASDAQ: CTTY ■ **Fax Area Code:* 734 ■ *Web:* www.catuity.com					
CeroView 3 Chrysler	Irvine	CA	92618	949-454-6500	454-2323
Web: www.ceroview.com					
Checkpoint Systems Inc 101 Wolf Dr	Thorofare	NJ	08086	856-848-1800	848-0937
NYSE: CKP ■ *TF:* 800-257-5540 ■ *Web:* www.checkpointsystems.com					
Comtrex Systems Corp 1247 N Church St Suite 7	Moorestown	NJ	08057	856-778-0090	778-9322
Web: www.comtrex.com					
Debitek Inc 2115 Chapman Rd Suite 159	Chattanooga	TN	37421	423-894-6177	855-7554
TF: 800-332-4835 ■ *Web:* www.debitek.com					
Dresser Inc Wayne Div 3814 Jarrett Way	Austin	TX	78728	512-388-8311	388-8429*
**Fax:* Hum Res ■ *TF:* 800-289-2963 ■ *Web:* www.wayne.com					
Fujitsu Transaction Solutions Inc 2801 Network Blvd	Frisco	TX	75034	972-963-2300	963-2651
TF: 800-538-8716 ■ *Web:* www.ftxs.fujitsu.com					
Hypercom Corp 2851 W Kathleen Rd	Phoenix	AZ	85053	602-504-5000	
NYSE: HYC ■ *TF:* 800-577-5501 ■ *Web:* www.hypercom.com					
Ingenico Corp 1003 Mansell Rd	Roswell	GA	30076	770-594-6000	594-6020
TF: 800-435-3014 ■ *Web:* www.ingenico-us.com					
Kiosk Information Systems Inc (KIS) 346 S Arthur Ave	Louisville	CO	80027	303-466-5471	466-6730
TF: 800-529-5471 ■ *Web:* www.kis-kiosk.com					
Micros Systems Inc 7031 Columbia Gateway Dr	Columbia	MD	21046	443-285-6000	285-0455*
NASDAQ: MCRS ■ **Fax:* Sales ■ *TF:* 800-937-2211 ■ *Web:* www.micros.com					
MTI Inc 1050 NW 229th Ave	Hillsboro	OR	97124	503-648-6500	648-7500
TF: 800-426-6844 ■ *Web:* www.mti-interactive.com					
NCR Corp 1700 S Patterson Blvd	Dayton	OH	45479	937-445-5000	445-5617*
NYSE: NCR ■ **Fax:* Cust Svc ■ *TF Cust Svc:* 800-531-2222 ■ *Web:* www.ncr.com					
Omron Systems Inc 55 E Commerce Dr	Schaumburg	IL	60173	847-884-0322	884-1866
TF Tech Supp: 800-706-6766 ■ *Web:* www.omronosi.com					
Pacer/CATS 355 Inverness Dr S	Englewood	CO	80112	303-649-9818	414-7805
Web: www.pacercats.com					
PAR Technology Corp 8383 Seneca Tpke	New Hartford	NY	13413	315-738-0600	738-0562
NYSE: PTC ■ *TF:* 800-448-6505 ■ *Web:* www.partech.com					
PSC Inc 959 Terry St	Eugene	OR	97402	541-683-5700	345-7140
TF: 800-695-5700 ■ *Web:* www.psc.com					
Radiant Systems Inc 3925 Brookside Pkwy	Alpharetta	GA	30022	770-576-6000	754-7790
NASDAQ: RADS ■ *TF:* 800-229-0991 ■ *Web:* www.radiants.com					
SeePoint Technology LLC 2619 Manhattan Beach Blvd	Redondo Beach	CA	90278	310-725-9660	535-9234
Web: www.seepoint.com					
TeamLinux 314 Leo St	Dayton	OH	45404	937-443-2400	443-2748
Toshiba TEC America 4401-A Bankers Cir	Atlanta	GA	30360	770-449-3040	449-1152
Web: www.toshibatecusa.com					
TouchSystems Corp 220 Tradesmen Dr	Hutto	TX	78634	512-846-2424	846-2425
TF: 800-320-5944 ■ *Web:* www.touchsystems.com					
Transaction Printer Group Inc 5893 Oberlin Dr Suite 103	San Diego	CA	92121	858-638-0000	320-0335
TF: 800-732-8950 ■ *Web:* www.tpgprinters.com					
Ultimate Technology Corp 100 Rawson Rd	Victor	NY	14564	585-924-9500	924-1434
TF: 800-349-0546 ■ *Web:* www.ultimatetechnology.com					
VeriFone Inc 2455 Augustine Dr	Santa Clara	CA	95054	408-232-7800	232-7811
NYSE: PAY ■ *TF:* 800-837-4366 ■ *Web:* www.verifone.com					
Wayne Div Dresser Inc 3814 Jarrett Way	Austin	TX	78728	512-388-8311	388-8429*
**Fax:* Hum Res ■ *TF:* 800-289-2963 ■ *Web:* www.wayne.com					

618 POLITICAL ACTION COMMITTEES

SEE ALSO Associations & Organizations - General - Civic & Political Organizations p. 1298

				Phone	Fax
21st Century Freedom PAC 355 Lexington Ave Suite 1001	New York	NY	10017	212-599-2121	370-0064
Action Committee for Rural Electrification (ACRE) 4301 Wilson Blvd	Arlington	VA	22203	703-907-5500	907-5516
Web: www.nreca.org/nreca/Policy/Legislative/ACRE					
Action Fund of Lehman Brothers Holdings Inc 2001 K St NW Suite 1125	Washington	DC	20006	202-452-4720	452-4791
AFL-CIO Committee on Political Education 815 16th St NW	Washington	DC	20006	202-637-5101	637-5058
AFLAC PAC (American Family Life Assurance Co PAC) 1300 Pennsylvania Ave Suite 300	Washington	DC	20004	202-289-6401	
Agricultural Retailers Assn PAC 1156 15th St NW Suite 302	Washington	DC	20005	202-457-0825	457-0864
Air Conditioning Contractors of America PAC (ACCA-PAC) 2800 Shirlington Rd Suite 300	Arlington	VA	22206	703-575-4477	575-4449
Aircraft Owners & Pilots Assn PAC 601 Pennsylvania Ave NW South Bldg Suite 875	Washington	DC	20004	202-737-7950	737-7951
American Academy of Ophthalmology PAC 1101 Vermont Ave NW Suite 700	Washington	DC	20005	202-737-6662	737-7061
American Academy of Physician Assistants PAC (AAPA PAC) 950 N Washington St	Alexandria	VA	22314	703-836-2272	684-1924
Web: www.aapa.org/gandp/pac					
American Airlines PAC 1101 17th St NW Suite 600	Washington	DC	20036	202-496-5666	496-5660
American Apparel & Footwear Assn PAC 1601 N Kent St Suite 1200	Arlington	VA	22209	703-524-1864	522-6741
American Assn of Crop Insurers PAC 1 Massachusetts Ave NW Suite 800	Washington	DC	20001	202-789-4100	408-7763
American Assn for Justice PAC 1050 31st St NW	Washington	DC	20007	202-965-3500	
Web: www.justice.org					
American Assn of Nurse Anesthetists PAC 412 1st St SE Suite 12	Washington	DC	20003	202-484-8400	484-8408
American Assn of Orthodontists PAC 401 N Lindbergh Blvd	Saint Louis	MO	63141	314-993-1700	997-1745
TF: 800-424-2841					
American Bakers Assn PAC 1300 'I' St NW Suite 700-W	Washington	DC	20005	202-789-0300	898-1164
American Bankers Assn PAC 1120 Connecticut Ave NW	Washington	DC	20036	202-663-5113	663-7544
American Beverage Assn PAC 1101 16th St NW	Washington	DC	20036	202-463-6732	463-8178
American Chiropractic Assn PAC (ACA-PAC) 1701 Clarendon Blvd	Arlington	VA	22209	703-276-8800	243-2593
TF: 800-986-4636					
American Dental PAC 1111 14th St NW Suite 1100	Washington	DC	20005	202-898-2424	898-2437
American Express PAC 801 Pennsylvania Ave NW Suite 650	Washington	DC	20004	202-434-0160	624-0775
American Family Life Assurance Co PAC (AFLAC PAC) 1300 Pennsylvania Ave Suite 300	Washington	DC	20004	202-289-6401	
American Federation of Teachers Committee on Political Education 555 New Jersey Ave NW	Washington	DC	20001	202-879-4400	879-4556*
**Fax:* PR ■ *TF:* 800-238-1133					
American Financial Services Assn PAC (AFSA PAC) 919 18th St NW Suite 300	Washington	DC	20006	202-296-5544	223-0321
American Frozen Food Institute PAC 2000 Corporate Ridge Suite 1000	McLean	VA	22102	703-821-0770	821-1350
American Health Care Assn PAC 1201 L St NW	Washington	DC	20005	202-842-4444	842-3860
American Home Furnishings Alliance PAC 1250 Connecticut Ave NW Suite 200	Washington	DC	20036	336-884-5000	261-3508*
**Fax Area Code:* 202 ■ *TF:* 877-278-2118 ■ *Web:* www.ahfa.us					
American Hospital Assn PAC 325 7th St NW Suite 700	Washington	DC	20004	202-638-1100	626-2345
American Insurance Assn PAC 1130 Connecticut Ave NW Suite 1000	Washington	DC	20036	202-828-7100	293-1219
American Intellectual Property Law Assn PAC (AIPLA PAC) 241 18th St S Suite 700	Arlington	VA	22202	703-415-0780	415-0786
American Iron & Steel Institute PAC 1140 Connecticut Ave NW Suite 705	Washington	DC	20036	202-452-7100	463-6573
American Meat Institute PAC 1150 Connecticut Ave NW	Washington	DC	20036	202-587-4200	587-4300
American Medical Assn PAC 1101 Vermont Ave NW 12th Fl	Washington	DC	20005	202-789-7400	789-7485
American Motorcyclist Assn PAC 101 Constitution Ave NW Suite 800-W	Washington	DC	20001	202-742-4301	
American Moving & Storage Assn PAC 1611 Duke St	Alexandria	VA	22314	703-683-7410	683-7527
Web: www.promover.org					
American Nurses Assn PAC (ANA PAC) 8515 Georgia Ave Suite 400	Silver Spring	MD	20910	301-628-5096	628-5001
American Pharmacists Assn PAC 2215 Constitution Ave NW	Washington	DC	20037	202-628-4410	783-2351
TF: 800-237-2742 ■ *Web:* www.aphanet.org/govt/govaffair.html					
American Postal Workers Union PAC (COPA) 1300 L St NW	Washington	DC	20005	202-842-4200	842-4283
American Resort Development Assn PAC (ARDA PAC) 1201 15th St NW Suite 400	Washington	DC	20005	202-371-6700	289-8544
American Society of Anesthesiologists PAC 1101 Vermont Ave NW Suite 606	Washington	DC	20005	202-289-2222	371-0384
American Society of Travel Agents PAC 1101 King St Suite 200	Alexandria	VA	22314	703-739-2782	684-8319
TF: 800-275-2782					
American Speech-Language-Hearing Assn PAC 10801 Rockville Pike	Rockville	MD	20852	301-897-5700	571-0457
TF: 800-638-8255					
American Sportfishing Assn PAC 225 Reinekers Ln Suite 420	Alexandria	VA	22314	703-519-9691	519-1872
Web: www.asafishing.org					
American Sugar Cane League PAC 206 E Bayon Rd	Thibodaux	LA	70301	985-448-3707	448-3722
American Supply Assn PAC 222 Merchandise Mart Plaza Suite 1400	Chicago	IL	60654	312-464-0090	464-0091
American Veterinary Medical Assn PAC 1910 Sunderland Pl NW	Washington	DC	20036	202-789-0007	842-4360
ANA PAC (American Nurses Assn PAC) 8515 Georgia Ave Suite 400	Silver Spring	MD	20910	301-628-5096	628-5001
ArchiPAC 1735 New York Ave NW	Washington	DC	20006	202-626-7300	626-7426
Ashland Inc PAC 499 S Capitol St SW Suite 600	Washington	DC	20003	202-289-9881	293-2913
Associated Builders & Contractors PAC (ABC-PAC) 4250 N Fairfax Dr 9th Fl	Arlington	VA	22203	703-812-2000	812-8203
Associated General Contractors PAC (AGC PAC) 333 John Carlyle St Suite 200	Alexandria	VA	22314	703-548-3118	548-3119
TF: 800-242-1766					
Association of Home Appliance Manufacturers PAC (AHAM PAC) 1111 19th St NW Suite 402	Washington	DC	20036	202-872-5955	872-9354
Bank of America PAC 1100 N King St	Wilmington	DE	19884	302-432-0956	432-0039
BellSouth Federal PAC 1155 Peachtree St NE	Atlanta	GA	30309	404-249-5966	
Black America's Political Action Committee 2029 P St NW Suite 202	Washington	DC	20036	202-785-9619	785-9621
TF: 877-722-6722 ■ *Web:* www.bampac.org					
Blue PAC 1310 G St NW 12th Fl	Washington	DC	20005	202-626-4780	626-4833
Bond Market Assn PAC 1399 New York Ave NW 8th Fl	Washington	DC	20005	202-434-8400	434-8456
Burlington Northern Santa Fe Corp RAILPAC 700 13th St NW	Washington	DC	20005	202-347-8662	347-8675
Business-Industry Political Action Committee (BIPAC) 888 16th St NW Suite 305	Washington	DC	20006	202-833-1880	833-2338
Web: www.bipac.org					
BUSPAC 700 13th St NW Suite 575	Washington	DC	20005	202-842-1645	842-0850
TF: 800-283-2877					
Campaign for Working Families 2800 Shirlington Rd Suite 930	Arlington	VA	22206	703-671-8800	671-8899
Web: www.campaignforfamilies.org					
Carpenter's Legislative Improvement Committee 101 Constitution Ave NW 10th Fl	Washington	DC	20001	202-546-6206	547-8979
Caterpillar Inc Employees PAC (CAT PAC) 100 NE Adams St	Peoria	IL	61629	309-675-4482	675-1753
Co-op PAC 50 F St NW Suite 900	Washington	DC	20001	202-626-8700	626-8722
COALPAC 101 Constitution Ave NW Suite 500E	Washington	DC	20001	202-463-2625	463-6152
Coca-Cola Nonpartisan Committee for Good Government PO Box 1734	Atlanta	GA	30301	404-676-5424	676-6792
College of American Pathologists PAC 1350 'I' St NW Suite 590	Washington	DC	20005	202-354-7100	354-7155
TF: 800-392-9994					
Committee for a Democratic Majority (CDM) 301 4th St NE Suite 202	Washington	DC	20002	202-544-4889	546-2285
Web: www.democraticmajority.com					
Committee for a Strong Economy 9300 Livingston Rd	Fort Washington	MD	20744	301-248-6200	248-7104
TF: 800-248-6862					
Committee on Letter Carriers Political Education (COLCPE) 100 Indiana Ave NW	Washington	DC	20001	202-393-4695	756-7400
Consumer Specialty Products Assn PAC 900 17th St NW Suite 300	Washington	DC	20006	202-872-8110	872-8114
Cosmetic Toiletry & Fragrance Assn PAC (CTFA PAC) 1101 17th St NW Suite 300	Washington	DC	20036	202-331-1770	331-1969
Credit Union Legislative Action Council of CUNA 601 Pennsylvania Ave NW South Bldg Suite 600	Washington	DC	20004	202-638-5777	638-7734
CSX Corp Good Government Fund 1331 Pennsylvania Ave NW Suite 560	Washington	DC	20004	202-783-8124	783-5929
Dairy Farmers of America PAC 10220 N Ambassador Dr Northpointe Tower	Kansas City	MO	64153	816-801-6455	801-6456
Dealers Election Action Committee 8400 Westpark Dr 3rd Fl MS 3	McLean	VA	22102	703-821-7110	442-3168
TF: 877-501-3322					
Democratic Leadership Council (DLC) 600 Pennsylvania Ave SE Suite 400	Washington	DC	20003	202-546-0007	544-5002
Web: www.dlc.org					
DGA-PAC 7920 W Sunset Blvd	Los Angeles	CA	90046	310-289-2000	289-2029
Direct Marketing Assn PAC 1111 19th St NW Suite 1100	Washington	DC	20036	202-955-5030	955-0085
DTE Energy Co PAC 2000 2nd Ave	Detroit	MI	48226	313-235-9195	235-6830
El Paso Corp PAC 1001 Louisiana St	Houston	TX	77002	713-420-2131	420-6969
Electric Power Supply Assn PAC (EPSA PAC) 1401 New York Ave NW 11th Fl	Washington	DC	20005	202-628-8200	628-8260
Electrical Contractors PAC 3 Bethesda Metro Ctr Suite 1100	Bethesda	MD	20814	301-657-3110	215-4500
Web: www.necanet.org/government					
ESOP Assn PAC 1726 M St NW Suite 501	Washington	DC	20036	202-293-2971	293-7568
ExxonMobil Corp PAC 2000 K St NW Suite 710	Washington	DC	20006	202-862-0200	862-0267
FedEx Corp Government Affairs 101 Constitution Ave NW Suite 801 E	Washington	DC	20001	202-218-3800	218-3803
FedPAC 801 Pennsylvania Ave NW Suite 245	Washington	DC	20004	202-624-1500	737-6462
FIREPAC 1750 New York Ave NW 3rd Fl	Washington	DC	20006	202-737-8484	737-8418
Web: www.iaff.org					
FishPac 7918 Jones Branch Dr Suite 700	McLean	VA	22102	703-524-8880	524-4619
FMC Corp PAC 1101 Pennsylvania Ave NW Suite 325	Washington	DC	20004	202-956-5200	956-5235
Food Marketing Institute PAC (FoodPAC) 655 15th St NW Suite 700	Washington	DC	20005	202-220-0600	429-4519
Footwear Distributors & Retailers of America PAC 1319 F St NW Suite 700	Washington	DC	20004	202-737-5660	638-2615
Ford Motor Co Civic Action Fund 1350 'I' St NW Suite 1000	Washington	DC	20005	202-962-5381	336-7228
FRAN-PAC 1501 K St Suite 350	Washington	DC	20005	202-628-8000	628-0812
TF: 800-543-1038 ■ *Web:* www.franchise.org					
Friends Committee on National Legislation 245 2nd St NE	Washington	DC	20002	202-547-6000	547-6019
Web: www.fcnl.org					
Friends of the Earth PAC 1717 Massachusetts Ave NW Suite 600	Washington	DC	20032	202-783-7400	783-0444
Web: foepac.org					
GASPAC 400 N Capitol St NW	Washington	DC	20001	202-824-7000	824-7115
General Dynamics Corp PAC 2941 Fairview Park Dr	Falls Church	VA	22042	703-876-3000	876-3125
General Electric Co PAC 1299 Pennsylvania Ave NW Suite 900	Washington	DC	20004	202-637-4000	637-4006
General Motors Corp PAC 25 Massachusetts Ave Suite 400	Washington	DC	20001	202-775-5090	775-5045
Web: www.gmpac.com					
Goodyear Tire & Rubber Co PAC 1420 New York Ave NW Suite 200	Washington	DC	20005	202-682-9250	682-1533
GOPAC 1101 16th St NW Suite 201	Washington	DC	20005	202-464-5170	464-5177
Web: www.gopac.org					
Harris Corp PAC 1201 E Abingdon Dr Suite 300	Alexandria	VA	22314	703-739-1942	739-2775
HotelPAC 1201 New York Ave NW Suite 600	Washington	DC	20005	202-289-3124	289-3185
Web: www.ahla.com/public_hotelpac.asp					
HSBC PAC 1401 I St NW Suite 520	Washington	DC	20005	202-466-3561	466-3583
Human Rights Campaign PAC 1640 Rhode Island Ave NW	Washington	DC	20036	202-628-4160	347-5323
TF: 800-777-4723					
IATSE PAC 1430 Broadway 20th Fl	New York	NY	10018	212-730-1770	730-7809
TF: 800-223-6972 ■ *Web:* www.iatse-intl.org/pac/pac.html					
Ice Cream Milk & Cheese PAC 1250 H St NW Suite 900	Washington	DC	20005	202-737-4332	331-7820
Independent Action Inc 1619 13th St NW	Washington	DC	20009	202-783-2900	783-3477
Web: www.independentaction.org					
Independent Community Bankers of America PAC 1615 L St Suite 900	Washington	DC	20036	202-659-8111	659-9216
TF: 800-422-8439					
Independent Insurance Agents & Brokers of America PAC (INSURPAC) 412 1st St SE Suite 300	Washington	DC	20003	202-863-7000	863-7015
Information Technology Assn of America PAC 1401 Wilson Blvd Suite 1100	Arlington	VA	22209	703-522-5055	525-2279
International Brotherhood of Electrical Workers PAC 900 7th St NW	Washington	DC	20001	202-833-7000	728-7676
International Chiropractors Assn PAC 1110 N Glebe Rd Suite 650	Arlington	VA	22201	703-528-5000	528-5023
International Council of Cruise Lines PAC 2111 Wilson Blvd 8th Fl	Arlington	VA	22201	703-522-8463	522-3811
International Council of Shopping Centers PAC 1399 New York Ave NW Suite 720	Washington	DC	20005	202-626-1400	626-1418
International Paper PAC 1101 Pennsylvania Ave NW Suite 200	Washington	DC	20004	202-628-1223	628-1368
Investment Company Institute PAC 1401 H St NW 12th Fl	Washington	DC	20005	202-326-5800	326-5985
Ironworkers Political Action League 1750 New York Ave NW Suite 400	Washington	DC	20006	202-383-4800	347-3569
TF: 800-368-0105					
JP Morgan Chase & Co PAC 270 Park Ave 9th Fl	New York	NY	10017	212-270-7260	622-4825

				Phone	Fax
Koch Industries PAC 655 15th St NW Suite 445	Washington	DC	20005	202-737-1977	737-8111
Lockheed Martin PAC 1550 Crystal Dr Suite 300	Arlington	VA	22202	703-413-5996	413-5846
Lucent Technologies Inc PAC					
1100 New York Ave NW Suite 640 West Tower	Washington	DC	20005	202-312-5901	
Magazine Publishers of America PAC					
1211 Connecticut Ave NW Suite 610	Washington	DC	20036	202-296-7277	296-0343
Manufactured Housing Institute PAC (MHI PAC)					
2101 Wilson Blvd Suite 610	Arlington	VA	22201	703-558-0400	558-0401
TF: 800-505-5500 ■ *Web:* www.manufacturedhousing.org					
Marriott International PAC 1 Marriott Dr	Washington	DC	20058	301-380-3000	380-7752
TF: 800-228-9290					
MassMutual PAC 1295 State St	Springfield	MA	01111	413-788-8411	744-6005
TF: 800-272-2216					
Mechanical Contractors Assn of America PAC					
1385 Piccard Dr	Rockville	MD	20850	301-869-5800	990-9690
TF: 800-556-3653					
Metropolitan Life Insurance Co Employees' Political Participation Fund 1620 L St NW Suite 800	Washington	DC	20036	202-659-3575	659-1026
MinePAC 101 Constitution Ave NW Suite 500 East	Washington	DC	20001	202-463-2625	463-2666
Morgan Stanley PAC 401 9th St NW Suite 650	Washington	DC	20004	202-654-2000	654-2100
Mortgage Bankers Assn PAC (MORPAC)					
1919 Pennsylvania Ave NW 8th Fl	Washington	DC	20006	202-557-2700	721-0249
Web: www.morpac.org					
Motion Picture Assn of America PAC 1600 'I' St NW	Washington	DC	20006	202-293-1966	293-7674
Motorola PAC 1350 'I' St NW Suite 400	Washington	DC	20005	202-371-6934	842-3578
NAADAC PAC 901 N Washington St Suite 600	Alexandria	VA	22314	703-741-7686	741-7698
TF: 800-548-0497					
NARAL Pro-Choice America PAC					
1156 15th St NW Suite 700	Washington	DC	20005	202-973-3000	973-3096
NASBIC PAC 666 11th St NW Suite 750	Washington	DC	20001	202-628-5055	628-5080
Web: www.nasbic.org/resources					
National Air Traffic Controllers Assn PAC (NATCA PAC)					
1325 Massachusetts Ave NW	Washington	DC	20005	202-628-5451	628-5767
National Assn of Chain Drug Stores PAC (NACDS PAC)					
413 N Lee St	Alexandria	VA	22314	703-549-3001	836-4869
TF: 800-678-6223					
National Assn of Convenience Stores PAC (NACS PAC)					
1600 Duke St	Alexandria	VA	22314	703-684-3600	836-4564
National Assn of Dental Plans PAC 8111 LBJ Fwy Suite 935	Dallas	TX	75251	972-458-6998	458-2258
National Assn of Home Builders PAC (Build PAC)					
1201 15th St NW	Washington	DC	20005	202-266-8200	266-8400
National Assn for Home Care & Hospice PAC					
228 7th St SE	Washington	DC	20003	202-547-7424	547-3540
National Assn of Insurance & Financial Advisors PAC					
2901 Telestar Ct	Falls Church	VA	22042	703-770-8100	770-8194
National Assn of REALTORS PAC (RPAC)					
500 New Jersey Ave NW	Washington	DC	20001	202-383-1000	383-7563
National Assn of Retired Federal Employees					
606 N Washington St	Alexandria	VA	22314	703-838-7760	838-7785
TF: 800-627-3394 ■ *Web:* www.narfe.org					
National Assn of Water Companies PAC (NAWC PAC)					
1725 K St NW Suite 200	Washington	DC	20006	202-833-8383	331-7442
National Assn of Wheat Growers PAC					
415 2nd St NE Suite 300	Washington	DC	20002	202-547-7800	546-2638
National Beer Wholesalers Assn PAC (NBWA PAC)					
1101 King St Suite 600	Alexandria	VA	22314	703-683-4300	683-8965
National Cable & Telecommunications Assn PAC (Cable PAC)					
25 Massachusetts Ave NW	Washington	DC	20001	202-222-2516	222-2517
Web: www.ncta.com					
National Cattlemen's Beef Assn PAC					
1301 Pennsylvania Ave NW Suite 300	Washington	DC	20004	202-347-0228	638-0607
Web: hill.beef.org					
National Chicken Council PAC 1015 15th St NW Suite 930	Washington	DC	20005	202-296-2622	293-4005
National Committee for an Effective Congress					
122 C St NW Suite 650	Washington	DC	20001	202-639-8300	639-5038
Web: www.ncec.org					
National Confectioners Assn PAC					
8320 Old Courthouse Rd Suite 300	Vienna	VA	22182	703-790-5750	790-5752
TF: 800-433-1200					
National Court Reporters Assn PAC 8224 Old Courthouse Rd	Vienna	VA	22182	703-556-6272	556-6291
TF: 800-272-6272 ■ *Web:* www.ncraonline.org					
National Federation of Independent Business SAFE Trust					
1201 F St NW Suite 200	Washington	DC	20004	202-554-9000	554-0496
TF: 800-552-6342					
National Fisheries Institute PAC					
7918 Jones Branch Dr Suite 700	McLean	VA	22102	703-524-8880	524-4619
National Funeral Directors Assn PAC 400 C St NE	Washington	DC	20002	202-547-0441	547-0726
National Grain & Feed Assn PAC					
1250 'I' St NW Suite 1003	Washington	DC	20005	202-289-0873	289-5388
Web: www.ngfa.org					
National Ground Water Assn PAC 601 Dempsey Rd	Westerville	OH	43081	614-898-7791	898-7786
TF: 800-551-7379					
National Milk Producers Federation PAC					
2101 Wilson Blvd Suite 400	Arlington	VA	22201	703-243-6111	841-9328
National Multi Housing Council PAC					
1850 M St NW Suite 540	Washington	DC	20036	202-974-2300	775-0112
National Organization for Women PAC					
1100 H St NW 3rd Fl	Washington	DC	20005	202-628-8669	785-8576
Web: www.nowpacs.org					
National Parking Assn PAC 1112 16th St NW Suite 300	Washington	DC	20036	202-296-4336	331-8523
National Pest Management Assn PAC 9300 Lee Hwy Suite 301	Fairfax	VA	22031	703-352-6762	352-3031
National Pork Producers Council PAC					
122 C St NW Suite 875	Washington	DC	20001	202-347-3600	347-5265
TF: 866-701-6388					
National Propane Gas Assn PAC					
1150 17th St NW Suite 310	Washington	DC	20036	202-466-7200	466-7205
National Restaurant Assn PAC 1200 17th St NW	Washington	DC	20036	202-331-5900	331-2429
TF: 800-424-5156 ■ *Web:* www.restaurant.org/government/nrapac/index.cfm					
National Right to Life PAC 512 10th St NW	Washington	DC	20004	202-626-8808	393-5433
National Roofing Contractors Assn PAC (NRCAPAC)					
324 4th St NE	Washington	DC	20002	202-546-7584	546-9289
National Stone Sand & Gravel Assn PAC 1605 King St	Alexandria	VA	22314	703-525-8788	525-7782
National Sunflower Assn PAC 4023 State St	Bismarck	ND	58503	701-328-5100	328-5101
TF: 888-718-7033					
National Tour Assn PAC 546 E Main St	Lexington	KY	40508	859-226-4250	226-4263
National Turkey Federation PAC					
1225 New York Ave NW Suite 400	Washington	DC	20005	202-898-0100	898-0203
National Venture Capital Assn PAC					
1655 N Fort Myer Dr Suite 850	Arlington	VA	22209	703-524-2549	524-3940
Web: www.nvca.org/venpac.html					
NATSO PAC 1737 King St Suite 200	Alexandria	VA	22314	703-549-2100	684-4525
NEA Fund for Children & Public Education					
1201 16th St NW	Washington	DC	20036	202-833-4000	822-7974
New Century Project (NCP)					
2021 E Dublin-Granville Rd Suite 161	Columbus	OH	43229	614-785-1600	785-1611
Web: www.newcenturyproject.org					
New Republican Majority Fund 201 N Union St Suite 530	Alexandria	VA	22314	703-299-6600	548-5954

				Phone	Fax
Northrop Grumman Corp PAC 1000 Wilson Blvd Suite 2300	Arlington	VA	22209	703-875-8400	276-0711
Northwest Airlines PAC 122 New York Ave NW Suite 200	Washington	DC	20005	202-842-3193	289-6834
NRA Institute for Legislative Action 11250 Waples Mill Rd	Fairfax	VA	22030	703-267-1000	267-3918
TF: 800-672-3888 ■ *Web:* www.nraila.org					
Nuclear Energy Institute Federal PAC					
1776 'I' St NW Suite 400	Washington	DC	20006	202-739-8000	785-4019
Outdoor Advertising Assn of America PAC					
1850 M St NW Suite 1040	Washington	DC	20036	202-833-5566	833-1522
Outdoor Amusement Business Assn PAC (OABA-PAC)					
1035 S Semoran Blvd Suite 1045A	Winter Park	FL	32792	407-681-9444	681-9445
Web: www.oaba.org					
Peace PAC 322 4th St NE	Washington	DC	20002	202-543-4100	543-6297
Petroleum Marketers Assn of America's Small Business Community 1901 N Fort Myer Dr Suite 500	Arlington	VA	22209	703-351-8000	351-9160
TF: 800-300-7622					
PG & E Corp PAC 1 Market Spear Tower Suite 2400	San Francisco	CA	94105	415-267-7000	267-7268
Philip Morris Cos Inc PAC (PHIL-PAC)					
101 Constitution Ave NW Suite 400W	Washington	DC	20001	202-354-1500	354-1535
Planned Parenthood Action Fund Inc					
1780 Massachusetts Ave NW	Washington	DC	20036	202-785-3351	296-3763
Web: www.ppaction.org/ppvotes					
Print PAC 601 13th St NW Suite 360-N	Washington	DC	20005	202-730-7970	730-7987
TF: 800-742-2666 ■ *Web:* www.printpaconline.org					
PTPAC 1111 N Fairfax St	Alexandria	VA	22314	703-684-2782	684-7343
Recording Industry Assn PAC 1025 F St NW	Washington	DC	20004	202-775-0101	775-7253
REITPAC 1875 'I' St NW Suite 600	Washington	DC	20006	202-739-9400	739-9401
Responsible Citizens Political League 3 Research Pl	Rockville	MD	20850	301-948-4910	330-7673
SBC Communications Inc Employee Federal PAC (SBC EMPAC) 1133 21st St NW Suite 900	Washington	DC	20036	202-463-4100	
Securities Industry Assn PAC (SIA-PAC)					
1425 K St NW 7th Fl	Washington	DC	20005	202-216-2000	216-2119
Web: www.sia.com/political_action					
Sierra Club PAC 85 2nd St 2nd Fl	San Francisco	CA	94105	415-977-5500	977-5797
Society of American Florists PAC 1601 Duke St	Alexandria	VA	22314	703-836-8700	836-8705
TF: 800-336-4743					
Southwest Airlines PAC 2702 Love Field Fr	Dallas	TX	75235	214-792-4000	792-5015
TF: 800-435-9792					
Television & Radio PAC 1771 'N' St NW	Washington	DC	20036	202-429-5300	775-2157
Textron Inc PAC 1101 Pennsylvania Ave NW Suite 400	Washington	DC	20004	202-637-3800	637-3865
Title Industry PAC 1828 L St NW Suite 705	Washington	DC	20036	202-296-3671	223-5843
TF: 800-787-2582					
Truck PAC 430 1st St SE 2nd Fl	Washington	DC	20003	202-544-6245	675-6568
Web: www.truckline.com					
UAW Voluntary Community Action Program (UAW V-CAP)					
8000 E Jefferson Ave	Detroit	MI	48214	313-926-5531	926-5691
United Parcel Service PAC					
316 Pennsylvania Ave SE Suite 300	Washington	DC	20003	202-675-4220	675-4230
United Steelworkers of America PAC 5 Gateway Ctr	Pittsburgh	PA	15222	412-562-2400	562-2445
United Technologies Corp PAC 1401 'I' St NW Suite 600	Washington	DC	20005	202-336-7400	336-7529
USAA Group PAC 9800 Fredericksburg Rd	San Antonio	TX	78288	210-498-2211	498-9940
UST Inc Executives Administrators & Managers PAC (USTeamPAC) 100 W Putnam Ave	Greenwich	CT	06830	203-661-1100	622-3493
Water PAC 2915 S 13th St	Duncan	OK	73533	580-252-0629	255-4476
Wine & Spirits Wholesalers of America PAC					
805 15th St NW Suite 430	Washington	DC	20005	202-371-9792	789-2405

POLITICAL LEADERS

SEE Government - US - Legislative Branch - US Senators, Representatives, Delegates p. 1760; Governors - State p. 1766

619 POLITICAL PARTIES (MAJOR)

SEE ALSO Associations & Organizations - General - Civic & Political Organizations p. 1298

				Phone	Fax
Communist Party USA 235 W 23rd St 7th Fl	New York	NY	10011	212-989-4994	
Web: www.cpusa.org					
Democratic National Committee 430 S Capitol St SE	Washington	DC	20003	202-863-8000	863-8063
TF: 800-934-8683 ■ *Web:* www.democrats.org					
Democratic Socialists of America 75 Maiden Ln Suite 505	New York	NY	10038	212-727-8610	
Web: www.dsausa.org					
Libertarian Party 2600 Virginia Ave NW Suite 200	Washington	DC	20037	202-333-0008	333-0072
TF: 800-682-1776 ■ *Web:* www.lp.org					
Republican National Committee 310 1st St SE	Washington	DC	20003	202-863-8500	863-8820
TF: 800-445-5768 ■ *Web:* www.gop.org					
Socialist Labor Party of America PO Box 218	Mountain View	CA	94042	408-280-7266	280-6964
Web: www.slp.org					
Socialist Party USA 339 Lafayette St Suite 303	New York	NY	10012	212-982-4586	982-4586
Web: sp-usa.org					

619-1 Democratic State Committees

				Phone	Fax
Alabama PO Box 950	Montgomery	AL	36104	334-262-2221	262-6474
TF: 800-995-3386 ■ *Web:* www.aladems.org					
Alaska PO Box 231230	Anchorage	AK	99523	907-258-3050	258-1626
Web: www.alaskademocrats.org					
Arizona 2910 N Central Ave	Phoenix	AZ	85012	602-298-4200	298-7117
Web: www.azdem.org					
Arkansas 1300 W Capitol Ave	Little Rock	AR	72201	501-374-2361	376-8409
Web: www.arkdems.org					
California 1401 21st St Suite 200	Sacramento	CA	95811	916-442-5707	
Web: www.cadem.org					
Colorado 777 Santa Fe Dr	Denver	CO	80204	303-623-4762	623-2443
Web: www.coloradodems.org					
Connecticut 179 Allyn St	Hartford	CT	06103	860-560-1775	560-1522
Web: www.ctdems.org					
Delaware 19 E Commons Blvd 2nd Fl	New Castle	DE	19720	302-328-9036	328-9386
Web: www.deldems.org					
District of Columbia 1341 G St NW Suite 720	Washington	DC	20005	202-347-7260	393-0095
Florida PO Box 1758	Tallahassee	FL	32302	850-222-3411	222-0916
TF: 800-925-3411 ■ *Web:* www.fladems.com					
Georgia 1100 Spring St Suite 710	Atlanta	GA	30309	404-870-8201	873-4396
TF: 800-894-1996 ■ *Web:* www.democraticpartyofgeorgia.org					

Democratic State Committees (Cont'd)

	City	State	Zip	Phone	Fax
Hawaii 770 Kapiolani Blvd Suite 115 *Web:* www.hawaiidemocrats.org	Honolulu	HI	96813	808-596-2980	596-2985
Idaho PO Box 445 *TF:* 800-542-4737 ■ *Web:* www.idaho-democrats.org	Boise	ID	83701	208-336-1815	336-1817
Indiana 1 N Capital St Suite 200 *TF:* 800-223-3387 ■ *Web:* www.indems.org	Indianapolis	IN	46204	317-231-7100	231-7129
Iowa 5661 Fleur Dr *Web:* www.iowademocrats.org	Des Moines	IA	50321	515-224-7292	244-5051
Kansas PO Box 1914 *Web:* www.ksdp.org	Topeka	KS	66601	785-234-0425	234-8420
Kentucky PO Box 694 *Web:* www.kydemocrat.com	Frankfort	KY	40602	502-695-4828	695-7629
Louisiana 701 Government St *Web:* www.lademo.org	Baton Rouge	LA	70802	225-336-4155	336-0046
Maine PO Box 5258 *Web:* www.mainedems.org	Augusta	ME	04332	207-622-6233	622-2657
Maryland 188 Main St Suite 1 *Web:* www.mddems.org	Annapolis	MD	21401	410-280-8818	280-8882
Massachusetts 10 Granite St 4th Fl *Web:* www.massdems.org	Quincy	MA	02169	617-472-0637	472-4391
Michigan 606 Townsend St *Web:* www.mi-democrats.com	Lansing	MI	48933	517-371-5410	371-2056
Minnesota 255 E Plato Blvd *TF:* 800-999-7457 ■ *Web:* www.dfl.org	Saint Paul	MN	55107	651-293-1200	251-6325
Mississippi PO Box 1583 *TF:* 888-674-3367 ■ *Web:* www.msdemocrats.net	Jackson	MS	39215	601-969-2913	354-1599
Missouri PO Box 719 *Web:* www.missouridems.org	Jefferson City	MO	65102	573-636-5241	634-8176
Montana PO Box 802 *Web:* www.montanademocrats.org	Helena	MT	59624	406-442-9520	442-9534
Nebraska 633 S 9th St Suite 201 *TF:* 800-677-7068 ■ *Web:* nebraskademocrats.org	Lincoln	NE	68508	402-434-2180	434-2188
New Hampshire 2 1/2 Beacon St *Web:* www.nh-democrats.org	Concord	NH	03301	603-225-6899	225-6797
New Jersey 196 W State St *Web:* www.njdems.org	Trenton	NJ	08608	609-392-3367	396-4778
New Mexico 1301 San Pedro Dr NE *Web:* www.dpnm.org	Albuquerque	NM	87110	505-830-3650	830-3645
New York 461 Park Ave S 10th Fl *Web:* www.nydems.org	New York	NY	10016	212-725-8825	725-8867
North Carolina 220 Hillsborough St *TF:* 800-229-3367 ■ *Web:* www.ncdp.org	Raleigh	NC	27603	919-821-2777	821-4778
North Dakota 1902 E Divide Ave *Web:* www.demnpl.com	Bismarck	ND	58501	701-255-0460	255-7823
Ohio 271 E State St *Web:* www.ohiodems.org	Columbus	OH	43215	614-221-6563	221-0721
Oklahoma 4100 N Lincoln Blvd *Web:* www.okdemocrats.org	Oklahoma City	OK	73105	405-427-3366	427-1310
Oregon 232 NE 9th Ave *Web:* www.dpo.org	Portland	OR	97232	503-224-8200	224-5335
Pennsylvania 510 N 3rd St *Web:* www.padems.com	Harrisburg	PA	17101	717-238-9381	233-3472
Puerto Rico PO Box 9065788	San Juan	PR	00906	787-721-2004	977-2045
Rhode Island 249 Roosevelt Ave Suite 202 *Web:* www.ridemocrats.org	Pawtucket	RI	02860	401-721-9900	724-5007
South Carolina PO Box 5965 *TF:* 800-841-1817 ■ *Web:* www.scdp.org	Columbia	SC	29250	803-799-7798	765-1692
South Dakota 207 E Capitol Ave Suite 103 *Web:* www.sddp.org	Pierre	SD	57501	605-224-1750	224-1759
Tennessee 223 8th Ave N Suite 200 *Web:* www.tndp.org	Nashville	TN	37203	615-327-9779	327-9759
Texas 707 Rio Grande St *Web:* www.txdemocrats.org	Austin	TX	78701	512-478-9800	480-2500
Utah 455 S 300 East Suite 301 *Web:* www.utdemocrats.org	Salt Lake City	UT	84111	801-328-1212	328-1238
Vermont 73 Main St Suite 36 PO Box 1220 *Web:* www.vtdemocrats.org	Montpelier	VT	05601	802-229-1783	229-1784
Virginia 1108 E Main St 2nd Fl *Web:* www.vademocrats.org	Richmond	VA	23219	804-644-1966	343-3642
Washington PO Box 4027 *Web:* www.wa-democrats.org	Seattle	WA	98194	206-583-0664	583-0301
West Virginia 5 Greenbrier St *Web:* www.wvdemocrats.com	Charleston	WV	25311	304-342-8121	342-8122
Wisconsin 222 W Washington Ave Suite 150 *Web:* www.wisdems.org	Madison	WI	53703	608-255-5172	255-8919
Wyoming 254 N Center St Suite 205 *TF:* 800-729-3367 ■ *Web:* www.wyomingdemocrats.com	Casper	WY	82601	307-473-1457	473-1459

619-2 Republican State Committees

	City	State	Zip	Phone	Fax
Alabama 3415 Independence Dr Suite 219 *TF:* 877-919-2002 ■ *Web:* www.algop.org	Birmingham	AL	35209	205-212-5900	212-5910
Alaska 1001 W Fireweed Ln *Web:* www.alaskarepublicans.com	Anchorage	AK	99503	907-276-4467	276-0425
Arizona 3501 N 24th St *TF:* 800-844-4065 ■ *Web:* www.azgop.org	Phoenix	AZ	85016	602-957-7770	224-0932
Arkansas 1201 W 6th St *Web:* www.arkansasgop.org	Little Rock	AR	72201	501-372-7301	372-1656
California 1903 W Magnolia Blvd *Web:* www.cagop.org	Burbank	CA	91506	818-841-5210	841-6668
Colorado 1777 S Harrison St Suite 100 *TF:* 800-236-3769 ■ *Web:* www.cologop.org	Denver	CO	80210	303-758-3333	753-4611
Connecticut 97 Elm St Rear *TF:* 888-982-8467 ■ *Web:* www.ctgop.org	Hartford	CT	06106	860-547-0589	278-8563
Delaware 3301 Lancaster Pike Suite 4B *Web:* www.delawaregop.com	Wilmington	DE	19805	302-651-0260	651-0270
District of Columbia 1275 K St NW Suite 102 *Web:* www.dcgop.com	Washington	DC	20005	202-289-8005	289-2197
Florida PO Box 311 *TF:* 800-777-7920 ■ *Web:* www.rpof.org	Tallahassee	FL	32302	850-222-7920	681-0184
Georgia 3110 Maple Dr Suite 200-E *TF:* 877-464-2467 ■ *Web:* www.gagop.org	Atlanta	GA	30305	404-257-5559	257-0779
Hawaii 725 Kapiolani Blvd Suite C105 *Web:* www.gophawaii.com	Honolulu	HI	96813	808-593-8180	593-7742
Idaho PO Box 2267 *TF:* 800-658-3898 ■ *Web:* www.idgop.org	Boise	ID	83701	208-343-6405	343-6414
Illinois 320 S 4th St *Web:* www.ilgop.org	Springfield	IL	62701	217-525-0011	753-4712
Indiana 47 S Meridian St Suite 200 *TF:* 800-466-1087 ■ *Web:* www.indgop.org	Indianapolis	IN	46204	317-635-7561	632-8510
Iowa 621 E 9th St *Web:* www.iowagop.org	Des Moines	IA	50309	515-282-8105	282-9019
Kansas 2025 SW Gage Blvd *TF:* 888-482-9051 ■ *Web:* www.ksgop.org	Topeka	KS	66604	785-234-3456	228-0353
Kentucky PO Box 1068 *Web:* www.rpk.org	Frankfort	KY	40602	502-875-5130	223-5625
Louisiana 11440 N Lake Sherwood Ave Suite A *Web:* www.lagop.com	Baton Rouge	LA	70816	225-928-2998	408-2798
Maine 9 Higgins St *Web:* www.mainegop.com	Augusta	ME	04330	207-622-6247	623-5322
Maryland 15 West St *Web:* www.mdgop.org	Annapolis	MD	21401	410-269-0113	269-5937
Massachusetts 85 Merrimac St Suite 400 *Web:* www.massgop.com	Boston	MA	02114	617-523-5005	523-6311
Michigan 2121 E Grand River Ave *TF:* 877-644-6704 ■ *Web:* www.migop.org	Lansing	MI	48912	517-487-5413	487-0090
Minnesota 525 Park St Suite 250 *Web:* www.mngop.org	Saint Paul	MN	55103	651-222-0022	224-4122
Mississippi PO Box 60 *Web:* www.msgop.org	Jackson	MS	39205	601-948-5191	354-0972
Missouri 204 E Dunklin St *Web:* www.mogop.org	Jefferson City	MO	65101	573-636-3146	636-3273
Montana 921 Euclid Ave *Web:* www.mtgop.org	Helena	MT	59601	406-442-6469	442-3293
Nebraska 1610 N St *TF:* 800-829-3459 ■ *Web:* www.negop.org	Lincoln	NE	68508	402-475-2122	475-3541
Nevada 8625 W Sahara Ave *Web:* www.nevadagop.org	Las Vegas	NV	89117	702-258-9182	258-9186
New Hampshire 134 N Main St *Web:* www.nhgop.org	Concord	NH	03301	603-225-9341	225-7498
New Jersey 150 W State St Suite 230 *Web:* www.njgop.org	Trenton	NJ	08608	609-989-7300	989-8685
New Mexico 2129 Osuna St NE Suite 101-B *Web:* www.gopnm.org	Albuquerque	NM	87113	505-298-3662	292-0755
New York 315 State St *Web:* www.nygop.org	Albany	NY	12210	518-462-2601	449-7443
North Carolina PO Box 12905 *Web:* www.ncgop.org	Raleigh	NC	27605	919-828-6423	899-3815
North Dakota PO Box 1917 *Web:* www.ndgop.org	Bismarck	ND	58502	701-255-0030	255-7513
Ohio 211 S 5th St *Web:* www.ohiogop.org	Columbus	OH	43215	614-228-2481	228-1093
Oklahoma 4031 N Lincoln Blvd *Web:* www.okgop.com	Oklahoma City	OK	73105	405-528-3501	521-9531
Oregon PO Box 789 *Web:* www.orgop.org	Salem	OR	97308	503-587-9233	587-9244
Pennsylvania 301 Market St *Web:* www.pagop.org	Harrisburg	PA	17101	717-234-4901	231-3828
Rhode Island 413 Knight St *Web:* www.rigop.org	Warwick	RI	02886	401-732-8282	921-2427
South Carolina 1508 Lady St *Web:* www.scgop.com	Columbia	SC	29201	803-988-8440	988-8444
South Dakota PO Box 1099 *Web:* www.southdakotagop.com	Pierre	SD	57501	605-224-7347	224-7349
Tennessee 2424 21st Ave Suite 200 *Web:* www.tngop.org	Nashville	TN	37212	615-269-4260	269-4261
Texas 900 Congress Ave Suite 300 *Web:* www.texasgop.org	Austin	TX	78701	512-477-9821	480-0709
Utah 117 E South Temple St *TF:* 800-230-8824 ■ *Web:* www.utahgop.org	Salt Lake City	UT	84111	801-533-9777	533-0327
Vermont PO Box 70 *Web:* www.vtgop.org	Montpelier	VT	05601	802-223-3411	229-1864
Virginia 115 E Grace St *Web:* www.rpv.org	Richmond	VA	23219	804-780-0111	343-1060
Washington 16400 Southcenter Pkwy Suite 200 *Web:* wsrp.org	Seattle	WA	98188	206-575-2900	575-1730
West Virginia 5019 MacCorkle Ave SW *Web:* www.wvgop.org	South Charleston	WV	25303	304-768-0493	768-6083
Wisconsin 148 E Johnson St *Web:* www.wisgop.org	Madison	WI	53701	608-257-4765	257-4141
Wyoming 400 E 1st St Suite 314 *Web:* www.wygop.org	Casper	WY	82601	307-234-9166	473-8640

620 PORTALS - VOICE

Voice portals permit users to access web-based messaging as well as various types of Internet information (e.g., weather, stock quotes, driving directions, etc.) via the telephone (wired or wireless).

	City	State	Zip	Phone	Fax
BeVocal Inc 685 Clyde Ave *TF:* 800-428-6225 ■ *Web:* www.bevocal.com	Mountain View	CA	94043	650-210-8600	210-9275
Genesys Telecommunications Laboratories Inc 1380 Rodrck Rd *Web:* www.genesyslab.com	Markham	ON	L3R4G5	905-968-3300	968-3400
GoSolo Technologies Inc 1901 Ulmerton Rd Suite 400 *TF:* 888-551-7656 ■ *Web:* www.gosolo.com	Clearwater	FL	33762	727-821-6565	898-9315
HeyAnita Inc 303 N Glenoaks Blvd Suite 500 *Web:* www.heyanita.com	Burbank	CA	91502	818-556-4400	556-4466
InternetSpeech.com 6980 Santa Teresa Blvd Suite 201 *Web:* www.internetspeech.com	San Jose	CA	95119	408-360-7730	360-7726
NetByTel Inc 1141 S Rogers Cir Suite 9 **Fax:* Hum Res ■ *TF:* 800-638-2983 ■ *Web:* www.netbytel.com	Boca Raton	FL	33487	561-988-5050	989-8299*
Tellme Networks Inc 1310 Villa St *TF:* 800-555-8355 ■ *Web:* www.tellme.com	Mountain View	CA	94041	650-930-9000	930-9101

621 PORTS & PORT AUTHORITIES

SEE ALSO Airports p. 1275; Cruise Lines p. 1583

	City	State	Zip	Phone	Fax
Alabama State Port Authority PO Box 1588 *Web:* www.asdd.com	Mobile	AL	36633	251-441-7200	441-7216
Ashtabula County Port Authority 17 N Market St	Jefferson	OH	44047	440-576-6069	576-5003
Bridgeport Port Authority 330 Water St *Web:* www.portofbridgeport.com	Bridgeport	CT	06604	203-384-9777	384-9686
Cleveland-Cuyahoga County Port Authority 1375 E 9th St Suite 2300 *Web:* www.portofcleveland.com	Cleveland	OH	44114	216-241-8004	241-8016

	City	State	Zip	Phone	Fax
Cordova Harbor & Port 114 Nickeloff Way	Cordova	AK	99574	907-424-6400	424-6446
Web: www.cityofcordova.net/harbor.htm					
Delaware River Port Authority 1 Port Center 2 Riverside Dr.	Camden	NJ	08101	856-968-2000	968-2458
Web: www.drpa.org					
Detroit-Wayne County Port Authority 8109 E Jefferson Ave	Detroit	MI	48214	313-331-3842	331-5457
TF: 800-249-7678 ■ *Web:* www.portdetroit.com					
Eastport Port Authority 3 Madison St	Eastport	ME	04631	207-853-4614	853-9584
Web: www.portofeastport.org					
Erie-Western Pennsylvania Port Authority 208 E Bayfront Pkwy Suite 201	Erie	PA	16507	814-455-7557	455-8070
Web: www.porterie.org					
Fall River Port Authority 1 Water St	Fall River	MA	02720	508-674-5707	675-7830
Fraser River Port Authority 100 The Point 999 Canada Pl	Vancouver	BC	V6C3T4	604-665-9000	284-4271*
**Fax Area Code:* 866 ■ *Web:* www.frpa.com					
Georgia Ports Authority PO Box 2406	Savannah	GA	31402	912-964-3811	964-3921
TF: 800-342-8012 ■ *Web:* www.gaports.com					
Greater Lafourche Port Commission PO Box 490	Galliano	LA	70354	985-632-6701	632-6703
Web: www.portfourchon.com					
Haines Harbor PO Box 1209	Haines	AK	99827	907-766-2448	766-3010
Halifax Port Authority 1215 Marginal Rd PO Box 336	Halifax	NS	B3J2P6	902-426-8222	426-7335
Web: www.portofhalifax.ca					
Hamilton Port Authority 605 James St N	Hamilton	ON	L8L1K1	905-525-4330	528-6554
Web: www.hamiltonport.ca					
Hawaii Dept of Transportation Harbors Div 79 S Nimitz Hwy	Honolulu	HI	96813	808-587-1927	587-1982
Web: www.hawaii.gov/dot/harbors					
Humboldt Bay Harbor District 601 Startare Dr	Eureka	CA	95501	707-443-0801	443-0800
Web: www.portofhumboldtbay.org					
Illinois International Port District 3600 E 95th St	Chicago	IL	60617	773-646-4400	221-7678
TF: 800-843-7678 ■ *Web:* www.illinoisinternationalportdistrict.com					
Indiana Port Commission 150 W Market St Suite 100	Indianapolis	IN	46204	317-232-9200	232-0137
TF: 800-232-7678 ■ *Web:* www.portsofindiana.com					
International Port of Dutch Harbor PO Box 610	Unalaska	AK	99685	907-581-1254	581-2519
Web: www.ci.unalaska.ak.us					
Juneau Harbor 155 S Seward St	Juneau	AK	99801	907-586-5255	586-2507
Web: www.juneau.org/harbors					
Ketchikan Ports & Harbors Dept 334 Front St	Ketchikan	AK	99901	907-228-5632	247-3610
Web: www.city.ketchikan.ak.us/departments/ports/index.html					
Key West Port Authority PO Box 6434	Key West	FL	33041	305-293-6439	293-6438
Web: www.keywestseaport.com					
Kodiak Port & Harbor 403 Marine Way	Kodiak	AK	99615	907-486-8080	486-8090
Web: www.city.kodiak.ak.us/harbor/index.shtml					
Manatee County Port Authority 300 Tampa Bay Way	Palmetto	FL	34221	941-722-6621	729-1463
Web: www.portmanatee.com					
Massachusetts Port Authority 1 Harborside Dr Suite 200S	East Boston	MA	02128	617-568-1000	568-1022
Web: www.massport.com					
Mississippi State Port Authority at Gulfport 2304 19th St Suite 102 PO Box 40	Gulfport	MS	39501	228-865-4300	865-4335
TF: 877-881-4367 ■ *Web:* www.shipmspa.com					
Montreal Port Authority Port of Montreal Bldg 2100 Pierre-Dupuy Ave Wing 1	Montreal	QC	H3C3R5	514-283-7011	283-0829
Web: www.port-montreal.com					
Nanaimo Port Authority 104 Front St	Nanaimo	BC	V9R5H7	250-753-4146	753-4899
Web: www.npa.ca					
New Bedford Harbor Development Commission 106 Co-Op Wharf	New Bedford	MA	02740	508-961-3000	979-1517
New Hampshire State Port Authority 555 Market St	Portsmouth	NH	03801	603-436-8500	436-2780
Web: www.portsmouthnh.com/port/nhpa.html					
North Carolina State Ports Authority 2202 Burnett Blvd PO Box 9002	Wilmington	NC	28402	910-763-1621	343-6225
TF: 800-334-0682 ■ *Web:* www.ncports.com					
Ogdensburg Bridge & Port Authority 1 Bridge Plaza	Ogdensburg	NY	13669	315-393-4080	393-7068
Web: www.ogdensport.com					
Oregon International Port of Coos Bay 125 Central Ave Suite 300 PO Box 1215	Coos Bay	OR	97420	541-267-7678	269-1475
Web: www.portofcoosbay.com					
Oshawa Harbour Commission 1050 Farewell Ave	Oshawa	ON	L1H6N6	905-576-0400	576-5701
Web: www.oshawaportauthority.com					
Panama City Port Authority 5321 W Hwy 98	Panama City	FL	32401	850-767-3220	767-3235
Web: www.portpanamacityusa.com					
Petersburg Harbor 223 Harbor Way	Petersburg	AK	99833	907-772-4688	772-4687
Philadelphia Regional Port Authority 3460 N Delaware Ave 2nd Fl	Philadelphia	PA	19134	215-426-2600	426-6800
Web: www.philaport.com					
Plaquemines Port Authority 124 Edna Lafrance Rd	Braithwaite	LA	70040	504-682-7920	682-0649
Port of Albany Albany Port District Commission 106 Smith Blvd	Albany	NY	12202	518-463-8763	463-8767
Web: www.portofalbany.com					
Port Alberni Port Authority 2750 Harbour Rd	Port Alberni	BC	V9Y7X2	250-723-5312	723-1114
Web: portalberniportauthority.ca					
Port of Anacortes PO Box 297	Anacortes	WA	98221	360-293-3134	293-9608
Web: portofanacortes.com					
Port of Anchorage 2000 Anchorage Port Rd	Anchorage	AK	99501	907-343-6200	277-5636
Web: www.muni.org/port					
Port of Astoria 1 Portway St	Astoria	OR	97103	503-325-4521	325-4525
TF: 800-860-4093 ■ *Web:* www.portofastoria.com					
Port Authority of New York/New Jersey 225 Park Ave S 15th Fl	New York	NY	10003	212-435-7000	
Web: www.panynj.gov					
Port of Baltimore Maryland Port Administration 401 E Pratt St World Trade Ctr	Baltimore	MD	21202	410-385-4484	333-3402
TF: 800-638-7519 ■ *Web:* www.mpa.state.md.us					
Port of Beaumont 1225 Main St	Beaumont	TX	77701	409-835-5367	835-0512
Web: www.portofbeaumont.com					
Port of Bellingham 1801 Roeder Ave	Bellingham	WA	98225	360-676-2500	671-6411
Web: www.portofbellingham.com					
Port of Brownsville 1000 Foust Rd	Brownsville	TX	78521	956-831-4592	831-5006
TF: 800-378-5395 ■ *Web:* www.portofbrownsville.com					
Port of Burns Harbor 6625 S Boundary Dr	Portage	IN	46368	219-787-8636	787-8842
Web: www.portsofindiana.com					
Port Canaveral 445 Challanger Rd	Cape Canaveral	FL	32920	321-783-7831	784-6223
TF: 888-767-8226 ■ *Web:* www.portcanaveral.org					
Port Colborne PO Box 129	Port Colborne	ON	L3K5V8	905-834-3644	834-7816
Port of Corpus Christi 222 Power St	Corpus Christi	TX	78401	361-882-5633	882-7110
TF: 800-580-7110 ■ *Web:* www.portofcorpuschristi.com					
Port of Duluth Duluth Seaway Port Authority 1200 Port Terminal Dr	Duluth	MN	55802	218-727-8525	727-6888
TF: 800-232-0703 ■ *Web:* www.duluthport.com					
Port of Everett 2911 Bond St Suite 202	Everett	WA	98201	425-259-3164	252-7366
TF: 800-729-7678 ■ *Web:* www.portofeverett.com					
Port Everglades 1850 Eller Dr	Fort Lauderdale	FL	33316	954-523-3404	525-1910
Web: www.porteverglades.org					
Port Freeport PO Box 615	Freeport	TX	77542	979-233-2667	233-5625
TF: 800-362-5473 ■ *Web:* www.portfreeport.com					
Port of Galveston 123 Rosenberg 8th Fl	Galveston	TX	77550	409-765-9321	766-6107
Web: www.portofgalveston.com					
Port of Grays Harbor 111 S Wooding St	Aberdeen	WA	98520	360-533-9528	533-9505
Web: www.portofgraysharbor.com					

	City	State	Zip	Phone	Fax
Port of Greater Baton Rouge Greater Baton Rouge Port Commission 2425 Ernest Wilson Dr	Port Allen	LA	70767	225-342-1660	342-1666
Web: www.portgbr.com					
Port of Green Bay 2561 S Broadway St	Green Bay	WI	54304	920-492-4950	492-4957
Port of Homer 4350 Homer Spit Rd	Homer	AK	99603	907-235-3160	235-3152
Web: port.ci.homer.ak.us					
Port of Houston 111 E Loop N	Houston	TX	77029	713-670-2400	670-2429
TF Cust Svc: 800-688-3625 ■ *Web:* www.portofhouston.com					
Port of Hueneme PO Box 608	Port Hueneme	CA	93044	805-488-3677	488-2620
Web: www.portofhueneme.org					
Port of Iberia 4611 S Lewis St PO Box 9986	New Iberia	LA	70562	337-364-1065	364-3136
Web: www.portofiberia.com					
Port Isabel-San Benito Navigation District 250 Industrial Dr	Port Isabel	TX	78578	956-943-7826	943-8922
Port of Jacksonville Jacksonville Port Authority 2831 Talleyrand Ave	Jacksonville	FL	32206	904-630-3080	798-2129
Web: www.jaxport.com					
Port of Kalama 380 W Marine Dr	Kalama	WA	98625	360-673-2325	673-1503
Web: www.portofkalama.com					
Port of Lake Charles 150 Marine St	Lake Charles	LA	70601	337-439-3661	493-3523
TF: 800-845-7678 ■ *Web:* www.portlc.com					
Port of Long Beach 925 Harbor Plaza	Long Beach	CA	90801	562-437-0041	901-1725
Web: www.polb.com					
Port of Longview 10 Port Way	Longview	WA	98632	360-425-3305	425-8650
Web: www.portoflongview.com					
Port of Los Angeles 425 S Palos Verdes St	San Pedro	CA	90731	310-732-7678	831-0439*
**Fax:* Hum Res ■ *Web:* www.portoflosangeles.org					
Port of Miami 1015 N America Way	Miami	FL	33132	305-371-7678	347-4843
Web: www.co.miami-dade.fl.us/portofmiami					
Port of Milwaukee 2323 S Lincoln Memorial Dr	Milwaukee	WI	53207	414-286-3511	286-8506
Web: www.port.mil.wi.us					
Port of Mobile Alabama State Docks Dept 250 N Water St	Mobile	AL	36602	251-441-7203	441-7216
Web: www.asdd.com					
Port of Monroe Monroe Port Commission 2929 E Front St PO Box 585	Monroe	MI	48161	734-241-6480	241-0813
Web: www.portofmonroe.com					
Port of New London Connecticut Bureau of Aviation & Ports State Pier Rd	New London	CT	06320	860-443-3856	437-7251
Port of New Orleans 1350 Port of New Orleans Pl	New Orleans	LA	70130	504-522-2551	524-4156
TF Mktg: 800-776-6652 ■ *Web:* www.portno.com					
Port of Newport 600 SE Bay Blvd	Newport	OR	97365	541-265-7758	265-4235
Web: www.portofnewport.com					
Port of Nome PO Box 281	Nome	AK	99762	907-443-6619	443-5473
Web: www.nomealaska.org/port/					
Port of Oakland Oakland Board of Port Commissioners 530 Water St	Oakland	CA	94607	510-627-1100	839-5104
Web: www.portofoakland.com					
Port of Olympia 915 Washington St NE	Olympia	WA	98501	360-528-8000	528-8090
Web: www.portolympia.com					
Port of Orange Orange County Navigation Port District 1201 Childers Rd	Orange	TX	77630	409-883-4363	883-5607
Web: www.portoforange.com					
Port of Oswego Authority 1 E 2nd St PO Box 387	Oswego	NY	13126	315-343-4503	343-5498
Web: www.portoswego.com					
Port of Palm Beach 1 E 11th St Suite 400	Riviera Beach	FL	33404	561-842-4201	842-4240
Web: www.portofpalmbeach.com					
Port of Pascagoula Jackson County Port Authority 3033 Pascagoula St	Pascagoula	MS	39567	228-762-4041	762-7476
Web: www.portofpascagoula.com					
Port of Pensacola 700 S Barracks St	Pensacola	FL	32502	850-436-5070	436-5076
Web: www.portofpensacola.com					
Port of Philadelphia & Camden 1 Port Center 2 Riverside Dr PO Box 1949	Camden	NJ	08101	856-968-2054	968-2056
Web: www.drpa.org					
Port of Pittsburgh 425 6th Ave Suite 2990	Pittsburgh	PA	15219	412-201-7330	201-7337
TF: 877-609-9870 ■ *Web:* www.port.pittsburgh.pa.us					
Port of Port Angeles 338 W 1st St PO Box 1350	Port Angeles	WA	98362	360-457-8527	452-3959
Web: www.portofpa.com					
Port of Port Arthur 221 Houston Ave	Port Arthur	TX	77640	409-983-2011	985-9312
Web: www.portofportarthur.com					
Port of Port Lavaca-Point Comfort Calhoun County Navigation District FM 2313 S	Point Comfort	TX	77978	361-987-2813	987-2189
Web: www.portofplpc.com					
Port of Portland 40 Commercial St Suite 100	Portland	ME	04101	207-541-6900	541-6905
Web: www.portofportlandmaine.com					
Port of Portland 121 NW Everett St	Portland	OR	97209	503-944-7000	944-7222
TF: 800-547-8411 ■ *Web:* www.portofportland.com					
Port of Prescott 3035 County Rd 2 PO Box 520	Prescott	ON	K0E1T0	613-925-4228	925-5022
Web: www.portofprescott.com					
Port of Redwood City 675 Seaport Blvd	Redwood City	CA	94063	650-306-4150	369-7636
Web: www.redwoodcityport.com					
Port of Richmond 1411 Harbor Way S	Richmond	CA	94804	510-215-4600	233-3105
Port of Richmond Commission 5000 Deepwater Terminal Rd	Richmond	VA	23234	804-646-2020	271-1524
Port of Sacramento 1110 W Capitol Ave	West Sacramento	CA	95691	916-371-8000	372-4802
TF: 888-258-7969 ■ *Web:* www.portofsacramento.com					
Port of Saint Helens 100 'E' St	Columbia City	OR	97018	503-397-2888	397-6924
Web: www.portsh.org					
Port of Saint Petersburg 250 8th Ave SE	Saint Petersburg	FL	33701	727-893-7329	893-7428
TF: 800-782-8350					
Port of San Diego PO Box 120488	San Diego	CA	92112	619-686-6200	686-6400*
**Fax:* Mktg ■ *TF:* 800-854-2757 ■ *Web:* www.portofsandiego.org					
Port of San Francisco Pier 1	San Francisco	CA	94111	415-274-0400	274-0528*
**Fax:* Mktg ■ *Web:* www.sfport.com					
Port of Seattle PO Box 1209	Seattle	WA	98111	206-728-3000	728-3280
TF: 800-426-7817 ■ *Web:* www.portseattle.org					
Port of Sept-Iles 1 quai Mgr-Blanche	Sept-Iles	QC	G4R5P3	418-968-1231	962-4445
Web: www.portsi.com					
Port of Seward PO Box 167	Seward	AK	99664	907-224-3138	224-7187
Web: www.cityofseward.net/harbor					
Port of South Louisiana 171 Belle Terre Blvd Suite 100	LaPlace	LA	70069	985-652-9278	652-9518
TF: 888-752-7678 ■ *Web:* www.portsl.com					
Port of Stockton 2201 W Washington St	Stockton	CA	95203	209-946-0246	465-7244
TF: 800-344-3213 ■ *Web:* www.portofstockton.com					
Port of Tacoma PO Box 1837	Tacoma	WA	98401	253-383-5841	593-4570
Web: www.portoftacoma.com					
Port of Valdez 412 Ferry Terminal Way	Valdez	AK	99686	907-835-4564	835-4479
Web: www.ci.valdez.ak.us/port					
Port of Vancouver 3103 NW Lower River Rd	Vancouver	WA	98660	360-693-3611	735-1565
Web: www.portvanusa.com					
Port of Virginia 600 World Trade Ctr	Norfolk	VA	23510	757-683-8000	683-2573
TF: 800-446-8098 ■ *Web:* www.vaports.com					
Port of Wilmington 1 Hausel Rd	Wilmington	DE	19801	302-472-7678	472-7740
Web: www.portofwilmingtonde.com					
Prince Rupert Port Authority 200-215 Cow Bay Rd	Prince Rupert	BC	V8J1A2	250-627-8899	627-8980
Web: www.rupertport.com					
Puerto Rico Ports Authority PO Box 362829	San Juan	PR	00936	787-729-8804	722-7867

Company	City	State	Zip	Phone	Fax
Quebec Port Authority 150 Dalhousie St PO Box 80 Station Haute-Ville *Web:* www.portquebec.ca	Quebec	QC	G1R4M8	418-648-3640	648-4160
Quonset Davisville Div Rhode Island Economic Development Corp 30 Enterprise Dr	North Kingstown	RI	02852	401-295-0044	295-8345
Rhode Island Economic Development Corp Quonset Davisville Div 30 Enterprise Dr	North Kingstown	RI	02852	401-295-0044	295-8345
Saguenay Port Authority 6600 Quai-Marcel-Dionne Rd *Web:* www.portsaguenay.ca	Ville de La Baie	QC	G7B3N9	418-697-0250	697-0243
Saint Bernard Port Harbor & Terminal District 9000 W St Bernard Hwy 200 Marlin Dr *Web:* www.stbernardport.state.la.us	Chalmette	LA	70043	504-277-8418	277-8471
Saint John Port Authority 133 Prince William St 5th Fl *Web:* www.sjport.com	Saint John	NB	E2L2B5	506-636-4869	636-4443
Saint John's Port Authority PO Box 6178 *Web:* www.sjpa.com	Saint John's	NL	A1C5X8	709-738-4780	738-4784
Saint Paul Harbor PO Box 901	Saint Paul	AK	99660	907-546-3140	546-3186
Sand Point Harbor PO Box 249	Sand Point	AK	99661	907-383-2331	383-5611
Sitka Harbor 617 Katlian St	Sitka	AK	99835	907-747-3439	747-6278
Skagway Harbor PO Box 415	Skagway	AK	99840	907-983-2628	983-3087
South Carolina State Ports Authority 176 Concord St *TF:* 800-845-7106 ■ *Web:* www.scspa.com	Charleston	SC	29401	843-723-8651	577-8626
South Jersey Port Corp 2nd & Beckett St *Web:* www.southjerseyport.com	Camden	NJ	08103	856-757-4969	757-4903
Tampa Port Authority 1101 Channelside Dr *TF:* 800-741-2297 ■ *Web:* www.tampaport.com	Tampa	FL	33602	813-905-7678	905-5109
Thunder Bay Port Authority 100 Main St *Web:* www.portauthority.thunder-bay.on.ca	Thunder Bay	ON	P7B6R9	807-345-6400	345-9058
Toledo-Lucas County Port Authority 1 Maritime Plaza *Web:* www.toledoportauthority.org	Toledo	OH	43604	419-243-8251	243-1835
Toronto Port Authority 60 Harbour St *Web:* www.torontoport.com	Toronto	ON	M5J1B7	416-863-2000	863-4830
Trois-Rivieres Port Authority 1545 Du Fleuve Suite 300 *Web:* www.porttr.com	Trois-Rivieres	QC	G9A6K4	819-378-2887	378-2487
Valleyfield Harbour Commission 950 Cadieux Blvd Suite 100	Salaberry-de-Valleyfield	QC	J6T6L4	450-373-4021	373-4026
Vancouver Fraser Port Authority 100 The Point 999 Canada Pl **Fax Area Code:* 866 ■ *Web:* www.vfpa.ca	Vancouver	BC	V6C3T4	604-665-9000	284-4271*
Vancouver Port Authority 100 The Point 999 Canada Pl **Fax Area Code:* 866 ■ *TF:* 888-767-8826 ■ *Web:* www.portvancouver.com	Vancouver	BC	V6C3T4	604-665-9000	284-4271*
Virginia Port Authority 600 World Trade Ctr *Web:* www.vaports.com	Norfold	VA	23510	757-683-8000	683-8500
Waukegan Port District 55 S Harbor Pl *Web:* www.waukeganport.com	Waukegan	IL	60085	847-244-3133	244-1348
Whittier Harbor PO Box 639	Whittier	AK	99693	907-472-2330	472-2472
Windsor Port Authority 251 Goyeau St Suite 502 *Web:* www.portwindsor.com	Windsor	ON	N9A6V2	519-258-5741	258-5905
Wrangell Harbor PO Box 531 *Web:* www.wrangell.com	Wrangell	AK	99929	907-874-3736	874-3197

622 POULTRY PROCESSING

SEE ALSO Meat Packing Plants p. 1952

Company	City	State	Zip	Phone	Fax
Allen Family Foods Inc 126 N Shipley St *TF:* 800-477-9136 ■ *Web:* www.allenfamilyfoods.com	Seaford	DE	19973	302-629-9136	629-9532
Amick Farms Inc PO Box 2309 *TF:* 800-926-4257 ■ *Web:* www.amickfarms.com	Leesville	SC	29070	803-532-1400	532-1492
Barber's Poultry Inc 4851 W 120th Ave *Web:* www.barberspoultry.com	Broomfield	CO	80020	303-466-7338	466-6960
Brown Produce Co PO Box 265	Farina	IL	62838	618-245-3301	
Butterball LLC 215 W Diehl Rd *Web:* www.butterball.com	Naperville	IL	60563	630-857-1000	512-1139
Butterfield Foods Co PO Box 229	Butterfield	MN	56120	507-956-5103	956-5751
Cagle's Inc 2000 Hills Ave NW *AMEX:* CGLa ■ *TF:* 800-476-2820 ■ *Web:* www.cagles.net	Atlanta	GA	30318	404-355-2820	355-9326
Cal-Maine Foods Inc PO Box 2960 *NASDAQ:* CALM ■ *Web:* www.calmainefoods.com	Jackson	MS	39207	601-948-6813	969-0905
Cargill Inc North America 15407 McGinty Rd *TF:* 800-227-4455	Wayzata	MN	55391	952-742-7575	
Cargill Turkey Products 1 Kratzer Rd *TF Cust Svc:* 800-233-8457	Harrisonburg	VA	22802	540-568-1400	568-1401
Case Farms Inc 121 Rand St	Morganton	NC	28655	828-438-6900	437-5205
Claxton Poultry Farms PO Box 428	Claxton	GA	30417	912-739-3181	
Coleman Natural Foods Snow Ball Div 1051 Sykes Ln *Web:* www.snowballfoods.com	Williamstown	NJ	08094	856-629-4081	728-4238
Columbia Farm Inc PO Box 3628	Leesville	SC	29070	803-532-4488	532-0056
Creekwood Farms Inc N5505 Crossman Rd Po Box 179	Lake Mills	WI	53551	920-648-2377	648-2869
Crescent Duck Processing Co 10 Edgar Ave PO Box 500	Aquebogue	NY	11931	631-722-8700	
Culver Duck Farms Inc PO Box 910 *Web:* www.culverduck.com	Middlebury	IN	46540	574-825-9537	825-2613
Downs Food Group 400 Armstrong Blvd N *TF:* 800-533-0452	Saint James	MN	56081	507-375-3111	375-3048
Durbin Marshall Co 2830 Commerce Blvd *Web:* www.marshalldurbin.com	Irondale	AL	35210	205-956-3505	380-3251
Durbin Marshall Food Corp 2830 Commerce Blvd *TF:* 800-768-2456 ■ *Web:* www.marshalldurbin.com	Irondale	AL	35210	205-956-3505	380-3251
Dutch Quality House 4110 Continental Dr **Fax Area Code:* 770 ■ *TF:* 800-392-0844 ■ *Web:* www.dutchqualityhouse.com	Oakwood	GA	30566	678-450-3100	534-9281*
Echo Lake Farm Produce Co 33102 S Honey Lake Rd PO Box 279 *TF:* 800-888-3447 ■ *Web:* www.echolakefoods.com	Burlington	WI	53105	262-763-9551	763-4593
Empire Kosher Poultry Inc RD 5 Box 228 *TF:* 800-233-7177 ■ *Web:* www.empirekosher.com	Mifflintown	PA	17059	717-436-5921	436-7070
Far Best Foods Inc 4689 S 400 W PO Box 480 *Web:* www.farbestfoods.com	Huntingburg	IN	47542	812-683-4200	683-4226
Farmers Pride Inc 154 W Main St PO Box 39 *Web:* www.bellandevans.com	Fredericksburg	PA	17026	717-865-6626	865-7046
Fieldale Farms Corp 555 Broiler Blvd *TF:* 800-241-5400 ■ *Web:* www.fieldale.com	Baldwin	GA	30511	706-778-5100	778-3767
Forest Packing Co Inc 345 Hwy 35 S	Forest	MS	39074	601-469-3321	469-2389
Foster Farms Inc 1000 Davis St PO Box 457 *Web:* www.fosterfarms.com	Livingston	CA	95334	209-394-7901	394-6342
Georges Inc PO Drawer G	Springdale	AR	72765	479-927-7000	927-7200
Gold Kist Inc 244 Perimeter Ctr Pkwy NE *NASDAQ:* GKIS ■ *Web:* goldkist.com	Atlanta	GA	30346	770-393-5000	393-5262
Golden Rod Broilers Inc PO Box 948 **Fax Area Code:* 334	Cullman	AL	35056	256-734-0941	739-4024*
Gold'n Plump Poultry 4150 2nd St S *TF:* 800-328-8236 ■ *Web:* www.goldnplump.com	Saint Cloud	MN	56301	320-251-6568	240-6250
Gress-Koch Foods LLC 329 Oak St NW Suite 001 *Web:* www.kochfoods.com	Gainesville	GA	30501	770-536-8818	536-4018
Harrison Poultry Inc Star St PO Box 550	Bethlehem	GA	30620	770-867-7511	867-0999
Henningsen Foods Inc 2700 Westchester Ave Suite 311 *Web:* www.henningsenfoods.com	Purchase	NY	10577	914-701-4020	701-4050
Holmes Foods Inc 101 S Liberty Ave	Nixon	TX	78140	830-582-1551	582-1090
House of Raeford Farms Inc PO Box 100 *TF:* 800-888-7539 ■ *Web:* www.houseofraeford.com	Raeford	NC	28376	910-875-5161	875-8300
ISE America Inc 33335 Galena Sassafras *TF:* 800-343-7926	Galena	MD	21635	410-755-6300	755-6367
Jennie-O Turkey Store 2505 Willmar Ave SW *TF:* 800-328-1756 ■ *Web:* www.jennieoturkeystore.com	Willmar	MN	56201	320-235-2622	231-7100
JFC Inc PO Box 1106 *TF:* 800-328-8236	Saint Cloud	MN	56302	320-251-3570	240-6250
Keystone Foods LLC 300 Bar Harbor Dr Suite 600 5 Tower Bridge *Web:* www.keystonefoods.com	West Conshohocken	PA	19428	610-667-6700	667-1460
Koch Foods Inc 3500 Western Blvd *TF:* 800-277-2473	Montgomery	AL	36108	334-281-0400	284-2998
Koch Foods Inc 1300 Higgins Rd Suite 100 *TF:* 800-837-2778	Park Ridge	IL	60068	847-384-5940	384-5961
Mar-Jac Poultry Inc PO Box 1017 *TF:* 800-226-0561 ■ *Web:* www.marjacpoultry.com	Gainesville	GA	30503	770-536-0561	531-5049
Marshall Durbin Co 2830 Commerce Blvd *Web:* www.marshalldurbin.com	Irondale	AL	35210	205-956-3505	380-3251
Marshall Durbin Food Corp 2830 Commerce Blvd *TF:* 800-768-2456 ■ *Web:* www.marshalldurbin.com	Irondale	AL	35210	205-956-3505	380-3251
Michael Foods Inc 301 Carlson Pkwy Suite 400 *TF:* 800-325-4270 ■ *Web:* www.michaelfoods.com	Minnetonka	MN	55305	952-258-4000	258-4940
Midwest Poultry Services LP 9951 W SR 25	Mentone	IN	46539	574-353-7651	353-7223
Mountaire Farms 17269 NC Hwy 71 N **Fax:* Hum Res ■ *TF:* 800-968-0720 ■ *Web:* www.mountaire.com	Lumber Bridge	NC	28357	910-843-5942	843-8840*
Northern Pride Inc PO Box 598	Thief River Falls	MN	56701	218-681-1201	681-7183
Oak Valley Farms Inc 705 20th Ave SW *Web:* www.oakvalleyfarms.com	Watertown	SD	57201	605-886-8025	882-2895
OK Foods Inc PO Box 1119 *TF:* 800-635-9441 ■ *Web:* www.okfoods.com	Fort Smith	AR	72902	479-783-0244	784-1280
Olymel LP 2200 Pratte Ave Pratte *Web:* www.olymel.com	Saint-Hyacinthe	QC	J2S4B6	450-771-0400	771-0519
Oskaloosa Food Products Corp 546 9th Ave E	Oskaloosa	IA	52577	641-673-3487	673-8684
Papetti's Hygrade Egg Products Inc 1 Papetti Plaza	Elizabeth	NJ	07206	908-282-7900	354-8660
Park Farms Inc 1925 30th St NE *TF:* 800-683-6511 ■ *Web:* www.parkfarms.com	Canton	OH	44705	330-455-0241	455-5820
PECO Foods Inc 3701 Kauloosa Ave *Web:* www.pecofoods.com	Tuscaloosa	AL	35403	205-345-3955	343-2401
Pennfield Corp 711 Rohrerstown Rd *TF:* 800-732-0467 ■ *Web:* www.dairyfeed.com	Lancaster	PA	17604	717-299-2561	295-8783
Perdue Farms Inc PO Box 1537 **Fax:* Sales ■ *TF:* 800-457-3738 ■ *Web:* www.perdue.com	Salisbury	MD	21802	410-543-3000	543-3212*
Petaluma Poultry Processors PO Box 7368 *TF:* 800-556-6789 ■ *Web:* www.petalumapoultry.com	Petaluma	CA	94955	707-763-1904	763-3924
Peterson Farms Inc 250 S Main St *Web:* www.petersonfarms.com	Decatur	AR	72722	479-752-5400	752-5650
Petit Jean Poultry Inc 1809 E 8th St	Danville	AR	72833	479-495-4300	495-4327
Pilgrim's Pride Corp 4845 US Hwy 271 PO Box 93 *NYSE:* PPC ■ *Web:* www.pilgrimspride.com	Pittsburg	TX	75686	903-434-1000	
Randall Foods Inc 2905 E 50th St **Fax:* Hum Res ■ *TF:* 800-372-6581	Vernon	CA	90058	323-587-2383	586-1587*
Rose Acre Farms Inc 351 Ronthor Dr *Web:* www.goodegg.com	Social Circle	GA	30025	770-464-2652	464-2998
Sanderson Farms Inc PO Box 988 *NASDAQ:* SAFM ■ *Web:* www.sandersonfarms.com	Laurel	MS	39441	601-649-4030	932-1461
Simmons Industries Inc 601 N Hico St *TF:* 888-831-7007 ■ *Web:* www.simmonsfoods.com	Siloam Springs	AR	72761	479-524-8151	524-6562
Siouxpreme Egg Products Inc 321 2nd Ave SW	Sioux Center	IA	51250	712-722-4787	722-3624
Snow Ball Div Coleman Natural Foods 1051 Sykes Ln *Web:* www.snowballfoods.com	Williamstown	NJ	08094	856-629-4081	728-4238
Sonstegard Foods Inc 707 E 41st St Suite 107 *TF:* 800-533-3184 ■ *Web:* www.sonstegard.com	Sioux Falls	SD	57105	605-338-4642	338-9765
Sunny Fresh Foods Inc 206 W 4th St *TF:* 800-872-3447 ■ *Web:* www.sunnyfreshfoods.com	Monticello	MN	55362	763-271-5600	271-5711
Tip Top Poultry Inc 327 Wallace Rd *TF:* 800-241-5230 ■ *Web:* www.tiptoppoultry.com	Marietta	GA	30062	770-973-8070	973-6897
Townsends Inc 919 N Market St Suite 420 *Web:* www.townsends.com	Wilmington	DE	19801	302-777-6650	777-6660
Turkey Valley Farms 112 S 6th St PO Box 200 *Web:* www.turkeyvalleyfarms.com	Marshall	MN	56258	507-337-3100	337-3009
Tyson Foods Inc 2210 W Oaklawn Dr *NYSE:* TSN ■ **Fax:* Hum Res ■ *TF:* 800-643-3410 ■ *Web:* www.tyson.com	Springdale	AR	72762	479-290-4000	290-4217*
Valley Fresh Inc 680 D St PO Box 339 *TF:* 800-526-3189 ■ *Web:* www.valleyfreshkitchen.com	Turlock	CA	95381	209-668-3695	668-0770
Wapsie Produce Inc 702 E Water St	Decorah	IA	52101	563-382-4271	382-8210
Watson Quality Food Inc PO Box 215 *TF:* 800-257-7870	Blackwood	NJ	08012	856-227-0594	228-1628
Wayne Farms Enterprises LLC 1020 County Rd 114 *TF:* 800-223-2569	Jack	AL	36346	334-897-3435	897-1000
West Central Turkeys Inc 704 N Broadway	Pelican Rapids	MN	56572	218-863-3131	863-3171
Willow Brook Foods Inc PO Box 50190 *TF:* 800-423-2366 ■ *Web:* www.wbfoods.com	Springfield	MO	65805	417-862-3612	837-1675
Zacky Farms Inc 13200 Crossroads Pkwy N Suite 25 *Web:* www.zacky.com	City of Industry	CA	91746	562-641-2900	641-2040

623 POWER TRANSMISSION EQUIPMENT - MECHANICAL

SEE ALSO Bearings - Ball & Roller p. 1373

Company	City	State	Zip	Phone	Fax
A-1 Carbide Corp 1649 Miraloma Ave *TF:* 800-222-9422	Placentia	CA	92870	714-630-9422	666-0648
Adams Co 8040 Chavenelle Rd *Web:* www.theadamscompany.com	Dubuque	IA	52002	563-583-3591	583-8048
Allied-Locke Industries 1088 Corregidor Rd *TF:* 800-435-7752 ■ *Web:* www.alliedlocke.com	Dixon	IL	61021	815-288-1471	288-7945
American Metal Bearing Co 7191 Acacia Ave *TF:* 800-888-3048 ■ *Web:* www.ambco.net	Garden Grove	CA	92841	714-892-5527	898-3217
AmeriDrives International 1802 Pittsburgh Ave *TF:* 800-352-0141 ■ *Web:* www.ameridrives.com	Erie	PA	16502	814-480-5100	453-5891
Barden Corp 200 Park Ave *TF:* 800-243-1060 ■ *Web:* www.bardenbearings.com	Danbury	CT	06810	203-744-2211	744-3756
Beemer Precision Inc 230 New York Dr PO Box 3080 *TF:* 800-836-2340 ■ *Web:* www.oilite.com	Fort Washington	PA	19034	215-646-8440	283-3397
Bird Precision 1 Spruce St PO Box 540569 *TF Cust Svc:* 800-454-7369 ■ *Web:* www.birdprecision.com	Waltham	MA	02454	781-894-0160	894-6308

				Phone	Fax
Bishop-Wisecarver Corp 2104 Martin Way	Pittsburg	CA	94565	925-439-8272	439-5931
TF: 888-580-8272 ■ *Web:* www.bwc.com					
Blount Forestry & Industrial Equipment Div 535 Mack Todd Rd	Zebulon	NC	27597	919-269-7421	269-2406
Web: www.blount-fied.com					
Brenco Inc 2580 Frontage Rd PO Box 389	Petersburg	VA	23804	804-732-0202	861-6989
TF: 800-238-4712 ■ *Web:* www.brencoqbs.com					
BW Elliott Mfg Inc 11 Beckwith Ave PO Box 733	Binghamton	NY	13902	607-772-0404	772-0431
Web: www.elliottmfg.com					
Cangro Industries Long Island Transmission Co 495 Smith St	Farmingdale	NY	11735	631-454-9000	454-9155
TF: 800-899-2264 ■ *Web:* www.cangroindustries.com					
Capitol Stampings Corp 2700 W North Ave	Milwaukee	WI	53208	414-372-3500	372-3535
Web: www.capitolstampings.com					
Carlyle Johnson Machine Co 291 Boston Tpke	Bolton	CT	06043	860-643-1531	646-2645
TF: 888-629-4867 ■ *Web:* www.cjmco.com					
Certified Power Inc 970 Campus Dr	Mundelein	IL	60060	847-573-3800	573-3832
TF: 800-877-8350 ■ *Web:* www.certifiedpower.com					
Coupling Products 1802 Pittsburgh Ave	Erie	PA	16502	814-480-5000	453-5891
TF: 800-352-0141 ■ *Web:* www.ameridrives.com/cplgprod.html					
Deere & Co John Deere Power Systems Div 3801 W Ridgeway Ave	Waterloo	IA	50701	319-292-5643	292-5364
Web: www.deere.com/en_US/rg					
Deublin Co 2050 Norman Dr W	Waukegan	IL	60085	847-689-8600	689-8690
Web: www.deublin.com					
Diamond Chain Co 402 Kentucky Ave	Indianapolis	IN	46225	317-638-6431	633-2243
TF Cust Svc: 800-872-4246 ■ *Web:* www.diamondchain.com					
Don Dye Co Inc 524 NW 20th Ave PO Box 107	Kingman	KS	67068	620-532-3131	532-2141
TF: 800-901-3131 ■ *Web:* www.dondyeco.com					
Drives Inc 1009 1st St	Fulton	IL	61252	815-589-2211	589-4420
TF: 800-435-0782 ■ *Web:* www.drivesinc.com					
Eaton Corp 1111 Superior Ave Eaton Center	Cleveland	OH	44114	216-523-5000	523-4787
NYSE: ETN ■ *Web:* www.eaton.com					
EC Styberg Engineering Co Inc 1600 Gold St PO Box 788	Racine	WI	53401	262-637-9301	637-1319
Web: www.styberg.com					
Elliott BW Mfg Inc 11 Beckwith Ave PO Box 733	Binghamton	NY	13902	607-772-0404	772-0431
Web: www.elliottmfg.com					
Emerson Power Transmission Corp 620 S Aurora St	Ithaca	NY	14850	607-272-7220	272-7239*
**Fax:* Sales ■ *Web:* www.emerson-ept.com					
Force Control Industries Inc 3660 Dixie Hwy	Fairfield	OH	45014	513-868-0900	868-2105
TF: 800-829-3244 ■ *Web:* www.forcecontrol.com					
Gear Products Inc 1111 N 161st East Ave	Tulsa	OK	74116	918-234-3044	234-3455
Web: www.gearproducts.com					
General Bearing Corp 44 High St	West Nyack	NY	10994	845-358-6000	358-6277
TF Sales: 800-431-1766 ■ *Web:* www.generalbearing.com					
GGB North America 700 Mid Atlantic Pkwy PO Box 189	Thorofare	NJ	08086	856-848-3200	848-5115*
**Fax:* Sales ■ *TF:* 800-222-0147 ■ *Web:* www.ggbearings.com					
GKN Rockford Inc 1200 Windsor Rd	Loves Park	IL	61111	815-633-7460	633-1311*
**Fax:* Sales ■ *Web:* www.rockfordpowertrain.com					
Helical Products Co Inc 901 W McCoy Ln PO Box 1069	Santa Maria	CA	93456	805-928-3851	928-2369
Web: www.heli-cal.com					
Hilliard Corp 100 W 4th St	Elmira	NY	14902	607-733-7121	733-3009
Web: www.hilliardcorp.com					
Horton Inc 2565 Walnut St	Roseville	MN	55113	651-361-6400	361-6804
TF: 800-843-7445 ■ *Web:* www.hortonww.com					
INA USA Corp 308 Springhill Farm Rd	Fort Mill	SC	29715	803-548-8500	548-8599
Web: www.ina.com/us					
Industrial Clutch Products 1701-3 Pearl St	Waukesha	WI	53186	262-547-3357	547-2949
Web: www.indclutch.com					
Ingersoll-Rand Co 155 Chestnut Ridge Rd	Montvale	NJ	07645	201-573-0123	573-3172
NYSE: IR ■ *Web:* www.irco.com					
John Deere Coffeyville Works Inc PO Box 577	Coffeyville	KS	67337	620-251-3400	252-3252
TF: 800-844-1337					
John Deere Power Systems Div Deere & Co 3801 W Ridgeway Ave	Waterloo	IA	50701	319-292-5643	292-5364
Web: www.deere.com/en_US/rg					
Kamatics Corp 1330 Blue Hills Ave	Bloomfield	CT	06002	860-243-9704	243-7993
TF: 800-468-4735 ■ *Web:* www.kamatics.com					
Kingsbury Inc 10385 Drummond Rd	Philadelphia	PA	19154	215-824-4000	824-4999
TF: 800-898-8912 ■ *Web:* www.kingsbury.com					
Linn Gear Co 100 N 8th St PO Box 397	Lebanon	OR	97355	541-259-1211	259-1299
TF: 800-547-2471 ■ *Web:* www.linngear.com					
Lovejoy Inc 2655 Wisconsin Ave	Downers Grove	IL	60515	630-852-0500	
TF: 800-334-9659 ■ *Web:* www.lovejoy-inc.com					
Magtrol Inc 70 Gardenville Pkwy W	Buffalo	NY	14224	716-668-5555	668-8705
TF: 800-828-7844 ■ *Web:* www.magtrol.com					
Mark IV Industries Inc 501 John James Audubon Pkwy	Amherst	NY	14226	716-689-4972	689-6098
Web: www.mark-iv.com					
Marland Clutch Products 16 W 485 S Frontage Rd Suite 330	Burr Ridge	IL	60527	708-352-3330	352-1403
TF: 800-216-3515 ■ *Web:* www.marland.com					
Martin Sprocket & Gear Inc 3100 Sprocket Dr PO Box 91588	Arlington	TX	76015	817-258-3000	258-3333
Web: www.martinsprocket.com					
Maurey Mfg Corp 410 S Industrial Park Rd	Holly Springs	MS	38635	662-252-1898	252-6364
TF: 800-284-2161 ■ *Web:* www.maurey.com					
Metallized Carbon Corp 19 S Water St	Ossining	NY	10562	914-941-3738	941-4050
Web: www.metcar.com					
Midwest Control Products Corp 590 E Main St	Bushnell	IL	61422	309-772-3163	772-2266
Web: www.midwestcontrol.com					
Nook Industries 4950 E 49th St	Cleveland	OH	44125	216-271-7900	271-7020
TF: 800-321-7800 ■ *Web:* www.nookindustries.com					
North American Clutch Corp					
4360 N Green Bay Ave PO Box 090228	Milwaukee	WI	53209	414-267-4000	267-4024
Web: www.noram-clutch.com					
NSK Corp 4200 Goss Rd	Ann Arbor	MI	48105	734-761-9500	913-7500
TF: 800-521-0605 ■ *Web:* www.nsk-corp.com					
NTN Bearing Corp of America 1600 E Bishop Ct	Mount Prospect	IL	60056	847-298-7500	699-9744
TF: 800-468-6528 ■ *Web:* www.ntnamerica.com					
OPW Engineered Systems Inc 2726 Henkle Dr	Lebanon	OH	45036	513-932-9114	245-8536*
**Fax Area Code:* 800 ■ **Fax:* Cust Svc ■ *TF Cust Svc:* 800-547-9393 ■ *Web:* www.opw-es.com					
Ormat Technologies Inc 6225 Neil Rd Suite 300	Reno	NV	89511	775-356-9029	356-9039
NYSE: ORA ■ *Web:* www.ormat.com					
Peer Bearing Co 2200 Norman Dr S	Waukegan	IL	60085	847-578-1000	578-1200
TF: 800-433-7337 ■ *Web:* www.peerbearing.com					
Pic Design Corp 86 Benson Rd PO Box 1004	Middlebury	CT	06762	203-758-8272	758-8271
TF: 800-243-6125 ■ *Web:* www.pic-design.com					
Ramsey Products Corp 3701 Performance Rd PO Box 668827	Charlotte	NC	28266	704-394-0322	394-9134
Web: www.ramseychain.com					
RBC Transport Dynamics Corp					
3131 W Segerstrom Ave PO Box 1953	Santa Ana	CA	92704	714-546-3131	545-9885
TF: 800-854-3922 ■ *Web:* www.rbcbearings.com					
Regal-Beloit Corp 200 State St	Beloit	WI	53511	608-364-8800	364-8818
NYSE: RBC ■ *Web:* www.regal-beloit.com					
Renold Ajax Inc 100 Bourne St	Westfield	NY	14787	716-326-3121	326-6121
Web: www.renold.com					
Siemens Power Transmission & Distribution Inc 7000 Siemens Rd	Wendell	NC	27591	919-365-2200	365-2201
TF: 800-347-6659 ■ *Web:* www.ptd.siemens.com					
SKF USA Inc 1111 Adams Ave	Norristown	PA	19403	610-630-2800	630-2801
Web: www.skfusa.com					
Speed Selector Inc 17050 Munn Rd	Chagrin Falls	OH	44023	440-543-8233	543-8527
Web: www.speedselector.com					
SS White Technologies Inc 151 Old New Brunswick Rd	Piscataway	NJ	08854	732-752-8300	752-8315
TF: 800-872-2673 ■ *Web:* www.sswt.com					
Stock Drive Products/Sterling Instrument 2101 Jericho Tpke	New Hyde Park	NY	11040	516-328-3300	326-8827
TF: 800-737-7436 ■ *Web:* www.sdp-si.com					
Styberg EC Engineering Co Inc 1600 Gold St PO Box 788	Racine	WI	53401	262-637-9301	637-1319
Web: www.styberg.com					
TB Wood's Inc 440 N 5th Ave	Chambersburg	PA	17201	717-264-7161	264-6420
NASDAQ: TBWC ■ *TF:* 888-829-6637 ■ *Web:* www.tbwoods.com					
Tuthill Corp 8500 S Madison St	Burr Ridge	IL	60527	630-382-4900	382-4999
TF: 800-888-4455 ■ *Web:* www.tuthill.com					
Tuthill Linkage Group 2110 Summit St	New Haven	IN	46774	260-749-5105	493-2387
Web: linkage.tuthill.com					
Twin Disc Inc 1328 Racine St	Racine	WI	53403	262-638-4000	
NASDAQ: TWIN ■ *Web:* www.twindisc.com					
Universal Bearings Inc 431 N Birkey St	Bremen	IN	46506	574-546-2261	546-5085
Web: www.univbrg.com					
US Tsubaki Inc 301 E Marquardt Dr	Wheeling	IL	60090	847-459-9500	
TF: 800-323-7790 ■ *Web:* www.ustsubaki.com					
Wampfler Inc 8091 Production Ave	Florence	KY	41042	859-814-2100	814-2110
TF: 800-326-2899 ■ *Web:* www.wampfler.com					
Warner Electric 449 Gardner St	South Beloit	IL	61080	815-389-3771	
TF: 800-234-3369 ■ *Web:* www.warnernet.com					
Waukesha Bearings Corp					
W 231 N 2811 Roundy Circle E Suite 200	Pewaukee	WI	53072	262-506-3000	506-3001
Web: www.waukbearing.com					
Wheeler Industries 7261 Investment Dr	North Charleston	SC	29418	843-552-1251	552-4790
TF Sales: 800-343-0803 ■ *Web:* www.wheeler-ind.com					
White SS Technologies Inc 151 Old New Brunswick Rd	Piscataway	NJ	08854	732-752-8300	752-8315
TF: 800-872-2673 ■ *Web:* www.sswt.com					
Whittet-Higgins Co 33 Higginson Ave PO Box 8	Central Falls	RI	02863	401-728-0700	728-0703
TF Sales: 800-972-8070 ■ *Web:* www.whittet-higgins.com					
Zero-Max Inc 13200 6th Ave N	Plymouth	MN	55441	763-546-4300	546-8260
TF: 800-533-1731 ■ *Web:* www.zero-max.com					

624 PRECISION MACHINED PRODUCTS

SEE ALSO Aircraft Parts & Auxiliary Equipment p. 1271; Machine Shops p. 1923

				Phone	Fax
A-1 Production Inc 5809 E Leighty Rd	Kendallville	IN	46755	260-347-0960	347-4727
Web: www.a1production.com					
Abbott Interfast Corp 190 Abbott Dr	Wheeling	IL	60090	847-459-6200	459-4076
Web: www.abbott-interfast.com					
Accellent Inc 200 W 7th Ave	Collegeville	PA	19426	610-489-0300	489-1150
TF: 800-321-6285 ■ *Web:* www.accellent.com					
Afco Products Inc 2074 S Mannheim Rd	Des Plaines	IL	60018	847-299-1055	299-8455
Web: www.afco-products.com					
AHF Ducommun Inc 268 E Gardena Blvd	Gardena	CA	90248	310-380-5390	380-5238
Web: www.ahfd.com					
Air-Matic Products Co Inc 22218 Telegraph Rd	Southfield	MI	48033	248-356-4200	356-0738
Web: www.air-matic.com					
Alco Mfg Corp 10584 Middle Ave	Elyria	OH	44035	440-458-5165	458-6821
Web: www.alcomfgcorp.com					
Alger Mfg Co Inc 724 S Bon View Ave	Ontario	CA	91761	909-986-4591	983-3351
TF: 800-854-9833 ■ *Web:* www.alger1.com					
Allan Tool & Machine Co Inc 1822 E Maple Rd	Troy	MI	48083	248-585-2910	585-7728
Allied Screw Products Inc 815 E Lowell Ave	Mishawaka	IN	46545	574-255-4718	255-4173
Web: www.aspi-nc.com					
Allied Swiss Screw Products Inc 2636 Vista Pacific Dr	Oceanside	CA	92056	760-941-1702	941-0044
Web: www.alliedswiss.com					
Allmetal Screw Products Corp 94A E Jefryn Blvd	Deer Park	NY	11729	631-243-5200	243-5307
Web: www.allmetalcorp.com					
Alpha Grainger Mfg Inc 20 Discovery Way	Franklin	MA	02038	508-520-4005	520-4185
Web: www.agmi.com					
American Products Co Inc 610 Rahway Ave	Union	NJ	07083	908-687-4100	687-0037
Web: www.amerprod.com					
American Turned Products Inc 7626 Klier Dr	Fairview	PA	16415	814-474-4200	474-4718
Web: www.atpteam.com					
Amsco-Wire Products Co 610 Grand Ave	Ridgefield	NJ	07657	201-945-5700	945-5618
TF: 800-255-7467					
Amtec Precision Products Inc 1875 Holmes Rd	Elgin	IL	60123	847-695-8030	695-8295
Web: www.amtecprecision.com					
Anchor Coupling Inc 5520 13th St	Menominee	MI	49858	906-863-2671	863-3242
TF: 800-662-5520 ■ *Web:* www.anchorcoupling.com					
Anderson Automatics Inc 6401 Welcome Ave N	Minneapolis	MN	55429	763-533-2206	533-0320
Web: www.andersonautomatics.com					
Anderson Precision Inc 20 Livingston Ave	Jamestown	NY	14701	716-484-1148	484-7779
Web: www.andersonprecision.com					
Ashley F Ward Inc 7490 Easy St	Mason	OH	45040	513-398-1414	398-1125
Web: www.ashleyward.com					
Astro Seal Inc 827-B Palmyrita Ave	Riverside	CA	92507	951-787-6670	787-6677
Web: www.astroseal.com					
ATEC Inc 12600 Executive Dr	Stafford	TX	77477	281-276-2700	240-2682
Web: www.atec.com					
Athanor Group Inc 921 E California Ave	Ontario	CA	91761	909-467-1205	467-1208
Web: www.athanorgroupinc.com					
Auer Precision Inc 1050 W Birchwood Ave	Mesa	AZ	85210	480-834-4637	964-8237
Web: www.auerprecision.com					
Automatic Machine Products Co 17 Wall St	Attleboro	MA	02703	508-222-2300	222-2307
Web: www.ampcomp.com					
Automatic Products Corp 2735 Forest Ln	Garland	TX	75042	972-272-6422	494-0533
Web: www.ap-corp.com					
Avanti Engineering Inc 200 W Lake Dr	Glendale Heights	IL	60139	630-260-1333	260-1762
Web: www.avantiengineering.com					
Barber-Nichols Inc 6325 W 55th Ave	Arvada	CO	80002	303-421-8111	420-4679
Web: www.barber-nichols.com					
Barton Products Corp PO Box 1060	West Bend	WI	53095	262-334-5583	334-0639
Web: www.bartonproducts.com					
Basler EJ Co 9511 W Ainslie St	Schiller Park	IL	60176	847-678-8880	678-8896
Web: www.ejbasler.com					
Bay Swiss Mfg Co Inc 5 Airpark Vista Blvd	Dayton	NV	89403	775-246-7100	246-7104
TF: 800-247-3207 ■ *Web:* www.bayswiss.com					
Berkley Screw Machine Products Inc					
2100 Royce Haley Dr	Rochester Hills	MI	48309	248-853-0044	853-1532
Berkshire Industries Inc 109 Apremont Way	Westfield	MA	01085	413-568-8676	562-0061
Web: www.berkshireindustries.com					
Betar Inc 1524 Millstone River Rd	Hillsborough	NJ	08844	908-359-4200	359-1010
TF: 800-841-8841 ■ *Web:* www,betar.net					
Betty Machine Co 324 Freehill Rd	Hendersonville	TN	37075	615-826-6004	826-6262
TF: 800-264-3480 ■ *Web:* www.bettymachine.com					

Company / Address	City	State	Zip	Phone	Fax
Biddle Precision Components Inc 701 S Main St	Sheridan	IN	46069	317-758-4451	758-5260
TF: 800-428-4387 ■ *Web:* www.bpcinc.biz					
Birken Mfg Co 3 Old Windsor Rd	Bloomfield	CT	06002	860-242-2211	242-2749
Web: www.birken.net					
Blackhawk Machine Products Inc 6 Industrial Dr	Smithfield	RI	02917	401-232-7563	732-0770
Web: www.blackhawk-machine.com					
BMI Inc 4541 Preslyn Dr	Raleigh	NC	27616	919-878-7776	878-0580
Web: www.bmi-inc.com					
Bracalente Mfg Co 20 W Creamery Rd PO Box 570	Trumbauersville	PA	18970	215-536-3077	536-4844
Web: www.bracalente.com					
Brucato Mfg Co 196 Mill St	Waterbury	CT	06706	203-756-3691	756-7202
Burgess-Norton Mfg Co 737 Peyton St	Geneva	IL	60134	630-232-4100	232-3700*
**Fax:* Hum Res ■ *Web:* www.burgessnorton.com					
Bystrom Brothers Inc 2200 Snelling Ave S	Minneapolis	MN	55404	612-721-7511	721-6745
Web: www.bystrombros.com					
Camcraft Inc 1080 Muirfield Dr	Hanover Park	IL	60133	630-582-6000	582-6019
Web: www.camcraft.com					
Cape Industries Inc 24055 Mound Rd	Warren	MI	48091	586-754-0898	754-7030
Web: www.capeind.net					
Cass Screw Machine Products Co 4800 N Lilac Dr	Minneapolis	MN	55429	763-535-0501	535-9238
Web: www.csmp.com					
CE Holden Inc 938 Rt 910	Cheswick	PA	15024	412-767-5050	767-9922
Web: www.ceholdeninc.com					
Charleston Metal Products Inc 350 Grant St	Waterloo	IN	46793	260-837-8211	837-8101
Web: www.charlestonmetal.com					
CNW Inc 4710 Madison Rd	Cincinnati	OH	45227	513-321-2775	321-2013
TF: 800-327-5900 ■ *Web:* www.cnwinc.com					
Cole Screw Machine Products Inc					
88 Great Hill Rd PO Box 1007	Naugatuck	CT	06770	203-723-1418	723-1252
Web: www.colescrew.com					
Contour Tool Inc 588 Ternes Ave	Elyria	OH	44035	440-365-7333	365-7335
Web: www.contourtool.com					
Corlett-Turner Co 2500 104th Ave	Zeeland	MI	49464	616-772-9082	772-1235
Cox Mfg Co 5500 N Loop 1604 E	San Antonio	TX	78247	210-657-7731	657-2345
TF: 800-900-7981 ■ *Web:* www.comaco.com					
CPI Aerostructures Inc 60 Heartland Blvd	Edgewood	NY	11717	631-586-5200	586-5814
AMEX: CVU ■ *Web:* www.cpiaero.com					
CSM Mfg Corp 24650 N Industrial Dr	Farmington Hills	MI	48335	248-471-0700	471-2714
Curtis Screw Co Inc 50 Thielman Dr	Buffalo	NY	14206	716-898-7800	898-7880
TF: 800-914-6276 ■ *Web:* www.curtisscrew.com					
D-Velco Mfg of Arizona 401 S 36th St	Phoenix	AZ	85034	602-275-4406	275-1071
Web: dvelco.northstar-aerospace.com					
Dabko Industries Inc 50 Emmett St	Bristol	CT	06010	860-589-0756	585-0874
Web: www.rgdtech.com					
DCG Precision Mfg Corp 9 Trowbridge Dr	Bethel	CT	06801	203-743-5525	791-1737
Web: www.dcgprecision.com					
Defiance Precision Products Inc 1125 Precision Way	Defiance	OH	43512	419-782-8955	782-4808
Web: www.defianceprecision.com					
Delo Screw Products Co 700 London Rd	Delaware	OH	43015	740-363-1971	363-0042
Web: www.deloscrew.com					
Dependable Screw Machine Products Inc					
244 Mill St PO Box 2179	Waterbury	CT	06706	203-756-5535	756-5536
Devon Precision Industries Inc 251 Munson Rd	Wolcott	CT	06716	203-879-1437	879-5556
Web: www.devonp.com					
Diamond Machine 150 Marr Ave	Marietta	GA	30060	770-590-0152	590-0235
TF: 800-556-6211 ■ *Web:* www.diamondroller.com					
Dirksen Screw Products Co 14490 23-Mile Rd	Shelby Township	MI	48315	586-247-5400	247-9507
Web: www.dirksenscrew.com					
Diversified Machine Inc 28059 Center Oaks Ct	Wixom	MI	48393	248-277-4400	277-4399
Web: www.divmi.com					
Dow Screw Products 3810 Paule Ave	Saint Louis	MO	63125	314-638-5100	638-4838
Web: www.dowscrew.com					
Duffin Mfg Co 316 Warden Ave PO Box 4036	Elyria	OH	44036	440-323-4681	323-7389
Web: www.duffinmfg.com					
DuPage Machine Products Inc 311 Longview Dr	Bloomingdale	IL	60108	630-690-5400	690-5504
Efficient Machine Products Corp 12133 Alameda Dr	Strongsville	OH	44149	440-268-0205	268-0215
Web: www.efficientmachineprod.com					
EJ Basler Co 9511 W Ainslie St	Schiller Park	IL	60176	847-678-8880	678-8896
Web: www.ejbasler.com					
Elyria Mfg Corp 145 Northrup St	Elyria	OH	44035	440-365-4171	365-4000
Web: www.elyriamfg.com					
Engineered Sinterings & Plastics Inc 140 Commercial St	Watertown	CT	06795	860-274-7546	274-4406
Web: www.engsint.com					
Enoch Mfg Co 14242 SE 82nd Dr PO Box 98	Clackamas	OR	97015	503-659-2660	659-4439
TF: 888-659-6565 ■ *Web:* www.enochmfg.com					
Fairchild Auto-mated Parts Inc 10 White St	Winsted	CT	06098	860-379-2725	379-5340
TF: 800-927-2545 ■ *Web:* www.fairchildparts.com					
Farrar Corp 142 W Burns St	Norwich	KS	67118	620-478-2212	478-2200
Web: www.farrarusa.com					
FC Phillips Inc 471 Washington St	Stoughton	MA	02072	781-344-9400	344-3440
Web: www.fcphillips.com					
FCI Inc 4661 Giles Rd	Cleveland	OH	44135	216-251-5200	251-5206
Web: www.fci-usa.com					
Federal Screw Works 20229 Nine-Mile Rd	Saint Clair Shores	MI	48080	586-443-4200	443-4210
Web: www.federalscrew.com					
Fischer Special Mfg Co 1188 Industrial Rd	Cold Spring	KY	41076	859-781-1400	781-4702
Web: www.fischerspecial.com					
Form Cut Industries Inc 197 Mt Pleasant Ave	Newark	NJ	07104	973-483-5154	483-4512
Web: www.formcut.com					
Fraen Machining Corp DBA Swisstronics 324 New Boston St	Woburn	MA	01801	781-205-5400	205-5472
Web: www.swisstronics.com					
Frisby PMC LLC 1500 Chase Ave	Elk Grove Village	IL	60007	847-439-1150	439-6463
Web: www.frisby-pmc.com					
Gates Albert Inc 3434 Union St	North Chili	NY	14514	585-594-9401	594-4305
Web: www.gatesalbert.com					
General Automotive Mfg LLC 5215 W Airways Ave	Franklin	WI	53132	414-423-6400	423-6415
Web: www.gamfg.com					
General Engineering Works 1515 W Wrightwood Ct	Addison	IL	60101	630-543-8000	543-8005
Web: www.gewinc.com					
General Machine & Tool Works Inc 313 W Chestnut St	Chicago	IL	60610	312-337-2177	337-0244
Gormac Products Inc 1836 Oakdale Ave	Racine	WI	53406	262-637-9146	637-1519
TF: 800-596-0156 ■ *Web:* www.gormacproducts.com					
Gregg Industries Inc 10460 Hickson St	El Monte	CA	91731	626-575-7664	401-0971
Web: www.greggind.com					
Greystone of Lincoln Inc 7 Wellington Rd	Lincoln	RI	02865	401-333-0444	334-5745
Griner Engineering Inc 2500 N Curry Pike	Bloomington	IN	47404	812-332-2220	332-2229
Web: www.griner.com					
H & H Swiss Screw Machine Products Co Inc					
1478 Chestnut Ave	Hillside	NJ	07205	908-688-6390	688-3503
TF: 800-826-9985 ■ *Web:* www.hhswiss.com					
H & L Tool Co Inc 32701 Dequindre Rd	Madison Heights	MI	48071	248-585-7474	585-5774
Web: www.hltool.com					
Hall Industries Inc 514 Mecklem Ln	Ellwood City	PA	16117	724-752-2000	758-1558
TF: 800-828-5519 ■ *Web:* www.hallind.com					
Herker Industries Inc N57 W13760 Carmen Ave	Menomonee Falls	WI	53051	262-781-4220	781-0931
Web: www.herker.com					
Hi-Shear Corp 2600 Skypark Dr	Torrance	CA	90509	310-326-8110	784-4144
Web: www.hi-shear.com					
High Precision Grinding & Machining Inc 1130 Pioneer Way	El Cajon	CA	92020	619-440-0303	440-2148
High Precision Inc PO Box 6157	Hamden	CT	06517	203-777-5395	773-1976
Web: www.highprecisioninc.com					
Highland Machine & Screw Products Co					
700 5th St PO Box 329	Highland	IL	62249	618-654-2103	654-8016
Web: www.highlandmachine.com					
Holden CE Inc 938 Rt 910	Cheswick	PA	15024	412-767-5050	767-9922
Web: www.ceholdeninc.com					
Horizon Enterprises LLC 4261 13th St	Wyandotte	MI	48192	734-246-2460	246-2467
Web: www.horizonet.com					
Horizon Mfg Industries Inc 11417 Cyrus Way Unit 1	Mukilteo	WA	98275	425-493-1220	
Web: www.horizonman.com					
Horspool & Romine Mfg Inc 5850 Marshall St	Oakland	CA	94608	510-652-1844	652-3455
TF: 800-446-2263 ■ *Web:* www.horspool.com					
Hudson Screw Machine Products Co 2305 Gardner Rd	Broadview	IL	60155	708-344-3030	344-5511
Huron Automatic Screw Co PO Box 610068	Port Huron	MI	48061	810-364-6636	364-6639
Web: www.huronauto.com					
Huron Inc 6554 Lakeshore Rd	Lexington	MI	48450	810-359-5344	359-7521
Hy-Level Industries Inc PO Box 368015	Cleveland	OH	44136	440-572-1540	572-5843
Web: www.hy-level.com					
Hyland Screw Machine Products 1900 Kuntz Rd	Dayton	OH	45404	937-233-8600	233-7067
Web: www.hylandmach.com					
Insaco Inc 1365 Canary Rd	Quakertown	PA	18951	215-536-3500	536-7750
TF: 800-497-4531 ■ *Web:* www.insaco.com					
Iseli Co 402 N Main St	Walworth	WI	53184	262-275-2108	275-6094
Web: www.iseli-co.com					
Jay Sons Screw Machine Products Inc					
197 Burritt St PO Box 674	Milldale	CT	06467	860-621-0141	621-0142
Web: www.jaysons.com					
Jessen Mfg Co Inc 1409 W Beardsley Ave PO Box 1729	Elkhart	IN	46515	574-295-3836	522-2962
Web: www.jessenmfg.com					
Jet Products Corp 9106 Balboa Ave	San Diego	CA	92123	858-278-8400	278-8768
Web: www.senioraerospace.com/Jet_Products					
John J Steuby Co 6002 N Lindbergh Blvd	Hazelwood	MO	63042	314-895-1000	895-9814
Web: www.steuby.com					
K & K Screw Products Inc 795 Kimberly Dr	Carol Stream	IL	60188	630-260-1735	260-4091
Web: www.kksp.com					
Kaddis Mfg Corp 1100 Beahan Rd PO Box 92985	Rochester	NY	14692	585-464-9000	464-0008
Web: www.kaddis.com					
Kerr Lakeside Inc 26841 Tungsten Rd	Euclid	OH	44132	216-261-2100	261-9798
TF: 800-487-5377 ■ *Web:* www.kerrlakeside.com					
Lakeshore Automatic Products Inc 1865 Industrial Park Dr	Grand Haven	MI	49417	616-846-5090	846-0790
TF: 800-851-6411 ■ *Web:* www.lakeshore-automatic.com					
LD Redmer Screw Products Inc 515 Thomas Dr	Bensenville	IL	60106	630-595-0404	595-0442
Lehr Precision Inc 11230 Deerfield Rd	Cincinnati	OH	45242	513-489-9800	489-2409
TF: 800-966-5060					
Lexington Machining 677 Buffalo Rd	Rochester	NY	14611	585-235-0880	235-7866
Liberty Brass Turning Co Inc 38-01 Queens Blvd	Long Island City	NY	11101	718-784-2911	784-2038
TF: 800-345-5939 ■ *Web:* www.libertybrass.com					
Lobaugh Rollin J Inc 240 Ryan Way	South San Francisco	CA	94080	650-583-9682	583-0445
Web: www.rjlobaugh.com					
LSC Co 100 Herrmann Rd	Pittsburgh	PA	15239	412-795-6400	795-6442
Web: www.lsccompany.com					
M & S Mfg Co Inc 550 E Main St	Hudson	MI	49247	517-448-2026	448-7200
Web: www.m-smanufacturing.com					
Maddox Foundry & Machine Works Inc 13370 SW 170th St	Archer	FL	32618	352-495-2121	495-3962
TF: 800-347-0789 ■ *Web:* www.maddoxfoundry.com					
MagStar Technologies 410 11th Ave S	Hopkins	MN	55343	952-935-6921	933-5803
TF: 800-473-8837 ■ *Web:* www.magstar.com					
Main Robert A & Sons Inc 555 Goffle Rd	Wyckoff	NJ	07481	201-447-3700	447-0302
Web: www.ramsco-inc.com					
Mantel Machine Products Inc					
W141 N9350 Fountain Blvd	Menomonee Falls	WI	53051	262-255-6780	255-9724
Web: www.mantelmachine.com					
Manth-Brownell Inc 1120 Fyler Rd	Kirkville	NY	13082	315-687-7263	687-6856
Web: www.manth.com					
MarathonNorco Aerospace Inc 8301 Imperial Dr	Waco	TX	76712	254-776-0650	776-6558
Web: www.mnaerospace.com					
Marox Corp 373 Whitney Ave	Holyoke	MA	01040	413-536-1300	534-1829
Web: www.marox.com					
Marshall Mfg Corp 611 Hawkins Dr PO Box 1729	Lewisburg	TN	37091	931-359-2573	359-5099
Web: www.marshallusa.com					
Marvel Screw Machine Products 58 Lafayette St	Waterbury	CT	06708	203-756-7058	754-0318
TF: 800-394-6767 ■ *Web:* www.marvelscrewmachine.com					
Meaden Screw Products Co 210 W 83rd St	Burr Ridge	IL	60527	630-655-0888	655-3012
Web: www.meaden.com					
Metric Machining Co 1425 S Vineyard Ave	Ontario	CA	91761	909-947-9222	923-1796
Web: www.metricorp.com					
Micro-Matics Corp 8050 Ranchers Rd	Minneapolis	MN	55432	763-780-2700	780-2706
Web: www.micro-matics.com					
Microbest Inc 670 Captain Neville Dr	Waterbury	CT	06705	203-597-0355	597-0655
Web: www.microbest.com					
Midwest Screw Products Inc 34700 Lakeland Blvd	Eastlake	OH	44095	440-951-2333	951-2336
Web: www.midwestllc.com					
Milford Automatics Inc 1553 Boston Post Rd	Milford	CT	06460	203-878-7465	874-4770
Mitchel & Scott Machine Co Inc 1841 Ludlow Ave	Indianapolis	IN	46201	317-639-5331	684-8245
Web: www.mitsco.com					
MKM Machine Tool Co Inc 100 Technology Way PO Box 2307	Jeffersonville	IN	47130	812-282-6627	280-4522
Web: www.mkmmachine.com					
Modern Machine & Engineering Corp 1707 Jefferson St NE	Minneapolis	MN	55413	612-781-3347	781-0030
TF: 800-218-8838					
Mount Vernon Screw Products Inc					
1020 N Canal St PO Box 250	Mount Vernon	IN	47620	812-838-5501	838-4038
TF: 800-880-5502 ■ *Web:* www.mvscrew.com					
MSK Precision Parts Inc 4100 NW 10th Ave	Fort Lauderdale	FL	33309	954-776-0770	776-3780
TF: 800-992-5018 ■ *Web:* www.mskprecision.com					
Multimatic Products Inc 390 Oser Ave	Hauppauge	NY	11788	631-231-1515	231-1625
TF: 800-767-7633 ■ *Web:* www.multimaticproducts.com					
National Technologies Inc 7641 S 10th St	Oak Creek	WI	53154	414-571-1000	571-1010
Web: www.nationaltechnologies.com					
New Castle Industries Inc PO Box 7359	New Castle	PA	16107	724-656-5600	656-5620
TF: 800-897-2830 ■ *Web:* www.newcas.com					
Northern Screw Machine Co Inc 300 Atwater St	Saint Paul	MN	55117	651-488-2568	488-6232
Northwest Swiss-Matic Inc 7600 32nd Ave N	Minneapolis	MN	55427	763-544-4222	544-6873
TF: 800-966-0178 ■ *Web:* www.nwswissmatic.com					
Ohio Screw Products Inc 818 Lowell St	Elyria	OH	44036	440-322-6341	322-0750
Web: www.ohioscrew.com					
P & C Quality Turned Components Inc PO Box 17009	Smithfield	RI	02917	401-231-7720	232-2370
Pacific Aerospace & Electronics Inc 434 Olds Station Rd	Wenatchee	WA	98801	509-667-9600	667-5311
Web: www.pacaero.com					
Pacific Rim Inc 4120 SE International Way	Portland	OR	97222	503-654-9543	654-8050
Web: www.pacificrimmfg.com					
Palladin Precision Products Inc 57 Bristol St	Waterbury	CT	06708	203-574-0246	756-9478
Web: www.palladin.com					
Peerless Screw Products Corp 286 Sandbank Rd	Cheshire	CT	06410	203-272-6413	271-2269

Company	City	State	Zip	Phone	Fax
PH Precision Products Corp 340 Commerce Way *Web:* www.phprecision.com	Pembroke	NH	03275	603-228-3321	228-3495
Phillips FC Inc 471 Washington St *Web:* www.fcphillips.com	Stoughton	MA	02072	781-344-9400	344-3440
Pohlman Inc 140 Long Rd *Web:* www.pohlman.com	Chesterfield	MO	63005	636-537-1909	537-1930
Precision Machine Works Inc 2024 Puyallup Ave *Web:* www.pmwinc.com	Tacoma	WA	98421	253-272-5119	272-6921
Precision Metal Products Co PO Box 1047 *Web:* www.pmpcscrewmach.com	Holland	MI	49422	616-392-3109	392-3100
Precision Plus Inc 840 Kootman Ln PO Box 168 *Web:* www.preplus.com	Elkhorn	WI	53121	262-743-1700	743-1701
Precision Screw Machine Products Inc PO Box 1944 *Web:* www.psmp.com	Biddeford	ME	04005	207-283-0121	283-4824
Precisionform Inc 148 W Airport Rd *TF:* 800-233-3821 ■ *Web:* www.precisionform.com	Lititz	PA	17543	717-560-7610	569-4792
Prime Screw Machine Products Inc 1012 Buckingham St PO Box 359 *Web:* www.primesmp.com	Watertown	CT	06795	860-274-6773	274-7939
Production Products Co 6176 E Molloy Rd *TF:* 800-800-6652 ■ *Web:* www.ppc-online.com	East Syracuse	NY	13057	315-431-7200	431-7201
Quality Control Corp 7315 W Wilson Ave *Web:* www.qccorp.com	Howard Heights	IL	60706	708-867-5400	887-5009
Rable Machine Inc 137 W Touby Ct *Web:* www.rablemachineinc.com	Mansfield	OH	44902	419-525-2255	525-2371
RB Royal Industries Inc 1350 S Hickory St PO Box 1168 *Web:* www.rbroyal.com	Fond du Lac	WI	54936	920-921-1550	921-4713
Redmer LD Screw Products Inc 515 Thomas Dr	Bensenville	IL	60106	630-595-0404	595-0442
Reino Tool & Mfg Co 3668 N Elston Ave	Chicago	IL	60618	773-588-5800	588-5810
Rima Mfg Co 3850 Munson Hwy *Web:* www.rimamfg.com	Hudson	MI	49247	517-448-8921	448-7142
Robert A Main & Sons Inc 555 Goffle Rd *Web:* www.ramsco-inc.com	Wyckoff	NJ	07481	201-447-3700	447-0302
Roberts Automatic Products Inc 880 Lake Dr *TF:* 800-879-9837 ■ *Web:* www.robertsautomatic.com	Chanhassen	MN	55317	952-949-1000	949-9240
Rollin J Lobaugh Inc 240 Ryan Way *Web:* www.rjlobaugh.com	South San Francisco	CA	94080	650-583-9682	583-0445
Roseland Metal Products Co 14753 Greenwood Rd *Web:* www.rosemet.com	Dolton	IL	60419	708-841-4400	841-6234
Royal Screw Machine Products Co PO Box 1325	Waterbury	CT	06721	203-755-6565	575-9001
RW Screw Products Inc PO Box 310	Massillon	OH	44648	330-837-9211	837-9223
Screwmatic Inc 925 W 1st St PO Box 518	Azusa	CA	91702	626-334-7831	334-6356
Selflock Screw Products Inc 114 Marcy St *Web:* www.selflockscrew.com	East Syracuse	NY	13057	315-437-3367	463-7131
Smithfield Mfg Inc 237 Kraft St *Web:* www.smithfieldmfg.com	Clarksville	TN	37040	931-552-4327	648-4460
Sorenson Engineering Inc 32032 Dunlap Blvd *Web:* www.sorensoneng.com	Yucaipa	CA	92399	909-795-2434	795-7190
Specialty Screw Machine Products Inc 1028 Dillerville Rd PO Box 4185 *Web:* www.ssmp-online.com	Lancaster	PA	17604	717-397-2867	397-5912
Speedring Inc PO Box 1588 *Web:* www.speedring.com	Cullman	AL	35056	256-737-5200	739-8298
Sperry Automatics Co Inc 1372 New Haven Rd PO Box 717 *Web:* www.sperryautomatics.com	Naugatuck	CT	06770	203-729-4589	729-7787
Stadco Corp 1931 N Broadway *Web:* www.stadco.com	Los Angeles	CA	90031	323-227-8888	222-0053
Standard Screw Products Co 1712 Langley Ave	Irvine	CA	92614	949-250-4727	250-4722
Standby Screw Machine Products Co Inc 1122 W Bagley Rd	Berea	OH	44017	440-243-8200	243-8310
Steuby John J Co 6002 N Lindbergh Blvd *Web:* www.steuby.com	Hazelwood	MO	63042	314-895-1000	895-9814
Superior Products Inc 3786 Ridge Rd *TF:* 877-483-2677 ■ *Web:* www.superiorprod.com	Cleveland	OH	44144	216-651-4031	651-4071
Supreme-Lake Mfg Inc 455 Atwater St PO Box 19 *Web:* www.supremelake.com	Plantsville	CT	06479	860-621-8911	628-9746
Supreme Machined Products Co Inc 18686 172nd Ave *Web:* www.supreme1.com	Spring Lake	MI	49456	616-842-6550	842-4481
Swift-Cor Precision Inc 344 W 157th St *Web:* www.swiftcor.com	Gardena	CA	90248	310-354-1200	323-2029
T & L Automatics Inc 770 Emerson St *Web:* www.tandlautomatics.com	Rochester	NY	14613	585-647-3717	647-1126
Talladega Machinery & Supply Co Inc 301 N Johnson Ave PO Box 736 *TF Cust Svc:* 800-289-8672 ■ *Web:* www.tmsco.com	Talladega	AL	35161	256-362-4124	761-2565
Tamer Industries 185 Riverside Ave *TF:* 800-882-6348 ■ *Web:* www.tamerind.com	Somerset	MA	02725	508-677-0900	677-2242
Tanko Screw Products Corp 515 Thomas Dr	Bensenville	IL	60106	630-787-0504	787-0507
Taylor Machine Products Inc 21300 Eureka Rd *Web:* www.taylormachine.com	Taylor	MI	48180	734-287-3550	287-4737
Taylor Metalworks Inc 3925 California Rd *Web:* www.taylorcnc.com	Orchard Park	NY	14127	716-662-3113	662-1096
Thorrez Industries Inc 4909 W Michigan Ave *Web:* www.thorrez.com	Jackson	MI	49201	517-750-3160	750-1792
Tomco Products Inc 51 Zima Park *Web:* www.tomcoquickcouplers.com	Spartanburg	SC	29305	864-574-7966	587-5608
Tompkins Products Inc 1040 W Grand Blvd *Web:* www.tompkinsproducts.com	Detroit	MI	48208	313-894-2222	894-2901
Torco Inc PO Box 4070 *Web:* www.torcoinc.com	Marietta	GA	30061	770-427-3704	426-9369
Trace-A-Matic Inc 1570 Commerce Ave *Web:* www.traceamatic.com	Brookfield	WI	53045	262-797-7300	797-9434
Trayer Products Inc 541 E Clinton St PO Box 88	Elmira	NY	14902	607-734-8124	732-1387
Triumph Components 203 N Johnson Ave *Web:* www.triumphgroup.com	El Cajon	CA	92020	619-440-2504	440-2509
Triumph Corp 2130 S Industrial Park Ave *Web:* www.triumphcorp.com/	Tempe	AZ	85282	480-967-3337	921-0446
V-S Industries Inc 900 S Chaddick Dr *Web:* www.v-s.com	Wheeling	IL	60090	847-520-1800	520-0269
Vallorbs Jewel Co 2599 Old Philadelphia Pike	Bird-in-Hand	PA	17505	717-392-3978	392-8947
Vanamatic Co 701 Ambrose Dr *Web:* www.vanamatic.com	Delphos	OH	45833	419-692-6085	692-3260
Waltco Engineering Co 401 W Redondo Beach Blvd **Fax:* Sales	Gardena	CA	90248	310-538-0321	516-6456*
Ward Ashley F Inc 7490 Easy St *Web:* www.ashleyward.com	Mason	OH	45040	513-398-1414	398-1125
Wells Mfg Co 2100 W Lake Shore Dr *TF:* 800-227-6455 ■ *Web:* www.wellsmanufacturing.com	Woodstock	IL	60098	815-338-3900	338-3950
Winslow Automatic Inc 23 St Clair Ave	New Britain	CT	06051	860-225-6321	224-1733
Xaloy Inc 102 Xaloy Way *TF:* 800-227-7357 ■ *Web:* www.xaloy.com	Pulaski	VA	24301	540-980-7560	980-5670

625 PREPARATORY SCHOOLS - BOARDING

SEE ALSO Preparatory Schools - Non-boarding p. 2137

Schools listed here are independent, college-preparatory schools that provide housing facilities for students and teachers. All are members of The Association of Boarding Schools (TABS), and many are considered to be among the top prep schools in the United States.

School	City	State	Zip	Phone	Fax
Academie Ste Cecile International School 925 Cousineau Rd *Web:* www.stececile.ca	Windsor	ON	N9G1V8	519-969-1291	969-7953
Admiral Farragut Academy 501 Park St N *Web:* www.farragut.org	Saint Petersburg	FL	33710	727-384-5500	347-5160
Albert College 160 Dundas St W *Web:* www.albertc.on.ca	Belleville	ON	K8P1A6	613-968-5726	968-9651
American Boychoir School 19 Lambert Dr *Web:* www.americanboychoir.org	Princeton	NJ	08540	609-924-5858	924-5812
Andrews School 38588 Mentor Ave *TF:* 800-753-4683 ■ *Web:* www.andrews-school.org	Willoughby	OH	44094	440-942-3606	954-5020
Annie Wright School 827 N Tacoma Ave *TF:* 800-847-1582 ■ *Web:* www.aw.org	Tacoma	WA	98403	253-272-2216	572-3616
Appleby College 540 Lakeshore Rd W *Web:* www.appleby.on.ca	Oakville	ON	L6K3P1	905-845-4681	845-9505
Army & Navy Academy 2605 Carlsbad Blvd PO Box 3000 *TF:* 888-762-2338 ■ *Web:* www.armyandnavyacademy.org	Carlsbad	CA	92018	760-729-2385	434-5948
Ashbury College 362 Mariposa Ave *Web:* www.ashbury.on.ca	Ottawa	ON	K1M0T3	613-749-5954	749-9724
Asheville School 360 Asheville School Rd *Web:* www.ashevilleschool.org	Asheville	NC	28806	828-254-6345	252-8666
Athenian School 2100 Mount Diablo Scenic Blvd *Web:* www.athenian.org	Danville	CA	94506	925-837-5375	831-1120
Avon Old Farms School 500 Old Farms Rd *TF:* 800-464-2866 ■ *Web:* www.avonoldfarms.com	Avon	CT	06001	860-404-4100	675-6051
Balmoral Hall School 630 Westminster Ave *Web:* www.balmoralhall.com	Winnipeg	MB	R3C3S1	204-784-1600	774-5534
Baylor School 177 Baylor School Rd *TF:* 800-222-9567 ■ *Web:* www.baylorschool.org	Chattanooga	TN	37405	423-267-5902	757-2525
Bement School 94 Main St *Web:* www.bement.org	Deerfield	MA	01342	413-774-7061	774-7863
Ben Lippen School 7401 Monticello Rd *TF:* 888-236-5476 ■ *Web:* www.benlippen.com	Columbia	SC	29203	803-786-7200	744-1387
Berkshire School 245 N Undermountain Rd *Web:* www.berkshireschool.org	Sheffield	MA	01257	413-229-8511	229-1016
Bethany Hills School 727 Bethany Hills Rd Box 10 *Web:* www.bethanyhills.on.ca	Bethany	ON	L0A1A0	705-277-2866	277-1279
Bishop Strachan School 298 Lonsdale Rd *Web:* www.bss.on.ca	Toronto	ON	M4V1X2	416-483-4325	481-5632
Bishop's College School 80 Moulton Hill Rd Box 5001 *Web:* www.bishopscollegeschool.com	Lennoxville	QC	J1M1Z8	819-566-0227	822-8917
Blair Academy 2 Park St PO Box 600 *Web:* www.blair.edu	Blairstown	NJ	07825	908-362-2024	362-7975
Blue Ridge School Rt 627 *Web:* www.blueridgeschool.com	Saint George	VA	22935	434-985-2811	985-7215
Bolles School 7400 San Jose Blvd *Web:* www.bolles.org	Jacksonville	FL	32217	904-733-5952	739-9929
Brandon Hall School 1701 Brandon Hall Dr *Web:* www.brandonhall.org	Atlanta	GA	30350	770-394-8177	804-8821
Branksome Hall 10 Elm Ave *Web:* www.branksome.on.ca	Toronto	ON	M4W1N4	416-920-9741	920-5390
Brehm Preparatory School 1245 E Grand Ave *Web:* www.brehm.org	Carbondale	IL	62901	618-457-0371	549-1248
Brenau Academy 500 Washingtron St SE *Web:* www.brenauacademy.org	Gainesville	GA	30501	770-534-6140	534-6298
Brentwood College School 2735 Mt Baker Rd *Web:* www.brentwood.bc.ca	Mill Bay	BC	V0R2P1	250-743-5521	743-2911
Brewster Academy 80 Academy Dr *TF:* 800-842-9961 ■ *Web:* www.brewsteracademy.org	Wolfeboro	NH	03894	603-569-7200	569-7272
Bridgton Academy PO Box 292 *Web:* www.bridgtonacademy.org	North Bridgton	ME	04057	207-647-3322	647-8513
Brooks School 1160 Great Pond Rd *Web:* www.brooksschool.org	North Andover	MA	01845	978-686-6101	725-6298
Cambridge School of Weston 45 Georgian Rd *Web:* www.csw.org	Weston	MA	02493	781-642-8650	899-3870
Canterbury School 105 Aspetuck Ave *Web:* www.cbury.org	New Milford	CT	06776	860-210-3800	350-1120
Canyonville Christian Academy 250 E 1st St PO Box 1100 *TF:* 888-222-6379 ■ *Web:* www.canyonville.net	Canyonville	OR	97417	541-839-4401	839-6228
Cardigan Mountain School 62 Alumni Dr *Web:* www.cardigan.org	Canaan	NH	03741	603-523-3510	523-3565
Carson Long Military Institute 200 N Carlisle St PO Box 98 *Web:* www.carsonlong.org	New Bloomfield	PA	17068	717-582-2121	582-8763
Cate School 1960 Cate Mesa Rd *Web:* www.cate.org	Carpinteria	CA	93013	805-684-4127	684-8940
CFS, The School at Church Farm PO Box 2000 *Web:* www.gocfs.net	Paoli	PA	19301	610-363-7500	280-6746
Chaminade College Preparatory School 425 S Lindbergh Blvd *TF:* 877-378-6847 ■ *Web:* www.chaminademo.com	Saint Louis	MO	63131	314-993-4400	993-5732
Chapel Hill-Chauncy Hall School 785 Beaver St *Web:* www.chch.org	Waltham	MA	02452	781-894-2644	894-5205
Chatham Hall 800 Chatham Hall Cir *Web:* www.chathamhall.org	Chatham	VA	24531	434-432-2941	432-2405
Cheshire Academy 10 Main St *Web:* www.cheshireacademy.org	Cheshire	CT	06410	203-272-5396	250-7209
Choate Rosemary Hall 333 Christian St *Web:* www.choate.edu	Wallingford	CT	06492	203-697-2239	697-2629
Christ School 500 Christ School Rd *TF:* 800-422-3212 ■ *Web:* www.christschool.org	Arden	NC	28704	828-684-6232	684-4869
Christchurch School 49 Seahorse Ln *TF:* 800-296-2306 ■ *Web:* www.christchurchschool.org	Christchurch	VA	23031	804-758-2306	758-0721
Colorado Rocky Mountain School 1493 County Rd 106 *Web:* www.crms.org	Carbondale	CO	81623	970-963-2562	963-9865
Concord Academy 166 Main St *Web:* www.concordacademy.org	Concord	MA	01742	978-402-2200	402-2210
Cotter High School 1115 W Broadway *Web:* www.winonacotter.org	Winona	MN	55987	507-453-5000	453-5406
Cranbrook Schools 39221 Woodward Ave *Web:* www.schools.cranbrook.edu	Bloomfield Hills	MI	48304	248-645-3610	645-3025
Crested Butte Academy 505 Whiterock Ave PO Box 1180 *TF:* 888-633-0222 ■ *Web:* www.crestedbutteacademy.com	Crested Butte	CO	81224	970-349-1805	349-0997
Culver Academies 1300 Academy Rd *TF:* 800-528-5837 ■ *Web:* www.culver.org	Culver	IN	46511	574-842-7000	842-8066
Cushing Academy 39 School St PO Box 8000 *Web:* www.cushing.org	Ashburnham	MA	01430	978-827-7000	827-6253

School	City	State	Zip	Phone	Fax
Dana Hall School 45 Dana Rd PO Box 9010	Wellesley	MA	02482	781-235-3010	235-0577
Web: www.danahall.org					
Darlington School 1014 Cave Spring Rd	Rome	GA	30161	706-235-6051	232-3600
TF: 800-368-4437 ■ *Web:* www.darlingtonschool.org					
Darrow School 110 Darrow Rd	New Lebanon	NY	12125	518-794-6000	794-7065
Web: www.darrowschool.org					
Deerfield Academy 7 Boyden Ln	Deerfield	MA	01342	413-772-0241	772-1100
Web: www.deerfield.edu					
Devereux Glenholme School 81 Sabbaday Ln	Washington	CT	06793	860-868-7377	868-7894
Web: www.theglenholmeschool.org					
Dublin School 18 Lehmann Way PO Box 522	Dublin	NH	03444	603-563-8584	563-8671
Web: www.dublinschool.org					
Dunn School 2555 Hwy 154 PO Box 98	Los Olivos	CA	93441	805-688-6471	686-2078
TF: 800-287-9197 ■ *Web:* www.dunnschool.org					
Eagle Hill School 242 Old Petersham Rd PO Box 116	Hardwick	MA	01037	413-477-6000	477-6837
Web: www.eaglehillschool.com					
Eaglebrook School 271 Pine Nook Rd	Deerfield	MA	01342	413-774-9111	774-9119
Web: www.eaglebrook.org					
Emma Willard School 285 Pawling Ave	Troy	NY	12180	518-833-1300	833-1805
Web: www.emmawillard.org					
Episcopal High School 1200 N Quaker Ln	Alexandria	VA	22302	703-933-4062	933-3016
TF: 877-933-4347 ■ *Web:* www.episcopalhighschool.org					
Ethel Walker School 230 Bushy Hill Rd	Simsbury	CT	06070	860-408-4200	408-4201
Web: www.ethelwalker.org					
Fay School 48 Main St	Southborough	MA	01772	508-485-0100	481-7872
TF: 800-933-2925 ■ *Web:* www.fayschool.org					
Fessenden School 250 Waltham St	West Newton	MA	02465	617-630-2300	630-2303
Web: www.fessenden.org					
Flintridge Sacred Heart Academy 440 Saint Katherine Dr	La Canada	CA	91011	626-685-8333	685-8520*
**Fax:* Admissions ■ *Web:* www.fsha.org					
Forman School 12 Norfolk Rd PO Box 80	Litchfield	CT	06759	860-567-1802	567-3501
Web: www.formanschool.org					
Fountain Valley School of Colorado					
6155 Fountain Valley School Rd	Colorado Springs	CO	80911	719-390-7035	390-7762
Web: www.fvs.edu					
Fox River Country Day School 1600 Dundee Ave	Elgin	IL	60120	847-888-7910	888-7947
Web: www.frcds.org					
Foxcroft School PO Box 5555	Middleburg	VA	20118	540-687-5555	687-3627
TF: 800-858-2364 ■ *Web:* www.foxcroft.org					
Fryeburg Academy 745 Main St	Fryeburg	ME	04037	207-935-2013	935-4292
TF: 877-935-2013 ■ *Web:* www.fryeburgacademy.org					
Garrison Forest School 300 Garrison Forest Rd	Owings Mills	MD	21117	410-363-1500	363-6841
Web: www.gfs.org					
George School 1690 Newtown-Langhorne Rd	Newtown	PA	18940	215-579-6547	579-6549
Web: www.georgeschool.org					
Georgetown Preparatory School 10900 Rockville Pike	North Bethesda	MD	20852	301-493-5000	493-6128
Web: www.gprep.org					
Gilmour Academy 34001 Cedar Rd	Gates Mills	OH	44040	440-442-1104	473-8010
Web: www.gilmour.org					
Girard College 2101 S College Ave Suite 311	Philadelphia	PA	19121	215-787-2600	787-4457
TF: 877-344-7273 ■ *Web:* www.girardcollege.com					
Gould Academy PO Box 860	Bethel	ME	04217	207-824-7777	824-2926
Web: www.gouldacademy.org					
Governor Dummer Academy 1 Elm St	Byfield	MA	01922	978-499-3120	462-1278
Web: www.thegovernorsacademy.org					
Gow School 2491 Emery Rd PO Box 85	South Wales	NY	14139	716-652-3450	652-3457
Web: www.gow.org					
Grand River Academy 3042 College St PO Box 222	Austinburg	OH	44010	440-275-2811	275-1825
Web: www.grandriver.org					
Greenwood School 14 Greenwood Ln	Putney	VT	05346	802-387-4545	387-5396
Web: www.thegreenwoodschool.org					
Grenville Christian College PO Box 610	Brockville	ON	K6V5V8	613-345-5521	345-3826
Web: www.grenvillecc.ca					
Grier School Rt 453 PO Box 308	Tyrone	PA	16686	814-684-3000	684-2177
Web: www.grier.org					
Groton School 282 Farmers Row Box 991	Groton	MA	01450	978-448-7510	448-9623
Web: www.groton.org					
Gunnery The 99 Green Hill Rd	Washington	CT	06793	860-868-7334	868-1614
Web: www.gunnery.org					
Hackley School 293 Benedict Ave	Tarrytown	NY	10591	914-631-0128	
Web: www.hackleyschool.org					
Hampshire Country School 28 Patey Cir	Rindge	NH	03461	603-899-3325	899-6521
Web: www.hampshirecountryschool.org					
Happy Valley School PO Box 850	Ojai	CA	93024	805-646-4343	464-6431
TF: 800-900-0437 ■ *Web:* www.hvalley.org					
Hargrave Military Academy 200 Military Dr	Chatham	VA	24531	434-432-2481	432-3129
TF: 800-432-2480 ■ *Web:* www.hargrave.edu					
Harvey School 260 Jay St	Katonah	NY	10536	914-232-3161	232-6034
Web: www.harveyschool.org					
Havergal College 1451 Avenue Rd	Toronto	ON	M5N2H9	416-483-3519	483-6796
Web: www.havergal.on.ca					
Hawaii Preparatory Academy 65-1692 Kohala Mountain Rd	Kamuela	HI	96743	808-881-4007	881-4045
Web: www.hpa.edu					
Hebron Academy Rt 119 PO Box 309	Hebron	ME	04238	207-966-2100	966-1111
TF: 888-432-7664 ■ *Web:* www.hebronacademy.org					
High Mowing School 222 Isaac Frye Hwy	Wilton	NH	03086	603-654-2391	654-6588
Web: www.highmowing.org					
Hill School 717 E High St	Pottstown	PA	19464	610-326-1000	705-1753
TF: 888-445-5150 ■ *Web:* www.thehill.org					
Hillside School 404 Robin Hill Rd	Marlborough	MA	01752	508-485-2824	485-4420
Web: www.hillsideschool.net					
Hockaday School 11600 Welch Rd	Dallas	TX	75229	214-363-6311	265-1649
Web: www.hockaday.org					
Holderness School Chapel Ln PO Box 1879	Plymouth	NH	03264	603-536-1747	536-2125
Web: www.holderness.org					
Hoosac School PO Box 9	Hoosick	NY	12089	518-686-7331	686-3370
Web: www.hoosac.com					
Hotchkiss School 11 Interlaken Rd PO Box 800	Lakeville	CT	06039	860-435-3102	435-0042
Web: www.hotchkiss.org					
Houghton Academy 9790 Thayer St	Houghton	NY	14744	585-567-8115	567-8048
Web: www.houghtonacademy.org					
Howe Military School PO Box 240	Howe	IN	46746	260-562-2131	562-3678
TF: 888-462-4693 ■ *Web:* www.howemilitary.com					
Hun School of Princeton 176 Edgerstoune Rd	Princeton	NJ	08540	609-921-7600	279-9398
Web: www.hunschool.org					
Hyde School 150 Rt 169 PO Box 237	Woodstock	CT	06281	860-963-4736	928-0612
Web: www.hyde.edu					
Hyde School 616 High St	Bath	ME	04530	207-443-5584	442-9346
Web: www.hyde.edu					
Idyllwild Arts Academy 52500 Temecula Rd PO Box 38	Idyllwild	CA	92549	951-659-2171	659-2058
Web: www.idyllwildarts.org					
Incarnate Word High School 727 E Hildebrand Ave	San Antonio	TX	78212	210-829-3100	829-3101
Web: www.incarnatewordhs.org					
Indian Mountain School 211 Indian Mountain Rd	Lakeville	CT	06039	860-435-0871	435-0641
Web: www.indianmountain.org					
Indian Springs School 190 Woodward Dr	Indian Springs	AL	35124	205-988-3350	988-3797
TF: 888-843-3477 ■ *Web:* www.indiansprings.org					

School	City	State	Zip	Phone	Fax
Kent School PO Box 2006	Kent	CT	06757	860-927-6111	927-6109
TF: 800-538-5368 ■ *Web:* www.kent-school.edu					
Kents Hill School Rt 17 PO Box 257	Kents Hill	ME	04349	207-685-4914	685-9529
Web: www.kentshill.org					
Kildonan School 425 Morse Hill Rd	Amenia	NY	12501	845-373-8111	373-2004
Web: www.kildonan.org					
Kimball Union Academy 57 Main St	Meriden	NH	03770	603-469-2000	469-2040
Web: www.kua.org					
Kiski School 1888 Brett Ln	Saltsburg	PA	15681	724-639-3586	639-8596
TF: 877-547-5448 ■ *Web:* www.kiski.org					
Knox School 541 Long Beach Rd	Saint James	NY	11780	631-686-1600	686-1651
Web: www.knoxschool.org					
La Lumiere School 6801 N Wilhelm Rd	La Porte	IN	46350	219-326-7450	325-3185
Web: www.lalumiere.org					
Lake Forest Academy 1500 W Kennedy Rd	Lake Forest	IL	60045	847-234-3210	615-3202
Web: www.lfanet.org					
Lakefield College School 4391 County Rd 29	Lakefield	ON	K0L2H0	705-652-3324	652-6320
Web: www.lakefieldcs.on.ca					
Landmark School 429 Hale St PO Box 227	Prides Crossing	MA	01965	978-236-3010	927-7268
Web: www.landmarkschool.org					
Lawrence Academy Powderhouse Rd PO Box 992	Groton	MA	01450	978-448-6535	448-9208
Web: www.lacademy.edu					
Lawrenceville School 2500 Main St PO Box 6008	Lawrenceville	NJ	08648	609-896-0400	895-2217
TF: 800-735-2030 ■ *Web:* www.lawrenceville.org					
Lee Academy 26 Winn Rd	Mee	ME	04455	207-738-2255	738-3257
TF: 888-433-2852 ■ *Web:* www.leeacademy.lee.me.us					
Leelanau School 1 Old Homestead Rd	Glen Arbor	MI	49636	231-334-5800	334-5898
TF: 800-533-5262 ■ *Web:* www.leelanau.org					
Linden Hall School for Girls 212 E Main St	Lititz	PA	17543	717-626-8512	627-1384
TF: 800-258-5778 ■ *Web:* www.lindenhall.org					
Linden Hill School 154 S Mountain Rd	Northfield	MA	01360	413-498-2906	498-2908
TF: 888-254-6336 ■ *Web:* www.lindenhs.org					
Linsly School 60 Knox Ln	Wheeling	WV	26003	304-233-1436	234-4614
Web: www.linsly.org					
Loomis Chaffee School 4 Batchelder Rd	Windsor	CT	06095	860-687-6400	298-8756
Web: www.loomischaffee.org					
Lowell Whiteman School 42605 RCR 36	Steamboat Springs	CO	80487	970-879-1350	879-0506
Web: www.lws.edu					
MacDuffie School 1 Ames Hill Dr	Springfield	MA	01105	413-734-4971	734-6693
Web: www.macduffie.com					
Madeira School 8328 Georgetown Pike	McLean	VA	22102	703-556-8200	
Web: www.madeira.org					
Maine Central Institute 125 S Main St	Pittsfield	ME	04967	207-487-3355	487-3512
Web: www.mci-school.org					
Marianapolis Preparatory School Rt 200 PO Box 304	Thompson	CT	06277	860-923-9565	923-3730
Web: www.marianapolis.org					
Marvelwood School 476 Skiff Mountain Rd PO Box 3001	Kent	CT	06757	860-927-0047	927-0021
TF: 800-440-9107 ■ *Web:* www.themarvelwoodschool.net					
Massanutten Military Academy 614 S Main St	Woodstock	VA	22664	540-459-2167	459-5421
Web: www.militaryschool.com					
Masters School The 49 Clinton Ave	Dobbs Ferry	NY	10522	914-479-6400	693-1230
Web: www.themastersschool.com					
Maur Hill-Mount Academy 1000 Green St	Atchison	KS	66002	913-367-5482	367-5096
Web: www.maurhillmountacademy.com					
McCallie School 500 Dodds Ave	Chattanooga	TN	37404	423-624-8300	493-5426
TF: 800-234-2163 ■ *Web:* www.mccallie.org					
Mercersburg Academy 300 E Seminary St	Mercersburg	PA	17236	717-328-6173	328-6319
Web: www.mercersburg.edu					
Mid-Pacific Institute 2445 Kaala St	Honolulu	HI	96822	808-973-5000	973-5099
Web: www.midpac.edu					
Middlesex School 1400 Lowell Rd	Concord	MA	01742	978-369-2550	402-1400
Web: www.mxschool.edu					
Midland School 5100 Figueroa Mountain Rd PO Box 8	Los Olivos	CA	93441	805-688-5114	686-2470
Web: www.midland-school.org					
Millbrook School 131 School Rd	Millbrook	NY	12545	845-677-8261	677-1265
Web: www.millbrook.org					
Miller School 1000 Samuel Miller Loop	Charlottesville	VA	22903	434-823-4805	823-6617
Web: www.millerschool.org					
Milton Academy 170 Centre St	Milton	MA	02186	617-898-1798	898-1701
Web: www.milton.edu					
Milton Hershey School PO Box 830	Hershey	PA	17033	717-520-2100	520-2117
TF: 800-322-3248 ■ *Web:* www.mhs-pa.org					
Miss Hall's School 492 Holmes Rd	Pittsfield	MA	01201	413-443-6401	448-2994
Web: www.misshalls.org					
Miss Porter's School 60 Main St	Farmington	CT	06032	860-409-3530	409-3531
Web: www.missporters.org					
Monte Vista Christian School 2 School Way	Watsonville	CA	95076	831-722-8178	722-6003
Web: www.mvcs.org					
Montverde Academy 17235 7th St	Montverde	FL	34756	407-469-2561	469-3711
Web: www.montverde.org					
National Sports Academy 821 Mirror Lake Dr	Lake Placid	NY	12946	518-523-3460	523-3488
Web: www.nationalsportsacademy.com					
New Hampton School 70 Main St PO Box 579	New Hampton	NH	03256	603-677-3400	677-3481
Web: www.newhampton.org					
New York Military Academy 78 Academy Ave	Cornwall-on-Hudson	NY	12520	845-534-3710	534-7699
TF: 888-275-6962 ■ *Web:* www.nyma.org					
North Country School PO Box 187	Lake Placid	NY	12946	518-523-9329	523-4858
Web: www.nct.org					
Northfield Mount Hermon School 206 Main St	Northfield	MA	01360	413-498-3227	498-3152
Web: www.nmhschool.org					
Northwest School 1415 Summit Ave	Seattle	WA	98122	206-682-7309	328-1776
Web: www.northwestschool.org					
Northwood School PO Box 1070	Lake Placid	NY	12946	518-523-3382	523-2073
Web: www.northwoodschool.com					
Oak Grove School 220 W Lomita Ave	Ojai	CA	93023	805-646-8236	646-6509
Web: www.oakgroveschool.com					
Oak Hill Academy 2635 Oak Hill Rd	Mouth of Wilson	VA	24363	276-579-2619	579-4722
Web: www.oak-hill.net					
Oakwood Friends School 22 Spackenkill Rd	Poughkeepsie	NY	12603	845-462-4200	462-4251
TF: 800-843-3341 ■ *Web:* www.oakwoodfriends.org					
Ojai Valley School 723 El Paseo Rd	Ojai	CA	93023	805-646-1423	646-0362
TF: 800-433-4687 ■ *Web:* www.ovs.org					
Oldfields School 1500 Glencoe Rd	Glencoe	MD	21152	410-472-4800	472-6839
Web: www.oldfieldsschool.org					
Olney Friends School 61830 Sandy Ridge Rd	Barnesville	OH	43713	740-425-3655	425-3202
TF: 800-303-4291 ■ *Web:* www.olneyfriends.org					
Oregon Episcopal School 6300 SW Nicol Rd	Portland	OR	97223	503-246-7771	768-3140
Web: www.oes.edu					
Orme School HC 63 Box 3040	Mayer	AZ	86333	928-632-7601	632-7601
Web: www.ormeschool.org					
Oxford Academy 1393 Boston Post Rd	Westbrook	CT	06498	860-399-6247	399-6805
Web: www.oxfordacademy.net					
Peddie School S Main St PO Box A	Hightstown	NJ	08520	609-490-7500	944-7901
Web: www.peddie.org					
Pennington School 112 W Delaware Ave	Pennington	NJ	08534	609-737-1838	730-1405
Web: www.pennington.org					

Phone Fax

Perkiomen School 200 Seminary St PO Box 130 .... Pennsburg PA 18073 215-679-9511 679-1146
Web: www.perkiomen.org
Phelps School 583 Sugartown Rd .... Malvern PA 19355 610-644-1754 644-6679
Web: www.thephelpsschool.org
Phillips Academy 180 Main St .... Andover MA 01810 978-749-4000 749-4068
Web: www.andover.edu
Phillips Exeter Academy 20 Main St .... Exeter NH 03833 603-772-4311 777-4399
Web: www.exeter.edu
Pickering College 16945 Bayview Ave .... Newmarket ON L3Y4X2 905-895-1700 895-9076
Web: www.pickeringcollege.on.ca
Piney Woods School 5096 Hwy 49 S PO Box 69 .... Piney Woods MS 39148 601-845-2214 845-2604
Web: www.pineywoods.org
Pomfret School 398 Pomfret St PO Box 128 .... Pomfret CT 06258 860-963-6100 963-2042
Web: www.pomfretschool.org
Portsmouth Abbey School 285 Cory's Ln .... Portsmouth RI 02871 401-683-2000 683-6766
Web: www.portsmouthabbey.org
Proctor Academy 204 Main St PO Box 500 .... Andover NH 03216 603-735-6000 735-6284
Web: proctoracademy.org
Purnell School 51 Pottersville Rd PO Box 500 .... Pottersville NJ 07979 908-439-2154 439-4088
Web: www.purnell.org
Putney School 418 Houghton Brook Rd .... Putney VT 05346 802-387-5566 387-6278
Web: www.putneyschool.org
Rabun Gap-Nacoochee School 339 Nacoochee Dr .... Rabun Gap GA 30568 706-746-7467 746-2594
TF: 800-543-7467 ■ *Web:* www.rabungap.org
Randolph-Macon Academy 200 Academy Dr .... Front Royal VA 22630 540-636-5200 636-5419
TF: 800-272-1172 ■ *Web:* www.rma.edu
Rectory School 528 Pomfret St PO Box 68 .... Pomfret CT 06258 860-928-7759 928-4961
Web: www.rectoryschool.org
Ridley College 2 Ridley Rd PO Box 3013 .... Saint Catharines ON L2R7C3 905-684-1889 684-8875
Web: www.ridley.on.ca
Riverside Military Academy 2001 Riverside Dr .... Gainesville GA 30501 770-532-6251 291-3364*
*Fax Area Code: 678 ■ *TF:* 800-462-2338 ■ *Web:* www.cadet.com
Rock Point School 1 Rock Point Rd .... Burlington VT 05408 802-863-1104 863-6628
Web: www.rockpoint.org
Rosseau Lake College 1967 Bright St .... Rosseau ON P0C1J0 705-732-4351 732-6319
Web: www.rosseaulakecollege.com
Rumsey Hall School 201 Romford Rd .... Washington Depot CT 06794 860-868-0535 868-7907
Web: www.rumseyhall.org
Saint Andrew's College 15800 Yonge St .... Aurora ON L4G3H7 905-727-3178 727-9032
TF: 877-378-1899 ■ *Web:* www.sac.on.ca
Saint Andrew's School 350 Noxontown Rd .... Middletown DE 19709 302-285-4231 378-7120
Web: www.standrews-de.org
Saint Andrew's School 3900 Jog Rd .... Boca Raton FL 33434 561-226-0214 487-4655
Web: www.saintandrewsschool.net
Saint Andrew's School 63 Federal Rd .... Barrington RI 02806 401-246-1230 246-0510
Web: www.standrews-ri.org
Saint Andrew's-Sewanee School 290 Quintard Rd .... Sewanee TN 37375 931-598-5651 598-0039
Web: www.sasweb.org
Saint Anne's-Belfield School 2132 Ivy Rd .... Charlottesville VA 22903 434-296-5106 979-1486
Web: www.stab.org
Saint Anthony's Catholic High School 3200 McCullough Ave .... San Antonio TX 78212 210-832-5600 832-5633
Web: www.sachs.org
Saint Bernard Preparatory School 1600 Saint Bernard Dr SE .... Cullman AL 35055 256-739-6682 734-2925
TF: 800-722-0999 ■ *Web:* www.stbernardprep.com
Saint Catherine's School 6001 Grove Ave .... Richmond VA 23226 804-288-2804 285-8169
TF: 800-648-4982 ■ *Web:* www.st.catherines.org
Saint George's School 3851 W 29th Ave .... Vancouver BC V6S1T6 604-224-1304 224-5820
Web: www.stgeorges.bc.ca
Saint George's School 372 Purgatory Rd .... Middletown RI 02842 401-842-6600 842-6600
Web: www.stgeorges.edu
Saint James School 17641 College Rd .... Saint James MD 21781 301-733-9330 739-1310
Web: www.stjames.edu
Saint John's Military School 110 E Otis Ave PO Box 5020 .... Salina KS 67402 785-823-7231 823-7236
TF: 866-704-5294 ■ *Web:* www.sjms.org
Saint John's Northwestern Military Academy 1101 N Genesee St .... Delafield WI 53018 262-646-7115 646-7128
TF: 800-752-2338 ■ *Web:* www.sjnma.org
Saint John's Preparatory School
1857 Watertower Rd PO Box 4000 .... Collegeville MN 56321 320-363-3321 363-3322
TF: 800-525-7737 ■ *Web:* www.sjprep.net
Saint John's-Ravenscourt School 400 South Dr .... Winnipeg MB R3T3K5 204-477-2400 477-2429
TF: 800-437-0040 ■ *Web:* www.sjr.mb.ca
Saint Johnsbury Academy 1000 Main St PO Box 906 .... Saint Johnsbury VT 05819 802-751-2130 748-5463
Web: www.stjohnsburyacademy.org
Saint Margaret's School 444 Water Ln PO Box 158 .... Tappahannock VA 22560 804-443-3357 443-6781
Web: www.sms.org
Saint Mark's School 25 Marlborough Rd .... Southborough MA 01772 508-786-6000 786-6120
Web: www.stmarksschool.org
Saint Mary's School 900 Hillsborough St .... Raleigh NC 27603 919-424-4100 424-4122
TF: 800-948-2557 ■ *Web:* www.saint-marys.edu
Saint Michael's University School 3400 Richmond Rd .... Victoria BC V8P4P5 250-592-2411 592-2812
TF: 800-661-5199 ■ *Web:* www.smus.bc.ca
Saint Paul's Preparatory Academy PO Box 32650 .... Phoenix AZ 85064 602-956-9090 956-3018
Web: www.stpaulsacademy.com
Saint Paul's School 325 Pleasant St .... Concord NH 03301 603-229-4600 229-4772
Web: www.sps.edu
Saint Stanislaus College 304 S Beach Blvd .... Bay Saint Louis MS 39520 228-467-9057 466-2972
TF: 800-517-6257 ■ *Web:* www.ststan.com
Saint Stephen's Episcopal School 2900 Bunny Run .... Austin TX 78746 512-327-1213 327-6771
TF: 888-377-7937 ■ *Web:* www.sstx.org
Saint Thomas Choir School 202 W 58th St .... New York NY 10019 212-247-3311 247-3393
Web: www.choirschool.org
Saint Thomas More School 45 Cottage Rd .... Oakdale CT 06370 860-823-3861 823-3863
Web: www.stthomasmoreschool.com
Saint Timothy's School 8400 Greenspring Ave .... Stevenson MD 21153 410-486-7400 486-1167
TF: 800-467-8846 ■ *Web:* www.sttims-school.org
Salem Academy 500 Salem Ave .... Winston-Salem NC 27101 336-721-2643 917-5340
TF: 877-407-2536 ■ *Web:* www.salemacademy.org
Salisbury School 251 Canaan Rd .... Salisbury CT 06068 860-435-5732 435-5750
Web: www.salisburyschool.org
San Domenico School 1500 Butterfield Rd .... San Anselmo CA 94960 415-258-1905 258-1906
Web: www.sandomenico.org
San Marcos Baptist Academy 2801 Ranch Rd 12 .... San Marcos TX 78666 512-753-8000 753-8031
TF: 800-428-5120 ■ *Web:* www.smba.org
Sandy Spring Friends School 16923 Norwood Rd .... Sandy Spring MD 20860 301-774-7455 924-1115
Web: www.ssfs.org
Santa Catalina School 1500 Mark Thomas Dr .... Monterey CA 93940 831-655-9300 655-7535
Web: www.santacatalina.org
Scattergood Friends School 1951 Delta Ave .... West Branch IA 52358 319-643-7628 643-7638
TF: 888-737-4636 ■ *Web:* www.scattergood.org
Sedbergh School 810 Cote Azelie .... Montebello QC J0V1L0 819-423-5523 423-5769
Web: www.sedbergh.com
Shady Side Academy 423 Fox Chapel Rd .... Pittsburgh PA 15238 412-968-3000 968-3213
Web: www.shadysideacademy.org
Shattuck-Saint Mary's School 1000 Shumway Ave PO Box 218 .... Faribault MN 55021 507-333-1616 333-1661
TF: 800-421-2724 ■ *Web:* www.s-sm.org
Shawnigan Lake School 1975 Renfrew Rd .... Shawnigan Lake BC V0R2W1 250-743-6207 743-6280
Web: www.sls.bc.ca

Phone Fax

Solebury School 6832 Phillips Mill Rd .... New Hope PA 18938 215-862-5261 862-3366
Web: www.solebury.org
South Kent School 40 Bull's Bridge Rd .... South Kent CT 06785 860-927-3539 927-1161
Web: www.southkentschool.net
Southwestern Academy 2800 Monterey Rd .... San Marino CA 91108 626-799-5010 799-0407
Web: www.southwesternacademy.edu
Stanstead College 450 Dufferin St .... Stanstead QC J0B3E0 819-876-2223 876-5891
Web: www.stansteadcollege.com
Stevenson School 3152 Forest Lake Rd .... Pebble Beach CA 93953 831-625-8300 625-5208
Web: www.rlstevenson.org
Stoneleigh-Burnham School 574 Bernardston Rd .... Greenfield MA 01301 413-774-2711 772-2602
Web: www.sbschool.org
Stony Brook School 1 Chapman Pkwy .... Stony Brook NY 11790 631-751-1800 751-4211
Web: www.stonybrookschool.org
Storm King School 314 Mountain Rd .... Cornwall-on-Hudson NY 12520 845-534-9860 534-9860
TF: 800-225-9144 ■ *Web:* www.sks.org
Stuart Hall School 235 E Frederick St PO Box 210 .... Staunton VA 24402 540-885-0356 886-2275
TF: 888-306-8926 ■ *Web:* www.stuart-hall.org
Subiaco Academy 405 N Subiaco Ave .... Subiaco AR 72865 479-934-1025 934-1033
TF: 800-364-7824 ■ *Web:* www.subi.org
Suffield Academy 185 N Main St PO Box 999 .... Suffield CT 06078 860-668-7315 668-2966
Web: www.suffieldacademy.org
Tabor Academy 66 Spring St .... Marion MA 02738 508-748-2000 748-0353
Web: www.taboracademy.org
Taft School 110 Woodbury Rd .... Watertown CT 06795 860-945-7777 945-7808
Web: www.taftschool.org
Tallulah Falls School 201 Campus Dr PO Box 10 .... Tallulah Falls GA 30573 706-754-0400 754-3595
Web: www.tallulahfalls.org
Texas Military Institute 20955 W Tejas Trail .... San Antonio TX 78257 210-698-7171 698-0715
Web: www.tmi-sa.org
Thacher School 5025 Thacher Rd .... Ojai CA 93023 805-640-3210 640-9377
Web: www.thacher.org
Thomas Jefferson School 4100 S Lindbergh Blvd .... Saint Louis MO 63127 314-843-4151 843-3527
Web: www.tjs.org
Thomas More Prep-Marian 1701 Hall St .... Hays KS 67601 785-625-6577 625-3912
Web: www.tmp-m.org
Tilton School 30 School St .... Tilton NH 03276 603-286-4342 286-1705
Web: www.tiltonschool.org
Trafalgar Castle School 401 Reynolds St .... Whitby ON L1N3W9 905-668-3358 668-4136
Web: www.castle-ed.com
Trinity College School 55 Deblaquire St N .... Port Hope ON L1A4K7 905-885-4565 885-7444
Web: www.tcs.on.ca
Trinity-Pawling School 700 Rt 22 .... Pawling NY 12564 845-855-3100 855-3816
Web: www.trinitypawling.org
Universal Ballet Academy 4301 Harewood Rd NE .... Washington DC 20017 202-832-1087 832-8995
Web: www.ubacademy.org
Upper Canada College 200 Lonsdale Rd .... Toronto ON M4V1W6 416-488-1125 484-8611
Web: www.ucc.on.ca
Valley Forge Military Academy & College 1001 Eagle Rd .... Wayne PA 19087 610-989-1300 688-1545*
*Fax: Admissions ■ *TF:* 800-234-8362 ■ *Web:* www.vfmac.edu
Vanguard School 22000 US Hwy 27 .... Lake Wales FL 33859 863-676-6091 676-8297
Web: www.vanguardschool.org
Verde Valley School 3511 Verde Valley School Rd .... Sedona AZ 86351 928-284-2272 284-0432
Web: www.verdevalleyschool.org
Vermont Academy PO Box 500 .... Saxtons River VT 05154 802-869-6229 869-6242
TF: 800-560-1876 ■ *Web:* www.vermontacademy.org
Villanova Preparatory School 12096 N Ventura Ave .... Ojai CA 93023 805-646-1464 646-4430
Web: www.villanovaprep.org
Virginia Episcopal School 400 VES Rd PO Box 408 .... Lynchburg VA 24503 434-385-3607 385-3603
Web: www.ves.org
Wasatch Academy 120 S 100 W .... Mount Pleasant UT 84647 435-462-1400 462-3380
TF: 800-634-4690 ■ *Web:* www.wacad.org
Washington Academy PO Box 190 .... East Machias ME 04630 207-255-8301 255-8303
Web: www.washingtonacademy.org
Wayland Academy 101 N University Ave .... Beaver Dam WI 53916 920-885-3373 887-3373
TF: 800-860-7725 ■ *Web:* www.wayland.org
Webb School PO Box 488 .... Bell Buckle TN 37020 931-389-9322 389-6657
TF: 888-733-9322 ■ *Web:* www.thewebbschool.com
Webb Schools 1175 W Baseline Rd .... Claremont CA 91711 909-482-5214 621-4582
Web: www.webb.org
West Nottingham Academy 1079 Firetower Rd .... Colora MD 21917 410-658-5556 658-9264
TF: 800-962-1744 ■ *Web:* www.wna.org
Western Reserve Academy 115 College St .... Hudson OH 44236 330-650-9717 650-9722
TF: 800-784-3776 ■ *Web:* www.wra.net
Westminster School 995 Hopmeadow St .... Simsbury CT 06070 860-408-3060 408-3042
Web: www.westminster-school.org
Westover School PO Box 847 .... Middlebury CT 06762 203-758-2423 577-4588
Web: www.westoverschool.org
Westtown School PO Box 1799 .... Westtown PA 19395 610-399-0123 399-3760
Web: www.westtown.edu
White Mountain School 371 W Farm Rd .... Bethlehem NH 03574 603-444-2928 444-5568
TF: 800-545-7813 ■ *Web:* www.whitemountain.org
Wilbraham & Monson Academy 423 Main St .... Wilbraham MA 01095 413-596-6811 596-2448
Web: wmacademy.org
Williston Northampton School 19 Payson Ave .... Easthampton MA 01027 413-529-3241 527-9497
Web: www.williston.com
Winchendon School 172 Ash St .... Winchendon MA 01475 978-297-4476 297-0911
Web: www.winchendon.org
Wolfeboro Camp School 93 Camp School Rd PO Box 390 .... Wolfeboro NH 03894 603-569-3451 569-4080
Web: www.wolfeboro.org
Woodhall School 58 Harrison Ln PO Box 550 .... Bethlehem CT 06751 203-266-7788 266-5896
Web: www.woodhallschool.org
Woodlands Academy of the Sacred Heart 760 E Westleigh Rd .... Lake Forest IL 60045 847-234-4300 234-0865
Web: www.woodlandsacademy.org
Woodside Priory School 302 Portola Rd .... Portola Valley CA 94028 650-851-8221 851-2839
Web: www.woodsidepriory.com
Worcester Academy 81 Providence St .... Worcester MA 01604 508-754-5302 752-2382
Web: www.worcesteracademy.org
Wyoming Seminary 201 N Sprague Ave .... Kingston PA 18704 570-270-2160 270-2191
TF: 877-996-7364 ■ *Web:* www.wyomingseminary.org

626 PREPARATORY SCHOOLS - NON-BOARDING

SEE ALSO Preparatory Schools - Boarding p. 2135

The schools listed here are among the leading private elementary and secondary schools in the U.S. None of these schools are boarding schools.

Phone Fax

Albuquerque Academy 6400 Wyoming Blvd NE .... Albuquerque NM 87109 505-828-3200 828-3320
Web: www.aa.edu

	City	State	Zip	Phone	Fax
Blake School 110 Blake Rd S *Web:* www.blakeschool.org	Hopkins	MN	55343	952-988-3400	988-3455
Brearley School 610 E 83rd St *Web:* www.brearley.org	New York	NY	10028	212-744-8582	472-8020
Chapin School 100 East End Ave *Web:* www.chapin.edu	New York	NY	10028	212-744-2335	
Iolani School 563 Kamoku St *Web:* www.iolani.org	Honolulu	HI	96826	808-949-5355	943-2297
Kinkaid School 201 Kinkaid School Dr *Web:* www.kinkaid.org	Houston	TX	77024	713-782-1640	782-3543
Latin School of Chicago 59 W North Blvd *Web:* www.latinschool.org	Chicago	IL	60610	312-582-6000	
Mary Institute & Saint Louis Country Day School 101 N Warson Rd *Web:* www.micds.org	Saint Louis	MO	63124	314-993-5100	
National Cathedral School 3609 Woodley Rd NW *Web:* www.ncs.cathedral.org	Washington	DC	20016	202-537-6339	537-5743
North Shore Country Day School 310 Green Bay Rd *Web:* www.nscds.org	Winnetka	IL	60093	847-446-0674	446-0675
Orchard School 615 W 64th St *Web:* www.orchard.org	Indianapolis	IN	46260	317-251-9253	254-8454
Punahou School 1601 Punahou St *Web:* www.punahou.edu	Honolulu	HI	96822	808-944-5711	944-5779
Roxbury Latin School 101 Saint Theresa Ave *Web:* www.roxburylatin.org	West Roxbury	MA	02132	617-325-4920	325-3585
Saint Albans School Mount Saint Alban *Web:* staweb.sta.cathedral.org	Washington	DC	20016	202-537-6435	537-5613
Saint Stephen's & Saint Agnes School 1000 Saint Stephen's Rd *Web:* www.sssas.org	Alexandria	VA	22304	703-751-2700	683-5930
Sidwell Friends School 3825 Wisconsin Ave NW *Web:* www.sidwell.edu	Washington	DC	20016	202-537-8100	537-8138
University School Hunting Valley Campus 2785 SOM Center Rd *Web:* www.us.edu	Hunting Valley	OH	44022	216-831-2200	292-7810
University School of Milwaukee 2100 W Fairy Chasm Rd *Web:* www.usm.k12.wi.us	Milwaukee	WI	53217	414-352-6000	352-8076
Westminster Schools 1424 W Paces Ferry Rd NW *Web:* www.westminster.net	Atlanta	GA	30327	404-355-8673	355-6606

627 PRESS CLIPPING SERVICES

	City	State	Zip	Phone	Fax
Allen's Press Clipping Bureau 657 Mission St Rm 602	San Francisco	CA	94105	415-392-2353	362-6208
BurrellesLuce 75 E Northfield Rd *TF:* 800-631-1160 ■ *Web:* www.burrellesluce.com	Livingston	NJ	07039	973-992-6600	992-7675
Cision US Inc 332 S Michigan Ave Suite 900 **Fax:* Cust Svc ■ *TF:* 866-639-5087 ■ *Web:* us.cision.com	Chicago	IL	60604	312-922-2400	922-3127*
Colorado Press Clipping Service 1336 Glenarm Pl *Web:* www.coloradopressassociation.com	Denver	CO	80204	303-571-5117	571-1803
CompetitivEdge 196 S Main St *TF:* 888-881-3343 ■ *Web:* www.clipresearch.com	Colchester	CT	06415	860-537-6731	537-6738
Florida Newsclips LLC PO Box 2190 *TF:* 800-442-0332 ■ *Web:* www.newsclipsonweb.com	Palm Harbor	FL	34682	727-726-5000	736-5005
Kentucky Press Assn 101 Consumer Ln *TF:* 800-264-5721 ■ *Web:* www.kypress.com	Frankfort	KY	40601	502-223-8821	226-3867
Magnolia Clipping Service 298 Commerce Park Dr Suite A *Web:* www.magnoliaclips.com	Ridgeland	MS	39157	601-856-0911	856-3340
New England Newsclip Agency Inc 5 Auburn St *TF:* 800-235-3879 ■ *Web:* www.newenglandnewsclip.com	Framingham	MA	01701	508-879-4460	872-0350
New Jersey Clipping Service 75 E Northfield Rd *TF:* 800-631-1160 ■ *Web:* www.njclippingservice.com	Livingston	NJ	07039	973-994-3333	533-6042
New York State Clipping Service 200 Central Park Ave N *TF:* 800-772-5477	Hartsdale	NY	10530	914-948-2525	948-3534
Newsclip 363 W Erie St 7th Fl *TF:* 800-544-8433 ■ *Web:* www.newsclip.com	Chicago	IL	60610	312-751-7300	751-7306
Oklahoma Press Service Inc 3601 N Lincoln Blvd *Web:* www.okpress.com	Oklahoma City	OK	73105	405-524-4421	524-2201
South Carolina Press Services Inc 421 Zimal Crest PO Box 11429 *TF:* 888-727-7377 ■ *Web:* www.scpress.org	Columbia	SC	29211	803-750-9561	551-0903
South Dakota Newspaper Services 527 Main Ave Suite 202 *TF:* 800-658-3697 ■ *Web:* www.sdna.com	Brookings	SD	57006	605-692-4300	692-6388
Virginia Press Services Inc 11529 Nuckols Rd *TF:* 800-849-8717 ■ *Web:* www.vpa.net	Glen Allen	VA	23059	804-521-7570	521-7590
West Virginia Press Services Inc 3422 Pennsylvania Ave *TF:* 800-235-6881 ■ *Web:* www.wvpress.org	Charleston	WV	25302	304-342-6908	343-5879

628 PRINTED CIRCUIT BOARDS

SEE ALSO Electronic Components & Accessories - Mfr p. 1609; Semiconductors & Related Devices p. 2312

	City	State	Zip	Phone	Fax
3Com Corp 350 Campus Dr *NASDAQ: COMS* ■ *Web:* www.3com.com	Marlborough	MA	01752	508-323-5000	323-1111
3Dlabs Inc 1901 McCarthy Blvd *TF:* 800-464-3348 ■ *Web:* www.3dlabs.com	Milpitas	CA	94035	408-432-6700	432-6701
Abelconn LLC 9210 Science Center Dr *Web:* www.abelconn.com	New Hope	MN	55428	763-533-3533	536-0349
ABIT Computer (USA) Corp 2901 Bayview Dr *Web:* www.abit-usa.com	Fremont	CA	94538	510-623-0500	623-1092
Acromag Inc 30765 S Wixom Rd *TF:* 800-881-0268 ■ *Web:* www.acromag.com	Wixom	MI	48393	248-624-1541	624-9234
Adaptec Inc 691 S Milpitas Blvd *NASDAQ: ADPT* ■ *TF Tech Supp:* 800-959-7274 ■ *Web:* www.adaptec.com	Milpitas	CA	95035	408-945-8600	262-2533
Analogic Corp 8 Centennial Dr *NASDAQ: ALOG* ■ **Fax:* Hum Res ■ *Web:* www.analogic.com	Peabody	MA	01960	978-977-3000	977-6810*
Antex Electronics Corp 19821 Hamilton Ave *TF:* 800-338-4231 ■ *Web:* www.antex.com	Torrance	CA	90502	310-532-3092	532-8509
Apex Micro Corp 8128 River Way *Web:* www.apexmicromfg.com	Delta	BC	V4G1K5	604-946-9666	942-0689
Apsco International 3700 Lane Rd *Web:* www.apscoinc.com	Perry	OH	44081	440-352-8961	354-7306
ASUSTeK Computer International 44370 Nobel Dr *Web:* www.asus.com	Fremont	CA	94538	510-739-3777	797-3579
ATI Technologies Inc 33 Commerce Valley Dr E *NASDAQ: ATYT* ■ *Web:* www.ati.com	Thornhill	ON	L3T7N6	905-882-2600	
AudioCodes Ltd 2099 Gateway Pl Suite 500 *NASDAQ: AUDC* ■ *Web:* www.audiocodes.com	San Jose	CA	95110	408-441-1175	451-9520
Benchmark Electronics Inc 3000 Technology Dr *NYSE: BHE* ■ *Web:* www.bench.com	Angleton	TX	77515	979-849-6550	848-5271
Best Data Products Inc 9650 DeSoto Ave *Web:* www.bestdata.com	Chatsworth	CA	91311	818-773-9600	773-9619
Bicom Inc 755 Main St *Web:* www.bicom-inc.com	Monroe	CT	06468	203-268-4484	268-3404
Bourns Inc 1200 Columbia Ave *TF:* 877-426-8767 ■ *Web:* www.bourns.com	Riverside	CA	92507	951-781-5690	781-5006
Centon Electronics Inc 15 Argonaut *TF:* 800-234-9292 ■ *Web:* www.centon.com	Aliso Viejo	CA	92656	949-855-9111	855-6553
Compunetics Inc 700 Seco Rd *TF:* 800-879-4266 ■ *Web:* www.compunetics.com	Monroeville	PA	15146	412-373-8110	373-8060
Computer Modules Inc 11409 W Bernardo Ct *Web:* www.computermodules.com	San Diego	CA	92127	858-613-1801	613-1815
Creative Labs Inc 1901 McCarthy Blvd *TF Cust Svc:* 800-998-1000 ■ *Web:* us.creative.com	Milpitas	CA	95035	408-428-6600	428-6611
Crucial Technology 3475 E Commercial Ct *TF:* 800-336-8915 ■ *Web:* www.crucial.com	Meridian	ID	83642	208-363-5790	363-5501
Cytec Corp 1017 William D Tate Ave Suite 107 *TF:* 888-349-8881 ■ *Web:* www.cytecsys.com	Grapevine	TX	76051	214-349-8881	
Data Translation Inc 100 Locke Dr *TF:* 800-525-8528 ■ *Web:* www.datx.com	Marlborough	MA	01752	508-481-3700	481-8620
Dataram Corp 186 Rt 571 *NASDAQ: DRAM* ■ *TF:* 800-328-2726 ■ *Web:* www.dataram.com	West Windsor	NJ	08550	609-799-0071	799-6734
DDi Corp 1220 Simon Cir *NASDAQ: DDIC* ■ *Web:* www.ddiglobal.com	Anaheim	CA	92806	714-688-7200	688-7500
Diamond Flower Electric Instrument Co USA Inc (DFI) 732-C Striker Ave *TF:* 800-909-4334 ■ *Web:* www.dfiusa.com	Sacramento	CA	95834	916-568-1234	568-1233
Diversified Technology Inc 476 Highland Colony Pkwy *TF:* 800-443-2667 ■ *Web:* www.dtims.com	Ridgeland	MS	39157	601-856-4121	856-2888
DRS Laurel Technologies 246 Airport Rd *Web:* www.drs.com	Johnstown	PA	15904	814-534-8900	534-8815
Dynaco Corp 1000 S Priest Dr *Web:* www.dynacocorp.com	Tempe	AZ	85281	480-968-2000	921-9830
Dynatem Inc 23263 Madero Suite C *TF:* 800-543-3830 ■ *Web:* www.dynatem.com	Mission Viejo	CA	92691	949-855-3235	770-3481
EDGE Tech Corp 327 E 14th St *Web:* www.edgetechcorp.com	Ada	OK	74820	580-332-6581	310-6518
EI Microcircuits Inc 1651 Pohl Rd *Web:* www.eimicro.com	Mankato	MN	56001	507-345-5786	345-7559
Electropac Co Inc 252 Willow St *Web:* www.electropac.com	Manchester	NH	03103	603-622-3711	622-1773
First International Computer Inc 50720 Brandon Ct *Web:* www.fica.com	Fremont	CA	94538	510-252-7777	252-8888
Flex Technology Inc 2 Industrial Dr *Web:* www.flextechnology.com	Hudson	NH	03051	603-883-1500	883-7919
GE Fanuc Embedded Systems Inc 7401 Snaproll NE *TF:* 800-727-1553 ■ *Web:* www.gefanucembedded.com	Albuquerque	NM	87109	505-875-0600	
Gigabyte Technology Inc 17358 Railroad St *Web:* www.giga-byte.com	City of Industry	CA	91748	626-854-9338	854-9340
GoldenRAM Computer Products 8 Whatney *TF:* 800-222-8861 ■ *Web:* www.goldenram.com	Irvine	CA	92618	949-460-9000	460-7600
Guillemot North America 5800 rue Saint-Denis Suite 1001 *Web:* us.guillemot.com	Montreal	QC	H2S3L5	514-279-9960	279-4954
Hauppauge Computer Works Inc 91 Cabot Ct *TF:* 800-443-6284 ■ *Web:* www.hauppauge.com	Hauppauge	NY	11788	631-434-1600	434-3198
Hauppauge Digital Inc 91 Cabot Ct *NASDAQ: HAUP* ■ *TF:* 800-443-6284 ■ *Web:* www.hauppauge.com	Hauppauge	NY	11788	631-434-1600	434-3198
Hitachi Computer Products (America) Inc (HICAM) 1800 E Imhoff Rd *TF:* 800-448-2244 ■ *Web:* www.hitachisoftware.com	Norman	OK	73071	405-360-5500	573-1299
I-Bus Corp 3350 Scott Blvd Bldg 54 *TF:* 877-777-4287 ■ *Web:* www.ibus.com	Santa Clara	CA	95054	408-450-7880	450-7881
IEC Electronics Corp 105 Norton St *Web:* www.iec-electronics.com	Newark	NY	14513	315-331-7742	331-3547
Intel Corp 2200 Mission College Blvd *NASDAQ: INTC* ■ *TF Cust Svc:* 800-628-8686 ■ *Web:* www.intel.com	Santa Clara	CA	95052	408-765-8080	
I/O Magic Corp 4 Marconi *Web:* www.iomagic.com	Irvine	CA	92618	949-707-4800	855-3550
ITW Chronomatic 700 High Grove Blvd *Web:* www.itwchronomatic.com	Glendale Heights	IL	60139	630-671-4700	671-4770
Jabil Circuit Inc 10560 ML King St N *NYSE: JBL* ■ *Web:* www.jabil.com	Saint Petersburg	FL	33716	727-577-9749	803-5401
Jaton Corp 556 S Milpitas Blvd **Fax:* Sales ■ *Web:* www.jaton.com	Milpitas	CA	95035	408-942-9888	942-9888*
Kimball Electronics Group 1038 E 15th St **Fax:* Sales ■ *TF:* 800-634-4005 ■ *Web:* www.kegroup.com	Jasper	IN	47549	812-634-4200	634-4330*
Kontron Communications Inc 616 Cure-Boivin *TF:* 800-387-4222 ■ *Web:* www.kontron.com	Boisbriand	QC	J7G2A7	450-437-5682	437-8053
Leadtek Research Inc 910 Auburn Ct *Web:* www.leadtek.com	Fremont	CA	94538	510-490-8076	490-7759
M-Wave Inc 475 Industrial Dr *NASDAQ: MWAV* ■ *Web:* www.mwav.com	West Chicago	IL	60185	630-562-5550	562-2430
Macrolink Inc 1500 N Kellogg Dr *Web:* www.macrolink.com	Anaheim	CA	92807	714-777-8800	777-8807
Matrox Electronic Systems Ltd 1055 St Regis Blvd *Web:* www.matrox.com	Dorval	QC	H9P2T4	514-822-6000	822-6000
McDonald Technologies International Inc 1920 Diplomat Dr *TF:* 800-678-7046 ■ *Web:* www.mcdonald-tech.com	Farmers Branch	TX	75234	972-243-6767	241-2643
Merix Corp 1521 Poplar Ln *NASDAQ: MERX* ■ **Fax:* Hum Res ■ *Web:* www.merix.com	Forest Grove	OR	97116	503-359-9300	357-1504*
Micro Industries Corp 8399 Green Meadow Dr N *TF:* 800-722-1845 ■ *Web:* www.microindustries.com	Westerville	OH	43081	740-548-7878	548-6184
Micro Memory Inc 9540 Vassar Ave *Web:* www.micromemory.com	Chatsworth	CA	91311	818-998-0070	998-4459
Micron Technology Inc 8000 S Federal Way *NYSE: MU* ■ *Web:* www.micron.com	Boise	ID	83707	208-368-4000	368-4617
Micron Technology Inc SpecTek Div 8000 S Federal Way *Web:* www.spectek.com	Boise	ID	83707	208-368-4000	
Motorola Computer Group 2900 S Diablo Way *TF:* 800-759-1107 ■ *Web:* www.motorola.com/computers	Tempe	AZ	85282	602-438-3000	438-5615
Motorola Inc 1301 E Algonquin Rd *NYSE: MOT* ■ **Fax:* Hum Res ■ *TF:* 800-331-6456 ■ *Web:* www.motorola.com	Schaumburg	IL	60196	847-576-5000	538-3617*
MSI Computer Corp 901 Canada Ct *Web:* www.msicomputer.com	City of Industry	CA	91748	626-913-0828	913-0818
National Semiconductor Corp 2900 Semiconductor Dr *NYSE: NSM* ■ *Web:* www.national.com	Santa Clara	CA	95051	408-721-5000	732-4880
Nitto Denko America Inc 48500 Fremont Blvd *TF:* 800-356-4880 ■ *Web:* www.nittousa.com	Fremont	CA	94538	510-445-5400	445-5480
NVIDIA Corp 2701 San Tomas Expy *NASDAQ: NVDA* ■ *TF:* 877-768-4342 ■ *Web:* www.nvidia.com	Santa Clara	CA	95050	408-486-2000	486-2200
Parallax Inc 599 Menlo Dr Suite 100 *TF:* 888-512-1024 ■ *Web:* www.parallaxinc.com	Rocklin	CA	95765	916-624-8333	624-8003
Park Electrochemical Corp 48 S Service Rd Suite 300 *NYSE: PKE* ■ *Web:* www.parkelectro.com	Melville	NY	11747	631-465-3600	465-3100

Company	City	State	Zip	Phone	Fax
Parlex Corp 1 Parlex Place *Web:* www.parlex.com	Methuen	MA	01844	978-685-4341	685-8809
PCI Inc 407 Lee Ave **Fax Area Code:* 847 ■ *Web:* www.pciltd.com	Highland Springs	VA	23075	804-737-7979	631-0799*
PEMSTAR Turtle Mountain 19 2nd St SE *Web:* www.pemstar.com/Dunseith.html	Dunseith	ND	58329	701-244-5242	244-5582
Pentek Inc 1 Park Way **Fax:* Acctg ■ *Web:* www.pentek.com	Upper Saddle River	NJ	07458	201-818-5900	818-5692*
Philway Products Inc 701 Virginia Ave **Fax:* Sales ■ *Web:* www.philway.com	Ashland	OH	44805	419-281-7777	289-3447*
Plexus Corp 2121 Harrison St *NASDAQ: PLXS* ■ *Web:* www.plexus.com	Neenah	WI	54957	920-722-3451	751-3252
PNC Inc 115 E Centre St *Web:* www.pnconline.com	Nutley	NJ	07110	973-284-1600	284-1925
Promise Technology Inc 580 Cottonwood Dr *TF Sales:* 800-888-0245 ■ *Web:* www.promise.com	Milpitas	CA	95035	408-228-1400	228-1099
Quatech Inc 5675 Hudson Industrial Pkwy *TF:* 800-553-1170 ■ *Web:* www.quatech.com	Hudson	OH	44236	330-655-9000	655-9070
Rabbit Semiconductor Inc 2900 Spafford St **Fax:* Mktg ■ *TF:* 888-362-3387 ■ *Web:* www.rabbitsemiconductor.com	Davis	CA	95616	530-757-8400	753-5141*
RadiSys Corp 5445 NE Dawson Creek Dr *NASDAQ: RSYS* ■ *TF:* 800-950-0044 ■ *Web:* www.radisys.com	Hillsboro	OR	97124	503-615-1100	615-1115
Ramp Industries Inc 1 N Floral Ave *Web:* www.rampindustries.com	Binghamton	NY	13905	607-729-5256	729-2977
Reptron Electronics Inc 13700 Reptron Blvd *TF:* 800-800-5441 ■ *Web:* www.reptronmfg.com	Tampa	FL	33626	813-854-2000	891-4056
Riverside Electronics Ltd 1 Riverside Dr *Web:* www.rellew.com	Lewiston	MN	55952	507-523-3220	523-2831
Sabtech Industries 23231 La Palma Ave *Web:* www.sabtech.com	Yorba Linda	CA	92887	714-692-3800	692-3838
Samsung Semiconductors Inc 3655 N 1st St *TF:* 800-726-7864 ■ *Web:* www.usa.samsungsemi.com	San Jose	CA	95134	408-544-4000	544-4980
Sanmina-SCI Corp 2700 N 1st St *NASDAQ: SANM* ■ *Web:* www.sanmina-sci.com	San Jose	CA	95134	408-964-3500	964-3636
Saturn Electronics & Engineering Inc 255 Rex Blvd *Web:* www.saturnee.com	Auburn Hills	MI	48326	248-853-5724	299-8570
SBS Technologies Inc 7401 Snaproll NE *NASDAQ: SBSE* ■ *TF:* 800-727-1553 ■ *Web:* www.sbs.com	Albuquerque	NM	87109	505-875-0600	875-0400
Sigma Designs Inc 1221 California Cir *NASDAQ: SIGM* ■ *TF Sales:* 800-845-8086 ■ *Web:* www.sdesigns.com	Milpitas	CA	95035	408-262-9003	957-9740
SigmaTron International Inc 2201 Landmeier Rd *NASDAQ: SGMA* ■ **Fax:* Hum Res ■ *Web:* www.sigmatronintl.com	Elk Grove Village	IL	60007	847-956-8000	956-9410*
SIIG Inc 6078 Stewart Ave *Web:* www.siig.com	Fremont	CA	94538	510-657-8688	657-5962
Socket Communications Inc 37400 Central Ct *NASDAQ: SCKT* ■ *TF:* 800-552-3300 ■ *Web:* www.socketcom.com	Newark	CA	94560	510-744-2700	744-2727
Solectron Corp 847 Gibraltar Dr *NYSE: SLR* ■ *Web:* www.solectron.com	Milpitas	CA	95035	408-957-8500	935-5925
Sparton Corp 2400 E Ganson St *NYSE: SPA* ■ *TF:* 800-248-9579 ■ *Web:* www.sparton.com	Jackson	MI	49202	517-787-8600	787-8046
SpecTek Div Micron Technology Inc 8000 S Federal Way *Web:* www.spectek.com	Boise	ID	83707	208-368-4000	
Spectrum Signal Processing by Vecima 2700 Production Way Suite 300 *NASDAQ: SSPI* ■ *TF:* 800-663-8986 ■ *Web:* www.spectrumsignal.com	Burnaby	BC	V5A4X1	604-421-5422	421-1764
Suntron Corp 2401 W Grandview Rd Suite 1 *NASDAQ: SUNN* ■ *TF:* 888-520-3382 ■ *Web:* www.suntroncorp.com	Phoenix	AZ	85023	602-789-6600	789-6600
Supermicro Computer Inc 980 Rock Ave *Web:* www.supermicro.com	San Jose	CA	95131	408-503-8000	503-8008
TechWorks 4030 W Braker Ln Suite 120 *TF Cust Svc:* 800-688-7466 ■ *Web:* www.techworks.com	Austin	TX	78759	512-794-8533	794-8520
Tekram Technology USA 2861 Saturn St Suite B *Web:* www.tekram.com	Brea	CA	92821	714-961-0800	961-0899
TTM Technologies Inc 17550 NE 67th Ct *NASDAQ: TTMI* ■ **Fax:* Sales ■ *Web:* www.ttmtechnologies.com	Redmond	WA	98052	425-883-7575	883-9676*
TYAN Computer Corp USA 3288 Laurelview Ct *Web:* www.tyan.com	Fremont	CA	94538	510-651-8868	651-7688
Tyco Electronics Corp 1050 Westlakes Dr *NYSE: TEL* ■ *Web:* www.tycoelectronics.com	Berwyn	PA	19312	610-893-9800	
Unigen Corp 45388 Warm Springs Blvd *TF:* 800-826-0808 ■ *Web:* www.unigen.com	Fremont	CA	94539	510-668-2088	661-2770
Universal Scientific of Illinois Inc 2101 Arthur Ave *Web:* www.usipcb.com	Elk Grove Village	IL	60007	847-228-6464	228-0523
Viasystems Group Inc 101 S Hanley Rd Suite 400 *Web:* www.viasystems.com	Saint Louis	MO	63105	314-727-2087	746-2233
Viking Components Inc 30200 Avenida de Las Banderas *TF:* 800-338-2361 ■ *Web:* www.vikingcomponents.com	Rancho Santa Margarita	CA	92688	949-643-7255	643-7250
VisionTek Inc 1610 Colonial Pkwy *Web:* www.visiontek.com	Inverness	IL	60067	224-836-3000	836-3600
VM Services Inc 6701 Mowry Ave	Newark	CA	94560	510-744-3720	744-3730
Voyetra Turtle Beach Inc 5 Odell Plaza *TF:* 800-233-9377 ■ *Web:* www.voyetra-turtle-beach.com	Yonkers	NY	10701	914-966-0600	966-1102
Western Electronics LLC 1550 S Tech Ln *TF:* 888-857-5775 ■ *Web:* www.westernelectronics.com	Meridian	ID	83642	208-377-1557	955-9752
Winnov 3285 Scott Blvd *Web:* www.winnov.com	Santa Clara	CA	95054	408-207-4400	562-9183
Wintec Industries Inc 4280 Technology Dr **Fax:* Tech Supp ■ *Web:* www.wintecindustries.com	Fremont	CA	94538	510-360-6300	770-9338*
Xetron Corp 460 W Crescentville Rd *TF:* 800-881-3275 ■ *Web:* www.xetron.com	Cincinnati	OH	45246	513-881-3100	881-3379
Xycom Automation Inc 750 N Maple Rd **Fax:* Sales ■ *TF:* 800-289-9266 ■ *Web:* www.xycom.com	Saline	MI	48176	734-429-4971	429-1010*
Zendex Corp 6780 Sierra Ct Suite A *Web:* www.zendex.com	Dublin	CA	94568	925-828-3000	828-1574

629 PRINTING COMPANIES - BOOK PRINTERS

Company	City	State	Zip	Phone	Fax
Adair Printing Technologies 7850 2nd St *TF:* 800-637-5025 ■ *Web:* www.adairprinting.com	Dexter	MI	48130	734-426-2822	426-4360
Bang Printing Inc 3323 Oak St *TF:* 800-328-0450 ■ *Web:* www.bangprinting.com	Brainerd	MN	56401	218-829-2877	829-7145
Banta Book Group PO Box 60 *TF:* 800-291-1171 ■ *Web:* www.banta.com/about/operations.html	Menasha	WI	54952	920-751-7771	751-7362
Berryville Graphics 25 Jack Enders Blvd PO Box 272 *TF:* 800-606-6467 ■ *Web:* www.bvgraphics.com	Berryville	VA	22611	540-955-2750	955-2633
Bertelsmann Printing & Mfg Corp 1540 Broadway	New York	NY	10036	212-782-7676	782-7600
Boyd Printing Co Inc 5 Sand Creek Rd Suite 2 *TF:* 800-877-2693 ■ *Web:* www.boydprinting.com	Albany	NY	12205	518-436-9686	436-7433
Bradford & Bigelow Inc 1 Electronic Ave Danvers Industrial Pk *TF:* 800-882-9503 ■ *Web:* www.bradford-bigelow.com	Danvers	MA	01923	978-777-1200	774-4021
Cadmus Communications Port City Press Div 1323 Greenwood Rd *TF:* 800-858-7678 ■ *Web:* www.portcitypress.com	Baltimore	MD	21208	410-486-3000	486-0706
CJK 3962 Virginia Ave *TF:* 800-598-7808 ■ *Web:* www.cjkusa.com	Cincinnati	OH	45227	513-271-6035	271-6082
Claitor's Law Books & Publishing Inc 3165 S Acadian Thwy *TF:* 800-274-1403 ■ *Web:* www.claitors.com	Baton Rouge	LA	70808	225-344-0476	344-0480
Command Web Offset Inc 100 Castle Rd *TF:* 800-466-2932	Secaucus	NJ	07094	201-863-8100	863-6693
Consolidated Printers Inc 2630 8th St *Web:* www.consoprinters.com	Berkeley	CA	94710	510-843-8524	486-0580
Cookbook Publishers Inc 10800 Lakeview Ave *TF:* 800-227-7282 ■ *Web:* www.cookbookpublishers.com	Lenexa	KS	66219	913-492-5900	492-5947
Courier Corp 15 Wellman Ave *NASDAQ: CRRC* ■ *Web:* www.courier.com	North Chelmsford	MA	01863	978-251-6000	251-0368
Courier Kendallville Inc 2500 Marion Dr *TF:* 800-228-9577 ■ *Web:* www.courier.com	Kendallville	IN	46755	260-347-3044	347-3507
Courier Stoughton 200 Shuman Ave *Web:* www.courier.com/ccorp/	Stoughton	MA	02072	781-341-1800	341-3973
Courier Westford Inc 22 Town Farm Rd *TF:* 800-666-8772 ■ *Web:* www.courier.com/ccorp/	Westford	MA	01886	978-692-6321	692-7292
Cushing-Malloy Inc 1350 N Main St *TF:* 888-295-7244 ■ *Web:* www.cushing-malloy.com	Ann Arbor	MI	48104	734-663-8554	663-5731
Darby Printing Co 6215 Purdue Dr *TF:* 800-241-5292 ■ *Web:* www.darbyprinting.com	Atlanta	GA	30336	404-344-2665	346-3332
DB Hess Co 1530 McConnell Rd PO Box 1209 *Web:* www.dbhess.com	Woodstock	IL	60098	815-338-6900	334-6191
Deaton-Kennedy Co Inc 927 Gardner St *TF:* 800-435-4068 ■ *Web:* www.deatonkennedy.com	Joliet	IL	60433	815-726-6234	726-1379
Edwards Brothers Inc 2500 S State St **Fax:* Cust Svc ■ *Web:* www.edwardsbrothers.com	Ann Arbor	MI	48104	734-769-1000	913-1338*
Fidlar Doubleday Inc 4570 Commercial Ave **Fax Area Code:* 800 ■ *TF:* 800-248-0888 ■ *Web:* www.fidlardoubleday.com	Portage	MI	49002	309-794-3300	884-9258*
Friesens Corp 1 Printers Way *Web:* www.friesens.com	Altona	MB	R0G0B0	204-324-6401	324-1333
Gospel Publishing House 1445 N Boonville Ave *TF Orders:* 800-641-4310 ■ *Web:* www.gospelpublishing.com	Springfield	MO	65802	417-862-2781	862-8558
Griffin Publishing Group 18022 Cowan *TF:* 800-472-9741 ■ *Web:* www.griffinpublishing.com	Irvine	CA	92614	949-263-3733	263-3734
Haddon Craftsmen Inc 4411 Old Berwick Rd	Bloomsburg	PA	17815	570-784-7394	784-3129
Hamilton Printing Co Inc PO Box 232 *TF:* 800-242-4222	Rensselaer	NY	12144	518-732-4491	732-7714
Henry John Co 5800 W Grand River Ave *TF:* 800-748-0517 ■ *Web:* www.jhc.com	Lansing	MI	48906	517-323-9000	323-4707
Joe Christensen Inc 1540 Adams St *TF:* 800-228-5030	Lincoln	NE	68521	402-476-7535	476-3094
John Henry Co 5800 W Grand River Ave *TF:* 800-748-0517 ■ *Web:* www.jhc.com	Lansing	MI	48906	517-323-9000	323-4707
Jostens Inc 3601 Minnesota Ave Suite 400 **Fax:* Hum Res ■ *TF:* 800-235-4774 ■ *Web:* www.jostens.com	Minneapolis	MN	55435	952-830-3300	830-3309*
Kirby Lithographic Co Inc 2900 S Eads St *TF:* 800-932-3594 ■ *Web:* www.kirbylitho.com	Arlington	VA	22202	703-684-7600	683-5918
Library Reproduction Service 14214 S Figueroa St *TF:* 800-255-5002 ■ *Web:* www.lrs-largeprint.com	Los Angeles	CA	90061	310-354-2610	354-2601
Malloy Inc 5411 Jackson Rd PO Box 1124 *TF:* 800-722-3231 ■ *Web:* www.malloy.com	Ann Arbor	MI	48106	734-665-6113	665-2326
Maple-Vail Book Mfg Group 480 Willow Springs Ln *Web:* www.maple-vail.com	York	PA	17406	717-764-5911	764-4702
McNaughton & Gunn Inc 960 Woodland Dr **Fax Area Code:* 800 ■ *Web:* www.mcnaughton-gunn.com	Saline	MI	48176	734-429-5411	677-2665*
Moran Printing Inc 5425 Florida Blvd *TF:* 800-211-8335 ■ *Web:* www.moranprinting.com	Baton Rouge	LA	70806	225-923-2550	923-1078
National Publishing Co 11311 Roosevelt Blvd *TF:* 888-333-1863 ■ *Web:* www.courier.com	Philadelphia	PA	19154	215-676-1863	856-9930
Offset Paperback Manufacturers Inc 101 Memorial Hwy *Web:* www.opm.com	Dallas	PA	18612	570-675-5261	675-8714
Page Litho Inc 6445 E Vernor Hwy *Web:* www.pagelithoinc.com	Detroit	MI	48207	313-921-6880	921-6771
Phillips Brothers Inc 1555 W Jefferson St *TF:* 800-637-9327 ■ *Web:* www.pbpweb.com	Springfield	IL	62702	217-787-3014	787-9624
Phoenix Color Corp 540 Western Maryland Pkwy *TF:* 800-632-4111 ■ *Web:* www.phoenixcolor.com	Hagerstown	MD	21740	301-733-0018	791-9560
Port City Press Div Cadmus Communications 1323 Greenwood Rd *TF:* 800-858-7678 ■ *Web:* www.portcitypress.com	Baltimore	MD	21208	410-486-3000	486-0706
Publishers Press Inc 100 Frank E Simon Ave *TF:* 800-627-5801 ■ *Web:* www.pubpress.com	Shepherdsville	KY	40165	502-955-6526	543-8808
RCL Enterprises 200 E Bethany Dr **Fax Area Code:* 800 ■ *TF:* 877-275-4725 ■ *Web:* www.rclweb.com	Allen	TX	75002	972-390-6400	688-8356*
Rose Printing Co Inc 2503 Jackson Bluff Rd *TF:* 800-227-3725 ■ *Web:* www.roseprinting.com	Tallahassee	FL	32304	850-576-4151	576-4153
RR Donnelley & Sons Co 111 S Wacker Dr *NYSE: RRD* ■ **Fax:* Mail Rm ■ *Web:* www.rrdonnelley.com	Chicago	IL	60601	312-326-8000	326-8543*
Schneidereith & Sons Inc 2905 Whittington Ave *TF:* 800-327-1982 ■ *Web:* www.schneidereith.com	Baltimore	MD	21230	410-525-0300	525-3797
Sheridan Books Inc 613 E Industrial Dr *TF:* 800-999-2665 ■ *Web:* www.sheridanbooks.com	Chelsea	MI	48118	734-475-9145	475-7337
Sheridan Group 11311 McCormick Rd Suite 260 *Web:* www.sheridan.com	Hunt Valley	MD	21031	410-785-7277	785-7217
Smith-Edwards-Dunlap Co 2867 E Allegheny Ave *TF:* 800-829-0020 ■ *Web:* www.sed.com	Philadelphia	PA	19134	215-425-8800	425-9110
Stinehour Press 853 Lancaster Rd *TF:* 800-331-7753 ■ *Web:* www.stinehourpress.com	Lunenburg	VT	05906	802-328-2507	328-3960
Thomson-Shore Inc 7300 W Joy Rd *Web:* www.tshore.com	Dexter	MI	48130	734-426-3939	426-6216
Transcontinental Inc 1 pl Ville Marie Bureau 3315 *TSX: TCL.a* ■ *Web:* www.transcontinental.com	Montreal	QC	H3B3N2	514-954-4000	954-4016
Transcontinental Printing Inc 395 Lebeau Blvd *TF:* 800-337-8560 ■ *Web:* www.transcontinental-gtc.com	Saint-Laurent	QC	H4N1S2	514-337-8560	339-5230
Tweddle Litho Co 24700 Maplehurst Dr *Web:* www.tweddle.com	Clinton Township	MI	48036	586-307-3700	307-3708
Typecraft Wood & Jones Inc 2040 E Walnut St *Web:* www.typecraft.com	Pasadena	CA	91107	626-795-7718	795-2423
United Graphics Inc 2916 Marshall Ave PO Box 559 *Web:* www.bookmanufacturing.com	Mattoon	IL	61938	217-235-7161	234-6274
Versa Press Inc 1465 Springbay Rd *TF:* 800-447-7829 ■ *Web:* www.versapress.com	East Peoria	IL	61611	309-822-8272	822-8141
Vicks Lithograph & Printing Co 5166 Commercial Dr PO Box 270 *Web:* www.vickslitho.com	Yorkville	NY	13495	315-736-9344	736-1901
Victor Graphics Inc 1211 Bernard Dr *TF:* 800-899-8303 ■ *Web:* www.victorgraphics.com	Baltimore	MD	21223	410-233-8300	233-8304
Von Hoffmann Corp 1000 Camera Ave *TF:* 800-325-2463 ■ *Web:* www.vonhoffmann.com	Saint Louis	MO	63126	314-966-0909	966-8670
Webcrafters Inc 2211 Fordem Ave **Fax:* Cust Svc ■ *TF:* 800-356-8200 ■ *Web:* www.webcrafters-inc.com	Madison	WI	53704	608-244-3561	244-3174*

	City	State	Zip	Phone	Fax
Whitehall Printing Co 4244 Corporate Sq *TF*: 800-321-9290 ■ *Web*: www.info@whitehallprinting.com	Naples	FL	34104	239-643-6464	643-6439
Williamson Law Book Co 790 Canning Pkwy *TF*: 800-733-9522 ■ *Web*: wlbonline.com	Victor	NY	14564	585-924-3400	924-4153
Worzalla Publishing Co 3535 Jefferson St *Web*: www.worzalla.com	Stevens Point	WI	54481	715-344-9600	344-2578
Wright Color Graphics 626 Sonora Ave *Web*: www.wrightcolor.com	Glendale	CA	91201	818-246-8877	246-8984

630 PRINTING COMPANIES - COMMERCIAL PRINTERS

	City	State	Zip	Phone	Fax
Acme Printing Co Inc 30 Industrial Way *TF*: 800-829-0800 ■ *Web*: www.quebecorworldinc.com	Wilmington	MA	01887	978-658-0800	658-3202
ADP Graphic Communications 100 Burma Rd *Web*: www.adpgc.com	Jersey City	NJ	07305	201-217-1990	333-8428
AdPlex Inc 650 Century Plaza Dr Suite 120 *Web*: www.adplex.com	Houston	TX	77073	281-443-4301	443-1040
Allegra Network LLC 21680 Haggerty Rd *TF*: 800-726-9050 ■ *Web*: www.allegranetwork.com	Northville	MI	48167	248-596-8600	596-8601
AlphaGraphics Inc 268 S State St Suite 300 *TF*: 800-955-6246 ■ *Web*: www.alphagraphics.com	Salt Lake City	UT	84111	801-595-7270	595-7271
American Banknote Corp 2200 Fletcher Ave *Web*: www.americanbanknote.com	Fort Lee	NJ	07024	201-592-3400	224-2762
American Color Graphics Inc 100 Winners Cir Suite 300 *TF*: 800-621-7746 ■ *Web*: www.americancolorgraphics.com	Brentwood	TN	37027	615-377-0377	377-0370
American Press LLC 1 American Pl *TF*: 800-289-4602 ■ *Web*: www.american-press.com	Gordonsville	VA	22942	540-832-2253	832-7253
American Spirit Graphics Corp 801 SE 9th St *Web*: www.asgc.com	Minneapolis	MN	55414	612-623-3333	623-9314
American Stationery Co Inc 100 N Park Ave *TF Sales*: 800-822-2577 ■ *Web*: www.americanstationery.com	Peru	IN	46970	765-473-4438	472-8510
Amidon Graphics 1966 Benson Ave *TF*: 800-328-6502 ■ *Web*: www.amidongraphics.com	Saint Paul	MN	55116	651-690-2401	690-4009
Anderson Lithograph Co 3217 S Garfield Ave *TF*: 800-727-5846 ■ *Web*: www.andlitho.com	Los Angeles	CA	90040	323-727-7767	215-2474
Arandell Corp N 82 W 13118 Leon Rd *TF*: 800-558-8724 ■ *Web*: www.arandell.com	Menomonee Falls	WI	53051	262-255-4400	253-3166
Balmar Inc 2818 Fallfax Dr **Fax*: Cust Svc ■ *Web*: www.balmar.com	Falls Church	VA	22042	703-289-9000	876-9606*
Banta Catalog Group 7401 Kilmer Ln *TF*: 888-882-2682 ■ *Web*: www.banta.com/catalog	Maple Grove	MN	55369	763-424-7446	315-8177
Banta Direct Marketing Group 2215 York Rd *TF Cust Svc*: 800-323-6112 ■ *Web*: www.banta.com/prodserv/direct.html	Oak Brook	IL	60523	630-575-2020	575-2010
Banta Publications Group 2215 York Rd Suite 400 *Web*: www.banta.com/prodserv/pub.html	Oak Brook	IL	60523	630-575-2020	323-0782
Berlin Industries Inc 175 Mercedes Dr *Web*: www.berlinindustries.com	Carol Stream	IL	60188	630-682-0600	682-3093
Bowne Business Communications Inc 215 County Ave *Web*: www.bowne.com	Secaucus	NJ	07094	201-271-1000	271-2060
Bowne & Co Inc 55 Water St 50th Fl *NYSE: BNE* ■ *Web*: www.bowne.com	New York	NY	10041	212-924-5500	229-7200
Brown Printing Co 2300 Brown Ave *TF*: 800-533-0475 ■ *Web*: www.brownprinting.com	Waseca	MN	56093	507-835-2410	835-0420
Cadmus Communications Corp Whitehall Group Div 2750 Whitehall Park Dr **Fax*: Sales ■ *TF*: 800-733-4318 ■ *Web*: www.cadmuswhitehall.com	Charlotte	NC	28273	704-583-6600	583-6781*
Cadmus Professional Communications 1801 Bayberry Ct Suite 200 *TF*: 877-422-3687 ■ *Web*: cjs.cadmus.com	Richmond	VA	23226	804-287-5680	287-5691
CadmusMack 2901 Byrdhill Rd *TF*: 800-888-2973 ■ *Web*: www.cadmus.com	Richmond	VA	23228	804-264-2711	515-5711
California Offset Printers Inc 620 W Elk Ave *Web*: www.copprints.com	Glendale	CA	91204	818-291-1100	291-1190
Canadian Bank Note Co Ltd 145 Richmond Rd *Web*: www.cbnco.com	Ottawa	ON	K1Z1A1	613-722-3421	722-2548
Cenveo Color-Art 10300 Watson Rd *TF*: 800-800-8845 ■ *Web*: www.colorart.com	Saint Louis	MO	63127	314-966-2000	966-4725
Cenveo Inc 1 Canterberry Green *NYSE: CVO* ■ *Web*: www.cenveo.com	Stamford	CT	06901	203-595-3000	595-3070
Champion Graphics 3901 Virginia Ave	Cincinnati	OH	45227	513-271-3800	271-5963
Champion Industries Inc 2450-90 1st Ave *NASDAQ: CHMP* ■ **Fax*: Cust Svc ■ *TF*: 800-624-3431 ■ *Web*: www.champion-industries.com	Huntington	WV	25703	304-528-2791	528-2746*
ColorDynamics 200 E Bethany Dr *TF*: 800-445-0017 ■ *Web*: www.colordynamics.com	Allen	TX	75002	972-390-6500	390-6699
ColorGraphics Inc 150 N Myers St *Web*: www.colorgraphics.com	Los Angeles	CA	90033	323-261-7171	261-7077
Concord Litho Group 92 Old Turnpike Rd *TF*: 800-258-3662 ■ *Web*: www.concordlitho.com	Concord	NH	03301	603-225-3328	225-6120
Consolidated Graphics Group Inc 1614 E 40th St *TF*: 888-884-9191 ■ *Web*: www.cgginc.com	Cleveland	OH	44103	216-881-9191	881-3442
Consolidated Graphics Inc 5858 Westheimer Rd Suite 200 *NYSE: CGX* ■ *Web*: www.consolidatedgraphics.com	Houston	TX	77057	713-787-0977	787-5188
Continental Web Press Inc 1430 Industrial Dr *Web*: www.continentalweb.com	Itasca	IL	60143	630-773-1903	773-1909
Cosmos Communications Inc 11-05 44th Dr *TF*: 800-223-5751 ■ *Web*: www.cosmoscommunications.com	Long Island City	NY	11101	718-482-1800	482-1968
Dingley Press 119 Lisbon St *TF*: 888-346-4539 ■ *Web*: www.dingley.com	Lisbon	ME	04250	207-353-4151	353-9886
Disc Graphics Inc 10 Gilpin Ave *Web*: www.discgraphics.com	Hauppauge	NY	11788	631-234-1400	234-1460
Document Security Systems Inc 28 E Main St Suite 1525 *AMEX: DMC* ■ *TF*: 877-276-0293 ■ *Web*: www.documentsecurity.com	Rochester	NY	14614	585-325-3610	325-2977
DuraColor 1840 Oakdale Ave *TF*: 877-899-7900 ■ *Web*: www.duracolor.net	Racine	WI	53406	262-636-0040	636-0070
E & D Web Inc 4633 W 16th St *TF*: 800-323-5733 ■ *Web*: www.eanddweb.com	Cicero	IL	60804	708-656-6600	656-8390
EarthColor 527 W 34th St *Web*: www.earthcolor.com	New York	NY	10001	212-967-9720	564-2500
EBSCO Media 801 5th Ave S *TF*: 800-765-0852 ■ *Web*: www.ebscomedia.com	Birmingham	AL	35233	205-323-1508	226-8400
EU Services 649 N Horners Ln *TF*: 800-230-3362 ■ *Web*: www.euservices.com	Rockville	MD	20850	301-424-3300	424-3696
FB Johnston Graphics 300 E Boundary St *TF*: 800-800-8160 ■ *Web*: www.fbjohnston.com	Chapin	SC	29036	803-345-5481	345-5512
FCL Graphics Inc 4600 N Olcott Ave *Web*: www.fclgraphics.com	Harwood Heights	IL	60706	708-867-5500	867-7768
FedEx Kinko's Office & Print Services Inc 13155 Noel Rd Suite 1600 *TF Cust Svc*: 800-254-6567 ■ *Web*: www.fedexkinkos.com	Dallas	TX	75240	214-550-7000	550-7001
Forest Corp 1665 Enterprise Pkwy *TF*: 800-637-6434 ■ *Web*: www.forestcorporation.com	Twinsburg	OH	44087	330-425-3805	425-9604
Fort Dearborn Co 6035 W Gross Point Rd *TF*: 888-332-7746 ■ *Web*: www.fortdearborn.com	Niles	IL	60714	773-774-4321	774-9105
Gannett Co Inc Gannett Offset Div 6883 Commercial Dr *TF*: 800-255-1457 ■ *Web*: www.gannettoffset.com	Springfield	VA	22159	703-642-1800	642-7392
Hennegan Co 7455 Empire Dr *Web*: www.hennegan.com	Florence	KY	41042	859-282-3600	282-3601
Henry Wurst Inc 1331 Saline St *TF*: 800-775-5851 ■ *Web*: www.henrywurst.com	North Kansas City	MO	64116	816-842-3113	472-6221
Hickory Printing Group Inc 725 Reese Dr SW *TF*: 800-442-5679 ■ *Web*: www.hickoryprinting.com	Conover	NC	28613	828-465-3431	465-2517
Holden Graphic Services 607 Washington Ave N *TF*: 800-423-1099 ■ *Web*: www.holdengraphics.com	Minneapolis	MN	55401	612-339-0241	349-0433
IGI Earth Color Group 527 W 34th St *Web*: www.earthcolor.com	New York	NY	10001	212-967-9720	967-2965
IntegraColor 3210 Innovative Way *TF*: 800-433-8247 ■ *Web*: www.integracolor.com	Mesquite	TX	75149	972-289-0705	285-4881
Intelligencer Printing Co 330 Eden Rd *TF*: 800-233-0107 ■ *Web*: www.intellprinting.com	Lancaster	PA	17601	717-291-3100	569-2752
Ivy Hill Corp 250 Park Ave S 8th Fl *TF*: 800-955-4893 ■ *Web*: www.ivyhill-cinram.com	New York	NY	10003	646-834-1500	834-1580
Japs-Olson Co 7500 Excelsior Blvd *TF*: 800-548-2897 ■ *Web*: www.japsolson.com	Saint Louis Park	MN	55426	952-932-9393	912-1900
John Roberts Co 9687 E River Rd *TF*: 800-551-1534 ■ *Web*: www.johnroberts.com	Coon Rapids	MN	55433	763-755-5500	754-4400
Johnston FB Graphics 300 E Boundary St *TF*: 800-800-8160 ■ *Web*: www.fbjohnston.com	Chapin	SC	29036	803-345-5481	345-5512
Journal Printing Co Inc 4848 Industrial Park Rd *Web*: www.journalprinting.com	Stevens Point	WI	54481	715-344-4084	344-0829
Keller Crescent Co Inc 1100 E Louisiana St **Fax*: Cust Svc ■ *TF*: 800-457-3837 ■ *Web*: www.kellercrescent.com	Evansville	IN	47711	812-464-2461	426-7601*
K/P Corp 12647 Alcosta Blvd Suite 425 *TF*: 877-957-2677 ■ *Web*: www.kpcorporation.com	San Ramon	CA	94583	925-543-5200	543-5252
Lake County Press Inc 98 Noll St *TF*: 800-369-4333 ■ *Web*: www.lakecountypress.com	Waukegan	IL	60085	847-336-4333	336-5846
Lane Press Inc PO Box 130 *TF*: 800-733-3740 ■ *Web*: www.lanepress.com	Burlington	VT	05402	802-863-5555	264-1485
Lehigh Press Inc 7001 N Park Dr **Fax*: Hum Res ■ *Web*: www.lehigh-press.com	Pennsauken	NJ	08109	856-665-5200	665-3810*
Litho-Krome Co 5700 Old Brim Dr *TF*: 800-572-8028 ■ *Web*: www.lithokrome.com	Midland	GA	31820	706-225-6600	225-6639
Lithographix Inc 12250 S Crenshaw Blvd *TF*: 800-848-2449 ■ *Web*: www.lithographix.com	Hawthorne	CA	90250	323-770-1000	720-6000
LP Thebault Co 249 Pomeroy Rd PO Box 169 **Fax*: Sales ■ *TF*: 800-843-2285 ■ *Web*: www.thebault.com	Parsippany	NJ	07054	973-884-1300	884-0169*
Merrill Corp 1 Merrill Cir *TF*: 800-688-4400 ■ *Web*: www.merrillcorp.com	Saint Paul	MN	55108	651-646-4501	649-3838
Merrill/Daniels Printing Co 40 Commercial St *TF*: 800-553-7733 ■ *Web*: www.merrillcorp.com	Everett	MA	02149	617-389-7900	389-5520
Meyers Co 7277 Boone Ave N *TF*: 800-927-9709 ■ *Web*: www.meyers.com	Brooklyn Park	MN	55428	763-533-9730	531-5771
Minuteman Press International Inc 61 Executive Blvd *TF*: 800-645-3006 ■ *Web*: minutemanpress.com	Farmingdale	NY	11735	631-249-1370	249-5618
Nahan Printing Inc 7000 Saukview Dr PO Box 697 *Web*: www.nahan.com	Saint Cloud	MN	56302	320-251-7611	259-1378
National Graphics Inc Rte 139 *Web*: www.natgraphics.com	North Branford	CT	06471	203-481-2351	483-0256
Nationwide Graphics Inc 2500 West Loop S Suite 500 *Web*: www.nationwidegraphics.com	Houston	TX	77027	713-961-4700	961-4701
Network Communications Inc 2305 New Point Pkwy *TF*: 800-841-3401 ■ *Web*: www.livingchoices.com	Lawrenceville	GA	30043	770-962-7220	822-4301
Newsweb Corp 1645 W Fullerton *Web*: www.newswebchicago.com	Chicago	IL	60614	773-975-0400	975-6975
Nielsen Co 7405 Industrial Rd *TF*: 800-877-7405 ■ *Web*: www.nielsenco.com	Florence	KY	41042	859-525-7405	525-7654
Outlook Group Corp 1180 American Dr PO Box 748 *NASDAQ: OUTL* ■ *Web*: www.outlookgroup.com	Neenah	WI	54957	920-722-2333	727-8529
Panel Prints Inc 1001 Moosic Rd *TF*: 800-557-2635 ■ *Web*: www.panelprints.com	Old Forge	PA	18518	570-457-8334	457-6440
PBM Graphics Inc PO Box 13603 *TF*: 800-849-8100 ■ *Web*: www.pbmgraphics.com	Durham	NC	27709	919-544-6222	544-6695
Penn Lithographics Inc 16221 Author St *Web*: www.pennlitho.com	Cerritos	CA	90703	562-926-0455	926-8955
Perry Judd's Inc 575 W Madison St *TF*: 800-737-7948 ■ *Web*: www.perryjudds.com	Waterloo	WI	53594	920-478-3551	478-1800
PIP Printing & Document Services Inc 26722 Plaza Dr Suite 200 *Web*: www.pip.com	Mission Viejo	CA	92691	949-282-3800	282-3899
Polytype America Corp 10 Industrial Ave *Web*: www.polytypeamerica.com	Mahwah	NJ	07430	201-995-1000	995-1080
Premier Print Holdings Inc 2500 West Loop S Suite 500 *Web*: www.nationwidegraphics.com	Houston	TX	77027	713-961-4700	961-4701
Press of Ohio 3765 Sunnybrook Rd *Web*: www.press-of-ohio.com	Brimfield	OH	44240	330-678-5868	677-3346
ProForma 8800 E Pleasant Valley Rd *TF*: 800-825-1525 ■ *Web*: www.proforma.com	Independence	OH	44131	216-520-8400	520-8444
Progress Printing Co 2677 Waterlick Rd *TF*: 800-572-7804 ■ *Web*: www.progprint.com	Lynchburg	VA	24502	434-239-9213	237-1618
Publishers Printing Co 100 Frank E Simon Ave *TF*: 800-627-5801 ■ *Web*: www.pubpress.com	Shepherdsville	KY	40165	502-543-2251	955-5586
Quad/Graphics Inc N63 W23075 Main St **Fax Area Code*: 262 ■ **Fax*: Hum Res ■ *Web*: www.qg.com	Sussex	WI	53089	414-566-6000	246-5123*
Quebecor World Inc 612 rue Saint-Jacques *NYSE: IQW* ■ *TF*: 800-567-7070 ■ *Web*: www.quebecorworldinc.com/en	Montreal	QC	H3C4M8	514-954-0101	954-9624
Quebecor World Inc Northeast Graphics 291 State St *Web*: www.quebecorworldinc.com	North Haven	CT	06473	203-288-2468	248-6478
Regency Thermographers Inc 725 Clayton Ave *TF*: 877-343-6291 ■ *Web*: www.regencythermo.com	Waynesboro	PA	17268	717-762-7161	765-3570
RR Donnelley & Sons Co 111 S Wacker Dr *NYSE: RRD* ■ **Fax*: Mail Rm ■ *Web*: www.rrdonnelley.com	Chicago	IL	60601	312-326-8000	326-8543*
Saint Ives Cleveland Inc 4437 E 49th St *TF*: 800-634-1262 ■ *Web*: www.st-ives-usa.com/clevmain.htm	Cleveland	OH	44125	216-271-5300	271-6203
Saint Ives Inc 2025 McKinley St **Fax*: Cust Svc ■ *Web*: www.st-ives-usa.com	Hollywood	FL	33020	954-920-7300	926-4885*
Saint Joseph Corp 50 MacIntosh Blvd *TF*: 877-660-3111 ■ *Web*: www.stjoseph.com	Concord	ON	L4K4P3	905-660-3111	660-9737
Sandy Alexander Inc 200 Entin Rd *Web*: www.sandyinc.com	Clifton	NJ	07014	973-470-8100	470-9269
Schawk Inc 1695 S River Rd *NYSE: SGK* ■ *TF*: 800-621-1909 ■ *Web*: www.schawk.com	Des Plaines	IL	60018	847-827-9494	827-1264
Schmidt Printing Inc 1101 Frontage Rd NW *Web*: www.schmidt.com	Byron	MN	55920	507-775-6400	775-6655
Shakopee Valley Printing 5101 Valley Industrial Blvd S *TF*: 800-752-9906	Shakopee	MN	55379	952-445-8260	445-5805
Sheridan Group 11311 McCormick Rd Suite 260 *Web*: www.sheridan.com	Hunt Valley	MD	21031	410-785-7277	785-7217
Shorewood Packaging Corp 277 Park Ave 30th Fl *Web*: www.shorewoodpackaging.com	New York	NY	10172	212-371-1500	752-5688

Company	City	State	Zip	Phone	Fax
Sir Speedy Inc 26722 Plaza Dr *TF:* 800-854-8297 ■ *Web:* www.sirspeedy.com	Mission Viejo	CA	92691	949-348-5000	348-5010
Smith Litho Inc 1029 E Gude Dr *TF:* 800-622-2577 ■ *Web:* www.smith-litho.com	Rockville	MD	20850	301-424-1400	762-2080
Solar Communications Inc 1120 Frontenac Rd *TF:* 800-323-2751 ■ *Web:* www.solarcommunications.com	Naperville	IL	60563	630-983-1400	983-1494
Spencer Press Inc 90 Spencer Dr *TF:* 800-765-0039 ■ *Web:* www.spencerpress.com	Wells	ME	04090	207-646-9926	646-5021
Stevens Graphics Inc 713 RD Abernathy Blvd *Web:* www.stevensgraphicsinc.com	Atlanta	GA	30310	404-753-1121	752-0514
Strathmore Co 2000 Gary Ln *Web:* www.strath.com	Geneva	IL	60134	630-232-9677	232-0198
Strine Printing Co Inc 30 Grumbacher Rd *TF:* 800-477-8746 ■ *Web:* www.strine.com	York	PA	17406	717-767-6602	764-3459
TanaSeybert LLC 525 W 52nd St *TF:* 800-606-6876 ■ *Web:* www.tanaseybert.com	New York	NY	10019	212-453-9300	633-9621
Times Printing Co Inc 100 Industrial Dr **Fax:* Cust Svc ■ *TF:* 800-236-4396 ■ *Web:* www.timesprintingco.com	Random Lake	WI	53075	920-994-4396	994-2059*
Toppan Printing Co America Inc 1100 Randolph Rd **Fax:* Sales ■ *Web:* www.ta.toppan.com	Somerset	NJ	08873	732-469-8400	469-1868*
Transcontinental Inc 1 pl Ville Marie Bureau 3315 *TSX:* TCL.a ■ *Web:* www.transcontinental.com	Montreal	QC	H3B3N2	514-954-4000	954-4016
Transcontinental Printing Inc 395 Lebeau Blvd *TF:* 800-337-8560 ■ *Web:* www.transcontinental-gtc.com	Saint-Laurent	QC	H4N1S2	514-337-8560	339-5230
Trend Offset Printing Services Inc 3791 Catalina St **Fax:* Cust Svc ■ *Web:* www.trendoffset.com	Los Alamitos	CA	90720	562-598-2446	430-2373*
Universal Printing Co 1234 S Kings Hwy *Web:* www.universalprintingco.com	Saint Louis	MO	63110	314-771-6900	771-7987
Valassis Communications Inc 19975 Victor Pkwy *NYSE:* VCI ■ **Fax:* Hum Res ■ *TF:* 800-437-0479 ■ *Web:* www.valassis.com	Livonia	MI	48152	734-591-3000	591-4994*
Vertis Inc 250 W Pratt St 18th Fl *TF:* 800-577-3569 ■ *Web:* www.vertisinc.com	Baltimore	MD	21201	410-528-9800	528-9289
Weldon Williams & Lick Inc PO Box 168 *TF:* 800-242-4995 ■ *Web:* www.wwlinc.com	Fort Smith	AR	72902	479-783-4113	783-7050
Wetmore Printing 1645 West Sam Houston Pkwy N *Web:* www.wetmore-printing.com	Houston	TX	77043	713-468-7175	468-8021
Whitehall Group Div Cadmus Communications Corp 2750 Whitehall Park Dr **Fax:* Sales ■ *TF:* 800-733-4318 ■ *Web:* www.cadmuswhitehall.com	Charlotte	NC	28273	704-583-6600	583-6781*
Williamson Printing Corp 6700 Denton Dr *TF:* 800-843-5423 ■ *Web:* www.wpcnet.com	Dallas	TX	75235	214-352-1122	352-1842

631 PRINTING & PHOTOCOPYING SUPPLIES

Company	City	State	Zip	Phone	Fax
Abco Distribution Inc 6282 Proprietors Rd *TF:* 800-821-9435 ■ *Web:* www.printingbyabco.com	Worthington	OH	43085	614-848-4899	848-4897
American Ribbon & Toner Co 6500 NW 15th Ave Suite 300 *TF:* 800-327-1013 ■ *Web:* www.ribbontoner.com	Fort Lauderdale	FL	33309	954-971-2999	971-2004
Atlantic Exchange Inc 10405 NW 37th Terr *TF:* 800-327-2822 ■ *Web:* www.atlex.com	Doral	FL	33178	305-593-1176	599-1653
Automated Office Products Inc 9730-EE ML King Jr Hwy *TF:* 800-929-2528 ■ *Web:* www.automatedonline.com	Lanham	MD	20706	301-731-4000	459-2783
Barouh Eaton Allen Corp 67 Kent Ave *TF:* 800-366-6767	Brooklyn	NY	11211	718-782-2601	486-6340
Buckeye Business Products Inc 3830 Kelley Ave *TF:* 800-837-4323 ■ *Web:* www.buckeyebusiness.com	Cleveland	OH	44114	216-391-6300	881-6105
Canon USA Inc 1 Canon Plaza *NYSE:* CAJ ■ **Fax:* Hum Res ■ *TF:* 800-828-4040 ■ *Web:* www.usa.canon.com	Lake Success	NY	11042	516-488-6700	328-4669*
Capital Imaging Co Inc 2745 W 5th North St *TF:* 800-868-6780 ■ *Web:* www.capitalimaging.com	Summerville	SC	29483	843-871-6084	873-3963
Chromaline Corp 4832 Grand Ave *TF:* 800-328-4261 ■ *Web:* www.chromaline.com	Duluth	MN	55807	218-628-2217	628-3245
Clover Technologies Group 4200 N Columbus St *TF:* 800-464-0272 ■ *Web:* www.clovertech.com	Ottawa	IL	61350	815-431-8100	431-8120
Codo Mfg Corp 7 Ave B	Leetsdale	PA	15056	412-741-2010	741-2785
Color Imaging Inc 4350 Peachtree Industrial Blvd Suite 100 **Fax Area Code:* 800 ■ *TF:* 800-783-1090 ■ *Web:* www.colorimaging.com	Norcross	GA	30071	770-840-1090	783-9010*
Corporate Express Imaging & Computer Graphic Supplies Inc 1096 E Newport Center Dr Suite 300 *TF:* 800-828-9949 ■ *Web:* imaging.cexp.com	Deerfield Beach	FL	33442	954-379-5500	379-5555
Curtis-Young Corp 2704 Cindel Dr *TF:* 800-282-6650	Cinnaminson	NJ	08077	856-665-6650	786-1705
Domino Amjet Inc 1290 Lakeside Dr *TF:* 800-444-4512 ■ *Web:* www.domino-printing.com	Gurnee	IL	60031	847-244-2501	244-1421
DuraLine Imaging Inc 110 Commercial Blvd *TF:* 800-982-3872 ■ *Web:* www.duralineimaging.com	Flat Rock	NC	28731	828-692-1301	
Encore Ribbon Inc 1010 N Dutton Ave *TF:* 800-431-4969 ■ *Web:* www.encoreribbon.com	Santa Rosa	CA	95401	707-206-9600	575-5295
Epson America Inc 3840 Kilroy Airport Way *TF Cust Svc:* 800-533-3731 ■ *Web:* www.epson.com	Long Beach	CA	90806	562-981-3840	290-5220
Frye Tech Inc 110 Industrial Rd **Fax Area Code:* 845 ■ *Web:* www.fryetech.com	New Windsor	NY	12553	800-705-3793	561-0415*
General Ribbon Corp 20650 Prairie St *TF:* 800-423-5400 ■ *Web:* www.printgrc.com	Chatsworth	CA	91311	818-709-1234	700-1209
Graphic Controls LLC 400 Exchange St *TF:* 800-669-1535 ■ *Web:* www.graphiccontrols.com	Buffalo	NY	14204	716-853-7500	847-7551
Guy Brown Products 9003 Overlook Blvd *TF:* 877-794-5906 ■ *Web:* www.guybrown.com	Brentwood	TN	37027	615-777-1500	777-1501
Hurst Chemical Co 16949 Wren Hill St *TF:* 800-723-2004 ■ *Web:* www.hurstchemical.com	Conroe	TX	77385	800-723-2004	723-2005
Image One Corp 13201 Capital Ave *TF:* 800-799-5377 ■ *Web:* www.imageonecorp.com	Oak Park	MI	48237	248-414-9955	414-9951
ImageTek Corp 420 E Easy St Suite 2 *TF:* 800-584-2503	Simi Valley	CA	93065	805-584-2100	584-1370
Ink Technology Corp 18320 Lanken Ave *TF:* 800-633-2826 ■ *Web:* www.inktechnology.com	Cleveland	OH	44119	216-486-6720	486-6003
International Communication Materials Inc Rt 119 S PO Box 716 **Fax Area Code:* 877 ■ *TF:* 800-438-2530 ■ *Web:* www.icmi-toner.com	Connellsville	PA	15425	724-628-1014	289-4264*
ITW Coding Products 111 W Park Dr *Web:* www.codingproducts.com	Kalkaska	MI	49646	231-258-5521	258-6120
Ko-Rec-Type Div Barouh Eaton Allen Corp 67 Kent Ave *TF:* 800-366-6767 ■ *Web:* www.korectype.com	Brooklyn	NY	11211	718-782-2601	486-6340
Kroy LLC 3830 Kelley Ave *TF:* 888-888-5769 ■ *Web:* www.kroy.com	Cleveland	OH	44114	216-426-5600	426-5601
LexJet Corp 1680 Fruitville Rd 3rd Fl *TF:* 800-453-9538 ■ *Web:* www.lexjet.com	Sarasota	FL	34236	941-330-1210	330-1220
Micro Solutions Enterprises 8201 Woodley Ave *TF:* 800-673-4968 ■ *Web:* www.mse-usa.com	Van Nuys	CA	91406	818-407-7500	407-7575
MKG Cartridge Systems Inc 1090 Lorimar Dr *TF:* 800-881-7545 ■ *Web:* www.mkg.org	Mississauga	ON	L5S1R8	905-564-9218	564-9225
NER Data Products Inc 307 S Delsea Dr **Fax Area Code:* 800 ■ *TF:* 800-257-5235 ■ *Web:* www.nerdata.com	Glassboro	NJ	08028	856-881-5524	637-2217*
Nukote International Inc 200 Beasley Dr **Fax:* Mail Rm ■ *TF:* 800-251-1910 ■ *Web:* www.nukote.com	Franklin	TN	37064	615-794-9000	236-5440*
Oasis Imaging Products Inc 460 Amherst St *TF:* 888-627-6555 ■ *Web:* www.oasis-imaging.com	Nashua	NH	03063	603-880-3991	598-4277
Perfecopy Co 103 W 61st St *TF Cust Svc:* 800-323-4030	Westmont	IL	60559	630-769-9901	769-1057
Rayven Inc 431 Griggs St N *TF Cust Svc:* 800-878-3776 ■ *Web:* www.rayven.com	Saint Paul	MN	55104	651-642-1112	642-9497
Ricoh Printing Systems America Inc 2635-A Park Center Dr *TF Cust Svc:* 800-887-8848 ■ *Web:* www.rpsa.ricoh.com	Simi Valley	CA	93065	805-578-4000	578-4001
Sercomp Corp 21050 Lassen St *TF:* 800-477-7372	Chatsworth	CA	91311	818-341-1680	341-9587
Texas Lift-Off Correction Ribbon 1700 Surveyor Blvd Suite 110	Carrollton	TX	75006	972-416-8100	416-9690
Tomoegawa USA Inc 742 Glenn Ave *Web:* www.tomoegawa.com	Wheeling	IL	60090	847-541-3001	541-3021
Western Numerical Control 41102 N Hudson Trail *TF:* 800-538-5108 ■ *Web:* www.westnc.com	Anthem	AZ	85086	623-594-4602	594-3769

632 PRINTING & PUBLISHING EQUIPMENT & SYSTEMS

SEE ALSO Computer Equipment - Printers p. 1503

Company	City	State	Zip	Phone	Fax
Baldwin Technology Co Inc 2 Trap Falls Rd Suite 402 *AMEX:* BLD ■ *Web:* www.baldwintech.com	Shelton	CT	06484	203-402-1000	402-5500
Brackett Inc PO Box 19306 *TF:* 800-255-3506 ■ *Web:* www.brackett-inc.com	Topeka	KS	66619	785-862-2205	862-1127
Brandtjen & Kluge Inc 539 Blanding Woods Rd *TF:* 800-826-7320 ■ *Web:* www.brandtjenandkluge.com	Saint Croix Falls	WI	54024	715-483-3265	483-1640
Burgess Industries Inc 2700 Campus Dr *TF Cust Svc:* 800-233-2589 ■ *Web:* www.burgessind.com	Plymouth	MN	55441	763-553-7800	553-9289
CODA Inc 30 Industrial Ave *Web:* www.codamount.com	Mahwah	NJ	07430	201-825-7400	825-8133
Craftsmen Machinery Co 840 Main St Suite 208	Millis	MA	02054	508-376-2001	376-2003
Dauphin Graphic Machines Inc PO Box 573 *TF:* 800-346-6119 ■ *Web:* www.dauphingraphic.com	Elizabethville	PA	17023	717-362-3243	362-4165
Day International Inc 130 W 2nd St Suite 1700 *Web:* www.dayintl.com	Dayton	OH	45401	937-224-4000	226-1466
Delphax Technologies Inc 6100 W 110th St *NASDAQ:* DLPX ■ **Fax:* Cust Svc ■ *Web:* www.delphax.com	Bloomington	MN	55338	952-939-9000	939-0798*
Diamond Roller 150 Marr Ave *TF:* 800-247-5290 ■ *Web:* www.diamondroller.com	Marietta	GA	30060	770-590-9991	590-0235
GMI (Graphics Microsystems Inc) 484 Oakmead Pkwy *TF:* 800-336-1464 ■ *Web:* www.gmicolor.com	Sunnyvale	CA	94085	408-731-2000	731-2100
Goss International Corp 3 Territorial Ct *Web:* www.gossinternational.com	Bolingbrook	IL	60440	630-755-9300	755-9301
Graphics Microsystems Inc (GMI) 484 Oakmead Pkwy *TF:* 800-336-1464 ■ *Web:* www.gmicolor.com	Sunnyvale	CA	94085	408-731-2000	731-2100
Gravograph-New Hermes Inc 2200 Northmont Pkwy **Fax Area Code:* 800 ■ *TF:* 800-843-7637 ■ *Web:* www.gravograph.com	Duluth	GA	30096	770-623-0331	533-7637*
Heidelberg USA Inc 1000 Gutenberg Dr *TF:* 800-437-7388 ■ *Web:* www.us.heidelberg.com	Kennesaw	GA	30144	770-419-6500	419-6550
Joseph Merritt & Co 650 Franklin Ave *TF:* 800-344-4477 ■ *Web:* www.jmerritt.com	Hartford	CT	06114	860-296-2500	296-0414
Kodak's Graphic Communications Group Canada 3700 Gilmore Way *TF:* 877-387-2736 ■ *Web:* graphics1.kodak.com	Burnaby	BC	V5G4M1	604-451-2700	437-9891
Kodak's Graphic Communications Group - Inkjet Printing Solutions 3000 Research Blvd *Web:* graphics1.kodak.com	Dayton	OH	45420	937-259-3000	259-3385
Konica Minolta Graphic Imaging USA Inc 5800 Foremost Dr SE *TF Cust Svc:* 800-282-5752 ■ *Web:* gi.konicaminolta.us	Grand Rapids	MI	49546	616-575-2800	285-7108
LasscoWizer Inc 485 Hague St *TF:* 800-854-6595 ■ *Web:* www.lasscowizer.com	Rochester	NY	14606	585-436-1934	464-8665
MAN Roland Inc 800 E Oak Hill Dr *TF:* 800-700-2344 ■ *Web:* www.manroland.com	Westmont	IL	60559	630-920-2000	920-9146
Mark Andy Inc 18081 Chesterfield Airport Rd **Fax:* Cust Svc ■ *TF:* 800-700-6275 ■ *Web:* www.markandy.com	Chesterfield	MO	63005	636-532-4433	532-4701*
Merritt Joseph & Co 650 Franklin Ave *TF:* 800-344-4477 ■ *Web:* www.jmerritt.com	Hartford	CT	06114	860-296-2500	296-0414
NUR America Inc 85 Oxford Dr *Web:* www.nur.com	Moonachie	NJ	07074	201-708-2100	708-2111
Pamarco Global Graphics 235 E 11th Ave *TF:* 800-526-2180 ■ *Web:* www.pamarcoglobal.com	Roselle	NJ	07203	908-241-1200	241-4237
Presstek Inc 55 Executive Dr *NASDAQ:* PRST ■ *TF:* 877-862-2227 ■ *Web:* www.presstek.com	Hudson	NH	03051	603-595-7000	594-8575
Rosback Co 125 Hawthorne Ave *TF:* 800-542-2420 ■ *Web:* www.rosbackcompany.com	Saint Joseph	MI	49085	269-983-2582	983-2516
Stevens Technology LLC 5700 E Belknap St *Web:* www.stevenstechnology.com	Fort Worth	TX	76117	817-759-4000	759-4080
Stolle Machinery Co LLC 6949 S Potomac St *TF:* 800-228-4593 ■ *Web:* www.stollemachinery.com	Centennial	CO	80112	303-708-9044	708-9045
Townsend Industries Inc 6650 NE 41st Ave *TF:* 877-868-3544 ■ *Web:* www.t-51.com	Altoona	IA	50009	515-967-4261	967-7519
Web Press Corp 22023 68th Ave S *TF:* 800-424-1411 ■ *Web:* www.webpresscorp.com	Kent	WA	98032	253-395-3343	395-4492
Xerox Corp 800 Long Ridge Rd *NYSE:* XRX ■ **Fax:* Mail Rm ■ *TF:* 800-842-0024 ■ *Web:* www.xerox.com	Stamford	CT	06904	203-968-3000	968-3508*

633 PRISON INDUSTRIES

Prison industries are programs established by federal and state governments that provide work for inmates while they are incarcerated as well as on-the-job training to help them become employable on release. At the same time, prison industries provide quality goods and services at competitive prices.

Company	City	State	Zip	Phone	Fax
Alabama Correctional Industries 1400 Lloyd St *TF:* 800-224-7007 ■ *Web:* www.doc.state.al.us/industries.htm	Montgomery	AL	36107	334-261-3600	240-3162
Arizona Correctional Industries 3701 W Cambridge Ave *Web:* www.adc.state.az.us/corrindu.htm	Phoenix	AZ	85009	602-272-7600	255-3108
Arkansas Correctional Industries 2403 E Harding St *Web:* www.acicatalog.com/info.html	Pine Bluff	AR	71601	870-850-8434	850-8440

Phone | Fax

Badger State Industries 3099 E Washington Ave ... Madison WI 53704 608-240-5200 240-3320
Web: www.buybsi.com
Big House Products & Services PO Box 47 ... Camp Hill PA 17001 717-731-7132 787-0132
TF: 877-673-3724 ■ *Web:* www.pci.state.pa.us/pci/site/default.asp
California Prison Industry Authority 560 E Natoma St ... Folsom CA 95630 916-358-2727 358-2660*
**Fax:* Cust Svc ■ *Web:* www.pia.ca.gov/piawebdev
Colorado Correctional Industries DBA Juniper Valley Products 2862 S Circle Dr ... Colorado Springs CO 80906 719-226-4206 226-4220
TF Cust Svc: 800-685-7891 ■ *Web:* www.cijvp.com
Corcraft Products 550 Broadway ... Albany NY 12204 518-436-6321 436-6007
Web: www.corcraft.org
Cornhusker State Industries 800 Pioneers Blvd ... Lincoln NE 68502 402-471-4597 471-1236
TF: 800-348-7537 ■ *Web:* www.corrections.state.ne.us/csi
Correctional Enterprises of Connecticut
24 Wolcott Hill Rd ... Wethersfield CT 06109 860-263-6839 263-6838
TF: 800-842-1146 ■ *Web:* www.ct.gov/doc/site/default.asp
Delaware Prison Industries 245 McKee Rd ... Dover DE 19904 302-739-5601 739-1608
DEPTCOR PO Box 867 ... Trenton NJ 08625 609-633-8100 633-2495
TF: 800-321-6524 ■ *Web:* www.state.nj.us/deptcor
Federal Prison Industries Inc DBA UNICOR 320 1st St NW ... Washington DC 20534 202-305-3501
Web: www.unicor.gov
Georgia Correctional Industries 2984 Clifton Springs Rd ... Decatur GA 30034 404-244-5100 244-5141
TF: 800-282-7130 ■ *Web:* www.gci-ga.com
Hawaii Correctional Industries 99-902 Mauna Loa Rd ... Aiea HI 96701 808-486-4883 488-4999
Idaho Correctional Industries 1299 N Orchard St Suite 110 ... Boise ID 83706 208-658-2175 658-2160
Web: www.ci.state.id.us
Illinois Correctional Industries 1301 Concordia Ct ... Springfield IL 62794 217-522-2666 522-1930
Web: www.idoc.state.il.us/subsections/industries
Inside Oregon Enterprises PO Box 12849 ... Salem OR 97309 503-373-7604 378-5592
Iowa Prison Industries 2323 Dean Ave ... Des Moines IA 50309 515-242-5778
Web: www.iaprisonind.com
Juniper Valley Products 2862 S Circle Dr ... Colorado Springs CO 80906 719-226-4206 226-4220
TF Cust Svc: 800-685-7891 ■ *Web:* www.cijvp.com
Kansas Correctional Industries PO Box 2 ... Lansing KS 66043 913-727-3249 727-2331
Web: www.accesskansas.org/lcf
Kentucky Correctional Industries 1041 Leestown Rd ... Frankfort KY 40601 502-573-1040 573-1045
Web: www.kcitoday.com
Louisiana Prison Enterprises PO Box 44314 ... Baton Rouge LA 70804 225-342-6633 342-5556
Maine State Prison Industries Program 807 Cushing Rd ... Warren ME 04864 207-273-5470 273-5474
Maryland Correctional Enterprises 7275 Waterloo Rd ... Jessup MD 20794 410-540-5400 540-5570
Web: www2.dpscs.state.md.us/sui
Massachusetts Correctional Industries PO Box 188 ... Norfolk MA 02056 617-727-3322 762-2971*
**Fax Area Code:* 781 ■ *Web:* www.mass.gov/doc/PROGRAMS/Corrind.htm
Michigan State Industries 5656 S Cedar St ... Lansing MI 48909 517-373-4277 241-9063*
**Fax:* Hum Res ■ *Web:* www.michigan.gov/corrections
MINNCOR Industries 1450 Energy Park Dr Suite 110 ... Saint Paul MN 55108 651-603-0118 603-0119
TF: 800-646-6267 ■ *Web:* www.minncor.com
Mississippi Prison Industries Corp 663 N State St ... Jackson MS 39202 601-969-5750 969-5757
Web: www.mpic.net
Missouri Vocational Enterprises PO Box 1898 ... Jefferson City MO 65102 573-751-6663 751-9197
TF Sales: 800-392-8486 ■ *Web:* www.corrections.state.mo.us
Montana Correctional Enterprises 300 Conley Lake Rd ... Deer Lodge MT 59722 406-846-1320 846-2954*
**Fax:* Orders ■ *TF:* 800-815-6252 ■ *Web:* www.cor.state.mt.us/About/MCE.asp
New Hampshire Correctional Industries
281 N State St PO Box 14 ... Concord NH 03302 603-271-1875 271-1116
Web: www.nh.gov/nhci
New Jersey Bureau of State Use Industries PO Box 867 ... Trenton NJ 08625 609-633-8100 633-2495
TF: 800-321-6524 ■ *Web:* www.state.nj.us/deptcor
New Mexico Correctional Industries 4337 SR 14 ... Santa Fe NM 87505 505-827-8838 827-8689*
**Fax:* Cust Svc ■ *TF:* 800-568-8789 ■ *Web:* www.state.nm.us/corrections/catelog.html
New York Correctional Industries DBA Corcraft Products
550 Broadway ... Albany NY 12204 518-436-6321 436-6007
Web: www.corcraft.org
North Carolina Correction Enterprises 2020 Yonkers Rd ... Raleigh NC 27604 919-716-3600 716-3974
Web: www.doc.state.nc.us/eprise/index.htm
Ohio Penal Industries 1221 McKinley Ave ... Columbus OH 43222 614-752-0287 752-0303
TF: 800-237-3454 ■ *Web:* www.opi.state.oh.us/
Oklahoma Correctional Industries 3402 ML King Blvd ... Oklahoma City OK 73111 405-425-7500 425-2838*
**Fax:* Cust Svc ■ *TF:* 800-522-3565 ■ *Web:* www.ocisales.com
PEN Products 6075 Lakeside Blvd ... Indianapolis IN 46278 317-388-8580 280-3001
Pennsylvania Bureau of Correctional Industries DBA Big House Products & Services PO Box 47 ... Camp Hill PA 17001 717-731-7132 787-0132
TF: 877-673-3724 ■ *Web:* www.pci.state.pa.us/pci/site/default.asp
Pheasantland Industries 1600 North Dr Box 5911 ... Sioux Falls SD 57117 605-367-5111 367-5102
Web: www.state.sd.us/corrections/corrections.html
PRIDE (Prison Rehabilitative Industries & Diversified Enterprises Inc) 12425 28th St N 3rd Fl ... Saint Petersburg FL 33716 727-572-1987 570-3366
TF: 800-643-8495 ■ *Web:* www.peol.com
Prison Rehabilitative Industries & Diversified Enterprises Inc (PRIDE) 12425 28th St N 3rd Fl ... Saint Petersburg FL 33716 727-572-1987 570-3366
TF: 800-643-8495 ■ *Web:* www.peol.com
Prisoner Employment Program 9101 Hesterberg Rd ... Eagle River AK 99577 907-696-7650 696-7651
Web: www.alaskaci.com
Rhode Island Correctional Industries 33 Power Rd ... Cranston RI 02920 401-462-2134 462-2135
Web: www.doc.state.ri.us
Rough Rider Industries 3303 E Main Ave ... Bismarck ND 58506 701-328-6161 328-6164
TF: 800-732-0557 ■ *Web:* www.roughriderindustries.com
Silver State Industries PO Box 7011 ... Carson City NV 89701 775-887-3303 883-6263
TF: 800-648-7578 ■ *Web:* www.silverstateindustries.com
South Carolina Prison Industries 4444 Broad River Rd ... Columbia SC 29210 803-896-8516 896-2173*
**Fax:* Cust Svc ■ *Web:* www.doc.sc.gov
Tennessee Rehabilitative Initiative in Correction (TRICOR)
240 Great Circle Rd Suite 310 ... Nashville TN 37228 615-741-5705 741-2747*
**Fax:* Cust Svc ■ *TF:* 800-958-7426 ■ *Web:* www.tricor.org
Texas Correctional Industries 861 I-45 ... Huntsville TX 77320 936-437-6048 437-6040
TF: 800-883-4302 ■ *Web:* www.tci.tdcj.state.tx.us
TRICOR (Tennessee Rehabilitative Initiative in Correction)
240 Great Circle Rd Suite 310 ... Nashville TN 37228 615-741-5705 741-2747*
**Fax:* Cust Svc ■ *TF:* 800-958-7426 ■ *Web:* www.tricor.org
UNICOR 320 1st St NW ... Washington DC 20534 202-305-3501
Web: www.unicor.gov
Utah Correctional Industries 14072 S Pony Express Rd ... Draper UT 84020 801-576-7700 523-9753
Web: uci.utah.gov
Vermont Correctional Industries 37 Commercial Dr ... Waterbury VT 05676 802-241-2268 241-1475
Web: www.vowp.com
Virginia Correctional Enterprises 8030 White Bark Terr ... Richmond VA 23237 804-743-4100 743-2206
Web: www.vcedigitalworks.com/vce
Washington Correctional Industries 801 88th Ave SE ... Tumwater WA 98512 360-725-9100 753-0219
Web: www.washingtonci.com
West Virginia Correctional Industries
617 Leon Sullivan Way ... Charleston WV 25301 304-558-6054 558-6056
TF: 800-525-5381 ■ *Web:* www.state.wv.us/wvdoc/industries.html

634 PROFESSIONAL EMPLOYER ORGANIZATIONS (PEOS)

Companies listed here contractually assume human resources responsibilities for client companies in exchange for a fee, thus allowing the client company to focus on its true company business. The PEO establishes and maintains an employer relationship with the workers assigned to its client companies, with the PEO and the client company each having specific rights and responsibilities toward the employees.

Phone | Fax

Accord Human Resources Inc 210 Park Ave Suite 1200 ... Oklahoma City OK 73102 405-232-9888 725-4049*
**Fax Area Code:* 800 ■ *TF:* 800-725-4004 ■ *Web:* www.accordhr.com
Adams Keegan Inc 6055 Primacy Pkwy Suite 300 ... Memphis TN 38119 901-683-5353 683-5392
TF: 800-621-1308 ■ *Web:* www.adamskeegan.com
Administaff Inc 19001 Crescent Springs Dr ... Kingwood TX 77339 281-358-8986 348-2849*
NYSE: ASF ■ **Fax:* Mktg ■ *TF:* 800-465-3800 ■ *Web:* www.administaff.com
ADP TotalSource Co 10200 Sunset Dr ... Miami FL 33173 305-630-1000 630-3006*
**Fax:* Hum Res ■ *TF:* 800-447-3237 ■ *Web:* www.adptotalsource.com
AdvanTech Solutions 4890 W Kennedy Blvd Suite 500 ... Tampa FL 33609 813-289-9442 636-8238
TF: 888-340-9442 ■ *Web:* www.advantechsolutions.com
Alcott Group 71 Executive Blvd ... Farmingdale NY 11735 631-420-0100 420-1894
TF: 888-425-2688 ■ *Web:* www.alcottgroup.com
All Staffing Inc 100 W Ridge St PO Box 219 ... Lansford PA 18232 570-645-5000 645-5255
TF: 800-442-4538 ■ *Web:* www.allstaffing.com
Allied Employer Group 4400 Buffalo Gap Rd Suite 4500 ... Abilene TX 79606 325-695-5822 692-9660
TF: 800-729-7823 ■ *Web:* www.coemployer.com
AlphaStaff Inc 800 Corporate Dr Suite 600 ... Fort Lauderdale FL 33334 954-267-1760 632-8090*
**Fax Area Code:* 866 ■ *TF:* 888-335-9545 ■ *Web:* www.alphastaff.com
ALTRES Inc 967 Kapiolani Blvd ... Honolulu HI 96814 808-591-4900 591-4914
TF: 800-373-1955 ■ *Web:* www.altres.com
AmStaff Human Resources Inc 6723 Plantation Rd ... Pensacola FL 32504 850-477-7022 478-4088
TF: 800-888-0472 ■ *Web:* www.amstaff.com
atWILL 9237 Ward Pkwy Suite 114 ... Kansas City MO 64114 816-444-1223 444-0505
Axiom HR Solutions 8345 Lenexa Dr Suite 100 ... Lenexa KS 66214 913-383-2999 383-2949
TF: 800-801-7557 ■ *Web:* www.axiomhrsolutions.com
Barrett Business Services Inc 4724 SW Macadam Ave ... Portland OR 97239 503-220-0988 220-0987
NASDAQ: BBSI ■ *TF:* 800-494-5669 ■ *Web:* www.barrettbusiness.com
Bowles Group of Cos DBA Workforce 2000
1903 Central Dr Suite 200 ... Bedford TX 76021 817-868-7277 868-7210
TF: 800-522-9778 ■ *Web:* www.workforcepeo.com
Century II Staffing Inc 278 Franklin Rd Suite 350 ... Brentwood TN 37027 615-665-9060 665-1833
TF: 800-972-9630 ■ *Web:* www.centuryiistaffing.com
Ceridian Corp 3311 E Old Shakopee Rd ... Minneapolis MN 55425 952-853-8100
NYSE: CEN ■ *TF:* 800-767-4969 ■ *Web:* www.ceridian.com
Certified HR Services 5101 NW 21st Ave Suite 350 ... Fort Lauderdale FL 33309 954-677-0202 677-1061
TF: 800-793-2872
Checks & Balances Inc 10328 Battleview Pkwy ... Manassas VA 20109 703-361-2220 368-1795
TF: 800-624-3698 ■ *Web:* www.checksbal.com
Co-Advantage Resources 111 W Jefferson St Suite 100 ... Orlando FL 32801 407-422-8448 422-4382
TF: 888-278-6055 ■ *Web:* www.coadvantage.com
Diversified Human Resources Inc 2735 E Camelback Rd ... Phoenix AZ 85016 480-941-5588 553-4684*
**Fax Area Code:* 602 ■ *TF:* 888-870-5588 ■ *Web:* www.dhr.net
Doherty Employment Group 7625 Parklawn Ave ... Edina MN 55435 952-832-8383 832-8371
TF: 800-910-8822 ■ *Web:* www.dohertyeg.com
EBDS (Employee Benefits Data Services Inc)
420 Fort Duquesne Blvd 1 Gateway Ctr Suite 1250 ... Pittsburgh PA 15222 412-394-6300 394-9669
TF: 800-472-2738 ■ *Web:* www.ebds.com
EHRI (Employer's Human Resources Inc) 75899 State Hwy 16 ... Wagoner OK 74467 918-485-9404 878-0953*
**Fax Area Code:* 800 ■ *TF:* 800-878-0515
Employee Benefits Data Services Inc (EBDS)
420 Fort Duquesne Blvd 1 Gateway Ctr Suite 1250 ... Pittsburgh PA 15222 412-394-6300 394-9669
TF: 800-472-2738 ■ *Web:* www.ebds.com
Employee Management Services 435 Elm St ... Cincinnati OH 45202 513-651-3244 381-2764
TF: 888-651-1536 ■ *Web:* www.emshro.com
Employee Professionals 6320 Trail Blvd ... Naples FL 34108 239-592-9700 592-9100
TF: 888-592-9700 ■ *Web:* www.employeepro.com
Employer's Human Resources Inc (EHRI) 75899 State Hwy 16 ... Wagoner OK 74467 918-485-9404 878-0953*
**Fax Area Code:* 800 ■ *TF:* 800-878-0515
Executive Staffing Group The 4101 Lake Boone Trail Suite 112 ... Raleigh NC 27607 919-783-6695 783-6351
TF: 888-374-4364 ■ *Web:* www.executivestaffing.com
Genesis Consolidated Services Inc 76 Blanchard Rd ... Burlington MA 01803 781-272-4900 273-6644
TF: 800-367-8367 ■ *Web:* www.genesis-cos.com
Gevity HR Inc 600 301 Blvd W ... Bradenton FL 34205 941-748-4540 741-4690*
NASDAQ: GVHR ■ **Fax:* Hum Res ■ *TF:* 800-243-8489 ■ *Web:* www.gevityhr.com
HR Affiliates 1930 Bishop Lane ... Louisville KY 40218 502-485-9675 485-1242
Web: www.hraffiliates.com
HR America 1833 Magnavox Way ... Fort Wayne IN 46804 260-436-3878 436-7692
TF: 800-837-4787 ■ *Web:* www.hramerica.net
Human Capital 18831 W 12 Mile Rd ... Southfield MI 48076 248-353-3444 353-3829
TF: 888-736-9071 ■ *Web:* www.human-capital.com
Human Resources Inc 2127 Espey Ct Suite 306 ... Crofton MD 21114 410-451-4202 451-4206
Web: www.hri-online.com
Kelly Staff Leasing 9444 Farnham St ... San Diego CA 92123 858-598-1800 243-1097*
**Fax Area Code:* 800 ■ *TF:* 800-877-8233 ■ *Web:* www.kellystaffleasing.com
KimStaff HR 17872 Cowan Ave ... Irvine CA 92614 949-752-2995 756-5015
TF: 800-601-4800 ■ *Web:* www.kimstaff.com
Merit Resources Inc 4165 120th St ... Des Moines IA 50323 515-278-1931 276-3813
TF: 800-336-1931 ■ *Web:* www.meritresources.com
Moresource Inc 401 Vandiver Dr Suite B ... Columbia MO 65202 573-443-1234 441-1225
TF: 800-495-5678 ■ *Web:* www.moresource-inc.com
NESCO Inc Service Group 6140 Parkland Blvd ... Mayfield Heights OH 44124 440-461-6000 449-3111
Oasis Outsourcing Inc
4400 N Congress Ave Suite 250 ... West Palm Beach FL 33407 888-627-4735 630-1410*
**Fax Area Code:* 561 ■ *TF:* 800-627-4735 ■ *Web:* www.oasisadvantage.com
Odyssey OneSource Inc 204 N Ector Dr ... Euless TX 76039 817-267-6090 508-7362
TF: 866-508-7361 ■ *Web:* www.odysseyonesource.com
Pay Plus Benefits Inc 1110 N Center Pkwy Suite B ... Kennewick WA 99336 509-735-1143 735-7668
TF: 888-531-5781 ■ *Web:* www.payplusbenefits.com
Paychex Business Solutions
10105 Dr Martin Luthur King Jr St N ... Saint Petersburg FL 33716 727-579-0505 579-0605
TF: 800-741-6277 ■ *Web:* www.paychex.com/products/pbs.html
PaySource Inc 251 New Karner Rd ... Albany NY 12205 518-452-9743 452-0472
TF: 888-452-9743 ■ *Web:* www.epaysource.com
PayTech 640 E Purdue Dr Suite 102 ... Phoenix AZ 85020 602-788-1317 971-6022
TF: 866-972-6064 ■ *Web:* www.pay-tech.com
People Lease Inc
689 Town Center Blvd Suite B PO Box 3303 ... Ridgeland MS 39158 601-987-3025 987-3029
TF: 800-723-3025 ■ *Web:* www.peoplelease.com
Persidion Solutions 1 Harbison Way Suite 201 ... Columbia SC 29212 803-781-7810 498-2963
TF: 800-493-2961
Personnel Management Inc PO Box 6657 ... Shreveport LA 71136 318-869-4555 841-4350
TF: 800-259-4126 ■ *Web:* www.pmiresource.com
Presidion Solutions 755 W Big Beaver Rd Suite 1700 ... Troy MI 48084 248-269-9600 269-5500
TF: 866-259-5434 ■ *Web:* www.presidionsolutions.com

	City	State	Zip	Phone	Fax
Professional Staff Management Inc 224 S 5th St. *TF:* 800-967-5515 ■ *Web:* www.psmin.com	Richmond	IN	47374	765-935-1515	962-6732
Progressive Employer Services 3106 Alternate 19 *TF:* 800-741-7848 ■ *Web:* www.progressiveemployer.com	Palm Harbor	FL	34683	727-712-9121	712-8051
Reserves Network The 22021 Brookpark Rd *TF:* 866-876-2020 ■ *Web:* www.thereservesnetwork.com	Fairview Park	OH	44126	440-779-1400	779-1493
Resource Management Inc 281 Main St Suite 5 *Web:* www.rmi-solutions.com	Fitchburg	MA	01420	978-343-6018	343-0719
RMPersonnel Inc 4707 Montana Ave *Web:* www.rmpersonnel.com	El Paso	TX	79903	915-565-7674	565-7687
Sequent Inc 222 E Campus View Blvd *TF:* 877-447-4111 ■ *Web:* www.sequenthr.com	Columbus	OH	43235	614-436-5880	436-5881
Shaw & Shaw 2421 N Glassell St *TF:* 800-933-6756 ■ *Web:* www.shawnshaw.com	Orange	CA	92865	714-921-5442	283-4686
Staff Management Inc 5919 Spring Creek Rd *TF:* 800-535-3518 ■ *Web:* www.staffmgmt.com	Rockford	IL	61114	815-282-3900	282-0826
Staff One Inc 1100 W Main St *TF:* 800-771-7823 ■ *Web:* www.staffone.com	Durant	OK	74701	580-920-1212	920-0863
Staff Resources Inc 870 Manzanita Ct Suite A *TF Sales:* 888-835-5774 ■ *Web:* www.staffresources.com	Chico	CA	95926	530-345-2487	894-8767
Staffing Plus 555 E Butterfield Rd Suite 330 *TF:* 800-782-3346	Lombard	IL	60148	630-515-0500	515-0510
Strategic Outsourcing Inc 5260 Parkway Plaza Blvd Suite 140 *TF:* 800-426-1121 ■ *Web:* www.soi.net	Charlotte	NC	28217	704-523-2191	523-2158
Tilson HR Inc 1499 Windhorst Way Suite 100 *TF:* 800-276-3976 ■ *Web:* www.tilsonhr.com	Greenwood	IN	46143	317-885-3838	807-1039
TriNet Group Inc 1100 San Leandro Blvd Suite 300 *TF:* 800-638-0461 ■ *Web:* www.trinet.com	San Leandro	CA	94577	510-352-5000	352-6480
USPersonnel 2300 Valley View Ln Suite 300 *TF:* 888-506-7785 ■ *Web:* www.uspersonnel.com	Irving	TX	75062	972-871-0400	871-0444
Wackenhut Resources Inc 4200 Wackenhut Dr Suite 100 **Fax: Hum Res*	Palm Beach Gardens	FL	33410	561-622-5656	691-6591*
Wausau Benefits Inc 115 W Wausau Ave *TF:* 800-826-9781 ■ *Web:* www.wausaubenefits.com	Wausau	WI	54402	715-841-2000	841-7373
Workforce 2000 1903 Central Dr Suite 200 *TF:* 800-522-9778 ■ *Web:* www.workforcepeo.com	Bedford	TX	76021	817-868-7277	868-7210

635 PUBLIC BROADCASTING ORGANIZATIONS

SEE ALSO Radio Networks p. 2164; Television Networks - Broadcast p. 2344

	City	State	Zip	Phone	Fax
Alabama Educational Television Commission 2112 11th Ave S Suite 400 *TF:* 800-239-5233 ■ *Web:* www.aptv.org	Birmingham	AL	35205	205-328-8756	251-2192
Alabama Public Television (APT) 2112 11th Ave S Suite 400 *TF:* 800-239-5233 ■ *Web:* www.aptv.org	Birmingham	AL	35205	205-328-8756	251-2192
Alaska One PO Box 755620 *TF:* 800-727-6543 ■ *Web:* www.alaskaone.org	Fairbanks	AK	99775	907-474-7491	474-5064
Alaska Public Broadcasting Commission PO Box 200009 *Web:* www.akpb.org	Anchorage	AK	99520	907-277-6300	277-6350
American Public Television (APT) 55 Summer St 4th Fl *Web:* www.aptvs.org	Boston	MA	02110	617-338-4455	338-5369
Annenberg Media c/o Learner Online 1301 Pennsylvania Ave NW Suite 302 *TF:* 800-532-7637 ■ *Web:* www.learner.org	Washington	DC	20004	202-783-0500	783-0333
Arkansas Educational Television Network (AETN) 350 S Donaghey Ave *TF:* 800-662-2386 ■ *Web:* www.aetn.org	Conway	AR	72034	501-682-2386	682-4122
Association of Independents in Radio (AIR) 42 Charles St 2nd Fl *Web:* www.airmedia.org	Dorchester	MA	02125	617-825-4400	
Association of Minnesota Public & Educational Radio Stations (AMPERS) 525 Park St Suite 310 *Web:* www.ampers.org	Saint Paul	MN	55103	651-293-0229	293-1709
Association of Public Television Stations (APTS) 2100 Crystal Dr Suite 700 *Web:* www.apts.org	Arlington	VA	22202	202-654-4200	654-4236
BBC Worldwide Americas 747 3rd Ave *TF:* 800-888-4741 ■ *Web:* www.bbcworldwide.com	New York	NY	10017	212-705-9300	888-0576
Blue Ridge Public Television 1215 McNeil Dr *TF:* 888-332-7788 ■ *Web:* www.blueridgepbs.org	Roanoke	VA	24015	540-344-0991	344-2148
Boise State Radio 1910 University Drive *TF:* 888-859-5278 ■ *Web:* radio.boisestate.edu	Boise	ID	83725	208-426-3663	344-6631
California Public Radio 4100 Vachell Ln	San Luis Obispo	CA	93401	805-781-3020	781-3025
Commonwealth Club of California 595 Market St 2nd Fl *TF:* 800-933-7548 ■ *Web:* www.commonwealthclub.org	San Francisco	CA	94105	415-597-6700	597-6729
Commonwealth Public Broadcasting DBA Community Idea Stations 23 Sesame St *Web:* www.ideastations.org	Richmond	VA	23235	804-320-1301	320-8729
Community Idea Stations 23 Sesame St *Web:* www.ideastations.org	Richmond	VA	23235	804-320-1301	320-8729
Connecticut Public Broadcasting Inc (CPBI) 1049 Asylum Ave *TF:* 800-683-2112 ■ *Web:* www.cpbi.org	Hartford	CT	06105	860-278-5310	244-9624
Corporation for Public Broadcasting (CPB) 401 9th St NW *TF:* 800-272-2190 ■ *Web:* www.cpb.org	Washington	DC	20004	202-879-9600	879-9700
Development Exchange Inc (DEI) 401 N 3rd St Suite 370 *TF:* 888-454-2314 ■ *Web:* www.deiworksite.org	Minneapolis	MN	55401	612-677-1505	677-1508
East Tennessee Public Communications Corp 1611 E Magnolia Ave *TF:* 800-595-0220 ■ *Web:* www.etptv.org	Knoxville	TN	37917	865-595-0220	595-0300
Florida Public Radio Network (FPRN) 1600 Red Barber Plaza *Web:* www.fsu.edu/wfsu_fm/fpr/index.htm	Tallahassee	FL	32310	850-487-3194	487-3293
Georgia Public Broadcasting (GPB) 260 14th St NW *TF:* 800-222-6006 ■ *Web:* www.gpb.org	Atlanta	GA	30318	404-685-4788	685-2431
GPB Education 260 14th St NW *TF:* 888-501-8960 ■ *Web:* www.gpb.org/peachstar	Atlanta	GA	30318	404-685-2550	685-2556
Hawaii Public Television (HPTV) 2350 Dole St *Web:* pbshawaii.org	Honolulu	HI	96822	808-973-1000	973-1090
Idaho Public Television (IPTV) 1455 N Orchard St *TF:* 800-543-6868 ■ *Web:* idptv.state.id.us	Boise	ID	83706	208-373-7220	373-7245
Independent Television Service (ITVS) 651 Brannan St Suite 410 *Web:* www.itvs.org	San Francisco	CA	94107	415-356-8383	356-8391
Indiana Higher Education Telecommunication System (IHETS) 714 N Senate Ave Rm 0100 *TF:* 800-776-4438 ■ *Web:* www.ihets.org	Indianapolis	IN	46202	317-263-8900	263-8831
Indiana Public Broadcasting Stations Inc Ball State University Telecommunications Dept *Web:* www.ipbs.org	Muncie	IN	47306	765-285-2466	285-1490
Intercollegiate Broadcasting System Inc (IBS) 367 Windsor Hwy *Web:* www.ibsradio.org	New Windsor	NY	12553	845-565-0003	565-7446
Iowa Public Television (IPTV) 6450 Corporate Dr PO Box 6450 *TF:* 800-532-1290 ■ *Web:* www.iptv.org	Johnston	IA	50131	515-242-3100	242-5830
Kentucky Educational Television (KET) 600 Cooper Dr *TF:* 800-432-0951 ■ *Web:* www.ket.org	Lexington	KY	40502	859-258-7000	258-7399
Louisiana Educational Television Authority 7733 Perkins Rd *TF:* 800-272-8161	Baton Rouge	LA	70810	225-767-5660	767-4299
Louisiana Public Broadcasting (LPB) 7733 Perkins Rd *TF:* 800-272-8161 ■ *Web:* www.lpb.org	Baton Rouge	LA	70810	225-767-5660	767-4299
Maine Public Broadcasting Network (MPBN) 65 Texas Ave *TF:* 800-884-1717 ■ *Web:* www.mpbn.net	Bangor	ME	04401	207-941-1010	942-2857
Maryland Public Television (MPT) 11767 Owings Mills Blvd *TF:* 800-223-3678 ■ *Web:* www.mpt.org	Owings Mills	MD	21117	410-356-5600	581-4338
Metropolitan Indianapolis Public Broadcasting Corp 1401 N Meridian St *Web:* www.wfyi.org	Indianapolis	IN	46202	317-636-2020	633-7418
Michigan Public Media 535 W William St Suite 110 *Web:* www.michiganradio.org	Ann Arbor	MI	48103	734-764-9210	647-3348
Minnesota Public Radio (MPR) 480 Cedar St *TF:* 800-228-7123 ■ *Web:* www.mpr.org	Saint Paul	MN	55101	651-290-1212	290-1260
Minnesota Public Television Assn 525 Park St Suite 310	Saint Paul	MN	55103	651-293-0229	293-1709
Mississippi Public Broadcasting 3825 Ridgewood Rd *TF:* 800-922-9698 ■ *Web:* www.etv.state.ms.us	Jackson	MS	39211	601-432-6565	432-6311
Montana Public Radio 32 Campus Dr University of Montana *TF:* 800-325-1565 ■ *Web:* www.mtpr.org	Missoula	MT	59812	406-243-4931	243-3299
Montana Public Television PO Box 173340 *TF:* 800-426-8243 ■ *Web:* www.montanapbs.org	Bozeman	MT	59717	406-994-3437	994-6545
National Captioning Institute Inc (NCI) 1900 Gallows Rd Suite 3000 *Web:* www.ncicap.org	Vienna	VA	22182	703-917-7600	917-9878
National Educational Telecommunications Assn (NETA) PO Box 50008 *Web:* www.netaonline.org	Columbia	SC	29250	803-799-5517	771-4831
National Public Radio (NPR) 635 Massachusetts Ave NW *Web:* www.npr.org	Washington	DC	20001	202-513-2000	513-3329
National Public Radio Chicago Bureau 65 E Wacker Pl Suite 1401	Chicago	IL	60601	312-516-3360	516-3377
National Public Radio New York Bureau 11 W 42nd St 19th Fl *Web:* www.npr.org	New York	NY	10036	212-880-3500	
Nebraska Educational Telecommunications (NET) 1800 N 33rd St *TF:* 800-634-6788 ■ *Web:* mynptv.org	Lincoln	NE	68503	402-472-3611	472-1785
New Hampshire Public Television (NHPTV) 268 Mast Rd *TF:* 800-639-8408 ■ *Web:* www.nhptv.org	Durham	NH	03824	603-868-1100	868-7552
New Jersey Public Broadcasting PO Box 777 *TF:* 800-792-8645 ■ *Web:* www.njn.net	Trenton	NJ	08625	609-777-5000	633-2912
New Mexico Commission on Public Broadcasting 2020 Coal Ave SE	Albuquerque	NM	87106	505-242-7163	277-2191
NJN Public Television & Radio PO Box 777 *TF:* 800-792-8645 ■ *Web:* www.njn.net	Trenton	NJ	08625	609-777-5000	633-2912
North Carolina Agency for Public Telecommunications 1316 Mail Service Ctr *Web:* www.ncapt.tv	Raleigh	NC	27699	919-733-6341	715-3569
NPR West 9909 Jefferson Blvd *Web:* www.npr.org	Culver City	CA	90232	310-815-4200	815-4329
Ohio Educational Telecommunications Network (OET) 2470 North Star Rd *Web:* www.oet.edu	Columbus	OH	43221	614-644-1714	644-3112
Oklahoma Educational TV Authority (OETA) 7403 N Kelley St *TF:* 800-879-6382 ■ *Web:* www.oeta.onenet.net	Oklahoma City	OK	73111	405-848-8501	841-9216
Oregon Public Broadcasting Inc (OPB) 7140 SW Macadam Ave *Web:* www.opb.org	Portland	OR	97219	503-244-9900	293-1919
Pennsylvania Public Television Network (PPTN) 24 Northeast Dr *Web:* www.pptn.state.pa.us	Hershey	PA	17033	717-533-6011	533-4236
Prairie Public Broadcasting Inc 207 N 5th St *TF:* 800-359-6900 ■ *Web:* www.prairiepublic.org	Fargo	ND	58102	701-241-6900	239-7650
PRI (Public Radio International) 100 N 6th St Suite 900A *Web:* www.pri.org	Minneapolis	MN	55403	612-338-5000	330-9222
Program Resources Group (PRG) 450 W 33rd St 7th Fl *Web:* www.programresourcesgroup.com	New York	NY	10001	212-974-2121	560-4921
Public Broadcast Marketing Inc (PBM) 1202 Lexington Ave Suite 307 *Web:* pbmnyc.com	New York	NY	10028	212-688-3530	888-0175
Public Broadcasting Council of Central New York PO Box 2400 *TF:* 800-451-9269 ■ *Web:* www.wcny.org	Syracuse	NY	13220	315-453-2424	451-8824
Public Broadcasting Northwest Pennsylvania 8425 Peach St *TF:* 800-727-8854 ■ *Web:* www.wqln.org	Erie	PA	16509	814-864-3001	864-4077
Public Broadcasting Service (PBS) 2100 Crystal Dr *Web:* www.pbs.org	Arlington	VA	22202	703-739-5000	739-0775
Puerto Rico Public Broadcasting Corp PO Box 190909	San Juan	PR	00919	787-766-0505	753-9846
Radio Research Consortium Inc (RRC) PO Box 1309 *Web:* www.rrconline.org	Olney	MD	20830	301-774-6686	774-0976
Rhode Island PBS 50 Park Lane *TF:* 800-613-8836 ■ *Web:* www.ripbs.org	Providence	RI	02907	401-222-3636	222-3407
Rocky Mountain Public Broadcasting Network (RMPB) 1089 Bannock St *TF:* 800-274-6666 ■ *Web:* www.rmpbn.org	Denver	CO	80204	303-892-6666	620-5600
Small Station Assn KRWG-TV PO Box 30001 MSCPB 22	Las Cruces	NM	88003	505-646-2222	646-1924
Smoky Hills Public Television (SHPTV) PO Box 9 *Web:* www.shptv.org	Bunker Hill	KS	67626	785-483-6990	483-4605
South Carolina Educational Television Commission 1101 George Rogers Blvd *Web:* www.scetv.org	Columbia	SC	29201	803-737-3200	737-3526
South Dakota Public Broadcasting (SDPB) 555 N Dakota St PO Box 5000 *TF:* 800-456-0766 ■ *Web:* www.sdpb.org	Vermillion	SD	57069	605-677-5861	677-5010
South Texas Public Broadcasting System Inc 4455 S Padre Island Dr Suite 38 *TF:* 800-307-5338 ■ *Web:* www.kedt.org	Corpus Christi	TX	78411	361-855-2213	855-3877
Station Resource Group (SRG) 6935 Laurel Ave Suite 202 *Web:* www.srg.org	Takoma Park	MD	20912	301-270-2617	270-2618
Texas Public Radio (TPR) 8401 Datapoint Dr Suite 800 *TF:* 800-622-8977 ■ *Web:* www.tpr.org	San Antonio	TX	78229	210-614-8977	614-8983
ThinkTV - Greater Dayton Public Television 110 S Jefferson St *TF:* 800-247-1614 ■ *Web:* www.thinktv.org	Dayton	OH	45402	937-220-1600	220-1642
TRAC Media Services 3961 E Speedway Blvd Suite 410 *TF:* 888-299-1866 ■ *Web:* www.tracmedia.org	Tucson	AZ	85712	520-299-1866	577-6077

Organization	City	State	Zip	Phone	Fax
Twin Cities Public TV Inc 172 E 4th St *Web:* www.tpt.org	Saint Paul	MN	55101	651-222-1717	229-1282
University of North Carolina Center for Public Television (UNC-TV) 10 TW Alexander Dr PO Box 14900 *TF:* 800-906-5050 ■ *Web:* www.unctv.org	Research Triangle Park	NC	27709	919-549-7000	549-7201
Vermont Public Television (VPT) 204 Ethan Allen Ave *TF:* 800-639-7811 ■ *Web:* www.vpt.org	Colchester	VT	05446	802-655-4800	655-6593
WAMC/Northeast Public Radio 318 Central Ave *TF:* 800-323-9262 ■ *Web:* www.wamc.org	Albany	NY	12206	518-465-5233	432-6974
West Central Illinois Educational Telecommunications Corporation PO Box 6248 *TF:* 800-232-3605 ■ *Web:* www.tkn.tv	Springfield	IL	62708	217-483-7887	483-1112
West Tennessee Public Television Council Inc PO Box 966 *TF:* 800-366-9558 ■ *Web:* www.wljt.org	Martin	TN	38237	731-881-7561	881-7566
West Virginia Public Broadcasting (WVPB) 600 Capitol St *Web:* www.wvpubcast.org	Charleston	WV	25301	304-556-4900	556-4980
WGBH Educational Foundation 1 Guest St Brighton Landing *Web:* main.wgbh.org	Brighton	MA	02135	617-300-2000	300-1026
Wisconsin Educational Communications Board 3319 W Beltline Hwy *Web:* www.ecb.org	Madison	WI	53713	608-264-9600	264-9622
Wisconsin Public Radio (WPR) 821 University Ave *TF:* 800-747-7444 ■ *Web:* www.wpr.org	Madison	WI	53706	608-263-2121	263-9763
Wisconsin Public Television (WPT) 821 University Ave *TF:* 800-422-9707 ■ *Web:* www.wpt.org	Madison	WI	53706	608-263-2121	263-9763
Wyoming Public Television 2660 Peck Ave *TF:* 800-495-9788 ■ *Web:* www.wyoptv.org	Riverton	WY	82501	307-856-6944	856-3893

636 PUBLIC INTEREST RESEARCH GROUPS (PIRGS) - STATE

SEE ALSO Associations & Organizations - General - Consumer Interest Organizations p. 1301

Organization	City	State	Zip	Phone	Fax
Alaska Public Interest Research Group (AkPIRG) PO Box 101093 *Web:* www.akpirg.org	Anchorage	AK	99510	907-278-3661	278-9300
California Public Interest Research Group (CAPIRG) 1107 9th St Suite 601 *Web:* www.calpirg.org	Sacramento	CA	95814	916-448-4516	448-4560
Colorado Public Interest Research Group (COPIRG) 1536 Wynkoop St Suite 10-D *Web:* www.copirg.org	Denver	CO	80202	303-573-7474	573-3780
Connecticut Public Interest Research Group (CONNPIRG) 198 Park Rd 2nd Floor *Web:* www.connpirg.org	West Hartford	CT	06119	860-233-7554	233-7574
Florida Public Interest Research Group (Florida PIRG) 926 E Park Ave *Web:* www.floridapirg.org	Tallahassee	FL	32301	850-224-3321	224-1310
Georgia Public Interest Research Group (Georgia PIRG) 1447 Peachtree St NE Suite 304 *Web:* www.georgiapirg.org	Atlanta	GA	30309	404-892-3573	892-5201
Illinois Public Interest Research Group (Illinois PIRG) 180 W Washington St Suite 500 *Web:* www.illinoispirg.org	Chicago	IL	60602	312-364-0096	364-0092
Indiana Student Public Interest Research Group (INPIRG) IMU Room 470A Indiana University *Web:* www.inpirg.org	Bloomington	IN	47405	812-856-4128	
Iowa Public Interest Research Group (Iowa PIRG) 3111 Ingersol Ave *Web:* www.iowapirg.org	Des Moines	IA	50312	515-282-4193	282-4196
Maryland Public Interest Research Group (MaryPIRG) 3121 Saint Paul St Suite 26 *Web:* www.marylandpirg.org	Baltimore	MD	21218	410-467-0439	366-2051
Massachusetts Public Interest Research Group (MASSPIRG) 44 Winter St 4th Fl *Web:* www.masspirg.org	Boston	MA	02108	617-292-4800	292-4800
Missouri State Public Interest Research Group (MoPIRG) 310-A N Euclid Ave *Web:* www.mopirg.org	Saint Louis	MO	63108	314-454-9560	454-0787
Montana Public Interest Research Group (MontPIRG) 360 Corbin Hall *Web:* www.montpirg.org	Missoula	MT	59812	406-243-2908	243-2910
New Hampshire Public Interest Research Group (NHPIRG) 80 N Main St *Web:* www.nhpirg.org	Concord	NH	03301	603-229-3222	229-3221
New Jersey Public Interest Research Group (NJPIRG) 11 N Willow St Citizen Lobby Law & Policy Center *Web:* www.njpirg.org	Trenton	NJ	08608	609-394-8155	989-9013
New Mexico Public Interest Research Group (NMPIRG) PO Box 40173 *Web:* www.nmpirg.org	Albuquerque	NM	87196	505-254-1244	254-2280
New York Public Interest Research Group (NYPIRG) 9 Murray St *Web:* www.nypirg.org	New York	NY	10007	212-349-6460	349-1366
North Carolina Public Interest Research Group (NCPIRG) 112 S Blount St *Web:* www.ncpirg.org	Raleigh	NC	27601	919-833-2070	839-0767
Ohio Public Interest Research Group (Ohio PIRG) 36 W Gay St Suite 315 *Web:* www.ohiopirg.org	Columbus	OH	43215	614-460-8732	
Oregon State Public Interest Research Group (OSPIRG) 1536 SE 11th Ave *Web:* www.ospirg.org	Portland	OR	97214	503-231-4181	231-4007
Pennsylvania Public Interest Research Group (PennPIRG) 1420 Walnut St Suite 650 *Web:* www.pennpirg.org	Philadelphia	PA	19107	215-732-3747	732-4599
Public Interest Research Group In Michigan (PIRGIM) 103 E Liberty St Suite 202 *Web:* www.pirgim.org	Ann Arbor	MI	48104	734-662-6597	662-8393
Rhode Island Public Interest Research Group (RIPIRG) 11 S Angell St Suite 337 *Web:* www.ripirg.org	Providence	RI	02906	401-421-6578	
Texas Public Interest Research Group (TexPIRG) 700 West Ave *Web:* www.texpirg.org	Austin	TX	78701	512-479-7287	479-0400
US Public Interest Research Group (US PIRG) 218 D St SE *Web:* www.uspirg.org	Washington	DC	20003	202-546-9707	546-2461
Vermont Public Interest Research Group (VPIRG) 141 Main St Suite 6 *Web:* www.vpirg.org	Montpelier	VT	05602	802-223-5221	223-6855
Washington State Public Interest Research Group (WashPIRG) 3240 Eastlake Ave E Suite 100 *Web:* www.washpirg.org	Seattle	WA	98102	206-568-2850	568-2858
Wisconsin Public Interest Research Group (WISPIRG) 210 N Bassett St Suite 200 *Web:* www.wispirg.org	Madison	WI	53703	608-251-1918	287-0865

637 PUBLIC POLICY RESEARCH CENTERS

Organization	City	State	Zip	Phone	Fax
AARP Public Policy Institute 601 'E' St NW *TF:* 888-687-2277 ■ *Web:* www.aarp.org/ppi	Washington	DC	20049	202-434-2277	434-7599
Acton Institute for the Study of Religion & Liberty 161 Ottawa Ave NW Suite 301 *TF:* 800-345-2286 ■ *Web:* www.acton.org	Grand Rapids	MI	49503	616-454-3080	454-9454
Allegheny Institute for Public Policy 305 Mt Lebanon Blvd Suite 208 *Web:* www.alleghenyinstitute.org	Pittsburgh	PA	15234	412-440-0079	440-0085
American Assembly 475 Riverside Dr Suite 456 *Web:* www.americanassembly.org	New York	NY	10115	212-870-3500	870-3555
American Enterprise Institute for Public Policy Research (AEI) 1150 17th St NW Suite 1100 *TF:* 800-862-5801 ■ *Web:* www.aei.org	Washington	DC	20036	202-862-5800	862-7177
Ashbrook Center 401 College Ave Ashland University *TF:* 877-289-5411 ■ *Web:* www.ashbrook.org	Ashland	OH	44805	419-289-5411	289-5425
Aspen Institute 1 DuPont Cir NW Suite 700 *Web:* www.aspeninstitute.org	Washington	DC	20036	202-736-5800	467-0790
Atlantic Council of the United States 1101 15th St NW 11th Fl *Web:* www.acus.org	Washington	DC	20005	202-463-7226	463-7241
Atlas Economic Research Foundation 2000 N 14th St Suite 550 *Web:* www.atlasusa.org	Arlington	VA	22201	703-934-6969	243-7715
Baker Institute for Public Policy Rice University 6100 Main St Baker Hall Suite 120 *Web:* www.bakerinstitute.org	Houston	TX	77005	713-348-4683	348-5993
Belfer Center for Science & International Affairs (BCSIA) Harvard Univ John F Kennedy School of Government 79 JFK St *Web:* bcsia.ksg.harvard.edu	Cambridge	MA	02138	617-495-1400	495-8963
Benton Foundation 1625 K St NW 11th Fl *Web:* www.benton.org	Washington	DC	20006	202-638-5770	638-5771
Berkeley Roundtable on the International Economy (BRIE) Univ of California Berkeley 2234 Piedmont Ave MC 2322 *Web:* brie.berkeley.edu	Berkeley	CA	94720	510-642-3067	643-6617
Brookings Institution 1775 Massachusetts Ave NW *TF:* 800-275-1447 ■ *Web:* www.brookings.edu	Washington	DC	20036	202-797-6000	797-6004
CAE (Center of the American Experiment) 12 S 6th St 1024 Plymouth Bldg *Web:* www.amexp.org	Minneapolis	MN	55402	612-338-3605	338-3621
Capital Research Center 1513 16th St NW *TF:* 800-459-3950 ■ *Web:* www.capitalresearch.org	Washington	DC	20036	202-483-6900	483-6902
Carnegie Council on Ethics & International Affairs Merrill House 170 E 64th St *Web:* www.cceia.org	New York	NY	10021	212-838-4120	752-2432
Carnegie Endowment for International Peace 1779 Massachusetts Ave NW *Web:* www.carnegieendowment.org	Washington	DC	20036	202-483-7600	483-1840
Carr Center for Human Rights Policy Harvard Univ John F Kennedy School of Government 79 JFK St *Web:* www.ksg.harvard.edu/cchrp	Cambridge	MA	02138	617-495-5819	495-4297
Carter Center 1 Copenhill Ave 453 Freedom Pkwy *Web:* www.cartercenter.org	Atlanta	GA	30307	404-331-3900	331-0283
Cascade Policy Institute 813 SW Alder St Suite 450 *Web:* www.cascadepolicy.org	Portland	OR	97205	503-242-0900	242-3822
Cato Institute 1000 Massachusetts Ave NW *Web:* www.cato.org	Washington	DC	20001	202-842-0200	842-3490
Center of the American Experiment (CAE) 12 S 6th St 1024 Plymouth Bldg *Web:* www.amexp.org	Minneapolis	MN	55402	612-338-3605	338-3621
Center for American Progress 1333 H St NW 10th Fl *Web:* www.americanprogress.org	Washington	DC	20005	202-682-1611	682-1867
Center for Animals & Public Policy Tufts Univ School of Veterinary Medicine 200 Westboro Rd *Web:* www.tufts.edu/vet/cfa	North Grafton	MA	01536	508-839-7920	839-2953
Center for Arts & Culture 4350 N Fairfax Dr Suite 740 *Web:* www.culturalpolicy.org	Arlington	VA	22203	703-248-0430	248-0414
Center on Budget & Policy Priorities 820 1st St NE Suite 510 *Web:* www.cbpp.org	Washington	DC	20002	202-408-1080	408-1056
Center for Business & Government Harvard Univ John F Kennedy School of Government Weil Hall 79 JFK St *Web:* www.ksg.harvard.edu/cbg/	Cambridge	MA	02138	617-384-7329	496-0063
Center for Cognitive Liberty & Ethics PO Box 73481 *Web:* www.cognitiveliberty.org	Davis	CA	95617	530-750-7912	
Center for Defense Information 1779 Massachusetts Ave NW Suite 615 *Web:* www.cdi.org	Washington	DC	20036	202-332-0600	462-4559
Center for Equal Opportunity (CEO) 14 Pidgeon Hill Dr Suite 500 *TF:* 800-819-2343 ■ *Web:* www.ceousa.org	Sterling	VA	20165	703-421-5443	421-6401
Center for Immigration Studies 1522 K St NW Suite 820 *Web:* www.cis.org	Washington	DC	20005	202-466-8185	466-8076
Center for International Development at Harvard University Harvard Univ John F Kennedy School of Government 1 Eliot St Bldg 79 JFK St *Web:* www.cid.harvard.edu	Cambridge	MA	02138	617-496-9683	
Center for International Private Enterprise 1155 15th St NW Suite 700 *Web:* www.cipe.org	Washington	DC	20005	202-721-9200	721-9250
Center for Law & Social Policy (CLASP) 1015 15th St NW Suite 400 *Web:* www.clasp.org	Washington	DC	20005	202-906-8000	842-2885
Center for Mathematical Studies in Economics & Management Sciences Northwestern University 2001 Sheridan Rd Leverone Hall Rm 580 *Web:* www.kellogg.northwestern.edu/research/math	Evanston	IL	60208	847-491-3527	491-2530
Center for Media & Public Affairs 2100 L St NW Suite 300 *Web:* www.cmpa.com	Washington	DC	20037	202-223-2942	872-4014

Phone Fax

Center for National Policy
1 Massachusetts Ave NW Suite 333 Washington DC 20001 202-682-1800 682-1818
Web: www.cnponline.org
Center for Neighborhood Technology 2125 W North Ave Chicago IL 60647 773-278-4800 278-3840
Web: www.cnt.org
Center for Nonproliferation Studies 460 Pierce St Monterey CA 93940 831-647-4154 647-3519
Web: www.cns.miis.edu
Center for Policy Research
Syracuse University Eggers Hall Rm 426 Syracuse NY 13244 315-443-3114 443-1081
Web: www-cpr.maxwell.syr.edu
Center for Public Integrity 910 17th St NW 7th Fl Washington DC 20006 202-466-1300 466-1101
Web: www.publicintegrity.org
Center for Public Leadership
Harvard Univ John F Kennedy School of Government 79
JFK St Cambridge MA 02138 617-496-8866 496-3337
Web: www.ksg.harvard.edu/leadership
Center for Responsive Politics
1101 14th St NW Suite 1030 Washington DC 20005 202-857-0044 857-7809
Web: www.opensecrets.org
Center for Security Policy
1901 Pennsylvania Ave NW Suite 201 Washington DC 20006 202-835-9077 835-9066
Web: www.centerforsecuritypolicy.org
Center for Strategic & International Studies
1800 K St NW Suite 400 Washington DC 20006 202-887-0200 775-3199
Web: www.csis.org
Century Foundation 41 E 70th St New York NY 10021 212-535-4441 535-7534
Web: www.tcf.org
Chicago Council on Foreign Relations
332 S Michigan Ave Suite 1100 Chicago IL 60604 312-726-3860 821-7555
Web: www.ccfr.org
Claremont Institute 937 W Foothill Blvd Suite E Claremont CA 91711 909-621-6825 626-8724
Web: www.claremont.org
Committee for Economic Development
2000 L St NW Suite 700 Washington DC 20036 202-296-5860 223-0776
Web: www.ced.org
Commonwealth Institute PO Box 398105 Cambridge MA 02139 617-547-4474 868-1267
Web: www.comw.org
Consortium for Policy Research in Education (CPRE)
University of Pennsylvania 3440 Market St Suite 560 Philadelphia PA 19104 215-573-0700 573-7914
Web: www.cpre.org
Council for Excellence in Government
1301 K St NW Suite 450 West Washington DC 20005 202-728-0418 728-0422
Web: www.excelgov.org
Council on Foreign Relations Inc
Harold Pratt House 58 E 68th St New York NY 10021 212-434-9400 434-9800
Web: www.cfr.org
Discovery Institute 208 Columbia St Seattle WA 98104 206-292-0401 682-5320
Web: www.discovery.org
Dole Institute of Politics 2350 Petefish Dr Lawrence KS 66045 785-864-4900 864-1414
Web: www.doleinstitute.org
Earth Policy Institute 1350 Connecticut Ave NW Suite 403 Washington DC 20036 202-496-9290 496-9325
Web: www.earth-policy.org
EastWest Institute 700 Broadway 2nd Fl New York NY 10003 212-824-4100 824-4149
Web: www.iews.org
EBRI (Employee Benefit Research Institute)
1100 13th St NW Suite 878 Washington DC 20005 202-659-0670 775-6312
Web: www.ebri.org
Economic Policy Institute
1333 H St NW Suite 300 East Tower Washington DC 20005 202-775-8810 775-0819
Web: www.epi.org
Economic Strategy Institute 3050 K St NW Suite 220 Washington DC 20007 202-965-9484 965-1104
Web: www.econstrat.org
Employee Benefit Research Institute (EBRI)
1100 13th St NW Suite 878 Washington DC 20005 202-659-0670 775-6312
Web: www.ebri.org
Employment Policies Institute
1090 Vermont Ave NW Suite 800 Washington DC 20005 202-463-7650 463-7107
Web: www.epionline.org
Ethics & Public Policy Center 1015 15th St NW Suite 900 Washington DC 20005 202-682-1200 408-0632
Web: www.eppc.org
Faith & Reason Institute 1413 K St NW Suite 1000 Washington DC 20005 202-289-8775 289-2502
Web: www.frinstitute.org
Food & Agricultural Policy Research Institute (FAPRI)
Iowa State University 578 Heady Hall Ames IA 50011 515-294-1183 294-6336
Web: www.fapri.iastate.edu
Food First 398 60th St Oakland CA 94618 510-654-4400 654-4551
Web: www.foodfirst.org
Foreign Policy Institute
Johns Hopkins Univ 1619 Massachusetts Ave NW Washington DC 20036 202-663-5773 663-5769
Web: www.sais-jhu.edu
Foreign Policy Research Institute (FPRI)
1528 Walnut St Suite 610 Philadelphia PA 19102 215-732-3774 732-4401
Web: www.fpri.org
Foundation for Economic Education (FEE)
30 S Broadway Irvington-on-Hudson NY 10533 914-591-7230 591-8910
TF: 800-960-4333 ■ *Web:* www.fee.org
Free Congress Foundation 717 2nd St NE Washington DC 20002 202-546-3000 543-5605
Web: www.freecongress.org
George Mason School of Public Policy
George Mason Univ 4400 University Dr MS 3C6 Fairfax VA 22030 703-993-2280 993-2284
Web: policy.gmu.edu
Goldwater Institute 500 E Coronado Rd Phoenix AZ 85004 602-462-5000 256-7045
Web: www.goldwaterinstitute.org
Hauser Center for Nonprofit Organizations
Harvard Univ John F Kennedy School of Government 79
JFK St Cambridge MA 02138 617-496-5675 495-0996
Web: www.ksg.harvard.edu/hauser
Heartland Institute 19 S LaSalle St Suite 903 Chicago IL 60603 312-377-4000 377-5000
Web: www.heartland.org
Heritage Foundation 214 Massachusetts Ave NE Washington DC 20002 202-546-4400 546-8328
TF: 800-546-2843 ■ *Web:* www.heritage.org
Hoover Institution on War Revolution & Peace
Stanford University 434 Galvez Mall Stanford CA 94305 650-723-1754 723-1687
TF: 877-466-8374 ■ *Web:* www.hoover.org
Hudson Institute 1015 15th St NW Suite 600 Washington DC 20005 202-974-2400 974-2410
TF: 800-483-7660 ■ *Web:* www.hudson.org
ICAP (International Center for Alcohol Policies)
1519 New Hampshire Ave NW Washington DC 20036 202-986-1159 986-2080
Web: www.icap.org
Independent Institute 100 Swan Way Oakland CA 94621 510-632-1366 568-6040
TF: 800-927-8733 ■ *Web:* www.independent.org
Institute for Contemporary Studies 3100 Harrison St Oakland CA 94611 510-238-5010 238-8440
Web: www.icspress.com
Institute on Education & the Economy
Teachers College Columbia University 525 W 120th St
Box 174 New York NY 10027 212-678-3091 678-3699
Web: www.tc.columbia.edu/iee

Phone Fax

Institute for Food & Development Policy 398 60th St Oakland CA 94618 510-654-4400 654-4551
Web: www.foodfirst.org
Institute for Foreign Policy Analysis Inc
675 Massachusetts Ave 10th Fl Cambridge MA 02139 617-492-2116 492-8242
Web: www.ifpa.org
Institute for the Future 124 University Ave Palo Alto CA 94301 650-854-6322 854-7850
Web: www.iftf.org
Institute of Government & Public Affairs
Univ of Illinois 1007 W Nevada St Urbana IL 61801 217-333-3340 244-4817
Web: www.igpa.uiuc.edu
Institute for Health Policy Studies
University of California San Francisco 3333 California
St Suite 265 Box 0936 San Francisco CA 94118 415-476-4921 476-0705
Web: ihps.ucsf.edu
Institute for Humane Studies 3301 N Fairfax Dr Suite 440 Arlington VA 22201 703-993-4880 993-4890
TF: 800-697-8799 ■ *Web:* www.theihs.org
Institute for International Economics
1750 Massachusetts Ave NW Washington DC 20036 202-328-9000 328-5432
Web: www.iie.com
Institute for Justice 901 N Glebe Rd Suite 900 Arlington VA 22203 703-682-9320 682-9321
Web: www2.ij.org
Institute for the North 935 W 3rd Ave Anchorage AK 99501 907-343-2444 343-2466
Web: www.institutenorth.org
Institute for Philosophy & Public Policy
Maryland School of Public Policy 3111 Van
Munching Hall College Park MD 20742 301-405-4753 314-9346
Web: www.puaf.umd.edu/IPPP
Institute for Policy Innovation (IPI)
1660 S Stemmons Fwy Suite 475 Lewisville TX 75067 972-847-5139 874-5144
Web: www.ipi.org
Institute for Policy Studies (IPS)
1112 16th St NW Suite 600 Washington DC 20036 202-234-9382 387-7915
Web: www.ips-dc.org
Institute of Politics
Harvard Univ John F Kennedy School of Government 79
JFK St Cambridge MA 02138 617-495-1360 496-4344
Web: www.iop.harvard.edu
Institute for Research on the Economics of Taxation (IRET)
1710 Rhode Island Ave NW 11th Fl Washington DC 20036 202-463-1400 463-6199
Web: www.iret.org
Institute of World Politics 1521 16th St NW Washington DC 20036 202-462-2101 464-0335
TF: 888-566-9497 ■ *Web:* www.iwp.edu
Inter-American Dialogue
1211 Connecticut Ave NW Suite 510 Washington DC 20036 202-822-9002 822-9553
Web: www.thedialogue.org
International Center for Alcohol Policies (ICAP)
1519 New Hampshire Ave NW Washington DC 20036 202-986-1159 986-2080
Web: www.icap.org
International Food Policy Research Institute (IFPRI)
2033 K St NW Washington DC 20006 202-862-5600 467-4439
Web: www.ifpri.org
James A Baker III Institute for Public Policy
Rice University 6100 Main St Baker Hall Suite 120 Houston TX 77005 713-348-4683 348-5993
Web: www.bakerinstitute.org
Joan Shorenstein Center on the Press Politics & Public Policy
Harvard Univ John F Kennedy School of Government 79
John F Kennedy St Cambridge MA 02138 617-495-8269 495-8696
Web: www.ksg.harvard.edu/presspol
Joint Center for Housing Studies
Harvard Univ 1033 Massachusetts Ave 5th Fl Cambridge MA 02138 617-495-7908 496-9957
Web: www.jchs.harvard.edu
Joint Center for Political & Economic Studies
1090 Vermont Ave NW Suite 1100 Washington DC 20005 202-789-3500 789-6385
Web: www.jointcenter.org
Keystone Center 1628 St John Rd Keystone CO 80435 970-513-5800 262-0152
Web: www.keystone.org
Leon & Sylvia Panetta Institute for Public Policy
California State University Monterey Bay 100 Campus Ctr
Bldg 86E Seaside CA 93955 831-582-4200 582-4082
Web: www.panettainstitute.org
Levy Economics Institute of Bard College
Blithewood Rd Bard College Annandale-on-Hudson NY 12504 845-758-7700 758-1149
Web: www.levy.org
Malcolm Wiener Center for Social Policy
John F Kennedy School of Government Harvard University
79 John F Kennedy St Cambridge MA 02138 617-495-1461 496-9053
Web: www.ksg.harvard.edu/socpol
Manhattan Institute for Policy Research
52 Vanderbilt Ave 3rd Fl New York NY 10017 212-599-7000 599-3494
Web: www.manhattan-institute.org
Manpower Demonstration Research Corp
16 E 34th St 19th Fl New York NY 10016 212-532-3200 684-0832
TF: 800-221-3165 ■ *Web:* www.mdrc.org
Margaret Chase Smith Policy Center
University of Maine York Complex Suite 4 Orono ME 04469 207-581-1648 581-1266
Web: www.umaine.edu/mcsc
Mershon Center 1501 Neil Ave Columbus OH 43201 614-292-1681 292-2407
Web: mershoncenter.osu.edu
Milken Institute 1250 4th St Santa Monica CA 90401 310-570-4600 570-4601
Web: www.milkeninstitute.org
National Academy on an Aging Society
1220 L St NW Suite 901 Washington DC 20005 202-842-1275 842-1150
Web: agingsociety.org
National Center on Institutions & Alternatives
7222 Ambassador Rd Baltimore MD 21244 410-265-1490
Web: www.ncianet.org
National Center for Policy Analysis 12770 Coit Rd Suite 800 Dallas TX 75251 972-386-6272 386-0924
Web: www.ncpa.org
National Center for Public Policy Research
501 Capitol Ct NE Suite 200 Washington DC 20002 202-543-4110 543-5975
Web: www.nationalcenter.org
National Defense Council Foundation (NDCF)
1220 King St Suite 230 Alexandria VA 22314 703-836-3443 836-5402
Web: www.ndcf.org
Nelson A Rockefeller Institute of Government 411 State St Albany NY 12203 518-443-5522 443-5788
Web: rockinst.org/
New America Foundation 1630 Connecticut Ave NW 7th Fl Washington DC 20009 202-986-2700 986-3696
Web: www.newamerica.net
Nixon Center 1615 L St NW Suite 1250 Washington DC 20036 202-887-1000 887-5222
Web: www.nixoncenter.org
Northeast-Midwest Institute (NMI) 50 F St NW Suite 950 Washington DC 20001 202-544-5200 544-0043
Web: www.nemw.org
Pacific Research Institute for Public Policy (PRI)
755 Sansome St Suite 450 San Francisco CA 94111 415-989-0833 989-2411
Web: www.pacificresearch.org

Phone | Fax

Panetta Institute
California State University Monterey Bay 100 Campus Ctr Bldg 86E Seaside CA 93955 831-582-4200 582-4082
Web: www.panettainstitute.org

Pepper Institute on Aging & Public Policy
Florida State Univ 207 Pepper Center 636 W Call St Tallahassee FL 32306 850-644-2831 644-2304
Web: www.pepperinstitute.org

Phoenix Center for Advanced Legal & Economic Public Policy Studies 5335 Wisconsin Ave NW Suite 440 Washington DC 20015 202-274-0235 244-8257
Web: www.phoenix-center.org

Princeton Institute for International & Regional Studies (PIIRS)
Princeton University Bendheim Hall Princeton NJ 08544 609-258-4852 258-3988
Web: www.princeton.edu/piirs

Progress & Freedom Foundation 1444 I St NW Suite 500 Washington DC 20005 202-289-8928 289-6079
Web: www.pff.org

Progressive Policy Institute (PPI)
600 Pennsylvania Ave SE Suite 400 Washington DC 20003 202-547-0001 544-5014
TF: 800-546-0027 ■ *Web:* www.ppionline.org

Public Agenda 6 E 39th St New York NY 10016 212-686-6610 889-3461
Web: www.publicagenda.org

RAND Corp 1700 Main St PO Box 2138 Santa Monica CA 90407 310-393-0411 393-4818
Web: www.rand.org

Reason Public Policy Institute
3415 S Sepulveda Blvd Suite 400 Los Angeles CA 90034 310-391-2245 391-4395
Web: www.reason.org

Renewable Energy Policy Project (REPP)
1612 K St NW Suite 202 Washington DC 20006 202-293-2898 293-5857
Web: www.repp.org

Resources for the Future 1616 P St NW Washington DC 20036 202-328-5000 939-3460
Web: www.rff.org

Robert J Dole Institute of Politics 2350 Petefish Dr Lawrence KS 66045 785-864-4900 864-1414
Web: www.doleinstitute.org

Rockford Institute 928 N Main St Rockford IL 61103 815-964-5053 964-9403
TF: 800-383-0680 ■ *Web:* www.rockfordinstitute.org

Schneider Institute for Health Policy
Brandeis University Heller Graduate School Box 9110 MS 035 Waltham MA 02454 781-736-3901 736-3905
Web: sihp.brandeis.edu

Science & Environmental Policy Project
1600 S Eads St Suite 712-S Arlington VA 22202 703-920-2744
Web: www.sepp.org

Shorenstein Center on the Press Politics & Public Policy
Harvard Univ John F Kennedy School of Government 79 John F Kennedy St Cambridge MA 02138 617-495-8269 495-8696
Web: www.ksg.harvard.edu/presspol

Smith Center for Private Enterprise Studies
California State Univ East Bay College of Business & Economics Hayward CA 94542 510-885-2640 885-4222
Web: thesmithcenter.org

Social Science Research Council (SSRC) 810 7th Ave New York NY 10019 212-377-2700 377-2727
Web: www.ssrc.org

Social Science Research Institute
Northern Illinois University 148 N 3rd St DeKalb IL 60115 815-753-1901 753-2305
Web: www.ssri.niu.edu

SSRC (Social Science Research Council) 810 7th Ave New York NY 10019 212-377-2700 377-2727
Web: www.ssrc.org

Taubman Center for State & Local Government
Harvard Univ John F Kennedy School of Government 79 JFK St Cambridge MA 02138 617-495-2199 496-1722
Web: www.ksg.harvard.edu/taubmancenter

Tellus Institute 11 Arlington St Boston MA 02116 617-266-5400 266-8303
Web: www.tellus.org

Urban Institute 2100 M St NW Washington DC 20037 202-833-7200 331-9747
Web: www.urban.org

Weatherhead Center for International Affairs
Harvard Univ 1737 Cambridge St Cambridge MA 02138 617-495-4420 495-8292
Web: www.wcfia.harvard.edu

Winrock International 38 Winrock Dr Morrilton AR 72110 501-727-5435 727-5242
Web: www.winrock.org

Woodrow Wilson International Center for Scholars
1 Woodrow Wilson Plaza 1300 Pennsylvania Ave NW Washington DC 20004 202-691-4000 691-4001
Web: wilsoncenter.org

World Policy Institute 220 5th Ave 9th Fl New York NY 10001 212-481-5005 481-5009
Web: worldpolicy.org

World Resources Institute (WRI) 10 G St NE Suite 800 Washington DC 20002 202-729-7600 729-7610
Web: www.wri.org

Worldwatch Institute 1776 Massachusetts Ave NW Washington DC 20036 202-452-1999 296-7365
TF: 877-539-9946 ■ *Web:* www.worldwatch.org

638 PUBLIC RECORDS SEARCH SERVICES

SEE ALSO Investigative Services p. 1873

Phone | Fax

Accufax PO Box 35563 Tulsa OK 74153 918-627-2226 622-9453
TF: 800-256-8898 ■ *Web:* www.accufax-us.com

All-Search & Inspection Inc 1108 E South Union Ave Midvale UT 84047 801-984-8160 984-8170
TF: 800-227-3152 ■ *Web:* www.all-search.com

American Background Information Services Inc
629 Cedar Creek Grade Suite C Winchester VA 22601 540-665-8056 722-4771
TF: 800-669-2247 ■ *Web:* www.americanbackground.com

American Driving Records Inc 2860 Gold Tailings Ct Rancho Cordova CA 95670 916-456-3200 456-3332
TF: 800-766-6877 ■ *Web:* www.mvrs.com

Ameridex Information Systems Inc PO Box 51314 Irvine CA 92619 714-731-2546
Web: www.ameridex.com

AmRent PO Box 771176 Houston TX 77215 713-266-1870 260-1290
TF: 800-324-4595 ■ *Web:* www.amrent.com

Applicant Insight Ltd PO Box 458 New Port Richey FL 34656 800-771-7703 890-6454
Web: www.ainsight.com

Apscreen Inc PO Box 80639 Rancho Santa Margarita CA 92688 949-646-4003 277-2733*
**Fax Area Code:* 888 ■ *TF:* 800-277-2733 ■ *Web:* www.apscreen.com

Background Bureau Inc 2019 Alexandria Pike Highland Heights KY 41076 859-781-3400 781-5888
TF: 800-854-3990 ■ *Web:* www.backgroundbureau.com

Background Information Services Inc 1800 30th St Suite 204 Boulder CO 80301 303-442-3960 442-1004
TF: 800-433-6010 ■ *Web:* www.bisi.com

Barry Shuster Information Services 1157 Tucker Rd North Dartmouth MA 02747 508-999-5436 852-7531*
**Fax Area Code:* 877 ■ *TF:* 877-852-2507

Best Reports Inc 209 W Jackson Blvd Suite 402 Chicago IL 60606 312-427-0900 427-0500
TF: 877-452-3781 ■ *Web:* www.bestreports.net

Canadian Securities Registration Systems
4126 Norland Ave Suite 200 Burnaby BC V5G3S8 604-637-4000 637-4001
TF: 800-561-1404 ■ *Web:* www.csrs.ca

Phone | Fax

Capitol Lien Records & Research Inc 1010 N Dale St Saint Paul MN 55117 651-488-0100 488-0200
TF: 800-845-4077 ■ *Web:* www.capitollien.com

Capitol Services Inc 800 Brazos St Suite 400 Austin TX 78701 512-474-8377 432-3622*
**Fax Area Code:* 800 ■ *TF:* 800-345-4647 ■ *Web:* www.capitolservices.com

CARCO Group Inc 5000 Corporate Ct Holtsville NY 11742 631-862-9300 584-7094
TF: 800-645-4556 ■ *Web:* www.carcogroup.com

CCH Legal Information Services 111 8th Ave New York NY 10011 212-894-8940
TF: 800-223-7567 ■ *Web:* www.cchlis.com/public/aboutCT.html

CCH Washington Service Bureau Inc
1015 15th St NW 10th Fl Washington DC 20005 202-312-6600 962-0152
TF: 800-955-5219 ■ *Web:* www.wsb.com

CDI Credit Inc 6160 Peachtree Dunwoody Rd NE Suite B-210 Atlanta GA 30328 770-350-5070 394-2197
TF: 800-633-3961 ■ *Web:* www.cdicredit.com

Charles Jones Inc PO Box 8488 Trenton NJ 08650 609-538-1000 883-0677
TF: 800-792-8888 ■ *Web:* www.cji.com

ChoicePoint Inc 1000 Alderman Dr Alpharetta GA 30005 770-752-6000
NYSE: CPS ■ *TF:* 877-317-5000 ■ *Web:* www.choicepointinc.com

Colby Attorneys Service Co Inc 41 State St Suite 106 Albany NY 12207 518-463-4426 434-2574
TF: 800-832-1220 ■ *Web:* www.colbyservice.com

Corporation Service Co 2711 Centerville Rd Suite 400 Wilmington DE 19808 302-636-5400 636-5454
TF: 800-927-9800 ■ *Web:* www.incspot.com

CT Corp 111 8th Ave New York NY 10011 212-894-8940
TF: 800-223-7567 ■ *Web:* www.cchlis.com/public/aboutCT.html

CT Corsearch 345 Hudson St 16th Fl New York NY 10014 917-408-5000 408-5006
TF: 800-732-7241 ■ *Web:* www.ctcorsearch.com

DCS Information Systems Inc 500 N Central Expy Suite 280 Plano TX 75074 972-422-3600 422-3621
TF: 800-299-3647 ■ *Web:* www.dnis.com

Doc-U-Search Inc 63 Pleasant St Concord NH 03301 603-224-2871 224-2794
TF: 800-332-3034 ■ *Web:* www.docusearchinc.com

Driving Records Facilities PO Box 1086 Glen Burnie MD 21061 410-761-5510 760-5837
TF: 800-772-5510 ■ *Web:* www.dr-rec-fac.com

Edge Information Management Inc 100 Rialto Pl Suite 800 Melbourne FL 32901 321-722-3343 780-3299*
**Fax Area Code:* 800 ■ **Fax:* Mktg ■ *TF:* 800-725-3343 ■
Web: www.edgeinformation.com

Employment Screening Services Inc
627 E Sprague St Suite 100 Spokane WA 99202 509-624-3851 321-2905*
**Fax Area Code:* 800 ■ *TF:* 800-473-7778 ■ *Web:* www.employscreen.com

Explore Information Services LLC 2945 Lone Oak Dr Suite 150 Eagan MN 55121 651-681-4460 681-4476
TF: 800-531-9125 ■ *Web:* www.exploredata.com

Federal Research Corp 1023 15th St NW Suite 401 Washington DC 20005 202-783-2700 783-0145
TF: 800-846-3190 ■ *Web:* www.federalresearch.com

Fidelifacts 42 Broadway 15th Fl New York NY 10004 212-425-1520 248-5619
TF: 800-509-8496 ■ *Web:* www.fidelifacts.com

Fidelity National Information Solutions Inc
601 Riverside Ave Jacksonville FL 32204 904-854-8100 854-4282
TF: 888-934-3354 ■ *Web:* www.fnis.com

First Advantage Corp 100 Carillon Pkwy Saint Petersburg FL 33716 727-214-3411 214-3410
TF: 800-321-4473 ■ *Web:* www.fadv.com

First Advantage SafeRent 7300 Westmore Rd Suite 3 Rockville MD 20850 301-881-8400
TF: 800-999-0350 ■ *Web:* www.fadvsaferent.com

First American Real Estate Solutions 1 First American Way Santa Ana CA 92707 714-250-5990 250-6915
TF: 800-426-1466 ■ *Web:* www.firstamres.com

Government Liaison Services Inc 200 N Glebe Rd Suite 321 Arlington VA 22203 703-524-8200 525-8451
TF: 800-642-6564 ■ *Web:* www.trademarkinfo.com

HRPlus 2902 Evergreen Pkwy Evergreen CO 80439 303-670-8177 670-8906
TF: 800-827-2479 ■ *Web:* www.hrplus.com

Human Resource Profile Inc 8506 Beechmont Ave Cincinnati OH 45255 513-388-4300 388-4320
TF: 800-969-4300 ■ *Web:* www.hrprofile.com

IMI Data Search Inc 275 E Hillcrest Dr Suite 102 Thousand Oaks CA 91360 805-495-1149 495-0310
TF: 800-860-7779 ■ *Web:* www.imidatasearch.com

Information Management Systems Inc
114 W Main St Suite 202 New Britain CT 06050 860-229-1119 225-5524
TF: 888-403-8347 ■ *Web:* www.imswebb.com

Information Source LLC 627 E Sprague Ave Suite 111 Spokane WA 99202 509-624-2229 458-8956
TF: 800-548-8847 ■ *Web:* www.tisource.com

InfoTrack Information Services Inc 111 Deerlake Rd Deerfield IL 60015 847-444-1177 274-5594*
**Fax Area Code:* 800 ■ *TF:* 800-275-5594 ■ *Web:* www.infotrackinc.com

Insured Aircraft Title Service Inc 4848 SW 36th St Oklahoma City OK 73179 405-681-6663 681-9299
TF: 800-654-4882 ■ *Web:* www.insuredaircraft.com

Jones Charles Inc PO Box 8488 Trenton NJ 08650 609-538-1000 883-0677
TF: 800-792-8888 ■ *Web:* www.cji.com

KnowX LLC 730 Peachtree St Suite 700 Atlanta GA 30303 404-541-0221 541-0244
TF: 877-317-5000 ■ *Web:* www.knowx.com

Kress Employment screening 320 Westcott St Suite 108 Houston TX 77007 713-880-3693 880-3694
TF: 888-636-3693 ■ *Web:* www.intelnetinc.com

Kroll Background America Inc 1900 Church St Suite 300 Nashville TN 37203 615-320-9800 321-9585
TF: 800-697-7189 ■ *Web:* www.baionline.net

Kroll Inc 900 3rd Ave 7th Fl New York NY 10022 212-593-1000 593-2631
TF: 800-675-3772 ■ *Web:* www.krollworldwide.com

Laborchex Co 2506 Lakeland Dr Suite 200 Jackson MS 39232 601-664-6760 844-2722*
**Fax Area Code:* 800 ■ *TF:* 800-880-0366 ■ *Web:* www.laborchex.com

Legal Data Resources Inc 2816 W Summerdale Ave Chicago IL 60625 773-561-2468 561-2488
TF: 800-735-9207 ■ *Web:* www.ldrsearch.com

LegalEase Inc 139 Fulton St Suite 1013 New York NY 10038 212-393-9070 393-9796
TF: 800-393-1277 ■ *Web:* www.legaleaseinc.com

LocatePLUS Inc 100 Cummings Center Suite 235M Beverly MA 01915 978-921-2727 524-8767
TF: 888-746-3463 ■ *Web:* www.locateplus.com

Merlin Information Services 215 S Complex Dr Kalispell MT 59901 406-755-8550 755-8568*
**Fax:* Cust Svc ■ *TF:* 800-367-6646 ■ *Web:* www.merlindata.com

MicroPatent LLC 250 Dodge Ave East Haven CT 06512 203-466-5055 466-5054
TF: 800-648-6787 ■ *Web:* www.micropatent.com

MLQ Attorney Services 2000 River Edge Pkwy Suite 885 Atlanta GA 30328 770-984-7007 984-7049
TF: 800-446-8794 ■ *Web:* www.mlqattorneyservices.com

National Data Access Corp 2 Office Park Ct Suite 103 Columbia SC 29223 803-699-6130 542-7499*
**Fax Area Code:* 800 ■ *TF:* 800-528-8790 ■ *Web:* www.n-dac.com

National Public Records Inc 4426 Hugh Howell Rd Suite B314 Tucker GA 30084 770-938-1050 808-8081
Web: www.findtherecord.com

Nationwide Information Services Inc 52 James St 5th Fl Albany NY 12207 518-449-8429 449-8522
TF: 800-873-3482

OPENonline 1650 Lake Shore Dr Suite 350 Columbus OH 43204 614-481-6999 481-6980
TF: 888-381-5656 ■ *Web:* www.openonline.com

Orange Tree Employment Screening
7301 Ohms Ln Suite 600 Minneapolis MN 55439 952-941-9040 941-9041
TF: 800-886-4777 ■ *Web:* www.orangetreescreening.com

Pacific Corporate & Title Services 914 S St Sacramento CA 95814 916-558-4988 441-2217
TF: 800-230-4988 ■ *Web:* www.paccorp.com

Parasec Inc 640 Bercut Dr Suite A Sacramento CA 95814 916-441-1001 603-5868*
**Fax Area Code:* 800 ■ *TF:* 800-533-7272 ■ *Web:* www.parasec.com

Penncorp Servicegroup Inc 600 N 2nd St Suite 401 Harrisburg PA 17101 717-234-2300 264-1137*
**Fax Area Code:* 800 ■ *TF:* 800-544-9050

Property Owners Exchange Inc
6630 Baltimore National Pike Suite 208 Baltimore MD 21228 410-719-0100 719-6715
TF: 800-869-3200 ■ *Web:* www.poeknows.com

Public Data Corp 519 8th Ave Suite 811 New York NY 10018 212-519-3063 519-3067
Web: www.pdcny.com

Questel Orbit 1725 Duke St Suite 625 Alexandria VA 22314 703-519-1820 519-1821
TF: 800-456-7248 ■ *Web:* www.questel.orbit.com

	City	State	Zip	Phone	Fax
Quick Search 4155 Buena Vista *TF:* 800-473-2840 ■ *Web:* www.quicksi.com	Dallas	TX	75204	214-358-2840	358-6057
Record Search America Inc 5481 Kendall St *TF:* 877-865-8003 ■ *Web:* www.researchforyou.com	Boise	ID	83706	208-375-1906	322-5469
Rental Research Services Inc 11300 Minnetonka Mills Rd *TF:* 800-328-0333 ■ *Web:* www.rentalresearch.com	Minnetonka	MN	55305	952-935-5700	935-9212
Search Co International 1535 Grant St Suite 140 *TF:* 800-727-2120 ■ *Web:* www.searchcompanyintl.com	Denver	CO	80203	303-863-1800	863-7767
Search Network Ltd 1503 42nd St Suite 210 *TF:* 800-383-5050 ■ *Web:* www.searchnetworkltd.com	West Des Moines	IA	50266	515-223-1153	223-2814
SearchTec Inc 211 N 13th St 6th Fl *TF:* 800-762-5018 ■ *Web:* www.searchtec.com	Philadelphia	PA	19107	215-963-0888	851-8775
Securitech Inc 8230 E Broadway Suite E-10 *TF:* 800-805-4473 ■ *Web:* www.hiresafe.com	Tucson	AZ	85710	520-721-0305	721-7706
Security Search & Abstract Co 111 Presidential Blvd Suite 159 **Fax Area Code:* 800 ■ *TF:* 800-345-9494 ■ *Web:* securitysearchabstract.com	Bala Cynwyd	PA	19004	610-664-5912	343-4294*
Sterling Testing Systems Inc 249 W 17th St 6th Fl **Fax Area Code:* 800 ■ *TF:* 800-899-2272 ■ *Web:* www.sterlingtesting.com	New York	NY	10011	212-736-5100	990-5578*
Superior Information Services Inc 300 Phillips Blvd Suite 500 *TF:* 800-792-8888 ■ *Web:* www.superiorinfo.com	Trenton	NJ	08618	609-883-7000	883-0677
TABB Inc PO Box 10 *TF:* 800-887-8222 ■ *Web:* www.tabb.net	Chester	NJ	07930	908-879-2323	879-8675
Thomson CompuMark 500 Victory Rd *TF:* 800-692-8833 ■ *Web:* www.thomson-thomson.com	North Quincy	MA	02171	617-479-1600	786-8273
Title First Agency Inc 555 S Front St Suite 400 *TF:* 800-837-4032 ■ *Web:* www.titlefirst.com	Columbus	OH	43215	614-224-9207	224-1423
TML Information Services Inc 116-55 Queens Blvd Suite 210 *TF:* 800-733-9777 ■ *Web:* www.tml.com	Forest Hills	NY	11375	718-793-3737	544-2853
UCC Direct 1232 Q St **Fax Area Code:* 800 ■ *TF:* 800-877-2877 ■ *Web:* www.uccdirect.com	Sacramento	CA	95814	916-443-0795	877-3877*
UCC Direct Services 2727 Allen Pkwy Suite 1000 **Fax:* Hum Res ■ *TF:* 800-833-5778 ■ *Web:* www.uccdirect.com	Houston	TX	77019	713-533-4600	527-0641*
UCC Filing & Search Services Inc 1574 Village Square Blvd Suite 100 **Fax Area Code:* 800 ■ *TF:* 800-822-5436	Tallahassee	FL	32309	850-681-6528	424-7979*
Unisearch Inc 1780 Barnes Blvd SW **Fax Area Code:* 800 ■ *TF:* 800-722-0708 ■ *Web:* www.unisearch.com	Tumwater	WA	98512	360-956-9500	531-1717*
US Datalink Inc 6711 Bayway Dr *TF:* 800-527-7930 ■ *Web:* www.usdatalink.net	Baytown	TX	77520	281-424-7223	424-3415
US Search.com Inc 600 Corporate Pointe Suite 220 *TF:* 877-327-2450 ■ *Web:* www.ussearch.com	Culver City	CA	90230	310-302-6300	822-7898
USIS 7799 Leesburg Pike Suite 1100-N *Web:* www.usis.com	Falls Church	VA	22043	703-448-0178	
USIS Commercial Services 4500 S 129th East Ave Suite 200 **Fax Area Code:* 918 ■ *TF:* 800-881-5993 ■ *Web:* www.usis.com/commercialservices	Tulsa	OK	74134	800-331-9175	665-3023*
Vantage Data Solutions 5889 S Greenwood Plaza Blvd Suite 201 *Web:* www.vantagedatasolutions.com	Greenwood Village	CO	80111	800-568-5665	799-5885
Vericon Resources Inc 2358 Perimeter Park Dr Suite 370 *TF:* 800-795-3784 ■ *Web:* www.vericon.com	Atlanta	GA	30341	770-457-9922	457-5006
Verified Credentials Inc 20890 Kenbridge Ct *TF:* 800-473-4934 ■ *Web:* www.verifiedcredentials.com	Lakeville	MN	55044	952-985-7200	985-7212
Washington Document Service Inc 1250 Connecticut Ave NW Suite 200-E **Fax Area Code:* 800 ■ *TF:* 800-728-5201 ■ *Web:* www.wdsdocs.com	Washington	DC	20036	202-628-5200	385-3823*
Westlaw Court Express 1100 13th St NW Suite 300 **Fax Area Code:* 888 ■ *TF:* 800-542-3320	Washington	DC	20005	877-362-7387	737-2640*

639 PUBLIC RELATIONS FIRMS

SEE ALSO Advertising Agencies p. 1257

	City	State	Zip	Phone	Fax
A & R Partners 201 Baldwin Ave *Web:* www.arpartners.com	San Mateo	CA	94401	650-762-2800	762-2801
Access Communications 101 Howard St *TF:* 800-393-7737 ■ *Web:* www.accesspr.com	San Francisco	CA	94105	415-904-7070	904-7055
Ackermann Public Relations & Marketing 1111 Northshore Dr Suite N-400 *TF:* 888-414-7787 ■ *Web:* www.ackermannpr.com	Knoxville	TN	37919	865-584-0550	588-3009
Alan Taylor Communications 225 W 34th St *Web:* www.alantaylor.com	New York	NY	10122	212-714-1280	695-5685
APCO Worldwide 700 12th St *Web:* www.apcoworldwide.com	Washington	DC	20005	202-778-1000	466-6002
B & B Media Group 109 S Main St *TF:* 800-927-0517 ■ *Web:* www.tbbmedia.com	Corsicana	TX	75110	903-872-0517	872-0518
Bader Rutter & Assoc Inc 13845 Bishops Dr *Web:* www.baderrutter.com	Brookfield	WI	53005	262-784-7200	938-5595
Bender/Helper Impact 11500 W Olympic Blvd Suite 655 *Web:* www.bhimpact.com	Los Angeles	CA	90064	310-473-4147	478-4727
Bite Communications 345 Spear St Suite 750 *TF:* 888-329-7059 ■ *Web:* www.bitepr.com	San Francisco	CA	94105	415-365-0222	365-0223
Bohle Co 1900 Ave of the Stars Suite 200 *Web:* www.bohle.com	Los Angeles	CA	90067	310-785-0515	277-2066
Booth M & Assoc Inc 300 Park Ave S 12th Fl *Web:* www.mbooth.com	New York	NY	10010	212-481-7000	481-9440
Brodeur Worldwide 855 Boylston St 2nd Fl *Web:* www.brodeur.com	Boston	MA	02116	617-587-2800	587-2828
Brotman-Winter-Fried Communications 111 Park Place *Web:* www.specialevent.com	Falls Church	VA	22046	703-534-4600	536-2255
Burson-Marsteller 230 Park Ave S *TF:* 800-342-5692 ■ *Web:* www.bm.com	New York	NY	10003	212-614-4000	598-6914
Carmichael Lynch Spong 800 Hennepin Ave *TF:* 800-835-9624 ■ *Web:* www.carmichaellynchspong.com	Minneapolis	MN	55403	612-334-6000	375-8501
Carter Ryley Thomas 101 W Commerce Rd *Web:* www.crtpr.com	Richmond	VA	23224	804-675-8100	675-8183
CCo Communications 3200 Greenfield St Suite 280 *Web:* www.pcgcampbell.com	Dearborn	MI	48120	313-336-9000	336-9029
Cerrell Assoc Inc 320 N Larchmont Blvd *Web:* www.cerrell.com	Los Angeles	CA	90004	323-466-3445	466-8653
Chandler Chicco Agency 450 W 15th St 7th Fl *Web:* www.ccapr.com	New York	NY	10011	212-229-8400	229-8496
Charles Ryan Assoc Inc 300 Summer St Suite 1100 *TF:* 877-342-0161 ■ *Web:* www.cryanassoc.com	Charleston	WV	25301	304-342-0161	342-1941
Citigate Cunningham 101 2nd St 22nd Fl Suite 2250 *Web:* www.citigatecunningham.com	San Francisco	CA	94105	415-618-8700	618-8702
Cohn & Wolfe 292 Madison Ave 9th Fl *Web:* www.cohnwolfe.com	New York	NY	10017	212-798-9700	329-9900
Cone Inc 855 Boylston St Suite 3 *TF:* 877-531-5578 ■ *Web:* www.conenet.com	Boston	MA	02116	617-227-2111	523-3955
Connect PR 580 Howard St Suite 204 *Web:* www.connectpr.com	San Francisco	CA	94105	415-222-9691	222-9694
Connors Communications 7 W 22nd St 7th Fl *Web:* www.connors.com	New York	NY	10010	212-807-7500	807-7503
Cramer-Krasselt 733 N Van Buren St 4th Fl *Web:* www.c-k.com	Milwaukee	WI	53202	414-227-3500	276-8710
Dan Klores Communications (DKC) 386 Park Ave S 10th Fl *Web:* www.dkcnews.com	New York	NY	10016	212-685-4300	685-9024
DeVries Public Relations 30 E 60th St 14th Fl *Web:* www.devries-pr.com	New York	NY	10022	212-891-0400	644-0291
DKC (Dan Klores Communications) 386 Park Ave S 10th Fl *Web:* www.dkcnews.com	New York	NY	10016	212-685-4300	685-9024
Duffey Communications Inc 3379 Peachtree Rd NE Suite 350 *Web:* www.duffey.com	Atlanta	GA	30326	404-266-2600	262-3198
Dye Van Mol & Lawrence 209 7th Ave N *Web:* www.dvl.com	Nashville	TN	37219	615-244-1818	780-3396
Edelman Financial 200 E Randolph Dr Suite 63 *Web:* www.edelman.com	Chicago	IL	60601	312-240-3000	240-2900
Edelman Public Relations Worldwide 200 E Randolph Dr Suite 6300 *Web:* www.edelman.com	Chicago	IL	60601	312-240-3000	240-2900
Edward Howard & Co 1100 Superior Ave Suite 1600 *TF:* 800-868-2045 ■ *Web:* www.edwardhoward.com	Cleveland	OH	44114	216-781-2400	781-8810
Environics Communications Inc 33 Bloor St E Suite 900 *TF:* 888-863-3377 ■ *Web:* eci.environics.net	Toronto	ON	M4W3H1	416-920-9000	920-1822
Equals Three Communications 7910 Woodmont Ave Suite 200 *Web:* www.equals3.com	Bethesda	MD	20814	301-656-3100	652-5264
Euro RSCG Magnet 110 5th Ave 6th Fl *Web:* www.magnet.com	New York	NY	10011	212-367-6800	367-7154
Euro RSCG Worldwide 350 Hudson St 6th Fl *TF:* 800-263-7590 ■ *Web:* www.eurorscg.com	New York	NY	10014	212-886-2000	886-2016
FD Morgen-Walke 88 Pine St	New York	NY	10005	212-850-5600	850-5790
FischerHealth Inc 5340 Alla Rd Suite 200 *Web:* www.fischerhealth.com	Los Angeles	CA	90066	310-577-7870	577-8151
FitzGerald Communications Inc 855 Boylston St 5th Fl *TF:* 888-494-9501 ■ *Web:* www.fitzgerald.com	Boston	MA	02116	617-488-9500	488-9501
Fleishman-Hillard Inc 200 N Broadway *Web:* www.fleishman.com	Saint Louis	MO	63102	314-982-1700	231-2313
French Richard & Assoc 112 E Hargett St	Raleigh	NC	27601	919-832-6300	832-8322
GCI Group Inc 825 3rd Ave 24th Fl *TF:* 800-883-9525 ■ *Web:* www.gcigroup.com	New York	NY	10022	212-537-8000	537-8050
Gibbs & Soell Public Relations 600 3rd Ave 6th Fl *Web:* www.gibbs-soell.com	New York	NY	10016	212-697-2600	697-2646
Gogerty Stark Marriott Inc 1501 4th Ave Suite 2900 *Web:* www.gsminc.com	Seattle	WA	98101	206-292-3000	292-2063
Golin/Harris International 111 E Wacker Dr 11th Fl *Web:* www.golinharris.com	Chicago	IL	60601	312-729-4000	729-4367
GPC International 100 Queen St *Web:* www.gpcinternational.com	Ottawa	ON	K1P1J9	613-238-2090	238-9380
GS Schwartz & Co Inc 470 Park Ave S 10th Fl *Web:* www.schwartz.com	New York	NY	10016	212-725-4500	725-9188
Hawthorn Group LC 1199 N Fairfax St Suite 1000 *Web:* www.hawthorngroup.com	Alexandria	VA	22314	703-299-4499	299-4488
Hill & Knowlton Inc 909 3rd Ave 10th Fl *Web:* www.hillandknowlton.com	New York	NY	10022	212-885-0300	885-0570
HLB Communications Inc 875 N Michigan Ave Suite 1340 *Web:* www.hlbcomm.com	Chicago	IL	60611	312-649-0371	649-1119
Hoffman Agency 70 N 2nd St *Web:* www.hoffman.com	San Jose	CA	95113	408-286-2611	286-0133
Horn Group Inc 612 Howard St Suite 100 *Web:* www.horngroup.com	San Francisco	CA	94105	415-905-4000	905-4001
Howard Edward & Co 1100 Superior Ave Suite 1600 *TF:* 800-868-2045 ■ *Web:* www.edwardhoward.com	Cleveland	OH	44114	216-781-2400	781-8810
Hunter Public Relations 41 Madison Ave 5th Fl *Web:* www.hunterpr.com	New York	NY	10010	212-679-6600	679-6607
InterActive Public Relations Inc 550 3rd St *Web:* www.interactive-pr.com	San Francisco	CA	94107	415-975-3350	975-2201
Jasculca/Terman & Assoc 730 N Franklin Suite 510 *Web:* www.jtpr.com	Chicago	IL	60610	312-337-7400	337-8189
KCSA Public Relations Worldwide 800 2nd Ave 5th Fl *Web:* www.kcsa.com	New York	NY	10017	212-682-6300	697-0910
Kemper Lesnik Communications 500 Skokie Blvd Suite 444 *Web:* www.klc.com	Northbrook	IL	60062	847-291-9666	291-0271
Ketchum 1285 Ave of the Americas *Web:* www.ketchum.com	New York	NY	10019	646-935-3900	935-4499
LaForce & Stevens 132 W 21st St 8th Fl *Web:* www.laforce-stevens.com	New York	NY	10011	212-242-9353	242-9565
Lois Paul & Partners 150 Presidential Way *Web:* www.loispaul.com	Woburn	MA	01801	781-782-5000	782-5999
M Booth & Assoc Inc 300 Park Ave S 12th Fl *Web:* www.mbooth.com	New York	NY	10010	212-481-7000	481-9440
Makovsky & Co Inc 575 Lexington Ave 15th Fl *Web:* www.makovsky.com	New York	NY	10022	212-508-9600	751-9710
Manning Selvage & Lee 1675 Broadway 9th Fl *Web:* www.mslpr.com	New York	NY	10019	212-468-4200	
Martin Public Relations 1 Shockoe Plaza *Web:* www.martinagency.com	Richmond	VA	23219	804-698-8800	698-8801
Marx Layne & Co 31420 Northwestern Hwy Suite 100 *Web:* www.marxlayne.com	Farmington Hills	MI	48334	248-855-6777	855-6719
McNeely Pigott & Fox 611 Commerce St Suite 2800 *TF:* 800-818-6953 ■ *Web:* www.mpf.com	Nashville	TN	37203	615-259-4000	259-4040
MCS Public Relations 1420 US Hwy 206 Suite 100 *TF:* 800-477-9626 ■ *Web:* www.mcspr.com	Bedminster	NJ	07921	908-234-9900	470-4490
Morgan & Myers Inc N 16 W 23233 Stone Ridge Dr Suite 200 *Web:* www.morganmyers.com	Weukesha	WI	53188	262-650-7260	650-7261
MWW Group 1 Meadowlands Plaza 6th Fl *TF:* 800-724-7602 ■ *Web:* www.mwwpr.com	East Rutherford	NJ	07073	201-507-9500	507-0092
Neale-May & Partners 409 Sherman Ave *Web:* www.nealemay.com	Palo Alto	CA	94306	650-328-5555	328-5016
Noonan/Russo Communications Inc 200 Madison Ave 7th Fl *Web:* www.noonanrusso.com	New York	NY	10016	212-845-4200	845-4260
Ogilvy Public Relations Worldwide 825 8th Ave 25th Fl *Web:* www.ogilvypr.com	New York	NY	10019	212-880-5200	370-4636
Pacifico Inc 3880 S Bascom Ave Suite 215 *Web:* www.pacifico.com	San Jose	CA	91525	408-559-8880	
Padilla Speer Beardsley Inc 1101 W River Pkwy Suite 400 *Web:* www.psbpr.com	Minneapolis	MN	55415	612-455-1700	455-1060
PainePR 19000 MacArthur Blvd 8th Fl *TF:* 866-724-6377 ■ *Web:* www.painepr.com	Irvine	CA	92612	949-809-6700	260-1116
PAN Communications 300 Brickstone Sq *Web:* www.pancommunications.com	Andover	MA	01810	978-474-1900	474-1903
Patrice Tanaka & Co Inc 320 W 13th St 7th Fl *Web:* www.ptanaka.com	New York	NY	10014	212-229-0500	229-0523
Paul Lois & Partners 150 Presidential Way *Web:* www.loispaul.com	Woburn	MA	01801	781-782-5000	782-5999

Company / Address	City	State	Zip	Phone	Fax
PepperCom Inc 470 Park Ave S 5th Fl *Web:* www.peppercom.com	New York	NY	10016	212-681-1333	931-6159
Porter Novelli International 75 Varick St 6th Fl *Web:* www.porternovelli.com	New York	NY	10013	212-601-8000	601-8101
PR21 215 Park Ave S 16th Fl *Web:* www.zenogroup.com	New York	NY	10003	212-299-8888	462-1026
Public Communications Inc 35 E Wacker Dr Suite 1254 *Web:* www.pcipr.com	Chicago	IL	60601	312-558-1770	558-5425
Publicis Dialog 14185 N Dallas Pkwy *Web:* www.publicisdialog.com	Dallas	TX	75254	972-628-7500	628-7790
Richard French & Assoc 112 E Hargett St	Raleigh	NC	27601	919-832-6300	832-8322
RMR Assoc Inc 5870 Hubbard Dr *Web:* www.rmr.com	Rockville	MD	20852	301-230-0045	230-0046
Rogers & Assoc 1875 Century Park E Suite 200 *TF:* 800-554-6901 ■ *Web:* www.rogersassoc.com	Los Angeles	CA	90067	310-552-6922	552-9052
Rowland Communications Worldwide 1675 Broadway *Web:* www.rowland.com/index_home.html	New York	NY	10019	212-527-8800	527-8989
Rubin Communications Group 421 Cedar Mountain Rd *Web:* www.rubincomm.com	Dahlonega	GA	30533	706-867-0271	
Ruder Finn 301 E 57th St 4th Fl *Web:* www.ruderfinn.com	New York	NY	10022	212-593-6400	593-6397
Ryan Charles Assoc Inc 300 Summer St Suite 1100 *TF:* 877-342-0161 ■ *Web:* www.cryanassoc.com	Charleston	WV	25301	304-342-0161	342-1941
Schwartz Communications Inc 230 3rd Ave *Web:* www.schwartz-pr.com	Waltham	MA	02451	781-684-0770	684-6500
Schwartz GS & Co Inc 470 Park Ave S 10th Fl *Web:* www.schwartz.com	New York	NY	10016	212-725-4500	725-9188
Sloane & Co 7 Times Square 17th Fl *Web:* www.sloanepr.com	New York	NY	10022	212-486-9500	702-9103
Southard Communications Inc 29 E 19th St 5th Fl *Web:* www.southardinc.com	New York	NY	10003	212-777-2220	777-7458
Stanton-Crenshaw Communications 460 Park AVe 8th Fl *Web:* www.stanton-crenshaw.com	New York	NY	10022	212-780-1900	780-4003
Strat@comm 1 Thomas Cir NW 10th Fl *Web:* www.stratacomm.net	Washington	DC	20005	202-289-2001	289-1327
Tanaka Patrice & Co Inc 320 W 13th St 7th Fl *Web:* www.ptanaka.com	New York	NY	10014	212-229-0500	229-0523
Taylor Alan Communications 225 W 34th St *Web:* www.alantaylor.com	New York	NY	10122	212-714-1280	695-5685
Text 100 North America 77 Maiden Ln 3rd Fl *Web:* www.text100.com	San Francisco	CA	94108	415-593-8400	593-8401
Tierney Communications 200 S Broad St *Web:* www.tierneyagency.com	Philadelphia	PA	19102	215-790-4100	790-4363
Townsend Agency Ltd 9700 W Higgins Rd Suite 600 *Web:* www.townagcy.com	Rosemont	IL	60018	847-318-9010	318-9036
Tunheim Partners 8009 34th Ave S Suite 1100 *Web:* www.tunheimpartners.com	Minneapolis	MN	55425	952-851-1600	851-1610
Vollmer Public Relations 808 Travis St Suite 501 *Web:* www.vollmerpr.com	Houston	TX	77002	713-970-2100	970-2140
Waggener Edstrom 3 Center Pt Dr Suite 300 *Web:* www.waggeneredstrom.com	Lake Oswego	OR	97035	503-443-7000	443-7001
Walt & Co Communications 2105 S Bascom Ave Suite 240 *Web:* www.walt.com	Campbell	CA	95008	408-369-7200	369-7201
Weber Shandwick Worldwide 640 5th Ave 8th Fl *Web:* www.webershandwick.com	New York	NY	10019	212-445-8000	445-8001
Widmeyer Communications 1825 Connecticut Ave NW 5th Fl *Web:* www.widmeyer.com	Washington	DC	20009	202-667-0901	667-0902
Zimmerman Agency 1821 Miccosukee Commons *Web:* www.zimmerman.com	Tallahassee	FL	32308	850-668-2222	656-4622

PUBLICATIONS

SEE Magazines & Journals p. 1926; Newsletters p. 2013; Newspapers p. 2019

640 PUBLISHING COMPANIES

SEE ALSO Book Producers p. 1389; Literary Agents p. 1916; Magazines & Journals p. 1926; Newsletters p. 2013; Newspapers p. 2019

640-1 Atlas & Map Publishers

Company / Address	City	State	Zip	Phone	Fax
American Hagstrom Langenscheidt DBA Hagstrom Map 36-36 33rd St Suite 401 *TF:* 800-432-6277 ■ *Web:* www.hagstrommap.com	Long Island City	NY	11106	718-784-0055	784-1216
Arrow Publishing Co 1800 Lovering Ave *TF:* 800-327-7992 ■ *Web:* www.arrowmap.com	Wilmington	DE	19806	302-998-6009	658-4598
DeLorme 2 DeLorme Dr **Fax Area Code:* 800 ■ **Fax:* Sales ■ *TF Sales:* 800-452-5931 ■ *Web:* www.delorme.com	Yarmouth	ME	04096	207-846-7000	575-2244*
George F Cram Co Inc 4719 W 62nd St *TF:* 800-227-4199 ■ *Web:* www.georgefcram.com	Indianapolis	IN	46268	317-635-5564	687-2840
Hagstrom Map 36-36 33rd St Suite 401 *TF:* 800-432-6277 ■ *Web:* www.hagstrommap.com	Long Island City	NY	11106	718-784-0055	784-1216
Hammond World Atlas Corp 95 Progress St *TF:* 800-526-4953 ■ *Web:* www.hammondmap.com	Union	NJ	07083	908-206-1300	206-1104
MARCOA Publishing Inc 9955 Black Mountain Rd *TF:* 800-854-2935 ■ *Web:* www.marcoa.com	San Diego	CA	92126	858-695-9600	695-9641
Nystrom 4719 W 62nd St *TF:* 800-621-8086 ■ *Web:* www.nystromnet.com	Indianapolis	IN	46268	317-612-3901	329-3305
Rand McNally & Co 8255 N Central Park Ave **Fax:* Cust Svc ■ *TF:* 800-333-0136 ■ *Web:* www.randmcnally.com	Skokie	IL	60076	847-329-8100	673-9935*
Sanborn Map Co 629 5th Ave *TF:* 800-930-3298 ■ *Web:* www.sanmap.com	Pelham	NY	10803	914-738-1649	738-1680
Universal Map 795 Progress Ct *TF:* 800-829-6277 ■ *Web:* www.universalmap.com	Williamston	MI	48895	517-655-5641	655-5739

640-2 Book Publishers

Company / Address	City	State	Zip	Phone	Fax
Abacus Software Inc 5130 Patterson St SE *TF Sales:* 800-451-4319 ■ *Web:* www.abacuspub.com	Grand Rapids	MI	49512	616-698-0330	698-0325
ABC-CLIO Inc 130 Cremona Dr *TF:* 800-368-6868 ■ *Web:* www.abc-clio.com	Santa Barbara	CA	93117	805-968-1911	685-9685
Abrams & Co Publishers Inc PO Box 10025 **Fax Area Code:* 800 ■ **Fax:* Cust Svc ■ *TF Cust Svc:* 800-227-9120 ■ *Web:* www.abramsandcompany.com	Waterbury	CT	06725	203-756-3580	737-3322*
Abrams Harry N Inc 115 W 18th St 6th Fl *TF:* 800-345-1359 ■ *Web:* www.hnabooks.com/abrams	New York	NY	10011	212-206-7715	519-1210
Adams Media Corp 57 Littlefield St *Web:* www.adamsmedia.com	Avon	MA	02322	800-872-5627	872-5628
Addison-Wesley Higher Education Group 75 Arlington St Suite 300 **Fax Area Code:* 800 ■ *TF:* 800-447-2226 ■ *Web:* www.aw-bc.com	Boston	MA	02116	617-848-5100	552-2499*
Advance Publications Inc 950 Fingerboard Rd	Staten Island	NY	10305	718-981-1234	981-5679
Albert Whitman & Co 6340 Oakton St *TF:* 800-255-7675 ■ *Web:* www.awhitmanco.com	Morton Grove	IL	60053	847-581-0033	581-0039
Alfred A Knopf Inc 1745 Broadway *Web:* www.randomhouse.com/knopf	New York	NY	10019	212-782-9000	
Algonquin Books PO Box 2225 *Web:* www.algonquin.com	Chapel Hill	NC	27515	919-967-0108	933-0272
Allyn & Bacon/Longman Publishers Pearson Education Inc 75 Arlington St Suite 300 *TF Orders:* 800-852-8024 ■ *Web:* www.ablongman.com	Boston	MA	02116	617-848-7090	848-7490
American Biographical Institute 5126 Bur Oak Cir *Web:* www.abiworldwide.com	Raleigh	NC	27612	919-781-8710	781-8712
American Printing House for the Blind 1839 Frankfort Ave PO Box 6085 *TF:* 800-223-1839 ■ *Web:* www.aph.org	Louisville	KY	40206	502-895-2405	899-2274
Antique Collectors' Club 116 Pleasant St Suite 8 Eastworks Bldg *TF:* 800-252-5231 ■ *Web:* www.antiquecc.com	Easthampton	MA	01027	413-529-0861	529-0862
Aspen Publishers Inc 111 8th Ave 7th Fl *TF Orders:* 800-447-1717 ■ *Web:* www.aspenpublishers.com	New York	NY	10011	212-771-0600	597-0335
Atlantic Publishing Co 1108 E 5th St *TF:* 800-672-1022 ■ *Web:* www.atlantic-pub.com	Tabor City	NC	28463	910-653-3153	653-9440
Auerbach Publications 600 Broken Sound Pkwy NW *TF Cust Svc:* 800-272-7737 ■ *Web:* www.auerbach-publications.com	Boca Raton	FL	33487	561-994-0555	
Author House 1663 Liberty Dr Suite 200 *TF:* 888-728-8467 ■ *Web:* www.authorhouse.com	Bloomington	IN	47403	812-339-6000	339-6554
Avalon Travel Publishing 1400 65th St Suite 250 *Web:* www.travelmatters.com	Emeryville	CA	94608	510-595-3664	595-4228
Avon Books Div HarperCollins Pubishers 10 E 53rd St *TF:* 800-242-7737 ■ *Web:* www.harpercollins.com	New York	NY	10022	212-207-7000	207-7901
Ballantine Del Rey Fawcett Books 1745 Broadway	New York	NY	10019	212-782-9000	782-8438
Bantam Dell Publishing Group Div Random House Inc 1745 Broadway *TF:* 800-726-0600 ■ *Web:* www.randomhouse.com/bantamdell	New York	NY	10019	212-782-9000	
Barron's Educational Series Inc 250 Wireless Blvd *TF:* 800-645-3476 ■ *Web:* www.barronseduc.com	Hauppauge	NY	11788	631-434-3311	434-3723
Bartleby.com Inc PO Box 13 *Web:* www.bartleby.com	New York	NY	10034	646-522-2474	
Beacon Press Inc 25 Beacon St **Fax Area Code:* 800 ■ *Web:* www.beacon.org	Boston	MA	02108	617-742-2110	225-3362*
Berkley Publishing Group 375 Hudson St *TF Cust Svc:* 800-631-8571	New York	NY	10014	212-366-2000	366-2385
Bernard C Harris Publishing Co Inc 2500 Westchester Ave Suite 400 **Fax Area Code:* 914 ■ *Web:* www.harrisconnect.com	Purchase	NY	10577	800-326-6600	641-3501*
Bertelsmann Publishing Group Inc 1745 Broadway *Web:* www.bertelsmann.com	New York	NY	10019	212-782-1000	782-1010
Black Classic Press PO Box 13414 *TF:* 800-476-8870 ■ *Web:* www.blackclassic.com	Baltimore	MD	21203	410-358-0980	358-0987
Blackwell Publishers Inc 350 Main St *TF:* 800-835-6770 ■ *Web:* www.blackwellpublishing.com	Malden	MA	02148	781-388-8250	388-8210
Blackwell Publishing Professional 2121 S State Ave *TF:* 800-862-6657 ■ *Web:* www.blackwellprofessional.com	Ames	IA	50014	515-292-0140	292-3348
BNA Books Div Bureau of National Affairs Inc 1231 25th St *TF Sales:* 800-960-1220 ■ *Web:* www.bna.com/bnabooks	Washington	DC	20037	202-452-4200	452-4997
BOA Editions Ltd 260 East Ave *Web:* www.boaeditions.org	Rochester	NY	14604	585-546-3410	546-3913
Books On Tape Inc 400 Hahn Rd **Fax Area Code:* 714 ■ *TF:* 800-882-6657 ■ *Web:* www.booksontape.com	Westminster	MD	21157	800-882-6657	825-0756*
BRB Publications Inc PO Box 27869 **Fax Area Code:* 800 ■ *TF:* 800-929-3811 ■ *Web:* www.brbpub.com	Tempe	AZ	85285	480-829-7475	929-3810*
Brooks/Cole Publishing Co 10 Davis Dr *TF:* 800-354-0092 ■ *Web:* www.brookscole.com	Belmont	CA	94002	650-595-2350	
Bureau of National Affairs Inc 1231 25th St NW *TF:* 800-372-1033 ■ *Web:* www.bna.com	Washington	DC	20037	202-452-4200	452-4610
Bureau of National Affairs Inc BNA Books Div 1231 25th St *TF Sales:* 800-960-1220 ■ *Web:* www.bna.com/bnabooks	Washington	DC	20037	202-452-4200	452-4997
Candlewick Press Inc 2067 Massachusetts Ave *Web:* www.candlewick.com	Cambridge	MA	02140	617-661-3330	661-0565
Carroll Publishing Co 4701 Sangamore Rd Suite S-155 *TF:* 800-336-4240 ■ *Web:* www.carrollpub.com	Bethesda	MD	20816	301-263-9800	263-9801
CCH Inc 2700 Lake Cook Rd *TF Cust Svc:* 800-835-5224 ■ *Web:* www.cch.com	Riverwoods	IL	60015	847-267-7000	267-2516
Charles C Thomas Publisher 2600 S 1st St *TF Sales:* 800-258-8980 ■ *Web:* www.ccthomas.com	Springfield	IL	62704	217-789-8980	789-9130
Children's Press PO Box 1795 *TF:* 800-621-1115	Danbury	CT	06816	203-797-3500	797-3657
Chronicle Books 680 2nd St 6th Fl **Fax Area Code:* 800 ■ *TF:* 800-722-6657 ■ *Web:* www.chroniclebooks.com	San Francisco	CA	94107	415-537-4200	858-7787*
Clarion Books 215 Park Ave S	New York	NY	10003	212-420-5800	420-5855
Congressional Quarterly Inc 1255 22nd St NW **Fax Area Code:* 800 ■ *TF:* 800-432-2250 ■ *Web:* www.cq.com	Washington	DC	20037	202-419-8500	380-3810*
Cornell Maritime Press PO Box 456 *TF:* 800-638-7641 ■ *Web:* www.cmptp.com	Centreville	MD	21617	410-758-1075	758-6849
Corwin Press Inc 2455 Teller Rd *TF Orders:* 800-818-7243 ■ *Web:* www.corwinpress.com	Thousand Oaks	CA	91320	805-499-9734	499-0871
CRC Press LLC 6000 Broken Sound Pkwy NW Suite 300 **Fax Area Code:* 800 ■ **Fax:* Cust Svc ■ *TF Cust Svc:* 800-272-7737 ■ *Web:* www.crcpress.com	Boca Raton	FL	33487	561-994-0555	374-3401*
Curriculum Assoc Inc PO Box 2001 *TF:* 800-225-0248 ■ *Web:* www.curriculumassociates.com	North Billerica	MA	01862	978-667-8000	667-5706
D & B 103 JFK Pkwy *NYSE:* DNB ■ *Web:* www.dnb.com/us/	Short Hills	NJ	07078	973-921-5500	921-5501
Dalmation Press 3101 Clairmont Rd Suite C *Web:* www.dalmatianpress.com	Atlanta	GA	30329	404-214-4300	
Davis FA Co 1915 Arch St *TF:* 800-323-3555 ■ *Web:* www.fadavis.com	Philadelphia	PA	19103	215-568-2270	568-5065
Dearborn Financial Publishing Inc DBA Dearborn A Kaplan Professional Co 30 S Wacker Dr *TF:* 800-621-9621 ■ *Web:* www.kaplanpublishing.com	Chicago	IL	60606	312-836-4400	836-9958
Dekker Marcel Inc 270 Madison Ave *TF Sales:* 800-228-1160 ■ *Web:* www.dekker.com	New York	NY	10016	212-696-9000	685-4540
Delacorte Press 1745 Broadway *TF:* 800-200-3552 ■ *Web:* www.randomhouse.com	New York	NY	10019	212-782-9000	302-7985

Company	City	State	Zip	Phone	Fax
Delmar Learning 5 Maxwell Dr	Clifton Park	NY	12065	518-348-2300	464-0342*
*Fax: Sales ■ TF: 800-998-7498 ■ Web: www.delmarlearning.com					
Disney Consumer Products 500 S Buena Vista St	Burbank	CA	91521	818-560-1000	560-1930*
*Fax: Cust Svc ■ TF PR: 800-723-4763					
Disney Publishing Worldwide Inc 114 5th Ave	New York	NY	10011	212-633-4400	633-4811
Web: disney.go.com/disneybooks					
Dolan Media Co 706 2nd Ave S Suite 1200	Minneapolis	MN	55402	612-317-9420	321-0563
Web: www.dolanmedia.com					
Donning Co Publishers 184 Business Pk Dr Suite 206	Virginia Beach	VA	23462	757-497-1789	497-2542
TF: 800-296-8572 ■ Web: www.donning.com					
Dorling Kindersley Publishing 375 Hudson St	New York	NY	10014	212-336-2000	689-4828
TF Cust Svc: 800-631-8571 ■ Web: www.dk.com					
Doubleday Broadway Publishing Group 1745 Broadway	New York	NY	10019	212-782-9000	659-2436*
*Fax Area Code: 800 ■ *Fax: Cust Svc ■ TF: 800-726-0600 ■ Web: www.randomhouse.com					
Douglas Publications Inc 2807 N Parham Rd Suite 200	Richmond	VA	23294	804-762-9600	217-8999
TF: 800-223-1797 ■ Web: www.douglaspublications.com					
Dover Publications Inc 31 E 2nd St	Mineola	NY	11501	516-294-7000	742-6953
TF: 800-223-3130 ■ Web: store.doverpublications.com					
Educators Publishing Service Inc PO Box 9031	Cambridge	MA	02139	617-547-6706	440-2665*
*Fax Area Code: 888 ■ TF: 800-225-5750 ■ Web: www.epsbooks.com					
Eerdmans William B Publishing Co 255 Jefferson Ave SE	Grand Rapids	MI	49503	616-459-4591	459-6540
TF: 800-253-7521 ■ Web: www.eerdmans.com					
EMC-Paradigm Publishing Co 875 Montreal Way	Saint Paul	MN	55102	651-290-2800	328-4564*
*Fax Area Code: 800 ■ TF: 800-328-1452 ■ Web: www.emcp.com					
Encyclopaedia Britannica Inc 331 N La Salle St	Chicago	IL	60610	312-347-7000	347-7906*
*Fax: PR ■ TF: 800-323-1229 ■ Web: www.eb.com					
F & W Publications Inc 4700 E Galbraith Rd	Cincinnati	OH	45236	513-531-2690	686-8174
TF Sales: 800-289-0963 ■ Web: www.fwpublications.com					
FA Davis Co 1915 Arch St	Philadelphia	PA	19103	215-568-2270	568-5065
TF: 800-323-3555 ■ Web: www.fadavis.com					
Facts on File Inc 132 W 31st St 17th Fl	New York	NY	10001	212-967-8800	678-3633*
*Fax Area Code: 800 ■ TF Cust Svc: 800-322-8755 ■ Web: www.factsonfile.com					
Farrar Straus & Giroux Inc 19 Union Sq W	New York	NY	10003	212-741-6900	633-9385
Web: www.fsgbooks.com					
Feminist Press at the City University of New York					
365 5th Ave 5th Fl	New York	NY	10016	212-817-7922	817-1593
Web: www.feministpress.org					
Financial Publishing Co PO Box 570	South Bend	IN	46624	574-243-6040	243-6060
TF Cust Svc: 800-433-0090 ■ Web: www.financial-publishing.com					
Fodor's Travel 1745 Broadway	New York	NY	10019	212-751-2600	
TF: 800-726-0600 ■ Web: www.fodors.com					
Forbes Inc 60 5th Ave	New York	NY	10011	212-620-2200	206-5534
TF: 800-888-9896 ■ Web: www.forbes.com					
Franklin Watts PO Box 1795	Danbury	CT	06816	203-797-3500	797-3657
TF Cust Svc: 800-621-1115					
Freeman WH & Co 41 Madison Ave 35th Fl	New York	NY	10010	212-576-9400	689-2383
TF: 800-903-3019 ■ Web: www.whfreeman.com					
Garland Publishing Inc 270 Madison Ave	New York	NY	10016	917-351-7100	564-7854*
*Fax Area Code: 212 ■ TF: 800-797-3803 ■ Web: www.garlandpub.com					
Glencoe/McGraw-Hill 8787 Orion Pl	Columbus	OH	43240	614-430-4000	430-4412*
*Fax: Hum Res ■ TF: 800-848-1567 ■ Web: www.glencoe.com					
Golden Books 1745 Broadway	New York	NY	10019	212-782-9000	
Web: www.randomhouse.com/golden					
Goodheart-Willcox Publisher 18604 W Creek Dr	Tinley Park	IL	60477	708-687-5000	409-3900*
*Fax Area Code: 888 ■ TF: 800-323-0440 ■ Web: www.goodheartwillcox.com					
Government Information Services 1725 K St NW Suite 700	Washington	DC	20006	202-872-4000	296-1091
TF: 800-677-3789					
Government Research Service PO Box 2067	Topeka	KS	66601	785-232-7720	232-1615
TF: 800-346-6898 ■ Web: www.thinktankdirectory.com					
Greenwillow Books 1350 Ave of the Americas	New York	NY	10019	212-261-6500	822-4090*
*Fax Area Code: 800 ■ TF: 800-242-7737 ■ Web: www.harpercollins.com					
Greenwood-Heinemann 361 Hanover St	Portsmouth	NH	03801	603-431-7894	431-7840
TF: 800-541-2086 ■ Web: www.heinemann.com					
Greenwood Publishing Group Inc 88 Post Rd W	Westport	CT	06881	203-226-3571	222-1502
TF Orders: 800-225-5800 ■ Web: www.greenwood.com					
Grey House Publishing 185 Millerton Rd PO Box 860	Millerton	NY	12546	518-789-8700	789-0556
TF: 800-562-2139 ■ Web: www.greyhouse.com					
Grolier Inc 90 Old Sherman Tpke	Danbury	CT	06816	203-797-3500	797-3197
Web: www.grolier.com					
Group360 Inc 10818 Midwest Industrial Blvd	Saint Louis	MO	63132	314-423-9300	423-6104
TF: 800-666-8243 ■ Web: www.group360.com					
Grove/Atlantic Inc 841 Broadway	New York	NY	10003	212-614-7860	614-7886
Web: www.groveatlantic.com					
Harcourt Achieve 6277 Sea Harbor Dr	Orlando	FL	32887	800-531-5015	699-9459
Web: www.harcourtachieve.com					
Harcourt Inc 6277 Sea Harbor Dr	Orlando	FL	32887	407-345-2000	345-3016*
*Fax: Cust Svc ■ TF: 800-782-4479 ■ Web: www.harcourt.com					
Harlequin Enterprises Ltd 225 Duncan Mill Rd	Don Mills	ON	M3B3K9	416-445-5860	445-8655
TF: 800-387-0112 ■ Web: www.eharlequin.com					
Harlequin-Silhouette Books 233 Broadway Suite 1001	New York	NY	10279	212-553-4200	227-8969
Web: www.eharlequin.com					
HarperCollins Canada Ltd 1995 Markham Rd	Scarborough	ON	M1B5M8	416-321-2241	321-3033
TF: 800-387-0117 ■ Web: www.harpercanada.com					
HarperCollins Children's Books Group					
1350 Ave of the Americas	New York	NY	10019	212-261-6500	822-4090*
*Fax Area Code: 800 ■ *Fax: Cust Svc ■ TF Cust Svc: 800-242-7737 ■ Web: www.harperchildrens.com					
HarperCollins Publishers Avon Books Div 10 E 53rd St	New York	NY	10022	212-207-7000	207-7901
TF: 800-242-7737 ■ Web: www.harpercollins.com					
HarperCollins Publishers Inc 10 E 53rd St	New York	NY	10022	212-207-7000	207-6998
Web: www.harpercollins.com					
Harris Bernard C Publishing Co Inc					
2500 Westchester Ave Suite 400	Purchase	NY	10577	800-326-6600	641-3501*
*Fax Area Code: 914 ■ Web: www.harrisconnect.com					
Harry N Abrams Inc 115 W 18th St 6th Fl	New York	NY	10011	212-206-7715	519-1210
TF: 800-345-1359 ■ Web: www.hnabooks.com/abrams					
Health Communications Inc (HCI) 3201 SW 15th St	Deerfield Beach	FL	33442	954-360-0909	360-0034
TF Cust Svc: 800-851-9100 ■ Web: www.hcibooks.com					
Hearst Corp 1345 6th Ave	New York	NY	10105	212-649-2000	280-1045*
*Fax Area Code: 646 ■ *Fax: Hum Res ■ Web: www.hearstcorp.com					
Hein William S & Co Inc 1285 Main St	Buffalo	NY	14209	716-882-2600	883-8100
TF: 800-828-7571 ■ Web: www.wshein.com					
Henry Holt & Co Inc 175 5th Ave	New York	NY	10010	646-307-5095	633-0748*
*Fax Area Code: 212 ■ Web: www.henryholt.com					
Herff Jones Inc 4501 W 62nd St	Indianapolis	IN	46268	317-297-3740	329-3308*
*Fax: Hum Res ■ TF: 800-427-3393 ■ Web: www.herff-jones.com					
Holt Rinehart & Winston Inc 10801 N MoPac Expy Bldg 3	Austin	TX	78759	512-721-7000	721-7770
TF: 800-992-1627 ■ Web: www.hrw.com					
Holtzbrinck Publishers 175 5th Ave	New York	NY	10010	212-674-5151	420-9314
TF: 800-221-7945 ■ Web: www.holtzbrinck.com/eng/index.html					
Houghton Mifflin Co 222 Berkeley St	Boston	MA	02116	617-351-5000	351-1100
Web: www.hmco.com					
Houghton Mifflin Co College Div 222 Berkeley St	Boston	MA	02116	617-351-5000	351-1100
Web: college.hmco.com					
Houghton Mifflin Co School Div 222 Berkeley St	Boston	MA	02116	617-351-5000	351-1100
Web: www.eduplace.com					
Houghton Mifflin Co Trade & Reference Div 222 Berkeley St	Boston	MA	02116	617-351-5000	351-1100
Web: www.houghtonmifflinbooks.com					
Howard W Sams 9850 E 30th St	Indianapolis	IN	46229	317-396-9850	552-3910*
*Fax Area Code: 800 ■ TF Cust Svc: 800-428-7267 ■ Web: www.samswebsite.com					
Human Kinetics 1607 N Market St	Champaign	IL	61820	217-351-5076	351-2674
TF: 800-747-4457 ■ Web: www.humankinetics.com					
HW Wilson Co 950 University Ave	Bronx	NY	10452	718-588-8400	590-1617*
*Fax: Cust Svc ■ TF: 800-367-6770 ■ Web: www.hwwilson.com					
Hyperion Books 77 W 66th St 11th Fl	New York	NY	10023	212-456-0100	
Web: www.hyperionbooks.com					
Inner Traditions International 1 Park St	Rochester	VT	05767	802-767-3174	767-3726
TF: 800-246-8648 ■ Web: www.innertraditions.com					
Island Press 1718 Connecticut Ave NW Suite 300	Washington	DC	20009	202-232-7933	234-1328
TF: 800-828-1302 ■ Web: www.islandpress.org					
iUniverse 2021 Pine Lake Rd Suite 100	Lincoln	NE	68512	402-323-7800	323-7824
TF: 800-288-4677 ■ Web: www.iuniverse.com					
J Weston Walch Publisher PO Box 658	Portland	ME	04104	207-772-2846	772-3105
TF: 800-558-2846 ■ Web: www.walch.com					
Jane's Information Group 110 N Royal St Suite 200	Alexandria	VA	22314	703-683-3700	836-0029
TF: 800-824-0768 ■ Web: www.janes.com					
Jeppesen Sanderson Inc 55 Inverness Dr E	Englewood	CO	80112	303-799-9090	353-2107
TF: 800-621-5377 ■ Web: www.jeppesen.com					
John Wiley & Sons Inc 111 River St	Hoboken	NJ	07030	201-748-6000	748-6088
NYSE: JWa ■ TF Sales: 800-225-5945 ■ Web: www.wiley.com					
Jossey-Bass & Pfeiffer 989 Market St 5th Fl	San Francisco	CA	94103	415-782-3100	433-0499
Web: www.josseybass.com					
Kalmbach Publishing Co 21027 Crossroads Cir	Waukesha	WI	53186	262-796-8776	796-1615
TF Cust Svc: 800-446-5489 ■ Web: www.kalmbach.com					
Kendall/Hunt Publishing Co 4050 Westmark Dr	Dubuque	IA	52002	563-589-1000	772-9165*
*Fax Area Code: 800 ■ *Fax: Cust Svc ■ TF Cust Svc: 800-228-0810 ■ Web: www.kendallhunt.com					
Kensington Publishing Corp 850 3rd Ave	New York	NY	10022	212-407-1500	935-0699
TF: 877-422-3665 ■ Web: www.kensingtonbooks.com					
Key Curriculum Press 1150 65th St	Emeryville	CA	94608	510-595-7000	541-2442*
*Fax Area Code: 800 ■ TF: 800-995-6284 ■ Web: www.keypress.com					
Klutz 450 Lambert Ave	Palo Alto	CA	94306	650-857-0888	857-9110
TF: 800-737-4123 ■ Web: klutz.com					
Knopf Alfred A Inc 1745 Broadway	New York	NY	10019	212-782-9000	
Web: www.randomhouse.com/knopf					
Lark Books 67 Broadway St	Asheville	NC	28801	828-253-0467	253-7952
Web: www.larkbooks.com					
Lawyers Diary & Manual 240 Mulberry St	Newark	NJ	07102	973-642-1440	642-4280*
*Fax: Cust Svc ■ TF: 800-444-4041 ■ Web: www.lawdiary.com					
Leadership Directories Inc 104 5th Ave 3rd Fl	New York	NY	10011	212-627-4140	645-0931
Web: www.leadershipdirectories.com					
Lerner Publishing Group 1251 Washington Ave N	Minneapolis	MN	55401	800-328-4929	332-1132
TF: 800-462-4703 ■ Web: www.lernerbooks.com					
LexisNexis Matthew Bender 744 Broad St	Newark	NJ	07102	973-820-2000	820-2007
TF: 800-252-9257 ■ Web: www.lexisnexis.com/matthewbender					
Lightning Source 1246 Heil Quaker Blvd	La Vergne	TN	37086	615-213-5815	213-4426
Web: www.lightningsource.com					
Linden Publishing 2006 S Mary St	Fresno	CA	93721	559-233-6633	233-6933
TF Sales: 800-345-4447 ■ Web: www.lindenpub.com					
Lippincott Williams & Wilkins 530 Walnut St	Philadelphia	PA	19106	215-521-8300	521-8902
Web: www.lww.com					
Little Brown & Co 1271 Ave of the Americas	New York	NY	10020	212-364-1100	522-0885
TF Cust Svc: 800-759-0190 ■ Web: www.twbookmark.com					
Llewellyn Worldwide Inc 2143 Wooddale Dr	Saint Paul	MN	55125	651-291-1970	291-1908
TF: 800-843-6666 ■ Web: www.llewellyn.com					
Lonely Planet Publications 150 Linden St	Oakland	CA	94607	510-893-8555	893-8563*
*Fax: Sales ■ TF: 800-275-8555 ■ Web: www.lonelyplanet.com					
LRP Publications 360 Hiatt Dr	Palm Beach Gardens	FL	33418	561-622-6520	622-2423
TF: 800-621-5463 ■ Web: www.lrp.com					
Marcel Dekker Inc 270 Madison Ave	New York	NY	10016	212-696-9000	685-4540
TF Sales: 800-228-1160 ■ Web: www.dekker.com					
Marquis Who's Who 890 Mountain Ave Suite 4	New Providence	NJ	07974	908-673-1000	673-1189
Web: www.marquiswhoswho.com					
Martha Stewart Living Omnimedia Inc 11 W 42nd St 23rd Fl	New York	NY	10036	212-827-8000	827-8204
NYSE: MSO ■ Web: www.marthastewart.com					
Matthew Bender & Co (now LexisNexis Matthew Bender)					
744 Broad St	Newark	NJ	07102	973-820-2000	820-2007
TF: 800-252-9257 ■ Web: www.lexisnexis.com/matthewbender					
McDougal Littell PO Box 1667	Evanston	IL	60204	847-869-2300	869-2598
TF: 800-323-5435 ■ Web: www.mcdougallittell.com					
McGraw-Hill Cos Inc 1221 Ave of the Americas	New York	NY	10020	212-512-2000	
NYSE: MHP ■ Web: www.mcgraw-hill.com					
McGraw-Hill Higher Education Group 1333 Burr Ridge Pkwy	Burr Ridge	IL	60527	630-789-4000	755-5654*
*Fax Area Code: 614 ■ TF: 800-634-3963 ■ Web: www.mhhe.com					
McGraw-Hill Professional Publishing Group					
2 Penn Plaza 11th Fl	New York	NY	10121	212-904-2000	904-4070
TF: 800-262-4729 ■ Web: books.mcgraw-hill.com					
ME Sharpe Inc 80 Business Park Dr Suite 202	Armonk	NY	10504	914-273-1800	273-2106
TF Orders: 800-541-6563 ■ Web: www.mesharpe.com					
Means RS Co Inc 63 Smiths Ln	Kingston	MA	02364	781-585-7880	585-8814*
*Fax: Cust Svc ■ TF: 800-448-8182 ■ Web: www.rsmeans.com					
Mel Bay Publications Inc 4 Industrial Dr	Pacific	MO	63069	636-257-3970	257-5062
TF: 800-863-5229 ■ Web: melbay.com					
Meredith Corp 1716 Locust St	Des Moines	IA	50309	515-284-3000	284-3806
NYSE: MDP ■ Web: www.meredith.com					
Merriam-Webster Inc PO Box 281	Springfield	MA	01102	413-734-3134	731-5979
TF: 800-201-5029 ■ Web: www.m-w.com					
Microsoft Press 1 Microsoft Way	Redmond	WA	98052	425-882-8080	936-7329
TF Cust Svc: 800-426-9400 ■ Web: www.microsoft.com/mspress					
Modern Library 1745 Broadway	New York	NY	10019	212-751-2600	659-2436*
*Fax Area Code: 800 ■ TF Cust Svc: 800-726-0600					
Moody's Corp 99 Church St	New York	NY	10007	212-553-0300	553-5376
NYSE: MCO ■ Web: www.moodys.com					
National Academy Press					
2101 Constitution Ave NW PO Box 285	Washington	DC	20055	202-334-3313	334-2451*
*Fax: Sales ■ TF: 800-624-6242 ■ Web: www.nap.edu					
National Braille Press Inc 88 Saint Stephens St	Boston	MA	02115	617-266-6160	437-0456
TF: 888-965-8965 ■ Web: www.nbp.org					
National Geographic Society 1145 17th St NW	Washington	DC	20036	202-857-7000	775-6141
TF Orders: 800-647-5463 ■ Web: www.nationalgeographic.com					
National Register Publishing Co					
890 Mountain Ave Suite 4	New Providence	NJ	07974	908-673-1000	673-1189
Web: www.nationalregisterpub.com					
National Underwriter Co 5081 Olympic Blvd	Erlanger	KY	41018	859-692-2100	692-2246
TF: 800-543-0874 ■ Web: www.nationalunderwriter.com					
Nerdy Books 135 Main St	Flemington	NJ	08822	908-788-4676	788-7097
TF: 866-843-8477 ■ Web: www.nerdybooks.com					
New Readers Press PO Box 35888	Syracuse	NY	13235	315-422-9121	894-2100*
*Fax Area Code: 866 ■ TF: 800-448-8878 ■ Web: www.newreaderspress.com					
Nightingale-Conant Corp 6245 W Howard St	Niles	IL	60714	847-647-0300	647-5552
TF Cust Svc: 800-323-3938 ■ Web: www.nightingale.com					
Nolo.com 950 Parker St	Berkeley	CA	94710	510-549-1976	548-5902
TF Cust Svc: 800-728-3555 ■ Web: www.nolo.com					

Book Publishers (Cont'd)

Company	City	State	Zip	Phone	Fax
Norton WW & Co Inc 500 5th Ave	New York	NY	10110	212-354-5500	869-0856
TF: 800-223-2584 ■ *Web:* www.wwnorton.com					
Oceana Publications Inc 198 Madison Ave	New York	NY	10016	212-726-6000	726-6458
TF Orders: 800-831-0758 ■ *Web:* www.oceanalaw.com					
Omnigraphics Inc PO Box 31-1640	Detroit	MI	48231	313-961-1340	961-1383
TF Orders: 800-234-1340 ■ *Web:* www.omnigraphics.com					
Open Court Publishing 220 E Daniel Dale Rd	DeSoto	TX	75115	972-224-1111	228-1982
Web: www.opencourtbooks.com					
Oxmoor House Inc 2100 Lakeshore Dr	Birmingham	AL	35209	205-445-6000	445-6078
TF: 800-633-4910 ■ *Web:* www.oxmoorhouse.com					
Pathway Press 1080 Montgomery Ave NE	Cleveland	TN	37311	423-476-4512	546-7590*
**Fax Area Code:* 800 ■ **Fax:* Sales ■ *TF Sales:* 800-553-8506 ■ *Web:* www.pathwaypress.org					
Peachpit Press 1249 8th St	Berkeley	CA	94710	510-524-2178	524-2221
TF: 800-283-9444 ■ *Web:* www.peachpit.com					
Pearson Education Inc 1 Lake St	Upper Saddle River	NJ	07458	201-236-7000	767-2993*
**Fax:* Cust Svc ■ *TF Cust Svc:* 800-922-0579 ■ *Web:* www.pearsoned.com					
Pearson Education Inc Allyn & Bacon/Longman Publishers 75 Arlington St Suite 300	Boston	MA	02116	617-848-7090	848-7490
TF Orders: 800-852-8024 ■ *Web:* www.ablongman.com					
Penguin Books Canada Ltd 90 Eglent Ave E Suite 700	Toronto	ON	M4P2Y3	416-925-2249	925-0068
TF: 800-810-3104 ■ *Web:* www.penguin.ca					
Penguin Group (USA) Inc 375 Hudson St	New York	NY	10014	212-366-2000	
TF Cust Svc: 800-631-8571 ■ *Web:* us.penguingroup.com					
Perseus Inc 387 Park Ave S	New York	NY	10016	212-340-8100	453-2884*
**Fax Area Code:* 800 ■ *TF:* 800-386-5656					
Peterson's Guides Inc Princeton Pike Corporate Ctr 2000 Lenox Dr	Lawrenceville	NJ	08648	609-896-1800	896-1811
TF: 800-338-3282 ■ *Web:* www.petersons.com					
Pike & Fischer Inc 1010 Wayne Ave Suite 1400	Silver Spring	MD	20910	301-562-1530	562-1521
TF: 800-255-8131 ■ *Web:* www.pf.com					
Pocket Books 1230 Ave of the Americas 13th Fl	New York	NY	10020	212-698-7000	
TF Cust Svc: 800-223-2336					
Praeger Publishers 88 Post Rd W	Westport	CT	06881	203-226-3571	222-1502
TF: 800-225-5800 ■ *Web:* www.praeger.com					
Prentice-Hall Inc 1 Lake St	Upper Saddle River	NJ	07458	201-236-7000	236-3381
TF: 800-947-7700 ■ *Web:* www.prenhall.com					
Prentice Hall-Professional Technical Reference 1 Lake St	Upper Saddle River	NJ	07458	201-236-7000	236-7123
TF: 800-922-0579 ■ *Web:* www.phptr.com					
Price Books & Forms Inc 751 N Coney Ave	Azusa	CA	91702	626-334-0348	334-8158
TF: 800-423-8961 ■ *Web:* www.autopricebooks.com					
Publications International Ltd 7373 N Cicero Ave	Lincolnwood	IL	60712	847-676-3470	676-3671
TF: 800-745-9299 ■ *Web:* www.pubint.com					
Quebecor Media Inc 612 rue Saint-Jacques	Montreal	QC	H3C4M8	514-877-9777	594-8844
Web: www.quebecor.com					
Rand McNally & Co 8255 N Central Park Ave	Skokie	IL	60076	847-329-8100	673-9935*
**Fax:* Cust Svc ■ *TF:* 800-333-0136 ■ *Web:* www.randmcnally.com					
Random House Inc 1745 Broadway	New York	NY	10019	212-782-9000	
TF Cust Svc: 800-733-3000 ■ *Web:* www.randomhouse.com					
Bantam Dell Publishing Group 1745 Broadway	New York	NY	10019	212-782-9000	
TF: 800-726-0600 ■ *Web:* www.randomhouse.com/bantamdell					
Random House Reference & Information Publishing 1745 Broadway	New York	NY	10019	212-751-2600	572-4997
TF: 800-733-3000 ■ *Web:* www.randomhouse.com					
Reader's Digest Assn Inc Reader's Digest Rd	Pleasantville	NY	10570	914-238-1000	238-4559
NYSE: RDA ■ *TF:* 800-635-5006 ■ *Web:* www.rd.com					
Reed Elsevier Inc 121 Chanlon Rd	New Providence	NJ	07974	908-464-6800	665-6688
TF: 800-526-4902 ■ *Web:* www.reed-elsevier.com					
Regnery Publishing Inc 1 Massachusetts Ave NW	Washington	DC	20001	202-216-0600	216-0612
TF: 888-219-4747 ■ *Web:* www.regnery.com					
RIA Group 395 Hudson St	New York	NY	10014	212-367-6300	337-4207
TF Cust Svc: 800-950-1205 ■ *Web:* ria.thomson.com					
Rizzoli International Publications Inc 300 Park Ave S 3rd Fl	New York	NY	10010	212-387-3400	387-3434
Web: www.rizzoliusa.com					
Rodale Inc 33 E Minor St	Emmaus	PA	18098	610-967-5171	813-6627*
**Fax Area Code:* 800 ■ **Fax:* Cust Svc ■ *TF Cust Svc:* 800-848-4735 ■ *Web:* www.rodale.com					
Rowman & Littlefield Publishers Inc 4501 Forbes Blvd Suite 200	Lanham	MD	20706	301-459-3366	429-5741*
**Fax:* Hum Res ■ *Web:* www.rowmanlittlefield.com					
RR Bowker LLC 630 Central Ave	New Providence	NJ	07974	908-286-1090	219-0098*
**Fax:* Cust Svc ■ *TF:* 800-521-8110 ■ *Web:* www.bowker.com					
RS Means Co Inc 63 Smiths Ln	Kingston	MA	02364	781-585-7880	585-8814*
**Fax:* Cust Svc ■ *TF:* 800-448-8182 ■ *Web:* www.rsmeans.com					
Running Press Book Publishers 125 S 22nd St	Philadelphia	PA	19103	215-567-5080	568-2919
TF: 800-345-5359 ■ *Web:* www.runningpress.com					
Rutledge Hill Press 15 Century Blvd Lakeview #2 Bldg	Nashville	TN	37214	615-889-9000	902-2340
TF: 800-251-4000 ■ *Web:* www.rutledgehillpress.com					
Sadlier William H Inc 14 Wall St	New York	NY	10005	212-227-2120	312-6080
TF: 800-582-5437 ■ *Web:* www.sadlier.com					
Sage Publications Inc 2455 Teller Rd	Thousand Oaks	CA	91320	805-499-9774	499-0871
TF: 800-818-7243 ■ *Web:* www.sagepub.com					
Saint Martin's Press Inc 175 5th Ave	New York	NY	10010	212-674-5151	420-9314
TF Cust Svc: 800-221-7945 ■ *Web:* www.stmartins.com					
Sams Technical Publishing 9850 E 30th St	Indianapolis	IN	46229	317-396-9850	552-3910*
**Fax Area Code:* 800 ■ *TF Cust Svc:* 800-428-7267 ■ *Web:* www.samswebsite.com					
Scholastic Corp 557 Broadway	New York	NY	10012	212-343-6100	
NASDAQ: SCHL ■ *TF Cust Svc:* 800-724-6527 ■ *Web:* www.scholastic.com					
School Annual Publishing Co 500 Science Pk Rd Suite B	State College	PA	16803	800-436-6030	436-6048
TF: 800-436-6030 ■ *Web:* www.schoolannual.com					
Scientific American Inc 415 Madison Ave	New York	NY	10017	212-451-8550	755-1976
TF Cust Svc: 800-333-1199 ■ *Web:* www.sciam.com					
Scott Foresman 1900 E Lake Ave	Glenview	IL	60025	847-729-3000	841-8939*
**Fax Area Code:* 800 ■ **Fax:* Cust Svc ■ *TF Cust Svc:* 800-554-4411 ■ *Web:* www.scottforesman.com					
Sharpe ME Inc 80 Business Park Dr Suite 202	Armonk	NY	10504	914-273-1800	273-2106
TF Orders: 800-541-6563 ■ *Web:* www.mesharpe.com					
Simon & Schuster Inc 1230 Ave of the Americas	New York	NY	10020	212-698-7000	943-9831*
**Fax Area Code:* 800 ■ *TF Cust Svc:* 800-223-2336 ■ *Web:* www.simonsays.com					
Slack Inc 6900 Grove Rd	Thorofare	NJ	08086	856-848-1000	853-5991
TF: 800-257-8290 ■ *Web:* www.slackinc.com					
South-Western Thomson Learning 5191 Natorp Blvd	Mason	OH	45040	513-229-1000	229-1020
Web: www.thomsonedu.com					
Springer-Verlag New York Inc 233 Spring St	New York	NY	10013	212-460-1500	460-1575
TF: 800-777-4643 ■ *Web:* www.springer-ny.com					
SRDS 1700 Higgins Rd	Des Plaines	IL	60018	847-375-5000	375-5001
TF: 800-851-7737 ■ *Web:* www.srds.com					
Stackpole Books 5067 Ritter Rd	Mechanicsburg	PA	17055	717-796-0411	796-0412
TF Sales: 800-732-3669 ■ *Web:* www.stackpolebooks.com					
Standard Educational Corp 900 Northshore Dr Suite 252	Lake Bluff	IL	60044	847-283-0301	283-0295
Web: www.fergpubco.com					
Standard & Poor's Corp 55 Water St	New York	NY	10041	212-438-2000	438-6675*
**Fax:* PR ■ *TF:* 800-289-8000 ■ *Web:* www.standardandpoors.com					
Steck-Vaughn Co 10801 N MoPac Expy Bldg 3	Austin	TX	78759	512-343-8227	343-6854
TF: 800-531-5015 ■ *Web:* www.steck-vaughn.com					
Sterling Publishing Co Inc 387 Park Ave S 5th Fl	New York	NY	10016	212-532-7160	213-2495
TF Cust Svc: 800-367-9692 ■ *Web:* www.sterlingpub.com					
Storey Communications Inc 210 Mass Moca Way	North Adams	MA	01247	413-346-2100	346-2196*
**Fax:* Edit ■ *TF:* 800-827-7444 ■ *Web:* www.storey.com					
Sunset Publishing Corp 80 Willow Rd	Menlo Park	CA	94025	650-321-3600	327-7537*
**Fax:* Edit ■ *TF:* 800-227-7346 ■ *Web:* www.sunset.com					
T & F Informa 6000 Broken Sound Pkwy NW Suite 300	Boca Raton	FL	33487	561-994-0555	361-6075
TF: 800-272-7737 ■ *Web:* www.taylorandfrancisgroup.com					
Taylor & Francis Group LLC DBA T & F Informa 6000 Broken Sound Pkwy NW Suite 300	Boca Raton	FL	33487	561-994-0555	361-6075
TF: 800-272-7737 ■ *Web:* www.taylorandfrancisgroup.com					
Taylor & Francis Routledge Publishers Inc 270 Madison Ave	New York	NY	10016	917-351-7100	564-7854*
**Fax Area Code:* 212 ■ *TF:* 800-634-7064 ■ *Web:* www.routledge-ny.com					
Taylor Publishing Co 1550 W Mockingbird Ln	Dallas	TX	75235	214-637-2800	819-8220
TF: 800-677-2800 ■ *Web:* www.taylorpub.com					
Technology Marketing Corp 1 Technology Plaza	Norwalk	CT	06854	203-852-6800	866-3326
TF Cust Svc: 800-243-6002 ■ *Web:* www.tmcnet.com					
Ten Speed Press PO Box 7123	Berkeley	CA	94707	510-559-1600	559-1629
TF: 800-841-2665 ■ *Web:* www.tenspeed.com					
TFH Publications Inc 3rd & Union Aves 1 TFH Plaza	Neptune	NJ	07753	732-988-8400	988-5466
TF: 800-631-2188 ■ *Web:* www.tfh.com					
Thomas Charles C Publisher 2600 S 1st St	Springfield	IL	62704	217-789-8980	789-9130
TF Sales: 800-258-8980 ■ *Web:* www.ccthomas.com					
Thomas Publishing Co 5 Penn Plaza	New York	NY	10001	212-695-0500	290-7365
TF: 800-699-9822 ■ *Web:* www.thomaspublishing.com					
Thomson Corp 1 Station Pl Metro Ctr	Stamford	CT	06902	203-539-8000	539-7734
TF: 800-354-9706 ■ *Web:* www.thomson.com					
Thomson Corp PO Box 24 Toronto-Dominion Ctr Suite 2706	Toronto	ON	M5K1A1	416-360-8700	360-8812
NYSE: TOC ■ *Web:* www.thomson.com					
Thomson Financial Publishing Inc 4709 W Golf Rd 6th Fl	Skokie	IL	60076	847-676-9600	933-8101
TF: 800-321-3373 ■ *Web:* www.tfp.com					
Thomson Gale 27500 Drake Rd	Farmington Hills	MI	48331	248-699-4253	363-4253*
**Fax Area Code:* 877 ■ *TF Cust Svc:* 800-877-4253 ■ *Web:* www.galegroup.com					
Thomson Learning 10650 Tobben Dr	Independence	KY	41051	859-525-2230	487-8488*
**Fax Area Code:* 800 ■ *TF:* 800-354-9706 ■ *Web:* www.thomson.com/learning/					
Thomson Learning Wadsworth PO Box 6904	Florence	KY	41022	859-525-2230	487-8488*
**Fax Area Code:* 800 ■ *TF:* 800-354-9706 ■ *Web:* www.wadsworth.com					
Thorndike Press 295 Kennedy Memorial Dr	Waterville	ME	04901	207-859-1000	859-1008
TF: 800-223-1244 ■ *Web:* www.gale.com/thorndike					
Time Inc 1271 Ave of the Americas	New York	NY	10020	212-522-1212	522-0555
Web: www.timeinc.com					
Time Warner Book Group Inc 1271 Ave of the Americas	New York	NY	10020	212-522-7200	467-2886
TF: 800-759-0190 ■ *Web:* www.twbookmark.com					
Tor Books 175 5th Ave 14th Fl	New York	NY	10010	212-388-0100	388-0191
Web: www.tor.com					
Torstar Corp 1 Yonge St Suite 600	Toronto	ON	M5E1P9	416-869-4010	869-4183
TSX: TS.B ■ *Web:* www.torstar.com					
Tribune Co 435 N Michigan Ave	Chicago	IL	60611	312-222-9100	329-0611
NYSE: TRB ■ *Web:* www.tribune.com					
Triumph Learning 136 Madison Ave	New York	NY	10016	212-652-0200	805-5723*
**Fax Area Code:* 866 ■ **Fax:* Cust Svc ■ *TF:* 800-221-9372 ■ *Web:* www.triumphlearning.com					
Tuttle Publishing 364 Innovation Dr Airport Industrial Pk	North Clarendon	VT	05759	802-773-8930	329-8885*
**Fax Area Code:* 800 ■ *TF Sales:* 800-526-2778 ■ *Web:* www.tuttlepublishing.com					
Unisystems Inc 155 E 55th St	New York	NY	10022	212-826-0850	759-9069
Web: www.modernpublishing.com					
United Communications Group 11300 Rockville Pike Suite 1100	Rockville	MD	20852	301-287-2700	816-8945
TF: 800-929-4824 ■ *Web:* www.ucg.com					
United Nations Publications 2 UN Plaza Suite DC2-853	New York	NY	10017	212-963-8302	
TF: 800-253-9646 ■ *Web:* www.un.org/Pubs					
University Press of America 4501 Forbes Blvd Suite 200	Lanham	MD	20706	301-459-3366	338-4550*
**Fax Area Code:* 800 ■ *TF:* 800-462-6420 ■ *Web:* www.univpress.com					
Uniworld Business Publications Inc 3 Clark Rd	Millis	MA	02054	508-376-6006	376-6006
Web: www.uniworldbp.com					
US Government Printing Office (GPO) 732 N Capitol St NW Suite 700	Washington	DC	20401	202-512-1800	512-2104
TF: 866-512-1800 ■ *Web:* www.gpoaccess.gov					
Vantage Press Inc 419 Park Ave S 18th Fl	New York	NY	10016	212-736-1767	736-2273
TF: 800-882-3273 ■ *Web:* www.vantagepress.com					
Verso Books 180 Varick St 10th Fl	New York	NY	10014	212-807-9680	807-9152
Web: www.versobooks.com					
Vintage Books 1745 Broadway	New York	NY	10019	212-751-2600	659-2436*
**Fax Area Code:* 800 ■ **Fax:* Cust Svc ■ *TF Orders:* 800-733-3000					
VNU Business Publications USA 770 Broadway	New York	NY	10003	646-654-5500	654-5518
TF: 800-451-1741 ■ *Web:* www.vnubusinessmedia.com					
Walch J Weston Publisher PO Box 658	Portland	ME	04104	207-772-2846	772-3105
TF: 800-558-2846 ■ *Web:* www.walch.com					
Walsworth Publishing Co Inc 306 N Kansas Ave	Marceline	MO	64658	660-376-3543	376-3444*
**Fax:* Hum Res ■ *TF:* 800-369-2646 ■ *Web:* www.walsworthyearbooks.com					
West Group 610 Opperman Dr	Eagan	MN	55123	651-687-7000	687-7551
TF Cust Svc: 800-328-4880 ■ *Web:* west.thomson.com					
Western Psychological Services 12031 Wilshire Blvd	Los Angeles	CA	90025	310-478-2061	478-7838
TF: 800-648-8857 ■ *Web:* www.wpspublish.com					
WH Freeman & Co 41 Madison Ave 35th Fl	New York	NY	10010	212-576-9400	689-2383
TF: 800-903-3019 ■ *Web:* www.whfreeman.com					
Wheatmark Inc 610 E Delano St Suite 104	Tucson	AZ	85705	520-798-0888	798-3394
TF: 888-934-0888 ■ *Web:* www.wheatmark.com					
White Wolf Publishing Co 1554 Litton Dr	Stone Mountain	GA	30083	404-292-1819	382-3882*
**Fax Area Code:* 678 ■ *TF Orders:* 800-454-9653 ■ *Web:* www.white-wolf.com					
Whitman Albert & Co 6340 Oakton St	Morton Grove	IL	60053	847-581-0033	581-0039
TF: 800-255-7675 ■ *Web:* www.awhitmanco.com					
Wiley John & Sons Inc 111 River St	Hoboken	NJ	07030	201-748-6000	748-6088
NYSE: JWa ■ *TF Sales:* 800-225-5945 ■ *Web:* www.wiley.com					
Wiley Publishing Inc 111 River St	Hoboken	NJ	07030	201-748-6000	748-6088
TF: 800-225-5945 ■ *Web:* www.wiley.com					
William B Eerdmans Publishing Co 255 Jefferson Ave SE	Grand Rapids	MI	49503	616-459-4591	459-6540
TF: 800-253-7521 ■ *Web:* www.eerdmans.com					
William H Sadlier Inc 14 Wall St	New York	NY	10005	212-227-2120	312-6080
TF: 800-582-5437 ■ *Web:* www.sadlier.com					
William Morrow & Co 10 E 53rd St	New York	NY	10022	212-207-7000	207-7203*
**Fax:* Edit ■ *TF:* 800-242-7737					
William S Hein & Co Inc 1285 Main St	Buffalo	NY	14209	716-882-2600	883-8100
TF: 800-828-7571 ■ *Web:* www.wshein.com					
Wilshire Book Co 9731 Variel Ave	Chatsworth	CA	91311	818-700-1522	700-1527
Web: www.mpowers.com					
Wilson HW Co 950 University Ave	Bronx	NY	10452	718-588-8400	590-1617*
**Fax:* Cust Svc ■ *TF:* 800-367-6770 ■ *Web:* www.hwwilson.com					
Wimmer Cos 4650 Shelby Air Dr	Memphis	TN	38118	901-362-8900	794-9806*
**Fax Area Code:* 800 ■ *TF:* 800-548-2537 ■ *Web:* www.wimmerco.com					
Wolters Kluwer US Corp 2700 Lake Cook Rd	Riverwood	IL	60015	847-580-5000	267-2516
Web: www.wolterskluwer.com					
Workman Publishing 225 Varick St 9th Fl	New York	NY	10014	212-254-5900	254-8098
TF: 800-722-7202 ■ *Web:* www.workmanweb.com					

	City	State	Zip	Phone	Fax
World Almanac Education Group 512 7th Ave 22nd Fl *Fax: Cust Svc ■ *Web:* www.worldalmanac.com	New York	NY	10018	646-312-6800	312-6839*
World Book Publishing 233 N Michigan Ave Suite 2000 *TF Sales:* 800-967-5325 ■ *Web:* www.worldbook.com	Chicago	IL	60601	312-729-5800	729-5600
Wright Group/McGraw-Hill 19201 120th Ave NE Suite 100 *Web:* www.wrightgroup.com	Bothell	WA	98011	425-486-8011	486-7868
WW Norton & Co Inc 500 5th Ave *TF:* 800-223-2584 ■ *Web:* www.wwnorton.com	New York	NY	10110	212-354-5500	869-0856
Xlibris Corp International Plaza 2 Suite 340 *TF:* 888-795-4274 ■ *Web:* www.xlibris.com	Philadelphia	PA	19113	610-915-5214	915-0294
Zaner-Bloser Inc PO Box 16764 *TF:* 800-421-3018 ■ *Web:* www.zaner-bloser.com	Columbus	OH	43216	614-486-0221	487-2699
Zebra Books Kensington Publishing Corp 850 3rd Ave *Fax: Sales ■ *TF:* 800-221-2647 ■ *Web:* www.kensingtonbooks.com	New York	NY	10022	212-407-1500	407-1589*
Ziff Davis Media Inc 28 E 28th St *TF:* 800-336-2423 ■ *Web:* www.ziffdavis.com	New York	NY	10016	212-503-3500	503-5696

640-3 Book Publishers - Religious & Spiritual Books

	City	State	Zip	Phone	Fax
Abbey Press Inc 200 Hill Dr *Fax: Mktg ■ *TF Sales:* 800-962-4760 ■ *Web:* www.abbeypress.com	Saint Meinrad	IN	47577	812-357-6611	357-8388*
American Bible Society 1865 Broadway *TF:* 800-242-5375 ■ *Web:* www.americanbible.org	New York	NY	10023	212-408-1200	408-1512
Augsburg Fortress Publishers PO Box 1209 *TF:* 800-426-0115 ■ *Web:* www.augsburgfortress.org	Minneapolis	MN	55440	612-330-3300	330-3455
Baker Book House Co Inc 6030 E Fulton St *TF Orders:* 800-877-2665 ■ *Web:* www.bakerbooks.com	Ada	MI	49301	616-676-9185	676-9573
Baker Book House Co Inc Revell Div 6030 E Fulton St *TF Orders:* 800-877-2665	Ada	MI	49301	616-676-9185	676-9573
Bethany House Publishers 11400 Hampshire Ave S *TF Cust Svc:* 800-328-6109 ■ *Web:* www.bethanyhouse.com	Bloomington	MN	55438	616-877-2665	676-9573
Brethren Press 1451 Dundee Ave *TF:* 800-441-3712 ■ *Web:* www.brethrenpress.com	Elgin	IL	60120	847-742-5100	742-6103
Broadman & Holman Publishers 1 Lifeway Plaza *Fax Area Code: 800 ■ *TF:* 800-251-3225 ■ *Web:* www.broadmanholman.com	Nashville	TN	37234	615-251-2000	296-4036*
Concordia Publishing House Inc 3558 S Jefferson Ave *TF Cust Svc:* 800-325-3040 ■ *Web:* www.cph.org	Saint Louis	MO	63118	314-268-1000	268-1329
Cook Communications Ministries 4050 Lee Vance View *TF:* 800-708-5550 ■ *Web:* www.davidccook.com	Colorado Springs	CO	80918	719-536-0100	536-3265
CRC Publications Co 2850 Kalamazoo Ave SE *Fax Area Code: 888 ■ *TF:* 800-333-8300 ■ *Web:* www.crcpublications.org	Grand Rapids	MI	49560	616-224-0727	642-8606*
Deseret Book Co PO Box 30178 *Fax Area Code: 800 ■ *TF Sales:* 800-453-4532 ■ *Web:* deseretbook.com	Salt Lake City	UT	84130	801-534-1515	453-3876*
DeVore & Sons Inc DBA Heirloom Bible Publishers PO Box 780189 *TF:* 800-676-2448	Wichita	KS	67278	316-267-3211	267-1850
E-Church Depot 3825 Hartzdale Dr *TF Orders:* 800-233-4443 ■ *Web:* www.echurchdepot.com	Camp Hill	PA	17011	717-761-7044	761-7273
Gospel Light Publications 1957 Eastman Ave *Fax: Mktg ■ *TF:* 800-235-3415 ■ *Web:* www.gospellight.com	Ventura	CA	93003	805-644-9721	677-6818*
Guideposts Inc 39 Seminary Hill Rd *TF Cust Svc:* 800-431-2344 ■ *Web:* www.guideposts.org	Carmel	NY	10512	845-225-3681	228-2115
Hay House Inc 2776 Loker Ave W PO Box 5100 *Fax Area Code: 800 ■ *TF:* 800-654-5126 ■ *Web:* www.hayhouse.com	Carlsbad	CA	92018	760-431-7695	650-5115*
Heirloom Bible Publishers PO Box 780189 *TF:* 800-676-2448	Wichita	KS	67278	316-267-3211	267-1850
Jewish Publication Society 2100 Arch St 2nd Fl *TF:* 800-234-3151 ■ *Web:* www.jewishpub.org	Philadelphia	PA	19103	215-832-0600	568-2017
Light & Life Communications PO Box 535002 *TF:* 800-348-2513	Indianapolis	IN	46253	317-244-3660	248-9055
Mennonite Publishing House 616 Walnut Ave *TF Sales:* 800-245-7894 ■ *Web:* www.mph.org	Scottdale	PA	15683	724-887-8500	887-3111
Multnomah Publishers 601 N Larch *Fax: Cust Svc ■ *TF:* 800-929-0910 ■ *Web:* www.multnomahbooks.com	Sisters	OR	97759	541-549-1144	549-0432*
NavPress 3820 N 30th St PO Box 6000 *Fax: Sales ■ *TF Cust Svc:* 800-366-7788 ■ *Web:* www.navpress.com	Colorado Springs	CO	80935	719-548-9222	598-0749*
Nazarene Publishing House Inc PO Box 419527 *TF:* 800-877-0700 ■ *Web:* www.nph.com	Kansas City	MO	64141	816-931-1900	753-4071
Nelson Bibles 501 Nelson Pl PO Box 141000 *TF:* 800-251-4000 ■ *Web:* www.nelsonbibles.com	Nashville	TN	37214	615-889-9000	391-5225
Nelson Thomas Inc 501 Nelson Pl PO Box 141000 *NYSE:* TNM ■ *TF:* 800-251-4000 ■ *Web:* www.thomasnelson.com	Nashville	TN	37214	615-889-9000	391-5225
Nelson Tommy 402 BNA Dr Bldg 100 Suite 600 *TF:* 800-251-4000 ■ *Web:* www.tommynelson.com	Nashville	TN	37217	615-889-9000	391-5225
New Leaf Publishing Group PO Box 726 *TF:* 800-999-3777 ■ *Web:* www.newleafpublishinggroup.com	Green Forest	AR	72638	870-438-5288	438-5120
New World Library 14 Pamaron Way *TF:* 800-972-6657 ■ *Web:* www.newworldlibrary.com	Novato	CA	94949	415-884-2100	884-2199
Northwestern Publishing House 1250 N 113th St *TF Orders:* 800-662-6022	Milwaukee	WI	53226	414-475-6600	475-7684
Oregon Catholic Press 5536 NE Hassalo St *TF:* 800-548-8749 ■ *Web:* www.ocp.org	Portland	OR	97213	503-281-1191	282-3486
Our Sunday Visitor Inc 200 Noll Plaza *TF:* 800-348-2440 ■ *Web:* www.osv.com	Huntington	IN	46750	260-356-8400	359-0029
Pacific Press Publishing Assn 1350 N Kings Rd *TF Cust Svc:* 800-545-2449 ■ *Web:* www.pacificpress.com	Nampa	ID	83687	208-465-2500	465-2531
Pauline Books & Media 50 Saint Paul's Ave *TF Sales:* 800-876-4463 ■ *Web:* www.pauline.org	Boston	MA	02130	617-522-8911	524-8035
Review & Herald Publishing Assn 55 W Oak Ridge Dr *TF:* 800-456-3991 ■ *Web:* www.rhpa.org	Hagerstown	MD	21740	301-393-3000	393-4055
Standard Publishing Co 8805 Governors Hill Dr Suite 400 *TF Orders:* 800-543-1353 ■ *Web:* www.standardpub.com	Cincinnati	OH	45249	513-931-4050	931-0904
Standex International Corp Consumer Group 8121 Hamilton Ave *Web:* www.standex.com/divisions/consumer.shtml	Cincinnati	OH	45231	513-931-4050	931-4045
Strang Communications 600 Rinehart Rd *Web:* www.strang.com	Lake Mary	FL	32746	407-333-0600	333-7100
Thomas Nelson Inc 501 Nelson Pl PO Box 141000 *NYSE:* TNM ■ *TF:* 800-251-4000 ■ *Web:* www.thomasnelson.com	Nashville	TN	37214	615-889-9000	391-5225
Tommy Nelson 402 BNA Dr Bldg 100 Suite 600 *TF:* 800-251-4000 ■ *Web:* www.tommynelson.com	Nashville	TN	37217	615-889-9000	391-5225
Tyndale House Publishers Inc 351 Executive Dr *TF:* 800-323-9400 ■ *Web:* www.tyndale.com	Carol Stream	IL	60188	630-668-8300	668-9092
United Methodist Publishing House PO Box 801 *TF Cust Svc:* 800-672-1789 ■ *Web:* www.umph.org	Nashville	TN	37202	615-749-6000	749-6079
W Publishing Group 501 Nelson Pl PO Box 141000 *TF Cust Svc:* 800-251-4000 ■ *Web:* www.wpublishinggroup.com	Nashville	TN	37214	615-889-9000	391-5225
Whitaker House/Anchor Distributors 1030 Hunt Valley Cir *TF Orders:* 800-444-4484 ■ *Web:* www.whitakerhouse.net	New Kensington	PA	15068	724-334-7000	334-1200
Zondervan 5300 Patterson Ave SE *Fax Area Code: 800 ■ *TF Cust Svc:* 800-727-1309 ■ *Web:* www.zondervan.com	Grand Rapids	MI	49530	616-698-6900	934-6381*

640-4 Book Publishers - University Presses

	City	State	Zip	Phone	Fax
Associated University Presses 2010 Eastpark Blvd *Web:* www.aupresses.com	Cranbury	NJ	08512	609-655-4770	655-8366
Cambridge University Press 32 6th Ave 17th Fl *Fax: Hum Res ■ *TF:* 800-221-4512 ■ *Web:* www.cambridge.org	New York	NY	10013	212-924-3900	691-3239*
Catholic University of America Press 620 Michigan Ave NE 240 Leahy Hall *Web:* www.cua.edu	Washington	DC	20064	202-319-5052	319-4985
Columbia University Press 61 W 62nd St 3rd Fl *TF:* 800-944-8648 ■ *Web:* www.columbia.edu/cu/cup	New York	NY	10023	212-459-0600	459-3677
Cornell University Press 750 Cascadilla St *TF Sales:* 800-666-2211 ■ *Web:* www.cornellpress.cornell.edu	Ithaca	NY	14850	607-277-2338	277-6292
Duke University Press 905 W Main St *Fax Area Code: 888 ■ *Fax: Cust Svc ■ *TF Cust Svc:* 888-651-0122 ■ *Web:* www.dukeupress.edu	Durham	NC	27701	919-687-3600	651-0124*
Edwin Mellen Press 415 Ridge St *Web:* www.mellenpress.com	Lewiston	NY	14092	716-754-2266	754-4056
Gallaudet University Press 800 Florida Ave NE *Web:* gupress.gallaudet.edu	Washington	DC	20002	202-651-5488	651-5489
Harvard Business School Publishing 60 Harvard Way *TF:* 800-545-7685 ■ *Web:* harvardbusinessonline.hbsp.harvard.edu	Boston	MA	02163	617-783-7400	783-7664
Harvard University Press 79 Garden St *TF Cust Svc:* 800-448-2242 ■ *Web:* www.hup.harvard.edu	Cambridge	MA	02138	617-495-2600	495-5898
Indiana University Press 601 N Morton St *TF:* 800-842-6796 ■ *Web:* www.iupress.indiana.edu	Bloomington	IN	47404	812-855-8817	855-7931
Johns Hopkins University Press 2715 N Charles St *Fax: Orders ■ *TF Orders:* 800-537-5487 ■ *Web:* www.press.jhu.edu	Baltimore	MD	21218	410-516-6900	516-6998*
Mellen Edwin Press 415 Ridge St *Web:* www.mellenpress.com	Lewiston	NY	14092	716-754-2266	754-4056
Mercer University Press 1400 Coleman Ave *TF:* 800-637-2378 ■ *Web:* www.mupress.org	Macon	GA	31207	478-301-2880	301-2264
Michigan State University Press 1405 S Harrison Rd Suite 25 *Fax Area Code: 800 ■ *TF:* 800-678-2120 ■ *Web:* msupress.msu.edu	East Lansing	MI	48823	517-355-9543	678-2120*
MIT Press 55 Hayward St *TF Sales:* 800-356-0343 ■ *Web:* mitpress.mit.edu	Cambridge	MA	02142	617-253-5646	258-6779
Naval Institute Press 291 Wood Rd *TF:* 800-233-8764 ■ *Web:* www.usni.org/press/press.html	Annapolis	MD	21402	410-268-6110	295-1049
Ohio State University Press 1070 Carmack Rd Pressey Hall Room 180 *Web:* www.ohiostatepress.org	Columbus	OH	43210	614-292-6930	292-2065
Ohio University Press Scott Quadrangle *TF Sales:* 800-621-2736 ■ *Web:* www.ohiou.edu/oupress	Athens	OH	45701	740-593-1155	593-4536
Oregon State University Press 500 Kerr Administration Bldg *TF Orders:* 800-426-3797 ■ *Web:* oregonstate.edu/dept/press/	Corvallis	OR	97331	541-737-3166	737-3170
Oxford University Press 198 Madison Ave *Fax: PR ■ *TF:* 800-334-4249 ■ *Web:* www.oup.com/us	New York	NY	10016	212-726-6000	726-6447*
Pennsylvania State University Press 820 N University Dr USB1 Suite C *TF:* 800-326-9180 ■ *Web:* www.psupress.org	University Park	PA	16802	814-865-1327	863-1408
Princeton University Press 41 William St *TF Sales:* 800-777-4726 ■ *Web:* pup.princeton.edu	Princeton	NJ	08540	609-258-4900	258-6305
Purdue University Press 509 Harrison St *TF Orders:* 800-247-6553 ■ *Web:* www.thepress.purdue.edu	West Lafayette	IN	47907	765-494-2038	496-2442
Rutgers University Press 100 Joyce Kilmer Ave *TF Orders:* 800-446-9323 ■ *Web:* rutgerspress.rutgers.edu	Piscataway	NJ	08854	732-445-7762	445-7039
Southern Illinois University Press 1915 University Press Dr *TF:* 800-346-2680 ■ *Web:* www.siu.edu/siupress	Carbondale	IL	62901	618-453-2281	453-3787
Southern Methodist University Press 6404 Hilltop Ln 314 Fondren Library W *TF:* 800-826-8911	Dallas	TX	75275	214-768-1432	768-1428
Stanford University Press 1450 Page Mill Rd *TF:* 800-621-2736 ■ *Web:* www.sup.org	Palo Alto	CA	94304	650-723-9434	725-3457
State University of New York Press 194 Washington Ave Suite 305 *TF Orders:* 800-666-2211 ■ *Web:* www.sunypress.edu	Albany	NY	12210	518-472-5000	472-5038
Temple University Press 1601 N Broad St USB 305 *Fax: Edit ■ *TF:* 800-447-1656 ■ *Web:* www.temple.edu/tempress	Philadelphia	PA	19122	215-204-8787	204-4719*
Texas A & M University Press John H Lindsey Bldg 4354 TAMUS *TF Orders:* 800-826-8911 ■ *Web:* www.tamu.edu/upress	College Station	TX	77843	979-845-1436	847-8752
Texas Tech University Press 2903 4th St *TF:* 800-832-4042 ■ *Web:* www.ttup.ttu.edu	Lubbock	TX	79409	806-742-2982	742-2979
University of Alabama Press 20 Research Dr Rm 201 McMillan Bldg *TF Orders:* 800-621-2736 ■ *Web:* www.uapress.ua.edu	Tuscaloosa	AL	35487	205-348-5180	348-9201
University of Alaska Press Box 756240 *TF:* 888-252-6657 ■ *Web:* www.uaf.edu/uapress	Fairbanks	AK	99775	907-474-5831	474-5502
University of Arizona Press 355 S Euclid Ave Suite 103 *TF Orders:* 800-426-3797 ■ *Web:* www.uapress.arizona.edu	Tucson	AZ	85719	520-621-1441	621-8899
University of Arkansas Press McIlroy House 201 Ozark Ave *TF:* 800-626-0090 ■ *Web:* www.uark.edu/~uaprinfo	Fayetteville	AR	72701	479-575-3246	575-6044
University of California Press 2120 Berkeley Way *TF:* 800-822-6657 ■ *Web:* www.ucpress.edu	Berkeley	CA	94704	510-642-4247	643-7127
University of Chicago Press 1427 E 60th St *TF Sales:* 800-621-2736 ■ *Web:* www.press.uchicago.edu	Chicago	IL	60637	773-702-7700	702-9756
University of Delaware Press 326 Hullihen Hall	Newark	DE	19716	302-831-1149	831-6549
University of Georgia Press 330 Research Dr Suite B-100 *TF Orders:* 800-266-5842 ■ *Web:* www.ugapress.uga.edu	Athens	GA	30602	706-369-6163	369-6131
University of Hawaii Press 2840 Kolowalu St *Fax Area Code: 800 ■ *TF:* 888-847-7377 ■ *Web:* www.uhpress.hawaii.edu	Honolulu	HI	96822	808-956-8255	650-7811*
University of Illinois Press 1325 S Oak St *TF Orders:* 800-545-4703 ■ *Web:* www.press.uillinois.edu	Champaign	IL	61820	217-333-0950	244-8082
University of Iowa Press 119 W Park Rd 100 Kuhl House *Web:* www.uiowa.edu/uiowapress	Iowa City	IA	52242	319-335-2000	335-2055
University of Massachusetts Press PO Box 429 *Fax Area Code: 800 ■ *Web:* www.umass.edu/umpress	Amherst	MA	01004	413-545-2217	488-1144*
University of Michigan Press 839 Greene St *Web:* www.press.umich.edu	Ann Arbor	MI	48104	734-764-4388	615-1540
University of Minnesota Press 111 3rd Ave S Suite 290 *TF:* 800-621-2736 ■ *Web:* www.upress.umn.edu	Minneapolis	MN	55401	612-627-1942	627-1980
University of Missouri Press 2910 LeMone Blvd *TF:* 800-828-1894 ■ *Web:* www.umsystem.edu/upress/	Columbia	MO	65201	573-882-7641	884-4498
University of Nebraska Press 1111 Lincoln Mall *Fax: Cust Svc ■ *TF:* 800-755-1105 ■ *Web:* nebraskapress.unl.edu	Lincoln	NE	68588	402-472-3581	472-6214*
University of Nevada Press MS 166 *TF Orders:* 877-682-6657 ■ *Web:* www.nvbooks.nevada.edu	Reno	NV	89557	775-784-6573	784-6200
University of New Mexico Press 1312 Basehart St *Fax Area Code: 800 ■ *TF Orders:* 800-249-7737 ■ *Web:* www.unmpress.com	Albuquerque	NM	87106	505-277-7771	622-8667*
University of North Carolina Press 116 S Boundary St *TF:* 800-848-6224 ■ *Web:* uncpress.unc.edu	Chapel Hill	NC	27514	919-966-3561	966-3829
University of North Texas Press 1820 Highland Ave Bain Hall Rm 101 *TF Sales:* 800-826-8911 ■ *Web:* www.unt.edu/untpress	Denton	TX	76201	940-565-2142	565-4590
University of Oklahoma Press 2800 Venture Dr *TF Orders:* 800-627-7377 ■ *Web:* www.ou.edu/oupress	Norman	OK	73069	405-325-2000	364-5798

Book Publishers - University Presses (Cont'd)

	City	State	Zip	Phone	Fax
University of Pennsylvania Press 3902 Spruce St. *TF Cust Svc:* 800-537-5487 ■ *Web:* www.upenn.edu/pennpress	Philadelphia	PA	19104	215-898-6261	898-0404
University of Pittsburgh Press 3400 Forbes Ave 5th Fl *TF Sales:* 800-666-2211 ■ *Web:* www.upress.pitt.edu	Pittsburgh	PA	15261	412-383-2456	383-2466
University Press of Colorado 5589 Arapahoe Ave Suite 206C *TF Mktg:* 800-627-7377 ■ *Web:* www.upcolorado.com	Boulder	CO	80303	720-406-8849	406-3443
University Press of Florida 15 NW 15th St *TF Sales:* 800-226-3822 ■ *Web:* www.upf.com	Gainesville	FL	32611	352-392-1351	392-7302
University Press of Kansas 2502 Westbrooke Cir *Web:* www.kansaspress.ku.edu	Lawrence	KS	66045	785-864-4154	864-4586
University Press of Kentucky 663 S Limestone St **Fax:* Mktg ■ *TF Sales:* 800-839-6855 ■ *Web:* www.uky.edu/UniversityPress	Lexington	KY	40508	859-257-8400	257-8481*
University Press of Mississippi 3825 Ridgewood Rd *TF:* 800-737-7788 ■ *Web:* www.upress.state.ms.us	Jackson	MS	39211	601-432-6205	432-6217
University Press of New England 1 Court St Suite 250 *TF Orders:* 800-421-1561 ■ *Web:* www.dartmouth.edu/upne	Lebanon	NH	03766	603-448-1533	448-9429
University Press of Virginia 210 Sprigg Ln *TF Sales:* 800-831-3406 ■ *Web:* www.upress.virginia.edu	Charlottesville	VA	22903	434-924-3469	982-2655
University of South Carolina Press 1600 Hampton St 5th Fl *TF Orders:* 800-768-2500 ■ *Web:* www.sc.edu/uscpress	Columbia	SC	29208	803-777-5243	777-0160
University of the South Press 735 University Ave Fulford Hall *TF:* 800-289-4919	Sewanee	TN	37383	931-598-1286	598-1667
University of Tennessee Press 110 Conference Ctr Bldg. *Web:* www.utpress.org	Knoxville	TN	37996	865-974-3321	974-3724
University of Texas Press 2100 Comal St *TF Sales:* 800-252-3206 ■ *Web:* www.utexas.edu/utpress	Austin	TX	78722	512-471-7233	232-7178
University of Utah Press 1795 E South Campus Drive Suite 101 *Web:* www.uofupress.com	Salt Lake City	UT	84112	801-581-6771	581-3365
University of Washington Press 1326 5th Ave Suite 555 *TF:* 800-441-4115 ■ *Web:* www.washington.edu/uwpress	Seattle	WA	98101	206-543-4050	543-3932
University of Wisconsin Press 1930 Monroe St 3rd Fl *Web:* www.wisc.edu/wisconsinpress	Madison	WI	53711	608-263-1110	263-1132
Vanderbilt University Press 214 Broadway Suite 320 Box 1813 Station B *Web:* www.vanderbilt.edu/vupress	Nashville	TN	37203	615-322-3585	343-8823
Wesleyan University Press 215 Long Ln *TF Orders:* 800-421-1561 ■ *Web:* www.wesleyan.edu/wespress	Middletown	CT	06459	860-685-7711	685-7712
Yale University Press 302 Temple St *TF Sales:* 800-987-7323 ■ *Web:* www.yale.edu/yup	New Haven	CT	06511	203-432-0960	432-0948
Yeshiva University Press 500 W 185th St *Web:* www.yu.edu	New York	NY	10033	212-960-5400	960-0043

640-5 Comic Book Publishers

	City	State	Zip	Phone	Fax
Archie Enterprises Inc 325 Fayette Ave *Web:* www.archiecomics.com	Mamaroneck	NY	10543	914-381-5155	381-2335
Dark Horse Comics Inc 10956 SE Main St *TF:* 800-862-0052 ■ *Web:* www.darkhorse.com	Milwaukie	OR	97222	503-652-8815	654-9440
DC Comics 1700 Broadway **Fax:* Mktg ■ *Web:* www.dccomics.com	New York	NY	10019	212-636-5400	636-5599*
Fantagraphics Books 7563 Lake City Way NE *TF:* 800-657-1100 ■ *Web:* www.fantagraphics.com	Seattle	WA	98115	206-524-1967	524-2104
Image Comics Inc 1942 University Ave Suite 305 *Web:* www.imagecomics.com	Berkeley	CA	94704	510-644-4980	
Marvel Enterprises Inc 417 5th Ave *NYSE: MVL* ■ *TF:* 800-217-9158 ■ *Web:* www.marvel.com	New York	NY	10016	212-576-4000	
Viz Media 295 Bay St *Web:* www.viz.com	San Francisco	CA	94133	415-546-7073	546-7086

640-6 Directory Publishers

	City	State	Zip	Phone	Fax
1-800-ATTORNEY Inc 186 Industrial Center Dr *TF:* 800-644-3458 ■ *Web:* www.1800attorney.com	Lake Helen	FL	32744	386-228-1000	228-0290
ALLTEL Publishing Corp 100 Executive Pkwy *TF:* 800-235-3386	Hudson	OH	44236	330-650-7100	650-7883
ASD Data Services LLC 180 Freedom Ave *TF:* 800-929-2612 ■ *Web:* www.asd.com	Murfreesboro	TN	37129	866-273-7297	
BellSouth Advertising & Publishing Corp 2247 Northlake Pkwy **Fax Area Code:* 678 ■ *TF:* 877-573-2597	Tucker	GA	30084	877-573-2597	406-5159*
Bresser's Cross Index Directory Co 684 W Baltimore St. *TF:* 800-878-3333 ■ *Web:* www.bressers.com	Detroit	MI	48202	313-874-0570	874-3510
BurrellesLuce 75 E Northfield Rd *TF:* 800-631-1160 ■ *Web:* www.burrellesluce.com	Livingston	NJ	07039	973-992-6600	992-7675
Capitol Advantage LLC 2751 Prosperity Ave 6th Fl *TF:* 800-659-8708 ■ *Web:* capitoladvantage.com	Fairfax	VA	22031	703-289-4670	289-4678
Cincinnati Bell Directory Inc 201 E 4th St *Web:* www.cincinnatibellyellowpages.com	Cincinnati	OH	45202	513-397-5775	784-1613
Cision US Inc 332 S Michigan Ave Suite 900 **Fax:* Cust Svc ■ *TF:* 866-639-5087 ■ *Web:* us.cision.com	Chicago	IL	60604	312-922-2400	922-3127*
Clarke Directory Publications Inc 5313 3rd St *Web:* www.clarkephonebook.com	Irwindale	CA	91706	626-338-6612	338-1387
Cole Information Services 901 W Bond St **Fax Area Code:* 800 ■ *TF:* 877-414-3332 ■ *Web:* www.coleinformation.com	Lincoln	NE	68521	402-323-3500	533-6591*
Commonwealth Business Media Inc 50 Millstone Rd Bldg 400 Suite 200 *TF:* 888-215-6084 ■ *Web:* www.cbizmedia.com	East Windsor	NJ	08520	609-371-7700	371-7873
Community Directory Publishing Service 2025 E Beltline Ave SE Suite 101 *TF:* 888-831-2800 ■ *Web:* www.cdps.com	Grand Rapids	MI	49546	616-831-2800	942-1038
Contractors Register Inc 800 E Main St *TF:* 800-431-2584 ■ *Web:* www.thebluebook.com	Jefferson Valley	NY	10535	914-245-0200	243-0287
CSG Information Services 3922 Coconut Palm Dr *TF:* 800-927-9292 ■ *Web:* www.csgis.com	Tampa	FL	33619	813-627-6800	627-6779
DAG Media Inc 125-10 Queens Blvd Suite 14 *NASDAQ: DAGM* ■ *TF:* 800-261-2799 ■ *Web:* www.newyellow.com	Kew Gardens	NY	11415	718-263-8454	793-2522
DataNational 3800 Concorde Pkwy Suite 500 *TF:* 800-888-7823 ■ *Web:* www.datanational.com	Chantilly	VA	20151	703-818-0120	818-1206
Dex Media Inc 198 Inverness Dr W *TF:* 800-243-2960 ■ *Web:* www.dexonline.com	Englewood	CO	80112	303-784-2900	
Dickman Directories Inc 6145 Columbus Pike *TF:* 877-836-4154	Lewis Center	OH	43035	740-548-6130	548-2217
DirectoryNet LLC 4555 Mansell Rd Suite 230 *TF:* 800-733-1212 ■ *Web:* www.directorynet.com	Alpharetta	GA	30022	770-521-0100	521-1295
Haines & Co Inc 8050 Freedom Ave NW *TF:* 800-843-8452 ■ *Web:* www.haines.com	North Canton	OH	44720	330-494-9111	494-3862
Harris InfoSource 2057 E Aurora Rd **Fax Area Code:* 800 ■ *TF:* 800-888-5900 ■ *Web:* www.harrisinfo.com	Twinsburg	OH	44087	330-425-9000	643-5997*
HealthLeaders-InterStudy 210 12th Ave S Suite 100 *TF:* 888-293-9675 ■ *Web:* home.healthleaders-interstudy.com	Nashville	TN	37203	615-385-4131	385-4979
Hill-Donnelly Information Services 10126 Windhorst Rd *TF:* 800-925-4654 ■ *Web:* www.hilldonn.com	Tampa	FL	33619	813-832-1600	832-1694
Hoover's Inc 5800 Airport Blvd *TF:* 800-486-8666 ■ *Web:* www.hoovers.com	Austin	TX	78752	512-374-4500	374-4501
LexisNexis Martindale-Hubbell 121 Chanlon Rd **Fax:* Edit ■ *TF:* 800-526-4902 ■ *Web:* www.martindale.com	New Providence	NJ	07974	908-464-6800	464-3553*
Manufacturers Group Inc 1084 Wellington Way PO Box 4310 *TF:* 800-264-3303 ■ *Web:* www.industrysearch.com	Lexington	KY	40544	859-223-6703	223-6709
Marc Publishing Co 600 Germantown Pike Suite B *TF:* 800-432-5478 ■ *Web:* www.marcpub.com	Lafayette Hill	PA	19444	610-834-8585	834-7707
Nelson Information 195 Broadway *TF:* 800-333-6357 ■ *Web:* www.nelsoninformation.com	New York	NY	10007	646-822-6499	
Oxbridge Communications Inc 186 5th Ave 6th Fl *Web:* www.oxbridge.com	New York	NY	10010	212-741-0231	633-2938
Real Yellow Pages Online 754 Peachtree St **Fax Area Code:* 404 ■ *TF:* 888-935-8818 ■ *Web:* www.realpageslive.com	Atlanta	GA	30308	877-573-2597	986-9425*
RH Donnelley Corp 1001 Winstead Dr *NYSE: RHD* ■ *Web:* www.rhd.com	Cary	NC	27513	919-297-1600	297-1285
Rich's California Business Directories Inc 2551 Casey Ave Suite A *TF:* 800-969-7424 ■ *Web:* www.norcalcompanies.com	Mountain View	CA	94043	650-564-9464	564-9465
SBC Smart Yellow Pages 100 E Big Beaver Rd *TF:* 800-434-7778	Troy	MI	48083	248-524-7300	740-5329
Stewart Directories Inc 10540 J York Rd *TF:* 800-311-0786 ■ *Web:* www.stewartdirectories.com	Cockeysville	MD	21030	410-628-5988	683-3153
SunShine Pages 3445 N Causeway Blvd Suite 1000 *TF:* 800-259-9835 ■ *Web:* www.sunshinepages.com	Metairie	LA	70002	504-832-9835	832-9931
T & F Informa 6000 Broken Sound Pkwy NW Suite 300 *TF:* 800-272-7737 ■ *Web:* www.taylorandfrancisgroup.com	Boca Raton	FL	33487	561-994-0555	361-6075
Taylor & Francis Group LLC DBA T & F Informa 6000 Broken Sound Pkwy NW Suite 300 *TF:* 800-272-7737 ■ *Web:* www.taylorandfrancisgroup.com	Boca Raton	FL	33487	561-994-0555	361-6075
United Communications Group 11300 Rockville Pike Suite 1100 *TF:* 800-929-4824 ■ *Web:* www.ucg.com	Rockville	MD	20852	301-287-2700	816-8945
United Yellow Pages Inc 12442 Knott St 2nd Fl *TF:* 800-343-2046 ■ *Web:* www.ypunited.com	Garden Grove	CA	92841	714-889-5200	889-5319
University Directories 88 VilCom Cir **Fax Area Code:* 800 ■ *TF:* 800-743-5556 ■ *Web:* www.universitydirectories.com	Chapel Hill	NC	27514	919-968-0225	743-0009*
Valley Yellow Pages 1850 N Gateway Blvd Suite 132 *TF:* 800-350-8887 ■ *Web:* www.valleyyellowpages.com	Fresno	CA	93727	559-251-8888	251-5392
Verizon Directories 2200 W Airfield Dr *TF Orders:* 800-888-8448 ■ *Web:* www.superpages.com	DFW Airport	TX	75261	972-453-7000	
Verizon Information Services 2200 W Airfield Dr *TF:* 877-814-6854 ■ *Web:* www.verizonyellowpages.com	DFW Airport	TX	75261	972-453-7000	453-7573
VNU Inc 770 Broadway *Web:* www.vnu.com	New York	NY	10003	646-654-5000	654-5001
Volt Directory Systems & Services 1 Sentry Pkwy Suite 1000 *TF:* 800-897-2508 ■ *Web:* voltdirectory.com	Blue Bell	PA	19422	610-825-7720	825-4719
West Legal Directory 610 Opperman Dr *TF:* 800-328-9378 ■ *Web:* lawyers.findlaw.com	Eagan	MN	55123	651-687-7000	
White Directory Publishers Inc 1945 Sheridan Dr *TF:* 800-388-8255 ■ *Web:* www.talkingphonebook.com	Buffalo	NY	14223	716-875-9100	874-4585
World Aviation Directory 1200 G St NW Suite 900 **Fax Area Code:* 202 ■ *TF:* 800-551-2015 ■ *Web:* www.wadaviation.com	Washington	DC	20005	609-426-5000	383-2478*
Worldwide Chamber of Commerce Directory Inc 200 E 7th St Suite 416 *Web:* www.chamberofcommerce.com	Loveland	CO	80537	970-663-3231	663-6187
Yellow Book USA 193 EAB Plaza **Fax:* Hum Res ■ *TF:* 877-512-7710 ■ *Web:* www.yellowbook.com	Uniondale	NY	11556	516-730-1900	730-1950*
YP Corp 4840 E Jasmine St Suite 105 *TF:* 800-300-3209 ■ *Web:* www.yp.com	Mesa	AZ	85205	480-654-9646	654-9727

640-7 Music Publishers

	City	State	Zip	Phone	Fax
Alfred Publishing Co 16320 Roscoe Blvd Suite 100 *TF:* 800-292-6122 ■ *Web:* www.alfred.com	Van Nuys	CA	91406	818-891-5999	891-2369
Brentwood Benson Music Publishing 741 Cool Springs Blvd *Web:* www.brentwood-bensonmusic.com	Franklin	TN	37067	615-261-6500	261-3385
Carl Fischer Inc 65 Bleecker St 8th Fl *TF:* 800-762-2328 ■ *Web:* www.carlfischer.com	New York	NY	10012	212-777-0900	477-6996
EMI Music Publishing 75 9th Ave 4th Fl *Web:* www.emimusicpub.com	New York	NY	10011	212-492-1200	
Famous Music Publishing Cos 1633 Broadway 11th Fl	New York	NY	10019	212-654-7433	654-4748
Hal Leonard Corp PO Box 227 **Fax:* Cust Svc ■ *TF:* 800-321-3408 ■ *Web:* www.halleonard.com	Winona	MN	55987	507-454-2920	454-8334*
Lorenz Corp PO Box 802 *TF:* 800-444-1144 ■ *Web:* www.lorenz.com	Dayton	OH	45401	937-228-6118	223-2042
Malaco Music Group Inc 3023 W Northside Dr *TF Cust Svc:* 800-272-7936 ■ *Web:* www.malaco.com	Jackson	MS	39213	601-982-4522	982-4528
Mel Bay Publications Inc 4 Industrial Dr *TF:* 800-863-5229 ■ *Web:* melbay.com	Pacific	MO	63069	636-257-3970	257-5062
Music Sales G Schirmer Inc 257 Park Ave S 20th Fl *Web:* www.schirmer.com	New York	NY	10010	212-254-2100	254-2013
Nazarene Publishing House Inc PO Box 419527 *TF:* 800-877-0700 ■ *Web:* www.nph.com	Kansas City	MO	64141	816-931-1900	753-4071
Sony-BMG Entertainment 1540 Broadway **Fax:* Sales ■ *Web:* www.sonybmg.com	New York	NY	10036	212-833-8000	930-4511*
Sony/ATV Music Publishing LLC 2100 Colorado Ave *Web:* www.sonyatv.com	Santa Monica	CA	90404	310-449-2120	449-2518
Theodore Presser Co 588 N Gulph Rd *Web:* www.presser.com	King of Prussia	PA	19406	610-592-1222	592-1229
Universal Music Publishing 8750 Wilshire Blvd *Web:* www.umpgmusicsearch.com	Beverly Hills	CA	90211	310-358-4700	
Walt Disney Music Publishing 500 S Buena Vista St MC 6174	Burbank	CA	91521	818-569-3228	
Warner/Chappell Music Inc 10585 Santa Monica Blvd *Web:* www.warnerchappell.com	Los Angeles	CA	90025	310-441-8600	441-8780
Wonderland Music Co Inc 500 S Buena Vista St MC 6174	Burbank	CA	91521	818-569-3228	

640-8 Newspaper Publishers

	City	State	Zip	Phone	Fax
ABC Inc 77 W 66th St *Web:* abc.go.com	New York	NY	10023	212-456-7777	456-2795
Acme Newspapers Inc 311 E Lancaster Ave	Ardmore	PA	19003	610-642-4300	642-6911
Ada Evening News Corp PO Box 489 *Web:* www.adaeveningnews.com	Ada	OK	74821	580-310-7500	332-8734
Advance Publications Inc 950 Fingerboard Rd	Staten Island	NY	10305	718-981-1234	981-5679
Afro-American Newspapers Co 2519 N Charles St *Web:* www.afro.com	Baltimore	MD	21218	410-554-8200	554-8213
Alameda Newspaper Group PO Box 28884 *TF:* 800-595-9595 ■ *Web:* www.newschoice.com	Oakland	CA	94604	510-208-6300	208-6477

	City	State	Zip	Phone	Fax
Albany Herald Publishing Co Inc 126 N Washington St *TF:* 800-685-4639 ■ *Web:* www.albanyherald.com	Albany	GA	31702	229-888-9300	888-9357
Albert Lea Newspapers Inc PO Box 60 *TF:* 800-657-4996 ■ *Web:* www.albertleatribune.com	Albert Lea	MN	56007	507-373-1411	373-0333
Americas Publishing Co 2900 NW 39th St	Miami	FL	33142	305-633-3341	635-4002
Amos Press Inc PO Box 4129 *TF:* 800-327-1259 ■ *Web:* www.amospress.com	Sidney	OH	45365	937-498-2111	498-0888
Arizona Publishing Cos PO Box 1950 *Web:* www.azcentral.com	Phoenix	AZ	85001	602-444-8000	444-8340
ASP Westward LP 523 N Sam Houston Pkwy E Suite 600	Houston	TX	77060	281-668-1100	668-1103
Athens Newspaper Inc PO Box 912 *Web:* onlineathens.com	Athens	GA	30603	706-549-0123	208-2246
Auburn Publishers Inc 25 Dill St *TF:* 800-878-5311 ■ *Web:* www.auburnpub.com	Auburn	NY	13021	315-253-5311	253-6031
Austin Daily Herald Inc 310 NE 2nd St *Web:* www.austindailyherald.com	Austin	MN	55912	507-433-8851	437-8644
Beacon Press Inc PO Box 627	Biddeford	ME	04005	207-282-1535	282-3138
Beckley Newspapers Inc 801 N Kanawha St *TF:* 800-950-0250	Beckley	WV	25801	304-255-4400	255-4427
Bee Publishing Co Inc PO Box 5503 *Web:* www.thebee.com	Newtown	CT	06470	203-426-3141	426-5169
Bell Globemedia Inc 9 Channel Nine Ct *Web:* www.bellglobemedia.ca	Toronto	ON	M1S4B5	416-332-5700	291-5537
Belo Corp 400 Record St *NYSE: BLC* ■ **Fax:* Mktg ■ *TF:* 800-431-0010 ■ *Web:* www.belo.com	Dallas	TX	75202	214-977-8222	977-6603*
Belo Corp Newspaper Group 400 S Record St *TF:* 800-431-0010 ■ *Web:* www.belo.com/companies/newsgroup.x2	Dallas	TX	75202	214-977-6606	977-6603
Bliss Communications Inc PO Box 5001 *TF:* 800-362-6712 ■ *Web:* www.blissnet.net	Janesville	WI	53547	608-752-7895	752-4438
Boone Newspapers Inc PO Box 2370 *Web:* www.boonenewspapers.com	Tuscaloosa	AL	35403	205-330-4100	330-4140
Booth Newspapers Inc PO Box 2168 *TF:* 800-886-5529 ■ *Web:* www.boothnewspapers.com	Grand Rapids	MI	49501	616-459-3824	222-5409
Breese Publishing Co 8060 Old Hwy 50 PO Box 405 *Web:* www.breesepub.com	Breese	IL	62230	618-526-7211	526-2590
Breeze Corp 2510 Del Prado Blvd *Web:* www.flguide.com	Cape Coral	FL	33904	239-574-1110	574-3403
Brehm Communications Inc PO Box 28429 *Web:* www.brehmcommunications.com	San Diego	CA	92198	858-451-6200	451-3814
Brethren Missionary Herald 1104 Kings Hwy *TF:* 800-348-2756	Winona Lake	IN	46590	574-267-7158	267-4745
Brooks Community Newspapers Inc 542 Westport Ave **Fax:* Sales ■ *Web:* www.bcnnews.com	Norwalk	CT	06851	203-849-1600	840-4844*
Brunswick Publishing Co PO Box 10 *Web:* www.timesrecord.com	Brunswick	ME	04011	207-729-3311	729-5728
Burlington Hawk Eye Co PO Box 10 *TF:* 800-397-1708 ■ *Web:* www.thehawkeye.com	Burlington	IA	52601	319-754-8461	754-6824
Butler TB Publishing Co 410 W Erwin St *TF:* 800-333-9141 ■ *Web:* www.tylerpaper.com	Tyler	TX	75702	903-597-8111	595-0335
Buylines Press 2465 Grand Ave *Web:* www.buylines.com	Baldwin	NY	11510	516-223-1274	867-4832
Byerly Publications Inc 1000 Armory Dr	Franklin	VA	23851	757-562-3187	562-6795
California Community News Corp 5091 4th St	Irwindale	CA	91706	626-472-5200	
Calkins Media Inc 8400 Rt 13	Levittown	PA	19057	215-949-4011	949-4021
Capital City Press Inc PO Box 588 **Fax:* Hum Res ■ *Web:* www.2theadvocate.com	Baton Rouge	LA	70821	225-383-1111	388-0397*
Capital-Gazette Communications Inc PO Box 911 *Web:* www.capitalgazette.com	Annapolis	MD	21404	410-268-5000	280-5953
Casa Grande Valley Newspaper Inc PO Box 15002 *TF:* 800-821-1746 ■ *Web:* www.trivalleycentral.com	Casa Grande	AZ	85230	520-836-7461	836-0343
Chattanooga Publishing Co 400 E 11th St *TF:* 800-733-2637 ■ *Web:* www.timesfreepress.com	Chattanooga	TN	37403	423-756-6900	757-6383
Chesapeake Publishing Corp 29088 Airpark Dr	Easton	MD	21601	410-822-1500	770-4019
Cheyenne Newspaper Inc 702 W Lincolnway *TF:* 800-561-6268 ■ *Web:* www.wyomingnews.com	Cheyenne	WY	82001	307-634-3361	633-3189
Christian Science Publishing Society 1 Norway St *TF:* 800-288-7090 ■ *Web:* www.csmonitor.com	Boston	MA	02115	617-450-2000	450-7575
Citizen Publishing Co Inc PO Box 309 *Web:* www.windomnews.com	Windom	MN	56101	507-831-3455	831-3740
Citizen Publishing Co Inc 805 Park Ave PO Box 558 **Fax:* Cust Svc ■ *TF:* 800-777-9470	Beaver Dam	WI	53916	920-887-0321	887-8790*
Cloquet Newspaper Inc 813 Cloquet Ave *Web:* www.cloquetmn.com	Cloquet	MN	55720	218-879-6761	879-2078
Coffee News USA PO Box 84444 *Web:* www.coffeenewsusa.com	Bangor	ME	04402	207-941-0860	941-1050
Collins William B Co 8 E Fulton St	Gloversville	NY	12078	518-725-8616	725-7350
Community Newspaper Co PO Box 9191 *Web:* www.townonline.com	Concord	MA	01742	978-369-2800	371-9058
Community Newspaper Co 254 2nd Ave **Fax:* Edit	Needham	MA	02494	781-433-6700	433-7879*
Community Newspaper Co Inc 72 Cherry Hill Dr *Web:* www.townonline.com	Beverly	MA	01915	978-739-1300	739-1392
Community Newspaper Holdings Inc 3500 Colonnade Pkwy Suite 600 *TF:* 800-951-2644 ■ *Web:* www.cnhi.com	Birmingham	AL	35243	205-298-7100	298-7102
Community Newspapers Inc 1325 SW Custer Dr	Portland	OR	97219	503-684-0360	620-3433
Community Press Newspapers 4910 Para Dr *Web:* news.communitypress.com	Cincinnati	OH	45237	513-242-4300	242-2649
Consolidated Publishing Co PO Box 189 *Web:* www.annistonstar.com	Anniston	AL	36202	256-236-1551	241-1991
Contra Costa Newspapers Inc 1700 Cavallo Rd *Web:* www.contracostatimes.com	Antioch	CA	94509	925-757-2525	754-9483
Copley Los Angeles Newspapers 7776 Ivanhoe Ave **Fax:* Hum Res	La Jolla	CA	92037	858-454-0411	729-7689*
Coulter Press Inc 156 Church St	Clinton	MA	01510	978-368-0176	368-1151
Country Media Inc 2640 Lazelle Rd *TF:* 800-253-3656 ■ *Web:* www.tsln.com	Sturgis	SD	57785	605-347-2585	347-2525
Courier Publications Inc 301 Park St PO Box 249 *Web:* www.courierpub.com	Rockland	ME	04841	207-594-4401	596-6981
Cox Newspapers Inc 6205 Peachtree Dunwoody Dr *TF:* 800-950-3739 ■ *Web:* www.coxnews.com	Atlanta	GA	30328	678-645-0000	645-5002
Cumberland Publishers PO Box 130	Carlisle	PA	17013	717-243-2611	243-3121
Daily Herald Co PO Box 930 *Web:* www.heraldnet.com	Everett	WA	98206	425-339-3000	339-3017
Daily Journal Corp 915 E 1st St *NASDAQ: DJCO* ■ *TF:* 800-788-7840 ■ *Web:* www.dailyjournal.com	Los Angeles	CA	90012	213-229-5300	680-3682
Daily Progress 685 W Rio Rd *Web:* www.dailyprogress.com	Charlottesville	VA	22901	434-978-7200	978-7252
Daily Record Co 11 E Saratoga St *TF:* 800-296-8181 ■ *Web:* www.mddailyrecord.com	Baltimore	MD	21202	410-752-3849	547-6705
Daily Record Inc 800 Jefferson Rd *Web:* www.dailyrecord.com	Parsippany	NJ	07054	973-428-6200	428-6666
Daily Reflector Inc PO Box 1967 *TF:* 800-849-6166 ■ *Web:* www.reflector.com	Greenville	NC	27835	252-752-6166	752-9583
Danbury Publishing Co 333 Main St *Web:* www.newstimes.com	Danbury	CT	06810	203-744-5100	792-8730
Day Publishing Co 47 Eugene O'Neill Dr *TF:* 800-542-3354 ■ *Web:* www.theday.com	New London	CT	06320	860-442-2200	442-5599
Dayton Newspapers Inc 45 S Ludlow St **Fax:* Mktg ■ *Web:* www.daytondailynews.com	Dayton	OH	45402	937-225-2000	225-2043*
Delphos Herald Inc 405 N Main St *TF:* 800-589-6950 ■ *Web:* www.delphosherald.com	Delphos	OH	45833	419-695-0015	692-7704
Denver Newspaper Agency 101 W Colfax Ave *Web:* www.denvernewspaperagency.com	Denver	CO	80204	303-954-1000	954-5260
Derrick Publishing Co 1510 W 1st St *TF:* 800-352-1002 ■ *Web:* www.thederrick.com	Oil City	PA	16301	814-676-7444	677-8351
Desert Sun Publishing Co PO Box 2734 *TF Advertising:* 800-233-3741 ■ *Web:* www.thedesertsun.com	Palm Springs	CA	92263	760-322-8889	778-4654
Detroit Legal News Co 2001 W Lafayette Blvd *TF:* 800-875-5275 ■ *Web:* www.legalnews.com	Detroit	MI	48216	313-961-3949	961-7817
Dispatch Printing Co 34 S 3rd St *TF:* 800-282-0263 ■ *Web:* www.dispatch.com	Columbus	OH	43215	614-461-5000	461-7580
DMG World Media 27 N Jefferson St *TF:* 800-876-5133 ■ *Web:* www.dmgworldmedia.com	Knightstown	IN	46148	765-345-5133	345-3398
Dow Jones & Co Inc 200 Liberty St *NYSE: DJ* ■ *Web:* www.dowjones.com	New York	NY	10281	212-416-2000	416-2658
Downers Grove Reporter Inc 922 Warren Ave	Downers Grove	IL	60515	630-969-0188	969-0228
Eagle Publications Inc 401 River Rd *TF:* 800-545-0347 ■ *Web:* www.eagletimes.com	Claremont	NH	03743	603-542-5121	542-9705
Eagle Publishing Co 75 S Church St *Web:* www.berkshireeagle.com	Pittsfield	MA	01201	413-447-7311	499-3419
East Coast Newspapers Inc PO Box 11707 *Web:* www.heraldonline.com	Rock Hill	SC	29731	803-329-4000	329-4021
East Hampton Star Inc PO Box 5002 *Web:* www.easthamptonstar.com	East Hampton	NY	11937	631-324-0002	324-7943
Eastern Middlesex Publications Inc 277 Commercial St	Malden	MA	02148	781-321-8000	321-8008
Eau Claire Press Co 701 S Farwell St *TF:* 800-236-8808 ■ *Web:* www.ecpc.com	Eau Claire	WI	54701	715-833-9200	833-9244
ECM Publishers Inc 1201 14th Ave S *Web:* www.ecm-inc.com	Princeton	MN	55371	763-389-4710	389-5228
Edward A Sherman Publishing Co 101 Malbone Rd *TF:* 800-320-2378	Newport	RI	02840	401-849-3300	849-3306
Enterprise Newspapers 4303 198th St SW *TF:* 800-944-3630 ■ *Web:* www.enterprisenewspapers.com	Lynnwood	WA	98036	425-673-6500	774-8622
Evening Post Publishing Co 134 Columbus St	Charleston	SC	29403	843-577-7111	937-5579
EW Scripps Co 312 Walnut St Suite 2800 *NYSE: SSP* ■ **Fax:* Hum Res ■ *TF:* 800-888-3000 ■ *Web:* www.scripps.com	Cincinnati	OH	45202	513-977-3000	977-3720*
Express-News Corp PO Box 2171 *TF:* 800-555-1551 ■ *Web:* www.mysanantonio.com	San Antonio	TX	78297	210-250-3000	250-3105
Fairfield Publishing Co 1250 Texas St *Web:* local.dailyrepublic.net	Fairfield	CA	94533	707-425-4646	425-5924
Feather Publishing Co Inc PO Box B *Web:* www.plumasnews.com	Quincy	CA	95971	530-283-0800	283-3952
Findlay Publishing Co 701 W Sandusky St *Web:* www.thecourier.com	Findlay	OH	45840	419-422-5151	422-2937
Finger Lakes Printing Co 218 Genesse St PO Box 393 *TF:* 800-388-6652 ■ *Web:* www.fltimes.com	Geneva	NY	14456	315-789-3333	789-4077
Flashes Publishers Inc 595 Jenner Dr *TF:* 800-968-4415 ■ *Web:* www.flashespublishers.com	Allegan	MI	49010	269-673-2141	673-4761
Fort Wayne Newspapers Inc 600 W Main St *TF:* 800-444-3303 ■ *Web:* www.fortwayne.com	Fort Wayne	IN	46802	260-461-8444	461-8817
Forum Communications Co 101 5th St N *TF:* 800-747-7311 ■ *Web:* www.forumcomm.com	Fargo	ND	58102	701-235-7311	241-5406
Forum Publishing Group 1701 Green Rd Suite B *TF:* 800-275-8820	Pompano Beach	FL	33064	954-698-6397	429-1207
Forward Publishing 45 E 33rd St *TF:* 800-266-0773 ■ *Web:* www.forward.com	New York	NY	10016	212-889-8200	447-6406
Foster George J Co Inc 333 Central Ave *TF:* 800-660-8310 ■ *Web:* www.fosters.com	Dover	NH	03820	603-742-4455	749-7079
Frankfort Publishing Co 1216 Wilkinson Blvd *Web:* www.state-journal.com	Frankfort	KY	40601	502-227-4556	227-2831
Freedom Communications Inc 17666 Fitch *Web:* www.freedom.com	Irvine	CA	92614	949-553-9292	474-7675
Galesburg Printing & Publishing Co PO Box 310 *Web:* www.register-mail.com	Galesburg	IL	61402	309-343-7181	343-2382
Gannett Co Inc 7950 Jones Branch Dr *NYSE: GCI* ■ *Web:* www.gannett.com	McLean	VA	22107	703-854-6000	
Gannett Co Inc Newspaper Div 7950 Jones Branch Dr *Web:* www.gannett.com/web/gan013.htm	McLean	VA	22107	703-854-6000	
Gateway Press Inc 610 Beatty Rd *Web:* www.gatewaynewspapers.com	Monroeville	PA	15146	412-856-7400	856-7954
Gazette Newspapers Inc 1200 Quince Orchard Blvd **Fax:* Hum Res ■ *TF:* 888-670-7100	Gaithersburg	MD	20878	301-948-3120	670-7138*
George J Foster Co Inc 333 Central Ave *TF:* 800-660-8310 ■ *Web:* www.fosters.com	Dover	NH	03820	603-742-4455	749-7079
George W Prescott Publishing Co Inc 400 Crown Colony Dr *Web:* www.southofboston.com	Quincy	MA	02169	617-786-7000	786-7025
Gesca Ltee 7 Rue Saint-Jacques	Montreal	QC	H2Y1K9	514-285-6859	
Gilmer Mirror Co PO Box 250 *Web:* www.gilmermirror.com	Gilmer	TX	75644	903-843-2503	843-5123
Glastonbury Citizen Inc PO Box 373 *Web:* www.glcitizen.com	Glastonbury	CT	06033	860-633-4691	657-3258
Glendale News Press 222 N Brand Ave *Web:* www.glendalenewspress.com	Glendale	CA	91203	818-637-3200	241-1975
Globe Publishing Co Inc 118 E McLeod Ave *Web:* www.ironwoodglobe.com	Ironwood	MI	49938	906-932-2211	932-4211
Gray Television Inc 4370 Peachtree Rd NE *NYSE: GTN* ■ *Web:* www.graycommunications.com	Atlanta	GA	30319	404-504-9828	261-9607
Greater Media Inc 35 Braintree Hill Pk Suite 300 *Web:* www.greater-media.com	Braintree	MA	02184	781-348-8600	348-8695
Guard Publishing Co PO Box 10188 *Web:* www.registerguard.com	Eugene	OR	97440	541-485-1234	984-4699
H & K Publications Inc PO Box 590 *Web:* www.pennysavers.com	Hamburg	NY	14075	716-649-4413	649-6374
Harris Enterprises Inc PO Box 748	Hutchinson	KS	67504	620-694-5830	694-5834
Hastings & Sons Publishing PO Box 951 *Web:* www.itemlive.com	Lynn	MA	01903	781-593-7700	598-2891
Hearst Corp 1345 6th Ave **Fax Area Code:* 646 ■ **Fax:* Hum Res ■ *Web:* www.hearstcorp.com	New York	NY	10105	212-649-2000	280-1045*
Hearst Newspapers 300 W 57th St 41st Fl *Web:* hearstcorp.com/newspapers	New York	NY	10005	212-649-2000	489-8239
Herald Mail Co Inc 100 Summit Ave *TF:* 888-851-2553 ■ *Web:* www.herald-mail.com	Hagerstown	MD	21740	301-733-5131	733-7264
Herald Palladium Publishing Co Inc PO Box 128 *Web:* www.heraldpalladium.com	Saint Joseph	MI	49085	269-429-2400	429-7661
Herald Publishing Co 1 Herald Sq	New Britain	CT	06050	860-225-4601	225-2611
Herald Publishing Co PO Box 11707 *Web:* www.heraldonline.com	Rock Hill	SC	29731	803-329-4000	329-4021
Herald Publishing Co PO Box 153	Houston	TX	77001	713-630-0391	630-0404
Herald-Star 401 Herald Sq *TF:* 800-526-7987 ■ *Web:* www.hsconnect.com	Steubenville	OH	43952	740-283-4711	284-7355
Herald-Sun Newspapers PO Box 2092 *TF:* 800-672-0061 ■ *Web:* www.heraldsun.com/durham/	Durham	NC	27702	919-419-6900	419-6889

Newspaper Publishers (Cont'd)

Company	City	State	Zip	Phone	Fax
Herald-Times Inc PO Box 909	Bloomington	IN	47402	812-332-4401	331-4285
Web: www.heraldtimesonline.com					
Heritage Newspapers Inc 1 Heritage Pl Suite 100	Southgate	MI	48195	734-246-0800	246-2727
Web: www.heritage.com					
Hersam Acorn Newspapers PO Box 1019	Ridgefield	CT	06877	203-438-6545	438-3395
TF: 800-372-2790 ■ *Web:* www.acorn-online.com					
Hersam Publishing Co 42 Vitti St	New Canaan	CT	06840	203-966-9541	966-8006
Web: www.acorn-online.com					
Hi-Desert Publishing Co PO Box 880	Yucca Valley	CA	92286	760-365-3315	365-2650
Web: www.hidesertstar.com					
Hickory Publishing Co Inc PO Box 968	Hickory	NC	28603	828-322-4510	324-8179
TF: 800-849-8586 ■ *Web:* www.hickoryrecord.com					
Hidalgo Publishing Co PO Box 148	Edinburg	TX	78540	956-383-2705	383-3172
High Plains Publishers Inc PO Box 760	Dodge City	KS	67801	620-227-7171	227-7173
TF: 800-452-7171 ■ *Web:* www.hpj.com					
Hills Newspapers 1516 Oak St	Alameda	CA	94501	510-748-1683	748-1680
Hollinger Inc 10 Toronto St	Toronto	ON	M5C2B7	416-363-8721	364-2088
TSX: HLGc ■ *Web:* www.hollinger.com					
Hollinger International Inc 401 N Wabash Ave Suite 740	Chicago	IL	60611	312-321-2299	321-0629
NYSE: HLR ■ *Web:* www.hollinger.com					
Home News Enterprises 333 2nd St	Columbus	IN	47201	812-372-7811	379-5706
TF: 800-876-7811					
HomeTown Communications Network Inc 36251 Schoolcraft Rd	Livonia	MI	48150	734-591-2300	591-7279
Web: www.homecomm.net					
Housatonic Publications 65 Bank St	New Milford	CT	06776	860-354-2261	354-2645
Houston Community Newspapers Inc 102 S Shaver Rd	Pasadena	TX	77506	713-477-0221	477-9783
Web: www.hcnonline.com					
Hubbard Publishing Co PO Box 40	Bellefontaine	OH	43311	937-592-3060	592-4463
Web: examiner.org					
Huckle Publishing Inc 135 W Pearl St	Owatonna	MN	55060	507-451-2840	451-6020
Web: www.owatonna.com					
Huse Publishing Co PO Box 977	Norfolk	NE	68702	402-371-1020	371-5802
TF: 800-672-8351 ■ *Web:* www.norfolkdailynews.com					
Hutchinson Leader Inc 36 Washington Ave W	Hutchinson	MN	55350	320-587-5000	587-6104
Web: www.hutchinsonleader.com					
Independent Newspapers Inc PO Box 737	Dover	DE	19903	302-674-3600	674-5910
Web: www2.newszap.com					
Independent Publishing Co 1000 Williamston Rd	Anderson	SC	29621	864-224-4321	260-1276
Web: www.independentmail.com					
Indiana Printing & Publishing Co 899 Water St PO Box 10	Indiana	PA	15701	724-465-5555	465-8267
Web: www.indianagazette.com					
Indianapolis Newspapers Inc 307 N Pennsylvania St	Indianapolis	IN	46204	317-633-1240	444-6600
TF: 800-669-7827					
Intercounty Newspaper Group 6220 Ridge Ave	Philadelphia	PA	19128	215-483-7300	483-2073
JH Zerbey Newspapers Inc 111 Mahantongo St	Pottsville	PA	17901	570-622-3456	628-6092
Journal Communications Inc 333 W State St	Milwaukee	WI	53203	414-224-2000	224-2469
NYSE: JRN ■ *TF:* 800-456-5943 ■ *Web:* www.jc.com					
Journal News Publishing Co Inc PO Box 998	Ephrata	WA	98823	509-754-4636	754-0996
Journal Publishing Co PO Box 909	Tupelo	MS	38802	662-842-2611	842-2233
TF: 800-264-6397 ■ *Web:* www.djournal.com					
Journal Register Co 790 Township Line Rd 12th Fl	Yardley	PA	19067	215-504-4200	
NYSE: JRC ■ *Web:* www.journalregister.com					
Journal & Topics Newspapers 622 Graceland Ave	Des Plaines	IL	60016	847-299-5511	298-8549
Web: www.journal-topics.com					
Keene Publishing Corp PO Box 546	Keene	NH	03431	603-352-1234	352-0437
TF: 800-765-9994 ■ *Web:* www.sentinelsource.com					
Kingsport Publishing Co 701 Lynn Garden Dr	Kingsport	TN	37660	423-246-8121	392-1385
TF: 800-251-0328					
Kline William J & Son Inc 1 Venner Rd	Amsterdam	NY	12010	518-843-1100	843-1338
TF: 800-453-6397 ■ *Web:* www.recordernews.com					
Knight Publishing Co 600 S Tryon St	Charlotte	NC	28202	704-358-5000	358-5707*
**Fax:* Hum Res ■ *TF:* 800-332-0686 ■ *Web:* www.charlotte.com					
Knight Ridder Inc 50 W San Fernando St Suite 1500	San Jose	CA	95113	408-938-7700	938-7766
NYSE: KRI ■ *Web:* www.kri.com					
Lake Charles American Press Inc PO Box 2893	Lake Charles	LA	70602	337-433-3000	494-4008
Web: www.americanpress.com					
Lakeville Journal Co LLC PO Box 1688	Lakeville	CT	06039	860-435-9873	435-4802
Web: www.tcextra.com					
Lakeway Publishers Inc PO Box 625	Morristown	TN	37815	423-581-5630	581-3061
Lancaster Newspapers Inc 8 W King St	Lancaster	PA	17603	717-291-8811	291-8728
TF: 800-809-4666 ■ *Web:* www.lancasteronline.com					
Landmark Community Newspapers Inc 601 Taylorsville Rd	Shelbyville	KY	40065	502-633-4334	633-4447
TF: 800-939-9322 ■ *Web:* www.lcni.com					
Law Bulletin Publishing Co 415 N State St	Chicago	IL	60610	312-644-7800	644-4255
Web: www.lawbulletin.com					
Lawrence Daily Journal-World Co 609 New Hampshire St	Lawrence	KS	66044	785-843-1000	843-4512
TF: 800-578-8748 ■ *Web:* www.ljworld.com					
Leader-Union Publishing Co 229 S 5th St	Vandalia	IL	62471	618-283-3374	283-0977
Web: www.leaderunion.com					
Leaf Chronicle Co 200 Commerce St	Clarksville	TN	37040	931-552-1808	648-8001
Web: www.theleafchronicle.com					
Lee Enterprises Inc 201 N Harrison Suite 600	Davenport	IA	52801	563-383-2100	323-9609
NYSE: LEE ■ *Web:* www.lee.net					
Lee Publications Inc 6113 State Hwy 5	Palatine Bridge	NY	13428	518-673-3237	673-3245
TF: 800-218-5586 ■ *Web:* www.leepub.com					
Legal Communications Corp 612 N 2nd St	Saint Louis	MO	63102	314-421-1880	421-0436
Lehman Communications Corp 350 Terry St	Longmont	CO	80501	303-776-2244	678-8615
TF: 800-796-8201					
Lerner Communications Newspapers 7331 N Lincoln Ave	Lincolnwood	IL	60712	847-329-2000	329-2060
Lewiston Daily Sun Corp 104 Park St	Lewiston	ME	04240	207-784-5411	777-3436
TF: 800-482-0753 ■ *Web:* www.sunjournal.com					
Liberty Group Publishing Inc 1101 W 31st St Suite 100	Downers Grove	IL	60515	630-368-1100	368-8809
Life Newspapers 7222 W Cermac Rd	North Riverside	IL	60546	708-447-9810	447-9871
Web: www.chicagosuburbannews.com					
Livingston County Daily Press & Argus PO Box 230	Howell	MI	48844	517-548-2000	548-2225
TF: 888-999-1288 ■ *Web:* www.livingstondaily.com					
Longview Newspapers Inc 320 E Methvin St	Longview	TX	75606	903-757-3311	757-3742
TF: 800-627-4716					
Los Angeles Newspaper Group 21221 Oxnard St	Woodland Hills	CA	91367	818-713-3000	437-7892*
**Fax Area Code:* 562 ■ *TF:* 877-289-5264 ■ *Web:* www.losangelesnewspapergroup.com					
Lowell Sun Publishing Co 491 Dutton St	Lowell	MA	01852	978-458-7100	970-4600*
**Fax:* Edit ■ *TF:* 800-694-7100 ■ *Web:* www.lowellsun.com					
Madison Newspapers Inc 1901 Fish Hatchery Rd	Madison	WI	53713	608-252-6200	252-6119
TF Classified: 800-252-7723 ■ *Web:* www.madison.com					
Magic Valley Newspapers 132 Fairfield St W	Twin Falls	ID	83301	208-733-0931	734-5538
TF: 800-658-3883 ■ *Web:* www.magicvalley.com					
Manhattan Media LLC 63 W 38th St Rm 206	New York	NY	10018	212-268-8600	268-0614
Web: www.manhattanmedia.com					
Marshall Independent Publishing Co 508 W Main St PO Box 411	Marshall	MN	56258	507-537-1551	537-1557
Web: www.marshallindependent.com					
Maverick Media Inc 123 W 17th St	Syracuse	NE	68446	402-269-2135	456-5158*
**Fax Area Code:* 800 ■ *TF:* 800-742-7662					

Company	City	State	Zip	Phone	Fax
McClatchy Co 2100 Q St	Sacramento	CA	95816	916-321-1855	321-1869
NYSE: MNI ■ *Web:* www.mcclatchy.com					
McClatchy Interactive 1101 Haynes St Suite 220	Raleigh	NC	27604	919-861-1200	
Web: www.mcclatchyinteractive.com					
McClatchy Newspapers Inc 2100 Q St	Sacramento	CA	95816	916-321-1000	321-1964
Web: www.mcclatchy.com					
McCormick & Co Inc 1201 3rd St	Alexandria	LA	71301	318-487-6397	487-6488
TF: 800-523-8391					
Media General Inc 333 E Franklin St	Richmond	VA	23219	804-649-6000	649-6898
NYSE: MEG ■ *Web:* www.media-general.com					
Media News Group 916 Cotting Ln	Vacaville	CA	95688	707-448-6401	447-8411
MediaNews Group Inc 1560 Broadway Suite 2100	Denver	CO	80202	303-563-6360	894-9327
Web: www.medianewsgroup.com					
Memphis Publishing Co 495 Union Ave	Memphis	TN	38103	901-529-2211	529-6445
TF Cust Svc: 800-444-6397					
Meridian Star Inc 814 22nd Ave	Meridian	MS	39301	601-693-1551	485-1275
TF: 800-232-2525					
Messenger Publishing Co 9300 Johnson Rd	Athens	OH	45701	740-592-6612	592-4647
TF: 800-233-6611 ■ *Web:* www.athensmessenger.com					
Metro Group Inc PO Box 211	Buffalo	NY	14225	716-668-5223	668-4526
TF: 800-836-7262 ■ *Web:* www.metrowny.com					
MetroActive Publishing Inc 550 S 1st St	San Jose	CA	95113	408-298-8000	298-0602
Web: www.metroactive.com					
Mid-America Publishing Corp 9 2nd St NW	Hampton	IA	50441	641-456-2585	456-2587
Milford Daily News Co 159 S Main St	Milford	MA	01757	508-473-1111	634-7514
Web: www.milforddailynews.com					
Mineral Daily News Tribune Inc 24 Armstrong St	Keyser	WV	26726	304-788-3333	788-3398
TF: 800-788-4026 ■ *Web:* www.newstribune.info					
Minnesota Sun Publications 10917 Valley View Rd	Eden Prairie	MN	55344	952-829-0797	392-6868
Web: www.mnsun.com					
Missourian Publishing Co 14 W Main St	Washington	MO	63090	636-239-7701	239-0915
TF: 888-239-7701 ■ *Web:* www.emissourian.com					
Mobile Press Register Inc PO Box 2488	Mobile	AL	36652	251-433-1551	219-5799
TF: 800-239-1340 ■ *Web:* www.mobileregister.com					
Moline Dispatch Publishing Co 1720 5th Ave	Moline	IL	61265	309-764-4344	797-0317
Morning Call Inc 101 N 6th St	Allentown	PA	18101	610-820-6500	820-6175*
**Fax:* Mktg ■ *TF:* 800-666-5492 ■ *Web:* www.mcall.com					
Morning Star Publishing Co 711 W Pickard St	Mount Pleasant	MI	48858	989-772-2971	773-0382
TF: 800-616-6397					
Morris Communications Co LLC 725 Broad St	Augusta	GA	30901	706-724-0851	823-3440
TF: 800-622-6358 ■ *Web:* www.morriscomm.com					
Morris Multimedia Inc 27 Abercorn St	Savannah	GA	31401	912-233-1281	232-4639
Web: www.morrismultimedia.com					
Murray Printing Co 155 E 4905 S	Murray	UT	84107	801-262-8091	262-5419
Natchez Newspapers Inc 503 N Canal St	Natchez	MS	39120	601-442-9101	442-7315
TF: 888-878-9101 ■ *Web:* www.natchezdemocrat.com					
Native American Times 570 E 141 St	Bartlesville	OK	74003	918-438-6548	438-6545
Web: nativetimes.com					
New Mass Media Inc 116 Pleasant St Suite 335	Easthampton	MA	01027	413-529-2840	529-2844
Web: www.newmassmedia.com					
New Media Printing 329 Broadway	Bethpage	NY	11714	516-681-0440	681-9354
TF: 888-626-4266 ■ *Web:* www.newmediaprinting.com					
New Mexico Newspapers Inc PO Box 450	Farmington	NM	87499	505-325-4545	564-4630
TF: 800-395-6397 ■ *Web:* www.daily-times.com					
New York News LP 450 W 33rd St 3rd Fl	New York	NY	10001	212-210-2100	643-7831
Web: www.nydailynews.com					
New York Times Co 620 8th Ave	New York	NY	10008	212-556-4317	428-2197*
NYSE: NYT ■ **Fax Area Code:* 646 ■ *Web:* www.nytco.com					
New York Times Co Regional Newspaper Group 2202 N Westshore Blvd Suite 370	Tampa	FL	33607	813-864-6000	281-2729
Newhouse Newspapers 950 Fingerboard Rd	Staten Island	NY	10305	718-981-1234	981-1456
News America Inc 1211 Ave of the Americas	New York	NY	10036	212-852-7000	
News Corp Ltd 1211 Ave of the Americas 7th Fl	New York	NY	10036	212-852-7000	852-7145*
NYSE: NWS ■ **Fax:* Investor Rel ■ *Web:* www.newscorp.com					
News Journal Co PO Box 15505	Wilmington	DE	19850	302-324-2500	324-5509
TF: 800-235-9100 ■ *Web:* www.delawareonline.com					
News-Journal Corp 901 6th St	Daytona Beach	FL	32117	386-252-1511	258-8465
Web: www.news-journalonline.com					
News Publishing Co PO Box 1633	Rome	GA	30162	706-291-6397	234-6478
Newspaper Agency Corp PO Box 45838	Salt Lake City	UT	84145	801-237-2800	237-2941
Web: www.nacorp.com/NAC2/index.html					
Newspapers of New England Inc PO Box 1177	Concord	NH	03302	603-224-5301	224-6949
Web: www.concordmonitor.com					
Newton Press Mentor Inc PO Box 151	Newton	IL	62448	618-783-2324	783-2325
Nittany Printing & Publishing Co 3400 E College Ave	State College	PA	16801	814-238-5000	238-1811
TF: 800-327-5500					
NJN Publishing 44 Veterans Memorial Dr E	Somerville	NJ	08876	908-575-6660	575-6683*
**Fax:* Edit					
North Jersey Media Group 150 River St	Hackensack	NJ	07601	201-646-4000	646-4310
Web: www.njmg.com					
Northeastern Publishing Co 425 Main St PO Box 5027	Bennington	VT	05201	802-447-7567	442-3413
Northwest Herald Inc PO Box 250	Crystal Lake	IL	60039	815-459-4040	459-5640
TF: 800-589-8910 ■ *Web:* www.nwherald.com					
Northwest Media Inc PO Box 90130	Bellevue	WA	98009	425-455-2222	450-1238*
**Fax:* Hum Res ■ *Web:* www.kingcountyjournal.com					
Northwest Publications 99 E State St	Rockford	IL	61104	815-987-1200	987-1365*
**Fax:* Edit ■ *TF:* 800-383-7827 ■ *Web:* www.rrstar.com					
Oakland Press Co 48 W Huron St	Pontiac	MI	48342	248-332-8181	332-8885
TF: 800-686-2236 ■ *Web:* www.theoaklandpress.com					
Observer Dispatch Inc 221 Oriskany Plaza	Utica	NY	13501	315-797-9150	792-5085*
**Fax:* Mktg					
Observer & Eccentric Newspapers 36251 Schoolcraft Rd	Livonia	MI	48150	734-591-2300	591-7279
Web: hometownlife.com					
Observer Publishing Co 122 S Main St	Washington	PA	15301	724-222-2200	225-2077
TF: 800-222-6397 ■ *Web:* www.observer-reporter.com					
Ocean County Newspapers Co 8 Robbins St	Toms River	NJ	08753	732-349-3000	557-5758
Ogden Newspapers Inc 1500 Main St	Wheeling	WV	26003	304-233-0100	233-9397
Web: www.oweb.com					
Ojai Valley News Inc PO Box 277	Ojai	CA	93024	805-646-1476	646-4281
Web: www.ojaivalleynews.com					
Oklahoma Publishing Co 9000 N Broadway Ext	Oklahoma City	OK	73114	405-475-3311	475-3513
TF: 800-375-3450					
Olympic Cascade Publishing Co Inc 3555 Erickson St	Gig Harbor	WA	98335	253-851-9921	851-3939
Oshkosh Northwestern Co 224 State St	Oshkosh	WI	54901	920-235-7700	235-1527
TF: 800-924-6168 ■ *Web:* www.thenorthwestern.com					
Ottaway Newspapers Inc 97 Rt 416 PO Box 401	Campbell Hall	NY	10916	845-294-8181	294-1659
Web: www.ottaway.com					
Our Sunday Visitor Inc 200 Noll Plaza	Huntington	IN	46750	260-356-8400	359-0029
TF: 800-348-2440 ■ *Web:* www.osv.com					
Pacific Palisades Post Co 839 Via de la Paz	Pacific Palisades	CA	90272	310-454-1321	454-1078
Web: www.palisadespost.com					
Pacific Publishing Co 4000 Aurora Ave N Suite 100	Seattle	WA	98103	206-461-1300	461-1289
Web: www.pacificpublishingcompany.com					
Paddock Publications Inc 155 E Algonquin Rd	Arlington Heights	IL	60005	847-427-4300	427-1301
Web: www.dailyherald.com					
Paducah Newspapers Inc PO Box 2300	Paducah	KY	42002	270-575-8600	442-7859
TF: 800-959-1771 ■ *Web:* www.paducah.com					

				Phone	Fax
Palm Beach Newspapers Inc PO Box 24700	West Palm Beach	FL	33416	561-820-4100	820-4407
TF: 800-432-7597 ■ *Web:* www.palmbeachpost.com					
Pamplin Communications Corp 10209 SE Division St	Portland	OR	97266	503-251-1597	262-3822*
*Fax: Hum Res					
Papers Inc PO Box 188	Milford	IN	46542	574-658-4111	658-4701
TF: 800-733-4111 ■ *Web:* auto-rv.com					
Patuxent Publishing Co 10750 Little Patuxent Pkwy	Columbia	MD	21044	410-730-3620	997-4564*
*Fax: News Rm ■ *TF:* 800-884-8797 ■ *Web:* www.patuxent.com					
Paxton Media Group PO Box 1680	Paducah	KY	42002	270-575-8614	442-8188
Penny Saver Publication Inc 6901 W 159th St	Tinley Park	IL	60477	708-633-6700	633-5927
Pennysaver 27101 Puerto Real Suite 250	Mission Viejo	CA	92691	949-614-2600	614-2727
TF: 800-873-5548 ■ *Web:* www.pennysaverusa.com					
Peoria Journal-Star Inc 1 News Plaza	Peoria	IL	61643	309-686-3000	686-3296
TF: 800-225-5757 ■ *Web:* www.pjstar.com					
Perry Publishing & Broadcasting 1701 W Pine Ave	Duncan	OK	73534	580-255-1350	470-9993
Web: www.blackchronicle.com					
Persis Corp 900 Fort Street Mall Suite 1725	Honolulu	HI	96813	808-599-8000	526-4114
Web: www.persiscorp.com					
PG Publishing Co 34 Blvd of the Allies	Pittsburgh	PA	15222	412-263-1100	263-1703
TF Cust Svc: 800-228-6397 ■ *Web:* www.post-gazette.com					
Philadelphia Tribune Co 520 S 16th St	Philadelphia	PA	19146	215-893-4050	735-3612
Phoenix Media Communications Group 126 Brookline Ave	Boston	MA	02215	617-536-5390	859-8201*
*Fax: Edit ■ *Web:* www.phx.com					
Phoenix Newspapers Inc 200 E Van Buren St	Phoenix	AZ	85004	602-444-8000	444-8044
TF: 800-331-9303					
Pioneer Group 115 N Michigan Ave	Big Rapids	MI	49307	231-796-4831	796-1152
Web: www.pioneergroup.net					
Pioneer Newspapers Inc 221 1st Ave W Suite 405	Seattle	WA	98119	206-284-4424	282-2143
Web: www.pioneernewspapers.com					
Pioneer Press Inc 3701 W Lake Ave	Glenview	IL	60026	847-486-9200	486-7451
Web: www.pioneerlocal.com					
Pipestone Publishing Co PO Box 277	Pipestone	MN	56164	507-825-3333	825-2168
TF: 800-325-6440 ■ *Web:* www.pipestonestar.com					
Pomerado Publishing Co PO Box 685	Poway	CA	92074	858-748-2311	748-7695
Web: www.pomeradonews.com					
Ponca City Publishing Inc PO Box 191	Ponca City	OK	74602	580-765-3311	762-6397
TF: 866-765-3311 ■ *Web:* www.poncacitynews.com					
Post Publishing Co PO Box 4639	Salisbury	NC	28145	704-633-8950	633-7373
TF: 800-633-8957 ■ *Web:* www.salisburypost.com					
Prescott George W Publishing Co Inc 400 Crown Colony Dr	Quincy	MA	02169	617-786-7000	786-7025
Web: www.southofboston.com					
Press of Atlantic City Media Group					
1000 W Washington Ave	Pleasantville	NJ	08232	609-272-7000	272-7724
Web: www.pressofatlanticcity.com					
Press Community Newspapers East & Northeast Group					
394 Wards Corner Suite 170	Loveland	OH	45140	513-248-8600	248-1938
Web: news.communitypress.com					
Press Community Newspapers West/Northwest Group					
5556 Cheviot Rd	Cincinnati	OH	45247	513-923-3111	923-1806
Web: news.communitypress.com					
Press-Enterprise Co PO Box 792	Riverside	CA	92502	951-684-1200	368-9022
TF: 800-933-1400 ■ *Web:* www.pe.com					
Press-Enterprise Inc 3185 Lackawanna Ave	Bloomsburg	PA	17815	570-784-2121	784-9226
TF: 800-228-3483 ■ *Web:* www.enterpe.com					
Press Publications 1101 W 31st St Suite 100	Downers Grove	IL	60515	630-368-1100	368-1188
Web: www.chicagosuburbannews.com					
Princeton Packet Inc PO Box 350	Princeton	NJ	08542	609-924-3244	924-3842
Web: www.pacpub.com					
Progressive Communications Corp 18 E Vine St	Mount Vernon	OH	43050	740-397-5333	397-1321
Web: www.mountvernonnews.com					
Progressive Publishing Co PO Box 291	Clearfield	PA	16830	814-765-5581	765-5165
Quebecor Media Inc 612 rue Saint-Jacques	Montreal	QC	H3C4M8	514-877-9777	594-8844
Web: www.quebecor.com					
Quincy Newspapers Inc 130 S 5th St	Quincy	IL	62301	217-223-5100	223-9757
TF: 800-373-9444 ■ *Web:* www.whig.com					
Recorder Publishing Co PO Box 687	Bernardsville	NJ	07924	908-766-3900	766-6365
Web: www.recordernewspapers.com					
Reminder Press Inc 130 Old Town Rd	Vernon	CT	06066	860-875-3366	872-4614
TF: 888-456-2211 ■ *Web:* www.remindernet.com					
Republican-American Inc 389 Meadow St	Waterbury	CT	06702	203-574-3636	596-9277
TF: 800-992-3232 ■ *Web:* www.rep-am.com					
Republican Co 1860 Main St	Springfield	MA	01103	413-788-1000	788-1301
Web: www.repub.com					
Richmond Newspapers Inc PO Box 85333	Richmond	VA	23293	804-649-6000	775-8046
TF: 800-468-3382 ■ *Web:* www.timesdispatch.com					
Rivertown Newspaper Group 2760 N Service Dr PO Box 15	Red Wing	MN	55066	651-388-8235	388-3404
TF: 800-535-1660 ■ *Web:* www.republican-eagle.com					
Roanoke Chowan Publishing PO Box 1325	Ahoskie	NC	27910	252-332-2123	332-3940
TF: 888-639-7437					
Rock Valley Publishing LLC 11512 N 2nd St	Machesney Park	IL	61115	815-877-4044	654-4857
Web: www.rvpublishing.com					
Rome Sentinel Co 333 W Dominick St	Rome	NY	13440	315-337-4000	339-6281
Web: www.rny.com					
Saint Joseph News Press & Gazette Co PO Box 29	Saint Joseph	MO	64502	816-271-8500	271-8692
TF: 800-779-6397					
Saint Lawrence County Newspapers PO Box 409	Ogdensburg	NY	13669	315-393-1000	393-5108
San Angelo Standard Times Inc PO Box 5111	San Angelo	TX	76902	325-653-1221	659-8173
TF: 800-588-1884 ■ *Web:* www.texaswest.com					
San Gabriel Valley Newspaper Group					
1210 N Azusa Canyon Rd	West Covina	CA	91790	626-962-8811	338-9157
Web: www.sgvn.com					
San Mateo Times Group Newspapers 1080 S Amphlett Blvd	San Mateo	CA	94402	650-348-4321	348-4446
TF: 800-843-6397					
Santa Barbara News-Press Publishing Co					
715 Anacapa St	Santa Barbara	CA	93101	805-564-5200	966-6258
TF: 800-654-3292 ■ *Web:* www.newspress.com					
Schurz Communications Inc 225 W Colfax Ave	South Bend	IN	46626	574-287-1001	287-2257
Web: www.schurz.com					
Scotsman Publishing Co 234 S Main St	Cambridge	MN	55008	763-689-1981	689-4372
TF: 800-473-1981 ■ *Web:* www.isanticountynews.com					
Scranton Times Co 149 Penn Ave	Scranton	PA	18503	570-348-9100	348-9135
TF: 800-228-4637 ■ *Web:* www.scrantontimes.com					
Scripps Howard Inc PO Box 5380	Cincinnati	OH	45202	513-977-3000	977-3721*
*Fax: PR ■ *TF:* 800-888-3000 ■ *Web:* www.scripps.com					
Scripps Marin Publishing Co PO Box 8	Novato	CA	94948	415-892-1516	897-0940
Web: www.novatoadvance.com					
Select Newspaper Group 138 Main St	Los Altos	CA	94022	650-948-4489	948-6647
Web: www.losaltosonline.com					
Sherman Edward A Publishing Co 101 Malbone Rd	Newport	RI	02840	401-849-3300	849-3306
TF: 800-320-2378					
Shore Line Newspapers 66 High St	Guilford	CT	06437	203-453-2711	453-4152
TF: 800-922-7066 ■ *Web:* www.shorelinetimes.com					
Singapore Press Holdings					
529 14th St NW National Press Bldg Suite 916	Washington	DC	20045	202-662-8726	662-8729
Web: www.sph.com.sg					
Sonoma Index-Tribune Inc 117 W Napa St	Sonoma	CA	95476	707-938-2111	938-1600
Web: www.sonomanews.com					
Sound Publishing Inc 7689 NE Day Rd	Bainbridge Island	WA	98110	206-842-8305	842-8030
Web: www.soundpublishing.com					
South Jersey Shopper's Guide Inc 8 Ranoldo Terr	Cherry Hill	NJ	08034	856-616-4900	616-0305
TF: 800-229-8775 ■ *Web:* www.theshoppersguide.com					
Southern Connecticut Newspapers Inc 75 Tresser Blvd	Stamford	CT	06901	203-964-2200	964-2345
Web: www.stamfordadvocate.com					
Southern Newspapers Inc 5701 Woodway Dr Suite 300	Houston	TX	77057	713-266-5481	266-1847
Web: www.sninews.com					
Star Community Publishing Group 250 Miller Pl	Hicksville	NY	11801	516-393-9300	812-3759
Web: www.starcpg.com					
Star-News Newspapers PO Box 840	Wilmington	NC	28402	910-343-2296	343-2229
TF: 800-222-2385 ■ *Web:* www.starnewsonline.com					
Star-News Publishing Co 321 E St	Chula Vista	CA	91910	619-427-3000	426-6346
Web: www.thestarnews.com					
Star Publications 6901 W 159th St	Tinley Park	IL	60477	708-802-8800	802-8088
Web: www.starnewspapers.com					
Stephens Media Group 1111 W Bonanza Rd	Las Vegas	NV	89106	702-383-0211	
Web: www.stephensmedia.com					
Stonebridge Press Inc 25 Elm St	Southbridge	MA	01550	508-764-4325	764-8015
TF: 800-536-5836					
Suburban Chicago Newspapers 1500 W Ogden Ave	Naperville	IL	60540	630-355-0063	416-5163
Web: www.suburbanchicagonews.com/sunpub					
Suburban News Publications 5257 Sinclair Rd	Columbus	OH	43229	614-785-1212	842-4760
Web: www.snponline.com					
Suburban Newspapers of Greater Saint Louis					
14522 S Outer 40 Dr	Town & Country	MO	63017	314-821-1110	821-0843
Suffolk Life Newspapers PO Box 9167	Riverhead	NY	11901	631-369-0800	591-5190
Sun Co 2239 Garnet Pkwy	San Bernardino	CA	92407	909-889-9666	885-8741
TF: 800-548-5448 ■ *Web:* www.sbsun.com					
Sun Media Corp 333 King St E	Toronto	ON	M5A3X5	416-947-2222	947-1664
Web: www.sunmedia.ca					
Sun Newspapers 5510 Cloverleaf Pkwy	Cleveland	OH	44125	216-986-2600	986-2380
TF: 800-362-8008 ■ *Web:* www.sunnews.com					
Sun Post Newspaper Group 1688 Meridian Ave Suite 404	Miami Beach	FL	33139	305-538-9700	538-6077
TF: 888-769-7678 ■ *Web:* www.miamisunpost.com					
Sun Publications 4370 W 109 St Suite 300	Overland Park	KS	66210	913-381-1010	381-9889
Web: www.sunpublications.com					
Sun Publishing Corp 201 N Thorp St	Hobbs	NM	88240	505-393-2123	393-5724
TF: 800-993-2123					
Sun-Sentinel Co 200 E Las Olas Blvd	Fort Lauderdale	FL	33301	954-356-4000	356-4559
TF: 800-548-6397 ■ *Web:* www.sun-sentinel.com					
Sunpress Inc PO Box 187	Dade City	FL	33526	352-567-5639	567-5640
Swift Newspapers Inc 500 Double Eagle Ct	Reno	NV	89521	775-850-7676	850-7677
Web: www.swiftnews.com					
Tacoma News Inc 1950 S State St	Tacoma	WA	98405	253-597-8742	597-8274
Web: www.thenewstribune.com					
TB Butler Publishing Co 410 W Erwin St	Tyler	TX	75702	903-597-8111	595-0335
TF: 800-333-9141 ■ *Web:* www.tylerpaper.com					
TDN Publishing Co 224 S Market St	Troy	OH	45373	937-335-5634	335-3552
Web: www.tdn-net.com					
Tennessee Valley Printing Co Inc PO Box 2213	Decatur	AL	35609	256-353-4612	340-2392
TF: 888-353-4612 ■ *Web:* www.decaturdaily.com					
Terry Newspapers Inc 108 W 1st St	Geneseo	IL	61254	309-944-2119	944-5615
TF: 888-422-3837					
This Week Community Newspapers 7801 N Central Dr	Lewis Center	OH	43035	740-888-6000	888-6006
Web: www.thisweeknews.com					
Tidings Inc 3424 Wilshire Blvd 6th Fl	Los Angeles	CA	90010	213-637-7360	637-6360
Web: www.the-tidings.com					
Time-Press Publishing Co 115 Oak St	Streator	IL	61364	815-673-3771	672-0623
Web: www.times-press.com					
Times Herald Inc 410 Markley St PO Box 591	Norristown	PA	19404	610-272-2500	272-0660
TF: 800-887-2501 ■ *Web:* www.timesherald.com					
Times News Publishing Co 707 S Main St	Burlington	NC	27215	336-227-0131	229-2462
TF: 800-488-0085 ■ *Web:* www.thetimesnews.com					
Times & News Publishing Co PO Box 3669	Gettysburg	PA	17325	717-334-1131	334-4243
Web: www.gettysburgtimes.com					
Times Publishing Co PO Box 1121	Saint Petersburg	FL	33731	727-893-8111	893-8675
Times Publishing Co 222 Lake St	Shreveport	LA	71101	318-459-3200	459-3528
TF: 800-525-4335 ■ *Web:* www.shreveporttimes.com					
Topics Newspapers 13095 Publishers Dr	Fishers	IN	46038	317-444-5500	444-5550
Web: www.topics.com					
Torstar Corp 1 Yonge St Suite 600	Toronto	ON	M5E1P9	416-869-4010	869-4183
TSX: TS.B ■ *Web:* www.torstar.com					
Trader Publications Inc 105 Kisco Ave	Mount Kisco	NY	10549	914-666-6222	666-6013
TF: 800-689-5933					
Tri-City Herald Co PO Box 2608	Tri-Cities	WA	99302	509-582-1500	582-1510
Web: www.tri-cityherald.com					
Tribune Co 435 N Michigan Ave	Chicago	IL	60611	312-222-9100	329-0611
NYSE: TRB ■ *Web:* www.tribune.com					
Tribune Review Publishing Co 622 Cabin Hill Dr	Greensburg	PA	15601	724-834-1151	838-5171
TF: 800-433-3045					
Troy Publishing Co 501 Broadway	Troy	NY	12180	518-270-1200	270-1251
TF: 800-934-4304					
Truth Publishing Co Inc 421 S 2nd St	Elkhart	IN	46516	574-294-1661	294-3895
TF: 800-585-5416 ■ *Web:* www.etruth.com					
Union-Tribune Publishing Co PO Box 120191	San Diego	CA	92112	619-299-3131	293-1896
TF: 800-244-6397					
Uniontown Newspapers Inc 8-18 E Church St	Uniontown	PA	15401	724-439-7500	439-7528
TF: 800-342-8254					
Village Voice Media Inc 36 Cooper Sq	New York	NY	10003	212-475-3300	475-8473
Web: villagevoicemedia.com					
Wappingers Falls Shopper Inc 84 E Main St	Wappingers Falls	NY	12590	845-297-3723	297-6810
Wave Newspaper Group 2401 Wilshire Blvd Suite 600	Los Angeles	CA	90010	323-556-5720	556-5704
Web: www.wavenewspapers.com					
Wayne Printing Co Inc 310 N Berkeley Blvd	Goldsboro	NC	27534	919-778-2211	778-5408
Web: www.newsargus.com					
Wehco Media Inc 115 E Capitol Ave	Little Rock	AR	72201	501-378-3543	372-4765
West Virginia Newspaper Publishing Co					
1251 Earl L Core Rd	Morgantown	WV	26505	304-292-6301	291-2326
TF: 800-654-4676 ■ *Web:* olive.dominionpost.com					
Western Communications Inc 1777 SW Chandler Ave	Bend	OR	97702	541-382-1811	383-0372
Web: www.bendbulletin.com					
Western States Weeklies Inc PO Box 600600	San Diego	CA	92160	619-280-2985	280-2989
TF: 800-280-2985 ■ *Web:* www.navydispatch.com					
Whitcom Partners 375 Park Ave 38th Fl	New York	NY	10152	212-582-2300	582-2310
Wick Communications Inc 333 W Wilcox Dr Suite 302	Sierra Vista	AZ	85635	520-458-0200	458-6166
TF: 800-777-9425 ■ *Web:* www.wickcommunications.com					
William B Collins Co 8 E Fulton St	Gloversville	NY	12078	518-725-8616	725-7350
William J Kline & Son Inc 1 Venner Rd	Amsterdam	NY	12010	518-843-1100	843-1338
TF: 800-453-6397 ■ *Web:* www.recordernews.com					
Wooster Republican Printing Co 212 E Liberty St	Wooster	OH	44691	330-264-1125	264-3756
Worcester Telegram & Gazette Inc PO Box 15012	Worcester	MA	01615	508-793-9100	793-9281
TF: 800-678-6680 ■ *Web:* www.telegram.com					
World Publishing Co 315 S Boulder Ave	Tulsa	OK	74102	918-583-2161	581-8353
Web: www.tulsaworld.com					
Yankton Printing Co PO Box 56	Yankton	SD	57078	605-665-7811	665-1721
TF: 800-743-2968 ■ *Web:* www.yankton.com					

Newspaper Publishers (Cont'd)

Phone | Fax

York Newspaper Co 1891 Loucks Rd ... York PA 17408 717-767-6397 764-6233
Web: www.ync.com
Yorktown Printing & Pennysaver Corp 1520 Front St ... Yorktown Heights NY 10598 914-962-3871 962-5123
Web: www.nypennysaver.com
Zerbey JH Newspapers Inc 111 Mahantongo St ... Pottsville PA 17901 570-622-3456 628-6092

640-9 Periodicals Publishers

Phone | Fax

1105 Media Inc 9121 Oakdale Ave Suite 101 ... Chatsworth CA 91311 818-734-1520 734-1522
Web: www.1105media.com
ABC Inc 77 W 66th St ... New York NY 10023 212-456-7777 456-2795
Web: abc.go.com
Access Intelligence LLC 4 Choke Cherry Rd 2nd Fl ... Rockville MD 20850 301-354-2000 738-8453
TF: 800-777-5006 ■ *Web:* www.accessintel.com
Advance Publications Inc 950 Fingerboard Rd ... Staten Island NY 10305 718-981-1234 981-5679
Advanstar Communications Inc 7500 Old Oak Blvd ... Cleveland OH 44130 440-243-8100 891-2651
TF: 800-225-4569 ■ *Web:* web.advanstar.com
Advanstar Veterinary Healthcare Communications 8033 Flint St ... Lenexa KS 66214 913-492-4300 492-4157
TF: 800-255-6864 ■ *Web:* www.vetmedpub.com
Advertising Specialties Institute 4800 Street Rd ... Trevose PA 19053 215-942-8600 829-9240*
**Fax Area Code:* 800 ■ *TF:* 800-546-1350 ■ *Web:* www.asicentral.com
Advisor Media Inc 4849 Viewridge Ave ... San Diego CA 92123 858-278-5600 278-0300
TF: 800-336-6060 ■ *Web:* advisor.com
Adweek Directories 770 Broadway ... New York NY 10003 646-654-5000 654-5362
Web: www.adweek.com
Affinity Group Inc 2575 Vista Del Mar ... Ventura CA 93001 805-667-4100 667-4298
Web: www.affinitygroup.com
Agora Publishing Inc 14 W Monument St ... Baltimore MD 21201 410-783-8499
TF: 800-433-1528 ■ *Web:* www.agora-inc.com
Alexander Communications Group Inc
712 Main St Suite 187-B ... Boonton NJ 07005 973-265-2300 402-6056
TF: 800-232-4317 ■ *Web:* www.alexcommgrp.com
Alexander Hamilton Institute Inc 70 Hilltop Rd ... Ramsey NJ 07446 201-825-3377 825-8696
TF Orders: 800-879-2441 ■ *Web:* www.ahipubs.com
American Banker Newsletters 1 State St Plaza 27th Fl ... New York NY 10004 212-803-8200 803-1592
TF: 800-221-1809 ■ *Web:* www.americanbanker.com
American Banker/Bond Buyer 1 State Street Plaza 26th Fl ... New York NY 10004 212-803-8200 264-6826*
**Fax Area Code:* 646 ■ **Fax:* Hum Res ■ *TF:* 800-362-3807 ■
Web: www.americanbanker.com
American City Business Journals Inc
120 W Moorehead St Suite 400 ... Charlotte NC 28202 704-973-1000 973-1001
TF: 800-704-3757 ■ *Web:* www.bizjournals.com
American Lawyer Media Inc 345 Park Ave S 8th Fl ... New York NY 10010 212-779-9200 481-8255
TF: 800-888-8300 ■ *Web:* www.alm.com
American Media Inc 1000 American Media Way ... Boca Raton FL 33464 561-997-7733 998-7235
TF: 800-749-7733
Americas Publishing Co 2900 NW 39th St ... Miami FL 33142 305-633-3341 635-4002
Amos Press Inc PO Box 4129 ... Sidney OH 45365 937-498-2111 498-0888
TF: 800-327-1259 ■ *Web:* www.amospress.com
Annual Reviews 4139 El Camino Way ... Palo Alto CA 94303 650-493-4400 855-9815
TF: 800-523-8635 ■ *Web:* www.annurev.org
APN Media LLC 1775 Broadway Suite 622 ... New York NY 10019 212-581-3380 245-4226
Web: www.americanparknetwork.com
Army Times Publishing Co 6883 Commercial Dr ... Springfield VA 22159 703-750-9000 750-8622
TF: 800-424-9335 ■ *Web:* www.atpco.com
AS Pratt & Sons 1725 K St NW Suite 700 ... Washington DC 20006 800-524-2003 739-9511*
**Fax Area Code:* 202 ■ *TF Cust Svc:* 800-945-6597 ■ *Web:* www.aspratt.com
Aspen Publishers Inc 111 8th Ave 7th Fl ... New York NY 10011 212-771-0600 597-0335
TF Orders: 800-447-1717 ■ *Web:* www.aspenpublishers.com
Athlon Sports Communications Inc 220 25th Ave N Suite 200 ... Nashville TN 37203 615-327-0747 327-1149
Web: www.athlonsports.com
Atlantic Information Services Inc
1100 17th St NW Suite 300 ... Washington DC 20036 202-775-9008 331-9542
TF: 800-521-4323 ■ *Web:* www.aishealth.com
Augsburg Fortress Publishers PO Box 1209 ... Minneapolis MN 55440 612-330-3300 330-3455
TF: 800-426-0115 ■ *Web:* www.augsburgfortress.org
Babcox Publications Inc 3550 Embassy Pkwy ... Akron OH 44333 330-670-1234 670-0874
Web: www.babcox.com
Bauer Publishing Co LP 270 Sylvan Ave ... Englewood Cliffs NJ 07632 201-569-6699 569-5303
Web: www.bauerpublishing.com
BCC Research 40 Washington St Suite 110 ... Wellesley MA 02481 781-489-7301 489-7308
TF: 866-285-7215 ■ *Web:* www.bccresearch.com
Becker Communications 119 Merchant St Suite 300 ... Honolulu HI 96813 808-533-4165 537-4990
Web: www.beckercommunications.com
Benjamin Franklin Literary & Medical Society Inc
1100 Waterway Blvd ... Indianapolis IN 46202 317-636-8881 637-0126
TF: 800-558-2376
Bertelsmann Publishing Group Inc 1745 Broadway ... New York NY 10019 212-782-1000 782-1010
Web: www.bertelsmann.com
Bland William F Co 709 Turmeric Ln ... Durham NC 27713 919-544-1717 544-1999
Bloomberg LP 731 Lexington Ave ... New York NY 10022 212-318-2000 893-5000
Web: www.bloomberg.com
Boardroom Inc 281 Tresser Blvd 8th Fl ... Stamford CT 06901 203-973-5900 967-3086
Web: www.boardroom.com
Bobit Business Media 3520 Challenger St ... Torrance CA 90503 310-533-2400 533-2508*
**Fax:* Hum Res ■ *Web:* www.bobit.com
Boucher Communications Inc
1300 Virginia Dr Suite 400 ... Fort Washington PA 19034 215-643-8000 643-3902
Web: www.boucher1.com
Bureau of National Affairs Inc 1231 25th St NW ... Washington DC 20037 202-452-4200 452-4610
TF: 800-372-1033 ■ *Web:* www.bna.com
Business & Legal Reports Inc 141 Mill Rock Rd E ... Old Saybrook CT 06475 860-510-0100 510-7225
TF: 800-727-5257 ■ *Web:* www.blr.com
Business News Publishing Co 2401 W Big Beaver Rd Suite 700 ... Troy MI 48084 248-362-3700 362-0317
TF: 800-837-7370 ■ *Web:* www.bnpmedia.com
Business Publishers Inc 2272 Airport Rd S ... Naples FL 34112 800-274-6737 587-1081*
**Fax Area Code:* 301 ■ *TF:* 800-274-6737 ■ *Web:* www.bpinews.com
Buyers Laboratory Inc 20 Railroad Ave ... Hackensack NJ 07601 201-488-0404 488-0461
Web: www.buyerslab.com
Careers & Colleges 2 LAN Dr Suite 100 ... Westford MA 01886 978-692-5092 692-4174
Web: www.careersandcolleges.com
CCH Inc 2700 Lake Cook Rd ... Riverwoods IL 60015 847-267-7000 267-2516
TF Cust Svc: 800-835-5224 ■ *Web:* www.cch.com
CD Publications 8204 Fenton St ... Silver Spring MD 20910 301-588-6380 588-0519
TF: 800-666-6380 ■ *Web:* www.cdpublications.com
Century Publishing Co 990 Grove St 4th Fl ... Evanston IL 60201 847-491-6440 491-0459
Web: www.centurysports.net
Challenge Publications Inc 9509 Vassar Ave Suite A ... Chatsworth CA 91311 818-700-6868 700-6282
TF: 800-562-9182 ■ *Web:* www.challengeweb.com
Chartcraft Inc 30 Church St ... New Rochelle NY 10801 914-632-0422 632-0335
Chemical Week Assoc 110 William St ... New York NY 10038 800-774-5733 621-4949*
**Fax Area Code:* 212 ■ *TF:* 800-774-5733 ■ *Web:* www.chemweek.com

Phone | Fax

Children's Better Health Institute 1100 Waterway Blvd ... Indianapolis IN 46202 317-636-8881 684-8094
TF: 800-558-2376 ■ *Web:* www.cbhi.org
Christian Board of Publication 1221 Locust St Suite 670 ... Saint Louis MO 63103 314-231-8500 231-8524
TF: 800-366-3383 ■ *Web:* www.cbp21.com
Christianity Today Inc 465 Gundersen Dr ... Carol Stream IL 60188 630-260-6200 260-0114
Web: www.christianitytoday.com
Cliggott Publishing Group 330 Boston Post Rd ... Darien CT 06820 203-662-6400 662-6776
CMP Media LLC 600 Community Dr ... Manhasset NY 11030 516-562-5000 562-5196*
**Fax:* Cust Svc ■ *TF:* 800-645-6278 ■ *Web:* www.cmp.com
Cobblestone Publishing Co 30 Grove St Suite C ... Peterborough NH 03458 603-924-7209 924-7380
TF: 800-821-0115 ■ *Web:* www.cobblestonepub.com
CollegeBound Network 1200 South Ave Suite 202 ... Staten Island NY 10314 718-761-4800 761-3300
Web: www.collegebound.net
Commodity Information Systems Inc
3030 Northwest Expy Suite 725 ... Oklahoma City OK 73112 405-604-8726 604-9696
TF: 800-231-0477 ■ *Web:* www.cis-okc.com
Commonwealth Business Media Inc
50 Millstone Rd Bldg 400 Suite 200 ... East Windsor NJ 08520 609-371-7700 371-7873
TF: 888-215-6084 ■ *Web:* www.cbizmedia.com
Communications International 630 5th Ave Suite 2109 ... New York NY 10111 212-218-7525 218-7527
Computer Economics Inc 2082 Business Center Dr Suite 240 ... Irvine CA 92612 949-831-8700 442-7688
Web: www.computereconomics.com
Conde Nast Publications Inc 4 Times Sq ... New York NY 10036 212-286-2860
TF: 800-223-0780 ■ *Web:* www.condenast.com
Congressional Quarterly Inc 1255 22nd St NW ... Washington DC 20037 202-419-8500 380-3810*
**Fax Area Code:* 800 ■ *TF:* 800-432-2250 ■ *Web:* www.cq.com
Connell Communications Inc 86 Elm St ... Peterborough NH 03458 603-924-7271 924-7013
TF: 800-677-8847
Conscious Media Inc 360 Interlocken Blvd Suite 300 ... Broomfield CO 80021 303-222-8200 222-3850
Web: www.consciousmedianetwork.com
Consumers Digest Inc 520 Lake Cook Rd Suite 500 ... Deerfield IL 60015 847-607-3000 763-0200
Consumers Union of US Inc 101 Truman Ave ... Yonkers NY 10703 914-378-2300 378-2906
TF: 800-234-1645 ■ *Web:* www.consumersunion.org
Cook Communications Ministries
4050 Lee Vance View ... Colorado Springs CO 80918 719-536-0100 536-3265
TF: 800-708-5550 ■ *Web:* www.davidccook.com
Cox Auto Trader Publishing Co 100 W Plume St ... Norfolk VA 23510 757-531-7700 470-5800
Web: www.traderonline.com
Crain Communications Inc 1155 Gratiot Ave ... Detroit MI 48207 313-446-6000 259-8454*
**Fax:* Hum Res ■ *Web:* www.crain.com
CRC Press LLC 6000 Broken Sound Pkwy NW Suite 300 ... Boca Raton FL 33487 561-994-0555 374-3401*
**Fax Area Code:* 800 ■ **Fax:* Cust Svc ■ *TF Cust Svc:* 800-272-7737 ■
Web: www.crcpress.com
Cutter Information Corp 37 Broadway Suite 1 ... Arlington MA 02474 781-648-8700 648-8707
TF: 800-964-5118 ■ *Web:* www.cutter.com
Cygnus Business Media Inc
3 Huntington Quadrangle Suite 301-N ... Melville NY 11747 631-845-2700 845-7109
TF: 800-547-7377 ■ *Web:* www.cygnusb2b.com
DataTrends Publications Inc PO Box 4460 ... Leesburg VA 20177 703-779-0574 779-2267
Web: www.stemcellresearchnews.com
Davis Dick Publishing Co PO Box 26774 ... Tamarac FL 33320 954-724-9826 724-2952
TF: 800-654-1514 ■ *Web:* www.dickdavis.com
Deal LLC 105 Madison Ave 4th Fl ... New York NY 10016 212-313-9200 313-9293
TF Cust Svc: 888-667-3325 ■ *Web:* www.thedeal.com
Dekker Marcel Inc 270 Madison Ave ... New York NY 10016 212-696-9000 685-4540
TF Sales: 800-228-1160 ■ *Web:* www.dekker.com
Dell Magazines 475 Park Ave S 11th Fl ... New York NY 10016 212-686-7188 686-7414
TF: 800-220-7443 ■ *Web:* www.dellmagazines.com
Desert Publications Inc
303 N Indian Canyon Dr PO Box 2724 ... Palm Springs CA 92262 760-325-2333 325-7008
TF: 800-775-7256 ■ *Web:* www.desertpublications.com
Dick Davis Publishing Co PO Box 26774 ... Tamarac FL 33320 954-724-9826 724-2952
TF: 800-654-1514 ■ *Web:* www.dickdavis.com
Disney Consumer Products 500 S Buena Vista St ... Burbank CA 91521 818-560-1000 560-1930*
**Fax:* Cust Svc ■ *TF PR:* 800-723-4763
Disney Magazine Publishing 114 5th Ave ... New York NY 10011 212-633-4400 633-4809
TF: 800-333-8734
Diversified Business Communications 121 Free St ... Portland ME 04101 207-842-5400 842-5505
TF: 800-842-5404 ■ *Web:* www.divbusiness.com
Doane Agricultural Services 77 Westport Plaza Suite 250 ... Saint Louis MO 63146 314-569-2700 569-1083
TF: 800-535-2342 ■ *Web:* www.doane.com
Earl G Graves Ltd 130 5th Ave 10th Fl ... New York NY 10011 212-242-8000 886-9610
TF: 800-727-7777
Economist Intelligence Unit 111 W 57th St 7th Fl ... New York NY 10019 212-554-0600 586-1181
TF: 800-938-4685 ■ *Web:* www.eiu.com
Editorial Projects in Education Inc
6935 Arlington Rd Suite 100 ... Bethesda MD 20814 301-280-3100 280-3200
Web: www.edweek.org
EGW Publishing Co Inc 4075 Papazian Way Suite 208 ... Fremont CA 94538 510-668-0268 668-0280
TF Cust Svc: 800-546-4754 ■ *Web:* www.egw.com
Ehlert Publishing Group Inc
6420 Sycamore Ln N Suite 100 ... Maple Grove MN 55369 763-383-4400 383-4499
TF: 800-848-6247 ■ *Web:* www.ehlertmedia.com
Eli Journals 2272 Airport Rd ... Naples FL 34112 239-280-2307 508-2592*
**Fax Area Code:* 800 ■ *TF:* 800-508-2582 ■ *Web:* www.elementkjournals.com
Elliott Wave International PO Box 1618 ... Gainesville GA 30503 770-536-0309 536-2514
TF Sales: 800-336-1618 ■ *Web:* www.elliottwave.com
Elsevier Science Ltd 360 Park Ave S ... New York NY 10010 212-989-5800 633-3990
TF: 888-437-4636 ■ *Web:* www.elsevier.com
Energy Intelligence Group 5 E 37th St 5th Fl ... New York NY 10016 212-532-1112 532-4838
TF: 888-427-7496 ■ *Web:* www.energyintel.com
Entrepreneur Media Inc 2445 McCabe Way Suite 440 ... Irvine CA 92614 949-261-2325 261-7729
Web: www.entrepreneur.com
EPM Communications Inc 160 Mercer St 3rd Fl ... New York NY 10012 212-941-0099 941-1622
TF: 888-852-9467 ■ *Web:* www.epmcom.com
Ernst Publishing Co LLC 1937 Delaware Tpke Suite B ... Clarksville NY 12041 800-345-3822 252-0906
Web: www.ernstpublishing.com
Essence Communications Inc 1500 Broadway 6th Fl ... New York NY 10036 212-642-0600 921-5173
TF Circ: 800-274-9398 ■ *Web:* www.essence.com
F & W Publications Inc 4700 E Galbraith Rd ... Cincinnati OH 45236 513-531-2690 686-8174
TF Sales: 800-289-0963 ■ *Web:* www.fwpublications.com
Fairchild Publications Inc 750 3rd Ave ... New York NY 10017 212-630-4000 630-3566*
**Fax:* Edit ■ *Web:* www.fairchildpub.com
Famfare Media Works Inc 25300 Rye Canyon Rd ... Valencia CA 91355 661-257-4000 600-0762
TF: 800-935-0090 ■ *Web:* www.fanfaremedia.com
Farm Progress Co Inc 191 S Gary Ave ... Carol Stream IL 60188 630-690-5600 462-2869
TF: 800-441-1410 ■ *Web:* www.farmprogress.com
FCN Publishing 1725 K St NW Suite 506 ... Washington DC 20006 202-887-6320 887-6335
TF: 888-732-7070 ■ *Web:* www.fcnpublishing.com
FDC Reports Inc 5635 Fishers Ln Suite 6000 ... Rockville MD 20852 240-221-4500 221-4400
TF: 800-332-2181 ■ *Web:* www.fdcreports.com
First Marketing 3300 Gateway Dr ... Pompano Beach FL 33069 954-979-0700 971-4884
TF: 800-641-9251 ■ *Web:* www.first-marketing.com
Flynt Larry Publications Inc 8484 Wilshire Blvd Suite 900 ... Beverly Hills CA 90211 323-651-5400 651-3525
Forbes Inc 60 5th Ave ... New York NY 10011 212-620-2200 206-5534
TF: 800-888-9896 ■ *Web:* www.forbes.com

Phone Fax

Forecast International/DMS Inc 22 Commerce Rd .... Newtown CT 06470 203-426-0800 426-4262
TF: 800-451-4975 ■ *Web:* www.forecast1.com
Forum Publishing Co 383 E Main St .... Centerport NY 11721 631-754-5000 754-0630
TF: 800-635-7654 ■ *Web:* www.forum123.com
Frequent Flyer Services 1930 Frequent Flyer Pt .... Colorado Springs CO 80915 719-597-8889 597-6855
TF: 800-209-2870 ■ *Web:* www.frequentflyerservices.com
Gannett Co Inc 7950 Jones Branch Dr .... McLean VA 22107 703-854-6000
NYSE: GCI ■ *Web:* www.gannett.com
Gardner Publications Inc 6915 Valley Ave .... Cincinnati OH 45244 513-527-8800 527-8801
TF: 800-950-8020 ■ *Web:* www.gardnerweb.com
Gemstar-TV Guide International Inc 6922 Hollywood Blvd .... Hollywood CA 90028 323-817-4600 817-4629
NASDAQ: GMST ■ *Web:* www.gemstartvguide.com
Government Information Services 1725 K St NW Suite 700 .... Washington DC 20006 202-872-4000 296-1091
TF: 800-677-3789
Grand View Media Group Inc 200 Croft St Suite 1 .... Birmingham AL 35242 205-408-3700 408-3798
TF: 888-431-2877 ■ *Web:* www.grandviewmedia.com
Grass Roots Publishing Co Inc
Hochman Assoc 908 Oaktree Rd Suite H .... South Plainfield NJ 07080 908-222-1811 222-8228
TF: 877-207-9007
Graves Earl G Ltd 130 5th Ave 10th Fl .... New York NY 10011 212-242-8000 886-9610
TF: 800-727-7777
Greater Washington Publishing Inc 1919 Gallows Rd Suite 200 .... Vienna VA 22182 703-992-1100 893-8356
Web: www.gwpi.net
Guest Informant Inc 21200 Erwin St .... Woodland Hills CA 91367 818-716-7484 716-7583
TF: 800-275-5885 ■ *Web:* www.guestinformant.com
Guideposts Inc 39 Seminary Hill Rd .... Carmel NY 10512 845-225-3681 228-2115
TF Cust Svc: 800-431-2344 ■ *Web:* www.guideposts.org
Gulf Publishing Co Inc 2 Greenway Plaza Suite 1020 .... Houston TX 77046 713-529-4301 520-4433
TF: 800-231-6275 ■ *Web:* www.gulfpub.com
Hachette Filipacchi Media US Inc 1633 Broadway .... New York NY 10019 212-767-6000 767-5600
Web: www.hfmus.com
Hanley-Wood LLC 1 Thomas Cir NW Suite 600 .... Washington DC 20005 202-452-0800 785-1974
TF: 800-636-0336 ■ *Web:* www.hanleywood.com
Hart Publications Inc 1616 S Voss Rd Suite 1000 .... Houston TX 77057 713-993-9320 840-8585
TF: 800-874-2544 ■ *Web:* www.hartenergynetwork.com
Hatton Brown Publishing Co 225 Hanrick St .... Montgomery AL 36104 334-834-1170 834-4525
TF: 800-669-5613 ■ *Web:* www.hattonbrown.com
Health Forum 1 N Franklin St 29th Fl .... Chicago IL 60606 312-893-6800 422-4506
TF: 800-621-6902
Healthy Directions LLC 7811 Montrose Rd .... Potomac MD 20854 301-340-2100 251-3758*
**Fax:* Hum Res ■ *TF:* 800-777-5015 ■ *Web:* www.healthydirections.com
Hearst Business Media 300 W 57th St .... New York NY 10019 212-649-2000
Web: hearstcorp.com/business_media
Hearst Corp 1345 6th Ave .... New York NY 10105 212-649-2000 280-1045*
**Fax Area Code:* 646 ■ **Fax:* Hum Res ■ *Web:* www.hearstcorp.com
Hearst Magazines Div 300 W 57th St .... New York NY 10019 212-649-2000
TF: 800-678-7767 ■ *Web:* hearstcorp.com/magazines
Highlights for Children Inc 1800 Watermark Dr .... Columbus OH 43215 614-486-0631 487-2700
TF Cust Svc: 800-255-9517 ■ *Web:* www.highlights.com
Hobsons CollegeView 50 E Business Way Suite 300 .... Cincinnati OH 45241 513-891-5444 891-6222
TF: 800-927-8439 ■ *Web:* www.collegeview.com
Homes & Land Magazine Affiliates LLC 1830 E Park Ave .... Tallahassee FL 32301 850-574-2111 575-9567
TF: 800-726-6683 ■ *Web:* www.homesandland.com
Honolulu Publishing Co Ltd 707 Richards St Suite 525 .... Honolulu HI 96813 808-524-7400 531-2306
TF: 800-272-5245 ■ *Web:* www.honpub.com
Horizon House Publications Inc 685 Canton St .... Norwood MA 02062 781-769-9750 762-9071
TF: 800-225-9977 ■ *Web:* www.horizonhouse.com
House of White Birches Inc 306 E Parr Rd .... Berne IN 46711 260-589-8741 589-8093
TF: 800-347-9887 ■ *Web:* www.whitebirches.com
HW Wilson Co 950 University Ave .... Bronx NY 10452 718-588-8400 590-1617*
**Fax:* Cust Svc ■ *TF:* 800-367-6770 ■ *Web:* www.hwwilson.com
IDG (International Data Group Inc) 1 Exeter Plaza 15th Fl .... Boston MA 02116 617-534-1200 859-8642
Web: www.idg.com
IEEE Computer Society Publications Office
10662 Los Vaqueros Cir .... Los Alamitos CA 90720 714-821-8380 821-4010
TF: 800-272-6657 ■ *Web:* www.computer.org/cspress
Information Today Inc 143 Old Marlton Pike .... Medford NJ 08055 609-654-6266 654-6760
TF: 800-300-9868 ■ *Web:* www.infotoday.com
InfoWorld Media Group Inc 501 2nd St Suite 120 .... San Francisco CA 94107 415-243-4344 453-2200
TF: 800-227-8365 ■ *Web:* www.infoworld.com
Inside Washington Publishers Inc
1225 South Clark St Suite 1400 .... Arlington VA 22202 703-416-8500 416-8543
TF: 800 424 9068 ■ *Web:* www.iwpnews.com
Institute of Management & Administration Inc (IOMA Inc)
3 Park Ave 30th Fl .... New York NY 10016 212-244-0360 564-0465
TF: 800-401-5937 ■ *Web:* www.ioma.com
Institutional Investor Inc 225 Park Ave S 7th Fl .... New York NY 10003 212-224-3300 224-3171
Web: www.dailyii.com
Institutional Investor Newsletters 225 Park Ave S 8th Fl .... New York NY 10003 212-224-3800 224-3491*
**Fax:* Cust Svc ■ *TF:* 800-715-9197 ■ *Web:* www.iinews.com
International Data Group Inc (IDG) 1 Exeter Plaza 15th Fl .... Boston MA 02116 617-534-1200 859-8642
Web: www.idg.com
International Scientific Communications Inc (ISC Inc)
30 Controls Dr PO Box 870 .... Shelton CT 06484 203-926-9300 926-9310
Web: www.iscpubs.com
Internet Business Network 303 Ross Dr .... Mill Valley CA 94941 415-377-2255 380-8245
Web: www.interbiznet.com
IOMA Inc (Institute of Management & Administration Inc)
3 Park Ave 30th Fl .... New York NY 10016 212-244-0360 564-0465
TF: 800-401-5937 ■ *Web:* www.ioma.com
ISC Inc (International Scientific Communications Inc)
30 Controls Dr PO Box 870 .... Shelton CT 06484 203-926-9300 926-9310
Web: www.iscpubs.com
Johnson Publishing Co Inc 820 S Michigan Ave .... Chicago IL 60605 312-322-9200 322-0951
Web: www.johnsonpublishing.com
Jossey-Bass & Pfeiffer 989 Market St 5th Fl .... San Francisco CA 94103 415-782-3100 433-0499
Web: www.josseybass.com
Journal of Commerce Group 33 Washington St 13th Fl .... Newark NJ 07102 973-848-7000 848-7167*
**Fax:* Edit ■ *TF Cust Svc:* 800-223-0243 ■ *Web:* www.joc.com
JR O'Dwyer Co 271 Madison Ave 6th Fl .... New York NY 10016 212-679-2471 683-2750
TF: 866-395-7710 ■ *Web:* www.odwyerpr.com
Kagan Research LLC 1 Lower Ragsdale Dr Bldg 1 Suite 130 .... Monterey CA 93940 831-624-1536 625-3225
TF: 800-307-2529 ■ *Web:* www.kagan.com
Kalmbach Publishing Co 21027 Crossroads Cir .... Waukesha WI 53186 262-796-8776 796-1615
TF Cust Svc: 800-446-5489 ■ *Web:* www.kalmbach.com
KCI Communications 7600 Leesburg Pike 300 West Bldg .... Falls Church VA 22043 703-905-8000 905-8100
TF Cust Svc: 800-832-2330 ■ *Web:* www.kci-com.com
Kennedy Information 1 Phoenix Mill Ln 3rd Fl .... Peterborough NH 03458 603-924-0900 924-4034
TF: 800-531-0007 ■ *Web:* www.kennedyinfo.com
Kiplinger Washington Editors Inc 1729 H St NW .... Washington DC 20006 202-887-6400 331-1206
TF: 800-544-0155 ■ *Web:* www.kiplinger.com
Krause Publications Inc 700 E State St .... Iola WI 54990 715-445-2214 445-4087
TF Cust Svc: 800-942-0673 ■ *Web:* www.krause.com
Laurin Publishing Co Inc 2 South St .... Pittsfield MA 01202 413-499-0514 442-3180
Web: www.photonics.com

Phone Fax

Lawrence Ragan Communications Inc
111 E Wacker Dr Suite 500 .... Chicago IL 60601 312-960-4100 861-3593
TF: 800-878-5331 ■ *Web:* www.ragan.com
Lebhar-Friedman Inc 425 Park Ave .... New York NY 10022 212-756-5000 756-5124*
**Fax:* Hum Res ■ *Web:* www.lf.com
Level 5 Communications 1283 Main St PO Box 1039 .... Dublin NH 03444 603-563-1631 563-8192
Web: www.deskeng.com
LFP Inc 8484 Wilshire Blvd Suite 900 .... Beverly Hills CA 90211 323-651-5400 651-3525
Liebert Mary Ann Publishers Inc 140 Huguenot St 3rd Fl .... New Rochelle NY 10801 914-740-2100 740-2101
TF: 800-654-3237 ■ *Web:* www.liebertpub.com
Line56 Media Inc 10940 Wilshire Blvd Suite 600 .... Los Angeles CA 90024 310-443-4226 443-4230
Web: www.line56.com
Lippincott Williams & Wilkins 530 Walnut St .... Philadelphia PA 19106 215-521-8300 521-8902
Web: www.lww.com
Liturgical Publications Inc 2875 S James Dr .... New Berlin WI 53151 262-785-1188 785-9567
TF: 800-876-4574 ■ *Web:* www.4lpi.com
LookSmart TV Listings 625 2nd St .... San Francisco CA 94107 415-348-7000 348-7050
LRP Publications 360 Hiatt Dr .... Palm Beach Gardens FL 33418 561-622-6520 622-2423
TF: 800-621-5463 ■ *Web:* www.lrp.com
M Shanken Communications Inc 387 Park Ave S 8th Fl .... New York NY 10016 212-684-4224 684-5424
TF: 800-866-0775
MAC Publishing LLC 501 2nd St .... San Francisco CA 94107 415-243-0505 882-0936
Web: www.macworld.com/info/aboutus
MacAddict Network 4000 Shoreline Ct Suite 400 .... South San Francisco CA 94080 650-238-2400 872-2207
TF Cust Svc: 888-771-6222 ■ *Web:* www.macaddict.com
MacFadden Publishing Inc 333 7th Ave 11th Fl .... New York NY 10001 212-979-4800 674-0101*
**Fax Area Code:* 646 ■ *TF:* 800-741-1289
Marcel Dekker Inc 270 Madison Ave .... New York NY 10016 212-696-9000 685-4540
TF Sales: 800-228-1160 ■ *Web:* www.dekker.com
Mary Ann Liebert Publishers Inc 140 Huguenot St 3rd Fl .... New Rochelle NY 10801 914-740-2100 740-2101
TF: 800-654-3237 ■ *Web:* www.liebertpub.com
McGraw-Hill Construction 2 Penn Plaza .... New York NY 10121 212-904-2000 216-0543*
**Fax Area Code:* 800 ■ *TF:* 800-221-0088 ■ *Web:* fwdodge.construction.com
McGraw-Hill Cos Inc 1221 Ave of the Americas .... New York NY 10020 212-512-2000
NYSE: MHP ■ *Web:* www.mcgraw-hill.com
McKnight's Long-Term Care News
570 Frontage Rd Suite 521 1 Northfield Plaza .... Northfield IL 60093 847-784-8706 784-9346
Web: www.mcknightsonline.com
Meister Publishing Co 37733 Euclid Ave .... Willoughby OH 44094 440-942-2000 942-0662
TF Orders: 800-572-7740 ■ *Web:* www.meistermedia.com
Meredith Corp 1716 Locust St .... Des Moines IA 50309 515-284-3000 284-3806
NYSE: MDP ■ *Web:* www.meredith.com
Mergent Inc 60 Madison Ave 6th Fl .... New York NY 10010 212-413-7700 413-7670
TF: 888-411-0893 ■ *Web:* www.mergent.com
Metal Bulletin Inc 230 Park Ave S 12th Fl .... New York NY 10003 212-213-6202 213-6273
TF: 800-638-2525 ■ *Web:* www.metalbulletin.com
Microsoft Press 1 Microsoft Way .... Redmond WA 98052 425-882-8080 936-7329
TF Cust Svc: 800-426-9400 ■ *Web:* www.microsoft.com/mspress
Miles Media Group Inc 6751 Professional Pkwy W Suite 200 .... Sarasota FL 34240 941-342-2300 907-0300
TF: 800-683-0010 ■ *Web:* www.see-florida.com
Miller Publishing Co 12400 Whitewater Dr Suite 160 .... Minnetonka MN 55343 952-931-0211 938-1832
Millin Publishing Group Inc 3217 Main St .... Barnstable MA 02630 508-362-4455
TF: 888-739-8500
Monarch Services Inc 4517 Harford Rd .... Baltimore MD 21214 410-254-9200 254-0991
Moody's Corp 99 Church St .... New York NY 10007 212-553-0300 553-5376
NYSE: MCO ■ *Web:* www.moodys.com
Morningstar Inc 225 W Wacker Dr .... Chicago IL 60606 312-696-6000 696-6001
NASDAQ: MORN ■ *TF Orders:* 800-735-0700 ■ *Web:* www.morningstar.com
National Auto Research Inc 2620 Barrett Rd .... Gainesville GA 30507 770-532-4111 357-3444*
**Fax Area Code:* 800 ■ *TF:* 800-554-1026
National Braille Press Inc 88 Saint Stephens St .... Boston MA 02115 617-266-6160 437-0456
TF: 888-965-8965 ■ *Web:* www.nbp.org
National Catholic Reporter Publishing Co
115 E Armour Blvd .... Kansas City MO 64111 816-531-0538 968-2280*
**Fax:* Edit ■ *TF:* 800-333-7373 ■ *Web:* www.natcath.com
National Geographic Society 1145 17th St NW .... Washington DC 20036 202-857-7000 775-6141
TF Orders: 800-647-5463 ■ *Web:* www.nationalgeographic.com
National Journal Group Inc
600 New Hampshire Ave NW 4th Fl .... Washington DC 20037 202-739-8400 833-8069
TF: 800-207-8001 ■ *Web:* nationaljournal.com
Nazarene Publishing House Inc PO Box 419527 .... Kansas City MO 64141 816-931-1900 753-4071
TF: 800-877-0700 ■ *Web:* www.nph.com
Nelson Publishing 2500 Tamiami Trail N .... Nokomis FL 34275 941-966-9521 966-2590
TF: 800 226 6113 ■ *Web:* www.nelsonpub.com
New York Times Co 620 8th Ave .... New York NY 10008 212-556-4317 428-2197*
NYSE: NYT ■ **Fax Area Code:* 646 ■ *Web:* www.nytco.com
News America Inc 1211 Ave of the Americas .... New York NY 10036 212-852-7000
News Corp Ltd 1211 Ave of the Americas 7th Fl .... New York NY 10036 212-852-7000 852-7145*
NYSE: NWS ■ **Fax:* Investor Rel ■ *Web:* www.newscorp.com
Newsweek Inc 251 W 57th St .... New York NY 10019 212-445-4000 445-4120
TF Cust Svc: 800-634-6842 ■ *Web:* www.newsweek.com
North American Publishing Co
1500 Springarden St Suite 1200 .... Philadelphia PA 19130 215-238-5482 238-5457
TF: 800-627-2689 ■ *Web:* www.napco.com
NORTHSTAR Travel Media LLC 100 Lighting Way .... Secaucus NJ 07094 201-902-2000 902-2037*
**Fax:* Hum Res ■ *TF:* 800-742-7076 ■ *Web:* www.northstartravelmedia.com
O'Dwyer JR Co 271 Madison Ave 6th Fl .... New York NY 10016 212-679-2471 683-2750
TF: 866-395-7710 ■ *Web:* www.odwyerpr.com
Omniprint 9700 Philadelphia Ct .... Lanham MD 20706 301-731-5200 731-7001
TF: 800-774-6809 ■ *Web:* www.omniprint.net
Open Horizons Publishing Co PO Box 2887 .... Taos NM 87571 505-751-3398 751-3100
Web: www.bookmarket.com
Our Sunday Visitor Inc 200 Noll Plaza .... Huntington IN 46750 260-356-8400 359-0029
TF: 800-348-2440 ■ *Web:* www.osv.com
Oxmoor House Inc 2100 Lakeshore Dr .... Birmingham AL 35209 205-445-6000 445-6078
TF: 800-633-4910 ■ *Web:* www.oxmoorhouse.com
Pace Communications Inc 1301 Carolina St Suite 200 .... Greensboro NC 27401 336-378-6065 378-8271
Web: www.pacecommunications.com
Pacific Press Publishing Assn 1350 N Kings Rd .... Nampa ID 83687 208-465-2500 465-2531
TF Cust Svc: 800-545-2449 ■ *Web:* www.pacificpress.com
Paisano Publications 28210 Dorothy Dr .... Agoura Hills CA 91301 818-889-8740 889-4726
TF: 800-247-6246 ■ *Web:* www.easyriders.com
Parade Publications Inc 711 3rd Ave .... New York NY 10017 212-450-7000 450-7287
Web: www.parade.com
Patch Communications 5211 S Washington Ave .... Titusville FL 32780 321-268-5010 267-7216
PC World Communications Inc 501 2nd St .... San Francisco CA 94107 415-243-0500 442-1891
TF: 800-997-2967 ■ *Web:* www.pcworld.com
PennWell Publishing Co 1421 S Sheridan Rd .... Tulsa OK 74112 918-835-3161 831-9497
TF: 800-331-4463 ■ *Web:* www.pennwell.com
Penton Media 249 W 17th St .... New York NY 10011 212-294-4200
Web: www.penton.com
Penton Media Inc 1300 E 9th St .... Cleveland OH 44114 216-696-7000 696-1752
Web: www.penton.com
Phillips International Inc 9420 Key West Ave 4th Fl .... Rockville MD 20850 301-279-4200
Web: www.phillips.com
Photosource International 1910 35th Rd Pine Lake Farm .... Osceola WI 54020 715-248-3800 248-7394
TF: 800-624-0266 ■ *Web:* www.photosource.com

Periodicals Publishers (Cont'd)

Phone | Fax

Pike & Fischer Inc 1010 Wayne Ave Suite 1400 .... Silver Spring MD 20910 301-562-1530 562-1521
TF: 800-255-8131 ■ *Web:* www.pf.com
Platts 2 Penn Plaza 25th Fl .... New York NY 10121 212-904-3070
TF: 800-752-8878 ■ *Web:* www.platts.com
Playboy Enterprises Inc 680 N Lake Shore Dr .... Chicago IL 60611 312-751-8000 751-2818
NYSE: PLA ■ *Web:* www.playboyenterprises.com
Pohly Co 99 Bedford St 5th Fl .... Boston MA 02111 617-451-1700 338-7767
TF: 877-687-6459 ■ *Web:* www.pohlyco.com/index.html
Pratt AS & Sons 1725 K St NW Suite 700 .... Washington DC 20006 800-524-2003 739-9511*
**Fax Area Code:* 202 ■ *TF Cust Svc:* 800-945-6597 ■ *Web:* www.aspratt.com
PRIMEDIA Inc 745 5th Ave .... New York NY 10151 212-745-0100 745-0121
NYSE: PRM ■ *Web:* www.primedia.com
PRIMEDIA Inc & Consumer Source Inc
3585 Engineering Dr Suite 100 .... Norcross GA 30092 678-421-3000
TF: 800-216-1423 ■ *Web:* www.primedia.com/divisions/cmmg
Professional Sports Publications 519 8th Ave 25th Fl .... New York NY 10018 212-697-1460 753-9481*
**Fax Area Code:* 646 ■ *Web:* www.pspsports.com
Publications & Communications Inc
13581 Pond Springs Rd Suite 450 .... Austin TX 78729 512-250-9023 331-3900
TF: 800-678-9724 ■ *Web:* www.pcinews.com
Publications International Ltd 7373 N Cicero Ave .... Lincolnwood IL 60712 847-676-3470 676-3671
TF: 800-745-9299 ■ *Web:* www.pubint.com
Publishing Group of America Inc
341 Cool Springs Blvd Suite 400 .... Franklin TN 37067 615-468-6000 468-6100
TF: 800-720-6323 ■ *Web:* www.pubgroupofamerica.com
Putman Media Inc 555 W Pierce Rd Suite 301 .... Itasca IL 60143 630-467-1300 467-0153*
**Fax:* Hum Res ■ *TF:* 800-984-7644 ■ *Web:* www.putmanmedia.com
Quebecor Media Inc 612 rue Saint-Jacques .... Montreal QC H3C4M8 514-877-9777 594-8844
Web: www.quebecor.com
R & R Inc PO Box 16555 .... North Hollywood CA 91615 800-562-2706 487-4550*
**Fax Area Code:* 818 ■ *TF:* 800-562-2706 ■ *Web:* www.radioandrecords.com
Radio & Records Inc PO Box 16555 .... North Hollywood CA 91615 800-562-2706 487-4550*
**Fax Area Code:* 818 ■ *TF:* 800-562-2706 ■ *Web:* www.radioandrecords.com
Ragan Lawrence Communications Inc
111 E Wacker Dr Suite 500 .... Chicago IL 60601 312-960-4100 861-3593
TF: 800-878-5331 ■ *Web:* www.ragan.com
Randall Publishing Co 3200 Rice Mine Rd NE .... Tuscaloosa AL 35406 205-349-2990 349-3765
TF Cust Svc: 800-633-5953 ■ *Web:* www.randallpub.com
Reader's Digest Assn Inc Reader's Digest Rd .... Pleasantville NY 10570 914-238-1000 238-4559
NYSE: RDA ■ *TF:* 800-635-5006 ■ *Web:* www.rd.com
Red Herring Communications Inc 19 Davis Dr .... Belmont CA 94002 650-428-2900 428-2901
Web: www.redherring.com
Reed Business Information 100 Enterprise Dr Suite 600 .... Rockaway NJ 07866 973-920-7000 920-7553*
**Fax:* Hum Res ■ *TF:* 800-446-6551 ■ *Web:* www.reedbusiness.com
Reed Elsevier Inc 121 Chanlon Rd .... New Providence NJ 07974 908-464-6800 665-6688
TF: 800-526-4902 ■ *Web:* www.reed-elsevier.com
Reiman Publications 5400 S 60th St .... Greendale WI 53129 414-423-0100 423-1143
TF: 800-344-6913 ■ *Web:* www.reimanpub.com
Remy Publishing Co 5315 N Clark St PMB 501 .... Chicago IL 60640 773-769-6760 769-6012
TF: 800-542-6670
Review & Herald Publishing Assn 55 W Oak Ridge Dr .... Hagerstown MD 21740 301-393-3000 393-4055
TF: 800-456-3991 ■ *Web:* www.rhpa.org
RIA Group 395 Hudson St .... New York NY 10014 212-367-6300 337-4207
TF Cust Svc: 800-950-1205 ■ *Web:* ria.thomson.com
Rodale Inc 33 E Minor St .... Emmaus PA 18098 610-967-5171 813-6627*
**Fax Area Code:* 800 ■ **Fax:* Cust Svc ■ *TF Cust Svc:* 800-848-4735 ■
Web: www.rodale.com
Rough Notes Co Inc 11690 Technology Dr .... Carmel IN 46032 317-582-1600 816-1000
TF: 800-428-4384 ■ *Web:* www.roughnotes.com
Sage Publications Inc 2455 Teller Rd .... Thousand Oaks CA 91320 805-499-9774 499-0871
TF: 800-818-7243 ■ *Web:* www.sagepub.com
Saint Croix Press Inc 1185 S Knowles Ave .... New Richmond WI 54017 715-246-5811 246-2486
TF: 800-826-6622 ■ *Web:* www.stcroixpress.com
Sandhills Publishing 120 W Harvest Dr .... Lincoln NE 68521 402-479-2181 479-2195
TF: 800-544-1382 ■ *Web:* www.sandhills.com
Saturday Evening Post Society 1100 Waterway Blvd .... Indianapolis IN 46202 317-634-1100 637-0126
TF: 800-558-2376 ■ *Web:* www.saturdayeveningpost.com
Schaeffer's Investment Research Inc
5151 Pfeiffer Rd Suite 250 .... Cincinnati OH 45242 513-589-3800 589-3810
TF: 800-448-2080 ■ *Web:* www.schaeffersresearch.com
Scholastic Corp 557 Broadway .... New York NY 10012 212-343-6100
NASDAQ: SCHL ■ *TF Cust Svc:* 800-724-6527 ■ *Web:* www.scholastic.com
Scientific American Inc 415 Madison Ave .... New York NY 10017 212-451-8550 755-1976
TF Cust Svc: 800-333-1199 ■ *Web:* www.sciam.com
Sesame Workshop 1 Lincoln Plaza .... New York NY 10023 212-595-3456 875-7359
Web: www.sesameworkshop.org
Shanken M Communications Inc 387 Park Ave S 8th Fl .... New York NY 10016 212-684-4224 684-5424
TF: 800-866-0775
Simba Information 60 Long Ridge Rd Suite 300 .... Stamford CT 06902 203-325-8193 325-8915
TF: 888-297-4622 ■ *Web:* www.simbainformation.com
Simmons-Boardman Publishing Corp 345 Hudson St 12th Fl .... New York NY 10014 212-620-7200 633-1165
TF: 800-895-4389 ■ *Web:* www.simmonsboardman.com
Singapore Press Holdings
529 14th St NW National Press Bldg Suite 916 .... Washington DC 20045 202-662-8726 662-8729
Web: www.sph.com.sg
Sky Publishing Corp 90 Sherman St .... Cambridge MA 02140 617-864-7360 864-6117
TF: 800-253-0245 ■ *Web:* skyandtelescope.com/aboutsky
Slack Inc 6900 Grove Rd .... Thorofare NJ 08086 856-848-1000 853-5991
TF: 800-257-8290 ■ *Web:* www.slackinc.com
Smithsonian Institution Business Ventures Div
600 Maryland Ave SW Suite 6001 .... Washington DC 20024 202-633-6080 633-6093
TF: 877-240-1183 ■ *Web:* www.si.edu
SNL Financial 1 SNL Plaza PO Box 2124 .... Charlottesville VA 22902 434-977-1600 977-4466
Web: www.snl.com
Source Media 1 State Street Plaza 27th Fl .... New York NY 10004 212-803-8200 843-9669
TF: 800-221-1809 ■ *Web:* www.sourcemedia.com
Southern Progress Corp 2100 Lakeshore Dr .... Birmingham AL 35209 205-445-6000 445-6085
TF: 800-366-4712 ■ *Web:* www.southernprogress.com
Springer-Verlag New York Inc 233 Spring St .... New York NY 10013 212-460-1500 460-1575
TF: 800-777-4643 ■ *Web:* www.springer-ny.com
ST Media Group International Inc 407 Gilbert Ave .... Cincinnati OH 45202 513-421-2050 421-5144
TF: 800-925-1110 ■ *Web:* www.stmediagroup.com
Stamats Communications Inc 615 5th St SE .... Cedar Rapids IA 52401 319-364-6167 365-5421
TF: 800-553-8878 ■ *Web:* www.stamats.com
Standard & Poor's Corp 55 Water St .... New York NY 10041 212-438-2000 438-6675*
**Fax:* PR ■ *TF:* 800-289-8000 ■ *Web:* www.standardandpoors.com
Standard Publishing Co 8805 Governors Hill Dr Suite 400 .... Cincinnati OH 45249 513-931-4050 931-0904
TF Orders: 800-543-1353 ■ *Web:* www.standardpub.com
State Capitals Newsletters PO Box 7376 .... Alexandria VA 22307 703-768-9600 768-9690
Web: www.statecapitals.com
Strafford Publications Inc PO Box 13729 .... Atlanta GA 30324 404-881-1141 881-0074
TF: 800-926-7926 ■ *Web:* www.straffordpub.com
Strang Communications 600 Rinehart Rd .... Lake Mary FL 32746 407-333-0600 333-7100
Web: www.strang.com

Phone | Fax

Sunset Publishing Corp 80 Willow Rd .... Menlo Park CA 94025 650-321-3600 327-7537*
**Fax:* Edit ■ *TF:* 800-227-7346 ■ *Web:* www.sunset.com
Sussex Publishers Inc 115 E 23rd St 9th Fl .... New York NY 10010 212-260-7210 260-7445*
**Fax:* Edit
Taunton Press Inc 63 S Main St .... Newtown CT 06470 203-426-8171 426-3434
TF: 800-283-7252 ■ *Web:* www.taunton.com
Tax Management Inc 1801 S Bell St .... Arlington VA 22202 703-341-3000 341-1623
TF: 800-372-1033 ■ *Web:* www.bnatax.com
Testa Communications 25 Willowdale Ave .... Port Washington NY 11050 516-767-2500 767-9335
TF: 800-937-7678 ■ *Web:* www.testa.com
Thompson American Health Consultants Inc
3525 Piedmont Rd NE Bldg 6 Suite 400 .... Atlanta GA 30305 404-262-7436 284-3291*
**Fax Area Code:* 800 ■ **Fax:* Cust Svc ■ *TF Cust Svc:* 800-688-2421 ■
Web: www.ahcpub.com
Thompson Publishing Group Inc 1725 K St NW Suite 700 .... Washington DC 20006 202-872-4000 296-1091
TF Cust Svc: 800-677-3789 ■ *Web:* www.thompson.com
Thomson Scientific 3501 Market St .... Philadelphia PA 19104 215-386-0100 386-2911
TF: 800-523-1850 ■ *Web:* www.thomsonscientific.com
Time Inc 1271 Ave of the Americas .... New York NY 10020 212-522-1212 522-0555
Web: www.timeinc.com
Times Mirror Magazines Inc 2Park Ave .... New York NY 10016 212-779-5000
TF: 800-227-2224
TL Enterprises Inc 2575 Vista Del Mar Dr .... Ventura CA 93001 805-667-4100 667-4485
TF: 800-765-1912
Transcontinental Inc 1 pl Ville Marie Bureau 3315 .... Montreal QC H3B3N2 514-954-4000 954-4016
TSX: TCL.a ■ *Web:* www.transcontinental.com
Transcontinental Media 1100 Rene-Levesque Blvd W 24th fl .... Montreal QC H3B4X9 514-392-9000 392-2040
TF: 800-461-3773 ■ *Web:* www.medias-transcontinental.com/en
TransWorld Media 353 Airport Rd .... Oceanside CA 92054 760-722-7777 722-0653
TF: 800-788-7072
Travelhost Inc 10701 N Stemmons Fwy .... Dallas TX 75220 972-556-0541 432-8729
TF: 800-527-1782 ■ *Web:* www.travelhost.com
TV Guide Inc 6922 Hollywood Blvd .... Hollywood CA 90028 323-817-4600 817-4629
NASDAQ: GMST ■ *Web:* www.gemstartvguide.com
United Advertising Publications Inc
2301 McDaniel Dr Suite 100 .... Carrollton TX 75006 972-280-0055
Web: www.unitedadvertising.com
United Communications Group
11300 Rockville Pike Suite 1100 .... Rockville MD 20852 301-287-2700 816-8945
TF: 800-929-4824 ■ *Web:* www.ucg.com
United Methodist Publishing House PO Box 801 .... Nashville TN 37202 615-749-6000 749-6079
TF Cust Svc: 800-672-1789 ■ *Web:* www.umph.org
United Nations Publications 2 UN Plaza Suite DC2-853 .... New York NY 10017 212-963-8302
TF: 800-253-9646 ■ *Web:* www.un.org/Pubs
University of Chicago Press Journals Div PO Box 37005 .... Chicago IL 60637 773-753-3347 753-0811
TF: 877-705-1878 ■ *Web:* www.journals.uchicago.edu
US Government Printing Office (GPO)
732 N Capitol St NW Suite 700 .... Washington DC 20401 202-512-1800 512-2104
TF: 866-512-1800 ■ *Web:* www.gpoaccess.gov
Value Line Inc 220 E 42nd St .... New York NY 10017 212-907-1500 818-9747
NASDAQ: VALU ■ *TF Cust Svc:* 800-634-3583 ■ *Web:* www.valueline.com
Vance Publishing Corp 400 Knightsbridge Pkwy .... Lincolnshire IL 60069 847-634-2600 634-4379
TF: 800-621-2845 ■ *Web:* www.vancepublishing.com
Vendome Group LLC 149 5th Ave Suite 10 .... New York NY 10010 212-812-8420 473-8786
TF: 800-519-3692 ■ *Web:* www.vendomegrp.com
Virgo Publishing Inc 3300 N Central Ave Suite 3000 .... Phoenix AZ 85012 480-990-1101 990-0819
Web: www.vpico.com
Viz Media 295 Bay St .... San Francisco CA 94133 415-546-7073 546-7086
Web: www.viz.com
Wakeman/Walworth Inc PO Box 7376 .... Alexandria VA 22307 703-768-9600 768-9690
Warren Communications News Inc 2115 Ward Ct NW .... Washington DC 20037 202-872-9200 318-8350
TF: 800-771-9202 ■ *Web:* www.warren-news.com
Washington Business Information Inc
300 N Washington St Suite 200 .... Falls Church VA 22046 703-538-7600 538-7676
TF: 888-838-5578 ■ *Web:* www.fdanews.com
Washington Crime News Service 2014 Woodland Rd .... Petersburg VA 23805 202-662-7035 662-7036
Watt Publishing Co 303 N Main St .... Rockford IL 61101 815-734-4171 966-6416
Web: www.wattnet.com
Weider Publications Inc 21100 Erwin St .... Woodland Hills CA 91367 818-884-6800 884-0371*
**Fax:* Hum Res ■ *TF:* 800-423-5590
Wenner Media Inc 1290 Ave of the Americas 2nd Fl .... New York NY 10104 212-484-1616 484-1621
Where International 79 Madison Ave 8th Fl .... New York NY 10016 212-636-2700 636-2787
Web: www.wheremagazine.com
Whitaker Newsletters Inc PO Box 224 .... Spencerville MD 20868 301-384-1573 879-8803
TF: 800-359-6049
William F Bland Co 709 Turmeric Ln .... Durham NC 27713 919-544-1717 544-1999
Wilson HW Co 950 University Ave .... Bronx NY 10452 718-588-8400 590-1617*
**Fax:* Cust Svc ■ *TF:* 800-367-6770 ■ *Web:* www.hwwilson.com
Windhover Information Inc 10 Hoyt St 2nd Fl .... Norwalk CT 06851 203-838-4401 838-3214
Web: www.windhoverinfo.com
Wolters Kluwer US Corp 2700 Lake Cook Rd .... Riverwood IL 60015 847-580-5000 267-2516
Web: www.wolterskluwer.com
Working Mother Media Inc 60 E 42nd St 27th .... New York NY 10165 212-351-6400 351-6487
TF: 800-627-0690 ■ *Web:* www.workingmother.com
Yankee Publishing Inc PO Box 520 .... Dublin NH 03444 603-563-8111 563-8252
TF: 800-729-9265
Ziff Davis Media Inc 28 E 28th St .... New York NY 10016 212-503-3500 503-5696
TF: 800-336-2423 ■ *Web:* www.ziffdavis.com

640-10 Publishers (Misc)

Phone | Fax

AM Best Co Ambest Rd .... Oldwick NJ 08858 908-439-2200 439-3363
Web: www.ambest.com
American Printing House for the Blind
1839 Frankfort Ave PO Box 6085 .... Louisville KY 40206 502-895-2405 899-2274
TF: 800-223-1839 ■ *Web:* www.aph.org
Art Publishing Group 165 Chubb Ave .... Lyndhurst NJ 07071 201-842-8500 842-8546
TF: 800-760-3058 ■ *Web:* www.theartpublishinggroup.com
Bernan Assoc 4611 F Assembly Dr .... Lanham MD 20706 301-459-2255 459-0056
TF: 800-865-3457 ■ *Web:* www.bernan.com
Best AM Co Ambest Rd .... Oldwick NJ 08858 908-439-2200 439-3363
Web: www.ambest.com
Britannica.com Inc 310 S Michigan Ave .... Chicago IL 60604 312-347-7000 347-7966
TF Cust Svc: 800-747-8503 ■ *Web:* www.britannica.com
Brodart Co Automation Div 500 Arch St .... Williamsport PA 17701 570-326-2461 327-9237
TF: 800-233-8467 ■ *Web:* www.books.brodart.com/products/automation.htm
Cathedral Press Inc 600 NE 6th St .... Long Prairie MN 56347 320-732-6143 732-3457
TF Cust Svc: 800-874-8332 ■ *Web:* www.cathedralpress.com
Chalk & Vermilion Fine Arts Inc 55 Old Post Rd #2 .... Greenwich CT 06830 203-869-9500 869-9520
TF: 800-877-2250 ■ *Web:* www.chalk-vermilion.com
Channing L Bete Co Inc 1 Community Pl .... South Deerfield MA 01373 413-665-7611 499-6464*
**Fax Area Code:* 800 ■ **Fax:* Cust Svc ■ *TF:* 800-628-7733 ■
Web: www.channing-bete.com
Clement Communications Inc 10 LaCrue Ave .... Concordville PA 19331 610-459-4200 459-0936
TF: 888-358-5858 ■ *Web:* www.clement.com

	City	State	ZIP	Phone	Fax
ClickZ Corp 475 Park Ave S 4th Fl	New York	NY	10016	212-547-7900	953-1733
Web: www.clickz.com					
CNET Networks Inc 235 2nd St	San Francisco	CA	94105	415-344-2000	395-9207
NASDAQ: CNET ■ *Web:* www.cnet.com					
Coastal Training Technologies Corp 500 Studio Dr	Virginia Beach	VA	23452	757-498-9014	498-3657
TF: 888-776-8268 ■ *Web:* www.coastal.com					
CoreData Group 4833 Rugby Ave	Bethesda	MD	20814	301-760-2500	654-5797
TF: 800-775-8118 ■ *Web:* www.coredatagroup.com					
CPP Inc 1055 Joaquin Rd Suite 200	Mountain View	CA	94043	650-969-8901	969-8608
TF: 800-624-1765 ■ *Web:* www.cpp.com					
CSS Industries Inc 1845 Walnut St Suite 800	Philadelphia	PA	19103	215-569-9900	569-9979
NYSE: CSS ■ *Web:* www.cssindustries.com					
Dorland Healthcare Information 1500 Walnut St Suite 1000	Philadelphia	PA	19102	215-875-1212	735-3966
TF: 800-784-2332 ■ *Web:* www.dorlandhealth.com					
Dow Jones Reuters Business Interactive LLC DBA Factiva					
PO Box 300	Princeton	NJ	08543	609-627-2000	627-2760*
**Fax:* Hum Res ■ *TF Cust Svc:* 800-369-7466 ■ *Web:* www.factiva.com					
Drivers License Guide Co 1492 Oddstad Dr	Redwood City	CA	94063	650-369-4849	364-8740
TF: 800-227-8827 ■ *Web:* www.driverslicenseguide.com					
EBSCO Information Services PO Box 1943	Birmingham	AL	35201	205-991-6600	991-1264
Web: www.ebsco.com					
EBSCO Publishing Inc 10 Estes St	Ipswich	MA	01938	978-356-6500	356-6565
TF: 800-653-2726 ■ *Web:* www.epnet.com					
Edmunds.com Inc 1620 26th St Suite 400 South Tower	Santa Monica	CA	90404	310-309-6300	309-6400
Web: www.edmunds.com					
Educational Communications Inc					
7211 Circle South Rd PO Box 149311	Austin	TX	78714	877-843-9946	447-1687*
**Fax Area Code:* 512 ■ *Web:* www.honoring.com					
Entertainment Publications Inc 1414 E Maple Rd	Troy	MI	48083	248-404-1000	404-1916
TF: 800-926-0565 ■ *Web:* www.entertainment.com					
Factiva PO Box 300	Princeton	NJ	08543	609-627-2000	627-2760*
**Fax:* Hum Res ■ *TF Cust Svc:* 800-369-7466 ■ *Web:* www.factiva.com					
Facts & Comparisons Inc 77 W Port Plaza Suite 450	Saint Louis	MO	63146	314-216-2100	878-5563
TF: 800-223-0554 ■ *Web:* www.factsandcomparisons.com					
Flyer Inc 201 Kelsey Ln	Tampa	FL	33619	813-622-7355	622-7571
Web: www.theflyer.net					
Forecast International/DMS Inc 22 Commerce Rd	Newtown	CT	06470	203-426-0800	426-4262
TF: 800-451-4975 ■ *Web:* www.forecast1.com					
Frames Data Inc 100 Ave of the Americas 14th Fl	New York	NY	10013	949-788-0150	
TF: 800-821-6069 ■ *Web:* www.framesdata.com					
Hadley Cos 4816 Nicollet Ave S	Minneapolis	MN	55419	952-943-8474	943-8098
TF Sales: 800-927-0880 ■ *Web:* www.hadleyhouse.com					
IGN Entertainment Inc 8000 Marina Blvd 4th Fl	Brisbane	CA	94005	415-508-2000	508-2001
TF: 800-994-2275 ■ *Web:* corp.ign.com					
Imaginova 470 Park Ave S 9th Fl	New York	NY	10016	212-703-5800	703-5900
Web: space.com					
InfoCommerce Group Inc 2 Bala Plaza Suite 300	Bala Cynwyd	PA	19004	610-649-1200	645-5360
Web: www.infocommercegroup.com					
Interactive Data Corp 22 Crosby Dr	Bedford	MA	01730	781-687-8500	687-8289
NYSE: IDC ■ *Web:* www.interactivedatacorp.com					
Intermix Media Inc 6060 Center Dr Suite 300	Los Angeles	CA	90045	310-215-1001	
Web: www.intermix.com					
Jordan Industries Inc Specialty Printing & Labeling Group					
1751 Lake Cook Rd Suite 550 ArborLake Center	Deerfield	IL	60015	847-945-5591	945-5698
Web: www.jordanindustries.com					
Jupitermedia Corp 23 Old Kings Hwy S	Darien	CT	06820	203-662-2800	655-4686
NASDAQ: JUPM ■ *Web:* www.jupitermedia.com					
Krames Communication/Staywell 780 Township Line Rd	Yardley	PA	19067	267-685-2500	685-2610
TF Sales: 800-333-3032 ■ *Web:* www.staywell.com					
Lifetouch Church Directories 1371 State Rt 598	Galion	OH	44833	419-468-4739	462-5688
TF: 800-521-4611					
Liturgical Publications of Saint Louis Inc 160 Old State Rd	Ballwin	MO	63021	636-394-7000	394-2501
TF: 800-876-7000 ■ *Web:* www.liturgical.com					
Mergent FIS Inc 60 Madison Ave 6th Fl	New York	NY	10010	212-413-7700	413-7777
TF: 800-342-5647 ■ *Web:* www.fisonline.com					
New York Graphic Society Ltd 129 Glover Ave	Norwalk	CT	06850	203-847-2000	846-2105
TF: 800-677-6947 ■ *Web:* www.nygs.com					
OAG Worldwide 3025 Highland Pkwy Suite 200	Downers Grove	IL	60515	630-515-5300	515-3933
TF: 800-323-3537 ■ *Web:* www.oag.com					
OneSource Information Services Inc 300 Baker Ave	Concord	MA	01742	978-318-4300	318-4690
TF: 800-333-8036 ■ *Web:* www.onesource.com					
Parish Publications Inc 6503 19 1/2 Mile Rd	Sterling Heights	MI	48314	586-997-4241	997-4494
TF: 800-521-4486 ■ *Web:* www.parishpub.com					
ProQuest Co 300 N Zeeb Rd	Ann Arbor	MI	48103	734-761-4700	761-3940*
NYSE: PQE ■ **Fax:* Cust Svc ■ *Web:* www.proquestcompany.com					
ProQuest Information & Learning Co 300 N Zeeb Rd	Ann Arbor	MI	48106	734-761-4700	997-4268*
**Fax:* Hum Res ■ *TF:* 800-521-0600 ■ *Web:* www.il.proquest.com					
Psychological Corp 19500 Bulverdy Rd	San Antonio	TX	78259	210-339-5000	339-5046
TF: 800-228-0752 ■ *Web:* www.psychcorp.com					
San Dieguito Printers 1880 Diamond St	San Marcos	CA	92078	760-744-0910	744-5379
TF: 800-321-5794 ■ *Web:* www.sd-print.com					
Somerset House Publishing PO Box 869	Fulshear	TX	77441	713-932-6847	878-2926*
**Fax Area Code:* 888 ■ *TF Sales:* 800-444-2540 ■ *Web:* www.somersethouse.com					
TechTarget 117 Kendrick St Suite 800	Needham	MA	02495	781-657-1000	657-1100
TF: 888-274-4111 ■ *Web:* www.techtarget.com					
Thomson CenterWatch Inc 22 Thomson Pl	Boston	MA	02210	617-856-5900	856-5901
TF Cust Svc: 800-765-9647 ■ *Web:* www.centerwatch.com					
VNU Business Publications 770 Broadway	New York	NY	10003	646-654-5500	654-5835
Web: www.vnubusinessmedia.com					
Washington Publishing Co 747 177th Ln NE	Bellevue	WA	98008	425-562-2245	239-2061*
**Fax Area Code:* 775 ■ *TF:* 800-972-4334 ■ *Web:* www.wpc-edi.com					
Winn Devon Art Group 6311 Westminster Hwy Unit 110	Richmond	BC	V7C4V4	800-663-1166	744-8275*
**Fax Area Code:* 888 ■ *Web:* www.winndevon.com					
Wonderlic Inc 1795 N Butterfield Rd	Libertyville	IL	60048	847-680-4900	680-9492
TF: 800-323-3742 ■ *Web:* www.wonderlic.com					
Workman Publishing 225 Varick St 9th Fl	New York	NY	10014	212-254-5900	254-8098
TF: 800-722-7202 ■ *Web:* www.workmanweb.com					
Zagat Survey LLC 4 Columbus Cir 3rd Fl	New York	NY	10019	212-977-6000	977-6488
TF: 800-333-3421 ■ *Web:* www.zagat.com					

640-11 Technical Publishers

	City	State	ZIP	Phone	Fax
Aircraft Technical Publishers 101 S Hill Dr	Brisbane	CA	94005	415-330-9500	468-1596*
**Fax:* Sales ■ *TF:* 800-227-4610 ■ *Web:* www.atp.com					
American Chemical Society Publications					
1155 16th St NW Publications Support Services	Washington	DC	20036	202-872-4600	872-6060
TF: 800-227-5558 ■ *Web:* www.pubs.acs.org					
American Technical Publishers Inc 1155 W 175th St	Homewood	IL	60430	708-957-1100	957-1137
TF: 800-323-3471 ■ *Web:* www.americantech.org					
Applied Computer Research Inc PO Box 41730	Phoenix	AZ	85080	602-216-9100	548-4800
TF: 800-234-2227 ■ *Web:* www.acrhq.com					
Books24x7.com Inc 100 River Ridge Dr	Norwood	MA	02062	781-440-0550	440-0560
Web: www.books24x7.com					
Buyers Laboratory Inc 20 Railroad Ave	Hackensack	NJ	07601	201-488-0404	488-0461
Web: www.buyerslab.com					
Cambridge Information Group 7200 Wisconsin Ave Suite 601	Bethesda	MD	20814	301-961-6700	961-6720
TF: 800-843-7751 ■ *Web:* www.csa.com					
Center for Communications Management Information					
11300 Rockville Pike Suite 1100	Rockville	MD	20852	301-287-2835	816-8945
TF: 888-275-2264 ■ *Web:* www.ccmi.com					
Cook Ken Co 9929 W Silver Springs Dr	Milwaukee	WI	53225	414-466-6060	466-0840
Web: www.kencook.com					
Course Technology 25 Thomson Pl	Boston	MA	02210	617-757-7900	757-7969
TF: 800-648-7450 ■ *Web:* www.course.com					
DCI Technical 475 Franklin Ave	Franklin Square	NY	11010	516-355-0464	355-0467
DevX Inc 150 Executive Pk Blvd Suite 4100	San Francisco	CA	94134	415-467-0305	467-0282
Web: www.devx.com					
Electronic Trend Publications 1975 Hamilton Ave Suite 6	San Jose	CA	95125	408-369-7000	369-8021
TF: 800-726-6858 ■ *Web:* www.electronictrendpubs.com					
Faulkner Information Services					
7905 Browning Rd Suite 116	Pennsauken	NJ	08109	856-662-2070	662-0905
TF: 800-843-0460 ■ *Web:* www.faulkner.com					
Fawcette Technical Publications					
2600 S El Camino Real Suite 300	San Mateo	CA	94403	650-378-7100	570-6307
TF: 800-848-5523 ■ *Web:* www.fawcette.com					
Health Forum 1 N Franklin St 29th Fl	Chicago	IL	60606	312-893-6800	422-4506
TF: 800-621-6902					
Information Gatekeepers Inc 320 Washington St Suite 302	Brighton	MA	02135	617-782-5033	782-5735
TF: 800-323-1088 ■ *Web:* www.igigroup.com					
JJ Keller & Assoc Inc PO Box 368	Neenah	WI	54957	920-722-2848	727-7516*
**Fax Area Code:* 800 ■ *TF:* 800-558-5011 ■ *Web:* www.jjkeller.com					
Keller JJ & Assoc Inc PO Box 368	Neenah	WI	54957	920-722-2848	727-7516*
**Fax Area Code:* 800 ■ *TF:* 800-558-5011 ■ *Web:* www.jjkeller.com					
Ken Cook Co 9929 W Silver Springs Dr	Milwaukee	WI	53225	414-466-6060	466-0840
Web: www.kencook.com					
knovel.com 13 Eaton Ave	Norwich	NY	13815	607-337-5600	334-9097
TF: 888-238-1626 ■ *Web:* www.knovel.com					
McGraw-Hill Osborne 2600 10th St	Berkeley	CA	94710	877-833-5524	549-6603*
**Fax Area Code:* 510 ■ *TF:* 800-227-0900 ■ *Web:* www.osborne.com					
McGraw-Hill Professional Publishing Group					
2 Penn Plaza 11th Fl	New York	NY	10121	212-904-2000	904-4070
TF: 800-262-4729 ■ *Web:* books.mcgraw-hill.com					
Miles-Samuelson Inc 475 Franklin Ave	Franklin Square	NY	11010	516-437-7330	488-8013
Web: www.miles-samuelson.com					
Mitchell 1 14145 Danielson St	Poway	CA	92064	858-391-5000	746-5250*
**Fax:* Sales ■ *TF:* 888-724-6742 ■ *Web:* www.mitchellrepair.com					
Mitchell International Inc 9889 Willow Creek Rd	San Diego	CA	92131	858-578-6550	578-4752
TF: 800-854-7030 ■ *Web:* www.mitchell.com					
O'Reilly & Assoc Inc 1005 Gravenstein Hwy N	Sebastopol	CA	95472	707-829-0515	829-0104
TF: 800-998-9938 ■ *Web:* www.oreilly.com					
SSC Media Corp PO Box 55549	Seattle	WA	98155	206-782-7733	782-7191
Web: www.ssc.com					
TeleGeography Inc 1909 K St NW Suite 380	Washington	DC	20006	202-741-0020	741-0021
Web: www.telegeography.com					
Thompson Publishing Group Inc 1725 K St NW Suite 700	Washington	DC	20006	202-872-4000	296-1091
TF Cust Svc: 800-677-3789 ■ *Web:* www.thompson.com					

641 PULP MILLS

SEE ALSO Paper Mills p. 2047; Paperboard Mills p. 2049

	City	State	ZIP	Phone	Fax
Alabama River Pulp Co 2373 Lena Landegger Hwy CR 39	Perdue Hill	AL	36470	251-575-2000	743-8425*
**Fax:* Hum Res					
Alberta-Pacific Forest Industries Inc Hwy 63 N	Boyle	AB	T0A0M0	780-525-8000	525-8423
TF: 800-661-5210 ■ *Web:* www.alpac.ca					
Boise Paper Solutions Corp 222 NE Park Plaza Dr Suite 105	Vancouver	WA	98684	360-891-8787	
Web: www.bc.com/paper					
Bowater Inc 55 E Camper Down Way	Greenville	SC	29601	864-271-7733	282-9591*
NYSE: BOW ■ **Fax:* Hum Res ■ *TF:* 800-845-6002 ■ *Web:* www.bowater.com					
Brant Allen Industries 80 Field Point Rd 3rd Fl	Greenwich	CT	06830	203-661-3344	661-3349
Buckeye Florida 1 Buckeye Dr	Perry	FL	32348	850-584-1121	584-1220
Canadian Forest Products Ltd					
5162 Northwood Pulp Mill Rd PO Box 6000	Prince George	BC	V2N2K3	250-962-3500	962-3533
Web: www.canfor.com					
Canfor Corp 1700 W 75th Ave Suite 100	Vancouver	BC	V6P6G2	604-661-5241	661-5226
TSX: CFP ■ *Web:* www.canfor.com					
Daishowa America Co Ltd PO Box 271	Port Angeles	WA	98362	360-457-4474	452-9004
TF Sales: 800-331-6314					
Domtar Inc 395 boul de Maisonneuve O	Montreal	QC	H3A1L6	514-848-5400	848-6609*
NYSE: DTC ■ **Fax:* Mktg ■ *TF:* 800-267-2040 ■ *Web:* www.domtar.com					
Georgia-Pacific Corp 133 Peachtree St NE	Atlanta	GA	30303	404-652-4000	230-5774
Web: www.gp.com					
International Paper Co 6400 Poplar Ave	Memphis	TN	38297	901-419-7000	
NYSE: IP ■ *TF Prod Info:* 800-223-1268 ■ *Web:* www.internationalpaper.com					
Kimberly-Clark Corp 351 Phelps Dr	Irving	TX	75038	972-281-1200	281-1435
NYSE: KMB ■ *TF:* 800-544-1847 ■ *Web:* www.kimberly-clark.com					
Longview Fibre Paper & Packaging Co					
300 Fibre Way PO Box 639	Longview	WA	98632	360-425-1550	575-5934
Web: www.longviewfibre.com					
MeadWestvaco Fiber Sales Courthouse Plaza NE	Dayton	OH	45463	937-495-3379	461-0318
TF: 800-345-6323 ■ *Web:* www.meadwestvaco.com					
Norbord Inc 1 Toronto St 6th Fl	Toronto	ON	M5C2W4	416-643-8820	365-3292
TSX: NBD ■ *TF:* 877-263-9367 ■ *Web:* www.norbord.com					
Ohio Pulp Mills Inc 2100 Losantiville Ave	Cincinnati	OH	45237	513-731-0208	351-2129
Parsons & Whittemore Inc 4 International Dr	Rye Brook	NY	10573	914-937-9009	937-2259
Pope & Talbot Inc 1500 SW 1st Ave Suite 200	Portland	OR	97201	503-228-9161	220-2755
NYSE: POP ■ *Web:* www.poptal.com					
Potlatch Corp 601 W 1st Ave Suite 1600	Spokane	WA	99201	509-835-1500	835-1555
NYSE: PCH ■ *Web:* www.potlatchcorp.com					
Potlatch Corp Pulp & Paperboard Div 805 Mill Rd	Lewiston	ID	83501	208-799-1429	750-7809*
**Fax:* Hum Res ■ *Web:* www.potlatchcorp.com					
Southern Cellulose Products Inc PO Box 2278	Chattanooga	TN	37409	423-821-1561	821-2624
Stora Enso Duluth Recycled Paper Mill 4920 Recycle Way	Duluth	MN	55807	218-628-5504	628-5510
Tembec Inc 800 boul Rene Levesque O Bureau 1050	Montreal	QC	H3B1X1	514-871-0137	397-0896
TSX: TBC ■ *Web:* www.tembec.ca					
West Fraser Timber Co Ltd 858 Beatty St Suite 501	Vancouver	BC	V6B1C1	604-895-2700	681-6061
TSX: WFT ■ *Web:* www.westfraser.com					
Western Forest Products Inc 435 Trunk Rd 3rd Fl	Duncan	BC	V9L2P9	250-748-3711	748-6630
TSX: WEF ■ *Web:* www.westernforest.com					
Weyerhaeuser Canada Ltd 925 W Georgia St	Vancouver	BC	V6C3L2	604-661-8000	

642 PUMPS - MEASURING & DISPENSING

				Phone	Fax
Bennett Pump Co 1218 E Pontaluna Rd *TF:* 800-423-6638 ■ *Web:* www.bennettusa.com	Spring Lake	MI	49456	231-798-1310	799-6202
Dresser Inc Wayne Div 3814 Jarrett Way **Fax:* Hum Res ■ *TF:* 800-289-2963 ■ *Web:* www.wayne.com	Austin	TX	78728	512-388-8311	388-8429*
Emsar Inc 125 Access Rd *Web:* www.emsargroup.com	Stratford	CT	06615	203-377-8100	377-0500
Gasboy International Inc 7300 W Friendly Ave **Fax Area Code:* 800 ■ **Fax:* Cust Svc ■ *TF Sales:* 800-444-5579 ■ *Web:* www.gasboy.com	Greensboro	NC	27420	336-547-5000	444-5569*
Gilbarco Inc 7300 W Friendly Ave **Fax:* Mktg ■ *Web:* www.gilbarco.com	Greensboro	NC	27420	336-547-5000	547-5890*
O'Day Equipment Inc 1301 40th St NW *TF:* 800-654-6329 ■ *Web:* www.odayequipment.com	Fargo	ND	58102	701-282-9260	281-9770
Tuthill Transfer Systems 8825 Aviation Dr *Web:* transfer.tuthill.com	Fort Wayne	IN	46809	260-747-7529	747-3159
Wayne Div Dresser Inc 3814 Jarrett Way **Fax:* Hum Res ■ *TF:* 800-289-2963 ■ *Web:* www.wayne.com	Austin	TX	78728	512-388-8311	388-8429*

643 PUMPS & MOTORS - FLUID POWER

				Phone	Fax
Applied Energy Co Inc 11431 Chairman Dr *TF:* 800-580-1171 ■ *Web:* www.appliedenergyco.com	Dallas	TX	75243	214-355-4200	355-4201
ARO Fluid Products Div Ingersoll-Rand Co 1 Aro Ctr PO Box 151 *TF Cust Svc:* 800-495-0276 ■ *Web:* www.arozone.com	Bryan	OH	43506	419-636-4242	633-1674
Bosch Rexroth Corp 5150 Prairie Stone Pkwy *TF:* 800-860-1055 ■ *Web:* www.boschrexroth-us.com	Hoffman Estates	IL	60192	847-645-3600	645-6201
Bosch Rexroth Corp Industrial Hydraulics Div 2315 City Line Rd *Web:* www.boschrexroth.com	Bethlehem	PA	18017	610-694-8300	694-8467
Bosch Rexroth Corp Piston Pump Div 8 Southchase Ct	Fountain Inn	SC	29644	864-967-2777	967-8900
Continental Hydraulics Div Continental Machines Inc 5502 W 123rd St *Web:* www.continentalhydraulics.com	Savage	MN	55378	952-894-8900	895-6444
Continental Machines Inc Continental Hydraulics Div 5502 W 123rd St *Web:* www.continentalhydraulics.com	Savage	MN	55378	952-894-8900	895-6444
Cross Mfg Inc 11011 King St Suite 210 *TF:* 800-542-7677 ■ *Web:* www.crossmfg.com	Overland Park	KS	66210	913-451-1233	451-1235
Delta Power Co 4484 Boeing Dr *Web:* www.delta-power.com	Rockford	IL	61109	815-397-6628	397-2526
Denison Hydraulics Inc 14249 Industrial Pkwy *Web:* www.denisonhydraulics.com	Marysville	OH	43040	937-644-3915	642-3738
Dynex Rivett Inc 770 Capitol Dr *Web:* www.dynexhydraulics.com	Pewaukee	WI	53072	262-691-0300	691-0312
Fluid Metering Inc 5 Aerial Way Suite 500 *TF:* 800-223-3388 ■ *Web:* www.fmipump.com	Syosset	NY	11791	516-922-6050	624-8261
Haldex Hydraulic Systems 2222 15th St *TF:* 800-572-7867 ■ *Web:* www.hbus.haldex.com	Rockford	IL	61104	815-398-4400	398-5977
Howden Airdynamics 2616 Research Dr *Web:* www.noa-fan.com	Corona	CA	92882	951-734-0070	734-2594
Hydreco 2915 Whitehall Park Dr *Web:* www.hydreco.com	Charlotte	NC	28273	704-295-7575	295-7574
Ingersoll-Rand Co ARO Fluid Products Div 1 Aro Ctr PO Box 151 *TF Cust Svc:* 800-495-0276 ■ *Web:* www.arozone.com	Bryan	OH	43506	419-636-4242	633-1674
ITT Fluid Technology Corp 10 Mountainview Rd 3rd Fl *Web:* www.ittfluidtechnology.com/home.html	Upper Saddle River	NJ	07458	201-760-9800	760-9692
ITT-Flygt Corp 35 Nutmeg Dr PO Box 1004 *Web:* www.flygt.com	Trumbull	CT	06611	203-380-4700	380-4705
ITT Industries Jabsco 666 E Dyer Rd *TF:* 800-845-7000 ■ *Web:* www.jabsco.com	Santa Ana	CA	92705	714-557-4700	628-8478
Jetstream of Houston LLP 4930 Cranswick *TF:* 800-231-8192 ■ *Web:* www.waterblast.com	Houston	TX	77041	713-462-7000	462-5387
Liquid Drive Corp 418 Hadley St *TF:* 800-523-4443 ■ *Web:* www.liquiddrive.com	Holly	MI	48442	248-634-5382	634-5720
Milton Roy USA 201 Ivyland Rd **Fax Area Code:* 860 ■ *Web:* www.miltonroy.com	Ivyland	PA	18974	215-441-0800	998-4192*
Monarch Hydraulics Inc 1316 Michigan St NE *Web:* www.monarchhyd.com	Grand Rapids	MI	49503	616-458-1306	458-1616
Nichols Portland Div Parker Hannifin Corp 2400 Congress St *Web:* www.parker.com/nichport	Portland	ME	04102	207-774-6121	774-3601
Oilgear Co PO Box 343924 *NASDAQ: OLGR* ■ *TF Sales:* 800-276-5356 ■ *Web:* www.oilgear.com	Milwaukee	WI	53234	414-327-1700	327-0532
Omhaline Hydraulic Co 106 Freedom Dr PO Box 19	North Sioux City	SD	57049	605-232-9060	232-4652
Parker Hannifin Corp Hydraulic Pump/Motor Div 2745 Snapps Ferry Rd *Web:* www.parker.com/pumpmotor	Greeneville	TN	37745	423-639-8151	787-2418
Parker Hannifin Corp Nichols Portland Div 2400 Congress St *Web:* www.parker.com/nichport	Portland	ME	04102	207-774-6121	774-3601
Permco Inc 1500 Frost Rd *TF:* 800-628-2801 ■ *Web:* www.permco.com	Streetsboro	OH	44241	330-626-2801	626-2805
Sauer-Sundstrand 2800 E 13th St	Ames	IA	50010	515-239-6000	239-6318
SPX Fluid Power 5885 11th St *Web:* www.spxfluidpower.com	Rockford	IL	61109	815-874-5556	874-7853
TII Network Technologies Inc 1385 Akron St *NASDAQ: TIII* ■ *TF:* 888-844-4720 ■ *Web:* www.tiinettech.com	Copiague	NY	11726	631-789-5000	789-5063
Viking Pump Inc 406 State St PO Box 8 *Web:* www.vikingpump.com	Cedar Falls	IA	50613	319-266-1741	273-8157
Voith Turbo Inc 25 Winship Rd *Web:* www.usa.voithturbo.com	York	PA	17406	717-767-3200	767-3210

644 PUMPS & PUMPING EQUIPMENT (GENERAL USE)

SEE ALSO Industrial Machinery, Equipment, & Supplies p. 1854

				Phone	Fax
Acme Dynamics Inc 3608 Sydney Rd *TF:* 800-622-9355 ■ *Web:* www.acmedynamics.com	Plant City	FL	33566	813-752-3137	752-4580
Aermotor Pumps Inc 293 Wright St *TF:* 800-265-7241 ■ *Web:* www.aermotor.com	Delavan	WI	53115	800-230-1816	230-1816
Afton Pumps Inc 7335 Ave N *TF:* 800-829-9731 ■ *Web:* www.aftonpumps.com	Houston	TX	77011	713-923-9731	923-3902
American Machine & Tool Co Inc 400 Spring St *TF:* 888-268-7867 ■ *Web:* www.amtpump.com	Royersford	PA	19468	610-948-3800	948-5300
Aqua-Dyne Inc 3620 W 11th St *Web:* www.aqua-dyne.com	Houston	TX	77008	713-864-6929	864-0313
AR Wilfley & Sons Inc 7350 E Progress Pl Suite 200 *TF:* 800-525-9930 ■ *Web:* www.wilfley.com	Englewood	CO	80111	303-779-1777	779-1277
Armstrong International Inc 2081 SE Ocean Blvd 4th Fl *Web:* www.armintl.com	Stuart	FL	34996	772-286-7175	286-1001
ASM Industries Inc Pacer Pumps Div 41 Industrial Cir *TF Cust Svc:* 800-233-3861 ■ *Web:* www.pacerpumps.com	Lancaster	PA	17601	717-656-2161	656-0477
Barney's Pumps Inc 2956 Barney's Pumps PL *Web:* www.barneyspumps.com	Lakeland	FL	33812	863-665-8500	666-3858
Beckett Corp 5931 Campus Circle Dr W *TF:* 888-232-5388 ■ *Web:* www.beckettpumps.com	Irving	TX	75063	972-871-8000	871-8888
Berkeley Pumps 293 Wright St **Fax Area Code:* 800 ■ **Fax:* Cust Svc ■ *TF Cust Svc:* 800-728-1240 ■ *Web:* www.berkeleypumps.com	Delavan	WI	53115	262-728-5551	426-9446*
Blackmer 1809 Century Ave *Web:* www.blackmer.com	Grand Rapids	MI	49503	616-241-1611	241-3752
Buffalo Pumps Inc 874 Oliver St *Web:* www.buffalopumps.com	North Tonawanda	NY	14120	716-693-1850	693-6303
Calvert Engineering Inc 28606 Livingston Ave *TF:* 800-225-1339 ■ *Web:* www.calpump.com	Valencia	CA	91355	661-257-7330	257-7331
Carver Pump Co 2415 Park Ave *Web:* www.carverpump.com	Muscatine	IA	52761	563-263-3410	262-7688
Cascade Pump Co 10107 S Norwalk Blvd *Web:* www.cascadepump.com	Santa Fe Springs	CA	90670	562-946-1414	941-3730
Cat Pumps 1681 94th Ln NE *Web:* www.catpumps.com	Minneapolis	MN	55449	763-780-5440	780-2958
Centrilift Inc 200 W Stuart Roosa Dr *TF:* 800-633-5088 ■ *Web:* www.bakerhughes.com/centrilift/	Claremore	OK	74017	918-341-9600	342-0260
CH & E Mfg Co 3849 N Palmer St *TF Cust Svc:* 800-236-0666	Milwaukee	WI	53212	414-964-3400	964-0677
CIRCOR International Inc 25 Corporate Dr Suite 130 *NYSE: CIR* ■ *Web:* www.circor.com	Burlington	MA	01803	781-270-1200	270-1299
Coffin Turbo Pump Inc 326 S Dean St *TF:* 800-568-9798 ■ *Web:* www.coffinturbopump.com	Englewood	NJ	07631	201-568-4700	568-4716
Cole Pattern & Engineering Co Inc 2817 Goshen Rd *Web:* colepattern.com	Fort Wayne	IN	46808	260-482-2958	482-2825
Colfax Corp 8730 Stony Point Pkwy Suite 150 *Web:* www.colfaxcorp.com	Richmond	VA	23235	804-560-4070	560-4076
Corcoran RS Co 500 N Vine St *TF:* 800-637-1067 ■ *Web:* www.corcoranpumps.com	New Lenox	IL	60451	815-485-2156	485-5840
Corken Inc 3805 NW 36th St *TF:* 800-631-4929 ■ *Web:* www.corken.com	Oklahoma City	OK	73112	405-946-5576	948-6664
Cornell Pump Co 16261 SE 130th Ave PO Box 6334 *Web:* www.cornellpump.com	Portland	OR	97228	503-653-0330	653-0338
Crane Co 100 1st Stamford Pl 4th Fl *NYSE: CR* ■ *Web:* www.craneco.com	Stamford	CT	06902	203-363-7300	363-7295
Crane Deming Pumps Co 420 Third Street *Web:* www.cranepumps.com	Piqua	OH	45356	937-778-8947	773-7157
Crane Pumps & Systems 420 3rd St *Web:* www.cranepumps.com	Piqua	OH	45356	937-773-2442	773-2238
David Brown Union Pumps Co 4600 W Dickman Rd *TF:* 800-877-7867 ■ *Web:* www.fhp.textron.com	Battle Creek	MI	49015	269-966-4600	966-4649
Dean Pump Div Met-Pro Corp 6040 Guion Rd *Web:* www.met-pro.com/html/dean.htm	Indianapolis	IN	46254	317-293-2930	297-7028
Dempster Industries Inc 711 S 6th St *TF:* 800-777-0212 ■ *Web:* www.dempsterinc.com	Beatrice	NE	68310	402-223-4026	228-4389
Dosmatic USA Inc 1230 Crowley Cir *TF:* 800-344-6767 ■ *Web:* www.dosmatic.com	Carrollton	TX	75006	972-245-9765	245-9000
Environment One Corp 2773 Balltown Rd *Web:* www.eone.com	Niskayuna	NY	12309	518-346-6161	
Evans-Hydro 18128 S Santa Fe Ave *TF:* 800-429-7867	Rancho Dominguez	CA	90221	310-608-5801	608-0685
Flint & Walling Inc 95 N Oak St *TF Sales:* 800-927-0360 ■ *Web:* www.flintandwalling.com	Kendallville	IN	46755	260-347-1600	347-0909
Flowserve Corp 5215 N O'Connor Blvd Suite 2300 *NYSE: FLS* ■ *Web:* www.flowserve.com	Irving	TX	75039	972-443-6500	443-6800
Fort Wayne Foundry Corp 4912 Lima Rd *Web:* www.fortwaynefoundry.com	Fort Wayne	IN	46808	260-483-0382	484-5719
Fybroc Div Met-Pro Corp 700 Emlen Way *TF:* 800-392-7621 ■ *Web:* www.fybroc.com	Telford	PA	18969	215-723-8155	723-2197
Gardner Denver Pump Div 4747 S 83rd E Ave *TF:* 800-637-8099 ■ *Web:* www.gardnerdenver.com	Tulsa	OK	74145	918-664-1151	664-6225
GIW Industries Inc 5000 Wrightsboro Rd *TF:* 800-241-2702 ■ *Web:* www.giwindustries.com	Grovetown	GA	30813	706-863-1011	860-5897
Gorman-Rupp Co 305 Bowman St *AMEX: GRC* ■ *Web:* www.gormanrupp.com	Mansfield	OH	44903	419-755-1011	755-1233
Gorman-Rupp Industries 180 Hines Ave *TF:* 800-998-3011 ■ *Web:* www.gripumps.com	Bellville	OH	44813	419-886-3001	886-2338
Goulds Pumps Inc 240 Fall St **Fax:* Sales ■ *Web:* www.goulds.com	Seneca Falls	NY	13148	315-568-2811	568-2418*
Graco Inc 88 11th Ave *NYSE: GGG* ■ **Fax:* Hum Res ■ *TF Cust Svc:* 800-328-0211 ■ *Web:* www.graco.com	Minneapolis	MN	55413	612-623-6000	623-6640*
Graymills Corp 3705 N Lincoln Ave *Web:* www.graymills.com	Chicago	IL	60613	773-477-4100	477-4133
Great Plains Industries Inc 5252 E 36th St N *TF Sales:* 800-835-0113 ■ *Web:* www.gpi.net	Wichita	KS	67220	316-686-7361	686-6746
Grundfos Pumps Corp 5900 E Shields Ave *TF Cust Svc:* 800-333-1366 ■ *Web:* www.grundfos.com/web/homeus.nsf	Fresno	CA	93727	559-292-8000	348-9628
Gusher Pumps Div Ruthman Pump & Engineering Inc 22 Ruthman Dr *Web:* www.gusher.com	Dry Ridge	KY	41035	859-824-5001	824-3011
Hale Products Inc 700 Spring Mill Ave **Fax:* Cust Svc ■ *TF:* 800-220-4253 ■ *Web:* www.haleproducts.com	Conshohocken	PA	19428	610-825-6300	825-6440*
Hamworthy Inc 1418 Edwards Ave Suite B *Web:* www.hamworthy.com	New Orleans	LA	70123	504-734-5525	734-5716
Harben Inc 2010 Ronald Regan Blvd *TF:* 800-327-5387 ■ *Web:* www.harben.com	Cumming	GA	30041	770-889-9535	887-9411
Haskel International Inc 100 E Graham Pl **Fax:* Sales ■ *TF:* 800-743-2720 ■ *Web:* www.haskel.com	Burbank	CA	91502	818-843-4000	841-4291*
Hayward Tyler Inc 480 Roosevelt Hwy *Web:* www.haywardtyler.com	Colchester	VT	05446	802-655-4444	655-4682
Houston Grinding & Mfg Inc 3544 W 12th St	Houston	TX	77008	713-869-3573	869-2660
Hypro 375 5th Ave NW **Fax:* Sales ■ *TF Cust Svc:* 800-424-9776 ■ *Web:* www.hypropumps.com	New Brighton	MN	55112	651-766-6300	766-6600*
IDEX Corp 630 Dundee Rd Suite 400 *NYSE: IEX* ■ *Web:* www.idexcorp.com	Northbrook	IL	60062	847-498-7070	498-3940
Imo Pump 1710 Airport Rd **Fax:* Sales ■ *Web:* www.imo-pump.com	Monroe	NC	28110	704-289-6511	289-9273*
Ingersoll-Rand Co 155 Chestnut Ridge Rd *NYSE: IR* ■ *Web:* www.irco.com	Montvale	NJ	07645	201-573-0123	573-3172
ITT A-C Pump N27 W 23293 Roundy Dr *Web:* www.ittacpump.com	Pewaukee	WI	53072	262-548-8181	548-8170
ITT Bell & Gossett 8200 N Austin Ave **Fax:* Mktg ■ *Web:* www.bellgossett.com	Morton Grove	IL	60053	847-966-3700	966-9052*

	City	State	Zip	Phone	Fax
ITT Fluid Technology Corp					
10 Mountainview Rd 3rd Fl	Upper Saddle River	NJ	07458	201-760-9800	760-9692
Web: www.ittfluidtechnology.com/home.html					
ITT-Flygt Corp 35 Nutmeg Dr PO Box 1004	Trumbull	CT	06611	203-380-4700	380-4705
Web: www.flygt.com					
ITT Industries Jabsco 666 E Dyer Rd	Santa Ana	CA	92705	714-557-4700	628-8478
TF: 800-845-7000 ■ *Web:* www.jabsco.com					
Kemlon Products & Development Co 1424 N Main St	Pearland	TX	77581	281-997-3300	997-1300
Web: www.kemlon.com					
Kerr Pump & Supply 12880 Cloverdale St	Oak Park	MI	48237	248-543-3880	543-3236
TF: 800-482-8259 ■ *Web:* www.kerrpump.com					
Kimray Inc 52 NW 42nd St	Oklahoma City	OK	73118	405-525-6601	525-7520
Web: www.kimray.com					
Krogh Pump Co 251 W Channel Rd	Benicia	CA	94510	707-747-7585	747-7599
TF: 800-225-7644 ■ *Web:* www.kroghpump.com					
KSB Inc 4415 Sarellen Rd	Richmond	VA	23231	804-222-1818	226-6961
TF: 800-945-7867 ■ *Web:* www.ksb-inc.com					
Lawrence Pumps Inc 371 Market St	Lawrence	MA	01843	978-682-5249	975-4291*
*Fax: Sales ■ *Web:* www.lawrencepumps.com					
Lewis Pumps 8625 Grant Rd	Saint Louis	MO	63123	314-843-4437	843-7964
Web: www.lewispumps.com					
Liquiflo Equipment Co 443 North Ave	Garwood	NJ	07027	908-518-0666	518-1847
Web: www.liquiflo.com					
Little Giant Pump Co 3810 N Tulsa Ave	Oklahoma City	OK	73112	405-947-2511	228-1587
TF: 800-621-7264 ■ *Web:* www.lgpc.com					
Maass Midwest Inc 11283 Dundee Rd	Huntley	IL	60142	847-669-5135	669-3230
TF: 800-323-6259 ■ *Web:* www.maassmidwest.com					
Madden Mfg Inc 1317 Princeton Blvd	Elkhart	IN	46516	574-295-4292	295-7562*
*Fax: Sales ■ *TF:* 800-369-6233 ■ *Web:* www.maddenmfg.com					
March Mfg Inc 1819 Pickwick Ave	Glenview	IL	60026	847-729-5300	729-7062
Web: www.marchpump.com					
McNally Industries LLC 340 W Benson Ave PO Box 129	Grantsburg	WI	54840	715-463-8300	463-5261
TF: 800-473-0053 ■ *Web:* www.northern-pump.com					
Met-Pro Corp Dean Pump Div 6040 Guion Rd	Indianapolis	IN	46254	317-293-2930	297-7028
Web: www.met-pro.com/html/dean.htm					
Met-Pro Corp Fybroc Div 700 Emlen Way	Telford	PA	18969	215-723-8155	723-2197
TF: 800-392-7621 ■ *Web:* www.fybroc.com					
Met-Pro Corp Sethco Div 800 Emlen Way	Telford	PA	18969	215-799-2577	799-0920
TF: 800-645-0500 ■ *Web:* www.sethco.com					
Micropump Inc 1402 NE 136th Ave	Vancouver	WA	98684	360-253-2008	253-8294
TF Sales: 800-671-6269 ■ *Web:* www.micropump.com					
Moyno Inc 1895 W Jefferson St	Springfield	OH	45506	937-327-3111	327-3177*
*Fax: Mktg ■ *TF:* 800-325-1331 ■ *Web:* www.moyno.com					
MP Pumps Inc 34800 Bennett Dr	Fraser	MI	48026	586-293-8240	293-8469
TF: 800-563-8006 ■ *Web:* www.mppumps.com					
MWI Corp 201 N Federal Hwy	Deerfield Beach	FL	33441	954-426-1500	426-1582
Web: www.mwicorp.com					
Nagle Pumps Inc 1249 Center Ave	Chicago Heights	IL	60411	708-754-2940	754-2944*
*Fax: Sales ■ *Web:* www.naglepumps.com					
Pacer Pumps Div ASM Industries Inc 41 Industrial Cir	Lancaster	PA	17601	717-656-2161	656-0477
TF Cust Svc: 800-233-3861 ■ *Web:* www.pacerpumps.com					
PACO Pumps Inc 902 Koomey Rd	Brookshire	TX	77423	281-994-2700	934-6082
TF: 800-955-5847 ■ *Web:* www.paco-pumps.net					
Patterson Pump Co 9201 Ayersville Rd	Toccoa	GA	30577	706-886-2101	886-0023
Web: www.pattersonpumps.com					
Peerless Pump Co 2005 ML King Jr St PO Box 7026	Indianapolis	IN	46207	317-925-9661	924-7388
TF: 800-879-0182 ■ *Web:* www.peerlesspump.com					
Pentair Inc 5500 Wayzata Blvd Suite 800	Golden Valley	MN	55416	763-545-1730	656-5400
NYSE: PNR ■ *TF:* 800-328-9626 ■ *Web:* www.pentair.com					
Pentair Water Pool & Spa 1620 Hawkins Ave	Sanford	NC	27330	919-566-8000	566-8910
TF: 800-831-7133 ■ *Web:* www.pentairpool.com					
Procon Products Co 910 Ridgely Rd	Murfreesboro	TN	37129	615-890-5710	896-7729
Web: www.proconpumps.com					
Pulsafeeder Inc 2883 Brighton-Henrietta Town Line Rd	Rochester	NY	14623	585-292-8000	424-5619
Web: www.pulsa.com					
Red Jacket Div Veeder-Root 125 Powder Forest Dr	Simsbury	CT	06070	860-651-2700	651-7140
TF: 800-873-3313 ■ *Web:* www.redjacket.com					
REDA PO Box 1181	Bartlesville	OK	74005	918-661-2000	661-2101
TF: 800-331-0970					
Robbins & Myers Inc Kettering Tower Suite 1400	Dayton	OH	45423	937-222-2610	225-3314
NYSE: RBN ■ *Web:* www.robn.com					
Roper Pump Co 3475 Old Maysville Rd PO Box 269	Commerce	GA	30529	706-335-5551	335-5490
TF Sales: 800-944-6769 ■ *Web:* www.roperpumps.com					
Roth Pump Co PO Box 4330	Rock Island	IL	61204	309-787-1791	787-5142
TF: 888-444-7684 ■ *Web:* www.rothpump.com					
RS Corcoran Co 500 N Vine St	New Lenox	IL	60451	815-485-2156	485-5840
TF: 800-637-1067 ■ *Web:* www.corcoranpumps.com					
Rupp Warren Inc 800 N Main St	Mansfield	OH	44902	419-524-8388	522-7867
Web: www.warrenrupp.com					
Ruthman Pump & Engineering Inc Gusher Pumps Div					
22 Ruthman Dr	Dry Ridge	KY	41035	859-824-5001	824-3011
Web: www.gusher.com					
Scot Pump 6437 Pioneer Rd	Cedarburg	WI	53012	262-377-7000	377-7330
TF: 888-835-0600 ■ *Web:* www.scotpump.com					
seepex Inc 511 Speedway Dr	Enon	OH	45323	937-864-7150	864-7157
TF: 800-695-3659 ■ *Web:* seepex.com					
Serfilco Ltd 2900 MacArthur Blvd	Northbrook	IL	60062	847-559-1777	559-1141
TF: 800-323-5431 ■ *Web:* www.serfilco.com					
Sethco Div Met-Pro Corp 800 Emlen Way	Telford	PA	18969	215-799-2577	799-0920
TF: 800-645-0500 ■ *Web:* www.sethco.com					
SHURflo Pump Mfg Co Inc 5900 Katella Ave Suite A	Cypress	CA	90630	562-795-5200	795-7554
TF: 800-854-3218 ■ *Web:* www.shurflo.com					
SIHI Pumps Inc 303 Industrial Blvd	Grand Island	NY	14072	716-773-6450	773-2330
Web: www.sihi-pumps.com					
Simflo Pumps Inc 754 E Maley St PO Box 849	Willcox	AZ	85644	520-384-2273	384-4042
Web: www.simflo.com					
SPX Process Equipment 611 Sugar Creek Rd	Delavan	WI	53115	262-728-1900	252-5012*
*Fax Area Code: 800 ■ *TF:* 800-252-5200 ■ *Web:* www.spxpe.com					
Standard Alloys & Mfg PO Box 969	Port Arthur	TX	77640	409-983-3201	983-7837
TF: 800-231-8240 ■ *Web:* www.standardalloys.com					
Sturm Rapid Response Center 1305 Main St	Barboursville	WV	25504	304-736-3476	736-4058
TF: 800-624-3485 ■ *Web:* www.sturm-inc.com					
Sulzer Pumps (US) Inc 2800 NW Front Ave	Portland	OR	97210	503-226-5200	226-5286
Web: www.sulzerpumps.com					
Syncroflo Inc 6700 Best Friend Rd	Norcross	GA	30071	770-447-4443	448-5120
Web: www.syncroflo.com					
Taco Inc 1160 Cranston St	Cranston	RI	02920	401-942-8000	248-0046*
*Fax: Cust Svc ■ *TF:* 800-822-6007 ■ *Web:* www.taco-hvac.com					
Textron Fluid & Power Inc 40 Westminster St	Providence	RI	02903	401-588-3400	621-5045
Web: www.textron.com					
Thompson Pump & Mfg Co Inc 4620 City Center Dr	Port Orange	FL	32129	386-767-7310	756-3217
TF: 800-767-7310 ■ *Web:* www.thompsonpumps.com					
Tramco Pump Co 1500 W Adams St	Chicago	IL	60607	312-243-5800	243-0702*
*Fax: Sales ■ *Web:* www.tramcopump.com					
Tuthill Corp 8500 S Madison St	Burr Ridge	IL	60527	630-382-4900	382-4999
TF: 800-888-4455 ■ *Web:* www.tuthill.com					
Tuthill Pump Group 12500 S Pulaski Rd	Alsip	IL	60803	708-389-2500	388-0869
Web: pump.tuthill.com					
Vanton Pump & Equipment Corp 201 Sweetland Ave	Hillside	NJ	07205	908-688-4216	686-9314
Web: www.vanton.com					
Vaughan Co Inc 364 Monte-Elma Rd	Montesano	WA	98563	360-249-4042	249-6155
TF: 888-249-2467 ■ *Web:* www.chopperpumps.com					
Veeder-Root Red Jacket Div 125 Powder Forest Dr	Simsbury	CT	06070	860-651-2700	651-7140
TF: 800-873-3313 ■ *Web:* www.redjacket.com					
Viking Pump Inc 406 State St PO Box 8	Cedar Falls	IA	50613	319-266-1741	273-8157
Web: www.vikingpump.com					
Warren Rupp Inc 800 N Main St	Mansfield	OH	44902	419-524-8388	522-7867
Web: www.warrenrupp.com					
Waterous Co 125 Hardman Ave	South Saint Paul	MN	55075	651-450-5000	450-5090
TF: 800-488-1228 ■ *Web:* www.waterousco.com					
Waukesha Cherry-Burrell Corp 611 Sugar Creek Rd	Delavan	WI	53115	262-728-1900	728-4988
TF: 800-252-5200 ■ *Web:* gowcb.com					
Weil Pump Co 6337 Western Rd PO Box 887	Cedarburg	WI	53012	262-377-1399	377-0515
Web: www.weilpump.com					
Weir Floway Pumps 2494 S Railroad Ave	Fresno	CA	93706	559-442-4000	442-3098
Web: www.weirclearliquid.com					
Weir Minerals 225 N Cedar St	Hazleton	PA	18201	570-455-7711	459-2586
Web: www.weirminerals.com					
Weir Slurry North America 2701 S Stoughton Rd	Madison	WI	53716	608-221-2261	221-5807
Web: www.weirslurry.com					
Weir Specialty Pumps 440 W 800 South	Salt Lake City	UT	84101	801-359-8731	355-9303
Web: www.wemcopump.com					
Whitten Pumps Inc 502 County Line Rd	Delano	CA	93215	661-725-0250	725-6553
TF: 800-287-4578					
Wilden Pump & Engineering Co 22069 Van Buren St	Grand Terrace	CA	92313	909-422-1730	783-3440
Web: www.wildenpump.com					
Wilfley AR & Sons Inc 7350 E Progress Pl Suite 200	Englewood	CO	80111	303-779-1777	779-1277
TF: 800-525-9930 ■ *Web:* www.wilfley.com					
Yeomans Chicago Corp 3905 Enterprise Ct	Aurora	IL	60504	630-236-5500	236-5511
Web: www.yccpump.com					
Zoeller Co 3649 Kane Run Rd	Louisville	KY	40211	502-778-2731	774-3624
TF: 800-928-7867 ■ *Web:* www.zoeller.com					

645 RACING & RACETRACKS

SEE ALSO Motor Speedways p. 1980

	City	State	Zip	Phone	Fax
Alameda County Fair 4501 Pleasanton Ave	Pleasanton	CA	94566	925-426-7600	426-7599
Arlington Park 2200 W Euclid Ave	Arlington Heights	IL	60006	847-255-4300	385-7251
Web: www.arlingtonpark.com					
Atlantic City Racing Course 4501 Black Horse Pike	Mays Landing	NJ	08330	609-641-2190	645-8309
Balmoral Park 26435 S Dixie Hwy	Crete	IL	60417	708-672-7544	672-5932
Web: www.balmoral.com					
Batavia Downs 8315 Park Rd	Batavia	NY	14020	585-343-3750	343-7773
TF: 800-724-2000 ■ *Web:* www.westernotb.com/batavia.asp					
Bay Meadows Racecourse 2600 S Delaware St	San Mateo	CA	94403	650-574-7223	573-4671
TF: 800-872-0873 ■ *Web:* www.baymeadows.com					
Bay Meadows Racing Assn 2600 S Delaware St	San Mateo	CA	94403	650-574-7223	345-6826
Web: www.baymeadows.com					
Belmont Park 2150 Hempstead Tpke	Elmont	NY	11003	516-488-6000	488-6016
Web: www.nyracing.com/belmont					
Beulah Park Race Track 3801 Southwest Blvd	Grove City	OH	43123	614-871-9600	871-0433
TF: 800-433-6905 ■ *Web:* www.beulahpark.com					
Brainerd International Raceway 5523 Birchdale Rd	Brainerd	MN	56401	218-824-7220	824-7240
Web: www.brainerdraceway.com					
Buffalo Raceway Hamburg Fairgrounds 5600 McKinley Pkwy	Hamburg	NY	14075	716-649-1280	649-0033
Web: www.buffaloraceway.com					
Burrillville Racing Assn Inc DBA Lincoln Park					
1600 Louisquisset Pike	Lincoln	RI	02865	401-723-3200	727-4770
Web: www.lincolnparkri.com					
Calder Race Course Inc 21001 NW 27th Ave	Miami	FL	33056	305-625-1311	620-2569
TF: 800-333-3227 ■ *Web:* www.calderracecourse.com					
Canterbury Park Holding Corp 1100 Canterbury Rd	Shakopee	MN	55379	952-445-7223	496-6400
AMEX: ECP ■ *TF:* 800-340-6361 ■ *Web:* www.canterburypark.com					
Cassia County Fairgrounds 1101 Elba Ave	Burley	ID	83318	208-678-9150	678-3612
Central Wyoming Fairgrounds 1700 Fairgrounds Rd	Casper	WY	82604	307-235-5775	266-4224
Web: www.centralwyomingfair.com					
Champ Car 5350 Lakeview Pkwy S Dr	Indianapolis	IN	46268	317-715-4100	715-4110
Web: www.cart.com					
Charles Town Races & Slots					
Flowing Springs Rd Rt 340 N	Charles Town	WV	25414	304-725-7001	725-6979
TF: 800-795-7001 ■ *Web:* www.ctownraces.com					
Churchill Downs Inc 700 Central Ave	Louisville	KY	40208	502-636-4400	636-4560
NASDAQ: CHDN ■ *TF:* 800-283-3729 ■ *Web:* www.churchilldowns.com					
Cloverleaf Kennel Club 2527 NW Frontage Rd	Loveland	CO	80538	970-667-6211	667-9106
Web: www.maccpe.com					
Coconino County Fair HCR 39 Box 3A	Flagstaff	AZ	86001	928-679-8000	774-2572
Colonial Holdings Inc 10515 Colonial Downs Pkwy	New Kent	VA	23124	804-966-7223	966-1565*
*Fax: PR ■ *TF:* 888-482-8722 ■ *Web:* www.colonialdowns.com					
Columbus Races 822 15th St	Columbus	NE	68601	402-564-0133	564-0990
TF: 800-314-2983					
Dairyland Greyhound Park 5522 104th Ave	Kenosha	WI	53144	262-657-8200	657-8231
TF: 800-233-3357 ■ *Web:* www.dairylandgreyhoundpark.com					
Del Mar Thoroughbred Club 2260 Jimmy Durante Blvd	Del Mar	CA	92014	858-755-1141	794-1004
Web: www.delmarracing.com					
Delaware North Cos Gaming & Entertainment 40 Fountain Plaza	Buffalo	NY	14202	716-858-5000	858-5926
TF: 800-828-7240 ■ *Web:* www.delawarenorth.com					
Delaware Park Racetrack & Slots Casino					
777 Delaware Park Blvd	Wilmington	DE	19804	302-994-2521	355-1298*
*Fax: Hum Res ■ *TF:* 800-417-5687 ■ *Web:* www.delawarepark.com					
Delaware Racing Assn 777 Delaware Park Blvd	Wilmington	DE	19804	302-994-2521	994-3567
TF Mktg: 800-441-5687 ■ *Web:* www.delpark.com					
Delta Downs Racetrack 2717 Delta Downs Dr	Vinton	LA	70668	337-589-7441	589-2399
TF: 800-589-7441 ■ *Web:* www.deltadowns.com					
Dover Downs 1131 N DuPont Hwy	Dover	DE	19901	302-674-4600	857-3253
TF: 800-711-5882 ■ *Web:* www.doverdowns.com/horseracing					
Dover Downs Gaming & Entertainment Inc 1131 N DuPont Hwy	Dover	DE	19901	302-674-4600	734-3124
NYSE: DDE ■ *TF:* 800-711-5882 ■ *Web:* www.doverdowns.com					
Dover Downs International Speedway					
1131 N DuPont Hwy PO Box 843	Dover	DE	19903	302-674-4600	741-8971
Web: www.doverspeedway.com					
Dover Motorsports Inc 1131 N Dupont Hwy	Dover	DE	19901	302-674-4600	672-0100
NYSE: DVD ■ *TF:* 800-441-7223 ■ *Web:* www.dovermotorsportsinc.com					
Dubuque Greyhound Park & Casino 1855 Greyhound Park Dr	Dubuque	IA	52001	563-582-3647	582-9074
TF: 800-373-3647 ■ *Web:* www.dgpc.com					
DuQuoin State Fair 655 Executive Dr	DuQuoin	IL	62832	618-542-1515	542-1541
Web: www.agr.state.il.us/dq					
Elko County Fairgrounds 13th St & Fairgrounds Rd	Elko	NV	89801	775-738-7925	778-3468

	City	State	Zip	Phone	Fax
Equus Gaming Co LP 650 Munoz Rivera Ave	Hato Rey	PR	00918	787-753-0676	758-2120
Eureka Downs 210 N Jefferson PO Box 228 *Web:* www.eurekadowns.com	Eureka	KS	67045	620-583-5528	583-5381
Fair Grounds Race Course 1751 Gentilly Blvd *Web:* www.fairgroundsracecourse.com	New Orleans	LA	70119	504-944-5515	944-1211
Fair Meadows at Tulsa 4609 E 21st St *Web:* www.fairmeadows.com	Tulsa	OK	74114	918-743-7223	743-8053
Fairmount Park 9301 Collinsville Rd *Web:* www.fairmountpark.com	Collinsville	IL	62234	618-345-4300	344-8218
Finger Lakes Gaming & Race Track 5857 Rt 96 *Web:* www.fingerlakesracetrack.com	Farmington	NY	14425	585-924-3232	924-3967
Finger Lakes Racing Assn 5857 Rt 96 *Web:* www.fingerlakesgaming.com	Farmington	NY	14425	585-924-3232	924-3967
Finish Line Management 1700 Joe Yenni Blvd	Kenner	LA	70065	504-466-8521	466-3908
Fonner Park 700 E Stolley Park Rd *Web:* www.fonnerpark.com	Grand Island	NE	68801	308-382-4515	384-2753
Fort Erie Race Track 230 Catherine St *TF:* 800-295-3770 ■ *Web:* www.forteriracing.com	Fort Erie	ON	L2A5N9	905-871-3200	994-3629
Freehold Raceway 130 Park Ave PO Box 6669 *TF:* 800-836-0462 ■ *Web:* www.freeholdraceway.com	Freehold	NJ	07728	732-462-3800	462-2920
Fresno District Fair 1121 S Chance Ave *Web:* www.fresnofair.com	Fresno	CA	93702	559-650-3247	650-3226
Gem County Fair 2199 S Johns Ave PO Box 443	Emmett	ID	83617	208-365-6828	365-0932
Gila County Fair Hwy 60	Globe	AZ	85502	928-425-5924	
Gillespie County Fairgrounds 530 Fair Dr PO Box 526 *Web:* www.gillespiefair.com	Fredericksburg	TX	78624	830-997-2359	997-4923
Golden Gate Fields 1100 Eastshore Hwy *Web:* www.goldengatefields.com	Berkeley	CA	94710	510-559-7345	559-7460
Graham County Fair 527 E Armory Rd	Safford	AZ	85546	928-428-7180	348-0023
Grants Pass Downs 1451 Fairgrounds Rd *Web:* www.jocofair.com	Grants Pass	OR	97527	541-476-3215	476-1027
Grays Harbor Raceway 32 Elma McCleary Rd PO Box 1229 *Web:* www.ghcfairgrounds.com	Elma	WA	98541	360-482-2651	482-3297
Greenetrack Inc I-59 at Exit 45 - Union Rd PO Drawer 471 *TF:* 800-633-5942 ■ *Web:* www.greenetrackpaysyoumoney.com	Eutaw	AL	35462	205-372-9318	372-4569
Greenlee County Fair 1258 Fairgrounds Rd PO Box 123	Duncan	AZ	85534	928-359-2032	359-2721
Harrington Raceway 15 W Rider Rd *Web:* www.harringtonraceway.com	Harrington	DE	19952	302-398-7223	398-3506
Hawthorne Race Course 3501 S Laramie Ave *TF:* 800-780-0701 ■ *Web:* www.hawthorneracecourse.com	Cicero	IL	60804	708-780-3700	780-3677
Hazel Park Raceway 1650 E 10 Mile Rd *Web:* www.hazelparkraceway.com	Hazel Park	MI	48030	248-398-1000	398-5236
Hinsdale Greyhound Park 688 Brattleboro Rd *TF:* 800-648-7225 ■ *Web:* www.hinsdalegreyhound.com	Hinsdale	NH	03451	603-336-5382	336-5477
Hippodrome de Montreal 7440 Decarie Blvd *Web:* www.hippodrome-montreal.ca	Montreal	QC	H4P2H1	514-739-2741	340-2025
Hippodrome de Quebec 250 Wilfrid-Hamel Blvd ExpoCite	Quebec	QC	G1K7M9	418-524-5283	524-0776
Historic Track-Goshen 44 Park Pl PO Box 121	Goshen	NY	10924	845-294-5333	294-3998
Hollywood Casino at Penn National Race Course 720 Bow Creek Rd *Web:* www.pennnational.com	Grantville	PA	17028	717-469-2211	469-2910
Hoosier Park 4500 Dan Patch Cir *TF:* 800-526-7223 ■ *Web:* www.hoosierpark.com	Anderson	IN	46013	765-642-7223	644-0467
Humboldt County Fair 1250 5th St *Web:* www.humboldtcountyfair.org	Ferndale	CA	95536	707-786-9511	786-9450
Illinois State Fairgrounds 801 E Sangamon Ave	Springfield	IL	62702	217-782-4231	524-6194
Indiana State Fairgrounds 1202 E 38th St *Web:* www.in.gov/statefair	Indianapolis	IN	46205	317-927-7500	927-7695
Indianapolis Motor Speedway Corp 4790 W 16th St *Web:* www.indyracingleague.com	Indianapolis	IN	46222	317-481-8500	492-6759
International Thoroughbred Breeders Inc 211 Benigno Blvd	Bellmawr	NJ	08031	856-931-8163	931-8165
Interstate Racing Assn 6200 Dahlia St *Web:* www.wembleyusa.com	Commerce City	CO	80022	303-288-1591	289-1640
Jackson Harness Raceway 200 W Ganson St *TF:* 877-316-0283 ■ *Web:* www.jacksonharnessraceway.com	Jackson	MI	49204	517-788-4500	788-6772
Jefferson County Kennel Club Inc 3079 N Jefferson St *Web:* www.jckcgreyhounds.com	Monticello	FL	32344	850-997-2561	997-3871
Jerome County Fairgrounds 200 N Fir *Web:* www.jeromecountyfair.com	Jerome	ID	83338	208-324-7209	
Lake Erie Speedway 1070 Delmas Dr *Web:* www.lakeeriespeedway.com/	North East	PA	16428	814-725-3303	
Laurel Park Rt 198 & Racetrack Rd *TF:* 800-638-1859 ■ *Web:* www.laurelpark.com	Laurel	MD	20724	301-725-0400	490-8194
Lebanon Raceway 665 N Broadway PO Box 58 *Web:* www.lebanonraceway.com	Lebanon	OH	45036	513-932-4936	932-7894
Lexington Trots Breeders Assn 1200 Red Mile Rd	Lexington	KY	40504	859-255-0752	231-0217
Lincoln Park 1600 Louisquisset Pike *Web:* www.lincolnparkri.com	Lincoln	RI	02865	401-723-3200	727-4770
Lone Star Park at Grand Prairie 1000 Lone Star Pkwy *TF:* 800-795-7223 ■ *Web:* www.lonestarpark.com	Grand Prairie	TX	75050	972-263-7223	237-5505
Los Alamitos Race Course 4961 Katella Ave *Web:* www.losalamitos.com/laqhr	Los Alamitos	CA	90720	714-820-2800	820-2820
Los Alamitos Racing Assn 4961 Katella Ave *Web:* www.losalamitos.com/laqhr	Los Alamitos	CA	90720	714-820-2800	820-2820
Los Angeles Turf Club Inc 285 W Huntington Dr *Web:* www.santaanita.com	Arcadia	CA	91007	626-574-7223	446-9565
Lowe's Motor Speedway 5555 Concord Pkwy S *Fax: Sales ■ *TF:* 800-455-3267 ■ *Web:* www.lowesmotorspeedway.com	Concord	NC	28027	704-455-3203	455-2272*
Magna Entertainment Corp 337 Magna Dr *NASDAQ: MECA* ■ *Web:* www.magnaentertainment.com	Aurora	ON	L4G7K1	905-726-2462	726-7164
Marias Fair 28082 Hwy 2	Shelby	MT	59474	406-434-2692	424-5395
Maryland Jockey Club at Pimlico 5201 Park Heights Ave *Web:* www.marylandracing.com	Baltimore	MD	21215	410-542-9400	466-2521
Maywood Park 8600 W North Ave *TF:* 800-748-5782 ■ *Web:* www.maywoodpark.com	Melrose Park	IL	60160	708-343-4800	343-2564
Meadowlands Racetrack 50 Rt 120 *Fax: Hum Res ■ *Web:* www.thebigm.com	East Rutherford	NJ	07073	201-935-8500	935-7121*
Meadows Racetrack Race Track Rd *Web:* www.themeadowsracing.com	Meadow Lands	PA	15347	724-225-9300	225-9347
Melbourne Greyhound Park 1100 N Wickham Rd *Web:* www.melbournegreyhoundpark.com	Melbourne	FL	32935	321-259-9800	259-3437
MetraPark 308 6th Ave N PO Box 2514 *TF:* 800-366-8538 ■ *Web:* www.metrapark.com	Billings	MT	59103	406-256-2422	256-2479
Midstate Raceway Inc 14 Ruth St PO Box 860 *TF:* 877-777-8559	Vernon	NY	13476	315-829-2201	829-2931
Mile High Greyhound Racing 6200 Dahlia St *Web:* www.mihiracing.com	Commerce City	CO	80022	303-288-1591	289-1640
Minidoka County Fairgrounds 75 E Baseline PO Box 151	Rupert	ID	83350	208-436-9748	436-8063
Mohave County Fair Assn 2600 Fairgrounds *Web:* www.mcfafairgrounds.org	Kingman	AZ	86401	928-753-2636	753-8383
Monmouth Park Racetrack 175 Oceanport Ave *Web:* www.monmouthpark.com	Oceanport	NJ	07757	732-222-5100	870-2814
Montana State Fair 400 3rd St NW	Great Falls	MT	59404	406-727-8900	452-8955
Monticello Raceway 204 Rt 17B *Web:* www.monticelloraceway.com	Monticello	NY	12701	845-794-4100	794-4110
Mount Pleasant Meadows 500 N Mission Rd	Mount Pleasant	MI	48858	989-773-0012	773-4632
Mountaineer Racetrack & Gaming Resort Rt 2 PO Box 358 *TF:* 800-804-0468 ■ *Web:* www.mtrgaming.com	Chester	WV	26034	304-387-2400	387-0084
MTR Gaming Group Inc PO Box 358 *NASDAQ: MNTG* ■ *TF:* 800-804-0468 ■ *Web:* www.mtrgaming.com	Chester	WV	26034	304-387-8300	387-8001
Naples/Fort Myers Greyhound Track 10601 Bonita Beach Rd *Web:* www.naplesfortmyersdogs.com	Bonita Springs	FL	34135	239-992-2411	947-9244
New Mexico State Fair 300 San Pedro NE *Web:* exponm.com	Albuquerque	NM	87108	505-265-1791	266-7784
New York City Off-Track Betting Corp 1501 Broadway 12th Fl *Web:* www.nycotb.com	New York	NY	10036	212-221-5200	221-8025
New York Racing Assn 110-00 Rockaway Blvd PO Box 90 *Web:* www.nyra.com	Jamaica	NY	11417	718-641-4700	835-5246
Northville Downs 301 S Center St *Web:* www.northvilledowns.com	Northville	MI	48167	248-349-1000	348-8955
Northwest Montana Fair 265 N Meridian Rd *Web:* www.nwmtfair.com	Kalispell	MT	59901	406-758-5810	756-8936
Oaklawn Park 2705 Central Ave *TF:* 800-625-5296 ■ *Web:* www.oaklawn.com	Hot Springs	AR	71901	501-623-4411	624-4950
Ocean Downs 10218 Racetrack Rd PO Box 11 *Web:* www.oceandowns.com	Berlin	MD	21811	410-641-0600	641-2711
Penn National Gaming Inc 825 Berkshire Blvd Suite 200 *NASDAQ: PENN* ■ *Web:* www.pnrc.com	Wyomissing	PA	19610	610-373-2400	373-4966
Pensacola Greyhound Track 951 Dog Track Rd *TF:* 800-345-3997 ■ *Web:* www.pensacolagreyhoundpark.com	Pensacola	FL	32506	850-455-8595	453-8883
Philadelphia Park Racetrack 3001 Street Rd PO Box 1000 *TF:* 800-523-6886 ■ *Web:* www.philadelphiapark.com	Bensalem	PA	19020	215-639-9000	639-0337
Phoenix Greyhound Park 3801 E Washington St *Web:* www.phoenixgreyhoundpark.com	Phoenix	AZ	85034	602-273-7181	273-6176
Pinnacle Entertainment Inc 3800 Howard Hughes Pkwy Suite 1800 *NYSE: PNK* ■ *Web:* www.pnkinc.com	Las Vegas	NV	89109	702-784-7777	784-7778
Pocatello Downs 10560 N Fairgrounds Rd	Pocatello	ID	83202	208-238-1721	
Portland International Raceway 1940 N Victory Blvd *Web:* www.portlandraceway.com	Portland	OR	97217	503-823-7223	823-5896
Portland Meadows Horse Track 1001 N Schmeer Rd *TF:* 800-944-3127 ■ *Web:* www.portlandmeadows.com	Portland	OR	97217	503-285-9144	286-9763
Ravalli County Fair 100 Old Corvallis Rd *Web:* www.ravallicountyfair.com	Hamilton	MT	59840	406-363-3411	375-9152
Remington Park Race Track 1 Remington Pl *TF:* 866-456-9880 ■ *Web:* www.remingtonpark.com	Oklahoma City	OK	73111	405-424-1000	425-3297
Retama Park 1 Retama Pkwy *Web:* www.retamapark.com	Selma	TX	78154	210-651-7000	651-7097
Rockingham Park Rockingham Park Blvd PO Box 47 *TF:* 800-639-4704 ■ *Web:* www.rockinghampark.com	Salem	NH	03079	603-898-2311	898-7163
Rosecroft Raceway 6336 Rosecroft Dr *TF:* 877-818-9467 ■ *Web:* www.rosecroft.com	Fort Washington	MD	20744	301-567-4000	567-9267
Ruidoso Downs Race Track 1461 Hwy 70 W PO Box 449 *Web:* ruidosodownsracing.com	Ruidoso Downs	NM	88346	505-378-4431	378-4631
Sam Houston Race Park 7575 N Sam Houston Pkwy W *TF:* 800-807-7223 ■ *Web:* www.shrp.com	Houston	TX	77064	281-807-8700	807-8777
San Joaquin County Fair 1658 S Airport Way *Web:* www.sanjoaquinfair.com	Stockton	CA	95206	209-466-5041	466-5739
Sandy Downs 1860 E 65 South	Idaho Falls	ID	83401	208-529-2276	612-8179
Santa Anita Park 285 W Huntington Dr *Web:* www.santaanita.com	Arcadia	CA	91007	626-574-7223	446-9565
Santa Cruz County Fair 3142 S Hwy 83 PO Box 85	Sonoita	AZ	85637	520-455-5553	455-5330
Saratoga Gaming & Raceway 342 Jefferson St PO Box 356 *Web:* www.saratogaraceway.com	Saratoga Springs	NY	12866	518-584-2110	583-1269
Saratoga Race Course Union Ave *Web:* www.nyracing.com/saratoga/	Saratoga Springs	NY	12866	718-641-4700	
Scarborough Downs Rt 1 PO Box 468 *Web:* www.scarboroughdowns.com	Scarborough	ME	04070	207-883-4331	883-2020
Solano County Fair 900 Fairgrounds Dr *Web:* www.scfair.com	Vallejo	CA	94589	707-551-2000	642-7947
Sonoma County Fairgrounds 1350 Bennett Valley Rd *Web:* www.sonomacountyfair.com	Santa Rosa	CA	95404	707-545-4200	573-9342
Southland Racing Corp 1550 N Ingram Blvd *TF:* 800-467-6182	West Memphis	AR	72301	870-735-3670	732-8335
Sports Creek Raceway 4290 Morrish Rd *TF:* 800-635-4582	Swartz Creek	MI	48473	810-635-3333	635-9711
State Fair Park 1800 State Fair Park Dr *Web:* www.statefair.org	Lincoln	NE	68508	402-473-4110	473-4114
Sun Downs 1500 S Oak St	Kennewick	WA	99337	509-586-9211	582-1894
Sunflower Racing Inc 9700 Leavenworth Rd *TF:* 800-695-7223	Kansas City	KS	66109	913-299-9797	299-9804
Sunland Park Racetrack 1200 Futurity Dr *Web:* www.sunland-park.com	Sunland Park	NM	88063	505-874-5200	589-1518
Syracuse Mile c/o Vernon Downs PO Box 860	Vernon	NY	13476	315-829-2201	829-2931
Tampa Bay Downs Inc 11225 Racetrack Rd *TF:* 800-200-4434 ■ *Web:* www.tampabaydowns.com	Tampa	FL	33626	813-855-4401	854-3539
Tampa Greyhound Track 8300 N Nebraska Ave *Web:* www.tampadogs.com	Tampa	FL	33604	813-932-4313	932-5048
Thistledown Racing Club Inc 21501 Emery Rd *Web:* www.thistledown.com	Cleveland	OH	44128	216-662-8600	662-5339
Thunder Ridge 164 Thunder Rd	Prestonsburg	KY	41653	606-886-7223	886-7225
Thunder Ridge Motor Speedway 1601 49th Ave SW *Web:* www.thunderridgemotorspdwy.com	Lanett	AL	36863	334-576-7233	
Tillamook County Fairgrounds 4603 E 3rd St PO Box 455 *Web:* www.wcn.net/tillamookfair	Tillamook	OR	97141	503-842-2272	842-3314
Turf Paradise Racetrack 1501 W Bell Rd *Web:* www.turfparadise.com	Phoenix	AZ	85023	602-942-1101	942-8659
Walla Walla Racetrack 9th & Orchard PO Box G	Walla Walla	WA	99362	509-527-3247	527-3259
Western Montana Fair 1101 South Ave W *Web:* www.westernmontanafair.com	Missoula	MT	59801	406-721-3247	728-7479
Woodlands The 9700 Leavenworth Rd *TF:* 800-695-7223 ■ *Web:* www.woodlandskc.com	Kansas City	KS	66109	913-299-9797	299-9804
Wyoming Downs 10180 Hwy 89 N *Web:* www.wyomingdowns.com	Evanston	WY	82930	307-789-0511	789-4614
Yavapai Downs at Prescott Valley 10501 Hwy 89A *Web:* www.yavapaidownsatpv.com	Prescott Valley	AZ	86314	928-775-8000	775-6084
Yonkers Raceway 810 Yonkers Ave *Web:* www.yonkersraceway.com	Yonkers	NY	10704	914-968-4200	968-4479
Yuma County Fair 2520 E 32nd St *Web:* www.yumafair.com	Yuma	AZ	85365	928-726-4420	344-3480

646 RADIO COMPANIES

	City	State	Zip	Phone	Fax
AAA Entertainment LLC 1110 Central Ave	Pawtucket	RI	02861	401-723-1063	728-1865

Phone Fax

ABC Radio Networks 444 Madison Ave New York NY 10022 212-735-1700 735-1799
Web: www.abcradio.com
Access 1 Communications Corp 208 N Thomas Dr Shreveport LA 71107 318-222-0636 459-1493
Albany Broadcasting Co 6 Johnson Rd Latham NY 12110 518-786-6600 786-6610
Allegheny Mountain Network PO Box 247 Tyrone PA 16686 814-684-3200 684-1220
American Family Radio PO Drawer 2440 Tupelo MS 38803 662-844-8888 842-6791
TF: 800-326-4543 ■ *Web:* www.afr.net
American General Media 1400 Easton Dr Suite 144-B Bakersfield CA 93309 661-328-1410 328-0873
Web: www.liveradio.com
Artistic Media Partners Inc 5520 E 75th St Indianapolis IN 46250 317-594-0600 594-9567
Web: www.artisticradio.com
Astral Media Radio 2 Saint Clair Ave W 2nd Fl Toronto ON M4V1L6 416-922-9999 872-8683
Web: www.astralmedia.com
Backyard Broadcasting 4237 Salisbury Rd Suite 225 Jacksonville FL 32216 904-674-0260 854-4596
Web: www.bybradio.com
Barnstable Broadcasting Inc 2 Newton Executive Pk Suite 302 Newton MA 02462 617-527-0062 630-0960
Beasley Broadcast Group Inc 3033 Riviera Dr Suite 200 Naples FL 34103 239-263-5000 263-8191
NASDAQ: BBGI ■ *Web:* www.bbgi.com
Bi-Coastal Media LLC 140 N Main St Lakeport CA 95453 707-263-6113 263-0939
Bible Broadcasting Network Inc 11530 Carmel Commons Blvd Charlotte NC 28226 704-523-5555 522-1967
TF: 800-888-7077 ■ *Web:* www.bbnradio.org/bbn
Birach Broadcasting Corp
21700 Northwestern Hwy Tower 14 Suite 1190 Southfield MI 48075 248-557-3500 557-2950
Web: www.birach.com
Black Crow Media 1711 Ellis Dr Valdosta GA 31601 229-244-8642 242-7620
Bliss Communications Inc PO Box 5001 Janesville WI 53547 608-752-7895 752-4438
TF: 800-362-6712 ■ *Web:* www.blissnet.net
Bonneville International Corp 55 N 300 West Salt Lake City UT 84180 801-575-7500 575-7548
Web: www.bonnint.com
Border Media Partners LLC 9426 Old Katy Rd Bldg 10 Houston TX 77055 713-968-4417 968-4518
Bott Radio Network 10550 Barkley St Suite 100 Overland Park KS 66212 913-642-7770 642-1319
TF: 800-875-1903 ■ *Web:* www.bottradionetwork.com
Brazos Valley Radio 1240 E Villa Maria Rd Bryan TX 77802 979-776-1240 776-6074
Brewer Broadcasting Inc 1305 Carter St Chattanooga TN 37402 423-265-9494 266-2335
Bristol Broadcasting Co Inc PO Box 1389 Bristol VA 24203 276-669-8112 669-0541
TF: 800-253-8112 ■ *Web:* www.bristolbroadcasting.com
Buckley Broadcasting Corp 166 W Putnam Ave Greenwich CT 06830 203-661-4307 622-7341
Web: www.buckleyradio.com
Canadian Broadcasting Corp (CBC) 181 Queen St Ottawa ON K1P1K9 613-288-6000
Web: cbc.radio-canada.ca
CBC (Canadian Broadcasting Corp) 181 Queen St Ottawa ON K1P1K9 613-288-6000
Web: cbc.radio-canada.ca
CBS Radio Inc 1515 Broadway 46th Fl New York NY 10036 212-846-3939 846-2315
Web: www.cbsradio.com
Cherry Creek Radio 501 S Cherry St Denver CO 80246 303-468-6500 468-6555
Web: www.cherrycreekradio.com
Citadel Broadcasting Corp
7201 W Lake Mead Blvd Suite 400 Las Vegas NV 89128 702-804-5200 804-5936
NYSE: CDL ■ *Web:* www.citadelbroadcasting.com
Clear Channel Radio 200 E Basse Rd San Antonio TX 78209 210-822-2828 822-2299
TF: 888-937-6131 ■ *Web:* www.clearchannel.com/radio
Commonwealth Broadcasting Corp 113 W Public Sq Suite 400 Glasgow KY 42141 270-659-2002 651-1771
Communications Corp of America
700 Saint John St Suite 300 Lafayette LA 70501 337-237-1142 237-1373
TF: 800-237-1142
Community Radio 2510 W 20th St Joplin MO 64804 417-781-1313 781-1316
Corus Entertainment Inc 181 Bay St Suite 1630 Toronto ON M5J2T3 416-642-3770 642-3779
NYSE: CJR ■ *TF:* 877-772-3770 ■ *Web:* www.corusent.com
Cox Radio Inc 6205 Peachtree Dunwoody Rd Atlanta GA 30328 678-645-0000 645-1889
NYSE: CXR ■ *Web:* coxradio.com
Crawford Broadcasting Co 2150 W 29th Ave Suite 300 Denver CO 80211 303-433-5500 433-1555
Web: www.crawfordbroadcasting.com
Cromwell Group Inc 1824 Murfreesboro Rd 2nd Fl Nashville TN 37217 615-361-7560 366-4313
CSN International PO Box 391 Twin Falls ID 83303 208-734-2049 736-1958
TF: 800-357-4226 ■ *Web:* www.csnradio.com
CTV Globe Media 1331 Yonge St Toronto ON M4T1Y1 416-925-6666 926-4026
Web: www.chumlimited.com
Cumulus Media Inc 3535 Piedmont Rd Bldg 14 Suite 1400 Atlanta GA 30305 404-949-0700 949-0740
NASDAQ: CMLS ■ *Web:* www.cumulus.com
Curtis Media Group 3012 Highwood Blvd Suite 201 Raleigh NC 27604 919-876-0674 790-8369
Web: www.curtismedia.com
Delmarva Broadcasting Co Inc PO Box 909 Salisbury MD 21803 410-219-3500 548-1543
Web: www.radiocenter.com
Disney Walt Co 500 S Buena Vista St Burbank CA 91521 818-560-1000 843-5346*
NYSE: DIS ■ **Fax:* Mail Rm ■ *Web:* corporate.disney.go.com
Eagle Communications Inc 2703 Hall St Suite 15 Hays KS 67601 785-625-4000 625-8030
Web: www.eaglecom.net
Eagle Radio Inc 2300 Hall PO Box 6 Hays KS 67601 785-625-2578 625-3632
TF: 800-569-0144
Educational Media Foundation DBA K-Love 2351 Sunset Blvd Rocklin CA 95765 916-251-1600 251-1650*
**Fax Area Code:* 919 ■ *TF:* 800-525-5683 ■ *Web:* www.klove.com
Emmis Communications Corp
40 Monument Cir 1 Emmis Plaza Suite 700 Indianapolis IN 46204 317-266-0100 631-3750
NASDAQ: EMMS ■ *Web:* www.emmis.com
Entercom Communications Corp 401 City Ave Suite 809 Bala Cynwyd PA 19004 610-660-5610 660-5620
NYSE: ETM ■ *Web:* www.entercom.com
Entravision Communications Corp
2425 Olympic Blvd Suite 6000 W Santa Monica CA 90404 310-447-3870 447-3899
NYSE: EVC ■ *Web:* www.entravision.com
Family Life Broadcasting System DBA Family Life Radio
7355 N Oracle Rd Tucson AZ 85704 520-742-6976 742-6979
TF: 800-776-1070 ■ *Web:* www.flc.org/flr
Family Radio 290 Hegenberger Rd Oakland CA 94621 510-568-6200 633-7983
TF: 800-543-1495 ■ *Web:* www.familyradio.com
Family Stations Radio Network 290 Hegenberger Rd Oakland CA 94621 510-568-6200 633-7983
TF: 800-543-1495 ■ *Web:* www.familyradio.com
Far East Broadcasting Co Inc PO Box 1 La Mirada CA 90637 562-947-4651 943-0160
TF: 800-523-3480 ■ *Web:* www.febc.org
First Media Radio LLC 863 Benner Pike Suite 200 State College PA 16801 814-231-0953 231-0950
Fisher Communications Inc 100 4th Ave N Suite 510 Seattle WA 98109 206-404-7000 404-6037
NASDAQ: FSCI ■ *TF:* 800-443-0073 ■ *Web:* www.fsci.com
Flinn Broadcasting 6080 Mt Moriah Rd Ext Memphis TN 38115 901-375-9324 795-4454
Web: www.flinn.com
Forever Broadcasting 1 Forever Dr Hollidaysburg PA 16648 814-941-9800 943-2754
Web: www.foreverradio.com
Galaxy Communications LP 235 Walton St Syracuse NY 13202 315-472-9111 472-1888
Web: www.galaxycommunications.com
Georgia-Carolina Radiocasting Cos LLC PO Drawer E Toccoa GA 30577 706-297-7264 297-7266
Web: www.gacaradio.com
Georgia Public Broadcasting (GPB) 260 14th St NW Atlanta GA 30318 404-685-4788 685-2431
TF: 800-222-6006 ■ *Web:* www.gpb.org
GHB Broadcasting Corp 1776 Briarcliff Rd NE Suite A Atlanta GA 30306 404-875-1110 875-1186
Golden West Radio Box 950 Altona MB R0G0B0 204-324-6464 324-8918
TF: 800-374-3315 ■ *Web:* www.gwr.goldenwestradio.ca
GPB (Georgia Public Broadcasting) 260 14th St NW Atlanta GA 30318 404-685-4788 685-2431
TF: 800-222-6006 ■ *Web:* www.gpb.org
Great Scott Broadcasting 224 Maugers Mill Rd Pottstown PA 19464 610-326-4000 326-4809

Phone Fax

Greater Media Inc 35 Braintree Hill Pk Suite 300 Braintree MA 02184 781-348-8600 348-8695
Web: www.greater-media.com
Hall Communications Inc PO Box 551 Norwich CT 06360 860-887-3511 886-7649
Web: www.hallradio.com
Inner City Broadcasting Corp 3 Park Ave 41st Fl New York NY 10016 212-447-1000 447-5194
International Broadcasting Bureau
330 Independence Ave SW Washington DC 20237 202-203-4500 203-4960
Web: www.ibb.gov
Jim Pattison Media Group 1067 W Cordova St Suite 1800 Vancouver BC V6C1C7 604-688-6764 694-6900
Web: www.jimpattison.com/medi/me__index.htm
Journal Broadcast Group Inc 720 E Capitol Dr Milwaukee WI 53212 414-332-9611 967-5400
Web: www.journalbroadcastgroup.com
K-Love 2351 Sunset Blvd Rocklin CA 95765 916-251-1600 251-1650*
**Fax Area Code:* 919 ■ *TF:* 800-525-5683 ■ *Web:* www.klove.com
Key Broadcasting PO Box 1227 Corbin KY 40702 606-528-8787 528-9924
Keymarket Communications LLC 123 Blaine Rd Brownsville PA 15417 724-938-2000 938-7824
Legend Communications 5074 Dorsey Hall Dr Suite 205 Ellicott City MD 21042 410-740-0250 740-7222
Leighton Enterprises Inc PO Box 1458 Saint Cloud MN 56302 320-251-1450 251-8952
Liberman Broadcasting Inc 1845 W Empire Ave Burbank CA 91504 818-563-5722 729-5678
Web: www.lbimedia.com
Lincoln Financial Media 100 N Greene St PO Box 21008 Greensboro NC 27420 336-691-3000 691-3938*
**Fax Area Code:* 704 ■ *Web:* www.lincolnfinancialmedia.com
LM Communications 401 W Main St Suite 301 Lexington KY 40507 859-233-1515 233-1517
Lotus Communications Corp 3301 Barham Blvd Suite 200 Los Angeles CA 90068 323-512-2225 512-2224
Web: www.lotuscorp.com
MacDonald Broadcasting Co 2000 Whittier St Saginaw MI 48601 989-752-8161 752-8102
Magic Broadcasting LLC 7106 Laird St Suite 102 Panama City Beach FL 32408 850-230-5855 230-6988
Web: www.magicbroadcasting.net
Magnum Radio Group Inc 1021 N Superior Ave Suite 5 Tomah WI 54660 608-372-9600 372-7566
Mahaffey Enterprises Inc PO Box 4584 Springfield MO 65808 417-883-9180 883-9096
TF: 800-725-9180
Main Line 25 Pencraft Ave Chambersburg PA 17201 717-263-0813 263-9649
Mapleton Communications 60 Garden Ct Suite 300 Monterey CA 93940 831-658-5200 658-5299
Maritime Broadcasting System 5121 Sackville St 7th Fl Halifax NS B3J1K1 902-425-1225 423-2093
Web: www.mbsradio.com
Maverick Media 136 Main St Suite 202 Westport CT 06880 203-227-2800 227-4819
Mega Communications LLC 8121 Georgia Ave 10th Fl Silver Spring MD 20910 301-588-6200 562-5850
Web: www.triplexespnradio.com
Mel Wheeler Inc 5009 S Hulen St Suite 101 Fort Worth TX 76132 817-294-7644 294-8519
Metropolitan Radio Group Inc 2010 S Stewart Ave Springfield MO 65804 417-862-0852 862-9079
TF: 800-961-5595 ■ *Web:* www.metropolitanradiogroup.net
Mid-America Radio Group Inc PO Box 1970 Martinsville IN 46151 765-349-1485 342-3569
Midwest Communications Inc 904 Grand Ave Wausau WI 54403 715-842-1437 842-7061*
**Fax:* Hum Res ■ *TF:* 877-903-2171 ■ *Web:* www.mwcradio.com
Midwest Family Broadcasting 319-B E Battlefield Springfield MO 65807 417-886-5677 886-2155
Web: www.mwfmarketing.fm
Midwestern Broadcasting Co 314 E Front St Traverse City MI 49684 231-947-7675 929-3988
Millenium Radio Group 109 Walters Ave Trenton NJ 08638 609-771-8181 406-7956
TF: 800-678-9599
Miller Communications Inc 51 Commerce St Sumter SC 29151 803-775-2321 773-4856
Web: www.miller.fm
Minnesota Public Radio (MPR) 480 Cedar St Saint Paul MN 55101 651-290-1212 290-1260
TF: 800-228-7123 ■ *Web:* www.mpr.org
Mississippi River Radio 324 Broadway Cape Girardeau MO 63701 573-335-8291 335-4806
Moody Broadcasting Network 820 N La Salle Blvd Chicago IL 60610 312-329-4300 329-4468
Web: www.mbn.org
Morris Communications Co LLC 725 Broad St Augusta GA 30901 706-724-0851 823-3440
TF: 800-622-6358 ■ *Web:* www.morriscomm.com
Mortenson Broadcasting Co 3270 Blazer Pkwy Suite 101 Lexington KY 40509 859-245-1000 245-1600
TF: 800-406-6333
Mount Rushmore Broadcasting Inc 218 N Wolcott St Casper WY 82601 307-265-1984 473-7461
Web: www.mrbradio.com
MPR (Minnesota Public Radio) 480 Cedar St Saint Paul MN 55101 651-290-1212 290-1260
TF: 800-228-7123 ■ *Web:* www.mpr.org
Multicultural Broadcasting Inc 449 Broadway New York NY 10013 212-966-1059 966-9580
Web: www.mrbi.net
Nassau Broadcasting Partners LP 619 Alexander Rd 3rd Fl Princeton NJ 08540 609-419-0300 419-0143
Web: www.nassaubroadcasting.com
New Northwest Broadcasters 1011 Western Ave Suite 920 Seattle WA 98104 206-204-0213 204-0214
Web: www.nnbradio.com
New South Communications Inc 265 Highpoint Dr Ridgeland MS 39157 601-956-0102 978-3980
Newcap Broadcasting Ltd 745 Windmill Rd Dartmouth NS B3B1C2 902-468-7557 468-7558
Web: www.ncc.ca
Newfoundland Capital Corp Ltd 745 Windmill Rd Dartmouth NS B3B1C2 902-468-7557 468-7558
Web: www.ncc.ca
Newradio Group E5680 State Rd 33 Reedsburg WI 53959 608-524-1400 524-8428
TF: 800-236-4105
Newspaper Radio Corp 1201 18th St Suite 200 Denver CO 80202 303-675-4680 296-7030
Web: www.nrcbroadcasting.com
NextMedia Group LLC
6312 S Fiddlers Green Cir Suite 360E Greenwood Village CO 80111 303-694-9118 694-4940
Web: www.nextmediagroup.net
Noalmark Broadcasting Corp 202 W 19th St El Dorado AR 71730 870-862-7777 862-0203
Northeast Broadcasting Corp 288 S River Rd Bedford NH 03110 603-668-6400 668-6470
Northern Star Broadcasting LLC 1356 Mackinaw Ave Cheboygan MI 49721 231-627-2341 627-7000
TF: 888-847-2346 ■ *Web:* www.nsbroadcasting.com
Pamal Broadcasting Ltd PO Box 310 Beacon NY 12508 845-831-8000 838-2109*
**Fax:* Sales ■ *Web:* www.pamal.com
Pamplin Communications Corp 10209 SE Division St Portland OR 97266 503-251-1597 262-3822*
**Fax:* Hum Res
Perry Publishing & Broadcasting 1701 W Pine Ave Duncan OK 73534 580-255-1350 470-9993
Web: www.blackchronicle.com
Prairie Communications LLP PO Box 448 DeKalb IL 60115 815-758-8686 756-9723
Quantum Communications Corp 3 Stamford Landing Suite 210 Stamford CT 06902 203-388-0048 388-0054
Quarnstrom Media Group LLC 1104 Cloquet Ave Cloquet MN 55720 218-879-4534 879-1962
TF: 888-404-9555
Radio One Inc 5900 Princess Garden Pkwy Suite 800 Lanham MD 20706 301-306-1111 306-9609
NASDAQ: ROIA ■ *Web:* www.radio-one.com
Radio Training Network Inc PO Box 7217 Lakeland FL 33807 863-644-3464 646-5326
Regent Communications Inc 100 E RiverCenter Blvd 9th Fl Covington KY 41011 859-292-0030 292-0352
NASDAQ: RGCI ■ *Web:* www.regentcomm.com
Renda Broadcasting Corp 900 Parish St 4th Fl Pittsburgh PA 15220 412-875-1800 875-1801
Web: www.rendabroadcasting.com
Results Radio LLC 1355 N Dutton Ave Suite 225 Santa Rosa CA 95401 707-546-9185 546-9188
Rogers Media Inc 777 Jarvis St Toronto ON M4Y3B7 416-935-8200 935-8202
Route 81 Radio LLC 780 E Market St Suite 265 West Chester PA 19382 610-696-8181 696-5072
Web: www.route81radio.com
Saga Communications Inc 73 Kercheval Ave Grosse Pointe Farms MI 48236 313-886-7070 886-7150
NYSE: SGA ■ *TF:* 888-886-7070 ■ *Web:* www.sagacommunications.com
Salem Communications Corp 4880 Santa Rosa Rd Camarillo CA 93012 805-987-0400 384-4511
NASDAQ: SALM ■ *Web:* www.salem.cc
Shamrock Communications Inc 149 Penn Ave Scranton PA 18503 570-348-9108 348-9109
TF: 800-228-4637
Shepherd Enterprises 300 W Reed St Moberly MO 65270 660-263-5800 263-2300
Web: www.regionalradio.com
Simmons Media Group Inc 515 S 700 East Suite 1C Salt Lake City UT 84102 801-524-2600 521-9234
Web: www.simmonsmedia.com

				Phone	Fax
Sorenson Broadcasting Corp 2804 Ridgeview Way	Sioux Falls	SD	57105	605-334-1117	
South Central Communications Corp PO Box 3848 *Web:* www.southcentralcommunications.net	Evansville	IN	47736	812-463-7950	463-7915
Spanish Broadcasting System Inc 2601 S Bayshore Dr PH 2 *NASDAQ: SBSA* ■ *Web:* www.spanishbroadcasting.com	Coconut Grove	FL	33133	305-441-6901	446-5148
Tejas Broadcasting 3639 Wolflin Ave	Amarillo	TX	79102	806-355-1044	457-0642
Telesouth Communications Inc 6311 Ridgewood Rd *Web:* www.telesouth.com	Jackson	MS	39211	601-957-1700	956-5228
Three Eagles Communications Co 1418 25th St *TF:* 800-651-5568 ■ *Web:* www.threeeagles.com	Columbus	NE	68601	402-564-2866	564-2867
Triad Broadcasting Co LLC 2511 Garden Rd Bldg A Suite 104 *Web:* www.triadbroadcasting.com	Monterey	CA	93940	831-655-6350	655-6355
Univision Radio 3102 Oak Lawn Ave Suite 215 *Web:* www.univision.net	Dallas	TX	75219	214-525-7700	525-7750
VerStandig Broadcasting PO Box 752 *TF:* 800-388-9782 ■ *Web:* www.valleyradio.com	Harrisonburg	VA	22803	540-434-0331	434-7087
Visionary Related Entertainment PO Box 1730	Rohnert Park	CA	94927	707-528-0339	664-9274
Waitt Media Inc 1125 S 103rd St Suite 200 *TF:* 888-656-0634 ■ *Web:* www.waittmedia.com	Omaha	NE	68124	402-697-8000	697-8024
Walt Disney Co 500 S Buena Vista St *NYSE: DIS* ■ **Fax:* Mail Rm ■ *Web:* corporate.disney.go.com	Burbank	CA	91521	818-560-1000	843-5346*
West Virginia Radio Corp 1251 Earl L Core Rd *Web:* www.wvradioadvertising.com	Morgantown	WV	26505	304-296-0029	296-3876
Willis Broadcasting 645 Church St Suite 400	Norfolk	VA	23510	757-622-4600	624-6515
Withers Broadcasting Co PO Box 1508 *TF:* 800-333-1577	Mount Vernon	IL	62864	618-242-3500	242-2490
Zimmer Radio Group 3215 Lemone Industrial Blvd Suite 200 *TF:* 800-455-1099	Columbia	MO	65201	573-875-1099	875-2439

647 RADIO NETWORKS

				Phone	Fax
ABC News Radio 125 West End Ave 6th Fl *Web:* www.abcradio.com	New York	NY	10023	212-456-5100	456-5150
Air America Radio 3 Park Ave *Web:* www.airamericaradio.com	New York	NY	10016	212-889-2965	889-3278
All Comedy Radio Network 8967 W Sunset Blvd *Web:* www.allcomedyradio.com	Los Angeles	CA	90069	310-859-9900	859-9987
American Family Radio PO Drawer 2440 *TF:* 800-326-4543 ■ *Web:* www.afr.net	Tupelo	MS	38803	662-844-8888	842-6791
American Public Media 480 Cedar St *TF:* 877-276-8400 ■ *Web:* americanpublicmedia.publicradio.org	Saint Paul	MN	55101	651-290-1225	290-1415
AP Broadcast Services 1825 K St NW Suite 800 *TF:* 800-821-4747 ■ *Web:* apbroadcast.com	Washington	DC	20006	202-736-1100	736-1199
Astral Media Inc 2100 Rue Sainte-Catherine O Bureau 1000 *TSX: ACM.A* ■ *Web:* www.astral.com	Montreal	QC	H3H2T3	514-939-5000	939-1515
Bible Broadcasting Network Inc 11530 Carmel Commons Blvd *TF:* 800-888-7077 ■ *Web:* www.bbnradio.org/bbn	Charlotte	NC	28226	704-523-5555	522-1967
Black Radio Network 166 Madison Ave 4th Fl	New York	NY	10016	212-686-6850	686-7308
Bloomberg Radio Network 499 Park Ave 15th Fl *TF:* 800-448-5678 ■ *Web:* www.bloomberg.com/media	New York	NY	10022	212-318-2000	940-1994
Bott Radio Network 10550 Barkley St Suite 100 *TF:* 800-875-1903 ■ *Web:* www.bottradionetwork.com	Overland Park	KS	66212	913-642-7770	642-1319
CBC Radio One PO Box 3220 Stn C *Web:* www.cbc.ca/radioone	Ottawa	ON	K1Y1E4	613-288-6000	
CBC Radio Two PO Box 3220 Stn C **Fax:* Mktg ■ *Web:* www.cbc.ca/radiotwo	Ottawa	ON	K1Y1E4	613-288-6000	724-5112*
CBS Corp 51 W 52nd St *NYSE: CBS* ■ *Web:* www.cbscorporation.com	New York	NY	10019	212-975-4321	975-4516
CBS Radio Network 524 W 57th St	New York	NY	10019	212-975-3615	975-6347
CNN en Espanol Radio 1 CNN Ctr *TF:* 800-331-7726 ■ *Web:* www.cnn.com/espanol	Atlanta	GA	30303	404-827-1220	827-1758
CNNRadio Network 1 CNN Ctr *Web:* www.cnnradio.com	Atlanta	GA	30303	404-827-2750	827-1758
Concert Music Network 100 Park Ave 5th Fl	New York	NY	10017	212-309-9370	309-9380
Crystal Media Networks 1100 Wilson Blvd Suite 3000	Arlington	VA	22209	703-247-7500	247-7505
CSN International PO Box 391 *TF:* 800-357-4226 ■ *Web:* www.csnradio.com	Twin Falls	ID	83303	208-734-2049	736-1958
Educational Media Foundation DBA K-Love 2351 Sunset Blvd **Fax Area Code:* 919 ■ *TF:* 800-525-5683 ■ *Web:* www.klove.com	Rocklin	CA	95765	916-251-1600	251-1650*
ESPN Radio Network ESPN 935 Middle St *Web:* www.espnradio.com	Bristol	CT	06010	860-766-2000	766-2213
Family Life Broadcasting System DBA Family Life Radio 7355 N Oracle Rd *TF:* 800-776-1070 ■ *Web:* www.flc.org/flr	Tucson	AZ	85704	520-742-6976	742-6979
Family Life Communications Inc 7355 N Oracle Rd PO Box 35300 *TF:* 800-776-1070 ■ *Web:* www.flc.org	Tucson	AZ	85740	520-742-6976	742-6979
Family Radio 290 Hegenberger Rd *TF:* 800-543-1495 ■ *Web:* www.familyradio.com	Oakland	CA	94621	510-568-6200	633-7983
Family Stations Radio Network 290 Hegenberger Rd *TF:* 800-543-1495 ■ *Web:* www.familyradio.com	Oakland	CA	94621	510-568-6200	633-7983
Far East Broadcasting Co Inc PO Box 1 *TF:* 800-523-3480 ■ *Web:* www.febc.org	La Mirada	CA	90637	562-947-4651	943-0160
Fox News Radio Network 1211 Ave of the Americas 18th Fl *Web:* www.foxnews.com/access/radio.html	New York	NY	10036	212-301-5800	301-5172
Fox Sports Radio Network 15260 Ventura Blvd Suite 500 *TF:* 800-533-8686	Sherman Oaks	CA	91403	818-461-8289	461-8219
Hispanic Communications Network 1126 16th St NW Suite 350 *Web:* www.hcnmedia.com/radio.html	Washington	DC	20036	202-637-8800	637-8801
Jones International Ltd 9697 E Mineral Ave **Fax:* Hum Res ■ *TF:* 800-525-7002 ■ *Web:* www.jones.com	Englewood	CO	80112	303-792-3111	784-8928*
Jones Media Networks Ltd 9697 E Mineral Ave *TF:* 800-525-7000 ■ *Web:* www.jones.com/jmg	Englewood	CO	80112	303-792-3111	
K-Love 2351 Sunset Blvd **Fax Area Code:* 919 ■ *TF:* 800-525-5683 ■ *Web:* www.klove.com	Rocklin	CA	95765	916-251-1600	251-1650*
La Chaîne culturelle FM PO Box 3220 Stn C	Ottawa	ON	K1Y1E4	613-288-6000	
La Radio de Radio-Canada PO Box 3220 Stn C **Fax:* Mktg ■ *Web:* www.radio-canada.ca	Ottawa	ON	K1Y1E4	613-288-6000	724-5112*
Launch Radio Networks 1065 Ave of the Americas 3rd Fl *Web:* www.launchradionetworks.com	New York	NY	10018	212-536-3600	536-3601
Marathon Media 980 N Michigan Ave Suite 1880	Chicago	IL	60611	312-204-9900	587-9466
Media Foundation DBA Relevant Radio 1496 Bellevue St Suite 202 *TF:* 800-342-0306 ■ *Web:* www.relevantradio.com	Green Bay	WI	54311	920-884-1460	884-3170
Metro Networks Inc 2800 Post Oak Blvd Suite 4000 *Web:* www.metronetworks.com	Houston	TX	77056	713-407-6000	407-6849
Moody Broadcasting Network 820 N La Salle Blvd *Web:* www.mbn.org	Chicago	IL	60610	312-329-4300	329-4468
Motor Racing Network 1801 W International Speedway Blvd *Web:* www.racingone.com/mrn	Daytona Beach	FL	32114	386-947-6400	947-6716
National Public Radio (NPR) 635 Massachusetts Ave NW *Web:* www.npr.org	Washington	DC	20001	202-513-2000	513-3329
NBC Radio Network 40 W 57th St	New York	NY	10019	212-641-2000	641-2155
New Dimensions Radio Broadcasting Network PO Box 569 *TF:* 800-935-8273 ■ *Web:* newdimensions.org	Ukiah	CA	95482	707-468-5215	
Pacifica Radio Foundation 1925 ML King Jr Way *Web:* www.pacifica.org	Berkeley	CA	94704	510-849-2590	849-2617
Public Radio International (PRI) 100 N 6th St Suite 900A *Web:* www.pri.org	Minneapolis	MN	55403	612-338-5000	330-9222
Q2 Media Group 111 Vallejo St *Web:* www.q2mediagroup.com	San Francisco	CA	94111	415-277-1710	435-7910
Radio America 1030 15th St NW Suite 1040 *TF:* 800-807-4703 ■ *Web:* www.radioamerica.org	Washington	DC	20005	202-408-0944	408-1087
Radio Disney 500 S Buena Vista St *Web:* radio.disney.go.com	Burbank	CA	91521	818-973-4680	973-4155
Radio Free Asia 2025 M St NW Suite 300 *Web:* www.rfa.org	Washington	DC	20036	202-530-4900	530-7794
Radio Free Europe/Radio Liberty (RFE/RL) 1201 Connecticut Ave NW 4th Fl *Web:* www.rferl.org	Washington	DC	20036	202-457-6900	457-6992
RFE/RL (Radio Free Europe/Radio Liberty) 1201 Connecticut Ave NW 4th Fl *Web:* www.rferl.org	Washington	DC	20036	202-457-6900	457-6992
Salem Communications Corp 4880 Santa Rosa Rd *NASDAQ: SALM* ■ *Web:* www.salem.cc	Camarillo	CA	93012	805-987-0400	384-4511
Salem Radio Network 6400 N Beltline Rd Suite 210 *Web:* www.srnonline.com	Irving	TX	75063	972-831-1920	831-8626
SCOLA 21557 270th St *Web:* www.scola.org	McClelland	IA	51548	712-566-2202	566-2502
Sirius Satellite Radio Inc 1221 Ave of the Americas *NASDAQ: SIRI* ■ *TF:* 888-539-7474 ■ *Web:* www.siriusradio.com	New York	NY	10020	212-584-5100	584-5200
Skylight Satellite Network 3003 Snelling Ave N *Web:* nwc.edu/radio/skylight1	Saint Paul	MN	55113	651-631-5000	631-5086
Sporting News Radio Network 1935 Techny Rd Suite 18 *Web:* radio.sportingnews.com	Northbrook	IL	60062	847-509-1661	509-1677
Sports Byline US 300 Broadway Suite 8 *Web:* www.sportsbyline.com	San Francisco	CA	94133	415-434-8300	391-2569
SRN Broadcasting PO Box 414 *Web:* internetfm.com	Lake Bluff	IL	60044	847-735-1995	
Tiger Financial News Network 601 Cleveland St Suite 618 *TF:* 877-518-9190 ■ *Web:* www.tfnn.com	Clearwater	FL	33755	727-518-9190	443-0869
Tribune Radio Network 435 N Michigan Ave *TF:* 800-654-8597 ■ *Web:* www.tribuneradio.com	Chicago	IL	60611	312-222-3342	222-4876
Trident Communications 31 Timber Ln	Hilton Head Island	SC	29926	843-837-4978	837-6898
United Stations Radio Network 1065 Ave of the Americas 3rd Fl *Web:* www.unitedstations.com	New York	NY	10018	212-869-1111	869-1115
Univision Radio 3102 Oak Lawn Ave Suite 215 *Web:* www.univision.net	Dallas	TX	75219	214-525-7700	525-7750
USA Radio Network 2290 Springlake Rd Suite 107 *TF:* 800-829-8111 ■ *Web:* www.usaradio.com	Dallas	TX	75234	972-484-3900	241-6826
Voice of America Radio Network International Broadcasting Bureau 330 Independence Ave SW *Web:* www.voanews.com	Washington	DC	20237	202-203-4000	619-1241
Waitt Radio Networks 1000 N 90th St Suite 105 *Web:* www.wrnonline.com	Omaha	NE	68114	402-952-7600	501-7060
Westwood One Inc 40 W 57th St 5th Fl *NYSE: WON* ■ *Web:* www.westwoodone.com	New York	NY	10019	212-641-2000	641-2172
WOR Radio Network 111 Broadway 3rd Fl *Web:* www.worradionet.com	New York	NY	10006	212-642-4533	642-4486
XM Satellite Radio Holdings Inc 1500 Eckington Pl NE *NASDAQ: XMSR* ■ *TF:* 877-967-2346 ■ *Web:* www.xmradio.com	Washington	DC	20002	202-380-4000	380-4500
Yesterday USA 2001 Plymouth Rock Dr *Web:* www.yesterdayusa.com	Richardson	TX	75081	972-889-9872	889-2329

648 RADIO STATIONS

SEE ALSO Internet Broadcasting p. 1870

AAA	Adult Album Alternative	**NAC**	New Adult Contemporary
AC	Adult Contemporary	**Nost**	Nostalgia
Alt	Alternative	**NPR**	National Public Radio
CBC	Canadian Broadcasting Corp	**Oldies**	Oldies/80s
CHR	Contemporary Hit Radio	**Rel**	Religious
Clas	Classical	**Rock**	Rock
CR	Classic Rock	**Span**	Spanish
Ctry	Country	**Sports**	Sports
Ethnic	Multilingual	**Urban**	Urban
N/T	News/Talk	**Var**	Variety

648-1 Abilene, TX

				Phone	Fax
KACU-FM 89.7 (NPR) ACU Box 27820 *Web:* www.kacu.org	Abilene	TX	79699	325-674-2441	674-2417
KBCY-FM 99.7 (Ctry) 2525 S Danville Dr *Web:* www.kbcy.com	Abilene	TX	79605	325-793-9700	692-1576
KCDD-FM 103.7 (Urban) 2525 S Danville Dr *Web:* www.power103.com	Abilene	TX	79605	325-793-9700	692-1576
KEAN-FM 105.1 (Ctry) 3911 S 1st St *TF:* 800-588-5326 ■ *Web:* www.keanradio.com	Abilene	TX	79605	325-676-7711	676-3851
KEYJ-FM 107.9 (Rock) 3911 S 1st St *Web:* www.keyj.com	Abilene	TX	79605	325-676-7711	676-3851
KFGL-FM 100.7 (Oldies) 3911 S 1st St	Abilene	TX	79605	325-676-7711	676-3851
KGNZ-FM 88.1 (Rel) 542 Butternut St *TF:* 800-588-8801 ■ *Web:* www.kgnz.com	Abilene	TX	79602	325-673-3045	672-7938
KGXL-FM 96.1 (Var) 1740 N 1st St *Web:* www.myxl96.com	Abilene	TX	79603	325-437-9596	673-1819
KHXS-FM 102.7 (CR) 2525 S Danville Dr *Web:* www.102thebear.com	Abilene	TX	79605	325-793-9700	692-1576
KKHR-FM 106.3 (Span) 402 Cypress St Suite 510 *Web:* www.radioabilene.com	Abilene	TX	79601	325-672-5442	672-6128
KORQ-FM 95.1 (CHR) 1740 N 1st St *Web:* www.95q.fm	Abilene	TX	79603	325-437-9596	673-1819
KTLT-FM 98.1 (Alt) 2525 S Danville Dr *Web:* www.98thelight.com/	Abilene	TX	79605	325-793-9700	692-1576
KULL-FM 92.5 (Oldies) 3911 S 1st St *TF:* 800-659-1965 ■ *Web:* www.kool92fm.com	Abilene	TX	79605	325-676-7711	676-3851

Station	City	State	ZIP	Phone	Fax
KVRP-FM 97.1 (Ctry) PO Box 1118 *TF:* 800-460-5877 ■ *Web:* www.kvrp.com	Haskell	TX	79521	940-864-8505	864-8001
KZQQ-AM 1560 (Sports) 402 Cypress St Suite 510 *Web:* www.radioabilene.com	Abilene	TX	79601	325-673-1455	672-6128

648-2 Akron, OH

Station	City	State	ZIP	Phone	Fax
WAKR-AM 1590 (N/T) 1795 W Market St *Web:* www.wakr.net	Akron	OH	44313	330-869-9800	864-6799
WAPS-FM 91.3 (AAA) 65 Steiner Ave *Web:* www.913thesummit.com	Akron	OH	44301	330-761-3099	761-3103
WARF-AM 1350 (Sports) 7755 Freedom Ave. *Web:* www.sportsradio1350.com	North Canton	OH	44720	330-836-4700	836-1350
WKDD-FM 98.1 (AC) 7755 Freedom Ave *Web:* www.wkdd.com	North Canton	OH	44720	330-836-4700	836-1350
WKSU-FM 89.7 (NPR) 1613 E Summit St *Web:* www.wksu.org	Kent	OH	44242	330-672-3114	672-4107
WNIR-FM 100.1 (N/T) PO Box 2170 *Web:* www.wnir.com	Akron	OH	44309	330-673-2323	673-0301
WONE-FM 97.5 (Rock) 1795 W Market St *Web:* www.wone.net	Akron	OH	44313	330-869-9800	864-6799
WQMX-FM 94.9 (Ctry) 1795 W Market St. *Web:* www.wqmx.com	Akron	OH	44313	330-869-9800	864-6799
WZIP-FM 88.1 (Rock) 302 E Buchtel Ave *Web:* www.wzip.fm	Akron	OH	44325	330-972-7105	972-5521

648-3 Albany, NY

Station	City	State	ZIP	Phone	Fax
WAJZ-FM 96.3 (Urban) 6 Johnson Rd. *Web:* jamz963.com	Latham	NY	12110	518-786-6600	786-6610
WAMC-FM 90.3 (NPR) 318 Central Ave. *TF:* 800-323-9262 ■ *Web:* www.wamc.org	Albany	NY	12206	518-465-5233	432-6974
WCDB-FM 90.9 (Var) 1400 Washington Ave SUNY Campus Center Rm 316 *Web:* www.wcdbfm.com	Albany	NY	12222	518-442-5234	442-4366
WFLY-FM 92.3 (CHR) 6 Johnson Rd *Web:* www.fly92.com	Latham	NY	12110	518-786-6600	786-6610
WGNA-FM 107.7 (Ctry) 1241 Kings Rd *TF:* 800-476-1077 ■ *Web:* www.wgna.com	Schenectady	NY	12303	518-881-1515	881-1516
WGY-AM 810 (N/T) 1203 Troy-Schenectady Rd Suite 201 Riverhill Center *TF:* 800-825-5949 ■ *Web:* www.wgy.com	Latham	NY	12110	518-452-4800	452-4855
WKLI-FM 100.9 (Nost) 6 Johnson Rd *Web:* www.albanymagic.com	Latham	NY	12110	518-786-6600	786-6610
WPYX-FM 106.5 (CR) 1203 Troy-Schenectady Rd Suite 201 Riverhill Center *Web:* www.pyx106.com	Latham	NY	12110	518-452-4800	452-4855
WQBK-FM 103.9 (Rock) 1241 Kings Rd *Web:* www.wqbk.com	Schenectady	NY	12303	518-881-1515	881-1516
WROW-AM 590 (N/T) 6 Johnson Rd *Web:* wrow.com	Latham	NY	12110	518-786-6600	786-6610
WRVE-FM 99.5 (AC) 1203 Troy-Schenectady Rd Suite 201 Riverhill Center *TF:* 800-995-9783 ■ *Web:* www.wrve.com	Latham	NY	12110	518-452-4800	452-4855
WTRY-FM 98.3 (Oldies) 1203 Troy-Schenectady Rd Suite 201 Riverhill Center *Web:* www.wtry.com	Latham	NY	12110	518-452-4800	452-4855
WYJB-FM 95.5 (AC) 6 Johnson Rd *Web:* b95.com	Latham	NY	12110	518-786-6600	786-6610

648-4 Albuquerque, NM

Station	City	State	ZIP	Phone	Fax
KABG-FM 98.5 (Oldies) 4125 Carlisle Ave NE *Web:* www.bigoldies.net	Albuquerque	NM	87107	505-878-0980	889-0619
KAGM-FM 106.3 (Ctry) 4125 Carlisle Blvd NE *Web:* www.1063therange.com	Albuquerque	NM	87107	505-878-0980	889-0619
KANW-FM 89.1 (NPR) 2020 Coal Ave SE *Web:* www.kanw.com	Albuquerque	NM	87106	505-242-7163	
KBQI-FM 107.9 (Ctry) 5411 Jefferson St NE Suite 100 *Web:* www.bigi1079.com	Albuquerque	NM	87109	505-830-6400	830-6543
KHFM-FM 95.5 (Clas) 4125 Carlisle Blvd NE *Web:* www.classicalkhfm.com	Albuquerque	NM	87107	505-878-0980	889-0619
KIOT-FM 102.5 (CR) 8009 Marble Ave NE.	Albuquerque	NM	87110	505-262-1142	262-9211
KJFA-FM 105.1 (Span) 8009 Marble Ave NE	Albuquerque	NM	87110	505-262-1142	254-7108
KKOB-AM 770 (N/T) 500 4th St NW Suite 500 *Web:* 770kkob.com	Albuquerque	NM	87102	505-767-6700	767-6767
KKOB-FM 93.3 (AC) 500 4th St NW Suite 500 *Web:* www.kobfm.com	Albuquerque	NM	87102	505-767-6700	767-6767
KKSS-FM 97.3 (CHR) 8009 Marble Ave NE *Web:* www.mykiss973.com	Albuquerque	NM	87110	505-262-1142	262-9211
KMGA-FM 99.5 (AC) 500 4th St NW Suite 500. *Web:* www.995magicfm.com	Albuquerque	NM	87102	505-767-6700	767-6767
KNML-AM 610 (Sports) 500 4th St NW Suite 500 *TF:* 888-922-0610 ■ *Web:* www.610thesportsanimal.com	Albuquerque	NM	87102	505-767-6700	767-6767
KRST-FM 92.3 (Ctry) 500 4th St NW Suite 500 *Web:* www.92.3krst.com	Albuquerque	NM	87102	505-767-6700	767-6767
KUNM-FM 89.9 (NPR) University of New Mexico MSC 06 3520 *Web:* www.kunm.org	Albuquerque	NM	87131	505-277-4806	277-6393
KZRR-FM 94.1 (Rock) 5411 Jefferson St NE Suite 100 *Web:* www.94rock.com	Albuquerque	NM	87109	505-830-6400	830-6543

648-5 Allentown, PA

Station	City	State	ZIP	Phone	Fax
WAEB-AM 790 (N/T) 1541 Alta Dr Suite 400. *Web:* www.waeb.com	Whitehall	PA	18052	610-434-1742	434-6288
WAEB-FM 104.1 (AC) 1541 Alta Dr Suite 400. *Web:* www.b104.com	Whitehall	PA	18052	610-434-1742	434-6288
WCTO-FM 96.1 (Ctry) 2158 Ave C Suite 100 *Web:* www.catcountry96.com	Bethlehem	PA	18017	610-266-7600	231-0400
WDIY-FM 88.1 (NPR) 301 Broadway 3rd Fl. *Web:* www.wdiyfm.org	Bethlehem	PA	18015	610-694-8100	954-9474
WGPA-AM 1100 (Var) 528 N New St. *Web:* www.wgpasunny1100.com	Bethlehem	PA	18018	610-866-8074	866-9381
WHOL-AM 1600 (Span) 1125 Colorado St. **Fax Area Code:* 484 ■ *Web:* www.whol1600.com	Allentown	PA	18103	610-434-4801	223-0088*
WLEV-FM 100.7 (AC) 2158 Ave C *Web:* www.wlevradio.com	Bethlehem	PA	18017	610-266-7600	231-0400
WODE-FM 99.9 (CR) 107 Paxinosa Rd W *Web:* www.999thehawk.com	Easton	PA	18040	610-258-6155	253-3384
WSAN-AM 1470 (Sports) 1541 Alta Dr Suite 400 *Web:* www.fox1470.com	Whitehall	PA	18052	610-434-1742	434-6288
WTKZ-AM 1320 (Sports) 107 Paxinosa Rd W	Easton	PA	18040	610-258-6155	253-3384
WZZO-FM 95.1 (Rock) 1541 Alta Dr Suite 400 *Web:* www.wzzo.com	Whitehall	PA	18052	610-434-1742	434-6288

648-6 Amarillo, TX

Station	City	State	ZIP	Phone	Fax
KACV-FM 89.9 (Alt) 2408 S Jackson St *TF:* 800-766-0176 ■ *Web:* www.kacvfm.org	Amarillo	TX	79109	806-371-5228	345-5576
KARX-FM 95.7 (CR) 301 S Polk St Suite 100 *Web:* www.karx.com	Amarillo	TX	79101	806-342-5200	342-5202
KATP-FM 101.9 (Ctry) 6214 W 34th Ave *Web:* www.katcountry1019.com	Amarillo	TX	79109	806-355-9777	355-5832
KBZD-FM 99.7 (Span) 3639 Wolflin Ave	Amarillo	TX	79102	806-355-1044	457-0642
KGNC-AM 710 (N/T) 3505 Olsen Blvd Suite 117 *TF:* 800-285-0710 ■ *Web:* www.kgncam.com	Amarillo	TX	79109	806-355-9801	354-8779
KGNC-FM 97.9 (Ctry) 3505 Olsen Blvd Suite 117 **Fax:* News Rm ■ *TF:* 877-765-9790 ■ *Web:* www.kgncfm.com	Amarillo	TX	79109	806-355-9801	354-9450*
KIXZ-AM 940 (News) 6214 W 34th St. *Web:* www.newsradio940.com	Amarillo	TX	79109	806-355-9777	355-5832
KMML-FM 96.9 (Ctry) 6214 W 34th St *Web:* www.969kmml.com	Amarillo	TX	79109	806-355-9777	355-5832
KMXJ-FM 94.1 (AC) 6214 W 34th St *Web:* www.mix941kmxj.com	Amarillo	TX	79109	806-355-9777	355-5832
KPRF-FM 98.7 (CHR) 6214 W 34th St. *Web:* www.power987.com	Amarillo	TX	79109	806-355-9777	355-5832
KPUR-FM 107.1 (Oldies) 301 S Polk St Suite 100 *Web:* www.kpur107.com	Amarillo	TX	79101	806-342-5200	342-5202
KQFX-FM 104.3 (Span) 3639 Wolflin Ave	Amarillo	TX	79102	806-355-1044	457-0642
KQIZ-FM 93.1 (CHR) 301 S Polk St Suite 100. *Web:* www.kqiz.com	Amarillo	TX	79101	806-342-5200	342-5202
KZRK-FM 107.9 (Rock) 301 S Polk St Suite 100	Amarillo	TX	79101	806-342-5200	342-5202

648-7 Anchorage, AK

Station	City	State	ZIP	Phone	Fax
KASH-FM 107.5 (Ctry) 800 E Dimond Blvd Suite 3-370 *Web:* www.kash1075.com	Anchorage	AK	99515	907-522-1515	743-5186
KATB-FM 89.3 (Rel) 6401 E Northern Lights Blvd *Web:* www.katb.org	Anchorage	AK	99504	907-333-5282	333-9851
KBBO-FM 92.1 (AC) 833 Gambell St *Web:* www.fmbob.com	Anchorage	AK	99501	907-344-4045	522-6053
KBFX-FM 100.5 (CR) 800 E Dimond Blvd Suite 3-370 *Web:* www.1005thefox.com	Anchorage	AK	99515	907-522-1515	743-5186
KBRJ-FM 104.1 (Ctry) 301 Arctic Slope Ave Suite 200 *Web:* www.kbrj.com	Anchorage	AK	99518	907-344-9622	349-3299
KBDZ-FM 102.1 (AC) 833 Gambell St *Web:* www.buzz1021.com	Anchorage	AK	99501	907-344-4045	522-6053
KEAG-FM 97.3 (Oldies) 301 Arctic Slope Ave Suite 200 *Web:* www.kool973.com	Anchorage	AK	99518	907-344-9622	349-3299
KENI-AM 650 (N/T) 800 E Dimond Blvd Suite 3-370. *Web:* www.650keni.com	Anchorage	AK	99515	907-522-1515	743-5186
KFAT-FM 92.9 (Urban) 833 Gambell *Web:* www.kfat929.com	Anchorage	AK	99501	907-344-4045	522-6053
KFQD-AM 750 (N/T) 301 Arctic Slope Ave Suite 200 *Web:* www.kfqd.com	Anchorage	AK	99518	907-344-9622	349-7326
KGOT-FM 101.3 (CHR) 800 E Dimond Blvd Suite 3-370 *Web:* www.kgot.com/main.html	Anchorage	AK	99515	907-272-5945	743-5183
KHAR-AM 590 (Nost) 301 Arctic Slope Ave Suite 200 *TF:* 800-896-1669	Anchorage	AK	99518	907-344-9622	349-7326
KLEF-FM 98.1 (Clas) 4700 Business Park Blvd Suite 44-A *Web:* www.klef.com	Anchorage	AK	99503	907-561-5556	562-4219
KMXS-FM 103.1 (AC) 301 Arctic Slope Ave *Web:* www.kmxs.com	Anchorage	AK	99518	907-344-9622	349-7326
KNBA-FM 90.3 (NPR) 3600 San Geronimo Suite 480 *TF:* 888-278-5622 ■ *Web:* www.knba.org	Anchorage	AK	99508	907-279-5622	793-3536
KNIK-FM 105.7 (NAC) 4700 Business Park Blvd Bldg E Suite 44A *Web:* www.knik.com	Anchorage	AK	99503	907-522-1018	522-1027
KSKA-FM 91.1 (NPR) 3877 University Dr *Web:* kska.org	Anchorage	AK	99508	907-550-8400	550-8403
KWHL-FM 106.5 (Rock) 301 Arctic Slope Ave *Web:* www.kwhl.com	Anchorage	AK	99518	907-344-9622	349-7326
KXLW-FM 96.3 (Rock) 833 Gambell St *Web:* 963thewolf.com	Anchorage	AK	99501	907-344-4045	522-6053
KYMG-FM 98.9 (AC) 800 E Dimond Blvd Suite 3-370 *Web:* www.magic989fm.com	Anchorage	AK	99515	907-522-1515	743-5186

648-8 Ann Arbor, MI

Station	City	State	ZIP	Phone	Fax
WAAM-AM 1600 (N/T) 4230 Packard Rd *Web:* www.waamannarbor.com	Ann Arbor	MI	48108	734-971-1600	973-2916
WCBN-FM 88.3 (Alt) University of Michigan 530 Student Activities Bldg. *Web:* wcbn.org	Ann Arbor	MI	48109	734-763-3500	647-4127
WDEO-AM 990 (Rel) PO Box 504 *Web:* www.wdeo.org	Ann Arbor	MI	48106	734-930-5200	930-3101
WFUM-FM 91.1 (NPR) 535 W William St Suite 110 *TF:* 800-728-9386 ■ *Web:* www.michiganradio.org	Ann Arbor	MI	48103	734-764-9210	647-3488
WQKL-FM 107.1 (AC) 1100 Victors Way Suite 100. *TF:* 866-525-9467 ■ *Web:* www.annarbors107one.com	Ann Arbor	MI	48108	734-302-8100	213-7508
WTKA-AM 1050 (N/T) 1100 Victors Way Suite 100. *TF:* 866-525-9467 ■ *Web:* www.wtka.com	Ann Arbor	MI	48108	734-302-8100	213-7508
WUOM-FM 91.7 (NPR) 535 W William St Suite 110 *Web:* www.michiganradio.org	Ann Arbor	MI	48103	734-764-9210	647-3488
WWWW-FM 102.9 (Ctry) 1100 Victors Way Suite 100 *TF:* 866-525-9467 ■ *Web:* www.w4country.com	Ann Arbor	MI	48108	734-302-8100	213-7508

648-9 Annapolis, MD

Station	City	State	ZIP	Phone	Fax
WBIS-AM 1190 (N/T) 1610 West St Suite 209 *Web:* www.wbis1190.com	Annapolis	MD	21401	410-269-0700	

Annapolis, MD (Cont'd)

Station	City	State	ZIP	Phone	Fax
WFSI-FM 107.9 (Rel) 918 Chesapeake Ave *Web:* www.familyradio.com	Annapolis	MD	21403	410-268-6200	268-0931
WNAV-AM 1430 (AC) PO Box 6726 *Web:* www.wnav.com	Annapolis	MD	21401	410-263-1430	268-5360
WRNR-FM 103.1 (AAA) 112 Main St 3rd Fl *Web:* www.wrnr.com	Annapolis	MD	21401	410-626-0103	267-7634

648-10 Asheville, NC

Station	City	State	ZIP	Phone	Fax
WCQS-FM 88.1 (NPR) 73 Broadway *TF:* 800-768-6698 ■ *Web:* www.wcqs.org	Asheville	NC	28801	828-253-6875	210-4801
WISE-AM 1310 (Sports) 1190 Patton Ave *Web:* www.1310bigwise.com	Asheville	NC	28806	828-259-9695	253-5619
WKJV-AM 1380 (Rel) 70 Adams Hill Rd *TF:* 800-809-9558 ■ *Web:* www.wkjv.com	Asheville	NC	28806	828-252-1380	259-9427
WKSF-FM 99.9 (Ctry) 13 Summerlin Rd *Web:* www.99kisscountry.com	Asheville	NC	28806	828-257-2700	255-7850
WNCW-FM 88.7 (AAA) PO Box 804 *Web:* www.wncw.org	Spindale	NC	28160	828-287-8000	287-8012
WPEK-AM 880 (N/T) 13 Summerlin Rd *Web:* www.880therevolution.com	Asheville	NC	28806	828-257-2700	255-7850
WQNQ-FM 104.3 (CR) 13 Summerlin Rd *Web:* www.star1043.com	Asheville	NC	28806	828-257-2700	255-7850
WSKY-AM 1230 (Rel) 40 Westgate Pkwy Suite F *Web:* www.wilkinsradio.com	Asheville	NC	28806	828-251-2000	251-2135
WWNC-AM 570 (N/T) 13 Summerlin Rd *Web:* www.wwnc.com	Asheville	NC	28806	828-257-2700	255-7850

648-11 Atlanta, GA

Station	City	State	ZIP	Phone	Fax
WABE-FM 90.1 (NPR) 740 Bismark Rd NE *Web:* www.wabe.org	Atlanta	GA	30324	678-686-0321	686-0356
WACG-FM 90.7 (NPR) 260 14th St NW *TF:* 800-222-4788 ■ *Web:* www.gpb.org/gpr	Atlanta	GA	30318	404-685-2690	685-2684
WALR-AM 1340 (N/T) 3535 Piedmont Rd Bldg 14 Suite 1200 *Web:* www.talkradio1340.com	Atlanta	GA	30305	404-688-0068	688-4262
WALR-FM 104.1 (AC) 1601 W Peachtree St NE *Web:* kiss1041fm.com	Atlanta	GA	30309	404-897-7500	897-6495
WAMJ-FM 102.5 (Urban) 101 Marietta St 12th Fl *Web:* www.1025atlanta.com	Atlanta	GA	30303	404-765-9750	688-7686
WAOK-AM 1380 (N/T) 1201 Peachtree St NE Suite 800 *Web:* www.waok.com	Atlanta	GA	30361	404-898-8900	898-8909
WAZX-FM 101.9 (Span) 1800 Lake Berk Dr Suite 99 *Web:* radiolaquebuena.com	Smyrna	GA	30080	770-436-6171	436-0100
WBTS-FM 95.5 (CHR) 1601 W Peachtree St NE *Web:* 955thebeat.com	Atlanta	GA	30309	404-897-7500	876-7363
WCLK-FM 91.9 (Jazz) 111 James P Brawley Dr SW *Web:* www.cau-wclk.com	Atlanta	GA	30314	404-880-8273	880-8869
WDCO-FM 89.7 (NPR) 260 14th St NW *TF:* 800-222-4788 ■ *Web:* www.gpb.org/gpr	Atlanta	GA	30318	404-685-2400	685-2684
WFSH-FM 104.7 (Rel) 2970 Peachtree Rd NW Suite 700 *Web:* www.thefishatlanta.com	Atlanta	GA	30305	404-995-7300	816-0748
WGST-AM 640 (N/T) 1819 Peachtree Rd NE Suite 700 *Web:* www.wgst.com	Atlanta	GA	30309	404-367-0640	367-1057
WHTA-FM 107.9 (Urban) 101 Marietta St 12th Fl *Web:* www.hot1079atl.com	Atlanta	GA	30303	404-765-9750	688-7686
WJSP-FM 88.1 (NPR) 260 14th St NW *TF:* 800-222-4788 ■ *Web:* www.gpb.org/gpr	Atlanta	GA	30318	404-685-2400	685-2684
WJZZ-FM 107.5 (NAC) 101 Marietta St 12th Fl *Web:* www.1075wjzz.com	Atlanta	GA	30303	404-765-9750	688-7686
WKHX-FM 101.5 (Ctry) 210 I-North Pkwy 6th Fl *Web:* www.wkhx.com	Atlanta	GA	30339	770-955-0101	953-4612
WKLS-FM 96.1 (Rock) 1819 Peachtree Rd NE Suite 700 *Web:* www.96rock.com	Atlanta	GA	30309	404-325-0960	325-8715
WNIV-AM 970 (Rel) 2970 Peachtree Rd NW Suite 700 *Web:* www.wniv.com	Atlanta	GA	30305	404-995-7300	816-0748
WNNX-FM 99.7 (Alt) 780 Johnson Ferry Rd NE 5th Fl *Web:* www.99x.com	Atlanta	GA	30342	404-497-4700	497-4735
WPZE-FM 97.5 (Rel) 101 Marietta St 12th Fl *Web:* www.praise975.com	Atlanta	GA	30303	404-765-9750	688-7686
WQXI-AM 790 (Sports) 3350 Peachtree Rd NE Suite 1600 *Web:* www.wqxi.com	Atlanta	GA	30326	404-261-2970	231-5923
WRAS-FM 88.5 (Var) Georgia State University 33 Gilmer St *Web:* www.wras.org	Atlanta	GA	30303	404-413-1630	463-9535
WRFG-FM 89.3 (Var) 1083 Austin Ave NE *Web:* www.wrfg.org	Atlanta	GA	30307	404-523-3471	523-8990
WSB-AM 750 (N/T) 1601 W Peachtree St NE *Web:* wsbradio.com	Atlanta	GA	30309	404-897-7500	897-7363
WSB-FM 98.5 (AC) 1601 W Peachtree St NE *Web:* b985.com	Atlanta	GA	30309	404-897-7500	897-7363
WSRV-FM 97.1 (AC) 1601 W Peachtree St *Web:* 971theriver.com	Atlanta	GA	30309	404-897-7500	897-7380
WSTR-FM 94.1 (CHR) 3350 Peachtree Rd NE Suite 1800 *Web:* www.star94.com	Atlanta	GA	30326	404-261-2970	365-9026
WUBL-FM 94.9 (Ctry) 1819 Peachtree Rd NE Suite 700 *Web:* www.peach949.com	Atlanta	GA	30309	404-367-0949	367-9490
WVEE-FM 103.3 (Urban) 1201 Peachtree St NE Suite 800 *Web:* www.v-103.com	Atlanta	GA	30361	404-898-8900	898-8909
WVFJ-FM 93.3 (Rel) 120 Peachtree East Shopping Center *Web:* www.j933.com	Peachtree City	GA	30269	770-487-4500	486-6400
WWVA-FM 105.7 (Span) 1819 Peachtree Rd NE Suite 700 *Web:* www.viva1053.com	Atlanta	GA	30309	404-607-1336	367-1105
WWWQ-FM 100.5 (CHR) 780 Johnson Ferry Rd NE 5th Fl *Web:* www.allthehitsq100.com	Atlanta	GA	30342	404-497-4700	497-4735
WYAY-FM 106.7 (Oldies) 210 I-North Pkwy 6th Fl *Web:* www.wyay.com	Atlanta	GA	30339	770-955-0101	563-8550
WZGC-FM 92.9 (CR) 1201 Peachtree St Suite 800 *Web:* www.929dave.fm	Atlanta	GA	30361	404-898-8900	898-8909

648-12 Atlantic City, NJ

Station	City	State	ZIP	Phone	Fax
WAYV-FM 95.1 (CHR) 8025 Black Horse Pike Suite 100 *Web:* www.951wayv.com	Pleasantville	NJ	08232	609-484-8444	646-6331
WFPG-FM 96.9 (AC) 950 Tilton Rd Suite 200 *TF:* 800-969-9374 ■ *Web:* www.literock969.com	Northfield	NJ	08225	609-645-9797	272-9228
WGBZ-FM 105.5 (CHR) 8025 Black Horse Pike Suite 100 *Web:* www.993thebuzz.com	Pleasantville	NJ	08232	609-484-8444	646-6331
WJSE-FM 102.7 (Alt) 1601 New Rd *Web:* www.wjse.com	Linwood	NJ	08221	609-653-1400	601-0450
WMGM-FM 103.7 (CR) 1601 New Rd *Web:* www.wmgm1037.com	Linwood	NJ	08221	609-653-1400	601-0450
WMID-AM 1340 (Nost) 8025 Black Horse Pike Suite 100 *Web:* www.classicoldieswmid.com	Pleasantville	NJ	08232	609-484-8444	646-6331
WOND-AM 1400 (N/T) 1601 New Rd *Web:* www.1400wond.com	Linwood	NJ	08221	609-653-1400	601-0450
WPUR-FM 107.3 (Ctry) 950 Tilton Rd Suite 200 *Web:* www.catcountry1073.com	Northfield	NJ	08225	609-645-9797	272-9228
WTKU-FM 98.3 (Oldies) 1601 New Rd *Web:* www.kool983.com	Linwood	NJ	08221	609-653-1400	601-0450
WTTH-FM 96.1 (Urban) 8025 Black Horse Pike Suite 100 *Web:* www.961wtth.com	Pleasantville	NJ	08232	609-484-8444	646-6331
WZXL-FM 100.7 (Rock) 8025 Black Horse Pike Suite 100 *Web:* www.wzxl.com	Pleasantville	NJ	08232	609-484-8444	646-6331

648-13 Augusta, GA

Station	City	State	ZIP	Phone	Fax
WAKB-FM 100.9 (Urban) 411 Radio Station Rd *Web:* www.1009magic.com	North Augusta	SC	29841	803-279-2330	279-8149
WBBQ-FM 104.3 (AC) 2743 Perimeter Pkwy Bldg 100 Suite 300 *Web:* www.wbbq.com	Augusta	GA	30909	706-396-6000	396-6010
WCHZ-FM 95.1 (Rock) 4051 Jimmie Dyess Pkwy *Web:* www.95rock.com	Augusta	GA	30909	706-396-7000	396-7100
WEKL-FM 105.7 (CR) 2743 Perimeter Pkwy Bldg 100 Suite 300	Augusta	GA	30909	706-396-6000	396-6010
WFAM-AM 1050 (Rel) 552 Laney Walker Blvd Ext	Augusta	GA	30901	706-722-6077	722-7066
WFXA-FM 103.1 (Urban) 411 Radio Station Rd *Web:* www.wfxa103jamz.com	North Augusta	SC	29841	803-279-2330	819-3781
WGAC-AM 580 (N/T) 4051 Jimmie Dyess Pkwy *Web:* www.wgac.com	Augusta	GA	30909	706-396-7000	396-7100
WGUS-FM 93.9 (Rel) 4051 Jimmie Dyess Pkwy	Augusta	GA	30909	706-396-7000	396-7100
WGUS-FM 102.7 (Rel) 4051 Jimmie Dyess Pkwy *Web:* www.1027wgus.com	Augusta	GA	30909	706-396-7000	396-7100
WHHD-FM 98.3 (AC) 4051 Jimmie Dyess Pkwy *Web:* www.hd983.com	Augusta	GA	30909	706-396-7000	396-7100
WIBL-FM 105.7 (Ctry) 2743 Perimeter Pkwy Bldg 100 Suite 300	Augusta	GA	30909	706-396-6000	396-6010
WKXC-FM 99.5 (Ctry) 4051 Jimmie Dyess Pkwy *Web:* www.kicks99.com	Augusta	GA	30909	706-396-7000	396-7100
WPRW-FM 107.7 (Urban) 2743 Perimeter Pkwy Bldg 100 Suite 300 *Web:* www.power107.net	Augusta	GA	30909	706-396-6000	396-6010

648-14 Augusta, ME

Station	City	State	ZIP	Phone	Fax
WABK-FM 104.3 (AC) 150 Whitten Rd *Web:* www.wabkfm.com	Augusta	ME	04330	207-623-9000	623-9007
WBCI-FM 105.9 (Rel) 122 Main St *Web:* www.wbci.fm	Topsham	ME	04086	207-725-9224	725-2686
WEBB-FM 98.5 (Ctry) 56 Western Ave Suite 13 *Web:* www.b985.fm	Augusta	ME	04330	207-623-4735	626-5948
WFAU-AM 1280 (Sports) 150 Whitten Rd	Augusta	ME	04330	207-623-9000	623-9007
WKCG-FM 101.3 (AC) 150 Whitten Rd *Web:* www.wkcgfm.com	Augusta	ME	04330	207-623-9000	623-9007
WMME-FM 92.3 (CHR) 56 Western Ave Suite 13 *Web:* www.92moose.fm	Augusta	ME	04330	207-623-4735	626-5948
WTOS-FM 105.1 (Rock) 150 Whitten Rd *Web:* www.tosrocks.com	Augusta	ME	04330	207-623-9000	623-9007

648-15 Austin, TX

Station	City	State	ZIP	Phone	Fax
KAMX-FM 94.7 (AC) 4301 Westbank Dr Bldg B 3rd Fl *Web:* www.mix947.com	Austin	TX	78746	512-327-9595	329-6252
KASE-FM 100.7 (Ctry) 3601 S Congress Ave Bldg F *Web:* www.kase101.com	Austin	TX	78704	512-684-7300	684-7441
KAZI-FM 88.7 (Var) 8906 Wall St Suite 203 *Web:* www.kazifm.org	Austin	TX	78754	512-836-9544	836-9563
KBPA-FM 103.5 (AC) 8309 N IH-35 *Web:* www.hibob.fm	Austin	TX	78753	512-832-4000	832-1579
KDHT-FM 93.3 (Urban) 8309 N IH-35 *Web:* www.hot933.fm	Austin	TX	78753	512-832-4000	832-1579
KFIT-AM 1060 (Rel) 110 Wild Basin Rd Suite 375	Austin	TX	78746	512-328-8400	328-8437
KFMK-FM 105.9 (Oldies) 3601 S Congress Ave Bldg F *Web:* www.jammin1059.com	Austin	TX	78704	512-684-7300	684-7441
KGSR-FM 107.1 (AAA) 8309 N IH-35 *Web:* www.kgsr.com	Austin	TX	78753	512-832-4000	832-1579
KHFI-FM 96.7 (CHR) 3601 S Congress Ave Bldg F *Web:* www.khfi.com	Austin	TX	78704	512-684-7300	684-7441
KHHL-FM 98.9 (Span) 912 S Capital of Texas Hwy Suite 400 *Web:* www.bmpradio.com	Austin	TX	78746	512-416-1100	314-7742
KINV-FM 107.7 (Span) 10801-2 N Mopac Expy Suite 250	Austin	TX	78759	512-340-7100	340-7107
KIXL-AM 970 (Rel) 11615 Angus Rd Suite 102 *Web:* www.relevantradio.com	Austin	TX	78759	512-390-5495	241-0510
KJCE-AM 1370 (N/T) 4301 Westbank Dr Bldg B 3rd Fl *Web:* www.talkradio1370am.com	Austin	TX	78746	512-327-9595	329-6288
KKMJ-FM 95.5 (AC) 4301 Westbank Dr Bldg B 3rd Fl *Web:* www.majic.com	Austin	TX	78746	512-327-9595	329-6252
KLBJ-AM 590 (N/T) 8309 N IH-35 *Web:* www.590klbj.com	Austin	TX	78753	512-832-4000	832-4081
KLBJ-FM 93.7 (Rock) 8309 N IH-35 *Web:* www.klbjfm.com	Austin	TX	78753	512-832-4000	832-4081
KMFA-FM 89.5 (Clas) 3001 N Lamar Blvd Suite 100 *TF:* 866-472-2221 ■ *Web:* www.kmfa.org	Austin	TX	78705	512-476-5632	474-7463
KOOP-FM 91.7 (Var) PO Box 2116 *TF:* 888-917-5667 ■ *Web:* www.koop.org	Austin	TX	78768	512-472-1369	472-6149
KPEZ-FM 102.3 (Rel) 3601 S Congress Ave Bldg F *Web:* www.channel1023.com	Austin	TX	78704	512-684-7300	684-7441
KROX-FM 101.5 (Alt) 8309 N IH-35 *Web:* www.krox.com	Austin	TX	78753	512-832-4000	832-4071
KUT-FM 90.5 (NPR) University of Texas 1 University Station Box A-0704 *TF:* 800-435-8836 ■ *Web:* www.kut.org	Austin	TX	78712	512-471-1631	471-3700
KVET-AM 1300 (Sports) 3601 S Congress Ave Bldg F *Web:* www.sportsradio1300.com	Austin	TX	78704	512-684-7300	684-7441
KVET-FM 98.1 (Ctry) 3601 S Congress Ave Bldg F *Web:* www.kvet.com	Austin	TX	78704	512-684-7300	684-7441

Phone Fax

KZNX-AM 1530 (Sports) 1050 E 11th St Suite 300 .... Austin TX 78702 512-346-8255 692-0599
Web: www.espnaustin.com

648-16 Bakersfield, CA

Phone Fax

KBFP-FM 105.3 (Span) 1100 Mohawk St Suite 280 .... Bakersfield CA 93309 661-322-9929 283-2963
Web: www.lapreciosa.com
KBKO-FM 96.5 (Ctry) 1100 Mohawk St Suite 280 .... Bakersfield CA 93309 661-322-9929 283-2963
Web: www.big965.com
KCWR-FM 107.1 (Ctry) 3223 Sillect Ave .... Bakersfield CA 93308 661-326-1011 328-7503
TF: 800-962-5590
KDFO-FM 98.5 (CR) 1100 Mohawk St Suite 280 .... Bakersfield CA 93309 661-322-9929 322-9239
Web: www.985thefox.com
KERI-AM 1180 (Rel) 1400 Easton Dr Suite 144-B .... Bakersfield CA 93309 661-328-1410 328-0873
Web: www.keri.com
KERN-AM 1410 (N/T) 1400 Easton Dr Suite 144-B .... Bakersfield CA 93309 661-328-1410 328-0873
Web: www.kernradio.com
KGFM-FM 101.5 (AC) 1400 Easton Dr Suite 144-B .... Bakersfield CA 93309 661-328-1410 328-0873
Web: www.kgfm.com
KHTY-AM 970 (CR) 1100 Mohawk St Suite 280 .... Bakersfield CA 93309 661-322-9929 283-2963
Web: www.mighty970.com
KISV-FM 94.1 (CHR) 1400 Easton Dr Suite 144-B .... Bakersfield CA 93309 661-328-1410 328-0873
Web: www.hot941.com
KIWI-FM 92.1 (Span) 5100 Commerce Dr .... Bakersfield CA 93309 661-327-9711 327-0797
Web: www.thespanishradio.com
KKBB-FM 99.3 (Oldies) 3651 Pegasus Dr Suite 107 .... Bakersfield CA 93308 661-393-1900 393-1915
Web: www.kkbb.com
KKXX-FM 93.1 (Var) 1400 Easton Dr Suite 144-B .... Bakersfield CA 93309 661-328-1410 328-0873
Web: www.bakersfieldpirateradio.com
KLHC-AM 1350 (Span) 3817 Wilson Rd Suite E .... Bakersfield CA 93309 661-847-1450 847-1452
Web: www.klhcradio.com
KLLY-FM 95.3 (AC) 3651 Pegasus Dr Suite 107 .... Bakersfield CA 93308 661-393-1900 393-1915
Web: www.klly.com
KMYX-FM 92.5 (Span) 6313 Schirra Ct .... Bakersfield CA 93313 661-837-0745 837-1612
Web: www.campesina.com
KNZR-AM 1560 (N/T) 3651 Pegasus Dr Suite 107 .... Bakersfield CA 93308 661-393-1900 393-1915
Web: www.knzr.com
KPSL-FM 102.9 (Span CHR) 5100 Commerce Dr .... Bakersfield CA 93309 661-327-9711 327-0797
Web: www.thespanishradio.com
KRAB-FM 106.1 (Rock) 1100 Mohawk St Suite 280 .... Bakersfield CA 93309 661-322-9929 283-2963
Web: www.krab.com
KSMJ-FM 97.7 (AC) 3651 Pegasus Dr Suite 107 .... Bakersfield CA 93308 661-393-1900 393-1915
TF: 866-977-5765 ■ *Web:* www.977thebreeze.com
KUZZ-FM 107.9 (Ctry) 3223 Sillect Ave .... Bakersfield CA 93308 661-326-1011 328-7503
Web: www.kuzz.com

648-17 Baltimore, MD

Phone Fax

WBAL-AM 1090 (N/T) 3800 Hooper Ave .... Baltimore MD 21211 410-467-3000 338-6675
Web: wbal.com
WBGR-AM 860 (Rel) 918 Chesapeake Ave .... Annapolis MD 21403 410-825-7700 268-0931
Web: www.familyradio.com
WBJC-FM 91.5 (Clas) 6776 Reisterstown Rd Suite 202 .... Baltimore MD 21215 410-580-5800
Web: www.wbjc.com
WCAO-AM 600 (Rel) 711 W 40th St Suite 350 .... Baltimore MD 21211 410-366-7600 467-0011
Web: www.heaven600.com
WCBM-AM 680 (N/T) 1726 Reisterstown Rd Suite 117 .... Baltimore MD 21208 410-580-6800 580-6810
Web: www.wcbm.com
WEAA-FM 88.9 (Jazz) 1700 E Cold Spring Ln .... Baltimore MD 21251 443-885-3564 885-8206
Web: www.weaa.org
WERQ-FM 92.3 (Urban) 1705 Whitehead Rd .... Baltimore MD 21207 410-332-8200 944-1282
Web: www.92qjams.com
WIYY-FM 97.9 (Rock) 3800 Hooper Ave .... Baltimore MD 21211 410-889-0098 675-7946
Web: 98online.com
WJFK-AM 1300 (N/T) 1423 Clarkview Rd Suite 100 .... Baltimore MD 21209 410-321-9535 823-0816
Web: www.1300wjfk.com
WLIF-FM 101.9 (AC) 1423 Clarkview Rd Suite 100 .... Baltimore MD 21209 410-296-1019 821-5482
WNST-AM 1570 (Sports) 1550 Hart Rd .... Towson MD 21286 410-821-9678 828-4698
Web: www.wnst.net
WOLB-AM 1010 (N/T) 1705 Whitehead Rd .... Baltimore MD 21207 410-332-8200 944-4230
Web: www.wolb1010.com
WPOC-FM 93.1 (Ctry) 711 W 40th St Suite 350 .... Baltimore MD 21211 410-366-7600 235-3899
Web: www.wpoc.com
WQSR-FM 105.7 (Var) 1423 Clarkview Rd Suite 100 .... Baltimore MD 21209 410-825-1000 821-8256
Web: www.wqsr.com
WRBS-FM 95.1 (Rel) 3600 Georgetown Rd .... Baltimore MD 21227 410-247-4100 247-4533
TF: 800-899-0951 ■ *Web:* www.wrbs.com
WSMJ-FM 104.3 (NAC) 711 W 40th St Suite 350 .... Baltimore MD 21211 410-366-7600 235-3899
Web: www.1043online.com
WTMD-FM 89.7 (AAA) 8000 York Rd Towson University .... Towson MD 21252 410-704-8938 704-2609
Web: wwwnew.towson.edu/wtmd
WWIN-AM 1400 (Rel) 1705 Whitehead Rd .... Baltimore MD 21207 410-332-8200 944-1282
Web: www.spirit1400.com
WWIN-FM 95.9 (Urban) 1705 Whitehead Rd .... Baltimore MD 21207 410-332-8200 944-1282
WWLG-AM 1370 (N/T) 1726 Reistertown Rd Suite 117 .... Baltimore MD 21208 410-580-6800 580-6810
WWMX-FM 106.5 (CHR) 1423 Clarkview Rd Suite 100 .... Baltimore MD 21209 410-825-1000 821-8256
Web: www.mix1065.fm
WYPR-FM 88.1 (NPR) 2216 N Charles St .... Baltimore MD 21218 410-235-1660 235-1161
TF: 866-661-9308 ■ *Web:* www.wypr.org
WZBA-FM 100.7 (CR)
11350 McCormick Rd Executive Plaza 3 Suite 701 .... Hunt Valley MD 21031 410-771-8484 771-1616
Web: www.wzbathebay.com

648-18 Bangor, ME

Phone Fax

WBFB-FM 104.7 (Ctry) 184 Target Industrial Cir .... Bangor ME 04401 207-947-9100 942-8039
WBQI-FM 107.7 (Clas) 98 Main St .... Ellsworth ME 04605 207-667-9800 667-3900
WBZN-FM 107.3 (CHR) 49 Acme Rd PO Box 100 .... Brewer ME 04412 207-989-5631 989-5685
Web: www.wbzn-fm.com
WDEA-AM 1370 (Nost) 49 Acme Rd PO Box 100 .... Brewer ME 04412 207-989-5631 989-5685
Web: www.am1370wdea.com
WERU-FM 89.9 (Var) PO Box 170 .... East Orland ME 04431 207-469-6600 469-8961
TF: 800-643-6273 ■ *Web:* www.weru.org
WEZQ-FM 92.9 (AC) 49 Acme Rd PO Box 100 .... Brewer ME 04412 207-989-5631 989-5685
Web: www.wezq-fm.com
WFZX-FM 101.7 (CR) 184 Target Industrial Cir .... Bangor ME 04401 207-947-9100 942-8039
Web: www.wfzxfm.com
WHCF-FM 88.5 (Rel) PO Box 5000 .... Bangor ME 04402 207-947-2751 947-0010
TF: 800-947-2577 ■ *Web:* www.whcffm.com

Phone Fax

WHSN-FM 89.3 (Alt) 1 College Cir .... Bangor ME 04401 207-941-7116 947-3987
Web: www.whsn-fm.com
WKIT-FM 100.3 (CR) 861 Broadway .... Bangor ME 04401 207-990-2800 990-2444
TF: 800-287-1003 ■ *Web:* www.zoneradio.com/wkit
WKSQ-FM 94.5 (AC) 184 Target Industrial Cir .... Bangor ME 04401 207-947-9100 942-8039
TF: 800-339-5477 ■ *Web:* www.kiss945fm.com/main.html
WLKE-FM 99.1 (Ctry) 24 Buttermilk Rd .... Ellsworth ME 04605 207-947-9100 942-8039
TF: 866-474-5087 ■ *Web:* www.lucky99.net
WMEH-FM 90.9 (NPR) 65 Texas Ave .... Bangor ME 04401 207-941-1010 761-0318
TF: 800-884-1717 ■ *Web:* www.mainepublicradio.org
WNSX-FM 97.7 (AC) 409 High St .... Ellsworth ME 04605 207-667-0002 667-0627
WQCB-FM 106.5 (Ctry) 49 Acme Rd PO Box 100 .... Brewer ME 04412 207-989-5631 989-5685
Web: www.wqcb-fm.com
WVOM-FM 103.9 (N/T) 184 Target Industrial Cir .... Bangor ME 04401 207-947-9100 942-8039
TF: 800-966-1039 ■ *Web:* www.wvomfm.com
WWBX-FM 97.1 (CHR) 184 Target Industrial Cir .... Bangor ME 04401 207-947-9100 942-8039
Web: www.b97hits.com
WWMJ-FM 95.7 (CR) 49 Acme Rd PO Box 100 .... Brewer ME 04412 207-989-5631 989-5685
Web: www.wwmj-fm.com
WZON-AM 620 (Sports) 861 Broadway .... Bangor ME 04401 207-990-2800 990-2444
Web: www.zoneradio.com/wzon

648-19 Baton Rouge, LA

Phone Fax

KNXX-FM 104.9 (Alt) 929-B Government St .... Baton Rouge LA 70802 225-388-9898 499-9800
Web: www.104thex.com
KQXL-FM 106.5 (Urban) 650 Wooddale Blvd .... Baton Rouge LA 70806 225-926-1106 928-1606
Web: www.q106dot5.com
KRDJ-FM 93.7 (AC) 202 Galbert Rd .... Lafayette LA 70506 337-232-1311 233-3779
Web: www.krdjfm.com
KRVE-FM 96.1 (AC) 5555 Hilton Ave Suite 500 .... Baton Rouge LA 70808 225-231-1860 231-1879*
*Fax: News Rm ■ *Web:* www.961theriver.com
WBKL-FM 92.7 (Rel) 7249 Florida Blvd .... Baton Rouge LA 70806 225-612-4927 612-4928
TF: 800-525-5683 ■ *Web:* www.klove.com
WBRH-FM 90.3 (Jazz) 2825 Government St .... Baton Rouge LA 70806 225-383-3243 379-7685
WCDV-FM 103.3 (AC) 650 Wooddale Blvd .... Baton Rouge LA 70806 225-926-1106 928-1606
Web: www.diva103.com
WDGL-FM 98.1 (CR) 929-B Government St .... Baton Rouge LA 70802 225-388-9898 499-9800
Web: www.eagle981.com
WEMX-FM 94.1 (Urban) 650 Wooddale Blvd .... Baton Rouge LA 70806 225-926-1106 928-1606
TF: 800-499-9410 ■ *Web:* www.max94one.com
WFMF-FM 102.5 (CHR) 5555 Hilton Ave Suite 500 .... Baton Rouge LA 70808 225-231-1860 231-1879
Web: www.wfmf.com
WJBO-AM 1150 (N/T) 5555 Hilton Ave Suite 500 .... Baton Rouge LA 70808 225-231-1860 231-1879
Web: www.wjbo.com
WPFC-AM 1550 (Rel) 6943 Titian Dr .... Baton Rouge LA 70806 225-926-1506 590-3238
Web: www.wpfc1550.com
WRKF-FM 89.3 (NPR) 3050 Valley Creek Dr .... Baton Rouge LA 70808 225-926-3050 926-3105
TF: 888-499-3050 ■ *Web:* www.wrkf.org
WSKR-AM 1210 (Sports) 5555 Hilton Ave Suite 500 .... Baton Rouge LA 70808 225-231-1860 231-1879
Web: www.thescore1210.com
WXOK-AM 1460 (Rel) 650 Wooddale Blvd .... Baton Rouge LA 70806 225-926-1106 928-1606
Web: www.heaven1460.com
WYNK-FM 101.5 (Ctry) 5555 Hilton Ave Suite 500 .... Baton Rouge LA 70808 225-231-1860 231-1879
Web: wynk.com
WYPY-FM 100.7 (Ctry) 929-B Government St .... Baton Rouge LA 70802 225-388-9898 499-9800
Web: www.newcountry1007.com

648-20 Billings, MT

Phone Fax

KBBB-FM 103.7 Var) 27 N 27th St 23rd Fl .... Billings MT 59101 406-248-7827 252-9577
Web: www.bee103.com
KBLG-AM 910 (N/T) 2075 Central Ave .... Billings MT 59102 406-652-8400 652-4899
Web: www.kblg.com
KBUL-AM 970 (N/T) 27 N 27th St 23rd Fl .... Billings MT 59101 406-248-7827 252-9577
Web: www.newsradio970.com
KCTR-FM 102.9 (Ctry) 27 N 27th St 23rd Fl .... Billings MT 59101 406-248-7827 252-9577
Web: www.kctr.com
KEMC-FM 91.7 (NPR) 1500 University Dr .... Billings MT 59101 406-657-2941 657-2977
TF: 800-441-2941 ■ *Web:* www.yellowstonepublicradio.org
KGHL-FM 98.5 (Ctry) 222 N 32nd St 10th Fl .... Billings MT 59101 406-238-1000 238-1038
Web: www.985thewolf.com
KKBR-FM 97.1 (Oldies) 27 N 27th St 23rd Fl .... Billings MT 59101 406-248-7827 252-9577
Web: www.kbear.com
KRKX-FM 94.1 (CR) 2075 Central Ave .... Billings MT 59102 406-652-8400 652-4899
TF: 866-627-5483 ■ *Web:* www.krkx.com
KRPM 107.5 (Rock) 222 N 32nd St 10th Fl .... Billings MT 59101 406-238-1000 238-1038
Web: www.theriver1075.com
KRSQ-FM 101.9 (Urban) 222 N 32nd St 10th Fl .... Billings MT 59101 406-238-1000 238-1038
Web: www.hot1019.com
KRZN-FM 96.3 (Rock) 2075 Central Ave .... Billings MT 59102 406-652-8400 652-4899
Web: www.thezone963.com
KURL-AM 730 (Rel) PO Box 31038 .... Billings MT 59107 406-245-3121 245-0822
Web: www.kurlradio.com
KYYA-FM 93.3 (AC) 2075 Central Ave .... Billings MT 59102 406-652-8400 652-4899
TF: 866-627-5483 ■ *Web:* www.y93.com

648-21 Birmingham, AL

Phone Fax

WAGG-AM 610 (Rel) 950 22nd St N Suite 1000 .... Birmingham AL 35203 205-322-2987 326-2526
Web: wagg610.com
WAPI-AM 1070 (N/T) 244 Goodwin Crest Dr Suite 300 .... Birmingham AL 35209 205-945-4646 917-1906
Web: www.wapi1070.com
WATV-AM 900 (Oldies) 3025 Ensley Ave .... Birmingham AL 35208 205-780-2014 780-4034
Web: www.900goldwatv.com
WBHJ-FM 95.7 (Urban) 950 22nd St N Suite 1000 .... Birmingham AL 35203 205-322-2987 326-2526
Web: 957jamz.com
WBHK-FM 98.7 (Urban) 950 22nd St N Suite 1000 .... Birmingham AL 35203 205-322-2987 326-2526
Web: 987kiss.com
WBHM-FM 90.3 (NPR) 650 11th St S .... Birmingham AL 35294 205-934-2606 934-5075
TF: 800-444-9246 ■ *Web:* www.wbhm.org
WBPT-FM 106.9 (AC) 301 Beacon Pkwy W Suite 200 .... Birmingham AL 35209 205-916-1100 916-1116
Web: birminghamseagle.com
WDJC-FM 93.7 (Rel) 120 Summit Pkwy .... Birmingham AL 35209 205-879-3324 941-1095
Web: www.wdjconline.com
WDXB-FM 102.5 (Ctry) 600 Beacon Pkwy W Suite 400 .... Birmingham AL 35209 205-439-9600 439-8390
Web: www.1025thebull.com
WENN-FM 105.5 (Rock) 600 Beacon Pkwy W Suite 400 .... Birmingham AL 35209 205-439-9600 439-8390
Web: www.hallelujah1055.com

Birmingham, AL (Cont'd)

Station	City	State	Zip	Phone	Fax
WERC-AM 960 (N/T) 600 Beacon Pkwy W Suite 400 *Web:* www.960werc.com	Birmingham	AL	35209	205-439-9600	439-8390
WJLD-AM 1400 (Var) PO Box 19123 *Web:* www.wjld1400.com	Birmingham	AL	35219	205-942-1776	942-4814
WJSR-FM 91.1 (CR) 2601 Carson Rd	Birmingham	AL	35215	205-856-7702	815-8499
WMJJ-FM 96.5 (AC) 600 Beacon Pkwy W Suite 400 *Web:* www.magic96fm.com	Birmingham	AL	35209	205-439-9600	439-8390
WNCB-FM 97.3 (Ctry) 301 Beacon Pkwy W Suite 200 *Web:* newcountry973.com	Birmingham	AL	35209	205-916-1100	916-1116
WQEN-FM 103.7 (CHR) 600 Beacon Pkwy W Suite 400 *Web:* www.1037theq.com	Birmingham	AL	35209	205-439-9600	439-8390
WSPZ-AM 690 (Sports) 244 Goodwin Crest Dr Suite 300 *Web:* www.690thesportsanimal.com	Birmingham	AL	35209	205-942-6690	917-1906
WYSF-FM 94.5 (AC) 244 Goodwin Crest Dr Suite 300 *Web:* www.softrock945.com	Birmingham	AL	35209	205-945-4646	945-3994
WZRR-FM 99.5 (CR) 244 Goodwin Crest Dr Suite 300 *Web:* www.wzrr.com	Birmingham	AL	35209	205-945-4646	942-8959
WZZK-FM 104.7 (Ctry) 301 Beacon Pkwy W Suite 200 *Web:* wzzk.com	Birmingham	AL	35209	205-916-1100	916-1116

648-22 Bismarck, ND

Station	City	State	Zip	Phone	Fax
KACL-FM 98.7 (Oldies) 1830 N 11th St *Web:* www.cool987fm.com	Bismarck	ND	58501	701-663-6411	663-8790
KBMR-AM 1130 (Ctry) 3500 E Rosser Ave *TF:* 800-766-5267 ■ *Web:* www.kbmr.com	Bismarck	ND	58501	701-255-1234	222-1131
KBYZ-FM 96.5 (CR) 1830 N 11th St *Web:* www.965thefox.com	Bismarck	ND	58501	701-663-6411	663-8790
KCND-FM 90.5 (NPR) 1814 N 15th St *TF:* 800-359-5566 ■ *Web:* www.prairiepublic.org/radio	Bismarck	ND	58501	701-224-1700	224-0555
KFYR-AM 550 (Var) 3500 E Rosser Ave *TF:* 800-766-5267 ■ *Web:* www.kfyr.com	Bismarck	ND	58501	701-258-5555	222-1131
KKCT-FM 97.5 (Ctry) 1830 N 11th St	Bismarck	ND	58501	701-663-6411	663-8790
KLXX-AM 1270 (N/T) 1830 N 11th St *Web:* www.supertalk1270.com	Bismarck	ND	58501	701-663-6411	663-8790
KNDR-FM 104.7 (Rel) 1400 NE 3rd St *TF:* 800-767-5095 ■ *Web:* kndr.fm	Mandan	ND	58554	701-663-2345	663-2347
KQDY-FM 94.5 (Ctry) 3500 E Rosser Ave *TF:* 800-825-5794 ■ *Web:* www.kqdy.com	Bismarck	ND	58501	701-255-1234	222-1131
KSSS-FM 101.5 (Rock) 3500 E Rosser Ave *TF:* 866-653-1015 ■ *Web:* www.1015.fm	Bismarck	ND	58501	701-255-1234	222-1131
KXMR-AM 710 (Sports) 3500 E Rosser Ave	Bismarck	ND	58501	701-255-1234	222-1131
KYYY-FM 92.9 (AC) 3500 E Rosser Ave *TF:* 866-929-9393 ■ *Web:* www.y93.fm	Bismarck	ND	58501	701-250-9393	222-1131

648-23 Boise, ID

Station	City	State	Zip	Phone	Fax
KBSX-FM 91.5 (NPR) 1910 University Dr *TF:* 888-859-5278 ■ *Web:* radio.boisestate.edu	Boise	ID	83725	208-947-5660	344-6631
KBXL-FM 94.1 (Rel) 1440 Weideman Ave *Web:* www.myfamilyradio.com	Boise	ID	83709	208-377-3790	377-3792
KGEM-AM 1140 (Nost) 5257 Fairview Ave Suite 260	Boise	ID	83706	208-344-3511	947-6765
KIDO-AM 580 (N/T) 827 E Park Blvd Suite 201 *Web:* www.580kido.com	Boise	ID	83712	208-344-6363	385-7385
KIZN-FM 92.3 (Ctry) 1419 W Bannock St *Web:* www.kizn.com	Boise	ID	83702	208-336-3670	336-3734
KJOT-FM 105.1 (Rock) 5257 Fairview Ave Suite 260 *Web:* www.j105.com	Boise	ID	83706	208-344-3511	947-6765
KKGL-FM 96.9 (CR) 1419 W Bannock St *Web:* www.96-9theeagle.com	Boise	ID	83702	208-336-3670	336-3734
KQFC-FM 97.9 (Ctry) 1419 W Bannock St *Web:* www.98kqfc.com	Boise	ID	83702	208-336-3670	336-3734
KQXR-FM 100.3 (Rock) 5257 Fairview Ave Suite 260 *Web:* www.xrock.com	Boise	ID	83706	208-344-3511	947-6765
KSAS-FM 103.3 (CHR) 827 E Park Blvd Suite 201 *Web:* www.1033kissfm.com	Boise	ID	83712	208-344-6363	385-7385
KTIK-AM 1350 (Sports) 1419 W Bannock St *Web:* www.ktik.com	Boise	ID	83702	208-336-3670	336-3734
KTMY-FM 104.3 (Ctry) 827 E Park Blvd Suite 201	Boise	ID	83712	208-344-6363	385-7385
KXLT-FM 107.9 (AC) 827 E Park Blvd Suite 201 *Web:* www.liteonline.com	Boise	ID	83712	208-344-6363	385-7385

648-24 Boston, MA

Station	City	State	Zip	Phone	Fax
WAAF-FM 107.3 (Rock) 20 Guest St 3rd Fl *Fax: Mktg ■ *Web:* www.waaf.com	Brighton	MA	02135	617-779-5800	779-5447*
WAMG-AM 890 (Sports) 529 Main St Suite 200 *Web:* www.espnboston.com	Charlestown	MA	02129	617-830-1000	242-8176
WBCN-FM 104.1 (Alt) 83 Leo Birmingham Pkwy *Web:* www.wbcn.com	Boston	MA	02135	617-746-1400	
WBMX-FM 98.5 (AC) 1200 Soldiers Field Rd *Web:* www.mix985.com	Boston	MA	02134	617-779-2000	779-2002
WBOS-FM 92.9 (AAA) 55 Morrissey Blvd *Web:* www.wbos.com	Boston	MA	02125	617-822-9600	822-6759
WBUR-FM 90.9 (NPR) 890 Commonwealth Ave *TF:* 800-909-9287 ■ *Web:* www.wbur.org	Boston	MA	02215	617-353-0909	353-9380
WBZ-AM 1030 (N/T) 1170 Soldiers Field Rd *Web:* www.wbz1030.com	Boston	MA	02134	617-787-7000	787-7060
WCIB-FM 101.9 (CR) 154 Barnstable Rd *TF:* 877-266-5102 ■ *Web:* www.cool102.com	Hyannis	MA	02601	508-778-2888	778-9651
WCRB-FM 99.5 (Clas) 750 South St *TF:* 800-400-9272 ■ *Web:* www.wcrb.com	Waltham	MA	02453	781-893-7080	893-0038
WEEI-AM 850 (Sports) 20 Guest St 3rd Fl *Fax: Mktg ■ *Web:* www.weei.com	Brighton	MA	02135	617-779-5800	779-5447*
WFNX-FM 101.7 (Alt) 25 Exchange St *Web:* fnxradio.com	Lynn	MA	01901	781-595-6200	595-3810
WGBH-FM 89.7 (NPR) 1 Guest St *Web:* www.wgbh.org	Boston	MA	02135	617-300-2000	300-1025
WHRB-FM 95.3 (Var) 389 Harvard St *Web:* www.whrb.org	Cambridge	MA	02138	617-495-4818	
WJDA-AM 1300 (N/T) 90 Everett Ave *Web:* www.wjda1300.com	Chelsea	MA	02150	617-884-4500	884-4515
WJIB-AM 740 (AC) 443 Concord Ave	Cambridge	MA	02138	617-868-7400	
WJMN-FM 94.5 (Urban) 10 Cabot Rd Suite 302 *Web:* www.jamn945.com	Medford	MA	02155	781-290-0009	290-0722
WKLB-FM 102.5 (Ctry) 55 Morrissey Blvd *Fax: News Rm ■ *TF:* 888-784-0995 ■ *Web:* www.wklb.com	Boston	MA	02125	617-822-9600	822-6659*
WMBR-FM 88.1 (Var) 3 Ames St *Web:* www.wmbr.org	Cambridge	MA	02142	617-253-4000	232-1384
WMJX-FM 106.7 (NAC) 55 Morrissey Blvd *Web:* www.magic1067.com	Boston	MA	02125	617-822-9600	822-6559
WMKK-FM 93.7 (Var) 20 Guest St 3rd Fl *Fax: Mktg ■ *Web:* www.star937fm.com	Brighton	MA	02135	617-779-5800	779-5447*
WNTN-AM 1550 (Var) 143 Rumford Ave *Web:* www.wntn.com	Newton	MA	02466	617-969-1550	969-1283
WODS-FM 103.3 (Oldies) 83 Leo Birmingham Pkwy *TF:* 800-336-1033 ■ *Web:* www.oldies1033.com	Boston	MA	02135	617-787-7500	787-7523
WPLM-FM 99.1 (AC) 17 Columbus Rd *Web:* www.wplm.fm	Plymouth	MA	02360	508-746-1390	830-1128
WRBB-FM 104.9 (Var) Northeastern University 360 Huntington Ave *Web:* wrbbradio.org	Boston	MA	02115	617-373-4338	
WRKO-AM 680 (N/T) 20 Guest St 3rd Fl *Fax: Mktg ■ *Web:* www.wrko.com	Brighton	MA	02135	617-779-5800	779-5447*
WROL-AM 950 (Rel) 500 Victory Rd *TF:* 888-659-0590 ■ *Web:* www.wrolradio.com	North Quincy	MA	02171	617-328-0880	328-0375
WROR-FM 105.7 (Oldies) 55 Morrissey Blvd *Web:* www.wror.com	Boston	MA	02125	617-822-9600	822-6459
WTKK-FM 96.9 (N/T) 55 Morrissey Blvd *Web:* www.969fmtalk.com	Boston	MA	02125	617-822-9600	822-6859
WUMB-FM 91.9 (Folk) 100 Morrissey Blvd *TF:* 800-573-2100 ■ *Web:* www.wumb.org	Boston	MA	02125	617-287-6900	287-6916
WWZN-AM 1510 (Sports) 308 Victory Rd *Web:* www.1510thezone.com	Quincy	MA	02171	617-237-1200	237-1177
WXKS-AM 1430 (Span) 10 Cabot Rd *Web:* www.am1430wxks.com	Medford	MA	02155	781-396-1430	290-0722
WXKS-FM 107.9 (CHR) 10 Cabot Rd *Web:* www.kiss108.com	Medford	MA	02155	781-396-1430	290-0722
WXRV-FM 92.5 (AAA) 30 How St *Web:* www.wxrv.com	Haverhill	MA	01830	978-374-4733	373-8023
WZBC-FM 90.3 (Var) Boston College 107 McElroy Commons *Web:* www.wzbc.org	Chestnut Hill	MA	02467	617-552-3511	552-1738
WZLX-FM 100.7 (CR) 83 Leo Birmingham Pkwy *Web:* www.wzlx.com	Brighton	MA	02135	617-746-5100	746-5105

648-25 Branson, MO

Station	City	State	Zip	Phone	Fax
KBCN-FM 104.3 (Ctry) 100 Bluebird St *TF:* 866-662-1043 ■ *Web:* www.kbcnradio.com	Harrison	AR	72601	870-743-1157	743-1168
KHOZ-FM 102.9 (Ctry) 1111 Radio Ave *TF:* 800-553-6103 ■ *Web:* khoz.com	Harrison	AR	72601	870-741-2301	741-3299
KLFC-FM 88.1 (Rel) 205 W Atlantic St *TF:* 877-334-5532 ■ *Web:* www.klfcradio.com	Branson	MO	65616	417-334-5532	335-2437
KOMC-AM 1220 (Rel) 202 Courtney St *Web:* hometownradioonline.com	Branson	MO	65616	417-334-6003	334-7141
KOMC-FM 100.1 (Nost) 202 Courtney St *Web:* hometownradioonline.com	Branson	MO	65616	417-334-6003	334-7141
KOZO-FM 89.7 (Rel) 301 Gibson Rd *TF:* 888-996-2747 ■ *Web:* www.oasisnetwork.org	Hollister	MO	65672	417-339-3388	339-3410
KRZK-FM 106.3 (Ctry) 202 Courtney St *Web:* hometownradioonline.com	Branson	MO	65616	417-334-6003	334-7141

648-26 Buffalo, NY

Station	City	State	Zip	Phone	Fax
CHTZ-FM 97.7 (Rock) 12 Yates St *Web:* www.htzfm.com	Saint Catharines	ON	L2R6Z4	905-688-0977	684-4800
CKEY-FM 101.1 (CHR) 4668 St Clair Ave PO Box 710	Niagara Falls	ON	L2E6X7	905-356-6710	356-0644
WBEN-AM 930 (N/T) 500 Corporate Pkwy Suite 200 *Web:* www.wben.com	Amherst	NY	14226	716-843-0600	832-3080
WBFO-FM 88.7 (NPR) 3435 Main St 205 Allen Hall *Web:* www.wbfo.org	Buffalo	NY	14214	716-829-2555	829-2277
WBLK-FM 93.7 (Urban AC) 14 Lafayette Sq Suite 1300 *Web:* www.wblk.com	Buffalo	NY	14203	716-852-9393	852-9390
WBNY-FM 91.3 (Alt) 1300 Elmwood Ave *Web:* www.buffalostate.edu/wbny	Buffalo	NY	14222	716-878-5104	878-6600
WBUF-FM 92.9 (Var) 14 Lafayette Sq Suite 1300 *Web:* www.wbuf.com	Buffalo	NY	14203	716-852-9292	852-9290
WDCX-FM 99.5 (Rel) 625 Delaware Ave Suite 308 *Web:* www.wdcxfm.com	Buffalo	NY	14202	716-883-3010	883-3606
WEDG-FM 103.3 (Alt) 50 James E Casey Dr *Web:* www.wedg.com	Buffalo	NY	14206	716-881-4555	884-2931
WGR-AM 550 (Sports) 500 Corporate Pkwy Suite 200 *Web:* www.wgr550.com	Amherst	NY	14226	716-843-0600	832-3080
WGRF-FM 96.9 (CR) 50 James E Casey Dr *Web:* www.97rock.com	Buffalo	NY	14206	716-881-4555	884-2931
WHTT-FM 104.1 (Oldies) 50 James E Casey Dr *Web:* www.whtt.com	Buffalo	NY	14206	716-881-4555	884-2931
WJYE-FM 96.1 (AC) 14 Lafayette Sq Suite 1200 *Web:* www.wjye.com	Buffalo	NY	14203	716-852-7444	852-0537
WKSE-FM 98.5 (CHR) 500 Corporate Pkwy Suite 200 *Web:* www.kiss985.com	Amherst	NY	14226	716-843-0600	832-3080
WLKK-FM 107.7 (CR) 500 Corporate Pkwy Suite 200 *Web:* www.1077thelake.com	Amherst	NY	14226	716-843-0600	832-3080
WMNY-AM 1120 (Rel) 50 James E Casey Dr	Buffalo	NY	14206	716-881-4555	848-9518
WNED-AM 970 (NPR) 140 Lower Terr *Web:* www.wned.org	Buffalo	NY	14202	716-845-7000	845-7043
WTSS-FM 102.5 (AC) 500 Corporate Pkwy Suite 200 *Web:* www.mystar1025.com	Amherst	NY	14226	716-843-0600	832-3080
WUFO-AM 1080 (Rel) 89 LaSalle Ave *Web:* www.wufoam.com	Buffalo	NY	14214	716-834-1080	837-1438
WWKB-AM 1520 (Oldies) 500 Corporate Pkwy Suite 200 *Web:* kb1520.com	Amherst	NY	14226	716-843-0600	832-3080
WWWS-AM 1400 (Urban) 500 Corporate Pkwy Suite 200 *Web:* www.am1400solidgoldsoul.com	Amherst	NY	14226	716-843-0600	832-3080
WXRL-AM 1300 (Ctry) 5426 Williams St PO Box 170 *Web:* www.wxrl.com	Lancaster	NY	14086	716-681-1313	681-7172
WYRK-FM 106.5 (Ctry) 14 Lafayette Sq Suite 1200 *Web:* www.wyrk.com	Buffalo	NY	14203	716-852-7444	852-5683

648-27 Burlington, VT

Station	City	State	Zip	Phone	Fax
WBTZ-FM 99.9 (Alt) 255 S Champlain St *Web:* www.999thebuzz.com	Burlington	VT	05401	802-860-2440	860-1818

Station	City	State	Zip	Phone	Fax
WCAT-AM 1390 (Sports) 372 Dorset St *TF:* 800-286-9537 ■ *Web:* www.wcat1390.com	South Burlington	VT	05403	802-863-1010	863-7256
WCPV-FM 101.3 (CR) 265 Hegeman Ave *Web:* www.champ1013.com	Colchester	VT	05446	802-655-0093	655-3224
WCVT-FM 101.7 (Clas) PO Box 550 *Web:* www.wcvtradio.com	Waterbury	VT	05676	802-244-7321	244-1771
WDEV-AM 550 (N/T) PO Box 550 *Web:* www.wdevradio.com	Waterbury	VT	05676	802-244-7321	244-1771
WEZF-FM 92.9 (AC) 265 Hegeman Ave *Web:* www.star929.com	Colchester	VT	05446	802-655-0093	655-0478
WIZN-FM 106.7 (Rock) 255 S Champlain St *Web:* www.wizn.com	Burlington	VT	05401	802-860-2440	860-1818
WJOY-AM 1230 (Nost) 70 Joy Dr *Web:* www.wjoy.com	South Burlington	VT	05403	802-658-1230	862-0786
WNCS-FM 104.7 (AAA) 169 River St *Web:* www.pointfm.com	Montpelier	VT	05602	802-223-5275	223-1520
WOKO-FM 98.9 (Ctry) 70 Joy Dr *TF:* 800-354-9890 ■ *Web:* www.woko.com	South Burlington	VT	05403	802-658-1230	862-0786
WORK-FM 107.1 (AC) 41 Jacques St *Web:* www.1071workfm.com	Barre	VT	05641	802-476-4168	479-5893
WRUV-FM 90.1 (Var) University of Vermont Davis Student Center *Web:* www.uvm.edu/~wruv	Burlington	VT	05405	802-656-0796	656-2281
WSKI-AM 1240 (Nost) 169 River St	Montpelier	VT	05602	802-223-5275	223-1520
WSNO-AM 1450 (N/T) 41 Jacques St *Web:* www.wsno1450.net	Barre	VT	05641	802-476-4168	479-5893
WVPS-FM 107.9 (NPR) 365 Troy Ave *TF:* 800-639-2192 ■ *Web:* www.vpr.net	Colchester	VT	05446	802-655-9451	655-2799
WWFY-FM 100.9 (Ctry) 41 Jacques St *Web:* www.froggy1009.com	Barre	VT	05641	802-476-4168	479-5893
WXXX-FM 95.5 (CHR) 118 Malletts Bay Ave *TF:* 888-805-9595 ■ *Web:* www.95triplex.com	Colchester	VT	05446	802-655-9550	655-1329

648-28 Calgary, AB

Station	City	Prov	Postal Code	Phone	Fax
CBR-AM 1010 (CBC) 1724 Westmount Blvd NW **Fax:* News Rm ■ *Web:* www.cbc.ca/calgary	Calgary	AB	T2N3G7	403-521-6000	521-6262*
CBR-FM 102.1 (CBC) 1724 Westmount Blvd NW *TF:* 866-306-4636 ■ *Web:* www.cbc.ca/calgary	Calgary	AB	T2N3G7	403-521-6000	521-6262
CFAC-AM 960 (Sports) 2723 37th Ave NE Suite 240 *Web:* www.fan960.com	Calgary	AB	T1Y5R8	403-291-0000	291-4368
CFFR-AM 660 (N/T) 2723 37th Ave NE *Web:* www.660news.com	Calgary	AB	T1Y5R8	403-291-0000	246-4368
CHFM-FM 95.9 (AC) 2723 37th Ave NE Suite 240 *Web:* www.lite96.ca	Calgary	AB	T1Y5R8	403-291-0000	291-4368
CHQR-AM 770 (N/T) 630 3rd Ave SW Suite 105 *TF:* 800-563-7770 ■ *Web:* www.qr77.com	Calgary	AB	T2P4L4	403-716-6500	716-2111
CJAY-FM 92.1 (CR) 1110 Center St NE Suite 300 *Web:* www.cjay92.com	Calgary	AB	T2E2R2	403-240-5850	240-5801
CJSW-FM 90.9 (Alt) 2500 University Dr NW MacEwan Hall Rm 127 *Web:* www.cjsw.com	Calgary	AB	T2N1N4	403-220-3902	289-8212
CKIK-FM 107.3 (CHR) 630 3rd Ave SW Suite 105 *TF:* 800-563-7770 ■ *Web:* www.q107fm.ca	Calgary	AB	T2P4L4	403-264-1073	716-2111
CKIS-FM 96.9 (CR) 2723 37th Ave NE Suite 240 *Web:* www.jackfm.ca	Calgary	AB	T1Y5R8	403-250-9797	291-4368
CKMX-AM 1060 (Ctry) 1110 Center St NE Suite 300 *Web:* www.classiccountryam1060.com	Calgary	AB	T2E2R2	403-240-5850	240-5801
CKRY-FM 105.1 (Ctry) 630 3rd Ave SW Suite 105 *TF:* 800-563-7770 ■ *Web:* www.country105.com	Calgary	AB	T2P4L4	403-508-9000	716-2111

648-29 Casper, WY

Station	City	State	Zip	Phone	Fax
KASS-FM 106.9 (CR) 218 N Wolcott St *Web:* www.wyomingradio.com/kass	Casper	WY	82601	307-265-1984	473-7461
KHOC-FM 102.5 (AC) 218 N Wolcott St *Web:* www.wyomingradio.com/khoc/	Casper	WY	82601	307-265-1984	473-7461
KMGW-FM 96.7 (AC) 150 N Nichols Ave *TF:* 800-832-0208	Casper	WY	82601	307-266-5252	235-9143
KMLD-FM 94.5 (Oldies) 218 N Wolcott St *Web:* www.wyomingradio.com/kmld/	Casper	WY	82601	307-265-1984	473-7461
KQLT-FM 103.7 (Ctry) 218 N Wolcott St *Web:* www.wyomingradio.com/kqlt	Casper	WY	82601	307-265-1984	473-7461
KRVK-FM 107.9 (Rock) 150 N Nichols Ave *Web:* www.theriver1079.com	Casper	WY	82601	307-266-5252	235-9143
KTRS-FM 104.7 (CHR) 150 N Nichols Ave *Web:* www.kissfm1047.com	Casper	WY	82601	307-266-5252	235-9143
KTWO-AM 1030 (Ctry) 150 N Nichols Ave *Web:* www.k2radio.com	Casper	WY	82601	307-266-5252	235-9143
KUWC-FM 91.3 (NPR) 1000 E University Ave PO Box 3984 *Web:* uwadmnweb.uwyo.edu/wpr	Laramie	WY	82071	307-766-4240	766-6184
KUYO-AM 830 (Rel) PO Box 50607 *Web:* www.kuyo.com	Casper	WY	82605	307-577-5896	
KVOC-AM 1230 (Nost) 218 N Wolcott St *Web:* www.wyomingradio.com/kvoc	Casper	WY	82601	307-265-1984	473-7461
KWYY-FM 95.5 (Ctry) 150 N Nichols Ave *Web:* www.mycountry955.com	Casper	WY	82601	307-266-5252	235-9143

648-30 Cedar Rapids, IA

Station	City	State	Zip	Phone	Fax
KCCK-FM 88.3 (Jazz) PO Box 2068 *TF:* 800-373-5225 ■ *Web:* www.kcck.org	Cedar Rapids	IA	52406	319-398-5446	398-5492
KDAT-FM 104.5 (AC) 425 2nd St SE 4th Fl *Web:* www.kdat.com	Cedar Rapids	IA	52401	319-365-9431	363-8062
KFMW-FM 107.9 (Rock) 514 Jefferson St **Fax:* News Rm ■ *Web:* www.rock108.com	Waterloo	IA	50701	319-234-2200	233-4946*
KHAK-FM 98.1 (Ctry) 425 2nd St SE 4th Fl *TF:* 800-747-5425 ■ *Web:* www.khak.com	Cedar Rapids	IA	52401	319-365-9431	363-8062
KKRQ-FM 100.7 (CR) 1 Stephen Atkins Dr *Web:* www.thefox.net	Iowa City	IA	52240	319-354-9500	354-9504
KMRY-AM 1450 (Nost) 1957 Blairs Ferry Rd NE *Web:* www.kmryradio.com	Cedar Rapids	IA	52402	319-393-1450	393-1407
KOKZ-FM 105.7 (Oldies) 514 Jefferson St **Fax:* News Rm ■ *Web:* www.cool1057.com	Waterloo	IA	50701	319-234-2200	233-4946*
KRNA-FM 94.1 (Rock) 425 2nd St SE 4th Fl *Web:* www.krna.com	Cedar Rapids	IA	52401	319-365-9431	363-8062
KZIA-FM 102.9 (CHR) 1110 26th Ave SW *Web:* www.kzia.com	Cedar Rapids	IA	52404	319-363-2061	363-2948
WMT-AM 600 (N/T) 600 Old Marion Rd *TF:* 800-332-5401 ■ *Web:* www.wmtradio.com	Cedar Rapids	IA	52402	319-395-0530	393-9600
WMT-FM 96.5 (AC) 600 Old Marion Rd NE *TF:* 800-258-0096 ■ *Web:* www.mix965.com	Cedar Rapids	IA	52402	319-395-0530	393-9600

648-31 Champaign, IL

Station	City	State	Zip	Phone	Fax
WBCP-AM 1580 (Urban) 904 N 4th St Suite D	Champaign	IL	61820	217-359-1580	359-1583
WBGL-FM 91.7 (Rel) 2108 W Springfield Ave *TF:* 800-475-9245 ■ *Web:* www.wbgl.org	Champaign	IL	61821	217-359-8232	359-7374
WCFF-FM 92.5 (Oldies) 2603 W Bradley Ave *Web:* www.925thechief.com	Champaign	IL	61821	217-352-4141	352-1256
WDWS-AM 1400 (N/T) 2301 S Neil St *TF:* 800-223-9397 ■ *Web:* www.wdws.com/wdws	Champaign	IL	61820	217-351-5300	351-5385
WEFT-FM 90.1 (Var) 113 N Market St *Web:* www.weft.org	Champaign	IL	61820	217-359-9338	
WGKC-FM 105.9 (CR) 4108 Fieldstone Rd Suite C *Web:* www.wgkc.net	Champaign	IL	61822	217-367-1195	367-3291
WHMS-FM 97.5 (AC) 2301 S Neil St *TF:* 800-223-9397 ■ *Web:* www.wdws.com/whms	Champaign	IL	61820	217-351-5300	351-5385
WILL-FM 90.9 (NPR) 300 N Goodwin Ave Campbell Hall *Web:* www.will.uiuc.edu	Urbana	IL	61801	217-333-0850	244-9586
WIXY-FM 100.3 (Ctry) 2603 W Bradley Ave *Web:* www.wixy.com	Champaign	IL	61821	217-352-4141	352-1256
WLRW-FM 94.5 (CHR) 2603 W Bradley Ave *Web:* www.mix945.com	Champaign	IL	61821	217-352-4141	352-1256
WPCD-FM 88.7 (Rock) 2400 W Bradley Ave *Web:* www.parkland.edu/WPCD/	Champaign	IL	61821	217-351-2450	
WPGU-FM 107.1 (Alt) 512 E Green St Suite 107 *Web:* www.wpgu.com	Champaign	IL	61820	217-337-3100	337-8303

648-32 Charleston, SC

Station	City	State	Zip	Phone	Fax
WAVF-FM 96.1 (Alt) 2294 Clements Ferry Rd *Web:* www.96wave.com	Charleston	SC	29492	843-972-1100	972-1200
WEZL-FM 103.5 (Ctry) 950 Houston Northcutt Blvd Suite 201 *Web:* www.wezlfm.com	Mount Pleasant	SC	29464	843-884-2534	884-1218
WIWF-FM 969 (Ctry) 4230 Faber Place Dr Suite 100 *Web:* 969thewolf.com	North Charleston	SC	29405	843-277-1200	277-1212
WMGL-FM 101.7 (Urban) 4230 Faber Place Dr Suite 100 *Web:* www.magic1017.com	North Charleston	SC	29405	843-277-1200	277-1212
WQSC-AM 1340 (Sports) 60 Markfield Dr Unit 4	Charleston	SC	29407	843-763-6631	766-1239
WRFQ-FM 104.5 (CR) 950 Houston Northcutt Blvd Suite 201 *Web:* www.wrfq.com	Mount Pleasant	SC	29464	843-884-2534	884-1218
WSCI-FM 89.3 (NPR) 1101 George Rogers Blvd *Web:* www.myetv.org/radio/	Columbia	SC	29201	803-737-3545	737-3552
WSSX-FM 95.1 (CHR) 4230 Faber Place Dr Suite 100 *Web:* www.95sx.com	North Charleston	SC	29405	843-277-1200	277-1212
WTMA-AM 1250 (N/T) 4230 Faber Place Dr Suite 100 *Web:* www.wtma.com	North Charleston	SC	29405	843-277-1200	277-1212
WWWZ-FM 93.3 (Urban) 4230 Faber Place Dr Suite 100 *Web:* www.z93jamz.com	North Charleston	SC	29405	843-277-1200	277-1212
WXLY-FM 102.5 (Oldies) 950 Houston Northcutt Blvd Suite 201 *Web:* www.wxly.com	Mount Pleasant	SC	29464	843-884-2534	884-1218
WXTC-AM 1390 (Rel) 2294 Clements Ferry Rd *Web:* www.heaven1390.com	Charleston	SC	29492	843-972-1100	972-1200
WYBB-FM 98.1 (Alt) 59 Windermere Blvd	Charleston	SC	29407	843-769-4799	769-4797

648-33 Charleston, WV

Station	City	State	Zip	Phone	Fax
WAMX-FM 106.3 (Rock) 134 4th Ave *Web:* www.x1063.com	Huntington	WV	25701	304-525-7788	525-6281
WCHS-AM 580 (N/T) 1111 Virginia St E *Web:* www.58wchs.com	Charleston	WV	25301	304-342-8131	344-4745
WKAZ-FM 107.3 (Var) 1111 Virginia St E *Web:* www.1073kaz.com	Charleston	WV	25301	304-342-8131	344-4745
WKLC-FM 105.1 (Rock) 100 Kanawha Terr *Web:* www.wklc.com	Saint Albans	WV	25177	304-722-3308	727-1300
WKWS-FM 96.1 (Ctry) 1111 Virginia St E *Web:* www.961thewolf.com	Charleston	WV	25301	304-342-8131	344-4745
WQBE-FM 97.5 (Ctry) 817 Suncrest Pl *Web:* www.wqbe.com	Charleston	WV	25303	304-342-3136	342-3118
WRVZ-FM 98.7 (CHR) 1111 Virginia St E *Web:* www.wlevradio.com	Charleston	WV	25301	304-342-8131	344-4745
WVAF-FM 99.9 (AC) 1111 Virginia St E *Web:* www.v100.fm	Charleston	WV	25301	304-342-8131	344-4745
WVNP-FM 89.9 (NPR) 600 Capitol St *TF:* 888-596-9729 ■ *Web:* www.wvpubrad.org	Charleston	WV	25301	304-556-4900	556-4981
WVPN-FM 88.5 (NPR) 600 Capitol St *TF:* 888-596-9729 ■ *Web:* www.wvpubrad.org	Charleston	WV	25301	304-556-4900	556-4981
WVSR-FM 102.7 (CHR) 817 Suncrest Pl *Web:* www.electric102.com	Charleston	WV	25303	304-342-3136	342-3118
WZJO-FM 94.5 (Alt) 817 Suncrest Pl *Web:* www.zrock945.com	Charleston	WV	25303	304-342-3136	342-3118

648-34 Charlotte, NC

Station	City	State	Zip	Phone	Fax
WBAV-FM 101.9 (Urban AC) 1520 South Blvd Suite 300 *Web:* www.v1019.com	Charlotte	NC	28203	704-342-2644	227-8985
WBT-AM 1110 (N/T) 1 Julian Price Pl *Web:* www.wbt.com	Charlotte	NC	28208	704-374-3500	374-3890
WEND-FM 106.5 (Alt) 801 Wood Ridge Center Dr *Web:* www.1065.com	Charlotte	NC	28217	704-714-9444	332-8805
WFAE-FM 90.7 (NPR) 8801 JM Keynes Dr Suite 91 *TF:* 800-876-9323 ■ *Web:* www.wfae.org	Charlotte	NC	28262	704-549-9323	547-8851
WFNZ-AM 610 (Sports) 1520 South Blvd Suite 300 *Web:* www.wfnz.com	Charlotte	NC	28203	704-342-2644	319-3934
WGIV-AM 1600 (Rel) 1520 South Blvd Suite 300	Charlotte	NC	28203	704-570-1672	
WKKT-FM 96.9 (Ctry) 801 Wood Ridge Center Dr *TF:* 800-332-1029 ■ *Web:* www.wkktfm.com	Charlotte	NC	28217	704-714-9444	332-8805
WLNK-FM 107.9 (AC) 1 Julian Price Pl *Web:* 1079thelink.com	Charlotte	NC	28208	704-374-3500	374-3889
WLYT-FM 102.9 (AC) 801 Wood Ridge Center Dr *TF:* 800-332-1029 ■ *Web:* www.wlyt.com	Charlotte	NC	28217	704-714-9444	332-8805

Charlotte, NC (Cont'd)

Station	City	State	ZIP	Phone	Fax
WMIT-FM 106.9 (Rel) PO Box 159 *TF:* 800-330-9648 ■ *Web:* www.wmit.org	Black Mountain	NC	28711	828-669-8477	669-6983*
WNKS-FM 95.1 (CHR) 4015 Stuart Andrew Blvd *Web:* www.kiss951.com	Charlotte	NC	28217	704-331-9510	331-9140
WNOW-AM 1030 (Span) 4201-J Stuart Andrew Blvd **Fax Area Code:* 208 ■ *Web:* www.wnow.com	Charlotte	NC	28217	704-665-9355	545-9888*
WPEG-FM 97.9 (Urban) 1520 South Blvd Suite 300 *TF:* 800-525-0098 ■ *Web:* www.power98fm.com	Charlotte	NC	28203	704-342-2644	227-8985
WQNC-FM 92.7 (Urban) 2303 W Morehead St *Web:* www.q927fm.com	Charlotte	NC	28208	704-358-0211	358-3752
WRCM-FM 91.9 (Rel) PO Box 17069 *Web:* www.wrcm.org	Charlotte	NC	28227	704-821-9293	821-9285
WRFX-FM 99.7 (CR) 801 Wood Ridge Center Dr *TF:* 800-332-1029 ■ *Web:* wrfx.com	Charlotte	NC	28217	704-714-9444	332-8805
WSIC-AM 1400 (N/T) 1117 Radio Rd *Web:* www.wsicweb.com	Statesville	NC	28677	704-872-6348	873-6921
WSOC-FM 103.7 (Ctry) 1520 South Blvd Suite 300 *Web:* www.wsocfm.com	Charlotte	NC	28203	704-342-2644	523-4800
WWMG-FM 96.1 (Urban) 801 Woodridge Center Dr	Charlotte	NC	28217	704-714-9444	334-9525
WXRC-FM 95.7 (CR) 1515 Mockingbird Ln Suite 205 *TF:* 800-282-9570 ■ *Web:* www.957theride.com	Charlotte	NC	28209	704-527-0957	527-2720

648-35 Chattanooga, TN

Station	City	State	ZIP	Phone	Fax
WBDX-FM 102.7 (Rel) 5512 Ringgold Rd Suite 214 *TF:* 877-262-5103 ■ *Web:* www.j103.com	Chattanooga	TN	37412	423-892-1200	892-1633
WDEF-AM 1370 (Sports) 2615 S Broad St	Chattanooga	TN	37408	423-321-6200	321-6270
WDEF-FM 92.3 (AC) 2615 S Broad St *Web:* www.sunny923.com	Chattanooga	TN	37408	423-321-6200	321-6270
WDOD-FM 96.5 (CHR) 2615 S Broad St *Web:* www.965themountain.com	Chattanooga	TN	37408	423-321-6200	321-6270
WGOW-FM 102.3 (N/T) 821 Pineville Rd *Web:* www.wgow.com	Chattanooga	TN	37405	423-756-6141	266-3629
WJTT-FM 94.3 (Urban) 1305 Carter St *Web:* power94.com	Chattanooga	TN	37402	423-265-9494	266-2335
WLND-FM 98.1 (Ctry) 7413 Old Lee Hwy *Web:* www.thelegendonline.com	Chattanooga	TN	37421	423-892-3333	899-7224
WMBW-FM 88.9 (Rel) PO Box 73026 *TF:* 800-621-9629 ■ *Web:* www.mbn.org	Chattanooga	TN	37407	423-629-8900	629-0021
WNOO-AM 1260 (Rel) 1108 Hendricks St *Web:* www.wnooradio.com	Chattanooga	TN	37406	423-698-8617	698-8796
WOGT-FM 107.9 (Ctry) 821 Pineville Rd *Web:* www.dukefm.com	Chattanooga	TN	37405	423-756-6141	266-3629
WRXR-FM 105.5 (Rock) 7413 Old Lee Hwy *Web:* www.rock105.net	Chattanooga	TN	37421	423-892-3333	899-7224
WSKZ-FM 106.5 (Rock) 821 Pineville Rd *Web:* www.kz106.com	Chattanooga	TN	37405	423-756-6141	266-3629
WUSY-FM 100.7 (Ctry) 7413 Old Lee Hwy *Web:* www.us101country.com	Chattanooga	TN	37421	423-892-3333	899-7224
WUTC-FM 88.1 (NPR) 615 McCallie Ave Dept 1151 *Web:* www.wutc.org	Chattanooga	TN	37403	423-265-9882	425-2379

648-36 Cheyenne, WY

Station	City	State	ZIP	Phone	Fax
KFBC-AM 1240 (N/T) 1806 Capitol Ave *TF:* 877-388-7353 ■ *Web:* www.kfbcradio.com	Cheyenne	WY	82001	307-634-4462	632-8586
KGAB-AM 650 (N/T) 1912 Capitol Ave Suite 300 *Web:* www.kgab.com	Cheyenne	WY	82001	307-632-4400	632-1818
KIGN-FM 101.9 (Rock) 1912 Capitol Ave Suite 300 *Web:* www.kign.com	Cheyenne	WY	82001	307-632-4400	632-1818
KJUA-AM 1380 (Span) 110 E 17th St Suite 205 *TF:* 888-896-1630	Cheyenne	WY	82001	307-635-8787	635-8788
KLEN-FM 106.3 (Ctry) 1912 Capitol Ave Suite 300 *Web:* www.1063klen.com	Cheyenne	WY	82001	307-632-4400	632-1818
KRAE-AM 1480 (Sports) 2109 E 10th St	Cheyenne	WY	82001	307-638-8921	638-8922
KRRR-FM 104.9 (Oldies) 2109 E 10th St *Web:* www.1049krrr.com	Cheyenne	WY	82001	307-638-8921	638-8922
KUWJ-FM 90.3 (NPR) 1000 E University Ave PO Box 3984 *Web:* uwadmnweb.uwyo.edu/wpr	Laramie	WY	82071	307-766-4240	766-6184
KUWR-FM 91.9 (NPR) 1000 E University Ave PO Box 3984 *Web:* uwadmnweb.uwyo.edu/wpr	Laramie	WY	82071	307-766-4240	766-6184

648-37 Chicago, IL

Station	City	State	ZIP	Phone	Fax
WBBM-AM 780 (N/T) 180 N Stetson Suite 1100 Prudential Plaza 2 *Web:* www.wbbm780.com	Chicago	IL	60601	312-297-7801	202-3676
WBBM-FM 96.3 (CHR) 180 N Stetson Suite 1100 Prudential Plaza 2 *Web:* www.b96.com	Chicago	IL	60601	312-297-7801	297-7822
WBEZ-FM 91.5 (NPR) 848 E Grand Ave Navy Pier *Web:* www.wbez.org	Chicago	IL	60611	312-948-4600	832-3158
WCFS-FM 105.9 (AC) 2 Prudential Plaza Suite 1059 *Web:* www.fresh1059.com	Chicago	IL	60601	312-240-7900	565-3181
WCGO-AM 1600 (Nost) 222 Vollmer Rd *Web:* www.wcgoradio.com	Chicago Heights	IL	60411	708-755-5900	755-5941
WDEK-FM 92.5 (AAA) 6012 S Pulaski Rd *Web:* www.weplayanything.com	Chicago	IL	60629	773-767-1000	767-1100
WDRV-FM 97.1 (CR) 875 N Michigan Ave Suite 1510 *Web:* www.971thedrive.com	Chicago	IL	60611	312-274-9710	274-1304
WFMT-FM 98.7 (Clas) 5400 N St Louis Ave *TF:* 800-872-9368 ■ *Web:* www.wfmt.com	Chicago	IL	60625	773-279-2000	279-2199
WGCI-FM 107.5 (Urban) 233 N Michigan Ave Suite 2800 **Fax:* Sales ■ *Web:* www.wgci.com	Chicago	IL	60601	312-540-2000	938-0692*
WGN-AM 720 (N/T) 435 N Michigan Ave *Web:* www.wgnradio.com	Chicago	IL	60611	312-222-4700	222-5165
WILV-FM 100.3 (AC) 130 E Randolph St 1 Prudential Plaza Suite 2780 *Web:* www.lovefm.fm	Chicago	IL	60601	312-297-5100	297-5155
WJMK-FM 104.3 (Oldies) 180 N Stetson Ave Suite 900 *Web:* www.wjmk.com	Chicago	IL	60601	312-870-6400	977-1859
WKQX-FM 101.1 (Alt) 230 Merchandise Mart Plaza *Web:* www.q101.com	Chicago	IL	60654	312-527-8348	527-3620
WKSC-FM 103.5 (CHR) 233 N Michigan Ave Suite 2800 **Fax:* Sales ■ *Web:* www.kiss1035.com	Chicago	IL	60601	312-540-2000	938-0692*
WLEY-FM 107.9 (Span) 150 N Michigan Ave Suite 1040 **Fax:* PR ■ *Web:* www.laley1079.com	Chicago	IL	60601	312-920-9500	920-9515*
WLIT-FM 93.9 (AC) 233 N Michigan Ave Suite 2800 *Web:* www.wlit.com	Chicago	IL	60601	312-540-2000	938-0111
WLS-AM 890 (N/T) 190 N State St 9th Fl *Web:* www.wlsam.com	Chicago	IL	60601	312-984-0890	984-5305
WLUP-FM 97.9 (CR) 222 Merchandise Mart Suite 230 *Web:* www.wlup.com	Chicago	IL	60654	312-440-5270	527-3620
WMBI-FM 90.1 (Rel) 820 N LaSalle Blvd *TF:* 800-600-9624 ■ *Web:* www.wmbi.org	Chicago	IL	60610	312-329-4300	329-4468
WMVP-AM 1000 (Sports) 190 N State St 7th Fl **Fax:* Sales ■ *Web:* www.espnradio1000.com	Chicago	IL	60601	312-980-1000	980-1010*
WNUA-FM 95.5 (NAC) 233 N Michigan Ave Suite 2800 *Web:* www.wnua.com	Chicago	IL	60601	312-540-2000	938-0111
WOJO-FM 105.1 (Span) 625 N Michigan Ave Suite 300 *TF:* 877-357-4786 ■ *Web:* www.univision.com	Chicago	IL	60611	312-981-1800	981-1840
WPWX-FM 92.3 (Urban) 6336 Calumet Ave **Fax Area Code:* 219 ■ *Web:* www.power92chicago.com	Hammond	IN	46324	773-734-4455	933-0323*
WRTO-AM 1200 (Span) 625 N Michigan Ave Suite 300 *Web:* www.univision.com	Chicago	IL	60611	312-981-1800	981-1840
WSCR-AM 670 (Sports) 455 N Cityfront Plaza *Web:* www.670thescore.com	Chicago	IL	60611	312-644-6767	425-6072
WTMX-FM 101.9 (AC) 130 E Randolph St Suite 2700 1 Prudential Plaza *Web:* www.wtmx.com	Chicago	IL	60601	312-946-1019	946-4747
WUSN-FM 99.5 (Ctry) 2 Prudential Plaza Suite 1000 *Web:* www.us99.com	Chicago	IL	60601	312-649-0099	856-9586
WVAZ-FM 102.7 (Urban AC) 233 N Michigan Ave Suite 2700 *Web:* www.v103.com	Chicago	IL	60604	312-540-2000	938-4477
WVON-AM 1690 (N/T) 1000 E 87th St *TF:* 877-591-1690 ■ *Web:* www.wvon.com	Chicago	IL	60619	773-247-6200	247-5366
WXRT-FM 93.1 (Alt) 4949 W Belmont Ave *Web:* www.wxrt.com	Chicago	IL	60641	773-777-1700	777-5031
WZZN-FM 94.7 (Oldies) 190 N State St 8th Fl *Web:* www.947chicago.com	Chicago	IL	60601	312-984-0890	984-5305

648-38 Cincinnati, OH

Station	City	State	ZIP	Phone	Fax
WAKW-FM 93.3 (Rel) 6275 Collegevue Pl Box 24126 *TF:* 888-542-9393 ■ *Web:* www.mystar933.com	Cincinnati	OH	45224	513-542-9258	542-9333
WCIN-AM 1480 (NAC) 4445 Lake Forest Dr Suite 420 *Web:* www.wcinam.com	Cincinnati	OH	45242	513-281-7180	281-5678
WCKY-AM 1530 (N/T) 8044 Montgomery Rd Suite 650 *Web:* www.wcky.com	Cincinnati	OH	45236	513-686-8300	241-0358
WCVX-AM 1050 (Rel) 635 W 7th St Suite 400 *Web:* www.wcvx.com	Cincinnati	OH	45203	513-533-2500	533-2527
WDJO-AM 1160 (Oldies) 635 W 7th St Suite 400 *Web:* www.oldies1160.com	Cincinnati	OH	45203	513-533-2500	533-2527
WEBN-FM 102.7 (Rock) 8044 Montgomery Rd Suite 650 *TF:* 800-616-9236 ■ *Web:* www.webn.com	Cincinnati	OH	45236	513-686-8300	749-3299
WGRR-FM 103.5 (Oldies) 895 Central Ave Suite 900 *Web:* www.wgrr.com	Cincinnati	OH	45202	513-241-9898	241-6689
WGUC-FM 90.9 (Clas) 1223 Central Pkwy *Web:* www.wguc.org	Cincinnati	OH	45214	513-241-8282	241-8456
WIZF-FM 100.9 (Urban) 705 Central Ave *Web:* www.wizfm.com	Cincinnati	OH	45202	513-679-6000	679-6014
WKFS-FM 107.1 (CHR) 8044 Montgomery Rd Suite 650 *Web:* www.kisscincinnati.com	Cincinnati	OH	45236	513-686-8300	421-3299
WKRC-AM 550 (N/T) 8044 Montgomery Rd Suite 650 *Web:* www.55krc.com	Cincinnati	OH	45236	513-686-8300	651-2555
WKRQ-FM 101.9 (CHR) 2060 Reading Rd *Web:* www.wkrq.com	Cincinnati	OH	45202	513-699-5102	699-5000
WLW-AM 700 (N/T) 8044 Montgomery Rd Suite 650 *Web:* www.700wlw.com	Cincinnati	OH	45236	513-686-8300	665-9700
WMOJ-FM 1003 (Urban) 705 Central Ave Suite 200 *Web:* www.wmoj.com	Cincinnati	OH	45202	513-679-6000	679-6014
WNNF-FM 94.1 (AC) 8044 Montgomery Rd Suite 650 *Web:* www.wvmx.com	Cincinnati	OH	45236	513-686-8300	421-3299
WOFX-FM 92.5 (CR) 8044 Montgomery Rd Suite 650 *Web:* www.wofx.com	Cincinnati	OH	45236	513-686-8300	784-1249
WRRM-FM 98.5 (AC) 895 Central Ave Suite 900 *Web:* www.warm98.com	Cincinnati	OH	45202	513-241-9898	241-6689
WSAI-AM 1530 (Sports) 8044 Montgomery Rd Suite 650 *Web:* www.wsai.com	Cincinnati	OH	45236	513-686-8300	241-0358
WUBE-FM 105.1 (Ctry) 2060 Reading Rd *Web:* www.wube.com	Cincinnati	OH	45202	513-699-5105	699-5000
WVXU-FM 91.7 (NPR) 1223 Central Pkwy *TF:* 800-230-3576 ■ *Web:* www.wvxu.org	Cincinnati	OH	45214	513-352-9170	241-8456
WYGY-FM 97.3 (Ctry) 2060 Reading Rd	Cincinnati	OH	45202	513-699-5102	699-5000

648-39 Cleveland, OH

Station	City	State	ZIP	Phone	Fax
WABQ-AM 1460 (Rel) 8000 Euclid Ave	Cleveland	OH	44103	216-231-8005	231-9803
WAKS-FM 96.5 (CHR) 6200 Oak Tree Blvd 4th Fl *Web:* www.kissfm965.com	Independence	OH	44131	216-520-2600	524-2600
WCLV-FM 104.9 (Clas) 26501 Renaissance Pkwy *Web:* www.wclv.com	Cleveland	OH	44128	216-464-0900	464-2206
WCPN-FM 90.3 (NPR) 1375 Euclid Ave *Web:* www.wcpn.org	Cleveland	OH	44115	216-916-6100	916-6101
WCRF-FM 103.3 (Rel) 9756 Barr Rd *TF:* 800-283-9273 ■ *Web:* wcrf.mbn.org	Cleveland	OH	44141	440-526-1111	526-1319
WDOK-FM 102.1 (AC) 1 Radio Ln *Web:* www.wdok.com	Cleveland	OH	44114	216-696-0123	363-7189
WENZ-FM 107.9 (Urban) 2510 St Clair Ave NE *Web:* www.z1079fm.com	Cleveland	OH	44114	216-579-1111	771-4164
WERE-AM 1490 (N/T) 2510 St Clair Ave NE *Web:* www.newstalk1490.com	Cleveland	OH	44114	216-579-1111	771-4164
WFHM-FM 95.5 (Rel) 4 Summit Park Dr Suite 150 *Web:* www.955thefish.com	Cleveland	OH	44131	216-901-0921	901-5517
WGAR-FM 99.5 (Ctry) 6200 Oak Tree Blvd 4th Fl **Fax:* Sales ■ *Web:* www.wgar.com	Independence	OH	44131	216-520-2600	524-2600*
WJMO-AM 1300 (Rel) 2510 St Clair Ave NE	Cleveland	OH	44114	216-579-1111	771-4164
WKNR-AM 850 (Sports) 1301 E 9th St Suite 232 *Web:* www.wknr.com	Cleveland	OH	44114	216-583-9901	583-0850
WKRK-FM 92.3 (Alt) 1041 Huron Rd *Web:* www.krockcleveland.com	Cleveland	OH	44115	216-861-0100	696-3710
WMJI-FM 105.7 (Oldies) 6200 Oak Tree Blvd 4th Fl *Web:* www.wmji.com	Independence	OH	44131	216-520-2600	524-2600
WMMS-FM 100.7 (Rock) 6200 Oak Tree Blvd 4th Fl *Web:* www.wmms.com	Independence	OH	44131	216-520-2600	524-2600
WMVX-FM 106.5 (AC) 6200 Oak Tree Blvd 4th Fl *TF:* 800-829-1065 ■ *Web:* www.wmvx.com	Independence	OH	44131	216-520-2600	524-2600

Station	City	State	ZIP	Phone	Fax
WNCX-FM 98.5 (CR) 1041 Huron Rd. *Web:* www.wncx.com	Cleveland	OH	44115	216-861-0100	696-0385
WNWV-FM 107.3 (NAC) 538 W Broad St 4th Fl *Web:* www.wnwv.com	Elyria	OH	44036	440-322-3761	236-3299
WQAL-FM 104.1 (AC) 1 Radio Ln *Web:* www.q104.com	Cleveland	OH	44114	216-696-0123	363-7104
WTAM-AM 1100 (N/T) 6200 Oak Tree Blvd 4th Fl. *Web:* www.wtam.com	Independence	OH	44131	216-520-2600	524-2600
WZAK-FM 93.1 (Urban) 2510 St Clair Ave NE. *Web:* www.931wzak.com	Cleveland	OH	44114	216-579-1111	771-4164

648-40 Colorado Springs, CO

Station	City	State	ZIP	Phone	Fax
KATC-FM 95.1 (Ctry) 6805 Corporate Dr Suite 130	Colorado Springs	CO	80919	719-632-1515	635-8455
KBIQ-FM 102.7 (Rel) 7150 Campus Dr Suite 150. *Web:* www.kbiqradio.com	Colorado Springs	CO	80920	719-531-5438	531-5588
KCCY-FM 96.9 (Ctry) 2864 S Circle Dr Suite 150. *Web:* www.kccyfm.com	Colorado Springs	CO	80906	719-540-9200	579-0882
KCMN-AM 1530 (Nost) 5050 Edison Ave Suite 218 *Web:* www.1530kcmn.com	Colorado Springs	CO	80915	719-570-1530	570-1007
KEPC-FM 89.7 (AAA) Pikes Peak Community College 5675 S Academy Blvd. *Web:* www.ppcc.cccoes.edu/dept/kepc	Colorado Springs	CO	80906	719-540-7489	
KILO-FM 94.3 (Rock) 1805 E Cheyenne Rd *Web:* www.kilo943.com	Colorado Springs	CO	80906	719-634-4896	634-5837
KKFM-FM 98.1 (CR) 6805 Corporate Dr Suite 130. *Web:* www.kkfm.com	Colorado Springs	CO	80919	719-593-2700	593-2727
KKLI-FM 106.3 (AC) 2864 S Circle Dr Suite 150 *Web:* kkli.com	Colorado Springs	CO	80906	719-540-9200	579-0882
KKMG-FM 98.9 (CHR) 6805 Corporate Dr Suite 130. *Web:* www.989magicfm.com	Colorado Springs	CO	80919	719-593-2700	593-2727
KKPK-FM 92.9 (AC) 6805 Corporate Dr Suite 130	Colorado Springs	CO	80919	719-593-2700	592-2727
KRCC-FM 91.5 (NPR) 912 N Weber St *TF:* 800-748-2727 ■ *Web:* www.krcc.org	Colorado Springs	CO	80903	719-473-4801	473-7863
KRDO-AM 1240 (N/T) 399 S 8th St *Web:* www.krdo.com	Colorado Springs	CO	80905	719-632-1515	635-8455
KSKX-FM 105.5 (N/T) 399 S 8th St. *Web:* www.krdo.com	Colorado Springs	CO	80905	719-632-1515	635-8455
KVOR-AM 740 (N/T) 6805 Corporate Dr Suite 130 *Web:* www.kvor.com	Colorado Springs	CO	80919	719-593-2700	593-2727
KVUU-FM 99.9 (AC) 2864 S Circle Dr Suite 150. *Web:* www.kvuu.com	Colorado Springs	CO	80906	719-540-9200	579-0882
KYZX-FM 103.9 (CR) 1805 E Cheyenne Rd *Web:* www.1039theeagle.com	Colorado Springs	CO	80906	719-634-4896	634-5837

648-41 Columbia, SC

Station	City	State	ZIP	Phone	Fax
WARQ-FM 93.5 (Rock) 1900 Pineview Rd. *Web:* www.warq.com	Columbia	SC	29209	803-695-8680	695-8605
WCOS-AM 1400 (Sports) 316 Greystone Blvd	Columbia	SC	29210	803-343-1100	252-9267
WCOS-FM 97.5 (Ctry) 316 Greystone Blvd *Web:* www.wcosfm.com	Columbia	SC	29210	803-343-1100	748-9267
WEPR-FM 90.1 (NPR) 1101 George Rogers Blvd *Web:* www.myetv.org/radio	Columbia	SC	29201	803-737-3545	737-3552
WFMV-FM 95.3 (Rel) 2440 Milwood Ave *Web:* www.wfmv.com	Columbia	SC	29205	803-939-9530	939-9469
WHMC-FM 90.1 (NPR) 1101 George Rogers Blvd.	Columbia	SC	29201	803-737-3545	737-3552
WHXT-FM 103.9 (Urban) 1900 Pineview Rd *TF:* 877-874-1039 ■ *Web:* www.hot1039fm.com	Columbia	SC	29209	803-376-1039	695-8605
WLTR-FM 91.3 (NPR) 1101 George Rogers Blvd *Web:* www.myetv.org/radio	Columbia	SC	29201	803-737-3545	737-3552
WLTY-FM 96.7 (AC) 316 Greystone Blvd. *Web:* www.wlty.com	Columbia	SC	29210	803-343-1100	
WLXC-FM 98.5 (Urban) 1801 Charleston Hwy Suite J *Web:* www.kiss985fm.com	Cayce	SC	29033	803-796-7600	796-5502
WMFX-FM 102.3 (CR) 1900 Pineview Rd *Web:* www.fox102.com	Columbia	SC	29209	803-695-8680	695-8605
WNOK-FM 104.7 (CHR) 316 Greystone Blvd *Web:* www.wnok.com	Columbia	SC	29210	803-343-1100	779-7874
WOIC-AM 1230 (Sports) 1900 Pineview Rd. *Web:* www.espn1230am.com	Columbia	SC	29209	803-695-8680	695-8605
WQXL-AM 1470 (Rel) PO Box 3277.	Columbia	SC	29230	803-779-7911	776-2853
WTCB-FM 106.7 (AC) 1801 Charleston Hwy Suite J. *Web:* www.b106fm.com	Columbia	SC	29250	803-796-7600	796-5502
WVOC-AM 560 (N/T) 316 Greystone Blvd *Web:* www.wvoc.com	Columbia	SC	29210	803-343-1100	256-5255
WWDM-FM 101.3 (Urban) 1900 Pineview Rd *Web:* www.thebigdm.com	Columbia	SC	29209	803-695-8680	695-8605

648-42 Columbus, GA

Station	City	State	ZIP	Phone	Fax
WAGH-FM 98.3 (Urban) 1501 13th Ave. *Web:* www.sunny100columbus.com	Columbus	GA	31901	706-576-3000	576-3010
WBFA-FM 98.3 (Urban) 1501 13th Ave.	Columbus	GA	31901	706-576-3000	576-3010
WCGQ-FM 107.3 (AC) 1353 13th Ave	Columbus	GA	31901	706-327-1217	596-4600
WDAK-AM 540 (N/T) 1501 13th Ave *Web:* www.newsradio540.com	Columbus	GA	31911	706-576-3000	576-3010
WEAM-AM 1580 (Rel) 2203 Wynnton Rd	Columbus	GA	31906	706-576-3565	576-3683
WFXE-FM 104.9 (Urban) 2203 Wynnton Rd *Web:* www.foxie105online.com	Columbus	GA	31906	706-576-3565	576-3683
WGSY-FM 100.1 (AC) 1501 13th Ave *Web:* www.sunny100columbus.com	Columbus	GA	31901	706-576-3000	576-3010
WHAL-AM 1460 (Span) 1501 13th Ave	Columbus	GA	31901	706-576-3000	576-3005
WKCN-FM 99.3 (Ctry) 1353 13th Ave *Web:* www.kissin993.com	Columbus	GA	31901	706-327-1217	596-4600
WOKS-AM 1340 (Urban) 2203 Wynnton Rd *Web:* www.woksam.com	Columbus	GA	31906	706-576-3565	576-3683
WRCG-AM 1420 (N/T) 1353 13th Ave *Web:* www.wrcg.com	Columbus	GA	31901	706-327-1217	596-4600
WRLD-FM 95.3 (Oldies) 1353 13th Ave. *Web:* www.boomer.fm	Columbus	GA	31901	706-327-1217	596-4600
WSTH-FM 106.1 (Ctry) 1501 13th Ave *TF:* 800-445-4106 ■ *Web:* www.rooster106online.com	Columbus	GA	31901	706-576-3000	576-3010
WVRK-FM 102.9 (Rock) 1501 13th Ave *Web:* www.rock103online.com	Columbus	GA	31901	706-576-3000	576-3010

648-43 Columbus, OH

Station	City	State	ZIP	Phone	Fax
WBNS-AM 1460 (Sports) 605 S Front St Suite 300 *Web:* www.1460thefan.com	Columbus	OH	43206	614-460-3850	460-2822
WBNS-FM 97.1 (AC) 605 S Front St Suite 300 *Web:* www.wbnsfm.com	Columbus	OH	43206	614-460-3850	460-2822
WCBE-FM 90.5 (NPR) 540 Jack Gibbs Blvd *Web:* wcbe.org	Columbus	OH	43215	614-365-5555	365-5060
WCKX-FM 107.5 (Urban) 350 E 1st Ave Suite 1000 *Web:* www.power1075.com	Columbus	OH	43201	614-487-1444	487-5862
WCLT-FM 100.3 (Ctry) PO Box 5150. *TF:* 800-837-9258 ■ *Web:* www.wclt.com	Newark	OH	43058	740-345-4004	345-5775
WCOL-FM 92.3 (Ctry) 2323 W 5th Ave Suite 200. *Web:* www.wcol.com	Columbus	OH	43204	614-486-6101	487-2554
WHOK-FM 95.5 (Ctry) 280 N Hight St. *Web:* www.whok.com	Columbus	OH	43215	614-225-9465	677-0116
WJYD-FM 106.3 (Rel) 350 E 1st Ave Suite 100 *Web:* www.joy106.com	Columbus	OH	43201	614-487-1444	487-5862
WJZA-FM 103.5 (NAC) 4401 Carriage Hill Ln *Web:* www.columbusjazz.com	Columbus	OH	43220	614-451-2191	451-1831
WLVQ-FM 96.3 (Rock) 280 N High St 2 Nationwide Plaza 10th Fl *Web:* www.qfm96.com	Columbus	OH	43215	614-227-9696	461-1059
WMNI-AM 920 (Nost) 1458 Dublin Rd. *Web:* www.wmni.com	Columbus	OH	43215	614-481-7800	481-8070
WNCI-FM 97.9 (CHR) 2323 W 5th Ave Suite 200 *Web:* www.wnci.com	Columbus	OH	43204	614-486-6101	487-2559
WNKK-FM 107.1 (Ctry) 280 N High St *Web:* www.wink1071.com	Columbus	OH	43215	614-255-9465	461-1059
WOSU-AM 820 (NPR) 2400 Olentangy River Rd *Web:* www.wosu.org	Columbus	OH	43210	614-292-9678	292-7625
WRKZ-FM 99.7 (Rock) 1458 Dublin Rd. *Web:* www.997wrkz.com	Columbus	OH	43215	614-481-7800	481-8070
WSNY-FM 94.7 (AC) 4401 Carriage Hill Ln *Web:* www.sunny95.com	Columbus	OH	43220	614-451-2191	451-1831
WTDA-FM 103.9 (N/T) 1458 Dublin Rd *Web:* www.eagle1039.com	Columbus	OH	43215	614-481-7800	481-8070
WTVN-AM 610 (N/T) 2323 W 5th Ave Suite 200 *Web:* www.610wtvn.com	Columbus	OH	43204	614-486-6101	487-2559
WUFM-FM 88.7 (Rel) 116 County Line Rd W *TF:* 877-272-3568 ■ *Web:* www.radiou.com	Westerville	OH	43082	614-890-9977	839-1329
WWCD-FM 101.1 (Alt) 503 S Front St Suite 101 *Web:* www.cd101.com	Columbus	OH	43215	614-221-9923	227-0021
WXMG-FM 98.9 (Urban) 350 E 1st Ave Suite 100 *Web:* www.magic989.com	Columbus	OH	43201	614-487-1444	487-5862
WYTS-FM 105.7 (N/T) 2323 W 5th Ave Suite 200 *Web:* www.1057thebrew.com	Columbus	OH	43204	614-486-6101	847-2559

648-44 Corpus Christi, TX

Station	City	State	ZIP	Phone	Fax
KEDT-FM 90.3 (NPR) 4455 S Padre Island Dr Suite 38 *TF:* 800-307-5338 ■ *Web:* www.kedt.org	Corpus Christi	TX	78411	361-855-2213	855-3877
KEYS-AM 1440 (N/T) 2117 Leopard St *Web:* www.1440keys.com	Corpus Christi	TX	78408	361-882-7411	882-9767
KFTX-FM 97.5 (Ctry) 1520 S Port Ave *TF:* 866-975-5389 ■ *Web:* www.kftx.com	Corpus Christi	TX	78405	361-883-5987	883-3648
KKBA-FM 92.7 (AC) 2117 Leopard St *Web:* www.927kkba.com	Corpus Christi	TX	78408	361-882-7411	882-9767
KLTG-FM 96.5 (AC) 1300 Antelope St *Web:* www.thebeach965.com	Corpus Christi	TX	78401	361-883-1600	883-9303
KLUX-FM 89.5 (AC) 1200 Lantana St *Web:* www.goccn.org/klux	Corpus Christi	TX	78407	361-289-2487	289-1420
KMXR-FM 93.9 (Oldies) 501 Tupper Ln *Web:* www.mix939.com	Corpus Christi	TX	78417	361-289-0111	289-5035
KNCN-FM 101.3 (Rock) 501 Tupper Ln. *Web:* www.c101.com	Corpus Christi	TX	78417	361-289-0111	289-5035
KOUL-FM 103.7 (Ctry) 1300 Antelope St. *Web:* www.countrynow.com/koul	Corpus Christi	TX	78401	361-883-1600	883-9303
KRYS-FM 99.1 (Ctry) 501 Tupper Ln. *Web:* www.krysfm.com	Corpus Christi	TX	78417	361-289-0111	289-5035
KSAB-FM 99.9 (Span) 501 Tupper Ln *Web:* www.ksabfm.com	Corpus Christi	TX	78417	361-289-0111	289-5035
KZFM-FM 95.5 (CHR) 2117 Leopard St. *Web:* www.hotz95.com	Corpus Christi	TX	78469	361-882-7411	882-9767

648-45 Dallas/Fort Worth, TX

Station	City	State	ZIP	Phone	Fax
KAAM-AM 770 (Nost) 3201 Royalty Row *Web:* www.kaamradio.com	Irving	TX	75062	972-445-1700	438-6574
KBFB-FM 97.9 (Urban) 13331 Preston Rd Suite 1180 *Web:* www.979thebeat.com	Dallas	TX	75240	972-331-5400	331-5560
KCBI-FM 90.9 (Rel) 411 Ryan Plaza Dr. *Web:* www.kcbi.org	Arlington	TX	76011	817-792-3800	277-9929
KDBN-FM 93.3 (CR) 3500 Maple Ave Suite 1310 *Web:* www.933thebone.com	Dallas	TX	75219	214-526-7400	525-2525
KDGE-FM 102.1 (Alt) 14001 N Dallas Pkwy Suite 300 *Web:* www.kdge.com	Dallas	TX	75240	214-866-8000	866-8008
KDMX-FM 102.9 (AC) 14001 N Dallas Pkwy Suite 300 *Web:* www.mix1029.com	Dallas	TX	75240	214-866-8000	866-8008
KDXX-FM 107.1 (Span AC) 7700 John Carpenter Fwy *Web:* kdxx.netmio.com	Dallas	TX	75247	214-525-0400	631-1196
KEGL-FM 97.1 (Rock) 14001 N Dallas Pkwy Suite 300 *Web:* www.kegl.com	Dallas	TX	75240	214-866-8000	866-8008
KERA-FM 90.1 (NPR) 3000 Harry Hines Blvd *TF:* 800-456-5372 ■ *Web:* www.kera.org/radio	Dallas	TX	75201	214-871-1390	754-0635
KESS-FM 107.9 (Span) 3102 Oak Lawn Ave Suite 215. *Web:* kess.netmio.com	Dallas	TX	75219	214-525-7700	525-7750
KHKS-FM 106.1 (CHR) 14001 N Dallas Pkwy Suite 300 *Web:* www.1061kissfm.com	Dallas	TX	75240	214-866-8000	866-8501
KHVN-AM 970 (Rel) 5787 S Hampton Rd Suite 285 *Fax Area Code: 214 ■ *Web:* www.khvnam.com	Dallas	TX	75232	972-572-5447	331-1908*
KJKK-FM 100.3 (Var) 7901 John Carpenter Fwy *Web:* www.jackontheweb.com	Dallas	TX	75247	214-525-7000	688-7760
KKDA-AM 730 (Oldies) 621 NW 6th St	Grand Prairie	TX	75050	972-263-9911	558-0010
KKDA-FM 104.5 (Urban) 621 NW 6th St. *Web:* www.k104fm.com	Grand Prairie	TX	75050	972-263-9911	558-0010
KLIF-AM 570 (N/T) 3500 Maple Ave Suite 1600 *TF:* 800-583-1570 ■ *Web:* www.klif.com	Dallas	TX	75219	214-526-2400	520-4343
KLNO-FM 94.1 (Span) 7700 John Carpenter Fwy	Dallas	TX	75247	214-525-0400	631-1196
KLTY-FM 94.9 (Rel) 6400 N Beltline Rd Suite 120 *Web:* www.klty.com	Irving	TX	75063	972-870-9949	490-8361

Dallas/Fort Worth, TX (Cont'd)

Station	City	State	Zip	Phone	Fax
KLUV-FM 98.7 (Oldies) 4131 N Central Expy Suite 1200 *Web:* www.kluv.com	Dallas	TX	75204	214-526-9870	443-1570
KMVK-FM 107.5 (Urban) 4131 N Central Expy Suite 1000 *Web:* www.movin1075.com	Dallas	TX	75204	214-525-7000	525-7145
KNON-FM 89.3 (Var) PO Box 710909 *Web:* knon.org	Dallas	TX	75371	214-828-9500	823-3051
KPLX-FM 99.5 (Ctry) 3500 Maple Ave Suite 1600 *Web:* www.995thewolf.com	Dallas	TX	75219	214-526-2400	520-4343
KRLD-AM 1080 (N/T) 4131 N Central Expy Suite 500 *TF:* 800-289-1080 ■ *Web:* www.krld.com	Dallas	TX	75204	214-443-6400	443-6572
KRNB-FM 105.7 (Urban) 621 NW 6th St *TF:* 800-310-1057 ■ *Web:* www.krnb.com	Grand Prairie	TX	75050	972-263-9911	558-0010
KSCS-FM 96.3 (Ctry) 2221 E Lamar Blvd Suite 300 *Web:* www.kscs.com	Arlington	TX	76006	817-640-1963	654-5727
KSKY-AM 660 (N/T) 6400 N Beltline Rd Suite 110 *TF:* 800-949-5973 ■ *Web:* www.ksky.com	Irving	TX	75063	214-561-9660	561-9662
KSOC-FM 94.5 (Urban) 13331 Preston Rd Suite 1180 *Web:* www.945ksoul.com	Dallas	TX	75240	972-331-5400	661-5728
KTCK-AM 1310 (Sports) 3500 Maple Ave Suite 1310 *Web:* www.theticket.com	Dallas	TX	75219	214-526-7400	525-2525
KTNO-AM 1440 (Span Rel) 5787 S Hampton Rd Suite 340 *TF:* 877-292-2431 ■ *Web:* www.ktnoam.com	Dallas	TX	75232	214-330-5866	230-9885
KVIL-FM 103.7 (AC) 4131 N Central Expy Suite 1o00 *Web:* 1037litefm.com	Dallas	TX	75204	214-526-9870	525-7157
KVTT-FM 91.7 (Rel) 11061 Shady Trail *TF:* 866-787-1917 ■ *Web:* www.kvtt.org	Dallas	TX	75229	214-351-6655	351-6809
KZPS-FM 92.5 (CR) 14001 N Dallas Pkwy Suite 300 *Web:* www.kzps.com	Dallas	TX	75240	214-866-8000	866-8008
WBAP-AM 820 (N/T) 2221 E Lamar Blvd Suite 300 *Web:* www.wbap.com	Arlington	TX	76006	817-640-1963	695-0018
WRR-FM 101.1 (Clas) PO Box 159001 *Web:* www.wrr101.com	Dallas	TX	75315	214-670-8888	670-8394

648-46 Dayton, OH

Station	City	State	Zip	Phone	Fax
WDAO-AM 1210 (Urban) 1012 W 3rd St *Web:* www.wdaoradio.com	Dayton	OH	45402	937-222-9326	461-6100
WDHT-FM 102.9 (Urban) 717 E David Rd *Web:* www.hot1029.com	Dayton	OH	45429	937-294-5858	297-5233
WDKF-FM 94.5 (CHR) 101 Pine St *Web:* www.channel945.com	Dayton	OH	45402	937-224-1137	224-3667
WDPR-FM 88.1 (Clas) 126 N Main St *Web:* www.dpr.org	Dayton	OH	45402	937-496-3850	496-3852
WFCJ-FM 93.7 (Rel) PO Box 937 *Web:* www.wfcj.com	Dayton	OH	45449	937-866-2471	866-2062
WGTZ-FM 92.9 (CHR) 717 E David Rd	Dayton	OH	45429	937-294-5858	297-5233
WHIO-AM 1290 (N/T) 1414 Wilmington Ave *Web:* 1290whio.com	Dayton	OH	45420	937-259-2111	259-2168
WHIO-FM 95.7 (N/T) 1414 Wilmington Ave *Web:* daytonspoint.com	Dayton	OH	45402	937-259-2111	259-2168
WHKO-FM 99.1 (Ctry) 1414 Wilmington Ave *Web:* k99online.com	Dayton	OH	45420	937-259-2111	259-2168
WING-AM 1410 (Sports) 717 E David Rd *Web:* www.wingam.com	Dayton	OH	45429	937-294-5858	297-5233
WLQT-FM 99.9 (AC) 101 Pine St *Web:* www.wlqt.com	Dayton	OH	45402	937-224-1137	222-5483
WMMX-FM 107.7 (AC) 101 Pine St *Web:* www.wmmx.com	Dayton	OH	45402	937-224-1137	224-3667
WONE-AM 980 (Sports) 101 Pine St *Web:* www.wone.com	Dayton	OH	45402	937-224-1137	224-3667
WPFB-FM 105.9 (Ctry) 4505 Central Ave *Web:* www.1059therebel.com	Middletown	OH	45044	513-422-3625	424-9732
WROU-FM 92.1 (Urban AC) 717 E David Rd *Web:* www.921wrou.com	Dayton	OH	45429	937-294-5858	297-5233
WTUE-FM 104.7 (Rock) 101 Pine St *Web:* www.wtue.com	Dayton	OH	45402	937-224-1137	224-3667
WXEG-FM 103.9 (Alt) 101 Pine St *Web:* www.wxeg.com	Dayton	OH	45402	937-224-1137	224-3667

648-47 Daytona Beach, FL

Station	City	State	Zip	Phone	Fax
WAPN-FM 91.5 (Rel) 1508 State Ave *Web:* www.wapn.net	Holly Hill	FL	32117	386-677-4272	673-3715
WELE-AM 1380 (N/T) 432 S Nova Rd *TF:* 866-672-1380 ■ *Web:* www.wele1380.com	Ormond Beach	FL	32174	386-677-4122	677-4123
WGNE-FM 99.9 (Ctry) 6440 Atlantic Blvd **Fax Area Code:* 386 ■ *Web:* www.999frog.com	Jacksonville	FL	32211	904-727-9696	677-2252*
WHOG-FM 95.7 (CR) 126 W International Speedway Blvd *Web:* www.whog.fm	Daytona Beach	FL	32114	386-257-1150	238-6488
WKRO-FM 93.1 (Ctry) 126 W International Speedway Blvd *Web:* www.wkro.fm	Daytona Beach	FL	32114	386-255-9300	238-6488
WKTO-FM 88.9 (Rel) 900 Old Mission Rd *TF:* 877-541-9586	New Smyrna Beach	FL	32168	386-427-1095	427-8970
WNDB-AM 1150 (N/T) 126 W International Speedway Blvd *Web:* www.wndb.am	Daytona Beach	FL	32114	386-355-9300	238-6488
WROD-AM 1340 (Nost) 2400 Ridgewood Ave Suite 51 *Web:* www.wrod.net	South Daytona Beach	FL	32119	386-253-0000	255-3178
WSBB-AM 1230 (Nost) 2400 Ridgewood Ave *Web:* www.wsbb.com	South Daytona	FL	32199	386-795-4956	255-3178
WVYB-FM 103.3 (CHR) 126 W International Speedway Blvd *Web:* www.wvyb.fm	Daytona Beach	FL	32114	386-257-6900	238-6488

648-48 Denver, CO

Station	City	State	Zip	Phone	Fax
KALC-FM 105.9 (AC) 4700 S Syracuse St Suite 1050 *Web:* www.alice1059.com	Denver	CO	80237	303-967-2700	967-2747
KBCO-FM 97.3 (AAA) 2500 Pearl St Suite 315 *Web:* www.kbco.com	Boulder	CO	80302	303-444-5600	449-3057
KBPI-FM 106.7 (Rock) 4695 S Monaco St *Web:* www.kbpi.com	Denver	CO	80237	303-713-8000	713-8734
KCFR-AM 1340 (NPR) 7409 S Alton Ct *TF:* 800-722-4449 ■ *Web:* www.cpr.org	Centennial	CO	80112	303-871-9191	733-3319
KEZW-AM 1430 (Nost) 4700 S Syracuse St Suite 1050 *Web:* www.kezw.com	Denver	CO	80237	303-967-2700	967-2747
KGNU-FM 88.5 (Var) 4700 Walnut St *TF:* 800-737-3030 ■ *Web:* www.kgnu.org	Boulder	CO	80301	303-449-4885	339-6340
KHOW-AM 630 (N/T) 4695 S Monaco St *Web:* www.khow.com	Denver	CO	80237	303-713-8000	713-8734
KIMN-FM 100.3 (AC) 1560 Broadway Suite 1100 *Web:* www.mix100.com	Denver	CO	80202	303-832-5665	832-7000
KJMN-FM 92.1 (Span AC) 777 Grant St 5th Fl *TF:* 888-874-2656 ■ *Web:* www.denverhispanicradio.com	Denver	CO	80203	303-832-0050	832-3410
KKFN-FM 104.3 (Sports) 7800 E Orchard Rd Suite 400 *Web:* www.fan950.com	Greenwood Village	CO	80111	303-321-0950	321-3383
KKZN-AM 760 (N/T) 4695 S Monaco St *Web:* www.am760.net	Denver	CO	80237	303-713-8000	713-8734
KMXA-AM 1090 (Span) 777 Grant St 5th Fl *TF:* 888-874-2656 ■ *Web:* www.denverhispanicradio.com	Denver	CO	80203	303-832-0050	832-3410
KNUS-AM 710 (N/T) 3131 S Vaughn Way Suite 601 *Web:* www.710knus.com	Aurora	CO	80014	303-750-5687	696-8063
KOA-AM 850 (N/T) 4695 S Monaco Ave *Web:* www.850koa.com	Denver	CO	80237	303-713-8000	713-8734
KOSI-FM 101.1 (AC) 4700 S Syracuse St Suite 1050 *Web:* www.kosi101.com	Denver	CO	80237	303-967-2700	967-2747
KPTT-FM 95.7 (CHR) 4695 S Monaco St	Denver	CO	80237	303-713-8000	713-8734
KQKS-FM 107.5 (Urban) 7800 E Orchard Rd Suite 400 *Web:* www.ks1075.com	Greenwood Village	CO	80111	303-321-0950	321-3383
KQMT-FM 99.5 (AAA) 4700 S Syracuse St Suite 1050 *Web:* www.995themountain.com	Denver	CO	80237	303-967-2700	967-2747
KRFX-FM 103.5 (CR) 4695 S Monaco St *Web:* www.thefox.com	Denver	CO	80237	303-713-8000	713-8734
KRKS-FM 94.7 (Rel) 3131 S Vaughn Way Suite 601 *Web:* www.krks.com	Aurora	CO	80014	303-750-5687	696-8063
KTCL-FM 93.3 (Alt) 4695 S Monaco St Suite 1300 *Web:* www.area93.com	Denver	CO	80237	303-713-8000	713-8734
KUVO-FM 89.3 (Jazz) PO Box 2040 *TF:* 800-574-5886 ■ *Web:* www.kuvo.org	Denver	CO	80201	303-480-9272	291-0757
KWLI-FM 92.5 (Ctry) 1560 Broadway Suite 1100 *Web:* www.willie925.com	Denver	CO	80202	303-832-5665	832-7000
KXKL-FM 105.1 (Oldies) 1560 Broadway Suite 1100 *Web:* www.kool105.com	Denver	CO	80202	303-832-5665	832-7000
KXPK-FM 96.5 (Span) 777 Grant St 5th Fl *TF:* 888-874-2656 ■ *Web:* www.denverhispanicradio.com	Denver	CO	80203	303-832-0050	832-3410
KYGO-FM 98.5 (Ctry) 7800 E Orchard Rd Suite 400 *Web:* www.kygo.com	Greenwood Village	CO	80111	303-321-0950	321-3383

648-49 Des Moines, IA

Station	City	State	Zip	Phone	Fax
KAZR-FM 103.3 (Rock) 1416 Locust St *Web:* www.lazer1033.com	Des Moines	IA	50309	515-280-1350	280-3011
KDRB-FM 100.3 (AC) 2141 Grand Ave *Web:* www.thebusfm.com	Des Moines	IA	50312	515-245-8900	245-8902
KGGO-FM 94.9 (CR) 4143 109th St *Web:* www.kggo.com	Urbandale	IA	50322	515-331-9200	331-9292
KHKI-FM 97.3 (Ctry) 4143 109th St *Web:* www.973thehawk.com	Urbandale	IA	50322	515-331-9200	331-9292
KIOA-FM 93.3 (Oldies) 1416 Locust St *Web:* www.kioa.com	Des Moines	IA	50309	515-280-1350	280-3011
KJJY-FM 92.5 (Ctry) 4143 109th St *Web:* www.kjjy.com	Urbandale	IA	50322	515-331-9200	331-9292
KKDM-FM 107.5 (AC) 2141 Grand Ave *Web:* www.kkdm.com	Des Moines	IA	50312	515-245-8900	245-8902
KLTI-FM 104.1 (AC) 1416 Locust St *Web:* www.lite1041.com	Des Moines	IA	50309	515-280-1350	280-3011
KNWI-FM 107.1 (Rel) 3737 Woodland Ave Suite 111 *Web:* knwi.nwc.edu	West Des Moines	IA	50266	515-327-1071	327-1073
KSTZ-FM 102.5 (AC) 1416 Locust St *Web:* www.star1025.com	Des Moines	IA	50309	515-280-1350	280-3011
KWKY-AM 1150 (Rel) PO Box 160 *Web:* www.kwky.com	Norwalk	IA	50211	515-223-1150	981-0840
KWQW-FM 98.3 (N/T) 4143 109th St *Web:* www.983wowfm.com	Urbandale	IA	50322	515-331-9200	331-9292
KZZQ-FM 99.5 (Rel) 33365 335th St *Web:* www.kzzq.com	Waukee	IA	50263	515-987-9995	987-9808
WHO-AM 1040 (N/T) 2141 Grand Ave *Web:* www.whoradio.com	Des Moines	IA	50312	515-245-8900	245-8902
WOI-AM 640 (NPR) Iowa State University 2022 Communications Bldg *TF:* 800-861-8000 ■ *Web:* www.woi.org	Ames	IA	50011	515-294-2025	294-1544
WOI-FM 90.1 (NPR) Iowa State University 2022 Communications Bldg *Web:* www.woi.org	Ames	IA	50011	515-294-2025	294-1544

648-50 Detroit, MI

Station	City	State	Zip	Phone	Fax
CIDR-FM 93.9 (AC) 1640 Ouellette Ave	Windsor	ON	N8X1L1	519-258-8888	258-0182
CIMX-FM 88.7 (Alt) 1640 Ouellette Ave *Web:* www.89xradio.com	Windsor	ON	N8X1L1	519-258-8888	258-0182
CKLW-AM 800 (N/T) 1640 Ouellette Ave *Web:* www.am800cklw.com	Windsor	ON	N8X1L1	519-258-8888	258-0182
CKWW-AM 580 (Nost) 1640 Ouellette Ave *Web:* www.am580radio.com	Windsor	ON	N8X1L1	519-258-8888	258-0182
WCAR-AM 1090 (Rel) 32500 Park Ln *TF:* 877-327-1090 ■ *Web:* www.catholicradio.org	Garden City	MI	48135	734-525-1111	525-3608
WCSX-FM 94.7 (CR) 1 Radio Plaza *Web:* www.wcsx.com	Ferndale	MI	48220	248-398-9470	541-9279
WDET-FM 101.9 (NPR) 4600 Cass Ave *Web:* www.wdetfm.org	Detroit	MI	48201	313-577-4146	577-1300
WDFN-AM 1130 (Sports) 27675 Halsted Rd *Web:* www.wdfn.com	Farmington Hills	MI	48331	248-324-5800	324-0356
WDMK-FM 105.9 (Urban) 3250 Franklin St *Web:* kissdetroit.com	Detroit	MI	48207	313-259-2000	259-7011
WDRQ-FM 93.1 (Var) 3011 W Grand Blvd Fisher Bldg Suite 800 *Web:* www.931dougfm.com	Detroit	MI	48202	313-871-9300	872-0190
WDTJ-FM 105.9 (Urban) 3250 E Franklin St	Detroit	MI	48207	313-259-2000	259-7011
WDTW-FM 106.7 (CR) 27675 Halsted Rd *Web:* www.foxspacelive.com	Farmington Hills	MI	48331	248-324-5800	324-0356
WDVD-FM 96.3 (AC) 3011 W Grand Blvd Fisher Bldg Suite 800 *Web:* www.963dvd.com	Detroit	MI	48202	313-871-3030	872-0190
WEMU-FM 89.1 (NPR) PO Box 980350 *TF:* 888-299-8910 ■ *Web:* www.wemu.org	Ypsilanti	MI	48198	734-487-2229	487-1015
WGPR-FM 107.5 (Urban) 3146 E Jefferson Ave *Web:* www.wgprdetroit.com	Detroit	MI	48207	313-259-8862	259-6662

Station	Address	City	State	ZIP	Phone	Fax
WJLB-FM 97.9 (Urban)	645 Griswold St Suite 633	Detroit	MI	48226	313-965-2000	965-3965
Web: www.fm98wjlb.com						
WJR-AM 760 (N/T)	3011 W Grand Blvd Fisher Bldg Suite 800	Detroit	MI	48202	313-875-4440	875-9022
Web: www.760wjr.com						
WKQI-FM 95.5 (CHR)	27675 Halsted Rd	Farmington Hills	MI	48331	248-324-5800	324-0356
Web: www.channel955.com						
WMGC-FM 105.1 (AC)	1 Radio Plaza	Ferndale	MI	48220	248-414-5600	524-7700
Web: www.detroitmagic.com						
WMUZ-FM 103.5 (Rel)	12300 Radio Pl	Detroit	MI	48228	313-272-3434	
Web: www.wmuz.com						
WMXD-FM 92.3 (Urban)	645 Griswold St Suite 633	Detroit	MI	48226	313-965-2000	965-3965
Web: www.wmxd923.com						
WNIC-FM 100.3 (AC)	27675 Halsted Rd	Farmington Hills	MI	48331	248-324-5800	324-0356
Web: www.wnic.com						
WOMC-FM 104.3 (Oldies)	2201 Woodward Heights	Ferndale	MI	48220	248-546-9600	546-5446
Web: www.womc.com/home.php						
WRIF-FM 101.1 (Rock)	1 Radio Plaza	Ferndale	MI	48220	248-547-0101	542-8800
Web: www.wrif.com						
WVMV-FM 98.7 (NAC)	26495 American Dr	Southfield	MI	48034	248-455-7200	455-7369
Web: www.v987.com						
WWJ-AM 950 (N/T)	26495 American Dr	Southfield	MI	48034	248-455-7200	304-4970
Web: wwj.com						
WXYT-AM 1270 (Sports)	26495 American Dr	Southfield	MI	48034	248-455-7200	455-7362
Web: www.wxyt.com						
WXYT-FM 97.1 (Sports)	31555 W 14 Mile Rd Suite 102	Farmington Hills	MI	48334	248-855-5100	855-1302
Web: www.wkrk.com						
WYCD-FM 99.5 (Ctry)	26555 Evergreen Rd Suite 675	Southfield	MI	48076	248-799-0600	358-9216
Web: www.wycd.com						

648-51 Dubuque, IA

Station	Address	City	State	ZIP	Phone	Fax
KATF-FM 92.9 (AC)	346 W 8th St	Dubuque	IA	52001	563-690-0800	588-5688
TF: 800-422-5384 ■ *Web:* www.katfm.com						
KDTH-AM 1370 (N/T)	346 W 8th St	Dubuque	IA	52001	563-690-0800	588-5688
TF: 800-422-5384 ■ *Web:* www.kdth.com						
KGRR-FM 97.3 (CR)	346 W 8th St	Dubuque	IA	52001	563-690-0800	588-5688
TF: 800-422-5384 ■ *Web:* www.kgrr.com						
KIYX-FM 106.1 (AC)	51 Means Dr	Platteville	WI	53818	608-349-2000	349-2002
TF: 800-362-2224						
KLYV-FM 105.3 (AC)	5490 Saratoga Rd	Dubuque	IA	52002	563-557-1040	583-4535
KXGE-FM 102.3 (CR)	5490 Saratoga Rd	Dubuque	IA	52002	563-557-1040	583-4535
WDBQ-AM 1490 (N/T)	5490 Saratoga Rd	Dubuque	IA	52002	563-557-1040	583-4535
WDBQ-FM 107.5 (Oldies)	5490 Saratoga Rd	Dubuque	IA	52002	563-557-1040	583-4535
WJOD-FM 103.3 (Ctry)	5490 Saratoga Rd	Dubuque	IA	52002	563-557-1040	583-4535

648-52 Duluth, MN

Station	Address	City	State	ZIP	Phone	Fax
KBMX-FM 107.7 (AC)	14 E Central Entrance	Duluth	MN	55811	218-727-4500	727-9356
TF: 866-266-2649 ■ *Web:* www.mix108.com						
KDAL-AM 610 (N/T)	715 E Central Entrance	Duluth	MN	55811	218-722-4321	722-5423
TF: 888-532-5610 ■ *Web:* www.kdal.am						
KDAL-FM 95.7 (AC)	715 E Central Entrance	Duluth	MN	55811	218-722-4321	722-5423
TF: 800-532-5610						
KDNW-FM 97.3 (Rel)	1101 E Central Entrance	Duluth	MN	55811	218-722-6700	722-1092
TF: 888-322-5369 ■ *Web:* www.kdnw.org						
KKCB-FM 105.1 (Ctry)	14 E Central Entrance	Duluth	MN	55811	218-727-4500	727-9356
TF: 800-928-2105 ■ *Web:* www.kkcb.com						
KLDJ-FM 101.7 (Oldies)	14 E Central Entrance	Duluth	MN	55811	218-727-4500	727-9356
TF: 888-564-1017 ■ *Web:* www.kool1017.com						
KRBR-FM 102.5 (Rock)	715 E Central Entrance	Duluth	MN	55811	218-722-4321	722-5423
TF: 888-532-5610 ■ *Web:* www.krbr.com						
KTCO-FM 98.9 (Ctry)	715 E Central Entrance	Duluth	MN	55811	218-722-4321	722-5423
TF: 888-532-5610 ■ *Web:* www.989ktco.com						
KUMD-FM 103.3 (Var)	1201 Ordean Ct Rm 130	Duluth	MN	55812	218-726-7181	726-6571
TF: 800-566-5863 ■ *Web:* www.kumd.org						
KUWS-FM 91.3 (NPR)	1800 Grand Ave PO Box 2000	Superior	WI	54880	715-394-8530	394-8404
TF: 800 300 8530 ■ *Web:* www.wpr.org						
KZIO-FM 104.3 (Alt)	501 Lake Ave S Suite 200-A	Duluth	MN	55802	218-728-9500	723-1499
WDSM-AM 710 (Sports)	715 E Central Entrance	Duluth	MN	55811	218-722-4321	722-5423
TF: 888-532-5610 ■ *Web:* www.wdsm.am						
WEBC-AM 560 (Sports)	14 E Central Entrance	Duluth	MN	55811	218-727-4500	727-9356
TF: 888-932-2560						
WJRF-FM 89.5 (Rel)	4604 Airpark Blvd	Duluth	MN	55811	218-722-3017	279-5010
TF: 800-727-4487 ■ *Web:* www.refugeradio.com						
WSCN-FM 100.5 (NPR)	207 W Superior St Suite 224	Duluth	MN	55802	218-722-9411	720-4900
Web: www.mpr.org						
WWAX-FM 92.1 (CHR)	501 Lake Ave S Suite 200-A	Duluth	MN	55802	218-728-9500	723-1499
TF: 877-921-5477						
WWJC-AM 850 (Rel)	1120 E McCuen St	Duluth	MN	55808	218-626-2738	626-2585
TF: 877-626-2738 ■ *Web:* www.wwjc.com						

648-53 Edmonton, AB

Station	Address	City	State	ZIP	Phone	Fax
CBX-AM 740 (CBC)	10062 102nd Ave 123 Edmonton City Center	Edmonton	AB	T5J2Y8	780-468-7500	468-7419
Web: www.cbc.ca/edmonton						
CBX-FM 90.9 (CBC)	10062 102nd Ave 123 Edmonton City Center	Edmonton	AB	T5J2Y8	780-468-7500	468-7419
Web: www.cbc.ca/edmonton						
CFBR-FM 100.3 (CR)	18520 Stony Plain Rd Suite 100	Edmonton	AB	T5S2E2	780-486-2800	489-6927
Web: www.thebearrocks.com						
CFCW-AM 790 (Ctry)	8882 178th St 2394 W Edmonton Mall	Edmonton	AB	T6H5G8	780-468-3939	436-9803
Web: www.cfcw.com						
CFRN-AM 1260 (Sports)	18520 Stony Plain Rd Suite 100	Edmonton	AB	T5S2E2	780-486-2800	489-6927
Web: www.cfrn.com						
CHED-AM 630 (N/T)	5204 84th St	Edmonton	AB	T6E5N8	780-424-8800	469-5937
Web: www.630ched.com						
CHFA-AM 680 (CBC)	10062 102nd Ave 123 Edmonton City Center	Edmonton	AB	T5J2Y8	780-468-7500	468-7849
Web: www.radio-canada.ca						
CHQT-AM 880 (AC)	5204 84th St	Edmonton	AB	T6E5N8	780-424-8800	469-5937
Web: www.cool880.com						
CIRK-FM 97.3 (CR)	8882 170th St 2394 W Edmonton Mall	Edmonton	AB	T5T4M2	780-437-4996	436-9803
Web: www.k-rock973.com						
CISN-FM 103.9 (Ctry)	5204 84th St	Edmonton	AB	T6E5N8	780-424-8800	469-5937
Web: www.cisnfm.com						
CJCA-AM 930 (Rel)	5316 Calgary Trail Suite 204	Edmonton	AB	T6H4J8	780-466-4930	469-5335
CJSR-FM 88.5 (Var)	University of Alberta Student Union Bldg Rm 0-09	Edmonton	AB	T6G2J7	780-492-2577	492-3121
Web: www.cjsr.com						
CKER-FM 101.7 (Rel)	5915 Gateway Blvd	Edmonton	AB	T6H2H3	780-702-1188	437-5129
Web: www.worldfm.ca						
CKNG-FM 92.5 (CHR)	5204 84th St	Edmonton	AB	T6E5N8	780-424-8800	468-6739
Web: www.joefm.ca						
CKRA-FM 96.3 (Ctry)	8882 178th St 2394 W Edmonton Mall	Edmonton	AB	T5T4M2	780-437-4996	436-9803
Web: www.bigearl963.com						
CKUA-AM 580 (Var)	10526 Jasper Ave 4th Fl	Edmonton	AB	T5J1Z7	780-428-7595	428-7624
Web: www.ckua.org						
CKUA-FM 94.9 (Var)	10526 Jasper Ave 4th Fl	Edmonton	AB	T5J1Z7	780-428-7595	428-7624
Web: www.ckua.org						

648-54 El Paso, TX

Station	Address	City	State	ZIP	Phone	Fax
KAMA-AM 750 (Span)	2211 E Missouri Ave Suite S-300	El Paso	TX	79903	915-544-9797	544-1247
TF: 800-880-9797 ■ *Web:* kama.netmio.com						
KBNA-FM 97.5 (Span AC)	2211 E Missouri Ave Suite S-300	El Paso	TX	79903	915-544-9797	544-1247
TF: 800-880-9797 ■ *Web:* kbna.netmio.com						
KELP-AM 1590 (Rel)	6900 Commerce St	El Paso	TX	79915	915-779-0016	779-6641
Web: www.kelpradio.com						
KGRT-FM 103.9 (Ctry)	1355 California St PO Box 968	Las Cruces	NM	88004	505-525-9298	525-9419
Web: www.kgrt.com						
KHEY-FM 96.3 (Ctry)	4045 N Mesa St	El Paso	TX	79902	915-351-5400	351-3136
Web: www.khey.com						
KHQT-FM 103.1 (CHR)	1355 California St PO Box 968	Las Cruces	NM	88004	505-525-9298	525-9419
Web: www.hot103.fm						
KHRO-AM 1650 (N/T)	5426 N Mesa St	El Paso	TX	79912	915-581-1126	532-4970
Web: www.airamerica.com						
KINT-FM 93.9 (Span)	5426 N Mesa St	El Paso	TX	79912	915-581-1126	532-4970
Web: www.lacalientefm.com						
KLAQ-FM 95.5 (Rock)	4180 N Mesa St	El Paso	TX	79902	915-544-8864	532-6342
Web: www.klaq.com						
KMVR-FM 104.9 (AC)	101 Perkins Dr	Las Cruces	NM	88005	505-527-1011	527-1100
KOBE-AM 1450 (N/T)	101 Perkins Dr	Las Cruces	NM	88005	505-527-1011	527-1100
KOFX-FM 92.3 (Oldies)	5426 N Mesa St	El Paso	TX	79912	915-581-1126	532-4970
KPRR-FM 102.1 (CHR)	4045 N Mesa St	El Paso	TX	79902	915-351-5400	351-3136
Web: www.kprr.com						
KROD-AM 600 (N/T)	4180 N Mesa St	El Paso	TX	79902	915-544-8864	532-6342
Web: www.krod.com						
KRWG-FM 90.7 (NPR)	PO Box 3000	Las Cruces	NM	88003	505-646-4525	646-1974
TF: 800-245-5794 ■ *Web:* www.krwgfm.org						
KSII-FM 93.1 (AC)	4180 N Mesa St	El Paso	TX	79902	915-544-8864	532-6342
Web: www.ksii.com						
KSNM-AM 570 (Var)	1355 California Ave PO Box 968	Las Cruces	NM	88004	505-525-9298	525-9419
Web: www.ksnm570.am						
KTEP-FM 88.5 (NPR)	500 W University Ave Cotton Memorial Bldg Rm 203	El Paso	TX	79968	915-747-5152	747-5641
Web: www.ktep.org						
KTSM-AM 690 (N/T)	4045 N Mesa St	El Paso	TX	79902	915-351-5400	351-3136
Web: www.ktsmradio.com						
KTSM-FM 99.9 (AC)	4045 N Mesa St	El Paso	TX	79902	915-351-5400	351-3136
Web: www.sunny999fm.com						
KVLC-FM 101.1 (Oldies)	101 Perkins Dr	Las Cruces	NM	88005	505-527-1111	527-1100
TF: 800-527-1170 ■ *Web:* www.101gold.com						
XHNZ-FM 107.5 (Span)	2100 Trawood Dr	El Paso	TX	79935	915-542-2969	542-2958
XHTO-FM 104.3 (CHR)	2100 Trawood Dr	El Paso	TX	79936	915-542-2969	542-2958
Web: www.hitfmradio.com						

648-55 Erie, PA

Station	Address	City	State	ZIP	Phone	Fax
WCTL-FM 106.3 (Rel)	10912 Peach St	Waterford	PA	16441	814-796-6000	796-3200
Web: www.wctl.org						
WFGO-FM 94.7 (Sports)	1 Boston Store Pl	Erie	PA	16501	814-461-1000	874-0011
Web: www.froggy947.com						
WFNN-AM 1330 (Sports)	1 Boston Store Pl	Erie	PA	16501	814-461-1000	874-0011
Web: www.sportsradio1330.com						
WJET-AM 1400 (N/T)	1 Boston Store Pl	Erie	PA	16501	814-461-1000	461-1500
Web: www.jetradio1400.com						
WQHZ-FM 102.3 (CR)	471 Robison Rd	Erie	PA	16509	814-868-5355	868-1876
Web: www.z102online.com						
WQLN-FM 91.3 (NPR)	8425 Peach St	Erie	PA	16509	814-864-3001	864-4077
TF: 800-727-8854 ■ *Web:* www.wqln.org						
WRIE-AM 1260 (Nost)	471 Robison Rd	Erie	PA	16509	814-868-5355	868-1876
WRKT-FM 100.9 (Rock)	1 Boston Store Pl	Erie	PA	16501	814-461-1000	455-1111
Web: www.rocket101.com						
WRTS-FM 103.7 (CHR)	1 Boston Store Pl	Erie	PA	16501	814-461-1000	455-6000
Web: www.star104.com						
WXKC-FM 99.9 (AC)	471 Robison Rd	Erie	PA	16509	814-868-5355	868-1876
Web: www.classy100.com						
WXTA-FM 97.9 (Ctry)	471 Robison Rd	Erie	PA	16509	814-868-5355	868-1876
Web: www.wxtacountry98.com						

648-56 Eugene, OR

Station	Address	City	State	ZIP	Phone	Fax
KDUK-FM 104.7 (CHR)	1500 Valley River Dr Suite 350	Eugene	OR	97401	541-485-1120	484-5769
Web: www.kduk.com						
KEUG-FM 105.5 (AC)	925 Country Club Rd Suite 200	Eugene	OR	97401	541-484-9400	344-9424
KKNU-FM 93.3 (Ctry)	925 Country Club Rd Suite 200	Eugene	OR	97401	541-484-9400	344-9424
Web: www.kknu.com						
KLCC-FM 89.7 (NPR)	4000 E 30th Ave	Eugene	OR	97405	541-463-6000	463-6046
Web: www.klcc.org						
KMGE-FM 94.5 (AC)	925 Country Club Rd Suite 200	Eugene	OR	97401	541-484-9400	344-9424
Web: www.kmge.fm						
KNRQ-FM 97.9 (Alt)	1200 Executive Pkwy Suite 440	Eugene	OR	97401	541-485-5846	485-0969
Web: www.nrq.com						
KODZ-FM 99.1 (Oldies)	1500 Valley River Dr Suite 350	Eugene	OR	97401	541-485-1120	484-5769
Web: www.oldies991.com						
KPNW-AM 1120 (N/T)	1500 Valley River Dr Suite 350	Eugene	OR	97401	541-485-1120	484-5769
Web: www.kpnw.com						
KUGN-AM 590 (N/T)	1200 Executive Pkwy Suite 440	Eugene	OR	97401	541-485-5846	485-0969
Web: www.kugn.com						
KZEL-FM 96.1 (CR)	1200 Executive Pkwy Suite 440	Eugene	OR	97401	541-485-5846	485-0969
Web: www.96kzel.com						

648-57 Evansville, IN

Station	Address	City	State	ZIP	Phone	Fax
WABX-FM 107.5 (CR)	1162 Mt Auburn Rd	Evansville	IN	47720	812-424-8284	426-7928
TF: 800-454-9459 ■ *Web:* www.wabx.net						

Evansville, IN (Cont'd)

Station	City	State	Zip	Phone	Fax
WDKS-FM 106.1 (CHR) 1133 Lincoln Ave	Evansville	IN	47714	812-425-4226	428-5895
Web: www.kissfmevansville.com					
WGBF-AM 1280 (N/T) 1133 Lincoln Ave	Evansville	IN	47714	812-425-4226	428-5895
WGBF-FM 103.1 (Rock) 1133 Lincoln Ave	Evansville	IN	47714	812-425-4226	428-5895
Web: www.103gbfrocks.com					
WIKY-FM 104.1 (AC) 1162 Mt Auburn Rd	Evansville	IN	47720	812-424-8284	426-7928
TF: 800-454-9459 ■ *Web:* www.wiky.com					
WJLT-FM 105.3 (Oldies) 1133 Lincoln Ave	Evansville	IN	47714	812-425-4226	428-5895
Web: www.espn949.com					
WKDQ-FM 99.5 (Ctry) 1133 Lincoln Ave	Evansville	IN	47714	812-425-4226	428-5895
Web: www.wkdq.com					
WLFW-FM 93.5 (Ctry) 1162 Mt Auburn Rd	Evansville	IN	47720	812-424-8284	426-7928
TF: 800-454-9459 ■ *Web:* www.wjps.com					
WNIN-FM 88.3 (NPR) 405 Carpenter St	Evansville	IN	47708	812-423-2973	428-7548
Web: www.wnin.org					
WSTO-FM 96.1 (CHR) 1162 Mt Auburn Rd	Evansville	IN	47720	812-424-8284	426-7928
TF: 800-454-9459 ■ *Web:* wsto.com					

648-58 Fairbanks, AK

Station	City	State	Zip	Phone	Fax
KAKQ-FM 101.1 (AC) 546 9th Ave	Fairbanks	AK	99701	907-450-1000	457-2128
Web: www.101magic.com					
KCBF-AM 820 (Sports) 819 1st Ave Suite A	Fairbanks	AK	99709	907-451-5910	451-5999
KFAR-AM 660 (N/T) 819 1st Ave Suite A	Fairbanks	AK	99709	907-451-5910	451-5999
Web: kfar660.com					
KFBX-AM 970 (N/T) 546 9th Ave	Fairbanks	AK	99701	907-450-1000	457-2128
Web: www.am970.com					
KIAK-FM 102.5 (Ctry) 546 9th Ave	Fairbanks	AK	99701	907-450-1000	457-2128
Web: www.kiak.com					
KKED-FM 104.7 (Rock) 546 9th Ave	Fairbanks	AK	99701	907-450-1000	457-2128
Web: www.1047theedge.com					
KSUA-FM 91.5 (Alt) PO Box 750113	Fairbanks	AK	99775	907-474-7054	474-6314
Web: ksua.uaf.edu					
KUAC-FM 89.9 (NPR)					
312 Tanana Dr Suite 202 PO Box 755620	Fairbanks	AK	99775	907-474-7491	474-5064
TF: 800-727-6543 ■ *Web:* www.kuac.org					
KWLF-FM 98.1 (CHR) 819 1st Ave Suite A	Fairbanks	AK	99709	907-451-5910	451-5999
Web: wolf98fm.com					
KXLR-FM 95.9 (CR) 819 1st Ave Suite A	Fairbanks	AK	99709	907-451-5910	451-5999

648-59 Fargo, ND

Station	City	State	Zip	Phone	Fax
KDSU-FM 91.9 (NPR) 207 5th St N	Fargo	ND	58102	701-241-6900	231-8899
TF: 800-359-6900 ■ *Web:* www.prairiepublic.org/radio					
KFGO-AM 790 (N/T) 1020 25th St S	Fargo	ND	58103	701-237-5346	235-4042
Web: www.kfgo.com					
KFJM-FM 90.7 (AAA) PO Box 8117	Grand Forks	ND	58202	701-777-4595	239-7650
TF: 800-359-4145 ■ *Web:* www.prairiepublic.org/radio					
KFNW-FM 97.9 (Rel) 5702 52nd Ave S	Fargo	ND	58104	701-282-5910	282-5781
TF: 800-979-1200 ■ *Web:* www.kfnw.org					
KKBX-FM 101.9 (CR) 1020 25th St S	Fargo	ND	58103	701-237-5346	235-4042
Web: www.thebox1019.com					
KLTA-FM 105.1 (AC) 2720 7th Ave S	Fargo	ND	58103	701-237-4500	235-9082
Web: www.fm1051.net					
KPFX-FM 107.9 (CR) 2720 7th Ave S	Fargo	ND	58103	701-237-4500	235-9082
Web: www.1079thefox.com					
KQWB-FM 98.7 (Rock) 2720 7th Ave S	Fargo	ND	58103	701-237-4500	235-9082
Web: www.q98.com					
KRVI-FM 95.1 (AC) 1020 25th St S	Fargo	ND	58103	701-237-5346	235-4042
Web: www.river95.com					
KVOX-FM 99.9 (Ctry) 2720 7th Ave S	Fargo	ND	58103	701-237-4500	235-9082
Web: www.froggyweb.com					
WDAY-AM 970 (N/T) 301 8th St S	Fargo	ND	58103	701-237-6500	241-5373
Web: www.in-forum.com/wday					
WDAY-FM 93.7 (CHR) 1020 25th St S	Fargo	ND	58103	701-237-5346	235-4042
Web: www.y94.com					

648-60 Flagstaff, AZ

Station	City	State	Zip	Phone	Fax
KAFF-AM 930 (Ctry) 1117 W Rt 66	Flagstaff	AZ	86001	928-774-5231	779-2988
TF: 888-893-5646 ■ *Web:* www.kaff.com					
KAFF-FM 92.9 (Ctry) 1117 W Rt 66	Flagstaff	AZ	86001	928-774-5231	779-2988
TF: 888-412-5233 ■ *Web:* www.kaff.com					
KFLX-FM 105.1 (AAA) 112 E Rt 66 Suite 105	Flagstaff	AZ	86001	928-779-1177	774-5179
TF: 877-600-5359 ■ *Web:* www.kflx.com					
KMGN-FM 93.9 (CR) 1117 W Rt 66	Flagstaff	AZ	86001	928-774-5231	779-2988
TF: 888-893-5646 ■ *Web:* www.kmgn.com					
KNAU-FM 88.7 (NPR) PO Box 5764 Bldg 83 NAU Campus	Flagstaff	AZ	86011	928-523-5628	523-7647
Web: www.knau.org					
KQST-FM 102.9 (CHR) 3405 E Hwy 89 A Bldg A	Cottonwood	AZ	86326	928-634-2286	634-2295
KSED-FM 107.5 (Ctry) 112 E Rt 66 Suite 105	Flagstaff	AZ	86001	928-779-1177	774-5179
TF: 800-799-5658 ■ *Web:* www.koltcountry.com					
KVNA-FM 100.1 (AC) 3405 E Hwy 89 A Bldg A	Cottonwood	AZ	86326	928-634-2286	634-2295
Web: www.radioflagstaff.com/Sunny/sunny.htm					
KZGL-FM 95.9 (Rock) 3405 E Hwy 89 A Bldg A	Cottonwood	AZ	86326	928-634-2286	634-2295
Web: www.radioflagstaff.com/kzgl/ZHome.htm					

648-61 Flint, MI

Station	City	State	Zip	Phone	Fax
WCRZ-FM 107.9 (AC) 3338 E Bristol Rd	Burton	MI	48529	810-743-1080	742-5170
Web: www.wcrz.com					
WDZZ-FM 92.7 (Urban) 6317 Taylor Dr	Flint	MI	48507	810-238-7300	238-7310
Web: www.wdzz.com					
WFBE-FM 95.1 (Ctry) G-4511 Miller Rd	Flint	MI	48507	810-720-9510	720-9513
Web: www.b95.fm					
WFLT-AM 1420 (Rel) 317 S Averill Ave	Flint	MI	48506	810-239-5733	239-7134
WFNT-AM 1470 (N/T) 3338 E Bristol Rd	Burton	MI	48529	810-743-1080	742-5170
Web: www.wfnt.com					
WHNN-FM 96.1 (Oldies) 1740 Champagne Dr N	Saginaw	MI	48604	989-776-2100	754-5990
TF: 877-479-9466 ■ *Web:* www.whnn.com					
WKCQ-FM 98.1 (Ctry) 2000 Whittier St	Saginaw	MI	48601	989-752-8161	752-8102
TF: 800-262-0098 ■ *Web:* www.98fmkcq.com					
WLSP-AM 1530 (Sports) 3338 E Bristol Rd	Burton	MI	48529	810-743-1080	742-5170
WOWE-FM 98.9 (Urban) 126 W Kearsley St	Flint	MI	48502	810-234-4335	234-7286
WRSR-FM 103.9 (CR) 6317 Taylor Dr	Flint	MI	48507	810-238-7300	238-7310
Web: www.classicfox.com					
WWBN-FM 101.5 (Rock) 3338 E Bristol Rd	Burton	MI	48529	810-743-1080	742-5170
Web: www.banana1015.com					
WWCK-FM 105.5 (CHR) 6317 Taylor Dr	Flint	MI	48507	810-238-7300	238-7310
Web: www.wwck.com					

648-62 Fort Collins, CO

Station	City	State	Zip	Phone	Fax
KCOL-AM 600 (N/T) 4270 Byrd Dr	Loveland	CO	80538	970-461-2560	461-0118
TF: 866-888-5449 ■ *Web:* www.kcol.com					
KIIX-AM 1410 (Sports) 4270 Byrd Dr	Loveland	CO	80538	970-461-2560	461-0118
Web: www.1410kiix.com					
KPAW-FM 107.9 (CR) 4270 Byrd Dr	Loveland	CO	80538	970-461-2560	461-0118
Web: www.1079thebear.com					
KQLF-FM 97.9 (AC) 4270 Byrd Dr	Loveland	CO	80538	970-461-2560	461-0118
KSME-FM 96.1 (CHR) 4270 Byrd Dr	Loveland	CO	80538	970-461-2560	461-0118
Web: www.kissfmcolorado.com					
KTRR-FM 102.5 (AC) 600 Main St	Windsor	CO	80550	970-686-2791	686-7491
TF: 800-964-1025 ■ *Web:* www.tri102.com					
KUAD-FM 99.1 (Ctry) 600 Main St	Windsor	CO	80550	970-686-2791	686-7491
TF: 800-500-2599 ■ *Web:* www.k99.com					

648-63 Fort Smith, AR

Station	City	State	Zip	Phone	Fax
KBBQ-FM 102.7 (Urban) 3104 S 70th St	Fort Smith	AR	72903	479-452-0681	452-0873
KEZA-FM 107.9 (AC) 2049 E Joyce Blvd Suite 101	Fayetteville	AR	72703	479-582-1079	587-8255
Web: www.magic1079.com					
KFPW-AM 1230 (N/T) 321 N Greenwood Ave	Fort Smith	AR	72901	479-783-5379	785-2638
TF: 800-352-1047 ■ *Web:* www.fortsmithradiogroup.com					
KISR-FM 93.7 (CHR) 601 N Greenwood Ave	Fort Smith	AR	72901	479-785-2526	782-9127
Web: www.kisr.net					
KKBD-FM 95.9 (CR) 311 Lexington Ave	Fort Smith	AR	72901	479-782-8888	785-5946
Web: www.bigdog959.com					
KLSZ-FM 100.7 (Rock) 3104 S 70th St	Fort Smith	AR	72903	479-452-0681	452-0873
KMAG-FM 99.1 (Ctry) 311 Lexington Ave	Fort Smith	AR	72901	479-782-8888	785-5946
Web: www.kmag991.com					
KOMS-FM 107.3 (Ctry) 3104 S 70th St	Fort Smith	AR	72903	479-452-0681	452-0873
KREU-FM 92.3 (Span) 601 N Greenwood Ave	Fort Smith	AR	72901	479-785-2526	782-9127
KTCS-FM 99.9 (Ctry) 5304 Hwy 45 E	Fort Smith	AR	72916	479-646-6151	646-3509
Web: www.ktcs.com					
KUAF-FM 91.3 (NPR) 747 W Dickson St Suite 2	Fayetteville	AR	72701	479-575-2556	575-8440
TF: 800-522-5823 ■ *Web:* www.kuaf.org					
KWHN-AM 1650 (N/T) 311 Lexington Ave	Fort Smith	AR	72901	479-782-8888	785-5946
Web: www.kwhn.com					
KZBB-FM 97.9 (CHR) 311 Lexington Ave	Fort Smith	AR	72901	479-782-8888	785-5946
Web: www.kzbb.com					
KZKZ-FM 106.3 (Rel) 6420 S Zero St	Fort Smith	AR	72903	479-646-6700	646-1373
TF: 800-583-7960 ■ *Web:* www.kzkzfm.com					

648-64 Fort Wayne, IN

Station	City	State	Zip	Phone	Fax
WAJI-FM 95.1 (AC) 347 W Berry St Suite 417	Fort Wayne	IN	46802	260-423-3676	422-5266
TF: 877-951-9254 ■ *Web:* www.waji.com					
WBCL-FM 90.3 (Rel) 1025 W Rudisill Blvd	Fort Wayne	IN	46807	260-745-0576	456-2913
Web: www.wbcl.org					
WBNI-FM 89.1 (NPR) 3204 Clairmont Ct	Fort Wayne	IN	46808	260-452-1189	452-1188
TF: 800-471-9264 ■ *Web:* www.wbni.org					
WBTU-FM 93.3 (Ctry) 2100 Goshen Rd Suite 232	Fort Wayne	IN	46808	260-482-9288	482-8655
Web: www.b93.fm					
WBYR-FM 98.9 (Rock) 1005 Production Rd	Fort Wayne	IN	46808	260-471-5100	471-5224
Web: www.989thebear.com					
WFWI-FM 92.3 (CR) 1005 Production Rd	Fort Wayne	IN	46808	260-471-5100	471-5224
Web: www.923thefort.com					
WJFX-FM 107.9 (Urban) 5936 E State Blvd	Fort Wayne	IN	46815	260-493-9539	749-5151
Web: www.hot1079online.com					
WLDE-FM 101.7 (Oldies) 347 W Berry St Suite 417	Fort Wayne	IN	46802	260-423-3676	422-5266
TF: 888-450-1017 ■ *Web:* www.wlde.com					
WMEE-FM 97.3 (AC) 2915 Maples Rd	Fort Wayne	IN	46816	260-447-5511	447-7546
Web: www.wmee.com					
WOWO-AM 1190 (N/T) 2915 Maples Rd	Fort Wayne	IN	46816	260-447-5511	447-7546
TF: 800-333-1190 ■ *Web:* www.wowo.com					
WQHK-FM 105.1 (Ctry) 2915 Maples Rd	Fort Wayne	IN	46816	260-447-5511	447-7546
Web: www.k105fm.com					
WXKE-FM 103.9 (CR) 2000 Lower Huntington Rd	Fort Wayne	IN	46819	260-747-1511	747-3999
WYBB-FM 106.3 (Oldies) 2100 Goshen Rd Suite 232	Fort Wayne	IN	46808	260-482-9288	482-8655

648-65 Fresno, CA

Station	City	State	Zip	Phone	Fax
KALZ-FM 96.7 (AC) 83 E Shaw Ave Suite 150	Fresno	CA	93710	559-230-4300	243-4301
KBOS-FM 94.9 (CHR) 83 E Shaw Ave Suite 150	Fresno	CA	93710	559-230-4300	243-4301
Web: www.b95forlife.com					
KEZL-AM 1340 (Sports) 83 E Shaw Ave Suite 150	Fresno	CA	93710	559-230-4300	243-4301
KFIG-AM 1430 (Sports) 351 W Cromwell Ave Suite 108	Fresno	CA	93711	559-447-3570	447-3579
Web: www.espn1430.com					
KFJK-FM 105.9 (Var) 1071 W Shaw Ave	Fresno	CA	93711	559-490-1019	490-5966
Web: www.1059jack.com					
KFRR-FM 104.1 (Rock) 1066 E Shaw Ave	Fresno	CA	93710	559-230-0104	230-0177
KJFX-FM 95.7 (CR) 1066 E Shaw Ave	Fresno	CA	93710	559-230-0104	230-0177
Web: www.957thefox.com					
KJWL-FM 99.3 (Nost) 675 Santa Fe Ave	Fresno	CA	93721	559-497-5118	497-9760
Web: www.kjwl.com					
KLBN-FM 105.1 (Span) 1110 E Olive Ave	Fresno	CA	93728	559-497-1100	497-1125
KMGV-FM 97.9 (Oldies) 1071 W Shaw Ave	Fresno	CA	93711	559-490-5800	490-5889
Web: www.mega979.com					
KMJ-AM 580 (N/T) 1071 W Shaw Ave	Fresno	CA	93711	559-490-5800	490-5997
TF: 800-776-5858 ■ *Web:* www.kmj580.com					
KPRX-FM 89.1 (NPR) 3437 W Shaw Ave Suite 101	Fresno	CA	93711	559-275-0764	275-2202
TF: 800-275-0764 ■ *Web:* www.kvpr.org					
KRZR-FM 103.7 (Rock) 83 E Shaw Ave Suite 150	Fresno	CA	93710	559-230-4300	243-4301
Web: www.krzr.com					
KSEQ-FM 97.1 (CHR) 617 W Tulare Ave	Visalia	CA	93277	559-627-9710	627-1590
Web: www.q97.com					
KSKS-FM 93.7 (Ctry) 1071 W Shaw Ave	Fresno	CA	93711	559-490-5800	490-5889
Web: www.ksks.com					

Station	City	State	Zip	Phone	Fax
KSOF-FM 98.9 (AC) 83 E Shaw Ave Suite 150 *Web:* www.softrock989.com	Fresno	CA	93710	559-230-4300	243-4301
KVPR-FM 89.3 (NPR) 3437 W Shaw Ave Suite 101 *TF:* 800-275-0764 ■ *Web:* www.kvpr.org	Fresno	CA	93711	559-275-0764	275-2202
KWYE-FM 101.1 (CHR) 1071 W Shaw Ave *Web:* www.y101hits.com	Fresno	CA	93711	559-490-1011	490-5990

648-66 Grand Forks, ND

Station	City	State	Zip	Phone	Fax
KCNN-AM 1590 (N/T) PO Box 13638 *Web:* www.kcnn.com	Grand Forks	ND	58208	701-775-4611	772-0540
KJKJ-FM 107.5 (Rock) 505 University Ave *Web:* www.kjkj.com	Grand Forks	ND	58203	701-746-1417	746-1410
KKXL-FM 92.9 (CR) 505 University Ave. *Web:* www.xl93.com	Grand Forks	ND	58203	701-746-1417	746-1410
KNOX-AM 1310 (N/T) PO Box 13638 *Web:* www.knoxradio.com	Grand Forks	ND	58208	701-775-4611	772-0540
KNOX-FM 94.7 (Ctry) PO Box 13638	Grand Forks	ND	58208	701-775-4611	772-0540
KQHT-FM 96.1 (CR) 505 University Ave *Web:* www.961thefox.com	Grand Forks	ND	58203	701-746-1417	746-1410
KROX-AM 1260 (Var) 208 S Main St. *TF:* 800-450-1140 ■ *Web:* www.kroxam.com	Crookston	MN	56716	218-281-1140	281-5036
KSNR-FM 100.3 (Ctry) 505 University Ave *Web:* www.ksnrfm100.com	Grand Forks	ND	58203	701-746-1417	746-1410
KYCK-FM 97.1 (Ctry) PO Box 13638 *Web:* www.97kyck.com	Grand Forks	ND	58208	701-775-4611	772-0540
KZLT-FM 104.3 (AC) PO Box 13638 *Web:* www.leightonbroadcasting.com	Grand Forks	ND	58208	701-775-4611	772-0540

648-67 Grand Rapids, MI

Station	City	State	Zip	Phone	Fax
WBBL-AM 1340 (Sports) 60 Monroe Center St NW 3rd Fl *TF:* 866-828-4843 ■ *Web:* www.wbbl.com	Grand Rapids	MI	49503	616-456-5461	451-3299
WBCT-FM 93.7 (Ctry) 77 Monroe Center St NW Suite 1000 *TF:* 800-633-9393 ■ *Web:* www.b93.com	Grand Rapids	MI	49503	616-459-1919	732-3330
WBFX-FM 101.3 (CR) 77 Monroe Center St NW Suite 1000 *Web:* www.101thefoxrocks.com	Grand Rapids	MI	49503	616-459-1919	242-9373
WCSG-FM 91.3 (Rel) 1159 E Beltline Ave NE *TF:* 800-968-4543 ■ *Web:* www.gospelcom.net/wcsg	Grand Rapids	MI	49525	616-942-1500	942-7078
WFGR-FM 98.7 (Oldies) 50 Monroe Ave NW Suite 500 *Web:* www.wfgr.com	Grand Rapids	MI	49503	616-451-4800	451-0113
WGRD-FM 97.9 (Rock) 50 Monroe Ave NW Suite 500 *TF:* 800-957-3979 ■ *Web:* www.wgrd.com	Grand Rapids	MI	49503	616-451-4800	451-0113
WGVU-FM 88.5 (NPR) 301 W Fulton St. *TF:* 800-442-2771 ■ *Web:* www.wgvu.org	Grand Rapids	MI	49504	616-331-6666	331-6625
WJNZ-AM 1140 (Urban) 1919 Eastern Ave *Web:* www.wjnz.com	Grand Rapids	MI	49507	616-475-4299	475-4335
WJQK-FM 99.3 (Rel) 425 Centerstone Ct *TF:* 888-993-1260 ■ *Web:* www.jq99.com	Zeeland	MI	49464	616-931-9930	931-1280
WKLQ-FM 107.3 (Rock) 60 Monroe Center St NW 3rd Fl. *TF:* 800-785-1073 ■ *Web:* www.wklq.com	Grand Rapids	MI	49503	616-774-8461	774-0351
WLAV-FM 96.9 (CR) 60 Monroe Center St NW 3rd Fl *Web:* www.wlav.com	Grand Rapids	MI	49503	616-774-8461	774-0351
WLHT-FM 95.7 (AC) 50 Monroe Ave NW Suite 500 *Web:* www.wlht.com	Grand Rapids	MI	49503	616-451-4800	451-0113
WOOD-AM 1300 (N/T) 77 Monroe Center St NW Suite 1000 *Web:* www.woodradio.com	Grand Rapids	MI	49503	616-459-1919	242-9373
WOOD-FM 105.7 (AC) 77 Monroe Center St NW Suite 1000 *Web:* www.ez1057.com	Grand Rapids	MI	49503	616-459-1919	732-3330
WSNX-FM 104.5 (CHR) 77 Monroe Center St NW Suite 1000 *Web:* www.wsnx.com	Grand Rapids	MI	49503	616-459-1919	242-9373
WTNR-FM 94.5 (Ctry) 60 Monroe Center St NW 3rd Fl	Grand Rapids	MI	49503	616-774-8461	774-0351

648-68 Great Falls, MT

Station	City	State	Zip	Phone	Fax
KAAK-FM 98.9 (AC) 20 3rd St N Suite 231 *Web:* www.k99radio.com	Great Falls	MT	59401	406-761-7600	761-5511
KEIN-AM 1310 (Nost) PO Box 1239	Great Falls	MT	59403	406-761-1310	454-3775
KLFM-FM 92.9 (Oldies) 20 3rd St N Suite 231	Great Falls	MT	59401	406-761-7600	761-5511
KMON-AM 560 (Ctry) 20 3rd St N Suite 231 *Web:* www.kmon.com	Great Falls	MT	59401	406-761-7600	761-5511
KMON-FM 94.5 (Ctry) 20 3rd St N Suite 231	Great Falls	MT	59401	406-761-7600	761-5511
KQDI-AM 1450 (N/T) 1300 Central Ave W *Web:* www.newstalk1450.com	Great Falls	MT	59404	406-761-2800	727-7218
KQDI-FM 106.1 (CR) 1300 Central Ave W *Web:* www.q106rocks.com	Great Falls	MT	59404	406-761-2800	727-7218
KTZZ-FM 93.7 (CR) PO Box 1239	Great Falls	MT	59403	406-761-1310	454-3775
KVVR-FM 97.9 (AC) 20 3rd St Suite 231	Great Falls	MT	59401	406-761-7600	761-5511
KXGF-AM 1400 (Sports) 1300 Central Ave W *Web:* www.classics1400.com	Great Falls	MT	59404	406-761-2800	727-7218

648-69 Green Bay, WI

Station	City	State	Zip	Phone	Fax
WAPL-FM 105.7 (Rock) PO Box 1519 *Web:* www.wapl.com	Appleton	WI	54912	920-431-0959	739-0494
WDUZ-AM 1400 (Sports) 810 Victoria St. *Web:* www.thefan1075.com	Green Bay	WI	54302	920-468-4100	468-0250
WIXX-FM 101.1 (CHR) PO Box 23333 *Web:* www.wixx.com	Green Bay	WI	54305	920-435-3771	444-1155
WKSZ-FM 95.9 (CHR) PO Box 1519 *Web:* www.959kissfm.com	Appleton	WI	54912	920-431-0959	739-0494
WNCY-FM 100.3 (Ctry) PO Box 23333 *Web:* www.wncy.com	Green Bay	WI	54305	920-435-3771	444-1155
WOGB-FM 103.1 (AC) 810 Victoria St. *Web:* www.greenbayoldies.com	Green Bay	WI	54302	920-468-4100	468-0250
WPNE-FM 89.3 (NPR) 2420 Nicolet Dr *TF:* 800-654-6228 ■ *Web:* www.wpr.org	Green Bay	WI	54311	920-465-2444	465-2576
WQLH-FM 98.5 (AC) 810 Victoria St *Web:* www.star98.net	Green Bay	WI	54302	920-468-4100	468-0250
WRVM-FM 102.7 (Rel) PO Box 212 *TF:* 888-225-9786 ■ *Web:* www.wrvm.org	Suring	WI	54174	920-842-2839	842-2704
WTAQ-AM 1360 (N/T) PO Box 23333 *Web:* www.wtaq.com	Green Bay	WI	54305	920-435-3771	444-1155
WZNN-FM 106.7 (Alt) 810 Victoria St	Green Bay	WI	54302	920-468-4100	468-0250

648-70 Greenville, SC

Station	City	State	Zip	Phone	Fax
WESC-FM 92.5 (Ctry) 101 N Main St Suite 1000 *TF:* 800-248-0863 ■ *Web:* www.wescfm.com	Greenville	SC	29601	864-242-4660	242-8813
WFBC-FM 93.7 (CHR) 25 Garlington Rd *Web:* www.b937online.com	Greenville	SC	29615	864-271-9200	242-1567
WHZT-FM 98.1 (CHR) 220 N Main St Suite 402 *TF:* 866-639-4689 ■ *Web:* hot981.com	Greenville	SC	29601	864-232-9810	370-3403
WJMZ-FM 107.3 (Urban) 220 N Main St Suite 402 *Web:* 1073jamz.com	Greenville	SC	29601	864-235-1073	370-3403
WLFJ-FM 89.3 (Rel) 2420 Wade Hampton Blvd *TF:* 800-447-7234 ■ *Web:* www.hisradio.com	Greenville	SC	29615	864-292-6040	292-8428
WMUU-FM 94.5 (Var) 920 Wade Hampton Blvd *Web:* www.wmuu.com	Greenville	SC	29609	864-242-6240	370-3829
WMYI-FM 102.5 (AC) 101 N Main St Suite 1000 *TF:* 800-248-0863 ■ *Web:* www.wmyi.com	Greenville	SC	29601	864-235-4660	242-8813
WORD-AM 1330 (N/T) 25 Garlington Rd *Web:* www.newsradioword.com	Greenville	SC	29615	864-271-9200	242-1567
WROQ-FM 101.1 (CR) 25 Garlington Rd Suite B3 *TF:* 800-476-9814 ■ *Web:* www.wroq.com	Greenville	SC	29615	864-271-9200	242-1567
WSPA-FM 98.9 (AC) 25 Garlington Rd *Web:* www.magic989online.com	Greenville	SC	29615	864-271-9200	242-1567
WSSL-FM 100.5 (Ctry) 101 N Main St Suite 1000 *TF:* 800-248-0863 ■ *Web:* www.wsslfm.com	Greenville	SC	29601	864-242-4660	242-8813
WTPT-FM 93.3 (Rock) 25 Garlington Rd. *Web:* www.newrock933.com	Greenville	SC	29615	864-271-9200	242-1567

648-71 Gulfport/Biloxi, MS

Station	City	State	Zip	Phone	Fax
WCPR-FM 97.9 (Rock) 1909 E Pass Rd Suite D-11 *TF:* 888-400-2771 ■ *Web:* www.wcprfm.com	Gulfport	MS	39507	228-388-2001	896-9736
WGCM-FM 102.3 (Oldies) PO Box 2639 *Web:* www.coast102.com	Gulfport	MS	39505	228-896-5500	896-0458
WHGO-FM 105.9 (CR) 1909 E Pass Rd Suite D-11 *TF:* 800-280-7625 ■ *Web:* www.wxrgfm.com	Gulfport	MS	39507	228-388-2001	896-9736
WJZD-FM 94.5 (Urban) 10211 Southpark Dr. *TF:* 866-945-9455 ■ *Web:* www.wjzd.com	Gulfport	MS	39503	228-896-5307	896-5703
WKNN-FM 99.1 (Ctry) 286 DeBuys Rd *TF:* 800-898-9900 ■ *Web:* www.k99fm.com	Biloxi	MS	39531	228-388-2323	388-2362
WMJY-FM 93.7 (AC) 286 DeBuys Rd *Web:* www.magic937.com	Biloxi	MS	39531	228-388-2323	388-2362
WOSM-FM 103.1 (Rel) 4720 Radio Rd	Ocean Springs	MS	39564	228-432-1032	875-6461
WTNI-AM 1640 (N/T) 1909 E Pass Rd Suite D-11 *TF:* 866-450-8255 ■ *Web:* www.1640wtni.com	Gulfport	MS	39507	228-388-2001	896-9736
WXYK-FM 107.1 (CHR) 1909 E Pass Rd Suite D-11 *TF:* 800-847-7361 ■ *Web:* www.monkeyradio.com	Gulfport	MS	39507	228-388-2001	896-9736
WZKX-FM 107.9 (Ctry) PO Box 2639 *Web:* www.kicker108.com	Gulfport	MS	39505	228-896-5500	896-0458

648-72 Halifax, NS

Station	City	State	Zip	Phone	Fax
CBH-FM 102.7 (CBC) PO Box 3000 *Web:* www.cbc.ca	Halifax	NS	B3J3E9	902-420-8311	420-4429
CBHA-FM 90.5 (CBC) PO Box 3000	Halifax	NS	B3J3E9	902-420-8311	420-4478
CFDR-AM 780 (Ctry) 2900 Agricola St.	Halifax	NS	B3K6A7	902-453-2524	453-3132
CFRQ-FM 104.3 (CR) 2900 Agricola St *Web:* www.q104.ca	Halifax	NS	B3K6A7	902-453-2524	453-3132
CHAL-FM 89.9 (Oldies) PO Box 400	Halifax	NS	B3J2R2	902-422-1651	422-5330
CHFX-FM 101.9 (Ctry) PO Box 400	Halifax	NS	B3J2R2	902-422-1651	422-5330
CIOO-FM 100.1 (AC) 2900 Agricola St. *Web:* www.c100fm.com	Halifax	NS	B3K6A7	902-453-2524	453-3132
CJCH-AM 920 (Oldies) 2900 Agricola St *Web:* www.cjch.ca	Halifax	NS	B3K6A7	902-453-2524	453-3132
CKDU-FM 88.1 (Alt) Dalhousie University 6136 University Ave *Web:* www.ckdu.ca	Halifax	NS	B3H4J2	902-494-6479	

648-73 Harrisburg, PA

Station	City	State	Zip	Phone	Fax
WAYZ-FM 104.7 (Ctry) 10960 John Wayne Dr *TF:* 888-950-1047 ■ *Web:* www.wayz.com	Greencastle	PA	17225	717-597-9200	597-9210
WCAT-FM 102.3 (Ctry) 515 S 32nd St *TF:* 800-932-0505 ■ *Web:* www.red1023.com	Camp Hill	PA	17011	717-635-7000	635-7551
WDAC-FM 94.5 (Rel) PO Box 3022 *Web:* www.wdac.com	Lancaster	PA	17604	717-284-4123	284-2300
WGET-AM 1320 (AC) 1560 Fairfield Rd PO Box 3179 *TF:* 800-366-9489 ■ *Web:* www.wget.com	Gettysburg	PA	17325	717-334-3101	334-5822
WGTY-FM 107.7 (Ctry) 1560 Fairfield Rd PO Box 3179 *TF:* 800-366-9489 ■ *Web:* www.wgty.com	Gettysburg	PA	17325	717-334-3101	334-5822
WHP-AM 580 (N/T) 600 Corporate Cir *TF:* 800-329-9562 ■ *Web:* www.whp580.com	Harrisburg	PA	17110	717-540-8800	540-9268
WHVR-AM 1280 (Ctry) 275 Radio Rd	Hanover	PA	17331	717-637-3831	637-9006
WITF-FM 89.5 (NPR) 4801 Lindle Rd *TF:* 800-366-9483 ■ *Web:* www.witf.org	Harrisburg	PA	17109	717-236-6000	236-4628
WKBO-AM 1230 (Rel) 600 Corporate Cir *TF:* 800-329-9562	Harrisburg	PA	17110	717-540-8800	540-9268
WLBR-AM 1270 (Var) 440 Rebecca Rd	Lebanon	PA	17046	717-272-7651	274-0161
WNNK-FM 104.1 (AC) 2300 Vartan Way *Web:* www.wink104.com	Harrisburg	PA	17110	717-238-1041	234-4842
WQXA-FM 105.7 (Rock) 515 S 32nd St *TF:* 800-932-0505 ■ *Web:* www.1057.com	Camp Hill	PA	17011	717-635-7000	635-7551
WRBT-FM 94.9 (Ctry) 600 Corporate Cir. *TF:* 800-329-9562 ■ *Web:* www.bobradio.com	Harrisburg	PA	17110	717-540-8800	540-9268
WROZ-FM 101.3 (AC) 1996 Auction Rd *Web:* www.roseradio.com	Manheim	PA	17545	717-653-0800	653-0122
WRVV-FM 97.3 (AC) 600 Corporate Cir. *TF:* 800-329-9562 ■ *Web:* www.river973.cc	Harrisburg	PA	17110	717-540-8800	540-9268
WTPA-FM 93.5 (CR) 2300 Vartan Way *Web:* www.wtpafm.com	Harrisburg	PA	17110	717-238-1041	234-4842
WWKL-FM 92.1 (CHR) 2300 Vartan Way *Web:* www.hot92.com	Harrisburg	PA	17110	717-238-1041	234-4842
WYCR-FM 98.5 (AC) 275 Radio Rd *Web:* www.98ycr.com	Hanover	PA	17331	717-637-3831	637-9006

Harrisburg, PA (Cont'd)

Station / Address	City	State	Zip	Phone	Fax
WZBT-FM 91.1 (Alt) 300 N Washington St Gettysburg College	Gettysburg	PA	17325	717-337-6315	

648-74 Hartford, CT

Station / Address	City	State	Zip	Phone	Fax
WCCC-FM 106.9 (Rock) 1039 Asylum Ave *Web:* www.wccc.com	Hartford	CT	06105	860-525-1069	246-9084
WDRC-AM 1360 (N/T) 869 Blue Hills Ave *Web:* www.wdrc.com	Bloomfield	CT	06002	860-243-1115	286-8257
WDRC-FM 102.9 (Oldies) 869 Blue Hills Ave *Web:* www.drcfm.com	Bloomfield	CT	06002	860-243-1115	286-8257
WEDW-FM 88.5 (NPR) 1049 Asylum Ave *Fax: News Rm	Hartford	CT	06105	860-278-5310	275-7403*
WHCN-FM 105.9 (CR) 10 Columbus Blvd *Web:* www.whcn.com	Hartford	CT	06106	860-723-6000	723-6106
WKSS-FM 95.7 (CHR) 10 Columbus Blvd *Web:* www.kiss957.com	Hartford	CT	06106	860-723-6000	723-6195
WLAT-AM 910 (Span) 330 Main St *TF:* 866-910-6342	Hartford	CT	06106	860-524-0001	524-0336
WMRQ-FM 104.1 (Alt) 10 Columbus Blvd *Web:* www.radio104.com	Hartford	CT	06106	860-723-6000	723-6078
WPKT-FM 90.5 (NPR) 1049 Asylum Ave *Web:* www.wnpr.org	Hartford	CT	06105	860-278-5310	275-7403
WPOP-AM 1410 (Sports) 10 Columbus Blvd *Web:* www.espnradio1410.com	Hartford	CT	06106	860-723-6000	723-6195
WRCH-FM 100.5 (AC) 10 Executive Dr *Web:* www.wrch.com	Farmington	CT	06032	860-677-6700	677-5483
WRTC-FM 89.3 (Var) Trinity College 300 Summit St *Web:* www.wrtcfm.com	Hartford	CT	06106	860-297-2439	297-5201
WTIC-AM 1080 (N/T) 10 Executive Dr *Web:* www.wtic.com	Farmington	CT	06032	860-677-6700	284-9842
WTIC-FM 96.5 (AC) 10 Executive Dr *Web:* www.ticfm.com	Farmington	CT	06032	860-677-6700	284-9650
WTMI-AM 1290 (Clas) 1039 Asylum Ave *Web:* www.beethoven.com	Hartford	CT	06105	860-525-1069	246-9084
WWYZ-FM 92.5 (Ctry) 10 Columbus Blvd *Web:* www.wwyz.com	Hartford	CT	06106	860-723-6000	723-6159
WZMX-FM 93.7 (Urban) 10 Executive Dr *Web:* www.hot937.com	Farmington	CT	06032	860-677-6700	674-8427

648-75 Hattiesburg, MS

Station / Address	City	State	Zip	Phone	Fax
WBBN-FM 95.9 (Ctry) 4580 Hwy 15 N PO Box 6408 *Web:* www.b95country.com	Laurel	MS	39441	601-649-0095	649-8199
WFOR-AM 1400 (Sports) 6555 Hwy 98 W Suite 8 *TF:* 877-993-0993	Hattiesburg	MS	39402	601-296-9800	271-8348
WHER-FM 99.3 (Ctry) 6555 Hwy 98 W Suite 8 *TF:* 877-993-0993 ■ *Web:* www.eagle99.com	Hattiesburg	MS	39402	601-296-9800	271-8348
WJKX-FM 102.5 (Urban) 6555 Hwy 98 W Suite 8 *TF:* 877-993-0993 ■ *Web:* www.102jkx.com	Hattiesburg	MS	39402	601-296-9800	271-8348
WJMG-FM 92.1 (Urban) 1204 Graveline St	Hattiesburg	MS	39401	601-544-1941	544-1947
WKZW-FM 94.3 (AC) 4580 Hwy 15 N PO Box 6408 *Web:* www.kz94.com	Laurel	MS	39441	601-649-0095	649-8199
WNSL-FM 100.3 (CHR) 6555 Hwy 98 W Suite 8 *TF:* 877-993-0993 ■ *Web:* www.sl100.com	Hattiesburg	MS	39402	601-296-9800	271-8348
WUSM-FM 88.5 (Var) 118 College Dr *Web:* www.wusm.usm.edu	Hattiesburg	MS	39406	601-266-4287	266-4288
WUSW-FM 103.7 (Rock) 6555 Hwy 98 W Suite 8 *TF:* 877-993-0993 ■ *Web:* www.thefoxrocks1037.com	Hattiesburg	MS	39402	601-296-9800	271-8348
WXHB-FM 96.5 (Rel) 4580 Hwy 15 N PO Box 6408 *Web:* www.solidgospel.com	Laurel	MS	39441	601-649-0095	649-8199
WXRR-FM 104.5 (Rock) 4580 Hwy 15 N PO Box 6408 *Web:* www.rock104fm.com	Laurel	MS	39441	601-649-0095	649-8199
WZLD-FM 106.3 (Urban) 6555 Hwy 98 W Suite 8 *TF:* 877-993-0993 ■ *Web:* www.wzldfm.com	Hattiesburg	MS	39402	601-296-9800	271-8348

648-76 Helena, MT

Station / Address	City	State	Zip	Phone	Fax
KBLL-AM 1240 (N/T) 110 E Broadway St	Helena	MT	59601	406-442-4490	442-7356
KBLL-FM 99.5 (Ctry) 110 E Broadway St	Helena	MT	59601	406-442-4490	442-7356
KGPR-FM 89.9 (NPR) PO Box 33343 *Web:* www.mtpr.net	Great Falls	MT	59403	406-268-3739	268-3736
KHKR-FM 104.1 (Ctry) 110 E Broadway St *Web:* www.khkr.com	Helena	MT	59601	406-442-4490	442-7356
KJFM-FM 91.7 (NPR) 32 Campus Dr University of Montana *TF:* 800-325-1565 ■ *Web:* www.mtpr.net	Missoula	MT	59812	406-243-4931	243-3299
KKGR-AM 680 (Oldies) 1400 11th Ave	Helena	MT	59601	406-443-5237	442-6916
KMBR-FM 95.5 (Rock) 750 Dewey Blvd Suite 1 *Web:* www.955kmbr.com	Butte	MT	59701	406-494-4442	494-6020
KMTX-FM 105.3 (AC) 516 Fuller Ave *Web:* www.hitsandfavorites.com	Helena	MT	59601	406-442-0400	442-0491
KVCM-FM 103.1 (Rel) PO Box 2426 *Web:* www.ynopradio.org	Havre	MT	59501	406-265-5845	265-8860
KZMT-FM 101.1 (CR) 110 E Broadway St *Web:* www.kzmt.com	Helena	MT	59601	406-442-4490	442-7356

648-77 Honolulu, HI

Station / Address	City	State	Zip	Phone	Fax
KAIM-FM 95.5 (Rel) 1160 N King St 2nd Fl *Web:* www.thefishhawaii.com	Honolulu	HI	96817	808-533-0065	524-2104
KCCN-FM 100.3 (CHR) 900 Fort St Suite 700 *Web:* kccnfm100.com	Honolulu	HI	96813	808-536-2728	536-2528
KDDB-FM 102.7 (CHR) 765 Amana St Suite 200 *Web:* www.dabombhawaii.com	Honolulu	HI	96814	808-947-1500	947-1506
KDNN-FM 98.5 (Island) 650 Iwilei Rd Suite 400 *Fax: Sales ■ *Web:* www.island985.com	Honolulu	HI	96817	808-550-9200	550-9504*
KGMZ-FM 107.9 (Oldies) 1160 N King St 2nd Fl *Web:* www.oldies1079honolulu.com	Honolulu	HI	96817	808-533-0065	524-2104
KHPR-FM 88.1 (NPR) 738 Kaheka St Suite 101 *Web:* www.hawaiipublicradio.org	Honolulu	HI	96814	808-955-8821	942-5477
KHVH-AM 830 (N/T) 650 Iwilei Rd Suite 400 *Fax: Sales ■ *Web:* www.khvh830am.com	Honolulu	HI	96817	808-550-9200	550-9288*
KIKI-FM 93.9 (CHR) 650 Iwilei Rd Suite 400 *Fax: Sales ■ *Web:* www.i-94.net	Honolulu	HI	96817	808-550-9200	550-9504*
KINE-FM 105.1 (AC) 900 Fort St Suite 700 *Web:* hawaiian105.com	Honolulu	HI	96813	808-536-2728	536-2528
KLHT-AM 1040 (Rel) 98 - 1016 Komo Mai Dr *Web:* www.klight.org	Aiea	HI	96701	808-524-1040	487-1040
KPHW-FM 104.3 (Urban) 900 Fort St Suite 700 *Web:* power1043.com	Honolulu	HI	96813	808-275-1000	536-2528
KPOI-FM 105.9 (CR) 765 Amana St Suite 200 *Web:* www.kpoifm.com/kpoi/	Honolulu	HI	96814	808-947-1500	947-1506
KQMQ-FM 93.1 (CHR) 765 Amana St Suite 200 *Web:* www.kqmq.net	Honolulu	HI	96814	808-947-1500	947-1506
KRTR-FM 96.3 (AC) 900 Fort St Suite 700 *Web:* krater96.com	Honolulu	HI	96813	808-275-1000	536-2528
KSSK-AM 590 (AC) 650 Iwilei Rd Suite 400 *Fax: Sales ■ *Web:* www.ksskradio.com	Honolulu	HI	96817	808-550-9200	550-9288*
KSSK-FM 92.3 (AC) 650 Iwilei Rd Suite 400 *Web:* www.ksskradio.com	Honolulu	HI	96817	808-550-9200	550-9288
KUCD-FM 101.9 (Alt) 650 Iwilei Rd Suite 400 *Fax: Sales ■ *Web:* www.star1019fm.com	Honolulu	HI	96817	808-550-9200	550-9504*
KUMU-FM 94.7 (AC) 765 Amana St Suite 206 *Web:* www.kumu.com	Honolulu	HI	96814	808-947-1500	947-1506

648-78 Hot Springs, AR

Station / Address	City	State	Zip	Phone	Fax
KBHS-AM 1420 (Ctry) 208 Buena Vista Rd *Web:* www.klazfm.com/kxow.html	Hot Springs	AR	71913	501-525-4600	525-4344
KBOK-AM 1310 (Ctry) 302 S Main	Malvern	AR	72104	501-332-6981	332-6984
KLAZ-FM 105.9 (CHR) 208 Buena Vista Rd *Web:* www.klaz.com	Hot Springs	AR	71913	501-525-4600	525-4344
KLXQ-FM 101.9 (CR) 125 Corporate Terr *TF:* 800-442-0097 ■ *Web:* www.1019therocket.com	Hot Springs	AR	71913	501-525-9700	525-9739
KQUS-FM 97.5 (Ctry) 125 Corporate Terr *TF:* 800-442-0097 ■ *Web:* www.us97country.com	Hot Springs	AR	71913	501-525-9700	525-9739
KVRE-FM 92.9 (AC) 122 Desoto Center Dr	Hot Springs Village	AR	71909	501-624-5994	922-6626
KYDL-FM 96.7 (AC) 125 Corporate Terr *TF:* 800-442-0097	Hot Springs	AR	71913	501-525-9700	525-9739
KZNG-AM 1340 (N/T) 125 Corporate Terr *TF:* 800-442-0097 ■ *Web:* www.kzng.net	Hot Springs	AR	71913	501-525-9700	525-9739

648-79 Houston, TX

Station / Address	City	State	Zip	Phone	Fax
KBME-AM 790 (Sports) 2000 West Loop S Suite 300 *Web:* www.espn790.com	Houston	TX	77027	713-212-8000	212-8790
KBXX-FM 97.9 (CHR) 24 Greenway Plaza Suite 900 *Web:* www.kbxx.com	Houston	TX	77046	713-623-2108	623-0344
KHJZ-FM 95.7 (NAC) 24 Greenway Plaza Suite 1900 *Web:* www.khjz.com	Houston	TX	77046	713-881-5100	881-5199
KHMX-FM 96.5 (CHR) 2000 West Loop S Suite 300 *Web:* www.khmx.com	Houston	TX	77027	713-212-8000	212-8963
KHPT-FM 106.9 (AC) 1990 Post Oak Blvd Suite 2300 *Web:* 1069thepoint.com	Houston	TX	77056	713-622-5533	993-9300
KHTC-FM 107.5 (Oldies) 1990 Post Oak Blvd Suite 2300 *Web:* 1075khits.com	Houston	TX	77056	713-963-1200	622-5457
KILT-AM 610 (Sports) 24 Greenway Plaza Suite 1900 *Web:* www.sportsradio610.com	Houston	TX	77046	713-881-5100	881-5199
KILT-FM 100.3 (Ctry) 24 Greenway Plaza Suite 1900 *Web:* www.kilt.com	Houston	TX	77046	713-881-5100	881-5199
KKBQ-FM 92.9 (Ctry) 1990 Post Oak Blvd Suite 2300 *Web:* kkbq.com	Houston	TX	77056	713-622-5533	993-9300
KKHT-FM 100.0 (Rel) 6161 Savoy Dr Suite 1200 *Web:* www.kkht.com	Houston	TX	77036	713-260-3600	260-3628
KKRW-FM 93.7 (CR) 2000 West Loop S Suite 300 *Web:* www.kkrw.com	Houston	TX	77027	713-212-8000	212-8963
KLAT-AM 1010 (Span N/T) 5100 SW Freeway Suite 550 *Web:* latremenda.netmio.com	Houston	TX	77056	713-407-1415	407-1400
KLOL-FM 101.1 (Span) 2000 West Loop S Suite 300 *Web:* mega101houston.com	Houston	TX	77027	713-212-8000	212-8101
KLTN-FM 102.9 (Span) 5100 SW Freeway *Web:* estereolatino.netmio.com	Houston	TX	77056	713-407-1415	965-2401
KMJQ-FM 102.1 (Urban) 24 Greenway Plaza Suite 900 *Web:* www.kmjq.com	Houston	TX	77046	713-623-2108	622-5267
KODA-FM 99.1 (AC) 2000 West Loop S Suite 300 *Web:* www.sunny99.com	Houston	TX	77027	713-212-8000	212-8963
KOVE-FM 106.5 (Span) 5100 SW Freeway Suite 550 *Web:* kove.netmio.com	Houston	TX	77056	713-407-1415	407-1400
KPRC-AM 950 (N/T) 2000 West Loop S Suite 300 *Web:* www.950kprc.com	Houston	TX	77027	713-212-8000	212-8963
KPTY-FM 104.9 (Urban) 5100 SW Freeway	Houston	TX	77056	713-407-1415	965-2401
KPVU-FM 91.3 (NPR) Prairie View A & M University MS 1415 PO Box 159 *Web:* www.pvamu.edu/kpvu	Prairie View	TX	77446	936-261-3750	261-3769
KQQK-FM 107.9 (Span AC) 3000 Bering Dr *Web:* www.xoradio.com	Houston	TX	77057	281-315-3400	
KRBE-FM 104.1 (CHR) 9801 Westheimer Rd Suite 700 *Web:* www.krbe.com	Houston	TX	77042	713-266-1000	954-2344
KSEV-AM 700 (N/T) 11451 Katy Fwy Suite 215 *Fax Area Code: 832 ■ *Web:* www.ksevradio.com	Houston	TX	77079	281-588-4800	358-8409*
KTBZ-FM 94.5 (Alt) 2000 West Loop S Suite 300 *Web:* www.thebuzz.com	Houston	TX	77027	713-212-8000	212-8963
KTHT-FM 97.1 (Ctry) 1990 Post Oak Blvd Suite 2300 *Web:* countrylegends971.com	Houston	TX	77056	713-622-5533	993-9300
KTRH-AM 740 (N/T) 2000 West Loop S Suite 300 *Web:* www.ktrh.com	Houston	TX	77027	713-212-8000	212-8958
KUHF-FM 88.7 (Clas) 4343 Elgin St 3rd Fl *Web:* www.kuhf.org	Houston	TX	77204	713-743-0887	743-0868

648-80 Huntsville, AL

Station / Address	City	State	Zip	Phone	Fax
WAHR-FM 99.1 (AC) 1555 The Boardwalk Suite 1 *Web:* www.star99.fm	Huntsville	AL	35816	256-536-1568	536-9447
WDRM-FM 102.1 (Ctry) 26869 Peoples Rd *Web:* www.wdrm.com	Madison	AL	35756	256-353-1750	350-2653
WEUP-FM 103.1 (Urban) 2609 Jordan Ln NW *TF:* 800-287-9387 ■ *Web:* www.103weup.com	Huntsville	AL	35816	256-837-9387	837-9404
WJAB-FM 90.9 (Jazz) Alabama A&M University Telecommunications Center PO Box 1687 *TF:* 800-845-9746 ■ *Web:* www.aamu.edu/wjab	Normal	AL	35762	256-372-5795	372-5907
WLOR-AM 1550 (Oldies) 1555 The Boardwalk Suite 1 *Web:* www.jammin1550.am	Huntsville	AL	35816	256-536-1568	536-4416

				Phone	Fax
WLRH-FM 89.3 (NPR) University of Alabama-Huntsville John Wright Dr	Huntsville	AL	35899	256-895-9574	830-4577
TF: 800-239-9574 ■ *Web:* www.wlrh.org					
WOCG-FM 90.1 (Rel) 4920 University Sq Suite J	Huntsville	AL	35806	256-722-9990	837-7918
Web: www.oakwood.edu/wocg					
WRSA-FM 96.9 (AC) 8402 Memorial Pkwy S	Huntsville	AL	35802	256-885-9797	885-9796
TF: 888-503-4969 ■ *Web:* www.lite969.com					
WRTT-FM 95.1 (Rock) 1555 The Boardwalk Suite 1	Huntsville	AL	35816	256-536-1568	536-4416
Web: www.rocket951.fm					
WTAK-FM 106.1 (CR) 26869 Peoples Rd	Madison	AL	35756	256-353-1750	350-2653
Web: www.wtak.com					
WUMP-AM 730 (Sports) 1717 Hwy 72 E	Athens	AL	35611	256-830-8300	232-6842
Web: www.730ump.com					
WVNN-AM 770 (N/T) 1717 Hwy 72 E	Athens	AL	35611	256-830-8300	232-6842
Web: www.wvnn.com					
WZYP-FM 104.3 (CHR) 1717 Hwy 72 E	Athens	AL	35612	256-830-8300	232-6842
Web: www.wzyp.net					

648-81 Indianapolis, IN

				Phone	Fax
WBWB-FM 96.7 (CHR) 304 SR 446	Bloomington	IN	47407	812-336-8000	336-7000
TF: 800-888-6499 ■ *Web:* www.wbwb.com					
WCBK-FM 102.3 (Ctry) 1639 Burton Ln	Martinsville	IN	46151	765-342-3394	342-5020
Web: www.wcbk.com					
WFBQ-FM 94.7 (CR) 6161 Fall Creek Rd	Indianapolis	IN	46220	317-257-7565	254-9619
Web: www.wfbq.com					
WFDM-FM 95.9 (N/T) 645 Industrial Dr	Franklin	IN	46131	317-736-4040	736-4781
WFHB-FM 91.3 (Var) 108 W 4th St	Bloomington	IN	47404	812-323-1200	323-0320
Web: www.wfhb.org					
WFIU-FM 103.7 (Clas) Indiana University 1229 E 7th St	Bloomington	IN	47405	812-855-1357	855-5600
TF: 877-285-9348 ■ *Web:* www.wfiu.org					
WFMS-FM 95.5 (Ctry) 6810 N Shadeland Ave	Indianapolis	IN	46220	317-842-9550	577-3361
Web: www.wfms.com					
WFYI-FM 90.1 (NPR) 1630 N Meridian St	Indianapolis	IN	46202	317-636-2020	633-7418
Web: www.wfyi.org					
WGCL-AM 1370 (N/T) 120 W 7th St 4th Fl	Bloomington	IN	47404	812-333-2665	331-4570
Web: www.am1370wgcl.com					
WHCC-FM 105.1 (Ctry) 304 SR 446 PO Box 7797	Bloomington	IN	47407	812-336-8000	336-7000
TF: 888-581-4487 ■ *Web:* www.whcc105.com					
WHHH-FM 96.3 (CHR) 21 E Saint Joseph St	Indianapolis	IN	46204	317-266-9600	328-3870
Web: www.hot963.com					
WIBC-AM 1070 (N/T) 40 Monument Cir Suite 400	Indianapolis	IN	46204	317-266-9422	684-2022
Web: www.wibc.com					
WJJK-FM 104.5 (Var) 6810 N Shadeland Ave	Indianapolis	IN	46220	317-842-9550	577-3361
WKKG-FM 101.5 (Ctry) 3212 Washington St	Columbus	IN	47203	812-372-4448	372-1061
Web: www.wkkg.com					
WKLU-FM 101.9 (CR) 8120 Knue Rd	Indianapolis	IN	46250	317-841-1019	841-5167
Web: www.wklu.net					
WLHK-FM 97.1 (Ctry) 40 Monument Cir Suite 600	Indianapolis	IN	46204	317-266-9700	684-2021
Web: www.wlsam.com					
WMYJ-AM 1540 (Rel) 1639 Burton Ln	Martinsville	IN	46151	765-342-3394	342-5020
WNDE-AM 1260 (Sports) 6161 Fall Creek Rd	Indianapolis	IN	46220	317-257-7565	254-9619
Web: www.wnde.com					
WNTR-FM 107.9 (AC) 9245 N Meridian St Suite 300	Indianapolis	IN	46260	317-816-4000	816-4060
Web: www.wtpi.com					
WRZX-FM 103.3 (Alt) 6161 Fall Creek Rd	Indianapolis	IN	46220	317-257-7565	254-9619
Web: www.x103.com					
WTLC-AM 1310 (Urban AC) 21 E Saint Joseph St	Indianapolis	IN	46204	317-266-9600	328-3870
WTLC-FM 106.7 (Urban) 21 E Saint Joseph St	Indianapolis	IN	46204	317-266-9600	328-3870
Web: www.wtlc.com					
WTTS-FM 92.3 (AAA) 400 One City Centre	Bloomington	IN	47404	812-332-3366	331-4570
Web: www.wttsfm.com					
WVNI-FM 95.1 (Rel) PO Box 1628	Bloomington	IN	47402	812-335-9500	335-8880
Web: www.spirit95fm.com					
WWFT-FM 93.9 (N/T) 6810 N Shadeland Ave	Indianapolis	IN	46220	317-842-9550	577-3361
Web: www.939thesong.com					
WXKU-FM 92.7 (Ctry) PO Box 806	Seymour	IN	47274	812-522-1390	522-9541
TF: 800-633-9370					
WXNT-AM 1430 (N/T) 9245 N Meridian St Suite 300	Indianapolis	IN	46260	317-816-4000	816-4060
Web: www.newstalk1430.com					
WYXB-FM 105.7 (AC) 40 Monument Cir Suite 600	Indianapolis	IN	46204	317-266-9700	684-2022
Web: www.b1057.com					
WZPL-FM 99.5 (AC) 9245 N Meridian St Suite 300	Indianapolis	IN	46260	317-816-4000	816-4060
Web: www.wzpl.com					

648-82 Jackson, MS

				Phone	Fax
WHLH-FM 95.5 (Rel) 1375 Beasley Rd	Jackson	MS	39206	601-982-1062	362-1905
WJDX-AM 620 (Sports) 1375 Beasley Rd	Jackson	MS	39206	601-982-1062	362-1905
Web: www.wjdx.com					
WJKK-FM 98.7 (AC) 265 Highpoint Dr	Ridgeland	MS	39157	601-956-0102	978-3980
Web: www.mix987.com					
WJMI-FM 99.7 (Urban) 731 S Pear Orchard Rd Suite 27	Ridgeland	MS	39157	601-957-1300	956-0516
Web: www.99jams.cc					
WJNT-AM 1180 (N/T) 731 S Pear Orchard Rd Suite 27	Ridgeland	MS	39157	601-957-1300	956-0516
Web: www.wjnt.com					
WJSU-FM 88.5 (Jazz) 1400 Lynch St	Jackson	MS	39217	601-979-2140	979-2878
WKXI-FM 107.5 (Urban) 731 S Pear Orchard Rd Suite 27	Ridgeland	MS	39157	601-957-1300	956-0516
Web: www.kixie107.com					
WMAE-FM 89.5 (NPR) 3825 Ridgewood Rd	Jackson	MS	39211	601-432-6565	432-6746
TF: 800-922-9698 ■ *Web:* www.mpbonline.org					
WMAH-FM 90.3 (NPR) 3825 Ridgewood Rd	Jackson	MS	39211	601-432-6800	432-6806
Web: www.mpbonline.org					
WMPN-FM 91.3 (NPR) 3825 Ridgewood Rd	Jackson	MS	39211	601-432-6800	432-6806
TF: 866-262-9643 ■ *Web:* www.mpbonline.org					
WMSI-FM 102.9 (Ctry) 1375 Beasley Rd	Jackson	MS	39206	601-982-1062	362-1905
Web: www.miss103.com					
WSTZ-FM 106.7 (CR) 1375 Beasley Rd	Jackson	MS	39206	601-982-1062	362-1905
Web: www.z106.com					
WUSJ-FM 96.3 (Ctry) 265 Highpoint Dr	Ridgeland	MS	39157	601-956-0102	978-3980
Web: www.us963.com					
WWJK-FM 94.7 (CR) 222 Beasley Rd	Jackson	MS	39206	601-957-3000	956-0370
Web: www.947jackfm.com					
WYOY-FM 101.7 (CHR) 265 Highpoint Dr	Ridgeland	MS	39157	601-956-0102	978-3980
Web: www.y101.com					

648-83 Jacksonville, FL

				Phone	Fax
WAPE-FM 95.1 (CHR) 8000 Belfort Pkwy Suite 100	Jacksonville	FL	32256	904-245-8500	245-8501
TF: 800-475-9595 ■ *Web:* wape951.com					
WAYL-FM 91.9 (AC) 4190 Belfort Rd Suite 450	Jacksonville	FL	32216	904-829-9200	296-1683
Web: www.riverradio.org					
WBOB-AM 1320 (N/T) 4190 Belfort Rd Suite 450	Jacksonville	FL	32216	904-470-4615	296-1683
Web: www.1320wbob.com					
WCGL-AM 1360 (Rel) 3890 Dunn Ave Suite 804	Jacksonville	FL	32218	904-766-9955	765-9214
Web: www.wcgl1360.com					
WEJZ-FM 96.1 (AC) 6440 Atlantic Blvd	Jacksonville	FL	32211	904-727-9696	721-9322
Web: www.wejz.com					
WFCF-FM 88.5 (Var) PO Box 1027 Flagler College	Saint Augustine	FL	32085	904-819-6449	826-0094
WFKS-FM 97.9 (CHR) 11700 Central Pkwy	Jacksonville	FL	32224	904-636-0507	636-7971*
**Fax:* Sales ■ *Web:* www.979kissfm.cc					
WFOY-AM 1240 (N/T) PO Box 3847	Saint Augustine	FL	32085	904-797-1955	797-3446
Web: www.1240news.com					
WFYV-FM 104.5 (CR) 8000 Belfort Pkwy Suite 100	Jacksonville	FL	32256	904-245-8500	245-8501
Web: rock105i.com					
WJAX-AM 1220 (Nost) 5353 Arlington Expy	Jacksonville	FL	32211	904-371-1184	
Web: www.wktz.jones.edu					
WJBT-FM 92.7 (Urban) 11700 Central Pkwy	Jacksonville	FL	32224	904-636-0507	636-7971*
**Fax:* Sales ■ *Web:* www.wjbt.com					
WJCT-FM 89.9 (NPR) 100 Festival Park Ave	Jacksonville	FL	32202	904-353-7770	358-6352
Web: www.wjct.org					
WJGL-FM 96.9 (CR) 8000 Belfort Pkwy	Jacksonville	FL	32256	904-245-8500	245-8501
Web: 969theeagle.com					
WKTZ-FM 90.9 (AC) 5353 Arlington Expy	Jacksonville	FL	32211	904-371-1184	
Web: wktz.jones.edu					
WMXQ-FM 102.9 (AC) 8000 Belfort Pkwy	Jacksonville	FL	32256	904-245-8500	245-8501
Web: 1029i.com					
WNCM-FM 88.1 (Rel) 4190 Belfort Rd Suite 450	Jacksonville	FL	32216	904-641-9626	645-9626
Web: www.fm88.org					
WOKV-AM 690 (N/T) 8000 Belfort Pkwy	Jacksonville	FL	32256	904-245-8500	245-8501
Web: wokv.com					
WPLA-FM 107.3 (Alt) 11700 Central Pkwy	Jacksonville	FL	32224	904-636-0507	636-7971*
**Fax:* Sales ■ *Web:* www.planet93.com					
WPLK-AM 800 (Nost) 1428 St John Ave	Palatka	FL	32177	386-325-5800	328-8725
Web: www.wplk.com					
WQIK-FM 99.1 (Ctry) 11700 Central Pkwy	Jacksonville	FL	32224	904-636-0507	636-7971*
**Fax:* Sales ■ *Web:* www.wqik.com					
WROO-FM 92.7 (Rel) 11700 Central Pkwy	Jacksonville	FL	32224	904-642-3030	636-7971*
**Fax:* Sales					
WSOL-FM 101.5 (Urban AC) 11700 Central Pkwy	Jacksonville	FL	32224	904-636-0507	636-7971*
**Fax:* Sales ■ *Web:* www.v1015.com					
WZAZ-AM 1400 (Rel) 4190 Belfort Rd Suite 450	Jacksonville	FL	32216	904-470-4707	652-1426
Web: www.wzaz.com					
WZNZ-AM 1460 (Rel) 4190 Belfort Rd Suite 450	Jacksonville	FL	32216	904-470-4615	296-1683

648-84 Jefferson City, MO

				Phone	Fax
KATI-FM 94.3 (Ctry) 3109 S Ten-Mile Dr	Jefferson City	MO	65109	573-893-5696	893-4137
Web: www.kat943.com					
KBBM-FM 100.1 (Alt) 503 Old 63 N	Columbia	MO	65201	573-449-4141	449-7770
Web: www.buzz.fm					
KBIA-FM 91.3 (NPR) 409 Jesse Hall	Columbia	MO	65211	573-882-3431	882-2636
TF: 800-292-9136 ■ *Web:* www.kbia.org					
KBXR-FM 102.3 (AAA) 503 Old 63 N	Columbia	MO	65201	573-449-4141	449-7770
Web: www.bxr.com					
KCLR-FM 99.3 (Ctry) 3215 Lemone Industrial Blvd Suite 200	Columbia	MO	65201	573-875-1099	875-2439
TF: 800-455-5257 ■ *Web:* www.clear99.com					
KCMQ-FM 96.7 (CR) 3215 Lemone Industrial Blvd Suite 200	Columbia	MO	65201	573-875-1099	875-2439
TF: 800-455-1967 ■ *Web:* www.kcmq.com					
KFAL-AM 900 (Ctry) 1805 Westminster Ave	Fulton	MO	65251	573-642-3341	642-3343
TF: 800-769-5274					
KFRU-AM 1400 (N/T) 503 Old 63 N	Columbia	MO	65201	573-449-4141	449-7770
Web: www.kfru.com					
KJLU-FM 88.9 (Jazz) 1004 E Dunklin St	Jefferson City	MO	65102	573-681-5301	681-5299
Web: www.kjlu.com					
KJMO-FM 97.5 (Oldies) 3605 Country Club Dr	Jefferson City	MO	65109	573-893-5100	893-8330
Web: www.kjmo.com					
KLIK-AM 1240 (N/T) 3605 Country Club Dr	Jefferson City	MO	65109	573-893-5100	893-8330
Web: www.klik1240.com					
KLOZ-FM 92.7 (AC) 160 Hwy 42	Kaiser	MO	65047	573-348-1958	348-1923
Web: www.z93-themix.com					
KMFC-FM 92.1 (Rel) 1249 E Hwy 22	Centralia	MO	65240	573-682-5525	682-2744
TF: 800-769-5632 ■ *Web:* www.kmfc.com					
KOPN-FM 89.5 (Var) 915 E Broadway	Columbia	MO	65201	573-874-5676	499-1662
Web: www.kopn.org					
KOQL-FM 106.1 (CHR) 503 Old 63 N	Columbia	MO	65201	573-449-4141	449-7770
KPLA-FM 101.5 (AC) 503 Old 63 N	Columbia	MO	65201	573-449-4141	449-7770
Web: www.kpla.com					
KTGR-AM 1580 (Sports) 3215 Lemone Industrial Blvd Suite 200	Columbia	MO	65201	573-875-1099	875-2439
Web: www.ktgr.com					
KTXY-FM 106.9 (AC) 3215 Lemone Industrial Blvd Suite 200	Columbia	MO	65201	573-875-1099	875-2439
TF: 800-500-9107 ■ *Web:* www.y107.com					
KWOS-AM 950 (N/T) 3109 S Ten-Mile Dr	Jefferson City	MO	65109	573-893-5696	893-4137
Web: www.kwos.com					
KWRT-AM 1370 (Ctry) 1600 Radio Hill Rd	Boonville	MO	65233	660-882-6686	882-6688
TF: 800-887-6686					
KWWC-FM 90.5 (Jazz) PO Box 2114	Columbia	MO	65215	573-876-7297	876-2330
Web: www.stephens.edu/campuslife/kwwc					
KWWR-FM 95.7 (Ctry) 1705 E Liberty St	Mexico	MO	65265	573-581-5500	581-1801
TF: 800-264-5997 ■ *Web:* www.country96.com					

648-85 Johnson City, TN

				Phone	Fax
WAEZ-FM 94.9 (CHR) 901 E Valley Dr	Bristol	VA	24201	276-669-8112	669-0541
TF: 888-937-4487 ■ *Web:* www.electric949.com					
WCQR-FM 88.3 (Rel) 2312 Oak St	Gray	TN	37615	423-477-5676	477-7060
TF: 888-477-5676 ■ *Web:* www.wcqr.org					
WETB-AM 790 (Rel) 231 Brandonwood Dr PO Box 4127	Johnson City	TN	37602	423-928-7131	928-8392
WETS-FM 89.5 (NPR) 89 Drive East Tennessee State University	Johnson City	TN	37614	423-439-6440	439-6449
TF: 888-895-9387 ■ *Web:* www.wets.org					
WGOC-AM 1320 (Ctry) 162 Freehill	Gray	TN	37615	423-477-1000	477-4747
Web: www.wgoc.com					
WJCW-AM 910 (N/T) 162 Freehill	Gray	TN	37615	423-477-1000	477-4747
Web: www.wjcw.com					
WKOS-FM 104.9 (Oldies) 162 Freehill	Gray	TN	37615	423-477-1000	477-4747
Web: www.wkos.com					
WKPT-AM 1400 (Nost) 222 Commerce St	Kingsport	TN	37660	423-246-9578	247-9836
Web: www.wkptam.com					
WOCQ-FM 103.9 (CHR) 20200 DuPont Blvd	Georgetown	DE	19947	302-856-2567	856-7633
TF: 888-780-0970 ■ *Web:* www.oc104.com					

Johnson City, TN (Cont'd)

Station	City	State	ZIP	Phone	Fax
WQUT-FM 101.5 (CR) 162 Freehill Rd *Web:* www.wqut.com	Gray	TN	37615	423-477-1000	477-4747
WRZK-FM 95.9 (Alt) 222 Commerce St *Web:* www.wrzk.com	Kingsport	TN	37660	423-246-9578	247-9836
WTFM-FM 98.5 (AC) 222 Commerce St *Web:* www.wtfm.com	Kingsport	TN	37660	423-246-9578	247-9836
WTZR-FM 99.3 (Alt) 901 E Valley Dr *TF:* 866-770-7625 ■ *Web:* www.zrock993.com	Bristol	VA	24201	276-669-8112	669-0541
WXBQ-FM 96.9 (Ctry) 901 E Valley Dr *TF:* 800-332-3697 ■ *Web:* www.wxbq.com	Bristol	VA	24201	276-669-8112	669-0541
WXIS-FM 103.9 (Urban) 101 Riverview Rd *Web:* www.x104.com	Erwin	TN	37650	423-743-6123	743-6122

648-86 Juneau, AK

Station	City	State	ZIP	Phone	Fax
KINY-AM 800 (AC) 1107 W 8th St Suite 2 *Web:* www.kinyradio.com	Juneau	AK	99801	907-586-1800	586-3266
KJNO-AM 630 (N/T) 3161 Channel Dr Suite 2 *Web:* www.kjno.com	Juneau	AK	99801	907-586-3630	463-3685
KTKU-FM 105.1 (Ctry) 3161 Channel Dr Suite 2 *Web:* www.taku105.com	Juneau	AK	99801	907-586-3630	463-3685
KTOO-FM 104.3 (NPR) 360 Egan Dr *TF:* 800-870-5866 ■ *Web:* www.ktoo.org/index.cfm	Juneau	AK	99801	907-586-1670	586-3612

648-87 Kansas City, KS & MO

Station	City	State	ZIP	Phone	Fax
KBEQ-FM 104.3 (Ctry) 4717 Grand Ave Suite 600 *Web:* www.youngcountryq104.com	Kansas City	MO	64112	816-753-4000	753-4045
KCCV-AM 760 (Rel) 10550 Barkley St Suite 112 *Web:* www.bottradionetwork.com	Overland Park	KS	66212	913-642-7600	642-2424
KCFX-FM 101.1 (CR) 5800 Foxridge Dr 6th Fl *Web:* www.kcfx.com	Mission	KS	66202	913-514-3000	514-3004
KCHZ-FM 95.7 (CHR) 5800 Foxridge Dr Suite 600 *Web:* www.z957.net	Mission	KS	66202	913-514-3000	262-3946
KCJK-FM 105.1 (AC) 5800 Foxridge Dr 6th Fl *Web:* www.1051jackfm.com	Mission	KS	66202	913-514-3000	514-3002
KCKC-FM 102.1 (AC) 508 Westport Rd Suite 202 *Web:* www.star102.com	Kansas City	MO	64111	816-561-9102	531-6547
KCMO-AM 710 (N/T) 5800 Foxridge Dr 6th Fl *Web:* www.710kcmo.com	Mission	KS	66202	913-514-3000	514-3004
KCMO-FM 94.9 (Oldies) 5800 Foxridge Dr 6th Fl *Web:* www.oldies95.com	Mission	KS	66202	913-514-3000	514-3004
KCSP-AM 610 (Sports) 7000 Squibb Rd *Web:* www.61sports.com	Mission	KS	66202	913-744-3600	
KCTE-AM 1510 (N/T) 6721 W 121st St *Web:* www.1510.com	Overland Park	KS	66209	913-344-1500	344-1599
KCUR-FM 89.3 (NPR) 4825 Troost Ave Suite 202 *Web:* www.kcur.org	Kansas City	MO	64110	816-235-1551	235-2864
KCXL-AM 1140 (N/T) 310 S La Frenz Rd *Web:* www.kcxl.com	Liberty	MO	64068	816-792-1140	792-8258
KFKF-FM 94.1 (Ctry) 4717 Grand Ave Suite 600 *Web:* www.kfkf.com	Kansas City	MO	64112	816-753-4000	753-4045
KGGN-AM 890 (Rel) 1734 E 63rd St Suite 600 *TF:* 800-924-3177 ■ *Web:* www.kggnam.com	Kansas City	MO	64110	816-333-0092	363-8120
KKFI-FM 90.1 (Var) 900 1/2 Westport Rd 2nd Fl *Web:* www.kkfi.org	Kansas City	MO	64171	816-931-3122	931-7078
KLJC-FM 88.5 (Rel) 15800 Calvary Rd *TF:* 800-466-5552 ■ *Web:* www.kljc.org	Kansas City	MO	64147	816-331-8700	331-3497
KMBZ-AM 980 (N/T) 7000 Squibb Rd *Web:* www.kmbz.com	Mission	KS	66202	913-744-3600	677-8901
KMJK-FM 107.3 (Urban) 5800 Foxridge Dr Suite 600 *Fax Area Code: 913 ■ *Web:* www.magic1073.com	Mission	KS	66202	816-576-7107	514-3004*
KMXV-FM 93.3 (CHR) 508 Westport Rd Suite 202 *Web:* www.mix93.com	Kansas City	MO	64111	816-561-9102	531-6547
KPRS-FM 103.3 (Urban) 11131 Colorado Ave *Web:* www.kprs.com	Kansas City	MO	64137	816-763-2040	966-1055
KPRT-AM 1590 (Rel) 11131 Colorado Ave *Web:* www.kprt.com	Kansas City	MO	64137	816-763-2040	966-1055
KQRC-FM 98.9 (Rock) 7000 Squibb Rd *Web:* www.989therock.com	Mission	KS	66202	913-744-3600	
KRBZ-FM 96.5 (Alt) 7000 Squibb Rd *Web:* www.965thebuzz.com	Mission	KS	66202	913-744-3600	677-8981
KUDL-FM 98.1 (AC) 7000 Squibb Rd *Web:* www.kudl.com	Mission	KS	66202	913-744-3600	677-8981
KXTR-AM 1660 (Clas) 7000 Squibb Rd	Mission	KS	66202	913-744-3600	677-8980
KYYS-FM 99.7 (CR) 7000 Squibb Rd *Web:* www.kyys.com	Mission	KS	66202	913-744-3600	677-8901
WDAF-FM 106.5 (Ctry) 7000 Squibb Rd *Web:* www.wdaf.com	Mission	KS	66202	913-744-3600	677-8061
WHB-AM 810 (Sports) 6721 W 121st St *Web:* www.810whb.com	Overland Park	KS	66209	913-344-1500	344-1599

648-88 Key West, FL

Station	City	State	ZIP	Phone	Fax
WAIL-FM 99.5 (Rock) 5450 MacDonald Ave Suite 10 *Web:* www.wail995.com	Key West	FL	33040	305-296-7511	296-0358
WCNK-FM 98.7 (Ctry) 30336 Overseas Hwy *Web:* www.conchcountry.com	Big Pine Key	FL	33043	305-872-9100	872-1603
WEOW-FM 92.7 (CHR) 5450 MacDonald Ave Suite 10 *Web:* www.weow927.com	Key West	FL	33040	305-296-7511	296-0358
WIIS-FM 107.1 (Alt) 1075 Duval St Suite C17	Key West	FL	33040	305-292-1133	292-6936
WJIR-FM 90.9 (Rel) 1209 United St *Web:* www.sosradio.net	Key West	FL	33040	305-296-5773	294-9547
WKEY-FM 93.5 (AC) 5450 MacDonald Ave Suite 10 *Web:* www.key93.com	Key West	FL	33040	305-296-7511	296-0358
WKIZ-AM 1500 (Span) 5016 5th Ave *Web:* www.wkizradio.com	Key West	FL	33040	305-293-9536	293-1793
WKWF-AM 1600 (Sports) 5450 MacDonald Ave Suite 10 *Web:* www.sportsradio1600.com	Key West	FL	33040	305-296-7511	296-0358
WPIK-FM 102.5 (Span) PO Box 420249	Summerland Key	FL	33042	305-745-9988	745-4165
WWUS-FM 104.1 (CR) 30336 Overseas Hwy *Web:* www.us1radio.com	Big Pine Key	FL	33043	305-872-9100	872-1603

648-89 Knoxville, TN

Station	City	State	ZIP	Phone	Fax
WFIV-FM 105.3 (AAA) 517 Watt Rd *Web:* www.wfiv.com/	Knoxville	TN	37934	865-675-4105	675-4859
WIMZ-FM 103.5 (CR) 1100 Sharps Ridge Rd *Web:* www.wimz.com	Knoxville	TN	37917	865-525-6000	525-2000
WITA-AM 1490 (Rel) 7212 Kingston Pike *Web:* www.wwcr.com/wita.html	Knoxville	TN	37919	865-588-2974	588-6720
WIVK-FM 107.7 (Ctry) 4711 Old Kingston Pike *Web:* www.wivk.com	Knoxville	TN	37919	865-588-9900	588-4218
WJBZ-FM 96.3 (Rel) 7101 Chapman Hwy *Web:* www.praise963.com	Knoxville	TN	37920	865-577-4885	579-4667
WJXB-FM 97.5 (AC) 1100 Sharps Ridge Rd *Web:* www.b975.com	Knoxville	TN	37917	865-525-6000	525-2000
WKGN-AM 1340 (Urban) 1017 Cox St	Knoxville	TN	37919	865-546-7900	546-7965
WMYU-FM 93.1 (Oldies) 1533 Amherst Rd *Web:* www.cool931fm.com	Knoxville	TN	37909	865-824-1021	824-1880
WNFZ-FM 94.3 (Alt) 1100 Sharps Ridge Rd *Web:* www.943extremeradio.com	Knoxville	TN	37917	865-525-6000	525-2000
WNML-AM 990 (Sports) 4711 Old Kingston Pike *Fax: News Rm ■ *Web:* www.wild987.net	Knoxville	TN	37919	865-558-9900	558-4218*
WNML-FM 99.1 (Sports) 4711 Old Kingston Pike *Web:* www.wild987.net	Knoxville	TN	37919	865-588-6511	656-9453
WNOX-FM 100.3 (N/T) 4711 Old Kingston Pike *Fax: News Rm ■ *Web:* www.wnoxnewstalk.com	Knoxville	TN	37919	865-558-9900	558-4218*
WOKI-FM 98.7 (AAA) 4711 Old Kingston Pike *Web:* www.theriver987.com	Knoxville	TN	37919	865-588-9900	588-4218
WUOT-FM 91.9 (NPR) 209 Communications Bldg *Web:* sunsite.utk.edu/wuot	Knoxville	TN	37996	865-974-5375	974-3941
WWST-FM 102.1 (CHR) 1533 Amherst Rd *Web:* www.star1021fm.com	Knoxville	TN	37909	865-824-1021	824-1880

648-90 Lafayette, LA

Station	City	State	ZIP	Phone	Fax
KAJN-FM 102.9 (Rel) 110 W 3rd St *TF:* 800-364-7238 ■ *Web:* www.kajn.com	Crowley	LA	70526	337-783-1560	783-1674
KANE-AM 1240 (Cajun) 145-B W Main *Web:* www.kane1240.com	New Iberia	LA	70560	337-365-3434	365-9117
KBON-FM 101.1 (Cajun) 109 S 2nd St *Web:* www.kbon.com	Eunice	LA	70535	337-546-0007	546-0097
KFTE-FM 96.5 (Rock) 1749 Bertrand Dr *Web:* www.planet965.com	Lafayette	LA	70506	337-233-6000	234-7360
KJCB-AM 770 (Urban) 604 Saint John St	Lafayette	LA	70501	337-233-4262	235-9681
KMDL-FM 97.3 (Ctry) 1749 Bertrand Dr	Lafayette	LA	70506	337-233-6000	234-7360
KNEK-FM 104.7 (Urban) 202 Galbert Rd *TF:* 866-896-5635 ■ *Web:* www.knek.com	Lafayette	LA	70506	337-232-1311	233-3779
KPEL-AM 1420 (Sports) 1749 Bertrand Dr	Lafayette	LA	70506	337-233-6000	234-7360
KPEL-FM 105.1 (N/T) 1749 Bertrand Dr *Web:* www.kpel1051news.com	Lafayette	LA	70506	337-233-6000	234-7360
KQIS-FM 102.1 (AC) 320 N Parkerson Ave *Web:* www.kqis.com	Crowley	LA	70526	337-783-2520	783-5744
KRKA-FM 107.9 (Urban) 1749 Bertrand Dr *Web:* www.1079ishot.com	Lafayette	LA	70506	337-233-6000	234-7360
KRRQ-FM 95.5 (Urban) 202 Galbert Rd *Web:* www.krrq.com	Lafayette	LA	70506	337-232-1311	233-3779
KRVS-FM 88.7 (NPR) PO Box 42171 *TF:* 800-892-6827 ■ *Web:* www.krvs.org	Lafayette	LA	70504	337-482-5787	482-6101
KSIG-AM 1450 (Oldies) 320 N Parkerson Ave	Crowley	LA	70526	337-783-2520	783-5744
KSMB-FM 94.5 (CHR) 202 Galbert Rd *TF:* 800-299-2100 ■ *Web:* www.ksmb.com	Lafayette	LA	70506	337-232-1311	233-3779
KTDY-FM 99.9 (AC) 1749 Bertrand Dr *Web:* www.999ktdy.com	Lafayette	LA	70506	337-233-6000	234-7360
KVOL-AM 1330 (N/T) 3225 Ambassador Caffery Pkwy *Web:* www.kvol1330.com	Lafayette	LA	70506	337-993-5500	993-5510
KXKC-FM 99.1 (Ctry) 202 Galbert Rd *Web:* www.kxkc.com	Lafayette	LA	70506	337-232-1311	233-3779

648-91 Lansing, MI

Station	City	State	ZIP	Phone	Fax
WFMK-FM 99.1 (AC) 3420 Pine Tree Rd *Web:* www.99wfmk.com	Lansing	MI	48911	517-394-7272	394-3565
WHZZ-FM 101.7 (AC) 600 W Cavanaugh Rd *Web:* www.z1017fm.com	Lansing	MI	48909	517-393-1320	393-0882
WILS-AM 1320 (Nost) 600 W Cavanaugh Rd *Web:* www.1320wils.com	Lansing	MI	48909	517-393-1320	393-0882
WITL-FM 100.7 (Ctry) 3420 Pine Tree Rd *TF:* 800-968-7749 ■ *Web:* www.witl.com	Lansing	MI	48911	517-393-1010	394-3565
WJIM-AM 1240 (N/T) 3420 Pine Tree Rd *Fax: News Rm ■ *Web:* www.wjimam.com	Lansing	MI	48911	517-394-7272	394-3565*
WJIM-FM 97.5 (CHR) 3420 Pine Tree Rd *Web:* www.oldies975.com	Lansing	MI	48911	517-394-7272	394-3565
WJXQ-FM 106.1 (Rock) 2495 N Cedar St *Web:* www.q106fm.com	Holt	MI	48842	517-699-0111	699-1880
WKAR-AM 870 (NPR) Michigan State University 283 Communications Arts & Sciences Bldg *Web:* wkar.org	East Lansing	MI	48824	517-355-6540	353-7124
WKAR-FM 90.5 (NPR) Michigan State University 283 Communications Arts & Sciences Bldg *Web:* wkar.org	East Lansing	MI	48824	517-355-6540	353-7124
WLNZ-FM 89.7 (Var) 400 N Capitol Ave Suite 001 *Web:* www.lcc.edu/wlnz	Lansing	MI	48933	517-483-1710	483-1894
WMMQ-FM 94.9 (CR) 3420 Pine Tree Rd *Web:* www.wmmq.com	Lansing	MI	48911	517-393-1010	394-3565
WQHH-FM 96.5 (Urban) 1011 Northcrest Rd Suite 4 *Web:* www.power965fm.com	Lansing	MI	48906	517-393-1320	484-9699
WQTX-FM 92.1 (Oldies) 2495 N Cedar St *Web:* www.wqtx.net	Holt	MI	48842	517-699-0111	699-1880
WVFN-AM 730 (Sports) 3420 Pine Tree Rd *Web:* www.730amthefan.com	Lansing	MI	48911	517-394-7272	394-3565

648-92 Las Vegas, NV

Station	City	State	ZIP	Phone	Fax
KCEP-FM 88.1 (Urban) 330 W Washington Ave *Web:* www.power88lv.com	Las Vegas	NV	89106	702-648-4218	647-0803
KCYE-FM 104.3 (Ctry) 1455 E Tropicana Ave Suite 800	Las Vegas	NV	89119	702-730-0300	736-8447
KDWN-AM 720 (N/T) 1455 E Tropicana Ave Suite 800 *Web:* www.kdwn.com	Las Vegas	NV	89119	702-385-7212	736-8447

Station	City	State	Zip	Phone	Fax
KENO-AM 1460 (Sports) 8755 W Flamingo Rd *Web:* foxsportsradio1460.com	Las Vegas	NV	89147	702-876-1460	876-6685
KISF-FM 103.5 (Span) 6767 W Tropicana Ave Suite 102 *Web:* kisf.netmio.com	Las Vegas	NV	89103	702-367-3322	284-6403
KKJJ-FM 100.5 (AC) 6655 W Sahara Ave Suite C216 *Web:* www.jackbaby.com	Las Vegas	NV	89146	702-889-5100	257-2936
KKLZ-FM 96.3 (CR) 1455 E Tropicana Ave Suite 800 *Web:* www.963kklz.com	Las Vegas	NV	89119	702-730-0300	736-8447
KKVV-AM 1060 (Rel) 3185 S Highland Dr Suite 13 *Web:* www.kkvv.com	Las Vegas	NV	89109	702-731-5588	731-5851
KLUC-FM 98.5 (CHR) 6655 W Sahara Ave Suite D208 *Web:* www.kluc.com	Las Vegas	NV	89146	702-253-9800	889-7373
KMXB-FM 94.1 (AC) 6655 W Sahara Ave Suite C216 *Web:* www.mix941.fm	Las Vegas	NV	89146	702-889-5100	257-2936
KNPR-FM 89.5 (NPR) 1289 S Torrey Pines Dr *TF:* 888-895-9895 ■ *Web:* www.knpr.org	Las Vegas	NV	89146	702-258-9895	258-5646
KNUU-AM 970 (N/T) 1455 E Tropicana Ave Suite 550 *Web:* 970knuu.com	Las Vegas	NV	89119	702-735-8644	734-4755
KOAS-FM 105.7 (NAC) 2725 E Desert Inn Rd Suite 180 *Web:* www.smoothjazz1057.com	Las Vegas	NV	89121	702-784-4000	784-4040
KOMP-FM 92.3 (Rock) 8755 W Flamingo Rd *Web:* www.komp.com	Las Vegas	NV	89147	702-876-1460	876-6685
KPLV-FM 93.1 (AC) 2880 Meade Ave Suite 250 *Web:* www.931theparty.com	Las Vegas	NV	89102	702-238-7300	732-4890
KQRT-FM 105.1 (Span N/T) 500 Pilot Rd Suite D	Las Vegas	NV	89119	702-597-3070	507-1084
KSNE-FM 106.5 (AC) 2880 Meade Ave Suite 250 *Web:* www.ksne.com	Las Vegas	NV	89102	702-238-7300	732-4890
KSTJ-FM 102.7 (Oldies) 1455 E Tropicana Ave Suite 800 *Web:* www.star1027fm.com	Las Vegas	NV	89119	702-730-0300	736-8447
KUNV-FM 91.5 (Jazz) 1515 E Tropicana Ave Suite 240 *Web:* kunv.unlv.edu	Las Vegas	NV	89119	702-798-9169	736-0983
KVEG-FM 97.5 (Urban) 3999 Las Vegas Blvd S Suite K *Web:* www.kvegas.com	Las Vegas	NV	89119	702-736-6161	736-2986
KWID-FM 101.9 (Span) 2880 Meade Ave Suite 250 *Web:* www.lapreciosa.com	Las Vegas	NV	89102	702-238-7300	732-4890
KWNR-FM 95.5 (Ctry) 2880 Meade Ave Suite 250 *Web:* www.kwnr.com	Las Vegas	NV	89102	702-238-7300	732-4890
KXNT-AM 840 (N/T) 6655 W Sahara Ave Suite D-110 *Web:* www.kxnt.com	Las Vegas	NV	89146	702-889-7300	889-7384
KXPT-FM 97.1 (CR) 8755 W Flamingo Rd *Web:* www.point97.com	Las Vegas	NV	89147	702-876-1460	876-6685
KXTE-FM 107.5 (Alt) 6655 W Sahara Ave Suite D-110 *Web:* www.xtremeradio.com	Las Vegas	NV	89146	702-257-1075	889-7575

648-93 Lexington/Frankfort, KY

Station	City	State	Zip	Phone	Fax
WBTF-FM 107.9 (Urban) 401 W Main St Suite 301	Lexington	KY	40507	859-233-1515	233-4248
WBUL-FM 98.1 (Ctry) 2601 Nicholasville Rd *Web:* www.wbul.com	Lexington	KY	40503	859-422-1000	422-1038
WEKU-FM 88.9 (Clas) 521 Lancaster Ave 102 Perkins Bldg-EKU *TF:* 800-621-8890	Richmond	KY	40475	859-622-1660	622-6276
WFKY-AM 1490 (Oldies) 115 W Main St	Frankfort	KY	40601	502-875-1130	875-1225
WGKS-FM 96.9 (AC) 401 W Main St Suite 301 *Web:* www.wgks.com	Lexington	KY	40507	859-233-1515	233-1517
WKED-AM 1130 (Nost) 115 W Main St	Frankfort	KY	40601	502-875-1130	875-1225
WKED-FM 103.7 (AC) 115 W Main St	Frankfort	KY	40601	502-875-1130	875-1225
WKQQ-FM 100.1 (Rock) 2601 Nicholasville Rd *Web:* www.wkqq.com	Lexington	KY	40503	859-422-1000	422-1038
WKYL-FM 102.1 (NAC) 88 C Michael Davenport Blvd	Frankfort	KY	40601	502-839-1021	
WKYW-FM 104.9 (Ctry) 115 W Main St	Frankfort	KY	40601	502-875-1130	875-1225
WLAP-AM 630 (N/T) 2601 Nicholasville Rd *Web:* www.wlap.com	Lexington	KY	40503	859-422-1000	422-1038
WLKT-FM 104.5 (CHR) 2601 Nicholasville Rd *Web:* www.wlkt.com	Lexington	KY	40503	859-422-1000	422-1038
WLXX-FM 92.9 (Ctry) 300 W Vine St *TF:* 877-777-9929 ■ *Web:* wlxxthebear.com	Lexington	KY	40507	859-253-5900	253-5940
WMKJ-FM 105.5 (Oldies) 2601 Nicholasville Rd *Web:* www.magic1055.com	Lexington	KY	40503	859-422-1000	422-1038
WMXL-FM 94.5 (AC) 2601 Nicholasville Rd *Web:* www.wmxl.com	Lexington	KY	40503	859-422-1000	422-1038
WUKY-FM 91.3 (NPR) 340 McVey Hall University of Kentucky *Web:* wuky.uky.edu	Lexington	KY	40506	859-257-3221	257-6291
WVLK-AM 590 (N/T) 300 W Vine St *TF:* 877-777-0590 ■ *Web:* www.wvlkam.com	Lexington	KY	40507	859-253-5900	253-5940
WVRB-FM 95.3 (Rel) 700 Lemons Mill Rd *TF:* 888-937-2471 ■ *Web:* www.air1.com	Georgetown	KY	40324	502-868-8879	868-9979
WXZZ-FM 103.3 (Rock) 300 W Vine St *TF:* 877-777-1033 ■ *Web:* www.zrock103.com	Lexington	KY	40507	859-253-5900	253-5940

648-94 Lincoln, NE

Station	City	State	Zip	Phone	Fax
KBBK-FM 107.3 (AC) 4343 'O' St *Web:* www.b1073.com	Lincoln	NE	68510	402-475-4567	479-1411
KFGE-FM 98.1 (Ctry) 4343 'O' St *Web:* www.froggy981.com	Lincoln	NE	68510	402-475-4567	479-1411
KFOR-AM 1240 (N/T) 3800 Cornhusker Hwy *Web:* www.kfor1240.com	Lincoln	NE	68504	402-466-1234	467-4095
KFRX-FM 106.3 (CHR) 3800 Cornhusker Hwy *Web:* www.kfrxfm.com	Lincoln	NE	68504	402-466-1234	467-4095
KIBZ-FM 104.1 (Rock) 3800 Cornhusker Hwy *Web:* www.kibz.com	Lincoln	NE	68504	402-466-1234	467-4095
KLIN-AM 1400 (N/T) 4343 'O' St *Web:* www.klin.com	Lincoln	NE	68510	402-475-4567	479-1411
KLNC-FM 105.3 (CR) 4343 'O' St *Web:* lincfm.com	Lincoln	NE	68510	402-475-4567	479-1411
KTGL-FM 92.9 (CR) 3800 Cornhusker Hwy *Web:* www.ktgl.com	Lincoln	NE	68504	402-466-1234	467-4095
KUCV-FM 91.1 (Var) 1800 N 33rd St *TF:* 888-638-7346 ■ *Web:* www.nprn.org	Lincoln	NE	68583	402-472-2200	472-2403
KZKX-FM 96.9 (Ctry) 3800 Cornhusker Hwy *Web:* www.kzkx.com	Lincoln	NE	68504	402-466-1234	467-4095

648-95 Little Rock, AR

Station	City	State	Zip	Phone	Fax
KABF-FM 88.3 (Var) 2101 S Main St Suite 200 *Web:* www.kabf.org	Little Rock	AR	72206	501-372-6119	375-5965
KABZ-FM 103.7 (N/T) 2400 Cottondale Ln *TF:* 800-477-1037 ■ *Web:* www.1037thebuzz.com	Little Rock	AR	72202	501-664-9410	664-5871
KARN-AM 920 (N/T) 700 Wellington Hills Rd *Web:* www.920karn.com	Little Rock	AR	72211	501-401-0200	401-0366
KHLR-FM 94.9 (Rel) 10800 Colonel Glenn Rd *Web:* www.949hallelujah.com	Little Rock	AR	72204	501-217-5000	228-9547
KHTE-FM 96.5 (CHR) 400 Hardin Rd Suite 150 *Web:* www.hot965.com	Little Rock	AR	72211	501-219-1919	225-4610
KIPR-FM 92.3 (Urban) 700 Wellington Hills Rd *Web:* www.power923.com	Little Rock	AR	72211	501-401-0200	401-0366
KKPT-FM 94.1 (CR) 2400 Cottondale Ln *TF:* 800-844-0094 ■ *Web:* www.kkpt.com	Little Rock	AR	72202	501-664-9410	664-5871
KLAL-FM 107.7 (CHR) 700 Wellington Hills Rd *Web:* www.alice1077.com	Little Rock	AR	72211	501-401-0200	401-0366
KMJX-FM 105.1 (CR) 10800 Colonel Glenn Rd *Web:* www.magic105fm.com	Little Rock	AR	72204	501-217-5000	228-9547
KOKY-FM 102.1 (Urban) 700 Wellington Hills Rd *Web:* www.koky.com	Little Rock	AR	72211	501-401-0200	401-0366
KSSN-FM 95.7 (Ctry) 10800 Colonel Glenn Rd *Web:* www.kssn.com	Little Rock	AR	72204	501-217-5000	228-9547
KTUV-AM 1440 (Span) 723 W Daisy Bates Dr *Web:* www.potencialatina.net	Little Rock	AR	72202	501-375-1440	375-0947
KUAR-FM 89.1 (NPR) 2801 S University Ave *TF:* 800-952-2528 ■ *Web:* www.ualr.edu/~kuar	Little Rock	AR	72204	501-569-8485	569-8488
KURB-FM 98.5 (AC) 700 Wellington Hills Rd *Web:* www.b98.com	Little Rock	AR	72211	501-401-0200	401-0366
KWBF-FM 101.1 (Oldies) 1 Shackleford Dr Suite 400	Little Rock	AR	72211	501-219-2400	604-8004
KYFX-FM 99.5 (Urban) 415 N McKinley St Suite 280-T *Web:* www.kyfx.com	Little Rock	AR	72205	501-666-9499	821-8823

648-96 Los Angeles, CA

Station	City	State	Zip	Phone	Fax
KABC-AM 790 (N/T) 3321 S La Cienega Blvd *Web:* www.kabc.com	Los Angeles	CA	90016	310-840-4900	838-5222
KBIG-FM 104.3 (AC) 3400 W Olive Ave Suite 550 *TF:* 866-544-6036 ■ *Web:* www.kbig104.com	Burbank	CA	91505	818-559-2252	955-8151
KBUE-FM 105.5 (Span) 1845 Empire Ave *Web:* www.aquisuena.com	Burbank	CA	91504	818-729-5300	729-5678
KCBS-FM 93.1 (Var) 5901 Venice Blvd *Web:* www.931jackfm.com	Los Angeles	CA	90034	323-937-9331	931-5198
KCRW-FM 89.9 (NPR) 1900 Pico Blvd *TF:* 888-600-5279 ■ *Web:* www.kcrw.com	Santa Monica	CA	90405	310-450-5183	450-7172
KFI-AM 640 (N/T) 3400 W Olive Ave Suite 550 *Web:* www.kfi640.com	Burbank	CA	91505	818-559-2252	729-2514
KFSH-FM 95.9 (Rel) 701 N Brand Blvd Suite 550 *TF:* 866-347-4959 ■ *Web:* www.thefish959.com	Glendale	CA	91203	818-956-5552	551-1110
KFWB-AM 980 (N/T) 5670 Wilshire Blvd Suite 200 *Web:* www.kfwb.com	Los Angeles	CA	90036	323-525-0980	464-6101
KHHT-FM 92.3 (Urban) 3400 W Olive Blvd Suite 550 *Web:* www.hot923.com	Burbank	CA	91505	818-559-2252	955-8178
KIIS-FM 102.7 (CHR) 3400 W Olive Ave Suite 550 *Web:* www.kiisfm.com	Burbank	CA	91505	818-559-2252	729-2502
KJLH-FM 102.3 (Urban) 161 N La Brea Ave *Web:* www.kjlhradio.com	Inglewood	CA	90301	310-330-5550	330-5555
KKGO-FM 105.1 (Ctry) PO Box 250028 *Web:* www.gocountry105.com	Los Angeles	CA	90025	310-478-5540	445-1439
KKJZ-FM 88.1 (Jazz) 1288 N Bellflower Blvd *TF:* 800-767-3688 ■ *Web:* www.jazzandblues.org	Long Beach	CA	90815	562-985-5566	985-2982
KLAC-AM 570 (Sports) 3400 W Olive Ave Suite 550 *Web:* www.570klac.com	Burbank	CA	91505	818-559-2252	260-9961
KLAX-FM 97.9 (Span) 10281 W Pico Blvd *Web:* www.979laraza.com	Los Angeles	CA	90064	310-203-0900	203-8989
KLOS-FM 95.5 (CR) 3321 S La Cienega Blvd *TF:* 800-955-5567 ■ *Web:* www.955klos.com	Los Angeles	CA	90016	310-840-4900	838-5222
KLSX-FM 97.1 (N/T) 5670 Wilshire Blvd Suite 200 *Web:* 971freefm.com	Los Angeles	CA	90036	323-971-9710	954-0971
KLVE-FM 107.5 (Span AC) 655 N Central Ave Suite 2500	Glendale	CA	91203	818-500-4500	500-4540
KLYY-FM 97.5 (Span) 5700 Wilshire Blvd Suite 250	Los Angeles	CA	90036	323-900-6100	900-6200
KNX-AM 1070 (N/T) 5670 Wilshire Blvd Suite 200 *Web:* www.knx1070.com	Los Angeles	CA	90036	323-964-8351	964-8398
KOST-FM 103.5 (AC) 3400 W Olive Ave Suite 550 *Web:* www.kost1035.com	Burbank	CA	91505	818-559-2252	260-9961
KPCC-FM 89.3 (NPR) 1570 E Colorado Blvd *Web:* www.scpr.org	Pasadena	CA	91106	626-585-7000	585-7916
KPWR-FM 105.9 (CHR) 2600 W Olive Ave Suite 850 *Web:* www.power106.fm	Burbank	CA	91505	818-953-4200	848-0961
KRBV-FM 100.3 (Rock) 5900 Wilshire Blvd Suite 1900 *Web:* www.thesoundla.com	Los Angeles	CA	90036	323-634-1800	634-1888
KRCD-FM 103.9 (Span) 655 N Central Ave Suite 2500 *Web:* krcd.netmio.com	Glendale	CA	91203	818-500-4500	500-4329
KROQ-FM 106.7 (Alt) 5901 Venice Blvd *TF:* 800-520-1067 ■ *Web:* www.kroq.com	Los Angeles	CA	90034	323-930-1067	931-1067
KRTH-FM 101.1 (Oldies) 5670 Wilshire Blvd Suite 200 *TF:* 800-232-5834 ■ *Web:* www.mykearth101.com	Los Angeles	CA	90036	323-936-5784	933-6072
KSCA-FM 101.9 (Span) 655 N Central Ave Suite 2500 *Web:* lanueva1019.netmio.com	Glendale	CA	91203	818-500-4500	500-4440
KSPN-AM 1110 (Sports) 3321 S La Cienega Blvd	Los Angeles	CA	90016	310-840-4900	558-5691
KSSE-FM 107.1 (Span) 5700 Wilshire Blvd Suite 250 *Web:* www.superestrella.com	Los Angeles	CA	90036	323-900-6100	900-6200
KTLK-AM 1150 (N/T) 3400 W Olive Ave Suite 550 *TF:* 866-987-8570 ■ *Web:* www.ktlk.com	Burbank	CA	91505	818-559-2252	
KTWV-FM 94.7 (NAC) 5670 Wilshire Blvd Suite 200 *TF:* 800-520-9283 ■ *Web:* www.947wave.com	Los Angeles	CA	90036	323-937-9283	549-9283
KUSC-FM 91.5 (Clas) PO Box 77913 *Web:* www.kusc.org	Los Angeles	CA	90007	213-225-7400	225-7410
KWIZ-FM 96.7 (Span) 3101 W 5th St	Santa Ana	CA	92703	714-554-5000	554-9362
KXOL-FM 96.3 (Span AC) 10281 W Pico Blvd *TF:* 877-963-0963 ■ *Web:* latino963.lamusica.com	Los Angeles	CA	90064	310-203-0900	203-8989
KYSR-FM 98.7 (AC) 3400 W Olive Ave Suite 550 *Web:* www.star987.com	Burbank	CA	91505	818-559-2252	955-8178
KZLA-FM 93.9 (AC) 2600 W Olive Ave 8th Fl *Web:* www.movin939.com	Burbank	CA	91505	818-525-5000	848-0961

648-97 Louisville, KY

Station	City	State	Zip	Phone	Fax
WAMZ-FM 97.5 (Ctry) 4000 One Radio Dr *Web:* www.wamz.com	Louisville	KY	40218	502-479-2222	479-2223
WAVG-AM 1450 (Sports) 9900 Corporate Campus Dr Suite 2600	Louisville	KY	40223	502-992-0939	992-0862
WDJX-FM 99.7 (CHR) 520 S 4th Ave 2nd Fl *Web:* www.wdjx.com	Louisville	KY	40202	502-625-1220	625-1253
WFIA-AM 900 (Rel) 9960 Corporate Campus Dr Suite 3600 *Web:* www.wfia-fm.com	Louisville	KY	40223	502-339-9470	423-3139
WFPK-FM 91.9 (AAA) 619 S 4th St *Web:* www.wfpk.org	Louisville	KY	40202	502-814-6500	814-6599

Louisville, KY (Cont'd)

Station	City	State	Zip	Phone	Fax
WFPL-FM 89.3 (NPR) 619 S 4th St *Web:* www.wfpl.org	Louisville	KY	40202	502-814-6500	814-6599
WGZB-FM 96.5 (Urban) 520 S 4th Ave 2nd Fl *Web:* www.b96jams.com	Louisville	KY	40202	502-625-1220	625-1253
WHAS-AM 840 (N/T) 4000 One Radio Dr *TF:* 800-444-8484 ■ *Web:* www.whas.com	Louisville	KY	40218	502-479-2222	479-2308
WLOU-AM 1350 (Rel) 2001 W Broadway Suite 13 *Web:* www.wlouam.com	Louisville	KY	40203	502-776-1240	776-1250
WLRS-FM 105.1 (Alt) 520 S 4th Ave 2nd Fl *Web:* www.wlrs.com	Louisville	KY	40202	502-625-1220	625-1253
WLUE-FM 100.5 (Var) 4000 One Radio Dr *Web:* www.louieonline.com	Louisville	KY	40218	502-479-2222	479-2227
WMJM-FM 101.3 (Oldies) 520 S 4th Ave 2nd Fl *Web:* www.1013online.com	Louisville	KY	40202	502-625-1220	625-1253
WMPI-FM 105.3 (Ctry) 22 E McClain Ave *TF:* 800-441-1053 ■ *Web:* www.i1053online.com	Scottsburg	IN	47170	812-752-3688	752-2345
WPTI-FM 103.9 (Ctry) 612 S 4th Ave Suite 100 *Web:* newcountry1039.com	Louisville	KY	40202	502-589-4800	583-4820
WQMF-FM 95.7 (CR) 4000 One Radio Dr *Web:* www.wqmf.com	Louisville	KY	40218	502-479-2222	479-2227
WRKA-FM 103.1 (Oldies) 612 S 4th Ave Suite 100 *Web:* wrka.com	Louisville	KY	40202	502-589-4800	583-4820
WRVI-FM 105.9 (Rel) 9960 Corporate Campus Dr Suite 3600 *Web:* www.salemradiogroup.com	Louisville	KY	40223	502-339-9470	423-3139
WSFR-FM 107.7 (CR) 612 S 4th Ave Suite 100 *Web:* 1077sfr.com	Louisville	KY	40202	502-589-4800	583-4820
WTFX-FM 93.1 (Rock) 4000 One Radio Dr	Louisville	KY	40218	502-479-2222	479-2227
WTMT-AM 620 (Span) 4109 Bardstown Rd Suite 104 *Web:* www.wtmt.com	Louisville	KY	40218	502-671-8407	671-8743
WVEZ-FM 106.9 (AC) 612 S 4th Ave Suite 100 *TF:* 866-566-2456 ■ *Web:* lite1069.com	Louisville	KY	40202	502-589-4800	583-4820
WXMA-FM 102.3 (AC) 520 S 4th Ave 2nd Fl *Web:* www.themaxfm.com	Louisville	KY	40202	502-625-1220	625-1255

648-98 Lubbock, TX

Station	City	State	Zip	Phone	Fax
KFMX-FM 94.5 (Rock) 4413 82nd St Suite 300 *Web:* www.kfmx.com	Lubbock	TX	79424	806-798-7078	798-7052
KFYO-AM 790 (N/T) 4413 82nd St Suite 300 *Web:* www.kfyo.com	Lubbock	TX	79424	806-798-7078	798-7052
KKAM-AM 1340 (Sports) 4413 82nd St Suite 300 *Web:* www.kkam.com	Lubbock	TX	79424	806-798-7078	798-7052
KKCL-FM 98.1 (Oldies) 4413 82nd St Suite 300 *Web:* www.98kool.com	Lubbock	TX	79424	806-798-7078	798-7052
KLLL-FM 96.3 (Ctry) 33 Briercroft Office Park *Web:* www.klll.com	Lubbock	TX	79412	806-762-3000	770-5363
KLZK-FM 104.3 (CHR) 9800 University Ave	Lubbock	TX	79423	806-745-3434	748-1949
KMMX-FM 100.3 (AC) 33 Briercroft Office Park *Web:* www.kmmx.com	Lubbock	TX	79412	806-762-3000	770-5363
KOHM-FM 89.1 (NPR) 1901 University Ave Suite 603 B *Web:* www.kohm.org	Lubbock	TX	79410	806-742-3100	742-3716
KONE-FM 101.1 (Rock) 33 Briercroft Office Park *Web:* www.rock101.fm	Lubbock	TX	79412	806-762-3000	770-5363
KQBR-FM 99.5 (Ctry) 4413 82nd St Suite 300 *Web:* www.kqbr.com	Lubbock	TX	79424	806-798-7078	798-7052
KRBL-FM 105.7 (Ctry) 916 Main St Suite 617 *Web:* www.krbl.net	Lubbock	TX	79401	806-749-1057	749-1177
KRFE-AM 580 (Nost) 6602 ML King Blvd *Web:* www.krfeam580.com	Lubbock	TX	79404	806-745-1197	745-1088
KZII-FM 102.5 (CHR) 4413 82nd St Suite 300 *Web:* www.z102.com	Lubbock	TX	79424	806-798-7078	798-7052

648-99 Macon, GA

Station	City	State	Zip	Phone	Fax
WAYS-FM 105.5 (Sports) 544 Mulberry St 5th Fl	Macon	GA	31201	478-746-6286	749-1393
WDDO-AM 1240 (Rel) 544 Mulberry St 5th Fl	Macon	GA	31201	478-746-6286	749-1393
WDEN-FM 99.1 (Ctry) 544 Mulberry St 7th Fl *Web:* www.wden.com	Macon	GA	31201	478-746-6286	749-1393
WEBL-FM 102.5 (Ctry) 7080 Industrial Hwy *Web:* www.bull1025.com	Macon	GA	31216	478-781-1063	781-6711
WFXM-FM 107.1 (Urban) 6174 Hwy 57	Macon	GA	31217	478-745-3301	742-2293
WIBB-FM 97.9 (Urban) 7080 Industrial Hwy *Web:* www.wibb.com	Macon	GA	31216	478-781-1063	781-6711
WLCG-AM 1280 (Rel) 7080 Industrial Hwy	Macon	GA	31216	478-781-1063	781-6711
WLZN-FM 92.3 (Urban) 544 Mulberry St Suite 700	Macon	GA	31201	478-746-6286	749-1393
WMAC-AM 940 (N/T) 544 Mulberry St Suite 500 *Web:* www.wmac-am.com	Macon	GA	31201	478-746-6286	749-1393
WMGB-FM 95.1 (CHR) 544 Mulberry St 5th Fl *Web:* www.allthehitsb951.com	Macon	GA	31201	478-746-6286	749-1393
WPEZ-FM 93.7 (AC) 544 Mulberry St 5th Fl *Web:* www.z937.com	Macon	GA	31201	478-746-6286	749-1393
WPGA-FM 100.9 (AC) 1691 Forsyth St *TF:* 800-247-4487	Macon	GA	31201	478-745-5858	745-5800
WQBZ-FM 106.3 (Rock) 7080 Industrial Hwy *Web:* www.q106.fm	Macon	GA	31216	478-781-1063	781-6711
WRBV-FM 101.7 (Urban AC) 7080 Industrial Hwy	Macon	GA	31216	478-781-1063	781-6711

648-100 Madison, WI

Station	City	State	Zip	Phone	Fax
WCHY-FM 105.1 (Var) 7601 Ganser Way *Web:* www.1051charliefm.com	Madison	WI	53719	608-826-0077	826-1244
WERN-FM 88.7 (NPR) 821 University Ave *TF:* 800-747-7444 ■ *Web:* www.wpr.org	Madison	WI	53706	608-263-2121	263-9763
WHA-AM 970 (NPR) 821 University Ave *TF:* 800-747-7444 ■ *Web:* www.wpr.org	Madison	WI	53706	608-263-2121	263-9763
WIBA-AM 1310 (N/T) 2651 S Fish Hatchery Rd *Web:* www.wiba.com	Madison	WI	53711	608-274-5450	274-5521
WIBA-FM 101.5 (CR) 2651 S Fish Hatchery Rd *Web:* www.wibafm.com	Madison	WI	53711	608-274-5450	274-5521
WJJO-FM 94.1 (Rock) 730 Rayovac Dr *Web:* www.wjjo.com	Madison	WI	53711	608-273-1000	271-8182
WMAD-FM 96.3 (Ctry) 2651 S Fish Hatchery Rd *Web:* www.wmad.com	Madison	WI	53711	608-274-5450	274-5521
WMGN-FM 98.1 (AC) 730 Rayovac Dr *Web:* www.magic98.com	Madison	WI	53711	608-273-1000	271-8182
WMMM-FM 105.5 (AAA) 7601 Ganser Way *Web:* www.1055triplem.com	Madison	WI	53719	608-826-0077	826-1244
WOLX-FM 94.9 (Oldies) 7601 Ganser Way *Web:* www.wolx.com	Madison	WI	53719	608-826-0077	826-1244
WTSO-AM 1070 (Sports) 2651 S Fish Hatchery Rd *Web:* www.espn1070.com	Madison	WI	53711	608-274-5450	274-5521
WTUX-AM 1550 (Nost) 730 Rayovac Dr *Web:* www.wtux.com	Madison	WI	53711	608-273-1000	271-8182
WWQM-FM 106.3 (Ctry) 730 Rayovac Dr *Web:* www.q106.com	Madison	WI	53711	608-273-1000	271-8182
WXXM-FM 92.1 (N/T) 2651 S Fish Hatchery Rd	Madison	WI	53711	608-274-5450	274-5521
WZEE-FM 104.1 (CHR) 2651 S Fish Hatchery Rd *Web:* www.z104fm.com	Madison	WI	53711	608-274-5450	274-5521

648-101 Manchester, NH

Station	City	State	Zip	Phone	Fax
WEVO-FM 89.1 (N/T) 207 N Main St *TF:* 800-262-1816 ■ *Web:* www.nhpr.org	Concord	NH	03301	603-228-8910	224-6052
WFEA-AM 1370 (Nost) 500 Commercial St *Web:* www.wfea1370.com	Manchester	NH	03101	603-669-5777	669-4641
WGIR-AM 610 (N/T) 195 McGregor St Suite 810 *Web:* www.wgiram.com	Manchester	NH	03102	603-625-6915	625-9255
WGIR-FM 101.1 (Rock) 195 McGregor St Suite 810 *Web:* www.rock101wgir.com	Manchester	NH	03102	603-625-6915	625-9255
WJYY-FM 105.5 (CHR) 11 Kimball Dr Unit 114 *TF:* 800-228-9664 ■ *Web:* www.wjyy.com	Hooksett	NH	03106	603-225-1160	225-5938
WMLL-FM 96.5 (CR) 500 Commercial St *Web:* www.themill965.com	Manchester	NH	03101	603-669-5777	669-4641
WNNH-FM 99.1 (Oldies) 11 Kimball Dr Unit 114 *TF:* 800-228-9664 ■ *Web:* www.wnnh.com	Hooksett	NH	03106	603-225-1160	225-5938
WOKQ-FM 97.5 (Ctry) 292 Middle Rd PO Box 576 *Web:* www.wokq.com	Dover	NH	03821	603-749-9750	749-1459
WTPL-FM 107.7 (N/T) 501 South St *Web:* www.wtplfm.com	Bow	NH	03304	603-545-0777	545-0781
WZID-FM 95.7 (AC) 500 Commercial St *Web:* www.wzid.com	Manchester	NH	03101	603-669-5777	669-4641

648-102 Memphis, TN

Station	City	State	Zip	Phone	Fax
KJMS-FM 101.1 (Urban) 2650 Thousand Oaks Blvd Suite 4100 *Web:* www.smooth101.com	Memphis	TN	38118	901-259-1300	259-6449
KWAM-AM 990 (N/T) 5495 Murray Rd *Web:* www.am990.com	Memphis	TN	38119	901-261-4200	261-4210
KXHT-FM 107.1 (CHR) 6080 Mt Moriah Rd Ext *Web:* www.hot1071.com	Memphis	TN	38115	901-375-9324	375-0041
WBBP-AM 1480 (Rel) 369 GE Patterson Ave *Web:* www.wbbp.org	Memphis	TN	38126	901-278-7878	332-1707
WCRV-AM 640 (Rel) 6401 Poplar Ave Suite 640 *TF:* 800-480-9278 ■ *Web:* www.bottradionetwork.com	Memphis	TN	38119	901-763-4640	763-4920
WDIA-AM 1070 (Urban) 2650 Thousand Oaks Blvd Suite 4100 *Web:* www.am1070wdia.com	Memphis	TN	38118	901-259-1300	259-6449
WEGR-FM 102.7 (CR) 2650 Thousand Oaks Blvd Suite 4100 *Web:* www.rock103.com	Memphis	TN	38118	901-259-1300	259-6449
WGKX-FM 105.9 (Ctry) 5629 Murray Rd *Web:* www.kix106.com	Memphis	TN	38119	901-680-9898	767-9531
WHAL-FM 95.7 (Rel) 2650 Thousand Oaks Blvd Suite 4100 *Web:* www.memphisoldies.com	Memphis	TN	38118	901-259-1300	259-6449
WHBQ-AM 560 (Sports) 6080 Mt Moriah Rd Ext *Web:* www.sports56whbq.com	Memphis	TN	38115	901-375-9324	375-0041
WHRK-FM 97.1 (Urban) 2650 Thousand Oaks Blvd Suite 4100 *Web:* www.k97fm.com	Memphis	TN	38118	901-259-1300	259-6449
WKIM-FM 98.9 (AC) 5629 Murray Rd *Web:* www.989kimfm.com	Memphis	TN	38119	901-680-9898	767-9531
WKNO-FM 91.1 (NPR) 900 Getwell Rd *TF:* 800-766-9566 ■ *Web:* www.wknofm.org	Memphis	TN	38124	901-325-6544	325-6506
WLOK-AM 1340 (Rel) 363 S 2nd St *Web:* www.wlok.com	Memphis	TN	38103	901-527-9565	528-0335
WMC-FM 99.7 (AC) 1960 Union Ave *Web:* www.fm100memphis.com	Memphis	TN	38104	901-726-0555	726-9580
WMFS-FM 92.9 (Alt) 1960 Union Ave *Web:* www.93xmemphis.com	Memphis	TN	38104	901-726-0555	726-9580
WRBO-FM 103.5 (Oldies) 5629 Murray Rd *Web:* www.soulclassics.com	Memphis	TN	38119	901-680-9898	767-9531
WREC-AM 600 (N/T) 2650 Thousand Oaks Blvd Suite 4100 *Web:* www.wrecradio.com	Memphis	TN	38118	901-259-1300	259-6449
WRVR-FM 104.5 (AC) 5904 Ridgeway Center Pkwy *Web:* www.wrvr.com	Memphis	TN	38120	901-767-0104	767-0582
WSMB-AM 680 (Sports) 5904 Ridgeway Center Pkwy	Memphis	TN	38120	901-767-0104	767-0582
WSNA-FM 94.1 (CHR) 5904 Ridgeway Center Pkwy *Web:* www.snap941.com	Memphis	TN	38120	901-767-0104	767-0582
WXMX-FM 98.1 (Rock) 5629 Murray Rd *Web:* www.981themax.com	Memphis	TN	38119	901-680-9898	767-9531

648-103 Miami/Fort Lauderdale, FL

Station	City	State	Zip	Phone	Fax
WAMR-FM 107.5 (Span AC) 800 S Douglas Rd Suite 111	Coral Gables	FL	33134	305-447-1140	643-1075
WAQI-AM 710 (Span N/T) 800 S Douglas Rd Suite 111	Coral Gables	FL	33134	305-447-1140	442-7676
WAVS-AM 1170 (Reggae) 6360 SW 41st Pl *Web:* www.wavs1170.com	Davie	FL	33314	954-584-1170	581-6441
WBGG-FM 105.9 (CR) 7601 Riviera Blvd *Web:* www.big1059.com	Miramar	FL	33023	954-862-2000	862-4212
WCMQ-FM 92.3 (Span) 1001 Ponce de Leon Blvd *Web:* www.clasica92fm.com	Coral Gables	FL	33134	305-444-9292	461-4951
WDNA-FM 88.9 (Jazz) 4848 SW 74th Ct *TF:* 866-688-9362 ■ *Web:* www.wdna.org	Miami	FL	33155	305-662-8889	662-1975
WEDR-FM 99.1 (Urban) 2741 N 29th Ave *Web:* wedr.com	Hollywood	FL	33020	305-444-4404	
WFLC-FM 97.3 (AC) 2741 N 29th Ave *TF:* 866-227-9730 ■ *Web:* coastfm.com	Hollywood	FL	33020	954-584-7117	847-3240
WHDR-FM 93.1 (Rock) 2741 N 29th Ave *Web:* 93rock.com	Hollywood	FL	33020	305-444-4404	
WHQT-FM 105.1 (Urban) 2741 N 29th Ave **Fax Area Code:* 954 ■ *Web:* hot105fm.com	Hollywood	FL	33020	305-444-4404	584-7117*
WHYI-FM 100.7 (CHR) 7601 Riviera Blvd *Web:* www.y100miami.com	Miramar	FL	33023	954-862-2000	862-4212
WINZ-AM 940 (N/T) 7601 Riviera Blvd *Web:* www.am940southflorida.com	Miramar	FL	33023	954-862-2000	862-4212
WIOD-AM 610 (N/T) 7601 Riviera Blvd *Web:* www.newsradio610.com	Miramar	FL	33023	954-862-2000	862-4212

Station	City	State	Zip	Phone	Fax
WKCP-FM 89.7 (Clas) 600 SW 3rd St Suite 2270 *TF:* 866-864-3806	Pompano Beach	FL	33060	954-545-7600	545-7630
WKIS-FM 99.9 (Ctry) 194 NW 187th St *Web:* www.wkis.com	Miami	FL	33169	305-654-1700	654-1717
WKPX-FM 88.5 (Alt) 8000 NW 44th St	Sunrise	FL	33351	754-322-1721	322-1830
WLQY-AM 1320 (Var) 10800 Biscayne Blvd Suite 810	North Miami	FL	33161	305-891-1729	891-1583
WLRN-FM 91.3 (NPR) 172 NE 15th St *Web:* www.wlrn.org	Miami	FL	33132	305-995-1717	995-2299
WLVE-FM 93.9 (NAC) 7601 Riviera Blvd *TF:* 877-456-8394 ■ *Web:* www.love94.com	Miramar	FL	33023	954-862-2000	862-4212
WLYF-FM 101.5 (AC) 20450 NW 2nd Ave *TF:* 800-469-1015 ■ *Web:* www.wlyf.com	Miami	FL	33169	305-521-5100	521-1414
WMBM-AM 1490 (Rel) 13242 NW 7th Ave *TF:* 888-599-9626 ■ *Web:* www.wmbm.com	North Miami	FL	33168	305-769-1100	769-9975
WMGE-FM 94.9 (Span CHR) 7601 Riviera Blvd *TF:* 877-634-2949 ■ *Web:* www.mega949.com	Miramar	FL	33023	954-862-2000	862-4212
WMIB-FM 103.5 (Urban) 7601 Riviera Blvd *Web:* www.thebeatmiami.com	Miramar	FL	33023	954-862-2000	862-4212
WMXJ-FM 102.7 (Oldies) 20450 NW 2nd Ave *TF:* 800-924-1027 ■ *Web:* www.majic1027.com	Miami	FL	33169	305-521-5100	521-1414
WPOW-FM 96.5 (CHR) 20295 NW 2nd Ave 3rd Fl *Web:* www.power96.com	Miami	FL	33169	305-653-6796	770-1456
WQAM-AM 560 (Sports) 20295 NW 2nd Ave 3rd Fl *Web:* wqam.com	Miami	FL	33169	305-653-6796	770-1456
WQBA-AM 1140 (N/T) 800 S Douglas Rd Suite 111	Coral Gables	FL	33134	305-447-1140	441-2454
WRMA-FM 106.7 (Span AC) 1001 Ponce de Leon Blvd *Web:* www.romancefm.com	Coral Gables	FL	33134	305-444-9292	461-4951
WRTO-FM 98.3 (Span) 800 S Douglas Rd Suite 111	Coral Gables	FL	33134	305-447-1140	443-4701
WSUA-AM 1260 (Span) 2100 Coral Way Suite 201 *TF:* 800-441-1260 ■ *Web:* www.caracol1260.com	Miami	FL	33145	305-285-7075	858-5907
WWFE-AM 670 (Span) 330 SW 27th Ave Suite 207 *TF:* 888-541-9933 ■ *Web:* www.lapoderosa.com	Miami	FL	33135	305-541-3300	541-2013
WXDJ-FM 95.7 (Span) 1001 Ponce de Leon Blvd *Web:* www.elzol.com	Coral Gables	FL	33134	305-444-9292	461-4951

648-104 Milwaukee, WI

Station	City	State	Zip	Phone	Fax
WAUK-AM 540 (Sports) 770 N Jefferson St *TF:* 888-273-3776 ■ *Web:* www.espnmilwaukee.com	Milwaukee	WI	53202	414-273-3776	291-3776
WHAD-FM 90.7 (NPR) 111 E Kilbourn Ave Suite 2375 *TF:* 800-486-8655 ■ *Web:* www.wpr.org	Milwaukee	WI	53202	414-227-2040	227-2043
WHQG-FM 102.9 (Rock) 5407 W McKinley Ave *Web:* www.1029thehog.com	Milwaukee	WI	53208	414-978-9000	978-9001
WISN-AM 1130 (N/T) 12100 W Howard Ave *Web:* www.newstalk1130.com	Greenfield	WI	53228	414-545-8900	546-9654
WJMR-FM 98.3 (Urban) 5407 W McKinley Ave *Web:* www.wjmr.com	Milwaukee	WI	53208	414-978-9000	978-9001
WJYI-AM 1340 (Rel) 5407 W McKinley Ave *Web:* www.joy1340.com	Milwaukee	WI	53208	414-978-9000	978-9001
WJZX-FM 106.9 (Jazz) 5407 W McKinley Ave *Web:* www.wfmr.com	Milwaukee	WI	53208	414-978-9000	978-9001
WKKV-FM 100.7 (Urban) 12100 W Howard Ave *Web:* www.v100.com	Greenfield	WI	53228	414-545-8900	546-9654
WKLH-FM 96.5 (CR) 5407 W McKinley Ave *Web:* www.wklh.com	Milwaukee	WI	53208	414-978-9000	978-9001
WKTI-FM 94.5 (AC) 720 E Capitol Dr *Web:* www.wkti.com	Milwaukee	WI	53212	414-332-9611	967-5266
WLDB-FM 93.3 (AC) N 72 West 12922 *Web:* www.b933fm.com	Menomonee Falls	WI	53051	414-778-1933	771-3036
WLUM-FM 102.1 (Rock) N 72 West 12922 *Web:* www.fm1021milwaukee.com	Menomonee Falls	WI	53051	414-771-1021	771-3036
WMCS-AM 1290 (Urban) 4222 W Capitol Dr *Web:* www.1290wmcs.com	Milwaukee	WI	53216	414-444-1290	444-1409
WMIL-FM 106.1 (Ctry) 12100 W Howard Ave *Web:* www.fm106.com	Greenfield	WI	53228	414-545-8900	546-9654
WMYX-FM 99.1 (AC) 11800 W Grange Ave *Web:* www.99wmyx.com	Hales Corners	WI	53130	414-529-1250	529-2122
WNOV-AM 860 (Urban) 2003 W Capitol Dr	Milwaukee	WI	53206	414-449-9668	449-9945
WOKY-AM 920 (Oldies) 12100 W Howard Ave *Web:* www.am920woky.com	Greenfield	WI	53228	414-545-8900	546-9654
WQBW-FM 97.3 (CR) 12100 W Howard Ave *Web:* www.973thebrew.com	Greenfield	WI	53228	414-545-8900	546-9654
WRIT-FM 95.7 (CR) 12100 W Howard Ave *Web:* www.oldies957.com	Greenfield	WI	53228	414-545-8900	546-9654
WTMJ-AM 620 (N/T) 720 E Capitol Dr *Web:* www.620wtmj.com	Milwaukee	WI	53212	414-332-9611	967-5298
WUWM-FM 89.7 (NPR) 161 W Wisconsin Ave Suite LL1000 *Web:* www.wuwm.com	Milwaukee	WI	53203	414-227-3355	270-1297
WXSS-FM 103.7 (CHR) 11800 W Grange Ave *Web:* www.1037kissfm.com	Hales Corners	WI	53130	414-529-1250	529-2122

648-105 Minneapolis/Saint Paul, MN

Station	City	State	Zip	Phone	Fax
KCMP-FM 89.3 (NPR) 480 Cedar St *Web:* minnesota.publicradio.org/radio	Saint Paul	MN	55101	651-290-1500	290-1295
KDWB-FM 101.3 (CHR) 1600 Utica Ave S Suite 400 *Web:* www.kdwb.com	Minneapolis	MN	55416	952-417-3000	417-3001
KEEY-FM 102.1 (Ctry) 1600 Utica Ave S Suite 400 *Web:* www.k102.com	Minneapolis	MN	55416	952-417-3000	417-3001
KFAN-AM 1130 (Sports) 1600 Utica Ave S Suite 400 *Web:* www.kfan.com	Minneapolis	MN	55416	952-417-3000	417-3001
KLBB-AM 1220 (Nost) 104 N Main St *Web:* www.klbbradio.com	Stillwater	MN	55082	651-439-5006	439-5015
KNOW-FM 91.1 (NPR) 480 Cedar St *TF:* 800-228-7123 ■ *Web:* minnesota.publicradio.org	Saint Paul	MN	55101	651-290-1500	290-1295
KQQL-FM 107.9 (Oldies) 1600 Utica Ave S Suite 400 *Web:* www.kool108.com	Minneapolis	MN	55416	952-417-3000	417-3001
KQRS-FM 92.5 (CR) 2000 SE Elm St *Web:* www.92kqrs.com	Minneapolis	MN	55414	612-617-4000	676-8292
KSTP-AM 1500 (N/T) 3415 University Ave *Web:* www.am1500.com	Saint Paul	MN	55114	651-647-1500	647-2904
KSTP-FM 94.5 (AC) 3415 University Ave *Web:* www.ks95.com	Saint Paul	MN	55114	651-642-4141	642-4148
KTCZ-FM 97.1 (AAA) 1600 Utica Ave S Suite 400 *Web:* www.cities97.com	Minneapolis	MN	55416	952-417-3000	417-3001
KTTB-FM 96.3 (Urban) 5300 Edina Industrial Blvd Suite 200 *Web:* www.b96online.com	Edina	MN	55439	952-842-7200	842-3333
KXXR-FM 93.7 (Rock) 2000 SE Elm St *Web:* www.93x.com	Minneapolis	MN	55414	612-617-4000	676-8292
KZJK-FM 104.1 (Var) 625 2nd Ave S Suite 550 *Web:* www.1041jackfm.com	Minneapolis	MN	55402	612-370-0611	370-0159
WCCO-AM 830 (N/T) 625 2nd Ave S Suite 200 *Web:* www.wccoradio.com	Minneapolis	MN	55402	612-370-0611	370-0159
WFMP-FM 107.1 (N/T) 3415 University Ave *Web:* www.fm107.fm	Saint Paul	MN	55114	651-642-4107	646-5367
WGVX-FM 105.7 (Alt) 2000 SE Elm St *Web:* www.love105.fm	Minneapolis	MN	55414	612-617-4000	676-8292
WLKX-FM 95.9 (Rel) 15226 W Freeway Dr *Web:* www.spirit.fm	Forest Lake	MN	55025	651-464-6796	464-3638
WLTE-FM 102.9 (AC) 625 2nd Ave S Suite 200 *Web:* www.wlte.com	Minneapolis	MN	55402	612-339-1029	339-5653
WWTC-AM 1280 (N/T) 2110 Cliff Rd *Web:* www.am1280thepatriot.com	Eagan	MN	55122	651-405-8800	405-8222

648-106 Mobile, AL

Station	City	State	Zip	Phone	Fax
WABB-FM 97.5 (CHR) 1551 Springhill Ave *TF:* 800-678-9736 ■ *Web:* www.wabb.com	Mobile	AL	36604	251-432-5572	438-4044
WBHY-FM 88.5 (Rel) PO Box 1328 *TF:* 888-473-8488 ■ *Web:* www.goforth.org	Mobile	AL	36633	251-473-8488	300-3130
WBLX-FM 92.9 (Urban) 2800 Dauphin St Suite 104 *Web:* www.thebigstation93blx.com	Mobile	AL	36606	251-652-2000	652-2001
WDLT-FM 92.3 (Urban AC) 2800 Dauphin St Suite 104	Mobile	AL	36606	251-652-2000	652-2001
WGOK-AM 900 (Rel) 2800 Dauphin St Suite 104	Mobile	AL	36606	251-652-2000	652-2001
WHIL-FM 91.3 (NPR) PO Box 8509 *TF:* 800-239-9445 ■ *Web:* www.whil.org	Mobile	AL	36689	251-380-4685	460-2189
WKSJ-FM 94.9 (Ctry) 555 Broadcast Dr 3rd Fl *Web:* www.95ksj.com	Mobile	AL	36606	251-450-0100	479-3418
WMXC-FM 99.9 (AC) 555 Broadcast Dr 3rd Fl *Web:* www.litemix.com	Mobile	AL	36606	251-450-0100	479-3418
WNSP-FM 105.5 (Sports) 1100 Dauphin St Suite E *TF:* 888-560-9754 ■ *Web:* www.wnsp.com	Mobile	AL	36604	251-438-5460	438-5462
WPMI-AM 710 (N/T) 555 Broadcast Dr 3rd Fl *Web:* www.newsradio710.com	Mobile	AL	36606	251-450-0100	479-3418
WRKH-FM 96.1 (CR) 555 Broadcast Dr 3rd Fl *Web:* www.961therocket.com	Mobile	AL	36606	251-450-0100	479-3418

648-107 Modesto, CA

Station	City	State	Zip	Phone	Fax
KABX-FM 97.5 (Oldies) 1020 W Main St *Web:* www.975kabx.com	Merced	CA	95340	209-723-2192	383-2950
KATM-FM 103.3 (Ctry) 1581 Cummins Dr Suite 135 *Web:* www.katm.com	Modesto	CA	95358	209-766-5000	522-2061
KCIV-FM 99.9 (Rel) 1031 15th St Suite 1 *TF:* 800-743-5248 ■ *Web:* www.bottradionetwork.com	Modesto	CA	95354	209-524-8999	524-9088
KESP-AM 970 (Sports) 1581 Cummins Dr Suite 135 *Web:* www.espnradio970.com	Modesto	CA	95358	209-766-5000	522-2061
KFIV-AM 1360 (N/T) 2121 Lancey Dr *Web:* www.kfiv1360.com	Modesto	CA	95355	209-551-1306	551-1359
KHKK-FM 104.1 (CR) 1581 Cummins Dr Suite 135 *Web:* www.104thehawk.com	Modesto	CA	95358	209-766-5000	522-2061
KHOP-FM 95.1 (CHR) 1581 Cummins Dr Suite 135 *Web:* www.khop.com	Modesto	CA	95358	209-766-5000	522-2061
KJSN-FM 102.3 (AC) 2121 Lancey Dr *Web:* www.sunny102fm.com	Modesto	CA	95355	209-551-1306	551-1359
KMRQ-AM 1280 (Span) 2121 Lancey Dr *Web:* www.lighthouse1280.com	Modesto	CA	95355	209-551-1306	551-1359
KMRQ-FM 96.7 (Span) 2121 Lancey Dr *Web:* kmrq-fm.clearchannel.com	Modesto	CA	95355	209-551-1306	551-1359
KOSO-FM 93.1 (AC) 2121 Lancey Dr *Web:* www.b931.com	Modesto	CA	95355	209-551-1306	551-1359
KQOD-FM 100.1 (Oldies) 2121 Lancey Dr *Web:* www.megajamminoldies.com	Modesto	CA	95355	209-551-1306	551-1359
KRVR-FM 105.5 (NAC) 961 N Emerald Ave Suite A *Web:* www.krvr.com	Modesto	CA	95351	209-544-1055	544-8105

648-108 Monterey, CA

Station	City	State	Zip	Phone	Fax
KAZU-FM 90.3 (NPR) 167 Central Ave *TF:* 800-903-6624 ■ *Web:* www.kazu.org	Pacific Grove	CA	93950	831-375-7275	375-0235
KBOQ-FM 95.5 (Clas) 60 Garden Ct Suite 300	Monterey	CA	93940	831-658-5200	658-5299
KCDU-FM 101.7 (AC) 60 Garden Ct Suite 300 *Web:* www.1017thebeach.com	Monterey	CA	93940	831-658-5200	658-5299
KDON-FM 102.5 (CHR) 903 N Main St *TF:* 888-558-5366 ■ *Web:* www.kdon.com	Salinas	CA	93906	831-755-8181	755-8193
KIDD-AM 630 (Nost) 5 Harris Ct Bldg C *Web:* www.magic63.com	Monterey	CA	93940	831-649-0969	649-3335
KLOK-FM 99.5 (Span) 67 Garden Ct *TF:* 888-874-2656	Monterey	CA	93940	831-333-9735	373-6700
KMBY-FM 103.9 (Alt) 60 Garden Ct Suite 300 *Web:* www.x1039fm.com	Monterey	CA	93940	831-658-5200	658-5299
KOCN-FM 105.1 (Urban) 903 N Main St *TF:* 888-896-5626	Salinas	CA	93906	831-755-8181	755-8193
KOTR-FM 93.5 (Oldies) 60 Garden Ct Suite 300	Monterey	CA	93940	831-658-5200	658-5299
KPIG-FM 107.5 (AAA) 1110 Main St Suite 16 *Web:* www.kpig.com	Watsonville	CA	95076	831-722-9000	722-7548
KRAY-FM 103.5 (Span) 548 E Alisal St	Salinas	CA	93905	831-757-1910	757-8015
KSEA-FM 107.9 (Span) 229 Pajaro St Suite 302D *Web:* campesina.net	Salinas	CA	93901	831-754-1469	754-1563
KSES-FM 107.1 (Span) 67 Garden Ct *TF:* 800-420-2757	Monterey	CA	93942	831-333-9735	333-9750
KTOM-FM 92.7 (Ctry) 903 N Main St *TF:* 888-660-5866 ■ *Web:* www.ktom.com	Salinas	CA	93906	831-755-8181	755-8193
KUSP-FM 88.9 (NPR) 203 8th Ave *TF:* 800-655-5877 ■ *Web:* www.kusp.org	Santa Cruz	CA	95062	831-476-2800	476-2802
KWAV-FM 96.9 (AC) 5 Harris Ct Bldg C *Web:* www.kwav.com	Monterey	CA	93940	831-649-0969	649-3335

648-109 Montgomery, AL

Station	City	State	Zip	Phone	Fax
WACV-AM 1170 (N/T) 4101-A Wall St *Web:* www.1170wacv.com	Montgomery	AL	36106	334-244-0961	279-9563
WBAM-FM 98.9 (Ctry) 4101-A Wall St *Web:* star989.com	Montgomery	AL	36106	334-244-0961	279-9563
WHHY-FM 101.9 (CHR) 1 Commerce St Suite 300 *Web:* www.y102montgomery.com	Montgomery	AL	36104	334-240-9274	240-9214
WHLW-FM 104.3 (Rel) 203 Gunn Rd *Web:* www.1043hallelujahfm.com	Montgomery	AL	36117	334-274-6464	274-6465
WJWZ-FM 97.9 (Urban) 4101-A Wall St *Web:* www.979jamz.com	Montgomery	AL	36106	334-244-0961	279-9563

Montgomery, AL (Cont'd)

Station	City	State	ZIP	Phone	Fax
WKXN-FM 95.9 (Urban) 563 Manningham Rd *Web:* www.wkxn.com	Greenville	AL	36037	334-382-6555	382-7770
WLWI-FM 92.3 (Ctry) 1 Commerce St Suite 300 *Web:* www.wlwi.com	Montgomery	AL	36104	334-240-9274	240-9214
WMSP-AM 740 (Sports) 1 Commerce St Suite 300 *Web:* www.sportsradio740.com	Montgomery	AL	36104	334-240-9274	240-9214
WMXS-FM 103.3 (AC) 1 Commerce St Suite 300 *Web:* www.mix103.com	Montgomery	AL	36104	334-240-9274	240-9214
WNZZ-AM 950 (Nost) 1 Commerce St Suite 300	Montgomery	AL	36104	334-240-9274	240-9214
WTSU-FM 89.9 (NPR) Troy State University Wallace Hall *TF:* 800-800-6616	Troy	AL	36082	334-670-3268	670-3934
WVAS-FM 90.7 (Jazz) 915 S Jackson St *Web:* www.alasu.edu/wvas	Montgomery	AL	36101	334-229-4287	269-4995
WWMG-FM 97.1 (Urban) 203 Gunn Rd *Web:* www.mymagic97.com	Montgomery	AL	36117	334-274-6464	274-6465
WXFX-FM 95.1 (Rock) 1 Commerce St Suite 300 *Web:* www.wxfx.com	Montgomery	AL	36104	334-240-9274	240-9214
WXVI-AM 1600 (Rel) 912 S Perry St *Web:* www.wxviradio.com	Montgomery	AL	36104	334-263-4141	263-9191
WZHT-FM 105.7 (Urban) 203 Gunn Rd *Web:* www.myhot105.com	Montgomery	AL	36117	334-274-6464	274-6465

648-110 Montreal, QC

Station	City	Prov	Postal Code	Phone	Fax
CBF-FM 100.7 (CBC) 1400 Rene Levesque Blvd E *Web:* www.cbc.ca/montreal	Montreal	QC	H2L2M2	514-597-6300	597-6510
CBM-FM 88.5 (CBC) 1400 Rene Levesque Blvd E *Web:* www.cbc.ca/montreal	Montreal	QC	H2L2M2	514-597-6300	597-6510
CFMB-AM 1280 (Ethnic) 35 York St *Web:* www.cfmb.ca	Montreal	QC	H3Z2Z5	514-483-2362	483-1362
CFQR-FM 92.5 (AC) 800 De La Gauchetiere W Suite 1100 *Web:* www.q92fm.com	Montreal	QC	H5A1M1	514-787-7799	787-7979
CHOM-FM 97.7 (CR) 1411 Fort St 3rd Fl *Web:* www.chom.com	Montreal	QC	H3H2R1	514-931-2466	846-4741
CIBL-FM 101.5 (Var) 1691 Pie IX Blvd *Web:* www.cibl.cam.org	Montreal	QC	H1V2C3	514-526-2581	526-3583
CINQ-FM 102.3 (Ethnic) 5212 Saint-Laurent Blvd *Web:* www.radiocentreville.com	Montreal	QC	H2T1S1	514-495-2597	495-2429
CITE-FM 107.3 (Rock) 1717 Rene Levesque Blvd E *Web:* www.rockdetente.com	Montreal	QC	H2L4T9	514-845-2483	288-1073
CJAD-AM 800 (N/T) 1411 Fort St 3rd Fl *Web:* www.cjad.com	Montreal	QC	H3H2R1	514-989-2523	989-3868
CJFM-FM 95.9 (CHR) 1411 Fort St *Web:* www.themix.com	Montreal	QC	H3H2R1	514-989-2536	989-2554
CKAC-AM 730 (N/T) 800 De La Gauchetiere W Suite 1100 *Web:* www.ckac.com	Montreal	QC	H5A1M1	514-845-5151	845-2224
CKMF-FM 94.3 (CHR) 1717 Rene-Levesque Blvd E *Web:* www.radioenergie.com	Montreal	QC	H2L4T9	514-529-3229	529-9308
CKOI-FM 96.9 (CHR) 800 rue De La Gauchetiere Suite 1100 *Web:* www.ckoi.com	Montreal	QC	H5A1M1	514-787-7799	
CKUT-FM 90.3 (Alt) 3647 University St *Web:* www.ckut.ca	Montreal	QC	H3A2B3	514-448-4041	398-8261

648-111 Morgantown, WV

Station	City	State	ZIP	Phone	Fax
WAJR-AM 1440 (N/T) 1251 Earl L Core Rd *Web:* www.wajr.com	Morgantown	WV	26505	304-296-0029	296-3876
WBRB-FM 101.3 (Ctry) 1065 Radio Park Dr *Web:* www.thebear1013.com	Mount Clare	WV	26048	304-623-6546	623-6547
WCLG-FM 100.1 (Rock) PO Box 885 *Web:* www.wclg.com	Morgantown	WV	26507	304-292-2222	292-2224
WDCI-FM 104.1 (AC) PO Box 360	Bridgeport	WV	26330	304-842-8644	842-8653
WFBY-FM 102.3 (CR) 1065 Radio Park Dr **Fax:* News Rm	Mount Clare	WV	26408	304-623-6546	623-6547*
WKKW-FM 97.9 (Ctry) 1251 Earl L Core Rd *Web:* wkkwfm.com	Morgantown	WV	26505	304-296-0029	296-3876
WPDX-FM 104.9 (Ctry) 59 Mountain Park Dr	Whitehall	WV	26554	304-624-6425	363-3852
WVAQ-FM 101.9 (CHR) 1251 Earl L Core Rd *Web:* www.wvaq.com	Morgantown	WV	26505	304-296-0029	296-3876
WVPM-FM 90.9 (NPR) 191 Scott Ave *TF:* 888-596-9729 ■ *Web:* www.wvpubcast.org	Morgantown	WV	26508	304-284-1440	284-1454
WWVU-FM 91.7 (Var) PO Box 6446 *Web:* www.wvu.edu/~u92	Morgantown	WV	26506	304-293-3329	293-7363

648-112 Myrtle Beach, SC

Station	City	State	ZIP	Phone	Fax
WDAI-FM 98.5 (Urban) 11640 Hwy 17 Bypass *Web:* www.985kissfm.net	Murrells Inlet	SC	29576	843-651-7869	651-3197
WEZV-FM 105.9 (AC) 3926 Wesley St Suite 301 *Web:* www.wezv.com	Myrtle Beach	SC	29579	843-903-9962	903-1797
WGTR-FM 107.9 (Ctry) 4841 Hwy 17 Bypass S *Web:* www.gator1079.com	Myrtle Beach	SC	29577	843-293-0107	293-1717
WKZQ-FM 101.7 (Rock) 1016 Ocala St *Web:* www.wkzq.net	Myrtle Beach	SC	29577	843-448-1041	626-5988
WMYB-FM 92.1 (AC) 1016 Ocala St *Web:* wmybstar92.net	Myrtle Beach	SC	29577	843-448-1041	626-5988
WQSD-FM 107.1 (CR) 4841 Hwy 17 Bypass S	Myrtle Beach	SC	29577	843-293-0107	293-1717
WRNN-FM 99.5 (N/T) 1016 Ocala St *Web:* wrnn.net	Myrtle Beach	SC	29577	843-448-1041	626-5988
WSYN-FM 106.5 (Oldies) 11640 Hwy 17 Bypass *Web:* www.sunny1065.net	Murrells Inlet	SC	29576	843-651-7869	651-3197
WVCO-FM 94.9 (Var) PO Box 3689 *Web:* www.949thesurf.com	North Myrtle Beach	SC	29582	843-445-9491	445-9490
WWXM-FM 97.7 (CHR) 4841 Hwy 17 Bypass S	Myrtle Beach	SC	29577	843-293-0107	293-1717
WYAK-FM 103.1 (Ctry) 11640 Hwy 17 Bypass *Web:* www.kcountry103.net	Murrells Inlet	SC	29576	843-651-7869	651-3197
WYAV-FM 104.1 (CR) 1016 Ocala St *Web:* www.wave104.com	Myrtle Beach	SC	29577	843-448-1041	626-5989
WYNA-FM 104.9 (Oldies) 3926 Wesley St Suite 301 *Web:* www.cool1049.com	Myrtle Beach	SC	29579	843-903-9962	903-1797

648-113 Naples, FL

Station	City	State	ZIP	Phone	Fax
WARO-FM 94.5 (CR) 2824 Palm Beach Blvd *Web:* www.classicrock945.com	Fort Myers	FL	33916	239-337-2346	332-0767
WAVV-FM 101.1 (AC) 11800 Tamiami Trail E *TF:* 866-310-9288 ■ *Web:* www.wavv101.com	Naples	FL	34113	239-775-9288	793-7000
WAYJ-FM 88.7 (Rel) 1860 Boyscout Dr Suite 202 *TF:* 888-936-1929 ■ *Web:* wayj.wayfm.com	Fort Myers	FL	33907	239-936-1929	936-5433
WBTT-FM 105.5 (Urban) 13320 Metro Pkwy Suite 1 *Web:* www.1055thebeat.com	Fort Myers	FL	33966	239-225-4300	225-4410
WCKT-FM 107.1 (Ctry) 13320 Metro Pkwy Suite 1 **Fax:* Hum Res ■ *Web:* www.wckt.com	Fort Myers	FL	33966	239-225-4300	225-4410*
WGCU-FM 90.1 (NPR) 10501 FGCU Blvd S *TF:* 888-824-0030 ■ *Web:* www.wgcu.org	Fort Myers	FL	33965	239-590-2500	590-2310
WINK-FM 96.9 (AC) 2824 Palm Beach Blvd *Web:* www.winkfm.com	Fort Myers	FL	33916	239-337-2346	332-0767
WJBX-FM 99.3 (Alt) 20125 S Tamiami Trail *TF:* 800-937-7465 ■ *Web:* www.99xwjbx.com	Estero	FL	33928	239-495-2100	992-8165
WJPT-FM 106.3 (Nost) 20125 S Tamiami Trail *Web:* www.wjpt.com	Estero	FL	33928	239-495-2100	948-0785
WNOG-AM 1270 (N/T) 2824 Palm Beach Blvd	Fort Myers	FL	33916	239-337-2346	332-0767
WOLZ-FM 95.3 (AC) 13320 Metro Pkwy Suite 1 *Web:* www.wolz.com	Fort Myers	FL	33966	239-225-4300	225-4410
WRQC-FM 92.5 (Rock) 2824 Palm Beach Blvd *Web:* www.realrock925.com	Fort Myers	FL	33916	239-337-2346	332-0767
WSGL-FM 104.7 (AC) 10915 K-Nine Dr *Web:* www.wsgl1047.com	Bonita Springs	FL	34135	239-495-8383	495-0883
WWGR-FM 101.9 (Ctry) 10915 K-Nine Dr *TF:* 877-787-1019 ■ *Web:* www.gatorcountry1019.com	Bonita Springs	FL	34135	239-495-8383	495-0883
WXKB-FM 103.9 (CHR) 20125 S Tamiami Trail *TF:* 866-608-3427 ■ *Web:* www.b1039.com	Estero	FL	33928	239-495-2100	948-0785

648-114 Nashville, TN

Station	City	State	ZIP	Phone	Fax
WAMB-AM 1200 (Nost) 1617 Lebanon Rd *Web:* www.wamb.net	Nashville	TN	37210	615-889-1960	902-9108
WBUZ-FM 102.9 (Alt) 1824 Murfreesboro Rd *Web:* www.1029thebuzz.com	Nashville	TN	37217	615-399-1029	361-9873
WCJK-FM 96.3 (Var) 504 Rosedale Ave *Web:* www.963jackfm.com	Nashville	TN	37211	615-259-9696	259-4594
WFFH-FM 94.1 (Rel) 402 BNA Dr Suite 400 *TF:* 800-826-3637 ■ *Web:* www.94fmthefish.net	Nashville	TN	37217	615-367-2210	367-0758
WGFX-FM 104.5 (Sports) 506 2nd Ave S *Web:* www.1045thezone.com	Nashville	TN	37210	615-244-9533	259-1271
WJXA-FM 92.9 (AC) 504 Rosedale Ave *Web:* www.mix929.com	Nashville	TN	37211	615-259-9696	259-4594
WKDF-FM 103.3 (Ctry) 506 2nd Ave S *Web:* www.103wkdf.com	Nashville	TN	37210	615-244-9533	259-1271
WLAC-AM 1510 (N/T) 55 Music Sq W *Web:* www.wlac.com	Nashville	TN	37203	615-664-2400	744-4743
WMBD-AM 880 (Rel) 209 10th Ave S Suite 342 *Web:* www.rejoice880.com	Nashville	TN	37203	615-242-1411	242-3823
WNRQ-FM 105.9 (CR) 55 Music Sq W *Web:* www.1059.com	Nashville	TN	37203	615-664-2400	742-1059
WNSR-AM 560 (Sports) 435 37th Ave N *TF:* 888-228-6123 ■ *Web:* www.wnsr.com	Nashville	TN	37209	615-844-1039	777-2284
WPLN-FM 90.3 (NPR) 630 Mainstream Dr *TF:* 877-760-2903 ■ *Web:* www.wpln.org	Nashville	TN	37228	615-760-2903	760-2904
WQQK-FM 92.1 (Urban) 10 Music Cir E *Web:* www.92qnashville.com	Nashville	TN	37203	615-321-1067	321-5771
WRLT-FM 100.1 (AAA) 1310 Clinton St Suite 200 *Web:* www.wrlt.com	Nashville	TN	37203	615-242-5600	296-9039
WRQQ-FM 97.1 (Oldies) 10 Music Cir E *Web:* www.star97.net	Nashville	TN	37203	615-321-1067	321-5771
WRVW-FM 107.5 (CHR) 55 Music Sq W *Web:* www.1075theriver.com	Nashville	TN	37203	615-664-2400	664-2434
WSIX-FM 97.9 (Ctry) 55 Music Sq W *Web:* www.wsix.com	Nashville	TN	37203	615-664-2400	664-2470
WSM-AM 650 (Ctry) 2804 Opryland Dr *TF:* 877-878-4650 ■ *Web:* www.wsmonline.com	Nashville	TN	37214	615-889-6595	458-2445
WSM-FM 95.5 (Ctry) 10 Music Cir E *Web:* www.955thewolf.com	Nashville	TN	37203	615-321-1067	321-5771
WUBT-FM 101.1 (Urban) 55 Music Sq W *Web:* www.101thebeat.com	Nashville	TN	37203	615-664-2400	664-2406
WVNS-FM 102.5 (AC) 1824 Murfreesboro Rd *Web:* www.1025theparty.com	Nashville	TN	37217	615-399-1029	361-9873
WWTN-FM 99.7 (N/T) 10 Music Cir E *Web:* www.997wtn.com	Nashville	TN	37203	615-321-1067	321-5771

648-115 New Haven, CT

Station	City	State	ZIP	Phone	Fax
WAVZ-AM 1300 (Sports) 495 Benham St *Web:* www.wavz.com	Hamden	CT	06514	203-248-8814	281-2795
WELI-AM 960 (N/T) 495 Benham St *Web:* www.weli.com	Hamden	CT	06514	203-248-8814	281-2795
WEZN-FM 99.9 (AC) 440 Wheelers Farm Rd Suite 302 *Web:* star999.com	Milford	CT	06461	203-783-8200	783-8399
WKCI-FM 101.3 (CHR) 495 Benham St *Web:* www.kc101.com	Hamden	CT	06514	203-248-8814	281-2795
WPLR-FM 99.1 (Rock) 440 Wheelers Farm Rd Suite 302 *Web:* wplr.com	Milford	CT	06461	203-783-8200	783-8399
WQUN-AM 1220 (Nost) 275 Mt Carmel Ave *Web:* www.quinnipiac.edu/x1353.xml	Hamden	CT	06518	203-582-8984	582-5372
WYBC-AM 1340 (Var) 142 Temple St Suite 203 *Web:* www.wybc.com	New Haven	CT	06510	203-776-4118	776-2446
WYBC-FM 94.3 (Urban) 142 Temple St Suite 203 *Web:* 943wybc.com	New Haven	CT	06510	203-776-4118	776-2446

648-116 New Orleans, LA

Station	City	State	ZIP	Phone	Fax
KKND-FM 106.7 (Ctry) 201 St Charles Ave Suite 201	New Orleans	LA	70170	504-581-7002	566-4857
KMEZ-FM 102.9 (Oldies) 201 St Charles Ave Suite 201 *Web:* www.oldschool1029.com	New Orleans	LA	70170	504-581-7002	566-4857
WDVW-FM 92.3 (AC) 201 St Charles Ave Suite 201 **Fax:* News Rm ■ *Web:* www.diva923.com	New Orleans	LA	70170	504-581-7002	566-4857*
WEZB-FM 97.1 (CHR) 400 Poydras St Suite 800 *Web:* www.b97.com	New Orleans	LA	70130	504-593-6376	593-2099
WGSO-AM 990 (N/T) 2250 E Gause Blvd Suite 205 *Web:* wgso.com	Slidell	LA	70461	985-639-3820	639-3869
WKBU-FM 95.7 (Rock) 400Poydras St Suite 800 *Web:* www.bayou957.com	New Orleans	LA	70130	504-593-6376	593-2099
WLMG-FM 101.9 (AC) 400 Poydras St Suite 800 *Web:* www.magic1019.com	New Orleans	LA	70130	504-593-6376	593-2099

Phone | Fax

WLNO-AM 1060 (Rel) 401 Whitney Ave Suite 160 — Gretna LA 70056 504-362-9800 362-5541
Web: www.wlno.com
WNOE-FM 101.1 (Ctry) 929 Howard Ave — New Orleans LA 70113 504-679-7300 679-7345
TF: 800-543-9663 ■ *Web:* www.wnoe.com
WODT-AM 1280 (Sports) 929 Howard Ave — New Orleans LA 70113 504-679-7300 679-7345
WQUE-FM 93.3 (Urban) 929 Howard Ave — New Orleans LA 70113 504-679-7300 679-7345
Web: www.q93.com
WRNO-FM 99.5 (N/T) 929 Howard Ave — New Orleans LA 70113 504-679-7300 679-7345
Web: www.wrno.com
WSHO-AM 800 (Rel) 365 Canal St Suite 1175 — New Orleans LA 70130 504-527-0800 527-0881
Web: www.wsho.com
WTIX-FM 94.3 (Oldies) 4539 N I-10 Service Rd 3rd Fl — Metairie LA 70006 504-454-9000 454-9002
Web: www.wtixfm.com
WWL-AM 870 (N/T) 400 Poydras St Suite 800 — New Orleans LA 70130 504-593-6376 593-2099
Web: www.wwl.com
WWL-FM 95.7 N/T) 400 Poydras St Suite 800 — New Orleans LA 70130 504-593-6376 593-2099
Web: www.wwl.com
WWNO-FM 89.9 (NPR)
University of New Orleans Lake Front Campus — New Orleans LA 70148 504-280-7000 280-6061
TF: 800-286-7002 ■ *Web:* www.wwno.org
WWOZ-FM 90.7 (Var) 1008 N Peters — New Orleans LA 70116 504-568-1239 558-9332
Web: www.wwoz.org
WYLD-AM 940 (Rel) 929 Howard Ave — New Orleans LA 70113 504-679-7300 679-7345
Web: www.am940.com
WYLD-FM 98.5 (Urban) 929 Howard Ave — New Orleans LA 70113 504-679-7300 679-7345
Web: www.wyldfm.com

648-117 New York, NY

Phone | Fax

WABC-AM 770 (N/T) 2 Penn Plaza 17th Fl — New York NY 10121 212-613-3800 613-3866
TF: 800-848-9222 ■ *Web:* www.wabcradio.com
WADO-AM 1280 (Span) 485 Madison Ave 3rd Fl — New York NY 10022 212-310-6000 888-3694
TF: 800-999-1280 ■ *Web:* www.univision.com
WALK-FM 97.5 (AC) 66 Colonial Dr — Patchogue NY 11772 631-475-5200 475-9016
Web: www.walkradio.com
WAXQ-FM 104.3 (CR) 32 Ave of the Americas — New York NY 10013 212-377-7900
TF: 888-872-1043 ■ *Web:* www.waxq.com
WBAB-FM 102.3 (Rock) 555 Sunrise Hwy — West Babylon NY 11704 631-587-1023 587-1282
Web: wbab.com
WBAI-FM 99.5 (N/T) 120 Wall St 10th Fl — New York NY 10005 212-209-2800 747-1698
Web: www.wbai.org
WBBR-AM 1130 (N/T) 731 Lexington Ave — New York NY 10022 212-318-2000 940-1994
Web: www.bloomberg.com/radio
WBGO-FM 88.3 (Jazz) 54 Park Pl — Newark NJ 07102 973-624-8880 824-8888
Web: www.wbgo.org
WBLI-FM 106.1 (CHR) 555 Sunrise Hwy — West Babylon NY 11704 631-587-1023 587-1282
Web: wbli.com
WBLS-FM 107.5 (Urban) 3 Park Ave 41st Fl — New York NY 10016 212-447-1000 447-5193
Web: www.wbls.com
WBON-FM 98.5 (Span)
3075 Veterans Memorial Hwy Suite 201 — Ronkonkoma NY 11779 631-648-2500 648-2550
Web: www.lafiestali.com
WBZO-FM 103.1 (Oldies) 234 Airport Plaza Suite 5 — Farmingdale NY 11735 631-770-4200 770-0110
Web: www.b103.com
WCAA-FM 105.9 (Span) 485 Madison Ave 3rd Fl — New York NY 10022 212-310-6000 888-3694
TF: 866-927-1059 ■ *Web:* wcaa.netmio.com
WCBS-AM 880 (N/T) 524 W 57th St 8th Fl — New York NY 10019 212-975-2127 975-1907*
*Fax: News Rm ■ *Web:* www.wcbs880.com
WCBS-FM 101.1 (Oldies) 40 W 57th St 15th Fl — New York NY 10019 212-846-5101 846-5188
Web: wcbsfm.com
WEPN-AM 1050 (Sports) 2 Penn Plaza 17th Fl — New York NY 10121 212-613-3800 615-3246
TF: 800-919-3776 ■ *Web:* www.1050espnradio.com
WFAN-AM 660 (Sports) 34-12 36th St — Astoria NY 11106 718-706-7690 383-5734
Web: www.wfan.com
WFUV-FM 90.7 (Var) 441 E Fordham Rd Fordham University — Bronx NY 10458 718-817-4550 365-9815
Web: www.wfuv.org
WHLI-AM 1100 (Nost) 234 Airport Plaza Suite 5 — Farmingdale NY 11735 631-770-4200 770-0110
Web: www.whli.com
WHTZ-FM 100.3 (CHR) PO Box 7100 — New York NY 10150 212-239-2300 239-2308
TF: 800-242-0100 ■ *Web:* www.z100.com
WINS-AM 1010 (N/T) 888 7th Ave 10th Fl — New York NY 10106 212-397-1010 247-7918
Web: www.1010wins.com
WKTU-FM 103.5 (CHR) 32 Ave of the Americas — New York NY 10013 212-377-7900 420-3787*
*Fax Area Code: 201 ■ *TF:* 800-245-1035 ■ *Web:* www.ktu.com
WLIB-AM 1190 (N/T) 641 6th Ave 4th Fl — New York NY 10011 212-889-1190 252-9574
Web: www.wlib.com
WLIR-FM 107.1 (Alt)
3075 Veterans Memorial Hwy Suite 201 — Ronkonkoma NY 11779 631-648-2500 648-2550
Web: www.wlir.fm
WLTW-FM 106.7 (AC) 32 Ave of the Americas 3rd Fl — New York NY 10013 212-377-7900 206-9169*
*Fax Area Code: 917 ■ *TF:* 800-222-1067 ■ *Web:* www.1067newyork.com
WNYC-AM 820 (NPR) 1 Centre St 24th Fl — New York NY 10007 212-669-7800 669-3312
Web: www.wnyc.org
WNYC-FM 93.9 (NPR) 1 Centre St 24th Fl — New York NY 10007 212-669-7800 669-3312
Web: www.wnyc.org
WOR-AM 710 (N/T) 111 Broadway 3rd Fl — New York NY 10006 212-642-4500 642-4486
Web: www.wor710.com
WPAT-AM 930 (Ethnic) 449 Broadway 2nd Fl — New York NY 10013 212-966-1059 966-9580
WPAT-FM 93.1 (Span AC) 26 W 56th St — New York NY 10019 212-541-9200 541-9239
TF: 800-246-9393 ■ *Web:* www.amorfm.com
WPLJ-FM 95.5 (AC) 2 Penn Plaza 17th Fl — New York NY 10121 212-613-8900 613-8956
TF: 800-321-9755 ■ *Web:* www.plj.com
WQCD-FM 101.9 (NAC) 395 Hudson St 7th Fl — New York NY 10014 212-352-1019 929-8559
TF: 800-423-1019 ■ *Web:* www.cd1019.com
WQHT-FM 97.1 (Urban) 395 Hudson St 7th Fl — New York NY 10014 212-229-9797 929-8559
TF: 800-223-9797 ■ *Web:* www.hot97.com
WQXR-FM 96.3 (Clas) 122 5th Ave 3rd Fl — New York NY 10011 212-633-7600 633-7666
Web: www.wqxr.com
WRKS-FM 98.7 (Urban) 395 Hudson St 7th Fl — New York NY 10014 212-242-9870 242-0706
TF: 800-288-5477 ■ *Web:* www.987kissfm.com
WSKQ-FM 97.9 (Span) 26 W 56th St — New York NY 10019 212-541-9200 541-9239
TF: 800-315-9790 ■ *Web:* www.lamega.com
WWFS-FM 102.7 (AC) 888 7th Ave 9th Fl — New York NY 10106 212-489-1027 957-9639
TF: 800-949-1027 ■ *Web:* mix1027fm.com
WWPR-FM 105.1 (Urban) 32 Ave of the Americas — New York NY 10013 212-377-7900 398-3299
TF: 800-585-1051 ■ *Web:* www.power1051fm.com
WWRV-AM 1330 (Span Rel) 419 Broadway — Paterson NJ 07509 973-881-8700 881-8324
Web: www.radiovision.net
WXRK-FM 92.3 (Rock) 40 W 57th St 14th Fl — New York NY 10019 212-314-9230 314-9338
TF: 888-313-3733 ■ *Web:* www.923freefm.com

648-118 Norfolk/Virginia Beach, VA

Phone | Fax

WAFX-FM 106.9 (CR) 870 Greenbrier Cir Suite 399 — Chesapeake VA 23320 757-366-9900 366-0022
Web: www.1069thefox.com
WCMS-AM 1310 (Sports) 5589 Greenwich Rd Suite 200 — Virginia Beach VA 23462 757-671-1000 671-1010
Web: www.espnradio1310.com
WCMS-FM 94.5 (Ctry) PO Box 1897 — Kill Devil Hills NC 27948 252-449-6065 441-4827
Web: www.wcms.com
WCWM-FM 90.7 (Var)
Campus Center PO Box 8795 College of William & Mary — Williamsburg VA 23187 757-221-3287 221-3451
Web: www.wcwm.org
WGH-FM 97.3 (Ctry) 5589 Greenwich Rd Suite 200 — Virginia Beach VA 23462 757-671-1000 671-1010
Web: www.eagle97.com
WGPL-AM 1350 (Rel) 645 Church St Suite 400 — Norfolk VA 23510 757-622-4600 624-6515
WHRO-FM 90.3 (Clas) 5200 Hampton Blvd — Norfolk VA 23508 757-889-9400 489-0007
Web: www.whro.org/radio/903
WHRV-FM 89.5 (NPR) 5200 Hampton Blvd — Norfolk VA 23508 757-889-9400 489-0007
Web: www.whro.org/radio/895
WJCD-FM 107.7 (AC) 1003 Norfolk Sq — Norfolk VA 23502 757-466-0009 466-7043
Web: www.wjcd.com
WJOI-AM 1230 (Nost) 870 Greenbrier Cir Suite 399 — Chesapeake VA 23320 757-366-9900 366-0022
WKGM-AM 940 (Rel) 13379 Great Spring Rd — Smithfield VA 23430 757-357-9546 365-0412
TF: 800-706-4769
WKUS-FM 105.3 (Urban) 1003 Norfolk Sq — Norfolk VA 23502 757-466-0009 466-7043
Web: www.1053kiss.com
WNIS-AM 790 (N/T)
999 Waterside Dr Dominion Tower Suite 500 — Norfolk VA 23510 757-640-8500 640-8552
Web: www.wnis.com
WNOR-FM 98.7 (Rock) 870 Greenbrier Cir Suite 399 — Chesapeake VA 23320 757-366-9900 366-0022
Web: www.fm99.com
WNSB-FM 91.1 (Urban) 700 Park Ave Suite 129 Spartan Station — Norfolk VA 23504 757-823-9672 823-2385
Web: www.nsu.edu/wnsb
WNVZ-FM 104.5 (CHR) 236 Clearfield Ave Suite 206 — Virginia Beach VA 23462 757-497-2000 456-5458
Web: www.z104.com
WOWI-FM 102.9 (Urban) 1003 Norfolk Sq — Norfolk VA 23502 757-466-0009 466-7043
Web: www.103jamz.com
WPCE-AM 1400 (Rel) 645 Church St Suite 400 — Norfolk VA 23510 757-622-4600 624-6515
Web: www.wpce1400.com
WPTE-FM 94.9 (AC) 236 Clearfield Ave Suite 206 — Virginia Beach VA 23462 757-497-2000 456-5458
Web: www.pointradio.com
WPYA-FM 93.7 (Var)
999 Waterside Dr Dominion Tower Suite 500 — Norfolk VA 23510 757-640-8500 640-8552
Web: www.bob-fm.com
WROX-FM 96.1 (Alt)
999 Waterside Dr Dominion Tower Suite 500 — Norfolk VA 23510 757-640-8500 640-8552
Web: 96xwrox.com
WTAR-AM 850 (N/T)
999 Waterside Dr Dominion Tower Suite 500 — Norfolk VA 23510 757-640-8500 640-8552
Web: www.wtar.com
WVBW-FM 92.9 (Oldies) 5589 Greenwich Rd Suite 200 — Virginia Beach VA 23462 757-671-1000 671-1010
Web: www.929thewave.com
WVKL-FM 95.7 (Urban) 236 Clearfield Ave Suite 206 — Virginia Beach VA 23462 757-497-2000 456-5458
Web: www.957rnb.com
WWDE-FM 101.3 (AC) 236 Clearfield Ave Suite 206 — Virginia Beach VA 23462 757-497-2000 456-5458
Web: www.2wd.com
WXEZ-FM 94.1 (Rel) 5589 Greenwich Rd Suite 200 — Virginia Beach VA 23462 757-671-1000 671-1010
Web: www.wxez941.com
WXGM-FM 99.1 (AC) PO Box 634 — Gloucester VA 23061 804-693-9946 693-2182
WYCS-FM 91.5 (Rel)
7330 George Washington Memorial Hwy Bldg J — Yorktown VA 23692 757-886-7490

648-119 Ocean City, MD

Phone | Fax

WGBG-FM 98.5 (CR) 20200 DuPont Blvd — Georgetown DE 19947 302-856-2567 856-7633
TF: 888-780-0970 ■ *Web:* www.bigclassicrock.com
WGMD-FM 92.7 (N/T) PO Box 530 — Rehoboth Beach DE 19971 302-945-2050 945-3781
TF: 800-933-9027 ■ *Web:* www.wgmd.com
WICO-AM 1320 (N/T) 919 Ellegood St — Salisbury MD 21801 410-742-3212 548-1543
Web: www.wicoam.com
WLBW-FM 92.1 (Oldies) 351 Tilghman Rd — Salisbury MD 21804 410-742-1923 742-2329
TF: 800-762-0105 ■ *Web:* www.isurfthewave.com
WNCL-FM 101.3 (Oldies) PO Box 808 — Milford DE 19963 302-422-7575 422-3069
Web: www.wxpz.com
WOCM-FM 98.1 (AAA) Irie Radio 117 W 49th St — Ocean City MD 21842 410-723-3683 723-4347
Web: www.irieradio.com
WOLC-FM 102.5 (Rel) 11890 Crisfield Ln PO Box 130 — Princess Anne MD 21853 410-543-9652 651-9652
TF: 877-569-9652 ■ *Web:* www.wolc.org
WOSC-FM 95.9 (Rock) 351 Tilghman Rd — Salisbury MD 21804 410-742-1923 742-2329
TF: 800-762-0105 ■ *Web:* www.96rocksyou.com
WQHQ-FM 104.7 (AC) 351 Tilghman Rd — Salisbury MD 21804 410-742-1923 742-2329
TF: 800-762-0105 ■ *Web:* www.q105fm.com
WQJZ-FM 97.1 (NAC) 919 Ellegood St — Salisbury MD 21801 410-219-3500 548-1543
Web: www.wqjz.com
WSBY-FM 98.9 (Urban AC) 351 Tilghman Rd — Salisbury MD 21804 410-742-1923 742-2329
TF: 800-762-0105 ■ *Web:* www.wsby.com
WSCL-FM 89.5 (NPR) PO Box 2596 Salisbury University — Salisbury MD 21802 410-543-6895 548-3000
TF: 800-543-6895 ■ *Web:* www.wscl.org
WWFG-FM 99.9 (Ctry) 351 Tilghman Rd — Salisbury MD 21804 410-742-1923 742-2329
TF: 800-762-0105 ■ *Web:* www.froggy999.com
WXJN-FM 105.9 (Ctry) 919 Ellegood St — Salisbury MD 21801 410-742-3212 548-1543
Web: www.catcountryradio.com
WYUS-AM 930 (Span) PO Box 808 — Milford DE 19963 302-422-7575 422-3069
WZBH-FM 93.5 (Rock) 20200 DuPont Blvd — Georgetown DE 19947 302-856-2567 856-7633
TF: 888-780-0970 ■ *Web:* www.max925.com
WZEB-FM 101.7 (AC) 20200 DuPont Blvd — Georgetown DE 19947 302-856-2567 856-7633
TF: 888-780-0970 ■ *Web:* www.musicontheb.com

648-120 Oklahoma City, OK

Phone | Fax

KATT-FM 100.5 (Rock) 4045 NW 64th St Suite 600 — Oklahoma City OK 73116 405-848-0100 843-5288
Web: www.katt.com
KGOU-FM 106.3 (NPR) 860 Van Vleet Oval Rm 300 — Norman OK 73019 405-325-3388 325-7129
Web: www.kgou.org
KHBZ-FM 94.7 (Rock) 50 Penn Pl Suite 1000 — Oklahoma City OK 73118 405-840-5271 858-5333
Web: www.947thebuzz.com
KJYO-FM 102.7 (CHR) 50 Penn Pl Suite 1000 — Oklahoma City OK 73118 405-840-5271 858-5333
Web: www.kj103fm.com
KKNG-FM 93.3 (Ctry) 5101 S Shields Blvd — Oklahoma City OK 73129 405-616-5500 616-5505
Web: www.kkng.com
KKWD-FM 97.9 (CHR) 4045 NW 64th St Suite 600 — Oklahoma City OK 73116 405-848-0100 843-5288
Web: www.wild979.com

Oklahoma City, OK (Cont'd)

Station	City	State	ZIP	Phone	Fax
KMGL-FM 104.1 (AC) 400 E Britton Rd *Web:* www.magic104.com/	Oklahoma City	OK	73114	405-478-5104	475-7021
KOMA-FM 92.5 (Oldies) 400 E Britton Rd *Web:* www.komaradio.com/	Oklahoma City	OK	73114	405-478-5104	475-7021
KQCV-AM 800 (Rel) 1919 N Broadway *TF:* 888-909-5728 ■ *Web:* www.bottradionetwork.com	Oklahoma City	OK	73103	405-521-0800	521-1391
KRXO-FM 107.7 (CR) 400 E Britton Rd *Web:* www.krxo.com/	Oklahoma City	OK	73114	405-478-5104	475-7021
KTOK-AM 1000 (N/T) 50 Penn Pl Suite 1000 *Web:* www.ktok.com	Oklahoma City	OK	73118	405-840-5271	858-5333
KTST-FM 101.9 (Ctry) 50 Penn Pl Suite 1000 *Web:* www.thetwister.com	Oklahoma City	OK	73118	405-840-5271	858-5333
KVSP-FM 103.5 (Urban) 1528 NE 23rd St *Web:* www.kvsp.com	Oklahoma City	OK	73111	405-425-4100	424-8811
KXXY-FM 96.1 (Ctry) 50 Penn Pl Suite 1000 *Web:* www.kxy.com	Oklahoma City	OK	73118	405-840-5271	858-5333
KYIS-FM 98.9 (AC) 4045 NW 64th St Suite 600 *Web:* www.kyis.com	Oklahoma City	OK	73116	405-848-0100	843-5288
WWLS-AM 640 (Sports) 4045 NW 64th Suite 600 *Web:* www.thesportsanimal.com	Oklahoma City	OK	73116	405-848-0100	843-5288

648-121 Omaha, NE

Station	City	State	ZIP	Phone	Fax
KEZO-FM 92.3 (Rock) 5030 N 72nd St Suite 192 **Fax:* Sales ■ *Web:* www.z92.com	Omaha	NE	68134	402-592-5300	592-9434*
KFAB-AM 1110 (N/T) 5010 Underwood Ave *Web:* www.kfab.com	Omaha	NE	68132	402-561-2000	556-8937
KGOR-FM 99.9 (Oldies) 5010 Underwood Ave *Web:* www.kgor.com	Omaha	NE	68132	402-561-2000	556-8937
KHUS-FM 93.3 (Ctry) 5010 Underwood Ave *Web:* www.thedamstation.com	Omaha	NE	68132	402-561-2000	556-8937
KIOS-FM 91.5 (NPR) 3230 Burt St *Web:* www.kios.org	Omaha	NE	68131	402-557-2777	557-2559
KKCD-FM 105.9 (CR) 5030 N 72nd St Suite 192 **Fax:* Sales ■ *Web:* www.cd1059.com	Omaha	NE	68134	402-592-5300	592-9434*
KLTQ-FM 101.9 (AC) 5011 Capitol Ave *Web:* www.literock1019.com	Omaha	NE	68132	402-342-2000	827-5293
KQBW-FM 96.1 (Rock) 5010 Underwood Ave	Omaha	NE	68132	402-558-9696	556-8937
KQCH-FM 94.1 (CHR) 5030 N 72nd St Suite 192 **Fax:* Sales ■ *Web:* www.channel941.com	Omaha	NE	68134	402-592-5300	592-9434*
KQKQ-FM 98.5 (CHR) 5011 Capitol Ave *Web:* www.sweet985.com	Omaha	NE	68132	402-342-2000	827-5293
KSRZ-FM 104.5 (AC) 5030 N 72nd St Suite 192 **Fax:* Sales ■ *Web:* www.104star.com	Omaha	NE	68134	402-592-5300	592-9434*
KXKT-FM 103.7 (Ctry) 5010 Underwood Ave *Web:* www.thekat.com	Omaha	NE	68132	402-561-2000	556-8937
KXSP-AM 590 (Sports) 5030 N 72nd St Suite 192 **Fax:* Sales ■ *Web:* www.bigsports590.com	Omaha	NE	68134	402-592-5300	592-9434*

648-122 Orlando, FL

Station	City	State	ZIP	Phone	Fax
WCFB-FM 94.5 (AC) 4192 N John Young Pkwy *TF:* 800-299-2945 ■ *Web:* star94fm.com	Orlando	FL	32804	407-294-2945	297-7595
WDBO-AM 580 (N/T) 4192 N John Young Pkwy *Web:* 580wdbo.com	Orlando	FL	32804	407-295-5858	291-4879
WFLF-FM 540 (N/T) 2500 Maitland Center Pkwy Suite 401	Maitland	FL	32751	407-916-7800	916-7406
WHOO-AM 1080 (Sports) 1160 S Semoran Blvd Suite A *Web:* www.espn1080.com	Orlando	FL	32807	407-380-9255	382-7565
WHTQ-FM 96.5 (CR) 4192 N John Young Pkwy *Web:* whtq.com	Orlando	FL	32804	407-422-9696	425-9696
WJHM-FM 101.9 (Urban) 1800 Pembrook Dr Suite 400 *Web:* www.102jamzorlando.com	Orlando	FL	32810	407-919-1000	919-1136
WJRR-FM 101.1 (Alt) 2500 Maitland Center Pkwy Suite 401 *Web:* www.wjrr.com	Maitland	FL	32751	407-916-7800	916-7406
WLOQ-FM 103.1 (NAC) 2301 Lucien Way Suite 180 *Web:* www.wloq.com	Maitland	FL	32751	407-647-5557	647-4495
WMFE-FM 90.7 (NPR) 11510 E Colonial Dr *Web:* www.wmfe.org/907	Orlando	FL	32817	407-273-2300	273-3613
WMGF-FM 107.7 (AC) 2500 Maitland Center Pkwy Suite 401 *Web:* www.magic107.com	Maitland	FL	32751	407-916-7800	916-7406
WMMO-FM 98.9 (AC) 4192 N John Young Pkwy *Web:* wmmo.com	Orlando	FL	32804	407-422-9890	422-6177
WNUE-FM 98.1 (Span) 337 S North Lake Blvd Suite 1024 *Web:* www.mega981.com	Altamonte Springs	FL	32701	407-331-1777	830-6223
WOCL-FM 105.9 (Rock) 1800 Pembrook Dr Suite 400 *TF:* 877-919-1059 ■ *Web:* www.orock1059.com	Orlando	FL	32810	407-919-1000	919-1190
WOMX-FM 105.1 (AC) 1800 Pembrook Dr Suite 400 *TF:* 877-919-1051 ■ *Web:* www.mix1051.com	Orlando	FL	32810	407-919-1000	919-1190
WONQ-AM 1030 (Span AC) 1355 E Altamonte Dr	Altamonte Springs	FL	32701	407-830-0800	260-6100
WPCV-FM 97.5 (Ctry) 404 W Lime St *TF:* 800-227-9797 ■ *Web:* www.wpcv.com	Lakeland	FL	33815	863-682-8184	683-2409
WPYO-FM 95.3 (CHR) 4192 N John Young Pkwy *Web:* 953party.com	Orlando	FL	32804	407-295-9595	291-6912
WQTM-AM 740 (Span) 2500 Maitland Center Pkwy Suite 401	Maitland	FL	32751	407-916-7800	916-7406
WTKS-FM 104.1 (N/T) 2500 Maitland Center Pkwy Suite 401 *Web:* www.wtks.com	Maitland	FL	32751	407-916-7800	916-7406
WTLN-AM 950 (Rel) 1188 Lakeview Dr *Web:* www.wtln.com	Altamonte Springs	FL	32714	407-682-9494	682-7005
WUCF-FM 89.9 (Jazz) PO Box 162199 *Web:* wucf.ucf.edu	Orlando	FL	32816	407-823-0899	823-6364
WWKA-FM 92.3 (Ctry) 4192 N John Young Pkwy *TF:* 800-749-9292 ■ *Web:* k92fm.com	Orlando	FL	32804	407-424-9236	291-6192
WXXL-FM 106.7 (CHR) 2500 Maitland Center Pkwy Suite 401 *Web:* www.wxxl.com	Maitland	FL	32751	407-916-7800	916-7406

648-123 Ottawa, ON

Station	City	Prov	Postal Code	Phone	Fax
CBO-FM 91.5 (CBC) PO Box 3220 Stn C *Web:* www.cbc.ca/ottawa	Ottawa	ON	K1Y1E4	613-288-6485	288-6490
CBOF-FM 90.7 (CBC) PO Box 3220 Stn C *Web:* radio-canada.ca/radio	Ottawa	ON	K1Y1E4	613-288-6600	288-6560
CBOQ-FM 103.3 (CBC) PO Box 3220 Stn C *Web:* www.cbc.ca/ottawa	Ottawa	ON	K1Y1E4	613-288-6000	562-8416
CFGO-AM 1200 (Sports) 87 George St *Web:* www.team1200.com	Ottawa	ON	K1N9H7	613-789-2486	738-5024
CFRA-AM 580 (N/T) 87 George St *Web:* www.cfra.com	Ottawa	ON	K1N9H7	613-789-2486	738-5024
CHEZ-FM 106.1 (CR) 2001 Thurston Dr *Web:* www.chez106.com	Ottawa	ON	K1G6C9	613-736-2001	736-2002
CHRI-FM 99.1 (Rel) 1010 Thomas Spratt Pl Suite 3 *TF:* 866-247-1440 ■ *Web:* www.chri.ca	Ottawa	ON	K1G5L5	613-247-1440	247-7128
CHUO-FM 89.1 (Var) 65 University Private Suite 0038 *Web:* www.chuo.fm	Ottawa	ON	K1N9A5	613-562-5965	562-5969
CIMF-FM 94.9 (Rock) 15 Taschereau *Web:* www.rockdetente.com	Gatineau	QC	J8Y2V6	819-770-2463	770-9338
CIWW-AM 1310 (Oldies) 2001 Thurston Dr *Web:* www.oldies1310.com	Ottawa	ON	K1G6C9	613-736-2001	736-2002
CJMJ-FM 100.3 (AC) 87 George St *Web:* www.majic100.fm	Ottawa	ON	K1N9H7	613-789-2486	738-5024
CJRC-FM 104.7 (N/T) 150 d'Edmonton St *Web:* www.cjrc1150.com	Gatineau	QC	J8Y3S6	819-561-8801	561-9439
CKBY-FM 101.1 (Ctry) 2001 Thurston Dr *Web:* www.y101.fm	Ottawa	ON	K1G6C9	613-736-2001	736-2002
CKCU-FM 93.1 (Var) University Center 1125 Colonel By Dr Rm 517 *Web:* www.ckcufm.com	Ottawa	ON	K1S5B6	613-520-2898	520-4060
CKKL-FM 93.9 (CHR) 87 George St *Web:* www.939bobfm.com	Ottawa	ON	K1N9H7	613-789-2486	738-5024
CKQB-FM 106.9 (Rock) 1504 Merivale Rd *Web:* www3.thebear.fm	Ottawa	ON	K2E6Z5	613-225-1069	226-3381
CKTF-FM 104.1 (CHR) 15 Taschereau *Web:* www.radioenergie.com	Gatineau	QC	J8Y2V6	819-243-5555	243-6828

648-124 Oxnard, CA

Station	City	State	ZIP	Phone	Fax
KBBY-FM 95.1 (AC) 1376 Walter St *Web:* www.b951.com	Ventura	CA	93003	805-642-8595	656-5838
KCAQ-FM 104.7 (CHR) 2284 S Victoria Ave Suite 2G *Web:* www.q1047.com	Ventura	CA	93003	805-289-1400	644-7906
KCLU-FM 88.3 (NPR) 60 W Olsen Rd Suite 4400 *Web:* www.kclu.org	Thousand Oaks	CA	91360	805-493-3900	
KDAR-FM 98.3 (Rel) 500 Esplanado Dr *Web:* www.kdar.com	Oxnard	CA	93030	805-485-8881	656-5330
KDB-FM 93.7 (Clas) 414 E Cota St *Web:* www.kdb.com	Santa Barbara	CA	93101	805-966-4131	966-4788
KHAY-FM 100.7 (Ctry) 1376 Walter St *Web:* www.khay.com	Ventura	CA	93003	805-642-8595	656-5838
KHJL-FM 92.7 (AC) 99 Long Ct Suite 200 *Web:* www.927jillfm.com	Thousand Oaks	CA	91360	805-497-8511	497-8514
KKZZ-AM 1400 (N/T) 2284 S Victoria Ave Suite 2G	Ventura	CA	93003	805-289-1400	644-7906
KMLA-FM 103.7 (Span) 355 S 'A' St Suite 103 *Web:* www.lam1037.com	Oxnard	CA	93030	805-385-5656	385-5690
KOCP-FM 95.9 (CR) 2284 S Victoria Ave Suite 2G *Web:* www.theoctopus959.com	Ventura	CA	93003	805-289-1400	644-7906
KXLM-FM 102.9 (Span) 200 S 'A' St Suite 400	Oxnard	CA	93030	805-487-0444	240-5960

648-125 Palm Springs, CA

Station	City	State	ZIP	Phone	Fax
KCLB-FM 93.7 (Rock) 1321 N Gene Autry Trail *Web:* www.desertfun.com	Palm Springs	CA	92262	760-322-7890	322-5493
KDES-FM 104.7 (Oldies) 2100 Tahquitz Canyon Way *Web:* www.kdes.com	Palm Springs	CA	92262	760-325-2582	322-3562
KDGL-FM 106.9 (AC) 1321 N Gene Autry Trail *Web:* www.theeagle1069.com	Palm Springs	CA	92262	760-322-7890	322-5493
KESQ-AM 1400 (N/T) 42-650 Melanie Pl	Palm Desert	CA	92211	760-568-6830	568-3984
KEZN-FM 103.1 (AC) 72-915 Parkview Dr *Web:* www.ez103.com	Palm Desert	CA	92260	760-340-9383	340-5756
KJJZ-FM 102.3 (NAC) 441 S Calle Encilia Suite 8 *Web:* www.102kjjz.com	Palm Springs	CA	92262	760-320-4550	320-3037
KKUU-FM 92.7 (CHR) 1321 N Gene Autry Trail *Web:* www.927kkuu.com	Palm Springs	CA	92262	760-322-7890	322-5493
KLOB-FM 94.7 (Span) 41601 Corporate Way *TF:* 888-331-2667 ■ *Web:* www.radiosuperestrella.com	Palm Desert	CA	92260	760-341-5837	341-0951
KMRJ-FM 99.5 (Alt) 1061 S Palm Canyon Dr *Web:* www.m995.com	Palm Springs	CA	92264	760-778-6995	778-1249
KNWZ-AM 970 (N/T) 1321 N Gene Autry Trail *Web:* www.desertfun.com	Palm Springs	CA	92262	760-322-7890	322-5493
KPLM-FM 106.1 (Ctry) 441 S Calle Encilia Suite 8 *Web:* www.thebig106.com	Palm Springs	CA	92262	760-320-4550	320-3037
KPSI-AM 920 (N/T) 2100 Tahquitz Canyon Way *Web:* www.newstalk920.com	Palm Springs	CA	92262	760-325-2582	325-4693
KPSI-FM 100.5 (AC) 2100 Tahquitz Canyon Way *TF:* 877-282-2648 ■ *Web:* www.mix1005.fm	Palm Springs	CA	92262	760-325-2582	322-3562
KUNA-FM 96.7 (Span) 42-650 Melanie Pl	Palm Desert	CA	92211	760-568-6830	568-3984
KWXY-FM 98.5 (Soft AC) 68700 Dinah Shore Dr *Web:* www.kwxy.com	Cathedral City	CA	92234	760-328-1104	328-7814

648-126 Pensacola, FL

Station	City	State	ZIP	Phone	Fax
WBSR-AM 1450 (AC) 1601 N Pace Blvd *Web:* www.wbsr.com	Pensacola	FL	32505	850-438-4982	433-7932
WCOA-AM 1370 (N/T) 6565 N 'W' St Suite 270 *Web:* www.wcoapensacola.com	Pensacola	FL	32505	850-478-6011	478-3971
WGCX-FM 95.7 (Rel) 2070 N Palafox St *TF:* 888-831-6335 ■ *Web:* www.praise95.net	Pensacola	FL	32501	850-434-1230	469-9698
WMEZ-FM 94.1 (AC) 6085 Quinette Rd *TF:* 888-741-0941 ■ *Web:* www.softrock941.com	Pace	FL	32571	850-994-5357	994-4169
WPCS-FM 89.5 (Rel) 250 Brent Ln *TF:* 800-726-1191 ■ *Web:* www.rejoice.org	Pensacola	FL	32503	850-479-6570	969-1638
WPNN-AM 790 (N/T) 3801 N Pace Blvd *TF:* 888-433-1141 ■ *Web:* www.cnnpensacola.com	Pensacola	FL	32505	850-433-1141	433-1142
WRNE-AM 980 (Urban) 312 E Nine-Mile Rd Suite 29D *TF:* 866-478-8866 ■ *Web:* www.wrne980.com	Pensacola	FL	32514	850-478-6000	484-8080
WTKE-FM 98.1 (Sports) 21 Miracle Strip Pkwy *TF:* 877-981-0981 ■ *Web:* www.sportstalktheticket.com	Fort Walton Beach	FL	32548	850-244-1400	243-1471
WTKX-FM 101.5 (Rock) 6485 Pensacola Blvd *TF:* 888-357-7625 ■ *Web:* www.tk101.com	Pensacola	FL	32505	850-473-0400	473-0907
WUWF-FM 88.1 (NPR) University of West Florida 11000 University Pkwy Bldg 88 *TF:* 800-239-9893 ■ *Web:* wuwf.org	Pensacola	FL	32514	850-474-2787	474-3283
WXBM-FM 102.7 (Ctry) 6085 Quintette Rd *TF:* 800-626-9926 ■ *Web:* www.wxbm.com	Pace	FL	32571	850-994-5357	994-4169
WYCL-FM 107.3 (Oldies) 6485 Pensacola Blvd *TF:* 888-345-1073 ■ *Web:* www.cool107.com	Pensacola	FL	32505	850-473-0400	473-0907

648-127 Peoria, IL

Station	City	State	Zip	Phone	Fax
WCBU-FM 89.9 (NPR) 1501 W Bradley Ave *TF:* 888-488-9228 ■ *Web:* www.bradley.edu/wcbu	Peoria	IL	61625	309-677-3690	677-3462
WCIC-FM 91.5 (Rel) 3902 W Baring Trace *TF:* 877-692-9242 ■ *Web:* www.wcicfm.org	Peoria	IL	61615	309-282-9191	692-9241
WDQX-FM 102.3 (CR) 331 Fulton St Suite 1200 *Web:* www.eagleclassichits.com	Peoria	IL	61602	309-637-3700	272-1476
WFYR-FM 97.3 (Ctry) 120 Eaton St *TF:* 866-673-0973 ■ *Web:* www.973rivercountry.com	Peoria	IL	61603	309-676-5000	676-2600
WGLO-FM 95.5 (CR) 120 Eaton St *TF:* 888-676-9595 ■ *Web:* www.955glo.com	Peoria	IL	61603	309-676-5000	676-2600
WIXO-FM 105.7 (Rock) 120 Eaton St *TF:* 877-495-9496 ■ *Web:* www.99xrocks.com	Peoria	IL	61603	309-676-5000	676-2600
WMBD-AM 1470 (N/T) 331 Fulton St Suite 1200 *TF:* 800-698-1470 ■ *Web:* www.wmbdradio.com	Peoria	IL	61602	309-637-3700	686-8655
WPBG-FM 93.3 (CH) 331 Fulton St Suite 1200 *TF:* 800-310-0930 ■ *Web:* www.bigoldies933.com	Peoria	IL	61602	309-637-3700	686-8655
WPEO-AM 1020 (Rel) 1708 Highview Rd *TF:* 800-728-1020 ■ *Web:* www.wpeo.com	East Peoria	IL	61611	309-698-9736	698-9740
WSWT-FM 106.9 (AC) 331 Fulton St Suite 1200 *TF:* 800-597-1069 ■ *Web:* www.literock107.com	Peoria	IL	61602	309-637-3700	686-8655
WWCT-FM 99.9 (AAA) 4234 N Brandywine Dr Suite D *Web:* www.rock965.com	Peoria	IL	61614	309-686-0101	686-0111
WXCL-FM 104.9 (Ctry) 331 Fulton St Suite 1200 *Web:* www.wxcl.com	Peoria	IL	61602	309-637-3700	272-1476
WZPW-FM 92.3 (Urban) 4234 N Brandywine Dr Suite D *Web:* www.power92.net	Peoria	IL	61614	309-686-0101	686-0111

648-128 Philadelphia, PA

Station	City	State	Zip	Phone	Fax
KYW-AM 1060 (N/T) 400 Market St 10th Fl *Web:* www.kyw1060.com	Philadelphia	PA	19106	215-238-1060	977-5658
WBEB-FM 101.1 (AC) 10 Presidential Blvd *Web:* www.b101radio.com	Bala Cynwyd	PA	19004	610-667-8400	667-6795
WDAS-FM 105.3 (Urban AC) 111 Presidential Blvd Suite 100 *TF:* 877-894-1053 ■ *Web:* www.wdasfm.com	Bala Cynwyd	PA	19004	610-784-3333	784-2098
WEMG-AM 1310 (Span) 1341 N Delaware Ave Suite 509	Philadelphia	PA	19125	215-426-1900	426-1550
WHAT-AM 1340 (Nost) 10 Shurs Ln Suite 204 *Web:* www.martiniloungeradio.com	Philadelphia	PA	19127	267-285-5161	285-5185
WHYY-FM 90.9 (NPR) 150 N 6th St *Web:* www.whyy.org	Philadelphia	PA	19106	215-351-9200	351-1211
WIOQ-FM 102.1 (CHR) 111 Presidential Blvd Suite 100 *TF:* 800-521-1021 ■ *Web:* www.q102philly.com	Bala Cynwyd	PA	19004	610-784-3333	
WIP-AM 610 (Sports) 2 Bala Plaza Suite 700 *Web:* www.610wip.com	Bala Cynwyd	PA	19004	610-949-7800	949-7889
WJJZ-FM 106.1 (NAC) 111 Presidential Blvd Suite 100 *Web:* www.wjjz.com	Bala Cynwyd	PA	19004	610-784-3333	784-2049
WMGK-FM 102.9 (CR) 1 Bala Plaza Suite 339 *Web:* www.wmgk.com	Bala Cynwyd	PA	19004	610-667-8500	664-9610
WMMR-FM 93.3 (Rock) 1 Bala Plaza Suite 424 *Web:* www.wmmr.com	Bala Cynwyd	PA	19004	610-771-0933	771-9610
WMWX-FM 95.7 (AC) 1 Bala Plaza Suite 339 *TF:* 866-957-2363 ■ *Web:* www.957benfm.com	Bala Cynwyd	PA	19004	610-667-8500	771-9610
WOGL-FM 98.1 (Oldies) 2 Bala Plaza Suite 800 *Web:* www.wogl.com	Bala Cynwyd	PA	19004	610-668-5900	667-1904
WPEN-AM 950 (Sports) 1 Bala Plaza Suite 339 *Web:* www.wpen.com	Bala Cynwyd	PA	19004	610-667-8500	664-9610
WPHI-FM 100.3 (Urban) 1000 River Rd Suite 400 *TF:* 800-232-1003 ■ *Web:* www.1003thebeatphilly.com	Conshohocken	PA	19428	610-276-1100	276-1139
WPHT-AM 1210 (N/T) 2 Bala Plaza Suite 800 *Web:* www.thebigtalker1210.com	Bala Cynwyd	PA	19004	610-668-5800	668-5885
WRDW-FM 96.5 (Urban) 555 City Line Ave Suite 330 *Web:* www.wired965.com	Bala Cynwyd	PA	19004	610-667-9000	667-2972
WRTI-FM 90.1 (NPR) 1509 Cecil B Moore Ave 3rd Fl *TF:* 800-245-8776 ■ *Web:* www.wrti.org	Philadelphia	PA	19122	215-204-8405	204-7027
WUSL-FM 98.9 (Urban) 111 Presidential Blvd *Web:* www.power99.com	Bala Cynwyd	PA	19004	610-784-3333	784-2049
WXPN-FM 88.5 (AAA) 3025 Walnut St *Web:* www.xpn.org	Philadelphia	PA	19104	215-898-6677	898-0707
WXTU-FM 92.5 (Ctry) 555 City Line Ave Suite 330 *Web:* www.wxtu.com	Bala Cynwyd	PA	19004	610-667-9000	667-5978
WYSP-FM 94.1 (Rock) 400 Market St 9th Fl *Web:* www.941freefm.com	Philadelphia	PA	19106	215-625-9460	625-6555

648-129 Phoenix, AZ

Station	City	State	Zip	Phone	Fax
KBAQ-FM 89.5 (Clas) 2323 W 14th St *Web:* kbaq.org	Tempe	AZ	85281	480-833-1122	774-8475
KDKB-FM 93.3 (Rock) 1167 W Javelina Ave **Fax:* Sales ■ *Web:* www.kdkb.com	Mesa	AZ	85210	480-897-9300	897-1964*
KEDJ-FM 103.9 (Alt) 4745 N 7th St Suite 410 *Web:* www.theedge1039.com	Phoenix	AZ	85014	602-648-9800	283-0923
KESZ-FM 99.9 (AC) 4686 E Van Buren St Suite 300 *Web:* www.kez999.com	Phoenix	AZ	85008	602-374-6000	374-6035
KFYI-AM 550 (N/T) 4686 E Van Buren St Suite 300 *Web:* www.kfyi.com	Phoenix	AZ	85008	602-374-6000	374-6035
KGME-AM 910 (Sports) 4686 E Van Buren Suite 300 *Web:* www.xtrasports910.com	Phoenix	AZ	85008	602-374-6000	374-6035
KHOT-FM 105.9 (Span) 4745 N 7th St Suite 140 *Web:* khot.netmio.com	Phoenix	AZ	85014	602-308-7900	308-7979
KJZZ-FM 91.5 (NPR) 2323 W 14th St *Web:* kjzz.org	Tempe	AZ	85281	480-834-5627	774-8475
KKFR-FM 98.3 (Urban) 4745 N 7th St Suite 410 *Web:* www.power983fm.com	Phoenix	AZ	85014	602-682-9200	283-0923
KLNZ-FM 103.5 (Span) 501 N 44th St Suite 425 *TF:* 888-874-2656 ■ *Web:* www.entravision.com	Phoenix	AZ	85008	602-266-2005	279-2921
KMLE-FM 107.9 (Ctry) 840 N Central Ave *Web:* www.kmle108.com	Phoenix	AZ	85004	602-258-8181	440-6530
KMXP-FM 96.9 (AC) 4686 E Van Buren Suite 300 *Web:* www.mix969.com	Phoenix	AZ	85008	602-374-6000	374-6035
KNIX-FM 102.5 (Ctry) 4686 E Van Buren St Suite 300 *Web:* www.knixcountry.com	Phoenix	AZ	85008	602-374-6000	374-6035
KOMR-FM 106.3 (Span) 4745 N 7th St Suite 140 *Web:* kmrr.netmio.com	Phoenix	AZ	85014	602-308-7900	308-7979
KOOL-FM 94.5 (Oldies) 840 N Central Ave *Web:* www.koolradio.com	Phoenix	AZ	85004	602-956-9696	285-1450
KOY-AM 1230 (Nost) 4686 E Van Buren St Suite 300 *Web:* www.am1230koy.com	Phoenix	AZ	85008	602-374-6000	374-6035
KPKX-FM 98.7 (CR) 5300 N Central Ave *Web:* www.987thepeak.com	Phoenix	AZ	85012	602-274-6200	266-3858
KSLX-FM 100.7 (CR) 4343 E Camelback Rd Suite 200 **Fax Area Code:* 602 ■ **Fax:* Sales ■ *Web:* www.kslx.com	Phoenix	AZ	85018	480-941-1007	808-2287*
KTAR-AM 620 (N/T) 5300 N Central Ave *Web:* www.620ktar.com	Phoenix	AZ	85012	602-274-6200	266-3858
KUPD-FM 97.9 (Rock) 1900 W Carmen St *Web:* www.98kupd.com	Tempe	AZ	85283	480-838-0400	820-8469
KVVA-FM 107.1 (Span AC) 501 N 44th St Suite 425 *TF:* 800-420-2656 ■ *Web:* www.superestrella.com	Phoenix	AZ	85008	602-266-2005	279-2921
KXEG-AM 1280 (Rel) 2800 N 44th St Suite 100 *Web:* www.1280kxeg.com	Phoenix	AZ	85008	602-254-5001	296-3624
KYOT-FM 95.5 (NAC) 4686 E Van Buren St Suite 300 *Web:* www.kyot.com	Phoenix	AZ	85008	602-374-6000	374-6035
KZON-FM 101.5 (Urban) 4745 N 7th St Suite 210 *Web:* www.kzon.com	Phoenix	AZ	85014	602-258-8181	440-3373
KZZP-FM 104.7 (CHR) 4686 E Van Buren St Suite 300 *Web:* www.kzzp.com	Phoenix	AZ	85008	602-374-6000	374-6035

648-130 Pierre, SD

Station	City	State	Zip	Phone	Fax
KCCR-AM 1240 (N/T) 106 W Capitol Ave	Pierre	SD	57501	605-224-1240	224-0095
KGFX-AM 1060 (Ctry) 214 W Pleasant Dr *TF:* 800-658-3534 ■ *Web:* www.dakotaradiogroup.com	Pierre	SD	57501	605-224-8686	224-8984
KGFX-FM 92.7 (AC) 214 W Pleasant Dr *TF:* 800-658-3534 ■ *Web:* www.dakotaradiogroup.com	Pierre	SD	57501	605-224-8686	224-8984
KLXS-FM 95.3 (AC) 106 W Capitol Ave	Pierre	SD	57501	605-224-1240	224-0095
KMLO-FM 100.7 (Ctry) 214 W Pleasant Dr *TF:* 800-658-3534	Pierre	SD	57501	605-224-8686	224-8984
KPLO-FM 94.5 (Ctry) 214 W Pleasant Dr *TF:* 800-658-3534	Pierre	SD	57501	605-224-8686	224-8984
KWYR-FM 93.7 (AC) PO Box 491 *TF:* 800-388-5997 ■ *Web:* www.kwyr.com	Winner	SD	57580	605-842-3333	842-3875

648-131 Pittsburgh, PA

Station	City	State	Zip	Phone	Fax
KDKA-AM 1020 (N/T) 1 Gateway Center *Web:* www.kdkaradio.com	Pittsburgh	PA	15222	412-575-2200	575-2874
KQV-AM 1410 (N/T) 650 Smithfield St Centre City Towers *TF:* 800-424-1410 ■ *Web:* www.kqv.com	Pittsburgh	PA	15222	412-562-5900	562-5903
WAMO-AM 860 (Urban) 960 Penn Ave Suite 200	Pittsburgh	PA	15222	412-456-4000	456-4077
WAMO-FM 106.7 (Urban) 960 Penn Ave Suite 200 *TF:* 800-369-9266 ■ *Web:* www.wamo.com	Pittsburgh	PA	15222	412-456-4000	456-4077
WBGG-AM 970 (Sports) 200 Fleet St *Web:* www.fox970.com	Pittsburgh	PA	15220	412-937-1441	923-0323
WDSY-FM 107.9 (Ctry) 651 Holiday Dr Foster Plaza 2nd Fl *Web:* www.y108.com	Pittsburgh	PA	15220	412-920-9400	920-9449
WDUQ-FM 90.5 (NPR) Duquesne University 600 Forbes Ave *Web:* www.wduq.org	Pittsburgh	PA	15282	412-396-6030	396-5061
WDVE-FM 102.5 (Rock) 200 Fleet St *Web:* www.dve.com	Pittsburgh	PA	15220	412-937-1441	923-0323
WEAE-AM 1250 (Sports) 400 Ardmore Blvd *Web:* www.espnradio1250.com	Pittsburgh	PA	15221	412-731-0996	244-4596
WJAS-AM 1320 (Nost) 900 Parish St 3rd Fl *Web:* www.1320wjas.com	Pittsburgh	PA	15220	412-875-9500	875-9474
WKST-FM 96.1 (CHR) 200 Fleet St 4th Fl *Web:* www.kissfm961.com	Pittsburgh	PA	15220	412-937-1441	923-0323
WLTJ-FM 92.9 (AC) 650 Smithfield St Suite 2200 *Web:* www.wltj.com	Pittsburgh	PA	15222	412-316-3342	316-3388
WMBS-AM 590 (Oldies) 44 S Mt Vernon Ave *TF:* 866-590-9627 ■ *Web:* www.wmbs590.com	Uniontown	PA	15401	724-438-3900	438-2406
WOGG-FM 94.9 (Ctry) 123 Blaine Rd *TF:* 866-937-6449 ■ *Web:* www.froggyland.com	Brownsville	PA	15417	724-938-2000	938-7824
WORD-FM 101.5 (Rel) 7 Parkway Center Suite 625 *TF:* 800-320-8255 ■ *Web:* www.wordfm.com	Pittsburgh	PA	15220	412-937-1500	937-1576
WPGB-FM 104.7 (N/T) 200 Fleet St *Web:* www.wpgb.com	Pittsburgh	PA	15220	412-937-1441	923-0323
WPTT-AM 1360 (N/T) 900 Parish St 3rd Fl *Web:* www.1360wptt.com	Pittsburgh	PA	15220	412-875-9500	875-9474
WQED-FM 89.3 (Clas) 4802 5th Ave *TF:* 800-876-1316 ■ *Web:* www.wqed.org/fm	Pittsburgh	PA	15213	412-622-1436	622-7073
WRRK-FM 96.9 (Var) 650 Smithfield St Suite 2200 *Web:* www.rrk.com	Pittsburgh	PA	15222	412-316-3342	316-3388
WSHH-FM 99.7 (AC) 900 Parish St 3rd Fl *Web:* www.wshh.com	Pittsburgh	PA	15220	412-875-9500	875-9474
WTZN-FM 93.7 (CHR) 651 Holiday Dr Foster Plaza 2nd Fl *Web:* www.937krock.com	Pittsburgh	PA	15220	412-920-9400	920-9449
WWSW-FM 94.5 (Oldies) 200 Fleet St *Web:* www.3wsradio.com	Pittsburgh	PA	15220	412-937-1441	923-0323
WXDX-FM 105.9 (Alt) 200 Fleet St *Web:* www.1059thex.com	Pittsburgh	PA	15220	412-937-1441	937-0323
WYEP-FM 91.3 (Var) 67 Bedford Sq *TF:* 877-381-9900 ■ *Web:* www.wyep.org	Pittsburgh	PA	15203	412-381-9131	381-9126
WZPT-FM 100.7 (AC) 651 Holiday Dr Suite 310 *Web:* www.1007.com	Pittsburgh	PA	15220	412-920-9400	920-9449

648-132 Pocatello, ID

Station	City	State	Zip	Phone	Fax
KCVI-FM 101.5 (Rock) PO Box 699 *Web:* www.kbear.fm	Blackfoot	ID	83221	208-785-1400	785-0184
KFTZ-FM 103.3 (CHR) PO Box 699 *Web:* www.z103.fm	Blackfoot	ID	83221	208-785-1400	785-0184
KISU-FM 91.1 (NPR) Idaho State University Campus Box 8014 *Web:* www.isu.edu/kisufm	Pocatello	ID	83209	208-282-3691	282-4600
KLCE-FM 97.3 (AC) PO Box 699 *Web:* www.klce.com	Blackfoot	ID	83221	208-785-1400	785-0184
KLLP-FM 98.5 (AC) 259 E Center St *TF:* 800-582-1240 ■ *Web:* www.kllp.com	Pocatello	ID	83201	208-233-1133	232-1240
KMGI-FM 102.5 (CR) 544 N Arthur Ave *Web:* www.102kmgi.com	Pocatello	ID	83204	208-233-2121	234-7682
KORR-FM 104.1 (AC) 436 N Main St	Pocatello	ID	83204	208-234-1290	234-9451
KOUU-AM 1290 (Ctry) 436 N Main St	Pocatello	ID	83204	208-234-1290	234-9451
KPKY-FM 94.9 (CR) 259 E Center St *TF:* 800-582-1240 ■ *Web:* www.kpky.com	Pocatello	ID	83201	208-233-1133	232-1240
KRTK-AM 1490 (Rel) 1633 Olympus Dr	Pocatello	ID	83201	208-237-9500	237-4600
KSEI-AM 930 (Sports) 544 N Arthur Ave	Pocatello	ID	83204	208-233-2121	234-7682
KWIK-AM 1240 (N/T) 259 E Center St *TF:* 800-582-1240 ■ *Web:* www.newsradio1240.com	Pocatello	ID	83201	208-233-1133	232-1240
KZBQ-FM 93.7 (Ctry) 436 N Main St	Pocatello	ID	83204	208-234-1290	234-9451

648-133 Portland, ME

Station / Address	City	State	ZIP	Phone	Fax
WBAE-AM 1490 (Nost) 420 Western Ave *Web:* www.1490thebay.com	South Portland	ME	04106	207-774-4561	774-3788
WBLM-FM 102.9 (CR) 1 City Center *Web:* www.wblm.com	Portland	ME	04101	207-774-6364	774-8707
WCYY-FM 94.3 (Alt) 1 City Center *Web:* www.wcyy.com	Portland	ME	04101	207-774-6364	774-8707
WGAN-AM 560 (N/T) 420 Western Ave *Web:* www.wgan.com	South Portland	ME	04106	207-774-4561	774-3788
WHOM-FM 94.9 (AC) 1 City Center *Web:* www.whom949.com	Portland	ME	04101	207-774-6364	774-8707
WJAB-AM 1440 (Sports) 779 Warren Ave *Web:* www.thebigjab.com	Portland	ME	04103	207-773-9695	761-4406
WJBQ-FM 97.9 (CHR) 1 City Center *Web:* www.wjbq.com	Portland	ME	04101	207-774-6364	774-8707
WMEA-FM 90.1 (NPR) 309 Marginal Way *TF:* 800-884-1717 ■ *Web:* www.mainepublicradio.org	Portland	ME	04101	207-874-6570	761-0318
WMGX-FM 93.1 (AC) 420 Western Ave *Web:* www.wmgx.com	South Portland	ME	04106	207-774-4561	774-3788
WPOR-FM 101.9 (Ctry) 420 Western Ave *Web:* www.wpor.com	South Portland	ME	04106	207-774-4561	774-3788
WRED-FM 95.9 (Urban) 779 Warren Ave *Web:* www.redhot959.com	Portland	ME	04106	207-773-9695	761-4406
WTHT-FM 99.9 (Ctry) 477 Congress St 3rd Fl Annex *TF:* 866-900-9653 ■ *Web:* www.999thewolf.com	Portland	ME	04101	207-797-0780	797-0368
WYNZ-FM 100.9 (Oldies) 420 Western Ave *Web:* www.wynz.com	South Portland	ME	04106	207-774-4561	774-3788

648-134 Portland/Salem, OR

Station / Address	City	State	ZIP	Phone	Fax
KBNP-AM 1410 (N/T) 278 SW Arthur St *Web:* www.kbnp.com	Portland	OR	97201	503-223-6769	223-4305
KBOO-FM 90.7 (Var) 20 SE 8th Ave *Web:* www.kboo.fm	Portland	OR	97214	503-231-8032	231-7145
KBPS-FM 89.9 (Clas) 515 NE 15th Ave *TF:* 888-306-5277 ■ *Web:* www.allclassical.org	Portland	OR	97232	503-943-5828	802-9456
KBVM-FM 88.3 (Rel) 5000 N Willamette Blvd Box 44 *Web:* www.kbvm.com	Portland	OR	97203	503-285-5200	285-3322
KBZY-AM 1490 (AC) 2659 Commercial St SE Suite 204 *Web:* www.kbzy.com	Salem	OR	97302	503-362-1490	362-6545
KEX-AM 1190 (N/T) 4949 SW Macadam Ave *TF:* 800-345-1190 ■ *Web:* www.1190kex.com	Portland	OR	97239	503-242-1190	323-6666
KFIS-FM 104.1 (Rel) 6400 SE Lake Rd Suite 350 *Web:* www.1041thefish.com	Portland	OR	97222	503-786-0600	786-1551
KFXX-AM 1080 (Sports) 0700 SW Bancroft St *Web:* www.1080thefan.com	Portland	OR	97239	503-223-1441	223-6909
KGON-FM 92.3 (CR) 0700 SW Bancroft St *TF:* 800-222-9236 ■ *Web:* www.kgon.com	Portland	OR	97239	503-223-1441	223-6909
KINK-FM 101.9 (AAA) 1501 SW Jefferson St *TF:* 877-567-5465 ■ *Web:* www.kink.fm	Portland	OR	97201	503-517-6000	517-6130
KKAD-AM 1550 (Oldies) 6605 SE Lake Rd *TF:* 866-517-1550 ■ *Web:* www.1550kkad.com	Portland	OR	97222	503-228-5523	294-0074
KKCW-FM 103.3 (AC) 4949 SW Macadam Ave *TF:* 800-333-0103 ■ *Web:* www.k103.com	Portland	OR	97239	503-222-5103	323-6664
KKRZ-FM 100.3 (CHR) 4949 SW Macadam Ave *TF:* 888-483-0100 ■ *Web:* www.z100portland.com	Portland	OR	97239	503-460-0100	323-6660
KLTH-FM 106.7 (AC) 222 SW Columbia Ave Suite 350 *Web:* www.khits1067.com	Portland	OR	97201	503-223-0300	517-6315
KNRK-FM 94.7 (Alt) 0700 SW Bancroft St *TF:* 800-777-0947 ■ *Web:* www.947.fm	Portland	OR	97239	503-223-1441	223-6909
KOOR-AM 1010 (Span) 5110 SE Stark St	Portland	OR	97251	503-234-5550	234-5583
KOPB-FM 91.5 (NPR) 7140 SW Macadam Ave *Web:* www.opb.org	Portland	OR	97219	503-293-1905	
KPDQ-FM 93.9 (Rel) 6400 SE Lake Rd Suite 350 *TF:* 800-845-2162 ■ *Web:* www.kpdq.com	Portland	OR	97222	503-786-0600	786-1551
KPOJ-AM 620 (N/T) 4949 SW Macadam Ave *TF:* 866-452-0620 ■ *Web:* www.620kpoj.com	Portland	OR	97239	503-323-6400	323-6664
KQOL-FM 105.9 (Oldies) 4949 SW Macadam Ave *Web:* www.kool1059.com	Portland	OR	97239	503-323-6400	323-6664
KRSK-FM 105.1 (AC) 0700 SW Bancroft St *Web:* www.1051thebuzz.com	Portland	OR	97239	503-223-1441	223-6909
KUFO-FM 101.1 (Rock) 2040 SW 1st Ave *TF:* 800-344-5836 ■ *Web:* www.kufo.com	Portland	OR	97201	503-222-1011	222-2047
KUPL-FM 98.7 (Ctry) 222 SW Columbia Ave Suite 350 *TF:* 800-533-5875 ■ *Web:* www.kupl.com	Portland	OR	97201	503-517-6200	223-6542
KVMX-FM 107.5 (AC) 2040 SW 1st Ave *TF:* 800-567-1075	Portland	OR	97201	503-222-1011	517-6401
KWBY-AM 940 (Span) 1665 James St	Woodburn	OR	97071	503-981-9400	981-3561
KWJJ-FM 99.5 (Ctry) 0700 SW Bancroft St *TF:* 866-239-9653 ■ *Web:* www.thewolfonline.com	Portland	OR	97239	503-223-1441	223-6909
KXJM-FM 95.5 (Sports) 0234 SW Bancroft St *Fax: News Rm ■ *TF:* 800-990-0750 ■ *Web:* www.955thegame.com	Portland	OR	97239	503-243-7595	417-7661*
KXL-AM 750 (N/T) 0234 SW Bancroft St *Fax: News Rm ■ *TF:* 800-990-0750 ■ *Web:* www.kxl.com	Portland	OR	97239	503-243-7595	417-7661*
KYCH-FM 97.1 (AC) 0700 SW Bancroft St *Web:* www.kisnfm.com	Portland	OR	97239	503-223-1441	223-6909
KYKN-AM 1430 (N/T) PO Box 1430 *Web:* www.kykn.com	Salem	OR	97308	503-390-3014	390-3728

648-135 Providence, RI

Station / Address	City	State	ZIP	Phone	Fax
WADK-AM 1540 (N/T) 15 Dr Marcus Wheatland Blvd *Web:* www.wadk.com	Newport	RI	02840	401-846-1540	846-1598
WARV-AM 1590 (Rel) 19 Luther Ave *Web:* www.warv.net	Warwick	RI	02886	401-737-0700	737-1604
WBRU-FM 95.5 (Alt) 88 Benevolent St *Web:* www.wbru.com	Providence	RI	02906	401-272-9550	272-9278
WCTK-FM 98.1 (Ctry) 75 Oxford St *Web:* www.wctk.com	Providence	RI	02905	401-467-4366	941-2795
WDOM-FM 91.3 (Var) 549 River Ave Providence College Slaven Center *Web:* studentweb.providence.edu/~wdom	Providence	RI	02918	401-865-2460	865-2522
WFHN-FM 107.1 (CHR) 22 Sconticut Neck Rd *Web:* www.fun107.com	Fairhaven	MA	02719	508-999-6690	999-1420
WHJJ-AM 920 (N/T) 75 Oxford St 3rd Fl *Web:* www.whjjam.com	Providence	RI	02905	401-781-9979	781-9329
WHJY-FM 94.1 (Rock) 75 Oxford St 3rd Fl *Web:* www.whjy.com	Providence	RI	02905	401-781-9979	781-9329
WPMZ-AM 1110 (Span) 1270 Mineral Springs Ave	North Providence	RI	02904	401-726-8413	726-8649
WPRO-AM 630 (N/T) 1502 Wampanoag Trail *TF:* 800-321-9776 ■ *Web:* www.630wpro.com	East Providence	RI	02915	401-433-4200	433-2932
WPRO-FM 92.3 (CHR) 1502 Wampanoag Trail *TF:* 800-638-0092 ■ *Web:* www.92profm.com	East Providence	RI	02915	401-433-4200	433-2932
WRNI-AM 1290 (NPR) 1 Union Stn *Web:* www.wrni.org	Providence	RI	02903	401-351-2800	351-0246
WSNE-FM 93.3 (AC) 75 Oxford St 3rd Fl *Web:* www.coast933.com	Providence	RI	02905	401-781-9979	781-9929
WWBB-FM 101.5 (Oldies) 75 Oxford St 3rd Fl *TF:* 800-808-2101 ■ *Web:* www.b101.com	Providence	RI	02905	401-781-9979	781-9329
WWKX-FM 106.3 (Urban) 1502 Wampanoag Trail *TF:* 888-224-1063 ■ *Web:* www.hot1063.com	East Providence	RI	02915	401-433-4200	433-5967
WWLI-FM 105.1 (AC) 1502 Wampanoag Trail *Web:* www.lite105.com	East Providence	RI	02915	401-433-4200	433-2932

648-136 Quebec City, QC

Station / Address	City	State	ZIP	Phone	Fax
CBV-FM 106.3 (CBC) PO Box 18800 *Web:* www.radio-canada.ca	Sainte-Foy	QC	G1K9L4	418-654-1341	691-3610
CBVE-FM 104.7 (CBC) 888 Saint Jean St *Web:* www.cbc.ca	Quebec City	QC	G1R5H6	418-691-3620	691-3610
CHIK-FM 98.9 (CHR) 900 Dyouville 1st Fl *Web:* www.radioenergie.com	Quebec	QC	G1R3P7	418-687-9900	687-3106
CHVD-FM 100.3 (AC) 1975 Walberg Blvd	Dolbeau-Mistassini	QC	G8L1Y5	418-276-3333	276-6755
CITF-FM 107.5 (Rock) 900 Dyouville 1st Fl *Web:* www.rockdetente.com	Quebec	QC	G1R3P7	418-527-3232	687-3106
CJMF-FM 93.3 (Var) 1305 ch Sainte-Foy Suite 402 *Fax: Sales ■ *Web:* www.cjmf.com	Quebec	QC	G1S4Y5	418-687-9330	687-0211*
CKIA-FM 88.3 (Var) 600 Cote d'Abraham *Web:* www.meduse.org/ckiafm	Quebec	QC	G1R1A1	418-529-9026	529-4156

648-137 Raleigh/Durham, NC

Station / Address	City	State	ZIP	Phone	Fax
WBBB-FM 96.1 (Rock) 3012 Highwoods Blvd Suite 200 *Web:* www.96rockonline.com	Raleigh	NC	27604	919-876-3831	876-9213
WDCG-FM 105.1 (CHR) 3100 Smoketree Ct Suite 700 *Web:* www.g105.com	Raleigh	NC	27604	919-878-1500	876-2929
WDNC-AM 620 (Sports) 4601 Six Forks Rd Suite 520 *Web:* www.620thebull.com	Raleigh	NC	27609	919-875-9100	510-6990
WFXC-FM 107.1 (Urban AC) 8001-101 Creedmoor Rd *TF:* 800-467-3699 ■ *Web:* www.foxyhits.com	Raleigh	NC	27613	919-848-9736	844-3947
WFXK-FM 104.3 (Urban AC) 8001-101 Creedmoor Rd *Web:* www.foxyhits.com	Raleigh	NC	27613	919-848-9736	844-3947
WKNC-FM 88.1 (Rock) NCSU Box 8607 343 Witherspoon Student Center *Web:* wknc.org	Raleigh	NC	27695	919-515-2401	513-2693
WKSL-FM 93.9 (CHR) 3100 Smoketree Ct Suite 700 *Web:* www.sunny939.com	Raleigh	NC	27604	919-878-1500	876-2929
WNCU-FM 90.7 (NPR) PO Box 19875 *Web:* www.wncu.org	Durham	NC	27707	919-530-7445	530-5031
WNNL-FM 103.9 (Rel) 8001-101 Creedmoor Rd *TF:* 877-310-9665 ■ *Web:* www.thelight1039.com	Raleigh	NC	27613	919-848-9736	844-3947
WPTF-AM 680 (N/T) 3012 Highwoods Blvd Suite 200 *TF:* 800-662-7979 ■ *Web:* www.wptf.com	Raleigh	NC	27604	919-876-0674	790-8369
WQDR-FM 94.7 (Ctry) 3012 Highwoods Blvd Suite 200 *TF:* 800-233-9497 ■ *Web:* www.947qdr.com	Raleigh	NC	27604	919-876-0674	790-8893
WQOK-FM 97.5 (Urban) 8001-101 Creedmoor Rd *TF:* 800-321-5975 ■ *Web:* www.k975.com	Raleigh	NC	27613	919-848-9736	844-3947
WRAL-FM 101.5 (AC) 711 Hillsborough St *TF:* 800-849-6101 ■ *Web:* www.wralfm.com	Raleigh	NC	27603	919-890-6101	890-6146
WRBZ-AM 850 (Sports) 4601 Six Forks Rd Suite 520 *Web:* www.850thebuzz.com	Raleigh	NC	27609	919-875-9100	510-6990
WRDU-FM 106.1 (Ctry) 3100 Smoketree Ct Suite 700 *Web:* www.1061rdu.com	Raleigh	NC	27604	919-878-1500	876-2929
WRJD-AM 1410 (Rel) 707 Leon St *Web:* www.1410wrjd.com	Durham	NC	27704	919-220-3226	220-0006
WRVA-FM 100.7 (AC) 3100 Smoketree Ct Suite 700 *Web:* www.1007theriver.com	Raleigh	NC	27604	919-878-1500	876-2929
WSHA-FM 88.9 (Jazz) 118 E South St *TF:* 800-241-0421 ■ *Web:* www.wshafm.org	Raleigh	NC	27601	919-546-8430	546-8315
WUNC-FM 91.5 (NPR) University of North Carolina Box 0915 *TF:* 800-962-9862 ■ *Web:* www.wunc.org	Chapel Hill	NC	27599	919-966-5454	
WWMY-FM 102.9 (Oldies) 3012 Highwoods Blvd Suite 201 *Web:* www.y1029.com	Raleigh	NC	27604	919-790-9392	790-8990
WXDU-FM 88.7 (Alt) PO Box 90689 *Web:* www.wxdu.duke.edu	Durham	NC	27708	919-684-2957	684-3260
WZTK-FM 101.1 (N/T) 1109 Tower Dr *TF:* 866-482-1011 ■ *Web:* www.fmtalk1011.com	Burlington	NC	27215	336-584-0126	584-0739

648-138 Rapid City, SD

Station / Address	City	State	ZIP	Phone	Fax
KBHE-FM 89.3 (NPR) 555 N Dakota St PO Box 5000 *TF:* 800-456-0766 ■ *Web:* www.sdpb.org	Vermillion	SD	57069	605-677-5861	677-5010
KFXS-FM 100.3 (CR) 660 Flormann St Suite 100 *Web:* www.foxradio.com	Rapid City	SD	57701	605-348-1100	343-9012
KIMM-AM 1150 (Ctry) 11 Main St	Rapid City	SD	57702	605-342-1150	343-1096
KIQK-FM 104.1 (Ctry) 306 1/2 E Saint Joseph St *TF:* 800-456-2613	Rapid City	SD	57701	605-343-0888	342-3075
KKLS-AM 920 (Oldies) 660 Flormann St Suite 100	Rapid City	SD	57701	605-343-6161	343-9012
KKMK-FM 93.9 (AC) 660 Flormann St Suite 100	Rapid City	SD	57701	605-343-6161	343-9012
KLMP-FM 88.3 (Rel) 1853 Fountain Plaza Dr *Web:* www.klmp.com	Rapid City	SD	57702	605-342-6822	342-0854
KOTA-AM 1380 (N/T) 518 Saint Joseph St *Web:* kotaradio.rapidnet.com	Rapid City	SD	57701	605-342-2000	342-7305
KOUT-FM 98.7 (Ctry) 660 Flormann St Suite 100 *Web:* www.katradio.com	Rapid City	SD	57701	605-348-1100	343-9012
KRCS-FM 93.1 (CHR) 660 Flormann St Suite 100 *Web:* www.hot931.com	Rapid City	SD	57701	605-343-6161	343-9012
KTOQ-AM 1340 (N/T) 306 1/2 E Saint Joseph St *TF:* 800-456-2613	Rapid City	SD	57701	605-343-0888	342-3075
KZLK-FM 106.3 (AC) 518 Saint Joseph St	Rapid City	SD	57701	605-342-2000	342-7305

648-139 Reno/Carson City, NV

Station / Address	City	State	ZIP	Phone	Fax
KBUL-FM 98.1 (Ctry) 595 E Plumb Ln *Web:* www.kbul.com	Reno	NV	89502	775-789-6700	789-6767
KDOT-FM 104.5 (Rock) 2900 Sutro St *Web:* www.kdot.com	Reno	NV	89512	775-329-9261	323-1450

				Phone	Fax
KJFK-AM 1230 (N/T) 961 Matley Ln Suite 120	Reno	NV	89502	775-829-1964	825-3183
Web: www.1230kjfk.com/					
KKOH-AM 780 (N/T) 595 E Plumb Ln	Reno	NV	89502	775-789-6700	789-6767
Web: www.kkoh.com					
KLCA-FM 96.5 (Alt) 961 Matley Ln Suite 120	Reno	NV	89502	775-829-1964	825-3183
Web: www.alice965.com					
KNIS-FM 91.3 (Rel) 6363 Hwy 50 E	Carson City	NV	89701	775-883-5647	
TF: 800-541-5647 ■ *Web:* www.pilgrimradio.com					
KODS-FM 103.7 (Oldies) 961 Matley Ln Suite 120	Reno	NV	89502	775-829-1964	825-3183
Web: www.river1037.com					
KOZZ-FM 105.7 (CR) 2900 Sutro St	Reno	NV	89512	775-329-9261	323-1450
Web: www.kozzradio.com					
KRNO-FM 106.9 (AC) 961 Matley Ln Suite 120	Reno	NV	89502	775-829-1964	825-3183
Web: www.sunny1069.com					
KRNV-FM 102.1 (Span) 300 S Wells Ave Suite 12	Reno	NV	89502	775-333-1017	333-9046
KRZQ-FM 100.9 (Alt) 300 E 2nd St Suite 1400	Reno	NV	89501	775-333-0123	322-7361
Web: www.krzqfm.com					
KTHX-FM 100.1 (AAA) 300 E 2nd St Suite 1400	Reno	NV	89501	775-333-0123	322-7361
Web: www.kthxfm.com					
KUNR-FM 88.7 (NPR) University of Nevada-Reno MS-294	Reno	NV	89557	775-327-5867	327-5386
Web: www.kunr.org					
KUUB-FM 94.5 (Ctry) 2900 Sutro St	Reno	NV	89512	775-329-9261	323-1450
Web: www.cubcountry945.com					

648-140 Richmond, VA

				Phone	Fax
WBBT-FM 107.3 (Oldies) 300 Arboretum Pl Suite 590	Richmond	VA	23236	804-327-9902	327-9911
Web: www.oldies1073.net					
WBTJ-FM 106.5 (Urban) 3245 Basie Rd	Richmond	VA	23228	804-474-0000	474-0096
Web: www.wbtj.com					
WCDX-FM 92.1 (Urban) 2809 Emerywood Pkwy Suite 300	Richmond	VA	23294	804-672-9299	672-9316
Web: www.power921jamz.com					
WCVE-FM 88.9 (NPR) 23 Sesame St	Richmond	VA	23235	804-320-1301	320-8729
Web: www.ideastations.org/wcvefm					
WDYL-FM 101.1 (Rock) 812 Moorefield Park Dr Suite 300	Richmond	VA	23236	804-330-5700	330-4079
Web: www.y101rocks.com					
WFTH-AM 1590 (Rel) 227 E Belt Blvd	Richmond	VA	23224	804-233-0765	233-3725
Web: www.faith1590.com					
WKHK-FM 95.3 (Ctry) 812 Moorefield Park Dr Suite 300	Richmond	VA	23236	804-330-5700	330-4079
Web: k95country.com					
WKJM-FM 99.3 (Urban) 2809 Emerywood Pkwy Suite 300	Richmond	VA	23294	804-672-9299	672-9316
WKJS-FM 105.7 (Urban) 2809 Emerywood Pkwy Suite 300	Richmond	VA	23294	804-672-9299	672-9316
Web: www.yestokiss.com					
WKLR-FM 96.5 (CR) 812 Moorefield Park Dr Suite 300	Richmond	VA	23236	804-330-5700	330-4079
Web: 965theplanet.com					
WLEE-AM 990 (N/T) 308 W Broad St	Richmond	VA	23220	804-643-0990	643-4990
Web: www.radiorichmond.com					
WLFV-FM 93.1 (Ctry) 300 Arboretum Pl Suite 590	Richmond	VA	23236	804-327-9902	327-9911
Web: www.931thewolf.com					
WMXB-FM 103.7 (AC) 812 Moorefield Park Dr Suite 300	Richmond	VA	23236	804-330-5700	330-4079
Web: mix1037.com					
WRNL-AM 910 (Sports) 3245 Basie Rd	Richmond	VA	23228	804-474-0000	474-0096
Web: www.sportsradio910.com					
WRVA-AM 1140 (N/T) 3245 Basie Rd	Richmond	VA	23228	804-474-0000	474-0096
Web: www.wrva.com					
WRVQ-FM 94.5 (CHR) 3245 Basie Rd	Richmond	VA	23228	804-474-0000	474-0096
Web: www.wrvq94.com					
WRXL-FM 102.1 (Rock) 3245 Basie Rd	Richmond	VA	23228	804-474-0000	474-0096
Web: www.1021thex.com					
WTVR-FM 98.1 (AC) 3245 Basie Rd	Richmond	VA	23228	804-474-0000	474-0096
Web: www.lite98.com					
WVNZ-AM 1320 (Span) 308 W Broad St	Richmond	VA	23220	804-643-0990	643-4990
Web: www.radiorichmond.com					
WXGI-AM 950 (Sports) 701 German School Rd	Richmond	VA	23225	804-233-7666	233-7681
Web: www.espn950am.com					

648-141 Riverside/San Bernardino, CA

				Phone	Fax
KCAL-AM 1410 (Span) 1950 S Sunwest Ln Suite 302	San Bernardino	CA	92408	909-825-5020	884-5844
Web: www.radiolazer.com					
KCAL-FM 96.7 (Rock) 1940 Orange Tree Ln Suite 200	Redlands	CA	92374	909-793-3554	798-6627
Web: www.kcalfm.com					
KCXX-FM 103.9 (Alt) 242 E Airport Dr Suite 106	San Bernardino	CA	92408	909-890-5904	890-9035
Web: www.x1039.com					
KDIF-AM 1440 (Span) 2030 Iowa Ave Suite A	Riverside	CA	92507	951-684-1991	274-4911
Web: www.kdif.com					
KFRG-FM 95.1 (Ctry) 900 E Washington St Suite 315	Colton	CA	92324	909-825-9525	825-0441
TF: 888-431-3764 ■ *Web:* www.kfrog.com					
KGGI-FM 99.1 (CHR) 2030 Iowa Ave Suite A	Riverside	CA	92507	951-684-1991	274-4911*
**Fax:* Sales ■ *Web:* www.kggiradio.com					
KKDD-AM 1290 (Kids) 2030 Iowa Ave Suite A	Riverside	CA	92507	951-684-1991	274-4911*
**Fax:* Sales					
KOLA-FM 99.9 (Clas) 1940 Orange Tree Ln Suite 200	Redlands	CA	92374	909-793-3554	793-7225
Web: www.kolafm.com					
KPRO-AM 1570 (Rel) 7351 Lincoln Ave	Riverside	CA	92504	951-688-1570	688-7009
Web: www.bristar.com/kpro/					
KSGN-FM 89.7 (Rel) 2048 Orange Tree Ln Suite 200	Redlands	CA	92354	909-583-2150	583-2170
TF: 800-321-5746 ■ *Web:* www.ksgn.com					
KUCR-FM 88.3 (Var) UC Riverside	Riverside	CA	92521	951-827-3737	827-3240
Web: www.kucr.org					
KVCR-FM 91.9 (NPR) 701 S Mt Vernon Ave	San Bernardino	CA	92410	909-384-4444	885-2116
Web: www.kvcr.org					
KXFG-FM 92.9 (Ctry) 900 E Washington St Suite 315	Colton	CA	92324	909-825-9525	825-0441
KXSB-FM 101.7 (Span) 345 W Fairway Blvd'	Big Bear	CA	92314	909-584-1069	584-1041
Web: www.radiolazer.com					

648-142 Roanoke, VA

				Phone	Fax
WFIR-AM 960 (N/T) 3934 Electric Rd SW	Roanoke	VA	24018	540-345-1511	342-2270
Web: www.wfir960.com					
WJJS-FM 106.1 (CHR) 3807 Brandon Ave SW Suite 2350	Roanoke	VA	24018	540-725-1220	725-1245
Web: www.wjjs.com					
WLLL-AM 930 (Rel) PO Box 11375	Lynchburg	VA	24506	434-385-9555	385-6073
TF: 888-224-9809 ■ *Web:* www.wlllradio.com					
WMGR-FM 104.9 (AC) 3305 Old Forest Rd	Lynchburg	VA	24501	434-385-8298	385-8991
Web: www.magicfm.cc					
WRIS-AM 1410 (Rel) 219 Luckett St NW	Roanoke	VA	24017	540-342-1410	342-5952
WROV-FM 96.3 (Rock) 3807 Brandon Ave SW Suite 2350	Roanoke	VA	24018	540-725-1220	725-1245
Web: www.96-3rov.com					
WSLC-FM 94.9 (Ctry) 3934 Electric Rd SW	Roanoke	VA	24018	540-387-0234	342-2270
Web: www.949starcountry.com					
WSLQ-FM 99.1 (AC) 3934 Electric Rd SW	Roanoke	VA	24018	540-387-0234	342-2270
Web: www.q99fm.com					
WSNV-FM 93.5 (AC) 3807 Brandon Ave SW Suite 2350	Roanoke	VA	24018	540-725-1220	725-1245
Web: www.sunny935.com					
WVTF-FM 89.1 (NPR) 3520 Kingsbury Ln	Roanoke	VA	24014	540-231-8900	776-2727
TF: 800-856-8900 ■ *Web:* www.wvtf.org					
WXLK-FM 92.3 (CHR) 3934 Electric Rd SW	Roanoke	VA	24018	540-774-9200	774-5667
Web: www.k92radio.com					
WYYD-FM 107.9 (Ctry) 3305 Old Forest Rd	Lynchburg	VA	24501	434-385-8298	385-8991
Web: www.wyyd.cc					

648-143 Rochester, MN

				Phone	Fax
KAUS-FM 99.9 (Ctry) 18431 State Hwy 105	Austin	MN	55912	507-437-7666	437-7669
KFSI-FM 92.9 (Rel) 4016 28th St SE	Rochester	MN	55904	507-289-8585	529-4017
Web: www.kfsi.org					
KLSE-FM 91.7 (Clas) 206 S Broadway Suite 735	Rochester	MN	55904	507-282-0910	282-2107
TF: 800-652-9700 ■ *Web:* www.mpr.org					
KNFX-AM 970 (Span) 1530 Greenview Dr SW Suite 200	Rochester	MN	55902	507-288-3888	288-7815
KOLM-AM 1520 (Sports) 122 SW 4th St	Rochester	MN	55902	507-286-1010	286-9370
KRCH-FM 101.7 (CR) 1530 Greenview Dr SW Suite 200	Rochester	MN	55902	507-288-3888	288-7815
Web: www.laser1017.net					
KROC-AM 1340 (N/T) 122 SW 4th St	Rochester	MN	55902	507-286-1010	286-9370
Web: www.kroc.com/kroc_am					
KROC-FM 106.9 (CHR) 122 SW 4th St	Rochester	MN	55902	507-286-1010	286-9370
Web: www.kroc.com/kroc_fm					
KWEB-AM 1270 (Sports) 1530 Greenview Dr SW Suite 200	Rochester	MN	55902	507-288-3888	288-7815
Web: www.fan1270.com					
KWWK-FM 96.5 (Ctry) 122 SW 4th St	Rochester	MN	55902	507-286-1010	286-9370
TF: 888-599-5965 ■ *Web:* www.kwwkfm.com					
KYBA-FM 105.3 (AC) 122 SW 4th St	Rochester	MN	55902	507-286-1010	286-9370
Web: www.y105fm.com					
KZSE-FM 90.7 (NPR) 206 S Broadway Suite 735	Rochester	MN	55904	507-282-0910	282-2107
TF: 800-652-9700 ■ *Web:* www.mpr.org					

648-144 Rochester, NY

				Phone	Fax
WBEE-FM 92.5 (Ctry) 70 Commercial St	Rochester	NY	14614	585-423-2900	423-2947
Web: www.wbee.com					
WBZA-FM 98.9 (CR) 70 Commercial St	Rochester	NY	14614	585-423-2900	423-2947
Web: www.rochesterbuzz.com					
WCMF-FM 96.5 (CR) 70 Commercial St	Rochester	NY	14614	585-423-2900	399-5750
Web: www.wcmf.com					
WDKX-FM 103.9 (Urban) 683 E Main St	Rochester	NY	14605	585-262-2050	262-2626
Web: www.wdkx.com					
WDVI-FM 100.5 (AC) 207 Midtown Plaza	Rochester	NY	14604	585-454-4884	454-5081
Web: www.mydrivefm.com					
WHAM-AM 1180 (N/T) 207 Midtown Plaza	Rochester	NY	14604	585-454-4884	454-5081
Web: www.wham1180.com					
WJZR-FM 105.9 (NAC) 1237 E Main St	Rochester	NY	14609	585-288-5020	
WKGS-FM 106.7 (CHR) 207 Midtown Plaza	Rochester	NY	14604	585-454-4884	454-5081
Web: www.kiss1067.com					
WNVE-FM 95.1 (Rock) 207 Midtown Plaza	Rochester	NY	14604	585-454-4884	454-5081
Web: www.fox951.com					
WPXY-FM 97.9 (CHR) 70 Commercial St	Rochester	NY	14614	585-423-2900	399-5750
Web: www.98pxy.com					
WRMM-FM 101.3 (AC) 1700 HSBC Plaza Suite 1700	Rochester	NY	14604	585-399-5700	399-5750
Web: www.warm1013.com					
WXXI-AM 1370 (NPR) PO Box 30021	Rochester	NY	14603	585-325-7500	258-0339
Web: www.wxxi.org					
WXXI-FM 91.5 (Clas) PO Box 30021	Rochester	NY	14603	585-325-7500	258-0339
Web: www.wxxi.org					
WZNE-FM 94.1 (Alt) 1700 HSBC Plaza Suite 1700	Rochester	NY	14604	585-399-5700	399-5750
Web: www.thezone941.com					

648-145 Rockford, IL

				Phone	Fax
WGEZ-AM 1490 (Oldies) 622 Public Ave	Beloit	WI	53511	608-365-8865	365-8867
WGFB-FM 103.1 (AC) 2830 Sandy Hollow Rd	Rockford	IL	61109	815-874-7861	874-2202
Web: www.b103fm.com					
WGSL-FM 91.1 (Rel) 5375 Pebble Creek Tr	Loves Park	IL	61111	815-654-1200	282-7779
Web: www.radio91.com					
WNIJ-FM 89.5 (NPR) 801 N 1st St	DeKalb	IL	60115	815-753-9000	753-9938
Web: www.northernpublicradio.org					
WNIU-FM 90.5 (Clas) 801 N 1st St	DeKalb	IL	60115	815-753-9000	753-9938
Web: www.northernpublicradio.org					
WNTA-AM 1330 (N/T) 2830 Sandy Hollow Rd	Rockford	IL	61109	815-874-7861	874-2202
Web: www.wnta.com					
WQFL-FM 100.9 (Rel) 5375 Pebble Creek Trail	Loves Park	IL	61111	815-654-1200	282-7779
Web: www.101qfl.com					
WROK-AM 1440 (N/T) 3901 Brendenwood Rd	Rockford	IL	61107	815-399-2233	399-8148
Web: www.wrok.com					
WTJK-AM 1380 (Sports) 1 Parker Pl Suite 485	Janesville	WI	53545	608-758-9025	758-9550
Web: www.espn1380.com					
WXRX-FM 104.9 (Rock) 2830 Sandy Hollow Rd	Rockford	IL	61109	815-874-7861	874-2202
Web: www.wxrx.com					
WXXQ-FM 98.5 (Ctry) 3901 Brendenwood Rd	Rockford	IL	61107	815-399-2233	399-8148
Web: www.wxxq.com					
WZOK-FM 97.5 (CHR) 3901 Brendenwood Rd	Rockford	IL	61107	815-399-2233	399-8148
Web: www.97zok.com					

648-146 Sacramento, CA

				Phone	Fax
KBMB-FM 103.5 (CHR) 1436 Auburn Blvd	Sacramento	CA	95815	916-646-4000	646-3237
Web: www.1035thebomb.com					
KCTC-AM 1320 (N/T) 5345 Madison Ave	Sacramento	CA	95841	916-334-7777	339-4591
KDND-FM 107.9 (CHR) 5345 Madison Ave	Sacramento	CA	95841	916-334-7777	339-4591
Web: www.endonline.com					
KFBK-AM 1530 (N/T) 1440 Ethan Way Suite 200	Sacramento	CA	95825	916-929-5325	921-5555
Web: www.kfbk.com					
KGBY-FM 92.5 (AC) 1440 Ethan Way Suite 200	Sacramento	CA	95825	916-929-5325	921-5555
Web: www.y92.com					
KHTK-AM 1140 (Sports) 5244 Madison Ave	Sacramento	CA	95841	916-338-9200	338-9155
TF: 800-920-1140 ■ *Web:* www.khtkam.com					

Sacramento, CA (Cont'd)

Station	City	State	Zip	Phone	Fax
KHYL-FM 101.1 (Oldies) 1440 Ethan Way Suite 200 *Web:* www.v1011fm.com	Sacramento	CA	95825	916-929-5325	921-5555
KKFS-FM 103.9 (Rel) 1425 River Park Dr Suite 520 *Web:* www.1039thefish.com	Sacramento	CA	95815	916-924-0710	924-1587
KMTY-FM 101.9 (Ctry) 1436 Auburn Blvd	Sacramento	CA	95815	916-646-4000	646-3237
KNCI-FM 105.1 (Ctry) 5244 Madison Ave *Fax: Sales ■ *TF:* 800-850-1051 ■ *Web:* www.kncifm.com	Sacramento	CA	95841	916-338-9200	338-9208*
KRXQ-FM 98.5 (Rock) 5345 Madison Ave *Web:* www.krxq.net	Sacramento	CA	95841	916-334-7777	339-4591
KSEG-FM 96.9 (CR) 5345 Madison Ave *Web:* www.eagle969.com	Sacramento	CA	95841	916-334-7777	339-4591
KSFM-FM 102.5 (Urban) 1750 Howe Ave Suite 500 *Web:* www.ksfm.com	Sacramento	CA	95825	916-920-1025	929-5341
KSSJ-FM 94.7 (NAC) 5345 Madison Ave *Web:* www.kssj.com	Sacramento	CA	95841	916-334-7777	339-4591
KSTE-AM 650 (N/T) 1440 Ethan Way Suite 200 *Web:* www.kste.com	Sacramento	CA	95825	916-929-5325	921-5555
KTKZ-AM 1380 (N/T) 1425 River Park Dr Suite 520 *Web:* www.ktkz.com	Sacramento	CA	95815	916-924-0710	924-1587
KUOP-FM 91.3 (NPR) 7055 Folsom Blvd *Web:* www.capradio.org	Sacramento	CA	95826	916-278-8900	278-8989
KWOD-FM 106.5 (Alt) 5345 Madison Ave *Web:* www.kwod.com	Sacramento	CA	95841	916-334-7777	339-4591
KXJZ-FM 88.9 (NPR) 7055 Folsom Blvd *TF:* 877-480-5900 ■ *Web:* www.capradio.org	Sacramento	CA	95826	916-278-8900	278-8989
KXPR-FM 90.9 (Clas) 7055 Folsom Blvd. *TF:* 877-480-5900 ■ *Web:* www.capradio.org	Sacramento	CA	95826	916-278-8900	278-8989
KXSE-FM 104.3 (Span AC) 1436 Auburn Blvd *TF:* 800-420-2757	Sacramento	CA	95815	916-646-4000	646-3237
KYMX-FM 96.1 (AC) 280 Commerce Cir *Web:* www.kymx.com	Sacramento	CA	95815	916-923-6800	923-9696
KZZO-FM 100.5 (AC) 280 Commerce Cir *Web:* www.radiozone.com	Sacramento	CA	95815	916-923-6800	927-6468

648-147 Saint Louis, MO

Station	City	State	Zip	Phone	Fax
KATZ-AM 1600 (Rel) 1001 Highlands Plaza Dr W Suite 100 *Web:* www.gospel1600.com	Saint Louis	MO	63110	314-333-8000	692-5125
KATZ-FM 100.3 (Urban) 1001 Highlands Plaza Dr W Suite 100 *TF:* 800-541-0036 ■ *Web:* www.katzfm.com	Saint Louis	MO	63110	314-333-8300	333-8200
KDHX-FM 88.1 (Var) 3504 Magnolia Ave *Web:* www.kdhx.org	Saint Louis	MO	63118	314-664-3955	664-1020
KEZK-FM 102.5 (AC) 3100 Market St *Web:* www.kezk.com	Saint Louis	MO	63103	314-531-0000	969-7638
KFNS-AM 590 (Sports) 8045 Big Bend Blvd *Fax: Sales ■ *Web:* www.kfns.com	Saint Louis	MO	63119	314-962-0590	962-7576*
KFNS-FM 100.7 (Sports) 8045 Big Bend Blvd *Web:* www.kfns.com	Saint Louis	MO	63119	314-962-0590	962-7576
KFUO-FM 99.1 (Clas) 85 Founders Ln. *TF:* 800-844-0524 ■ *Web:* www.classic99.com	Clayton	MO	63105	314-505-7899	725-3801
KLOU-FM 103.3 (Oldies) 1001 Highlands Plaza Dr W *Web:* www.klou.com	Saint Louis	MO	63110	314-333-8000	333-8200
KMJM-FM 104.9 (Urban AC) 1001 Highlands Plaza Dr W Suite 100 *Web:* www.majic105fm.com	Saint Louis	MO	63110	314-333-8000	333-8200
KMOX-AM 1120 (N/T) 1 Memorial Dr *TF:* 800-436-7900 ■ *Web:* www.kmox.com	Saint Louis	MO	63102	314-621-2345	444-3298
KPNT-FM 105.7 (Alt) 800 St Louis Union Stn *Web:* www.kpnt.com	Saint Louis	MO	63103	314-621-0095	621-3000
KSD-FM 93.7 (Ctry) 1001 Highlands Plaza Dr W Suite 100 *Web:* www.thebullrocks.com	Saint Louis	MO	63110	314-333-8000	333-8200
KSHE-FM 94.7 (Rock) 800 St Louis Union Stn *Web:* www.kshe95.com	Saint Louis	MO	63103	314-621-0095	621-3000
KSLZ-FM 107.7 (CHR) 1001 Highlands Plaza Dr W Suite 100 *Web:* www.z1077.com	Saint Louis	MO	63110	314-333-8000	333-8200
KTRS-AM 550 (N/T) 638 W Port Plaza *TF:* 888-550-5877 ■ *Web:* www.ktrs.com	Saint Louis	MO	63146	314-453-5500	453-9704
KWMU-FM 90.7 (NPR) 8001 Natural Bridge Rd *Web:* www.kwmu.org	Saint Louis	MO	63121	314-516-5968	516-5993
KYKY-FM 98.1 (AC) 3100 Market St *Web:* www.y98.com	Saint Louis	MO	63103	314-531-0000	531-9855
WARH-FM 106.5 (CR) 11647 Olive Blvd *Web:* www.1065thearch.com	Saint Louis	MO	63141	314-983-6000	994-9421
WEW-AM 770 (Var) 2740 Hampton Ave *Web:* www.wewradio.com	Saint Louis	MO	63139	314-781-9397	781-8545
WHHL-FM 104.1 (CHR) 9666 Olive Blvd Suite 610	Saint Louis	MO	63132	314-989-9550	989-9551
WIL-FM 92.3 (Ctry) 11647 Olive Blvd *Web:* www.wil92.com	Saint Louis	MO	63141	314-983-6000	994-9421
WVRV-FM 101.1 (AC) 11647 Olive Blvd *Web:* www.wvrv.com	Saint Louis	MO	63141	314-983-6000	994-9447

648-148 Salt Lake City, UT

Station	City	State	Zip	Phone	Fax
KALL-AM 700 (N/T) 515 S 700 East Suite 1-C *Web:* www.hotticket700.com	Salt Lake City	UT	84102	801-524-2600	908-1499
KBEE-FM 98.7 (AC) 434 Bearcat Dr. *Web:* www.b987.com	Salt Lake City	UT	84115	801-485-6700	487-5369
KBER-FM 101.1 (Rock) 434 Bearcat Dr. *Web:* www.kber.com	Salt Lake City	UT	84115	801-485-6700	487-5369
KBZN-FM 97.9 (NAC) 257 E 200 South Suite 400 *Web:* www.kbzn.com	Salt Lake City	UT	84111	801-670-9079	364-8068
KCPW-FM 88.3 (NPR) PO Box 510730 *TF:* 888-359-5279 ■ *Web:* www.kcpw.org	Salt Lake City	UT	84151	801-359-5279	746-2708
KEGA-FM 101.5 (Ctry) 515 S 700 East Suite 1C *Web:* www.1015theeagle.com	Salt Lake City	UT	84102	801-524-2600	364-1811
KENZ-FM 107.5 (AAA) 434 Bearcat Dr. *Web:* www.1075.com	Salt Lake City	UT	84115	801-485-6700	487-5369
KEYY-AM 1450 (Rel) 307 S 1600 West *Web:* www.keyy.com	Provo	UT	84601	801-374-5210	374-2910
KFNZ-AM 1320 (Sports) 434 Bearcat Dr *Web:* www.1320kfan.com	Salt Lake City	UT	84115	801-485-6700	487-5369
KJMY-FM 99.5 (Rock) 2801 S Decker Lake Dr. *Web:* www.my995fm.com	Salt Lake City	UT	84119	801-908-1300	908-1310
KLO-AM 1430 (N/T) 4155 Harrison Blvd Suite 206 *TF:* 866-627-1430 ■ *Web:* www.kloradio.com	Ogden	UT	84403	801-627-1430	627-0317
KNRS-AM 570 (N/T) 2801 S Decker Lake Dr. *Web:* www.knrs.com	Salt Lake City	UT	84119	801-908-1300	908-1499
KODJ-FM 94.1 (Oldies) 2801 S Decker Lake Dr *Web:* www.kodj.com	Salt Lake City	UT	84119	801-908-1300	908-1429
KOSY-FM 106.5 (AC) 2801 S Decker Lake Dr *Web:* www.kosy.com	Salt Lake City	UT	84119	801-908-1300	908-1310
KRSP-FM 103.5 (CR) 55 N 300 West *Web:* www.arrow1035.com	Salt Lake City	UT	84180	801-595-1003	526-1070
KSFI-FM 100.3 (AC) 55 N 300 West *Web:* www.fm100.com	Salt Lake City	UT	84180	801-595-1003	526-1070
KSL-AM 1160 (N/T) 55 N 300 West PO Box 1160 *Web:* www.ksl.com	Salt Lake City	UT	84180	801-575-7600	575-5560
KSL-FM 102.7 (N/T) 55 N 300 West *Web:* www.ksl.com	Salt Lake City	UT	84180	801-575-5555	575-5560
KSOP-AM 1370 (Ctry) 1285 W 2320 South	Salt Lake City	UT	84119	801-972-1043	974-0868
KSOP-FM 104.3 (Ctry) 1285 W 2320 South *Web:* www.ksopcountry.com	Salt Lake City	UT	84119	801-972-1043	974-0868
KSVN-AM 730 (Span) 4215 W 4000 South	West Haven	UT	84401	801-292-1799	731-4445
KTCE-FM 92.3 (Urban) 2835 E 3300 South *Web:* www.u92online.com	Salt Lake City	UT	84109	801-412-6040	412-6041
KUBL-FM 93.3 (Ctry) 434 Bearcat Dr *Web:* www.kbull93.com	Salt Lake City	UT	84115	801-485-6700	487-5369
KUDD-FM 107.9 (CHR) 2835 E 3300 South *Web:* www.1079themix.com	Salt Lake City	UT	84109	801-412-6040	412-6041
KUER-FM 90.1 (NPR) 101 S Wasatch Dr Rm 270 *TF:* 800-313-5837 ■ *Web:* www.kuer.org	Salt Lake City	UT	84112	801-581-6625	581-6758
KUUU-FM 92.5 (Urban) 2835 E 3300 South *Web:* www.u92online.com	Salt Lake City	UT	84109	801-412-6040	412-6041
KWCR-FM 88.1 (CHR) 2188 University Cir *Web:* departments.weber.edu/kwcr/	Ogden	UT	84408	801-626-6450	626-6935
KXRK-FM 96.3 (Alt) 515 S 700 East Suite 1C *Web:* www.x96.com	Salt Lake City	UT	84102	801-524-2600	521-9234
KXRV-FM 105.7 (Ctry) 2801 S Decker Lake Dr. *Web:* www.mycountry.com	Salt Lake City	UT	84119	801-908-1300	908-1310
KZHT-FM 97.1 (CHR) 2801 S Decker Lake Dr *Web:* www.971zht.com	Salt Lake City	UT	84119	801-908-1300	908-1310
KZNS-AM 1280 (Sports) 515 S 700 East Suite 1C *Web:* www.1280kzn.com	Salt Lake City	UT	84102	801-524-2600	521-9234

648-149 San Antonio, TX

Station	City	State	Zip	Phone	Fax
KAJA-FM 97.3 (Ctry) 6222 NW IH-10 *TF:* 800-707-5597 ■ *Web:* www.kj97.com	San Antonio	TX	78201	210-736-9700	735-8811
KBBT-FM 98.5 (Urban) 1777 NE Loop 410 Suite 400 *Web:* www.thebeatsa.com	San Antonio	TX	78217	210-829-1075	804-7820
KCYY-FM 100.3 (Ctry) 8122 Datapoint Dr Suite 600 *Web:* y100fm.com	San Antonio	TX	78229	210-615-5400	615-5331
KGSX-FM 95.1 (Span) 1777 NE Loop 410 Suite 400	San Antonio	TX	78217	210-829-1075	804-7820
KISS-FM 99.5 (Rock) 8122 Datapoint Dr Suite 600 *Web:* kissrocks.com	San Antonio	TX	78229	210-615-5400	615-5331
KJXK-FM 102.7 (Var) 4050 Eisenhauer Rd *Web:* www.hellojack.com	San Antonio	TX	78218	210-654-5100	855-5039
KKYX-AM 680 (Ctry) 8122 Datapoint Dr Suite 600 *Web:* kkyx.com	San Antonio	TX	78229	210-615-5400	615-5331
KLEY-FM 95.7 (Span) 4050 Eisenhower Rd	San Antonio	TX	78218	210-654-5100	855-5076
KLUP-AM 930 (N/T) 9601 McAllister Fwy Suite 1200 *TF:* 866-308-8867 ■ *Web:* www.klup.com	San Antonio	TX	78216	210-344-8481	340-1213
KONO-AM 860 (Oldies) 8122 Datapoint Dr Suite 600 *Web:* kono1011.com	San Antonio	TX	78229	210-615-5400	615-5300
KONO-FM 101.1 (Oldies) 8122 Datapoint Dr Suite 600 *Web:* kono1011.com	San Antonio	TX	78229	210-615-5400	615-5300
KPWT-FM 106.7 (Urban) 8122 Datapoint Dr Suite 600 *Web:* z1067fm.com	San Antonio	TX	78229	210-615-5400	615-5331
KQXT-FM 101.9 (AC) 6222 NW IH-10 *Web:* www.softrock1019.com	San Antonio	TX	78201	210-736-9700	735-8811
KROM-FM 92.9 (Span) 1777 NE Loop 410 Suite 400	San Antonio	TX	78217	210-829-1075	822-2372
KSLR-AM 630 (Rel) 9601 McAllister Fwy Suite 1200 *TF:* 877-630-5757 ■ *Web:* www.kslr.com	San Antonio	TX	78216	210-344-8481	340-1213
KSMG-FM 105.3 (AC) 8122 Datapoint Dr Suite 600 *Web:* magic1053.com	San Antonio	TX	78229	210-615-5400	871-6116
KSTX-FM 89.1 (NPR) 8401 Datapoint Dr Suite 800 *TF:* 800-622-8977 ■ *Web:* www.tpr.org	San Antonio	TX	78229	210-614-8977	614-8983
KTKR-AM 760 (Sports) 6222 NW IH-10 *Web:* www.ticket760.com	San Antonio	TX	78201	210-736-9700	735-8811
KTSA-AM 550 (N/T) 4050 Eisenhauer Rd. *TF:* 800-299-5872 ■ *Web:* www.ktsa.com	San Antonio	TX	78218	210-654-5100	599-5588
KXTN-FM 107.5 (Span) 1777 NE Loop 410 Suite 400 *Web:* www.kxtn.com	San Antonio	TX	78217	210-829-1075	804-7820
KXXM-FM 96.1 (CHR) 6222 NW IH-10 *Web:* www.mix961.com	San Antonio	TX	78201	210-736-9700	735-8811
KZEP-FM 104.5 (CR) 427 E 9th St *Web:* www.kzep.com/kzep	San Antonio	TX	78215	210-226-6444	225-5736
WOAI-AM 1200 (N/T) 6222 NW IH-10 *TF:* 800-373-9700 ■ *Web:* www.ksjl.com	San Antonio	TX	78201	210-736-9700	735-8811

648-150 San Diego, CA

Station	City	State	Zip	Phone	Fax
KBZT-FM 94.9 (Alt) 1615 Murray Canyon Rd Suite 710 *Web:* www.fm949sd.com	San Diego	CA	92108	619-291-9797	543-1353
KFMB-AM 760 (N/T) 7677 Engineer Rd. *TF:* 800-760-5362 ■ *Web:* www.760kfmb.com	San Diego	CA	92111	858-292-7600	279-7676
KFMB-FM 100.7 (AC) 7677 Engineer Rd. *Web:* www.sandiegojack.com	San Diego	CA	92111	858-292-7600	279-7676
KGB-FM 101.5 (CR) 9660 Granite Ridge Dr Suite 100 *Web:* www.101kgb.com	San Diego	CA	92123	858-292-2000	560-0742
KHTS-FM 93.3 (CHR) 9660 Granite Ridge Dr *Web:* www.channel933.com	San Diego	CA	92123	858-292-2000	294-2916
KIFM-FM 98.1 (NAC) 1615 Murray Canyon Rd Suite 710 *Web:* www.kifm.com	San Diego	CA	92108	619-291-9797	543-1353
KIOZ-FM 105.3 (Rock) 9660 Granite Ridge Dr Suite 100 *Web:* www.kioz.com	San Diego	CA	92123	858-292-2000	560-0742
KLNV-FM 106.5 (Span) 600 W Broadway Suite 2150 *TF:* 866-702-1065 ■ *Web:* www.univision.com	San Diego	CA	92101	619-235-0600	744-4300
KLQV-FM 102.9 (Span AC) 600 W Broadway Suite 2150 *TF:* 877-702-1029 ■ *Web:* www.univision.com	San Diego	CA	92101	619-235-0600	744-4300
KLSD-AM 1360 (N/T) 9660 Granite Ridge Dr.	San Diego	CA	92123	858-292-2000	715-3303
KMYI-FM 94.1 (AC) 9660 Granite Ridge Dr Suite 100 *Web:* www.my941.com	San Diego	CA	92123	858-292-2000	294-2916
KOCL-FM 99.3 (Span) 9660 Granite Ridge Dr. *Web:* www.lapreciosa.com	San Diego	CA	92123	858-292-2000	715-3607
KOGO-AM 600 (N/T) 9660 Granite Ridge Dr *Web:* www.kogo.com	San Diego	CA	92123	858-292-2000	715-3675
KPBS-FM 89.5 (NPR) San Diego State University 5200 Campanile Dr. *Web:* www.kpbs.org	San Diego	CA	92182	619-594-8100	594-3812

Station / Address	City	State	ZIP	Phone	Fax
KPRI-FM 102.1 (AAA) 9710 Scranton Rd Suite 200	San Diego	CA	92121	858-678-0102	320-7024
Web: www.kprifm.com					
KSCF-FM 103.7 (N/T) 8033 Linda Vista Rd	San Diego	CA	92111	858-571-7600	571-0326
Web: 1037freefm.com					
KSDS-FM 88.3 (Jazz) 1313 Park Blvd	San Diego	CA	92101	619-234-1062	230-2928
Web: www.jazz88online.org					
KSON-FM 97.3 (Ctry) 1615 Murray Canyon Rd Suite 710	San Diego	CA	92108	619-291-9797	543-1353
TF: 800-243-1973 ■ *Web:* www.kson.com					
KUSS-FM 95.7 (Ctry) 9660 Granite Ridge Dr Suite 100	San Diego	CA	92123	858-292-2000	278-7957
Web: www.us957.com					
KYXY-FM 96.5 (AC) 8033 Linda Vista Rd	San Diego	CA	92111	858-571-7600	571-0326
Web: www.kyxy.com					
XEMO-AM 860 (Span) 5030 Camino de la Siesta Suite 403	San Diego	CA	92108	619-497-0600	497-1019
XHRM-FM 92.5 (Oldies) 9660 Granite Rdige Dr Suite 200	San Diego	CA	92123	858-495-9100	336-4925*
**Fax Area Code:* 619 ■ *Web:* www.magic925.com					
XHTZ-FM 90.3 (Urban) 9660 Granite Ridge Dr Suite 200	San Diego	CA	92123	858-495-9100	499-1750
Web: www.z90.com					
XLTN-FM 104.5 (Span AC) 401 Mile of Cars Suite 370	National City	CA	91950	619-336-7800	420-1092
Web: www.1045radiolatina.com					
XTRA-FM 91.1 (Alt) 9660 Granite Ridge Dr Suite 200	San Diego	CA	92123	858-495-9100	499-1805
TF: 866-690-1150 ■ *Web:* www.91x.com					

648-151 San Francisco, CA

Station / Address	City	State	ZIP	Phone	Fax
KALW-FM 91.7 (NPR) 500 Mansell St	San Francisco	CA	94134	415-841-4121	841-4125
Web: www.kalw.org					
KBLX-FM 102.9 (Urban AC) 55 Hawthorne St Suite 900	San Francisco	CA	94105	415-284-1029	764-4959
Web: www.kblxfm.com					
KBWF-FM 95.7 (Ctry) 201 3rd St Suite 1200	San Francisco	CA	94103	415-957-0957	356-8394
TF: 888-266-9653 ■ *Web:* kbwf.radiotown.com					
KCBS-AM 740 (N/T) 865 Battery St 3rd Fl	San Francisco	CA	94111	415-391-9970	765-4146
Web: www.kcbs.com					
KCSM-FM 91.1 (Jazz) 1700 W Hillsdale Blvd	San Mateo	CA	94402	650-574-6586	524-6975
Web: www.kcsm.org					
KDFC-FM 102.1 (Clas) 201 3rd St Suite 1200	San Francisco	CA	94103	415-764-1021	777-2291*
**Fax Area Code:* 650 ■ *Web:* www.kdfc.com					
KFFG-FM 97.7 (CH) 55 Hawthorne St Suite 1100	San Francisco	CA	94105	415-981-5726	995-6867
TF: 800-300-5364 ■ *Web:* www.kfog.com					
KFOG-FM 104.5 (CH) 55 Hawthorne St Suite 1100	San Francisco	CA	94105	415-981-5726	995-6867
Web: www.kfog.com					
KFRC-AM 610 (Oldies) 865 Battery St	San Francisco	CA	94111	415-391-9970	765-4146
Web: www.kfrc.com					
KFRC-FM 99.7 (Oldies) 865 Battery St 2nd Fl	San Francisco	CA	94111	415-391-9970	765-4146
TF: 888-456-5372 ■ *Web:* www.kfrc.com					
KGO-AM 810 (N/T) 900 Front St	San Francisco	CA	94111	415-954-8100	954-8686
Web: www.kgoam810.com					
KIOI-FM 101.3 (AC) 340 Townsend St 4th Fl	San Francisco	CA	94107	415-975-5555	538-1000
TF: 800-800-1013 ■ *Web:* www.star1013fm.com					
KISQ-FM 98.1 (Urban AC) 340 Townsend St 4th Fl	San Francisco	CA	94107	415-975-5555	538-1000
TF: 888-354-7736 ■ *Web:* www.981kissfm.com					
KITS-FM 105.3 (Alt) 865 Battery St	San Francisco	CA	94111	415-391-9970	765-4146
Web: www.live105.com					
KKSF-FM 103.7 (NAC) 340 Townsend St 4th Fl	San Francisco	CA	94107	415-975-5555	538-1000
TF: 866-900-1037 ■ *Web:* www.kksf.com					
KMEL-FM 106.1 (Urban) 340 Townsend St 4th Fl	San Francisco	CA	94107	415-975-5555	538-1060
TF: 800-955-5635 ■ *Web:* www.106kmel.com					
KMKY-AM 1310 (Kids) 900 Front St	San Francisco	CA	94111	650-637-8800	
KMVQ-FM 99.7 (AC) 865 Battery St	San Francisco	CA	94111	415-391-9970	765-4146
Web: www.kbay.com					
KNBR-AM 1050 (Sports) 55 Hawthorne St Suite 1100	San Francisco	CA	94105	415-981-5726	995-6867
Web: www.knbr.com					
KOIT-FM 96.5 (AC) 201 3rd St Suite 1200	San Francisco	CA	94103	415-777-0965	896-0965
TF: 800-564-8965 ■ *Web:* www.koit.com					
KQED-FM 88.5 (NPR) 2601 Mariposa St	San Francisco	CA	94110	415-864-2000	
Web: www.kqed.org					
KSAN-FM 107.7 (Alt) 55 Hawthorne St Suite 1100	San Francisco	CA	94105	415-981-5726	995-6867
TF: 888-303-2663 ■ *Web:* www.1077thebone.com					
KSFO-AM 560 (N/T) 900 Front St	San Francisco	CA	94111	415-954-7449	658-5401
Web: www.ksfo560.com					
KSOL-FM 98.9 (Span) 750 Battery St Suite 200	San Francisco	CA	94111	415-733-5765	733-5766
TF: 000-000-5705 ■ *Web:* ksol.netmio.com					
KVVF-FM 105.7 (Span AC) 750 Battery St Suite 200	San Francisco	CA	94111	415-733-5765	733-5766
TF: 888-415-2553					
KYLD-FM 94.9 (Urban) 340 Townsend St 4th Fl	San Francisco	CA	94107	415-975-5555	538-1000
TF: 888-333-9490 ■ *Web:* www.wild949.com					

648-152 San Jose, CA

Station / Address	City	State	ZIP	Phone	Fax
KBAY-FM 94.5 (AC) 190 Park Center Plaza Suite 200	San Jose	CA	95113	408-287-5775	293-3341
TF: 800-948-5229 ■ *Web:* www.kbay.com					
KBRG-FM 100.3 (Span AC) 750 Battery St Suite 200	San Francisco	CA	94111	415-989-5765	
KCNL-FM 104.9 (Alt) 1420 Koll Cir Suite A	San Jose	CA	95112	408-453-5400	452-1330
Web: www.channel1049.com					
KEZR-FM 106.5 (AC) 190 Park Center Plaza Suite 200	San Jose	CA	95113	408-287-5775	293-3341
Web: www.kezr.com					
KFAX-AM 1100 (Rel) PO Box 8125	Fremont	CA	94537	510-713-1100	505-1448
Web: www.kfax.com					
KLOK-AM 1170 (Span N/T) 750 Battery St Suite 200	San Francisco	CA	94111	415-989-5765	733-5766
KOHL-FM 89.3 (CHR) 43600 Mission Blvd	Fremont	CA	94539	510-659-6221	659-6001
Web: www.kohlradio.com					
KRTY-FM 95.3 (Ctry) 750 Story Rd	San Jose	CA	95122	408-293-8030	995-0823
Web: www.krty.com					
KSJO-FM 92.3 (Span) 1420 Koll Cir Suite A	San Jose	CA	95112	408-453-5400	452-1330
Web: www.lapreciosa.com					
KUFX-FM 98.5 (CR) 1420 Koll Cir Suite A	San Jose	CA	95112	408-453-5400	452-1330
Web: www.kufx.com					

648-153 Santa Fe, NM

Station / Address	City	State	ZIP	Phone	Fax
KBAC-FM 98.1 (AAA) 2502 Camino Entrada Suite C	Santa Fe	NM	87507	505-988-5222	989-3881
Web: www.kbac.com					
KBOM-FM 94.7 (CHR) 2502 Camino Entrada Suite C	Santa Fe	NM	87507	505-471-1067	473-2667
KSWV-AM 810 (Span) 102 Taos St	Santa Fe	NM	87505	505-989-7441	989-7607
TF: 800-794-5798					
KTRC-AM 1260 (N/T) 2502 Camino Entrada Suite C	Santa Fe	NM	87507	505-471-1067	473-2667
Web: www.airamerica.com					

648-154 Savannah, GA

Station / Address	City	State	ZIP	Phone	Fax
WAEV-FM 97.3 (AC) 245 Alfred St	Savannah	GA	31408	912-964-7794	964-9414
Web: www.973kissfm.com					
WEAS-FM 93.1 (Urban) 214 Television Cir	Savannah	GA	31406	912-961-9000	961-7070
Web: www.e93.com					
WFXH-AM 1130 (Sports) 1 St Augustine Pl	Hilton Head Island	SC	29928	843-785-9569	842-3369
WFXH-FM 106.1 (Rock) 1 St Augustine Pl	Hilton Head Island	SC	29928	843-785-9569	842-3369
Web: www.rock1061.com					
WGCO-FM 98.3 (Var) 401 Mall Blvd Suite 101D	Savannah	GA	31406	912-351-9830	352-4821
TF: 800-332-0983 ■ *Web:* www.adventureradio.fm					
WGZO-FM 103.1 (AC) 401 Mall Blvd Suite 101D	Savannah	GA	31406	912-351-9830	352-4821
TF: 888-844-1031 ■ *Web:* www.star1031.com					
WGZR-FM 106.9 (Ctry) 1 St Augustine Pl	Hilton Head Island	SC	29928	843-785-9569	842-3369
Web: www.104.9thegator.com					
WIXV-FM 95.5 (Rock) 214 Television Cir	Savannah	GA	31406	912-961-9000	961-7070
Web: www.rockofsavannah.com					
WJCL-FM 96.5 (Ctry) 214 Television Cir	Savannah	GA	31406	912-961-9000	961-7070
Web: www.kix96.com					
WLOW-FM 107.9 (Nost) 1 St Augustine Pl	Hilton Head Island	SC	29928	843-785-9569	842-3369
Web: www.wlow.com					
WLVH-FM 101.1 (Urban AC) 245 Alfred St	Savannah	GA	31408	912-964-7794	964-9414
Web: www.love1011.com					
WQBT-FM 94.1 (Urban) 245 Alfred St	Savannah	GA	31408	912-964-7794	964-9414
Web: www.941thebeat.com					
WRHQ-FM 105.3 (Rock) 1102 E 52nd St	Savannah	GA	31404	912-234-1053	354-6600
Web: www.wrhq.com					
WSOK-AM 1230 (Rel) 245 Alfred St	Savannah	GA	31408	912-964-7794	964-9414
WSVH-FM 91.1 (NPR) 12 Ocean Science Cir	Savannah	GA	31411	912-598-3300	
TF: 800-673-7332 ■ *Web:* www.wsvh.org					
WTKS-AM 1290 (N/T) 245 Alfred St	Savannah	GA	31408	912-964-7794	964-9414
Web: www.newsradio1290wtks.com					
WYKZ-FM 98.7 (AC) 245 Alfred St	Savannah	GA	31408	912-964-7794	964-9414
Web: www.987theriver.com					
WZAT-FM 102.1 (CHR) 214 Television Cir	Savannah	GA	31406	912-961-9000	961-7070

648-155 Scranton, PA

Station / Address	City	State	ZIP	Phone	Fax
WBHT-FM 97.1 (CHR) 600 Baltimore Dr	Wilkes-Barre	PA	18702	570-824-9000	820-0520
TF: 800-447-5000 ■ *Web:* www.97bht.com					
WEJL-AM 630 (Sports) 149 Penn Ave	Scranton	PA	18503	570-346-6555	346-6038
Web: www.wejl-wbax.com					
WEZX-FM 106.9 (Rock) 149 Penn Ave	Scranton	PA	18503	570-346-6555	346-6038
Web: www.rock107.com					
WGGY-FM 101.3 (Ctry) 305 Hwy 315	Pittston	PA	18640	570-883-9850	883-9851
Web: www.froggy101.com					
WILK-AM 980 (N/T) 305 Hwy 315	Pittston	PA	18640	570-883-9850	883-9851
Web: www.wilknetwork.com					
WKRZ-FM 98.5 (CHR) 305 Hwy 315	Pittston	PA	18640	570-883-9850	883-9851
Web: www.wkrz.com					
WMGS-FM 92.9 (AC) 600 Baltimore Dr	Wilkes-Barre	PA	18702	570-824-9000	820-0520
TF: 800-447-5000 ■ *Web:* www.magic93fm.com					
WNAK-AM 730 (Span) 84 S Prospect St	Nanticoke	PA	18634	570-735-0730	735-4844
Web: www.wnakam.com					
WQFN-FM 92.1 (Var) 149 Penn Ave	Scranton	PA	18503	570-346-6555	346-6038
WVIA-FM 89.9 (NPR) 100 WVIA Way	Pittston	PA	18640	570-826-6144	655-1180
Web: www.wvia.org					
WVMW-FM 91.7 (Alt) 2300 Adams Ave Marywood University	Scranton	PA	18509	570-348-6202	961-4769
WWRR-FM 104.9 (AC) 1049 N Sekol Rd	Scranton	PA	18504	570-344-1221	344-0996
TF: 888-577-4487 ■ *Web:* www.105theriver.net					

648-156 Seattle/Tacoma, WA

Station / Address	City	State	ZIP	Phone	Fax
KBKS-FM 106.1 (CHR) 1000 Dexter Ave N Suite 100	Seattle	WA	98109	206-805-1110	805-0923
TF: 888-343-1061 ■ *Web:* kissfmseattle.com/					
KBSG-FM 97.3 (Oldies) 1820 Eastlake Ave E	Seattle	WA	98102	206-726-7000	726-7001
TF: 877-668-9797 ■ *Web:* www.kbsg.com					
KCMS-FM 105.3 (Rel) 19319 Fremont Ave N	Shoreline	WA	98133	206-546-7350	546-7372
Web: www.spirit1053.com					
KFNK-FM 104.9 (Alt) 351 Elliott Ave W Suite 300	Seattle	WA	98119	206-494-2000	286-2376
TF: 800-482-1049 ■ *Web:* www.funkymonkey1049.fm					
KGY-AM 1240 (AC) 1700 Marine Dr NE	Olympia	WA	98501	360-943-1240	352-1222
TF: 800-310-7625 ■ *Web:* www.kgyradio.com					
KGY-FM 96.9 (Ctry) 1700 Marine Dr NE	Olympia	WA	98501	360-943-1240	352-1222
TF: 800-962-5590 ■ *Web:* www.kgyradio.com					
KHHO-AM 850 (Sports) 351 Elliott Ave W Suite 300	Seattle	WA	98119	206-285-2295	286-2376
Web: www.foxsports850.com					
KING-FM 98.1 (Clas) 10 Harrison St Suite 100	Seattle	WA	98109	206-691-2981	691-2982
Web: www.king.org					
KIRO-AM 710 (N/T) 1820 Eastlake Ave E	Seattle	WA	98102	206-726-7000	726-5446
Web: www.kiro710.com					
KISW-FM 99.9 (Rock) 1100 Olive Way Suite 1650	Seattle	WA	98101	206-285-7625	215-9355
TF: 800-783-7625 ■ *Web:* www.kisw.com					
KIXI-AM 880 (Nost) 3650 131st Ave SE Suite 550	Bellevue	WA	98006	425-373-5536	653-1088
TF: 866-880-5494 ■ *Web:* www.kixi.com					
KJAQ-FM 96.5 (Var) 1000 Dexter Ave N Suite 100	Seattle	WA	98109	206-805-1100	805-0932
TF: 866-416-5225 ■ *Web:* www.965jackfm.com					
KJR-AM 950 (Sports) 351 Elliott Ave W Suite 300	Seattle	WA	98119	206-285-2295	286-2376
TF: 800-829-0950 ■ *Web:* www.kjram.com					
KJR-FM 95.7 (CR) 351 Elliott Ave W Suite 300	Seattle	WA	98119	206-285-2295	286-2376
TF: 866-901-9595 ■ *Web:* www.957kjrfm.com					
KKWF-FM 100.7 (Ctry) 1100 Olive Way Suite 1650	Seattle	WA	98101	206-285-7625	381-0997
TF: 866-328-9653 ■ *Web:* www.seattlewolf.com					
KMPS-FM 94.1 (Ctry) 1000 Dexter Ave N Suite 100	Seattle	WA	98109	206-805-1100	805-0911
TF: 800-464-9436 ■ *Web:* www.kmps.com					
KMTT-FM 103.7 (AAA) 1100 Olive Way Suite 1650	Seattle	WA	98101	206-233-1037	233-8979
Web: www.kmtt.com					
KNDD-FM 107.7 (Alt) 1100 Olive Way Suite 1650	Seattle	WA	98101	206-622-3251	682-8349
TF: 800-423-1077 ■ *Web:* www.1077theend.com					
KOMO-AM 1000 (N/T) 140 4th Ave N Suite 340	Seattle	WA	98109	206-404-4000	404-3646
TF: 877-869-6469 ■ *Web:* komoradio.com					
KPLU-FM 88.5 (NPR) Pacific Lutheran University	Tacoma	WA	98447	253-535-7758	535-8332
TF: 800-677-5758 ■ *Web:* www.kplu.org					
KPLZ-FM 101.5 (AC) 140 4th Ave N Suite 340	Seattle	WA	98109	206-404-4000	404-3644
TF: 888-821-1015 ■ *Web:* www.star1015.com					
KPTK-AM 1090 (N/T) 1000 Dexter Ave N Suite 100	Seattle	WA	98109	206-805-1090	805-0922
TF: 877-753-1090 ■ *Web:* www.am1090seattle.com					
KQMV-FM 92.5 (AC) 3650 131st Ave SE Suite 550	Bellevue	WA	98006	425-653-9462	653-9464
TF: 866-668-4692 ■ *Web:* www.movin925.fm					
KRWM-FM 106.9 (AC) 3650 131st Ave SE Suite 550	Bellevue	WA	98006	425-373-5536	653-1199
Web: www.warm1069.com					

Seattle/Tacoma, WA (Cont'd)

Phone Fax

KUBE-FM 93.3 (AC) 351 Elliott Ave W Suite 300 .... Seattle WA 98119 206-285-2295 286-2376
TF: 877-933-9393 ■ *Web:* www.kube93.com
KUOW-FM 94.9 (NPR) 4518 University Way NE Suite 310 .... Seattle WA 98105 206-543-2710 543-2720
TF: 800-289-5869 ■ *Web:* www.kuow.org
KVI-AM 570 (N/T) 140 4th Ave N Suite 340 .... Seattle WA 98109 206-404-4000 404-3648
TF: 877-312-5757 ■ *Web:* www.570kvi.com
KWJZ-FM 98.9 (NAC) 3650 131st Ave SE Suite 550............... Bellevue WA 98006 425-373-5536 653-1133
Web: www.kwjz.com
KXXO-FM 96.1 (AC) 119 NE Washington St .... Olympia WA 98501 360-943-9937 352-3643
Web: www.mixx96.com
KZOK-FM 102.5 (CR) 1000 Dexter Ave N Suite 100 .... Seattle WA 98109 206-805-1100 805-0919
TF: 800-252-1025 ■ *Web:* www.kzok.com

648-157 Shreveport, LA

Phone Fax

KBTT-FM 103.7 (CHR) 208 N Thomas Dr .... Shreveport LA 71107 318-222-3122 459-1493
KDAQ-FM 89.9 (NPR) 1 University Pl. .... Shreveport LA 71115 318-797-5150 797-5153
TF: 800-552-8502 ■ *Web:* www.redriverradio.com
KDKS-FM 102.1 (Urban) 208 N Thomas Dr. .... Shreveport LA 71107 318-222-3122 459-1493
Web: www.kdks.fm
KEEL-AM 710 (N/T) 6341 W Port Ave .... Shreveport LA 71129 318-688-1130 687-8574
Web: www.710keel.com
KLKL-FM 95.7 (Oldies) 208 N Thomas Dr. .... Shreveport LA 71107 318-222-3122 459-1493
Web: www.oldies957.fm
KMJJ-FM 99.7 (Urban AC) 270 Plaza Loop. .... Bossier City LA 71111 318-549-8500 549-8505
KRMD-AM 1340 (N/T) 270 Plaza Loop. .... Bossier City LA 71111 318-549-8500 549-8505
KRMD-FM 101.1 (Ctry) 270 Plaza Loop .... Bossier City LA 71111 318-549-8500 549-8505
KRUF-FM 94.5 (CHR) 6341 W Port Ave. .... Shreveport LA 71129 318-688-1130 687-8574
Web: www.k945.com
KTAL-FM 98.1 (CR) 208 N Thomas Dr .... Shreveport LA 71107 318-222-3122 459-1493
Web: www.98rocks.fm
KTUX-FM 98.9 (Rock) 6341 W Port Ave. .... Shreveport LA 71129 318-688-1130 687-8574
Web: www.ktux.com
KVKI-FM 96.5 (AC) 6341 W Port Ave .... Shreveport LA 71129 318-688-1130 687-8574
Web: www.965kvki.com
KWKH-AM 1130 (Sports) 6341 W Port Ave. .... Shreveport LA 71129 318-688-1130 687-8574
Web: www.am1130thefan.com
KXKS-FM 93.7 (Ctry) 6341 W Port Ave. .... Shreveport LA 71129 318-688-1130 687-8574
Web: www.kisscountry937.com

648-158 Sioux Falls, SD

Phone Fax

KCSD-FM 90.9 (NPR) 555 N Dakota St PO Box 5000 .... Vermillion SD 57069 605-677-5861 677-5010
TF: 800-456-0766 ■ *Web:* www.sdpb.org
KELO-AM 1320 (N/T) 500 S Phillips Ave .... Sioux Falls SD 57104 605-331-5350 336-0415
TF: 800-529-5356 ■ *Web:* www.keloam.com
KELO-FM 92.5 (AC) 500 S Phillips Ave .... Sioux Falls SD 57104 605-331-5350 336-0415
TF: 800-529-5356 ■ *Web:* www.kelofm.com
KIKN-FM 100.5 (Ctry) 5100 S Tennis Ln. .... Sioux Falls SD 57108 605-339-1140 339-2735
Web: www.kikn.com
KKLS-FM 104.7 (CHR) 5100 S Tennis Ln .... Sioux Falls SD 57108 605-339-1140 339-2735
Web: www.hot1047.com
KMXC-FM 97.3 (AC) 5100 S Tennis Ln. .... Sioux Falls SD 57108 605-339-1140 339-2735
Web: www.mix97-3.com
KNWC-AM 1270 (Rel) 6300 S Tallgrass Ave .... Sioux Falls SD 57108 605-339-1270 339-1271
Web: www.knwc.org
KRRO-FM 103.7 (Rock) 500 S Phillips Ave. .... Sioux Falls SD 57104 605-331-5350 336-0415
TF: 800-529-5356 ■ *Web:* www.krro.com
KRSD-FM 88.1 (Clas) Augustana College Box 737 .... Sioux Falls SD 57197 605-335-6666 335-1259
KSOO-AM 1140 (N/T) 5100 S Tennis Ln .... Sioux Falls SD 57108 605-339-1140 339-2735
Web: www.ksoo.com
KTSD-FM 91.1 (NPR) 555 N Dakota St PO Box 5000 .... Vermillion SD 57069 605-677-5861 677-5010
TF: 800-456-0766 ■ *Web:* www.sdpb.org
KTWB-FM 101.9 (Ctry) 500 S Phillips Ave .... Sioux Falls SD 57104 605-331-5350 336-0415
TF: 800-529-5356 ■ *Web:* www.ktwb.com
KXRB-AM 1000 (Ctry) 5100 S Tennis Ln. .... Sioux Falls SD 57108 605-339-1140 339-2735
Web: www.kxrb.com
KYBB-FM 102.7 (CR) 5100 S Tennis Ln .... Sioux Falls SD 57108 605-339-1140 339-2735
Web: www.b1027.com

648-159 South Bend, IN

Phone Fax

WAOR-FM 95.3 (CR) 237 W Edison Rd .... Mishawaka IN 46545 574-258-5483 258-0930
Web: www.waor.com
WBYT-FM 100.7 (Ctry) 237 W Edison Rd .... Mishawaka IN 46545 574-258-5483 258-0930
Web: www.b100.com
WFRN-AM 1270 (Rel) 25802 CR 26 .... Elkhart IN 46517 574-875-5166 875-6662
TF: 800-522-9376 ■ *Web:* wfrn.com
WHPZ-FM 96.9 (Rel) 61300 S Ironwood Rd .... South Bend IN 46614 574-291-8200 291-9043
Web: www.pulsefm.com
WNDV-FM 92.9 (CHR) 3371 Cleveland Rd Suite 300 .... South Bend IN 46628 574-273-9300 273-9090
Web: www.u93.com
WNSN-FM 101.5 (AC) 202 S Michigan St 3rd Fl. .... South Bend IN 46601 574-233-3141 239-4231
Web: www.sunny1015.com
WRBR-FM 103.9 (Rock) 237 W Edison Rd .... Mishawaka IN 46545 574-258-5483 258-0930
Web: www.wrbr.com
WSBT-AM 960 (N/T) 202 S Michigan St 3rd Fl .... South Bend IN 46601 574-233-3141 239-4231
Web: www.wsbtradio.com
WSMK-FM 99.1 (Urban) 925 N 5th St. .... Niles MI 49120 269-683-4343 683-7759
Web: www.wsmkradio.com
WVPE-FM 88.1 (NPR) 2424 California Rd .... Elkhart IN 46514 574-262-5660 262-5700
TF: 888-399-9873 ■ *Web:* www.wvpe.org
WZOC-FM 94.3 (Oldies) 112 W Washington St. .... Plymouth IN 46563 574-936-4096 936-6776

648-160 Spokane, WA

Phone Fax

KAQQ-AM 1280 (Nost) 808 E Sprague Ave .... Spokane WA 99202 509-242-2400 242-1160
Web: www.q59.com
KBBD-FM 103.9 (AC) 1601 E 57th Ave .... Spokane WA 99223 509-448-1000 448-7015
KDRK-FM 93.7 (Ctry) 1601 E 57th Ave .... Spokane WA 99223 509-448-1000 448-7015
Web: www.catcountry94.com
KEYF-FM 101.1 (Oldies) 1601 E 57th Ave .... Spokane WA 99223 509-448-1000 448-7015
Web: www.oldies1011.com

Phone Fax

KGA-AM 1510 (N/T) 1601 E 57th Ave .... Spokane WA 99223 509-448-1000 448-7015
Web: www.1510kga.com
KHTQ-FM 92.5 (Rock) 500 W Boone Ave .... Spokane WA 99201 509-324-4200 352-0676
Web: www.rock945.com
KISC-FM 98.1 (AC) 808 E Sprague Ave. .... Spokane WA 99202 509-242-2400 242-1160
Web: www.literockkiss.com
KJRB-AM 790 (Sports) 1601 E 57th Ave .... Spokane WA 99223 509-448-1000 448-7015
Web: www.790kfan.com
KKZX-FM 98.9 (CR) 808 E Sprague Ave .... Spokane WA 99202 509-242-2400 242-1160
Web: www.kkzx.com
KPBX-FM 91.1 (NPR) 2319 N Monroe St .... Spokane WA 99205 509-328-5729 328-5764
TF: 800-328-5729 ■ *Web:* www.kpbx.org
KTSL-FM 101.9 (Rel) 1212 N Washington St Suite 124 .... Spokane WA 99201 509-326-9500 326-1560
Web: www.spirit1019.com
KXLY-AM 920 (N/T) 500 W Boone Ave .... Spokane WA 99201 509-324-4200 325-0676
Web: www.kxly.com
KXLY-FM 99.9 (AC) 500 W Boone Ave .... Spokane WA 99201 509-324-4200 325-0676
Web: www.classy99.com
KZBD-FM 105.7 (Rock) 1601 E 57th Ave .... Spokane WA 99223 509-448-1000 448-7015
TF: 800-718-7874 ■ *Web:* www.1057thebuzzard.com
KZZU-FM 92.9 (CHR) 500 W Boone Ave .... Spokane WA 99201 509-324-4200 325-0676
Web: www.kzzu.com

648-161 Springfield, IL

Phone Fax

WDBR-FM 103.7 (CHR) 3501 E Sangamon Ave. .... Springfield IL 62707 217-753-5400 753-7902
Web: www.wdbr.com
WFMB-AM 1450 (Sports) 3055 S 4th St .... Springfield IL 62703 217-544-9855 528-5348
Web: www.sportsradio1450.com
WFMB-FM 104.5 (Ctry) 3055 S 4th St .... Springfield IL 62703 217-544-9855 528-5348
Web: www.wfmb.com
WMAY-AM 970 (N/T) 1510 N 3rd St .... Riverton IL 62561 217-629-7077 629-7952
Web: www.wmay.com
WNNS-FM 98.7 (AC) 1510 N 3rd St .... Riverton IL 62561 217-629-7077 629-7952
Web: www.wnns.com
WQLZ-FM 92.7 (Rock) 1510 N 3rd St .... Riverton IL 62561 217-629-7077 629-7952
Web: www.wqlz.com
WQQL-FM 101.9 (Oldies) 3501 E Sangamon Ave .... Springfield IL 62707 217-753-5400 753-7902
Web: www.cool1019.com
WTAX-AM 1240 (N/T) 3501 E Sangamon Ave .... Springfield IL 62707 217-753-5400 753-7902
Web: www.wtax.com
WUIS-FM 91.9 (NPR)
University of Illinois at Springfield 1 University
Plaza WUIS-130 .... Springfield IL 62703 217-206-6516 206-6527
TF: 866-206-9847 ■ *Web:* wuis.org
WXAJ-FM 99.7 (CHR) 3055 S 4th St. .... Springfield IL 62703 217-528-3033 528-5348
Web: www.997kissfm.com
WYMG-FM 100.5 (CR) 3501 E Sangamon Ave .... Springfield IL 62707 217-753-5400 753-7902
Web: www.wymg.com

648-162 Springfield, MA

Phone Fax

WACE-AM 730 (Rel) 326 Chicopee St .... Chicopee MA 01013 413-594-6654
Web: www.waceradio.com
WAQY-FM 102.1 (CR) 45 Fisher Ave .... East Longmeadow MA 01028 413-525-4141 525-4334
Web: www.rock102.com
WEIB-FM 106.3 (NAC) 8 N King St .... Northampton MA 01060 413-585-1112 585-9138
Web: www.weibfm.com
WFCR-FM 88.5 (NPR)
University of Massachusetts 131 County Cir. .... Amherst MA 01003 413-545-0100 545-2546
Web: www.wfcr.org
WHYN-AM 560 (N/T) 1331 Main St 4th Fl .... Springfield MA 01103 413-781-1011 734-4434
TF: 800-331-9496 ■ *Web:* www.whyn.com
WHYN-FM 93.1 (AC) 1331 Main St 4th Fl .... Springfield MA 01103 413-781-1011
TF: 888-293-9310 ■ *Web:* www.mix931.com
WLZX-FM 99.3 (Rock) 45 Fisher Ave .... East Longmeadow MA 01028 413-525-4141 525-4334
Web: www.lazer993.com
WMAS-AM 1450 (Nost) 101 West St. .... Springfield MA 01104 413-737-1414 737-1488
TF: 800-937-9627
WMAS-FM 94.7 (AC) 101 West St. .... Springfield MA 01104 413-737-1414 737-1488
TF: 800-937-9627 ■ *Web:* www.947wmas.com
WNNZ-AM 640 (NPR) 1331 Main St 4th Fl. .... Springfield MA 01103 413-781-1011
Web: www.wnnz.com
WPKX-FM 97.9 (Ctry) 1331 Main St 4th Fl .... Springfield MA 01103 413-781-1011 734-4434
TF: 800-345-9759 ■ *Web:* www.kix979.com
WRNX-FM 100.9 (AAA) 1331 Main St 4th Fl .... Springfield MA 01103 413-781-1011 536-1153
TF: 800-977-1009 ■ *Web:* www.wrnx.com
WSCB-FM 89.9 (Urban) 263 Alden St .... Springfield MA 01109 413-748-3712 748-3473
WTCC-FM 90.7 (Var) 1 Armory Sq .... Springfield MA 01105 413-781-6628 755-6305
Web: www.wtccfm.org

648-163 Springfield, MO

Phone Fax

KADI-FM 99.5 (Rel) 5431 W Sunshine St .... Brookline Station MO 65619 417-831-0995 831-4026
Web: www.kadi.com
KGBX-FM 105.9 (AC) 1856 S Glenstone Ave. .... Springfield MO 65804 417-890-5555 890-5050
TF: 800-445-1059 ■ *Web:* www.kgbx.com
KGMY-AM 1400 (Sports) 1856 S Glenstone Ave. .... Springfield MO 65804 417-890-5555 890-5050
TF: 800-996-9653
KKLH-FM 104.7 (CR) 319 E Battlefield St Suite B .... Springfield MO 65807 417-886-5677 886-2155
Web: www.kklh.fm
KOSP-FM 105.1 (Oldies) 319 E Battlefield St Suite B .... Springfield MO 65807 417-886-5677 886-2155
Web: www.kosp.fm
KSMS-FM 90.5 (NPR)
Missouri State University 901 S National Ave .... Springfield MO 65897 417-836-5878 836-5889
TF: 800-767-5768
KSMU-FM 91.1 (NPR)
Missouri State University 901 S National Ave .... Springfield MO 65897 417-836-5878 836-5889
TF: 800-767-5768 ■ *Web:* www.ksmu.org
KSPW-FM 96.5 (CHR) 2330 W Grand St .... Springfield MO 65802 417-865-6614 865-9643
Web: www.power965jams.com
KSWF-FM 100.5 (Ctry) 1856 S Glenstone Ave .... Springfield MO 65804 417-890-5555 890-5050
Web: www.1005thewolf.com
KTOZ-FM 95.5 (AC) 1856 S Glenstone Ave .... Springfield MO 65804 417-890-5555 890-5050
TF: 800-757-9550 ■ *Web:* www.alice955.com
KTTS-FM 94.7 (Ctry) 2330 W Grand St .... Springfield MO 65802 417-865-6614 865-9643
TF: 800-765-5887 ■ *Web:* www.ktts.com
KTXR-FM 101.3 (AC) 3000 E Chestnut Expy .... Springfield MO 65802 417-862-3751 869-7675
TF: 800-749-8001 ■ *Web:* www.ktxrfm.com

	City	State	ZIP	Phone	Fax
KWTO-AM 560 (N/T) 3000 E Chestnut Expy	Springfield	MO	65802	417-862-3751	869-7675
TF: 800-749-8001 ■ *Web:* www.newstalk560.com					
KXUS-FM 97.3 (CR) 1856 S Glenstone Ave	Springfield	MO	65804	417-890-5555	890-5050
TF: 800-494-8858 ■ *Web:* www.us97.com					

648-164 Stamford/Bridgeport, CT

	City	State	ZIP	Phone	Fax
WCUM-AM 1450 (Span) 1862 State St Ext	Bridgeport	CT	06605	203-335-1450	331-9378
WEBE-FM 107.9 (AC) 2 Lafayette Sq	Bridgeport	CT	06604	203-333-9108	384-0600
Web: www.webe108.com					
WICC-AM 600 (N/T) 2 Lafayette Sq	Bridgeport	CT	06604	203-333-9108	384-0600
Web: www.wicc600.com					
WKHL-FM 96.7 (Oldies) 444 Westport Ave	Norwalk	CT	06851	203-845-3030	845-3097
Web: kool967.com					
WPKN-FM 89.5 (Var) 244 University Ave	Bridgeport	CT	06604	203-331-9756	
Web: www.wpkn.org					
WSHU-FM 91.1 (NPR) 5151 Park Ave	Fairfield	CT	06825	203-365-6604	371-7991
TF: 800-937-6045 ■ *Web:* www.wshu.org					
WSTC-AM 1400 (N/T) 444 Westport Ave	Norwalk	CT	06851	203-845-3030	845-3097
Web: wstcwnlk.com					

648-165 Stockton, CA

	City	State	ZIP	Phone	Fax
KCVR-AM 1570 (Span) 6820 Pacific Ave 3rd Fl	Stockton	CA	95207	209-474-0154	474-0316
KJOY-FM 99.3 (AC) 4643 Quail Lakes Dr Suite 100	Stockton	CA	95207	209-476-1230	957-1839
Web: www.993kjoy.com					
KMIX-FM 100.9 (Span) 6820 Pacific Ave 3rd Fl	Stockton	CA	95207	209-474-0154	474-0316
KSTN-AM 1420 (Oldies) 2171 Ralph Ave	Stockton	CA	95206	209-948-5786	
KSTN-FM 107.3 (Span) 2171 Ralph Ave	Stockton	CA	95206	209-948-5786	
KWIN-FM 97.7 (CHR) 4643 Quail Lakes Dr Suite 100	Stockton	CA	95207	209-476-1230	951-0030
Web: www.kwin.com					
KWNN-FM 98.3 (CHR) 4643 Quail Lakes Dr Suite 100	Stockton	CA	95207	209-476-1230	951-0030
Web: www.kwin.com					
KYCC-FM 90.1 (Rel) 9019 West Ln	Stockton	CA	95210	209-477-3690	477-2762
TF: 800-654-5254 ■ *Web:* www.kycc.org					

648-166 Syracuse, NY

	City	State	ZIP	Phone	Fax
WAER-FM 88.3 (Jazz) 795 Ostram Ave	Syracuse	NY	13244	315-443-4021	443-2148
TF: 888-918-3688 ■ *Web:* www.waer.org					
WAQX-FM 95.7 (Rock) 1064 James St	Syracuse	NY	13203	315-472-0200	478-5625
Web: www.waqx.com					
WBBS-FM 104.7 (Ctry) 500 Plum St Suite 100	Syracuse	NY	13204	315-472-9797	472-2323
Web: www.b1047.net					
WCNY-FM 91.3 (NPR) 506 Old Liverpool Rd	Liverpool	NY	13088	315-453-2424	451-8824
TF: 800-451-9269 ■ *Web:* www.wcny.org					
WHEN-AM 620 (Sports) 500 Plum St Suite 100	Syracuse	NY	13204	315-472-9797	472-2323
Web: www.sportsradio620.com					
WJPZ-FM 89.1 (CHR) 316 Waverly Ave	Syracuse	NY	13210	315-443-4689	443-4379
Web: www.z89.com					
WKRL-FM 100.9 (Alt) 235 Walton St	Syracuse	NY	13202	315-472-9111	472-1888
Web: www.krock.com					
WLTI-FM 105.9 (AC) 1064 James St	Syracuse	NY	13203	315-472-0200	478-5625
Web: www.lite1059.com					
WMHR-FM 102.9 (Rel) 4044 Makyes Rd	Syracuse	NY	13215	315-469-5051	469-4066
TF: 800-677-1881					
WNTQ-FM 93.1 (CHR) 1064 James St	Syracuse	NY	13203	315-472-0200	478-5625
Web: www.93q.com					
WPHR-FM 106.9 (Urban) 500 Plum St Suite 100	Syracuse	NY	13204	315-472-9797	472-2323
Web: www.power1069jamz.com					
WSEN-FM 92.1 (CR) 8456 Smokey Hollow Rd PO Box 1050	Baldwinsville	NY	13027	315-635-3971	635-3490
Web: www.wsenfm.com					
WSYR-AM 570 (N/T) 500 Plum St Suite 100	Syracuse	NY	13204	315-472-9797	472-2323
Web: www.wsyr.com					
WTKW-FM 99.5 (CR) 235 Walton St	Syracuse	NY	13202	315-472-9111	472-1888
Web: www.classicrock.com					
WWHT-FM 107.9 (CHR) 500 Plum St Suite 100	Syracuse	NY	13204	315-472-9797	472-2323
Web: www.hot1079.com					
WYYY-FM 94.5 (AC) 500 Plum St Suite 100	Syracuse	NY	13204	315-472-9797	472-2323
Web: www.y94fm.com					

648-167 Tallahassee, FL

	City	State	ZIP	Phone	Fax
WAIB-FM 103.1 (Ctry) 3000 Olson Rd	Tallahassee	FL	32308	850-386-8004	422-1897
Web: newcountryb103.com					
WBZE-FM 98.9 (AC) 3411 W Tharpe St	Tallahassee	FL	32304	850-201-3000	201-2329
Web: www.mystar98.com					
WFSQ-FM 91.5 (Clas) 1600 Red Barber Plaza	Tallahassee	FL	32310	850-487-3086	487-2611
TF: 800-829-8809 ■ *Web:* www.fsu.edu/~wfsu_fm					
WFSU-FM 88.9 (NPR) 1600 Red Barber Plaza	Tallahassee	FL	32310	850-487-3086	487-2611
TF: 800-829-8809 ■ *Web:* www.wfsu.org					
WGLF-FM 104.1 (CR) 3411 W Tharpe St	Tallahassee	FL	32304	850-201-3000	201-2329
Web: www.gulf104.com					
WHBX-FM 96.1 (Urban AC) 3411 W Tharpe St	Tallahassee	FL	32304	850-201-3000	201-2329
Web: www.961jamz.com					
WHTF-FM 104.9 (CHR) 3000 Olsen Rd	Tallahassee	FL	32308	850-386-8004	422-1897
Web: www.hot1049.com					
WNLS-AM 1270 (Sports) 325 John Knox Rd Bldg G	Tallahassee	FL	32303	850-422-3107	383-0747
Web: www.wnls.com					
WSLA-FM 100.7 (N/T) 325 John Knox Rd Bldg G	Tallahassee	FL	32303	850-422-3107	383-0747
WTLY-FM 107.1 (AC) 325 John Knox Rd Bldg G	Tallahassee	FL	32303	850-422-3107	383-0747
Web: www.magic1071.com					
WTNT-FM 94.9 (Ctry) 325 John Knox Rd Bldg G	Tallahassee	FL	32303	850-422-3107	383-0747
Web: www.wtntfm.com					
WUTL-FM 106.1 (Rock) 3000 Olson Rd	Tallahassee	FL	32308	850-386-8004	422-1897
Web: www.u1061.com					
WXSR-FM 101.5 (Alt) 325 John Knox Rd Bldg G	Tallahassee	FL	32303	850-422-3107	383-0747
Web: www.x1015.com					

648-168 Tampa/Saint Petersburg, FL

	City	State	ZIP	Phone	Fax
WBTB-FM 95.7 (Urban) 4002 W Gandy Blvd	Tampa	FL	33611	813-839-9393	832-1045
Web: www.957thebeat.com					
WDAE-AM 620 (Sports) 4002 W Gandy Blvd	Tampa	FL	33611	813-839-9393	837-0300
TF: 888-546-4620 ■ *Web:* www.620wdae.com					
WDUV-FM 105.5 (AC) 11300 4th St N Suite 300	Saint Petersburg	FL	33716	727-577-7131	578-2477
TF: 888-723-9388 ■ *Web:* wduv.com					
WFLA-AM 970 (N/T) 4002 W Gandy Blvd	Tampa	FL	33611	813-839-9393	837-0300
Web: www.970wfla.com					
WFLZ-FM 93.3 (CHR) 4002 W Gandy Blvd	Tampa	FL	33611	813-839-9393	831-3299
Web: www.933flz.com					
WFUS-FM 103.5 (Ctry) 4002 W Gandy Blvd	Tampa	FL	33611	813-839-9393	831-3299
Web: www.us1035.com					
WGUL-AM 860 (N/T) 5211 W Laurel St Suite 101	Tampa	FL	33607	813-639-1903	639-1272
Web: www.860wgul.com					
WHPT-FM 102.5 (CR) 11300 4th St N Suite 300	Saint Petersburg	FL	33716	727-577-7131	579-2662
TF: 800-771-1025 ■ *Web:* theboneonline.com					
WLLD-FM 98.7 (CHR) 9721 Executive Center Dr N Suite 200	Saint Petersburg	FL	33702	727-579-1925	579-9250
Web: www.wild987.com					
WMTX-FM 100.7 (AC) 4002 W Gandy Blvd	Tampa	FL	33611	813-839-9393	831-3299
Web: www.mixmeansvariety.com					
WPOI-FM 101.5 (CR) 11300 4th St N Suite 300	Saint Petersburg	FL	33716	727-577-7131	578-1015
TF: 877-999-1015 ■ *Web:* 1015thepoint.com					
WQYK-AM 1010 (Ctry) 9721 Executive Center Dr N Suite 200	Saint Petersburg	FL	33702	727-579-1925	636-0995*
**Fax Area Code:* 813 ■ *Web:* www.wqyk.com					
WQYK-FM 99.5 (Ctry) 9721 Executive Center Dr N Suite 200	Saint Petersburg	FL	33702	727-579-1925	636-0995*
**Fax Area Code:* 813 ■ *Web:* www.wqyk.com					
WRBQ-FM 104.7 (Oldies) 9721 Executive Center Dr N Suite 200	Saint Petersburg	FL	33702	727-579-1925	579-9250
Web: www.oldies1047.com					
WRXB-AM 1590 (Urban) 2060 1st Ave N	Saint Petersburg	FL	33713	727-327-9792	321-3025
TF: 877-900-1590 ■ *Web:* www.wrxb.us					
WSJT-FM 94.1 (NAC) 9721 Executive Center Dr N Suite 200	Saint Petersburg	FL	33702	727-579-1925	579-9250
Web: www.wsjt.com					
WSUN-FM 97.1 (Alt) 11300 4th St N Suite 300	Saint Petersburg	FL	33716	727-577-7131	578-2477
TF: 877-327-9797 ■ *Web:* 97xonline.com					
WTBN-AM 570 (Rel) 5211 W Laurel St Suite 101	Tampa	FL	33607	813-639-1903	639-1272
Web: www.bayword.com					
WTMP-AM 1150 (Urban) 5207 Washington Blvd	Tampa	FL	33619	813-620-1300	628-0713
Web: www.wtmp.com					
WUSF-FM 89.7 (NPR) 4202 E Fowler Ave WRB 219	Tampa	FL	33620	813-974-8700	974-5016
TF: 800-741-9090 ■ *Web:* www.wusf.usf.edu/wusf-fm					
WWRM-FM 94.9 (AC) 11300 4th St N Suite 300	Saint Petersburg	FL	33716	727-577-7131	578-2477
Web: 949online.com					
WXGL-FM 107.3 (AC) 11300 4th St N Suite 300	Saint Petersburg	FL	33716	727-577-7131	579-2662
Web: 1073theeagle.com					
WXTB-FM 97.9 (Rock) 4002 W Gandy Blvd	Tampa	FL	33611	813-839-9393	831-3299
Web: www.98rock.com					
WYUU-FM 92.5 (Span) 9721 Executive Center Dr N Suite 200	Saint Petersburg	FL	33702	727-579-1925	
Web: www.lanueva925.com					

648-169 Toledo, OH

	City	State	ZIP	Phone	Fax
WCWA-AM 1230 (Sports) 125 S Superior St	Toledo	OH	43604	419-244-8321	244-7631
Web: www.wcwa.com					
WDMN-AM 1520 (Rel) 1510 S Reynolds Rd	Maumee	OH	43537	419-725-9366	725-2600
Web: www.toledo1520am.com					
WGTE-FM 91.3 (NPR) 1270 S Detroit Ave PO Box 30	Toledo	OH	43614	419-380-4600	380-4710
TF: 800-243-9483 ■ *Web:* www.wgte.org					
WIMX-FM 95.7 (Urban/AC) 5744 Southwyck Blvd Suite 200	Toledo	OH	43614	419-868-7914	868-8765
Web: www.mix957.org					
WIOT-FM 104.7 (Rock) 125 S Superior St	Toledo	OH	43604	419-244-8321	244-7631
Web: www.wiot.com					
WJUC-FM 107.3 (Urban) 5902 Southwyck Blvd Suite 101	Toledo	OH	43614	419-861-9582	861-2866
Web: www.thejuice1073.com					
WKKO-FM 99.9 (Ctry) 3225 Arlington Ave	Toledo	OH	43614	419-385-2507	385-2902
Web: www.k100country.com					
WLQR-AM 1470 (Sports) 3225 Arlington Ave	Toledo	OH	43614	419-385-2507	385-2902
Web: www.1470theticket.com					
WRQN-FM 93.5 (Oldies) 3225 Arlington Ave	Toledo	OH	43614	419-385-2507	385-2902
Web: www.935wrqn.com					
WRVF-FM 101.5 (AC) 125 S Superior St	Toledo	OH	43604	419-244-8321	244-7631
Web: www.1015theriver.com					
WSPD-AM 1370 (N/T) 125 S Superior St	Toledo	OH	43604	419-244-8321	244-7631
Web: www.wspd.com					
WTWR-FM 98.3 (CHR) 14930 LaPlaisance Rd Suite 113	Monroe	MI	48161	734-242-6600	242-6599
TF: 888-578-0098					
WVKS-FM 92.5 (CHR) 125 S Superior St	Toledo	OH	43604	419-244-8321	244-7631
TF: 877-547-7366 ■ *Web:* www.925kissfm.com					
WWWM-FM 105.5 (AC) 3225 Arlington Ave	Toledo	OH	42614	419-385-2507	385-2902
Web: www.star105toledo.com					
WXKR-FM 94.5 (CR) 3225 Arlington Ave	Toledo	OH	43614	419-385-2507	385-2902
Web: www.wxkr.com					

648-170 Topeka, KS

	City	State	ZIP	Phone	Fax
KANU-FM 91.5 (NPR) 1120 W 11th St University of Kansas	Lawrence	KS	66044	785-864-4530	864-5278
TF: 888-577-5268 ■ *Web:* kanu.ku.edu					
KDVV-FM 100.3 (Rock) 825 S Kansas Ave Suite 100	Topeka	KS	66612	785-272-2122	272-6219
TF: 866-297-1003 ■ *Web:* www.v100rocks.com					
KLZR-FM 105.9 (AC) 3125 W 6th St	Lawrence	KS	66049	785-843-1320	841-5924
Web: www.lazer.com					
KMAJ-AM 1440 (N/T) 825 S Kansas Ave Suite 100	Topeka	KS	66612	785-272-2122	272-6219
TF: 877-297-1077 ■ *Web:* www.kmaj.com					
KMAJ-FM 107.7 (AC) 825 S Kansas Ave Suite 100	Topeka	KS	66612	785-272-2122	272-6219
TF: 877-297-1077 ■ *Web:* www.kmaj.com					
KTOP-AM 1490 (Nost) 825 S Kansas Ave Suite 100	Topeka	KS	66612	785-272-2122	272-6219
KTPK-FM 106.9 (Ctry) 2121 SW Chelsea Dr	Topeka	KS	66614	785-273-1069	273-0123
TF: 888-291-1069 ■ *Web:* www.ktpk1069.com					
KWIC-FM 99.3 (Oldies) 825 S Kansas Ave Suite 100	Topeka	KS	66612	785-272-2122	272-6219
Web: www.eagle993.com					
WIBW-AM 580 (N/T) 1210 SW Executive Dr PO Box 1818	Topeka	KS	66601	785-272-3456	228-7282
Web: www.am580wibw.com					
WIBW-FM 94.5 (Ctry) 1210 SW Executive Dr PO Box 1818	Topeka	KS	66601	785-272-3456	228-7282
Web: www.94country.com					

648-171 Toronto, ON

	City	State	ZIP	Phone	Fax
CBL-FM 94.1 (Clas) PO Box 500 Stn A	Toronto	ON	M5W1E6	416-205-3311	205-2841*
**Fax:* Hum Res ■ *Web:* www.cbc.ca/toronto					

Toronto, ON (Cont'd)

Phone | Fax

CBLA-FM 99.1 (CBC) PO Box 500 Stn A — Toronto ON M5W1E6 416-205-3311 205-6336
Web: www.cbc.ca/programguide/radio

CFNY-FM 102.1 (Alt) 1 Dundas St W Suite 1600 — Toronto ON M5G1Z3 416-221-0107 847-3300
Web: www.edge.ca

CFRB-AM 1010 (N/T) 2 St Clair Ave W 2nd Fl — Toronto ON M4V1L6 416-924-5711 323-6816
Web: www.cfrb.com

CFTR-AM 680 (N/T) 777 Jarvis St — Toronto ON M4Y3B7 416-935-8200 363-2387
Web: www.680news.com

CHFI-FM 98.1 (AC) 777 Jarvis St — Toronto ON M4Y3B7 416-935-8298 363-2387
Web: www.chfi.com

CHIN-AM 1540 (Ethnic) 622 College St 4th Fl — Toronto ON M6G1B6 416-531-9991 531-5274
TF: 888-944-2446 ■ *Web:* www.chinradio.com

CHIN-FM 100.7 (Ethnic) 622 College St 4th Fl — Toronto ON M6G1B6 416-531-9991 531-5274
TF: 888-944-2446 ■ *Web:* www.chinradio.com

CHUM-AM 1050 (Oldies) 1331 Yonge St — Toronto ON M4T1Y1 416-925-6666 926-4026
Web: www.1050chum.com

CHUM-FM 104.5 (AC) 1331 Yonge St — Toronto ON M4T1Y1 416-925-6666 926-4026
Web: www.chumfm.com

CILQ-FM 107.1 (CR) 1 Dundas St W Suite 1600 — Toronto ON M5G1Z3 416-221-0107 847-3300
Web: www.q107.com

CING-FM 95.3 (Ctry) 875 Main St W Suite 900 — Hamilton ON L8S4R1 905-521-9900 521-2306
Web: www.country953.com

CJEZ-FM 97.3 (AC) 2 St Clair Ave W 2nd Fl — Toronto ON M4V1L6 416-482-0973 486-5696
Web: www.ezrock.com

CJRT-FM 91.1 (Jazz) 4 Pardee Ave Unit 100 — Toronto ON M6K3H5 416-595-0404 595-9413
TF: 888-595-0404 ■ *Web:* www.jazz.fm

CJXY-FM 107.9 (CR) 875 Main St W Suite 900 — Hamilton ON L8S4R1 905-521-9900 521-2306
Web: www.y108.ca

CKFM-FM 99.9 (AC) 2 St Clair Ave W 2nd Fl — Toronto ON M4V1L6 416-922-9999 323-6800
Web: www.mix999.com

CKLN-FM 88.1 (Alt) 55 Gould St — Toronto ON M5B1E9 416-595-5251 595-0226
Web: www.ckln.fm

648-172 Trenton, NJ

Phone | Fax

WBUD-AM 1260 (Oldies) 109 Walters Ave — Trenton NJ 08638 609-771-8181 406-7954
TF: 800-678-9599

WIMG-AM 1300 (Rel) 1842 S Broad St — Trenton NJ 08610 609-695-1300 278-1588
Web: www.wimg1300.com

WKXW-FM 101.5 (N/T) 109 Walters Ave — Trenton NJ 08638 609-771-8181 406-7956
TF: 800-678-9599 ■ *Web:* www.nj1015.com

WNJN-FM 89.7 (NPR) PO Box 777 — Trenton NJ 08625 609-777-5000 633-2927
TF: 800-792-8645 ■ *Web:* www.njn.net/radio

WNJT-FM 88.1 (NPR) PO Box 777 — Trenton NJ 08625 609-777-5000 633-2927
Web: www.njn.net/radio

WPST-FM 94.5 (CHR) 619 Alexander Rd 3rd Fl — Princeton NJ 08540 609-419-0300 419-0143
Web: www.wpst.com

WTSR-FM 91.3 (Alt)
College of New Jersey Kendall Hall PO Box 7718 — Ewing NJ 08628 609-771-3200 637-5113
Web: www.wtsr.org

WWFM-FM 89.1 (Clas) PO Box B — Trenton NJ 08690 609-587-8989 570-3863
TF: 888-232-1212 ■ *Web:* www.wwfm.org

648-173 Tucson, AZ

Phone | Fax

KEVT-AM 1210 (Span) 2955 E Broadway Blvd Suite 230 — Tucson AZ 85716 520-889-8904 889-8573

KFFN-AM 1490 (Sports) 3438 N Country Club Rd — Tucson AZ 85716 520-795-1490 327-2260

KFMA-FM 92.1 (Alt) 3871 N Commerce Dr — Tucson AZ 85705 520-622-6711 407-4600
Web: www.kfma.com

KGMS-AM 940 (Rel) 3222 S Richey Ave — Tucson AZ 85713 520-790-2440 790-2937
TF: 866-725-5467 ■ *Web:* www.kgms.com

KHYT-FM 107.5 (CR) 575 W Roger Rd — Tucson AZ 85705 520-887-1000 887-6397
Web: www.rock1075.com

KIIM-FM 99.5 (Ctry) 575 W Roger Rd — Tucson AZ 85705 520-887-1000 887-6397
Web: www.kiimfm.com

KLPX-FM 96.1 (Rock) 3871 N Commerce Dr — Tucson AZ 85705 520-622-6711 407-4600
Web: www.klpx.com

KMXZ-FM 94.9 (AC) 3438 N Country Club Rd — Tucson AZ 85716 520-795-1490 327-2260
Web: www.mixfm.com

KNST-AM 790 (N/T) 3202 N Oracle Rd — Tucson AZ 85705 520-618-2100 618-2135
Web: www.knst.com

KOHT-FM 98.3 (Urban) 3202 N Oracle Rd — Tucson AZ 85705 520-618-2100 618-2135
Web: www.hot983.com

KOYT-FM 92.9 (Ctry) 3202 N Oracle Rd — Tucson AZ 85705 520-618-2100 618-2135
Web: www.929coyotecountry.com

KRQQ-FM 93.7 (CHR) 3202 N Oracle Rd — Tucson AZ 85705 520-618-2100 618-2135
Web: www.krq.com

KTUC-AM 1400 (Nost) 575 W Roger Rd — Tucson AZ 85705 520-887-1000 887-6397
Web: www.1400ktuc.net

KUAT-FM 90.5 (Clas) PO Box 210067 — Tucson AZ 85721 520-621-5828 621-3360
TF: 800-521-5828 ■ *Web:* kuatfm.org/classical.cfm

KUAZ-FM 89.1 (NPR) PO Box 210067 — Tucson AZ 85721 520-621-5828 621-3360
TF: 800-521-5828 ■ *Web:* www.kuaz.org

648-174 Tulsa, OK

Phone | Fax

KAKC-AM 1300 (Sports) 2625 S Memorial Dr — Tulsa OK 74129 918-664-2810 665-0555

KBEZ-FM 92.9 (AC) 7030 S Yale Ave Suite 711 — Tulsa OK 74136 918-496-9336 495-1850
Web: www.kbez.com

KFAQ-AM 1170 (N/T) 4590 E 29th St — Tulsa OK 74114 918-743-7814 743-7613
Web: www.1170kfaq.com

KHTT-FM 106.9 (CHR) 7030 S Yale Ave Suite 711 — Tulsa OK 74136 918-492-2020 496-2681
Web: www.khits.com

KJSR-FM 103.3 (CR) 7136 S Yale Ave Suite 500 — Tulsa OK 74136 918-493-7400 493-2376
Web: star103fm.com

KMOD-FM 97.5 (Rock) 2625 S Memorial Dr — Tulsa OK 74129 918-664-2810 665-0555
Web: www.kmod.com

KMYZ-FM 104.5 (Alt) 5810 E Skelly Dr Suite 801 — Tulsa OK 74135 918-665-3131 663-6622
Web: www.edgetulsa.com

KQLL-FM 106.1 (Oldies) 2625 S Memorial Dr — Tulsa OK 74129 918-664-2810 665-0555
Web: www.kooltulsa.com

KRAV-FM 96.5 (AC) 7136 S Yale Ave Suite 500 — Tulsa OK 74136 918-493-7400 493-2376
Web: mix96tulsa.com

KRMG-AM 740 (N/T) 7136 S Yale Ave Suite 500 — Tulsa OK 74136 918-493-7400 493-2376
Web: krmg.com

KTBT-FM 101.5 (Urban) 2625 S Memorial Dr — Tulsa OK 74129 918-664-2810 665-0555
Web: www.1015thebeat.com

KTBZ-AM 1430 (Sports) 2625 S Memorial Dr — Tulsa OK 74129 918-388-5100 665-0555
Web: www.1430thebuzz.com

KVOO-FM 98.5 (Ctry) 4590 E 29th St — Tulsa OK 74114 918-743-7814 743-7613
Web: www.kvoo.com

KWEN-FM 95.5 (Ctry) 7136 S Yale Ave Suite 500 — Tulsa OK 74136 918-493-7400 493-2376
Web: k955fm.com

KWGS-FM 89.5 (NPR) 600 S College Ave — Tulsa OK 74104 918-631-2577 631-3695
TF: 888-594-5947 ■ *Web:* www.kwgs.org

KXOJ-FM 100.9 (Rel) 2448 E 81st St Suite 5500 — Tulsa OK 74137 918-492-2660 492-8840
Web: www.kxoj.com

648-175 Tupelo, MS

Phone | Fax

WAFR-FM 88.3 (Rel) 107 Parkgate Dr PO Box 2440 — Tupelo MS 38803 662-844-8888 842-6791
Web: www.afr.net/newafr/default.asp

WATP-FM 90.7 (Rel) PO Box 2440 — Tupelo MS 38803 662-844-8888 842-6791
Web: www.afr.net

WBVV-FM 99.3 (Rel) 5026 Cliff Gookin Blvd — Tupelo MS 38801 662-728-5301 728-2572

WESE-FM 92.5 (Urban) 5026 Cliff Gookin Blvd — Tupelo MS 38801 662-842-1067 842-0725
Web: www.925jamz.com

WFTA-FM 101.9 (AC) 1241 Cliff Gookin Blvd — Tupelo MS 38803 662-862-3191 842-9568

WMXU-FM 106.1 (Urban)
601 2nd Ave N Suite 202 Court Sq Towers — Columbus MS 39701 662-327-1183 328-1122

WSEL-FM 96.7 (Rel) PO Box 3788 — Tupelo MS 38803 662-489-0297 489-0297

WSMS-FM 99.9 (CR)
601 2nd Ave N Suite 202 Court Sq Towers — Columbus MS 39701 662-327-1183 328-1122

WSYE-FM 93.3 (AC) 2214 S Gloster St — Tupelo MS 38801 662-842-7658 842-0197
Web: www.sunny93fm.com

WTUP-AM 1490 (Sports) 5026 Cliff Gookin Blvd — Tupelo MS 38801 662-842-1067 842-0725
Web: www.wtup1490.com

WWKZ-FM 103.9 (CHR) 5026 Cliff Gookin Blvd — Tupelo MS 38801 662-842-1067 842-0725
Web: www.kz103.com

WWMS-FM 97.5 (Ctry) 2214 S Gloster St — Tupelo MS 38802 662-842-7658 842-0197
Web: www.miss98.com

WWZD-FM 106.7 (Ctry) 5026 Cliff Gookin Blvd — Tupelo MS 38801 662-842-1067 842-0725
Web: www.wizard106.com

WZLQ-FM 98.5 (AC) 2214 S Gloster St — Tupelo MS 38802 662-842-7658 842-0197

648-176 Tuscaloosa, AL

Phone | Fax

WACT-AM 1420 (Sports) 2121 9th St Suite B — Tuscaloosa AL 35401 205-344-4589 366-9774

WBEI-FM 101.7 (AC) 142 Skyland Blvd — Tuscaloosa AL 35405 205-345-7200 349-1715
Web: www.b1017.fm

WDGM-FM 99.1 (Oldies) 142 Skyland Blvd — Tuscaloosa AL 35405 205-345-7200 349-1715

WJOX-FM 100.5 (Sports) 244 Goodwin Crst Dr Suite 300 — Birmingham AL 35209 205-917-1930 942-8959
Web: www.wrax.com

WQZZ-FM 104.3 (Urban AC) 601 Greensboro Ave Suite 507 — Tuscaloosa AL 35401 205-345-4787 345-4790

WRTR-FM 105.5 (Rock) 2121 9th St Suite B — Tuscaloosa AL 35402 205-344-4589 366-9774
Web: www.rock105online.com

WTBC-AM 1230 (N/T) 2110 McFarland Blvd E Suite C — Tuscaloosa AL 35404 205-758-5523 752-9696
TF: 800-518-1977 ■ *Web:* www.wtbc1230.com

WTSK-AM 790 (Rel) 142 Skyland Blvd — Tuscaloosa AL 35405 205-345-7200 349-1715

WTUG-FM 92.9 (Urban) 142 Skyland Blvd — Tuscaloosa AL 35405 205-345-7200 349-1715
Web: www.wtug.com

WTXT-FM 98.1 (Ctry) 2121 9th St Suite B — Tuscaloosa AL 35402 205-344-4589 366-9774
Web: www.98txt.com

WUAL-FM 91.5 (NPR)
University of Alabama Phifer Hall Suite 166 — Tuscaloosa AL 35487 205-348-6644 348-6648
TF: 800-654-4262 ■ *Web:* www.wual.ua.edu

WWPG-AM 1280 (Rel) 601 Greensboro Ave Suite 507 — Tuscaloosa AL 35401 205-345-4787 345-4790

WZBQ-FM 94.1 (CHR) 2121 9th St Suite B — Tuscaloosa AL 35402 205-344-4589 366-9774
Web: www.941zbq.com

648-177 Vancouver, BC

Phone | Fax

CBU-AM 690 (CBC) PO Box 4600 — Vancouver BC V6B4A2 604-662-6000 662-6106
TF: 866-306-4636 ■ *Web:* www.cbc.ca/radioone

CFMI-FM 101.1 (CR) 700 W Georgia St Suite 2000 — Vancouver BC V7Y1K9 604-331-2808 331-2722
Web: www.rock101.com

CFOX-FM 99.3 (Rock) 700 W Georgia St Suite 2000 — Vancouver BC V7Y1K9 604-684-7221 331-2722
Web: www.cfox.com

CFUN-AM 1410 (N/T) 380 W 2nd Ave Suite 300 — Vancouver BC V5Y1C8 604-871-9000 871-2901
Web: www.cfun.com

CHQM-FM 103.5 (AC) 380 W 2nd Ave Suite 300 — Vancouver BC V5Y1C8 604-871-9000 871-2901
Web: www.qmfm.com

CISL-AM 650 (Oldies) 11151 Horseshoe Way Suite 20 — Richmond BC V7A4S5 604-272-6500 272-0917
Web: www.650cisl.com

CITR-FM 101.9 (Var)
6138 Sub Blvd Student Union Bldg Rm 233 — Vancouver BC V6T1Z1 604-822-3017 822-9364
Web: www.ams.ubc.ca/citr

CJJR-FM 93.7 (Ctry) 1401 W 8th Ave Suite 300 — Vancouver BC V6H1C9 604-731-7772 731-0493
Web: www.jrfm.com

CJVB-AM 1470 (Ethnic) 4151 Hazel Bridgeway Rm 2090 — Richmond BC V6X4J7 604-295-1234 295-1201
Web: www.am1470.com

CKBD-AM 600 (Nost) 1401 W 8th Ave Suite 300 — Vancouver BC V6H1C9 604-731-6111 731-0493
Web: www.600am.com

CKLG-FM 96.9 (Var) 2440 Ash St — Vancouver BC V5Z4J6 604-872-2557 873-0877*
**Fax:* News Rm ■ *Web:* www.jackfm.com

CKNW-AM 980 (N/T) 700 W Georgia St Suite 2000 — Vancouver BC V7Y1K9 604-331-2711 331-2722
Web: www.cknw.com

CKST-AM 1040 (Sports) 380 W 2nd Ave Suite 300 — Vancouver BC V5Y1C8 604-871-9000 871-2901
TF: 866-266-8326 ■ *Web:* www.team1040.ca

CKWX-AM 1130 (N/T) 2440 Ash St — Vancouver BC V5Z4J6 604-873-2599 873-0877
Web: www.news1130.com

CKZZ-FM 95.3 (AC) 11151 Horseshoe Way Suite 20 — Richmond BC V7A4S5 604-241-0953 272-0917
Web: www.z95.com

648-178 Washington, DC

Phone | Fax

WAMU-FM 88.5 (NPR)
4000 Brandywine St NW American University Radio — Washington DC 20016 202-885-1200 885-1269
Web: www.wamu.org

WASH-FM 97.1 (AC) 1801 Rockville Pike 6th Fl — Rockville MD 20852 301-984-9710 255-4344
TF: 866-927-4361 ■ *Web:* www.washfm.com

Station	City	State	Zip	Phone	Fax
WAVA-AM 780 (Rel) 1901 N Moore St Suite 200 *TF:* 800-738-2356 ■ *Web:* www.wava.com	Arlington	VA	22209	703-807-2266	807-2248
WAVA-FM 105.1 (Rel) 1901 N Moore St Suite 200 *TF:* 888-293-9282 ■ *Web:* www.wava.com	Arlington	VA	22209	703-807-2266	807-2248
WBIG-FM 100.3 (Oldies) 1801 Rockville Pike 6th Fl *TF:* 800-493-1003 ■ *Web:* www.wbig.com	Rockville	MD	20852	301-231-8231	770-0236
WETA-FM 90.9 (NPR) 2775 S Quincy St *Web:* www.weta.org/fm	Arlington	VA	22206	703-998-2600	998-3401
WETH-FM 89.1 (NPR) 2775 S Quincy St *Web:* www.weta.org/fm	Arlington	VA	22206	703-998-2600	998-3401
WFAX-AM 1220 (Rel) 161-B Hillwood Ave *Web:* www.wfaxam.com	Falls Church	VA	22046	703-532-1220	533-7572
WFRE-FM 99.9 (Ctry) 5966 Grove Hill Rd *TF:* 877-999-9373 ■ *Web:* www.wfre.com	Frederick	MD	21703	301-663-4181	682-8018
WGTS-FM 91.9 (Rel) 7600 Flower Ave *TF:* 877-948-7919 ■ *Web:* www.wgts.org	Takoma Park	MD	20912	301-891-4200	270-9191
WHFS-FM 105.7 (N/T) 1423 Clarkview Rd Suite 100 *Web:* www.whfs.com	Balitmore	MD	21209	410-828-7722	821-8256
WHUR-FM 96.3 (Urban AC) 529 Bryant St NW *TF:* 800-221-9487 ■ *Web:* www.whur.com	Washington	DC	20059	202-806-3500	806-3522
WIHT-FM 99.5 (CHR) 1801 Rockville Pike 6th Fl *TF:* 877-995-4681 ■ *Web:* www.hot995.com	Rockville	MD	20852	301-747-2700	
WJFK-FM 106.7 (N/T) 10800 Main St *Web:* www.1067wjfk.com	Fairfax	VA	22030	703-691-1900	352-0111
WJZW-FM 105.9 (NAC) 4400 Jenifer St NW 4th Fl *TF:* 800-779-1059 ■ *Web:* www.smoothjazz1059.com	Washington	DC	20015	202-686-3100	686-3064
WKYS-FM 93.9 (Urban) 5900 Princess Garden Pkwy 8th Fl *Web:* www.939wkys.com	Lanham	MD	20706	301-306-1111	306-9609
WMAL-AM 630 (N/T) 4400 Jenifer St NW 4th Fl *TF:* 888-630-9625 ■ *Web:* www.wmal.com	Washington	DC	20015	202-686-3100	686-3061
WMMJ-FM 102.3 (Urban AC) 5900 Princess Garden Pkwy 8th Fl *Web:* www.majic1023.com	Lanham	MD	20706	301-306-1111	306-9609
WMZQ-FM 98.7 (Ctry) 1801 Rockville Pike 6th Fl *TF:* 800-505-0098 ■ *Web:* www.wmzq.com	Rockville	MD	20852	301-231-8231	984-4895
WOL-AM 1450 (N/T) 5900 Princess Garden Pkwy 8th Fl	Lanham	MD	20706	301-306-1111	306-1149
WPGC-AM 1580 (Rel) 4200 Parliament Pl Suite 300 *TF:* 888-432-1580 ■ *Web:* www.heaven1580am.com	Latham	MD	20706	301-918-0955	731-1583
WPGC-FM 95.5 (CHR) 4200 Parliament Pl Suite 300 *TF:* 877-955-5267 ■ *Web:* www.wpgc955.com	Lanham	MD	20706	301-918-0955	459-9557
WPRS-FM 104.1 (Rel) 5900 Princess Garden Pkwy	Lanham	MD	20706	301-306-1111	306-9540
WRQX-FM 107.3 (AC) 4400 Jenifer St NW 4th Fl *Web:* www.mix1073fm.com	Washington	DC	20015	202-686-3100	686-3091
WTEM-AM 980 (Sports) 1801 Rockville Pike *Web:* www.sportstalk980.com	Rockville	MD	20852	301-231-7798	881-8025
WTGB-FM 94.7 (CR) 4200 Parliament Pl Suite 300 *Web:* www.947thearrow.com	Lanham	MD	20706	301-683-0947	881-8746
WTLP-FM 103.9(N/T) 3400 Idaho Ave NW *TF:* 800-987-2104	Washington	DC	20016	202-895-5000	895-5149
WTOP-FM 103.5 (N/T) 3400 Idaho Ave NW *Web:* www.wtopnews.com	Washington	DC	20016	202-895-5000	895-5149
WWDC-FM 101.1 (Rock) 1801 Rockville Pike Suite 405 *Web:* www.dc101.com	Rockville	MD	20852	301-255-4489	587-0225
WWRC-AM 1260 (N/T) 1801 Rockville Pike *Web:* www.wrcam1260.com	Rockville	MD	20852	301-231-7798	565-3329
WWWT-FM 107.7 (N/T) 3400 Idaho Ave NW *Web:* www.wtopnews.com	Washington	DC	20016	202-895-5000	895-5149
WYCB-AM 1340 (Rel) 5900 Princess Garden Pkwy Suite 800	Lanham	MD	20706	301-306-1111	306-1149

648-179 West Palm Beach, FL

Station	City	State	Zip	Phone	Fax
WAYF-FM 88.1 (Rel) 800 Northpoint Pkwy Suite 881 *Web:* wayf.wayfm.com	West Palm Beach	FL	33407	561-881-1929	840-1929
WBZT-AM 1230 (N/T) 3071 Continental Dr *Web:* www.wbzt.com	West Palm Beach	FL	33407	561-616-6600	616-6677
WDJA-AM 1420 (N/T) 2710 W Atlantic Ave *Web:* www.wdja.com	Delray Beach	FL	33445	561-278-1420	278-1898
WEAT-FM 104.3 (AC) 701 Northpoint Pkwy Suite 500 *TF:* 800-579-1043 ■ *Web:* www.sunny1043.com	West Palm Beach	FL	33407	561-686-9505	686-0157
WIRK-FM 107.9 (Ctry) 701 Northpoint Pkwy Suite 500 *TF:* 800-919-1079 ■ *Web:* www.wirk.com	West Palm Beach	FL	33407	561-686-9505	686-0157
WJNO-AM 1290 (N/T) 3071 Continental Dr *Web:* www.wjno.com	West Palm Beach	FL	33407	561-616-6600	616-6677
WKGR-FM 98.7 (CR) 3071 Continental Dr *Web:* www.gater.com	West Palm Beach	FL	33407	561-616-6600	616-6677
WLDI-FM 95.5 (CHR) 3071 Continental Dr *Web:* www.wild955.com	West Palm Beach	FL	33407	561-616-6600	616-6677
WMBX-FM 102.3 (Urban) 701 Northpoint Pkwy Suite 500 *TF:* 800-969-1023 ■ *Web:* www.thenewx1023.com	West Palm Beach	FL	33407	561-686-9505	686-0157
WOLL-FM 105.5 (AC) 3071 Continental Dr *TF:* 888-415-1055 ■ *Web:* www.kool1055.com	West Palm Beach	FL	33407	561-616-6600	616-6677
WPBZ-FM 103.1 (Alt) 701 Northpoint Pkwy Suite 500 *TF:* 866-951-7625 ■ *Web:* www.buzz103.com	West Palm Beach	FL	33407	561-686-9505	686-0157
WRMF-FM 97.9 (AC) 477 S Rosemary Ave Suite 302 *Web:* www.wrmf.com	West Palm Beach	FL	33401	561-868-1100	868-1111
WXEL-FM 90.7 (NPR) PO Box 6607 *TF:* 800-915-9935 ■ *Web:* www.wxel.org	West Palm Beach	FL	33405	561-737-8000	369-3067
WZZR-FM 94.3 (N/T) 3771 SE Jennings Rd *TF:* 877-927-6969 ■ *Web:* www.wzzr.com	Port Saint Lucie	FL	34952	772-335-9300	335-3291

648-180 Wheeling, WV

Station	City	State	Zip	Phone	Fax
WBBD-AM 1400 (Nost) 1015 Main St *TF:* 800-668-7426	Wheeling	WV	26003	304-232-1170	234-0041
WEGW-FM 107.5 (Rock) 1015 Main St *TF:* 800 668 7426 ■ *Web:* www.wegwfm.com	Wheeling	WV	26003	304-232-1170	234-0041
WKWK-FM 97.3 (AC) 1015 Main St *TF:* 800-668-7426 ■ *Web:* www.wk973.com	Wheeling	WV	26003	304-232-1170	234-0041
WOGH-FM 103.5 (Ctry) 320 Market St *TF:* 800-874-1035 ■ *Web:* www.froggyland.com	Steubenville	OH	43952	740-283-4747	283-3655
WOMP-AM 1290 (Sports) 56325 High Ridge Rd *Web:* www.wompam.com	Bellaire	OH	43906	740-676-5661	676-2742
WOVK-FM 98.7 (Ctry) 1015 Main St *TF:* 800-668-7426 ■ *Web:* www.wovk.com	Wheeling	WV	26003	304-232-1170	234-0041
WVKF-FM 95.7 (CHR) 1015 Main St *TF:* 800-668-7426 ■ *Web:* www.kisswheeling.com	Wheeling	WV	26003	304-232-1170	234-0036
WVKF-FM 105.5 (CHR) 1015 Main St *TF:* 800-668-7426 ■ *Web:* www.wvkffm.com	Wheeling	WV	26003	304-232-1170	234-0041
WWVA-AM 1170 (N/T) 1015 Main St *TF:* 800-668-7426 ■ *Web:* www.wwva.com	Wheeling	WV	26003	304-232-1170	234-0041
WYJK-FM 100.5 (Var) 56325 High Ridge Rd *Web:* www.wyjkfm.com	Bellaire	OH	43906	740-676-5661	676-2742

648-181 Wichita, KS

Station	City	State	Zip	Phone	Fax
KDGS-FM 93.9 (CHR) 2120 N Woodlawn St Suite 352 *Web:* www.power939.com	Wichita	KS	67208	316-685-2121	685-3408
KEYN-FM 103.7 (Oldies) 2120 N Woodlawn St Suite 352 *Web:* www.keyn.com	Wichita	KS	67208	316-685-2121	685-3408
KFBZ-FM 105.3 (AC) 2120 N Woodlawn St Suite 352 *Web:* www.1053thebuzz.com	Wichita	KS	67208	316-685-2121	685-3408
KFDI-FM 101.3 (Ctry) 4200 N Old Lawrence Rd *Web:* www.kfdi.com	Wichita	KS	67219	316-838-9141	838-3607
KFH-AM 1240 (N/T) 2120 N Woodlawn St Suite 352 *Web:* www.kfhradio.com	Wichita	KS	67208	316-685-2121	685-3408
KFTI-AM 1070 (Ctry) 4200 N Old Lawrence Rd *Web:* www.kfdi.com	Wichita	KS	67219	316-838-9141	838-3607
KHCC-FM 90.1 (NPR) 815 N Walnut St Suite 300 *TF:* 800-723-4657 ■ *Web:* www.radiokansas.org	Hutchinson	KS	67501	620-662-6646	
KICT-FM 95.1 (Rock) 4200 N Old Lawrence Rd *Web:* www.t95.com	Wichita	KS	67219	316-838-9141	838-3607
KMUW-FM 89.1 (NPR) 3317 E 17th St N *Web:* www.kmuw.org	Wichita	KS	67208	316-978-6789	978-3946
KNSS-AM 1330 (N/T) 2120 N Woodlawn St Suite 352 *Web:* www.knssradio.com	Wichita	KS	67208	316-685-2121	685-3408
KRBB-FM 97.9 (AC) 9323 E 37th St N *Web:* www.b98fm.com	Wichita	KS	67226	316-494-6600	494-6730
KTHR-FM 107.3 (CR) 9323 E 37th St N *Web:* www.1073theroad.com	Wichita	KS	67226	316-494-6600	494-6730
KTLI-FM 99.1 (Rel) 125 N Market St Suite 1900 *TF:* 800-525-5683	Wichita	KS	67202	316-303-9999	303-9900
KZCH-FM 96.3 (CHR) 9323 E 37th St N *Web:* www.channel963.com	Wichita	KS	67226	316-494-6600	494-6730
KZSN-FM 102.1 (Ctry) 9323 E 37th St N *Web:* www.kzsn.com	Wichita	KS	67226	316-494-6600	494-6730

648-182 Wilmington/Dover, DE

Station	City	State	Zip	Phone	Fax
WAFL-FM 97.7 (AC) PO Box 808	Milford	DE	19963	302-422-7575	422-3069
WDEL-AM 1150 (N/T) 2727 Shipley Rd *TF:* 800-544-1150 ■ *Web:* www.wdel.com	Wilmington	DE	19810	302-478-2700	478-0100
WDOV-AM 1410 (N/T) 1575 McKee Rd Suite 206 *Web:* www.wdov.com	Dover	DE	19904	302-674-1410	674-8621
WDSD-FM 92.9 (Ctry) 1575 McKee Rd Suite 206 *TF:* 888-929-9373 ■ *Web:* www.wdsd.com	Dover	DE	19904	302-674-1410	674-5978
WILM-AM 1450 (N/T) 920 W Basin Rd Suite 400 *Web:* www.wilm.com	New Castle	DE	19720	302-395-9800	395-9808
WJBR-AM 1290 (Sports) 920 W Basin Rd Suite 400 *Web:* www.am1290.com	Claymont	DE	19720	302-395-9800	395-9808
WJBR-FM 99.5 (AC) 812 Philadelphia Pike *Web:* www.wjbr.com	Wilmington	DE	19809	302-765-1160	765-1192
WMPH-FM 91.7 (CHR) 5201 Washington St Ext *Web:* www.wmph.org	Wilmington	DE	19809	302-762-7199	762-7042
WRDX-FM 94.7 (CR) 920 W Basin Rd Suite 400 *Web:* www.wrdx.com	Claymont	DE	19720	302-395-9800	395-9808
WSTW-FM 93.7 (CHR) 2727 Shipley Rd *TF:* 800-544-9370 ■ *Web:* www.wstw.com	Wilmington	DE	19810	302-478-2700	478-0100
WVCH-AM 740 (Rel) 308 Dutton Mill Rd PO Box A *Web:* www.wvch.com	Brookhaven	PA	19015	610-872-8861	872-8865
WXCY-FM 103.7 (Ctry) 707 Revolution St *TF:* 800-788-9929 ■ *Web:* www.1037wxcy.com	Havre de Grace	MD	21078	410-939-1100	939-1104

648-183 Winnipeg, MB

Station	City	State	Zip	Phone	Fax
CBW-AM 990 (CBC) 541 Portage Ave *Web:* www.cbc.ca/manitoba	Winnipeg	MB	R3B2G1	204-788-3222	788-3227
CBW-FM 98.3 (Clas) 541 Portage Ave *Web:* www.cbc.ca/manitoba	Winnipeg	MB	R3B2G1	204-788-3222	788-3227
CFQX-FM 104.1 (Ctry) 177 Lombard Ave 3rd Fl *Web:* www.qx104fm.com	Winnipeg	MB	R3B0W5	204-944-1031	943-7687
CFST-AM 1290 (Oldies) 1445 Pembina Hwy	Winnipeg	MB	R3T5C2	204-477-5120	453-8777
CHIQ-FM 94.3 (AC) 1445 Pembina Hwy *Web:* www.q94fm.com	Winnipeg	MB	R3T5C2	204-477-5120	453-8777
CITI-FM 92.1 (CR) 4-166 Osborne St *Web:* www.92citifm.ca	Winnipeg	MB	R3L1Y8	204-788-3400	788-3401
CJKR-FM 97.5 (Rock) 930 Portage Ave *Web:* www.power97.com	Winnipeg	MB	R3G0P8	204-786-2471	783-4512
CJOB-AM 680 (N/T) 930 Portage Ave *Web:* www.cjob.com	Winnipeg	MB	R3G0P8	204-786-2471	783-4512
CKJS-AM 810 (Ethnic) 520 Corydon Ave *Web:* www.ckjs.com	Winnipeg	MB	R3L0P1	204-477-1221	453-8244
CKMM-FM 103.1 (CHR) 177 Lombard Ave 3rd Fl *Web:* www.hot103live.com	Winnipeg	MB	R3B0W5	204-944-1031	989-5291
CKY-FM 102.3 (AC) 4-166 Osborne St *Web:* www.102clearfm.com	Winnipeg	MB	R3L1Y8	204-788-3400	788-3401

648-184 Winston-Salem, NC

Station	City	State	Zip	Phone	Fax
WBFJ-FM 89.3 (Rel) 1249 Trade St *Web:* www.wbfj.org	Winston-Salem	NC	27101	336-721-1560	777-1032
WFDD-FM 88.5 (NPR) PO Box 8850 *TF:* 800-262-8850 ■ *Web:* www.wfdd.org	Winston-Salem	NC	27109	336-758-8850	758-5193
WJMH-FM 102.1 (Urban) 7819 National Service Rd Suite 401 *Web:* www.102jamz.com	Greensboro	NC	27409	336-605-5200	605-5219
WKRR-FM 92.3 (CR) 192 E Lewis St *TF:* 800-762-5923 ■ *Web:* www.rock92.com	Greensboro	NC	27406	336-274-8042	274-5745
WKZL-FM 107.5 (CHR) 192 E Lewis St *TF:* 800-682-1075 ■ *Web:* www.1075kzl.com	Greensboro	NC	27406	336-274-8042	274-1629
WMAG-FM 99.5 (AC) 2-B PAI Park *Web:* www.wmagradio.com	Greensboro	NC	27409	336-822-2000	887-0104
WMQX-FM 93.1 (Oldies) 7819 National Service Rd Suite 401 *Web:* www.oldies93.net	Greensboro	NC	27409	336-605-5200	605-5221
WNAA-FM 90.1 (Jazz) North Carolina A&T State University Price Hall Suite 200 *Web:* wnaalive.ncat.edu	Greensboro	NC	27411	336-334-7936	334-7960
WOZN-FM 98.7 (AC) 7819 National Service Rd Suite 401 *Web:* www.987thezone.com	Greensboro	NC	27409	336-605-5200	387-7214
WPET-AM 950 (Rel) 7819 National Service Rd Suite 401 *Web:* www.wpetam950.com	Greensboro	NC	27409	336-605-5200	387-7206

Winston-Salem, NC (Cont'd)

Phone | Fax

WPOL-AM 1340 (Rel) 4405 Providence Ln ... Winston-Salem NC 27106 336-759-0363 759-0366
Web: www.1340thelight.com
WQMG-FM 97.1 (Urban AC) 7819 National Service Rd Suite 401 ... Greensboro NC 27409 336-605-5200 605-0138
Web: www.wqmg.com
WSJS-AM 600 (N/T) 875 W 5th St ... Winston-Salem NC 27101 336-777-3900 777-3915
Web: www.wsjs.com
WTHZ-FM 94.1 (AC) 200 Radio Dr ... Lexington NC 27292 336-248-2716 248-2800
Web: www.hitz94.com
WTOB-AM 1380 (Span) 4405 Providence Ln ... Winston-Salem NC 27106 336-759-0363 759-0366
WTQR-FM 104.1 (Ctry) 2-B PAI Park ... Greensboro NC 27409 336-822-2000 887-0104
Web: www.wtqr.com
WVBZ-FM 100.3 (Rock) 2-B PAI Park ... Greensboro NC 27409 336-822-2000 887-0104
Web: www.buzzardrocks.com

648-185 Worcester, MA

Phone | Fax

WCRN-AM 830 (N/T) 1049 Main St ... Worcester MA 01603 508-792-5803 770-0659
Web: www.wcrnradio.com
WCUW-FM 91.3 (Var) 910 Main St ... Worcester MA 01610 508-753-1012
Web: www.wcuw.com
WICN-FM 90.5 (NPR) 50 Portland St ... Worcester MA 01608 508-752-0700 752-7518
Web: www.wicn.org
WKOX-AM 1200 (N/T) 10 Cabot Rd ... Medford MA 02155 781-396-1430 391-3064
WORC-AM 1310 (Span) 122 Green St Suite 2-R ... Worcester MA 01604 508-791-2111 752-6897
Web: www.power1310.com
WSRS-FM 96.1 (AC) 96 Stereo Ln ... Paxton MA 01612 508-795-0580 757-1779
Web: www.wsrs.com
WTAG-AM 580 (N/T) 96 Stereo Ln ... Paxton MA 01612 508-795-0580 757-1779
Web: www.wtag.com
WVNE-AM 760 (Rel) 70 James St Suite 201 ... Worcester MA 01603 508-831-9863 831-7964
Web: www.wvne.net
WWFX-FM 100.1 (CR) 250 Commercial St ... Worcester MA 01608 508-752-1045 793-0824
Web: www.thefoxfm.com
WXLO-FM 104.5 (AC) 250 Commercial St ... Worcester MA 01608 508-752-1045 793-0824
Web: www.wxlo.com

648-186 Youngstown, OH

Phone | Fax

WAKZ-FM 95.9 (CHR) 7461 South Ave ... Youngstown OH 44512 330-965-0057 729-9991
Web: www.959kiss.com
WBBG-FM 106.1 (Oldies) 7461 South Ave ... Boardman OH 44512 330-740-9300 729-9991
Web: www.wbbgfm.com
WBBW-AM 1240 (Sports) 4040 Simon Rd ... Youngstown OH 44512 330-783-1000 783-0060
Web: www.wbbw.com
WGFT-AM 1500 (Rel) 20 Federal Plaza W 1st Fl ... Youngstown OH 44503 330-744-5115 744-4020
WHOT-FM 101.1 (CHR) 4040 Simon Rd ... Youngstown OH 44512 330-783-1000 783-0060
TF: 800-989-9468 ■ *Web:* www.hot101.com
WKBN-AM 570 (N/T) 7461 South Ave ... Boardman OH 44512 330-965-0057 729-9991
Web: www.wkbnradio.com
WKTX-AM 830 (Var) 11906 Madison Ave ... Lakewood OH 44107 216-221-0330 221-3638
WMXY-FM 98.9 (AC) 7461 South Ave ... Youngstown OH 44512 330-965-0057 729-9991
Web: www.mix989.com
WNCD-FM 93.3 (Rock) 7461 South Ave ... Youngstown OH 44512 330-965-0057 729-9991
Web: www.cd933.com
WNIO-AM 1390 (Nost) 7461 South Ave ... Boardman OH 44512 330-740-9300 729-9991
Web: www.wnio.com
WQXK-FM 105.1 (Ctry) 4040 Simon Rd ... Youngstown OH 44512 330-783-1000 783-0060
Web: www.k105country.com
WRBP-FM 101.9 (Urban) 20 Federal Plaza W 1st Fl ... Youngstown OH 44503 330-744-5115 744-4020
WYFM-FM 102.9 (CR) 4040 Simon Rd ... Youngstown OH 44512 330-783-1000 783-0060
Web: www.y-103.com
WYSU-FM 88.5 (Clas) Youngstown State University 1 University Plaza ... Youngstown OH 44555 330-941-3363 941-1501
Web: www.wysu.org

649 RADIO SYNDICATORS

Phone | Fax

AARP Broadcast Dept 601 'E' St NW ... Washington DC 20049 202-434-2600 434-6469
TF: 888-687-2277
Agrinet Farm Radio Network 104 Radio Rd ... Powells Point NC 27966 252-491-2414 491-2939
Web: www.agrinetradio.com
American Urban Radio Networks 960 Penn Ave Suite 200 ... Pittsburgh PA 15222 412-456-4030 456-4040
Web: www.aurn.com
AP Broadcast Services 1825 K St NW Suite 800 ... Washington DC 20006 202-736-1100 736-1199
TF: 800-821-4747 ■ *Web:* apbroadcast.com
B & B Media Group 109 S Main St ... Corsicana TX 75110 903-872-0517 872-0518
TF: 800-927-0517 ■ *Web:* www.tbbmedia.com
Bill Harris Syndicate 6662 Whitley Terr ... Hollywood CA 90068 323-874-9040 874-9241
Black Radio Network 166 Madison Ave 4th Fl ... New York NY 10016 212-686-6850 686-7308
Bloomberg Radio Network 499 Park Ave 15th Fl ... New York NY 10022 212-318-2000 940-1994
TF: 800-448-5678 ■ *Web:* www.bloomberg.com/media
Business TalkRadio Network 1490 Dayton Ave ... Greenwich CT 06831 203-422-2800 422-2288
Web: www.businesstalkradio.net
Car Clinic Productions 5675 N Davis Hwy ... Pensacola FL 32503 850-478-3139 477-0862
TF: 800-264-5454 ■ *Web:* www.carclinicnetwork.com
Cox Radio Inc 6205 Peachtree Dunwoody Rd ... Atlanta GA 30328 678-645-0000 645-1889
NYSE: CXR ■ *Web:* coxradio.com
Crystal Media Networks 1100 Wilson Blvd Suite 3000 ... Arlington VA 22209 703-247-7500 247-7505
Environmental Media Broadcasting Radio Network 7302 Pierce Ave ... Whittier CA 90607 562-945-6469 945-1802
TF: 800-963-9927 ■ *Web:* www.thingsgreen.com
FamilyNet 6350 West Fwy ... Fort Worth TX 76116 817-737-4011 737-8209
TF: 800-292-2287 ■ *Web:* www.familynet.com
Focus on the Family 8605 Explorer Dr ... Colorado Springs CO 80920 719-531-3400 548-4670
TF Sales: 800-232-6459 ■ *Web:* www.family.org
Harris Bill Syndicate 6662 Whitley Terr ... Hollywood CA 90068 323-874-9040 874-9241
Jameson Broadcast Inc 1644 Hawthorne St ... Sarasota FL 34239 941-906-8800 906-8801
Web: www.jamesonbroadcast.com
Joanna Langfield's Entertainment Reports 340 W 55th St Suite 8-C ... New York NY 10019 212-757-7654
Web: www.themovieminute.com
Jones Media Networks Ltd 9697 E Mineral Ave ... Englewood CO 80112 303-792-3111
TF: 800-525-7000 ■ *Web:* www.jones.com/jmg
Jones MediaAmerica Inc 11 W 42nd St 11th Fl ... New York NY 10036 212-302-1100 556-9402
Web: www.mediaamerica.com
Lichtenstein Creative Media Inc 1 Broadway 3rd Fl ... Cambridge MA 02142 617-682-3700 682-3710
Web: lcmedia.com
Media Syndication Services 236 Massachusetts Ave NE Suite 510 ... Washington DC 20002 202-544-4457 546-8435
MediaTracks Communications 2250 E Devon Ave Suite 151 ... Des Plaines IL 60018 847-299-9500 299-9501
Web: www.mediatracks.com
National Public Radio (NPR) 635 Massachusetts Ave NW ... Washington DC 20001 202-513-2000 513-3329
Web: www.npr.org
New Dimensions Radio Broadcasting Network PO Box 569 ... Ukiah CA 95482 707-468-5215
TF: 800-935-8273 ■ *Web:* newdimensions.org
North American Network Inc 7910 Woodmont Ave Suite 1400 ... Bethesda MD 20814 301-654-9810 654-9828
Web: www.radiospace.com
Pentacom Productions 1375 N Wetherly Dr ... Los Angeles CA 90069 310-276-7001 276-7002
Premiere Radio Networks Inc 15260 Ventura Blvd Suite 500 ... Sherman Oaks CA 91403 818-377-5300 377-5333
TF: 800-533-8686 ■ *Web:* www.premrad.com
Radio America 1030 15th St NW Suite 1040 ... Washington DC 20005 202-408-0944 408-1087
TF: 800-807-4703 ■ *Web:* www.radioamerica.org
Radio Express Inc 1415 W Magnolia Blvd Suite 201 ... Burbank CA 91506 818-295-5800 295-5801
Web: www.radioexpress.com
Salem Radio Network 6400 N Beltline Rd Suite 210 ... Irving TX 75063 972-831-1920 831-8626
Web: www.srnonline.com
Strand Media Group Inc 22 Fawn Ridge Ln Suite 2 ... Southport CT 06890 203-254-9914 254-9924
Web: www.somethingyoushouldknow.net
Success Journal Corp 8700 Waukegan Rd Suite 250 ... Morton Grove IL 60053 847-583-9000 677-8450
Web: www.successjournal.com
Superadio LLC 1661 Worcester Rd ... Framingham MA 01701 508-620-0006 628-1590
Web: www.superadio.com
Syndicated Solutions Inc PO Box 1078 ... Ridgefield CT 06877 203-431-0790 431-0792
Web: www.syndsolutions.com
Talk Radio Network PO Box 3755 ... Central Point OR 97502 541-664-8827 664-6250
TF: 888-383-3733 ■ *Web:* www.talkradionetwork.com
TM Century Inc 2002 Academy Ln ... Dallas TX 75234 972-406-6800 406-6890
Web: www.tmcentury.com
Transmedia Productions Inc 500 Washington St ... San Francisco CA 94111 415-956-3118 956-8098
TF: 800-229-7234 ■ *Web:* www.transmediasf.com
Tribune Radio Network 435 N Michigan Ave ... Chicago IL 60611 312-222-3342 222-4876
TF: 800-654-8597 ■ *Web:* www.tribuneradio.com
Trident Communications 31 Timber Ln ... Hilton Head Island SC 29926 843-837-4978 837-6898
WCLV/Seaway Productions 26501 Renaissance Pkwy ... Cleveland OH 44128 216-464-0900 464-2206
TF: 800-491-8863 ■ *Web:* www.wclv.com
WestStar Talk Radio Networks 2711 N 24th St ... Phoenix AZ 85008 602-381-8200 381-8221
Web: www.weststar.com
Westwood One Inc 40 W 57th St 5th Fl ... New York NY 10019 212-641-2000 641-2172
NYSE: WON ■ *Web:* www.westwoodone.com
WOR Radio Network 111 Broadway 3rd Fl ... New York NY 10006 212-642-4533 642-4486
Web: www.worradionet.com

650 RADIO & TELEVISION BROADCASTING & COMMUNICATIONS EQUIPMENT

SEE ALSO Audio & Video Equipment p. 1355; Telecommunications Equipment & Systems p. 2339

Phone | Fax

Acrodyne Industries Inc 200 Schell Ln ... Phoenixville PA 19460 610-917-1300 917-8148
TF: 800-523-2596 ■ *Web:* www.acrodyne.com
AeroAstro Inc 20145 Ashbrook Pl ... Ashburn VA 20147 703-723-9800 723-9850
TF: 800-669-5437 ■ *Web:* www.aeroastro.com
AheadTek Inc 6410 Via Del Oro ... San Jose CA 95119 408-226-9991 226-9195
TF: 800-971-9191 ■ *Web:* www.aheadtek.com
Andersen Mfg Inc 3125 N Yellowstone Hwy ... Idaho Falls ID 83401 208-523-6460 523-6562
Web: www.andersenInc.com
Andrew Corp 3 Westbrook Corporate Ctr Suite 900 ... Westchester IL 60154 708-236-6600 349-5444
NASDAQ: ANDW ■ *TF Cust Svc:* 800-255-1479 ■ *Web:* www.andrew.com
Antedo Inc 1475 Saratoga Ave Suite 790 ... San Jose CA 95129 408-253-1870 253-1871
Web: www.antedo.com
Antenna Products Corp 101 SE 25th Ave ... Mineral Wells TX 76067 940-325-3301 325-0716
Web: www.antennaproducts.com
Antennas for Communications 350 Cypress Rd ... Ocala FL 34472 352-687-4121 687-1203
Web: www.afcsat.com
Apex Airtronics Inc 2465 Atlantic Ave ... Brooklyn NY 11207 718-485-8560 485-8564
AR Worldwide 160 Schoolhouse Rd ... Souderton PA 18964 215-723-8181 723-5688
Web: www.ar-worldwide.com
ArrayComm Inc 2480 N 1st St Suite 200 ... San Jose CA 95131 408-428-9080 428-9083
Web: www.arraycomm.com
Arris Group Inc 3871 Lakefield Dr ... Suwanee GA 30024 770-622-8400
NASDAQ: ARRS ■ *TF:* 800-469-6569 ■ *Web:* www.arrisi.com
Artel Video Systems Corp 330 Codman Hill Rd ... Boxborough MA 01719 978-263-5775 263-9755
TF: 800-225-0228 ■ *Web:* www.artel.com
Associated Industries 11347 Vanowen St ... North Hollywood CA 91605 818-760-1000 760-2142
TF: 800-775-2000 ■ *Web:* www.associated-ind.com
Avtech Corp 3400 Wallingford Ave N ... Seattle WA 98103 206-634-2540 634-3011
Web: www.avtcorp.com
Axcera Corp 103 Freedom Dr ... Lawrence PA 15055 724-873-8100 873-8105
TF: 800-215-2614 ■ *Web:* www.axcera.com
Ball Aerospace & Technologies Corp 1600 Commerce St ... Boulder CO 80301 303-939-4000 460-2315*
**Fax:* Mail Rm ■ *Web:* www.ballaerospace.com
Barker & Williamson 603 Cidco Rd ... Cocoa FL 32926 321-639-1510 639-2545
Web: www.bwantennas.com
Blonder Tongue Laboratories Inc 1 Jake Brown Rd ... Old Bridge NJ 08857 732-679-4000 679-4353
AMEX: BDR ■ *TF:* 800-523-6049 ■ *Web:* www.blondertongue.com
Broadcast Electronics Inc 4100 N 24th St ... Quincy IL 62305 217-224-9600 224-9607
Web: www.bdcast.com
C-COR Inc 60 Decibel Rd ... State College PA 16801 814-238-2461 238-4065
NASDAQ: CCBL ■ *TF:* 800-233-2267 ■ *Web:* www.c-cor.com
CalAmp Corp 1401 N Rice Ave ... Oxnard CA 93030 805-987-9000 482-5842*
NASDAQ: CAMP ■ **Fax:* Hum Res ■ *TF:* 888-767-7988 ■ *Web:* www.calamp.com
Cattron-Theimeg Inc 58 W Shenango St ... Sharpsville PA 16150 724-962-3571 962-4310
Web: www.cattron.com
Celerity Systems Inc 1650 Tysons Blvd Suite 1100 ... McLean VA 22102 703-848-1900 848-2139
Web: www.celerity.com
Centurion Wireless Technologies Inc 3425 N 44th St ... Lincoln NE 68504 402-467-4491 467-5973
TF: 800-228-4563 ■ *Web:* www.centurion.com
Channell Commercial Corp 26040 Ynez Rd ... Temecula CA 92591 951-719-2600 296-2322
NASDAQ: CHNL ■ *TF:* 800-423-1863 ■ *Web:* www.channellcomm.com
Chelton Inc 1955 Lakeway Dr Suite 200 ... Lewisville TX 75057 972-221-1783 436-2716
Web: www.chelton.com
CIC International Ltd 5 Marine View Plaza ... Hoboken NJ 07030 201-792-1800 792-5755
Web: www.cic-international.com

Company / Address	City	State	Zip	Phone	Fax
Circuit Research Labs Inc 7970 S Kyrene Rd *TF:* 800-535-7648	Tempe	AZ	85284	480-403-8300	403-8301
Cobham Defense Electronic Systems Atlantic Microwave Div 58 Main St Rt 117 *Web:* www.atlanticmicrowave.com	Bolton	MA	01740	978-779-6963	779-2906
Cobra Electronics Corp 6500 W Cortland St *NASDAQ: COBR* ■ *Web:* www.cobraelec.com	Chicago	IL	60707	773-889-8870	889-4453
Cohu Inc 12367 Crosthwaite Cir *NASDAQ: COHU* ■ *Web:* www.cohu.com	Poway	CA	92064	858-848-8100	848-8185
Cohu Inc Electronics Div 3912 Calle Fortunada *TF:* 800-735-2648 ■ *Web:* www.cohu-cameras.com	San Diego	CA	92123	858-277-6700	277-0221
Communications & Power Industries Inc Beverly Microwave Div **DBA CPI Inc Beverly Microwave Div** 150 Sohier Rd *Web:* www.cpii.com/bmd	Beverly	MA	01915	978-922-6000	922-8914
Comtech Systems Inc 2900 Titan Row Suite 142 *Web:* www.comtechsystems.com	Orlando	FL	32809	407-854-1950	851-6960
Comtech Telecommunications Corp 68 S Service Rd Suite 230 *NASDAQ: CMTL* ■ *Web:* www.comtechtel.com	Melville	NY	11747	631-962-7000	962-7001
Concurrent 4375 River Green Pkwy Suite 100 *NASDAQ: CCUR* ■ *TF:* 877-978-7363 ■ *Web:* www.ccur.com	Duluth	GA	30096	678-258-4000	258-4300
Conolog Corp 5 Columbia Rd *NASDAQ: CNLG* ■ *TF:* 800-526-3984 ■ *Web:* www.conolog.com	Somerville	NJ	08876	908-722-8081	722-5461
Continental Electronics Corp 4212 S Buckner Blvd *TF:* 800-733-5011 ■ *Web:* www.contelec.com	Dallas	TX	75227	214-381-7161	381-4949
Cushcraft Corp 48 Perimeter Rd *Web:* www.cushcraft.com	Manchester	NH	03103	603-627-7877	627-1764
Dage-MTI Inc 701 N Roeske Ave *Web:* www.dagemti.com	Michigan City	IN	46360	219-872-5514	872-5559
DAQ Electronics Inc 262B Old New Brunswick Rd *Web:* www.daq.net	Piscataway	NJ	08854	732-981-0050	981-0058
Datron World Communications Inc 3030 Enterprise Ct *TF Sales:* 800-405-0744 ■ *Web:* www.dtwc.com	Vista	CA	92081	760-734-5454	597-1510
Dayton-Granger Inc 3299 SW 9th Ave *Web:* www.daytongranger.com	Fort Lauderdale	FL	33315	954-463-3451	761-3172
Diamond Antenna & Microwave Corp 59 Porter Rd *Web:* www.diamondantenna.com	Littleton	MA	01460	978-486-0039	486-0079
Dielectric Communications 22 Tower Rd *TF Sales:* 800-341-9678 ■ *Web:* www.dielectric.com	Raymond	ME	04071	207-655-4555	655-4669
Digital Angel Corp 490 Villaume Ave S *AMEX: DOC* ■ *TF:* 800-328-0118 ■ *Web:* www.digitalangelcorp.com	South Saint Paul	MN	55075	651-455-1621	455-0413
DIRECTV Group Inc 2230 E Imperial Hwy *NYSE: DTV* ■ *Web:* www.directv.com	El Segundo	CA	90245	310-964-0700	535-5225
Drake RL Co 230 Industrial Dr *Web:* www.rldrake.com	Franklin	OH	45005	937-746-4556	806-1507
DRS C3 systems LLC 1200 E Mermaid Ln *Web:* www.drs.com	Wyndmoor	PA	19038	215-233-4100	233-9947
DRS Codem Systems (West) 788 Palomar Ave *Web:* www.drs-cs.com	Sunnyvale	CA	94085	408-852-0800	852-0801
Eagle Comtronics Inc 7665 Henry Clay Blvd *TF:* 800-448-7474 ■ *Web:* www.eaglecomtronics.com	Liverpool	NY	13088	315-622-3402	622-3800
Earmark LLC 1125 Dixwell Ave *TF Cust Svc:* 888-327-6275 ■ *Web:* www.earmark.com	Hamden	CT	06514	203-777-2130	777-2886
EDO Antenna Products & Technologies 585 Johnson Ave *Web:* www.edocorp.com	Bohemia	NY	11716	631-218-5500	218-7096
EDO Defense Systems 1500 New Horizons Blvd *Web:* www.edocorp.com	North Amityville	NY	11701	631-630-4000	630-0470
EMS Technologies Inc 660 Engineering Dr Technology Park Atlanta *NASDAQ: ELMG* ■ *Web:* www.elmg.com	Norcross	GA	30092	770-263-9200	263-9207
GAI-Tronics Corp PO Box 1060 *TF:* 800-492-1212 ■ *Web:* www.gai-tronics.com	Reading	PA	19607	610-777-1374	775-6540
General Dynamics SATCOM Technologies 1500 Prodelin Dr *TF:* 888-836-1979 ■ *Web:* www.rsicom.com	Newton	NC	28658	828-464-4141	464-5725
Globecomm Systems Inc 45 Oser Ave *NASDAQ: GCOM* ■ *TF:* 888-231-9800 ■ *Web:* www.globecommsystems.com	Hauppauge	NY	11788	631-231-9800	231-1557
Goodrich Corp Space Flight Systems Div 6600 Gulton Ct NE *Web:* www.isr.goodrich.com/SpaceFlightSystems.shtml	Albuquerque	NM	87109	505-345-9031	344-9879
HAL Communications Corp 1201 W Kenyon Rd *Web:* www.halcomm.com	Urbana	IL	61801	217-367-7373	
Harmonic Inc 549 Baltic Way *NASDAQ: HLIT* ■ *TF:* 800-788-1330 ■ *Web:* www.harmonicinc.com	Sunnyvale	CA	94089	408-542-2500	542-2511
Harris Corp 1025 W NASA Blvd *NYSE: HRS* ■ *TF:* 800-442-7747 ■ *Web:* www.harris.com	Melbourne	FL	32919	321-727-9100	
Harris Corp Broadcast Communications Div 3200 Wismann Ln *TF:* 800-622-0022 ■ *Web:* www.broadcast.harris.com	Quincy	IL	62301	217-222-8200	222-7082
Harris Corp Government Communication Systems Div 1025 W Nasa Blvd *Web:* www.govcomm.harris.com	Melbourne	FL	32902	321-727-4000	
Harris Corp Microwave Communications Div 350 Twin Dolphin Dr *TF:* 800-227-8332 ■ *Web:* www.microwave.harris.com	Redwood Shores	CA	94065	650-594-3000	594-3110
Harris Corp RF Communications Div 1680 University Ave *TF:* 800-288-4277 ■ *Web:* www.rfcomm.harris.com	Rochester	NY	14610	585-244-5830	242-4755
Hitachi Kokusai Electric America Ltd 150 Crossways Park Dr *Web:* www.hitachikokusai.us	Woodbury	NY	11797	516-921-7200	496-3718
Hughes Network Systems LLC 11717 Exploration Ln *Web:* www.hns.com	Germantown	MD	20876	301-428-5500	428-1868
ICOM America Inc 2380 116th Ave NE *TF:* 800-872-4266 ■ *Web:* www.icomamerica.com	Bellevue	WA	98004	425-454-8155	454-1509
ICTV Inc 14600 Winchester Blvd *TF:* 800-926-8398 ■ *Web:* www.ictv.com	Los Gatos	CA	95032	408-364-9200	364-9300
ID Systems Inc 1 University Plaza Suite 600 *NASDAQ: IDSY* ■ *TF:* 866-410-0152 ■ *Web:* www.id-systems.com	Hackensack	NJ	07601	201-996-9000	996-9144
Ikegami Electronics USA Inc 37 Brook Ave *TF:* 800-368-9171 ■ *Web:* www.ikegami.com	Maywood	NJ	07607	201-368-9171	569-1626
Integral Systems Inc 5000 Philadelphia Way Suite A *NASDAQ: ISYS* ■ *Web:* www.integ.com	Lanham	MD	20706	301-731-4233	731-9606
Intelect Technologies Inc 1225 Commerce Dr *TF:* 888-477-7272 ■ *Web:* www.intelectinc.com	Richardson	TX	75081	972-367-2100	367-2200
Iteris Inc 1515 S Manchester Ave *AMEX: ITI* ■ *Web:* www.iteris.com	Anaheim	CA	92802	714-774-5000	780-7287
ITT Aerospace/Communications Div 1919 W Cook Rd *Web:* www.acd.itt.com	Fort Wayne	IN	46818	260-451-6000	451-6033
ITT Defense 1650 Tysons Blvd Suite 1700 *Web:* defense.itt.com	McLean	VA	22102	703-790-6300	790-6360
Jampro Antennas Inc 6340 Sky Creek Dr *Web:* www.jampro.com	Sacramento	CA	95828	916-383-1177	383-1182
Jaybeam Wireless 730 21st Street Dr SE *Web:* www.jaybeamwireless.com	Hickory	NC	28658	828-324-6971	327-6027
Kenwood USA Corp 2201 E Flamingo St PO Box 22745 **Fax:* Hum Res ■ *TF:* 800-536-9663 ■ *Web:* www.kenwoodusa.com	Long Beach	CA	90801	310-639-9000	608-5445*
Kongsberg Maritime Inc 7225 Langtry St Suite 700 *Web:* www.kongsbergmaritime.com	Houston	TX	77040	713-934-8885	934-8886
KVH Industries Inc 50 Enterprise Center *NASDAQ: KVHI* ■ *TF:* 888-584-4773 ■ *Web:* www.kvh.com	Middletown	RI	02842	401-847-3327	849-0045
L-3 Communications Corp 600 3rd Ave 34-35 Fl *NYSE: LLL* ■ *TF:* 866-463-6555 ■ *Web:* www.l-3com.com	New York	NY	10016	212-697-1111	867-5249
L-3 Communications ESSCO (ESSCO) 48 Old Powder Mill Rd *Web:* www.l-3com.com/essco	Concord	MA	01742	978-369-7200	369-7641
L-3 Communications Narda Microwave East 435 Moreland Rd *TF:* 800-666-7060 ■ *Web:* www.nardamicrowave.com	Hauppauge	NY	11788	631-272-5600	272-1711
L-3 Communications Telemetry East Div 1515 Grundy's Ln *Web:* www.l-3com.com/te	Bristol	PA	19007	267-545-7000	545-0100
L-3 Communications Telemetry West Div 9020 Balboa Ave *TF:* 800-351-8483 ■ *Web:* www.l-3com.com/tw	San Diego	CA	92123	858-694-7500	694-7538
Laird Technologies 3481 Rider Trail S *TF:* 800-843-4556 ■ *Web:* www.lairdtech.com	Saint Louis	MO	63045	314-344-9300	344-9333
Larcan Inc 228 Ambassador Dr *Web:* www.larcan.com	Mississauga	ON	L5T2J2	905-564-9222	564-9244
MCL Inc 501 S Woodcreek Rd *TF Support:* 800-743-4625 ■ *Web:* www.mcl.com	Bolingbrook	IL	60440	630-759-9500	771-7381
MDI Security Systems Inc 9725 Datapoint Dr Suite 200 *NASDAQ: MDII* ■ *TF:* 866-435-7634 ■ *Web:* www.mdisecure.com	San Antonio	TX	78229	210-477-5400	477-5401
MFJ Enterprises Inc 300 Industrial Park Rd *TF:* 800-647-1800 ■ *Web:* www.mfjenterprises.com	Starkville	MS	39759	662-323-5869	323-6551
Microphase Corp 587 Connecticut Ave *Web:* www.microphase.com	Norwalk	CT	06854	203-866-8000	866-6727
Microwave Radio Communications 101 Billerica Ave Bldg 6 *TF:* 800-490-5700 ■ *Web:* www.mrcbroadcast.com	North Billerica	MA	01862	978-671-5700	671-5800
Miller RA Industries Inc 14500 168th Ave *TF:* 888-845-9450 ■ *Web:* www.rami.com	Grand Haven	MI	49417	616-842-9450	842-2771
Minerva Networks Inc 2111 Tasman Dr *TF:* 800-806-9594 ■ *Web:* www.minervanetworks.com	Santa Clara	CA	95054	408-567-9400	567-0747
Mitsubishi International Corp 655 3rd Ave *Web:* www.micusa.com	New York	NY	10017	212-605-2000	
Morcom International Inc 3656 Centerview Dr Unit 1 *Web:* www.morcom.com	Chantilly	VA	20151	703-263-9305	263-9308
Moseley Assoc Inc 111 Castilian Dr *Web:* www.moseleysb.com	Santa Barbara	CA	93117	805-968-9621	685-9638
Motorola Inc Broadband Communications Sector 101 Tournament Dr *TF:* 800-523-6678 ■ *Web:* broadband.motorola.com	Horsham	PA	19044	215-323-1000	
Narco Avionics 270 Commerce Dr *TF Sales:* 800-223-3636 ■ *Web:* www.narco-avionics.com	Fort Washington	PA	19034	215-643-2900	643-0197
Narda Microwave East 435 Moreland Rd *TF:* 800-666-7060 ■ *Web:* www.nardamicrowave.com	Hauppauge	NY	11788	631-272-5600	272-1711
NCT Group Inc 375 Bridgeport Ave 2nd Fl *TF:* 800-278-3526 ■ *Web:* www.nctgroupinc.com	Shelton	CT	06484	203-944-9533	944-9733
Orbit/FR Inc 506 Prudential Rd *TF:* 800-672-4859 ■ *Web:* www.orbitfr.com	Horsham	PA	19044	215-674-5100	674-5108
ParkerVision Inc 7915 Baymeadows Way *NASDAQ: PRKR* ■ *TF:* 800-532-8034 ■ *Web:* www.parkervision.com	Jacksonville	FL	32256	904-737-1367	731-0958
Pelco 3500 Pelco Way **Fax Area Code:* 800 ■ *TF:* 800-289-9100 ■ *Web:* www.pelco.com	Clovis	CA	93612	559-292-1981	289-9150*
Pico Macom Inc 6260 Sequence Dr *TF:* 800-421-6511 ■ *Web:* www.piconet.com	San Diego	CA	92121	858-546-5050	546-5051
Powerwave Technologies Inc 1801 E Saint Andrew Pl *NASDAQ: PWAV* ■ *TF:* 888-797-9283 ■ *Web:* www.powerwave.com	Santa Ana	CA	92705	714-466-1000	466-5800
Prodelin Corp 1500 Prodelin Dr *TF:* 888-836-1979 ■ *Web:* www.prodelin.com	Newton	NC	28658	828-464-4141	464-5725
PTS Corp 5233 Hwy 37 S **Fax:* Cust Svc ■ *TF:* 800-844-7871 ■ *Web:* www.ptscorp.com	Bloomington	IN	47401	812-824-9331	824-2848*
RA Miller Industries Inc 14500 168th Ave *TF:* 888-845-9450 ■ *Web:* www.rami.com	Grand Haven	MI	49417	616-842-9450	842-2771
Radio Holland USA Inc 8943 Gulf Fwy *Web:* www.radiohollandusa.com	Houston	TX	77017	713-943-3325	378-2101
Rantec Microwave Systems Inc 24003 Ventura Blvd *Web:* www.rantecmdm.com	Calabasas	CA	91302	818-223-5000	223-5089
Raytheon Co Space & Airborne Systems 2000 East El Segundo Blvd *Web:* www.raytheon.com/businesses/rsas/index.html	El Segundo	CA	90245	310-647-1000	647-0785
RELM Wireless Corp 7100 Technology Dr *AMEX: RWC* ■ *TF Cust Svc:* 800-648-0947 ■ *Web:* www.relm.com	West Melbourne	FL	32904	321-984-1414	676-4403
RF Products Inc Davis & Copewood Sts *Web:* www.rfproductsinc.com	Camden	NJ	08103	856-365-5500	342-9757
RF Scientific Inc 5644 Commerce Dr *TF:* 800-741-5465 ■ *Web:* www.rfscientific.com	Orlando	FL	32839	407-856-1050	855-7640
RL Drake Co 230 Industrial Dr *Web:* www.rldrake.com	Franklin	OH	45005	937-746-4556	806-1507
Rockwell Collins Inc 400 Collins Rd NE *NYSE: COL* ■ **Fax:* PR ■ *Web:* www.rockwellcollins.com	Cedar Rapids	IA	52498	319-295-1000	295-9347*
Satellite Systems Corp 101 Malibu Dr *Web:* www.satsyscorp.com	Virginia Beach	VA	23452	757-463-3553	463-3891
Scientific-Atlanta Inc - A Cisco Co 5030 Sugarloaf Pkwy *TF Sales:* 800-722-2009 ■ *Web:* www.sciatl.com	Lawrenceville	GA	30044	770-236-5000	
SCM Microsystems Inc 466 Kato Terr *NASDAQ: SCMM* ■ *Web:* www.scmmicro.com	Fremont	CA	94539	510-360-2300	360-0211
SeaChange International Inc 50 Nagog Park *NASDAQ: SEAC* ■ *TF:* 888-732-2641 ■ *Web:* www.schange.com	Acton	MA	01720	978-897-0100	897-0132
SEA/Datamarine Inc 7030 220th St SW *TF:* 800-426-1330 ■ *Web:* www.sea-dmi.com	Mountlake Terrace	WA	98043	425-771-2182	771-2650
Sensor Systems Inc 8929 Fullbright Ave *Web:* www.sensorantennas.com	Chatsworth	CA	91311	818-341-5366	341-9059
Shively Labs 188 Harrison Rd PO Box 389 *TF:* 888-744-8359 ■ *Web:* www.shively.com	Bridgton	ME	04009	207-647-3327	647-8273
SkyStream Networks Inc 455 DeGuigne Dr *TF Cust Svc:* 877-475-9787 ■ *Web:* www.skystream.com	Sunnyvale	CA	94085	408-616-3300	616-3400
Space Systems/Loral 3825 Fabian Way *TF:* 800-332-6490 ■ *Web:* ssloral.com	Palo Alto	CA	94303	650-852-4000	852-4788
Sunair Electronics Inc 3005 SW 3rd Ave *AMEX: SNR* ■ *Web:* www.sunairhf.com	Fort Lauderdale	FL	33315	954-525-1505	765-1322
Technology for Communications International Inc 47300 Kato Rd *TF:* 800-827-2661 ■ *Web:* www.tcibr.com	Fremont	CA	94538	510-687-6100	687-6101
Tecom Industries Inc 375 Conejo Ridge Ave *TF:* 800-959-0495 ■ *Web:* www.tecom-ind.com	Thousand Oaks	CA	91361	805-267-0100	267-0181
Teledyne Technologies Inc 12333 W Olympic Blvd *NYSE: TDY* ■ *Web:* www.teledynetechnologies.com	Los Angeles	CA	90064	310-893-1600	893-1613
Telephonics Corp 815 Broad Hollow Rd *TF:* 877-755-7700 ■ *Web:* www.telephonics.com	Farmingdale	NY	11735	631-755-7000	755-7046
Ten-Tec Inc 1185 Dolly Parton Pkwy *TF Cust Svc:* 800-833-7373 ■ *Web:* www.tentec.com	Sevierville	TN	37862	865-453-7172	428-4483
Thales Broadcast & Multimedia Inc 104 Feeding Hills Rd *TF:* 800-266-9283 ■ *Web:* www.thomcast.com	Southwick	MA	01077	413-569-0116	569-0679
Thales Communications Inc 22605 Gateway Center Dr *TF:* 800-258-4420 ■ *Web:* www.thalescommunications.com	Clarksburg	MD	20871	240-864-7000	864-7249
TPL Communications 3370 San Fernando Rd Unit 206 *TF:* 800-447-6937 ■ *Web:* www.tplcom.com	Los Angeles	CA	90065	323-256-3000	254-3210
Transcript International 3900 NW 12th St Suite 200 *TF:* 800-228-0226	Lincoln	NE	68521	402-474-4800	479-8472

	City	State	Zip	Phone	Fax
Ultra Electronics-DNE Technologies Inc 50 Barnes Park N. *TF:* 800-370-4485 ■ *Web:* www.dnetech.com	Wallingford	CT	06492	203-265-7151	265-9101
Ultra Electronics Flightline Systems Inc 7625 Omni Tech Pl *Web:* www.flightline-systems.com	Victor	NY	14564	585-924-4000	924-5732
Van Ordt Inc 10875 S Grand Ave	Ontario	CA	91762	909-628-4791	287-0692
ViaSat Inc 6155 El Camino Real *NASDAQ: VSAT* ■ *Web:* www.viasat.com	Carlsbad	CA	92009	760-476-2200	929-3941
Vicon Industries Inc 89 Arkay Dr *AMEX: VII* ■ *TF Cust Svc:* 800-645-9116 ■ *Web:* www.vicon-cctv.com	Hauppauge	NY	11788	631-952-2288	951-2288
Videotek Inc 243 Shoemaker Rd *TF Sales:* 800-800-5719 ■ *Web:* www.videotek.com	Pottstown	PA	19464	610-327-2292	327-9295
Viewsonics Inc 3103 N Andrews Ave Ext *TF:* 800-645-7600 ■ *Web:* www.viewsonics.com	Pompano Beach	FL	33064	954-971-8439	971-4422
Ward Products LLC 633 Nassau St *TF:* 877-732-4095	North Brunswick	NJ	08902	732-846-7500	846-2261
Wegener Communications Inc 11350 Technology Cir *TF:* 800-848-9467 ■ *Web:* www.wegener.com	Duluth	GA	30097	770-623-0096	623-0698
Wilcom Inc 73 Daniel Webster Hwy *TF:* 800-222-1898 ■ *Web:* www.wilcominc.com	Belmont	NH	03220	603-524-2622	524-3735
Winegard Co 3000 Kirkwood St *TF Cust Svc:* 800-288-8094 ■ *Web:* www.winegard.com	Burlington	IA	52601	319-754-0600	754-0787
WJ Communications Inc 401 River Oaks Pkwy *NASDAQ: WJCI* ■ *TF:* 800-951-4401 ■ *Web:* www.wj.com	San Jose	CA	95134	408-577-6200	577-6621
Zetron Inc 12034 134th Ct NE *Web:* www.zetron.com	Redmond	WA	98052	425-820-6363	820-7031

651 RAIL TRANSPORT SERVICES

SEE ALSO Logistics Services (Transportation & Warehousing) p. 1918

	City	State	Zip	Phone	Fax
Aberdeen & Rockfish Railroad Co 101 E Main St *TF:* 800-849-5713 ■ *Web:* www.aberdeen-rockfish.com	Aberdeen	NC	28315	910-944-2341	944-9738
AN Railway LLC 190 Railroad Shop Rd PO Box 250	Port Saint Joe	FL	32457	850-229-7411	229-2755
Angelina & Neches River Railroad 225 Spence St PO Box 1328 *Web:* www.anrrr.com	Lufkin	TX	75902	936-634-4403	639-3879
Apache Railway Co 13 W Hwy 277 PO Box 857	Snowflake	AZ	85937	928-536-4697	536-4260
Arkansas Louisiana & Mississippi Railroad 140 Plywood Rd PO Box 757 *TF:* 866-907-6245	Crossett	AR	71635	870-364-9009	364-4521
Atlantic & Western Railway LP 317 Chatham St	Sanford	NC	27330	919-776-7521	774-4621
Birmingham Southern Railroad Co 6200 EJ Oliver Blvd PO Box 579	Fairfield	AL	35064	205-783-2821	783-4507
BNSF (Burlington Northern & Santa Fe Railway) 2650 Lou Menk Dr **Fax Area Code:* 817 ■ *Web:* www.bnsf.com	Fort Worth	TX	76131	800-795-2673	352-7171*
Buffalo & Pittsburgh Railroad 1200-C Scottsville Rd Suite 200 *TF:* 800-603-3385 ■ *Web:* www.gwrr.com	Rochester	NY	14624	585-463-3308	463-3317
Burlington Northern & Santa Fe Railway (BNSF) 2650 Lou Menk Dr **Fax Area Code:* 817 ■ *Web:* www.bnsf.com	Fort Worth	TX	76131	800-795-2673	352-7171*
Canadian National Railway Co 935 rue de la Gauchetiere O *NYSE: CNI* ■ *Web:* www.cn.ca	Montreal	QC	H3B2M9	514-399-5430	
Canadian Pacific Railway Co Gulf Canada Sq 401 9th Ave SW *NYSE: CP* ■ **Fax:* Hum Res ■ *TF:* 888-333-6370 ■ *Web:* www8.cpr.ca	Calgary	AB	T2P4Z4	403-319-7000	319-7479*
Cedar Rapids & Iowa City Railway Co 2330 12th St SW *Web:* www.crandic.com	Cedar Rapids	IA	52404	319-786-3696	786-3671
Chattahoochee Industrial Railroad Inc Hwy 370 PO Box 253	Cedar Springs	GA	39832	229-793-4530	793-4548
CHEP USA 8517 S Park Cir *TF:* 800-432-2437 ■ *Web:* www.chep.com	Orlando	FL	32819	407-370-2437	355-6211
Chicago Southshore & South Bend Railroad 505 N Carroll Ave *Web:* www.southshorefreight.com	Michigan City	IN	46360	219-874-9000	879-3754
Colorado & Wyoming Railway Co 2100 S Freeway	Pueblo	CO	81004	719-561-6358	561-6837
Columbus & Greenville Railway Co 201 19th St N PO Box 6000 *TF:* 888-601-1222 ■ *Web:* www.cagy.com/cgrail.htm	Columbus	MS	39703	662-327-8664	329-7729
Conrail Inc 2001 Market St 2 Commerce Sq 8th Fl *Web:* www.conrail.com	Philadelphia	PA	19103	215-209-5014	209-4819
Consolidated Rail Corp 2001 Market St 2 Commerce Sq 8th Fl *Web:* www.conrail.com	Philadelphia	PA	19103	215-209-5014	209-4819
CSX Transportation Inc 500 Water St *TF:* 877-744-7279 ■ *Web:* www.csxt.com	Jacksonville	FL	32202	904-359-3100	359-1899
Dardanelle & Russellville Railroad Co 4416 S Arkansas Ave *TF:* 800-530-7526	Russellville	AR	72801	479-968-6455	968-2634
Delray Connecting Railroad Co 7819 W Jefferson St	Detroit	MI	48209	313-841-2851	841-2470
El Dorado & Wesson Railway Co 900 S West Ave	El Dorado	AR	71730	870-863-7100	863-7130
Elgin Joliet & Eastern Railway Co 1141 Maple Rd	Joliet	IL	60432	815-740-6903	740-6729
Florida East Coast Industries Inc 1 Malaga St *NYSE: FLA* ■ *TF:* 800-342-1131 ■ *Web:* www.feci.com	Saint Augustine	FL	32084	904-829-3421	826-2338
Florida East Coast Railway 1 Malaga St *TF:* 800-342-1131 ■ *Web:* www.feci.com	Saint Augustine	FL	32084	904-829-3421	826-2338
Genesee & Wyoming Inc 66 Field Point Rd *NYSE: GWR* ■ *TF:* 800-528-7296 ■ *Web:* www.gwrr.com	Greenwich	CT	06830	203-629-3722	661-4106
Georgetown Railroad Co 5300 S IH-35 PO Box 529 *TF:* 800-772-8272	Georgetown	TX	78627	512-863-2538	869-2649
Guilford Rail Systems Iron Horse Park High St *TF:* 800-955-9208 ■ *Web:* www.guilfordrail.com	North Billerica	MA	01862	978-663-1130	663-1143
Illinois & Midland Railroad Inc 1500 N Grand Ave E *Web:* www.gwrr.com	Springfield	IL	62705	217-788-8601	788-8630
Iowa Interstate Railroad 5900 6th St SW *TF:* 800-321-3884 ■ *Web:* www.iaisrr.com	Cedar Rapids	IA	52404	319-298-5400	298-5454
Kansas City Southern Railway Co 114 W 11th St *TF:* 800-468-6527 ■ *Web:* www.kcsi.com	Kansas City	MO	64105	816-983-1303	
Lake State Railway Co 323 Newman St PO Box 232 *Web:* www.lsrc.com	East Tawas	MI	48730	989-362-0207	362-4677
Lake Superior & Ishpeming Railroad Co PO Box 2000	Ishpeming	MI	49849	906-475-3471	
Long Island Railroad 930-2 Sutphin Blvd **Fax:* PR	Jamaica	NY	11435	718-558-7400	558-6824*
Louisiana & Delta Railroad Inc 402 W Washington St *Web:* www.gwrr.com	New Iberia	LA	70560	337-364-9625	369-1487
McCloud Railway Co 801 Industrial Way PO Box 1500 *Web:* www.mctrain.com	McCloud	CA	96057	530-964-2141	964-2250
Mississippi Export Railroad Co 4519 McInnis Ave *TF:* 866-353-3322 ■ *Web:* www.mserailroad.com	Moss Point	MS	39563	228-475-3322	475-3337
Modesto & Empire Traction Co 530 11th St *Web:* www.metrr.com	Modesto	CA	95354	209-524-4631	529-0336
Montana Rail Link Inc 101 International Way *TF:* 800-338-4750 ■ *Web:* www.montanarail.com	Missoula	MT	59808	406-523-1500	523-1493
Montreal Maine & Atlantic Railway Ltd 15 Iron Rd *TF:* 800-422-6760 ■ *Web:* www.mmarail.com	Hermon	ME	04401	207-848-4280	848-4232
New England Central Railroad 2 Federal St Suite 201 *TF Cust Svc:* 800-800-3450 ■ *Web:* www.railamerica.com/railmaps/NECR.htm	Saint Albans	VT	05478	802-527-3450	527-3488
New York Susquehanna & Western Railway Corp 1 Railroad Ave *TF:* 800-366-6979 ■ *Web:* www.nysw.com	Cooperstown	NY	13326	607-547-2555	547-9834
Norfolk Southern Railway Co 3 Commercial Pl *TF:* 800-635-5768 ■ *Web:* www.nscorp.com	Norfolk	VA	23510	757-629-2600	
Pioneer Railcorp 1318 S Johanson Rd *TF:* 800-914-3810 ■ *Web:* www.pioneer-railcorp.com	Peoria	IL	61607	309-697-1400	697-5387
Prescott & Northwestern Railroad Co 2000 Mill Rd PO Box 610	Prescott	AR	71857	870-887-3103	887-3779
Providence & Worcester Railroad Co 75 Hammond St *AMEX: PWX* ■ *TF:* 800-447-2003 ■ *Web:* www.pwrr.com	Worcester	MA	01610	508-755-4000	753-5548
RailAmerica Inc 5300 Broken Sound Blvd NW 2nd Fl *NYSE: RRA* ■ *TF:* 800-211-7245 ■ *Web:* www.railamerica.com	Boca Raton	FL	33487	561-994-6015	994-4629
Sandersville Railroad Co 206 N Smith St PO Box 269	Sandersville	GA	31082	478-552-5151	552-1118
Somerset Railroad Corp 7725 Lake Rd	Barker	NY	14012	716-795-9501	795-3672
Triple Crown Services 2720 Dupont Commerce Ct Suite 200 *TF:* 800-325-6510 ■ *Web:* www.triplecrownsvc.com	Fort Wayne	IN	46825	260-416-3600	416-3771
Union Pacific Railroad Co 1400 Douglas St **Fax Area Code:* 402 ■ *TF:* 888-870-8777 ■ *Web:* www.uprr.com	Omaha	NE	68179	888-870-8777	271-2256*
Union Railroad Co 1200 Penn Ave *Web:* www.tstarinc.com	Pittsburgh	PA	15222	412-433-7090	
Winston-Salem Southbound Railway Co 4550 Overdale Rd *TF:* 888-631-8223	Winston-Salem	NC	27107	336-788-9407	788-9085
York Railroad Co 2790 W market St	York	PA	17404	717-771-1700	854-6275

652 RAIL TRAVEL

SEE ALSO Mass Transportation (Local & Suburban) p. 1947

	City	State	Zip	Phone	Fax
Amtrak 60 Massachusetts Ave NE *TF:* 800-872-7245 ■ *Web:* www.amtrak.com	Washington	DC	20002	202-906-3000	
National Railroad Passenger Corp DBA Amtrak 60 Massachusetts Ave NE *TF:* 800-872-7245 ■ *Web:* www.amtrak.com	Washington	DC	20002	202-906-3000	
VIA Rail Canada Inc 3 Place Ville-Marie Suite 500 *TF:* 800-681-2561 ■ *Web:* www.viarail.ca	Montreal	QC	H3B2C9	514-871-6000	871-6104

653 RAILROAD EQUIPMENT - MFR

SEE ALSO Transportation Equipment & Supplies - Whol p. 2380

	City	State	Zip	Phone	Fax
A Stucki Co 2600 Neville Rd *TF:* 800-771-7302 ■ *Web:* www.stucki.com	Pittsburgh	PA	15225	412-771-7300	771-7308
ACF Industries Inc 101 Clark St *Web:* www.acfindustries.com	Saint Charles	MO	63301	636-949-2399	949-2825
Adams & Westlake Ltd 940 N Michigan St PO Box 4524 *Web:* www.adlake.com	Elkhart	IN	46514	574-264-1141	264-1146
American Railcar Industries Inc 100 Clark St *NASDAQ: ARII* ■ *TF:* 800-933-7937 ■ *Web:* www.americanrailcar.com	Saint Charles	MO	63301	636-940-6000	940-6030
AMSTED Industries Inc 180 N Stetson St Suite 1800 **Fax:* Hum Res ■ *Web:* www.amsted.com	Chicago	IL	60601	312-645-1700	819-8504*
Barber Brake Beam LLC 4133 S M-139 *Web:* www.brakebeams.com	Saint Joseph	MI	49085	269-408-0011	408-0012
Bombardier Transportation Equipment Group-North America 1101 Parent St *Web:* www.transportation.bombardier.com	Saint-Bruno	QC	J3V6E6	450-441-2020	441-1515
Cardwell Westinghouse Co 8400 S Stewart Ave **Fax:* Cust Svc ■ *Web:* www.wabtec.com/subsidiaries/subsidiaries.asp?id=2	Chicago	IL	60620	773-483-7575	483-9302*
Curran Group Inc 7502 S Main St *Web:* www.currangroup.com	Crystal Lake	IL	60014	815-455-5100	455-7894
Dayton-Phoenix Group Inc 1619 Kuntz Rd *TF:* 800-657-0707 ■ *Web:* www.dayton-phoenix.com	Dayton	OH	45404	937-496-3807	496-3969
Electro-Motive Diesel Inc 9301 W 55th St *TF:* 800-255-5355 ■ *Web:* www.emdiesels.com	La Grange	IL	60525	708-387-6000	387-6626
Foster LB Co 415 Holiday Dr *NASDAQ: FSTR* ■ **Fax:* Sales ■ *TF:* 800-255-4500 ■ *Web:* www.lbfoster.com	Pittsburgh	PA	15220	412-928-3400	928-3427*
FreightCar America Inc 17 Johns St *NASDAQ: RAIL* ■ **Fax Area Code:* 814 ■ *Web:* www.freightcaramerica.com	Johnstown	PA	15901	800-458-2235	533-5010*
GE Aviation 1 Neumann Way *Web:* www.geaviation.com	Cincinnati	OH	45215	513-243-2000	
GE Transportation Rail 2901 E Lake Rd **Fax:* Hum Res ■ *TF Prod Info:* 800-626-2000 ■ *Web:* www.getransportation.com	Erie	PA	16531	814-875-2234	875-2620*
Graham-White Mfg Co 1242 Colorado St PO Box 1099 *Web:* www.grahamwhite.com	Salem	VA	24153	540-387-5600	387-5697
Greenbrier Co 1 Centerpointe Dr Suite 200 *NYSE: GBX* ■ *TF:* 800-343-7188 ■ *Web:* www.gbrx.com	Lake Oswego	OR	97035	503-684-7000	684-7553
Gunderson Inc 4350 NW Front Ave *TF:* 800-253-4350 ■ *Web:* www.gundersoninc.com	Portland	OR	97210	503-972-5700	972-5987
Harsco Track Technologies (HTT) 2401 Edmund Rd Box 20 *TF:* 800-345-9160 ■ *Web:* www.harscotrack.com	West Columbia	SC	29171	803-822-9160	822-7471
Holland Co 1000 Holland Dr *TF:* 800-899-7754 ■ *Web:* www.hollandco.com	Crete	IL	60417	708-672-2300	672-0119
HTT (Harsco Track Technologies) 2401 Edmund Rd Box 20 *TF:* 800-345-9160 ■ *Web:* www.harscotrack.com	West Columbia	SC	29171	803-822-9160	822-7471
Knorr Brake Corp 861 Baltimore Blvd **Fax:* Mktg ■ *Web:* www.knorrbrakecorp.com	Westminster	MD	21157	410-875-0900	875-1210*
LB Foster Co 415 Holiday Dr *NASDAQ: FSTR* ■ **Fax:* Sales ■ *TF:* 800-255-4500 ■ *Web:* www.lbfoster.com	Pittsburgh	PA	15220	412-928-3400	928-3427*
Miner Enterprises Inc 1200 E State St *TF:* 800-323-0625 ■ *Web:* www.minerent.com	Geneva	IL	60134	630-232-3000	232-3123
MotivePower 4600 Apple St *TF:* 800-272-7702	Boise	ID	83716	208-947-4800	947-4820
National Railway Equipment Co (NREC) 14400 S Robey St *TF:* 800-253-2905 ■ *Web:* www.nationalrailway.com	Dixmoor	IL	60426	708-388-6002	388-2487
New York Air Brake Co 748 Starbuck Ave **Fax:* Sales ■ *TF:* 888-836-6922 ■ *Web:* www.nyab.com	Watertown	NY	13601	315-786-5200	786-5675*
Nolan Co 1016 9th St SW *TF:* 800-298-2832 ■ *Web:* www.nolancompany.com	Canton	OH	44707	330-453-7922	453-7449

				Phone	Fax
NREC (National Railway Equipment Co) 14400 S Robey St	Dixmoor	IL	60426	708-388-6002	388-2487
TF: 800-253-2905 ■ *Web:* www.nationalrailway.com					
Plasser American Corp 2001 Myers Rd PO Box 5464	Chesapeake	VA	23324	757-543-3526	543-4330
Web: www.plasseramerican.com					
Portec Rail Products Inc 900 Old Freeport Rd PO Box 38250	Pittsburgh	PA	15238	412-782-6000	782-1037
NASDAQ: PRPX ■ *TF:* 800-722-9960 ■ *Web:* www.portecrail.com					
Q-Tron Ltd 4600 Apple St	Boise	ID	83716	208-947-4800	947-4812
Racine Railroad Products Inc 1524 Frederick St PO Box 044577	Racine	WI	53404	262-637-9681	637-9069
Web: www.racinerailroad.com					
Salco Products Inc 20W201 101st St Suite A	Lemont	IL	60439	630-783-2570	792-8186
TF: 800-535-8990 ■ *Web:* www.salcoproducts.com					
Siemens Transportation Systems Inc 7464 French Rd	Sacramento	CA	95828	916-681-3000	681-3006
Web: www.sts.siemens.com					
Stucki A Co 2600 Neville Rd	Pittsburgh	PA	15225	412-771-7300	771-7308
TF: 800-771-7302 ■ *Web:* www.stucki.com					
Trackmobile Inc 1602 Executive Dr	LaGrange	GA	30240	706-884-6651	884-0390
Web: www.trackmobile.com					
Transco Railway Products Inc 820 Hopley Ave PO Box 231	Bucyrus	OH	44820	419-562-1031	562-3684
Web: www.transcorailway.com					
Trinity Mining Service 109 48th St	Pittsburgh	PA	15201	412-682-4700	682-4725
TF: 800-245-6206 ■ *Web:* www.trin-mine.com					
Trinity Rail Group Inc 2525 Stemmons Fwy	Dallas	TX	75207	214-631-4420	589-8501
TF: 800-631-4420 ■ *Web:* www.trinityrail.com					
Union Tank Car Co 175 W Jackson Blvd Suite 2100	Chicago	IL	60604	312-431-3111	347-5020
TF: 800-635-3770 ■ *Web:* www.utlx.com					
Vapor Bus International 1010 Johnson Dr	Buffalo Grove	IL	60089	847-777-6400	520-2220
TF: 800-631-9200 ■ *Web:* www.vapordoors.com					
Vapor Rail 10655 Henri-Bourassa W	Saint-Laurent	QC	H4S1A1	514-335-4200	335-4231
Web: www.wabtec.com					
WABCO Freight Car Products Ltd 475 Seaman Dr	Stoney Creek	ON	L8E2R2	905-561-8700	799-2819*
**Fax Area Code:* 877 ■ *TF:* 877-757-2226 ■ *Web:* www.wabtec.com					
WABCO Locomotive Products 1001 Air Brake Ave	Wilmerding	PA	15148	412-825-1000	825-1019
TF: 800-784-6816 ■ *Web:* www.wabtec.com					
WABCO Transit Div Wabtec Corp PO Box 11	Spartanburg	SC	29304	864-433-5900	433-0176
Web: www.wabtec.com					
Wabtec Corp 1001 Air Brake Ave	Wilmerding	PA	15148	412-825-1000	825-1019
NYSE: WAB ■ *TF:* 800-784-6816 ■ *Web:* www.wabtec.com					
Wabtec Corp WABCO Transit Div PO Box 11	Spartanburg	SC	29304	864-433-5900	433-0176
Web: www.wabtec.com					

654 RAILROAD SWITCHING & TERMINAL SERVICES

				Phone	Fax
Belt Railway Co of Chicago 6900 S Central Ave	Bedford Park	IL	60638	708-496-4000	496-3037
Web: www.beltrailway.com					
Central California Traction Co					
2201 W Washington St Suite 12	Stockton	CA	95203	209-466-6927	466-1204
Web: www.cctrailroad.com					
Chicago Rail Link LLC 2728 E 104th St	Chicago	IL	60617	773-721-4000	374-6605
East Erie Commercial Railroad 1030 Lawrence Pkwy	Erie	PA	16511	814-875-6572	875-5858
Indiana Harbor Belt Railroad Co 2721 161st St	Hammond	IN	46323	219-989-4703	989-4967*
**Fax:* Hum Res ■ *Web:* www.ihbrr.com					
Los Angeles Junction Railway Co 4433 Exchange Ave	Los Angeles	CA	90058	323-277-2004	277-2009
Manufacturers Junction Railway LLC 2335 S Cicero Ave	Cicero	IL	60502	773-721-4000	863-1719*
**Fax Area Code:* 708					
Manufacturers Railway Co 2850 S Broadway	Saint Louis	MO	63118	314-577-1703	
Minnesota Commercial Railway 508 Cleveland Ave N	Saint Paul	MN	55114	651-646-2010	646-8337
OmniTRAX Inc 50 S Steele St Suite 250	Denver	CO	80209	303-398-4500	398-4540
Web: www.omnitrax.com					
Pittsburgh & West Virginia Railroad 2 Port Amherst Dr	Charleston	WV	25306	304-926-1124	926-1136
AMEX: PW					
Portland Terminal Railroad Co 3500 NW Yeon Ave	Portland	OR	97210	503-241-9898	241-9885
Public Belt Railroad Commission 4822 Tchoupitulas St	New Orleans	LA	70115	504-896-7410	896-7452
TF Cust Svc: 800-524-3421					
Rail Link Inc 4337 Pablo Oaks Ct Suite 104	Jacksonville	FL	32224	904-223-1110	223-8710
TF: 888-902-7245					
Railserve Inc 1691 Phoenix Blvd Suite 110	Atlanta	GA	30349	770-996-6838	996-6830
TF: 800-345-7245 ■ *Web:* www.railserveinc.com					
Rescar Inc 1101 31st St Suite 250	Downers Grove	IL	60515	630-963-1114	963-6342
TF: 800-851-5196 ■ *Web:* www.rescar.com					
Terminal Railroad Assn of Saint Louis					
1000 St Louis Union Station Suite 200	Saint Louis	MO	63103	314-231-5196	621-3673
Web: www.terminalrailroad.com					

655 REAL ESTATE AGENTS & BROKERS

				Phone	Fax
Aronov Realty 3500 Eastern Blvd	Montgomery	AL	36116	334-277-1000	272-0747
Web: www.aronov.com					
Assist-2-Sell Inc 1610 Meadow Wood Ln	Reno	NV	89502	775-688-6060	688-6069
TF: 800-528-7816 ■ *Web:* www.assist2sell.com					
Baird & Warner Inc 120 S LaSalle St Suite 2000	Chicago	IL	60603	312-368-1855	368-1490
Web: www.bairdwarner.com					
Buy Owner 1192 E Newport Center Dr Suite 200	Deerfield Beach	FL	33442	954-771-7777	745-7777
TF: 800-940-7777 ■ *Web:* www.buyowner.com					
Carlson Real Estate Co Inc 301 Carlson Pkwy Suite 100	Minnetonka	MN	55305	952-404-5000	404-5001
Web: www.carlsonrealestate.org					
Casto Don M Organization 191 W Nationwide Blvd Suite 200	Columbus	OH	43215	614-228-5331	469-8376
Web: www.donmcasto.com					
CB Richard Ellis Group Inc					
100 N Sepulveda Blvd Suite 1050	El Segundo	CA	90245	310-606-4700	613-3005*
NYSE: CBG ■ **Fax Area Code:* 213 ■ *Web:* www.cbre.com					
Century 21 Commercial Investment Network 1 Campus Dr	Parsippany	NJ	07054	973-428-9700	407-5806
TF: 800-221-2765					
Century 21 Real Estate Corp 1 Campus Dr	Parsippany	NJ	07054	973-428-9700	496-5966*
**Fax:* Hum Res ■ *TF:* 800-992-8023 ■ *Web:* www.century21.com					
Chelsea Moore Co 8940 Glendale Milford Rd	Loveland	OH	45140	513-561-5454	561-5497
TF: 888-621-1161 ■ *Web:* www.chelseamoore.com					
Codina Realty Services Inc 355 Alhambra Cir Suite 900	Coral Gables	FL	33134	305-520-2300	520-2350
Web: www.codina.com/rs.home.aspx					
Cohen-Esrey Real Estate Services Inc					
1100 Main St Suite 2700	Kansas City	MO	64105	816-531-8100	531-4470
Web: www.cohenesrey.com					
Coldwell Banker Gundaker					
2458 Old Dorsett Rd Suite 300	Maryland Heights	MO	63043	314-298-5000	298-5059
TF: 800-325-1978 ■ *Web:* www.gundaker.com					
Coldwell Banker Real Estate Corp 1 Campus Dr	Parsippany	NJ	07054	973-496-2653	496-7217
Web: www.coldwellbanker.com					
Coldwell Banker Relocation					
27271 Las Ramblas Suite 233	Mission Viejo	CA	92691	800-292-2656	207-6724*
**Fax Area Code:* 310 ■ *TF:* 800-733-1380					
Coldwell Banker Residential Brokerage					
8490 E Crescent Pkwy Suite 250	Greenwood Village	CO	80111	303-409-1500	409-6336
TF: 800-525-3030					
Coldwell Banker Residential Real Estate 5951 Cattleridge Ave	Sarasota	FL	34232	941-378-8211	378-8250
TF: 800-624-5292 ■ *Web:* www.floridamoves.com					
Colliers International 50 Milk St 20th Fl	Boston	MA	02109	617-722-0221	722-0224
Web: www.colliers.com					
Colliers Pinkard 100 Light St Suite 1400	Baltimore	MD	21202	410-752-4285	576-9031
Web: www.colliers.com/Markets/Baltimore/					
Colliers Towle Turley Martin Tucker					
200 S 6th St Suite 1400	Minneapolis	MN	55402	612-341-4444	347-9389
Web: www.colliers.com/Markets/Minneapolis					
Commercial Realty & Resources Corp					
1415 Wyckoff Rd PO Box 1468	Wall	NJ	07719	732-938-1111	938-6735
Crye-Leike Inc 6525 Quail Hollow Rd	Memphis	TN	38120	901-756-8900	758-5641
Web: www.crye-leike.com					
Curry Investment Co 2700 Kendallwood Pkwy Suite 208	Gladstone	MO	64119	816-454-6688	452-4757
Web: www.curryre.com					
Cushman & Wakefield Inc 51 W 52nd St	New York	NY	10019	212-841-7500	841-7867
Web: www.cushwake.com					
Daugherty John Realtors 14094 Memorial Dr	Houston	TX	77079	281-497-3055	497-2155
Web: www.jdaugherty.com					
Daum Commercial Real Estate Services					
4675 McArthur Ct Suite 220	Newport Beach	CA	92660	949-724-1900	474-1771
TF: 888-659-3286 ■ *Web:* daumcommercial.com					
Divaris Real Estate Inc 1 Columbus Center Suite 700	Virginia Beach	VA	23462	757-497-2113	497-1338
TF: 888-373-0023 ■ *Web:* www.divaris.com					
Dodge NP Real Estate 8701 W Dodge Rd Suite 300	Omaha	NE	68114	402-397-4900	398-5202
TF: 800-642-5008 ■ *Web:* www.npdodge.com					
Don M Casto Organization 191 W Nationwide Blvd Suite 200	Columbus	OH	43215	614-228-5331	469-8376
Web: www.donmcasto.com					
ERA Franchise Systems Inc 1 Campus Dr	Parsippany	NJ	07054	973-428-9700	261-6275*
**Fax Area Code:* 800 ■ *TF:* 800-869-1260 ■ *Web:* www.era.com					
Esslinger-Wooten-Maxwell Realtors 1360 S Dixie Hwy	Coral Gables	FL	33146	305-667-8871	662-5646
Web: www.ewm.com					
First Hartford Realty Corp 149 Colonial Rd PO Box 1270	Manchester	CT	06045	860-646-6555	646-8572
TF: 888-646-6555 ■ *Web:* www.firsthartford.com					
First Service Realty Inc 13155 SW 42nd St Suite 200	Miami	FL	33175	305-551-9400	551-4965
TF: 800-899-8477 ■ *Web:* www.firstservicerealty.com					
Grubb & Ellis Co 2215 Sanders Rd Suite 400	Northbrook	IL	60062	847-753-9010	753-9034
Web: www.grubb-ellis.com					
Grubb & Ellis/Harrison & Bates Inc					
6606 W Broad St Suite 400	Richmond	VA	23230	804-788-1000	782-1145
Web: www.harrison-bates.com					
GVA Advantis 101 W Main St Suite 900	Norfolk	VA	23510	757-627-0661	627-1901
Web: www.gvaadvantis.com					
Hart Corp International 900 Jaymor Rd	Southampton	PA	18966	215-322-5100	322-5840
Web: www.hartcorp.com					
Heitman LLC 191 N Wacker Dr Suite 2500	Chicago	IL	60606	312-855-5700	251-4807
TF: 800-225-5435 ■ *Web:* www.heitman.com					
Help-U-Sell Real Estate 900 W Castleton Rd Suite 230	Castle Rock	CO	80109	303-814-1400	814-3400
TF: 800-366-1177 ■ *Web:* www.helpusell.com					
HomeGain.com Inc 1250 45th St Suite 200	Emeryville	CA	94608	510-655-0800	655-0848
TF: 888-542-0800 ■ *Web:* www.homegain.com					
HomeServices.com Inc 6800 France Ave S Suite 600	Edina	MN	55435	952-928-5900	928-5725
Web: www.homeservices.com					
Inland Group Inc 2901 Butterfield Rd	Oak Brook	IL	60523	630-218-8000	218-4917
TF: 800-828-8999 ■ *Web:* www.inlandgroup.com					
Inland Real Estate Sales Inc 2901 Butterfield Rd	Oak Brook	IL	60523	630-218-8000	218-4917
TF: 800-828-8999 ■ *Web:* www.inlandgroup.com/ires					
Iowa Realty Co Inc 3501 Westown Pkwy	West Des Moines	IA	50266	515-453-6222	453-5786
TF: 800-247-2430 ■ *Web:* www.iowarealty.com					
John Daugherty Realtors 14094 Memorial Dr	Houston	TX	77079	281-497-3055	497-2155
Web: www.jdaugherty.com					
John L Scott Inc 3380 146th Pl SE Suite 450	Bellevue	WA	98007	206-230-7600	230-7550
TF: 800-368-4278 ■ *Web:* www.johnlscott.com					
Jones Lang LaSalle Leasing & Management Services					
200 E Randolph Dr Suite 4600	Chicago	IL	60601	312-782-5800	782-4339
Joyner Fine Properties 2727 Enterprise Pkwy PO Box 31355	Richmond	VA	23294	804-270-9440	967-2770
TF: 800-446-3858 ■ *Web:* www.joynerfineproperties.com					
K & J Properties 924 SE 3rd Ave	Delray Beach	FL	33483	954-622-1115	
Keller Williams Realty Inc 807 Las Cimas Pkwy Suite 200	Austin	TX	78746	512-327-3070	328-1433
Web: www.kw.com					
Lincoln Property Co 500 N Akard St Suite 3300	Dallas	TX	75201	214-740-3300	740-3313
Web: www.lincolnproperty.com					
Long & Foster Realtors 11351 Random Hills Rd	Fairfax	VA	22030	703-359-1500	359-1902*
**Fax:* Hum Res ■ *TF:* 800-237-8800 ■ *Web:* www.longandfoster.com					
Marcus & Millichap Real Estate Investment Brokerage Co					
2626 Hanover St	Palo Alto	CA	94304	650-494-8900	494-0213
Web: www.mmreibc.com					
Mason-McDuffie Real Estate Inc DBA Prudential California Realty 5724 W Las Positas Blvd Suite 100	Pleasanton	CA	94588	925-924-4600	924-1852
Web: www.prudentialcal.com					
MAXXAM Property Co 1330 Post Oak Blvd Suite 2000	Houston	TX	77056	713-267-3750	267-3703
Miller WC & AN Realtors					
4910 Massachusetts Ave NW Suite 119	Washington	DC	20016	202-362-1300	362-3164
TF: 877-362-1300 ■ *Web:* www.wcanmiller.com					
Mitsui Fudosan America Inc					
1251 Ave of the Americas Suite 800	New York	NY	10020	212-403-5600	403-5657
Web: www.mitsuifudosan.co.jp					
NP Dodge Real Estate 8701 W Dodge Rd Suite 300	Omaha	NE	68114	402-397-4900	398-5202
TF: 800-642-5008 ■ *Web:* www.npdodge.com					
Olive Real Estate Group					
102 N Cascade Ave Suite 250	Colorado Springs	CO	80903	719-598-3000	578-0089
Web: www.olivereg.com					
Oxbow Realty Services Inc 725 Canton St	Norwood	MA	02062	781-769-2222	769-8186
Web: www.oxbowrealty.com					
Patterson-Schwartz & Assoc Inc					
7234 Lancaster Pike Suite 200A	Hockessin	DE	19707	302-234-5250	
TF: 877-408-1166 ■ *Web:* www.pattersonschwartz.com					
Prudential California Realty					
5724 W Las Positas Blvd Suite 100	Pleasanton	CA	94588	925-924-4600	924-1852
Web: www.prudentialcal.com					
Prudential Fox & Roach Realtors 431 W Lancaster Ave	Devon	PA	19333	610-889-7760	889-3064
Web: www.prufoxroach.com					
Prudential MacPherson's Real Estate					
18551 Aurora Ave N Suite 100	Seattle	WA	98133	206-542-6363	542-6566
Web: www.prudentialmacphersons.com					
Prudential Northwest Real Estate 2497 Bethel Rd SE	Port Orchard	WA	98366	360-876-5522	876-4833
TF: 800-463-7768 ■ *Web:* www.pnwre.com					
Prudential Real Estate Affiliates Inc					
3333 Michelson Dr Suite 1000	Irvine	CA	92612	949-794-7900	794-7036*
**Fax:* Mktg ■ *TF:* 800-999-1120 ■ *Web:* www.prudential.com/realestate					

				Phone	Fax
Real Estate One Inc 25800 Northwestern Hwy Suite 100	Southfield	MI	48075	248-851-2600	263-5966
TF: 800-521-0508 ■ *Web:* www.realestateone.com					
Real Living Inc 77 E Nationwide Blvd	Columbus	OH	43215	614-459-7400	457-6807
TF: 800-848-7400 ■ *Web:* www.realliving.com					
Realogy Corp 1 Campus Dr	Parsippany	NJ	07054	973-407-2000	407-7004
Web: www.realogy.com					
Realty Executives International Inc					
2398 E Camelback Rd Suite 900	Phoenix	AZ	85016	602-957-0747	224-5542
TF: 800-252-3366 ■ *Web:* www.realtyexecutives.com					
Realty One 800 W St Clair	Cleveland	OH	44113	216-328-2500	328-5035*
**Fax:* Hum Res ■ *TF:* 877-328-2500 ■ *Web:* www.realtyone.com					
Reece & Nichols Realtors 11500 Granada Ln	Leawood	KS	66211	913-491-1001	491-0930
Web: www.reeceandnichols.com					
Re/MAX Equity Group Inc 8405 SW Nimbus Ave	Beaverton	OR	97008	503-670-3000	670-1138
TF: 800-283-3358 ■ *Web:* www.equitygroup.com					
RE/MAX International Inc					
8390 E Crescent Pkwy Suite 500	Greenwood Village	CO	80111	303-770-5531	796-3599
TF Cust Svc: 800-525-7452 ■ *Web:* www.remax.com					
RE/MAX Ontario-Atlantic 7101 Syntex Dr	Mississauga	ON	L5N6H5	905-542-2400	542-3340
TF: 888-542-2499 ■ *Web:* www.remax-oa.com					
RE/MAX Quebec Inc 1500 Cunard St	Laval	QC	H7S2B7	450-668-7743	668-2115
TF: 800-361-9325 ■ *Web:* www.remax-quebec.com					
RE/MAX of Western Canada Inc 1060 Manhattan Dr Suite 340	Kelowna	BC	V1Y9X9	250-860-3628	860-7424
TF: 800-563-3622 ■ *Web:* www.remax.ca/index_western.html					
Royal LePage Estate Services Ltd 39 Wynford Dr	Don Mills	ON	M3C3K5	416-510-5800	510-5856
Web: www.royallepage.com					
Scott John L Inc 3380 146th Pl SE Suite 450	Bellevue	WA	98007	206-230-7600	230-7550
TF: 800-368-4278 ■ *Web:* www.johnlscott.com					
Semonin Realtors 4967 US Hwy 42 Suite 200	Louisville	KY	40222	502-425-4760	339-8950
TF: 800-548-1650 ■ *Web:* www.semonin.com					
Sotheby's International Realty 38 E 61st St	New York	NY	10021	212-606-4100	606-4199
TF: 800-848-2541 ■ *Web:* www.sothebysrealty.com					
Staubach Co 15601 Dallas Pkwy Suite 400	Addison	TX	75001	972-361-5000	361-5910
TF: 800-944-0012 ■ *Web:* www.staubach.com					
Stiles Realty Co 300 SE 2nd St	Fort Lauderdale	FL	33301	954-627-9300	627-9305
Web: www.stiles.com					
Studley Inc 300 Park Ave 3rd Fl	New York	NY	10022	212-326-1000	326-1034
Web: www.studley.com					
Towne Realty Inc 710 N Plankinton Ave 12th Fl	Milwaukee	WI	53203	414-273-2200	274-2728*
**Fax:* Cust Svc ■ *TF:* 800-945-4450 ■ *Web:* www.homesbytowne.com					
Trammell Crow Co 2001 Ross Ave Suite 3400	Dallas	TX	75201	214-863-3000	863-3138
NYSE: TCC ■ *Web:* www.trammellcrow.com					
United Properties Inc 404 N 31st St Suite 100	Billings	MT	59101	406-255-7100	255-7125
Watne Inc Realtors 408 N Broadway	Minot	ND	58703	701-852-1156	839-8966
TF: 800-568-5311 ■ *Web:* www.watne.com					
Watson Realty Co 5701 Truxtun Ave Suite 100	Bakersfield	CA	93309	661-327-5161	861-7474
Web: www.watsonrealty.com					
WC & AN Miller Realtors					
4910 Massachusetts Ave NW Suite 119	Washington	DC	20016	202-362-1300	362-3164
TF: 877-362-1300 ■ *Web:* www.wcanmiller.com					
Weichert Realtors 225 Littleton Rd	Morris Plains	NJ	07950	973-359-8377	292-1428
TF: 800-872-7653 ■ *Web:* www.weichert.com					
Westdale Realty Co 300 E Beltline Ave NE	Grand Rapids	MI	49506	616-949-9400	949-6579
TF: 800-968-8770 ■ *Web:* www.westdaleworks.com					
Weston Cos 1715 Aaron Brenner Dr Suite 500 PO Box 17847	Memphis	TN	38187	901-682-9100	684-6357
Web: www.westonco.com					
ZipRealty Inc 2000 Powell St Suite 300	Emeryville	CA	94608	510-735-2600	735-2850
NASDAQ: ZIPR ■ *TF:* 800-225-5947 ■ *Web:* www.ziprealty.com					

656 REAL ESTATE DEVELOPERS

SEE ALSO Construction - Building Contractors - Non-Residential p. 1528; Construction - Building Contractors - Residential p. 1531

				Phone	Fax
A & B Properties Inc 822 Bishop St	Honolulu	HI	96813	808-525-6611	525-6652
Web: www.abprop.com					
Abbey Group Ltd 714 Enterprise Dr	Oakbrook	IL	60523	630-573-8200	573-1415
AG Spanos Cos 10100 Trinity Pkwy 5th Fl	Stockton	CA	95219	209-478-7954	478-3309
Web: www.agspanos.com					
AG Spanos Development Inc 10100 Trinity Pkwy 5th Fl	Stockton	CA	95219	209-478-7954	478-3309
Web: www.agspanos.com					
Al Neyer Inc 302 W 3rd St Suite 800	Cincinnati	OH	45202	513-271-6400	271-1350
TF: 877-271-6400 ■ *Web:* www.neyer.com					
Allen & O'Hara Inc 530 Oak Court Dr Suite 300	Memphis	TN	38117	901-259-2500	259-2594
Web: www.aoinc.com					
Alter Group 5500 W Howard St	Skokie	IL	60077	847-676-4300	676-4302
TF: 800-637-4842 ■ *Web:* www.altergroup.com					
Amelia Island Co 1501 Lewis St	Amelia Island	FL	32034	904-261-6161	277-5159
TF: 888-261-6161 ■ *Web:* www.aipfl.com					
Amerco Real Estate Co 2727 N Central Ave Suite 500	Phoenix	AZ	85004	602-263-6555	277-5824
American Invsco Corp 1028 N Clark St	Chicago	IL	60610	312-431-8311	431-1125
TF: 800-340-3420 ■ *Web:* www.invsco.com					
American West Homes 250 Pilot Rd Suite 140	Las Vegas	NV	89119	702-736-6434	736-7970
Web: www.americanwesthomes.com					
Amfac/JMB Hawaii LLC 700 Bishop St Suite 2002	Honolulu	HI	96813	808-543-8900	543-8918
AMLI Residential Properties Trust					
125 S Wacker Dr Suite 3100	Chicago	IL	60606	312-443-1477	443-0909
NYSE: AML ■ *Web:* www.amlires.com					
AMREP Corp 505 Park Ave 7th Fl	New York	NY	10022	212-705-4700	705-4666
NYSE: AXR					
AMREP Southwest Inc 333 Rio Rancho Dr NE	Rio Rancho	NM	87124	505-892-9200	896-9180*
**Fax:* Cust Svc ■ *Web:* www.amrepsouthwest.com					
Astoria Homes 10655 Park Run Dr	Las Vegas	NV	89134	702-257-1188	257-1681
Web: www.astoriahomes.com					
Atlantic Builders Inc 7800 Belfort Pkwy Suite 200	Jacksonville	FL	32256	904-279-9500	279-9559
Web: www.atlanticbuilders.net					
Ausherman Homes 721 Corporate Ct Suite B	Frederick	MD	21703	301-663-6104	663-3929
Web: www.ausherman.com					
Avatar Holdings Inc 201 Alhambra Cir 12th Fl	Coral Gables	FL	33134	305-442-7000	448-9929
NASDAQ: AVTR ■ *TF:* 800-736-6660 ■ *Web:* www.avatar-holdings.com					
Barratt American Inc 5950 Priestly Dr Suite 101	Carlsbad	CA	92008	760-431-0800	929-6430
TF: 800-675-0440 ■ *Web:* www.barrattamerican.com					
Beazer Homes 9202 N Meridian St Suite 300	Indianapolis	IN	46260	317-843-9514	846-0398
Web: www.beazer.com					
Beazer Homes USA Inc 1000 Abernathy Rd Suite 1200	Atlanta	GA	30328	770-829-3700	481-0431
NYSE: BZH ■ *Web:* www.beazer.com					
Bellemead Development Corp 85 Livingstone Ave	Roseland	NJ	07068	973-740-1110	740-0126*
**Fax:* Hum Res					
Belz Enterprises 100 Peabody Pl Suite 1400	Memphis	TN	38103	901-767-4780	271-7238
Web: www.belz.com					
BF Enterprises Inc 100 Bush St Suite 1250	San Francisco	CA	94104	415-989-6580	788-5756
NASDAQ: BFEN					

				Phone	Fax
BPG Properties Ltd 1500 Market St Suite 3000	Philadelphia	PA	19102	215-496-0400	496-0431
Web: www.bpgltd.com					
Branigar Organization Inc 108 Traders Cross Suite 102	Bluffton	SC	29909	843-706-4000	706-4020
Brehm Cos 1935 Camino Vida Roble Suite 200	Carlsbad	CA	92008	760-448-2420	448-2421
Web: www.brehm.net					
Bresler & Reiner Inc 11200 Rockville Pike Suite 502	Rockville	MD	20852	301-945-4300	945-4301
Web: www.breslerandreiner.com					
Breslin Realty Development Corp					
500 Old Country Rd Suite 200	Garden City	NY	11530	516-741-7400	741-7128
Web: www.breslinrealty.com					
Brighton Builders 13111 Northwest Fwy Suite 310	Houston	TX	77040	713-460-0264	460-8634
Brisben Cos 7800 E Kemper Rd	Cincinnati	OH	45249	513-489-1990	489-2780
Web: www.brisben.com					
Brooks Resources Corp 409 NW Franklin Ave Suite A	Bend	OR	97702	541-382-1662	385-3285
TF: 888-773-7553 ■ *Web:* www.brooksresources.com					
Brown Family Communities 2164 E Broadway Rd Suite 300	Tempe	AZ	85282	480-921-1400	921-0545
Web: www.homebfc.com					
Bruce Gunstra Builders Inc 2150 Market Sq	Lafayette	IN	47904	765-447-2134	447-0332
Web: www.gunstrabuilders.com					
Buchan John F Homes 2821 Northup Way Suite 100	Bellevue	WA	98004	425-827-2266	827-0462
TF: 866-528-2426 ■ *Web:* www.buchan.com					
Butler Real Estate 1540 Genessee St	Kansas City	MO	64102	816-968-3000	968-3720
Web: www.butlermfg.com					
Cadillac Fairview Ltd 20 Queen St W 5th Fl	Toronto	ON	M5H3R4	416-598-8200	598-8607*
**Fax:* Hum Res ■ *Web:* www.cadillacfairview.com					
Cafaro Co 2445 Belmont Ave	Youngstown	OH	44505	330-747-2661	743-2902
Web: www.cafarocompany.com					
California Coastal Communities Inc 6 Executive Cir Suite 250	Irvine	CA	92614	949-250-7700	250-7705
NASDAQ: CALC					
California Pacific Homes 38 Executive Park Suite 200	Irvine	CA	92614	949-833-6000	833-6133
TF: 800-999-0629 ■ *Web:* www.calpacifichomes.com					
Capeletti Brothers Inc 16401 NW 58th Ave PO Box 4944	Miami Lakes	FL	33014	305-823-9500	823-0942
Capo Group 1150 NW 72 Ave PH 1	Miami	FL	33126	305-513-0501	513-9108
Cappelli Development Corp 115 E Stevens Ave	Valhalla	NY	10595	914-769-6500	769-2179
Web: www.cappelli-inc.com					
Caribe Homes Corp 11755 SW 90th St Suite 210	Miami	FL	33186	305-273-1303	273-7513
Web: www.caribehomes.com					
Carl M Freeman Assoc Inc 18330 Village Center Dr 2nd Fl	Olney	MD	20832	240-779-8000	779-8180
Web: www.freemancommunities.com					
Casden Properties 9090 Wilshire Blvd 3rd Fl	Beverly Hills	CA	90211	310-274-5553	276-6486
Castle & Cooke Inc 10900 Wilshire Blvd Suite 1600	Los Angeles	CA	90024	310-208-3636	824-2159
Web: www.castlecooke.com					
Centex Development Co 2728 N Harwood St	Dallas	TX	75201	214-981-6770	981-6786
Centex Homes 2728 N Harwood St	Dallas	TX	75201	214-981-5000	981-6000*
**Fax:* Sales ■ *Web:* www.centexhomes.com					
Centex Real Estate Corp DBA Centex Homes 2728 N Harwood St	Dallas	TX	75201	214-981-5000	981-6000*
**Fax:* Sales ■ *Web:* www.centexhomes.com					
Century Builders Group Inc 2301 NW 87 Ave 6th Fl	Doral	FL	33172	305-599-8100	470-1900
Web: www.centuryhomebuilders.com					
Century Homebuilders LLC 7270 NW 12th St Suite 410	Miami	FL	33126	305-599-8100	470-1900
Web: www.centurybuildersgroup.com					
CFC Inc 320 W 8th St Suite 200	Bloomington	IN	47404	812-332-0053	333-4680
Web: www.cfcincorporated.com					
Choice Homes of Texas PO Box 1048	Arlington	TX	76004	817-652-4900	633-3330
Web: www.choice-homes.com					
Christensen Group 4400 SE Columbia Way	Vancouver	WA	98661	360-696-0381	695-4762
Codina Development Co 355 Alhambra Cir Suite 900	Coral Gables	FL	33134	305-520-2300	520-2467
Web: www.codina.com/dev.home.aspx					
Codina Group Inc 355 Alhambra Cir Suite 900	Coral Gables	FL	33134	305-520-2300	520-2467
Web: www.codina.com					
Coleman Homes Inc 5251 Office Pk Dr Suite 200	Bakersfield	CA	93309	661-326-1141	326-1139
Web: www.colemanhomes.com					
Colony Homes 110 Londonderry Ct Suite 136	Woodstock	GA	30188	770-928-0092	486-4584*
**Fax Area Code:* 678 ■ *Web:* www.colonyhomes.com					
Comstock Homebulding Cos Inc					
11465 Sunny Hills Rd Suite 510	Reston	VA	20190	703-883-1700	760-1520
NASDAQ: CHCI ■ *Web:* www.comstockhomebuilding.com					
Connell Realty & Development Co 100 Connell Dr	Berkeley Heights	NJ	07922	908-673-3700	673-3800
TF: 800-233-3240 ■ *Web:* www.connellco.com/REALTY.htm					
Conner Homes Co 846 108th Ave NE	Bellevue	WA	98004	425-455-9280	462-0426
Web: www.connerhomes.com					
Continental Real Estate Cos 150 E Broad St	Columbus	OH	43215	614-221-1800	221-6365
Web: www.continental-realestate.com					
Cooper Communities Inc 903 N 47th St	Rogers	AR	72756	479-246-6500	
TF: 800-648-6401 ■ *Web:* www.cooper-communities.com					
Coppenbarger Homes 7700 Square Lake Blvd	Jacksonville	FL	32256	904-363-1414	363-1994
Web: www.coppenbargerhomes.com					
Corcoran Jennison Development Co					
150 Mt Vernon St Bayside Office Ctr Suite 500	Boston	MA	02125	617-822-7350	822-7352
Web: www.corcoranjennison.com					
Cornerstone Group 2121 Ponce de Leon Blvd PH 2	Coral Gables	FL	33134	305-443-8288	443-9339
TF: 800-421-1148 ■ *Web:* www.cornerstonegrp.com					
CountryTyme Inc 1660 Gateway Cir	Grove City	OH	43123	614-875-1423	875-1084
TF: 800-388-1349 ■ *Web:* www.countrytyme.com					
Craftmark Homes 6820 Elm St Suite 102	McLean	VA	22101	703-734-9855	749-9758
Web: www.craftmarkhomes.com					
Crescent Resources Inc 400 S Tryon St Suite 1300	Charlotte	NC	28202	980-321-6000	
Web: www.crescent-resources.com					
Crosland Group Inc 125 Scaleybark Rd	Charlotte	NC	28209	704-523-0272	523-7110
Web: www.croslandgroup.com					
Crosswinds Communities 41050 Vincenti Ct	Novi	MI	48375	248-615-1313	615-4129
Web: www.crosswinds.com					
Crown Henry Co 222 N LaSalle St Suite 2000	Chicago	IL	60601	312-236-6300	984-1458
Darling Homes 2500 Legacy Dr Suite 100	Frisco	TX	75034	972-624-4100	624-4106
Web: www.darlinghomes.com					
David Weekley Homes Inc 1111 N Post Oak Rd	Houston	TX	77055	713-963-0500	963-0322
Web: davidweekleyhomes.com					
Davis Homes Inc 3755 E 82nd St Suite 120	Indianapolis	IN	46240	317-595-2800	595-2918
TF: 888-595-2800 ■ *Web:* www.davishomes.com					
De Anza Land & Leisure Corp 1615 Cordova St	Los Angeles	CA	90007	323-734-9951	734-2531
Del Webb Corp 15111 N Pima Rd Suite 100	Scottsdale	AZ	85260	480-391-6000	391-6100
TF: 800-808-8088 ■ *Web:* www.delwebb.com					
Deltona Corp 8014 SW 135th St Rd	Ocala	FL	34473	352-347-2322	307-8103
TF: 800-935-6378 ■ *Web:* www.deltona.com					
Developers of Nevada 7448 W Sahara Ave Suite 101	Las Vegas	NV	89117	702-222-1410	227-0746
Development Services of America					
4025 Delridge Way SW Suite 500	Seattle	WA	98106	206-933-4888	933-4889
TF: 800-372-3663					
DiVosta & Co 4500 PGA Blvd Suite 400	Palm Beach Gardens	FL	33418	561-627-2112	775-9121
Web: www.divosta.com					
Dixon Builders & Developers Inc 7924 Jessie's Way	Hamilton	OH	45011	513-887-6400	887-6643
TF: 877-442-5888 ■ *Web:* www.dixonbuilders.com					
Dominion Homes Inc 5000 Tuttle Crossing Blvd	Dublin	OH	43016	614-761-6000	761-6899
NASDAQ: DHOM ■ *Web:* www.dominionhomes.com					
Donohoe Cos Inc 2101 Wisconsin Ave NW	Washington	DC	20007	202-333-0880	342-3924
TF: 877-366-6463 ■ *Web:* www.donohoe.com					

Company	City	State	Zip	Phone	Fax
Double Diamond Co 10100 N Central Expy Suite 600 *TF:* 800-324-7438 ■ *Web:* www.ddresorts.com	Dallas	TX	75231	214-706-9801	706-9878
DR Horton Inc 301 Commerce St Suite 500 *NYSE: DHI* ■ *TF:* 800-846-7866 ■ *Web:* www.drhorton.com	Fort Worth	TX	76102	817-390-8200	390-1717
Duffel Financial & Construction Co 1430 Willow Pass Rd Suite 220	Concord	CA	94520	925-603-8444	603-8440
Duffy Homes 8724 Olde Worthington Rd *Web:* www.duffyhomes.com	Westerville	OH	43082	614-410-4100	410-4104
Eagle Hospitality Properties Trust Inc 100 E RiverCenter Blvd Suite 480 *NYSE: EHP* ■ *Web:* www.eaglehospitality.com	Covington	KY	41011	859-581-5900	292-5599
EBSCO Development Co 5 Mt Laurel Ave *TF:* 888-408-8696	Birmingham	AL	35242	205-408-8696	408-8991
Echelon Real Estate Services Inc 235 3rd St S Suite 300 *Web:* www.echelonre.com	Saint Petersburg	FL	33701	727-803-8200	803-8203
EJM Development Co 9061 Santa Monica Blvd *Web:* www.ejmdevelopment.com	Los Angeles	CA	90069	310-278-1830	278-2965
Elan Development 211 Highland Cross Dr Suite 101	Houston	TX	77073	281-821-5556	482-1652
Elliott Homes 80 Iron Point Cir Suite 110 *Web:* elliotthomes.com	Folsom	CA	95630	916-984-1300	984-1322
Embrey Partners Ltd 1020 NE Loop 410 Suite 700 *Web:* www.embreypropertiesltd.com	San Antonio	TX	78209	210-824-6044	824-7656
Emmer Group 2801 SW Archer Rd *Web:* www.emmergroup.com	Gainesville	FL	32608	352-376-2444	376-2260
Ennis Homes 643 N Westwood St *Web:* www.ennishomes.com	Porterville	CA	93257	559-781-8888	781-3606
Ensign-Bickford Industries Inc 100 Grist Mill Rd *TF:* 800-828-9814 ■ *Web:* www.ensign-bickfordind.com	Simsbury	CT	06070	860-843-2000	843-1510
Epoch Properties Inc 359 Carolina Ave *Web:* www.epochproperties.com	Winter Park	FL	32789	407-644-9055	644-9845
Ergon Properties Inc 2829 Lakeland Dr PO Box 23038 **Fax:* Hum Res ■ *TF:* 800-824-2626	Jackson	MS	39225	601-933-3000	933-3355*
Estridge Cos 1041 W Main St *TF:* 800-473-7326 ■ *Web:* www.estridge.com	Carmel	IN	46032	317-846-7311	
Fairfield Homes 6420 E Tanque Verde Rd *TF:* 877-868-7125 ■ *Web:* www.fairfieldhomes.net	Tucson	AZ	85701	520-622-8771	622-8876
Farnsworth Development Co 460 S Greenfield Rd Suite 2	Mesa	AZ	85206	480-830-7784	641-4481
Fieldstone Communities Inc 14 Corporate Plaza *TF:* 800-665-0661 ■ *Web:* www.fieldstone-homes.com	Newport Beach	CA	92660	949-759-5810	759-5032
First Hartford Realty Corp 149 Colonial Rd PO Box 1270 *TF:* 888-646-6555 ■ *Web:* www.firsthartford.com	Manchester	CT	06045	860-646-6555	646-8572
Flagship Properties Corp 1 Greenway Plaza Suite 750 *TF:* 866-849-7701 ■ *Web:* www.flagshipco.com	Houston	TX	77046	713-623-6000	623-0009
Flournoy Development Co 900 Brookstone Center Pkwy *Web:* www.flournoydevelopment.com	Columbus	GA	31904	706-324-4000	324-4150
Ford Motor Land Development Corp 550 Town Ctr Dr Suite 200	Dearborn	MI	48126	313-323-3100	594-7215
Forecast Group DBA Forecast Homes 3536 Concours St Suite 100 *TF:* 800-229-4117 ■ *Web:* www.forecasthomes.com	Ontario	CA	91764	909-483-7320	980-7305
Forest City Commercial Group 50 Public Sq Terminal Tower Suite 1130 *Web:* www.fceinc.com	Cleveland	OH	44113	216-621-6060	263-6209
Forest City Enterprises Inc 50 Public Sq Terminal Tower Suite 1100 *NYSE: FCEa* ■ **Fax:* Hum Res ■ *Web:* www.fceinc.com	Cleveland	OH	44113	216-621-6060	263-4808*
Forest City Land Group 50 Public Sq Terminal Tower Suite 1050 *Web:* www.fceinc.com	Cleveland	OH	44113	216-621-6060	263-4809
Forest City Ratner Cos 1 MetroTech Center N 11th Fl *Web:* www.fcrc.com/	Brooklyn	NY	11201	718-923-8400	
Forest City Residential Development Inc 50 Public Sq Terminal Tower Suite 1170 *Web:* www.fceinc.com/	Cleveland	OH	44113	216-621-6060	263-6207
Fox & Jacobs Homes 9229 LBJ Fwy Suite 100 **Fax Area Code:* 214 ■ **Fax:* Sales ■ *Web:* foxandjacobs.com	Dallas	TX	75243	972-416-1447	764-9920*
Fralin & Waldron Inc 2917 Penn Forest Blvd *TF:* 888-238-7459 ■ *Web:* www.fwinc.com	Roanoke	VA	24018	540-774-4415	774-4582
Freeman Carl M Assoc Inc 18330 Village Center Dr 2nd Fl *Web:* www.freemancommunities.com	Olney	MD	20832	240-779-8000	779-8180
Friendswood Development Co 550 Greens Pkwy Suite 100	Houston	TX	77067	281-875-1552	872-4207
Gambone Brothers Development Co PO Box 287 *Web:* www.gambone.com	Fairview Village	PA	19409	610-277-4220	539-0498
Gehan Homes 14901 Quorum Dr Suite 300 *Web:* www.gehanhomes.com	Dallas	TX	75254	972-383-4300	383-4399
General Real Estate Corp 8500 SW 8th St Suite 228	Miami	FL	33144	305-262-6533	262-4118
Genesee Co 9990 Pk Meadows Dr *Web:* www.geneseeco.com	Lone Tree	CO	80124	303-754-0600	526-2975
Gentry Homes Ltd 560 N Nimitz Hwy **Fax:* Sales ■ *Web:* www.gentryhawaii.com	Honolulu	HI	96809	808-599-5558	533-2949*
Gilbane Properties Inc 7 Jackson Walkway *Web:* www.gilbaneproperties.com	Providence	RI	02903	401-456-5890	456-5996
Ginsburg Development Corp 245 Saw Mill River Rd *Web:* www.gdc-homes.com	Hawthorne	NY	10532	914-747-3600	747-1608
GL Homes of Florida Corp 1600 Sawgrass Corporate Pkwy Suite 300 *Web:* www.glhomes.com	Sunrise	FL	33323	954-753-1730	753-4509
Goldrich & Kest Industries 5150 Overland Ave *Web:* www.gkind.com	Culver City	CA	90230	310-204-2050	204-1900
Goodnight Homes Inc PO Box 276	Killeen	TX	76540	254-634-0491	634-5619
Grand Homes Inc 15950 N Central Expy Suite 600 *Web:* www.grandhomes.com	Dallas	TX	75206	214-750-6528	750-6849
Grubb & Ellis Co 2215 Sanders Rd Suite 400 *Web:* www.grubb-ellis.com	Northbrook	IL	60062	847-753-9010	753-9034
Gumberg JJ Co Inc 1051 Brinton Rd *Web:* www.jjgumberg.com	Pittsburgh	PA	15221	412-244-4000	244-9133
Gunstra Bruce Builders Inc 2150 Market Sq *Web:* www.gunstrabuilders.com	Lafayette	IN	47904	765-447-2134	447-0332
Haas & Haynie Corp 395 Oyster Point Blvd Suite 309 *Web:* www.hh1898.com	South San Francisco	CA	94080	650-588-5600	873-9150
Hamlet Homes 308 E 4500South Suite 200 *Web:* www.hamlethomes.com	Salt Lake City	UT	84107	801-281-2223	281-2224
Harbour Homes 1300 Dexter Ave N Suite 500 *Web:* www.harbourhomes.com	Seattle	WA	98109	206-352-2020	352-2010
Hartz Construction Co Inc 9026 Heritage Pkwy *Web:* www.hartzhomes.com	Woodridge	IL	60517	630-228-3800	228-4800
Hartz Mountain Real Estate 400 Plaza Dr *Web:* www.hartzmountain.com	Secaucus	NJ	07094	201-348-1200	348-4358
Haubert Homes Inc 15 Central Blvd *Web:* www.hauberthomes.com	Camp Hill	PA	17011	717-761-7951	761-4125
Hayden Homes Inc 7 The Pines Ct *Web:* www.haydenhomes.com	Saint Louis	MO	63141	314-434-0995	434-5951*
Henry Crown Co 222 N LaSalle St Suite 2000	Chicago	IL	60601	312-236-6300	984-1458
Heritage Development Group Inc 465 Heritage Rd PO Box 873 *Web:* www.heritagedevelopmentgroup.com	Southbury	CT	06488	203-264-8291	264-3347
Highland Homes 12850 Hillcrest Rd Suite 200 *Web:* www.highlandhomes.com	Dallas	TX	75230	972-387-7905	385-0403
Hills Communities Inc 4901 Hunt Rd Suite 300 *Web:* www.hillsinc.com	Cincinnati	OH	45242	513-984-0300	618-7694
Hines Interest LP 2800 Post Oak Blvd 48th Fl *Web:* www.hines.com	Houston	TX	77056	713-621-8000	966-2055
HJ Kalikow Inc 101 Park Ave 25th Fl *Web:* www.hjkalikow.com	New York	NY	10178	212-808-7000	573-6380
Hoffman Homes Inc 320 W NW Hwy *Web:* www.hoffmanhomes.com	Arlington Heights	IL	60004	847-590-0100	590-1989
Hofmann Co 1380 Galaxy Way *Web:* www.hofmannhomes.com	Concord	CA	94520	925-682-4830	682-4771
Holiday Builders Inc 2293 W Eau Gallie Blvd *Web:* www.holidaybuilders.com	Melbourne	FL	32935	321-259-3130	751-9198
Horton DR Inc 301 Commerce St Suite 500 *NYSE: DHI* ■ *TF:* 800-846-7866 ■ *Web:* www.drhorton.com	Fort Worth	TX	76102	817-390-8200	390-1717
Hovnanian Enterprises Inc 10 Hwy 35 *NYSE: HOV* ■ *Web:* www.khov.com	Red Bank	NJ	07701	732-747-7800	747-7159
Howard Hughes Corp 10000 W Charleston Blvd Suite 200 *Web:* www.howardhughes.com	Las Vegas	NV	89135	702-791-4000	791-4450
Hunt Building Co Ltd 4401 N Mesa St *Web:* www.huntelp.com	El Paso	TX	79902	915-533-1122	545-2631
Hunt Midwest Enterprises Inc 8300 NE Underground Dr *TF:* 800-551-6877 ■ *Web:* www.huntmidwest.com	Kansas City	MO	64161	816-455-2500	
Hunt Midwest Residential Development 8300 NE Underground Dr *TF:* 800-551-6877 ■ *Web:* www.huntcommunities.com	Kansas City	MO	64161	816-455-2500	455-8701
IDI Group Cos 1700 N Moore St Suite 2020 *Web:* www.idigroup.com	Arlington	VA	22209	703-558-7300	558-7377
Inland Real Estate Development Corp 2901 Butterfield Rd *TF:* 800-828-8999 ■ *Web:* www.inlandgroup.com	Oak Brook	IL	60523	630-218-8000	218-4917
International Rivercenter 2 Poydras St 2nd Fl Riverside	New Orleans	LA	70140	504-584-3901	584-3955
Interstate General Co LP 105 W Washington St *Web:* www.igclp.com	Middleburg	VA	20117	540-687-3177	687-3179
Intervest Construction Inc 2379 Beville Rd *Web:* www.homesbyici.com	Daytona Beach	FL	32119	386-788-0820	760-2237
Irvine Co 550 Newport Center Dr **Fax:* Hum Res ■ *Web:* www.irvinecompany.com	Newport Beach	CA	92660	949-720-2000	720-2501*
Ivory Homes 970 E Woodoak Ln *Web:* www.ivoryhomes.com	Salt Lake City	UT	84117	801-268-0700	747-7090
JJ Gumberg Co Inc 1051 Brinton Rd *Web:* www.jjgumberg.com	Pittsburgh	PA	15221	412-244-4000	244-9133
JMB Realty Corp 900 N Michigan Ave 14th Fl	Chicago	IL	60611	312-440-4800	915-2310
JMB/Urban Retail Properties Co 900 N Michigan Ave Suite 1300	Chicago	IL	60611	312-440-4800	915-3180
JMC Communities 2201 4th St N Suite 200 *TF:* 800-741-4106 ■ *Web:* www.jmcdev.com	Saint Petersburg	FL	33704	727-823-0022	821-2007
John F Buchan Homes 2821 Northup Way Suite 100 *TF:* 866-528-2426 ■ *Web:* www.buchan.com	Bellevue	WA	98004	425-827-2266	827-0462
John F Long Properties LLLP 5035 W Camelback Rd **Fax Area Code:* 623 ■ *Web:* www.jflong.com	Phoenix	AZ	85031	602-272-0421	846-7208*
John Kavanagh Homes 1810 Pembroke Rd *TF:* 800-940-9904 ■ *Web:* www.kavanaghhomes.com	Greensboro	NC	27408	336-272-9904	370-4137
John Wieland Homes & Neighborhoods Inc 1950 Sullivan Rd *TF:* 800-376-4663 ■ *Web:* www.jwhomes.com	Atlanta	GA	30337	770-996-2400	904-3481
JPI 600 E Las Colinas Blvd Suite 1800 *Web:* www.jpi.com	Irving	TX	75039	972-556-1700	444-2102
Jupiter Realty Corp 401 Michigan Ave Suite 1300 *TF:* 800-910-2276 ■ *Web:* www.jupiterrealty.com	Chicago	IL	60611	312-642-6000	642-2316
K Hovnanian Homes 1802 Brightseat Rd *TF:* 800-342-5944 ■ *Web:* www.washingtonhomes.com	Landover	MD	20785	301-772-8900	772-1380
Kaiser Ventures LLC 3633 E Inland Empire Blvd Suite 480 *TF:* 800-889-3652 ■ *Web:* www.kaiserventures.com	Ontario	CA	91764	909-483-8500	944-6605
Kalikow HJ Inc 101 Park Ave 25th Fl *Web:* www.hjkalikow.com	New York	NY	10178	212-808-7000	573-6380
Kapalua Land Co Ltd 129 Bay Dr *TF Sales:* 800-545-8439 ■ *Web:* www.kapaluarealty.com	Kapalua	HI	96761	808-669-5622	669-5454
Kavanagh John Homes 1810 Pembroke Rd *TF:* 800-940-9904 ■ *Web:* www.kavanaghhomes.com	Greensboro	NC	27408	336-272-9904	370-4137
KB Home 10990 Wilshire Blvd 7th Fl *NYSE: KBH* ■ *TF:* 800-344-6637 ■ *Web:* www.kbhome.com	Los Angeles	CA	90024	310-231-4000	231-4222
Keauhou-Kona Resort Co 78-128 Ehukai St	Kailua-Kona	HI	96740	808-930-4900	930-4800
Kennedy Group of Cos 1051 E Main St Suite 109 *Web:* www.kennedyhomebuilders.com	East Dundee	IL	60118	847-844-8600	844-8606
Kettler Brothers Inc 9426 Stewartown Rd Suite 3B	Montgomery Village	MD	20886	301-948-4000	948-9749
Keystone Builders Resource Group Inc 1207 Roseneath Rd Suite 200 *Web:* www.keybuild.com	Richmond	VA	23230	804-354-8830	358-6976
Killearn Inc 135 N Park Pl Suite 100 *Web:* www.killearn.com	Stockbridge	GA	30281	770-389-2020	389-2010
Kimball Hill Homes 5999 New Wilke Rd Suite 504 *Web:* www.kimballhillhomes.com	Rolling Meadows	IL	60008	847-364-7300	439-0875
Knight Development Inc 9497 Thornton Blvd *Web:* www.knighthomes.com	Jonesboro	GA	30236	770-471-4751	603-0904
Koren Development Inc 9200 Rumsey Rd Suite 210	Columbia	MD	21045	410-740-1010	992-5573
Kravco Co 234 Mall Blvd *Web:* www.kravco.com	King of Prussia	PA	19406	610-768-6300	768-6444
KSI Services Inc 1751 Pinnacle Dr Suite 700 *Web:* www.ketsco.com	McLean	VA	22102	703-641-9000	641-9630
Lakewood Homes 2700 W Higgins Rd Suite 100 *Web:* www.lakewoodhomes.com	Hoffman Estates	IL	60195	847-884-8800	884-8986
Lancia Construction 9430 Lima Rd Suite A *TF:* 800-752-6242 ■ *Web:* www.lanciahomes.com	Fort Wayne	IN	46818	260-489-4433	489-0325
Landstar Development Corp 120 Fairway Woods Blvd *TF:* 800-327-9105 ■ *Web:* www.landstarhomes.com	Orlando	FL	32824	407-240-0044	857-2267
Larwin Co 16633 Ventura Blvd Suite 1300	Encino	CA	91436	818-986-8890	784-2891
LCOR Inc 100 Berwyn Pk Suite 110 *Web:* www.lcor.com	Berwyn	PA	19312	610-251-9110	408-4420
LeCesse Development Corp 650 S Northlake Blvd Suite 450	Altamonte Springs	FL	32701	407-645-5575	645-0553
Lefrak Organization 97-77 Queens Blvd *Web:* www.lefrak.com	Rego Park	NY	11374	718-459-9021	575-4816
Lennar Homes of Arizona Inc 5151 E Broadway Suite 1100 *Web:* www.lennar.com	Tucson	AZ	85711	520-747-0997	
Lennar Homes of California Inc 25 Enterprise *Web:* www.lennarcalifornia.com	Mission Viejo	CA	92656	949-349-8000	349-0798
Lennar Homes Inc 700 NW 107th Ave Suite 400 *TF:* 800-741-4663 ■ *Web:* www.lennar.com	Miami	FL	33172	305-559-4000	226-4158
Lester Group 101 E Commerce Pkwy *Web:* www.lestergroup.com	Barnesville	VA	24102	276-632-2195	632-2117
Lewis TW 850 W Elliot Rd Suite 101 **Fax Area Code:* 602 ■ *Web:* www.twlewis.com	Tempe	AZ	85284	480-820-0807	820-1455*
Lifestyle Homes Inc 17865-Georgetown Dr *Web:* www.woodlandvillagehomes.com	Cold Springs	NV	89506	775-673-9000	674-4030

				Phone	Fax
Louis Dreyfus Group 20 Westport Rd	Wilton	CT	06897	203-761-2000	761-2375
Web: www.louisdreyfus.com					
Lozier Homes Corp 1203 114th Ave SE	Bellevue	WA	98004	425-454-8690	646-8695
Web: www.lozierhomes.com					
Martin Stanley Cos Inc 11111 Sunset Hills Rd Suite 200	Reston	VA	20190	703-715-7800	715-8076
TF: 800-446-4807 ■ *Web:* www.stanleymartin.com					
Matrix Development Corp 12755 SW 69th Ave Suite 100	Portland	OR	97223	503-620-8080	598-8900
Matzel & Mumford Organization Inc 100 Village Ct	Hazlet	NJ	07730	732-888-1055	888-2192*
**Fax:* Mktg ■ *Web:* www.khov.com					
Maui Land & Pineapple Co Ltd 120 Kane St PO Box 187	Kahului	HI	96733	808-877-3351	871-0953
AMEX: MLP ■ *Web:* www.mauiland.com					
MAXXAM Property Co 1330 Post Oak Blvd Suite 2000	Houston	TX	77056	713-267-3750	267-3703
McGuyer Homebuilders Inc 7676 Woodway Dr Suite 104	Houston	TX	77063	713-952-6767	952-5637
Web: www.mcguyerhomebuilders.com					
McKee Group 940 W Sproul Rd Suite 301	Springfield	PA	19064	610-604-9800	328-5023
Web: www.mckeebuilders.com					
McMillin Cos 2750 Womble Ave	San Diego	CA	92106	619-477-4117	794-1604
TF: 800-781-0401 ■ *Web:* www.mcmillin.com					
McStain Enterprises Inc 400 Centennial Pkwy Suite 200	Louisville	CO	80027	303-494-5900	494-4933
Web: www.mcstain.com					
Mercedes Homes Inc 6905 N Wickham Rd Suite 403	Melbourne	FL	32940	321-259-6972	242-1789
Web: www.merhomes.com					
Meritage Homes Corp 17851 N 85th St Suite 300	Scottsdale	AZ	85255	480-515-8100	515-7904
NYSE: MTH ■ *Web:* www.meritagecorp.com					
M/I Homes Inc 3 Easton Oval	Columbus	OH	43219	614-418-8000	418-8080
NYSE: MHO ■ *Web:* www.mihomes.com					
Mid-West Terminal Warehouse Co Inc					
1700 N Universal Ave	Kansas City	MO	64120	816-231-8811	231-0020
Web: www.mwtco.com					
Miller & Smith Cos 8401 Greensboro Dr Suite 300	McLean	VA	22102	703-821-2500	356-1933
Web: www.millerandsmith.com					
Miller Valentine Group 4000 Miller Valentine Ct	Dayton	OH	45439	937-293-0900	299-1564
TF: 877-684-7687 ■ *Web:* www.mvg.com					
Minto Builders 4400 W Sample Rd Suite 200	Coconut Creek	FL	33073	954-973-4490	974-7452
TF: 800-767-4490 ■ *Web:* www.minto.com					
Mission West Properties 10050 Bandley Dr	Cupertino	CA	95014	408-725-0700	725-1626
AMEX: MSW ■ *TF:* 800-222-5401 ■ *Web:* www.missionwest.com					
Mitchell Co Inc					
41 W I-65 Service Rd N Colonial Bank Center 3rd Fl	Mobile	AL	36608	251-380-2929	345-1264
Web: www.mitchellcompany.com					
Mitsubishi Estate NY Inc 1221 Ave of the Americas 17th Fl	New York	NY	10020	212-698-2200	698-2211
Web: www.mec.co.jp/index_ef.htm					
Moceri Development Corp 3005 University Dr Suite 100	Auburn Hills	MI	48326	248-340-9400	340-9401
Web: www.moceri.com					
Montalbano Builders Inc 2208 Midwest Rd	Oak Brook	IL	60523	630-571-8877	481-4290
Web: www.montalbanohomes.com					
Morrison Homes 3655 Brookside Pkwy Suite 400	Alpharetta	GA	30022	770-360-8700	360-8701
Web: www.morrisonhomes.com					
NESCO Inc Real Estate Group 6140 Parkland Blvd	Mayfield Heights	OH	44124	440-461-6000	449-3111
Neumann Homes 4355 Weaver Pkwy	Warrenville	IL	60555	630-281-2000	281-2177
Web: www.neumannhomes.com					
Newhall Land & Farming Co 23823 Valencia Blvd	Valencia	CA	91355	661-255-4000	255-3960
TF: 800-342-3612 ■ *Web:* www.valencia.com					
Neyer Al Inc 302 W 3rd St Suite 800	Cincinnati	OH	45202	513-271-6400	271-1350
TF: 877-271-6400 ■ *Web:* www.neyer.com					
Norwood Builders 7458 N Harlem Ave	Chicago	IL	60631	773-775-5400	775-4433
Web: www.norwoodbuilders.com					
NTS Development Co 10172 Linn Station Rd	Louisville	KY	40223	502-426-4800	426-4994
Web: www.ntsdevelopment.com					
NTS Realty Holdings LP 10172 Linn Station Rd	Louisville	KY	40223	502-426-4800	426-4994
AMEX: NLP ■ *Web:* www.ntsdevelopment.com					
O Hill Partners 1 Upper Newport Plaza	Newport Beach	CA	92660	949-752-0700	752-0885
Olympia Development LLC 2211 Woodward Ave	Detroit	MI	48201	313-983-6200	983-6199
Oriole Homes Corp 6400 Congress Ave Suite 2000	Boca Raton	FL	33487	561-999-1860	988-9490
TF: 800-964-6631 ■ *Web:* www.oriolehomes.com					
Orleans Homebuilders Inc					
3333 Street Rd 1 Greenwood Sq Suite 101	Bensalem	PA	19020	215-245-7500	633-2352
AMEX: OHB ■ *Web:* www.orleanshomes.com					
Pacific Properties & Development LLC					
5440 W Sahara Ave 3rd Fl	Las Vegas	NV	89146	702-948-1200	948-1201
Paparone Corp 702 N White Horse Pike	Stratford	NJ	08084	856-784-0550	627-0650
Web: www.paparonenewhomes.com					
Paramount Development Assoc Inc 73 Mt Wayte Ave	Framingham	MA	01701	508-628-2410	628-2920
Park Square Enterprises Inc 5200 Vineland Rd Suite 200	Orlando	FL	32811	407-529-3000	529-3100
Web: www.parksquarehomes.com					
Parker Lancaster Corp 711 Moorefield Park Dr Suite E	Richmond	VA	23236	804-323-3100	330-7198
Peebles Atlantic Development Corp					
550 Biltmore Way Suite 970	Coral Gables	FL	33134	305-442-4342	442-4345
Web: www.padcorp.com					
Peterson Cos 10000 W 75th St Suite 100	Shawnee Mission	KS	66204	913-384-3800	384-9605
Phoenix Developers 605 Silverleaf Dr	Joliet	IL	60431	815-730-0008	730-6814
Web: www.phoenixdevelopers.com					
Picerne Real Estate Group 75 Lambert Lind Hwy	Warwick	RI	02886	401-732-3700	738-6452
Web: www.picerne.com					
Pineloch Management Inc 102 W Pineloch Ave Suite 10	Orlando	FL	32806	407-859-3550	650-0303
Web: www.pineloch.com					
Pittway Real Estate PO Box 7018	Wesley Chapel	FL	33543	813-973-3685	973-0115
Plaster Development Co Inc DBA Signature Homes					
801 S Rancho Dr Suite E-4	Las Vegas	NV	89106	702-385-5031	385-6567
Web: www.signaturehomes.com					
Polygon Northwest Co 11624 SE 5th St Suite 200	Bellevue	WA	98005	425-586-7700	688-0500
TF: 800-765-9466 ■ *Web:* www.polygonhomes.com					
Porten Cos 5515 Security Ln Suite 550	Rockville	MD	20852	301-881-0040	881-2191
Web: www.portencompanies.com					
Post Properties Inc 4401 Northside Pkwy Suite 800	Atlanta	GA	30327	404-846-5000	846-6161*
NYSE: PPS ■ **Fax:* Hum Res ■ *Web:* www.postproperties.com					
Princeville Corp PO Box 223040	Princeville	HI	96722	808-826-3040	826-9592
Pringle Development Inc 2801 S Bay St	Eustis	FL	32726	352-483-8000	483-8001
TF: 800-325-4471 ■ *Web:* www.pringle.com					
Puget Western Inc 19515 N Creek Pkwy Suite 310	Bothell	WA	98011	425-487-6550	487-6565
Pulte Home Corp 100 Bloomfield Hills Pkwy Suite 300	Bloomfield Hills	MI	48304	248-644-7300	433-4598
TF: 800-777-8583 ■ *Web:* www.pulte.com					
Quadrangle Development Corp 1001 G St NW Suite 700-W	Washington	DC	20001	202-393-1999	393-0548
Web: www.quadrangledevcorp.com					
Quadrant Corp 14725 SE 36 St Suite 300	Bellevue	WA	98006	425-455-2900	646-8377
Web: www.quadranthomes.com					
Questar Properties Inc 124 Slade Ave Suite 200	Baltimore	MD	21208	410-486-1234	486-6346*
**Fax:* Sales ■ *Web:* www.questar.net/qpi.html					
Realty Investment Co Ltd 345 Kekuanaoa St Suite 20	Hilo	HI	96720	808-961-5252	935-8099
Web: www.rinvest.com					
Reeves-Williams Inc 8727 Northwest Dr Suite 3	Southaven	MS	38671	662-393-4250	393-4298
Web: www.reeveswilliams.com					
Related Group of Florida 2828 Coral Way PH 1	Miami	FL	33145	305-460-9900	460-9911
Web: www.relatedgroup.com					
Related Midwest 350 W Hubbard St Suite 300	Chicago	IL	60610	312-595-7400	595-1898
Web: www.relatedmidwest.com					
Reliable Development 816 N 360 West	Valparaiso	IN	46385	219-762-2118	762-1978

				Phone	Fax
Resource Properties Inc 1845 Walnut St 10th Fl	Philadelphia	PA	19103	215-546-5005	546-5388
Web: www.resourceamerica.com					
Richman Group of Cos 599 W Putnam Ave	Greenwich	CT	06830	203-869-0900	869-1034
TF: 800-333-3509					
Richmond American Homes Inc					
6550 S Greenwood Plaza Blvd	Centennial	CO	80111	303-773-2727	220-4492
TF: 888-402-4663 ■ *Web:* www.richmondamerican.com					
Roberts Properties 450 Northridge Pkwy Suite 300	Atlanta	GA	30350	770-394-6000	396-0706
Robson Communities 9532 E Riggs Rd	Sun Lakes	AZ	85248	480-895-9200	895-0136
TF: 800-732-9949 ■ *Web:* www.robson.com					
Rottlund Co Inc 3065 Centre Pt Dr	Roseville	MN	55113	651-638-0500	638-0501
Web: www.rottlundhomes.com					
Royce Homes LP 7850 N Sam Houston Pkwy W	Houston	TX	77064	281-440-5091	440-2910
Web: www.roycebuilders.com					
Ryder Homes of Nevada Inc 290 Gentry Way Suite 5	Reno	NV	89502	775-823-3788	823-3799
Web: www.ryderhomes.com					
Ryland Group Inc 24025 Park Sorrento Suite 400	Calabasas	CA	91302	818-223-7500	223-7667
NYSE: RYL ■ *TF:* 800-267-0998 ■ *Web:* www.ryland.com					
S & A Custom Built Homes					
2121 Old Gatesburg Rd Suite 200	State College	PA	16803	814-231-4780	272-8821
Web: www.sahomebuilder.com					
Sabey Corp 12201 Tukwila International Blvd 4th Fl	Seattle	WA	98168	206-281-8700	282-9951
Web: www.sabey.com					
Sabine Investment Co of Texas Inc 736 Crown Colony Dr	Lufkin	TX	75901	936-637-6300	637-3768
Web: www.sabineinvestment.com					
Saint Joe Co 245 Riverside Ave Suite 500	Jacksonville	FL	32202	904-396-6600	301-4201
NYSE: JOE ■ *Web:* www.joe.com					
Saint Joe Towns & Resorts 7900 Glades Rd Suite 200	Boca Raton	FL	33434	561-479-1100	479-1226
Web: www.joetowns.com					
Santa Anita Enterprises Inc 285 W Huntington Dr	Arcadia	CA	91007	626-574-7223	446-9565
Schatten Properties Management Co Inc 1514 South St	Nashville	TN	37212	615-329-3011	327-2343
TF: 800-892-1315 ■ *Web:* www.schattenproperties.com					
Sea Pines Plantation Co Inc 32 Greenwood Dr	Hilton Head Island	SC	29928	843-785-3333	842-1475
TF: 800-925-4653 ■ *Web:* www.seapines.com					
Sea Ranch Properties Inc 312 SE 17th St Suite 300	Fort Lauderdale	FL	33316	954-527-0880	527-0904
Seago Group Inc 3446 Marinatown Ln	North Fort Myers	FL	33903	239-997-7711	997-6407
SEDA Construction Co 2120 Corporate Sq Blvd Suite 3	Jacksonville	FL	32216	904-724-7800	727-9500
Web: www.sedaconstruction.com					
Shapell Industries Inc 8383 Wilshire Blvd Suite 700	Beverly Hills	CA	90211	323-655-7330	655-4349
TF: 800-655-9502 ■ *Web:* www.shapell.com					
Shea Homes Inc 8800 N Gainey Center Dr Suite 350	Scottsdale	AZ	85258	480-348-6000	948-8806
Web: www.sheahomes.com					
Shodeen Inc 17 N 1st St	Geneva	IL	60134	630-232-8570	232-8581
Web: www.shodeen.com					
Signature Homes 801 S Rancho Dr Suite E-4	Las Vegas	NV	89106	702-385-5031	385-6567
Web: www.signaturehomes.com					
Simpson Housing LP 8110 E Union Ave Suite 200	Denver	CO	80237	888-330-5951	
Web: www.simpsonhousing.com					
Singh Homes Inc 7125 Orchard Lake Rd Suite 200	West Bloomfield	MI	48322	248-865-1600	865-1630
Web: www.singhweb.com					
Skanska USA Inc 16-16 Whitestone Expy	Whitestone	NY	11357	718-767-2600	767-2663
Web: www.skanska.com					
South Shore Harbor Development Ltd					
2525 S Shore Blvd Suite 205	League City	TX	77573	281-334-7501	334-7506
Web: www.southshoreharbour.com					
Space Center Inc 2501 Rosegate	Saint Paul	MN	55113	651-604-4200	604-4222
TF: 800-548-9737 ■ *Web:* www.spacecenterinc.com					
Spanos AG Cos 10100 Trinity Pkwy 5th Fl	Stockton	CA	95219	209-478-7954	478-3309
Web: www.agspanos.com					
Spanos AG Development Inc 10100 Trinity Pkwy 5th Fl	Stockton	CA	95219	209-478-7954	478-3309
Web: www.agspanos.com					
Stanley Martin Cos Inc 11111 Sunset Hills Rd Suite 200	Reston	VA	20190	703-715-7800	715-8076
TF: 800-446-4807 ■ *Web:* www.stanleymartin.com					
Stiles Corp 300 SE 2nd St	Fort Lauderdale	FL	33301	954-627-9300	627-9305
Web: www.stiles.com					
Stiles Development Co 300 SE 2nd St	Fort Lauderdale	FL	33301	954-627-9300	627-9305
Web: www.stiles.com/development_about_us.htm					
Stratus Properties Inc 98 San Jacinto Blvd Suite 220	Austin	TX	78701	512-478-5788	478-6340
NASDAQ: STRS ■ *TF:* 800-690-0315 ■ *Web:* www.stratusprop.com					
Suarez Housing Corp 9950 Princess Palm Ave Suite 212	Tampa	FL	33619	813-664-1100	622-6813
Web: www.suarezhousing.com					
SunCor Development Co 80 E Rio Salado Pkwy Suite 410	Tempe	AZ	85281	480-317-6800	317-6934
Web: www.suncoraz.com					
Susquehanna Real Estate 140 E Market St	York	PA	17401	717-848-5500	771-1430
Web: www.susquehanna-realestate.com					
Swerdlow Real Estate Group 3390 Mary St Suite 200	Coconut Grove	FL	33133	305-476-0100	476-0108
Web: www.swerdlowgroup.com					
TA Forsberg Inc 2422 Jolly Rd Suite 200	Okemos	MI	48864	517-349-9330	349-7131
Web: www.taforsberg.com					
Taylor-Morley Homes					
17107 Chesterfield Airport Rd Suite 200	Chesterfield	MO	63005	314-434-9000	434-1390
TF: 888-297-3155 ■ *Web:* www.taylormorley.com					
Taylor Woodrow Homes Inc 15 Cushing	Irvine	CA	92618	949-341-1200	341-1400
Web: www.taylorwoodrow.com					
TELACU Industries Inc 5400 E Olympic Blvd Suite 300	Los Angeles	CA	90022	323-721-1655	724-3372
Web: www.telacu.com					
Tishman Speyer Properties Inc 520 Madison Ave	New York	NY	10022	212-715-0300	319-1745
Web: www.tishmanspeyer.com					
Toll Brothers Inc 250 Gibraltar Rd	Horsham	PA	19044	215-938-8000	938-8217*
NYSE: TOL ■ **Fax:* Mktg ■ *TF:* 800-289-8655 ■ *Web:* www.tollbrothers.com					
Trammell Crow Co 2001 Ross Ave Suite 3400	Dallas	TX	75201	214-863-3000	863-3138
NYSE: TCC ■ *Web:* www.trammellcrow.com					
Trammell Crow Residential 2859 Paces Ferry Rd Suite 1100	Atlanta	GA	30339	770-801-1600	801-1256
Web: www.tcresidential.com					
TransCon Builders Inc 25250 Rockside Rd	Bedford Heights	OH	44146	440-439-3400	439-6710
TF: 800-362-0371 ■ *Web:* www.transconbuilders.com					
Transeastern Properties Inc					
3300 N University Dr Suite 001	Coral Springs	FL	33065	954-346-9700	346-9704
TF: 877-352-4635 ■ *Web:* www.transeasternhomes.com					
Trizec Properties Inc 1114 Ave of the Americas 31st Fl	New York	NY	10036	212-382-9300	382-9334
NYSE: TRZ ■ *Web:* www.trz.com					
TW Lewis 850 W Elliot Rd Suite 101	Tempe	AZ	85284	480-820-0807	820-1455*
**Fax Area Code:* 602 ■ *Web:* www.twlewis.com					
United Properties Inc 404 N 31st St Suite 100	Billings	MT	59101	406-255-7100	255-7125
US Home Corp 10707 Clay Rd	Houston	TX	77041	713-877-2311	877-2452
Web: www.lennar.com/ushome					
Van Daele Development Corp 2900 Adams St Suite C-25	Riverside	CA	92504	951-354-2121	354-2996
Web: www.vandaele.com					
Van Metre Cos 5252 Lyngate Ct	Burke	VA	22015	703-425-2600	425-2261
Viera Co 7380 Murrell Rd Suite 201	Viera	FL	32940	321-242-1200	253-1800
Village Builders 550 Greens Pkwy Suite 200	Houston	TX	77067	281-873-4663	872-4210
Web: www.lennar.com/village					
Village Green Cos 30833 Northwestern Hwy Suite 300	Farmington Hills	MI	48334	248-851-9600	851-6161
Web: www.villagegreen.com					
Village Homes of Colorado Inc					
100 Inverness Terr Suite E-200	Englewood	CO	80112	303-795-1976	
TF: 866-752-2322 ■ *Web:* www.villagehomes.com					

Company / Address	City	State	Zip	Phone	Fax
Villages of Lake Sumter Inc 1100 Main St	The Villages	FL	32159	352-753-2270	753-6224*
*Fax: Sales ■ *TF:* 800-346-4556 ■ *Web:* www.thevillages.com					
Walt Disney Imagineering 1401 Flower St PO Box 25020	Glendale	CA	91221	818-544-6500	544-7995
Walton Associated Co Inc DBA Walton Co 2001 Financial Way Suite 200	Glendora	CA	91741	626-963-8505	914-7016
Walton Co 2001 Financial Way Suite 200	Glendora	CA	91741	626-963-8505	914-7016
Warmington Group 3090 Pullman St	Costa Mesa	CA	92626	714-557-5511	641-9337
TF: 800-925-9709 ■ *Web:* www.warmingtonhomes.com					
Wathen-Castanos Inc 7259 N 1st St Suite 101	Fresno	CA	93720	559-432-8181	432-8595
Web: www.wathen-castanos.com					
Watkins Associated Developers 1948 Monroe Dr NE PO Box 1738	Atlanta	GA	30301	404-872-8666	872-8806
Watson Land Co 22010 S Wilmington Ave Suite 400	Carson	CA	90745	310-952-6400	522-8788
Web: www.watsonlandcompany.com					
WCI Communities Inc 24301 Walden Center Dr	Bonita Springs	FL	34134	239-947-2600	498-8278*
NYSE: WCI ■ *Fax: Hum Res ■ *TF:* 800-924-2290 ■ *Web:* www.wcicommunities.com					
Webb Del Corp 15111 N Pima Rd Suite 100	Scottsdale	AZ	85260	480-391-6000	391-6100
TF: 800-808-8088 ■ *Web:* www.delwebb.com					
Weekley David Homes Inc 1111 N Post Oak Rd	Houston	TX	77055	713-963-0500	963-0322
Web: davidweekleyhomes.com					
Weiss Homes Inc 828 E Jefferson Blvd	South Bend	IN	46617	574-234-7373	282-2987
TF: 888-336-7373 ■ *Web:* www.weisshomes.com					
Wellsford Real Estate 535 Madison Ave	New York	NY	10022	212-838-3400	421-7244
Web: wellsford.com					
Wellsford Real Properties Inc 535 Madison Ave	New York	NY	10022	212-838-3400	421-7244
AMEX: WRP ■ *Web:* www.wellsford.com					
Wensmann Homes Inc 1895 Plaza Dr Suite 200	Eagan	MN	55122	651-406-4400	905-3678
Web: www.wensmann.com					
Weston Cos 1715 Aaron Brenner Dr Suite 500 PO Box 17847	Memphis	TN	38187	901-682-9100	684-6357
Web: www.westonco.com					
Westrum Development Co Inc 370 Commerce Dr	Fort Washington	PA	19034	215-283-2190	283-0991
TF: 800-937-8786 ■ *Web:* www.westrum.com					
Weyerhaeuser Co 33663 Weyerhaeuser Way S	Federal Way	WA	98003	253-924-2345	924-2685
NYSE: WY ■ *TF:* 800-525-5440 ■ *Web:* www.weyerhaeuser.com					
Whitlatch & Co 8848 Commons Blvd Suite 101 PO Box 363	Twinsburg	OH	44087	330-425-3500	425-7813
Web: www.whitlatch.com					
Wieland John Homes & Neighborhoods Inc 1950 Sullivan Rd	Atlanta	GA	30337	770-996-2400	904-3481
TF: 800-376-4663 ■ *Web:* www.jwhomes.com					
Wilshire Homes 8200 N Mopac Expy Suite 300	Austin	TX	78759	512-502-2050	338-4163
Web: www.buffingtonhomes.com					
Wispark LLC 301 W Wisconsin Ave Suite 400	Milwaukee	WI	53203	414-274-4600	274-4640
Web: www.wispark.com					
Woodside Homes of Nevada 5888 W Sunset Rd Suite 200	Las Vegas	NV	89118	702-889-7800	889-0801
Web: www.woodsidegroupinc.com					
Wooldridge Organization 395 Taylor Blvd Suite 120	Pleasant Hill	CA	94523	925-680-7979	680-7685
Worthington Communities 9341 Marketplace Rd Suite 2	Fort Myers	FL	33912	239-561-4666	561-4676
TF: 877-560-4666 ■ *Web:* www.worthingtoncommunities.com					
Wynne Building Corp 12804 SW 122nd Ave	Miami	FL	33186	305-235-3175	378-9716
Zaremba Group 14600 Detroit Ave Suite 1500	Lakewood	OH	44107	216-221-6600	221-0105
TF: 800-252-3222 ■ *Web:* www.zarembagroup.com					
Zicka Walker Homes Inc 7861 E Kemper Rd	Cincinnati	OH	45249	513-247-3500	247-3512
TF: 800-652-1745 ■ *Web:* www.zickawalkerhomes.com					

657 REAL ESTATE INVESTMENT TRUSTS (REITS)

Company / Address	City	State	Zip	Phone	Fax
Acadia Realty Trust 1311 Mamaroneck Ave Suite 260	White Plains	NY	10605	914-288-8100	428-2380
NYSE: AKR ■ *TF:* 800-227-5570 ■ *Web:* www.acadiarealty.com					
Affordable Residential Communities Inc 7887 E Belleview Ave Suite 200	Englewood	CO	80111	303-291-0222	294-9946
NYSE: ARC ■ *TF:* 800-245-5415 ■ *Web:* www.aboutarc.com					
Agree Realty Corp 31850 Northwestern Hwy	Farmington Hills	MI	48334	248-737-4190	737-9110
NYSE: ADC ■ *Web:* www.agreerealty.com					
Alesco Financial Inc 2929 Arch St 17th Fl	Philadelphia	PA	19104	215-701-9555	701-8281
NYSE: AFN ■ *Web:* www.alescofinancial.com					
Alexander's Inc 210 Rt 4 E	Paramus	NJ	07652	201-587-8541	587-0600
NYSE: ALX ■ *TF:* 800-242-4119 ■ *Web:* www.alx-inc.com					
Alexandria Real Estate Equities Inc 385 E Colorado Blvd Suite 299	Pasadena	CA	91101	626-578-0777	578-0770
NYSE: ARE					
All Capital/GPT Properties 13625 California St Suite 310	Omaha	NE	68154	402-391-0010	391-4144
NYSE: GPT ■ *Web:* www.allco.com.					
AMB Property Corp Pier 1 Bay 1	San Francisco	CA	94111	415-394-9000	394-9001
NYSE: AMB ■ *Web:* www.amb.com					
America First Apartment Investors Inc 1004 Farnam St Suite 100	Omaha	NE	68102	402-557-6360	557-6399
NASDAQ: APRO ■ *Web:* www.apro-reit.com					
American Campus Communities Inc 805 Las Cimas Pkwy Suite 400	Austin	TX	78746	512-732-1000	732-2450
NYSE: ACC ■ *Web:* www.studenthousing.com					
American Community Properties Trust 222 Smallwood Village Ctr	Saint Charles	MD	20602	301-843-8600	870-8481
AMEX: APO ■ *Web:* www.acptrust.com					
American Financial Realty Trust 680 Old York Rd	Jenkintown	PA	19046	215-887-2280	887-2585
NYSE: AFR ■ *Web:* www.afrg.com					
American Land Lease Inc 29399 US 19 N Suite 320	Clearwater	FL	33761	727-726-8868	725-4391
NYSE: ANL ■ *TF:* 800-826-6069 ■ *Web:* www.americanlandlease.com					
American Mortgage Acceptance Co 625 Madison Ave 5th Fl	New York	NY	10022	212-317-5700	751-3550
AMEX: AMC ■ *Web:* www.americanmortgageco.com					
AMLI Residential Properties Trust 125 S Wacker Dr Suite 3100	Chicago	IL	60606	312-443-1477	443-0909
NYSE: AML ■ *Web:* www.amlires.com					
AmREIT 8 Greenway Plaza Suite 1000	Houston	TX	77046	713-850-1400	850-0498
AMEX: AMY ■ *TF:* 800-888-4400 ■ *Web:* www.amreit.com					
Annaly Mortgage Management Inc 1211 Ave of the Americas Suite 2902	New York	NY	10036	212-696-0100	696-9809
NYSE: NLY ■ *TF:* 800-487-9947 ■ *Web:* www.annaly.com					
Anthracite Capital Inc 40 E 52nd St	New York	NY	10022	212-409-3333	
NYSE: AHR ■ *Web:* www.blackrock.com/anthracite					
Anworth Mortgage Asset Corp 1299 Ocean Ave 2nd Fl	Santa Monica	CA	90401	310-255-4493	434-0070
NYSE: ANH ■ *Web:* www.anworth.com					
Apartment Investment & Management Co 4582 S Ulster Street Pkwy Suite 1100	Denver	CO	80237	303-757-8101	759-3226
NYSE: AIV ■ *TF:* 888-789-8600 ■ *Web:* www.aimco.com					
Arbor Realty Trust Inc 333 Earle Ovington Blvd Suite 900	Uniondale	NY	11553	516-832-8002	832-8045
NYSE: ABR ■ *TF:* 800-272-6710 ■ *Web:* www.arborrealtytrust.com					
ARC Corporate Realty Trust Inc 1401 Broad St 2nd Fl	Clifton	NJ	07013	973-249-1000	249-1001
Web: www.arcproperties.com					
Archstone-Smith Trust 9200 E Panorama Cir Suite 400	Englewood	CO	80112	303-708-5959	858-0023
NYSE: ASN ■ *TF:* 877-272-4786 ■ *Web:* www.archstonesmith.com					
Arden Realty Inc 11601 Wilshire Blvd 4th Fl	Los Angeles	CA	90025	310-966-2600	966-2699
NYSE: ARI ■ *Web:* www.ardenrealty.com					
Arizona Land Income Corp 2999 N 44th St Suite 100	Phoenix	AZ	85018	602-952-6800	952-0924
AMEX: AZL ■ *TF:* 800-999-1818					
Ashford Hospitality Trust Inc 14185 Dallas Pkwy Suite 1100	Dallas	TX	75254	972-490-9600	980-2705
NYSE: AHT ■ *Web:* www.ahtreit.com					
Associated Estates Realty Corp 1 AEC Pkwy	Richmond Heights	OH	44143	216-261-5000	289-9600
NYSE: AEC ■ *TF:* 800-440-2372 ■ *Web:* www.aecrealty.com					
AutoStar 180 Glastonbury Blvd Suite 201	Glastonbury	CT	06033	860-815-5900	815-5901
Web: www.autostar.com					
AvalonBay Communities Inc 2900 Eisenhower Ave Suite 300	Alexandria	VA	22314	703-329-6300	329-1459*
NYSE: AVB ■ *Fax: Investor Rel ■ *Web:* www.avalonbay.com					
Babcock & Brown Residential LLC 301 S College St Suite 3850	Charlotte	NC	28202	704-944-0100	944-2039
AMEX: BNP ■ *Web:* www.bnproperties.com					
Berkshire Income Realty Inc 1 Beacon St	Boston	MA	02108	617-523-7722	646-2375
AMEX: BIR_pa ■ *TF:* 888-867-0100 ■ *Web:* www.berkshireincomerealty.com					
BioMed Realty Trust Inc 17140 Bernardo Center Dr Suite 222	San Diego	CA	92128	858-485-9840	485-9843
NYSE: BMR ■ *Web:* www.biomedrealty.com					
Boardwalk Real Estate Investment Trust 1501 1st St SW Suite 200	Calgary	AB	T2P0W1	403-531-9255	531-9565
TSX: BEI ■ *Web:* www.boardwalkreit.com					
Boston Properties Inc 800 Boylston St Suite 1900	Boston	MA	02199	617-236-3300	236-3684
NYSE: BXP ■ *Web:* www.bostonproperties.com					
Brandywine Realty Trust 555 E Lancaster Ave Suite 100	Radnor	PA	19087	610-325-5600	325-5622
NYSE: BDN ■ *TF:* 866-426-5400 ■ *Web:* www.brandywinerealty.com					
BRE Properties Inc 525 Market St 4th Fl	San Francisco	CA	94105	415-445-6530	445-6505
NYSE: BRE ■ *Web:* www.breproperties.com					
BRT Realty Trust 60 Cutter Mill Rd Suite 303	Great Neck	NY	11021	516-466-3100	466-3132
NYSE: BRT ■ *TF:* 800-450-5816 ■ *Web:* www.brtrealty.com					
Cal-American Properties Trust 1925 Century Park E Suite 2100	Los Angeles	CA	90067	310-277-6318	277-0738
Camden Property Trust 3 E Greenway Plaza Suite 1300	Houston	TX	77046	713-354-2500	354-2700*
NYSE: CPT ■ *Fax: Mktg ■ *TF:* 800-922-6336 ■ *Web:* www.camdenliving.com					
Canadian Real Estate Investment Trust 175 Bloor St E Suite 500	Toronto	ON	M4W3R8	416-628-7771	628-7777
TSX: REF ■ *Web:* www.creit.ca					
Capital Alliance Income Trust Ltd 100 Pine St Suite 2450	San Francisco	CA	94111	415-288-9575	288-9590
AMEX: CAA ■ *Web:* www.caitreit.com					
Capital Automotive Real Estate Services Inc 8270 Greensboro Dr Suite 950	McLean	VA	22102	703-288-3075	288-3375
TF: 877-422-7288 ■ *Web:* www.capitalautomotive.com					
Capital Lease Funding Inc 1065 Ave of the Americas 19th Fl	New York	NY	10018	212-217-6300	217-6301
NYSE: LSE ■ *Web:* www.caplease.com					
Capital Trust Inc 410 Park Ave 14th Fl	New York	NY	10022	212-655-0220	655-0044
NYSE: CT ■ *Web:* www.capitaltrust.com					
CAPREIT Inc 11200 Rockville Pike Suite 100	Rockville	MD	20852	301-231-8700	468-8392
Web: capreit.com					
Capstead Mortgage Corp 8401 N Central Expy Suite 800	Dallas	TX	75225	214-874-2323	874-2398
NYSE: CMO ■ *TF:* 800-358-2323 ■ *Web:* www.capstead.com					
CBL & Assoc Properties Inc CBL Ctr 2030 Hamilton Place Blvd Suite 500	Chattanooga	TN	37421	423-855-0001	490-8662
NYSE: CBL ■ *Web:* www.cblproperties.com					
Cedar Shopping Centers Inc 44 S Bayles Ave Suite 304	Port Washington	NY	11050	516-767-6492	767-6497
NYSE: CDR ■ *TF:* 800-564-3128 ■ *Web:* www.cedarshoppingcenters.com					
CenterPoint Properties Trust 1808 Swift Dr	Oak Brook	IL	60523	630-586-8000	586-8010
NYSE: CNT ■ *Web:* www.centerpoint-prop.com					
Centro Properties Group 131 Dartmouth St	Boston	MA	02116	617-247-2200	266-0885
Web: www.centroproperties.net					
Centro Properties Group 420 Lexington Ave 7th Fl	New York	NY	10170	646-344-8600	869-3989*
*Fax Area Code: 212 ■ *TF:* 800-468-7526 ■ *Web:* www.centroprop.com					
Centro Properties Group 580 W Germantown Pike Suite 200	Plymouth Meeting	PA	19462	610-825-7100	834-8110
Web: www.centroprop.com					
Chelsea Property Group Inc 105 Eisenhower Pkwy	Roseland	NJ	07068	973-228-6111	228-3891
Web: www.cpgi.com					
Church Loans & Investment Trust PO Box 8203	Amarillo	TX	79114	806-358-3666	358-1430
TF: 800-692-1111 ■ *Web:* www.churchloans.com					
CNL Hospitality Properties Inc 450 S Orange Ave	Orlando	FL	32801	407-650-1000	540-2211
TF: 866-312-2490 ■ *Web:* www.cnlservice.com					
Cogdell Spencer Inc 4401 Barclay Downs Dr Suite 300	Charlotte	NC	28209	704-940-2900	940-2957
NYSE: CSA ■ *Web:* www.cogdellspencer.com					
Colonial Properties Trust 2101 6th Ave N Suite 750	Birmingham	AL	35203	205-250-8700	250-8890
NYSE: CLP ■ *Web:* www.colonialprop.com					
Commercial Properties Realty Trust 5630 Bankers Ave	Baton Rouge	LA	70808	225-924-7206	924-1235
TF: 800-648-9064 ■ *Web:* www.cpdcbr.com					
Community Development Trust 1350 Broadway Suite 700	New York	NY	10018	212-271-5080	271-5079
Web: www.commdevtrust.com					
Corporate Office Properties Trust 6711 Columbia Gateway Dr Suite 300	Columbia	MD	21046	443-285-5400	285-7650
NYSE: OFC ■ *Web:* www.copt.com					
Cousins Properties Inc 191 Peachtree St NE Suite 3600	Atlanta	GA	30303	404-407-1000	407-1002
NYSE: CUZ ■ *TF:* 800-926-8746 ■ *Web:* www.cousinsproperties.com					
Crescent Real Estate Equities Co 777 Main St Suite 2100	Fort Worth	TX	76102	817-321-2100	321-2000
NYSE: CEI ■ *Web:* www.crescent.com					
CRIIMI MAE Inc 701 13th St NW Suite 1000	Washington	DC	20005	202-715-9500	
TF: 800-266-0535 ■ *Web:* www.cwcapital.com					
Developers Diversified Realty Corp 3300 Enterprise Pkwy	Beachwood	OH	44122	216-755-5500	755-1500
NYSE: DDR ■ *TF:* 800-258-7289 ■ *Web:* www.ddrc.com					
DiamondRock Hospitality Co 6903 Rockledge Dr Suite 800	Bethesda	MD	20817	240-744-1150	744-1199
NYSE: DRH ■ *Web:* www.drhc.com					
Digital Realty Trust Inc 560 Mission St Suite 2900	San Francisco	CA	94105	415-738-6500	738-6501
NYSE: DLR ■ *Web:* www.digitalrealtytrust.com					
Dividend Capital Trust 518 17th St Suite 1700	Denver	CO	80202	303-228-2200	228-2201
TF: 866-324-7348 ■ *Web:* www.dividendcapitaltrust.com					
Donahue Schriber Realty Group Inc 200 E Baker St Suite 100	Costa Mesa	CA	92626	714-545-1400	545-4222
Web: www.donahueschriber.com					
Duke Realty Corp 600 E 96th St Suite 100	Indianapolis	IN	46240	317-808-6000	808-6794
NYSE: DRE ■ *TF:* 800-875-3366 ■ *Web:* www.dukerealty.com					
Dynex Capital Inc 4551 Cox Rd Suite 300	Glen Allen	VA	23060	804-217-5800	217-5860
NYSE: DX ■ *Web:* www.dynexcapital.com					
EastGroup Properties Inc 188 E Capitol St Suite 300	Jackson	MS	39201	601-354-3555	352-1441
NYSE: EGP ■ *TF:* 800-337-5602 ■ *Web:* www.eastgroup.net					
ECC Capital Corp 2040 Main St Suite 800	Irvine	CA	92606	949-856-8300	856-7358
NYSE: ECR ■ *TF:* 800-899-0926 ■ *Web:* www.ecccapital.com					
Education Realty Trust Inc 530 Oak Court Dr Suite 300	Memphis	TN	38117	901-259-2500	259-2594
NYSE: EDR					
Entertainment Properties Trust 30 W Pershing Rd Suite 201	Kansas City	MO	64108	816-472-1700	472-5794
NYSE: EPR ■ *TF:* 888-377-7348 ■ *Web:* www.eprkc.com					
Equity Inns Inc 7700 Wolf River Blvd	Germantown	TN	38138	901-754-7774	754-2374
NYSE: ENN ■ *Web:* www.equityinns.com					
Equity Lifestyle Properties Inc 2 N Riverside Plaza Suite 800	Chicago	IL	60606	312-279-1400	279-1710
NYSE: ELS ■ *Web:* www1.mhchomes.com					
Equity Office Properties Trust 2 N Riverside Plaza Suite 2100	Chicago	IL	60606	312-466-3300	454-0332
NYSE: EOP ■ *Web:* www.equityoffice.com					

Company	City	State	ZIP	Phone	Fax
Equity One Inc 1696 NE Miami Gardens Dr *NYSE: EQY* ■ *TF:* 800-867-2777 ■ *Web:* www.equityone.net	North Miami Beach	FL	33179	305-947-1664	947-1734
Equity Residential 2 N Riverside Plaza Suite 400 *NYSE: EQR* ■ *Web:* www.equityapartments.com	Chicago	IL	60606	312-474-1300	454-8703
Essex Property Trust Inc 925 E Meadow Dr *NYSE: ESS* ■ *Web:* www.essexproperties.com	Palo Alto	CA	94303	650-494-3700	494-8743
Federal Realty Investment Trust 1626 E Jefferson St *NYSE: FRT* ■ *TF:* 800-658-8980 ■ *Web:* www.federalrealty.com	Rockville	MD	20852	301-998-8100	998-3700
FelCor Lodging Trust Inc 545 E John Carpenter Fwy Suite 1300 *NYSE: FCH* ■ *Web:* www.felcor.com	Irving	TX	75062	972-444-4900	444-4949
Feldman Mall Properties Inc 2201 E Camelback Rd Suite 350 *NYSE: FMP* ■ *Web:* www.feldmanmall.com	Phoenix	AZ	85016	602-277-5559	277-7774
First Industrial Realty Trust Inc 311 S Wacker Dr Suite 4000 *NYSE: FR* ■ *TF:* 800-894-8778 ■ *Web:* www.firstindustrial.com	Chicago	IL	60606	312-344-4300	922-6320
First Potomac Realty Trust 7600 Wisconsin Ave Suite 1100 *NYSE: FPO* ■ *Web:* www.first-potomac.com	Bethesda	MD	20814	301-986-9200	986-5554
First REIT of New Jersey 505 Main St	Hackensack	NJ	07602	201-488-6400	487-7881
Franklin Street Properties Corp 401 Edgewater Pl Suite 200 *AMEX: FSP* ■ *TF:* 877-686-9496 ■ *Web:* www.franklinstreetproperties.com	Wakefield	MA	01880	781-557-1300	246-2807
Friedman Billings Ramsey Group Inc 1001 19th St N 18th Fl *NYSE: FBR* ■ *TF:* 800-846-5050 ■ *Web:* www.fbr.com	Arlington	VA	22209	703-312-9500	312-9501
G & L Realty Corp 439 N Bedford Dr *Web:* www.glrealty.com	Beverly Hills	CA	90210	310-273-9930	248-2222
Gables Residential Trust 777 Yamato Rd Suite 510 *Web:* www.gables.com	Boca Raton	FL	33431	561-997-9700	241-9506
GE Capital Solutions Franchise Finance 450 S Orange Ave *TF:* 877-667-4769 ■ *Web:* gecapsol.com	Orlando	FL	32801	407-540-2000	540-2004
General Growth Properties Inc 110 N Wacker Dr *NYSE: GGP* ■ *Web:* www.generalgrowth.com	Chicago	IL	60606	312-960-5000	960-5475
Glenborough Realty Trust Inc 400 S El Camino Real Suite 1100 *NYSE: GLB* ■ *Web:* www.glenborough.com	San Mateo	CA	94402	650-343-9300	343-9690
Glimcher Realty Trust 150 E Gay St 24th Fl *NYSE: GRT* ■ *TF:* 800-987-8786 ■ *Web:* www.glimcher.com	Columbus	OH	43215	614-621-9000	621-9311
Gramercy Capital Corp 420 Lexington Ave *NYSE: GKK* ■ *Web:* www.gramercycapitalcorp.com	New York	NY	10170	212-297-1000	297-1090
Hanover Capital Mortgage Holdings Inc 55 Broadway Suite 3002 *AMEX: HCM* ■ *Web:* www.hanovercapitalholdings.com	New York	NY	10006	212-227-0075	227-5434
Health Care Property Investors Inc 3760 Kilroy Airport Way Suite 300 *NYSE: HCP* ■ *TF:* 888-604-1990 ■ *Web:* www.hcpi.com	Long Beach	CA	90806	562-733-5100	733-5200
Health Care REIT Inc 1 SeaGate Suite 1500 *NYSE: HCN* ■ *Web:* www.hcreit.com	Toledo	OH	43603	419-247-2800	247-2826
Healthcare Realty Trust Inc 3310 West End Ave Suite 700 *NYSE: HR* ■ *Web:* www.healthcarerealty.com	Nashville	TN	37203	615-269-8175	269-8260
Hersha Hospitality Trust 1909 N Front St *AMEX: HT* ■ *Web:* www.hersha.com	Harrisburg	PA	17102	717-236-4400	774-7383
Highland Hospitality Corp 8405 Greensboro Dr Suite 500 *NYSE: HIH* ■ *Web:* www.highlandhospitality.com	McLean	VA	22102	703-336-4901	336-4905
Highwoods Properties Inc 3100 Smoketree Ct Suite 600 *NYSE: HIW* ■ *TF:* 866-449-6637 ■ *Web:* www.highwoods.com	Raleigh	NC	27604	919-872-4924	876-2448
HMG/Courtland Properties Inc 1870 S Bayshore Dr *AMEX: HMG*	Coconut Grove	FL	33133	305-854-6803	856-7342
Home Properties Inc 850 Clinton Sq *NYSE: HME* ■ *Web:* www.homeproperties.com	Rochester	NY	14604	585-546-4900	546-5433
Horizon Group Properties Inc 5000 Hakes Dr *Web:* www.horizongroup.com	Muskegon	MI	49441	231-798-9100	798-5100
Hospitality Properties Trust 400 Centre St *NYSE: HPT* ■ *Web:* www.hptreit.com	Newton	MA	02458	617-964-8389	969-5730
Host Hotels & Resorts Inc 6903 Rockledge Dr Suite 1500 *NYSE: HST* ■ *TF:* 800-724-4268 ■ *Web:* www.hosthotels.com	Bethesda	MD	20817	240-744-1000	744-5125
HRPT Properties Trust 400 Centre St *NYSE: HRP* ■ *Web:* www.hrpreit.com	Newton	MA	02458	617-332-3990	332-2261
Impac Mortgage Holdings Inc 19500 Jamboree Rd *NYSE: IMH* ■ *TF:* 800-597-4101 ■ *Web:* www.impaccompanies.com	Irvine	CA	92612	949-475-3600	
Income Opportunity Realty Investors Inc 1800 Valley View Ln Suite 300 *AMEX: IOT* ■ *Web:* www.incomeopp-realty.com	Dallas	TX	75234	469-522-4200	522-4299
ING Clarion Partners 230 Park Ave 12th Fl *TF:* 800-776-4696 ■ *Web:* www.ingclarion.com	New York	NY	10169	212-883-2500	883-2700
Ing Real Estate Canada 202 Brownlow Ave Tower 2 Suite D200 *TF:* 866-786-6481 ■ *Web:* www.ingrealestate.ca	Dartmouth	NS	B3B1T5	902-421-1222	420-0559
Inland Real Estate Corp 2901 Butterfield Rd *NYSE: IRC* ■ **Fax:* Investor Rel ■ *TF:* 888-331-4732 ■ *Web:* www.inlandrealestate.com	Oak Brook	IL	60523	630-218-8000	218-7357*
Innkeepers USA Trust 340 Royal Poinciana Plaza *NYSE: KPA* ■ *Web:* www.innkeepersusa.com	Palm Beach	FL	33480	561-835-1800	835-0457
InnSuites Hospitality Trust 1615 E Northern Ave Suite 102 *AMEX: IHT* ■ *Web:* www.innsuitestrust.com	Phoenix	AZ	85020	602-997-6285	678-0281
Investors Real Estate Trust 12 S Main St *NASDAQ: IRETS* ■ *Web:* www.irets.com	Minot	ND	58702	701-837-4738	838-7785
iStar Financial Inc 1114 Ave of the Americas 39th Fl *NYSE: SFI* ■ *Web:* www.istarfinancial.com	New York	NY	10036	212-930-9400	930-9494
Kilroy Realty Corp 12200 W Olympic Blvd Suite 200 *NYSE: KRC* ■ *Web:* www.kilroyrealty.com	Los Angeles	CA	90064	310-481-8400	481-6501
Kimco Realty Corp 3333 New Hyde Pk Rd Suite 100 *NYSE: KIM* ■ *TF:* 800-645-6292 ■ *Web:* www.kimcorealty.com	New Hyde Park	NY	11042	516-869-9000	869-9001
Kite Realty Group Trust 30 S Meridian St Suite 1100 *NYSE: KRG* ■ *TF:* 888-577-5600 ■ *Web:* www.kiterealty.com	Indianapolis	IN	46204	317-577-5600	577-5605
KKR Financial Corp 555 California St Suite 5000 *NYSE: KFN* ■ *Web:* www.kkrfinancial.com	San Francisco	CA	94104	415-315-3620	391-3077
La Quinta Properties Inc 909 Hidden Ridge Suite 600 *TF:* 877-204-9204	Irving	TX	75038	214-492-6600	492-6971
LaSalle Hotel Properties 3 Bethesda Metro Center Suite 1200 *NYSE: LHO* ■ *Web:* www.lasallehotels.com	Bethesda	MD	20814	301-941-1500	941-1553
Lexington Corporate Properties Trust 1 Penn Plaza Suite 4015 *NYSE: LXP* ■ *Web:* www.lxp.com	New York	NY	10119	212-692-7260	594-6600
Lexington Realty Trust Inc 1 Penn Plaza Suite 4015 *Web:* www.lxp.com	New York	NY	10119	212-692-7200	594-6600
Liberty Property Trust 500 Chesterfield Pkwy *NYSE: LRY* ■ *Web:* www.libertyproperty.com	Malvern	PA	19355	610-648-1700	644-4129
Lillibridge Healthcare Real Estate Trust 200 W Madison St Suite 3200 *Web:* lillibridge.com	Chicago	IL	60606	312-408-1370	408-1415
LTC Properties Inc 31365 Oak Crest Dr Suite 200 *NYSE: LTC* ■ *Web:* www.ltcproperties.com	Westlake Village	CA	91361	805-981-8655	981-8663
Luminent Mortgage Capital Inc 101 California St Suite 1350 *NYSE: LUM* ■ *Web:* www.luminentcapital.com	San Francisco	CA	94111	415-217-4500	217-4518
Macerich Co 401 Wilshire Blvd Suite 700 *NYSE: MAC* ■ *TF:* 800-421-7237 ■ *Web:* www.macerich.com	Santa Monica	CA	90401	310-394-6911	395-2791
Mack-Cali Realty Corp 343 Thornall St *NYSE: CLI* ■ *Web:* www.mack-cali.com	Edison	NJ	08837	732-590-1000	205-8237
Madison Park Financial Corp 409 13th St 8th Fl *Web:* www.mpfcorp.com	Oakland	CA	94612	510-452-2944	452-2973
Maguire Properties Inc 333 S Grand Ave Suite 400 *NYSE: MPG* ■ *Web:* www.maguirepartners.com	Los Angeles	CA	90071	213-626-3300	687-4758
Maxus Realty Trust Inc 104 Armour Rd *NASDAQ: MRTI*	North Kansas City	MO	64116	816-303-4500	221-1829
Medical Properties Trust Inc 1000 Urban Center Dr Suite 501 *NYSE: MPW* ■ *Web:* www.medicalpropertiestrust.com	Birmingham	AL	35242	205-969-3755	969-3756
Meredith Enterprises Inc 3000 Sand Hill Rd Bldg 2 Suite 120 *Web:* www.meredithreit.com	Menlo Park	CA	94025	650-233-7140	233-7160
MFA Mortgage Investments Inc 350 Park Ave 21st Fl *NYSE: MFA* ■ *Web:* www.mfa-reit.com	New York	NY	10022	212-207-6400	207-6420
MHI Hospitality Corp 4801 Courthouse St Suite 201 *AMEX: MDH* ■ *Web:* www.mhihospitality.com	Williamsburg	VA	23188	757-229-5648	564-8801
Mid-America Apartment Communities Inc 6584 Poplar Ave Suite 300 *NYSE: MAA* ■ *Web:* www.maac.net	Memphis	TN	38138	901-682-6600	682-6667
Monmouth Real Estate Investment Corp 3499 Rt 9 N Suite 3C *NASDAQ: MNRTA* ■ *Web:* www.mreic.com	Freehold	NJ	07728	732-577-9997	577-9981
National Health Investors Inc 100 Vine St *NYSE: NHI* ■ *Web:* www.nhinvestors.com	Murfreesboro	TN	37130	615-890-9100	890-0123
National Health Realty Inc 100 Vine St *AMEX: NHR* ■ *Web:* www.nationalhealthrealty.com	Murfreesboro	TN	37130	615-890-2020	890-0123
National Retail Properties 450 S Orange Ave Suite 900 *TF:* 800-666-7348	Orlando	FL	32801	407-265-7348	206-2194
Nationwide Health Properties Inc 610 Newport Ctr Dr Suite 1150 *NYSE: NHP* ■ *Web:* www.nhp-reit.com	Newport Beach	CA	92660	949-718-4400	759-6876
NB Capital Corp 65 E 55th St *NYSE: NBD*	New York	NY	10022	212-632-8532	632-8789
New York Mortgage Trust Inc 1301 Ave of the Americas 7th Fl *NYSE: NTR* ■ *TF:* 800-491-6962 ■ *Web:* www.nymtrust.com	New York	NY	10019	212-634-9400	655-6269
Newcastle Investment Corp 1345 Ave of the Americas 46th Fl *NYSE: NCT* ■ *Web:* www.newcastleinv.com	New York	NY	10105	212-798-6100	
NorthStar Realty Finance Corp 399 Park Ave 18th Fl *NYSE: NRF* ■ *Web:* www.nrfc.com	New York	NY	10022	212-547-2600	547-2700
Novastar Financial Inc 8140 Ward Pkwy Suite 300 *NYSE: NFI* ■ **Fax Area Code:* 913 ■ *TF:* 800-469-4270 ■ *Web:* www.novastarmortgage.com	Kansas City	MO	64114	816-237-7000	237-7515*
Omega Healthcare Investors Inc 9690 Deereco Rd Suite 100 *NYSE: OHI* ■ *TF:* 866-226-6342 ■ *Web:* www.omegahealthcare.com	Timonium	MD	21093	410-427-1700	427-8800
One Liberty Properties Inc 60 Cutter Mill Rd Suite 303 *NYSE: OLP* ■ *TF:* 800-450-5816 ■ *Web:* www.1liberty.com	Great Neck	NY	11021	516-466-3100	466-3132
Parkway Properties Inc 188 E Capitol St Suite 1000 *NYSE: PKY* ■ *TF:* 800-748-1667 ■ *Web:* www.pky.com	Jackson	MS	39201	601-948-4091	949-4077
Pennsylvania Real Estate Investment Trust 200 S Broad St 3rd Fl *NYSE: PEI* ■ *Web:* www.preit.com	Philadelphia	PA	19102	215-875-0700	546-7311
Plum Creek Timber Co Inc 999 3rd Ave Suite 4300 *NYSE: PCL* ■ *Web:* www.plumcreek.com	Seattle	WA	98104	206-467-3600	467-3795
PMC Commercial Trust 17950 Preston Rd Suite 600 *AMEX: PCC* ■ *TF:* 800-486-3223 ■ *Web:* www.pmctrust.com	Dallas	TX	75252	972-349-3200	349-3265
Post Properties Inc 4401 Northside Pkwy Suite 800 *NYSE: PPS* ■ **Fax:* Hum Res ■ *Web:* www.postproperties.com	Atlanta	GA	30327	404-846-5000	846-6161*
Presidential Realty Corp 180 S Broadway *AMEX: PDL/A* ■ *TF:* 800-948-2977	White Plains	NY	10605	914-948-1300	948-1327
Prime Group Realty Trust 77 W Wacker Dr Suite 3900 *NYSE: PGE* ■ *Web:* www.pgrt.com	Chicago	IL	60601	312-917-1300	917-1310
Prime Retail LP 217 E Redwood St 20th Fl **Fax:* Hum Res ■ *TF:* 800-980-7467 ■ *Web:* www.primeretail.com	Baltimore	MD	21202	410-234-0782	234-0402*
ProLogis 4545 Airport Way *NYSE: PLD* ■ *TF:* 800-566-2706 ■ *Web:* www.prologis.com	Denver	CO	80239	303-375-9292	567-5600
PS Business Parks Inc 701 Western Ave *AMEX: PSB* ■ *TF:* 800-567-0759 ■ *Web:* www.psbusinessparks.com	Glendale	CA	91201	818-244-8080	242-0566
Public Storage Inc 701 Western Ave *NYSE: PSA* ■ **Fax:* Mail Rm ■ *TF Cust Svc:* 800-567-0759 ■ *Web:* www.publicstorage.com	Glendale	CA	91201	818-244-8080	291-1015*
RAIT Investment Trust 2929 Arch St Suite 1703 *NYSE: RAS* ■ *TF:* 800-826-6096 ■ *Web:* www.raitinvestmenttrust.com	Philadelphia	PA	19104	215-701-9555	701-8282
Ramco-Gershenson Properties Trust 31500 Northwestern Hwy Suite 300 *NYSE: RPT* ■ *TF:* 800-225-6765 ■ *Web:* www.ramcogershenson.com	Farmington Hills	MI	48334	248-350-9900	350-9925
Realty Income Corp 220 W Crest St *NYSE: O* ■ *TF:* 800-375-6700 ■ *Web:* www.realtyincome.com	Escondido	CA	92025	760-741-2111	741-8674
Redwood Trust Inc 1 Belvedere Pl Suite 300 *NYSE: RWT* ■ *Web:* www.redwoodtrust.com	Mill Valley	CA	94941	415-389-7373	381-1773
Regency Centers 1 Independent Dr Suite 114 *NYSE: REG* ■ *TF:* 800-950-6333 ■ *Web:* www.regencyrealty.com	Jacksonville	FL	32202	904-598-7000	634-3428
Republic Property Trust 13861 Sunrise Valley Dr Suite 410 *NYSE: RPB* ■ *Web:* www.republicpropertytrust.com	Herndon	VA	20171	703-880-2900	880-2901
Resource Capital Corp 712 5th Ave 10th Fl *NYSE: RSO*	New York	NY	10019	212-974-1708	245-6372
Retirement Residences Real Estate Investment Trust 55 Standish Ct 8th Fl *TSX: RRR.UN* ■ *Web:* www.retirementreit.com	Mississauga	ON	L5R4B2	289-360-1200	360-1201
Revenue Properties (America) Inc 2542 Williams Blvd *Web:* www.sizeler.net	Kenner	LA	70062	504-904-8500	904-8555
Rex Corp Realty 625 Rex Corp Plaza *TF:* 888-732-5766 ■ *Web:* www.rexcorprealty.com	Uniondale	NY	11556	516-506-6000	506-6800
RioCan Real Estate Investment Trust 130 King St W Suite 700 *TSX: REI.UN* ■ *TF:* 800-465-2733 ■ *Web:* www.riocan.com	Toronto	ON	M5X1E2	416-866-3033	866-3020
Roberts Realty Investors Inc 450 Northridge Pkwy Suite 302 *AMEX: RPI*	Atlanta	GA	30350	770-394-6000	551-5914
Royal Host Real Estate Investment Trust 808 42nd Ave SE Suite 103 *TSX: RYL* ■ *Web:* www.royalhost.com	Calgary	AB	T2G1Y9	403-259-9800	259-8580
Saul Centers Inc 7501 Wisconsin Ave Suite 1500 *NYSE: BFS* ■ *Web:* www.saulcenters.com	Bethesda	MD	20814	301-986-6000	986-6079
Senior Housing Properties Trust 400 Centre St *NYSE: SNH* ■ *Web:* www.snhreit.com	Newton	MA	02458	617-796-8350	796-8349
Simon Property Group Inc 225 W Washington St *NYSE: SPG* ■ **Fax:* Cust Svc ■ *Web:* www.simon.com	Indianapolis	IN	46204	317-636-1600	263-7658*
SL Green Realty Corp 420 Lexington Ave *NYSE: SLG* ■ *Web:* www.slgreen.com	New York	NY	10170	212-594-2700	216-1790
Spirit Finance Corp 14631 N Scottsdale Rd Suite 200 *NYSE: SFC* ■ *TF:* 866-557-7474 ■ *Web:* www.spiritfinance.com	Scottsdale	AZ	85254	480-606-0820	606-0826
Starwood Hotels & Resorts Worldwide Inc 1111 Westchester Ave *NYSE: HOT* ■ *TF Cust Svc:* 877-443-4585 ■ *Web:* www.starwoodhotels.com	White Plains	NY	10604	914-640-8100	640-8310
Strategic Hotels & Resorts 77 W Wacker Dr Suite 4600 *NYSE: SLH* ■ *Web:* www.strategichotels.com	Chicago	IL	60601	312-658-5000	658-5799
Sun Communities Inc 27777 Franklin Rd Suite 200 *NYSE: SUI* ■ *Web:* www.suncommunities.com	Southfield	MI	48034	248-208-2500	208-2640

Phone | Fax

Sunstone Hotel Investors LLC
903 Calle Amanecer Suite 100 ... San Clemente CA 92673 949-369-4000 369-4010
NYSE: SHO ■ *Web:* www.sunstonehotels.com
Supertel Hospitality Inc 309 N 5th St PO Box 1448 ... Norfolk NE 68701 402-371-2520 371-5783
NASDAQ: SPPR ■ *Web:* www.supertelinc.com
Tanger Factory Outlet Centers Inc
3200 Northline Ave Suite 360 ... Greensboro NC 27408 336-292-3010 852-2096
NYSE: SKT ■ *TF:* 800-438-8474 ■ *Web:* www.tangeroutlet.com
Taubman Centers Inc 200 E Long Lake Rd Suite 300 ... Bloomfield Hills MI 48303 248-258-6800 258-7683
NYSE: TCO ■ *TF:* 800-828-2626 ■ *Web:* www.taubman.com
Thayer Lodging Group 410 Severn Ave Suite 314 ... Annapolis MD 21403 410-268-0515 268-1582
Web: www.thayerlodging.com
Thornburg Mortgage Co 150 Washington Ave Suite 302 ... Santa Fe NM 87501 505-989-1900 989-8156
NYSE: TMA ■ *TF:* 888-898-8698 ■ *Web:* www.thornburgmortgage.com
Transcontinental Realty Investors Inc
1800 Valley View Ln 1 Hickory Ctr ... Dallas TX 75234 469-522-4200 522-4299
NYSE: TCI ■ *TF:* 800-400-6407 ■ *Web:* www.transconrealty-invest.com
United Dominion Realty Trust Inc 400 E Cary St ... Richmond VA 23219 804-780-2691 343-1912
NYSE: UDR ■ *TF:* 800-800-2691 ■ *Web:* www.udrt.com
United Mobile Homes Inc 3499 Rt 9 N Suite 3C ... Freehold NJ 07728 732-577-9997 577-9980
AMEX: UMH ■ *Web:* www.umh.com
Universal Health Realty Income Trust
Universal Corporate Ctr 367 S Gulph Rd ... King of Prussia PA 19406 610-768-3300 382-4407
NYSE: UHT ■ *Web:* www.uhrit.com
Urstadt Biddle Properties Inc 321 Railroad Ave ... Greenwich CT 06830 203-863-8200 861-6755
NYSE: UBP ■ *TF:* 800-323-8216 ■ *Web:* www.ubproperties.com
Ventas Inc 10350 Ormsby Pk Pl Suite 300 ... Louisville KY 40223 502-357-9000 357-9029
NYSE: VTR ■ *TF:* 877-483-6827 ■ *Web:* www.ventasreit.com
Vornado Realty Trust 210 Rt 4 E ... Paramus NJ 07652 201-587-1000 587-0600
NYSE: VNO ■ *TF:* 800-242-4119 ■ *Web:* www.vno.com
Washington Real Estate Investment Trust
6110 Executive Blvd Suite 800 ... Rockville MD 20852 301-984-9400 984-9610
NYSE: WRE ■ *TF:* 800-565-9748 ■ *Web:* www.washreit.com
Watson Land Co 22010 S Wilmington Ave Suite 400 ... Carson CA 90745 310-952-6400 522-8788
Web: www.watsonlandcompany.com
Weingarten Realty Investors 2600 Citadel Plaza Dr Suite 300 ... Houston TX 77008 713-866-6000 866-6049
NYSE: WRI ■ *TF:* 800-688-8865 ■ *Web:* www.weingarten.com
Wells Real Estate Investment Trust 6200 The Corners Pkwy ... Norcross GA 30092 770-449-7800 243-8450
TF: 800-282-1581 ■ *Web:* www.wellsref.com
Westfield America Inc 11601 Wilshire Blvd 11th Fl ... Los Angeles CA 90025 310-478-4456 478-1267
Web: www.westfield.com
Wilmorite Properties Inc 1265 Scottsville Rd ... Rochester NY 14624 585-464-9400 464-0706
Web: www.wilmorite.com
Windrose Medical Properties Trust
3502 Woodview Trace Suite 100 ... Indianapolis IN 46268 317-860-8180 860-9190
NYSE: WRS ■ *Web:* www.windroseintl.com
Winston Hotels Inc 2626 Glenwood Ave Suite 200 ... Raleigh NC 27608 919-510-6010 510-6832
NYSE: WXH ■ *Web:* www.winstonhotels.com
Winthrop Realty Trust 7 Bulfinch Pl Suite 500 ... Boston MA 02114 617-570-4614 570-4746
NYSE: FUR ■ *Web:* www.winthropreit.com
WP Carey & Co LLC 50 Rockefeller Plaza 2nd Fl ... New York NY 10020 212-492-1100 492-8922
NYSE: WPC ■ *TF:* 800-972-2739 ■ *Web:* www.wpcarey.com

658 REAL ESTATE MANAGERS & OPERATORS

SEE ALSO Hotels & Hotel Companies p. 1832; Retirement Communities p. 2297

Phone | Fax

Acadia Realty Trust 1311 Mamaroneck Ave Suite 260 ... White Plains NY 10605 914-288-8100 428-2380
NYSE: AKR ■ *TF:* 800-227-5570 ■ *Web:* www.acadiarealty.com
Agree Realty Corp 31850 Northwestern Hwy ... Farmington Hills MI 48334 248-737-4190 737-9110
NYSE: ADC ■ *Web:* www.agreerealty.com
Alexander Muss & Sons 35 Sea Coast Terr Suite 1-W ... Brooklyn NY 11235 718-646-3800
Alexander Summer LLC E 80 Rt 4 Suite 300 ... Paramus NJ 07652 201-712-1000 712-1274
Web: www.alexandersummer.com
Alexander's Inc 210 Rt 4 E ... Paramus NJ 07652 201-587-8541 587-0600
NYSE: ALX ■ *TF:* 800-242-4119 ■ *Web:* www.alx-inc.com
Alexandria Real Estate Equities Inc
385 E Colorado Blvd Suite 299 ... Pasadena CA 91101 626-578-0777 578-0770
NYSE: ARE
Allied Realty Co 20 26th St ... Huntington WV 25703 304-525-9125 697-5511
Allred Douglas Co 11512 El Camino Real Suite 100 ... San Diego CA 92130 858-793-0202 793-5363
TF: 800-555-6214 ■ *Web:* www.douglasallredco.com
AMB Property Corp Pier 1 Bay 1 ... San Francisco CA 94111 415-394-9000 394-9001
NYSE: AMB ■ *Web:* www.amb.com
America First Apartment Investors Inc
1004 Farnam St Suite 100 ... Omaha NE 68102 402-557-6360 557-6399
NASDAQ: APRO ■ *Web:* www.apro-reit.com
American Golf Corp 2951 28th St ... Santa Monica CA 90405 310-664-4000 664-6160
TF: 800-345-4259 ■ *Web:* www.americangolf.com
American Land Lease Inc 29399 US 19 N Suite 320 ... Clearwater FL 33761 727-726-8868 725-4391
NYSE: ANL ■ *TF:* 800-826-6069 ■ *Web:* www.americanlandlease.com
American Motel Management 2200 Northlake Pkwy Suite 277 ... Tucker GA 30084 770-939-1801 939-1419
Web: www.americanmotelonline.com
American Real Estate Partners LP
445 Hamilton Ave Suite 1210 White Plains Plaza ... White Plains NY 10601 914-614-7000 614-7001
NYSE: ACP ■ *TF:* 800-255-2737 ■ *Web:* www.areplp.com
American Realty Investors Inc 1800 Valley View Ln Suite 300 ... Dallas TX 75234 469-522-4200 522-4299
NYSE: ARL ■ *Web:* www.amrealtytrust.com
American Spectrum Realty Inc 5850 San Felipe Suite 450 ... Houston TX 77057 713-706-6200 706-6201
AMEX: AQQ ■ *Web:* www.americanspectrum.com
AmREIT 8 Greenway Plaza Suite 1000 ... Houston TX 77046 713-850-1400 850-0498
AMEX: AMY ■ *TF:* 800-888-4400 ■ *Web:* www.amreit.com
Amurcon Corp 30215 Southfield Rd Suite 200 ... Southfield MI 48076 248-646-0202 646-0482
ANG Management Co 7779 New York Ln ... Glen Burnie MD 21061 410-766-8900 766-6557
Apartment Investment & Management Co
4582 S Ulster Street Pkwy Suite 1100 ... Denver CO 80237 303-757-8101 759-3226
NYSE: AIV ■ *TF:* 888-789-8600 ■ *Web:* www.aimco.com
ARC Corporate Realty Trust Inc 1401 Broad St 2nd Fl ... Clifton NJ 07013 973-249-1000 249-1001
Web: www.arcproperties.com
Archstone-Smith Trust 9200 E Panorama Cir Suite 400 ... Englewood CO 80112 303-708-5959 858-0023
NYSE: ASN ■ *TF:* 877-272-4786 ■ *Web:* www.archstonesmith.com
Arden Realty Inc 11601 Wilshire Blvd 4th Fl ... Los Angeles CA 90025 310-966-2600 966-2699
NYSE: ARI ■ *Web:* www.ardenrealty.com
Aronov Realty 3500 Eastern Blvd ... Montgomery AL 36116 334-277-1000 272-0747
Web: www.aronov.com
Associated Estates Realty Corp 1 AEC Pkwy ... Richmond Heights OH 44143 216-261-5000 289-9600
NYSE: AEC ■ *TF:* 800-440-2372 ■ *Web:* www.aecrealty.com
AvalonBay Communities Inc 2900 Eisenhower Ave Suite 300 ... Alexandria VA 22314 703-329-6300 329-1459*
NYSE: AVB ■ **Fax: Investor Rel* ■ *Web:* www.avalonbay.com
Babcock & Brown Residential LLC
301 S College St Suite 3850 ... Charlotte NC 28202 704-944-0100 944-2039
AMEX: BNP ■ *Web:* www.bnproperties.com

Phone | Fax

Belz Enterprises 100 Peabody Pl Suite 1400 ... Memphis TN 38103 901-767-4780 271-7238
Web: www.belz.com
Ben Carter Properties LLC 950 E Paces Ferry Rd Suite 900 ... Atlanta GA 30326 404-869-2700 869-7171
Web: www.bencarterproperties.com
Benderson Development Co Inc 8441 Cooper Creek Blvd ... University Park FL 34201 941-359-8303 359-1836
Web: www.benderson.com
Berkshire Income Realty Inc 1 Beacon St ... Boston MA 02108 617-523-7722 646-2375
AMEX: BIR_pa ■ *TF:* 888-867-0100 ■ *Web:* www.berkshireincomerealty.com
Berkshire Property Advisors LLC 1 Beacon St Suite 1550 ... Boston MA 02108 617-646-2300 646-2375
TF: 888-867-0100 ■ *Web:* www.berkshireapartments.com
Berwind Natural Resources Corp
1500 Market St 3000 Centre Sq W ... Philadelphia PA 19102 215-563-2800 563-8347
Web: www.berwind.com
Berwind Realty Services Inc
1500 Market St West Tower 30th Fl ... Philadelphia PA 19102 215-563-2800 496-0431
Web: www.bpgltd.com
Blue Ridge Real Estate Co PO Box 707 ... Blakeslee PA 18610 570-443-8433
Blumberg Larry & Assoc 2733 Ross Clark Cir ... Dothan AL 36301 334-793-6855 793-1707
Web: www.lbaproperties.com
Bob Harris Oil Co 905 S Main St ... Cleburne TX 76031 817-641-4771 641-3074
Boston Properties Inc 800 Boylston St Suite 1900 ... Boston MA 02199 617-236-3300 236-3684
NYSE: BXP ■ *Web:* www.bostonproperties.com
Boyle Investment Co 5900 Poplar Ave Suite 100 ... Memphis TN 38119 901-767-0100 766-4299
TF: 888-862-6953 ■ *Web:* www.boyle.com
Bozzuto Group 7850 Walker Dr Suite 400 ... Greenbelt MD 20770 301-220-0100 220-3738
TF: 800-718-0200 ■ *Web:* www.bozzuto.com
BPO Properties Ltd 181 Bay St Suite 330 ... Toronto ON M5J2T3 416-359-8555 359-8596
TSX: BPP ■ *Web:* www.bpoproperties.com
Bradford Cos 9400 N Central Expy Suite 500 ... Dallas TX 75231 972-776-7000 776-7083
Web: www.bradford.com
Brandywine Realty Trust 555 E Lancaster Ave Suite 100 ... Radnor PA 19087 610-325-5600 325-5622
NYSE: BDN ■ *TF:* 866-426-5400 ■ *Web:* www.brandywinerealty.com
BRE Properties Inc 525 Market St 4th Fl ... San Francisco CA 94105 415-445-6530 445-6505
NYSE: BRE ■ *Web:* www.breproperties.com
Bresler & Reiner Inc 11200 Rockville Pike Suite 502 ... Rockville MD 20852 301-945-4300 945-4301
Web: www.bresleranreiner.com
Breslin Realty Development Corp
500 Old Country Rd Suite 200 ... Garden City NY 11530 516-741-7400 741-7128
Web: www.breslinrealty.com
Brookfield Properties Corp 181 Bay St Suite 330 ... Toronto ON M5J2T3 416-369-2300 369-2301
NYSE: BPO ■ *Web:* www.brookfieldproperties.com
Brooklyn Navy Yard Development Corp
63 Flushing Ave Bldg 292 3rd Fl ... Brooklyn NY 11205 718-907-5900 643-9296
Web: www.brooklynnavyyard.com
Burger Eugene Management Corp 6600 Hunter Dr ... Rohnert Park CA 94928 707-584-5123 584-5124
Web: www.ebmc.com
Cadillac Fairview Ltd 20 Queen St W 5th Fl ... Toronto ON M5H3R4 416-598-8200 598-8607*
**Fax: Hum Res* ■ *Web:* www.cadillacfairview.com
Calista Corp 301 Calista Ct Suite A ... Anchorage AK 99518 907-279-5516 272-5060
TF: 800-277-5516 ■ *Web:* www.calistacorp.com
Camden Property Trust 3 E Greenway Plaza Suite 1300 ... Houston TX 77046 713-354-2500 354-2700*
NYSE: CPT ■ **Fax: Mktg* ■ *TF:* 800-922-6336 ■ *Web:* www.camdenliving.com
Capital Properties Inc 100 Dexter Rd ... East Providence RI 02914 401-435-7171 435-7179
AMEX: CPI
CAPREIT Inc 11200 Rockville Pike Suite 100 ... Rockville MD 20852 301-231-8700 468-8392
Web: capreit.com
Casto Don M Organization 191 W Nationwide Blvd Suite 200 ... Columbus OH 43215 614-228-5331 469-8376
Web: www.donmcasto.com
CBL & Assoc Properties Inc
CBL Ctr 2030 Hamilton Place Blvd Suite 500 ... Chattanooga TN 37421 423-855-0001 490-8662
NYSE: CBL ■ *Web:* www.cblproperties.com
Cedar Shopping Centers Inc
44 S Bayles Ave Suite 304 ... Port Washington NY 11050 516-767-6492 767-6497
NYSE: CDR ■ *TF:* 800-564-3128 ■ *Web:* www.cedarshoppingcenters.com
Cencor Realty Services Inc 3102 Maple Ave Suite 500 ... Dallas TX 75201 214-954-0300 953-0860
TF: 800-256-5296 ■ *Web:* www.cencorrealty.com
CenterPoint Properties Trust 1808 Swift Dr ... Oak Brook IL 60523 630-586-8000 586-8010
NYSE: CNT ■ *Web:* www.centerpoint-prop.com
Centro Properties Group 131 Dartmouth St ... Boston MA 02116 617-247-2200 266-0885
Web: www.centroproperties.net
Centro Properties Group 420 Lexington Ave 7th Fl ... New York NY 10170 646-344-8600 869-3989*
**Fax Area Code: 212* ■ *TF:* 800-468-7526 ■ *Web:* www.centroprop.com
Centro Properties Group
580 W Germantown Pike Suite 200 ... Plymouth Meeting PA 19462 610-825-7100 834-8110
Web: www.centroprop.com
Century 21 Commercial Investment Network 1 Campus Dr ... Parsippany NJ 07054 973-428-9700 407-5806
TF: 800-221-2765
CFC Inc 320 W 8th St Suite 200 ... Bloomington IN 47404 812-332-0053 333-4680
Web: www.cfcincorporated.com
Charles E Lakin Enterprises 8990 W Dodge Rd Suite 225 ... Omaha NE 68114 402-393-5550
Charlwood International 1199 W Pender St Suite 900 ... Vancouver BC V6E2R1 604-718-2600 718-2678
Chelsea Property Group Inc 105 Eisenhower Pkwy ... Roseland NJ 07068 973-228-6111 228-3891
Web: www.cpgi.com
Clayton Homes Inc PO Box 9780 ... Maryville TN 37802 865-380-3000 380-3788
Web: www.clayton.net
Clover Financial Corp
4300 Haddonfield Rd Suite 314 Fairway Corp Ctr 1 ... Pennsauken NJ 08109 856-662-1116 662-6303
ClubCorp Inc 3030 LBJ Fwy ... Dallas TX 75234 972-243-6191 888-7555
TF: 800-346-7621 ■ *Web:* www.clubcorp.com
ClubLink Corp 15675 Dufferin St ... King City ON L7B1K5 905-841-3730 841-8068
TSX: LNK ■ *TF:* 800-661-1818 ■ *Web:* www.clublink.ca
Codding Enterprises California LP
1400 Valley House Dr Suite 100 ... Rohnert Park CA 94928 707-795-3550 665-2882
TF: 800-273-6833 ■ *Web:* www.codding.com
Codina Real Estate Management
355 Alhambra Cir Suite 900 ... Coral Gables FL 33134 305-520-2403 520-2467
Web: www.codina.com/management.home.aspx
Cogdell Spencer Inc 4401 Barclay Downs Dr Suite 300 ... Charlotte NC 28209 704-940-2900 940-2957
NYSE: CSA ■ *Web:* www.cogdellspencer.com
Coldwell Banker Commercial 1 Campus Dr ... Parsippany NJ 07054 973-407-7651 407-6615
TF: 800-222-2162 ■ *Web:* www.coldwellbankercommercial.com
Colliers International 50 Milk St 20th Fl ... Boston MA 02109 617-722-0221 722-0224
Web: www.colliers.com
Colonial Properties Trust 2101 6th Ave N Suite 750 ... Birmingham AL 35203 205-250-8700 250-8890
NYSE: CLP ■ *Web:* www.colonialprop.com
Combined Properties Inc 300 Commercial St ... Malden MA 02148 781-321-7800 321-5144
Web: www.combinedproperties.com
Community Development Trust 1350 Broadway Suite 700 ... New York NY 10018 212-271-5080 271-5079
Web: www.commdevtrust.com
Continental Group Inc 2950 N 28th Terrace ... Hollywood FL 33020 954-378-2300 378-2298
Corporate Office Properties Trust
6711 Columbia Gateway Dr Suite 300 ... Columbia MD 21046 443-285-5400 285-7650
NYSE: OFC ■ *Web:* www.copt.com
Cousins Properties Inc 191 Peachtree St NE Suite 3600 ... Atlanta GA 30303 404-407-1000 407-1002
NYSE: CUZ ■ *TF:* 800-926-8746 ■ *Web:* www.cousinsproperties.com
Crescent Real Estate Equities Co 777 Main St Suite 2100 ... Fort Worth TX 76102 817-321-2100 321-2000
NYSE: CEI ■ *Web:* www.crescent.com

				Phone	Fax
Crombie Properties Ltd 115 King St.	Stellarton	NS	B0K1S0	902-755-4440	755-6477
Web: www.crombieproperties.ca					
Crown Golf Properties LP 2700 Patriot Blvd Suite 410	Glenview	IL	60026	847-832-1800	832-1830
Web: www.crown-golf.com					
Crye-Leike Property Management Inc 890 Willow Tree Cir Suite 1	Cordova	TN	38018	901-758-5678	758-5671
Web: www.cryeleikerentals.com					
Curry Investment Co 2700 Kendallwood Pkwy Suite 208	Gladstone	MO	64119	816-454-6688	452-4757
Web: www.curryre.com					
Cushman & Wakefield Inc 51 W 52nd St	New York	NY	10019	212-841-7500	841-7867
Web: www.cushwake.com					
Daniel Corp 3595 Grandview Pkwy PO Box 43250	Birmingham	AL	35243	205-443-4500	
Web: www.danielcorp.com					
Developers Diversified Realty Corp 3300 Enterprise Pkwy	Beachwood	OH	44122	216-755-5500	755-1500
NYSE: DDR ■ *TF:* 800-258-7289 ■ *Web:* www.ddrc.com					
Divaris Real Estate Inc 1 Columbus Center Suite 700	Virginia Beach	VA	23462	757-497-2113	497-1338
TF: 888-373-0023 ■ *Web:* www.divaris.com					
Don M Casto Organization 191 W Nationwide Blvd Suite 200	Columbus	OH	43215	614-228-5331	469-8376
Web: www.donmcasto.com					
Donahue Schriber Realty Group Inc 200 E Baker St Suite 100	Costa Mesa	CA	92626	714-545-1400	545-4222
Web: www.donahueschriber.com					
Douglas Allred Co 11512 El Camino Real Suite 100	San Diego	CA	92130	858-793-0202	793-5363
TF: 800-555-6214 ■ *Web:* www.douglasallredco.com					
Douglas Elliman Property Management 675 3rd Ave 6th Fl	New York	NY	10017	212-350-2800	455-4726
Web: www.ellimanpm.com					
Draper & Kramer Inc 33 W Monroe St Suite 1900	Chicago	IL	60603	312-346-8600	346-2177
TF: 800-621-0776 ■ *Web:* www.dklends.com					
Duke Realty Corp 600 E 96th St Suite 100	Indianapolis	IN	46240	317-808-6000	808-6794
NYSE: DRE ■ *TF:* 800-875-3366 ■ *Web:* www.dukerealty.com					
DVL Inc 70 E 55th St 7th Fl	New York	NY	10022	212-350-9900	350-9911
EastGroup Properties Inc 188 E Capitol St Suite 300	Jackson	MS	39201	601-354-3555	352-1441
NYSE: EGP ■ *TF:* 800-337-5602 ■ *Web:* www.eastgroup.net					
Echelon Real Estate Services Inc 235 3rd St S Suite 300	Saint Petersburg	FL	33701	727-803-8200	803-8203
Web: www.echelonre.com					
Entertainment Properties Trust 30 W Pershing Rd Suite 201	Kansas City	MO	64108	816-472-1700	472-5794
NYSE: EPR ■ *TF:* 888-377-7348 ■ *Web:* www.eprkc.com					
Epoch Management Inc 359 Carolina Ave	Winter Park	FL	32789	407-629-5004	629-4264
Web: www.epochmanagement.com					
Epoch Properties Inc 359 Carolina Ave	Winter Park	FL	32789	407-644-9055	644-9845
Web: www.epochproperties.com					
Equity Inns Inc 7700 Wolf River Blvd	Germantown	TN	38138	901-754-7774	754-2374
NYSE: ENN ■ *Web:* www.equityinns.com					
Equity Lifestyle Properties Inc 2 N Riverside Plaza Suite 800	Chicago	IL	60606	312-279-1400	279-1710
NYSE: ELS ■ *Web:* www1.mhchomes.com					
Equity Office Properties Trust 2 N Riverside Plaza Suite 2100	Chicago	IL	60606	312-466-3300	454-0332
NYSE: EOP ■ *Web:* www.equityoffice.com					
Equity One Inc 1696 NE Miami Gardens Dr	North Miami Beach	FL	33179	305-947-1664	947-1734
NYSE: EQY ■ *TF:* 800-867-2777 ■ *Web:* www.equityone.net					
Equity Residential 2 N Riverside Plaza Suite 400	Chicago	IL	60606	312-474-1300	454-8703
NYSE: EQR ■ *Web:* www.equityapartments.com					
Ergon Properties Inc 2829 Lakeland Dr PO Box 23038	Jackson	MS	39225	601-933-3000	933-3355*
**Fax:* Hum Res ■ *TF:* 800-824-2626					
Essex Property Trust Inc 925 E Meadow Dr	Palo Alto	CA	94303	650-494-3700	494-8743
NYSE: ESS ■ *Web:* www.essexproperties.com					
Eugene Burger Management Corp 6600 Hunter Dr	Rohnert Park	CA	94928	707-584-5123	584-5124
Web: www.ebmc.com					
Farb Harold Investments PO Box 27741	Houston	TX	77227	713-629-9977	629-4552
Federal Realty Investment Trust 1626 E Jefferson St	Rockville	MD	20852	301-998-8100	998-3700
NYSE: FRT ■ *TF:* 800-658-8980 ■ *Web:* www.federalrealty.com					
FelCor Lodging Trust Inc 545 E John Carpenter Fwy Suite 1300	Irving	TX	75062	972-444-4900	444-4949
NYSE: FCH ■ *Web:* www.felcor.com					
Ferland Corp 85 Douglas Pike	Smithfield	RI	02917	401-233-8900	233-8930
Web: www.ferlandmgt.com					
Festival Cos 9841 Airport Blvd Suite 700	Los Angeles	CA	90045	310-665-9600	665-9009
TF: 800-800-1816 ■ *Web:* www.festivalcos.com					
First Hartford Realty Corp 149 Colonial Rd PO Box 1270	Manchester	CT	06045	860-646-6555	646-8572
TF: 888-646-6555 ■ *Web:* www.firsthartford.com					
First Industrial Realty Trust Inc 311 S Wacker Dr Suite 4000	Chicago	IL	60606	312-344-4300	922-6320
NYSE: FR ■ *TF:* 800-894-8778 ■ *Web:* www.firstindustrial.com					
First Realty Management Corp 151 Tremont St	Boston	MA	02111	617-423-7000	482-6617
Web: www.frmboston.com					
First REIT of New Jersey 505 Main St	Hackensack	NJ	07602	201-488-6400	487-7881
First Republic Corp of America 302 5th Ave	New York	NY	10001	212-279-6100	629-6848
TF: 800-578-2254					
Flatley Co 50 Braintree Hill Office Pk Suite 400	Braintree	MA	02184	781-848-2000	849-4400
Web: www.flatleyco.com					
Forest City Commercial Group 50 Public Sq Terminal Tower Suite 1130	Cleveland	OH	44113	216-621-6060	263-6209
Web: www.fceinc.com					
Forest City Enterprises Inc 50 Public Sq Terminal Tower Suite 1100	Cleveland	OH	44113	216-621-6060	263-4808*
NYSE: FCEa ■ **Fax:* Hum Res ■ *Web:* www.fceinc.com					
Forest City Residential Group Inc 50 Public Sq Terminal Tower Suite 1100	Cleveland	OH	44113	216-621-6060	263-6205
TF: 800-726-1800 ■ *Web:* www.fceinc.com					
Fortune International Realty 2666 Brickell Ave	Miami	FL	33129	305-856-2600	857-3636*
**Fax:* Hum Res ■ *Web:* www.fortunemiami.com					
Frederick Ross Co 717 17th St Suite 2000	Denver	CO	80202	303-892-1111	892-6338
Web: www.frederickross.com					
Freeport Center Assoc PO Box 160466 Bldg A-1	Clearfield	UT	84016	801-825-9741	825-3587
Web: www.freeportcenter.com					
G & B Real Estate Cos 201 W North River Dr Suite 200	Spokane	WA	99201	509-459-6109	325-7324
Web: www.g-b.com					
G & L Realty Corp 439 N Bedford Dr	Beverly Hills	CA	90210	310-273-9930	248-2222
Web: www.glrealty.com					
Gene B Glick Co Inc 8425 Woodfield Crossing Blvd Suite 300-W	Indianapolis	IN	46240	317-469-0400	469-8142
Web: www.genebglick.com					
General Growth Properties Inc 110 N Wacker Dr	Chicago	IL	60606	312-960-5000	960-5475
NYSE: GGP ■ *Web:* www.generalgrowth.com					
Gentry & Morris Properties 127 Phoenix Village	Fort Smith	AR	72901	479-646-7889	646-7880
Glenborough Realty Trust Inc 400 S El Camino Real Suite 1100	San Mateo	CA	94402	650-343-9300	343-9690
NYSE: GLB ■ *Web:* www.glenborough.com					
Glick Gene B Co Inc 8425 Woodfield Crossing Blvd Suite 300-W	Indianapolis	IN	46240	317-469-0400	469-8142
Web: www.genebglick.com					
Glimcher Realty Trust 150 E Gay St 24th Fl	Columbus	OH	43215	614-621-9000	621-9311
NYSE: GRT ■ *TF:* 800-987-8786 ■ *Web:* www.glimcher.com					
Grady Management Inc 8630 Fenton St Suite 625	Silver Spring	MD	20910	301-587-3330	588-5040*
**Fax:* Acctg ■ *TF:* 800-544-7239 ■ *Web:* www.gradymgt.com					
Graham Cos 6843 Main St	Miami Lakes	FL	33014	305-821-1130	557-0313
Gundaker Property Management 2458 Old Dorsett Rd Suite 300	Maryland Heights	MO	63043	314-298-5000	298-5096
TF: 800-325-1978 ■ *Web:* www.gundaker.com					
GVA Advantis 101 W Main St Suite 900	Norfolk	VA	23510	757-627-0661	627-1901
Web: www.gvaadvantis.com					
Gyrodyne Co of America Inc 1 Flowerfield Suite 24	Saint James	NY	11780	631-584-5400	584-7075
NASDAQ: GYRO ■ *Web:* www.gyrodyne.com					
H & R Retail Inc 9475 Deereco Rd Suite 300	Timonium	MD	21093	410-308-0800	308-0676
Web: www.hrretail.com					
Hall Financial Group 6801 Gaylord Pkwy Suite 100	Frisco	TX	75034	972-377-1100	377-6694
Web: www.hallfinancial.com					
Hallwood Commercial Real Estate LLC 3710 Rawlins St Suite 1500	Dallas	TX	75219	214-528-5588	528-8855
TF: 800-225-0135 ■ *Web:* www.hallwood.com/hcre/index.php					
Harold Farb Investments PO Box 27741	Houston	TX	77227	713-629-9977	629-4552
Harris Bob Oil Co 905 S Main St	Cleburne	TX	76031	817-641-4771	641-3074
Hawaii Reserves Inc 55-510 Kamehameha Hwy	Laie	HI	96762	808-293-9201	293-6456
Web: www.hawaiireserves.com					
Health Care Property Investors Inc 3760 Kilroy Airport Way Suite 300	Long Beach	CA	90806	562-733-5100	733-5200
NYSE: HCP ■ *TF:* 888-604-1990 ■ *Web:* www.hcpi.com					
Health Care REIT Inc 1 SeaGate Suite 1500	Toledo	OH	43603	419-247-2800	247-2826
NYSE: HCN ■ *Web:* www.hcreit.com					
Healthcare Realty Trust Inc 3310 West End Ave Suite 700	Nashville	TN	37203	615-269-8175	269-8260
NYSE: HR ■ *Web:* www.healthcarerealty.com					
Heitman LLC 191 N Wacker Dr Suite 2500	Chicago	IL	60606	312-855-5700	251-4807
TF: 800-225-5435 ■ *Web:* www.heitman.com					
Helmsley-Spear Inc 60 E 42nd St 53rd Fl	New York	NY	10165	212-880-0100	687-6437
Web: www.helmsleyspear.com/					
Hemstreet Development Co 16100 NW Cornell Rd Suite 100	Beaverton	OR	97006	503-531-4000	531-4001
Web: www.hemstreet.com					
Herbert H Redl 80 Washington St Suite 100	Poughkeepsie	NY	12601	845-471-3388	471-3851
Heritage Realty Management Inc 131 Dartmouth St	Boston	MA	02116	617-247-2200	266-0885
Web: www.heritage-realty.com					
Hersha Enterprises 44 Hersha Dr	Harrisburg	PA	17102	717-236-4400	774-7383
Web: www.hersha.com					
Hersha Hospitality Trust 1909 N Front St	Harrisburg	PA	17102	717-236-4400	774-7383
AMEX: HT ■ *Web:* www.hersha.com					
Hickel Investment Co 939 W 5th Ave PO Box 101700	Anchorage	AK	99510	907-343-2400	343-2211
Highwoods Properties Inc 3100 Smoketree Ct Suite 600	Raleigh	NC	27604	919-872-4924	876-2448
NYSE: HIW ■ *TF:* 866-449-6637 ■ *Web:* www.highwoods.com					
Holiday Retirement Corp 2250 McGilchrist St SE	Salem	OR	97302	503-370-7070	364-5716
TF: 888-370-7071 ■ *Web:* www.holidaytouch.com					
Holladay Corp 3400 Idaho Ave NW Suite 500	Washington	DC	20016	202-362-2400	364-0844
Home Properties 6 Garrison View Rd	Owings Mills	MD	21117	410-356-3320	356-0324
Web: www.homeproperties.com					
Home Properties Inc 850 Clinton Sq	Rochester	NY	14604	585-546-4900	546-5433
NYSE: HME ■ *Web:* www.homeproperties.com					
Horizon Group Properties Inc 5000 Hakes Dr	Muskegon	MI	49441	231-798-9100	798-5100
Web: www.horizongroup.com					
Horning Brothers 1350 Connecticut Ave NW Suite 800	Washington	DC	20036	202-659-0700	659-9489
Web: www.horningbrothers.com					
Hospitality Properties Trust 400 Centre St	Newton	MA	02458	617-964-8389	969-5730
NYSE: HPT ■ *Web:* www.hptreit.com					
HQ Global Workplaces Inc 15305 N Dallas Pkwy Suite 1400	Addison	TX	75001	972-361-8100	361-8101
Web: www.hq.com					
HRPT Properties Trust 400 Centre St	Newton	MA	02458	617-332-3990	332-2261
NYSE: HRP ■ *Web:* www.hrpreit.com					
Hunt Midwest Enterprises Inc 8300 NE Underground Dr	Kansas City	MO	64161	816-455-2500	
TF: 800-551-6877 ■ *Web:* www.huntmidwest.com					
Hunt Midwest Real Estate Development Inc 8300 NE Underground Dr	Kansas City	MO	64161	816-455-2500	455-8701
Web: www.huntmidwest.com					
Inland Group Inc 2901 Butterfield Rd	Oak Brook	IL	60523	630-218-8000	218-4917
TF: 800-828-8999 ■ *Web:* www.inlandgroup.com					
Inland Real Estate Corp 2901 Butterfield Rd	Oak Brook	IL	60523	630-218-8000	218-7357*
NYSE: IRC ■ **Fax:* Investor Rel ■ *TF:* 888-331-4732 ■ *Web:* www.inlandrealestate.com					
Investors Real Estate Trust 12 S Main St	Minot	ND	58702	701-837-4738	838-7785
NASDAQ: IRETS ■ *Web:* www.irets.com					
Irvine Co Apartment Communities 110 Innovation Dr	Irvine	CA	92617	949-720-5500	720-5601
Web: www.rental-living.com					
Jacobs Richard E Group Inc 25425 Center Ridge Rd	Cleveland	OH	44145	440-871-4800	808-6903
TF: 800-852-9558 ■ *Web:* www.rejacobsgroup.com					
Jim Wilson & Assoc Inc 2660 E Chase Ln Suite 100	Montgomery	AL	36117	334-260-2500	260-2533
Web: www.jwamalls.com					
JJ Gumberg Co Inc 1051 Brinton Rd	Pittsburgh	PA	15221	412-244-4000	244-9133
Web: www.jjgumberg.com					
JMG Realty Inc 5605 Glenridge Dr Suite 1010	Atlanta	GA	30342	404-847-0111	995-1112
Web: www.jmgrealty.com					
John F Long Properties LLLP 5035 W Camelback Rd	Phoenix	AZ	85031	602-272-0421	846-7208*
**Fax Area Code:* 623 ■ *Web:* www.jflong.com					
Jonas Equities 725 Church Ave	Brooklyn	NY	11218	718-871-4840	871-4324
Web: www.jonasequities.com					
Jones Lang LaSalle Inc 200 E Randolph Dr suite 4600	Chicago	IL	60601	312-782-5800	782-4339
NYSE: JLL ■ *Web:* www.joneslanglasalle.com					
Jones Lang LaSalle Leasing & Management Services 200 E Randolph Dr Suite 4600	Chicago	IL	60601	312-782-5800	782-4339
JPI 600 E Las Colinas Blvd Suite 1800	Irving	TX	75039	972-556-1700	444-2102
Web: www.jpi.com					
JW Mays Inc 9 Bond St	Brooklyn	NY	11201	718-624-7400	935-0378
NASDAQ: MAYS ■ *Web:* www.jwmays.com					
Kaempfer Co 1501 K St NW Suite 300	Washington	DC	20005	202-331-4300	331-4313
Web: kaempfer.com					
Kilroy Realty Corp 12200 W Olympic Blvd Suite 200	Los Angeles	CA	90064	310-481-8400	481-6501
NYSE: KRC ■ *Web:* www.kilroyrealty.com					
Kimco Realty Corp 3333 New Hyde Pk Rd Suite 100	New Hyde Park	NY	11042	516-869-9000	869-9001
NYSE: KIM ■ *TF:* 800-645-6292 ■ *Web:* www.kimcorealty.com					
Koren Development Inc 9200 Rumsey Rd Suite 210	Columbia	MD	21045	410-740-1010	992-5573
Kraus-Anderson Realty Co 4210 W Old Shakopee Rd	Bloomington	MN	55437	952-881-8166	881-8114
TF: 800-399-4220 ■ *Web:* www.krausanderson.com/ka-realty.html					
Kravco Co 234 Mall Blvd	King of Prussia	PA	19406	610-768-6300	768-6444
Web: www.kravco.com					
L & B Realty Advisors LLP 8750 N Central Expy Suite 800	Dallas	TX	75231	214-989-0800	989-0600
Web: www.lbgroup.com					
La Quinta Corp 909 Hidden Ridge Suite 600	Irving	TX	75038	214-492-6600	
NYSE: LQI ■ *TF:* 877-204-9204 ■ *Web:* www.lq.com					
La Quinta Properties Inc 909 Hidden Ridge Suite 600	Irving	TX	75038	214-492-6600	492-6971
TF: 877-204-9204					
Lakin Charles E Enterprises 8990 W Dodge Rd Suite 225	Omaha	NE	68114	402-393-5550	
Larry Blumberg & Assoc 2733 Ross Clark Cir	Dothan	AL	36301	334-793-6855	793-1707
Web: www.lbaproperties.com					
Lefrak Organization 97-77 Queens Blvd	Rego Park	NY	11374	718-459-9021	575-4816
Web: www.lefrak.com					
Levin Management Corp 893 Rt 22 W	North Plainfield	NJ	07060	908-755-2401	755-7194
TF: 800-488-0768 ■ *Web:* www.levinmgt.com					
Lexington Center Corp 430 W Vine St	Lexington	KY	40507	859-233-4567	253-2718
Web: www.lexingtoncenter.com					

	City	State	ZIP	Phone	Fax
Lexington Corporate Properties Trust 1 Penn Plaza Suite 4015 *NYSE: LXP* ■ *Web:* www.lxp.com	New York	NY	10119	212-692-7260	594-6600
Liberty Property Trust 500 Chesterfield Pkwy *NYSE: LRY* ■ *Web:* www.libertyproperty.com	Malvern	PA	19355	610-648-1700	644-4129
Lillibridge Healthcare Real Estate Trust 200 W Madison St Suite 3200 *Web:* lillibridge.com	Chicago	IL	60606	312-408-1370	408-1415
Lincoln Property Co 500 N Akard St Suite 3300 *Web:* www.lincolnproperty.com	Dallas	TX	75201	214-740-3300	740-3313
LNR Property Corp 1601 Washington Ave Suite 800 *TF:* 800-784-6380 ■ *Web:* www.lnrproperty.com	Miami Beach	FL	33139	305-695-5600	695-5499
Lowe Enterprises 11777 San Vicente Blvd Suite 900 *Web:* www.loweenterprises.com	Los Angeles	CA	90049	310-820-6661	207-1132
Macerich Co 401 Wilshire Blvd Suite 700 *NYSE: MAC* ■ *TF:* 800-421-7237 ■ *Web:* www.macerich.com	Santa Monica	CA	90401	310-394-6911	395-2791
Mack-Cali Realty Corp 343 Thornall St *NYSE: CLI* ■ *Web:* www.mack-cali.com	Edison	NJ	08837	732-590-1000	205-8237
Madison Marquette 909 Montgomery St Suite 200 *Web:* www.madisonmarquette.com	San Francisco	CA	94133	415-277-6800	217-5368
Madison Park Financial Corp 409 13th St 8th Fl *Web:* www.mpfcorp.com	Oakland	CA	94612	510-452-2944	452-2973
Madison Square Garden Corp 2 Pennsylvania Plaza 16th Fl **Fax:* Hum Res ■ *Web:* www.thegarden.com	New York	NY	10121	212-465-6000	465-6026*
Majestic Realty Co 13191 Crossroads Pkwy N 6th Fl *Web:* www.majesticrealty.com	City of Industry	CA	91746	562-692-9581	695-2329
Maxus Realty Trust Inc 104 Armour Rd *NASDAQ: MRTI*	North Kansas City	MO	64116	816-303-4500	221-1829
Mays JW Inc 9 Bond St *NASDAQ: MAYS* ■ *Web:* www.jwmays.com	Brooklyn	NY	11201	718-624-7400	935-0378
Mid-America Apartment Communities Inc 6584 Poplar Ave Suite 300 *NYSE: MAA* ■ *Web:* www.maac.net	Memphis	TN	38138	901-682-6600	682-6667
Milestone Properties Inc 200 Congress Pk Dr Suite 103 *Web:* www.milestonepropertiesinc.com	Delray Beach	FL	33445	561-394-9533	394-6748
Miller Valentine Group 4000 Miller Valentine Ct *TF:* 877-684-7687 ■ *Web:* www.mvg.com	Dayton	OH	45439	937-293-0900	299-1564
Miller WC & AN Development Co 4315 50th St NW *Web:* www.wcanmiller.com	Washington	DC	20016	202-895-2700	895-2735
Monmouth Real Estate Investment Corp 3499 Rt 9 N Suite 3C *NASDAQ: MNRTA* ■ *Web:* www.mreic.com	Freehold	NJ	07728	732-577-9997	577-9981
Muss Alexander & Sons 35 Sea Coast Terr Suite 1-W	Brooklyn	NY	11235	718-646-3800	
National Health Realty Inc 100 Vine St *AMEX: NHR* ■ *Web:* www.nationalhealthrealty.com	Murfreesboro	TN	37130	615-890-2020	890-0123
National Retail Properties 450 S Orange Ave Suite 900 *TF:* 800-666-7348	Orlando	FL	32801	407-265-7348	206-2194
Nationwide Health Properties Inc 610 Newport Ctr Dr Suite 1150 *NYSE: NHP* ■ *Web:* www.nhp-reit.com	Newport Beach	CA	92660	949-718-4400	759-6876
NESCO Inc Real Estate Group 6140 Parkland Blvd	Mayfield Heights	OH	44124	440-461-6000	449-3111
New Boston Garden Corp 1 FleetCenter Pl Suite 200	Boston	MA	02114	617-624-1101	624-1111
New England Development 1 Wells Ave *Web:* www.nedevelopment.com	Newton	MA	02459	617-965-8700	243-7085
Newcastle Investment Corp 1345 Ave of the Americas 46th Fl *NYSE: NCT* ■ *Web:* www.newcastleinv.com	New York	NY	10105	212-798-6100	
NTS Realty Holdings LP 10172 Linn Station Rd *AMEX: NLP* ■ *Web:* www.ntsdevelopment.com	Louisville	KY	40223	502-426-4800	426-4994
Omega Healthcare Investors Inc 9690 Deereco Rd Suite 100 *NYSE: OHI* ■ *TF:* 866-226-6342 ■ *Web:* www.omegahealthcare.com	Timonium	MD	21093	410-427-1700	427-8800
One Liberty Properties Inc 60 Cutter Mill Rd Suite 303 *NYSE: OLP* ■ *TF:* 800-450-5816 ■ *Web:* www.1liberty.com	Great Neck	NY	11021	516-466-3100	466-3132
Oxbow Realty Services Inc 725 Canton St *Web:* www.oxbowrealty.com	Norwood	MA	02062	781-769-2222	769-8186
Oxford Development Co 1 Oxford Ctr Suite 4500 *Web:* www.oxford-pgh.com	Pittsburgh	PA	15219	412-261-1500	642-7543
Pappas Properties Inc 655 Summer St	Boston	MA	02210	617-330-9797	439-9717
Parkway Properties Inc 188 E Capitol St Suite 1000 *NYSE: PKY* ■ *TF:* 800-748-1667 ■ *Web:* www.pky.com	Jackson	MS	39201	601-948-4091	949-4077
Peek Properties 510 University Village	Richardson	TX	75081	972-783-6040	669-0586
Penn Virginia Resource Partners LP 100 Matsonford Rd Suite 300 3 Radnor Corp Ctr *NYSE: PVR* ■ *Web:* www.pvresource.com	Radnor	PA	19087	610-687-8900	687-3688
Pennsylvania Real Estate Investment Trust 200 S Broad St 3rd Fl *NYSE: PEI* ■ *Web:* www.preit.com	Philadelphia	PA	19102	215-875-0700	546-7311
Perini Management Services Inc 73 Mt Wayte Ave *Web:* www.perini.com/pmsi/specialized_body.htm	Framingham	MA	01701	508-628-2000	628-2960
Persis Corp 900 Fort Street Mall Suite 1725 *Web:* www.persiscorp.com	Honolulu	HI	96813	808-599-8000	526-4114
Peterson Cos 12500 Fair Lakes Cir Suite 400 *Web:* www.petersoncos.com	Fairfax	VA	22033	703-227-2000	631-6481
Picerne Real Estate Group 75 Lambert Lind Hwy *Web:* www.picerne.com	Warwick	RI	02886	401-732-3700	738-6452
Pier 39 LP Inc Beach & Embarcadero Sts Stairway 2 Level 3 *Web:* www.pier39.com	San Francisco	CA	94133	415-705-5500	981-8808
PM Realty Group 1000 Main St Suite 2400 **Fax:* Hum Res ■ *Web:* www.pmrealtygroup.com	Houston	TX	77002	713-209-5800	209-5786*
Pocahontas Land Corp 800 Princeton Ave *Web:* www.nscorp.com	Bluefield	WV	24701	304-324-2429	324-2461
Polinger Shannon & Luchs Co 5530 Wisconsin Ave Suite 1000 *Web:* www.recgov.org/polinger/polinger.html	Chevy Chase	MD	20815	301-657-3600	986-9533
Portman Cos 303 Peachtree St NE Suite 4600 *Web:* www.portmanholdings.com	Atlanta	GA	30308	404-614-5252	614-5400
PRC Group 40 Monmouth Pk Hwy *Web:* www.prcgroup.com	West Long Branch	NJ	07764	732-222-5062	222-6410
Price Edwards & Co 210 Park Ave Suite 1000 *TF:* 800-316-7811 ■ *Web:* www.priceedwards.com	Oklahoma City	OK	73102	405-843-7474	236-1849
Prime Group Realty Trust 77 W Wacker Dr Suite 3900 *NYSE: PGE* ■ *Web:* www.pgrt.com	Chicago	IL	60601	312-917-1300	917-1310
Prime Management Group Inc 6300 Park of Commerce Blvd *Web:* www.prime-mgt.com	Boca Raton	FL	33487	561-997-4045	997-5684
Prime Retail LP 217 E Redwood St 20th Fl **Fax:* Hum Res ■ *TF:* 800-980-7467 ■ *Web:* www.primeretail.com	Baltimore	MD	21202	410-234-0782	234-0402*
Professional Community Management Inc 23726 Birtcher Dr **Fax:* Cust Svc ■ *TF:* 800-369-7260 ■ *Web:* www.pcm-ca.com	Lake Forest	CA	92630	949-768-7261	859-3729*
ProLogis 4545 Airport Way *NYSE: PLD* ■ *TF:* 800-566-2706 ■ *Web:* www.prologis.com	Denver	CO	80239	303-375-9292	567-5600
PS Business Parks Inc 701 Western Ave *AMEX: PSB* ■ *TF:* 800-567-0759 ■ *Web:* www.psbusinessparks.com	Glendale	CA	91201	818-244-8080	242-0566
Pyramid Cos 4 Clinton Sq *Web:* www.pyramidmg.com	Syracuse	NY	13202	315-422-7000	472-4035
Ramco-Gershenson Properties Trust 31500 Northwestern Hwy Suite 300 *NYSE: RPT* ■ *TF:* 800-225-6765 ■ *Web:* www.ramcogershenson.com	Farmington Hills	MI	48334	248-350-9900	350-9925
RD Management LLC 810 7th Ave 28th Fl *Web:* www.rdmanagement.com	New York	NY	10019	212-265-6600	459-9133
Realty Income Corp 220 W Crest St *NYSE: O* ■ *TF:* 800-375-6700 ■ *Web:* www.realtyincome.com	Escondido	CA	92025	760-741-2111	741-8674
Redl Herbert H 80 Washington St Suite 100	Poughkeepsie	NY	12601	845-471-3388	471-3851
Regency Centers 1 Independent Dr Suite 114 *NYSE: REG* ■ *TF:* 800-950-6333 ■ *Web:* www.regencyrealty.com	Jacksonville	FL	32202	904-598-7000	634-3428
ResortQuest International Inc 1 Gaylord Dr *Web:* www.resortquest.com	Nashville	TN	37214	615-316-6000	316-6290
Revenue Properties (America) Inc 2542 Williams Blvd *Web:* www.sizeler.net	Kenner	LA	70062	504-904-8500	904-8555
Rex Corp Realty 625 Rex Corp Plaza *TF:* 888-732-5766 ■ *Web:* www.rexcorprealty.com	Uniondale	NY	11556	516-506-6000	506-6800
Richard E Jacobs Group Inc 25425 Center Ridge Rd *TF:* 800-852-9558 ■ *Web:* www.rejacobsgroup.com	Cleveland	OH	44145	440-871-4800	808-6903
Roberts Realty Investors Inc 450 Northridge Pkwy Suite 302 *AMEX: RPI*	Atlanta	GA	30350	770-394-6000	551-5914
Rochdale Village Inc 169-65 137th Ave	Jamaica	NY	11434	718-276-5700	723-0963
Rosen Assoc Management Corp 33 S Service Rd *Web:* www.rosenmgmt.com	Jericho	NY	11753	516-333-2000	333-7555
Rosenberg Investment Co 3400 E Bayaud Ave Suite 390	Denver	CO	80209	303-320-6067	320-0137
Ross Frederick Co 717 17th St Suite 2000 *Web:* www.frederickross.com	Denver	CO	80202	303-892-1111	892-6338
Rossmar & Graham Community Assn Management Co 9362 E Raintree Dr *Web:* www.rossmar.com	Scottsdale	AZ	85260	480-551-4300	551-6000
Royal American Group 27181 Euclid Ave	Euclid	OH	44132	216-289-0600	261-6716
Ruffin Cos 1522 S Florence St *Web:* www.ruffinco.com	Wichita	KS	67209	316-942-7940	942-0216
Sabey Corp 12201 Tukwila International Blvd 4th Fl *Web:* www.sabey.com	Seattle	WA	98168	206-281-8700	282-9951
Saint Joe Towns & Resorts 7900 Glades Rd Suite 200 *Web:* www.joetowns.com	Boca Raton	FL	33434	561-479-1100	479-1226
Samson Management LLC 97-77 Queens Blvd Suite 710	Rego Park	NY	11374	718-830-0131	897-4387
Sares-Regis Group 18802 Bardeen Ave *Web:* www.sares-regis.com	Irvine	CA	92612	949-756-5959	756-5955
Saul Centers Inc 7501 Wisconsin Ave Suite 1500 *NYSE: BFS* ■ *Web:* www.saulcenters.com	Bethesda	MD	20814	301-986-6000	986-6079
Schatten Properties Management Co Inc 1514 South St *TF:* 800-892-1315 ■ *Web:* www.schattenproperties.com	Nashville	TN	37212	615-329-3011	327-2343
Sea Island Co PO Box 30351 *TF:* 800-732-4752 ■ *Web:* www.seaisland.com	Sea Island	GA	31561	912-638-3611	634-3961
Selig Enterprises Inc 1100 Spring St NW Suite 550 *TF:* 800-830-9965 ■ *Web:* www.seligenterprises.com	Atlanta	GA	30309	404-876-5511	875-2629
Seligman & Assoc 1 Town Sq Suite 1913 *TF:* 866-864-9824	Southfield	MI	48076	248-862-8000	351-4888
Sen Plex Corp 938 Kohou St *TF:* 800-552-4553	Honolulu	HI	96817	808-848-0111	848-0210
Senior Housing Properties Trust 400 Centre St *NYSE: SNH* ■ *Web:* www.snhreit.com	Newton	MA	02458	617-796-8350	796-8349
Sentinel Real Estate Corp 1251 Ave of the Americas 35th Fl *Web:* www.sentinelcorp.com	New York	NY	10020	212-408-2900	603-4965
Shorenstein Co LLC 555 California St Suite 4900 *Web:* www.shorenstein.com	San Francisco	CA	94104	415-772-7000	398-2280
Simon Property Group Inc 225 W Washington St *NYSE: SPG* ■ **Fax:* Cust Svc ■ *Web:* www.simon.com	Indianapolis	IN	46204	317-636-1600	263-7658*
SL Green Realty Corp 420 Lexington Ave *NYSE: SLG* ■ *Web:* www.slgreen.com	New York	NY	10170	212-594-2700	216-1790
SonomaWest Holdings Inc 2064 Gravenstein Hwy N	Sebastopol	CA	95472	707-824-2534	829-4630
SR Weiner & Assoc Inc 1330 Boylston St Suite 212 *Web:* www.srweiner.com	Chestnut Hill	MA	02467	617-232-8900	738-4661
Stadium Management Co 3600 Van Rick Dr *Web:* www.wingsstadium.com	Kalamazoo	MI	49001	269-345-1125	345-6452
Stanmar Inc 130 Boston Post Rd *Web:* www.stanmar-inc.com	Sudbury	MA	01776	978-443-9922	443-0479
Staubach Co 15601 Dallas Pkwy Suite 400 *TF:* 800-944-0012 ■ *Web:* www.staubach.com	Addison	TX	75001	972-361-5000	361-5910
Stiles Capital Group 300 SE 2nd St *Web:* www.stiles.com/capital_about_us.htm	Fort Lauderdale	FL	33301	954-627-9300	627-9399
Stiles Property Management 300 SE 2nd St *Web:* www.stiles.com/propmgt_about_us.htm	Fort Lauderdale	FL	33301	954-627-9300	627-9188
Stirling Properties 109 Northpark Blvd Suite 300 *TF:* 888-261-2022 ■ *Web:* www.stirlingprop.com	Covington	LA	70433	985-898-2022	898-2077
Sun Communities Inc 27777 Franklin Rd Suite 200 *NYSE: SUI* ■ *Web:* www.suncommunities.com	Southfield	MI	48034	248-208-2500	208-2640
Sunstone Hotel Investors LLC 903 Calle Amanecer Suite 100 *NYSE: SHO* ■ *Web:* www.sunstonehotels.com	San Clemente	CA	92673	949-369-4000	369-4010
Supertel Hospitality Inc 309 N 5th St PO Box 1448 *NASDAQ: SPPR* ■ *Web:* www.supertelinc.com	Norfolk	NE	68701	402-371-2520	371-5783
Susquehanna Real Estate 140 E Market St *Web:* www.susquehanna-realestate.com	York	PA	17401	717-848-5500	771-1430
Tanger Factory Outlet Centers Inc 3200 Northline Ave Suite 360 *NYSE: SKT* ■ *TF:* 800-438-8474 ■ *Web:* www.tangeroutlet.com	Greensboro	NC	27408	336-292-3010	852-2096
Tarragon Corp 423 W 55th St 12th Fl *NASDAQ: TARR* ■ *Web:* www.tarragoncorp.com	New York	NY	10019	212-949-5000	949-8001
Taubman Centers Inc 200 E Long Lake Rd Suite 300 *NYSE: TCO* ■ *TF:* 800-828-2626 ■ *Web:* www.taubman.com	Bloomfield Hills	MI	48303	248-258-6800	258-7683
Topa Management Co 1800 Ave of the Stars Suite 1400 *Web:* www.topa.com	Los Angeles	CA	90067	310-203-9199	286-1817
Tower Properties Co 911 Main St Suite 100 **Fax:* Hum Res ■ *Web:* www.towerproperties.com	Kansas City	MO	64105	816-421-8255	374-0624*
Towne Properties 1055 St Paul Pl *Web:* www.towneprop.com	Cincinnati	OH	45202	513-381-8696	345-6971
Towne Realty Inc 710 N Plankinton Ave 12th Fl **Fax:* Cust Svc ■ *TF:* 800-945-4450 ■ *Web:* www.homesbytowne.com	Milwaukee	WI	53203	414-273-2200	274-2728*
Trammell Crow Co 2001 Ross Ave Suite 3400 *NYSE: TCC* ■ *Web:* www.trammellcrow.com	Dallas	TX	75201	214-863-3000	863-3138
Trammell Crow Residential 2859 Paces Ferry Rd Suite 1100 *Web:* www.tcresidential.com	Atlanta	GA	30339	770-801-1600	801-1256
Transcontinental Realty Investors Inc 1800 Valley View Ln 1 Hickory Ctr *NYSE: TCI* ■ *TF:* 800-400-6407 ■ *Web:* www.transconrealty-invest.com	Dallas	TX	75234	469-522-4200	522-4299
Transwestern Commercial Services 1900 W Loop S Suite 1300 *Web:* www.transwestern.net	Houston	TX	77027	713-270-7700	271-8063
Trillium Corp 4350 Cordata Pkwy *TF:* 800-546-7317 ■ *Web:* www.trilliumcorp.com	Bellingham	WA	98226	360-676-9400	676-7736
Trizec Properties Inc 1114 Ave of the Americas 31st Fl *NYSE: TRZ* ■ *Web:* www.trz.com	New York	NY	10036	212-382-9300	382-9334
Tucson Realty & Trust Co 335 N Wilmont Rd Suite 505 *TF:* 877-254-5740 ■ *Web:* www.tucsonrealty.com	Tucson	AZ	85711	520-577-7000	918-3031

				Phone	Fax
Ukpeagvik Inupiat Corp 1250 Agvik St PO Box 890 *Web:* www.ukpik.com	Barrow	AK	99723	907-852-4460	852-4459
United Capital Corp 9 Park Pl 4th Fl *AMEX: AFP*	Great Neck	NY	11021	516-466-6464	829-4301
United Dominion Realty Trust Inc 400 E Cary St. *NYSE: UDR* ■ *TF:* 800-800-2691 ■ *Web:* www.udrt.com	Richmond	VA	23219	804-780-2691	343-1912
United Mobile Homes Inc 3499 Rt 9 N Suite 3C *AMEX: UMH* ■ *Web:* www.umh.com	Freehold	NJ	07728	732-577-9997	577-9980
Universal Health Realty Income Trust Universal Corporate Ctr 367 S Gulph Rd. *NYSE: UHT* ■ *Web:* www.uhrit.com	King of Prussia	PA	19406	610-768-3300	382-4407
University City Housing 3418 Sansom St. *Web:* www.uchweb.com	Philadelphia	PA	19104	215-382-2986	222-5449
Urban Retail Properties Co 900 N Michigan Ave 13th Fl. *Web:* www.urbanretail.com	Chicago	IL	60611	312-915-2000	
Urstadt Biddle Properties Inc 321 Railroad Ave *NYSE: UBP* ■ *TF:* 800-323-8216 ■ *Web:* www.ubproperties.com	Greenwich	CT	06830	203-863-8200	861-6755
USAA Real Estate Co 9830 Colonnade Blvd Suite 600. *TF:* 800-531-8182 ■ *Web:* realco.usaa.com	San Antonio	TX	78230	210-498-3222	498-0311
Vann Realty Co 10330 Regency Pkwy Dr Suite 301 *Web:* www.vannrealtyco.com	Omaha	NE	68114	402-734-4800	734-5248
VCG Holding Corp 390 Union Blvd Suite 540. *AMEX: PTT* ■ *Web:* www.ptsshowclub.com	Lakewood	CO	80228	303-934-2424	922-0746
Ventas Inc 10350 Ormsby Pk Pl Suite 300 *NYSE: VTR* ■ *TF:* 877-483-6827 ■ *Web:* www.ventasreit.com	Louisville	KY	40223	502-357-9000	357-9029
Vestar Development 2425 E Camelback Rd Suite 750. *Web:* www.vestar.com	Phoenix	AZ	85016	602-866-0900	955-2298
Village Green Cos 30833 Northwestern Hwy Suite 300. *Web:* www.villagegreen.com	Farmington Hills	MI	48334	248-851-9600	851-6161
Vinings Investment Properties Trust 2839 Paces Ferry Rd NW Suite 880 **Fax:* Cust Svc ■ *TF:* 800-849-5868	Atlanta	GA	30339	770-984-9500	984-1951*
Vornado Realty Trust 210 Rt 4 E *NYSE: VNO* ■ *TF:* 800-242-4119 ■ *Web:* www.vno.com	Paramus	NJ	07652	201-587-1000	587-0600
Wal-Mart Realty 2001 SE 10th St **Fax Area Code:* 800 ■ *TF:* 800-925-6278 ■ *Web:* www.wal-martrealty.com	Bentonville	AR	72716	479-273-4000	966-6546*
Warren Properties Inc PO Box 469114 *TF:* 877-927-7361 ■ *Web:* www.warrenproperties.com	Escondido	CA	92046	760-480-6211	480-6404
Washington Real Estate Investment Trust 6110 Executive Blvd Suite 800 *NYSE: WRE* ■ *TF:* 800-565-9748 ■ *Web:* www.washreit.com	Rockville	MD	20852	301-984-9400	984-9610
WC & AN Miller Development Co 4315 50th St NW *Web:* www.wcanmiller.com	Washington	DC	20016	202-895-2700	895-2735
Weiner SR & Assoc Inc 1330 Boylston St Suite 212 *Web:* www.srweiner.com	Chestnut Hill	MA	02467	617-232-8900	738-4661
Weingarten Realty Investors 2600 Citadel Plaza Dr Suite 300 *NYSE: WRI* ■ *TF:* 800-688-8865 ■ *Web:* www.weingarten.com	Houston	TX	77008	713-866-6000	866-6049
Wentworth Group Inc 901 S Trooper Rd *TF:* 800-222-7569 ■ *Web:* www.wentworth-mgt.com	Norristown	PA	19403	610-650-0600	650-0700
Westcor Partners 11411 N Tatum Blvd *Web:* www.westcor.com	Phoenix	AZ	85028	602-953-6200	953-1964
Westfield America Inc 11601 Wilshire Blvd 11th Fl *Web:* www.westfield.com	Los Angeles	CA	90025	310-478-4456	478-1267
Westgate Management Co Inc 133 Franklin Corner Rd.	Lawrenceville	NJ	08648	609-895-8890	895-0058
Weston Cos 1715 Aaron Brenner Dr Suite 500 PO Box 17847 *Web:* www.westonco.com	Memphis	TN	38187	901-682-9100	684-6357
White Co 1600 S Brentwood Blvd Suite 770 *TF:* 888-221-9679 ■ *Web:* www.white-co.com	Saint Louis	MO	63144	314-961-4480	961-5903
Wilson Jim & Assoc Inc 2660 E Chase Ln Suite 100 *Web:* www.jwamalls.com	Montgomery	AL	36117	334-260-2500	260-2533
Wilwat Properties 1946 Monroe Dr NE	Atlanta	GA	30324	404-872-3841	872-8806
Windrose Medical Properties Trust 3502 Woodview Trace Suite 100. *NYSE: WRS* ■ *Web:* www.windroseintl.com	Indianapolis	IN	46268	317-860-8180	860-9190
Winston Hotels Inc 2626 Glenwood Ave Suite 200 *NYSE: WXH* ■ *Web:* www.winstonhotels.com	Raleigh	NC	27608	919-510-6010	510-6832
Winthrop Realty Trust 7 Bulfinch Pl Suite 500. *NYSE: FUR* ■ *Web:* www.winthropreit.com	Boston	MA	02114	617-570-4614	570-4746
Woodmont Real Estate Services 1050 Ralston Ave. *Web:* www.wres.com	Belmont	CA	94002	650-592-3960	598-9094
WP Carey & Co LLC 50 Rockefeller Plaza 2nd Fl *NYSE: WPC* ■ *TF:* 800-972-2739 ■ *Web:* www.wpcarey.com	New York	NY	10020	212-492-1100	492-8922
Wright Runstad & Co 1201 3rd Ave Suite 2700. *Web:* www.wrightrunstad.com	Seattle	WA	98101	206-447-9000	223-8791
Zamias Services Inc 300 Market St *Web:* www.zamias.com	Johnstown	PA	15901	814-535-3563	536-5505
Zions Securities Corp 5 Triad Center Suite 450. *Web:* www.zsc.com	Salt Lake City	UT	84180	801-321-8700	320-4600

659 REALTOR ASSOCIATIONS - STATE

SEE ALSO Associations & Organizations - Professional & Trade - Real Estate Professionals Associations p. 1338

Listed here are the state branches of the National Association of Realtors.

				Phone	Fax
Alabama 522 Washington Ave. *Web:* www.alabamarealtors.com	Montgomery	AL	36104	334-262-3808	263-9650
Alaska 4205 Minnesota Dr *Web:* www.alaskarealtors.com	Anchorage	AK	99503	907-563-7133	561-1779
Arizona 255 E Osborne Rd Suite 200 *TF:* 800-426-7274 ■ *Web:* www.aaronline.com	Phoenix	AZ	85012	602-248-7787	351-2474
Arkansas 204 Executive Ct Suite 300 *TF:* 888-333-2206 ■ *Web:* www.arkansasrealtors.com	Little Rock	AR	72205	501-225-2020	225-7131
California 525 S Virgil Ave *Web:* www.car.org	Los Angeles	CA	90020	213-739-8200	480-7724
Capital Area (Greater) 8757 Georgia Ave Suite 600. *Web:* www.gcaar.com	Silver Spring	MD	20910	301-590-2000	590-2248
Colorado 309 Inverness Way S. *TF:* 800-944-6550 ■ *Web:* coloradorealtors.com	Englewood	CO	80112	303-790-7099	790-7299
Connecticut 111 Founders Plaza Suite 1101 *TF:* 800-335-4862 ■ *Web:* www.ctrealtor.com	East Hartford	CT	06108	860-290-6601	290-6615
Delaware 134 E Water St *TF:* 800-305-4445 ■ *Web:* www.delawarerealtor.com	Dover	DE	19901	302-734-4444	734-1341
Florida PO Box 725025 *Web:* www.floridarealtors.org	Orlando	FL	32872	407-438-1400	438-1411
Georgia 3200 Presidential Dr. *TF:* 866-280-0576 ■ *Web:* www.garealtor.com	Atlanta	GA	30340	770-451-1831	458-6992
Hawaii 1136 12th Ave Suite 220. *TF:* 866-693-6767 ■ *Web:* www.hawaiirealtors.com	Honolulu	HI	96816	808-737-4000	737-4977
Idaho 301 S Capitol Blvd. *TF:* 800-621-7553 ■ *Web:* www.idahorealtors.com	Boise	ID	83702	208-342-3585	336-7958
Illinois 522 W 5th St. *Web:* www.illinoisrealtor.org	Springfield	IL	62701	217-529-2600	529-3904
Indiana 7301 N Shadeland Ave Suite A. *Web:* www.indianarealtors.com	Indianapolis	IN	46250	317-842-0890	842-1076
Iowa 1370 NW 114th St Suite 100 *TF:* 800-532-1515 ■ *Web:* www.iowarealtors.com	Clive	IA	50325	515-453-1064	453-1070
Kansas 3644 SW Burlingame Rd *TF:* 800-366-0069 ■ *Web:* www.kansasrealtor.com	Topeka	KS	66611	785-267-3610	267-1867
Kentucky 161 Prosperous Pl. *TF:* 800-264-2185 ■ *Web:* www.kar.com	Lexington	KY	40509	859-263-7377	263-7565
Louisiana 4639 Bennington Ave *TF:* 800-266-8538 ■ *Web:* www.larealtors.org	Baton Rouge	LA	70808	225-923-2210	926-5922
Maine 19 Community Dr. *Web:* www.mainerealtors.com	Augusta	ME	04330	207-622-7501	623-3590
Maryland 2594 Riva Rd. **Fax Area Code:* 301 ■ *TF:* 800-638-6425 ■ *Web:* www.mdrealtor.org	Annapolis	MD	21401	410-841-6080	261-8369*
Massachusetts 256 2nd Ave. *TF:* 800-725-6272 ■ *Web:* www.marealtor.com	Waltham	MA	02451	781-890-3700	890-4919
Michigan 720 N Washington Ave *TF:* 800-454-7842 ■ *Web:* www.mirealtors.com	Lansing	MI	48906	517-372-8890	334-5568
Minnesota 5750 Lincoln Dr. *TF:* 800-862-6097 ■ *Web:* www.mnrealtor.com	Edina	MN	55436	952-935-8313	835-3815
Mississippi PO Box 321000 *TF:* 800-747-1103 ■ *Web:* ms.living.net	Jackson	MS	39232	601-932-9325	932-0382
Missouri 2601 Bernadette Pl. *TF:* 800-403-0101 ■ *Web:* www.missourirealtor.org	Columbia	MO	65203	573-445-8400	445-7865
Montana 208 N Montana Ave Suite 203. *TF:* 800-477-1864 ■ *Web:* www.montanarealtors.org	Helena	MT	59601	406-443-4032	443-4220
Nebraska 145 S 56th St Suite 100 *TF:* 800-777-5231 ■ *Web:* www.nebraskarealtors.com	Lincoln	NE	68510	402-323-6500	323-6501
Nevada 760 Margrave Dr Suite 200 *TF:* 800-748-5526 ■ *Web:* www.nvar.org	Reno	NV	89502	775-829-5911	829-5915
New Hampshire 115A Airport Rd *Web:* nhar.org	Concord	NH	03301	603-225-5549	228-0385
New Jersey 295 Pierson Ave. *Web:* www.njar.com	Edison	NJ	08837	732-494-5616	494-4723
New Mexico 2201 Brothers Rd *TF:* 800-224-2282 ■ *Web:* www.nmrealtor.com	Santa Fe	NM	87505	505-982-2442	983-8809
New York 130 Washington Ave. *TF:* 800-422-2501 ■ *Web:* www.nysar.com	Albany	NY	12210	518-463-0300	462-5474
North Carolina 4511 Weybridge Ln. *TF:* 800-443-9956 ■ *Web:* www.ncrealtors.org	Greensboro	NC	27407	336-294-1415	299-7872
North Dakota 318 W Apollo Ave *TF:* 800-279-2361 ■ *Web:* www.ndrealtors.com	Bismarck	ND	58503	701-355-1010	258-7211
Ohio 200 East Town St *Web:* www.ohiorealtors.org	Columbus	OH	43215	614-228-6675	228-2601
Oklahoma 9807 N Broadway *TF:* 800-375-9944 ■ *Web:* www.oklahomarealtors.com	Oklahoma City	OK	73114	405-848-9944	848-9947
Oregon 2110 Mission St SE. *TF:* 800-252-9115 ■ *Web:* www.oregonrealtors.org	Salem	OR	97308	503-362-3645	362-9615
Pennsylvania 4501 Chambers Hill Rd. *Web:* www.parealtor.org	Harrisburg	PA	17111	717-561-1303	561-8796
Rhode Island 100 Bignall St *Web:* www.riliving.com	Warwick	RI	02888	401-785-9898	941-5360
South Carolina 3780 Fernandina Rd *TF:* 800-233-6381 ■ *Web:* www.screaltors.com	Columbia	SC	29210	803-772-5206	798-6650
South Dakota 204 N Euclid Ave *Web:* www.sdrealtor.org	Pierre	SD	57501	605-224-0554	224-8975
Tennessee 901 19th Ave S Suite 201. **Fax:* Tech Supp ■ *Web:* www.tarnet.com	Nashville	TN	37212	615-321-1477	321-4905*
Texas 1115 San Jacinto Blvd Suite 200 *TF:* 800-873-9155 ■ *Web:* www.texasrealtors.com	Austin	TX	78701	512-480-8200	370-2390
Utah 230 W Towne Ridge Pkwy Suite 500 *TF:* 800-594-8933 ■ *Web:* www.utahrealtors.com	Sandy	UT	84070	801-676-5200	676-5225
Vermont 148 State St *TF:* 877-229-0523 ■ *Web:* www.vtrealtor.com	Montpelier	VT	05602	802-229-0513	229-0995
Virginia 10231 Telegraph Rd. *TF:* 800-755-8271 ■ *Web:* www.varealtor.com	Glen Allen	VA	23059	804-264-5033	262-0497
Washington 504 E 14th Ave *TF:* 800-562-6024 ■ *Web:* www.warealtor.com	Olympia	WA	98501	360-943-3100	357-6627
West Virginia 2110 Kanawha Blvd E. *TF:* 800-445-7600 ■ *Web:* www.wvrealtors.com	Charleston	WV	25311	304-342-7600	343-5811
Wisconsin 4801 Forest Run Rd Suite 201 *TF:* 800-279-1972 ■ *Web:* www.wra.org	Madison	WI	53704	608-241-2047	241-2901
Wyoming 951 Werner Ct Suite 300. *TF:* 800-676-4085 ■ *Web:* www.wyorealtors.com	Casper	WY	82601	307-237-4085	237-7929

660 RECORDING COMPANIES

				Phone	Fax
A & M Records 2220 Colorado Ave *Web:* www.amrecords.com	Santa Monica	CA	90404	310-865-1000	865-5633
Abkco Music & Records Inc 1700 Broadway 41st Fl. *Web:* www.abkco.com	New York	NY	10019	212-399-0300	582-5090
Alligator Records & Artist Management Inc PO Box 60234. *Web:* www.alligator.com	Chicago	IL	60660	773-973-7736	973-2088
American Gramaphone LLC 9130 Mormon Bridge Rd *TF:* 800-348-3434 ■ *Web:* www.amgram.com	Omaha	NE	68152	402-457-4341	457-4332
Angel Records 150 5th Ave. **Fax:* Mail Rm ■ *Web:* www.angelrecords.com	New York	NY	10011	212-786-8600	253-3099*
Artemis Records 130 5th Ave 7th Fl.	New York	NY	10011	212-433-1800	414-1703
Astralwerks Records 104 W 29th St 4th Fl *Web:* www.astralwerks.com	New York	NY	10001	212-886-7500	643-5563
Back Porch Records 4650 N Port Washington Rd. *TF:* 800-966-3699 ■ *Web:* www.backporchrecords.com	Milwaukee	WI	53212	414-961-8350	961-8351
Bad Boy Entertainment 1710 Broadway *Web:* www.badboyonline.com	New York	NY	10019	212-381-1540	381-1599
Balboa Records Inc 10900 Washington Blvd *Web:* www.balboarecords.com	Culver City	CA	90232	310-204-3792	204-0886
Blue Note Records 150 5th Ave **Fax:* Mail Rm ■ *Web:* www.bluenote.com	New York	NY	10011	212-786-8600	253-3099*
BMG Heritage 550 Madison Ave *TF:* 877-264-7744 ■ *Web:* www.bmgheritage.com	New York	NY	10022	212-833-8000	930-6706
BNA Records Label 1400 18th Ave S *Web:* bnarecords.com	Nashville	TN	37212	615-301-4400	301-4347
Buena Vista Music Group 500 S Buena Vista St	Burbank	CA	91521	818-560-1000	560-5737
Cambria Music Box 374 *Web:* cambriamus.com	Lomita	CA	90717	310-831-1322	833-7442
Capitol Records Inc 1750 N Vine St. *Web:* www.capitolrecords.com	Hollywood	CA	90028	323-462-6252	871-5123
Capitol Records Nashville 3322 West End Ave 11th Fl *Web:* www.capitol-nashville.com	Nashville	TN	37203	615-269-2050	269-2023

				Phone	Fax
Century Media 2323 W El Segundo Blvd *TF:* 800-250-4600 ■ *Web:* www.centurymedia.com	Hawthorne	CA	90250	323-418-1400	418-0118
Columbia Records 550 Madison Ave *Web:* www.columbia-records.com	New York	NY	10022	212-833-8000	
Concord Records Inc 270 N Canon Dr Suite 1212 *TF:* 800-551-5299 ■ *Web:* www.concordrecords.com	Beverly Hills	CA	90210	310-385-4455	385-4466
Curb Records 48 Music Sq E **Fax:* PR ■ *Web:* www.curb.com	Nashville	TN	37203	615-321-5080	321-5377*
Def Jam Records 825 8th Ave *Web:* www.defjam.com	New York	NY	10019	212-333-8000	
Def Soul Records 825 8th Ave *Web:* www.defsoul.com	New York	NY	10019	212-333-8000	
Dualtone Music Group 1614 17th Ave S *Web:* www.dualtone.com	Nashville	TN	37212	615-320-0620	320-0692
EMI Music Canada 3109 American Dr *Web:* www.emimusic.ca	Mississauga	ON	L4V1B2	905-677-5050	677-1651
Epic Records Group 550 Madison Ave 21st Fl *Web:* www.epicrecords.com	New York	NY	10022	212-833-8000	
Epitaph Records 2798 Sunset Blvd *Web:* www.epitaph.com	Los Angeles	CA	90026	213-413-7353	413-9678
Essential Records 741 Cool Springs Blvd **Fax:* Hum Res ■ *Web:* www.essentialrecords.com	Franklin	TN	37067	615-261-6450	261-5909*
Fantasy Inc 2600 10th St *TF:* 800-227-0466 ■ *Web:* www.fantasyjazz.com	Berkeley	CA	94710	510-549-2500	486-2015
Forefront Records PO Box 5085 *Web:* www.forefrontrecords.com	Brentwood	TN	37024	615-371-4300	
Geffen Records 2220 Colorado Ave **Fax:* Sales ■ *Web:* www.geffenrecords.com	Santa Monica	CA	90404	310-865-4000	865-5940*
HighBridge Audio 33 S 6th St CC-2205 *TF:* 800-755-8532 ■ *Web:* www.highbridgeaudio.com	Minneapolis	MN	55402	612-304-7163	304-7175
Higher Octave Music 4650 N Port Washington Rd *TF:* 800-966-3699 ■ *Web:* www.higheroctave.com	Milwaukee	WI	53212	414-961-8350	961-8351
HighTone Records 220 4th St Suite 101 *Web:* www.hightone.com	Oakland	CA	94607	510-763-8500	763-8558
Hollywood Records 500 S Buena Vista St *Web:* www.hollywoodrecords.go.com	Burbank	CA	91521	818-560-5670	560-5737
Integrity Media Inc 1000 Cody Rd S *TF Orders:* 800-533-6912 ■ *Web:* www.integritymusic.com	Mobile	AL	36695	251-633-9000	776-5134
Interscope Records 2220 Colorado Ave *TF:* 800-982-1812 ■ *Web:* www.interscope.com	Santa Monica	CA	90404	310-865-1000	865-7096
Island Def Jam Music Group 825 8th Ave **Fax:* Mktg ■ *Web:* www.islanddefjam.com	New York	NY	10019	212-333-8000	603-7941*
Island Records 825 8th Ave *Web:* www.islandrecords.com	New York	NY	10019	212-333-8000	603-7941
J Records 745 5th Ave 6th Floor *Web:* www.jrecords.com	New York	NY	10151	646-840-5600	840-5679
Jive Records 137-139 W 25th St *Web:* www.jiverecords.com	New York	NY	10001	212-727-0016	645-3783
K-Tel International Inc 2655 Cheshire Ln N Suite 100 *TF:* 800-328-6640 ■ *Web:* www.k-tel.com	Plymouth	MN	55447	763-559-5566	559-5505
Koch Entertainment Distribution 22 Harbor Pk Dr *TF:* 800-332-7553 ■ *Web:* www.kochdistribution.com	Port Washington	NY	11050	516-484-1000	484-4746
LaFace Records 137-139 W 25th St *Web:* www.laface.com	New York	NY	10001	212-727-0016	
Lava Records 1290 Ave of the Americas *Web:* www.lavarecords.com	New York	NY	10104	212-707-2000	405-5561
Legacy Recordings 550 Madison Ave *Web:* www.legacyrecordings.com	New York	NY	10022	212-833-8000	
Lost Highway Records 54 Music Sq E Suite 300 *Web:* www.umgnashville.com	Nashville	TN	37203	615-524-7500	524-7600
Lyric Street Records 1100 Demonbreun St Suite 100 *TF:* 888-814-4934 ■ *Web:* lyricstreet.go.com	Nashville	TN	37203	615-963-4848	963-4846
Malaco Music Group Inc 3023 W Northside Dr *TF Cust Svc:* 800-272-7936 ■ *Web:* www.malaco.com	Jackson	MS	39213	601-982-4522	982-4528
Matador Records 625 Broadway 12th Fl *Web:* www.matadorrecords.com	New York	NY	10012	212-995-5882	995-5883
Maverick Reprise & Warner Brothers 3300 Warner Blvd *Web:* www.maverickrc.com	Burbank	CA	91505	310-385-7800	
MCA Nashville 60 Music Sq E **Fax:* PR ■ *Web:* www.mca-nashville.com	Nashville	TN	37203	615-244-8944	880-7440*
Mercury Nashville 54 Music Sq E Suite 300 *Web:* www.umgnashville.com	Nashville	TN	37203	615-524-7500	524-7600
Mosaic Records 35 Melrose Pl *Web:* www.mosaicrecords.com	Stamford	CT	06902	203-327-7111	323-3526
Motown Record Co 1755 Broadway 7th Fl *Web:* www.motown.com	New York	NY	10019	212-373-0600	
Narada Productions Inc 4650 N Port Washington Rd *TF:* 800-966-3699 ■ *Web:* www.narada.com	Milwaukee	WI	53212	414-961-8350	961-8351
Naxos of America Inc 416 Mary Lindsay Polk Dr Suite 509 *TF:* 877-629-6723 ■ *Web:* www.naxos.com	Franklin	TN	37067	615-771-9393	771-6747
Nightingale-Conant Corp 6245 W Howard St *TF Cust Svc:* 800-323-3938 ■ *Web:* www.nightingale.com	Niles	IL	60714	847-647-0300	647-5552
Nitro Records 7071 Warner Ave Suite F-736 *Web:* www.nitrorecords.com	Huntington Beach	CA	92647	714-842-8897	847-3028
Nonesuch Records 1290 Ave of the Americas 23rd Fl *Web:* www.nonesuch.com	New York	NY	10104	212-707-2900	707-3205
Putumayo World Music 411 Lafayette St 4th Fl *TF:* 888-788-8629 ■ *Web:* www.putumayo.com	New York	NY	10003	212-995-9400	460-0095
RCA Label Group Nashville 1400 18th Ave S *Web:* www.rcalabelgroup.com	Nashville	TN	37212	615-858-1200	301-4347
RCA Records 550 Madison Ave *Web:* www.rcarecords.com	New York	NY	10022	212-833-8000	930-4447
Real World Records 4650 N Port Washington Rd *TF:* 800-966-3699 ■ *Web:* www.realworldusa.com	Milwaukee	WI	53212	414-961-8350	961-8351
Record Plant Inc 1032 N Sycamore Ave *Web:* www.recordplant.com	Hollywood	CA	90038	323-993-9300	466-8835
Reprise Records 3300 Warner Blvd *Web:* www.repriserec.com	Burbank	CA	91505	818-846-9090	846-8474
Republic Records 1755 Broadway 6th Fl *Web:* www.republicrecords.com	New York	NY	10019	212-841-5100	841-8012
Reunion Records 741 Cool Springs Blvd E *Web:* www.reunionrecords.com	Franklin	TN	37067	615-261-6500	261-5909
Rhino Records 3400 W Olive Ave *TF:* 800-827-4466 ■ *Web:* www.rhino.com	Burbank	CA	91505	818-238-6100	562-9231
Righteous Babe Records PO Box 95 Ellicott Station *TF:* 800-664-3769 ■ *Web:* righteousbabe.com	Buffalo	NY	14205	716-852-8020	852-2741
Rounder Records 1 Camp St *TF:* 800-768-6337 ■ *Web:* www.rounder.com	Cambridge	MA	02140	617-354-0700	491-1970
RuffNation Records 1080 N Delaware Ave *Web:* www.ruffnation.com	Philadelphia	PA	19125	215-426-5536	426-6099
Rykodisc Inc 30 Irving Pl *Web:* www.rykodisc.com	New York	NY	10003	212-287-6100	
Sire Records 1296 Ave of the Americas *Web:* www.sirerecords.com	New York	NY	10104	212-707-3200	
Skaggs Family Records 329 Rockland Rd *Web:* www.skaggsfamilyrecords.com	Hendersonville	TN	37075	615-264-8877	264-8899

				Phone	Fax
Smithsonian Folkways Recordings 600 Maryland Ave SW Suite 200 *TF:* 800-410-9815 ■ *Web:* www.folkways.si.edu	Washington	DC	20024	202-633-6450	633-6477
So So Def Records 137-139 W 25th St *Web:* www.soso-def.com	New York	NY	10001	212-727-0016	
Sony-BMG Entertainment 1540 Broadway **Fax:* Sales ■ *Web:* www.sonybmg.com	New York	NY	10036	212-833-8000	930-4511*
Sony-BMG Masterworks 550 Madison Ave *Web:* www.bmgclassics.com	New York	NY	10022	212-833-8000	930-4511
Sony-BMG Music Canada 190 Liberty St Suite 100 *Web:* click2music.ca	Toronto	ON	M6K3L5	416-586-0022	589-3001
Sony BMG Music Entertainment 550 Madison Ave *Web:* www.sonybmg.com	New York	NY	10022	212-833-8000	
Sony Classical 550 Madison Ave *Web:* www.sonyclassical.com	New York	NY	10022	212-833-8000	
Sony Music Canada 1121 Leslie St *Web:* www.sonybmg.ca	Toronto	ON	M3C2J9	416-391-3311	447-6973
Sony Music Nashville 1400 18th Ave S *Web:* www.sonynashville.com	Nashville	TN	37212	615-858-1300	301-4347
Sony Wonder 550 Madison Ave *Web:* www.sonywonder.com	New York	NY	10022	212-833-8100	833-5414
Sound of America Records (SOAR) 5200 Constitution Ave NE *TF:* 800-890-7627 ■ *Web:* www.soundofamerica.com	Albuquerque	NM	87110	505-268-6110	268-0237
Sparrow Label Group PO Box 5010 *TF:* 800-347-4777 ■ *Web:* www.sparrowrecords.com	Brentwood	TN	37024	615-371-6800	371-6997
SubPop Records 2013 4th Ave 3rd Fl *Web:* www.subpop.com	Seattle	WA	98121	206-441-8441	441-8245
Sugar Hill Records 120 31st Ave N *TF:* 800-996-4455 ■ *Web:* www.sugarhillrecords.com	Nashville	TN	37203	615-297-6890	297-9945
Telarc International Corp 23307 Commerce Pk Rd *TF:* 800-801-5810 ■ *Web:* www.telarc.com	Cleveland	OH	44122	216-464-2313	360-9663
Tommy Boy Music Inc 902 Broadway 13th Fl *Web:* www.tommyboy.com	New York	NY	10010	212-388-8300	388-8400
Universal Music Group 1755 Broadway *Web:* new.umusic.com	New York	NY	10019	212-373-0600	
Verity Records 137-139 W 25th St *Web:* www.verityrecords.com	New York	NY	10001	212-727-0016	
Verve Music Group 1755 Broadway 3rd Fl *Web:* www.vervemusicgroup.com	New York	NY	10019	212-373-0600	
Victory Records Inc 346 N Justine St Suite 504 *Web:* www.victoryrecords.com	Chicago	IL	60607	312-666-8661	666-8665
Virgin Music Canada 3109 American Dr *Web:* www.virginmusic.ca	Mississauga	ON	L4V1B2	905-678-4488	677-9565
Virgin Records 150 5th Ave *Web:* www.virginrecords.com	New York	NY	10011	212-786-8200	253-3099
Walt Disney Records 500 S Buena Vista St *Web:* disney.go.com/DisneyRecords	Burbank	CA	91521	818-560-1000	
Warner Bros Nashville 20 Music Sq E *Web:* www.wbrnashville.com	Nashville	TN	37203	615-748-8000	214-1567
Warner Bros Records 3300 Warner Blvd *Web:* www.warnerbrosrecords.com	Burbank	CA	91505	818-846-9090	846-8474
Warner Music Group Corp 75 Rockefeller Plaza 30th Fl *NYSE:* WMG ■ *Web:* www.wmg.com	New York	NY	10019	212-275-2041	
Wind-up Records 72 Madison Ave 8th Fl *Web:* www.winduprecords.com	New York	NY	10016	212-251-9665	895-3200
Word Entertainment 25 Music Sq W *Web:* www.wordrecords.com	Nashville	TN	37203	615-251-0600	252-8864

661 RECORDING MEDIA - MAGNETIC & OPTICAL

SEE ALSO Photographic Equipment & Supplies p. 2113

				Phone	Fax
Allied Vaughn Inc 7951 Computer Ave *TF:* 800-323-0281 ■ *Web:* www.alliedvaughn.com	Bloomington	MN	55435	952-832-3200	832-3179
Americ Disc Inc 2525 rue Canadien *TF:* 800-263-0419 ■ *Web:* www.americdisc.com	Drummondville	QC	J2C7W2	819-474-2655	478-4575
Ampex Corp 1228 Douglas Ave *NASDAQ:* AMPX ■ **Fax:* Hum Res ■ *TF:* 800-227-8333 ■ *Web:* www.ampex.com	Redwood City	CA	94063	650-367-2011	367-3077*
Athana Inc 24045 Frampton Ave *TF:* 800-421-1591 ■ *Web:* www.athana.com	Harbor City	CA	90710	310-539-7280	539-6596
Cine Magnetics Inc 100 Business Pk Dr Suite 1 *TF:* 800-431-1102 ■ *Web:* www.cinemagnetics.com	Armonk	NY	10504	914-273-7500	273-7575
Cinram International Inc 2255 Markham Rd *TF:* 800-387-5146 ■ *Web:* www.cinram.com	Scarborough	ON	M1B2W3	416-298-8190	298-0612
Digital Excellence 300 York Ave *TF:* 800-608-8008 ■ *Web:* www.digx.com	Saint Paul	MN	55101	651-772-5100	771-5629
Duplication Factory Inc 4275 Norex Dr *TF:* 800-279-2009 ■ *Web:* www.duplicationfactory.com	Chaska	MN	55318	952-448-9912	448-3983
Forge Recording Studios Inc 100 Mill Rd *TF:* 800-331-0405 ■ *Web:* www.forgerecording.com	Oreland	PA	19075	610-935-1422	935-1940
Fuji Photo Film USA Inc 200 Summit Lake Dr *TF:* 800-755-3854 ■ *Web:* www.fujifilm.com	Valhalla	NY	10595	914-789-8100	789-8295
Imation Corp 1 Imation Pl *NYSE:* IMN ■ *TF:* 888-466-3456 ■ *Web:* www.imation.com	Oakdale	MN	55128	651-704-4000	704-7100
Inoveris LLC 7001 Metatec Blvd *Web:* www.inoveris.com	Dublin	OH	43017	614-761-2000	761-4258
JVC Disc America Co 2 JVC Rd *TF:* 800-223-5081 ■ *Web:* www.jvcdiscusa.com	Tuscaloosa	AL	35405	205-556-7111	554-5500
Komag Inc 1710 Automation Pkwy *NASDAQ:* KOMG ■ *TF:* 800-576-2000 ■ *Web:* www.komag.com	San Jose	CA	95131	408-576-2000	944-9255
LaserCard Corp 1875 N Shoreline Blvd *NASDAQ:* LCRD ■ *Web:* www.lasercard.com	Mountain View	CA	94043	650-969-4428	969-3140
Maxell Corp of America 22-08 Rt 208 *TF:* 800-533-2836 ■ *Web:* www.maxell.com	Fair Lawn	NJ	07410	201-794-5900	796-8790
Optical Disc Solutions Inc 1767 Sheridan St *TF:* 800-704-7648 ■ *Web:* www.odiscs.com	Richmond	IN	47374	765-935-7574	935-0174
Peripheral Mfg Inc 4775 Paris St *TF:* 800-468-6888 ■ *Web:* www.periphman.com	Denver	CO	80239	303-371-8651	371-8643
Quantegy Inc 2230 Marvyn Pkwy PO Box 190 *Web:* www.quantegy.com	Opelika	AL	36803	334-745-7643	749-7665
TDK Electronics Corp 901 Franklin Ave *TF:* 800-835-8273 ■ *Web:* www.tdk.com	Garden City	NY	11530	516-535-2600	294-7931
TDK USA Corp 901 Franklin Ave PO Box 9302 **Fax:* Sales ■ *TF:* 800-835-8273 ■ *Web:* www.tdk.com	Garden City	NY	11530	516-535-2600	294-7751*
Transco Products Corp PO Box 1025 *TF:* 800-876-0039 ■ *Web:* www.transcousa.com	Linden	NJ	07036	908-862-0030	862-0035
US Optical Disc Inc 1 Eagle Dr *TF:* 800-743-1124 ■ *Web:* www.usod.com	Sanford	ME	04073	207-324-1124	490-1707

	City	State	Zip	Phone	Fax
USA Dubs 29 W 38th St *TF:* 800-872-3821 ■ *Web:* www.usadubs.com	New York	NY	10018	212-398-6400	398-4145
Verbatim Corp 1200 West WT Harris Blvd *TF:* 800-538-8589 ■ *Web:* www.verbatimcorp.com	Charlotte	NC	28262	704-547-6500	547-6767
VU Media Duplication 1420 Blake St *TF:* 800-637-4336 ■ *Web:* www.vumedia.com	Denver	CO	80202	303-534-5503	595-4630
Wabash Computer Products Inc 4720 W 90th St *TF Cust Svc:* 800-323-9868 ■ *Web:* www.wabashcomp.com	Tulsa	OK	74132	918-808-3867	
Zomax Inc 5353 Nathan Ln N *NASDAQ: ZOMX* ■ *Web:* www.zomax.com	Plymouth	MN	55442	763-553-9300	553-0826

662 RECREATION FACILITY OPERATORS

SEE ALSO Bowling Centers p. 1395

	City	State	Zip	Phone	Fax
Clicks Billiards 3100 Monticello Ave Suite 350 *Web:* clicks.com	Dallas	TX	75205	214-521-7001	521-1449
Dave & Buster's Inc 2481 Manana Dr *NYSE: DAB* ■ *TF:* 800-842-5369 ■ *Web:* www.daveandbusters.com	Dallas	TX	75220	214-357-9588	350-0941
GameWorks 600 N Brand Blvd 5th Fl *Web:* www.gameworks.com	Glendale	CA	91203	818-254-4263	254-4306
Jeepers! Inc 800 South St Suite 355 *TF:* 800-533-7377 ■ *Web:* www.jeepers.com	Waltham	MA	02453	781-890-1800	891-4916
Jillian's Entertainment Corp 2481 Manana Dr *Web:* www.jillians.com	Dallas	TX	75220	214-357-9588	350-0941
New Horizon Kids Quest Inc 16355 36th Ave N Suite 700 *TF:* 800-941-1007 ■ *Web:* www.kidsquest.com	Plymouth	MN	55446	763-557-1111	383-6101
Palace Entertainment Inc 4950 MacArthur Rd Suite 400 *Web:* www.palaceentertainment.com	Newport Beach	CA	92660	949-261-0404	261-1414
Pump It Up 1249 Quarry Ln Suite 150 *TF:* 866-325-9663 ■ *Web:* www.pumpitupparty.com	Pleasanton	CA	94566	925-397-1300	600-0279
Putt-Putt LLC 6350 Quadrangle Dr Suite 210 *TF:* 866-788-8788 ■ *Web:* www.puttputt.com	Chapel Hill	NC	27517	919-493-9999	402-9902
SEGA GameWorks LLC 600 N Brand Blvd 5th Fl *Web:* www.gameworks.com	Glendale	CA	91203	818-254-4263	254-4306

663 RECYCLABLE MATERIALS RECOVERY

Included here are companies that recycle post-consumer trash, tires, appliances, batteries, etc. as well as industrial recyclers of plastics, paper, wood, glass, solvents, and so on.

	City	State	Zip	Phone	Fax
ACC Recycling Corp 1190 20th St N *TF:* 800-282-1153	Saint Petersburg	FL	33713	727-896-9600	822-4923
Active Recycling Co Inc 2000 W Slauson Ave	Los Angeles	CA	90047	323-295-7774	292-2114
Advanced Environmental Recycling Technologies Inc 914 N Jefferson St *NASDAQ: AERTA* ■ *TF:* 800-951-5117 ■ *Web:* www.aertinc.com	Springdale	AR	72764	479-756-7400	756-7410
All American Recycling Corp 2 Hope St	Jersey City	NJ	07307	201-656-3363	656-8188
American Paper Recycling Corp 301 W Lake St *TF Cust Svc:* 800-762-6790	Northlake	IL	60164	708-344-6789	344-0262
Anheuser-Busch Recycling Co 3636 S Geyer Rd	Saint Louis	MO	63127	314-957-9500	957-9319
Appliance Recycling Centers of America Inc 7400 Excelsior Blvd *NASDAQ: ARCI* ■ *TF:* 800-452-8680 ■ *Web:* www.appliancesmart.com	Minneapolis	MN	55426	952-930-9000	930-1800
Automated Material Handling Co 655 Christian Ln PO Box 7146	Kensington	CT	06037	860-223-3601	225-3166
Batliner Paper Stock Co 2501 Front St *TF:* 800-821-8512 ■ *Web:* www.batlinerpaperstock.com	Kansas City	MO	64120	816-483-3343	241-9736
Better Management Corp (BMC) 41738 Esterly Dr *TF:* 877-293-4300 ■ *Web:* www.bmcohio.com	Columbiana	OH	44408	330-482-7070	482-5929
Canusa Hershman Recycling Co 9 Business Park Dr Unit 8 *Web:* www.chrecycling.com	Branford	CT	06405	203-488-0887	488-9499
Clean Earth of North Jersey Inc 115 Jacobus Ave	South Kearny	NJ	07032	973-344-4004	344-8652
Community Recycling Inc 3840 NW 37th Ct	Miami	FL	33142	305-633-3100	634-4272
Continental Paper Grading Co Inc 1623 S Lumber St	Chicago	IL	60616	312-226-2010	226-2025
Energy Answers Corp 79 N Pearl St *Web:* www.energyanswers.com	Albany	NY	12207	518-434-1227	436-6343
Excell Minerals 2 Gateway Ctr 603 Stanwix St Suite 1825 *Web:* www.excellminerals.com	Pittsburgh	PA	15222	412-434-5700	434-5600
FCR 809 W Hill St *Web:* www.casella.com/locations/fcr	Charlotte	NC	28208	704-697-2000	376-1625
Federal International Inc 7935 Clayton Rd *TF:* 800-972-7277 ■ *Web:* www.federalinternational.com	Saint Louis	MO	63117	314-721-3377	721-2007
GreenMan Technologies Inc 7 Kimball Ln Bldg A *AMEX: GRN* ■ *Web:* www.greenman.biz	Lynnfield	MA	01940	781-224-2411	224-0114
Hummelstein Iron & Metal Inc Recycling Div 806 Burke Ave *TF:* 800-323-4333 ■ *Web:* www.hummelstein.com/recycle.htm	Jonesboro	AR	72401	870-932-8361	935-4044
International Metals Reclamation Co Inc 1 Inmetco Dr *Web:* www.inmetco.com	Ellwood City	PA	16117	724-758-2800	758-2845
Macon Iron & Paper Stock Co Inc 950 Lower Poplar Rd *TF:* 800-342-1933 ■ *Web:* www.thescrapmarket.com	Macon	GA	31202	478-743-6773	743-9965
Mervis Industries Inc 3295 E Main St *TF:* 800-637-3016 ■ *Web:* www.mervis.com	Danville	IL	61834	217-442-5300	477-9245
Metro Recycling Co Inc 2424 Beekman St *TF:* 800-235-4843	Cincinnati	OH	45214	513-251-1800	251-5239
Mid America Recycling 2742 E Market St *Web:* www.midamericarecycling.com	Des Moines	IA	50317	515-265-1208	262-2209
Minergy Corp 1512 S Commercial St *Web:* www.minergy.com	Neenah	WI	54956	920-727-1919	727-1418
North Shore Recycled Fibers Inc 53 Jefferson Ave	Salem	MA	01970	978-744-4330	744-8857
Pall Corp 2200 Northern Blvd *NYSE: PLL* ■ *TF:* 800-645-6532 ■ *Web:* www.pall.com	East Hills	NY	11548	516-484-5400	484-5228
Paper Tigers Inc 2121 Waukegan Rd Suite 130 *TF:* 800-621-1774 ■ *Web:* www.papertigers.com	Bannockburn	IL	60015	847-919-6500	919-6501
Potential Industries Inc 922 E 'E' St	Wilmington	CA	90744	310-549-5901	513-1361
Rock-Tenn Co 504 Thrasher St PO Box 4098 *NYSE: RKT* ■ *TF:* 800-762-5836 ■ *Web:* www.rocktenn.com	Norcross	GA	30091	770-448-2193	263-4483
Smurfit-Stone Container Corp Recycling Div 8182 Maryland Ave *Web:* www.smurfit-stone.com	Clayton	MO	63105	314-746-1100	
South Coast Recycling Inc 4560 Doran St **Fax Area Code:* 818	Los Angeles	CA	90039	323-245-5133	548-8814*
Strategic Materials Inc 16365 Park Ten Pl Suite 200 *Web:* www.strategicmaterials.com	Houston	TX	77084	281-647-2700	647-2710
Sun Valley Paper Stock Inc 11166 Pendleton St	Sun Valley	CA	91352	818-767-8984	767-1323
US Rubber Reclaiming Inc 2000 Rubber Way Rd *TF:* 800-842-6043 ■ *Web:* www.usrubberreclaiming.com	Vicksburg	MS	39180	601-636-7071	638-0151
wTe Corp 7 Alfred Cir *Web:* www.wte.com	Bedford	MA	01730	781-275-6400	275-8612

664 RECYCLED PLASTICS PRODUCTS

SEE ALSO Flooring - Resilient p. 1640

	City	State	Zip	Phone	Fax
Aeolian Enterprises Inc PO Box 888 *TF:* 800-269-4672 ■ *Web:* www.aeo1.com	Latrobe	PA	15650	724-539-9460	539-0572
Allen Ventures Inc 517 State Farm Rd *TF:* 877-423-9800 ■ *Web:* www.allenventures.com	Deerfield	WI	53531	608-423-9800	423-9804
American Recycled Plastic Inc 1500 Main St *TF:* 866-674-1525 ■ *Web:* www.itsrecycled.com	Palm Bay	FL	32905	321-674-1525	674-2365
Bedford Technology LLC 2424 Armour Rd PO Box 609 *Web:* www.bedfordtech.com	Worthington	MN	56187	507-372-5558	372-5726
Carefree Recycled Products 10290 S Progress Way Suite 102 *Web:* www.carefreerecycled.com	Parker	CO	80134	303-805-7809	805-7812
Cascades Re-Plast Inc 1350 ch Quatre-Saisons PO Box 514 *TF:* 888-313-2440 ■ *Web:* www.cascadesreplast.com	Notre-Dame-du-Bon-Conseil	QC	J0C1A0	819-336-2440	336-2442
Everlast Plastic Lumber Inc 800 W Market St PO Box 367 *Web:* www.everlastlumber.com	Auburn	PA	17922	570-754-7440	754-7441
GreenEarth Products Inc 2424 Hamilton Mill Rd	Charlotte	NC	28270	704-365-4964	
Koller Craft Plastic Products 1400 S Old Hwy 141 *Web:* www.koller-craft.com	Fenton	MO	63026	636-343-9220	343-1034
MacLumber Inc 4154 Faust St *Web:* www.maclumber.com	Bamberg	SC	29003	803-245-1700	245-1701
NEW Plastics Corp Renew Plastics Div 112 4th St PO Box 480 *TF:* 800-666-5207 ■ *Web:* www.renewplastics.com	Luxemburg	WI	54217	920-845-2326	845-2335
North American Technologies Group Inc 3000 Brittmoore Rd Suite D *Web:* www.natk.com	Houston	TX	77043	713-462-0303	934-8238
Northern Plastic Lumber 77 Saint David St *TF:* 888-255-1222 ■ *Web:* www.northernplasticlumber.com	Lindsay	ON	K9V1N8	705-878-5700	878-5702
Parkland Plastics Inc 104 Yoder Dr PO Box 339 *TF:* 800-835-4110 ■ *Web:* www.parklandplastics.com	Middlebury	IN	46540	574-825-4336	825-4338
PlasTEAK 3563 Copley Rd PO Box 4290 *TF:* 800-320-1841 ■ *Web:* www.plasteak.com	Akron	OH	44321	330-668-2587	666-0844
Plastic Lumber Co Inc 115 W Bartges St *TF:* 800-886-8990 ■ *Web:* www.plasticlumber.com	Akron	OH	44311	330-762-8989	762-1613
Plastic Lumberyard LLC 220 E Washington St *Web:* www.plasticlumberyard.com	Norristown	PA	19401	610-277-3900	277-3970
Plastic Pilings Inc 1485 S Willow Ave *Web:* www.plasticpilings.com	Rialto	CA	92376	909-874-4080	874-4860
Plastic Recycling of Iowa Falls Inc 10252 Hwy 65 *Web:* www.hammersplastic.com	Iowa Falls	IA	50126	641-648-5073	648-5074
Plastival 1685 Holmes Rd *TF:* 800-585-4988 ■ *Web:* www.plastival.com	Elgin	IL	60123	847-931-4771	931-1771
Recycled Plastic Man Inc PO Box 609 *TF:* 800-253-7742 ■ *Web:* www.recycledplasticman.com	Placida	FL	33946	941-698-1060	698-1038
Recycled Plastic Products Inc 1600 W Evans Ave Unit J *TF:* 800-235-7940 ■ *Web:* www.pfproducts.com	Englewood	CO	80110	303-975-0033	975-0050
Renew Plastics Div NEW Plastics Corp 112 4th St PO Box 480 *TF:* 800-666-5207 ■ *Web:* www.renewplastics.com	Luxemburg	WI	54217	920-845-2326	845-2335
Resco Plastics Inc 93783 Newport Ln *TF:* 800-266-5097 ■ *Web:* www.rescoplastics.com	Coos Bay	OR	97420	541-269-5485	269-2572
Saint Jude Polymer Corp 6 Industrial Park *Web:* www.stjudepolymer.com	Frackville	PA	17931	570-874-1220	874-2980
Trex Co Inc 160 Exeter Dr *NYSE: TWP* ■ *TF:* 800-289-8739 ■ *Web:* www.trex.com	Winchester	VA	22603	540-678-4070	542-6880

665 REFRACTORIES - CLAY

	City	State	Zip	Phone	Fax
ANH Refractories Co 400 Fairway Dr Cherrington Corporate Center **Fax:* Cust Svc ■ *Web:* www.hwr.com	Moon Township	PA	15108	412-375-6600	375-6860*
BNZ Materials Inc 6901 S Pierce St Suite 260 *TF:* 800-999-0890 ■ *Web:* www.bnzmaterials.com	Littleton	CO	80128	303-978-1199	978-0308
Christy Refractories Co 4641 McRee Ave *Web:* www.christyco.com/refract.html	Saint Louis	MO	63110	314-773-7500	773-8371
DFC Ceramics Inc 515 S 9th St *TF:* 888-372-1876 ■ *Web:* www.dfcceramics.com	Canon City	CO	81212	719-275-7525	275-2051
Freeport Brick Co PO Drawer F	Freeport	PA	16229	724-295-2111	295-5210
Harbison-Walker Refractories Co 400 Fairway Dr *Web:* www.hwr.com	Moon Township	PA	15108	412-375-6600	375-6962
MINTEQ International Inc 405 Lexington Ave 19th Fl *TF:* 888-801-1031 ■ *Web:* www.mineralstech.com/minteq.html	New York	NY	10174	212-878-1800	878-1952
Mount Savage Specialty Refractories Co 736 W Ingomar Rd *TF:* 800-437-6777 ■ *Web:* www.mtsavage.com	Ingomar	PA	15127	412-367-9100	367-2228
Permatech Inc 911 E Elm St *Web:* www.permatech.net	Graham	NC	27253	336-578-0701	578-7758
Reftech Div RENO Refractories Inc 601 Reno Dr **Fax Area Code:* 205 ■ *Web:* www.reftechnology.com	Morris	AL	35116	800-741-7366	647-2115*
RENO Refractories Inc 601 Reno Dr *TF:* 800-741-7366 ■ *Web:* www.renorefractories.com	Morris	AL	35116	205-647-0240	647-2115
RENO Refractories Inc Reftech Div 601 Reno Dr **Fax Area Code:* 205 ■ *Web:* www.reftechnology.com	Morris	AL	35116	800-741-7366	647-2115*
Resco Products Inc 2 Penn Center W Suite 430 *TF:* 888-283-5505 ■ *Web:* www.rescoproducts.com	Pittsburgh	PA	15276	412-494-4491	494-4571
Riverside Refractories Inc 201 Truss Ferry Rd *TF:* 800-226-4542 ■ *Web:* www.riversiderefractories.com	Pell City	AL	35128	205-338-3366	338-7456
Saxonburg Ceramics Inc 100 N Isabella St PO Box 688 *TF:* 800-245-1270 ■ *Web:* www.saxonburgceramics.com	Saxonburg	PA	16056	724-352-1561	352-3580
Shenango Advanced Ceramics LLC 606 McCleary Ave *Web:* www.shenangoceramics.com	New Castle	PA	16101	724-652-6668	652-6664
Utah Refractories Corp 2200 North 1100 W *TF:* 800-345-6808	Lehi	UT	84043	801-768-3591	768-2684
Whitacre Greer Fireproofing Inc 1400 S Mahoning Ave *TF:* 800-947-2837 ■ *Web:* www.wgpaver.com	Alliance	OH	44601	330-823-1610	823-5502

666 REFRACTORIES - NONCLAY

	City	State	Zip	Phone	Fax
Allied Mineral Products Inc 2700 Scioto Pkwy *Web:* www.alliedmineral.com	Columbus	OH	43221	614-876-0244	876-0981
American Flux & Metal 352 E Fleming Pike PO Box 74	Winslow	NJ	08095	609-561-7500	561-3724
C-E Minerals Inc 901 E 8th Ave *Web:* www.ceminerals.com	King of Prussia	PA	19406	610-265-6880	337-8122
Christy Refractories Co 4641 McRee Ave *Web:* www.christyco.com/refract.html	Saint Louis	MO	63110	314-773-7500	773-8371
Corhart Refractories Corp 1600 W Lee St *TF:* 800-233-1421	Louisville	KY	40210	502-778-3311	775-7300
Fedmet Resources Corp 4060 Saint Catherine St W Suite 630 *TF:* 800-609-5711 ■ *Web:* www.fedmet.com	Montreal	QC	H3Z2Z3	514-931-5711	931-8378
Inland Refractories Co 38600 Chester Rd *TF:* 800-321-0767 ■ *Web:* www.inlandrefractories.com	Avon	OH	44011	440-934-6600	934-6601
LWB Refractories Co PO Box 1189 *TF:* 800-233-1991	York	PA	17405	717-848-1501	848-2294
Minerals Technologies Inc 405 Lexington Ave 20th Fl *NYSE: MTX* ■ *Web:* www.mineralstech.com	New York	NY	10174	212-878-1800	878-1801
MINTEQ International Inc 405 Lexington Ave 19th Fl *TF:* 888-801-1031 ■ *Web:* www.mineralstech.com/minteq.html	New York	NY	10174	212-878-1800	878-1952
Monofrax Inc 1870 New York Ave *Web:* www.monofrax.com	Falconer	NY	14733	716-483-7200	665-2478
Morganite Crucible Inc 22 N Plains Industrial Rd Suite 1 *TF:* 800-936-7550 ■ *Web:* www.morganitecrucible.com	Wallingford	CT	06492	203-697-0808	265-6267
Mount Savage Specialty Refractories Co 736 W Ingomar Rd *TF:* 800-437-6777 ■ *Web:* www.mtsavage.com	Ingomar	PA	15127	412-367-9100	367-2228
New Castle Refractories Co 915 Industrial St *Web:* www.ncrci.com	New Castle	PA	16102	724-654-7711	654-6322
Norton Co Refractories Div 1 New Bond St Box 15008 *TF:* 800-543-4335 ■ *Web:* www.nortonabrasives.com	Worcester	MA	01615	508-795-5000	795-2051
Permatech Inc 911 E Elm St *Web:* www.permatech.net	Graham	NC	27253	336-578-0701	578-7758
Plibrico Co 1010 N Hooker St *TF:* 800-511-6203 ■ *Web:* www.plibrico-usa.com	Chicago	IL	60622	312-337-9000	337-9003
Ransom & Randolph Co 3535 Briarfield Blvd *TF:* 800-800-7496 ■ *Web:* www.ransom-randolph.com	Maumee	OH	43537	419-865-9497	865-9997
Reftech Div RENO Refractories Inc 601 Reno Dr **Fax Area Code: 205* ■ *Web:* www.reftechnology.com	Morris	AL	35116	800-741-7366	647-2115*
RENO Refractories Inc 601 Reno Dr *TF:* 800-741-7366 ■ *Web:* www.renorefractories.com	Morris	AL	35116	205-647-0240	647-2115
RENO Refractories Inc Reftech Div 601 Reno Dr **Fax Area Code: 205* ■ *Web:* www.reftechnology.com	Morris	AL	35116	800-741-7366	647-2115*
Rex Roto Corp 5600 E Grand River PO Box 980 *Web:* www.rexroto.com	Fowlerville	MI	48836	517-223-3787	223-6822
TYK America Inc 301 Brickyard Rd *Web:* www.tykamerica.com	Clairton	PA	15025	412-384-4259	384-4242
Vesuvius McDanel Co 510 9th Ave *Web:* www.ceramics.com/vesuvius	Beaver Falls	PA	15010	724-843-8300	843-5644
Wahl Refractories Inc 767 SR 19 S *TF:* 800-837-9245 ■ *Web:* www.wahlref.com	Fremont	OH	43420	419-334-2658	334-9445
Wulfrath Refractories Inc 6th & Center Sts PO Box 28 *TF:* 800-245-1801	Tarentum	PA	15084	724-224-8800	224-3353

667 REFRIGERATION EQUIPMENT - MFR

SEE ALSO Air Conditioning & Heating Equipment - Commercial/Industrial p. 1267

	City	State	Zip	Phone	Fax
Advance Energy Technologies Inc 1 Solar Dr *TF:* 800-724-0198 ■ *Web:* www.advanceet.com	Clifton Park	NY	12065	518-371-2140	371-0737
Aluma Shield Industries Inc Butcher Boy Doors Div 725 Summerhill Dr *TF:* 888-882-5862	DeLand	FL	32724	386-626-6789	626-6884
American Panel Corp 5800 SE 78th St *TF:* 800-327-3015 ■ *Web:* www.americanpanel.com	Ocala	FL	34472	352-245-7055	245-0726
Applied Process Cooling Corp 1408 Grove St *Web:* www.apcco.net	Healdsburg	CA	95448	707-433-9471	433-1310
Arctic Star Refrigeration Mfg Co Inc 3540 W Pioneer Pkwy *TF:* 800-229-6562 ■ *Web:* arcticstarmfg.com	Arlington	TX	76013	817-274-1396	277-4828
Berg Co 2160 Industrial Dr *Web:* www.berg-controls.com	Monona	WI	53713	608-221-4281	221-1416
Brown WA & Son Inc 209 Long Meadow Dr *TF:* 800-438-2316 ■ *Web:* www.wabrown.com	Salisbury	NC	28147	704-636-5131	637-0919
Burch Industries Inc 16780 Airbase Rd *TF:* 800-322-3688 ■ *Web:* www.burchindustries.com	Maxton	NC	28364	910-844-3688	844-3689
Butcher Boy Doors Div Aluma Shield Industries Inc 725 Summerhill Dr *TF:* 888-882-5862	DeLand	FL	32724	386-626-6789	626-6884
Continental Materials Corp 200 S Wacker Dr Suite 4000 *AMEX: CUO*	Chicago	IL	60606	312-541-7200	541-8089
CrownTonka Inc 10700 Hwy 55 Suite 300 *TF:* 800-523-7337 ■ *Web:* www.crowntonka.com	Plymouth	MN	55441	763-541-1410	541-1563
Custom Coolers LLC 5609 Azle Ave *TF:* 800-627-0488 ■ *Web:* www.cccoolers.com	Fort Worth	TX	76114	817-626-3737	626-1213
Delfield Co 980 S Isabella Rd *TF:* 800-733-8821 ■ *Web:* www.delfield.com	Mount Pleasant	MI	48858	989-773-7981	773-3210
Dole Refrigerating Co 1420 Higgs Rd *TF:* 800-251-8990 ■ *Web:* www.doleref.com/	Lewisburg	TN	37091	931-359-6211	359-8664
Edey Mfg Co Inc 2159 E 92nd St *TF:* 800-333-9634	Los Angeles	CA	90002	323-566-6151	566-0262
Eliason Corp 9229 Shaver Rd *TF Cust Svc:* 800-828-3655 ■ *Web:* www.eliasoncorp.com	Portage	MI	49024	269-327-7003	327-7006
Federal Industries Div Standex Corp 215 Federal Ave PO Box 290 *TF:* 800-356-4206 ■ *Web:* www.federalind.com	Belleville	WI	53508	608-424-3331	424-3234
Follett Corp 801 Church Ln *TF Cust Svc:* 800-523-9361 ■ *Web:* www.follettice.com	Easton	PA	18040	610-252-7301	250-0169
Gem Refrigerator Co 650 E Erie Ave *TF:* 800-922-1422 ■ *Web:* www.gemrefrigeratorco.com	Philadelphia	PA	19134	215-426-8700	426-8731
Harris Environmental Systems Inc 11 Connector Rd *TF:* 888-771-4200 ■ *Web:* www.harris-env.com	Andover	MA	01810	978-475-0104	475-7903
Haws Corp 1455 Kleppe Ln *TF:* 888-640-4297 ■ *Web:* www.hawsco.com	Sparks	NV	89431	775-359-4712	359-7424
Heatcraft Refrigeration Products 2175 W Park Place Blvd *TF:* 800-321-1881 ■ *Web:* www.heatcraftrpd.com	Stone Mountain	GA	30087	770-465-5600	465-5990
Hill PHOENIX Inc 709 Sigman Rd *TF:* 800-518-6630 ■ *Web:* www.hillphoenix.com	Conyers	GA	30013	770-388-0706	285-3071
Howe Corp 1650 N Elston Ave *Web:* www.howecorp.com	Chicago	IL	60622	773-235-0200	235-1530
Hussmann Corp 12999 St Charles Rock Rd *TF:* 800-879-1152 ■ *Web:* www.hussmann.com	Bridgeton	MO	63044	314-291-2000	298-4756
Ice-O-Matic 11100 E 45th Ave *TF:* 800-423-3367 ■ *Web:* www.iceomatic.com	Denver	CO	80239	303-371-3737	371-6296
IMI Cornelius Inc 101 Broadway St W *TF:* 800-238-3600 ■ *Web:* www.cornelius.com	Osseo	MN	55369	763-488-8200	488-4298
International Cold Storage Co Inc 215 E 13th St *TF:* 800-835-0001 ■ *Web:* www.icsco.com	Andover	KS	67002	316-733-1385	733-2434
KDIndustries 1525 E Lake Rd *TF:* 800-840-9577 ■ *Web:* www.kold-draft.com	Erie	PA	16511	814-453-6761	455-6336
Kloppenberg & Co 2627 W Oxford Ave *TF:* 800-346-3246 ■ *Web:* www.kloppenberg.com	Englewood	CO	80110	303-761-1615	789-1741
Kolpak Inc 2915 Tennessee Ave N *TF:* 800-826-7036 ■ *Web:* www.kolpak.com	Parsons	TN	38363	731-847-6361	847-5387
Kysor Panel Systems 4201 N Beach St *TF:* 800-633-3426 ■ *Web:* www.kysorpanel.com	Fort Worth	TX	76137	817-281-5121	281-5521
Lancer Corp 6655 Lancer Blvd *TF:* 800-729-1500 ■ *Web:* www.lancercorp.com	San Antonio	TX	78219	210-310-7000	310-7250
Leer LP 206 Leer St *TF Cust Svc:* 800-766-5337 ■ *Web:* www.leerlp.com	New Lisbon	WI	53950	608-562-3161	562-3203
Manitowoc Ice Inc 2110 S 26th St **Fax:* Sales ■ *TF:* 800-545-5720 ■ *Web:* www.manitowocice.com	Manitowoc	WI	54220	920-682-0161	683-7589*
McCann's Engineering & Mfg Co 4570 W Colorado Blvd *TF:* 800-423-2429 ■ *Web:* www.mccannseng.com	Los Angeles	CA	90039	818-637-7200	637-7222
Micro Matic USA Inc 10726 N 2nd St **Fax:* Sales ■ *TF:* 800-435-6950 ■ *Web:* www.micro-matic.com	Machesney Park	IL	61115	815-968-7557	968-0363*
MicroMetl Corp 3035 N Shadeland Ave Suite 300 *TF:* 800-662-4822 ■ *Web:* www.micrometl.com	Indianapolis	IN	46226	317-524-5400	524-5499
Morris & Assoc Inc 803 Morris Dr *Web:* www.morris-associates.com	Garner	NC	27529	919-779-1250	779-3466
Mr Winter Inc 8080 W 26th Ct *TF:* 800-327-3371 ■ *Web:* www.mrwinterinc.com	Hialeah	FL	33016	305-556-6741	821-1084
Multi-Flow Dispensers LP 1434 County Line Rd	Huntingdon Valley	PA	19006	215-322-1800	322-6883
National Refrigeration Co 563 Corbin Rd *TF:* 800-845-9800 ■ *Web:* www.kelv-air.com	Honea Path	SC	29654	864-369-1665	369-1668
Nor-Lake Inc 727 2nd St PO Box 248 *TF:* 800-388-5253 ■ *Web:* www.norlake.com	Hudson	WI	54016	715-386-2323	386-6149
Perlick Corp 8300 W Good Hope Rd *TF:* 800-558-5592 ■ *Web:* www.perlick.com	Milwaukee	WI	53223	414-353-7060	353-7069
Scotsman Ice Systems 775 Corporate Woods Pkwy *TF:* 800-726-8762 ■ *Web:* www.scotsman-ice.com	Vernon Hills	IL	60061	847-215-4500	913-9844
Seattle Refrigeration & Mfg Co 1057 S Director St *TF:* 800-228-8881 ■ *Web:* www.seafrig.com	Seattle	WA	98108	206-762-7740	762-1730
Semco Mfg Co 705 E Business 83 *Web:* www.semcomfgco.com	Pharr	TX	78577	956-787-4203	781-0620
Silver King Refrigeration Inc 1600 Xenium Ln N *TF:* 800-328-3329 ■ *Web:* www.silverking.com	Minneapolis	MN	55441	763-923-2441	553-1209
Springer Penguin Inc 460 Grand Blvd *TF:* 800-529-4375 ■ *Web:* www.springer-penguin.com	Westbury	NY	11590	516-333-4400	333-4759
Standex Corp Federal Industries Div 215 Federal Ave PO Box 290 *TF:* 800-356-4206 ■ *Web:* www.federalind.com	Belleville	WI	53508	608-424-3331	424-3234
Starrett Corp 6203 Johns Rd Suite 8 *TF:* 800-237-8350 ■ *Web:* www.leerlp.com/starretm.html	Tampa	FL	33634	813-882-3616	882-3702
Toromont Industries Ltd 3131 Hwy 7 W *TSX: TIH* ■ *Web:* www.toromont.com	Concord	ON	L4K1B7	416-667-5511	667-5555
True Mfg Co 2001 E Terra Ln *TF:* 800-325-6152 ■ *Web:* www.truemfg.com	O'Fallon	MO	63366	636-240-2400	
Turbo Refrigerating LLC 1815 Shady Oaks Dr *TF:* 800-775-8648 ■ *Web:* www.vogtice.com	Denton	TX	76205	940-387-4301	382-0364
Tyler Refrigeration 1329 Lake St *TF:* 800-992-3744 ■ *Web:* www.tylerrefrigeration.com	Niles	MI	49120	269-683-2000	684-9802
Victory Refrigeration Inc 110 Woodcrest Rd *TF:* 800-523-5008 ■ *Web:* www.victory-refrig.com	Cherry Hill	NJ	08003	856-428-4200	428-7299
Vilter Mfg LLC 5555 S Packard Ave PO Box 8904 *TF Orders:* 800-862-2677 ■ *Web:* www.vilter.com	Cudahy	WI	53110	414-744-0111	744-3483
Vogt Tube Ice 1000 W Ormsby Ave Suite 19 *TF:* 800-853-8648 ■ *Web:* www.tubeice.com	Louisville	KY	40210	502-635-3000	634-0479
WA Brown & Son Inc 209 Long Meadow Dr *TF:* 800-438-2316 ■ *Web:* www.wabrown.com	Salisbury	NC	28147	704-636-5131	637-0919
York Refrigeration Systems Frick 100 CV Ave *TF:* 800-487-2653 ■ *Web:* www.frickcold.com	Waynesboro	PA	17268	717-762-2121	762-8624

668 REFRIGERATION EQUIPMENT - WHOL

SEE ALSO Plumbing, Heating, Air Conditioning Equipment & Supplies - Whol p. 2126

	City	State	Zip	Phone	Fax
Abco Refrigeration Supply Corp 49-70 31st St *TF:* 800-786-2075 ■ *Web:* www.abcorefrig.com	Long Island City	NY	11101	718-937-9000	392-1296
Allied Supply Co Inc 1100 E Monument Ave *TF:* 800-589-5690 ■ *Web:* www.alliedsupply.com	Dayton	OH	45402	937-224-9833	224-5648
American Refrigeration Supplies PO Box 21127 *Web:* www.ars-net.com	Phoenix	AZ	85036	602-243-2792	243-2893
Automatic Ice & Beverage Inc PO Box 110159 *TF:* 800-476-4242	Birmingham	AL	35211	205-787-9640	787-9659
Baker Distributing Co 14610 Breakers Dr *TF:* 800-217-4698 ■ *Web:* www.bakerdist.com	Jacksonville	FL	32258	904-733-9633	407-4511
Dennis Supply Co PO Box 3376 *TF:* 800-352-4618 ■ *Web:* www.dennissupply.com	Sioux City	IA	51102	712-255-7637	255-4913
Don Stevens Inc 980 Discovery Rd *TF:* 800-444-2299	Eagan	MN	55121	651-452-0872	452-4189
Ernest F Mariani Co Inc 614 W 600 South *TF:* 800-453-2927	Salt Lake City	UT	84104	801-359-3744	531-9615
Gulf Refrigeration Supply Inc of Tampa 8920 Sabal Industrial Blvd *TF:* 888-683-2111	Tampa	FL	33619	813-626-5111	621-2329
Gustave A Larson Co PO Box 910 *TF:* 800-829-9609 ■ *Web:* www.galarson.com	Pewaukee	WI	53072	262-542-0200	542-1400
Hart & Price Corp PO Box 36368 *TF:* 800-777-9129 ■ *Web:* www.hartprice.com	Dallas	TX	75235	214-521-9129	350-4143
Harvey Sid Industries Inc 605 Locust St **Fax Area Code: 800* ■ *Web:* www.sidharvey.com	Garden City	NY	11530	516-745-9200	268-6542*
Insco Distributing Inc 12501 Network Blvd *TF:* 800-203-8400 ■ *Web:* www.inscohvac.com	San Antonio	TX	78249	210-690-8400	690-1524
ISI Commercial Refrigeration LP 9136 Viscount Row *TF:* 800-777-5070 ■ *Web:* www.isi-texas.com	Dallas	TX	75247	214-631-7980	631-6813
Larson Gustave A Co PO Box 910 *TF:* 800-829-9609 ■ *Web:* www.galarson.com	Pewaukee	WI	53072	262-542-0200	542-1400

Phone | Fax

Lewis RE Refrigeration Inc 803 S Lincoln St PO Box 92 .... Creston IA 50801 641-782-8183 782-8156
TF: 800-264-0767 ■ *Web:* www.relewisinc.com

Mariani Ernest F Co Inc 614 W 600 South ....Salt Lake City UT 84104 801-359-3744 531-9615
TF: 800-453-2927

Michel RE Co Inc 1 RE Michel Dr........................ Glen Burnie MD 21060 410-760-4000 761-3703
TF: 800-283-7362 ■ *Web:* www.remichel.com

Midlands Carrier Transicold Inc 13986 Valley Ridge Dr........... Omaha NE 68138 402-895-5500 895-7773
TF: 800-655-9382 ■ *Web:* www.midlandscarrier.com

Modern Ice Equipment & Supply Co DBA Modern Tour Inc
109 May Dr ....Harrison OH 45030 513-367-2101 367-5762
TF: 800-543-1581 ■ *Web:* www.modernice.com

Modern Tour Inc 109 May Dr ....Harrison OH 45030 513-367-2101 367-5762
TF: 800-543-1581 ■ *Web:* www.modernice.com

Preston Refrigeration Co Inc 3200 Fiberglass Rd............. Kansas City KS 66115 913-621-1813 621-6962
TF: 800-621-1813 ■ *Web:* www.prestonrefrigeration.com

RE Lewis Refrigeration Inc 803 S Lincoln St PO Box 92 .... Creston IA 50801 641-782-8183 782-8156
TF: 800-264-0767 ■ *Web:* www.relewisinc.com

RE Michel Co Inc 1 RE Michel Dr........................ Glen Burnie MD 21060 410-760-4000 761-3703
TF: 800-283-7362 ■ *Web:* www.remichel.com

Redico Inc 1850 S Lee Ct.. Buford GA 30518 770-614-1401 614-1403
TF: 800-242-3920 ■ *Web:* www.redicoinc.com

Refricenter of Miami Inc 7101 NW 43rd St......................Miami FL 33166 305-477-8880 599-9323
Web: www.refricenter.net

Refrigeration Supplies Distributor
1201 Monterey Pass Rd.............................Monterey Park CA 91754 323-264-2800 264-5205
Web: www.rsd-tc.com

Refron Inc 38-18 33rd St .... Long Island City NY 11101 718-392-8002 392-8006
TF: 800-473-3766 ■ *Web:* www.refron.com

Rogers Supply Co Inc PO Box 740..........................Champaign IL 61824 217-356-0166 356-1768
TF: 800-252-0406 ■ *Web:* www.rogerssupply.com

Sid Harvey Industries Inc 605 Locust St .... Garden City NY 11530 516-745-9200 268-6542*
*Fax Area Code: 800 ■ *Web:* www.sidharvey.com

Southern Refrigeration Corp 3140 Shenandoah Ave ....Roanoke VA 24017 540-342-3493 343-2163
TF: 800-763-4433 ■ *Web:* www.southernrefcorp.com

Stafford-Smith Inc 3414 S Burdick St ....Kalamazoo MI 49001 269-343-1240 343-2509
TF: 800-968-2442 ■ *Web:* www.staffordsmith.com

Supermarket Systems Inc PO Box 472513..................... Charlotte NC 28247 704-542-6000 542-6999
TF: 800-553-1905

SWH Supply Co 242 E Main St .... Louisville KY 40202 502-589-9287 585-3812
TF: 800-866-6672 ■ *Web:* www.swhsupply.com

Taylor Freezer Sales Co Inc 2032 Atlantic Ave .... Chesapeake VA 23324 757-545-7900 545-7908
TF: 800-768-6945 ■ *Web:* www.taylorfreezer.com

Taylor Freezers of Southern California
6825 E Washington Blvd ....Commerce CA 90040 323-889-8700 888-9292
TF: 800-927-7704 ■ *Web:* www.taylorfreezers.com

Taylor Industries Inc 1533 E Euclid Ave.................... Des Moines IA 50313 515-262-8221 262-6080
TF: 800-362-2500 ■ *Web:* www.taylorind.com

Transport Refrigeration Inc 301 Lawrence Dr ....De Pere WI 54115 920-339-5700 339-5717

United Refrigeration Inc 11401 Roosevelt Blvd..............Philadelphia PA 19154 215-698-9100
TF: 800-852-5132 ■ *Web:* www.uri.com

Western Pacific Distributors Inc 1739 Sabre St ....Hayward CA 94545 510-732-0100 732-0155
Web: www.teamwpd.com

Wittichen Supply Co Inc 1600 3rd Ave S......................Birmingham AL 35233 205-251-8203 251-9004
TF: 800-239-5294 ■ *Web:* www.wittichen-supply.com

669 RELOCATION CONSULTING SERVICES

Phone | Fax

Arizona Insights Relocation Center Inc
10446 N 74th St Suite 100 .... Scottsdale AZ 85258 480-481-8401 850-3030
TF: 800-899-7356

Cartus Corp 40 Apple Ridge Rd ....Danbury CT 06810 203-205-3400 748-3704
Web: www.cartus.com

Century 21 Real Estate Corp 1 Campus Dr..................Parsippany NJ 07054 973-428-9700 496-5966*
*Fax: Hum Res ■ *TF:* 800-992-8023 ■ *Web:* www.century21.com

Coldwell Banker Gundaker
2458 Old Dorsett Rd Suite 300.....................Maryland Heights MO 63043 314-298-5000 298-5059
TF: 800-325-1978 ■ *Web:* www.gundaker.com

Coldwell Banker Real Estate Corp 1 Campus Dr..............Parsippany NJ 07054 973-496-2653 496-7217
Web: www.coldwellbanker.com

Crye-Leike Inc 6525 Quail Hollow Rd......................... Memphis TN 38120 901-756-8900 758-5641
Web: www.crye-leike.com

Daugherty John Realtors 14094 Memorial Dr ....Houston TX 77079 281-497-3055 497-2155
Web: www.jdaugherty.com

GMAC Global Relocation Services 900 S Frontage Rd ....Woodridge IL 60517 866-465-0323 972-2287*
*Fax Area Code: 630 ■ *TF:* 800-589-7858 ■ *Web:* www.gmacglobalrelocation.com

Hewitt Relocation Services Inc
7901 Stoneridge Dr Suite 390...........................Pleasanton CA 94588 925-734-3434 734-3440
TF: 800-831-3444 ■ *Web:* www.reloaction.com

John Daugherty Realtors 14094 Memorial Dr ....Houston TX 77079 281-497-3055 497-2155
Web: www.jdaugherty.com

Joyner Fine Properties 2727 Enterprise Pkwy PO Box 31355..... Richmond VA 23294 804-270-9440 967-2770
TF: 800-446-3858 ■ *Web:* www.joynerfineproperties.com

Options/Resource Careers 343 W Bagley Rd Suite 302............. Berea OH 44017 440-243-2810 243-7082
TF Cust Svc: 800-899-1770 ■ *Web:* www.optionsrc.com

Prudential Real Estate Affiliates Inc
3333 Michelson Dr Suite 1000 .... Irvine CA 92612 949-794-7900 794-7036*
*Fax: Mktg ■ *TF:* 800-999-1120 ■ *Web:* www.prudential.com/realestate

Realogy Corp 1 Campus Dr.................................Parsippany NJ 07054 973-407-2000 407-7004
Web: www.realogy.com

RELO Direct Inc 161 N Clark St Suite 1250 .... Chicago IL 60601 312-424-0400 384-5988
TF: 800-548-4492 ■ *Web:* www.relodirect.com

Relocation America 25800 Northwestern Hwy Suite 210 ....Southfield MI 48075 248-208-2900 263-0093
TF Cust Svc: 800-521-0508 ■ *Web:* www.relocationamerica.com

Re/MAX Equity Group Inc 8405 SW Nimbus Ave..................Beaverton OR 97008 503-670-3000 670-1138
TF: 800-283-3358 ■ *Web:* www.equitygroup.com

Re/MAX International Relocation Services Inc
8390 E Crescent Pkwy Suite 500......................Greenwood Village CO 80111 303-770-5531 796-3599
TF: 800-442-3501 ■ *Web:* www.remax.com/corpreloc

Runzheimer International Runzheimer Pk ....Rochester WI 53167 262-971-2200 971-2254
TF: 800-558-1702 ■ *Web:* www.runzheimer.com

SIRVA Inc 700 Oakmont Ln.................................... Westmont IL 60559 630-570-3000 570-3606
NYSE: SIR ■ *TF:* 800-234-2788 ■ *Web:* www.sirva.com

Weichert Relocation Resources Inc 120 Longwater Dr............Norwell MA 02061 781-871-4500 982-9740*
*Fax: Mktg ■ *TF:* 800-926-8774 ■ *Web:* www.wrri.com

Welcome Wagon 245 Newtown Rd Suite 500 PO Box 9101 .... Plainview NY 11803 800-779-3526
Web: www.homestore.com/shop/welcomewagon

Windermere Relocation Inc
4040 Lake Washington Blvd NE Suite 201 .... Kirkland WA 98033 425-216-7100 216-7140
TF: 800-735-7029 ■ *Web:* www.windermererelocation.com

670 REMEDIATION SERVICES

SEE ALSO Associations & Organizations - General - Environmental Organizations p. 1304; Consulting Services - Environmental p. 1551; Waste Management p. 2412

Remediation services include clean-up, restorative, and corrective work to repair or minimize environmental damage caused by lead, asbestos, mining, petroleum, chemicals, and other pollutants.

Phone | Fax

3CI Complete Compliance Corp
1517 W North Carrier Pkwy Suite 104 .... Grand Prairie TX 75050 972-375-0006 660-3493
TF: 800-863-0345 ■ *Web:* www.american3ci.com

Allstate Power Vac Inc 928 E Hazelwood Ave.................. Rahway NJ 07065 732-815-0220 815-9892
TF: 800-876-9699 ■ *Web:* www.allstatepv.com

American Ecology Corp 300 E Mallard Dr Suite 300 .... Boise ID 83706 208-331-8400 331-7900
NASDAQ: ECOL ■ *Web:* www.americanecology.com

Aquagenix Inc 1460 SW 3rd St Suite B2 ....Pompano Beach FL 33069 954-943-5118 943-2994
TF: 800-832-5253

Brook Environmental & Engineering Corp
11419 Cronridge Dr Suite 10............................ Owings Mills MD 21117 410-356-4875 356-5073
TF: 800-381-4434 ■ *Web:* www.brookeng.com

Carylon Corp 2500 W Arthington St .... Chicago IL 60612 312-666-7700 666-5810
TF: 800-621-4342 ■ *Web:* www.caryloncorp.com

Chem-Nuclear Systems Inc 140 Stoneridge Dr .... Columbia SC 29210 803-256-0450 799-4470
TF: 800-925-1592 ■ *Web:* www.duratekinc.com

Chemical Waste Management Inc 1001 Fannin St Suite 4000...... Houston TX 77002 713-512-6200 513-6299

Clean Harbors Inc 1501 Washington St PO Box 859048.......... Braintree MA 02185 781-849-1800 794-1770
NASDAQ: CLHB ■ *TF:* 800-282-0058 ■ *Web:* www.cleanharbors.com

Clean Venture/Cycle Chem Inc 201 S 1st St.....................Elizabeth NJ 07206 908-355-5800 355-0562
TF: 800-347-7672 ■ *Web:* www.cyclechem.com

Commodore Applied Technologies Inc
2151 Jamieson Ave Suite 308 .... Alexandria VA 22314 703-567-1284 566-7526
Web: www.commodore.com

Contaminant Recovery Systems 9 Rocky Hill Rd................Smithfield RI 02917 401-231-3770 231-3360
Web: www.conrec.net

Conti Cos 3001 S Clinton Ave.......................... South Plainfield NJ 07080 908-561-7600 754-3283
Web: www.conticorp.com

Crosby & Overton Inc 1610 W 17th St..................... Long Beach CA 90813 562-432-5445 436-7540
TF: 800-827-6729 ■ *Web:* www.crosbyoverton.com

Cyn Environmental Services Inc 100 Tosca Dr PO Box 119...... Stoughton MA 02072 781-341-5108 344-3318
Web: www.cynenv.com

Delta Environmental Consultants Inc 5910 Rice Creek Pkwy ..... Shoreview MN 55126 651-639-9449 639-9497
TF: 800-477-7411 ■ *Web:* www.deltaenv.com

Duratek Inc 10100 Old Columbia Rd .... Columbia MD 21046 410-312-5100 290-9070
NASDAQ: DRTK ■ *TF:* 800-638-3838 ■ *Web:* www.duratekinc.com

Ecology Control Industries Inc 255 Parr Blvd .... Richmond CA 94801 510-235-1393 235-3709
TF: 800-788-1393 ■ *Web:* www.ecologycontrol.com

Envirite Inc 2050 Central Ave SE .... Canton OH 44707 330-456-6238 456-2801
Web: www.envirite.com

Environmental Enterprises Inc 10163 Cincinnati Dayton Rd.......Cincinnati OH 45241 513-772-2818 782-8950
TF: 800-722-2818 ■ *Web:* www.eeienv.com

Handex Group Inc 30941 Suneagle Dr .... Mount Dora FL 32757 352-735-1800 735-5990
TF: 800-989-3753 ■ *Web:* www.handex.com

JE Services Technologies Inc 125 Broadway Ave .... Oak Ridge TN 37830 865-220-4800 220-6033

Kemron Environmental Services Inc 8150 Leesburg Pike Suite 1410 ... Vienna VA 22182 703-893-4106 893-5636
TF: 800-777-1042 ■ *Web:* www.kemron.com

LVI Services Inc 80 Broad St 3rd Fl.........................New York NY 10004 212-951-3660 481-9895
Web: www.lviservices.com

MARCOR Remediation Inc 246 Cockeysville Rd Suite 1......... Hunt Valley MD 21030 410-785-0001 771-0348
TF: 800-547-0128 ■ *Web:* www.marcor.com

Marisol Inc 213 W Union Ave.............................. Bound Brook NJ 08805 732-469-5100 469-1957
TF: 877-627-4765 ■ *Web:* www.marisolinc.com

Nuclear Fuel Services Inc 1205 Banner Hill Rd.................... Erwin TN 37650 423-743-9141 743-9025
Web: www.atnfs.com

OVI Services Inc 10500 Telephone Rd........................Houston TX 77075 713-991-0480 991-2814

Pacific Ecosolutions Inc 2025 Battell Blvd ....Richland WA 99352 509-375-5160 375-0613

Pangea Inc 2604 S Jefferson St..........................Saint Louis MO 63118 314-333-0600 333-0601
Web: www.pangea-group.com

PDG Environmental Inc 1386 Beulah Rd Bldg 801.............. Pittsburgh PA 15235 412-243-3200 243-4900
TF: 800-972-7341 ■ *Web:* www.pdge.com

Perma-Fix Environmental Services Inc 1940 NW 67th Pl........ Gainesville FL 32653 352-373-4200 372-8963
NASDAQ: PESI ■ *TF:* 800-365-6066 ■ *Web:* www.perma-fix.com

Petroclean Inc PO Box 92 ....Carnegie PA 15106 412-279-9556 279-7082
TF: 800-247-3592 ■ *Web:* www.petroclean.com

PW Stephens Inc 15201 Pipeline Ln Unit B .... Huntington Beach CA 92649 714-892-2028 891-9807
TF: 800-937-1521 ■ *Web:* www.pwstephensinc.com

Romic Environmental Technologies Corp 2081 Bay Rd ...... East Palo Alto CA 94303 650-324-1638 462-2411
TF: 800-766-4248 ■ *Web:* www.romic.com

Safety-Kleen Corp 5400 Legacy Dr Cluster 2 Bldg 3................ Plano TX 75024 972-265-2000 265-2990
TF: 800-669-5740 ■ *Web:* www.safety-kleen.com

SEACOR Holdings Inc 460 Park Ave 12th Fl....................New York NY 10022 212-307-6633 582-8522
NYSE: CKH ■ *Web:* www.seacorsmit.com

Sevenson Environmental Services Inc 2749 Lockport Rd...... Niagara Falls NY 14305 716-284-0431 284-1796
TF: 800-777-3836 ■ *Web:* www.sevenson.com

Sigma Environmental Services Inc 1300 W Canal St .... Milwaukee WI 53233 414-643-4200 643-4210
TF: 800-732-4671 ■ *Web:* www.thesigmagroup.com

United Oil Recovery Inc 14-16 W Main St........................ Meriden CT 06451 203-238-6745 238-6772
TF: 888-276-0887

UXB International Inc 1715 Pratt Dr Suite 1300 ....Blacksburg VA 24060 540-443-3700 443-3790
TF: 800-422-4892 ■ *Web:* www.uxb.com

Waste Control Specialists LLC 5430 LBJ Fwy Suite 1700............Dallas TX 75240 972-450-4226 448-1447
Web: www.wcstexas.com

Winter Environmental Services Inc 1300 Spring St NW............ Atlanta GA 30309 404-588-3300 946-6494*
*Fax: Hum Res ■ *Web:* www.wintercompanies.com/envprofile.html

WRR Environmental Services Co Inc 5200 SR-93...............Eau Claire WI 54701 715-834-9624 836-8785
TF: 800-727-8760 ■ *Web:* www.wrres.com

671 RESEARCH CENTERS & INSTITUTIONS

SEE ALSO Market Research Firms p. 1946; Public Policy Research Centers p. 2144; Testing Facilities p. 2360

Phone | Fax

Aaron Diamond AIDS Research Center 455 1st Ave 7th Fl ....New York NY 10016 212-448-5000 725-1126
Web: www.adarc.org

Phone | Fax

Advanced Light Source 1 Cyclotron Rd MS 6-2100 ... Berkeley CA 94720 510-486-7745 486-4773
Web: www-als.lbl.gov
Advanced Technology for Large Structural Systems Center (ATLSS) Lehigh University 117 ATLSS Dr ... Bethlehem PA 18015 610-758-3525 758-5902
Web: www.atlss.lehigh.edu
Aerodyne Research Inc 45 Manning Rd ... Billerica MA 01821 978-663-9500 663-4918
Web: www.aerodyne.com
Aeronautical Systems Center (ASC)
1865 4th St Rm 240 ... Wright-Patterson AFB OH 45433 937-255-3334 656-4022
Web: www.wpafb.af.mil/asc
Aerospace Corp PO Box 92957 ... Los Angeles CA 90009 310-336-5000 336-1467
Web: www.aero.org
AFRRI (Armed Forces Radiobiology Research Institute)
8901 Wisconsin Ave ... Bethesda MD 20889 301-295-1953 295-4967
Web: www.afrri.usuhs.mil
Agricultural Research Service (ARS)
US Dept of Agriculture 1400 Independence Ave SW ... Washington DC 20250 202-720-3656 720-5427
Web: www.ars.usda.gov
Air Force Office of Scientific Research (AFOSR)
875 N Randolph St Suite 325 Rm 3112 ... Arlington VA 22203 703-696-7551 696-9556
Web: www.afosr.af.mil
Air Force Research Laboratory (AFRL)
AFRL/PA 1864 4th St Bldg 15 Rm 225 ... Wright-Patterson AFB OH 45433 937-904-9851
Web: www.afrl.af.mil
Air Resources Laboratory
NOAA/OAR/ARL 1315 East-West Hwy Bldg 3 Rm 3316 ... Silver Spring MD 20910 301-713-0684 713-0119
Web: www.arl.noaa.gov
Alaska Fisheries Science Center (AFSC)
National Marine Fisheries Service 7600 Sand Point Way NE Bldg 4 ... Seattle WA 98115 206-526-4000 526-4004
Web: www.afsc.noaa.gov
Albany International Research Co 777 West St ... Mansfield MA 02048 508-339-7300 339-4996
Web: www.albint.com
Albert Einstein Cancer Center (AECC)
Yeshiva University Albert Einstein College of Medicine 1300 Morris Park Ave ... Bronx NY 10461 718-430-2302 430-8550
Web: www.aecom.yu.edu/cancer
AMC Cancer Research Center 1600 Pierce St ... Denver CO 80214 303-233-6501 239-3400
TF: 800-321-1557 ■ *Web:* www.amc.org
American Institute for Cancer Research 1759 R St NW ... Washington DC 20009 202-328-7744 328-7226
TF: 800-843-8114 ■ *Web:* www.aicr.org
American Institutes for Research
1000 Thomas Jefferson St NW ... Washington DC 20007 202-342-5000 403-5001
Web: www.air.org
American Type Culture Collection (ATCC)
10801 University Blvd PO Box 1549 ... Manassas VA 20108 703-365-2700 365-2701
TF: 800-638-6597 ■ *Web:* www.atcc.org
Ames Laboratory Iowa State University 111 TASF ... Ames IA 50011 515-294-9557 294-3226
Web: www.external.ameslab.gov
Ames Research Center ... Moffett Field CA 94035 650-604-5000
Web: www.nasa.gov/centers/ames
Applied Physics Laboratory (APL-UW)
University of Washington 1013 NE 40th St Box 355640 ... Seattle WA 98105 206-543-1300 543-6785
Web: www.apl.washington.edu
Applied Physics Laboratory Johns Hopkins University
11100 Johns Hopkins Rd ... Laurel MD 20723 240-228-5000 228-1093
Web: www.jhuapl.edu
Applied Research Laboratory
Pennsylvania State University PO Box 30 ... State College PA 16804 814-865-6531 865-3105
Web: www.arl.psu.edu
Arctic Region Supercomputing Center
University of Alaska-Fairbanks 909 Kayukuk Dr Suite 105 PO Box 756020 ... Fairbanks AK 99775 907-450-8600 450-8601
Web: www.arsc.edu
Arctic Research Consortium of the US (ARCUS)
3535 College Rd Suite 101 ... Fairbanks AK 99709 907-474-1600 474-1604
Web: www.arcus.org
Argonne National Laboratory (ANL) 9700 S Cass Ave ... Argonne IL 60439 630-252-2000 252-9396
Web: www.anl.gov
Armed Forces Institute of Pathology (AFIP) 6825 16th St NW ... Washington DC 20306 202-782-2111 782-9376
Web: www.afip.org
Armed Forces Radiobiology Research Institute (AFRRI)
8901 Wisconsin Ave ... Bethesda MD 20889 301-295-1953 295-4967
Web: www.afrri.usuhs.mil
Arthropod-Borne Animal Diseases Research Laboratory
USDA/ARS ABADRL College of Agriculture Dept 3354 1000 E University Ave ... Laramie WY 82071 307-766-3600 766-3500
Arthur G James Cancer Hospital & Richard J Solove Research Institute 300 W 10th Ave ... Columbus OH 43210 614-293-5485 293-3132
TF: 888-293-5066 ■ *Web:* www.jamesline.com
Atlantic Oceanographic & Meteorological Laboratory (AOML)
NOAA/R/AOML 4301 Rickenbacker Cswy ... Miami FL 33149 305-361-4300 361-4449
Web: www.aoml.noaa.gov
Autism Research Institute (ARI) 4182 Adams Ave ... San Diego CA 92116 619-281-7165 563-6840
Web: www.autism.com
Baker Institute for Animal Health
Cornell University College of Veterinary Medicine Hungerford Hill Rd ... Ithaca NY 14853 607-256-5600 256-5608
Web: bakerinstitute.vet.cornell.edu
Barbara Ann Karmanos Cancer Institute 4110 John R St ... Detroit MI 48201 313-833-0710 831-6535
TF: 800-527-6266 ■ *Web:* www.karmanos.org
Battelle Memorial Institute Inc 505 King Ave ... Columbus OH 43201 614-424-6424 424-5263
Web: www.battelle.org
Bell Labs Inc 600 Mountain Ave ... Murray Hill NJ 07974 908-582-8500 508-8080
TF: 877-894-4647 ■ *Web:* www.alcatel-lucent.com
Belle W Baruch Institute for Marine & Coastal Sciences
University of South Carolina 607 EWS Bldg ... Columbia SC 29208 803-777-5288 777-3935
Web: www.cas.sc.edu/baruch
Beltsville Agricultural Research Center (BARC)
USDA/ARS BARC-West Bldg 003 Rm 223 10300 Baltimore Ave ... Beltsville MD 20705 301-504-6078 504-5863
Web: www.ars.usda.gov/main/site_main.htm?modecode=12-00-00-00
Beltsville Human Nutrition Research Center
USDA/ARS BARC-East Bldg 307-C Rm 117 10300 Baltimore Blvd ... Beltsville MD 20705 301-504-8157 504-9381
Web: www.ars.usda.gov/main/site_main.htm?modecode=12-35-00-00
Berkeley Sensor & Actuator Center
University of California 497 Cory Hall MC 1774 ... Berkeley CA 94720 510-643-6690 643-6637
Web: www-bsac.eecs.berkeley.edu
Bernard Schwartz Center for Economic Policy Analysis
New School of Social Research 79 5th Ave 11th Fl ... New York NY 10003 212-229-5717 229-5903
Web: www.newschool.edu/cepa
Bettis Laboratory 814 Pittsburgh-McKeesport Blvd ... West Mifflin PA 15122 412-476-5000 476-7509*
**Fax:* Hum Res ■ *TF:* 800-296-5002 ■ *Web:* www.bettislab.com
Biotechnology Center
2613 Institute for Genomic Biology 1206 W Gregory MC-195 ... Urbana IL 61801 217-333-1695 244-0466
Web: www.biotech.uiuc.edu

Phone | Fax

Biotechnology Center for Agriculture & the Environment
Rutgers The State University of New Jersey Foran Hall Cook College 59 Dudley Rd ... New Brunswick NJ 08901 732-932-8165 932-6535
Web: aesop.rutgers.edu/~biotech
Biotechnology Research & Development Corp 1815 N University St ... Peoria IL 61604 309-688-1188 688-1292
Web: www.biordc.com
Boyce Thompson Institute for Plant Research Inc
Cornell University Tower Rd ... Ithaca NY 14853 607-254-1234 254-1242
Web: bti.cornell.edu
Brain Research Institute
University of California Los Angeles 1506 Gonda Ctr Box 951761 ... Los Angeles CA 90095 310-825-5061 206-5855
Web: www.bri.ucla.edu
Brookhaven National Laboratory (BNL) PO Box 5000 ... Upton NY 11973 631-344-8000 344-3000
Web: www.bnl.gov/world/
Bumpers Dale Small Farms Research Center
USDA/ARS 6883 S State Hwy 23 ... Booneville AR 72927 479-675-3834 675-2940
Web: www.ars.usda.gov/Main/docs.htm?docid=2354
Bureau of Economic Analysis (BEA)
US Dept of Commerce 1441 L St NW ... Washington DC 20230 202-606-9900 606-5311
Web: www.bea.gov
Burnham Institute for Medical Research 10901 N Torrey Pines Rd ... La Jolla CA 92037 858-646-3100 646-3199
Web: www.burnham.org
Caelum Research Corp 1700 Research Blvd Suite 250 ... Rockville MD 20850 301-424-8205 424-8183
Web: www.caelum.com
California National Primate Research Center (CNPRC)
1 Shields Ave University of California ... Davis CA 95616 530-752-0447 752-2880
Web: www.cnprc.ucdavis.edu
California Pacific Medical Center Research Institute
475 Brannan St Suite 220 ... San Francisco CA 94107 415-600-1601 600-1753
Web: www.cpmc.org/professionals/research
Cancer Research Center of Hawaii
University of Hawaii 1236 Lauhala St ... Honolulu HI 96813 808-586-3013 586-3052
Web: www.crch.org
Cardiovascular Research Institute
University of California 400 Parnassus Ave Rm A-6110 Box 0957 ... San Francisco CA 94143 415-353-2357 353-2669
Web: cvri.ucsf.edu
Caribbean Marine Research Center
Perry Institute for Marine Science Caribbean Marine Research Center 100 N US Hwy 1 Suite 201 ... Jupiter FL 33477 561-741-0192 741-0193
Web: www.cmrc.org
Carnegie Institution of Washington 1530 P St NW ... Washington DC 20005 202-387-6400 387-8092
Web: www.carnegieinstitution.org
CBR Institute for Biomedical Research Inc 800 Huntington Ave ... Boston MA 02115 617-278-3000 278-3493
TF: 800-850-2466 ■ *Web:* cbr.med.harvard.edu
Center for Advanced Biotechnology & Medicine
Rutgers The State University of New Jersey 679 Hoes Ln W ... Piscataway NJ 08854 732-235-5300 235-5318
Web: cabm.umdnj.edu
Center for Advanced Food Technology
Rutgers University 63 Dudley Rd ... New Brunswick NJ 08901 732-932-8306 932-8690
Web: foodsci.rutgers.edu/caft
Center for Automation Research
University of Maryland AV Williams Bldg 115 Rm 4417 ... College Park MD 20742 301-405-4526 314-9115
Web: www.cfar.umd.edu
Center for Biofilm Engineering
Montana State University 366 EPS Bldg Box 173980 ... Bozeman MT 59717 406-994-4770 994-6098
Web: www.erc.montana.edu
Center for Biophysical Sciences & Engineering (CBSE)
University of Alabama CBSE 100 1530 3rd Ave S ... Birmingham AL 35294 205-934-5329 934-0480
Web: www.cbse.uab.edu
Center for Crops Utilization Research
Iowa State University 1041 Food Sciences Bldg ... Ames IA 50011 515-294-0160 294-6261
Web: www.ag.iastate.edu/centers/ccur
Center on Drug & Alcohol Research (CDAR)
University of Kentucky 643 Maxwelton Ct ... Lexington KY 40506 859-257-2355 323-1193
Web: cdar.uky.edu
Center for Education
Rice University 320 IBC Bldg 6100 Main St MS 147 ... Houston TX 77005 713-348-5145 348-4229
Web: centerforeducation.rice.edu
Center on Education & Training for Employment
Ohio State University 1900 Kenny Rd ... Columbus OH 43210 614-292-4353 292-1260
TF: 800-848-4815 ■ *Web:* www.cete.org
Center for Electromechanics
University of Texas at Austin 10100 Burnet Rd Bldg 133 ... Austin TX 78758 512-471-4496 471-0781
Web: www.utexas.edu/research/cem
Center for Engineering Logistics & Distribution (CELDi)
University of Arkansas Dept of Industrial Engineering 4207 Bell Engineering Ctr ... Fayetteville AR 72701 479-575-2124 575-8431
Web: www.celdi.ineg.uark.edu
Center for Global Change & Arctic System Research
University of Alaska-Fairbanks PO Box 757740 ... Fairbanks AK 99775 907-474-5818 474-6722
Web: www.cgc.uaf.edu
Center for Global Change Science
Massachusetts Institute of Technology 77 Massachusetts Ave Bldg 54-1312 ... Cambridge MA 02139 617-253-4902 253-0354
Web: web.mit.edu/cgcs/www
Center for High Performance Software Research (HiPerSoft)
Rice University 6100 Main St MS-41 ... Houston TX 77005 713-348-5186 348-3111
Web: www.hipersoft.rice.edu
Center on Human Development & Disability
University of Washington 1962 Columbia Rd Box 357920 ... Seattle WA 98195 206-543-2832 543-3561
Web: depts.washington.edu/chdd
Center for Information Systems Research (CISR)
Massachusetts Institute of Technology NE20-336 3 Cambridge Ctr ... Cambridge MA 02142 617-253-2348 253-4424
Web: mitsloan.mit.edu/cisr
Center for Integrative Toxicology
Michigan State University 165C Food Safety & Toxicology Bldg ... East Lansing MI 48824 517-353-6469 355-4603
Web: www.cit.msu.edu
Center for International Trade in Forest Products (CINTRAFOR)
University of Washington Box 352100 ... Seattle WA 98195 206-543-8684 685-0790
Web: www.cintrafor.org
Center for Lesbian & Gay Studies
City Univ of New York 365 5th Ave Rm 7115 ... New York NY 10016 212-817-1955 817-2985
Web: web.gc.cuny.edu/clags
Center for Medical Agricultural & Veterinary Entomology
1600 SW 23rd Dr ... Gainesville FL 32608 352-374-5901 374-5852
Web: www.ars.usda.gov/saa/cmave
Center for Nanophysics & Advanced Materials
University of Maryland Physics Bldg 082 ... College Park MD 20742 301-405-6129 405-3779
Web: www.csr.umd.edu
Center for Population Research
National Institute of Child Health & Human Development 6100 Executive Blvd MSC 7510 ... Bethesda MD 20892 301-496-1101 496-0962
Web: www.nichd.nih.gov/cpr

				Phone	Fax

Center for Radiophysics & Space Research
Cornell University 104 Space Sciences Bldg — Ithaca NY 14853 607-255-4341 255-3433
Web: astrosun.tn.cornell.edu

Center for Research on the Context of Teaching
Stanford University Galvez Mall CERAS Bldg 520 Rm 411 — Stanford CA 94305 650-725-1845 736-2296
Web: www.stanford.edu/group/CRC

Center for Research on Education Diversity & Excellence (CREDE) University of California Berkeley Graduate School of Education 1640 Tolman Hall — Berkeley CA 94720 510-643-9024
Web: www.crede.org

Center for Research on Learning
University of Kansas 1122 W Campus Rd Rm 517 — Lawrence KS 66045 785-864-4780 864-5728
Web: www.ku-crl.org

Center for Research in Mathematics and Science Education
San Diego State University 6475 Alvarado Rd Suite 206 — San Diego CA 92120 619-594-5090 594-1581
Web: www.sci.sdsu.edu/CRMSE

Center for Research for Mothers & Children
National Institute of Child Health & Human Development 6100 Executive Blvd MSC 7510 — Bethesda MD 20892 301-496-5097 480-7773
Web: www.nichd.nih.gov/about/crmc

Center for Space Exploration Power Systems
Auburn University Space Research Institute 231 Leach Ctr — Auburn AL 36849 334-844-5894 844-5900
Web: www.auburn.edu/research/vpr/sri

Center for Space Plasma & Aeronomic Research
University of Alabama Huntsville UAH Technology Hall S101 — Huntsville AL 35899 256-824-6413 824-6382
Web: cspar.uah.edu

Center for Space Research
University of Texas 3925 W Braker Ln Suite 200 — Austin TX 78759 512-471-5573 471-3570
Web: www.csr.utexas.edu

Center for the Study of Aging & Human Development
Duke University Medical Ctr Box 3003 — Durham NC 27710 919-660-7500 684-8569
Web: www.geri.duke.edu

Center for the Study of Language & Information
Stanford University Cordura Hall 210 Panama St — Stanford CA 94305 650-725-3286 723-0758
Web: www-csli.stanford.edu

Center for the Study of Teaching & Policy (CTP)
University of Washington Box 353600 — Seattle WA 98195 206-221-4114 616-8158
Web: depts.washington.edu/ctpmail

Center for Sustainable Environmental Technologies
Iowa State University 411 Marston — Ames IA 50011 515-294-7936 294-3091
Web: csetweb.me.iastate.edu

Center for Transportation Research
University of Tennessee 309 Conference Ctr Bldg 600 Henley St — Knoxville TN 37996 865-974-5255 974-3889
Web: ctr.utk.edu

Centers for Disease Control & Prevention (CDC)
National Center for Environmental Health
4770 Buford Hwy Bldg 101 — Chamblee GA 30341 770-498-0004 488-0083
TF: 888-232-6789 ■ *Web:* www.cdc.gov/nceh
National Center for HIV/AIDS Viral Hepatitis STD & TB Prevention
1108 Corporate Sq Bldg 8 — Atlanta GA 30329 404-639-8187 639-8609
Web: www.cdc.gov/nchstp/od/nchstp.html
National Institute for Occupational Safety & Health
200 Independence Ave SW — Washington DC 20201 202-401-6997
TF: 800-356-4674 ■ *Web:* www.cdc.gov/niosh

Centers for Disease Control & Prevention National Center for Zoonotic Vector-Borne & Enteric Diseases 1600 Clifton Rd MS D-76 — Atlanta GA 30333 404-639-3311
Web: www.cdc.gov/nczved

CERT (Computer Emergency Response Team)
Software Engineering Institute Carnegie Mellon University 4500 5th Ave — Pittsburgh PA 15213 412-268-7090 268-6989
Web: www.cert.org

Charles River Laboratories Inc 251 Ballardvale St — Wilmington MA 01887 978-658-6000 658-7132
NYSE: CRL ■ *TF:* 800-522-7287 ■ *Web:* www.criver.com

Charles Stark Draper Laboratory Inc 555 Technology Sq — Cambridge MA 02139 617-258-1000 258-1131
TF: 800-676-1977 ■ *Web:* www.draper.com

Children's Nutrition Research Center
USDA/ARS Baylor College of Medicine 1100 Bates St — Houston TX 77030 713-798-7022 798-7046
Web: www.bcm.edu/cnrc

Children's Research Institute
Children's National Medical Center 111 Michigan Ave NW Research Fl 5 — Washington DC 20010 202-476-3898 884-3985
Web: www.dcchildrens.com/cnmcresearch

Chiron Novartis Vaccines and Diagnostics 4560 Horton St — Emeryville CA 94608 510-655-8730 923-3864
Web: www.chiron.com

CIIT Centers for Health Research
6 Davis Dr PO Box 12137 — Research Triangle Park NC 27709 919-558-1200 558-1300
Web: www.ciit.org

Cincinnati Children's Hospital Research Foundation
Children's Hospital Medical Center 3333 Burnet Ave — Cincinnati OH 45229 513-636-4588 636-8453
TF: 800-344-2462 ■ *Web:* www.cincinnatichildrens.org/research

CNA Corp 4825 Mark Center Dr — Alexandria VA 22311 703-824-2000 824-2949
TF: 800-344-0007 ■ *Web:* www.cna.org

Coal Research Center
Southern Illinois University 405 W Grand Ave — Carbondale IL 62901 618-536-5521 453-7346
Web: www.crc.siu.edu

Coastal & Marine Institute
San Diego State University 5500 Campanile Dr — San Diego CA 92182 619-594-5142 594-6381
Web: www.sci.sdsu.edu/CMI

Cold Spring Harbor Laboratory (CSHL)
1 Bungtown Rd — Cold Spring Harbor NY 11724 516-367-8800 367-8846*
**Fax:* PR ■ *Web:* www.cshl.edu

Colorado Center for Astrodynamics Research (CCAR)
University of Colorado CB 431 ECNT 323 — Boulder CO 80309 303-492-6677 492-2825
Web: ccar.colorado.edu

Columbia Environmental Research Center (CERC)
4200 New Haven Rd — Columbia MO 65201 573-875-5399 876-1896
Web: www.cerc.usgs.gov

Columbia Institute for Tele-Information (CITI)
Columbia University 3022 Broadway Uris Hall Suite 1A — New York NY 10027 212-854-4222 854-1471
Web: www.citi.columbia.edu

Columbus Children's Research Institute 700 Children's Dr — Columbus OH 43205 614-722-2700 722-2716
Web: www.columbuschildrens.com

Computer Emergency Response Team (CERT)
Software Engineering Institute Carnegie Mellon University 4500 5th Ave — Pittsburgh PA 15213 412-268-7090 268-6989
Web: www.cert.org

Computer & Information Technology Institute
Rice University MS 39 6100 S Main St — Houston TX 77251 713-348-5823 348-6182
Web: www.citi.rice.edu

Computer Science & Artificial Intelligence Laboratory (CSAIL)
Massachusetts Institute of Technology 32 Vassar St Bldg 32 — Cambridge MA 02139 617-253-5851 258-8682
Web: www.csail.mit.edu

COMSAT Laboratories
20511 Seneca Meadows Pkwy Suite 200 — Germantown MD 20876 240-686-4420 686-4800
Web: www.viasat.com/comsat

Conservation & Production Research Laboratory
USDA/ARS PO Drawer 10 — Bushland TX 79012 806-356-5724 356-5750
Web: www.cprl.ars.usda.gov

Cooperative Institute for Arctic Research (CIFAR)
University of Alaska Fairbanks PO Box 757740 — Fairbanks AK 99775 907-474-5818 474-6722
Web: www.cifar.uaf.edu

Cooperative Institute for Limnology & Ecosystems Research (CILER) CILER/University of Michigan 2038-A Dana Bldg 440 Church St — Ann Arbor MI 48109 734-763-3010 763-8965
Web: ciler.snre.umich.edu

Cooperative State Research Education & Extension Service
US Dept of Agriculture 1400 Independence Ave SW MS 2201 — Washington DC 20250 202-720-7441 720-8987
Web: www.csrees.usda.gov

Coriell Institute for Medical Research 403 Haddon Ave — Camden NJ 08103 856-757-9758 757-9737
TF: 800-752-3805 ■ *Web:* www.coriell.org

Cornell NanoScale Science & Technology Facility (CNF)
Cornell University 250 Duffield Hall — Ithaca NY 14853 607-255-2329 255-8601
Web: www.cnf.cornell.edu

Courant Institute of Mathematical Sciences
New York University 251 Mercer St — New York NY 10012 212-998-3000 995-4121
Web: www.cims.nyu.edu

Creare Inc PO Box 71 — Hanover NH 03755 603-643-3800 643-4657
Web: www.creare.com

CTC Inc Public Safety Technology Center
134 Flanders Rd Suite 375 — Westborough MA 01581 508-870-0042 366-0101
TF: 800-328-8801 ■ *Web:* www.ctc.org

Curriculum Research & Development Group
University of Hawaii 1776 University Ave — Honolulu HI 96822 808-956-7961 956-9486
Web: www.hawaii.edu/crdg

Dale Bumpers Small Farms Research Center
USDA/ARS 6883 S State Hwy 23 — Booneville AR 72927 479-675-3834 675-2940
Web: www.ars.usda.gov/Main/docs.htm?docid=2354

Dana-Farber Cancer Institute 44 Binney St — Boston MA 02115 617-632-3000 632-5520*
**Fax:* PR ■ *TF:* 800-757-3324 ■ *Web:* www.dana-farber.org

Data Storage Systems Center (DSSC)
Carnegie Mellon University ECE Dept 5000 Forbes Ave — Pittsburgh PA 15213 412-268-6600 268-3497
Web: www.dssc.ece.cmu.edu

Defense Advanced Research Projects Agency (DARPA)
3701 N Fairfax Dr — Arlington VA 22203 703-696-2400 696-2209
Web: www.darpa.mil

DEKA Research & Development Corp
340 Commercial St Suite 401 — Manchester NH 03101 603-669-5139 624-0573
Web: www.dekaresearch.com

Delta States Research Center
USDA/ARS Experiment Station Rd PO Box 225 — Stoneville MS 38776 662-686-5265 686-5459
Web: www.ars.usda.gov/main/site_main.htm?modecode=64-02-00-00

Desert Research Institute 2215 Raggio Pkwy — Reno NV 89512 775-673-7300 673-7397
Web: www.dri.edu

Diabetes & Endocrinology Research Center
University of California San Francisco 513 Parnassus Ave Box 0534 — San Francisco CA 94143 415-514-3734 502-1447
Web: derc.diabetes.ucsf.edu

Diabetes Research Institute
University of Miami Leonard M Miller School of Medicine 1450 NW 10th Ave — Miami FL 33136 305-243-5300 243-4404
Web: www.diabetesresearch.org

Dryden Flight Research Center PO Box 273 — Edwards CA 93523 661-276-3311 276-3566
Web: www.dfrc.nasa.gov

Dupree Harry K Stuttgart National Aquaculture Research Center
USDA/ARS 2955 Hwy 130E PO Box 1050 — Stuttgart AR 72160 870-673-4483 673-7710
Web: ars.usda.gov/main/site_main.htm?modecode=62251000

Earth Sciences & Resources Institute
901 Sumter St Byrnes International Center Suite 402 — Columbia SC 29208 803-777-6484 777-6437
Web: www.esri.sc.edu

Earth System Research Laboratory NOAA/ESRL 325 Broadway — Boulder CO 80305 303-497-6643 497-6951
Web: www.esrl.noaa.gov

Eastern Regional Research Center (ERRC)
USDA/ARS 600 E Mermaid Ln — Wyndmoor PA 19038 215-233-6400 233-6559
Web: www.ars.usda.gov/main/site_main.htm?modecode=19350000

Economic Research Service (ERS)
US Dept of Agriculture 1800 M St NW — Washington DC 20036 202-694-5050 694-5757
Web: www.ers.usda.gov

Edgewood Chemical Biological Center
ATTN: AMSRD-ECB-AP-B 5183 Blackhawk Rd Bldg E3330 — Aberdeen Proving Ground MD 21010 410-436-3610 436-2014
Web: www.ecbc.army.mil

Edison Biotechnology Institute
Ohio University 101 Konneker Research Laboratories Bldg 25 The Ridges — Athens OH 45701 740-593-4713 593-4795
Web: www.ohiou.edu/biotech

Einstein Albert Cancer Center
Yeshiva University Albert Einstein College of Medicine 1300 Morris Park Ave — Bronx NY 10461 718-430-2302 430-8550
Web: www.aecom.yu.edu/cancer

Eleanor Roosevelt Institute 1899 Gaylord St — Denver CO 80206 303-333-4515 333-8423
Web: www.nsm.du.edu/eri

Electric Power Research Institute 3412 Hillview Ave — Palo Alto CA 94304 650-855-2000
Web: www.epri.com

ELORET Corp 465 S Mathilda Ave Suite 103 — Sunnyvale CA 94086 408-732-3028 732-2482
Web: www.eloret.com

Encorium Group Inc 1275 Drummers Ln Suite 100 — Wayne PA 19087 610-975-9533 975-9556
NASDAQ: ENCO ■ *Web:* www.covalentgroup.com

Energy & Environmental Research Center (EERC)
University of North Dakota 15 N 23rd St PO Box 9018 — Grand Forks ND 58202 701-777-5000 777-5181
Web: www.eerc.und.nodak.edu

Energy Institute
Pennsylvania State University Coal Utilization Laboratory Rm C211 — University Park PA 16802 814-863-5984 863-7432
Web: www.energy.psu.edu

Engineering Research Center for Advanced Electronic Materials Processing North Carolina State University 2410 Campus Shore Dr Rm 421 MRC Campus Box 7920 — Raleigh NC 27695 919-515-5153 515-3027
Web: www.aemp.ncsu.edu

Engineering Research Center for Net Shape Manufacturing
Ohio State University 1971 Neil Ave Rm 339 — Columbus OH 43210 614-292-5063 292-7219
Web: nsmwww.eng.ohio-state.edu

Enrico Fermi Institute University of Chicago 5640 S Ellis Ave — Chicago IL 60637 773-702-7823 702-8038
Web: efi.uchicago.edu

Environmental & Occupational Health Sciences Institute (EOHSI) 170 Frelinghuysen Rd — Piscataway NJ 08854 732-445-0200 445-0131
Web: www.eohsi.rutgers.edu

EPRI 3412 Hillview Ave — Palo Alto CA 94304 650-855-2000
Web: www.epri.com

Phone Fax

Ernest B Yeager Center for Electrochemical Sciences
Case Western Reserve University 10900 Euclid Ave Dept of Chemistry ... Cleveland OH 44106 216-368-3622 368-3006
Web: electrochem.cwru.edu

Eunice Kennedy Shriver Center 200 Trapelo Rd ... Waltham MA 02452 781-642-0001 894-9968
Web: www.umassmed.edu/shriver

Exponent Inc 149 Commonwealth Dr ... Menlo Park CA 94025 650-326-9400 326-8072
NASDAQ: EXPO ■ *TF:* 888-656-3976 ■ *Web:* www.exponent.com

Families & Work Institute 267 5th Ave 2nd Fl ... New York NY 10016 212-465-2044 465-8637
Web: www.familiesandwork.org

Federal Aviation Administration (FAA) Office of Aviation Research 800 Independence Ave SW Rm 528A ... Washington DC 20591 202-267-9251 267-5320
Web: research.faa.gov/aar

Federal Judicial Center
Thurgood Marshall Federal Judiciary Bldg 1 Columbus Cir NE ... Washington DC 20002 202-502-4000 502-4099
Web: www.fjc.gov

Fels Institute for Cancer Research & Molecular Biology
Temple Univ School of Medicine 3307 N Broad St Rm 150 ... Philadelphia PA 19140 215-707-4300 707-4588
Web: www.medschool.temple.edu/Research

Fermi National Accelerator Laboratory (Fermilab) PO Box 500 ... Batavia IL 60510 630-840-3000 840-4343
Web: www.fnal.gov

Florida Resources & Environmental Analysis Center
Florida State University UCC 2200 FSU ... Tallahassee FL 32306 850-644-2007 644-7360
Web: www.freac.fsu.edu

Florida Solar Energy Center
University of Central Florida 1679 Clearlake Rd ... Cocoa FL 32922 321-638-1000 638-1010
Web: www.fsec.ucf.edu

Fogarty International Center 31 Center Dr MSC 2220 ... Bethesda MD 20892 301-496-2075 594-1211
Web: www.fic.nih.gov

Food Research Institute
University of Wisconsin Madison 1550 Linden Dr ... Madison WI 53706 608-263-7777 263-1114
Web: www.wisc.edu/fri

Forest Products Laboratory
USDA Forest Service 1 Gifford Pinchot Dr ... Madison WI 53726 608-231-9200 231-9592
Web: www.fpl.fs.fed.us

Fox Chase Cancer Center 333 Cottman Ave ... Philadelphia PA 19111 215-728-6900 728-2594
TF: 888-369-2427 ■ *Web:* www.fccc.edu

Framingham Heart Study 73 Mt Wayte Ave Suite 2 ... Framingham MA 01702 508-935-3439 626-1262
Web: www.nhlbi.nih.gov/about/framingham

Francis Bitter Magnet Laboratory
Massachusetts Institute of Technology 150 Albany St NW 14 ... Cambridge MA 02139 617-253-5478 253-5405
Web: web.mit.edu/fbml

Fred Hutchinson Cancer Research Center
1100 Fairview Ave N PO Box 19024 ... Seattle WA 98109 206-667-5000 667-4051
Web: www.fhcrc.org

Friends Research Institute Inc 505 Baltimore Ave ... Baltimore MD 21204 410-823-5116 823-5131
TF: 800-822-3677 ■ *Web:* www.friendsresearch.org
Social Research Center 1040 Park Ave Suite 103 ... Baltimore MD 21201 410-837-3977 752-4218
Web: www.frisrc.org

Gas Technology Institute (GTI) 1700 S Mt Prospect Rd ... Des Plaines IL 60018 847-768-0500 768-0501
Web: www.gastechnology.org

Gatorade Sports Science Institute 617 W Main St ... Barrington IL 60010 847-381-1980
TF: 800-616-4774 ■ *Web:* www.gssiweb.com

General Atomics 3550 General Atomics Ct PO Box 85608 ... San Diego CA 92186 858-455-3000 455-3621
Web: www.ga.com

Geophysical Fluid Dynamics Laboratory (GFDL)
NOAA/OAR/GFDL 201 Forrestal Rd ... Princeton NJ 08540 609-452-6500 987-5063
Web: www.gfdl.noaa.gov

Georgia Tech Fusion Research Center 900 Atlantic Dr Rm G106 ... Atlanta GA 30332 404-894-3758 894-3733
Web: www.frc.gatech.edu

Georgia Tech Research Institute (GTRI) 400 10th St NW ... Atlanta GA 30332 404-894-3400 894-9875
Web: www.gtri.gatech.edu

Gerontology Research Center
Johns Hopkins Bayview Medical Ctr 5600 Nathan Shock Dr ... Baltimore MD 21224 410-558-8110
Web: www.grc.nia.nih.gov

Glenn Research Center Lewis Field 21000 Brookpark Rd ... Brookpark OH 44135 216-433-4000 433-8000
Web: www.nasa.gov/centers/glenn/home/index.html

Goddard Institute for Space Studies 2880 Broadway ... New York NY 10025 212-678-5500 678-5552
Web: www.giss.nasa.gov

Goddard Space Flight Center Greenbelt Rd ... Greenbelt MD 20771 301-286-2000 286-1707*
**Fax:* PR ■ *Web:* www.nasa.gov/centers/goddard

Grain Marketing & Production Research Center
USDA/ARS 1515 College Ave ... Manhattan KS 66502 785-776-2701 776-2789
TF: 800-627-0388 ■ *Web:* www.ars.usda.gov/main/site_main.htm?modecode=54300000

Grand Forks Human Nutrition Research Center
USDA/ARS 2420 2nd Ave N PO Box 9034 ... Grand Forks ND 58202 701-795-8353 795-8395
Web: www.ars.usda.gov/Main/docs.htm?docid=3898

Great Lakes Environmental Research Laboratory (GLERL)
NOAA/OAR/GLERL 2205 Commonwealth Blvd ... Ann Arbor MI 48105 734-741-2235 741-2055
Web: www.glerl.noaa.gov

Gregory Fleming James Cystic Fibrosis Research Center
University of Alabama 1530 3rd Ave S MCLM 790 ... Birmingham AL 35294 205-934-7210 934-7593
Web: www.cfcenter.uab.edu

GTI (Gas Technology Institute) 1700 S Mt Prospect Rd ... Des Plaines IL 60018 847-768-0500 768-0501
Web: www.gastechnology.org

Gulf Coast Research Laboratory 703 E Beach Dr ... Ocean Springs MS 39564 228-872-4200 872-4204
Web: www.coms.usm.edu

H Lee Moffitt Cancer Center & Research Institute
University of South Florida 12902 Magnolia Dr ... Tampa FL 33612 813-972-4673 745-8495
TF: 800-456-3434 ■ *Web:* www.moffittcancercenter.com

Harbor Branch Oceanographic Institution 5600 US 1 N ... Fort Pierce FL 34946 772-465-2400 465-7156
Web: www.hboi.edu

HARC (Houston Advanced Research Center)
4800 Research Forest Dr ... The Woodlands TX 77381 281-367-1348 363-7914
Web: www.harc.edu

Harry K Dupree Stuttgart National Aquaculture Research Center
USDA/ARS 2955 Hwy 130E PO Box 1050 ... Stuttgart AR 72160 870-673-4483 673-7710
Web: ars.usda.gov/main/site_main.htm?modecode=62251000

Harry Reid Center for Environmental Studies
University of Nevada 4505 Maryland Pkwy Box 454030 ... Las Vegas NV 89154 702-895-3382 895-3094
Web: hrcweb.lv-hrc.nevada.edu

Harvard-Smithsonian Center for Astrophysics 60 Garden St ... Cambridge MA 02138 617-495-7000 495-7468
Web: cfa-www.harvard.edu

Hatfield Marine Science Center
Oregon State University 2030 SE Marine Science Dr ... Newport OR 97365 541-867-0100 867-0138
Web: hmsc.oregonstate.edu

Hawaii Agriculture Research Center (HARC)
99-193 Aiea Heights Dr Suite 300 ... Aiea HI 96701 808-487-5561 486-5020
Web: www.hawaiiag.org/harc

Hawaii Insitute of Geophysics & Planetology
University of Hawaii 1680 East-West Rd Post 602B ... Honolulu HI 96822 808-956-8760 956-3188
Web: www.higp.hawaii.edu

Hawaii Undersea Research Laboratory
University of Hawaii at Manoa 1000 Pope Rd MSB Rm 303 ... Honolulu HI 96822 808-956-6335 956-9772
Web: www.soest.hawaii.edu/HURL

Hazen Research Inc 4601 Indiana St ... Golden CO 80403 303-279-4501 278-1528
Web: www.hazenusa.com

High Performance Computing Collaboratory
Mississippi State University HPC Bldg Box 9627 ... Mississippi State MS 39762 662-325-8278 325-7692
Web: www.erc.msstate.edu

Hill Top Research Inc 6088 Main & Mill Sts PO Box 138 ... Miamiville OH 45147 513-831-3114 831-1217
TF: 800-785-2693 ■ *Web:* www.hill-top.com

Holifield Radioactive Ion Beam Facility
Oak Ridge National Laboratory Bldg 6000 PO Box 2008 ... Oak Ridge TN 37831 865-574-4114 574-1268
Web: www.phy.ornl.gov/hribf

Holland Jerome H Laboratory for the Biomedical Sciences
American Red Cross Biomedical Sciences 15601 Crabbs Branch Way ... Rockville MD 20855 301-738-0600 738-0660
Web: www.redcross.org/services/youth/lab/holland.html

Hopkins Population Center
Johns Hopkins University 615 N Wolfe St Suite E-4644 ... Baltimore MD 21205 410-955-7803 502-5831
Web: www.jhsph.edu/popcenter

Houston Advanced Research Center (HARC)
4800 Research Forest Dr ... The Woodlands TX 77381 281-367-1348 363-7914
Web: www.harc.edu

Howard Hughes Medical Institute 4000 Jones Bridge Rd ... Chevy Chase MD 20815 301-215-8500 215-8558
Web: www.hhmi.org

Hughes Howard Medical Institute 4000 Jones Bridge Rd ... Chevy Chase MD 20815 301-215-8500 215-8558
Web: www.hhmi.org

Human Resources Research Organization (HumRRO)
66 Canal Ctr Plaza Suite 400 ... Alexandria VA 22314 703-549-3611 549-9025
Web: www.humrro.org

HumRRO (Human Resources Research Organization)
66 Canal Ctr Plaza Suite 400 ... Alexandria VA 22314 703-549-3611 549-9025
Web: www.humrro.org

Huntingdon Life Sciences Inc
Princeton Research Centre PO Box 2360 Mettlers Rd ... East Millstone NJ 08875 732-873-2550 873-3992
Web: www.huntingdon.com

Hydrologic Engineering Center 609 2nd St ... Davis CA 95616 530-756-1104 756-8250
Web: www.hec.usace.army.mil

IBM Almaden Research Center 650 Harry Rd ... San Jose CA 95120 408-927-1000 927-2100
Web: www.almaden.ibm.com

ICAIR (International Center for Advanced Internet Research)
750 N Lake Shore Dr Suite 600 ... Chicago IL 60611 312-503-0735
Web: www.icair.org

Idaho National Laboratory (INL) PO Box 1625 ... Idaho Falls ID 83415 866-495-7440 526-5408*
**Fax Area Code:* 208 ■ *TF:* 800-708-2680 ■ *Web:* www.inl.gov

Ideas International Inc 800 Westchester Ave Suite S620 ... Rye Brook NY 10573 914-937-4302 937-2485
TF: 800-253-1799 ■ *Web:* www.ideasinternational.com

IIT Research Institute (IITRI) 10 W 35th St ... Chicago IL 60616 312-567-4000 567-4067*
**Fax:* Hum Res ■ *Web:* www.iitri.org

Indiana Molecular Biology Institute
Indiana University 800 E 3rd St ... Bloomington IN 47405 812-855-4183 855-6082
Web: imbi.bio.indiana.edu

Industrial Partnership for Research in Interfacial & Materials Engineering (IPRIME) University of Minnesota
151 Amundson Hall 421 Washington Ave SE ... Minneapolis MN 55455 612-626-9509 626-1686
Web: www.iprime.umn.edu

Industrial Relations Center
University of Minnesota Carlson School of Management 321 19th Ave S Suite 3-300 ... Minneapolis MN 55455 612-624-2500 624-8360
Web: www.irc.csom.umn.edu

Innovative Nuclear Space Power & Propulsion Institute
University of Florida 2800 SW Archer Rd Bldg 554 PO Box 116502 ... Gainesville FL 32611 352-392-1427 392-8656
Web: www.inspi.ufl.edu

Institute of Arctic & Alpine Research (INSTAAR)
University of Colorado 1560 30th St CB 450 ... Boulder CO 80309 303-492-6387 492-6388
Web: instaar.colorado.edu

Institute for Astronomy
University of Hawaii 2680 Woodlawn Dr ... Honolulu HI 96822 808-956-8312 988-2790
Web: www.ifa.hawaii.edu

Institute for Basic Research in Developmental Disabilities
1050 Forest Hill Rd ... Staten Island NY 10314 718-494-0600 698-3803
Web: www.omr.state.ny.us/ws/ws_ibr_resources.jsp

Institute of Behavioral Science
University of Colorado 1416 Broadway ... Boulder CO 80302 303-492-8147 492-6924
Web: www.colorado.edu/IBS

Institute for Biotechnology & Life Science Technologies
Cornell University Biotechnology Bldg Rm 130 ... Ithaca NY 14853 607-255-2300 255-6249
Web: www.biotech.cornell.edu

Institute for Defense Analyses (IDA) 4850 Mark Center Dr ... Alexandria VA 22311 703-845-2000 845-2588
Web: www.ida.org

Institute for Diabetes Obesity & Metabolism (IDOM)
University of Pennsylvania 700 Clinical Research Bldg ... Philadelphia PA 19104 215-898-4365 898-5408
Web: www.med.upenn.edu/pdc/

Institute of Ecosystem Studies (IES)
2801 Sharon Tpke Box AB ... Millbrook NY 12545 845-677-5343 677-5976
Web: www.ecostudies.org

Institute of Education Sciences
US Dept of Education 555 New Jersey Ave NW Rm 600 ... Washington DC 20208 202-219-1385 219-1466
Web: www.ed.gov/about/offices/list/ies

Institute of Gerontology
University of Michigan 300 N Ingalls St ... Ann Arbor MI 48109 734-764-3493 936-2116
Web: www.iog.umich.edu

Institute of Human Origins (IHO)
Arizona State Univ PO Box 874101 ... Tempe AZ 85287 480-727-6580 727-6570
Web: www.asu.edu/clas/iho

Institute of Marine Science University of Alaska Fairbanks ... Fairbanks AK 99775 907-474-7829 474-7204
Web: www.ims.uaf.edu

Institute of Materials Science
University of Connecticut 97 N Eagleville Rd ... Storrs CT 06269 860-486-4623 486-4745
Web: www.ims.uconn.edu

Institute for Molecular Manufacturing (IMM)
555 Bryant St Suite 354 ... Palo Alto CA 94301 650-917-1120
Web: www.imm.org

Institute for Molecular Virology
University of Wisconsin Bock Laboratories Rm 413 1525 Linden Dr ... Madison WI 53706 608-262-4540 262-7414
Web: www.virology.wisc.edu/IMV

Institute for Physical Research & Technology (IPRT)
Iowa State University 305 TASF ... Ames IA 50011 515-294-8902 294-4456
Web: www.iprt.iastate.edu

Institute for Research on Poverty
University of Wisconsin Madison 1180 Observatory Dr 3412 Social Science Bldg ... Madison WI 53706 608-262-6358 265-3119
Web: www.irp.wisc.edu

Institute for Scientific Analysis 390 4th St 2nd Fl ... San Francisco CA 94107 415-777-2352 563-9940
Web: www.scientificanalysis.org

Phone Fax

Institute for Simulation & Training 3100 Technology Pkwy ... Orlando FL 32826 407-882-1300 658-5059
Web: www.ist.ucf.edu

Institute for Social Behavioral & Economic Research
University of California 2201 N Hall ... Santa Barbara CA 93106 805-893-2548 893-7995
Web: www.isber.ucsb.edu

Institute for Social Research
University of Michigan 426 Thompson St ... Ann Arbor MI 48104 734-764-8363 936-9708
Web: www.isr.umich.edu

Institute for Systems Research
University of Maryland 2173 AV Williams Bldg ... College Park MD 20742 301-405-6615 314-9920
Web: www.isr.umd.edu

Institute for Telecommunications Sciences 325 Broadway ... Boulder CO 80305 303-497-5216
Web: www.its.bldrdoc.gov

Integrated Media Systems Center
University of Southern California 734 W Adams Blvd ... Los Angeles CA 90089 213-743-2314 743-4519
Web: imsc.usc.edu

International Arctic Research Center (IARC)
930 Koyukuk Dr PO Box 757340 ... Fairbanks AK 99775 907-474-7413 474-5662
Web: www.iarc.uaf.edu

International Center for Advanced Internet Research (iCAIR)
750 N Lake Shore Dr Suite 600 ... Chicago IL 60611 312-503-0735
Web: www.icair.org

International Diabetes Center at Park Nicollet
Park Nicollet Clinic - St Louis Park 3800 Park Nicollet Blvd ... Saint Louis Park MN 55416 952-993-3393 993-3634
TF: 888-825-6315 ■ *Web:* www.parknicollet.com/diabetes

International Institute of Tropical Forestry
USDA Forest Service Jardin Botanico Sur 1201 Calle Ceiba ... San Juan PR 00926 787-766-5335 766-6302
Web: www.fs.fed.us/global/iitf

IPRIME (Industrial Partnership for Research in Interfacial & Materials Engineering) University of Minnesota 151 Amundson Hall 421 Washington Ave SE ... Minneapolis MN 55455 612-626-9509 626-1686
Web: www.iprime.umn.edu

Jamie Whitten Delta States Research Center
USDA/ARS Experiment Station Rd PO Box 225 ... Stoneville MS 38776 662-686-5265 686-5459
Web: www.ars.usda.gov/main/site_main.htm?modecode=64-02-00-00

Jean Mayer USDA Human Nutrition Research Center on Aging
Tufts University 711 Washington St ... Boston MA 02111 617-556-3000 556-3344
Web: www.hnrc.tufts.edu

Jerome H Holland Laboratory for the Biomedical Sciences
American Red Cross Biomedical Sciences 15601 Crabbs Branch Way ... Rockville MD 20855 301-738-0600 738-0660
Web: www.redcross.org/services/youth/lab/holland.html

Jet Propulsion Laboratory (JPL) 4800 Oak Grove Dr ... Pasadena CA 91109 818-354-4321
Web: www.jpl.nasa.gov

John A Volpe National Transportation Systems Center
55 Broadway ... Cambridge MA 02142 617-494-2000
Web: www.volpe.dot.gov

John Wayne Cancer Institute 2200 Santa Monica Blvd ... Santa Monica CA 90404 800-262-6259 449-5259*
**Fax Area Code:* 310 ■ *Web:* www.jwci.org

Johns Hopkins University Applied Physics Laboratory
11100 Johns Hopkins Rd ... Laurel MD 20723 240-228-5000 228-1093
Web: www.jhuapl.edu

Johnson Space Center 2101 NASA Pkwy ... Houston TX 77058 281-483-0123 483-9192
Web: www.nasa.gov/centers/johnson

Joint Institute for Laboratory Astrophysics (JILA)
University of Colorado CB 440 ... Boulder CO 80309 303-492-7789 492-5235
Web: jilawww.colorado.edu

Joint Institute for Marine & Atmospheric Research (JIMAR)
University of Hawaii 1000 Pope Rd MSB Rm 312 ... Honolulu HI 96822 808-956-8083 956-4104
Web: ilikai.soest.hawaii.edu/JIMAR

Joint Institute for Marine Observations (JIMO)
Scripps Institution of Oceanography University of California San Diego 9500 Gilman Dr ... La Jolla CA 92093 858-534-4100
Web: www.jimo.ucsd.edu

Joseph P & Rose F Kennedy Institute of Ethics
Georgetown University Healy Hall 4th Fl 37th & 'O' St NW ... Washington DC 20057 202-687-8099 687-8089
Web: kennedyinstitute.georgetown.edu

Joseph Stokes Jr Research Institute
Children's Hospital of Philadelphia 3615 Civic Center Blvd ... Philadelphia PA 19104 215-590-3800 590-3804
Web: stokes.chop.edu

Joslin Diabetes Center 1 Joslin Pl ... Boston MA 02215 617-732-2400 732-2542
Web: www.joslin.org

JPL (Jet Propulsion Laboratory) 4800 Oak Grove Dr ... Pasadena CA 91109 818-354-4321
Web: www.jpl.nasa.gov

Kaiser Permanente Center for Health Research
3800 N Interstate Ave ... Portland OR 97227 503-335-2400 335-2424
Web: www.kpchr.org

Karmanos Barbara Ann Cancer Institute 4110 John R St ... Detroit MI 48201 313-833-0710 831-6535
TF: 800-527-6266 ■ *Web:* www.karmanos.org

Kavali Institute for Astrophysics & Space Research
Massachusetts Institute of Technology 77 Massachusetts Ave ... Cambridge MA 02139 617-253-6104 253-0861
Web: space.mit.edu

Keck WM Center for Comparative & Functional Genomics
340 Edward R Madigan Laboratory 1201 W Gregory Dr ... Urbana IL 61801 217-265-5057 265-5066
Web: www.biotec.uiuc.edu/centers/Keck

Kendle International Inc 441 Vine St 1200 Carew Tower ... Cincinnati OH 45202 513-381-5550 381-5870
NASDAQ: KNDL ■ *TF:* 800-733-1572 ■ *Web:* www.kendle.com

Kennedy Institute of Ethics
Georgetown University Healy Hall 4th Fl 37th & 'O' St NW ... Washington DC 20057 202-687-8099 687-8089
Web: kennedyinstitute.georgetown.edu

Kennedy Space Center Public Inquiries ... Kennedy Space Center FL 32899 321-867-5000
TF: 800-561-8618 ■ *Web:* www.nasa.gov/centers/kennedy

Keweenaw Research Center
Michigan Technological University 1400 Townsend Dr ... Houghton MI 49931 906-487-2750 487-2202
Web: www.mtukrc.org

Kika de la Garza Subtropical Agricultural Research Center
USDA/ARS 2413 E Hwy 83 Bldg 200 ... Weslaco TX 78596 956-447-6301 447-6345
Web: www.ars.usda.gov/spa/weslaco

Kline Nathan S Institute for Psychiatric Research
140 Old Orangeburg Rd Bldg 35 ... Orangeburg NY 10962 845-398-5500 398-5419
Web: www.rfmh.org/nki

Knolls Atomic Power Laboratory (KAPL) PO Box 1072 ... Schenectady NY 12301 518-395-4000 395-4658
Web: www.kaplinc.com

Kresge Hearing Research Institute (KHRI)
University of Michigan Medical School 1301 E Ann St Rm 5032 ... Ann Arbor MI 48109 734-764-8110 764-0014
Web: www.khri.med.umich.edu

Kurzweil Technologies Inc 15 Walnut St Suite 200 ... Wellesley Hills MA 02481 781-263-0000 263-9999
TF: 877-365-9633 ■ *Web:* www.kurzweiltech.com

L-3 Communications Titan Group 11955 Freedom Dr ... Reston VA 20190 703-434-4000 434-5075
Web: www.titan.com

Phone Fax

Laboratory for Laser Energetics
University of Rochester 250 E River Rd ... Rochester NY 14623 585-275-5101 275-5960
Web: www.lle.rochester.edu

Laboratory for Nuclear Science
Massachusetts Institute of Technology 77 Massachusetts Ave Bldg 26 Rm 505 ... Cambridge MA 02139 617-253-2361 253-0111
Web: www.lns.mit.edu

Lamont-Doherty Earth Observatory PO Box 1000 61 Rte 9W ... Palisades NY 10964 845-359-2900 359-2931
Web: www.ldeo.columbia.edu

Langley Research Center ... Hampton VA 23681 757-864-1000
Web: www.nasa.gov/centers/langley

Lawrence Berkeley National Laboratory Advanced Light Source
1 Cyclotron Rd MS 6-2100 ... Berkeley CA 94720 510-486-7745 486-4773
Web: www-als.lbl.gov

Lawrence Berkeley National Laboratory (LBNL) 1 Cyclotron Rd ... Berkeley CA 94720 510-486-4000 486-7000
Web: www.lbl.gov

Lawrence Livermore National Laboratory (LLNL)
7000 East Ave PO Box 808 ... Livermore CA 94550 925-422-1100 422-1370
Web: www.llnl.gov

Learning Research & Development Center (LRDC)
University of Pittsburgh 3939 O'Hara St ... Pittsburgh PA 15260 412-624-7020 624-9149
Web: www.lrdc.pitt.edu

Learning Systems Institute
Florida State University 4600 University Ctr Bldg C ... Tallahassee FL 32306 850-644-2570 644-4952
Web: www.lsi.fsu.edu

Lerner Research Institute
Cleveland Clinic Foundation 9500 Euclid Ave MS NB 21 ... Cleveland OH 44195 216-444-3900 444-3279
TF: 800-223-2273 ■ *Web:* www.lerner.ccf.org

LIMRA International Inc 300 Day Hill Rd ... Windsor CT 06095 860-688-3358 298-9555
Web: www.limra.com

Lincoln Laboratory
Massachusetts Institute of Technology 244 Wood St ... Lexington MA 02420 781-981-5500 981-7086*
**Fax:* Hum Res ■ *Web:* www.ll.mit.edu

Lister Hill National Center for Biomedical Communications
8600 Rockville Pike Bldg 38A 7th Fl ... Bethesda MD 20894 301-496-4441 480-3035
Web: lhncbc.nlm.nih.gov

Lodestar Research Corp 2400 Central Ave Suite P-5 ... Boulder CO 80301 303-449-9691 449-3865
Web: www.lodestar.com

Long Term Ecological Research Network (LTER)
1 University of New Mexico UNM Dept of Biology MSCo3 2020 ... Albuquerque NM 87131 505-277-2597 277-2541
Web: www.lternet.edu/sites/lno

Los Alamos National Laboratory (LANL)
Bikini Atoll Rd PO Box 1663 ... Los Alamos NM 87545 505-667-7000
Web: www.lanl.gov

Los Angeles Biomedical Research Institute
1124 W Carson St ... Torrance CA 90502 877-452-2674
TF: 877-452-2674 ■ *Web:* www.labiomed.org

Lovelace Respiratory Research Institute (LRRI)
2425 Ridgecrest Dr SE ... Albuquerque NM 87108 505-348-9400 348-8541
Web: www.lrri.org

Mahoney Institute of Neurological Sciences
University of Pennsylvania School of Medicine Stemmler Hall Rm 215 ... Philadelphia PA 19104 215-898-0869 573-2015
Web: www.med.upenn.edu/ins

Mailman Research Center McLean Hospital 115 Mill St ... Belmont MA 02478 617-855-2000 855-3479
Web: www.mclean.harvard.edu/research/mrc

Marine Biological Laboratory (MBL) 7 MBL St ... Woods Hole MA 02543 508-548-3705 540-6902
Web: www.mbl.edu

Marine Environmental Research Institute
MERI Center for Marine Studies 55 Main St PO Box 652 ... Blue Hill ME 04614 207-374-2135 374-2931
Web: www.meriresearch.org

Marine Science Institute University of California ... Santa Barbara CA 93106 805-893-3765 893-8062
Web: www.msi.ucsb.edu

Marshall Space Flight Center ... Huntsville AL 35812 256-544-2121 544-7476
Web: www.nasa.gov/centers/marshall

Massey Cancer Center
Virginia Commonwealth University 401 College St PO Box 980037 ... Richmond VA 23298 804-828-0450 828-8453
Web: www.massey.vcu.edu

MBI International PO Box 27609 ... Lansing MI 48909 517-337-3181 337-2122
Web: www.mbi.org

McArdle Laboratory for Cancer Research
University of Wisconsin Dept of Oncology 1400 University Ave ... Madison WI 53706 608-262-2177 262-2824
Web: mcardle.oncology.wisc.edu

McCrone Assoc Inc 850 Pasquinelli Dr ... Westmont IL 60559 630-887-7100 887-7417
Web: www.mccroneassociates.com

MCEER SUNY Red Jacket Quadrangle ... Buffalo NY 14261 716-645-3391 645-3399
Web: mceer.buffalo.edu

Measurement & Control Engineering Center
University of Tennessee College of Engineering 510 E Stadium Hall ... Knoxville TN 37996 865-974-2375 974-4995
Web: mcec.engr.utk.edu

Mechanical Technology Inc 431 New Karner Rd ... Albany NY 12205 518-533-2200 533-2201
NASDAQ: MKTY ■ *TF:* 800-828-8210 ■ *Web:* www.mechtech.com

Memorial Sloan-Kettering Cancer Center 1275 York Ave ... New York NY 10021 212-639-2000 432-2331*
**Fax:* Admitting ■ *TF:* 800-525-2225 ■ *Web:* www.mskcc.org

Mental Retardation Research Center
UCLA Neuropsychiatric Institute & Hospital 760 Westwood Plaza Rm 58-258 ... Los Angeles CA 90024 310-825-0404 206-5060
Web: www.mrrc.npi.ucla.edu

Miami Project to Cure Paralysis
PO Box 016960 Mail Locator R-48 ... Miami FL 33101 305-243-6001 243-6017
TF: 800-782-6387 ■ *Web:* www.miamiproject.miami.edu

Michigan Manufacturing Technology Center
47911 Halyard Dr ... Plymouth MI 48170 888-414-6682 451-4201*
**Fax Area Code:* 734 ■ *Web:* www.mmtc.org

Micro & Nanotechnology Laboratory
University of Illinois Urbana-Champaign 208 N Wright St ... Urbana IL 61801 217-333-3097 244-6375
Web: www.micro.uiuc.edu

Microelectronics Research Center
Georgia Institute of Technology 791 Atlantic Dr NW MC 0269 ... Atlanta GA 30332 404-894-5100 894-5028
Web: www.mirc.gatech.edu

Mid-Atlantic Bight National Undersea Research Center
Institute of Marine & Coastal Sciences Rutgers University 71 Dudley Rd ... New Brunswick NJ 08901 732-932-6555 932-8578
Web: www.marine.rutgers.edu/nurp/mabnurc.html

Mid-Continent Research for Education and Learning (McREL)
4601 DTC Blvd Suite 500 ... Denver CO 80237 303-337-0990 337-3005
Web: www.mcrel.org

Midwest Research Institute (MRI) 425 Volker Blvd ... Kansas City MO 64110 816-753-7600 753-8420
Web: www.mriresearch.org

MIT Center for Materials Science & Engineering (CMSE)
Massachusetts Institute of Technology 77 Massachusetts Ave Bldg 13 Rm 2106 ... Cambridge MA 02139 617-253-6850 258-6478
Web: web.mit.edu/cmse

Phone Fax

MIT Media Laboratory
Massachusetts Institute of Technology 77 Massachusetts Ave Bldg E15 ... Cambridge MA 02139 617-253-5960 258-6264
Web: www.media.mit.edu

MITRE Corp 202 Burlington Rd ... Bedford MA 01730 781-271-2000 271-2271
Web: www.mitre.org

Monell Chemical Senses Center 3500 Market St ... Philadelphia PA 19104 215-519-4700 898-2084
Web: www.monell.org

Mote Marine Laboratory 1600 Ken Thompson Pkwy ... Sarasota FL 34236 941-388-4441 388-4312
TF: 800-690-6083 ■ *Web:* www.mote.org

MSU-DOE Plant Research Laboratory
Michigan State University 106 Plant Biology ... East Lansing MI 48824 517-353-2270 353-9168
Web: www.prl.msu.edu

NAHB Research Center 400 Prince Georges Blvd ... Upper Marlboro MD 20774 301-249-4000 430-6180
TF: 800-638-8556 ■ *Web:* www.nahbrc.org

NASA Ames Research Center ... Moffett Field CA 94035 650-604-5000
Web: www.nasa.gov/centers/ames

NASA Dryden Flight Research Center PO Box 273 ... Edwards CA 93523 661-276-3311 276-3566
Web: www.dfrc.nasa.gov

NASA Glenn Research Center
Lewis Field 21000 Brookpark Rd ... Brookpark OH 44135 216-433-4000 433-8000
Web: www.nasa.gov/centers/glenn/home/index.html

NASA Goddard Institute for Space Studies 2880 Broadway ... New York NY 10025 212-678-5500 678-5552
Web: www.giss.nasa.gov

NASA Goddard Space Flight Center Greenbelt Rd ... Greenbelt MD 20771 301-286-2000 286-1707*
**Fax:* PR ■ *Web:* www.nasa.gov/centers/goddard

NASA Langley Research Center ... Hampton VA 23681 757-864-1000
Web: www.nasa.gov/centers/langley

NASA Marshall Space Flight Center ... Huntsville AL 35812 256-544-2121 544-7476
Web: www.nasa.gov/centers/marshall

NASA Stennis Space Center Blach Blvd Bldg 1100 ... Stennis Space Center MS 39529 228-688-2211 688-1094*
**Fax:* PR ■ *Web:* www.nasa.gov/centers/stennis

Nathan S Kline Institute for Psychiatric Research
140 Old Orangeburg Rd Bldg 35 ... Orangeburg NY 10962 845-398-5500 398-5419
Web: www.rfmh.org/nki

Natick Labs ATTN: PAO Kansas St ... Natick MA 01760 508-233-4300 233-5390
Web: www.natick.army.mil

National Animal Disease Center (NADC)
USDA/ARS 2300 Dayton Rd ... Ames IA 50010 515-663-7200 663-7458
Web: www.nadc.ars.usda.gov

National Astronomy & Ionosphere Center (NAIC)
Cornell University Space Sciences Bldg ... Ithaca NY 14853 607-255-3735 255-8803
Web: www.naic.edu

National Biodynamics Laboratory (NBDL)
Univ of New Orleans College of Engineering 2000 Lakeshore Dr Rm 910 ... New Orleans LA 70148 504-257-3918 257-5456
Web: www.nbdl.org

National Bureau of Economic Research
1050 Massachusetts Ave ... Cambridge MA 02138 617-868-3900 868-2742
Web: www.nber.org

National Cancer Institute
Public Inquiries Office 6116 Executive Blvd Rm 3036A ... Bethesda MD 20892 301-435-3848 402-2594
TF: 800-422-6237 ■ *Web:* www.cancer.gov

National Cancer Institute at Frederick
1050 Boyles St PO Box B ... Frederick MD 21702 301-846-1108 846-1494
Web: www.ncifcrf.gov

National Center for Agricultural Utilization Research
USDA/ARS 1815 N University St ... Peoria IL 61604 309-685-4011 681-6686
Web: www.ars.usda.gov/Main/docs.htm?docid=3153

National Center for Atmospheric Research (NCAR)
1850 Table Mesa Dr ... Boulder CO 80305 303-497-1000 497-8610*
**Fax:* PR ■ *Web:* www.ncar.ucar.edu

National Center for Complementary & Alternative Medicine
National Institutes of Health 31 Center Dr Bldg 31 ... Bethesda MD 20892 301-519-3153 464-3616*
**Fax Area Code:* 866 ■ *TF:* 888-644-6226 ■ *Web:* nccam.nih.gov

National Center for Computational Toxicology
US Environmental Protection Agency 109 TW Alexander Dr ... Research Triangle Park NC 27709 919-541-3850
Web: www.epa.gov/comptox

National Center for Ecological Analysis & Synthesis (NCEAS) University of California Santa Barbara 735 State St Suite 300 ... Santa Barbara CA 93101 805-892-2500 892-2510
Web: www.nceas.ucsb.edu

National Center for Education Statistics 1990 K St NW ... Washington DC 20006 202-502-7300 502-7466
Web: nces.ed.gov

National Center for Electron Microscopy (NCEM)
Lawrence Berkeley National Laboratory MS 72-150 ... Berkeley CA 94720 510-486-6036 486-5888
Web: ncem.lbl.gov

National Center for Environmental Research (NCER)
US Environmental Protection Agency 1025 F St NW ... Washington DC 20004 202-343-9800 233-0680
Web: es.epa.gov/ncer

National Center for Genetic Resources Preservation
USDA/ARS 1111 S Mason St ... Fort Collins CO 80521 970-495-3200 221-1427
Web: www.ars.usda.gov/npa/ftcollins/ncgrp

National Center for Genome Resources 2935 Rodeo Park Dr E ... Santa Fe NM 87505 505-982-7840 995-4432
TF: 800-450-4854 ■ *Web:* www.ncgr.org

National Center for Manufacturing Sciences (NCMS)
3025 Boardwalk ... Ann Arbor MI 48108 734-995-0300 995-1150
TF: 800-222-6267 ■ *Web:* www.ncms.org

Veterans Health Administration National Center for Post-Traumatic Stress Disorder 215 N Main St ... White River Junction VT 05009 802-296-5132 296-5135
Web: www.ncptsd.va.gov

National Center for Research on Evaluation Standards & Student Testing (CRESST) UCLA 300 Charles E Young Dr N GSE&IS Bldg Suite 301 Mail Box 951522 ... Los Angeles CA 90095 310-206-1532 825-3883
Web: www.cse.ucla.edu

National Center on Sleep Disorders Research
National Heart Lung & Blood Institute 6701 Rockledge Dr Bldg 2 ... Bethesda MD 20892 301-435-0199 480-3451
Web: www.nhlbi.nih.gov/about/ncsdr

National Center for Supercomputing Applications
University of Illinois Urbana-Champaign 1205 W Clark St Rm 1008 MC-257 ... Urbana IL 61801 217-244-0072 244-8195
Web: www.ncsa.uiuc.edu

National Center for Toxicological Research 3900 NCTR Rd ... Jefferson AR 72079 870-543-7000 543-7576
TF: 800-638-3321 ■ *Web:* www.fda.gov/nctr

National Development & Research Institutes Inc
71 W 23rd St 8th Fl ... New York NY 10010 212-845-4400 438-0894*
**Fax Area Code:* 917 ■ *Web:* www.ndri.org

National Energy Research Scientific Computing Center (NERSC)
Lawrence Berkeley National Laboratory 1 Cyclotron Rd MS 50C3396 ... Berkeley CA 94720 510-486-5849 486-7520
TF: 800-847-6070 ■ *Web:* www.nersc.gov

National Energy Technology Laboratory (NETL)
US Dept of Energy 626 Cochrans Mill Rd PO Box 10940 ... Pittsburgh PA 15236 412-386-6000 386-4604
Web: www.netl.doe.gov

Phone Fax

National Energy Technology Laboratory (NETL)
US Dept of Energy 3610 Collins Ferry Rd PO Box 880 ... Morgantown WV 26507 304-285-4764 285-4403
TF: 800-432-8330 ■ *Web:* www.netl.doe.gov

National Exposure Research Laboratory (NERL)
US Environmental Protection Agency TW Alexander ... Research Triangle Park NC 27709 919-541-2106 541-0445
Web: www.epa.gov/nerl

National Eye Institute 2020 Vision Pl ... Bethesda MD 20892 301-496-5248
Web: www.nei.nih.gov

National Hansen's Disease Program (NHDP)
1770 Physicians Park Dr ... Baton Rouge LA 70816 800-642-2477
Web: www.hrsa.gov/hansens

National Health & Environmental Effects Research Laboratory (NHEERL) US Environmental Protection Agency 109 TW Alexander Dr MC B305-01 ... Research Triangle Park NC 27709 919-541-2281 541-4324
Web: www.epa.gov/nheerl

National Heart Lung & Blood Institute
31 Center Dr Bldg 31 Rm 5A48 MSC 2486 ... Bethesda MD 20892 301-496-5166 402-0818
Web: www.nhlbi.nih.gov

National High Magnetic Field Laboratory (NHMFL)
Florida State University 1800 E Paul Dirac Dr ... Tallahassee FL 32310 850-644-0311 644-8350*
**Fax:* PR ■ *Web:* www.magnet.fsu.edu

National Homeland Security Research Center
US Environmental Protection Agency 26 W Martin Luther King Dr ... Cincinnati OH 45268 513-569-7907 487-2555
Web: www.epa.gov/nhsrc

National Human Genome Research Institute
31 Center Dr Bldg 31 Rm 4B09 ... Bethesda MD 20892 301-402-0911 402-2218
Web: www.genome.gov

National Institute on Aging
31 Center Dr Bldg 31 Rm 5C27 MSC 2292 ... Bethesda MD 20892 301-496-1752 496-1072
Web: www.nia.nih.gov

National Institute on Alcohol Abuse & Alcoholism
5635 Fishers Ln MSC 9304 ... Bethesda MD 20892 301-443-3885
Web: www.niaaa.nih.gov

National Institute of Allergy & Infectious Diseases
6610 Rockledge Dr MSC 6612 ... Bethesda MD 20892 301-496-5717 402-3573
Web: www.niaid.nih.gov

National Institute of Arthritis & Musculoskeletal & Skin Diseases 31 Center Dr MSC 2350 Bldg 31 Rm 4C02 ... Bethesda MD 20892 301-496-8190 480-2814
Web: www.niams.nih.gov

National Institute of Biomedical Imaging & Bioengineering
6707 Democracy Blvd ... Bethesda MD 20892 301-496-8859 480-0679
Web: www.nibib.nih.gov

National Institute of Child Health & Human Development
31 Center Dr Bldg 31 Rm 2A32 ... Bethesda MD 20892 301-496-5133 496-7101
TF: 800-370-2943 ■ *Web:* www.nichd.nih.gov

National Institute on Deafness & Other Communication Disorders 31 Center Dr MSC 2320 ... Bethesda MD 20892 301-496-7243 402-0018
Web: www.nidcd.nih.gov

National Institute of Dental & Craniofacial Research
31 Center Dr ... Bethesda MD 20892 301-496-3571
Web: www.nidcr.nih.gov

National Institute of Diabetes & Digestive & Kidney Diseases
31 Center Dr MSC 2560 ... Bethesda MD 20892 301-496-3583 496-4722
Web: www.niddk.nih.gov

National Institute on Disability & Rehabilitation Research (NIDRR) 400 Maryland Ave SW MS PCP-6056 ... Washington DC 20202 202-245-7640 245-7323
Web: www.ed.gov/about/offices/list/osers/nidrr

National Institute on Drug Abuse
6001 Executive Blvd Rm 5274 ... Bethesda MD 20892 301-443-6480 443-8908
Web: www.nida.nih.gov

National Institute of Environmental Health Sciences PO Box 12233 ... Research Triangle Park NC 27709 919-541-3201 541-2260
Web: www.niehs.nih.gov

National Institute of General Medical Sciences
45 Center Dr MSC 6200 ... Bethesda MD 20892 301-496-7301
Web: www.nigms.nih.gov

National Institute of Mental Health
6001 Executive Blvd Rm 8184 MSC 9663 ... Bethesda MD 20892 301-443-4513 443-4279
TF: 866-615-6464 ■ *Web:* www.nimh.nih.gov

National Institute of Neurological Disorders & Stroke
PO Box 5801 ... Bethesda MD 20824 301-496-5751
TF: 800-352-9424 ■ *Web:* www.ninds.nih.gov

National Institute of Nursing Research
31 Center Dr Bldg 31 Rm 5B05 ... Bethesda MD 20892 301-496-8230
Web: www.nih.gov/ninr

National Institute for Occupational Safety & Health
200 Independence Ave SW ... Washington DC 20201 202-401-6997
TF: 800-356-4674 ■ *Web:* www.cdc.gov/niosh

National Institute of Standards & Technology (NIST)
100 Bureau Dr MS 2500 ... Gaithersburg MD 20899 301-975-6478 926-1630
Web: www.nist.gov
Boulder Laboratories 325 Broadway MS 104 ... Boulder CO 80305 303-497-5507
Web: www.boulder.nist.gov

National Institutes of Health (NCI-Frederick) National Cancer Institute at Frederick 1050 Boyles St PO Box B ... Frederick MD 21702 301-846-1108 846-1494
Web: www.ncifcrf.gov

National Institutes of Health (NIH) 9000 Rockville Pike ... Bethesda MD 20892 301-496-4000
Web: www.nih.gov
Clinical Center 10 Center Dr Bldg 10 ... Bethesda MD 20892 301-496-2563 402-2984
Web: www.cc.nih.gov
John E Fogarty International Center 31 Center Dr MSC 2220 ... Bethesda MD 20892 301-496-2075 594-1211
Web: www.fic.nih.gov
National Cancer Institute
Public Inquiries Office 6116 Executive Blvd Rm 3036A ... Bethesda MD 20892 301-435-3848 402-2594
TF: 800-422-6237 ■ *Web:* www.cancer.gov
National Center for Complementary & Alternative Medicine
National Institutes of Health 31 Center Dr Bldg 31 ... Bethesda MD 20892 301-519-3153 464-3616*
**Fax Area Code:* 866 ■ *TF:* 888-644-6226 ■ *Web:* nccam.nih.gov
National Eye Institute 2020 Vision Pl ... Bethesda MD 20892 301-496-5248
Web: www.nei.nih.gov
National Heart Lung & Blood Institute
31 Center Dr Bldg 31 Rm 5A48 MSC 2486 ... Bethesda MD 20892 301-496-5166 402-0818
Web: www.nhlbi.nih.gov
National Human Genome Research Institute
31 Center Dr Bldg 31 Rm 4B09 ... Bethesda MD 20892 301-402-0911 402-2218
Web: www.genome.gov
National Institute on Aging
31 Center Dr Bldg 31 Rm 5C27 MSC 2292 ... Bethesda MD 20892 301-496-1752 496-1072
Web: www.nia.nih.gov
National Institute on Alcohol Abuse & Alcoholism
5635 Fishers Ln MSC 9304 ... Bethesda MD 20892 301-443-3885
Web: www.niaaa.nih.gov

	City	State	Zip	Phone	Fax
National Institute of Allergy & Infectious Diseases 6610 Rockledge Dr MSC 6612	Bethesda	MD	20892	301-496-5717	402-3573
Web: www.niaid.nih.gov					
National Institute of Arthritis & Musculoskeletal & Skin Diseases 31 Center Dr MSC 2350 Bldg 31 Rm 4C02	Bethesda	MD	20892	301-496-8190	480-2814
Web: www.niams.nih.gov					
National Institute of Biomedical Imaging & Bioengineering 6707 Democracy Blvd	Bethesda	MD	20892	301-496-8859	480-0679
Web: www.nibib.nih.gov					
National Institute of Child Health & Human Development 31 Center Dr Bldg 31 Rm 2A32	Bethesda	MD	20892	301-496-5133	496-7101
TF: 800-370-2943 ■ *Web:* www.nichd.nih.gov					
National Institute on Deafness & Other Communication Disorders 31 Center Dr MSC 2320	Bethesda	MD	20892	301-496-7243	402-0018
Web: www.nidcd.nih.gov					
National Institute of Dental & Craniofacial Research 31 Center Dr	Bethesda	MD	20892	301-496-3571	
Web: www.nidcr.nih.gov					
National Institute of Diabetes & Digestive & Kidney Diseases 31 Center Dr MSC 2560	Bethesda	MD	20892	301-496-3583	496-4722
Web: www.niddk.nih.gov					
National Institute on Drug Abuse 6001 Executive Blvd Rm 5274	Bethesda	MD	20892	301-443-6480	443-8908
Web: www.nida.nih.gov					
National Institute of Environmental Health Sciences PO Box 12233	Research Triangle Park	NC	27709	919-541-3201	541-2260
Web: www.niehs.nih.gov					
National Institute of General Medical Sciences 45 Center Dr MSC 6200	Bethesda	MD	20892	301-496-7301	
Web: www.nigms.nih.gov					
National Institute of Mental Health 6001 Executive Blvd Rm 8184 MSC 9663	Bethesda	MD	20892	301-443-4513	443-4279
TF: 866-615-6464 ■ *Web:* www.nimh.nih.gov					
National Institute of Neurological Disorders & Stroke PO Box 5801	Bethesda	MD	20824	301-496-5751	
TF: 800-352-9424 ■ *Web:* www.ninds.nih.gov					
National Institute of Nursing Research 31 Center Dr Bldg 31 Rm 5B05	Bethesda	MD	20892	301-496-8230	
Web: www.nih.gov/ninr					
National Marine Mammal Laboratory National Marine Fisheries Service 7600 Sand Point Way NE Bldg 4	Seattle	WA	98115	206-526-4045	526-6615
Web: nmml.afsc.noaa.gov					
National Optical Astronomy Observatories 950 N Cherry Ave	Tucson	AZ	85719	520-318-8002	318-8360
Web: www.noao.edu					
National Peanut Research Laboratory USDA/ARS 1011 Forrester Dr SE PO Box 509	Dawson	GA	39842	229-995-7400	995-7416
Web: arsserv0.tamu.edu/main/site_main.htm?modecode=66-04-00-00					
National Protection Center (NPC) US Army Soldier Systems Center ATTN: PAO Kansas St	Natick	MA	01760	508-233-5340	
Web: www.natick.army.mil/soldier/npc					
National Radio Astronomy Observatory (NRAO) 520 Edgemont Rd	Charlottesville	VA	22903	434-296-0211	296-0278
Web: www.nrao.edu					
National Renewable Energy Laboratory (NREL) 1617 Cole Blvd	Golden	CO	80401	303-275-3000	275-4053
Web: www.nrel.gov					
National Research Center for Coal & Energy West Virginia University Evansdale Dr PO Box 6064	Morgantown	WV	26506	304-293-2867	293-3749
TF: 800-624-8301 ■ *Web:* www.nrcce.wvu.edu					
National Research Center on English Learning & Achievement (CELA) School of Education University of Albany B9 1400 Washington Ave	Albany	NY	12222	518-442-5026	442-5933
Web: cela.albany.edu/					
National Research Center on the Gifted & Talented (NRC/GT) University of Connecticut 2131 Hillside Rd Unit 3007	Storrs	CT	06269	860-486-4676	486-2900
Web: www.gifted.uconn.edu/nrcgt.html					
National Risk Management Research Laboratory (NRMRL) US Environmental Protection Agency 26 Martin Luther King Dr	Cincinnati	OH	45268	513-569-7418	569-7680
Web: www.epa.gov/ordntrnt/ORD/NRMRL					
National Science Foundation (NSF) 4201 Wilson Blvd	Arlington	VA	22230	703-292-5111	292-9232
Web: www.nsf.gov					
National Sedimentation Laboratory USDA/ARS 598 McElroy Dr PO Box 1157	Oxford	MS	38655	662-232-2900	281-5713
Web: www.ars.usda.gov/main/site_main.htm?modecode=64-08-05-00					
National Severe Storms Laboratory (NSSL) 120 David L Boren Blvd	Norman	OK	73072	405-325-3620	
Web: www.nssl.noaa.gov					
National Soil Dynamics Laboratory USDA/ARS 411 S Donahue Dr	Auburn	AL	36832	334-887-8596	887-8597
Web: www.ars.usda.gov/main/site_main.htm?modecode=64-20-05-00					
National Soil Erosion Research Laboratory USDA/ARS 275 S Russell St	West Lafayette	IN	47907	765-494-8673	494-5948
Web: www.ars.usda.gov/main/site_main.htm?modecode=36021500					
National Soil Tilth Laboratory USDA/ARS 2110 University Blvd	Ames	IA	50011	515-294-5723	294-8125
Web: www.ars.usda.gov/main/site_main.htm?modecode=36-25-15-00					
National Technical Information Service (NTIS) 5285 Port Royal Rd	Springfield	VA	22161	703-605-6000	605-6900
TF Orders: 800-553-6847 ■ *Web:* www.ntis.gov					
National Technology Transfer Center Wheeling Jesuit University 316 Washington Ave	Wheeling	WV	26003	304-243-2455	243-2523
TF: 800-678-6882 ■ *Web:* www.nttc.edu					
National Toxicology Program (NTP) PO Box 12233	Research Triangle Park	NC	27709	919-541-3419	541-3687
Web: ntp-server.niehs.nih.gov					
National Undersea Research Center for the Caribbean Perry Institute for Marine Science Caribbean Marine Research Center 100 N US Hwy 1 Suite 201	Jupiter	FL	33477	561-741-0192	741-0193
Web: www.cmrc.org					
National Undersea Research Center for Hawaii & the Western Pacific University of Hawaii at Manoa 1000 Pope Rd MSB Rm 303	Honolulu	HI	96822	808-956-6335	956-9772
Web: www.soest.hawaii.edu/HURL					
National Undersea Research Center for the Mid-Atlantic Bight Institute of Marine & Coastal Sciences Rutgers University 71 Dudley Rd	New Brunswick	NJ	08901	732-932-6555	932-8578
Web: www.marine.rutgers.edu/nurp/mabnurc.html					
National Undersea Research Center for the North Atlantic & Great Lakes University of Connecticut at Avery Point 1080 Shennecossett Rd	Groton	CT	06340	860-405-9121	445-2969
Web: www.nurc.uconn.edu					
National Undersea Research Center for the Southeastern US & Gulf of Mexico University of North Carolina at Wilmington 5600 Marvin K Moss Ln	Wilmington	NC	28409	910-962-2301	962-2444
Web: www.uncwil.edu/nurc					
Florida Keys Research Program 515 Caribbean Dr	Key Largo	FL	33037	305-451-0233	453-9719
Web: www.uncwil.edu/nurc					
National Undersea Research Center for the West Coast & Polar Regions University of Alaska-Fairbanks 209 O'Neill Bldg PO Box 757220	Fairbanks	AK	99775	907-474-5870	474-5804
Web: www.westnurc.uaf.edu					
National Water Resources Institutes Program (NWRI) US Geological Survey National Center 12201 Sunrise Valley Dr	Reston	VA	20192	703-648-6800	
Web: wrri.nmsu.edu/niwr/niwr.html					
National Wetlands Research Center 700 Cajundome Blvd	Lafayette	LA	70506	337-266-8500	266-8513
Web: www.nwrc.usgs.gov					
National Wildlife Health Center 6006 Schroeder Rd	Madison	WI	53711	608-270-2400	270-2415
Web: www.nwhc.usgs.gov					
National Wildlife Research Center 4101 LaPorte Ave	Fort Collins	CO	80521	970-266-6000	266-6032
Web: www.aphis.usda.gov/ws/nwrc					
Natural Hazards Center University of Colorado CB 482	Boulder	CO	80309	303-492-6818	492-2151
Web: www.colorado.edu/hazards					
Natural Resource Ecology Laboratory Colorado State University Campus Delivery 1499	Fort Collins	CO	80523	970-491-1982	491-1965
Web: www.nrel.colostate.edu					
Natural Resources Research Institute (NRRI) University of Minnesota Duluth 5013 Miller Trunk Hwy	Duluth	MN	55811	218-720-4294	720-4219
TF: 800-234-0054 ■ *Web:* www.nrri.umn.edu					
Naval Aerospace Medical Research Laboratory (NAMRL) 280 Fred Bauer St Naval Air Stn	Pensacola	FL	32508	850-452-3486	452-4479
Web: www.namrl.navy.mil					
Naval Health Research Center (NHRC) PO Box 85122	San Diego	CA	92186	619-553-8400	553-9389
Web: www.nhrc.navy.mil					
Naval Institute for Dental & Biomedical Research (NDRI) 310-A B St Bldg 1-H	Great Lakes	IL	60088	847-688-5647	688-4279
Web: www.nmrc.navy.mil/nidbr.htm					
Naval Medical Research Center (NMRC) 503 Robert Grant Ave	Silver Spring	MD	20910	301-319-7401	319-7410
Web: www.nmrc.navy.mil					
Naval Research Laboratory (NRL) 4555 Overlook Ave SW Code 1000	Washington	DC	20375	202-767-3403	404-7419
Web: www.nrl.navy.mil					
Naval Submarine Medical Research Laboratory (NSMRL) PO Box 900	Groton	CT	06349	860-694-3263	694-4809
Web: www.nhrc.navy.mil/nsmrl					
Naval Surface Warfare Center (NSWC) 1333 Isaac Hull Ave SE MS 7101	Washington Navy Yard	DC	20376	202-781-2975	
Web: www.nswcdc.navy.mil					
Carderock Div 9500 MacArthur Blvd	West Bethesda	MD	20817	301-227-1137	227-3574
Web: www.dt.navy.mil					
Dahlgren Div 17320 Dahlgren Rd	Dahlgren	VA	22448	540-653-8291	653-8975
Web: www.nswc.navy.mil					
Naval Undersea Warfare Center (NUWC) 1176 Howell St	Newport	RI	02841	401-832-3611	832-4661
Web: www.nuwc.navy.mil					
Keyport Div 610 Dowell St	Keyport	WA	98345	360-396-2699	396-2387
Web: www-keyport.kpt.nuwc.navy.mil					
Newport Div 1176 Howell St	Newport	RI	02841	401-832-3611	832-4661
Web: www.npt.nuwc.navy.mil					
Navy Clothing & Textile Research Facility (NCTRF) Bldg 86 DSN 256-4172 Kansas St	Natick	MA	01760	508-233-4172	233-4783
Web: www.navy-nex.com/command/nctrf/nctrf-index.html					
NBDL (National Biodynamics Laboratory) Univ of New Orleans College of Engineering 2000 Lakeshore Dr Rm 910	New Orleans	LA	70148	504-257-3918	257-5456
Web: www.nbdl.org					
Nebraska Center for Materials & Nanoscience University of Nebraska Brace Lab Rm 111	Lincoln	NE	68588	402-472-7886	472-2879
Web: www.unl.edu/ncmn					
NEC Laboratories America Inc 4 Independence Way	Princeton	NJ	08540	609-520-1555	951-2481
TF: 888-777-6324 ■ *Web:* www.nec-labs.com					
New Brunswick Laboratory (NBL) 9800 S Cass Ave Bldg 350	Argonne	IL	60439	630-252-2442	252-6256
Web: www.nbl.doe.gov					
New England Primate Research Center (NEPRC) 1 Pine Hill Dr PO Box 9102	Southborough	MA	01772	508-624-8002	460-0612
Web: www.hms.harvard.edu/nerprc					
NIDRR (National Institute on Disability & Rehabilitation Research) 400 Maryland Ave SW MS PCP-6056	Washington	DC	20202	202-245-7640	245-7323
Web: www.ed.gov/about/offices/list/osers/nidrr					
Noblis 3150 Fairview Park Dr S	Falls Church	VA	22042	703-610-2002	
Web: www.noblis.org					
Northeast Fisheries Science Center National Marine Fisheries Service 166 Water St	Woods Hole	MA	02543	508-495-2000	495-2258
Web: www.nefsc.noaa.gov					
Northern Grain Insects Research Laboratory (NGIRL) USDA/ARS 2923 Medary Ave	Brookings	SD	57006	605-693-3241	693-5240
Web: www.ars.usda.gov/Main/docs.htm?docid=2357					
Northern Plains Agricultural Research Laboratory USDA/ARS 1500 N Central Ave	Sidney	MT	59270	406-433-2020	433-5038
Web: www.ars.usda.gov/main/site_main.htm?modecode=54360000					
Northern Prairie Wildlife Research Center 8711 37th St SE	Jamestown	ND	58401	701-253-5500	253-5553
Web: www.npwrc.usgs.gov					
Northern Research Station USDA Forest Service 11 Campus Blvd Suite 200	Newtown Square	PA	19073	610-557-4017	557-4095
Web: www.nrs.fs.fed.us					
Northwest Fisheries Science Center 2725 Montlake Blvd E	Seattle	WA	98112	206-860-3200	860-3217
Web: www.nwfsc.noaa.gov					
Notre Dame Radiation Laboratory University of Notre Dame	Notre Dame	IN	46556	574-631-6163	631-8068
Web: www.rad.nd.edu					
NSF (National Science Foundation) 4201 Wilson Blvd	Arlington	VA	22230	703-292-5111	292-9232
Web: www.nsf.gov					
NUWC (Naval Undersea Warfare Center)					
Keyport Div 610 Dowell St	Keyport	WA	98345	360-396-2699	396-2387
Web: www-keyport.kpt.nuwc.navy.mil					
Newport Div 1176 Howell St	Newport	RI	02841	401-832-3611	832-4661
Web: www.npt.nuwc.navy.mil					
Oak Ridge National Laboratory (ORNL) PO Box 2008	Oak Ridge	TN	37831	865-576-2900	574-0595*
**Fax:* PR ■ *Web:* www.ornl.gov					
Oceanic Institute 41-202 Kalanianaole Hwy	Waimanalo	HI	96795	808-259-7951	259-5971
Web: www.oceanicinstitute.org					
Office of Naval Research (ONR) 1 Liberty Center 875 N Randolph St Suite 1425	Arlington	VA	22203	703-696-5031	696-5940*
**Fax:* PR ■ *Web:* www.onr.navy.mil					
Office of Population Research Princeton University Wallace Hall 2nd Fl	Princeton	NJ	08544	609-258-4870	258-1039
Web: opr.princeton.edu					
Ohio Agricultural Research & Development Center Ohio State University 1680 Madison Ave	Wooster	OH	44691	330-263-3700	263-3688
Web: www.oardc.ohio-state.edu					
Oklahoma Medical Research Foundation (OMRF) 825 NE 13th St	Oklahoma City	OK	73104	405-271-6673	271-3980
TF: 800-522-0211 ■ *Web:* www.omrf.org					
Omnicare Clinical Research 630 Allendale Rd	King of Prussia	PA	19406	484-679-2400	679-2505
TF: 800-290-5766 ■ *Web:* www.omnicarecr.com					

Phone Fax

Oregon National Primate Research Center (ONPRC)
Oregon Health & Science University 505 NW 185th Ave .... Beaverton OR 97006 503-645-1141 690-5532
Web: onprc.ohsu.edu

Pacific Disaster Center 1305 N Holopono St Suite 2 .... Kihei HI 96753 808-891-0525 891-0526
TF: 888-808-6688 ■ *Web:* www.pdc.org

Pacific Institute for Research & Evaluation (PIRE)
11720 Beltsville Dr Suite 900 .... Calverton MD 20705 301-755-2700 755-2799
Web: www.pire.org

Pacific International Center for High Technology Research (PICHTR) 1440 Kapiolani Blvd Suite 1225 .... Honolulu HI 96814 808-943-9581 943-9582
Web: www.pichtr.org

Pacific Island Ecosystems Research Center
677 Ala Moana Blvd Suite 615 .... Honolulu HI 96813 808-587-7452 587-7451
Web: biology.usgs.gov/pierc

Pacific Marine Environmental Laboratory (PMEL)
NOAA/OAR/PMEL 7600 Sand Point Way NE .... Seattle WA 98115 206-526-6810 526-4576
Web: www.pmel.noaa.gov

Pacific Northwest National Laboratory (PNNL)
902 Battelle Blvd PO Box 999 .... Richland WA 99354 509-375-2121 375-2507*
**Fax:* Mail Rm ■ *TF:* 888-375-7665 ■ *Web:* www.pnl.gov

Pacific Northwest Research Station
USDA Forest Service 333 SW 1st Ave........................ Portland OR 97208 503-808-2592 808-2130
Web: www.fs.fed.us/pnw

Pacific Southwest Research Station
USDA Forest Service 800 Buchanan St........................ Albany CA 94710 510-559-6300 559-6440
Web: www.fs.fed.us/psw

Palo Alto Research Center Inc (PARC) 3333 Coyote Hill Rd....... Palo Alto CA 94304 650-812-4000 812-4970
Web: www.parc.xerox.com

PARC (Palo Alto Research Center Inc) 3333 Coyote Hill Rd....... Palo Alto CA 94304 650-812-4000 812-4970
Web: www.parc.xerox.com

PAREXEL International Corp 195 West St .... Waltham MA 02451 781-487-9900 487-0525
NASDAQ: PRXL ■ *TF:* 800-727-3935 ■ *Web:* www.parexel.com

Patrick Center for Environmental Research
1900 Benjamin Franklin Pkwy .... Philadelphia PA 19103 215-299-1080 299-1079
Web: www.ansp.org/research/pcer

Patuxent Wildlife Research Center 12100 Beech Forest Rd.......... Laurel MD 20708 301-497-5500 497-5505
Web: www.pwrc.usgs.gov

Pittsburgh Supercomputing Center 300 S Craig St............. Pittsburgh PA 15213 412-268-4960 268-5832
TF: 800-221-1641 ■ *Web:* www.psc.edu

Plasma Science & Fusion Center
Massachusetts Institute of Technology 167 Albany St
NW 16-288.. Cambridge MA 02139 617-253-8100 253-0238
Web: www.psfc.mit.edu

Plum Island Animal Disease Center USDA/ARS PO Box 848 ...... Greenport NY 11944 631-323-3200 323-2507
Web: www.ars.usda.gov/main/site_main.htm?modecode=19400000

Polisher Research Institute
Abramson Center for Jewish Life 1425 Horsham Rd .... North Wales PA 19454 215-371-3000 371-3015
Web: www.pgc.org/PRI

Population Council 1 Dag Hammarskjold Plaza 9th Fl........... New York NY 10017 212-339-0500 755-6052
Web: www.popcouncil.org

Population Research Center
University of Chicago 1155 E 60th St....................... Chicago IL 60637 773-256-6302 256-6313
Web: www.src.uchicago.edu/prc

Population Research Institute
Pennsylvania State University 601 Oswald Tower........ University Park PA 16802 814-865-0486 863-8342
Web: www.pop.psu.edu

PPD Inc 3151 S 17th St .... Wilmington NC 28412 910-251-0081 762-5820
NASDAQ: PPDI ■ *Web:* www.ppdi.com

Princeton Plasma Physics Laboratory (PPPL)
Princeton University James Forrestal Campus PO Box 451 ...... Princeton NJ 08543 609-243-2750 243-2751
Web: www.pppl.gov

Public Health Research Institute (PHRI)
International Center for Public Health 225 Warren St............ Newark NJ 07103 973-854-3100 854-3101
Web: www.phri.org

QRDC Inc 125 Columbia Ct Suite 6............................ Chaska MN 55318 952-556-5205 556-5206
Web: www.qrdc.com

Quintiles Transnational Corp PO Box 13979 .... Research Triangle Park NC 27709 919-998-2000 998-9113
TF: 800-875-2888 ■ *Web:* www.quintiles.com

Red River Valley Agricultural Research Center
USDA/ARS 1307 18th St N .... Fargo ND 58105 701-239-1370 239-1395
Web: www.ars.usda.gov/main/site_main.htm?modecode=54-42-00-00

Regional Research Institute for Human Services
Portland State University 1600 SW 4th Ave Suite 900........... Portland OR 97201 503-725-4040 725-4180
Web: www.rri.pdx.edu

Reid Harry Center for Environmental Studies
University of Nevada 4505 Maryland Pkwy Box 454030........ Las Vegas NV 89154 702-895-3382 895-3094
Web: hrcweb.lv-hrc.nevada.edu

Renaissance Computing Institute (RENCI)
100 Europa Dr Suite 540.................................... Chapel Hill NC 27517 919-445-9640 445-9669
Web: www.renci.org

RENCI (Renaissance Computing Institute)
100 Europa Dr Suite 540.................................... Chapel Hill NC 27517 919-445-9640 445-9669
Web: www.renci.org

Research for Better Schools Inc 112 N Broad St .... Philadelphia PA 19102 215-568-6150 568-7260
Web: www.rbs.org

Research & Innovative Technology Administration (RITA)
400 7th St SW Suite 3103.................................. Washington DC 20590 202-366-7582 493-2381
Web: www.rita.dot.gov

Research Institute on Addictions 1021 Main St .... Buffalo NY 14203 716-887-2566 887-2252
Web: www.ria.buffalo.edu

Research Institute for Advanced Computer Science (RIACS)
NASA Ames Research Ctr MS T35-B-1........................ Moffett Field CA 94035 650-966-5020 966-5021
Web: www.riacs.edu

Research Laboratory of Electronics
Massachusetts Institute of Technology 77 Massachusetts
Ave Rm 36-413 .... Cambridge MA 02139 617-253-2519 253-1301
Web: rleweb.mit.edu

Research Triangle Institute
3040 Cornwallis Rd PO Box 12194............. Research Triangle Park NC 27709 919-541-6000 541-5985
TF: 800-334-8571 ■ *Web:* www.rti.org

RIACS (Research Institute for Advanced Computer Science)
NASA Ames Research Ctr MS T35-B-1........................ Moffett Field CA 94035 650-966-5020 966-5021
Web: www.riacs.edu

Ricerca Biosciences LLC 7528 Auburn Rd PO Box 1000 .... Concord OH 44077 440-357-3300 357-4939
TF: 888-742-3722 ■ *Web:* www.ricerca.com

Richard B Russell Agricultural Research Center
USDA/ARS 950 College Station Rd .... Athens GA 30605 706-546-3152 546-3367

Riverside Research Institute 156 William St 9th Fl............. New York NY 10038 212-563-4545 502-1742
Web: www.rri-usa.org

Robert H Lurie Comprehensive Cancer Center
Northwestern University 303 E Chicago Ave Olson Pavilion
Suite 8250 .... Chicago IL 60611 312-908-5250 908-1372
Web: www.cancer.northwestern.edu/Home/Index.cfm

Robotics Institute
Carnegie Mellon University 5000 Forbes Ave .... Pittsburgh PA 15213 412-268-3818 268-6436
Web: www.ri.cmu.edu

Phone Fax

Rocky Mountain Research Station
US Forest Service 2150 Centre Ave Bldg A................. Fort Collins CO 80526 970-295-5926 295-5927
Web: www.fs.fed.us/rm

Rodale Institute 611 Siegfriedale Rd .... Kutztown PA 19530 610-683-1400 683-8548
Web: www.rodaleinstitute.org

Roman L Hruska US Meat Animal Research Center (MARC)
USDA/ARS PO Box 166 .... Clay Center NE 68933 402-762-4100 762-4148
Web: www.ars.usda.gov/

Roosevelt Eleanor Institute 1899 Gaylord St..................... Denver CO 80206 303-333-4515 333-8423
Web: www.nsm.du.edu/eri

Rose F Kennedy Center for Research in Mental Retardation & Developmental Disabilities Yeshiva University Albert Einstein
College of Medicine 1410 Pelham Pkwy S .... Bronx NY 10461 718-430-4229 918-7505
Web: kennedy.aecom.yu.edu

Roswell Park Cancer Institute Elm & Carlton Sts................. Buffalo NY 14263 716-845-2300 845-8335
TF: 877-275-7724 ■ *Web:* www.roswellpark.org

Roy J Carver Biotechnology Center
2613 Institute for Genomic Biology 1206 W Gregory MC-195...... Urbana IL 61801 217-333-1695 244-0466
Web: www.biotech.uiuc.edu

Russell Richard B Agricultural Research Center
USDA/ARS 950 College Station Rd .... Athens GA 30605 706-546-3152 546-3367

Russell Sage Foundation 112 E 64th St........................ New York NY 10021 212-750-6000 371-4761
Web: www.russellsage.org

Safety Analysis & Forensic Engineering 495 Pine Ave Suite A .... Goleta CA 93117 805-964-0676 964-7669
Web: www.saferesearch.com

SAIC Inc 10260 Campus Point Dr.......................... San Diego CA 92121 858-826-6000 826-6634
Web: www.saic.com

Saint Jude Children's Research Hospital 332 N Lauderdale St .... Memphis TN 38105 901-495-3300 495-5297*
**Fax:* Admitting ■ *TF:* 866-278-5833 ■ *Web:* www.stjude.org

Salk Institute for Biological Studies PO Box 85800 .... San Diego CA 92186 858-453-4100 552-8285
Web: www.salk.edu

San Diego Supercomputer Center (SDSC)
University of California San Diego 9500 Gilman Dr.............. La Jolla CA 92093 858-534-5000 534-5056
Web: www.sdsc.edu

Sandia National Laboratories - California (SNL)
7011 East Ave PO Box 969 .... Livermore CA 94551 925-294-3000
Web: www.ca.sandia.gov

Sandia National Laboratories - New Mexico (SNL)
1515 Eubank SE PO Box 5800 .... Albuquerque NM 87185 505-844-5678
Web: www.sandia.gov

Sarnoff Corp 201 Washington Rd PO Box 5300................. Princeton NJ 08543 609-734-2000 734-2221
Web: www.sarnoff.com

Savannah River Ecology Laboratory Drawer E......................... Aiken SC 29803 803-725-2472 725-3309
Web: www.uga.edu/~srel

Savannah River National Laboratory Savannah River Site............ Aiken SC 29808 803-725-3994 725-1660
Web: srnl.doe.gov

Schiefelbusch Institute for Life Span Studies
Univ of Kansas Robert Dole Human Development Ctr Rm
1052 1000 Sunnyside Ave................................. Lawrence KS 66045 785-864-4295 864-5323
Web: www.lsi.ku.edu/lsi

Schwartz Bernard Center for Economic Policy Analysis
New School of Social Research 79 5th Ave 11th Fl............ New York NY 10003 212-229-5717 229-5903
Web: www.newschool.edu/cepa

Science Applications International Corp
10260 Campus Point Dr.................................... San Diego CA 92121 858-826-6000 826-6634
Web: www.saic.com

Scripps Institution of Oceanography (SIO)
9500 Gilman Dr Dept 0233 .... La Jolla CA 92093 858-534-3624 534-5306
Web: www-sio.ucsd.edu

Scripps Research Institute 10550 N Torrey Pines Rd............. La Jolla CA 92037 858-784-1000 784-8071*
**Fax:* Hum Res ■ *Web:* www.scripps.edu

SEDL 4700 Mueller Blvd... Austin TX 78723 512-476-6861 476-2286
Web: www.sedl.org

SEMATECH 2706 Montopolis Dr .... Austin TX 78741 512-356-3500 356-3086*
**Fax:* Hum Res ■ *Web:* www.sematech.org

SERVE PO Box 5367 .... Greensboro NC 27435 336-315-7400 315-7457
TF: 800-755-3277 ■ *Web:* www.serve.org

Shiley-Marcos Alzheimer's Disease Research Center
8950 Villa La Jolla Dr Suite C129 .... La Jolla CA 92037 858-622-5800 622-1012
Web: adrc.ucsd.edu

Sidney Kimmel Comprehensive Cancer Center at Johns Hopkins
401 N Broadway Suite 1100 .... Baltimore MD 21231 410-955-5222 955-6787
Web: www.hopkinskimmelcancercenter.org

Siteman Cancer Center 4921 Parkview Pl .... Saint Louis MO 63110 314-362-5196
TF: 800-600-3606 ■ *Web:* www.siteman.wustl.edu

Sloan-Kettering Cancer Center 1275 York Ave .... New York NY 10021 212-639-2000 432-2331*
**Fax:* Admitting ■ *TF:* 800-525-2225 ■ *Web:* www.mskcc.org

Smith-Kettlewell Eye Research Institute
2318 Fillmore St.. San Francisco CA 94115 415-345-2000 345-8455
Web: www.ski.org

Smithsonian Environmental Research Center
PO Box 28 647 Contees Wharf Rd .... Edgewater MD 21037 443-482-2200 482-2380
Web: www.serc.si.edu

Smithsonian Tropical Research Institute
PO Box 37012 Quad Suite 3123 705......................... Washington DC 20013 202-633-4014 786-2557
Web: www.stri.org

Social & Economic Sciences Research Center
Washington State University Wilson Hall Rm 133 PO
Box 644014 .... Pullman WA 99164 509-335-1511 335-0116
TF: 800-833-0867 ■ *Web:* www.sesrc.wsu.edu/sesrcsite

Software Engineering Institute (SEI)
Carnegie Mellon University 4500 5th Ave .... Pittsburgh PA 15213 412-268-5800 268-6257*
**Fax:* Cust Svc ■ *Web:* www.sei.cmu.edu

Southeast Fisheries Science Center
National Marine Fisheries Service 75 Virginia Beach Dr .... Miami FL 33149 305-361-4200 361-4219
Web: www.sefsc.noaa.gov

Southern California Earthquake Center
USC 3651 Trousdale Pkwy Science Hall Rm
169 MC0742.. Los Angeles CA 90089 213-740-5843 740-0011
Web: www.scec.org

Southern Plains Agricultural Research Center
USDA/ARS 2881 F & B Rd .... College Station TX 77845 979-260-9372 260-9377
Web: www.sparc.ars.usda.gov

Southern Regional Research Center (SRRC)
USDA/ARS 1100 Robert E Lee Blvd PO Box 19687 .... New Orleans LA 70179 504-286-4200 286-4419
Web: www.ars.usda.gov/main/site_main.htm?modecode=64350000

Southern Research Institute 2000 9th Ave S................. Birmingham AL 35205 205-581-2000 581-2726
TF: 800-967-6774 ■ *Web:* www.sri.org

Southern Research Station
USDA Forest Service 200 Weaver Blvd .... Asheville NC 28804 828-257-4300 257-4840
Web: www.srs.fs.usda.gov

Southwest Fisheries Science Center
National Marine Fisheries Service 8604 La Jolla Shores Dr .... La Jolla CA 92037 858-546-7000 546-7003
Web: swfsc.noaa.gov

Southwest National Primate Research Center
PO Box 760549 .... San Antonio TX 78245 210-258-9400
Web: www.sfbr.org/pages/snprc_index.php

Organization / Address	City	State	Zip	Phone	Fax
Southwest Research Institute (SwRI) 6220 Culebra Rd. *Fax: Hum Res ■ *Web:* www.swri.edu	San Antonio	TX	78238	210-684-5111	522-3990*
Space Dynamics Laboratory 1695 N Research Pkwy *Web:* www.sdl.usu.edu	North Logan	UT	84341	435-797-4600	797-4495
Space & Naval Warfare Systems Center (SPAWAR SYSCEN) 53560 Hull St *Web:* www.spawar.navy.mil/sandiego	San Diego	CA	92152	619-553-2717	553-2726
Space Physics Research Laboratory 2455 Hayward St University of Michigan *Web:* www.sprl.umich.edu	Ann Arbor	MI	48109	734-936-7775	763-0437
Space Research Institute Auburn University 231 Leach Center *Web:* www.auburn.edu/research/vpr/sri	Auburn	AL	36849	334-844-5894	844-5900
Space Science & Engineering Center University of Wisconsin 1225 W Dayton St *Web:* www.ssec.wisc.edu	Madison	WI	53706	608-262-0544	262-5974
Space Telescope Science Institute 3700 San Martin Dr *Web:* www.stsci.edu	Baltimore	MD	21218	410-338-4700	338-4767
SRI International 333 Ravenswood Ave *Web:* www.sri.com	Menlo Park	CA	94025	650-859-2000	326-5512
Stanford Cancer Center 875 Lake Blake Wilbur Dr *Web:* cancer.stanford.edu	Stanford	CA	94305	650-498-6000	725-9113
Stanford Linear Accelerator Center (SLAC) 2575 Sand Hill Rd *Web:* www.slac.stanford.edu	Menlo Park	CA	94025	650-926-3300	926-4999
Stanford Prevention Research Center Hoover Pavilion MC-5705 211 Quarry Rd *Web:* prevention.stanford.edu	Stanford	CA	94305	650-723-6254	725-6906
Stanford Synchrotron Radiation Laboratory 2575 Sand Hill Rd MS 69 *Web:* www-ssrl.slac.stanford.edu	Menlo Park	CA	94025	650-926-3153	926-4100
Stennis Space Center Blach Blvd Bldg 1100 *Fax: PR ■ *Web:* www.nasa.gov/centers/stennis	Stennis Space Center	MS	39529	228-688-2211	688-1094*
Supercomputing Institute for Digital Simulation and Advanced Computation University of Minnesota 599 Walter Library 117 Pleasant St SE *Web:* www.msi.umn.edu	Minneapolis	MN	55455	612-625-1818	624-8861
Synchrotron Radiation Center (SRC) University of Wisconsin Madison 3731 Schneider Dr *Web:* www.src.wisc.edu	Stoughton	WI	53589	608-877-2000	877-2001
Syracuse Research Corp (SRC) 6225 Running Ridge Rd *Fax: Hum Res ■ *TF:* 800-724-0451 ■ *Web:* www.syrres.com	North Syracuse	NY	13212	315-452-8000	452-8090*
TCTI Hazardous Substance Research Center PO Box 10613	Beaumont	TX	77710	409-880-8768	880-2397
Technology Management Research Center Rutgers University 180 University Ave *Web:* business.rutgers.edu/default.aspx?id=645	Newark	NJ	07102	973-353-5982	
Technology Service Corp 962 Wayne Ave Suite 800 *Web:* www.tsc.com	Silver Spring	MD	20910	301-565-2970	565-0673
TERC 2067 Massachusetts Ave 2nd Fl *Web:* www.terc.edu	Cambridge	MA	02140	617-547-0430	349-3535
Texas Center for Superconductivity University of Houston 202 Houston Science Center *Web:* www.tcsuh.uh.edu	Houston	TX	77204	713-743-8200	743-8201
Thomas Jefferson National Accelerator Facility (JLab) 12000 Jefferson Ave MS12-G *Web:* www.jlab.org	Newport News	VA	23606	757-269-7100	269-7363
Thompson Boyce Institute for Plant Research Inc Cornell University Tower Rd *Web:* bti.cornell.edu	Ithaca	NY	14853	607-254-1234	254-1242
Thurston Arthritis Research Center University of North Carolina 3330 Thurston Bldg CB 7280 *Web:* www.med.unc.edu/mac	Chapel Hill	NC	27599	919-966-0552	966-1739
Transportation Research Center Inc (TRC Inc) 10820 Rt 347 PO Box B-67 *TF:* 800-837-7872 ■ *Web:* www.trcpg.com	East Liberty	OH	43319	937-666-2011	666-5066
Transportation Technology Center Inc 55500 DOT Rd PO Box 11130 *Web:* www.aar.com	Pueblo	CO	81001	719-584-0750	584-0711
Trex Enterprises Corp 10455 Pacific Center Ct *TF:* 800-626-5885 ■ *Web:* www.trexenterprises.com	San Diego	CA	92121	858-646-5300	646-5301
Tulane National Primate Research Center 18703 Three Rivers Rd *Web:* www.tpc.tulane.edu	Covington	LA	70433	504-862-8040	
Turner-Fairbank Highway Research Center 6300 Georgetown Pike *Web:* www.tfhrc.gov	McLean	VA	22101	202-493-3165	493-3170
UAB Comprehensive Cancer Center University of Alabama at Birmingham 1824 6th Ave S *Web:* www3.ccc.uab.edu	Birmingham	AL	35294	800-822-0933	
UNC Neuroscience Center University of North Carolina 105 Mason Farm Rd CB 7250 *Web:* www.neuroscience.unc.edu	Chapel Hill	NC	27599	919-966-4068	966-1844
University of Chicago Cancer Research Center 5841 S Maryland Ave MC1140 *Web:* www-uccrc.bsd.uchicago.edu	Chicago	IL	60637	773-834-7490	
University of Maryland Biotechnology Institute 9600 Gudelsky Dr *Web:* www.umbi.umd.edu	Rockville	MD	20850	240-314-6000	314-6255
University of Maryland Center for Environmental Science (UMCES) 2020 Horn Point Rd *Web:* www.umces.edu	Cambridge	MD	21613	410-228-9250	228-3843
University of Michigan Transportation Research Institute (UMTRI) 2901 Baxter Rd *Web:* www.umtri.umich.edu	Ann Arbor	MI	48109	734-764-6504	936-1081
University of Texas Institute for Geophysics (UTIG) JJ Pickle Research Campus Bldg 196 10100 Burnet Rd (RR2200) *Web:* www.ig.utexas.edu	Austin	TX	78758	512-471-6156	471-8844
US Arid-Land Agricultural Research Center USDA/ARS 21881 N Cardon Ln *Web:* www.ars.usda.gov/main/site_main.htm?modecode=53-47-00-00	Mariposa	AZ	85239	520-316-6310	
US Army Aeromedical Research Laboratory (USAARL) MCMR-UAC 6901 Farrel Rd *Web:* www.usaarl.army.mil	Fort Rucker	AL	36362	334-255-6900	255-6937
US Army Armament Research Development & Engineering Center (ARDEC) Technical Research Center Bldg 59 *Web:* www.pica.army.mil	Picatinny	NJ	07806	973-724-5898	724-3044
US Army Aviation & Missile Research Development & Engineering Center (AMRDEC) AMSAM-PA *Web:* www.redstone.army.mil/amrdec	Redstone Arsenal	AL	35898	256-876-4161	955-0133
US Army Benet Laboratories Watervliet Arsenal 1 Buffington St AMSTA-AR-CCB Bldg 40 *Web:* www.benet.wva.army.mil	Watervliet	NY	12189	518-266-5418	266-3612
US Army Center for Environmental Health Research ATTN: MCMR-CDE-Z 568 Doughten Dr *Web:* usacehr.amedd.army.mil	Fort Detrick	MD	21702	301-619-7685	619-7606

Organization / Address	City	State	Zip	Phone	Fax
US Army Communications-Electronics Research Development & Engineering Center (CERDEC) ATTN: AMSRD-CER-D Myers Center Bldg 2700 *Web:* www.cerdec.army.mil	Fort Monmouth	NJ	07703	732-532-5225	532-0749
US Army Engineer Research & Development Center (ERDC) 3909 Halls Ferry Rd ATTN: CEERD-PA-Z *TF:* 800-522-6937 ■ *Web:* www.erdc.usace.army.mil	Vicksburg	MS	39180	601-634-2502	634-2388
US Army Institute of Surgical Research (USAISR) MCMR-USZ 3400 Rawley E Chambers Ave *Web:* www.usaisr.amedd.army.mil	Fort Sam Houston	TX	78234	210-916-3219	227-8502
US Army Medical Research Institute of Chemical Defense (USAMRICD) MCMR-CDZ 3100 Ricketts Point Rd *Web:* usamricd.apgea.army.mil	Aberdeen Proving Ground	MD	21010	410-436-3276	436-4150
US Army Medical Research Institute of Infectious Diseases (USAMRIID) ATTN: MCMR-UIZ-R 1425 Porter St *Web:* www.usamriid.army.mil	Frederick	MD	21702	301-619-2285	
US Army Medical Research & Materiel Command 504 Scott St *Web:* mrmc-www.army.mil	Fort Detrick	MD	21702	301-619-2736	
US Army Natick Research Development & Engineering Center ATTN: PAO Kansas St *Web:* www.natick.army.mil	Natick	MA	01760	508-233-4300	233-5390
US Army Research Institute for the Behavioral & Social Sciences (ARI) 2511 Jefferson Davis Hwy *Web:* www.hqda.army.mil/ari	Arlington	VA	22202	703-602-8049	
US Army Research Institute of Environmental Medicine (USARIEM) MCMR-UEMZ Bldg 42 Kansas St *Web:* www.usariem.army.mil	Natick	MA	01760	508-233-4811	233-5298
US Army Research Laboratory (ARL) ATTN: AMSRD-ARL-O-PA 2800 Powder Mill Rd *TF:* 800-276-9522 ■ *Web:* www.arl.army.mil	Adelphi	MD	20783	301-394-3590	394-1174
US Army Tank-Automotive Research Development & Engineering Center (TARDEC) AMSTA-CS-P 6501 E 11-Mile Rd *Web:* tardec.army.mil	Warren	MI	48397	586-574-5494	574-5097
US Coast Guard Research & Development Center 1082 Shennecossett Rd *Web:* www.rdc.uscg.gov	Groton	CT	06340	860-441-2600	441-2792
US Dairy Forage Research Center (DFRC) 1925 Linden Dr W *Web:* www.dfrc.ars.usda.gov	Madison	WI	53706	608-890-0050	
US Horticultural Research Laboratory USDA/ARS 2001 S Rock Rd *Web:* www.ars.usda.gov/Main/docs.htm?docid=7376	Fort Pierce	FL	34945	772-462-5800	462-5986
US Meat Animal Research Center USDA/ARS PO Box 166 *Web:* www.ars.usda.gov/	Clay Center	NE	68933	402-762-4100	762-4148
US Salinity Laboratory USDA/ARS 450 W Big Springs Rd *Web:* www.ars.usda.gov/AboutUs/AboutUs.htm?modecode=53-10-20-00	Riverside	CA	92507	951-369-4814	369-4818
US Vegetable Laboratory USDA/ARS 2700 Savannah Hwy *Web:* www.ars.usda.gov/Main/docs.htm?docid=5953	Charleston	SC	29414	843-402-5300	
USC Information Sciences Institute 4676 Admiralty Way Suite 1001 *Web:* www.isi.edu	Marina del Rey	CA	90292	310-822-1511	823-6714
USGS Forest & Rangeland Ecosystem Science Center 777 NW 9th St Suite 400 *Web:* fresc.usgs.gov	Corvallis	OR	97330	541-750-1030	750-1069
USGS Great Lakes Science Center 1451 Green Rd *Web:* www.glsc.usgs.gov	Ann Arbor	MI	48105	734-994-3331	994-8780
USGS Leetown Science Center 11649 Leetown Rd *Web:* www.lsc.usgs.gov	Kearneysville	WV	25430	304-724-4400	724-4410
USGS Northern Rocky Mountain Science Center Montana State University PO Box 173492 *Web:* nrmsc.usgs.gov	Bozeman	MT	59717	406-994-5304	994-6556
USGS Southwest Biological Science Center 2255 N Gemini Dr MS-9394 *Web:* sbsc.wr.usgs.gov	Flagstaff	AZ	86001	928-556-7094	556-7092
USGS Upper Midwest Environmental Sciences Center 2630 Fanta Reed Rd *Web:* www.umesc.usgs.gov	La Crosse	WI	54603	608-783-6451	783-6066
USGS Western Fisheries Research Center US Geological Survey 6505 NE 65th St *Web:* wfrc.usgs.gov	Seattle	WA	98115	206-526-6282	526-6654
Vanderbilt Kennedy Center for Research on Human Development Peabody College Box 40 230 Appleton Pl Vanderbilt University *Web:* kc.vanderbilt.edu/kennedy	Nashville	TN	37203	615-322-8240	322-8236
Virginia Institute of Marine Science Rt 1208 Great Rd PO Box 1346 *Web:* www.vims.edu	Gloucester Point	VA	23062	804-684-7000	684-7097
Visidyne Inc 10 Corporate Pl S Bedford St *Web:* www.visidyne.com	Burlington	MA	01803	781-273-2820	272-1068
Volpe National Transportation Systems Center 55 Broadway *Web:* www.volpe.dot.gov	Cambridge	MA	02142	617-494-2000	
Wadsworth Center Biggs Laboratory New York Department of Health Empire State Plaza PO Box 509 *Web:* www.wadsworth.org	Albany	NY	12201	518-474-2160	
Waisman Center University of Wisconsin 1500 Highland Ave *Web:* www.waisman.wisc.edu	Madison	WI	53705	608-263-5940	263-0529
Walter Reed Army Institute of Research (WRAIR) MCMR-UWZ 503 Robert Grant Ave *Web:* wrair-www.army.mil	Silver Spring	MD	20910	301-319-9100	319-9227
Washington National Primate Research Center 1705 NE Pacific St Box 357330 HSB I-421 *Web:* www.wanprc.org/WaNPRC	Seattle	WA	98195	206-543-0440	685-0305
Weis Center for Research 100 N Academy Ave *Web:* www.geisinger.org/professionals/research/wcr	Danville	PA	17822	570-271-6659	271-5886
West Coast & Polar Regions Undersea Research Center University of Alaska-Fairbanks 209 O'Neill Bldg PO Box 757220 *Web:* www.westnurc.uaf.edu	Fairbanks	AK	99775	907-474-5870	474-5804
WestEd 730 Harrison St 5th Fl *Web:* www.wested.org	San Francisco	CA	94107	415-565-3000	565-3012
Western Human Nutrition Research Center WSDA/ARS/WHNRC 430 W Health Sciences 1 Shields Ave University of California *Web:* www.ars.usda.gov/main/site_main.htm?modecode=53-06-25-00	Davis	CA	95616	530-752-5276	752-5271
Western Regional Research Center (WRRC) USDA/ARS 800 Buchanan St *Web:* www.ars.usda.gov/Main/docs.htm?docid=5819	Albany	CA	94710	510-559-5600	559-5963
Western Research Institute 365 N 9th St *TF:* 888-436-6974 ■ *Web:* wri.uwyo.edu	Laramie	WY	82072	307-721-2011	721-2345
Whitaker Institute of Biomedical Engineering Univ of California San Diego 9500 Gilman Dr SERF Rm 228 MC 0435 *Web:* www-bioeng.ucsd.edu/wibe	La Jolla	CA	92093	858-822-4278	822-1160

	City	State	Zip	Phone	Fax
Wisconsin Center for Education Research University of Wisconsin Madison 1025 W Johnson St *Web:* www.wcer.wisc.edu	Madison	WI	53706	608-263-4200	263-6448
Wisconsin National Primate Research Center 1220 Capitol Ct. *Web:* www.primate.wisc.edu	Madison	WI	53715	608-263-3500	263-4031
Wistar Institute 3601 Spruce St *TF:* 800-724-6633 ■ *Web:* www.wistar.upenn.edu	Philadelphia	PA	19104	215-898-3700	898-3715
WM Keck Center for Comparative & Functional Genomics 340 Edward R Madigan Laboratory 1201 W Gregory Dr *Web:* www.biotec.uiuc.edu/centers/Keck	Urbana	IL	61801	217-265-5057	265-5066
WM Keck Observatory 65-1120 Mamalahoa Hwy. *Web:* www.keckobservatory.org	Kamuela	HI	96743	808-885-7887	885-4464
Woods Hole Oceanographic Institution 86 Water St. **Fax:* Hum Res ■ *Web:* www.whoi.edu	Woods Hole	MA	02543	508-548-1400	457-2173*
Yale Child Study Center Yale University 230 S Frontage Rd *Web:* info.med.yale.edu/chldstdy	New Haven	CT	06520	203-785-2513	785-7611
Yerkes National Primate Research Center Emory University 954 Gatewood Rd *Web:* www.yerkes.emory.edu	Atlanta	GA	30322	404-727-7732	727-3108

672 RESORTS & RESORT COMPANIES

SEE ALSO Casinos p. 1409; Dude Ranches p. 1592; Hotels & Hotel Companies p. 1832; Hotels - Conference Center p. 1830; Spas - Hotel & Resort p. 2319

Alabama

	City	State	Zip	Phone	Fax
Joe Wheeler Resort Lodge & Convention Center Joe Wheeler State Park 4401 McLean Dr *TF:* 800-544-5639 ■ *Web:* www.joewheelerstatepark.com	Rogersville	AL	35652	256-247-5461	247-5471
Perdido Beach Resort 27200 Perdido Beach Blvd *TF:* 800-634-8001 ■ *Web:* www.perdidobeachresort.com	Orange Beach	AL	36561	251-981-9811	981-5670
StillWaters Resort 797 Moonbrook Dr *TF:* 800-687-3732 ■ *Web:* www.stillwatersgolf.com	Dadeville	AL	36853	256-825-7021	825-4147

Alaska

	City	State	Zip	Phone	Fax
Alyeska Prince Hotel & Resort PO Box 249 *TF:* 800-880-3880 ■ *Web:* www.alyeskaresort.com	Girdwood	AK	99587	907-754-1111	754-2200
Pybus Point Lodge PO Box 33497 *Web:* www.pybus.com	Juneau	AK	99801	907-790-4866	790-4866
Whalers' Cove Sportfishing Lodge Mile 1 Killisnoo Rd PO Box 101 *TF:* 800-423-3123 ■ *Web:* www.whalerscovelodge.com	Angoon	AK	99820	907-788-3123	788-3104

Alberta

	City	State	Zip	Phone	Fax
Delta Lodge at Kananaskis 1 Centennial Dr. *TF:* 866-432-4322 ■ *Web:* www.deltahotels.com/hotels/hotels.php?hotelId=30	Kananaskis Village	AB	T0L2H0	403-591-7711	591-7770
Fairmont Banff Springs PO Box 960 *TF:* 800-441-1414 ■ *Web:* www.fairmont.com	Banff	AB	T1L1J4	403-762-2211	762-5755
Fairmont Chateau Lake Louise 111 Lake Louise Dr *TF:* 800-441-1414 ■ *Web:* www.fairmont.com	Lake Louise	AB	T0L1E0	403-522-3511	522-3834
Fairmont Jasper Park Lodge 1 Lodge Rd. *TF:* 800-441-1414 ■ *Web:* www.fairmont.com	Jasper	AB	T0E1E0	780-852-3301	852-5107
Rimrock Resort Hotel 300 Mountain Ave PO Box 1110 *TF:* 800-661-1587 ■ *Web:* www.rimrockresort.com	Banff	AB	T1L1J2	403-762-3356	762-4132
Waterton Lakes Resort Box 4 101 Clematis Ave *TF:* 888-985-6343 ■ *Web:* www.watertonlakeslodge.com	Waterton Park	AB	T0K2M0	403-859-2150	859-2229

Arizona

	City	State	Zip	Phone	Fax
Arizona Biltmore Resort & Spa 2400 E Missouri *TF:* 800-950-0086 ■ *Web:* www.arizonabiltmore.com	Phoenix	AZ	85016	602-955-6600	381-7600
Arizona Golf Resort & Conference Center 425 S Power Rd *TF:* 800-528-8282 ■ *Web:* www.arizonagolfresort.com	Mesa	AZ	85206	480-832-3202	981-0151
Boulders Resort & Golden Door Spa 34631 N Tom Darlington Dr PO Box 2090 *TF:* 866-397-6520 ■ *Web:* www.theboulders.com	Carefree	AZ	85377	480-488-9009	488-4118
Camelback Inn JW Marriott Resort Golf Club & Spa 5402 E Lincoln Dr *TF:* 800-242-2635 ■ *Web:* www.camelbackinn.com	Scottsdale	AZ	85253	480-948-1700	596-7029
Canyon Ranch Tucson 8600 E Rockcliff Rd *TF:* 800-742-9000 ■ *Web:* www.canyonranch.com/tucson	Tucson	AZ	85750	520-749-9655	749-1646
Chaparral Suites Resort & Conference Center 5001 N Scottsdale Rd *TF:* 800-528-1456 ■ *Web:* www.chaparralsuites.com	Scottsdale	AZ	85250	480-949-1414	947-2675
CopperWynd Resort & Club 13225 N Eagle Ridge Dr *TF:* 877-707-7760 ■ *Web:* www.copperwynd.com	Fountain Hills	AZ	85268	480-333-1900	333-1901
Doubletree Paradise Valley Resort 5401 N Scottsdale Rd *TF:* 800-222-8733 ■ *Web:* www.doubletree.com	Scottsdale	AZ	85250	480-947-5400	946-1524
Enchantment Resort 525 Boynton Canyon Rd *TF:* 800-826-4180 ■ *Web:* www.enchantmentresort.com	Sedona	AZ	86336	928-282-2900	282-9249
Esplendor Resort at Rio Rico 1069 Camino Caralampi *TF:* 800-288-4746 ■ *Web:* www.esplendor-resort.com	Rio Rico	AZ	85648	520-281-1901	281-7132
Fairmont Scottsdale Princess 7575 E Princess Dr *TF:* 800-344-4758 ■ *Web:* www.fairmont.com	Scottsdale	AZ	85255	480-585-4848	585-0086
FireSky Resort & Spa 4925 N Scottsdale Rd *TF:* 800-528-7867 ■ *Web:* www.fireskyresort.com	Scottsdale	AZ	85251	480-945-7666	946-4056
Four Seasons Resort Scottsdale at Troon North 10600 E Crescent Moon Dr *TF:* 800-332-3442 ■ *Web:* www.fourseasons.com/scottsdale	Scottsdale	AZ	85262	480-515-5700	515-5599
Francisco Grande Hotel & Golf Resort 26000 Gila Bend Hwy. *TF:* 866-589-3411 ■ *Web:* www.franciscogrande.com/	Phoenix	AZ	85222	520-836-6444	421-0544
Gold Canyon Golf Resort 6100 S Kings Ranch Rd. *TF:* 800-624-6445 ■ *Web:* www.gcgr.com	Gold Canyon	AZ	85218	480-982-9090	830-5211
Hacienda del Sol Guest Ranch Resort 5601 Hacienda del Sol Rd *TF:* 800-728-6514 ■ *Web:* www.haciendadelsol.com/	Tucson	AZ	85718	520-299-1501	299-5554
Harrah's Ak-Chin Casino Resort 15406 Maricopa Rd *TF:* 888-302-3293 ■ *Web:* www.harrahs.com	Maricopa	AZ	85239	480-802-5000	802-5048
Hilton Sedona Resort & Spa 90 Ridge Trail Dr *TF:* 800-222-8733 ■ *Web:* www.hilton.com	Sedona	AZ	86351	928-284-4040	284-6940
JW Marriott Desert Ridge Resort & Spa 5350 E Marriott Dr *TF:* 800-898-4527 ■ *Web:* www.marriott.com/hotels/travel/phxdr	Phoenix	AZ	85054	480-293-5000	293-3600
Lake Powell Resorts & Marinas 100 Lakeshore Dr *TF:* 800-528-6154 ■ *Web:* www.touroklahoma.com/parks.asp	Page	AZ	86040	928-645-2433	645-1031
L'Auberge de Sedona 301 L'Auberge Ln *TF Resv:* 800-272-6777 ■ *Web:* www.lauberge.com	Sedona	AZ	86336	928-282-1661	282-2885
Legacy Golf Resort 6808 S 32nd St *TF:* 888-828-3673 ■ *Web:* www.legacygolfresort.com	Phoenix	AZ	85042	602-305-5500	305-5501
Lodge at Ventana Canyon - A Wyndham Luxury Resort 6200 N Clubhouse Ln *TF:* 800-828-5701 ■ *Web:* www.thelodgeatventanacanyon.com	Tucson	AZ	85750	520-577-1400	577-4065
Loews Ventana Canyon Resort 7000 N Resort Dr *TF:* 800-234-5117 ■ *Web:* www.loewshotels.com/hotels/tucson	Tucson	AZ	85750	520-299-2020	299-6832
Los Abrigados Resort 160 Portal Ln *TF:* 800-521-3131 ■ *Web:* www.losabrigados.com	Sedona	AZ	86336	928-282-1777	282-2614
Millennium Resort Scottsdale McCormick Ranch 7401 N Scottsdale Rd *TF:* 800-243-1332 ■ *Web:* www1.millenniumhotels.com	Scottsdale	AZ	85253	480-948-5050	991-5572
Omni Tucson National Golf Resort & Spa 2727 W Club Dr *Web:* www.tucsonnational.com	Tucson	AZ	85742	520-297-2271	297-7544
Orange Tree Golf & Conference Resort 10601 N 56th St *TF:* 800-228-0386 ■ *Web:* www.orangetreegolfresort.com	Scottsdale	AZ	85254	480-948-6100	483-6074
Phoenician The 6000 E Camelback Rd *TF:* 800-888-8234 ■ *Web:* www.thephoenician.com	Scottsdale	AZ	85251	480-941-8200	947-4311
Pointe Hilton Resort at Tapatio Cliffs 11111 N 7th St *TF:* 800-876-4683 ■ *Web:* www.pointehilton.com	Phoenix	AZ	85020	602-866-7500	993-0276
Pointe Hilton at Squaw Peak Resort 7677 N 16th St *TF:* 800-685-0550 ■ *Web:* www.pointehilton.com	Phoenix	AZ	85020	602-997-2626	997-2391
Pointe South Mountain Resort 7777 S Pointe Pkwy *TF:* 877-800-4888 ■ *Web:* www.pointesouthmtn.com	Phoenix	AZ	85044	602-438-9000	431-6535
Radisson Fort McDowell Resort 10438 N Fort McDowell Rd *TF:* 800-333-3333 ■ *Web:* www.radissonfortmcdowellresort.com	Scottsdale	AZ	85264	480-789-5300	836-5333
Radisson Poco Diablo Resort 1752 S Hwy 179 *Web:* www.radisson.com	Sedona	AZ	86336	928-282-7333	282-2090
Rancho de los Caballeros 1551 S Vulture Mine Rd *TF:* 800-684-5030 ■ *Web:* www.sunc.com	Wickenburg	AZ	85390	928-684-5484	684-2267
Renaissance Scottsdale Resort 6160 N Scottsdale Rd *Web:* www.renaissancehotel.com/phxsr	Scottsdale	AZ	85253	480-991-1414	951-3350
Resort Suites of Scottsdale 7677 E Princess Blvd *TF:* 800-541-5203 ■ *Web:* www.resortsuites.com	Scottsdale	AZ	85255	480-585-1234	585-1457
Ritz-Carlton Phoenix 2401 E Camelback Rd *TF:* 800-241-3333 ■ *Web:* www.ritzcarlton.com/hotels/phoenix/	Phoenix	AZ	85016	602-468-0700	468-0793
Royal Palms Resort & Spa 5200 E Camelback Rd *TF:* 800-672-6011 ■ *Web:* www.royalpalmshotel.com	Phoenix	AZ	85018	602-840-3610	840-6927
Saguaro Lake Ranch 13020 Bush Hwy *Web:* www.saguarolakeranch.com	Mesa	AZ	85215	480-984-2194	380-1489
Sanctuary on Camelback Mountain 5700 E McDonald Dr *TF:* 800-245-2051 ■ *Web:* www.sanctuaryoncamelback.com	Paradise Valley	AZ	85253	480-948-2100	948-7314
Scottsdale Camelback Resort 6302 E Camelback Rd *TF:* 800-891-8585 ■ *Web:* www.scottsdalecamelback.com	Scottsdale	AZ	85251	480-947-3300	994-0594
Scottsdale Plaza Resort 7200 N Scottsdale Rd *TF:* 800-832-2025 ■ *Web:* www.scottsdaleplaza.com	Scottsdale	AZ	85253	480-948-5000	998-5971
Sedona Rouge Resort & Spa 2250 W Hwy 89A *TF:* 866-589-3411 ■ *Web:* www.sedonarouge.com	Sedona	AZ	86336	928-203-4111	203-9040
Sheraton San Marcos Golf Resort & Conference Center 1 San Marcos Pl *TF:* 800-528-8071 ■ *Web:* www.sanmarcosresort.com	Chandler	AZ	85225	480-812-0900	963-6777
Sheraton Wild Horse Pass Resort & Spa 5594 W Wild Horse Pass Blvd. *TF:* 888-218-8989 ■ *Web:* www.wildhorsepassresort.com	Chandler	AZ	85226	602-225-0100	225-0300
Tanque Verde Guest Ranch 14301 E Speedway Blvd *TF:* 800-234-3833 ■ *Web:* www.tvgr.com	Tucson	AZ	85748	520-296-6275	721-9426
Westward Look Resort 245 E Ina Rd *TF:* 800-722-2500 ■ *Web:* www.westwardlook.com/	Tucson	AZ	85704	520-297-1151	297-9023
Wigwam Golf Resort & Spa 300 Wigwam Blvd *TF:* 800-327-0396 ■ *Web:* www.wigwamresort.com	Litchfield Park	AZ	85340	623-935-3811	935-3737

Arkansas

	City	State	Zip	Phone	Fax
Arlington Resort Hotel & Spa 239 Central Ave *TF:* 800-643-1502 ■ *Web:* www.arlingtonhotel.com	Hot Springs	AR	71901	501-623-7771	623-2243
Best Western Inn of the Ozarks 207 W Van Buren *TF:* 800-552-3785 ■ *Web:* www.bestwestern.com	Eureka Springs	AR	72632	479-253-9768	253-9768
Gaston's White River Resort 1777 River Rd *Web:* www.gastons.com	Lakeview	AR	72642	870-431-5202	431-5216
Lake Hamilton Resort 2803 Albert Pike Rd *Web:* www.lakehamiltonresort.com	Hot Springs	AR	71913	501-767-8606	767-8576

British Columbia

	City	State	Zip	Phone	Fax
Aerie Resort PO Box 108 *TF:* 800-518-1933 ■ *Web:* www.aerie.bc.ca	Malahat	BC	V0R2L0	250-743-7115	743-4766
Coast Hotels & Resorts Canada 1090 W Georgia St Suite 900 *Web:* www.coasthotels.com	Vancouver	BC	V6E3V7	604-682-7982	682-7982
Delta Victoria Ocean Pointe Resort & Spa 45 Songhees Rd *TF:* 800-667-4677 ■ *Web:* www.deltahotels.com/hotels	Victoria	BC	V9A6T3	250-360-2999	360-1041
Delta Whistler Village Suites 4308 Main St *TF:* 888-244-8666 ■ *Web:* www.deltahotels.com/hotels/hotels.php?hotelId=23	Whistler	BC	V0N1B4	604-905-3987	938-6500
Echo Valley Ranch & Spa Clinton PO Box 16 *TF:* 800-253-8831 ■ *Web:* www.evranch.com	Jesmond	BC	V0K1K0	250-459-2386	459-0086
Fairmont Chateau Whistler 4599 Chateau Blvd *TF:* 800-441-1414 ■ *Web:* www.fairmont.com	Whistler	BC	V0N1B4	604-938-8000	938-2291
Fairmont Empress 721 Government St *TF:* 800-441-1414 ■ *Web:* www.fairmont.com	Victoria	BC	V8W1W5	250-384-8111	381-4334
Four Seasons Resort Whistler 4591 Blackcomb Way *Web:* www.fourseasons.com/whistler	Whistler	BC	V0N1B4	604-935-3400	935-3455
Harrison Hot Springs Resort & Spa 100 Esplanade Ave *TF:* 800-663-2266 ■ *Web:* www.harrisonresort.com	Harrison Hot Springs	BC	V0M1K0	604-796-2244	796-3682
Hilton Whistler Resort & Spa 4050 Whistler Way *TF:* 888-244-8666 ■ *Web:* www.hiltonwhistler.com	Whistler	BC	V0N1B4	604-932-1982	932-7332
Holiday Inn SunSpree Resort Whistler Village 4295 Blackcomb Way *TF:* 800-229-3188 ■ *Web:* www.ichotelsgroup.com/h/d/hi/home	Whistler	BC	V0N1B4	604-938-0878	938-9943
Intrawest ULC 200 Burrard St Suite 800 *Web:* www.intrawest.com	Vancouver	BC	V6C3L6	604-669-9777	683-6778
O'Neill Hotels & Resorts Management Ltd 401 W Georgia St Suite 1690 *Web:* www.oneillhotels.com	Vancouver	BC	V6B5A1	604-684-0444	684-0482
Pan Pacific Whistler Mountainside 4320 Sundial Crescent *TF:* 888-905-9995 ■ *Web:* whistler.panpacific.com	Whistler	BC	V0N1B4	604-905-2999	905-2995

British Columbia (Cont'd)

Phone Fax

River Rock Casino Resort 8811 River Rd. Richmond BC V6X3P8 604-247-8900 247-2641
TF: 866-748-3718 ■ *Web:* www.greatcanadiancasinos.com/riverrock
Tantalus Resort Lodge 4200 Whistler Way Whistler BC V0N1B4 604-932-4146 932-2405
TF: 888-633-4046 ■ *Web:* www.tantaluslodge.com
Whistler Blackcomb Mountain Ski Resort
4545 Blackcomb Way Whistler BC V0N1B4 604-932-3434 938-7527
TF: 800-766-0449 ■ *Web:* www.whistlerblackcomb.com

California

Phone Fax

Alisal Guest Ranch & Resort 1054 Alisal Rd Solvang CA 93463 805-688-6411 688-2510
TF: 800-425-4725 ■ *Web:* www.alisal.com
Alpine Meadows Ski Resort
2600 Alpine Meadows Rd PO Box 5279 Tahoe City CA 96145 530-583-4232 583-0963
TF: 800-441-4423 ■ *Web:* www.skialpine.com
Bacara Resort & Spa 8301 Hollister Ave Santa Barbara CA 93117 805-968-0100 968-1800
TF: 877-422-4245 ■ *Web:* www.bacararesort.com
Bahia Resort Hotel 998 W Mission Bay Dr San Diego CA 92109 858-488-0551 488-7055
TF: 800-576-4229 ■ *Web:* www.bahiahotel.com
Balboa Bay Club & Resort 1221 W Coast Hwy Newport Beach CA 92663 949-645-5000 630-4315
TF: 888-445-7153 ■ *Web:* www.balboabayclub.com
Barona Valley Ranch Resort & Casino
1932 Wildcat Canyon Rd Lakeside CA 92040 619-443-2300 443-1794
TF: 888-722-7662 ■ *Web:* www.barona.com
Bear Mountain Ski & Golf Resort
43101 Gold Mine Dr PO Box 77 Big Bear Lake CA 92315 909-585-2519 585-6805
Web: www.bigbearmountainresorts.com
Booth Creek Ski Holdings Inc 12257 Business Park Dr Suite 8 Truckee CA 96161 530-550-5100 550-5116
Web: www.boothcreek.com
Calistoga Ranch 580 Lommel Rd Calistoga CA 94515 707-254-2800 254-2825
TF: 800-942-4220 ■ *Web:* www.calistogaranch.com
Carmel Valley Ranch Resort 1 Old Ranch Rd Carmel CA 93923 831-625-9500 624-2858
TF: 866-282-4745 ■ *Web:* www.carmelvalleyranch.com
Casa Palmero 1518 Cypress Dr Pebble Beach CA 93953 831-647-7500 644-7955
TF: 800-654-9300 ■ *Web:* www.pebble-beach.com/2e.html
Catalina Canyon Resort & Spa 888 Country Club Dr. Avalon CA 90704 310-510-0325 510-0900
TF: 888-478-7829 ■ *Web:* catalina-canyon-resort.pacificahost.com
Chaminade 1 Chaminade Ln Santa Cruz CA 95065 831-475-5600 476-4798
TF: 800-283-6569 ■ *Web:* www.chaminade.com
Claremont Resort & Spa 41 Tunnel Rd Berkeley CA 94705 510-843-3000 848-6208
TF: 800-551-7266 ■ *Web:* www.claremontresort.com
Costanoa Coastal Lodge & Camp 2001 Rossi Rd Pescadero CA 94060 650-879-1100 879-2275
TF: 877-262-7848 ■ *Web:* www.costanoa.com
Desert Hot Springs Spa Hotel 10805 Palm Dr Desert Hot Springs CA 92240 760-329-6000 329-6915
TF: 800-808-7727 ■ *Web:* www.dhsspa.com
Desert Springs Marriott Resort & Spa
74855 Country Club Dr Palm Desert CA 92260 760-341-2211 341-1872
TF: 800-331-3112 ■ *Web:* www.desertspringsresort.com
Doral Desert Princess Palm Springs Resort
67-967 Vista Chino Cathedral City CA 92234 760-322-7000 322-6853
TF: 888-386-4677 ■ *Web:* www.doralpalmsprings.com
Double Eagle Resort & Spa 5587 Hwy 158 PO Box 736 June Lake CA 93529 760-648-7004 648-8225
Web: www.doubleeagleresort.com
Doubletree Golf Resort San Diego 14455 Penasquitos Dr. San Diego CA 92129 858-672-9100 672-9187
Web: www.doubletree.com
Dr Wilkinson's Hot Springs Resort 1507 Lincoln Ave Calistoga CA 94515 707-942-4102 942-4412
Web: www.drwilkinson.com
Estancia La Jolla Hotel & Spa 9700 N Torrey Pines Rd La Jolla CA 92037 858-550-1000 550-1001
Web: www.estancialajolla.com
Fairmont Hotels & Resorts Inc 650 California St 12th Fl San Francisco CA 94108 415-772-7800 772-7805
Web: www.fairmont.com
Fairmont Sonoma Mission Inn & Spa
100 Boyes Blvd Boyes Hot Springs CA 95416 707-938-9000 938-4250
TF: 800-862-4945 ■ *Web:* www.fairmont.com
Fess Parker's Doubletree Resort 633 E Cabrillo Blvd Santa Barbara CA 93103 805-564-4333 564-4964
TF: 800-222-8733 ■ *Web:* www.fpdtr.com
Flamingo Resort Hotel & Conference Center 2777 4th St Santa Rosa CA 95405 707-545-8530 528-1404
TF: 800-848-8300 ■ *Web:* www.flamingohotel.com
Four Seasons Resort Aviara 7100 Four Seasons Pt. Carlsbad CA 92009 760-603-6800 603-6801
TF: 800-332-3442 ■ *Web:* www.fourseasons.com/aviara
Four Seasons Resort Santa Barbara 1260 Channel Dr Santa Barbara CA 93108 805-969-2261 565-8321
TF: 888-424-5866 ■ *Web:* www.fourseasons.com/santabarbara
Furnace Creek Inn & Ranch Resort Hwy 190 Death Valley CA 92328 760-786-2345 786-2514
Web: www.furnacecreekresort.com
Gardiner's Resort 114 Carmel Valley Rd Carmel Valley CA 93924 831-659-2207 659-2492
TF: 800-453-6225 ■ *Web:* www.gardiners-resort.com
Grand Pacific Palisades Resort & Hotel 5805 Armada Dr Carlsbad CA 92008 760-827-3200 827-3210
TF: 800-725-4723 ■ *Web:* www.grandpacificpalisades.com
Greenhorn Creek Resort 711 McCauley Ranch Rd Angels Camp CA 95222 209-736-6201 736-6210
TF: 888-736-5900 ■ *Web:* www.greenhorncreek.com
Handlery Hotel & Resort 950 Hotel Cir N San Diego CA 92108 619-298-0511 298-9793
TF: 800-676-6567 ■ *Web:* www.handlery.com
Harrah's Rincon Casino & Resort
777 Harrah's Rincon Way Valley Center CA 92082 760-751-3100 751-3200
TF: 877-777-2457 ■ *Web:* www.harrahs.com/our_casinos/rin
Hilton Palm Springs Resort 400 E Tahquitz Canyon Way Palm Springs CA 92262 760-320-6868 320-2126
TF: 800-522-6900 ■ *Web:* www.hiltonpalmsprings.com
Hilton San Diego Resort 1775 E Mission Bay Dr San Diego CA 92109 619-276-4010 275-8944
TF: 877-414-8019 ■ *Web:* www.hilton.com
Hilton Waterfront Beach Resort
21100 Pacific Coast Hwy Huntington Beach CA 92648 714-845-8000 845-8424
TF: 800-822-7873 ■ *Web:* www.hilton.com
Hotel Del Coronado 1500 Orange Ave Coronado CA 92118 619-522-8000 522-8262
TF: 800-582-2595 ■ *Web:* www.hoteldel.com
Indian Springs Resort & Spa 1712 Lincoln Ave Calistoga CA 94515 707-942-4913 942-4919
Web: www.indianspringscalistoga.com
Indian Wells Resort Hotel 76-661 Hwy 111 Indian Wells CA 92210 760-345-6466 772-5083
TF: 800-248-3220 ■ *Web:* www.indianwellsresort.com
Inn at Rancho Santa Fe
5951 Linea Del Cielo PO Box 869 Rancho Santa Fe CA 92067 858-756-1131 759-1604
TF: 800-843-4661 ■ *Web:* www.theinnatrsf.com
Inn at Spanish Bay 2700 17-Mile Dr. Pebble Beach CA 93953 831-647-7500 644-7955
TF: 800-654-9300 ■ *Web:* www.pebble-beach.com
Knott's Berry Farm Resort 7675 Crescent Ave Buena Park CA 90620 714-995-1111 952-9545*
*Fax: Resv ■ *TF:* 866-752-2444 ■ *Web:* www.radisson.com/buenaparkca
La Casa del Zorro 3845 Yaqui Pass Rd Borrego Springs CA 92004 760-767-5323 767-5963
TF: 800-824-1884 ■ *Web:* www.lacasadelzorro.com
La Costa Resort & Spa 2100 Costa del Mar Rd Carlsbad CA 92009 760-438-9111 438-3758
TF: 800-854-5000 ■ *Web:* www.lacosta.com
La Jolla Beach & Tennis Club 2000 Spindrift Dr. La Jolla CA 92037 858-454-7126 456-3805
TF: 800-237-5211 ■ *Web:* www.ljbtc.com

Phone Fax

La Quinta Resort & Club 49-499 Eisenhower Dr La Quinta CA 92253 760-564-4111 564-7625
TF: 800-598-3828 ■ *Web:* www.laquintaresort.com
Laguna Cliffs Marriott Resort 25135 Park Lantern Dana Point CA 92629 949-661-5000 661-5358
TF: 800-228-9290 ■ *Web:* www.lagunacliffs.com
Lake Arrowhead Resort & Spa 27984 Hwy 189 Lake Arrowhead CA 92352 909-336-1511 744-3088
TF: 800-800-6792 ■ *Web:* www.laresort.com/
Lakeland Village Beach & Mountain Resort
3535 Lake Tahoe Blvd South Lake Tahoe CA 96150 530-544-1685 544-0193
TF: 800-822-5969 ■ *Web:* www.lakeland-village.com
L'Auberge Del Mar Resort & Spa 1540 Camino del Mar Del Mar CA 92014 858-259-1515 755-4940
TF: 800-553-1336 ■ *Web:* www.laubergedelmar.com
Lawrence Welks Desert Oasis
34567 Cathedral Canyon Dr Cathedral City CA 92234 760-321-9000 321-6200
TF: 800-824-8224 ■ *Web:* www.welkresort.com
Le Parker Meridien Palm Springs
4200 E Palm Canyon Dr Palm Springs CA 92264 760-770-5000 324-2188
Web: www.starwoodhotels.com/lemeridien
Leisure Sports Inc 7077 Koll Center Pkwy Suite 110 Pleasanton CA 94566 925-600-1966 600-1144
Web: www.leisuresportsinc.com
Lodge at Pebble Beach 1500 Cypress Dr Pebble Beach CA 93953 831-624-3811 625-8598
TF: 800-654-9300
Lodge at Sonoma - A Renaissance Resort & Spa
1325 Broadway Sonoma CA 95476 707-935-6600 935-6829
TF: 888-710-8008 ■ *Web:* www.thelodgeatsonoma.com
Lodge at Torrey Pines Inn 11480 N Torrey Pines Rd La Jolla CA 92037 858-453-4420 550-3908
Web: www.lodgeattorreypines.com
Loews Coronado Bay Resort 4000 Coronado Bay Rd Coronado CA 92118 619-424-4000 424-4400
TF: 800-815-6397 ■ *Web:* www.loewshotels.com/hotels/sandiego
Mammoth Mountain Resort 1 Minaret Rd PO Box 24 Mammoth Lakes CA 93546 760-934-2571 934-0615
TF: 800-626-6684 ■ *Web:* www.mammoth-mtn.com
Meadowood Napa Valley 900 Meadowood Ln Saint Helena CA 94574 707-963-3646 963-3532
TF: 800-458-8080 ■ *Web:* www.meadowood.com
Miramonte Resort & Spa 45000 Indian Wells Ln Indian Wells CA 92210 760-341-2200 568-0541
TF: 800-237-2926 ■ *Web:* www.miramonteresort.com
Montage Resort & Spa 30801 S Coast Hwy Laguna Beach CA 92651 949-715-6001 715-6070
TF: 866-271-6953 ■ *Web:* www.montagelagunabeach.com
Montage Resort & Spa Laguna Beach
30801 S Coast Hwy Laguna Beach CA 92651 949-715-6000 715-6100
Web: www.montagelagunabeach.com
Morgan Run Resort & Club 5690 Cancha de Golf Rancho Santa Fe CA 92091 858-756-2471 756-3013
TF: 800-378-4653 ■ *Web:* www.morganrun.com
Morongo Casino Resort & Spa
49500 Seminole Dr PO Box 366 Cabazon CA 92230 951-849-3080 849-3181
TF: 800-252-4499 ■ *Web:* www.morongocasinoresort.com
Mount Shasta Resort 1000 Siskiyou Lake Blvd Mount Shasta CA 96067 530-926-3030 926-0333
TF: 800-958-3363 ■ *Web:* www.mountshastaresort.com
Northstar-at-Tahoe PO Box 129 Truckee CA 96160 530-562-1010 562-3812
TF: 800-466-6784 ■ *Web:* www.northstarattahoe.com
Oasis Villa Resort Hotel 4190 E Palm Canyon Dr Palm Springs CA 92264 760-328-1499 328-3359
TF: 800-247-4664
Ojai Valley Inn & Spa 905 Country Club Rd Ojai CA 93023 805-646-5511 640-0305
TF: 800-422-6524 ■ *Web:* www.ojairesort.com
Pacific Palms Conference Resort 1 Industry Hills Pkwy City of Industry CA 91744 626-810-4455 964-9535
TF: 800-524-4557 ■ *Web:* www.pacificpalmsresort.com
Pala Casino Resort & Spa 11154 Hwy 76 PO Box 40 Pala CA 92059 760-510-5100 510-5190
TF: 877-946-7252 ■ *Web:* www.palacasino.com
Pala Mesa Resort 2001 Old Hwy 395 Fallbrook CA 92028 760-728-5881 723-8292
TF: 800-722-4700 ■ *Web:* www.palamesa.com
Palm Mountain Resort & Spa 155 S Belardo Rd Palm Springs CA 92262 760-325-1301 323-8937
TF: 800-622-9451 ■ *Web:* www.palmmountainresort.com
Pan Pacific Hotels & Resorts 500 Post St San Francisco CA 94102 415-732-7747 732-5800
TF: 800-327-8585 ■ *Web:* www.panpacific.com
Paradise Point Resort & Spa 1404 W Vacation Rd San Diego CA 92109 858-274-4630 581-5929
TF: 800-344-2626 ■ *Web:* www.paradisepoint.com
Pechanga Resort & Casino 45000 Pechanga Pkwy Temecula CA 92592 951-693-1819 695-7410
TF: 877-711-2946 ■ *Web:* www.pechanga.com
Post Ranch Inn Hwy 1 Big Sur CA 93920 831-667-2200 667-2824
TF: 800-527-2200 ■ *Web:* www.postranchinn.com
Quail Lodge Resort & Golf Club 8205 Valley Greens Dr Carmel CA 93923 831-624-2888 624-3726
TF: 800-538-9516 ■ *Web:* www.quaillodge.com
Rancho Bernardo Inn 17550 Bernardo Oaks Dr San Diego CA 92128 858-675-8500 675-8501
TF: 877-517-9342 ■ *Web:* www.ranchobernardoinn.com
Rancho Las Palmas Marriott Resort & Spa
41000 Bob Hope Dr Rancho Mirage CA 92270 760-568-2727 568-5845
TF: 888-772-5809 ■ *Web:* www.marriotthotels.com/PSPCA
Rancho Valencia Resort
5921 Valencia Cir PO Box 9126 Rancho Santa Fe CA 92067 858-756-1123 756-0165
TF: 800-548-3664 ■ *Web:* www.ranchovalencia.com
Renaissance Esmeralda Resort 44-400 Indian Wells Ln Indian Wells CA 92210 760-773-4444 346-9308
TF: 800-552-4386 ■ *Web:* www.renaissanceesmeralda.com
Resort at Squaw Creek 400 Squaw Creek Rd Olympic Valley CA 96146 530-583-6300 581-6632
TF: 800-327-3353 ■ *Web:* www.squawcreek.com
Ritz-Carlton Half Moon Bay 1 Miramontes Pt Rd Half Moon Bay CA 94019 650-712-7000 712-7015
TF: 800-244-3333 ■ *Web:* www.ritzcarlton.com/resorts/half_moon_bay/
Ritz-Carlton Huntington Hotel & Spa 1401 S Oak Knoll Ave Pasadena CA 91106 626-568-3900 568-3700
TF: 800-241-3333 ■ *Web:* www.ritzcarlton.com/hotels/huntington/spa/
Ritz-Carlton Laguna Niguel 1 Ritz Carlton Dr Dana Point CA 92629 949-240-2000 240-1061
TF: 800-241-3333 ■ *Web:* www.ritzcarlton.com/resorts/laguna_niguel/
Saint Regis Monarch Beach Resort & Spa
3300 Niguel Rd 1 Monarch Beach Resort Dana Point CA 92629 949-234-3200 234-3201
TF: 800-722-1543 ■ *Web:* www.stregismonarchbeach.com
San Vicente Inn & Golf Course 24157 San Vicente Rd Ramona CA 92065 760-789-8290 788-6115
TF: 800-776-1289 ■ *Web:* www.sanvicenteresort.com
San Ysidro Ranch 900 San Ysidro Ln Montecito CA 93108 805-969-5046 565-1995
TF: 800-368-6788 ■ *Web:* www.sanysidroranch.com
Sea Venture Resort 100 Ocean View Ave Pismo Beach CA 93449 805-773-4994 773-0924
TF: 800-662-5545 ■ *Web:* www.seaventure.com
Shadow Mountain Resort & Club 45-750 San Luis Rey Palm Desert CA 92260 760-346-6123 346-6518
TF: 800-472-3713 ■ *Web:* www.shadow-mountain.com
Silverado Resort 1600 Atlas Peak Rd Napa CA 94558 707-257-0200 257-2867
TF: 800-532-0500 ■ *Web:* www.silveradoresort.com
Snow Valley Mountain Resort
35100 Hwy 18 PO Box 2337 Running Springs CA 92382 909-867-2751 867-7687
Web: www.snow-valley.com
Spa Resort The 100 N Indian Canyon Dr Palm Springs CA 92262 760-325-1461 325-3344
TF: 800-854-1279 ■ *Web:* www.sparesortcasino.com
Spa Resort Casino 401 E Amado Rd Palm Springs CA 92262 760-883-1000 883-1250
TF: 800-854-1279 ■ *Web:* www.sparesortcasino.com
Squaw Valley USA PO Box 2007 Olympic Valley CA 96146 530-583-6985 581-7106
TF: 800-545-4350 ■ *Web:* www.squaw.com
Stonepine 150 E Carmel Valley Rd Carmel Valley CA 93924 831-659-2245 659-5160
Web: www.stonepinecalifornia.com
Sycuan Resort & Casino 3007 Dehesa Rd El Cajon CA 92019 619-442-3425 442-9574
TF: 800-457-5568 ■ *Web:* www.sycuan.com/sycuan_resort
Tahoe Seasons Resort 3901 Saddle Rd South Lake Tahoe CA 96150 530-541-6700 541-0653
TF: 800-540-4874 ■ *Web:* www.tahoeseasons.com

				Phone	Fax
Temecula Creek Inn 44501 Rainbow Canyon Rd	Temecula	CA	92592	951-694-1000	676-8961
TF: 800-962-7335 ■ *Web:* www.temeculacreekinn.com					
Town & Country Resort & Convention Center 500 Hotel Cir N	San Diego	CA	92108	619-291-7131	291-3584
TF: 800-772-8527 ■ *Web:* www.towncountry.com					
Two Bunch Palms Resort & Spa 67425 Two Bunch Palms Trail	Desert Hot Springs	CA	92240	760-329-8791	329-1874
TF: 800-472-4334 ■ *Web:* www.twobunchpalms.com					
Ventana Inn 48123 Hwy 1	Big Sur	CA	93920	831-667-2331	667-2419
TF: 800-628-6500 ■ *Web:* www.ventanainn.com					
Welk Resort San Diego 8860 Lawrence Welk Dr	Escondido	CA	92026	760-749-3000	749-9537
TF: 800-932-9355 ■ *Web:* www.welkresort.com					
Winner's Circle Resort 550 Via de la Valle	Solana Beach	CA	92075	858-755-6666	481-3706
Web: www.winnerscircleresort.com					

Colorado

				Phone	Fax
Aspen Meadows Resort 845 Meadows Rd	Aspen	CO	81611	970-925-4240	925-7790
TF: 800-452-4240 ■ *Web:* aspenmeadowsresort.dolce.com					
Aspen Skiing Co LLC PO Box 1248	Aspen	CO	81612	970-925-1220	429-3219*
**Fax:* Sales ■ *TF Sales:* 800-525-6200 ■ *Web:* www.aspensnowmass.com					
Beaver Run Resort & Conference Center 620 Village Rd	Breckenridge	CO	80424	970-453-6000	453-2454
TF: 800-525-2253 ■ *Web:* www.beaverrun.com					
Breckenridge Ski Resort 351 County Rd 708	Breckenridge	CO	80424	970-453-5000	453-3202
TF: 800-789-7669 ■ *Web:* www.breckenridge.com					
Broadmoor The 1 Lake Ave	Colorado Springs	CO	80906	719-634-7711	577-5738
TF: 800-634-7711 ■ *Web:* www.broadmoor.com					
C Lazy U Ranch 3640 Colorado Hwy 125 PO Box 379	Granby	CO	80446	970-887-3344	887-3917
Web: www.clazyu.com					
Copper Mountain Resort 509 Copper Rd PO Box 3001	Copper Mountain	CO	80443	970-968-2882	968-3300
TF: 888-219-2441 ■ *Web:* www.coppercolorado.com					
Crested Butte Mountain Resort 12 Snowmass Rd PO Box 5700	Mount Crested Butte	CO	81225	970-349-2201	349-2250
TF: 800-810-7669 ■ *Web:* www.crestedbutteresort.com					
Destination Hotels & Resorts Inc 10333 E Dry Creek Rd Suite 450	Englewood	CO	80112	303-799-3830	799-6011
TF: 800-633-8347 ■ *Web:* www.destinationhotels.com					
Durango Mountain Resort 1 Skier Pl	Durango	CO	81301	970-247-9000	385-2106
TF: 800-693-0175 ■ *Web:* www.durangomountainresort.com					
Gold Lake Mountain Resort & Spa 3371 Gold Lake Rd	Ward	CO	80481	303-459-3544	459-9077
TF: 800-450-3544 ■ *Web:* www.goldlake.com					
Grand Lodge Crested Butte 6 Emmons Loop	Mount Crested Butte	CO	81225	970-349-8000	349-8050
TF: 888-823-4446 ■ *Web:* www.grandlodgecrestedbutte.com					
Hot Springs Lodge & Pool 415 E 6th St PO Box 308	Glenwood Springs	CO	81602	970-945-6571	947-2950
TF: 800-537-7946 ■ *Web:* www.hotspringspool.com					
Indian Springs Resort 302 Soda Creek Rd	Idaho Springs	CO	80452	303-989-6666	567-9304
Web: www.indianspringsresort.com					
Inn at Beaver Creek 10 Elk Track Ln	Beaver Creek	CO	81620	970-845-7800	845-5279
TF: 800-859-8242					
Inverness Hotel & Golf Club 200 Inverness Dr W	Englewood	CO	80112	303-799-5800	799-5874
TF: 800-346-4891 ■ *Web:* www.invernesshotel.com					
Keystone Resort 21996 Hwy 6 PO Box 38	Keystone	CO	80435	970-496-2316	496-4215
TF: 800-239-1639 ■ *Web:* keystone.snow.com					
Lion Square Lodge & Conference Center 660 W Lionshead Pl	Vail	CO	81657	970-476-2281	476-7423
TF: 800-525-5788 ■ *Web:* www.lionsquare.com					
Lodge at Tamarron 40292 Hwy 550 N	Durango	CO	81301	970-259-2000	382-7899
TF: 800-678-1000 ■ *Web:* www.lodgeattamarron.com					
Lodge at Vail 174 E Gore Creek Dr	Vail	CO	81657	970-476-5011	476-7425
TF: 800-331-5634 ■ *Web:* lodgeatvail.rockresorts.com/					
Manor Vail Lodge 595 E Vail Valley Dr	Vail	CO	81657	970-476-5651	476-4982
TF: 800-950-8245 ■ *Web:* www.manorvail.com					
Millennium Hotels & Resorts 6560 Greenwood Plaza Blvd Suite 300	Greenwood Village	CO	80111	303-779-2000	779-2001
Web: www.millenniumhotels.com					
Monarch Mountain Lodge 22720 W US Hwy 50	Monarch	CO	81227	719-539-2581	539-7652
TF: 888-996-7669 ■ *Web:* www.monarchmountainlodge.com					
Mountain Lodge at Telluride 457 Mountain Village Blvd	Telluride	CO	81435	970-369-5000	369-4317
TF: 866-368-6867 ■ *Web:* www.mountainlodgetelluride.com					
Omni Interlocken Resort 500 Interlocken Blvd	Broomfield	CO	80021	303-438-6600	464-3236
TF: 800-843-6664 ■ *Web:* www.omnihotels.com					
Park Hyatt Beaver Creek Resort & Spa 136 E Thomas Pl	Beaver Creek	CO	81620	[illegible]	[illegible]
TF: 800-233-1234 ■ *Web:* beavercreek.hyatt.com					
Peaks Resort & Golden Door Spa 136 Country Club Dr	Telluride	CO	81435	800-789-2220	728-6175*
**Fax Area Code:* 970 ■ *TF:* 866-282-4557 ■ *Web:* www.thepeaksresort.com					
Ritz-Carlton Bachelor Gulch 0130 Daybreak Ridge	Avon	CO	81620	970-748-6200	343-1070
TF: 800-241-3333 ■ *Web:* www.ritzcarlton.com					
Saint Regis Resort Aspen 315 E Dean St	Aspen	CO	81611	970-920-3300	925-8998
TF: 888-454-9005 ■ *Web:* www.stregisaspen.com					
Sheraton Steamboat Resort & Conference Center 2200 Village Inn Ct	Steamboat Springs	CO	80487	970-879-2220	879-7686
TF: 800-325-3535 ■ *Web:* www.steamboat-sheraton.com					
Snowmass Club PO Box G-2	Snowmass Village	CO	81615	970-923-5600	923-6944
TF: 800-525-0710 ■ *Web:* www.snowmassclub.com					
Sonnenalp Resort of Vail 20 Vail Rd	Vail	CO	81657	970-476-5656	476-1639
TF: 800-654-8312 ■ *Web:* www.sonnenalp.com					
Steamboat Grand Resort Hotel & Conference Center 2300 Mt Werner Cir	Steamboat Springs	CO	80487	970-871-5500	871-5501
TF: 877-269-2628 ■ *Web:* www.steamboatgrand.com					
Steamboat Resorts 1847 Ski Times Square Dr PO Box 772995	Steamboat Springs	CO	80487	970-879-8000	879-8060
TF: 800-525-5502 ■ *Web:* www.steamboatresorts.com					
Steamboat Ski & Resort Corp 2305 Mt Werner Cir	Steamboat Springs	CO	80487	970-879-6111	879-4757
TF: 877-237-2628 ■ *Web:* www.steamboat.com					
Tall Timber Resort 1 Silverton Star	Durango	CO	81301	970-259-4813	259-4813
Web: www.talltimberresort.com					
Torian Plum Condo Resort 1855 Ski Time Square Dr	Steamboat Springs	CO	80487	970-879-8811	879-7374
TF: 800-228-2458 ■ *Web:* www.torianplum.com					
Vail Cascade Resort & Spa 1300 Westhaven Dr	Vail	CO	81657	970-476-7111	479-7020
TF: 800-420-2424 ■ *Web:* www.vailcascade.com					
Vail Resorts Management Co 137 Benchmark Rd	Avon	CO	81620	970-476-5601	845-2465
NYSE: MTN ■ *Web:* www.snow.com					
Village at Breckenridge Resort 535 S Park Ave	Breckenridge	CO	80424	970-453-2000	453-5116
TF: 800-332-0424 ■ *Web:* breckresorts.com/villageatbreckenridge/					
Winter Park Resort 150 Alpenglobe Way PO Box 36	Winter Park	CO	80482	303-892-0961	892-5823
TF: 800-979-0332 ■ *Web:* www.skiwinterpark.com					

Connecticut

				Phone	Fax
Foxwoods Resort Casino 39 Norwich Westerly Rd	Ledyard	CT	06339	860-312-3000	396-3639
TF: 800-752-9244 ■ *Web:* www.foxwoods.com					
Heritage Hotel 522 Heritage Rd	Southbury	CT	06488	203-264-8200	264-5035
TF: 800-932-3466 ■ *Web:* www.heritagesouthbury.com					
Interlaken Inn 74 Interlaken Rd	Lakeville	CT	06039	860-435-9878	435-2980
TF: 800-222-2909 ■ *Web:* www.interlakeninn.com					
Mohegan Sun Resort & Casino 1 Mohegan Sun Blvd	Uncasville	CT	06382	860-862-8000	862-7824
TF: 888-226-7711 ■ *Web:* www.mohegansun.com					
Saybrook Point Inn & Spa 2 Bridge St	Old Saybrook	CT	06475	860-395-2000	388-1504
TF: 800-243-0212 ■ *Web:* www.saybrook.com					
Water's Edge Resort & Spa 1525 Boston Post Rd	Westbrook	CT	06498	860-399-5901	399-6172
TF: 800-222-5901 ■ *Web:* www.watersedgeresortandspa.com					

District of Columbia

				Phone	Fax
JW Marriott Hotels & Resorts 1 Marriott Dr	Washington	DC	20058	301-380-3000	
TF: 888-236-2427 ■ *Web:* marriott.com/jwmarriott					
Marriott Hotels & Resorts 1 Marriott Dr	Washington	DC	20058	301-380-3000	380-3090
TF: 800-228-9290 ■ *Web:* marriott.com/marriott					
Renaissance Hotels & Resorts 1 Marriott Dr	Washington	DC	20058	301-380-3000	380-4055
Web: marriott.com/renaissancehotels					

Florida

				Phone	Fax
Admiral Lehigh Golf Resort & Spa 225 E Joel Blvd	Lehigh Acres	FL	33972	239-369-2121	368-1660
TF: 888-465-3222 ■ *Web:* www.flagolfgetaway.com					
Alden Beach Resort 5900 Gulf Blvd	Saint Pete Beach	FL	33706	727-360-7081	360-5957
TF: 800-237-2530 ■ *Web:* www.aldenbeachresort.com					
Amelia Island Plantation 1501 Lewis St	Amelia Island	FL	32034	904-261-6161	277-5159
TF: 800-874-6878 ■ *Web:* www.aipfl.com					
Americano Beach Resort 1260 N Atlantic Ave	Daytona Beach	FL	32118	386-255-7431	253-9513
TF: 800-874-1824 ■ *Web:* www.americanobeachresort.com					
Bahia Mar Beach Resort & Yachting Center 801 Seabreeze Blvd	Fort Lauderdale	FL	33316	954-764-2233	523-5424
TF: 888-802-2442 ■ *Web:* bahiamarhotel.com					
Banana Bay Resort 2319 N Roosevelt Blvd	Key West	FL	33040	305-296-6925	296-2004
TF: 800-226-2621 ■ *Web:* www.bananabay.com					
Banyan Resort 323 Whitehead St	Key West	FL	33040	305-296-7786	294-1107
TF: 800-853-9937 ■ *Web:* www.thebanyanresort.com					
Bay Hill Golf Club & Lodge 9000 Bay Hill Blvd	Orlando	FL	32819	407-876-2429	876-1035
TF: 888-422-9445 ■ *Web:* www.bayhill.com					
Bay Point Resort Village Marriott Golf & Yacht Club 4200 Marriott Dr	Panama City Beach	FL	32408	850-236-6000	236-6158
TF: 800-874-7105 ■ *Web:* marriotthotels.com/PFNBP					
Beachcomber Resort Hotel & Villas 1200 S Ocean Blvd	Fort Lauderdale	FL	33062	954-941-7830	942-7680
TF: 800-231-2423 ■ *Web:* www.beachcomberresort.com					
Belleview Biltmore Resort & Spa 25 Belleview Blvd	Clearwater	FL	33756	727-442-6171	441-4173
TF: 800-237-8947 ■ *Web:* www.belleviewbiltmore.com					
Biltmore Hotel & Conference Center of the Americas 1200 Anastasia Ave	Coral Gables	FL	33134	305-445-1926	913-3159
TF: 800-727-1926 ■ *Web:* www.biltmorehotel.com					
Bluewater Bay Resort 1940 Bluewater Blvd	Niceville	FL	32578	850-897-3613	897-2424
TF: 800-874-2128 ■ *Web:* www.bwbresort.com					
Boca Raton Resort & Club 501 E Camino Real	Boca Raton	FL	33432	561-447-3000	394-3961
TF: 800-327-0101 ■ *Web:* www.bocaresort.com					
Breakers The 1 S County Rd	Palm Beach	FL	33480	561-655-6611	659-8403
TF: 800-833-3141 ■ *Web:* www.thebreakers.com					
Buena Vista Hospitality Group Inc 10100 International Dr Suite 2001	Orlando	FL	32821	407-352-7161	352-2413
Web: www.bvhg.com					
Buena Vista Palace Hotel & Spa 1900 Buena Vista Dr	Lake Buena Vista	FL	32830	407-827-2727	827-6034
TF: 866-397-6516 ■ *Web:* www.buenavistapalace.com					
Casa Del Mar Beach Resort 621 S Atlantic Ave	Ormond Beach	FL	32176	386-672-4550	672-1418
Casa Marina Resort & Beach Club 1500 Reynolds St	Key West	FL	33040	305-296-3535	296-4633
TF: 866-397-6342 ■ *Web:* www.casamarinaresort.com					
Casa Ybel Resort 2255 W Gulf Dr	Sanibel	FL	33957	239-472-3145	472-2109
TF: 800-276-4753 ■ *Web:* www.casaybelresort.com					
Castaways Beach Resort 2043 S Atlantic Ave	Daytona Beach Shores	FL	32118	386-254-8480	253-6554
TF: 866-254-2722 ■ *Web:* www.castawaysbeachresort.com					
Charter Club Resort on Naples Bay 1000 10th Ave S	Naples	FL	34102	239-261-5559	261-6782
TF: 800-494-5559 ■ *Web:* www.islandone.com/ior/ccr.html					
Cheeca Lodge & Spa MM 82 81801 Overseas Hwy	Islamorada	FL	33036	305-664-4651	664-2893
TF: 800-327-2888 ■ *Web:* www.cheeca.com					
Club Med Inc 75 Valencia Ave	Coral Gables	FL	33134	305-925-9000	443-0562*
**Fax:* Mail Rm ■ *TF:* 800-258-2633 ■ *Web:* www.clubmed.com					
Club Med Sandpiper 4500 SE Pine Valley St	Port Saint Lucie	FL	34952	772-398-5100	398-5103
TF: 800-258-2633 ■ *Web:* www.clubmed.com					
Colony Beach & Tennis Resort 1620 Gulf of Mexico Dr	Longboat Key	FL	34228	941-383-6464	383-7549
TF: 800-426-5669 ■ *Web:* www.colonybeachresort.com					
Colony Reef Club 4670 A1A S	Saint Augustine	FL	32080	904-471-2233	471-6429
TF: 800-624-5965 ■ *Web:* www.colonyreef.com					
Deauville Beach Resort 6701 Collins Ave	Miami Beach	FL	33141	305-865-8511	865-8154
TF: 800-327-6656 ■ *Web:* www.deauvillebeachresort.com					
Diplomat Country Club & Spa 501 Diplomat Pkwy	Hallandale Beach	FL	33009	954-883-4000	883-4009
TF: 800-327-1212 ■ *Web:* www.diplomatcountryclub.com					
Disney's All-Star Movies Resort 1991 W Buena Vista Dr	Lake Buena Vista	FL	32830	407-939-7000	939-7111
Web: disneyworld.disney.go.com					
Disney's All-Star Music Resort 1801 W Buena Vista Dr	Lake Buena Vista	FL	32830	407-939-6000	939-7222
Web: disneyworld.disney.go.com					
Disney's All-Star Sports Resort 1701 W Buena Vista Dr	Lake Buena Vista	FL	32830	407-939-5000	939-7333
Web: disneyworld.disney.go.com					
Disney's Animal Kingdom Lodge 2901 Osceola Pkwy	Lake Buena Vista	FL	32830	407-938-3000	938-4799
Web: disneyworld.disney.go.com					
Disney's Beach Club Resort 1800 Epcot Resort Blvd	Lake Buena Vista	FL	32830	407-934-8000	934-3850
Web: disneyworld.disney.go.com					
Disney's BoardWalk Resort 2101 N Epcot Resort Blvd	Lake Buena Vista	FL	32830	407-939-5100	939-5150
Web: disneyworld.disney.go.com					
Disney's BoardWalk Villas 2101 N Epcot Resort Blvd	Lake Buena Vista	FL	32830	407-939-5100	939-5150
Web: disneyworld.disney.go.com					
Disney's Caribbean Beach Resort 900 Cayman Way	Lake Buena Vista	FL	32830	407-934-3400	934-3288
Web: disneyworld.disney.go.com					
Disney's Contemporary Resort 4600 N World Dr	Lake Buena Vista	FL	32830	407-824-1000	824-3539
Web: disneyworld.disney.go.com					
Disney's Coronado Springs Resort 1001 W Buena Vista Dr	Lake Buena Vista	FL	32830	407-939-1000	939-1001
Web: disneyworld.disney.go.com					
Disney's Fort Wilderness Resort & Campground 4510 Fort Wilderness Trail	Lake Buena Vista	FL	32830	407-824-2900	824-3508
Web: disneyworld.disney.go.com/					
Disney's Grand Floridian Resort & Spa 4401 Grand Floridian Way	Lake Buena Vista	FL	32830	407-824-3000	824-3186
Web: disneyworld.disney.go.com					
Disney's Old Key West Resort 1510 N Cove Rd	Lake Buena Vista	FL	32830	407-827-7700	827-7710
Web: disneyworld.disney.go.com					

Florida (Cont'd)

Phone | Fax

Disney's Polynesian Resort 1600 Seven Seas Dr ... Lake Buena Vista FL 32830 407-824-2000 824-3174
Web: disneyworld.disney.go.com
Disney's Pop Century Resort 1050 Century Dr ... Lake Buena Vista FL 32830 407-938-4000 938-4040
Disney's Port Orleans Resort-French Quarter
2201 Orleans Dr ... Lake Buena Vista FL 32830 407-934-5000 934-5353
Web: disneyworld.disney.go.com/waltdisneyworld/resorts/resortshomeindex?
Disney's Port Orleans Resort-Riverside
1251 Riverside Dr ... Lake Buena Vista FL 32830 407-934-6000 934-5777
Web: disneyworld.disney.go.com
Disney's Wilderness Lodge 901 Timberline Dr ... Lake Buena Vista FL 32830 407-824-3200 824-3232
Web: disneyworld.disney.go.com
Disney's Yacht Club Resort 1700 EPCOT Resorts Blvd ... Lake Buena Vista FL 32830 407-934-7000 934-3850
Web: disneyworld.disney.go.com
Don CeSar Beach Resort - A Loews Hotel
3400 Gulf Blvd ... Saint Pete Beach FL 33706 727-360-1881 363-5034*
**Fax:* Sales ■ *TF:* 866-563-9792 ■ *Web:* www.doncesar.com
Don Shula's Hotel & Golf Club 7601 Miami Lakes Dr ... Miami Lakes FL 33014 305-821-1150 820-8087
TF: 800-247-4852 ■ *Web:* www.donshulahotel.com
Doral Golf Resort & Spa 4400 NW 87th Ave ... Miami FL 33178 305-592-2000 594-4682
TF: 800-713-6725 ■ *Web:* www.doralgolf.com
Doubletree Grand Key Resort 3990 S Roosevelt Blvd ... Key West FL 33040 305-293-1818 296-6962
TF: 888-844-0454 ■ *Web:* grandkeyresort.com
Eden Roc - A Renaissance Beach Resort & Spa
4525 Collins Ave ... Miami Beach FL 33140 305-531-0000 674-5555
TF: 800-228-9290 ■ *Web:* www.edenrocresort.com
Fairmont Turnberry Isle Resort & Club
19999 W Country Club Dr ... Aventura FL 33180 305-932-6200 933-6554
TF: 800-327-7028 ■ *Web:* www.turnberryisle.com
Fisher Island Hotel & Resort 1 Fisher Island Dr ... Fisher Island FL 33109 305-535-6080 535-6003
TF: 800-537-3708 ■ *Web:* www.fisherisland-florida.com
Fishermen's Village 1200 W Retta Esplanade ... Punta Gorda FL 33950 941-639-8721 637-1054
TF: 800-639-0020 ■ *Web:* www.fishville.com
Fontainebleau Hilton Resort 4441 Collins Ave ... Miami Beach FL 33140 305-538-2000 531-2845
TF: 800-548-8886 ■ *Web:* www.fontainebleau.hilton.com
Fort Lauderdale Grande Hotel & Yacht Club
1881 SE 17th St ... Fort Lauderdale FL 33316 954-463-4000 527-6705
TF: 866-380-1110 ■ *Web:* www.fortlauderdalegrande.com
Four Seasons Resort Palm Beach 2800 S Ocean Blvd ... Palm Beach FL 33480 561-582-2800 547-1374
TF: 800-432-2335 ■ *Web:* www.fourseasons.com/palmbeach
Galleon Resort & Marina 617 Front St ... Key West FL 33040 305-296-7711 296-0821
TF: 800-544-3030 ■ *Web:* www.galleonresort.com
Gaylord Palms Resort & Convention Center
6000 W Osceola Pkwy ... Kissimmee FL 34746 407-586-0000 586-2199
Web: www.gaylordpalms.com
Grand Palms Hotel & Golf Resort 110 Grand Palms Dr ... Pembroke Pines FL 33027 954-431-8800 435-5988
TF: 800-327-9246 ■ *Web:* www.grandpalmsresort.com/
Grenelefe Golf & Tennis Resort 3200 SR-546 ... Haines City FL 33844 863-422-7511 421-5000
TF: 888-808-7410 ■ *Web:* www.grenelefe.com
Hard Rock Hotel at Universal Orlando Resort
5800 Universal Blvd ... Orlando FL 32819 407-503-2000 503-2010
TF: 800-232-7827 ■ *Web:* www.loewshotels.com
Hawk's Cay Resort & Marina 61 Hawk's Cay Blvd ... Duck Key FL 33050 305-743-7000 743-5215
TF: 800-432-2242 ■ *Web:* www.hawkscay.com
Hilton Longboat Key Beach Resort
4711 Gulf of Mexico Dr ... Longboat Key FL 34228 941-383-2451 383-7979
TF: 800-445-8667 ■ *Web:* www.hilton.com
Hilton Marco Island Beach Resort 560 S Collier Blvd ... Marco Island FL 34145 239-394-5000 394-5251
TF: 800-443-4550 ■ *Web:* www.hilton.com/en/hi/hotels/index.jhtml?ctyhocn=MRKMHHF
Hilton Sandestin Beach Golf Resort & Spa
4000 Sandestin Blvd S ... Destin FL 32550 850-267-9500 267-3076
TF: 800-367-1271 ■ *Web:* www.hilton.com
Holiday Inn SunSpree Resort Lake Buena Vista 13351 SR 535 ... Orlando FL 32821 407-239-4500 239-8463
TF: 800-366-6299 ■ *Web:* www.kidsuites.com
Holiday Inn SunSpree Resort Marina Cove
6800 Sunshine Skyway Ln ... Saint Petersburg FL 33711 727-867-1151 864-4494
TF: 800-227-8045 ■ *Web:* www.ichotelsgroup.com/h/d/hi/home
Holiday Isle Beach Resort & Marina 84001 Overseas Hwy ... Islamorada FL 33036 305-664-2321 664-2703
TF: 800-327-7070 ■ *Web:* www.holidayisle.com
Innisbrook Resort & Golf Club 36750 US Hwy 19 N ... Palm Harbor FL 34684 727-942-2000 942-5576
TF: 800-456-2000 ■ *Web:* www.innisbrookgolfresort.com
Inverrary Plaza Resort 3501 Inverrary Blvd ... Fort Lauderdale FL 33319 954-485-0500 733-0236
TF: 800-241-0363 ■ *Web:* www.inverrary.org
Janus Hotels & Resorts Inc
2300 Corporate Blvd NW Suite 232 ... Boca Raton FL 33431 561-997-2325 997-5331
Web: www.janushotels.com
Jupiter Beach Resort 5 N Hwy A1A ... Jupiter FL 33477 561-746-2511 744-1741
TF: 800-228-8810 ■ *Web:* www.jupiterbeachresort.com
JW Marriott Orlando Grande Lakes Resort
4040 Central Florida Pkwy ... Orlando FL 32837 407-206-2300 206-2301
TF: 800-576-5750 ■ *Web:* www.grandelakes.com
Key Largo Bay Marriott Beach Resort 103800 Overseas Hwy ... Key Largo FL 33037 305-453-0000 453-0093
TF: 866-849-3753 ■ *Web:* www.marriotthotels.com/MTHKL
Key Largo Grande Resort & Beach Club
97000 S Overseas Hwy ... Key Largo FL 33037 305-852-5553 852-8669
TF: 866-597-5397 ■ *Web:* www.keylargogrande.com
La Cita Country Club 777 Country Club Dr ... Titusville FL 32780 321-383-2582 267-4209
Web: www.lacitacc.com
La Playa Beach & Golf Resort 9891 Gulf Shore Dr ... Naples FL 34108 239-597-3123 597-6278
TF: 800-237-6883 ■ *Web:* www.laplayaresort.com
Lago Mar Resort & Club 1700 S Ocean Ln ... Fort Lauderdale FL 33316 954-523-6511 524-6627
TF: 800-524-6627 ■ *Web:* www.lagomar.com
Le Meridien Sunny Isles Beach 18683 Collins Ave ... Sunny Isles Beach FL 33160 305-503-6000 503-6001
Web: www.starwoodhotels.com/lemeridien
Little Palm Island 28500 Overseas Hwy MM 28.5 ... Little Torch Key FL 33042 305-872-2524 872-1752
TF: 800-343-8567 ■ *Web:* www.littlepalmisland.com
Lodge & Club at Ponte Vedra Beach
607 Ponte Vedra Blvd ... Ponte Vedra Beach FL 32082 904-273-9500 273-0210
TF: 800-243-4304 ■ *Web:* www.pvresorts.com
Longboat Key Club 301 Gulf of Mexico Dr ... Longboat Key FL 34228 941-383-8821 383-5308
TF: 800-237-8821 ■ *Web:* www.longboatkeyclub.com
Marco Beach Ocean Resort 480 S Collier Blvd ... Marco Island FL 34145 239-393-1400 393-1401
TF: 877-220-6642 ■ *Web:* www.marcoresort.com
Marriott Golf & Yacht Club Bay Point Resort Village
4200 Marriott Dr ... Panama City Beach FL 32408 850-236-6000 236-6158
TF: 800-874-7105 ■ *Web:* marriotthotels.com/PFNBP
Miami Beach Resort & Spa 4833 Collins Ave ... Miami Beach FL 33140 305-532-3600 534-7409
TF: 866-767-6060 ■ *Web:* www.miamibeachresortandspa.com
Miccosukee Resort & Convention Center 500 SW 177th Ave ... Miami FL 33194 305-925-2555 925-2556
TF: 877-242-6464 ■ *Web:* www.miccosukee.com
Mission Inn Golf & Tennis Resort 10400 CR 48 ... Howey in the Hills FL 34737 352-324-3101 324-2636
TF: 800-874-9053 ■ *Web:* www.missioninnresort.com
Naples Bay Resort 1800 Tamiami Trail E ... Naples FL 34112 239-530-1199 436-8024
TF: 866-605-1199 ■ *Web:* www.naplesbayresort.com

Phone | Fax

Naples Beach Hotel & Golf Club 851 Gulf Shore Blvd N ... Naples FL 34102 239-261-2222 261-7380
TF: 800-237-7600 ■ *Web:* www.naplesbeachhotel.com
Naples Grande Resort & Club 475 Seagate Dr ... Naples FL 34103 239-597-3232 594-6777
TF: 888-422-6177 ■ *Web:* www.naplesgranderesort.com
Nickelodeon Family Suites by Holiday Inn
14500 Continental Gateway ... Orlando FL 32821 407-387-5437 387-1488
TF: 877-387-5437 ■ *Web:* www.nickhotel.com
Occidental Hotels & Resorts 6303 Blue Lagoon Dr Suite 250 ... Miami FL 33126 305-262-5909 266-7845
TF: 800-858-2258 ■ *Web:* www.occidentalhotels.com
Ocean Hammock Resort 105 16th Rd ... Palm Coast FL 32137 386-445-3000 445-2947
TF: 800-654-6538 ■ *Web:* www.oceanhammock.com
Ocean Key Resort & Spa Zero Duval St ... Key West FL 33040 305-296-7701 292-7685
TF: 800-328-9815 ■ *Web:* www.oceankey.com
Ocean Manor Resort 4040 Galt Ocean Dr ... Fort Lauderdale FL 33308 954-566-7500 564-3075
TF: 800-955-0444 ■ *Web:* www.oceanmanor.com
Ocean Sands Resort & Spa 1350 N Ocean Blvd ... Pompano Beach FL 33062 954-590-1000 590-1101
TF: 800-583-3500 ■ *Web:* www.theoceansandsresortandspa.com
Ocean Waters 2025 S Atlantic Ave ... Daytona Beach Shores FL 32118 386-257-1950 253-9935
TF: 800-874-7420 ■ *Web:* www.daytonahotels.com
Omni Orlando Resort at Championsgate
1500 Masters Blvd ... Champions Gate FL 33896 407-390-6664 390-6600
TF: 800-843-6664 ■ *Web:* www.omnihotels.com
Orlando World Center Marriott Resort & Convention Center
8701 World Center Dr ... Orlando FL 32821 407-239-4200 238-8777
TF: 800-621-0638 ■ *Web:* www.marriotthotels.com/MCOWC
Palm Plaza Oceanfront Resort
3301 S Atlantic Ave ... Daytona Beach Shores FL 32118 386-767-1711 756-8394
TF: 800-329-8662 ■ *Web:* www.daytonahotels.com/PalmPlaza/index.php
Palms The 3025 Collins Ave ... Miami Beach FL 33140 305-534-0505 534-0515
TF: 800-550-0505 ■ *Web:* www.thepalmshotel.com
Park Shore Resort 600 Neapolitan Way ... Naples FL 34103 239-263-2222 263-0946
TF: 888-627-1595 ■ *Web:* www.parkshorefl.com
PGA National Resort & Spa
400 Ave of the Champions ... Palm Beach Gardens FL 33418 561-627-2000 227-2595
TF: 800-633-9150 ■ *Web:* www.pgaresort.com
Pier House Resort & Caribbean Spa 1 Duval St ... Key West FL 33040 305-296-4600 296-7569
TF: 800-327-8340 ■ *Web:* www.pierhouse.com
Plantation Inn & Golf Resort 9301 W Fort Island Trail ... Crystal River FL 34429 352-795-4211 795-1156
TF: 800-632-6262 ■ *Web:* www.plantationinn.com
Plaza Resort & Spa 600 N Atlantic Ave ... Daytona Beach FL 32118 386-255-4471 238-7984
TF: 800-874-7420 ■ *Web:* www.plazaresortandspa.com
Ponte Vedra Inn & Club 200 Ponte Vedra Blvd ... Ponte Vedra Beach FL 32082 904-285-1111 285-2111
TF: 800-234-7842 ■ *Web:* www.pvresorts.com
Portofino Bay Hotel at Universal Orlando - A Loews Hotel
5601 Universal Blvd ... Orlando FL 32819 407-503-1000 503-1010
TF: 800-232-7827 ■ *Web:* www.loewshotels.com
Portofino Island Resort & Spa 10 Portofino Dr ... Pensacola Beach FL 32561 850-916-5000 916-5010
TF: 877-484-3405 ■ *Web:* www.portofinoisland.com
Quality Inn & Suites Naples Golf Resort
4100 Golden Gate Pkwy ... Naples FL 34116 239-455-1010 455-4038
TF: 800-277-0017 ■ *Web:* www.naplesgolfresort.com
Radisson Palm Beach Shores Resort & Vacation Villas 181 Ocean Ave ... Palm Beach Shores FL 33404 561-863-4000 845-3245
Web: www.radisson.com
Radisson Resort Parkway 2900 Parkway Blvd ... Kissimmee FL 34747 407-396-7000 396-6792
TF: 800-333-3333 ■ *Web:* www.radisson.com/orlando_disneymaingate
Reach Resort 1435 Simonton St ... Key West FL 33040 305-296-5000 296-2830
TF: 866-397-6427 ■ *Web:* www.reachresort.com
Renaissance Orlando Resort at SeaWorld 6677 Sea Harbor Dr ... Orlando FL 32821 407-351-5555 351-9991
TF: 800-380-7917 ■ *Web:* www.renaissancehotel.com/mcosr
Renaissance Resort at World Golf Village
500 S Legacy Trail ... Saint Augustine FL 32092 904-940-8000 940-8008
TF: 888-740-7020 ■ *Web:* www.renaissancehotel.com/jaxbr
Renaissance Vinoy Resort & Golf Club
501 5th Ave NE ... Saint Petersburg FL 33701 727-894-1000 822-2785
TF: 800-468-3571 ■ *Web:* www.renaissancehotel.com/tpasr
Resort & Club at Little Harbor 611 Destiny Dr ... Ruskin FL 33570 813-645-3291 641-1589
TF: 800-327-2773 ■ *Web:* www.staylittleharbor.com/
Resort at Singer Island 3800 N Ocean Dr ... Singer Island FL 33404 561-340-1700 340-1705
TF: 800-325-3589
Ritz-Carlton Amelia Island 4750 Amelia Island Pkwy ... Amelia Island FL 32034 904-277-1100 261-9064
TF: 800-241-3333 ■ *Web:* www.ritzcarlton.com/resorts/amelia_island/
Ritz-Carlton Key Biscayne 455 Grand Bay Dr ... Key Biscayne FL 33149 305-365-9575 365-4505
TF: 800-241-3333 ■ *Web:* www.ritzcarlton.com/resorts/key_biscayne/
Ritz-Carlton Naples 280 Vanderbilt Beach Rd ... Naples FL 34108 239-598-3300 598-6690
TF: 800-241-3333 ■ *Web:* www.ritzcarlton.com/resorts/naples/
Ritz-Carlton Naples Golf Resort 2600 Tiburon Dr ... Naples FL 34109 239-593-2000 254-3300
TF: 888-856-2164 ■ *Web:* www.ritzcarlton.com
Ritz-Carlton Orlando Grande Lakes 4012 Central Florida Pkwy ... Orlando FL 32837 407-206-2400 206-2401
TF: 800-576-5760 ■ *Web:* www.ritzcarlton.com/en/Properties/Orlando/
Ritz-Carlton Palm Beach 100 S Ocean Blvd ... Manalapan FL 33462 561-533-6000 588-4202
TF: 800-241-3333 ■ *Web:* www.ritzcarlton.com/resorts/palm_beach/
Ritz-Carlton Sarasota 1111 Ritz-Carlton Dr ... Sarasota FL 34236 941-309-2000 309-2100
TF: 800-241-3333 ■ *Web:* www.ritzcarlton.com
Rosen Hotels & Resorts Inc 9840 International Dr ... Orlando FL 32819 407-996-9840 996-0865
TF: 800-204-7234 ■ *Web:* www.rosenhotels.com
Royal Pacific Resort at Universal Orlando - A Loews Hotel
6300 Hollywood Way ... Orlando FL 32819 407-503-3000 503-3010
TF: 800-232-7827 ■ *Web:* www.loewshotels.com
Saddlebrook Resort 5700 Saddlebrook Way ... Wesley Chapel FL 33543 813-973-1111 973-4504
TF: 800-729-8383 ■ *Web:* www.saddlebrook.com
Safety Harbor Resort & Spa 105 N Bayshore Dr ... Safety Harbor FL 34695 727-726-1161 726-4268
TF: 888-237-8772 ■ *Web:* www.safetyharborspa.com
Sandals Resorts International 4950 SW 72nd Ave ... Miami FL 33155 305-284-1300 666-5332*
**Fax:* PR ■ *TF:* 888-726-3257 ■ *Web:* www.sandals.com
Sandestin Golf & Beach Resort 9300 Emerald Coast Pkwy W ... Sandestin FL 32550 850-267-8000 267-8221
TF: 800-277-0800 ■ *Web:* www.sandestin.com
Sanibel Harbour Resort & Spa 17260 Harbour Pointe Dr ... Fort Myers FL 33908 239-466-4000 466-2274
TF: 800-767-7777 ■ *Web:* www.sanibel-resort.com
Sawgrass Marriott Resort & Beach Club
1000 PGA Tour Blvd ... Ponte Vedra Beach FL 32082 904-285-7777 285-0906
TF: 800-228-9290 ■ *Web:* www.marriott.com
Sea Gardens Beach & Tennis Resort
615 N Ocean Blvd ... Pompano Beach FL 33062 954-943-6200 783-0047
Web: www.seagardens.com
Seabonay Beach Resort 1159 Hillsboro Mile ... Hillsboro Beach FL 33062 954-427-2525 427-3228
TF: 800-777-1961
Seascape Resort 100 Seascape Dr ... Destin FL 32550 850-837-9181 837-4769
TF: 800-874-9106 ■ *Web:* www.seascape-resort.com
Seminole Hard Rock Hotel & Casino Hollywood
1 Seminole Way ... Hollywood FL 33314 954-327-7625 327-7655
TF: 800-937-0010 ■ *Web:* www.seminolehardrock.com
Seminole Hard Rock Hotel & Casino Tampa 5223 N Orient Rd ... Tampa FL 33610 813-621-1302 623-6862
TF: 800-282-7016 ■ *Web:* www.hardrockhotelcasinotampa.com
Sheraton Sand Key Resort 1160 Gulf Blvd ... Clearwater Beach FL 33767 727-595-1611 596-8488
TF: 800-325-3535 ■ *Web:* www.sheratonsandkey.com/

				Phone	Fax
Sirata Beach Resort & Conference Center 5300 Gulf Blvd *TF:* 866-587-8538 ■ *Web:* www.sirata.com	Saint Pete Beach	FL	33706	727-363-5100	363-5195
South Seas Island Resort 5400 Plantation Rd *TF:* 877-205-1293 ■ *Web:* www.southseas.com	Captiva	FL	33924	239-472-5111	472-7541
Standard The 40 Island Ave *TF:* 800-327-8363 ■ *Web:* www.lidospa.com	Miami Beach	FL	33139	305-673-1717	673-8181
Summer Beach Resort 5456 First Coast Hwy *TF:* 800-862-9297 ■ *Web:* www.summerbeach.com	Amelia Island	FL	32034	904-277-0905	261-1065
Sundial Beach & Golf Resort 1451 Middle Gulf Dr *TF:* 866-565-5093 ■ *Web:* www.sundialresort.com	Sanibel	FL	33957	239-472-4151	472-8892
Sunset Beach Resort 3287 W Gulf Dr *TF:* 866-565-5091 ■ *Web:* www.sanibelcollection.com	Sanibel Island	FL	33957	239-472-1700	
Sunset Key Guest Cottages at Hilton Key West Resort 245 Front St *TF:* 888-477-7786 ■ *Web:* www.hilton.com	Key West	FL	33040	305-292-5300	292-5395
TradeWinds Island Grand Beach Resort 5500 Gulf Blvd *TF:* 800-360-4016 ■ *Web:* www.tradewindsresort.com	Saint Pete Beach	FL	33706	727-367-6461	363-2221
TradeWinds Resorts Inc 5600 Gulf Blvd *Web:* www.tradewindsresort.com	Saint Pete Beach	FL	33706	727-363-2371	
Trump International Sonesta Beach Resort 18101 Collins Ave *TF:* 800-766-3782 ■ *Web:* www.sonesta.com/SunnyIsles/	Sunny Isles Beach	FL	33160	305-692-5600	692-5601
Vanderbilt Beach Resort 9225 Gulf Shore Dr N *TF:* 800-243-9076 ■ *Web:* www.vanderbiltbeachresort.com	Naples	FL	34108	239-597-3144	597-2199
Villas of Grand Cypress 1 N Jacaranda *TF:* 800-835-7377 ■ *Web:* www.grandcypress.com	Orlando	FL	32836	407-239-4700	239-7219
Walt Disney World Dolphin 1500 Epcot Resorts Blvd *TF:* 800-227-1500 ■ *Web:* www.swandolphin.com	Lake Buena Vista	FL	32830	407-934-4000	934-4884
Walt Disney World Resorts PO Box 10000 *Web:* disneyworld.disney.go.com	Lake Buena Vista	FL	32830	407-824-2222	827-2096
Walt Disney World Swan 1200 Epcot Resorts Blvd *TF:* 800-248-7926 ■ *Web:* www.swandolphin.com	Lake Buena Vista	FL	32830	407-934-3000	934-1888
West Wind Inn 3345 W Gulf Dr *TF:* 800-824-0476 ■ *Web:* www.westwindinn.com	Sanibel	FL	33957	239-472-1541	472-8134
Westin Key West Resort & Marina 245 Front St *TF:* 866-716-8108 ■ *Web:* www.westinkeywestresort.com	Key West	FL	33040	305-294-4000	294-4086

Georgia

				Phone	Fax
Barnsley Gardens 597 Barnsley Gardens Rd *TF:* 877-773-2447 ■ *Web:* www.barnsleyinn.com	Adairsville	GA	30103	770-773-7480	773-1779
Brasstown Valley Resort 6321 US Hwy 76 *TF:* 800-201-3205 ■ *Web:* www.brasstownvalley.com	Young Harris	GA	30582	706-379-9900	379-9999
Callaway Gardens PO Box 2000 *TF:* 800-225-5292 ■ *Web:* www.callawaygardens.com	Pine Mountain	GA	31822	706-663-2281	663-6812
Chateau Elan Resort & Conference Center 100 rue Charlemagne *TF:* 800-233-9463 ■ *Web:* www.chateauelan.com	Braselton	GA	30517	678-425-0900	425-6000
Cloister The 100 Salt Marsh Ln *TF:* 800-732-4752 ■ *Web:* www.cloister.com	Saint Simons	GA	31522	912-638-3611	638-5159
Crowne Plaza Hotels & Resorts 3 Ravinia Dr Suite 100 *Web:* www.crowneplaza.com	Atlanta	GA	30346	770-604-2000	604-5403
Emerald Pointe Resort 7000 Holiday Rd **Fax Area Code:* 678 ■ *TF:* 800-768-5253 ■ *Web:* www.lakelanierislands.com	Lake Lanier Islands	GA	30518	770-945-8787	318-2005*
Evergreen Marriott Conference Resort 4021 Lakeview Dr *TF:* 800-228-9290 ■ *Web:* www.evergreenresort.com	Stone Mountain	GA	30083	770-879-9900	465-3264
Forrest Hills Mountain Resort & Conference Center 135 Forrest Hills Rd *TF:* 800-654-6313 ■ *Web:* www.foresths.com	Dahlonega	GA	30533	706-864-6456	864-0757
Holiday Inn Hotels & Resorts 3 Ravinia Dr Suite 100 *Web:* www.holidayinn.com	Atlanta	GA	30346	770-604-2000	604-5403
InterContinental Hotels & Resorts 3 Ravinia Dr Suite 100 *Web:* www.intercontinental.com	Atlanta	GA	30346	770-604-2000	604-5403
Jekyll Island Club Hotel 371 Riverview Dr *TF:* 800-535-9547 ■ *Web:* www.jekyllclub.com	Jekyll Island	GA	31527	912-635-2600	635-2818
King & Prince Beach & Golf Resort 201 Arnold Rd *TF:* 800-342-0212 ■ *Web:* www.kingandprince.com	Saint Simons Island	GA	31522	912-638-3631	634-1720
Marietta Conference Center & Resort 500 Powder Springs St **Fax Area Code:* 070 ■ *TF:* 800-685-2500 ■ *Web:* www.mariettaresort.com	Marietta	GA	30064	770-427-2500	819-3224*
Reynolds Plantation 100 Linger Longer Rd *TF:* 800-800-5250 ■ *Web:* www.reynoldsplantation.com	Greensboro	GA	30642	706-467-3151	467-3071
Ritz-Carlton Lodge Reynolds Plantation 1 Lake Oconee Trail *TF:* 800-826-1945 ■ *Web:* www.ritzcarlton.com	Greensboro	GA	30642	706-467-0600	467-7124
Sea Palms Golf & Tennis Resort 5445 Frederica Rd *TF:* 800-841-6268 ■ *Web:* www.seapalms.com	Saint Simons Island	GA	31522	912-638-3351	634-8029
Sky Valley Golf Course Resort 696 Sky Valley Way *TF:* 800-437-2416 ■ *Web:* www.skyvalley.com	Sky Valley	GA	30537	706-746-5302	746-5198
Villas by the Sea Resort 1175 N Beachview Dr *TF:* 800-841-6262 ■ *Web:* www.jekyllislandga.com	Jekyll Island	GA	31527	912-635-2521	635-2569

Hawaii

				Phone	Fax
Castle Resorts & Hotels 500 Ala Moana Blvd Suite 555 3 Waterfront Plaza *TF:* 800-733-7753 ■ *Web:* www.castleresorts.com	Honolulu	HI	96813	808-524-0900	521-9994
Fairmont Kea Lani Maui 4100 Wailea Alanui Dr *TF:* 800-659-4100 ■ *Web:* www.fairmont.com	Maui	HI	96753	808-875-4100	875-1200
Fairmont Orchid Hawaii 1 N Kaniku Dr *TF:* 800-845-9905 ■ *Web:* www.fairmont.com/orchid	Kohala	HI	96743	808-885-2000	885-5778
Four Seasons Resort Hualalai 100 Ka'upulehu Dr *TF:* 888-340-5662 ■ *Web:* www.fourseasons.com/hualalai	Ka'upulehu-Kona	HI	96740	808-325-8000	325-8200
Four Seasons Resort Maui at Wailea 3900 Wailea Alanui Dr *TF:* 800-334-6284 ■ *Web:* www.fourseasons.com/maui	Wailea	HI	96753	808-874-8000	874-2244
Grand Wailea Resort & Spa 3850 Wailea Alanui Dr *TF:* 800-888-6100 ■ *Web:* www.grandwailea.com	Wailea	HI	96753	808-875-1234	879-4077
Hanalei Bay Resort & Suites 5380 Honoiki Rd *TF:* 800-827-4427 ■ *Web:* www.hanaleibayresort.com	Princeville	HI	96722	808-826-6522	826-6680
Hapuna Beach Prince Hotel 62-100 Kauna'oa Dr *TF:* 800-882-6060 ■ *Web:* www.hapunabeachhotel.com	Kamuela	HI	96743	808-880-1111	880-3142
Hawaii Prince Hotel Waikiki 100 Holomoana St *TF:* 800-321-6248 ■ *Web:* princeresortshawaii.com/hawaii-prince-hotel.php	Honolulu	HI	96815	808-956-1111	946-0811
Hilton Hawaiian Village 2005 Kalia Rd *TF:* 800-445-8667 ■ *Web:* www.hilton.com	Honolulu	HI	96815	808-949-4321	951-5458
Hilton Waikoloa Village 425 Waikoloa Beach Dr *TF:* 866-223-6574 ■ *Web:* www.hiltonwaikoloavillage.com	Waikoloa	HI	96738	808-886-1234	886-2900
Hotel Hana-Maui PO Box 9 *TF:* 800-321-4262 ■ *Web:* www.hanacoast.com/hotel.html	Hana	HI	96713	808-248-8211	248-7202
Hyatt Regency Kauai Resort & Spa 1571 Poipu Rd *TF:* 800-233-1234 ■ *Web:* kauai.hyatt.com	Koloa	HI	96756	808-742-1234	742-1557
Hyatt Regency Maui Resort & Spa 200 Nohea Kai Dr *TF:* 800-233-1234 ■ *Web:* maui.hyatt.com	Lahaina	HI	96761	808-661-1234	667-4497
JW Marriott Resort Ihilani 92-1001 Olani St *TF:* 800-626-4446 ■ *Web:* www.ihilani.com	Kapolei	HI	96707	808-679-0079	679-0080
Kapalua Resort 300 Kapalua Dr *TF:* 877-527-2582 ■ *Web:* www.kapaluamaui.com	Kapalua	HI	96761	808-669-8044	669-4956
Kapalua Villas The 500 Office Rd *TF:* 800-545-0018 ■ *Web:* www.kapaluavillas.com	Maui	HI	96761	808-669-8088	669-5234
Kaua'i Marriott Resort & Beach Club 3610 Rice St *TF:* 800-220-2925 ■ *Web:* marriotthotels.com/LIHHI	Lihue	HI	96766	808-245-5050	245-5049
Kona Village Resort Queen Kaahumanu Hwy *TF:* 800-367-5290 ■ *Web:* www.konavillage.com	Kaupulehu-Kona	HI	96740	808-325-5555	325-5124
Lodge at Koele PO Box 631380 *TF:* 800-321-4666 ■ *Web:* www.lodgeatkoele.com	Lanai City	HI	96763	808-565-7300	565-4561
Makena Resort Maui Prince Hotel 5400 Makena Alanui *TF:* 800-321-6248 ■ *Web:* www.mauiprince.com/mph/	Kihei	HI	96753	808-874-1111	944-4491
Manele Bay Hotel 1 Manele Rd *TF:* 800-321-4666 ■ *Web:* www.manelebayhotel.com	Lanai City	HI	96763	808-565-7700	565-2483
Marc Resorts Hawaii 810 Richards St 2nd Fl City Center *TF:* 800-535-0085 ■ *Web:* www.marcresorts.com	Honolulu	HI	96813	808-926-5900	922-2421
Marriott Kaua'i Resort & Beach Club 3610 Rice St *TF:* 800-220-2925 ■ *Web:* marriotthotels.com/LIHHI	Lihue	HI	96766	808-245-5050	245-5049
Marriott Maui Resort 100 Nohea Kai Dr *TF:* 800-763-1333 ■ *Web:* marriotthotels.com/HNMHI	Lahaina	HI	96761	808-667-1200	667-8300
Maui Prince Hotel 5400 Makena Alanui *TF:* 800-321-6248 ■ *Web:* www.mauiprince.com/mph/	Kihei	HI	96753	808-874-1111	944-4491
Mauna Kea Beach Hotel 62-100 Maunakea Beach Dr *TF:* 800-882-6060 ■ *Web:* www.maunakeabeachhotel.com	Kamuela	HI	96743	808-882-7222	882-5700
Mauna Lani Bay Hotel & Bungalows 68-1400 Mauna Lani Dr *TF:* 800-367-2323 ■ *Web:* www.maunalani.com	Kohala Coast	HI	96743	808-885-6622	881-7000
Napili Kai Beach Club 5900 Honoapiilani Rd *TF:* 800-367-5030 ■ *Web:* www.napilikai.com	Lahaina	HI	96761	808-669-6271	669-0086
OHANA Hotels & Resorts 2375 Kuhio Ave *TF:* 800-462-6262 ■ *Web:* www.ohanahotels.com	Honolulu	HI	96815	808-921-6600	
Outrigger Hotels & Resorts 2375 Kuhio Ave **Fax:* Sales ■ *TF:* 800-688-7444 ■ *Web:* www.outrigger.com	Honolulu	HI	96815	808-921-6600	926-4368*
Outrigger Kanaloa at Kona 78-261 Manukai St *TF:* 800-688-7444 ■ *Web:* outrigger.com	Kailua-Kona	HI	96740	808-322-9625	322-3818
Outrigger Reef on the Beach 2169 Kalia Rd *TF:* 800-688-7444 ■ *Web:* outrigger.com	Honolulu	HI	96815	808-923-3111	924-4957
Prince Resorts Hawaii 100 Holomoana St *TF:* 800-774-6234 ■ *Web:* www.princehawaii.com	Honolulu	HI	96815	808-956-1111	943-4158
Princeville Resort 5520 Ka Haku Rd *TF:* 800-826-1260 ■ *Web:* www.princeville.com	Princeville	HI	96722	808-826-9644	826-1166
Renaissance Wailea Beach Resort 3550 Wailea Alanui Dr *TF:* 800-992-4532 ■ *Web:* www.renaissancehotel.com/hnmrn	Kihei	HI	96753	808-879-4900	891-7086
ResortQuest Hawaii 2155 Kalakaua Ave Suite 500 **Fax:* Hum Res ■ *TF:* 866-774-2924 ■ *Web:* www.resortquesthawaii.com	Honolulu	HI	96815	808-931-1400	931-1565*
Ritz-Carlton Kapalua 1 Ritz-Carlton Dr *TF:* 800-262-8440 ■ *Web:* www.ritzcarlton.com/resorts/kapalua/	Lahaina	HI	96761	808-669-6200	669-1566
Royal Hawaiian 2259 Kalakaua Ave *Web:* www.royal-hawaiian.com	Honolulu	HI	96815	808-923-7311	931-7098
Royal Lahaina Resort 2780 Kekaa Dr *TF:* 800-447-6925 ■ *Web:* www.hawaiianhotels.com	Lahaina	HI	96761	808-661-3611	661-6150
Sheraton Kauai Resort 2440 Hoonani Rd *TF:* 888-847-0208 ■ *Web:* www.sheraton-kauai.com	Koloa	HI	96756	808-742-1661	742-4041
Sheraton Maui Resort 2605 Kaanapali Pkwy *TF:* 888-782-9488 ■ *Web:* www.sheraton-maui.com	Lahaina	HI	96761	808-661-0031	661-0458
Sheraton Moana Surfrider 2365 Kalakaua Ave *TF:* 800-325-3535 ■ *Web:* www.moana-surfrider.com	Honolulu	HI	96815	808-922-3111	924-4799
Sheraton Waikiki 2255 Kalakaua Ave *TF:* 800-325-3535 ■ *Web:* www.sheraton-waikiki.com	Honolulu	HI	96815	808-922-4422	923-8785
Turtle Bay Resort 57-091 Kamehameha Hwy *TF:* 800-203-3650 ■ *Web:* www.turtlebayresort.com	Kahuku	HI	96731	808-293-8811	293-9147
Wailea Beach Marriott Resort & Spa 3700 Wailea Alanui Dr *TF:* 800-367-2960 ■ *Web:* marriott.com	Wailea	HI	96753	808-879-1922	874-7802

Idaho

				Phone	Fax
Coeur d'Alene Resort 115 S 2nd St PO Box 7200 *TF:* 800-688-5253 ■ *Web:* www.cdaresort.com	Coeur d'Alene	ID	83814	208-765-4000	664-7276
Elkhorn Golf Club 1 Elkhorn Rd PO Box 6029 *Web:* www.elkhorngolfclub.com	Sun Valley	ID	83354	208-622-3309	622-7052
Premier Resorts Sun Valley PO Box 659 *TF:* 800-635-4444 ■ *Web:* www.premier-sunvalley.com	Sun Valley	ID	83353	208-727-4000	727-4040
Red Lion Templin's Hotel on the River 414 E 1st Ave *TF:* 800-283-6754 ■ *Web:* redlion.rdln.com/	Post Falls	ID	83854	208-773-1611	773-4192
Sun Valley Resort 1 Sun Valley Rd *TF:* 800-786-8259 ■ *Web:* www.sunvalley.com	Sun Valley	ID	83353	208-622-2001	622-2015

Illinois

				Phone	Fax
Eagle Ridge Inn & Resort 444 Eagle Ridge Dr *TF:* 800-892-2269 ■ *Web:* www.eagleridge.com	Galena	IL	61036	815-777-2444	777-4502
Eaglewood Resort & Spa 1401 Nordic Rd *TF:* 877-285-6150 ■ *Web:* www.eaglewoodresort.com	Itasca	IL	60143	630-773-1400	773-1709
Hyatt Resorts 71 S Wacker Dr *TF:* 800-233-1234 ■ *Web:* www.hyatt.com/hyatt/resorts	Chicago	IL	60606	312-750-1234	780-5289
Indian Lakes Resort 250 W Schick Rd *TF:* 800-334-3417 ■ *Web:* www.indianlakesresort.com	Bloomingdale	IL	60108	630-529-0200	529-9271
Pheasant Run Resort & Spa 4051 E Main St *TF:* 800-999-3319 ■ *Web:* www.pheasantrun.com	Saint Charles	IL	60174	630-584-6300	584-4693
Preferred Hotels & Resorts Worldwide Inc 311 S Wacker Dr Suite 1900 *TF:* 800-323-7500 ■ *Web:* www.preferredhotels.com	Chicago	IL	60606	312-913-0400	913-0444
Summit Hotels & Resorts 311 S Wacker Dr Suite 1900 *TF:* 800-457-4000 ■ *Web:* www.summithotels.com	Chicago	IL	60606	312-913-0400	913-5124

Indiana

				Phone	Fax
Belterra Casino Resort 777 Belterra Dr **Fax:* Hum Res ■ *TF Resv:* 888-235-8377 ■ *Web:* www.belterracasino.com	Florence	IN	47020	812-427-7777	427-7812*
Brickyard Crossing Golf Resort & Inn 4400 W 16th St *Web:* www.brickyardcrossing.com/hotel	Indianapolis	IN	46222	317-241-2500	492-2715
Eagle Pointe Golf Resort 2250 E Pointe Rd *TF:* 877-324-7683 ■ *Web:* www.eaglepointe.com	Bloomington	IN	47401	812-824-4040	824-6860

Indiana (Cont'd)

				Phone	Fax
Fourwinds Resort & Marina 9301 Fairfax Rd *TF:* 800-538-1187 ■ *Web:* www.fourwindsresort.com	Bloomington	IN	47401	812-824-9904	824-9816
French Lick Springs Resort & Spa 8670 W SR-56 *TF:* 800-457-4042 ■ *Web:* www.frenchlick.com	French Lick	IN	47432	812-936-9300	936-2100
Grand Victoria Casino & Resort by Hyatt 600 Grand Victoria Dr *TF:* 800-472-6311 ■ *Web:* www.hyatt.com	Rising Sun	IN	47040	812-438-1234	438-5151
Potawatomi Inn Pokagan State Park 6 Lane 100A Lake James *TF:* 877-768-2928 ■ *Web:* www.in.gov/dnr/parklake/inns/potawatomi/	Angola	IN	46703	260-833-1077	833-4087

Iowa

				Phone	Fax
Grand Harbor Resort & Waterpark 350 Bell St *TF:* 866-690-4006 ■ *Web:* www.grandharborresort.com	Dubuque	IA	52001	563-690-4000	690-0558

Kansas

				Phone	Fax
Great Wolf Lodge & Indoor Waterpark 10401 Cabela Dr *TF:* 800-608-9653 ■ *Web:* kc.greatwolflodge.com	Kansas City	KS	66111	913-299-7001	299-7002
Terradyne Resort Hotel & Country Club 1400 Terradyne Dr *Web:* www.terradyne-resort.com	Andover	KS	67002	316-733-2582	733-9149

Kentucky

				Phone	Fax
Barren River Lake State Resort Park 1149 State Park Rd **Fax Area Code: 270* ■ *TF:* 800-325-0057 ■ *Web:* www.parks.ky.gov/resortparks/br	Lucas	KY	42156	800-325-0057	646-3645*
Carter Caves State Resort Park 344 Caveland Dr *TF:* 800-325-0059 ■ *Web:* parks.ky.gov	Olive Hill	KY	41164	606-286-4411	286-0471
General Butler State Resort Park PO Box 325 *TF:* 866-462-8853 ■ *Web:* parks.ky.gov/findparks/resortparks/gb/	Carrollton	KY	41008	502-732-4384	732-4270
Griffin Gate Marriott Resort 1800 Newtown Pike *TF:* 800-228-9290 ■ *Web:* www.marriotthotels.com/LEXKY	Lexington	KY	40511	859-231-5100	255-9944
Kentucky Dam Village State Resort Park 166 Upper Village Dr *Web:* www.parks.ky.gov/resortparks/kd	Gilbertsville	KY	42044	800-325-0146	
Lake Barkley State Resort Park 3500 State Park Rd Box 790 *TF:* 800-325-1708 ■ *Web:* www.state.ky.us/agencies/parks/lakebark.htm	Cadiz	KY	42211	270-924-1131	924-0013
Lake Cumberland State Resort Park 5465 State Park Rd *TF:* 800-325-1709 ■ *Web:* www.state.ky.us/agencies/parks/lakecumb.htm	Jamestown	KY	42629	270-343-3111	343-5510
Park Mammoth Resort 22850 Louisville Rd PO Box 307	Park City	KY	42160	270-749-4101	749-2524

Louisiana

				Phone	Fax
Emerald Hills Golf Resort 42618 Hwy 171 S *TF:* 800-533-5031 ■ *Web:* www.emeraldhillsresort.com	Florien	LA	71429	318-586-4661	586-4804

Maine

				Phone	Fax
Atlantic Oakes 119 Eden St *TF:* 800-336-2463 ■ *Web:* www.barharbor.com	Bar Harbor	ME	04609	207-288-5801	288-8402
Bar Harbor Inn Oceanfront Resort Newport Dr Box 7 *TF:* 800-248-3351 ■ *Web:* www.barharborinn.com	Bar Harbor	ME	04609	207-288-3351	288-8454
Bethel Inn & Country Club 21 Broad St PO Box 49 *TF:* 800-654-0125 ■ *Web:* www.bethelinn.com	Bethel	ME	04217	207-824-2175	824-2233
Black Point Inn Resort 510 Black Point Rd *TF:* 800-258-0003 ■ *Web:* www.blackpointinn.com	Scarborough	ME	04074	207-883-2500	883-9976
Cliff House Resort & Spa 591 Shore Rd *Web:* www.cliffhousemaine.com	Cape Neddick	ME	03902	207-361-1000	361-2122
Colony Hotel 140 Ocean Ave *TF:* 800-552-2363 ■ *Web:* www.thecolonyhotel.com	Kennebunkport	ME	04046	207-967-3331	967-8738
Holiday Inn SunSpree Bar Harbor Regency Resort 123 Eden St *TF:* 800-234-6835 ■ *Web:* www.barharborregency.com/	Bar Harbor	ME	04609	207-288-9723	288-3089
Inn by the Sea 40 Bowery Beach Rd *TF:* 800-888-4287 ■ *Web:* www.innbythesea.com	Cape Elizabeth	ME	04107	207-799-3134	799-4779
Samoset Resort 220 Warrenton St *TF:* 800-341-1650 ■ *Web:* www.samoset.com	Rockport	ME	04856	207-594-2511	594-0722
Sebasco Harbor Resort 29 Keynon Rd *TF:* 800-225-3819 ■ *Web:* www.sebasco.com	Sebasco Estates	ME	04562	207-389-1161	389-2004
Spruce Point Inn 88 Grandview Ave PO Box 237 *TF:* 800-553-0289 ■ *Web:* www.sprucepointinn.com	Boothbay Harbor	ME	04538	207-633-4152	633-7138
Stage Neck Inn 8 Stage Neck Rd Rt 1A Box 70 *TF:* 800-222-3238 ■ *Web:* www.stageneck.com	York Harbor	ME	03911	207-363-3850	363-2221
Sugarloaf/USA 5092 Access Rd *TF:* 800-843-5623 ■ *Web:* www.sugarloaf.com	Carrabassett Valley	ME	04947	207-237-2000	237-3768
Sunday River Ski Resort 15 S Ridge Rd *TF:* 800-543-2754 ■ *Web:* www.sundayriver.com	Newry	ME	04261	207-824-3000	824-5110

Maryland

				Phone	Fax
Coconut Malorie Resort 200 59th St *TF:* 800-767-6060 ■ *Web:* www.coconutmalorie.com	Ocean City	MD	21842	410-723-6100	524-9327
Francis Scott Key Family Resort 12806 Ocean Gateway PO Box 468 *TF:* 800-213-0088 ■ *Web:* www.fskmotel.com	Ocean City	MD	21842	410-213-0088	213-2854
Harbourtowne Golf Resort & Conference Center 9784 Martingham Dr *TF:* 800-446-9066 ■ *Web:* www.harbourtowne.com	Saint Michaels	MD	21663	410-745-9066	745-9124
Turf Valley Resort & Conference Center 2700 Turf Valley Rd *TF:* 800-666-8873 ■ *Web:* www.turfvalley.com	Ellicott City	MD	21042	410-465-1500	465-9282
Wisp Mountain Resort Hotel & Conference Center Deep Creek Lake 290 Marsh Hill Rd *TF:* 800-462-9477 ■ *Web:* www.wispresort.com	McHenry	MD	21541	301-387-5581	542-0041

Massachusetts

				Phone	Fax
Bayside Resort Hotel 225 Main St *TF:* 800-243-1114 ■ *Web:* www.baysideresort.com	West Yarmouth	MA	02673	508-775-5669	775-8862
Best Western Blue Rock Golf Resort 39 Todd Rd *TF:* 800-227-3263 ■ *Web:* www.bluerockresort.com	South Yarmouth	MA	02664	508-398-6962	398-1830
Blue Water Resort 291 S Shore Dr *TF:* 800-367-9393 ■ *Web:* www.redjacketresorts.com/resorts/blue-water-resort.php	South Yarmouth	MA	02664	508-398-2288	398-1010
Canyon Ranch Lenox 165 Kemble St *TF Resv:* 800-742-9000 ■ *Web:* www.canyonranch.com/lenox	Lenox	MA	01240	413-637-4100	637-0057
Cape Codder Resort & Spa 1225 Iyanough Rd *TF:* 888-297-2200 ■ *Web:* www.capecodderresort.com	Hyannis	MA	02601	508-771-3000	790-8145
Captain Gosnold Village 230 Gosnold St *Web:* www.captaingosnold.com	Hyannis	MA	02601	508-775-9111	
Chatham Bars Inn 297 Shore Rd *TF:* 800-527-4884 ■ *Web:* www.chathambarsinn.com	Chatham	MA	02633	508-945-0096	945-5491
Cranwell Resort Spa & Golf Club 55 Lee Rd *TF:* 800-272-6935 ■ *Web:* www.cranwell.com	Lenox	MA	01240	413-637-1364	637-4364
Harbor House Village South Beach St PO Box 1130 *TF:* 800-475-2637 ■ *Web:* www.harborhousevillage.com	Nantucket	MA	02554	508-228-1500	228-7639
New Seabury Resort 20 Red Brook Rd *TF:* 800-999-9033 ■ *Web:* www.newseabury.com	Mashpee	MA	02649	508-477-9111	539-8634
Ocean Edge Resort & Golf Club 2907 Main St *TF:* 800-343-6074 ■ *Web:* www.oceanedge.com	Brewster	MA	02631	508-896-9000	896-9123
Ocean Mist Resort 97 S Shore Dr *TF:* 800-248-6478 ■ *Web:* www.capecodtravel.com/oceanmist	South Yarmouth	MA	02664	508-398-2633	760-3151
Sea Crest Resort & Conference Center 350 Quaker Rd *TF:* 800-225-3110 ■ *Web:* www.seacrest-resort.com	North Falmouth	MA	02556	508-540-9400	548-0556
Sonesta International Hotels Corp 116 Huntington Ave 9th Fl *NASDAQ: SNSTA* ■ *TF:* 800-766-3782 ■ *Web:* www.sonesta.com	Boston	MA	02116	617-421-5400	421-5402
Wequassett Inn Resort & Golf Club 2173 Rt 28 *TF:* 800-225-7125 ■ *Web:* www.wequassett.com	East Harwich	MA	02645	508-432-5400	432-1915

Michigan

				Phone	Fax
Bay Valley Hotel & Resort 2470 Old Bridge Rd *TF:* 800-292-5028 ■ *Web:* www.bayvalley.com	Bay City	MI	48706	989-686-3500	686-6931
Boyne Highlands Resort 600 Highlands Dr *TF:* 800-462-6963 ■ *Web:* www.boynehighlands.com	Harbor Springs	MI	49740	231-526-3000	526-3100
Boyne Mountain Resort PO Box 19 *TF:* 800-462-6963 ■ *Web:* www.boynemountain.com	Boyne Falls	MI	49713	231-549-6000	549-6093
Boyne USA Resorts PO Box 19 *TF:* 800-462-6963 ■ *Web:* www.boyneusa.com	Boyne Falls	MI	49713	231-549-6000	549-6094
Crystal Mountain Resort 12500 Crystal Mountain Dr *TF:* 800-968-7686 ■ *Web:* www.crystalmountain.com	Thompsonville	MI	49683	231-378-2000	378-2998
Garland Resort 4700 N Red Oak Rd *TF:* 800-968-0042 ■ *Web:* www.garlandusa.com	Lewiston	MI	49756	989-786-2211	786-2254
Grand Hotel 286 Grand Dr *TF:* 800-334-7263 ■ *Web:* www.grandhotel.com	Mackinac Island	MI	49757	906-847-3331	847-3259
Grand Traverse Resort & Spa 6300 US 31 N *TF:* 800-748-0303 ■ *Web:* www.grandtraverseresort.com	Acme	MI	49610	231-534-6000	534-6670
Homestead Resort The Wood Ridge Rd *Web:* www.thehomesteadresort.com	Glen Arbor	MI	49636	231-334-5000	334-5246
Indianhead Mountain Resort 500 Indianhead Rd *TF:* 800-346-3426 ■ *Web:* www.indianheadmtn.com	Wakefield	MI	49968	906-229-2229	229-5134
Inn at Bay Harbor 3600 Village Harbor Dr *TF:* 800-462-6963 ■ *Web:* www.innatbayharbor.com	Bay Harbor	MI	49770	231-439-4000	439-4094
Lakewood Shores Resort 7751 Cedar Lake Rd *TF:* 800-882-2493 ■ *Web:* www.lakewoodshores.com	Oscoda	MI	48750	989-739-2073	739-1351
Marsh Ridge Resort 4815 Old US Hwy 27 S *TF:* 800-743-7529 ■ *Web:* www.marshridge.com	Gaylord	MI	49735	989-732-5552	732-2134
McGuire's Resort 7880 Mackinaw Trail *TF:* 800-632-7302 ■ *Web:* www.mcguiresresort.com	Cadillac	MI	49601	231-775-9947	775-9621
Mission Point Resort 1 Lake Shore Dr PO Box 430 *TF:* 800-833-7711 ■ *Web:* www.missionpoint.com	Mackinac Island	MI	49757	906-847-3312	847-3408
Otsego Club 696 M-32 E Main St PO Box 556 *TF:* 800-752-5510 ■ *Web:* www.otsegoclub.com	Gaylord	MI	49734	989-732-5181	732-0497
Shanty Creek Resort 1 Shanty Creek Rd *TF:* 800-678-4111 ■ *Web:* www.shantycreek.com	Bellaire	MI	49615	231-533-8621	533-7020
Soaring Eagle Casino & Resort 6800 E Soaring Eagle Blvd *TF:* 877-232-4532 ■ *Web:* www.soaringeaglecasino.com	Mount Pleasant	MI	48858	989-775-5777	775-5483
Treetops Resort 3962 Wilkinson Rd *TF:* 800-444-6711 ■ *Web:* www.treetops.com	Treetops Village	MI	49735	989-732-6711	732-8459

Minnesota

				Phone	Fax
Arrowwood Resort & Conference Center 2100 Arrowwood Ln NW *TF:* 866-386-5263 ■ *Web:* www.arrowwoodresort.com	Alexandria	MN	56308	320-762-1124	762-0133
Breezy Point Resort 9252 Breezy Point Dr *TF:* 800-432-3777 ■ *Web:* breezypointresort.com	Breezy Point	MN	56472	218-562-7811	562-4930
Caribou Highlands Lodge 371 Ski Hill Rd *TF:* 800-642-6036 ■ *Web:* www.caribouhighlands.com	Lutsen	MN	55612	218-663-7241	663-7920
Cascade Lodge 3719 W Hwy 61 *TF:* 800-322-9543 ■ *Web:* www.cascadelodgemn.com	Lutsen	MN	55612	218-387-1112	387-1113
Cragun's Conference & Golf Resort 11000 Cragun's Dr *TF:* 800-272-4867 ■ *Web:* www.craguns.com	Brainerd	MN	56401	218-829-3591	829-9188
Driftwood Resort 6020 Driftwood Ln *TF:* 800-950-3540 ■ *Web:* www.driftwoodresort.com	Pine River	MN	56474	218-568-4221	568-4222
Eagle's Nest Resort 6103 Lavaque Rd *TF:* 800-348-4575	Duluth	MN	55803	218-721-4147	
Fair Hills Resort 24270 County Hwy 20 *TF:* 800-323-2849 ■ *Web:* www.fairhillsresort.com	Detroit Lakes	MN	56501	218-847-7638	532-2068
Grand Casino Hinckley 777 Lady Luck Dr *TF:* 800-472-6321 ■ *Web:* www.grandcasinomn.com	Hinckley	MN	55037	320-384-7777	384-4775
Grand Casino Mille Lacs 777 Grand Ave PO Box 343 *TF:* 800-626-5825 ■ *Web:* www.grandcasinomn.com	Onamia	MN	56359	320-532-7777	532-8103
Grand Portage Lodge & Casino PO Box 233 *TF:* 800-543-1384 ■ *Web:* www.grandportage.com	Grand Portage	MN	55605	218-475-2401	475-2309
Grand View Lodge 23521 Nokomis Ave *TF:* 800-432-3788 ■ *Web:* www.grandviewlodge.com	Nisswa	MN	56468	218-963-2234	963-2269
Izatys Golf & Yacht Club 40005 85th Ave *TF:* 800-533-1728 ■ *Web:* www.izatys.com	Onamia	MN	56359	320-532-3101	532-3208
Lake Breeze Motel Resort 9000 Congdon Blvd *TF:* 800-738-5884 ■ *Web:* www.lakebreeze.com	Duluth	MN	55804	218-525-6808	525-2986
Lutsen Resort 5700 W Hwy 61 PO Box 9 *TF:* 800-258-8736 ■ *Web:* www.lutsenresort.com	Lutsen	MN	55612	218-663-7212	663-0145
Madden's on Gull Lake 11266 Pine Beach Peninsula *TF:* 800-247-1040 ■ *Web:* www.maddens.com	Brainerd	MN	56401	218-829-2811	829-6583
Park Plaza Hotels & Resorts PO Box 59159 *Web:* www.carlsonhotelsmedia.tekgroup.com	Minneapolis	MN	55459	763-212-1000	212-6631

				Phone	Fax
Radisson Hotels & Resorts PO Box 59159 *TF:* 800-333-3333 ■ *Web:* www.radisson.com	Minneapolis	MN	55459	763-212-5526	212-3400
Ruttger's Bay Lake Lodge 25039 Tame Fish Lake Rd Box 400 *TF:* 800-450-4545 ■ *Web:* www.ruttgers.com	Deerwood	MN	56444	218-678-2885	678-2864
Superior Shores Resort 1521 Superior Shores Dr *TF:* 800-242-1988 ■ *Web:* www.superiorshores.com	Two Harbors	MN	55616	218-834-5671	834-5677

Mississippi

				Phone	Fax
Beau Rivage Resort & Casino 875 Beach Blvd *TF:* 888-750-7111 ■ *Web:* www.beaurivage.com	Biloxi	MS	39530	228-386-7111	386-7414
Grand Casino Biloxi 280 Beach Blvd *TF:* 800-946-2946 ■ *Web:* www.harrahs.com	Biloxi	MS	39530	228-436-2946	436-2896
Grand Casino Tunica 13615 Old Hwy 61 N *TF:* 800-946-4946 ■ *Web:* www.harrahs.com	Robinsonville	MS	38664	662-363-2788	357-3464
Gulf Hills Hotel 13701 Paso Rd *TF:* 866-875-4211 ■ *Web:* www.gulfhillshotel.com	Ocean Springs	MS	39564	228-875-4211	875-4213
IP Casino Resort & Spa 850 Bayview Ave *TF:* 800-436-3000 ■ *Web:* www.ipbiloxi.com	Biloxi	MS	39530	228-436-3000	432-3260
Treasure Bay Casino & Hotel 1980 Beach Blvd *TF:* 800-747-2839 ■ *Web:* treasurebay.com	Biloxi	MS	39531	228-385-6000	385-6082

Missouri

				Phone	Fax
Best Western Dogwood Hills Resort Inn & Golf Club 1252 State Hwy KK *TF:* 800-528-1234 ■ *Web:* www.dogwoodhillsresort.com	Osage Beach	MO	65065	573-348-1735	348-0014
Big Cedar Lodge 612 Devil's Pool Rd *Web:* www.big-cedar.com	Ridgedale	MO	65739	417-335-2777	335-2340
Indian Point Lodge 71 Dogwood Park Trail *TF:* 800-888-1891 ■ *Web:* www.indianpoint.com	Branson	MO	65616	417-338-2250	338-3507
Lilleys' Landing Resort 367 River Ln *TF:* 800-284-2916 ■ *Web:* www.lilleyslanding.com	Branson	MO	65616	417-334-6380	334-6311
Lodge of Four Seasons 315 Four Seasons Dr PO Box 215 *TF:* 800-843-5253 ■ *Web:* www.4seasonsresort.com	Lake Ozark	MO	65049	573-365-3000	365-8525
Plantation at Fall Creek Resort 1 Fall Creek Dr *TF:* 800-510-7472 ■ *Web:* www.sunterra.com	Branson	MO	65616	417-334-6404	335-3255
Resort at Port Arrowhead The 3080 Bagnell Dam Blvd PO Box 1930 *TF:* 800-532-3575 ■ *Web:* www.lakeoftheozarksgetaway.com	Lake Ozark	MO	65049	573-365-2334	365-6887
Tan-Tar-A Resort Golf Club & Spa PO Box 188 TT *TF Resv:* 800-826-8272 ■ *Web:* www.tan-tar-a.com	Osage Beach	MO	65065	573-348-3131	348-3206
Thousand Hills Golf Resort 245 S Wildwood Dr *TF:* 800-864-4145 ■ *Web:* www.thousandhills.com	Branson	MO	65616	417-336-5873	337-5740
Welk Resort Branson 1984 State Hwy 165 *TF:* 800-505-9355 ■ *Web:* www.welkresortbranson.com	Branson	MO	65616	417-336-3575	339-3176

Montana

				Phone	Fax
Big EZ Lodge PO Box 160070 7000 Beaver Creek Rd *TF:* 877-244-3299 ■ *Web:* www.bigezlodge.com	Big Sky	MT	59716	406-995-7000	995-7007
Big Sky Resort 1 Lone Mountain Trail PO Box 160001 *TF:* 800-548-4486 ■ *Web:* www.bigskyresort.com	Big Sky	MT	59716	406-995-5000	995-5002
Fairmont Hot Springs Resort 1500 Fairmont Rd *TF:* 800-332-3272 ■ *Web:* www.fairmontmontana.com	Fairmont	MT	59711	406-797-3241	797-3260
Glacier Park Inc PO Box 2025 *Web:* www.glacierparkinc.com	Columbia Falls	MT	59912	406-892-2525	892-1375
Meadow Lake Resort 100 St Andrews Dr *TF:* 800-321-4653 ■ *Web:* www.meadowlake.com	Columbia Falls	MT	59912	406-892-8700	892-0330
Rock Creek Resort HC 49 Box 3500 *TF:* 800-667-1119 ■ *Web:* www.rockcreekresort.com	Red Lodge	MT	59068	406-446-1111	237-9851
Triple Creek Ranch 5551 West Fork Rd *Web:* www.triplecreekranch.com	Darby	MT	59829	406-821-4600	821-4666
Winter Sports Inc 3812 Big Mountain Rd PO Box 1400 *TF:* 800-858-5439 ■ *Web:* www.bigmtn.com	Whitefish	MT	59937	406-862-1900	862-2955

Nevada

				Phone	Fax
Alexis Park Resort 375 E Harmon Ave *TF:* 800-582-2228 ■ *Web:* www.alexispark.com	Las Vegas	NV	89169	702-796-3300	796-3354
Aquarius Casino Resort 1900 S Casino Dr *TF:* 888-662-5825 ■ *Web:* www.aquariuscasinoresort.com	Laughlin	NV	89029	702-298-5111	
Atlantis Casino Resort 3800 S Virginia St *TF:* 800-723-6500 ■ *Web:* www.atlantiscasino.com	Reno	NV	89502	775-825-4700	332-2211
Bally's Las Vegas 3645 Las Vegas Blvd S *TF Resv:* 800-225-5977 ■ *Web:* www.harrahs.com	Las Vegas	NV	89109	702-739-4111	967-4405
Bellagio Hotel & Casino 3600 Las Vegas Blvd S *TF:* 888-987-7111 ■ *Web:* www.bellagio.com	Las Vegas	NV	89109	702-693-7111	693-8585
Buffalo Bill's Resort & Casino 31700 S Las Vegas Blvd *TF:* 800-386-7867 ■ *Web:* www.primmvalleyresorts.com/pages/bb_home.asp	Primm	NV	89019	702-382-1111	679-7766
Cal-Neva Resort Spa & Casino 2 Stateline Rd PO Box 368 *TF:* 800-225-6382 ■ *Web:* www.calnevaresort.com	Crystal Bay	NV	89402	775-832-4000	831-9007
Casablanca Resort 950 W Mesquite Blvd *TF:* 800-459-7529 ■ *Web:* www.casablancaresort.com	Mesquite	NV	89027	702-346-7529	346-6888
Club Cal Neva Hotel Casino 133 N Virginia St *TF:* 877-777-7303 ■ *Web:* www.clubcalneva.com	Reno	NV	89501	775-323-1046	335-2614
Don Laughlin's Riverside Resort & Casino 1650 Casino Dr *TF:* 800-227-3849 ■ *Web:* www.riversideresort.com	Laughlin	NV	89029	702-298-2535	298-2695
Flamingo Las Vegas 3555 Las Vegas Blvd S *TF Resv:* 800-732-2111 ■ *Web:* www.harrahs.com	Las Vegas	NV	89109	702-733-3111	733-3528
Golden Nugget Hotel 129 E Fremont St *TF:* 800-634-3454 ■ *Web:* www.goldennugget.com	Las Vegas	NV	89101	702-385-7111	385-7111
Golden Nugget Laughlin 2300 S Casino Dr *TF:* 800-237-1739 ■ *Web:* www.goldennugget.com/laughlin/	Laughlin	NV	89029	702-298-7111	298-7122
Grand Sierra Resort & Casino 2500 E 2nd St *TF:* 800-501-2651 ■ *Web:* www.grandsierraresort.com	Reno	NV	89595	775-789-2000	789-1678
Hard Rock Hotel & Casino 4455 Paradise Rd *TF:* 800-473-7625 ■ *Web:* www.hardrockhotel.com	Las Vegas	NV	89169	702-693-5000	693-5557
Harrah's Las Vegas 3475 Las Vegas Blvd S *TF:* 800-427-7247 ■ *Web:* www.harrahs.com/our_casinos/	Las Vegas	NV	89109	702-369-5000	369-6014
Harrah's Laughlin 2900 S Casino Dr *TF:* 800-427-7247 ■ *Web:* www.harrahs.com/our_casinos/	Laughlin	NV	89029	702-298-4600	298-6802
John Ascuaga's Nugget Hotel Casino 1100 Nugget Ave *TF:* 800-648-1177 ■ *Web:* www.janugget.com	Sparks	NV	89431	775-356-3300	356-3434
JW Marriott Resort Las Vegas 221 N Rampart Blvd *TF:* 877-869-8777 ■ *Web:* www.marriott.com	Las Vegas	NV	89145	702-869-7777	869-7339
Las Vegas Sands Corp 3355 Las Vegas Blvd S *NYSE: LVS* ■ *Web:* www.lasvegassands.com	Las Vegas	NV	89109	702-733-5728	733-5620
Loews Lake Las Vegas Resort 101 Montelago Blvd *TF:* 800-235-6397 ■ *Web:* www.loewshotels.com	Henderson	NV	89011	702-567-6000	567-6067
Mandalay Bay Resort & Casino 3950 Las Vegas Blvd S *TF:* 877-632-7800 ■ *Web:* www.mandalaybay.com	Las Vegas	NV	89119	702-632-7777	632-7234
MGM Grand Hotel & Casino 3799 Las Vegas Blvd S *TF:* 800-929-1111 ■ *Web:* www.mgmgrand.com	Las Vegas	NV	89109	702-891-1111	891-3036
MGM Mirage Inc 3600 Las Vegas Blvd S *NYSE: MGM* ■ *Web:* www.mgmmirage.com	Las Vegas	NV	89109	702-693-7120	693-8626
Mirage The 3400 Las Vegas Blvd S *TF:* 800-627-6667 ■ *Web:* www.mirage.com	Las Vegas	NV	89109	702-791-7111	791-7414
Monarch Casino & Resort Inc 1175 W Moana Ln Suite 200 *NASDAQ: MCRI* ■ *Web:* www.monarchcasino.com	Reno	NV	89509	775-825-3355	825-7705
Monte Carlo Resort & Casino 3770 Las Vegas Blvd S *TF:* 800-311-8999 ■ *Web:* www.montecarlo.com	Las Vegas	NV	89109	702-730-7777	730-7200
Oasis Resort Casino Golf & Spa 897 W Mesquite Blvd *TF:* 800-621-0187 ■ *Web:* www.oasisresort.com	Mesquite	NV	89027	702-346-5232	346-2746
Planet Hollywood Resort & Casino 3667 Las Vegas Blvd S *TF:* 866-919-7472 ■ *Web:* www.planethollywoodresort.com	Las Vegas	NV	89109	702-785-5555	785-9600
Primm Valley Resort & Casino 31900 S Las Vegas Blvd *TF:* 800-386-7867 ■ *Web:* www.primmvalleyresorts.com	Primm	NV	89019	702-386-7867	679-5424
Ridge Tahoe 400 Ridge Club Dr PO Box 5790 *TF:* 800-334-1600 ■ *Web:* www.ridgetahoeresort.com	Stateline	NV	89449	775-588-3553	588-1551
Rio All-Suite Hotel & Casino 3700 W Flamingo Rd *TF:* 888-746-7482 ■ *Web:* www.harrahs.com/our-casinos/	Las Vegas	NV	89103	702-777-7777	777-6565
Ritz-Carlton Lake Las Vegas 1610 Lake Las Vegas Pkwy *TF:* 800-241-3333 ■ *Web:* www.ritzcarlton.com	Henderson	NV	89011	702-567-4700	567-4777
Riviera Hotel & Casino 2901 Las Vegas Blvd S *TF Resv:* 800-634-6753 ■ *Web:* www.rivierahotel.com	Las Vegas	NV	89109	702-734-5110	794-9663
Sahara Hotel & Casino 2535 Las Vegas Blvd S *TF:* 888-696-2121 ■ *Web:* www.saharavegas.com	Las Vegas	NV	89109	702-737-2111	737-1017
Silver Legacy Resort & Casino 407 N Virginia St *TF:* 800-687-8733 ■ *Web:* www.silverlegacy.com	Reno	NV	89501	775-329-4777	325-7474
Treasure Island Hotel & Casino 3300 Las Vegas Blvd S *TF:* 800-944-7444 ■ *Web:* www.treasureisland.com	Las Vegas	NV	89109	702-894-7111	894-7414
Tropicana Resort & Casino 3801 Las Vegas Blvd S *TF Resv:* 888-826-8767 ■ *Web:* tropicanalv.com	Las Vegas	NV	89109	702-739-2222	739-3648
Venetian Resort Hotel & Casino 3355 Las Vegas Blvd S *TF:* 877-283-6423 ■ *Web:* www.venetian.com	Las Vegas	NV	89109	702-414-1000	414-1100
Wynn Resorts Ltd 3131 Las Vegas Blvd S *NASDAQ: WYNN* ■ *TF:* 877-321-9966 ■ *Web:* www.wynnresorts.com	Las Vegas	NV	89109	702-770-7000	770-1571

New Brunswick

				Phone	Fax
Fairmont Algonquin 184 Adolphus St *TF:* 800-441-1414 ■ *Web:* www.fairmont.com	Saint Andrews	NB	E5B1T7	506-529-8823	529-7162

New Hampshire

				Phone	Fax
BALSAMS The 1000 Cold Springs Rd *TF:* 800-255-0600 ■ *Web:* www.thebalsams.com	Dixville Notch	NH	03576	603-255-3400	255-4221
Cranmore Mountain Resort 1 Skimobile Rd PO Box 1640 *TF:* 800-786-6754 ■ *Web:* www.cranmore.com	North Conway	NH	03860	603-356-5544	356-8526
Margate on Winnipesaukee 76 Lake St *TF:* 800-627-4283 ■ *Web:* www.themargate.com	Laconia	NH	03246	603-524-5210	528-4485
Mount Washington Hotel & Resort 310 Mt Washington Hotel Rd *TF:* 800-314-1752 ■ *Web:* www.mtwashington.com	Bretton Woods	NH	03575	603-278-1000	278-8828
Valley Inn Tecumseh Rd PO Box 1 *TF:* 800-343-0969 ■ *Web:* www.valleyinn.com	Waterville Valley	NH	03215	603-236-8425	236-4294
Waterville Valley Resort 1 Ski Area Rd PO Box 540 *TF:* 800-468-2553 ■ *Web:* www.waterville.com	Waterville Valley	NH	03215	603-236-8311	236-4344
White Mountain Hotel & Resort West Side Rd PO Box 1828 *TF:* 800-533-6301 ■ *Web:* www.whitemountainhotel.com	North Conway	NH	03860	603-356-7100	356-7100

New Jersey

				Phone	Fax
Atlantic City Hilton Casino Resort Pacific & Boston *TF:* 877-432-7139 ■ *Web:* www.hiltonac.com	Atlantic City	NJ	08401	609-347-7111	340-7128
Bally's Atlantic City 1900 Boardwalk *TF:* 800-772-7777 ■ *Web:* www.harrahs.com	Atlantic City	NJ	08401	609-340-2000	340-1725
Caesars Atlantic City Hotel Casino 2100 Pacific Ave *TF:* 800-443-0104 ■ *Web:* www.harrahs.com	Atlantic City	NJ	08401	609-348-4411	343-2405
Dolce International 28 W Grand Ave *TF:* 888-993-6523 ■ *Web:* www.dolce.com	Montvale	NJ	07645	201-307-8700	307-8837
Legends Resort & Country Club 430 Rt 517 PO Box 637 *TF:* 800-835-2555 ■ *Web:* www.golegends.com	McAfee	NJ	07428	973-827-6000	827-7198
Montreal Inn Beach Dr & Madison Ave *TF:* 800-525-7011 ■ *Web:* www.montreal-inn.com	Cape May	NJ	08204	609-884-7011	884-4559
Mountain Creek Resort 200 Rt 94 **Fax:* Hum Res ■ *Web:* www.mountaincreek.com	Vernon	NJ	07462	973-827-2000	209-3342*
Ocean Place Resort & Spa 1 Ocean Blvd *TF:* 800-411-6493 ■ *Web:* www.oceanplaceresort.com	Long Branch	NJ	07740	732-571-4000	229-0931
Resorts Atlantic City 1133 Boardwalk *TF:* 800-336-6378 ■ *Web:* www.resortsac.com	Atlantic City	NJ	08401	609-344-6000	340-6847
Seaview Marriott Resort & Spa 401 S New York Rd *TF:* 800-228-9290 ■ *Web:* www.seaviewmarriott.com	Galloway	NJ	08205	609-652-1800	652-2307
Showboat Atlantic City 801 Boardwalk *TF:* 800-427-7247 ■ *Web:* www.harrahs.com/our_casinos/sac	Atlantic City	NJ	08401	609-343-4000	343-3409
Tropicana Casino & Resort 2831 Boardwalk *TF:* 800-843-8767 ■ *Web:* www.tropicana.net	Atlantic City	NJ	08401	609-340-4000	340-4457
Trump Taj Mahal Casino Resort 1000 Boardwalk & Virginia Ave *TF Resv:* 800-825-8786 ■ *Web:* www.trumptaj.com	Atlantic City	NJ	08401	609-449-1000	449-6818
Wyndham Hotels & Resorts 1 Sylvan Way *TF Resv:* 877-999-3223 ■ *Web:* www.wyndham.com	Parsippany	NJ	07054	973-753-6600	
Wyndham Hotel Group Wyndham Hotels & Resorts 1 Sylvan Way *TF Resv:* 877-999-3223 ■ *Web:* www.wyndham.com	Parsippany	NJ	07054	973-753-6600	

New Mexico

				Phone	Fax
Angel Fire Resort PO Box 130 *TF:* 800-633-7463 ■ *Web:* www.angelfireresort.com	Angel Fire	NM	87710	505-377-6401	377-4200

New Mexico (Cont'd)

	City	State	ZIP	Phone	Fax
Bishop's Lodge Resort & Spa 2197 Bishop's Lodge Rd PO Box 2367 *TF:* 800-732-2240 ■ *Web:* www.bishopslodge.com	Santa Fe	NM	87501	505-983-6377	989-8739
El Monte Sagrado Living Resort & Spa 317 Kit Carson Rd *TF:* 800-828-8267 ■ *Web:* www.elmontesagrado.com	Taos	NM	87571	505-758-3502	737-2985
Inn of the Mountain Gods 287 Carrizo Canyon Rd *TF:* 800-545-9011 ■ *Web:* www.innofthemountaingods.com	Mescalero	NM	88340	505-464-5141	464-6173
La Posada de Santa Fe Resort & Spa 330 E Palace Ave *TF:* 800-727-5276 ■ *Web:* laposada.rockresorts.com/	Santa Fe	NM	87501	505-986-0000	982-9646
Lifts West Condominium Resort Hotel PO Box 330 *TF:* 800-221-1859 ■ *Web:* www.redrivernm.com/liftswest	Red River	NM	87558	505-754-2778	754-6617
Lodge at Cloudcroft 1 Corona Pl *TF:* 800-395-6343 ■ *Web:* www.thelodgeresort.com	Cloudcroft	NM	88317	505-682-2566	682-2715

New York

	City	State	ZIP	Phone	Fax
Bonnie Castle Resort 31 Holland St *TF:* 800-955-4511 ■ *Web:* www.bonniecastle.com	Alexandria Bay	NY	13607	315-482-4511	482-9600
Canoe Island Lodge 3820 Lakeshore Dr *Web:* www.canoeislandlodge.com	Diamond Point	NY	12824	518-668-5592	668-2012
Concord Resort & Golf Club Concord Rd *TF:* 888-448-9686 ■ *Web:* www.concordresort.com	Kiamesha Lake	NY	12751	845-794-4000	794-6944
Doral Arrowwood Conference Resort 975 Anderson Hill Rd *TF:* 800-223-6725 ■ *Web:* www.arrowwood.com	Rye Brook	NY	10573	914-939-5500	323-5500
Friar Tuck Resort & Convention Center 4858 SR-32 *TF:* 800-832-7600 ■ *Web:* www.friartuck.com	Catskill	NY	12414	518-678-2271	678-2214
Gurney's Inn Resort & Spa 290 Old Montauk Hwy *TF:* 800-848-7639 ■ *Web:* www.gurneys-inn.com	Montauk	NY	11954	631-668-2345	668-3576
Hampshire Hotels & Resorts LLC 1251 Ave of the Americas Suite 934 *Web:* www.hampshirehotels.com	New York	NY	10019	212-474-9800	474-9801
Hilton Lake Placid Resort 1 Mirror Lake Dr *TF:* 800-755-5598 ■ *Web:* www.lphilton.com	Lake Placid	NY	12946	518-523-4411	523-1120
Holiday Valley Resort PO Box 370 Rt 219 *TF:* 800-323-0020 ■ *Web:* www.holidayvalley.com	Ellicottville	NY	14731	716-699-2345	699-5204
Kutsher's Country Club Resort Kutchers Rd PO Box 432 *TF:* 800-431-1273 ■ *Web:* www.kutshers.com	Monticello	NY	12701	845-794-6000	794-0157
Le Meridien 1111 Westchester Ave *TF:* 888-625-5144 ■ *Web:* www.starwoodhotels.com/lemeridien	White Plains	NY	10604	914-640-8100	640-8310
Lodge at Woodcliff 199 Woodcliff Dr *TF:* 800-365-3065 ■ *Web:* www.woodclifflodge.com	Fairport	NY	14450	585-381-4000	381-2673
Mirror Lake Inn Resort & Spa 77 Mirror Lake Dr *Web:* www.mirrorlakeinn.com	Lake Placid	NY	12946	518-523-2544	523-2871
Mohonk Mountain House 1000 Mountain Rest Rd *TF:* 800-772-6646 ■ *Web:* www.mohonk.com	New Paltz	NY	12561	845-255-1000	256-2161
Montauk Yacht Club Resort & Marina 32 Star Island Rd *TF:* 888-692-8668 ■ *Web:* www.montaukyachtclub.com	Montauk	NY	11954	631-668-3100	668-6181
Nevele Grande Resort & Country Club 1 Nevele Rd *TF:* 800-647-6000 ■ *Web:* www.nevele.com	Ellenville	NY	12428	845-647-6000	647-9884
Otesaga The 60 Lake St *TF:* 800-348-6222 ■ *Web:* www.otesaga.com	Cooperstown	NY	13326	607-547-9931	547-9675
Peek 'n Peak Resort 1405 Olde Rd PO Box 360 *Web:* www.pknpk.com	Findley Lake	NY	14736	716-355-4141	355-4542
Pine Tree Point Resort 70 Anthony St PO Box 99 *TF:* 888-746-3229 ■ *Web:* www.pinetreepointresort.com	Alexandria Bay	NY	13607	315-482-9911	482-6420
Point The PO Box 1327 *TF:* 800-255-3530 ■ *Web:* www.thepointresort.com	Saranac Lake	NY	12983	518-891-5674	891-1152
Roaring Brook Ranch & Tennis Resort PO Box 671 *Web:* www.roaringbrookranch.com	Lake George	NY	12845	518-668-5767	668-4019
Rocking Horse Ranch Resort 600 Rt 44-55 *TF:* 800-647-2624 ■ *Web:* www.rhranch.com	Highland	NY	12528	845-691-2927	691-6434
Sagamore The 110 Sagamore Rd *TF:* 800-358-3585 ■ *Web:* www.thesagamore.com	Bolton Landing	NY	12814	518-644-9400	743-6036
Saint Regis Hotels & Resorts 1111 Westchester Ave *Web:* www.starwood.com/stregis	White Plains	NY	10604	914-640-8100	640-8310
Sheraton Hotels & Resorts 1111 Westchester Ave *TF:* 800-325-3535 ■ *Web:* www.starwood.com/sheraton	White Plains	NY	10604	914-640-8100	640-8310
Thousand Islands Country Club 46433 CR 100 PO Box 290 *Web:* www.ticountryclub.com	Wellesley Island	NY	13640	315-482-9454	482-9321
Villa Roma Resort & Conference Center 356 Villa Roma Rd *TF:* 800-727-8455 ■ *Web:* www.villaroma.com	Callicoon	NY	12723	845-887-4880	887-4824
Westin Hotels & Resorts 1111 Westchester Ave *TF:* 877-443-4585 ■ *Web:* www.starwood.com/westin	White Plains	NY	10604	914-640-8100	640-8310
Whiteface Club & Resort 373 Whiteface Inn Ln *TF:* 800-422-6757 ■ *Web:* www.whitefaceclub.com	Lake Placid	NY	12946	518-523-2551	523-4278

North Carolina

	City	State	ZIP	Phone	Fax
Ballantyne Resort Hotel 10000 Ballantyne Commons Pkwy *TF:* 866-248-4824 ■ *Web:* www.ballantyneresort.com	Charlotte	NC	28277	704-248-4000	248-4005
Chetola Resort PO Box 17 N Main St *TF:* 800-243-8652 ■ *Web:* www.chetola.com	Blowing Rock	NC	28605	828-295-5500	295-5529
Divi Resorts Inc 6340 Quadrangle Dr Suite 300 *TF:* 800-367-3484 ■ *Web:* www.diviresorts.com	Chapel Hill	NC	27517	919-419-3484	419-2075
Eseeola Lodge 175 Linville Ave PO Box 99 *TF:* 800-742-6717 ■ *Web:* www.eseeola.com	Linville	NC	28646	828-733-4311	733-3227
Fontana Village Resort Hwy 28 PO Box 68 *TF:* 800-849-2258 ■ *Web:* www.fontanavillage.com	Fontana Dam	NC	28733	828-498-2211	498-2345
Greystone Inn Greystone Ln *TF:* 800-824-5766 ■ *Web:* www.greystoneinn.com	Lake Toxaway	NC	28747	828-966-4700	862-5689
Grove Park Inn Resort & Spa 290 Macon Ave *TF:* 800-438-5800 ■ *Web:* www.groveparkinn.com	Asheville	NC	28804	828-252-2711	253-7053
High Hampton Inn & Country Club 1525 Hwy 107 S *TF:* 800-334-2551 ■ *Web:* www.highhamptoninn.com	Cashiers	NC	28717	828-743-2450	743-5991
Holiday Inn SunSpree Resort Wrightsville Beach 1706 N Lumina Ave *TF:* 877-330-5050 ■ *Web:* www.ichotelsgroup.com/h/d/hi/home	Wrightsville Beach	NC	28480	910-256-2231	256-9208
Hound Ears Lodge & Club PO Box 188 *Web:* www.houndears.com	Blowing Rock	NC	28605	828-963-4321	963-8030
Maggie Valley Resort & Country Club 1819 Country Club Dr *TF:* 800-438-3861 ■ *Web:* www.maggievalleyresort.com	Maggie Valley	NC	28751	828-926-1616	926-2906
Mid Pines Inn & Golf Club 1010 Midland Rd *TF:* 800-323-2114 ■ *Web:* www.pineneedles-midpines.com	Southern Pines	NC	28387	910-692-2114	692-4615
Pine Needles Lodge & Golf Club PO Box 88 *TF:* 800-747-7272 ■ *Web:* www.pineneedles-midpines.com/	Southern Pines	NC	28388	910-692-7111	692-5349
Pinehurst Resort & Country Club 80 Carolina Vista Dr *TF:* 800-487-4653 ■ *Web:* www.pinehurst.com	Pinehurst	NC	28374	910-295-6811	295-8466
Pinnacle Inn Resort 303 Pinnacle Inn Rd *TF:* 800-405-7888	Banner Elk	NC	28604	828-387-2231	387-3745
Sanderling Resort & Spa 1461 Duck Rd *TF:* 800-701-4111 ■ *Web:* www.sanderlinginn.com	Duck	NC	27949	252-261-4111	261-1638
Waynesville Country Club Inn 176 Country Club Dr *TF:* 800-627-6250 ■ *Web:* www.wccinn.com	Waynesville	NC	28786	828-456-3551	456-3555
Wolf Laurel Ski Resort 578 Valley View Cir *TF:* 800-817-4111 ■ *Web:* www.skiwolflaurel.com	Mars Hill	NC	28754	828-689-4111	689-9819

North Dakota

	City	State	ZIP	Phone	Fax
Prairie Knights Casino & Resort 7932 Hwy 24 *TF:* 800-425-8277 ■ *Web:* www.prairieknights.com	Fort Yates	ND	58538	701-854-7777	854-7786

Nova Scotia

	City	State	ZIP	Phone	Fax
Inverary Resort PO Box 190 *TF:* 800-565-5660 ■ *Web:* www.capebretonresorts.com/inverary.asp	Baddeck	NS	B0E1B0	902-295-3500	295-3527
Oak Island Resort Spa & Convention Center 36 Treasure Dr *TF:* 800-565-5075 ■ *Web:* www.oakislandresortandspa.com	Western Shore	NS	B0J3M0	902-627-2600	627-2020
Pines Resort The 103 Shore Rd PO Box 70 *TF:* 800-667-4637 ■ *Web:* www.signatureresorts.com/pines	Digby	NS	B0V1A0	902-245-2511	245-6133

Ohio

	City	State	ZIP	Phone	Fax
Atwood Lake Resort 2650 Lodge Rd *TF:* 800-362-6406 ■ *Web:* www.atwoodlakeresort.com	Sherrodsville	OH	44675	330-735-2211	735-2562
Avalon Inn & Resort 9519 E Market St *TF:* 800-828-2566 ■ *Web:* www.avaloninn.com	Warren	OH	44484	330-856-1900	856-2248
Deer Creek Resort & Conference Center 22300 State Park Rd *TF:* 877-678-3777 ■ *Web:* www.visitdeercreek.com	Mount Sterling	OH	43143	740-869-2020	869-4059
Glenmoor Country Club 4191 Glenmoor Rd NW *TF:* 888-456-6667 ■ *Web:* www.glenmoorcc.com	Canton	OH	44718	330-966-3600	966-3611
Hueston Woods Resort & Conference Center 5201 Lodge Rd *Web:* www.huestonwoodsresort.com	College Corner	OH	45003	513-664-3500	523-1522
Renaissance Quail Hollow Resort 11080 Concord-Hambden Rd *TF:* 800-792-0258 ■ *Web:* www.renaissancehotel.com/cleqh	Painesville	OH	44077	440-497-1100	497-1111
Sawmill Creek Resort 400 Sawmill Creek Dr *TF:* 800-729-6455 ■ *Web:* www.sawmillcreek.com	Huron	OH	44839	419-433-3800	433-7610

Oklahoma

	City	State	ZIP	Phone	Fax
Cherokee Casino & Resort 777 W Cherokee St *TF:* 800-760-6700 ■ *Web:* www.cherokeecasino.com	Catoosa	OK	74015	918-384-7800	266-3038
Fin & Feather Resort Inc Rt 1 Box 194 *Web:* www.finandfeatherresort.com	Gore	OK	74435	918-487-5148	487-5025
Lake Murray Resort Park 3323 Lodge Rd *TF:* 800-257-0322 ■ *Web:* www.touroklahoma.com/parks.asp	Ardmore	OK	73401	580-223-6600	226-9613
Lake Texoma Resort Park PO Box 248 *TF:* 800-528-0593 ■ *Web:* www.touroklahoma.com/parks.asp	Kingston	OK	73439	580-564-2311	564-9322
Quartz Mountain Resort & Conference Center 22469 Lodge Rd *TF:* 877-999-5567 ■ *Web:* www.quartzmountainresort.com	Lone Wolf	OK	73655	580-563-2424	563-2422
Shangri-La Resort 57401 E Hwy 125 *TF:* 800-331-4060	Afton	OK	74331	918-257-4204	257-5614

Ontario

	City	State	ZIP	Phone	Fax
Deerhurst Resort 1235 Deerhurst Dr *TF:* 800-461-4390 ■ *Web:* www.deerhurstresort.com	Huntsville	ON	P1H2E8	705-789-6411	789-2431
Delta Hotels Ltd 100 Wellington St W Suite 1200 *TF Resv:* 800-268-1133 ■ *Web:* www.deltahotels.com	Toronto	ON	M5K1J3	416-874-2000	874-2001
Delta Meadowvale Resort & Conference Centre 6750 Mississauga Rd *TF:* 800-268-1133 ■ *Web:* www.deltahotels.com/hotels	Mississauga	ON	L5N2L3	905-821-1981	542-4036
Fairmont Hotels & Resorts Inc 100 Wellington St W TD Centre Suite 1600 *NYSE: FHR* ■ *TF:* 800-866-5577 ■ *Web:* www.fairmont.com	Toronto	ON	M5K1B7	416-874-2600	874-2601
Niagara Fallsview Casino Resort 6380 Fallsview Blvd *TF:* 888-325-5788 ■ *Web:* www.fallsviewcasinoresort.com	Niagara Falls	ON	L2G7X5	905-358-3255	371-7952
Pinestone Resort PO Box 809 *TF:* 800-461-0357 ■ *Web:* www.deltahotels.com	Haliburton	ON	K0M1S0	705-457-1800	457-1783
White Oaks Conference Resort & Spa 253 Taylor Rd *TF:* 800-263-5766 ■ *Web:* www.whiteoaksresort.com	Niagara-on-the-Lake	ON	L0S1J0	905-688-2550	688-2220

Oregon

	City	State	ZIP	Phone	Fax
Black Butte Ranch 12930 Hawks Beard Rd PO Box 8000 *TF:* 800-452-7455 ■ *Web:* www.blackbutteranch.com	Black Butte Ranch	OR	97759	541-595-6211	595-2077
Gearhart By The Sea PO Box 2700 *TF:* 800-547-0115 ■ *Web:* gearhartresort.com	Gearhart	OR	97138	503-738-8331	738-0881
Mount Bachelor Village Resort & Conference Center 19717 Mt Bachelor Dr *TF:* 800-452-9846 ■ *Web:* www.mtbachelorvillage.com	Bend	OR	97702	541-389-5900	388-7401
Resort at the Mountain 68010 E Fairway Ave *TF:* 800-669-7666 ■ *Web:* www.theresort.com	Welches	OR	97067	503-622-3101	622-2222
Salishan Lodge & Golf Resort PO Box 118 *TF:* 800-452-2300 ■ *Web:* www.salishan.com	Gleneden Beach	OR	97388	541-764-2371	764-3681
Seventh Mountain Resort 18575 SW Century Dr *TF:* 800-452-6810 ■ *Web:* www.seventhmountain.com	Bend	OR	97702	541-382-8711	382-3517
Sunriver Resort 17600 Center Dr PO Box 3609 *TF:* 800-547-3922 ■ *Web:* www.sunriver-resort.com	Sunriver	OR	97707	541-593-1000	593-4685
Timberline Lodge 88 Hwy 150 *TF:* 800-547-1406 ■ *Web:* www.timberlinelodge.com	Timberline Lodge	OR	97028	503-272-3311	622-0710
Village Green Resort & Gardens 725 Row River Rd *TF:* 800-343-7666 ■ *Web:* www.villagegreenresortandgardens.com	Cottage Grove	OR	97424	541-942-2491	942-2386

Pennsylvania

Resort	City	State	Zip	Phone	Fax
Allenberry Resort 1559 Boiling Springs Rd *TF:* 800-430-5468 ■ *Web:* www.allenberry.com	Boiling Springs	PA	17007	717-258-3211	960-5280
Brookdale on the Lake 1 Brookdale Rd & Rt 611 *TF:* 800-233-4141 ■ *Web:* www.caesarspoconoresorts.com	Scotrun	PA	18355	570-839-8843	839-0490
Caesars Cove Haven Resort 194 Lakeview Dr *TF:* 800-233-4141 ■ *Web:* www.caesarspoconoresorts.com	Lakeville	PA	18438	570-226-4506	226-4697
Caesars Paradise Stream Rt 940 PO Box 99 *TF:* 800-233-4141 ■ *Web:* www.caesarspoconoresorts.com	Mount Pocono	PA	18344	570-839-8881	839-1842
Caesars Pocono Palace Resort Rt 209 *TF:* 800-233-4141 ■ *Web:* www.caesarspoconoresorts.com	Marshalls Creek	PA	18335	570-588-6692	588-0754
Carroll Valley Golf Resort 121 Sanders Rd *TF:* 800-548-8504 ■ *Web:* www.carrollvalley.com	Fairfield	PA	17320	717-642-8211	642-5529
Felicita Resort 2201 Fishing Creek Valley Rd *TF:* 888-321-3713 ■ *Web:* www.felicitaresort.com	Harrisburg	PA	17112	717-599-5301	599-7714
Fernwood Resort & Country Club Rt 209 *TF:* 888-337-6966 ■ *Web:* resortsusa.com/fernwood.php	Bushkill	PA	18324	570-588-9500	588-0403
Heritage Hills Golf Resort & Conference Center 2700 Mount Rose Ave *TF:* 877-782-9752 ■ *Web:* www.hhgr.com	York	PA	17402	717-755-0123	840-2647
Hershey Entertainment & Resorts Co 27 W Chocolate Ave *TF:* 800-437-7439 ■ *Web:* www.hersheypa.com	Hershey	PA	17033	717-534-3131	534-3324
Hidden Valley Resort & Conference Center 1 Craighead Dr *TF:* 800-458-0175 ■ *Web:* www.hiddenvalleyresort.com	Hidden Valley	PA	15502	814-443-8000	443-1907
Hotel Hershey 100 Hotel Rd *TF:* 800-533-3131 ■ *Web:* www.thehotelhershey.com/	Hershey	PA	17033	717-533-2171	534-8887
Lancaster Host Resort 2300 Lincoln Hwy E *TF Resv:* 800-233-0121 ■ *Web:* www.lancasterhost.com	Lancaster	PA	17602	717-299-5500	295-5104
Liberty Mountain Resort & Conference Center 78 Country Club Trail *Web:* www.libertymountainresort.com	Carroll Valley	PA	17320	717-642-8282	742-6534
Mountain Laurel Resort & Spa Rt 940 PO Box 9 *TF:* 888-243-9300 ■ *Web:* www.mountainlaurelresort.com	White Haven	PA	18661	570-443-8411	443-5518
Nemacolin Woodlands Resort & Spa 1001 Lafayette Dr *TF:* 800-422-2736 ■ *Web:* www.nwlr.com	Farmington	PA	15437	724-329-8555	329-6198
Penn Hills Resort Rt 447 & 191 PO Box 309 *TF:* 800-233-8240 ■ *Web:* www.pennhillsresort.com	Analomink	PA	18320	570-421-6464	424-0310
Pocono Manor Golf Resort & Spa Rt 314 *TF:* 800-233-8150 ■ *Web:* www.theinnatpoconomanor.com	Pocono Manor	PA	18349	570-839-7111	839-0708
Ritz-Carlton Philadelphia 10 Ave of the Arts *TF:* 888-505-3914 ■ *Web:* www.ritzcarlton.com/hotels/philadelphia/	Philadelphia	PA	19102	215-523-8000	568-0942
Seven Springs Mountain Resort 777 Waterwheel Dr *TF:* 800-452-2223 ■ *Web:* www.7springs.com	Champion	PA	15622	814-352-7777	352-7911
Shadowbrook Inn & Resort 615 SR 6 E *TF:* 800-955-0295 ■ *Web:* www.shadowbrookresort.com	Tunkhannock	PA	18657	570-836-2151	836-5655
Shawnee Inn & Golf Resort PO Box 67 1 River Rd *TF:* 800-742-9633 ■ *Web:* www.shawneeinn.com	Shawnee on Delaware	PA	18356	570-424-4000	424-9168
Skytop Lodge 1 Skytop *TF:* 800-345-7759 ■ *Web:* www.skytop.com	Skytop	PA	18357	570-595-7401	595-9618
Split Rock Resort 1 Lake Dr *TF:* 800-255-7625 ■ *Web:* www.splitrockresort.com	Lake Harmony	PA	18624	570-722-9111	722-8831
Tamiment Resort & Conference Center Bushkill Falls Rd *TF:* 800-532-8280 ■ *Web:* www.tamiment.com	Tamiment	PA	18371	570-588-6652	
Toftrees Golf Resort & Conference Center 1 Country Club Ln *TF:* 800-252-3551 ■ *Web:* www.toftrees.com	State College	PA	16803	814-234-8000	238-4404
Willow Valley Resort & Conference Center 2416 Willow Street Pike *TF:* 800-444-1714 ■ *Web:* www.willowvalley.com	Lancaster	PA	17602	717-464-2711	464-4784
Woodlands Inn & Resort 1073 Hwy 315 *TF:* 800-762-2222 ■ *Web:* www.thewoodlandsresort.com	Wilkes-Barre	PA	18702	570-824-9831	824-8865

Puerto Rico

Resort	City	State	Zip	Phone	Fax
Candalero Resort at Palmas Del Mar 270 Harborside Dr Suite 1 *TF:* 800-725-6273 ■ *Web:* www.palmasresort.com	Humacao	PR	00791	787-852-6000	852-6370
Caribe Hilton Los Rosales St San Geronimo Grounds *TF:* 800-445-8667 ■ *Web:* www.hilton.com	San Juan	PR	00901	787-721-0303	725-8849
El Conquistador Resort & Golden Door Spa 1000 El Conquistador Ave *TF:* 866-317-8932 ■ *Web:* www.elconresort.com	Fajardo	PR	00738	787-863-1000	863-6500
InterContinental San Juan Resort & Casino 5961 Isla Verde Ave *TF:* 800-443-2009 ■ *Web:* www.ichotelsgroup.com/h/d/ic/1/en/hd/sjuha	Carolina	PR	00979	787-791-6100	253-2510
Las Casitas Village & Golden Door Spa 1000 El Conquistador Ave *TF:* 800-996-3426 ■ *Web:* lascasitasvillage.com	Fajardo	PR	00738	787-863-1000	863-6831
Ritz-Carlton San Juan Hotel Spa & Casino 6961 Ave of the Governors *TF:* 800-241-3333 ■ *Web:* www.ritzcarlton.com/hotels/san_juan/	Carolina	PR	00979	787-253-1700	253-1777
Wyndham Condado Plaza Hotel & Casino 999 Ashford Ave *TF:* 800-468-5228	San Juan	PR	00907	787-721-1000	721-4613

Quebec

Resort	City	State	Zip	Phone	Fax
Fairmont Le Chateau Montebello 392 Notre Dame St *TF:* 800-441-1414 ■ *Web:* www.fairmont.com	Montebello	QC	J0V1L0	819-423-6341	423-1133
Gray Rocks Resort & Convention Center 2322 rue Labelle *TF:* 800-567-6767 ■ *Web:* www.grayrocks.com	Mont-Tremblant	QC	J8E1T8	819-425-2771	425-3006
Hotel Cheribourg 2603 ch du Parc *TF:* 800-567-6132 ■ *Web:* www.cheribourg.com	Orford	QC	J1X8C8	819-843-3308	843-2639
Hotel Club Tremblant 121 rue Cuttle *TF:* 800-567-8341 ■ *Web:* www.clubtremblant.com	Mont-Tremblant	QC	J8E1B9	819-425-2731	425-5617
Manoir du Lac Delage 40 du Lac Ave *TF:* 888-202-3242 ■ *Web:* www.lacdelage.com	Lac Delage	QC	G0A4P0	418-848-2551	848-1352
Mont Sainte-Anne Resort 500 du Beau-Pre Blvd *TF:* 800-463-4467	Beaupre	QC	G0A1E0	418-827-5211	827-5072
Westin Resort Tremblant 100 ch Kandahar *TF:* 800-937-8461 ■ *Web:* www.starwood.com/westin	Mont-Tremblant	QC	J8E1E2	819-681-8000	681-8001

Rhode Island

Resort	City	State	Zip	Phone	Fax
Castle Hill Inn & Resort 590 Ocean Dr *TF:* 888-466-1355 ■ *Web:* www.castlehillinn.com	Newport	RI	02840	401-849-3800	849-3885
Inn on the Harbor 359 Thames St *TF:* 800-225-3522	Newport	RI	02840	401-849-6789	849-2680
Inn on Long Wharf 142 Long Wharf *TF:* 800-225-3522	Newport	RI	02840	401-847-7800	845-0127

South Carolina

Resort	City	State	Zip	Phone	Fax
Barefoot Resort & Golf 4980 Barefoot Resort Bridge Rd *TF:* 800-856-0501 ■ *Web:* www.barefootgolf.com	North Myrtle Beach	SC	29582	843-390-3200	390-3213
Bay Watch Resort & Conference Center 2701 S Ocean Blvd *TF:* 866-270-2172 ■ *Web:* www.patricia.com/myrtle-beach-resorts/bay-watch-resort	North Myrtle Beach	SC	29582	843-272-4600	272-4440
Beach Colony Resort 5308 N Ocean Blvd *TF:* 800-222-2141 ■ *Web:* www.beachcolony.com	Myrtle Beach	SC	29577	843-449-4010	449-2810
Blue Water Resort 2001 S Ocean Blvd *TF:* 800-845-6994 ■ *Web:* www.bluewaterresort.com	Myrtle Beach	SC	29577	843-626-8345	448-2310
Breakers Resort 2006 N Ocean Blvd *TF:* 800-952-4507 ■ *Web:* www.breakers.com	Myrtle Beach	SC	29578	843-444-4444	626-5001
Caravelle Resort Hotel & Villas 6900 N Ocean Blvd *TF:* 800-367-4518 ■ *Web:* www.thecaravelle.com	Myrtle Beach	SC	29572	843-918-8000	918-8199
Caribbean Resort & Villas 3000 N Ocean Blvd *TF:* 800-552-8509 ■ *Web:* www.caribbeanresort.com	Myrtle Beach	SC	29577	843-448-7181	448-3224
Compass Cove Ocean Resort 2311 S Ocean Blvd *TF:* 800-228-9894 ■ *Web:* www.compasscove.com	Myrtle Beach	SC	29577	843-448-8373	448-5444
Coral Beach Resort & Suites 1105 S Ocean Blvd *TF:* 800-843-2684 ■ *Web:* www.coral-beach.com	Myrtle Beach	SC	29577	843-448-8421	626-0156
Disney's Hilton Head Island Resort 22 Harborside Ln *Web:* dvc.disney.go.com/dvc	Hilton Head Island	SC	29928	843-341-4100	341-4130
Fairfield Ocean Ridge Resort 1 King Cotton Rd *TF:* 877-296-6335 ■ *Web:* www.wyndhamvacationresorts.com/	Edisto Beach	SC	29438	843-869-2561	869-2384
Harbour Town Resort & Yacht Club 149 Lighthouse Rd *TF:* 800-541-7375 ■ *Web:* www.harbourtownresorts.com	Hilton Head Island	SC	29928	843-671-1400	671-0422
Hilton Charleston Harbor Resort & Marina 20 Patriots Point Rd *TF:* 800-445-8667 ■ *Web:* www.hilton.com	Mount Pleasant	SC	29464	843-856-0028	856-8333
Hilton Head Island Beach & Tennis Resort 40 Folly Field Rd *TF:* 800-475-2631 ■ *Web:* www.hhibeachandtennis.com	Hilton Head Island	SC	29928	843-842-4402	842-3323
Hilton Myrtle Beach Resort 10000 Beach Club Dr *TF:* 877-887-9549 ■ *Web:* www.hilton.com	Myrtle Beach	SC	29572	843-449-5000	449-3216
Hilton Oceanfront Resort Hilton Head Island 23 Ocean Ln *TF:* 800-845-8001 ■ *Web:* www.hilton.com	Hilton Head Island	SC	29928	843-842-8000	341-8034
Holiday Inn Oceanfront at Surfside Beach 1601 N Ocean Blvd *TF:* 866-661-5139 ■ *Web:* www.ichotelsgroup.com/h/d/hi/home	Surfside Beach	SC	29575	843-238-5601	238-4758
Kiawah Island Golf Resort 1 Sanctuary Dr *TF:* 800-654-2924 ■ *Web:* www.kiawahresort.com/golf/	Kiawah Island	SC	29455	843-768-2121	768-9339
Landmark Resort 1501 S Ocean Blvd *TF:* 800-845-0658 ■ *Web:* www.landmarkresort.com	Myrtle Beach	SC	29577	843-448-9441	448-6701
Legends Resort 1500 Legends Dr PO Box 2038 *TF:* 888-246-9809 ■ *Web:* www.legendsgolf.com	Myrtle Beach	SC	29578	843-236-9318	236-0516
Litchfield Beach & Golf Resort 14276 Ocean Highway *TF:* 800-845-1897 ■ *Web:* www.litchfieldbeach.com	Pawleys Island	SC	29585	843-237-3000	237-4282
Myrtle Beach Marriott Resort at Grande Dunes 8400 Costa Verde Dr *Web:* www.marriott.com	Myrtle Beach	SC	29572	843-449-8880	449-8669
Myrtle Beach Resort 5905 S Kings Hwy *TF:* 888-627-3767 ■ *Web:* www.myrtle-beach-resort.com	Myrtle Beach	SC	29578	843-238-1559	238-2424
Mystic Sea Resort 2105 S Ocean Blvd *TF:* 800-443-7050 ■ *Web:* www.mysticsea.com	Myrtle Beach	SC	29577	843-448-8446	626-2024
Ocean Dunes Resort & Villas 201 75th Ave N *TF:* 800-845-0635 ■ *Web:* www.sandsresorts.com/resorts/oceandunes	Myrtle Beach	SC	29578	843-449-7441	449-0558
Ocean Forest Villa Resort 5601 N Ocean Blvd *TF:* 800-845-0347 ■ *Web:* www.sandsresorts.com/resorts/oceanforestvilla/	Myrtle Beach	SC	29577	843-449-9661	449-9207
Ocean Reef Resort 7100 N Ocean Blvd *TF:* 888-322-6411 ■ *Web:* www.oceanreefmyrtlebeach.com	Myrtle Beach	SC	29572	843-449-4441	497-3041
Palmetto Dunes Resort 4 Quoon Folly Rd *TF:* 800-845-6130 ■ *Web:* www.palmettodunes.com	Hilton Head Island	SC	29938	843-842-7000	842-4482
Palms Resort 2500 N Ocean Blvd *TF:* 800-528-0451 ■ *Web:* www.palmsresort.com	Myrtle Beach	SC	29577	843-626-8334	448-1950
Patricia Grand Resort 2710 N Ocean Blvd *TF:* 800-255-4763 ■ *Web:* www.patricia.com	Myrtle Beach	SC	29577	843-448-8453	448-3080
Pawleys Plantation 70 Tanglewood Dr *TF:* 800-367-9959 ■ *Web:* www.sandsresorts.com	Pawleys Island	SC	29585	843-237-6009	237-0418
Player's Club Resort 35 Deallyon Ave *TF:* 800-497-7529	Hilton Head Island	SC	29928	843-785-8000	785-9185
Reef Resort 2101 S Ocean Blvd *TF:* 800-845-1212 ■ *Web:* www.reefmyrtlebeach.com	Myrtle Beach	SC	29577	843-448-1765	626-9971
Resort at Seabrook Island 3772 Seabrook Island Rd *Web:* www.discoverseabrook.com	Seabrook Island	SC	29455	843-768-2500	768-7524
Sand Dunes Resort Hotel 201 74th Ave N *TF:* 800-845-6701 ■ *Web:* www.sandsresorts.com	Myrtle Beach	SC	29572	843-449-3313	692-5178
Sea Mist Resort 1200 S Ocean Blvd *TF:* 800-732-6478 ■ *Web:* www.myrtlebeachseamist.com/	Myrtle Beach	SC	29577	843-448-1551	893-1108
Sea Pines Resort 32 Greenwood Dr *TF:* 800-732-7463 ■ *Web:* www.seapines.com	Hilton Head Island	SC	29928	843-785-3333	842-1475
Seacrest Oceanfront Resort on the South Beach 803 S Ocean Blvd *TF:* 800-845-1112 ■ *Web:* www.gotomyrtle.com	Myrtle Beach	SC	29577	843-913-5800	913-5801
Shore Crest Vacation Villas 4709 S Ocean Blvd *Web:* www.bluegreenrentals.com	North Myrtle Beach	SC	29582	843-361-3600	361-3601
Tropical Winds 705 S Ocean Blvd *TF:* 800-843-3466 ■ *Web:* www.tropicalwinds.com	Myrtle Beach	SC	29577	843-448-4304	448-0015
Wild Dunes Resort 5757 Palm Blvd *TF:* 800-845-8880 ■ *Web:* www.wilddunes.com	Isle of Palms	SC	29451	843-886-6000	886-2916
Woodlands Resort & Inn 125 Parsons Rd *TF:* 800-774-9999 ■ *Web:* www.woodlandsinn.com	Summerville	SC	29483	843-875-2600	875-2603

South Dakota

Resort	City	State	Zip	Phone	Fax
Blue Bell Lodge & Resort 25453 S Dakota Hwy Custer State Park *TF:* 800-658-3530 ■ *Web:* www.custerresorts.com	Custer	SD	57730	605-255-4535	255-4752
Spearfish Canyon Resort 10619 Roughlock Falls Rd *TF:* 877-975-6343 ■ *Web:* www.spfcanyon.com	Lead	SD	57754	605-584-3435	584-3990
Spring Creek Resort 610 N Jackson St *Web:* www.springcreekresortsd.com	Pierre	SD	57501	605-224-8336	

South Dakota (Cont'd)

Tennessee

Phone / Fax

Blackberry Farm 1471 W Millers Cove Rd — Walland TN 37886 — 865-380-2260 — 681-7753
TF: 800-273-6004 ■ *Web:* www.blackberryfarm.com

Brookside Resort 463 East Pkwy — Gatlinburg TN 37738 — 865-436-5611 — 436-0039
TF: 800-251-9597 ■ *Web:* www.brooksideresort.com

Fairfield Glade Resort 109 Fairfield Blvd PO Box 1500 — Fairfield Glade TN 38558 — 931-484-7521 — 484-3788
Web: www.fairfieldresorts.com/ffr/resort/details.do

Texas

Phone / Fax

Bahia Mar Resort & Conference Center
6300 Padre Blvd — South Padre Island TX 78597 — 956-761-1343 — 761-6287
TF: 800-997-2373 ■ *Web:* www.bahiamar.com

Barton Creek Conference Resort 8212 Barton Club Dr — Austin TX 78735 — 512-329-4000 — 329-4597
TF: 800-336-6158 ■ *Web:* www.bartoncreek.com

Benchmark Hospitality International
2170 Buckthorne Pl Suite 400 — The Woodlands TX 77380 — 281-367-5757 — 367-1407
Web: www.benchmark-hospitality.com

Columbia Lakes Resort & Conference Center
180 Freeman Blvd — West Columbia TX 77486 — 979-345-5151 — 345-3049
TF: 800-231-1030 ■ *Web:* www.columbia-lakes.com

Four Seasons Resort & Club Dallas at Las Colinas
4150 N MacArthur Blvd — Irving TX 75038 — 972-717-0700 — 717-2550
TF: 800-332-3442 ■ *Web:* www.fourseasons.com/dallas

Hilton Galveston Island Resort 5400 Seawall Blvd — Galveston TX 77551 — 409-744-5000 — 740-2209
TF: 800-475-3386 ■ *Web:* www.hilton.com

Holiday Inn SunSpree Resort South Padre Island
100 Padre Blvd — South Padre Island TX 78597 — 956-761-5401 — 761-1560
TF: 800-531-7405 ■ *Web:* www.ichotelsgroup.com/h/d/hi/home

Houstonian Hotel Club & Spa 111 N Post Oak Ln — Houston TX 77024 — 713-680-2626 — 680-2992
TF: 800-231-2759 ■ *Web:* www.houstonian.com

Inn of the Hills River Resort 1001 Junction Hwy — Kerrville TX 78028 — 830-895-5000 — 895-6020
TF: 800-292-5690 ■ *Web:* www.innofthehills.com

Lakeway Inn & Resort 101 Lakeway Dr — Austin TX 78734 — 512-261-6600 — 261-7311
TF: 800-525-3929 ■ *Web:* lakeway.dolce.com

Quorum Hotels & Resorts 12770 Merit Dr Suite 700 — Dallas TX 75251 — 972-458-7265 — 991-5647
Web: www.quorumhotels.com

Radisson Resort South Padre Island 500 Padre Blvd — South Padre Island TX 78597 — 956-761-6511 — 761-1602
TF: 800-333-3333 ■ *Web:* www.radisson.com/southpadretx

Rancho Viejo Resort & Country Club 1 Rancho Viejo Dr — Rancho Viejo TX 78575 — 956-350-4000 — 350-5696
TF: 800-531-7400 ■ *Web:* www.playrancho.com

Rosewood Hotels & Resorts 500 Crescent Ct Suite 300 — Dallas TX 75201 — 214-880-4200 — 880-4201
TF: 888-767-3966 ■ *Web:* www.rosewoodhotels.com

San Luis Resort Spa & Conference Center
5222 Seawall Blvd — Galveston Island TX 77551 — 409-744-1500 — 744-8452
TF: 800-445-0090 ■ *Web:* www.sanluisresort.com

South Shore Harbour Resort & Conference Center
2500 S Shore Blvd — League City TX 77573 — 281-334-1000 — 334-1157
TF: 800-442-5005 ■ *Web:* www.sshr.com

Tanglewood Resort Hotel & Conference Center
290 Tanglewood Cir — Pottsboro TX 75076 — 903-786-2968 — 786-2128
TF: 800-833-6569 ■ *Web:* www.tanglewoodresort.com

Tapatio Springs Golf Resort & Conference Center PO Box 550 — Boerne TX 78006 — 830-537-4611 — 537-4962
TF: 800-999-3299 ■ *Web:* www.tapatio.com

Waterwood National Resort 1 Waterwood Pkwy — Huntsville TX 77320 — 936-891-5211 — 891-5011
TF: 877-441-5211 ■ *Web:* www.waterwoodnational.com

Woodlands Resort & Conference Center
2301 N Millbend Dr — The Woodlands TX 77380 — 281-367-1100 — 364-6275
TF: 800-433-2624 ■ *Web:* www.woodlandsresort.com

Utah

Phone / Fax

Alta Lodge PO Box 8040 — Alta UT 84092 — 801-742-3500 — 742-3504
TF: 800-707-2582 ■ *Web:* www.altalodge.com

American Skiing Co 136 Heber Ave Suite 303 — Park City UT 84060 — 435-615-0340
Web: www.peaks.com

Brighton Ski Resort 12601 E Big Cottonwood Canyon — Brighton UT 84121 — 801-532-4731 — 649-1787*
*Fax Area Code: 435 ■ *TF:* 800-873-5512 ■ *Web:* www.brightonresort.com

Canyons Resort 4000 The Canyons Resort Dr — Park City UT 84098 — 435-649-5400 — 649-7374
TF: 888-226-9667 ■ *Web:* www.thecanyons.com

Deer Valley Lodging 1375 Deer Valley Dr S — Park City UT 84060 — 435-649-4040 — 645-8419
TF: 888-976-2732 ■ *Web:* www.deervalleylodging.com

Green Valley Resort 1871 W Canyon View Dr — Saint George UT 84770 — 435-628-8060 — 673-4084
TF: 800-237-1068 ■ *Web:* www.gvresort.com

Homestead The 700 N Homestead Dr — Midway UT 84049 — 435-654-1102 — 654-5087
TF: 800-327-7220 ■ *Web:* homesteadresort.com

Inn on the Creek 375 Rainbow Lane PO Box 1000 — Midway UT 84049 — 435-654-0892 — 654-5871
TF: 800-654-0892 ■ *Web:* www.innoncreek.com

Little America Hotels & Resorts 500 S Main St — Salt Lake City UT 84101 — 801-363-6781 — 596-5911
TF Resv: 800-453-9450 ■ *Web:* www.littleamerica.com

Park City Mountain Resort 1310 Lowell Ave PO Box 39 — Park City UT 84060 — 435-649-8111 — 647-5374
TF: 800-222-7275 ■ *Web:* www.parkcitymountain.com

Premier Resorts International
PO Box 4800 1375 Deer Valley Dr S — Park City UT 84060 — 435-655-4800 — 655-4848
TF: 888-774-3533 ■ *Web:* www.premier-resorts.com

Rustler Lodge 10380 E Hwy 210 PO Box 8030 — Alta UT 84092 — 801-742-2200 — 742-3832
TF: 888-532-2582 ■ *Web:* www.rustlerlodge.com

Snowbasin Ski Resort 3925 E Snowbasin Rd — Huntsville UT 84317 — 801-399-1135 — 620-1314
TF: 888-437-5488 ■ *Web:* www.snowbasin.com

Snowbird Ski & Summer Resort Hwy 210 PO Box 929000 — Snowbird UT 84092 — 801-742-2222 — 947-8227
TF: 800-453-3000 ■ *Web:* www.snowbird.com

Solitude Mountain Ski Resort 12000 Big Cottonwood Canyon — Solitude UT 84121 — 801-534-1400 — 517-7705
TF: 800-748-4754 ■ *Web:* www.skisolitude.com

Stein Eriksen Lodge 7700 Stein Way — Park City UT 84060 — 435-649-3700 — 649-5825
TF: 800-453-1302 ■ *Web:* www.steinlodge.com

Sundance Ski Resort North Fork Provo Canyon — Provo UT 84604 — 801-225-4107 — 226-1937
TF: 800-892-1600 ■ *Web:* www.sundanceresort.com

Vermont

Phone / Fax

Ascutney Mountain Resort 485 Hotel Rd PO Box 699 — Brownsville VT 05037 — 802-484-7711 — 484-3117
TF: 800-243-0011 ■ *Web:* www.ascutney.com

Basin Harbor Club 4800 Basin Harbor Rd — Vergennes VT 05491 — 802-475-2311 — 475-6545
TF: 800-622-4000 ■ *Web:* www.basinharbor.com

Equinox The 3567 Main St — Manchester Village VT 05254 — 802-362-4700 — 362-4868
TF: 800-362-4747 ■ *Web:* www.equinoxresort.com

Hawk Inn & Mountain Resort HCR 70 Box 64 — Plymouth VT 05056 — 802-672-3811 — 672-5585
TF: 800-685-4295 ■ *Web:* www.hawkresort.com

Inn at Stratton Mountain 61 Middle Ridge Rd — Stratton Mountain VT 05155 — 802-297-2500 — 297-1778
TF: 800-777-1700 ■ *Web:* www.strattonmountain.com

Jay Peak Ski & Summer Resort 4850 Rt 242 — Jay VT 05859 — 802-988-2611 — 988-4049
TF: 800-451-4449 ■ *Web:* www.jaypeakresort.com

Killington Resort & Pico Mountain 4763 Killington Rd — Killington VT 05751 — 802-422-6200 — 422-6113
TF: 800-621-6867 ■ *Web:* www.killington.com

Lake Morey Resort Club House Ln PO Box 48 — Fairlee VT 05045 — 802-333-4311 — 333-4553
TF: 800-423-1211 ■ *Web:* www.lakemoreyresort.com

Mount Snow Resort Rt 100 — West Dover VT 05356 — 802-464-3333 — 464-4141
TF: 800-451-4211 ■ *Web:* www.mountsnow.com

Smugglers' Notch Resort 4323 Vermont Rt 108 S — Jeffersonville VT 05464 — 802-644-8851 — 644-1230
TF: 800-451-8752 ■ *Web:* www.smuggs.com

Stowe Mountain Resort 5781 Mountain Rd — Stowe VT 05672 — 802-253-3000 — 253-3406
TF: 800-253-4754 ■ *Web:* www.stowe.com

Stoweflake Mountain Resort & Spa
1746 Mountain Rd PO Box 369 — Stowe VT 05672 — 802-253-7355 — 253-6858
TF: 800-253-2232 ■ *Web:* www.stoweflake.com

Sugarbush Resort & Inn 1840 Sugarbush Access Rd — Warren VT 05674 — 802-583-6300 — 583-6390
TF: 800-537-8427 ■ *Web:* www.sugarbush.com

Topnotch at Stowe Resort & Spa 4000 Mountain Rd — Stowe VT 05672 — 802-253-8585 — 253-9263
TF: 800-451-8686 ■ *Web:* www.topnotch-resort.com

Trapp Family Lodge 700 Trapp Hill Rd PO Box 1428 — Stowe VT 05672 — 802-253-8511 — 253-5740
TF: 800-826-7000 ■ *Web:* www.trappfamily.com

Tyler Place Family Resort
175 Old Dock Rd PO Box 254 — Highgate Springs VT 05460 — 802-868-4000 — 868-5621
Web: www.tylerplace.com

Woodstock Inn & Resort 14 The Green — Woodstock VT 05091 — 802-457-1100 — 457-6699
TF: 800-448-7900 ■ *Web:* www.woodstockinn.com

Virginia

Phone / Fax

Alamar Resort Inn 311 16th St — Virginia Beach VA 23451 — 757-823-4056 — 428-4857
TF: 800-346-5681 ■ *Web:* www.va-beach.com/alamarresort

Boar's Head Inn 200 Ednam Dr — Charlottesville VA 22903 — 434-296-2181 — 972-6024
TF: 800-476-1988 ■ *Web:* www.boarsheadinn.com

Breakers Resort Inn 1503 Atlantic Ave — Virginia Beach VA 23451 — 757-428-1821 — 422-9602
TF: 800-237-7532 ■ *Web:* www.breakersresort.com

Cavalier Hotel 4201 Atlantic Ave — Virginia Beach VA 23451 — 757-425-8555 — 425-0629
TF: 800-446-8199 ■ *Web:* www.cavalierhotel.com

Crestline Hotels & Resorts 8405 Greensboro Dr Suite 500 — McLean VA 22102 — 571-382-1800 — 382-1860
Web: www.crestlinehotels.com

Great Wolf Lodge Williamsburg 549 E Rochambeau Dr — Williamsburg VA 23188 — 757-229-9700 — 229-9780
TF: 800-551-9653 ■ *Web:* williamsburg.greatwolflodge.com

Holiday Inn SunSpree Resort Virginia Beach
3900 Atlantic Ave — Virginia Beach VA 23451 — 757-428-1711 — 425-7872
TF: 800-942-3224 ■ *Web:* www.ichotelsgroup.com/h/d/hi/home

Homestead The 7696 Sam Snead Hwy PO Box 2000 — Hot Springs VA 24445 — 540-839-1766 — 839-7656
TF: 800-838-1766 ■ *Web:* www.thehomestead.com

Interstate Hotels & Resorts Inc 4501 N Fairfax Dr — Arlington VA 22033 — 703-387-3100 — 387-3101
NYSE: IHR ■ *Web:* www.ihrco.com

Kingsmill Resort & Spa 1010 Kingsmill Rd — Williamsburg VA 23185 — 757-253-1703 — 253-8246
TF: 800-832-5665 ■ *Web:* www.kingsmill.com

Lansdowne Resort 44050 Woodridge Pkwy — Leesburg VA 20176 — 703-729-8400 — 729-4096
TF: 800-541-4801 ■ *Web:* www.lansdowneresort.com

Massanutten Resort 1822 Resort Dr — McGaheysville VA 22840 — 540-289-9441 — 289-6981
Web: www.massresort.com

Shenvalee Golf Resort 9660 Fairway Dr PO Box 930 — New Market VA 22844 — 540-740-3181 — 740-8931
TF: 888-339-3181 ■ *Web:* www.shenvalee.com

Tides Resort 480 King Carter Dr — Irvington VA 22480 — 804-438-5000 — 438-5222
TF: 800-843-3746 ■ *Web:* www.the-tides.com

Turtle Cay Resort 600 Atlantic Ave — Virginia Beach VA 23451 — 757-437-5565 — 437-9104
TF: 888-989-7788 ■ *Web:* www.turtlecayresort.com

Virginia Beach Resort Hotel & Conference Center
2800 Shore Dr — Virginia Beach VA 23451 — 757-481-9000 — 496-7429
TF: 800-468-2722 ■ *Web:* www.virginiabeachresort.com

Virginia Crossings Resort 1000 Virginia Center Pkwy — Glen Allen VA 23059 — 804-262-1010 — 262-2332
TF: 888-444-6553 ■ *Web:* www.virginiacrossingsresort.com

Williamsburg Inn 136 E Francis St — Williamsburg VA 23185 — 757-229-1000 — 220-7096
TF: 800-447-8679 ■ *Web:* www.colonialwilliamsburg.com

Washington

Phone / Fax

Alderbrook Resort & Spa 7101 E SR-106 — Union WA 98592 — 360-898-2200 — 898-4610
TF: 800-622-9370 ■ *Web:* www.alderbrookresort.com

Campbell's Resort PO Box 278 — Chelan WA 98816 — 509-682-2561 — 682-2177
TF: 800-553-8225 ■ *Web:* www.campbellsresort.com

Carson Hot Mineral Springs Resort 372 St Martin Rd — Carson WA 98610 — 509-427-8292 — 427-7242
TF: 800-607-3678 ■ *Web:* www.carsonhotspringsresort.com

Coast Hotels & Resorts USA 2003 Western Ave Suite 500 — Seattle WA 98121 — 206-826-2700 — 826-2701
Web: www.coasthotels.com

Desert Canyon Golf Resort 1201 Desert Canyon Blvd — Orondo WA 98843 — 509-784-1111 — 784-2701
TF: 800-258-4173 ■ *Web:* www.desertcanyon.com

Freestone Inn at Wilson Ranch 31 Early Winters Dr — Mazama WA 98833 — 509-996-3906 — 996-3907
TF: 800-639-3809 ■ *Web:* www.freestoneinn.com

Lake Quinault Lodge 345 S Shore Rd PO Box 7 — Quinault WA 98575 — 360-288-2900 — 288-2901
TF: 800-562-6672 ■ *Web:* www.visitlakequinault.com

Little Creek Casino Resort W 91 Hwy 108 — Shelton WA 98584 — 360-427-7711 — 427-7868
TF: 800-667-7711 ■ *Web:* www.little-creek.com

Polynesian Resort The 615 Ocean Shores Blvd NW — Ocean Shores WA 98569 — 360-289-3361 — 289-0294
TF: 800-562-4836 ■ *Web:* www.thepolynesian.com

Resort at Deer Harbor 31 Jack & Jill Ln PO Box 200 — Deer Harbor WA 98243 — 360-376-4420 — 376-5523
TF: 888-376-4480 ■ *Web:* www.deerharbor.com

Resort Semiahmoo 9565 Semiahmoo Pkwy — Blaine WA 98230 — 360-318-2000 — 318-2087
TF: 800-770-7992 ■ *Web:* www.semiahmoo.com

Rosario Resort & Spa 1400 Rosario Rd — Eastsound WA 98245 — 360-376-2222 — 376-2289
TF: 800-562-8820 ■ *Web:* www.rosarioresort.com

Salish Lodge & Spa 6501 Railroad Ave DE PO Box 1109 — Snoqualmie WA 98065 — 425-888-2556 — 888-2533
TF: 800-826-6124 ■ *Web:* www.salishlodge.com

Sun Mountain Lodge 604 Patterson Lake Rd PO Box 1000 — Winthrop WA 98862 — 509-996-2211 — 996-3133
TF: 800-572-0493 ■ *Web:* www.sunmountainlodge.com

West Virginia

Phone / Fax

Canaan Valley Resort & Conference Center HC 70 Box 330 — Davis WV 26260 — 304-866-4121 — 866-2172
TF: 800-622-4121 ■ *Web:* www.canaanresort.com

	City	State	Zip	Phone	Fax
Coolfont Resort 3621 Cold Run Valley Rd *TF:* 800-888-8768 ■ *Web:* www.coolfont.com	Berkeley Springs	WV	25411	304-258-4500	258-5499
Glade Springs Resort 255 Resort Dr. *TF:* 800-634-5233 ■ *Web:* www.gladesprings.com	Daniels	WV	25832	304-763-2000	763-3398
Greenbrier The 300 W Main St. *TF:* 800-453-4858 ■ *Web:* www.greenbrier.com	White Sulphur Springs	WV	24986	304-536-1110	536-7854
Lakeview Scanticon Resort & Conference Center 1 Lakeview Dr *TF:* 800-624-8300 ■ *Web:* www.lakeviewresort.com	Morgantown	WV	26508	304-594-1111	594-9472
Oglebay Resort & Conference Center Rt 88 N Oglebay Park *TF:* 800-624-6988 ■ *Web:* www.oglebay-resort.com	Wheeling	WV	26003	304-243-4000	243-4070
Pipestem Resort State Park PO Box 150 *Web:* www.pipestemresort.com	Pipestem	WV	25979	304-466-1800	466-2803
Snowshoe Mountain Resort 10 Snowshoe Dr *TF:* 877-441-4386 ■ *Web:* www.snowshoemtn.com	Snowshoe	WV	26209	304-572-1000	572-5407
Stonewall Resort 940 Resort Dr. *TF:* 888-278-8150 ■ *Web:* www.stonewallresort.com	Roanoke	WV	26447	304-269-7400	269-8818
Woods Resort & Conference Center Mountain Lake Rd PO Box 5 *TF:* 800-248-2222 ■ *Web:* www.thewoodsresort.com	Hedgesville	WV	25427	304-754-7977	754-8146

Wisconsin

	City	State	Zip	Phone	Fax
Abbey Resort & Fontana Spa 269 Fontana Blvd *TF:* 800-558-2405 ■ *Web:* www.theabbeyresort.com	Fontana	WI	53125	262-275-6811	275-3264
Alpine Resort 7715 Alpine Rd. *Web:* www.alpineresort.com	Egg Harbor	WI	54209	920-868-3000	868-2576
American Club The 419 Highland Dr *TF:* 800-344-2838 ■ *Web:* www.destinationkohler.com	Kohler	WI	53044	920-457-8000	457-0299
Chanticleer Inn 1458 E Dollar Lake Rd *TF:* 800-752-9193 ■ *Web:* www.chanticleerinn.com	Eagle River	WI	54521	715-479-4486	479-0004
Chula Vista Theme Resort 25011 N River Rd *TF:* 800-388-4782 ■ *Web:* www.chulavistaresort.com	Wisconsin Dells	WI	53965	608-254-8366	254-7653
Devil's Head Resort & Convention Center S6330 Bluff Rd *TF:* 800-472-6670 ■ *Web:* www.devilsheadresort.com	Merrimac	WI	53561	608-493-2251	493-2176
Fox Hills Resort & Convention Center 250 W Church St *TF:* 800-950-7615 ■ *Web:* www.fox-hills.com	Mishicot	WI	54228	920-755-2376	755-2186
Grand Geneva Resort & Spa 7036 Grand Geneva Way *TF:* 800-558-3417 ■ *Web:* www.grandgeneva.com	Lake Geneva	WI	53147	262-248-8811	249-4587
Great Wolf Resorts Inc 122 W Washington Ave *NASDAQ: WOLF* ■ *Web:* www.greatwolfresorts.com	Madison	WI	53703	608-251-6400	661-4701
Heidel House Resort 643 Illinois Ave *TF:* 800-444-2812 ■ *Web:* www.heidelhouse.com	Green Lake	WI	54941	920-294-3344	294-6128
Holiday Acres Resort & Conference Center 4060 S Shore Dr PO Box 460 *TF:* 800-261-1500 ■ *Web:* www.holidayacres.com	Rhinelander	WI	54501	715-369-1500	369-3665
Inn on Woodlake 705 Woodlake Rd *TF:* 800-919-3600	Kohler	WI	53044	920-452-7800	452-6288
Lake Lawn Resort 2400 E Geneva St *TF:* 800-338-5253 ■ *Web:* www.lakelawnresort.com	Delavan	WI	53115	262-728-7950	728-2347
Landmark Resort 7643 Hillside Rd *TF:* 800-273-7877 ■ *Web:* www.thelandmarkresort.com	Egg Harbor	WI	54209	920-868-3205	868-2569
Marcus Hotels & Resorts 100 E Wisconsin Ave Suite 1900 *Web:* www.marcusresorts.com	Milwaukee	WI	53202	414-905-1200	905-2250
Maxwelton Braes Golf Resort 7670 Hwy 57 *Web:* www.maxwelton-braes.com	Baileys Harbor	WI	54202	920-839-2321	839-2729
Olympia Resort & Spa 1350 Royale Mile Rd *TF:* 800-558-9573 ■ *Web:* www.olympiaresort.com	Oconomowoc	WI	53066	262-567-0311	369-4998
Osthoff Resort 101 Osthoff Ave *TF:* 800-876-3399 ■ *Web:* www.osthoff.com	Elkhart Lake	WI	53020	920-876-3366	876-3228
Tundra Lodge Resort & Waterpark 865 Lombardi Ave *TF:* 877-886-3725 ■ *Web:* www.tundralodge.com	Green Bay	WI	54304	920-405-8700	405-1997

Wyoming

	City	State	Zip	Phone	Fax
Amangani Resort 1535 NE Butte Rd *TF:* 877-734-7333 ■ *Web:* www.amanresorts.com	Jackson	WY	83001	307-734-7333	734-7332
Cowboy Village Resort at Togwotee 27655 Hwy 26 & 287 PO Box 91 *TF:* 800-543-2847 ■ *Web:* www.cowboyvillage.com	Moran	WY	83013	307-543-2847	543-2391
Four Seasons Resort Jackson Hole 7680 Granite Loop Rd PO Box 544 *Web:* www.fourseasons.com/jacksonhole	Teton Village	WY	83025	307-732-5000	732-5001
Grand Targhee Resort 3300 E Ski Hill Rd *TF:* 800-827-4433 ■ *Web:* www.grandtarghee.com	Alta	WY	83414	307-353-2300	353-8619
Grand Teton Lodge Co PO Box 240 *TF:* 800-628-9988 ■ *Web:* www.gtlc.com	Moran	WY	83013	307-543-3100	543-3046
Jackson Hole Mountain Resort PO Box 290 *TF:* 888-333-7766 ■ *Web:* www.jacksonhole.com	Teton Village	WY	83025	307-733-2292	733-2660
Jackson Hole Racquet Club Resort 3535 Moose-Wilson Rd. *TF:* 800-443-8613 ■ *Web:* www.jhrl.com	Wilson	WY	83014	307-733-3990	733-5551
Jackson Lake Lodge PO Box 250 *TF:* 800-628-9988 ■ *Web:* www.gtlc.com/lodgeJac.htm	Moran	WY	83013	307-543-2811	543-3143
Jenny Lake Lodge PO Box 250 *TF:* 800-628-9988 ■ *Web:* www.gtlc.com/lodgeJen.htm	Moran	WY	83013	307-733-4647	543-3358
Rusty Parrot Lodge & Spa PO Box 1657 *TF:* 800-458-2004 ■ *Web:* www.rustyparrot.com	Jackson	WY	83001	307-733-2000	733-5566
Signal Mountain Lodge PO Box 50 *Web:* www.signalmtnlodge.com	Moran	WY	83013	307-543-2831	543-2569
Snake River Lodge & Spa 7710 Granite Loop Rd *TF:* 800-445-4655 ■ *Web:* snakeriverlodge.rockresorts.com	Teton Village	WY	83025	307-733-3657	732-6009
Snow King Resort 400 E Snow King Ave PO Box SKI *TF:* 800-522-5464 ■ *Web:* www.snowking.com	Jackson	WY	83001	307-733-5200	733-4086
Teton Pines Resort & Country Club 3450 N Clubhouse Dr *TF:* 800-238-2223 ■ *Web:* www.tetonpines.com	Wilson	WY	83014	307-733-1005	733-2860

673 RESTAURANT COMPANIES

SEE ALSO Bakeries p. 1367; Food Service p. 1664; Franchises p. 1672; Ice Cream & Dairy Stores p. 1851

	City	State	Zip	Phone	Fax
4B's Corp 3495 W Broadway *Web:* www.4-bs.com	Missoula	MT	59807	406-543-8265	
5 & Diner Franchise Corp 1140 E Greenway St Suite 1 *Web:* www.5anddiner.com	Mesa	AZ	85203	480-962-7104	962-0159
94th Aero Squadron Restaurants 8191 E Kaiser Blvd *Web:* www.specialtyrestaurants.com	Anaheim	CA	92808	714-279-6100	998-4962
A & W Restaurants Inc 1441 Gardiner Ln *Web:* www.awrestaurants.com	Louisville	KY	40213	502-874-8300	874-3183
Abuelo's Mexican Food Embassy 2575 S Loop 289 *Web:* www.abuelos.com	Lubbock	TX	79423	806-785-8686	785-8866
Acapulco Restaurants Inc 4001 Via Oro Ave Suite 200 *TF:* 800-735-3501 ■ *Web:* www.acapulcorestaurants.com	Long Beach	CA	90810	310-513-7500	522-4350
AFC Enterprises Inc 5555 Glenridge Connector NE Suite 300 *NASDAQ: AFCE* ■ *TF:* 866-232-4401 ■ *Web:* www.afc-online.com	Atlanta	GA	30342	404-459-4450	459-4533
AJS Assoc 1003 Jordan Ln *TF:* 800-227-0340 ■ *Web:* www.ajskfc.com	Huntsville	AL	35816	256-830-2423	830-2882
Al Copeland Investments 1405 Airline Hwy *TF:* 800-401-0401 ■ *Web:* www.alcopeland.com	Metairie	LA	70001	504-830-1000	832-8918
Ale House Management Inc 612 N Orange Ave Suite C-6 *TF:* 866-743-2299 ■ *Web:* www.alehouseinc.com	Jupiter	FL	33458	561-743-2299	743-7210
Aloha Restaurants Inc 17320 Redhill Ave Suite 190	Irvine	CA	92614	949-250-0331	250-5735
American Cafe 150 W Church Ave *TF:* 800-325-0755 ■ *Web:* www.americancafe.com	Maryville	TN	37801	865-379-5700	379-6830
American Hospitality LLC 226 Bailey Ave Suite 101	Fort Worth	TX	76107	817-332-4761	877-0420
American Restaurant Group Inc 4410 El Camino Real Suite 201	Los Altos	CA	94022	650-949-6400	917-9207
American Restaurant Partners LP 3020 N Cypress Rd Suite 100	Wichita	KS	67226	316-634-1190	634-1662
Anthony's Seafood Group 5232 Lovelock St. *Web:* www.gofishanthonys.com	San Diego	CA	92110	619-291-7254	298-1212
Applebee's International Inc 4551 W 107th St *NASDAQ: APPB* ■ *Web:* www.applebees.com	Overland Park	KS	66207	913-967-4000	341-1694
Arby's Restaurant Group Inc 1155 Perimeter Center W. *TF:* 800-487-2729 ■ *Web:* www.arbys.com	Atlanta	GA	30338	678-514-4100	
Arctic Circle Restaurants Inc 411 W 7200 South Suite 200 *Web:* www.arcticcirclerest.com	Midvale	UT	84047	801-561-3620	561-9646
Ark Restaurants Corp 85 5th Ave 14th Fl. *NASDAQ: ARKR* ■ *Web:* www.arkrestaurants.com	New York	NY	10003	212-206-8800	206-8845
Aunt Sarah's LLC 9010 Brook Rd	Glen Allen	VA	23060	804-264-9189	266-1255
Aunt Sarah's Pancake House 9010 Brooks Rd	Glen Allen	VA	23060	804-264-9189	266-1255
Aurelio's Pizza 18162 Harwood Ave *Web:* www.aureliospizza.com	Homewood	IL	60430	708-798-8050	798-6692
Austin Grills Inc 2404 Wisconsin Ave NW *Web:* www.austingrill.com	Washington	DC	20007	202-337-8080	338-5598
Avado Brands Inc 150 Hancock St *TF:* 800-609-1255 ■ *Web:* www.avado.com	Madison	GA	30650	706-342-4552	342-4057
Azteca Mexican Restaurants 133 SW 158th St. *Web:* www.aztecamex.com	Seattle	WA	98166	206-243-7021	246-0429
BAB Inc 500 Lake Cook Rd Suite 475 **Fax Area Code: 847* ■ *TF:* 800-251-6101 ■ *Web:* www.babcorp.com	Deerfield	IL	60015	800-251-6101	405-8140*
Back Bay Restaurant Group Inc 284 Newberry St. *TF:* 800-367-2424 ■ *Web:* www.bbrginc.com	Boston	MA	02115	617-536-2800	236-4175
Back Yard Burgers Inc 1657 Shelby Oaks Dr N Suite 105 *NASDAQ: BYBI* ■ *TF:* 800-292-6939 ■ *Web:* www.backyardburgers.com	Memphis	TN	38134	901-367-0888	367-0999
Bahama Breeze 5900 Lake Ellenor Dr. *TF:* 866-475-5666 ■ *Web:* www.bahamabreeze.com	Orlando	FL	32809	407-245-4000	245-5189
Bailey's Sports Grill 1551 N Waterfront Pkwy Suite 310 *TF:* 800-229-2118	Wichita	KS	67206	316-634-0505	634-6060
Baja Fresh Mexican Grill 100 Moody Ct Suite 200 *TF:* 800-932-5309 ■ *Web:* www.bajafresh.com	Thousand Oaks	CA	91360	805-495-4704	374-1144
Baker's Burgers Inc 1875 Business Ctr Dr. *Web:* www.bakersdrivethru.com	San Bernardino	CA	92408	909-884-7241	885-4059
Bakers Square Restaurants Inc 400 W 48th Ave. **Fax:* Cust Svc ■ *TF:* 800-800-3644 ■ *Web:* www.vicorpinc.com	Denver	CO	80216	303-296-2121	672-2676*
Bandido's Inc 6060 E State Blvd.	Fort Wayne	IN	46815	260-493-0607	493-0806
Barbato's Italian Restaurants 3512 Buffalo Rd *Web:* www.barbatos.com	Erie	PA	16510	814-899-3423	899-5293
Barnhill's Buffet Inc 226 Palafox Pl 5th Fl. *TF:* 888-738-3808 ■ *Web:* www.barnhills.com	Pensacola	FL	32502	850-435-9914	435-9229
Battleground Restaurant Group Inc (BRG) PO Box 10398 *Web:* www.brginc.com	Greensboro	NC	27404	336-272-9355	272-5568
Beef O'Bradys Inc 5510 W LaSalle St Suite 200 *TF:* 800-728-8878 ■ *Web:* www.beefobradys.com	Tampa	FL	33607	813-226-2333	226-0030
Bellacino's Corp 10096 Shaver Rd. *TF:* 877-379-0700 ■ *Web:* www.bellacinos.com	Portage	MI	49024	269-329-0782	329-0930
Benihana Inc 8685 NW 53rd Terr Suite 201 *NASDAQ: BNHN* ■ *TF:* 800-327-3369 ■ *Web:* www.benihana.com	Miami	FL	33166	305-593-0770	592-6371
Bennett's Bar-B-Que Inc 12503 E Euclid Dr Suite 80 *Web:* www.bennettsbbq.com	Centennial	CO	80111	303-792-3088	792-5801
Bennigan's 6500 International Pkwy Suite 1000 **Fax:* Cust Svc ■ *TF:* 800-727-8355 ■ *Web:* www.bennigans.com	Plano	TX	75093	972-588-5000	588-5280*
Bertolini's 350 N LaSalle Suite 500 *TF:* 800-486-4791 ■ *Web:* www.mortons.com/berto	Chicago	IL	60610	312-923-0030	923-0090
Bertucci's Restaurant Corp 155 Otis St. *Web:* www.bertuccis.com	Northborough	MA	01532	508-351-2500	393-1231
Beverly Hills Cafe Inc 18500 NE 5th Ave.	North Miami Beach	FL	33179	305-652-7008	652-7017
BF Nashville 1101 Kermit Dr Suite 310	Nashville	TN	37217	615-399-9700	399-3373
Biaggi's Ristorante Italiano 1705 Clearwater Ave *Web:* www.biaggis.com	Bloomington	IL	61704	309-664-2148	664-2149
Bice Restaurant 551 Madison AVe Suite 1601 *Web:* www.bicenewyork.com	New York	NY	10022	212-593-0665	593-0671
Bickford's Family Restaurants Inc 1330 Soldiers Field Rd *TF:* 800-969-5653 ■ *Web:* www.bickfordsrestaurants.com	Boston	MA	02135	617-782-4010	783-2554
Big Bowl 6820 LBJ Fwy. *TF:* 800-983-4637 ■ *Web:* www.bigbowl.com	Dallas	TX	75240	972-980-9917	770-9593
Big Boy Restaurants International LLC 4199 Marcy St. **Fax:* Cust Svc ■ *TF:* 800-837-3003 ■ *Web:* www.bigboy.com	Warren	MI	48091	586-759-6000	755-8531*
Big Boy Restaurants International LLC 4199 Marcy St. **Fax:* Cust Svc ■ *TF:* 800-837-3003 ■ *Web:* www.bigboy.com	Warren	MI	48091	586-759-6000	755-8531*
Big Buck Brewery & Steakhouse Inc 550 S Wisconsin Ave *Web:* www.bigbuck.com	Gaylord	MI	49735	989-731-0401	731-2788
Big Town Hero Franchising Corp 912 SW 3rd Ave *Web:* www.bth.com	Portland	OR	97204	503-228-4376	228-4376
Bill Miller Bar-B-Q 430 S Santa Rosa St **Fax:* Sales ■ *TF:* 800-339-3111 ■ *Web:* www.kcmrestaurants.com	San Antonio	TX	78207	210-225-4461	302-1533*
Bill Thomas' Halo Burger Inc 800 S Saginaw St.	Flint	MI	48502	810-238-1839	238-7358
Bishop's Buffet 1520 Midland Ct NE Suite 300 *TF:* 866-393-4766	Cedar Rapids	IA	52402	319-393-4766	393-4866
BJ's Restaurants Inc 16162 Beach Blvd Suite 100 *NASDAQ: BJRI* ■ *TF:* 800-223-1255 ■ *Web:* www.bjsbrewhouse.com	Huntington Beach	CA	92647	714-848-3747	848-5587
Black-Eyed Pea Restaurants 1210 Briarville Rd	Madison	TN	37115	615-277-1234	277-1220
Blake's Lotaburger LLC 3205 Richmond Dr NE PO Box 3648 *Web:* www.lotaburger.com	Albuquerque	NM	87190	505-884-2160	884-2164
Blimpie International Inc 7730 E Greenway Rd Suite 104 *TF:* 800-447-6258 ■ *Web:* www.blimpie.com	Scottsdale	AZ	85260	480-443-0200	443-1972
Bob Evans Farms Inc 3776 S High St *NASDAQ: BOBE* ■ **Fax:* Hum Res ■ *TF:* 800-272-7675 ■ *Web:* www.bobevans.com	Columbus	OH	43207	614-491-2225	497-4318*
Bobby Cox Cos Inc 4055 International Plaza Suite 450 *TF:* 800-897-8723 ■ *Web:* www.bobbycox.com	Fort Worth	TX	76109	817-377-6200	377-6201
Bobby McGee's Conglomeration 8501 N 27th Ave *Web:* www.bobbymcgees.com	Phoenix	AZ	85051	602-995-5982	995-7547
Bobby Rubino's Place for Ribs 1990 E Sunrise Blvd.	Fort Lauderdale	FL	33304	954-763-1478	

Phone | Fax

Boddie-Noell Enterprises Inc 1021 Noell Ln Rocky Mount NC 27804 252-937-2800 937-6991
Web: www.bneinc.com

Bojangles' Restaurants Inc 9432 Southern Pine Blvd Charlotte NC 28273 704-527-2675 523-6676
TF: 800-366-9921 ■ *Web:* www.bojangles.com

Bonanza Restaurants 6500 International Pkwy Suite 1000 Plano TX 75093 972-588-5000 588-5325*
*Fax: Cust Svc ■ *TF:* 800-727-8355 ■ *Web:* www.bonanzarestaurants.com

Bonefish Grill 2202 N West Shore Blvd Tampa FL 33607 813-282-1225 282-1209
TF: 866-880-2226 ■ *Web:* www.bonefishgrill.com

Bongos Cuban Cafe 420 Jefferson Ave Miami Beach FL 33139 305-534-4330 534-5220
Web: www.bongoscubancafe.com

Bono's Pit Bar-B-Q 10645 Phillips Hwy Bldg 200 Jacksonville FL 32256 904-880-8310 880-8373
Web: www.bonosbarbq.com

Boomerang Grille 1800 N Interstate Dr Suite 200 Norman OK 73072 405-321-2600 321-2992

Boston Beanery Restaurants Inc 2931-B University Ave Morgantown WV 26505 304-598-8828 598-7201
Web: www.bostonbeanery.com

Boston Market Corp 14103 Denver West Pkwy Golden CO 80401 303-278-9500 216-5335
TF: 800-877-2870 ■ *Web:* www.bostonmarket.com

Boston Pizza International Inc 5500 Parkwood Way Richmond BC V6V2M4 604-270-1108 270-4168
Web: www.bostonpizza.com

Boston Pizza Restaurants LP 1501 LBJ Fwy Suite 450 Dallas TX 75234 972-484-9022 484-7630
Web: www.bostonsgourmet.com

Boston Restaurant Assoc Inc 6 Kimball Ln Suite 210 Lynnfield MA 01940 781-231-7575 231-5225
Web: www.pizzeriaregina.com

Boulder Creek Steakhouse 1701 Sunrise Hwy Bay Shore NY 11706 631-968-9696 968-9698
Web: www.bouldercreeksteakhouses.net

BR Assoc Inc 4201 Mannheim Rd Suite A Jasper IN 47546 812-482-3212 482-4013
Web: www.brsidal.com

Bravo Cucina Italiana 4644 Kenny Rd Columbus OH 43220 614-326-7944 626-4009*
*Fax Area Code: 866 ■ *TF:* 888-452-7286 ■ *Web:* www.bravoitalian.com

Bravo! Development Inc 777 Goodale Blvd Suite 100 Columbus OH 43212 614-326-7944 626-4009*
*Fax Area Code: 866 ■ *TF:* 888-452-7286 ■ *Web:* www.bestitalianusa.com

Breadeaux Pizza Inc 2300 Frederick St Saint Joseph MO 64506 816-364-1088 364-3739
TF: 800-835-6534 ■ *Web:* www.breadeauxpizza.com

BRG (Battleground Restaurant Group Inc) PO Box 10398 Greensboro NC 27404 336-272-9355 272-5568
Web: www.brginc.com

Briad Group 78 Okner Pkwy Livingston NJ 07039 973-597-6433 597-6422
Web: www.briad.com

Bridgeman Foods Inc 1903 Stanley Gault Pkwy Louisville KY 40223 502-254-7130 254-7031
TF: 800-254-7130

Bridgetown Grill 689 Peachtree St NE Atlanta GA 30308 404-873-2996 873-2014
Web: www.bridgetowngrill.com

Brigantine Restaurants Inc 7889 Ostrow St San Diego CA 92111 858-268-1030 268-5727
Web: www.brigantine.com

Brinker International Inc 6820 LBJ Fwy Dallas TX 75240 972-980-9917 770-9593
NYSE: EAT ■ *TF:* 800-983-4637 ■ *Web:* www.brinker.com

Brio Tuscan Grille 777 Goodale Blvd Suite 100 Columbus OH 43212 614-326-7944 626-4009*
*Fax Area Code: 866 ■ *TF:* 888-452-7286 ■ *Web:* www.brioitalian.com

Bristol Bar & Grill 8700 State Line Rd Leawood KS 66206 913-901-2500 901-2651
Web: www.houlihans.com

Bristol Bar & Grille Inc 1308 Bardstown Rd Louisville KY 40204 502-456-6762 456-6784
Web: www.bristolbarandgrille.com

Brown's Chicken & Pasta Inc 489 W Fullerton Ave Elmhurst IL 60126 630-617-8800 617-5900
TF: 888-582-7700 ■ *Web:* www.brownscatering.com

Bruchi's Cheesesteaks & Subs 6115 NE 114th Ave Vancouver WA 98662 360-882-8823 882-5988
TF: 877-488-9045 ■ *Web:* www.bruchis.com

Bubba Gump Shrimp Co LLC
209 Avenida Fabricante Suite 200 San Clemente CA 92672 949-366-6260 366-6261
TF: 877-729-4867 ■ *Web:* www.bubbagump.com

Buca di Beppo 1300 Nicollet Mall Suite 5003 Minneapolis MN 55403 612-288-2382 827-6446
Web: www.bucadibeppo.com

Buca Inc 1300 Nicollet Mall Suite 5003 Minneapolis MN 55403 612-288-2382 827-6446
NASDAQ: BUCA ■ *TF:* 800-273-1388 ■ *Web:* www.bucainc.com

Buckhead Life Restaurant Group 265 Pharr Rd Atlanta GA 30305 404-237-2060 237-2160
Web: www.buckheadrestaurants.com

Buck's Pizza Franchising Corp Inc 53 Industrial Dr Du Bois PA 15801 814-371-3076 371-4214
TF: 800-310-8848 ■ *Web:* www.buckspizza.com

Buddy's Bar-B-Q 5806 Kingston Pike Knoxville TN 37919 865-584-1924 588-7211
TF: 800-368-9208 ■ *Web:* www.buddysbarbq.com

Buffalo Wild Wings Inc 1600 Utica Ave S Suite 700 Minneapolis MN 55416 952-593-9943 593-9787
NASDAQ: BWLD ■ *TF:* 800-499-9586 ■ *Web:* www.buffalowildwings.com

Buffalo's Franchise Concepts Inc
707 Whitlock Ave SW Bldg H Suite 13 Marietta GA 30064 770-420-1800 420-1810*
*Fax: Cust Svc ■ *TF:* 800-459-4647 ■ *Web:* www.buffaloscafe.com

Buffet Partners LP 2701 E Plano Pkwy Plano TX 75074 214-291-2900 291-2476
TF: 800-804-7151 ■ *Web:* www.furrs.net

Buffets Inc 1460 Buffet Way Eagan MN 55121 651-994-8608 365-2356
Web: www.buffet.com

Bugaboo Creek Steak House Inc 8215 Roswell Rd Bldg 600 Atlanta GA 30350 770-399-9595 901-6628
TF: 800-434-6245 ■ *Web:* www.bugaboocreeksteakhouse.com

Bullets Corp of America Inc 456-A Southlake Blvd Richmond VA 23236 804-378-0046 378-1517
Web: www.bulletsnet.com

Burger King Corp 5505 Blue Lagoon Dr Miami FL 33126 305-378-7011 378-7262
Web: www.bk.com

Burger King Restaurants of Canada Inc
401 The West Mall 7th Fl Etobicoke ON M9C5J4 416-626-6464 626-6684*
*Fax: Mktg ■ *TF:* 888-252-8280

Burgerville USA 109 W 17th St Vancouver WA 98660 360-694-1521 694-9114
Web: www.burgerville.com

Cafe Express LLC 5858 Westheimer Rd Suite 110 Houston TX 77057 713-977-1922 977-9519
TF: 800-552-1999 ■ *Web:* www.cafe-express.com

Cajun & Grill of America 4104 Aurora St Coral Gables FL 33146 305-476-1611 476-9622
TF: 800-662-1668 ■ *Web:* www.kellyscajungrill.com

California Cafe Restaurants 2200 Powell St Suite 750 Emeryville CA 94608 510-594-4262 654-8295
Web: www.californiacafe.com

California Pizza Kitchen Inc
6053 W Century Blvd Suite 1100 Los Angeles CA 90045 310-342-5000 342-4602*
NASDAQ: CPKI ■ *Fax: Hum Res ■ *TF:* 800-275-8255 ■ *Web:* www.cpk.com

Camille's Sidewalk Cafe 8801 S Yale Suite 400 Tulsa OK 74137 800-230-7004 497-1916*
*Fax Area Code: 918 ■ *Web:* www.camillescafe.com

Capital Grille 8215 Roswell Rd Bldg 600 Atlanta GA 30350 770-399-9595 901-6628
TF: 800-434-6245 ■ *Web:* www.thecapitalgrille.com

Capital Restaurant Concepts Ltd 1305 Wisconsin Ave NW Washington DC 20007 202-333-7336 333-6395
Web: www.capitalrestaurants.com

Captain D's LLC 1717 Elm Hill Pike Suite A-1 Nashville TN 37210 615-391-5461 231-2309
TF: 800-314-4819 ■ *Web:* www.captainds.com

Captain Tony's Inc 2607 S Woodland Blvd Suite 300 DeLand FL 32720 386-736-9855 736-7237
TF: 800-332-8669 ■ *Web:* www.captain-tonys.wati.com

Cara Operations Ltd 6303 Airport Rd Mississauga ON L4V1R8 905-405-6500 405-6777
TF: 800-860-4082 ■ *Web:* www.cara.com

Carey Hilliard's Restaurants 11111 Abercorn St Savannah GA 31419 912-925-2131 925-1699

Carisch Inc 681 E Lake St Suite 262 Wayzata MN 55391 952-473-4291 476-7293
TF: 800-952-7297

Carlos O'Kelly's 1877 N Rock Rd Wichita KS 67206 316-683-2611 681-2481
Web: www.carlosokellys.com

Carl's Jr Restaurants 6307 Carpinteria Ave Suite A Carpinteria CA 93013 714-774-5796 778-7183
TF Cust Svc: 877-799-7827 ■ *Web:* www.carlsjr.com

Carlson Restaurants Worldwide Inc 4201 Marsh Ln Carrollton TX 75007 972-662-5400 662-5739
TF: 800-374-3297 ■ *Web:* www.fridays.com/companyinfo.htm

Carrabba's Italian Grill 2202 N Westshore Blvd 5th Fl Tampa FL 33607 813-288-8286 288-1779
Web: www.carrabbas.com

Carrols Corp 968 James St Syracuse NY 13203 315-424-0513 425-8874*
*Fax: Mktg ■ *Web:* www.carrols.com

Carrows Restaurants 5780 Fleet St Suite 250 Carlsbad CA 92008 760-804-5750 476-5141
Web: www.carrows.com

Carson's Inc 5970 N Ridge Ave Chicago IL 60660 773-271-4000 271-3699
TF: 888-999-7427 ■ *Web:* www.ribs.com

Carvers 10200 Willow Creek Rd San Diego CA 92131 858-689-2333 689-2289

Casa Ole 1135 Edgebrook St Houston TX 77034 713-943-7574 943-9554
TF: 800-741-7574 ■ *Web:* www.mexicanrestaurantsinc.com

Casey's Bar & Grill 10 Kingsbridge Garden Cir Suite 600 Mississauga ON L5R3K6 905-568-0000 568-0080
TF: 800-361-3111 ■ *Web:* www.caseysbar-grill.com

Cask 'n' Cleaver 8651 Madrone Ave Rancho Cucamonga CA 91730 909-981-5771 981-9734
Web: www.casknclever.com

Cassano's Inc 1700 E Stroop Rd Kettering OH 45429 937-294-8400 294-8107
Web: www.cassanos.com

Catalina Restaurant Group Inc 5780 Fleet St Suite 250 Carlsbad CA 92008 760-804-5750 476-5141
Web: www.catalinarestaurantgroup.com

Cattle Baron Restaurants Inc 201 E College Blvd Roswell NM 88201 505-622-3311 623-8801
Web: www.cattlebaron.com

Cattlemens 250 Dutton Ave Santa Rosa CA 95407 707-528-1040 571-7762
Web: www.beststeakinthewest.com

CB & Potts 10013 59th Ave SW PO Box 99010 Lakewood WA 98499 253-588-1788 588-0713
TF: 888-898-4050 ■ *Web:* www.cbpotts.com

CEC Entertainment Inc 4441 W Airport Fwy Irving TX 75062 972-258-8507 258-8545
NYSE: CEC ■ *Web:* www.chuckecheese.com

Central Park America Inc 5751 Uptain Rd Suite 210 Chattanooga TN 37411 423-855-0991 899-5923
Web: www.centralparkamerica.com

Champps Entertainment Inc
10375 Park Meadows Dr Suite 560 Littleton CO 80124 303-804-1333 804-8477
NASDAQ: CMPP ■ *TF:* 800-461-5965 ■ *Web:* www.champps.com

Champps Restaurants & Bar
10375 Park Meadows Dr Suite 560 Littleton CO 80124 303-804-1333 804-8477
TF: 800-461-5965 ■ *Web:* www.champps.com

Chao Praya International 1880 Lakeland Dr Suite 3 Jackson MS 39216 601-982-2863 982-2895

Char-O Chicken Systems Inc 2134 Main St Suite 220 Huntington Beach CA 92648 714-960-2348 374-1889
Web: www.charochicken.com

Charleston's Restaurant 1800 N Interstate Dr Suite 200 Norman OK 73072 405-321-2600 321-2992

Charley's Eating & Drinking Saloon 284 Newbury St Boston MA 02115 617-536-2800 236-4175
TF: 800-424-2753 ■ *Web:* www.backbayrestaurantgroup.com

Charley's Grilled Subs 2500 Farmers Dr Suite 140 Columbus OH 43235 614-923-4700 923-4701
TF: 800-437-8325 ■ *Web:* www.charleys.com

Charley's Steakery 2500 Farmers Dr Columbus OH 43235 614-923-4700 923-4701
TF: 800-437-8325 ■ *Web:* www.charleyssteakery.com

Charlie Brown's Steakhouse Inc 1450 Rt 22 W Mountainside NJ 07092 908-518-1800 518-1509
TF: 800-518-1855 ■ *Web:* www.charliebrowns.com

Chart House Restaurants 1510 W Loop South Houston TX 77027 713-850-1010 386-7707
TF: 800-552-6379 ■ *Web:* www.chart-house.com

Checkers Drive-In Restaurants Inc
4300 W Cypress St Suite 600 Tampa FL 33607 813-283-7000 283-7001
NASDAQ: CHKR ■ *TF:* 800-800-8072 ■ *Web:* www.checkers.com

Cheddar's Casual Cafe 6600 Campus Circle Dr E Suite 560 Irving TX 75063 214-596-6700

Cheeburger Cheeburger Restaurants Inc
15951 McGregor Blvd Suite 2A Fort Myers FL 33908 239-437-1611 437-1512
TF: 800-487-6211 ■ *Web:* www.cheeburger.com

Cheesecake Factory Inc 26950 Agoura Rd Calabasas Hills CA 91301 818-880-9323 871-3100
NASDAQ: CAKE ■ *Web:* www.thecheesecakefactory.com

Chefs International Inc 62 Broadway Point Pleasant Beach NJ 08742 732-295-0350 295-4514
Web: jackbakerslobstershanty.com

Chelo's Inc 1725 Mendon Rd Suite 205 Cumberland RI 02864 401-312-6500 312-6501
Web: www.chelos.com

Chequer's 8700 Stateline Rd Leawood KS 66206 913-901-2500 901-2651

Chesapeake Bay Seafood House Assoc LLC
1960 Gallows Rd Suite 200 Vienna VA 22182 703-827-0320 893-1536
Web: www.chesapeakerestaurants.com

Chester's International LLC
3500 Colonnade Pkwy Suite 325 Birmingham AL 32543 800-288-1555 298-0332*
*Fax Area Code: 205 ■ *Web:* www.chestersinternational.com

Chevys Inc 5660 Katella Ave Suite 100 Cypress CA 90631 562-346-1200 346-1470
TF: 800-424-3897 ■ *Web:* www.chevys.com

Chick-fil-A Inc 5200 Buffington Rd Atlanta GA 30349 404-765-8000 765-8140*
*Fax: Mktg ■ *TF:* 800-232-2677 ■ *Web:* www.chick-fil-a.com

Chicken Out Rotisserie 15952 Shady Grove Rd Gaithersburg MD 20877 301-921-0600 869-2386
TF: 800-328-4663 ■ *Web:* www.chickenout.com

Chili's Grill & Bar 6820 LBJ Fwy Dallas TX 75240 972-980-9917
TF: 800-983-4637 ■ *Web:* www.chilis.com

China Grill Inc 60 W 53rd St New York NY 10019 212-262-0028 956-7062
Web: www.chinagrillmgt.com

Chinese Cafes of America 4104 Aurora St Coral Gables FL 33146 305-476-1611 476-9622
TF: 800-662-1668

Chipotle Mexican Grill Inc 1543 Wazee St Suite 200 Denver CO 80202 303-595-4000 595-4014
NYSE: CMG ■ *Web:* www.chipotle.com

ChopHouse & Brewery 248 Centennial Pkwy Louisville CO 80027 303-664-4000 664-4199
TF: 800-273-9827 ■ *Web:* www.bennettsbbq.com

Christo's Inc 782 Crescent St Brockton MA 02302 508-588-4200 583-6946

Chuck E Cheese's 4441 W Airport Fwy Irving TX 75062 972-258-8507 258-8545
Web: www.chuckecheese.com

Chuck's Steak House Inc 1003 Orange Ave West Haven CT 06516 203-934-5300 934-3635
Web: www.chuckssteakhouse.com

Church's Chicken Inc 980 Hammond Dr NE Suite 1100 Atlanta GA 30328 770-350-3800 512-3920
Web: www.churchs.com

Chuy's Comida Deluxe 1623 Toomey Rd Austin TX 78704 512-473-2783 473-8684
TF: 800-439-2489 ■ *Web:* www.chuys.com

CiCi Enterprises LP 1080 W Bethel Rd Coppell TX 75019 972-745-4200 745-4204
Web: www.cicispizza.com

City Bites Inc 2600 E Memorial Rd Edmond OK 73013 405-607-8100 607-8200
Web: www.citybites.com

CKE Restaurants Inc 401 W Carl Karcher Way Anaheim CA 92801 714-774-5796 778-7183*
NYSE: CKR ■ *Fax: Mail Rm ■ *TF:* 800-758-2275 ■ *Web:* www.ckr.com

Claim Jumper Restaurants 16721 Millikan Ave Irvine CA 92606 949-756-9001 756-8733
TF: 800-949-4538 ■ *Web:* www.claimjumper.com

Clancy's Inc 15570 Stoney Creek Way Noblesville IN 46060 317-773-3284 776-6869

Claremont Restaurant Group 129 Fast Ln Mooresville NC 28117 704-660-5939 799-6199
TF: 877-704-5939 ■ *Web:* www.sagebrushsteakhouse.com

Clock Restaurants 902 Clint Moore Rd Suite 126 Boca Raton FL 33487 561-994-3440 994-3655

Clyde's Restaurant Group 3236 M St NW Washington DC 20007 202-333-9180 625-7429
Web: www.clydes.com

Coco's Bakery Restaurants 5780 Fleet St Suite 250 Carlsbad CA 92008 760-804-5750 476-5141
Web: www.cocosbakery.com

Colter's Bar-B-Q 7502 Greenville Ave Suite 500 Dallas TX 75231 214-987-5910 890-9230
Web: www.coltersbbq.com

Consolidated Restaurant Operations Inc
12200 N Stemmons Fwy Suite 100 Dallas TX 75234 972-241-5500 888-8198
TF: 800-275-1337 ■ *Web:* www.croinc.com

Company	City	State	Zip	Phone	Fax
Copeland Al Investments 1405 Airline Hwy TF: 800-401-0401 ■ Web: www.alcopeland.com	Metairie	LA	70001	504-830-1000	832-8918
Copeland's of New Orleans 1405 Airline Dr TF: 800-401-0401 ■ Web: www.copelands.net	Metairie	LA	70001	504-830-1000	832-8918
Cosi Inc 1751 Lake Cook Rd NASDAQ: COSI ■ Web: www.getcosi.com	Deerfield	IL	60015	847-597-5800	597-8884
Cotton Patch Cafe Inc 4825 W Royal Ln Web: www2.themetro.com/cottonpatchcafe	Irving	TX	75063	972-929-2806	929-0252
Country Market Restaurant & Buffet 1104 Country Hills Dr Web: www.flyingj.com/restaurant	Ogden	UT	84403	801-624-1000	624-1170
Country Pride Restaurants 24601 Center Ridge Rd Suite 200 *Fax: Mktg ■ TF: 800-872-7024	Westlake	OH	44145	440-808-9100	808-3303*
Cousins Subs Inc N 83 W 13400 Leon Rd TF: 800-238-9736 ■ Web: www.cousinssubs.com	Menomonee Falls	WI	53051	262-253-7700	253-7710
Cozymel's Mexican Grill 5720 LBJ Fwy Suite 190 Web: www.cozymels.com	Dallas	TX	75240	214-443-2000	443-2001
Crab House 1510 W Loop South TF: 800-552-6379 ■ Web: www.crabhouseseafood.com	Houston	TX	77027	713-850-1010	850-7274
Cracker Barrel Old Country Store Inc 305 Hartmann Dr TF: 800-333-9566 ■ Web: www.crackerbarrelocs.com	Lebanon	TN	37087	615-444-5533	235-4064
Cucina! Cucina! Inc 555 116th Ave NE Suite 220 Web: www.cucinacucina.com	Bellevue	WA	98004	425-635-3575	637-7055
Culver Franchising System Inc 540 Water St Web: www.culvers.com	Prairie du Sac	WI	53578	608-643-7980	643-7982
Daily Grill 11661 San Vincente Blvd Suite 404 TF: 888-999-9156 ■ Web: www.dailygrill.com	Los Angeles	CA	90049	310-820-5559	820-6530
Dairy Belle Inc 8140 Zinfandel Way Web: www.dairybelle.com	Somerset	CA	95684	530-620-2414	
D'Angelo Sandwich Shops 600 Providence Hwy TF: 800-727-2446 ■ Web: www.dangelos.com	Dedham	MA	02026	781-461-1200	461-1896
Darden Restaurants Inc 5900 Lake Ellenor Dr NYSE: DRI ■ Web: www.dardenrestaurants.com	Orlando	FL	32809	407-245-4000	245-5114
Darryl's Restaurant & Bar 8700 State Line Rd Suite 100 Web: www.houlihans.com	Leawood	KS	66206	913-901-2500	901-2651
Davanni's Inc 1100 Xenium Ln N Web: www.davannis.com	Plymouth	MN	55441	952-927-2300	927-2323
DavCo Restaurants Inc 1657 Crofton Blvd TF: 800-523-1411 ■ Web: www.davcorestaurants.com	Crofton	MD	21114	410-721-3770	793-0754
Dave & Buster's Inc 2481 Manana Dr NYSE: DAB ■ TF: 800-842-5369 ■ Web: www.daveandbusters.com	Dallas	TX	75220	214-357-9588	350-0941
Del Frisco's 224 E Douglas Ave TF: 800-234-0888 ■ Web: www.lonestarsteakhouse.com	Wichita	KS	67202	316-264-8899	264-5988
Del Taco Inc 25521 Commercentre Dr Suite 200 TF Cust Svc: 800-852-7204 ■ Web: www.deltaco.com	Lake Forest	CA	92630	949-462-9300	462-7444
Deli Management Inc 2400 Broadway	Beaumont	TX	77702	409-838-1976	838-1906
Denny's Corp 203 E Main St NASDAQ: DENN ■ *Fax: Mktg ■ TF Cust Svc: 800-733-6697 ■ Web: www.dennys.com	Spartanburg	SC	29319	864-597-8000	597-7230*
Denny's Inc 203 E Main St *Fax: Mktg ■ Web: www.dennys.com	Spartanburg	SC	29319	864-597-8000	597-8780*
Desert Moon Cafe 612 Corporate Way Suite 1M TF: 877-564-6362 ■ Web: www.desertmooncafe.com	Valley Cottage	NY	10989	845-267-3300	267-2548
Diamond Dave's Mexican Restaurants 201 S Clinton St Suite 281 Web: www.diamonddaves.com	Iowa City	IA	52240	319-354-6794	337-4707
Dickey's Barbecue Restaurants Inc 4514 Cole Ave Suite 1100 TF: 866-340-6188 ■ Web: www.dickeys.com	Dallas	TX	75205	972-248-9899	248-8667
Dick's Last Resort 4514 Travis St Suite 220 Web: www.dickslastresort.com	Dallas	TX	75205	214-572-8000	572-8008
Dino's Pizza 11018 Southwalk Ln	Raleigh	NC	27614	919-676-1080	676-1081
Dixie Restaurants Inc 1215 Rebsamen Pk Rd TF: 800-508-1242 ■ Web: www.dixiecafe.com	Little Rock	AR	72202	501-666-3494	666-8900
Doctor's Assoc Inc 325 Bic Dr TF: 800-888-4848	Milford	CT	06460	203-877-4281	783-7293
Dolly's Pizza Franchising Inc 1097-B Union Lake Rd TF: 866-336-5597 ■ Web: www.dollyspizza.com	White Lake	MI	48386	248-360-6440	360-7020
Domino's Pizza Inc 30 Frank Lloyd Wright Dr NYSE: DPZ ■ *Fax: Mail Rm ■ TF: 888-366-4667 ■ Web: www.dominos.com	Ann Arbor	MI	48106	734-930-3030	930-3580*
Don Cherry's Grapevine Restaurants Inc 500 Ray Lawson Blvd Web: www.doncherrys.com	Brampton	ON	L6Y5B3	905-451-5197	451-1980
Don Pablo's Mexican Kitchen 150 Hancock St TF: 800-765-7894 ■ Web: www.donpablos.com	Madison	GA	30650	706-342-4552	342-7893
Donatos Pizza 935 Taylor Stn Rd TF: 000-300-2807 ■ Web: www.donatos.com	Columbus	OH	43230	614-864-2444	575-4466
Don's Restaurants 8905 Lake Ave Web: www.strangcorp.com	Cleveland	OH	44102	216-961-6767	961-1966
Duff's Restaurant Inc 1451-A Missouri Ave N	Largo	FL	33770	727-585-2695	586-4938
Durango Steakhouse 2325 Ulmerton Rd Suite 20 TF: 800-525-8643 ■ Web: www.durangosteakhouse.com	Clearwater	FL	33762	727-576-6424	572-8342
Dutchman Hospitality Group 4985 Walnut St Web: www.dhgroup.com	Walnut Creek	OH	44687	330-893-2926	893-2637
Dynaco Inc 2246 E Date Ave TF: 800-230-4985 ■ Web: www.dynacofoods.com	Fresno	CA	93706	559-485-8520	485-3704
Dynamic Management LLC 1210 Briarville Rd TF: 800-306-1748 ■ Web: dynamicusa.com	Madison	TN	37115	615-277-1234	277-1220
East of Chicago Pizza Co 512 E Tiffin St Web: www.eastofchicago.com	Willard	OH	44890	419-935-3033	935-3278
Eat at Joe's Ltd 670 White Plains Rd Suite 120 Web: www.eatatjoesltd.com	Scarsdale	NY	10583	914-725-2700	725-8663
Eateries Inc 1220 S Santa Fe Ave Web: www.eats-inc.com	Edmond	OK	73003	405-705-5000	705-5001
Eat'n Park Hospitality Group Inc 285 E Waterfront Dr PO Box 3000 TF: 800-947-4033 ■ Web: www.eatnpark.com	Pittsburgh	PA	15230	412-461-2000	461-6000
Edo Japan International Inc 4838-32 St SE Web: www.edojapan.com	Calgary	AB	T2B2S6	403-215-8800	215-8801
Edwardo's Natural Pizza Restaurants 600 W Jackson Blvd Suite 200 TF: 800-344-5455	Chicago	IL	60661	312-463-1210	798-6761
Eegee's Inc 3360 E Ajo Way Web: www.eegees.com	Tucson	AZ	85713	520-294-3333	889-4340
El Arroyo 1616 W 5th St Web: www.elarroyo.com	Austin	TX	78703	512-478-2577	474-7172
El Centro Foods Inc 6930 1/2 Tujunga Ave	North Hollywood	CA	91605	818-766-4395	766-1496
El Fenix Corp 11075 Harry Hines Blvd TF: 877-591-1918 ■ Web: www.elfenix.com	Dallas	TX	75229	972-241-2171	241-3031
El Paso Bar-B-Que Co 8541 E Anderson Dr Suite 106 Web: www.elpasobarbeque.com	Scottsdale	AZ	85255	480-921-2260	377-9224
El Pollo Loco 3333 Michelson Dr Suite 550 Web: www.elpolloloco.com	Irvine	CA	92612	949-399-2000	399-2175
El Torito Restaurants Inc 5660 Katella Ave Suite 100 TF: 800-735-3501 ■ Web: www.eltorito.com	Cypress	CA	90630	562-346-1200	346-1470
Elephant Bar Restaurant 4630 Candlewood St Web: www.elephantbar.com	Lakewood	CA	90712	562-529-3200	
Elephant & Castle Group Inc 1190 Hornby St 12th Fl Web: www.elephantcastle.com	Vancouver	BC	V6Z2K5	604-684-6451	684-8595
Elmer's Restaurants Inc 11802 SE Stark St TF: 800-325-5188 ■ Web: www.elmers-restaurants.com	Portland	OR	97216	503-252-1485	257-7448
Embers America 2561 Territorial Rd Web: www.embersamerica.com	Saint Paul	MN	55114	651-645-6473	645-6866
Emeril's Homebase 829 St Charles Ave Web: www.emerils.com	New Orleans	LA	70130	504-524-4241	558-3937
Empress Chili 10592 Taconic Terr	Cincinnati	OH	45215	513-771-1441	771-1442
Erik's Deli Cafe 365 Coral St Web: www.eriksdelicafe.com	Santa Cruz	CA	95060	831-458-1818	458-9797
Escape Enterprises Inc 222 Neilston St Web: www.steakescape.com	Columbus	OH	43215	614-224-0300	224-6460
Estefan Enterprises Inc 420 Jefferson Ave	Miami Beach	FL	33139	305-534-4330	534-5220
Extreme Pita 2187 Dunwin Dr TF: 888-729-7482 ■ Web: www.extremepita.com	Mississauga	ON	L5L1X2	905-820-7887	820-8448
Fado Pubs Inc 309 E Paces Ferry Rd Suite 800 Web: fadoirishpub.com	Atlanta	GA	30305	404-848-8433	848-9984
Family Sports Concepts Inc 5510 W La Salle St Suite 200 TF: 800-728-8878 ■ Web: www.beefobradys.com	Tampa	FL	33607	813-226-2333	226-0030
Family Steak Houses of Florida Inc 2113 Florida Blvd	Neptune Beach	FL	32266	904-249-4197	249-1466
Famous Dave's of America Inc 12701 Whitewater Dr Suite 200 NASDAQ: DAVE ■ TF: 800-210-4040 ■ Web: www.famousdaves.com	Minnetonka	MN	55343	952-294-1300	294-0242
Famous Sam's Inc 16012 Metcalf Ave Suite 1 Web: www.famoussams.com	Overland Park	KS	66085	913-239-0266	239-9768
Fatburger North America Inc 301 Arizona Ave Suite 200 Web: www.fatburger.com	Santa Monica	CA	90401	310-319-1850	319-1863
Fatz Cafe 4324 Wade Hampton Blvd Web: www.fatzcafe.com	Taylors	SC	29687	864-322-1331	322-1332
Fausto's Fried Chicken Inc 905 E 4th St	Dequincy	LA	70633	337-786-7264	
Faz Restaurants Inc 5121 Hopyard Rd Web: www.fazrestaurants.com	Pleasanton	CA	94588	925-469-1600	469-1604
Fieldstone Restaurants Corp Hwy 65 S PO Box 969 Web: www.fieldstonerestaurants.com	Albert Lea	MN	56007	507-377-3805	377-8118
Figaro's Italian Pizza Inc 1500 Liberty St SE Suite 160 TF: 888-344-2767 ■ Web: figaros.com	Salem	OR	97302	503-371-9318	363-5364
Fired Up Inc 7500 Rialto Blvd Suite 250 Web: www.firedupinc.com	Austin	TX	78735	512-263-0800	263-8055
Firehouse Subs 3410 Kori Rd TF: 800-388-3473 ■ Web: www.firehousesubs.com	Jacksonville	FL	32257	904-886-8300	886-2111
Firehouse Restaurant Group Inc DBA Firehouse Subs 3410 Kori Rd TF: 800-388-3473 ■ Web: www.firehousesubs.com	Jacksonville	FL	32257	904-886-8300	886-2111
First Watch Inc 9027 Town Center Pkwy TF: 800-774-0724 ■ Web: www.firstwatch.com	Bradenton	FL	94202	941-907-9800	907-8933
Flamers Charbroiled Hamburgers 1515 International Pkwy Web: www.flamersgrill.com	Heathrow	FL	32746	407-936-1765	333-8852
Flanigan's Enterprises Inc 5059 NE 18th Ave AMEX: BDL ■ Web: www.flanigans.net	Fort Lauderdale	FL	33334	954-377-1961	377-1980
Fleming's Prime Steakhouse & Wine Bar 455 Newport Center Dr Web: www.flemingssteakhouse.com	Newport Beach	CA	92660	949-222-2223	222-0313
Flying J Travel Plaza Restaurants 1104 Country Hills Dr Web: www.flyingj.com	Ogden	UT	84403	801-624-1000	624-1170
Fogo de Chao 15028 Beltway Dr Web: www.fogodechao.com	Addison	TX	75001	972-960-9533	960-9877
Folks Restaurant Management Group 3120 Medlock Bridge Rd Bldg C Web: www.folkskitchen.com	Norcross	GA	30071	770-446-5998	446-6272
Food Concepts International LP 2575 S Loop 289 Web: www.abuelos.com	Lubbock	TX	79423	806-785-8686	785-8866
Foodee's Franchising Inc 2 S Main St	Concord	NH	03301	603-225-3834	224-2421
Fosters Freeze LLC 8300 Utica Ave Suite 157 Web: www.fostersfreeze.com	Rancho Cucamonga	CA	91730	909-635-2030	
Fox & Hound English Pub & Grille 1551 N Waterfront Pkwy Suite 30 Web: www.fhrg.com	Wichita	KS	67206	316-634-0505	634-6060
Fox & Hound Restaurant Group 1551 N Waterfront Pkwy Suite 310 NASDAQ: FOXX ■ TF: 800-229-2118 ■ Web: www.fhrg.com	Wichita	KS	67206	316-634-0505	634-6060
Fox's Pizza Den Inc 3243 Old Frankstown Rd TF: 800-899-3697 ■ Web: www.foxspizza.com	Pittsburgh	PA	15239	724-733-7888	325-5479
Fresh Choice Inc 8371 Central Ave Suite A TF: 800-859-8693 ■ Web: www.freshchoice.com	Newark	CA	94560	510-857-1230	857-1269
Fresh Enterprises Inc 100 Moody Ct Suite 200 TF: 877-225-2373 ■ Web: www.bajafresh.com	Thousand Oaks	CA	91360	805-495-4704	374-1144
Freshens Frozen Treats 1750 The Exchange TF: 800-633-4519 ■ Web: www.freshens.com	Atlanta	GA	30339	678-627-5400	627-5454
Fricker's USA 4963 Springboro Pike Web: www.frickers.com	West Carrollton	OH	45439	937-298-1423	298-9745
Friendly Ice Cream Corp 1855 Boston Rd AMEX: FRN ■ Web: www.friendlys.com	Wilbraham	MA	01095	413-543-2400	543-3966
Frisch's Restaurants Inc 2800 Gilbert Ave AMEX: FRS ■ TF: 800-873-3633 ■ Web: www.frischs.com	Cincinnati	OH	45206	513-961-2660	559-5160
Frullati Cafe & Bakery 7730 E Greenway Rd Suite 104 TF: 800-438-2590 ■ Web: www.frullati.com	Scottsdale	AZ	85260	480-443-0200	443-1972
Fuddruckers Inc 5700 MopaC Expy S Bldg C Suite 300 Web: www.fuddruckers.com	Austin	TX	78749	512-275-0400	275-0670
Garcia's Mexican Restaurants 1220 S Santa Fe Ave Web: www.eateriesinc.com	Edmond	OK	73003	405-705-5000	705-5001
Garden Fresh Restaurant Corp 15822 Bernardo Ctr Dr Suite A TF: 800-874-1600 ■ Web: www.gardenfreshcorp.com	San Diego	CA	92127	858-675-1600	675-1616
Garduno's 10555 Montgomery Blvd NE Suite 90 Web: www.gardunosrestaurants.com	Albuquerque	NM	87111	505-298-5514	323-4445
Garfield's Restaurant & Pub 1220 S Santa Fe Ave	Edmond	OK	73003	405-705-5000	705-5001
Gastronomy Inc 48 W Market St Suite 250 Web: www.gastronomyinc.com	Salt Lake City	UT	84101	801-322-2020	363-5275
Gates Bar-B-Q 4621 Paseo Blvd TF: 800-662-7427 ■ Web: www.gatesbbq.com	Kansas City	MO	64110	816-923-0900	923-3922
GCF Food Services Inc 5415 Dundas St W Suite 110 TF: 800-465-3324 ■ Web: www.holeechow.com	Toronto	ON	M9B1B5	416-778-8028	778-6818
Gigglebees 519 S Minnesota Ave Web: www.gigglebees.com	Sioux Falls	SD	57104	605-331-4242	334-4514
Giordano's Pizza 308 W Randolph Ave Web: www.giordanos.com	Chicago	IL	60606	312-641-6500	641-1505
Giorgio Restaurants 222 Saint Laurent Blvd Web: www.giorgio.ca	Montreal	QC	H2Y2Y3	514-845-4221	844-0071
Giovanni's Pizza 6926 US Rt 60	Ashland	KY	41102	606-928-6459	929-5709
Gold Star Chili 650 Lunken Pk Dr TF: 800-643-0465 ■ Web: www.goldstarchili.com	Cincinnati	OH	45226	513-231-4541	624-4415
Golden Chick 11488 Luna Rd Suite 100B Web: www.goldenchick.com	Dallas	TX	75234	972-831-0911	831-0401
Golden Corral Corp 5151 Glenwood Ave TF: 800-284-5673 ■ Web: www.goldencorral.net	Raleigh	NC	27612	919-781-9310	881-4485
Golden Franchising Corp 11488 Luna Rd Suite 100B Web: www.goldenchick.com	Dallas	TX	75234	972-831-0911	831-0401

Phone | Fax

Golden Griddle Corp 305 Milner Ave Suite 900 ... Toronto ON M1B3V4 416-609-2200 609-2207
Web: www.goldengriddlecorp.com

Good Eats Inc 12200 Stemmons Fwy Suite 100 ... Dallas TX 75234 972-241-5500 888-8198
TF: 800-275-1337 ■ *Web:* www.goodeatsgrill.com

Good Times Restaurants Inc 601 Corporate Circle ... Golden CO 80401 303-384-1400 273-0177
NASDAQ: GTIM ■ *Web:* www.goodtimesburgers.com

Gordon Biersch Brewery Restaurants
PO Box 5907 Suite 600 ... Chattanooga TN 37406 423-424-2000 752-1973
Web: www.gordonbiersch.com

Gorin's Homemade Cafe & Grill 4 Executive Pk E Suite 315 ... Atlanta GA 30329 404-248-9900 248-0180
TF: 888-489-7277

Gorin's Homemade Inc 4 Executive Pk E Suite 315 ... Atlanta GA 30329 404-248-9900 248-0180
Web: www.greatwraps.com

Grady's American Grill 4220 Edison Lakes Pkwy ... Mishawaka IN 46545 574-271-4600 271-4612
TF: 800-589-3820

Granite City Food & Brewery Ltd
5402 Parkdale Dr Suite 101 ... Saint Louis Park MN 55426 952-215-0660 215-0661
NASDAQ: GCFB ■ *Web:* www.gcfb.net

Great Steak & Potato Co 188 N Brookwood Ave Suite 100 ... Hamilton OH 45013 513-896-9695 896-3750
Web: www.thegreatsteak.com

Great Wraps! Inc 4 Executive Pk E Suite 315 ... Atlanta GA 30329 404-248-9900 248-0180
TF: 888-489-7277 ■ *Web:* www.greatwraps.com

Greco Pizza Donair 105 Walker St ... Truro NS B2N5G9 902-893-4141 895-7635
Web: www.greco.ca

Greek's Pizzeria 1600 University Ave ... Muncie IN 47303 765-284-5655

Green Burrito 401 Carl Karcher Way ... Anaheim CA 92801 714-774-5796 490-3630
TF: 800-422-4141

Green Mill Restaurants Inc 3900 N Woods Dr ... Arden Hills MN 55112 651-203-3100 203-3101
Web: www.greenmill.com

Gregory's Restaurants 1133 E Missouri Ave Suite L ... Phoenix AZ 85014 602-248-7950 265-6581

Griff's of America Inc 1202 Richardson Dr Suite 312 ... Richardson TX 75080 972-238-9561 238-9564

Grill Concepts Inc 11661 San Vincente Blvd Suite 404 ... Los Angeles CA 90049 310-820-5559 820-6530
NASDAQ: GRIL ■ *TF:* 888-999-9156 ■ *Web:* dailygrill.zgraph.net/news.cfm

Grindstone Charley's 15570 Stoney Creek Way ... Noblesville IN 46060 317-773-3284 776-6869

Grinner's Food Systems Ltd 105 Walker St PO Box 1040 ... Truro NS B2N5G9 902-893-4141 895-7635
Web: www.greco.ca

Grisanti's Inc 9300 Shelbyville Rd Suite 508 ... Louisville KY 40222 502-429-0341 426-1236
TF: 800-436-6323

Grotto Pizza Inc 4075 Hwy 1 ... Rehoboth Beach DE 19971 302-227-3567 227-4566
Web: www.grottopizza.com

Groupe d Alimentation MTY Inc 3465 Thimens Blvd ... Sainte-Laurent QC H4R1V5 514-336-8885 336-9222
Web: www.mtygroup.com

Gumby's Pizza International 7731 W Newberry Rd Suite A3 ... Gainesville FL 32606 352-332-4141 332-4193

Gunther Toody's LLC
6200 S Syracuse Way Suite 125 ... Greenwood Village CO 80111 303-773-7151 773-7152
Web: www.gunthertoodys.com

Hacienda Mexican Restaurants 1501 N Ironwood Dr ... South Bend IN 46635 574-272-5922 272-6055
TF: 800-541-3227 ■ *Web:* www.haciendafiesta.com

Haddad Restaurant Group Inc 4717 Grand Ave Suite 200 ... Kansas City MO 64112 816-931-2261 931-9044

Hal Smith Restaurant Group Inc 1800 N Interstate Dr Suite 200 ... Norman OK 73072 405-321-2600 321-2992

Happy Chef Systems Inc 51646 US Hwy 169 ... Mankato MN 56001 507-345-4571 345-4585
Web: www.happychef.com

Happy Joe's Inc 2705 Happy Joe Dr ... Bettendorf IA 52722 563-332-8811 332-5822
Web: www.happyjoes.com

Hard Rock Cafe International Inc 6100 Old Park Ln ... Orlando FL 32835 407-445-7625 445-7869
TF: 800-235-7625 ■ *Web:* www.hardrock.com

Hard Times Cafe Inc 6320 Augusta Dr Suite 801 ... Springfield VA 22150 703-451-7555 451-9292
Web: www.hardtimes.com

Hardee's Food Systems Inc 505 N 7th St Suite 2000 ... Saint Louis MO 63101 314-259-6200 259-6300*
**Fax:* Cust Svc ■ *TF Cust Svc:* 877-799-7827 ■ *Web:* www.hardees.com

Harlon's Bar-B-Que 11403 ML King Blvd ... Houston TX 77048 713-230-0111 230-0118
Web: www.harlonsbbq.com

Harman Management Corp 199 1st St Suite 212 ... Los Altos CA 94022 650-941-5681 948-7532

Hartz Restaurants 14451 Cornerstone Village Dr Suite 250 ... Houston TX 77014 281-583-0020 580-3752

Harvey's 6303 Airport Rd ... Mississauga ON L4V1R8 905-405-6500 405-6650
TF: 877-439-1125 ■ *Web:* www.harveys.ca

Heart of America Restaurants & Inns LLC 1501 River Dr ... Moline IL 61265 309-797-9300 797-8700
Web: www.hoari.com

Heartland Food Corp 1400 Opus Pl Suite 900 ... Downers Grove IL 60515 630-598-3300 598-2211
Web: www.heartlandfoodcorp.com

Heidi's Family Restaurant Inc 106 E Adams St Suite 206 ... Carson City NV 89706 775-884-1415 884-2091

Hibachi-San Japanese Grill 1683 Walnut Grove Ave ... Rosemead CA 91770 626-799-9898 927-9888
TF: 800-487-2632 ■ *Web:* www.hibachisan.com

High Plains Pizza Inc 7 W Parkway Blvd ... Liberal KS 67901 620-624-5638 624-5411

Ho-Lee-Chow 5415 Dundes St W Suite 110 ... Toronto ON M9B1B5 416-778-8028 778-6818
TF: 800-465-3324 ■ *Web:* www.holeechow.com

Hobee's California Restaurants 4224 El Camino Real ... Palo Alto CA 94306 650-493-7823 493-0756
Web: www.hobees.com

Hof's Hut Restaurants Inc 2601 E Willow St ... Signal Hill CA 90755 562-596-0200 430-0480
Web: www.hofshut.com

Hogi Yogi Corp 4833 N Edgewood Dr ... Provo UT 84604 801-222-9004 222-0977
TF: 800-653-4581 ■ *Web:* www.hogiyogi.com

Holland Inc 109 W 17th St ... Vancouver WA 98660 360-694-1521 694-9114
Web: www.hollandinc.com

Home Run Inn Inc 1300 Internationale Pkwy ... Woodridge IL 60517 630-783-9696 783-0069
TF: 800-636-9696 ■ *Web:* www.homeruninn.com

HomeTown Buffet Restaurants 1460 Buffet Way ... Eagan MN 55121 651-994-8608 365-2356
Web: www.buffet.com

Hooters Restaurants 1815 The Exchange ... Atlanta GA 30339 770-951-2040 618-7031*
**Fax:* Hum Res ■ *Web:* www.hooters.com

Hops Grillhouse & Brewery 150 Hancock St ... Madison GA 30650 706-342-4552 342-4057
Web: www.hopsrestaurants.com

Hoss's Steak & Sea House 170 Patch Way Rd ... Duncansville PA 16635 814-695-7600 695-3865
TF: 800-992-4677 ■ *Web:* www.hosss.com

Hot Dog on a Stick 5601 Palmer Way ... Carlsbad CA 92010 760-930-0456 930-0420
TF: 800-321-8400 ■ *Web:* www.hotdogonastick.com

Hot 'n Now 4205 Charlar Dr Suite 3 ... Holt MI 48842 517-694-4240 694-6370

Houlihan's Restaurant Group Inc
8700 State Line Rd Suite 100 ... Leawood KS 66206 913-901-2500 901-2651
Web: www.houlihans.com

House of Blues Entertainment Inc 6255 Sunset Blvd 16th Fl ... Hollywood CA 90028 323-769-4600 769-4792
TF: 800-843-2583 ■ *Web:* www.hob.com

Houston's Restaurants 2425 E Camelback Rd Suite 200 ... Phoenix AZ 85016 602-553-2111 553-2170
TF: 866-418-8583 ■ *Web:* www.houstons.com

Huddle House Inc 2969 E Ponce de Leon Ave ... Decatur GA 30030 404-377-5700 377-4142
TF: 800-418-9555 ■ *Web:* www.huddlehouse.com

Hudson's Grill of America Inc 16970 Dallas Pkwy Suite 402 ... Dallas TX 75248 972-931-9237 931-1326
Web: www.hudsonsgrill.com

Humperdinks 10013 59th Ave SW ... Lakewood WA 98499 253-588-1788 588-0713
TF: 888-898-4050

Humpty's Restaurants International Inc 2505 Macleod Tr S ... Calgary AB T2G5J4 403-269-4675 266-1973
TF: 800-661-7589 ■ *Web:* www.humptys.com

Hungry Howie's Pizza & Subs Inc
30300 Stephenson Hwy Suite 200 ... Madison Heights MI 48071 248-414-3300 414-3301
TF: 800-624-8122 ■ *Web:* www.hungryhowies.com

Hungry Hunter 10200 Willow Creek Rd ... San Diego CA 92131 858-689-2333 689-0433*
**Fax:* Mktg ■ *Web:* paragonsteak.com

Hyde Park Grille 9724 Ravenna Rd Suite 100 ... Twinsburg OH 44087 330-405-5658 405-5659
Web: www.hydeparkgrille.com

Hyde Park Restaurant Systems 26300 Chagrin Blvd Suite 1 ... Beachwood OH 44122 216-514-1777 514-1995
Web: www.hydeparkrestaurants.com

Hy's of Canada Ltd 1523 Davie St 3rd Fl ... Vancouver BC V6G3A2 604-684-3311 684-3535
Web: www.hyssteakhouse.com

I Can't Believe It's Yogurt 210 Shields Ct ... Markham ON L3R8V2 905-479-8762 479-5235
TF: 800-528-0727 ■ *Web:* www.yogenfruz.com

IHOP Corp 450 N Brand Blvd 7th Fl ... Glendale CA 91203 818-240-6055 543-4178
NYSE: IHP ■ *TF:* 800-241-4467 ■ *Web:* www.ihop.com

Il Fornaio America Corp 770 Tamalpais Dr Suite 400 ... Corte Madera CA 94925 415-945-0500 924-0906
TF: 800-291-1505 ■ *Web:* www.ilfornaio.com

Imo's Pizza 1610 Des Peres Rd Suite 160 ... Saint Louis MO 63131 314-822-7227 822-5278
Web: www.imospizza.com

In-N-Out Burger Inc 4199 Campus Dr Suite 900 ... Irvine CA 92612 949-509-6200 509-6300
TF Cust Svc: 800-786-1000 ■ *Web:* www.in-n-out.com

Interfoods of America Inc 9400 S Dadeland Blvd Suite 720 ... Miami FL 33156 305-670-0746 670-0767
TF: 866-476-7393

International Dairy Queen Inc 7505 Metro Blvd ... Minneapolis MN 55439 952-830-0200 830-0270
TF: 866-793-7582 ■ *Web:* www.idq.com

International Restaurant Management Group Inc
4104 Aurora St ... Coral Gables FL 33146 305-476-1611 476-9622
TF: 800-662-1668

Iron Hill Brewery & Restaurant 2502 W 6th St ... Wilmington DE 19805 302-888-2739 652-4115
Web: www.ironhillbrewery.com

Iron Skillet 6080 Surety Dr ... El Paso TX 79905 915-779-4711 774-4360
TF: 800-331-8809 ■ *Web:* www.petrotruckstops.com/iron_skillet.asp

Isaac's Deli Inc 354 N Prince St Suite 220 ... Lancaster PA 17603 717-394-0623 393-0955
Web: www.isaacsdeli.com

Islands Restaurants 5750 Fleet St Suite 120 ... Carlsbad CA 92008 760-268-1800 918-1500
Web: www.islandsrestaurants.com

J Alexander's Corp 3401 West End Ave Suite 260 ... Nashville TN 37203 615-269-1900 269-1999
AMEX: JAX ■ *TF:* 888-285-2539 ■ *Web:* www.jalexanders.com

J Gilbert's Wood Fired Steaks 8700 State Line Rd Suite 100 ... Leawood KS 66206 913-901-2500 901-2650
Web: www.jgilberts.com

Jack in the Box 9330 Balboa Ave ... San Diego CA 92123 858-571-2121 571-2101
TF: 800-500-5225 ■ *Web:* www.jackinthebox.com

Jack in the Box Inc 9330 Balboa Ave ... San Diego CA 92123 858-571-2121 571-2101
NYSE: JBX ■ *TF:* 800-500-5225 ■ *Web:* www.jackinthebox.com

Jack's Family Restaurants Inc 124 W Oxmoor Rd ... Birmingham AL 35209 205-945-8167 945-9820
TF: 800-422-3893 ■ *Web:* www.eatatjacks.com

Jake's Over the Top 4605 Harrison Blvd ... Ogden UT 84403 801-476-9780 476-9788
TF: 800-207-5804

Jake's Pizza Enterprises Inc
1931 Rohlwing Rd Suite B ... Rolling Meadows IL 60008 847-368-1990 368-1995
TF: 800-425-2537 ■ *Web:* www.jakespizza.com

James Coney Island Inc 11111 Katy Frwy Suite 700 ... Houston TX 77079 713-932-1500 932-0061
Web: www.jamesconeyisland.com

Jan Cos 35 Sockanosset Cross Rd ... Cranston RI 02920 401-946-4000 946-4392
TF: 800-937-1800 ■ *Web:* www.jancompanies.com

Jason Deli Co 2400 Broadway ... Beaumont TX 77702 409-838-1976 838-0370
Web: www.jasonsdeli.com

JB's Restaurants Inc 2207 S 48th St Suite A ... Tempe AZ 85282 602-426-0477 426-0480

Jerry's Famous Deli Inc 12711 Ventura Blvd Suite 400 ... Studio City CA 91604 818-766-8311 766-8315
Web: www.jerrysfamousdeli.com

Jerry's Subs & Pizza 15942 Shady Grove Rd ... Gaithersburg MD 20877 301-921-8777 948-3508
TF: 800-990-9176 ■ *Web:* www.jerrys-subs.com

Jerry's Systems Inc 15942 Shady Grove Rd ... Gaithersburg MD 20877 301-921-8777 948-3508
Web: www.jerrys-subs.com

Jet's America Inc 37177 Mound Rd ... Sterling Heights MI 48130 586-268-5870 268-6762
TF: 888-446-5870 ■ *Web:* www.jetspizza.com

Jillian's Restaurants 4500 Bowling Blvd Suite 200 ... Louisville KY 40207 502-638-9008 638-0984
TF: 888-594-8231 ■ *Web:* www.jillians.com

Jimmy John's Franchise Inc 2212 Fox Dr ... Champaign IL 61820 217-356-9900 359-2956
TF: 800-546-6904 ■ *Web:* www.jimmyjohns.com

Jim's Restaurants 8520 Crownhill Blvd ... San Antonio TX 78209 210-828-1493 822-8606
Web: www.jimsrestaurants.com

JJ North's Grand Buffet PO Box 1340 ... Medford OR 97501 541-779-6610 779-6739
Web: www.norths.com

Jocks & Jills LLC
1201 Peachtree St NE 400 Colony Sq Suite 1500 ... Atlanta GA 30361 404-892-7967 875-3712
Web: www.jocks-frankies.com

Joe's American Bar & Grille 284 Newbury St ... Boston MA 02115 617-536-2800 236-4175
Web: www.backbayrestaurantgroup.com

Joe's Crab Shack 1510 W Loop South ... Houston TX 77027 713-850-1010 850-7205
TF: 800-552-6379 ■ *Web:* www.joescrabshack.com

Joey's Only Seafood Franchising Corp 514-42nd Ave SE ... Calgary AB T2G1Y6 403-243-4584 243-8989
TF: 800-661-2123 ■ *Web:* www.joeys-only.com

John Harvard's Brew House 33 Dunster St ... Cambridge MA 02138 617-868-3585 868-4341
Web: www.johnharvards.com

Johnny Rockets Group Inc
25550 Commerce Centre Dr Suite 200 ... Lake Forest CA 92630 949-643-6100 643-6200
TF: 888-236-9100 ■ *Web:* www.johnnyrockets.com

Johnny's Pizza House Inc 2920 N 7th St ... West Monroe LA 71291 318-323-0518 322-3191
TF: 800-256-5453 ■ *Web:* www.johnnys-pizza.com

Johnson WB Properties 100 W Paces Ferry Rd ... Atlanta GA 30305 404-237-7300 365-9800

Jonny Carino's Country Italian 7500 Rialto Blvd Suite 250 ... Austin TX 78735 512-263-0800 263-8055
Web: www.carinos.com

JRN Inc 201 W 7th St ... Columbia TN 38401 931-381-3000 490-4801
TF: 800-251-8035

K Bob's Steakhouse 2235 Main St SE Suite B ... Los Lunas NM 87031 505-866-5555 886-7777
Web: www.kbobs.com

K-Mac Enterprises Inc 1820 S Zero St ... Fort Smith AR 72906 479-646-2053 646-8748
TF: 800-345-5622 ■ *Web:* www.kmaccorp.com

Kahala Corp 7730 E Greenway Rd Suite 104 ... Scottsdale AZ 85260 480-443-0200 443-1972
Web: www.kahalacorp.com

Kahunaville Management Inc 500 S Madison St ... Wilmington DE 19801 302-571-6200 571-6212
TF: 888-453-3990 ■ *Web:* www.kahunaville.com

KC Masterpiece Restaurants 10985 Metcalf Ave ... Overland Park KS 66062 913-345-2255 888-2852

Keg Restaurants Ltd 10100 Shellbridge Way ... Richmond BC V6X2W7 604-276-0242 276-2681
Web: www.kegsteakhouse.com

Kelly's Cajun Grill 4104 Aurora St ... Coral Gables FL 33146 305-476-1611 476-9622
Web: www.kellyscajungrill.com

Kenny Rogers Roasters 1400 Old Country Rd Suite 400 ... Westbury NY 11590 516-338-8500 338-7220
TF: 800-628-4267 ■ *Web:* www.nathansfamous.com/rogers/

Kettle Country Kitchen Inc 350 Oaks Trail Suite 142 ... Garland TX 75043 972-203-6222
TF: 800-929-2391 ■ *Web:* www.kettle.com

KFC Corp 1441 Gardiner Ln ... Louisville KY 40213 502-874-8300 874-2759
TF: 800-544-5774 ■ *Web:* www.kfc.com

Kimpton Hotel & Restaurant Group LLC
222 Kearny St Suite 200 ... San Francisco CA 94108 415-397-5572 296-8031
TF: 800-546-2686 ■ *Web:* www.kimptonhotels.com

Kincaid's Fish Chop & Steak House 1818 N Northlake Way ... Seattle WA 98103 206-634-3082 632-3533

King Taco Restaurants Inc 3421 E 14th St ... Los Angeles CA 90023 323-268-2267 266-6565
Web: www.kingtaco.com

Kings Family Restaurants 1180 Long Run Rd ... White Oak PA 15131 412-751-0700 751-9008*
**Fax:* Hum Res ■ *Web:* www.kingsfamily.com

Phone Fax

King's Fish House 100 W Broadway Ave Suite 550 Long Beach CA 90802 562-432-7463 436-5432
Web: www.kingsfishhouse.com
King's Seafood Co 3185 Airway Ave Bldg 8 Costa Mesa CA 92626 714-432-0400 432-0111
Web: www.kingsseafood.com
Kobe Japanese Steakhouse Inc 468 W Hwy 436 Altamonte Springs FL 32714 407-862-2888 788-8887
Web: www.kobesteakhouse.com
Kojo Inc 408 E Axton Rd Bellingham WA 98226 360-671-4290 392-0999
Web: www.kojo.com
Kona Grill Inc 7150 E Camelback Rd Suite 220 Scottsdale AZ 85251 480-922-8100 991-6811
NASDAQ: KONA ■ *Web:* www.konagrill.com
Koo Koo Roo 5700 MopaC Expy S Bldg C Suite 300 Austin TX 78749 512-275-0400 275-0670
Web: www.kookooroo.com
Krystal Co 1 Union Sq Chattanooga TN 37402 423-757-1550 757-5644
TF: 800-458-5841 ■ *Web:* www.krystalco.com
L & L Hawaiian Barbecue 931 University Ave Suite 202 Honolulu HI 96826 808-951-9888 951-0888
Web: www.hawaiianbarbecue.com
L & L Franchise Inc DBA L & L Hawaiian Barbecue
931 University Ave Suite 202 Honolulu HI 96826 808-951-9888 951-0888
Web: www.hawaiianbarbecue.com
L & L Hawaiian Barbecue 931 University Ave Suite 202 Honolulu HI 96826 808-951-9888 951-0888
Web: www.hawaiianbarbecue.com
La Madeleine Inc 6688 N Central Expy Suite 700 Dallas TX 75206 214-696-6962 696-0485*
**Fax: Cust Svc* ■ *TF:* 800-400-5840 ■ *Web:* www.lamadeleine.com
La Pizza Loca 9550 Firestone Blvd Suite 105 Downey CA 90241 562-862-4470 862-7989
Web: www.lapizzaloca.com
La Salsa Inc 6307 Carpinteria Ave Suite A Carpinteria CA 93013 805-745-7500
TF: 800-527-2572 ■ *Web:* www.lasalsa.com
La Senorita 1135 Edgebrook St Houston TX 77034 713-943-7574 943-9554
TF: 800-741-7574 ■ *Web:* www.lasenorita.com
La Shish Inc 13250 Rotunda Dr Dearborn MI 48120 313-441-2900 441-4432
Web: www.lashish.com
LaBelle Management Inc 405 S Mission Rd Mount Pleasant MI 48858 989-772-2902 773-7521
Web: www.labellemgt.com
Lambert's Cafe Inc 36 Papa Holler Ln Sikeston MO 63801 573-471-8795 471-7563
Web: www.throwedrolls.com
Lamppost Pizza Franchise Corp 3002 Dow Ave Suite 320 Tustin CA 92780 714-731-6171 731-0951
Web: www.lamppostpizza.com
Landry's Restaurants Inc 1510 W Loop South Houston TX 77027 713-850-1010 850-7205
NYSE: LNY ■ *TF:* 800-552-6379 ■ *Web:* www.landrysrestaurants.com
LaRosa's Inc 2334 Boudinot Ave Cincinnati OH 45238 513-347-5660 922-2776
Web: www.larosas.com
Lawry's Restaurants Inc 234 E Colorado Blvd Suite 500 Pasadena CA 91101 626-440-5234 440-5232
Web: www.lawrysonline.com
Le Peep Restaurant 2500 E Arapahoe Rd Littleton CO 80122 303-973-3202 779-5909
Web: www.lepeep.com
LEDO Pizza System Inc 2001 Tidewater Colony Dr Suite 203 Annapolis MD 21401 410-721-6887 266-6888
Web: www.ledopizza.com
Leeann Chin Inc 3600 American Blvd W Suite 418 Bloomington MN 55431 952-896-3606 896-3615
TF: 800-784-0029 ■ *Web:* www.leeannchin.com
Legal Sea Foods Inc 1 Seafood Way Boston MA 02210 617-783-8088 530-9023
TF: 800-477-5342 ■ *Web:* www.legalseafoods.com
Leona's Pizzeria Inc 3931 S Leavitt St Chicago IL 60609 773-523-7676 890-1462
Web: www.leonas.com
Lettuce Entertain You Enterprises Inc 5419 N Sheridan Rd Chicago IL 60640 773-878-7340 878-7667
Web: www.leye.com
Levy Restaurants 980 N Michigan Ave Suite 400 Chicago IL 60611 312-664-8200 280-2739
Web: www.levyrestaurants.com
Libby Hill Seafood Restaurants Inc 4517-B W Market St Greensboro NC 27407 336-294-0505 292-6005
TF: 800-452-2071 ■ *Web:* www.libbyhill.com
Li'l Dino Corp 5601 Roanne Way Suite 100 Greensboro NC 27409 336-297-4440 297-4449
TF: 800-525-6782 ■ *Web:* www.lildino.com
Little Caesars Inc 2211 Woodward Ave Detroit MI 48201 313-983-6000 983-6166*
**Fax: Cust Svc* ■ *TF:* 800-722-3727 ■ *Web:* www.littlecaesars.com
Little King Inc 11811 'I' St Omaha NE 68137 402-330-8019 330-3221
TF: 800-788-9478 ■ *Web:* www.littlekinginc.com
Lobster Shanty 62 Broadway Point Pleasant Beach NJ 08742 732-295-0350 295-4514
Logan's Roadhouse Inc 3011 Armory Dr Suite 300 Nashville TN 37211 615-885-9056 885-9057
TF: 800-815-9056 ■ *Web:* www.logansroadhouse.com
Lone Star Steakhouse & Saloon Inc 224 E Douglas Ave Wichita KS 67202 316-264-8899 264-5988
NASDAQ: STAR ■ *TF:* 800-234-0888 ■ *Web:* www.lonestarsteakhouse.com
Lone Star Texas Grill 472 Morden Rd Suite 101 Oakville ON L6K3W4 905-845-5852 845-7091
Web: www.lonestartexasgrill.com
Long John Silver's Restaurants Inc 1441 Gardiner Ln Louisville KY 40213 502-874-8300 874-8306
Web: www.ljsilvers.com
LongHorn Steakhouse 8215 Roswell Rd Bldg 600 Atlanta GA 30350 770-399-9595 901-6628
TF: 800-434-6245 ■ *Web:* www.longhornsteakhouse.com
Luby's Inc PO Box 33069 San Antonio TX 78265 210-654-9000 871-7867
NYSE: LUB ■ *TF:* 800-886-4600 ■ *Web:* www.lubys.com
Lunan Corp 414 N Orleans St Suite 402 Chicago IL 60610 312-645-9898 645-0654
Web: arbysrestaurants.com
Lundy Enterprises LLC 10555 Lake Forest Blvd Suite 1J New Orleans LA 70127 504-241-6658 241-9531
Luther's Bar-B-Q Inc 2611 FM 1960 W Suite B-101 Houston TX 77068 281-537-8895 537-8908
Macayo Mexican Restaurants 3117 N 16th St Phoenix AZ 85016 602-212-2424 277-1795
Web: www.macayo.com
Machine Shed 1501 River Dr Moline IL 61265 309-797-9300 797-8700
Web: www.machineshed.com
Maggiano's Little Italy 6820 LBJ Fwy Dallas TX 75240 972-980-9917 770-9593
Web: www.maggianos.com
Magic Restaurants LLC 4407 Monterey Blvd Suite 100 Austin TX 78749 512-275-0400 275-0670
Magic Time Machine 8520 Crownhill Blvd San Antonio TX 78209 210-828-1493 822-8830
Web: www.magictimemachine.com
Magic Wok Inc 6540 W Central Ave Suite L Toledo OH 43617 419-841-1818 841-1899
Main Street Management LLC 1308 Bardstown Rd Louisville KY 40204 502-456-6762 456-6784
Malnati Organization Inc 3685 Woodhead Dr Northbrook IL 60062 847-562-1814 562-1950
TF: 800-568-8646 ■ *Web:* www.loumalnatis.com
Mancha Development Co 2275 Sampson Ave Suite 201 Corona CA 92879 951-271-4100 271-4110
Manchu Wok 85 Citizen Ct Unit 9 Markham ON L6G1A8 905-946-7200 946-7201
TF: 800-361-8864 ■ *Web:* www.manchuwok.com
Manchu Wok Canada Inc 85 Citizen Ct Unit 9 Markham ON L6G1A8 905-946-7200 946-7201
TF: 800-361-8864
Marco's Franchising LLC 5252 Monroe St Toledo OH 43623 419-885-7000 885-5215
TF: 800-262-7267 ■ *Web:* www.marcos.com
Margaritaville Inc 424-A Fleming St Key West FL 33040 305-296-9089 296-1084
TF: 800-262-6835 ■ *Web:* margaritaville.com
Marie Callender Inc 27081 Aliso Creek Rd Suite 200 Aliso Viejo CA 92656 949-448-5300 448-5315
TF: 800-776-7437 ■ *Web:* www.mariecallender.com
Mark II Family Restaurant Inc
1020 Wikesburg Township Blvd Wilkes-Barre PA 18702 570-823-0121 825-6157
Maui Tacos International Inc
180 Interstate N Pkwy SE Suite 500 Atlanta GA 30339 770-226-8226 541-2300
TF: 888-628-4822 ■ *Web:* www.mauitacos.com
Maui Wowi Inc 5445 DTC Pkwy Suite 1050 Greenwood Village CO 80111 303-781-7800 781-2438
Web: www.mauiwowi.com
Max & Erma's Restaurants Inc 4849 Evanswood Dr Columbus OH 43229 614-431-5800 431-4100
NASDAQ: MAXE ■ *Web:* www.maxandermas.com
Max's Opera Cafe 120 E Grand Ave South San Francisco CA 94080 650-873-6297 873-6461
Web: www.maxsworld.com

Phone Fax

McAlister's Corp 731 S Pear Orchard Rd Suite 51 Ridgeland MS 39157 601-952-1100 957-0964
TF: 888-855-3354 ■ *Web:* www.mcalistersdeli.com
McCormick & Schmick's Seafood Restaurant Inc
720 SW Washington St Suite 550 Portland OR 97205 503-226-3440 228-5074
NASDAQ: MSSR ■ *Web:* www.mccormickandschmicks.com
McDonald's Corp 1 McDonald's Plaza Oak Brook IL 60523 630-623-3000 623-5500
NYSE: MCD ■ *TF:* 800-234-6227 ■ *Web:* www.mcdonalds.com
McDonald's Restaurants of Canada Ltd 1 McDonald's Pl Toronto ON M3C3L4 416-443-1000 446-3376
Web: www.mcdonalds.ca
McGrath's Fish House 1935 Davcor St SE Salem OR 97302 503-399-8456 391-2846
Web: www.mcgrathsfishhouse.com
McGuffey's Restaurant Inc 370 N Louisiana Ave Suite H-2 Asheville NC 28806 828-252-3300 254-3907
MCL Cafeterias Inc 2730 E 62nd St Indianapolis IN 46220 317-257-5425 252-8504
TF: 800-530-9625 ■ *Web:* www.mclcafe.com
Me-N-Ed's Pizzerias 5701 N West Ave Fresno CA 93711 559-432-0399 432-0398
TF: 888-636-3373 ■ *Web:* milano-ri.com
Melting Pot Restaurants Inc 8810 Twin Lakes Blvd Tampa FL 33614 813-881-0055 889-9361
TF: 800-783-0867 ■ *Web:* www.meltingpot.com
Meritage Hospitality Group Inc
1971 E Beltline NE Suite 200 Grand Rapids MI 49525 616-776-2600 776-2776
AMEX: MHG ■ *Web:* www.meritagehospitality.com
Metromedia Restaurant Group
6500 International Pkwy Suite 1000 Plano TX 75093 972-588-5000 588-5203
Web: www.metromediarestaurants.com
Metz & Assoc Ltd 2 Woodland Dr Dallas PA 18612 570-675-8100 675-0919
Web: www.metzltd.com
Mexican Restaurants Inc 1135 Edgebrook St Houston TX 77034 713-943-7574 943-9554
NASDAQ: CASA ■ *TF:* 800-741-7574 ■ *Web:* www.mexicanrestaurantsinc.com
Mighty Taco Inc 9362 Transit Rd East Amherst NY 14051 716-636-1097 636-4520
Milio's Sandwiches 5585 Guilford Rd Madison WI 53711 608-277-9000 277-9363
Web: www.milios.com
Millie's 565 W Lambert Rd Suite C Brea CA 92821 714-671-0772 671-7957
Web: www.millies.com
Mimi's Cafe 17852 E 17th St South Bldg Suite 108 Tustin CA 92780 714-544-4826 544-7663
Web: www.mimiscafe.com
Mirabile Investment Corp 1900 Whitten Rd Memphis TN 38133 901-324-0450 312-3280
Web: www.mic-memphis.com
Moe's Southwest Grill LLC 2915 Peachtree Rd Atlanta GA 30305 404-351-3500 442-8320
Web: www.moes.com
Monical Pizza Corp 530 N Kinzie Ave Bradley IL 60915 815-937-1890 937-9828
TF: 800-929-3227 ■ *Web:* www.monicals.com
Montana's Cookhouse Saloon 6303 Airport Rd Mississauga ON L4V1R8 905-405-6500 405-5063
TF: 800-860-4082 ■ *Web:* www.montanas.ca
Monterey's Little Mexico 1135 Edgebrook St Houston TX 77034 713-943-7574 943-9554
TF: 800-741-7574 ■ *Web:* www.montereys.com
Monterey's Tex-Mex Cafe 1135 Edgebrook St Houston TX 77034 713-943-7574 943-9554
TF: 800-741-7574
Morgan's Foods Inc 24200 Chagrin Blvd Suite 126 Beachwood OH 44122 216-360-7500 360-0299
TF: 800-869-8691 ■ *Web:* www.morgansfoods.com
Morton's Restaurant Group Inc
3333 New Hyde Park Rd Suite 210 New Hyde Park NY 11042 516-627-1515 627-2050
NYSE: MRT ■ *Web:* www.mortons.com
Morton's The Steakhouse 400 Post St San Francisco CA 94102 415-986-5830 986-5829
Web: www.mortons.com
Mo's Enterprises Inc 657 SW Bay Blvd Newport OR 97365 541-265-7512 265-9323
Web: www.moschowder.com
Mountain Jack 10200 Willow Creek Rd San Diego CA 92131 858-689-2333 689-2289
TF: 800-570-9159 ■ *Web:* paragonsteak.com
Mountain Mike's Corp 9845 Horn Rd Suite 160 Sacramento CA 95827 916-857-0650 857-0830
Web: www.mountainmikes.com
Mozzarella's Cafe 150 W Church Ave Maryville TN 37801 865-379-5700 379-6830
TF: 800-325-0755
Mr Gatti's Inc 5912 Balcones Dr Austin TX 78751 512-459-4796 454-4990
Web: www.mrgattis.com
Mr Goodcents Franchise Systems Inc 8997 Commerce Dr DeSoto KS 66018 913-583-8400 583-3500
TF: 800-648-2368 ■ *Web:* www.mrgoodcents.com
Mr Hero Restaurants 7010 Engle Rd Suite 100 Middleburg Heights OH 44130 440-625-3080 625-3081
TF: 888-860-5082 ■ *Web:* www.mrhero.com
Mr Jim's Pizza Inc 4276 Kellway Cir Addison TX 75001 972-267-5467 267-5463
TF: 800-583-5960 ■ *Web:* www.mrjimspizza.net
Mr Mike's Grill 1500 W George St 19th Fl Vancouver BC V6G2Z6 604-684-6901 684-6948
Web: www.mrmikes.ca
Mr Sub 4576 Yonge St Suite 600 Toronto ON M2N6P1 416-225-5545 225-5536
TF: 000 000-7027 ■ *Web:* www.mrsub.ca
Mr Subb Franchise Corp 601 Columbia St Cohoes NY 12047 518-783-0276 783-0294
TF: 800-267-7822 ■ *Web:* www.mrsubb.com
Mrs Winner's Chicken & Biscuits 6055 Barfield Rd Suite 200 Atlanta GA 30328 404-459-5805 514-4677*
**Fax Area Code: 678* ■ *TF:* 877-733-5577
MTY Food Group Inc 3465 Thimens Blvd Sainte-Laurent QC H4R1V5 514-336-8885 336-9222
Web: www.mtygroup.com
My Friend's Place 904 Bombay Ln Roswell GA 30076 770-817-4200
TF: 800-882-9436 ■ *Web:* www.myfriendsplacedeli.com
Myriad Restaurant Group Inc 180 Franklin St New York NY 10013 212-219-9500 219-2380
Web: www.myriadrestaurantgroup.com
Nancy's Pizzeria 8200 W 185th St Suite J Tinley Park IL 60478 708-444-4411 444-4422
TF: 800-626-2977 ■ *Web:* www.nancyspizza.com
Napa Valley Grill 2200 Powell St Suite 750 Emeryville CA 94608 510-594-4262 654-8295
TF: 800-294-9323 ■ *Web:* www.napavalleygrille.com
Nathan's Famous Inc 1400 Old Country Rd Suite 400 Westbury NY 11590 516-338-8500 338-7220
NASDAQ: NATH ■ *TF:* 800-628-4267 ■ *Web:* www.nathansfamous.com
National Coney Island Inc 27947 Groesback Hwy Roseville MI 48066 586-771-7744 771-9578
Web: www.nationalconeyisland.com
National Restaurants Management Inc DBA Riese Restaurants
560 5th Ave New York NY 10036 212-563-7440 629-0942
Nature's Table Franchise Co 800 N Magnolia Ave Orlando FL 32803 407-481-2544 843-6057
TF: 800-222-6090 ■ *Web:* www.naturestable.com
New King Inc 874 Silas Deane Hwy Wethersfield CT 06109 860-257-9000 257-9248
New World Restaurant Group Inc 1687 Cole Blvd Golden CO 80401 303-568-8000
Web: www.newworldrestaurantgroup.com
New York Fries 1220 Yonge St Suite 400 Toronto ON M4T1W1 416-963-5005 963-4920
Web: www.newyorkfries.com
Newport Bay Restaurants 7165 SW Fir Loop Suite 200 Portland OR 97223 503-684-2803 620-6149
Web: www.newportbay.com
Nickels Restaurants 1955 Cote-de-liesse Suite 205 Saint-Laurent QC H4N3A8 514-856-5555 856-6050
Web: www.nickelsrestaurants.com
Ninety-Nine Restaurant & Pubs 160 Olympia Ave Woburn MA 01801 781-933-8999 933-0821
Web: www.99restaurants.com
Noble Roman's Pizza Inc 1 Virginia Ave Suite 800 Indianapolis IN 46204 317-634-3377 636-3207
TF: 800-585-0669 ■ *Web:* www.nobleromans.com
Noodles & Co 2590 Pearl St Boulder CO 80302 720-214-1900 214-1933
Web: www.noodles.com
Norsan Group 4824 N Royal Dr Tucker GA 30085 770-414-5026 414-5839
Web: www.norsangroup.com
North Beach Pizza Inc 1499 Grant Ave San Francisco CA 94133 415-433-2444 433-7217
Web: www.northbeachpizza.com
North's Restaurants Inc 1005 N Riverside Ave Suite 300 Medford OR 97501 541-779-6610 779-6739
Web: www.norths.com

Phone | Fax

NPC International Inc 720 W 20th St. Pittsburgh KS 66762 620-231-3390 232-3692
Web: www.npcinternational.com

Nu-Ventures Inc 1324 W Milham St. Portage MI 49024 269-226-4400 226-4466
TF: 888-432-8379 ■ *Web:* samuelmancinos.com

O'Charley's Inc 3038 Sidco Dr. Nashville TN 37204 615-256-8500 782-5043
NASDAQ: CHUX ■ *Web:* www.ocharleys.com

Office Beer Bar & Grill 1450 Rt 22 W. Mountainside NJ 07092 908-518-1800 518-1509
TF: 800-518-1855 ■ *Web:* www.office-beerbar.com

Old Chicago Restaurants 248 Centennial Pkwy. Louisville CO 80027 303-664-4000 664-4199
TF: 800-273-9827 ■ *Web:* www.oldchicago.com

Old Country Buffet Restaurants 1460 Buffet Way. Eagan MN 55121 651-994-8608 365-2356
Web: www.buffet.com

Old Spaghetti Factory Inc 0715 SW Bancroft St. Portland OR 97239 503-225-0433 226-6214
Web: www.osf.com

Olga's Kitchen Inc 1940 Northwood Dr. Troy MI 48084 248-362-0001 362-2013
TF: 800-336-5427 ■ *Web:* www.olgaskitchen.com

Olive Garden 5900 Lake Ellenor Dr. Orlando FL 32809 407-245-4000 245-5389*
**Fax:* Mail Rm ■ *Web:* www.olivegarden.com

On the Border Mexican Cafe 6820 LBJ Fwy. Dallas TX 75240 972-980-9917 770-9593
TF: 800-983-4637 ■ *Web:* www.ontheborder.com

Orange Julius of America 7505 Metro Blvd PO Box 39286. Minneapolis MN 55439 952-830-0200 830-0480*
**Fax:* Mktg ■ *TF:* 800-679-6556 ■ *Web:* www.orangejulius.com

Original Gino's East of Chicago 600 W Jackson Blvd Suite 200. Chicago IL 60661 312-463-1210 798-6761

Original Pancake House Franchising Inc 8601 SW 24th Ave. Portland OR 97219 503-246-9007 245-2396
Web: www.originalpancakehouse.com

Outback Steakhouse Inc 2202 N West Shore Blvd 5th Fl. Tampa FL 33607 813-282-1225 282-1209
NYSE: OSI ■ *Web:* www.outback.com

Pacific Coast Restaurants Inc 7165 SW Fir Loop Suite 200. Portland OR 97223 503-684-2803 620-6149
Web: www.pacificcoastrestaurants.com

PacPizza LLC 220 Porter Dr Suite 100. San Ramon CA 94583 925-838-8567 838-5801

Palm Management Corp
1730 Rhode Island Ave NW Suite 900. Washington DC 20036 202-775-7256 775-8292
TF: 800-388-7256 ■ *Web:* www.thepalm.com

Palm Restaurant 1730 Rhode Island Ave NW Suite 900. Washington DC 20036 202-775-7256 775-8292
TF: 800-795-7256 ■ *Web:* www.thepalm.com

Palomino Euro-Bistro 1818 N Northlake Way. Seattle WA 98103 206-634-0550 632-3533

Panchero's Mexican Grill 2475 Coral Ct Suite B. Coraville IA 52241 319-545-6565 545-6570
TF: 888-639-2378 ■ *Web:* www.pancheros.com

Pancho's Management Inc 2855 Lamb Pl. Memphis TN 38118 901-362-9691 362-8487

Pancho's Mexican Buffet Inc 3500 Noble Ave. Fort Worth TX 76111 817-831-0081 838-1480
TF: 800-433-7670 ■ *Web:* www.panchosmexicanbuffet.com

Panda Express 1683 Walnut Grove Ave. Rosemead CA 91770 626-799-9898 927-9888
TF: 800-487-2632 ■ *Web:* www.pandaexpress.com

Panda Inn 1683 Walnut Grove Ave. Rosemead CA 91770 626-799-9898 927-9888
TF: 800-487-2632 ■ *Web:* www.pandainn.com

Panda Restaurant Group 1683 Walnut Grove Ave. Rosemead CA 91770 626-799-9898 927-9888
TF: 800-877-8988 ■ *Web:* www.pandarg.com

Paolo's 1305 Wisconsin Ave NW. Washington DC 20007 202-333-7336 333-6395

Papa Gino's Inc 600 Providence Hwy. Dedham MA 02026 781-461-1200 461-1896
TF: 800-727-2446 ■ *Web:* www.papaginos.com

Papa John's International Inc 2002 Papa John's Blvd. Louisville KY 40299 502-261-7272 261-4331*
NASDAQ: PZZA ■ **Fax:* Cust Svc ■ *TF:* 877-547-7272 ■ *Web:* www.papajohns.com

Papa Murphy's International Inc
8000 NE Parkway Dr Suite 350. Vancouver WA 98662 360-260-7272 260-0500
Web: www.papamurphys.com

Papa Razzi 284 Newbury St. Boston MA 02115 617-536-2800 236-4175
TF: 800-424-2753 ■ *Web:* www.backbayrestaurantgroup.com

Papa's Pizza-To-Go Inc 4465 Commerce Dr Suite 101. Buford GA 30518 770-614-6676 614-9095
Web: www.papaspizzatogo.com

Pappadeaux Seafood Kitchen 642 Yale St. Houston TX 77007 713-869-0151 869-4932
TF: 877-277-2748 ■ *Web:* www.pappadeaux.com

Pappas Restaurants Inc 642 Yale St. Houston TX 77007 713-869-0151 869-4932
TF: 877-277-2748 ■ *Web:* www.pappas.com

Pappas Seafood House 642 Yale St. Houston TX 77077 713-869-0151 869-4932
TF: 877-277-2748 ■ *Web:* www.pappas.com

Pappasito's Cantina 642 Yale St. Houston TX 77007 713-869-0151 869-4932
TF: 877-277-2748 ■ *Web:* www.pappas.com

Paragon Steakhouse Restaurants Inc
10200 Willow Creek Rd. San Diego CA 92131 858-689-2333 689-2289
Web: www.paragonsteak.com

Pasta House Co 1143 Macklind Ave. Saint Louis MO 63110 314-535-6644 531-2499
TF: 800-467-2782 ■ *Web:* www.pastahouse.com

Pasta Pomodoro Inc 1550 Bryant St Suite 100. San Francisco CA 94103 415-431-2681 431-8940
Web: pastapomodoro.com

Pat & Mario's 10 Kingsbridge Garden Cir Suite 600. Mississauga ON L5R3K6 905-568-0000 568-0080
TF: 800-361-3111

Pat O'Brien's International Inc 718 Saint Peter St. New Orleans LA 70116 504-525-4823 582-6918
TF: 800-597-4823 ■ *Web:* www.patobriens.com

Pat & Oscar's 10679 Westview Pkwy. San Diego CA 92126 858-695-8500
Web: www.breadstick.com

Patina Group 400 S Hope St Suite 950. Los Angeles CA 90071 213-239-2500 239-2501
Web: www.patinagroup.com

Paul Revere's Pizza International Ltd 1570 42nd St NE. Cedar Rapids IA 52402 319-395-9113 395-9115
Web: www.paulreverespizza.com

Pei Wei 7676 E Pinnacle Peak Rd. Scottsdale AZ 85255 602-957-8986 957-8998
Web: www.peiwei.com

Penguin Point Franchise Systems Inc 2691 E US 30. Warsaw IN 46580 574-267-3107 267-3154
TF: 800-577-5755 ■ *Web:* www.penguinpoint.com

Penn Station Inc 8276 Beechmont Ave. Cincinnati OH 45255 513-474-5957 474-7116
Web: www.penn-station.com

Pepe's Inc 1325 W 15th St. Chicago IL 60608 312-733-2500 733-2564
Web: www.pepes.com

Pepperoni Grill 1220 S Santa Fe Ave. Edmond OK 73003 405-705-5000 705-5001
TF: 800-679-3607

Perkins Restaurant & Bakery 6075 Poplar Ave Suite 800. Memphis TN 38119 901-766-6400 766-6482
TF: 800-877-7375 ■ *Web:* www.perkinsrestaurants.com

Perko's Cafe 2246 E Date Ave. Fresno CA 93706 559-485-8520 485-3704
TF: 800-230-4985 ■ *Web:* www.perkos.com

Peter Piper Inc 14635 N Kierland Blvd Suite 160. Scottsdale AZ 85254 480-609-6400 609-6523
TF: 800-899-3425 ■ *Web:* www.peterpiperpizza.com

Petro's Chili & Chips 5614 Kingston Pike 2nd Fl. Knoxville TN 37919 865-588-1076 588-0916
TF: 800-738-7639 ■ *Web:* www.petros.com

PF Chang's China Bistro Inc 7676 E Pinnacle Peak Rd. Scottsdale AZ 85255 602-957-8986 957-8998
NASDAQ: PFCB ■ *Web:* www.pfchangs.com

Phillips Seafood Restaurants 1215 E Fort Ave. Baltimore MD 21230 443-263-1200 837-8525*
**Fax Area Code:* 410 ■ *TF:* 800-648-7067 ■ *Web:* www.phillipsfoods.com

Philly Connection 120 Interstate N Pkwy E Suite 112. Atlanta GA 30339 770-952-6152 952-3168
TF: 800-886-8826 ■ *Web:* www.phillyconnection.com

Philly Franchising Co DBA Philly Connection
120 Interstate N Pkwy E Suite 112. Atlanta GA 30339 770-952-6152 952-3168
TF: 800-886-8826 ■ *Web:* www.phillyconnection.com

Piatti Restaurant Co 625 Redwood Hwy. Mill Valley CA 94941 415-380-2511 380-2535
Web: www.piatti.com

Piccadilly Cafeterias Inc 3232 Sherwood Forest Blvd. Baton Rouge LA 70816 225-293-9440 296-8370
TF: 800-535-9974 ■ *Web:* www.piccadilly.com

Piccadilly Circus Pizza 1007 Okoboji Ave. Milford IA 51351 712-338-2771 338-2263
TF: 800-338-4340 ■ *Web:* www.pcpizza.com

Pick Up Stix Inc 1330 Calle Avanzado. San Clemente CA 92673 949-361-3189 361-7749
TF: 800-400-7849 ■ *Web:* www.pickupstix.com

Pitt Grill Inc 928 Shady Ln. Lake Charles LA 70601 337-479-1320 582-4297

Pizza Boli's 5725 Falls Rd. Baltimore MD 21209 800-234-2654 464-9226*
**Fax Area Code:* 410 ■ *Web:* www.pizzabolis.com

Pizza Factory Inc 49430 Rd 426. Oakhurst CA 93644 559-683-3377 683-6879
TF: 800-654-4840 ■ *Web:* www.pizzafactoryinc.com

Pizza Hut Inc 14841 N Dallas Pkwy. Dallas TX 75254 972-338-7700 338-6869*
**Fax:* Cust Svc ■ *TF:* 800-948-8488 ■ *Web:* www.pizzahut.com

Pizza Inn Inc 3551 Plano Pkwy. The Colony TX 75056 469-384-5000 384-5054
NASDAQ: PZZI ■ *TF:* 800-880-9955 ■ *Web:* www.pizzainn.com

Pizza King Inc 221 Farabee Dr. Lafayette IN 47905 765-447-2172 447-5491

Pizza Man-He Delivers 6930 1/2 Tujunga Ave. North Hollywood CA 91605 818-766-4395 766-1496

Pizza Pizza Ltd 580 Jarvis St. Toronto ON M4Y2H9 416-967-1010 967-0891
TF: 800-265-9762 ■ *Web:* www.pizzapizza.ca

Pizza Plus Pizza Inc PO Box 629. Blountville TN 37617 423-652-2336 652-2190
TF: 800-675-1220 ■ *Web:* www.pizzaplusinc.com

Pizza Pro Inc 2107 N 2nd St PO Box 1285. Cabot AR 72023 501-605-1175 605-1204
TF: 800-777-7554 ■ *Web:* www.pizzapro.com

Pizza Ranch Inc 1121 Main St. Hull IA 51239 712-439-1150 439-1125
TF: 800-321-3401 ■ *Web:* www.pizzaranch.com

Pizzeria Regina 999 Broadway Suite 400. Saugus MA 01906 781-231-7575 231-5225
Web: www.pizzeriaregina.com

PJ America Inc 2300 Resource Dr. Birmingham AL 35242 205-980-6483 981-2881

Planet Hollywood International Inc 7598 W Sand Lake Rd. Orlando FL 32819 407-903-5500 352-7310
Web: www.planethollywood.com

PoFolks Restaurants 508 Harmon Ave. Panama City FL 32401 850-763-0501 872-0072
TF: 888-876-3655 ■ *Web:* www.pofolks.com

Pollo Tropical Inc 7300 N Kendall Dr 8th Fl. Miami FL 33156 305-670-7696 670-6403
TF: 888-778-7696 ■ *Web:* www.pollotropical.com

Ponderosa Steakhouses 6500 International Pkwy Suite 1000. Plano TX 75093 972-588-5000 588-5973*
**Fax:* Cust Svc ■ *TF:* 800-727-8355 ■ *Web:* www.ponderosasteakhouses.com

Popeyes Chicken & Biscuits
5555 Glenridge Connector NE Suite 300. Atlanta GA 30342 404-459-4450 459-4533
TF: 866-232-4403 ■ *Web:* www.popeyes.com

Port of Subs Inc 5365 Mae Anne Ave Suite A-29. Reno NV 89523 775-747-0555 747-1510
TF: 800-245-0245 ■ *Web:* www.portofsubs.com

Portillo Restaurant Group 2001 Spring Rd Suite 500. Oak Brook IL 60523 630-954-3773 954-5851
Web: www.portillos.com

Potbelly Sandwich Works
222 Merchandise Mart Plaza Suite 2300. Chicago IL 60654 312-951-0600 951-0300
Web: www.potbelly.com

Premier Restaurant Management Co
3620 Walnut Hills Ave. Orange Village OH 44122 216-464-6900 464-8430

Pretzelmaker 2855 E Cottonwood Pkwy Suite 400. Salt Lake City UT 84121 801-736-5600 736-5970
TF: 800-266-5437 ■ *Web:* pretzelmaker.com

Prime Pubs Inc 10 Kingsbridge Garden Cir Suite 600. Mississauga ON L5R3K6 905-568-0000 568-0080
TF: 800-361-3111 ■ *Web:* www.primepubs.com

Prime Restaurant Group Inc
10 Kingsbridge Garden Cir Suite 600. Mississauga ON L5R3K6 905-568-0000 568-0080
TF: 800-613-1111 ■ *Web:* www.primepubs.com

Prime Sirloin Steak House 129 Fast Ln. Mooresville NC 28117 704-660-5939 799-6199
TF: 877-704-5939

Prism LP 101 Exchange Ave. Vaughan ON L4K5R6 416-739-2900

Pry-Wing LLC 808 Stevens Creek Rd. Augusta GA 30907 706-860-0510 860-4640

Qdoba Mexican Grill 4865 Ward Rd Suite 500. Wheat Ridge CO 80033 720-898-2300 898-2396
TF: 877-261-4783 ■ *Web:* www.qdoba.com

Qdoba Restaurant Corp DBA Qdoba Mexican Grill
4865 Ward Rd Suite 500. Wheat Ridge CO 80033 720-898-2300 898-2396
TF: 877-261-4783 ■ *Web:* www.qdoba.com

Quality Dining Inc 4220 Edison Lakes Pkwy. Mishawaka IN 46545 574-271-4600 271-4612
TF: 800-589-3820 ■ *Web:* www.qdi.com

Quiznos Corp 1475 Lawrence St Suite 400. Denver CO 80202 720-359-3300 359-3399
Web: www.quiznos.com

Rafferty's Inc 1750 Scottsville Rd Suite 2. Bowling Green KY 42104 270-781-2834 781-2860
Web: www.raffertys.com

Rainforest Cafe 1510 W Loop South. Houston TX 77027 713-850-1010 850-7205
TF: 800-552-6379 ■ *Web:* www.rainforestcafe.com

Rally's Hamburgers Inc 4300 W Cypress St Suite 600. Tampa FL 33607 813-283-7000 283-7001
TF: 800-800-8072 ■ *Web:* www.rallyshamburgers.com

Ram The 10013 59th Ave SW. Lakewood WA 98499 253-588-1788 588-0713
TF: 888-898-4050 ■ *Web:* www.theram.com

Ram International Ltd 10013 59th Ave Sw. Lakewood WA 98499 253-588-1788 588-0713
Web: www.theram.com

Ram's Horn Restaurant Inc 24225 W Nine-Mile Rd. Southfield MI 48034 248-350-3430 350-1024

Rare Hospitality International Inc 8215 Roswell Rd Bldg 600. Atlanta GA 30350 770-399-9595 901-6628*
NASDAQ: RARE ■ **Fax:* Cust Svc ■ *TF:* 800-434-6245 ■ *Web:* www.rarehospitality.com

Rascal House Pizza Systems Inc 2064 Euclid Ave. Cleveland OH 44115 216-781-0904 781-9243
Web: www.rascalhousepizza.com

Razzoo's LP 5080 Spectrum Dr Suite 806. Addison TX 75001 972-233-6399 233-1540
Web: www.razzoos.com

Red Hot & Blue Restaurants Inc
1701 Clarendon Blvd Suite 105. Arlington VA 22209 703-276-8833 528-4789
TF: 800-723-0745 ■ *Web:* www.redhotandblue.com

Red Lobster 5900 Lake Ellenor Dr. Orlando FL 32809 407-245-4000 245-5389
Web: www.redlobster.com

Red Robin Gourmet Burgers Inc
6312 S Fiddlers Green Cir Suite 200-N. Greenwood Village CO 80111 303-846-6000 846-6013
NASDAQ: RRGB ■ *Web:* www.redrobin.com

Redfish America LLC 5050 N 40th St Suite 200. Phoenix AZ 85018 602-852-9000 852-0001
TF: 888-677-5080 ■ *Web:* www.redfishamerica.com

Renzio's Inc 4690 S Yosemite St. Greenwood Village CO 80111 303-267-0300 220-7899
Web: www.renzios.com

Restaurant Assoc Inc 120 W 45th St 16th Fl. New York NY 10036 212-789-8100 302-8032
Web: www.restaurantassociates.com

Restaurant Developers Corp 5755 Granger Rd Suite 200. Independence OH 44131 216-398-1101 398-0707
TF: 800-837-9599 ■ *Web:* www.mrhero.com

Restaurants Unlimited Inc 1818 N Northlake Way. Seattle WA 98103 206-634-0550 632-3533
TF: 877-855-6106 ■ *Web:* www.r-u-i.com

Rib Crib Corp 4535 S Harvard Ave. Tulsa OK 74135 918-712-7427 728-6945
TF: 800-275-9677 ■ *Web:* www.ribcrib.com

Rick's Cabaret International Inc 10959 Cutten Rd. Houston TX 77066 281-397-6730 397-6765
NASDAQ: RICK ■ *Web:* www.ricks.com

Riese Restaurants 560 5th Ave. New York NY 10036 212-563-7440 629-0942

Rigel Corp 7545 Pacific St. Omaha NE 68114 402-392-2904 392-1645

Riscky's Barbecue 2314 Azle Ave. Fort Worth TX 76106 817-624-8662 624-3777

RJ Boar's Franchising Corp 3127 Brady St Suite 3. Davenport IA 52803 563-322-2627 322-1947
TF: 877-395-8910 ■ *Web:* www.rjboars.com

RJ Gator's Hometown Grill & Bar 609 Hepburn Ave Suite 103. Jupiter FL 33458 561-575-0326 575-9220
TF: 800-438-4286 ■ *Web:* www.rjgators.com

Rock Bottom Restaurants Inc 248 Centennial Pkwy. Louisville CO 80027 303-664-4000 664-4199
TF: 800-273-9827 ■ *Web:* www.rockbottom.com

Rock-Ola Restaurants 1337 Winstad Pl. Greensboro NC 27408 336-272-9355 272-5568
Web: www.rock-olacafe.com

Rockfish Seafood Grill 5307 E Mockingbird Ln Suite 1001. Dallas TX 75206 214-887-9400 821-0138
Web: www.rockfishseafood.com

				Phone	Fax
Rocky Rococo 105 E Wisconsin Ave	Oconomowoc	WI	53066	262-569-5580	569-5591
TF: 800-888-7625 ■ Web: www.rockyrococo.com					
Romacorp Inc 9304 Forest Ln Suite 200	Dallas	TX	75243	214-343-7800	343-2680
TF: 800-286-7662					
Romano's Macaroni Grill 6820 LBJ Fwy	Dallas	TX	75240	972-980-9917	770-9593
TF: 800-983-4637 ■ Web: www.macaronigrill.com					
Ronzio Pizza 111 John St	Lincoln	RI	02865	401-334-9750	312-0378
Web: www.ronziopizza.com					
Rosati's Pizza 7020 Greenleaf St	Niles	IL	60714	847-663-0870	965-8324
Web: www.rosatispizza.com					
Rosebud Restaurant 1419 W Diversey Pkwy	Chicago	IL	60614	773-325-9700	325-9708
Web: www.rosebudrestaurants.com					
Royal Fork Buffet Restaurant 6874 Fairview Ave	Boise	ID	83704	208-322-5600	322-0149
Roy's Restaurants 1300 Dove St Suite 105	Newport Beach	CA	962660	949-261-2424	261-2626
Web: www.roysrestaurants.com					
RPM Pizza LLC 15384 5th St	Gulfport	MS	39503	228-832-4000	832-1092
TF: 800-622-6000 ■ Web: www.rpmpizza.com					
Rubio's Restaurants Inc 1902 Wright Pl Suite 300	Carlsbad	CA	92008	760-929-8226	929-8203
NASDAQ: RUBO ■ Web: www.rubios.com					
Ruby Tuesday Inc 150 W Church Ave	Maryville	TN	37801	865-379-5700	379-6826*
NYSE: RI ■ *Fax: Mktg ■ TF: 800-325-0755 ■ Web: www.ruby-tuesday.com					
Ruby's Diner Inc 660 Newport Ctr Dr Suite 850	Newport Beach	CA	92660	949-644-7829	644-4625
TF: 800-439-7829 ■ Web: www.rubys.com					
Runza Drive-Ins of America Inc 5931 S 58th St Suite D	Lincoln	NE	68516	402-423-2394	423-5726
TF: 800-929-2394 ■ Web: www.runza.com					
Russ' Restaurants Inc 390 E 8th St	Holland	MI	49423	616-396-6571	396-6755
TF: 800-521-1778 ■ Web: www.russrestaurants.com					
Rusty Pelican 209 Avenida Fabricante Suite 200	San Clemente	CA	92672	949-366-6260	366-6261
TF: 877-729-4867 ■ Web: www.rustypelican.com					
Rusty's Pizza Parlors Inc 228 W Carrillo St Suite F	Santa Barbara	CA	93101	805-963-9127	962-5054
Web: www.rustyspizza.com					
Ruth's Chris Steak House 3321 Hessmer Ave	Metairie	LA	70002	504-454-6560	454-9060
NASDAQ: RUTH ■ TF: 800-487-4785 ■ Web: www.ruthschris.com					
Ryan's Restaurant Group Inc 405 Lancaster Ave	Greer	SC	29650	864-879-1000	877-0974
NASDAQ: RYAN ■ Web: www.ryansinc.com					
S & S Cafeterias 2124 Riverside Dr	Macon	GA	31204	478-745-4759	746-8233
TF: 800-841-5385 ■ Web: www.sscafeterias.com					
Sagebrush Steakhouse 129 Fast Ln	Mooresville	NC	28117	704-660-5939	799-6199
TF: 877-704-5939 ■ Web: www.sagebrushsteakhouse.com					
Saladworks Inc					
Eight Tower Bridge 161 Washington St Suite 225	Conshohocken	PA	19428	610-825-3080	825-3280
Web: www.saladworks.com					
Saltgrass Steak House Corp 1510 W Loop South	Houston	TX	77027	713-850-1010	850-7274
TF: 800-552-6379 ■ Web: www.saltgrass.com					
Sandella's LLC 9 Brookside Pl	West Redding	CT	06896	203-544-9984	544-9981
TF: 888-544-9984 ■ Web: www.sandellas.com					
Sasnak Management Corp 1877 N Rock Rd	Wichita	KS	67206	316-683-2611	681-2481
Sbarro Inc 401 Broadhollow Rd	Melville	NY	11747	631-715-4100	715-4181
TF Cust Svc: 800-766-4949 ■ Web: www.sbarro.com					
Schwartz Brothers Restaurants 325 118th Ave SE Suite 106	Bellevue	WA	98005	425-455-3948	451-3573
Web: www.schwartzbros.com					
Scotto Management Corp 1895 Greentree Rd	Cherry Hill	NJ	08003	856-424-4260	424-9278
Seed Restaurant Group 2470 Palumbo Dr	Lexington	KY	40509	859-268-1668	268-2263
Web: www.fazolis.com					
Select Restaurants Inc 2000 Auburn Dr Suite 410	Cleveland	OH	44122	216-464-6606	464-8565
Web: www.selectrestaurants.com					
Semolina International Pasta Restaurants Inc					
5080 Pontchartrain Blvd	New Orleans	LA	70118	504-482-2288	482-2267
Web: www.semolina.com					
Shakey's USA 2200 W Valley Blvd	Alhambra	CA	91803	626-576-0737	576-2114
TF: 888-444-6686 ■ Web: www.shakeys.com					
Shari's Restaurants 9400 SW Gemini Dr	Beaverton	OR	97008	503-605-4299	605-4294
TF: 800-433-5334 ■ Web: www.sharis.com					
Shells Seafood Restaurants Inc					
16313 N Dale Mabry Hwy Suite 100	Tampa	FL	33618	813-961-0944	960-9059
Web: www.shellsseafood.com					
Shoney's Restaurants Inc 1717 Elm Hill Pike Suite B1	Nashville	TN	37210	615-391-5395	231-2498
TF: 877-474-6639 ■ Web: www.shoneys.com					
Shula's Steak House 7601 Miami Lakes Dr	Miami Lakes	FL	33014	305-820-8102	820-8175
TF: 800-247-4852 ■ Web: www.donshula.com					
Silver Diner Inc 11806 Rockville Pike	Rockville	MD	20852	301-770-1444	770-1940
Web: www.silverdiner.com					
Simm's Restaurants 7985 Santa Monica Blvd Suite 200	Los Angeles	CA	90046	323-656-0874	656-7898
Sirloin Stockade International 2908 N Plum St	Hutchinson	KS	67502	620-669-9372	669-0531
Web: www.stockadecompanies.com					
Sixx Holdings Inc 3878 Oak Lawn Suite 500	Dallas	TX	75219	214-855-8800	855-8808
Sizzler Restaurants					
15301 Ventura Blvd Bldg B Suite 300	Sherman Oaks	CA	91403	818-662-9800	662-9870
Web: www.sizzler.com					
Sizzling Wok International Inc 6551 #3 Rd Unit 1538	Richmond	BC	V6Y2B6	604-207-8871	207-9893
Skipper's Inc 170 W Dayton St Suite 204	Edmonds	WA	98020	425-563-9200	563-9201
Web: www.skippers.net					
Skyline Chili Inc 4180 Thunderbird Ln	Fairfield	OH	45014	513-874-1188	874-3591
TF: 800-443-4371 ■ Web: www.skylinechili.com					
Slaymaker Group 404 E 4500 South Suite A-12	Salt Lake City	UT	84107	801-261-3700	261-1615
Smith Brothers Restaurant Corp 16 N Marengo Ave Suite 609	Pasadena	CA	91101	626-577-2400	577-8330
Web: www.smithbrothersrestaurants.com					
Smith Hal Restaurant Group Inc 1800 N Interstate Dr Suite 200	Norman	OK	73072	405-321-2600	321-2992
Smith & Sons Foods Inc 2124 Riverside Dr	Macon	GA	31204	478-745-4759	746-8233
TF: 800-841-5385 ■ Web: www.sscafeterias.com					
Smith & Wollensky Restaurant Group Inc					
1114 1st Ave 6th Fl	New York	NY	10021	212-838-2061	355-0120
NASDAQ: SWRG ■ Web: www.smithandwollensky.com					
Smitty's Canada Ltd 600-501 18th Ave SW	Calgary	AB	T2S0C7	403-229-3838	229-3899
Web: www.smittys.ca					
Smokey Bones BBQ 5900 Lake Ellenor Dr	Orlando	FL	32809	407-245-4000	245-5189
TF: 800-421-3035 ■ Web: www.darden.com					
Smokey's Place 425 NW 43rd Way	Deerfield Beach	FL	33442	954-622-1115	
Smoothie King Franchises Inc 2400 Veterans Blvd Suite 110	Kenner	LA	70062	504-467-4006	469-1274
TF: 800-577-4200 ■ Web: www.smoothieking.com					
Snappy Tomato Pizza Co 7230 Turfway Rd	Florence	KY	41042	859-525-4680	525-4686
TF: 888-463-7627 ■ Web: www.snappytomato.com					
Sobik's Subs 1515 International Pkwy Suite 2013	Heathrow	FL	32746	407-333-8998	333-8852
Web: www.sobiks.com					
Sonic Corp 300 Johnny Bench Dr	Oklahoma City	OK	73104	405-280-7654	225-5969
NASDAQ: SONC ■ TF: 800-569-6656 ■ Web: www.sonicdrivein.com					
Sonic Drive-in Restaurants 300 Johnny Bench Dr	Oklahoma City	OK	73104	405-225-5000	225-5963
TF: 800-569-6656 ■ Web: www.sonicdrivein.com					
Sonny Bryan's Smokehouse 3890 W Northwest Hwy Suite 200	Dallas	TX	75220	214-350-1800	350-3738
Web: www.sonnybryans.com					
Sonny's Real Pit Bar-B-Q 2605 Maitland Ctr Pkwy Suite C	Maitland	FL	32751	407-660-8888	660-9050
Web: www.sonnysbbq.com					
Souper Salad Inc 140 Heimer Rd Suite 400	San Antonio	TX	78232	210-495-9644	495-9655
TF: 800-346-7687 ■ Web: www.soupersalad.com					
Souplantation 15822 Bernardo Ctr Dr Suite A	San Diego	CA	92127	858-675-1600	675-1616
TF: 800-874-1600 ■ Web: www.soupplantation.com					
Southern Multifoods Inc 101 E Cherokee St	Jacksonville	TX	75766	903-586-1524	586-9644
Web: www.smi-tex.com					
Spaghetti Warehouse Inc 12200 Stemmons Fwy Suite 100	Dallas	TX	75234	972-241-5500	888-4200
TF Cust Svc: 800-929-4000 ■ Web: www.meatballs.com					
Spangles Inc 437 N Hillside St	Wichita	KS	67214	316-685-8817	685-1671
Web: www.spanglesinc.com					
Spear's Food Service Co 1930 N Woodlawn St	Wichita	KS	67208	316-686-5173	687-5253
Specialty Restaurants Corp 8191 E Kaiser Blvd	Anaheim	CA	92808	714-279-6100	998-7574
Web: www.specialtyrestaurants.com					
Spectra Hospitality Group Inc 1880 W 1st Ave 2nd Fl	Vancouver	BC	V6J1G5	604-714-6500	730-5508
Web: www.spectragroup.com					
Spoons Restaurants Inc 18500 Von Karman Ave Suite 380	Irvine	CA	92612	949-225-5460	225-5482
Web: www.spoonsgrillandbar.com					
Stanford's Restaurant & Bar 7165 SW Fir Loop Suite 200	Portland	OR	97223	503-684-2803	620-6149
Web: www.stanfords.com					
Star Buffet Inc 1312 N Scottsdale Rd	Scottsdale	AZ	85257	480-425-0397	425-0494
NASDAQ: STRZ					
Steak & Ale 6500 International Pkwy Suite 1000	Plano	TX	75093	972-588-5000	588-5325
TF: 800-727-8355 ■ Web: www.steakale.com					
Steak Escape 222 Neilston St	Columbus	OH	43215	614-224-0300	224-6460
Web: www.steakescape.com					
Steak n Shake Co 36 S Pennsylvania St Suite 500	Indianapolis	IN	46204	317-633-4100	633-4105
NYSE: SNS ■ TF: 800-437-2406 ■ Web: www.steaknshake.com					
Steakhouse Partners Inc 10200 Willow Creek Rd	San Diego	CA	92131	858-689-2333	689-2289
Strang Corp 8905 Lake Ave	Cleveland	OH	44102	216-961-6767	961-1966
Web: www.strangcorp.com					
Strategic Restaurants Inc 3000 Executive Pkwy Suite 515	San Ramon	CA	94583	925-328-3300	328-3333
Web: www.strategicrestaurants.com					
Straw Hat Co-op Corp 18 Crow Canyon Ct Suite 150	San Ramon	CA	94583	925-837-3400	820-1080
Web: www.strawhatpizza.com					
Stuart Anderson's Black Angus					
4410 El Camino Real Suite 201	Los Altos	CA	94022	650-949-6400	949-6425
TF: 800-750-0211 ■ Web: www.stuartanderson.com					
Stuckey's Corp 8555 16th St Suite 850	Silver Spring	MD	20910	301-585-8222	585-8997
TF: 800-423-6171 ■ Web: www.stuckeyscorp.com					
Stuft Pizza Franchise Corp 50855 Washington St Suite 210	La Quinta	CA	92253	760-777-1660	777-1948
Web: www.stuftpizza.com					
Sub Station II Inc 425 N Main St	Sumter	SC	29150	803-773-4711	775-2220
TF: 800-779-2970 ■ Web: www.substationii.com					
Subway Restaurants 325 Bic Dr	Milford	CT	06460	203-877-4281	783-7614
TF: 800-888-4848 ■ Web: www.subway.com					
Sullivan's 224 E Douglas Ave	Wichita	KS	67227	316-264-8899	264-5988
TF: 800-234-0888 ■ Web: www.lonestarsteakhouse.com					
SunShine Cafe Restaurants 7112 Zionsville Rd	Indianapolis	IN	46268	317-299-3391	299-3390
TF: 800-808-4774					
Super Subby's Inc 8924 N Dixie Dr	Dayton	OH	45414	937-898-0996	898-2367
Web: www.subbys.com					
Sushi Doraku 8685 NW 53rd Terr Suite 201	Miami	FL	33166	305-593-0770	592-6371
TF: 800-327-3369 ■ Web: www.dorakusushi.com					
Sweet Tomatoes 15822 Bernardo Ctr Dr Suite A	San Diego	CA	92127	858-675-1600	675-1616
TF: 800-874-1600 ■ Web: www.soupplantation.com					
Swensen's Ice Cream Co 4175 Veterans Memorial Hwy	Ronkonkoma	NY	11779	631-737-9898	737-9792
TF: 800-423-2763					
Swiss Chalet Rotisserie & Grill 6303 Airport Rd	Mississauga	ON	L4V1R8	905-405-6500	405-6648
TF: 800-860-4082 ■ Web: www.swisschalet.com					
Tacala LLC 4268 Cahaba Heights Ct	Birmingham	AL	35243	205-443-9600	443-9796
Web: www.tacala.com					
Taco Bell Corp 17901 Von Karman Ave	Irvine	CA	92614	949-863-4500	863-2214
Web: www.tacobell.com					
Taco Bueno Restaurants Inc 3033 Kellway Dr Suite 122	Carrollton	TX	75006	972-417-4800	417-4811
TF: 800-440-0778					
Taco Cabana Inc 8918 Tesoro Dr Suite 200	San Antonio	TX	78217	210-804-0990	804-1970
TF: 800-357-9924 ■ Web: www.tacocabana.com					
Taco Casa International Ltd 1607 SW 37th Terr	Topeka	KS	66609	785-267-2548	267-2652
Web: www.tacocasafranchise.com					
Taco Land Co 456 Broadway	Kingston	NY	12401	845-334-8775	334-8775
Taco Maker Inc 4605 Harrison Blvd PO Box 84415	Ogden	UT	84403	801-476-9780	476-9788
TF: 800-207-5804 ■ Web: www.tacomaker.com					
Taco Mayo Inc 10405 Greenbriar Pl	Oklahoma City	OK	73159	405-691-8226	691-2572
TF: 800-291-8226 ■ Web: www.tacomayo.com					
Taco Tico Inc 2118 N Tyler St Suite B-100	Wichita	KS	67212	316-681-0220	681-0582
TF: 877-681-0220 ■ Web: www.tacotico.com					
Taco Time International Inc 7730 E Greenway Rd Suite 104	Scottsdale	AZ	85260	480-443-0200	443-1972
TF: 800-547-8907 ■ Web: www.tacotime.com					
Tacone 950 S Flower St Suite 105	Los Angeles	CA	90015	213-236-0950	236-0951
TF: 877-482-2663 ■ Web: www.tacone.com					
Tacos Mexico Inc 5120 E Olympic Blvd	Los Angeles	CA	90022	323-266-0482	266-1721
Tavistock Restaurants LLC 2200 Powell St Suite 750	Emeryville	CA	94608	510-594-4262	654-8295
Web: www.tavistockrestaurants.com					
TDL Group Corp 874 Sinclair Rd	Oakville	ON	L6K2Y1	905-845-6511	845-0265
NYSE: THI ■ TF: 888-601-1616 ■ Web: www.timhortons.com					
Ted's Hot Dogs 95 Roger Chaffee Dr	Amherst	NY	14228	716-691-3731	691-3776
Web: www.tedsonline.com					
Tee Jaye's Country Place Restaurants					
1363 Parsons Ave PO Box 06359	Columbus	OH	43206	614-443-1938	443-0613
Web: www.teejayes.com					
Temple Square Hospitality Corp					
15 E South Temple St 9th Fl	Salt Lake City	UT	84150	801-539-3101	596-0107
Web: www.templesquarehospitality.com					
Texas Land & Cattle Co 224 E Douglas Suite 700	Wichita	KS	67202	316-264-8899	358-2826*
*Fax Area Code: 214 ■ Web: www.texaslandandcattle.com					
Texas Roadhouse Inc 6040 Dutchmans Ln Suite 400	Louisville	KY	40205	502-426-9984	426-9924
NASDAQ: TXRH ■ TF: 800-839-7623 ■ Web: www.texasroadhouse.com					
Texas Steakhouse & Saloon 1021 Noell Ln PO Box 1908	Rocky Mount	NC	27804	252-937-2800	937-4909
Web: www.texassteakhouse.com					
TGI Friday's Worldwide Inc 4201 Marsh Ln	Carrollton	TX	75007	972-662-5400	662-5739*
*Fax: Mktg ■ TF: 800-374-3297 ■ Web: www.tgifridays.com					
Thompson Hospitality 505 Huntmar Pk Dr Suite 350	Herndon	VA	20170	703-709-0145	964-0505
TF: 800-842-2737 ■ Web: www.thompsonhospitality.com					
Thundercloud Subs 1102 W 6th St	Austin	TX	78703	512-479-8805	479-8806
TF: 800-256-7895 ■ Web: www.thundercloud.com					
Tia's Tex Mex 1101 N Union Bower Rd Suite 160	Irving	TX	75061	972-554-6886	554-6888
TF: 800-486-5322					
Tim Hortons Inc 874 Sinclair Rd	Oakville	ON	L6K2Y1	905-845-6511	845-0265
NYSE: THI ■ TF: 888-601-1616 ■ Web: www.timhortons.com					
Timber Lodge Steakhouses Inc					
1801 American Blvd E Suite 27	Bloomington	MN	55425	952-929-9353	929-5658
Web: www.timberlodgesteakhouse.com					
Toarmina's Pizza Inc 673 Barbara St	Westland	MI	48185	734-729-9067	729-1882
Web: www.toarminaspizza.com					
Todai Franchising LLC 3700 Wilshire Blvd Suite 560	Los Angeles	CA	90010	909-869-7727	
TF: 888-558-6324 ■ Web: www.todai.com					
Tony Roma's Inc 9304 Forest Ln Suite 200	Dallas	TX	75243	214-343-7800	343-2680
TF: 800-286-7662 ■ Web: www.tonyromas.com					
TooJays Original Gourmet Deli 3654 Georgia Ave	West Palm Beach	FL	33405	561-659-9011	659-9703
Web: www.toojays.com					

Company	City	State	Zip	Phone	Fax
Tortuga Coastal Cantina 1135 Edgebrook St	Houston	TX	77034	713-943-7574	943-9554
TF: 800-741-7574					
Trader Vic's Inc 2 Fifer Ave Suite 130	Corte Madera	CA	94925	415-927-9788	927-9688
TF: 877-762-4824 ■ *Web:* www.tradervics.com					
Trail Dust Steak Houses Inc 2300 E Lamar Blvd	Arlington	TX	70006	817-633-4996	
Web: www.traildust.com					
Travaglini Enterprises 231 Chestnut St	Meadville	PA	16335	814-724-4880	337-2630
Trigild Inc 12707 High Bluff Dr Suite 300	San Diego	CA	92130	858-720-6700	720-6707
Web: www.trigild.com					
Tripps Restaurants 1337 Winstead Pl	Greensboro	NC	27408	336-272-9355	272-5568
Web: www.trippsrestaurants.com/					
Tropical Smoothie Cafe 4100 Legendary Dr Suite 250	Destin	FL	32541	850-269-9850	269-9845
Web: www.tropicalsmoothie.com					
TS Restaurants of California & Hawaii 2530 Kekaa Dr Suite C2	Lahaina	HI	96761	808-667-4800	667-4802
Web: www.hulapie.com					
Tubby's Inc 35807 Moravian	Clinton Township	MI	48035	586-792-2369	792-4250
TF: 800-752-0644 ■ *Web:* www.tubby.com					
Tudor's Biscuit World PO Box 3603	Charleston	WV	25536	304-343-4026	727-1111
Web: www.tudorsbiscuitworld.com					
Tumbleweed Inc 2301 River Rd Suite 200	Louisville	KY	40206	502-893-0323	893-6676
Web: www.tumbleweedrestaurants.com					
Ultimate Franchise Systems Inc					
300 International Pkwy Suite 100	Heathrow	FL	32746	407-333-8998	444-8852
Web: www.ufsi.net					
Una Mas Restaurants Inc 25064 Viking St	Hayward	CA	94545	408-747-7000	744-1051
TF: 888-862-2627 ■ *Web:* www.unamas.com					
Uno Chicago Grill 100 Charles Park Rd	Boston	MA	02132	617-323-9200	469-3949
TF: 866-600-8667 ■ *Web:* www.unos.com					
Uno Restaurant Corp 100 Charles Pk Rd	West Roxbury	MA	02132	617-323-9200	323-6906
Web: www.unos.com					
V & J Holding Cos Inc 6933 W Brown Deer Rd	Milwaukee	WI	53223	414-365-9003	365-9467
Val Ltd Inc 2601 S 70th St	Lincoln	NE	68506	402-434-9350	434-9325
TF: 800-556-8150 ■ *Web:* www.valentinos.com					
Valentino's 2601 S 70th St	Lincoln	NE	68506	402-434-9350	434-9325
TF: 888-240-8257 ■ *Web:* www.valentinos.com					
VICORP Restaurants Inc 400 W 48th Ave	Denver	CO	80216	303-296-2121	672-2664*
**Fax:* Mktg ■ *Web:* www.vicorpinc.com					
Villa Enterprises Management Ltd Inc 25 Washington St	Morristown	NJ	07960	973-285-4800	285-5252
Web: www.villapizza.com					
Village Inn 400 W 48th Ave	Denver	CO	80216	303-296-2121	672-2676*
**Fax:* Cust Svc ■ *TF:* 800-800-3644 ■ *Web:* www.vicorpinc.com					
Viva Burrito Co 860 E 16th St	Tucson	AZ	85718	520-882-8713	620-6468
Vocelli Pizza 2101 Greentree Rd Suite A-202	Pittsburgh	PA	15220	412-279-9100	279-9781
Web: www.vocellipizza.com					
Waffle House Inc 5986 Financial Dr	Norcross	GA	30071	770-729-5700	729-5758
TF: 800-882-9235 ■ *Web:* www.wafflehouse.com					
Wahoo's Fish Taco 2855 Pullman St	Santa Ana	CA	92705	949-222-0670	222-0750
Web: www.wahoos.com					
Waid's Family Restaurants 4717 Grand Ave Suite 200	Kansas City	MO	64112	816-931-2261	931-9044
Wall Street Deli Inc 14 Penn Plaza Suite 1305	New York	NY	10122	516-358-0600	359-3601*
**Fax Area Code:* 212 ■ *Web:* www.wallstreetdeli.com					
Ward's Food Systems Inc 5293 Old Hwy 11	Hattiesburg	MS	39402	601-268-9273	268-9283
Web: www.wardsrestaurants.com					
WB Johnson Properties 100 W Paces Ferry Rd	Atlanta	GA	30305	404-237-7300	365-9800
Weathervane Seafood Restaurant 31 Badgers Island W	Kittery	ME	03904	207-439-0335	439-7754
TF: 800-654-4639 ■ *Web:* www.weathervaneseafoods.com					
Wendy's International Inc 1 Dave Thomas Blvd	Dublin	OH	43017	614-764-3100	764-3459
NYSE: WEN ■ *Web:* www.wendys.com					
Western Sizzlin Corp 1338 Plantation Rd	Roanoke	VA	24012	540-345-3195	345-0831
TF: 800-247-8325 ■ *Web:* www.western-sizzlin.com					
Western Steer Family Steakhouse					
129 Fast Ln PO Box 3130	Mooresville	NC	28117	704-660-5939	799-6199
TF: 877-704-5939 ■ *Web:* www.primesirloin.com					
Whataburger Inc 1 Whataburger Way	Corpus Christi	TX	78411	361-878-0650	878-0401
Web: www.whataburger.com					
White Castle System Inc 555 W Goodale St	Columbus	OH	43215	614-228-5781	464-0596
TF: 866-272-8372 ■ *Web:* www.whitecastle.com					
White Lodging Services Corp 1000 E 80th Pl Suite 600-N	Merrillville	IN	46410	219-769-3267	756-2902
Web: www.whitelodging.com					
Wienerschnitzel 4450 Von Karman Ave Suite 220	Newport Beach	CA	92660	949-752-5800	
Web: www.wienerschnitzel.com					
Willie G's 1510 W Loop South	Houston	TX	77027	713-850-1010	850-7274
TF: 800-552-6379 ■ *Web:* www.williegs.com					
Wing Zone Franchise Corp 900 Circle 75 Pkwy Suite 930	Atlanta	GA	30339	404-875-5045	875-6631
TF: 877-946-4966 ■ *Web:* www.wingzone.com					
Winger's Franchising Inc 404 E 4500 South Suite A-12	Salt Lake City	UT	84107	801-261-3700	261-1615
Web: www.wingers.info					
Wings To Go Inc 846 Ritchie Hwy Suite 1 B	Severna Park	MD	21146	800-552-9464	
Web: www.wingstogo.com					
Wingstop Restaurants Inc 1101 E Arapaho Rd Suite 150	Richardson	TX	75081	972-686-6500	686-6502
Web: www.wingstop.com					
Winstead's Restaurants 4717 Grand Ave Suite 200	Kansas City	MO	64112	816-931-2261	931-9044
Web: www.winsteads.com					
Wolfgang Puck Worldwide Inc					
100 N Crescent Dr Suite 100	Beverly Hills	CA	90210	310-432-1500	432-1630
Web: www.wolfgangpuck.com					
Wolfgang Puck's Express 100 N Cresent Dr Suite 100	Beverly Hills	CA	90210	310-432-1500	432-1630
Web: www.wolfgangpuck.com/rest/index.html					
Woody's Bar-B-Q 4745 Sutton Pk Ct Suite 301	Jacksonville	FL	32224	904-992-0556	992-0551
Web: www.woodysbarbq.com					
World Wrapps 401 2nd Ave S Suite 150	Seattle	WA	98104	206-233-9727	233-0539
TF: 888-233-9727 ■ *Web:* www.worldwrapps.com					
Yard House 8001 Irvine Center Dr Suite 1170	Irvine	CA	92618	949-727-0959	727-0831
Web: www.yardhouse.com					
Yaya's Flame Broiled Chicken 521 S Dort Hwy	Flint	MI	48503	810-235-6550	235-5210
TF: 800-754-1242 ■ *Web:* www.yayas.com					
Yoshinoya Beef Bowl 1603 W Sepulveda Blvd	Torrance	CA	90501	310-539-8319	
TF: 800-576-8017 ■ *Web:* www.yoshinoyausa.com					
Yours Truly Restaurants 30 N Main St	Chagrin Falls	OH	44022	440-247-8338	247-2131
Web: www.ytr.com					
Yum! Brands Inc 1441 Gardiner Ln	Louisville	KY	40213	502-874-8300	874-8790
NYSE: YUM ■ *TF:* 800-225-5532 ■ *Web:* www.yum.com					
Zaxby's Franchising Inc 1040 Founder's Blvd	Athens	GA	30606	706-353-8107	548-6002
TF: 866-892-9297 ■ *Web:* www.zaxbys.com					
Zero's Subs 2859 Virginia Beach Blvd Suite 105	Virginia Beach	VA	23452	757-486-8338	486-9755
TF: 800-588-0782 ■ *Web:* www.zeros.com					
Zio's Italian Kitchen 4441 S 72nd East Ave	Tulsa	OK	74145	918-663-8880	641-1236
Web: www.zios.com					
Zippy's Restaurant Inc 1765 S King St 2nd Fl	Honolulu	HI	96826	808-973-0880	973-0888
Web: www.zippys.com					
Zyng Inc PO Box 72108 RPO Atwater	Montreal	QC	H3J2Z6	514-288-8800	939-8808
TF: 888-966-6353 ■ *Web:* www.zyng.com					

674 RESTAURANTS (INDIVIDUAL)

SEE ALSO Attractions - Shopping/Dining/Entertainment Districts p. 1353; Restaurant Companies p. 2229

Individual restaurants are organized by city names within state and province groupings. (Canadian provinces are interfiled among the US states, in alphabetical order.)

Alabama

Restaurant	City	State	Zip	Phone	Fax
Boque's Restaurant 3028 Clairmont Ave S	Birmingham	AL	35205	205-254-9780	
Bottega 2240 Highland Ave S	Birmingham	AL	35205	205-939-1000	939-1536
Web: www.bottegarestaurant.com					
Cafe Ciao 2031 Cahaba Rd	Birmingham	AL	35223	205-871-2423	
Daniel George 2837 Culver Rd	Birmingham	AL	35223	205-871-3266	871-7266
Web: www.birminghammenus.com/danielgeorge					
Dragon Restaurant 114 Wildwood Pkwy	Birmingham	AL	35209	205-345-8711	
Dreamland BBQ 1427 14th Ave S	Birmingham	AL	35205	205-933-2133	933-9770
Web: www.dreamlandbbq.com					
Fire Restaurant & Bar 212 Country Club Park	Birmingham	AL	35213	205-802-1410	
Web: www.fire-restaurant.com					
Fleming's Prime Steakhouse & Wine Bar 103 Summit Blvd	Birmingham	AL	35243	205-262-9463	262-9461
Web: www.flemingssteakhouse.com					
Golden Palace 7001 Crestwood Blvd	Birmingham	AL	35210	205-595-6868	595-6969
Highlands Bar & Grill 2011 11th Ave S	Birmingham	AL	35205	205-939-1400	939-1405
Web: www.highlandsbarandgrill.com					
Hot & Hot Fish Club 2180 11th Ct S	Birmingham	AL	35205	205-933-5474	933-6243
Web: www.birminghammenus.com/hotandhot/					
Ichiban Japanese Steakhouse 620 Olde Town Rd	Birmingham	AL	35216	205-822-4646	822-4512
J Alexanders 3320 Galleria Cir	Birmingham	AL	35244	205-733-9995	733-8461
Web: www.jalexanders.com					
Jim-n-Nick's 1810 Montgomery Hwy S	Birmingham	AL	35244	205-733-1300	733-1314
Web: www.birminghammenus.com/jimnnicks					
Johnny Ray's Bar-B-Que 316 Valley Ave	Birmingham	AL	35209	205-945-7437	945-7419
La Dolce Vita 1851 Montgomery Hwy S Suite 107	Birmingham	AL	35244	205-985-2909	
Little Savannah 3811 Clairmont Ave	Birmingham	AL	35222	205-591-1119	592-0415
Web: birminghammenus.com/littlesavannah/					
(local) Restaurant & Cocktail Bar 700 Montgomery Hwy	Birmingham	AL	35216	205-949-0886	
Web: www.birminghammenus.com/local/					
Los Angeles 2801 7th Ave S	Birmingham	AL	35233	205-328-7160	322-1708
Web: www.birminghammenus.com/losangeles					
Ming's Cuisine 514 Cahaba Park Cir	Birmingham	AL	35242	205-991-3803	
Nabeel's Cafe 1706 Oxmoor Rd	Birmingham	AL	35209	205-879-9292	879-9291
Web: www.nabeels.com					
Niki's West 233 Finley Ave W	Birmingham	AL	35204	205-252-5751	252-8163
Ocean 1218 20th St S	Birmingham	AL	35205	205-933-0999	933-0998
Web: www.birminghammenus.com/ocean					
PF Chang's China Bistro 233 Summit Blvd	Birmingham	AL	35243	205-967-0040	967-3661
Web: www.pfchangs.com					
Ruth's Chris Steak House 2300 Woodcrest Pl	Birmingham	AL	35209	205-879-9995	879-8883
Web: www.ruthschris.com					
Sabor Latino 112 Green Springs Hwy	Birmingham	AL	35209	205-942-9480	942-9428
Sekisui Japanese Restaurant					
700 Montgomery Hwy Suite 178	Birmingham	AL	35216	205-978-7775	978-7756
Web: www.sekisuiusa.com					
Shula's Steak House 1000 Riverchase Galleria	Birmingham	AL	35244	205-444-5750	987-0454
Web: www.donshula.com					
Sol Y Luna 2811 7th Ave S	Birmingham	AL	35233	205-322-1186	322-1708
Web: www.birminghammenus.com/solyluna					
Standard Bistro 3 Mt Laurel Ave	Birmingham	AL	35242	205-995-0512	995-1854
Web: www.birminghammenus.com/standardbistro					
Stix 3250 Galleria Cir	Birmingham	AL	35244	205-982-3070	982-3073
Web: www.stixdining.com					
Surin West 1918 11th Ave S	Birmingham	AL	35205	205-324-1928	
Web: www.surinwest.com					
Taste of Thailand 3321 Lorna Rd	Birmingham	AL	35216	205-978-6863	978-6857
Ted's Montana Grill 3440 Galleria Cir	Birmingham	AL	35244	205-987-6093	987-6094
Web: www.tedsmontanagrill.com					
Village Tavern 101 Summit Blvd	Birmingham	AL	35243	205-970-1640	970-1641
Web: www.villagetavern.com					
Cocina Superior 587 Brookwood Village	Homewood	AL	35209	205-259-1980	
Web: www.thecocinasuperior.com					
Grey House Grille 1830 29th Ave S Suite S-160	Homewood	AL	35259	205-414-1755	414-1756
Web: www.greyhousegrille.com					
801 Franklin 801 Franklin St	Huntsville	AL	35801	256-519-8019	519-6801
Web: www.801franklin.com					
Big Spring Cafe 2906 Governors Dr	Huntsville	AL	35805	256-539-9994	
Cafe 302 2700 Winchester Rd NE	Huntsville	AL	35811	256-852-3442	
Cajun Grill 2801 Memorial Pkwy SW	Huntsville	AL	35801	256-534-7225	
Clem's BBQ & Fishery 3700 Blue Spring Rd NW	Huntsville	AL	35810	256-852-6661	
Dreamland Bar-B-Que Ribs 3855 University Dr	Huntsville	AL	35816	256-539-7427	
Web: www.dreamlandbbq.com					
El Camino Real 4116 University Dr NW	Huntsville	AL	35816	256-830-1188	830-1188
Korea House Restaurant 405 Jordan Ln NW	Huntsville	AL	35805	256-837-9207	
La Alameda 3807 University Dr NW	Huntsville	AL	35816	256-539-6244	
Landry's Seafood House 5101 Governor's House Dr	Huntsville	AL	35805	256-864-0000	864-0001
Web: www.landrysseafoodhouse.com					
Little Diner The 1219 Jordan Ln NW	Huntsville	AL	35816	256-837-6971	
Logan's Roadhouse 4249 Balmoral Dr SW	Huntsville	AL	35801	256-881-0584	881-3296
Web: www.logansroadhouse.com					
Mikato Japanese Steak House 4061 Independence Dr NW	Huntsville	AL	35816	256-830-1700	830-1873
Miyako 10013 S Memorial Pkwy	Huntsville	AL	35803	256-880-9879	
Po Boy Factory 815 Andrew Jackson Way N	Huntsville	AL	35801	256-539-3616	
Rolo's Cafe 975 Airport Rd	Huntsville	AL	35802	256-883-7656	
Scrugg's Barbeque 7529 Moore Mill Rd	Huntsville	AL	35811	256-859-6800	
Tellini's 1515 Perimeter Pkwy NW	Huntsville	AL	35806	256-726-9006	837-3276
Thai Garden 800 Wellman Ave NE	Huntsville	AL	35801	256-534-0122	564-7341
Web: www.geocities.com/thaigarden_2000/					
WildFlour Bistro 501 Jordan Ln	Huntsville	AL	35805	256-722-9401	
Web: www.wildflourbistro.com					
Bama Belles Country Restaurant 3651 Government Blvd	Mobile	AL	36693	251-661-8700	
Banana Docks Cafe 36 Hillcrest Rd	Mobile	AL	36608	251-342-2775	342-1924
Bilotti's Italian Cafe 1850 Airport Blvd	Mobile	AL	36606	251-476-6777	476-9060
Brick Pit 5456 Old Shell Rd	Mobile	AL	36608	251-343-0001	
Web: www.brickpit.com					
Cafe 615 615 Dauphin St	Mobile	AL	36602	251-432-8434	433-9885
Delhi Palace 3674 Airport Blvd	Mobile	AL	36608	251-341-6171	341-6121
Downtowners 107 Dauphin St	Mobile	AL	36602	251-433-8868	433-8867
Guido's 351 George St	Mobile	AL	36604	251-694-0606	
Hunan Restaurant 7765 Airport Blvd Suite 819	Mobile	AL	36608	251-633-9700	633-9639

Name / Address	City	State	Zip	Phone	Fax
JR's Smokehouse 3843 Airport Blvd	Mobile	AL	36608	251-343-1853	
Web: www.jrssmokehouse.com					
Lakeside Lodge 650 Cody Rd S	Mobile	AL	36602	251-343-2211	
Oliver's 251 Government St	Mobile	AL	36602	251-432-8000	
Picklefish The 251 Dauphin St	Mobile	AL	36602	251-434-0000	
Pillars The 1757 Government St	Mobile	AL	36604	251-471-3411	
Web: www.thepillarsmobile.com					
Riverview Cafe & Grill 64 S Water St	Mobile	AL	36602	251-438-4000	415-0123
Ruth's Chris Steak House 2058 Airport Blvd	Mobile	AL	36606	251-476-0516	476-0518
Web: www.ruthschris.com					
Saucy-Q Bar B Que 1111 Government St	Mobile	AL	36604	251-433-7427	433-7428
Ala Thai 1361 Federal Dr	Montgomery	AL	36107	334-262-5830	
Bonefish Grill 7020 Eastchase Pkwy	Montgomery	AL	36117	334-396-1770	396-1787
Web: www.bonefishgrill.com					
City Grill 8147 Vaughn Rd	Montgomery	AL	36116	334-244-0960	409-0068
Dreamland Bar-B-Que Ribs 109 East Blvd	Montgomery	AL	36117	334-273-7427	273-7857
Web: www.dreamlandbbq.com					
Emperors Garden 3447 McGehee Rd	Montgomery	AL	36111	334-284-1888	288-8578
Gator's Plaza Cafe 5040 Vaughn Rd	Montgomery	AL	36116	334-274-0330	
Island Delight Caribbean Restaurant 323 Airbase Blvd	Montgomery	AL	36108	334-264-0041	
Ixtapa 6132 Atlanta Hwy	Montgomery	AL	36117	334-272-5232	
King Buffet 2727 Bell Rd	Montgomery	AL	36117	334-273-8883	273-8880
La Jolla 6854 E Chase Pkwy	Montgomery	AL	36117	334-356-2600	356-2610
Web: www.lajollarestaurant.com					
Lek's Taste of Thailand 5421 Atlanta Hwy	Montgomery	AL	36109	334-244-8994	244-8994
Web: www.leksrailroadthai.com					
Martha's Place 458 Sayre St	Montgomery	AL	36104	334-263-9135	
Mings Garden 1741 Eastern Bypass	Montgomery	AL	36117	334-277-8188	277-8266
Montgomery Brewing Co 12 W Jefferson St	Montgomery	AL	36104	334-834-2739	834-1110
Web: www.thebrewpub.info					
Nobles Restaurant & Lounge 129 Montgomery St	Montgomery	AL	36104	334-262-3326	
Web: www.noblesandoliveroom.com					
Olive Room 121 Montgomery St	Montgomery	AL	36104	334-262-2763	
Peyton's Place 5355 Atlanta Hwy	Montgomery	AL	36109	334-396-3630	
Shogun Japanese Steak & Sushi 5215 Carmichael Rd	Montgomery	AL	36106	334-271-6999	
Tequila Grill 2152 Cobbs Ford Rd	Montgomery	AL	36054	334-285-3500	
Vintage Year 405 Cloverdale Rd	Montgomery	AL	36106	334-264-8463	269-5700
Web: www.vintageyearonline.com					
Zoes Kitchen 7218 EastChase Pkwy	Montgomery	AL	36117	334-270-9115	270-9116
Web: zoeskitchen.com					
Globe The 430 Main Ave	Northport	AL	35476	205-391-0949	
Web: www.theglobe restaurant.net					
Felix's Fish Camp at Pier 4 1530 Battleship Pkwy	Spanish Fort	AL	36527	251-626-6710	626-6794
Web: www.felixsfishcamp.com					
Roussos 30500 State Hwy 181 Eastern Shore Center	Spanish Fort	AL	36527	251-625-3386	625-3440
Web: www.roussosrestaurant.com					
15th Street Diner 1036 15th St	Tuscaloosa	AL	35401	205-750-8750	758-4751
Web: www.dinerrestaurants.com					
Benkei Japanese Steakhouse 1223 McFarland Blvd NE	Tuscaloosa	AL	35406	205-759-5300	
Bento 1306 University Blvd Suite D	Tuscaloosa	AL	35401	205-758-7426	
Buffalo Phil's 1149 University Blvd	Tuscaloosa	AL	35401	205-758-3318	758-3310
Cafe Venice 2321 University Blvd	Tuscaloosa	AL	35401	205-366-1209	366-8762
Cancun Restaurant 2200 McFarland Blvd E	Tuscaloosa	AL	35404	205-758-0875	758-0871
China Fun 2600 University Blvd	Tuscaloosa	AL	35401	205-553-2435	
Cypress Inn 501 Rice Mine Rd N	Tuscaloosa	AL	35406	205-345-6963	345-6997
Web: www.cypressinnrestaurant.com					
DePalma's Italian Cafe 2300 University Blvd	Tuscaloosa	AL	35401	205-759-1879	
Dreamland Bar-B-Que Ribs 5335 15th Ave	Tuscaloosa	AL	35401	205-758-8135	
Web: www.dreamlandbbq.com					
Epiphany Cafe 519 Greenborough Ave	Tuscaloosa	AL	35401	205-344-5583	344-5033
Evangeline's 1653 McFarland Blvd N	Tuscaloosa	AL	35406	205-752-0830	752-0355
Web: www.evangelinesdining.com					
Jalapeno's Bar & Grill 405 23rd Ave E	Tuscaloosa	AL	35401	205-343-2422	
Kozy's 3510 Loop Rd	Tuscaloosa	AL	35404	205-556-0665	633-4034
Web: www.kozysrestaurant.com					
Lai Lai 1205 University Blvd	Tuscaloosa	AL	35401	205-345-2472	
Los Tarascos 1759 Skyland Blvd	Tuscaloosa	AL	35405	205-553-8896	
Pepito's 1203 University Blvd	Tuscaloosa	AL	35401	205-391-9028	
Pottery Grill Hwy 11	Tuscaloosa	AL	35453	205-554-1815	
Rama Jama's 1000 Paul Bryant Dr	Tuscaloosa	AL	35401	205-750-0901	
Wilhagan's Sports Grille 2209 4th St	Tuscaloosa	AL	35401	205-366-0913	
Wing's Sports Grille 500 Harper Lee Dr	Tuscaloosa	AL	35401	205-556-5658	556-5639
Web: www.wingssportsgrille.com					
Sol Azteca 1360 Montgomery Hwy Suite 128	Vestavia Hills	AL	35216	205-979-4002	979-9140
Borderline Cafe 60 Village Loop	Wetumpka	AL	36093	334-514-8646	
Casa Napoli 2215 US Hwy 231	Wetumpka	AL	36093	334-567-7777	
Web: www.napoli2.com					

Alaska

Name / Address	City	State	Zip	Phone	Fax
Aladdin's 4240 Old Seward Hwy	Anchorage	AK	99503	907-561-2373	563-5117
Web: www.aladdinsak.com					
Benihana 1100 W 8th Ave	Anchorage	AK	99501	907-222-5212	
Black Angus Steakhouse 300 W Tudor Rd	Anchorage	AK	99503	907-562-2844	562-2632
Web: www.blackangus.com					
Bombay Deluxe 555 W Northern Lights Blvd	Anchorage	AK	99503	907-277-1200	
Web: www.bombaydeluxe.com					
Bradley House 11321 Old Seward Hwy	Anchorage	AK	99517	907-336-7177	336-7178
Club Paris 417 W 5th Ave	Anchorage	AK	99501	907-277-6332	277-6544
Web: www.clubparisrestaurant.com					
Corsair 944 W 5th Ave	Anchorage	AK	99501	907-278-4502	274-0333
Web: www.corsairrestaurant.com					
Crow's Nest 939 W 5th Ave Hotel Captain Cook	Anchorage	AK	99501	907-276-6000	
Web: www.captaincook.com/restaurants.htm					
Don Jose's 2052 E Northern Lights Blvd	Anchorage	AK	99508	907-279-5111	279-2053
Web: www.alaskadonjoses.com					
Glacier Brew House 737 W 5th Ave	Anchorage	AK	99501	907-274-2739	277-1033
Web: www.glacierbrewhouse.com					
Gweenie's Old Alaska Restaurant 4333 Spenard Rd	Anchorage	AK	99517	907-243-2090	
Humpy's Great Alaskan Alehouse 610 W 6th Ave	Anchorage	AK	99501	907-276-2337	258-0780
Web: www.humpys.com					
Jen's Restaurant 701 W 36th Ave	Anchorage	AK	99503	907-561-5367	561-5325
Web: www.jensrestaurant.com					
Kincaid Grill 6700 Jewel Lake Rd	Anchorage	AK	99502	907-243-0507	243-5110
Web: www.kincaidgrill.com					
Kumagoro Restaurant 533 W 4th Ave	Anchorage	AK	99501	907-272-9905	272-0573
La Cabana 312 E 4th Ave	Anchorage	AK	99501	907-272-0135	
Little Italy 2300 E 88th Ave	Anchorage	AK	99507	907-344-1515	344-1538
Los Arcos 2000 E Dowling St	Anchorage	AK	99507	907-562-0477	
Marx Brothers Cafe 627 W 3rd Ave	Anchorage	AK	99501	907-278-2133	258-6279
Web: www.marxcafe.com					
Mick's at the Inlet 1200 L St Inlet Towers Hotel	Anchorage	AK	99501	907-222-8787	258-4914
Organic Oasis 2610 Spenard Rd	Anchorage	AK	99503	907-277-7882	277-7881
Web: www.alaska.net/~organicoasis/					
Orso Ristorante 737 W 5th Ave	Anchorage	AK	99501	907-222-3232	792-3701
Web: www.orsoalaska.com					
Peking Wok 4000 W Dimond Blvd	Anchorage	AK	99515	907-248-1648	245-2491
Phyllis' Cafe & Salmon Bake 436 D St	Anchorage	AK	99501	907-274-6576	
Ptarmigan Grille 401 E 6th Ave Sheraton Anchorage Hotel	Anchorage	AK	99501	907-343-3150	
Sacks Cafe 328 G St	Anchorage	AK	99501	907-276-3546	
Sea Galley 4101 Credit Union Dr	Anchorage	AK	99503	907-563-3520	563-6382
Web: www.seagalleyalaska.com					
Simon & Seafort's Saloon & Grill 420 L St	Anchorage	AK	99501	907-274-3502	274-2487
Web: www.simonandseaforts.com					
Snow Goose Restaurant 717 W 3rd Ave	Anchorage	AK	99501	907-277-7727	277-0606
Web: www.alaskabeers.com					
Sorrento's Restaurant 610 E Fireweed Ln	Anchorage	AK	99503	907-278-3439	258-2261
Sourdough Mining Co 5200 Juneau St	Anchorage	AK	99518	907-563-2272	
Southside Bistro 1320 Huffman Park Dr	Anchorage	AK	99515	907-348-0088	348-0089
Web: www.southsidebistro.com					
Sullivan's Steakhouse 320 W 5th Ave Suite 100	Anchorage	AK	99501	907-258-2882	258-2808
Top of the World 500 W 3rd Ave	Anchorage	AK	99501	907-265-7111	
Touch of Russia 333 W 4th Ave	Anchorage	AK	99501	907-276-5907	
Villa Nova Restaurant 5121 Arctic Blvd Suite I	Anchorage	AK	99503	907-561-1660	
Alaska Salmon Bake In Alaskaland Airport Way & Peger Rd	Fairbanks	AK	99709	907-452-7274	
Web: www.akvisit.com					
Asiana Teriyaki 2001 Airport Way	Fairbanks	AK	99701	907-457-3333	451-6689
Chena's Fine Dining & Deck 4200 Boat St	Fairbanks	AK	99709	907-474-3644	474-8023
Cookie Jar 1006 Cadillac Ct	Fairbanks	AK	99701	907-479-8319	479-8329
Gambardella's Pasta Bella 706 2nd Ave	Fairbanks	AK	99701	907-456-3417	456-3425
Web: www.gambardellas.com					
Geraldo's 701 College Rd	Fairbanks	AK	99701	907-452-2299	452-7634
Hong Kong Hai 1900 Airport Way	Fairbanks	AK	99701	907-451-1100	452-2530
Ivory Jack's 2581 Goldstream Rd	Fairbanks	AK	99709	907-455-6666	455-4254
Web: www.mosquitonet.com/~ivoryjacks/ij					
Koreana 1528 S Cushman St	Fairbanks	AK	99701	907-451-0651	
Lavelle's Bistro 575 1st Ave	Fairbanks	AK	99701	907-450-0555	450-0444
Web: www.lavellesbistro.com					
Musher's Roadhouse 1411 Airport Way Captain Bartlett Inn	Fairbanks	AK	99701	907-452-1888	452-7674
Web: www.captainbartlettinn.com					
Pikes Landing 4438 Airport Way	Fairbanks	AK	99706	907-479-7113	479-6513
Pump House The 796 Chena Pump Rd	Fairbanks	AK	99709	907-479-8452	
Web: www.ptialaska.net/~pumphse/					
Red Lantern Steak & Spirits Westmark Hotel 813 Noble St	Fairbanks	AK	99701	907-459-7725	
Soapy Smith's Pioneer Restaurant 543 2nd Ave	Fairbanks	AK	99701	907-451-8380	451-8383
Thai House 412 5th Ave	Fairbanks	AK	99701	907-452-6123	452-6124
Turtle Club 10 Mile Old Steese Hwy	Fairbanks	AK	99712	907-457-3883	457-4789
Vallata 2190 Goldstream Rd	Fairbanks	AK	99709	907-455-6600	
Zach's 1717 University Ave S	Fairbanks	AK	99709	907-479-3650	479-7951
Seven Glaciers Restaurant 1000 Arlberg Ave	Girdwood	AK	99587	907-754-2237	754-2180
Turnagain House Mile 103 Seward Hwy	Indian	AK	99540	907-653-7500	
Breakwater Inn Restaurant & Lounge 1711 Glacier Ave	Juneau	AK	99801	907-586-6303	463-4820
Web: www.breakwaterinn.com					
Canton House 8585 Old Dairy Rd	Juneau	AK	99801	907-789-5075	790-2172
Capital Cafe 127 N Franklin St	Juneau	AK	99801	907-586-2660	
DocWater's Pub 2 Marine Way Suite 225	Juneau	AK	99801	907-586-3627	
Web: www.docwaterspub.com					
El Sombrero 157 S Franklin St	Juneau	AK	99801	907-586-6770	586-6772
Glacier Restaurant 1873 Shell Simmons Dr Suite 220	Juneau	AK	99801	907-789-9538	789-3090
Gold Room 127 N Franklin St	Juneau	AK	99801	907-586-2660	586-8315
Grandma's Feather Bed Restaurant 2348 Mendenhall Loop Rd	Juneau	AK	99801	907-789-5566	789-2818
Hangar On The Wharf 2 Marine Way Suite 106	Juneau	AK	99801	907-586-5018	586-8173
Mi Casa 9200 Glacier Hwy	Juneau	AK	99801	907-789-3636	789-1969
Olivia's De Mexico 222 Seward St	Juneau	AK	99801	907-586-6870	
Web: www.juneau.airseago.com/olivias					
Red Dog Saloon 278 S Franklin St	Juneau	AK	99801	907-463-3658	
Web: www.reddogsaloon.cc					
Seong's Sushi Bar 740 W 9th St	Juneau	AK	99801	907-586-4778	
Thane Ore House Salmon Bake 4400 Thane Rd	Juneau	AK	99801	907-586-3442	
TK Maguire's 375 Whittier St	Juneau	AK	99801	907-586-3737	586-1204
Web: www.prospectorhotel.com/restaurant.htm					
Twisted Fish Co 550 S Franklin St	Juneau	AK	99801	907-463-5033	586-8173
Web: www.twistedfishco.com					
Mambo Grill Latin Cuisine 300 N Santa Clause Ln	North Pole	AK	99705	907-490-6868	490-6658
Web: www.themambogrill.com					

Alberta

Name / Address	City	Prov	Postal Code	Phone	Fax
Abruzzo Ristorante 402 8th St SW	Calgary	AB	T2P1Z9	403-237-5660	237-5661
Aida's Mediterranean Bistro 2208 4th St SW	Calgary	AB	T2S1W9	403-541-1189	541-5398
Antonio's Garlic Clove 2206 4th St SW	Calgary	AB	T2S1W9	403-228-0866	
Web: www.garlicclove.net					
Belvedere The 107 8th Ave SW	Calgary	AB	T2P1B4	403-265-9595	
Web: www.thebelvedere.ca					
Bonterra Trattoria 1016 8th St SW	Calgary	AB	T2R1K2	403-262-8480	262-6541
Web: www.bonterra.ca					
Bow Bul Go Gui House 3515A 17th Ave SW	Calgary	AB	T3E0B6	403-686-6826	
Broken Plate The 10816 MacLeod Trail SE	Calgary	AB	T2J5N8	403-225-9650	225-9691
Web: www.brokenplate.ca					
Buddha's Veggie Restaurant 5802 MacLeod Trail SW	Calgary	AB	T2J0J8	403-252-8830	
Web: www.buddhasveggie.com					
Buon Giorno Ristorante Italiano 823 17th Ave SW	Calgary	AB	T2T0A1	403-244-5522	244-5631
Cactus Club Cafe 7010 MacLeod Trail S	Calgary	AB	T2H0L3	403-255-1088	255-1049
Web: www.cactusclubcafe.com					
Caesar's Steak House 512 4th Ave SW	Calgary	AB	T2P0J6	403-264-1222	264-9933
Carver's Steakhouse 2620 32nd Ave NE	Calgary	AB	T1Y6B8	403-250-6327	
Catch Oyster Bar/Seafood Restaurant 100 8th Ave SE	Calgary	AB	T2G0K6	403-206-0000	206-0005
Web: www.catchrestaurant.ca					
Charly Chan's 1140 Kensington Rd NW	Calgary	AB	T2N3P3	403-283-6165	
Web: www.charlychans.com					
Chianti Cafe 1438 17th Ave SW	Calgary	AB	T2T0C8	403-229-1600	228-9699
Web: www.chianticafe.ca					
China Rose Restaurant 228 28th St SE	Calgary	AB	T2A6J9	403-248-2711	248-6810
Web: www.chinaroserestaurant.ca					
Cilantro 338 17th Ave SW	Calgary	AB	T2S0A8	403-229-1177	245-5239
Web: www.crmr.com/cilantro/					
Co Do 1411 17th Ave SW	Calgary	AB	T2T0C6	403-228-7798	228-7739
Web: www.codo.ca					
Coup The 924B 17th Ave SW	Calgary	AB	T2T0A2	403-541-1041	
Web: www.thecoup.ca					
Da Guido Ristorante 2001 Centre St N	Calgary	AB	T2E2S9	403-276-1365	230-1102
Web: www.daguido.com					
Da Paolo Ristorante 121 17th Ave SE	Calgary	AB	T2G1H3	403-228-5556	229-0550
Ed's Restaurant 202 17th Ave SE	Calgary	AB	T2G1H4	403-262-3500	261-7810
Web: www.edsrestaurant.com					
El Sombrero 520 17th Ave SW	Calgary	AB	T2S0B1	403-228-0332	228-0540
Web: www.elsombrero.ca					
Essence 320 4th Ave SW Westin Hotel	Calgary	AB	T2P2S6	403-266-1611	233-7471
Fiore Cantina Italiana 638 17th Ave SW	Calgary	AB	T2S0B4	403-244-6603	244-6615
Web: www.fiore.ca					
Hana Sushi 1803 4th St SW	Calgary	AB	T2S1W2	403-229-1499	229-1517
Hawkwood Palace 555 Hawkwood Blvd NW	Calgary	AB	T3G3K2	403-241-1888	239-1045

Alberta (Cont'd)

Name / Address	City	State	Postal Code	Phone	Fax
Il Sogno 24 4th St NE	Calgary	AB	T2E3R7	403-232-8901	232-8816
Web: www.ilsogno.org					
James Joyce Authentic Irish Pub 114 8th Ave SW	Calgary	AB	T2P1B3	403-262-0708	262-0709
Web: www.jamesjoycepub.com					
Japanese Village Restaurant 317 10th Ave SW	Calgary	AB	T2R0E5	403-262-2738	265-4307
Joey Tomato's 208 Barclay Parade SW	Calgary	AB	T2P4R5	403-263-6336	263-6385
Web: www.joeysrestaurants.com					
Juan's 232 8th Ave SW	Calgary	AB	T2P1B7	403-266-0051	
Kashmir 507 17th Ave SW	Calgary	AB	T2S0A9	403-244-2294	
Keg Steakhouse & Bar 7104 MacLeod Trail S	Calgary	AB	T2H0L3	403-253-2534	253-2875
Web: www.kegsteakhouse.com					
King & I 822 11th Ave SW	Calgary	AB	T2R0E5	403-264-7241	264-8490
Web: www.kingandi.ca					
Kyoto 17 908 17th Ave SW	Calgary	AB	T2M0P2	403-245-3188	228-3191
La Chaumiere 139 17th Ave SW	Calgary	AB	T2S0A1	403-228-5690	228-4448
Web: www.lachaumiere.ca					
La Paella 800 6th Ave SW	Calgary	AB	T2P3G3	403-269-5911	269-5913
Web: www.lapaella.ca					
La Viena 2139 Kensington Rd NW	Calgary	AB	T2N3R8	403-283-3063	
Leo Fu's 511 70th Ave SW	Calgary	AB	T2V0P5	403-255-2528	
Limerick Traditional Public House 7304 MacLeod Trail S	Calgary	AB	T2H0L9	403-252-9190	252-9174
Web: www.calgarysbestpubs.com/Limericks/limericks.htm					
Marathon Ethiopian Restaurant 130 10th St NW	Calgary	AB	T2N1V3	403-283-6796	283-1104
Maurya 1204 Kensington Rd NW	Calgary	AB	T2N3P5	403-270-3133	
Melrose Cafe & Bar 730 17th Ave SW	Calgary	AB	T2S0B7	403-228-3566	228-5708
Web: www.melrosecalgary.com					
Molly Malone's Irish Pub 1153 Kensington Crescent NW	Calgary	AB	T2N1X7	403-296-3220	
Moti Mahal 1805 14 St SW	Calgary	AB	T2T2T1	403-228-9990	
Web: www.motimahal.ca					
Oriental Phoenix 104 58th Ave SE	Calgary	AB	T2H0N7	403-253-8383	253-8382
Pegasus 1101 14th St SW	Calgary	AB	T3C1C2	403-229-1231	228-7120
Web: www.ourpegasus.com					
Q Haute Cuisine 100 La Caille Pl SW	Calgary	AB	T2P5E2	403-262-5554	
Web: www.qhautecuisine.com/					
Rajdoot 2424 4th St SW	Calgary	AB	T2S2T4	403-245-0181	228-7194
Redwater Rustic Grille 9223 MacLeod Trail S	Calgary	AB	T2J0P5	403-253-4266	253-9045
Web: www.redwatergrille.com					
River Cafe 200 Barclay Parade SW	Calgary	AB	T2P4R5	403-261-7670	261-8795
Web: www.river-cafe.com					
Rouge 1240 8th Ave SE	Calgary	AB	T2G0M7	403-531-2767	
Web: www.rougecalgary.com					
Sakana Grill 116 2nd Ave SW	Calgary	AB	T2P0B9	403-290-1118	290-1120
Salt & Pepper 6515 Bowness Rd NW	Calgary	AB	T2B0H6	403-247-4402	
Web: www.saltnpepper.ca					
Santa Fe Grill 9250 MacLeod Trail S	Calgary	AB	T2J0P5	403-253-9096	253-9095
Santorini Greek Taverna 1502 Centre St N	Calgary	AB	T2E2R9	403-276-8363	276-8399
Silver Dragon Restaurant 106 3rd Ave SE	Calgary	AB	T2G0B6	403-264-5326	
Singapore Sam's 555 11th Ave SW Suite 101	Calgary	AB	T2R1P6	403-234-8088	266-6883
Web: www.singaporesams.com					
Smuggler's Inn 6920 MacLeod Trail S	Calgary	AB	T2H0L3	403-253-5355	259-4787
Web: www.smugglers-inn.com					
Sushi Kawa 2204 4th St SW	Calgary	AB	T2S1W9	403-802-0058	
Tandoori Hut 217 10th St NW	Calgary	AB	T2N1V5	403-270-4012	
Thai Boat 108-2323 32nd Ave NE	Calgary	AB	T2E6Z3	403-291-9887	
Thai Sa-On 351 10th Ave SW	Calgary	AB	T2R0A5	403-264-3526	
Web: www.thai-sa-on.com					
Villa Firenze 610 1st Ave NE	Calgary	AB	T2E3B6	403-264-4297	365-1990
Vintage Chophouse & Tavern 322 11th Ave SW	Calgary	AB	T2R0C5	403-262-7262	262-7263
Web: www.vintagechophouse.com/					
Wa's 1721 Centre St NW	Calgary	AB	T2E2S3	403-277-2077	277-2109
Wellington's 10325 Bonaventure Dr SE	Calgary	AB	T2J7E4	403-278-5250	271-3809
Wildwood 2417 4th St SW	Calgary	AB	T2S1X5	403-228-0100	228-0076
Allegro Italian Kitchen 10011 109th St	Edmonton	AB	T5J3F8	780-424-6644	424-8844
Web: www.allegroitaliankitchen.ca					
Ban Thai 15726 100th Ave	Edmonton	AB	T5P0L1	780-444-9345	484-8496
Barb & Ernie's 9906 72nd Ave	Edmonton	AB	T6E0Z3	780-433-3242	
Billingsgate Lighthouse Cafe 7331 104th St	Edmonton	AB	T6E4B9	780-433-0091	439-0099
Web: www.billingsgate.com					
Blue Pear 10643 123rd St NW	Edmonton	AB	T5N1P3	780-482-7178	
Web: www.thebluepear.com					
Bua Thai Restaurant 10049 113th St NW	Edmonton	AB	T5K1N9	780-482-2277	
Bul-Go-Gi House 8813 92nd St	Edmonton	AB	P6C3P9	780-466-2330	469-8178
Cafe Mosaics 10844 82nd Ave	Edmonton	AB	P6E2B3	780-433-9702	
Cafe de Ville 10137 124th St	Edmonton	AB	T5N1P5	780-488-9188	488-2829
Web: www.cafedeville.com					
Characters 10257 105th St	Edmonton	AB	T5J1E3	780-421-4100	425-1550
Web: www.characters.ca					
Chiante Cafe 10501 82nd Ave	Edmonton	AB	P6E2A4	780-439-9829	
Creperie The 10220 103rd St	Edmonton	AB	T5J0Y8	780-420-6656	426-5026
Web: www.thecreperie.com					
Dan Shing 15912 Stony Plain Rd	Edmonton	AB	P5P3Z8	780-483-1143	
Double Greeting Won Ton 10212 96th St	Edmonton	AB	T5H2G7	780-424-2486	
Fuji Japanese Restaurant 8025 104th St NW	Edmonton	AB	T6E4E3	780-944-1388	
Furusato 10012 82nd Ave	Edmonton	AB	T6E3Z1	780-439-1335	
Hardware Grill 9698 Jasper Ave	Edmonton	AB	T5H3V5	780-423-0969	423-4739
Web: www.hardwaregrill.com					
Il Pasticcio Trattoria 11520 100th Ave	Edmonton	AB	T5K0J7	780-488-9543	482-7956
India Grill 4620 99th St	Edmonton	AB	T6E5H5	780-436-8267	438-1204
Web: www.indiagrill.ca					
Jack's Grill 5842 111th St	Edmonton	AB	T6H3G1	780-434-1113	433-0276
Web: www.jacksgrill.ca					
Japanese Village 10126 100th St	Edmonton	AB	T5J0N8	780-422-6083	425-0099
Julio's Barrio 10450 82nd Ave	Edmonton	AB	T6E2A2	780-431-0774	433-0575
Web: www.juliosbarrio.com					
Keg Steakhouse & Bar 8020 105th St	Edmonton	AB	T6E4Z4	780-432-7494	439-6165
Web: www.kegsteakhouse.com					
Khazana 10177 107th St	Edmonton	AB	T5J1J5	780-702-0330	
Web: www.khazana.ab.ca					
Koutouki Restaurant 10719 124th St NW	Edmonton	AB	T5M0H1	780-452-5383	
Louisiana Purchase Restaurant 10320 111th St	Edmonton	AB	T5K1L2	780-420-6779	
Web: www.louisianapurchase.ca					
Moose Factory The 4810 Calgary Trail Southbound NW	Edmonton	AB	T6H5H5	780-437-5862	437-1956
New Asian Village 10143 Saskatchewan Dr	Edmonton	AB	P6E6B6	780-433-3804	433-8476
Web: www.newasianvillage.com					
Noodle Noodle 10008 106th Ave	Edmonton	AB	T5H0N7	780-422-6862	424-8112
Normand's 11639 A Jasper Ave	Edmonton	AB	T5K0M9	780-482-2600	488-3286
Web: www.normands.com					
Parkallen 7018 109th St	Edmonton	AB	T6H3C1	780-436-8080	430-0469
Web: www.parkallen.com					
Pearl River 4728 99th St NW	Edmonton	AB	T6E5H5	780-435-2015	431-2758
Red Ox Inn 9420 91st St NW	Edmonton	AB	T6C3P4	780-465-5727	
Web: www.theredoxinn.com					
Sorrentino's On 95th 10844 95th St	Edmonton	AB	T5H2E4	780-425-0960	421-9123
Web: www.sorrentinos.com					
Tasty Tom's Bistro 9965 82nd Ave NW	Edmonton	AB	T6E1Z1	780-437-5761	
Tropika Malaysian Cuisine 6004 104th St NW	Edmonton	AB	T6H2K3	780-439-6699	439-6644
West Palace 103-6104 172nd St	Edmonton	AB	T6M1G9	780-481-9898	487-2787
Yianni's Taverna 10444 82nd Ave	Edmonton	AB	T6E2A2	780-433-6768	436-8883
Web: www.eatmorelamb.com					

Arizona

Name / Address	City	State	Zip	Phone	Fax
August Moon Chinese Restaurant 1300 S Milton Rd	Flagstaff	AZ	86001	928-774-5280	
Beaver Street Brewery 11 S Beaver St	Flagstaff	AZ	86001	928-779-0079	
Web: www.beaverstreetbrewery.com					
Black Barts Steakhouse Saloon 2760 E Butler Ave	Flagstaff	AZ	86004	928-779-3142	774-1113
Web: www.blackbartssteakhouse.com					
Brandy's 1500 E Cedar Ave Suite 70	Flagstaff	AZ	86004	928-779-2187	779-0004
Web: www.brandysrestaurant.com					
Buster's Restaurant & Bar 1800 S Milton Rd	Flagstaff	AZ	86001	928-774-5155	774-5156
Web: www.busters-restaurant.com					
Cafe Espress 16 N San Francisco St	Flagstaff	AZ	86001	928-774-0541	774-6830
Collins Irish Pub 2 E Rt 66	Flagstaff	AZ	86001	928-214-7363	226-7389
Cottage Place 126 W Cottage Ave	Flagstaff	AZ	86001	928-774-8431	774-0374
Web: www.cottageplace.com					
Dara Thai 14 S San Francisco St	Flagstaff	AZ	86001	928-774-0047	
Dehli Palace Cuisine of India 2700 S Woodlands Village Blvd	Flagstaff	AZ	86001	928-556-0019	
El Capitan Fresh Mexican Grill 1800 S Milton Rd Suite 21	Flagstaff	AZ	86001	928-774-1083	774-0447
Web: www.elcapitanfmg.com					
El Charro Cafe 409 S San Francisco St	Flagstaff	AZ	86001	928-779-0552	779-3034
Granny's Closet 218 S Milton Rd	Flagstaff	AZ	86001	928-774-8331	774-9594
Web: www.grannys-closet.com					
Horsemen Lodge 8500 Hwy 89 N	Flagstaff	AZ	86004	928-526-2655	526-1586
Web: www.horsemenlodge.com					
Hunan West 1302 S Plaza Way	Flagstaff	AZ	86001	928-779-2229	773-8987
Jackson's Grill at the Springs 7055 S Hwy 89A	Flagstaff	AZ	86001	928-213-9332	213-9360
Josephine's 503 N Humphreys St	Flagstaff	AZ	86001	928-779-3400	226-0910
Web: www.josephinesrestaurant.com					
La Fonda 1900 N 2nd St	Flagstaff	AZ	86004	928-779-0296	773-9060
Little Thai Kitchen 1051 S Milton Rd	Flagstaff	AZ	86001	928-226-9422	226-9421
Mamma Luisa 2710 N Steves Blvd Suite 14	Flagstaff	AZ	86004	928-526-6809	526-6325
Miz Zips Cafe 2924 E Rt 66	Flagstaff	AZ	86001	928-526-0104	
Mogollon Brewing Co 15 N Agassiz St	Flagstaff	AZ	86001	928-773-8950	779-3140
Mountain Oasis 11 E Aspen Ave	Flagstaff	AZ	86001	928-214-9270	214-0020
Sakura 1175 W Rt 66	Flagstaff	AZ	86001	928-773-9118	773-0597
Szechuan 1451 S Milton Rd	Flagstaff	AZ	86001	928-774-8039	774-8335
Romeo's Euro Cafe 207 N Gilbert Rd Suite 105	Gilbert	AZ	85234	480-962-4224	558-2033
Web: www.eurocafe.com					
Ajo Al's 7458 W Bell Rd	Glendale	AZ	85308	623-334-9899	
Web: www.ajoals.com					
Babbo's 20211 N 67th Ave	Glendale	AZ	85308	623-566-9898	566-5561
Bill Johnson's Big Apple 7322 W Bell Rd	Glendale	AZ	85308	623-776-1900	776-0657
Web: www.billjohnsons.com					
Bistro Di Napoli 5830 W Thunderbird Rd	Glendale	AZ	85306	602-298-6767	298-6766
Web: www.bistrodinapoli.com					
Bitz-Ee Mama's 7023 N 58th Ave	Glendale	AZ	85301	623-931-0562	
Web: www.bitzeemamas.com					
Black Bear Diner 6039 W Bell Rd	Glendale	AZ	85306	602-843-1921	
Web: www.blackbeardiner.com					
Caramba 5421 W Glendale Ave	Glendale	AZ	85301	623-934-8888	487-1934
Carvers Steakhouse 8172 W Bell Rd	Glendale	AZ	85308	623-412-0787	412-0454
Chanpen 13828 N 51st Ave	Glendale	AZ	85306	602-993-2046	993-2047
Cocono's 8280 W Union Hills Dr	Glendale	AZ	85308	623-362-8000	
Web: www.coconos.com					
Cucina Tagliani 17045 N 59th Ave	Glendale	AZ	85308	602-547-2782	547-9934
Web: www.cucinatagliani.com					
El Paso Barbeque 4303 W Peoria Ave	Glendale	AZ	85302	623-931-2438	931-2038
Web: www.elpasobarbeque.com					
Haus Murphy's 5739 W Glendale Ave	Glendale	AZ	85301	623-939-2480	
Web: www.hausmurphys.com					
Kiss the Cook Restaurant 4915 W Glendale Ave	Glendale	AZ	85301	623-939-4663	939-2989
La Perla Cafe 5912 W Glendale Ave	Glendale	AZ	85301	623-939-7561	
Web: www.laperlacafe.net					
Long Wong's 5270 N 59th St Suite 101	Glendale	AZ	85301	623-934-4455	
Maharaja Palace 5775 W Bell Rd	Glendale	AZ	85308	602-547-1000	
Mimi's Cafe 7450 W Bell Rd	Glendale	AZ	85308	623-979-4500	979-4339
Web: www.mimiscafe.com					
Pedro's 4938 W Glendale Ave	Glendale	AZ	85301	623-937-0807	551-8069
Rosario Ristorante 9250 N 43rd Ave	Glendale	AZ	85302	623-931-1810	
Web: www.rosarioristorante.com					
Spicery Restaurant & Tea Room 7141 N 59th Ave	Glendale	AZ	85301	623-937-6534	937-6543
Web: www.thespicery.com					
Ah-So 1919 S Gilbert Rd	Mesa	AZ	85204	480-497-1114	497-1115
Aloha Kitchen 2950 S Alma School Rd Suite 12	Mesa	AZ	85210	480-897-2451	897-7295
Web: www.alohakitchen.com					
Anzio Landing 2613 N Thunderbird Cir	Mesa	AZ	85215	480-832-1188	924-4954
Web: anziolanding.com					
Bavarian Point 4815 E Main St	Mesa	AZ	85205	480-830-0999	830-0530
Benchwarmers Grill 801 S Power Rd Suite 101	Mesa	AZ	85206	480-854-8670	854-9950
Blue Adobe Grille 144 N Country Club Dr	Mesa	AZ	85201	480-962-1000	962-1110
Web: www.blueadobegrille.com					
Brunello of Mesa 1954 S Dobson Rd	Mesa	AZ	85202	480-897-0140	897-0253
Web: www.brunellorestaurant.net					
Cafe Roma 2011 N Recker Rd	Mesa	AZ	85215	480-654-0558	
Charleston's 1623 S Stapely Dr	Mesa	AZ	85204	480-635-9500	635-9503
Web: www.charlestons.com					
Golden Gate 2640 W Baseline Rd	Mesa	AZ	85202	480-897-1335	345-8416
Hodori 1116 S Dobson Rd	Mesa	AZ	85202	480-668-7979	668-9898
Ichi Ban 2015 S Alma School Rd	Mesa	AZ	85210	480-777-8433	777-8432
Johnny Rockets 1445 W Southern Ave	Mesa	AZ	85202	480-844-2408	844-1585
Web: www.johnnyrockets.com					
Julio's Too 1935 S Val Vista Dr	Mesa	AZ	85296	480-497-6600	497-6618
Landmark Restaurant 809 W Main St	Mesa	AZ	85201	480-962-4652	
Web: www.landmarkrestaurant.com					
On the Border Mexican Cafe 1710 S Power Rd	Mesa	AZ	85206	480-654-5711	654-6925
Web: www.ontheborder.com					
Rosa's Mexican Grill 328 E University Dr	Mesa	AZ	85201	480-964-5451	964-3273
SN Pacific Rim Asian Kitchen 1236 E Baseline Rd	Mesa	AZ	85204	480-892-0688	
Waldo's BBQ 4500 E Main St	Mesa	AZ	85205	480-807-1645	985-3373
Web: www.waldosbbq.com					
Alexi's Grill 3550 N Central Ave Suite 120	Phoenix	AZ	85012	602-279-0982	279-0984
Alice Cooper's Town Sports Bar & Grill 101 E Jackson St	Phoenix	AZ	85004	602-253-7337	253-4866
Web: www.alicecooperstown.com					
Avanti's 2728 E Thomas Rd	Phoenix	AZ	85016	602-956-0900	468-1913
Web: www.avanti-az.com					
Baby Kay's Cajun Kitchen 2119 E Camelback Rd	Phoenix	AZ	85016	602-955-0011	955-2288
Bamboo Club 2596 E Camelback Rd	Phoenix	AZ	85016	602-955-1288	955-0062
Web: www.thebambooclub.com					
Barrio Cafe 2814 N 16th St	Phoenix	AZ	85006	602-636-0240	636-0385
Web: www.barriocafe.com					

	City	State	Zip	Phone	Fax
Christopher's Fermier Bistro 2584 E Camelback Rd	Phoenix	AZ	85016	602-522-2344	468-0314
Web: www.fermier.com					
Coronado Cafe 2201 N 7th St	Phoenix	AZ	85006	602-258-5149	258-7455
Coup des Tartes 4626 N 16th St	Phoenix	AZ	85016	602-212-1082	212-1138
Desert Jade 3215 E Indian School Rd	Phoenix	AZ	85018	602-954-0048	954-4038
Different Pointe of View 11111 N 7th St	Phoenix	AZ	85020	602-866-6350	866-6358
Web: www.pointehilton.com					
Durant's Restaurant 2611 N Central Ave	Phoenix	AZ	85004	602-264-5967	264-5112
Web: www.durantsaz.com					
Fish Market Restaurant 1720 E Camelback Rd	Phoenix	AZ	85016	602-277-3474	277-2543
Web: www.thefishmarket.com					
George & Dragon 4240 N Central Ave	Phoenix	AZ	85012	602-241-0018	234-3841
Giuseppe's Italian Kitchen 2824 E Indian School Rd	Phoenix	AZ	85016	602-381-1237	381-3669
Web: www.giuseppes-restaurant.com					
Hard Rock Cafe 3 S 2nd St	Phoenix	AZ	85004	602-261-7625	261-7635
Web: www.hardrock.com					
India Palace 3202 E Greenbay Way	Phoenix	AZ	85032	602-942-4224	942-0719
Kincaid's Fish Chop & Steak House 2 S 3rd St	Phoenix	AZ	85004	602-340-0000	254-8881
Web: www.kincaids.com					
La Pinata 3330 N 19th Ave	Phoenix	AZ	85015	602-279-1763	200-0931
Majerle's Sports Grill 24 N 2nd St	Phoenix	AZ	85004	602-253-9004	
Web: www.majerles.com					
Melting Pot The 3626 E Ray Rd	Phoenix	AZ	85044	480-704-9206	704-2973
Web: www.meltingpot.com					
Michelina's 3241 E Shea Blvd	Phoenix	AZ	85028	602-996-8977	996-9041
Morton's The Steakhouse 2501 E Camelback Rd	Phoenix	AZ	85016	602-955-9577	955-9670
Web: www.mortons.com					
Pizzeria Bianco 623 E Adams St	Phoenix	AZ	85004	602-258-8300	
Web: www.pizzeriabianco.com					
Roy's 5350 E Marriott Dr	Phoenix	AZ	85054	480-419-7697	419-7720
Web: www.roysrestaurant.com					
Ruth's Chris Steak House 2201 E Camelback Rd	Phoenix	AZ	85016	602-957-9600	224-1948
Web: www.ruthschris.com					
Sam's Cafe 2566 E Camelback Rd Suite 201	Phoenix	AZ	85016	602-954-7100	954-7404
Web: www.canyoncafe.com					
Such is Life 3602 N 24th St	Phoenix	AZ	85016	602-955-7822	
T Cook's 5200 E Camelback Rd	Phoenix	AZ	85018	602-808-0766	840-6927
Web: www.royalpalmsresortandspa.com/tcooks.htm					
Tarbell's 3213 E Camelback Rd	Phoenix	AZ	85018	602-955-8100	955-8181
Web: www.tarbells.com					
That's Italiano 3717 E Indian School Rd	Phoenix	AZ	85018	602-778-9100	
Vincent Guerithault on Camelback 3930 E Camelback Rd	Phoenix	AZ	85018	602-224-0225	956-5400
Web: www.vincentsoncamelback.com					
Zen 32 3160 E Camelback Rd	Phoenix	AZ	85016	602-954-8700	667-9510
Web: www.zen32.com					
Arcadia Farms Cafe 7014 E 1st Ave	Scottsdale	AZ	85251	480-941-5665	
Arizona Rib Co 10885 N Frank Lloyd Wright Blvd	Scottsdale	AZ	85259	480-314-0550	
Web: www.azribco.com					
Atlas Bistro 2515 N Scottsdale Rd	Scottsdale	AZ	85257	480-990-2433	
Bandera Scottsdale 3821 N Scottsdale Rd	Scottsdale	AZ	85251	480-994-3524	
Barcelona 15440 Greenway-Hayden Loop	Scottsdale	AZ	85260	480-603-0367	
Web: www.barcelonadining.com					
Bloom 8877 N Scottsdale Rd Suite 402	Scottsdale	AZ	85253	480-922-5666	
Web: www.tasteofbloom.com					
Bravo Bistro 4327 N Scottsdale Rd	Scottsdale	AZ	85251	480-481-7614	946-8205
Web: www.bravobistro.com					
Chaparral Room 5402 E Lincoln Dr	Scottsdale	AZ	85253	480-948-1700	
Web: www.camelbackinn.com/dining/dining.asp					
Chart House Restaurant 7255 McCormick Pkwy	Scottsdale	AZ	85258	480-951-2550	
Web: www.scottsdalecharthouse.com					
Cowboy Ciao Wine Bar & Grill 7133 E Stetson Dr	Scottsdale	AZ	85251	480-946-3111	
Web: www.cowboyciao.com					
Coyote Grill 7077 E Bell Rd	Scottsdale	AZ	85254	480-922-8424	
Don & Charlie's 7501 E Camelback Rd	Scottsdale	AZ	85251	480-990-0900	
Web: www.donandcharlies.com					
Earls 15784 N Pima Rd	Scottsdale	AZ	85260	480-607-1941	
Web: www.earls.ca					
Eddie V's Edgewater Grille 20715 N Pima Rd	Scottsdale	AZ	85255	480-538-8468	
Web: www.eddiev.com					
El Chorro Lodge 5550 E Lincoln Dr	Scottsdale	AZ	85253	480-948-5170	
Web: www.elchorrolodge.com					
Fleming's Prime Steakhouse & Wine Bar 6333 N Scottsdale Rd	Scottsdale	AZ	85250	480-596-8265	
Web: www.flemingssteakhouse.com					
George & Sons 11291 E Via Linda St	Scottsdale	AZ	85259	480-661-6336	661-8104
Web: www.georgeandsons.com					
Ibiza Cafe & Bar 4400 N Scottsdale Rd	Scottsdale	AZ	85251	480-994-3377	
Jalapeno's Mexican Cafe 23587 N Scottsdale	Scottsdale	AZ	85255	480-585-6442	
Jewel of the Crown 7373 Scottsdale Mall Suite 1	Scottsdale	AZ	85251	480-949-8000	970-9035
Kazimierz World Wine Bar 7137 E Stetson Dr	Scottsdale	AZ	85251	480-946-3004	
Kona Grill & Sushi Bar 7014 E Camelback Rd	Scottsdale	AZ	85251	480-429-1100	
Los Olivos Mexican Patio 7328 2nd St	Scottsdale	AZ	85251	480-946-2256	
Mancuso's Restaurant 6166 N Scottsdale Rd Suite 500	Scottsdale	AZ	85253	480-948-9988	
Web: www.mancusosrestaurant.com					
Mary Elaine's 6000 E Camelback Rd	Scottsdale	AZ	85251	480-423-2410	
Web: www.thephoenician.com/dining/dine_marymenu.html					
Mastro's Ocean Club 15045 N Kierland Blvd	Scottsdale	AZ	85254	480-443-8555	
Mastro's Steakhouse 8852 E Pinnacle Peak Rd	Scottsdale	AZ	85255	480-585-9500	
Web: www.mastrossteakhouse.com					
Morton's The Steakhouse 15233 Kierland Blvd	Scottsdale	AZ	85254	480-951-4440	
Web: www.mortons.com					
Mosaic 10600 E Jomax Rd	Scottsdale	AZ	85255	480-563-9600	
Web: www.mosaic-restaurant.com					
Palm Court The 7700 E McCormick Pkwy	Scottsdale	AZ	85258	480-991-3400	
Pane E Vino 8900 E Pinnacle Peak Rd	Scottsdale	AZ	85255	480-473-7900	
Pepin 7363 E Scottsdale Mall	Scottsdale	AZ	85251	480-990-9026	
PF Chang's China Bistro 7014 E Camelback Rd	Scottsdale	AZ	85251	480-949-2610	
Pinon Grill 7401 N Scottsdale Rd	Scottsdale	AZ	85253	480-367-2422	991-5572
Rancho Pinot Grill 6208 N Scottsdale Rd	Scottsdale	AZ	85253	480-367-8030	443-7616
Web: www.ranchopinot.com					
Remington's 7200 N Scottsdale Rd	Scottsdale	AZ	85253	480-951-5101	951-5108
Web: www.scottsdaleplaza.com/dining_remingtons.htm					
Roaring Fork 7243 E Camelback Rd	Scottsdale	AZ	85251	480-947-0795	
Web: www.roaringfork.com					
Roy's 7001 N Scottsdale Rd	Scottsdale	AZ	85253	480-905-1155	
Web: www.roysrestaurant.com					
Ruth's Chris Steak House 7001 N Scottsdale Rd Suite 290	Scottsdale	AZ	85253	480-991-5988	
Web: www.ruthschris.com					
Salt Cellar 550 N Hayden Rd	Scottsdale	AZ	85257	480-947-1963	
Sapporo 14344 N Scottsdale Rd	Scottsdale	AZ	85254	480-607-1114	
Web: www.sappororestaurant.com					
Sassi Ristorante 10455 E Pinnacle Peak Pkwy	Scottsdale	AZ	85255	480-502-9095	
Web: www.sassi.biz					
Sushi on Shea 7000 E Shea Blvd	Scottsdale	AZ	85254	480-483-7799	
Taggia 4925 N Scottsdale Rd	Scottsdale	AZ	85251	480-424-6095	425-8966
Web: www.taggiascottsdale.com					
Thaifoon 8777 N Scottsdale Rd	Scottsdale	AZ	85253	480-998-0011	
Veneto Trattoria 6137 N Scottsdale Rd	Scottsdale	AZ	85250	480-948-9928	
Windows on the Green 6000 E Camelback Rd	Scottsdale	AZ	85251	480-423-2530	
Web: www.thephoenician.com/dining					
L'Auberge de Sedona 301 L'Auberge Ln	Sedona	AZ	86336	928-282-1661	282-2885
Web: www.lauberge.com					
Blue Iguana 1849 N Scottsdale Rd	Tempe	AZ	85281	480-421-2525	421-2526
Blue Nile Cafe 933 E University Dr Suite 112	Tempe	AZ	85281	480-377-1113	
Byblos Restaurant 3332 S Mill Ave	Tempe	AZ	85282	480-894-1945	
Web: www.amdest.com/az/tempe/br/byblos.html					
Caffe Boa 398 S Mill Ave	Tempe	AZ	85281	480-968-9112	
Web: www.cafeboa.com					
Casey Moore's Oyster House 850 S Ash Ave	Tempe	AZ	85281	480-968-9935	968-6193
Cervantes 3318 S Mill Ave	Tempe	AZ	85282	480-921-9113	
Char's Thai Restaurant 927 E University Dr	Tempe	AZ	85281	480-967-6013	
Dimonte's Grille 818 W Broadway	Tempe	AZ	85282	480-557-8300	557-6815
House of Tricks 114 E 7th St	Tempe	AZ	85281	480-968-1114	968-0080
Web: www.houseoftricks.com					
John Henry's 909 E Elliot Rd	Tempe	AZ	85283	480-730-9009	831-2487
Web: www.johnhenrysrestaurant.com					
Longhitano's Restaurant 1835 E Elliot Rd	Tempe	AZ	85284	480-820-2786	820-1987
Monti's La Casa Vieja 1 W Rio Salado Pkwy	Tempe	AZ	85281	480-967-7594	967-8129
Web: www.montis.com					
Papa Razzini's 1825 E Guadalupe Rd	Tempe	AZ	85283	480-345-6560	345-6558
Web: www.paparazzinis.netfirms.com					
Pita Jungle 1250 E Apache Blvd	Tempe	AZ	85281	480-804-0234	
Rainforest Cafe 5000 S Arizona Mills Cir Suite 573	Tempe	AZ	85282	480-752-9100	752-9101
Web: www.rainforestcafe.com					
Urban Cafe 1212 E Apache Blvd	Tempe	AZ	85281	480-968-8888	
Wong's Place 1825 E Baseline Rd	Tempe	AZ	85283	480-838-8988	
Z'Tejas 20 W 6th St	Tempe	AZ	85281	480-377-1170	377-1167
Anthony's in the Catalinas 6440 N Campbell Ave	Tucson	AZ	85718	520-299-1771	299-6635
Web: www.anthonyscatalinas.com					
Arizona Inn 2200 E Elm St	Tucson	AZ	85719	520-325-1541	881-5830
Web: www.arizonainn.com/dining.htm					
Athens on Fourth Avenue 500 N 4th Ave	Tucson	AZ	85705	520-624-6886	
Beer Bottoms Bistro 5151 S Country Club	Tucson	AZ	85706	520-239-1300	239-1699
Bistro Zin 1865 E River Rd	Tucson	AZ	85718	520-299-7799	615-4534
Web: www.tasteofbistrozin.com					
Cafe Poca Cosa 88 E Broadway Blvd	Tucson	AZ	85701	520-622-6400	
Cafe Terra Cotta 3500 E Sunrise Dr	Tucson	AZ	85718	520-577-8100	577-9015
Web: www.dineterracotta.com					
Casa Molina 4240 E Grant Rd	Tucson	AZ	85712	520-326-6663	326-9937
Web: www.casamolina.com					
Char Thai 5039 E 5th St	Tucson	AZ	85711	520-795-1715	
Delectables 533 N 4th Ave	Tucson	AZ	85705	520-884-9289	628-7948
Web: www.delectables.com					
El Charro 311 N Court Ave	Tucson	AZ	85701	520-622-5465	624-4118
Web: www.elcharrorestaurant.com					
El Corral 2201 E River Rd	Tucson	AZ	85718	520-299-6092	
Elle 3048 E Broadway Blvd	Tucson	AZ	85716	520-327-0500	327-2353
Web: www.elletucson.com					
Feast 4122 E Speedway Blvd	Tucson	AZ	85712	520-326-9363	326-9245
Web: www.eatatfeast.com					
Fuego Bar & Grill 6958 E Tanque Verde Rd	Tucson	AZ	85715	520-886-1745	
Web: www.fuegorestaurant.com					
Gandhi 150 W Fort Lowell Rd	Tucson	AZ	85705	520-292-1738	
Gavi 7865 E Broadway Blvd	Tucson	AZ	85710	520-290-8380	
Gold Room 245 E Ina Rd	Tucson	AZ	85704	520-297-1151	297-9023
Grill at Hacienda del Sol 5601 N Hacienda del Sol Rd	Tucson	AZ	85718	520-529-3500	
Web: www.haciendadelsol.com/grill/					
J Bar 3770 E Sunrise Dr	Tucson	AZ	85718	520-615-6100	615-3334
Janos 3770 E Sunrise Dr	Tucson	AZ	85718	520-615-6100	615-3334
Web: www.janos.com					
Jonathan's Tucson Cork 6320 E Tanque Verde Rd	Tucson	AZ	85715	520-296-1631	296-0765
Web: www.jonathanscork.com					
Kingfisher Bar & Grill 2564 E Grant Rd	Tucson	AZ	85716	520-323-7739	795-7810
Web: www.kingfisherbarandgrill.com					
Le Rendez-vous 3844 E Fort Lowell Rd	Tucson	AZ	85716	520-323-7373	
Web: www.lerendez-vous.com/restaurant.htm					
Metro Grill Park Place 5870 E Broadway Blvd Suite 520	Tucson	AZ	85711	520-571-7111	571-1067
Web: www.metrorestaurants.com					
Mi Nidito Cafe 1813 S 4th Ave	Tucson	AZ	85713	520-622-5081	
Web: www.minidito.net					
Michelangelo 420 W Magee Rd	Tucson	AZ	85704	520-297-5772	
Web: www.michelangelotucson.com					
Pastiche Modern Eatery 3025 N Campbell Ave	Tucson	AZ	85718	520-325-3333	
Web: pasticheme.com					
PF Chang's China Bistro 1805 E River Rd	Tucson	AZ	85718	520-615-8788	
Web: www.pfchangs.com					
Sushi Ten 4500 E Speedway Blvd	Tucson	AZ	85712	520-324-0010	
Thunder Canyon Brewery 7401 N La Cholla Blvd	Tucson	AZ	85741	520-797-2652	797-2589
Web: www.thundercanyonbrewery.com					
Ventana Room 7000 N Resort Dr	Tucson	AZ	85750	520-299-2020	
Web: www.ventanaroom.com					
Vivace 4310 N Campbell Rd	Tucson	AZ	85718	520-795-7221	
Wildflower 7037 N Oracle Rd	Tucson	AZ	85704	520-219-4230	
Yama 5425 N Kolb Rd	Tucson	AZ	85750	520-615-1031	
Yoshimatsu 2660 N Campbell Ave	Tucson	AZ	85719	520-320-1574	

Arkansas

	City	State	Zip	Phone	Fax
Bella Italia 407 N 8th St	Fort Smith	AR	72901	479-785-1550	785-1558
Calico County 2401 S 56th St	Fort Smith	AR	72903	479-452-3299	452-4286
Web: www.calicocounty.net					
Catfish Cove 1615 Phoenix Ave	Fort Smith	AR	72901	479-646-8835	646-8835
Jerry Neel's Bar-B-Que 1823 Phoenix St	Fort Smith	AR	72901	479-646-8085	696-0555
Light House Inn 6000 Midland Blvd	Fort Smith	AR	72904	479-783-9420	
Red Barn Steak House 3716 Newlon Rd	Fort Smith	AR	72904	479-783-4075	
Taliano's Restaurant 201 N 14th St	Fort Smith	AR	72901	479-785-2292	785-2640
Web: www.talianosrestaurant.com					
Back Porch Grill 4810 Central Ave	Hot Springs	AR	71901	501-525-0885	
Web: www.backporchgrill.com					
Cafe 1217 1217 Malvern Ave	Hot Springs	AR	71901	501-318-1094	
Cafe Pompeii 2012 Central Ave	Hot Springs	AR	71901	501-318-3287	318-3288
Cafe Santa Clare 323 Whittington Ave	Hot Springs	AR	71901	501-624-0166	
Cajun Boilers 2806 Albert Pike Rd	Hot Springs	AR	71913	501-767-5695	
Chef Paul's 4330 Central Ave	Hot Springs	AR	71913	501-520-4187	520-4334
Web: www.cpauls.com					
Chuck's Southern Bar-B-Que 1118 Airport Rd	Hot Springs	AR	71913	501-760-3223	
Coy's 300 Coy St	Hot Springs	AR	71901	501-321-1414	321-1497
Web: www.coyssteakhouse.com					
Don Juan 1311A Albert Pike Rd	Hot Springs	AR	71913	501-321-0766	
Fountain Room Grill 239 Central Ave	Hot Springs	AR	71901	501-623-7771	623-2243
Hamilton House 132 Van Lyell Dr	Hot Springs	AR	71913	501-520-4040	520-4023
Web: www.hamiltonhouseestate.com					

Arkansas (Cont'd)

				Phone	Fax
King's 3310 Central Ave	Hot Springs	AR	71903	501-318-1888	318-3888
La Hacienda 3836 Central Ave	Hot Springs	AR	71913	501-525-8203	520-4397
Magnolia's on Central 510 Central Ave	Hot Springs	AR	71901	501-624-5500	
Web: www.magnoliasoncentral.com/					
McClard's Bar-B-Q 505 Albert Pike Rd	Hot Springs	AR	71913	501-624-9586	622-2527
Web: www.mcclards.com					
Mickey's BBQ 1622 Park Ave	Hot Springs	AR	71901	501-624-1247	
Web: www.mickeysbbq.net					
Mollie's Restaurant 538 W Grand Ave	Hot Springs	AR	71901	501-623-6582	623-6704
1620 Restaurant 1620 Market St	Little Rock	AR	72212	501-221-1620	221-1921
Acadia 3000 Kavanaugh Blvd	Little Rock	AR	72205	501-603-9630	
Alley Oops 11900 Kanis Rd Suite D10	Little Rock	AR	72211	501-221-9400	
Anderson's Cajun Wharf 2400 Cantrell Rd	Little Rock	AR	72202	501-375-5351	
Ashley's 111 W Markham St	Little Rock	AR	72201	501-374-7474	
Black Angus 10907 N Rodney Parham Rd	Little Rock	AR	72212	501-228-7800	
Brave New Restaurant 2300 Cottondale Ln	Little Rock	AR	72205	501-663-2677	
Web: www.bravenewrestaurant.com					
Bruno's Little Italy 315 N Bowman Rd	Little Rock	AR	72211	501-224-4700	
Buffalo Grill 1611 Rebsamen Park Rd	Little Rock	AR	72202	501-663-2158	
Capers 14502 Cantrell Rd	Little Rock	AR	72223	501-868-7600	
Web: www.capersrestaurant.com					
Capriccio 200 W Markam	Little Rock	AR	72201	501-906-4000	399-8073
Dave's Place 210 Center St	Little Rock	AR	72201	501-372-3283	
Web: www.davesplacerestaurant.com					
Doe's Eat Place 1023 W Marckham St	Little Rock	AR	72201	501-376-1195	374-1190
Web: www.doeseatplace.net					
El Chico 8409 I-30	Little Rock	AR	72209	501-562-3762	
El Dorado Mexican Restaurant 5820 Asher Ave	Little Rock	AR	72204	501-562-1025	
Faded Rose 400 N Bowman Rd	Little Rock	AR	72211	501-224-3377	224-4546
Web: www.thefadedrose.com					
Fu Lin Chinese Restaurant 200 N Bowman Rd	Little Rock	AR	72211	501-225-8989	
Graffiti's 7811 Cantrell Rd	Little Rock	AR	72227	501-224-9079	224-9161
Web: www.littlerockgraffitis.com					
Juanita's 1300 S Main St	Little Rock	AR	72202	501-372-1228	374-9735
Web: www.juanitas.com					
Kabab & Curry Indian Restaurant					
11121 N Rochey Parham Rd Suite 36B	Little Rock	AR	72212	501-978-8920	978-8921
Loca Luna 3519 Old Cantrell Rd	Little Rock	AR	72202	501-663-4666	
Web: www.localuna.com					
Markham Street Grill & Pub 11321 W Markham St	Little Rock	AR	72211	501-224-2010	
Shogun Japanese Steak House 2815 Cantrell Rd	Little Rock	AR	72202	501-666-7070	666-7077
Web: www.shogunlr.com					
Shorty Small's Great American Restaurant					
11100 N Rodney Parham Rd	Little Rock	AR	72212	501-224-3344	
Sonny Williams' Steak Room 500 President Clinton Ave	Little Rock	AR	72201	501-324-2999	324-4888
Web: www.sonnywilliamssteakroom.com					
Trio's 8201 Cantrell Rd	Little Rock	AR	72227	501-221-3330	221-1002
Web: www.triosrestaurant.com					
Star of India 301 N Shackleford Rd Suite C4	West Little Rock	AR	72211	501-227-9900	

British Columbia

				Phone	Fax
Accents 1967 W Broadway	Vancouver	BC	V6J1Z3	604-734-6660	
Web: www.accentsrestaurant.com					
Afghan Horseman 1833 Anderson St	Vancouver	BC	V6H4E5	604-873-5923	
Athene's 3618 W Broadway	Vancouver	BC	V6R2B7	604-731-4135	
Bacchus Ristorante 845 Hornby St	Vancouver	BC	V6Z1V1	604-689-7777	
Banana Leaf 820 W Broadway	Vancouver	BC	V5Z1J8	604-731-6333	
Web: www.bananaleaf-vancouver.com					
Baru Latino Tapas Lounge 2535 Alma St	Vancouver	BC	V6R3R8	604-222-9171	
Bin 941 Tapas Parlour 941 Davie St	Vancouver	BC	V6Z1B9	604-683-1246	
Web: www.bin941.com					
Bishop's 2183 W 4th Ave	Vancouver	BC	V6K1N7	604-738-2025	
Web: www.bishopsonline.com					
Bistro Pastis 2153 4th Ave W	Vancouver	BC	V6K1N7	604-731-5020	
Web: www.bistropastis.com					
Blue Water Cafe & Raw Bar 1095 Hamilton St	Vancouver	BC	V6B5T4	604-688-8078	688-8978
Web: www.bluewatercafe.net					
Bridges Restaurant 1676 Duranleau St	Vancouver	BC	V6H3S4	604-687-4400	
Web: www.bridgesrestaurant.com					
C Restaurant 1600 Howe St Suite 2	Vancouver	BC	V6Z2L9	604-681-1164	605-8263
Web: www.crestaurant.com					
Caffe de Medici 1025 Robson St Suite 109	Vancouver	BC	V6E1A9	604-669-9322	
Web: www.caffedemedici.com					
Candia Taverna 4510 W 10th Ave	Vancouver	BC	V6R2J1	604-228-9512	
Cannery Seafood Restaurant 2205 Commissioner St	Vancouver	BC	V5L1A4	604-254-9606	
Web: www.canneryseafood.com					
Capone's 1141 Hamilton St	Vancouver	BC	B6B5P6	604-684-7900	
Web: www.caponesrestaurant.net					
Cardero's 1583 Coal Harbour Quay	Vancouver	BC	B6G3E7	604-669-7666	
Web: www.vancouverdine.com/carderos					
Chambar 562 Beatty St	Vancouver	BC	V6B2L3	604-879-7119	
Web: www.chambar.com					
Ch'i 1796 Nanaimo St	Vancouver	BC	V5N5B9	604-215-0078	
CinCin Ristorante 1154 Robson St	Vancouver	BC	V6E1B5	604-688-7338	
Web: www.cincin.net/cincin/					
Cioppino's Enoteca 1129 Hamilton St	Vancouver	BC	V6B5P6	604-685-8462	
Cioppino's Mediterranean Grill 1133 Hamilton St	Vancouver	BC	V6B5P6	604-688-7466	
Cloud Nine Revolving Restaurant 1400 Robson St	Vancouver	BC	V6G1B9	604-687-0511	
Coast 1257 Hamilton St	Vancouver	BC	V6B6K3	604-685-5010	
Web: www.coastrestaurant.ca					
Diva at the Met 645 Howe St	Vancouver	BC	V6C2Y9	604-602-7788	
Web: www.metropolitan.com/diva					
Five Sails Restaurant 999 Canada Pl Suite 300	Vancouver	BC	V6C3B5	604-891-2892	
Web: www.fivesails.ca					
Glowbal Grill & Satay Bar 1079 Mainland St	Vancouver	BC	V6B5P9	604-602-0835	
Web: www.glowbalgrill.com					
Go Fish! Ocean Emporium 1505 W 1st Ave	Vancouver	BC	V6J1E8	604-730-5040	
Gotham Steakhouse & Cocktail Bar 615 Seymour St	Vancouver	BC	V6B3K3	604-605-8282	
Web: www.gothamsteakhouse.com					
Hapa Izakaya 1479 Robson St	Vancouver	BC	V6G1C1	604-689-4272	
Hy's Encore 637 Hornby St	Vancouver	BC	V6C2G3	604-683-7671	
Imperial Chinese Seafood Restaurant 355 Burrard St	Vancouver	BC	V6C2G8	604-688-8191	
Web: www.imperialrest.com					
Kamei Royal 211-1030 W Georgia St	Vancouver	BC	V6E2Y3	604-687-8588	
Kettle of Fish 900 Pacific St	Vancouver	BC	V6Z2E3	604-682-6661	
Web: www.akettleoffish.net					
La Bodega Restaurante & Tapa Bar 1277 Howe St	Vancouver	BC	V6Z1R3	604-684-8814	
Web: www.labodegavancouver.com					
Las Margaritas Restaurante 1999 W 4th Ave	Vancouver	BC	V6J1M7	604-734-7117	
Web: www.lasmargaritas.com					
Le Gavroche Restaurant 1616 Alberni St	Vancouver	BC	V6G1A6	604-685-3924	
Web: www.legavroche.com					
Living Room Bistro 2958 W 4th Ave	Vancouver	BC	V6K1R4	604-737-7529	
Lumiere Restaurant 2551 W Broadway	Vancouver	BC	V6K2E9	604-739-8185	
Maurya Indian Cuisine 1643 W Broadway	Vancouver	BC	V6J1W9	604-742-0622	
Memphis Blues Barbecue House 1465 W Broadway	Vancouver	BC	V6H1H6	604-738-6806	
Web: www.memphisbluesbbq.com					
Montri's 3629 Broadway W	Vancouver	BC	V6R2B8	604-738-9888	
Morton's The Steakhouse 750 Cordova St W	Vancouver	BC	V6C1A1	604-915-5105	915-5110
Web: www.mortons.com					
Mr Pickwick's 8620 Granville St	Vancouver	BC	V6P5A1	604-266-2340	
Web: www.mrpickwicks.bc.ca					
Original Tandoori Kitchen King 689 E 65th Ave	Vancouver	BC	V5X2P7	604-327-8900	
Web: www.originaltandoori.ca					
Osaka Teppanyaki 103-1788 W Broadway	Vancouver	BC	V6J1Y1	604-733-8258	
Ouest 2881 Granville St	Vancouver	BC	V6H3J4	604-738-8938	
Ouisi Bistro 3014 Granville St	Vancouver	BC	V6H3J8	604-732-7550	
Panos Greek Taverna 654 SE Marine Dr	Vancouver	BC	V5X2T4	604-322-7117	
Pho Thai Hoa 1625 Kingsway	Vancouver	BC	V5N2S2	604-873-2348	
Pink Pearl Chinese Seafood 1132 E Hastings St	Vancouver	BC	P6A1S2	604-253-4316	
Web: www.pinkpearl.com					
Raincity Grill 1193 Denman St	Vancouver	BC	V6G2N1	604-685-7337	
Web: www.raincitygrill.com					
Reef The 4172 Main St	Vancouver	BC	V5V3P7	604-874-5375	
Web: www.thereefrestaurant.com					
Sawasdee Thai 4250 Main St	Vancouver	BC	V5V3P9	604-876-4030	
Sequoia Grill at the Teahouse 1583 Cole Harbor Key	Vancouver	BC	V6G2E7	604-669-3281	
Web: www.vancouverdine.com					
Shanghai Chinese Bistro 548 W Broadway	Vancouver	BC	V6E1A5	604-873-1816	
Simply Thai 1211 Hamilton St	Vancouver	BC	V6B6K3	604-642-0123	
Star Anise Restaurant 1485 W 12th Ave	Vancouver	BC	V6H1M6	604-737-1485	
Web: www.staranise.ca					
Stepho's 1124 Davie St	Vancouver	BC	V6E1N1	604-683-2555	
Sun Sui Wah Seafood Restaurant 3888 Main St	Vancouver	BC	V5V3N9	604-872-8822	
Web: www.sunsuiwah.com					
Tojo's 777 W Broadway Suite 202	Vancouver	BC	V6H1G1	604-872-8050	
Web: www.tojos.com					
Vij's Restaurant & Curry Art Gallery 1480 W 11th Ave	Vancouver	BC	V6H1L1	604-736-6664	
William Tell Restaurant 765 Beatty St	Vancouver	BC	V6B2M4	604-688-3504	
Yew Restaurant & Bar 791 W Georgia St 2nd Fl	Vancouver	BC	V6C2T4	604-692-4939	
Yuji Tapas 2059 4th Ave W	Vancouver	BC	V6J1N3	604-734-4990	
Zin Restaurant & Lounge 1277 Robson St	Vancouver	BC	V6E1C4	604-408-1700	
Web: www.zin-restaurant.com					

California

				Phone	Fax
Cuban Bistro 28 W Main St	Alhambra	CA	91801	626-308-3350	308-3161
Web: www.cubanbistro.com					
Anaheim White House 887 S Anaheim Blvd	Anaheim	CA	92805	714-772-1381	772-7062
Web: www.anaheimwhitehouse.com					
Benihana 2100 E Ball Rd	Anaheim	CA	92806	714-774-4940	774-4943
Web: www.benihana.com					
Catal Restaurant & Uva Bar					
1580 Disneyland Dr Downtown Disney	Anaheim	CA	92803	714-774-4442	
Catch The 1929 S State College Blvd	Anaheim	CA	92806	714-935-0101	935-0105
Web: www.catchanaheim.com					
El Ortega's 2561 W Ball Rd	Anaheim	CA	92804	714-828-2830	
Gustav's Jaegerhaus 2525 E Ball Rd	Anaheim	CA	92806	714-520-9500	
Hibachi Steak House 108 S Fairmont Blvd	Anaheim	CA	92807	714-998-4110	921-9926
Hook's Pointe 1150 Magic Way Disneyland Hotel	Anaheim	CA	92802	714-778-6600	
Inka Anaheim 400 S Euclid St	Anaheim	CA	92802	714-772-2263	
Web: www.inkaanaheim.com					
JT Schmid's Restaurant & Brewery 2610 E Katella Ave	Anaheim	CA	92806	714-634-9200	635-0816
Web: www.jtschmids.com					
JW's Steakhouse 700 W Convention Way	Anaheim	CA	92802	714-750-8000	750-8000
Merhaba 2801 W Ball Rd	Anaheim	CA	92804	714-826-8859	
Mr Stox 1105 E Katella Ave	Anaheim	CA	92805	714-634-2994	634-0561
Web: www.mrstox.com					
Napa Rose 1600 S Disneyland Dr	Anaheim	CA	92802	714-781-3463	
Naples 1550 Disneyland Dr Downtown Disney	Anaheim	CA	92801	714-776-6200	776-6200
Web: www.patinagroup.com/naples					
Pepe's 2429 W Ball Rd	Anaheim	CA	92804	714-952-9410	
Pho Republic 30 S Anaheim Blvd	Anaheim	CA	92805	714-999-1200	
Web: www.pho-republic.com					
Rainforest Cafe 1515 S Disneyland Dr Downtown Disney	Anaheim	CA	92802	714-772-0413	772-3024
Ralph Brennan's Jazz Kitchen					
1590 S Disneyland Dr Downtown Disney	Anaheim	CA	92802	714-776-5200	776-5300
Web: www.rbjazzkitchen.com					
Rosine's 721 S Weir Canyon Rd	Anaheim	CA	92808	714-283-5141	283-0158
Web: www.rosines.com					
Steakhouse 55 1150 Magic Way	Anaheim	CA	92802	714-956-6402	956-6597
Tortilla Jo's 1510 Disneyland Dr Downtown Disney	Anaheim	CA	92803	714-535-5000	535-5700
Web: www.patinagroup.com/tortillaJos					
Ciao Italian Kitchen 416 N Lakeview Ave	Anaheim Hills	CA	92807	714-282-2220	
Basque Cafe The 4420 Coffee Rd	Bakersfield	CA	93308	661-587-9055	587-9088
Benji's 4001 Rosedale Hwy	Bakersfield	CA	93308	661-328-0400	328-0423
Bill Lee's Bamboo Chopsticks 1203 18th St	Bakersfield	CA	93301	661-324-9441	324-7811
Web: www.billlees.com					
Bit Of Germany 1901 Flower St	Bakersfield	CA	93305	661-325-8874	872-0854
Buck Owens' Crystal Palace Steakhouse					
2800 Buck Owens Blvd	Bakersfield	CA	93308	661-328-7560	328-7565
Web: www.buckowens.com					
Cactus Valley 4215 Rosedale Hwy	Bakersfield	CA	93308	661-633-1948	322-3234
Cafe Med 4809 Scottdale Hwy	Bakersfield	CA	93309	661-834-4433	834-0188
Web: www.cafemedrestaurant.com					
Chalet Basque 200 Oak St	Bakersfield	CA	93304	661-327-2915	
Web: www.chaletbasque.net					
China Palace 4142 California Ave	Bakersfield	CA	93309	661-326-8202	
Chuy's Mesquite Broiler 2500 New Stine Rd	Bakersfield	CA	93309	661-833-3469	833-3130
Coconut Joe's Island Grill House 4158 California Ave	Bakersfield	CA	93309	661-327-1378	
Web: www.coconutjoes.com					
Cope's Knotty Pine Cafe 1530 Norris Rd	Bakersfield	CA	93308	661-399-0120	
Grand China 3770 Ming Ave	Bakersfield	CA	93309	661-831-6300	
Imperial Chinese Restaurant 4525 Ming Ave	Bakersfield	CA	93309	661-836-0288	
Izumo Sushi 4412 Ming Ave	Bakersfield	CA	93309	661-398-0608	
Jake's Tex-Mex Cafe 1710 Oak St	Bakersfield	CA	93301	661-322-6380	322-3731
Lamina 354 Oak St	Bakersfield	CA	93304	661-322-1087	322-3509
Las Costa Mariscos 716 21st St	Bakersfield	CA	93301	661-322-2655	
Mama Tosca's 9000 Ming Ave Suite K3	Bakersfield	CA	93309	661-831-1242	663-7436
Web: www.mamatoscas.com					
Mossman's Southwest 3610 Wible Rd	Bakersfield	CA	93309	661-832-5130	832-4783
Mr Tibbs Ribs 3508 New Stine Rd	Bakersfield	CA	93309	661-397-4030	397-5706
Sorella Ristorante 7800 McNair Ct	Bakersfield	CA	93313	661-396-8603	396-9649
Stuart Anderson's Black Angus 3601 Rosedale Hwy	Bakersfield	CA	93308	661-324-0814	324-3109

				Phone	Fax
Tahoe Joe's 9000 Ming Ave	Bakersfield	CA	93311	661-664-8723	664-7732
Web: www.tahoejoes.com					
Texas Cattle Co 1429 N China Lake Blvd	Bakersfield	CA	93555	760-446-6602	
Uricchio's Trattoria 1400 17th St	Bakersfield	CA	93301	661-326-8870	326-8829
Wool Growers 620 E 19th St	Bakersfield	CA	93305	661-327-9584	
Belvedere The 9882 S Santa Monica Blvd	Beverly Hills	CA	90212	310-788-2306	788-2319
Crustacean 9646 Little Santa Monica Blvd	Beverly Hills	CA	90210	310-205-8990	271-0737
Hokusai 8400 Wilshire Blvd	Beverly Hills	CA	90211	323-782-9717	782-9908
Web: www.hokusairestaurant.com					
La Scala 434 N Canon Dr	Beverly Hills	CA	90210	310-275-0579	246-9099
Lawry's The Prime Rib 100 N La Cienega Blvd	Beverly Hills	CA	90211	310-652-2827	657-5463
Web: www.lawrysonline.com/theprimerib.asp					
Mastro's Steakhouse 246 N Canon Dr	Beverly Hills	CA	90210	310-888-8782	
Web: www.mastrossteakhouse.com					
Matsuhisa 129 N La Cienega Blvd	Beverly Hills	CA	90211	310-659-9639	659-0492
Web: www.nobumatsuhisa.com					
Morton's The Steakhouse 435 S La Cienega Blvd	Beverly Hills	CA	90048	310-246-1501	246-1203
Web: www.mortons.com					
Porterhouse Bistro 8635 Wilshire Blvd	Beverly Hills	CA	90211	310-659-1099	659-2099
Web: www.porterhousebistro.com					
Ruth's Chris Steak House 224 S Beverly Dr	Beverly Hills	CA	90212	310-859-8744	859-2576
Web: www.ruthschris.com					
Spago 176 N Canon Dr	Beverly Hills	CA	90210	310-385-0880	385-0880
Web: www.wolfgangpuck.com					
Tanzore 50 N La Cienega Blvd	Beverly Hills	CA	90211	310-652-3838	652-0163
Web: www.tanzore.com					
Kuleto's Trattoria 1095 Rollins Rd	Burlingame	CA	94010	650-342-4922	344-3376
Web: www.kuletostrattoria.com/					
Anton & Michel Mission St	Carmel	CA	93921	831-624-2406	625-1542
Web: www.carmelsbest.com/antonmichel/					
Bahama Billy's 3690 The Barnyard	Carmel	CA	93923	831-626-0430	626-5820
Web: www.bahamabillys.com					
Bouchee Mission St	Carmel	CA	93921	831-626-7880	626-7883
Web: www.boucheecarmel.com					
Carmel Chop House 5th Ave & San Carlos St	Carmel	CA	93921	831-625-1199	625-0984
Web: www.carmelchophouse.com					
Casanova 5th St-between Mission & San Carlos	Carmel	CA	93921	831-625-0501	625-9799
Web: www.casanovarestaurant.com					
Covey The 8205 Valley Greens Dr	Carmel	CA	93923	831-624-2888	624-3726
Flying Fish Grill Mission St	Carmel	CA	93921	831-625-1962	
French Poodle The Junipero & 5th Ave	Carmel	CA	93921	831-624-8643	
Grasing's 6th & Mission Sts	Carmel	CA	93921	831-624-6562	624-7431
Web: www.grasings.com					
Pacific's Edge 120 Highland Dr	Carmel	CA	93923	831-622-5445	
Rio Grill 101 Crossroads Blvd	Carmel	CA	93923	831-625-5436	625-2950
Web: www.riogrill.com					
Robata Grill 3658 The Barnyard	Carmel	CA	93923	831-624-2643	624-0360
Anthony's Fish Grotto 215 W Bay Blvd	Chula Vista	CA	91910	619-425-4200	425-8370
Web: www.gofishanthonys.com					
Aunt Emma's 700 'E' St	Chula Vista	CA	91910	619-427-2722	727-4440
Web: www.aunt-emmas.com					
Baja Lobster 1060 Broadway Ave	Chula Vista	CA	91911	619-425-2512	425-2519
Cilantro Live! 315 1/2 3rd Ave	Chula Vista	CA	91910	619-827-7401	827-7403
Web: www.cilantrolive.com					
La Costa Azul 1037 Broadway Ave	Chula Vista	CA	91911	619-691-9812	
La Nena 975 Broadway Ave	Chula Vista	CA	91911	619-420-1625	420-1689
Meakwan 230 3rd Ave	Chula Vista	CA	91910	619-426-5172	
Pescados y Mariscos Hector's 1177 Broadway Ave	Chula Vista	CA	91911	619-585-0773	585-7732
Web: www.pescadosymariscoshectors.com					
RJ's Restaurant 89 Bonita Rd	Chula Vista	CA	91910	619-426-8323	691-8465
Tango Grille 635 Broadway Ave	Chula Vista	CA	91910	619-420-0384	
Web: www.tangogrille.com					
Valentines 655 H St	Chula Vista	CA	91910	619-425-1219	
Zorba's Family Restaurant 100 Broadway	Chula Vista	CA	91910	619-422-8853	422-0104
Web: www.zorbasgreekbuffet.com					
Azzura Point 4000 Coronado Bay Rd	Coronado	CA	92118	619-424-4477	
Rainforest Cafe 3333 Bristol St Suite 1073	Costa Mesa	CA	92626	714-424-9200	
Web: www.rainforestcafe.com					
Slocum House 7992 California Ave	Fair Oaks	CA	95628	916-961-7211	961-5710
Web: www.slocum-house.com					
Carmen & Family Bar-B-Q 41986 Fremont Blvd	Fremont	CA	94538	510-657-5464	657-9125
China Chili 39116 State St	Fremont	CA	95438	510-791-1688	791-5181
Country Way 5325 Mowry Ave	Fremont	CA	94536	510-797-3188	
El Patio Restaurant 37311 Fremont Blvd	Fremont	CA	94536	510-796-1733	796-0833
Web: www.elpatiooriginal.com					
Fremont Market Broiler 39195 Farwell Dr	Fremont	CA	94538	510-791-8675	791-6172
Web: www.marketbroiler.com					
Habibi 3906 Washington Blvd	Fremont	CA	94538	510-659-9600	659-9034
Web: www.habibirestaurant.com					
Ho Chow Restaurant 47966 Warm Springs Blvd	Fremont	CA	94539	510-657-0683	
Kimaree 39620 Mission Blvd	Fremont	CA	94539	510-742-5152	
La Casita 41240 Fremont Blvd	Fremont	CA	94538	510-657-8602	
Massimo's 5200 Mowry Ave	Fremont	CA	94538	510-792-2000	792-7041
Web: www.massimos.com					
Mughal Cuisine 4812A Thornton Dr	Fremont	CA	94536	510-792-4200	
Web: www.mughalcuisine.com					
Norman's Family Restaurant 4949 Stevenson Blvd	Fremont	CA	94538	510-226-7777	
Papillon Restaurant 37296 Mission Blvd	Fremont	CA	94536	510-793-6331	793-2789
Web: www.papillonrestaurant.com					
Ristorante Il Porcino 3339 Walnut Ave	Fremont	CA	94538	510-791-7383	
Salang Pass 37462 Fremont Blvd	Fremont	CA	94536	510-795-9200	792-4408
Southern Heritage BBQ 40645 Fremont Blvd Suite 23	Fremont	CA	94538	510-668-1850	
Star Buffett 34755 Ardenwood Blvd	Fremont	CA	94555	510-797-7181	797-7182
Yuri Japanese Restaurant 3810 Mowry Ave	Fremont	CA	94538	510-795-6701	
Bangkok Restaurant 1627 E Ashlan Ave	Fresno	CA	93704	559-227-9776	
Campagnia 1185 E Champlain Dr	Fresno	CA	93720	559-433-3300	433-3066
Web: www.campagnia.net					
Chopsticks 4783 E Olive Ave	Fresno	CA	93702	559-255-0489	
Elbow Room 731 W San Jose Ave	Fresno	CA	93704	559-227-1234	227-1843
Web: www.elbow-room.com					
Fong's 4608 E Tulare St	Fresno	CA	93702	559-255-0682	
Giulia's 3050 W Shaw Ave	Fresno	CA	93711	559-276-3573	277-7552
La Rocca's Ristorante 6735 N 1st St Suite 111	Fresno	CA	93710	559-431-1278	435-7884
Landmark The 644 E Olive Ave	Fresno	CA	93728	559-233-6505	233-9662
Livingstone's Restaurant & Pub 831 E Fern Ave	Fresno	CA	93728	559-485-5198	485-3439
Max's 1784 W Bullard Ave	Fresno	CA	93711	559-439-6900	439-7206
Web: www.maxsbistro.com					
Pacific Seafood 1055 E Herndon Ave	Fresno	CA	93720	559-439-2778	439-2651
Richard's 1609 E Belmont Ave	Fresno	CA	93701	559-266-4077	498-3946
Ripe Tomato 5064 N Palm Ave	Fresno	CA	93704	559-225-1850	
Sequoia Brewing Co 777 E Olive St	Fresno	CA	93728	559-264-5521	
Thai House 1069 E Shaw Ave	Fresno	CA	93710	559-221-7245	
Tokyo Garden 1711 Fulton St	Fresno	CA	93721	559-268-3596	
Yanagi 1901 E Shields Ave	Fresno	CA	93726	559-224-0396	
Yoshino Restaurant 6226 N Blackstone Ave	Fresno	CA	93710	559-431-2205	431-0377
Anaheim Suites Grill 12017 Harbor Blvd Anaheim Marriott Suites	Garden Grove	CA	92840	714-383-6000	383-6050
Azteca 12911 Main St	Garden Grove	CA	92840	714-638-3790	638-3737
Web: www.elvislounge.com					
Buca de Beppo 11757 Harbor Blvd	Garden Grove	CA	92840	714-740-2822	740-1556
California Grill 11999 Harbor Blvd Hyatt Regency Orange County	Garden Grove	CA	92840	714-750-1234	740-0465
Carolina's 12045 Chapman Ave	Garden Grove	CA	92840	714-971-5551	971-5552
Casa De Soto 8562 Garden Grove Blvd	Garden Grove	CA	92844	714-530-4200	
Web: www.casadesoto.com					
Copa D'Oro 12021 Harbor Blvd Crowne Plaza Anaheim Resort	Garden Grove	CA	92840	714-867-5555	
Furiwa Seafood 13826 Brookhurst St	Garden Grove	CA	92843	714-534-3996	534-5327
Gennaro's 5244 Lampson Ave	Garden Grove	CA	92845	714-892-2705	901-0403
Joe's Crab Shack 12011 Harbor Blvd	Garden Grove	CA	92840	714-703-0505	703-0252
Web: www.joescrabshack.com					
King Harbor 13018 Harbor Blvd	Garden Grove	CA	92843	714-636-9103	636-3033
Los Sanchez 11906 Garden Grove Blvd	Garden Grove	CA	92843	714-590-9300	590-9339
Web: www.lossanchez.com					
Pho 79 9941 Hazard Ave	Garden Grove	CA	92844	714-531-2490	
Web: www.pho79.com					
Seafood Cove 8547 Westminster Blvd	Garden Grove	CA	92844	714-895-7964	
Spring Garden Restaurant & Sushi Bar 10022 Garden Grove Blvd	Garden Grove	CA	92844	714-534-1818	539-9930
Tokyo Love 12565 S Harbor Blvd	Garden Grove	CA	92840	714-534-4751	534-4158
Vien Dong 14271 Brookhurst St	Garden Grove	CA	92843	714-531-8253	
Wong's 10642 Westminster Ave	Garden Grove	CA	92843	714-537-4920	
Barragan's 814 S Central Ave	Glendale	CA	91204	818-243-1103	243-2637
Carousel 304 N Brand Blvd	Glendale	CA	91203	818-246-7775	246-6627
Web: www.carouselrestaurant.com					
Damon's Steak House 317 N Brand Blvd	Glendale	CA	91203	818-507-1510	240-0087
Web: www.damonsglendale.com					
Far Niente Ristorante 204 1/2 N Brand Blvd	Glendale	CA	91203	818-242-3835	242-2956
Fresco Ristorante 514 S Brand Blvd	Glendale	CA	91204	818-247-5541	247-1964
Web: www.frescoristorante.com					
Gauchos Village Churrascaria & Bar 411 N Brand Blvd	Glendale	CA	91203	818-550-1430	550-1429
Web: www.gauchosvillage.com					
Gennaro's Ristorante 1109 N Brand Blvd	Glendale	CA	91202	818-243-6231	254-0080
Web: www.gennarosristorante.com					
La Cabanita 3447 N Verdugo Rd	Glendale	CA	91208	818-957-2711	
Maurizio's 135 N Maryland Ave	Glendale	CA	91206	818-247-5600	247-7692
Web: www.mauriziosbar.com					
Max's of Manila 313 W Broadway	Glendale	CA	91204	818-637-7751	637-2325
Notte Luna 113 N Maryland Ave	Glendale	CA	91206	818-552-4100	552-3522
Web: www.notteluna.com					
Panda Inn 111 E Wilson Ave	Glendale	CA	91206	818-502-1234	502-1730
Web: www.pandainn.com					
Scarantino's 1524 E Colorado St	Glendale	CA	91205	818-247-9777	247-5344
Web: www.scarantinos.com					
Shiraz 211 S Glendale Ave	Glendale	CA	91205	818-500-4948	
Tep Thai 209 W Wilson Ave	Glendale	CA	91203	818-246-0380	
Web: www.tepthai.com					
Two Guys From Italy 405 N Verdugo Rd	Glendale	CA	91206	818-240-0370	240-0972
Varouj's Kabobs 1110 S Glendale Ave	Glendale	CA	91205	818-243-9870	
Vert 6801 Hollywood Blvd 4th Fl	Hollywood	CA	90028	323-491-1300	491-1293
Arbor's 6060 Warner Ave	Huntington Beach	CA	92647	714-842-5111	843-5768
Web: www.arborsrestaurantinc.com					
Baci 18748 Beach Blvd	Huntington Beach	CA	92648	714-965-1194	965-4106
Web: www.bacirestaurant.com					
Baja Willie's 7891 Warner Ave	Huntington Beach	CA	92647	714-842-8955	842-6778
Web: www.bajawillies.net					
Beachfront 301 301 Main St	Huntington Beach	CA	92648	714-374-3399	
Web: www.beachfront301.com					
BJ's Restaurant & Brewhouse 200 Main St	Huntington Beach	CA	92648	714-374-2224	374-0015
Web: www.bjsrestaurants.com					
Bukhara Cuisine Of India 7594 Edinger Ave	Huntington Beach	CA	92647	714-842-3171	
Californian The 21500 Pacific Coast Hwy	Huntington Beach	CA	92648	714-698-1234	845-4990
Capone's Cucina 19688 Beach Blvd	Huntington Beach	CA	92648	714-593-2888	
Web: www.caponescucina.com					
Chimayo at the Beach 315 Pacific Coast Hwy	Huntington Beach	CA	92648	714-374-7273	374-7263
Web: www.culinaryadventures.com					
Daimon 16232 Pacific Coast Hwy	Huntington Beach	CA	92649	562-592-4862	
Duke's Huntington Beach 317 Pacific Coast Hwy	Huntington Beach	CA	92648	714-374-6446	374-6546
Web: www.hulapie.com					
Kung Pao Chinese Restaurant 4911 Warner Ave Suite 109	Huntington Beach	CA	92649	714-840-5721	
La Fontana 18344 Beach Blvd	Huntington Beach	CA	92648	714-841-0059	
Longboard Restaurant & Pub 217 Main St	Huntington Beach	CA	92648	714-960-1896	960-8447
Web: longboardpub.com					
Lou's Oak Oven 21501 Brookhurst St Suite D	Huntington Beach	CA	92646	714-965-5200	
Web: www.lousbbq.com					
Mario's Restaurant 18603 Main St	Huntington Beach	CA	92648	714-842-5811	
Matsu Restaurant 18035 Beach Blvd	Huntington Beach	CA	92648	714-848-4404	842-4049
Palm Court 21100 Pacific Coast Hwy	Huntington Beach	CA	92648	714-960-7873	845-8424
Ruby's Diner 1 Main St	Huntington Beach	CA	92648	714-969-7829	696-1630
Web: www.rubys.com					
Sea Siam Restaurant 16103 Bolsa Chica St	Huntington Beach	CA	92649	714-846-8986	846-4543
Spark Woodfire Grill 300 Pacific Coast Hwy Suite 202	Huntington Beach	CA	92648	714-960-0996	960-7332
Web: www.sparkwoodfiregrill.com					
Surf City Sunset Grill 21500 Pacific Coast Hwy Hyatt Huntington Beach	Huntington Beach	CA	92648	714-698-1234	845-4620
Tsunami 17236 Pacific Coast Hwy	Huntington Beach	CA	92649	562-592-5806	592-4437
Tuna Town 221 Main St	Huntington Beach	CA	92648	714-536-3194	536-3473
Web: www.tunatownsushibar.com					
West Coast Club 21100 Pacific Coast Hwy Hilton Waterfront Beach Resort	Huntington Beach	CA	92648	714-845-8000	845-8424
Zubie's Dry Dock 9059 Adams Ave	Huntington Beach	CA	92646	714-963-6362	
Marine Room 2000 Spindrift Dr	La Jolla	CA	92037	858-459-7222	551-4673
Web: www.ljbtc.com/marineroom					
Piatti 2182 Avenida de la Playa	La Jolla	CA	92037	858-454-1589	454-1799
Roppongi 875 Prospect St	La Jolla	CA	92037	858-551-5252	551-7712
Web: www.roppongiusa.com					
Sky Room 1132 Prospect St	La Jolla	CA	92037	858-454-0771	
Web: www.lavalencia.com/dining_sky.asp					
Tapenade 7612 Fay Ave	La Jolla	CA	92037	858-551-7500	551-9913
Napoli Italian Restaurant 24960 Redlands Blvd	Loma Linda	CA	92354	909-796-3770	478-7756
555 East 555 E Ocean Blvd	Long Beach	CA	90802	562-437-0626	
Web: www.555east.com					
Alegria Cocina Latina Restaurant 115 Pine Ave	Long Beach	CA	90802	562-436-3388	436-9108
Web: www.alegriacocinalatina.com					
Bangkok Cuisine 3426 E 4th St	Long Beach	CA	90814	562-433-0093	
Web: www.geocities.com/bkthaicuisine/					
Belmont Brewing Company 25 39th Pl	Long Beach	CA	90803	562-433-3891	434-0604
Web: www.belmontbrewing.com					
Cafe Piccolo 3222 E Broadway	Long Beach	CA	90803	562-438-1316	
Web: www.cafepiccolo.com					
Caffe La Strada 4716 E 2nd St	Long Beach	CA	90803	562-433-8100	

California (Cont'd)

Restaurant	City	State	ZIP	Phone	Fax
Christy's 3937 E Broadway	Long Beach	CA	90803	562-433-7133	621-1471
Web: www.christysristorante.com					
Crab Pot The 215 N Marina Dr	Long Beach	CA	90803	562-430-0272	799-0686
Web: www.thecrabpot.com					
Daphne's Greek Cafe 7535 Carson Blvd	Long Beach	CA	90808	562-627-3966	627-0926
Web: www.daphnesgreekcafe.com					
Delius 2951 Cherry Ave	Long Beach	CA	90807	562-426-0694	
Web: www.deliusrestaurant.com					
Four Olives Cafe 4276 Atlantic Ave	Long Beach	CA	90807	562-595-1131	595-1151
Web: fourolivescafe.com					
Frenchy's Bistro 4137 E Anaheim St	Long Beach	CA	90804	562-494-8787	494-1613
Web: www.frenchysbistro.com					
George's Greek Cafe 5316 E 2nd St	Long Beach	CA	90803	562-433-1755	
Green Field Churrascaria 5305 E Pacific Coast Hwy	Long Beach	CA	90804	562-597-0906	597-0916
Web: www.greenfieldchurrascaria.com					
Joe's Crab Shack 6550 Marina Dr	Long Beach	CA	90803	562-594-6551	
Johnny Rebs' Southern Roadhouse 4663 Long Beach Blvd	Long Beach	CA	90805	562-423-7327	422-9681
Web: www.johnnyrebs.com					
Kelly's 5716 E 2nd St	Long Beach	CA	90803	562-433-4983	
Khoury's 110 Marina Dr	Long Beach	CA	90803	562-598-6800	598-0079
Web: www.khourys.net					
King's Fish House 100 W Broadway	Long Beach	CA	90802	562-432-7463	435-6143
Web: www.kingsfishhouse.com					
La Traviata 301 Cedar Ave	Long Beach	CA	90802	562-432-8022	432-6222
Web: www.latraviata301.com					
Lasher's 3441 E Broadway	Long Beach	CA	90803	562-433-0153	433-2735
Web: www.lashersrestaurant.com					
L'Opera 101 Pine Ave	Long Beach	CA	90802	562-491-0066	436-1108
Web: www.lopera.com					
Lucille's Smokehouse Bar-B-Que 7411 Carson St	Long Beach	CA	90808	562-938-7427	627-1947
Madison 102 Pine Ave	Long Beach	CA	90802	562-628-8866	628-8870
McKenna's on the Bay 190 Marina Dr	Long Beach	CA	90803	562-342-9411	493-5399
Web: www.mckennasonthebay.com					
Nino's 3853 Atlantic Ave	Long Beach	CA	90807	562-427-1003	427-3093
Parker's Lighthouse 435 Shoreline Village Dr	Long Beach	CA	90802	562-432-6500	436-3551
Phil Trani's 3490 Long Beach Blvd	Long Beach	CA	90807	562-426-3668	426-1218
Web: www.philtranis.com					
Reef The 880 S Harbor Scenic Dr	Long Beach	CA	90802	562-435-8013	432-6823
Web: www.reefrestaurant.com					
Roscoe's House of Chicken & Waffles 730 E Broadway	Long Beach	CA	90802	562-437-8355	437-2454
Web: www.roscoeschickenandwaffles.com					
Sir Winston's 1126 Queens Hwy	Long Beach	CA	90802	562-435-3511	
Web: www.queenmary.com					
Sky Room 40 S Locust Ave	Long Beach	CA	90802	562-983-2722	
Sushi of Naples 5470 E 2nd St	Long Beach	CA	90803	562-434-1122	434-0319
Web: www.sushiofnaples.com					
Utopia 445 E 1st St	Long Beach	CA	90802	562-432-6888	432-8687
Web: www.utopiarestaurant.net					
Yard House 401 Shoreline Village Dr	Long Beach	CA	90802	562-628-0455	435-5544
Web: www.yardhouse.com					
Shenandoah at the Arbor 10631 Los Alamitos Blvd	Los Alamitos	CA	90720	562-431-1990	431-1910
Web: www.shenandoahatthearbor.com					
410 Boyd 410 Boyd St	Los Angeles	CA	90013	213-617-2491	617-0157
ABC Seafood 205 Ord St	Los Angeles	CA	90012	213-680-2887	
Amalfi 143 N Brea Ave	Los Angeles	CA	90036	323-938-2504	938-2252
Web: www.amalfiristorante.com					
Angeli Caffe 7274 Melrose Ave	Los Angeles	CA	90046	323-936-9086	938-9873
Web: www.angelicaffe.com					
Angelini Osteria 7313 Beverly Blvd	Los Angeles	CA	90036	323-297-0070	297-0072
Web: www.angeliniosteria.com					
Angelique Cafe 840 S Spring St	Los Angeles	CA	90014	213-623-8698	
Web: www.angeliquecafe.com					
AOC 8022 W 3rd St	Los Angeles	CA	90048	323-653-6359	653-1390
Web: www.aocwinebar.com					
Bamboo 10835 Venice Blvd	Los Angeles	CA	90034	310-287-0668	287-0229
Web: www.bamboorestaurant.net					
Ca'Brea 346 S La Brea Ave	Los Angeles	CA	90036	323-938-2863	938-8659
Web: www.cabrearestaurant.com					
Cafe La Boheme 8400 Santa Monica Blvd	Los Angeles	CA	90069	323-848-2367	
Cafe Pinot 700 W 5th St	Los Angeles	CA	90071	213-239-6500	
Web: www.patinagroup.com/cafePinot					
Cafe Stella 3932 Sunset Blvd	Los Angeles	CA	90027	323-666-0265	
Campanile 624 S La Brea Ave	Los Angeles	CA	90036	323-938-1447	938-5840
Web: www.campanilerestaurant.com					
Carlitos Gardel 7963 Melrose Ave	Los Angeles	CA	90046	323-655-0891	655-1576
Web: www.carlitosgardel.com					
Cha Cha Cha 656 N Virgil Ave	Los Angeles	CA	90004	323-664-7723	664-7769
Web: www.theoriginalchachacha.com					
Checkers 535 S Grand Ave	Los Angeles	CA	90071	213-624-0000	
Web: www.hiltoncheckers.com/diningCD.php					
Chi Dynasty 2112 Hillhurst Ave	Los Angeles	CA	90027	323-667-3388	667-3393
Web: www.chidynasty.com					
Ciao Trattoria 815 W 7th St	Los Angeles	CA	90017	213-624-2244	624-7788
Web: www.ciaotrattoria.com					
Cicada 617 S Olive St	Los Angeles	CA	90014	213-488-9488	488-9546
Web: www.cicadarestaurant.com					
Ciudad 445 S Figueroa St	Los Angeles	CA	90071	213-486-5171	486-5172
Web: www.ciudad-la.com					
Cobras & Matadors 7615 W Beverly Blvd	Los Angeles	CA	90048	323-932-6178	
Cynthia's 8370 W 3rd St	Los Angeles	CA	90048	323-658-7851	658-7535
Web: www.cynthias-restaurant.com					
Doughboys 8136 W 3rd St	Los Angeles	CA	90048	323-651-4202	467-8225
Web: www.doughboys.net					
Empress Pavilion 988 N Hill St	Los Angeles	CA	90012	213-617-9898	617-8114
Encounter 209 World Way	Los Angeles	CA	90045	310-215-5151	
Web: www.encounterrestaurant.com					
Engine Co No 28 644 S Figueroa St	Los Angeles	CA	90017	213-624-6996	623-9278
Web: www.engineco.com					
Farfalla Trattoria 1978 Hillhurst Ave	Los Angeles	CA	90027	323-661-7365	661-5956
Web: www.farfallatrattoria.com					
Gardens 300 S Doheny Dr Four Seasons Hotel	Los Angeles	CA	90048	310-273-2222	786-2242
Genghis Cohen 740 N Fairfax Ave	Los Angeles	CA	90046	323-653-0640	653-0701
Web: www.genghiscohen.com					
Grace 7360 Beverly Blvd	Los Angeles	CA	90036	323-934-4400	934-0485
Web: www.gracerestaurant.com					
Guelaguetza 11127 Palms Blvd	Los Angeles	CA	90034	310-837-1153	837-1034
Gumbo Pot 6333 W 3rd St	Los Angeles	CA	90036	323-933-0358	932-6820
Web: www.thegumbopotla.com					
Hamasaku 11043 Santa Monica Blvd	Los Angeles	CA	90024	310-479-7636	479-3116
Web: www.hamasakula.com					
Harold & Belle's 2920 W Jefferson Blvd	Los Angeles	CA	90018	323-735-9023	735-8770
House of Blues 8439 W Sunset Blvd	Los Angeles	CA	90069	323-650-0247	
Hu's Szechwan 10450 National Blvd	Los Angeles	CA	90034	310-837-0252	
Web: www.husrestaurant.com					
Il Grano 11359 Santa Monica Blvd	Los Angeles	CA	90025	310-477-7886	477-7775
India's Oven 7233 Beverly Blvd	Los Angeles	CA	90036	323-936-1000	936-1792
Web: www.indiasovenla.com					
India's Tandoori 5947 W Pico Blvd	Los Angeles	CA	90035	323-936-2050	936-0187
Web: www.indiastandoori.com					
Indo Cafe 10428 1/2 National Blvd	Los Angeles	CA	90034	310-815-1290	815-9011
Ita-Cho 7311 Beverly Blvd	Los Angeles	CA	90036	323-938-9009	
Ivy The 113 N Robertson Blvd	Los Angeles	CA	90048	310-274-8303	
JAR 8225 Beverly Blvd	Los Angeles	CA	90048	323-655-6566	655-6577
Web: www.thejar.com					
Jitlada 5233 1/2 W Sunset Blvd	Los Angeles	CA	90027	323-667-9809	663-3104
Kendall's Brasserie & Bar 135 N Grand Ave	Los Angeles	CA	90012	213-972-7322	972-7331
Web: www.patinagroup.com/kendallsBrasserie					
Kitchen The 4348 Fountain Ave	Los Angeles	CA	90029	323-664-3663	
Web: www.thekitchen-silverlake.com					
La Barca 2414 S Vermont Ave	Los Angeles	CA	90007	323-735-6567	735-0309
Little Door 8164 W 3rd St	Los Angeles	CA	90048	323-951-1210	951-0487
Web: www.thelittledoor.com					
Locanda Veneta 8638 W 3rd St	Los Angeles	CA	90048	310-274-1893	274-4217
Web: www.locandaveneta.com					
L'Orangerie 903 N La Cienega Blvd	Los Angeles	CA	90069	310-652-9770	
Web: www.orangerie.com					
Loteria! Grill 6333 W 3rd St	Los Angeles	CA	90036	323-930-2211	930-2208
Web: www.loteriagrill.com					
Louise's Trattoria 4500 Los Seliz Blvd	Los Angeles	CA	90027	323-667-0777	644-0083
Manna 3377 W Olympic Blvd	Los Angeles	CA	90019	323-733-8516	
Marino 6001 Melrose Ave	Los Angeles	CA	90038	323-466-8812	466-9010
Mario's Peruvian 5786 Melrose Ave	Los Angeles	CA	90038	323-466-4181	
Marouch 4905 Santa Monica Blvd	Los Angeles	CA	90029	323-662-9325	
Web: www.marouchrestaurant.com					
Michelia 8738 W 3rd St	Los Angeles	CA	90048	310-276-8288	276-6788
Web: www.micheliabistro.com					
Milky Way 9108 W Pico Blvd	Los Angeles	CA	90035	310-859-0004	859-1094
Mimosa 8009 Beverly Blvd	Los Angeles	CA	90048	323-655-8895	655-9178
Web: www.mimosarestaurant.com					
Moishe's 6333 W 3rd St	Los Angeles	CA	90036	323-936-4998	
Mori Sushi 11500 W Pico Blvd	Los Angeles	CA	90064	310-479-3939	479-2525
Web: www.morisushi.org					
Nick & Stef's Steakhouse 330 S Hope St	Los Angeles	CA	90071	213-680-0330	680-0052
Noe 251 S Olive St	Los Angeles	CA	90012	213-356-4100	356-4009
Ocean Seafood 750 N Hill St	Los Angeles	CA	90012	213-687-3088	687-8549
Web: www.oceansf.com					
Orso 8706 W 3rd St	Los Angeles	CA	90048	310-274-7144	273-4643
Pacific Dining Car 1310 W 6th St	Los Angeles	CA	90017	213-483-6000	483-4545
Web: www.pacificdiningcar.com					
Palm The 9001 Santa Monica Blvd	Los Angeles	CA	90069	310-550-8811	278-5334
Web: www.thepalm.com					
Palms Thai 5273 Hollywood Blvd	Los Angeles	CA	90027	323-462-5073	
Pane e Vino 8265 Beverly Blvd	Los Angeles	CA	90048	323-651-4600	651-1651
Web: www.panevinola.com					
Papa Cristos 2771 W Pico Blvd	Los Angeles	CA	90006	323-737-2970	737-3571
Web: www.papacristo.com					
Pastis 8114 Beverly Blvd	Los Angeles	CA	90048	323-655-8822	655-1457
Patina 141 S Grand Ave	Los Angeles	CA	90012	213-972-3331	972-3531
Web: www.patinagroup.com					
R-23 923 E 2nd St	Los Angeles	CA	90013	213-687-7178	687-7187
Web: www.r23.com					
Rambutan Thai 2835 W Sunset Blvd	Los Angeles	CA	90026	213-273-8424	
Web: www.rambutanthai.com					
Seoul Jung 930 Wilshire Blvd	Los Angeles	CA	90017	213-688-7880	612-3976
Shabu Shabu House 127 Japanese Village Plaza Mall	Los Angeles	CA	90012	213-680-3890	810-1348
Simon LA 8555 Beverly Blvd Hotel Sofitel	Los Angeles	CA	90048	310-278-5444	
Sonora Cafe 180 S LaBrea Ave	Los Angeles	CA	90036	323-857-1800	857-1883
Web: www.sonoracafe.com					
Soot Bull Jeep 3136 8th St	Los Angeles	CA	90005	213-387-3865	
Surya India 8048 W 3rd St	Los Angeles	CA	90048	323-653-5151	
Web: www.surya-india.com					
Table 8 7661 Melrose Ave	Los Angeles	CA	90038	323-782-8258	782-8259
Web: www.table8la.com					
Tam O'Shanter Inn 2980 Los Feliz Blvd	Los Angeles	CA	90039	323-664-0228	664-4915
Web: www.lawrysonline.com					
Tantra 3705 W Sunset Blvd	Los Angeles	CA	90026	323-663-8268	666-5522
Web: www.tantrasunset.com					
Taylor's Steak House 3361 W 8th St	Los Angeles	CA	90005	213-382-8449	
Web: www.taylorssteakhouse.com					
Tesoro Trattoria 300 S Grand Ave	Los Angeles	CA	90071	213-680-0000	
Web: www.tesorotrattoria.com/					
Thousand Cranes A 120 S Los Angeles St New Otani	Los Angeles	CA	90012	213-253-9255	253-9280
Traxx 800 N Alameda St	Los Angeles	CA	90012	213-625-1999	625-2999
Web: www.traxxrestaurant.com					
Tuk Tuk Thai 8875 W Pico Blvd	Los Angeles	CA	90035	310-860-1872	492-0003
Vermont 1714 N Vermont Ave	Los Angeles	CA	90027	323-661-6163	661-6206
Web: www.vermontrestaurantonline.com					
Versailles 10319 Venice Blvd	Los Angeles	CA	90034	310-558-3168	558-1870
Water Grill 544 S Grand Ave	Los Angeles	CA	90071	213-891-0900	629-1891
Web: www.watergrill.com					
Yang Chow 819 N Broadway	Los Angeles	CA	90012	213-625-0811	625-7901
Web: www.yangchow.com					
Zen Grill 8432 W 3rd St	Los Angeles	CA	90048	323-655-9991	655-9890
Zucca Ristorante 801 S Figueroa St	Los Angeles	CA	90017	213-614-7800	614-7887
Web: www.patinagroup.com/zuccaRistorante					
Nobu 3835 Crosscreek Rd	Malibu	CA	90265	310-317-9140	317-9136
Web: www.nobumatsuhisa.com					
Appetez 825 W Roseburg Ave	Modesto	CA	95350	209-577-5099	577-5598
Web: www.appetez.com					
Dewz 1101 'I' St	Modesto	CA	95354	209-549-1101	549-0454
Early Dawn Cattle Enterprises 1000 Kansas Ave	Modesto	CA	95351	209-577-5833	577-4050
El Rosal 3430 Tully Rd	Modesto	CA	95350	209-523-7871	
Falafel Hut 917 Yosemite Blvd	Modesto	CA	95354	209-557-9454	
Farmers Catfish House 4937 Beckwith Rd	Modesto	CA	95358	209-526-0969	
Fruit Yard 7948 Yosemite Blvd	Modesto	CA	95357	209-577-3093	577-0600
Web: www.thefruityard.com					
Fuzio Universal Pasta 1020 10th St Suite 100	Modesto	CA	95354	209-557-9711	557-9717
Web: www.fuzio.com					
Galletto Ristorante 1101 J St	Modesto	CA	95354	209-523-4500	523-1213
Web: www.galletto.biz					
Hazel's Elegant Dining 431 12th St	Modesto	CA	95354	209-578-3463	578-0403
Web: www.hazelsmodesto.com					
India Pallat 915 Yosemite Blvd	Modesto	CA	95354	209-523-0324	523-2559
La Morenita 1667 E Hatch Rd	Modesto	CA	95351	209-537-7900	538-3837
Marcella Restaurant 3507 Tully Rd	Modesto	CA	95350	209-577-3777	
Miki 180 Leveland Ln	Modesto	CA	95350	209-524-3555	524-3555
Minnie's 107 McHenry Ave	Modesto	CA	95354	209-524-4621	524-6043
Noah's Hof Brau 1311 J St	Modesto	CA	95354	209-527-1090	527-8039
Orient House 609 Tully Rd	Modesto	CA	95350	209-577-2099	
Papachino's 1212 J St	Modesto	CA	95354	209-578-5225	
Papapavlo's 1320 Standiford Ave	Modesto	CA	95350	209-525-3995	525-3795

Name / Address	City	State	Zip	Phone	Fax
Pub Wexford's 3313 McHenry Ave	Modesto	CA	95350	209-576-7939	576-7934
Web: pwexfords.com					
Restaurant 15-O-Five 1505 J St	Modesto	CA	95354	209-571-1505	571-1555
Web: www.restaurant1505.com					
Strings Italian Cafe 2601 Oakdale Rd	Modesto	CA	95355	209-578-9777	578-5266
Tasty Thai 1401 Coffee Rd	Modesto	CA	95355	209-571-8424	571-8164
Torii Japanese Restaurant 2401 E Orangeburg Ave Suite 590	Modesto	CA	95355	209-529-9881	
Velvet Grill & Creamery 2204 McHenry Ave	Modesto	CA	95350	209-544-9029	
Web: www.velvetgrill.net					
Verona's Cucina Italiana 1700 McHenry Ave	Modesto	CA	95354	209-549-8876	549-8869
Abalonetti Seafood Trattoria 57 Fisherman's Wharf Suite 1	Monterey	CA	93940	831-373-1851	373-2058
Web: restauranteur.com/abalonetti/					
Blue Moon 654 Cannery Row	Monterey	CA	93940	831-375-4155	375-6501
Web: www.pisto.com					
Bubba Gump Shrimp Co 720 Cannery Row	Monterey	CA	93940	831-373-1884	373-0354
Web: www.bubbagump.com/html/monterey.html					
Bullwacker's 653 Cannery Row	Monterey	CA	93940	831-373-1353	373-0196
Web: www.bullwackers.com					
Cafe Fina 47 Fisherman's Wharf	Monterey	CA	93940	831-372-5200	372-5209
Web: www.cafefina.com					
Chart House 444 Cannery Row	Monterey	CA	93940	831-372-3362	372-1277
Web: www.chart-house.com					
Chef Lee's 2031 N Fremont Blvd	Monterey	CA	93940	831-375-9551	656-9376
Domenico's on the Wharf 50 Fisherman's Wharf # 1	Monterey	CA	93940	831-372-3655	372-2073
Web: www.restauranteur.com/domenicos/					
Duck Club The 400 Cannery Row	Monterey	CA	93940	831-646-1700	646-0285
Epsilon Greek Restaurant 422 Tyler St	Monterey	CA	93940	831-655-8108	655-1791
Fresh Cream 99 Pacific St Suite 100C	Monterey	CA	93940	831-375-9798	375-2283
Web: www.freshcream.com					
Gilbert's on the Wharf 30 Fisherman's Wharf	Monterey	CA	93940	831-375-3113	375-3124
Indian Summer 220 Olivier St	Monterey	CA	93940	831-372-4744	
Jugem Japanese Restaurant 409 Alvarado St	Monterey	CA	93940	831-373-6463	
Montrio 414 Calle Principal	Monterey	CA	93940	831-648-8880	648-8241
Web: www.montrio.com					
Old Fishermans Grotto 39 Fishermans Wharf	Monterey	CA	93940	831-375-4604	375-0391
Web: www.oldfishermansgrotto.com					
Rosine's 434 Alvarado St	Monterey	CA	93940	831-375-1400	375-2636
Web: www.rosinesmonterey.com					
Sardine Factory 701 Wave St	Monterey	CA	93940	831-373-3775	373-4241
Web: www.sardinefactory.com					
Stokes Restaurant & Bar 500 Hartnell St	Monterey	CA	93940	831-373-1110	373-1202
Web: www.stokesadobe.com					
Tarpy's Roadhouse 2999 Monterey-Salinas Hwy	Monterey	CA	93940	831-647-1444	647-1103
Web: www.tarpys.com					
Thai Cafe 731 Munras Ave	Monterey	CA	93940	831-655-9797	655-4867
Whaling Station Prime Steaks & Seafood 763 Wave St	Monterey	CA	93940	831-373-3778	373-2460
Web: whalingstationmonterey.com					
A Cote 5478 College Ave	Oakland	CA	94618	510-655-6469	
Web: www.acoterestaurant.com					
Banana Blossom Thai 4228 Park Blvd	Oakland	CA	94602	510-336-0990	
Web: www.bananablossomthai.com					
Battambang 850 Broadway	Oakland	CA	94607	510-839-8815	
Bay Wolf Restaurant 3853 Piedmont Ave	Oakland	CA	94611	510-655-6004	
Web: www.baywolf.com					
Blackberry Bistro 4240 Park Blvd	Oakland	CA	94602	510-336-1088	
Web: www.blackberrybistro.com					
Citron 5484 College Ave	Oakland	CA	94618	510-653-5484	653-9915
Web: www.citronrestaurant.com					
Dopo 4293 Piedmont Ave	Oakland	CA	94611	510-652-3676	
El Huarache Azteca 3842 International Blvd	Oakland	CA	94601	510-332-2395	
Everett & Jones Barbeque 126 Broadway	Oakland	CA	94607	510-663-2350	663-8856
Web: www.eandjbbq.com					
Garibaldi's 5356 College Ave	Oakland	CA	94618	510-595-4000	594-2218
Web: www.garibaldis-eastbay.com					
Holy Land 677 Rand Ave	Oakland	CA	94610	510-272-0535	
Jojo 3859 Piedmont Ave	Oakland	CA	94611	510-985-3003	985-3033
Web: www.jojorestaurant.com					
Jordan's at the Claremont 41 Tunnel Rd	Oakland	CA	94623	510-549-8510	
Kincaid's Bay House 1 Franklin St	Oakland	CA	94607	510-835-8600	835-2032
Web: www.kincaids.com/					
Koryo Wooden Charcoal BBQ 4390 Telegraph Ave	Oakland	CA	94609	510-652-6007	
La Taza de Cafe 3909 Grand Ave	Oakland	CA	94610	510-658-2373	339-7100
Web: www.latazadecafe.com					
Le Cheval Restaurant 1007 Clay St	Oakland	CA	94607	510-763-8495	763-7610
Web: www.lecheval.com					
Legendary Palace 708 Franklin St	Oakland	CA	94607	510-663-9188	
Mama's Royal Cafe 4012 Broadway	Oakland	CA	94611	510-547-7600	
Marica Seafood Restaurant 5301 College Ave	Oakland	CA	94618	510-985-8388	
Mezze 3407 Lakeshore Ave	Oakland	CA	94610	510-663-2500	
Web: www.mezze.com					
Milano Ristorante 3425 Grand Ave	Oakland	CA	94610	510-763-0300	763-1171
Web: www.milanooakland.com					
Nan Yang Rockridge Restaurant 6048 College Ave	Oakland	CA	94618	510-655-3298	
Oliveto Cafe & Restaurant 5655 College Ave	Oakland	CA	94618	510-547-4381	
Web: www.oliveto.com					
Pho84 354 17th St	Oakland	CA	94612	510-832-1338	
Quinn's Lighthouse 1951 Embarcadero Cove	Oakland	CA	94606	510-536-2050	532-4156
Web: www.quinnslighthouse.com					
Restaurant Peony 388 9th St Suite 288	Oakland	CA	94607	510-286-8866	286-8868
Scott's 2 Broadway	Oakland	CA	94607	510-444-3456	444-6917
Web: www.scottsrestaurants.com					
Soi Four Bangkok Eatery 5421 College Ave	Oakland	CA	94618	510-655-0889	
Soizic 300 Broadway	Oakland	CA	94607	510-251-8100	
Web: www.soizicbistro.com					
Spettro 3355 Lakeshore Ave	Oakland	CA	94610	510-465-8320	
Sushi Zone 388 9th St	Oakland	CA	94607	510-893-9663	
TJ's Gingerbread House 741 5th St	Oakland	CA	94607	510-444-7373	444-2204
Web: www.tjsgingerbread.com					
Uzen 5415 College Ave	Oakland	CA	94618	510-654-7753	
Ameci 1929 Patterson Rd	Oxnard	CA	93035	805-382-8888	
Baja Fresh 2340 Vineyard Ave	Oxnard	CA	93030	805-988-7878	988-7979
Web: www.bajafresh.com					
Big Daddy O's Beach BBQ 2333 Roosevelt Blvd	Oxnard	CA	93035	805-984-0014	
BJ's Restaurant & Brewery 461 W Esplanade Dr	Oxnard	CA	93030	805-485-1124	485-5293
Web: www.bjsbrewhouse.com					
Cabo Seafood Grill & Cantina 1041 S Oxnard Blvd	Oxnard	CA	93030	805-487-6933	487-6954
Web: caboseafoodgrill.com					
Capistrano's 2101 Mandalay Beach Rd	Oxnard	CA	93035	805-984-2500	985-6930
Web: www.capistranos.com					
El Ranchero 131 W 2nd St	Oxnard	CA	93030	805-486-5665	
Green Burrito 1801 E Ventura Blvd	Oxnard	CA	93030	805-983-7117	
Kampai Japanese Restaurant 2367 N Oxnard Blvd	Oxnard	CA	93030	805-988-0252	988-1482
Web: www.kampairestaurant.com/					
Korean Barbeque Swan 2061 N Oxnard Blvd	Oxnard	CA	93030	805-278-9611	
Lobster Trap Restaurant 3605 Peninsula Rd	Oxnard	CA	93035	805-985-6361	
Pepe's 200 Rossmore Dr	Oxnard	CA	93035	805-985-2880	
Pilar's Cafe 746 S 'A' St	Oxnard	CA	93030	805-487-1444	

Name / Address	City	State	Zip	Phone	Fax
Pirates Grub & Grog 450 S Victoria Ave	Oxnard	CA	93030	805-984-0046	382-6945
Plaza Grill 600 Esplanade Dr	Oxnard	CA	93030	805-485-9666	485-2061
Port Royal Steak & Lobster House 3900 Bluefin Cir	Oxnard	CA	93035	805-382-7678	382-4829
Sal's Mexican Inn 1450 S Oxnard Blvd	Oxnard	CA	93030	805-483-9015	483-4766
Tomas Cafe 622 S 'A' St	Oxnard	CA	93030	805-483-6633	
Yolanda's 2801 Saviers Rd	Oxnard	CA	93033	805-487-3895	487-6365
Web: www.yolandasmexicancafe.com					
Favaloro's 542 Lighthouse Ave	Pacific Grove	CA	93950	831-373-8523	
Web: www.favaloros.com					
Passionfish 701 Lighthouse Ave	Pacific Grove	CA	93950	831-655-3311	
Web: www.passionfish.net					
Vito's 1180 Forest Ave	Pacific Grove	CA	93950	831-375-3070	
Pearl Dragon 15229 W Sunset Blvd	Pacific Palisades	CA	90272	310-459-9790	459-9560
Web: www.thepearldragon.com					
Al Dente Pasta 491 N Palm Canyon Dr	Palm Springs	CA	92262	760-325-1160	325-2199
Web: www.aldente-palmsprings.com					
Chop House 252 S Palm Canyon Dr	Palm Springs	CA	92262	760-320-4500	320-6940
Crazy Bones Barbeque 262 S Palm Canyon Dr	Palm Springs	CA	92262	760-325-5200	320-6940
Edgardo's Cafe Veracruz 494 N Palm Canyon Dr	Palm Springs	CA	92262	760-320-3558	
El Mirasol Regional Cuisines of Mexico 140 E Palm Canyon Dr	Palm Springs	CA	92264	760-323-0721	323-0692
Enzo's Ristorante 140 S Palm Canyon Dr	Palm Springs	CA	92262	760-416-4418	
Europa Restaurant 1620 S Indian Trail	Palm Springs	CA	92262	760-327-2314	322-3794
Web: www.palmsprings.com/dine/europa/					
Falls Prime Steakhouse 155 S Palm Canyon Dr 2nd Fl	Palm Springs	CA	92262	760-416-8664	416-8656
Web: www.thefallsprimesteakhouse.com					
Fisherman's Market & Grill 235 S Indian Canyon Dr	Palm Springs	CA	92262	760-327-1766	416-8641
Web: www.fishermansmarketandgrill.com					
Johanne's 196 S Indian Canyon Dr	Palm Springs	CA	92262	760-778-0017	778-1447
Web: www.johannesrestaurants.com					
John Henry's Cafe 1785 E Tahquitz Canyon Way	Palm Springs	CA	92262	760-327-7667	
Kaiser Grille 205 S Palm Canyon Dr	Palm Springs	CA	92262	760-323-1003	
Las Casuelas Terraza 222 S Palm Canyon Dr	Palm Springs	CA	92262	760-325-2794	327-4174
Web: www.lascasuelasterraza.com					
Le Vallauris 385 W Tahquitz Canyon Way	Palm Springs	CA	92262	760-325-5059	325-7602
Web: palmsprings.com/dine/levallauris/					
Leon's Bar & Grill 1800 E Palm Canyon Dr	Palm Springs	CA	92264	760-416-4421	416-1902
LG's Prime Steakhouse 255 S Palm Canyon Dr	Palm Springs	CA	92262	760-416-1779	416-1719
Lyons English Grill 233 E Palm Canyon Dr	Palm Springs	CA	92264	760-327-1551	322-9833
Melvyn's 200 W Ramon Rd	Palm Springs	CA	92264	760-325-0045	325-3052
Native Foods 1775 E Palm Canyon Dr	Palm Springs	CA	92262	760-416-0070	416-2888
Web: www.nativefoods.com					
Norma's 4200 E Palm Canyon Dr	Palm Springs	CA	92264	760-770-5000	342-2188
Web: www.starwoodhotels.com/lemeridien					
Palm Springs Cedar Creek Inn 1555 S Palm Canyon Dr	Palm Springs	CA	92264	760-325-7300	325-2592
Web: www.palmsprings.com/dine/cedarcreekinn/					
Riccio's 2155 N Palm Canyon Dr	Palm Springs	CA	92262	760-325-2369	
Saint James at the Vineyard 265 S Palm Canyon Dr	Palm Springs	CA	92262	760-320-8041	
Web: www.palmsprings.com/dine/stjames/					
Spencer's 701 W Barista Rd	Palm Springs	CA	92262	760-327-3446	327-5125
Web: www.spencersrestaurant.com					
Teriyaki Yogi 555 S Palm Canyon Dr	Palm Springs	CA	92264	760-323-1162	
Thai Smile 651 N Palm Canyon Dr	Palm Springs	CA	92262	760-320-5503	320-5584
Arroyo Chop House 536 S Arroyo Pkwy	Pasadena	CA	91105	626-577-7463	577-1089
Web: www.arroyochophouse.com					
Parkway Grill 510 S Arroyo Pkwy	Pasadena	CA	91105	626-795-1001	796-6221
Web: www.theparkwaygrill.com					
Akina Sushi - Teppan Restaurant 195 E Alessandro Blvd	Riverside	CA	92508	951-789-2621	
Babylon 4085 Vine St	Riverside	CA	92507	951-784-3033	784-3206
Web: www.gothookah.com					
Bombay Restaurant 1725 University Ave	Riverside	CA	92507	951-788-4994	
Bossa Nova Grill 1690 Spruce St	Riverside	CA	92507	951-781-6682	
Chan's 1445 University Ave	Riverside	CA	92507	951-788-6360	788-0172
Chen Ling Palace 9856 Magnolia Ave	Riverside	CA	92503	951-351-8511	351-8162
Ciao Bella 1630 Spruce St	Riverside	CA	92507	951-781-8840	781-1970
City Cuisine The 3425 Mission Inn Ave	Riverside	CA	92501	951-682-9566	682-8649
Duane's 3649 Mission Inn Ave	Riverside	CA	92501	951-341-6767	328-6915
Web: www.missioninn.com					
Garden Cafe 6060 Magnolia Ave	Riverside	CA	92506	951-686-4143	
Gerard's 9814 Magnolia Ave	Riverside	CA	92503	951-687-4882	687-2433
Web: www.dineatgerards.com					
Ho Ho 3411 Madison St	Riverside	CA	92504	951-637-2411	
Kountry Folks 3653 La Sierra Ave	Riverside	CA	92505	951-354-0409	354-7720
Web: www.kountry.com					
Las Campanas 3649 Mission Inn Ave	Riverside	CA	92501	951-784-0300	328-6915
Little Emperor 5225 Canyon Crest Dr	Riverside	CA	92507	951-683-1073	
Mario's Place 3646 Mission Inn Ave	Riverside	CA	92501	951-684-7755	
Web: www.mariosplace.com					
Millie's Country Kitchen 3580 Adams St	Riverside	CA	92504	951-351-1500	351-0859
Web: www.millies.com					
Pepito's 6539 Magnolia Ave	Riverside	CA	92506	951-683-1511	
Sevilla 3252 Mission Inn Ave	Riverside	CA	92507	951-778-0611	530-0083
Web: www.cafesevilla.com					
33rd Street Bistro 3301 Folsom Blvd	Sacramento	CA	95816	916-455-2233	457-2189
Web: www.33rdstreetbistro.com					
Aces Supperclub 5323 Date Ave	Sacramento	CA	95841	916-348-5656	
Aioli Bodega Espanola 1800 L St	Sacramento	CA	95814	916-447-9440	
Alamar Restaurant 5999 Garden Hwy	Sacramento	CA	95837	916-922-0200	
Web: www.alamarmarina.com					
Amarin Thai Cuisine 900 12th St	Sacramento	CA	95814	916-447-9063	441-7884
Web: www.amarinsacramento.com					
Bandera 2232 Fair Oaks Blvd	Sacramento	CA	95825	916-922-3524	922-9196
Biba 2801 Capitol Ave	Sacramento	CA	95816	916-455-2422	455-0452
Web: biba-restaurant.com					
Bravo 2333 Fair Oaks Blvd	Sacramento	CA	95825	916-568-0494	
Caballo Blanco Restaurante 5604 Franklin Blvd	Sacramento	CA	95824	916-428-6706	
California Fats 1015 Front St	Sacramento	CA	95814	916-441-7966	447-3900
Casablanca 3516 Fair Oaks Blvd	Sacramento	CA	95864	916-979-1160	
Da Big Kahuna's 1128 8th St	Sacramento	CA	95814	916-497-0600	497-0101
El Novillero 4216 Franklin Blvd	Sacramento	CA	95820	916-456-4287	456-4149
Web: www.elnov.com					
Enotria Cafe & Wine Bar 1431 Del Paso Blvd	Sacramento	CA	95815	916-922-6792	
Ernesto's 1901 16th St	Sacramento	CA	95814	916-441-5850	441-2154
Web: www.ernestosmexicanfood.com					
Esquire Grill 1213 K St	Sacramento	CA	95814	916-448-8900	
Web: www.esquiregrill.com					
Firedance Bar & Grill 8704 La Riviera Dr	Sacramento	CA	95826	916-366-3657	
Firehouse The 1112 2nd St	Sacramento	CA	95814	916-442-4772	442-6617
Web: www.firehouseoldsac.com/					
Frank Fat's 806 L St	Sacramento	CA	95814	916-442-7092	442-0117
Gonuls J Street Cafe 3839 J St	Sacramento	CA	95816	916-457-1155	457-4492
Greek Village Inn 65 University Dr	Sacramento	CA	95864	916-922-6334	922-2321
Hana Tsubaki 5006 J St	Sacramento	CA	95819	916-456-2849	
Hard Rock Cafe 545 Downtown Plaza Suite C-103	Sacramento	CA	95814	916-441-5591	441-5597
Web: www.hardrockcafe.com					
House of Chang 1589 W El Camino Ave	Sacramento	CA	95833	916-925-2138	

California (Cont'd)

Restaurant	City	State	ZIP	Phone	Fax
Il Fornaio 400 Capitol Mall	Sacramento	CA	95814	916-446-4100	
Web: www.ilfornaio.com					
Isabela's 1119 21st St	Sacramento	CA	95814	916-492-9565	
JR's Texas Bar-B-Que 180 Otto Cir.	Sacramento	CA	95822	916-424-3520	424-9915
Web: www.jrtexasbbq.com					
Kamon 2210 16th St	Sacramento	CA	95818	916-443-8888	
Kaveri Madras Cuisine 1148 Fulton Ave.	Sacramento	CA	95825	916-481-9970	
Web: www.kaverimadrascuisine.com					
Kitchen The 2225 Hurley Way	Sacramento	CA	95825	916-568-7171	
Lemon Grass 601 Munroe St.	Sacramento	CA	95825	916-486-4891	486-1627
Web: www.lemongrassrestaurant.com					
Lucca 1615 J St.	Sacramento	CA	95814	916-669-5300	669-2848
Web: www.luccarestaurant.com					
Mace's 501 Pavilion Ln.	Sacramento	CA	95825	916-922-0222	
MacQue's 8101 Elder Creek Rd.	Sacramento	CA	95824	916-381-4119	381-3723
Web: www.macques.com					
Marrakech 1833 Fulton Ave	Sacramento	CA	95825	916-486-1944	
Web: www.marrakechrestaurant.com					
Mikuni 1530 J St.	Sacramento	CA	95814	916-447-2111	447-6908
Web: www.mikunisushi.com					
Morton's The Steakhouse 521 L St	Sacramento	CA	95814	916-442-5091	442-7877
Web: www.mortons.com					
Mother India 1030 J St.	Sacramento	CA	95814	916-491-4072	
Nishiki Sushi 1501 16th St	Sacramento	CA	95814	916-446-3629	
PF Chang's China Bistro 1530 J St Suite 100	Sacramento	CA	95814	916-288-0970	288-0979
Web: www.pfchangs.com					
Piatti 571 Pavilions Ln	Sacramento	CA	95825	916-649-8885	649-8907
Web: www.piatti.com					
Rio City Cafe 1110 Front St	Sacramento	CA	95814	916-442-8226	
Web: www.riocitycafe.com					
Riverside Clubhouse 2633 Riverside Blvd	Sacramento	CA	95818	916-448-9988	448-9388
Web: www.riversideclubhouse.com					
Scott's Seafood Grill & Bar 545 Munroe St.	Sacramento	CA	95825	916-489-1822	489-2447
Web: www.scottsseafood.net					
Seoul Palace 9336 La Riviera Dr	Sacramento	CA	95826	916-369-0600	
Sofia Restaurant 815 11th St	Sacramento	CA	95814	916-558-1580	
Tapa the World 2115 J St.	Sacramento	CA	95816	916-442-4353	442-4348
Texas Mexican Restaurant 1114 8th St.	Sacramento	CA	95814	916-443-2030	
Texas West Bar-B-Que 1600 Fulton Ave.	Sacramento	CA	95825	916-483-7427	483-8636
Web: www.texaswestbbq.com					
Thai Basil 2431 J St	Sacramento	CA	95816	916-442-7690	442-7680
Web: www.thaibasil.com					
Thai Palms 943 Howe Ave	Sacramento	CA	95825	916-929-5915	
Tower Cafe 1518 Broadway	Sacramento	CA	95818	916-441-0222	
Web: www.towercafe.com					
Waterboy The 2000 Capitol Ave	Sacramento	CA	95814	916-498-9891	498-9893
Web: www.waterboyrestaurant.com					
Zinfandel Grille 2384 Fair Oaks Blvd	Sacramento	CA	95825	916-485-7100	484-7728
Costa Azul 7218 Franklin Blvd.	Sacremento	CA	95823	916-424-9608	
Alfredo's Pizza & Pasta 251 W Baseline St.	San Bernardino	CA	92410	909-885-0218	
Bamboo Garden 228 W Hospitality Ln	San Bernardino	CA	92408	909-890-0077	890-0112
Castaway The 670 Kendall Dr.	San Bernardino	CA	92407	909-881-1502	881-2548
Crabby Bob's Grill 239 E Hospitality Ln	San Bernardino	CA	92408	909-381-3518	
Guadalaharry's 280 E Hospitality Ln.	San Bernardino	CA	92408	909-889-8555	
Isabella's Ristorante Italiano 201 N 'E' St	San Bernardino	CA	92401	909-884-2534	
Le Rendez-Vous 4775 N Sierra Way	San Bernardino	CA	92407	909-883-1231	
Web: www.lerendezvous.com					
Lotus Garden 111 E Hospitality Ln	San Bernardino	CA	92408	909-381-6171	381-1757
Mediterranean 1300 E Highland Ave	San Bernardino	CA	92404	909-882-2505	
Mexico Restaurant 892 E Highland Ave	San Bernardino	CA	92404	909-882-3000	
Potiniere The 285 E Hospitality Ln.	San Bernardino	CA	92408	909-889-0133	
Addison The Grand Del Mar 5200 Grand Del Mar Way	San Diego	CA	92130	858-314-1900	
Web: www.addisondelmar.com/addison/					
Albie's Beef Inn 1201 Hotel Cir S.	San Diego	CA	92108	619-291-1103	
Alfiere Mediterranean Bistro 1590 Harbor Island Dr.	San Diego	CA	92101	619-692-2778	
Web: www.alfiereonline.com					
Andiamo 5950 Santo Rd	San Diego	CA	92124	858-277-3501	
Web: www.andiamo-ristorante.com					
Andre's 1235 Morena Blvd	San Diego	CA	92110	619-275-4114	276-4245
Web: www.andresres.com					
Anthony's Fish Grotto 1360 N Harbor Dr.	San Diego	CA	92101	619-232-5104	
Web: www.gofishanthonys.com					
Arterra 11966 El Camino Real	San Diego	CA	92130	858-369-6032	359-6088
Web: www.arterrarestaurant.com					
Ashoka the Great 9474 Black Mountain Rd	San Diego	CA	92126	858-695-9749	695-9279
Bandar 825 4th Ave.	San Diego	CA	92101	619-238-0101	232-7348
Web: www.bandarrestaurant.com					
Bernard'O 12457 Rancho Bernardo Rd.	San Diego	CA	92128	858-487-7171	487-7185
Web: www.bernardorestaurant.com					
Berta's 3928 Twiggs St.	San Diego	CA	92110	619-295-2343	
Web: www.bertasinoldtown.com					
Bertrand at Mister A's 2550 5th Ave 12th Fl.	San Diego	CA	92103	619-239-1377	
Blue Point Coastal Cuisine 565 5th Ave	San Diego	CA	92101	619-233-6623	
Buon Appetito 1609 India St.	San Diego	CA	92101	619-238-9880	
Cafe Cerise 1125 6th Ave.	San Diego	CA	92101	619-595-0153	595-0154
Web: www.cafecerise.com					
Cafe Japengo 8960 University Center Ln	San Diego	CA	92122	858-450-3355	552-6104
Web: www.cafejapengo.com					
Cafe Lautrec 7644 Girard Ave.	San Diego	CA	92037	858-459-9940	
Web: www.cafelautrec.com					
Cafe Pacifica 2414 San Diego Ave.	San Diego	CA	92110	619-291-6666	291-0122
Web: www.cafepacifica.com					
Cafe on Park 3831 Park Blvd	San Diego	CA	92103	619-293-7275	
Cafe Zucchero 1731 India St	San Diego	CA	92101	619-531-1731	
Web: www.cafezucchero.signonsandiego.com					
Candelas 416 3rd Ave.	San Diego	CA	92101	619-702-4455	
Web: www.candelas.signonsandiego.com					
Celadon 540 University Ave.	San Diego	CA	92103	619-297-8424	
Web: celadonrestaurant.com					
Chateau Orleans 926 Turquoise St.	San Diego	CA	92109	858-488-6744	488-3745
Web: www.chateauorleans.com					
Corvette Diner 3946 5th Ave.	San Diego	CA	92103	619-542-1001	
Croce's 802 5th Ave	San Diego	CA	92101	619-233-4355	
Web: www.croces.com					
Crocodile Cafe 7007 Friars Rd	San Diego	CA	92108	619-297-3247	
Web: www.crocodilecafe.com/					
Dakota Grill & Spirits 901 5th Ave.	San Diego	CA	92101	619-234-5554	
Web: www.cohnrestaurants.com					
De Medici 815 5th Ave	San Diego	CA	92101	619-702-7228	
Dobson's 956 Broadway Cir.	San Diego	CA	92101	619-231-6771	
Web: www.dobsonsrestaurant.com					
Donovan's Steak & Chop House 4340 La Jolla Village Dr	San Diego	CA	92122	858-450-6666	
Web: www.donovanssteakhouse.com					
Edgewater Grill 861 W Harbor Dr.	San Diego	CA	92101	619-232-7581	
Web: www.edgewatergrill.com					
El Bizcocho 17550 Bernardo Oaks Dr.	San Diego	CA	92128	858-487-1611	675-8443
Web: www.ranchobernardoinn.com/dining.htm					
Emerald Chinese Seafood Restaurant 3709 Convoy St.	San Diego	CA	92111	858-565-6888	565-6688
Web: www.emeraldrestaurant.com					
Field The 544 5th Ave.	San Diego	CA	92101	619-232-9840	
Web: www.thefield.com					
Fifth & Hawthorne 515 Hawthorne St.	San Diego	CA	92101	619-544-0940	
Fleming's Prime Steakhouse & Wine Bar 8970 University Center Ln	San Diego	CA	92122	858-535-0078	535-0096
French Market Grille 15717 Bernardo Heights Pkwy	San Diego	CA	92128	858-485-8055	673-5471
George's on Fifth 835 5th Ave	San Diego	CA	92101	619-702-0444	
Web: www.georgesonfifth.com					
Georgia's Greek Cuisine 3550 Rosecrans St	San Diego	CA	92110	619-523-1007	523-2455
Greek Palace 8878 Clairmont Mesa Blvd	San Diego	CA	92123	858-573-0155	
Web: www.greekpalace.com					
Greystone the Steakhouse 658 5th Ave.	San Diego	CA	92101	619-232-0225	233-3606
Web: www.greystonethesteakhouse.com					
Gulf Coast Grill 4130 Park Blvd	San Diego	CA	92103	619-295-2244	
Hob-Nob Hill 2271 1st Ave	San Diego	CA	92101	619-239-8176	
Humphrey's by the Bay 2241 Shelter Island Dr	San Diego	CA	92106	619-224-3411	523-1064
Web: www.humphreysbythebay.com					
Ichiban 1449 University Ave	San Diego	CA	92103	619-299-7203	
Indigo Grill 1536 India St	San Diego	CA	92101	619-234-6802	234-6868
Web: www.cohnrestaurants.com					
Islandia 1441 Quivira Rd.	San Diego	CA	92109	619-221-4810	
Jack & Giulio's 2391 San Diego Ave	San Diego	CA	92110	619-294-2074	
Jasmine 4609 Convoy St.	San Diego	CA	92111	858-268-0888	268-7729
JSix Restaurant 616 J St	San Diego	CA	92101	619-531-8744	531-8747
Web: www.jsixsandiego.com/					
Kemo Sabe 3958 5th Ave	San Diego	CA	92103	619-220-6802	
La Gran Tapa 611 B St	San Diego	CA	92101	619-234-8272	
Lamont Street Grill 4445 Lamont St.	San Diego	CA	92109	858-270-3060	
Laurel 505 Laurel St	San Diego	CA	92101	619-239-2222	
Le Fontainbleau 1055 2nd Ave.	San Diego	CA	92101	619-238-1818	
Lou & Mickey's 224 5th Ave.	San Diego	CA	92101	619-237-4900	233-4977
Web: www.louandmickeys.com					
Mandarin Dynasty 1458 University Ave	San Diego	CA	92103	619-298-8899	
Morton's The Steakhouse 285 J St	San Diego	CA	92101	619-696-3369	
Web: www.mortons.com					
Old Trieste 2335 Morena Blvd	San Diego	CA	92110	619-276-1841	
Web: www.oldtriesterestaurant.com					
Ole Madrid 755 5th Ave	San Diego	CA	92101	619-557-0146	
Web: www.olemadrid.com					
Osteria Panevino 722 5th Ave	San Diego	CA	92101	619-595-7959	233-3606
Web: www.osteriapanevino.com					
Pampas Bar & Grill 8690 Aero Dr	San Diego	CA	92123	858-278-5971	278-9674
Web: Pampas.signonsandiego.com					
Panda Inn 506 Horton Plaza	San Diego	CA	92101	619-233-7800	
Parallel 33 741 W Washington St	San Diego	CA	92103	619-260-0033	
Web: www.parallel33sd.com					
Park House Eatery 4574 Park Blvd.	San Diego	CA	92116	619-295-7275	295-6458
Web: www.parkhouseeatery.com					
PF Chang's China Bistro 7077 Friars Rd	San Diego	CA	92108	619-260-8484	260-0808
Web: www.pfchangs.com					
Phil's BBQ 4030 Goldfinch St	San Diego	CA	92103	619-688-0559	
Web: www.philsbbq.com					
Princess Pub & Grille 1665 India St	San Diego	CA	92101	619-702-3021	
Web: www.princesspub.com					
Rainwater's 1202 Kettner Blvd	San Diego	CA	92101	619-233-5757	
Web: www.rainwaters.com					
Rama 327 4th Ave	San Diego	CA	92101	619-501-8424	546-5304
Web: www.ramarestaurant.com					
Rei do Gado 939 4th Ave	San Diego	CA	92101	619-702-8464	
Web: www.reidogado.net					
Roy's 8670 Genesee Ave.	San Diego	CA	92122	858-455-1616	
Web: www.roysrestaurant.com					
Ruth's Chris Steakhouse 1355 N Harbor Dr.	San Diego	CA	92101	619-233-1422	
Web: www.ruthschris.com					
Saigon on Fifth 3900 5th Ave Suite 120	San Diego	CA	92103	619-220-8828	
Shien of Osaka 16769 Bernardo Center Dr Suite K-11	San Diego	CA	92128	858-451-0074	451-2485
Star of India 423 F St.	San Diego	CA	92101	619-234-8000	
Web: www.starofindia.com					
Star of the Sea 1360 N Harbor Dr	San Diego	CA	92101	619-232-7408	
Sushi Ota 4529 Mission Bay Dr	San Diego	CA	92109	858-270-5670	
Taka Restaurant 555 5th Ave.	San Diego	CA	92101	619-338-0555	
Web: www.takasushi.com					
Tapas Picasso 3923 4th Ave.	San Diego	CA	92103	619-294-3061	
Web: www.tapaspicasso.com					
Taste of Thai 527 University Ave	San Diego	CA	92103	619-291-7525	
Terra 3900 Block of Vermont	San Diego	CA	92103	619-293-7088	293-7193
Web: www.terra.signonsandiego.com					
Thee Bungalow 4996 W Point Loma Blvd	San Diego	CA	92107	619-224-2884	224-3563
Web: www.theebungalow.com					
Tom Ham's Lighthouse 2150 Harbor Island Dr.	San Diego	CA	92101	619-291-9110	
Web: www.tomhamslighthouse.com					
Trattoria La Strada 702 5th Ave.	San Diego	CA	92101	619-239-3400	
Web: www.trattorialastrada.com					
WineSellar & Brasserie 9550 Waples St Suite 115	San Diego	CA	92121	858-450-9557	
Web: www.winesellar.com					
Zen Cafe 615 Broadway	San Diego	CA	92101	619-231-0011	231-0061
Zio Mario's 2121 Adams Ave	San Diego	CA	92116	619-297-3354	
Web: www.ziomarios.com					
1550 Hyde Cafe & Wine Bar 1550 Hyde St	San Francisco	CA	94109	415-775-1550	
2223 Restaurant & Bar 2223 Market St.	San Francisco	CA	94114	415-431-0692	
Web: www.2223restaurant.com					
A Sabella's 2766 Taylor St	San Francisco	CA	94133	415-771-6775	771-6777
Web: www.asabellas.com					
Absinthe Brasserie & Bar 398 Hayes St.	San Francisco	CA	94102	415-551-1590	
Web: www.absinthe.com					
Acquerello 1722 Sacramento St	San Francisco	CA	94109	415-567-5432	567-6432
Web: www.acquerello.com					
Albona Ristorante Istriano 545 Francisco St	San Francisco	CA	94133	415-441-1040	
Alfred's Steakhouse 659 Merchant St	San Francisco	CA	94111	415-781-7058	
Web: www.alfredssteakhouse.com					
Ana Mandara 891 Beach St.	San Francisco	CA	94109	415-771-6800	
Web: www.anamandara.com					
Antica Trattoria 2400 Polk St.	San Francisco	CA	94109	415-928-5797	
Anzu 222 Mason St Hotel Nikko	San Francisco	CA	94102	415-394-1100	394-1102
Web: www.restaurantanzu.com					
Aqua 252 California St.	San Francisco	CA	94111	415-956-9662	
Web: www.aqua-sf.com					
asiaSF 201 9th St	San Francisco	CA	94103	415-255-2742	
Web: www.asiasf.com					
Aziza 5800 Geary Blvd	San Francisco	CA	94121	415-752-2222	
Web: www.aziza-sf.com					

Name / Address	City	State	Zip	Phone	Fax
Bacar Restaurant & Wine Saloon 448 Brannan St	San Francisco	CA	94107	415-904-4100	
Web: www.bacarsf.com					
Baraka 288 Connecticut St	San Francisco	CA	94110	415-255-0387	
Web: www.barakasf.net					
Betelnut 2030 Union St	San Francisco	CA	94123	415-929-8855	
Web: www.betelnutrestaurant.com					
Big Four Restaurant 1075 California St	San Francisco	CA	94108	415-771-1140	
Bistro Aix 3340 Steiner St	San Francisco	CA	94123	415-202-0100	202-0153
Web: www.bistroaix.com					
Bix 56 Gold St	San Francisco	CA	94133	415-433-6300	
Web: www.bixrestaurant.com					
Blue Mermaid Chowder House & Bar 471 Jefferson St	San Francisco	CA	94109	415-771-2222	447-4014
Web: www.bluemermaidsf.com/					
Blue Plate 3218 Mission St	San Francisco	CA	94110	415-282-6777	282-6777
Web: www.blueplatesf.com					
Boulevard 1 Mission St	San Francisco	CA	94105	415-543-6084	
Web: www.boulevardrestaurant.com					
Cafe Jacqueline 1454 Grant Ave	San Francisco	CA	94133	415-981-5565	
Cafe Kati 1963 Sutter St	San Francisco	CA	94115	415-775-7313	
Web: www.cafekati.com					
Campton Place Restaurant 340 Stockton St	San Francisco	CA	94108	415-781-5555	
Chapeau! 1408 Clement St	San Francisco	CA	94118	415-750-9787	
Chaya Brasserie 132 The Embarcadero	San Francisco	CA	94105	415-777-8688	
Web: www.thechaya.com					
Chenery Park 683 Chenery St	San Francisco	CA	94131	415-337-8537	
Web: www.chenerypark.com					
Chez Papa Bistrot 1401 18th St	San Francisco	CA	94107	415-255-0387	
Web: www.chezpapasf.com					
Chez Spencer 82 14th St	San Francisco	CA	94103	415-864-2191	864-2199
Clementine 126 Clement St	San Francisco	CA	94118	415-387-0408	
Coco 500 500 Brannan St	San Francisco	CA	94107	415-543-2222	
Web: www.coco500.com/					
Cortez 550 Geary St Adagio Hotel	San Francisco	CA	94102	415-292-6360	923-0906
Web: www.cortezrestaurant.com					
Cosmopolitan Cafe 121 Spear St	San Francisco	CA	94105	415-543-4001	
Web: www.cosmopolitancafe.citysearch.com					
Crustacean 1475 Polk St 3rd Fl	San Francisco	CA	94109	415-776-2722	
Web: www.anfamily.com					
Delfina 3621 18th St	San Francisco	CA	94110	415-552-4055	
Dining Room The 600 Stockton St	San Francisco	CA	94108	415-296-7465	773-6198
Dottie's True Blue Cafe 522 Jones St	San Francisco	CA	94102	415-885-2767	
Ebisu 1283 9th Ave	San Francisco	CA	94122	415-566-1770	
Web: www.ebisusushi.com					
Eos 901 Cole St	San Francisco	CA	94117	415-566-3063	
Web: www.eossf.com					
Farallon 450 Post St	San Francisco	CA	94102	415-956-6969	
Web: www.farallonrestaurant.com					
Fior D'Italia 2237 Mason St	San Francisco	CA	94133	415-986-1886	
Web: www.fior.com					
Firefly 4288 24th St	San Francisco	CA	94114	415-821-7652	
Web: www.fireflyrestaurant.com					
Fleur de Lys 777 Sutter St	San Francisco	CA	94109	415-673-7779	
Web: www.fleurdelyssf.com					
Foreign Cinema 2534 Mission St	San Francisco	CA	94110	415-648-7600	
Web: www.foreigncinema.com					
Fournou's Ovens 905 California St	San Francisco	CA	94108	415-989-1910	
Frascati 1901 Hyde St	San Francisco	CA	94109	415-928-1406	
Web: www.frascatisf.com					
Fringale 570 4th St	San Francisco	CA	94107	415-543-0573	
Web: www.fringalesf.com					
Garcon Restaurant 1101 Valencia St	San Francisco	CA	94110	415-401-8959	
Web: www.garconsf.com/					
Garibaldis 347 Presidio Ave	San Francisco	CA	94115	415-563-8841	563-3731
Grand Cafe 501 Geary St	San Francisco	CA	94102	415-292-0101	
Web: grandcafe.citysearch.com					
Greens					
Buchanan St & Marina Blvd Fort Mason Center Bldg A	San Francisco	CA	94123	415-771-6222	
Web: www.greensrestaurant.com					
Harris' Restaurant 2100 Van Ness Ave	San Francisco	CA	94109	415-673-1888	673-8817
Web: www.harrisrestaurant.com					
Hog Island Oyster Co & Bar					
Foot of Market St 1 Ferry Bldg Suite 11A	San Francisco	CA	94105	415-391-7117	
Web: www.hogislandoysters.com					
House 1230 Grant Ave	San Francisco	CA	94133	415-900-0012	001-8818
Web: www.thehse.com					
House of Prime Rib 1906 Van Ness Ave	San Francisco	CA	94109	415-885-4605	
Hyde Street Seafood House 1509 Hyde St	San Francisco	CA	94109	415-931-3474	
Iluna Basque 701 Union St	San Francisco	CA	94133	415-402-0011	402-0099
Web: www.ilunabasque.com					
Incanto 1550 Church St	San Francisco	CA	94131	415-641-4500	
Web: www.incanto.biz					
Indian Oven 233 Fillmore St	San Francisco	CA	94117	415-626-1628	553-3259
Web: www.indianovensf.com					
Isa 3324 Steiner St	San Francisco	CA	94123	415-567-9588	409-1879
Web: www.isarestaurant.com					
Jardiniere 300 Grove St	San Francisco	CA	94102	415-861-5555	
Web: www.jardiniere.com					
Jeanty at Jack's 615 Sacramento St	San Francisco	CA	94111	415-693-0941	693-0947
Web: www.jeantyatjacks.com					
Kabuto Sushi 5121 Geary St	San Francisco	CA	94118	415-752-5652	
Khan Toke Thai House 5937 Geary Blvd	San Francisco	CA	94121	415-668-6654	
Kokkari Estiatorio 200 Jackson St	San Francisco	CA	94111	415-981-0983	
Web: kokkari.com					
Kyo-ya 2 New Montgomery St	San Francisco	CA	94105	415-546-5090	
La Folie 2316 Polk St	San Francisco	CA	94109	415-776-5577	776-3431
Web: www.lafolie.com					
Les Imas 568 Sacramento St	San Francisco	CA	94111	415-291-9145	
Little Nepal 925 Cortland Ave	San Francisco	CA	94110	415-643-3881	643-8088
Web: www.littlenepalsf.com					
Ma Tante Sumi 4243 18th St	San Francisco	CA	94111	415-626-7864	
Manora's Thai Cuisine 1600 Folsom St	San Francisco	CA	94103	415-861-6224	
Masa's Restaurant 648 Bush St	San Francisco	CA	94108	415-989-7154	
Web: www.masasrestaurant.com					
Maya 303 2nd St	San Francisco	CA	94107	415-543-2928	
Web: www.mayasf.net					
Maykadeh 470 Green St	San Francisco	CA	94133	415-362-8286	
Mecca 2029 Market St	San Francisco	CA	94114	415-621-7000	
Web: www.sfmecca.com					
Millennium 580 Geary St	San Francisco	CA	94102	415-345-3900	345-3941
Web: www.millenniumrestaurant.com					
Moose's 1652 Stockton St	San Francisco	CA	94133	415-989-7800	
Web: www.mooses.com					
Morton's The Steakhouse 400 Post St	San Francisco	CA	94102	415-986-5830	986-5829
Web: www.mortons.com					
One Market 1 Market St	San Francisco	CA	94105	415-777-5577	
Web: www.onemarket.com					
Ozumo 161 Steuart St	San Francisco	CA	94105	415-882-1333	
Web: www.ozumo.com					
Pacific 500 Post St	San Francisco	CA	94102	415-771-8600	
Pane e Vino 1715 Union St	San Francisco	CA	94123	415-346-2111	
Web: www.paneevinotrattoria.com					
Park Grill 333 Battery St	San Francisco	CA	94111	415-296-2933	296-2919
Pesce 2227 Polk St	San Francisco	CA	94109	415-928-8025	
Piperade 1015 Battery St	San Francisco	CA	94111	415-391-2555	391-1159
Web: www.piperade.com					
PlumpJack Cafe 3127 Fillmore St	San Francisco	CA	94123	415-563-4755	
Web: www.plumpjack.com					
Ponzu Restaurant 401 Taylor St	San Francisco	CA	94102	415-775-7979	351-7656
Web: www.ponzurestaurant.com/					
Postrio 545 Post St	San Francisco	CA	94102	415-776-7825	
Web: www.postrio.com					
Public The 1489 Folsom St	San Francisco	CA	94103	415-552-3065	
Web: www.thepublicsf.com					
Puccini & Pinetti 129 Ellis St	San Francisco	CA	94102	415-392-5500	392-1635
Web: www.pucciniandpinetti.com/					
Quince 1701 Octavia St	San Francisco	CA	94109	415-775-8500	
Web: www.quincerestaurant.com					
Restaurant Azie 826 Folsom St	San Francisco	CA	94107	415-538-0918	538-0916
Web: www.restaurantlulu.com					
Restaurant Gary Danko 800 N Point St	San Francisco	CA	94109	415-749-2060	
Web: www.garydanko.com					
Ristorante Bacco 737 Diamond St	San Francisco	CA	94114	415-282-4969	282-1315
RNM 598 Haight St	San Francisco	CA	94117	415-551-7900	
Web: www.rnmrestaurant.com					
Roy's 575 Mission St	San Francisco	CA	94105	415-777-0277	777-0377
Web: www.roysrestaurant.com					
Rubicon 558 Sacramento St	San Francisco	CA	94111	415-434-4100	421-7648
Web: www.myriadrestaurantgroup.com					
Ruth's Chris Steak House 1601 Van Ness Ave	San Francisco	CA	94109	415-673-0557	673-5309
Web: www.ruthschris.com					
Scala's Bistro 432 Powell St	San Francisco	CA	94102	415-395-8555	395-8549
Web: www.scalasbistro.com					
Schroeder's Cafe 240 Front St	San Francisco	CA	94111	415-421-4778	
Web: www.schroederssf.com					
Seasons 757 Market St	San Francisco	CA	94103	415-633-3838	633-3001
Senses 1152 Valencia St	San Francisco	CA	94110	415-648-6000	
Silks 222 Sansome St	San Francisco	CA	94104	415-986-2020	
Slanted Door 1 Ferry Bldg	San Francisco	CA	94111	415-861-8032	
Web: www.slanteddoor.com					
Sociale 3665 Sacramento St	San Francisco	CA	94118	415-921-3200	
South Park Cafe 108 S Park St	San Francisco	CA	94107	415-495-7275	
Straits Restaurant 845 Market St Suite 597	San Francisco	CA	94103	415-668-1783	
Web: www.straitsrestaurants.com					
Terrace The 600 Stockton St	San Francisco	CA	94108	415-773-6198	951-8730
Tommy Toy's Cuisine Chinoise 655 Montgomery St	San Francisco	CA	94111	415-397-4888	397-0469
Web: www.tommytoys.com					
Town Hall 342 Howard St	San Francisco	CA	94105	415-908-3900	908-3700
Web: www.townhallsf.com					
Trattoria Contadina 1800 Mason St	San Francisco	CA	94133	415-982-5728	
Web: www.trattcontadina.citysearch.com					
Tsunami Sushi & Sake Bar 1306 Fulton St	San Francisco	CA	94117	415-567-7664	
Web: www.tsunami-sf.com					
TWO 22 Hawthorne St	San Francisco	CA	94105	415-777-9779	777-9782
Web: www.two-sf.com					
Venticello 1257 Taylor St	San Francisco	CA	94108	415-922-2545	
Yabbies Coastal Kitchen 2237 Polk St	San Francisco	CA	94109	415-474-4088	
Web: www.yabbiesrestaurant.com					
Yank Sing 49 Stevenson St	San Francisco	CA	94105	415-541-4949	
Web: www.yanksing.com					
Zuni Cafe & Grill 1658 Market St	San Francisco	CA	94102	415-552-2522	
Web: www.zunicafe.com					
71 Sainte Peter 71 N San Pedro St	San Jose	CA	95110	408-971-8523	938-3440
Web: www.71saintpeter.com					
840 North First 840 N 1st St	San Jose	CA	95112	408-282-0840	
Web: www.840.com					
Amber India 1140 Olsen Dr	San Jose	CA	95128	408-248-5400	248-5401
Web: www.amber-india.com					
Anise Cafe 1663 W San Carlos Ave	San Jose	CA	95128	408-298-8178	
Web: www.anisecafe.com					
AP Stumps 163 W Santa Clara St	San Jose	CA	95113	408-292-9928	292-9927
Web: www.apstumps.com					
Aqui Cal-Mex Grill 1145 Lincoln Ave	San Jose	CA	95125	408-995-0381	995-0385
Web: www.aquicalmex.com					
Arcadia 100 W San Carlos St	San Jose	CA	95113	408-278-4555	278-4556
Armadillo Willy's BBQ 878 Blossom Hill Rd	San Jose	CA	95123	408-224-7427	224-2210
Web: www.armadillowillys.com					
Bella Mia 58 S 1st St	San Jose	CA	95113	408-280-1993	280-5624
Web: www.bellamia.com					
Blowfish 355 Santana Row	San Jose	CA	95128	408-345-3848	345-3855
Web: www.blowfishsushi.com					
Cajun Crab House 826 S Winchester Blvd	San Jose	CA	95128	408-244-2528	
Web: www.cajuncrabhouse.com/					
Chaat Cafe 834 Blossom Hill Rd	San Jose	CA	95123	408-225-2233	516-9059
Web: www.chaatcafes.com					
Chacho's 18 S Almaden Ave	San Jose	CA	95113	408-293-1387	293-9913
Web: www.chachos.net					
Cheesecake Factory 925 Blossom Hill Rd	San Jose	CA	95123	408-225-6948	225-6957
Web: www.thecheesecakefactory.com					
Delfin 1202 E Santa Clara St	San Jose	CA	95116	408-295-8477	
E & O Trading Co 96 S 1st St	San Jose	CA	95113	408-938-4100	938-4164
Web: www.eotrading.com					
Emile's 545 S 2nd St	San Jose	CA	95112	408-289-1960	998-1245
Web: www.emiles.com					
Eulipia Restaurant 374 S 1st St	San Jose	CA	95113	408-280-6161	280-1639
Web: www.eulipia.com					
Gecko Grill 855 N 13th St	San Jose	CA	95112	408-971-1826	971-1809
Grill on the Alley 172 S Market St	San Jose	CA	95113	408-294-2244	294-2255
Henry's Hi-life 301 W Saint John St	San Jose	CA	95110	408-295-5414	295-5431
House of Siam 151 S 2nd St	San Jose	CA	95113	408-295-3397	
Korean Palace 2297A Stevens Creek Blvd	San Jose	CA	95128	408-279-9686	941-1887
Web: www.koreanpalace.com					
Krung Thai 640 S Winchester Ave	San Jose	CA	95128	408-260-8224	
La Foret 21747 Bertram Rd	San Jose	CA	95120	408-997-3458	
Web: www.laforetrestaurant.com					
La Pastaia 233 W Santa Clara St	San Jose	CA	95113	408-286-8686	286-8787
Web: www.lapastaia.com					
Le Papillon 410 Saratoga Ave	San Jose	CA	95129	408-296-3730	247-7812
Web: www.lepapillon.com					
Left Bank 377 Santana Row	San Jose	CA	95128	408-984-3500	984-0300
Web: www.leftbank.com					
Menara 41 E Gish Rd	San Jose	CA	95112	408-453-1983	
Original Joe's 301 S 1st St	San Jose	CA	97113	408-292-7030	
Web: www.originaljoes.com					

California (Cont'd)

				Phone	Fax
Pagoda The 170 S Market St	San Jose	CA	95113	408-998-3937	
Paolo's 333 W San Carlos St Suite 150	San Jose	CA	95110	408-294-2558	294-2595
Web: www.paolosrestaurant.com					
PF Chang's China Bistro 98 S 2nd St	San Jose	CA	95113	408-961-5250	961-5260
Web: www.pfchangs.com					
Picasso's 62 W Santa Clara St	San Jose	CA	95113	408-298-4400	267-8662
Plaza Garibaldi 1170 E Santa Clara St	San Jose	CA	95116	408-298-0121	
Rosy's Fish City 2882 Story Rd	San Jose	CA	95127	408-272-2088	272-2000
Sahand 4628 Meridian Ave	San Jose	CA	95124	408-267-1288	
Seven 754 The Alameda	San Jose	CA	95101	408-280-1644	280-7818
Web: www.7restaurant.us					
Spiedo 151 W Santa Clara St	San Jose	CA	95113	408-971-6096	971-6090
Web: www.spiedo.com					
Straits Cafe 333 Santana Row Suite 1100	San Jose	CA	95128	408-246-6320	246-6397
Web: www.straitsrestaurants.com					
Sushi Factory Japanese Restaurant 4632 Meridian Ave	San Jose	CA	95124	408-723-2598	723-2579
Web: www.sushifactorysj.com					
Teske's Germania 255 N 1st St	San Jose	CA	95131	408-292-0291	292-0347
Web: www.teskes-germania.com					
Tokyo Sushi 1716 Lundy Ave	San Jose	CA	95131	408-452-8868	452-8869
Tomisushi 4336 Moorpark Ave	San Jose	CA	95129	408-257-4722	
Vung Tau 535 E Santa Clara St	San Jose	CA	95112	408-288-9055	288-9083
50 Forks 3601 Sunflower Ave	Santa Ana	CA	92704	714-429-0918	
Antonello Ristorante 3800 S Plaza Dr	Santa Ana	CA	92704	714-751-7153	
Web: www.antonello.com					
Bluewater Grill 1621 W Sunflower Ave	Santa Ana	CA	92704	714-546-3474	
Web: www.bluewatergrill.com					
Colima 130 N Fairview St	Santa Ana	CA	92703	714-836-1254	
Dayra Restaurant 1611 W Sunflower Ave	Santa Ana	CA	92704	714-557-6600	
El Gallo Giro 1442 S Bristol St	Santa Ana	CA	92704	714-549-2011	
Favori 3502 W 1st St	Santa Ana	CA	92703	714-531-6838	
Web: www.favorirestaurant.com					
Ferdussi 3605 S Bristol St	Santa Ana	CA	92704	714-545-9096	
Web: www.ferdussi.com					
George's Thai Bistro 3732 S Bristol St	Santa Ana	CA	92704	714-979-8366	
Green Parrot Cafe 2035 N Main St	Santa Ana	CA	92706	714-550-6040	
Web: www.greenparrotcafe.net					
Gypsy Den 125 N Broadway	Santa Ana	CA	92701	714-835-8840	835-8327
Web: www.gypsyden.com					
Hacienda The 1725 College Ave	Santa Ana	CA	92706	714-558-1304	
Web: www.the-hacienda.com					
Memphis 201 N Broadway	Santa Ana	CA	92701	714-564-1064	
Morton's The Steakhouse 1641 W Sunflower Ave	Santa Ana	CA	92704	714-444-4834	
Web: www.mortons.com					
Olde Ship The 1120 W 17th St	Santa Ana	CA	92706	714-550-6700	550-6702
Web: www.theoldeship.com					
Polly's 2660 N Main St	Santa Ana	CA	92705	714-547-9681	547-5302
Web: www.pollypies.com					
Royal Khyber 1621 W Sunflower Ave	Santa Ana	CA	92706	714-436-1010	
Ruth's Place 1236 Civic Center Dr W Suite C	Santa Ana	CA	92703	714-953-9454	953-1102
Spoons California Grill 2601 Hotel Terr	Santa Ana	CA	92705	714-556-0700	
Super Antonjitos 1130 W Warner Ave	Santa Ana	CA	92707	714-662-2035	
Tangata 2002 N Main St	Santa Ana	CA	92706	714-550-0906	
Taqueria De Anda 1029 E 4th St	Santa Ana	CA	92701	714-558-0856	
Yellow Basket Restaurant 2860 S Main St	Santa Ana	CA	92707	714-545-8219	
Web: www.yellowbasket.com					
3 on Fourth 1432-A 4th St	Santa Monica	CA	90401	310-395-6765	395-6850
Web: www.3onfourth.com					
Border Grill 1445 4th St	Santa Monica	CA	90401	310-451-1655	394-2049
Web: www.bordergrill.com					
Chinois on Main 2709 Main St	Santa Monica	CA	90405	310-392-9025	396-5102
Web: www.wolfgangpuck.com					
Ivy at the Shore 1535 Ocean Ave	Santa Monica	CA	90401	310-393-3113	
JiRaffe Restaurant 502 Santa Monica Blvd	Santa Monica	CA	90401	310-917-6671	917-6677
Web: www.jirafferestaurant.com					
Josie 2424 Pico Blvd	Santa Monica	CA	90405	310-581-9888	581-4202
Web: www.josierestaurant.com					
Melisse 1104 Wilshire Blvd	Santa Monica	CA	90401	310-395-0881	395-3810
Web: www.melisse.com					
Ocean Avenue Seafood 1401 Ocean Ave	Santa Monica	CA	90401	310-394-5669	394-7322
Web: www.oceanave.com					
Rockenwagner 2435 Main St	Santa Monica	CA	90405	310-399-6504	
Web: www.rockenwagner.com					
Valentino 3115 Pico Blvd	Santa Monica	CA	90405	310-829-4313	315-2791
Web: www.welovewine.com					
Thai Nakorn 11951 Beach Blvd	Stanton	CA	90680	714-799-2031	799-2032
Angelina's 1563 E Fremont St	Stockton	CA	95205	209-948-6609	948-2477
Web: www.angelinas.com					
Bangkok 3255 W Hammer Ln Suite 18	Stockton	CA	95209	209-476-8616	
Web: www.stocktonbangkok.com					
Basil's 2324 Grand Canal Blvd	Stockton	CA	95207	209-478-6290	
Black Angus Steakhouse 2605 W March Ln	Stockton	CA	95207	209-951-8900	951-2364
Web: www.blackangus.com					
Breadfruit Tree 8095 N Rio Blanco Rd	Stockton	CA	95219	209-952-7361	
Web: www.breadfruittree.com					
Bud's Seafood Grill 314 Lincoln Center	Stockton	CA	95207	209-956-0270	956-0275
Web: www.budsseafood.com					
Casa Flores 201 E Weber Ave	Stockton	CA	95202	209-462-2272	
China Palace 5052 West Ln	Stockton	CA	95210	209-955-0888	952-8871
Chitiva's Salsa & Sports Bar & Grille 445 W Weber Ave	Stockton	CA	95202	209-941-8605	
Web: www.chitiva.net					
Cocoro Bistro & Sushi Bar 2105 Pacific Ave	Stockton	CA	95204	209-941-6053	
Dave Wong's 2828 W March Ln	Stockton	CA	95219	209-951-4152	951-5106
El Rancho Steak House 1457 E Mariposa Rd	Stockton	CA	95205	209-467-1529	
El Zarape Restaurant 36 N California St	Stockton	CA	95202	209-462-6664	
Ernie's on the Brick Walk 296 Lincoln Center	Stockton	CA	95207	209-951-3311	951-4068
Garlic Brothers 6629 Embarcadero Dr	Stockton	CA	95219	209-474-6585	474-0741
Web: www.garlic-brothers.com					
Hana Sushi 1101 E March Ln	Stockton	CA	95210	209-477-1667	
House of Shaw 227 Dorris Pl	Stockton	CA	95204	209-948-4300	
Le Bistro 3121 W Benjamin Holt Dr	Stockton	CA	95219	209-951-0885	951-3976
Web: www.lebistrostockton.com					
Le Kim's 631 N Center St	Stockton	CA	95202	209-943-0308	
Mallard's Restaurant 3409 Brookside Rd	Stockton	CA	95219	209-952-3825	952-1818
Web: www.mallardsrestaurant.com					
Mi Ranchito Cafe 425 S Center St	Stockton	CA	95203	209-946-9257	939-0227
Miguel's 7555 Pacific Ave	Stockton	CA	95207	209-951-1931	
Papapavlos Mediterranean Bistro 7555 Pacific Ave	Stockton	CA	95207	209-477-6855	
Saigon 1904 Pacific Ave	Stockton	CA	95204	209-463-2274	
Sho Mi 419 Lincoln Center	Stockton	CA	95207	209-951-3525	951-3628
Stockton Joe's 236 Lincoln Center	Stockton	CA	95207	209-951-2980	951-5900
Susy's Mexican Food 120 W Harding Way	Stockton	CA	95204	209-463-0360	
Yasso Yani Restaurant 326 E Main St	Stockton	CA	95202	209-464-3108	
Yen Ching 6511 Pacific Ave	Stockton	CA	95207	209-957-0913	

				Phone	Fax
Katsu-ya 11680 Ventura Blvd	Studio City	CA	91604	818-985-6976	
Pinot Bistro 12969 Ventura Blvd	Studio City	CA	91604	818-990-0500	
Web: www.patinagroup.com/pinotBistro					
Sushi Nozawa 11288 Ventura Blvd Suite C	Studio City	CA	91604	818-508-7017	
Ca'del Sole 4100 Cahuenga Blvd	Toluka Lake	CA	91602	818-985-4669	985-5696
Web: www.cadelsole.com					
Chaya Brasserie 8741 Alden Dr	West Hollywood	CA	90048	310-859-8833	859-4991
Web: www.thechaya.com					
Ketchup 8590 Sunset Blvd	West Hollywood	CA	90069	310-289-8590	289-8510
Web: www.dolcegroup.com/ketchup/					
Lucques 8474 Melrose Ave	West Hollywood	CA	90069	323-655-6277	655-3925
Web: www.lucques.com					
Madeo 8897 Beverly Blvd	West Hollywood	CA	90048	310-859-4903	859-0313
Nishimura 8684 Melrose Ave	West Hollywood	CA	90069	310-659-4770	659-4963
Vivoli Cafe & Trattoria 7994 Sunset Blvd	West Hollywood	CA	90046	323-656-5050	656-0419
Web: www.vivolicafe.com					
Wa Restaurant 1106 N La Cienega Blvd	West Hollywood	CA	90069	310-854-7285	
Eduardo's Border Grill 1830 Westwood Blvd	West Los Angeles	CA	90025	310-475-2410	
Sushi Sasabune 12400 Wilshire Blvd	West Los Angeles	CA	90025	310-268-8380	
Sunnin 1779 Westwood Blvd	Westwood	CA	90025	310-477-2358	
Web: www.sunnin.com					
Bistro Jeanty 6510 Washington St	Yountville	CA	94599	707-944-0103	944-0370
Web: www.bistrojeanty.com/					

Colorado

				Phone	Fax
Cache Cache Bistro 205 S Mill St	Aspen	CO	81611	970-925-3835	544-8248
Campo de Fiori 205 S Mill St	Aspen	CO	81611	970-920-7717	920-3098
Web: www.campodefiori.net					
China Thai Asian Cuisine 308 S Hunter St	Aspen	CO	81611	970-544-9888	
Hickory House Ribs 730 W Main St	Aspen	CO	81611	970-925-2313	920-3819
Web: www.hickoryhouseribs.com					
Matsuhisa 303 E Main St	Aspen	CO	81611	970-544-6628	544-6630
Montagna 675 E Durant St	Aspen	CO	81611	970-920-6330	920-6328
TF: 888-843-6355					
Pine Creek Cookhouse 11399 Castle Creek Rd	Aspen	CO	81611	970-925-1044	925-7939
Web: www.pinecreekcookhouse.com					
Pinons 105 S Mill St	Aspen	CO	81611	970-920-2021	
Web: www.pinons.net					
Syzygy 520 E Hyman Ave	Aspen	CO	81611	970-925-3700	925-5593
Web: www.syzygyrestaurant.com					
Takah Sushi 320 S Mill St	Aspen	CO	81611	970-925-8588	925-4255
Web: www.takahsushi.com					
Antonio's Mexican Grill 18581 E Hampden Ave	Aurora	CO	80013	303-627-8226	627-0331
Web: www.antoniosmexicangrill.com					
Armando's Ristorante 16611 E Smoky Hill Rd	Aurora	CO	80015	303-690-6660	
Aurora Summit 2700 S Havana St	Aurora	CO	80014	303-751-2112	369-8028
Web: www.aurorasummit.com					
Bender's Brat Haus 15343 E 6th Ave	Aurora	CO	80011	303-344-2648	344-2060
Dozens 2180 S Havana St	Aurora	CO	80014	303-337-6627	
Web: www.dozensrestaurant.com					
East Cafe Chinese Restaurant 15140 E Mississippi Ave	Aurora	CO	80012	303-369-6103	
El Alamo 1708 S Chambers Rd	Aurora	CO	80017	303-614-9806	
Emil-Lene's Sirloin House 16000 Smith Rd	Aurora	CO	80011	303-366-6674	360-8886
Web: www.sirloinhouse.com					
Helga's German Restaurant 728 Peoria St	Aurora	CO	80011	303-344-5488	344-5101
Web: www.helgasdeli.com					
Joe's Crab Shack 14025 E Evans Ave	Aurora	CO	80014	303-306-7070	306-7201
Web: www.joescrabshack.com					
La Cueva 9742 E Colfax Ave	Aurora	CO	80010	303-367-1422	367-1422
Web: www.lacueva.net					
Luigi's Bent Noodle 3055 S Parker Rd	Aurora	CO	80014	303-337-2733	751-1424
Web: www.bentnoodle.com					
Masalaa 3140 S Parker Rd	Aurora	CO	80014	303-755-6272	
Rock The 22934 E Smoky Hill Rd	Aurora	CO	80016	303-690-7934	690-1476
Royal Hilltop 18581 E Hampden Ave	Aurora	CO	80013	303-690-7738	690-7742
Web: www.royalhilltop.com					
Sam's No 3 2580 S Havana St	Aurora	CO	80014	303-751-0347	696-2025
Web: www.samsno3.com					
Senor Ric's 13200 E Mississippi Ave	Aurora	CO	80012	303-750-9000	750-9006
Sonoda's 3108 S Parker Rd	Aurora	CO	80014	303-337-3800	750-5567
Web: www.sonodassushi.com					
Ted's Montana Grill 16495 E 40th Cir	Aurora	CO	80011	720-374-7220	374-7221
Web: www.tedsmontanagrill.com					
14th St Bar & Grill 1400 Pearl St	Boulder	CO	80302	303-444-5854	
Ajuua 627 S Broadway St	Boulder	CO	80303	303-494-9204	499-0450
Web: www.ajuua.com					
Bacaro 921 Pearl St	Boulder	CO	80302	303-444-4888	445-2422
Web: www.bacaro.com					
Bombay Bistro 1800 Broadway Suite 110	Boulder	CO	80302	303-444-4721	
Boulder ChopHouse & Tavern 921 Walnut St	Boulder	CO	80302	303-443-1188	443-4876
Web: www.chophouse.com					
Boulder Cork 3295 30th St	Boulder	CO	80301	303-443-9505	443-0193
Web: www.bouldercork.com					
Buff Restaurant 1725 28th St	Boulder	CO	80301	303-442-9150	442-8302
Web: www.buffrestaurant.com					
Carelli's of Boulder 645 30th St	Boulder	CO	80303	303-938-9300	938-4077
Web: www.carellis.com					
Casa Alvarez 3161 Walnut St	Boulder	CO	80301	303-546-0630	
Web: www.casaalvarezcolorado.com/					
Chautauqua Dining Hall 900 Baseline Rd	Boulder	CO	80302	303-440-3776	440-0926
Web: www.chautauquadininghall.com					
Chez Thuy 2655 28th St	Boulder	CO	80301	303-442-1700	
Web: www.chezthuy.com					
Dolan's Restaurant 2319 Arapahoe Ave	Boulder	CO	80302	303-444-8758	786-7197
Web: www.dolansrestaurant.com					
Falafel King Restaurant 1314 Pearl St	Boulder	CO	80302	303-449-9321	
Flagstaff House 1138 Flagstaff Rd	Boulder	CO	80302	303-442-4640	442-8924
Web: www.flagstaffhouse.com					
Greenbriar Inn 8735 N Foothills Hwy	Boulder	CO	80302	303-440-7979	449-2054
Web: www.greenbriarinn.com					
Illegal Pete's 1447 Pearl St	Boulder	CO	80302	303-440-3955	440-6191
Japango 1136 Pearl St	Boulder	CO	80302	303-938-0330	938-0101
Web: www.japonsushi.com					
Jax Fish House 928 Pearl St	Boulder	CO	80302	303-444-1811	444-1007
Web: www.jaxfishhouseboulder.com					
John's 2328 Pearl St	Boulder	CO	80302	303-444-5232	
Web: www.johnsrestaurantboulder.com					
L'Atelier 1739 Pearl St	Boulder	CO	80302	303-442-7233	652-3564
Web: www.latelierboulder.com					
Laudisio 1710 29th St	Boulder	CO	80301	303-442-1300	442-6617
Web: laudisio.com					
Lucile's 2124 14th St	Boulder	CO	80302	303-442-4743	939-9848
Web: www.luciles.com					
Orchid Pavillion 1050 Walnut St	Boulder	CO	80302	303-449-4353	449-4272

				Phone	Fax
Pasta Jays 1001 Pearl St	Boulder	CO	80302	303-444-5800	443-2699
Web: www.pastajays.com					
Q's Restaurant 2115 13th St	Boulder	CO	80302	303-442-4880	
Web: www.qsboulder.com					
Ras Kassa's Ethiopian Restaurant 2111 30th St	Boulder	CO	80301	303-447-2919	
Web: www.raskassas.com					
Red Lion Restaurant 38472 Boulder Canyon Dr	Boulder	CO	80302	303-442-9368	447-0986
Web: www.redlionrestaurant.com					
Rio Grande Restaurant 1101 Walnut St	Boulder	CO	80302	303-444-3690	
Sushi Tora 2014 10th St	Boulder	CO	80302	303-444-2280	
Web: www.sushitora.net					
Sushi Zanmai 1221 Spruce St	Boulder	CO	80302	303-440-0733	440-6676
Web: www.sushizanmai.com					
Taj Restaurant 2630 Baseline Rd	Boulder	CO	80303	303-494-5216	
Thyme on the Creek 1345 28th St	Boulder	CO	80302	303-998-3835	443-1480
Walnut Brewery 1123 Walnut St	Boulder	CO	80302	303-447-1345	447-0067
Web: www.walnutbrewery.com					
Walnut Cafe 3073 Walnut St	Boulder	CO	80301	303-447-2315	
Web: www.walnutcafe.com					
Zolo Grill 2525 Arapahoe Ave	Boulder	CO	80302	303-449-0444	
Six89 Kitchen & Wine Bar 689 Main St	Carbondale	CO	81623	970-963-6890	963-4350
Amanda's Fonda 3625 W Colorado Ave	Colorado Springs	CO	80904	719-227-1975	
Antonio's Italiano Ristorante 4475 Northpark Dr	Colorado Springs	CO	80907	719-531-7177	531-5622
Web: www.antoniosital.com					
Bamboo Court 4935 Centennial Blvd	Colorado Springs	CO	80919	719-599-7383	
Blue Star The 1645 S Tejon St	Colorado Springs	CO	80906	719-632-1086	632-6284
Web: www.thebluestar.net					
Cafe El Paso 3840 N Nevada Ave	Colorado Springs	CO	80907	719-634-3940	
Charles Court 1 Lake Ave	Colorado Springs	CO	80901	719-577-5774	
Web: www.broadmoor.com/charlescourt.html					
Charlie's Pit Bar-B-Que 2819 N Nevada Ave	Colorado Springs	CO	80907	719-636-2200	636-2201
China Town 326 S Nevada Ave	Colorado Springs	CO	80903	719-632-5151	
Chopsticks 120 E Cheyenne Mountain Blvd	Colorado Springs	CO	80906	719-579-9111	579-9161
Web: www.chopsticksasianbistro.com					
Edelweiss 34 E Ramona Ave	Colorado Springs	CO	80906	719-633-2220	471-8413
Web: restauranteur.com/edelweiss					
El Palenque 2165 N Academy Pl	Colorado Springs	CO	80909	719-570-0326	570-0473
El Tesoro Restaurant 10 N Sierra Madre St	Colorado Springs	CO	80903	719-471-0106	
Web: www.el-tesoro.com					
Flying W Ranch 3330 Chuckwagon Rd	Colorado Springs	CO	80919	719-598-4000	598-4600
Web: www.flyingw.com					
Fratelli 124 N Nevada Ave	Colorado Springs	CO	80903	719-575-9571	
Web: www.fratelliristorante.com					
Giuseppe's Old Depot Restaurant					
10 S Sierra Madre St	Colorado Springs	CO	80903	719-635-3111	444-0857
Web: www.giuseppes-depot.com					
Ichiban Suehiro 4331 N Academy Blvd	Colorado Springs	CO	80918	719-593-1800	
Il Vicino 11 S Tejon St	Colorado Springs	CO	80903	719-475-9224	
Web: www.ilvicino.com					
Jake & Telly's 2616 W Colorado Ave	Colorado Springs	CO	80904	719-633-0406	473-1153
Web: www.jakeandtellys.com					
Jun Japanese Restaurant					
1760 Dublin at Academy Blvd	Colorado Springs	CO	80918	719-531-9368	531-0089
La Carreta 35 Iowa Ave	Colorado Springs	CO	80909	719-477-1157	
La Creperie Bistro 204 N Tejon St	Colorado Springs	CO	80903	719-632-0984	
La Petite Maison 1015 W Colorado Ave	Colorado Springs	CO	80904	719-632-4887	632-0340
Web: www.restauranteur.com/maison					
Luigi's 947 S Tejon St	Colorado Springs	CO	80903	719-632-0700	
MacKenzie's Chop House 128 S Tejon St	Colorado Springs	CO	80903	719-633-3230	635-1225
Web: www.mackenzieschophouse.com					
Maggie Mae's 2405 E Pikes Peak Ave	Colorado Springs	CO	80909	719-475-1623	475-1623
Marigold Cafe 4605 Centennial Blvd	Colorado Springs	CO	80919	719-599-4776	262-9521
Mason Jar 2925 W Colorado Ave	Colorado Springs	CO	80904	719-632-4820	632-0392
Web: www.masonjarcolorado.com					
Penrose Room 1 Lake Ave	Colorado Springs	CO	80906	719-634-7711	
Peppertree 888 W Moreno Ave	Colorado Springs	CO	80905	719-471-4888	471-0997
Web: www.peppertreecs.com					
PF Chang's China Bistro 1725 Briargate Pkwy	Colorado Springs	CO	80920	719-593-8580	593-8836
Web: www.pfchangs.com					
Phantom Canyon Brewing Co 2 E Pikes Peak Ave	Colorado Springs	CO	80903	719-635-2800	635-9930
Web: www.phantomcanyon.com					
Uwes German Restaurant 31 N Iowa Ave	Colorado Springs	CO	80909	719-475-1611	
1515 On Market 1515 Market St	Denver	CO	80202	303-571-0011	
Web: www.1515restaurant.com					
Aix Restaurant 719 E 17th Ave	Denver	CO	80203	303-831-1296	
Web: www.restaurantaix.com					
Andre's 370 S Garfield St	Denver	CO	80209	303-322-8871	322-2096
Barolo Grill 3030 E 6th Ave	Denver	CO	80206	303-393-1040	333-9240
Web: www.barologrilldenver.com					
Bella Vista 127 E 20th Ave	Denver	CO	80205	303-297-9020	297-8866
Bistro Vendome 1420 Larimer Sq	Denver	CO	80202	303-825-3232	825-3240
Web: www.bistrovendome.com					
Broker The 821 17th St	Denver	CO	80202	303-292-5065	292-2652
Web: www.brokerrestaurant.com					
Cafe Brazil 4408 Lowell Blvd	Denver	CO	80211	303-480-1877	
Web: www.cafebrazildenver.com					
Capital Grille 1450 Larimer St	Denver	CO	80202	303-539-2500	539-2700
Web: www.thecapitalgrille.com					
Carmine's on Penn 92 S Pennsylvania St	Denver	CO	80209	303-777-6443	777-4129
Casa Bonita 6715 W Colfax Ave	Denver	CO	80214	303-232-5115	232-7801
Web: www.casabonitadenver.com					
Celtic Tavern The 1801 Blake St	Denver	CO	80202	303-308-1795	
Corkhouse The 4900 E Colfax Ave	Denver	CO	80220	303-355-4488	355-1336
Web: www.corkhousedenver.com					
Damascus 2276 S Colorado Blvd	Denver	CO	80222	303-757-3515	
Denver Chophouse & Brewery 1735 19th St	Denver	CO	80202	303-296-0800	296-2800
Web: www.chophouse.com					
El Taco de Mexico 714 Santa Fe Dr	Denver	CO	80204	303-623-3926	
Fado Irish Pub 1735 19th St Suite 250	Denver	CO	80202	303-297-0066	297-0055
Web: www.fadoirishpub.com					
Hapa Sushi Grill & Sake Bar 2780 E 2nd Ave	Denver	CO	80206	303-322-9554	355-3449
Web: www.hapasushi.com					
Highlands Garden Cafe 3927 W 32nd Ave	Denver	CO	80212	303-458-5920	477-6695
Web: www.highlandsgardencafe.com					
India's 3333 S Tamarac Dr	Denver	CO	80231	303-755-4284	752-9814
Web: indiasrestaurant.com					
Jax Fish House 1539 17th St	Denver	CO	80202	303-292-5767	292-0530
Web: www.jaxfishhousedenver.com					
La Loma 2527 W 26th Ave	Denver	CO	80211	303-433-8300	433-8309
Web: www.lalomarestaurant.com					
Le Central 112 E 8th Ave	Denver	CO	80203	303-863-8094	863-0219
Web: www.lecentral.com					
Little India 330 E 6th Ave	Denver	CO	80203	303-871-9777	871-4126
Luca d'Italia 711 Grant St	Denver	CO	80203	303-832-6600	823-3532
Web: www.lucadenver.com					
M & D's Bar-B-Que & Fish Palace 2000 E 28th Ave	Denver	CO	80205	303-296-1760	296-1606
Maggiano's Little Italy 500 16th St	Denver	CO	80202	303-260-7707	260-7683
Web: www.maggianos.com					
McCormick's Fish House & Bar 1659 Wazee St	Denver	CO	80202	303-825-1107	825-1106
Mizuna 225 E 7th Ave	Denver	CO	80203	303-832-4778	832-3532
Web: www.mizunadenver.com					
Mori Sushi Bar & Tokyo Cuisine 2019 Market St	Denver	CO	80205	303-298-1864	
Morton's The Steakhouse 1710 Wynkoop St	Denver	CO	80202	303-825-3353	825-1248
Web: www.mortons.com					
New Saigon 630 S Federal Blvd	Denver	CO	80219	303-936-4954	
Pagliacci's 1440 W 33rd Ave	Denver	CO	80211	303-458-0530	
Web: www.ipagliaccio.com					
Palace Arms 321 17th St Brown Palace Hotel	Denver	CO	80202	303-297-3111	
Palomino Euro Bistro 1515 Arapahoe St Suite 150	Denver	CO	80202	303-534-7800	534-7001
Web: www.palomino.com					
Panzano 909 17th St	Denver	CO	80202	303-296-3525	296-1818
Web: www.panzano-denver.com					
Parisi 4401 Tennyson St	Denver	CO	80212	303-561-0234	480-5514
Web: www.parisidenver.com					
Pearl Street Grill 1477 S Pearl St	Denver	CO	80210	303-778-6475	778-0430
Web: www.pearlstreetgrilldenver.com					
PF Chang's China Bistro 1415 15th St	Denver	CO	80202	303-260-7222	260-7223
Web: www.pfchangs.com					
Pho Fusion 8800 E Hampden Ave	Denver	CO	80231	303-843-6080	
Web: www.phofusion.com					
Potager 1109 Ogden St	Denver	CO	80218	303-832-5788	861-8985
Restaurant Kevin Taylor 1106 14th St	Denver	CO	80202	303-820-2600	893-1293
Web: www.restaurantkevintaylor.com					
Ruth's Chris Steakhouse 1445 Market St	Denver	CO	80202	303-446-2233	446-2244
Web: www.ruthschris.com					
Solera 5410 E Colfax Ave	Denver	CO	80220	303-388-8429	333-0553
Web: www.solerarestaurant.com					
Stars Restaurant 201 Steele St 3rd Fl	Denver	CO	80206	303-333-4569	
Sullivan's Steakhouse 1745 Wazee St	Denver	CO	80202	303-295-2664	295-2698
Web: www.sullivansteakhouse.com					
Sushi Den 1487 S Pearl St	Denver	CO	80210	303-777-0826	777-3916
Web: www.sushiden.net					
Tamayo 1400 Larimer St	Denver	CO	80202	720-946-1433	946-1434
Web: www.modernmexican.com/tamayode					
Tuscany 4150 E Mississippi Ave	Denver	CO	80246	303-782-9300	758-6542
Venice Ristorante & Wine Bar 1700 Wynkoop St	Denver	CO	80202	303-534-2222	
Web: www.veniceristorante.com/					
Wellshire Inn 3333 S Colorado Blvd	Denver	CO	80222	303-759-3333	759-3487
Wynkoop Brewing Co 1634 18th St	Denver	CO	80202	303-297-2700	297-2958
Web: www.wynkoop.com					
Yanni's 2223 S Monaco Pkwy	Denver	CO	80222	303-692-0404	
Zengo 1610 Little Raven St	Denver	CO	80202	720-904-0965	904-0966
Web: www.zengorestaurant.com					
Ariano's 150 E College Dr	Durango	CO	81301	970-247-8146	
Bar D Chuckwagon Suppers 8080 County Rd 250	Durango	CO	81301	970-247-5753	247-2010
TF: 888-800-5753 ■ *Web:* www.bardchuckwagon.com					
Brickhouse Cafe 1849 Main Ave	Durango	CO	81301	970-247-3760	
Web: www.brickhousecafe.com					
Carver Brewing Co 1022 Main Ave	Durango	CO	81301	970-259-2545	385-7268
Web: www.carverbrewing.com					
Chez Grand-mere 3 Depot Pl	Durango	CO	81301	970-247-7979	
Web: chezgrand-mere.com					
Christina's Grill & Bar 21382 Hwy 160 W	Durango	CO	81303	970-382-3844	382-3865
Web: www.christinasgrill.com					
Cyprus Cafe 725 E 2nd Ave	Durango	CO	81301	970-385-6884	259-4530
Web: www.cypruscafe.com					
East by Southwest 160 E College Dr	Durango	CO	81301	970-247-5533	247-2647
Web: www.eastbysouthwest.com					
Farquahrts & Pizza Mia 725 Main Ave	Durango	CO	81301	970-247-5440	259-7726
Web: www.farquahrts.com					
Francisco's Restaurante y Cantina 619 Main Ave	Durango	CO	81301	970-247-4098	247-1373
Gazpacho 431 E 2nd Ave	Durango	CO	81301	970-259-9494	
Ken & Sue's 636 Main Ave	Durango	CO	81301	970-385-1810	385-1801
Lady Falconburgh's Barley Exchange 640 Main Ave	Durango	CO	81301	970-382-9664	382-9625
Web: www.ladyfalconburgh.com					
Mahogany Grille 699 Main Ave	Durango	CO	81301	970-247-4433	259-2208
Web: www.mahoganygrille.com					
Purgy's Slopeside Bar & Restaurant 1 Skier Pl	Durango	CO	81301	970-247-9000	
Randy's 152 E College Dr	Durango	CO	81301	970-247-9083	247-0191
Web: www.randycroctaurant.com					
Red Snapper 144 E 9th St	Durango	CO	80301	970-259-3417	259-3441
Web: www.redsnapperdurango.com					
Alsalam 822 S College Ave	Fort Collins	CO	80524	970-484-3198	484-3152
Austin's American Grill 100 W Mountain Ave	Fort Collins	CO	80524	970-224-9691	
Web: www.austinsamericangrill.com					
Bisetti's Italian Restaurant 120 S College Ave	Fort Collins	CO	80524	970-493-0086	493-1701
Enzio's Italian Kitchen 126 W Mountain Ave	Fort Collins	CO	80524	970-484-8466	484-8490
Web: www.enzios.com					
Jasmine Garden 2721 S College Rd	Fort Collins	CO	80525	970-223-6211	
Jay's Bistro 135 W Oak St	Fort Collins	CO	80524	970-482-1876	482-1897
Web: www.jaysbistro.net					
Little Saigon Cafe 3500 S College Ave	Fort Collins	CO	80525	970-225-6630	225-1738
Los Tarascos 626 S College Ave	Fort Collins	CO	80524	970-416-0265	416-8455
Moot House 2626 S College Ave	Fort Collins	CO	80525	970-226-2121	223-8436
Nate's Steak & Seafood Place 3620 S Mason St	Fort Collins	CO	80525	970-223-9200	
Nico's Catacombs 115 S College Ave	Fort Collins	CO	80524	970-484-6029	224-2843
Web: www.nicoscatacombs.com					
Nimo's 1220 W Elizabeth St	Fort Collins	CO	80521	970-221-1040	
Rainbow Restaurant 212 W Laurel St	Fort Collins	CO	80521	970-221-2664	221-2699
Renzio's 215 E Foothills Pkwy	Fort Collins	CO	80525	970-282-8818	
South China 4613 S Mason St Unit D-1	Fort Collins	CO	80525	970-225-6886	
SportsCaster Bar & Grill 165 E Boardwalk Dr	Fort Collins	CO	80525	970-223-3553	223-0838
Web: www.sportscasterbar.com					
Suehiro 223 Linden St	Fort Collins	CO	80524	970-482-3734	
Young's Cafe 3307 S College Rd	Fort Collins	CO	80525	970-223-8000	223-4923
Web: www.youngscafe.com					
Sam Taylor's Barbeque 435 S Cherry St	Glendale	CO	80246	303-388-9300	388-2230
240 Union 240 Union Blvd	Lakewood	CO	80228	303-989-3562	989-3565
Web: www.240union.com					
Briarhurst Manor 404 Manitou Ave	Manitou Springs	CO	80829	719-685-1864	314-4017
Web: www.briarhurst.com					
Butch's Lobster Bar 264 Snowmelt Rd	Snowmass Village	CO	81615	970-923-4004	923-3036
Web: www.butchslobsterbar.com					
Krabloonik 4250 Divide Rd	Snowmass Village	CO	81615	970-923-3953	923-0246
Web: www.krabloonik.com					

Connecticut

				Phone	Fax
Black Rock Castle 2895 Fairfield Ave	Bridgeport	CT	06605	203-336-3990	
Web: www.blackrockcastle.com					

Connecticut (Cont'd)

Name / Address	City	State	ZIP	Phone	Fax
Bloodroot 85 Ferris St	Bridgeport	CT	06605	203-576-9168	
Web: www.bloodroot.com					
Captain's Cove 1 Bostwick Ave	Bridgeport	CT	06605	203-335-7104	335-6793
Web: www.captainscoveseaport.com					
Field Restaurant & Bar The 3001 Fairfield Ave	Bridgeport	CT	06605	203-333-0043	
Web: www.thefieldrestaurant.net/					
Joseph's Steakhouse 360 Fairfield Ave	Bridgeport	CT	06604	203-337-9944	337-9996
Web: www.josephssteakhouse.com					
King & I 545 Broadbridge Rd	Bridgeport	CT	06610	203-374-2081	371-2293
Web: www.kingandict.com					
La Scogliera Restaurant 697 Madison Ave	Bridgeport	CT	06606	203-333-0673	333-1014
Web: www.lascoglierarestaurant.com					
Ralph 'N Rich's 815 Main St	Bridgeport	CT	06604	203-366-3597	
Roberto's 899 Main St	Bridgeport	CT	06604	203-368-6599	368-0926
Tony's Huntington Inn 437 Huntington Tpke	Bridgeport	CT	06610	203-374-5541	396-0179
Web: www.huntington-inn.com					
Tuscany 1084 Madison Ave	Bridgeport	CT	06606	203-331-9884	
Vazzy's Brick Oven Restaurant 513 Broadbridge Rd	Bridgeport	CT	06610	203-371-8046	371-4293
Web: www.vazzysrest.com					
Barcelona Restaurant & Wine Bar 4180 Black Rock Tpke	Fairfield	CT	06824	203-255-0800	255-0225
Web: www.barcelonawinebar.com					
La Colline Verte 75 Hillside Rd	Fairfield	CT	06430	203-256-9242	256-0306
Ole Mole 2074 Black Rock Tpke	Fairfield	CT	06430	203-333-0400	333-0325
Saint Tropez Bistro 52 Sanford St	Fairfield	CT	06430	203-254-8094	254-8209
Web: www.saint-tropez-bistro.com					
Sarabande 12 Unquowa Pl	Fairfield	CT	06824	203-259-8084	259-1493
Sherman 70 Reef Rd	Fairfield	CT	06430	203-254-2070	256-9569
Shiki Sushi Restaurant 222 Post Rd	Fairfield	CT	06824	203-259-5950	259-5428
Asiana Cafe 130 E Putnam Ave	Greenwich	CT	06830	203-622-6833	861-2680
Barcelona Restaurant & Wine Bar 18 W Putnam Ave	Greenwich	CT	06830	203-983-6400	983-6087
Web: www.barcelonawinebar.com					
Elm Street Oyster House 11 W Elm St	Greenwich	CT	06830	203-629-5795	629-8515
Web: www.elmstoysterhouse.com					
Gaia 253 Greenwich Ave	Greenwich	CT	06830	203-661-3443	661-3588
Web: www.gaiarestaurant.com					
Jean-Louis 61 Lewis St	Greenwich	CT	06830	203-622-8450	
Web: www.restaurantjeanlouis.com					
L'Escale 500 Steamboat Rd Delamar Hotel	Greenwich	CT	06830	203-661-4600	661-4601
Web: www.lescalerestaurant.com					
Meli-Melo 362 Greenwich Ave	Greenwich	CT	06830	203-629-6153	
Penang Grill 55 Lewis St	Greenwich	CT	06830	203-861-1988	861-0003
Polpo 554 Old Post Rd	Greenwich	CT	06830	203-629-1999	629-1718
Web: www.polporestaurant.com					
Rebeccas 265 Glenville Rd	Greenwich	CT	06831	203-532-9270	532-9271
Tengda Asian Bistro 21 Field Point Rd	Greenwich	CT	06830	203-625-5338	625-5343
Web: www.tengdaasianbistro.com					
Thomas Henkelmann Restaurant 420 Field Point Rd	Greenwich	CT	06830	203-869-7500	869-7502
Wild Ginger 328 Pemberwick Rd	Greenwich	CT	06831	203-531-3322	531-4800
Web: www.wildginger-ct.com					
Aibonitos 517 Park St	Hartford	CT	06106	860-525-8160	
Carbone's Ristorante 588 Franklin Ave	Hartford	CT	06114	860-296-9646	296-2785
Web: www.carbonesct.com					
Casa Mia Ristorante 381 Franklin Ave	Hartford	CT	06114	860-296-3441	563-4271
Web: www.tomad.net					
Chef Eugene 428 Franklin Ave	Hartford	CT	06114	860-296-4540	
Web: www.chefeugene.com					
City Steam Brewery Cafe 942 Main St	Hartford	CT	06103	860-525-1600	244-2255
Web: www.citysteambrewerycafe.com					
Costa del Sol 901 Wethersfield Ave	Hartford	CT	06114	860-296-1714	296-9250
Web: www.costadelsolrestaurant.net					
Coyote Flaco 635 New Britain Ave	Hartford	CT	06106	860-953-1299	953-1954
Web: www.coyoteflaco.com					
Ficara's 577 Franklin Ave	Hartford	CT	06114	860-296-3238	
First & Last Tavern 939 Maple Ave	Hartford	CT	06114	860-956-6000	956-9783
Hot Tomato's 1 Union Pl	Hartford	CT	06103	860-249-5100	524-8120
Web: www.hottomatos.net					
Ichiban Japanese Steak House 530 Farmington Ave	Hartford	CT	06105	860-236-5599	236-2669
Web: www.ichibanhartford.com					
Kashmir Restaurant 481 Wethersfield Ave	Hartford	CT	06114	860-296-9685	
King & I 1901 Park St	Hartford	CT	06106	860-232-5471	
Koji 17 Asylum St	Hartford	CT	06103	860-247-5654	
Web: www.kojidowntown.com/					
Max Downtown 185 Asylum St	Hartford	CT	06103	860-522-2530	246-5279
Web: www.maxrestaurantgroup.com					
Morton's The Steakhouse 30 State House Sq	Hartford	CT	06103	860-724-0044	724-0661
Web: www.mortons.com					
Museum Cafe at the Wadsworth Antheneum Museum of Art 600 Main St	Hartford	CT	06103	860-838-4042	
New Park 1615 Park St	Hartford	CT	06106	860-232-1565	233-7894
Oporto 2074 Park St	Hartford	CT	06106	860-233-3184	231-8112
Web: www.oportohartford.com					
Peppercorn's Grill 357 Main St	Hartford	CT	06106	860-547-1714	724-7612
Web: www.peppercornsgrill.com					
Pierpont's Restaurant 1 Haynes St	Hartford	CT	06103	860-522-4935	247-4576
Sally's Fish Camp 201 Ann St	Hartford	CT	06103	860-278-8852	278-8854
Web: www.sallysfishcamp.com					
Spris 10 Constitution Plaza	Hartford	CT	06103	860-247-7747	246-1212
Web: www.spris.cc					
Szechuan Tokyo 1245 New Britain Ave	Hartford	CT	06110	860-561-0180	
Web: www.asianfusion.net					
Tapas on Ann 126-130 Ann St	Hartford	CT	06103	860-525-5988	525-5354
Web: www.tapasonline.com					
Trumbull Kitchen 150 Trumbull St	Hartford	CT	06103	860-493-7412	493-7416
Web: www.maxrestaurantgroup.com/home.html					
Vito's by the Park 26 Trumbull St	Hartford	CT	06103	860-244-2200	244-2210
Web: www.vitosct.com					
VIVO Seasonal Trattoria 200 Columbus Blvd	Hartford	CT	06103	860-760-2333	
Cavey's 45 E Center St	Manchester	CT	06040	860-643-2751	
Web: www.caveysrestaurant.com					
Adriana's 771 Grand Ave	New Haven	CT	06511	203-865-6474	865-4846
Akasaka 1450 Whalley Ave	New Haven	CT	06515	203-387-4898	397-3069
Archie Moore's Bar & Restaurant 188 1/2 Willow St	New Haven	CT	06511	203-773-9870	
Web: www.archiemoores.com					
Bangkok Garden 172 York St	New Haven	CT	06511	203-789-8684	789-0336
Bentara 76 Orange St	New Haven	CT	06510	203-562-2511	562-0892
Web: www.bentara.com					
Brasi's Italian Restaurant 201 Food Terminal Plaza	New Haven	CT	06511	203-498-2488	
Caffe Adulis 228 College St	New Haven	CT	06511	203-777-5081	562-4126
Carmen Anthony Steakhouse 660 State St	New Haven	CT	06511	203-773-1444	772-4853
Web: www.carmenanthony.com					
Carmine's Tuscan Grill Ristorante 1500 Whalley Ave	New Haven	CT	06515	203-389-2805	389-1071
Web: www.carminestuscangrill.com/					
Central Steakhouse 919 Orange St	New Haven	CT	06510	203-787-7885	787-9662
Web: www.centralsteakhouse.com/					
Christopher Martin's 860 State St	New Haven	CT	06511	203-776-8835	777-8875
Web: www.christophermartins.com					
Claire's Corner Copia 1000 Chapel St	New Haven	CT	06510	203-562-3888	
Web: www.clairescornercopia.com					
Consiglio's 165 Wooster St	New Haven	CT	06511	203-865-4489	865-3197
Web: www.consiglios.com					
D'Amato's 271 Grand Ave	New Haven	CT	06513	203-777-9897	777-9543
Fireside Restaurant 810 Woodward Ave	New Haven	CT	66512	203-466-1919	
Gunung Tahan 1451 Whalley Ave	New Haven	CT	06515	203-389-1280	389-1329
House of Chao 898 Whalley Ave	New Haven	CT	06515	203-389-6624	
Mamoun's Falafel Restaurant 85 Howe St	New Haven	CT	06511	203-562-8444	562-1474
Web: www.mamounsfalafel.com					
Miya 68 Howe St	New Haven	CT	06511	203-777-9760	
Playwright 144 Temple St	New Haven	CT	06510	203-752-0450	772-3465
Web: www.playwrightirishpub.com					
Roomba 1044 Chapel St	New Haven	CT	06510	203-562-7666	
Sage American Bar & Grill 100 S Water St	New Haven	CT	06519	203-787-3466	777-8274
Web: www.sageamerican.com					
Tre Scalini 100 Wooster St	New Haven	CT	06511	203-777-3373	787-5360
Web: www.trescalinirestaurant.com					
Union League Cafe 1032 Chapel St	New Haven	CT	06510	203-562-4299	562-6712
Web: www.unionleaguecafe.com					
Zaroka 148 York St	New Haven	CT	06511	203-776-8644	776-0051
Web: www.zaroka.com					
Zinc 964 Chapel St	New Haven	CT	06510	203-624-0507	624-9156
Web: www.zincfood.com					
Ruth's Chris Steak House 2513 Berlin Tpke	Newington	CT	06111	860-666-2202	665-7246
Web: www.ruthschris.com					
Bennett's Steak & Fish House 24-26 Spring St	Stamford	CT	06901	203-978-7995	406-2078
Web: www.bennettssteakandfish.com					
Bobby Valentine's Sports Gallery Cafe 225 Main St	Stamford	CT	06901	203-348-0010	359-9395
Web: www.bobbyv.com/					
Brasitas 954 E Main St	Stamford	CT	06902	203-323-3176	
Web: www.brasitas.com					
Chez Jean-Pierre 188 Bedford St	Stamford	CT	06901	203-357-9526	357-9618
Web: www.chezjeanpierre.com					
Columbus Park Trattoria 205 Main St	Stamford	CT	06901	203-967-9191	
Web: www.columbusparktrattoria.com					
Court Square Diner Cafe 108 Prospect St	Stamford	CT	06901	203-406-0060	
Crab Shell 46 Southfield Ave	Stamford	CT	06902	203-967-7229	967-7233
Web: www.crabshell.com					
Dakshin 68 Broad St	Stamford	CT	06901	203-964-1010	358-8848
Eclisse Restaurant 700 Canal St	Stamford	CT	06902	203-325-3773	327-2308
Web: www.eclisserestaurant.com					
Egane 135 Bedford St	Stamford	CT	06901	203-975-0209	
Web: www.eganerestaurant.com					
Fio's 299 Long Ridge Rd	Stamford	CT	06902	203-964-9802	964-9804
Web: www.fiosristorante.com					
Grand 15 Bank St	Stamford	CT	06901	203-323-3232	323-3236
Web: www.stamfordgrand.com					
Hugo's Restaurant 161 Stillwater Ave	Stamford	CT	06902	203-323-5577	
Il Falco 59 Broad St	Stamford	CT	06901	203-327-0002	967-8315
Kotobuki 457 Summer St	Stamford	CT	06901	203-359-4747	357-7522
Web: www.kotobukijapaneserestaurant.com					
La Bretagne 2010 W Main St	Stamford	CT	06902	203-324-9539	961-9468
Web: www.labretagnerestaurant.com					
La Hacienda 222 Summer St	Stamford	CT	06901	203-324-0577	
Morton's The Steakhouse 377 N State St	Stamford	CT	06901	203-324-3939	324-4336
Web: www.mortons.com					
Ocean 211 211 Summer St	Stamford	CT	06901	203-973-0494	973-0495
Web: www.ocean211.com					
Ole Mole 1030 High Ridge Rd	Stamford	CT	06905	203-461-9962	329-7438
Plateau 25 Bank St	Stamford	CT	06901	203-961-9875	961-9877
Quattro Regali 245 Hope St	Stamford	CT	06906	203-964-1801	588-9188
Royal Green 1349 Newfield Ave	Stamford	CT	06905	203-322-6244	
Sabatiello's Italian Grille 269 Bedford St	Stamford	CT	06901	203-353-3300	327-4720
Web: www.sabatiellos.com					
Siena 519 Summer St	Stamford	CT	06901	203-351-0898	351-0899
Telluride 245 Bedford St	Stamford	CT	06901	203-357-7679	
Web: www.telluriderestaurant.com					
Zinc Bistro & Bar 222 Summer St	Stamford	CT	06901	203-252-2352	252-2353
Web: www.zincstamford.com					
Arugula 953 Farmington Ave	West Hartford	CT	06107	860-561-4888	
Bricco 78 LaSalle Rd	West Hartford	CT	06107	860-233-0220	233-7503
Web: www.restaurantbricco.com					
Chengdu 179 Park Rd	West Hartford	CT	06119	860-232-6455	232-3002
Grant's 977 Farmington Ave	West Hartford	CT	06107	860-236-1930	570-1431
Max's Oyster Bar 964 Farmington Ave	West Hartford	CT	06107	860-236-6299	233-6969
Web: www.maxrestaurantgroup.com					
Murasaki 23 LaSalle Rd	West Hartford	CT	06107	860-236-7622	236-7626
Web: www.murasakijapaneserestaurant.com					
Pond House Cafe 1555 Asylum Ave	West Hartford	CT	06117	860-231-8823	231-8731
Web: www.pondhousecafe.com					

Delaware

Name / Address	City	State	ZIP	Phone	Fax
Captain's Table Restaurant 3206 Hwy 1	Dewey Beach	DE	19971	302-227-6203	
Crabber's Cove Restaurant 113 Dickinson St	Dewey Beach	DE	19971	302-227-4888	226-2402
Lighthouse Restaurant 115 Dickinson St	Dewey Beach	DE	19971	302-227-4333	
Mama Maria's Italian Restaurant 1608 Hwy 1	Dewey Beach	DE	19971	302-227-3242	
Web: www.mamamaria.com					
Rusty Rudder Restaurant 113 Dickinson St	Dewey Beach	DE	19971	302-227-3888	226-2402
Two Seas Restaurant Van Dyke Ave & Rt 1	Dewey Beach	DE	19971	302-227-2610	
Venus on the Half Shell Dagsworthy St	Dewey Beach	DE	19971	302-227-3317	
Cool Springs Fish Bar 2463 S State St	Dover	DE	19901	302-698-1955	
Hibachi Japanese Steak House 691 N DuPont Hwy	Dover	DE	19901	302-734-5900	734-5671
Iron Gate Inn 1151 S Bay Rd	Dover	DE	19901	302-678-9666	
La Tolteca 859 N DuPont Hwy	Dover	DE	19901	302-734-3444	734-1777
Lonestar Steakhouse & Saloon 365 N DuPont Hwy	Dover	DE	19901	302-736-5836	
Web: www.lonestarsteakhouse.com/					
Marimonti 107 Gagway West	Dover	DE	19904	302-674-0966	674-8070
Niko's 1115 S Governors Ave	Dover	DE	19904	302-730-3551	
Roma Italian Restaurant 3 President Dr	Dover	DE	19901	302-678-1041	678-1045
Web: www.romadover.com					
Sambo's Tavern 284 Front St	Dover	DE	19904	302-674-9724	
Schucker's Pier 13 Restaurant 889 N DuPont Hwy	Dover	DE	19901	302-674-1190	674-2965
Viet Kieu 510 Jefferic Blvd	Dover	DE	19901	302-744-9300	
Where Pigs Fly 617 E Loockerman St	Dover	DE	19901	302-678-0586	
Village Inn 3726 S Little Creek Rd	Little Creek	DE	19961	302-734-3245	
Sail Loft 1517 Bay Rd	Milford	DE	19963	302-422-5858	422-7208
Web: www.sailloftrestaurant.com					
1776 Eastern Shore Steakhouse & Bar 6 Midway Shopping Center	Rehoboth Beach	DE	19971	302-645-9355	645-0854
Web: www.1776steakhouse.com					
Adriatico Italian Restaurant 30 Baltimore Ave	Rehoboth Beach	DE	19971	302-227-9255	

Name / Address	City	State	ZIP	Phone	Fax
Avenue Restaurant 110 Rehoboth Ave	Rehoboth Beach	DE	19971	302-226-0132	
Big Fish Grill 4117 Hwy 1	Rehoboth Beach	DE	19971	302-227-9007	227-1705
Web: www.bigfishgrill.com					
Blue Moon Restaurant 35 Baltimore Ave	Rehoboth Beach	DE	19971	302-227-6515	227-3702
Web: www.bluemoonrehoboth.com					
Catcher's Restaurant & Raw Bar 249 Rehoboth Ave	Rehoboth Beach	DE	19971	302-227-1808	
Celsius Restaurant 50-C Wilmington Ave	Rehoboth Beach	DE	19971	302-227-5767	227-8346
Chez La Mer 210 2nd St	Rehoboth Beach	DE	19971	302-227-6494	227-6797
Web: www.chezlamer.com					
Crabby Dick's 4534 Hwy 1	Rehoboth Beach	DE	19971	302-645-9132	
Web: www.crabby-dicks.com/					
Dos Locos 10 Wilmington Ave	Rehoboth Beach	DE	19971	302-227-3353	227-2213
Web: www.rehoboth.com/doslocos					
Fusion 50 Wilmington Ave	Rehoboth Beach	DE	19971	302-226-1940	
Jake's Seafood House Restaurant 29 Baltimore Ave	Rehoboth Beach	DE	19971	302-227-6237	226-5137
Web: www.jakesseafood.com					
Ristorante Zebra 32 Lake Ave	Rehoboth Beach	DE	19971	302-226-1160	226-4985
Roadhouse Steak Joint 4572 Hwy 1	Rehoboth Beach	DE	19971	302-645-8273	645-8275
Web: www.roadhousesteakjoint.com					
Starboard Restaurant 2009 Hwy 1	Rehoboth Beach	DE	19971	302-227-4600	
Victoria's Restaurant 2 Olive Ave Boardwalk Plaza Hotel	Rehoboth Beach	DE	19971	302-227-0615	
Web: www.boardwalkplaza.com/restaurant.htm					
Wahoo Raw Bar & Crab Co 19598 Coastal Hwy	Rehoboth Beach	DE	19971	302-227-6700	227-6711
Yong Hua Chinese Restaurant 4377 Hwy 1	Rehoboth Beach	DE	19971	302-227-1549	
Thomas England House 1165 S DuPont Blvd	Smyrna	DE	19977	302-653-1420	
Bean Bag Cafe 913 N Market St	Wilmington	DE	19801	302-888-2444	427-2700
Bertucci's 3596 Concord Pike	Wilmington	DE	19803	302-529-0800	529-7144
Web: www.bertuccis.com					
Blue Parrott Bar & Grille 1934 W 6th St	Wilmington	DE	19805	302-655-8990	655-9488
Web: www.blueparrotgrille.com					
Bonhouse 4713 Kirkwood Hwy	Wilmington	DE	19808	302-633-1218	633-3928
Brandywine Room 1100 Market St	Wilmington	DE	19801	302-594-3156	594-3070
TF: 800-338-3404					
Bull's Eye Saloon & Restaurant 3734 Kirkwood Hwy	Wilmington	DE	19808	302-633-6557	998-9151
Web: www.bullseyesaloon.com					
China Royal 1845 Marsh Rd	Wilmington	DE	19810	302-475-3686	
Corner Bistro 3604 Silverside Rd	Wilmington	DE	19810	302-477-1778	477-1779
Culinaria 1812 Marsh Rd	Wilmington	DE	19810	302-475-4860	
Deep Blue 111 W 11th St	Wilmington	DE	19801	302-777-2040	777-1012
Web: www.deepbluebarandgrill.com					
Eclipse Bistro 1020 N Union St	Wilmington	DE	19805	302-658-1588	661-1080
Web: www.eclipsebistro.com					
Golden Castle Diner-Restaurant 2722 Concord Pike	Wilmington	DE	19803	302-478-7701	478-7710
Web: www.goldencastlediner.com					
Green Room at the Hotel duPont 1100 Market St	Wilmington	DE	19801	302-594-3154	594-3070
Web: www.dupont.com/hotel/dining.htm					
Harry's Savoy Grill 2020 Naamans Rd	Wilmington	DE	19810	302-475-3000	475-9990
Web: www.harrys-savoy.com					
Harry's Seafood Grill 101 S Market St	Wilmington	DE	19801	302-777-1500	777-2406
Web: www.harrysseafoodgrill.com					
Hibachi Japanese Steak House 5607 Concord Pike	Wilmington	DE	19803	302-477-0194	477-0319
Jasmine 3654 Concord Pike	Wilmington	DE	19803	302-479-5618	
Jimmy's Restaurant 703 Philadelphia Pike	Wilmington	DE	19809	302-764-1702	
Lamberti's Cucina 514 Philadelphia Pike	Wilmington	DE	19809	302-762-9094	762-8608
Web: www.lambertis.com					
LaTolteca 4015 Concord Pike	Wilmington	DE	19803	302-478-9477	
Web: www.lastoltecas.com					
Luigi Vitrone's Pastabilities 415 N Lincoln St	Wilmington	DE	19805	302-656-9822	
Web: ljv-pastabilities.com					
Madeline's Italian Restaurant 531 N DuPont St	Wilmington	DE	19805	302-652-9373	
Web: www.madelinesitalianrestaurant.com					
Melting Pot The 1601 Concord Pike	Wilmington	DE	19803	302-652-6358	652-8101
Web: www.meltingpot.com					
Mexican Post 3100 Naamans Rd	Wilmington	DE	19810	302-478-3939	478-5599
Web: www.mexicanpost.com/wilmingtonde.cfm					
Mikimoto's 1212 N Washington St	Wilmington	DE	19801	302-656-8638	656-7423
Web: www.mikimotos.com					
Moro 1307 N Scott St	Wilmington	DE	19806	302-777-1800	
Web: www.mororestaurant.net					
Mrs Robino's Restaurant 520 N Union St	Wilmington	DE	19805	302-652-9223	
Web: www.mrsrobinos.com					
Nonna Ristorante 4621 Stanton Ogleton Rd	Wilmington	DE	19713	302-737-9999	737-4410
Web: www.nonnaristorante.com					
Restaurant 821 821 Market St	Wilmington	DE	19801	302-652-8821	652-4481
Web: www.restaurant821.com					
Scrimmages Restaurant 4723 Concord Pike	Wilmington	DE	19803	302-478-8638	
Stanley's Tavern 2038 Foulk Rd	Wilmington	DE	19810	302-475-1887	475-0904
Web: www.stanleystavern.com					
Sullivan's Steakhouse 5525 Concord Pike	Wilmington	DE	19803	302-479-7970	479-7991
Toscana Kitchen & Bar 1412 N DuPont St	Wilmington	DE	19806	302-654-8001	654-8250
Web: www.bigchefguy.com					
Union City Grille 805 N Union St	Wilmington	DE	19805	302-654-9780	654-0238
Utage 1601 Concord Pike	Wilmington	DE	19803	302-652-1230	
Valle Cucina Italiana 4752 Limestone Rd	Wilmington	DE	19808	302-998-9999	
Web: www.vallecucina.com					
Walter's Steak House & Saloon 802 N Union St	Wilmington	DE	19805	302-652-6780	

District of Columbia

Name / Address	City	State	ZIP	Phone	Fax
15 ria 1515 Rhode Island Ave NW	Washington	DC	20005	202-742-0015	332-8436
Web: www.15ria.com/					
701 701 Pennsylvania Ave NW	Washington	DC	20004	202-393-0701	393-0242
Web: www.701restaurant.com					
1789 Restaurant 1226 36th St NW	Washington	DC	20007	202-965-1789	337-1541
Web: www.1789restaurant.com					
Al Tiramisu 2014 P St NW	Washington	DC	20036	202-467-4466	467-4468
Web: www.altiramisu.com					
Aquarelle 2650 Virginia Ave NW Watergate Hotel	Washington	DC	20037	202-298-4455	965-1173
Ardeo 3311 Connecticut Ave NW	Washington	DC	20008	202-244-6750	
Web: www.ardeorestaurant.com					
Asia Nora 2213 M St NW	Washington	DC	20037	202-797-4860	797-1300
Web: www.noras.com					
Bangkok Bistro 3251 Prospect St NW	Washington	DC	20007	202-337-2424	337-2222
Web: www.bangkokbistrodc.com					
Barolo 223 Pennsylvania Ave SE	Washington	DC	20003	202-547-5011	
Bistro Bis 15 'E' St NW	Washington	DC	20001	202-661-2700	661-2747
Web: www.bistrobis.com					
Bombay Club 815 Connecticut Ave NW	Washington	DC	20006	202-659-3727	659-5012
Web: www.bombayclubdc.com					
Bombay Palace 2020 K St NW	Washington	DC	20006	202-331-4200	331-1505
Busara 2340 Wisconsin Ave NW	Washington	DC	20007	202-337-2340	333-1364
Web: www.busara.com					
Butterfield 9 600 14th St NW	Washington	DC	20005	202-289-8810	
Web: www.butterfield9.com					

Name / Address	City	State	ZIP	Phone	Fax
Cactus Cantina 3300 Wisconsin Ave NW	Washington	DC	20016	202-686-7222	362-5649
Web: www.cactuscantina.com					
Cafe 15 806 15th St NW	Washington	DC	20005	202-737-8800	730-8500
Cafe Atlantico 405 8th St NW	Washington	DC	20004	202-393-0812	393-0555
Web: www.cafeatlantico.com					
Capital Grille 601 Pennsylvania Ave NW	Washington	DC	20004	202-737-6200	637-8821
Web: www.thecapitalgrille.com					
Cashion's Eat Place 1819 Columbia Rd NW	Washington	DC	20009	202-797-1819	797-0048
Web: www.cashionseatplace.com					
Caucus Room 401 9th St NW	Washington	DC	20004	202-393-1300	393-6066
Web: www.thecaucusroom.com					
Ceiba 701 14th St NW	Washington	DC	20005	202-393-3983	393-1863
Web: www.ceibarestaurant.com					
Charlie Palmer Steak 101 Constitution Ave NW	Washington	DC	20001	202-547-8100	547-6607
Web: www.charliepalmer.com/steak_dc					
Citronelle 3000 M St NW	Washington	DC	20007	202-625-2150	339-6326
Web: www.citronelledc.com					
City Lights of China 1731 Connecticut Ave NW	Washington	DC	20009	202-265-6688	263-1369
Web: www.citylightsofchina.com					
Coeur de Lion 926 Massachusetts Ave NW	Washington	DC	20001	202-414-0500	414-0513
Corduroy 1201 K St NW	Washington	DC	20005	202-589-0699	589-0688
DC Coast 1401 K St NW	Washington	DC	20005	202-216-5988	371-2221
Web: www.dccoast.com					
Equinox 818 Connecticut Ave NW	Washington	DC	20006	202-331-8118	331-0809
Web: www.equinoxrestaurant.com					
Filomena Ristorante 1063 Wisconsin Ave NW	Washington	DC	20007	202-338-8800	338-8806
Web: www.filomenadc.com					
Gerard's Place 915 15th St NW	Washington	DC	20005	202-737-4445	737-5555
Web: www.gerardsplacedc.net					
Hard Rock Cafe 999 'E' St NW	Washington	DC	20004	202-737-7625	628-6595
Web: www.hardrock.com					
Heritage India 1337 Connecticut Ave NW	Washington	DC	20036	202-331-1414	331-8788
Web: www.heritageindia.biz					
I Ricchi 1220 19th St NW	Washington	DC	20036	202-835-0459	872-1220
Web: www.iricchi.net					
Indique 3512-14 Connecticut Ave NW	Washington	DC	20008	202-244-6600	
Web: www.indique.com					
Jaleo 480 7th St NW	Washington	DC	20004	202-628-7949	628-7952
Web: www.jaleo.com					
Johnny's Half Shell 400 N Capitol St	Washington	DC	20001	202-737-0400	737-3026
Jyoti 2433 18th St NW	Washington	DC	20009	202-518-5892	
Kaz Sushi Bistro 1915 'I' St NW	Washington	DC	20006	202-530-5500	530-5501
Web: kazsushibistro.com					
Kinkead's 2000 Pennsylvania Ave NW	Washington	DC	20006	202-296-7700	296-7688
Web: www.kinkead.com					
Komi 1509 17th St NW	Washington	DC	20036	202-332-9200	
Lebanese Taverna 2641 Connecticut Ave NW	Washington	DC	20008	202-265-8681	483-3007
Web: www.lebanese-taverna.com					
Little Fountain Cafe 2339 18th St NW	Washington	DC	20009	202-462-8100	
Web: www.littlefountaincafe.com					
Makoto 4822 MacArthur Blvd NW	Washington	DC	20007	202-298-6866	
Marcel's 2401 Pennsylvania Ave NW	Washington	DC	20037	202-296-1166	296-6466
Web: www.marcelsdc.com					
Marrakesh 617 New York Ave NW	Washington	DC	20001	202-393-9393	737-3737
Web: www.marrakesh.us					
Matisse 4934 Wisconsin Ave NW	Washington	DC	20016	202-244-5222	244-1039
McCormick & Schmick's 1652 K St NW	Washington	DC	20006	202-861-2233	822-4679
Web: www.mccormickandschmicks.com					
Mendocino Grille & Wine Bar 2917 M St NW	Washington	DC	20007	202-333-2912	625-7888
Web: www.mendocinodc.com					
Montmarte 327 7th St SE	Washington	DC	20003	202-544-1244	544-4038
Morrison-Clark Inn 1015 L St NW	Washington	DC	20001	202-898-1200	289-8576
Web: www.morrisonclark.com					
Morton's The Steakhouse 1050 Connecticut Ave NW	Washington	DC	20036	202-955-5997	955-5889
Web: www.mortons.com					
New Heights 2317 Calvert St NW	Washington	DC	20008	202-234-4110	
Web: www.newheightsrestaurant.com					
Nora 2132 Florida Ave NW	Washington	DC	20008	202-462-5143	234-6232
Web: www.noras.com					
Obelisk 2029 P St NW	Washington	DC	20036	202-872-1180	
Occidental Grill 1475 Pennsylvania Ave NW	Washington	DC	20004	202-783-1475	783-1475
Web: www.occidental.com					
Oceanaire Seafood Room 1201 F St NW	Washington	DC	20004	202-347-2277	347-9858
Web: www.thoceanaire.com					
Old Ebbitt Grill 675 15th St NW	Washington	DC	20005	202-347-4800	347-6136
Web: www.ebbitt.com					
Olives DC 1600 K St NW	Washington	DC	20005	202-452-1866	452-1245
Web: www.toddenglish.com					
Palena 3529 Connecticut Ave NW	Washington	DC	20008	202-537-9250	
Web: www.palenarestaurant.com					
Palette 15th & M Sts NW	Washington	DC	20005	202-587-2700	587-2705
Web: www.palettedc.com					
Palm The 1225 19th St NW	Washington	DC	20036	202-293-9091	775-1468
Web: www.thepalm.com					
Peacock Cafe 3251 Prospect St NW	Washington	DC	20007	202-625-2740	625-1402
Web: www.peacockcafe.com					
Pesce 2016 P St NW	Washington	DC	20036	202-466-3474	466-8302
Web: www.pescebistro.com					
Posh Restaurant & Supper Club 730 11th St NW	Washington	DC	20001	202-393-0975	393-1390
Web: www.poshdc.com/					
Prime Rib The 2020 K St NW	Washington	DC	20006	202-466-8811	466-2010
Web: www.theprimerib.com					
Restaurant Kolumbia 1801 K St NW	Washington	DC	20006	202-331-5551	331-4700
Web: www.restaurantkolumbia.com					
Rice 1608 14th St NW	Washington	DC	20009	202-234-2400	234-2737
Ruth's Chris Steak House 1801 Connecticut Ave NW	Washington	DC	20009	202-797-0033	667-4257
Web: www.ruthschris.com					
Sakana 2026 P St NW	Washington	DC	20036	202-887-0900	
Sake Club 2635 Connecticut Ave NW	Washington	DC	20008	202-332-2711	332-2712
Web: www.sakeclub.net					
Sam & Harry's 1200 19th St NW	Washington	DC	20036	202-296-4333	785-1070
Web: www.samandharrys.com					
Sea Catch 1054 31st St NW	Washington	DC	20007	202-337-8855	337-7159
Web: www.seacatchrestaurant.com					
Seasons 2800 Pennsylvania Ave NW	Washington	DC	20007	202-342-0810	944-2086
Smith & Wollensky 1112 19th St NW	Washington	DC	20036	202-466-1100	728-2020
Web: www.smithandwollensky.com					
Sushi-Ko 2309 Wisconsin Ave NW	Washington	DC	20007	202-333-4187	333-7594
Web: www.sushiko.us					
Sushi Taro 1503 17th St NW	Washington	DC	20036	202-462-8999	328-3756
Web: www.sushitaro.com					
Tabard Inn 1739 'N' St NW	Washington	DC	20036	202-331-8528	785-6173
Web: www.tabardinn.com					
Taberna Del Alabardero 1776 'I' St NW	Washington	DC	20006	202-429-2200	775-3713
Web: www.alabardero.com					
Teatro Goldoni 1909 K St NW	Washington	DC	20006	202-955-9494	955-5584
Web: www.teatrogoldoni.com					

District of Columbia (Cont'd)

Restaurant	City	State	ZIP	Phone	Fax
TenPenh 1001 Pennsylvania Ave NW	Washington	DC	20004	202-393-4500	393-4744
Web: www.tenpenh.com					
Tosca 1112 F St NW	Washington	DC	20004	202-367-1990	367-1999
Web: www.toscadc.com					
Vidalia 1990 M St NW	Washington	DC	20036	202-659-1990	223-8572
Web: www.vidaliadc.com/vidalia/					
Willard Room 1401 Pennsylvania Ave NW	Washington	DC	20004	202-637-7440	637-7326
Zaytinya 701 9th St NW	Washington	DC	20001	202-638-0800	638-6969
Web: www.zaytinya.com					
Zola 800 F St NW	Washington	DC	20004	202-654-0999	654-0974
Web: www.zoladc.com					

Florida

Restaurant	City	State	ZIP	Phone	Fax
Chef Allen's 19088 NE 29th Ave	Aventura	FL	33180	305-935-2900	935-9062
Web: chefallens.com					
Palm Restaurant 9650 E Bay Harbor Dr	Bay Harbor Islands	FL	33154	305-868-7256	
Addison The 2 E Camino Real	Boca Raton	FL	33432	561-395-9335	393-6255
Web: www.theaddison.com					
Arturo's 6750 N Federal Hwy	Boca Raton	FL	33487	561-997-7373	988-7259
Web: www.arturosrestaurant.com					
Johannes 47 E Palmetto Park Rd	Boca Raton	FL	33432	561-394-0007	
Kathy's Gazebo Cafe 4199 N Federal Hwy	Boca Raton	FL	33431	561-395-6033	
Web: www.kathysgazebo.com					
Ke-e Grill 17940 N Military Trail	Boca Raton	FL	33496	561-995-5044	995-5024
La Vieille Maison 770 E Palmetto Park Rd	Boca Raton	FL	33432	561-391-6701	368-4507
Le Vieux Paris 170 W Camino Real	Boca Raton	FL	33432	561-368-7910	
Web: www.levieuxparis.us					
Lucca 501 E Camino Real	Boca Raton	FL	33432	561-447-5822	
Web: www.myriadrestaurantgroup.com					
Mario's Tuscan Grill 1450 N Federal Hwy	Boca Raton	FL	33432	561-362-7407	
Web: www.mariostuscangrill.com					
Mark's at the Park 344 Plaza Real	Boca Raton	FL	33432	561-395-0770	
Web: www.chefmark.com/miznerpark					
Max's Grille 404 Plaza Real	Boca Raton	FL	33432	561-368-0080	392-1907
Web: www.maxsgrille.com					
New York Prime 2350 NW Executive Center Dr	Boca Raton	FL	33431	561-998-3881	
Web: www.newyorkprime.com					
Sapori 301 Via de Palmas	Boca Raton	FL	33432	561-367-9779	367-9779
Uncle Tai's 5250 Town Center Cir	Boca Raton	FL	33428	561-368-8806	
Roy's 26831 S Bay Dr	Bonita Springs	FL	34134	239-498-7697	495-3985
Web: www.roysrestaurant.com					
Sandbar Seafood & Spirits 100 Spring Ave	Bradenton	FL	34216	941-778-0444	778-3997
Sun House The 111 Gulf Dr S	Bradenton Beach	FL	34217	941-782-1122	
Web: www.thesunhouserestaurant.com					
Island Way Grill 20 Island Way	Clearwater Beach	FL	33767	727-461-6617	461-0158
Web: www.islandwaygrill.com					
Baleen 4 Grove Isle Dr	Coconut Grove	FL	33133	305-858-8300	858-6634
Bizcaya Grill 3300 SW 27th Ave	Coconut Grove	FL	33133	305-644-4675	644-4681
Cacao 141 Giralda Ave	Coral Gables	FL	33134	305-445-1001	445-1053
Web: www.cacaorestaurant.com					
Caffe Abbracci 318 Aragon Ave	Coral Gables	FL	33134	305-441-0700	441-0781
Caffe Vialetto 4019 S Le Jeune Rd	Coral Gables	FL	33146	305-446-5659	446-3532
Christy's 3101 Ponce de Leon Blvd	Coral Gables	FL	33134	305-446-1400	446-3257
Web: www.christysrestaurant.com					
Francesco 325 Alcazar Ave	Coral Gables	FL	33134	305-446-1600	446-3364
Web: www.francescorestaurant.com					
Les Halles 2415 Ponce de Leon Blvd	Coral Gables	FL	33134	305-461-1099	461-9912
Web: www.leshalles.net					
Maroosh 223 Valencia Ave	Coral Gables	FL	33134	305-476-9800	476-3999
Web: www.maroosh.com					
Miss Saigon Bistro 148 Giralda Ave	Coral Gables	FL	33134	305-446-8006	446-3085
Web: www.misssaigonbistro.com					
Norman's 21 Almeria Ave	Coral Gables	FL	33134	305-446-6767	446-7909
Web: www.normans.com					
Ortanique 278 Miracle Mile	Coral Gables	FL	33134	305-446-7710	446-9895
Pascal's on Ponce 2611 Ponce de Leon Blvd	Coral Gables	FL	33134	305-444-2024	444-9798
Web: www.pascalmiami.com					
Restaurant Saint Michel 162 Alcazar Ave	Coral Gables	FL	33134	305-446-6572	446-3966
Ruth's Chris Steak House 2320 Salzedo St	Coral Gables	FL	33134	305-461-8360	461-8363
Web: www.ruthschris.com					
Runyon's 9810 W Sample Rd	Coral Springs	FL	33065	954-752-2333	
Islamorada Fish Co 220 Gulf Stream Way	Dania Beach	FL	33004	954-927-7737	924-5108
Web: www.ifcstonecrab.com					
Shorty's Bar-B-Q 5989 S University Dr	Davie	FL	33328	954-680-9900	
Web: www.shortys.com					
Adobe Gilas 250 N Atlantic Ave	Daytona Beach	FL	32118	386-481-1000	481-1002
Aku Tiki Traders 2225 S Atlantic Ave	Daytona Beach	FL	32118	386-253-8338	252-1198
Angell & Phelps Cafe 156 S Beach St	Daytona Beach	FL	32114	386-257-2677	
Web: www.angellandphelpscafe.com					
Anna's Trattoria 304 Seabreeze Blvd	Daytona Beach	FL	32118	386-239-9624	
Cancun Lagoon Bar & Grill					
1735 W International Speedway Blvd	Daytona Beach	FL	32114	386-255-6500	239-0537
Web: www.cancunlagoon.com					
Caribbean Jack's 721 Ballough Rd	Daytona Beach	FL	32114	386-523-3000	252-7362
Web: caribbeanjacks.com					
Cellar The 220 Magnolia Ave	Daytona Beach	FL	32114	386-258-0011	258-0117
Web: www.thecellarrestaurant.com					
Chart House 1100 Marina Point Dr	Daytona Beach	FL	32114	386-255-9022	255-5362
Web: www.chart-house.com					
Gene's Steak House					
3674 W International Speedway Blvd	Daytona Beach	FL	32124	386-255-2059	255-5460
Gilly's Pub 44 Riverfront 115 Main St	Daytona Beach	FL	32118	386-226-3000	248-4700
Web: www.pub44.com					
Il Bacio 631 N Grandview Ave	Daytona Beach	FL	32118	386-255-9822	
Italian Village 1500 Beville Rd Suite 406	Daytona Beach	FL	32114	386-257-2250	
Maria Bonita 1784 S Ridgwood Ave S	Daytona Beach	FL	32119	386-767-9512	
Ocean Deck 127 S Ocean Ave	Daytona Beach	FL	32118	386-253-5224	253-7226
Web: www.oceandeck.com					
Oyster Pub 555 Seabreeze Blvd	Daytona Beach	FL	32118	386-255-6348	258-7489
Web: www.oysterpub.com					
Pasha 919 W International Speedway Blvd	Daytona Beach	FL	32114	386-257-7753	255-3421
Porto-Fino Restaurant 3124 S Atlantic Ave	Daytona Beach	FL	32118	386-767-9484	
Top Of Daytona Restaurant 2625 S Atlantic Ave	Daytona Beach	FL	32118	386-767-5791	322-1601
Web: www.topofdaytona.com					
Crabby Joe's Deck & Grill 3701 S Atlantic Ave	Daytona Beach Shores	FL	32127	386-788-3364	756-9878
Web: www.sunglowpier.com					
Teauila's Hawaiian Dinner Theater					
2301 S Atlantic Ave	Daytona Beach Shores	FL	32118	386-255-5411	763-1901
Web: www.teauilashawaii.com					
Baja Cafe Dos 1310 S Federal Hwy	Deerfield Beach	FL	33441	954-596-1305	596-1306
Web: www.bajacafe.com					
Brooks 500 S Federal Hwy	Deerfield Beach	FL	33441	954-427-9302	427-9811
Web: www.brooksrestaurant.com					
Tamarind Asian Grill & Sushi Bar 949 S Federal Hwy	Deerfield Beach	FL	33441	954-428-8009	418-0939
Web: www.tamarindasiangrill.com					
32 East 32 E Atlantic Ave	Delray Beach	FL	33444	561-276-7868	
Web: www.32east.com					
Fifth Avenue Grill 821 S Federal Hwy	Delray Beach	FL	33483	561-265-0122	265-0633
Web: www.fifthavenuegrill.net					
Gotham City Restaurant & Bar 16950 Jog Rd	Delray Beach	FL	33446	561-381-0200	
Web: www.gothamcityrestaurant.com					
Kyoto Sushi 25 NE 2nd Ave Suite 208	Delray Beach	FL	33444	561-330-2275	330-2276
Web: www.kyotosushisake.com					
Old Calypso 900 E Atlantic Ave	Delray Beach	FL	33483	561-279-2300	279-0100
Pineapple Grille 800 Palm Trail	Delray Beach	FL	33483	561-265-1368	
Web: www.pineapplegrille.com					
Splendid Blendeds Cafe 432 E Atlantic Ave	Delray Beach	FL	33483	561-265-1035	
15th Street Fisheries 1900 SE 15th St	Fort Lauderdale	FL	33316	954-763-2777	
Web: www.15streetfisheries.com					
3030 Ocean 3030 Holiday Dr	Fort Lauderdale	FL	33316	954-765-3030	765-3136
Web: www.3030ocean.com					
Ambry 3016 E Commercial Blvd	Fort Lauderdale	FL	33308	954-771-7342	771-7378
Web: www.ambryrestaurant.com					
Anthony's Runway 84 330 SR-84	Fort Lauderdale	FL	33315	954-467-8484	467-7822
Bahia Cabana 3001 Harbor Dr	Fort Lauderdale	FL	33316	954-524-1555	764-5951
Web: www.bahiacabanaresort.com/restaurant.htm					
Bahia Mar Bar & Grill 801 Seabreeze Blvd	Fort Lauderdale	FL	33316	954-764-2233	627-6313
Web: www.bahiamarhotel.com/recreation_dining.htm					
Bangkok Bistro 1507 N Federal Hwy	Fort Lauderdale	FL	33304	954-630-0030	
Bistro 17 1617 SE 17th St	Fort Lauderdale	FL	33316	954-626-1701	626-1752
Bistro Mezzaluna 741 SE 17th St	Fort Lauderdale	FL	33316	954-522-6620	522-3080
Web: www.bistromezzaluna.com					
Black Orchid Cafe 2985 N Ocean Blvd	Fort Lauderdale	FL	33308	954-561-9398	561-4182
Web: www.blackorchidcafe.com					
Cafe Martorano 3343 E Oakland Park Blvd	Fort Lauderdale	FL	33308	954-561-2554	
Web: www.cafemartorano.com					
Cafe Seville 2768 E Oakland Park Blvd	Fort Lauderdale	FL	33306	954-565-1148	
Web: www.cafeseville.com					
Cafe Vico 1125 N Federal Hwy	Fort Lauderdale	FL	33304	954-565-9681	565-6978
Web: www.cafevicorestaurant.com					
Canyon 1818 E Sunrise Blvd	Fort Lauderdale	FL	33304	954-765-1950	
Web: www.canyonfl.com					
Casa D'Angelo 1201 N Federal Hwy	Fort Lauderdale	FL	33304	954-564-1234	564-1235
Casablanca Cafe 3049 Alhambra St	Fort Lauderdale	FL	33304	954-764-3500	764-3815
Catalina 3331 NE 33rd St	Fort Lauderdale	FL	33308	954-564-6770	
Creolina's 209 SW 2nd St	Fort Lauderdale	FL	33301	954-524-2003	
Eduardo de San Angel 2822 E Commercial Blvd	Fort Lauderdale	FL	33308	954-772-4731	772-0794
Web: www.eduardodesanangel.com					
Grandma's French Cafe 3354 N Ocean Blvd	Fort Lauderdale	FL	33308	954-564-3671	206-0292
Web: www.grandmasfrenchcafe.com					
Greek Islands Taverna 3300 N Ocean Blvd	Fort Lauderdale	FL	33308	954-565-5505	
Web: www.greekislandstaverna.com					
Grill Room 620 E Las Olas Blvd Riverside Hotel	Fort Lauderdale	FL	33301	954-467-2555	
Web: www.grillroomonlasolas.com					
Hi-Life Cafe 3000 N Federal Hwy	Fort Lauderdale	FL	33306	954-563-1395	563-1615
Web: www.hilifecafe.com					
Himmarshee Bar & Grille 210 SW 2nd St	Fort Lauderdale	FL	33301	954-524-1818	524-1813
Web: www.himmarshee.com					
Il Mulino 1800 E Sunrise Blvd	Fort Lauderdale	FL	33304	954-524-1800	524-3811
Web: www.ilmulinofl.com					
Jackson's Steakhouse 450 E Las Olas Blvd	Fort Lauderdale	FL	33301	954-522-4450	522-1911
Web: www.jacksonssteakhouse.com					
Johnny V 625 E Las Olas Blvd	Fort Lauderdale	FL	33301	954-761-7920	761-3495
Web: www.johnnyvlasolas.com					
Las Vegas 2807 E Oakland Park Blvd	Fort Lauderdale	FL	33306	954-564-1370	564-8837
Web: www.lasvegascubancuisine.com					
Mango's 904 E Las Olas Blvd	Fort Lauderdale	FL	33301	954-523-5001	523-5355
Web: www.mangosonlasolas.com					
Max's Beach Place 17 S Ft Lauderdale Beach Blvd	Fort Lauderdale	FL	33316	954-525-5022	
Web: www.maxsgrill.net					
Max's Grille 300 SW 1st Ave	Fort Lauderdale	FL	33301	954-779-1800	
Web: www.maxsgrille.net					
Mulligan's 101 E Commercial Blvd	Fort Lauderdale	FL	33308	954-351-1900	351-1238
Nick's 3496 N Ocean Blvd	Fort Lauderdale	FL	33308	954-563-6441	563-9232
Web: www.nicksitalian.com					
Old Florida Seafood House 1414 NE 26th St	Fort Lauderdale	FL	33305	954-566-1044	
PF Chang's China Bistro 2418 E Sunrise Blvd	Fort Lauderdale	FL	33304	954-565-5877	
Web: www.pfchangs.com/					
Primavera Restaurant 830 E Oakland Park Blvd	Fort Lauderdale	FL	33334	954-564-6363	564-0372
Web: www.restaurantprimavera.com					
Rainbow Palace 2787 E Oakland Park Blvd	Fort Lauderdale	FL	33306	954-565-5652	565-4175
Reed's River House 301 SW 3rd Ave	Fort Lauderdale	FL	33312	954-525-7661	525-8389
Rosey Baby					
4587 N University Dr Sun Village Shopping Center	Fort Lauderdale	FL	33351	954-749-5627	749-5733
Web: www.roseybaby.com/fl/index.html					
Rustic Inn 4331 Anglers Ave	Fort Lauderdale	FL	33312	954-584-1637	581-4365
Web: www.garliccrab.com					
Ruth's Chris Steak House 2525 N Federal Hwy	Fort Lauderdale	FL	33305	954-565-2338	565-8078
Web: www.ruthschris.com					
Sage 2378 N Federal Hwy	Fort Lauderdale	FL	33305	954-565-2299	565-3309
Web: www.sagecafe.net					
Samba Room 350 E Las Olas Blvd	Fort Lauderdale	FL	33330	954-468-2000	468-1459
Sea Watch Restaurant 6002 N Ocean Blvd	Fort Lauderdale	FL	33308	954-781-2200	783-0282
Web: www.seawatchfl.com					
Shula's On the Beach					
321 N Fort Lauderdale Beach Blvd	Fort Lauderdale	FL	33304	954-355-4000	462-2342
Sloppy Joe's 17 S Fort Lauderdale Beach Blvd	Fort Lauderdale	FL	33316	954-522-7553	522-0940
Web: www.sloppy-howl.com					
Stuffed Grape Leaf The 900 NE 20th Ave	Fort Lauderdale	FL	33304	954-764-6868	764-3998
Web: www.thestuffedgrapeleaf.com					
Sublime 1431 N Federal Hwy	Fort Lauderdale	FL	33304	954-615-1431	
Web: www.sublimerestaurant.com					
Sunfish Grill 2761 E Oakland Park Blvd	Fort Lauderdale	FL	33306	954-788-2434	
Web: www.sunfishgrill.com					
Sushi Rock Cafe 1515 E Las Olas Blvd	Fort Lauderdale	FL	33301	954-462-5541	
Taverna Opa 3051 NE 32nd Ave	Fort Lauderdale	FL	33308	954-567-1630	567-1672
Web: www.tavernaoparestaurant.com					
Thai on the Beach 901 N Fort Lauderdale Beach Blvd	Fort Lauderdale	FL	33304	954-565-0015	
Web: www.thaionthebeach.com					
Thai Spice 1514 E Commercial Blvd	Fort Lauderdale	FL	33334	954-771-4535	771-5678
Web: www.thaispicefla.com					
Timpano Italian Chophouse 450 E Las Olas Blvd	Fort Lauderdale	FL	33301	954-462-9119	462-9109
Web: www.crww.com/timpano					
Tokyo Sushi 1499 SE 17th St	Fort Lauderdale	FL	33316	954-767-9922	
Tom Jenkins' Bar-B-Q 1236 S Federal Hwy	Fort Lauderdale	FL	33316	954-522-5046	522-7687
Web: www.tomjenkinsbbq.com					
Trina 601 N Fort Lauderdale Beach Blvd	Fort Lauderdale	FL	33304	954-567-8070	567-8040
Web: www.theatlantichotelfortlauderdale.com/trina					

Name / Address	City	State	Zip	Phone	Fax
Zuckerello's 3017 E Commercial Blvd	Fort Lauderdale	FL	33308	954-776-4282	776-6096
Web: www.zuckerellos.com					
Origami 13300-41 S Cleveland Ave	Fort Myers	FL	33907	239-428-2126	482-7420
Web: www.origamisushi.biz					
Alan's Cubana 1712 W University Ave	Gainesville	FL	32603	352-375-6969	373-6969
Amelia's 235 S Main St	Gainesville	FL	32601	352-373-1919	374-8565
Bahn Thai 1902 SW 13th St	Gainesville	FL	32608	352-335-1204	
Web: www.bahnthai.com					
Cedar River 1621 SW 13th St	Gainesville	FL	32608	352-376-0351	376-5075
David's Barbecue 5121 NW 39th Ave	Gainesville	FL	32606	352-373-2002	372-8492
Dinner at Thornebrook 2441 NW 43rd St Suite 13	Gainesville	FL	32606	352-377-0996	377-2270
Web: www.dinneratthornebrook.com					
Dragonfly 201 SE 2nd Ave Suite 104	Gainesville	FL	32601	352-371-3359	371-3329
Web: www.dragonflysushi.com					
Emiliano's Cafe 7 SE 1st Ave	Gainesville	FL	32601	352-375-7381	373-1437
Web: www.emilianoscafe.com					
Golden Lights 4150 NW 16th Blvd	Gainesville	FL	32605	352-371-9365	371-9388
Ivey's Grille 3303 W University Ave	Gainesville	FL	32605	352-371-4839	
Joe's Place 5109 NW 39th Ave Suite J	Gainesville	FL	32606	352-377-1365	377-1008
Web: www.panamajoesplace.com					
La Fiesta 7038 NW 10th Pl	Gainesville	FL	32605	352-332-0878	332-0878
Las Margaritas 4401 NW 25th Pl	Gainesville	FL	32606	352-374-6699	264-8822
Leonardo's 706 706 W University Ave	Gainesville	FL	32601	352-378-2001	373-6239
Market Street Pub 120 SW 1st Ave	Gainesville	FL	32601	352-377-2927	377-3308
Web: www.marketstreetpub.com					
Mildred's 3445 W University Ave	Gainesville	FL	32607	352-371-1711	335-2788
Web: www.mildredsbigcityfood.com					
Miya Sushi 3222 SW 35th Blvd	Gainesville	FL	32608	352-335-3030	335-2288
Mr Han's 6944 NW 10th Pl	Gainesville	FL	32605	352-331-6400	332-5681
Northwest Grille 5115 NW 39th Ave	Gainesville	FL	32606	352-376-0500	376-0018
Schezuan Panda 3830 SW 13th St	Gainesville	FL	32608	352-336-6464	373-6251
Sovereign Restaurant 12 SE 2nd Ave	Gainesville	FL	32601	352-378-6307	
Steve's Cafe Americain 12 W University Ave	Gainesville	FL	32601	352-377-9337	377-0593
Web: www.stevescafeamericain.com					
Sushi Matsuri 3418 SW Archer Rd	Gainesville	FL	32608	352-335-1875	
Web: www.matsuritime.com					
Tim's Thai 501 NW 23rd Ave Suite A	Gainesville	FL	32609	352-372-5424	372-5424
Web: www.timsthairestaurant.com					
Yamato Japanese Steak House 526 NW 60th St	Gainesville	FL	32607	352-332-4466	332-7799
Flanigan's 1550 W 84th St	Hialeah	FL	33015	305-821-0993	821-7012
Web: www.flanigans.net					
Koky's Bar-B-Q Ranch 4950 W 12th Ave	Hialeah	FL	33012	305-558-5512	
Las Culebrinas 4590 W 12th Ave	Hialeah	FL	33012	305-823-5828	822-2341
Molina's 4090 E 8th Ave	Hialeah	FL	33013	305-687-0008	693-9255
Thai Cafe 6845 Main St	Hialeah	FL	33014	305-825-7752	
Dave & Buster's Oakwood Plaza 3000 Oakwood Blvd	Hollywood	FL	33020	954-923-5505	929-6643
Web: www.daveandbusters.com					
bb's 1019 Hendricks Ave	Jacksonville	FL	32207	904-306-0100	306-0118
Biscotti's 3556 St Johns Ave	Jacksonville	FL	32205	904-387-2060	387-0051
Web: www.biscottis.net					
Bistro Aix 1440 San Marco Blvd	Jacksonville	FL	32207	904-398-1949	398-9386
Web: www.bistrox.com					
Chart House 1501 Riverplace Blvd	Jacksonville	FL	32207	904-398-3353	396-6876
Web: www.chart-house.com					
Corner Brasserie 1430 San Marco Blvd	Jacksonville	FL	32207	904-396-1414	396-1114
Web: www.thecornerbrasserie.com					
Dave & Buster's 7025 Salisbury Rd S	Jacksonville	FL	32256	904-296-1525	296-9005
Web: www.daveandbusters.com					
JJ's Bistro de Paris 7643 Gate Pkwy Suite 105	Jacksonville	FL	32256	904-996-7557	996-7577
Web: www.jjbistro.com					
Marker 32 14549 Beach Blvd	Jacksonville	FL	32250	904-223-1534	223-7763
Web: www.marker32.com					
Matthew's 2107 Hendricks Ave	Jacksonville	FL	32207	904-396-9922	396-5222
Web: www.matthewsrestaurant.com					
Morton's The Steakhouse 1510 Riverplace Blvd	Jacksonville	FL	32207	904-399-3933	399-1230
Web: www.mortons.com					
Pastiche 4260 Herschel St	Jacksonville	FL	32210	904-387-6213	387-0609
Web: www.mypastiche.com					
Row The 1521 Riverside Ave	Jacksonville	FL	32204	904-354-5080	354-6854
Roy's 2400-101 3rd St S	Jacksonville	FL	32250	904-241-7697	241-7698
Web: www.roysrestaurant.com					
Ruth's Chris Steak House 1201 Riverplace Blvd	Jacksonville	FL	32207	904-396-6200	396-4559
Web: www.ruthschris.com					
Wine Cellar 1314 Prudential Dr	Jacksonville	FL	32207	904-398-8989	398-3964
Web: www.winecellarjax.com					
Chizu Japanese Steak & Seafood House 1227 3rd St S	Jacksonville Beach	FL	32250	904-241-8455	
Dolphin Depot 704 1st St N	Jacksonville Beach	FL	32250	904-270-1424	
Dwight's 1527 Penman Rd	Jacksonville Beach	FL	32250	904-241-4496	
Web: www.dwightsbistro.com					
Eleven South 216 11th Ave S	Jacksonville Beach	FL	32250	904-241-1112	241-1109
Web: www.elevensouth.com					
Giovanni's 1161 Beach Blvd	Jacksonville Beach	FL	32250	904-249-7787	249-6203
Web: www.giovannirestaurant.com					
Max's 1316 Beach Blvd	Jacksonville Beach	FL	32250	904-247-6820	246-8743
Old Siam 1716 3rd St N	Jacksonville Beach	FL	32250	904-247-7763	247-9569
Thai Room 1286 3rd St S	Jacksonville Beach	FL	32250	904-249-8444	
Web: www.thai-room.com					
Lan 8332 S Dixie Hwy	Kendall	FL	33143	305-661-8141	661-7643
A & B Lobster House 700 Front St	Key West	FL	33040	305-294-5880	294-6871
Web: www.aandblobsterhouse.com					
Alice's Key West 1114 Duval St	Key West	FL	33040	305-292-5733	292-5727
Web: aliceskeywest.com					
Ambrosia 1100 Packer St	Key West	FL	33040	305-293-0304	
Antonia's 615 Duval St	Key West	FL	33040	305-294-6565	294-3888
Web: www.antoniaskeywest.com					
Bagatelle 115 Duval St	Key West	FL	33040	305-296-6609	294-7304
Web: www.bagatelle-keywest.com					
Blue Heaven 729 Thomas St	Key West	FL	33040	305-296-8666	296-9052
Web: blueheavenkw.homestead.com/Blue_Heaven_Restaurant_Key_West.html					
BO's Fish Wagon 801 Caroline St	Key West	FL	33040	305-294-9272	
Cafe Marquesa 600 Fleming St	Key West	FL	33040	305-292-1244	
Web: www.marquesa.com/cafe.htm					
Cafe Med 425 Grinnell St	Key West	FL	33040	305-294-1117	
Cafe Sole 1029 Southard St	Key West	FL	33040	305-294-0230	296-8286
Web: www.cafesole.com					
Camille's 1202 Simonton St	Key West	FL	33040	305-296-4811	294-8983
Chico's Cantina 5230 US Hwy 1	Key West	FL	33040	305-296-4714	296-1485
Web: www.chicoscantina.com					
Conch Republic Seafood Co 631 Greene St	Key West	FL	33040	305-294-4403	296-4330
Web: www.conchrepublicseafood.com/					
Duffy's Steak & Lobster House 1007 Simonton St	Key West	FL	33040	305-296-4900	
El Siboney 900 Catherine St	Key West	FL	33040	305-296-4184	296-8850
Web: www.elsiboneyrestaurant.com					
Grand Cafe Key West 314 Duval St	Key West	FL	33040	305-292-4740	
Web: www.grandcafekeywest.com/					
Harbor Lights Seafood Palm Ave	Key West	FL	33040	305-295-3350	
Hard Rock Cafe 313 Duval St	Key West	FL	33040	305-293-0230	293-0267
Web: www.hardrockcafe.com					
Hog's Breath Saloon 400 Front St Suite C	Key West	FL	33040	305-296-4222	292-8472
Web: hogsbreath.com					
Jimmy Buffet's Margaritaville 500 Duval St	Key West	FL	33040	305-292-1435	294-9147
Web: margaritaville.com					
Kelly's Caribbean Bar Grill & Brewery 301 Whitehead St	Key West	FL	33040	305-293-8484	296-0047
Web: www.kellyskeywest.com					
La Trattoria 524 Duval St	Key West	FL	33040	305-296-1075	296-4941
Web: www.latrattoria.us					
Latitudes Beach Cafe 245 Front St	Key West	FL	33040	305-292-5394	
Louie's Backyard 700 Waddell Ave	Key West	FL	33040	305-294-1061	294-0002
Web: louiesbackyard.com					
Mangia Mangia 900 Southard St	Key West	FL	33040	305-294-2469	
Web: www.mangia-mangia.com					
Mangoes 700 Duval St	Key West	FL	33040	305-292-4606	292-7958
Web: www.mangoeskeywest.com					
Meteor Smokehouse 404 Southard St	Key West	FL	33040	305-294-5602	294-9462
Web: www.meteorsmokehouse.com					
Michael's 532 Margaret St	Key West	FL	33040	305-295-1300	295-1378
Web: www.michaelskeywest.com					
Mo's 1116 White St	Key West	FL	33040	305-296-8955	
Opera 613 Duval St	Key West	FL	33040	305-295-2705	
Web: www.operarestaurant.com					
Pier House 1 Duval St	Key West	FL	33040	305-296-4600	296-7568
Web: www.pierhouse.com					
Pisces 1007 Simonton St	Key West	FL	33040	305-294-7100	
Web: www.pisceskeywest.com					
Seven Fish 632 Olivia St	Key West	FL	33040	305-296-2777	
Web: www.7fish.com					
Sloppy Joe's 201 Duval St	Key West	FL	33040	305-294-8585	
Web: www.sloppyjoes.com					
Square One 1075 Duval St Suite C12	Key West	FL	33040	305-296-4300	292-5039
Web: www.squareonerestaurant.com					
Turtle Kraals Restaurant & Bar 231 Margaret St	Key West	FL	33040	305-294-2640	294-7985
Web: www.turtlekraals.com					
All Star Cafe 690 S Victory Way	Lake Buena Vista	FL	32830	407-827-8326	
Arthur's 27 1900 Buena Vista Dr	Lake Buena Vista	FL	32830	407-827-3450	
Artist Point 901 Timberline Dr	Lake Buena Vista	FL	32830	407-824-1081	824-5230
Benihana 1751 Hotel Plaza Blvd	Lake Buena Vista	FL	32830	407-827-4865	827-6030
Web: www.benihana.com					
bluezoo 1500 Epcot Resorts Blvd	Lake Buena Vista	FL	32830	407-934-1111	934-4882
Web: www.toddenglish.com/Restaurants.html					
Boma 2901 Osceola Pkwy	Lake Buena Vista	FL	32830	407-938-4722	
Bongos Cuban Cafe 1498 E Buena Vista Dr	Lake Buena Vista	FL	32830	407-828-0999	828-0999
Web: www.bongoscubancafe.com					
California Grill 4600 N World Dr	Lake Buena Vista	FL	32830	407-824-1576	824-3254
Citricos 4401 Grand Floridian Way Disney's Grand Floridian Resort & Spa	Lake Buena Vista	FL	32830	407-939-3463	
Flying Fish Cafe 2101 N Epcot Resorts Blvd	Lake Buena Vista	FL	32830	407-939-3463	
House of Blues 1490 E Lake Buena Vista Dr	Lake Buena Vista	FL	32830	407-934-2583	
Web: www.hob.com					
Jiko 2901 Osceola Pkwy Disney's Animal Kingdom Lodge	Lake Buena Vista	FL	32830	407-939-3463	
Narcoossee's 4401 Grand Floridian Way Disney's Grand Floridian Resort & Spa	Lake Buena Vista	FL	32830	407-939-3463	
Ohana 1600 Seven Seas Dr	Lake Buena Vista	FL	32830	407-824-2000	824-3174
Planet Hollywood 1506 E Buena Vista Dr	Lake Buena Vista	FL	32830	407-827-7827	827-7847
Rainforest Cafe 1800 E Buena Vista Dr	Lake Buena Vista	FL	32830	407-827-8500	827-8308
Web: www.rainforestcafe.com					
Victoria & Albert's 40001 Floridian Way	Lake Buena Vista	FL	32830	407-824-2383	
Wolfgang Puck Cafe 1482 E Buena Vista Dr	Lake Buena Vista	FL	32830	407-938-9653	828-0090
Web: www.wolfgangpuck.com					
Mississippi Sweets BBQ 6604 Hypoluxo Rd	Lake Worth	FL	33467	561-432-8555	432-8589
Taqueria Elvira 3618 Lantana Rd	Lantana	FL	33462	561-965-2117	
Benihana 276 E Commerical Blvd	Lauderdale-by-the-Sea	FL	33308	954-776-0111	
Web: www.benihana.com					
Blue Moon Fish Co 4405 W Tradewinds Ave	Lauderdale-by-the-Sea	FL	33308	954-267-9888	267-9006
Web: www.bluemoonfishco.com					
Cap's Place Island Restaurant 2765 NE 28th Ct	Lighthouse Point	FL	33064	954-941-0418	941-2346
Web: www.capsplace.com					
Le Bistro 4626 N Federal Hwy	Lighthouse Point	FL	33064	954-946-9240	
Web: www.lebistrorestaurant.com					
Seafood World 4602 N Federal Hwy	Lighthouse Point	FL	33064	954-942-0740	942-0771
Web: www.seafood-world.com					
Chart House 201 Gulf of Mexico Dr	Longboat Key	FL	34228	941-383-5593	383-5879
Web: www.chart-house.com					
Colony Dining Room 1620 Gulf of Mexico Dr Colony Beach & Tennis Resort	Longboat Key	FL	34228	941-383-5558	387-0250
TF: 800-425-5669 ■ *Web:* www.colonybeachresort.com					
Euphemia Haye 5540 Gulf of Mexico Dr	Longboat Key	FL	34228	941-383-3633	387-8336
Web: www.euphemiahaye.com					
Harry's Continental Kitchens 525 St Judes Dr	Longboat Key	FL	34228	941-383-0777	383-2029
Web: www.harryskitchen.com					
Pattigeorge's 4120 Gulf of Mexico Dr	Longboat Key	FL	34228	941-383-5111	
La Vie en Rose Cafe 2950 N State Rd 7	Margate	FL	33063	954-977-0110	
Anokha 3195 Commodore Plaza	Miami	FL	33133	786-552-1030	
Azul 500 Brickell Key Dr	Miami	FL	33131	305-913-8254	913-3825
Bal Harbor Bistro 9700 Collins Ave	Miami	FL	33154	305-861-4544	861-5344
Bali Cafe 109 NE 2nd Ave	Miami	FL	33132	305-358-5751	358-4777
Bongos Cuban Cafe 601 Biscayne Blvd	Miami	FL	33132	786-777-2100	
Web: www.bongoscubancafe.com					
Bubba Gump Shrimp Co 401 Biscayne Blvd Bayside Marketplace	Miami	FL	33132	305-379-8866	379-9699
Web: www.bubbagump.com/html/miami.html					
Cafe Sambal 500 Brickell Key Dr Mandarin Oriental Hotel	Miami	FL	33131	305-913-8251	913-3825
Cancun Grill 15406 NW 77th Ct	Miami	FL	33016	305-826-8571	826-7994
Capital Grille 444 Brickell Ave	Miami	FL	33131	305-374-4500	374-2777
Web: www.thecapitalgrille.com					
Casa Juancho 2436 SW 8th St	Miami	FL	33135	305-642-2452	642-2524
Web: www.casajuancho.com					
Casa Larios 7705 W Flagler St	Miami	FL	33144	305-266-5494	266-5894
Casa Panza 1620 SW 8th St	Miami	FL	33135	305-643-5343	643-9747
Chispa 11500 NW 41st St	Miami	FL	33178	305-591-7166	591-7167
Web: www.chisparestaurant.com/					
Garcia's 398 NW North River Dr	Miami	FL	33128	305-375-0765	375-0167
Graziano's 9227 SW 40th St	Miami	FL	33165	305-225-0008	221-1949
Hard Rock Cafe 401 Biscayne Blvd Suite R-200	Miami	FL	33132	305-377-3110	374-0058
Web: www.hardrock.com					
Hy-Vong 3458 SW 8th St	Miami	FL	33135	305-446-3674	662-4128
Web: www.hyvongcuisine.com					
La Loggia 68 W Flagler St	Miami	FL	33130	305-373-4800	373-7350
Web: www.laloggiaristorante.com					
Las Culebrinas 4700 W Flagler St	Miami	FL	33134	305-445-2337	445-4320
Lila's 8518 Coral Way	Miami	FL	33155	305-553-6061	553-6062

Florida (Cont'd)

Name / Address	City	State	ZIP	Phone	Fax
Lombardi's 401 Biscayne Blvd	Miami	FL	33132	305-381-9580	381-9366
Magnum 709 NE 79th St	Miami	FL	33138	305-757-3368	
Melting Pot The 11520 Sunset Dr	Miami	FL	33173	305-279-8816	598-8931
Web: www.meltingpot.com					
Miyako 9533 S Dixie Hwy	Miami	FL	33156	305-668-9367	
Morton's The Steakhouse 1200 Brickell Ave	Miami	FL	33131	305-400-9990	400-9899
Web: www.mortons.com					
Mosaico 1000 S Miami Ave	Miami	FL	33130	305-371-3473	371-3430
Web: www.mosaicorestaurant.com					
Old Lisbon 1698 SW 22nd St	Miami	FL	33142	305-854-0039	854-3677
Web: www.oldlisbon.com					
Pacific Time 915 Lincoln Rd	Miami	FL	33139	305-534-5979	534-1607
Web: www.pacifictime.biz					
Perricone's Marketplace & Cafe 15 SE 10th St	Miami	FL	33131	305-374-9449	374-9667
Web: www.perricones.com					
PF Chang's China Bistro 8888 SW 136th St Suite 100	Miami	FL	33176	305-234-2338	234-0944
Web: www.pfchangs.com					
Porcao Churrascaria 801 S Brickell Bay Dr	Miami	FL	33131	305-373-2777	373-1177
Web: www.porcaous.com/miami/					
Romeo's Cafe 2257 SW 22nd St	Miami	FL	33145	305-859-2228	
Sushi Siam 801 Brickell Bay Dr	Miami	FL	33131	305-579-9944	579-0297
Tony Chan's Water Club 1717 N Bayshore Dr Suite 131	Miami	FL	33132	305-374-8888	
Web: www.tonychans.com					
Tropical Chinese Restaurant 7991 SW 40th St	Miami	FL	33155	305-262-7576	262-5172
Web: www.tropical-chinese.com					
Tutto Pasta 1751 SW 3rd Ave	Miami	FL	33129	305-857-0709	365-2805
Web: www.tuttopasta.org					
Versailles 3555 SW 8th St	Miami	FL	33135	305-444-0240	444-0774
Zuperpollo 1247 SW 22nd St	Miami	FL	33142	305-856-9494	859-9985
Web: www.zuperpollo.com					
1220 at the Tides 1220 Ocean Dr	Miami Beach	FL	33139	305-604-5130	604-5177
Web: www.tidesmiami.com/dining/1220.html					
A Fish Called Avalon 700 Ocean Dr	Miami Beach	FL	33139	305-532-1727	913-6818
Web: www.afishcalledavalon.com					
AltaMar 1223 Lincoln Rd	Miami Beach	FL	33139	305-532-3061	
Barton G 1427 West Ave	Miami Beach	FL	33139	305-672-8881	672-8781
Web: www.bartong.com					
Blue Sea 1685 Collins Ave	Miami Beach	FL	33139	305-674-6400	
Bond Street Lounge 150 20th St	Miami Beach	FL	33139	305-534-3800	534-3811
Cafe Prima Pasta 414 71st St	Miami Beach	FL	33141	305-867-0106	867-0761
Web: www.primapasta.com					
Carpaccio 9700 Collins Ave Shops of Bal Harbour	Miami Beach	FL	33154	305-867-7777	
Casa Tua 1700 James Ave	Miami Beach	FL	33139	305-673-1010	673-0974
China Grill 404 Washington Ave	Miami Beach	FL	33139	305-534-2211	534-2565
El Rancho Grande 1626 Pennsylvania Ave	Miami Beach	FL	33139	305-673-0480	673-0424
Web: www.elranchograndemexicanrestaurant.com					
Emeril's Miami Beach 1601 Collins Ave	Miami Beach	FL	33139	305-695-4550	695-4551
Web: www.emerils.com/restaurants/miamibeach_emerils					
Escopazzo 1311 Washington Ave	Miami Beach	FL	33139	305-674-9450	532-8770
Web: www.escopazzo.com					
Forge The 432 41st St	Miami Beach	FL	33140	305-538-8533	538-7733
Web: www.theforge.com					
Grillfish 1444 Collins Ave	Miami Beach	FL	33139	305-538-9908	538-2203
Web: www.grillfish.com					
Hosteria Romana 429 Espanola Way	Miami Beach	FL	33139	305-532-4299	673-2570
Web: www.hosteriaromana.com					
Icebox Cafe 1657 Michigan Ave	Miami Beach	FL	33139	305-538-8448	538-6405
Web: www.iceboxcafe.com					
Joe Allen 1787 Purdy Ave	Miami Beach	FL	33139	305-531-7007	531-7075
Web: www.joeallenrestaurant.com					
Joe's Stone Crab 11 Washington Ave	Miami Beach	FL	33139	305-673-0365	673-0295
Web: www.joesstonecrab.com					
Macaluso's 1747 Alton Rd	Miami Beach	FL	33139	305-604-1811	
Maiko 1255 Washington Ave	Miami Beach	FL	33139	305-531-6369	672-2773
Web: www.maikosushi.com					
Mr Chu's Hong Kong Cuisine 890 Washington Ave	Miami Beach	FL	33139	305-538-8424	672-0114
Web: www.mrchu.net					
Nemo 100 Collins Ave	Miami Beach	FL	33139	305-532-4550	532-4187
Web: www.nemorestaurant.com					
News Cafe 800 Ocean Dr	Miami Beach	FL	33139	305-538-6397	538-7817
Web: www.newscafe.com					
Nobu 1901 Collins Ave	Miami Beach	FL	33139	305-695-3232	695-3246
Web: www.nobumatsuhisa.com					
Novecento 1080 Alton Rd	Miami Beach	FL	33139	305-531-0900	531-0072
Osteria Del Teatro 1443 Washington Ave	Miami Beach	FL	33139	305-538-7850	477-2830
Pearl Restaurant & Champagne Lounge 1 Ocean Dr	Miami Beach	FL	33139	305-538-1111	
Web: www.pearlsouthbeach.com					
Pelican Cafe 826 Ocean Dr	Miami Beach	FL	33139	305-673-1000	673-3255
Prime 112 112 Ocean Dr	Miami Beach	FL	33139	305-532-8112	674-7317
Web: www.prime112.com					
Puerto Sagua 700 Collins Ave	Miami Beach	FL	33139	305-673-1115	
Shoji 100 Collins Ave	Miami Beach	FL	33139	305-532-4245	
Web: www.shojisushi.com					
Shula's Steak House 5225 Collins Ave	Miami Beach	FL	33140	305-865-6500	341-6553
Web: www.donshula.com					
Smith & Wollensky 1 Washington Ave	Miami Beach	FL	33139	305-673-1708	673-5943
Web: www.smithandwollensky.com					
Sushi Rock Cafe 1351 Collins Ave	Miami Beach	FL	33139	305-532-2133	
SushiSamba 600 Lincoln Rd	Miami Beach	FL	33139	305-673-5337	673-5451
Web: www.sushisamba.com					
Tamarind Thai 946 Normandy Dr	Miami Beach	FL	33141	305-861-6222	861-8822
Web: www.tamarindthai.us					
Tantra 1445 Pennsylvania Ave	Miami Beach	FL	33139	305-672-4765	624-2084
Web: www.tantrarestaurant.com					
Tap Tap 819 5th St	Miami Beach	FL	33139	305-672-2898	672-0550
Taverna Opa 36 Ocean Dr	Miami Beach	FL	33139	305-673-6730	673-1180
Web: www.tavernaoparestaurant.com					
Toni's Sushi Bar 1208 Washington Ave	Miami Beach	FL	33139	305-673-9368	
Web: www.tonisushi.com					
Touch 910 Lincoln Rd	Miami Beach	FL	33139	305-532-8003	532-0551
Web: www.touchrestaurant.com					
Tuscan Steak 433 Washington Ave	Miami Beach	FL	33139	305-534-2233	534-5715
Wish 801 Collins Ave	Miami Beach	FL	33139	305-674-9474	695-9539
Web: www.wishrestaurant.com					
World Resources 719 Lincoln Rd	Miami Beach	FL	33139	305-535-8987	604-9673
Web: www.worldresourcecafe.com					
Yuca 501 Lincoln Rd	Miami Beach	FL	33139	305-532-9822	673-8276
Web: www.yuca.com					
Beverly Hills Cafe 7321 Miami Lakes Dr	Miami Lakes	FL	33014	305-558-8201	822-2503
Canton Chinese Restaurant 16780 NW 67th Ave	Miami Lakes	FL	33015	305-821-1111	821-8711
El Novillo 15450 New Barn Rd	Miami Lakes	FL	33014	305-819-2755	819-7570
Web: www.elnovillo.com					
Johnny Rockets 6769-6770 Main St	Miami Lakes	FL	33014	305-827-0055	827-1108
Web: www.johnnyrockets.com					

Name / Address	City	State	ZIP	Phone	Fax
Lakes Cafe 15462 NW 77th Ct	Miami Lakes	FL	33015	305-557-0775	
Michael's 16927 NW 67th Ave	Miami Lakes	FL	33015	305-556-8094	556-4230
Shula's Steak 2 6842 Main St	Miami Lakes	FL	33014	305-820-8047	820-8039
Web: www.donshula.com					
Shula's Steak House 7601 Miami Lakes Dr	Miami Lakes	FL	33014	305-820-8102	821-1175
Web: www.donshula.com					
Bistro 821 821 5th Ave S	Naples	FL	34102	239-261-5821	261-1972
Web: www.bistro821.com					
Campiello 1177 3rd St S	Naples	FL	34102	239-435-1166	435-1689
Web: www.campiello.damico.com					
Chop's City Grill 837 5th Ave S	Naples	FL	34102	239-262-4677	430-2227
Web: www.chopscitygrill.com					
Cloyde's Steak & Lobster House 4050 Gulf Shore Blvd	Naples	FL	34103	239-261-0622	261-7554
Web: www.cloydes.com					
Club at Edgewater The 1901 Gulf Shore Blvd N	Naples	FL	34102	239-403-2000	403-2100
Dining Room The 280 Vanderbilt Beach Rd	Naples	FL	34108	239-598-6644	598-6644
Dock at Crayton Cove 845 12th Ave S	Naples	FL	34102	239-263-9940	261-5074
Web: www.dockcraytoncove.com					
Grill The 280 Vanderbilt Beach Rd	Naples	FL	34108	239-598-3300	598-6658
Jasmine 7231 Radio Rd	Naples	FL	34104	239-352-5528	352-5285
Lemonia 2600 Tiburon Dr	Naples	FL	34109	239-254-3373	254-3452
Marie-Michelle's Restaurant on the Bay					
4236 Gulf Shore Blvd N	Naples	FL	34103	239-263-0900	
Web: www.mariemichelle.com/					
Maxwell's on the Bay 4300 Gulf Shore Blvd N	Naples	FL	34103	239-263-1662	263-3509
Web: www.naples.com/maxwells/					
McCabe's Irish Pub 699 5th Ave S	Naples	FL	34102	239-403-7170	403-8778
Pazzo! 853 5th Ave S	Naples	FL	34102	239-434-8494	649-5222
PF Chang's China Bistro 10840 Tamiami Trail N	Naples	FL	34108	239-596-2174	596-3369
Web: www.pfchangs.com					
Pier 41 1200 5th Ave S	Naples	FL	34102	239-649-5858	649-8647
Rancho Grande 4859 Golden Gate Pkwy	Naples	FL	34116	239-348-8180	348-0715
Ristorante Ciao 835 4th Ave S	Naples	FL	34102	239-263-3889	263-3658
Web: www.ristoranteciao.com					
Shula's Steak House 5111 Tamiami Trail N	Naples	FL	34103	239-430-4999	430-8299
Web: www.donshula.com					
Watermark Grille 11280 Tamiami Trail N	Naples	FL	34110	239-596-1400	596-1402
Web: www.watermarkgrille.com					
Yabba Island Grill 711 5th Ave S	Naples	FL	34102	239-262-5787	262-7767
Web: www.yabbaislandgrill.com					
Zizi Restaurant & Lounge 221 9th St S	Naples	FL	34102	239-262-4835	649-6233
Heelsha 1550 NE 165th St	North Miami Beach	FL	33162	305-919-8393	
Web: www.heelsha.com					
Le Mistral 12189 US Hwy 1	North Palm Beach	FL	33408	561-622-3009	296-3592
Web: www.lemistralrestaurant.net					
Ruth's Chris Steak House 661 N Federal Hwy	North Palm Beach	FL	33408	561-863-0660	
Web: www.ruthschris.com					
By Word of Mouth 3200 NE 12th Ave	Oakland Park	FL	33334	954-564-3663	564-1901
Web: www.bywordofmouthfoods.com					
Ayothaya Thai Cuisine 7555 W Sand Lake	Orlando	FL	32819	407-345-0040	345-0495
Web: www.orlandocitybeat.com/dining					
Bahama Breeze 8849 International Dr	Orlando	FL	32819	407-248-2499	248-2494
Web: www.bahamabreeze.com					
Barney's Steak & Seafood 1615 E Colonial Dr	Orlando	FL	32803	407-896-6864	896-4392
Web: www.barneyssteakhouse.com					
Bill Wong's Restaurant 5668 International Dr	Orlando	FL	32819	407-352-5373	363-4678
Boheme The 325 S Orange Ave	Orlando	FL	32801	407-581-4700	313-9001
Web: www.grandbohemianhotel.com/theboheme/					
Bonefish Grill 7830 W Sand Lake Rd	Orlando	FL	32819	407-355-7707	355-7705
Web: www.bonefishgrill.com					
Bravissimo Wine Bar & Cafe 337 N Shine Ave	Orlando	FL	32803	407-898-7333	
Web: www.cafebravissimo.com					
Bubbalou's Bodacious BBQ 5818 Conroy Rd	Orlando	FL	32835	407-295-1212	295-9090
Web: www.bubbalous.com					
Cafe Tu Tu Tango 8625 International Dr	Orlando	FL	32819	407-248-2222	352-3696
Web: www.cafetututango.com					
Cariera's Cucina Italiana 7600 Dr Phillips Blvd	Orlando	FL	32819	407-351-1187	351-1565
Web: www.carieras.com					
Cedar's 7732 W Sand Lake Rd	Orlando	FL	32819	407-351-6000	355-0607
Web: www.cedarsoforlando.com					
Charley's Steak House 8255 International Dr	Orlando	FL	32819	407-363-0228	354-4617
Chatham's Place 7575 Doctor Philips Blvd	Orlando	FL	32819	407-345-2992	345-0307
Web: www.chathamsplace.com					
Cheesecake Factory 4200 Conroy Rd	Orlando	FL	32839	407-226-0333	226-9020
Web: www.cheesecakefactory.com					
Christini's 7600 Dr Phillips Blvd	Orlando	FL	32819	407-345-8770	345-8700
Web: www.christinis.com					
Ciao Italia 6149 Westwood Blvd	Orlando	FL	32821	407-354-0770	370-0124
Web: www.ciaoitaliaonline.com					
Dux 9801 International Dr	Orlando	FL	32819	407-345-4550	
Emeril's Orlando 6000 Universal Blvd Suite 702	Orlando	FL	32819	407-224-2424	224-2525
Web: www.emerils.com/restaurants					
Emeril's Tchoup Chop					
Universal Orlando's Royal Pacific Resort 6300 Hollywood Way	Orlando	FL	32819	407-503-2467	503-3344
Web: www.emerils.com/restaurants/orlando_tchoupchop					
Fuji Sushi 6700 Conroy Rd	Orlando	FL	32835	407-298-2989	
Fusian 12281 University Blvd	Orlando	FL	32817	407-736-8987	737-0803
Web: www.myfusian.com					
Hard Rock Cafe 6050 Universal Blvd	Orlando	FL	32819	407-351-7625	351-3983
Web: www.hardrock.com					
Harvey's Bistro 390 N Orange Ave	Orlando	FL	32801	407-246-6560	246-6561
Hemingway's 1 Grand Cypress Blvd	Orlando	FL	32836	407-239-1234	239-3800
Hemisphere 9300 Airport Blvd	Orlando	FL	32827	407-825-1234	849-9652
Hue 629 E Central Blvd	Orlando	FL	32801	407-849-1800	872-3348
Web: www.huerestaurant.com					
Ichiban 19 S Orange Ave	Orlando	FL	32801	407-423-2688	
Web: www.ichibanrestaurant.com					
Journeys World Inspired Cuisine 1831 W State Rd 434	Orlando	FL	32750	407-629-2221	
Web: www.journeysrestaurant.net					
Julie's Waterfront 4201 S Orange Ave	Orlando	FL	32806	407-240-2557	857-5850
Web: www.julieswaterfront.com					
K Restaurant & Wine Bar 2401 Edgewater Dr	Orlando	FL	32804	407-872-2332	872-7983
Web: www.krestaurantwinebar.com					
Kobe Japanese Steakhouse & Wine Bar 8350 International Dr	Orlando	FL	32819	407-352-1811	352-1158
Web: www.kobesteakhouse.com					
La Coquina 1 Grand Cypress Blvd	Orlando	FL	32836	407-239-1234	239-3800
Le Coq au Vin 4800 S Orange Ave	Orlando	FL	32806	407-851-6980	248-0658
Web: www.lecoqauvinrestaurant.com					
Linda's La Cantina 4721 E Colonial Dr	Orlando	FL	32803	407-894-4491	894-6415
Web: www.lindaslacantina.com					
Little Saigon 1106 E Colonial Dr	Orlando	FL	32803	407-423-8539	
Manuel's on the 28th 390 N Orange Ave 28th Fl	Orlando	FL	32801	407-246-6580	246-6575
Web: www.manuelsonthe28th.com					
Margarita's Grill 587 S Chicasaw Trail	Orlando	FL	32825	407-380-2600	380-8998
McCormick & Schmick's 4200 Conroy Rd Suite 146	Orlando	FL	32839	407-226-6515	226-6516
Web: www.mccormickandschmicks.com					

				Phone	Fax
Ming Court 9188 International Dr	Orlando	FL	32819	407-351-9988	252-2524
MoonFish 7525 W Sand Lake Rd	Orlando	FL	32819	407-363-7262	345-0097
Web: www.fishfusion.com					
Morton's The Steakhouse 7600 Dr Phillips Blvd	Orlando	FL	32819	407-248-3485	248-8559
Web: www.mortons.com					
NASCAR Cafe 6000 Universal Blvd Universal CityWalk	Orlando	FL	32819	407-224-7223	224-2001
Web: www.nascarcafe.com					
Palm 5800 Universal Blvd Hard Rock Hotel	Orlando	FL	32819	407-503-7256	503-2383
Web: www.thepalm.com					
Roy's 7760 W Sand Lake Rd	Orlando	FL	32819	407-352-4844	352-3733
Web: www.roysrestaurant.com					
Ruth's Chris Steak House 7501 W Sand Lake Rd	Orlando	FL	32819	407-226-3900	226-3108
Web: www.ruthschris.com					
Seasons 52 7700 W Sand Lake Rd	Orlando	FL	32819	407-354-5212	345-1109
Web: www.seasons52.com					
Straub's Fine Seafood 5101 E Colonial Dr	Orlando	FL	32803	407-273-9330	823-8921
Web: www.straubsseafood.com					
Sushi House of Orlando 1311 Florida Mall Ave	Orlando	FL	32809	407-812-9767	
Web: www.sushihouseorlando.com					
Thai House 2117 E Colonial Dr	Orlando	FL	32803	407-898-0820	898-1375
Trey Yuen Restaurant 6800 Visitors Cir	Orlando	FL	32819	407-352-6822	226-0281
Viet Garden 1237-1239 E Colonial Dr	Orlando	FL	32803	407-896-4154	
Web: www.vietgardenorlando.com					
Vito's Chop House 8633 International Dr	Orlando	FL	32819	407-354-2467	226-0914
Web: www.vitoschophouse.com					
Bice 313 1/2 Worth Ave	Palm Beach	FL	33480	561-835-1600	
Cafe Boulud 301 Australian Ave	Palm Beach	FL	33480	561-655-6060	655-5060
Web: www.danielnyc.com/cafeboulud					
Cafe Cellini 2505 S Ocean Blvd	Palm Beach	FL	33480	561-588-1871	
Cafe L'Europe 331 S County Rd	Palm Beach	FL	33480	561-655-4020	659-6619
Web: www.cafeleurope.com					
Chez Jean-Pierre Bistro 132 N County Rd	Palm Beach	FL	33480	561-833-1171	
Echo 230A Sunrise Ave	Palm Beach	FL	33480	561-802-4222	
Web: www.echopalmbeach.com					
Flagler Steakhouse 2 S County Rd	Palm Beach	FL	33480	561-659-8471	659-8485
L'Escalier at the Florentine Room 1 S County Rd	Palm Beach	FL	33480	561-659-8480	655-2947
Renato's 87 Via Mizner	Palm Beach	FL	33480	561-655-9752	
Web: www.ninos-vincents.com					
Restaurant The 2800 S Ocean Blvd	Palm Beach	FL	33480	561-582-2800	
Trevini 150 Worth Ave	Palm Beach	FL	33480	561-833-3883	835-9115
Web: www.treviniristorante.com					
Cafe Chardonnay 4533 PGA Blvd	Palm Beach Gardens	FL	33418	561-627-2662	627-3413
Web: www.cafechardonnay.com					
River House The 2373 PGA Blvd	Palm Beach Gardens	FL	33410	561-694-1188	
Web: www.riverhouse-restaurant.com					
Shula's Steak House 400 Avenue of the Champions	Palm Beach Gardens	FL	33418	561-627-2000	624-3117
Web: www.donshula.com					
Capriccio 2424 N University Dr	Pembroke Pines	FL	33024	954-432-7001	
Web: www.capriccios.net					
Angus The 1101 Scenic Hwy	Pensacola	FL	32503	850-432-0539	433-9060
Web: www.anguspensacola.com/					
Brews Brothers 847 N Navy Blvd	Pensacola	FL	32507	850-456-2537	
Cazadores 8183 W Fairfield Dr	Pensacola	FL	32506	850-457-4747	457-2823
Copeland's 400 E Chase St	Pensacola	FL	32501	850-432-7738	432-0138
Fish House The 600 S Barracks St	Pensacola	FL	32501	850-470-0003	470-0694
Web: www.goodgrits.com					
Hall's Seafood 920 E Gregory St	Pensacola	FL	32501	850-438-9019	436-2676
Horizen 3102 E Strong St	Pensacola	FL	32503	850-432-7899	
Hunan Garden 1708 W Fairfield Dr	Pensacola	FL	32501	850-432-3433	
Jackson's 400 S Palafox St	Pensacola	FL	32501	850-469-9898	469-8198
Web: www.jacksonsrestaurant.com					
Jamie's French Restaurant 424 E Zarragossa St	Pensacola	FL	32501	850-434-2911	434-8180
Los Rancheros 7250 Plantation Rd	Pensacola	FL	32504	850-476-1623	
McGuire's Irish Pub 600 E Gregory St	Pensacola	FL	32501	850-433-6789	434-5400
Web: www.mcguiresirishpub.com					
Melting Pot The 418 Gregory St	Pensacola	FL	32501	850-438-4030	433-7664
Web: www.meltingpot.com					
Monterrey's Mexican Grill 5030 Bayou Blvd	Pensacola	FL	32503	850-479-7351	494-1891
Oscar's Restaurant 2805 W Cervantes St	Pensacola	FL	32505	850-432-8388	
Petrella's Italian Cafe 2174 W Nine Mile Rd	Pensacola	FL	32534	850-471-9444	417-9336
Web: www.petrellasitaliancafe.com					
Siam Thai 6403 N 9th Ave	Pensacola	FL	32504	850-479-2882	479-2769
Skopelos on the Bay 670 Scenic Hwy	Pensacola	FL	32503	850-432-6565	438-9396
Web: skopelosrestaurant.com/					
Tokyo Japanese Steakhouse 312 E Nine Mile Rd	Pensacola	FL	32514	850-479-9111	479-5881
Web: www.tokyopensacola.com					
Vallarta 8971 Pensacola Blvd	Pensacola	FL	32534	850-476-5262	
Yamato Oriental Cuisine 131 N New Warrington Rd	Pensacola	FL	32506	850-453-3461	
Web: www.yamatodining.com/					
Captain's Tavern 9621 S Dixie Hwy	Pinecrest	FL	33156	305-666-5979	665-9753
Fleming A Taste of Denmark 8511 SW 136th St	Pinecrest	FL	33156	305-232-6444	232-5834
Web: www.flemingatasteofdenmark.com					
Caspian Persian Grill 7821 W Sunrise Blvd	Plantation	FL	33322	954-236-9955	382-4027
India House 1711 N University Dr	Plantation	FL	33311	954-565-5701	
Web: www.indiahouserestaurant.com					
Cafe Maxx 2601 E Atlantic Blvd	Pompano Beach	FL	33062	954-782-0606	782-0648
Web: www.cafemaxx.com					
Booth's Bowery 3657 S Nova Rd	Port Orange	FL	32129	386-761-9464	761-7518
Web: www.boothsbowery.com					
Kiwi's Down Under 65 Dunlawton Ave	Port Orange	FL	32127	386-322-1708	322-1780
95 Cordova 95 Cordova St	Saint Augustine	FL	32084	904-810-6810	810-6811
Web: www.95cordova.com					
Acapulco Restaurant 1835 US 1 S Suites 133-135	Saint Augustine	FL	32084	904-826-0191	
Web: www.acabay.com					
Amici's 1915-B A1A S	Saint Augustine	FL	32084	904-461-0102	461-3457
Barnacle Bill's 14 Castillo Dr	Saint Augustine	FL	32084	904-824-3663	
Web: www.barnaclebillsonline.com					
Beachcomber Restaurant 2 A St	Saint Augustine	FL	32080	904-471-3744	
Cap's 4325 Myrtle St	Saint Augustine	FL	32095	904-824-8794	829-0709
Web: www.capsonthewater.com					
Columbia Restaurant 98 Saint George St	Saint Augustine	FL	32084	904-824-3341	824-1361
Web: www.columbiarestaurant.com					
Conch House Restaurant 57 Comares Ave Conch House Marina Resort	Saint Augustine	FL	32080	904-829-8646	829-5414
Web: www.conch-house.com/restrnt2.htm					
Cortesse's Bistro 172 San Marco Ave	Saint Augustine	FL	32084	904-825-6775	
Web: www.cortessesbistro.com					
Creekside Dinery 160 Nix Boat Yard Rd	Saint Augustine	FL	32086	904-829-6113	
Fiddlers Green 2750 Anahma Dr	Saint Augustine	FL	32084	904-824-8897	824-5227
Fusion Point 237 San Marco Ave	Saint Augustine	FL	32084	904-823-1444	823-1445
Web: www.fusioncuisine.com					
Gypsy Cab Co 828 Anastasia Blvd	Saint Augustine	FL	32084	904-824-8244	829-9080
Web: www.gypsycab.com					
Jewel of the Sea 7601 A1A S	Saint Augustine	FL	32080	904-461-8841	461-4881
Kingfish Grill 252 Yacht Club Dr	Saint Augustine	FL	32084	904-824-2111	819-6765
Web: www.kingfishgrill.com					

				Phone	Fax
Kings Head British Pub 6460 US Hwy 1 N	Saint Augustine	FL	32095	904-823-9787	823-1466
La Parisienne 60 Hypolita St	Saint Augustine	FL	32084	904-829-0055	
Web: www.laparisienne.net					
Le Pavillon 45 San Marco Ave	Saint Augustine	FL	32084	904-824-6202	824-1024
Web: www.lepav.com					
Manatee Cafe 525 SR 16 Suite 106	Saint Augustine	FL	32084	904-826-0210	826-4080
Web: www.manateecafe.com					
Mikado Steak House 1092 S Ponce de Leon Blvd	Saint Augustine	FL	32086	904-824-7064	
Oasis Deck & Restaurant 4000 A1A S	Saint Augustine	FL	32084	904-471-3424	471-2739
Web: www.worldfamousoasis.com					
Opus 39 39 Cordova St	Saint Augustine	FL	32084	904-824-0402	824-5009
Web: www.opus39.com					
O'Steen's 205 Anastasia Blvd	Saint Augustine	FL	32080	904-829-6974	
Raintree 102 San Marco Ave	Saint Augustine	FL	32084	904-824-7211	824-8909
Web: www.raintreerestaurant.com/					
Reef The 4100 Coastal Hwy	Saint Augustine	FL	32084	904-824-8008	824-9991
Web: www.thereefstaugustine.com					
Salt Water Cowboy's 299 Dondanville Rd	Saint Augustine	FL	32084	904-471-2332	471-8997
Web: www.saltwatercowboys.com					
Santa Maria Restaurant 135 Avenida Menendez	Saint Augustine	FL	32084	904-829-6578	824-9214
South Beach Grill 45 Cubbedge Rd	Saint Augustine	FL	32086	904-471-8700	471-6762
Web: www.southbeachgrill.net					
Sunset Grill 421 A1A Beach Blvd	Saint Augustine	FL	32084	904-471-5555	
Villa Santa Monica 105 D St	Saint Augustine Beach	FL	32080	904-826-0209	
Maritana Grille 3400 Gulf Blvd	Saint Pete Beach	FL	33706	727-360-1881	363-5034
9 Bangkok Restaurant 571 Central Ave	Saint Petersburg	FL	33701	727-894-5990	826-6164
Alfredino's on the Beach 7141 Gulf Blvd	Saint Petersburg	FL	33706	727-367-9999	
Web: www.alfredinosonthebeach.com					
Arigato Japanese Steak House 3600 66th St N	Saint Petersburg	FL	33710	727-343-5200	344-3869
Athenian Garden 6940 22nd Ave N	Saint Petersburg	FL	33710	727-345-7040	
Basta's Fine Italian Cuisine 1625 4th St S	Saint Petersburg	FL	33701	727-894-7880	
Web: www.bastas.net					
Bonefish Grill 5901 4th St N	Saint Petersburg	FL	33703	727-521-3434	
Web: www.bonefishgrill.com					
Carmelita's 5211 Park St	Saint Petersburg	FL	33709	727-545-2956	545-8569
Chateau France 136 4th Ave NE	Saint Petersburg	FL	33701	727-894-7163	894-0221
Web: www.chateaufrancecuisine.com					
Chattaway 358 22nd Ave S	Saint Petersburg	FL	33705	727-823-1594	
Cody's Original Roadhouse 7022 22nd Ave N	Saint Petersburg	FL	33710	727-345-1022	381-4604
Web: www.codysoriginalroadhouse.com					
Columbia Restaurant 800 2nd Ave NE 4th Fl	Saint Petersburg	FL	33701	727-822-8000	821-9125
Web: www.columbiarestaurant.com					
Crazy Conch Cafe 1110 Pinellas Bay Way S	Saint Petersburg	FL	33715	727-865-0633	
Dave's 2339 9th St N	Saint Petersburg	FL	33704	727-895-6057	
Fresco's Waterfront Bar & Grill 300 2nd Ave NE	Saint Petersburg	FL	33701	727-894-4429	894-0377
Web: www.frescosrestaurant.com					
Garden Bistro 217 Central Ave	Saint Petersburg	FL	33701	727-896-3800	
Julian's 256 2nd St N	Saint Petersburg	FL	33701	727-823-6382	822-4826
Marbo of Fourth Street 8123 4th St N	Saint Petersburg	FL	33702	727-578-3080	
Marchand's Grill 501 5th Ave NE Renaissance Vinoy Resort	Saint Petersburg	FL	33701	727-894-1000	824-5044
Mattison's American Bistro 111 2nd Ave NE	Saint Petersburg	FL	33701	727-895-2200	
Web: www.mattisons.com					
Melting Pot The 2221 4th St N	Saint Petersburg	FL	33704	727-895-6358	894-7383
Web: www.meltingpot.com					
Pacific Wave 211 2nd St S	Saint Petersburg	FL	33701	727-822-5235	822-5456
Web: www.pacificwaveonline.com					
Pepin 4125 4th St N	Saint Petersburg	FL	33703	727-821-3773	822-5991
Red Mesa Restaurant 4912 4th St N	Saint Petersburg	FL	33703	727-527-8728	537-4798
Web: www.redmesarestaurant.com					
Redwoods 247 Central Ave	Saint Petersburg	FL	33701	727-896-5118	
Saffron's Restaurant & Catering 1700 Park St N	Saint Petersburg	FL	33710	727-345-6400	384-5612
Web: www.saffronscuisine.com					
Siam Garden 3125 9th St N	Saint Petersburg	FL	33704	727-822-0613	
Web: www.siamgardenthai1.com					
Skyway Jack's 2795 34th St S	Saint Petersburg	FL	33711	727-867-1907	
Spoto's Steak Joint 4871 Park St N	Saint Petersburg	FL	33709	727-545-9481	545-4615
Tangelo's Grille 226 1st Ave N	Saint Petersburg	FL	33701	727-894-1695	821-7027
Ted Peter's 1350 Pasadena Ave S	Saint Petersburg	FL	33707	727-381-7931	
Tokyo Bay 5901 Sun Blvd	Saint Petersburg	FL	33715	727-867-0770	
Web: www.tokyobay.verizonsupersite.com					
Bijou Cafe 1287 1st St	Sarasota	FL	34236	941-366-8111	366-7510
Web: www.bijoucafe.net					
Cafe Amici 1371 Main St	Sarasota	FL	34236	941-951-6896	
Cafe Baci 4001 S Tamiami Trail	Sarasota	FL	34231	941-921-4848	923-8643
Web: www.cafebaci.net					
Cafe L'Europe 431 St Armands Cir	Sarasota	FL	34237	941-388-4415	388-2362
Captain Brian's 8421 N Tamiami Trail	Sarasota	FL	34243	941-351-4492	
Chutney's Etc 1944 Hillview St	Sarasota	FL	34239	941-954-4444	
Web: www.chutneysetc.com					
Columbia 411 St Armands Cir	Sarasota	FL	34236	941-388-3987	388-3321
Web: www.columbiarestaurant.com					
Demetrio's 4410 S Tamiami Trail	Sarasota	FL	34231	941-922-1585	
Fred's 1917 S Osprey Ave	Sarasota	FL	34239	941-364-5811	
Marie's Italian Kitchen 5767 Beneva Rd	Sarasota	FL	34233	941-923-1000	923-7677
Web: www.marieskitchen.com					
Mediterraneo 1970 Main St	Sarasota	FL	34236	941-365-4122	954-0106
Michael's on East 1212 East Ave S	Sarasota	FL	34237	941-366-0007	
Morel 3809 S Tuttle Ave	Sarasota	FL	34239	941-927-8716	922-3390
Web: www.morelrestaurant.com					
Old Salty Dog 1601 Ken Thompson Pkwy	Sarasota	FL	34236	941-388-4311	
Web: www.theoldsaltydog.com					
Patricks 1400 Main St	Sarasota	FL	34236	941-952-1170	
Phillippi Creek Village Restaurant & Oyster Bar 5353 S Tamiami Trail	Sarasota	FL	34231	941-925-4444	923-2861
Web: www.creekseafood.com/					
Ruth's Chris Steak House 5700 S Tamiami Trail	Sarasota	FL	34231	941-924-9442	924-8982
TF: 800-544-0808 ■ *Web:* www.ruthschris.com					
Saga Japanese Steak House 8383 S Tamiami Trail	Sarasota	FL	34238	941-924-2800	
Selva Grill 1345 Main St	Sarasota	FL	34236	941-362-4427	556-0989
Web: www.selvagrill.com					
Tandoor 3440 Clark Rd S	Sarasota	FL	34231	941-926-3077	
Zoria 1991 Main St Suite 118	Sarasota	FL	34236	941-955-4457	955-4328
Web: www.zoria.net					
Ophelia's on the Bay 9105 Midnight Pass Rd	Siesta Key	FL	34242	941-349-2212	349-3328
Web: www.opheliasonthebay.net					
Martini's Chophouse 1815 S Ridgewood Ave	South Daytona	FL	32119	386-763-1090	
Web: www.martinischophouse.com					
Songkran Thai Restaurant 2309 S Ridgewood Ave	South Daytona Beach	FL	32119	386-760-0300	
Two Chefs 8287 S Dixie Hwy	South Miami	FL	33143	305-663-2100	
Legal Sea Foods 2602 Sawgrass Mills Cir	Sunrise	FL	33323	954-846-9011	846-1162
Web: www.legalseafood.com					
Rainforest Cafe 12801 W Sunrise Blvd	Sunrise	FL	33322	954-851-1015	851-1016
Web: www.rainforestcafe.com					
Cafe Ragazzi 9500 Harding Ave	Surfside	FL	33154	305-866-4495	
Albert's Provence 1415 Timberline Rd	Tallahassee	FL	32312	850-894-9003	893-8996

Florida (Cont'd)

Name / Address	City	State	Zip	Phone	Fax
Andrew's 228 228 S Adams St	Tallahassee	FL	32301	850-222-3444	222-2433
Web: www.andrewsdowntown.com					
Angelo's 2910 Kerry Forest Pkwy	Tallahassee	FL	32309	850-894-9997	
Anthony's 1950 Thomasville Rd	Tallahassee	FL	32303	850-224-1447	561-8332
Web: www.anthonysitalianrestaurant.net					
Bahn Thai Restaurant 1319 S Monroe St	Tallahassee	FL	32301	850-224-4765	
Bamboo House 112 E 6th Ave	Tallahassee	FL	32303	850-224-9099	
Barnacle Bill's 1830 N Monroe St	Tallahassee	FL	32303	850-385-8734	385-6298
Bonefish Grill 3491 Thomasville Rd	Tallahassee	FL	32308	850-297-0460	297-0465
Web: www.bonefishgrill.com					
Cabo's Island Grill & Bar 1221 Apalachee Pkwy	Tallahassee	FL	32301	850-878-3332	878-7835
Web: www.cabosgrill.com					
Cafe Cabernet 1019 N Monroe St	Tallahassee	FL	32303	850-224-1175	
Web: www.cafecabernet.com					
Carlos' Cuban Cafe 402 E Tennessee St	Tallahassee	FL	32301	850-222-8581	
Chez Pierre 1215 Thomasville Rd	Tallahassee	FL	32303	850-222-0936	681-3507
Web: www.chezpierre.com					
Chou's Dynasty 3507 Maclay Blvd	Tallahassee	FL	32312	850-906-0990	906-0967
Clusters & Hops 707 N Monroe St	Tallahassee	FL	32303	850-222-2669	
Web: www.winencheese.com					
Crystal River Seafood 1968 W Tennessee St	Tallahassee	FL	32304	850-575-4418	
Cypress The 320 E Tennessee St	Tallahassee	FL	32301	850-513-1100	
Web: www.cypressrestaurant.com					
Food Glorious Food 1950 Thomasville Rd Betton Pl	Tallahassee	FL	32303	850-224-9974	224-4673
Web: www.foodgloriousfood.com					
Georgio's 3425 Thomasville Rd	Tallahassee	FL	33209	850-893-4161	668-2674
Julie's Place 2901 N Monroe St	Tallahassee	FL	32303	850-386-7181	422-3619
Web: www.juliesplace.net					
Kitcho 1415 Timberlane Rd Suite 121	Tallahassee	FL	32312	850-893-7686	
Longhorn Steakhouse 2400 N Monroe St	Tallahassee	FL	32304	850-385-4028	383-0466
Los Compadres 2102 W Pensacola St	Tallahassee	FL	32304	850-576-8946	576-7900
Marie Livingston's Steakhouse & Saloon 2714 Graves Rd	Tallahassee	FL	32303	850-562-2525	562-0262
Melting Pot The 1832 N Monroe St	Tallahassee	FL	32303	850-386-7440	386-8410
Web: www.meltingpot.com					
Mom & Dad's 4175 Apalachee Pkwy	Tallahassee	FL	32311	850-877-4518	
Nino 6497 Apalachee Pkwy	Tallahassee	FL	32311	850-878-8141	
Web: mynetworkusa.com/nino/					
Osaka Japanese Steak House 1690 Raymond Diehl Rd	Tallahassee	FL	32308	850-531-0022	
Samrat 2529 Apalachee Pkwy	Tallahassee	FL	32301	850-942-1993	942-8091
San Miguel 200 W Tharpe St	Tallahassee	FL	32303	850-385-3346	
Scales & Tails 2741 Capital Cir NE	Tallahassee	FL	32308	850-385-9992	385-5589
Silver Slipper 531 Silver Slipper Ln	Tallahassee	FL	32303	850-386-9366	422-0825
Web: www.thesilverslipper.com					
Smokey Bones BBQ 3131 Capital Cir NE	Tallahassee	FL	32308	850-386-2480	386-3914
Web: www.smokeybones.com					
Z Bardhi 3596 Kinhega Dr	Tallahassee	FL	32312	850-894-9919	894-2466
3 Palms Grille & Gallery 8203 N Armenia Ave	Tampa	FL	33604	813-933-2401	932-9202
Web: 3palms.hgolub.com/3palms/					
Angithi 2047 E Fowler Ave	Tampa	FL	33612	813-979-4889	972-0401
Armani's 2900 Bayport Dr	Tampa	FL	33607	813-207-6800	207-6804
Web: www.armanisrestaurant.com					
Bamboo Club 2223 N Westshore Blvd Suite 212	Tampa	FL	33607	813-353-0326	353-0367
Web: www.thebambooclub.com					
Bern's Steak House 1208 S Howard Ave	Tampa	FL	33606	813-251-2421	
Web: www.bernssteakhouse.com					
Boizao Steakhouse 4606 W Boy Scout Blvd	Tampa	FL	33607	813-286-7100	286-7113
Web: www.boizao.com					
Byblos Cafe 2832 S MacDill Ave	Tampa	FL	33629	813-805-7977	837-0951
Web: www.bybloscafe.com					
Cafe Anna 3671 S Westshore Blvd	Tampa	FL	33629	813-831-0694	
Web: www.cafeanna.net					
Cafe BT 3324 W Gandy Blvd	Tampa	FL	33611	813-831-9254	
Caffe Amaretto 5915 N Memorial Hwy Suite R	Tampa	FL	33615	813-885-4700	885-9326
Caffe Paridiso 4205 S MacDill Ave	Tampa	FL	33611	813-835-6622	
Capdevila at Lateresita 3248 W Columbus Dr	Tampa	FL	33607	813-879-9704	871-2321
Castaways The 7720 Courtney Campbell Cswy	Tampa	FL	33607	813-281-0770	281-2215
Charley's Steakhouse 4444 W Cypress St	Tampa	FL	33607	813-353-9706	353-9510
Donatello 232 N Dale Mabry Hwy	Tampa	FL	33609	813-875-6660	876-3644
Web: www.donatellorestaurant.com/					
Fleming's Prime Steakhouse & Wine Bar 4322 W Boy Scout Blvd	Tampa	FL	33607	813-874-9463	673-8661
Web: www.flemingssteakhouse.com					
Ichiban 2786A E Fowler Ave	Tampa	FL	33612	813-978-8095	
Jackson's Bistro 601 S Harbor Island Blvd	Tampa	FL	33602	813-277-0112	277-0114
Web: www.jacksonsbistro.com					
Jasmine 13248 N Dale Mabry Hwy	Tampa	FL	33618	813-968-1501	
Jimbo's Pit BBQ 4103 W Kennedy Blvd	Tampa	FL	33609	813-289-9724	
Kojak's House of Ribs 2808 W Gandy Blvd	Tampa	FL	33611	813-837-3774	837-2179
Web: www.kojaksbbq.com					
Mangroves Bar & Grille 208 S Howard Ave	Tampa	FL	33602	813-258-3302	250-9802
Web: www.mangrovesseafoodgrille.com					
Melting Pot The 13164 N Dale Mabry Hwy	Tampa	FL	33618	813-962-6936	962-0125
Web: www.meltingpot.com					
Mise En Place 442 W Kennedy Blvd	Tampa	FL	33606	813-254-5373	
Web: www.miseonline.com					
Palm The 205 Westshore Plaza Dr	Tampa	FL	33609	813-849-7256	849-0878
Web: www.thepalm.com					
PF Chang's China Bistro 219 Westshore Plaza	Tampa	FL	33069	813-289-8400	289-8403
Web: www.pfchangs.com					
Polo's Italian Grill 19040 Bruce B Downs Blvd	Tampa	FL	33647	813-615-0087	
Web: www.polositaliangrill.com					
Roy's 4342 W Boy Scout Blvd	Tampa	FL	33607	813-873-7697	
Web: www.roysrestaurant.com					
Rusty Pelican 2425 N Rocky Point Dr	Tampa	FL	33607	813-281-1943	289-3782
Ruth's Chris Steak House 1700 N Westshore Blvd	Tampa	FL	33607	813-282-1118	281-0982
Web: www.ruthschris.com					
Sam Seltzer's Steakhouse 4744 N Dale Mabry Hwy	Tampa	FL	33614	813-873-7267	879-4744
Web: www.samseltzers.com					
Sawatdee Thai Cuisine 10938 N 56th St	Tampa	FL	33617	813-985-2071	
Shula's Steak House 4860 W Kennedy Blvd	Tampa	FL	33609	813-286-4366	286-4034
Web: www.donshula.com					
Sidebern's 2208 W Morrison Ave	Tampa	FL	33606	813-258-2233	259-9463
Web: www.bernssteakhouse.com					
Six Tables 4267 Henderson Blvd	Tampa	FL	33629	813-207-0527	
Web: www.sixtablestampa.com					
Taj Indian Cuisine 2734 E Fowler Ave	Tampa	FL	33612	813-971-8483	972-3587
TC Choy's 301 S Howard Ave	Tampa	FL	33608	813-521-1191	
Thai Terrace 2055-C N Dale Mabry Hwy	Tampa	FL	33607	813-877-8955	
Zaeem Palace 3333 S Westshore Blvd	Tampa	FL	33629	813-832-1188	832-4004
Web: zaeempalace.com					
Bimini Twist 8480 Okeechobee Blvd	West Palm Beach	FL	33411	561-784-2660	784-2633
Cabana 118 S Clematis St	West Palm Beach	FL	33401	561-833-4773	514-0655
Cafe Protege 2400 Metrocentre Blvd	West Palm Beach	FL	33407	561-687-2433	
Web: www.cafeprotege.com					
Capri Blu 116 N Dixie Hwy	West Palm Beach	FL	33401	561-832-4300	832-0900
Web: www.capriblulflorida.com					
City Cellar Wine Bar & Grill 700 S Rosemary Ave	West Palm Beach	FL	33401	561-366-0071	366-8541
La Sirena 6316 S Dixie Hwy	West Palm Beach	FL	33405	561-585-3128	
Leila 120 S Dixie Hwy	West Palm Beach	FL	33401	561-659-7373	
Maison Carlos 207 Clematis St	West Palm Beach	FL	33401	561-659-6524	
Morton's The Steakhouse 777 S Flagler Dr	West Palm Beach	FL	33401	561-835-9664	835-4806
Web: www.mortons.com					
Nando's Beefeeder's Steakhouse 3208 Forest Hill Blvd	West Palm Beach	FL	33406	561-649-4545	
Okeechobee Steakhouse 2854 Okeechobee Blvd	West Palm Beach	FL	33409	561-683-5151	684-7402
Painted Horse Cafe 2417 S Dixie Hwy	West Palm Beach	FL	33401	561-833-1490	
Web: www.paintedhorsecafe.com					
PF Chang's China Bistro 3101 PGA Blvd	West Palm Beach	FL	33410	561-691-1610	691-0147
Web: www.pfchangs.com					
Raindancer Steak House 2300 Palm Beach Lakes Blvd	West Palm Beach	FL	33409	561-684-2810	
Web: www.raindancersteakhouse.com					
Rhythm Cafe 3800 S Dixie Hwy	West Palm Beach	FL	33405	561-833-3406	
Web: www.rhythmcafe.cc					
Spoto's Oyster Bar 125 Datura St	West Palm Beach	FL	33401	561-835-1828	
Stresa 2710 Okeechobee Blvd	West Palm Beach	FL	33409	561-615-0200	615-0350
Sushi Rok 106 N Olive St	West Palm Beach	FL	33401	561-802-9906	802-9908
Tsunami 651 Okeechobee Blvd	West Palm Beach	FL	33401	561-835-9696	
Boondocks Restaurant 3948 S Peninsula Dr	Wilbur by the Sea	FL	32127	386-760-9001	
Houston's 215 S Orlando Ave	Winter Park	FL	32789	407-740-4005	740-4050
Web: www.houstons.com					
Columbia Restaurant 2117 E 7th Ave	Ybor City	FL	33605	813-248-4961	248-1718
Web: www.columbiarestaurant.com					

Georgia

Name / Address	City	State	Zip	Phone	Fax
Di Paolo Cucina 8560 Holcomb Bridge Rd	Alpharetta	GA	30022	770-587-1051	587-1195
Web: www.dipaolorestaurant.com					
5 Seasons Brewing Co 5600 Roswell Rd Suite 21	Atlanta	GA	30342	404-255-5911	255-5966
Web: www.5seasonsbrewing.com					
10 Degrees South 4183 Roswell Rd NE	Atlanta	GA	30342	404-705-8870	
Web: www.10degreessouth.com					
Agave 242 Boulevard SE	Atlanta	GA	30312	404-588-0006	588-0909
Web: www.agaverestaurant.com					
Ali-Oli 3535 Peachtree Rd Suite 105	Atlanta	GA	30326	404-266-0414	266-3855
Web: www.aliolirestaurant.com					
Anis Cafe & Bistro 2974 Grandview Ave	Atlanta	GA	30305	404-233-9889	233-4894
Web: www.anisbistro.com					
Annie's Thai Castle 3195 Roswell Rd	Atlanta	GA	30305	404-264-9546	
Anthony's Plantation Restaurant 3109 Piedmont Rd NE	Atlanta	GA	30305	404-262-7379	261-6009
Web: www.anthonysfinedining.com					
Antica Posta 519 E Paces Ferry Rd	Atlanta	GA	30305	404-262-7112	262-7335
Web: www.anticaposta.com					
Aria Restaurant 490 E Paces Ferry Rd NE	Atlanta	GA	30305	404-233-7673	262-5208
Web: www.aria-atl.com					
Atlanta Fish Market 265 Pharr Rd NE	Atlanta	GA	30305	404-262-3165	601-1315
Web: www.buckheadrestaurants.com					
Atlanta Grill 181 Peachtree St NE	Atlanta	GA	30303	404-221-6550	215-4672
Atmosphere 1620 Piedmont Ave	Atlanta	GA	30324	678-702-1620	702-1621
Web: www.atmospherebistro.com					
Babette's Cafe 573 N Highland Ave	Atlanta	GA	30307	404-523-9121	523-7909
Web: www.babettescafe.com					
Bacchanalia 1198 Howell Mill Rd	Atlanta	GA	30318	404-365-0410	365-8020
Bangkok Thai 1492 Piedmont Ave NE	Atlanta	GA	30309	404-874-2514	
Baraonda 710 Peachtree St	Atlanta	GA	30308	404-879-9962	892-3973
Web: www.baraondaatlanta.com					
Basil's Restaurant & Bar 2985 Grandview Ave NE	Atlanta	GA	30305	404-233-9755	
Web: www.basils.net					
Beautiful 2260 Cascade Rd SW	Atlanta	GA	30311	404-752-5931	758-4767
Web: www.beautifulrestaurant-atlanta.com					
Benihana 229 Peachtree St NE	Atlanta	GA	30303	404-522-9629	522-4834
Web: www.benihana.com					
Blue Ridge Grill 1261 W Paces Ferry Rd	Atlanta	GA	30327	404-233-5030	233-5023
Web: www.blueridgegrill.com					
BluePointe 3455 Peachtree Rd	Atlanta	GA	30326	404-237-9070	237-2387
Web: www.buckheadrestaurants.com/bluepointe/					
Bone's Restaurant 3130 Piedmont Rd NE	Atlanta	GA	30305	404-237-2663	233-5704
Web: www.bonesrestaurant.com					
Brasserie Le Coze 30 Ivan Allen Blvd	Atlanta	GA	30308	404-266-1440	266-1436
Web: www.brasserieatlanta.com					
Buckhead Bowl 3717 Roswell Rd NE	Atlanta	GA	30342	404-231-4433	237-6826
Buckhead Diner 3073 Piedmont Rd NE	Atlanta	GA	30305	404-262-3336	262-3593
Web: www.buckheadrestaurants.com					
Cafe The 3434 Peachtree Rd NE Ritz-Carlton Buckhead	Atlanta	GA	30326	404-237-2700	239-0078
Cafe Prego 4279 Roswell Rd	Atlanta	GA	30342	404-252-0032	
Cafe Sunflower 2140 Peachtree Rd	Atlanta	GA	30309	404-352-8859	352-2556
Web: www.cafesunflower.com					
Canoe 4199 Paces Ferry Rd NW	Atlanta	GA	30339	770-432-2808	433-2542
Web: www.canoe-atl.com					
Capital Grille The 255 E Paces Ferry Rd	Atlanta	GA	30305	404-262-1162	262-1163
Web: www.thecapitalgrille.com					
Chequers Seafood Grill 236 Perimeter Center Pkwy	Atlanta	GA	30346	770-391-9383	394-2055
Web: www.chequersseafood.com					
China Cooks 215 Northwood Dr	Atlanta	GA	30342	404-252-6611	256-8221
Chops/Lobster Bar 70 West Paces Ferry Rd NW	Atlanta	GA	30305	404-262-2675	240-6645
Web: www.buckheadrestaurants.com					
Chopstix 4279 Roswell Rd NE	Atlanta	GA	30342	404-255-4868	
Web: chopstixatlanta.net					
City Grill 50 Hurt Plaza	Atlanta	GA	30303	404-524-2489	529-9474
Web: www.citygrillatlanta.com					
Dailey's Restaurant 17 Andrew Young International Blvd	Atlanta	GA	30303	404-681-3303	681-6643
Web: www.daileysrestaurant.com					
Dish 870 N Highland Ave	Atlanta	GA	30306	404-897-3463	874-2886
Web: dish-atlanta.com					
Eclipse di Luna 764 Miami Cir	Atlanta	GA	30324	404-846-0449	869-7418
Web: www.eclipsediluna.com					
Emeril's Atlanta 3500 Lenox Rd 1 Alliance Center	Atlanta	GA	30326	404-564-5600	564-5611
Web: www.emerils.com					
Eno Restaurant & Wine Bar 800 Peachtree St Suite A	Atlanta	GA	30308	404-685-3191	685-3199
Web: www.enorestaurant.com					
Fat Matt's Rib Shack 1811 Piedmont Ave	Atlanta	GA	30324	404-607-1622	
Web: www.fatmattsribshack.com					
Figo Pasta/Osteria del Figo 1170B Collier Rd	Atlanta	GA	30318	404-351-9667	351-9677
Web: www.figopasta.com					
Fishmonger 4969 Roswell Rd Pier 160	Atlanta	GA	30342	404-459-9003	459-9006
Web: www.fishmongerseafoodgrill.com					
Floataway Cafe 1123 Zonolite Rd Suite 15	Atlanta	GA	30306	404-892-1414	892-8833
Web: www.starprovisions.com/float/					

Name / Address	City	State	Zip	Phone	Fax
Flying Biscuit Cafe 1655 McLendon Ave	Atlanta	GA	30307	404-687-8888	687-8838
Web: www.flyingbiscuit.com					
Fogo de Chao 3101 Piedmont Rd	Atlanta	GA	30326	404-266-9988	995-9983
Web: www.fogodechao.com					
Food Studio 887 W Marietta St NW	Atlanta	GA	30318	404-815-6677	815-4811
Web: www.thefoodstudio.com					
Fratelli di Napoli 2101 Tula St NW Suite B	Atlanta	GA	30309	404-351-1533	351-1204
Web: www.fratelli.net					
Fritti 311 N Highland Ave	Atlanta	GA	30307	404-880-9559	880-0462
Web: www.frittirestaurant.com					
Fuego Spanish Grill 1136 Crescent Ave NE	Atlanta	GA	30309	404-389-0660	389-0662
Web: www.fuegocafe.com					
Georgia Grille 2290 Peachtree Rd	Atlanta	GA	30309	404-352-3517	841-9964
Web: www.georgiagrille.com					
Goldfish 4400 Ashford Dunwoody Rd	Atlanta	GA	30346	770-671-0100	671-1887
Grand China 2975 Peachtree Rd NE	Atlanta	GA	30305	404-231-8690	231-5415
Web: www.grandchinaatl.com					
Hal's on Old Ivy 30 Old Ivy Rd	Atlanta	GA	30342	404-261-0025	814-1248
Web: hals.net					
Harmony 4897 Buford Hwy	Atlanta	GA	30341	770-457-7288	
Harold's Barbecue 171 McDonough Blvd SE	Atlanta	GA	30315	404-627-9268	627-0672
Web: www.haroldsbarbecue.com					
Harry & Sons 820 N Highland Ave	Atlanta	GA	30306	404-873-2009	
Web: www.harryandsonsrestaurant.com					
Haven 1441 Dresden Dr NE	Atlanta	GA	30319	404-969-0700	969-0701
Web: www.havenrestaurant.com					
Horseradish Grill 4320 Powers Ferry Rd	Atlanta	GA	30342	404-255-7277	847-0603
Web: www.horseradishgrill.com					
Hsu's Gourmet Chinese Restaurant 192 Peachtree Center Ave	Atlanta	GA	30303	404-659-2788	577-3456
Web: www.hsus.com					
Joel 3290 Northside Pkwy	Atlanta	GA	30327	404-233-3500	467-4750
Web: www.joelrestaurant.com					
Kyma 3085 Piedmont Rd	Atlanta	GA	30305	404-262-0702	841-9924
Web: www.buckheadrestaurants.com/kyma					
La Grotta 2637 Peachtree Rd	Atlanta	GA	30305	404-231-1368	231-1274
Web: www.la-grotta.com					
La Tavola Trattoria 992 Virginia Ave NE	Atlanta	GA	30306	404-873-5430	873-5410
Web: www.latavolatrattoria.com					
Le Giverny 1641 Clifton Rd	Atlanta	GA	30329	404-325-7252	325-8414
Web: www.legiverny.net					
Malaya 857 Collier Rd	Atlanta	GA	30318	404-609-9991	609-9892
Web: www.malayacuisine.com					
Mali Restaurant 961 Amsterdam Ave NE	Atlanta	GA	30306	404-874-1411	874-5112
Web: www.geocities.com/themali2001					
McCormick & Schmick's 190 Marietta St NW	Atlanta	GA	30318	404-521-1236	521-1236
Web: www.mccormickandschmicks.com					
McKendrick's Steak House 4505 Ashford Dunwoody Rd NE	Atlanta	GA	30346	770-512-8888	379-1470
Web: www.mckendricks.com					
MF Sushibar 265 Ponce de Leon Ave	Atlanta	GA	30308	404-815-8844	
Web: www.mfsushibar.com					
Mitra 818 Juniper St	Atlanta	GA	30308	404-875-5515	875-5510
Web: www.mitrarestaurant.com					
Morton's The Steakhouse 303 Peachtree Center Ave	Atlanta	GA	30308	404-577-4366	577-4687
Web: www.mortons.com					
Mu Lan 824 Juniper St NE	Atlanta	GA	30308	404-877-5797	877-5798
Web: www.mulanatl.com					
Nakato 1776 Cheshire Bridge Rd	Atlanta	GA	30324	404-873-6582	874-7897
Web: www.nakatorestaurant.com					
Nam 931 Monroe Dr NE	Atlanta	GA	30308	404-541-9997	
Web: www.namrestaurant.com					
Nan Thai 1350 Spring St NW	Atlanta	GA	30309	404-870-9933	870-9955
Web: www.nanfinedining.com					
Nava 3060 Peachtree Rd	Atlanta	GA	30305	404-240-1984	240-1381
Web: www.buckheadrestaurants.com					
New York Prime 3424 Peachtree Rd NE	Atlanta	GA	30326	404-846-0644	846-8584
Web: www.newyorkprime.com					
Nikolai's Roof 255 Courtland St	Atlanta	GA	30303	404-221-6362	221-6811
Web: www.nikolaisroof.com					
Nino's 1931 Cheshire Bridge Rd NE	Atlanta	GA	30324	404-874-6505	
Web: www.ninosatlanta.com					
Nuevo Laredo 1495 Chattahoochee Ave	Atlanta	GA	30318	404-352-9009	352-9202
Web: www.nuevolaredocantina.com					
Oscar's Villa Capri 2090 Dunwoody Club Dr	Atlanta	GA	30350	770-392-7940	
Web: www.oscarsvillacapri.com					
Pacific Rim Bistro 303 Peachtree Center Ave	Atlanta	GA	30308	404-893-0018	893-0020
Web: www.pacificrimbistro.com					
Palm Restaurant 3391 Peachtree Rd NE	Atlanta	GA	30326	404-814-1955	814-1985
Web: www.thepalm.com					
Pano's & Paul's 1232 W Paces Ferry Rd NW	Atlanta	GA	30327	404-261-3662	261-4512
Web: www.buckheadrestaurants.com					
Park 75 75 14th St	Atlanta	GA	30309	404-253-3840	253-3935
Paul's Restaurant 10 King Cir	Atlanta	GA	30305	404-231-4113	231-4710
PF Chang's China Bistro 500 Ashwood Pkwy	Atlanta	GA	30338	770-352-0500	352-0525
Web: www.pfchangs.com					
Portofino 3199 Paces Ferry Pl	Atlanta	GA	30305	404-231-1136	231-4773
Web: www.portofinobistro.com					
Pricci 500 Pharr Rd	Atlanta	GA	30305	404-237-2941	261-0058
Web: www.buckheadrestaurants.com					
Prime 3393 Peachtree Rd	Atlanta	GA	30326	404-812-0555	812-0225
Pura Vida 656 North Highland Ave NE	Atlanta	GA	30306	404-870-9797	870-9795
Web: www.puravidatapas.com					
Rathbun's 112 Krog St Suite R	Atlanta	GA	30307	404-524-8280	524-8580
Web: www.rathbunsrestaurant.com					
Ray's in the City 240 Peachtree St	Atlanta	GA	30303	404-524-9224	524-9229
Ritz-Carlton Dining Room 3434 Peachtree Rd NE	Atlanta	GA	30326	404-237-2700	
River Room 4403 Northside Pkwy NW	Atlanta	GA	30327	404-233-5455	233-3073
Web: www.riverroom.com					
Rolling Bones Premium Pit BBQ 377 Edgewood Ave SE	Atlanta	GA	30312	404-222-2324	221-1174
Web: www.rollingbonesbbq.com					
Roy's 3475 Piedmont Rd NE	Atlanta	GA	30305	404-231-3232	231-5956
Web: www.roysrestaurant.com					
Rustic Gourmet 1145 Zonolite Rd NE	Atlanta	GA	30306	404-881-1288	
Web: www.rusticgourmet.com					
Ruth's Chris Steak House 267 Marietta St	Atlanta	GA	30313	404-223-6500	223-1155
Web: www.ruthschrisatlanta.com					
Savu 111 Perimeter Center W	Atlanta	GA	30346	770-280-0700	
Soleil Bistro 3081 Maple Dr	Atlanta	GA	30305	404-467-1790	467-1430
Web: www.soleilbistro.com					
Sotto Sotto Cucina Italiana 313 N Highland Ave	Atlanta	GA	30307	404-523-6678	880-0462
Web: www.sottosottorestaurant.com					
South City Kitchen 1144 Crescent Ave	Atlanta	GA	30309	404-873-7358	873-0317
Web: www.southcitykitchen.com					
Sundown Cafe 2165 Cheshire Bridge Rd	Atlanta	GA	30324	404-321-1118	
Web: www.sundowncafe.com					
Surin of Thailand 810 N Highland Ave NE	Atlanta	GA	30306	404-892-7789	
Web: www.surinofthailand.com					

Name / Address	City	State	Zip	Phone	Fax
Taka 375 Pharr Rd NE	Atlanta	GA	30305	404-869-2802	926-0750
Web: www.taka-atlanta.com					
Tamarind 80 14th St NW	Atlanta	GA	30309	404-873-4888	
Thai Chili 2169 Briarcliff Rd NE	Atlanta	GA	30329	404-315-6750	315-9367
Web: www.thaichilicuisine.com					
Tierra 1425 Piedmont Ave NE	Atlanta	GA	30309	404-874-5951	874-5235
Web: www.tierrarestaurant.com					
Toni's Casa Napoli 2486 Mt Vernon Rd	Atlanta	GA	30338	770-394-9359	393-1842
Web: www.toniscasanapoli.com					
Top Spice 3007 N Druid Hills Rd	Atlanta	GA	30329	404-728-0588	728-1132
Web: www.topspicetocohills.com					
Tringali's Restaurant & Bar 94 Upper Prior St SW	Atlanta	GA	30303	404-522-6568	
Web: www.tringalisatlanta.com					
Veni-Vidi-Vici 41 14th St	Atlanta	GA	30309	404-875-8424	875-6533
Web: www.buckheadrestaurants.com/vvv.html					
Vinings Inn 3011 Paces Mill Rd SE	Atlanta	GA	30339	770-438-2282	438-0653
Web: www.viningsinn.com					
Vinocity Wine Bar & Restaurant 1963 Josea Williams Blvd	Atlanta	GA	30309	404-870-8886	702-0250*
*Fax Area Code: 678 ■ *Web:* www.vinocitywinebar.com					
Wisteria 471 N Highland Ave	Atlanta	GA	30307	404-525-3363	525-3313
Web: www.wisteria-atlanta.com					
Woodfire Grill 1782 Cheshire Bridge Rd	Atlanta	GA	30324	404-347-9055	347-9566
Web: www.woodfiregrill.com					
Augustino's 2 10th St	Augusta	GA	30901	706-823-6521	
Web: www.augustinos.net					
Bamboo Garden 819 15th St	Augusta	GA	30901	706-722-7300	
Beamie's 865 Reynolds St	Augusta	GA	30901	706-724-6593	724-7466
Bill's Family Restaurant 2518 Peach Orchard Rd	Augusta	GA	30906	706-790-4613	
Boll Weevil Cafe 10 9th St	Augusta	GA	30904	706-722-7772	722-7722
Web: www.uniquelyaugusta.com					
California Dreaming 3241 Washington Rd	Augusta	GA	30907	706-860-6206	860-4699
Web: www.californiadreamings.com					
Calvert's 475 Highland Ave	Augusta	GA	30909	706-738-4514	312-2121
Web: www.calvertsrestaurant.com					
Fat Man's Cafe 1717 Laney Walker Blvd	Augusta	GA	30904	706-733-1740	364-5696
Web: www.fatmans.com/cafe.asp					
Formosa's 3830 Washington Rd	Augusta	GA	30907	706-855-8998	855-9742
French Market Grille 425 Highland Ave	Augusta	GA	30909	706-737-4865	733-0275
Hot Foods by Calvin 2027 Broad St	Augusta	GA	30904	706-738-5666	738-5688
La Maison on Telfair 404 Telfair St	Augusta	GA	30901	706-722-4805	722-5177
Web: www.lamaisontelfair.com					
Luigi's 590 Broad St	Augusta	GA	30901	706-722-4056	
Web: www.luigisinc.com					
Ming Wah 920 Baker Ave	Augusta	GA	30904	706-733-0740	
Miyabi Kyoto Japanese Steak House 1315 Augusta West Pkwy	Augusta	GA	30909	706-210-2600	210-2618
Rhinehart's Oyster Bar 3051 Washington Rd	Augusta	GA	30907	706-860-2337	
Sconyer's Bar-B-Que 2250 Sconyers Way	Augusta	GA	30906	706-790-5411	790-1505
Shangri-La 3847 Washington Rd	Augusta	GA	30907	706-854-9791	
T-Bonz 1654 Gordon Hwy	Augusta	GA	30906	706-796-1875	796-1745
Web: www.tbonz.com					
T's Restaurant 3416 Mike Pagett Hwy	Augusta	GA	30906	706-798-4145	793-8474
Web: www.tsrestaurant.com					
Vallarta 2808 Washington Rd	Augusta	GA	30909	706-733-5584	737-1999
Verandah Grill 2110 Walton Way Partridge Inn	Augusta	GA	30904	706-737-8888	731-0826
Web: www.partridgeinn.com/dining					
Villa Europa 3044 Deans Bridge Rd	Augusta	GA	30906	706-798-6211	798-0066
Web: www.villaeuropa.com					
Ambra 148 W Main St	Cartersville	GA	30120	770-386-1960	
Web: www.ambradining.com					
Cafe Amici 2301 Airport Thwy Suite E2	Columbus	GA	31904	706-653-6361	653-6357
Chef Lee's Peking Chinese Restaurant 4248 Buena Vista Rd	Columbus	GA	31907	706-568-7554	569-6473
Country's Barbecue 3137 Mercury Dr	Columbus	GA	31906	706-563-7604	563-8839
Web: www.countrysbarbecue.com					
Don Chuco's 5770 Milgen Rd	Columbus	GA	31907	706-561-3040	
El Vaquero Restaurant 3135 Cross Country Plaza	Columbus	GA	31906	706-569-1420	569-8265
Los Amigos Mexican Restaurant 5592 Whitesville Rd	Columbus	GA	31904	706-322-1993	
Macon Road Barbecue 2703 Avalon Rd	Columbus	GA	31907	706-563-0542	563-0208
Mediterranean Cafe 5300 Sidney Simons Blvd	Columbus	GA	31904	706-320-9111	320-9112
Web: www.med-cafe.com					
Mikata Japanese Steakhouse 5300 Sidney Simons Blvd	Columbus	GA	31904	706-327-5100	
Web: www.mikatasteakhouse.com					
O'Charley's 1528 Bradley Park Dr	Columbus	GA	31904	706-324-2929	324-4656
Web: www.ocharleys.com					
Panda Garden 5600 Milgen Rd	Columbus	GA	31907	706-569-8487	
Saigon Oriental Restaurant 4403 17th Ave	Columbus	GA	31904	706-653-8540	653-8541
Shogun Japanese Steakhouse 1808 Manchester Expy	Columbus	GA	31904	706-327-4856	
Back Burner 2461 Riverside Dr	Macon	GA	31204	478-746-3336	746-2611
Bert's 442 Cherry St	Macon	GA	31201	478-742-9100	
Caliente's 6255 Zebulon Rd Suite 260	Macon	GA	31210	478-471-8110	471-8148
Web: www.calientesburritoshop.com					
Dawson's Kitchen 3360 Brookdale Ave	Macon	GA	31204	478-742-9852	
Downtown Grill 562 Mulberry Street Ln	Macon	GA	31201	478-742-5999	742-9708
El Azteca 169 Tom Hill Sr Blvd	Macon	GA	31210	478-475-9199	475-4409
Web: www.elaztecacantina.com					
Fincher's Barbeque 5267 Houston Rd	Macon	GA	31216	478-781-6998	
India Garden 5033 Brookhaven Rd	Macon	GA	31206	478-785-8540	785-0858
Logan's Roadhouse 3933 Arkwright Rd	Macon	GA	31210	478-477-8806	477-8637
Web: www.logansroadhouse.com					
Marco 4581 Forsyth Rd	Macon	GA	31210	478-405-5660	405-5668
Web: www.marcomacon.com					
Natalia's 2720 Riverside Plaza	Macon	GA	31204	478-741-1380	743-9388
Rain The 4632-A Presidential Pkwy	Macon	GA	31206	478-476-8895	
Saleem Fish Supreme 2198 Pio Nono Ave	Macon	GA	31206	478-788-8600	
San Marcos 2460 Riverside Dr	Macon	GA	31204	478-755-8858	755-0737
Tic Toc Room 408 ML King Jr Blvd	Macon	GA	31201	478-744-0123	744-0124
Edmund's 3935 Washington Rd	Martinez	GA	30907	706-863-4277	863-1185
Monterrey 4018 Washington Rd	Martinez	GA	30907	706-855-9949	855-6962
Aqua Blue 1564 Holcomb Bridge Rd	Roswell	GA	30076	770-643-8886	643-8851
Web: www.atlantaaquablue.com					
Dick & Harry's 1570 Holcomb Bridge Rd Suite 810	Roswell	GA	30076	770-641-8757	641-8884
Web: www.dickandharrys.com					
17 Hundred 90 Restaurant 307 E President St	Savannah	GA	31401	912-236-7122	
Web: www.17hundred90.com					
45 Bistro 123 E Broughton St	Savannah	GA	31401	912-644-7896	234-3334
Web: www.marshallhouse.com/dining.shtml					
45 South 20 E Broad St	Savannah	GA	31401	912-233-1881	234-1212
Alligator Soul 114 Barnard St	Savannah	GA	31401	912-232-7899	232-7898
Web: www.alligatorsoul.com					
Aquastar 1 Resort Dr	Savannah	GA	31421	912-201-2000	
Belford's 315 W Saint Julian St	Savannah	GA	31401	912-233-2626	233-6741
Bistro Savannah 309 W Congress St	Savannah	GA	31401	912-233-6266	232-7957
Cancun 5500 Abercorn St Suite 30	Savannah	GA	31405	912-356-1333	
Casbah 118 E Broughton St	Savannah	GA	31401	912-234-6168	
Web: www.casbahrestaurant.com					
Chart House 202 W Bay St	Savannah	GA	31401	912-234-6686	234-6686
Web: www.chart-house.com					

Georgia (Cont'd)

Restaurant	City	State	Zip	Phone	Fax
Elizabeth on 37th 105 E 37th St	Savannah	GA	31401	912-236-5547	232-1095
Web: www.elizabethon37th.com					
Exchange Tavern & Restaurant 201 E River St	Savannah	GA	31401	912-232-7088	
Garibaldi Cafe 315 W Congress St	Savannah	GA	31401	912-232-7118	232-7957
Huey's 115 E River St	Savannah	GA	31401	912-234-7385	234-7307
Il Pasticcio 2 E Broughton St	Savannah	GA	31401	912-231-8888	
Lady & Sons The 102 W Congress St	Savannah	GA	31401	912-233-2600	233-8283
Web: www.ladyandsons.com					
Loves Seafood & Steaks 6817 Chief of Love Rd	Savannah	GA	31419	912-925-3616	925-1900
Mediterranean 2308 Skidaway Rd	Savannah	GA	31404	912-233-3337	
Olde Pink House 23 Abercorn St	Savannah	GA	31401	912-232-4286	
Pearl's Elegant Pelican 7000 LaRoche Ave	Savannah	GA	31406	912-352-8221	
Pirates' House 20 E Broad St	Savannah	GA	31401	912-233-5757	234-1212
Web: www.thepirateshouse.com					
River House 125 W River St	Savannah	GA	31401	912-234-1900	234-7007
Web: www.riverhouseseafood.com					
Sapphire Grill 110 W Saint Julian St	Savannah	GA	31401	912-443-9962	
Web: www.sapphiregrill.com					
Shellhouse 8 Gateway Blvd	Savannah	GA	31419	912-927-3280	920-4814
Six Pence Pub 245 Bull St	Savannah	GA	31401	912-233-3156	
Toucan Cafe 531 Stephenson Ave	Savannah	GA	31406	912-352-2233	352-2258
Web: www.toucancafe.com					
Tubby's Tank House 2909 River Dr	Savannah	GA	31404	912-354-9040	
Uncle Bubba's Seafood & Oyster House 104 Bryan Woods Rd	Savannah	GA	31410	912-897-6101	897-6811
Web: www.unclebubbasoysterhouse.com					
Uncle Yogi's Italian Grille 7054 Hodgson Memorial Dr	Savannah	GA	31406	912-352-1060	
Wilkes Dining Room 107 W Jones St	Savannah	GA	31401	912-232-5997	

Hawaii

Restaurant	City	State	Zip	Phone	Fax
Bravo 98-115 Kaonohi St	Aiea	HI	96701	808-487-5544	486-3837
Web: www.bravorestaurant.com					
3660 on the Rise 3660 Waialae Ave	Honolulu	HI	96816	808-737-1177	735-6105
Web: www.3660.com					
Aaron's 410 Atkinson Dr 36th Fl	Honolulu	HI	96814	808-955-4466	955-4249
Web: www.tri-star-restaurants.com					
Alan Wong's 1857 S King St	Honolulu	HI	96826	808-949-2526	951-9520
Web: www.alanwongs.com					
Auntie Pasto's 1099 S Beretania St	Honolulu	HI	96814	808-523-8855	524-6267
Web: www.auntiepastos.com					
Bali By-the-Sea 2005 Kalia Rd	Honolulu	HI	96815	808-949-4321	947-7926
Bistro at Century Center 1750 Kalakaua Ave	Honolulu	HI	96815	808-943-6500	
Bubba Gump Shrimp Co 1450 Ala Moana Blvd Suite 3253	Honolulu	HI	96814	808-949-4867	952-0400
Web: www.bubbagump.com/html/oahu.html					
Chef Mavro 1969 S King St	Honolulu	HI	96813	808-944-4714	944-3903
Web: www.chefmavro.com					
Chuck's Steak House 2552 Kalakaua Ave	Honolulu	HI	96815	808-922-5744	924-2373
Compadres Mexican Bar & Grill 1200 Ala Moana Blvd	Honolulu	HI	96814	808-591-8307	593-2901
Diamond Head Grill 2885 Kalakaua Ave	Honolulu	HI	96815	808-922-3734	791-5164
Web: www.diamondheadgrill.com					
Duke's Waikiki Restaurant & Barefoot Bar 2335 Kalakaua Ave	Honolulu	HI	96815	808-922-2268	923-4204
El Burrito 550 Piikoi St	Honolulu	HI	96814	808-596-8225	
Genki Sushi Hawaii 885 Kapahulu Ave	Honolulu	HI	96816	808-735-7700	735-7708
Web: www.genkisushiusa.com					
Golden Dragon 2005 Kalia Rd	Honolulu	HI	96815	808-946-5336	947-7926
Gyotaku 1824 S King St	Honolulu	HI	96826	808-949-4584	946-6529
Hard Rock Cafe 1837 Kapiolani Blvd	Honolulu	HI	96826	808-955-7383	949-6040
Web: www.hardrockcafe.com					
Hee Hing 449 Kapahulu Ave	Honolulu	HI	96815	808-735-5544	732-6026
Hiroshi Eurasian Tapas 500 Ala Moana Blvd	Honolulu	HI	96813	808-533-4476	
Web: www.hiroshihawaii.com/					
Hoku's 5000 Kahala Ave	Honolulu	HI	96816	808-739-8779	739-8800
Hy's Steak House 2440 Kuhio Ave	Honolulu	HI	96815	808-922-5555	926-5089
Web: www.hyshawaii.com					
Indigo 1121 Nuuanu Ave	Honolulu	HI	96817	808-521-2900	537-4164
Web: www.indigo-hawaii.com					
John Dominis 43 Ahui St	Honolulu	HI	96813	808-523-0955	526-3758
Web: www.johndominis.com					
Keo's 2028 Kuhio Ave	Honolulu	HI	96815	808-951-9355	734-4642
Web: www.keosthaicuisine.com					
Kincaid's Fish Chop & Steak House 1050 Ala Moana Blvd	Honolulu	HI	96814	808-591-2005	591-2501
Web: www.kincaids.com					
La Mer 2199 Kalia Rd Halekulani Hotel	Honolulu	HI	96815	808-923-2311	931-5315
Longhi's 1450 Ala Moana Blvd Suite 3001	Honolulu	HI	96814	808-947-9899	944-3733
Web: www.longhis.com					
Mariposa 1450 Ala Moana Blvd	Honolulu	HI	96814	808-951-3420	951-3419
Mekong Thai 1295 S Beretania St	Honolulu	HI	96814	808-591-8841	591-8842
Michel's 2895 Kalakaua Ave Colony Surf Hotel	Honolulu	HI	96815	808-923-8056	526-3758
Web: www.michelshawaii.com					
Morton's The Steakhouse 1450 Ala Moana Blvd Suite 2001	Honolulu	HI	96814	808-949-1300	947-9512
Web: www.mortons.com					
Nick's Fishmarket 2070 Kalakaua Ave	Honolulu	HI	96815	808-955-6333	946-0478
Web: www.nicksfishmarket.com					
Oceanarium 2490 Kalakaua Ave	Honolulu	HI	96815	808-921-6111	926-2218
Olive Tree Cafe 4614 Kilauea Ave	Honolulu	HI	96816	808-737-0303	
Orchids 2199 Kalia Rd Halekulani Hotel	Honolulu	HI	96815	808-923-2311	931-5315
Pineapple Room 1450 Ala Moana Blvd	Honolulu	HI	96814	808-945-6573	945-5246
Planet Hollywood 2155 Kalakaua Ave Suite 200	Honolulu	HI	96815	808-924-7877	924-7811
Web: www.planethollywood.com					
Roy's 6600 Kalanianaole Hwy	Honolulu	HI	96825	808-396-7697	396-8706
Web: www.roysrestaurant.com					
Ruth's Chris Steak House 500 Ala Moana Blvd Suite 6C	Honolulu	HI	96813	808-599-3860	533-0786
Web: www.ruthschris.com					
Ryan's Grill at Ward Centre 1200 Ala Moana Blvd	Honolulu	HI	96814	808-591-9132	591-0034
Web: www.ryansgrill.com					
Sam Choy's Diamond Head 449 Kapahulu Ave Suite 201	Honolulu	HI	96815	808-732-8645	732-8683
Sansei Seafood Restaurant & Sushi Bar 2552 Kalakauna Ave	Honolulu	HI	96815	808-931-6286	
Web: www.sanseihawaii.com					
Shorebird Beach Broiler 2169 Kalia Rd Outrigger Reef Hotel	Honolulu	HI	96815	808-922-2887	926-5372
Side Street Inn 1225 Hopaka St	Honolulu	HI	96814	808-591-0253	
Sorabol 805 Keeaumoku St	Honolulu	HI	96814	808-947-3113	
Stage Restaurant 1250 Kapiolani Blvd	Honolulu	HI	96814	808-237-5429	
Tanaka of Tokyo 131 Kaiulani Ave 3rd Fl	Honolulu	HI	96815	808-922-4233	922-6948
Web: www.tanakaoftokyohawaii.com					
Willows The 901 Hausten St	Honolulu	HI	96826	808-952-9200	952-0050
Web: www.willowshawaii.com					
Assaggio 95-1249 Meheula Pkwy	Mililani	HI	96789	808-623-5115	623-4693
Big Island Steakhouse 250 Waikoloa Beach Dr Suite C-1	Waikoloa	HI	96738	808-886-8805	886-0455
Spago 3900 Wailea Alaui Dr	Wailea	HI	96753	808-879-2999	879-2995

Idaho

Restaurant	City	State	Zip	Phone	Fax
Aladdin 111 Broadway Ave	Boise	ID	83702	208-368-0880	
Web: www.aladdin-egypt.com					
Angell's Bar & Grill 999 W Main St One Capital Center	Boise	ID	83702	208-342-4900	342-3971
Web: www.angellsbarandgrill.com					
Barbacoa Grill 276 Bobwhite Ct	Boise	ID	83706	208-338-5000	
Web: www.barbacoa-boise.com/					
Bitter Creek Ale House 246 N 8th St	Boise	ID	83702	208-345-1813	345-3788
Web: www.bittercreekalehouse.com					
Brick Oven Bistro 801 Main St	Boise	ID	83702	208-342-3456	384-0266
Web: www.brickovenbistro.com					
Casa Mexico 10332 Fairview Ave	Boise	ID	83704	208-375-0342	
Web: www.casamexicoidaho.com					
Cazba 211 N 8th St	Boise	ID	83702	208-381-0222	
Web: www.cazba.com					
Cottonwood Grille 913 W River St	Boise	ID	83702	208-333-9800	333-1450
Web: www.cottonwoodgrille.com					
Dong Khanh 139 Broadway	Boise	ID	83702	208-345-0980	
Fujiyama 283 N Milwaukee St	Boise	ID	83704	208-672-8227	672-8247
Gamekeeper 1109 Main St	Boise	ID	83702	208-343-4611	381-0695
Gino's 150 N 8th St Suite 217	Boise	ID	83702	208-331-3771	331-0476
Goodwood Barbecue Co 7849 W Spectrum Dr	Boise	ID	83709	208-658-7173	658-7176
Web: www.goodwoodbbq.com					
Joe's Crab Shack 2288 N Garden St	Boise	ID	83706	208-336-9370	336-6029
Web: www.joescrabshack.com					
Mai Thai 750 W Idaho St	Boise	ID	83702	208-344-8424	344-2445
Web: www.maithaiboise.com					
Melting Pot The 200 N 6th St	Boise	ID	83712	208-383-0900	383-0901
Web: www.meltingpot.com					
MilkyWay 205 N 10th St	Boise	ID	83702	208-343-4334	319-0123
Mortimer's 110 S 5th St	Boise	ID	83702	208-338-6550	424-0475
Web: www.mortimersidaho.com					
Reef 105 S 6th St	Boise	ID	83702	208-287-9200	287-9203
Web: www.reefboise.com/reef/					
Shige Japanese Cuisine 100 N 8th St Suite 215	Boise	ID	83702	208-338-8423	
Smoky Mountain Pizza & Pasta 1805 W State St	Boise	ID	83702	208-387-2727	387-3596
Web: www.smokymountainpizza.com					
Taj Mahal 10548 W Fairview Ave	Boise	ID	83704	208-327-4500	327-4501
Web: www.tajmahalofboise.com					
Yen Ching 305 N 9th St	Boise	ID	83702	208-384-0384	336-0707
Bamboo Garden 1200 Yellowstone Ave	Pocatello	ID	83201	208-238-2331	238-7662
Buddy's Italian Restaurant 626 E Lewis St	Pocatello	ID	83201	208-233-1172	
Butterburrs 917 Yellowstone Ave	Pocatello	ID	83201	208-232-3296	478-0147
Chapala 117 W Burnside Ave	Pocatello	ID	83202	208-238-3365	237-1712
Continental Bistro 140 S Main St	Pocatello	ID	83204	208-233-4433	233-4082
Web: www.continentalbistro.com					
Mama Inez 390 Yellowstone Ave	Pocatello	ID	83201	208-234-7674	234-2707
Mandarin House 675 Yellowstone Ave	Pocatello	ID	83201	208-233-6088	
New Hong Kong 548 E Center St	Pocatello	ID	83201	208-236-6637	
Oliver's 130 S 5th Ave	Pocatello	ID	83201	208-234-0672	234-4185
Remo's Steak Seafood & Pasta 160 W Cedar St	Pocatello	ID	83201	208-233-1710	233-1438
Web: www.remosrestaurant.com					
Sandpiper 1400 Bench Rd	Pocatello	ID	83201	208-233-1000	233-1006
Winger's 696 Yellowstone Ave	Pocatello	ID	83201	208-232-0420	232-0566
Web: www.wingersdiner.com					

Illinois

Restaurant	City	State	Zip	Phone	Fax
Alexander's Steak House 202 W Anthony Dr	Champaign	IL	61821	217-359-1789	359-9117
Bacaro 113 N Walnut St	Champaign	IL	61820	217-398-6982	355-1662
Basil Thai Cafe 410 E Green St	Champaign	IL	61820	217-344-9130	344-9140
Basmati 302 S 1st St	Champaign	IL	61820	217-351-8877	351-2008
Dom's Patio Villa 301 S Locust St	Champaign	IL	61820	217-352-8444	
Dos Reales 1407 N Prospect Ave	Champaign	IL	61820	217-351-6879	351-1156
Empire Chinese Restaurant 410 E Green St	Champaign	IL	61820	217-328-0832	
Fiesta Cafe 216 1st St	Champaign	IL	61820	217-352-5902	
Web: www.fiestacafe.com					
Great Impasta 114 W Church St	Champaign	IL	61820	217-359-7377	366-0199
Web: www.greatimpastarestaurant.com					
Kamakura 715 S Neil St	Champaign	IL	61820	217-351-9898	
Li'l Porgy's Bar-B-Q 1917 W Springfield Ave	Champaign	IL	61821	217-398-6811	
Web: www.lilporgysbbq.com/					
Radio Maria 119 N Walnut St	Champaign	IL	61820	217-398-7729	398-4865
Web: www.radio-maria.net					
Ryan's Family Steak House 1004 W Anthony Dr	Champaign	IL	61821	217-352-7403	352-8344
Web: www.ryans.com					
Sea Boat Restaurant 1114 N Market St	Champaign	IL	61820	217-351-6209	351-1530
Taffie's 301 S Mattis Ave	Champaign	IL	61821	217-359-4201	359-4213
A Tavola 2148 W Chicago Ave	Chicago	IL	60622	773-276-7567	
Web: www.atavola-restaurant.com					
Adobo Grill 1610 N Wells St	Chicago	IL	60614	312-266-7999	266-9299
Web: www.adobogrill.com					
Alinea 1723 N Halsted St	Chicago	IL	60614	312-867-0110	
Amarit Thai Restaurant 600 S Dearborn	Chicago	IL	60611	312-649-0500	
Ambria 2300 N Lincoln Park West	Chicago	IL	60614	773-472-5959	472-9077
Web: www.leye.com					
Amelia's Mexican Grill 1235 W Grand Ave	Chicago	IL	60622	312-421-2000	
Amore 1330 W Madison St	Chicago	IL	60607	312-829-3333	829-0123
Web: www.amorechicago.com					
Angelina's 3561 N Broadway St	Chicago	IL	60657	773-935-5933	
Web: www.angelinasristorante.com					
Aria 200 N Columbus Dr	Chicago	IL	60601	312-565-8000	856-1032
Web: www.ariachicago.com					
Arun's 4156 N Kedzie Ave	Chicago	IL	60618	773-539-1909	539-2125
Web: www.arunsthai.com					
Atwood Cafe 1 W Washington St	Chicago	IL	60602	312-368-1900	357-2875
Web: atwood.citysearch.com/					
Avec 615 W Randolph St	Chicago	IL	60661	312-377-2002	377-2008
Web: www.avecrestaurant.com					
Avenues 108 E Superior St	Chicago	IL	60611	312-573-6754	573-6697
Bacchanalia 2413 S Oakley Ave	Chicago	IL	60608	773-254-6555	254-6565
Web: www.bacchanaliachicago.com					
Ben Pao 52 W Illinois St	Chicago	IL	60610	312-222-1888	222-0925
Web: www.benpao.com/					
BIN 36 339 N Dearborn St	Chicago	IL	60610	312-755-9463	755-9410
Web: www.bin36.com					
Bistrot Margot 1437 N Wells St	Chicago	IL	60610	312-587-3660	587-3668
Web: www.bistrotmargot.com					
Blackbird 619 W Randolph St	Chicago	IL	60606	312-715-0708	715-0774
Web: www.blackbirdrestaurant.com					
Bongo Room 1470 N Milwaukee Ave	Chicago	IL	60622	773-489-0690	489-0710
Web: www.bongoroom.com					
Brasserie Jo 59 W Hubbard St	Chicago	IL	60610	312-595-0800	595-0808
Web: www.brasseriejo.com					

Name / Address	City	State	ZIP	Phone	Fax
Buona Terra 2535 N California Ave	Chicago	IL	60647	773-289-3800	289-3838
Web: www.buona-terra.com					
Cafe Absinthe 1954 W North Ave	Chicago	IL	60622	773-278-4488	278-5291
Cafe Matou 1846 N Milwaukee Ave	Chicago	IL	60647	773-384-8911	384-8749
Web: www.cafematou.com					
Caliterra 633 N Saint Clair St	Chicago	IL	60611	312-274-4444	
Capital Grille 633 N Saint Clair St	Chicago	IL	60611	312-337-9400	337-1259
Web: www.thecapitalgrille.com					
Charlie Trotter's 816 W Armitage Ave	Chicago	IL	60614	773-248-6228	248-6088
Web: www.charlietrotters.com					
Chicago Chop House 60 W Ontario St	Chicago	IL	60610	312-787-7100	787-3219
Web: www.chicagochophouse.com					
Coco Pazzo 300 W Hubbard St	Chicago	IL	60610	312-836-0900	836-0257
Web: www.cocopazzochicago.com					
Cornelia's 750 W Cornelia Ave	Chicago	IL	60657	773-248-8333	248-7537
Web: www.ilovecornelias.com					
Crofton on Wells 535 N Wells St	Chicago	IL	60610	312-755-1790	755-1850
Web: www.croftononwells.com					
Erwin 2925 N Halsted St	Chicago	IL	60657	773-528-7200	528-1931
Web: www.erwincafe.com					
Everest 440 S La Salle St 40th Fl	Chicago	IL	60605	312-663-8920	663-8802
Web: www.leye.com					
Fat Willy's 2416 W Schubert Ave	Chicago	IL	60647	773-782-1800	782-1818
Web: www.fatwillysribshack.com/					
Fogo de Chao 661 N LaSalle St	Chicago	IL	60610	312-932-9330	932-9388
Web: www.fogodechao.com					
Francesca's on Taylor 1400 W Taylor St	Chicago	IL	60607	312-829-2828	
Web: www.francescarestaurants.com					
Frontera Grill 445 N Clark St	Chicago	IL	60610	312-661-1434	661-1830
Web: www.fronterakitchens.com					
Geja's Cafe 340 W Armitage Ave	Chicago	IL	60614	773-281-9101	281-0849
Web: www.gejascafe.com					
Gene & Georgetti 500 N Franklin St	Chicago	IL	60610	312-527-3718	527-2039
Web: www.geneandgeorgetti.com					
Gibsons Steakhouse 1028 N Rush St	Chicago	IL	60611	312-266-8999	787-1108
Web: www.gibsonssteakhouse.com					
Green Zebra 1460 W Chicago Ave	Chicago	IL	60622	312-243-7100	226-3360
Web: www.greenzebrachicago.com					
Hugo's Frog Bar & Fish House 1024 N Rush St	Chicago	IL	60611	312-640-0999	266-3327
Web: www.hugosfrogbar.com					
Indian Garden 2546 W Devon Ave	Chicago	IL	60659	773-338-2929	338-3930
Web: www.theindiangarden.org					
Japonais 600 W Chicago Ave	Chicago	IL	60610	312-822-9600	822-9623
Web: www.japonaischicago.com					
Jin Ju 5203 N Clark St	Chicago	IL	60640	773-334-6377	
Joe's Seafood Prime Steak & Stone Crab 60 E Grand Ave	Chicago	IL	60611	312-379-5637	494-9787
Web: leye.com					
Kevin 9 W Hubbard St	Chicago	IL	60610	312-595-0055	923-9487
Web: www.kevinrestaurant.com					
Kiki's Bistro 900 N Franklin St	Chicago	IL	60610	312-335-5454	335-0614
Web: www.kikisbistro.com					
Klay Oven 414 N Orleans St	Chicago	IL	60610	312-527-3999	527-1563
Web: www.klayovenrestaurant.com					
La Petite Folie 1504 E 55th St	Chicago	IL	60615	773-493-1394	493-1450
Web: www.lapetitefolie.com					
Lawry's The Prime Rib 100 E Ontario St	Chicago	IL	60611	312-787-5000	787-1264
Web: www.lawrysonline.com/theprimerib.asp					
Le Colonial 937 N Rush St	Chicago	IL	60611	312-255-0088	255-1108
Web: www.lecolonialchicago.com					
Le Lan 749 N Clark St	Chicago	IL	60610	312-280-9100	280-9107
Web: lelanrestaurant.com/					
Les Nomades 222 E Ontario St	Chicago	IL	60611	312-649-9010	649-0608
Web: www.lesnomades.net					
Lobby The 108 E Superior St 5th Fl	Chicago	IL	60611	312-573-6760	573-6907
M Henry 5707 N Clark St	Chicago	IL	60660	773-356-1600	561-1635
Web: www.mhenry.net/					
Marche 833 W Randolph St	Chicago	IL	60607	312-226-8399	226-4169
Web: www.marche-chicago.com					
Mas 1670 W Division St	Chicago	IL	60622	773-276-8700	276-8717
Web: www.masrestaurant.com					
Matsuya 3469 N Clark St	Chicago	IL	60657	773-248-2677	281-8803
Meritage Cafe & Wine Bar 2118 N Damen Ave	Chicago	IL	60647	773-235-6434	235-6318
Web: www.meritagecafe.com					
Merlo 16 W Maple St	Chicago	IL	60610	312-335-8200	335-8205
Web: www.merlochicago.com					
Mia Francesca 3311 N Clark St	Chicago	IL	60657	773-281-3310	281-6671
Web: www.miafrancesca.com					
Mike Ditka's Restaurant 100 E Chestnut St	Chicago	IL	60611	312-587-8989	587-8980
Web: www.mikeditkaschicago.com					
Mirai Sushi 2020 W Division St	Chicago	IL	60622	773-862-8500	862-8510
mk Restaurant 868 N Franklin St	Chicago	IL	60610	312-482-9179	482-9171
Web: www.mkchicago.com					
Mon Ami Gabi 2300 N Lincoln Park West	Chicago	IL	60614	773-348-8886	472-9077
Web: www.monamigabi.com					
Morton's The Steakhouse 1050 N State St	Chicago	IL	60610	312-266-4820	266-4852
Web: www.mortons.com					
N9ne 440 W Randolph St	Chicago	IL	60606	312-575-9900	575-9801
Web: www.n9ne.com/home.asp					
Nacional 27 325 W Huron St	Chicago	IL	60610	312-664-2727	649-0256
Web: leye.com					
Naha 500 N Clark St	Chicago	IL	60610	312-321-6242	321-7561
Web: www.naha-chicago.com					
Nick's Fishmarket 51 S Clark St	Chicago	IL	60603	312-621-0200	621-1118
Web: www.nicksfishmarketchicago.com					
NoMI 800 N Michigan Ave	Chicago	IL	60611	312-239-4030	239-4121
North Pond 2610 N Cannon Dr	Chicago	IL	60614	773-477-5845	427-3234
Web: www.northpondrestaurant.com					
One SixtyBlue 1400 W Randolph St	Chicago	IL	60607	312-850-0303	829-3046
Web: www.onesixtyblue.com					
Opera 1301 S Wabash Ave	Chicago	IL	60605	312-461-0161	226-6112
Web: www.opera-chicago.com					
Palm The 323 E Wacker Dr	Chicago	IL	60601	312-616-1000	616-3717
Web: www.thepalm.com/					
Pane Caldo 72 E Walton St	Chicago	IL	60611	312-649-0055	274-0540
Web: pane-caldo.com					
Parthenon The 314 S Halsted St	Chicago	IL	60661	312-726-2407	726-3203
Web: www.theparthenon.com					
Petterino's 150 N Dearborn St	Chicago	IL	60601	312-422-0150	
Pump Room 1301 N State Pkwy	Chicago	IL	60610	312-266-0360	266-1798
Web: www.pumproom.com					
Quartino 626 N State St	Chicago	IL	60610	312-698-5000	
Web: www.quartinochicago.com					
Rhapsody 65 E Adams St	Chicago	IL	60603	312-786-9911	786-1718
Web: www.rhapsodychicago.com					
Rise Sushi & Sake Lounge 3401 N Southport Ave	Chicago	IL	60657	773-525-3535	
Ritz-Carlton Cafe 160 E Pearson St 12 Fl	Chicago	IL	60611	312-573-5160	
Rockwell's Neighborhood Grill 4632 N Rockwell St	Chicago	IL	60625	773-509-1871	509-1877
Web: www.rockwellsgrill.com					
Roy's 720 N State St	Chicago	IL	60610	312-787-7599	787-7297
Web: www.roysrestaurant.com					
Ruth's Chris Steak House 431 N Dearborn St	Chicago	IL	60610	312-321-2725	321-1365
Web: www.ruthschris.com					
Sabatino's 4441 W Irving Park Rd	Chicago	IL	60641	773-283-8331	283-0603
Web: www.sabatinoschicago.com					
Sai Cafe 2010 N Sheffield Ave	Chicago	IL	60614	773-472-8080	472-0699
Web: www.saicafe.com					
Saloon Steakhouse The 200 E Chestnut St	Chicago	IL	60611	312-280-5454	280-6980
Web: www.saloonsteakhouse.com					
Salpicon 1252 N Wells St	Chicago	IL	60610	312-988-7811	988-7715
Web: salpicon.com					
Seasons 120 E Delaware Pl 7th Fl	Chicago	IL	60611	312-649-2349	649-2372
Shanghai Terrace 108 E Superior St 4th Fl	Chicago	IL	60611	312-573-6744	573-6697
Shaw's Crab House 21 E Hubbard St	Chicago	IL	60611	312-527-2722	527-4740
Web: www.shawscrabhouse.com					
Soul Vegetarian East 205 E 75th St	Chicago	IL	60619	773-224-0104	224-6667
South Water Kitchen 225 N Wabash Ave	Chicago	IL	60602	312-236-9300	960-8538
Web: www.southwaterkitchen.com/					
Spiaggia 980 N Michigan Ave	Chicago	IL	60611	312-280-2750	943-8560
Web: www.levyrestaurants.com					
Spring Restaurant 2039 W North Ave	Chicago	IL	60647	773-395-7100	394-3360
Web: www.springrestaurant.net					
Suparossa 4256 N Central Ave	Chicago	IL	60634	773-736-5828	736-1372
Web: www.suparossa.com					
Sushi Loop 810 W Jackson Blvd	Chicago	IL	60607	312-714-1234	714-1120
Sushi Wabi 842 W Randolph St	Chicago	IL	60607	312-563-1224	563-9579
Web: www.sushiwabi.com					
Topolobampo 445 N Clark St	Chicago	IL	60610	312-661-1434	661-1830
Web: www.fronterakitchens.com					
Trattoria No 10 10 N Dearborn St	Chicago	IL	60602	312-984-1718	984-1525
Web: www.trattoriaten.com					
Tre Kronor 3258 W Foster Ave	Chicago	IL	60625	773-267-9888	
Tru 676 N Saint Claire St	Chicago	IL	60611	312-202-0001	
Web: www.trurestaurant.com					
University Club of Chicago 76 E Monroe St	Chicago	IL	60603	312-726-2840	726-0620
Web: www.ucco.com/					
Vivere 71 W Monroe St	Chicago	IL	60603	312-332-4040	332-2656
Web: www.italianvillage-chicago.com/factsviv.html					
Vong Thai's Kitchen 6 W Hubbard St	Chicago	IL	60610	312-644-8664	644-9551
Web: www.jean-georges.com					
West Town Tavern 1329 W Chicago Ave	Chicago	IL	60622	312-666-6175	666-6178
Web: www.westtowntavern.com					
Wildfire 159 W Erie St	Chicago	IL	60610	312-787-9000	787-9123
Web: www.wildfirerestaurant.com					
Yoshi's Cafe 3257 N Halsted St	Chicago	IL	60657	773-248-6160	248-1860
Web: www.yoshiscafe.com					
Zealous 419 W Superior St	Chicago	IL	60610	312-475-9112	
Web: www.zealousrestaurant.com					
Bittersweet on the Bluff 7010 Donna's Dr	East Dubuque	IL	61025	815-747-2360	
Web: www.bittersweetonthebluff.com					
Captain Merry Guesthouse & Fine Dining 399 Sinsinawa Ave	East Dubuque	IL	61025	815-747-3644	747-3645
Web: www.captainmerry.com					
Agatucci's 2607 N University St	Peoria	IL	61604	309-688-8200	
Alexander's Steak House 100 Alexander St	Peoria	IL	61603	309-688-0404	688-0409
Alley Cats Eatery 1301 W Pioneerr Pkwy	Peoria	IL	61615	309-692-1059	
Carnegie's 501 Main St	Peoria	IL	61602	309-637-6500	
Fairview Farms 5911 Heuermann Rd	Peoria	IL	61607	309-697-4111	697-1887
Web: www.fairview-farm.com					
Fish House The 4919 N University St	Peoria	IL	61614	309-691-9358	
Flagstones 117 N Western Ave	Peoria	IL	61604	309-673-8040	
Flat Top Grill 5201 W War Memorial Dr	Peoria	IL	61615	309-693-9966	693-9846
Web: www.flattopgrill.com/					
Haddad Restaurant 1024 W Main St	Peoria	IL	61606	309-672-5339	
Jim's Downtown Steakhouse 110 SW Jefferson St	Peoria	IL	61602	309-673-5300	
Ponte Vecchio 4125 N Sheridan Rd	Peoria	IL	61614	309-682-3994	
Sushigawa 2601 W Lake Ave	Peoria	IL	61615	309-679-9300	
Vonachen's Old Place 5934 N Knoxville Ave	Peoria	IL	61614	309-692-7033	
Bacchus 515 E State St	Rockford	IL	61104	815-968-9463	968-9792
Web: www.bacchusrockford.com					
Capri 313 E State St	Rockford	IL	61104	815-965-0341	965-8202
Cliffbreakers River Restaurant 700 W Riverside Blvd	Rockford	IL	61103	815-282-3033	637-4704
Web: www.cliffbreakers.com					
Dos Reales 5855 E State St	Rockford	IL	61108	815-227-4979	
Garrett's Cafe 1631 N Bell School Rd	Rockford	IL	61107	815-484-9473	
Web: www.garrettscafe.com/					
Giovanni's 610 N Bell School Rd	Rockford	IL	61107	815-398-6411	398-6416
Web: www.giodine.com					
Great Wall Restaurant 4228 E State St	Rockford	IL	61108	815-226-0982	
Hoffman House 7550 E State St	Rockford	IL	61108	815-397-5800	397-0175
Imperial Palace 3415 E State St	Rockford	IL	61108	815-227-1442	227-5281
JMK Nippon 2551 N Perryville Rd	Rockford	IL	61107	815-877-0505	877-0681
Maria's Italian Restaurant 828 Cunningham St	Rockford	IL	61102	815-968-6781	
Mary's Market 1659 N Alpine Rd	Rockford	IL	61107	815-394-0765	394-0787
Octane Interlounge 124 N Main St	Rockford	IL	61101	815-965-4012	
Olympia Tavern 2327 N Main St	Rockford	IL	61103	815-962-8758	
Paragon on State 205 W State St	Rockford	IL	61101	815-963-1660	
Web: www.paragononstate.com					
Parisi's 6164 E Riverside Blvd	Rockford	IL	61111	815-633-4899	
Rathskeller The 1132 Auburn St	Rockford	IL	61103	815-963-2922	963-9185
Shogun 293 Executive Pkwy	Rockford	IL	61107	815-394-0007	
Table 13 1313 Auburn St	Rockford	IL	61103	815-964-1300	
Web: www.table-13.com					
Alexander's 620 Bruns Ln	Springfield	IL	62702	217-793-0440	793-0453
Augie's Front Burner 2 W Old State Capitol Plaza	Springfield	IL	62701	217-544-6979	544-7088
Web: augiesfrontburner.com/augies/					
Bianco's Supper Club 1926 Clear Lake Ave	Springfield	IL	62703	217-544-4491	
Cafe Brio 524 E Monroe St	Springfield	IL	62701	217-544-0574	544-2558
Capitol Steakhouse 620 S 1st St	Springfield	IL	62704	217-744-3333	525-0872
Web: www.capitolsteakhouse.com					
Capitol Teletrack 1766 Wabash Ave	Springfield	IL	62704	217-546-2111	
Chesapeake Seafood House 3045 Clear Lake Ave	Springfield	IL	62702	217-522-5220	522-5993
Web: www.chesapeakeseafoodhouse.com					
Corky's Ribs & BBQ 3458 Freedom Dr	Springfield	IL	62704	217-787-2227	787-2229
Web: www.corkys-springfield.com					
Fritz's Wagon Wheel Restaurant 2709 S MacArthur Blvd	Springfield	IL	62704	217-546-9888	
Golden Dragon 425 N Grand Ave East	Springfield	IL	62703	217-753-2996	
Indigo 3013 Lindbergh Blvd	Springfield	IL	62704	217-726-3487	
La Sorella 3325 Robbins Rd	Springfield	IL	62704	217-546-1680	
Lime Street Cafe 951 S Durkin Dr	Springfield	IL	62704	217-793-1905	793-7860
Maldaner's 222 S 6th St	Springfield	IL	62701	217-522-4313	522-1720
Web: www.maldaners.com					
Sebastian's Hide-Out 221 S 5th St	Springfield	IL	62701	217-789-8988	
Tai Pan 2636 Stevenson Dr	Springfield	IL	62703	217-529-8089	

Illinois (Cont'd)

Name	City	State	Zip	Phone	Fax
Taste Of Thai Restaurant 3053 S Dirksen Pkwy	Springfield	IL	62703	217-529-8393	
Tokyo of Japan 2225 Stevenson Dr	Springfield	IL	62703	217-585-0088	
Tuscany 3123 Robbins Rd	Springfield	IL	62704	217-726-5343	726-5344
Web: www.tuscanyitalianrestaurant.net					
Courier Cafe 111 N Race St	Urbana	IL	61801	217-328-1811	328-1880
Web: www.couriersilvercreek.com					
Kennedy's at Stone Creek 2560 S Stone Creek Blvd	Urbana	IL	61802	217-384-8111	384-4823
Web: www.kennedysatstonecreek.com					
Miko Restaurant 407 W University Ave	Urbana	IL	61801	217-367-0822	367-0818
Web: www.restaurantmiko.com					
Milo's Restaurant 156-D Lincoln Square Mall	Urbana	IL	61801	217-344-8946	344-8922
Timpone's 710 S Goodwin Ave	Urbana	IL	61801	217-344-7619	344-7648
Web: www.timpones-urbana.com					

Indiana

Name	City	State	Zip	Phone	Fax
Buffa Louie's 114 S Indiana Ave	Bloomington	IN	47408	812-333-3030	334-3945
Web: www.buffalouies.com					
Cafe Django 116 N Grant St	Bloomington	IN	47408	812-335-1297	
Chapman's Restaurant 300 SR 446	Bloomington	IN	47401	812-337-9999	336-0436
Web: www.chapmansrestaurant.com					
Cloverleaf Family Restaurant 2500 W 3rd St	Bloomington	IN	47404	812-334-1077	
Crazy Horse 214 W Kirkwood Ave	Bloomington	IN	47404	812-336-8877	336-8011
Dragon Chinese Restaurant 3261 W 3rd St	Bloomington	IN	47404	812-332-6610	335-8389
Esan Thai 221 E Kirkwood Ave	Bloomington	IN	47408	812-333-8424	
Web: www.esanthairestaurant.com					
Fairfax Inn 8660 S Fairfax Rd	Bloomington	IN	47401	812-824-8552	824-2634
Gratzi 106 W 6th St	Bloomington	IN	47401	812-323-0303	
Irish Lion 212 W Kirkwood Ave	Bloomington	IN	47404	812-336-9076	876-6435
Web: www.irishlion.com					
Laughing Planet Cafe 322 E Kirkwood Ave	Bloomington	IN	47408	812-323-2233	
Le Petit Cafe 308 W 6th St	Bloomington	IN	47404	812-334-9747	
Limestone Grille 2920 E Covenanter Dr	Bloomington	IN	47401	812-335-8110	
Web: www.limestonegrille.com					
Malibu Grill 106 N Walnut St	Bloomington	IN	47402	812-332-4334	332-2282
Web: www.malibuhospitality.com					
Michael's Uptown Cafe 102 E Kirkwood Ave	Bloomington	IN	47408	812-339-0900	331-6027
Web: www.michaelsuptowncafe.com					
Mikado 895 S College Mall Rd	Bloomington	IN	47401	812-333-1950	
Nick's English Hut 423 E Kirkwood Ave	Bloomington	IN	47408	812-332-4040	339-0282
Web: www.nicksenglishhut.com					
Restaurant Tallent 208 N Walnut	Bloomington	IN	47404	812-330-9801	330-9803
Web: restauranttallent.com					
Scholars Inn Gourmet Cafe 717 N College Ave	Bloomington	IN	47404	812-323-1531	355-8785
Web: www.scholarsinn.com					
Trojan Horse 100 E Kirkwood Ave	Bloomington	IN	47408	812-332-1101	330-7092
Web: www.thetrojanhorse.com					
Upland Brewing Co 350 W 11th St	Bloomington	IN	47404	812-336-2337	330-7421
Web: www.uplandbeer.com/					
Yogi's Grill & Bar 519 E 10th St	Bloomington	IN	47408	812-323-9644	323-8898
Web: www.yogis.com					
Glass Chimney 12901 N Old Meridian St	Carmel	IN	46032	317-844-0921	574-1360
Web: www.glasschimneyanddeeters.com					
Angelo's 305 Main St	Evansville	IN	47708	812-428-6666	428-6699
Biaggi's 6401 E Lloyd Expy Suite 3	Evansville	IN	47715	812-421-0800	421-0801
Web: www.biaggis.com					
Canton Inn 947 N Park Dr	Evansville	IN	47710	812-428-6611	428-4962
Chopstick House 5412 E Indiana St	Evansville	IN	47715	812-473-5551	
Hacienda 711 1st Ave	Evansville	IN	47710	812-423-6355	
Web: www.haciendafiesta.com/					
Jacob's Pub & Restaurant 4428 N 1st Ave	Evansville	IN	47710	812-423-0050	
Lorenzo's Bread Bistro 972 S Hebron Ave	Evansville	IN	47714	812-475-9477	475-9478
Web: www.lorenzosbistro.com					
Los Bravos 834 Tutor Ln	Evansville	IN	47715	812-474-9078	474-9756
Moe's Southwest Grill 6401 E Lloyd Expy Suite 5	Evansville	IN	47715	812-491-6637	
Web: www.moes.com					
Raffi's 1100 N Burkehardt Rd	Evansville	IN	47715	812-479-9166	491-0318
Web: raffis.evvit.com					
Raffis Italian Cuisine 4025 E Morgan Ave	Evansville	IN	47715	812-479-9166	
Turoni's Forget-Me-Not Inn 4 N Weinbach Ave	Evansville	IN	47711	812-477-7500	471-3029
Western Rib-Eye & Ribs 1401 N Boeke Rd	Evansville	IN	47711	812-476-5405	473-4850
Wolf's Bar-B-Q Restaurant 6600 1st Ave	Evansville	IN	47710	812-424-8891	424-8905
Yen Ching 406 S Green River Rd	Evansville	IN	47715	812-474-0181	479-5561
Web: www.yenchingrestaurant.com					
Baan Thai 4634 Coldwater Rd	Fort Wayne	IN	46825	260-471-2929	471-2020
Bandido's 6536 E State Blvd	Fort Wayne	IN	46815	260-749-0485	748-2052
Web: www.bandidos.com					
Biaggi's 4010 W Jefferson Blvd	Fort Wayne	IN	46804	260-459-6700	459-6701
Web: www.biaggis.com					
Casa Grille 411 E DuPont Rd	Fort Wayne	IN	46825	260-490-4745	497-9411
Web: www.casa4pasta.com					
Catablu 2441 Broadway	Fort Wayne	IN	46807	260-456-6563	456-9155
Chappell's Coral Grill & Seafood Market 2723 Broadway	Fort Wayne	IN	46807	260-456-9652	744-1120
Club Soda 235 E Superior St	Fort Wayne	IN	46802	260-426-3442	426-4214
Web: www.clubsodafortwayne.com					
Cork'N Cleaver 221 E Washington Center Rd	Fort Wayne	IN	46825	260-484-7772	482-8471
Don Hall's Old Gas House 305 E Superior St	Fort Wayne	IN	46802	260-426-3411	424-2903
Web: www.donhalls.com					
Double Dragon 117 W Wayne St	Fort Wayne	IN	46802	260-422-6426	
Eddie Merlot's 1502 Illinois Rd S	Fort Wayne	IN	46804	260-459-2222	459-8896
Web: www.eddiemerlots.com					
Flanagan's Restaurant & Pub 6525 Covington Rd	Fort Wayne	IN	46804	260-432-6666	432-6799
Flat Top Grill 4150 W Jefferson Blvd	Fort Wayne	IN	46804	260-432-4100	432-8708
Web: www.flattopgrill.com					
Logan's Roadhouse 6617 Lima Rd	Fort Wayne	IN	46818	260-487-9944	
Web: www.logansroadhouse.com					
Mi Pueblo IV 2419 W Jefferson Blvd	Fort Wayne	IN	46802	260-432-6462	459-2542
Opus 24 6328 W Jefferson Blvd	Fort Wayne	IN	46804	260-459-2459	436-5864
Park Place Grill 200 E Main St Suite 120	Fort Wayne	IN	46802	260-420-7275	424-3128
Rib Room 1235 E State Blvd	Fort Wayne	IN	46805	260-483-9767	
Web: www.theribroom.com					
Sakura 5828 W Jefferson Blvd	Fort Wayne	IN	46804	260-459-2022	
Taj Mahal 6410 W Jefferson Blvd	Fort Wayne	IN	46804	260-432-8993	432-8486
Takaoka of Japan 305 E Superior St	Fort Wayne	IN	46802	260-424-3183	
Yokohama 918 Woodland Plaza Suite G	Fort Wayne	IN	46825	260-497-7130	
Acropolis Restaurant & Lounge 1625 E Southport Rd	Indianapolis	IN	46227	317-787-8883	
Agio 635 Massachusetts Ave	Indianapolis	IN	46204	317-488-0359	488-0361
Web: www.agiorestaurant.net					
Amalfi 1351 W 86th St	Indianapolis	IN	46260	317-253-4034	253-1267
Amici's 601 E New York St	Indianapolis	IN	46202	317-634-0440	
Bonefish Grill 4501 E 82nd St	Indianapolis	IN	46250	317-863-3474	863-0067
Web: www.bonefishgrill.com					
Cafe Nora 1300 E 86th St	Indianapolis	IN	46240	317-571-1000	575-1705
Web: www.cafenora.com					
Cafe Patachou 4911 N Pennsylvania St	Indianapolis	IN	46205	317-925-2823	
Web: www.cafepatachou.com					
Cancun Mexican 8311 N Michigan Ave	Indianapolis	IN	46268	317-876-9995	876-9222
Cheesecake Factory 8701 Keystone Crossing Blvd	Indianapolis	IN	46240	317-566-0100	566-0200
Web: www.cheesecakefactory.com					
Circle City Bar & Grille 350 W Maryland St	Indianapolis	IN	46225	317-405-6100	822-1002
Web: www.circlecitygrille.com					
Dunaway's 351 S East St	Indianapolis	IN	46204	317-638-7663	638-7677
Web: www.dunaways.com					
Eagle's Nest Restaurant 1 S Capitol Ave	Indianapolis	IN	46204	317-632-1234	616-6175
El Jaripeo 10417 E Washington St	Indianapolis	IN	46229	317-898-3921	
El Torito Grill 8650 Keystone Crossing	Indianapolis	IN	46240	317-848-5202	575-0068
Web: www.etgrill.com					
Fujiyama Japanese Steakhouse 5149 Victory Dr	Indianapolis	IN	46203	317-787-7900	784-5682
Web: www.fujiyama-indy.com					
Greek Islands Restaurant 906 S Meridian St	Indianapolis	IN	46225	317-636-0700	636-2347
Web: www.greekislandsrestaurant.com					
Hard Rock Cafe 49 S Meridian St	Indianapolis	IN	46204	317-636-2550	636-2551
Web: www.hardrock.com					
Hollyhock Hill 8110 N College Ave	Indianapolis	IN	46240	317-251-2294	251-2295
Web: www.hollyhockhill.com					
Iaria's Italian Restaurant 317 S College Ave	Indianapolis	IN	46202	317-638-7706	687-9232
Web: www.iariasrestaurant.com					
India Garden 830 Broad Ripple Ave	Indianapolis	IN	46220	317-253-6060	
Web: www.indiagardenindy.com					
India Palace 4213 Lafayette Rd	Indianapolis	IN	46254	317-298-0773	298-1823
Web: www.indiapalaceindy.com					
Iron Skillet 2489 W 30th St	Indianapolis	IN	46222	317-923-6353	
Web: www.ironskillet.net					
Kona Jack's Fish Market & Sushi Bar 9419 N Meridian St	Indianapolis	IN	46260	317-843-1609	571-6987
Web: www.konajacksindy.com					
Le Peep 301 N Illinois St	Indianapolis	IN	46204	317-237-3447	
Web: www.lepeep.com					
Maggiano's Little Italy 3550 E 86th St	Indianapolis	IN	46240	317-814-0700	814-0707
Web: www.maggianos.com					
Mama Carolla's Old Italian Restaurant 1031 E 54th St	Indianapolis	IN	46220	317-259-9412	
Marker The 2544 Executive Dr	Indianapolis	IN	46241	317-381-6146	381-6170
Melting Pot The 5650 E 86th St Suite F	Indianapolis	IN	46250	317-841-3601	841-1207
Web: www.meltingpot.com					
Mikado Japanese Restaurant 148 S Illinois St	Indianapolis	IN	46225	317-972-4180	972-4191
Morton's The Steakhouse 41 E Washington St	Indianapolis	IN	46204	317-229-4700	229-4704
Web: www.mortons.com					
Mo's 47 S Pennsylvania St	Indianapolis	IN	46204	317-636-5418	624-0721
Web: www.mosindy.com					
Oakley's Bistro 1464 W 86th St	Indianapolis	IN	46260	317-824-1231	824-0938
Web: www.oakleysbistro.com					
Oceanaire Seafood Room 30 S Meridian St Suite 100	Indianapolis	IN	46204	317-955-2277	955-2278
Web: www.theoceanaire.com					
Oh Yumm! Bistro 5615 N Illinois St	Indianapolis	IN	46208	317-251-5656	255-1840
Web: www.ohyummbistro.com					
Palomino Euro Bistro 49 W Maryland St Suite 189	Indianapolis	IN	46204	317-974-0400	974-1865
Web: www.palomino.com					
PF Chang's China Bistro 8601 Keystone Crossing	Indianapolis	IN	46240	317-815-8773	815-8774
Web: www.pfchangs.com					
Plump's Last Shot 6416 Cornell Ave	Indianapolis	IN	46220	317-257-5867	
R Bistro 888 Massachusetts Ave	Indianapolis	IN	46204	317-423-0312	423-0348
Web: www.rbistro.com					
Rathskeller Restaurant 401 E Michigan St	Indianapolis	IN	46204	317-636-0396	636-2013
Web: www.rathskeller.com					
Restaurant at the Canterbury 123 S Illinois St	Indianapolis	IN	46225	317-634-3000	685-2519
Web: www.canterburyhotel.com/go/restaurant.html					
Rick's Cafe Boatyard 4050 Dandy Trail	Indianapolis	IN	46254	317-290-9300	291-1043
Ruth's Chris Steak House 9445 Threel Rd	Indianapolis	IN	46240	317-844-1155	574-9306
Web: www.ruthschris.com					
Saint Elmo Steak House 127 S Illinois St	Indianapolis	IN	46225	317-637-1811	687-9162
Web: www.stelmos.com					
Sakura 7201 N Keystone Ave	Indianapolis	IN	46240	317-259-4171	253-7846
Scholars Inn 725 Massachusetts Ave	Indianapolis	IN	46204	317-536-0707	536-0650
Web: www.scholarsinn.com					
Shula's Steak House 50 S Capitol Ave	Indianapolis	IN	46204	317-262-8100	231-3924
Web: www.donshula.com					
Thai House 8431 N Michigan Rd	Indianapolis	IN	46268	317-871-0023	
Udupi Cafe 4225 Lafayette Rd	Indianapolis	IN	46254	317-299-2127	280-4087
Yen Ching 9150 N Michigan Rd	Indianapolis	IN	46268	317-228-0868	228-0886
Bonefish Grill 620 W Edison Ave Suite 100	Mishawaka	IN	46545	574-259-2663	259-7725
Web: www.bonefishgrill.com					
Hana Yori 3601 Grape Rd	Mishawaka	IN	46545	574-258-5817	
Main Street Grille 112 N Main St	Mishawaka	IN	46544	574-254-4995	254-4999
Web: www.mainstgrille.com/					
Backstage Grill The 222 S Michigan St	South Bend	IN	46601	574-232-0222	234-5544
Web: www.222italiansteakhouse.com					
Canton House Restaurant 25590 SR 2	South Bend	IN	46619	574-232-8182	
Carriage House 24460 Adams Rd	South Bend	IN	46628	574-272-9220	272-6179
Web: www.carriagehousedining.com					
Frankie's Barbecue 1621 Circle Ave	South Bend	IN	46628	574-287-8993	
Web: www.frankiesbbq.com					
Hacienda 4650 Miami St	South Bend	IN	46614	574-291-2566	968-0609
Web: www.haciendafiesta.com					
Honkers 3939 S Michigan St	South Bend	IN	46614	574-291-2115	291-1145
LaSalle Grill 115 W Colfax Ave	South Bend	IN	46601	574-288-1155	288-2012
Web: www.lasallegrill.com					
Matuba 2930 McKinley Ave	South Bend	IN	46615	574-251-0674	251-0675
Parisi's Italian Ristorante 1412 S Bend Ave	South Bend	IN	46617	574-232-4244	232-4257
Web: www.parisisrestaurant.com					
Rocco's 537 N St Louis Blvd	South Bend	IN	46617	574-233-2464	288-0168
Siam Thai Restaurant 211 N Main St	South Bend	IN	46601	574-232-4445	232-3799
Web: www.siamthairestaurant.com					
Simeri's Old Town Tap 1505 W Indiana Ave	South Bend	IN	46613	574-289-1361	
Web: www.simerisoldtowntap.com					
Tippecanoe Place 620 W Washington St	South Bend	IN	46601	574-234-9077	
Web: www.tippe.com					
Volcano Restaurant 3700 Lincoln Way W	South Bend	IN	46628	574-287-5775	

Iowa

Name	City	State	Zip	Phone	Fax
Biaggi's Ristorante 320 Collins Rd NE	Cedar Rapids	IA	52402	319-393-6593	393-6593
Web: www.biaggis.com					
Bonanza Steakhouse 3505 16th Ave SW	Cedar Rapids	IA	52404	319-396-1876	
Web: www.bonanzasteakhouses.com/					
El Rancho 2747 16th Ave SW	Cedar Rapids	IA	52404	319-298-8844	298-2845
Genghis Grill 2230 Edgewood Rd SW	Cedar Rapids	IA	52404	319-390-5426	390-5420
Web: www.genghisgrill.com					
Irish Democrat Pub & Grill 3207 1st Ave SE	Cedar Rapids	IA	52403	319-364-9896	368-8020

	City	State	ZIP	Phone	Fax
Olive Tree Restaurant 2201 16th Ave SW	Cedar Rapids	IA	52404	319-364-0781	
Papa Juans 5505 Center Point Rd NE	Cedar Rapids	IA	52402	319-393-0258	378-8953
Pei's Mandarin 5350 Council St NE	Cedar Rapids	IA	52402	319-395-9741	
Web: www.peismandarin.com					
Texas Roadhouse 2605 Edgewood Rd SW	Cedar Rapids	IA	52404	319-396-3300	
Web: www.texasroadhouse.com/					
Third Base Sports Bar & Brewery 500 Blairs Ferry Rd NE	Cedar Rapids	IA	52402	319-378-9090	378-9697
Vernon Inn 2663 Mount Vernon Rd SE	Cedar Rapids	IA	52403	319-366-7817	366-2109
Vino's 3611 1st Ave SE	Cedar Rapids	IA	52402	319-363-7550	
Web: www.vinosristorante.com					
Vito's 4100 River Ridge Dr NE	Cedar Rapids	IA	52402	319-393-8727	393-3981
Zindrick Czech Restaurant 86 16th Ave SW	Cedar Rapids	IA	52404	319-369-3940	
Zio Johno's Spaghetti House 2925 Williams Blvd SW	Cedar Rapids	IA	52404	319-396-1700	
Cosi Cucina 1975 NW 86th St	Clive	IA	50325	515-278-8148	278-2262
Taste of Italy 8421 University Blvd	Clive	IA	50325	515-221-0743	309-3156
801 Steak & Chop House Ltd 801 Grand Ave Suite 200	Des Moines	IA	50309	515-288-6000	288-4083
Web: www.801steakandchop.com					
A Dong 1511 High St	Des Moines	IA	50309	515-284-5632	
AK O'Connors 4050 Urbandale Ave	Des Moines	IA	50310	515-277-2227	
Barattas 2320 S Union St	Des Moines	IA	50315	515-243-4516	243-5324
Web: www.barattas.com					
Buzzard Billy's Flying Carp Cafe 100 Court Ave	Des Moines	IA	50309	515-280-6060	280-3815
Web: www.buzzardbillys.com					
Cheesecake Factory 101 Jordan Creek Pkwy	Des Moines	IA	50266	515-457-9888	457-9890
Web: www.thecheesecakefactory.com					
China Chef Restaurant 5010 SW 9th St	Des Moines	IA	50315	515-256-8005	
Chuck's Restaurant 3610 6th Ave	Des Moines	IA	50313	515-244-4104	
Court Avenue Brewing Co 309 Court Ave	Des Moines	IA	50309	515-282-2739	282-3789
Web: www.courtavebrew.com					
Crimmins Cattle Co 1201 E Army Post Rd	Des Moines	IA	50315	515-287-6611	287-0382
Felix & Oscars 4050 Merle Hay Rd	Des Moines	IA	50310	515-278-8887	
Web: www.felixandoscars.com					
Forty-Three Restaurant & Bar 1000 Walnut St	Des Moines	IA	50309	515-362-5224	243-4317
Web: www.hotelfortdesmoines.com/fortythreerestaurantandbar					
Gino's 2809 6th Ave	Des Moines	IA	50313	515-282-4029	
Iowa Beef Steakhouse 1201 E Euclid Ave	Des Moines	IA	50316	515-262-1138	
Web: www.iowabeefsteakhouse.com					
Latin King 2200 Hubbell Ave	Des Moines	IA	50317	515-266-4466	264-1096
Web: www.tursislatinking.com					
Manterrey 8801 University Ave	Des Moines	IA	50325	515-457-8900	457-7964
Raccoon River Brewing Co 200 10th St	Des Moines	IA	50309	515-362-5222	243-4347
Web: www.raccoonbrew.com					
Riccelli's Restaurant 3803 Indianola Ave	Des Moines	IA	50320	515-288-7755	
Sage 6587 University Ave	Des Moines	IA	50311	515-255-7722	
Web: www.sagetherestaurant.com					
Thai Flavors 1254 E 14th St	Des Moines	IA	50316	515-262-4658	262-0033
Bridge Restaurant 31 Locust St	Dubuque	IA	52001	563-557-7280	
Davinci's Ristorante & Pub 395 W 9th St	Dubuque	IA	52001	563-582-7057	
Web: www.davincisdubuque.com					
Hoffman House 3100 Dodge St Best Western Midway	Dubuque	IA	52003	563-557-8000	557-7692
Mario's Restaurant 1298 Main St	Dubuque	IA	52001	563-556-9424	582-0904
Pepper Sprout 378 Main St	Dubuque	IA	52001	563-556-2167	583-6428
Web: www.peppersprout.com					
Point Restaurant 2370 Rhomberg Ave	Dubuque	IA	52001	563-582-2418	582-0586
Yen Ching 926 Main St	Dubuque	IA	52001	563-556-2574	
Trostel's Greenbrier Restaurant 5810 Merle Hay Rd	Johnston	IA	50131	515-253-0124	
Iowa Machine Shed Restaurant 11151 Hickman Rd	Urbandale	IA	50322	515-270-6818	270-0832
Web: www.machineshed.com					
Biaggi's 5990 University Ave	West Des Moines	IA	50266	515-221-9900	221-9901
Web: www.biaggis.com					
Rock Bottom Restaurant & Brewery 4508 University Ave	West Des Moines	IA	50266	515-267-8900	267-1400
Web: www.rockbottom.com					
Waterfront Seafood Market 2900 University Ave	West Des Moines	IA	50266	515-223-5106	

Kansas

	City	State	ZIP	Phone	Fax
Arthur Bryant Barbecue 1702 Village West Pkwy	Kansas City	KS	66111	913-788-7500	788-2333
Casa De Hernandez 1817 Park Dr	Kansas City	KS	66102	913-342-6226	342-3981
Cheeseburger in Paradise 1705 Village West Pkwy	Kansas City	KS	66111	913-334-4500	334-4507
Web: www.cheeseburgerinparadise.com					
Felitza's Fine Italian Cuisine 402 N 5th St	Kansas City	KS	66101	913-281-1569	281-1522
Gates & Sons Bar-B-Que 1026 State Ave	Kansas City	KS	66102	913-621-1134	
Lone Star Steakhouse & Saloon 1501 Village West Pkwy	Kansas City	KS	66111	913-334-9995	
Web: www.lonestarsteakhouse.com					
Los Amigos 2610 State Ave	Kansas City	KS	66102	913-281-4547	
Oklahoma Joe's BBQ & Catering 3002 W 47th Ave	Kansas City	KS	66103	913-722-3366	722-6644
Web: www.oklahomajoesbbq.com					
Rosedale Barbeque 600 Southwest Blvd	Kansas City	KS	66103	913-262-0343	
Sol Azteca Mexican Grill 542 Southwest Blvd	Kansas City	KS	66103	913-362-0817	677-1699
Taste of China 570 S 4th St	Kansas City	KS	66111	913-422-2565	422-2569
Vietnam Cafe 2200 W 39th St	Kansas City	KS	66103	913-262-8552	262-8193
Yukon Base Camp Restaurant 10300 Cabela Dr	Kansas City	KS	66111	913-328-0322	328-0348
Fiorella's Jack Stack 9520 Metcalf Ave	Overland Park	KS	66212	913-385-7427	385-5020
Web: jackstackbbq.com					
Garozzo's 9950 W College Blvd	Overland Park	KS	66210	913-491-8300	491-9797
Web: www.garozzos.com					
Ruchi 11168 Antioch Rd	Overland Park	KS	66210	913-661-9088	338-3662
Thai Place 9359 Santa Fe Dr	Overland Park	KS	66212	913-649-5420	649-4257
Web: www.kcthaiplace.com					
Blind Tiger Brewery & Restaurant 417 SW 37th St	Topeka	KS	66611	785-267-2739	267-7527
Web: www.blindtiger.com/					
Casa 3320 S Topeka Blvd	Topeka	KS	66611	785-266-4503	266-4539
Web: www.casatopeka.com					
China Inn 2010 NW Central Ave	Topeka	KS	66608	785-233-2319	233-1901
Frances O'Dooley's Irish Pub & Grille 1930 Westport Rd	Topeka	KS	66604	785-273-0131	271-6267
Kiku Japanese Steak House 5331 SW 22nd Pl	Topeka	KS	66614	785-272-6633	
New City Cafe 4005 SW Gage Center Dr	Topeka	KS	66604	785-271-8646	271-8636
Paisano's 4043 SW 10th St	Topeka	KS	66604	785-273-0100	273-3674
Pat's Pig 5900 SW Topeka Blvd	Topeka	KS	66619	785-862-7427	
Pepe & Chela's 1001 SW Tyler St	Topeka	KS	66612	785-357-8332	
Rosa's 2025 SE California Ave	Topeka	KS	66607	785-233-9842	
Sarapes 1521 SW 21st St	Topeka	KS	66604	785-232-7231	232-7232
Shogun 5632 SW 29th St	Topeka	KS	66614	785-273-7979	
Sun's 2121 SW Belle Ave	Topeka	KS	66614	785-272-6090	
Timberline Steakhouse & Grill 1425 SW Wanamaker	Topeka	KS	66614	785-228-1155	228-1187
Web: www.timberlinesteakhouse.com					
Topeka Steak House 526 Dupont Rd	Topeka	KS	66542	785-379-9994	
Web: www.topekasteakhouse.com					
Boss Hawg's 2833 SW 29th St	Topkea	KS	66614	785-273-7300	273-0077
Web: www.bosshawgsbbq.com					
Angelo's 1930 E Oliver St	Wichita	KS	67211	316-682-1473	
Bamboo Stix 2243 N Tyler Rd Suite 101	Wichita	KS	67205	316-722-8886	462-0888
Web: www.bamboostix.com					
Bella Donna 2121 N Webb Rd	Wichita	KS	67206	316-315-0000	315-0054
Cafe Bel Ami 229 E William St	Wichita	KS	67202	316-267-3433	267-3070
Canterbury 5805 W Kellogg	Wichita	KS	67209	316-942-7911	942-0854
Chelsea Bar & Grill 2949 N Rock Rd	Wichita	KS	67226	316-636-1103	
Cibola 1900 N Rock Rd	Wichita	KS	67202	316-631-3700	
Felipe's 2241 N Woodlawn	Wichita	KS	67220	316-652-0027	618-9465
Fox & Hound 1421 Waterfront Pkwy	Wichita	KS	67206	316-634-2123	634-1741
Web: www.fhrg.com					
Great Wall 410 N Hillside Ave	Wichita	KS	67214	316-688-0881	612-4825
Il Vicino 4817 E Douglas	Wichita	KS	67218	316-612-7085	
Imbiss Grille 315 N Mead St	Wichita	KS	67202	316-263-9062	263-9063
Web: www.imbissgrille.com					
Kwan Court 1443 N Rock Rd	Wichita	KS	67206	316-634-1828	
La Chinita 1451 N Broadway St	Wichita	KS	67214	316-267-1552	267-7097
La Mesa 6960 W 21st St	Wichita	KS	67205	316-722-0955	722-0977
Larkspur Restaurant & Grill 904 E Douglas St	Wichita	KS	67202	316-262-5275	262-1292
Web: www.larkspuronline.com					
Legends 2098 Airport Rd	Wichita	KS	67209	316-945-5272	945-7620
Mamadeaux Seafood House 606 N Winterset	Wichita	KS	67212	316-944-1114	
Nu Way Restaurant 1416 W Douglas Ave	Wichita	KS	67203	316-267-1131	
Web: www.nuwaycafe.com/					
PF Chang's China Bistro 1401 Waterfront Pkwy	Wichita	KS	67206	316-634-2211	634-0480
Web: www.pfchangs.com					
Saigon 1103 N Broadway St	Wichita	KS	67214	316-262-8134	267-3360
Sal's Japanese Steakhouse 6829 E Kellogg Dr	Wichita	KS	67207	316-682-8880	
Savute's 3303 N Broadway St	Wichita	KS	67219	316-838-0455	
Web: www.savutes.com					
Southwinds Bar & Grill 400 W Waterman	Wichita	KS	67202	316-293-1234	293-1200
Sweet Basil 2424 N Woodlawn St	Wichita	KS	67220	316-651-0123	651-0220
Ted's Montana Grill 2142 N Tyler Rd	Wichita	KS	67212	316-773-4443	773-4449
Web: www.tedsmontanagrill.com					
Texas Roadhouse 6707 W Kellogg Dr	Wichita	KS	67209	316-943-8722	
Web: www.texasroadhouse.com					
Timberline Steakhouse & Grill 2243 N Tyler Rd	Wichita	KS	67205	316-773-3111	
Web: www.timberlinesteakhouse.com/					
Tommy's Restaurant & Lounge 2121 N Tyler Rd	Wichita	KS	67212	316-722-7687	
Upper Crust The 7038 E Lincoln St	Wichita	KS	67211	316-683-8088	
Yen Ching 430 N Rock Rd	Wichita	KS	67206	316-686-9510	
Yia Yia's Euro Bistro 8115 E 21st St North	Wichita	KS	67206	316-634-1000	634-2263

Kentucky

	City	State	ZIP	Phone	Fax
Pho Paris 318 Greenup St	Covington	KY	41001	859-643-1234	643-1900
Web: www.phoparis.com					
Casa Fiesta 801 Louisville Rd	Frankfort	KY	40601	502-226-5010	696-0960
China Wok 111 E Wood Shopping Center	Frankfort	KY	40601	502-695-9388	695-0788
Forks at Elkhorn Creek The 3710 Georgetown Rd	Frankfort	KY	40601	502-695-0078	
Jim's Seafood 950 Wilkinson Blvd	Frankfort	KY	40601	502-223-7448	227-7419
La Fiesta Grande 314 Versailles Rd	Frankfort	KY	40601	502-695-8378	695-8378
Nema's Grille 334 Saint Clair St	Frankfort	KY	40601	502-227-3456	
New China 1309 US Hwy 127 S	Frankfort	KY	40601	502-226-3400	226-3800
A La Lucie 159 N Limestone St	Lexington	KY	40507	859-252-5277	225-5027
Web: www.alalucie.net					
Anna Belle's Bistro 127 N Limestone St	Lexington	KY	40507	859-381-0900	381-1336
Bella Notte 3715 Nicholasville Rd	Lexington	KY	40503	859-245-1789	245-2072
Web: www.bellalexington.com					
Billy's Hickory Pit Bar B-Q 101 Cochran Rd	Lexington	KY	40502	859-269-9593	266-7865
Bistro 147 147 N Limestone St	Lexington	KY	40507	859-225-8883	
Charlie Brown's Restaurant 816 E Euclid Ave	Lexington	KY	40502	859-269-5701	
Cheapside Bar & Grill 131 Cheapside St	Lexington	KY	40507	859-254-0046	233-2146
Web: www.cheapsidebarandgrill.com					
DeSha's 101 N Broadway	Lexington	KY	40507	859-259-3771	254-1602
Web: www.deshas.com					
Dudley's 380 S Mill St	Lexington	KY	40508	859-252-1010	253-9383
Web: www.dudleysrestaurant.com					
Durango's 2121 Richmond Rd	Lexington	KY	40502	859-268-0723	269-0396
Hunan 115 Southland Dr	Lexington	KY	40503	859-278-3811	
Jalapeno's 295 New Circle Rd NW	Lexington	KY	40505	859-299-8299	294-9739
Joe Bologna's 117 W Maxwell St	Lexington	KY	40508	859-259-0495	259-0496
Web: www.joebolognas.com					
Jonathan at Gratz Park 120 W 2nd St	Lexington	KY	40507	859-252-4949	252-4949
Ketch The 2012 Regency Rd	Lexington	KY	40503	859-277-5919	277-6304
Web: www.theketch.info					
Malone's 3347 Tates Creek Rd	Lexington	KY	40502	859-335-6500	335-1815
Web: www.malonesrestaurant.com					
Mandarin Oriental Cafe 2220 Nicholasville Rd	Lexington	KY	40503	859-275-1666	275-1666
Mansion at Griffin Gate 1800 Newtown Pike	Lexington	KY	40511	859-288-6142	255-9944
Merrick Inn 3380 Tates Creek Rd	Lexington	KY	40502	859-269-5417	269-5934
Web: www.murrays-merrick.com					
Natasha's Cafe 108 Esplanade St	Lexington	KY	40507	859-259-2694	
Web: www.natashascafe.com					
Panda Garden 531 W New Circle Rd	Lexington	KY	40511	859-299-9798	
Portofino 249 E Main St	Lexington	KY	40507	859-253-9300	258-2488
Web: www.portofinolexington.com					
Ramsey's 500 E High St	Lexington	KY	40507	859-259-2708	
Seki 1093 S Broadway	Lexington	KY	40504	859-254-5289	
Tachibana 785 Newtown Ct	Lexington	KY	40511	859-254-1911	231-3804
2 Hahns Mongolian Grill 9148 Taylorsville Rd	Louisville	KY	40299	502-493-0234	495-1001
211 Clover Lane 211 Clover Ln	Louisville	KY	40207	502-896-9570	896-9591
Web: www.211cloverlane.com					
610 Magnolia 610 Magnolia Ave	Louisville	KY	40208	502-636-0783	636-0787
Web: www.610magnolia.com					
Artemisia 620 E Market St	Louisville	KY	40202	502-583-4177	584-4178
Web: www.artemisiarestaurant.com					
Asiatique 1767 Bardstown Rd	Louisville	KY	40205	502-451-2749	451-2797
Web: www.asiatique.bigstep.com					
August Moon 2269 Lexington Rd	Louisville	KY	40206	502-456-6569	456-4669
Web: www.augustmoonbistro.com					
Avalon 1314 Bardstown Rd	Louisville	KY	40204	502-454-5336	
Azalea 3612 Brownsboro Rd	Louisville	KY	40207	502-895-5493	895-4822
Web: tosabe.com/azalea					
Bazo's Fresh Mexican Grill 323 Wallace Ave	Louisville	KY	40207	502-899-9600	
Bristol Bar & Grille 300 N Hurstbourne Pkwy	Louisville	KY	40222	502-426-0627	426-9318
Browning's Restaurant & Brewery 401 E Main St Louisville Slugger Field	Louisville	KY	40220	502-515-0174	515-0175
Buck's 425 W Ormsby Ave	Louisville	KY	40203	502-637-5284	637-7883
Cafe Kilimanjaro 649 S 4th St	Louisville	KY	40202	502-583-4332	583-3143
Web: www.cafekilimanjaro.com					
Cafe Metro 1700 Bardstown Rd	Louisville	KY	40205	502-458-4830	458-4252
Web: www.cafemetrolouisville.com					
Club Grotto 2116 Bardstown Rd	Louisville	KY	40205	502-459-5275	473-7186
De La Torre's 1606 Bardstown Rd	Louisville	KY	40205	502-456-4955	
Web: www.delatorres.com					
El Mundo 2345 Frankfort Ave	Louisville	KY	40206	502-899-9930	
Web: www.502elmundo.com					
English Grill 335 W Broadway St	Louisville	KY	40202	502-583-1234	

Kentucky (Cont'd)

Restaurant	City	State	Zip	Phone	Fax
Equus 122 Sears Ave	Louisville	KY	40207	502-897-9721	897-0535
Web: www.equusrestaurant.com					
Jarfi's Bistro 501 W Main St	Louisville	KY	502562075	02-589-5060	562-0785
Kashmir 1285 Bardstown Rd	Louisville	KY	40204	502-473-8765	
Web: www.kashmirlouisville.com					
Lilly's 1147 Bardstown Rd	Louisville	KY	40204	502-451-0447	
Web: www.lillyslapeche.com					
Limestone Falls Restaurant 10001 Forest Green Blvd	Louisville	KY	40223	502-426-7477	426-7479
Web: www.limestonerestaurant.com					
Lynn's Paradise Cafe 984 Barret Ave	Louisville	KY	40204	502-583-3447	583-0211
Web: www.lynnsparadisecafe.com					
Morton's The Steakhouse 626 W Main St	Louisville	KY	40202	502-584-0421	584-7463
Web: www.mortons.com					
Napa River Grill 3938 DuPont Cir	Louisville	KY	40207	502-893-0141	899-5893
Oakroom The 500 S 4th Ave	Louisville	KY	40202	502-807-3463	585-9239
Park Place 401 E Main St	Louisville	KY	40202	502-515-0172	515-0176
Web: www.parkplaceonmain.com					
Pat's Steak House 2437 Brownsboro Rd	Louisville	KY	40206	502-896-9234	893-2062
Porcini 2730 Frankfort Ave	Louisville	KY	40206	502-894-8686	899-1798
Ruth's Chris Steak House 6100 Dutchman's Ln 16th Fl	Louisville	KY	40205	502-479-0026	451-5340
Web: www.ruthschris.com					
Uptown Cafe 1624 Bardstown Rd	Louisville	KY	40205	502-458-4212	458-4252
Vincenzo's 150 S 5th St	Louisville	KY	40202	502-580-1350	580-1355
Web: www.vincenzosdining.biz					
Winston's 3101 Bardstown Rd	Louisville	KY	40205	502-456-0980	456-0040
Yang Kee Noodle 7900 Shelbyville Rd	Louisville	KY	40222	502-426-0800	426-9080
Web: www.yangkeenoodle.com					
Patron The 3400 Frankfort Ave	Saint Matthews	KY	40207	502-896-1661	896-1643
Web: www.thepatron.org					

Louisiana

Restaurant	City	State	Zip	Phone	Fax
Albasha 5454 Bluebonnet Rd Suite G	Baton Rouge	LA	70809	225-292-7988	291-2739
Web: www.albashabr.com/					
Boutin's 8322 Bluebonnet Blvd	Baton Rouge	LA	70810	225-819-9862	819-9759
Web: www.boutins.com					
Brunet's Cajun Restaurant 135 S Flannery Rd	Baton Rouge	LA	70815	225-272-6226	272-0353
Web: www.brunetscajunrestaurant.com					
Chimes Restaurant & Tap Room 3357 Highland Rd	Baton Rouge	LA	70802	225-383-1754	387-5413
Web: www.thechimes.com					
Copelands of New Orleans 4957 Essen Ln	Baton Rouge	LA	70809	225-769-1800	769-1812
Web: www.copelands.net					
Don's Seafood & Steak House 6823 Airline Hwy	Baton Rouge	LA	70805	225-357-0601	357-9543
Fleming's Prime Steakhouse & Wine Bar 7321 Corporate Blvd	Baton Rouge	LA	70809	225-925-2710	925-9523
Web: www.flemingssteakhouse.com					
Gino's 4542 Bennington Ave	Baton Rouge	LA	70808	225-927-7156	927-7146
Web: www.ginosrestaurant.com					
India's 5230 Essen Ln	Baton Rouge	LA	70809	225-769-0600	769-2683
Juban's 3739 Perkins Rd	Baton Rouge	LA	70808	225-346-8422	387-2601
Web: www.jubans.com					
Kiva's 7622 Old Hammond Hwy	Baton Rouge	LA	70809	225-923-3222	923-8222
Web: www.kivasbr.com					
Koto of Japan 3023 College Dr	Baton Rouge	LA	70808	225-924-1980	925-8530
Web: www.kotoofjapan.com					
Mansur's 5720 Corporate Blvd	Baton Rouge	LA	70808	225-923-3366	923-2976
Web: www.mansursontheboulevard.com					
Melting Pot The 5294 Corporate Blvd	Baton Rouge	LA	70808	225-928-5677	928-5622
Web: www.meltingpot.com					
Mike Anderson's Seafood Restaurant 1031 W Lee Dr	Baton Rouge	LA	70820	225-766-3728	766-3205
Web: www.mikeandersonsseafood.com					
Ninfa's Restaurant 4738 Constitution Ave	Baton Rouge	LA	70808	225-924-0377	924-5620
Nino's 7512 Bluebonnet Blvd	Baton Rouge	LA	70810	225-757-9300	757-9302
Portobello's Grill 1072 W Lee Dr	Baton Rouge	LA	70808	225-761-5005	763-9447
Web: www.portobellos.net					
Ruth's Chris Steak House 4836 Constitution Ave	Baton Rouge	LA	70808	225-925-0163	927-0368
Web: www.ruthschris.com					
Sullivan's Steakhouse 5252 Corporate Blvd	Baton Rouge	LA	70808	225-925-1161	925-2348
Web: www.sullivansteakhouse.com					
Thai Kitchen 4335 Perkins Rd	Baton Rouge	LA	70808	225-346-1230	346-5113
Web: www.thaikitchenexpress.com					
TJ Ribs 2324 S Acadian Thwy	Baton Rouge	LA	70808	225-383-7427	346-1227
L'Italiano 701 Barksdale Blvd	Bossier City	LA	71111	318-747-7777	
Lucky Palace 750 Isle of Capri Blvd	Bossier City	LA	71111	318-752-1888	752-1177
Nicky's 1400 Airline Dr	Bossier City	LA	71112	318-746-8811	746-0829
Web: www.nickysmexicanrestaurant.com					
Ralph & Kacoo's 1700 Old Minden Rd	Bossier City	LA	71111	318-747-6660	747-9816
Nash's 101 E 2nd St	Broussard	LA	70518	337-839-9333	839-9330
Web: www.nashsrestaurant.com					
Antoni's Italian Cafe 1118 Coolidge Blvd Suite A	Lafayette	LA	70503	337-232-8384	232-4311
Web: www.antoniscafe.com					
Bailey's Seafood & Grill 5520A Johnston St	Lafayette	LA	70503	337-988-6464	988-6494
Bella Figura 340-C Kaliste Saloom Rd	Lafayette	LA	70508	337-216-6660	
Cafe Vermilionville 1304 W Pinhook Rd	Lafayette	LA	70503	337-237-0100	233-5599
Web: www.cafev.com					
Casa Ole 2312 Kaliste Saloom Rd	Lafayette	LA	70508	337-993-9900	
Charley G's Seafood Grill 3809 Ambassador Caffery Pkwy	Lafayette	LA	70503	337-981-0108	981-5899
Web: www.charleygs.com					
Country Cuisine 709 N University Ave	Lafayette	LA	70506	337-269-1653	
Don's Seafood & Steakhouse 301 E Vermilion St	Lafayette	LA	70501	337-235-3551	235-6707
I Monelli Italian Restaurant 4017 Johnston St	Lafayette	LA	70503	337-989-9291	981-5618
Lafayette's 1025 Kaliste Saloom Rd	Lafayette	LA	70508	337-216-9024	216-9067
Web: www.lafayettes.com					
LaFonda 3809 Johnston St	Lafayette	LA	70503	337-984-5630	984-5639
Picante Mexican Restaurant 3235 NW Evangeline Thwy	Lafayette	LA	70507	337-896-1200	896-1202
Prejean's Restaurant 3480 I-49 N	Lafayette	LA	70507	337-896-3247	896-9193
Web: www.prejeans.com					
Ruth's Chris Steak House 620 W Pinhook Rd	Lafayette	LA	70503	337-237-6123	237-8013
Web: www.ruthschris.com					
Tsunami 412 Jefferson St	Lafayette	LA	70501	337-234-3474	234-3426
Web: www.servingsushi.com					
Acropolis Cuisine 3841 Veterans Memorial Blvd	Metairie	LA	70002	504-888-9046	888-9012
Anselmo's 3401 N Hullen St	Metairie	LA	70002	504-889-1212	889-1792
Ardoise 4300 Veterans Memorial Blvd	Metairie	LA	70006	504-885-5566	
Bozo's 3117 21st St	Metairie	LA	70002	504-831-8666	
Carreta's Grill 2320 Veterans Memorial Blvd	Metairie	LA	70002	504-837-6696	
Casa Garcia 8814 Veterans Memorial Blvd	Metairie	LA	70003	504-464-0354	
Cuco's 5048 Veterans Memorial Blvd	Metairie	LA	70006	504-454-5005	
Deanie's Seafood 1713 Lake Ave	Metairie	LA	70005	504-834-1225	837-2166
Web: www.deanies.com					
Drago's 3232 N Arnoult Rd	Metairie	LA	70002	504-888-9254	888-9255
Web: www.dragosrestaurant.com					
Fausto's Bistro 530 Veterans Memorial Blvd	Metairie	LA	70005	504-833-7121	
Web: www.faustosbistro.com					
Impastato's 3400 16th St	Metairie	LA	70002	504-455-1545	833-1816
Web: www.impastatos.com					
La Thai Cuisine 933 Metairie Rd	Metairie	LA	70005	504-828-3080	
Little Tokyo 1521 N Causeway Blvd	Metairie	LA	70001	504-831-6788	831-6672
Peppermill Restaurant 3524 Severn Ave	Metairie	LA	70002	504-455-2266	
Ruth's Chris Steak House 3633 Veterans Memorial Blvd	Metairie	LA	70002	504-888-3600	885-6422
Web: www.ruthschris.com					
Sake Cafe 4201 Veterans Memorial Blvd	Metairie	LA	70003	504-779-7253	
Serrano's Salsa Co 4436 Veterans Memorial Blvd Suite 36	Metairie	LA	70002	504-780-2354	780-2358
Web: www.serranossalsacompany.com					
Siamese Restaurant 6601 Veterans Memorial Blvd	Metairie	LA	70003	504-454-8752	454-8751
Web: www.siamesecuisine.com					
Sun Ray Grill 619 Pink St	Metairie	LA	70005	504-837-0055	835-2555
Web: www.sunraygrill.com					
Texas Bar-B-Que 3320 Houma Blvd	Metairie	LA	70006	504-456-2832	
Vega Tapas Cafe 2051 Metairie Rd	Metairie	LA	70005	504-836-2007	833-0907
Web: vegatapascafe.com					
Vincent's 4411 Chastant St	Metairie	LA	70006	504-885-2984	
Acme Oyster House 724 Iberville St	New Orleans	LA	70130	504-522-5973	524-1595
Web: www.acmeoyster.com					
Antoine's 713 Saint Louis St	New Orleans	LA	70130	504-581-4044	581-2152
Web: www.antoines.com					
Arnaud's 813 Bienville St	New Orleans	LA	70112	504-523-5433	581-7908
Web: www.arnauds.com					
August 301 Tchoupitoulas St	New Orleans	LA	70130	504-299-9777	299-1199
Web: www.rest-august.com					
Bacco 310 Chartres St	New Orleans	LA	70130	504-522-2426	521-8323
Web: www.bacco.com					
Bayona 430 Dauphine St	New Orleans	LA	70112	504-525-4455	522-0589
Web: www.bayona.com					
Begue's 300 Bourbon St	New Orleans	LA	70130	504-553-2278	
Bon Ton Cafe 401 Magazine St	New Orleans	LA	70130	504-524-3386	
Bourbon House Seafood & Oyster Bar 144 Bourbon St	New Orleans	LA	70130	504-522-0111	522-0333
Web: www.bourbonhouse.com					
Brigtsen's 723 Dante St	New Orleans	LA	70118	504-861-7610	866-7397
Web: www.brigtsens.com					
Broussard's Restaurant 819 rue Conti	New Orleans	LA	70112	504-581-3866	581-3873
Web: www.broussards.com					
Byblos 3218 Magazine St	New Orleans	LA	70115	504-894-1233	894-1239
Cafe Degas 3127 Esplanade Ave	New Orleans	LA	70119	504-945-5635	943-5255
Web: www.cafedegas.com					
Cafe Giovanni 117 Decatur St	New Orleans	LA	70130	504-529-2154	529-3352
Web: cafegiovanni.com					
Casamento's 4330 Magazine St	New Orleans	LA	70115	504-895-9761	
Ciro's Cote Sud 7918 Maple St	New Orleans	LA	70118	504-866-9551	
Clancy's 6100 Annunciation St	New Orleans	LA	70118	504-895-1111	
Cuvee 322 Magazine St	New Orleans	LA	70130	504-587-9001	587-9006
Web: www.restaurantcuvee.com					
Dick & Jenny's 4501 Tchoupitoulas St	New Orleans	LA	70115	504-894-9880	895-5636
Web: www.dickandjennys.com					
Dominique's 1001 Toulouse St	New Orleans	LA	70112	504-586-8000	648-6106
Web: dominiquesrestaurant.com					
Elizabeth's 601 Gallier St	New Orleans	LA	70117	504-944-9272	
Emeril's 800 Tchoupitoulas St	New Orleans	LA	70130	504-528-9393	558-3925
Web: www.emerils.com/restaurants					
Emeril's Delmonico 1300 St Charles Ave	New Orleans	LA	70130	504-525-4937	595-2206
Web: www.emerils.com/restaurants					
Galatoire's 209 Bourbon St	New Orleans	LA	70130	504-525-2021	525-5900
Web: www.galatoires.com					
GW Fins 808 Bienville St	New Orleans	LA	70012	504-581-3467	565-5459
Web: www.gwfins.com					
Herbsaint 701 St Charles Ave	New Orleans	LA	70130	504-524-4114	522-1679
Web: www.herbsaint.com					
Horinoya 920 Poydras St	New Orleans	LA	70112	504-561-8914	561-8919
Irene's Cuisine 539 Saint Phillip St	New Orleans	LA	70116	504-529-8811	527-5273
Jacques-Imo's Cafe 8324 Oak St	New Orleans	LA	70118	504-861-0886	314-1585
Web: www.jacquesimoscafe.com					
K-Paul's Louisiana Kitchen 416 Chartres St	New Orleans	LA	70130	504-524-7394	596-2540
Web: www.kpauls.com					
Kyoto 4920 Prytania St	New Orleans	LA	70115	504-891-3644	891-3694
La Crepe Nanou 1410 Robert St	New Orleans	LA	70115	504-899-2670	
Liborio's 321 Magazine St	New Orleans	LA	70130	504-581-9680	
Web: www.liboriocuban.com					
Lilette 3637 Magazine St	New Orleans	LA	70115	504-895-1636	895-3622
Web: www.liletterestaurant.com					
Lolita 3312 Esplanade Ave	New Orleans	LA	70119	504-488-6946	
Louisiana Bistro 337 Dauphine St	New Orleans	LA	70112	504-525-3335	
Martinique Bistro 5908 Magazine St	New Orleans	LA	70115	504-891-8495	891-2622
Mat & Naddie's Restaurant 937 Leonidas St	New Orleans	LA	70118	504-861-9600	865-8094
Web: www.matandnaddies.com					
Morton's The Steakhouse 365 Canal St	New Orleans	LA	70130	504-566-0221	566-8326
Web: www.mortons.com					
Mr B's Bistro 201 Royal St	New Orleans	LA	70130	504-523-2078	521-8304
Web: www.mrbsbistro.com/					
Muriel's 801 Chartres St	New Orleans	LA	70116	504-568-1885	568-9795
Web: www.muriels.com					
New Orleans Grill 300 Gravier St	New Orleans	LA	70130	504-522-1992	596-4513
Ninja 8433 Oak St	New Orleans	LA	70118	504-866-1119	
NOLA 534 Saint Louis St	New Orleans	LA	70130	504-522-6652	524-6178
Web: www.emerils.com/restaurants/neworleans_nola/					
Orleans Grapevine Wine Bar & Bistro 720 Orleans Ave	New Orleans	LA	70116	504-523-1930	523-1245
Web: www.orleansgrapevine.com					
Palace Cafe 605 Canal St	New Orleans	LA	70130	504-523-1661	
Web: www.palacecafe.com					
Pelican Club 312 Exchange Alley	New Orleans	LA	70130	504-523-1504	522-2331
Web: www.pelicanclub.com					
Peristyle 1041 Dumaine St	New Orleans	LA	70016	504-593-9535	
Petunias 817 Saint Louis St	New Orleans	LA	70112	504-522-6440	528-9042
Web: www.petuniasrestaurant.com					
Port of Call 838 Esplanade Ave	New Orleans	LA	70116	504-523-0120	529-7678
Red Fish Grill 115 Bourbon St	New Orleans	LA	70130	504-598-1200	598-1211
Web: www.redfishgrill.com					
Rib Room 621 Saint Louis St	New Orleans	LA	70140	504-529-7045	529-7089
RioMar 800 S Peters St	New Orleans	LA	70130	504-525-3474	
Web: www.riomarseafood.com					
Sake Cafe 2830 Magazine St	New Orleans	LA	70115	504-894-0033	894-1546
Web: www.sakecafeuptown.com					
Sara's 724 Dublin St	New Orleans	LA	70118	504-861-0565	
Web: www.sarasrestaurant.com					
Stella! 1032 Chartres St	New Orleans	LA	70116	504-587-0091	587-0092
Web: www.restaurantstella.com					
Sun Ray Grill 1051 Annunciation St	New Orleans	LA	70130	504-566-0021	566-0041
Web: www.sunraygrill.com					
Upperline 1413 Upperline St	New Orleans	LA	70115	504-891-9822	
Web: www.upperline.com					

				Phone	Fax
Veranda Restaurant 444 St Charles Ave	New Orleans	LA	70130	504-525-5566	
Vincent's 7839 St Charles Ave	New Orleans	LA	70118	504-866-9313	861-8972
Web: www.vincentsitaliancuisine.com					
Wasabi 900 Frenchman St	New Orleans	LA	70116	504-943-9433	943-4579
Web: www.wasabirestaurant.com					
Bella Fresca Restaurant 6307 Line Ave	Shreveport	LA	71101	318-865-6307	865-6362
Bistro 6301 6301 Line Ave	Shreveport	LA	71106	318-865-6301	
Web: www.bistro6301.com					
Chianti Restaurant 6535 Line Ave	Shreveport	LA	71106	318-868-8866	865-7119
Copeland's of New Orleans 1665 E Industrial Loop	Shreveport	LA	71106	318-797-0143	797-7135
Web: www.copelands.net					
Don's Seafood & Steak House 3100 Highland Ave	Shreveport	LA	71104	318-865-4291	869-1925
Earthereal Restaurant 3309 Line Ave	Shreveport	LA	71104	318-865-8947	
Ernest's Orleans Restaurant 1601 Spring St S	Shreveport	LA	71101	318-226-1325	425-0900
Web: ernestsorleans.com					
Jayne Marie on Cross Lake 5301 S Lakeshore Dr	Shreveport	LA	71105	318-631-0919	
Web: www.jaynemarieoncrosslake.com					
Kon Tiki 5815 Youree Dr	Shreveport	LA	71105	318-869-2316	868-7688
Mabry House 1540 Irving Pl	Shreveport	LA	71101	318-227-1121	227-1121
Ming Garden 1250 Shreveport Barksdale Hwy	Shreveport	LA	71105	318-861-2741	865-7222
Monjunis 1315 Louisiana Ave	Shreveport	LA	71101	318-227-0847	
Web: www.monjunis.com					
Noble Savage Tavern 417 Texas St	Shreveport	LA	71101	318-221-1781	
Superior Bar & Grill 6123 Line Ave	Shreveport	LA	71106	318-869-3243	868-7688
Trejo's 9122 Mansfield Rd	Shreveport	LA	71118	318-687-6192	687-8187
Village Grille 1313 Louisiana Ave	Shreveport	LA	71101	318-424-2874	

Maine

				Phone	Fax
Augusta House of Pancakes 100 Western Ave	Augusta	ME	04330	207-623-9775	
Capital Buffet 208 Western Ave	Augusta	ME	04330	207-623-8878	626-3568
Ground Round 110 Community Dr	Augusta	ME	04330	207-623-0022	621-2860
Margaritas 390 Western Ave	Augusta	ME	04330	207-622-7874	622-7908
Web: www.margs.com					
Red Barn 455 Riverside Dr	Augusta	ME	04330	207-623-9485	623-9520
Riverfront Barbeque & Grill 300 Water St	Augusta	ME	04330	207-622-8899	
Senator Oyster Bar & Grill 284 Outer Western Ave	Augusta	ME	04330	207-622-0320	622-8803
Tea House 8 Shuman Ave	Augusta	ME	04330	207-622-7500	622-7500
Thai Star 75 Airport Rd	Augusta	ME	04330	207-621-8575	621-8576
Vickery Cafe 261 Water St	Augusta	ME	04330	207-623-7670	
Bugaboo Creek Steak House 24 Bangor Mall Blvd	Bangor	ME	04401	207-945-5515	945-5445
Web: www.bugaboocreeksteakhouse.com					
Captain Nick's 1165 Union St	Bangor	ME	04401	207-942-6444	947-8630
China Light 571 Broadway	Bangor	ME	04401	207-947-6759	
China Wall 930 Stillwater Ave	Bangor	ME	04401	207-941-9331	990-2898
Geaghan's Restaurant & Pub 570 Main St	Bangor	ME	04401	207-945-3730	941-6758
Web: www.geaghanspub.com					
Governor's Restaurant & Bakery 643 Broadway	Bangor	ME	04401	207-947-3113	942-2209
Web: www.governorsrestaurant.com					
Ichiban 226 Union St	Bangor	ME	04401	207-262-9308	262-9310
Momma Baldacci's 12 Alden St	Bangor	ME	04401	207-945-5813	990-1757
New Moon 49 Park St	Bangor	ME	04401	207-990-2233	990-6070
Web: www.newmoondining.com					
Opus 193 Broad St	Bangor	ME	04401	207-945-5100	
Web: opusme.com					
Oriental Jade 555 Stillwater Ave	Bangor	ME	04401	207-947-6969	942-7170
Web: www.orientaljade.com					
Panda Garden 123 Franklin St	Bangor	ME	04401	207-942-2704	942-2704
Pepino's 570 Stillwater Ave	Bangor	ME	04401	207-947-1233	947-1233
Web: www.pepinosrestaurant.com					
Sea Dog Brewing Co 26 Front St	Bangor	ME	04401	207-947-8004	947-8720
Web: seadogbrewing.com					
Thistle's 175 Exchange St	Bangor	ME	04401	207-945-5480	990-3836
Web: www.thistlesrestaurant.com					
Whig & Courier Pub 18 Broad St	Bangor	ME	04401	207-947-4095	947-4095
Wright Bros American Grill & Lounge 308 Godfrey Blvd	Bangor	ME	04401	207-947-6721	941-9761
Cafe Blue Fish 122 Cottage St	Bar Harbor	ME	04609	207-288-3696	
Web: www.cafebluefishbarharbor.com					
China Joy 195 Main St	Bar Harbor	ME	04609	207-288-8666	288-8662
Freddies Route 66 21 Cottage St	Bar Harbor	ME	04609	207-288-3708	
Web: www.bhroute66.com					
Geddy's Pub 19 Main St	Bar Harbor	ME	04609	207-288-5077	288-9927
Web: www.geddys.com					
Havana 318 Main St	Bar Harbor	ME	04609	207-288-2822	
Maggie's Classic Scales 6 Summer St	Bar Harbor	ME	04609	207-288-9007	
Web: www.maggiesbarharbor.com					
Mama Di Matteo's 34 Kennebec Pl	Bar Harbor	ME	04609	207-288-3666	
Web: www.mamadimatteos.com					
Michelle's 194 Main St	Bar Harbor	ME	04609	207-288-0038	
Web: www.ivymanor.com					
Parkside Restaurant 185 Main St	Bar Harbor	ME	04609	207-288-3700	288-4929
Poor Boy's Gourmet 300 Main St	Bar Harbor	ME	04609	207-288-4148	
Web: www.poorboysgourmet.com					
Rosalie's 46 Cottage St	Bar Harbor	ME	04609	207-288-5666	
Rupununi Bar & Grill 119 Main St	Bar Harbor	ME	04609	207-288-2886	
Web: www.rupununi.com					
Stewman's Lobster Pound 123 Eden St	Bar Harbor	ME	04609	207-288-9723	288-9723
Web: www.stewmans.com					
West Street Cafe 76 West St	Bar Harbor	ME	04609	207-288-5242	
Web: www.weststreetcafe.com					
Audubon Room 40 Bowery Beach Rd	Cape Elizabeth	ME	04107	207-767-0888	767-0891
Web: www.innbythesea.com					
Hattie's Chowder House 103 Water St	Hallowell	ME	04347	207-621-4114	621-2622
Web: www.hattieslobsterstew.com					
Lucky Garden 218 Water St	Hallowell	ME	04347	207-622-3465	
Bar Harbor Lobster Bakes 10 State Hwy 3	Hulls Cove	ME	04644	207-288-4055	288-5767
Web: www.barharborlobsterbakes.com					
Back Bay Grill 65 Portland St	Portland	ME	04101	207-772-8833	
Web: www.backbaygrill.com					
Benkay 2 India St	Portland	ME	04101	207-773-5555	
Bintliff's American Cafe 98 Portland St	Portland	ME	04101	207-774-0005	774-2505
Web: www.bintliffscafe.com					
Blue Spoon 89 Congress St	Portland	ME	04101	207-773-1116	773-1119
Cafe Uffa 190 State St	Portland	ME	04101	207-775-3380	
Web: www.uffarestaurant.com					
Cinque Terre 36 Wharf St	Portland	ME	04101	207-347-6154	347-6157
Web: www.cinqueterremaine.com					
David's Creative Cuisine 22 Monument Sq	Portland	ME	04101	207-773-4340	773-4425
Web: www.davidsrestaurant.com/					
DiMillo's Floating Restaurant 25 Long Wharf	Portland	ME	04101	207-772-2216	772-1082
Web: www.dimillos.com					
Duckfat 43 Middle St	Portland	ME	04101	207-774-8080	774-0262
Web: www.duckfat.com					
Eve's 468 Fore St	Portland	ME	04101	207-523-2045	775-9990
Web: www.portlandharborhotel.com					
Federal Spice 225 Federal St	Portland	ME	04101	207-774-6404	
Fore Street 288 Fore St	Portland	ME	04101	207-775-2717	
Fuji 29 Exchange St	Portland	ME	04101	207-773-2900	773-7096
Web: www.fujimaine.com					
Gilbert's Chowder House 92 Commercial St	Portland	ME	04101	207-871-5636	
Hugo's Restaurant 88 Middle St	Portland	ME	04101	207-774-8538	
Web: www.hugos.net					
Katahdin Restaurant 106 High St	Portland	ME	04101	207-774-1740	774-1740
Web: www.katahdinrestaurant.com					
Maria's 337 Cumberland Ave	Portland	ME	04101	207-772-9232	
Mims Brasserie 205 Commercial St	Portland	ME	04101	207-347-7478	
Pat's Cafe 484 Stevens Ave	Portland	ME	04103	207-874-0706	
Web: cafeatpats.com					
Pepperclub 78 Middle St	Portland	ME	04101	207-772-0531	
Porthole 20 Custom House Wharf	Portland	ME	04101	207-780-6533	
Portland Lobster Co 180 Commercial St	Portland	ME	04112	207-775-2112	
Web: www.portlandlobstercompany.com					
Ri Ra Irish Pub & Restaurant 72 Commercial St	Portland	ME	04101	207-761-4446	761-4447
Web: www.rira.com					
Ribollita 41 Middle St	Portland	ME	04101	207-774-2972	
Roma The 769 Congress St	Portland	ME	04102	207-773-9873	756-6768
Web: www.theromacafe.com					
Saigon Thinh Thanh 608 Congress St	Portland	ME	04101	207-773-2932	773-3084
Sapporo 230 Commercial St	Portland	ME	04101	207-772-1233	871-9275
Web: www.sappororestaurant.com					
Siam City Cafe 339 Fore St	Portland	ME	04101	207-773-8389	773-6369
Web: www.siamportland.com					
Walter's Cafe 15 Exchange St	Portland	ME	04101	207-871-9258	871-1018
Web: www.walterscafe.com					
Joe's Boathouse 1 Spring Point Dr	South Portland	ME	04106	207-741-2780	347-5718
Web: www.joesboathouse.com					

Manitoba

				Phone	Fax
529 Wellington 529 Wellington Crescent	Winnipeg	MB	R2M5G8	204-487-8325	
Alycias 559 Cathedral Ave	Winnipeg	MB	R2W0Y6	204-582-8789	
Amici 326 Broadway	Winnipeg	MB	R3C0S5	204-943-4997	943-0369
Web: www.amiciwpg.com					
Bailey's 185 Lombard Ave	Winnipeg	MB	R3B0W4	204-944-1180	
Bella Vista 53 Maryland St	Winnipeg	MB	R3G1K6	204-775-4485	
Bombolini 326 Broadway	Winnipeg	MB	R3C0S5	204-943-5066	943-0369
Branigan's 162-1 Forks Market Rd	Winnipeg	MB	R3C4L8	204-948-0020	
Web: www.bdgrestaurantgroup.com/branigans/					
Cafe Carlo 243 Lilac St	Winnipeg	MB	R3M2S2	204-477-5544	477-1652
Web: www.cafecarlo.com					
Chianti's Fine Dining 680 St Anne's Rd Suite D	Winnipeg	MB	R2N3M6	204-257-0630	
Delicious Vegetarian 1467 Pembina Hwy	Winnipeg	MB	R3T2C5	204-477-1530	
Dim Sum Garden 277 Rupert Ave	Winnipeg	MB	R3B0N5	204-942-8297	947-5834
East India Co 349 York Ave	Winnipeg	MB	R3C3S9	204-947-3097	
Web: www.eastindiaco.com					
Edohei 355 Ellice Ave	Winnipeg	MB	R3B1X8	204-943-0427	
Web: www.edohei.mb.ca					
Elephant & Castle 350 St Mary Ave	Winnipeg	MB	R3C3J2	204-942-5555	947-0275
Web: www.elephantcastle.com					
Fusion Grill 550 Academy Rd	Winnipeg	MB	R3N0E3	204-489-6963	
Web: www.fusiongrill.mb.ca					
Gasthaus Gutenberger 2583 Portage Ave	Winnipeg	MB	R2Y0V3	204-888-3133	
Web: www.gasthaus-gutenberger.com					
Good Earth Chop Suey House 1849 Portage Ave	Winnipeg	MB	R2J0G8	204-889-8880	889-8882
Hy's Steak House 1 Lombard St	Winnipeg	MB	R3B0X3	204-942-1000	947-3588
Web: www.hyssteakhouse.com					
Ichiban 189 Carlton St	Winnipeg	MB	R3C3H7	204-925-7400	957-1697
Web: www.ichiban.ca					
King's Head Pub 120 King St	Winnipeg	MB	R3B1H9	204-957-7710	253-6520
La Vieille Gare 630 Des Meurons St	Winnipeg	MB	R2H2P9	204-237-5015	
Web: www.lavieillegare.com					
Liberty Grill 177 Lombard Ave	Winnipeg	MB	R3B0W5	204-947-0660	
Web: fae-wpg.com/liberty/libertygrill.htm					
Luce 635 Corydon Ave	Winnipeg	MB	R3M0W3	204-452-3037	
Marigold 2591 Portage Ave	Winnipeg	MB	R3J0P5	204-888-5665	
Maxime 1131 St Mary's Rd	Winnipeg	MB	R2M3T9	204-257-1521	
Mei Ji Sushi 454 River Ave	Winnipeg	MB	R3L0C7	204-284-3996	452-3749
Mona Lisa 1697 Corydon Ave	Winnipeg	MB	R3N0J9	204-488-3687	
Mondragon 91 Albert St	Winnipeg	MB	R3B1G5	204-946-5241	956-1505
Web: www.a-zone.org/mondragon/					
Orlando's Seafood Grill 709 Corydon Ave	Winnipeg	MB	R3M0W4	204-477-5899	
Pasta La Vista 66-333 St Mary Ave	Winnipeg	MB	R3C4A5	204-956-2229	942-6770
Web: www.wowhospitality.ca					
Pembina Village Restaurant 333 Pembina Hwy	Winnipeg	MB	R3L2E4	204-477-5439	
Restaurant Dubrovnik 390 Assiniboine Ave	Winnipeg	MB	R3C0Y1	204-944-0594	
Web: www.restaurantdubrovnik.com					
Sawatdee 555 Osborne St	Winnipeg	MB	R3L2B3	204-284-8424	
Spicy Noodle House 102-99 Osborne St	Winnipeg	MB	R3L2R4	204-287-2388	
Step'n Out Eclectic Cuisine 157 Provencher Blvd	Winnipeg	MB	R2H0G2	204-956-7837	
Tavern in the Park 55 Pavilion Crescent	Winnipeg	MB	R3P2N6	204-896-7275	896-9101
Web: www.taverninthepark.ca					
Toad in the Hole 112 Osborne St	Winnipeg	MB	R3L1Y5	204-284-7201	
Tre Visi 173 McDermot Ave	Winnipeg	MB	R3B0S1	204-949-9032	943-7540
Tropikis 878 Ellice Ave	Winnipeg	MB	R3G0C6	204-788-4733	772-7935
Velvet Glove The 2 Lombard Pl	Winnipeg	MB	R2C0A1	204-957-1350	
Vesuvio 696 Osborne St	Winnipeg	MB	R3L2B9	204-452-6084	
Wasabi Restaurant & Sushi Bistro 105-121 Osborne St	Winnipeg	MB	R3L1Y4	204-474-2332	
White Tower 3670 Roblin Blvd	Winnipeg	MB	R3R0E1	204-896-0406	837-3873

Maryland

				Phone	Fax
Adam's Ribs East 921C Chesapeake Ave	Annapolis	MD	21403	410-267-0064	626-1077
Web: www.adamsribseast.com/					
Aqua Terra 164 Main St	Annapolis	MD	21401	410-263-1985	263-1986
Web: www.aquaterraofannapolis.com					
Cafe Normandie 185 Main St	Annapolis	MD	21401	410-263-3382	263-8824
Cantler's Riverside Inn 458 Forest Beach Rd	Annapolis	MD	21409	410-757-1311	757-6784
Web: www.cantlers.com					
Castlebay Irish Pub 193A Main St	Annapolis	MD	21401	410-626-0165	626-0827
Famous Dave's Barbeque 181 Jennifer Rd	Annapolis	MD	21401	410-224-2207	224-2088
Web: www.famousdaves.com					
Federal House Bar & Grille 22 Market Space	Annapolis	MD	21401	410-268-2576	280-0195
Galway Bay 61-63 Maryland Ave	Annapolis	MD	21401	410-263-8333	263-8989
Web: www.galwaybayannapolis.com					
Harry Browne's 66 State Cir	Annapolis	MD	21401	410-263-4332	263-8049
Web: www.harrybrownes.com					
Jalapenos 85 Forest Dr	Annapolis	MD	21401	410-266-7580	266-7582
Web: www.jalapenosonline.com					

Maryland (Cont'd)

				Phone	Fax
Joss Cafe & Sushi Bar 195 Main St *Web:* www.josscafe-sushibar.com	Annapolis	MD	21401	410-263-4688	263-4764
La Mona Lisa 2444 Solomons Island Rd	Annapolis	MD	21401	410-266-7595	266-6425
Lebanese Taverna 2478 Solomons Island Rd *Web:* www.lebanesetaverna.com	Annapolis	MD	21037	410-897-1111	897-9099
Les Folies 2552 Riva Rd *Web:* www.lesfoliesbrasserie.com	Annapolis	MD	21401	410-573-0970	573-9131
Lewnes' Steakhouse 401 4th St *Web:* www.lewnessteakhouse.com	Annapolis	MD	21403	410-263-1617	
Main Ingredient 914 Bay Ridge Rd *Web:* www.themainingredient.com	Annapolis	MD	21403	410-626-0388	626-0204
Mangia 81 Main St *Web:* www.mangiagrille.com	Annapolis	MD	21401	410-268-1350	268-6420
Maria's Italian Ristorante 12 Market Space *Web:* www.mariasristorante.com	Annapolis	MD	21401	410-268-2112	280-1355
Melting Pot The 2348 Solomons Island Rd *Web:* www.meltingpot.com	Annapolis	MD	21401	410-266-8004	266-8431
Metropolitan 169 West St	Annapolis	MD	21401	410-268-7733	
Mexican Cafe 975 Bay Ridge Rd *Web:* www.mexicancafe.com	Annapolis	MD	21401	410-626-1520	
Northwoods 609 Melvin Ave *Web:* www.northwoodsrestaurant.com	Annapolis	MD	21401	410-268-2609	268-0930
O'Brien's Oyster Bar & Restaurant 113 Main St *Web:* www.obriensoysterbar.com	Annapolis	MD	21401	410-268-6288	267-7767
O'Leary's Seafood Restaurant 310 3rd St	Annapolis	MD	21403	410-263-0884	263-5859
Osteria 177 177 Main St *Web:* osteria177.com	Annapolis	MD	21401	410-267-7700	267-9999
Paul's Homewood Cafe 919 West St	Annapolis	MD	21401	410-267-7891	267-8004
Piccola Roma 200 Main St	Annapolis	MD	21401	410-268-7898	
Red Hot & Blue 200 Old Mill Bottom Rd S *Web:* www.redhotandblue.com	Annapolis	MD	21401	410-626-7427	757-5095
Reynolds Tavern 7 Church Cir *Web:* www.reynoldstavern.org	Annapolis	MD	21401	410-295-9555	295-9559
Riordan's Saloon & Restaurant 26 Market Space *Web:* www.riordans.com	Annapolis	MD	21401	410-263-5449	268-5768
Rockfish The 400 6th St *Web:* www.rockfishmd.com/	Annapolis	MD	21403	410-267-1800	
Ruth's Chris Steak House 301 Severn Ave *Web:* www.ruthschris.com	Annapolis	MD	21403	410-990-0033	269-6700
Sam's on the Waterfront 2020 Chesapeake Harbour Dr E *Web:* www.samsonthewaterfront.com	Annapolis	MD	21403	410-263-3600	263-3654
Tsunami 51 West St *Web:* www.tsunami51.com	Annapolis	MD	21401	410-990-9868	990-4939
Yin Yankee Cafe 105 Main St *Web:* www.yinyankee.com	Annapolis	MD	21401	410-268-8703	990-4322
Abacrombie 58 W Biddle St *Web:* www.abacrombie.net	Baltimore	MD	21201	410-244-7227	244-8415
Akbar 823 N Charles St *Web:* www.akbar-restaurant.com/	Baltimore	MD	21201	410-539-0944	539-0308
Aldo's 306 S High St *Web:* www.aldositaly.com	Baltimore	MD	21202	410-727-0700	625-3700
Ambassador Dining Room 3811 Canterbury Rd *Web:* www.ambassadordiningroom.com	Baltimore	MD	21218	410-366-1484	
Amicci's of Little Italy 231 S High St *Web:* www.amiccis.com	Baltimore	MD	21202	410-528-1096	685-6259
b 1501 Bolton St *Web:* www.b-bistro.com	Baltimore	MD	21217	410-383-8600	383-1017
Babalu Grill 32 Market Pl *Web:* www.babalugrill.com	Baltimore	MD	21202	410-234-9898	234-8028
Ban Thai 340 N Charles St *Web:* www.banthaibaltimore.com	Baltimore	MD	21201	410-727-7971	727-0125
Bicycle 1444 Light St *Web:* www.bicyclebistro.com/	Baltimore	MD	21230	410-234-1900	878-7146
Birches 641 S Montford Ave *Web:* www.birchesrestaurant.com	Baltimore	MD	21224	410-732-3000	
Black Olive 814 S Bond St *Web:* www.theblackolive.com	Baltimore	MD	21231	410-276-7141	276-7143
Blue Moon Cafe 1621 Aliceanna St	Baltimore	MD	21231	410-522-3940	
Blue Sea Grill 614 Water St *Web:* www.blueseagrill.com	Baltimore	MD	21202	410-837-7300	837-7200
Boccaccio 925 Eastern Ave *Web:* www.boccaccio-restaurant.com	Baltimore	MD	21202	410-234-1322	727-6318
Brass Elephant 924 N Charles St *Web:* www.brasselephant.com	Baltimore	MD	21201	410-547-8480	783-2933
Brewers Art 1106 N Charles St	Baltimore	MD	21201	410-547-9310	547-7417
Brighton's 550 Light St	Baltimore	MD	21202	410-347-9750	659-5925
Cafe Zen 438 E Belvedere Ave *Web:* www.cafezen.com	Baltimore	MD	21212	410-532-0022	
Carlyle Club 500 W University Pkwy	Baltimore	MD	21210	410-243-5454	
Chameleon Cafe 4341 Harford Rd *Web:* www.thechameleoncafe.com	Baltimore	MD	21214	410-254-2376	254-9437
Charleston 1000 Lancaster St *Web:* www.charlestonrestaurant.com	Baltimore	MD	21202	410-332-7373	332-8425
Chinatown Cafe 323 Park Ave	Baltimore	MD	21201	410-727-5599	727-6556
Ciao Bella 236 S High St *Web:* www.cbella.com	Baltimore	MD	21202	410-685-7733	625-4847
Copra 313 N Charles St	Baltimore	MD	21201	410-727-6080	727-6081
Cork's 1026 S Charles St *Web:* www.corksrestaurant.com	Baltimore	MD	21230	410-752-3810	752-0639
Cosmopolitan Bar & Grill 2933 O'Donnell St	Baltimore	MD	21224	410-563-5000	563-2947
Da Mimmo Italian Cuisine 217 S High St *Web:* www.damimmo.com	Baltimore	MD	21202	410-727-6876	727-1927
Dalesio's of Little Italy 829 Eastern Ave *Web:* www.dalesios.com	Baltimore	MD	21202	410-539-1965	576-8749
Della Note Ristorante 801 Eastern Ave *Web:* www.dellanotte.com	Baltimore	MD	21202	410-837-5500	837-2600
Dukem 1100 Maryland Ave **Fax Area Code: 202* ■ *Web:* www.dukemrestaurant.com	Baltimore	MD	21201	410-385-0318	667-2488*
Faidley's Seafood 203 N Paca St *Web:* www.faidleyscrabcakes.com	Baltimore	MD	21201	410-727-4898	
Fleming's Prime Steakhouse & Wine Bar 720 Aliceanna St *Web:* www.flemingssteakhouse.com	Baltimore	MD	21202	410-332-1666	332-0436
Gertrude's 10 Art Museum Dr	Baltimore	MD	21218	410-889-3399	889-9689
Helen's Garden 2908 O'Donnell St *Web:* www.helensgarden.com	Baltimore	MD	21224	410-276-2233	675-8132
Helmand The 806 N Charles St *Web:* www.helmand.com	Baltimore	MD	21201	410-752-0311	752-0511
Henninger's Tavern 1812 Bank St *Web:* www.henningerstavern.com	Baltimore	MD	21231	410-342-2172	
Holy Frijoles 908 W 36th St	Baltimore	MD	21211	410-235-2326	
Hull Street Blues 1222 Hull St *Web:* www.hullstreetblues.com	Baltimore	MD	21230	410-727-7476	576-2343
Ikaros 4805 Eastern Ave *Web:* www.ikarosrestaurant.com	Baltimore	MD	21224	410-633-3750	633-7881
Ixia 518 N Charles St *Web:* www.ixia-online.com	Baltimore	MD	21201	410-727-1800	727-1887
Kali's Court 1606 Thames St *Web:* www.kaliscourt.com	Baltimore	MD	21231	410-276-4700	276-2420
Kali's Mezze 1606 Thames St *Web:* www.kalismezze.com	Baltimore	MD	21231	410-563-7600	276-2420
La Scala 1012 Eastern Ave *Web:* www.lascaladining.com	Baltimore	MD	21202	410-727-3437	783-5949
La Tavola 248 Albemarle St *Web:* www.la-tavola.com	Baltimore	MD	21202	410-685-1859	685-1891
Little Havana 1325 Key Hwy *Web:* www.littlehavanas.com	Baltimore	MD	21230	410-837-9903	332-0775
Louisiana 1708 Aliceanna St	Baltimore	MD	21231	410-327-2610	327-0372
Mama's on the Half Shell 2901 O'Donnell St *Web:* www.mamasonthehalfshell.com	Baltimore	MD	21224	410-276-3160	327-7140
Martick's 214 W Mulberry St	Baltimore	MD	21201	410-752-5155	
Matsuri Restaurant 1105 S Charles St *Web:* www.matsuri.us	Baltimore	MD	21230	410-752-8561	752-9919
McCormick & Schmick's 711 Eastern Ave *Web:* www.mccormickandschmicks.com	Baltimore	MD	21202	410-234-1300	234-1430
Minato Restaurant 800 N Charles St *Web:* www.minatorestaurant.com	Baltimore	MD	21201	410-332-0332	547-5613
Morton's The Steakhouse 300 S Charles St *Web:* www.mortons.com	Baltimore	MD	21201	410-547-8255	547-8244
Mughal Garden 920 N Charles St	Baltimore	MD	21201	410-547-0001	547-0002
Nacho Mama's 2907 O'Donnell St	Baltimore	MD	21224	410-675-0898	
One World Cafe 100 W University Pkwy *Web:* www.one-world-cafe.com	Baltimore	MD	21210	410-235-5777	235-5815
Peter's Inn 504 S Ann St *Web:* www.petersinn.com	Baltimore	MD	21231	410-675-7313	
Petit Louis Bistro 4800 Roland Ave *Web:* www.petitlouis.com	Baltimore	MD	21210	410-366-9393	366-9019
Pisces 300 Light St	Baltimore	MD	21202	410-605-2835	605-2870
Prime Rib 1101 N Calvert St *Web:* www.theprimerib.com	Baltimore	MD	21202	410-539-1804	837-0244
Red Maple 930 N Charles St **Fax Area Code: 443* ■ *Web:* www.930redmaple.com	Baltimore	MD	21201	410-385-0520	524-1995*
Rocco's Capriccio 846 Fawn St	Baltimore	MD	21202	410-685-2710	
Roy's 720B Aliceanna St *Web:* www.roysrestaurant.com	Baltimore	MD	21202	410-659-0099	659-0075
Ruth's Chris Steak House 600 Water St *Web:* www.ruthschris.com	Baltimore	MD	21202	410-783-0033	783-0049
Sabatino's 901 Fawn St *Web:* www.sabatinos.com	Baltimore	MD	21202	410-727-9414	837-6540
Saffron 802 N Charles St *Web:* www.saffronusa.com	Baltimore	MD	21201	410-528-1616	528-1310
Samos 600 Oldham St *Web:* www.samosrestaurant.com	Baltimore	MD	21224	410-675-5292	
San Sushi 2748 Lighthouse Pt	Baltimore	MD	21224	410-534-8888	534-8665
Sascha's 527 527 N Charles St *Web:* www.saschas.com	Baltimore	MD	21201	410-539-8880	539-6105
Sotto Sopra 405 N Charles St *Web:* www.sottosoprainc.com	Baltimore	MD	21201	410-625-0534	625-2642
Suzie's Soba 1009 W 36th St	Baltimore	MD	21211	410-243-0051	243-3838
Tapas Teatro 1711 N Charles St *Web:* www.tapasteatro.net	Baltimore	MD	21201	410-332-0110	323-1229
Thai 3316-18 Greenmount Ave	Baltimore	MD	21218	410-889-6002	889-6003
Thai Arroy 1019 Light St *Web:* www.thaiarroy.com	Baltimore	MD	21230	410-385-8587	
Thai Landing 1207 N Charles St *Web:* www.thailanding.us	Baltimore	MD	21201	410-727-1234	
Timothy Dean's Bistro 1717 Eastern Ave *Web:* www.tdbistro.com	Baltimore	MD	21231	410-534-5650	534-2452
Tio Pepe 10 E Franklin St	Baltimore	MD	21202	410-539-4675	837-7288
Viccino Bistro 1317 N Charles St *Web:* www.viccino.com	Baltimore	MD	21201	410-347-0349	783-1938
Windows 202 E Pratt St 5th Fl *Web:* www.windowsharbor.com	Baltimore	MD	21202	410-685-8439	783-9676
Angler Restaurant 312 Talbot St *Web:* www.theangleroc.com	Ocean City	MD	21842	410-289-7424	
BJ's On The Water 115 75th St *Web:* www.ocean-city.com/bjs.htm	Ocean City	MD	21842	410-524-7575	524-7624
Boardwalk Joe's 401 N Atlantic Ave	Ocean City	MD	21842	410-289-5104	
Bonfire 7009 Coastal Hwy	Ocean City	MD	21842	410-524-7171	524-4228
Buxy's Salty Dog 2707 Philadelphia Ave *Web:* www.buxyssaltydog.com	Ocean City	MD	21842	410-289-0973	289-0038
Captain's Galley 12817 Harbor Rd	Ocean City	MD	21842	410-213-2525	213-0702
Castaway's Bar & Grill 105 64th St *Web:* www.castawaysoc.com	Ocean City	MD	21842	410-524-9090	
Conners of Ocean City 211 N Boardwalk	Ocean City	MD	21842	410-289-4105	
Coral Reef Restaurant 1701 Atlantic Ave	Ocean City	MD	21842	410-289-2612	289-3381
Crab Alley 9703 Golf Course Rd *Web:* www.craballey.com	Ocean City	MD	21842	410-213-7800	213-1048
Croc's Sports Steak House 11427 Coast Hwy	Ocean City	MD	21842	410-723-1697	
Fager's Island Restaurant 201 60th St *Web:* www.fagers.com	Ocean City	MD	21842	410-524-5500	723-2055
Galaxy Bar & Grille 6601 Coastal Hwy *Web:* www.galaxy66barandgrille.com	Ocean City	MD	21842	410-723-6762	723-1387
Greene Turtle 11601 Coastal Hwy *Web:* www.greeneturtle.com	Ocean City	MD	21842	410-723-2128	
Hall's Restaurant 5909 Coastal Hwy *Web:* www.halls-oc.com	Ocean City	MD	21842	410-524-5008	524-5377
Harrison's Harbor Watch Restaurant 806 S Boardwalk	Ocean City	MD	21842	410-289-5121	
Horizons 101st St & Oceanfront	Ocean City	MD	21842	410-524-3535	524-3834
Jonah & the Whale 26th St & Boardwalk	Ocean City	MD	21842	410-524-2722	
JR's Place for Ribs 131st St & Coastal *Web:* www.jrsribs.com	Ocean City	MD	21842	410-250-3100	250-3104
Jules 11805 Coastal Hwy	Ocean City	MD	21842	410-524-3396	
La Hacienda Restaurant 8003 Coastal Hwy *TF:* 800-297-8081 ■ *Web:* www.beach-net.com/laha	Ocean City	MD	21842	410-524-8080	
Macky's Bayside Bar & Grill 5311 Coastal Hwy *Web:* www.mackys.com	Ocean City	MD	21842	410-723-5565	723-4445
Marina Deck 306 Dorchester St *Web:* www.marinadeckrestaurant.com	Ocean City	MD	21842	410-289-4411	289-6449
Marlin Moon Grille 12806 Ocean Gateway *Web:* www.marlinmoongrille.com	Ocean City	MD	21842	410-213-1618	
Nick's Original House of Ribs 14410 Coastal Hwy *Web:* www.nickshouseofribs.com	Ocean City	MD	21842	410-250-1984	250-2770
Ocean Club 10100 Coastal Hwy	Ocean City	MD	21842	410-524-7500	
Phillips Crab House 2004 N Philadelphia Ave *Web:* www.phillipsoc.com	Ocean City	MD	21842	410-289-6821	289-4258
Phillips by the Sea Restaurant 1301 Atlantic Ave Phillips Beach Plaza Hotel	Ocean City	MD	21842	410-289-9121	289-3041
Reflections Restaurant & Wine Bar 67th St & Coastal Hwy	Ocean City	MD	21842	410-524-5252	
Tequila Mockingbird 12919 Coastal Hwy	Ocean City	MD	21842	410-250-4424	
Tutti Gusti 3322 Coastal Hwy *Web:* www.ocean-city.com/tuttigusti.htm	Ocean City	MD	21842	410-289-3318	

Massachusetts

Phone | Fax

Outermost Inn 81 Lighthouse Rd .... Aquinnah MA 02535 508-645-3511
Web: www.outermostinn.com
29 Newbury 29 Newbury St .... Boston MA 02116 617-536-0290
Web: www.29newbury.com/
75 Chestnut 75 Chestnut St .... Boston MA 02108 617-227-2175 227-3675
Web: www.75chestnut.com
Abe & Louie's 793 Boylston St .... Boston MA 02116 617-536-6300 437-6291
Web: www.bbrginc.com/al/
Addis Red Sea 544 Tremont St .... Boston MA 02116 617-426-8727 695-3677
Web: www.addisredsea.com
Antico Forno 93 Salem St .... Boston MA 02113 617-723-6733
Web: www.anticofornoboston.com
Aquitaine 569 Tremont St .... Boston MA 02118 617-424-8577 424-0249
Web: aquitaineboston.com/
Assaggio 29 Prince St .... Boston MA 02113 617-227-7380 742-3512
Web: www.assaggioboston.com
Atlantic Fish Co 761 Boylston St .... Boston MA 02116 617-267-4000 267-0755
Web: www.bbrginc.com/afco
Aujourd'hui 200 Boylston St .... Boston MA 02116 617-351-2172 351-2293
Azure 61 Exeter St .... Boston MA 02116 617-933-4800 933-4802
Web: www.azureboston.com
B & G Oysters 550 Tremont St .... Boston MA 02116 617-423-0550 423-3533
Web: www.bandgoysters.com
Bangkok Blue 651 Boylston St .... Boston MA 02116 617-266-1010 266-9747
Web: www.bkkblueboston.com
Bhindi Bazaar 95 Mass Ave .... Boston MA 02115 617-450-0660 450-0320
Web: www.bhindibazaar.com
Bin 26 Enoteca 26 Charles St .... Boston MA 02114 617-723-5939
Web: www.bin26.com
Blu 4 Avery St .... Boston MA 02111 617-375-8550 375-8201
Web: www.blurestaurant.com
Bricco 241 Hanover St .... Boston MA 02113 617-248-6800 367-0666
Web: www.bricco.com
Bristol The 200 Boylston St .... Boston MA 02116 617-338-4400 423-0154
Brown Sugar Cafe 129 Jersey St .... Boston MA 02215 617-266-2928 266-2928
Web: www.brownsugarcafe.com
Butcher Shop The 552 Tremont St .... Boston MA 02118 617-423-4800 423-4840
Web: www.thebutchershopboston.com
Cafe Fleuri 250 Franklin St .... Boston MA 02110 617-451-1900 423-2844
Cantina Italiana 346 Hanover St .... Boston MA 02113 617-723-4577 723-6357
Web: www.cantinaitaliana.com
Capital Grille 359 Newbury St .... Boston MA 02115 617-262-8900 262-9449
Web: www.thecapitalgrille.com
Carmen 33 North Sq .... Boston MA 02113 617-742-6421 742-1880
Casa Romero 30 Gloucester St .... Boston MA 02115 617-536-4341 536-6191
Web: www.casaromero.com
Clio 370-A Commonwealth Ave .... Boston MA 02215 617-536-7200 578-0394
Web: www.cliorestaurant.com
Davide 326 Commercial St .... Boston MA 02109 617-227-5745 227-8976
Web: www.daviderestaurant.com
Dom's 100 Salem St .... Boston MA 02113 617-367-8979
East Ocean City 25 Beach St .... Boston MA 02111 617-542-2504 348-2878
Excelsior 272 Boylston St .... Boston MA 02116 617-426-7878 426-9253
Web: www.excelsiorrestaurant.com
Federalist The 15 Beacon St .... Boston MA 02108 617-670-2515 670-2525
Web: www.federalistrestaurant.com
Figs 42 Charles St .... Boston MA 02114 617-742-3447
Web: www.toddenglish.com/Restaurants.html
Fleming's Prime Steakhouse & Wine Bar 217 Stuart St .... Boston MA 02116 617-292-0808 482-3025
Web: www.flemingssteakhouse.com
Franklin Cafe 278 Shawmut Ave .... Boston MA 02118 617-350-0010 350-5115
Web: www.franklincafe.com
Giacomo's 431 Columbus Ave .... Boston MA 02116 617-536-5723
Ginza 16 Hudson St .... Boston MA 02111 617-338-2261 426-3563
Web: www.ginzaboston.com
Great Bay 500 Commonwealth Ave Hotel Commonwealth .... Boston MA 02215 617-532-5300 266-5251
Web: www.gbayrestaurant.com
Grill 23 & Bar 161 Berkeley St .... Boston MA 02116 617-542-2255 896-1042
Web: www.grill23.com
Grotto 37 Bowdoin St .... Boston MA 02114 617-227-3434 227-4616
Web: www.grottorestaurant.com
Hamersley's Bistro 553 Tremont St .... Boston MA 02116 617-423-2700 423-7710
Web: www.hamersleysbistro.com
House of Siam 542 Columbus Ave .... Boston MA 02118 617-267-1755 267-2984
Web: www.houseofsiam.com
Icarus 3 Appleton St .... Boston MA 02116 617-426-1790 426-2150
Web: www.icarusrestaurant.com
India Quality 484 Commonwealth Ave .... Boston MA 02215 617-267-4499 267-4477
Web: www.indiaquality.com
Kashmir 279 Newbury St .... Boston MA 02116 617-536-1695 536-1598
Web: www.kashmirspices.com
Kingfish Hall 188 Market Bldg 6 .... Boston MA 02109 617-523-8862 523-8860
Web: www.toddenglish.com
KO Prime 90 Tremont St .... Boston MA 02108 617-772-0202 772-5810
Web: www.koprimeboston.com
Lala Rokh 97 Mt Vernon St .... Boston MA 02108 617-720-5511
Web: www.lalarokh.com
Legal Sea Foods 26 Park Sq .... Boston MA 02116 617-426-4444 338-7629
Web: www.legalseafoods.com
Les Zygomates 129 South St .... Boston MA 02111 617-542-5108 482-8806
Web: www.winebar.com
L'Espalier 30 Gloucester St .... Boston MA 02115 617-262-3023 375-9297
Web: www.lespalier.com
Locke-Ober 3 Winter Pl .... Boston MA 02108 617-542-1340 542-6452
Web: www.lockeober.com
Lucca 226 Hanover St .... Boston MA 02113 617-742-9200 723-2081
Web: www.luccaboston.com
Mamma Maria's 3 North Sq .... Boston MA 02113 617-523-0077 523-4348
Web: www.mammamaria.com
Mantra Restaurant 52 Temple Pl .... Boston MA 02111 617-542-8111 542-8666
Web: www.mantrarestaurant.com
Meritage 70 Rowes Wharf .... Boston MA 02210 617-439-3995 439-0464
Web: www.meritagetherestaurant.com
Metropolis Cafe 584 Tremont St .... Boston MA 02118 617-247-2931 247-2495
Mistral 223 Columbus Ave .... Boston MA 02116 617-867-9300 351-2601
Web: www.mistralbistro.com
Monica's 143 Richmond St .... Boston MA 02109 617-227-0311 227-3381
Web: www.monicasonline.com
Montien 63 Stuart St .... Boston MA 02116 617-338-5600 338-5348
Web: www.montien-boston.com
Morton's The Steakhouse 699 Boylston at Exeter .... Boston MA 02116 617-266-5858 266-9521
Web: www.mortons.com
New Shanghai 21 Hudson St .... Boston MA 02111 617-338-6688 338-0732
Web: www.newshanghaiboston.com

Phone | Fax

No 9 PARK 9 Park St .... Boston MA 02108 617-742-9991 742-9993
Web: www.no9park.com
o ya 9 East St .... Boston MA 02111 617-654-9900
Oak Room 138 St James Ave .... Boston MA 02116 617-267-5300 375-9648
Oishii Boston 1166 Washington St .... Boston MA 02118 617-482-8868
Web: oishiiboston.com/
Palm The 200 Dartmouth St .... Boston MA 02116 617-867-9292 867-0789
Web: www.thepalm.com/
Peach Farm 4 Tyler St .... Boston MA 02111 617-482-3332 482-1116
Piccola Venezia 263 Hanover St .... Boston MA 02113 617-523-3888 742-2960
Web: www.piccolaveneziaboston.com
Pigalle 75 Charles St S .... Boston MA 02116 617-423-4944 423-6766
Web: www.pigalleboston.com
Prezza 24 Fleet St .... Boston MA 02113 617-227-1577 227-1587
Web: www.prezza.com
Radius 8 High St .... Boston MA 02110 617-426-1234 426-2526
Web: www.radiusrestaurant.com
Restaurant L 234 Berkeley St .... Boston MA 02116 617-266-4680 266-4686
Web: www.louisboston.com
Ruby Room 155 Portland St .... Boston MA 02114 617-557-9950 557-0005
Web: www.rubyroomboston.com/
Sage Restaurant 1395 Washington St .... Boston MA 02118 617-248-8814 248-1879
Web: www.sageboston.com
Sakurabana 57 Broad St .... Boston MA 02109 617-542-4311 542-2320
Web: www.sakurabanaboston.com
Seasons 26 North St .... Boston MA 02109 617-523-3600 523-2454
Sel de la Terre 255 State St .... Boston MA 02109 617-720-1300 227-1579
Web: www.seldelaterre.com
Sonsie 327 Newbury St .... Boston MA 02115 617-351-2500 351-2565
Strega 379 Hanover St .... Boston MA 02113 617-523-8481 523-2475
Web: www.stregaristorante.com
Tapeo 266 Newbury St .... Boston MA 02116 617-267-4799 267-1602
Web: www.tapeo.com
Taranta 210 Hanover St .... Boston MA 02113 617-720-0052 507-0492
Web: www.tarantarist.com
Teatro 177 Tremont St .... Boston MA 02111 617-778-6841 778-6845
Web: www.teatroboston.com
Terramia Ristorante 98 Salem St .... Boston MA 02113 617-523-3112
Web: www.terramiaristorante.com
Tresca 233 Hanover St .... Boston MA 02113 617-742-8240 742-8246
Web: www.trescanorthend.com
Troquet 140 Boylston St .... Boston MA 02116 617-695-9463
Web: www.troquetboston.com
Umbria 295 Franklin St .... Boston MA 02110 617-338-1000 338-4112
Web: www.umbriaristorante.com
Union Bar & Grille 1357 Washington St .... Boston MA 02118 617-423-0555 423-6055
Web: www.unionrestaurant.com
Via Matta 79 Park Plaza .... Boston MA 02116 617-422-0008 422-0014
Web: www.viamattarestaurant.com
Wagamama Quincy Market .... Boston MA 02109 617-742-9242
Web: www.wagamama.us/
Bramble Inn 2019 Main St .... Brewster MA 02631 508-896-7644 896-9332
Web: www.brambleinn.com
Chillingsworth 2449 Main St .... Brewster MA 02631 508-896-3640
Web: www.chillingsworth.com
Fireplace 1634 Beacon St .... Brookline MA 02446 617-975-1900 975-1600
Web: www.fireplacerest.com
East Coast Grill & Raw Bar 1271 Cambridge St .... Cambridge MA 02114 617-491-6568 868-4278
Web: www.eastcoastgrill.net
Elephant Walk 2067 Massachusetts Ave .... Cambridge MA 02140 617-492-6900 492-3907
Web: www.elephantwalk.com
Harvest 44 Brattle St .... Cambridge MA 02138 617-868-2255
Web: www.harvestcambridge.com
Helmand 143 1st St .... Cambridge MA 02142 617-492-4646 497-6507
Web: www.helmandrestaurantcambridge.com
Oleana 134 Hampshire St .... Cambridge MA 02139 617-661-0505 661-3336
Web: www.oleanarestaurant.com
Courtyard Restaurant & Bar 1337 County Rd .... Cataumet MA 02556 508-563-1818
Theo's Inn at Blueberry Hill 74 North Rd .... Chilmark MA 02535 508-645-3322 645-3799
Web: www.blueberryinn.com
Regatta of Cotuit at the Crocker House 4631 Falmouth Rd Rt 28 .... Cotuit MA 02635 508-428-5715 428-5742
Web: www.regattarestaurant.com
Red Pheasant 905 Main St .... Dennis MA 02638 508-385-2133
Nauset Beach Club 222 Main St .... East Orleans MA 02643 508-255-8547 255-8872
Web: www.nausetbeachclub.com
Atria 137 Main St .... Edgartown MA 02539 508-627-5850 627-7325
Web: www.atriamv.com
Coach House 131 N Water St .... Edgartown MA 02539 508-627-7000 627-8417
L'etoile 22 N Water St .... Edgartown MA 02539 508-627-5187
Web: www.letoile.net
Firefly Woodfire Grill & Bar 271 Main St .... Falmouth MA 02540 508-548-7953
Web: www.fireflywoodfiregrill.com/
La Cucina Sul Mare 237 Main St .... Falmouth MA 02540 508-548-5600
Web: www.lacucinasulmare.com
Ay Caramba Cafe 703 Main St .... Harwich MA 02645 508-432-9800 432-9977
Web: www.aycarambacafe.com
Buca's Tuscan Roadhouse 4 Depot Rd .... Harwich MA 02645 508-432-6900
Web: www.bucasroadhouse.com/
L'Alouette 787 Rte 28 .... Harwich Port MA 02646 508-430-0405
Web: www.lalouettebistro.com
Delaney House Rt 5 Smith's Ferry .... Holyoke MA 01040 413-532-1800 533-7137
Web: www.delaneyhouse.com
Baxter's Boathouse 117 Pleasant St .... Hyannis MA 02601 508-775-4490
Web: www.baxterscapecod.com/
Brazilian Grill 680 Main St .... Hyannis MA 02601 508-771-0109 771-1070
Cooke's Seafood 1120 Rte 132 .... Hyannis MA 02601 508-775-0450
Web: www.cookesseafood.com
Fazio's Trattoria 294 Main St .... Hyannis MA 02601 508-775-9400
Web: www.fazio.net
Misaki 379 W Main St .... Hyannis MA 02601 508-771-3771 771-4431
Web: www.misakisushi.com
Naked Oyster Bistro & Raw Bar 20 Independence Dr .... Hyannis MA 02601 508-778-6500 778-5704
Web: www.nakedoyster.com
Paddock The 20 Scudder Ave .... Hyannis MA 02601 508-775-7677 771-9517
Web: www.paddockcapecod.com
Roobar 586 Main St .... Hyannis MA 02601 508-778-6515
Web: www.theroobar.com
Sam Diego's 950 Iyanough Rd .... Hyannis MA 02601 508-771-8816 771-0174
Web: www.samdiegos.com
Tiki Port 714 Iyanough Rd .... Hyannis MA 02601 508-771-5220 771-2775
Centre Street Cafe 669 A Centre St .... Jamaica Plain MA 02130 617-524-9217 522-4028
Beach Plum Inn 50 Beach Plum Ln .... Menemsha MA 02552 508-645-9454 645-3718
TF: 877-645-7398 ■ *Web:* www.beachpluminn.com
Brant Point Grill 50 Easton St PO Box 1139 .... Nantucket MA 02554 508-228-2500
Company of the Cauldron 5 India St .... Nantucket MA 02554 508-228-4016
Web: www.companyofthecauldron.com

Massachusetts (Cont'd)

	City	State	ZIP	Phone	Fax
DeMarco 9 India St	Nantucket	MA	02554	508-228-1836	228-9437
Web: www.demarcorestaurant.com					
Le Languedoc Bistro 24 Broad St	Nantucket	MA	02554	508-228-2552	228-4682
Web: www.lelanguedoc.com					
Pearl 12 Federal St	Nantucket	MA	02554	508-228-9701	
Straight Wharf 6 Harbor Sq	Nantucket	MA	02554	508-228-4499	
Topper's 120 Wauwinet Rd	Nantucket	MA	02554	508-228-8768	
Woodbox The 36 Fair St	Nantucket	MA	02554	508-228-0587	
Lumiere 1293 Washington St	Newton	MA	02465	617-244-9199	
Web: www.lumiererestaurant.com/					
Abba 89 Old Colony Way	Orleans	MA	02653	508-255-8144	
Academy Ocean Grille 2 Academy Pl	Orleans	MA	02653	508-240-1585	240-1344
Web: www.academyoceangrille.com					
Captain Linnell House 137 Skaket Beach Rd	Orleans	MA	02653	508-255-3400	255-5377
Web: www.linnell.com					
Chester 404 Commercial St	Provincetown	MA	02657	508-487-8200	
Enzo 186 Commercial St	Provincetown	MA	02657	508-487-7555	487-6611
Web: www.fireflywoodfiregrill.com/					
Front Street 230 Commercial St	Provincetown	MA	02657	508-487-9715	487-7748
Web: www.frontstreetrestaurant.com					
Lorraine's 133 Commercial St	Provincetown	MA	02657	508-487-6074	
Web: www.lorrainesrestaurant.com					
Mews Restaurant & Cafe 429 Commercial St	Provincetown	MA	02657	508-487-1500	487-3700
Web: www.mews.com					
Red Inn 15 Commercial St	Provincetown	MA	02657	508-487-7334	487-5115
Web: www.theredinn.com					
Ross' Grill 237 Commercial St	Provincetown	MA	02657	508-487-8878	
Daniel Webster Inn 149 Main St	Sandwich	MA	02563	508-888-3622	888-5156
TF: 800-444-3566 ■ *Web:* www.danlwebsterinn.com/dining.html					
Dali Restaurant 415 Washington St	Somerville	MA	02143	617-661-3254	661-2813
Web: www.dalirestaurant.com					
902 Main Restaurant 902 Rt 28	South Yarmouth	MA	02664	508-398-9902	
Web: www.902main.com					
Ardeo 23V Whites Path	South Yarmouth	MA	02664	508-760-1500	760-1504
Web: www.ardeocapecod.com					
Riverway Lobster House 1338 Rte 28	South Yarmouth	MA	02664	508-398-2172	398-7111
Web: www.riverwaylobsterhouse.com					
Aqui-me-quedo Restaurant 13 Locust St	Springfield	MA	01108	413-737-2827	
Bamboo House 676 Belmont Ave	Springfield	MA	01108	413-732-0741	
Big Mamou 63 Liberty St	Springfield	MA	01103	413-732-1011	
Cafe Lebanon 1390 Main St	Springfield	MA	01103	413-737-7373	737-5773
Web: www.cafelebanon.com					
Casa De Nana 995 Boston Rd	Springfield	MA	01119	413-783-1549	
China Gourmet 1374 Allen St	Springfield	MA	01118	413-796-1888	439-0403
Cobalt 1 Worthington St	Springfield	MA	01103	413-731-5454	734-3334
Web: www.cobaltdowntown.com					
Currents 1500 Main St	Springfield	MA	01104	413-781-7111	731-8932
Lido's 555 Worthington St	Springfield	MA	01105	413-736-9433	781-7970
Web: www.lidosrestaurant.com					
L'uva 1676 Main St	Springfield	MA	01103	413-734-1010	
Web: www.luva.us					
Max's Tavern 1000 W Columbus Blvd	Springfield	MA	01105	413-746-6299	746-6211
Web: www.maxrestaurantgroup.com/					
Pazzo Ristorante 1000 W Columbus Ave	Springfield	MA	01105	413-737-5800	737-0217
Web: www.pazzohof.com					
Peter's Grill 1 Monarch Pl	Springfield	MA	01144	413-781-1010	734-3264
Pho Saigon 398 Dickinson St	Springfield	MA	01108	413-781-4488	
Salvatore's 1333 Boston Rd	Springfield	MA	01119	413-782-9968	796-7601
Sitar Restaurant 1688 Main St	Springfield	MA	01103	413-732-8011	788-7868
Student Prince & Fort Restaurant 8 Fort St	Springfield	MA	01103	413-734-7475	739-7303
Web: www.studentprince.com					
Theodore's Booze Blues & BBQ 201 Worthington St	Springfield	MA	01103	413-736-6000	
Web: www.theobbq.com					
Touch of Garlic 427 White St	Springfield	MA	01108	413-739-0236	
Typical Sicilian 497 Belmont Ave	Springfield	MA	01108	413-739-7100	
Wong Wok 749 Sumner Ave	Springfield	MA	01108	413-746-8084	
Zaffino's Italian Restaurant 711 Dwight St	Springfield	MA	01104	413-781-0900	
Il Capriccio 888 Main St	Waltham	MA	02451	781-894-2234	891-3227
Web: www.bostonchefs.com					
Blue Ginger 583 Washington St	Wellesley	MA	02484	781-283-5790	283-5772
Web: www.ming.com					
Bistro 5 5 Playstead Rd	West Medford	MA	02115	781-395-7464	395-0130
Web: bistro5.com					
B'Shara's Restaurant 1268 Riverdale Rd	West Springfield	MA	01089	413-732-4740	732-5968
Web: www.bsharas.com/					
Cal's Wood-Fired Grill & Bar 1068 Riverdale St	West Springfield	MA	01105	413-827-9353	
Web: www.calswoodfiredgrill.com/					
Debbie Wong 878 Memorial Ave	West Springfield	MA	01089	413-781-1711	
Pintus 217 Elm St	West Springfield	MA	01089	413-788-4929	214-6506
Web: www.pintusrestaurant.com					
111 Chop House 111 Shrewsbury St	Worcester	MA	01604	508-799-4111	
Web: www.111chophouse.com/					
Beijing Palace 321 W Boylston St	Worcester	MA	01606	508-853-8880	853-8841
Block 5 139 Green St	Worcester	MA	01604	508-767-3483	
Web: block5bistro.com					
Boynton Family Restaurant 117 Highland St	Worcester	MA	01609	508-756-8458	756-8208
Brisa's Tropical Restaurant 976 Main St	Worcester	MA	01603	508-797-3900	
Cactus Pete's Steak House & Saloon 400 Park Ave	Worcester	MA	01610	508-752-3038	798-7001
Web: www.ameristarcasinos.com/cactus/					
Caesar's Bistro 70 S Bridge St	Worcester	MA	01608	508-791-1400	
Christo's 97 Stafford St	Worcester	MA	01603	508-752-3765	
Coral Seafood Restaurant & Fish Market 112-114 Green St	Worcester	MA	01604	508-755-8331	
Dalat Restaurant 425 Park Ave	Worcester	MA	01610	508-753-6036	
Dino's 13 Lord St	Worcester	MA	01604	508-753-9978	753-5646
El Basha 424 Belmont St	Worcester	MA	01604	508-797-0884	797-1728
Web: www.elbasharestaurant.com					
Flying Rhino Cafe 278 Shrewsbury St	Worcester	MA	01604	508-757-1450	754-8102
Web: www.flyingrhinocafe.com					
House of India 439 Park Ave	Worcester	MA	01610	508-752-1330	792-1187
Leo's Ristorante 11 Bracket Ct	Worcester	MA	01605	508-753-9490	797-5123
Maria's Kitchen 826 Main St	Worcester	MA	01610	508-797-3380	
Maxwell Silverman's Toolhouse 25 Union St	Worcester	MA	01608	508-755-1200	791-5317
Nancy Chang 372 Chandler St	Worcester	MA	01602	508-752-8899	798-6688
Web: www.nancychang.com					
O'Connor's Restaurant & Bar 1160 W Boylston St	Worcester	MA	01606	508-853-0789	853-2879
One Eleven Chop House 111 Shrewsbury St	Worcester	MA	01604	508-799-4111	791-7224
Web: www.111chophouse.com					
Ping's Garden Restaurant 60 Madison St	Worcester	MA	01608	508-791-9577	752-2911
Porto Bello 156 Shrewsbury St	Worcester	MA	01604	508-753-9865	
Quan Yin 56 Hamilton St	Worcester	MA	01604	508-831-1322	
Sahara Cafe & Restaurant 143 Highland St	Worcester	MA	01609	508-798-2181	798-9164
Sakura 640 Park Ave	Worcester	MA	01603	508-792-1078	
Seoul Leecci 385 Main St	Worcester	MA	01608	508-363-0891	
Sole Proprietor 118 Highland St	Worcester	MA	01609	508-798-3474	753-4889
Web: www.thesole.com					
Struck Cafe 344 Chandler St	Worcester	MA	01602	508-757-1670	752-0375
Web: www.struckcafe.com					
Thai Cha-Da 266 Park Ave	Worcester	MA	01603	508-752-2211	752-2211
Web: www.thaicha-da.com					
Thymes Square on Hudson 455 Pleasant St	Worcester	MA	01609	508-791-6102	755-8002
Web: www.thymessquare.com					
Tortilla Sams 107 Highland St	Worcester	MA	01609	508-791-1746	
Viva Bene 144 Commercial St	Worcester	MA	01608	508-797-0007	752-4334
Web: www.viva-bene.com					
Webster House Restaurant 1 Webster St	Worcester	MA	01603	508-757-7208	
Web: www.websterhouseweb.com					
Zipango Sushi Bar 270 Shrewsbury St	Worcester	MA	01604	508-754-8047	
Abbicci 43 Main St	Yarmouth Port	MA	02675	508-362-3501	362-7802
Web: www.abbicci.com					
Inaho 157 Rt 6A	Yarmouth Port	MA	02675	508-362-5522	
Colonial House Inn 277 Main St	Yarmouthport	MA	02675	508-362-4348	362-8034
TF: 800-999-3416 ■ *Web:* www.colonialhousecapecod.com/dine.html					

Michigan

	City	State	ZIP	Phone	Fax
Amadeus 122 E Washington St	Ann Arbor	MI	48104	734-665-8767	
Web: www.amadeusrestaurant.com					
Arbor Brewing Co 114 E Washington St	Ann Arbor	MI	48104	734-213-1393	213-2835
Web: www.arborbrewing.com					
Argiero's 300 Detroit St	Ann Arbor	MI	48104	734-665-0444	665-2653
Web: www.argierosrestaurant.com					
Banh Na 4837 Washtenaw Ave	Ann Arbor	MI	48108	734-528-2336	528-2629
Bella Ciao 118 W Liberty St	Ann Arbor	MI	48104	734-995-2107	995-5004
Web: www.bellaciao.com					
Blue Nile 221 E Washington St	Ann Arbor	MI	48104	734-998-4746	998-4750
Web: www.bluenilemi.com					
Chia Shiang 2016 Packard St	Ann Arbor	MI	48104	734-741-0778	
Chop House The 322 S Main St	Ann Arbor	MI	48104	734-669-9977	669-7177
Earle The 121 W Washington St	Ann Arbor	MI	48104	734-994-0211	994-3466
Web: www.theearle.com					
Eve 415 N 5th Ave	Ann Arbor	MI	48103	734-222-0711	222-4035
Web: www.evetherestaurant.com					
Gandy Dancer 401 Depot St	Ann Arbor	MI	48104	734-769-0592	769-0415
Web: www.muer.com					
Gratzi 326 S Main St	Ann Arbor	MI	48104	734-663-5555	668-7261
Great Lakes Chinese Seafood 2910 Carpenter Rd	Ann Arbor	MI	48108	734-973-6666	973-0030
Grizzly Peak Brewing Co 120 W Washington St	Ann Arbor	MI	48104	734-741-7325	741-4976
Web: www.grizzlypeak.net					
Jerusalem Garden 307 S 5th Ave	Ann Arbor	MI	48104	734-995-5060	995-9843
Web: www.jerusalemgarden.net					
Knight's Steak House 2324 Dexter Ave	Ann Arbor	MI	48103	734-665-8644	665-7948
Web: www.knightsrestaurants.com					
La Shish 2370 Carpenter Rd	Ann Arbor	MI	48108	734-973-2737	
Mediterrano 2900 S State St	Ann Arbor	MI	48104	734-332-9700	332-9702
Web: www.mediterrano.com					
Metzeger's 305 N Zeeb Rd	Ann Arbor	MI	48103	734-668-8987	668-9028
Middle Kingdom 332 S Main St	Ann Arbor	MI	48104	734-668-6638	668-6621
Web: www.annarbormiddlekingdom.com					
Miki Japanese Restaurant 106 S 1st St	Ann Arbor	MI	48104	734-665-8226	665-1301
Web: www.mikirestaurant.com					
MisSaigon 4085 Stoneschool Rd	Ann Arbor	MI	48108	734-971-8880	
Web: www.missaigononline.com/					
Pacific Rim 114 W Liberty St	Ann Arbor	MI	48104	734-662-9303	662-8397
Web: www.pacificrimbykana.com					
Paesano's 3411 Washtenaw Ave	Ann Arbor	MI	48104	734-971-0484	971-0419
Web: www.paesanosannarbor.com					
Palio 347 S Main St	Ann Arbor	MI	48104	734-930-6156	930-0332
Web: www.paliorestaurant.com					
Parthenon 226 S Main St	Ann Arbor	MI	48104	734-994-1012	994-7073
Web: www.parthenonrestaurant.net					
Prickly Pear Southwest Cafe 328 S Main St	Ann Arbor	MI	48104	734-930-0047	
Raja Rani 400 S Division St	Ann Arbor	MI	48104	734-995-1545	995-5999
Real Seafood Co 341 S Main St	Ann Arbor	MI	48104	734-769-5960	769-5749
Sabor Latino 211 N Main St	Ann Arbor	MI	48104	734-214-7775	214-7776
Seoul Garden 3125 Boardwalk St	Ann Arbor	MI	48108	734-997-2120	
Seva Restaurant 314 E Liberty St	Ann Arbor	MI	48104	734-662-1111	662-8447
Shalimar 307 S Main St	Ann Arbor	MI	48104	734-663-1500	929-9129
Web: www.shalimarrestaurant.com					
Smokehouse Blues 4855 Washtenaw Ave	Ann Arbor	MI	48108	734-434-5554	434-4969
Web: www.smokehouseblues.com					
Tuptim 4896 Washtenaw Ave	Ann Arbor	MI	48108	734-528-5588	528-2569
Web: www.tuptim.com					
Vinology 110 S Main St	Ann Arbor	MI	48104	734-222-9841	
Weber's 3050 Jackson Rd	Ann Arbor	MI	48103	734-665-3636	769-4743
Web: www.webersinn.com/restaurant.html					
West End Grill 120 W Liberty Ave	Ann Arbor	MI	48104	734-747-6260	665-6493
Web: www.westendgrilla2.com					
Zingerman's Roadhouse 2501 Jackson Rd	Ann Arbor	MI	48103	734-663-3663	
Web: www.zingermansroadhouse.com					
Alley Grille 555 E Lafayette St	Detroit	MI	48226	313-223-2999	
Andiamo 400 Renaissance Center Suite A403	Detroit	MI	48243	313-567-6700	567-6701
Web: www.andiamoitalia.com					
Armando's Mexican Restaurant 4242 W Vernor Hwy	Detroit	MI	48209	313-554-0666	
Web: www.mexicantown.com/					
Atlas Global Bistro 3111 Woodward Ave	Detroit	MI	48201	313-831-2241	831-4023
Web: www.atlasglobalbistro.com					
Atwater Brewing Co 237 Joseph Campau	Detroit	MI	48207	313-877-9205	877-9206
Carl's Chop House 3020 Grand River Ave	Detroit	MI	48201	313-833-0700	831-2390
Web: www.carlschophouse.com					
Caucus Club 150 W Congress St	Detroit	MI	48226	313-965-4970	
Century Grille 333 Madison Ave	Detroit	MI	48226	313-963-9800	963-9873
Clubhouse Tavern 3011 W Grand Blvd	Detroit	MI	48221	313-874-4653	
Coach Insignia 100 Renaissance Center	Detroit	MI	48226	313-567-2622	567-9598
Cuisine 670 Lothrop Rd	Detroit	MI	48202	313-872-5110	872-3801
Web: www.cuisinedetroit.com					
Cyprus Taverna 579 Monroe St	Detroit	MI	48226	313-961-1550	961-2241
Web: www.cyprustaverna.com					
DaEdoardo Foxtown Grille 2203 Woodward Ave	Detroit	MI	48201	313-471-3500	471-3499
Web: www.daedoardo.com					
Dona Lola 1312 Springwells St	Detroit	MI	48209	313-843-4129	
El Comal 3456 W Vernor Ave	Detroit	MI	48216	313-841-7753	841-7071
El Zocalo Mexican Restaurant 3400 Bagley St	Detroit	MI	48216	313-841-3700	
Web: www.elzocalodetroit.com/					
Evie's Tamales 3454 Bagley St	Detroit	MI	48216	313-843-5056	843-5143
Giovanni's Ristorante 330 S Oakwood Blvd	Detroit	MI	48217	313-841-0122	841-3947
Web: www.giovannisristorante.com					
Hard Rock Cafe 45 Monroe St	Detroit	MI	48226	313-964-7625	964-5064
Web: www.hardrock.com					

Name / Address	City	State	Zip	Phone	Fax
Hockeytown Cafe 2301 Woodward Ave	Detroit	MI	48201	313-965-9500	471-3466
Iridescence 2901 Grand River Ave	Detroit	MI	48201	313-237-7711	961-0966
La Dolce Vita 17546 Woodward	Detroit	MI	48203	313-865-0331	867-3568
Laffrey's Steaks on the Hearth 24201 W Seven-Mile Rd	Detroit	MI	48219	313-538-4688	538-2105
Louisiana Creole Gumbo 2053 Gratiot Ave	Detroit	MI	48207	313-446-9639	396-1708
Magnolia 1440 E Franklin St	Detroit	MI	48207	313-393-0018	393-3783
Mario's 4222 2nd Ave	Detroit	MI	48201	313-832-1616	832-1460
Web: www.mariosdetroit.com					
New Hellas Cafe 583 Monroe St	Detroit	MI	48226	313-961-5544	
Opus One 565 E Larned St	Detroit	MI	48226	313-961-7766	961-9243
Web: www.opus-one.com					
Pegasus Taverna 558 Monroe St	Detroit	MI	48226	313-964-6800	964-0869
Rattlesnake Club 300 River Pl	Detroit	MI	48207	313-567-4400	567-2063
Web: www.rattlesnakeclub.com					
Roma Cafe 3401 Riopelle St	Detroit	MI	48207	313-831-5940	831-2253
Web: www.romacafe.com					
Sala Thai 1541 E Lafayette St	Detroit	MI	48207	313-567-8424	
Seldom Blues 400 Renaissance Center	Detroit	MI	48243	313-567-7301	567-7501
Web: www.seldomblues.com					
Senor Lopez Taqueria 7146 Michigan Ave	Detroit	MI	48210	313-551-0685	849-4427
Small Plates 1521 Broadway St	Detroit	MI	48226	313-963-0497	963-0702
Web: www.smallplates.com					
Sweet Georgia Brown 1045 Brush St	Detroit	MI	48226	313-965-1245	965-1234
Web: www.sweetgb.com					
Sweet Lorraine's Cafe & Bar 333 E Jefferson Ave	Detroit	MI	48226	313-223-3933	
Web: www.sweetlorraines.com					
Taqueria Mi Pueblo 7278 Dix St	Detroit	MI	48209	313-841-3315	841-3015
Web: www.mipueblorestaurant.com					
Tom's Oyster Bar 519 E Jefferson Ave	Detroit	MI	48226	313-964-4010	964-4025
Web: www.tomsoysterbar.com					
Union Street 4145 Woodward Ave	Detroit	MI	48201	313-831-3965	831-2553
Web: www.unionstreetdetroit.com					
Vincente's 1250 Library St	Detroit	MI	48226	313-962-8800	962-0898
Whitney The 4421 Woodward Ave	Detroit	MI	48201	313-832-5700	832-2159
Web: www.thewhitney.com					
Xochimilco Restaurant 3409 Bagley St	Detroit	MI	48216	313-843-0179	
Rose's on Reeds Lake 550 Lakeside Dr SE	East Grand Rapids	MI	49506	616-458-1122	458-3411
Beggar's Banquet 218 Abbott Rd	East Lansing	MI	48823	517-351-4573	351-3585
Web: www.beggarsbanquet.com					
Hershey's Steak & Seafood 2682 E Grand River Ave	East Lansing	MI	48823	517-337-7324	337-8004
Web: www.hersheyssteakandseafood.com					
English Inn 677 S Michigan Rd	Eaton Rapids	MI	48827	517-663-2500	663-2643
Web: www.englishinn.com					
Blue Nile 545 W Nine-Mile Rd	Ferndale	MI	48220	248-547-6699	547-3165
Web: www.bluenilemi.com					
Badawest 4018 Corruna Rd	Flint	MI	48532	810-232-2479	232-3326
Big Eazy Grill 5311 Corunna Rd	Flint	MI	48532	810-732-4600	732-5176
Canton Chinese Restaurant 5313 Fenton Rd	Flint	MI	48507	810-232-8710	
Churchill's Food & Spirits 340 S Saginaw St	Flint	MI	48502	810-238-3800	
El Charritos 2804 Richfield Rd	Flint	MI	48506	810-736-9550	736-7410
Golden Moon 4527 Miller Rd	Flint	MI	48507	810-733-7030	
Grand Blanc Inn 5313 S Dort Hwy	Flint	MI	48507	810-694-0010	694-9408
La Familia 725 Garland St	Flint	MI	48503	810-341-6888	341-9510
Latina Restaurant & Pizzeria 1370 W Bristol Rd	Flint	MI	48507	810-767-8491	
Luigi's 2132 Davison Rd	Flint	MI	48506	810-234-9545	234-3153
Mario's G5227 Fenton Rd	Flint	MI	48507	810-232-6535	
Mr Browns 4031 Richfield Rd	Flint	MI	48506	810-736-1900	736-1311
Red Rooster Makuchs 3302 Davison Rd	Flint	MI	48506	810-742-9310	
Redwood Lodge 5304 Gateway Center Dr	Flint	MI	48507	810-233-8000	233-8833
Rib City Grill 4150 Miller Rd	Flint	MI	48507	810-230-0094	
Web: www.ribcityflint.com/					
Roma Pizzeria & Restaurant G5227 N Saginaw St	Flint	MI	48505	810-787-1061	787-6788
Web: www.romaspizza.com					
Salvatore Scallopini Restaurant G-3227 Miller Rd	Flint	MI	48507	810-732-1070	732-1538
Web: www.salvatorescallopini.com					
White Horse Tavern 621 W Court St	Flint	MI	48503	810-234-3811	234-9073
Bavarian Inn 713 S Main St	Frankenmuth	MI	48734	989-652-9941	652-3481
Web: www.bavarianinn.com					
1913 Room 187 Monroe Ave NW	Grand Rapids	MI	49503	616-774-2000	776-6489
Adobe Restaurant 617 W Fulton	Grand Rapids	MI	49504	616-454-2992	
Bangkok View 1233 28th St SW	Grand Rapids	MI	49509	616-531-8070	
Beltline Bar 16 28th St SE	Grand Rapids	MI	49548	616-245-0494	245-3955
Bentham's Riverfront Restaurant 187 Monroe St NW	Grand Rapids	MI	49503	616-774-2000	
Bistro Bella Vita 44 Grandville Ave SW	Grand Rapids	MI	49503	616-222-4600	222-4601
Web: www.bistrobellavita.com/					
Bombay Cuisine 1420 Lake Dr	Grand Rapids	MI	49506	616-456-7055	
Brann's Steakhouse & Grille 401 Leonard St NW	Grand Rapids	MI	49504	616-454-9368	454-7702
Web: www.branns.com					
Charley's Crab Restaurant 63 Market St SW	Grand Rapids	MI	49503	616-459-2500	459-8142
Web: www.muer.com					
China Chef 4335 Lake Michigan Dr NW	Grand Rapids	MI	49544	616-791-4488	
Cygnus 187 Monroe Ave NW	Grand Rapids	MI	49503	616-776-6425	
Web: www.amwaygrand.com/cygnus.html					
Gill's Fish House 20 Monroe Ave NW	Grand Rapids	MI	49503	616-356-2000	
Hunan Chinese Restaurant 1740 44th St SW	Grand Rapids	MI	49509	616-530-3377	458-2130
Maggie's Kitchen 615 Bridge St NW	Grand Rapids	MI	49504	616-458-8583	458-1370
Web: www.gibsonsrestaurant.com					
Mikado 3971 28th St SE	Grand Rapids	MI	49512	616-285-7666	977-0509
Noto's Old World Italian 6600 28th St SE	Grand Rapids	MI	49546	616-493-6686	493-6682
Web: www.notosoldworld.com					
One Trick Pony 136 E Fulton St	Grand Rapids	MI	49503	616-235-7669	454-9809
Web: www.onetrick.biz					
San Chez 38 W Fulton St	Grand Rapids	MI	49503	616-774-8272	774-9954
Web: www.sanchezbistro.com					
Sayfee's 3555 Lake Eastbrook Blvd SE	Grand Rapids	MI	49546	616-949-5750	
Seoul Garden 3321 28th St	Grand Rapids	MI	49512	616-956-1522	956-1801
Spinnaker 4747 28th St SE	Grand Rapids	MI	49512	616-957-1111	
Taps Sports Bar 8 Ionia Ave SW	Grand Rapids	MI	49503	616-774-3338	774-7182
Web: www.tapssb.com					
Tillman's 1245 Monroe Ave NW	Grand Rapids	MI	49505	616-451-9266	451-2227
Tokyo Grill 4478 Breton Rd SE	Grand Rapids	MI	49508	616-455-3433	455-0385
Tre Cugini 122 Monroe Center NW	Grand Rapids	MI	49503	616-235-9339	235-9449
Web: www.trecugini.com					
XO Asian Cuisine 58 Monroe Center NW	Grand Rapids	MI	49503	616-235-6969	235-2801
Web: www.xoasiancuisine.com					
Z's Bar & Restaurant 168 Louis Campau Promenade NW	Grand Rapids	MI	49503	616-454-3141	454-2075
Web: www.zsbar.com					
Antonio's 20311 Mack Ave	Grosse Pointe	MI	48236	313-884-0253	
Apple Jade 300 N Clippert St	Lansing	MI	48912	517-332-8010	
Bangkok House Restaurant 420 E Saginaw Hwy	Lansing	MI	48906	517-487-6900	
Capitol City Grille 111 N Grand Ave Radisson Hotel Lansing	Lansing	MI	48933	517-267-3459	
Christie's Bistro 925 S Creyts Rd	Lansing	MI	48917	517-323-4190	323-2180
Web: www.sheratonlansing.com					
Clara's 637 E Michigan Ave	Lansing	MI	48912	517-372-7120	372-0157
Web: www.claras.com					
Deluca's Restaurant 2006 W Willow St	Lansing	MI	48917	517-487-6087	487-3633
Web: www.delucaspizza.com					
El Azteco 1016 W Saginaw St	Lansing	MI	48915	517-485-4589	485-2420
Emil's 2012 E Michigan Ave	Lansing	MI	48912	517-482-4430	482-9390
Firm Food & Spirits The 227 S Washington Sq	Lansing	MI	48933	517-487-3663	
Web: www.thefirmlounge.com					
Golden Harvest Restaurant 1625 N Turner St	Lansing	MI	48906	517-485-3663	
House of Ing 4113 S Cedar St	Lansing	MI	48910	517-393-4848	393-6868
Web: www.houseofing.com					
Kelly's Downtown 203 S Washington Ave	Lansing	MI	48933	517-484-5007	
Web: www.kellysdowntown.com					
Knight Cap 320 E Michigan Ave	Lansing	MI	48933	517-484-7676	
Web: www.theknightcap.com					
La Senorita 2706 Lake Lansing Rd	Lansing	MI	48912	517-485-0166	485-8350
Web: www.lasenorita.com					
Midori Sushi & Korean BBQ 436 Elmwood Rd	Lansing	MI	48911	517-323-7991	
Mitchell's Fish Market 2975 Preyde Blvd	Lansing	MI	48912	517-482-3474	482-3474
Web: www.cameronmitchell.com					
New China Restaurant 6250 S Cedar St	Lansing	MI	48911	517-882-7755	882-6223
PF Chang's China Bistro 2425 Lake Lansing Rd	Lansing	MI	48912	517-267-3833	267-3834
Web: www.pfchangs.com					
Piazzano's 1825 N Grand River Ave	Lansing	MI	48906	517-484-9922	484-2744
Web: www.piazzanos.com					
Dusty's Cellar 1839 E Grand River Ave	Okemos	MI	48864	517-349-8680	349-8416
Web: www.dustyscellar.com					
Dalat Restaurant 100 W Michigan Ave	Ypsilanti	MI	48197	734-487-7600	

Minnesota

Name / Address	City	State	Zip	Phone	Fax
Kincaid's Fish Chop & Fish House 8400 Normandale Lake Blvd	Bloomington	MN	55437	952-921-2255	921-2252
Web: www.kincaids.com					
Angie's Cantina 11 Buchanan St	Duluth	MN	55802	218-727-6117	727-8235
Web: www.grandmasrestaurants.com					
Beijing Restaurant 1219 E Superior St	Duluth	MN	55802	218-724-2627	724-2578
Bellisio's 405 Lake Ave S	Duluth	MN	55802	218-727-4921	
Web: www.grandmasrestaurants.com					
Bennett's on the Lake 600 E Superior St	Duluth	MN	55802	218-722-2829	722-7303
Web: www.bennettsonthelake.com					
Chef Yee's 319 W 1st St	Duluth	MN	55802	218-722-3993	722-1121
Chinese Dragon 108 E Superior St	Duluth	MN	55802	218-723-4036	
Duluth Athletic Club Bar & Grill 21 N 4th Ave West	Duluth	MN	55802	218-720-4445	720-4689
Web: www.duluthathleticclub.net					
Fitger's Brewery Complex 600 E Superior St	Duluth	MN	55802	218-722-8826	
TF: 800-348-4377 ■ *Web:* www.brewhouse.net					
Grandma's Saloon & Grill 522 Lake Ave S	Duluth	MN	55802	218-727-4192	723-1986
Web: www.grandmasrestaurants.com					
Grandma's Sports Garden Bar & Grill 425 Lake Ave S	Duluth	MN	55802	218-722-4722	720-3804
Web: www.grandmasrestaurants.com					
Green Mill Restaurant & Bar 340 Lake Ave S	Duluth	MN	55802	218-727-7000	723-8510
Web: www.greenmill.com					
Hacienda del Sol 319 E Superior St	Duluth	MN	55802	218-722-7296	
Web: www.hacienda-del-sol.com					
India Palace 319 W Superior St	Duluth	MN	55802	218-727-8767	
Jade Fountain 305 N Central Ave	Duluth	MN	55807	218-624-4212	624-4212
Lake Avenue Cafe 394 Lake Ave S	Duluth	MN	55802	218-722-2355	
Web: www.lakeavenuecafe.com					
Lakeview Castle Dining Room 5135 N Shore Dr	Duluth	MN	55804	218-525-1014	
Web: www.lakeviewcastleduluth.com					
Le Grand Supper Club 5906 Old Miller Trunk Hwy	Duluth	MN	55811	218-729-7973	729-1144
Maya 1725 Miller Trunk Hwy	Duluth	MN	55811	218-722-0360	
New Scenic Cafe 5461 North Shore Dr	Duluth	MN	55804	218-525-6274	525-0737
Web: www.sceniccafe.com					
Old Chicago 327 Lake Ave S	Duluth	MN	55802	218-720-2966	720-2930
Web: www.oldchicago.com					
Pickwick 508 E Superior St	Duluth	MN	55802	218-727-8901	786-0228
Web: www.pickwickrestaurant.com					
Porter's 200 W 1st St	Duluth	MN	55802	218-727-6746	722-0233
Saigon Cafe 2224 Mountain Shadow Dr Suite 2400	Duluth	MN	55811	218-727-3987	
Sir Benedict's Tavern 805 E Superior St	Duluth	MN	55802	218-728-1192	728-9878
Web: www.sirbenedicts.com					
Sneakers Sports Bar & Grill 207 W 1st St	Duluth	MN	55802	218-727-7494	
Thai Krathong 114 W 1st St	Duluth	MN	55802	218-733-9774	
Web: www.thaikrathong.com					
Timber Lodge Steakhouse 325 Lake Ave S	Duluth	MN	55802	218-722-2624	722-3844
Web: www.timberlodgesteakhouse.com					
Top of the Harbor 505 W Superior St Radisson Hotel Duluth Harborview	Duluth	MN	55802	218-727-8981	
Hubbell House Hwy 57 & 5th Ave	Mantorville	MN	55955	507-635-2331	635-5280
Alma 528 University Ave SE	Minneapolis	MN	55414	612-379-4909	
Web: www.restaurantalma.com					
Azia 2550 Nicollet Ave	Minneapolis	MN	55404	612-813-1200	870-8496
Web: www.aziarestaurant.com					
Black Forest Inn 1 E 26th St	Minneapolis	MN	55404	612-872-0812	872-0826
Web: www.blackforestinnmpls.com					
Brit's Pub & Eating Establishment 1110 Nicollet Mall	Minneapolis	MN	55403	612-332-3908	332-8032
Web: www.britspub.com					
Broders Southside Pasta Bar 5000 Penn Ave S	Minneapolis	MN	55419	612-925-9202	
Web: www.broders.com					
Cafe Barbette 1600 W Lake St	Minneapolis	MN	55408	612-827-5710	822-6305
Web: www.barbette.com					
Cafe Brenda 300 1st Ave N	Minneapolis	MN	55401	612-342-9230	342-0155
Web: www.cafebrenda.com					
Cafe Di Napoli 816 Hennepin Ave	Minneapolis	MN	55403	612-333-4949	
Cafe Lurcat 1624 Harmon Pl	Minneapolis	MN	55403	612-486-5500	
Web: www.cafelurcat.com					
Cafe Twenty-Eight 2724 W 43rd St	Minneapolis	MN	55410	612-926-2800	926-2804
Web: www.cafetwentyeight.com					
California Cafe Bar & Grill 368 South Blvd	Minneapolis	MN	55425	952-854-2233	
Campiello 1320 W Lake St	Minneapolis	MN	55408	612-825-2222	
Web: www.campiello.damico.com					
Capital Grille The 801 Hennepin Ave	Minneapolis	MN	55402	612-692-9000	692-9002
Web: www.thecapitalgrille.com					
Cave Vin 5555 Xerxes Ave S	Minneapolis	MN	55410	612-922-0100	
Christo's 2632 Nicollet Ave S	Minneapolis	MN	55408	612-871-2111	871-8129
Web: www.christos.com					
Cosmos 601 1st Ave	Minneapolis	MN	55402	612-312-1158	677-1200
Web: www.cosmosrestaurant.com					
Cue 806 2nd St S	Minneapolis	MN	54415	612-225-6499	
Dakota Jazz Club & Restaurant 1010 Nicollet Ave	Minneapolis	MN	55403	612-332-1010	332-7070
Web: www.dakotacooks.com					
D'Amico Cucina 100 N 6th St	Minneapolis	MN	55403	612-338-2401	337-5130
Erte 1304 University Ave NE	Minneapolis	MN	55413	612-623-4211	
Famous Dave's Bar-B-Que 3001 Hennepin Ave	Minneapolis	MN	55408	612-822-9900	822-9221
Web: www.famousdaves.com					
Figlio 3001 Hennepin Ave S	Minneapolis	MN	55408	612-822-1688	822-0433
Web: www.figlio.com					

Minnesota (Cont'd)

Restaurant	City	State	Zip	Phone	Fax
FireLake Grill House & Cocktail Bar 31 S 7th St	Minneapolis	MN	55402	612-216-3473	547-6240
Web: www.firelakerestaurant.com					
Fuji-Ya 600 W Lake St	Minneapolis	MN	55408	612-871-4055	
Web: www.fujiyasushi.com					
Gardens of Salonica 19 NE 5th St	Minneapolis	MN	55413	612-378-0611	378-0611
Joe's Garage 1610 Harmon Pl	Minneapolis	MN	55403	612-904-1163	904-1260
Web: www.joes-garage.com					
JP American Bistro 2937 Lyndale Ave S	Minneapolis	MN	55408	612-824-9300	824-9301
Web: www.jpamericanbistro.com					
Khan's Mongolian Barbecue 500 E 78th St	Minneapolis	MN	55423	612-861-7991	
Kikugawa 43 Main St SE	Minneapolis	MN	55414	612-378-3006	
King & I 1346 La Salle Ave	Minneapolis	MN	55403	612-332-6928	338-4293
Web: www.kingandithai.com					
La Belle Vie 510 Groveland Ave	Minneapolis	MN	55403	612-874-6440	
Web: www.labellevie.us/					
Local The 931 Nicollet Mall	Minneapolis	MN	55402	612-904-1000	904-1005
Web: www.the-local.com					
Lucia's 1432 W 31st St	Minneapolis	MN	55408	612-825-1572	824-4553
Web: www.lucias.com					
Mandarin Kitchen 8766 Lyndale Ave S	Minneapolis	MN	55420	952-884-5356	
Manny's Steak House 1300 Nicollet Mall	Minneapolis	MN	55403	612-339-9900	341-2373
Web: www.mannyssteakhouse.com					
McCormick & Schmick's 800 Nicollet Mall	Minneapolis	MN	55402	612-338-3300	338-3314
Web: www.mccormickandschmicks.com					
Melting Pot The 80 S 9th St	Minneapolis	MN	55402	612-338-9900	312-2855
Web: www.meltingpot.com					
Mission American Kitchen 77 S 7th St	Minneapolis	MN	55402	612-339-1000	339-8700
Web: www.missionamerican.com					
Modern Cafe 337 13th Ave NE	Minneapolis	MN	55413	612-378-9882	
Morton's The Steakhouse 555 Nicollet Mall	Minneapolis	MN	55402	612-673-9700	673-0853
Web: www.mortons.com					
Murray's 26 S 6th St	Minneapolis	MN	55402	612-339-0909	339-2310
Web: www.murraysrestaurant.com					
Nalapak 4920 Central Ave NE	Minneapolis	MN	55421	763-574-1113	574-1116
Web: www.nalapak.com/					
Nami 251 N 1st Ave	Minneapolis	MN	55402	612-333-1999	333-7449
Web: www.namisushi.com					
Nicollet Island Inn 95 Merriam St	Minneapolis	MN	55401	612-331-3035	331-5667
Web: www.nicolletislandinn.com					
Oak Grill 700 Nicollet Mall	Minneapolis	MN	55402	612-375-2938	375-3323
Oceanaire Seafood Room 1300 Nicollet Mall	Minneapolis	MN	55403	612-333-2277	305-1923
Web: www.theoceanaire.com					
Oddfellows 401 E Hennepin Ave	Minneapolis	MN	55414	612-378-3188	
Origami 30 N 1st St	Minneapolis	MN	55401	612-333-8430	333-8974
Web: www.origamirestaurant.com					
Palomino Euro Bistro 825 Hennepin Ave	Minneapolis	MN	55402	612-339-3800	339-1628
Web: www.palomino.com					
Pane Vino Dolce 819 W 50th St	Minneapolis	MN	55419	612-825-3201	
Peking Garden 2324 University Ave SE	Minneapolis	MN	55414	612-623-3989	623-4629
Prima 5325 Lyndale Ave S	Minneapolis	MN	55419	612-827-7376	827-7534
Web: www.primamn.com					
Quang 2719 Nicollet Ave S	Minneapolis	MN	55408	612-870-4739	879-4739
Web: www.quangrestaurant.com					
Rainbow Chinese 2739 Nicollet Ave S	Minneapolis	MN	55408	612-870-7084	872-6204
Web: www.rainbowrestaurant.com					
Rice Paper 2726 W 43rd St	Minneapolis	MN	55410	612-926-8650	
Rock Bottom Brewery 825 Hennepin Ave	Minneapolis	MN	55402	612-332-2739	332-1508
Web: www.rockbottom.com					
Ruth's Chris Steak House 920 2nd Ave S	Minneapolis	MN	55402	612-672-9000	672-9102
Web: www.ruthschris.com					
Salsa a la Salsa 1420 Nicollet Ave S	Minneapolis	MN	55403	612-813-1970	813-1972
Web: www.salsaalasalsa.com					
Sapor Cafe & Bar 428 Washington Ave N	Minneapolis	MN	55401	612-375-1971	375-1974
Web: www.saporcafe.com					
Sawatdee 607 Washington Ave S	Minneapolis	MN	55415	612-338-6451	338-6498
Web: www.sawatdee.com					
Solera 900 Hennepin Ave	Minneapolis	MN	55403	612-338-0062	338-8871
Web: www.solera-restaurant.com					
True Thai 2627 Franklin Ave E	Minneapolis	MN	55406	612-375-9942	
Web: www.truethairestaurant.com					
Vincent Restaurant 1100 Nicollet Mall	Minneapolis	MN	55403	612-630-1189	343-5907
Web: www.vincentrestaurant.com					
Zelo 831 Nicollet Mall	Minneapolis	MN	55402	612-333-7000	333-7707
Broken Axe The 700 1st Ave N	Moorhead	MN	56560	218-287-0080	287-0090
Web: www.thebrokenaxe.com					
Speak Easy 1001 30th Ave S	Moorhead	MN	56560	218-233-1326	233-6012
Web: www.speakeasyrestaurant.com					
Broadstreet Cafe 300 1st Ave NW	Rochester	MN	55901	507-281-2451	
Canadian Honker 1203 2nd St SW	Rochester	MN	55902	507-282-6572	
Web: www.canadianhonker.com					
Chardonnay 723 2nd St SW	Rochester	MN	55902	507-252-1310	252-1178
China Dynasty 701 S Broadway	Rochester	MN	55904	507-289-2333	289-2553
City Cafe 216 1st Ave SW	Rochester	MN	55902	507-289-1949	
Web: cccrmg.com/city_cafe.htm					
Famous Dave's Bar-B-Que 431 NW 16th Ave	Rochester	MN	55901	507-282-4200	
Web: www.famousdaves.com					
Fazoli's 5550 Hwy 52 N	Rochester	MN	55901	507-286-8763	286-8764
Web: www.fazolis.com					
Fiesta Mexicana 1645 N Broadway	Rochester	MN	55906	507-288-1116	
Great China 4214 Hwy 52 N	Rochester	MN	55901	507-280-9092	
Hunan 844 S Broadway	Rochester	MN	55904	507-287-0002	287-0141
India Garden 1107 N Broadway	Rochester	MN	55906	507-288-6280	
Jaspers Alsatian Bistro & Wine Bar 14 Historic 3rd St SW	Rochester	MN	55902	507-280-6446	
Jenpachi Japanese Steak House 3160 Wellner NE	Rochester	MN	55906	507-292-1688	
Michael's 15 S Broadway	Rochester	MN	55904	507-288-2020	288-5553
Web: www.michaelsfinedining.com					
Redwood Room 300 1st Ave NW	Rochester	MN	55901	507-281-2978	
Web: www.cccrmg.com/redwoodroom.htm					
Roscoe's Root Beer & Ribs 603 4th St SE	Rochester	MN	55904	507-285-0501	
Sky Dragon Buffet 34 17th Ave NW	Rochester	MN	55901	507-281-1813	
Timber Lodge Steakhouse 4144 Hwy 52 N	Rochester	MN	55901	507-252-8075	252-8074
Web: www.timberlodgesteakhouse.com					
Victoria's 7 1st Ave NW	Rochester	MN	55902	507-280-6232	280-6288
Web: www.victoriasmn.com					
Zorba's 924 7th St NW	Rochester	MN	55901	507-281-1540	281-0720
Kahn's Mongolian Barbeque 2720 Snowing Ave	Roseville	MN	55113	651-631-3398	
128 Cafe 128 Cleveland Ave N	Saint Paul	MN	55104	651-645-4128	
A Rebours 410 Saint Peter St	Saint Paul	MN	55102	651-665-0656	665-0755
Beirut Restaurant 1385 Robert St S	Saint Paul	MN	55118	651-457-4886	
Web: www.beirutrestaurantanddeli.com					
Cafe Latte 850 Grand Ave	Saint Paul	MN	55105	651-224-5687	
Web: www.cafelatte.com					
Chang O'Hara's 498 Selby Ave	Saint Paul	MN	55102	651-290-2338	
El Amanecer 194 Concord St	Saint Paul	MN	55107	651-291-0758	225-1719
Web: www.elamanecerrestaurant.com					
El Burrito Mercado 175 Concord St	Saint Paul	MN	55107	651-227-2192	227-2411
Everest on Grand 1278 Grand Ave	Saint Paul	MN	55105	651-696-1666	698-6662
Forepaugh's 276 S Exchange St	Saint Paul	MN	55102	651-224-5606	224-5607
Web: www.forepaughs.com					
Fuji-Ya 465 N Wabasha St	Saint Paul	MN	55102	651-310-0111	
Web: www.fujiyasushi.com/					
Heartland 1806 St Clair Ave	Saint Paul	MN	55105	651-699-3536	
Web: www.heartlandrestaurant.com					
Kincaid's Fish Chop & Steak House 380 Saint Peters St Suite A	Saint Paul	MN	55102	651-602-9000	602-9158
Web: www.kincaids.com					
La Grolla 452 Selby Ave	Saint Paul	MN	55102	651-221-1061	
Lexington The 1096 Grand Ave	Saint Paul	MN	55105	651-222-5878	222-8230
Web: www.the-lexington.com					
Lindey's Prime Steak House 3610 Snelling Ave N	Saint Paul	MN	55112	651-633-9813	633-2222
Luci Ancora 2060 Randolph Ave	Saint Paul	MN	55105	651-698-6889	698-6696
Mai Village 394 University Ave	Saint Paul	MN	55103	651-290-2585	
Mancini's Char House 531 7th St W	Saint Paul	MN	55102	651-224-7345	224-9367
Web: www.mancinis.com					
Moscow on the Hill 371 Selby Ave	Saint Paul	MN	55102	651-291-1236	
Web: www.moscowonthehill.com					
Muffuletta Cafe 2260 Como Ave	Saint Paul	MN	55108	651-644-9116	644-5329
Web: www.muffuletta.com					
Pad Thai Grand Cafe 1681 Grand Ave	Saint Paul	MN	55105	651-690-1393	
Pazzaluna 360 Saint Peter St	Saint Paul	MN	55102	651-223-7000	227-1296
River Room 411 Cedar St	Saint Paul	MN	55101	651-292-5174	
Saint Paul Grill 350 Market St	Saint Paul	MN	55102	651-224-7455	
Web: www.saintpaulgrill.com					
Saji-Ya 695 Grand Ave	Saint Paul	MN	55105	651-292-0444	225-4881
Web: www.sajiya.com					
Sakura Japanese Restaurant 350 Saint Peter St	Saint Paul	MN	55102	651-224-0185	225-9350
Web: www.sakurastpaul.com					
Tavern on Grand 656 Grand Ave	Saint Paul	MN	55105	651-228-9030	229-0090
Web: www.tavernongrand.com					
Trattoria da Vinci 400 Sibley St	Saint Paul	MN	55101	651-222-4050	224-4545
Web: www.trattoriadavinci.com					
Vintage & Wine Bar The 579 Selby Ave	Saint Paul	MN	55102	651-222-7000	
Wild Onion 788 Grand Ave	Saint Paul	MN	55105	651-291-2525	291-5215
Web: www.wild-onion.net					
Yang's 1568 Woodlane Dr	Saint Paul	MN	55125	651-731-3212	
Zander Cafe 525 Selby Ave	Saint Paul	MN	55102	651-222-5224	312-1193
Web: www.zandercafe.com					

Mississippi

Restaurant	City	State	Zip	Phone	Fax
32 850 Bayview Ave Imperial Palace Hotel & Casino	Biloxi	MS	39530	228-436-3000	432-3262
BR Prime Steakhouse 875 Beach Blvd Beau Rivage Resort & Casino	Biloxi	MS	39530	228-386-7111	
Jazzeppi's 195 B Porter Ave	Biloxi	MS	39530	228-374-9660	374-9692
Web: www.jazzeppis.com					
Jia 875 Beach Blvd Beau Rivage Resort & Casino	Biloxi	MS	39530	228-386-7111	
Mary Mahoney's Old French House 116 Rue Magnolia	Biloxi	MS	39530	228-374-0163	432-1387
Web: www.marymahoneys.com					
Mr Greek 1670 H Pass Rd	Biloxi	MS	39531	228-432-7888	432-8379
Olives 875 Beach Blvd Beau Rivage Resort & Casino	Biloxi	MS	39530	228-386-7111	
Blow Fly Inn 9415 Hwy 49	Gulfport	MS	39503	228-896-9812	248-0048
Web: www.blowflyinn.com					
El Mexicano Inn 1215 30th Ave	Gulfport	MS	39501	228-863-3691	
Emeril's Gulf Coast Fish House 3300 W Beach Blvd	Gulfport	MS	39501	228-314-1515	
Lil Ray's 500A Courthouse Rd	Gulfport	MS	39501	228-896-9601	896-9622
South China 548 Courthouse Rd	Gulfport	MS	39507	228-896-9832	
206 Front 206 E Front St	Hattiesburg	MS	39401	601-545-5677	545-2025
Web: www.206front.com					
Chesterfield's 2507 Hardy St	Hattiesburg	MS	39401	601-582-2778	582-3942
Copeland's of New Orleans 4591 Hardy St	Hattiesburg	MS	39402	601-296-9300	296-9388
Web: www.alcopeland.com					
Cuco's Mexican Cafe 6104 Hwy 49 S	Hattiesburg	MS	39401	601-545-8241	545-8244
Donanelle's Bar & Grill 4321 Hwy 49	Hattiesburg	MS	39401	601-545-3860	545-7822
Web: www.donanelles.com					
Front Porch 205 Thornhill Dr	Hattiesburg	MS	39402	601-264-3536	268-0991
Garfield's 1000 Turtle Creek Dr	Hattiesburg	MS	39402	601-264-7000	
La Fiesta Brava 4404 Hardy St	Hattiesburg	MS	39401	601-271-6070	271-8348
Web: www.lafiestabrava.net					
Leatha's Bar-B-Que Inn 6374 US Hwy 98 Suite D	Hattiesburg	MS	39402	601-271-6003	
Web: www.leathas.com					
Mandarin House 4400 Hardy St Suite A7	Hattiesburg	MS	39402	601-268-1776	268-1773
Panino's 3801 Hardy St	Hattiesburg	MS	39402	601-264-0605	264-0602
Purple Parrot Cafe 3810 Hardy St	Hattiesburg	MS	39402	601-264-0656	264-0681
Rayner's Seafood House 7343 Hwy 49	Hattiesburg	MS	39402	601-268-2639	
Sakura 6194 Hwy 49	Hattiesburg	MS	39401	601-545-9393	545-9394
Walnut Circle Grill 115 Walnut St	Hattiesburg	MS	39401	601-544-2202	271-6004
Web: www.walnutcirclegrill.com					
Bonsai Japanese Steak House 1925 Lakeland Dr	Jackson	MS	39216	601-981-0606	
Bravo 244 Highland Village Suite 244	Jackson	MS	39211	601-982-8111	981-1463
Web: www.bravobuzz.com					
Creschale's 3107 Hwy 80 W	Jackson	MS	39204	601-355-1840	
CS's Restaurant 1359 1/2 N West St	Jackson	MS	39202	601-969-9482	969-9021
E & L Bar-B-Que 1111 Bailey Ave	Jackson	MS	39213	601-355-5035	
El Torrero 4337 Lakeland Dr	Jackson	MS	39208	601-932-0030	
Elite Restaurant 141 E Capitol St	Jackson	MS	39201	601-352-5606	
Fenian's Pub 901 E Fortification St	Jackson	MS	39202	601-948-0055	948-1155
Web: www.fenianspub.com					
Hal & Mal's 200 S Commerce St	Jackson	MS	39201	601-948-0888	355-1790
Web: www.halandmals.com					
Keifer's 705 Poplar Blvd	Jackson	MS	39202	601-355-6825	355-0380
La Cazuela Mexican Grill 1401 E Fortification St	Jackson	MS	39202	601-353-3014	353-3015
Nick's 1501 Lakeland Dr	Jackson	MS	39216	601-981-8017	982-9640
Web: www.nicksrestaurant.com					
Peking Chinese Restaurant 5315 I-55 N	Jackson	MS	39206	601-362-7000	
Penn's Fish House 2085 Lakeland Dr	Jackson	MS	39216	601-982-9004	982-0910
Que Sera Sera 2801 N State St	Jackson	MS	39216	601-981-2520	981-2522
Sakura Bana 4800 I-55 N LeFleur's Gallery	Jackson	MS	39211	601-982-3035	982-3075
Steak-Out 4680 I-55 N	Jackson	MS	39211	601-366-1100	366-4004
Web: www.steakout.com					
Thai House Restaurant 1405 Old Square Rd	Jackson	MS	39211	601-982-9991	
Cock of the Walk 141 Madison Landing Cir	Ridgeland	MS	39157	601-856-5500	856-5502
Cancun Mexican Restaurant 201 N Gloster St	Tupelo	MS	38801	662-842-9557	
Casa Monterrey Grill & Cantina 700 W Main St	Tupelo	MS	38801	662-844-0440	844-7723
China Capital 530 N Gloster St	Tupelo	MS	38804	662-841-0484	
Gentry's on Gloster 205 N Gloster St	Tupelo	MS	38804	662-842-7205	
Harvey's 424 S Gloster St	Tupelo	MS	38801	662-842-6763	844-4251
Web: www.eatwithus.com/harveys					
Hunan Chinese Restaurant 365 S Gloster St	Tupelo	MS	38801	662-842-8888	

				Phone	Fax
Ichiban Japanese Grill 603 N Gloster St	Tupelo	MS	38804	662-842-3838	
IV's 150 S Industrial Rd	Tupelo	MS	38801	662-407-0096	
Web: www.ivsrestaurant.com					
Las Margaritas 123 Industrial Rd	Tupelo	MS	38801	662-844-7399	
Web: www.lasmargaritas.com					
Logan's Roadhouse 3954 N Gloster St	Tupelo	MS	38804	662-840-7552	840-8308
Web: www.logansroadhouse.com					
Malone's Fish & Steak House 1369 Rd 41	Tupelo	MS	38801	662-842-2747	
Park Heights 825 W Jefferson St	Tupelo	MS	38804	662-842-5665	844-7172
Web: www.eatwithus.com/park_heights					
Sun Kai 775 E Main St	Tupelo	MS	38804	662-844-7047	
Tellini's 504 S Gloster St	Tupelo	MS	38801	662-620-9955	620-9951
Web: www.meltingpot.com					
Vanelli's 1302 N Gloster St	Tupelo	MS	38804	662-844-4410	
Web: www.vanellis.com					
Woody's 619 N Gloster St	Tupelo	MS	38801	662-840-0460	

Missouri

				Phone	Fax
Baldknobbers Restaurant 2845 W Hwy 76	Branson	MO	65616	417-334-7202	339-3505
Web: www.baldknobbers.com					
Branson Cafe 120 W Main St	Branson	MO	65616	417-334-3021	
BT Bones 2280 Shepherd Hill Expy	Branson	MO	65616	417-335-2002	338-8554
Web: www.btbones.com					
Buckingham's Restaurant & Oasis 2820 W Hwy 76	Branson	MO	65616	417-337-7777	337-5335
Candlestick Inn 127 Taney St	Branson	MO	65616	417-334-3633	336-4348
Web: www.candlestickinn.com					
Casa Fuentes 1107 W Hwy 76	Branson	MO	65616	417-339-3888	
Web: www.casafuentes.com					
Charlie's Steak-Ribs-Ale 3009 W State Hwy 76	Branson	MO	65616	417-334-6090	336-4038
Chateau Grille 415 N State Hwy 265	Branson	MO	65616	417-334-1161	339-5566
Web: www.chateauonthelake.com					
Farmhouse Restaurant 119 W Main St	Branson	MO	65616	417-334-9701	334-5222
Gilley's Texas Cafe 3457 W State Hwy 76	Branson	MO	65616	417-335-2755	335-2749
Web: www.gilleys.com					
Landry's Seafood House 2900 State Hwy 76	Branson	MO	65616	417-339-1010	339-3801
Web: www.landrysseafoodhouse.com					
Lotus Valley 3129 W Hwy 76	Branson	MO	65616	417-334-3427	
Pasta House 2690 Green Mountain Dr	Branson	MO	65616	417-337-9882	339-2671
Web: www.pastahouse.com					
Plantation Restaurant 3460 W State Hwy 76	Branson	MO	65616	417-334-7800	334-6365
Plaza View 245 N Wildwood Dr	Branson	MO	65616	417-335-2798	335-7907
Rocky's Italian Restaurant 120 N Sycamore St	Branson	MO	65616	417-335-4765	
Sadies Sideboard Restaurant 2830 W Hwy 76	Branson	MO	65616	417-334-3619	334-5841
Shogun Japanese Steak Sushi & Cocktail Lounge					
3265 Falls Pkwy	Branson	MO	65616	417-332-0260	332-0994
Whipper Snapper's 236 Shepherd of the Hills Expy	Branson	MO	65616	417-334-3282	
Web: www.whippersnappersrestaurant.com					
Cardwell's 8100 Maryland Ave	Clayton	MO	63105	314-726-5055	726-1909
Web: www.cardwellsinclayton.com					
Morton's The Steakhouse 7822 Bonhomme Ave	Clayton	MO	63105	314-725-4008	725-1261
Web: www.mortons.com					
63 Diner 5801 Hwy 763 N	Columbia	MO	65202	573-443-2331	815-0017
Web: www.63diner.com					
Addison's 709 Cherry St	Columbia	MO	65201	573-256-1995	256-2836
Web: www.addisonssophias.com					
Angelo's 4107 S Providence Rd	Columbia	MO	65203	573-443-6100	
Bambino's 203 Hitt St	Columbia	MO	65201	573-443-4473	442-2683
Web: www.bambinositaliancafe.com					
Bangkok Gardens 811 Cherry St	Columbia	MO	65201	573-874-3284	
Web: www.bangkokgardens.com					
Buckingham Smokehouse Bar-B-Que 213 Business Loop 70 E	Columbia	MO	65203	573-449-7782	
Chris McD's Restaurant & Wine Bar 1400 Forum Blvd	Columbia	MO	65203	573-446-6237	445-9441
Churchill's					
2200 I-70 Dr SW Holiday Inn Select Executive Center	Columbia	MO	65203	573-445-8531	445-7607
CJ's 704 E Broadway	Columbia	MO	65201	573-442-7777	
Ernie's Cafe 1005 E Walnut St	Columbia	MO	65201	573-874-7804	
Everett's Restaurant & Lounge 1601 Rangeline St	Columbia	MO	65201	573-443-6200	443-3518
Web: www.everettssteakhouse.com					
Flat Branch Pub & Brewing Co 115 S 5th St	Columbia	MO	65201	573-499-0400	
Web: www.flatbranch.com					
Forge & Vine 119 W 7th St	Columbia	MO	65201	573-443-6743	
Web: www.forgeandvine.com					
Formosa Restaurant 913 E Broadway Suite A	Columbia	MO	65201	573-449-3339	
Gaucho's Churrascaria & Steakhouse 10 Southampton	Columbia	MO	65203	573-443-3259	256-8566
Web: www.gauchos.us					
Great Wall 2005 W Worley St	Columbia	MO	65203	573-446-3888	
Hong Kong Restaurant 106 Business Loop 70 W	Columbia	MO	65203	573-442-7350	472-7360
India's Rasoi 1101 E Broadway	Columbia	MO	65201	573-817-2009	874-3018
International Cafe 209 Hitt St	Columbia	MO	65201	573-449-4560	499-1535
Italian Village Pizza 711 Vandiver Dr Suite B	Columbia	MO	65202	573-442-8821	442-3571
Jack's Gourmet Restaurant 1903 Business Loop 70 E	Columbia	MO	65201	573-449-3927	442-9881
Web: www.jacksgourmetrestaurant.com					
Jimmy's Family Steak House 3101 S Providence Rd	Columbia	MO	65203	573-443-1796	
Loon Sheng 2716 Paris Rd	Columbia	MO	65202	573-886-0166	
Murry's 3107 Green Meadows Way	Columbia	MO	65203	573-442-4969	
Osaka 120 E Nifong Blvd Suite A	Columbia	MO	65203	573-875-8588	875-8580
Web: www.osakacolumbia.com					
Pasta Factory 1020 E Broadway	Columbia	MO	65201	573-449-3948	815-0155
Q's 4004 Peach Ct	Columbia	MO	65203	573-442-5342	
Web: www.qs-chinese.biz					
Sake Japanese Bistro & Bar 16 S 10th St	Columbia	MO	65201	573-256-7252	
Sophia's 3915 S Providence Rd	Columbia	MO	65203	573-874-8009	874-4990
Taj Mahal 19 N 5th St	Columbia	MO	65201	573-256-6800	442-7146
Trattoria Strada Nova 21 N 9th St	Columbia	MO	65201	573-442-8992	
Web: www.trattoriastradanova.com					
Wine Cellar & Bistro 505 Cherry St	Columbia	MO	65201	573-442-7281	441-8318
Web: www.winecellarbistro.com					
54th Street Grill 18700 E 38th Terr	Independence	MO	64057	816-795-7077	
Web: www.54thstreetgrill.com					
Bamboo Hut 10111 E 40 Hwy	Independence	MO	64055	816-353-9472	
Cafe Verona 206 W Lexington St	Independence	MO	64050	816-833-0044	833-0603
El Maguey 3738 S Noland Rd	Independence	MO	64055	816-252-6868	
Englewood Cafe 10904 E Winner Rd	Independence	MO	64050	816-461-9588	
Gates Bar-B-Q 10440 E 40 Hwy	Independence	MO	64055	816-353-5880	923-3922
Web: www.gatesbbq.com					
Little Richard's Restaurant 301 N 291 Hwy	Independence	MO	64056	816-257-7295	
Ophelia 201 N Main St	Independence	MO	64050	816-836-4004	836-4248
Rheinland Restaurant 208 N Main St	Independence	MO	64050	816-461-5383	461-9159
Web: www.rheinlandrestaurant.com					
Salty Iguana 17717 E 40 Hwy	Independence	MO	64055	816-350-8003	350-8003
Web: www.saltyiguana.com					
Salvatore Garozzo's 12801 E 40 Hwy	Independence	MO	64055	816-737-2400	356-6622
Samurai Chef Japanese Steakhouse & Sushi Bar					
12712 E Hwy 40	Independence	MO	64055	816-350-3777	350-3149
Web: www.kc-samuraichef.com					

				Phone	Fax
South Chinese Restaurant 1020 S Sterling Ave	Independence	MO	64054	816-461-3564	461-3572
Trolley Inn 11400 E Truman Rd	Independence	MO	64050	816-461-9857	
V's 10819 E US Hwy 40	Independence	MO	64055	816-353-1241	353-0004
Web: www.vsrestaurant.com					
Zio's Italian Kitchen 3901 S Bolger Dr	Independence	MO	64055	816-350-1011	350-1211
Web: www.zios.com/					
Alexandro's 2125 Missouri Blvd	Jefferson City	MO	65109	573-634-7740	
Cajun Catfish House 6819 Hwy 50 W	Jefferson City	MO	65109	573-893-4665	893-8580
Capital City Steak House 127 E High St	Jefferson City	MO	65101	573-893-3888	
China Garden 311 E High St	Jefferson City	MO	65101	573-636-4977	636-7993
Das Stein Haus 1436 South Ridge Dr	Jefferson City	MO	65109	573-634-3869	834-8909
Web: www.dassteinhaus.com					
Dragon Kitchen 2219-D Missouri Blvd	Jefferson City	MO	65109	573-635-8838	636-8368
El Jimador 1410 Missouri Blvd	Jefferson City	MO	65109	573-761-1616	761-4118
Happy Garden 2803 W Truman Blvd	Jefferson City	MO	65109	573-893-7818	893-7028
Hunan Restaurant 1416 Missouri Blvd	Jefferson City	MO	65109	573-634-5253	634-8230
Jasmine Garden 2021 Missouri Blvd	Jefferson City	MO	65109	573-659-9135	
Madison's Cafe 216 Madison St	Jefferson City	MO	65101	573-634-2988	634-3740
Web: www.madisonscafe.com					
Mel's Country Cafe 2421 Industrial Dr	Jefferson City	MO	65109	573-893-9115	
Park Place Restaurant 415 W McCarty St	Jefferson City	MO	65101	573-635-1234	635-4565
Yen Ching Restaurant 2208 Missouri Blvd	Jefferson City	MO	65109	573-635-5225	638-8893
1924 Main 1924 Main St	Kansas City	MO	64108	816-472-1924	472-1925
Web: www.1924main.com					
Aixois 251 E 55th St	Kansas City	MO	64113	816-333-3305	333-3990
Web: www.aixois.com					
Arthur Bryant's Barbeque 1727 Brooklyn Ave	Kansas City	MO	64127	816-231-1123	421-7427
Web: www.arthurbryantsbbq.com					
BB's Lawnside Bar-B-Q 1205 E 85th St	Kansas City	MO	64131	816-822-7427	
Web: www.bbslawnsidebbq.com					
Bell Street Mama's 1726 W 39th St	Kansas City	MO	64111	816-531-6422	
Benton's Steak & Chop House 1 E Pershing Rd	Kansas City	MO	64108	816-391-4460	
Web: www.bentonskc.com/					
Blue Bird Bistro 1700 Summit St	Kansas City	MO	64108	816-221-7559	221-7901
Bluestem 900 Westport Rd	Kansas City	MO	64111	816-561-1101	561-5726
Web: www.kansascitymenus.com/bluestem					
Bo Ling's 4800 Main St	Kansas City	MO	64112	816-753-1718	753-8819
Web: www.bolings.com					
Brio Tuscan Grille 502 Nichols Dr	Kansas City	MO	64112	816-561-5888	
Web: www.brioitalian.com/					
Cafe Al Dente 412D Delaware	Kansas City	MO	64105	816-472-9444	472-9779
Cafe Sebastienne 4420 Warwick Blvd	Kansas City	MO	64111	816-561-7740	960-3674
Californos 4124 Pennsylvania Ave	Kansas City	MO	64111	816-531-7878	531-1894
Web: www.californos.com					
Capital Grille The 4740 Jefferson St	Kansas City	MO	64112	816-531-8345	531-8348
Web: www.thecapitalgrille.com					
Cascone's 3737 N Oak Trafficway	Kansas City	MO	64116	816-454-7977	454-8041
Web: www.cascones.com					
Chappell's Restaurant & Sports Museum 323 Armour Rd	Kansas City	MO	64108	816-421-0002	472-7141
City Tavern 101 W 22nd St	Kansas City	MO	64108	816-421-3696	421-0704
Web: www.citytavern.net					
Cupini's Fresh Pasta & Panini 1809 Westport Rd	Kansas City	MO	64111	816-753-7662	753-7564
Web: www.cupinis.com					
Danny Edwards' Famous Kansas City Barbecue					
1227 Grand Blvd	Kansas City	MO	64106	816-283-0880	
EBT 1310 Carondelet Dr	Kansas City	MO	64114	816-942-8870	941-8532
Web: www.ebtrestaurant.com					
Europa! 323 E 55th St	Kansas City	MO	64113	816-523-1212	
Fiorella's Jack Stack Barbecue 13441 Holmes Rd	Kansas City	MO	64145	816-942-9141	941-8762
Web: www.shilohsfinefoods.com					
Garozzo's 526 Harrison St	Kansas City	MO	64106	816-221-2455	221-7174
Web: www.garozzos.com					
George Brett's 210 W 47th St	Kansas City	MO	64112	816-561-6565	561-2336
Web: www.georgebretts.com					
Grand Street Cafe 4740 Grand Ave	Kansas City	MO	64112	816-561-8000	561-9156
Web: www.kansascitymenus.com/grandstcafe/					
Grille on Broadway 3605 Broadway St	Kansas City	MO	64111	816-531-0700	361-9089
Grinders 417 E 18th St	Kansas City	MO	64108	816-472-5454	
Hereford House 2 E 20th St	Kansas City	MO	64108	816-842-1080	842-5107
Web: www.herefordhouse.com					
Houston's 4640 Wornall Rd	Kansas City	MO	64112	816-561-8542	561-0423
Jardine's 4536 Main St	Kansas City	MO	64111	816-561-6480	561-2885
Web: www.jardines4jazz.com					
Jasper's 1201 W 103rd St	Kansas City	MO	64114	816-941-6600	941-4121
Web: www.jasperskc.com					
Jess & Jim's Steakhouse 517 E 135th St	Kansas City	MO	64145	816-941-9499	942-6348
Web: www.jessandjims.com					
JJ's 910 W 48th St	Kansas City	MO	64112	816-561-7136	561-5490
Web: www.jjs-restaurant.com					
Joe D's 6227 Brookside Plaza	Kansas City	MO	64113	816-333-6116	
Web: www.kansascitymenus.com/joeds/					
Kato 6340 NW Barry Rd	Kansas City	MO	64154	816-584-8883	
La Bodega 703 Southwest Blvd	Kansas City	MO	64108	816-472-8272	471-5250
Web: www.kansascitymenus.com/labodega/					
Le Fou Frog 400 E 5th St	Kansas City	MO	64106	816-474-6060	474-3066
Web: www.kansascitymenus.com/lefoufrog/					
Lidia's Kansas City 101 W 22nd St	Kansas City	MO	64108	816-221-3722	842-1960
Web: www.lidiasitaly.com					
Majestic Steakhouse 931 Broadway	Kansas City	MO	64105	816-471-8484	471-7906
Web: www.kansascitymenus.com/majesticsteakhouse					
Malay Cafe 6003 NW Barry Rd	Kansas City	MO	64154	816-741-3616	
McCormick & Schmick's 448 W 47th St	Kansas City	MO	64112	816-531-6800	531-2090
Web: www.mccormickandschmicks.com					
Morton's The Steakhouse 2475 Grand Ave	Kansas City	MO	64108	816-474-0555	474-4474
Web: www.mortons.com					
New Peking 540 Westport Rd	Kansas City	MO	64111	816-531-6969	531-9188
Osteria Il Centro 5101 Main St	Kansas City	MO	64112	816-561-2369	561-0511
Web: www.osteria-ilcentro.com					
Peach Tree 1512 E 18th St	Kansas City	MO	64108	816-472-8733	472-1573
Web: www.peachtreerestaurant.com					
PF Chang's China Bistro 102 W 47th St	Kansas City	MO	64112	816-931-9988	931-2830
Web: www.pfchangs.com					
Pierpont's at Union Station 30 W Pershing Rd Suite 900	Kansas City	MO	64108	816-221-5111	221-9779
Web: www.herefordhouse.com/ppdefault.htm					
PotPie 904 Westport Rd	Kansas City	MO	64111	816-561-2702	
Web: www.kcpotpie.com					
Red Snapper 8430 Ward Pkwy	Kansas City	MO	64114	816-333-8899	333-8893
Web: www.kcredsnapper.com					
Ruth's Chris Steak House 700 W 47th St	Kansas City	MO	64112	816-531-4800	931-2094
Web: www.ruthschris.com					
Scotty's on 39th 1403 W 39th St	Kansas City	MO	64111	816-561-0100	561-0145
Shiraz 320 Southwest Blvd	Kansas City	MO	64108	816-472-0015	
Sienna Bistro 303 W 10th St	Kansas City	MO	64105	816-527-0221	
Smokin' Guns BBQ 1218 Swift Ave	Kansas City	MO	64116	816-221-2535	221-2606
Web: www.smokingunsbbq.com					
Starker's Reserve 201 W 47th St	Kansas City	MO	64112	816-753-3565	753-3844
Web: www.starkersreserve.com					

Missouri (Cont'd)

Name / Address	City	State	ZIP	Phone	Fax
Streetcar Named Desire 2450 Grand Ave	Kansas City	MO	64108	816-472-5959	
Stroud's Oak Ridge Manor 5410 NE Oak Ridge Rd	Kansas City	MO	64119	816-454-9600	454-0718
Web: www.stroudsrestaurant.com					
Taj Mahal 7521 Wornall Rd	Kansas City	MO	64114	816-361-1722	361-1654
Web: www.kctajmahal.com					
Thomas Restaurant 1815 W 39th St	Kansas City	MO	64111	816-561-3663	756-3265
Web: www.thomaskc.com					
Blue Owl Restaurant 2nd & Mill Sts	Kimmswick	MO	63053	636-464-3128	
Web: www.saucecafe.com/blueowl/					
Blue Water Grill 343 S Kirkwood Rd	Kirkwood	MO	63122	314-821-5757	821-4565
Al's 1200 N 1st St	Saint Louis	MO	63102	314-421-6399	421-0357
Web: www.alsrestaurant.net					
An American Place 822 Washington Ave	Saint Louis	MO	63102	314-418-5800	
Bandana's Bar-B-Q 11750 Gravois Rd	Saint Louis	MO	63127	314-849-1162	729-1126
Web: www.bandanasbbq.com					
Bar Italian Ristorante-Caffe 13 Maryland Plaza	Saint Louis	MO	63108	314-361-7010	361-6131
Web: www.baritaliastl.com					
Broadway Oyster Bar 736 S Broadway	Saint Louis	MO	63102	314-621-8811	621-1995
Web: broadwayoysterbar.com/					
Cafe Balaban 405 N Euclid Ave	Saint Louis	MO	63108	314-361-8085	361-5740
Web: www.cafebalaban.com					
Carmine's Steak House 20 S 4th St	Saint Louis	MO	63101	314-241-1631	231-2952
Web: www.lombardosrestaurants.com					
Chez Leon 4580 Laclede Ave	Saint Louis	MO	63108	314-361-1589	
Web: www.chezleon.com					
Clark Street Grill 811 Spruce St	Saint Louis	MO	63102	314-621-2000	552-5749
Web: www.clarkstreetgrill.com					
Crossing The 7823 Forsyth Blvd	Saint Louis	MO	63105	314-721-7375	721-3646
Cunetto House of Pasta 5453 Magnolia Ave	Saint Louis	MO	63139	314-781-1135	781-5674
Web: www.cunetto.com					
Dierdorf & Hart's Steak House					
701 Market St Suite 100 Gateway One Bldg	Saint Louis	MO	63101	314-421-1772	621-7217
Web: www.dierdorfharts.com					
Duff's 392 N Euclid Ave	Saint Louis	MO	63108	314-361-0522	
Web: www.dineatduffs.com					
Faust's 315 Chestnut St	Saint Louis	MO	63102	314-241-7400	241-6618
Frazer's 1811 Pestalozzi St	Saint Louis	MO	63118	314-773-8646	773-8615
Web: www.frazergoodeats.com					
Gian-Tony's 5356 Daggett Ave	Saint Louis	MO	63110	314-772-4893	772-1004
Giovanni's 5201 Shaw Ave	Saint Louis	MO	63110	314-772-5958	772-0343
Web: www.giovannisonthehill.com					
Giuseppe's 4141 S Grand Blvd	Saint Louis	MO	63118	314-832-8013	832-7598
Web: www.giuseppesongrand.com					
Happy China 12919 Olive Blvd	Saint Louis	MO	63141	314-878-6660	
Harry's Restaurant & Bar 2144 Market St	Saint Louis	MO	63103	314-421-6969	241-2755
Web: www.harrysrestaurantandbar.com					
House of India 8501 Delmar Blvd	Saint Louis	MO	63124	314-567-6850	
Web: www.hoistl.com					
I Love Mr. Sushi 9443 Olive Blvd	Saint Louis	MO	63132	314-432-8898	432-6590
Kemoll's 211 N Broadway	Saint Louis	MO	63102	314-421-0555	436-9692
Web: www.kemolls.com					
King & I 3157 S Grand Blvd	Saint Louis	MO	63118	314-771-1777	771-3265
Web: www.thaispicy.com					
King Louie's 3800 Chouteau Ave	Saint Louis	MO	63110	314-865-3662	865-0151
Web: www.kinglouies.com					
Kreis' Restaurant 535 S Lindbergh Blvd	Saint Louis	MO	63131	314-993-0735	993-3020
Web: www.kreisrestaurant.com					
Liluma 236 N Euclid Ave	Saint Louis	MO	63108	314-361-7771	
Lorenzo's Trattoria 1933 Edwards St	Saint Louis	MO	63139	314-773-2223	773-0689
Web: www.lorenzostrattoria.com					
LoRusso's Cucina 3121 Watson Rd	Saint Louis	MO	63139	314-647-6222	647-2821
Web: www.lorussos.com					
Mike Shannon's 620 Market St	Saint Louis	MO	63101	314-421-1540	241-5642
Web: www.shannonsteak.com					
Modesto 5257 Shaw Ave	Saint Louis	MO	63110	314-772-8272	
Web: www.saucecafe.com/modesto					
Nobu's 8643 Olive Blvd	Saint Louis	MO	63132	314-997-2303	
Norton's Cafe 808 Geyer St	Saint Louis	MO	63104	314-436-0828	436-3188
Web: www.nortonscafe.com					
Pho Grand 3195 S Grand Blvd	Saint Louis	MO	63118	314-664-7435	771-5169
Web: www.phogrand.com					
Riddles Penultimate Cafe & Wine Bar 6307 Delmar Blvd	Saint Louis	MO	63130	314-725-6985	725-1153
Saint Louis Fish Market 901 N 1st St	Saint Louis	MO	63102	314-621-4612	241-6513
Web: www.stlouisfishmarket.com					
Sam's Steakhouse 10205 Gravois Rd	Saint Louis	MO	63123	314-849-3033	849-0423
Web: www.samssteakhouse.com					
Sansui 4955 W Pine Blvd	Saint Louis	MO	63108	314-367-2020	367-2529
Sidney Street Cafe 2000 Sidney St	Saint Louis	MO	63104	314-771-5777	771-7016
Web: www.sidneystreetcafe.com					
Soulard's Restaurant 1731 S 7th St	Saint Louis	MO	63104	314-241-7956	241-7956
Web: www.soulards.com					
Spiro's 3122 Watson Rd	Saint Louis	MO	63139	314-645-8383	781-0968
Web: www.spiros-restaurant.com					
SqWire's 1415 S 18th St	Saint Louis	MO	63104	314-865-3522	865-3524
Web: www.sqwires.com					
Tenderloin Room 232 N Kingshighway Blvd	Saint Louis	MO	63108	314-361-0900	
Web: www.tenderloinroom.com					
Tony's 410 Market St	Saint Louis	MO	63102	314-231-7007	231-4740
Top of the Riverfront 200 S 4th St 28th Fl	Saint Louis	MO	63102	314-241-3191	
Trattoria Marcella 3600 Watson Rd	Saint Louis	MO	63109	314-352-7706	352-0848
Tucker's Place 2117 S 12th St	Saint Louis	MO	63104	314-772-5977	773-3775
Web: www.tuckersplace.com					
Vin de Set Rooftop Bar & Bistro 2017 Chouteau Ave	Saint Louis	MO	63103	314-241-8989	621-5550
Web: www.1111-m.com/					
Yemanja Brasil 2900 Missouri Ave	Saint Louis	MO	63118	314-771-7457	
Web: www.brazildining.com					
Zia's 5256 Wilson Ave	Saint Louis	MO	63110	314-776-0020	776-5778
Web: www.zias.com					
Dominic's 5101 Wilson Ave	South Saint Louis	MO	63110	314-771-1632	771-1695
Web: www.dominicsrestaurant.com					
Agrario 311 S Patton Ave	Springfield	MO	65806	417-865-4255	799-0204
Web: www.agrariorestaurant.com					
Bamboo Inn 948 S Glenstone Ave	Springfield	MO	65802	417-869-2506	
Bangkok City 1129 E Walnut St	Springfield	MO	65806	417-799-1221	
Bijan's Sea & Grille 209 E Walnut St	Springfield	MO	65806	417-831-1480	
Web: www.bijans.com					
Buckingham Smokehouse BBQ 2002 S Campbell Ave	Springfield	MO	65807	417-886-9979	
Canton Inn 205 W Sunshine St	Springfield	MO	65807	417-862-5444	862-5934
Carriage House 1772 S Glenstone Ave	Springfield	MO	65804	417-823-9904	
Cartoon's Oyster Bar & Grill 1614 S Glenstone	Springfield	MO	65804	417-882-5752	882-3353
Web: www.cartoonman.com					
Cheddar's Casual Cafe 1950 E Primrose Ln	Springfield	MO	65804	417-889-8998	
China Star 1444 E Republic Rd	Springfield	MO	65804	417-887-9779	
Cielito Lindo Mexicano 2953 S National Ave	Springfield	MO	65804	417-886-3320	
Clary's 3014-A E Sunshine St	Springfield	MO	65804	417-886-1940	227-9425
Web: www.clarysrestaurant.com					
El Chico 2639 S Glenstone St	Springfield	MO	65804	417-886-4768	886-6867
Gem of India 211 W Battlefield St	Springfield	MO	65807	417-881-9558	
Gilardi's 820 E Walnut St	Springfield	MO	65806	417-862-6400	
Hemingway's Blue Water Cafe 1935 S Campbell Ave	Springfield	MO	65898	417-891-5100	887-5204
J Parrino's 1550 E Battlefield St	Springfield	MO	65804	417-882-1808	882-2445
Lucy's Chinese Food 3330 S Campbell Ave Suite C	Springfield	MO	65807	417-882-5383	
Metropolitan Grill 2931 E Battlefield	Springfield	MO	65804	417-889-4951	889-2728
Nakato Japanese Steak House 2615 S Glenstone Ave	Springfield	MO	65804	417-881-7171	881-4443
Web: www.nakatos.com					
Nonna's Italian American Cafe 306 South Ave	Springfield	MO	65806	417-831-1222	
Pappy's Place 943 N Main Ave	Springfield	MO	65802	417-866-8744	
Schultz & Dooley's 2210 W Chesterfield St	Springfield	MO	65807	417-885-0060	
Shanghai Inn 1937 N Glenstone Ave	Springfield	MO	65803	417-865-5111	
Silk Road 310 W Battlefield St	Springfield	MO	65807	417-886-0999	
Springfield Brewing Co 305 S Market Ave	Springfield	MO	65806	417-832-8277	
Web: www.springfieldbrewingco.com					
Ziggie's Cafe 2222 S Campbell Ave	Springfield	MO	65807	417-883-0900	
Web: ziggiescafe.com					
Saleem's 6501 Delmar Blvd	University City	MO	63130	314-721-7947	721-2295

Montana

Name / Address	City	State	ZIP	Phone	Fax
Bruno's Italian Specialties 2658 Grand Ave	Billings	MT	59102	406-652-4416	652-0024
Don Luis 15 N 26th St	Billings	MT	59101	406-256-3355	256-3359
Enzo 1502 Rehberg Ln	Billings	MT	59102	406-651-0999	
Four Seas 1005 Grand Ave	Billings	MT	59102	406-254-1886	254-1186
George Henry's Restaurant 404 N 30th St	Billings	MT	59101	406-245-4570	245-3745
Guadalajara Family Mexican 17 N 29th St	Billings	MT	59101	406-259-8930	259-8950
Gusick's 760 S 20th St W	Billings	MT	59102	406-652-5441	652-4663
Jade Palace 2021 Overland Ave	Billings	MT	59102	406-656-8888	
Jake's 2701 1st Ave N	Billings	MT	59101	406-259-9375	259-1142
Juliano's 2912 7th Ave N	Billings	MT	59101	406-248-6400	
Lucky Diamond 27 N 27th St The Crown Plaza	Billings	MT	59101	406-252-7400	
Montana Brewing Co 113 N 28th St	Billings	MT	59101	406-252-9200	259-3329
Rex The 2401 Montana Ave	Billings	MT	59101	406-245-7477	248-6469
Windmill Club 3429 Transtech Way	Billings	MT	59102	406-252-8100	651-0249
3-D International 1825 Smelter Ave	Black Eagle	MT	59414	406-453-6561	453-9947
Borrie's 1800 Smelter Ave	Black Eagle	MT	59414	406-761-0300	761-2021
Bar-S Supper Club 8535 US Hwy 89	Great Falls	MT	59405	406-761-9550	
Breaks Alehouse & Grill 202 2nd Ave S	Great Falls	MT	59405	406-453-5980	
Cattlemen's Cut Supper Club 369 Vaughn Frontage Rd S	Great Falls	MT	59404	406-452-0702	452-0408
Dante's Creative Cuisine 1325 8th Ave N	Great Falls	MT	59401	406-453-9599	453-9599
Eddie's Supper Club 3725 2nd Ave N	Great Falls	MT	59401	406-453-1616	
El Comedor 1120 25th St S	Great Falls	MT	59405	406-761-5500	761-5502
Kickers 600 Central Ave	Great Falls	MT	59401	406-453-5292	
Loft Restaurant 4800 10th Ave S	Great Falls	MT	59405	406-727-8988	
Maple Garden 5401 9th Ave S	Great Falls	MT	59401	406-727-0310	452-5906
Maria's Mexican Restaurant 2501 10th Ave S	Great Falls	MT	59405	406-453-5303	
Prime Cut Restaurant 3219 10th Ave S	Great Falls	MT	59405	406-727-2141	
Sting The 1826 10th Ave S	Great Falls	MT	59405	406-727-7972	727-7972
Willow Creek Steakhouse 1700 Fox Farm Rd	Great Falls	MT	59404	406-761-1900	761-0136
Bert & Ernie's Saloon 361 N Last Chance Gulch	Helena	MT	59601	406-443-5680	443-7857
Web: www.bertanderniesofhelena.com					
Brewhouse Brew Pub & Grill 939 1/2 Getchell St	Helena	MT	59601	406-457-9390	457-9296
Chinese Kitchen & Oriental Shop 901 Euclid Ave	Helena	MT	59601	406-442-2302	
Emiliano's 632 Euclid Ave	Helena	MT	59601	406-443-5478	
Jade Garden 3128 N Montana Ave	Helena	MT	59602	406-443-8899	443-8390
Web: www.jadegardenhelena.co					
Jorgenson's 1720 11th Ave	Helena	MT	59601	406-442-6380	442-7693
Mediterranean Grill 42 S Park Ave	Helena	MT	59601	406-495-1212	443-5252
Miller's Crossing 52 S Park Ave	Helena	MT	59601	406-442-3290	442-1715
Web: www.millerscrossing.biz					
Montana Club 24 W 6th Ave	Helena	MT	59601	406-442-5980	442-0276
Web: www.mtclub.org					
On Broadway 106 Broadway	Helena	MT	59601	406-443-1929	
Staggering Ox 400 Euclid Ave	Helena	MT	59601	406-443-1729	449-0400
Web: www.staggeringox.com					
Toi's 423 N Last Chance Gulch	Helena	MT	59601	406-443-6656	
Windbag Saloon & Grill 19 S Last Chance Gulch	Helena	MT	59601	406-443-9669	
Marysville House 153 Main St	Marysville	MT	59640	406-443-6677	
Web: www.marysvillehouse.net					

Nebraska

Name / Address	City	State	ZIP	Phone	Fax
1st Ave Bar & Grill 2310 N 1st St	Lincoln	NE	68521	402-475-4600	475-1281
Web: www.1stavebargrill.com					
Arturo's 803 Q St	Lincoln	NE	68508	402-475-8226	
Billy's 1301 H St	Lincoln	NE	68508	402-474-0084	474-3391
Web: www.billysrestaurant.com					
Carlos O'Kelly's Mexican Cafe 4455 N 27th St	Lincoln	NE	68521	402-438-4455	
Web: www.carlosokellys.com/					
Doozy's 101 N 14th St	Lincoln	NE	68508	402-438-1616	
El Sitio 17 Van Dorn St	Lincoln	NE	68502	402-476-0414	
El Toro 2600 S 48th St	Lincoln	NE	68506	402-488-3939	488-7746
Famous Dave's Bar-B-Que 2750 Pine Lake Rd	Lincoln	NE	68516	402-421-3434	421-3488
Web: www.famousdaves.com					
Green Gateau 330 S 10th St	Lincoln	NE	68508	402-477-0330	477-0782
Web: www.greengateau.com					
Imperial Palace 701 N 27th St	Lincoln	NE	68503	402-474-2688	
La Paz 321 N Cotner Blvd	Lincoln	NE	68505	402-466-9111	466-9244
Web: www.lapazmexican.biz					
Lazlo's Brewery & Grill 210 N 7th St	Lincoln	NE	68508	402-434-5636	434-3291
Mazatlan 211 N 70th St	Lincoln	NE	68505	402-464-7201	464-7527
Misty's Steakhouse & Brewery 200 N 11th St	Lincoln	NE	68508	402-476-7766	476-7796
Web: www.mistyslincoln.com					
Oven The 201 N 8th St	Lincoln	NE	68508	402-475-6118	475-1281
Parthenon 5500 S 56th St	Lincoln	NE	68516	402-423-2222	423-2228
Web: www.theparthenon.net					
Rib Ranch 6440 'O' St	Lincoln	NE	68510	402-467-5110	467-5128
Sher-E-Punjab 1601 Q St	Lincoln	NE	68508	402-477-3090	477-2282
Shogun 3700 S 9th St Suite F	Lincoln	NE	68502	402-421-7100	
Skeeter Barnes 5800 S 58th St	Lincoln	NE	68516	402-421-3340	421-3504
Web: www.skeeterbarnes.com					
Steak House The 3441 Adams St	Lincoln	NE	68504	402-466-2472	466-4897
Web: www.thesteakhouselincoln.com					
Tandoor 3530 Village Dr	Lincoln	NE	68516	402-423-2007	423-2995
Terrace Grille 333 S 13th St	Lincoln	NE	68508	402-479-8292	474-1847
Tico's 317 S 17th St	Lincoln	NE	68508	402-475-1048	475-3291
Web: www.ticosoflincoln.com					
Vincenzo's 808 P St	Lincoln	NE	68505	402-435-3889	

	City	State	Zip	Phone	Fax
Wind Chimes 3520 Village Dr	Lincoln	NE	68516	402-420-7171	720-7172
Web: www.yourwindchimes.com					
Ahmad's Persian 1006 Howard St	Omaha	NE	68102	402-341-9616	
Anthony's 7220 F St	Omaha	NE	68127	402-331-7575	331-1497
Web: www.anthonyssteakhouse.com					
Bangkok Cuisine 1905 Farnam St	Omaha	NE	68102	402-346-5874	
Biaggi's Ristorante Italiano 13655 California St	Omaha	NE	68154	402-965-9800	
Blue Sushi Sake Grill 14450 Eagle Run Dr Suite 240	Omaha	NE	68116	402-445-2583	445-4985
Web: www.bluesushisakegrill.com					
Bohemian Cafe 1406 S 13th St	Omaha	NE	68108	402-342-9838	
Web: www.bohemiancafe.net					
Brother Sebastian's Steak House 1350 S 119th St	Omaha	NE	68144	402-330-0300	330-4814
Web: www.brothersebastians.com					
Caniglia's Venice Inn 6920 Pacific St	Omaha	NE	68106	402-556-3111	
Web: www.veniceinn.com					
Cascio's Steak House 1620 S 10th St	Omaha	NE	68108	402-345-8313	
Web: www.casciossteakhouse.com					
Charlie's on the Lake 4150 S 144th St	Omaha	NE	68137	402-894-9411	894-9415
Web: www.charliesonthelake.net					
Fleming's Prime Steakhouse & Wine Bar 140 Regency Pkwy	Omaha	NE	68114	402-393-0811	393-0958
Web: www.flemingssteakhouse.com					
Fox & Hound English Pub & Grille 17602 Wright St	Omaha	NE	68130	402-334-3133	334-1911
Gorat's 4917 Center St	Omaha	NE	68106	402-551-3733	551-3735
Web: www.goratssteakhouse.com					
Greek Islands 3821 Center St	Omaha	NE	68105	402-346-1528	345-7428
Grisantis Restaurant 10875 W Dodge Rd	Omaha	NE	68154	402-330-0440	
Hiro Sushi 3655 N 129th St	Omaha	NE	68164	402-933-0091	
Web: www.hirosushiomaha.com					
House of Hunan 2405 S 132nd St	Omaha	NE	68144	402-334-5382	
Indian Oven 1010 Howard St	Omaha	NE	68102	402-342-4856	342-2526
Jack & Mary's Restaurant 655 N 114th St	Omaha	NE	68154	402-496-2090	
Jaipur The 10922 Elm St	Omaha	NE	68144	402-392-7331	392-7338
Web: www.jaipurbrewhouse.com					
Jams American Grill 7814 W Dodge Rd	Omaha	NE	68114	402-399-8300	392-1765
Web: www.jamseats.com					
Jazz A Louisiana Kitchen 1421 Farnam St	Omaha	NE	68102	402-342-3662	
Jim & Jennie's Greek Village 3026 N 90th St	Omaha	NE	68134	402-571-2857	
Johnny's Cafe 4702 S 27th St	Omaha	NE	68107	402-731-4774	
Web: www.johnnyscafe.com					
Le Cafe de Paris 1228 S 6th St	Omaha	NE	68108	402-344-0227	
Lo Sole Mio 3001 S 32nd Ave	Omaha	NE	68105	402-345-5656	345-5859
Web: www.losolemio.com					
McFoster's Natural Kind Cafe 302 S 38th St	Omaha	NE	68131	402-345-7477	345-4585
Mediterranean Bistro 1712 N 120th St	Omaha	NE	68154	402-493-3080	493-3097
Web: www.medbistro.com					
Melting Pot The 17151 Davenport St	Omaha	NE	68118	402-391-6358	504-4620
Web: www.themeltingpot.com					
Mimi's Cafe 301 N 175th Plaza	Omaha	NE	68118	402-289-9610	
Web: www.mimiscafe.com/					
Mister C's Steakhouse 5319 N 30th St	Omaha	NE	68111	402-451-1998	451-1910
Web: www.mistercs.com					
M's Pub 422 S 11th St	Omaha	NE	68102	402-342-2550	342-3035
Web: www.mspubomaha.com					
Piccolo Pete's 2202 S 20th St	Omaha	NE	68108	402-342-9038	
Web: www.piccolopetesrestaurant.com					
Sean O'Casey's 10730 Q St	Omaha	NE	68127	402-593-1746	
Shanghai 3118 Tower 24 St	Omaha	NE	68108	402-342-2244	
Taste of Thailand 15712 W Center Rd	Omaha	NE	68130	402-691-9991	
Web: www.totomaha.com					
Thai Spice 2933 N 108th St	Omaha	NE	68164	402-492-8808	492-8808
Web: www.thaispiceomaha.com					
Timber Lodge Steakhouse 14460 W Maple Rd	Omaha	NE	68116	402-491-0000	614-3089
Upstream Brewing Co 514 S 11th St	Omaha	NE	68102	402-344-0200	344-0451
Web: www.upstreambrewing.com					
Vincenzo's Ristorante 1207 Harney St	Omaha	NE	68102	402-342-4010	991-8149
Web: www.vincenzos-ne.com					

Nevada

	City	State	Zip	Phone	Fax
Adele's 1112 N Carson St	Carson City	NV	89706	775-882-3353	882-0437
Web: www.adelesrestaurantandlounge.com					
B'Sghetti's 318 N Carson St	Carson City	NV	89701	775-887-8879	887-1942
Web: www.bsghettis.com					
China East 1810 Hwy 50 E	Carson City	NV	89701	775-885-6996	885-2138
Garibaldi's 307 N Carson St	Carson City	NV	89701	775-884-4574	246-4529
Glen Eagles 3700 N Carson St	Carson City	NV	89703	775-884-4414	884-4447
Grandma Hattie's 2811 S Carson St	Carson City	NV	89701	775-882-4900	
Heidi's 1020 N Carson St	Carson City	NV	89701	775-882-0486	884-2091
Ming's 2330 S Carson St	Carson City	NV	89701	775-887-8878	887-0570
Panda Kitchen 1986 Hwy 50 E	Carson City	NV	89701	775-882-8128	882-3236
Web: www.pandakitchenrestaurant.com					
Playa Azul 415 E William St	Carson City	NV	89701	775-883-2244	
Red's Old 395 Grill 1055 S Carson St	Carson City	NV	89701	775-887-0395	887-5640
Taqueria Uruaban 4601 Goni Rd	Carson City	NV	89706	775-883-7609	
Thai Spice Kitchen 111 E Telegraph St	Carson City	NV	89701	775-841-8999	841-9099
Thurman's Ranch House 2943 Hwy 50 E	Carson City	NV	89701	775-883-1773	
Tito's 444 E William St	Carson City	NV	89701	775-885-0309	
Viet Pho 1214 N Carson St	Carson City	NV	89701	775-883-6668	
808 3570 Las Vegas Blvd S Caesar's Palace	Las Vegas	NV	89109	702-731-7110	866-1700
TF: 800-634-6001					
Alex 3131 Las Vegas Blvd S	Las Vegas	NV	89109	702-770-9966	
Alize at the Top of the Palms 4321 W Flamingo Rd	Las Vegas	NV	89103	702-951-7000	651-7002
Web: www.alizelv.com					
America 3790 Las Vegas Blvd S	Las Vegas	NV	89119	702-740-6451	740-6453
Andiamo 3000 Paradise Rd	Las Vegas	NV	89109	702-732-5664	732-5318
Andre's 401 S 6th St	Las Vegas	NV	89101	702-385-5016	384-8574
Web: www.andrelv.com					
Antonio's 3700 W Flamingo Rd	Las Vegas	NV	89103	702-777-7777	777-7932
Archi's Thai Kitchen 6360 W Flamingo Rd	Las Vegas	NV	89103	702-880-5550	870-5551
Aureole 3950 Las Vegas Blvd S	Las Vegas	NV	89119	702-632-7401	632-7440
Web: www.charliepalmer.com					
Bartolotta Ristorante diMare 3131 Las Vegas Blvd S	Las Vegas	NV	89109	702-770-9966	
Benihana 3000 Paradise Rd	Las Vegas	NV	89109	702-732-5755	732-5662
Web: www.benihana.com					
Blackstone's Steak House 3770 Las Vegas Blvd S	Las Vegas	NV	89109	702-730-7405	730-7203
Border Grill Las Vegas					
3950 Las Vegas Blvd S Mandalay Bay Resort & Casino	Las Vegas	NV	89119	702-632-7403	632-6945
Web: www.bordergrill.com					
Bouchon 3355 Las Vegas Blvd S	Las Vegas	NV	89109	702-414-6200	
Bradley Ogden at Caesar's Palace 3570 Las Vegas Blvd S	Las Vegas	NV	89109	702-731-7413	
Web: www.larkcreek.com/bolv.htm					
Buzio's 3700 W Flamingo Rd	Las Vegas	NV	89103	702-252-7697	777-7932
Canaletta 3377 Las Vegas Blvd S	Las Vegas	NV	89109	702-733-0070	
Capital Grille 3200 Las Vegas Blvd S	Las Vegas	NV	89109	702-932-6631	
Web: www.vivathecapitalgrille.com/					
Carluccio's Tivoli Gardens 1775 E Tropicana Ave	Las Vegas	NV	89119	702-795-3236	795-0283
Charlie Palmer Steak					
Four Seasons Hotel 3960 Las Vegas Blvd S	Las Vegas	NV	89119	702-632-5120	632-5459
Web: www.charliepalmer.com					
Chicago Joe's 820 S 4th St	Las Vegas	NV	89101	702-382-5637	
Web: www.chicagojoesrestaurant.com					
China Grill 3950 Las Vegas Blvd S	Las Vegas	NV	89109	702-632-7404	632-6906
Web: www.chinagrillmgt.com					
Craftsteak 3799 Las Vegas Blvd S	Las Vegas	NV	89109	702-891-7318	891-5899
Del Frisco's Double Eagle Steak House 3925 Paradise Rd	Las Vegas	NV	89109	702-796-0063	796-0081
Web: www.delfriscos.com					
Delmonico Steakhouse					
3355 Las Vegas Blvd S Venetian Resort Hotel & Casino	Las Vegas	NV	89109	702-414-3737	414-3838
Web: www.emerils.com					
Eiffel Tower Restaurant 3655 Las Vegas Blvd S	Las Vegas	NV	89019	702-948-6937	942-0004
Web: www.eiffeltowerrestaurant.com					
Emeril's New Orleans Fish House					
3799 Las Vegas Blvd S MGM Grand Hotel	Las Vegas	NV	89109	702-891-7374	
Web: www.emerils.com					
Empress Court 3570 Las Vegas Blvd S	Las Vegas	NV	89109	702-731-7888	
Ferraro's 5900 W Flamingo Rd	Las Vegas	NV	89103	702-364-5300	871-2721
Web: www.ferraroslasvegas.com					
Fiamma Trattoria 3799 Las Vegas Blvd S	Las Vegas	NV	89109	702-891-7600	
Fleming's Prime Steakhouse & Wine Bar					
8721 W Charleston Blvd	Las Vegas	NV	89117	702-838-4774	838-6639
Web: www.flemingssteakhouse.com					
Fleur de Lys 3950 Las Vegas Blvd S	Las Vegas	NV	89109	702-632-9400	
Gandhi India's Cuisine 4080 Paradise Rd	Las Vegas	NV	89109	702-734-0094	734-3444
Web: www.gandhicuisine.com					
Grotto Ristorante 129 E Fremont St	Las Vegas	NV	89101	702-385-7111	
Web: www.goldennugget.com/home/dining/grotto/					
Hugo's Cellar 202 Fremont St	Las Vegas	NV	89101	702-385-4011	387-5120
Hyakumi 3570 Las Vegas Blvd S	Las Vegas	NV	89109	702-731-7110	697-5788
Il Mulino New York 3500 Las Vegas Blvd S	Las Vegas	NV	89109	702-492-6000	
Web: www.ilmulino.com/					
Inka Si Senor 2797 S Maryland Pkwy	Las Vegas	NV	89109	702-731-0826	731-9749
Web: www.sisenor.org/isshome.htm					
Jasmine 3600 Las Vegas Blvd S	Las Vegas	NV	89109	702-693-7111	
Lawry's the Prime Rib 4043 Howard Hughes Pkwy	Las Vegas	NV	89109	702-893-2223	
Web: www.lawrysonline.com					
Le Cirque 3600 Las Vegas Blvd S	Las Vegas	NV	89109	702-693-8100	693-8106
Web: www.osteriadelcirco.com					
Lillie's Noodle House 129 E Fremont St	Las Vegas	NV	89101	702-385-7111	
Web: www.goldennugget.com/home/dining					
Lotus of Siam 953 E Sahara Ave	Las Vegas	NV	89104	702-735-3033	735-3033
Web: www.saipinchutima.com					
Luxor Steakhouse 3900 Las Vegas Blvd S	Las Vegas	NV	89109	702-262-4778	262-4788
Mayflower Cuisinier 4750 W Sahara Ave Suite 326	Las Vegas	NV	89102	702-870-8432	259-8493
Web: www.mayflowercuisinier.com					
McCormick & Schmick's 335 Hughes Center Dr	Las Vegas	NV	89109	702-836-9000	836-9500
Web: www.mccormickandschmicks.com					
Mesa Grill 3570 Las Vegas Blvd S Caesars Palace	Las Vegas	NV	89109	702-731-7731	650-5962
Michael Mina 3600 Las Vegas Blvd S	Las Vegas	NV	89109	702-693-7111	693-8512
Web: www.michaelmina.net					
Michael's 9777 Las Vegas Blvd S	Las Vegas	NV	89183	702-796-7111	797-8216
Mon Ami Gabi 3655 Las Vegas Blvd S	Las Vegas	NV	89109	702-944-4224	
Web: www.monamigabi.com					
Morton's The Steakhouse 600 E Flamingo Rd	Las Vegas	NV	89109	702-893-0703	893-3020
Web: www.mortons.com					
N9ne Steakhouse 4321 W Flamingo Rd	Las Vegas	NV	89103	702-933-9900	942-8072
Web: www.n9negroup.com					
Nob Hill 3799 Las Vegas Blvd S MGM Grand Hotel	Las Vegas	NV	89109	702-891-1111	891-7336
Nobu 4455 Paradise Rd	Las Vegas	NV	89109	702-693-5090	693-5091
Web: www.nobumatsuhisa.com					
Okada 3131 Las Vegas Blvd S	Las Vegas	NV	89109	702-770-9966	
Olives 3600 Las Vegas Blvd S	Las Vegas	NV	89117	702-693-8181	
Onda 3400 Las Vegas Blvd S	Las Vegas	NV	89109	702-791-7223	
Osaka 4205 W Sahara Ave	Las Vegas	NV	89102	702-876-4988	876-0259
Web: www.lasvegas-sushi.com					
Osteria Del Circo 3600 Las Vegas Blvd S	Las Vegas	NV	89109	702-693-8150	693-8106
Web: www.osteriadelcirco.com					
Palm The 3500 Las Vegas Blvd S Suite A-7	Las Vegas	NV	89109	702-732-7256	
Pamplemousse 400 E Sahara Ave	Las Vegas	NV	89104	702-733-2066	733-9139
Web: www.pamplemousserestaurant.com					
PF Chang's China Bistro 3667 Las Vegas Blvd S	Las Vegas	NV	89128	702-836-0955	836-1963
Web: www.pfchangs.com					
Picasso 3600 Las Vegas Blvd S	Las Vegas	NV	89109	702-693-7223	
Piero's Restaurant 355 Convention Center Dr	Las Vegas	NV	89109	702-369-2305	735-5699
Web: www.pieroscuisine.com					
Pinot Brasserie 3355 Las Vegas Blvd S	Las Vegas	NV	89109	702-414-8888	414-3885
Web: www.patinagroup.com/pinotBrasserie					
Postrio 3377 Las Vegas Blvd S	Las Vegas	NV	89109	702-796-1110	796-1112
Prime Steakhouse					
3600 Las Vegas Blvd S Bellagio Hotel & Casino	Las Vegas	NV	89109	702-693-7111	
Pullman Grille					
200 N Main St Main Street Station Hotel & Casino	Las Vegas	NV	89101	702-387-1896	386-4406
Rosemary's 8125 W Sahara Ave Suite 110	Las Vegas	NV	89107	702-869-2251	869-2283
Web: www.rosemarysrestaurant.com					
Roy's 620 E Flamingo Rd	Las Vegas	NV	89119	702-691-2053	691-2072
Web: www.roysrestaurants.com					
Rumjungle 3950 Las Vegas Blvd S	Las Vegas	NV	89119	702-632-7408	632-6906
Web: www.chinagrillmgt.com					
Ruth's Chris Steak House 3900 Paradise Rd	Las Vegas	NV	89109	702-791-7011	791-0284
Web: www.ruthschris.com					
Second Street Grill 200 E Fremont St	Las Vegas	NV	89125	702-385-6277	
Shintaro 3600 Las Vegas Blvd S Bellagio Resort & Casino	Las Vegas	NV	89109	702-693-8141	693-8512
Simon Kitchen & Bar 4455 Paradise Rd	Las Vegas	NV	89109	702-693-5000	693-5532
Smith & Wollensky 3767 Las Vegas Blvd S	Las Vegas	NV	89109	702-862-4100	933-3931
Web: www.smithandwollensky.com					
Spago 3500 Las Vegas Blvd S Suite G1	Las Vegas	NV	89109	702-369-6300	369-0361
Web: www.wolfgangpuck.com					
Steak House 2880 Las Vegas Blvd S	Las Vegas	NV	89109	702-794-3767	
Sterling Brunch 3645 Las Vegas Blvd S	Las Vegas	NV	89109	702-739-4111	
STRIPSTEAK 3950 Las Vegas Blvd S Mandalay Bay Hotel	Las Vegas	NV	89119	702-632-7400	632-7456
Sushi Roku 3500 Las Vegas Blvd S	Las Vegas	NV	89109	702-733-7373	
SW Steakhouse 3131 Las Vegas Blvd S	Las Vegas	NV	89109	702-770-9966	
Swiss Cafe 3175 E Tropicana Ave	Las Vegas	NV	89121	702-454-2270	
Thai Spice 4433 W Flamingo Rd	Las Vegas	NV	89103	702-362-5308	
Tillerman 2245 E Flamingo Rd	Las Vegas	NV	89119	702-731-4036	731-1560
Web: www.tillerman.com					
Top of the World 2000 Las Vegas Blvd S	Las Vegas	NV	89101	702-380-7711	
Web: www.topoftheworldlv.com					
Trattoria Del Lupo 3950 Las Vegas Blvd S	Las Vegas	NV	89119	702-740-5522	740-5533
Tsunami Asian Grill 3377 Las Vegas Blvd S	Las Vegas	NV	89109	702-414-1980	414-1981
Valentino Las Vegas					
3355 Las Vegas Blvd S Venetian Resort Hotel & Casino	Las Vegas	NV	89109	702-414-3000	414-3099
Web: pieroselvaggio.com					

Nevada (Cont'd)

Restaurant	City	State	ZIP	Phone	Fax
Verandah 3960 Las Vegas Blvd S	Las Vegas	NV	89119	702-632-5000	632-5195
Voodoo Cafe & Lounge 3700 W Flamingo Rd 50th Fl	Las Vegas	NV	89103	702-247-7800	
Willy & Jose's Mexican Cantina 5111 Boulder Hwy	Las Vegas	NV	89122	702-456-7777	
Wolfgang Puck's Bar & Grill 3799 Las Vegas Blvd S	Las Vegas	NV	89109	702-891-3000	891-3263
Web: www.wolfgangpuck.com					
Zeffirino Ristorante 3355 Las Vegas Blvd S	Las Vegas	NV	89109	702-414-3500	
Web: www.zeffirinolasvegas.com/					
4th Street Bistro 3065 W 4th St	Reno	NV	89503	775-323-3200	323-3391
Asian Garden 1945 S Virginia St	Reno	NV	89502	775-825-5510	825-1169
Atlantis Seafood Steakhouse 3800 S Virginia St Atlantis Casino Resort	Reno	NV	89502	800-723-6500	
Bavarian World 595 Valley Rd	Reno	NV	89512	775-323-7646	
Beaujolais Bistro 130 West St	Reno	NV	89501	775-323-2227	
Web: www.beaujolaisbistro.com					
Bertha Miranda's 336 Mill St	Reno	NV	89502	775-786-9697	786-2525
Web: www.berthamirandas.com					
Beto's 575 W 5th St	Reno	NV	89503	775-324-0632	
Black Bear Diner 2323 S Virginia St	Reno	NV	89509	775-827-5570	
Web: www.blackbeardiner.com/					
Brew House Pub & Grill 6395 S McCarran Blvd	Reno	NV	89509	775-828-2700	828-2716
Bricks 1695 S Virginia St	Reno	NV	89502	775-786-2277	
Cafe de Thai 7499 Longly Ln	Reno	NV	89511	775-829-8424	
Cantina Los Tres Hombres 7111 S Virginia St	Reno	NV	89511	775-852-0202	852-5714
Web: www.cantinalth.com					
China East Restaurant 1086A S Virginia St	Reno	NV	89502	775-348-7020	348-1956
Flowing Tide Pub 10580 N McCarran Blvd	Reno	NV	89503	775-747-7707	
Galena Forest Restaurant 17025 Mt Rose Hwy	Reno	NV	89511	775-849-2100	849-2197
Web: www.galenaforestrestaurant.com					
Golden Flower 205 W 5th St	Reno	NV	89503	775-323-1628	
Harrah's Steak House 219 N Center St	Reno	NV	89501	775-788-2929	788-2962
India Garden 1565 S Virginia St	Reno	NV	89502	775-337-8002	379-8022
Johnny's 4245 W 4th St	Reno	NV	89503	775-747-4511	
La Strada 345 N Virginia St	Reno	NV	89501	775-348-9297	
Louis' Basque Corner 301 E 4th St	Reno	NV	89512	775-323-7203	
Luciano's 719 S Virginia St	Reno	NV	89501	775-322-7373	
Mi Casa Too 2205 W 4th St	Reno	NV	89509	775-323-6466	323-6502
Odett's 6800 Pembroke	Reno	NV	89502	775-857-2894	
Paisan's 4826 Longley Ln	Reno	NV	89502	775-826-9444	
Palais de Jade 960 W Moana Ln	Reno	NV	89509	775-827-5233	
PF Chang's China Bistro 5180 Kietzke Ln	Reno	NV	89511	775-825-9800	825-9825
Web: www.pfchangs.com					
Pho 777 Vietnamese Restaurant 201 E 2nd St	Reno	NV	89501	775-323-7777	
Pneumatic Diner 501 W 1st St	Reno	NV	89503	775-786-8888	
Rapscallion Seafood House 1555 S Wells Ave	Reno	NV	89502	775-323-1211	323-6096
Web: www.rapscallion.com					
Romanza 2707 S Virginia St Peppermill Hotel Casino	Reno	NV	89502	775-826-2121	
Silver Peak Grill & Taproom 135 N Sierra St	Reno	NV	89501	775-284-3300	284-3301
Sterling's Seafood Steakhouse 4th & Virginia Sts	Reno	NV	89505	775-325-7573	
Sushi Club 294 E Moana Ln	Reno	NV	89502	775-828-7311	828-5426
Sushi Pier 1290 E Plumb Ln	Reno	NV	89502	775-825-6776	
Viaggio 2309 Kietzke Ln	Reno	NV	89502	775-828-2708	828-2741
Washoe Grill 4201 W 4th St	Reno	NV	89503	775-786-1323	786-1314
Web: www.washoesteakhouse.com					
White Orchid 2707 S Virginia St	Reno	NV	89502	775-826-2121	
Yen Ching 565 W Moana Ln	Reno	NV	89509	775-825-2451	829-2222

New Hampshire

Restaurant	City	State	ZIP	Phone	Fax
Bedford Village Inn 2 Olde Bedford Way	Bedford	NH	03110	603-472-2001	472-2379
Web: www.bedfordvillageinn.com					
Chen Yang Li 520 South St	Bow	NH	03304	603-228-8508	228-8308
Web: www.chenyangli.com					
Alan's Restaurant & Lounge 133 N Main St	Concord	NH	03303	603-753-6631	
Angelina's Ristorante Italiano 11 Depot St	Concord	NH	03301	603-228-3313	228-3775
Web: www.angelinasrestaurant.com					
Barley House 132 N Main St	Concord	NH	03301	603-228-6363	228-6565
Web: www.thebarleyhouse.com					
Capitol Grille 1 Eagle Sq	Concord	NH	03301	603-228-6608	223-2387
Web: www.capitol-grille.com					
Cat N' Fiddle 118 Manchester St	Concord	NH	03301	603-228-8911	226-2350
Web: www.catnfiddle.com					
Cheers 17 Depot St	Concord	NH	03301	603-228-0180	226-3459
Web: www.cheersnh.com					
Common Man The 25 Water St	Concord	NH	03301	603-228-3463	224-5722
Web: www.thecman.com					
Corner View Restaurant 80 1/2 South St	Concord	NH	03301	603-229-4554	229-0932
Franklin Pierce Dining Room 96 Pleasant St	Concord	NH	03301	603-225-7102	225-5031
Green Martini 6 Pleasant St Ext	Concord	NH	03301	603-223-6672	
Hermanos Cocina Mexicana 11 Hills Ave	Concord	NH	03301	603-224-5669	
Web: www.hermanosmexican.com					
House of India 6 Pleasant St	Concord	NH	03301	603-227-5266	227-5266
Makris Lobster & Steak House Rt 106	Concord	NH	03301	603-225-7665	224-4375
Web: www.eatalobster.com					
Man Yee Restaurant 79 South St	Concord	NH	03301	603-226-0001	226-0003
Margarita's 1 Bicentennial Sq	Concord	NH	03301	603-224-2821	224-3023
Web: www.margs.com					
Moritomo 32 Fort Eddy Rd	Concord	NH	03301	603-224-8363	224-8038
Red Blazer 72 Manchester St	Concord	NH	03301	603-224-4101	224-7118
Web: www.redblazer.cc					
Siam Orchid 158 N Main St	Concord	NH	03301	603-228-1529	228-0571
Web: www.siamorchid.net					
Szechuan Garden Restaurant 108 Fisherville Rd	Concord	NH	03301	603-226-2650	226-2650
Tea Garden Restaurant 184 N Main St	Concord	NH	03301	603-228-4420	224-9820
Andy's Place 342 Cypress St	Manchester	NH	03103	603-645-1889	
Belmont Hall & Restaurant 718 Grove St	Manchester	NH	03103	603-625-8540	
Black Brimmer American Bar & Grill 1087 Elm St	Manchester	NH	03101	603-669-5523	
Web: www.blackbrimmer.com/					
Cactus Jacks Southwest Grill 782 S Willow St	Manchester	NH	03103	603-627-8600	627-3200
Web: www.t-bones.com/cj_home.html					
Chateau Restaurant 201 Hanover St	Manchester	NH	03104	603-627-2677	
Commercial Street Fishery 33 S Commercial St	Manchester	NH	03101	603-296-0706	296-0710
Web: www.csfishery.com					
Cotton 75 Arms St	Manchester	NH	03101	603-622-5488	627-4529
Web: www.cottonfood.com/home.html					
Derryfield Restaurant 625 Mammoth Rd	Manchester	NH	03104	603-623-2880	623-6850
Web: www.thederryfield.com					
Don Quijote 362 Union St	Manchester	NH	03103	603-622-2246	
Fratello's Ristorante Italiano 155 Dow St	Manchester	NH	03101	603-624-2022	629-9465
Web: www.fratellos.com					
Gauchos Churrascaria 620 Lowell St	Manchester	NH	03101	603-669-9460	
Web: www.gauchosbraziliansteakhouse.com					
India Palace 575 S Willow St	Manchester	NH	03103	603-641-8413	641-8583
Korean Place 110 Hanover St	Manchester	NH	03101	603-622-9377	
La Carreta 545 Daniel Webster Hwy	Manchester	NH	03104	603-628-6899	628-6890
Web: www.lacarretamexican.com					
Lakorn Thai Restaurant 470 S Main St	Manchester	NH	03102	603-626-4545	626-4545
Piccola Italia 815 Elm St	Manchester	NH	03101	603-606-5100	
Web: www.piccolaitalianh.com					
Richard's Bistro 36 Lowell St	Manchester	NH	03101	603-644-1180	624-6082
Web: www.richardsbistro.com					
Shogun Japanese Steak House 545 Daniel Webster Hwy N	Manchester	NH	03104	603-669-8122	
Shorty's 1050 Bicentennial Dr	Manchester	NH	03104	603-625-1730	625-1770
Spatts 2264 Candia Rd	Manchester	NH	03109	603-627-9959	629-9731
Szechuan House 245 Maple St	Manchester	NH	03103	603-669-8811	622-7318
Taste of Europe 827 Elm St	Manchester	NH	03101	603-296-0292	
Thousand Crane 1000 Elm St	Manchester	NH	03101	603-634-0000	634-0040
Yard The 1211 S Mammoth Rd	Manchester	NH	03109	603-623-3545	625-8420
Web: www.theyardrestaurant.com					
Puritan Backroom Restaurant 245 Hooksett Rd	North Manchester	NH	03104	603-669-6890	623-3788
Web: www.puritanbackroom.com					

New Jersey

Restaurant	City	State	ZIP	Phone	Fax
Rams Head Inn 9 W White Horse Pike	Absecon	NJ	08201	609-652-1700	652-2605
Angelo's Fairmount Tavern 2300 Fairmount Ave	Atlantic City	NJ	08401	609-344-2439	348-1043
Web: angelosfairmounttavern.com					
Atlantic City Bar & Grill 1219 Pacific Ave	Atlantic City	NJ	08401	609-348-8080	348-8466
Web: www.acbarandgrill.com					
Billy Ho's Imperial East 7800 Ventnor Ave	Atlantic City	NJ	08402	609-487-1040	
Bobby Flay Steak 1 Borgata Way	Atlantic City	NJ	08401	609-317-1000	
Web: www.bobbyflaysteak.com/					
Cuba Libre 2001 Pacific Ave	Atlantic City	NJ	08401	609-348-6700	348-6704
Web: www.cubalibrerestaurant.com					
Dock's Oyster House 2405 Atlantic Ave	Atlantic City	NJ	08401	609-345-0092	345-7893
Web: www.docksoysterhouse.com					
Farinacci 3004 Atlantic Ave	Atlantic City	NJ	08401	609-344-6767	
Web: www.farinaccirestaurant.com					
Girasole Ristorante 3108 Pacific Ave	Atlantic City	NJ	08401	609-345-5554	344-0091
Web: www.girasoleac.com					
Hard Rock Cafe Boardwalk at Virginia Ave	Atlantic City	NJ	08401	609-441-0007	449-1836
Web: www.hardrock.com					
Knife & Fork Inn The 29 S Albany Ave	Atlantic City	NJ	08401	609-344-1133	344-3533
Web: www.knifeandforkinn.com					
Los Amigos 1926 Atlantic Ave	Atlantic City	NJ	08401	609-344-2293	344-2373
Web: www.losamigosrest.com					
Mexico 3810 Ventor Ave	Atlantic City	NJ	08406	609-344-0366	
Mia Restaurant 2100 Pacific Ave	Atlantic City	NJ	08401	609-441-2345	
Web: www.miaac.com					
Old Homestead 1 Borgata Way	Atlantic City	NJ	08401	609-317-1000	317-1100
Ombra 1 Borgata Way	Atlantic City	NJ	08401	609-317-1000	317-1100
Palm The 2801 Pacific Ave	Atlantic City	NJ	08401	609-344-7256	
Peregrines' Boston Ave	Atlantic City	NJ	08401	609-340-7400	
PF Chang's China Bistro 2801 N Pacific Ave	Atlantic City	NJ	08401	609-348-4600	
Web: www.pfchangs.com					
Red Square 2801 Pacific Ave	Atlantic City	NJ	08401	609-344-9100	344-9105
Sea Blue 1 Borgata Way	Atlantic City	NJ	08401	609-317-8220	
Specchio 1 Borgata Way	Atlantic City	NJ	08401	609-317-1000	317-1100
Waterfront Buffet 777 Harrah's Blvd Harrah's Hotel & Casino	Atlantic City	NJ	08401	609-441-5576	
Wolfgang Puck American Grille 1 Borgata Way	Atlantic City	NJ	08401	609-317-1000	
Banzai 3690 Quakerbridge Rd	Hamilton	NJ	08619	609-587-5454	
Web: www.banzairestaurant.com					
Oddfellows Rest 80 River St	Hoboken	NJ	07030	201-656-9009	656-0484
Web: www.oddfellowsrest.com					
Amelia's Bistro 187 Warren St	Jersey City	NJ	07303	201-332-2200	
Amiya 160 Green St Harborside Financial Center Plaza 5	Jersey City	NJ	07311	201-433-8000	433-8866
Web: www.amiyarestaurant.com					
Baja 117 Montgomery St	Jersey City	NJ	07302	201-915-0062	915-1880
Web: www.bajamexicancuisine.com					
Casa Dante 737 Newark Ave	Jersey City	NJ	07306	201-795-2750	795-1225
Web: www.casadante.com					
Confucius Asian Bistro 558 Washington Blvd	Jersey City	NJ	07306	201-386-8898	386-8896
Iron Monkey 97 Greene St	Jersey City	NJ	07302	201-435-5756	433-0762
Just Sonny 169 Sterling Ave	Jersey City	NJ	07305	201-434-9413	
Web: www.justsonny.com/					
Komegashi 103 Montgomery St	Jersey City	NJ	07302	201-433-4567	333-8946
Web: www.komegashi.com					
Laico's 67 Terhune Ave	Jersey City	NJ	07305	201-434-9853	434-4116
Liberty House 76 Audrey Zapp Dr	Jersey City	NJ	07304	201-395-0300	395-0065
Web: www.libertyhouserestaurant.com					
Light Horse Tavern 199 Washington St	Jersey City	NJ	07302	201-946-2028	946-2029
Web: www.lighthorsetavern.com					
Madame Claude Cafe 364 1/2 4th St	Jersey City	NJ	07302	201-876-8800	
Web: www.madameclaudecafe.com					
Marco & Pepe 289 Grove St	Jersey City	NJ	07302	201-860-9688	
Web: www.marcoandpepe.com					
Marker's Harborside Grill 153 Plaza Two	Jersey City	NJ	07311	201-433-6275	433-0399
Web: www.markersrestaurant.com					
Merchant The 279 Grove St	Jersey City	NJ	07302	201-200-0202	200-9945
Web: www.themerchantnj.com					
Nha Tranh Place 249 Newark Ave	Jersey City	NJ	07302	201-239-1988	
Pointe 2 Chapel Ave	Jersey City	NJ	07302	201-985-9854	
Puccini's 1064 Westside Ave	Jersey City	NJ	07306	201-432-4111	432-9026
Web: www.puccinisrestaurant.com					
Rita & Joe's 142 Broadway	Jersey City	NJ	07306	201-451-3606	
Web: rita-joes.com					
South City Grill 70 Town Square Pl	Jersey City	NJ	07302	201-610-9225	610-1010
Web: www.southcitygrill.com					
Vu 2 Exchange Pl	Jersey City	NJ	07303	201-469-4650	432-4491
Acacia 2637 Lawrenceville Rd	Lawrenceville	NJ	08648	609-895-9885	895-9874
Steve & Cookies By the Bay 9700 Amherst Ave	Margate	NJ	08402	609-823-1163	823-9571
Web: www.steveandcookies.com					
Adega Grill 130 Ferry St	Newark	NJ	07105	973-589-8830	741-0778
Web: www.adegagrill.com					
Bentley's 1 Gateway Center	Newark	NJ	07102	973-622-5000	
Brasilia Restaurante 132 Ferry St	Newark	NJ	07105	973-465-1227	
Campino Restaurant 70 Jabez St	Newark	NJ	07105	973-589-4004	589-8880
Casa Vasca 141 Elm St	Newark	NJ	07105	973-465-1350	465-7335
Don Pepe Restaurant & Catering 844 McCarter Hwy	Newark	NJ	07102	973-623-4662	623-5402
Web: www.donpeperestaurant.com					
Fernandes Steak House 158 Felming Ave	Newark	NJ	07105	973-589-4344	589-6312
Web: www.fernandessteakhouse.com					
Fornos of Spain 47 Ferry St	Newark	NJ	00751	973-589-4767	589-1482
Web: www.fornosrestaurant.com					
Iberia Peninsula Restaurant 67 Ferry St	Newark	NJ	07105	973-344-5611	344-2067
Je's 34 Williams St	Newark	NJ	07105	973-623-8848	623-1743

Name / Address	City	State	Zip	Phone	Fax
John's Place 24 Wright St	Newark	NJ	07114	973-824-9233	824-2038
Maize 50 Park Pl	Newark	NJ	07102	973-639-1200	639-1600
Web: www.maizerestaurant.com					
Pronto Cena Ristorante 1 Riverfront Plaza	Newark	NJ	07102	973-824-8999	
Seabra's Rodizio 1034 McCarter Hwy	Newark	NJ	07105	973-622-6221	623-0820
Spain 419 Market St	Newark	NJ	07105	973-344-0994	344-2669
Web: www.spainrestaurant.com					
Spanish Sangria 157 Magazine St	Newark	NJ	07105	973-344-9286	344-1310
Spanish Tavern 103 McWhorter St	Newark	NJ	07105	973-589-4959	589-4148
Web: www.spanishtavern.com					
Theater Square Grill 1 Center St	Newark	NJ	07102	973-642-1226	297-5877
Web: www.theatersquaregrill.com					
Tio Pepe Restaurant 118 Stockton St	Newark	NJ	07105	973-344-1927	
Tony da Caneca 72 Elm Rd	Newark	NJ	07105	973-589-6882	589-0036
Web: www.tonydacaneca.com					
Albasha 1076 Main St	Paterson	NJ	07503	973-345-3700	345-6001
Web: www.albashaonline.com					
Bonfire 999 Market St	Paterson	NJ	07513	973-278-2400	278-1380
Web: www.bonfirerestaurant.com					
Brownstone House 351 W Broadway	Paterson	NJ	07522	973-595-8582	595-1141
Web: www.thebrownstone.com					
Cortina Ristorante 118 Berkshire Ave	Paterson	NJ	07502	973-942-1750	942-9590
Web: www.cortinarestaurant.com					
D'Classico 58-60 Ellison St	Paterson	NJ	07501	973-569-4300	
E & V Restaurant 320 Chamberlain Ave	Paterson	NJ	07502	973-942-4664	942-0060
Web: www.evrestaurant.com					
Getty Avenue Grill 169 Crooks Ave	Paterson	NJ	07503	973-278-7999	
Hacienda Restaurant 102 McLean Blvd	Paterson	NJ	07514	973-345-1255	345-5502
Web: www.haciendarestaurant.com					
Kikiriki 215 Market St	Paterson	NJ	07505	973-225-0336	
King Wok 712 Main St	Paterson	NJ	07503	973-881-8818	881-8878
Patsy's 72 7th Ave	Paterson	NJ	07524	973-742-9596	
Seven Brothers Grill 846 Market St	Paterson	NJ	07513	973-684-2579	
Tierras Colombians 395 21st Ave	Paterson	NJ	07513	973-742-3736	742-3736
Big Fish Seafood Bistro 3535 US Rt 1 S	Princeton	NJ	08540	609-919-1179	919-0674
Blue Point Grill 258 Nassau St	Princeton	NJ	08542	609-921-1211	
Crab Trap 2 Broadway	Somers Point	NJ	08244	609-927-7377	927-5979
Web: www.thecrabtrap.com					
Amici Milano Restaurant 600 Chesnut Ave	Trenton	NJ	08611	609-396-6300	396-3926
Web: www.amicimilano.com					
Blue Danube 538 Adeline St	Trenton	NJ	08621	609-393-6133	
Capalbo's 1218 S Clinton Ave	Trenton	NJ	08611	609-396-4188	396-4962
Casino Restaurant 15 Anderson St	Trenton	NJ	08611	609-393-5875	
Gervasios 1644 Whitehorse Mercerville Rd	Trenton	NJ	08619	609-586-1166	586-8969
Homestead Inn 800 Kuser Rd	Trenton	NJ	08619	609-890-9851	
John Henry's Seafood Restaurant 2 Mifflin St	Trenton	NJ	08611	609-396-3083	396-4060
Web: www.johnhenrysseafood.com					
Katmandu 50 Riverview Executive Park	Trenton	NJ	08611	609-393-7300	695-8737
Web: www.katmandutrenton.com					
Malaga Spanish Restaurant 511 Lalor St	Trenton	NJ	08610	609-396-8878	396-5514
Web: www.malagarestaurant.com					
Marsilio's 541 Roebling Ave	Trenton	NJ	08611	609-695-1916	
Passage to India 2495 US Hwy 1	Trenton	NJ	08648	609-637-0800	637-0880
Sal Deforte's 200 Fulton St	Trenton	NJ	08611	609-396-6856	393-8607
Web: www.saldefortes.com					
Villa Maria 3800 Quakerbridge Rd	Trenton	NJ	08619	609-587-4445	587-6539
Yoshi Sono Japanese Restaurant 643 Eagle Rock Ave Suite A	West Orange	NJ	07052	973-325-2005	
On the Border Mexican Cafe 1738 US Rt 46 W	West Paterson	NJ	07424	973-785-9188	785-9226
Web: www.ontheborder.com					
Taste of China 500 McBride Ave	West Paterson	NJ	07424	973-523-8805	

New Mexico

Name / Address	City	State	Zip	Phone	Fax
66 Diner 1405 Central Ave NE	Albuquerque	NM	87106	505-247-1421	247-0882
Web: www.66diner.com					
ABQ Nick's Crossroads Cafe 400 Central SW	Albuquerque	NM	87102	505-242-6447	242-8379
Ambrozia Cafe & Wine Bar 108 Rio Grande Blvd NE	Albuquerque	NM	87104	505-242-6560	242-6502
Web: www.ambroziacafe.com					
Amerasia 301 Cornell Dr SE	Albuquerque	NM	87106	505-266-8400	
Antiquity 112 Romero St NW	Albuquerque	NM	87104	505-247-3545	
Artichoke Cafe 424 Central Ave SE	Albuquerque	NM	87102	505-243-0200	243-3365
Web: www.artichokecafe.com					
Bangkok Cafe 5901 Central Ave NE	Albuquerque	NM	87108	505-255-5036	255-9177
Barry's Oasis Restaurant 4451 Osuna Rd NE	Albuquerque	NM	87109	505-884-2324	
Web: www.barrysoasis.com					
Cajun Kitchen 4500 Osuna Rd NE Suite 155	Albuquerque	NM	87109	505-344-5355	344-5955
Cantina 1901 University NE Hilton Hotel	Albuquerque	NM	87102	505-884-2500	889-9118
Chama River Brewery Co 4939 Pan American Fwy	Albuquerque	NM	87109	505-342-1800	342-2018
Web: www.chamariverbrewery.com					
Charlie's Front & Back Door 8224 Menaul Blvd NE	Albuquerque	NM	87110	505-294-3130	
China Town 5001 Central Ave NE	Albuquerque	NM	87108	505-265-8859	266-3324
County Line 9600 Tramway Blvd NE	Albuquerque	NM	87122	505-856-7477	856-7479
Web: www.countyline.com					
East Ocean Chinese Seafood 3601 Carlisle Blvd NE	Albuquerque	NM	87110	505-889-9315	830-1066
El Pinto 10500 4th St NW	Albuquerque	NM	87114	505-898-1771	
Gardunos of Mexico 5400 Academy Rd NE	Albuquerque	NM	87109	505-821-3030	823-1628
Web: www.gardunosrestaurants.com					
Geezamboni's 3851 Rio Grande Blvd NW	Albuquerque	NM	87107	505-345-3354	345-2777
Gold Street Caffe 218 Gold Ave SW	Albuquerque	NM	87102	505-765-1633	
Great American Steakhouse 1550 Tramway Blvd NE	Albuquerque	NM	87112	505-292-1510	292-0407
Web: www.steakandwine.com					
High Finance Restaurant 40 Tramway Rd NE	Albuquerque	NM	87122	505-243-9742	247-8501
Web: www.highfinancerestaurant.com					
Il Vicino 3403 Central Ave NE	Albuquerque	NM	87106	505-266-7855	266-5133
Web: www.ilvicino.com					
India Kitchen 6910 Montgomery Blvd NE	Albuquerque	NM	87109	505-884-2333	
India Palace 4410Q Wyoming NE	Albuquerque	NM	87111	505-271-5009	271-5042
Japanese Kitchen 6521 Americas Pkwy NE	Albuquerque	NM	87110	505-884-8937	884-8938
La Familiar 1611 4th St NW	Albuquerque	NM	87102	505-242-9661	
Lin's Restaurant 1035 Juan Tabo Blvd NE	Albuquerque	NM	87112	505-292-5438	
McGrath's 330 Tijeras Ave NW Hyatt Regency Albuquerque	Albuquerque	NM	87102	505-842-1234	843-2710
Melting Pot The 2011 Mountain Rd NW	Albuquerque	NM	87104	505-843-6358	883-3941
Web: www.meltingpot.com					
Monte Vista Fire Station 3201 Central Ave NE	Albuquerque	NM	87106	505-255-2424	255-2521
Mr Powdrell's Barbeque House 11301 Central Ave NE	Albuquerque	NM	87123	505-298-6766	298-0025
Pelican's Restaurant 9800 Montgomery Blvd NE	Albuquerque	NM	87111	505-298-7678	293-9953
Ragin' Shrimp 3619 Copper Ave NE	Albuquerque	NM	87108	505-254-1544	
Web: www.raginshrimp.com					
Ranchers Club of New Mexico 1901 University Blvd NE Hilton Hotel	Albuquerque	NM	87102	505-884-2500	889-9118
Robb's Ribbs 3000-C San Pedro Dr NE	Albuquerque	NM	87110	505-884-7422	884-3250
Web: www.robbsribbs.com					
Sadie's 6230 4th St NW	Albuquerque	NM	87107	505-345-5339	345-9440
Web: www.sadiessalsa.com					
Samurai Grill & Sushi Bar 9500 Montgomery Blvd NE	Albuquerque	NM	87111	505-275-6601	275-4146
Web: www.abqsamurai.com					
Sandiago's Mexican Grill at the Tram 40 Tramway Rd NE	Albuquerque	NM	87122	505-856-6692	856-6364
Web: www.sandiagos.com					
Scalo Northern Italian Grill 3500 Central Ave SE	Albuquerque	NM	87106	505-255-8781	265-7850
Web: www.scalonobhill.com					
Seasons Rotisserie & Grill 2031 Mountain Rd NW	Albuquerque	NM	87104	505-766-5100	766-5252
Web: www.seasonsonthenet.com					
Trattoria Trombino 5415 Academy Rd NE	Albuquerque	NM	87109	505-821-5974	
Yanni's Mediterranean Bar & Grill 3109 Central Ave NE	Albuquerque	NM	87106	505-268-9250	268-9178
Zinc Wine Bar & Bistro 3009 Central Ave NE	Albuquerque	NM	87106	505-254-9462	
Prairie Star The Pueblo of Santa Ana 255 Prairie Star Rd	Bernalillo	NM	87004	505-867-3327	
Carillos Cafe 330 S Church St	Las Cruces	NM	88001	505-523-9913	
Casa Luna 1340 E Lohman Ave	Las Cruces	NM	88001	505-523-0111	
Cattle Baron 790 S Telshor Blvd	Las Cruces	NM	88001	505-522-7533	521-3300
Web: www.cattlebaron.com					
Cattlemen's Steak House 3375 Bataan Memorial W	Las Cruces	NM	88012	505-382-9051	
Chilito's 2405 S Valley Dr	Las Cruces	NM	88005	505-526-4184	532-1104
Web: www.chilitosrestaurant.com					
El Sombrero 363 S Espina St	Las Cruces	NM	88001	505-524-9911	526-4394
Farley's 3499 Foothills Dr	Las Cruces	NM	88011	505-522-0466	521-3523
Web: www.farleyspub.com					
Joy Luck 3530 Foothills Rd	Las Cruces	NM	88011	505-532-0157	
Lemongrass 2540 El Paseo Rd	Las Cruces	NM	88001	505-523-8778	523-8777
Lorenzo's 741 N Alameda Suite 16	Las Cruces	NM	88005	505-524-2850	521-3753
Los Compas Cafe 603 S Nevarez St	Las Cruces	NM	88001	505-523-1778	527-5590
Mesilla Valley Kitchen 2001 E Lohman Ave Suite 103	Las Cruces	NM	88001	505-523-9311	
Meson de Mesilla 1803 Avenida de Mesilla	Las Cruces	NM	88005	505-525-9212	527-4196
Web: www.mesondemesilla.com					
Mix 1001 E University Ave Suite D4	Las Cruces	NM	88001	505-532-2042	532-2046
Nellie's Cafe 1226 W Hadley Ave	Las Cruces	NM	88005	505-524-9982	
New China 850 N Telshor Blvd	Las Cruces	NM	88011	505-522-8989	532-6200
Nopalito 2605 Missouri Ave	Las Cruces	NM	88011	505-522-0440	
Purple Sage Restaurant 4100 Dripping Springs Rd	Las Cruces	NM	88011	505-532-1765	
Ranchway 604 N Valley Dr	Las Cruces	NM	88005	505-523-7361	
Roberto's 908 E Amador Ave	Las Cruces	NM	88001	505-523-1851	
Si Senor 1551 E Amador Ave	Las Cruces	NM	88001	505-527-0817	527-0412
Web: www.sisenor.com					
Spanish Kitchen 2960 N Main St	Las Cruces	NM	88001	505-526-4275	526-2275
Teriyaki Chicken House 805 El Paseo Rd	Las Cruces	NM	88001	505-541-1696	
Double Eagle Restaurant 2355 Calle de Guadelupe	Mesilla	NM	88046	505-523-6700	
Web: www.double-eagle-mesilla.com/					
Anasazi 113 Washington Ave	Santa Fe	NM	87501	505-988-3236	
Andiamo 322 Garfield St	Santa Fe	NM	87501	505-995-9595	
Web: www.andiamorestaurant.com					
Annapurna Chai House 905 W Alameda St	Santa Fe	NM	87501	505-988-9688	988-9914
Blue Corn Cafe & Brewery 133 Water St	Santa Fe	NM	87501	505-984-1800	984-2104
Web: www.bluecorncafe.com					
Bull Ring 150 Washington Ave	Santa Fe	NM	87501	505-983-3328	982-8254
Cafe Paris 31 Burro Alley St	Santa Fe	NM	87501	505-986-9162	986-0504
Cafe San Estevan 428 Agua Fria	Santa Fe	NM	87501	505-995-1996	995-0160
Chow's Contemporary Chinese Food 720 St Michaels Dr	Santa Fe	NM	87505	505-471-7120	
Web: www.mychows.com					
Cleopatra Cafe 418 Cerrillos Rd	Santa Fe	NM	87501	505-820-7381	
Coyote Cafe 132 W Water St	Santa Fe	NM	87501	505-983-1615	989-9026
Web: www.coyotecafe.com					
El Farol 808 Canyon Rd	Santa Fe	NM	87501	505-983-9912	
Web: www.elfarolsf.com					
Fuego 330 E Palace Ave	Santa Fe	NM	87501	505-986-0000	982-6850
Garduno's of Santa Fe 130 Lincoln Ave	Santa Fe	NM	87501	505-983-9797	984-0332
Geronimo 724 Canyon Rd	Santa Fe	NM	87501	505-982-1500	
Web: www.geronimorestaurant.com					
Harry's Roadhouse 96B Old Las Vegas Hwy	Santa Fe	NM	87505	505-989-4629	
Il Piatto 95 W Marcy St	Santa Fe	NM	87501	505-984-1091	983-6939
Web: www.ilpiattorestaurant.com					
Il Vicino 321 W San Francisco St	Santa Fe	NM	87501	505-986-8700	820-0524
Web: www.ilvicino.com					
India Palace 227 Don Gaspar Ave	Santa Fe	NM	87501	505-986-5859	986-5856
Web: www.indiapalace.com					
Julian's 221 Shelby St	Santa Fe	NM	87501	505-988-2355	988-5071
Web: www.juliansofsantafe.com					
Kohnami 313 S Guadalupe St	Santa Fe	NM	87501	505-984-2002	
Maria's New Mexican Kitchen 555 W Cordova Rd	Santa Fe	NM	87501	505-983-7929	
Web: www.marias-santafe.com					
Mariscos La Playa 2875 Cerrillos Rd	Santa Fe	NM	87501	505-982-2790	
Mu Du Noodles 1494 Cerrillos Rd	Santa Fe	NM	87505	505-983-1411	
Web: www.mudunoodles.com					
Old House 309 W San Francisco St	Santa Fe	NM	87501	505-988-4455	
Pasqual's 121 Don Gaspar Ave	Santa Fe	NM	87501	505-983-9340	988-4645
Web: www.pasquals.com					
Rio Chama Steakhouse 414 Old Santa Fe Trail	Santa Fe	NM	87501	505-955-0765	955-8579
Web: www.riochamasteakhouse.com					
Santacafe 231 Washington Ave	Santa Fe	NM	87501	505-984-1788	
Web: www.santacafe.com					
Shed The 113 1/2 E Palace Ave	Santa Fe	NM	87501	505-982-9030	982-0902
Web: www.sfshed.com					
Tecolote Cafe 1203 Cerrillos Rd	Santa Fe	NM	87505	505-988-1362	
Tomasita's Santa Fe Station 500 S Guadalupe St	Santa Fe	NM	87501	505-983-5721	983-0780
Tortilla Flats 3139 Cerrillos Rd	Santa Fe	NM	87505	505-471-8685	471-8686
Web: www.santafenow.com/rest/tortilla/					
El Nido County Rd 591 & Bishop's Lodge Rd	Tesuque	NM	87574	505-988-4340	

New York

Name / Address	City	State	Zip	Phone	Fax
Butcher Block 1632A Central Ave	Albany	NY	12212	518-456-1653	456-2179
Web: www.butcherblockrestaurant.com					
Cafe Capriccio 49 Grand St	Albany	NY	12207	518-465-0439	465-6822
Web: www.cafecapriccio.com					
Caffe Italia Ristorante 662 Central Ave	Albany	NY	12206	518-459-8029	
CH Evans Brewing Co-The Pump Station 19 Quackenbush Sq	Albany	NY	12207	518-447-9000	465-1410
Web: www.evansale.com					
El Loco Mexican Cafe 465 Madison Ave	Albany	NY	12210	518-436-1855	
El Mariachi 144 Washington Ave	Albany	NY	12206	518-465-2568	463-1930
Gandhi 1 Central Ave	Albany	NY	12210	518-449-5577	449-8941
Web: www.albanygandhi.com					
Hiros 1933 Central Ave	Albany	NY	12205	518-456-1180	
Ichiban 338 Central Ave	Albany	NY	12206	518-432-0358	432-6038
Jack's Oyster House 42 State St	Albany	NY	12207	518-465-8854	434-2134
Web: www.jacksoysterhouse.com					
Justin's 301 Lark St	Albany	NY	12210	518-436-7008	432-4122
Web: www.justinsonlark.com					
Kirker's Steak & Seafood 959 Loudon Rd	Albany	NY	12110	518-785-3653	
Lark Tavern 453 Madison Ave	Albany	NY	12210	518-463-9779	
Web: www.larktavern.com/					
McGuire's 353 State St	Albany	NY	12210	518-463-2100	463-2094

New York (Cont'd)

Name / Address	City	State	ZIP	Phone	Fax
Miss Albany Diner 893 Broadway	Albany	NY	12207	518-465-9148	
Web: www.missalbanydiner.com					
My Linh 272 Delaware Ave	Albany	NY	12209	518-465-8899	465-8898
Web: www.mylinhrestaurant.com					
Nicole's Bistro 25 Quackenbush Sq	Albany	NY	12207	518-465-1111	465-3911
Web: www.nicolesbistro.com					
Pearl 1 Steuben Pl.	Albany	NY	12207	518-433-0011	433-0012
Web: www.pearlalbany.com					
Provence 1475 Western Ave Stuyvesant Plaza	Albany	NY	12203	518-689-7777	689-7780
Web: www.provence-restaurant.net					
Real Seafood Co 195 Wolf Rd	Albany	NY	12205	518-458-2068	482-3471
Web: www.realseafood.com					
Saso's Japanese Noodle House 218 Central Ave	Albany	NY	12205	518-436-7789	439-0159
Web: www.sasos.com					
Scrimshaw The 660 Albany-Shaker Rd	Albany	NY	12211	518-869-8100	452-4454
Web: www.desmondhotelsalbany.com					
Sushi House 6 New Scotland Ave	Albany	NY	12208	518-935-2270	462-3860
Taste of Greece 193 Lark St.	Albany	NY	12207	518-426-9000	465-6099
Web: www.atasteofgreece.biz					
Bing's 1952 Kensington Ave	Amherst	NY	14215	716-839-5788	839-5336
Scotch & Sirloin 3999 Maple Rd	Amherst	NY	14226	716-837-4900	837-0987
Web: www.frontstreetrestaurant.com					
Roberto's 603 Crescent Ave	Bronx	NY	10458	718-733-9503	733-2724
Web: www.usmenuguide.com/Robertos.htm					
360 360 Van Brunt St	Brooklyn	NY	11231	718-246-0360	
Web: www.360brooklyn.com					
Elia 8611 3rd Ave	Brooklyn	NY	11209	718-748-9891	748-9879
Frankies 457 Court Street Spuntino 457 Court St.	Brooklyn	NY	11231	718-403-0033	403-9260
Web: www.frankies457.com					
Garden Cafe 620 Vanderbilt Ave	Brooklyn	NY	11238	718-857-8863	
Grocery The 288 Smith St.	Brooklyn	NY	11231	718-596-3335	
Web: www.thegroceryrestaurant.com					
Ici 246 DeKalb Ave	Brooklyn	NY	11205	718-789-2778	
Web: www.icirestaurant.com					
Peter Luger Steak House 178 Broadway	Brooklyn	NY	11211	718-387-7400	387-3523
Web: www.peterluger.com					
River Cafe 1 Water St	Brooklyn	NY	11201	718-522-5200	875-0037
Web: www.rivercafe.com					
Saul 140 Smith St	Brooklyn	NY	11201	718-935-9844	
Web: www.saulrestaurant.com					
Acropolis Family Restaurant 708 Elmwood Ave	Buffalo	NY	14222	716-886-2977	886-4802
Ambrosia 467 Elmwood Ave	Buffalo	NY	14222	716-881-2196	881-2220
Bijou Grille 643 Main St	Buffalo	NY	14203	716-847-1512	852-3041
Web: www.bijougrille.com					
Billy Ogden's Lovejoy Grill 1834 William St.	Buffalo	NY	14206	716-896-8018	896-4932
Web: www.billyogdens.com					
Blackthorn Restaurant & Pub 2134 Seneca St	Buffalo	NY	14210	716-825-9327	
Duff's 3651 Sheridan Dr	Buffalo	NY	14226	716-834-6234	831-5513
Fat Bob's Smokehouse 41 Virginia Pl.	Buffalo	NY	14202	716-887-2971	332-1201
Web: www.fatbobs.com/					
Fiddle Heads Restaurant 62 Allen St	Buffalo	NY	14202	716-883-4166	
Web: www.fiddleheads.us					
Frank & Teressa's Anchor Bar & Restaurant 1047 Main St.	Buffalo	NY	14209	716-886-8920	883-6124
Web: www.anchorbar.com					
Friar's Table 301 Cleveland Dr	Buffalo	NY	14215	716-833-5554	833-5560
Web: www.thefriarstable.com					
Gigi's Restaurant 257 E Ferry St	Buffalo	NY	14208	716-883-1438	
Harry's Harbour Place Grille 2192 Niagara St	Buffalo	NY	14207	716-874-5400	874-0132
Web: www.harrysharbour.com					
Hutch's 1375 Delaware Ave.	Buffalo	NY	14209	716-885-0074	881-0222
Web: www.hutchsrestaurant.com					
Ilio DiPaolo's 3785 S Park Ave.	Buffalo	NY	14219	716-825-3675	825-1054
Web: www.iliodipaolos.com					
La Dolce Vita Caffe & Bistro 1472 Hertel Ave.	Buffalo	NY	14216	716-446-5690	
Web: www.iloveladolcevita.com					
Left Bank 511 Rhode Island St.	Buffalo	NY	14213	716-882-3509	881-5895
Web: www.leftbankrestaurant.com					
Marco's 1085 Niagara St.	Buffalo	NY	14213	716-886-8776	885-4399
Mother's 33 Virginia Pl	Buffalo	NY	14202	716-882-2989	
Oliver's 2095 Delaware Ave.	Buffalo	NY	14216	716-877-9662	877-8291
Web: www.oliverscuisine.com					
Pearl Street Grill & Brewery 76 Pearl St	Buffalo	NY	14202	716-856-2337	849-0839
Web: www.pearlstreetgrill.com					
Rue Franklin 341 Franklin St.	Buffalo	NY	14202	716-852-4416	
Web: www.ruefranklin.com					
Santasiero's 1329 Niagara St	Buffalo	NY	14213	716-886-9197	884-9338
Web: www.santasieros.com					
Scharf's Schiller Park Restaurant 34 S Crossman St.	Buffalo	NY	14211	716-895-7249	894-1992
Web: www.scharfsrest.com					
Tandoori at Transit 7740 Transit Rd	Buffalo	NY	14221	716-632-1112	632-1130
Web: www.tandooris.com					
Salvatore's Italian Gardens 6461 Transit Rd	Depew	NY	14043	716-683-7990	684-9229
Web: www.salvatores.net					
Horizons 199 Woodcliff Dr.	Fairport	NY	14450	585-248-4825	381-5673
Jovi's 2795 Delaware Ave	Kenmore	NY	14217	716-874-9103	
Casa Mono 52 Irving Pl.	Manhattan	NY	10017	212-253-2773	253-5318
Cru 24 5th Ave.	Manhattan	NY	10011	212-529-1700	529-6300
Web: www.cru-nyc.com					
Jewel Bako 239 E 5th St.	Manhattan	NY	10003	212-979-1012	
Kittichai 60 Thompson St.	Manhattan	NY	10012	212-219-2000	925-2971
Web: www.kittichairestaurant.com					
Modern The 9 W 53rd St	Manhattan	NY	10019	212-333-1220	408-6322
Web: www.themodernnyc.com					
Shanghai Pavilion 1378 3rd Ave.	Manhattan	NY	10021	212-585-3388	288-9235
Sugiyama 251 W 55th St.	Manhattan	NY	10019	212-956-0670	956-0671
Web: www.sugiyama-nyc.com					
Sushi Zen 108 W 44th St	Manhattan	NY	10036	212-302-0707	944-7710
Web: www.sushizen-ny.com					
Tomoe Sushi 172 Thompson St	Manhattan	NY	10012	212-777-9346	
Ada 208 E 58th St.	New York	NY	10022	212-371-6060	371-8182
Web: www.adanyc.com					
Aix 2398 Broadway	New York	NY	10024	212-874-7400	874-7643
Web: www.aixnyc.com/					
Aki 181 W 4th St.	New York	NY	10014	212-989-5440	
Alain Ducasse at the Essex House 145 W 58th St	New York	NY	10019	212-265-7300	
Web: www.alain-ducasse.com					
Alfama 551 Hudson St	New York	NY	10014	212-645-2500	645-1476
Web: www.alfamarestaurant.com					
Annisa 13 Barrow St	New York	NY	10014	212-741-6699	
Web: www.annisarestaurant.com					
Aquagrill 210 Spring St.	New York	NY	10012	212-274-0505	274-0587
Web: www.aquagrill.com					
Aquavit 65 E 55th St	New York	NY	16022	212-307-7311	
Web: www.aquavit.org					
Artisanal 2 Park Ave	New York	NY	10016	212-725-8585	481-5455
Web: www.artisanalbistro.com					
Asia de Cuba 237 Madison Ave	New York	NY	10016	212-726-7755	726-7755
Atelier 50 Central Park S.	New York	NY	10019	212-521-6125	
Atlantic Grill 1341 3rd Ave.	New York	NY	10021	212-988-9200	452-1447
August 359 Bleecker St	New York	NY	10014	212-929-4774	
Web: www.augustny.com					
Aureole 34 E 61st St.	New York	NY	10021	212-319-1660	755-3126
Web: www.charliepalmer.com/aureole_ny					
Babbo 110 Waverly Pl	New York	NY	10011	212-777-0303	
Web: www.babbonyc.com					
Balthazar 80 Spring St	New York	NY	10012	212-965-1414	
Web: www.balthazarny.com					
Bar Americain 152 W 52nd St	New York	NY	10019	212-265-9700	
Web: www.baramericain.com					
Barbuto 775 Washington St	New York	NY	10014	212-924-9700	924-9300
Web: www.barbutonyc.com					
Beacon Restaurant & Bar 25 W 56th St	New York	NY	10019	212-332-0500	
Web: www.beaconnyc.com					
Biltmore Room 290 8th Ave	New York	NY	10001	212-807-0111	807-0074
Web: www.thebiltmoreroom.com					
BLT Prime 111 E 22nd St	New York	NY	10010	212-995-8500	460-5881
Web: www.bltprime.com					
Blue Fin 1567 Broadway	New York	NY	10036	212-918-1400	918-1300
Web: www.brguestrestaurants.com/restaurants/blue_fin/					
Blue Hill 75 Washington Pl	New York	NY	10011	212-539-1776	539-0959
Web: www.bluehillnyc.com					
Blue Mahoe The 243 E 14th St.	New York	NY	10003	212-358-0012	505-1247
Web: www.bluemahoenyc.com					
Blue Ribbon 97 Sullivan St	New York	NY	10012	212-274-0404	274-1318
Web: www.blueribbonrestaurants.com					
Blue Water Grill 31 Union Sq W.	New York	NY	10003	212-675-9500	675-1899
Bolo 23 E 22nd St	New York	NY	10010	212-228-2200	228-2239
Web: www.bolorestaurant.com					
Bond Street 6 Bond St	New York	NY	10012	212-777-2500	777-6530
Boom 152 Spring St.	New York	NY	10012	212-431-3663	431-3643
Bouley 120 W Broadway	New York	NY	10013	212-964-2525	219-3443
Web: www.bouley.net					
Cafe des Artistes 1 W 67th St	New York	NY	10023	212-877-3500	877-7754
Web: www.cafenyc.com					
Cafe Boulud 20 E 76th St	New York	NY	10021	212-772-2600	772-7755
Web: www.danielnyc.com/cafeboulud					
Cafe Carlyle 35 E 76th St.	New York	NY	10021	212-744-1600	717-4682
Cafe Centro 200 Park Ave.	New York	NY	10166	212-818-1222	949-8266
Cafe Gray 10 Columbus Cir 3rd Fl	New York	NY	10019	212-823-6338	823-6221
Web: www.cafegray.com					
Cafe Pierre 2 E 61st St.	New York	NY	10021	212-940-8195	
Capsouto Freres 451 Washington St	New York	NY	10013	212-966-4900	925-5296
Web: www.capsoutofreres.com					
Caviar Russe 538 Madison Ave 2nd Fl	New York	NY	10022	212-980-5908	871-1842
Web: www.caviarrusse.com					
Chanterelle 2 Harrison St	New York	NY	10013	212-966-6960	966-6143
Web: www.chanterellenyc.com					
China Grill 60 W 53rd St	New York	NY	10019	212-333-7788	581-9299
Churrascaria Plataforma 316 W 49th St	New York	NY	10019	212-245-0505	974-8250
Web: www.churrascariaplataforma.com					
Craft 43 E 19th St	New York	NY	10003	212-780-0880	780-0580
Web: www.craftrestaurant.com					
Daniel 60 E 65th St	New York	NY	10021	212-288-0033	396-9014
Web: www.danielnyc.com					
Danube 30 Hudson St	New York	NY	10013	212-791-3771	693-7490
Davidburke & Donatella 133 E 61st St.	New York	NY	10021	212-813-2121	486-2322
Web: www.dbdrestaurant.com					
Dawat 210 E 58th St	New York	NY	10022	212-355-7555	355-1735
db Bistro Moderne 55 W 44th St	New York	NY	10036	212-391-2400	391-1188
Web: danielnyc.com/dbbistro					
Del Frisco's Double Eagle Steak House 1221 Ave of the Americas	New York	NY	10020	212-575-5129	575-4873
Web: www.delfriscos.com					
Del Posto 85 10th Ave.	New York	NY	10011	212-497-8090	
Web: www.delposto.com					
Devi 8 E 18th St	New York	NY	10003	212-691-1300	691-1695
Web: www.devinyc.com					
DISTRICT 130 W 46th St	New York	NY	10036	212-485-2999	
Web: www.districtnyc.com/					
Donguri 309 E 83rd St.	New York	NY	10028	212-737-5656	
Eleven Madison Park 11 Madison Ave	New York	NY	10010	212-889-0905	
Web: www.elevenmadisonpark.com					
Erminia 250 E 83rd St.	New York	NY	10028	212-879-4284	
Web: www.erminiarestaurant.com					
Estiatorio Milos 125 W 55th St	New York	NY	10019	212-245-7400	245-4828
Web: www.milos.ca					
Felidia 243 E 58th St	New York	NY	10022	212-758-1479	935-7687
Web: felidia.lidiasitaly.com					
Fiamma 206 Spring St.	New York	NY	10012	212-653-0100	653-0101
Firebird 365 W 46th St	New York	NY	10036	212-586-0244	957-2983
Web: www.firebirdrestaurant.com					
Fleur de Sel 5 E 20th St	New York	NY	10003	212-460-9100	460-8319
Web: www.fleurdeselnyc.com					
Four Seasons 99 E 52nd St.	New York	NY	10022	212-754-9494	754-1077
Web: www.fourseasonsrestaurant.com					
Gordon Ramsay at the London 151 W 54th St.	New York	NY	10019	212-468-8888	
Web: www.thelondonnyc.com/gordon_ramsay/					
Gotham Bar & Grill 12 E 12th St	New York	NY	10003	212-620-4020	627-7810
Web: www.gothambarandgrill.com					
Gramercy Tavern 42 E 20th St	New York	NY	10003	212-477-0777	477-1160
Web: www.gramercytavern.com					
Hangawi 12 E 32nd St.	New York	NY	10016	212-213-0077	689-0780
Web: www.hangawirestaurant.com					
Harrison 355 Greenwich St	New York	NY	10013	212-274-9310	274-9376
Web: www.theharrison.com/harrison.html					
Il Mulino 86 W 3rd St.	New York	NY	10012	212-673-3783	673-9875
Web: www.ilmulinonewyork.com					
Il Nido 251 E 53rd St.	New York	NY	10022	212-753-8450	224-0155
Web: ilnidonyc.com					
Il Palazzo 151 Mulberry St	New York	NY	10013	212-343-7000	343-1508
Jean Georges 1 Central Park W	New York	NY	10023	212-299-3900	299-3914
Web: starchefs.com/JeanGeorges/jean_georges.htm					
JoJo 160 E 64th St	New York	NY	10021	212-223-5656	755-9038
Kai 822 Madison Ave 2nd Fl	New York	NY	10021	212-988-7277	507-4500
Web: www.itoen.com/kai					
Kuruma Zushi 7 E 47th St 2nd Fl	New York	NY	10017	212-317-2802	317-2803
La Grenouille 3 E 52nd St.	New York	NY	10022	212-752-1495	593-4964
Web: www.la-grenouille.com					
L'Absinthe 227 E 67th St	New York	NY	10021	212-794-4950	794-1589
Web: labsinthe.com					

	City	State	Zip	Phone	Fax
Le Bernardin 155 W 51st St	New York	NY	10019	212-489-1515	554-1100
Web: www.le-bernardin.com					
Le Perigord 405 E 52nd St	New York	NY	10022	212-755-6244	
Web: www.leperigord.com					
Lever House Restaurant Bar 390 Park Ave	New York	NY	10022	212-888-2700	
Web: www.leverhouse.com					
L'Impero 45 Tudor City Pl	New York	NY	10017	212-599-5045	599-5043
Web: www.limpero.com					
Lucy Latin Kitchen 35 E 18th St	New York	NY	10003	212-777-6211	598-3020
Web: www.lucylatinkitchen.com					
Lupa Osteria Romana 170 Thompson St	New York	NY	10012	212-982-5089	982-5490
Web: www.luparestaurant.com					
Maloney & Porcelli 37 E 50th St	New York	NY	10022	212-750-2233	750-2252
Web: www.maloneyandporcelli.com					
Mas 39 Downing St	New York	NY	10014	212-255-1790	255-0279
Masa 10 Columbus Cir Time Warner Center 4th Fl	New York	NY	10019	212-823-9800	
Web: www.masanyc.com					
Megu 62 Thomas St	New York	NY	10013	212-964-7777	
Web: www.megunyc.com					
Mercer Kitchen 99 Prince St	New York	NY	10012	212-966-5454	965-3855
Web: www.jean-georges.com					
Mesa Grill 102 5th Ave	New York	NY	10011	212-807-7400	989-0039
Web: www.mesagrill.com					
Metrazur Grand Central Terminal East Balcony	New York	NY	10017	212-687-4600	687-5671
Web: www.charliepalmer.com/metrazur					
Mexican Mama 525 Hudson St	New York	NY	10014	212-924-4119	
Michael Jordan's Steak House 23 Vanderbilt Ave	New York	NY	10017	212-655-2300	655-4915
Michael's New York 24 W 55th St	New York	NY	10019	212-767-0555	581-6778
Web: www.michaelsnewyork.com					
Montrachet 239 W Broadway	New York	NY	10013	212-219-2777	274-9508
Web: www.myriadrestaurantgroup.com					
Nish 405 E 58th St	New York	NY	10022	212-754-6272	838-5108
Web: www.waynenish.net					
Nobu 105 Hudson St	New York	NY	10013	212-219-0500	
Web: www.nobumatsuhisa.com					
Oceana 55 E 54th St	New York	NY	10022	212-759-5941	759-6076
Web: www.oceanarestaurant.com					
Olives New York 201 Park Ave S	New York	NY	10003	212-353-8345	353-9592
One if by Land Two if by Sea 17 Barrow St	New York	NY	10014	212-255-8649	206-7855
Web: www.oneifbyland.com					
Ouest 2315 Broadway	New York	NY	10024	212-580-8700	580-1360
Web: www.ouestny.com					
Palm Restaurant 837 2nd Ave	New York	NY	10017	212-687-2953	983-4584
Web: www.thepalm.com					
Pampano 209 E 49th St	New York	NY	10017	212-751-4545	
Web: www.modernmexican.com					
Park Avenue Cafe 100 E 63rd St	New York	NY	10021	212-644-1900	688-0373
Web: www.parkavenuecafe.com					
Pearl Oyster Bar 18 Cornelia St	New York	NY	10014	212-691-8211	691-8210
Web: www.pearloysterbar.com					
Peasant 194 Elizabeth St	New York	NY	10012	212-965-9511	965-8174
Web: www.peasantnyc.com					
Per Se 10 Columbus Cir 4th Fl	New York	NY	10019	212-823-9335	823-9497
Periyali 35 W 20th St	New York	NY	10011	212-463-7890	924-9403
Web: www.periyali.com					
Petrossian 182 W 58th St	New York	NY	10019	212-245-2214	245-2812
Picholine 35 W 64th St	New York	NY	10023	212-724-8585	875-8979
Web: www.picholinenyc.com					
Po 31 Cornelia St	New York	NY	10014	212-645-2189	367-9448
Web: www.porestaurant.com					
Poke 305 E 85th St	New York	NY	10028	212-249-0569	
Post House The 28 E 63rd St	New York	NY	10021	212-935-2888	371-9264
Web: www.theposthouse.com					
Prime Grill 60 E 49th St	New York	NY	10017	212-692-9292	
Web: www.theprimegrill.com					
Provence 38 MacDougal St	New York	NY	10012	212-475-7500	602-9772*
*Fax Area Code: 646 ■ *Web:* provence.citysearch.com					
Remi 145 W 53rd St	New York	NY	10019	212-581-4242	581-5948
Rene Pujol 321 W 51st St	New York	NY	10019	212-246-3023	245-5206
Web: www.renepujol.com					
Rothmann's Steakhouse & Grill 3 E 54th St	New York	NY	10022	212-319-5500	319-5540
Web: www.rothmannssteakhouse.com					
Roy's 130 Washington St	New York	NY	10006	212-266-6262	
Web: www.roysrestaurant.com					
Scalini Fedeli 165 Duane St	New York	NY	10013	212-528-0400	587-8773
Web: www.scalinifedeli.com					
Sea Grill Restaurant 19 W 49th St	New York	NY	10020	212-332-7610	332-7677
Shun Lee Palace 155 E 55th St	New York	NY	10022	212-371-8844	752-1936
Web: shunleepalace.com					
Silverleaf Tavern 43 E 38th St	New York	NY	10036	212-973-2550	973-2551
Web: www.silverleaftavern.com/					
Smith & Wollensky 797 3rd Ave	New York	NY	10022	212-753-1530	751-5446
Web: www.smithandwollensky.com					
Sparks Steak House 210 E 46th St	New York	NY	10017	212-687-4855	557-7409
Web: www.sparkssteakhouse.com					
Spice Market 403 W 13th St	New York	NY	10014	212-675-2322	675-4365
Web: www.jean-georges.com					
Strip House 13 E 12th St	New York	NY	10003	212-328-0000	337-0233
Sushi of Gari 402 E 78th St	New York	NY	10021	212-517-5340	
Sushi Seki 1143 1st Ave	New York	NY	10021	212-371-0238	
Sushi Yasuda 204 E 43rd St	New York	NY	10017	212-972-1001	972-1717
Web: www.sushiyasuda.com					
Tabla 11 Madison Ave	New York	NY	10010	212-889-0667	889-3865
Web: www.tablany.com					
Tamarind 41-43 E 22nd St	New York	NY	10010	212-674-7400	674-4449
Web: www.tamarinde22.com					
Tasting Room 72 E 1st St	New York	NY	10003	212-358-7831	358-8432
Web: www.thetastingroomnyc.com					
Tavern on the Green W 67th St & Central Park W	New York	NY	10023	212-873-3200	
Web: www.tavernonthegreen.com					
Terrace in the Sky 400 W 119th St	New York	NY	10027	212-666-9490	666-3471
Web: www.terraceinthesky.com					
Thalia 828 8th Ave	New York	NY	10019	212-399-4444	399-3268
Web: www.restaurantthalia.com					
Tocqueville 1 W 15th St	New York	NY	10003	212-647-1515	647-7148
Web: www.tocquevillerestaurant.com					
Town 15 W 56th St	New York	NY	10019	212-582-4445	852-5535
Web: www.townnyc.com					
Trattoria dell'Arte 900 7th Ave	New York	NY	10106	212-245-9800	265-3296
Web: www.trattoriadellarte.com					
Triomphe 49 W 44th St	New York	NY	10036	212-453-4233	827-0464
Web: www.triomphe-newyork.com					
Union Square Cafe 21 E 16th St	New York	NY	10003	212-243-4020	627-2673
Veritas 43 E 20th St	New York	NY	10003	212-353-3700	353-1632
Web: www.veritas-nyc.com					
Vong 200 E 54th St	New York	NY	10022	212-486-9592	826-4169

	City	State	Zip	Phone	Fax
Wallse 344 W 11th St	New York	NY	10014	212-352-2300	645-7127
Web: www.wallse.com					
Wolfgang's Steakhouse 4 Park Ave	New York	NY	10016	212-889-3369	889-6845
Web: www.wolfgangssteakhouse.com					
Erawan 42-31 Bell Blvd	Queens	NY	11361	718-428-2112	428-2098
Web: www.erawanthai.com					
Sapori d'Ischia 55-15 37th Ave	Queens	NY	11377	718-446-1500	446-0134
Sripraphai 64-13 39th Ave	Queens	NY	11377	718-899-9599	
Trattoria L'incontro 21-76 31st St	Queens	NY	11105	718-721-3532	626-3375
Web: www.trattorialincontro.com					
Agatina's 2967 Buffalo Rd	Rochester	NY	14624	585-426-0510	
Web: www.agatinas.com					
Aladdin's Natural Eatery 646 Monroe Ave	Rochester	NY	14607	585-442-5000	442-0550
Web: www.aladdinsnaturaleatery.com					
Athena 3576 Mt Read Blvd	Rochester	NY	14616	585-621-4494	
Bacco's 263 Park Ave	Rochester	NY	14607	585-442-5090	
Basha 798 S Clinton Ave	Rochester	NY	14620	585-256-1370	
Bathtub Billy's 630 Ridge Rd W	Rochester	NY	14615	585-865-6510	865-6323
Web: www.bathtubbillys.com					
Benucci's 3349 Monroe Ave	Rochester	NY	14618	585-264-1300	264-1926
Web: www.benuccis.com					
Bernard's Grove 187 Long Pond Rd	Rochester	NY	14612	585-227-6405	723-5915
Web: www.bernardsgrove.com					
Big Apple Cafe 682 Park Ave	Rochester	NY	14607	585-271-1039	271-6410
Brook House 920 Elmridge Center Dr	Rochester	NY	14626	585-723-9988	723-9993
California Rollin' 274 N Goodman St	Rochester	NY	14607	585-271-8990	
Dinosaur Bar-B-Que 99 Court St	Rochester	NY	14604	585-325-7090	325-7125
Web: www.dinosaurbarbque.com					
Edibles Restaurant & Bar 704 University Ave	Rochester	NY	14607	585-271-4910	
Web: www.ediblesrestaurant.com					
El Conquistador 1939 Clifford Ave	Rochester	NY	14609	585-288-4160	288-9188
Elmwood Inn The 1256 Mt Hope Ave	Rochester	NY	14620	585-271-5195	271-6689
Grill at Strathallan The 550 East Ave	Rochester	NY	14607	585-454-1880	
Web: www.strathallan.com/htm/thegrill.htm					
Hogan's Hideaway 197 Park Ave	Rochester	NY	14607	585-442-4293	461-4965
Web: www.hoganshideaway.com					
House of Poon 2185 Monroe Ave	Rochester	NY	14618	585-271-7371	
India House 998 S Clinton Ave	Rochester	NY	14620	585-461-0880	461-5918
India Palace 1900 S Clinton Ave	Rochester	NY	14618	585-271-2100	271-3627
Web: www.ipretaurant.com					
Lucano 1815 East Ave	Rochester	NY	14610	585-244-3460	
Mamasan 309 University Ave	Rochester	NY	14607	585-262-4580	
Mario's Via Abruzzi 2740 Monroe Ave	Rochester	NY	14618	585-271-1111	
Web: www.mariosviaabruzzi.com					
Martini Grille 176 S Goodman	Rochester	NY	14607	585-244-6526	
Web: www.martinigrille.net					
Oasis Mediterranean Bistro 687 Monroe Ave	Rochester	NY	14607	585-473-0050	
Web: www.oasisbistro.com					
Pakistan House 2411 W Henrietta Rd	Rochester	NY	14623	585-427-8797	427-0348
Web: www.pakistanhouserestaurant.com					
Phillips European Restaurant 26 Corporate Woods	Rochester	NY	14623	585-272-9910	272-1778
Web: www.phillipseuropean.com					
Portobello Ristorante 2171 W Henrietta Rd	Rochester	NY	14623	585-427-0110	424-1283
Web: www.portobelloristorante.com					
Remington's 425 Merchants Rd	Rochester	NY	14609	585-482-4434	244-0710
Web: www.remingtonsrochester.com					
Salena's 274 N Goodman St	Rochester	NY	14607	585-256-5980	256-7428
Web: www.salenas.com					
Skippy's 742 South Ave	Rochester	NY	14620	585-271-7590	
Web: www.skippysvegout.com					
1060 at the Genesee Grande 1060 E Genesee St	Syracuse	NY	13214	315-476-9000	
Alto Cinco 526 Westcott St	Syracuse	NY	13210	315-422-6399	
Web: www.alto-cinco.com					
Ambrosia 201 Walton St	Syracuse	NY	13202	315-426-8800	
Angotti's 725 Burnet Ave	Syracuse	NY	13203	315-472-8403	
Antonio's 700 N Salina St	Syracuse	NY	13208	315-425-1946	
Blue Tusk 165 Walton St	Syracuse	NY	13218	315-472-1934	
Web: www.bluetusk.com					
Casa Di Copani 3414 Burnet Ave	Syracuse	NY	13206	315-463-1031	
Daniel Jack's Entertainment Restaurant 218 Walton St	Syracuse	NY	13208	315-475-8357	
Web: danieljacks.com					
Delmonico's Italian Steakhouse 2950 Erie Blvd E	Syracuse	NY	13224	315-445-1111	445-0257
Web: www.delmonicositaliansteakhouse.com					
Dinosaur Bar-B-Que 246 W Willow St	Syracuse	NY	13202	315-476-4937	
Web: www.dinosaurbarbque.com					
Gentile's 305 Burnet Ave	Syracuse	NY	13204	315-474-8258	
Joey's Restaurant 6594 Thompson Rd	Syracuse	NY	13206	315-432-0315	
Juanita's Mexican Kitchen 600 Court St	Syracuse	NY	13208	315-478-2185	
King David's 129 Marshall St	Syracuse	NY	13210	315-471-5000	
Web: www.kingdavids.com					
L'Adour 110 Montgomery St	Syracuse	NY	13202	315-475-7653	
Web: www.ladour.com					
Lemon Grass 238 W Jefferson St	Syracuse	NY	13202	315-475-1111	475-3287
Web: www.lemongrass-238bistro.com					
Little Thai House 2863 Erie Blvd E	Syracuse	NY	13224	315-251-1366	
Luigi's 1524 Valley Dr	Syracuse	NY	13207	315-492-9997	
Mission The 304 E Onondaga St	Syracuse	NY	13202	315-475-7344	475-7340
Pascale Wine Bar & Restaurant 204 W Fayette St	Syracuse	NY	13202	315-471-3040	
Phoebe's 900 E Genesee St	Syracuse	NY	13210	315-475-5154	
Web: www.phoebessyracuse.com					
Redfield's 701 E Genesee St	Syracuse	NY	13210	315-479-7000	
Riley's 312 Park St	Syracuse	NY	13203	315-471-7111	
Saratoga Steaks & Seafood 200 Waring Rd	Syracuse	NY	13224	315-445-1976	446-2094
Syracuse Suds Factory 320 S Clinton St	Syracuse	NY	13202	315-471-2253	
Web: www.sudsfactory.com					
Tokyo-Seoul 3180 Erie Blvd E	Syracuse	NY	13214	315-449-2688	
Jasmine 1330 Niagara Falls Blvd	Tonawanda	NY	14150	716-838-3011	332-0280
Web: www.jasminethairestaurant.com					
Ferrara's Seafood-Pasta Grill 2150 Central Park Ave	Yonkers	NY	10710	914-961-8908	961-8908
Hunan Village Restaurant 1828 Central Park Ave	Yonkers	NY	10710	914-779-2272	779-0164
Web: www.hunanvillage.com					
Kang Suh 2375 Central Park Ave	Yonkers	NY	10710	914-771-4066	
La Lanterna 23 Grey Oaks Ave	Yonkers	NY	10710	914-476-3060	375-7477
Web: www.lalanterna.com					
Louie's 187 S Broadway	Yonkers	NY	10701	914-969-8821	963-2418
Nyauta 27 Meyers Ave	Yonkers	NY	10704	914-476-1910	476-8878
Web: www.nyauta.com					
Patang 2223 Central Park Ave	Yonkers	NY	10710	914-793-8888	961-5300
Web: www.patangcuisine.com					
Renegades Bar & Grill 748 Yonkers Ave	Yonkers	NY	10704	914-375-2233	
Web: www.renegadessportsbar.com					
Rory Dolan's 890 McLean Ave	Yonkers	NY	10704	914-776-2946	776-6538
Web: www.rorydolans.com					
Spiritoso 811 McLean Ave	Yonkers	NY	10704	914-237-4075	237-5713
Web: www.spiritosoristorante.com					
Tombolino Restaurant 356 Kimball Ave	Yonkers	NY	10704	914-237-1266	237-1254
Web: www.tombolinorestaurant.com					

New York (Cont'd)

				Phone	Fax
Valentino's of America Inc 132 Bronx River Rd	Yonkers	NY	10704	914-776-6731	
Ya Hala 326 S Broadway	Yonkers	NY	10705	914-476-4200	
Web: www.yahalarestaurant.com					
Zuppa 59 Main St	Yonkers	NY	10701	914-376-6500	376-4900
Web: www.zupparestaurant.com					

North Carolina

				Phone	Fax
Battery Park Bistro 22 Battery Park Ave	Asheville	NC	28801	828-253-2158	
Blue Ridge Dining Room 290 Macon Ave	Asheville	NC	28804	828-252-2711	252-7053
Cafe Bouchon 62 N Lexington Ave	Asheville	NC	28801	828-350-1140	
Cafe on the Square 1 Biltmore Ave Pack Sq	Asheville	NC	28801	828-251-5565	251-0846
Web: www.cafeonthesquare.com					
Charlotte Street Grill & Pub 157 Charlotte St	Asheville	NC	28801	828-253-5348	
Web: charlottestreetgrill.com					
Cottonwood Cafe 122 College St	Asheville	NC	28801	828-281-0710	281-3549
Doc Chey's Noodle House 37 Biltmore Ave	Asheville	NC	28801	828-252-8220	
Web: www.doccheys.com					
Gabrielle's 87 Richmond Hill Dr	Asheville	NC	28806	828-252-7313	252-8726
Web: www.richmondhillinn.com/dining.html					
Greenery The 148 Tunnel Rd	Asheville	NC	28805	828-253-2809	254-0645
Web: www.greeneryrestaurant.com					
Heiwa Shokudo 87 N Lexington Ave	Asheville	NC	28801	828-254-7761	
India Garden 156 S Tunnel Rd	Asheville	NC	28805	828-298-5001	298-5007
La Caterina Trattoria 39 Elm St	Asheville	NC	28801	828-254-1148	281-1051
Web: www.lacaterina.com					
Laughing Seed Cafe 40 Wall St	Asheville	NC	28801	828-252-3445	252-0104
Web: www.laughingseed.com					
Magnolia's Raw Bar & Grille 26 Walnut St	Asheville	NC	28801	828-251-5211	
Market Place The 20 Wall St	Asheville	NC	28801	828-252-4162	253-3120
Web: www.marketplace-restaurant.com					
Moose Cafe 570 Brevard Rd	Asheville	NC	28806	828-255-0920	255-0042
Rio Burrito 11 Broadway Ave	Asheville	NC	28801	828-253-2422	
Ristorante da Vincenzo 10 N Market St	Asheville	NC	28801	828-254-4698	
Salsa 6 Patton Ave	Asheville	NC	28801	828-252-9805	252-9805
Savoy Restaurant & Martini Bar 641 Merrimon Ave	Asheville	NC	28804	828-253-1077	252-6776
Web: www.savoyasheville.com					
Sorrento 875 Tunnel Rd	Asheville	NC	28805	828-299-1928	
Southside Cafe 1800 Hendersonville Rd	Asheville	NC	28803	828-274-4413	274-4910
Sunset Terrace 290 Macon Ave	Asheville	NC	28804	828-252-2711	252-6442
Web: www.groveparkinn.com					
Tripps 311 College St	Asheville	NC	28801	828-254-9163	252-8448
Tupelo Honey Cafe 12 College St	Asheville	NC	28801	828-255-4863	255-4864
Web: www.tupelohoneycafe.com					
Yoshida Japanese Steak House 4 Regent Park Blvd	Asheville	NC	28806	828-252-5903	258-3514
Zambra! 85 W Walnut St	Asheville	NC	28801	828-232-1060	
Web: www.zambratapas.com					
Baoding 4722 Sharon Rd Suite F	Charlotte	NC	28210	704-552-8899	552-8828
Barrington's 7822 Fairview Rd	Charlotte	NC	28226	704-364-5755	364-5732
Web: www.barringtonsrestaurant.com					
Big Ben British Pub & Restaurant 801 Providence Rd	Charlotte	NC	28207	704-334-6338	334-6233
Web: bigbenpub.com					
Bill Spoon's Barbecue 5524 South Blvd	Charlotte	NC	28217	704-525-8865	
Blue 206 N College St	Charlotte	NC	28202	704-927-2583	927-0555
Web: www.bluecharlotte.com					
Bonterra Dining & Wine Room 1829 Cleveland Ave	Charlotte	NC	28203	704-333-9463	372-9463
Web: www.bonterradining.com					
Caffe Siena 230 N College St	Charlotte	NC	28202	704-602-2750	376-4921
Web: www.caffesienacharlotte.com					
Cajun Queen 1800 E 7th St	Charlotte	NC	28204	704-377-9017	
Web: www.cajunqueen.net					
Carpe Diem 1535 Elizabeth Ave	Charlotte	NC	28204	704-377-7976	377-7975
Web: www.carpediemrestaurant.com					
Charleston House on the Plaza 3128 The Plaza	Charlotte	NC	28205	704-333-4441	
Dakotas 8140 Providence Rd	Charlotte	NC	28277	704-541-9990	541-1163
Web: www.dakotasdining.com					
Greek Isles 200 E Bland St	Charlotte	NC	28203	704-444-9000	373-2883
Web: www.greekislesrestaurant.com					
Ilios Noche 11508 Providence Rd	Charlotte	NC	28277	704-814-9882	
Jaimama Restaurant 1626 East Blvd	Charlotte	NC	28203	704-358-8188	
Web: www.jaimamarestaurant.com					
Latorre's 118 W 5th St	Charlotte	NC	28202	704-377-4448	377-4449
Web: www.latorresrestaurant.com					
LaVecchia's Seafood Grille 225 E 6th St	Charlotte	NC	28202	704-370-6776	370-0016
Web: www.lavecchias.com					
Luce Ristorante & Bar 214 N Tryon St	Charlotte	NC	28202	704-344-9222	
Web: www.luceristorante.net/					
Mama Ricotta's 601 S Kings Dr	Charlotte	NC	28204	704-343-0148	377-7461
McCormick & Schmick's 200 S Tryon St	Charlotte	NC	28202	704-377-0201	377-0208
Web: www.mccormickandschmicks.com					
McIntosh's Steak & Seafood 1812 South Blvd	Charlotte	NC	28203	704-342-1088	335-0063
Web: www.mcintoshs1.com					
McNinch House 511 N Church St	Charlotte	NC	28202	704-332-6159	376-0212
Web: www.mcninchhouserestaurant.com					
Melting Pot The 901 S Kings Dr	Charlotte	NC	28204	704-334-4400	334-0535
Web: www.meltingpot.com					
Mert's Heart & Soul 214 N College St	Charlotte	NC	28202	704-342-4222	342-4499
Web: www.merts.com					
Mickey & Mooch 8128 Providence Rd Suite 1200	Charlotte	NC	28277	704-752-8080	752-8822
Web: www.mickeyandmooch.com					
Mimosa Grill 327 S Tryon St	Charlotte	NC	28202	704-343-0700	343-9002
Web: www.mimosagrill.com					
Miro 7804A Red Rd Suite A	Charlotte	NC	28277	704-540-7374	540-7388
Web: www.mirospanishgrille.com					
Morton's The Steakhouse 227 W Trade St	Charlotte	NC	28202	704-333-2602	333-3204
Web: www.mortons.com					
Musashi 10110 Johnston Rd	Charlotte	NC	28210	704-543-5181	
Web: www.musashi-nc.com					
Nikko 1300-F South Blvd	Charlotte	NC	28203	704-370-0100	
Web: www.nikkosushibar.net/					
Noble's 6801 Morrison Blvd	Charlotte	NC	28211	704-367-9463	367-9443
Web: www.noblesrestaurants.com					
Old Hickory House Restaurant 6538 N Tryon St	Charlotte	NC	28213	704-596-8014	596-0922
Palm The 6705-B Phillips Place Ct	Charlotte	NC	28210	704-552-7256	552-9313
Web: www.thepalm.com					
Patou French Bistro 1315 East Blvd	Charlotte	NC	28203	704-376-2233	376-8658
Web: www.patoubistro.com					
Pewter Rose 1820 South Blvd	Charlotte	NC	28203	704-332-8149	333-7075
Web: pewterose.com					
PF Chang's China Bistro 6809 Phillips Place Ct	Charlotte	NC	28210	704-552-6644	552-9909
Web: www.pfchangs.com					
Pho 98 5937 South Blvd	Charlotte	NC	28217	704-643-1243	643-1307
Portofino 3124 Eastway Dr	Charlotte	NC	28205	704-568-7933	
Restaurant i 1524 East Blvd	Charlotte	NC	28203	704-333-8118	
Web: www.restaurant-i.com					
Salute 613 Providence Rd	Charlotte	NC	28207	704-343-9095	
Senor Tequila 6414 Rea Rd	Charlotte	NC	28277	704-543-0706	
Sonoma 100 N Tryon St	Charlotte	NC	28202	704-377-1333	322-1134
Web: www.sonomarestaurants.net					
Sullivan's Steakhouse 1928 South Blvd	Charlotte	NC	28203	704-335-8228	333-8797
Web: www.sullivansteakhouse.com					
Taverna 100 100 N Tryon St	Charlotte	NC	28202	704-344-0515	344-4773
Web: www.taverna100.com					
Thai Orchid 4223 Providence Rd	Charlotte	NC	28211	704-364-1134	
Web: www.thaiorchidcharlotte.com					
Tomi 7741 Colony Rd	Charlotte	NC	28226	704-759-1288	
Toscana 6401 Morrison Blvd	Charlotte	NC	28211	704-367-1808	367-0854
town 710 W Trade St	Charlotte	NC	28202	704-379-7555	379-7580
Upstream 6902 Phillips Place Ct	Charlotte	NC	28210	704-556-7730	552-2793
Web: www.upstreamit.com					
Villa Antonio 4707 South Blvd	Charlotte	NC	28217	704-523-1594	523-5697
Web: www.villaantonio.com					
Volare Ristorante Italiano 1523 Elizabeth Ave	Charlotte	NC	28204	704-370-0208	370-2584
Web: www.volareristoranteitaliano.com					
Woodlands Pure Vegetarian 7128A Albemarle Rd	Charlotte	NC	28227	704-569-9193	
Web: www.woodlands-usa.com					
Zebra 4521 Sharon Rd	Charlotte	NC	28211	704-442-9525	442-9546
Web: www.zebrarestaurant.net					
Another Thyme 109 N Gregson St	Durham	NC	27701	919-682-5225	
Web: www.anotherthyme.com					
Bennett Pointe Grill 4625 Hillsborough Rd	Durham	NC	27705	919-382-9431	382-8073
Web: www.bpgrill.com					
Blue Corn Cafe 716-B 9th St	Durham	NC	27705	919-286-9600	416-0862
Web: www.bluecorn-tosca.com					
Bullock's Bar-B-Que 3330 Quebec Dr	Durham	NC	27705	919-383-3211	383-6202
Web: www.bullocksbbq.com					
Cafe Parizade 2200 W Main St	Durham	NC	27705	919-286-9712	416-9706
Web: www.parizaderestaurant.com					
Cosmic Cantina 1920 1/2 Perry St	Durham	NC	27705	919-286-1875	416-9575
Dillard's Bar-B-Que 3921 Fayetteville St	Durham	NC	27713	919-544-1587	364-3410
Web: www.dillardsbarbecue.com					
El Rodeo 4215 University Dr	Durham	NC	27707	919-402-9190	
Elmo's Diner 776 9th St	Durham	NC	27705	919-416-3823	416-1246
Web: www.elmosdiner.com					
Fairview Restaurant 3001 Cameron Blvd	Durham	NC	27705	919-493-6699	681-3514
Fishmonger's 806 W Main St	Durham	NC	27701	919-682-0128	
Web: www.fishmongers.net					
Four Square 2701 Chapel Hill Rd	Durham	NC	27707	919-401-9877	401-9878
Web: www.foursquarerestaurant.com					
George's Garage 737 9th St	Durham	NC	27705	919-286-4131	286-4950
Web: www.food-passion.com/George'sGarage					
Hog Heaven Bar-B-Q 2419 Guess Rd	Durham	NC	27705	919-286-7447	286-2829
Web: www.hogheavenbarbecue.com					
Jamaica Jamaica 4853 Hwy 55	Durham	NC	27713	919-544-1532	
Kanki Japanese House of Steaks 3504 Mt Moriah Rd	Durham	NC	27707	919-401-6908	401-6843
Web: www.kanki.com					
Kemp's Seafood House 115 Page Point Cir	Durham	NC	27703	919-957-7155	957-0758
Kurama Seafood & Steakhouse 3644 Chapel Hill Blvd	Durham	NC	27707	919-489-2669	
Web: www.kuramarestaurants.com					
Magnolia Grill 1002 9th St	Durham	NC	27705	919-286-3609	
Web: www.magnoliagrill.net					
Nana's 2514 University Dr	Durham	NC	27707	919-493-8545	403-8487
Web: www.nanasdurham.com					
Neo-China 4015 University Dr	Durham	NC	27707	919-489-2828	489-9898
Web: www.neo-china.com					
Pao Lim Asian Bistro & Bar 2505 Durham Chapel Hill Blvd	Durham	NC	27707	919-419-1771	419-1772
Web: www.paolim.net					
Papas Grill 1821 Hillandale Rd	Durham	NC	27705	919-383-8502	382-9529
Web: www.papasgrille.com					
Pop's Italian Trattoria 810 W Peabody St	Durham	NC	27701	919-956-7677	688-0098
Web: www.pops-durham.com					
Q Shack The 2510 University Dr	Durham	NC	27707	919-402-4227	
Restaurant Starlu 3211 Shannon Rd	Durham	NC	27707	919-489-1500	
Web: www.starlu.com					
Satisfaction Restaurant 905 W Main St Brightleaf Square	Durham	NC	27701	919-682-7397	682-6642
Web: satisfaction.citysearch.com					
Shanghai Restaurant 3433 Hillsborough Rd	Durham	NC	27705	919-383-7581	
Web: shanghai.citysearch.com					
Shiki Sushi 207 W Hwy 54	Durham	NC	27713	919-484-4108	484-4168
Web: www.shikisushionline.com					
Spice & Curry 2105 E Hwy 54	Durham	NC	27713	919-544-7555	544-7110
Web: www.spicencurry.net					
Torero's 800 W Main St	Durham	NC	27701	919-682-4197	682-2662
Tosca Ristorante Italiano 604 W Morgan St	Durham	NC	27701	919-680-6333	
Web: www.bluecorn-tosca.com/tr_home.asp					
Vin Rouge Bistro 2010 Hillsborough Rd	Durham	NC	27705	919-416-0406	
Web: www.vinrougerestaurant.com					
Acropolis Restaurant 416 N Eugene St	Greensboro	NC	27401	336-273-3306	273-3353
Anton's 1628 Battleground Ave	Greensboro	NC	27408	336-273-1386	273-1225
Asahi 4520 W Market St	Greensboro	NC	27407	336-855-8883	
Bangkok Cafe 1203-C S Holden Rd	Greensboro	NC	24707	336-855-9370	
Bert's Seafood Grille 4608 W Market St	Greensboro	NC	27407	336-854-2314	297-4885
Web: www.bertsseafood.com					
Bianca's 1901 Spring Garden St	Greensboro	NC	27403	336-273-8114	
Web: www.biancasitalianrestaurant.com					
Binh Minh 5211-C W Market St	Greensboro	NC	27409	336-851-1527	851-1552
Boba House 332 S Tate St	Greensboro	NC	27403	336-379-7444	
Web: www.bobahouse.com					
Bonefish Grill 2100 Koury Blvd	Greensboro	NC	27407	336-851-8900	851-8910
Web: www.bonefishgrill.com					
Cafe Pasta 305 State St	Greensboro	NC	27408	336-272-1308	
Web: www.cafepasta.com					
Casaldi's Cafe 1310 Westover Terr	Greensboro	NC	27408	336-379-8191	379-0341
Web: www.casaldiscafe.com					
Cooper's Ale House 5340 W Market St	Greensboro	NC	27409	336-294-0575	292-8603
Web: www.coopers-ale-house.com					
Darryl's 3300 High Point Rd	Greensboro	NC	27407	336-294-1781	294-2242
Frosty's Barbeque 4836 Summit Ave	Greensboro	NC	27405	336-375-4089	954-5476
Gate City Chop House 106 S Holden Rd	Greensboro	NC	27407	336-294-9977	294-1048
Web: www.gatecitychophouse.com					
George K's Continental Cuisine 2108 Cedar Fork Dr	Greensboro	NC	27407	336-854-0007	854-7841
Web: www.georgeks.net					
Green Valley Grill 622 Green Valley Rd	Greensboro	NC	27408	336-854-2015	544-9000
Web: www.greenvalleygrill.com					
Greenhouse Restaurant 3927-B High Point Rd	Greensboro	NC	27407	336-852-2244	
Hugo's Food Sports & Spirits 3011-A Spring Garden St	Greensboro	NC	27403	336-852-9421	852-7061
Web: www.hugosmenu.com					

	City	State	Zip	Phone	Fax
India Palace 413 Tate St.	Greensboro	NC	27403	336-379-0744	
Web: www.indiapalacegreensboro.com					
Kabob & Curry 3008 High Point Rd	Greensboro	NC	27403	336-297-9544	
Leblon 4512 W Market St	Greensboro	NC	27407	336-294-2605	294-2606
Web: www.leblonbraziliansteakhouse.com					
Liberty Oak Wine & Cheese 100D W Washington St.	Greensboro	NC	27041	336-273-7057	273-7111
Web: www.libertyoakrestaurant.com					
Lucky 32 1421 Westover Terr	Greensboro	NC	27408	336-370-0707	574-0037
Web: www.lucky32.com					
Mahi's Seafood Grill 4721 Lawndale Dr.	Greensboro	NC	27455	336-282-8112	
Marisol 5834 High Point Rd	Greensboro	NC	27407	336-852-3303	852-0347
Web: www.themarisol.com					
Melting Pot The 2924 Battleground Ave.	Greensboro	NC	27408	336-545-6233	545-6449
Web: www.meltingpot.com					
Monterrey 3724 Battleground Ave.	Greensboro	NC	27410	336-282-5588	282-7794
Rearn Thai Restaurant 5120 W Market St	Greensboro	NC	27409	336-292-5901	
Red Oak Browing Pub 714 Francis King St.	Greensboro	NC	27410	336-299-3649	
Revival Grill 604 Milner Dr	Greensboro	NC	27410	336-297-0950	297-4606
Web: www.revivalgrill.com					
Saigon 4205 High Point Rd	Greensboro	NC	27407	336-294-9286	294-9994
Web: www.saigonrestaurant.net					
Sapporo Japanese Steak House 2939 C Battleground Ave	Greensboro	NC	27408	336-282-5345	282-5379
Solaris Tapas Restaurant & Bar 125 Summit Ave.	Greensboro	NC	27401	336-378-0198	378-4459
Southern Lights 105 Smyres Pl	Greensboro	NC	27403	336-379-9414	273-3875
Stamey's Barbecue 2206 High Point Rd.	Greensboro	NC	27403	336-299-9888	294-2599
Web: www.stameys.com					
Taste of Thai 1500 Mill St	Greensboro	NC	27408	336-273-1318	273-0180
Web: www.tasteofthairestaurant.net					
Undercurrent The 600 S Elm St	Greensboro	NC	27406	336-370-1266	
Web: www.undercurrentrestaurant.com					
Village Tavern 1903 Westridge Rd	Greensboro	NC	27410	336-282-3063	545-1953
Web: www.villagetavern.com					
Villarosa Italian Restaurant & Grill 6010 Landmark Center Blvd.	Greensboro	NC	27407	336-294-8688	294-8688
Web: www.villarosaitalian.com					
Lucky 32 832 Spring Forest Rd.	North Raleigh	NC	27609	919-876-9932	876-1744
Web: www.lucky32.com					
518 West 518 W Jones St.	Raleigh	NC	27603	919-829-2518	829-0248
Web: www.518west.com					
Angus Barn 9401 Glenwood Ave	Raleigh	NC	27617	919-781-2444	783-5568
Web: www.angusbarn.com					
Bella Monica 3121-103 Edwards Mill Rd	Raleigh	NC	27612	919-881-9778	881-1241
Web: www.bellamonica.com					
Bistro 607 607 Glenwood Ave.	Raleigh	NC	27603	919-828-0840	
Web: www.bistro607.com					
Bloomsbury Bistro 509-101 W Whitaker Mill Rd	Raleigh	NC	27608	919-834-9011	834-9096
Web: www.bloomsburybistro.com					
Cafe Cyclo 2020 Cameron St	Raleigh	NC	27605	919-829-3773	
Web: www.cafecyclo.com					
Caffe Luna 136 E Hargett St	Raleigh	NC	27601	919-832-6090	832-0176
Web: cafeluna.com					
Cappers 4421 Six Forks Rd.	Raleigh	NC	27609	919-787-8963	878-8979
Carvers Creek 2711 Capital Blvd.	Raleigh	NC	27604	919-872-2300	
Web: www.carverscreek.com					
Cooper's Barbeque 109 E Davie St.	Raleigh	NC	27601	919-832-7614	
Dalat 2109-120 Avent Ferry Rd.	Raleigh	NC	27606	919-832-7449	832-9620
Duck & Dumpling The 222 S Blount St	Raleigh	NC	27601	919-838-0085	838-0087
Web: www.theduckanddumpling.com					
Enoteca Vin 410 Glenwood Ave Suite 350	Raleigh	NC	27603	919-834-3070	
Web: www.enotecavin.com					
Est! Est! Est! 19 W Hargett St	Raleigh	NC	27601	919-890-4500	834-4998
Web: www.estest.com					
Fins 7713 Lead Mine Rd Suite 39.	Raleigh	NC	27615	919-847-4119	
Frazier's Bistro 2418 Hillsborough St.	Raleigh	NC	27607	919-828-6699	821-2489
Web: www.fraziersbistro.com					
Irregardless Cafe 901 W Morgan St.	Raleigh	NC	27603	919-833-8898	
Kanki Japanese House of Steaks 4500 Old Wake Forest Rd	Raleigh	NC	27609	919-876-4157	876-7699
Web: www.kanki.com					
Melting Pot The 3100 Wake Forest Rd.	Raleigh	NC	27609	919-878-0477	878-0815
Web: www.meltingpot.com					
Nana's Chophouse 328 W Davie St.	Raleigh	NC	27601	919-829-1212	
Web: www.nanaschophouse.com					
Neo China of Raleigh 6602 Glenwood Ave.	Raleigh	NC	27612	919-783-8383	783-8353
Web: www.neo-china.com					
Nina's 8801 Lead Mine Rd	Raleigh	NC	27615	919-845-1122	
PF Chang's China Bistro 4325 Glenwood Ave	Raleigh	NC	27612	919-787-7754	787-7683
Web: www.pfchangs.com					
Prime Only Steak & Seafood 13200 Strickland Rd	Raleigh	NC	27613	919-844-1216	844-1219
Web: www.primeonly.com					
Red Palace 3945 New Bern Ave	Raleigh	NC	27610	919-231-3788	231-8143
Rey's 1130 Buck Jones Rd	Raleigh	NC	27606	919-380-0122	380-0411
Web: www.reysrestaurant.com					
Ristorante Cinelli 7361 Six Forks Rd	Raleigh	NC	27615	919-844-8160	844-8235
Web: www.cinellis.com					
Ruth's Chris Steakhouse 2010 Renaissance Park Pl	Raleigh	NC	27513	919-677-0033	677-8633
Web: www.ruthschris.com					
Saint-Jacques 6112 Falls of the Neuse Rd	Raleigh	NC	27609	919-862-2770	862-2771
Second Empire 330 Hillsborough St	Raleigh	NC	27603	919-829-3663	
Web: www.second-empire.com					
ShabaShabu 3080 Wake Forest Rd	Raleigh	NC	27609	919-501-7755	501-7479
Sullivan's Steakhouse 414 Glenwood Ave Suite 103	Raleigh	NC	27603	919-833-2888	833-2889
Web: www.sullivansteakhouse.com					
Sushi Blues 301 Glenwood Ave.	Raleigh	NC	27603	919-664-8061	664-8070
Web: sushibluescafe.com					
Underground 861 W Morgan St	Raleigh	NC	27603	919-664-8704	
Web: www.comeunderground.com					
Waraji 5910 Duraleigh Rd Suite 147	Raleigh	NC	27612	919-783-1883	783-0693
Zely & Ritz 301 Glenwood Ave	Raleigh	NC	27603	919-828-0018	828-2937
Web: www.zelyandritz.com					
1703 1703 Robin Hood Rd	Winston-Salem	NC	27104	336-725-5767	725-5768
Arigato Japanese Steak House 585 Bethesda St	Winston-Salem	NC	27103	336-765-7798	765-4053
Bayberry The 420 High St.	Winston-Salem	NC	27101	336-777-3000	
Bernardin's 373 Jonestown Rd	Winston-Salem	NC	27104	336-768-9365	
Web: www.bernardinsfinedining.com					
Cha-Da Thai 420-J Jonestown Rd.	Winston-Salem	NC	27104	336-659-8466	659-8458
East China 216 Summit Square Blvd	Winston-Salem	NC	27105	336-377-9191	
Fabian's 1100 Reynolda Rd	Winston-Salem	NC	27104	336-723-7700	
Forsyth Seafood Cafe 108 ML King Dr.	Winston-Salem	NC	27101	336-748-0793	
Franco's 420 Jonestown Rd	Winston-Salem	NC	27104	336-659-7778	659-7778
Hill's Lexington Barbecue 4005 Patterson Ave	Winston-Salem	NC	27105	336-767-2184	
Ishi 121 Stark St	Winston-Salem	NC	27103	336-774-0433	774-0451
Joanie B's Family Restaurant 6110 University Pkwy.	Winston-Salem	NC	27105	336-377-9914	
Mayflower Seafood Restaurant 850 Peters Creek Pkwy	Winston-Salem	NC	27103	336-725-3261	725-2555
Midtown Cafe & Dessertery 151 S Stratford Rd	Winston-Salem	NC	27104	336-724-9800	724-9830
Web: www.midtowncafedelivery.com					
Monterrey 3028 Healy Dr	Winston-Salem	NC	27103	336-765-2933	
Newab Indian Cuisine 129 S Stratford Rd	Winston-Salem	NC	27104	336-725-3949	725-8434
Newtown Bistro & Bar 420 Jonestown Rd Suite U	Winston-Salem	NC	27104	336-659-8062	659-9835
Web: www.newtownbistro.com					
Noble's Grill 380 Knollwood St.	Winston-Salem	NC	27103	336-777-8477	777-0322
Web: www.noblesrestaurant.com					
Old Fourth Street Filling Station The 871 W 4th St	Winston-Salem	NC	27101	336-724-7600	724-6300
Web: www.theoldfourthstreetfillingstation.com					
Par 3 Bistro 3870 Bethania Station Rd	Winston-Salem	NC	27106	336-924-5850	
Paul's Fine Italian Dining 3443-B Robinhood Rd	Winston-Salem	NC	27106	336-768-2645	
Ryan's 719 Coliseum Dr	Winston-Salem	NC	27106	336-724-6132	724-5761
Web: www.ryansrestaurant.com					
Sampan Chinese Restaurant 985 Peters Creek Pkwy.	Winston-Salem	NC	27103	336-777-8266	
South by Southwest 241 S Marshall St	Winston-Salem	NC	27101	336-727-0800	
Web: www.triaddiner.com					
Sweet Potatoes 529 N Trade St	Winston-Salem	NC	27101	336-727-4844	727-4808
Web: www.sweetpotatoes-arestaurant.com					
Szechuan Palace 3040 Healy Dr.	Winston-Salem	NC	27103	336-768-7123	
Tansoshii 1555 Hanes Mall Blvd	Winston-Salem	NC	27103	336-760-0206	760-0920
Tequila 2802 Reynolda Rd	Winston-Salem	NC	27106	336-727-9547	
Tokyo Japanese Steakhouse 1111 Salisbury Ridge Rd	Winston-Salem	NC	27127	336-722-5009	722-5059
Web: www.tjsteakhouse.com					
Village Tavern 2000 Griffith Rd	Winston-Salem	NC	27103	336-760-8686	774-0001
Web: www.villagetavern.com					
Vincenzo's 3449 Robinhood Rd	Winston-Salem	NC	27106	336-765-3176	
Yacht House 4881 Country Club Rd	Winston-Salem	NC	27104	336-768-3370	760-4144

North Dakota

	City	State	Zip	Phone	Fax
Bistro An American Cafe 1103 E Front Ave	Bismarck	ND	58504	701-224-8800	224-0398
Web: www.bistro1100.com					
Captain Meriwether's Landing 1700 River Rd	Bismarck	ND	58501	701-258-0666	255-1598
China Garden 1929 N Washington St	Bismarck	ND	58501	701-224-0698	
DiDonna's 505 E Bismarck Expy	Bismarck	ND	58504	701-223-0012	
East 40 Chophouse & Tavern 1401 E Interchange Ave	Bismarck	ND	58501	701-258-7222	258-7228
Famous Dave's 401 E Bismarck Expy	Bismarck	ND	58504	701-223-3422	223-2485
Web: www.famousdaves.com					
Fiesta Villa 411 E Main Ave	Bismarck	ND	58501	701-222-8075	222-4255
Fortune Cookie 658 Kirkwood Mall	Bismarck	ND	58504	701-222-1518	222-1519
Hong Kong 1055 E Interstate Ave	Bismarck	ND	58501	701-223-2130	
Jack's Steakhouse 1201 S 12th St.	Bismarck	ND	58504	701-221-9120	221-2264
Web: www.jackssteakhouse.net					
Little Cottage Cafe 2513 E Main Ave	Bismarck	ND	58501	701-223-4949	
Los Amigos 431 S 3rd St	Bismarck	ND	58504	701-223-7580	
Minerva's Restaurant & Bar 1800 N 12th St.	Bismarck	ND	58501	701-222-1402	
North American Steak Buffet 2000 N 12th St	Bismarck	ND	58501	701-223-1107	224-9921
Paradiso 2620 State St	Bismarck	ND	58501	701-224-1111	223-4689
Peacock Alley 422 E Main St	Bismarck	ND	58501	701-255-7917	255-7231
Web: www.peacock-alley.com					
Seasons Cafe 800 S 3rd St	Bismarck	ND	58504	701-258-7700	224-8212
Space Aliens Grill & Bar 1304 E Century Ave	Bismarck	ND	58503	701-223-6220	223-2252
Web: www.spacealiens.cc					
Walrus The 1136 Arrowhead Plaza	Bismarck	ND	58502	701-250-0020	
Wood House Restaurant 1825 N 13th St	Bismarck	ND	58501	701-255-3654	
Bison Turf 1211 N University Dr	Fargo	ND	58102	701-235-9118	
Cafe Aladdin 530 6th Ave N	Fargo	ND	58102	701-298-0880	
Giant Panda 1331 Gateway Dr S	Fargo	ND	58103	701-298-8558	237-4511
Granite City 1636 42nd St SW	Fargo	ND	58103	701-293-3000	492-0724
Web: www.gcfb.com					
Great Wall 1617 University Dr S	Fargo	ND	58103	701-232-8288	
Juano's 402 Broadway	Fargo	ND	58102	701-232-3123	241-9085
Lone Star Steakhouse & Saloon 4328 13th Ave SW	Fargo	ND	58103	701-282-6642	282-6275
Web: www.lonestarsteakhouse.com					
Mexican Village 814 Main Ave	Fargo	ND	58103	701-293-0120	298-2911
Web: www.fargoweb.com/mexicanvillage/					
Mr Steak 1150 36th St S	Fargo	ND	58103	701-232-2400	
Nine Dragons Restaurant 3228 13th Ave SW	Fargo	ND	58103	701-232-2411	232-9312
Paradiso 801 38th St SW	Fargo	ND	58103	701-282-5747	281-8570
Royal Fork Buffet Restaurant 4325 13th Ave S	Fargo	ND	58103	701-282-9539	281-2938
Santa Lucia 1109 38th St S	Fargo	ND	58103	701-281-8656	
Web: www.santaluciainc.com					
Seasons at Rose Creek 1500 Rose Creek Pkwy E	Fargo	ND	58104	701-235-5000	235-3010
Web: www.seasonsatrosecreek.com					
Shang Hai 3051 25th St SW	Fargo	ND	58103	701-280-5818	232-9433
Space Aliens Grill & Bar 1840 45th St SW	Fargo	ND	58103	701-281-2033	282-0956
Web: www.spacealiens.cc					
Timberlodge Steakhouse 1111 38th St SW	Fargo	ND	58103	701-282-8990	282-8987
Web: www.timberlodgesteakhouse.com					
Trollwood Cafe 3105 N Broadway	Fargo	ND	58102	701-237-6593	
Valley Kitchen Restaurant 3535 Main Ave.	Fargo	ND	58103	701-237-0731	364-9165
Bronze Boot Steakhouse & Lounge 1804 N Washington St	Grand Forks	ND	58203	701-746-5433	
Web: www.bronzeboot.com					
China Garden 2550 32nd Ave S	Grand Forks	ND	58201	701-772-0660	
Eagle's Crest Grill 5301 S Columbia Rd.	Grand Forks	ND	58201	701-787-3491	787-3494
Emerald Grill 1200 47th St N	Grand Forks	ND	58203	701-780-0888	780-0866
GF Goodribs 4223 12th Ave N	Grand Forks	ND	58203	701-746-7115	775-1051
Italian Moon 810 S Washington St	Grand Forks	ND	58201	701-772-7277	335-2493
Web: www.gcfb.com					
Paradiso 905 S Washington St	Grand Forks	ND	58201	701-772-3000	772-7848
Web: www.paradiso.com					
Red Pepper 1011 University Ave	Grand Forks	ND	58203	701-775-9671	746-7268
Web: www.redpepper.com					
Royal Fork Buffet 2800 S Columbia Rd	Grand Forks	ND	58201	701-746-0869	746-0925
Sanders 1907 22 S 3rd St	Grand Forks	ND	58201	701-746-8970	
Web: www.sanders1907.com					
Shangri-La Restaurant 4220 5th Ave N	Grand Forks	ND	58203	701-775-5549	
Suite 49 2950 10th Ave N	Grand Forks	ND	58203	701-746-8966	746-5043
Web: www.suite49.com					

Nova Scotia

	City	Prov.	Postal Code	Phone	Fax
Anatolia Turkish Cuisine 1518 Dresden Row	Halifax	NS	B3J2K2	902-492-4568	492-0851
Baan Thai 1569 Dresden Row 2nd Fl	Halifax	NS	B3J2K4	902-446-4301	
Bish World Cuisine 1475 Lower Water St	Halifax	NS	B3J3Z2	902-425-7993	
Cafe Chianti 5165 South St	Halifax	NS	B3J2A6	902-423-7471	422-9801
Web: www.cafechianti.ca					
Chives 1537 Barrington St.	Halifax	NS	B3J1Z4	902-420-9626	422-7238
Web: www.chives.ca					
Cousin's 3545 Robie St	Halifax	NS	B3K4S7	902-455-8931	
Web: www.cousinsrestaurant.tk					
Da Maurizio 1496 Lower Water St	Halifax	NS	B3J1R7	902-423-0859	496-5913
Web: www.damaurizio.ca					
Dharma Sushi 1576 Argyle St	Halifax	NS	B3J2B3	902-425-7785	425-7290
Economy Shoe Shop Cafe & Bar 1663 Argyle St	Halifax	NS	B3J2B5	902-423-7463	423-5880

Nova Scotia (Cont'd)

Restaurant	City	Prov	Postal Code	Phone	Fax
Fid 1569 Dresden Row	Halifax	NS	B3J2K4	902-422-9162	422-0018
Five Fishermen 1740 Argyle St	Halifax	NS	B3J2W1	902-422-4421	422-4503
Web: www.fivefishermen.com					
Great Wall 1649 Bedford Row	Halifax	NS	B3J1T1	902-422-6153	
Web: www.thegreatwall.ca					
Halliburton House Inn 5184 Morris St	Halifax	NS	B3J1B3	902-420-0658	423-2324
Web: www.thehalliburton.com					
Hamachi House 5190 Morris St	Halifax	NS	B3J1B3	902-425-7711	484-7868
Web: www.hamachihouse.com					
I Love Sushi 5232 Blowers St	Halifax	NS	B3J1J7	902-429-6168	
Jane's on the Common 2394 Robie St	Halifax	NS	B3K4M7	902-431-5683	
Web: www.janesonthecommon.com					
Keg The 1712 Market St	Halifax	NS	B3J2E3	902-425-8355	492-9792
Web: www.kegsteakhouse.com					
McKelvie's 1680 Lower Water St	Halifax	NS	B3J1S4	902-421-6161	425-8949
Web: www.mckelvies.ca					
Mexicali Rosa's 5680 Spring Garden Rd	Halifax	NS	B3J1H5	902-422-7672	
Mexico Lindo 3635 Dutch Village Rd	Halifax	NS	B3N2T1	902-445-0996	
Montana's Cook House & Bar 194B Chain Lake Dr	Halifax	NS	B3S1C5	902-450-1011	
Web: www.montanas.ca					
Murphy's on the Water 1751 Lower Water St	Halifax	NS	B3J3E4	902-420-1015	423-7942
Web: www.murphysonthewater.com					
Onyx Dining Room & Cocktail Bar 5680 Spring Garden Rd	Halifax	NS	B3J1H5	902-428-5680	428-5175
Web: www.onyxdining.com					
Opa! Greek Taverna 1565 Argyle St	Halifax	NS	B3J2B2	902-492-7999	431-9310
Web: www.opataverna.com					
Satisfaction Feast & Vegetarian Restaurant 1581 Grafton St	Halifax	NS	B3J2C3	902-422-3540	429-5234
Web: www.satisfactionfeast.com					
Sweet Basil Bistro 1866 Upper Water St	Halifax	NS	B3J1S8	902-425-2133	
Taj Mahal 5175 South St	Halifax	NS	B3J1A2	902-492-8251	
Web: www.tajmahal7wonders.com					
Trinity 1333 South Park St	Halifax	NS	B3J2K9	902-423-8428	425-3379
Wooden Monkey 1685 Argyle St	Halifax	NS	B3J2B5	902-444-3844	444-3693
Web: www.thewoodenmonkey.ca					
Your Father's Moustache 5686 Spring Garden Rd	Halifax	NS	B3J1H5	902-423-6766	422-0054
Web: www.yourfathersmoustache.ca					

Ohio

Restaurant	City	State	Zip	Phone	Fax
Bialy's at the Lake 493 Portage Lakes Dr	Akron	OH	44319	330-644-7177	644-1747
Bill Hwang's Restaurant 879 Canton Rd	Akron	OH	44312	330-784-7167	
Bricco 1 W Exchange St	Akron	OH	44308	330-475-1600	475-1604
Web: www.briccoakron.com					
Dakota's Grille 2727 Manchester Rd	Akron	OH	44319	330-848-2426	
Dontino's La Vita Gardens 555 E Cuyahoga Falls Ave	Akron	OH	44310	330-928-9530	
Web: www.dontinos.com					
Duffy's Restaurant 231 Darrow Rd	Akron	OH	44305	330-784-5043	
El Rincon 1485 S Arlington St	Akron	OH	44306	330-785-3724	785-2816
Gasoline Alley 870 N Cleveland Massillon Rd	Akron	OH	44333	330-666-2670	
Gus' Chalet Restaurant 938 E Tallmadge Ave	Akron	OH	44310	330-633-2322	633-8775
House of Hunan 2717 W Market St	Akron	OH	44308	330-253-1888	
Hyde Park Grille 4073 Medina Rd	Akron	OH	44333	330-670-6303	670-6174
Web: www.hydeparkrestaurants.com					
Ido Bar & Grille 1537 S Main St	Akron	OH	44301	330-773-1724	
Web: www.idobar.com					
Jasper's 662 Canton Rd	Akron	OH	44312	330-784-9570	784-9528
Ken Stewart's Grille 1970 W Market St	Akron	OH	44313	330-867-2555	867-5858
Web: www.kenstewartsgrille.com					
Lanning's 826 N Cleveland-Massillon Rd	Akron	OH	44333	330-666-1159	
Web: www.lannings-restaurant.com					
Larry's Main Entrance 1964 W Market St	Akron	OH	44313	330-864-8162	
Luigi's 105 N Main St	Akron	OH	44308	330-253-2999	762-9140
New Era Restaurant 10 Massillon Rd	Akron	OH	44312	330-784-0087	784-7906
Web: www.newerarestaurant.net					
Nick Anthe's 1008 N Main St	Akron	OH	44310	330-929-6425	929-3532
North Side Grill 111 N Main St	Akron	OH	44308	330-434-7625	
Olde Harbor Inn 562 Portage Lakes Dr	Akron	OH	44319	330-644-1664	644-1441
Otani Japanese Seafood & Steakhouse 1684 Merriman Rd	Akron	OH	44313	330-836-1500	
Papa Joe's 1561 Akron Peninsula Rd	Akron	OH	44313	330-923-7999	923-8009
Parasson's Italian Restaurant 501 N Main St	Akron	OH	44310	330-376-2117	724-2118
Platinum Dragon 814 1/2 W Market St	Akron	OH	44303	330-434-8108	434-1908
Two Amigos 804 W Market St	Akron	OH	44303	330-762-8226	
Vaccaro's Trattoria 1000 Ghent Rd	Akron	OH	44312	330-666-6158	666-4558
Web: www.vaccarostrattoria.com					
Antone's Italian Cafe 4837 Mahoning Ave	Austintown	OH	44515	330-793-0707	793-2857
Scacchetti's Italian Steakhouse 3781 Mahoning Ave	Austintown	OH	44515	330-799-1316	799-1405
Benihana 23611 Chagrin Blvd	Beachwood	OH	44122	216-464-7575	464-7575
Web: www.benihana.com					
Asuka 7381 Market St	Boardman	OH	44512	330-629-8088	629-6880
Blue Moon 79 S Main St	Centerville	OH	45458	937-436-3925	436-3921
Web: www.bluemoonbistro.com					
Ambar 350 Ludlow Ave	Cincinnati	OH	45220	513-281-7000	281-7001
Amol India 354 Ludlow Ave	Cincinnati	OH	45220	513-961-3600	961-3665
Andy's Mediterranean Grille 906 Nassau St	Cincinnati	OH	45206	513-281-9791	
Web: www.andyskabob.com					
Bacall's Cafe 6118 Hamilton Ave	Cincinnati	OH	45224	513-541-8804	541-8145
Web: www.bacallscafe.com					
Ban Thai 792 Eastgate South Dr	Cincinnati	OH	45245	513-752-3200	752-8424
Barresi's 4111 Webster Ave	Cincinnati	OH	45236	513-793-2540	
Web: www.barresis.com					
BBQ Revue 4725 Madison Rd	Cincinnati	OH	45227	513-871-3500	
Web: www.bbqrevue.com					
Beluga 3520 Edwards Rd	Cincinnati	OH	45208	513-533-4444	533-0943
Web: www.belugasushi.com					
Big Art's BBQ 2796 Struble Rd	Cincinnati	OH	45251	513-825-4811	
Boca 3200 Madison Rd	Cincinnati	OH	45209	513-542-2022	321-2366
Web: www.bocarest.com					
Bonefish Grill 2737 Madison Rd	Cincinnati	OH	45209	513-321-5222	321-6102
Web: www.bonefishgrill.com					
Brown Dog Cafe 5893 Pfeiffer Rd	Cincinnati	OH	45242	513-794-1610	794-1613
Web: www.browndogcafe.com					
Celestial Restaurant 1071 Celestial St	Cincinnati	OH	45202	513-241-4455	241-4855
Web: www.thecelestial.com					
China Gourmet 3340 Erie Ave	Cincinnati	OH	45208	513-871-6612	
Cumin 3520 Erie Ave	Cincinnati	OH	45208	513-871-8714	871-3287
Web: www.cuminrestaurant.com					
Daveed's at 934 934 Hatch St	Cincinnati	OH	45202	513-721-2665	721-0185
Delight Thai Cafe & Sushi Bar 11928 Montgomery Rd	Cincinnati	OH	45249	513-677-6175	
Web: www.delighthaicafe.com					
El Coyote 7404 State Rd	Cincinnati	OH	45230	513-232-5757	232-3094
Web: www.elcoyoterestaurant.com					
Grand Finale 3 E Sharon Ave	Cincinnati	OH	45246	513-771-5925	772-3079
Web: www.grandfinale.info					
Hibachi Master 8160 Beechmont Ave	Cincinnati	OH	45255	513-474-9888	
Iron Horse Inn 40 Village Sq	Cincinnati	OH	45246	513-771-4787	
Web: www.ironhorseinn.com					
Jean-Robert at Pigall's 127 W 4th St	Cincinnati	OH	45202	513-721-1345	352-6010
Web: www.jean-robertatpigalls.com					
JeanRo 413 Vine St	Cincinnati	OH	45202	513-621-1465	621-2701
Web: www.bistrojeanro.com					
Jeff Ruby's Steakhouse 700 Walnut St	Cincinnati	OH	45202	513-784-1200	723-4455
Web: jeffruby.com					
Kona Bistro 3012 Madison Rd	Cincinnati	OH	45209	513-842-5662	
Montgomery Inn 9440 Montgomery Rd	Cincinnati	OH	45242	513-791-3482	985-2049
Web: www.montgomeryinn.com					
Morton's The Steakhouse 28 W 4th St	Cincinnati	OH	45202	513-241-4104	241-3666
Web: www.mortons.com					
Mt Adams Fish House 940 Pavilion St	Cincinnati	OH	45202	513-421-3250	421-1446
Web: www.mtadamsfishhouse.com					
Nectar Restaurant 1000 Delta Ave	Cincinnati	OH	45208	513-929-0525	929-0301
Web: www.thenectarrestaurant.com					
Nicholson's Tavern & Pub 625 Walnut St	Cincinnati	OH	45202	513-564-9111	564-0123
Web: www.nicholsonspub.com					
Nicola's 1420 Sycamore St	Cincinnati	OH	45202	513-721-6200	721-1777
Web: nicolasrestaurant.com					
Palace The 601 Vine St	Cincinnati	OH	45202	513-381-6006	651-0256
Web: www.palacecincinnati.com					
Palomino Euro Bistro 505 Vine St	Cincinnati	OH	45202	513-381-1300	381-1303
Web: www.palomino.com					
PF Chang's China Bistro 2633 Edmondson Rd	Cincinnati	OH	45209	513-531-4567	531-4679
Web: www.pfchangs.com					
Precinct The 311 Delta Ave	Cincinnati	OH	45226	513-321-5454	321-8010
Web: jeffruby.com					
Primavista 810 Matson Pl	Cincinnati	OH	45204	513-251-6467	251-4669
Web: www.pvista.com					
Restaurant at the Phoenix 812 Race St	Cincinnati	OH	45202	513-721-8901	721-1475
Web: www.thephx.com/restaurant/					
Shanghai Mama's 216 E 6th St	Cincinnati	OH	45202	513-241-7777	247-1309
Web: www.shanghaimamas.com					
Slims 4046 Hamilton Ave	Cincinnati	OH	45223	513-681-6500	
Web: www.slimsrestaurant.com					
Teak Thai 1049-51 Saint Gregory St	Cincinnati	OH	45202	513-665-9800	665-9861
Tink's Cafe 3410 Telford Ave	Cincinnati	OH	45220	513-961-6500	961-2585
Web: www.tinkscafe.com					
Trio 7565 Kenwood Rd	Cincinnati	OH	45236	513-984-1905	984-3873
Web: www.triobistro.com					
Agostino's 4218 Ridge Rd	Cleveland	OH	44144	216-741-6522	741-7104
Baricelli Inn 2203 Cornell Rd	Cleveland	OH	44106	216-791-6500	791-9131
Web: www.baricelli.com/					
Battuto 12405 Mayfield Rd	Cleveland	OH	44106	216-707-1055	707-1124
Web: www.battuto.net					
Blue Point Grille 700 W St Clair Ave	Cleveland	OH	44113	216-875-7827	902-8175
Bo Loong Restaurant 3922 St Clair Ave	Cleveland	OH	44114	216-391-3113	391-8407
Cafe Limbo 12706 Larchmere Blvd	Cleveland	OH	44120	216-707-3333	
Web: www.cafelimbo.com					
China Jade 2190 Brookpark Rd	Cleveland	OH	44134	216-749-4720	
Don's Lighthouse Grille 8905 Lake Ave	Cleveland	OH	44102	216-961-6700	961-1966
Web: www.donslighthouse.com					
Fahrenheit 2417 Professor Ave	Cleveland	OH	44113	216-781-8858	781-8867
Web: www.fahrenheittremont.com					
Fat Cats 2061 W 10th St	Cleveland	OH	44113	216-579-0200	579-0588
Fire 13220 Shaker Sq	Cleveland	OH	44120	216-921-3473	921-1957
Web: www.firefoodanddrink.com					
Flying Fig 2523 Market St	Cleveland	OH	44113	216-241-4243	241-0255
Web: www.theflyingfig.com					
Frank Sterles Slovenian Restaurant 1401 E 55th St	Cleveland	OH	44103	216-881-4181	
Web: www.sterlescountryhouse.com					
Gene's Place 3730 Rocky River Dr	Cleveland	OH	44111	216-252-1741	252-1742
Ginza Sushi House 1105 Carnegie Ave	Cleveland	OH	44115	216-589-8503	589-9768
Web: www.ginzasushi.com					
Great Lakes Brewing Co 2516 Market Ave	Cleveland	OH	44113	216-771-4404	771-4466
Web: www.greatlakesbrewing.com					
Gusto 12022 Mayfield Rd	Cleveland	OH	44106	216-791-9900	791-9903
Web: www.gustolittleitaly.com					
Harp The 4408 Detroit Ave	Cleveland	OH	44113	216-939-0200	939-0068
Web: www.the-harp.com					
Hyde Park Steakhouse 123 Prospect Ave W	Cleveland	OH	44115	216-344-2444	344-2726
Web: www.hydeparkrestaurants.com					
John Q's Steakhouse 55 Public Sq	Cleveland	OH	44113	216-861-0900	861-1237
Web: www.johnqssteakhouse.com					
Johnny's Bar on Fulton 3164 Fulton Rd	Cleveland	OH	44109	216-281-0055	631-6890
Johnny's Bistro 1400 W 6th St	Cleveland	OH	44113	216-774-0055	623-1248
Johnny's Downtown 1406 W 6th St	Cleveland	OH	44113	216-623-0055	623-1248
Web: www.johnnyscleveland.com					
Lemon Grass 2179 Lee Rd	Cleveland	OH	44118	216-321-0210	321-2180
Web: www.lemongrassrestaurant.net					
Li Wah 2999 Payne Ave	Cleveland	OH	44114	216-696-6556	696-6581
Light Bistro 2801 Bridge Ave	Cleveland	OH	44113	216-771-7130	771-8130
Web: www.lightbistro.com					
Lolita 900 Literary Rd	Cleveland	OH	44113	216-771-5652	771-5633
Web: www.lolabistro.com					
Mallorca 1390 W 9th St	Cleveland	OH	44113	216-687-9494	687-9493
Web: www.mallorcacleveland.com					
Mekong River 1918 Lee Rd	Cleveland	OH	44118	216-371-9575	
Mi Pueblo 11611 Euclid Ave	Cleveland	OH	44106	216-791-8226	791-1676
Momocho 1835 Fulton Rd	Cleveland	OH	44113	216-694-2122	696-7139
Web: www.momocho.com					
Mortons the Steakhouse 1600 W 2nd St	Cleveland	OH	44113	216-621-6200	621-7745
Web: www.mortons.com					
Muse Restaurant 1515 W 3rd St 6th Fl	Cleveland	OH	44113	216-623-1300	623-0515
One Walnut Restaurant 1 Walnut Ave	Cleveland	OH	44114	216-575-1111	579-4349
Web: www.onewalnut.com					
Otani 1625 Golden Gate Plaza	Cleveland	OH	44124	440-442-7098	442-7138
Web: www.otanirestaurant.com					
Parallax 2179 W 11th St	Cleveland	OH	44113	216-583-9999	583-0720
Web: www.parallaxtremont.com					
Pearl of the Orient 20121 Van Aken Blvd	Cleveland	OH	44122	216-751-8181	283-8810
Web: www.pearl-east.com					
Phnom Penh 13124 Lorain Ave	Cleveland	OH	44111	216-251-0210	
Saffron Patch 20600 Chagrin Blvd Suite 150	Cleveland	OH	44122	216-295-0400	295-1320
Sans Souci 24 Public Sq	Cleveland	OH	44113	216-696-5600	696-0432
Web: www.sanssoucicleveland.com					
Sergio's in University Circle 1903 Ford Dr	Cleveland	OH	44106	216-231-1234	231-5700
Web: www.sergioscleveland.com					
Siam Cafe 3951 St Clair Ave	Cleveland	OH	44114	216-361-2323	361-9191
Snicker's Tavern 5800 Detroit Ave	Cleveland	OH	44102	216-631-7555	651-5720
Sun Luck Garden 1901 S Taylor Rd	Cleveland	OH	44118	216-397-7676	289-4554
Sushi 86 144 Euclid Ave	Cleveland	OH	44114	216-621-8686	

Name / Address	City	State	Zip	Phone	Fax
Sushi Rock 1276 W 6th St	Cleveland	OH	44113	216-623-1212	623-1218
Web: www.sushirockohio.com					
Taytu 6125 St Clair Ave	Cleveland	OH	44103	216-391-9400	
Tommy's 1824 Coventry Rd	Cleveland	OH	44118	216-321-7757	321-8377
Web: www.tommyscoventry.com					
Villa Y Zapata 8505 Madison Ave	Cleveland	OH	44102	216-961-4369	961-0574
Vivo 347 Euclid Ave	Cleveland	OH	44114	216-621-4678	621-4802
Web: www.vivo-cleveland.com					
XO 500 W St Claire Ave	Cleveland	OH	44113	216-861-1919	861-0374
Aladdin's Eatery 12447 Cedar Rd	Cleveland Heights	OH	44106	216-932-4333	932-9312
Web: www.aladdinseatery.com					
Cafe Tandoor 2096 S Taylor Rd	Cleveland Heights	OH	44118	216-371-8500	371-8560
Mad Greek 2466 Fairmount Blvd	Cleveland Heights	OH	44106	216-421-3333	421-8821
Web: www.madgreekcleveland.com					
Aladdin's Eatery 2931 N High St	Columbus	OH	43202	614-262-2414	262-2450
Web: www.aladdinseatery.com					
Alana's Food & Wine 2333 N High St	Columbus	OH	43202	614-294-6783	
Web: www.alanas.com					
Anatolia Cafe 1097 Worthington Woods Blvd	Columbus	OH	43085	614-781-0700	
Web: www.anatoliacafe.net					
Anna's 7370 Sawmill Rd	Columbus	OH	43235	614-799-2207	799-2207
Web: www.annasgreekcuisine.com					
Barcelona 263 E Whittier St	Columbus	OH	43206	614-443-3699	444-0539
Web: www.barcelonacolumbus.com					
Barley's Smokehouse & Brewpub 1130 Dublin Rd	Columbus	OH	43215	614-485-0227	485-0166
Web: www.barleysbrewing.com					
Basi Italia 811 Highland St	Columbus	OH	43215	614-294-7383	294-1236
Benevolence 41 W Swan St	Columbus	OH	43215	614-221-9330	
Web: www.benevolencecafe.com					
Brio Tuscan Grille 3993 Easton Station St	Columbus	OH	43219	614-416-4745	416-4747
Web: www.brioitalian.com					
Cafe Istanbul 3983 Worth Ave	Columbus	OH	43219	614-473-9144	473-9133
Web: www.cafeistanbul.com					
Cafe Shish Kebab 1450 Bethel Rd	Columbus	OH	43220	614-273-4444	326-4668
Cap City 1299 Olentangy River Rd	Columbus	OH	43212	614-291-3663	291-0336
Web: www.cameronmitchell.com					
China Dynasty 1689 W Lane Ave	Columbus	OH	43221	614-486-7126	
Web: www.chinadynasty-cmh.com					
Columbus Fish Market 1245 Olentangy River Rd	Columbus	OH	43212	614-291-3474	291-7258
Due Amici 67 E Gay St	Columbus	OH	43215	614-224-9373	227-0015
Web: www.due-amici.com					
El Vaquero 2195 Riverside Dr	Columbus	OH	43221	614-486-4547	486-4050
G Michael's Bistro 595 S 3rd St	Columbus	OH	43215	614-464-0575	
Web: www.gmichaelsbistro.com					
Haiku Poetic Food & Art 800 N High St	Columbus	OH	43215	614-294-8168	294-3868
Web: www.haikupoeticfood.com					
Handke's Cuisine 520 S Front St	Columbus	OH	43215	614-621-2500	621-2626
Web: www.chefhandke.com					
Hunan House 2350 E Dublin Granville Rd	Columbus	OH	43229	614-895-3330	895-3073
Hyde Park Prime Steakhouse 569 N High St	Columbus	OH	43215	614-224-2204	
Indian Oven 427 E Main St	Columbus	OH	43215	614-220-9390	
Web: www.indianoven.com					
J Alexander's 7550 Vantage Dr	Columbus	OH	43235	614-847-1166	847-1332
Web: www.jalexanders.com					
Japanese Steak House 479 N High St	Columbus	OH	43215	614-228-3030	228-0504
Kikyo 3706 Riverside Dr	Columbus	OH	43221	614-457-5277	
L'Antibes 772 N High St Suite 106	Columbus	OH	43215	614-291-1666	
Web: www.melrosecalgary.com					
Latitude 41 50 N 3rd St	Columbus	OH	43215	614-233-7541	
Lemongrass 641 N High St	Columbus	OH	43215	614-224-1414	221-2535
Web: www.lemongrassfusion.com					
Lindey's 169 E Beck St	Columbus	OH	43206	614-228-4343	228-8920
Web: www.lindeys.com					
M 2 Miranova PL	Columbus	OH	43215	614-629-0000	221-5020
Web: www.cameronmitchell.com					
Martini Italian Bistro 445 N High St	Columbus	OH	43215	614-224-8259	224-8780
Web: www.martini-italian-bistro.com					
Mitchell's Ocean Club 4002 Easton Stn	Columbus	OH	43219	614-416-2582	416-2800
Web: www.mitchellsoceanclub.com					
Mitchell's Steakhouse 45 N 3rd St	Columbus	OH	43215	614-621-2333	621-2898
Web: www.cameronmitchell.com					
Morton's The Steakhouse 280 N High St 280 Plaza	Columbus	OH	43215	614-464-4442	464-2940
Web: www.mortons.com					
Otani 5900 Roche Dr	Columbus	OH	43229	614-431-3333	840-9755
Web: www.otanisushi.com					
PF Chang's China Bistro 4040 Townsfair Way	Columbus	OH	43219	614-416-4100	416-4101
Web: www.pfchangs.com					
Refectory 1092 Bethel Rd	Columbus	OH	43220	614-451-9774	451-4434
Web: www.therefectoryrestaurant.com					
Rigsby's Kitchen 698 N High St	Columbus	OH	43215	614-461-7888	228-5639
Web: www.rigsbyskitchen.com					
Rossi Bar & Kitchen 895 N High St	Columbus	OH	43201	614-299-2810	299-2801
Ruth's Chris Steak House 7550 High Cross Blvd	Columbus	OH	43235	614-885-2910	885-5740
Web: www.ruthschris.com					
Schmidt's Sausage Haus 240 E Kossuth St	Columbus	OH	43206	614-444-6808	449-4039
Shoku 1312 Grandview Ave	Columbus	OH	43212	614-485-9490	
Smith & Wollensky 4145 The Strand W	Columbus	OH	43219	614-416-2400	416-2401
Web: www.smithandwollensky.com					
Thai Taste 1178 Kenny Centre Mall	Columbus	OH	43220	614-451-7605	451-7605
Web: www.taste-for-thai.com					
Trattoria Roma 1447 Grandview Ave	Columbus	OH	43212	614-488-2104	488-4452
Web: www.trattoria-roma.com					
Windward Passage 4739 Reed Rd	Columbus	OH	43220	614-451-2497	
Akashi Sushi Bar 2020 Harshman Rd	Dayton	OH	45424	937-233-8005	233-8845
Amber Rose 1400 Valley St	Dayton	OH	45404	937-228-2511	222-0479
Web: www.theamberrose.com					
Barnsider 5202 N Main St	Dayton	OH	45415	937-277-1332	277-0567
Cafe Boulevard 329 E 5th St	Dayton	OH	45402	937-824-2722	824-2810
Web: www.cafeboulevard.com					
Citilites 109 N Main St Suite 305	Dayton	OH	45402	937-222-0623	222-1504
Web: www.citilites.net					
Dublin Pub 300 Wayne Ave	Dayton	OH	45410	937-224-7822	224-0355
Web: www.dubpub.com					
Elsa's 3618 Linden Ave	Dayton	OH	45410	937-252-9635	
Fox & Hound English Pub & Grille 667 Lyons Rd	Dayton	OH	45459	937-432-9904	432-9905
Franco's Ristorante Italiano 824 E 5th St	Dayton	OH	45402	937-222-0204	222-1380
Web: www.francos-italiano.com					
Grub Steak 1410 N Main St	Dayton	OH	45405	937-276-4193	277-3764
I-Zu 5252 N Dixie Dr	Dayton	OH	45414	937-277-9596	
J Alexander's 7970 Washington Village	Dayton	OH	45459	937-435-4441	435-7723
Web: www.jalexanders.com					
Jay's 225 E 6th St	Dayton	OH	45402	937-222-2892	222-7547
Web: www.jays.com					
Las Piramides 101 W Franklin St	Dayton	OH	45459	937-291-0900	291-1910
North China 6090 Far Hills Ave	Dayton	OH	45459	937-433-6837	
Old Hickory 4029 N Main St	Dayton	OH	45405	937-276-2002	276-3001
Pine Club The 1926 Brown St	Dayton	OH	45409	937-228-7463	228-5371
Web: www.thepineclub.com					
Sake 7260 Miller Ln	Dayton	OH	45414	937-898-9834	898-9835
Thai9 11 Brown St	Dayton	OH	45402	937-222-3227	222-3235
Web: www.thai9restaurant.com					
Thai Orchid 7654 Sawmill Rd	Dublin	OH	43017	614-792-1112	792-1115
Web: www.thaiorchidcolumbus.com					
La Petite France 3177 Glendale-Milford Rd	Evendale	OH	45241	513-733-8383	733-0038
Web: www.lapetitefrance.biz					
Max & Erma's 3750 W Market St	Fairlawn	OH	44333	330-666-1002	666-3001
Mama DiSalvo's 1375 E Stroop Rd	Kettering	OH	45429	937-299-5831	299-1752
356th Fighter Group 4919 Mt Pleasant Rd	North Canton	OH	44720	330-494-3500	494-5509
Web: www.starcom2.com/356thFG					
Cousino's Steak House 1842 Woodville Rd	Oregon	OH	43616	419-693-0862	
Web: www.cousinos-restaurants.com/steakhouse					
Avenue Bistro 6710 W Central Ave	Sylvania	OH	43615	419-841-5944	842-1435
Beirut 4082 Monroe St	Toledo	OH	43606	419-473-0885	
Connie Jr's 4330 W Central Ave	Toledo	OH	43615	419-531-3103	
Cousino's Old Navy Bistro 26 Main St	Toledo	OH	43605	419-697-6289	697-6333
Web: www.cousinosnavybistro.com					
Diva 329 N Huron St	Toledo	OH	43604	419-324-0000	242-5709
Dolly & Joe's 1045 S Reynolds St	Toledo	OH	43615	419-385-2441	
Dorr Street Cafe 5243 Dorr St	Toledo	OH	43615	419-531-4446	
Eddie Lee's 4700 Nantucket Dr	Toledo	OH	43623	419-882-0616	
El Camino Real 2500 W Sylvania Ave	Toledo	OH	43613	419-472-0700	
Fifi's 1423 Bernath Pkwy	Toledo	OH	43615	419-866-6777	
Web: www.fifisrestaurant.com					
Fritz & Alfredo's 3025 N Summit St	Toledo	OH	43611	419-729-9775	
Georgio's Cafe International 426 N Superior St	Toledo	OH	43604	419-242-2424	242-2155
Web: www.georgiostoledo.com					
Gumbo's 18 Main St	Toledo	OH	43605	419-697-8700	697-9998
HJ's Prime Cut 505 E Alexis Rd	Toledo	OH	43612	419-476-1616	476-1602
J Alexander's 4315 Talmadge Rd	Toledo	OH	43623	419-474-8620	474-9187
Web: www.jalexanders.com					
Joe's Crab Shack 1435 Baronial Plaza	Toledo	OH	43615	419-866-8877	866-4652
Web: www.joescrabshack.com					
Mancy's 953 Phillips Ave	Toledo	OH	43612	419-476-4154	
Web: www.mancys.com					
Mango Tree 217 S Reynolds Rd	Toledo	OH	43615	419-536-2883	
Manos Greek Restaurant & Bar 1701 Adams St	Toledo	OH	43624	419-244-4479	255-8881
Web: www.manosgreekrestaurant.com					
Marsyl's 2633 Bancroft St	Toledo	OH	43606	419-531-8327	536-7278
Web: www.marsyls.com					
Matthew's Creative Cuisine 4400 Heatherdowns Blvd	Toledo	OH	43614	419-382-2559	
Real Seafood Co 22 Main St	Toledo	OH	43605	419-697-5427	697-4404
Web: www.realseafoodcorestaurant.com					
Rockwell's 27 Broadway	Toledo	OH	43602	419-241-1253	243-9256
Rose Thai 5333 Monroe St	Toledo	OH	43623	419-841-8467	843-6060
Shorty's Bar-B-Cue 5111 Monroe St	Toledo	OH	43623	419-841-9505	843-2158
Web: www.mancys.com/shortys					
Spaghetti Warehouse 42 S Superior St	Toledo	OH	43602	419-255-5038	255-9225
Web: www.meatballs.com					
Thai Kitchen 1515 S Byrne Rd	Toledo	OH	43614	419-380-9333	
Tommy's 5520 W Central Ave	Toledo	OH	43615	419-535-1271	
Tony Packo's 1902 Front St	Toledo	OH	43605	419-691-6054	
Web: www.tonypacko.com/					
Tropics Restaurant & Lounge 1583 Sylvania Ave	Toledo	OH	43612	419-478-8592	
Ventura's 7742 W Bancroft St	Toledo	OH	43617	419-841-7523	
Zia's 20 Main St	Toledo	OH	43605	419-697-7138	697-4565
Web: www.ziasrestaurant.com					
Aladdin's Eatery 7325 South Ave	Youngstown	OH	44512	330-629-6450	629-6453
Web: www.aladdinseatery.com					
Anthony's on the River 15 Oak Hill Ave	Youngstown	OH	44502	330-744-7888	
Blue Light Restaurant & Lounge 3136 Belmont Ave	Youngstown	OH	44505	330-759-8484	
Cancun Restaurant 4055 Belmont Ave	Youngstown	OH	44505	330-759-3301	
Cedars Lounge & Restaurant 23 N Hazel St	Youngstown	OH	44503	330-743-6560	743-9686
Fifth Season 7098 Mahoning Ave	Youngstown	OH	44515	330-799-3483	799-3485
Web: www.fifthseasoninc.com					
Golden Dawn 1245 Logan Ave	Youngstown	OH	44505	330-746-0393	
Golden Hunan Restaurant 3111 Belmont Ave	Youngstown	OH	44505	330-759-7197	
Joe's Restaurant 2921 Belmont Ave	Youngstown	OH	44505	330-759-8890	
Lucianno's Restaurant 1732 S Raccoon Rd	Youngstown	OH	44515	330-792-5975	792-4711
Web: www.luciannosrestaurant.com					
Main Moon 1760 Belmont Ave	Youngstown	OH	44504	330-743-1638	743-8336
Nicolinni's 1912 S Raccoon Rd	Youngstown	OH	44515	330-799-9999	
Web: www.nicolinnis.com					
Riverbend 1105 Poland Ave	Youngstown	OH	44706	330-746-3300	
Station Square Restaurant 4250 Belmont Ave	Youngstown	OH	44505	330-759-8802	
Upstairs 4500 Mahoning Ave	Youngstown	OH	44515	330-793-5577	259-0658
Youngstown Crab Co 3917 Belmont Ave	Youngstown	OH	44505	330-759-5480	759-7811
Web: www.youngstowncrabco.com					
Youngstown Roadhouse 2537 South Ave	Youngstown	OH	44502	330-782-8033	782-9157

Oklahoma

Name / Address	City	State	Zip	Phone	Fax
Ajanta 11921 N Pennsylvania Ave	Oklahoma City	OK	73120	405-752-5283	
Web: www.ajantaokc.com					
Alavarado's 11641 S Western Ave	Oklahoma City	OK	73170	405-692-2007	
Applewoods Restaurant 2747 W Memorial Rd	Oklahoma City	OK	73134	405-752-4484	752-4486
Web: www.applewoodfarmhouserestaurant.com					
Bangkok Restaurant 7906 N MacArthur Blvd	Oklahoma City	OK	73132	405-728-4822	
Bricktown Brewery 1 N Oklahoma Ave	Oklahoma City	OK	73104	405-232-2739	232-0531
Web: www.bricktownbrewery.com					
Cattlemans Steakhouse 1309 S Agnew Ave	Oklahoma City	OK	73108	405-236-0416	235-1969
Charleston's 5907 NW Expressway St	Oklahoma City	OK	73132	405-721-0060	720-0039
Web: www.charlestons.com					
Coach House 6437 Avondale Dr	Oklahoma City	OK	73116	405-842-1000	842-1000
Web: www.restaurant-row.org/coach					
Deep Fork Grill 5418 N Western Ave	Oklahoma City	OK	73118	405-848-7678	840-0624
Web: www.deepforkgrill.com					
Dot Wo 3101 N Portland Ave	Oklahoma City	OK	73112	405-942-1376	
Earl's Rib Place 6816 N Western Ave	Oklahoma City	OK	73116	405-843-9922	
Eddy's of Oklahoma City 4227 N Meridian Ave	Oklahoma City	OK	73112	405-787-2944	
Web: www.eddyssteakhouseokc.com					
Ground Floor Cafe 211 Robinson Leadership Sq	Oklahoma City	OK	73102	405-232-2233	
Haunted House 7101 Miramar Blvd	Oklahoma City	OK	73111	405-478-1417	
Juniors Supper Club 2601 NW Expressway St	Oklahoma City	OK	73112	405-848-5597	848-5850
Web: www.juniorsokc.com					
Kona Ranch Steakhouse 2037 S Meridian Ave	Oklahoma City	OK	73108	405-681-1000	681-0265
Web: www.kona-ranch.com					
Mantel at Bricktown 201 E Sheridan Ave	Oklahoma City	OK	73104	405-236-8040	236-4123
Web: www.themantelokc.com					
Metro Wine Bar & Bistro 6418 N Western Ave	Oklahoma City	OK	73116	405-840-9463	840-5963
Web: www.restaurant-row.org/metro/					

Oklahoma (Cont'd)

Name / Address	City	State	Zip	Phone	Fax
Mickey Mantle's Steakhouse 7 Mickey Mantle Dr.	Oklahoma City	OK	73104	405-272-0777	232-7111
Web: www.mickeymantlesteakhouse.com					
Musashi's Japanese Steakhouse 4315 N Western Ave	Oklahoma City	OK	73118	405-602-5575	602-4474
Web: www.musashis.com					
Papa Dio's 10712 N May Ave	Oklahoma City	OK	73120	405-755-2255	755-5522
Pearl's Oyster Bar 928 NW 63rd St	Oklahoma City	OK	73116	405-848-8008	842-8443
Pelicans 291 N Air Depot Blvd	Oklahoma City	OK	73110	405-732-4392	732-5700
Web: www.pelicansrestaurantokc.com					
PF Chang's China Bistro 13700 N Pennsylvania Ave	Oklahoma City	OK	73134	405-748-4003	748-5247
Web: www.pfchangs.com					
Ranch Steakhouse 3000 W Birtton Rd	Oklahoma City	OK	73120	405-755-3501	751-3134
Web: www.ranchsteakhouse.com					
Redrock Canyon Grill 9221 Lake Hefner Pkwy	Oklahoma City	OK	73120	405-749-1995	749-2556
Web: www.redrockcanyongrill.com					
Royal Bavaria Brewery 3401 S Sooner Rd	Oklahoma City	OK	73165	405-799-7666	
Web: www.royal-bavaria.com					
Shogun Steakhouse 6301 N Meridian Ave	Oklahoma City	OK	73112	405-722-6844	
Sushi Neko 4318 N Western Ave	Oklahoma City	OK	73118	405-528-8862	521-9877
Web: www.sushineko.com					
Ted's Cafe Escondido 2836 NW 68th St	Oklahoma City	OK	73116	405-848-8337	840-5865
Tokyo Japanese Restaurant 7516 N Western Ave	Oklahoma City	OK	73116	405-848-6733	
Web: www.tokyookc.com					
Trapper's Fishcamp & Grill 4300 W Reno St	Oklahoma City	OK	73107	405-943-9111	942-0694
Web: www.funfresh.com/trappers.html					
Zio's Italian Kitchen 2035 S Meridian Ave	Oklahoma City	OK	73108	405-680-9999	685-7740
Web: www.zios.com					
Albert G's Bar-BQ 2748 S Harvard Ave	Tulsa	OK	74114	918-747-4799	747-6438
Web: www.albertgs.com					
Atlantic Sea Grill 8321 E 61st St Suite A	Tulsa	OK	74133	918-252-7966	
Avalon Steak House 6304 S 54th West Ave	Tulsa	OK	74131	918-446-9917	
Web: www.avalonsteakhouse.com					
Big Al's 3303 E 15th St	Tulsa	OK	74112	918-744-5085	
Binh-Le 5903 E 31st St	Tulsa	OK	74135	918-835-7722	
Bodean Seafood Restaurant 3323 E 51st St Suite B	Tulsa	OK	74135	918-743-3861	747-9352
Web: www.bodean.net					
Bourbon Street Cafe 8246 S Lewis Ave	Tulsa	OK	74137	918-298-0000	298-0439
Web: www.bourbonstreetcafe.com					
Brookside by Day 3313 S Peoria Ave	Tulsa	OK	74105	918-745-9989	
Cardigan's in London Square 6000 S Lewis	Tulsa	OK	74105	918-749-9070	712-9843
Casa Laredo 1411 E 41st St	Tulsa	OK	74105	918-743-3744	
Chalkboard The 1324 S Main St	Tulsa	OK	74119	918-582-1964	382-6013
Web: www.thechalkboard-tulsa.com					
Chimi's 1304 E 15th St	Tulsa	OK	74120	918-587-4411	587-0402
Doe's Eat Place 1350 E 15th St	Tulsa	OK	74120	918-585-3637	585-9309
Web: www.doestulsa.com					
Flavors 6104 E 71st St	Tulsa	OK	74136	918-492-7767	
Web: www.flavorsrestaurant.com					
Fleming's Prime Steakhouse & Wine Bar 1976 E 21st St South	Tulsa	OK	74114	918-712-7500	712-7505
Web: www.flemingssteakhouse.com					
French Hen The 7143 S Yale Ave	Tulsa	OK	74136	918-492-2596	
Fuji 8226 E 71st St	Tulsa	OK	74133	918-250-1821	459-5012
Web: www.fujisushibar.com					
Green Onion 4532 E 51st St	Tulsa	OK	74135	918-481-3338	
Web: www.greenoniontulsa.com					
In the Raw 3321 S Peoria	Tulsa	OK	74105	918-744-1300	744-1311
Web: www.intheraw-tulsa.com					
India Palace Restaurant 6963 S Lewis Ave	Tulsa	OK	74136	918-492-8040	
Joe's Crab Shack 7646 E 61st St	Tulsa	OK	74133	918-252-1010	254-0319
Kilkenny's Irish Pub & Eatery 1413 E 15th St	Tulsa	OK	74120	918-582-8282	582-3931
Web: www.kilkennysirishpub.net					
Lanna Thai 3535 E 51st St	Tulsa	OK	74135	918-712-3273	
Mahogany Prime Steak House 6823 S Yale Ave	Tulsa	OK	74136	918-494-4043	494-0209
Web: www.mahoganyprime.com					
Margaret's 5107 S Sheridan St	Tulsa	OK	74145	918-622-3747	
McGill's 1560 E 21st St	Tulsa	OK	74114	918-742-8080	742-8099
New Hong Kong Restaurant 2623 E 11th St	Tulsa	OK	74104	918-585-5328	
Paddy's Irish Restaurant & Pub 8056 S Memorial Dr	Tulsa	OK	74133	918-250-3626	
PF Chang's China Bistro 1978 E 21st St	Tulsa	OK	74114	918-747-6555	747-6575
Web: www.pfchangs.com					
Polo Grill 2038 Utica Sq	Tulsa	OK	74114	918-744-4280	749-7082
Web: www.pologrill.com					
Rendezvous Restaurant 1400 Gilcrease Museum Rd	Tulsa	OK	74127	918-596-2720	
Ricardo's 5629 E 41st St	Tulsa	OK	74135	918-622-2668	622-2669
Senor Tequila 3525 E 51st St	Tulsa	OK	74135	918-742-1499	742-2671
Spudder The 6536 E 50th St	Tulsa	OK	74145	918-665-1416	477-7719
Table Ten 3512 S Peoria	Tulsa	OK	74105	918-749-3310	
Web: www.tabletentulsa.com					
Taste of China 11360 E 31st St	Tulsa	OK	74146	918-664-2252	
Tsunami Sushi 309 E 2nd St	Tulsa	OK	74120	918-582-4100	
White Lion Pub 6927 S Canton Ave	Tulsa	OK	74136	918-491-6533	
Zio's 7111 S Mingo Rd	Tulsa	OK	74133	918-250-5999	252-1287

Ontario

Name / Address	City	Prov	Postal Code	Phone	Fax
Al's Steak & Seafood House 327 Elgin St	Ottawa	ON	K2P1M5	613-233-7111	
Web: www.alssteakhouse.ca					
Beckta Dining & Wine 226 Nepean St	Ottawa	ON	K2P0B8	613-238-7063	231-7474
Web: www.beckta.com					
Big Daddy's Crab Shack & Oyster Bar 339 Elgin St	Ottawa	ON	K2P1M9	613-569-5200	
Web: www.bigdaddys.ca					
Bistro 115 110 Murray St	Ottawa	ON	K1N5M6	613-562-7244	
Web: www.bistro115.com					
Black Tomato 11 George St	Ottawa	ON	K1N8W5	613-789-8123	
Blue Cactus Bar & Grill 2 ByWard Market	Ottawa	ON	K1N7A1	613-241-7061	
Web: www.bluecactusbarandgrill.com					
Cafe Spiga 271 Dalhousie St	Ottawa	ON	K1N7E5	613-241-4381	
Web: www.cafespiga.com					
Capone's 831 Industrial Ave	Ottawa	ON	K1V8Y5	613-738-0900	
Web: www.capones.com					
Chahaya Malaysia 1690 Montreal Rd	Ottawa	ON	K1J6N5	613-742-0242	
Coriander 282 Kent St	Ottawa	ON	K1V8Y5	613-233-2828	
D'Arcy McGee's Irish Pub 44 Sparks St	Ottawa	ON	K1P5A8	613-230-4433	
Web: www.darcymcgees.ca					
Don Alfonso 434 Bank St	Ottawa	ON	K2P1Y8	613-236-7750	
Fairouz 343 Somerset W	Ottawa	ON	K1V8Y5	613-233-1536	
Web: www.fairouz.ca					
Fratelli 749 Bank St	Ottawa	ON	K1S3V3	613-237-1658	237-1079
Web: www.fratelli.ca					
Giovanni's 362 Preston St	Ottawa	ON	K1S4M7	613-234-3156	238-7461
Web: www.giovannis-restaurant.com					
Golden Palace 2195 Carling Ave	Ottawa	ON	K2B7E8	613-820-8444	
Greek Souvlaki House 1200 Prince of Wales Dr	Ottawa	ON	K2C3Y4	613-225-1144	
Green Door 198 Main St	Ottawa	ON	K1S1C6	613-234-9597	234-6771
Green Papaya 256 Preston St	Ottawa	ON	K1R7R5	613-231-8424	
Web: www.greenpapaya.ca					
Haveli Restaurant 39 Clarence St	Ottawa	ON	K1N5P4	613-241-1700	241-8491
Web: www.haveli.com					
Heart & Crown 67 Clarence St	Ottawa	ON	K1N5P5	613-562-0674	
Web: www.irishvillage.ca					
Horn of Africa 364 Rideau St	Ottawa	ON	K1N5Y8	613-789-0025	
Ichibei 197 Bank	Ottawa	ON	K2P1W7	613-563-2375	
Il Piccolino 449 Preston St	Ottawa	ON	K1S4N5	613-236-8158	
Web: www.ilpiccolino.ca					
Indian Biriyani House 1589 Bank St	Ottawa	ON	K1H7Z3	613-260-3893	
Island Jerk 1800 Bank St	Ottawa	ON	K1V8Y5	613-737-5163	
Juniper 1293 Wellington St	Ottawa	ON	K1Y3B1	613-728-0220	728-2993
Web: www.juniperdining.ca					
Kinki 41 York St	Ottawa	ON	K1N5S7	613-789-7559	789-0505
Web: www.kinki.ca					
Korea Garden 470 Rideau St	Ottawa	ON	K1N5Z4	613-789-5496	
Le Caveau de Szechuan 129 York	Ottawa	ON	K1N5T4	613-562-2882	562-2884
Luxe Bistro 47 York St	Ottawa	ON	K1N7A1	613-241-8805	241-8886
Web: www.luxebistro.com					
Mamma Grazzi's Kitchen 25 George St	Ottawa	ON	K1N8W5	613-241-8656	241-5738
Web: www.mammagrazzis.com					
Manx The 370 Elgin St	Ottawa	ON	K2P1N1	613-231-2070	
Mekong 637 Somerset St W	Ottawa	ON	K1R5K3	613-237-7717	
Web: www.mekong.ca					
Merlot Rooftop Grill 100 Kent St	Ottawa	ON	K1P5R7	613-783-4212	783-4228
Web: www.merlotottawa.com					
Mezzanotte Cafe 50 Murray St	Ottawa	ON	K1N9K1	613-562-3978	
Web: www.mezzanotte-bistro.com					
New Dubrovnik Dining Lounge 1170 Carling Ave	Ottawa	ON	K1Z7K2	613-722-1490	722-3249
Web: www.newdubrovnik.com					
New Mee Fung 350 Booth St	Ottawa	ON	K1R7K4	613-567-8228	
Nokham Thai 747 Richmond Rd	Ottawa	ON	K2A0G6	613-724-6135	724-6620
Pancho Villa 361 Elgin St	Ottawa	ON	K2P1M7	613-234-8872	
Pho Bo Ga 2 843B Somerset St W	Ottawa	ON	K1R6R6	613-234-7089	
Web: www.phoboga2.com					
Pub Italia 434 1/2 Preston St	Ottawa	ON	K1S4N4	613-232-2326	
Web: www.pubitalia.ca					
Royal Thai 272 Dalhousie St	Ottawa	ON	K1N7E6	613-562-8818	
Saigon 85 Clarence St	Ottawa	ON	K1N5P5	613-789-7934	
Sante Restaurant 45 Rideau St	Ottawa	ON	K1N5W8	613-241-7113	
Web: www.santerestaurant.com					
Savana Cafe 431 Gilmour St	Ottawa	ON	K2P0R5	613-233-9159	
Shanghai 651 Somerset St W	Ottawa	ON	K1R5K3	613-233-4001	
Shawarma King 331 Elgin St	Ottawa	ON	K2P1M5	613-233-5000	
Suisha Garden Japanese Restaurant 208 Slater St	Ottawa	ON	K1V8Y5	613-236-9602	
Web: www.japaninottawa.ca					
Sweet Basil 1585 Bank St	Ottawa	ON	K1H7Z3	613-731-8424	
Sweetgrass Aboriginal Bistro 108 Murray St	Ottawa	ON	K1N5M6	613-562-3683	562-4674
Web: www.sweetgrassbistro.ca					
Tosca Ristorante 144 O'Connor St	Ottawa	ON	K2P2G7	613-565-3933	565-0312
Web: www.tosca-ristorante.ca/					
Vietnam Palace Restaurant 819 Somerset St W	Ottawa	ON	K1R6R4	613-238-6758	
Vineyards Wine Bar Bistro 54 York St	Ottawa	ON	K1N5T1	613-241-4270	241-5538
Web: www.vineyards.ca					
Vittoria Trattoria 35 William St	Ottawa	ON	K1N6Z9	613-789-8959	730-5239
Web: www.vittoriatrattoria.com					
Yangtze 700 Somerset W	Ottawa	ON	K1R6P6	613-236-0555	236-6825
Web: www.yangtze.ca/					
360 Revolving Restaurant 301 Front St W	Toronto	ON	M5V2T6	416-362-5411	
Accents 955 Bay St	Toronto	ON	M5S2A2	416-324-5633	
Acqua Ristorante Bar 10 Front St W	Toronto	ON	M5J2T3	416-368-7171	
Web: www.acqua.ca					
Adega 33 Elm St	Toronto	ON	M5G1H1	416-977-4338	
Web: www.adegarestaurante.ca					
Avalon 270 Adelaide St W	Toronto	ON	M5H1X6	416-979-9918	
Bangkok Garden 18 Elm St	Toronto	ON	M5G1G7	416-977-6748	
Web: www.bangkokgarden.ca					
Barberian's Steak House 7 Elm St	Toronto	ON	M5G1H1	416-597-0335	
Biagio 155 King St E	Toronto	ON	M5C1G9	416-366-4040	
Big Daddy's Crab Shack & Oyster Bar 212 King St W	Toronto	ON	M5H1K5	416-599-5200	
Web: www.bigdaddys.ca					
Cafe 668 668 Dundas St W	Toronto	ON	M5T1H9	416-703-0668	
Web: www.cafe668.com					
Cafe Brussel 124 Danforth Ave	Toronto	ON	M4K2P7	416-465-7363	
Web: www.cafebrussel.com					
Cafe Nervosa 75 Yorkville Ave	Toronto	ON	M5R1B8	416-961-4642	
Web: www.cafenervosa.ca					
Canoe Restaurant & Bar					
66 Wellington St W TD Bank Tower 54th Fl	Toronto	ON	M5K1H6	416-364-0054	
Carman's 26 Alexander St	Toronto	ON	M4Y1B4	416-924-8697	
Web: carmans.sites.toronto.com/					
Celestin 623 Mount Pleasant Rd	Toronto	ON	M4S2M9	416-544-9035	
Centro Grill & Wine Bar 2472 Yonge St	Toronto	ON	M4P2H5	416-483-2211	
Chiado 864 College St	Toronto	ON	M6H1A3	416-538-1910	
Web: www.chiadorestaurant.com					
Coppi 3363 Yonge St	Toronto	ON	M4N2M6	416-484-4464	
Corner House 501 Davenport Rd	Toronto	ON	M4W1B8	416-923-2604	
Web: cornerhouse.sites.toronto.com					
Courthouse Market Grille 57 Adelaide St E	Toronto	ON	M5C1K6	416-214-9379	
Courtyard Cafe 18 Saint Thomas St	Toronto	ON	M5S3E7	416-921-2921	
Dhaba 309 King St W	Toronto	ON	M5V1J5	416-740-6622	
Web: www.dhaba.ca					
Easy & the Fifth 225 Richmond St W	Toronto	ON	M5V1W2	416-979-3000	
Web: www.easyandthefifth.com					
Edo 484 Eglinton Ave W	Toronto	ON	M5N1A5	416-322-3033	
Edo-ko 431 Spadina Rd	Toronto	ON	M5P2W3	416-482-8973	
El Sol 1448 Danforth Ave	Toronto	ON	M4J1N4	416-405-8074	
Far Niente Napa Grill 187 Bay St	Toronto	ON	M3H6A7	416-214-9922	
Web: www.farnientegrill.com					
Gandhi 554 Queen St W	Toronto	ON	M5V2B5	416-504-8155	
George 111C Queen St E	Toronto	ON	M5C1S2	416-863-6006	
Giovanna 637 College St	Toronto	ON	M6G1B5	416-538-2098	
Golden Thai 105 Church St	Toronto	ON	M5C2G3	416-868-6668	
Gonzo's 977 O'Connor Dr	Toronto	ON	M4B2T1	416-750-9424	
Grappa 797 College St	Toronto	ON	M6G1C7	416-535-3337	
Web: www.grappa.redto.com/grappa/					
Harbour Sixty Steakhouse 60 Harbour St	Toronto	ON	M5J1B7	416-777-2111	
Web: www.harboursixty.com					
Hemispheres Restaurant & Bistro 110 Chestnut St	Toronto	ON	M5G1R3	416-599-8000	
Il Gatto Nero 720 College St	Toronto	ON	M6G1C3	416-536-3132	
Web: www.ilgattonero.ca					
Joso's 202 Davenport Rd	Toronto	ON	M5R1J2	416-925-1903	
Web: www.josos.com					
JOV Bistro 1701 Bayview Ave	Toronto	ON	M3H6A7	416-322-0530	

				Phone	Fax
JW's 525 Bay St	Toronto	ON	M5G2L2	416-597-9200	
La Bodega 30 Baldwin St	Toronto	ON	M5T1L3	416-977-1287	
Web: www.bodegarestaurant.com					
La Fenice 319 King St W	Toronto	ON	M5V1J5	416-585-2377	
Web: www.lafenice.ca					
Lai Wah Heen 108 Chestnut St	Toronto	ON	M5G1R3	416-977-9899	
Web: www.metropolitan.com/lwh/					
Laide 138 Adelaide St E	Toronto	ON	M5C1K9	416-850-2726	
Lakes Bar & Grill 1112 Yonge St	Toronto	ON	M4W2L6	416-966-0185	
Le Papillon Restaurant 16 Church St	Toronto	ON	M5E1M1	416-363-0838	
Web: www.lepapillon.ca					
Le Petit Liban 580 Church St	Toronto	ON	M4Y2E5	416-963-2222	
Web: www.lepetitliban.com					
Le Saint Tropez 315 King St W	Toronto	ON	M5B2A3	416-591-3600	
Web: www.marcels.com					
Lee 603 King St W	Toronto	ON	M5W1M5	416-504-7867	
Linda 335 Yonge St	Toronto	ON	M5B1R7	416-971-7041	
Web: www.saladking.com					
Lone Star Texas Grill 200 Front St W	Toronto	ON	M5V3J1	416-408-4064	
Web: www.lonestartexasgrill.com					
Mandarin 2206 Eglinton Ave E	Toronto	ON	M1B1A1	416-288-1177	
Web: www.mandarinbuffet.com					
Marcel's 315 King St W	Toronto	ON	M5V1J5	416-591-8600	
Web: www.marcels.com					
Messis 97 Harbord St	Toronto	ON	M5S1G4	416-920-2186	
Web: www.messis.ca					
Mi Tierra 828 St Clair Ave W	Toronto	ON	M6C1C1	416-654-8886	
Monsoon Restaurant 100 Simcoe St	Toronto	ON	M5H3G2	416-979-7172	
Web: www.monsoonrestaurant.ca					
Morton's of Chicago 4 Avenue Rd	Toronto	ON	M5R2E8	416-925-0648	
Web: www.mortons.com					
New Generation Sushi 493 Bloor St W	Toronto	ON	M5S1Y2	416-963-8861	
North 44 Degrees 2537 Yonge St	Toronto	ON	M4P2H9	416-487-4897	
Web: www.north44restaurant.com					
Opus 37 Prince Arthur Ave	Toronto	ON	M5R1B2	416-921-3105	
Web: www.opusrestaurant.com					
Oro 45 Elm St	Toronto	ON	M3H6A7	416-597-0155	
Panagaea 1221 Bay St	Toronto	ON	M5R3P5	416-920-2323	
Phil's Original BBQ 838 College St	Toronto	ON	M5H1A2	416-532-8161	
Web: www.philsoriginalbbq.com					
Prego della Piazza 150 Bloor St W	Toronto	ON	M5S2X9	416-920-9900	
Web: www.pregodellapiazza.ca					
Provence 12 Amelia St	Toronto	ON	M4X1E1	416-924-9901	
Web: www.provencerestaurant.com					
Red's Bistro & Bar 77 Adelaide St W	Toronto	ON	M5X1B1	416-862-7337	
Web: www.redsbistro.com					
Rodney's Oyster House 469 King St W	Toronto	ON	M5V1K4	416-363-8105	
Web: www.rodneysoysterhouse.com					
Rol San 323 Spadina Ave	Toronto	ON	M5T2E9	416-977-1128	
Rosewater Supper Club 19 Toronto St	Toronto	ON	M5C2R1	416-214-5888	
Ruth's Chris Steak House 145 Richmond St W	Toronto	ON	M3H6A7	416-955-1455	
Web: www.ruthschris-toronto.com					
Sassafraz 100 Cumberland St	Toronto	ON	M5R1A6	416-964-2222	
Web: www.sassafraz.ca					
Scaramouche Restaurant 1 Benvenuto Pl	Toronto	ON	M4V2L1	416-961-8011	
Web: www.scaramoucherestaurant.com					
Segovia 5 Saint Nicholas St	Toronto	ON	M4Y1W5	416-960-1010	
Web: www.segovia.ca					
Signatures 22 Bloor St W	Toronto	ON	M5S1T8	416-324-5885	
Sotto Sotto 116A Avenue Rd	Toronto	ON	M5R2H4	416-962-0011	
Southern Accent 595 Markham St	Toronto	ON	M3H6A7	416-536-3211	
Web: www.southernaccent.com					
Splendido's 88 Harbord St	Toronto	ON	M5S1G5	416-929-7788	
Web: www.splendido.ca					
Spuntini 116 Avenue Rd	Toronto	ON	M5R2H4	416-962-1110	
Web: www.spuntini.ca					
Truffles 21 Avenue Rd	Toronto	ON	M5R2G1	416-928-7331	
Young Thailand 81 Church St	Toronto	ON	M5C2G2	416-368-1368	
Web: www.youngthailand.com					
Zucca 2150 Yonge St	Toronto	ON	M4S2A8	416-488-5774	

Oregon

				Phone	Fax
Merenda Restaurant & Wine Bar 900 NW Wall St	Bend	OR	97701	541-330-2304	330-2348
Web: www.merendarestaurant.com/					
Adam's Place 30 E Broadway	Eugene	OR	97401	541-344-6948	344-1266
Web: www.adamsplacerestaurant.com					
Ambrosia Restaurant 174 E Broadway	Eugene	OR	97401	541-342-4141	345-6965
Web: www.ambrosiarestaurant.com					
Anatolia's 992 Willamette St	Eugene	OR	97401	541-343-9661	
Beppe & Gianni's Tratorria 1646 E 19th Ave	Eugene	OR	97403	541-683-6661	485-9698
Broadway The 200 W Broadway	Eugene	OR	97401	541-685-0790	345-1235
Cafe Soriah 384 W 13th Ave	Eugene	OR	97401	541-342-4410	
Web: www.soriah.com					
Cafe Zenon 898 Pearl St	Eugene	OR	97401	541-343-3005	
Chanterelle 207 E 5th Ave Suite 109	Eugene	OR	97401	541-484-4065	
Chao Praya 580 Adams St	Eugene	OR	97402	541-344-1706	344-1181
Chapala 136 Oakway Rd	Eugene	OR	97401	541-434-6113	434-6267
El Jarro Azul 764 Blair Blvd	Eugene	OR	97402	541-344-0650	
Fisherman's Market 830 W 7th Ave	Eugene	OR	97402	541-484-2722	
High Street Brewery & Cafe 1243 High St	Eugene	OR	97401	541-345-4905	686-4320
Iraila 2435 Hilyard	Eugene	OR	97405	541-684-8400	
Web: www.iraila.com					
Jade Palace 906 W 7th Ave	Eugene	OR	97402	541-344-9523	
Koho Bistro 2101 Bailey Hill Rd	Eugene	OR	97405	541-681-9335	
Web: www.kohobistro.com					
Lotus Garden 810 Charnelton St	Eugene	OR	97401	541-344-1928	
Maple Garden 1275 Alder St	Eugene	OR	97401	541-683-8128	683-1126
Marche 296 E 5th Ave	Eugene	OR	97401	541-342-3612	342-3611
Web: www.marcherestaurant.com					
Mazzi's Restaurant 3377 E Amazon Dr	Eugene	OR	97405	541-687-2252	687-2291
Web: www.mazzis.com					
McGrath's Fish House 1036 Valley River Way	Eugene	OR	97401	541-342-6404	342-6079
Web: www.mcgrathsfishhouse.com					
Mekala's 1796 Franklin Blvd	Eugene	OR	97403	541-342-4872	
Web: www.mekalas.com					
Misako 5 E 8th Ave	Eugene	OR	97401	541-686-3464	
Morning Glory Cafe 450 Willamette St	Eugene	OR	97401	541-687-0709	
Ocean Sky 1601 Chambers St	Eugene	OR	97402	541-342-4848	
Oregon Electric Station 27 E 5th Ave	Eugene	OR	97401	541-485-4444	484-6149
Red Agave 454 Willamette St	Eugene	OR	97401	541-683-2206	
Ring of Fire 1099 Chambers St	Eugene	OR	97402	541-344-6475	684-0732
Web: www.ringoffirerestaurant.com					
Sixth Street Grill 55 W 6th Ave	Eugene	OR	97401	541-485-2961	485-3080
Web: www.sixthstreetgrill.com					
Steelhead Brewery & Cafe 199 E 5th Ave	Eugene	OR	97401	541-686-2739	342-5338
Web: www.steelheadbrewery.com					
Sushi Station 199 E 5th Ave	Eugene	OR	97401	541-484-1334	
Taste of India 2495 Hilyard St	Eugene	OR	97405	541-485-9698	485-9698
Turtles Bar & Grill 2690 Willamette St	Eugene	OR	97405	541-465-9038	465-9051
Vintage Restaurant the 839 Lincoln St	Eugene	OR	97401	541-349-9181	
West Brothers River Ranch Barbeque & Steaks 2123 Franklin Blvd	Eugene	OR	97403	541-686-2020	344-6564
3 Doors Down Cafe 1429 SE 37th St	Portland	OR	97214	503-236-6886	235-9221
Web: www.3doorsdowncafe.com					
Acadia 1303 NE Fremont St	Portland	OR	97212	503-249-5001	288-4383
Web: www.creolapdx.com					
Amalfi's 4703 NE Fremont St	Portland	OR	97213	503-284-6747	
Web: www.amalfisrestaurant.com					
Andina 1314 NW Glisan	Portland	OR	97209	503-228-9535	228-0788
Web: www.andinarestaurant.com					
Assaggio 7742 SE 13th Ave	Portland	OR	97202	503-232-6151	715-4981
Web: www.assaggiorestaurant.com					
Basta's Trattoria 410 NW 21st Ave	Portland	OR	97209	503-274-1572	
Berlin Inn 3131 SE 12th Ave	Portland	OR	97202	503-236-6761	238-4068
Web: www.berlininn.com					
Bluehour 250 NW 13th Ave	Portland	OR	97209	503-226-3394	221-5005
Web: www.bluehouronline.com					
Bombay Cricket Club Restaurant 1925 SE Hawthorne Blvd	Portland	OR	97214	503-231-0740	
Web: www.bombaycricketclubrestaurant.com					
Cafe du Berry 6439 SW MacAdam Ave	Portland	OR	97201	503-244-5551	
Cafe Castagna 1752 SE Hawthorne Blvd	Portland	OR	97214	503-231-9959	231-7474
Web: www.castagnarestaurant.com					
Caffe Mingo 807 NW 21st Ave	Portland	OR	97209	503-226-4646	295-2040
Campbell's Bar-B-Q 8701 SE Powell Blvd	Portland	OR	97266	503-777-9795	
Web: campbellsbbq.com					
Canton Grill 2610 SE 82nd Ave	Portland	OR	97202	503-774-1135	
Caprial's Bistro 7015 SE Milwaukee Ave	Portland	OR	97202	503-236-6457	238-8554
Castagna 1752 SE Hawthorne Blvd	Portland	OR	97214	503-231-7373	231-7474
Web: www.castagnarestaurant.com					
Cha! Cha! Cha! 1208 N Glisan St	Portland	OR	97209	503-221-2111	
Chart House 5700 SW Terwilliger Blvd	Portland	OR	97201	503-246-6963	246-8437
Web: www.chart-house.com					
Clay's Smokehouse Grill 2932 SE Division St	Portland	OR	97202	503-235-4755	
El Gaucho 319 SW Broadway	Portland	OR	97201	503-227-8794	227-3412
Web: www.elgaucho.com					
El Palermo 320 SW Alder St	Portland	OR	97204	503-227-3376	
Esparza's Tex-Mex Cafe 2725 SE Ankeny St	Portland	OR	97214	503-234-7909	
Fife 4440 NE Fremont St	Portland	OR	97213	971-222-3433	222-0042
Web: www.fiferestaurant.com					
Fratelli 1230 NW Hoyt St	Portland	OR	97209	503-241-8800	
Web: www.fratellicucina.com					
Genoa 2832 SE Belmont St	Portland	OR	97214	503-238-1464	238-9786
Web: genoarestaurant.com					
Giorgio's 1131 NW Hoyt St	Portland	OR	97209	503-221-1888	
Web: www.giorgiospdx.com					
Giuseppe's 17937 SE Stark St	Portland	OR	97233	503-669-8767	492-4665
Harrison Portland 838 SW Park Ave	Portland	OR	97214	503-299-6161	299-2171
Web: www.harrisonrestaurant.net					
Heathman Restaurant 1001 SW Broadway	Portland	OR	97205	503-241-4100	790-7105
Higgins Restaurant & Bar 1239 SW Broadway	Portland	OR	97205	503-222-9070	
Hugo's Cafe & Restaurant 2130 NE Broadway	Portland	OR	97232	503-287-7490	249-2012
Web: www.hugosonbroadway.com					
Il Piatto 2348 SE Ankeny St	Portland	OR	97214	503-236-4997	
Web: www.ilpiatto.citysearch.com					
Iron Horse 6034 SE Milwaukie Ave	Portland	OR	97202	503-232-1826	236-3988
Web: www.portlandironhorse.com					
Jake's Famous Crawfish 401 SW 12th Ave	Portland	OR	97205	503-226-1419	220-1856
Web: www.jakesfamouscrawfish.com					
Jake's Grill 611 SW 10th Ave	Portland	OR	97205	503-220-1850	226-8365
Web: www.jakesgrill.com					
Kell's 112 SW 2nd Ave	Portland	OR	97204	503-227-4057	593-1227
Web: www.kellsirish.com/portland/pdx.html					
Koji Osakaya 606 SW Broadway	Portland	OR	97205	503-294-1169	294-1169
Web: www.koji.com					
Le Bouchon 517 NW 14th Ave	Portland	OR	97209	503-248-2193	
Lemongrass 1705 NE Couch St	Portland	OR	97232	503-231-5780	
London Grill 309 SW Broadway	Portland	OR	97205	503-295-4110	471-3924
Lucy's Table 706 NW 21st Ave	Portland	OR	97209	503-226-6126	274-7122
Web: www.lucystable.com					
McCormick & Schmick's 235 SW 1st Ave	Portland	OR	97201	503-224-7522	220-1881
Web: www.mccormickandschmicks.com					
McCormick & Schmick's Harborside 309 SW Montgomery	Portland	OR	97201	503-220-1865	220-1855
Web: www.mccormickandschmicks.com					
Mint Restaurant & Bar 816 N Russell St	Portland	OR	97227	503-284-5518	284-5519
Web: www.mintrestaurant.com					
Mio Sushi 2271 NW Johnson St	Portland	OR	97210	503-221-1469	827-4932
Morton's The Steakhouse 213 SW Clay St	Portland	OR	97201	503-248-2100	218-2005
Web: www.mortons.com					
Mother's Bistro & Bar 212 SW Stark St	Portland	OR	97204	503-464-1122	525-5877
Web: www.mothersbistro.com					
Noble Rot 2724 SE Ankeny St	Portland	OR	97214	503-233-1999	233-5999
Web: www.noblerotpdx.com					
Oba! 555 NW 12th Ave	Portland	OR	97209	503-228-6161	228-2673
OM Seafood Restaurant 7632 SE Powell Blvd	Portland	OR	97206	503-788-3128	471-2101
Paley's Place 1204 NW 21st Ave	Portland	OR	97209	503-243-2403	223-8041
Web: paleysplace.citysearch.com					
Pambiche 2811 NE Glisan St	Portland	OR	97232	503-233-0511	233-0495
Web: www.pambiche.com					
Pho Van 1012 NW Glisan St	Portland	OR	97216	503-248-2172	
Piazza Italia 1129 NW Johnson St	Portland	OR	97209	503-478-0619	
Web: www.piazzaportland.com					
Plainfield's Mayur 852 SW 21st Ave	Portland	OR	97205	503-223-2995	
Web: www.plainfields.com					
Portland City Grill 111 SW 5th Ave Unico US Bank Tower 30th Fl	Portland	OR	97204	503-450-0030	525-5265
Web: www.portlandcitygrill.com					
Red Star Tavern & Roast House 503 SW Alder St	Portland	OR	97204	503-222-0005	417-3334
Web: www.redstartavern.com					
Restaurant Murata 200 SW Market St	Portland	OR	97201	503-227-0080	
Ringside The 2165 W Burnside St	Portland	OR	97210	503-223-1513	223-6908
Web: www.ringsidesteakhouse.com					
Ruth's Chris Steak House 309 SW 3rd Ave	Portland	OR	97204	503-221-4518	221-7766
Web: www.ruthschris.com					
Saburo's Sushi House 1667 SE Bybee Blvd	Portland	OR	97202	503-236-4237	
Santorini 11525 SW Barns Rd	Portland	OR	97225	503-646-6889	671-0402
Saucebox 214 SW Broadway	Portland	OR	97205	503-241-3393	
Web: www.saucebox.com					
Sin Ju 1022 NW Johnson St	Portland	OR	97209	503-223-6535	223-6536
Web: www.sinjurestaurant.com					
Southpark Seafood Grill & Wine Bar 901 SW Salmon St	Portland	OR	97205	503-326-1300	326-1301
Web: www.southpark.citysearch.com					

Oregon (Cont'd)

Restaurant	City	State	ZIP	Phone	Fax
Stickers Asian Cafe 6808 SE Milwaukie Ave *Web:* www.stickersasiancafe.com	Portland	OR	97217	503-239-8739	230-9884
Sungari 735 SW 1st Ave *Web:* sungarirestaurant.com	Portland	OR	97204	503-224-0800	224-8567
Sweet Basil 3135 NE Broadway *Web:* www.sweetbasilor.com	Portland	OR	97232	503-281-8337	
Taqueria Nueve 28 NE 28th Ave *Web:* www.taco9.com	Portland	OR	97232	503-236-6195	233-0966
Thai Orchid 10075 SW Barbur Blvd *Web:* www.thaiorchidrestaurant.com	Portland	OR	97219	503-452-2544	
Todai 340 SW Morrison St *Web:* www.todai.com	Portland	OR	97204	503-294-0007	294-0009
Tuscany Grill 811 NW 21st Ave *Web:* tuscanygrill.com	Portland	OR	97209	503-243-2757	242-0118
Typhoon! 400 SW Broadway Imperial Hotel *Web:* www.typhoon.com	Portland	OR	97205	503-224-8285	224-3468
Veritable Quandary 1220 SW 1st Ave	Portland	OR	97204	503-227-7342	227-5142
Wildwood Restaurant & Bar 1221 NW 21st Ave *Web:* wildwoodrestaurant.com	Portland	OR	97209	503-248-9663	225-0030
Ya Hala 8005 SE Stark St *Web:* www.yahalarestaurant.com	Portland	OR	97215	503-256-4484	
Adam's Rib 1210 State St	Salem	OR	97301	503-362-2194	362-2196
Alessandro's Park Plaza 120 Commercial St NE *Web:* www.alessandros120.com	Salem	OR	97301	503-370-9951	375-3412
Almost Home Restaurant & Steakhouse 3310 Market St NE	Salem	OR	97301	503-378-0100	315-7155
Amadeus Cafe 5121 Skyline Village Loop S Suite 190	Salem	OR	97306	503-362-8830	
Arbor Cafe 380 High St NE	Salem	OR	97301	503-588-2353	371-9532
Casa Baez 1292 Lancaster Dr NE	Salem	OR	97301	503-371-3867	371-9568
Da Vinci 180 High St	Salem	OR	97301	503-399-1413	
El Mirador East 1660 Lancaster Dr NE	Salem	OR	97301	503-566-7232	391-8244
Eng's Garden 4645 Commercial St SE	Salem	OR	97302	503-585-8380	
Eola Inn Riverview Restaurant 4250 Salem-Dallas Hwy NW *Web:* www.eolainn.com	Salem	OR	97304	503-363-8580	
Flight Deck Restaurant & Lounge 2680 Aerial Way *Web:* www.flightdeckrestaurant.com/	Salem	OR	97302	503-581-5721	
India Palace 377 Court St	Salem	OR	97301	503-371-4808	
J James 325 High St SE *Web:* www.jjamesrestaurant.com	Salem	OR	97301	503-362-0888	362-8077
Jonathan's Oyster Bar 445 State St	Salem	OR	97301	503-362-7219	
La Margarita Co 545 Ferry St SE	Salem	OR	97301	503-362-8861	
Los Arcos Mexican Grill 4120 Commercial St SE	Salem	OR	97302	503-581-2740	
Los Baez 2920 Commercial St SE	Salem	OR	97302	503-363-3109	
Lucky Fortune 1401 Lancaster Dr NE	Salem	OR	97301	503-399-9189	581-7810
Lum-Yuen 3190 Portland Rd NE	Salem	OR	97303	503-581-2912	581-2903
Macedonia 189 Liberty St NE	Salem	OR	97301	503-316-9997	
Marco Polo Global Restaurant 210 Liberty St SE	Salem	OR	97301	503-364-4833	
McGrath's Fish House 350 Chemeketa St NE	Salem	OR	97301	503-362-0736	362-7306
Mortons Bistro Northwest 1128 Edgewater St NW	Salem	OR	97304	503-585-1113	
Ram Big Horn Brewery 515 12th St SE *Web:* www.theram.com	Salem	OR	97301	503-363-1904	
Smokin' Swine Publick House 2809 Market St NE *Web:* www.smokinswine.com	Salem	OR	97302	503-399-1995	
Soprano's Italian Steak House 189 Liberty St NE	Salem	OR	97302	503-364-1515	
Thompson's Brewery & Public House 3575 Liberty Rd S	Salem	OR	97302	503-363-7286	363-7827

Pennsylvania

Restaurant	City	State	ZIP	Phone	Fax
Altland House Rt 30 N & Rt 94 Center Sq *Web:* www.altlandhouse.com	Abbottstown	PA	17301	717-259-9535	259-9956
Aladdin 651 Union Blvd	Allentown	PA	18103	610-437-4023	437-9841
Bay Leaf 935 Hamilton St *Web:* www.allentownbayleaf.com	Allentown	PA	18101	610-433-4211	433-2652
Brass Rail Restaurant 3015 Lehigh St *Web:* www.brassrailrestaurant.com	Allentown	PA	18103	610-797-1927	797-5530
Charlie's Brown's Steakhouse 1908 Walbert Ave *Web:* www.charliebrowns.com	Allentown	PA	18104	610-437-1070	437-1189
Federal Grill 536 Hamilton St *Web:* www.federalgrill.com	Allentown	PA	18101	610-776-7600	776-3660
Gregory's 2201 Schoenersville Rd *Web:* www.gregoryssteaks.com	Allentown	PA	18103	610-264-9301	264-7394
Henry's Salt of the Sea 1926 W Allen St	Allentown	PA	18104	610-434-2628	
House of Chen 732 Hamilton Mall	Allentown	PA	18101	610-439-1330	433-4219
Hunan Springs 4939 Hamilton Blvd	Allentown	PA	18106	610-366-8338	366-7184
Ichiban 1916 Catasauqua Rd	Allentown	PA	18109	610-266-7781	266-7783
Jack Creek Steakhouse 1900 Catasauqua Rd *Web:* jackcreeksteakhouse.com	Allentown	PA	18103	610-264-8888	264-0670
La Mexicana Grill 407 N 7th St	Allentown	PA	18102	610-776-1910	966-1870
Louie's 1207 Chew St *Web:* www.louiesrestaurant.com	Allentown	PA	18102	610-434-2340	776-1201
New China Buffet 1680 S 4th St	Allentown	PA	18103	610-797-7768	797-7781
Oasis Restaurant 2355 Schoenersville Rd	Allentown	PA	18103	610-264-1955	
Pho Vung Tau 1500 Union Blvd	Allentown	PA	18103	610-433-3405	433-1726
Ritz Barbecue 302 17th St	Allentown	PA	18104	610-432-0952	
Robata Of Tokyo 39 S 9th St *Web:* www.robataoftokyo.com	Allentown	PA	18102	610-821-6900	
Sunset Grille 6751 Ruppsville Rd *Web:* www.sunset-grille.com	Allentown	PA	18106	610-395-9622	398-0697
Wert's Cafe 515 N 18th St	Allentown	PA	18104	610-439-0951	439-1131
Youell's Oyster House 2249 Walnut St *Web:* www.youellsoysterhouse.com	Allentown	PA	18104	610-439-1203	
Cashtown Inn Restaurant 1325 Old Rt 30 *TF:* 800-367-1797	Cashtown	PA	17310	717-334-9722	334-4679
Angelo Bistocchi's Restaurant 1120 Wheeler Ave	Dunmore	PA	18510	570-961-9112	
Barbato's 1707 State St	Erie	PA	16501	814-459-2158	
Bertrand's 18 N Park Row	Erie	PA	16501	814-871-6477	464-9029
Calamari's Squid Row 1317 State St *Web:* www.calamaris-squidrow.com	Erie	PA	16501	814-459-4276	455-5635
China Garden Restaurant 6801 Peach St	Erie	PA	16509	814-868-2695	
Colao's Ristorante 2826 Plum St	Erie	PA	16508	814-866-9621	
Colony Pub & Grille 2670 W 8th St	Erie	PA	16505	814-838-2162	838-9804
Danny's 5653 Peach St	Erie	PA	16509	814-868-4486	
El Canelo 2709 W 12th St	Erie	PA	16505	814-835-2290	836-0334
Hector's 802 W 18th St	Erie	PA	16502	814-454-9130	
Hibachi Japanese Steak House 3000 W 12th St *Web:* www.hibachijapan.com	Erie	PA	16505	814-838-2495	
Hoss's Steak & Sea House 3302 W 26th St *Web:* www.hosss.com	Erie	PA	16506	814-838-6718	838-5071
Joe Roots Grill 35 Peninsula Dr	Erie	PA	16505	814-836-7668	
Matthew's Trattoria 153 E 13th St *Web:* www.matthewstrattoria.com	Erie	PA	16503	814-459-6458	452-2585
Max & Erma's 2078 Interchange Rd *Web:* www.maxandermas.com	Erie	PA	16509	814-860-3332	860-3430
Molly Brannigan's Irish Pub 506 State St *Web:* www.mollybrannigans.com/	Erie	PA	16501	814-453-7800	480-8330
Nunzie's Place 2330 E 38th St	Erie	PA	16510	814-825-1051	
Oscar's Pub & Restaurant 2147 W 12th St	Erie	PA	16505	814-454-4325	455-7659
Panos Restaurant 1504 W 38th St	Erie	PA	16508	814-866-0517	
Papermoon 1325 State St	Erie	PA	16501	814-455-7766	455-7768
Petra 3602 W Lake Rd *Web:* www.petrarestaurant.com	Erie	PA	16505	814-838-7197	833-9543
Pio's Italian Restaurant 815 East Ave	Erie	PA	16503	814-456-8866	
Pufferbelly 414 French St	Erie	PA	16507	814-454-1557	455-6138
Ricardo's 2112 E Lake Rd	Erie	PA	16511	814-455-4947	461-9177
Smokey Bones BBQ 2074 Interchange Rd *Web:* www.smokeybones.com	Erie	PA	16565	814-868-3388	864-9907
Sullivan's Pub & Eatery 301 French St	Erie	PA	16507	814-452-3446	
Syd's Place 2992 W Lake Rd	Erie	PA	16505	814-838-3089	
Valerio's 3205 Pittsburgh Ave	Erie	PA	16509	814-833-2959	
Waterfall Restaurant & Lounge 5735 E Lake Rd *Web:* www.waterfallrestaurant.com	Erie	PA	16511	814-899-8173	899-9895
Avenue Restaurant 21 Steinwehr Ave	Gettysburg	PA	17325	717-334-3235	334-5209
Blue Parrot Bistro 35 Chambersburg St	Gettysburg	PA	17325	717-337-3739	338-9345
Centuries on the Square 1 Lincoln Sq Best Western Gettysburg Hotel	Gettysburg	PA	17325	717-337-2000	337-2075
Dobbin House Tavern 89 Steinwehr Ave *Web:* www.dobbinhouse.com	Gettysburg	PA	17325	717-334-2100	334-6905
Dunlap's 90 Buford Ave *Web:* www.dunlapsrestaurant.com	Gettysburg	PA	17325	717-334-4816	334-2053
Ernie's Texas Lunch 58 Chambersburg St	Gettysburg	PA	17325	717-334-1970	
Farnsworth House Inn 401 Baltimore St *Web:* www.farnsworthhouseinn.com/dining-room.html	Gettysburg	PA	17325	717-334-8838	334-5862
General Pickett's Buffet 571 Steinwehr Ave	Gettysburg	PA	17325	717-334-7580	334-3701
Gingerbread Man 217 Steinwehr Ave *Web:* thegingerbreadman.net	Gettysburg	PA	17325	717-334-1100	
Herr Tavern 900 Chambersburg Rd *Web:* www.herrtavern.com	Gettysburg	PA	17325	717-334-4332	334-3332
La Bella Italia 402 York St	Gettysburg	PA	17325	717-334-1978	334-0781
Mamma Ventura 13 Chambersburg St	Gettysburg	PA	17325	717-334-5548	334-7231
O'Rorke's Eatery & Spirits 44 Steinwehr Ave	Gettysburg	PA	17325	717-334-2333	
Ping's Cafe 34 Baltimore St *Web:* www.pingscafe.com	Gettysburg	PA	17325	717-334-2234	337-2289
Plaza Restaurant 2-8 Baltimore St	Gettysburg	PA	17325	717-334-1999	
Aangan 3500 Walnut St *Web:* www.aanganindianrestaurant.com	Harrisburg	PA	17109	717-909-7777	909-7979
Appalachian Brewing Co 50 N Cameron St *Web:* abcbrew.com	Harrisburg	PA	17101	717-221-1080	221-1083
Benihana 2517 Paxton St *Web:* www.benihana.com	Harrisburg	PA	17111	717-232-6731	232-6740
El Rodeo 4659 Jonestown Rd	Harrisburg	PA	17109	717-652-5340	
Fuji Do Restaurant 1701 Paxton St	Harrisburg	PA	17104	717-561-1380	
Gabriella 3907 Jonestown Rd	Harrisburg	PA	17109	717-540-0040	
Golden Sheaf 1 N 2nd St	Harrisburg	PA	17101	717-237-6400	233-6271
Haydn's on Pine 215 Pine St	Harrisburg	PA	17101	717-920-1800	920-5630
Isaac's 421 Friendship Rd *Web:* www.isaacsdeli.com	Harrisburg	PA	17111	717-920-5757	920-3955
Marco Polo Gardens 4071 Chambers Hill Rd	Harrisburg	PA	17111	717-564-5382	
McGrath's Pub & Restaurant 202 Locust St	Harrisburg	PA	17101	717-232-9914	
Miyako 227 N 2nd St	Harrisburg	PA	17101	717-234-3250	
Molly Brannigans 31 N 2nd St *Web:* www.mollybrannigans.com	Harrisburg	PA	17101	717-260-9242	260-9244
Morgan's Place 4425 N Front St *Web:* www.morgans-place.com	Harrisburg	PA	17110	717-234-8103	260-0166
Passage to India 525 S Front St *Web:* www.passagetoindiapa.com	Harrisburg	PA	17104	717-233-1202	
Pavone's 300 S Hershey Rd *Web:* pavones1.com	Harrisburg	PA	17112	717-545-2338	671-9393
Raspberries 1 N 2nd St	Harrisburg	PA	17101	717-237-6419	233-6271
Scott's Bar & Grill 212 Locust St *Web:* www.scottsgrill.com	Harrisburg	PA	17101	717-234-7599	901-9966
Stocks on Second 211 N 2nd St *Web:* www.stocksonsecond.com	Harrisburg	PA	17101	717-233-6699	441-1119
Ted's Bar & Grill 6197 Allentown Blvd	Harrisburg	PA	17112	717-652-3832	671-1806
Tuscan Bistro 7011 Allentown Blvd	Harrisburg	PA	17112	717-920-5550	
Vietnamese Garden 304 Reily St	Harrisburg	PA	17102	717-238-9310	
Wharf The 6852 Derry St *Web:* www.thewharfbarandgrill.com	Harrisburg	PA	17111	717-564-9920	
Sullivan's Steakhouse 700 W DeKalb Pike *Web:* www.sullivansteakhouse.com	King of Prussia	PA	19406	610-878-9025	878-9248
Carr's Restaurant 50 W Grant St *Web:* www.carrsrestaurant.com/	Lancaster	PA	17603	717-299-7090	
Cove The 680 Milcross Rd	Lancaster	PA	17601	717-299-0159	390-8779
Damon's 680 Park City Center *Web:* www.damons.com	Lancaster	PA	17601	717-481-9800	481-9831
Doc Holliday's Steakhouse 931 Harrisburg Pike *Web:* www.dhollidays.com	Lancaster	PA	17603	717-397-3811	397-3622
El Serrano 2151 Columbia Ave *Web:* www.elserrano.com	Lancaster	PA	17603	717-397-6191	397-6180
Florentino's 1411 Columbia Ave	Lancaster	PA	17603	717-295-4964	
Gibraltar 931 Harrisburg Pike	Lancaster	PA	17603	717-397-2790	
La Fleur 2285 Lincoln Hwy E Continental Inn *Web:* www.continentalinn.com/laFleur.asp	Lancaster	PA	17602	717-299-0421	
Lemon Grass Thai 2481 Lincoln Hwy E	Lancaster	PA	17602	717-295-1621	295-2419
Loft Restaurant The 201 W Orange St *Web:* www.theloftlancaster.com/	Lancaster	PA	17603	717-299-0661	299-2010
Log Cabin 11 Lehoy Forest Dr *Web:* www.logcabinrestaurant.com	Lancaster	PA	17540	717-626-1181	626-1181
Lombardo's 216 Harrisburg Ave *Web:* www.lombardosrestaurant.com	Lancaster	PA	17603	717-394-3749	394-7179
Olde Greenfield Inn 595 Greenfield Rd *Web:* www.theoldegreenfieldinn.com	Lancaster	PA	17601	717-393-0668	393-0908
Pressroom Restaurant 26-28 W King St *Web:* www.pressroomrestaurant.com	Lancaster	PA	17603	717-399-5400	399-5463
Symposium 125 S Centerville Rd *Web:* www.symposiumrestaurant.com	Lancaster	PA	17603	717-391-7656	391-0749
Taj Mahal 2080 Bennet Ave *Web:* www.tajlancaster.com	Lancaster	PA	17601	717-295-1434	295-7413
Tony Wang's 2217 Lincoln Hwy E	Lancaster	PA	17602	717-399-1915	399-8475
Walnut Street Grille at Lancaster Brewing Co 302 N Plum St *Web:* www.lancasterbrewing.com	Lancaster	PA	17602	717-391-6258	391-6015
Amber 3505 Birney Ave	Moosic	PA	18507	570-344-7100	
Hacienda 4151 Birney Ave	Moosic	PA	18507	570-451-3663	
Nana's Pasta House 1223 Springbrook Ave	Moosic	PA	18507	570-457-9612	
Hickory Bridge Farm 96 Hickory Bridge Rd *TF:* 800-642-1766 ■ *Web:* www.hickorybridgefarm.com	Orrtanna	PA	17353	717-642-5261	624-6419
Alma de Cuba 1623 Walnut St *Web:* www.almadecubarestaurant.com	Philadelphia	PA	19103	215-988-1799	988-0807
Anjou 206 Market St	Philadelphia	PA	19106	215-923-1600	923-4981
Azure 931 N 2nd St *Web:* www.azurerestaurant.net	Philadelphia	PA	19123	215-629-0500	629-0555

				Phone	Fax
Barclay Prime 237 S 18th St	Philadelphia	PA	19103	215-732-7560	732-7564
Bistro Romano 120 Lombard St	Philadelphia	PA	19147	215-925-8880	925-9888
Web: www.bistroromano.com					
Brasserie Perrier 1619 Walnut St	Philadelphia	PA	19103	215-568-3000	568-7855
Web: www.brasserieperrier.com/index.cfm					
Buddakan 325 Chestnut St	Philadelphia	PA	19106	215-574-9440	574-8994
Web: www.buddakan.com					
Capital Grille The 1338 Chestnut St	Philadelphia	PA	19107	215-545-9588	545-6419
Web: www.thecapitalgrille.com					
Charles Plaza 234 N 10th St	Philadelphia	PA	19107	215-829-4383	
Chloe 232 Arch St	Philadelphia	PA	19106	215-629-2337	
Web: www.chloebyob.com					
Citrus 8136 Germantown Ave	Philadelphia	PA	19118	215-247-8188	
Continental The 138 Market St	Philadelphia	PA	19106	215-923-6069	923-2955
Web: www.continentalmartinibar.com					
Cuba Libre Restaurant 10 S 2nd St	Philadelphia	PA	19106	215-627-0666	627-6193
Web: www.cubalibrerestaurant.com					
Cucina Forte 768 S 8th St	Philadelphia	PA	19147	215-238-0778	
Dahlak 4708 Baltimore Ave	Philadelphia	PA	19143	215-726-6464	726-0996
Web: www.dahlakrestaurant.com					
Deux Cheminees 1221 Locust St	Philadelphia	PA	19107	215-790-0200	790-0202
Django 526 S 4th St	Philadelphia	PA	19147	215-922-7151	
Dmitri's 2227 Pine St	Philadelphia	PA	19103	215-985-3680	985-0278
El Vez 121 S 13th St	Philadelphia	PA	19107	215-928-9800	928-9889
Web: www.elvezrestaurant.com					
Fork 306 Market St	Philadelphia	PA	19106	215-625-9425	625-9435
Web: www.forkrestaurant.com					
Fountain Restaurant 1 Logan Sq	Philadelphia	PA	19103	215-963-1500	963-2748
Frederick's 757 S Front St	Philadelphia	PA	19147	215-271-3733	271-6888
Friday Saturday Sunday 261 S 21st St	Philadelphia	PA	19103	215-546-4232	940-1028
Web: www.frisatsun.com					
Grill The 10 S Broad St	Philadelphia	PA	19103	215-523-8000	523-8277
Hikaru 607 S 2nd St	Philadelphia	PA	19147	215-627-7110	
Il Cantuccio 701 N 3rd St	Philadelphia	PA	19123	215-627-6573	627-6573
Il Portico 1519 Walnut St	Philadelphia	PA	19102	215-587-7000	587-7005
Web: www.il-portico.com					
Jake's 4365 Main St	Philadelphia	PA	19127	215-483-0444	487-7122
Web: www.jakesrestaurant.com					
Karma 114 Chestnut St	Philadelphia	PA	19106	215-925-1444	925-1472
Web: www.thekarmarestaurant.com					
Kristian's 1100 Federal St	Philadelphia	PA	19147	215-468-0104	336-6229
Web: www.kristiansrestaurant.com					
L2 Restaurant & Bar 2201 South St	Philadelphia	PA	19146	215-732-7878	732-5278
Web: www.l2restaurant.com					
La Famiglia 8 S Front St	Philadelphia	PA	19106	215-922-2803	922-7495
Web: www.lafamiglia.com					
Lacroix at the Rittenhouse					
Rittenhouse Hotel 210 W Rittenhouse Sq	Philadelphia	PA	19103	215-790-2533	546-9858
Web: www.rittenhousehotel.com/lacroix.cfm					
L'Angolo 1415 Porter St	Philadelphia	PA	19145	215-389-4252	389-4525
Le Bar Lyonnais 1523 Walnut St	Philadelphia	PA	19102	215-567-1000	568-1151
Le Bec-Fin 1523 Walnut St	Philadelphia	PA	19102	215-567-1000	568-1151
Web: www.lebecfin.com/index.cfm					
Little Fish 600 Catherine St	Philadelphia	PA	19147	215-413-3464	
Web: www.littlefishphilly.com					
Los Catrines & Tequila's Bar 1602 Locust St	Philadelphia	PA	19103	215-546-0181	546-9953
Macaroni's 9315 Old Bustleton Ave	Philadelphia	PA	19115	215-464-3040	
Mama Yolanda's 746 S 8th St	Philadelphia	PA	19147	215-592-0195	
Marrakesh 517 S Leithgow St	Philadelphia	PA	19147	215-925-5929	627-6107
Matyson 37 S 19th St	Philadelphia	PA	19103	215-564-2925	564-2926
Web: www.matyson.com					
McCormick & Schmick's 1 S Broad St	Philadelphia	PA	19107	215-568-6888	568-2066
Web: www.mccormickandschmicks.com					
Melograno 2201 Spruce St	Philadelphia	PA	19103	215-875-8116	
Meritage Philadelphia 500 S 20th St	Philadelphia	PA	19146	215-985-1922	985-0455
Web: www.meritagephiladelphia.com					
Monte Carlo Living Room 150 South St	Philadelphia	PA	19147	215-925-2220	925-9956
Web: www.montecarlolivingroom.com					
Morimoto 723 Chestnut St	Philadelphia	PA	19106	215-413-9070	413-9075
Web: www.morimotorestaurant.com					
Morning Glory Diner 735 S 10th St	Philadelphia	PA	19147	215-413-3999	
Web: www.morningglorydiner.com					
Morton's The Steakhouse 1411 Walnut St	Philadelphia	PA	19106	215-557-0724	557-9741
Web: www.mortons.com					
Nan 4000 Chestnut St	Philadelphia	PA	19104	215-382-0818	
Web: www.nanrestaurant.com					
Old Original Bookbinders 125 Walnut St	Philadelphia	PA	19106	215-925-7027	925-7028
Web: www.bookbinders.biz					
Osaka 8605 Germantown Ave	Philadelphia	PA	19118	215-242-5900	242-4085
Overtures Restaurant 609 E Passyunk Ave	Philadelphia	PA	19147	215-627-3455	
Palm Restaurant 200 S Broad St	Philadelphia	PA	19102	215-546-7256	546-3088
Web: www.thepalm.com					
Paloma 6516 Castor Ave	Philadelphia	PA	19149	215-533-0356	
Web: www.palomarestaurant.com					
Pasion 211 S 15th St	Philadelphia	PA	19102	215-875-9895	875-9935
Web: www.pasionrestaurant.com					
Pif 1009 S 8th St	Philadelphia	PA	19149	215-625-2923	
Pod Restaurant 3636 Sansom St	Philadelphia	PA	19104	215-387-1803	387-1809
Web: www.podphiladelphia.com					
Prime Rib 1701 Locust St	Philadelphia	PA	19103	215-772-1701	790-9979
Web: www.theprimerib.com					
Radicchio 314 York Ave	Philadelphia	PA	19106	215-627-6850	627-6801
Web: www.radicchio-cafe.com					
Rib Crib 6333 Germantown Ave	Philadelphia	PA	19144	215-438-6793	
Ristorante Panorama 14 N Front St	Philadelphia	PA	19106	215-922-7800	922-7642
Rose Tattoo Cafe 1847 Callowhill St	Philadelphia	PA	19130	215-569-8939	947-9786
Web: www.rosetattoocafe.com					
Roy's 124-34 S 15th St	Philadelphia	PA	19102	215-988-1814	988-1867
Web: www.roysrestaurant.com					
Ruth's Chris Steakhouse 260 S Broad St	Philadelphia	PA	19102	215-790-1515	790-9480
Web: www.ruthschris.com					
Saloon 750 S 7th St	Philadelphia	PA	19147	215-627-1811	627-6265
Web: www.saloonrestaurant.net					
Sansom Street Oyster House 1516 Sansom St	Philadelphia	PA	19102	215-567-7683	567-0476
Web: www.sansomoysters.com					
Scannicchio 2500 S Broad St	Philadelphia	PA	19145	215-468-3900	468-3900
Web: www.scannicchio.com					
Shiao Lan Kung 930 Race St	Philadelphia	PA	19107	215-928-0282	
Siam Lotus 931 Spring Garden St	Philadelphia	PA	19123	215-769-2031	769-2032
Web: www.siamlotuscuisine.com					
Smith & Wollensky 210 W Rittenhouse Sq	Philadelphia	PA	19103	215-545-1700	545-8918
Web: www.smithandwollensky.com					
Sovalo 702 N 2nd St	Philadelphia	PA	19123	215-413-7770	413-7771
Web: www.sovalo.com					
Standard Tap 901 N 2nd St	Philadelphia	PA	19123	215-238-0630	238-0493
Web: www.standardtap.com					

				Phone	Fax
Susanna Foo 1512 Walnut St	Philadelphia	PA	19102	215-545-2666	546-9106
Web: www.susannafoo.com					
Swann Lounge 1 Logan Sq	Philadelphia	PA	19103	215-963-1500	963-9506
Sweet Lucy's Smokehouse 7500 State Rd	Philadelphia	PA	19136	215-331-3112	331-3185
Web: www.sweetlucys.com					
Tai Lake Restaurant 134 N 10th St	Philadelphia	PA	19107	215-922-0698	922-0347
Web: www.tailakerestaurant.com					
Tangerine 232 Market St	Philadelphia	PA	19106	215-627-5116	627-5117
Web: www.tangerinerestaurant.com					
Tre Scalini 1915 Passyunk Ave	Philadelphia	PA	19148	215-551-3870	
Twenty21 2005 Market St	Philadelphia	PA	19103	215-851-6262	851-6270
Web: www.twenty-21.com					
Umbria 7131 Germantown Ave	Philadelphia	PA	19119	215-242-6470	
Valanni Restaurant & Lounge 1229 Spruce St	Philadelphia	PA	19107	215-790-9494	790-9642
Web: www.valanni.com					
Vetri 1312 Spruce St	Philadelphia	PA	19107	215-732-3478	732-3487
Web: www.vetriristorante.com					
Vientiane Cafe 4728 Baltimore Ave	Philadelphia	PA	19143	215-726-1095	
Vietnam Restaurant 221 N 11th St	Philadelphia	PA	19107	215-592-1163	
Web: www.eatatvietnam.com					
White Dog Cafe 3420 Sansom St	Philadelphia	PA	19104	215-386-9224	
Web: www.whitedog.com					
Zanzibar Blue 200 S Broad St	Philadelphia	PA	19102	215-732-5200	
Web: www.zanzibarblue.com					
1902 Landmark Tavern 24 Market Sq	Pittsburgh	PA	15222	412-471-1902	
Ali Baba 404 S Craig St	Pittsburgh	PA	15213	412-682-2829	682-0926
Web: www.ibp.com/pitt/ali-baba					
Amel's 435 McNeilly Rd	Pittsburgh	PA	15226	412-563-3466	
Web: www.amelsrestaurant.com					
Bruschetta's 1831 E Carson St	Pittsburgh	PA	15203	412-431-3535	488-9703
Web: www.bruschettas.com					
Cafe Allegro 51 S 12th St	Pittsburgh	PA	15203	412-481-7788	481-4520
Web: www.cafeallegropittsburgh.com					
Cafe du Jour 1107 E Carson St	Pittsburgh	PA	15203	412-488-9695	
Cafe Zao 649 Penn Ave	Pittsburgh	PA	15222	412-325-7007	
Carlton Restaurant 500 Grant St 1 Mellon Bank Center	Pittsburgh	PA	15219	412-391-4099	281-1704
Web: www.thecarltonrestaurant.com					
Casbah 229 S Highland Dr	Pittsburgh	PA	15206	412-661-5656	
Web: www.bigburrito.com/casbah					
China Palace 5440 Walnut St	Pittsburgh	PA	15232	412-687-7423	687-5555
Web: www.chinapalacepittsburgh.com					
Christos Mediterranean Grille 130 6th St	Pittsburgh	PA	15222	412-261-6442	
Church Brew Works 3525 Liberty Ave	Pittsburgh	PA	15201	412-688-8200	688-8201
Web: www.churchbrew.com					
Del's 4428 Liberty Ave	Pittsburgh	PA	15224	412-683-1448	683-3863
Web: www.delsrest.com					
Eleven 1150 Smallman St	Pittsburgh	PA	15222	412-201-5656	201-5655
Web: www.bigburrito.com					
Grand Concourse 100 W Station Square Dr	Pittsburgh	PA	15219	412-261-1717	261-6041
Web: www.muer.com					
Gypsy Cafe 1330 Bingham St	Pittsburgh	PA	15203	412-381-4977	
Web: www.gypsycafe.net					
India Garden 328 Atwood St	Pittsburgh	PA	15213	412-682-3000	682-3130
Web: www.indiagarden.net					
Jimmy Tsang's 5700 Centre Ave	Pittsburgh	PA	15206	412-661-4226	661-8659
Kaya 2000 Smallman St	Pittsburgh	PA	15222	412-261-6565	261-1526
Web: www.bigburrito.com					
Kiku 225 W Station Square Dr	Pittsburgh	PA	15219	412-765-3200	765-3202
La Cucina Flegrea 2114 Murray Ave	Pittsburgh	PA	15217	412-521-2082	
Laforet 5701 Bryant St	Pittsburgh	PA	15206	412-665-9000	
Le Pommier 2104 E Carson St	Pittsburgh	PA	15203	412-431-1901	
Web: www.lepommier.com					
Lidia's 1400 Smallman St	Pittsburgh	PA	15222	412-552-0150	
Web: www.lidiasitaly.com					
Mallorca 2228 E Carson St	Pittsburgh	PA	15203	412-488-1818	488-1320
Web: www.mallorcarestaurant.com					
Max's Allegheny Tavern 537 Suismon St	Pittsburgh	PA	15212	412-231-1899	231-5099
Web: www.maxsalleghenytavern.com					
Monterey Bay Fish Grotto 1411 Grandview Ave	Pittsburgh	PA	15211	412-481-4414	481-4448
Web: montereybayfishgrotto.com					
Morton's The Steakhouse 625 Liberty Ave	Pittsburgh	PA	15222	412-261-7141	261-7151
Web: www.mortons.com					
Mullaney's Harp & Fiddle 24th St & Penn Ave	Pittsburgh	PA	15222	412-642-6622	
Web: www.harpandfiddle.com					
Nakama Japanese Steakhouse 1611 E Carson St	Pittsburgh	PA	15203	412-381-6000	381-6643
Web: www.eatatnakama.com					
Old Europe 1209 E Carson St	Pittsburgh	PA	15203	412-488-1700	
Opus 107 6th St	Pittsburgh	PA	15222	412-992-2005	992-2080
Web: www.dineatopus.com					
Original Fish Market 1001 Liberty Ave	Pittsburgh	PA	15222	412-227-3657	227-3658
Web: www.originalfishmarket.com					
Palomino 4 Gateway Center	Pittsburgh	PA	15222	412-642-7711	642-7731
Web: www.palomino.com					
Penn Brewery 800 Vinial St	Pittsburgh	PA	15212	412-237-9402	237-9106
Web: www.pennbrew.com					
Pittsburgh Steak Co 1924 E Carson St	Pittsburgh	PA	15203	412-381-5505	488-6628
Web: www.pghsteak.com					
Pleasure Bar & Restaurant 4729 Liberty Ave	Pittsburgh	PA	15224	412-682-9603	
Primanti Brothers 46 18th St	Pittsburgh	PA	15222	412-263-2142	
Web: www.primantibrothers.com					
Ruth's Chris Steak House 6 PPG Pl	Pittsburgh	PA	15222	412-391-4800	263-0121
Web: www.ruthschris.com					
Sesame Inn 715 Washington Rd	Pittsburgh	PA	15228	412-341-2555	341-6887
Web: www.sesameinn.net					
Soba 5847 Ellsworth Ave	Pittsburgh	PA	15232	412-362-5656	
Web: www.bigburrito.com					
Spice Island Tea House 253 Atwood St	Pittsburgh	PA	15213	412-687-8821	
Steelhead Grill 112 Washington Pl	Pittsburgh	PA	15219	412-394-3474	281-4797
Web: www.steelhead-grill.com					
Sushi Kim 1241 Penn Ave	Pittsburgh	PA	15222	412-281-9956	
Web: www.sushikim.com					
Tessaro's 4601 Liberty Ave	Pittsburgh	PA	15224	412-682-6809	
Thai Me Up 1925 E Carson St	Pittsburgh	PA	15203	412-488-8893	
Thai Place 5528 Walnut St	Pittsburgh	PA	15232	412-687-8586	687-7970
Web: www.thaiplacepgh.com					
Tram's Kitchen 4050 Penn Ave	Pittsburgh	PA	15224	412-682-2688	
Typhoon 242 S Highland Ave	Pittsburgh	PA	15206	412-362-2005	362-1040
Umi 5849 Ellsworth Ave	Pittsburgh	PA	15232	412-362-6198	
Wilson's Bar-B-Q 700 N Taylor Ave	Pittsburgh	PA	15212	412-322-7427	
Jad's Place Rt 315	Pittston Township	PA	18640	570-655-1234	
Banshee 320 Penn Ave	Scranton	PA	18503	570-969-4248	
Web: www.thebansheepub.com					
Carmen's 700 Lackawanna Ave	Scranton	PA	18503	570-342-8300	
Casa De Mama 1829 Bundy St	Scranton	PA	18508	570-961-2202	
Cooper's Seafood House 701 N Washington Ave	Scranton	PA	18509	570-346-6883	
Web: www.coopers-seafood.com					
Foliage 122 N Main Ave	Scranton	PA	18504	570-347-1071	

Pennsylvania (Cont'd)

Name / Address	City	State	Zip	Phone	Fax
Fresno's 914 Scranton Carbondale Hwy	Scranton	PA	18508	570-383-9400	
Web: www.fresnos.com					
Kelly's Pub & Eatery 1802 Cedar Ave	Scranton	PA	18505	570-346-9758	
La Trattoria 522 Moosic St	Scranton	PA	18505	570-961-1504	
Le Thai 1008 Scranton Carbondale Hwy	Scranton	PA	18508	570-341-5311	
Lone Star Steakhouse 1 Viewmont Dr	Scranton	PA	18508	570-963-0846	
Web: www.lonestarsteakhouse.com					
Osaka 244 Adams Ave	Scranton	PA	18503	570-341-9600	
Russell's 1918 Ash St	Scranton	PA	18510	570-961-8949	
Sibio's 1240 Quincy Ave	Scranton	PA	18510	570-961-9274	
Smith's Restaurant 1402 Cedar Ave	Scranton	PA	18505	570-961-9192	
Stirna's 120 W Market St	Scranton	PA	18508	570-343-5742	

Quebec

Name / Address	City	State	Postal Code	Phone	Fax
3 Amigos 1657 Ste Catherine W	Montreal	QC	H3H1L9	514-939-3329	
Anise 104 Laurier W	Montreal	QC	H2T2N7	514-276-6999	
Arahova 256 Saint-Viateur St W	Montreal	QC	H2V1X9	514-274-7828	
Au Bistro Gourmet 2 4007 St-Denis	Montreal	QC	H2W2M4	514-844-0555	
Web: www.aubistrogourmet.com					
Bangkok Cuisine 1616 Sainte-Catherine St W	Montreal	QC	H3H1L7	514-935-2178	
Baton Rouge 180 Sainte-Catherine St W	Montreal	QC	H5B1B5	514-282-7444	
Web: www.batonrougerestaurants.com					
Beijing 92 de la Gauchetiere W	Montreal	QC	H3W1K3	514-861-2003	
Berlin 101 Fairmount W	Montreal	QC	H2T2M4	514-270-3000	
Bohemia 1725 ch des Priaires	Montreal	QC	J4X1G5	450-444-5464	
Bombay Mahal 1001 Jean-Talon St W	Montreal	QC	H3N1T2	514-273-3331	
Buffet Maharaja 1481 Rene Levesque Blvd W	Montreal	QC	H3G1T8	514-934-0655	932-2515
Carlos & Pepe's 1420 Peel St	Montreal	QC	H3A1S8	514-288-3090	288-3092
Web: www.carlosandpepes.com/en					
Casa Napoli 6728 St-Laurent Blvd	Montreal	QC	H2S3C7	514-274-4351	
Chalet Bar-B-Q 5456 Sherbrooke St W	Montreal	QC	H4A1V9	514-489-7235	
Web: www.chaletbbq.com					
Chao Praya 50 Laurier W	Montreal	QC	H2T2N4	514-272-5339	272-7793
Chez Leveque 1030 Laurier W	Montreal	QC	H1A1A1	514-279-7355	
Chez la Mere Michel 1209 Guy St	Montreal	QC	H3H2K5	514-934-0473	
Web: www.chezlameremichel.com					
Chu Chai 4088 St Denis	Montreal	QC	H2W2M5	514-843-4194	
Coco Rico 3907 St-Laurent Blvd	Montreal	QC	H2W1X9	514-849-5554	
Da Vinci 1180 Bishop	Montreal	QC	H3G2E3	514-874-2001	
Europea 1227 de la Montagne	Montreal	QC	H3G1Z2	514-398-9229	
Web: www.europea.ca					
Ferreira Cafe Trattoria 1446 Peel St	Montreal	QC	H3A1S8	514-848-0988	
Web: www.ferreiracafe.com					
Frite Alors! 1562 Laurier E	Montreal	QC	H1A1A1	514-524-6336	
Web: www.fritealors.com					
Gandhi 230 St-Paul W	Montreal	QC	H2Y1Z9	514-845-5866	
Web: www.restaurantgandhi.com					
Gibby's 298 d'Youville Pl	Montreal	QC	H2Y2B6	514-282-1837	282-9771
Web: www.gibbys.com					
Globe Bar-Restaurant 3455 Saint-Laurent Blvd	Montreal	QC	H2X2T6	514-284-3823	284-3531
Web: www.restaurantglobe.com					
Hwang-Kum 5908 Sherbrooke St W	Montreal	QC	H4A1X7	514-487-1712	
Jano 3883 St-Laurent Blvd	Montreal	QC	H2W1X9	514-849-0646	849-3628
Kaizen Sushi Bar 4075 Ste-Catherine W	Montreal	QC	H3Z3J8	514-707-8744	932-4274
Web: www.70sushi.com					
Katsura 2170 de la Montagne St	Montreal	QC	H3G1Z7	514-849-1172	849-1705
Keg Steakhouse 25 St Paul E	Montreal	QC	H2V2Z7	514-871-9093	871-9818
Web: www.kegsteakhouse.com					
La Buona Forchetta 2407 Mont-Royal E	Montreal	QC	H2H1L2	514-521-6766	
La Chronique 99 Laurier Ave W	Montreal	QC	H2T2N6	514-271-3095	
Web: www.lachronique.qc.ca					
La Colombe 554 Duluth E	Montreal	QC	H2L1A9	514-849-8844	
La Maree 404 Jacques Cartier Pl	Montreal	QC	H2Y3B2	514-861-8126	
La Mer 1065 Papineau St	Montreal	QC	H2K4G9	514-522-2889	
La Sila 2040 Saint-Denis St	Montreal	QC	H2X3K7	514-844-5083	282-6519
La Sirene de la Mer 114 Dresden	Montreal	QC	H3P2B6	514-345-0345	345-0407
La Tarantella 184 Jean Talon E	Montreal	QC	H2R1S7	514-278-3067	278-3068
Web: www.restaurantlatarantella.com					
La Troika 2171 Crescent St	Montreal	QC	H3G2C1	514-849-9333	
Web: www.thetroika.com					
Laloux 250 Pine Ave E	Montreal	QC	H2W1P3	514-287-9127	281-0682
Web: www.laloux.com					
Le Mas Des Oliviers 1216 rue Bishop	Montreal	QC	H3G2E3	514-861-6733	861-7838
Web: www.lemasdesoliviers.ca					
Le Nil Bleu 3706 St-Denis	Montreal	QC	H2X3L7	514-285-4628	
Le Pacifique 1605 Saint-Denis St	Montreal	QC	H2X3K3	514-285-8820	
Le Petit Moulinsart 139 St Paul W	Montreal	QC	H2Y1Z5	514-843-7432	843-4779
Web: www.lepetitmoulinsart.com					
Le Piemontais 1145A de Bullion	Montreal	QC	H3X2Z2	514-861-8122	
L'Entrecote St-Jean 2022 Peel St	Montreal	QC	H3A2W5	514-281-6492	
Les Caprices de Nicolas 2072 Drummond St	Montreal	QC	H3G1W9	514-282-9790	288-0249
Web: www.lescaprices.com					
Les Chenets 2075 rue Bishop	Montreal	QC	H1A1A1	514-844-1842	844-0552
Web: www.leschenets.com					
Les Remparts 93 de la Commune E	Montreal	QC	H2V1J1	514-392-1649	
L'Estaminet 1340 Fleury E	Montreal	QC	H2C1R3	514-389-0596	
L'Express 3927 Saint-Denis St	Montreal	QC	H2W2M4	514-845-5333	
Maestro SVP 3615 St Laurent Blvd	Montreal	QC	H2X2V5	514-842-6447	
Web: www.maestrosvp.com					
Maison VIP 1077 Clark St	Montreal	QC	H2Z1K3	514-861-1943	
Mediterraneo Grill & Wine Bar 3500 Saint-Laurent Blvd	Montreal	QC	H2X2V1	514-844-0027	
Milos 5357 du Parc Ave	Montreal	QC	H2V4G9	514-272-3522	272-0778
Web: milos.ca					
Moishes Steakhouse 3961 Saint-Laurent Blvd	Montreal	QC	H2W1Y4	514-845-3509	845-9504
Web: www.moishes.ca					
Molivos 2310 Guy St	Montreal	QC	H3H2M2	514-846-8818	846-1263
Web: molivos.qc.ca					
Mysore Indian Cuisine 4216 St Laurent	Montreal	QC	H2W1Z3	514-844-4733	
Nuances 1 du Casino Ave	Montreal	QC	H3C4W7	514-392-2708	
Oishii Sushi 277 Bernard St W	Montreal	QC	H2V1T5	514-271-8863	
Pho Bang New York 1001 St-Laurent Blvd	Montreal	QC	H2Z1J3	514-954-2032	
Pub St-Paul 124 Saint-Paul St E	Montreal	QC	H2Y1G6	514-874-0485	874-9801
Web: www.pubstpaul.com					
Restaurant SOTIA 2556 Centre	Montreal	QC	H3K1J8	514-934-3282	
Ristorante Bar Luce 8693 Saint-Denis St	Montreal	QC	H2P2H4	514-858-5823	
Rotisserie Italienne 1933 Sainte-Catherine St W	Montreal	QC	H3H1M3	514-935-4436	
Toque 900 Jean-Paul Rio Pell	Montreal	QC	H2Z2B2	514-499-2084	
Upstairs Jazz Bar & Grill 1254 MacKay	Montreal	QC	H3G2H4	514-931-6808	931-5213
Web: www.upstairsjazz.com					
YOY Sushi Bar 4526 Saint-Denis St W	Montreal	QC	H2J2L3	514-844-9884	
ZYNG Nouillerie 1748 St Denis	Montreal	QC	H1A1A1	514-284-2016	284-3348
Web: www.zyng.com					
Au Parmesan 38 Saint-Louis St	Quebec	QC	G1R3Z1	418-692-0341	
Au Petit Coin Breton 1029 Saint-Jean St	Quebec	QC	G1R1R9	418-694-0758	
Auberge Louis-Hebert 668 Grande Allee E	Quebec	QC	G1R2K5	418-525-7812	
Web: www.louishebert.com					
Auberge du Tresor 20 Sainte-Anne St	Quebec	QC	G1R3X2	418-694-1876	
Web: www.aubergedutresor.com					
Aux Anciens Canadiens 34 Saint-Louis St	Quebec	QC	G1R4P3	418-692-1627	
Web: www.auxancienscanadiens.qc.ca					
Cafe d'Europe 27 Sainte-Angele St	Quebec	QC	G1R4G5	418-692-3835	
Cafe de la Paix 44 des Jardins St	Quebec	QC	G1R4L7	418-692-1430	
Web: www.restoquebec.com/cafedelapaix/					
Charles Baillairge 57 Sainte-Anne St	Quebec	QC	G1R3X4	418-692-2480	
Cochon Dingue Le 46 Champlain Blvd	Quebec	QC	G1K4H7	418-692-2013	
Web: www.cochondingue.com					
Cosmos Cafe 575 Grande Allee E	Quebec	QC	G1R2K4	418-640-0606	
D'Orsay Restaurant Pub 65 Buade St	Quebec	QC	G1R4A2	418-694-1582	
Entrecote Saint Jean 1080 Saint-Jean St	Quebec	QC	G1R1R8	418-694-0234	
Web: www.entrecotesaintjean.com					
Initiale 54 St-Pierre St	Quebec	QC	G1K3Z9	418-694-1818	
Web: www.restaurantinitiale.com					
La Cremaillere 73 Sainte Anne St	Quebec	QC	G1R3X4	418-692-2216	
La Grolla 815 Cote d'Abraham	Quebec	QC	G1R1A4	418-529-8107	
Web: www.restaurantlagrolla.com					
L'Astral 1225 cours du General-de-Montcalm	Quebec	QC	G1R4W6	418-647-2222	
Laurie Raphael 117 Dalhousie St	Quebec	QC	G1K4B9	418-692-4555	
Web: www.laurieraphael.com					
L'Aviatic Club 450 de la Gare-du-Palais	Quebec	QC	G1K3X2	418-522-3555	
Le Beffroi Steakhouse 775 Honore-Mercier Ave	Quebec	QC	G1R6A5	418-380-2638	
Le Champlain 1 des Carrieres St	Quebec	QC	G1R4P5	418-692-3861	
Le Charbon 450 de la Gare-Du-Palais St	Quebec	QC	G1K3X2	418-522-0133	
Le Continental 26 Saint-Louis St	Quebec	QC	G1R3Y9	418-694-9995	
Web: www.restaurantlecontinental.com					
Le Patriarche 17 Saint-Stanislas St	Quebec	QC	G1R4G7	418-692-5488	
Le Saint-Amour 48 Sainte-Ursule St	Quebec	QC	G1R4E2	418-694-0667	
L'Echaude 73 du Sault-au-Matelot St	Quebec	QC	G1K3Y9	418-692-1299	
Web: www.echaude.com					
Marie-Clarisse 12 du Petit-Champlain St	Quebec	QC	G1K4H4	418-692-0857	
Pub Saint-Alexandre 1087 Saint-Jean St	Quebec	QC	G1R1S3	418-694-0015	
Web: www.pubstalexandre.com					
Pub Thomas Dunn 369 Saint-Paul St	Quebec	QC	G1K3X3	418-692-4693	
Saint-James Resto Bistro 44 Cote du Palais	Quebec	QC	G1R4H8	418-692-1030	
Voodoo Grill 575 Grande Allee E	Quebec	QC	G1R2K4	418-647-2000	
Web: www.voodoogrill.com					
Apsara 71 D'Auteuil	Quebec City	QC	G1R433	418-694-0232	
Chez Rabelais 2 Petit-Champlain	Quebec City	QC	G1K4H4	418-694-9460	
Ciccio Cafe 875 Claire-Fontaine	Quebec City	QC	G1R3A8	418-525-6161	
Il Teatro 972 St-Jean	Quebec City	QC	G1R1R5	418-694-9996	
Le Lapin Saute 52 ru du Petit-Champlain	Quebec City	QC	G1S1X6	418-692-5325	
Mistral Gagnant 160 St-Paul	Quebec City	QC	G1K3W1	418-692-4260	
Poisson D'Avril 115 quai St Andre	Quebec City	QC	G1K3Y3	418-692-1010	
Restaurant Le Graffiti 1191 Cartier Ave	Quebec City	QC	G1R2C9	418-529-4949	
Serge Bruyere 1200 St-Jean St	Quebec City	QC	G1R1S8	418-694-0618	

Rhode Island

Name / Address	City	State	Zip	Phone	Fax
Basta 2195 Broad St	Cranston	RI	02905	401-461-0330	
22 Bowen's 22 Bowen's Wharf	Newport	RI	02840	401-841-8884	841-8883
Web: www.22bowens.com					
Alva 41 Mary St	Newport	RI	02840	401-846-6200	846-0701
Black Pearl Bannister's Wharf	Newport	RI	02840	401-846-5264	846-0360
Web: www.blackpearlnewport.com					
Brick Alley Pub & Restaurant 140 Thames St	Newport	RI	02840	401-849-6334	848-5640
Web: www.brickalley.com					
Cafe Zelda 528 Lower Thames St	Newport	RI	02840	401-849-4002	846-4578
Web: www.cafezelda.com					
Castle Hill Inn & Resort 590 Ocean Ave	Newport	RI	02840	401-849-3800	849-3838
Web: www.castlehillinn.com					
Christie's of Newport 14 Perry Mill Wharf	Newport	RI	02840	401-847-5400	
Web: www.christiesofnewport.com					
Clarke Cooke House Bannister's Wharf	Newport	RI	02840	401-849-2900	849-8750
Web: www.clarkecooke.com					
Elizabeth's Dining Room 404 Thames St	Newport	RI	02840	401-846-6862	
Loca 109 Long Wharf	Newport	RI	02840	401-843-8300	843-8301
Mamma Luisa 673 Thames St	Newport	RI	02840	401-848-5257	849-8415
Web: www.mammaluisa.com					
Mooring The Sayer's Wharf	Newport	RI	02840	401-846-2260	846-8950
Web: www.mooringrestaurant.com					
Mudville Pub 8 Marlboro St	Newport	RI	02840	401-849-1408	
Red Parrot 348 Thames St	Newport	RI	02840	401-847-3140	845-2530
Web: www.redparrotrestaurant.com					
Restaurant Bouchard 505 Thames St	Newport	RI	02840	401-846-0123	
Web: www.restaurantbouchard.com					
Salas' Dining Room 345 Thames St	Newport	RI	02840	401-846-8772	846-7428
Salvation Cafe 140 Broadway	Newport	RI	02840	401-847-2620	847-8967
Web: www.salvationcafe.com					
Sardella's 30 Memorial Blvd W	Newport	RI	02840	401-849-6312	848-0190
Web: www.sardellas.com					
Scales & Shells Restaurant & Raw Bar 527 Thames St	Newport	RI	02840	401-846-3474	848-7706
Web: www.scalesandshells.com					
Spiced Pear 117 Memorial Blvd	Newport	RI	02840	401-847-2244	847-3620
Web: www.spicedpear.com					
Thai Cuisine at Thames 517 Thames St	Newport	RI	02840	401-841-8822	845-8338
Tucker's Bistro 150 Broadway	Newport	RI	02840	401-846-3449	
Web: www.tuckersbistro.com					
White Horse Tavern 26 Marlborough St	Newport	RI	02840	401-849-3600	849-7317
Web: www.whitehorsetavern.com					
Al Forno Restaurant 577 S Main St	Providence	RI	02903	401-273-9760	
Andreas 268 Thayer St	Providence	RI	02906	401-331-7879	331-7300
Beyondindia 123 Dorrance St	Providence	RI	02903	401-278-2000	
Big Fish 370 Richmond St	Providence	RI	02903	401-751-3474	751-3495
Web: www.bigfishri.com					
Blue Grotto 210 Atwells Ave	Providence	RI	02903	401-272-9030	272-4818
Web: www.bluegrottorestaurant.com					
Cafe Nuovo 1 Citizens Plaza	Providence	RI	02903	401-421-2525	621-7126
Web: www.cafenuovo.com					
Camille's 71 Bradford St	Providence	RI	02903	401-751-4812	
Web: www.camillesonthehill.com/					
Capital Grille 1 Union Station	Providence	RI	02903	401-521-5600	331-8997
Web: www.thecapitalgrille.com					
Capriccio 2 Pine St	Providence	RI	02903	401-421-1320	331-8732
Web: www.capriccios.com					
Cassarino's Restaurant 177 Atwells Ave	Providence	RI	02903	401-751-3333	
Web: www.cassarinosri.com/					

Name / Address	City	State	ZIP	Phone	Fax
CAV 14 Imperial Pl.	Providence	RI	02903	401-751-9164	274-9107
Web: www.cavrestaurant.com					
Chez Pascal 960 Hope St	Providence	RI	02905	401-421-4422	
Web: www.chez-pascal.com					
Chilangos 447 Manton Ave	Providence	RI	02909	401-383-4877	
Classic Cafe 865 Westminster St	Providence	RI	02903	401-273-0707	273-0757
Cuban Revolution 149 Washington St	Providence	RI	02903	401-331-8829	
Web: www.thecubanrevolution.com					
Don Jose Tequila's 351 Atwells Ave	Providence	RI	02903	401-454-8951	
Web: www.donjoseteq.com					
Downcity Food & Cocktails 151 Weybosett St	Providence	RI	02903	401-331-9217	331-7260
Web: www.downcityfood.com					
Gracie's Place 194 Washington St	Providence	RI	02903	401-272-7811	
Haruki East 172 Wayland Ave	Providence	RI	02906	401-223-0332	490-3243
Hemenway's Seafood Grille					
121 S Main St Providence Washington Plaza	Providence	RI	02903	401-351-8570	331-8997
Web: www.hemenwaysrestaurant.com					
Julian's 318 Broadway	Providence	RI	02909	401-861-1770	831-3706
Web: www.juliansprovidence.com					
Lot 401 44 Hospital St	Providence	RI	02903	401-490-3980	
Web: www.lot401.com					
Mandarin Garden 555 Chalkstone Ave	Providence	RI	02908	401-751-0144	
Mill's Tavern 101 N Main St	Providence	RI	02903	401-272-3331	272-4453
New Japan Restaurant 145 Washington St	Providence	RI	02903	401-351-0300	
New Rivers Restaurant 7 Steeple St	Providence	RI	02903	401-751-0350	751-9669
Web: www.newriversrestaurant.com					
Nick's on Broadway 500 Broadway	Providence	RI	02903	401-421-0286	
Not Just Snacks 833 Hope St	Providence	RI	02906	401-831-1150	351-1166
Olives 108 N Main St	Providence	RI	02903	401-751-1200	861-4249
Opa 244 Atwells Ave	Providence	RI	02903	401-351-8282	351-4666
Pakarang 303 S Main St	Providence	RI	02903	401-453-3660	453-3661
Web: www.pakarangrestaurant.com					
Pane e Vino 365 Atwells Ave	Providence	RI	02903	401-223-2230	223-4322
Web: www.panevino.net					
Parkside Rotisserie & Bar 76 S Main St	Providence	RI	02903	401-331-0003	454-1600
Web: www.parksideprovidence.com					
Pot Au Feu 44 Custom House St	Providence	RI	02903	401-273-8953	273-8963
Providence Oyster Bar 283 Atwells Ave	Providence	RI	02903	401-272-8866	
Web: www.providenceoysterbar.com					
Raphael Bar-Ristro 1 Union Station	Providence	RI	02909	401-421-4646	421-4698
Sawaddee Thai Restaurant 93 Hope St	Providence	RI	02906	401-831-1122	831-1121
Web: sawaddeerestaurant.com					
Taste of India 230 Wickenden St	Providence	RI	02903	401-421-4355	751-1432
Web: www.tasteofindiari.com					
Ten Prime Steak & Sushi 55 Pine St	Providence	RI	02903	401-453-2333	453-5217
Web: www.tenprimesteakandsushi.com					
Tokyo Restaurant 388 Wickenden St	Providence	RI	02903	401-331-5330	
Waterman Grille The 4 Richmond Sq	Providence	RI	02906	401-521-9229	521-9351
Web: www.watermangrille.com					
Wes' Rib House 38 Dike St	Providence	RI	02909	401-421-9090	
Web: www.wesribhouse.com					
XO Steakhouse 125 N Main St	Providence	RI	02903	401-273-9090	273-0187
Web: www.xocafe.com					
Tuscan Tavern 632 Metacom Ave	Warren	RI	02885	401-247-9200	246-1755
Web: www.tuscantavern.net					

South Carolina

Name / Address	City	State	ZIP	Phone	Fax
39 Rue De Jean 39 John St	Charleston	SC	29401	843-722-8881	722-8835
Web: www.39ruedejean.com					
82 Queen 82 Queen St	Charleston	SC	29401	843-723-7591	577-7463
Web: www.82queen.com					
Amuse Tapas Restaurant & Wine Bar					
1720 Sam Rittenberg Blvd	Charleston	SC	29407	843-573-8778	
Anson's 12 Anson St	Charleston	SC	29401	843-577-0551	720-1955
Web: www.ansonrestaurant.com					
AW Shuck's 72 State St	Charleston	SC	29401	843-723-1151	720-2102
Web: www.a-w-shucks.com					
Barbadoes Room The 115 Meeting St	Charleston	SC	29401	843-577-2400	722-2112
TF: 800-874-9600 ■ *Web:* www.millshouse.com					
Basil 460 King St	Charleston	SC	29403	843-724-3490	724-3536
Web: www.basilthairestaurant.com					
Blossom Restaurant 171 E Bay St	Charleston	SC	29401	843-722-9200	937-4019
Boathouse The 549 E Bay St	Charleston	SC	29403	843-577-7171	577-7173
Web: www.boathouserestaurants.com					
Bubba Gump Shrimp Co 99 S Market St	Charleston	SC	29401	843-723-5665	723-5220
Web: www.bubbagump.com/html/charleston.html					
California Dreaming 1 Ashley Pointe Dr	Charleston	SC	29407	843-766-1644	571-2232
Web: www.centraarchy.com					
Carolina's 10 Exchange St	Charleston	SC	29401	843-724-3800	722-9473
Web: www.crewcarolina.com					
Charleston Grill 224 King St	Charleston	SC	29401	843-577-4522	724-8405
Web: www.charlestongrill.com					
Cintra 16 N Market St	Charleston	SC	29401	843-377-1090	377-1093
Circa 1886 149 Wentworth St	Charleston	SC	29401	843-853-7828	720-5292
Web: www.circa1886.com					
Coast 39-D John St	Charleston	SC	29403	843-722-8838	722-8835
Web: www.coastbarandgrill.com					
Cordavi Restaurant 14 N Market St	Charleston	SC	29401	843-577-0090	577-0272
Web: www.cordavi.com					
Cru Cafe 18 Pinckney St	Charleston	SC	29401	843-534-2434	534-2439
Web: www.crucafe.com					
Cypress Lowcountry Grille 167 E Bay St	Charleston	SC	29401	843-727-0111	853-6073
Web: www.magnolias-blossom-cypress.com/cypress					
FIG 232 Meeting St	Charleston	SC	29401	843-805-5900	805-5996
Web: www.eatatfig.com					
Fish 442 King St	Charleston	SC	29403	843-722-3474	937-0406
Web: www.fishrestaurant.net					
Fulton Five 5 Fulton St	Charleston	SC	29401	843-853-5555	853-6212
Gaulart & Maliclet 98 Broad St	Charleston	SC	29401	843-577-9797	723-1018
Web: www.fastandfrench.org					
Great Wall Express 1077 King St	Charleston	SC	29403	843-722-8834	722-8834
Grill 225 225 E Bay St	Charleston	SC	29401	843-266-4222	723-4320
Web: www.grill225.com					
Hank's Seafood Restaurant 10 Hayne St	Charleston	SC	29401	843-723-3474	
Web: www.hanksseafoodrestaurant.com					
Harbor View Restaurant 301 Savannah Hwy	Charleston	SC	29407	843-556-7100	556-6176
High Cotton Maverick Bar & Grill 199 E Bay St	Charleston	SC	29401	843-724-3815	724-3816
Web: www.high-cotton.net					
Hominy Grill 207 Rutledge Ave	Charleston	SC	29403	843-937-0930	937-0931
Web: www.hominygrill.com/					
Il Cortile Del Re 193A King St	Charleston	SC	29401	843-853-1888	
Jack's 41 George St	Charleston	SC	29401	843-723-5237	
Jestine's Kitchen 251 Meeting St	Charleston	SC	29401	843-722-7224	722-1133
Kim's Korean Japanese Steak House 1716 Hwy 171	Charleston	SC	29407	843-571-5100	
Magnolia's 185 E Bay St	Charleston	SC	29401	843-577-7771	722-0035
Web: www.magnolias-blossom-cypress.com/magnolias					
McCrady's 2 Unity Alley	Charleston	SC	29401	843-577-0025	577-3681
Web: www.mccradysrestaurant.com					
Middleton Place 4300 Ashley River Rd	Charleston	SC	29414	843-556-6020	766-4460
Web: www.middletonplace.org					
Mistral Restaurant 99 S Market St	Charleston	SC	29401	843-722-5708	
North Towne Grill & Seafood 2093 Eagle Landing Rd	Charleston	SC	29406	843-863-1001	863-1002
Web: www.northtownetogo.com					
Peninsula Grill 112 N Market St Planters Inn Historic Hotel	Charleston	SC	29401	843-723-0700	577-2125
Web: www.peninsulagrill.com					
Poogan's Porch 72 Queen St	Charleston	SC	29401	843-577-2337	577-2493
Web: www.poogansporch.com					
Robert's of Charleston 182 E Bay St	Charleston	SC	29401	843-577-7565	889-2953*
**Fax Area Code: 866* ■ *Web:* www.robertsofcharleston.com					
Slightly North of Broad 192 E Bay St	Charleston	SC	29401	843-723-3424	724-3811
Web: www.mavericksouthernkitchens.com/snob.html					
Sticky Fingers 235 Meeting St	Charleston	SC	29401	843-853-7427	853-0136
Web: www.stickyfingersonline.com					
Sushi Hiro 298 King St	Charleston	SC	29401	843-723-3628	723-0199
Tristan 55 S Market St	Charleston	SC	29401	843-534-2155	254-2156
Web: www.tristandining.com					
Trotter's 2008 Savannah Hwy	Charleston	SC	29407	843-571-1000	766-9444
Vickery's Bar & Grill 15 Beaufain St	Charleston	SC	29401	843-577-5300	577-5020
Web: www.vickerysbarandgrill.com					
Wasabi 61 State St	Charleston	SC	29401	843-577-5222	577-5001
Web: www.wasabicharleston.com					
Baan Sawan 2135 Devine St	Columbia	SC	29205	803-252-8992	252-8992
Web: www.baansawan.com					
Bert's Grill & Diner 6820 Main St	Columbia	SC	29203	803-786-4432	
Blue Marlin 1200 Lincoln St	Columbia	SC	29201	803-799-3838	799-5606
Web: www.bluemarlincolumbia.com					
California Dreaming 401 South Main St	Columbia	SC	29201	803-254-6767	254-0158
Web: www.californiadreamings.com					
Camon 1332 Assembly St	Columbia	SC	29201	803-254-5400	
Captain Tom's Seafood 1904 Broad River Rd	Columbia	SC	29210	803-772-7811	772-0907
Charleston Crab House 7201 Two Notch Rd	Columbia	SC	29223	803-462-1618	865-7363
Web: www.charlestoncrabhouse.com					
Delhi Palace 1029 Briargate Cir	Columbia	SC	29210	803-750-0866	750-2262
Web: www.delhipalacesc.com					
Dianne's on Devine 2400 Devine St	Columbia	SC	29205	803-254-3535	254-3445
Web: www.diannesondevine.com					
Eric's San Jose 6118 Garners Ferry Rd	Columbia	SC	29209	803-783-6650	
Garibaldi's 2013 Green St	Columbia	SC	29205	803-771-8888	771-8889
Gervais & Vine 620-A Gervais St	Columbia	SC	29201	803-799-8463	799-8442
Web: www.gervine.com					
Hampton Street Vineyard 1201 Hampton St	Columbia	SC	29201	803-252-0850	931-0193
Web: www.hamptonstreetvineyard.com					
Kyoto Japanese Steak House 1999 N Beltline Blvd	Columbia	SC	29204	803-782-1064	
Melting Pot The 1410 Colonial Life Blvd	Columbia	SC	29210	803-731-8500	731-8569
Web: www.meltingpot.com					
Miyo's Gourmet Shanghai & Szechuan Cuisine 922 S Main St	Columbia	SC	29201	803-779-6496	
Web: www.miyos.com					
Motor Supply Co Bistro 920 Gervais St	Columbia	SC	29201	803-256-6687	799-5146
Web: www.motorsupplycobistro.com					
Mr Friendly's New Southern Cafe 2001 Greene St Suite A	Columbia	SC	29205	803-254-7828	254-8219
Web: www.mrfriendlys.com/					
Palmetto Pig 530 Devine St	Columbia	SC	29201	803-733-2556	733-5860
Piggie Shack 5609 Farrow Rd	Columbia	SC	29203	803-691-4406	691-4383
SakiTumi Grill & Sushi Bar 807 Gervais St	Columbia	SC	29201	803-931-0700	799-7749
Saluda's 751 Saluda Ave	Columbia	SC	29205	803-799-9500	779-5997
Web: www.saludas.com					
Thai Lotus 612 Ashland Park St Andrews Rd	Columbia	SC	29210	803-561-0006	
Villa Tronco 1213 Blanding St	Columbia	SC	29201	803-256-7677	256-4336
Web: www.villatronco.com					
Village Gourmet 1410 Colonial Life Blvd W Suite 150	Columbia	SC	29210	803-798-6300	798-2226
Web: www.thevillagegourmet.net					
Yamato Steak House of Japan 360 Columbian Dr	Columbia	SC	29212	803-407-0033	407-6645
Web: www.yamatoinc.com					
Yesterday's 2030 Devine St	Columbia	SC	29205	803-799-0196	256-0860
Web: www.yesterdayssc.com					
Zorba's 6169 St Andrews Rd	Columbia	SC	29212	803-772-4617	772-0342
Addy's Dutch Cafe & Restaurant 17 E Coffee St	Greenville	SC	29601	864-232-2339	
Web: www.addys.net					
Augusta Grill 1818 Augusta St	Greenville	SC	29605	864-242-0316	232-0151
Web: www.augustagrill.com					
Bistro Europa 219 N Main St	Greenville	SC	29601	864-467-9975	232-7199
Web: www.bistro219.com					
Blue Ridge Brewing Co 217 N Main St	Greenville	SC	29601	864-232-4677	232-4680
Web: www.blueridgebrewing.com					
Caesar's 225 S Pleasantburg Dr	Greenville	SC	29607	864-233-4094	233-5801
Cafe & Then Some 101 College St	Greenville	SC	29601	864-232-2287	
Chicora Alley 608B S Main St	Greenville	SC	29601	864-232-4100	
Web: www.chicoraalley.com					
Chophouse '47 36 Beacon Dr	Greenville	SC	29615	864-286-8700	286-8733
Web: www.chophouse47.com					
City Range Steakhouse Grill 615 Haywood Rd	Greenville	SC	29607	864-286-9018	286-8139
Web: www.cityrange.com					
Greek Grille 3235 D-4 N Pleasantville Dr	Greenville	SC	29609	864-232-4033	232-7898
Web: www.greekgrille.com					
Henry's Smokehouse 240 Wade Hampton Blvd	Greenville	SC	29609	864-232-7774	232-7237
Web: www.henryssmokehouse.com					
Irashiai Sushi Pub & Japanese Restaurant					
420 N Pleasantburg Dr	Greenville	SC	29607	864-244-2008	
Web: www.irashiai.com					
Italian Market & Grill 534 Woods Lake Rd	Greenville	SC	29607	864-234-8464	234-8460
Web: www.italianmarketandgrill.com					
Joy of Tokyo 215 Pelham Rd	Greenville	SC	29615	864-232-2888	232-4323
Kanpai of Tokyo 533 Haywood Rd	Greenville	SC	29607	864-234-0334	234-0165
Web: www.kanpaioftokyo.com					
Khaki's 3795 E North St	Greenville	SC	29615	864-244-7733	
Larkin's on the River 318 S Main St	Greenville	SC	29601	864-467-9777	467-3028
Web: www.larkinsontheriver.com					
Latitude 631 S Main St	Greenville	SC	29601	864-467-1101	467-0788
Web: www.latitude-westend.com					
Lemongrass 106 N Main St	Greenville	SC	29601	864-241-9988	241-0503
Web: www.lemongrassthai.net					
Melting Pot The 475-5 Haywood Rd	Greenville	SC	29607	864-297-5035	
Web: www.meltingpot.com/					
Peter David's Fine Dining 921 Grove Rd	Greenville	SC	29605	864-242-0404	232-5028
Web: www.peterdavids.com					
Portofino's 3795 E North St	Greenville	SC	29615	864-268-9432	
Restaurant O 116 S Main St	Greenville	SC	29601	864-331-0007	
Web: www.restauranto.com/					
Royal Thai 104 Mauldin Rd	Greenville	SC	29605	864-299-0806	
Saskatoon 477 Haywood Rd	Greenville	SC	29607	864-297-7244	297-3614
Web: www.saskatoonrestaurant.com					

South Carolina (Cont'd)

Name / Address	City	State	ZIP	Phone	Fax
Soby's 207 S Main St	Greenville	SC	29601	864-232-7007	232-5282
Web: www.sobys.com					
Trattoria Giorgio 121 S Main St	Greenville	SC	29601	864-271-9166	
Web: www.trattoriagiorgio.net					
Westwood Restaurant 1601A Cedar Lane Rd	Greenville	SC	29617	864-246-8880	246-8987
Web: www.eatatwestwood.com/					
Alexander's Seafood Restaurant 76 Queens Folly Rd	Hilton Head Island	SC	29928	843-785-4999	785-2117
Web: www.alexandersrestaurant.com					
Alligator Grille Seafood & Sushi Bar 33 Office Park Rd	Hilton Head Island	SC	29928	843-842-4888	
Antonio's Restaurant 1000 William Hilton Pkwy Village at Wexford Suite G-2	Hilton Head Island	SC	29928	843-842-5505	842-8280
Web: www.antonios.net					
Aunt Chilada's Easy Street Cafe 69 Pope Ave	Hilton Head Island	SC	29928	843-785-7700	842-9936
Barony The 2 Grass Lawn Ave	Hilton Head Island	SC	29926	843-681-4000	
Boathouse II 397 Squire Pope Rd	Hilton Head Island	SC	29926	843-681-3663	342-2288
Web: www.celebrationusa.com					
Charley's Crab 2 Hudson Rd	Hilton Head Island	SC	29926	843-342-9066	342-9546
Charlie's L'Etoile Verte 8 New Orleans Rd	Hilton Head Island	SC	29928	843-785-9277	
Web: www.charliesofhiltonhead.com					
CQ's Restaurant 140-A Lighthouse Rd Harbour Town	Hilton Head Island	SC	29928	843-671-2779	671-6787
Web: www.cqsrestaurant.com					
Crane's Tavern & Steakhouse 26 New Orleans Rd	Hilton Head Island	SC	29928	843-341-2333	341-3089
Crazy Crab 149 Lighthouse Rd	Hilton Head Island	SC	29928	843-363-2722	363-6025
Web: www.thecrazycrab.com					
Del Vecchio's 890 William Hilton Pkwy	Hilton Head Island	SC	29928	843-842-8700	842-3400
Fiesta Fresh Mexican Grill 51 New Orleans Rd Suite 4	Hilton Head Island	SC	29928	843-785-4788	
Harbourmaster's Restaurant 1 Shelter Cove Ln	Hilton Head Island	SC	29928	843-785-3030	842-2252
Home Port The 106 Helmsman Way	Hilton Head Island	SC	29928	843-785-9666	
Web: eugeneswaterfront.com					
Hudson's on the Docks 3 Hudsons Rd	Hilton Head Island	SC	29926	843-681-2772	681-2774
Web: www.hudsonsonthedocks.com					
It's Greek to Me Inc 1 New Orleans Rd Suite G	Hilton Head Island	SC	29928	843-341-3556	341-3558
Jaxx Restaurant The 45 Pembroke Dr 105 Festival Center	Hilton Head Island	SC	29926	843-342-2400	
Web: www.jaxxofhiltonhead.com					
Juleps Restaurant 14 Greenwood Dr Suite G	Hilton Head Island	SC	29928	843-842-5857	842-2893
Web: www.julepsofhiltonhead.com/					
Jump & Phil's Bar & Grill 7-B Greenwood Dr Suite 3	Hilton Head Island	SC	29928	843-785-9070	785-8298
Just Pasta 1 Coligny Plaza	Hilton Head Island	SC	29928	843-686-3900	
Kenny B's French Quarter Cafe 70 Circle Center	Hilton Head Island	SC	29926	843-785-3315	785-3327
Kingfisher Seafood & Steak House 18 Harborside Ln Shelter Cove Harbour	Hilton Head Island	SC	29928	843-785-4442	785-6792
Web: www.kingfisherseafood.com					
Mangiamo 1107 Main St	Hilton Head Island	SC	29926	843-682-2444	682-3355
Web: mangiamo.net					
Market Street Cafe 1 N Forest Beach Blvd	Hilton Head Island	SC	29928	843-686-4976	
Web: www.marketstreetcafe.com/					
Marley's Island Grille 35 Office Park Rd	Hilton Head Island	SC	29928	843-686-5800	686-4765
Web: www.marleysislandgrille.com					
Mi Tierra Mexican Restaurant 160 William Hilton Pkwy Suite 6	Hilton Head Island	SC	29926	843-342-3409	
Michael Anthony's 37 New Orleans Rd Suite L	Hilton Head Island	SC	29928	843-785-6272	671-3513
Web: www.hiltonheaddlc.com/michaelanthony.htm					
Mostly Seafood 23 Ocean Ln	Hilton Head Island	SC	29938	843-341-8004	
Old Fort Pub 65 Skull Creek Dr	Hilton Head Island	SC	29926	843-681-2386	681-9287
Old Oyster Factory 101 Marshland Rd	Hilton Head Island	SC	29926	843-681-6040	
Web: www.oldoysterfactory.com					
Plantation Cafe 81 Pope Ave	Hilton Head Island	SC	29928	843-785-9020	785-8457
Red Fish 8 Archer Rd	Hilton Head Island	SC	29938	843-686-3388	
Web: www.redfishofhiltonhead.com					
Sage Room 81 Pope Ave	Hilton Head Island	SC	29928	843-785-5352	785-5354
Web: www.thesageroom.com					
Salty Dog Cafe 232 S Sea Pines Dr	Hilton Head Island	SC	29928	843-671-5199	671-6498
Web: saltydog.com					
Santa Fe Cafe 807 William Hilton Pkwy	Hilton Head Island	SC	29928	843-785-3838	785-2496
Scott's Fish Market Restaurant 1 Shelter Cove Ln	Hilton Head Island	SC	29928	843-785-7575	785-6658
Signe's Bakery & Cafe 93 Arrow Rd	Hilton Head Island	SC	29928	843-785-9118	785-6144
Web: www.signesbakery.com					
Smokehouse The 102 Pope Ave	Hilton Head Island	SC	29928	843-842-4227	842-4245
Web: www.smokehousehhi.com					
Spice Lounge & Restaurant Village at Wexford Suite B-6	Hilton Head Island	SC	29928	843-785-4850	
Web: www.spicehhi.com					
Steamer Seafood Co 1 N Forest Beach Dr Suite 28 Calligny Plaza	Hilton Head Island	SC	29928	843-785-2070	
Web: www.steamerseafood.com					
Sticky Fingers 34 Palmetto Bay Rd	Hilton Head Island	SC	29928	843-686-7427	686-6988
Web: www.stickyfingersonline.com					
Stripes 32 Office Park Rd	Hilton Head Island	SC	29928	843-686-4747	
Studio The 20 Pope Executive Park	Hilton Head Island	SC	29928	843-785-6000	785-5999
Web: www.studiodining.com					
Tapas Restaurant 11 Northridge Plaza	Hilton Head Island	SC	29926	843-681-8590	
Web: www.tapasrestaurant.com/					
Taste of Thailand 807 William Hilton Pkwy Suite 1200	Hilton Head Island	SC	29928	843-341-6500	342-5327
Truffles Cafe 71 Lighthouse Rd	Hilton Head Island	SC	29928	843-671-6136	671-6194
Web: www.trufflescafe.com/					
Water Front Cafe 160 Lighthouse Rd	Hilton Head Island	SC	29928	843-671-3399	
Web: www.waterfrontcafehhi.com/					
Bovine's 3979 Hwy 17 Business	Murrells Inlet	SC	29576	843-651-2888	651-0211
Angelo's Steak & Pasta 2011 S Kings Hwy	Myrtle Beach	SC	29577	843-626-2800	
Bangkok House 318 N Kings Hwy	Myrtle Beach	SC	29577	843-626-5384	
Bella Napoli 3901 Dick Pond Rd	Myrtle Beach	SC	29588	843-215-8777	
Big D's 350 George Bishop Pkwy	Myrtle Beach	SC	29579	843-236-4666	
Captain George's 1401 29th Ave	Myrtle Beach	SC	29577	843-916-2278	443-9097
Web: www.captaingeorges.com					
Caruso's Italian Restaurant 4700 Hwy 17 Bypass S	Myrtle Beach	SC	29588	843-293-8682	
China Buffet 9668 N Kings Hwy	Myrtle Beach	SC	29572	843-692-0238	692-9366
El Cerro Grande 108 S Kings Hwy	Myrtle Beach	SC	29577	843-946-9562	448-4431
Farm House 500 N Kings Hwy	Myrtle Beach	SC	29577	843-448-2743	
Farmer & Fisherman 9924 Hwy 17 N	Myrtle Beach	SC	29572	843-839-3474	
Fiesta Del Burroloco 960 Jason Blvd	Myrtle Beach	SC	29577	843-626-1756	626-1860
Web: www.fiestadelburroloco.com					
Flamingo Grille 7050 N Kings Hwy	Myrtle Beach	SC	29572	843-449-5388	449-4551
Giant Crab 9597 N Kings Hwy	Myrtle Beach	SC	29572	843-449-1097	449-3575
Web: www.giantcrab.com					
J Edwards Great Ribs & More 2300 S Kings Hwy	Myrtle Beach	SC	29577	843-626-9986	626-9988
Web: www.jedwardsgreatribs.com					
Melting Pot The 5001 N Kings Hwy	Myrtle Beach	SC	29577	843-692-9003	692-9004
Web: www.meltingpot.com					
Miyabi 9732 N Kings Hwy	Myrtle Beach	SC	29572	843-449-9294	692-2274
NASCAR Cafe 1808 21st Ave N	Myrtle Beach	SC	29577	843-946-7223	916-0314
Web: www.nascarcafe.com					
New China Buffet 9601 N Kings Hwy	Myrtle Beach	SC	29572	843-497-0100	
Original Benjamin's The 9593 N Kings Hwy	Myrtle Beach	SC	29572	843-449-0821	
Web: www.originalbenjamins.com					
Planet Hollywood 2915 Hollywood Dr	Myrtle Beach	SC	29577	843-916-0411	448-7828
Web: www.planethollywood.com					
Sea Captain's House 3000 N Ocean Blvd	Myrtle Beach	SC	29577	843-448-8082	
Web: www.seacaptains.com					
Senor Frogs 1304 Celebrity Cir Bldg R-8	Myrtle Beach	SC	29577	843-444-5506	
Web: www.senorfrogs.com					
Spring House Restaurant 2600 N Kings Hwy	Myrtle Beach	SC	29577	843-626-5941	
Sugami 4813 N Kings Hwy	Myrtle Beach	SC	29577	843-692-7709	692-7639
Thoroughbreds 9706 N Kings Hwy	Myrtle Beach	SC	29572	843-497-2636	497-6474
Web: www.thoroughbredsrest.com					
Yamato Steak House of Japan 1213 Celebrity Cir Suite R-5	Myrtle Beach	SC	29577	843-448-1959	448-6811
Web: www.yamato-inc.com					
Sea Blue 501 Hwy 17 N	North Myrtle Beach	SC	29582	843-249-8800	
Web: www.seablueonline.com/					
Crabby Mike's Calabash Seafood 290 Hwy 17 N	Surfside Beach	SC	29575	843-444-2722	238-3526
Web: www.crabbymikes.com					

South Dakota

Name / Address	City	State	ZIP	Phone	Fax
Cattleman's Club Steakhouse & Lounge 29608 SD Hwy 34	Pierre	SD	57501	605-224-9774	
Guadalajara 314 W Sioux Ave	Pierre	SD	57501	605-224-2771	224-2720
Jake's Good Time Place 620 S Cleveland	Pierre	SD	57501	605-945-0485	
La Minestra 106 E Dakota Ave	Pierre	SD	57501	605-224-8090	945-2696
Web: www.laminestra.com					
Lighthouse Bistro 19602 Lake Pl	Pierre	SD	57501	605-224-9340	
Web: www.lighthousepointe.com					
Longbranch Restaurant & Lounge 351 S Pierre St	Pierre	SD	57501	605-224-6166	945-2240
Web: www.geocities.com/longbranchbar					
Mad Mary's Steakhouse & Saloon 110 E Dakota Ave	Pierre	SD	57501	605-224-6469	
Outpost Lodge 28229 Cow Creek Rd	Pierre	SD	57501	605-264-5450	264-5369
Web: www.theoutpostlodge.com					
Pier 347 Capitol Cafe 347 S Pierre St	Pierre	SD	57501	605-224-2400	
Saint Charles Restaurant & Cactus Lounge 207 E Capitol Ave	Pierre	SD	57501	605-224-4546	
Web: www.stcharlesrestaurant.com/					
Smokee's BBQ 1415 E Wells Ave	Pierre	SD	57501	605-224-7427	
Sunset Lodge Steakhouse 28181 182nd St	Pierre	SD	57501	605-264-5480	264-5487
Botticelli Italian Restaurant 523 Main St	Rapid City	SD	57701	605-348-0089	
Casa del Rey 1902 Mt Rushmore Rd	Rapid City	SD	57701	605-348-5679	348-9671
Colonial House 2501 Mt Rushmore Rd	Rapid City	SD	57701	605-342-4640	341-0445
Diamond Dave's 2200 N Maple Ave	Rapid City	SD	57701	605-342-0556	
Web: www.diamonddaves.com					
Firehouse Brewing Co 610 Main St	Rapid City	SD	57701	605-348-1915	
Fireside Inn 23021 Hisega Rd	Rapid City	SD	55702	605-342-3900	
Golden Phoenix 2421 W Main St	Rapid City	SD	57702	605-348-4195	
Great Wall 315 E North St	Rapid City	SD	57701	605-348-1060	
Hong Kong Buffet 927 E North St	Rapid City	SD	57701	605-716-4664	
Hunan 1720 Mt Rushmore Rd	Rapid City	SD	57701	605-341-3888	
La Costa Mexican Restaurant 643 Omaha St	Rapid City	SD	57701	605-388-8780	
Landmark Restaurant 523 6th St	Rapid City	SD	57701	605-342-1210	
Minerva's 2111 N Lacrosse St	Rapid City	SD	57701	605-394-9505	394-8945
Mongolian Grill 1415 Lacrosse St	Rapid City	SD	57701	605-388-3187	
Ristorante Marsala 609 Main St	Rapid City	SD	57701	605-341-3088	
Saigon 221 E North St	Rapid City	SD	57701	605-348-8523	
601 Arota 601 W 33rd St	Sioux Falls	SD	57105	605-338-6801	
Web: www.601arota.com					
Carolina Cafe 222 S Philips Ave	Sioux Falls	SD	57104	605-339-0118	331-4218
Casa Del Rey 901 W Russell St	Sioux Falls	SD	57104	605-338-6078	
Cherry Creek Grill 3104 E 26th St	Sioux Falls	SD	57103	605-336-2333	336-1999
CJ Callaway's 500 E 69th St	Sioux Falls	SD	57108	605-334-8888	334-1998
Web: www.cjcallaways.com					
Dynasty 5326 W 26th St	Sioux Falls	SD	57106	605-362-8888	
Falls Landing 200 E 8th St	Sioux Falls	SD	57103	605-336-2290	
Famous Dave's 2700 S Minnesota Ave	Sioux Falls	SD	57105	605-334-8800	334-8822
Web: www.famousdaves.com					
Granite City Food & Brewery 2620 S Louise Ave	Sioux Falls	SD	57106	605-362-0000	362-0029
Web: www.gcfb.net					
Incas 3312 S Holly Ave	Sioux Falls	SD	57105	605-367-1992	367-1993
La Fiesta 2039 W 41st St	Sioux Falls	SD	57105	605-332-0330	332-5257
Minerva's 301 S Phillips Ave	Sioux Falls	SD	57104	605-334-0386	334-9585
River Walk 196 E 6th St	Sioux Falls	SD	57104	605-339-4824	274-0086
Web: www.theriverwalkcafe.com					
Sanaa's 401 E 8th St	Sioux Falls	SD	57104	605-275-2516	
Spezia 1716 S Western Ave	Sioux Falls	SD	57105	605-334-7491	334-7574
Web: www.ciaodown.com					
Surf's Up Crab Shack & Smokehouse 220 S Philips Ave	Sioux Falls	SD	57104	605-336-5040	331-4218
Sushi Masa 423 S Phillips Ave	Sioux Falls	SD	57104	605-977-6968	
Szechwan 415 N Minnesota Ave	Sioux Falls	SD	57104	605-332-2010	332-4010
Timberlodge Steakhouse 3509 W 41st St	Sioux Falls	SD	57106	605-361-8899	362-9531
Web: www.timberlodgesteakhouse.com					
Touch of Europe 337 S Phillips Ave	Sioux Falls	SD	57104	605-336-3066	

Tennessee

Name / Address	City	State	ZIP	Phone	Fax
Corky's 100 Franklin Rd	Brentwood	TN	37027	615-373-1020	371-1638
Terra Nostra 105 Frazier Ave	Chattanooga	TN	37405	423-634-0238	634-0268
Web: terranostra.rootresources.com					
212 Market Restaurant 212 Market St	Chattanooga	TN	37402	423-265-1212	267-6757
Web: www.212market.com					
Acropolis The 2213 Hamilton Place Blvd	Chattanooga	TN	37421	423-899-5341	899-6587
Web: www.acropolisgrill.com					
Amigo Mexican Restaurant 3805 Ringgold Rd	Chattanooga	TN	37412	423-624-4345	
Back Inn Cafe 412 E 2nd St	Chattanooga	TN	37403	423-265-5033	
Broad Street Grille at the Chattanoogan 1201 Broad St	Chattanooga	TN	37402	423-424-3700	756-3404
Web: www.chattanooganhotel.com/dining/					
China Moon 5600 Brainerd Rd	Chattanooga	TN	37411	423-893-8088	
Chop House The 2011 Gunbarrel Rd	Chattanooga	TN	37421	423-892-1222	
Web: www.thechophouse.com/					
Formosa Restaurant 5425 Hwy 153	Chattanooga	TN	37343	423-875-6953	875-4727
Web: www.formosa-restaurant.com					
India Mahal 5970 Brainerd Rd	Chattanooga	TN	37421	423-510-9651	
J Alexander's 2215 Hamilton Place Blvd	Chattanooga	TN	37421	423-855-5559	855-5559
Web: www.jalexanders.com					
Kanpai of Tokyo Hamilton Crossing 2200 Hamilton Place Blvd	Chattanooga	TN	37421	423-855-8204	855-9687
Web: www.kanpaioftokyo.com					
Logan's Roadhouse 2119 Gunbarrel Rd	Chattanooga	TN	37421	423-499-4339	499-4350
Web: www.logansroadhouse.com					

Restaurant	City	State	ZIP	Phone	Fax
Mount Vernon 3535 Broad St	Chattanooga	TN	37409	423-266-6591	
Na Go Ya 4921 Brainerd Rd	Chattanooga	TN	37411	423-899-9252	899-9252
Porker's BBQ 1251 Market St	Chattanooga	TN	37402	423-267-2726	
Web: www.porkersbbq.com					
Provino's 5084 South Terrace Plaza	Chattanooga	TN	37412	423-899-2559	
Web: www.provinos.com					
Riverside Catfish House 18039 Hwy 41	Chattanooga	TN	37419	423-821-9214	
Saint John's 1278 Market St	Chattanooga	TN	37402	423-266-4400	267-3004
Web: www.stjohnsrestaurant.com					
Sekisui of Chattanooga 200 Market St	Chattanooga	TN	37402	423-267-4600	267-4610
Web: www.sekisuiusa.com/					
Southern Star 1206 Market St	Chattanooga	TN	37402	423-267-8899	
Web: www.southernstarrestaurant.com					
Southside Grill 1400 Cowart St	Chattanooga	TN	37408	423-266-9211	266-0927
Web: www.southsidegrill.com					
Station House 1400 Market St	Chattanooga	TN	37402	423-266-5000	
Sticky Fingers 420 Broad St	Chattanooga	TN	37402	423-265-7427	265-3107
Web: www.stickyfingersonline.com					
Sushi Nabe of Kyoto 110 River St	Chattanooga	TN	37421	423-634-0171	
Web: www.sushinabechattanooga.com					
Sweet Basil 5845 Brainerd Rd	Chattanooga	TN	37411	423-485-8836	485-9545
Thai Smile 3 219 Market St	Chattanooga	TN	37402	423-266-2333	266-7198
Tony's Pasta Shop & Trattoria 212 High St	Chattanooga	TN	37403	423-265-5033	
Alta Cucina 1200 N Roan St	Johnson City	TN	37601	423-928-2092	928-3684
Amigo III 3211 Peoples St	Johnson City	TN	37604	423-952-0551	
Bello Vita 2927 N Roan St Bldg 2	Johnson City	TN	37601	423-282-8600	
Cafe 111 111 Broyles Dr	Johnson City	TN	37601	423-283-4633	283-0550
Cafe Pacific 1033 W Oakland Ave	Johnson City	TN	37604	423-610-0117	610-0117
Charley's Steakery 2011 N Roan St	Johnson City	TN	37601	423-283-0784	
Dixie Barbecue Co 3301 N Roan St	Johnson City	TN	37601	423-283-7447	
El Chico 2929 N Roan St	Johnson City	TN	37601	423-282-4080	282-0801
Web: www.elchico.com					
El Matador 2904 Bristol Hwy	Johnson City	TN	37601	423-282-8111	283-5480
Firehouse Restaurant 627 W Walnut St	Johnson City	TN	37604	423-929-7377	929-2080
Web: www.thefirehouse.com					
Harbor House Seafood 2510 N Roan St	Johnson City	TN	37601	423-282-5122	282-0428
Web: www.harborhousejc.com					
Horseshoe Restaurant & Lounge 908 W Market St	Johnson City	TN	37604	423-928-8992	929-1511
House of Ribs 3100 Kingsport Hwy	Johnson City	TN	37601	423-282-8077	282-0540
Logan's Roadhouse 3112 Browns Mill Rd	Johnson City	TN	37604	423-915-1122	915-1022
Web: www.logansroadhouse.com					
Misaki Seafood & Steak House of Japan 3104 Bristol Hwy	Johnson City	TN	37601	423-282-5451	
Moto Japanese Restaurant 2607 N Roan St	Johnson City	TN	37601	423-282-6686	282-0132
Office Lounge 2406 N Roan St	Johnson City	TN	37601	423-283-0050	282-2488
Peerless Steak House 2531 N Roan St	Johnson City	TN	37601	423-282-2351	283-0439
Web: www.thepeerlessinc.com					
Red Pig Bar-B-Q 2201 Ferguson Rd	Johnson City	TN	37604	423-282-6585	282-6309
Sushi Blues 1805 N Roan St Suite E-3	Johnson City	TN	37601	423-232-1289	
Web: www.sushiblues.net					
Vito's Italian Connection 3103 N Roan St	Johnson City	TN	37601	423-926-6161	
Baker-Peters Jazz Club 9000 Kingston Pike	Knoxville	TN	37923	865-690-8110	690-4022
Web: www.bakerpetersjazzclub.com/BP					
Bayou Bay Seafood House 7117 Chapman Hwy	Knoxville	TN	37920	865-573-7936	
Bonefish Grill 6610 Kingston Pike	Knoxville	TN	37919	865-558-5743	909-0915
Web: www.bonefishgrill.com					
Bravo Cucina Italiana 106 Major Reynolds Pl	Knoxville	TN	37919	865-584-5510	584-5804
Web: www.bestitalianusa.com					
Buddy's Bar-B-Q 4401 Chapman Hwy	Knoxville	TN	37920	865-579-1747	579-3315
By the Tracks Bistro 5200 Kingston Pike	Knoxville	TN	37919	865-558-9500	584-7786
Web: www.bythetracksbistro.com					
Calhoun's 10020 Kingston Pike	Knoxville	TN	37922	865-673-3444	673-3446
Web: www.calhouns.com					
Cancun 4829 N Broadway St	Knoxville	TN	37918	865-688-4030	
Chesapeake's 500 Henley St	Knoxville	TN	37902	865-673-3433	673-3435
Web: www.chesapeakes.com					
Chop House 9700 Kingston Pike	Knoxville	TN	37922	865-531-2467	693-4814
Copper Cellar 1807 Cumberland Ave	Knoxville	TN	37916	865-673-3411	673-3413
Web: www.coppercellar.com/cc/index.htm					
Downtown Grill & Brewery 424 S Gay St	Knoxville	TN	37902	865-633-8111	633-8954
Web: www.downtownbrewery.com					
Italian Market & Grill 9648 Kingston Pike Suite 4	Knoxville	TN	37922	865-690-2600	539-4356
Web: www.italianmarketandgrill.com					
Kashmir 711 17th St SW	Knoxville	TN	37916	865-524-1982	524-1699
King Tut's Grill 4132 Martin Mill Pike	Knoxville	TN	37920	865-573-6021	
Litton's Market & Restaurant 2803 Essary Dr	Knoxville	TN	37918	865-687-8788	687-8788
Mandarin House 8111 Gleason Rd	Knoxville	TN	37919	865-694-0340	
Melting Pot The 111 N Central Ave	Knoxville	TN	37902	865-971-5400	971-3006
Web: www.meltingpot.com					
Miyabi Japanese Steakhouse 8207 Kingston Pike	Knoxville	TN	37919	865-691-3121	691-3218
Monterrey Mexican Grill 11151 Kingston Pike	Knoxville	TN	37927	865-671-3119	
Nama Sushi Bar 135 S Gay St	Knoxville	TN	37902	865-633-8539	633-8533
Web: www.namasushibar.com					
Naples Italian Restaurant 5500 Kingston Pike	Knoxville	TN	37919	865-584-5033	584-9415
Oodles 20 Market Sq	Knoxville	TN	37902	865-521-0600	546-2256
Orangery The 5412 Kingston Pike	Knoxville	TN	37919	865-588-2964	588-5499
Web: www.theorangeryrestaurant.com					
Pelanchos Mexican Grill 1516 Downtown West Blvd	Knoxville	TN	37919	865-694-9060	692-9666
Web: www.pelanchos.com					
PF Chang's China Bistro 6741 Kingston Pike	Knoxville	TN	37919	865-212-5514	212-4258
Web: www.pfchangs.com					
Puleo's Grille 260 N Peters Rd	Knoxville	TN	37923	865-691-1960	691-1969
Web: www.puleosgrille.com					
Regas 318 N Gay St	Knoxville	TN	37917	865-637-3427	637-7799
Sam & Andy's Fountain City 4813 N Broadway	Knoxville	TN	37918	865-281-9539	281-9642
Savelli's 3055 Sutherland Ave	Knoxville	TN	37919	865-521-9085	
Sitar Indian Cuisine 6004 Kingston Pike	Knoxville	TN	37919	865-588-1828	
Web: www.sitarknox.com					
Stir Fry Cafe 7240 Kingston Pike	Knoxville	TN	37919	865-588-2064	584-1841
Web: www.stirfrycafe.com					
Sunspot 1909 Cumberland Ave	Knoxville	TN	37916	865-637-4663	637-4373
Taste of Thai 213 N Peters Rd	Knoxville	TN	37923	865-691-4442	
Tomato Head 12 Market Sq	Knoxville	TN	37902	865-637-4067	637-4019
Web: www.thetomatohead.com					
Wasabi Japanese Steak House 226 Lovell Rd	Knoxville	TN	37922	865-675-0201	675-0202
Web: www.wasabi-steakhouse.com					
Wong's Palace 4009 Chapman Hwy	Knoxville	TN	37920	865-573-4580	573-9798
Ye Olde Steak House 6838 Chapman Hwy	Knoxville	TN	37920	865-577-9328	
Web: www.yeoldesteakhouse.com					
A Tan 3445 Poplar Ave	Memphis	TN	38111	901-452-4477	452-4484
Amerigo 1239 Ridgeway St	Memphis	TN	38119	901-761-4000	761-4001
Web: www.amerigo.net					
Arcade The 540 S Main St	Memphis	TN	38103	901-526-5757	526-5726
Automatic Slim's Tonga Club 83 S 2nd St	Memphis	TN	38103	901-525-7948	526-6642
Bar-B-Q Shop The 1782 Madison Ave	Memphis	TN	38104	901-272-1277	272-9085
BB King's Blues Club & Restaurant 143 Beale St	Memphis	TN	38103	901-524-5464	524-5454
Web: www.bbkingsclub.com					
Benihana 912 Ridgelake Blvd	Memphis	TN	38120	901-683-7390	683-6946
Web: www.benihana.com					
Bhan Thai 1324 Peabody Ave	Memphis	TN	38104	901-272-1538	272-2487
Web: www.bhanthairestaurant.com					
Bonefish Grill 1250 N Germantown Pkwy	Memphis	TN	38016	901-753-2220	753-2220
Web: www.bonefishgrill.com					
Boscos Squared 2120 Madison Ave	Memphis	TN	38104	901-432-2222	432-8030
Web: www.boscosbeer.com					
Brushmark The 1934 Poplar Ave	Memphis	TN	38104	901-544-6225	725-4071
Buckley's 5355 Poplar Ave	Memphis	TN	38119	901-683-4538	
Web: www.buckleysgrill.com/					
Butcher Shop 101 S Front St	Memphis	TN	38103	901-521-0856	525-6657
Cafe 1912 243 S Cooper St	Memphis	TN	38104	901-722-2700	
Cafe Society 212 N Evergreen St	Memphis	TN	38112	901-722-2177	722-2186
Catfish Cabin 2846 Airways Blvd	Memphis	TN	38142	901-345-2015	
Celtic Crossing Irish Pub & Restaurant 903 S Cooper St	Memphis	TN	38104	901-274-5151	274-5159
Web: www.celticcrossingmemphis.com					
Central BBQ 2249 Central Ave	Memphis	TN	38104	901-272-9377	728-5850
Corky's Bar-B-Q 743 W Poplar Ave	Memphis	TN	38107	901-405-4999	273-2084
Cupboard The 1400 Union Ave	Memphis	TN	38104	901-276-8015	728-5518
Web: www.thecupboardrestaurant.com					
Dish Restaurant 948 S Cooper St	Memphis	TN	38104	901-276-0002	276-7799
Web: www.dishmemphis.com					
Erling Jensen Restaurant 1044 S Yates Rd	Memphis	TN	38119	901-763-3700	763-3800
Web: www.ejensen.com					
Folk's Folly Prime Steak House 551 S Mendenhall Rd	Memphis	TN	38117	901-762-8200	328-2287
Web: www.folksfolly.com					
Frank Grisanti's 1022 Shady Grove Rd	Memphis	TN	38120	901-761-9462	761-2245
Web: www.frankgrisanti-embassy.com					
Golden India 2097 Madison Ave	Memphis	TN	38104	901-728-5111	728-5112
Grill83 83 Madison Ave	Memphis	TN	38103	901-333-1224	333-1210
Web: www.grill83.com/					
Grove Grill 4550 Poplar Ave	Memphis	TN	38117	901-818-9951	818-9953
Web: www.thegrovegrill.com					
Houston's 5000 Poplar Ave	Memphis	TN	38117	901-683-0915	683-5330
Huey's 1927 Madison Ave	Memphis	TN	38104	901-726-4372	278-9073
Web: www.hueyburger.com					
India Palace 1720 Poplar Ave	Memphis	TN	38304	901-278-1199	278-1977
Web: www.indiapalaceinc.com					
Jarrett's 5689 Quince Rd	Memphis	TN	38119	901-763-2264	
Web: www.jarretts.com					
Jim Neely's Interstate Barbeque 2265 S 3rd St	Memphis	TN	38109	901-775-2304	775-3149
Web: www.jimneelysinterstatebarbecue.com					
Jim's Place East 5560 Shelby Oaks Dr	Memphis	TN	38134	901-388-7200	
Web: www.jimsplaceeast.com					
King's Palace Cafe 162 Beale St	Memphis	TN	38107	901-521-1851	
La Tourelle 2146 Monroe Ave	Memphis	TN	38104	901-726-5771	
Web: www.latourellememphis.com					
Le Chardonnay 2100-5 Overton Sq	Memphis	TN	38104	901-725-1375	
Web: www.lechardonnay.com					
McEwen's on Monroe 122 Monroe Ave	Memphis	TN	38103	901-527-7085	527-0334
Web: www.mcewensonmonroe.com					
Melting Pot The 2828 Wolfcreek Pkwy	Memphis	TN	38133	901-380-9500	380-9510
Web: www.themeltingpot.com					
Mikasa Japan 6150 Poplar Ave	Memphis	TN	38119	901-683-0000	
Mollie's La Casita Restaurant 2006 Madison Ave	Memphis	TN	38104	901-726-1873	726-1876
Owen Brennan's Restaurant 6150 Poplar Ave	Memphis	TN	38119	901-761-0990	761-9177
Web: www.brennansmemphis.com					
Paulette's 2110 Madison Ave	Memphis	TN	38104	901-726-5128	726-5670
Web: www.paulettes.net					
Pete & Sam's 3886 Park Ave	Memphis	TN	38111	901-458-0694	458-9607
PF Chang's China Bistro 1181 Ridgeway Rd	Memphis	TN	38119	901-818-3889	818-3890
Web: www.pfchangs.com					
Rendezvous 52 S 2nd St	Memphis	TN	38103	901-523-2746	525-7688
Web: www.hogsfly.com					
Ronnie Grisanti & Sons 2855 Poplar Ave	Memphis	TN	901323000	901-323-0007	323-0070
Ruth's Chris Steak House 6120 Poplar Ave	Memphis	TN	38120	901-761-0055	763-4856
Web: www.ruthschris.com					
Saigon Le 51 N Cleveland St	Memphis	TN	38104	901-276-5326	
Salsa 6150 Poplar Ave Suite 129	Memphis	TN	38119	901-683-6325	767-4953
Sekisui 25 S Belvedere Blvd	Memphis	TN	38104	901-725-0005	
Web: www.sekisuiusa.com					
Silky O'Sullivan's 183 Beale St	Memphis	TN	38103	901-522-9596	522-8462
Web: www.silkyosullivans.com					
Stella 39 S Main St	Memphis	TN	38103	901-526-4950	536-4941
Web: www.stellamemphis.com					
Texas de Brazil 150 Peabody Pl Suite 103	Memphis	TN	38103	901-526-7600	526-7615
Web: www.texasdebrazil.com					
Santa Fe Cantina 1824 Old Fort Pkwy	Murfreesboro	TN	37129	615-890-3030	
Acorn The 114 28th Ave N	Nashville	TN	37203	615-320-4399	320-4397
Web: www.theacornrestaurant.com					
Amerigo 1920 West End Ave	Nashville	TN	37203	615-320-1740	320-0644
Web: www.amerigo.net					
Anatolia 48 White Bridge Rd	Nashville	TN	37205	615-356-1556	356-1551
Web: www.anatolia-restaurant.com					
Antonios' of Nashville 7097 Old Harding Rd	Nashville	TN	37221	615-646-9166	
Big River Grille & Brewing Works 111 Broadway	Nashville	TN	37201	615-251-4677	742-3500
Web: www.gordonbiersch.com					
Blackstone Restaurant & Brewery 1918 West End Ave	Nashville	TN	37203	615-327-9969	327-4131
Web: www.blackstonebrewery.com					
Bound'ry 911 20th Ave S	Nashville	TN	37212	615-321-3043	321-0984
Web: www.pansouth.net/boundry-index.htm					
Chinatown 3900 Hillsboro Pike	Nashville	TN	37215	615-269-3275	
Cock of the Walk 2624 Music Valley Dr	Nashville	TN	37214	615-889-1930	889-0047
Web: www.cockofthewalkrestaurant.com					
Copper Kettle Cafe 4004 Granny White Pike	Nashville	TN	37204	615-383-7242	383-7949
Cuisine of India 1500 21st Ave S	Nashville	TN	37212	615-320-1315	320-1330
F Scott's 2210 Crestmoor Rd	Nashville	TN	37215	615-269-5861	269-8948
Web: www.fscotts.com					
Finezza Trattoria 5405 Harding Rd	Nashville	TN	37205	615-356-9398	356-7256
Fleming's Prime Steakhouse & Wine Bar 2525 West End Ave	Nashville	TN	37203	615-342-0131	342-0134
Web: www.flemingssteakhouse.com					
Florida Seafood Kitchen 2719 Lebanon Rd	Nashville	TN	37214	615-316-0933	316-0900
Goten Japanese Steak & Sushi Bar 1719 W End Ave Suite 101W	Nashville	TN	37203	615-321-4537	321-3105
Hog Heaven 115 27th Ave N	Nashville	TN	37203	615-329-1234	
Web: www.hogheaven.com					
Horn of Africa 1041 Murfreesboro Pike	Nashville	TN	37217	615-366-3468	
Web: www.hornofafrica-restaurant.com					
J Alexander's 73 White Bridge Rd Suite 130	Nashville	TN	37205	615-352-0981	356-4793
Web: www.jalexanders.com					
Jack's Bar-B-Que 334 W Trinity Ln	Nashville	TN	37207	615-228-4600	
Jim 'N Nick's 7004 Charlotte Pike	Nashville	TN	37209	615-352-5777	
Jimmy Kelly's 217 Louise Ave	Nashville	TN	37203	615-329-4349	320-7882
Web: www.jimmykellys.com					
Kalamata's 3764 Hillsboro Rd	Nashville	TN	37215	615-383-8700	383-8788
Web: www.bigfatgreekolives.com					

Tennessee (Cont'd)

Name / Address	City	State	ZIP	Phone	Fax
Ken's 2007 Division St	Nashville	TN	37203	615-321-2444	321-2455
Kien Giang 5825 Charlotte Pike	Nashville	TN	37209	615-353-1250	
Kobe 210 25th Ave N	Nashville	TN	37203	615-327-9081	327-9083
Web: kobe-steaks.com					
Korea House 6410 Charlotte Pike Suite 108	Nashville	TN	37209	615-352-2790	
La Paz Restaurante Cantina 3808 Cleghorn Ave	Nashville	TN	37215	615-383-5200	
Web: www.lapaz.com					
Mad Platter The 1239 6th Ave N	Nashville	TN	37208	615-242-2563	
Mambu 1806 Hayes St	Nashville	TN	37203	615-329-1293	329-1203
Margot Cafe & Bar 1017 Woodland St	Nashville	TN	37206	615-227-4668	
Market Street Brewery & Public House 134 2nd Ave N	Nashville	TN	37201	615-259-9611	
Melting Pot The 166 2nd Ave N	Nashville	TN	37201	615-742-4970	726-6328
Web: www.meltingpot.com					
Midtown Cafe 102 19th Ave S	Nashville	TN	37203	615-320-7176	320-0920
Web: www.midtowncafe.com					
Morton's The Steakhouse 618 Church St	Nashville	TN	37219	615-259-4558	726-2760
Web: www.mortons.com					
New Orleans Manor 1400 Murfreesboro Rd	Nashville	TN	37217	615-367-2777	
Web: www.neworleansmanor.com					
Palm The 140 5th Ave S	Nashville	TN	37206	615-742-7256	742-9028
Web: www.thepalm.com					
Park Cafe 4403 Murphy Rd	Nashville	TN	37209	615-383-4409	383-4829
PF Chang's China Bistro 2525 West End Ave	Nashville	TN	37203	615-329-8901	329-8904
Web: www.pfchangs.com					
Rotier's 2413 Elliston Pl	Nashville	TN	37203	615-327-9892	
Royal Thai 120 19th Ave N	Nashville	TN	37203	615-321-6104	321-6108
Ru San's 505 12th Ave S	Nashville	TN	37203	615-252-8787	
Ruth's Chris Steak House 2100 West End Ave	Nashville	TN	37203	615-320-0163	329-0062
Web: www.ruthschris.com					
Shalimar 3711 Hillsboro Pike	Nashville	TN	37215	615-269-8577	292-0330
Shintomi 2184 Brandywood Dr	Nashville	TN	37215	615-386-3022	665-9586
Siam Cafe 316 McCall St	Nashville	TN	37211	615-834-3181	
Sitar 116 21st Ave N	Nashville	TN	37203	615-321-8889	321-2688
Web: www.sitarnashville.com					
Sonobana Japanese Restaurant & Grocery 40 White Bridge Rd	Nashville	TN	37205	615-356-6600	
Web: sonobananashville.com					
South Street 907 20th Ave S	Nashville	TN	37203	615-320-5555	
Web: www.pansouth.net/southstreet-index.htm					
Sperry's 5109 Harding Rd	Nashville	TN	37205	615-353-0809	353-0814
Web: www.sperrys.com					
Stock-Yard Restaurant 901 2nd Ave N	Nashville	TN	37201	615-255-6464	255-9561
Web: stock-yardrestaurant.com					
Sunset Grill 2001 Belcourt Ave	Nashville	TN	37212	615-386-3663	
Web: www.sunsetgrill.com					
Sylvan Park 4502 Murphy Rd	Nashville	TN	37209	615-292-9275	
Tang's 5814 Nolensville Rd Suite 110	Nashville	TN	37211	615-831-1171	
Tayst 2100 21st Ave S	Nashville	TN	37212	615-383-1953	
Web: www.tayst.info					
Tin Angel 3201 W End Ave	Nashville	TN	37203	615-298-3444	
Valentino's 1907 West End Ave	Nashville	TN	37203	615-327-0148	327-9482
Web: www.valentinosnashville.com					
Yellow Porch 734 Thompson Ln	Nashville	TN	37204	615-386-0260	
Zola 3001 West End Ave	Nashville	TN	37203	615-320-7778	
Web: www.restaurantzola.com					

Texas

Name / Address	City	State	ZIP	Phone	Fax
Alfredo's Mexican Food 2849 S 14th St	Abilene	TX	79605	325-698-0104	
Bedford Street Restaurant 1882 S Clack St	Abilene	TX	79605	325-695-1770	
Cahoots 301 S 11th St	Abilene	TX	79605	325-672-6540	672-3151
Carino's 4157 Buffalo Gap Rd	Abilene	TX	79605	325-698-4950	698-0498
Web: www.carinos.com/					
Casa Herrera 4109 Ridgemont Dr	Abilene	TX	79606	325-692-7065	692-7868
Catfish Corner 780 S Treadaway Blvd	Abilene	TX	79602	325-672-3620	672-4027
China Garden 2525 S 14th St	Abilene	TX	79605	325-692-3872	
Cotton Patch Cafe 3302 S Clack St	Abilene	TX	79606	325-691-0509	691-1058
Web: www.cottonpatch.com					
Cypress Street Station 158 Cypress St	Abilene	TX	79601	325-676-3463	676-6715
Web: www.cypress-street.com					
Eckos Restaurant 2701 S 1st St	Abilene	TX	79605	325-672-3792	
Enrique's 4358 Sayles Blvd	Abilene	TX	79605	325-795-2750	795-2730
Farolito Restaurant 209 Cottonwood St	Abilene	TX	79601	325-672-0002	676-4855
Fuji Japanese Steak House 3110 S 27th St	Abilene	TX	79605	325-695-9233	
Harlow's Smokehouse 2002 N Clack St	Abilene	TX	79603	325-672-2132	
Harold's 1305 Walnut St	Abilene	TX	79601	325-672-4451	
Joe Allen's Pit Bar-B-Que 303 S 11th St	Abilene	TX	79602	325-672-6082	
Web: www.joeallens.com					
Little Panda 1035 N Judge Ely Blvd	Abilene	TX	79601	325-670-9393	670-9392
Web: www.littlepandaonline.com					
Los Arcos 1902 Ambler Ave	Abilene	TX	79603	325-670-9801	
Lytle Land & Cattle Co 1150 E S 11th St	Abilene	TX	79605	325-677-1925	677-0951
Web: www.lytlelandandcattle.com					
Ronnie Ingle Pit Bar-B-Que 3910 S Treadway Blvd	Abilene	TX	79602	325-695-9924	
Spano's 4534 Buffalo Gap Rd	Abilene	TX	79606	325-698-3704	695-0598
Web: www.spanositalianrestaurant.com					
Tamolly's 4400 Ridgemont Dr	Abilene	TX	79606	325-698-2000	
Web: www.tamollys.com					
Texas Roadhouse 1381 S Danville Rd	Abilene	TX	79605	325-690-0145	690-0159
Web: www.texasroadhouse.com					
Towne Crier Steak House 818 Hwy 80 E	Abilene	TX	79601	325-673-4551	673-0065
Web: www.townecriersteakhouse.com					
Clay Pit 4460 Belt Line Rd	Addison	TX	75001	972-233-0111	233-0141
Web: www.claypit.com					
Abuelo's Mexican Food Embassy 3501 W 45th Ave	Amarillo	TX	79109	806-354-8294	
Web: www.abuelos.com					
Amarillo Club 600 S Tyler St	Amarillo	TX	79101	806-373-4361	372-2606
Web: www.amarilloclub.com/					
Big Texan Steak Ranch 7701 I-40 E	Amarillo	TX	79118	806-372-7000	371-0099
TF: 800-657-7177 ■ *Web:* www.bigtexan.com					
BL Bistro 2203 S Austin St	Amarillo	TX	79109	806-355-7838	373-8481
Web: www.blbistro.com					
Boondocks Bar & Grill 711 W 10th Ave	Amarillo	TX	79101	806-373-3727	
Buns Over Texas 3440 Bell St	Amarillo	TX	79109	806-358-6808	
Calico County 2410 Paramount Blvd	Amarillo	TX	79109	806-358-7664	358-7692
Cattle Call 7701 I-40 W Suite 398	Amarillo	TX	79121	806-353-1227	353-9084
Web: www.cattlecall.com					
Coyote Bluff Cafe 2417 S Grand St	Amarillo	TX	79103	806-373-4640	
David's Steaks & Seafood 2721 Virginia Cir	Amarillo	TX	79109	806-355-8171	
Doug's Hickory Pit Bar B Que 3313 S Georgia St	Amarillo	TX	79109	806-352-8471	
Golden Light Cafe 2908 W 6th Ave	Amarillo	TX	79106	806-374-0097	
Web: www.goldenlightcafe.com					
Hoffbrau Steaks 7203 I-40 W	Amarillo	TX	79106	806-358-6595	354-8411
Web: www.hoffbrausteaks.com					
Hummer's Sports Cafe 2600 Paramount Blvd	Amarillo	TX	79109	806-353-0723	353-4249
Joe's Crab Shack 8300 I-40 W	Amarillo	TX	79106	806-351-0349	351-1325
Web: www.joescrabshack.com					
Jorge's Taco Garcia Mexican Cafe 1100 S Ross St	Amarillo	TX	79102	806-371-0411	371-0538
Web: www.tacosgarcia.com					
Kabuki Japanese Steakhouse 3319 I-40 W	Amarillo	TX	79109	806-358-7799	
Macaroni Joe's 1619 S Kentucky St Suite 1500-D	Amarillo	TX	79102	806-358-8990	433-1325
Web: www.macaronijoes.com					
Montana Mike's Steakhouse 4332 W 45th Ave	Amarillo	TX	79109	806-353-3339	356-9243
My Thai 2029 Coulter Dr	Amarillo	TX	79106	806-355-9541	379-9732
Pacific Rim 2061 Paramount Blvd	Amarillo	TX	79109	806-353-9179	
Web: www.pacificrimam.com					
Plaza Restaurant 3415 Bell St	Amarillo	TX	79109	806-358-4897	358-4038
Ruby Tequila's 2108 Paramount Blvd	Amarillo	TX	79109	806-358-7829	358-0086
Web: www.rubytequilas.com					
Zen 721 614 S Polk St	Amarillo	TX	79101	806-372-1909	
Web: www.zen721.com					
Abuelo's Mexican Food Embassy 1041 W I-20	Arlington	TX	76017	817-468-2622	468-7221
Web: www.abuelos.com					
Arlington Steak House 1724 W Division St	Arlington	TX	76012	817-275-7881	
Bigotes 1821 E Abram St	Arlington	TX	76010	817-274-1350	
Buck N' Loons Cafe 3517 S Cooper St	Arlington	TX	76015	817-466-2825	466-2900
Web: www.bucknloons.com					
Cacherel 2221 E Lamar Blvd	Arlington	TX	76006	817-640-9981	633-5737
Web: www.cacharel.net					
Candlelite Inn Restaurant 1202 E Division St	Arlington	TX	76011	817-275-9613	459-3288
Web: www.candlelite-inn.com					
Joe's Crab Shack 1520 Nolan Ryan Expy	Arlington	TX	76011	817-261-4696	274-2657
Web: www.joescrabshack.com					
Khaki's Fresh Food 4401 Little Rd	Arlington	TX	76016	817-478-4666	483-9255
Web: www.khakisfreshfood.com					
La Isla 611 W Park Row	Arlington	TX	76010	817-460-1180	
Mariano's 2614 Majesty Dr	Arlington	TX	76011	817-640-5118	633-3894
Web: www.marianosrestaurant.com					
My Martini Wine & Bistro 859 NE Green Oaks Blvd	Arlington	TX	76006	817-461-4424	795-4840
Web: www.mymartinibistro.com/					
Nagoya 4040 S Cooper St	Arlington	TX	76015	817-466-3688	466-3684
Web: www.nagoyatx.com					
Pappadeaux Seafood Kitchen 1304 E Copeland Rd	Arlington	TX	76011	817-543-0545	543-0548
Web: www.pappadeaux.com					
Pappasito's Cantina 321 W Rd to Six Flags	Arlington	TX	76011	817-795-3535	795-5865
Web: www.pappas.com					
Piccolo Mondo 829 E Lamar Blvd	Arlington	TX	76011	817-265-9174	226-3474
Web: www.piccolomondo.com					
Piranha 851 NE Green Oaks Blvd	Arlington	TX	76006	817-261-1636	
Web: www.piranhakillersushi.com/					
Portofino Ristorante 226 Lincoln Sq	Arlington	TX	76011	817-861-8300	861-1987
Web: www.portofinoristorante.com					
Red Hot & Blue 1350 E Copeland Rd	Arlington	TX	76011	817-795-7427	795-3291
Web: www.redhotandblue.com					
Simply Fondue 770 E Road to Six Flags	Arlington	TX	76011	817-274-7909	274-1607
Web: www.simplyfondue.com					
Sukhothai 423 Fielder North Plaza	Arlington	TX	76012	817-860-4107	860-0421
Sushi Zone 915 E Road to Six Flags	Arlington	TX	76011	817-226-4055	226-2265
Tandoor 532 N Fielder Rd	Arlington	TX	76012	817-261-6604	548-9026
Taste of Thai 2535 E Arkansas Ln	Arlington	TX	76010	817-543-0110	
Texas Land & Cattle Co 2009 E Copeland Rd	Arlington	TX	76011	817-461-1500	801-6600
Web: www.txlc.com					
Thanh Thanh 2515 E Arkansas Ln	Arlington	TX	76014	817-275-2449	275-7920
TL Kowloon 100 W Pioneer Pkwy	Arlington	TX	76010	817-261-6699	
888 911 W Anderson Ln	Austin	TX	78757	512-302-5433	
Alborz Persian Cuisine 3300 W Anderson Ln Suite 303	Austin	TX	78757	512-420-2222	
Web: www.alborzpersiancuisine.com					
Aquarelle 606 Rio Grande St	Austin	TX	78701	512-479-8117	206-0077
Web: www.aquarellerestaurant.com					
Asti Trattoria 408C E 43rd St	Austin	TX	78751	512-451-1218	451-2233
Web: www.astiaustin.com					
Austin Land & Cattle Co 1205 N LaMar Blvd	Austin	TX	78703	512-472-1813	472-1815
Web: www.austinlandandcattlecompany.com					
Bistro 88 2712 Bee Caves Rd	Austin	TX	78746	512-328-8888	328-1740
Web: bistro88.com					
Cafe at the Four Seasons 98 San Jacinto Blvd	Austin	TX	78701	512-478-4500	685-7892
Casa de Luz 1701 Toomey Rd	Austin	TX	78704	512-476-2535	476-0198
Web: www.casadeluz.org					
Castle Hill Cafe 1101 W 5th St	Austin	TX	78703	512-476-7218	476-0055
Web: www.castlehillcafe.com					
Chez Nous 510 Neches St	Austin	TX	78701	512-473-2413	236-8468
Chez Zee American Bistro 5406 Balcones Dr	Austin	TX	78731	512-454-2666	454-0034
Web: www.chezzee.com					
Clay Pit 1601 Guadalupe St	Austin	TX	78701	512-322-5131	322-9514
Web: www.claypit.com					
County Line 6500 W Bee Caves Rd	Austin	TX	78746	512-327-1742	328-9478
Web: www.countyline.com					
Curra's Grill 614 E Oltorf St	Austin	TX	78704	512-444-0012	444-2542
Web: www.currasgrillsouth.com					
Cypress Grill 4404 W William Cannon Dr Suite L	Austin	TX	78749	512-358-7474	358-7472
Web: www.cypressgrill.net					
Din Ho's Chinese BBQ 8557 Research Blvd	Austin	TX	78758	512-832-8788	
Dog & Duck Pub 406 W 17th St	Austin	TX	78701	512-479-0598	
Web: www.dogandduckpub.com					
Dona Emilia's South American Bar & Grill 101 San Jacinto Blvd	Austin	TX	78701	512-478-2520	478-2531
Driskill Grill 604 Brazos St	Austin	TX	78701	512-391-7162	391-7059
Web: www.driskillgrill.com					
Eastside Cafe 2113 Manor Rd	Austin	TX	78722	512-476-5858	477-5847
Web: www.eastsidecafeaustin.com					
Eddie V's Edgewater Grille 301 E 5th St	Austin	TX	78701	512-472-1860	477-9794
Web: www.eddiev.com					
El Azteca 2600 E 7th St	Austin	TX	78702	512-477-4701	
El Sol y La Luna 1224 S Congress Ave	Austin	TX	78704	512-444-7770	444-4554
Emerald Restaurant 13614 Hwy 71 W	Austin	TX	78738	512-263-2147	
Web: www.theemerald.com					
Fado's Irish Pub 214 W 4th St	Austin	TX	78701	512-457-0172	457-0519
Web: www.fadoirishpub.com					
Fonda San Miguel 2330 W North Loop Blvd	Austin	TX	78756	512-459-4121	459-5792
Web: www.fondasanmiguel.com					
Green Pastures 811 W Live Oak St	Austin	TX	78704	512-444-4747	444-3912
Gumbo's Louisiana Style Cafe 710 Colorado St	Austin	TX	78701	512-480-8053	480-8063
Web: www.gumbosaustin.com					
Habana 709 E 6th St	Austin	TX	78701	512-443-4252	472-4042
Web: www.habana.com					
Hoover's Cooking 2002 Manor Rd	Austin	TX	78722	512-479-5006	479-0889
Web: www.hooverscooking.com					
Hudson's on the Bend 3509 Ranch Rd 620 N	Austin	TX	78734	512-266-1369	266-1399
Web: www.hudsonsonthebend.com					

	City	State	Zip	Phone	Fax
Hula Hut 3825 Lake Austin Blvd	Austin	TX	78703	512-476-4852	477-1604
Web: www.hulahut.com					
Hunan 1940 W William Cannon Dr	Austin	TX	78745	512-443-8848	
Web: www.hunanaustin.com					
Hyde Park Bar & Grill 4206 Duval St	Austin	TX	78751	512-458-3168	458-6722
Web: www.hydeparkbarandgrill.com					
Ill Forks 111 Lavaca St	Austin	TX	78701	512-474-1776	
Web: www.3forks.com/					
Jeffrey's Restaurant 1204 W Lynn St	Austin	TX	78703	512-477-5584	474-7279
Web: www.jeffreysofaustin.com					
Kenichi 419 Colorado St	Austin	TX	78701	512-320-8883	320-8882
Web: www.kenichiaustin.com					
Kim Phung 7601 N Lamar Blvd Suite I	Austin	TX	78752	512-451-2464	451-8083
Korea House 2700 W Anderson Ln	Austin	TX	78757	512-458-2477	
Kyoto Japanese Restaurant 315 Congress Ave Suite 200	Austin	TX	78701	512-482-9010	472-3915
Web: www.kyotodowntown.com					
La Traviata 314 Congress Ave	Austin	TX	78701	512-479-8131	479-8545
Madam Mam's 2514 Guadalupe St	Austin	TX	78705	512-472-8306	236-4030
Madras Pavillion 9025 Research Blvd	Austin	TX	78758	512-719-5575	719-4527
Magnolia Cafe 2304 Lake Austin Blvd	Austin	TX	78703	512-478-8645	494-1722
Web: www.cafemagnolia.com					
Marakesh Mediterranean Cafe 906 Congress Ave	Austin	TX	78701	512-476-7735	
Mars 1400 S Congress Ave	Austin	TX	78704	512-472-3901	
Web: www.marsaustin.com					
Mikado Ryotei 9033 Research Blvd	Austin	TX	78758	512-833-8188	833-8145
Web: www.mikadoryotei.com					
Mirabelle 8127 Mesa Dr Suite A-100	Austin	TX	78759	512-346-7900	346-9900
Web: www.mirabellerestaurant.com					
Moonshine Patio Bar & Grill 303 Red River St	Austin	TX	78701	512-236-9599	236-8816
Web: www.moonshinegrill.com					
Musashino Sushi Dokoro 3407 Greystone Dr	Austin	TX	78731	512-795-8593	
Web: www.musashinosushi.com					
Noodle-ism 107 W 5th St	Austin	TX	78701	512-275-9988	275-9987
Web: www.noodle-ism.com					
Oasis The 6550 Comanche Trail	Austin	TX	78732	512-266-2442	266-9296
Web: www.oasis-austin.com					
PF Chang's China Bistro 201 San Jacinto Blvd	Austin	TX	78701	512-457-8300	457-8313
Web: www.pfchangs.com					
Polvos 2004 S 1st St	Austin	TX	78704	512-441-5446	
Roaring Fork 701 Congress Ave	Austin	TX	78701	512-583-0000	583-0005
Web: www.eddiev.com/					
Rocco's Grill 900 Ranch Rd 620 S Suite A106	Austin	TX	78734	512-263-8204	263-5332
Web: www.roccosgrill.com/					
Romeo's 1500 Barton Springs Rd	Austin	TX	78704	512-476-1090	476-5107
Web: www.austinromeos.com					
Roy's 340 E 2nd St	Austin	TX	78701	512-391-1500	391-1514
Web: www.roysrestaurant.com					
Ruth's Chris Steak House 107 W 6th St	Austin	TX	78701	512-477-7884	
Web: www.ruthschris-austin.com					
Satay 3202 W Anderson Ln	Austin	TX	78757	512-467-6731	467-9640
Web: www.satayusa.com					
Shoreline Grill 98 San Jacinto Blvd	Austin	TX	78701	512-477-3300	477-6392
Web: www.shorelinegrill.com					
Star of India 2900 W Anderson Ln	Austin	TX	78757	512-452-8199	
Web: www.starofindiaaustin.com					
Starlite 407 Colorado St	Austin	TX	78701	512-374-9012	299-9209
Sullivan's Steakhouse 300 Colorado St	Austin	TX	78701	512-495-6504	495-6509
Web: www.sullivansteakhouse.com					
Sunflower 8557 Research Blvd	Austin	TX	78758	512-339-7860	
Sushi Japon 6801 N IH-35	Austin	TX	78752	512-323-6663	323-6789
Web: www.sushijaponbar.com					
Suzi's Chinese Kitchen 7858 Shoal Creek Blvd	Austin	TX	78757	512-302-4600	302-3858
T & S Seafood 10014 N Lamar Blvd	Austin	TX	78754	512-339-8434	339-7751
Texicalli Grill 534 E Oltorf St	Austin	TX	78704	512-442-2799	
Thai Kitchen 801 E William Cannon Dr	Austin	TX	78745	512-445-4844	
Web: www.thaikitchenofaustin.com					
Thai Noodles Etc House 2602 Guadelupe St	Austin	TX	78705	512-494-1011	474-2562
Thai Passion 620 Congress Ave	Austin	TX	78701	512-472-1244	472-1876
Web: www.thaipassion.com					
Threadgill's 6416 N Lamar Blvd	Austin	TX	78752	512-451-5440	451-5033
Web: www.threadgills.com					
Tien Hong 8301 Burnet Rd	Austin	TX	78757	512-458-2263	458-2268
Web: www.tienhong.net					
TRIO 98 San Jacinto Blvd	Austin	TX	78701	512-685-8300	
Trudy's 409 W 30th St	Austin	TX	78705	512-477-2935	477-1805
Web: www.trudys.com					
Uchi 801 S Lamar Blvd	Austin	TX	78704	512-916-4808	916-4806
Web: www.uchiaustin.com					
Umi Sushi Bar & Grill 5510 S IH-35 Suite 400	Austin	TX	78745	512-383-8681	383-8802
Veggie Heaven 1914 Guadalupe St	Austin	TX	78705	512-457-1013	
Vespaio 1610 S Congress Ave	Austin	TX	78704	512-441-6100	441-7746
Vin Bistro 1601 W 38th St	Austin	TX	78731	512-377-5252	377-2299
Web: www.vinbistro.com					
Wink Restaurant 1014 N Lamar Blvd	Austin	TX	78703	512-482-8868	482-9477
Web: www.winkrestaurant.com					
Z Tejas Grill 9400-A Arboreum Blvd	Austin	TX	78759	512-346-3506	346-6328
Web: www.ztejas.com					
Zoot 509 Hearn St	Austin	TX	78703	512-477-6535	476-7649
Web: www.zootrestaurant.com					
Antonio's Mexican Village 840 Paredes Rd	Brownsville	TX	78521	956-542-6504	542-1125
Big J's 5805 FM 802 Suite A	Brownsville	TX	78521	956-831-6884	
Blue Mermaid Cafe 119 Billy Mitchell Blvd	Brownsville	TX	78521	956-544-2157	
Canton Chinese Restaurant 2489 Boca Chica Blvd	Brownsville	TX	78521	956-982-1888	504-3139
Cobbleheads Bar & Grill 3154 Central Blvd	Brownsville	TX	78520	956-546-6224	546-6772
Web: cobbleheads.com					
El Pato Restaurant 2425 Paredes Line Rd	Brownsville	TX	78526	956-547-9100	
Ho's Garden 1552 Palm Blvd Palm Village Shopping Center	Brownsville	TX	78520	956-544-3009	
Isabella's Restaurant 1156 Market Sq	Brownsville	TX	78520	956-542-4782	
La Fonda Chiquita 1435 Southmost Rd	Brownsville	TX	78521	956-504-5258	
Los Camperos 125 N FM 511	Brownsville	TX	78575	956-546-8172	546-8506
Lotus Inn 905 North Expy	Brownsville	TX	78520	956-542-5715	541-6973
Lula's 2235 Central Blvd	Brownsville	TX	78520	956-541-4911	
Oyster Bar I 1057 E Levee St	Brownsville	TX	79520	956-542-9786	
Palm Court Restaurant 2200 Boca Chica Blvd Suite 124	Brownsville	TX	78521	956-542-3575	548-0761
Sylvia's Restaurant 1843 Southmost Rd	Brownsville	TX	78521	956-542-9220	
Vermillion The 115 Paredes Line Rd	Brownsville	TX	78521	956-542-9893	541-4221
Web: www.thevermillion.com					
Deutschlander Freshwater Catfish Co 502 Houston St	Buffalo Gap	TX	79508	325-572-3486	572-3432
Ancient Mariner 4366 S Alameda St	Corpus Christi	TX	78412	361-992-7371	992-8812
Crawdaddy's 414 Starr St	Corpus Christi	TX	78401	361-883-5432	888-8892
D Noodlehouse 4701 Ayers St	Corpus Christi	TX	78415	361-855-6096	
El Rinconcitos 4025 Prescott St	Corpus Christi	TX	78416	361-851-8020	
Executive Surf Club 309 N Water St	Corpus Christi	TX	78401	361-884-7873	884-2865
Web: www.executivesurfclub.com					
Joe's Crab Shack 5025 S Padre Island Rd	Corpus Christi	TX	78411	361-980-0023	
Web: www.joescrabshack.com/					
Kiko's 5514 Everhart Rd	Corpus Christi	TX	78411	361-991-1211	
Kobe Japanese Seafood 5134 Carroll Ln	Corpus Christi	TX	78415	361-851-2555	851-2555
Web: www.kobecc.com					
Little Manila Lumpia House 2124 Waldron Rd	Corpus Christi	TX	78418	361-937-5651	
Mamma Mia's 128 N Mesquite St	Corpus Christi	TX	78401	361-883-3773	
Origami 1220 Airline Rd	Corpus Christi	TX	78412	361-993-3966	993-8308
Peoples 9738 Up River Rd	Corpus Christi	TX	78410	361-241-8087	241-8089
Pier 99 2822 N Shoreline Blvd	Corpus Christi	TX	78402	361-887-0764	
Republic of Texas Bar & Grill 900 N Shoreline Blvd	Corpus Christi	TX	78401	361-886-3515	886-3530
Rosita's 5253 S Staples St	Corpus Christi	TX	78411	361-906-1007	906-1017
Snoopy's Pier 13313 S Padre Island Dr	Corpus Christi	TX	78418	361-949-8815	
Thai Spice 601 N Shoreline Blvd	Corpus Christi	TX	78401	361-883-8884	883-8881
Web: www.thaispicecc.com					
Torch Restaurant 4425 S Alameda St	Corpus Christi	TX	78412	361-992-7491	
Two George's 5884 Everhart Rd	Corpus Christi	TX	78413	361-993-8008	993-0094
Vietnam Restaurant 701 N Water St	Corpus Christi	TX	78401	361-853-2682	
Web: www.vietnam-restaurant.com					
Water Street Oyster Bar 309 N Water St	Corpus Christi	TX	78401	361-881-9448	888-7783
Web: www.waterstreetco.com					
Water Street Seafood Co 309 N Water St	Corpus Christi	TX	78401	361-882-8683	
2900 2900 Thomas Ave	Dallas	TX	75204	214-303-0400	
Web: www.2900restaurant.com					
Abacus 4511 McKinney Ave	Dallas	TX	75205	214-559-3111	559-3113
Web: www.abacus-restaurant.com					
Al Biernat's 4217 Oak Lawn Ave	Dallas	TX	75219	214-219-2201	219-2093
Web: www.albiernats.com					
Ali Baba Cafe 1905 Greenville Ave	Dallas	TX	75206	214-823-8235	
Web: www.alibabacafe.com					
Amore 6931 Snider Plaza	Dallas	TX	75205	214-739-0502	739-0577
Anderson's BBQ House 5410 Harry Hines Blvd	Dallas	TX	75235	214-630-0735	630-1686
Web: www.mikeandersonsbbq.com					
Arcodoro & Pomodoro 2708 Routh St	Dallas	TX	75201	214-871-1924	871-3141
Asian Mint 11617 N Central Expy Suite 135	Dallas	TX	75243	214-363-6655	363-6686
Web: www.asianmint.com					
August Moon 15030 Preston Rd	Dallas	TX	75254	972-385-7227	385-7617
Web: august-moon.com					
Aurora 4216 Oak Lawn Ave	Dallas	TX	75219	214-528-9400	528-9503
Web: www.auroradallas.net					
Avila's 4714 Maple Ave	Dallas	TX	75219	214-520-2700	
Aw Shucks 3601 Greenville Ave	Dallas	TX	75206	214-821-9449	821-4581
Web: www.awshucksdallas.com					
Blue Fish 3519 Greenville Ave	Dallas	TX	75206	214-824-3474	
Web: www.thebluefishsushi.com					
Bob's Steak & Chop House 4300 Lemmon Ave	Dallas	TX	75219	214-528-9446	526-8159
Web: www.bobs-steakandchop.com					
Cafe Istanbul 5450 W Lovers Ln	Dallas	TX	75209	214-902-0919	
Web: www.cafe-istanbul.net					
Cafe Izmir 3711 Greenville Ave	Dallas	TX	75206	214-826-7788	827-4359
Web: www.izmirgroup.com					
Cafe Madrid 4501 Travis St	Dallas	TX	75205	214-528-1731	522-8752
Web: www.cafemadrid-dallas.com					
Cafe Pacific 24 Highland Park Village	Dallas	TX	75205	214-526-1170	526-0332
Capital Grille The 500 Crescent Ct Suite 135	Dallas	TX	75201	214-303-0500	303-0523
Web: www.thecapitalgrille.com					
Celebration Restaurant & Catering 4503 W Lovers Ln	Dallas	TX	75209	214-358-0612	904-1716
Web: www.celebrationrestaurant.com					
City Cafe 5757 W Lovers Ln	Dallas	TX	75209	214-351-2233	351-1936
Web: www.thecitycafedallas.com					
Ciudad DF 3888 Oak Lawn Ave Suite 135	Dallas	TX	75219	214-219-3141	219-3291
Web: www.ciudaddf.com					
Cosmic Cafe 2912 Oak Lawn Ave	Dallas	TX	75219	214-521-6157	
Web: www.cosmiccafedallas.com					
Cuba Libre 2822 N Henderson Ave	Dallas	TX	75206	214-827-2820	827-2189
Web: consilientrestaurants.com					
De Tapas 5100 Belt Line Rd	Dallas	TX	75240	972-233-8553	233-9565
Web: www.detapasrestaurant.com					
Deep Sushi 2624 Elm St	Dallas	TX	75226	214-651-1177	
Web: www.deepsushi.com					
Del Frisco's Double Eagle Steak House 5251 Spring Valley Rd	Dallas	TX	75254	972-490-9000	934-0867
Web: www.delfriscos.com					
East Wind Vietnamese Restaurant 2800 Routh St	Dallas	TX	75201	214-745-5554	
Web: www.eastwinddallas.com/					
Fadi's Mediterranean Grill 3001 Knox St	Dallas	TX	75205	214-528-1800	528-1807
Web: www.fadiscuisine.com					
Fearing's 2121 McKinney Ave	Dallas	TX	75201	214-922-4848	
Web: www.fearingsrestaurant.com/					
French Room 1321 Commerce St	Dallas	TX	75202	214-742-8200	651-3575
Fuji Steakhouse & Sushi Bar 12817 Preston Rd	Dallas	TX	75230	972-661-5662	
Grape The 2808 Greenville Ave	Dallas	TX	75206	214-828-1981	826-2187
Web: www.thegraperestaurant.com					
Green Papaya 3211 Oak Lawn Ave	Dallas	TX	75219	214-521-4811	521-4685
Web: www.greenpapayarestaurants.com					
Greenville Avenue Seafood & Jazz 2104 Greenville Ave	Dallas	TX	75206	214-826-6376	
Web: greenvilleavenueseafoodandjazz.com/					
Hibiscus 2927 N Henderson Ave	Dallas	TX	75206	214-827-2927	
Web: www.hibiscusdallas.com/					
Hotel St Germain 2516 Maple Ave	Dallas	TX	75201	214-871-2516	871-0740
Web: www.hotelstgermain.com					
III Forks Steakhouse 17776 Dallas Pkwy	Dallas	TX	75287	972-267-1776	267-1799
Web: www.iiiforks.com					
Il Sole 4514 Travis St	Dallas	TX	75205	214-559-3888	559-3990
Web: www.ilsole-dallas.com					
India Palace Restaurant 12817 Preston Rd	Dallas	TX	75230	972-392-0190	392-3188
Web: www.indiapalacedallas.com					
Jade Garden 4800 Bryan St	Dallas	TX	75204	214-821-0675	
Javier's Gourmet Mexicano 4912 Cole Ave	Dallas	TX	75205	214-521-4211	521-5239
Web: www.javiers.net					
Kathleen's Art Cafe 4424 Lovers Ln	Dallas	TX	75225	214-691-2355	
Web: www.kathleensartcafe.com					
La Duni Latin Cafe 4264 Oak Lawn Ave	Dallas	TX	75219	214-520-6888	
Web: www.laduni.com					
La Madeleine 8319 Preston Rd	Dallas	TX	75225	214-346-9733	265-1061
Web: www.lamadeleine.com					
L'Ancestral 4514 Travis St	Dallas	TX	75205	214-528-1081	528-1142
Lavendou 19009 Preston Rd Suite 200	Dallas	TX	75252	972-248-1911	248-1660
Web: www.lavendou.com					
Lola 2917 Fairmount St	Dallas	TX	75201	214-855-0700	871-7202
Web: www.lola4dinner.com					
Luna de Noche 7927 Forest Ln	Dallas	TX	75230	972-233-1880	726-0390
Web: www.lunadenoche.net					
Mansion on Turtle Creek 3411 Gillespie St	Dallas	TX	75219	214-559-2100	526-5345
Web: www.mansiononturtlecreek.com					
May Dragon 4848 Beltline Rd	Dallas	TX	75254	972-392-9998	490-5023
Web: www.maydragon.com					
Mercury Grill The 11909 Preston Rd Suite 1418	Dallas	TX	75230	972-960-7774	960-7988
Web: www.mcrowd.com					
Monica's Aca y Alla 2914 Main St	Dallas	TX	75226	214-748-7140	748-3291
Web: www.monicas.com					

Texas (Cont'd)

Phone Fax

Morton's The Steakhouse 501 Elm St ..... Dallas TX 75202 214-741-2277 748-6360
Web: www.mortons.com
Nana 2201 Stemmons Fwy ..... Dallas TX 75207 214-761-7479 761-7819
Web: www.nanarestaurant.com
Nick & Sam's 3008 Maple Ave ..... Dallas TX 75201 214-871-7444 871-7663
Web: www.nick-sams.com
Oceanaire Seafood Room 1334 Dallas Pkwy ..... Dallas TX 75240 972-759-2277 759-0706
Web: www.theoceanaire.com
Oishii 2525 Wycliff Ave ..... Dallas TX 75219 214-599-9448 599-9468
Old Warsaw The 2610 Maple Ave ..... Dallas TX 75201 214-528-0032
Web: www.theoldwarsaw.com
Palm The Restaurant 701 Ross Ave ..... Dallas TX 75202 214-698-0470
Web: www.thepalm.com
Palomino Euro Bistro 500 Crescent Ct Suite 165 ..... Dallas TX 75201 214-999-1222 999-1115
Web: www.palomino.com
Pappadeaux Seafood Kitchen 3520 Oak Lawn Ave ..... Dallas TX 75219 214-521-4700 521-4726
Web: www.pappadeaux.com
Pappas Bros Steakhouse 10477 Lombardy Ln ..... Dallas TX 75220 214-366-2000 366-2222
Web: www.pappasbros.com
Perry's 2911 Routh St ..... Dallas TX 75201 214-871-9991 871-0302
Web: www.perrys-dallas.com
PF Chang's China Bistro 225 Northpark Center ..... Dallas TX 75225 214-265-8669 265-8836
Web: www.pfchangs.com
Primo's 3309 McKinney Ave ..... Dallas TX 75204 214-220-0510 220-2786
Web: www.primosdallas.com
Pyramid Grill 1717 N Akard St ..... Dallas TX 75201 214-720-5249 720-5282
Quan Kien Giang 9560 Skillman St ..... Dallas TX 75243 214-221-0043 221-3977
Royal Thai 5500 Greenville Ave ..... Dallas TX 75206 214-691-3555
Ruth's Chris Steak House 17840 Dallas Pkwy ..... Dallas TX 75287 972-250-2244 250-1590
Web: www.ruthschris.com
S & D Oyster Co 2701 McKinney Ave ..... Dallas TX 75204 214-880-0111
Saint Martin's Wine Bistro 3020 Greenville Ave ..... Dallas TX 75206 214-826-0940
Web: www.stmartinswinebistro.com
Samba Room 4514 Travis St ..... Dallas TX 75205 214-522-4137 522-4442
Sammy's Barbeque 2126 Leonard St ..... Dallas TX 75201 214-880-9064 871-7597
Web: www.sammysbbq.com
Sevy's Grill 8201 Preston Rd Suite 100 ..... Dallas TX 75225 214-265-7389 265-8949
Web: www.sevys.com
Steel 3102 Oaklawn Ave ..... Dallas TX 75219 214-219-9908 219-9929
Web: www.steeldallas.com
Suze 4535 W Northwest Hwy ..... Dallas TX 75220 214-350-6135 350-6178
Web: www.suzerestaurant.net
Tei Tei Robata Bar 2906 N Henderson St ..... Dallas TX 75206 214-828-2400
Web: www.teiteirobata.com
Tejano 110 W Davis St ..... Dallas TX 75208 214-943-8610 946-4779
Teppo Yakitori & Sushi Bar 2014 Greenville Ave ..... Dallas TX 75206 214-826-8989 826-1913
Web: www.teppo.com
Texas de Brazil 2727 Cedar Springs Rd ..... Dallas TX 75201 214-720-1414 720-7155
Web: www.texasdebrazil.com
Tin Star 2626 Howell St ..... Dallas TX 75204 214-999-0059 999-0049
Web: www.tinstar.us
Tipperary Inn 5815 Live Oak St ..... Dallas TX 75206 214-821-6500
Web: www.tippinn.com
Tramontana 8220B Westchester Dr ..... Dallas TX 75225 214-368-4188
Web: www.mybistro.net
Truluck's 2401 McKinney Ave ..... Dallas TX 75201 214-220-2401 220-2801
Web: www.trulucks.com
Watel's 2207 Allen St ..... Dallas TX 75204 214-720-0323
YO Ranch Steakhouse 702 Ross Ave ..... Dallas TX 75201 214-744-3287 748-7957
Web: www.yoranchsteakhouse.com
York Street 6047 Lewis St ..... Dallas TX 75206 214-826-0968 826-0182
Web: www.yorkstreetdallas.com
Ziziki's Restaurant & Bar 4514 Travis St Suite 122 ..... Dallas TX 75205 214-521-2233 521-2722
Web: www.zizikis.com
Salt Lick 18300 FM 1826 ..... Driftwood TX 78619 512-858-4959 858-2038
Web: www.saltlickbbq.com
Azulejo's 101 S El Paso St ..... El Paso TX 79901 915-534-3000 534-3024
Bella Napoli 6331 N Mesa St ..... El Paso TX 79912 915-584-3321 584-3466
Web: www.bellanapoliristorante.com
Cafe Central 109 N Oregon St ..... El Paso TX 79901 915-545-2233 545-2884
Web: www.cafecentral.com
Cappetto's 2716 Montana Ave ..... El Paso TX 79903 915-566-9357
Web: www.cappettos.com
Casa Jurado 226 Cincinnati Ave ..... El Paso TX 79902 915-532-6429
Cattle Baron 1700 Airway Blvd ..... El Paso TX 79925 915-779-6633 779-3147
Web: www.cattlebaron.com
Dome The 101 S El Paso St ..... El Paso TX 79901 915-534-3000
Dominic's 6901 Montana Ave ..... El Paso TX 79925 915-778-0011 778-0098
Web: www.dominicsitalianrestaurant.com
Dona Lupe Cafe 2919 Pershing Dr ..... El Paso TX 79903 915-566-9833 566-1175
Edge of Texas Steakhouse 8690 Edge of Texas ..... El Paso TX 79934 915-822-3343 822-3348
Forti's Mexican Elder 321 Chelsea St ..... El Paso TX 79905 915-772-0066 772-0067
Japanese Kitchen 4024 N Mesa St ..... El Paso TX 79902 915-533-4267
Jaxon's 4799 N Mesa St ..... El Paso TX 79912 915-544-1188 577-0638
Web: www.jaxons.com
Julio's Cafe Corona 8050 Gateway Blvd E ..... El Paso TX 79907 915-591-7676 592-1294
L & J Cafe 3622 E Missouri St ..... El Paso TX 79903 915-566-8418 566-4070
Landry's Seafood House 6801 Gateway Blvd W ..... El Paso TX 79925 915-779-2900 779-0600
Mediterranean Cuisine 4111 N Mesa St ..... El Paso TX 79902 915-542-1012
Michelinos 3615 Rutherglen St ..... El Paso TX 79925 915-592-1700
Web: www.michelinos.com
New Clock Restaurant 8409 Dyer St ..... El Paso TX 79904 915-751-6367
Peking Garden 3306 Fort Blvd ..... El Paso TX 79930 915-565-9090 565-9091
Pelican's West 130 Shadow Mountain Rd ..... El Paso TX 79912 915-581-1392
PF Chang's China Bistro 760 Sunland Park Dr ..... El Paso TX 79912 915-845-0166 845-0180
Web: www.pfchangs.com
Pho Tre Bien 8838 Viscount Blvd ..... El Paso TX 79925 915-598-0166
Seafood Galley 1130 Geronimo Dr ..... El Paso TX 79925 915-778-8388 778-6035
Senor Fish 9530 Viscount Blvd Suite 1A ..... El Paso TX 79925 915-598-3630 598-3608
Shogun Steakhouse 1201 Airway Blvd Suite A-4 ..... El Paso TX 79925 915-775-1282 771-9248
State Line 1222 Sunland Park Dr ..... El Paso TX 79922 915-581-3371 833-4843
Web: www.airribs.com/
State Line The 1222 Sunland Park Dr ..... El Paso TX 79922 915-581-3371
Web: www.countyline.com
Sushi Place 2604 N Mesa St ..... El Paso TX 79902 915-838-8088
Trattoria Bella Sera 9449 Montana Ave ..... El Paso TX 79925 915-598-7948
Web: trattoriabellasera.com/
True Thai 4309 Fred Wilson St ..... El Paso TX 79904 915-564-4300
Cattleman's Steakhouse Indian Cliff's Ranch PO Box 1056 ..... Fabens TX 79838 915-544-3200 764-4168
Web: www.cattlemanssteakhouse.com
Bella Italia West 5139 Camp Bowie Blvd ..... Fort Worth TX 76107 817-738-1700
Bistro Louise 2900 S Hulen St ..... Fort Worth TX 76109 817-922-9244 922-8148
Web: www.bistrolouise.com

Phone Fax

Blue Mesa Grill 1600 S University Dr ..... Fort Worth TX 76107 817-332-6372 332-6398
Web: www.bluemesagrill.com
Bonnell's 4259 Bryant Irvin Rd ..... Fort Worth TX 76019 817-738-5489
Web: www.bonnellsrestaurant.com
Byblos 1406 N Main St ..... Fort Worth TX 76106 817-625-9667 625-8319
Web: www.byblostx.com
Cafe Aspen 6103 Camp Bowie Blvd ..... Fort Worth TX 76116 817-738-0838 738-3217
Web: www.cafeaspen.com
Cafe Modern 3200 Darnell St ..... Fort Worth TX 76107 817-840-2157 735-1161
Web: www.themodern.org
Caro's 3505 Bluebonnet Cir ..... Fort Worth TX 76109 817-924-9977
Web: www.caros.biz
Celaborelle Phoenician Buffet 2257 Hemphill St ..... Fort Worth TX 76110 817-922-8118
Web: www.celaborelle.com
Del Frisco's Double Eagle Steak House 812 Main St ..... Fort Worth TX 76102 817-877-3999 877-4499
Web: www.delfriscos.com
Dixie House Cafe 6200 E Lancaster Ave ..... Fort Worth TX 76112 817-451-6180 451-4763
Web: www.dixiehousecafe.com
Edelweiss 3801 SW Blvd A ..... Fort Worth TX 76116 817-738-5934 738-6946
Web: www.edelweissrestaurant.com
El Rancho Grande Restaurante 1400 N Main St ..... Fort Worth TX 76106 817-624-9206 626-8681
Fizzi 500 Commerce St ..... Fort Worth TX 76102 817-336-3499 336-5696
Web: www.fizzis.com
Fort Worth Chop House 301 Main St ..... Fort Worth TX 76102 817-336-4129 332-6773
H3 Ranch 109 E Exchange Ave Stockyards Hotel ..... Fort Worth TX 76106 817-624-1246 624-2571
Web: www.h3ranch.com
Hui Chuan Sushi 6100 Camp Bowie Blvd Suite 12 ..... Fort Worth TX 76116 817-989-8886
Web: www.huichuansushi.com
Joe T Garcia's 2201 N Commerce St ..... Fort Worth TX 76106 817-626-4356 626-0581
Web: www.joets.com
Keg The 5760 SW Loop 820 ..... Fort Worth TX 76132 817-731-3534 732-2817
Web: www.kegsteakhouse.com
La Familia Restaurant 841 Foch St ..... Fort Worth TX 76107 817-870-2002
Web: www.lafamilia-fw.com/
Lanny's Alta Cocina Mexicana 3405 W 7th St ..... Fort Worth TX 76107 817-850-9996 850-9989
Web: www.lannyskitchen.com
Lonesome Dove Western Bistro 2406 N Main St ..... Fort Worth TX 76106 817-740-8810 740-8632
Web: www.lonesomedovebistro.com
Los Molcajetes 4320 Western Center Blvd ..... Fort Worth TX 76137 817-306-9000 306-9033
Web: www.losmolcajetes.com
Lucille's Stateside Bistro 4700 Camp Bowie Blvd ..... Fort Worth TX 76107 817-738-4761
Maharaja Restaurant 6308 Hulen Bend Blvd ..... Fort Worth TX 76132 817-263-7156
Mi Cocina 509 Main St ..... Fort Worth TX 76102 817-877-3600 332-4182
Ocean Rock 3468 Blue Bonnet Cir ..... Fort Worth TX 76109 817-922-8080 923-3144
PF Chang's China Bistro 400 Throckmorton St ..... Fort Worth TX 76102 817-840-2450 840-2455
Web: www.pfchangs.com
Piranha 335 W 3rd St ..... Fort Worth TX 76102 817-348-0200
Web: www.piranhakillersushi.com/
Railhead Smokehouse 2900 Montgomery St ..... Fort Worth TX 76107 817-738-9808 732-4059
Reata 310 Houston St ..... Fort Worth TX 76102 817-336-1009 336-2661
Web: www.reata.net
Ristorante La Piazza 1600 S University Dr ..... Fort Worth TX 76107 817-334-0000 338-0945
Saint Emilion 3617 W 7th St ..... Fort Worth TX 76107 817-737-2781
Sapristi! 2418 Forest Park Blvd ..... Fort Worth TX 76110 817-924-7231
Web: www.sapristibistro.com
Sardines Ristorante Italiano 509 University Dr ..... Fort Worth TX 76107 817-332-9937 332-6708
Silver Fox Steakhouse 1651 S University Dr ..... Fort Worth TX 76107 817-332-9060 332-9073
Web: www.silverfoxsteakhouse.com
Spiral Diner 1314 W Magnolia Ave ..... Fort Worth TX 76104 817-332-8834
Web: www.spiraldiner.com
Texas de Brazil 101 N Houston St ..... Fort Worth TX 76102 817-882-9500 882-9503
Web: www.texasdebrazil.com
Tokyo Cafe 5121 Pershing Ave ..... Fort Worth TX 76107 817-737-8568
Web: www.thetokyocafe.com
Tres Jose's 4004 White Settlement Rd ..... Fort Worth TX 76107 817-763-0456 763-0911
West Side Cafe 7950 Camp Bowie W ..... Fort Worth TX 76116 817-560-1996
Yum Yum 4954 Overton Ridge Blvd ..... Fort Worth TX 76132 817-370-0688
Web: www.yumyumrestaurant.com
Arc-en-Ciel 3555 W Walnut St ..... Garland TX 75042 972-272-2188 276-9796
Babe's Chicken Dinner House 1456 Belt Line Rd Suite 171 ..... Garland TX 75044 972-496-1041 495-8026
Web: www.babeschicken.com
Baker's Ribs 488 W I-30 ..... Garland TX 75043 972-226-7447 203-9443
Web: www.bakersribs.com
China City Restaurant 6022 Broadway Blvd ..... Garland TX 75043 972-303-0373
China Star 2425 W Walnut St Suite 222 ..... Garland TX 75042 972-487-8311
Crazy Catfish 1410 W Buckingham Rd ..... Garland TX 75042 972-487-2100
Desperado's 3443 W Campbell Rd ..... Garland TX 75044 972-530-8886
Ernesto's 1202 Northwest Hwy ..... Garland TX 75041 972-681-8112
Fish City Grill 445 Coneflower Dr ..... Garland TX 75040 972-675-1600
Web: www.fishcitygrill.com/
General Pao Chinese Restaurant 1311 Plaza Dr ..... Garland TX 75041 972-686-8691 686-8692
Lucky China Buffet 1102 Northwest Hwy ..... Garland TX 75041 972-270-3430 270-8839
Luna de Noche 7602 N Jupiter Rd ..... Garland TX 75044 972-414-3616 414-2654
Web: www.lunadenoche.net
On The Border Cafe 1350 Northwest Hwy ..... Garland TX 75041 972-686-7867 613-0235
Pupusas Mama Tita 618 W Walnut St ..... Garland TX 75042 972-272-5818
Rick's Smoke House Barbecue 1417 Jupiter Rd ..... Garland TX 75042 972-276-4353 487-1101
Web: www.rickssmokehousebbq.com
Saigon Kitchen 3555 Walnut St ..... Garland TX 75042 972-276-2214
Scooter's 1401 Northwest Hwy Suite 121 ..... Garland TX 75041 972-864-1063
Soulman's Barbeque 3410 Broadway Blvd ..... Garland TX 75043 972-271-6885
Spring Creek BBQ 3335 N George Bush Fwy ..... Garland TX 75040 972-675-2920 675-5320
Uncle Wing Chinese Restaurant 107 N 1st St ..... Garland TX 75040 972-272-2775
Yen China Cafe 1225 Belt Line Rd ..... Garland TX 75040 972-495-9779 495-4929
Rainforest Cafe 3000 Grapevine Mills Pkwy ..... Grapevine TX 76051 972-539-5001
Web: www.rainforestcafe.com
Grey Moss Inn 19010 Scenic Loop Rd ..... Grey Forest TX 78023 210-695-8301 695-3237
Web: www.grey-moss-inn.com
Americas 1800 Post Oak Blvd Suite 164 ..... Houston TX 77056 713-961-1492 626-2701
Web: www.cordua.com/Americas_hm.htm
Arcodoro 5000 Westheimer Rd Suite 120 ..... Houston TX 77056 713-621-6888 621-6886
Web: www.arcodoro.com
Armandos 2630 Westheimer Rd ..... Houston TX 77098 713-520-1738 520-5748
Web: www.armandoshouston.com
Artista 800 Bagby St ..... Houston TX 77002 713-278-4782 315-2445
Ashiana 12610 Briar Forest ..... Houston TX 77070 281-679-5555 493-0981
Web: www.ashiana.cc
Babin's Seafood House 17485 Tomball Pkwy ..... Houston TX 77064 281-477-9300 477-9322
Web: www.babinsseafood.com
Backstreet Cafe 1103 S Shepherd Dr ..... Houston TX 77019 713-521-2239 520-5724
Web: www.backstreetcafe.net
Baker's Ribs 2223 S Voss Rd ..... Houston TX 77057 713-977-8725
Web: www.bakersribs.com
Barbecue Inn 116 W Crosstimbers St ..... Houston TX 77018 713-695-8112
Benjy's 2424 Dunstan Rd Suite 125 ..... Houston TX 77005 713-522-7602 522-7655
Web: www.benjys.com

Name / Address	City	State	ZIP	Phone	Fax
Bistro Moderne 2525 West Loop S	Houston	TX	77027	713-297-4383	297-4326
Web: www.bistromoderne.com					
Bistro Vino 819 W Alabama St	Houston	TX	77006	713-526-5500	526-7170
Web: www.bistrovino.net					
Bocados 1312 W Alabama St	Houston	TX	77006	713-523-5230	
Bonnie's Beef & Seafood Co 6867 Gulf Fwy	Houston	TX	77087	713-641-2397	641-4235
Web: www.bonniesbeefandseafood.com					
Bossa 610 Main St	Houston	TX	77002	713-223-2622	223-2629
Brennan's of Houston 3300 Smith St	Houston	TX	77006	713-522-9711	522-9508
Web: www.brennanshouston.com					
Brenner's Steakhouse 10911 Katy Fwy	Houston	TX	77079	713-465-2901	877-3116
Web: www.brennerssteakhouse.com					
Brownstone The 2736 Virginia St	Houston	TX	77098	713-520-5666	520-7001
Web: www.brownstone-houston.com					
Burns BBQ 8397 De Priest	Houston	TX	77088	281-445-7574	
Cafe Annie 1728 Post Oak Blvd	Houston	TX	77056	713-840-1111	850-1558
Web: www.cafe-annie.com					
Cafe Rabelais 2462 Bolsover St	Houston	TX	77005	713-526-6841	
Web: www.caferabelais.com					
Cafe Red Onion 12041 Northwest Fwy	Houston	TX	77092	713-957-0957	957-1338
Capital Grille 5365 Westheimer Rd	Houston	TX	77056	713-623-4600	623-4606
Web: www.thecapitalgrille.com					
Carmelo's 14795 Memorial Dr	Houston	TX	77079	281-531-0696	
Web: www.carmelosrestaurant.com					
Charivari 2521 Bagby St	Houston	TX	77006	713-521-7231	521-4697
Web: www.charivarirest.com					
Churrasco's 2055 Westheimer Rd	Houston	TX	77098	713-527-8300	527-0847
Web: www.churrascos.com					
Da Marco 1520 Westheimer Rd	Houston	TX	77006	713-807-8857	807-8301
Web: www.damarcohouston.com					
Damian's Cucina Italiana 3011 Smith St	Houston	TX	77006	713-522-0439	522-4408
Web: www.damians.com					
El Tiempo Cantina 3130 Richmond Ave	Houston	TX	77098	713-807-1600	807-1616
Web: www.eltiempocantina.com					
Empire Turkish Grill 12448 Memorial Dr	Houston	TX	77024	713-827-7475	463-7719
Web: www.theempireturkishgrill.com					
Fabio's Bar & Grille 212 Westheimer Rd	Houston	TX	77006	713-528-4212	523-8212
Web: www.fabiosbarandgrill.com					
Fadi's Mediterranean Cuisine 8383 Westheimer Rd	Houston	TX	77063	713-532-0666	532-0677
Web: www.fadiscuisine.com					
Farrago 318 Gray St	Houston	TX	77002	713-523-6404	523-6405
Web: www.farrago.tv					
Felix 904 Westheimer Rd	Houston	TX	77006	713-529-3949	529-0508
Fleming's Prime Steakhouse & Wine Bar 2405 W Alabama St	Houston	TX	77098	713-520-5959	520-8840
Web: www.flemingssteakhouse.com					
Fogo de Chao 8250 Westheimer Rd	Houston	TX	77063	713-978-6500	978-6501
Web: www.fogodechao.com					
Frenchie's 1041 NASA Pkwy	Houston	TX	77058	281-486-7144	486-3952
Fuad's 6100 Westheimer Rd	Houston	TX	77057	713-785-0130	785-2215
Fung's Kitchen 7320 Southwest Fwy	Houston	TX	77074	713-779-2288	271-2288
Web: www.fungskitchen.com					
Goode Co Seafood 2621 Westpark Dr	Houston	TX	77098	713-523-7154	523-0774
Goode Co Texas Barbecue 5109 Kirby Dr	Houston	TX	77098	713-522-2530	522-3873
Web: www.goodecompany.com					
Hard Rock Cafe 570 Texas Ave	Houston	TX	77002	713-227-1392	228-2689
Web: www.hardrockcafe.com					
Hugo's 1600 Westheimer Rd	Houston	TX	77006	713-524-7744	524-7719
Web: www.hugosrestaurant.net					
Hunan Village 3311 S Shepherd Dr	Houston	TX	77098	713-528-4651	
Ibiza Food & Wine Bar 2450 Louisiana St	Houston	TX	77006	713-524-0004	520-7369
Web: www.ibizafoodandwinebar.com					
Indika 516 Westheimer Rd	Houston	TX	77006	713-524-2170	984-1755
Web: www.indikausa.com					
Jasmine Asian Cuisine 9938 Bellaire Blvd Suite D	Houston	TX	77036	713-272-8188	272-8187
Kam's 4500 Montrose Blvd	Houston	TX	77006	713-529-5057	529-5486
Kiran's Restaurant & Bar 4100 Westheimer Rd	Houston	TX	77027	713-960-8472	993-0739
Web: www.kiranshouston.com/					
Kubo's Sushi Bar & Grill 2414 University Blvd	Houston	TX	77005	713-528-7878	528-9150
Web: www.kubos-sushi.com					
La Colombe D'Or 3410 Montrose Blvd	Houston	TX	77006	713-524-7999	524-8923
Web: www.lacolombedorhouston.com/					
La Griglia 2002 W Gray St	Houston	TX	77019	713-526-4700	526-9249
Los Tios 9527 Westheimer St	Houston	TX	77063	713-784-0380	784-5211
Lynn's Steakhouse 955 Dairy Ashford	Houston	TX	77079	281-870-0807	870-0888
Web: www.lynnssteakhouse.com					
Madras Pavilion 3910 Kirby Dr	Houston	TX	77098	713-521-2617	521-2647
Web: www.madraspavilion.us					
Maggiano's Little Italy Restaurant 2019 Post Oak Blvd	Houston	TX	77056	713-961-2700	961-4550
Web: www.maggianos.com					
Magic Island 2215 Southwest Fwy	Houston	TX	77098	713-526-2442	526-8309
Web: www.themagicisland.com					
Magnolia Bar & Grill 6000 Richmond Ave	Houston	TX	77057	713-781-6207	781-8061
Web: www.magnolia-grill.com					
Mai Thai 3819 Kirby Dr	Houston	TX	77098	713-522-6707	522-4806
Mark's American Cuisine 1658 Westheimer Rd	Houston	TX	77006	713-523-3800	523-9292
Web: www.marks1658.com					
Masraff's 1025 S Post Oak Ln	Houston	TX	77056	713-355-1975	355-1965
Web: www.masraffs.com					
Massa's 1160 Smith St	Houston	TX	77002	713-650-0837	650-0165
Web: www.massas.com					
Mockingbird Bistro 1985 Welch St	Houston	TX	77019	713-533-0200	533-0215
Web: www.mockingbirdbistro.com					
Morton's The Steakhouse 5000 Westheimer Rd	Houston	TX	77056	713-629-1946	629-4348
Web: www.mortons.com					
Mykonos Island 2181 Richmond Ave	Houston	TX	77098	713-523-4114	523-0759
Nino's 2817 W Dallas St	Houston	TX	77019	713-522-5120	
Web: www.ninos-vincents.com					
Noe Restaurant & Bar 4 Riverway	Houston	TX	77056	713-871-8177	871-0719
Old Heidelberg 1810 Fountain View	Houston	TX	77057	713-781-3581	781-3350
Web: www.theoldheidelberg.com					
Osaka Japanese Restaurant 515 Westheimer Rd	Houston	TX	77006	713-533-9098	
Palm Restaurant 6100 Westheimer Rd	Houston	TX	77057	713-977-2544	977-3503
Web: www.thepalm.com					
Pappas Brothers Steakhouse 5839 Westheimer Rd	Houston	TX	77057	713-917-0090	780-8119
Web: www.pappasbros.com					
Pesce 3029 Kirby Dr	Houston	TX	77098	713-522-4858	522-9666
Web: www.pescehouston.com					
PF Chang's China Bistro 11685 Westheimer Rd	Houston	TX	77077	281-920-3553	920-3567
Web: www.pfchangs.com					
Piatto Ristorante 4925 W Alabama St	Houston	TX	77056	713-871-9722	871-9190
Web: www.piattoristorante.com					
Prego 2520 Amherst St	Houston	TX	77005	713-529-2420	526-3181
Web: www.prego-houston.com					
Prime Time Steakhouse 9275 FM 1960 W	Houston	TX	77070	281-469-1234	
Web: www.primetimesteakhouse.com					
Quattro 1300 Lamar St	Houston	TX	77010	713-650-1300	276-4720
Rainbow Lodge 2011 Ella Blvd	Houston	TX	77008	713-861-8666	861-8405
Web: www.rainbow-lodge.com					
Reef 2600 Travis St	Houston	TX	77006	713-526-8282	
Web: www.reefhouston.com/					
Remington The 1919 Briar Oaks Ln	Houston	TX	77027	713-403-2631	840-0616
Web: www.theremingtonrestaurant.com					
Rio Ranch 9999 Westheimer Rd	Houston	TX	77042	713-952-5000	952-2263
Web: www.rioranch.com					
Ruggles Grill 903 Westheimer Rd	Houston	TX	77006	713-524-3839	524-7396
Web: www.rugglesgrill.com					
Ruth's Chris Steak House 6213 Richmond Ave	Houston	TX	77057	713-789-2333	789-4136
Web: www.ruthschris.com					
Sabor! 5712 Bellaire Blvd	Houston	TX	77081	713-667-6001	
Saltgrass Steak House 520 Meyerland Plaza Mall	Houston	TX	77096	713-665-2226	877-3176
Shiva 2514 Times Blvd	Houston	TX	77005	713-523-4753	523-4754
Web: www.shivarestaurant.com					
Simposio 5591 Richmond Ave	Houston	TX	77056	713-532-0550	532-7712
Web: www.simposiorestaurant.com					
Spanish Flower 4701 N Main St	Houston	TX	77009	713-869-1706	869-1734
Spindletop 1200 Louisiana St	Houston	TX	77002	713-375-4775	
T'afia 3701 Travis St	Houston	TX	77002	713-524-6922	
Web: www.tafia.com					
Taste of Texas Restaurant 10505 Katy Fwy	Houston	TX	77024	713-932-6901	461-6177
Web: www.tasteoftexas.com					
Thai Pepper 2049 W Alabama St	Houston	TX	77098	713-520-8225	
Web: tealas.com					
Tony Mandola's Gulf Coast Kitchen 1962 W Gray St	Houston	TX	77019	713-528-3474	528-4438
Web: www.tonymandolas.com					
Tony's 3755 Richmond St	Houston	TX	77056	713-622-6778	
Tropical Grill 6521 Bissonnet St	Houston	TX	77074	713-771-3399	
Vic & Anthony's 1510 Texas Ave	Houston	TX	77002	713-228-1111	228-1114
Web: www.vicandanthonys.com					
Vieng Thai 6929 Long Point St	Houston	TX	77055	713-688-9910	
Zula 705 Main St Suite B	Houston	TX	77002	713-227-7052	227-7056
Web: www.zulahouston.com					
Benihana 5400 Whitehall St	Irving	TX	75038	972-550-0060	
Web: www.benihana.com					
Blue Fish 925 W John Carpenter Fwy	Irving	TX	75039	972-385-3474	910-0130
Web: www.thebluefishsushi.com					
Bruno's 9462 N MacArthur Blvd	Irving	TX	75063	972-556-2465	
Cafe Cipriani 220 E Las Colinas Blvd	Irving	TX	75039	972-869-0713	869-2281
Web: www.cafecipriani.com					
Cafe on the Green 4150 N MacArthur Blvd	Irving	TX	75038	972-717-0700	717-2550
Cool River Cafe 1045 Hidden Ridge	Irving	TX	75038	972-871-8881	871-8882
Web: www.coolrivercafe.com					
Danal's 508 N O'Connor Rd	Irving	TX	75061	972-254-2666	259-7483
Web: www.danalsmexmex.com					
Empress of China 2648 N Belt Line Rd	Irving	TX	75062	972-252-7677	258-6776
Hanasho 2938 N Belt Line Rd	Irving	TX	75062	972-258-0250	257-1243
Web: www.hanasho.com					
Haveli 1800 Valley View Ln	Irving	TX	75061	972-313-0144	
I Fratelli 7701 N McArthur	Irving	TX	75063	972-501-9700	501-9704
Web: www.ifratelli.net					
Isshin Sushi Bar & Grill 7600 N MacArthur Blvd	Irving	TX	75063	972-506-9906	506-3183
Italian Cafe 387 Las Colinas Blvd E	Irving	TX	75039	972-401-0000	401-9193
Jinbeh 301 E Las Colinas Blvd	Irving	TX	75039	972-869-4011	869-4311
Web: www.jinbeh.com/lascolinas.htm					
Keg Steakhouse & Bar 859 W John Carpenter Fwy	Irving	TX	75039	972-556-9188	506-0591
Web: www.kegsteakhouse.com					
Le Peep 4835 N O'Connor Rd	Irving	TX	75062	972-717-0422	650-1446
Web: www.lepeep.com					
Mi Cocina 7750 N MacArthur Blvd Suite 150	Irving	TX	75063	469-621-0452	621-0455
Midori Sushi 4020 N MacArthur Blvd	Irving	TX	75038	972-887-1818	717-3836
Pasand Indian Cuisine 2600 N Belt Line Rd	Irving	TX	75062	972-594-0693	594-8935
Pei Wei Asian Diner 7600 N MacArthur Blvd	Irving	TX	75063	972-373-8000	
Piman Asian Bistro 4835 N O'Connor Rd	Irving	TX	75062	972-650-0001	
Web: www.pimanasian.com					
Red Hot & Blues Barbecue 5910 N MacArthur Blvd	Irving	TX	76039	972-402-0225	
Web: www.redhotandblue.com					
Rockfish Seafood Grill 7400 N MacArthur Blvd	Irving	TX	75603	214-574-4111	
Web: www.rockfish.com					
Ruen Thai Cuisine 3310 W Rochelle Rd	Irving	TX	75062	972-570-7716	
Sonny Bryan's Smoke House 4030 N MacArthur Blvd Suite 222	Irving	TX	75038	972-650-9564	
Web: www.sonnybryans.com					
Spring Creek Barbeque 3514 W Airport Fwy	Irving	TX	75062	972-313-0987	313-1174
Web: www.springcreekbarbeque.com					
Texadelphia 7601 N MacArthur Blvd	Irving	TX	75063	972-432-0725	373-8810
Web: www.texadelphia.com					
Thai Chili 397 E Las Colinas Blvd	Irving	TX	75039	972-831-0797	
Trevi's 221 Las Colinas Blvd E	Irving	TX	75039	972-869-5550	
Via Real Restaurant 4020 N MacArthur Blvd	Irving	TX	75038	972-650-9001	541-0215
Web: www.viareal.com					
50 Yard Line Steakhouse 2549 Loop 289 S	Lubbock	TX	79423	806-745-3991	
Abuelo's Mexican Food Embassy 4401 82nd St	Lubbock	TX	79414	806-794-1762	794-4179
Web: www.abuelos.com					
Benaglio's 4210 82nd St	Lubbock	TX	79423	806-793-4433	
Web: www.benaglios.com					
Bless Your Heart 3701 19th St	Lubbock	TX	79410	806-791-2211	
Cagle Steaks 108 N FM 179	Lubbock	TX	79416	806-795-3879	
Web: www.caglesteaks.com					
Cattle Baron 8201 Quaker Ave Suite 170	Lubbock	TX	79424	806-798-7033	
Web: www.cattlebaron.com					
Chez Suzette 4423 50th St	Lubbock	TX	79423	806-795-6796	
China Star 1919 50th St	Lubbock	TX	79412	806-749-2100	
Chinese Kitchen 3715 19th St	Lubbock	TX	79410	806-792-4636	
Choochai Thai Cuisine 2330 19th St	Lubbock	TX	79401	806-747-1767	
Cricket Grill & Draft House 2412 Broadway	Lubbock	TX	79401	806-744-4677	
Delhi Palace 5401 Aberdeen Ave	Lubbock	TX	79414	806-799-6772	
Don Pablo's 4625 50th St	Lubbock	TX	79414	806-793-7204	
Fortune Cookie 7006 University Ave Suite 6	Lubbock	TX	79413	806-745-2205	
Gardski's 2009 Broadway	Lubbock	TX	79401	806-744-2391	
Great Wall 1625 University Ave	Lubbock	TX	79401	806-747-1264	
Jake's Sports Cafe 5025 50th St	Lubbock	TX	79414	806-687-5253	
Web: www.jakes-sportscafe.com					
Jazz Restaurant 3703 19th St Suite C	Lubbock	TX	79410	806-799-2124	799-7870
Web: www.jazzkitchen.com					
Joe's Crab Shack 5802 W Loop South 289	Lubbock	TX	79414	806-797-8600	
Web: www.joescrabshack.com					
La Fiesta 1519 34th St Suite B	Lubbock	TX	79411	806-744-9151	
Montelongo's 3021 Clovis Rd	Lubbock	TX	79415	806-762-3068	
Orlando's 2402 Ave Q	Lubbock	TX	79405	806-747-5998	
Web: www.orlandos.com					
Picantes 3814 34th St	Lubbock	TX	79410	806-793-8304	
Rudy's Country Store & Bar BQ 4930 S Loop 289	Lubbock	TX	79414	806-797-1777	
Web: www.rudys.com					
Texas Cafe & Bar 3604 50th St	Lubbock	TX	79413	806-792-8544	

Texas (Cont'd)

Name / Address	City	State	Zip	Phone	Fax
Texas Land & Cattle Steak House 7202 Indiana Ave	Lubbock	TX	79423	806-791-0555	
Web: www.txlc.com					
Texas Roadhouse 4810 S Loop 289 Service Rd	Lubbock	TX	79414	806-799-9900	
Web: www.texasroadhouse.com					
Thai Thai 5018 50th St	Lubbock	TX	79414	806-791-0024	
Tokyo Japanese Restaurant 4637 50th St	Lubbock	TX	79414	806-799-8998	
Awaji 4701 W Park Blvd	Plano	TX	75093	972-519-1688	
Bavarian Grill 221 W Parker Rd	Plano	TX	75023	972-881-0705	
Web: www.bavariangrill.com					
Big Easy The 1915 N Central Expy	Plano	TX	75075	972-424-5261	
Blue Goose Cantina 4757 W Park Blvd	Plano	TX	75093	972-596-8882	596-8722
Web: www.bluegoosecantina.com					
Bob's Steak & Chop House 5760 Legacy Dr Suite B1	Plano	TX	75024	972-608-2627	
Web: www.bobs-steakandchop.com					
Cathy's Wok 3948 Legacy Dr	Plano	TX	75023	972-491-7267	
Chettinaad Palace 2205 N Central Expy	Plano	TX	75075	469-229-9100	
Web: www.chettinaadpalace.com					
Covino's 3265 Independence Pkwy	Plano	TX	75075	972-519-0345	
Fishmonger's Seafood 1915 N Central Expy	Plano	TX	75074	972-423-3699	
Greek Isles Tavern & Restaurant 3309 N Central Expy Suite 370	Plano	TX	75023	972-423-7778	
Jade Palace 820 W Spring Creek Pkwy Suite 212	Plano	TX	75023	972-424-5578	
Japon Steak House & Sushi Bar 4021 Preston Rd	Plano	TX	75093	972-781-2818	
Web: www.japonsteakhouseandsushi.com					
Joe's Crab Shack 3320 N Central Expy	Plano	TX	75074	972-423-2800	
Jorg's Cafe Vienna 1037 E 15th St	Plano	TX	75074	972-509-5966	
Kirby's Steakhouse 3408 Preston Rd	Plano	TX	75093	972-867-2122	
Web: www.kirbyssteakhouse.com					
Kosta's Cafe 4621 W Park Blvd	Plano	TX	75093	972-596-8424	
Web: www.kostascafe.com					
La Madeleine 5000 W Park Blvd	Plano	TX	75093	972-407-1878	
Love & War In Texas 601 E Plano Pkwy	Plano	TX	75074	972-422-6201	
Web: www.loveandwarintexas.com					
Mango's Thai Cuisine 4701 W Park Blvd	Plano	TX	75093	972-599-0289	599-7013
Web: www.mangoplano.com					
Mario's Chiquita 3310 N Central Expy	Plano	TX	75074	972-423-2977	
Naan Restaurant 7161 Bishop Rd	Plano	TX	75024	972-943-9288	
Web: www.naan-restaurant.com/					
Nakamoto 3309 N Central Expy	Plano	TX	75023	972-881-0328	578-8965
Ocean Seafood & Grill 3115 W Parker Rd	Plano	TX	75023	972-758-1232	
Ojeda's 1915 N Central Expy	Plano	TX	75075	972-422-5677	
Web: www.bigbenojeda.com					
Osaka Sushi 5012 W Park Blvd	Plano	TX	75093	972-931-8898	
Paesano's 508 E 14th St	Plano	TX	75074	972-578-2727	578-1105
Web: www.paesanosrestaurant.com					
Papaya's 3033 W Parker Rd	Plano	TX	75023	972-985-7527	867-9371
Patrizio's 1900 Preston Rd	Plano	TX	75093	972-964-2200	596-1743
Picasso's 3948 Legacy Dr	Plano	TX	75023	972-618-4143	
Posados Cafe 3421 N Central Expy	Plano	TX	75023	972-509-4999	
Rockfish Seafood Grill 4701 W Park Blvd Suite 105	Plano	TX	75093	972-599-2190	964-6898
Roy's 2840 Dallas Pkwy	Plano	TX	75093	972-473-6263	
Web: www.roysrestaurant.com					
Steve Fields Steak & Lobster Lounge 5013 W Park Blvd	Plano	TX	75093	972-596-7100	599-3950
Web: www.stevefieldsrestaurant.com					
Taste of the Islands 909 W Spring Creek Pkwy	Plano	TX	75023	972-517-5900	
Texas Land & Cattle Co 3945 Central Expy	Plano	TX	75023	972-578-8707	578-0097
Web: www.texaslandandcattle.com					
Tin Star 2208 Dallas Pkwy	Plano	TX	75093	972-403-1765	
Web: www.tinstar.us					
Vincent's 2432 Preston Rd	Plano	TX	75093	972-612-6208	612-0969
Web: www.vincentsseafood.com					
Alamo Cafe 10060 W IH-10	San Antonio	TX	78230	210-691-8827	691-0056
Web: www.alamocafe.com					
Amy's Tex-Mex Cafe 9775 Culebra Rd	San Antonio	TX	78251	210-520-1661	
Anaqua Grill 555 S Alamo St	San Antonio	TX	78205	210-229-1000	229-1418
Biga on the Banks 203 S Saint Mary's St	San Antonio	TX	78205	210-225-0722	
Web: www.biga.com					
Bistro Vatel 218 E Olmos Dr	San Antonio	TX	78212	210-828-3141	
Web: www.bistrovatel.com					
Boardwalk Bistro 4011 Broadway	San Antonio	TX	78209	210-824-0100	
Web: www.boardwalkbistro.net/					
Bohanan's 219 E Houston St Suite 275	San Antonio	TX	78205	210-472-2600	
Web: www.bohanans.com					
Boudro's On The Riverwalk 421 E Commerce St	San Antonio	TX	78205	210-224-8484	225-2839
Web: www.boudros.com					
Cappy's 5011 Broadway St	San Antonio	TX	78209	210-828-9669	828-3041
Web: www.cappysrestaurant.com					
Cheesecake Factory 7400 San Pedro St	San Antonio	TX	78216	210-798-2222	798-2232
Web: www.cheesecakefactory.com					
Chris Madrid's 1900 Blanco Rd	San Antonio	TX	78212	210-735-3552	
Citrus 150 E Houston St 2nd Fl	San Antonio	TX	78205	210-230-8412	227-9701
County Line 10101 W IH-10	San Antonio	TX	78230	210-641-1998	641-1345
Web: www.countyline.com					
Cove The 606 W Cypress St	San Antonio	TX	78212	210-227-2683	
Web: www.thecove.us					
Crumpets 3920 Harry Wurzbach St	San Antonio	TX	78209	210-821-5454	821-5624
Web: www.crumpetsa.com					
Demo's 2501 N Saint Mary's St	San Antonio	TX	78212	210-732-7777	731-9002
Web: www.demosgreekfood.com					
El Mirador 722 S Saint Mary's St	San Antonio	TX	78205	210-225-9444	
Fig Tree 515 Villita St	San Antonio	TX	78205	210-224-1976	271-9180
Web: www.figtreerestaurant.com					
Formosa Garden 1011 NE Loop 410	San Antonio	TX	78209	210-828-9988	826-2566
Web: www.formosagarden.com					
Golden Wok 8822 Wurzbach Rd	San Antonio	TX	78240	210-615-8282	
Golfo de Mexico 603 Bandera Rd	San Antonio	TX	78228	210-434-8662	
Hard Rock Cafe 111 W Crocket St	San Antonio	TX	78205	210-224-7625	224-7693
Web: www.hardrockcafe.com					
India Oven 1031 Patricia St Suite 106	San Antonio	TX	78213	210-366-1030	366-1033
Web: www.indiaoven.com					
India Palace 8440 Fredericksburg Rd	San Antonio	TX	78229	210-692-5262	
J Alexander's 255 E Basse Rd	San Antonio	TX	78209	210-824-0275	824-0770
Web: www.jalexanders.com					
La Fogata 2427 Vance Jackson Rd	San Antonio	TX	78213	210-340-1337	349-6467
Web: www.lafogata.com					
La Fonda on Main 2415 N Main Ave	San Antonio	TX	78212	210-733-0621	
Web: www.lafondaonmain.com					
L'Etoile 6106 Broadway St	San Antonio	TX	78209	210-826-4551	826-0653
Web: www.letoilesa.com					
Little Rhein Steakhouse 231 S Alamo St	San Antonio	TX	78205	210-225-2111	271-9180
Web: www.littlerheinsteakhouse.com					
Lodge of Castle Hills The 1746 Lockhill Selma Rd	San Antonio	TX	78213	210-349-8466	
Melting Pot The 14855 Blanco Rd Suite 110	San Antonio	TX	78216	210-479-6358	
Web: www.meltingpot.com					
Menciu's Gourmet Hunan Chinese Restaurant 7959 Fredericksburg Rd	San Antonio	TX	78229	210-615-1288	615-6558
Meson European Dining 5999 De Zavala Rd	San Antonio	TX	78249	210-690-5811	
Web: www.mesoneuropeandining.com					
Morton's The Steakhouse 300 E Crockett St	San Antonio	TX	78205	210-228-0700	228-0778
Web: www.mortons.com					
Old San Francisco Steak House 10223 Sahara Dr	San Antonio	TX	78216	210-342-2321	
Web: www.osfsteakhouse.com					
Paesano's 555 E Basse Rd	San Antonio	TX	78209	210-828-5191	
Web: www.joesfood.com					
Pappadeaux Seafood Kitchen 76 NE Loop 410	San Antonio	TX	78216	210-340-7143	340-0572
Web: www.pappadeaux.com					
Pesca on the River 212 W Crockett St	San Antonio	TX	78205	210-396-5817	
Web: www.watermarkhotel.com/restaurant					
PF Chang's China Bistro 255 E Basse Rd	San Antonio	TX	78209	210-507-1000	507-1001
Web: www.pfchangs.com					
Piatti 255 E Basse Rd Suite 500	San Antonio	TX	78209	210-832-0300	832-0303
Web: www.piatti.com					
Picante Grill 3810 Broadway	San Antonio	TX	78209	210-822-3797	
Restaurant Le Reve 152 E Pecan St	San Antonio	TX	78205	210-212-2221	
Web: www.restaurantlereve.com/					
Rio Rio Cantina 421 E Commerce St	San Antonio	TX	78205	210-226-8462	226-8443
Web: www.rioriocantina.com					
Rudy's Country Store & Bar-B-Q 24152 W IH-10	San Antonio	TX	78257	210-698-2141	698-0995
Ruth's Chris Steak House 7720 Jones-Maltsberger Rd	San Antonio	TX	78216	210-821-5051	821-5095
Web: www.ruthschris.com					
Silo 1133 Austin Hwy	San Antonio	TX	78209	210-824-8686	805-8452
Web: www.siloelevatedcuisine.com					
Sushi Zushi 203 S Saint Mary's St	San Antonio	TX	78205	210-472-2900	
Web: www.sushizushi.com					
Texas Land & Cattle Steak House 9911 IH-10 W	San Antonio	TX	78230	210-699-8744	
Web: www.txlc.com					
Thai Kitchen 100 Villita St	San Antonio	TX	78205	210-226-2970	
Zio's 12858 W IH-10	San Antonio	TX	78249	210-697-7222	697-7333
Web: www.zios.com					

Utah

Name / Address	City	State	Zip	Phone	Fax
La Caille at Quail Run 9565 Wasatch Blvd	Little Cottonwood Canyon	UT	84092	801-942-1751	
Web: www.lacaille.com					
Athenian 252 25th St	Ogden	UT	84401	801-621-4911	395-2468
Bistro 258 258 25th St	Ogden	UT	84401	801-394-1595	
Web: www.bistro258.com					
China Nite Cafe 2783 Washington Blvd	Ogden	UT	84401	801-393-1031	
Eastern Winds 3740 Washington Blvd	Ogden	UT	84403	801-627-2739	
El Matador 2564 Ogden Ave	Ogden	UT	84401	801-393-3151	
Golden Dynasty 3433 Washington Blvd	Ogden	UT	84401	801-621-6789	
Jasoh 4590 Harrison Blvd	Ogden	UT	84403	801-399-0088	
Web: www.jasoh.com					
Javiers 703 Washington Blvd	Ogden	UT	84404	801-393-4747	
Jeremiah's 1307 W 1200 S	Ogden	UT	84404	801-394-3273	627-6579
Web: www.jeremiahsogden.com					
Pantheon Cafe 1045 N Washington Blvd	Ogden	UT	84404	801-782-5303	
Prairie Schooner Restaurant 445 Park Blvd	Ogden	UT	84401	801-621-5511	
Web: www.prairieschoonerrestaurant.com					
Rooster's 253 25th St	Ogden	UT	84401	801-627-6171	622-1353
Web: www.roostersbrewingco.com					
Ruby River Steak House 4286 Riverdale Rd	Ogden	UT	84405	801-622-2320	622-2420
Web: www.rubyriver.com					
Temari 3035 Washington Blvd	Ogden	UT	84401	801-399-9536	
Timber Mine 1701 Park Blvd	Ogden	UT	84401	801-393-2155	
Web: www.timbermine.com					
Tona 210 25th St	Ogden	UT	84401	801-622-8662	
Web: www.tonarestaurant.com					
Union Grill 2501 Wall Ave	Ogden	UT	84401	801-621-2830	621-7946
Web: www.uniongrillogden.com					
Windy's Sukiyaki 3809 Riverdale Rd	Ogden	UT	84405	801-621-4505	
Web: www.windyssukiyaki.com					
Yu's Maple Garden 3798 Washington Blvd	Ogden	UT	84403	801-621-1888	
Bajio 4801 N University Ave	Provo	UT	84606	801-224-6668	
Bombay House 463 N University Ave	Provo	UT	84601	801-373-6677	
Brick Oven 111 E 800 North	Provo	UT	84606	801-374-8800	
Web: brickovenpizza.biz					
Cafe Rio 2250 N University Pkwy	Provo	UT	84604	801-375-5133	375-5176
Web: www.caferio.com					
Demae Japanese Restaurant 82 W Center St	Provo	UT	84601	801-374-0306	
Happy Sumo at the Riverwoods 4801 N University Ave	Provo	UT	84604	801-225-9100	
Web: www.happysumosushi.com					
Joe Vera's Mexican Fiestaurant 250 W Center St	Provo	UT	84601	801-375-6714	
La Dolce Vita 61 N 100 East	Provo	UT	84606	801-373-8482	
Web: www.ladolcevitaprovo.com					
Osaka Japanese Restaurant 46 W Center St	Provo	UT	84601	801-373-1060	
Ottavio's 71 E Center St	Provo	UT	84606	801-377-9555	377-1316
Web: www.ottavios.com					
Ozz 490 N Freedom Blvd	Provo	UT	84601	801-818-9000	
Web: www.ozzpool.com					
Ruby River Steakhouse 1454 S University Ave	Provo	UT	84601	801-371-0648	
Web: www.rubyriver.com					
Saigon Cafe 440 W 300 South	Provo	UT	84601	801-812-1173	
Web: www.saigoncafeprovo.com					
Sam Hawk 660 N Freedom Blvd	Provo	UT	84601	801-377-7766	
Tepanyaki Japanese Steak House 1240 N State St	Provo	UT	84604	801-374-0633	
Web: www.mytepanyaki.com					
Thai Ruby 744 E 820 North	Provo	UT	84606	801-375-6840	
Training Table 2230 N University Pkwy	Provo	UT	84604	801-377-3939	
Tucanos Brazilian Grill 4801 N University Ave Unit 790	Provo	UT	84604	801-224-4774	
Web: www.tucanos.com					
Aristo's 224 S 1300 East	Salt Lake City	UT	84102	801-581-0888	
Web: www.aristosgreekrestaurant.com					
Atlantic Cafe 325 S Main St	Salt Lake City	UT	84111	801-524-9900	
Baba Afghan Restaurant 55 E 400 South	Salt Lake City	UT	84111	801-596-0786	
Baci Trattoria 134 W Pierpont Ave	Salt Lake City	UT	84101	801-328-1500	
Web: www.gastronomyinc.com/baci					
Bambara Restaurant 202 S Main St	Salt Lake City	UT	84101	801-363-5454	
Web: www.bambara-slc.com					
Bangkok Thai 1400 S Foothill Dr Suite 210	Salt Lake City	UT	84108	801-582-8424	
Web: www.bangkokthai.com					
Benihana of Tokyo 165 S West Temple	Salt Lake City	UT	84101	801-322-2421	
Web: www.benihana.com					
Blue Iguana 165 S West Temple	Salt Lake City	UT	84101	801-533-8900	
Web: www.blueiguanarestaurant.net					
Bombay House 2731 E Parleys Way	Salt Lake City	UT	84108	801-581-0222	
Web: www.bombayhouse.com					
Cafe Madrid 2080 E 3900 South	Salt Lake City	UT	84124	801-273-0837	

Restaurant	City	State	Zip	Phone	Fax
Cafe Rio 3025 E 3300 South	Salt Lake City	UT	84109	801-463-7250	
Web: www.caferio.com					
Cafe Sha Sha 175 E 400 South	Salt Lake City	UT	84101	801-322-4949	
Cafe Trang 818 S Main St	Salt Lake City	UT	84101	801-539-1638	
Web: www.cafetrangutah.com					
Cafe Trio 6405 S 3000 East	Salt Lake City	UT	84121	801-733-6600	
Web: www.triodining.com					
Caffe Molise 55 W 100 South	Salt Lake City	UT	84101	801-364-8833	
Web: www.caffemolise.com					
Christopher's Seafood & Steak House 110 W Broadway	Salt Lake City	UT	84101	801-519-8515	
Cinegrill 344 S 300 East	Salt Lake City	UT	84111	801-328-4900	
Citris Grill 2991 E 3300 South	Salt Lake City	UT	84109	801-466-1202	
Web: www.citrisgrill.com					
Cucina Toscana 307 W Pierpont Ave	Salt Lake City	UT	84101	801-328-3463	
Web: www.cucina-toscana.com					
Desert Edge Brewery 273 Trolley Sq	Salt Lake City	UT	84102	801-521-8917	
Em's 271 N Center St	Salt Lake City	UT	84101	801-596-0566	
Web: www.emsrestaurant.com					
Fleming's Prime Steakhouse & Wine Bar 20 S 400 West	Salt Lake City	UT	84101	801-355-3704	
Web: www.flemingssteakhouse.com					
Formosa Grill 2115 E 2100 South	Salt Lake City	UT	84109	801-461-0661	
Web: www.formosagrill.com					
Fresco Italian Cafe 1513 S 1500 East	Salt Lake City	UT	84105	801-486-1300	
Web: www.frescoitaliancafe.com					
Ginza 209 W 200 South	Salt Lake City	UT	84101	801-322-2224	
Hong Kong Tea House 565 W 200 South	Salt Lake City	UT	84101	801-531-7010	
Ichiban Sushi & Japanese Cuisine 336 S 400 East	Salt Lake City	UT	84111	801-532-7522	
Koyo 2275 E 33rd South	Salt Lake City	UT	84109	801-466-7111	
Kyoto 1100 E 1300 South	Salt Lake City	UT	84105	801-487-3525	
La Puente 3434 S State St	Salt Lake City	UT	84115	801-466-1194	
Lamb's Grill Cafe 169 S Main St	Salt Lake City	UT	84111	801-364-7166	
Web: www.lambsgrill.com					
Log Haven 6451 E Milcreek Canyon	Salt Lake City	UT	84109	801-272-8255	
Web: www.log-haven.com					
Lugano Restaurant 3364 S 2300 East	Salt Lake City	UT	84109	801-412-9994	
Web: www.luganorestaurant.com					
Market Street Broiler 260 S 1300 East	Salt Lake City	UT	84102	801-583-8808	
Market Street Grill 48 Market St	Salt Lake City	UT	84101	801-322-4668	
Market Street Oyster Bar 54 Market St	Salt Lake City	UT	84101	801-531-6044	
Martine 22 E 100 South	Salt Lake City	UT	84111	801-363-9328	
Mazza 1515 S 1500 East	Salt Lake City	UT	84105	801-484-9259	
Web: www.mazzacafe.com					
Metropolitan 173 W Broadway	Salt Lake City	UT	84101	801-364-3472	
Web: www.themetropolitan.com					
Michelangelo Ristorante 2156 S Highland Dr	Salt Lake City	UT	84106	801-466-0961	
Mikado 67 W 100 South	Salt Lake City	UT	84101	801-328-0929	
Web: www.latituderg.com					
Monsoon Thai Bistro 1615 S Foothill Dr	Salt Lake City	UT	84108	801-583-5339	
Web: www.monsoonthai.com					
New Yorker 60 W Market St	Salt Lake City	UT	84101	801-363-0166	
Oasis Cafe 151 S 500 East	Salt Lake City	UT	84102	801-322-0404	
Old Salt City Jail 460 S 1000 East	Salt Lake City	UT	84102	801-359-6090	
Pagoda Restaurant 26 'E' St	Salt Lake City	UT	84103	801-355-8155	
Paris Bistro 1500 S 1500 East	Salt Lake City	UT	85105	801-486-5585	
Web: www.theparis.net					
Passages Restaurant 71 W South Temple	Salt Lake City	UT	84101	801-536-7200	
PF Chang's China Bistro 174 W 300 South	Salt Lake City	UT	84111	801-539-0500	
Web: www.pfchangs.com					
Red Iguana 736 W North Temple St	Salt Lake City	UT	84116	801-322-1489	
Web: www.rediguana.com					
Red Rock Brewing Co 254 S 200 West	Salt Lake City	UT	84101	801-521-7446	
Web: www.redrockbrewing.com					
Rino's 2302 E Parleys Way	Salt Lake City	UT	84109	801-484-0901	
Rio Grande Cafe 270 S Rio Grande St	Salt Lake City	UT	84101	801-364-3302	
Rodizio Grill 459 Trolley Sq	Salt Lake City	UT	84102	801-220-0500	
Web: www.rodiziogrill.com					
Rumbi Island Grill 358 S 700 East	Salt Lake City	UT	84102	801-530-1000	
Sage's Cafe 473 E Broadway	Salt Lake City	UT	84111	801-322-3790	
Web: www.sagescafe.com					
Sampan 675 E 2100 South	Salt Lake City	UT	84106	801-467-3663	
Web: www.esampan.com					
Shogun 321 Main St	Salt Lake City	UT	84111	801-364-7142	
Spencer's for Steaks & Chops 255 S West Temple St	Salt Lake City	UT	84101	801-238-4748	
Web: www.spencersforsteaksandchops.com					
Squatter's Pub Brewery 147 W Broadway	Salt Lake City	UT	84101	801-363-2739	
Web: www.squatters.com					
Sugarhouse Barbecue Co 2207 S 700 East	Salt Lake City	UT	84106	801-463-4800	
Web: www.sugarhousebbq.com					
Thai Siam 1435 S State St	Salt Lake City	UT	84115	801-474-3322	
Web: www.thaisiam.net					
Tuscany 2832 E 6200 South	Salt Lake City	UT	84121	801-277-9919	
Web: www.tuscanyslc.com					

Vermont

Restaurant	City	State	Zip	Phone	Fax
Auggies Island Grill 213 College St	Burlington	VT	05401	802-865-2800	
Web: auggiesislandgrill.com					
Bangkok Bistro 144 Church St	Burlington	VT	05401	802-951-5888	951-5858
Bove's of Vermont 68 Pearl St	Burlington	VT	05401	802-864-6651	
Web: www.boves.com					
Cannon's 1127 North Ave Suite 20	Burlington	VT	05401	802-652-5151	652-5155
Web: www.cannonsitalian.com					
Daily Planet 15 Center St	Burlington	VT	05401	802-862-9647	862-6693
Web: www.dailyplanet15.com					
Halvorson's Upstreet Cafe 16 Church St	Burlington	VT	05401	802-658-0278	
India House Restaurant 207 Colchester Ave	Burlington	VT	05401	802-862-7800	862-9191
L'Amante 126 College St	Burlington	VT	05401	802-863-5200	
Web: www.lamante.com					
Leunig's Bistro 115 Church St	Burlington	VT	05401	802-862-5306	658-6332
Web: www.leunigsbistro.com					
New World Tortilla 10 N Winooski Ave	Burlington	VT	05401	802-865-1058	
Web: www.newworldtortilla.com					
Parlima 185 Pearl St	Burlington	VT	05401	802-864-7917	
Pauline's 1834 Shelburne Rd	Burlington	VT	05403	802-862-1081	
Web: www.paulinescafe.com					
Ri Ra 123 Church St	Burlington	VT	05401	802-860-9401	
Web: www.rira.com					
Rusty Scuffer 148 Church St	Burlington	VT	05401	802-864-9451	
Sakura 2 Church St	Burlington	VT	05401	802-863-1988	860-0496
Web: www.sakuravt.com					
Single Pebble 133 Bank St	Burlington	VT	05401	802-865-5200	
Web: www.asinglepebble.com					
Smokejacks 156 Church St	Burlington	VT	05401	802-658-1119	658-0730
Web: www.smokejacks.com					
Souza's 131 Main St	Burlington	VT	05401	802-864-2433	
Web: www.souzasrestaurant.com					
Sweetwaters 120 Church St	Burlington	VT	05401	802-864-9800	
Web: www.sweetwatersvt.com					
Trattoria Delia 152 Saint Paul St	Burlington	VT	05401	802-864-5253	
Web: www.trattoriadelia.com					
Black Door Bar & Bistro 44 Main St 2nd & 3rd Fls	Montpelier	VT	05602	802-223-7070	223-7003
Web: www.blackdoorvt.com					
Chef's Table 118 Main St	Montpelier	VT	05602	802-229-9202	
China Star Chinese Restaurant 15 Main St	Montpelier	VT	05602	802-223-0808	
House of Tang 114 River St	Montpelier	VT	05602	802-223-6020	223-3388
J Morgan's Steakhouse 100 State St	Montpelier	VT	05602	802-223-5252	229-5427
Julio's Restaurant 54 State St	Montpelier	VT	05602	802-229-9348	
Main Street Grill & Bar 118 Main St	Montpelier	VT	05602	802-223-3188	
McGillicuddy's Irish Pub 14 Langdon St	Montpelier	VT	05602	802-223-2721	
Rhapsody 28 Main St	Montpelier	VT	05602	802-229-6112	
Royal Orchid 38 Elm St	Montpelier	VT	05602	802-223-0436	223-0457
Sarducci's 3 Main St	Montpelier	VT	05602	802-223-0229	
Web: www.sarduccisrestaurant.com					
Thrush Tavern 107 State St	Montpelier	VT	05602	802-223-2030	
Web: www.thrushtavern.com					
Orchid 5 Market St	South Burlington	VT	05403	802-658-3626	658-3513
Web: www.orchidrest.com					
Trader Duke's 1117 Williston Rd	South Burlington	VT	05403	802-660-7523	660-7523
Tuscan Kitchen 1080 Shelburne Rd	South Burlington	VT	05403	802-862-1300	862-5215
Web: www.reelhospitality.com					
Peking Duck House 79 W Canal St	Winooski	VT	05404	802-655-7474	
Web: www.pekingduckhousevt.com					

Virginia

Restaurant	City	State	Zip	Phone	Fax
219 219 King St	Alexandria	VA	22314	703-549-1141	549-1928
Web: www.219restaurant.com					
A La Lucia 315 Madison St	Alexandria	VA	22314	703-836-5123	548-9463
Web: www.alalucia.com					
Afghan Restaurant 2700 Jefferson Davis Hwy	Alexandria	VA	22301	703-548-0022	548-0673
Akasaka Japanese Restaurant 514-C S Van Dorn St	Alexandria	VA	22304	703-751-3133	
Atlantis Restaurant 3648 King St	Alexandria	VA	22302	703-671-0250	
Bistrot Lafayette 1118 King St	Alexandria	VA	22314	703-548-2525	548-0222
Web: www.bistrotlafayette.com					
Bombay Curry Co 3102 Mt Vernon Ave	Alexandria	VA	22305	703-836-6363	
Web: www.bombaycurrycompany.com					
Cafe Monti 3250 Duke St	Alexandria	VA	22314	703-370-3632	
Web: www.cafemonti.com					
Cafe Salsa 808 King St	Alexandria	VA	22314	703-684-4100	684-4188
Web: www.cafesalsarestaurant.com					
Chart House Restaurant 1 Cameron St	Alexandria	VA	22314	703-684-5080	684-7364
Web: www.chart-house.com					
Dancing Peppers Cantina 4111 Duke St	Alexandria	VA	22304	703-823-1167	823-1111
Web: www.dancingpepperscantina.com					
Del Merei Grille 3106 Mount Vernon Ave	Alexandria	VA	22305	703-739-4335	739-4991
Web: www.delmereigrille.com					
Evening Star Cafe 2000 Mount Vernon Ave	Alexandria	VA	22301	703-549-5051	549-8520
Web: www.eveningstarcafe.net					
Farrah Olivia 600 Franklin St	Alexandria	VA	22314	703-739-0404	778-2236
Web: www.farraholiviarestaurant.com					
Finn & Porter 5000 Seminary Rd	Alexandria	VA	22311	703-379-2346	845-7662
Web: www.finnandporter.com					
Fish Market 105 King St	Alexandria	VA	22314	703-836-5676	684-9424
Web: www.fishmarketoldtown.com					
Geranio Ristorante 722 King St	Alexandria	VA	22314	703-548-0088	548-0091
Web: www.geranio.net					
Grille The 116 S Alfred St	Alexandria	VA	22314	703-838-8000	519-7709
Hana Tokyo Seafood & Steak House 4603 Duke St	Alexandria	VA	22304	703-823-3168	823-3161
Web: www.hanatokyo.com					
Hector's Place Ristorante 3112 Mt Vernon Ave	Alexandria	VA	22305	703-837-0666	837-0067
Web: www.hectorsplaceristorante.com					
Hee Been 6231 Little River Tpke	Alexandria	VA	22003	703-941-3737	
Web: www.heebeen.com					
House of Dynasty 7550 Telegraph Rd	Alexandria	VA	22315	703-922-5210	922-5211
Web: www.houseofdynasty.com					
Il Porto Ristorante 121 King St	Alexandria	VA	22314	703-836-8833	836-8836
Web: www.ilporto.com					
La Bergerie 218 N Lee St	Alexandria	VA	22314	703-683-1007	519-6114
Web: www.labergerie.com					
La Piazza 535 E Braddock Rd	Alexandria	VA	22314	703-519-7711	
Web: www.lapiazzaoldtown.com					
Landini Brothers 115 King St	Alexandria	VA	22314	703-836-8404	549-3596
Web: www.landinibrothers.com					
Las Tapas Restaurant 710 King St	Alexandria	VA	22314	703-836-4000	836-4668
Web: www.lastapas.us					
Le Gaulois Cafe 1106 King St	Alexandria	VA	22314	703-739-9494	548-1273
Web: legauloiscafe.com					
Le Refuge Restaurant 127 N Washington St	Alexandria	VA	22314	703-548-4661	
Web: www.lerefugealexandria.com					
Majestic Cafe 911 King St	Alexandria	VA	22314	703-837-9117	548-6681
Web: www.majesticcafe.com					
Mike's Italian Restaurant 8368 Richmond Hwy	Alexandria	VA	22309	703-780-5966	780-2604
Morrison House 116 S Alfred St	Alexandria	VA	22314	703-838-8000	684-6283
Web: www.morrisonhouse.com					
Murphy's Grand Irish Pub 713 King St	Alexandria	VA	22314	703-548-1717	739-4583
Web: www.murphyspub.com					
Po Siam 3807 Mt Vernon Ave	Alexandria	VA	22305	703-548-3925	548-4683
Potowmack Landing Restaurant 1 Marina Dr	Alexandria	VA	22314	703-548-0001	548-2296
Web: www.potowmacklanding.com					
Restaurant Eve 110 S Pitt St	Alexandria	VA	22314	703-706-0450	706-0968
Web: www.restauranteve.com					
Rocklands 25 S Quaker Ln	Alexandria	VA	22314	703-778-8000	778-8007
Web: www.rocklands.com					
RT's 3804 Mount Vernon Ave	Alexandria	VA	22305	703-684-6010	548-0417
Web: www.rtsrestaurant.net					
Satay Sarinah 512A S Van Dorn St	Alexandria	VA	22304	703-370-4313	370-9672
Web: www.sataysarinah.com					
Savio's 516 S Van Dorn St	Alexandria	VA	22304	703-212-9651	212-9652
Web: www.saviosrestaurant.com					
Shooter McGees 5239 Duke St	Alexandria	VA	22304	703-751-9266	
Web: www.shootermcgees.com					
Simply Fish 1700 Fern St	Alexandria	VA	22302	703-778-3474	778-2940
Web: www.simplyfish.biz					
Southside 815 815 S Washington St	Alexandria	VA	22314	703-836-6222	549-6985
Web: www.southside815.com					
Stardust Restaurant 608 Montgomery St	Alexandria	VA	22314	703-548-9864	548-4442
Web: www.stardustrestaurant.com					
Taqueria el Poblano 2400B Mt Vernon Ave	Alexandria	VA	22310	703-548-8226	548-2824
Web: www.taqueriapoblano.com					

Virginia (Cont'd)

Name / Address	City	State	Zip	Phone	Fax
Taverna Cretekou 818 King St	Alexandria	VA	22314	703-548-8688	683-2739
Web: www.tavernacretekou.com					
Tempo Restaurant 4231 Duke St	Alexandria	VA	22304	703-370-7900	370-7902
Web: www.temporestaurant.com					
Thai Lemon Grass Restaurant 506 S Van Dorn St	Alexandria	VA	22304	703-751-4627	
Thai Old Town Restaurant 300 King St	Alexandria	VA	22314	703-684-6503	684-7979
Union Street Public House 121 S Union St	Alexandria	VA	22314	703-548-1785	548-0705
Web: www.usphalexandria.com					
Vermilion 1120 King St	Alexandria	VA	22314	703-684-9669	684-9614
Web: www.vermilionrestaurant.com					
Warehouse Bar & Grill 214 King St	Alexandria	VA	22314	703-683-6868	683-6928
Web: warehousebarandgrill.com					
Wharf The 119 King St	Alexandria	VA	22314	703-836-2836	836-2830
Web: www.wharfrestaurant.com					
Yamazato 6303 Little River Tpke	Alexandria	VA	22312	703-914-8877	914-8833
Web: www.yamazato.net					
Alpine Restaurant 4770 Lee Hwy	Arlington	VA	22207	703-528-7600	528-7625
Athena Pallas 556 22nd St S	Arlington	VA	22202	703-521-3870	521-3877
Web: www.athenapallas.com					
Bangkok 54 2919 Columbia Pike	Arlington	VA	22204	703-521-4070	521-4069
Web: www.bangkok54restaurant.com					
Cafe Asia 1550 Wilson Blvd	Arlington	VA	22209	703-741-0870	741-7666
Web: www.cafeasia.com					
Cafe Parisian Express 4520 Lee Hwy	Arlington	VA	22207	703-525-3332	525-3340
Caribbean Grill 5183 Lee Hwy	Arlington	VA	22207	703-241-8947	
Carlyle 4000 S 28th St	Arlington	VA	22206	703-931-0777	931-9420
Web: www.greatamericanrestaurants.com					
China Garden 1100 Wilson Blvd	Arlington	VA	22209	703-525-5317	525-5568
Clarendon Grill 1101 N Highland St	Arlington	VA	22201	703-524-7455	524-9598
Web: www.cgrill.com					
Crystal Thai 4819 1st St N	Arlington	VA	22203	703-522-1311	522-1331
Web: www.crystalthai.com					
El Paso Cafe 4235 N Pershing Dr	Arlington	VA	22203	703-243-9811	243-0064
Web: www.elpasocafe.net					
El Pollo Rico 932 N Kennmore St	Arlington	VA	22201	703-522-3220	522-3282
Freddie's Beach Bar & Restaurant 555 23rd St S	Arlington	VA	22202	703-685-0555	685-0877
Web: www.freddiesbeachbar.com					
Grill The 1250 S Hayes St	Arlington	VA	22202	703-415-5000	415-5060
Guajillo 1727 Wilson Blvd	Arlington	VA	22201	703-807-0840	
Web: www.guajillogrill.com					
Harry's Tap Room 2800 Clarendon Blvd	Arlington	VA	22201	703-778-7788	778-8888
Web: www.harrystaproom.com					
Hunan Gate 4233 N Fairfax Dr	Arlington	VA	22203	703-243-5678	
Jaleo 2250A Crystal Dr	Arlington	VA	22202	703-413-8181	413-5566
Web: www.jaleo.com					
Johnny Rockets 1100 S Hayes St	Arlington	VA	22202	703-415-3510	
La Cote d'Or Cafe 6876 Lee Hwy	Arlington	VA	22213	703-538-3033	573-0409
Web: www.lacotedorcafe.com					
Laylalina 5216 Wilson Blvd	Arlington	VA	22205	703-525-1170	525-6561
Web: www.laylalinarestaurant.com					
Legal Sea Foods 2301 Jefferson Davis Hwy	Arlington	VA	22202	703-415-1200	415-1464
Web: www.legalseafoods.com					
Matuba 2915 Columbia Pike	Arlington	VA	22204	703-521-2811	
Web: www.matuba-sushi.com					
McCormick & Schmick's 2010 Crystal Dr	Arlington	VA	22202	703-413-6400	413-7118
Web: www.mccormickandschmicks.com					
Melting Pot The 1110 N Glebe Rd	Arlington	VA	22201	703-243-4490	243-4545
Web: www.meltingpot.com					
Mexicali Blues 2933 Wilson Blvd	Arlington	VA	22201	703-812-9352	
Web: www.mexicali-blues.com					
Minh's 2500 Wilson Blvd	Arlington	VA	22201	703-525-2828	525-2829
Morton's The Steakhouse 1750 Crystal Dr	Arlington	VA	22202	703-418-1444	418-1199
Web: www.mortons.com					
Pho 75 1721 Wilson Blvd	Arlington	VA	22209	703-525-7355	525-0597
Portabellos 2109 N Pollard St	Arlington	VA	22207	703-528-1557	528-2126
Web: www.portabellosrestaurant.com					
Ray's the Steaks 1725 Wilson Blvd	Arlington	VA	22209	703-841-7297	
Red Hot & Blue 1600 Wilson Blvd	Arlington	VA	22209	703-276-7427	276-7609
Web: www.redhotandblue.com					
Rhodeside Grill 1836 Wilson Blvd	Arlington	VA	22201	703-243-0145	243-8454
Web: www.rhodesidegrill.com					
Rio Grande Cafe 4301 N Fairfax Dr	Arlington	VA	22203	703-528-3131	
Ristorante Murali 1201 S Joyce St	Arlington	VA	22202	703-415-0411	415-0410
Web: www.muraliva.com					
Ruth's Chris Steak House 2231 Crystal Dr 11th Fl	Arlington	VA	22202	703-979-7275	
Web: www.ruthschris.com					
Sala Thai 2900 N 10th St	Arlington	VA	22201	703-465-2900	465-4406
Web: www.salathaidc.com					
SoBe Seafood Co 3100 Clarendon Blvd	Arlington	VA	22210	703-528-0033	
Web: www.sobeseafood.com					
Taqueria el Poblano 2503 N Harrison St	Arlington	VA	22301	703-237-8250	237-9502
Web: www.taqueriapoblano.com					
Tara Thai 4001 N Fairfax Dr	Arlington	VA	22203	703-908-4999	408-9009
THAI 4029 28th St S	Arlington	VA	22206	703-931-3203	
Web: www.thaiinshirlington.com					
Thaiphoon 1301 S Joy St	Arlington	VA	22202	703-413-8200	413-8868
Web: www.thaiphoon.com					
Tivoli Restaurant 1700 N Moore St	Arlington	VA	22209	703-524-8900	524-4971
Tutto Bene 501 N Randolph St	Arlington	VA	22203	703-522-1005	527-0863
Web: www.tuttobeneitalian.com					
Village Bistro 1723 Wilson Blvd	Arlington	VA	22209	703-522-0284	522-7797
Web: www.villagebistro.com					
3 Amigos 200 N Battlefield Blvd	Chesapeake	VA	23320	757-548-4105	549-4295
Web: www.3amigosrestaurant.com					
Andrea's Italian Restaurant 138 S Battlefield Blvd	Chesapeake	VA	23320	757-482-4600	482-3272
Atlas Bar & Grill 1432 Greenbrier Pkwy	Chesapeake	VA	23320	757-420-6222	420-8003
Court House Cafe 350 S Battlefield Blvd	Chesapeake	VA	23322	757-482-7077	
Cugini's 1729 Parkview Dr	Chesapeake	VA	23320	757-366-9696	
Daikichi Sushi Japanese Bistro 1400 N Battlefield Blvd	Chesapeake	VA	23320	757-549-0200	549-0200
Web: www.welovesushi.net					
El Loro 801 Volvo Pkwy	Chesapeake	VA	23320	757-436-3415	436-3181
Grand China Buffet 1329 Battlefield Blvd	Chesapeake	VA	23320	757-549-6868	549-8383
Web: www.grandchinabuffetrestaurant.com					
Great Bridge BBQ 800 Battlefield Blvd S Suite 112	Chesapeake	VA	23322	757-546-2270	
Ho-Ho Chinese Restaurant 202 S Battlefield Blvd	Chesapeake	VA	23322	757-482-2242	
Web: www.hohorestaurant.biz					
Jade Garden Restaurant 1200 Battlefield Blvd N	Chesapeake	VA	23320	757-436-1010	
Joe's Crab Shack 1568 Crossways Blvd	Chesapeake	VA	23320	757-420-8330	
Kelly's Tavern 1412 Greenbrier Pkwy Suite 10	Chesapeake	VA	23320	757-523-1781	
Web: www.kellystavern.com					
Kyoto Japanese Steak House & Sushi Bar					
1412 Greenbrier Pkwy Suite 129	Chesapeake	VA	23320	757-420-0950	420-0692
Web: www.kyotochesapeake.com/					
Locks Pointe 136 N Battlefield Blvd	Chesapeake	VA	23320	757-547-9618	

Name / Address	City	State	Zip	Phone	Fax
Nagoya Sushi 109 Gainsborough Sq	Chesapeake	VA	23320	757-549-7977	549-3458
Pirate's Cove 109 Gainsborough Sq	Chesapeake	VA	23320	757-549-7272	
Rancho Grande 1320 S Military Hwy	Chesapeake	VA	23320	757-366-5128	366-5241
Rose Bay 805 Battlefield Blvd N Suite 101	Chesapeake	VA	23320	757-548-9300	548-9318
Smokey Bones BBQ & Grill 1405 Greenbrier Pkwy	Chesapeake	VA	23320	757-361-6843	361-6849
Web: www.smokeybones.com					
Tida Thai Cuisine 1937 S Military Hwy	Chesapeake	VA	23320	757-543-9116	543-8872
Polo Grill 7784 Gunston Plaza Dr	Lorton	VA	22079	703-550-0002	550-0283
Web: www.pologrill.net					
Fleming's Prime Steakhouse & Wine Bar					
1960-A Chain Bridge Rd	McLean	VA	22102	703-442-8384	442-3828
Web: www.flemingssteakhouse.com					
Kabuto Steak House 13158 Midlothian Tpke	Midlothian	VA	23113	804-379-7979	
Alfresco 11710-A & B Jefferson Ave	Newport News	VA	23606	757-873-0644	873-2355
Web: www.alfrescoitalianrestaurant.com					
Barclay's 943 J Clyde Morris Blvd	Newport News	VA	23601	757-952-1122	
Web: www.barclays.bz					
Bill's Seafood House 10900 Warwick Blvd	Newport News	VA	23601	757-595-4320	
Blue Cactus Cafe 10367 Warwick Blvd Hilton Village	Newport News	VA	23601	757-596-7372	
Chung Oak 15320 A & B Warwick Blvd	Newport News	VA	23608	757-874-3505	
Das Waldcafe 12529 Warwick Blvd	Newport News	VA	23602	757-930-1781	
Japan Samurai 12233 Jefferson Ave	Newport News	VA	23602	757-249-4400	
Light Restaurant & Bar					
3150 William Styron Sq N Port Warwick	Newport News	VA	23606	757-599-5800	599-5652
Web: www.lightrestaurant.com					
Matadore Sports Pub 7015 Huntington Ave	Newport News	VA	23607	757-723-6927	
Web: www.matadore.com					
Mitty's Italian Ristorante 1000 Omni Blvd	Newport News	VA	23606	757-873-6664	873-1732
Nara of Japan Steak & Seafood 10608 Warwick Blvd	Newport News	VA	23601	757-595-7399	
Plaza Azteca 12428 Warwick Blvd	Newport News	VA	23606	757-599-6727	
Web: www.plazaazteca.com					
Port Arthur 11137 Warwick Blvd	Newport News	VA	23601	757-599-6474	
RJ's Restaurant & Sports Pub 12743 Jefferson Ave	Newport News	VA	23602	757-874-4246	
Schlesinger's Chop House 1106 William Stryon Sq	Newport News	VA	23606	757-599-4700	599-4707
Web: www.schlesingerssteaks.com					
So Ya Japanese Restaurant 12715 Warwick Blvd Suite J	Newport News	VA	23606	757-930-0156	930-2208
219 Restaurant 219 Granby St	Norfolk	VA	23510	757-627-2896	
Web: www.the219.com					
456 Fish 456 Granby St	Norfolk	VA	23507	757-625-4444	626-3692
Web: www.456fish.com					
Banque The 1849 E Little Creek Rd	Norfolk	VA	23518	757-480-3600	
Blue Crab Bar & Grill 4521 Pretty Lake Ave	Norfolk	VA	23518	757-362-3133	362-3681
Web: www.thebluecrabrestaurant.com					
Bodega 442 Granby St	Norfolk	VA	23510	757-622-8527	622-8529
Web: www.bodegaongranby.com					
Club Soda 111 Tazewell St	Norfolk	VA	23510	757-200-7632	412-2671
Dawat 888 N Military Hwy	Norfolk	VA	23504	757-455-8080	
Web: www.dawat.us					
Domo 273 Granby St	Norfolk	VA	23510	757-628-8282	
Empire Little Bar & Bistro The 245 Granby St	Norfolk	VA	23510	757-626-3100	626-3124
Fellini's 3910 Colley Ave	Norfolk	VA	23508	757-625-3000	625-0717
Franco's 6200 N Military Hwy	Norfolk	VA	23518	757-853-0177	853-8377
Freemason Abbey 209 W Freemason St	Norfolk	VA	23510	757-622-3966	622-3592
Web: www.freemasonabbey.com					
Granby North 9619 Granby St	Norfolk	VA	23503	757-588-6728	
Web: www.granbynorth.com					
Havana's 255 Granby St	Norfolk	VA	23227	757-627-5800	962-0296
Web: www.liquidassetsrestaurants.com					
Kin's Wok 222 W 21st St	Norfolk	VA	23517	757-623-2933	
Kotobuki 721 W 21st St	Norfolk	VA	23517	757-628-1025	628-9281
La Galleria Ristorante 120 College Pl	Norfolk	VA	23510	757-623-3939	623-9106
Web: www.lagalleriaristorante.com					
Luna Maya 2000 Colonial Ave	Norfolk	VA	23517	757-622-6986	
Magnolia Steak 749 W Princess Anne Rd	Norfolk	VA	23517	757-625-0400	625-0114
Web: www.magnoliasteak.com					
Max & Erma's Restaurant 1500 N Military Hwy	Norfolk	VA	23503	757-466-8000	
Mi Hogar 4201 Granby St	Norfolk	VA	23504	757-640-7705	640-1526
Omar's Carriage House 313 W Bute St	Norfolk	VA	23510	757-622-4990	622-8122
Orapax Inn 1300 Redgate Ave	Norfolk	VA	23507	757-627-8041	
Web: www.theorapax.com					
Painted Lady 112 E 17th St	Norfolk	VA	23517	757-623-8872	623-0635
Web: www.thepaintedlady.com					
Rajput Foods 742 W 21st St	Norfolk	VA	23517	757-625-4634	622-2955
Web: www.rajputfoods.com					
Regino's 3816 E Little Creek Rd	Norfolk	VA	23518	757-588-4300	
Sai Gai Japanese Steakhouse 7521 Granby St	Norfolk	VA	23505	757-423-1000	
San Antonio Sams 1501 Colley Ave	Norfolk	VA	23517	757-623-0233	623-9577
Web: www.sanantoniosams.com/					
Siam 21 742 W 21st St	Norfolk	VA	23517	757-624-2455	624-2457
Web: www.siam21.com					
Sirena 455 Granby St	Norfolk	VA	23510	757-623-6622	623-6623
Web: www.sirenanorfolk.com					
Sterling's 245 Granby St	Norfolk	VA	23510	757-625-3366	
Web: www.sterlingssteakhouse.com					
Surf Rider 8180 Shore Dr	Norfolk	VA	23518	757-480-5000	
Web: www.surfridergroup.com					
Todd Jurich's Bistro 150 W Main St Suite 100	Norfolk	VA	23510	757-622-3210	962-7638
Web: www.toddjurichsbistro.com					
Uptown Buffet 1050 N Military Hwy	Norfolk	VA	23502	757-893-9293	
Velvet 25 332 Granby St	Norfolk	VA	23510	757-961-7143	398-8740
Voila! 509 Botetourt St	Norfolk	VA	23510	757-640-0343	
Acacia 3325 W Cary St	Richmond	VA	23221	804-354-6060	
Web: www.acaciarestaurant.com					
Akida 814 N Robinson St	Richmond	VA	23220	804-359-8036	
Amici 3343 W Cary St	Richmond	VA	23221	804-353-4700	
Web: www.amiciristorante.net					
Bella Italia 6407 Iron Bridge Rd	Richmond	VA	23234	804-743-1116	
Web: www.bellaitalia.cc					
Blue Fire Steakhouse 500 E Broad St	Richmond	VA	23219	804-643-3400	
Capital Ale House 623 E Main St	Richmond	VA	23219	804-643-2537	
Web: www.capitalalehouse.com					
Cheesecake Factory 11800 W Broad St	Richmond	VA	23233	804-364-4300	
Web: www.thecheesecakefactory.com					
Copper Grill 11800 W Broad St	Richmond	VA	23233	804-364-9408	
Web: www.coppergrill.com					
Davis & Main 2501 W Main St	Richmond	VA	23220	804-353-6641	
Fleming's Prime Steakhouse & Wine Bar					
9200 Stony Point Pkwy	Richmond	VA	23235	804-272-7755	
Web: www.flemingssteakhouse.com					
Franco's Ristorante 9031 W Broad St	Richmond	VA	23294	804-270-9124	
Web: www.francosristorante.com					
Full Kee 6400 Horespen Rd	Richmond	VA	23226	804-673-2233	
Grafiti Grille 403B Ridge Rd	Richmond	VA	23229	804-288-0633	
Web: www.grafitigrille.com					
Hana Zushi 1309 E Cary St	Richmond	VA	23219	804-225-8801	
Helen's 2527 W Main St	Richmond	VA	23220	804-358-4370	
India K'Raja 9051-5 W Broad St	Richmond	VA	23294	804-965-6345	

				Phone	Fax
Indochine 2923 W Cary St	Richmond	VA	23221	804-353-5799	
Julian's 2617 W Broad St	Richmond	VA	23220	804-359-0605	
Web: www.juliansrestaurant.net					
Kabab Grille 1580-B W Koger Center Dr	Richmond	VA	23235	804-378-3394	378-3396
Web: www.kababgrille.com/					
La Casita 5204 Brook Rd	Richmond	VA	23227	804-264-9896	
Web: www.lacasitarestaurant.com					
La Petite France 2108 Maywill St	Richmond	VA	23230	804-353-8729	
Web: www.lapetitefrance.net					
La Siesta 9900 Midlothian Tpke	Richmond	VA	23235	804-272-7333	
Web: www.lasiestarestaurant.com					
Lemaire 101 W Franklin St	Richmond	VA	23220	804-788-8000	
L'Italia 10610 Patterson Ave	Richmond	VA	23233	804-740-1165	
Mamma 'Zu 501 S Pine St.	Richmond	VA	23220	804-788-4205	
Mekong 6004 W Broad St.	Richmond	VA	23230	804-288-8929	
Web: www.mekong-restaurant.com					
Melting Pot The 9704 Gayton Rd	Richmond	VA	23233	804-741-3120	
Web: www.meltingpot.com					
Millie's 2603 E Main St.	Richmond	VA	23223	804-643-5512	
Web: www.milliesdiner.com					
Morton's The Steakhouse 111 Virginia St	Richmond	VA	23219	804-648-1662	
Web: www.mortons.com					
Old Original Bookbinder's 2306 E Cary St	Richmond	VA	23223	804-643-6900	
Palani Drive 401 Libbie Ave	Richmond	VA	23226	804-285-3200	
Web: www.palanidrive.com					
Pasta Luna 8902 W Broad St	Richmond	VA	23294	804-762-9029	
Web: www.pastaluna.com					
PF Chang's China Bistro 9212 Stony Point	Richmond	VA	23235	804-253-0492	
Pomegranate 1209 E Cary St	Richmond	VA	23219	804-643-9354	
Web: www.pomegranate-eurobistro.com					
Roma's 6017 Nine Mile Rd	Richmond	VA	23223	804-737-3104	
Sam Miller's Restaurant 1210 E Cary St	Richmond	VA	23219	804-643-1301	
Web: www.sammillers.com					
Sine 1327 E Cary St.	Richmond	VA	23219	804-649-7767	
Web: www.sineirishpub.com					
Skilligalee 5416 Glenside Dr.	Richmond	VA	23228	804-672-6200	
Web: www.skilligalee.com					
Sticky Rice 2232 W Main St.	Richmond	VA	23220	804-358-7870	
Web: www.ilovestickyrice.com					
Strawberry Street Cafe 421 N Strawberry St	Richmond	VA	23220	804-353-6860	
Web: www.strawberrystreetcafe.com					
Tandoor 7801 W Broad St.	Richmond	VA	23294	804-755-4400	
Tobacco Co 1201 E Cary St	Richmond	VA	23219	804-782-9431	
Web: www.thetobaccocompany.com					
Track The 2915 W Cary St	Richmond	VA	23221	804-359-4781	
White Dog The 2329 W Main St	Richmond	VA	23220	804-340-1975	
Web: thewhitedog.com					
Zeus Gallery Cafe 201 N Belmont Ave	Richmond	VA	23221	804-359-3219	
Zorba's 9068 W Broad St	Richmond	VA	23294	804-270-6026	
419 West 3865 Electric Rd	Roanoke	VA	24018	540-776-0419	
Alexander's 105 S Jefferson St.	Roanoke	VA	24011	540-982-6983	
Awful Arthur's 108 Campbell Ave SE	Roanoke	VA	24011	540-344-2997	
Web: www.awfularthurs.com					
Billy's Ritz 102 Salem Ave	Roanoke	VA	24011	540-342-3937	
Carlos Brazilian International Cuisine 4167 Electric Rd SW	Roanoke	VA	24014	540-776-1117	
Web: www.carlosbrazilian.com					
Coach & Four 5206 Williamson Rd NW	Roanoke	VA	24012	540-362-4220	
Web: www.coachandfour.com					
DJ's Brasserie 117 Duke of Gloucester St	Roanoke	VA	24014	540-342-4773	
Double Dragon 7232 Williamson Rd	Roanoke	VA	24019	540-265-0393	
El Rodeo 4301 Brambleton Ave SW	Roanoke	VA	24015	540-772-2927	
El Toreo 3790 Peter's Creek Rd Ext SW	Roanoke	VA	24018	540-342-7060	
Flat Rock Grille 5033 Valley View Blvd NW	Roanoke	VA	24012	540-265-6901	
Web: www.flatrockgrille.com					
Frankie Rowland's Steakhouse 104 Jefferson St.	Roanoke	VA	24011	540-527-2333	
Green Dolphin Grille 127 Campbell Ave SE	Roanoke	VA	23011	540-857-0688	
Kabuki Japanese Steak House 3503 Franklin Rd SW	Roanoke	VA	24014	540-981-0222	
Kobe Japanese Steak House 3214 Electric Rd.	Roanoke	VA	24018	540-776-0008	
Luigi's 3301 Brambleton Ave SW	Roanoke	VA	24018	540-989-6277	
Metro! 14 Campbell Ave SE	Roanoke	VA	24011	540-345-6645	
Montano's 3733 Franklin Rd SW.	Roanoke	VA	24014	540-344-8960	
Web: www.montanos.com					
Nawab Indian Cuisine 118A Campbell Ave.	Roanoke	VA	24011	540-345-5150	
Web: nawabonline.com					
Ragazzi's 3843 Electric Rd	Roanoke	VA	24018	540-989-9022	
Web: www.ragazzis.com					
Red Coyote Mexican Grill 32 Market Sq SE.	Roanoke	VA	24011	540-345-2180	
Regency Room The 110 Shenandoah Ave.	Roanoke	VA	24016	540-985-5900	
Szechuan 5207 Bernard Dr	Roanoke	VA	24018	540-989-7947	
Texas Steak House & Saloon 5025 Valley View Blvd NW	Roanoke	VA	24012	540-265-1809	
Web: www.texassteakhouse.com					
Ye Olde English Inn 6063 Bent Mountain Rd	Roanoke	VA	24018	540-774-2670	
Woo Lae Oak 8240 Leesburg Pike	Vienna	VA	22182	703-827-7300	827-7302
Web: www.woolaeoak.com					
22nd Street Raw Bar & Grill 202 22nd St	Virginia Beach	VA	23451	757-491-2222	
Aberdeen Barn 5805 Northampton Blvd	Virginia Beach	VA	23455	757-464-1580	
Web: www.aberdeenbarn.com					
Albie's 2401 Seaboard Rd	Virginia Beach	VA	23456	757-301-3326	
Web: albieseatery.com					
Aldo's Ristorante 1860 Laskin Rd	Virginia Beach	VA	23454	757-491-1111	
Alexander's on the Bay 4536 Ocean View Ave.	Virginia Beach	VA	23455	757-464-4999	
Web: www.alexandersonthebay.com					
Angelo's By the Sea 2809 Atlantic Ave.	Virginia Beach	VA	23451	757-425-0347	
Blue Pete's Restaurant 1400 Muddy Creek Rd	Virginia Beach	VA	23456	757-426-2005	
Web: www.bluepetes.com					
Boulevard Cafe 2935 Virginia Beach Blvd.	Virginia Beach	VA	23452	757-463-1311	
Bubba's Crabhouse Seafood Restaurant 3323 Shore Dr.	Virginia Beach	VA	23451	757-481-0907	
Captain George's Seafood 2272 Old Pungo Ferry Rd	Virginia Beach	VA	23457	757-721-3463	
Cheesecake Factory 265 Central Park Ave.	Virginia Beach	VA	23462	757-473-2900	
Web: www.cheesecakefactory.com					
Coastal Grill 1427 N Great Neck Rd	Virginia Beach	VA	23454	757-496-3348	
Coyote Cafe Cantina 972A Laskin Rd	Virginia Beach	VA	23451	757-425-8705	
Web: www.coyotecafevb.com					
Croc's Restaurant 620 19th St	Virginia Beach	VA	23451	757-428-5444	
Web: www.crocsrestaurant.com					
Ellington's on the Ocean 2901 Atlantic Ave	Virginia Beach	VA	23451	757-428-4585	
Ensenada 2824 Virginia Beach Blvd	Virginia Beach	VA	23452	757-631-1090	
Five 01 City Grill 501 N Birdneck Rd	Virginia Beach	VA	23451	757-425-7195	
Frankie's Ribs & More 408 Laskin Rd	Virginia Beach	VA	23451	757-428-7631	
Web: frankiesribs.com					
Frederico 357 Independence Blvd	Virginia Beach	VA	23462	757-497-1445	
GF Keagan's 1550 Laskin Rd	Virginia Beach	VA	23451	757-422-9545	
Hooplas Bar & Grill 5760 Northampton Blvd	Virginia Beach	VA	23455	757-460-2100	
Hot Tuna Bar & Grill 2817 Shore Dr	Virginia Beach	VA	23455	757-481-2888	
Web: www.hottunavb.com					
Il Giardino 910 Atlantic Ave.	Virginia Beach	VA	23451	757-422-6464	
Web: www.ilgiardino.com					

				Phone	Fax
Imperial Palace 4878 Princess Anne Rd	Virginia Beach	VA	23462	757-493-8838	
Laverne's 701 Atlantic Ave	Virginia Beach	VA	23451	757-428-6836	
Lucky Star 1608 Pleasure House Rd.	Virginia Beach	VA	23455	757-363-8410	
Web: www.theluckystarrestaurant.net					
Lynnhaven Fish House 2350 Starfish Rd	Virginia Beach	VA	23451	757-481-0003	
Web: www.lynnhavenfishhouse.net					
Mahi Mah's 615 Atlantic Ave	Virginia Beach	VA	23451	757-437-8030	
Web: www.mahimahs.com					
Melting Pot The 1564 Laskin Rd	Virginia Beach	VA	23451	757-425-3463	
Web: www.meltingpot.com					
Mi Casita 3600 Bonney Rd	Virginia Beach	VA	23452	757-463-3819	
Mo Mo Sushi 1385 Fordham Dr	Virginia Beach	VA	23464	757-366-3188	
Nara Sushi 717 Independence Blvd	Virginia Beach	VA	23455	757-456-5111	
Web: www.getfoodtoday.com/nara					
One Fish - Two Fish 2109 W Great Neck Rd	Virginia Beach	VA	23451	757-496-4350	
Web: www.onefish-twofish.com					
Otani 1532 Laskin Rd	Virginia Beach	VA	23454	757-425-0404	
Web: www.gootani.com					
PF Chang's China Bistro 4551 Virginia Beach Blvd	Virginia Beach	VA	23462	757-473-9028	
Web: www.pfchangs.com					
Plaza Azteca 4292 Holland Rd	Virginia Beach	VA	23452	757-431-8135	
Reginella's 4000 Virginia Beach Blvd	Virginia Beach	VA	23452	757-498-9770	
Shogun Japanese Steakhouse 550 First Colonial Rd	Virginia Beach	VA	23451	757-422-5150	
Steinhilbers Thalia 653 Thalia Rd.	Virginia Beach	VA	23452	757-340-1156	
Surf Rider Restaurant 928 Diamond Springs Rd	Virginia Beach	VA	23455	757-497-3534	
Web: www.surfridergroup.com					
Tautog's 205 23rd St.	Virginia Beach	VA	23451	757-422-0081	
Web: www.tautogs.com					
Timbuktu 3107 Atlantic Ave.	Virginia Beach	VA	23451	757-491-1800	
Tradewinds 2800 Shore Dr	Virginia Beach	VA	23451	757-481-9000	
Waterman's Grill 415 Atlantic Ave	Virginia Beach	VA	23451	757-428-3644	
Web: www.watermans.com					
Zia Marie 4497 Lookout Rd	Virginia Beach	VA	23455	757-460-0715	
Inn at Little Washington Middle & Main Sts	Washington	VA	22747	540-675-3800	
Web: www.theinnatlittlewashington.com					
A Carroll's Bistro 601 Prince George St.	Williamsburg	VA	23185	757-258-8882	
Aberdeen Barn 1601 Richmond Rd.	Williamsburg	VA	23185	757-229-6661	
Web: www.aberdeen-barn.com					
Blue Talon Bistro 420 Prince George St.	Williamsburg	VA	23185	757-476-2583	
Web: www.bluetalonbistro.com/					
Bray Bistro 1010 Kingsmill Rd	Williamsburg	VA	23185	757-253-1703	
Web: www.kingsmill.com/dining.html					
Captain George's Seafood Buffet 5363 Richmond Rd.	Williamsburg	VA	23188	757-565-2323	
Web: www.captaingeorges.com					
Casa Maya 1660 Richmond Rd.	Williamsburg	VA	23185	757-259-2470	
Christiana Campbell's Tavern Waller St.	Williamsburg	VA	23185	757-229-2141	
Cities Grille 4511C John Tyler Hwy	Williamsburg	VA	23185	757-564-3955	
Web: www.citiesgrilles.com					
Dining Room at Ford's Colony 240 Ford's Colony Dr	Williamsburg	VA	23188	757-258-4107	
Web: www.fordscolony.com/dining/dining.html					
Doraldo 1915 Pocahontas Trail	Williamsburg	VA	23185	757-220-0795	
Fat Canary 410 Duke of Gloucester St	Williamsburg	VA	23185	757-229-3333	
Giuseppe's Italian Cafe 5601 Richmond Rd	Williamsburg	VA	23188	757-565-1977	
Jefferson Restaurant 1453 Richmond Rd	Williamsburg	VA	23185	757-229-2296	
King's Arms Tavern 416 E Duke of Gloucester St	Williamsburg	VA	23185	757-229-2141	
Kitchen at Powhatan Plantation 3601 Ironbound Rd	Williamsburg	VA	23188	757-253-7893	
La Tolteca 5611 Richmond Rd	Williamsburg	VA	23188	757-253-2939	
Le Yaca 1915 Pocahontas Trail	Williamsburg	VA	23185	757-220-3616	
Mirabella's 207 Bypass Rd	Williamsburg	VA	23185	757-253-8550	
Nawab Indian Cuisine					
204 Monticello Ave Monticello Shopping Center	Williamsburg	VA	23185	757-565-3200	
Web: www.nawabonline.com					
Old Chickahominy House 1211 Jamestown Rd	Williamsburg	VA	23185	757-229-4689	
Papillon Bistro					
415 Richmond Rd Williamsburg Hospitality House	Williamsburg	VA	23185	757-229-4020	
Peking 120 Waller Mill Rd	Williamsburg	VA	23185	757-229-2288	
Pierce's Pitt Bar-B-Que 477 E Rochambeau Dr	Williamsburg	VA	23185	757-565-2955	
Web: www.pierces.com					
Regency Room 136 E Francis St	Williamsburg	VA	23187	757-229-2141	
Sal's 1242 Richmond Rd	Williamsburg	VA	23185	757-220-2641	
Web: www.salsbyvictor.com					
Seafare The 1632 Richmond Rd	Williamsburg	VA	23185	757-229-0099	
Second Street Restaurant & Tavern 140 2nd St	Williamsburg	VA	23185	757-220-2286	
Web: www.secondst.com					
Trellis Restaurant 403 Duke of Gloucester St	Williamsburg	VA	23185	757-229-8610	
Web: www.thetrellis.com					
Whaling Co The 494 McLaws Cir	Williamsburg	VA	23185	757-229-0275	
Web: www.paragonsteak.com					
Whitehall Restaurant 1325 Jamestown Rd	Williamsburg	VA	23185	757-229-4677	
Web: www.thewhitehall.com					
Yorkshire Steak & Seafood Restaurant 700 York St.	Williamsburg	VA	23185	757-229-9790	
Web: www.yorkshire-wmbg.com					

Washington

				Phone	Fax
Anthony's Homeport 704 Columbia St NW	Olympia	WA	98501	360-357-9700	357-8023
Web: www.anthonys.com					
Bavarian Corner 8910-D Martin Way E.	Olympia	WA	98516	360-456-5066	
Budd Bay Cafe 525 N Columbia St	Olympia	WA	98501	360-357-6963	786-8474
Web: www.buddbaycafe.com/					
Capitale Fusion Grill 514 Capitol Way S	Olympia	WA	98501	360-352-8007	
Casa Mia 716 Plum St S	Olympia	WA	98501	360-352-0440	
Web: www.casamiarestaurants.com					
El Sarape 4043 Martin Way E	Olympia	WA	98506	360-459-5525	
Emperor's Palace 400 Cooper Point Rd SW	Olympia	WA	98502	360-352-0777	754-2188
Web: www.eprestaurant.com					
Fishbowl Brew Pub & Cafe 515 Jefferson St SE	Olympia	WA	98501	360-943-3650	943-6983
Web: www.fishbowl.com					
Gardner's Seafood & Pasta 111 Thurston Ave NW	Olympia	WA	98501	360-786-8466	
Koibito 1707 Harrison Ave NW	Olympia	WA	98502	360-352-4751	
Lemon Grass Restaurant 212 4th Ave W	Olympia	WA	98501	360-705-1832	
Little Saigon Cuisine 237 Division St NW	Olympia	WA	98502	360-943-8013	
Mayan Family 4520 Pacific Ave SE	Olympia	WA	98503	360-491-8244	413-0564
Mekong 125 Columbia St NW	Olympia	WA	98501	360-352-9620	
Mercato 111 Market St NE	Olympia	WA	98501	360-528-3663	528-3665
Oyster House 320 4th Ave W	Olympia	WA	98502	360-753-7000	753-7077
Web: www.oysterhouse.com					
Peppers South Of The Border 114 Cherry St	Olympia	WA	98501	360-943-1111	
Portofino Ristorante 101 Division St NW	Olympia	WA	98502	360-352-2803	
Racha Noodles & Thai Cuisine 625 Black Lake Blvd SW	Olympia	WA	98502	360-943-8883	
Web: www.rachathai.com					
Ramblin Jack's 520 4th Ave E	Olympia	WA	98501	360-754-8909	
Web: www.ramblinjacks.com					
Saigon Rendez-vous 117 5th Ave SW	Olympia	WA	98501	360-352-1989	
Spar The 114 4th Ave E.	Olympia	WA	98501	360-357-6444	

Washington (Cont'd)

Name / Address	City	State	ZIP	Phone	Fax
Trinacria Ristorante 113 Capitol Way N	Olympia	WA	98501	360-352-8892	
Tumwater Valley Bar & Grill 4611 Tumwater Valley Dr SE	Olympia	WA	98501	360-753-6020	
Urban Onion 116 Legion Way SE	Olympia	WA	98501	360-943-9242	
13 Coins 125 Boren Ave N	Seattle	WA	98109	206-682-2513	
Web: www.13coins.com					
611 Supreme 611 E Pine St	Seattle	WA	98122	206-328-0292	
1200 Bistro & Lounge 1200 E Pike St	Seattle	WA	98122	206-320-1200	325-6913
Web: www.1200bistro.com					
Agua Verde Cafe 1303 NE Boat St	Seattle	WA	98105	206-545-8570	
Web: www.aguaverde.com					
Al Boccalino 1 Yesler Way	Seattle	WA	98104	206-622-7688	
Alki Homestead 2717 61st Ave SW	Seattle	WA	98116	206-935-5678	
Andaluca 405 Olive Way	Seattle	WA	98101	206-382-6999	382-6997
Web: www.andaluca.com					
Anthony's Pier 66 2201 Alaskan Way	Seattle	WA	98121	206-448-6688	728-2500
Web: www.anthonys.com					
Assaggio Ristorante 2010 4th Ave	Seattle	WA	98121	206-441-1399	
Web: www.assaggioseattle.com					
Asteroid Cafe 3601 Fremont Ave N	Seattle	WA	98103	206-547-2514	
Web: www.asteroidcafe.com					
Blue Onion Bistro 5801 Roosevelt Way NE	Seattle	WA	98105	206-729-0579	
Web: www.theblueonionbistro.com					
BluWater Bistro 1001 Fairview Ave N	Seattle	WA	98109	206-447-0769	
Web: www.bluwaterbistro.com					
Brad's Swingside Cafe 4212 Fremont Ave N	Seattle	WA	98103	206-633-4057	
Brasa 2107 3rd Ave	Seattle	WA	98121	206-728-4220	
Web: www.brasa.com					
Brasserie Margaux 401 Lenora St	Seattle	WA	98121	206-777-1990	
Web: www.margauxseattle.com					
Brooklyn Seafood Steak & Oyster House 1212 2nd Ave	Seattle	WA	98101	206-224-7000	224-7088
Cactus 4220 E Madison St	Seattle	WA	98112	206-324-4140	
Web: www.cactusrestaurants.com					
Cafe Flora 2901 E Madison St	Seattle	WA	98112	206-325-9100	
Web: www.cafeflora.com					
Cafe Lago 2305 24th Ave E	Seattle	WA	98112	206-329-8005	329-8053
Web: www.cafelago.com					
Cafe Stellina 1429 12th Ave	Seattle	WA	98122	206-322-2688	
Campagne 86 Pine St	Seattle	WA	98101	206-728-2800	443-3804
Web: www.campagnerestaurant.com					
Canlis Restaurant 2576 Aurora Ave N	Seattle	WA	98109	206-283-3313	
Web: www.canlis.com					
Carmelita 7314 Greenwood Ave N	Seattle	WA	98103	206-706-7703	
Cascadia Restaurant 2328 1st Ave	Seattle	WA	98121	206-448-8884	
Web: www.cascadiarestaurant.com					
Chandler's Crabhouse 901 Fairview Ave N	Seattle	WA	98109	206-223-2722	223-9380
Web: www.schwartzbros.com/chandlers.cfm					
Chez Shea 94 Pike St Suite 34	Seattle	WA	98101	206-467-9990	
Web: www.chezshea.com					
Chinook's at Salmon Bay 1900 W Nickerson St Suite 103	Seattle	WA	98119	206-283-4665	283-3705
Chiso Restaurant 3520 Fremont Ave N	Seattle	WA	98103	206-632-3430	632-3429
Web: www.chisoseattle.com					
Chutney's Grille on the Hill 605 15th Ave E	Seattle	WA	98112	206-726-1000	
Coldwater Bar & Grill 1900 5th Ave Westin Seattle	Seattle	WA	98101	206-728-1000	
Cutters Bayhouse 2001 Western Ave	Seattle	WA	98121	206-448-4884	
Web: www.cuttersbayhouse.com					
Dahlia Lounge 2001 4th Ave	Seattle	WA	98121	206-682-4142	467-0568
Web: www.tomdouglas.com/dahlia					
Daniel's Broiler 809 Fairview Pl N	Seattle	WA	98109	206-621-8262	748-7765
Web: www.schwartzbros.com/daniels.cfm					
Dragonfish Asian Cafe 722 Pine St	Seattle	WA	98101	206-467-7777	467-8891
Web: www.dragonfishcafe.com					
Dulces Latin Bistro 1430 34th Ave	Seattle	WA	98122	206-322-5453	
Web: www.dulceslatinbistro.com					
Earth & Ocean 1112 4th Ave	Seattle	WA	98101	206-264-6060	264-6070
Web: www.earthocean.net					
El Gaucho 2505 1st Ave	Seattle	WA	98121	206-728-1337	
Web: www.elgaucho.com					
El Greco 219 Broadway Ave E	Seattle	WA	98102	206-328-4604	
Web: www.elgrecorestaurant.com					
Elemental @ Gasworks 3309 Wallingford Ave N	Seattle	WA	98103	206-547-2317	
Web: www.elementalatgasworks.com/					
Elliott's Oyster House Pier 56 1201 Alaskan Way	Seattle	WA	98101	206-623-4340	224-0154
Web: www.elliottsoysterhouse.com					
Etta's Seafood 2020 Western Ave	Seattle	WA	98121	206-443-6000	443-0648
Web: www.tomdouglas.com/ettas					
Eva 2227 N 56th St	Seattle	WA	98103	206-633-3538	
Fish Club 2100 Alaskan Way	Seattle	WA	98121	206-256-1040	256-1100
Web: www.toddenglish.com/Restaurants.html					
Flying Fish 2234 1st Ave	Seattle	WA	98121	206-728-8595	728-1551
Web: www.flyingfishseattle.com					
Galerias 611 Broadway E	Seattle	WA	98102	206-322-5757	
Web: www.galeriasgourmet.net					
Gaudi Braseria 3410 NE 55th St	Seattle	WA	98105	206-527-3400	
Geneva 1106 8th Ave	Seattle	WA	98101	206-624-2222	
Web: www.genevarestaurant.com					
Georgian Room 411 University St	Seattle	WA	98101	206-621-7889	
Harvest Vine 2701 E Madison St	Seattle	WA	98112	206-320-9771	
Web: www.harvestvine.com					
Hunt Club The 900 Madison St	Seattle	WA	98104	206-622-6400	
Icon Grill 1933 5th Ave	Seattle	WA	98101	206-441-6330	441-7037
Web: www.icongrill.net					
Il Bistro 93-A Pike St	Seattle	WA	98101	206-682-3049	223-0234
Web: www.ilbistro.net					
Il Fornaio 600 Pine St	Seattle	WA	98101	206-264-0994	264-0715
Web: www.ilfornaio.com					
Il Terrazzo Carmine 411 1st Ave S	Seattle	WA	98104	206-467-7797	
Web: ilterrazzocarmine.com/					
India Bistro 2301 NW Market St	Seattle	WA	98107	206-783-5080	297-9069
Web: www.seattleindiabistro.com					
Ivar's Acres of Clams 1001 Alaskan Way Pier 54	Seattle	WA	98104	206-624-6852	624-4895
Web: www.ivars.net/Acres_Home/acres.html					
JaK's Grill 3701 NE 45th St	Seattle	WA	98116	206-985-8545	985-8552
Web: www.jaksgrill.com					
Kabul Afghan Cuisine 2301 N 45th St	Seattle	WA	98103	206-545-9000	
Web: www.kabulrestaurant.com					
Kingfish Cafe 602 19th Ave E	Seattle	WA	98112	206-320-8757	320-0021
La Medusa 4857 Rainier Ave S	Seattle	WA	98118	206-723-2192	
Web: www.lamedusarestaurant.com					
La Rustica 4100 Beach Dr SW	Seattle	WA	98116	206-932-3020	
La Vita E Bella 2400 2nd Ave	Seattle	WA	98121	206-441-5322	
Web: www.lavitaebella.us					
Lampreia 2400 1st Ave	Seattle	WA	98121	206-443-3301	
Le Gourmand 425 NW Market St	Seattle	WA	98107	206-784-3463	
Le Pichet 1933 1st Ave	Seattle	WA	98101	206-256-1499	
Lola 2000-B 4th Ave	Seattle	WA	98121	206-441-1430	441-5224
Web: www.tomdouglas.com/lola					
Madison Park Cafe 1807 42nd Ave E	Seattle	WA	98112	206-324-2626	328-0432
Web: madisonparkcafe.citysearch.com/					
Maneki 304 6th Ave S	Seattle	WA	98122	206-622-2631	
Marco's Supperclub 2510 1st Ave	Seattle	WA	98121	206-441-7801	
Web: www.marcossupperclub.com					
Market Street Grill 1744 NW Market St	Seattle	WA	98107	206-789-6766	
Web: www.marketstreetgrill.net					
Mashiko 4725 California Ave SW	Seattle	WA	98116	206-935-4339	
Matt's in the Market 94 Pike St Suite 32	Seattle	WA	98101	206-467-7909	
Web: www.mattsinthemarket.com					
McCormick's Fish House & Bar 722 4th Ave	Seattle	WA	98104	206-682-3900	667-0081
Web: www.mccormickandschmicks.com					
Metropolitan Grill 820 2nd Ave	Seattle	WA	98104	206-624-3287	389-0042
Web: www.themetropolitangrill.com					
Mistral Restaurant 113 Blanchard St	Seattle	WA	98121	206-770-7799	
Web: www.mistralseattle.com					
Monsoon 615 19th Ave E	Seattle	WA	98112	206-325-2111	
Morton's The Steakhouse 1511 6th Ave	Seattle	WA	98101	206-223-0550	223-0507
Web: www.mortons.com					
Nell's 6804 East Green Lake Way N	Seattle	WA	98115	206-524-4044	
Nishino 3130 E Madison St	Seattle	WA	98112	206-322-5800	
Noodle Ranch 2228 2nd Ave	Seattle	WA	98121	206-728-0463	
Oceanaire Seafood Room 1700 7th Ave	Seattle	WA	98101	206-267-2277	
Web: www.theoceanaire.com					
Ototo Sushi 7 Boston St	Seattle	WA	98109	206-691-3838	
Web: www.ototosushi.com					
Pabla Indian Cuisine 1516 2nd Ave	Seattle	WA	98101	206-623-2868	
Web: www.pablaindiancuisine.com					
Palace Kitchen 2030 5th Ave	Seattle	WA	98121	206-448-2001	
Web: www.tomdouglas.com/palace/					
Palisade 2601 W Marina Pl	Seattle	WA	98199	206-285-1000	285-7087
Web: www.palisaderestaurant.com					
Palomino 1420 5th Ave	Seattle	WA	98101	206-623-1300	467-1386
Web: www.palomino.com					
Paseo 4225 Fremont Ave N	Seattle	WA	98103	206-545-7440	
PF Chang's China Bistro 400 Pine St Suite 136	Seattle	WA	98101	206-393-0070	393-0075
Web: www.pfchangs.com					
Phoenecia at Alki 2716 Alki Ave SW	Seattle	WA	98116	206-935-6550	
Pink Door The 1919 Post Alley	Seattle	WA	98101	206-443-3241	443-3341
Web: www.thepinkdoor.net					
Place Pigalle 81 Pike St	Seattle	WA	98101	206-624-1756	
Ponti Seafood Grill 3014 3rd Ave N	Seattle	WA	98109	206-284-3000	284-4768
Web: www.pontiseafoodgrill.com					
Queen City Grill 2201 1st Ave	Seattle	WA	98121	206-443-0975	
Web: www.queencitygrill.com					
Ray's Boathouse 6049 Seaview Ave NW	Seattle	WA	98107	206-789-3770	
Web: www.rays.com					
Restaurant Zoe 2137 2nd Ave	Seattle	WA	98121	206-256-2060	
Web: www.restaurantzoe.com					
Rock Salt Steak House 1232 Westlake Ave N	Seattle	WA	98109	206-284-1047	
Web: www.rocksaltlakeunion.com					
Rover's 2808 E Madison St	Seattle	WA	98112	206-325-7442	
Web: www.rovers-seattle.com					
Ruth's Chris Steak House 727 Pine St	Seattle	WA	98101	206-624-8524	624-6268
Web: www.ruthschris.com					
Saito's Japanese Cafe & Bar 2122 2nd Ave	Seattle	WA	98121	206-728-1333	
Salty's on Alki Beach 1936 Harbor Ave SW	Seattle	WA	98126	206-937-1600	937-1430
Web: www.saltys.com					
Salumi 309 3rd Ave	Seattle	WA	98104	206-621-8772	223-0817
Sazerac 1101 4th Ave	Seattle	WA	98101	206-624-7755	624-0050
Serafina 2043 Eastlake Ave E	Seattle	WA	98102	206-323-0807	325-2766
Web: www.serafinaseattle.com					
Shiro's 2401 2nd Ave	Seattle	WA	98121	206-443-9844	
Web: www.shiros.com					
SkyCity Restaurant 400 Broad St	Seattle	WA	98109	206-443-2100	
Web: spaceneedle.com/restaurant					
Sostanza Trattoria 1927 43rd Ave E	Seattle	WA	98112	206-324-9701	324-9462
Web: www.sostanzaseattle.com					
Sunfish 2800 Alki Ave SW	Seattle	WA	98116	206-938-4112	
Szmania's 3321 W McGraw St	Seattle	WA	98199	206-284-7305	283-7303
Web: www.szmanias.com					
Tango 1100 Pike St	Seattle	WA	98101	206-583-0382	
Ten Mercer 10 Mercer St	Seattle	WA	98109	206-691-3723	
Web: www.tenmercer.com					
Thai Heaven 352 Roy St	Seattle	WA	98109	206-285-1596	
Tilth Restaurant 1411 N 45th St	Seattle	WA	98103	206-633-0801	633-0801
Web: www.tilthrestaurant.com					
Tulio Ristorante 1100 5th Ave	Seattle	WA	98101	206-624-5500	
Web: www.tulio.com					
Typhoon! 1400 Western Ave	Seattle	WA	98101	206-262-9797	
Web: www.typhoonrestaurants.com					
Union Bay Cafe 3515 NE 45th St	Seattle	WA	98105	206-527-8364	
Web: www.unionbaycafe.com					
Union Square Grill 621 Union St	Seattle	WA	98101	206-224-4321	224-4331
Web: www.unionsquaregrill.com					
Volterra 5411 Ballard Ave NW	Seattle	WA	98107	206-789-5100	
Web: www.volterrarestaurant.com					
Waterfront Seafood Grill 2801 Alaskan Way Pier 70	Seattle	WA	98121	206-956-9171	956-8090
Web: www.waterfrontpier70.com					
Wild Ginger Asian Restaurant 1401 3rd Ave	Seattle	WA	98101	206-623-4450	623-8265
Web: www.wildginger.net					
Yanni's Restaurant 7419 Greenwood Ave N	Seattle	WA	98103	206-783-6945	
Ankeny's Restaurant 515 W Sprague Ave	Spokane	WA	99201	509-838-2711	
Azar's 2501 N Monroe St	Spokane	WA	99205	509-326-7171	
Azteca 245 W Spokane Falls Blvd	Spokane	WA	99206	509-456-0350	
Web: www.aztecamex.com					
Cafe Marron 144 Cannon St	Spokane	WA	99204	509-456-8660	
Web: www.cafemarronbrownes.com					
Catacombs Pub 110 S Monroe St	Spokane	WA	99201	509-838-4610	
Web: www.catacombspub.com					
Cathay Inn 3714 N Division St	Spokane	WA	99207	509-326-2226	
Web: www.cathayinn.com					
China Dragon 27 E Queen Ave	Spokane	WA	99207	509-483-5209	
Clinkerdagger 621 W Mallon Ave	Spokane	WA	99201	509-328-5965	
Web: www.clinkerdagger.com					
Cyrus O'Leary's 516 W Main Ave	Spokane	WA	99201	509-624-9000	
Web: www.cyrusolearys.com					
Downriver Grill 3315 W Northwest Blvd	Spokane	WA	99205	509-323-1600	
Elk Public House 1931 W Pacific Ave	Spokane	WA	99204	509-363-1973	
Europa 125 S Wall St	Spokane	WA	99201	509-455-4051	
Garden Grill 3022 N Division St	Spokane	WA	99207	509-326-7741	
Kim Do 2018 N Hamilton St	Spokane	WA	99207	509-487-7700	
Linnie Thai Cuisine 1301 W 3rd Ave	Spokane	WA	99201	509-838-0626	
Longhorn BBQ 2315 N Argonne Rd	Spokane	WA	99212	509-924-9600	
Web: www.longhornbarbecue.com					

Name / Address	City	State	ZIP	Phone	Fax
Luigi's 245 W Main St	Spokane	WA	99201	509-624-5226	
Web: www.luigis-spokane.com					
Luna 5620 S Perry St	Spokane	WA	99223	509-448-2383	
Web: www.lunaspokane.com					
Mamma Mia's 420 W Francis Ave	Spokane	WA	99205	509-467-7786	
Marrakesh 2008 Northwest Blvd	Spokane	WA	99205	509-328-9733	
Ming Wah 1618 W 3rd Ave	Spokane	WA	99204	509-455-9474	
Mizuna 214 N Howard St	Spokane	WA	99201	509-747-2004	
Web: www.mizuna.com					
Mustard Seed 4750 N Division St	Spokane	WA	99207	509-483-1500	
Web: www.mustardseedcafe.com					
Niko's Greek Restaurant & Wine Bar 725 W Riverside Ave	Spokane	WA	99201	509-624-7444	
Web: www.nikosspokane.com					
O'Doherty's Irish Grill 525 W Spokane Falls Blvd	Spokane	WA	99201	509-747-0322	
Rancho Chico 2023 W Northwest Blvd	Spokane	WA	99205	509-327-2723	
Ripples on the River 700 N Division St	Spokane	WA	99202	509-326-5577	
Shogun 821 E 3rd Ave	Spokane	WA	99202	509-534-7777	
Spencer's 322 N Spokane Falls Ct	Spokane	WA	99201	509-455-9600	
Web: www.spencersforsteaksandchops.com					
Taste of India 3110 N Division St	Spokane	WA	99207	509-327-7313	
Thai Kitchen 621 S Pines Rd	Spokane	WA	99206	509-926-8161	
Tomato Street North 6220 N Division St	Spokane	WA	99207	509-484-4500	
Web: www.tomatostreet.com					
Twigs Bistro & Bar 808 W Main Ave	Spokane	WA	99201	509-232-3376	
Web: www.twigsbistro.com					
Altezzo's 1320 Broadway Plaza	Tacoma	WA	98402	253-572-3200	
Anthony's at Point Defiance 5910 N Waterfront Dr	Tacoma	WA	98407	253-752-9700	752-1929
Web: www.anthonys.com					
Azteca 4801 Tacoma Mall Blvd	Tacoma	WA	98409	253-472-0246	
Bai Poe 10515 Pacific Hwy SW	Tacoma	WA	98422	253-983-8217	
Dock Street Landing 535 E Dock St	Tacoma	WA	98402	253-272-5004	
East & West Cafe 5319 Tacoma Mall Blvd	Tacoma	WA	98409	253-475-7755	
Web: www.eastandwestcafe.com					
El Gaucho 2119 Pacific Ave	Tacoma	WA	98402	253-272-1510	
Web: www.elgaucho.com					
Europa Bistro 2515 N Proctor St	Tacoma	WA	98403	253-761-5660	
Web: www.europabistro.net					
Galanga 1129 Broadway	Tacoma	WA	98402	253-272-3393	
Web: www.galangathai.com					
Harmon Brewing Co 1938 Pacific Ave	Tacoma	WA	98402	253-383-2739	
Web: www.harmonbrewing.com					
Hidalgo 806 72nd St E	Tacoma	WA	98404	253-476-1097	
Il Fiasco 2717 6th Ave	Tacoma	WA	98406	253-272-6688	
Web: www.ilfiasco.com					
Indochine Asian Dining Lounge 1924 Pacific Ave	Tacoma	WA	98402	253-272-8200	
Web: www.indochinedowntown.com/					
Johnny's Dock 1900 E 'D' St	Tacoma	WA	98421	253-627-3186	
Web: www.johnnysdock.com					
Kabuki Japanese Restaurant 2919 S 38th St Suite B	Tacoma	WA	98409	253-474-1650	
La Costa Mexican Restaurant 928 Pacific Ave	Tacoma	WA	98402	253-272-0300	
Web: www.lacostatacoma.net					
Le-Le 1012 S Martin Luther King Jr Way	Tacoma	WA	98405	253-572-9491	
Lobster Shop South 4015 Ruston Way	Tacoma	WA	98402	253-759-2165	
Web: www.lobstershop.com					
Marzano 516 Garfield St S	Tacoma	WA	98444	253-537-4191	
Mekong 2901 S 47th St	Tacoma	WA	98409	253-474-2728	
Melting Pot The 2121 Pacific Ave	Tacoma	WA	98402	253-535-3939	
Web: www.meltingpot.com					
Moctezuma's 4102 S 56th St	Tacoma	WA	98409	253-474-5593	
Web: www.moctezumas.com					
North China Garden 2303 6th Ave	Tacoma	WA	98403	253-572-5106	
Old House Cafe 2717 N Proctor St	Tacoma	WA	98407	253-759-7336	
Primo Grill 601 S Pine St	Tacoma	WA	98405	253-383-7000	
Web: www.primogrilltacoma.com					
Ravenous Restaurant 785 Broadway	Tacoma	WA	98402	253-572-6374	
Sakura Japanese Steakhouse 3630 S Cedar St	Tacoma	WA	98409	253-475-1300	
Skippers Seafood & Chowder House 4710 Pacific Ave	Tacoma	WA	98408	253-475-5255	
Web: www.skippers.net					
Southern Kitchen 1716 6th Ave	Tacoma	WA	98405	253-627-4282	
Web: www.southernkitchenrestaurant.net					
Stanley & Seafort's 115 E 34th St	Tacoma	WA	98404	253-473-7300	
Web: www.stanleyandseaforts.com					
Sushi Tama 3919 6th Ave	Tacoma	WA	98406	253-761-1014	
Taqueria Guaymas 2630 S 38th St	Tacoma	WA	98409	253-471-2224	
Vuelve a la Vida 5310 Pacific Ave	Tacoma	WA	98408	253-473-7068	
Falls Terrace 106 S Deschutes Way	Tumwater	WA	98501	360-943-7830	943-7830
Web: www.fallsterracerestaurant.com					
Bacchus 3200 SE 16th Ave	Vancouver	WA	98683	360-882-9672	
Cactus Ya Ya 15704 SE Mill Plain Blvd	Vancouver	WA	98684	360-944-9292	
Cafe D Vine 6709 NE 63rd St	Vancouver	WA	98661	360-695-2529	
Canton Chinese Buffet 1118 NE 78th St	Vancouver	WA	98665	360-576-8699	
Carol's Corner Cafe 7800 NE St Johns Blvd	Vancouver	WA	98665	360-573-6357	
Dragon King 1401 NE 78th St	Vancouver	WA	98665	360-574-6684	
El Presidente Mexican Restaurant & Cantina 312 E Evergreen Blvd	Vancouver	WA	98660	360-750-7475	
Fa Fa Gourmet Chinese Restaurant 11712 NE 4th Plain Rd	Vancouver	WA	98682	360-260-1378	
Hudson's Bar & Grill 7805 NW Greenwood Dr	Vancouver	WA	98662	360-816-6100	
Web: www.hudsonsbarandgrill.com					
Jerusalem Restaurant & Cafe 106 E Evergreen Blvd	Vancouver	WA	98660	360-906-0306	
Joe's Crab Shack 101 E Columbia Way	Vancouver	WA	98661	360-693-9211	
Little Italy's Trattoria 901 Washington St	Vancouver	WA	98660	360-737-2363	
Web: www.littleitalystrattoria.com					
McMenamins on the Columbia 1801 SE Columbia River Dr	Vancouver	WA	98661	360-699-1521	
Namaste 6300 NE 117th Ave	Vancouver	WA	98662	360-891-5857	
Web: www.namasteindiancuisine.com					
Patrick's Hawaiian Cafe 316 SE 123rd Ave	Vancouver	WA	98683	360-885-0881	
Web: www.hawaiiancafe.com					
Stuart Anderson's Black Angus & Cattle Co 415 E 13th St	Vancouver	WA	98660	360-695-1506	
Thai Little Home 3214 E Fourth Plain Blvd	Vancouver	WA	98661	360-693-4061	
Thai Orchid 1004 Washington St	Vancouver	WA	98660	360-695-7786	
Web: www.thaiorchidrestaurant.com					
Tiger's Garden 312 W 8th St	Vancouver	WA	98660	360-693-9585	
Who-Song & Larry's 111 SE Columbia Way	Vancouver	WA	98661	360-695-1198	
Web: www.eltorito.com					
Beaches Restaurant & Bar 1919 SE Columbia River Dr	Vancover	WA	98661	360-699-1592	
Web: www.beachesrestaurantandbar.com					
Herbfarm The 14590 NE 145th St	Woodenville	WA	98072	206-784-2222	
Web: www.theherbfarm.com					

West Virginia

Name / Address	City	State	ZIP	Phone	Fax
Aladdin 3024 Chesterfield Ave	Charleston	WV	25304	304-345-0052	343-3364
Chesapeake Crabhouse Grill 600 Kanawha Blvd E Holiday Inn	Charleston	WV	25301	304-344-4092	345-6331
Chop House The 1003 Charleston Town Center	Charleston	WV	25389	304-344-3954	344-3959
Fifth Quarter 201 Clendenin St	Charleston	WV	25301	304-345-3933	
Gratzi 1061 Charleston Town Center	Charleston	WV	25389	304-344-4824	344-4831
Web: www.gratzirestaurant.com					
Joe Fazio's 1008 Bullitt St	Charleston	WV	25301	304-344-3071	
Laury's 350 MacCorkle Ave SE	Charleston	WV	25314	304-343-0055	343-0078
Leonoro's Spaghetti House 1507 Washington St E	Charleston	WV	25311	304-343-1851	
Main Kwong 1407 Washington St E	Charleston	WV	25301	304-342-8899	
Rio Grande 60 Court St	Charleston	WV	25301	304-344-8616	345-6458
Sam's Uptown Cafe 28 Capitol St	Charleston	WV	25301	304-346-6222	
Sitar of India 702 Lee St E	Charleston	WV	25301	304-346-3745	
Southern Kitchen MacCorkle Avenue at 53rd St	Charleston	WV	25304	304-925-3154	925-0809
Texas Steak House 2815 Mountaineer Blvd	Charleston	WV	25309	304-744-1255	744-1250
Web: www.texassteakhouse.com					
Tidewater Grill 1060 Charleston Town Center	Charleston	WV	25389	304-345-2620	
Web: www.tidewatergrillrestaurant.com					
Whitewater Grille 200 Lee St E	Charleston	WV	25301	304-353-3636	353-3727
Asian Garden Restaurant 3109 University Ave	Morgantown	WV	26505	304-599-1888	
Back Bay 1869 Mileground Rd	Morgantown	WV	26505	304-296-3027	
Cafe Bacchus 76 High St	Morgantown	WV	26505	304-296-9234	
Casa D'Amici 485 High St	Morgantown	WV	26505	304-292-4400	
Web: casadamici.com					
Dimitri's 2506 Cranberry Sq	Morgantown	WV	26508	304-594-0777	594-0030
Flying Fish & Co 1111 Van Voorhis Rd	Morgantown	WV	26505	304-225-3474	
Foosheen 450 Beechurst Ave	Morgantown	WV	26505	304-296-6999	
Gibbie's Pub & Eatery 368 High St	Morgantown	WV	26505	304-296-4427	
Glasshouse Grille 709 Beechurst Ave	Morgantown	WV	26505	304-296-8460	
Web: www.theglasshousegrille.com					
Great Chinese Buffet 5000 Greenbag Rd	Morgantown	WV	26501	304-296-4050	
Hibachi Japanese Steak House 3091 University Ave	Morgantown	WV	26505	304-598-7140	
Web: www.mangoeskeywest.com					
Los Mariachi's 1137 Van Voorhis Rd	Morgantown	WV	26505	304-598-3715	
Madeleine's Restaurant-Cellar 140 High St	Morgantown	WV	26505	304-296-6230	
Maxwell's 1 Wall St	Morgantown	WV	26505	304-292-0982	
Oliverio's Ristorante on the Wharf 52 Clay St	Morgantown	WV	26505	304-296-2565	296-2564
Web: oliverios.sites.morgantowns.com					
Peking House 1125 Van Voorhis Rd	Morgantown	WV	26505	304-598-3333	
Puglioni's 1137 Van Voorhis Rd	Morgantown	WV	26505	304-599-7521	
Tiberio's Rt 857 N	Morgantown	WV	26505	304-594-0832	
Voyagers Restaurant 110 Hartfield Rd	Morgantown	WV	26505	304-292-4701	
West Virginia Brewing Co 1291 University Ave	Morgantown	WV	26505	304-296-2739	296-2781
Web: mountainlair.com/WVBrewPub					
Wellington's 1 Dairy Rd	Poca	WV	25159	304-755-8219	755-3229
Web: restaurant.com/wellingtons					
Colasante's 416 Fairmont Rd	Westover	WV	26505	304-296-7689	
Web: www.colasantes.com					
Abbeys 145 Zane St	Wheeling	WV	26003	304-233-0729	
Bella Via 1 Burkham Ct	Wheeling	WV	26003	304-242-8181	
Coleman's Fish Market 2226 Centre Market	Wheeling	WV	26003	304-232-8510	
Ernie's Cork & Bottle 39 12th St	Wheeling	WV	26003	304-232-4400	
Figaretti's 1035 Mt de Chantel Rd	Wheeling	WV	26003	304-243-5625	
Generations 338 National Rd	Wheeling	WV	26003	304-232-7917	
Web: www.generationswhg.com					
Golden Chopsticks 329 N York St	Wheeling	WV	26003	304-232-2888	
Hoss' Steak & Sea House 10 Elm Grove Mall	Wheeling	WV	26003	304-243-9303	242-9544
Web: www.hosss.com					
Keg Und Kraut 167 16th St	Wheeling	WV	26003	304-232-5654	
Panda Chinese Kitchen 1133 Market St	Wheeling	WV	26003	304-232-7572	
River City Ale Works 1400 Main St	Wheeling	WV	26003	304-233-4555	

Wisconsin

Name / Address	City	State	ZIP	Phone	Fax
River Lane Inn 4313 W River Ln	Brown Deer	WI	53223	414-354-1995	
Angelina 117 N Adams St	Green Bay	WI	54301	920-437-7248	
Brett Favre's Steakhouse 1004 Brett Favre Pass	Green Bay	WI	54304	920-499-6874	405-6896
Web: www.foodspot.com/brettfavresteakhouse					
China Palace 213 N Washington St	Green Bay	WI	54301	920-433-0688	433-9043
Eve's Supper Club 2020 Riverside Dr	Green Bay	WI	54301	920-435-1571	435-2899
Web: www.evessupperclub.com					
Grazies Pasta Co 2851 S Oneida St	Green Bay	WI	54304	920-499-6365	499-7983
Hinterland Brewery & Restaurant 313 Dousman St	Green Bay	WI	54303	920-438-8050	438-8053
Web: www.hinterlandbeer.com					
Kavarna 112 S Broadway	Green Bay	WI	54303	920-430-3200	
Web: www.kavarna.com					
Krolls East 1658 Main St	Green Bay	WI	54302	920-468-4422	
Krolls West 1990 S Ridge Rd	Green Bay	WI	54304	920-497-1111	497-0237
Web: www.krollswest.com					
Lee's Cantonese House 2247 University Ave	Green Bay	WI	54302	920-468-9500	468-4530
Legends Brewhouse & Eatery 2840 Shawano Ave	Green Bay	WI	54313	920-662-1111	
Little Tokyo 121B N Broadway	Green Bay	WI	54303	920-433-9323	433-9523
Los Banditos 1258 Main St	Green Bay	WI	54302	920-432-6460	
Web: www.foodspot.com/losbanditos					
Luigi's Italian Bistro 2733 Mantiwoc Rd	Green Bay	WI	54311	920-468-4900	
Mackinaws Grill & Spirits 2925 Voyager Dr	Green Bay	WI	54311	920-406-8000	406-8840
Web: www.mackinaws.com					
Mandarin Garden 2394 S Oneida St	Green Bay	WI	54304	920-499-4459	429-2992
Patrick's on the Bay 2607 Nicolet Dr	Green Bay	WI	54311	920-965-2483	965-2485
Web: www.patricksgb.net					
Prime Quarter Steak House 2610 S Oneida St	Green Bay	WI	54304	920-498-8701	498-2624
Web: www.primequarter.com					
River's Bend 792 N Riverview Dr	Green Bay	WI	54303	920-434-1383	434-9742
Web: www.riversbendrestaurant.com					
Rock Garden 1951 W Bond St	Green Bay	WI	54303	920-497-4701	499-5242
Timsan's Japanese Steak House 1654 E Mason St	Green Bay	WI	54302	920-465-6295	
Titletown Brewing Co 200 S Dousman St	Green Bay	WI	54303	920-437-2337	437-2739
Web: www.titletownbrewing.com					
Victoria's 2610 Bay Settlement Rd	Green Bay	WI	54311	920-468-8070	468-8125
Wellington Restaurant 1060 Hansen Rd	Green Bay	WI	54304	920-499-2000	
Admiralty Room 666 Wisconsin Ave	Madison	WI	53703	608-256-9071	
Angelic Brewing Co 322 W Johnson St	Madison	WI	53703	608-257-2707	
Web: www.angelicbrewing.com					
Avenue Bar 1128 E Washington Ave	Madison	WI	53703	608-257-6877	
Babe's Grill & Bar 5614 Schroeder Rd	Madison	WI	53711	608-274-7300	274-3201
Web: www.babesmadison.com					
Bahn Thai Restaurant 944 Williamson St	Madison	WI	53703	608-256-0202	
Web: www.bahnthai.741.com					
Bandung Indonesian Restaurant 600 Williamson St	Madison	WI	53703	608-255-6910	
Web: www.bandungrestaurant.com					
Bellini Lounge & Restaurant 401 E Washington	Madison	WI	53703	608-250-0097	
Biaggi's 601 Junction Rd	Madison	WI	53703	608-664-9288	664-0024
Web: www.biaggis.com					
Blue Marlin 101 N Hamilton St	Madison	WI	53703	608-255-2255	204-0043
Web: www.thebluemarlin.net					
Blue Moon Bar & Grill 2535 University Ave	Madison	WI	53705	608-233-0441	
Web: www.bluemoonbar.com					
Capitol Chophouse 9 E Wilson St	Madison	WI	53703	608-255-0165	

Wisconsin (Cont'd)

	City	State	ZIP	Phone	Fax
Chautara 334 State St	Madison	WI	53703	608-251-3626	
Dardanelles 1851 Monroe St	Madison	WI	53711	608-256-8804	
Eldorado Grill 744 Williamson St	Madison	WI	53703	608-280-9378	
Eno Vino Wine Bar & Bistro 601 Junction Rd	Madison	WI	53717	608-664-9565	664-9563
Web: www.eno-vino.com					
Essen Haus 514 E Wilson St	Madison	WI	53703	608-255-4674	
Web: www.essen-haus.com					
Famous Dave's Bar-B-Que 900 S Park St	Madison	WI	53715	608-286-9400	286-9402
Web: www.famousdaves.com					
Ginza of Tokyo 6734 Odana Rd	Madison	WI	53719	608-833-8282	
Great Dane Pub & Brewing Co 123 E Doty St	Madison	WI	53703	608-284-0000	284-0990
Web: www.greatdanepub.com					
Hong Kong Cafe 2 S Mills St	Madison	WI	53715	608-259-1668	259-0368
Husnu's 547 State St	Madison	WI	53703	608-256-0900	
Imperial Garden 4214 E Washington Ave	Madison	WI	53714	608-249-0466	249-1526
Johnny Delmonico's 130 S Pinckney St	Madison	WI	53703	608-257-8325	257-8324
Web: www.foodfightinc.com/jd.asp					
Jolly Bob's 1210 Williamson St	Madison	WI	53703	608-251-3902	
JT Whitney's Pub & Brewery 674 S Whitney Way	Madison	WI	53711	608-274-1776	274-6773
Web: www.jtwhitneys.com					
La Hacienda 515 S Park St	Madison	WI	53715	608-255-8227	
Lao Laan-Xang 1146 Williamson St	Madison	WI	53703	608-280-0104	
Laredo's 694 S Whitney Way	Madison	WI	53711	608-278-0585	
L'Etoile 25 N Pinckney St	Madison	WI	53703	608-251-0500	251-7577
Web: www.letoile-restaurant.com					
Lombardino's 2500 University Ave	Madison	WI	53705	608-238-1922	
Web: www.lombardinos.com					
Maharaja 6713 Odana Rd	Madison	WI	53719	608-833-1824	803-2657
Mariner's Inn The 5339 Lighthouse Bay Dr	Madison	WI	53704	608-246-3120	
Nau-Ti-Gal 5360 Westport Rd	Madison	WI	53704	608-246-3130	
Ocean Grill 117 MLK Jr Blvd	Madison	WI	53703	608-285-2582	
Web: www.foodfightinc.com/ocean.asp					
Otto's Restaurant & Bar 6405 Mineral Point Rd	Madison	WI	53705	608-274-4044	
Web: www.madison.com/otto					
Paisan's 131 W Balsam St	Madison	WI	53705	608-257-3832	
Pedro's Mexican Restaurante 3555 E Washington Ave	Madison	WI	53704	608-241-8110	241-8248
Web: www.pedrosmexicanrestaurant.com					
Porta Bella 425 N Frances St	Madison	WI	53703	608-256-3186	
Web: www.portabellarestaurant.biz					
Prime Quarter Steak House 3520 E Washington Ave	Madison	WI	53704	608-244-3520	244-3527
Web: www.primequarter.com					
Restaurant Magnus 120 E Wilson St	Madison	WI	53703	608-258-8787	
Web: www.restaurantmagnus.com					
Restaurant Muramoto 106 King St	Madison	WI	53703	608-260-2680	
Web: www.muramoto.biz					
Sa Bai Thong 2840 University Ave	Madison	WI	53705	608-238-3100	
Web: www.sabaithong.com					
Smokey Jon's No 1 B-B-Q 2310 Packers Ave	Madison	WI	53704	608-249-7427	249-7798
Smoky's Club 3005 University Ave	Madison	WI	53705	608-233-2120	
State Street Brats 603 State St	Madison	WI	53703	608-255-5544	
Web: www.statestreetbrats.com					
Taj 1256 S Park St	Madison	WI	53715	608-268-0772	268-0774
Web: www.tajmadison.com					
Takara Japanese Restaurant 315 State St	Madison	WI	53703	608-268-0188	268-0189
Tornado Club Steak House 116 S Hamilton St	Madison	WI	53704	608-256-3570	
Tutto Pasta 305 State St	Madison	WI	53703	608-294-1000	255-2773
Wasabi Japanese Restaurant 449 State St	Madison	WI	53703	608-255-5020	
Web: madisonwasabi.fc2web.com					
Captain Bill's Seafood Co 2701 Century Harbor Rd	Middleton	WI	53562	608-831-7327	831-0634
Web: www.capbills.com					
Abu's 1978 N Farwell Ave	Milwaukee	WI	53202	414-277-0485	277-0491
African Hut 1107 N Old World 3rd St	Milwaukee	WI	53203	414-765-1110	765-0772
Web: www.africanpresentations.com					
Alioto's 3041 N Mayfair Rd	Milwaukee	WI	53222	414-476-6900	476-6902
Web: www.foodspot.com/aliotos/					
Apollo Cafe 1310 E Brady St	Milwaukee	WI	53202	414-272-2233	272-2344
Web: www.apollocafe.com					
Bacchus Restaurant 925 E Wells St	Milwaukee	WI	53202	414-765-1166	765-1161
Web: www.bacchusmke.com					
Beans & Barley 1901 E North Ave	Milwaukee	WI	53202	414-278-7878	278-6013
Web: www.beansandbarley.com					
Botanas 816 S 5th St	Milwaukee	WI	53204	414-672-3755	672-2771
Web: www.botanasrestaurant.com					
Caterina's 9104 W Oklahoma Ave	Milwaukee	WI	53227	414-541-4200	541-4221
Web: www.caterinasrestaurant.com					
Celia 424 E Wisconsin Ave	Milwaukee	WI	53202	414-273-8222	390-3869
Cempazuchi 1205 E Brady St	Milwaukee	WI	53202	414-291-5233	291-5254
Web: www.cempazuchi.com					
Coast 931 E Wisconsin Ave	Milwaukee	WI	53202	414-727-5555	727-0777
Web: www.coastrestaurant.com					
Coerper's Five-O'Clock Club House 2416 W State St	Milwaukee	WI	53233	414-342-3553	342-3511
Coquette Cafe 316 N Milwaukee St	Milwaukee	WI	53202	414-291-2655	291-2657
Web: www.coquettecafe.com					
County Clare 1234 N Astor St	Milwaukee	WI	53202	414-272-5273	290-6300
Web: www.countyclare-inn.com					
Crawdaddy's 6414 W Greenfield Ave	Milwaukee	WI	53214	414-778-2228	778-0250
Web: www.foodspot.com/crawdaddys					
Dancing Ganesha 1692-94 N Van Buren St	Milwaukee	WI	53202	414-220-0202	220-0264
Web: www.dancingganesha.com					
Don Quijote 704 S 2nd St	Milwaukee	WI	53204	414-221-9850	
Dream Dance 1721 W Canal St	Milwaukee	WI	53233	414-847-7883	847-7871
Eagan's on Water 1030 N Water St	Milwaukee	WI	53202	414-271-6900	226-3225
Web: www.eagansonwater.com					
Eddie Martini's 8612 Watertown Plank Rd	Milwaukee	WI	53213	414-771-6680	771-5034
Web: www.foodspot.com/eddiemartinis					
Elliot's Bistro 2321 N Murray Ave	Milwaukee	WI	53211	414-273-1488	273-1480
Web: www.elliotsbistro.com					
Elsa's on the Park 833 N Jefferson St	Milwaukee	WI	53202	414-765-0615	
Web: www.elsas.com					
Emperor of China 1010 E Brady St	Milwaukee	WI	53202	414-271-8889	
Web: www.emperorofchinarestaurant.com					
Historic Turner Restaurant 1034 N 4th St	Milwaukee	WI	53203	414-276-4844	276-0442
Web: www.foodspot.com/turner					
Il Mito 605 W Virginia St	Milwaukee	WI	53204	414-276-1414	276-2191
Web: www.ilmito.com					
Izumi's 2150 N Prospect Ave	Milwaukee	WI	53202	414-271-5278	287-0196
Web: www.izumis.com					
Jack Pandl's Whitefish Bay Inn 1319 E Henry Clay St	Milwaukee	WI	53217	414-964-3800	962-9309
Web: www.jackpandls.com					
Jackson Grill 3736 W Mitchell St	Milwaukee	WI	53215	414-384-7384	
Karl Ratzsch's Old World Restaurant 320 E Mason St	Milwaukee	WI	53202	414-276-2720	
Web: www.karlratzsch.com					
Kegels German Inn 5901 W National Ave	Milwaukee	WI	53214	414-257-9999	774-4517
King & I 830 N Old World 3rd St	Milwaukee	WI	53203	414-276-4181	276-4387
Web: www.kingandirestaurant.com					
La Fuente 625 S 5th St	Milwaukee	WI	53204	414-271-8595	271-8594
Web: www.ilovelafuente.com					
La Perla 734 S 5th St	Milwaukee	WI	53204	414-645-9888	
Web: www.laperla.com					
Lake Park Bistro 3133 E Newberry Blvd	Milwaukee	WI	53211	414-962-6300	962-4248
Web: www.lakeparkbistro.com					
Louise's Trattoria 801 N Jefferson St	Milwaukee	WI	53202	414-273-4224	273-5225
Web: www.louiseswisconsin.com					
Mader's German Restaurant 1037 N Old World 3rd St	Milwaukee	WI	53203	414-271-3377	271-0515
Web: www.maders.com					
Maharaja 1550 N Farwell Ave	Milwaukee	WI	53202	414-276-2250	
Web: www.restaurantmaharaja.com					
Milwaukee Chop House 633 N 5th St	Milwaukee	WI	53203	414-226-2467	390-4889
Web: www.milwaukeechophouse.com					
Mimma's Cafe 1307 E Brady St	Milwaukee	WI	53202	414-271-7337	272-4543
Web: www.mimmas.com					
Mo's A Place for Steaks 720 N Plankinton Ave	Milwaukee	WI	53203	414-272-0720	272-2714
Web: www.mosaplaceforsteaks.com					
Nanakusa Japanese Restaurant 408 E Chicago St	Milwaukee	WI	53202	414-223-3200	347-0414
North Shore Bistro 8649 N Port Washington Rd	Milwaukee	WI	53217	414-351-6100	351-1443
Web: www.northshorebistro.com					
Old Town 522 W Lincoln Ave	Milwaukee	WI	53207	414-672-0206	
Osteria del Mondo 1028 E Juneau Ave	Milwaukee	WI	53202	414-291-3770	291-0840
Web: www.osteria.com					
Packing House 900 E Layton Ave	Milwaukee	WI	53207	414-483-5054	483-3481
Web: www.foodspot.com/thepackinghouse/					
Palms 221 N Broadway	Milwaukee	WI	53202	414-298-3000	
Pasta Tree 1503 N Farwell Ave	Milwaukee	WI	53202	414-276-8867	
Pieces of Eight 550 N Harbor Dr	Milwaukee	WI	53202	414-271-0597	
Polaris Revolving Rooftop Restaurant 333 W Kilbourn Ave	Milwaukee	WI	53203	414-276-1234	
Restaurant Hama 333 W Brown Deer Rd	Milwaukee	WI	53217	414-352-5051	
Safe House The 779 N Front St	Milwaukee	WI	53202	414-271-2007	271-2676
Web: www.safe-house.com					
Sanford 1547 N Jackson St	Milwaukee	WI	53202	414-276-9608	278-8509
Web: www.sanfordrestaurant.com					
Saraphino's 3074 E Layton Ave	Milwaukee	WI	53235	414-744-0303	
Web: www.saraphinos.com					
Savoy Room 1962 N Prospect Ave	Milwaukee	WI	53202	414-270-9933	270-9923
Saz's 5539 W State St	Milwaukee	WI	53208	414-453-2410	256-8778
Web: www.sazs.com					
Shahrazad 2847 N Oakland Ave	Milwaukee	WI	53211	414-964-5475	964-5471
Web: www.shahrazadrestaurant.com					
Speed Queen BBQ 1130 W Walnut St	Milwaukee	WI	53205	414-265-2900	265-7001
Web: www.foodspot.com/speedqueen/					
Swig 1227 N Water St	Milwaukee	WI	53202	414-431-7944	
Web: www.swigmilwaukee.com					
Tandoor 1117 S 108th St	Milwaukee	WI	53214	414-777-1600	777-1577
Tess 2499 N Bartlett Ave	Milwaukee	WI	53211	414-964-8377	964-7790
Thai Palace 838 N Old World 3rd St	Milwaukee	WI	53203	414-224-7076	
Third Ward Caffe 225 E Saint Paul Ave	Milwaukee	WI	53202	414-224-0895	
Web: www.foodspot.com/thirdwardcaffe/					
Three Brothers 2414 S Saint Clair St	Milwaukee	WI	53207	414-481-7530	481-8652
TJ Aliota's 261 E Hampton Ave	Milwaukee	WI	53217	414-332-4555	
Trocadero 1758 N Water St	Milwaukee	WI	53202	414-272-0205	272-0252
Web: www.ztrocadero.com					
Water Street Brewery 1101 N Water St	Milwaukee	WI	53202	414-272-1195	272-0406
Web: www.waterstreetbrewery.com					
Polonez 4016 S Packard Ave	Saint Frances	WI	53235	414-482-0080	482-0084
Hammond Steakhouse 1402 N 5th St	Superior	WI	54880	715-392-3269	392-8374
Lan-Chi's Restaurant 1320 Belknap St	Superior	WI	54880	715-394-4496	
Famous Dave's 2137 E Moreland Blvd	Waukesha	WI	53186	262-522-3210	
Web: www.famousdaves.com					
Bartolotta 7616 W State St	Wauwatosa	WI	53213	414-771-7910	771-1589
Web: www.bartolottas.com					
Filippo's 6915 W Lincoln Ave	West Allis	WI	53219	414-321-4040	
Singha Thai 2237 S 108th St	West Allis	WI	53227	414-541-1234	541-0683
Web: www.singhathairestaurant.com					

Wyoming

	City	State	ZIP	Phone	Fax
19th Hole Restaurant & Lounge 2120 Allendale Blvd	Casper	WY	82609	307-237-9470	235-8330
303 303 S Wolcott St	Casper	WY	82601	307-233-4303	234-7005
Web: www.303grill.com					
Armor's Silver Fox Restaurant & Lounge 3422 S Energy Ln	Casper	WY	82604	307-235-3000	234-5324
Bosco's 847 E 'A' St	Casper	WY	82601	307-265-9658	
Colonial Restaurant & Lounge 4370 S Poplar St	Casper	WY	82601	307-234-6839	237-6180
Dorn's Fireside 1745 Cy Ave	Casper	WY	82604	307-235-6831	235-6304
Goose Egg Inn 10580 Goose Egg Rd	Casper	WY	82604	307-473-8838	
Guadalajara 3355 Cy Ave	Casper	WY	82604	307-234-4699	234-5018
JS Chinese 116 W 2nd St	Casper	WY	82601	307-577-0618	577-0678
La Costa 1600 E 2nd St	Casper	WY	82601	307-235-6599	
Ming House 233 E 2nd St	Casper	WY	82601	307-265-1838	
Mongolian Grill 4801 E 2nd St Suite 110	Casper	WY	82609	307-473-1033	
Poor Boys Steakhouse 739 N Center St	Casper	WY	82601	307-237-8325	
Web: www.poorboyssteakhouse.net					
Sanford's Grub & Pub 241 Center St	Casper	WY	82601	307-234-4555	265-6449
Avanti 4620 Grandview Ave	Cheyenne	WY	82009	307-634-3432	
Casa de Trujillo 122 W 6th St	Cheyenne	WY	82007	307-635-1227	
Cheyenne Cattle Co 1700 W Lincolnway	Cheyenne	WY	82001	307-775-7303	
Cheyenne Smokehouse 219 E 18th St	Cheyenne	WY	82001	307-773-8621	
Cloud 9 300 E 8th Ave	Cheyenne	WY	82001	307-634-4333	
Good Friends 507 E Lincolnway	Cheyenne	WY	82001	307-778-7088	
Guadalajara 1745 Dell Range Blvd	Cheyenne	WY	82009	307-432-6803	
Korean House 3219 Snyder Ave	Cheyenne	WY	82001	307-638-7938	
Little Bear Inn 1700 Little Bear Rd	Cheyenne	WY	82009	307-634-3684	
Los Amigos 620 Central Ave	Cheyenne	WY	82007	307-638-8591	
Renzios Greek Food 1400 Dell Range Blvd	Cheyenne	WY	82009	307-637-5411	
T-Joe's Steakhouse & Saloon 12700 I-80 Service Rd	Cheyenne	WY	82009	307-634-8750	
Teriyaki Grill 1720 Capitol Ave	Cheyenne	WY	82001	307-637-4393	
Twin Dragons 1809 Carey Ave	Cheyenne	WY	82001	307-637-6622	632-1168
Bar-T-5 Covered Wagon Cook Out & Wild West Show 812 Cache Creek Dr	Jackson	WY	83001	307-733-5386	739-9183
Web: www.bart5.com					
Blue Lion Restaurant 160 N Millward St	Jackson	WY	83001	307-733-3912	733-3915
Web: www.bluelionrestaurant.com					
BonAppeThai 245 W Pearl St	Jackson	WY	83001	307-734-0245	
Bubba's 515 W Broadway	Jackson	WY	83001	307-733-2288	733-8990
Bunnery The 130 N Cache Dr	Jackson	WY	83001	307-733-5474	
Cadillac Grille 55 N Cache St	Jackson	WY	83001	307-733-3279	739-0110
Calico Restaurant & Bar Teton Village Rd	Jackson	WY	83001	307-733-2460	734-0451
Web: www.calicorestaurant.com					
Chinatown 850 W Broadway	Jackson	WY	83001	307-733-8856	739-1904
Granary at Spring Creek Ranch The 1800 Spirit Dance Rd	Jackson	WY	83001	307-733-8833	733-1964
Web: www.springcreekranch.com/dining.html					

	City	State	Zip	Phone	Fax
Grill The 1535 NE Butte Rd	Jackson	WY	83001	307-734-7333	734-7332
Gun Barrel Steak & Game House 862 W Broadway	Jackson	WY	83002	307-733-3287	733-6090
Web: www.gunbarrel.com					
Horse Creek Station 9800 S Hwy 89	Jackson	WY	83001	307-733-0810	
Nikai Sushi 225 N Cache St	Jackson	WY	83002	307-734-6490	
Web: www.nikaisushi.com					
Ocean City 340 W Broadway	Jackson	WY	83001	307-734-9768	734-0454
Old Yellowstone Garage 175 Center St	Jackson	WY	83001	307-734-6161	734-6753
Rendezvous Bistro 380 S Broadway	Jackson	WY	83001	307-739-1100	734-0494
Web: www.rendezvousbistro.com					
Snake River Brewing Co 265 S Millward St	Jackson	WY	83001	307-739-2337	739-2296
Web: www.snakeriverbrewing.com					
Snake River Grill 84 E Broadway	Jackson	WY	83001	307-733-0557	733-5767
Web: www.snakerivergrill.com					
Sweetwater Restaurant 85 King St	Jackson	WY	83001	307-733-3553	733-4463
Web: www.sweetwaterrest.com					
Teton Steakhouse 40 W Pearl St	Jackson	WY	83001	307-733-2639	739-4586
Web: www.tetonsteakhouse.com					
Thai Me Up 75 E Pearl St	Jackson	WY	85001	307-733-0005	
Mangy Moose PO Box 590	Teton Village	WY	83025	307-733-4913	734-9436
Web: mangymoose.net					

675 RETIREMENT COMMUNITIES

SEE ALSO Long-Term Care Facilities p. 1919

Listed here are senior communities where the majority of residents live independently but where nursing care and/or other personal care is available on-site. The listings in this category are organized alphabetically by state names.

	City	State	Zip	Phone	Fax
Galleria Woods 3850 Galleria Woods Dr	Birmingham	AL	35244	205-985-7537	987-2146
Web: www.arclp.com					
Westminster Village 500 Spanish Fort Blvd	Spanish Fort	AL	36527	251-626-7007	626-8529
Beatitudes Campus of Care 1610 W Glendale Ave	Phoenix	AZ	85021	602-995-2611	995-4854
Web: www.beatitudescampus.org					
Campana del Rio 1550 E River Rd	Tucson	AZ	85718	520-299-1941	529-2572
Web: www.atriaseniorliving.com					
Chandler Villas 101 S Yucca St	Chandler	AZ	85224	480-899-7650	899-4485
Web: www.atriaseniorliving.com					
Forum at Desert Harbor 13840 N Desert Harbor Dr	Peoria	AZ	85381	623-972-0995	977-5271
Forum Pueblo Norte 7100 E Mescal St	Scottsdale	AZ	85254	480-948-3990	951-7245
Forum at Tucson 2500 N Rosemont Blvd	Tucson	AZ	85712	520-325-4800	319-4076
Friendship Village of Tempe 2645 E Southern Ave	Tempe	AZ	85282	480-831-5000	413-0285
TF: 800-824-1112 ■ *Web:* www.friendshipvillageaz.com					
Glencroft Retirement Community 8641 N 67th Ave	Glendale	AZ	85302	623-939-9475	842-9588
Web: www.glencroft.com					
La Posada at Park Centre 350 E Morningside Rd	Green Valley	AZ	85614	520-648-8131	648-8397
Web: www.laposadagv.com					
Terraces of Phoenix 7550 N 16th St	Phoenix	AZ	85020	602-944-4455	943-2611
TF: 877-279-6207 ■ *Web:* www.theterracesphoenix.com					
Butterfield Trail Village 1923 E Joyce Blvd	Fayetteville	AR	72703	479-442-7220	442-2019
TF: 800-441-9996 ■ *Web:* www.butterfieldtrailvillage.com					
Concordia of Bella Vista 1 Concordia Dr	Bella Vista	AR	72714	479-855-3714	855-6688
Web: www.concordiahomesinc.com					
Alhambra Retirement Community 2400 S Fremont Ave	Alhambra	CA	91803	626-289-6211	570-5254
Atherton Baptist Homes 214 S Atlantic Blvd	Alhambra	CA	91801	626-289-4178	576-0857
Web: www.abh.org					
Bixby Knolls Towers 3737 Atlantic Ave	Long Beach	CA	90807	562-426-6123	426-1506
California Christian Home 8417 Mission Dr	Rosemead	CA	91770	626-287-0438	287-3361
Web: www.calchristianhm.com					
Carlsbad by the Sea 2855 Carlsbad Blvd	Carlsbad	CA	92008	760-729-2377	729-0938*
**Fax:* Mktg ■ *TF:* 800-255-1556 ■ *Web:* www.carlsbadbythesea.com					
Carmel Valley Manor 8545 Carmel Valley Rd	Carmel	CA	93923	831-624-1281	622-4553
TF: 800-544-5546 ■ *Web:* www.cvmanor.com					
Casa Dorinda 300 Hot Springs Rd	Santa Barbara	CA	93108	805-969-8011	969-8686
Web: www.casadorinda.com					
Castle Hill Retirement Village 3575 N Moorpark Rd	Thousand Oaks	CA	91360	805-492-2471	492-7431
Web: www.castlehill.com					
Channing House 850 Webster St	Palo Alto	CA	94301	650-327-0950	324-7585
Covenant Village of Turlock 2125 N Olive Ave	Turlock	CA	95382	209-632-9976	632-7885
TF: 800-485-7844 ■ *Web:* www.covenantretirement.com					
Eskaton Inc 5105 Manzanita Ave	Carmichael	CA	95608	916-334-0810	338-1248
Web: www.eskaton.com					
Eskaton Village 3939 Walnut Ave	Carmichael	CA	95608	916-974-2000	974-2022
TF: 800-300-3929 ■ *Web:* www.eskaton.com					
Forum at Rancho San Antonio 23500 Cristo Rey Dr	Cupertino	CA	95101	650-944-0100	903-5920
Web: www.theforum-cupertino.com					
Freedom Village 23442 El Toro Rd	Lake Forest	CA	92630	949-472-4700	587-9711
TF: 800-584-8084 ■ *Web:* www.freedomvillage.org					
Grand Lake Gardens 401 Santa Clara Ave	Oakland	CA	94610	510-893-8897	893-0114
Hillcrest Homes 2705 Mountain View Dr	La Verne	CA	91750	909-593-4917	596-5538
TF Mktg: 800-566-4636 ■ *Web:* www.livingathillcrest.org					
Kensington Place 1580 Geary Rd	Walnut Creek	CA	94597	925-943-1121	943-6705
Web: www.kensingtonplace.com					
Lake Park Retirement Residences 1850 Alice St	Oakland	CA	94612	510-835-5511	273-0529
Los Gatos Meadows 110 Wood Rd	Los Gatos	CA	95030	408-354-0211	354-4193
Web: www.ehf.org/lgm/index.htm					
Morningside of Fullerton 800 Morningside Dr	Fullerton	CA	92835	714-529-2952	256-2469
TF: 800-499-6010 ■ *Web:* www.morningsideoffullerton.com					
Mount Miguel Covenant Village 325 Kempton St	Spring Valley	CA	91977	619-479-4790	479-2337
Mount San Antonio Gardens 900 E Harrison Ave	Pomona	CA	91767	909-624-5061	621-3327
O'Connor Woods 3400 Wagner Heights Rd	Stockton	CA	95209	209-956-3400	952-6201
TF: 800-249-6637 ■ *Web:* www.oconnorwoods.org					
Park Lane Classic Residence by Hyatt 200 Glenwood Cir	Monterey	CA	93940	831-373-6126	373-0863
TF: 800-782-5730 ■ *Web:* www.hyattclassic.com/monterey/index.html					
Peninsula Regent 1 Baldwin Ave	San Mateo	CA	94401	650-579-5500	579-0446
Web: www.peninsularegent.com					
Piedmont Gardens 110 41st St	Oakland	CA	94611	510-654-7172	658-6866
Web: www.piedmontgardens.com					
Pilgrim Haven 373 Pine Ln	Los Altos	CA	94022	650-948-8291	941-0372
TF: 877-284-7635 ■ *Web:* www.abhow.com/multi/pilgrim_haven					
Plymouth Village 900 Salem Dr	Redlands	CA	92373	909-793-1233	798-5504
Quaker Gardens 12151 Dale St	Stanton	CA	90680	714-530-9100	530-0945*
**Fax:* Mktg ■ *Web:* www.quakergardens.com					
Rancho Park Villa 801 Cypress Way	San Dimas	CA	91773	626-339-5426	339-1755
Redwood Terrace 710 W 13th Ave	Escondido	CA	92025	760-747-4306	480-2759
TF Mktg: 800-842-6775 ■ *Web:* www.redwoodterrace.com					
Regents Point 19191 Harvard Ave	Irvine	CA	92612	949-854-9500	725-9132
Web: www.regentspoint.com					
Remington Club 16925 Hierba Dr	San Diego	CA	92128	858-673-6300	673-6318
Rosewood Retirement Community 1301 New Stine Rd	Bakersfield	CA	93309	661-834-0620	834-0280
Royal Oaks Manor 1763 Royal Oaks Dr N	Bradbury	CA	91010	626-359-9371	357-9723
Saint Paul's Towers 100 Bay Pl	Oakland	CA	94610	510-835-4700	891-8110
Web: www.ehf.org					
Samarkand The 2550 Treasure Dr	Santa Barbara	CA	93105	805-687-0701	687-3386
San Joaquin Gardens 5555 N Fresno St	Fresno	CA	93710	559-439-4770	439-2457
Web: www.sanjoaquingardens.com					
Sequoias Portola Valley 501 Portola Rd	Portola Valley	CA	94028	650-851-1501	851-5007
Web: www.ncphs.org					
Sequoias San Francisco 1400 Geary Blvd	San Francisco	CA	94109	415-922-9700	567-2576
Web: www.ncphs.org					
Smith Ranch Homes 500 Deer Valley Rd	San Rafael	CA	94903	415-492-4900	492-4901
TF Mktg: 800-772-6264 ■ *Web:* www.smithranchhomes.com					
Solheim Lutheran Home 2236 Merton Ave	Eagle Rock	CA	90041	323-257-7518	255-3544
Web: www.solheimlh.org					
Spring Lake Village 5555 Montgomery Dr	Santa Rosa	CA	95409	707-538-8400	579-6997
TF: 800-795-1267 ■ *Web:* www.lifecare.org					
Sunrise Villa Valencia 24552 Paseo de Valencia	Laguna Hills	CA	92653	949-581-6111	837-1082
Web: www.sunriseseniorliving.com					
Tamalpais The 501 Via Casitas	Greenbrae	CA	94904	415-461-2300	461-0241
Web: www.ncphs.org					
Terraces of Los Gatos 800 Blossom Hill Rd	Los Gatos	CA	95032	408-356-1006	356-9647
Valle Verde 900 Calle de los Amigos	Santa Barbara	CA	93105	805-687-1571	687-5540
Web: www.valleverdesb.com					
Villa Gardens 842 E Villa St	Pasadena	CA	91101	626-796-8162	568-9606
Villa Marin 100 Thorndale Dr	San Rafael	CA	94903	415-499-8711	499-1061
Web: www.villa-marin.com					
Village The 2200 W Acacia Ave	Hemet	CA	92545	951-658-3369	658-4295
Web: www.thevillagehemet.com					
Vista del Monte 3775 Modoc Rd	Santa Barbara	CA	93105	805-687-0793	687-6350
White Sands of La Jolla 7450 Olivetas Ave	La Jolla	CA	92037	858-454-4201	450-5298
TF: 800-892-7817					
Englewood Meridian 3455 S Corona St	Englewood	CO	80113	303-761-0300	762-2154
Web: www.meridians.com					
Heritage Club 2020 S Monroe St	Denver	CO	80210	303-757-1404	758-3738
TF: 877-756-0025					
Parkplace 111 Emerson St	Denver	CO	80218	303-744-0400	744-2118
Web: www.arclp.com					
Villa Pueblo Towers 1111 Bonforte Blvd	Pueblo	CO	81001	719-545-5911	544-1354
Villas at Sunny Acres 2501 E 104th Ave	Denver	CO	80233	303-452-4181	452-7993
TF: 800-447-2092					
3030 Park 3030 Park Ave	Bridgeport	CT	06604	203-374-5611	374-2871
Web: www.3030park.com					
Arbors The 403 W Center St	Manchester	CT	06040	860-647-9343	647-7509
TF: 888-227-2677 ■ *Web:* www.arborsct.com					
Ashlar Village 22 Masonic Ave PO Box 70	Wallingford	CT	06492	203-679-5900	679-6405
Web: www.masonicare.org					
Covenant Village of Cromwell & Pilgrim Manor 52 Missionary Rd	Cromwell	CT	06416	860-635-2690	632-2407
Web: www.covenantretirement.com					
Duncaster 40 Loeffler Rd	Bloomfield	CT	06002	860-726-2000	242-8004
TF: 800-545-5065 ■ *Web:* www.duncaster.org					
East Hill Woods 611 E Hill Rd	Southbury	CT	06488	203-262-6161	262-8002*
**Fax:* Mktg ■ *TF:* 800-435-4249 ■ *Web:* www.easthillwoods.com					
Elim Park Place 150 Cook Hill Rd	Cheshire	CT	06410	203-272-3547	250-6282
Essex Meadows 30 Bokum Rd	Essex	CT	06426	860-767-7201	767-0014
Web: www.essexmeadows.com					
Evergreen Woods 88 Notch Hill Rd	North Branford	CT	06471	203-488-8000	488-9429
Web: www.evergreenwoods.com					
McAuley The 275 Steele Rd	West Hartford	CT	06117	860-236-6300	232-4077
Web: www.themcauleyct.com					
Pomperaug Woods 80 Heritage Rd	Southbury	CT	06488	203-262-6555	264-2155
Web: www.pomperaugwoods.com					
Sterling Glen of Stamford 77 3rd St	Stamford	CT	06905	203-327-4551	353-9105
TF: 800-443-3245 ■ *Web:* www.sterlingglen.com/senior-communities/stamford/index.asp					
Whitney Center 200 Leeder Hill Dr	Hamden	CT	06517	203-281-6745	288-3789
Web: www.whitneycenter.com					
Cokesbury Village 726 Loveville Rd	Hockessin	DE	19707	302-235-6000	239-2650
Methodist Country House 4830 Kennett Pike	Wilmington	DE	19807	302-654-5101	426-8108
Methodist Manor House 1001 Middleford Rd	Seaford	DE	19973	302-629-4593	629-6520
TF: 800-775-4593					
Stonegates 4031 Kennett Pike	Greenville	DE	19807	302-658-6200	658-1510
Web: www.stonegates.com					
Westminster Village 191 Westminster Dr	Dover	DE	19904	302-744-3600	744-3540
TF: 866-710-3101 ■ *Web:* www.wmvdover.org					
Ingleside Rock Creek 3050 Military Rd NW	Washington	DC	20015	202-363-8310	363-0950
Web: www.ircdc.org					
Knollwood 6200 Oregon Ave NW	Washington	DC	20015	202-541-0400	364-2856
Web: www.armydistaff.org					
Sunrise at Thomas Circle 1330 Massachusetts Ave NW	Washington	DC	20005	202-628-2092	638-0649
Web: www.sunriseseniorliving.com					
Abbey Delray 2000 Lowson Blvd	Delray Beach	FL	33445	561-454-2000	278-8956
TF: 800-936-7397 ■ *Web:* www.abbeydelray.com					
Atria Meridian Retirement Community 3061 Donnelly Dr	Lantana	FL	33462	561-965-7200	965-3542
Azalea Trace 10100 Hillview DR	Pensacola	FL	32514	850-478-5200	474-0558
TF: 800-828-8274 ■ *Web:* www.azaleatrace.org					
Bay Village 8400 Vamo Rd	Sarasota	FL	34231	941-966-5611	966-4040
Web: www.bayvillage.org					
Classic Bentley Village Inc 561 Bentley Village Ct	Naples	FL	34110	239-598-3153	598-3357
Covenant Village of Florida 9201 W Broward Blvd	Plantation	FL	33324	954-472-2860	472-5934
Web: www.covenantretirement.com					
East Ridge Retirement Village 19301 SW 87th Ave	Miami	FL	33157	305-256-3564	256-1911
TF: 800-605-7778 ■ *Web:* www.eastridgerc.com					
Edgewater Pointe Estates 23315 Blue Water Cir	Boca Raton	FL	33433	561-391-6305	367-8526
Fleet Landing Retirement Community 1 Fleet Landing Blvd	Atlantic Beach	FL	32233	904-246-9900	246-9447
TF: 800-872-8761 ■ *Web:* www.fleetlanding.com					
Florida Presbyterian Homes 16 Lake Hunter Dr	Lakeland	FL	33803	863-682-7787	682-4644
Web: www.fphi.org					
Forum at Deer Creek 3001 Country Club Blvd	Deerfield Beach	FL	33442	954-698-9004	428-3074
Web: www.sunriseseniorliving.com					
Freedom Village 6501 17th Ave W	Bradenton	FL	34209	941-798-8122	798-8193
TF: 800-841-4676 ■ *Web:* www.freedomvillage.com					
Gulf Coast Village 1333 Santa Barbara Blvd	Cape Coral	FL	33991	239-772-1333	772-0242*
**Fax:* Mktg ■ *Web:* www.gulfcoastvillage.com					
Harbour's Edge 401 E Linton Blvd	Delray Beach	FL	33483	561-272-7979	243-0038
TF: 800-232-1358 ■ *Web:* www.harboursedge.com					
Indian River Estates 2250 Indian Creek Blvd W	Vero Beach	FL	32966	772-562-7400	778-7747
TF Mktg: 800-544-0277					
John Knox Village 651 Lakeside Cir	Pompano Beach	FL	33060	954-783-4000	783-4044
Web: www.johnknoxvillage.com					
Lake Seminole Square 8333 Seminole Blvd	Seminole	FL	33772	727-391-0500	392-9497
Mayflower Retirement Community 1620 Mayflower Ct	Winter Park	FL	32792	407-672-1620	671-6336
TF: 800-228-6518 ■ *Web:* www.themayflower.com					
Mease Manor 700 Mease Plaza	Dunedin	FL	34698	727-733-1161	736-6306
Web: www.measemanor.com					
Moorings Park 120 Moorings Park Dr	Naples	FL	34105	239-261-1616	262-7040
Web: www.mooringspark.org					

				Phone	Fax
Oaks at Clearwater 420 Bay Ave	Clearwater	FL	33756	727-445-4700	462-9902
Web: www.theoaksofclearwater.com					
Park Summit of Coral Springs 8500 Royal Palm Blvd	Coral Springs	FL	33065	954-752-9500	755-9559
Plymouth Harbor 700 John Ringling Blvd	Sarasota	FL	34236	941-361-7514	957-1812
Web: www.plymouthharbor.org					
Saint Andrews Estates 6152 Verde Trail N.	Boca Raton	FL	33433	561-487-5500	883-3823
TF Mktg: 800-850-2287 ■ *Web:* www.acts-retirement.org					
Saint Mark Village 2655 Nebraska Ave	Palm Harbor	FL	34684	727-785-2576	786-6835
Shell Point Village 15000 Shell Point Blvd	Fort Myers	FL	33908	239-466-1111	454-2220
TF Mktg: 800-780-1131 ■ *Web:* www.shellpoint.org					
Stratford Court 45 Katherine Blvd	Palm Harbor	FL	34684	727-787-1500	787-1506
TF: 800-772-2622 ■ *Web:* www.sunriseseniorliving.com					
Village on the Green 500 Village Pl	Longwood	FL	32779	407-788-2300	682-3893*
**Fax:* Mktg ■ *TF Mktg:* 800-432-8833 ■ *Web:* www.villageonthegreenrc.com					
Village on the Isle 920 Tamiami Trail S.	Venice	FL	34285	941-484-9753	484-0407
Waterford The 601 Universe Blvd	Juno Beach	FL	33408	561-627-3800	694-0242
Web: www.thewaterford.com					
Westminster Bradenton Manor 1700 21st Ave W	Bradenton	FL	34205	941-748-4161	748-6673
Westminster Oaks 4449 Meandering Way	Tallahassee	FL	32308	850-878-1136	942-4924
Web: www.westminsterretirement.com					
Westminster Towers 70 W Lucerne Cir	Orlando	FL	32801	407-841-1310	849-0900
Web: www.westminsterretirement.com					
Winter Park Towers 1111 S Lakemont Ave	Winter Park	FL	32792	407-647-4083	645-4409
Web: www.westminsterretirement.com					
Clairmont Place 2100 Clairmont Lake	Decatur	GA	30033	404-633-8875	633-9417
Lenbrook Square 3747 Peachtree Rd NE	Atlanta	GA	30319	404-233-3000	264-3380
Web: www.lenbrook-atlanta.com					
Savannah Commons 1 Peachtree Dr	Savannah	GA	31419	912-927-0500	920-9890
Web: www.kiscoseniorliving.com					
Arcadia Retirement Residence 1434 Punahou St	Honolulu	HI	96822	808-941-0941	949-4965
Web: www.arcadia-hi.org					
Admiral at the Lake 909 W Foster Ave	Chicago	IL	60640	773-561-2900	561-2573
Web: www.admiralatthelake.com					
Brookdale Senior Living Inc 330 N Wabash Ave Suite 1400	Chicago	IL	60611	312-977-3700	977-3701
NYSE: BKD ■ *Web:* www.brookdaleliving.com					
Church Creek 1250 W Central Rd	Arlington Heights	IL	60005	847-506-3200	506-2598
Web: www.sunriseseniorliving.com					
Clark-Lindsey Village 101 W Windsor Rd	Urbana	IL	61802	217-344-2144	344-9147
TF: 800-998-2581 ■ *Web:* www.clark-lindsey.com					
Covenant Village of Northbrook 2625 Techny Rd	Northbrook	IL	60062	847-480-6380	480-7666
Web: www.covenantretirement.com					
Devonshire The 1700 Robin Ln.	Lisle	IL	60532	630-963-1880	963-8074
Web: www.thedevonshireoflisle.com					
Fairview Village 210 Village Dr	Downers Grove	IL	60516	630-769-6000	769-6020
Web: www.fairview-inc.com					
Friendship Manor 1209 21st Ave	Rock Island	IL	61201	309-786-9667	786-5611
Web: www.friendshipmanor.org					
Hallmark The 2960 N Lake Shore Dr	Chicago	IL	60657	773-880-2960	880-2966
Web: www.thehallmarkofchicago.com					
Holmstad The 700 W Fabyan Pkwy	Batavia	IL	60510	630-879-4000	879-1153
Web: www.covenantretirement.org					
Moorings The 811 E Central Rd	Arlington Heights	IL	60005	847-437-6700	956-4451
Web: www.presbyterianhomes.org					
Oak Crest DeKalb Area Retirement Center					
2944 Greenwood Acres Dr	DeKalb	IL	60115	815-756-8461	756-6515
Web: www.oakcrestdekalb.org					
Senior Lifestyle Corp 111 E Wacker Dr Suite 2200	Chicago	IL	60601	312-673-4333	673-4440
Web: www.senr.com					
Westminster Place 3200 Grant St	Evanston	IL	60201	847-492-4800	492-2850
TF: 800-896-9095 ■ *Web:* www.presbyterianhomes.org					
Westminster Village 2025 E Lincoln St	Bloomington	IL	61701	309-663-6474	663-1069
Concord Village 6723 S Anthony Blvd	Fort Wayne	IN	46816	260-447-1591	447-7369
Four Seasons Retirement Center 1901 Taylor Rd	Columbus	IN	47203	812-372-8481	378-6184
Web: www.fourseasonsretirement.com					
Greencroft PO Box 819	Goshen	IN	46527	574-537-4000	537-4185
Web: www.greencroft.org					
Greenwood Village South 295 Village Ln	Greenwood	IN	46143	317-881-2591	881-1299
Hoosier Village 5300 W 96th St	Indianapolis	IN	46268	317-873-3349	873-8224
Web: www.hoosiervillage.com					
Marquette Manor 8140 Township Line Rd	Indianapolis	IN	46260	317-875-9700	875-7504
Web: www.retirement-living.org					
Meadowood Retirement Community 2455 Tamarack Trail	Bloomington	IN	47408	812-336-7060	333-8917
Web: meadowoodrc.com					
Towne Centre 7250 Arthur Blvd	Merrillville	IN	46410	219-736-2900	736-2209
Towne House The 2209 St Joe Ctr Rd	Fort Wayne	IN	46825	260-483-3116	969-8072
Web: www.townehouse.org					
Wesley Manor 1555 N Main St	Frankfort	IN	46041	765-659-1811	654-5596
Westminster Village 1120 E Davis Dr	Terre Haute	IN	47802	812-232-7533	232-3304
Friendship Village 600 Park Ln	Waterloo	IA	50702	319-291-8100	291-8324
Web: www.friendshipvillageiowa.com					
Meth-Wick Community 1224 13th St NW	Cedar Rapids	IA	52405	319-365-9171	363-5312
Web: www.methwick.org					
Western Home Communities 420 E 11th St	Cedar Falls	IA	50613	319-277-2141	277-5158
Web: www.westernhomecommunities.org					
Aldersgate Village 7220 SW Asbury Dr	Topeka	KS	66614	785-478-9440	478-9104
Web: www.umhomes.org					
Brewster Place 1205 SW 29th St	Topeka	KS	66611	785-267-1666	267-9355
Heatherwood Village 1035 SE 3rd St	Newton	KS	67114	316-283-6600	283-6375
Larksfield Place 7373 E 29th St N	Wichita	KS	67226	316-636-1000	636-5790
TF: 877-636-1234 ■ *Web:* www.larksfieldplace.org					
Wesley Towers 700 Monterey Pl	Hutchinson	KS	67502	620-663-9175	663-2961
Web: www.wesleytowers.com					
Forum at Brookside 200 Brookside Dr	Louisville	KY	40243	502-245-3048	244-6327*
**Fax:* Mktg					
Treyton Oak Towers 211 W Oak St	Louisville	KY	40203	502-589-3211	589-7263
Saint James Place 333 Lee Dr	Baton Rouge	LA	70808	225-769-1407	215-4515
Web: www.stjamesplace.com					
Asbury Methodist Village 201 Russell Ave	Gaithersburg	MD	20877	301-330-3000	216-4269
TF: 800-327-2879 ■ *Web:* www.asburymethodistvillage.org					
Bedford Court 3701 International Dr	Silver Spring	MD	20906	301-598-2900	598-0715
Web: www.sunriseseniorliving.com					
Broadmead 13801 York Rd	Cockeysville	MD	21030	410-527-1900	527-0259
Web: www.broadmead.org					
Carroll Lutheran Village 300 Saint Luke Cir	Westminster	MD	21158	410-848-0090	848-8133
Web: www.clvillage.org					
Charlestown Retirement Community 719 Maiden Choice Ln	Catonsville	MD	21228	410-247-3400	737-8841
Web: www.ericksonretirement.com/cci					
Classic Residence by Hyatt 8100 Connecticut Ave	Chevy Chase	MD	20815	301-907-8895	907-4627*
**Fax:* Mktg ■ *Web:* www.hyattclassic.com					
Collington Episcopal Community 10450 Lottsford Rd	Mitchellville	MD	20721	301-925-9610	925-7357
Edenwald 800 Southerly Rd	Baltimore	MD	21286	410-339-6000	583-8786
Web: www.edenwald.org					
Fairhaven 7200 3rd Ave	Sykesville	MD	21784	410-795-8800	549-6788
TF: 800-241-9997 ■ *Web:* www.fairhavenccrc.org					
Ginger Cove 4000 River Crescent Dr	Annapolis	MD	21401	410-266-7300	266-6144
Web: www.gingercove.com					
Glen Meadows 11630 Glen Arm Rd	Glen Arm	MD	21057	410-592-5310	592-6175
Web: www.glenmeadows.org					
Heron Point of Chestertown 501 E Campus Ave	Chestertown	MD	21620	410-778-7300	778-0053
TF: 800-327-9138 ■ *Web:* www.heronpoint.com					
Homewood at Williamsport 16505 Virginia Ave	Williamsport	MD	21795	301-582-1472	582-1805
Web: www.homewood.com					
Roland Park Place 830 W 40th St	Baltimore	MD	21211	410-243-5800	243-4929
Web: www.rolandparkplace.org					
Brookhaven at Lexington 1010 Waltham St	Lexington	MA	02421	781-863-9660	863-9944
Web: www.aboutbrookhaven.org					
Carleton-Willard Village 100 Old Billerica Rd	Bedford	MA	01730	781-275-8700	275-5787
Web: www.carleton-willard.org					
Fox Hill Village 10 Longwood Dr	Westwood	MA	02090	781-329-4433	461-2464
Loomis Communities 246 N Main St	South Hadley	MA	01075	413-532-5325	532-8676
TF: 800-865-7655 ■ *Web:* www.loomiscommunities.org					
New Pond Village 180 Main St	Walpole	MA	02081	508-660-1555	668-8893
Willows The 1 Lyman St	Westborough	MA	01581	508-366-4730	366-1930
TF: 800-464-4730 ■ *Web:* www.salmonfamily.com					
Burcham Hills Retirement Center 2700 Burcham Dr	East Lansing	MI	48823	517-351-8377	351-1738
Friendship Village 1400 N Drake Rd	Kalamazoo	MI	49006	269-381-0560	381-5354
TF: 800-613-3984					
Glacier Hills 1200 Earhart Rd	Ann Arbor	MI	48105	734-663-5202	769-3613
Web: www.glacierhills.org					
Porter Hills 3600 E Fulton St	Grand Rapids	MI	49546	616-949-4971	954-1795
Web: www.porterhills.org					
Vista Grande Villa 2251 Springport Rd	Jackson	MI	49202	517-787-0222	787-6909
Web: www.vistagrandevilla.com					
Covenant Village of Golden Valley 5800 St Croix Ave	Minneapolis	MN	55422	763-546-6125	546-8529
Web: www.covenantretirement.com/sb_index.asp?cmps_id=10					
Friendship Village 8100 Highwood Dr	Bloomington	MN	55438	952-831-7500	830-9893
Web: www.friendshipvillagemn.com					
Armed Forces Retirement Home - Gulfport 1800 Beach Dr	Gulfport	MS	39507	228-604-2205	897-4013
TF: 800-332-3527 ■ *Web:* www.afrh.gov					
Seashore Retirement Community 1450 Beach Blvd	Biloxi	MS	39530	228-435-3861	435-9957
Web: www.umssm.org/methodist.html					
Trinity Place Retirement Community 300 Airline Rd	Columbus	MS	39702	662-327-6716	327-5873
Web: www.umssm.org/trinity.html					
Foxwood Springs 1500 W Foxwood Dr	Raymore	MO	64083	816-331-3111	331-2490
Friendship Village of South County 12503 Village Circle Dr	Saint Louis	MO	63127	314-842-6840	525-7500
Web: www.friendshipvillagesouth.com					
John Knox Village 400 NW Murray Rd	Lee's Summit	MO	64081	816-524-8400	246-7812
TF: 800-892-5669 ■ *Web:* www.johnknoxvillage.org					
Kingswood Senior Living Community 10000 Wornall Rd	Kansas City	MO	64114	816-942-0994	942-8131
Web: www.kingswoodathome.org					
Laclede Groves Retirement Community					
723 S Laclede Station Rd	Saint Louis	MO	63119	314-968-5570	968-8504
TF: 877-363-1211 ■ *Web:* www.lssmo.org/laclede.html					
Parkside Meadows Retirement Community					
2150 W Randolph St	Saint Charles	MO	63301	636-946-4966	940-0214
Web: www.parkside.org					
Village North Retirement Community					
11160 Village North Dr	Saint Louis	MO	63136	314-355-8010	653-4801
Eastmont Towers 6315 'O' St	Lincoln	NE	68510	402-489-6591	486-2331
Web: www.eastmonttowers.com					
Northfield Villa & Residency 2550 21st St	Gering	NE	69341	308-436-3101	436-3493
Skyline Retirement Community 7350 Graceland Dr	Omaha	NE	68134	402-572-5750	572-5777
Classic Residence by Hyatt 3201 Plumas St	Reno	NV	89509	775-825-1105	829-1052
Web: www.hyattclassic.com					
Havenwood-Heritage Heights Havenwood Campus					
33 Christian Ave	Concord	NH	03301	603-224-5363	229-1188
Web: www.hhhinfo.com					
Hillcrest Terrace 200 Alliance Way	Manchester	NH	03102	603-645-6500	626-7724
TF: 800-862-9490 ■ *Web:* www.hillcrestterrace.com					
Kendal at Hanover 80 Lyme Rd	Hanover	NH	03755	603-643-8900	643-7099
RiverMead Retirement Community 150 RiverMead Rd	Peterborough	NH	03458	603-924-0062	924-6507
TF: 800-200-5433 ■ *Web:* www.rivermead.org					
RiverWoods at Exeter 7 RiverWoods Dr	Exeter	NH	03833	603-772-4700	778-9623
Web: www.riverwoodsrc.org					
Applewood Estates 1 Applewood Dr	Freehold	NJ	07728	732-780-7370	303-1240
TF Mktg: 800-438-0888 ■ *Web:* www.applewoodestates.com					
Cadbury Retirement Community 2150 Rt 38	Cherry Hill	NJ	08002	856-667-4550	667-3653
TF: 800-422-3287 ■ *Web:* www.cadbury.org					
Classic Residence by Hyatt 655 Pomander Walk	Teaneck	NJ	07666	201-836-7474	836-9435
TF: 800-292-7474 ■ *Web:* www.hyattclassic.com					
Crestwood Manor 50 Lacey Rd	Whiting	NJ	08759	732-849-4900	849-4342
TF: 800-526-1665					
Evergreens The 309 Bridgeboro Rd	Moorestown	NJ	08057	856-439-2000	439-2112*
**Fax:* Mktg ■ *TF:* 800-371-4918 ■ *Web:* www.evergreens.org					
Franciscan Oaks 19 Pocono Rd	Denville	NJ	07834	973-586-6000	586-6030
Harrogate 400 Locust St	Lakewood	NJ	08701	732-905-7070	905-2824
Web: www.harrogate-lifecare.org					
Leisure Park at Lakewood 1400 Rt 70 E	Lakewood	NJ	08701	732-370-0444	370-1783
Meadowlakes 300 Meadow Lakes	Hightstown	NJ	08520	609-448-4100	448-5380
TF: 800-222-0609					
Medford Leas 1 Medford Leas Way	Medford	NJ	08055	609-654-3000	654-7894
TF: 800-331-4302 ■ *Web:* www.medfordleas.org					
Monroe Village 1 David Brainerd Dr	Monroe Township	NJ	08831	732-521-6400	521-6540
TF: 800-833-4447 ■ *Web:* www.phsnet.org					
La Vida Llena 10501 Lagrima de Oro NE	Albuquerque	NM	87111	505-293-4001	291-3199
TF: 800-922-1344 ■ *Web:* www.lavidallena.com					
Montebello The 10500 Academy Rd NE	Albuquerque	NM	87111	505-294-9944	294-1808
Andrus on Hudson 185 Old Broadway	Hastings-on-Hudson	NY	10706	914-478-3700	478-3541
Fountains at Millbrook 79 Flint Rd	Millbrook	NY	12545	845-677-8550	677-8630
TF: 800-433-6092 ■ *Web:* www.thefountains.com					
Kendal at Ithaca 2230 N Triphammer Rd	Ithaca	NY	14850	607-266-5300	266-5353
TF: 800-253-6325 ■ *Web:* www.kendal.org					
Arbor Acres 1240 Arbor Rd	Winston-Salem	NC	27104	336-724-7921	721-0271
Web: www.arboracres.org					
Bermuda Village 142 Bermuda Village Dr	Advance	NC	27006	336-998-6535	940-2140*
**Fax:* Mktg ■ *TF Mktg:* 800-843-5433 ■ *Web:* www.bermudavillage.com					
Carol Woods Retirement Community 750 Weaver Dairy Rd	Chapel Hill	NC	27514	919-968-4511	918-3349
TF: 800-518-9333 ■ *Web:* www.carolwoods.org					
Carolina Meadows 100 Carolina Meadows	Chapel Hill	NC	27517	919-942-4014	929-7808
TF: 800-458-6756 ■ *Web:* www.carolinameadows.org					
Carolina Village 600 Carolina Village Rd	Hendersonville	NC	28792	828-692-6275	692-7876
Web: www.carolinavillage.com					
Covenant Village 1351 Robinwood Rd	Gastonia	NC	28054	704-867-2319	861-8893
Deerfield Episcopal Retirement Community					
1617 Hendersonville Rd	Asheville	NC	28803	828-274-1531	274-0238
Web: www.deerfieldwnc.org					
Forest at Duke 2701 Pickett Rd	Durham	NC	27705	919-490-8000	490-0887
Web: www.forestduke.com					
Friends Homes West 6100 W Friendly Ave	Greensboro	NC	27410	336-292-9952	294-0129
Pines at Davidson 400 Avinger Ln	Davidson	NC	28036	704-896-1100	896-1119
Web: www.thepinesatdavidson.org					
Presbyterian Home of High Point 201 Greensboro Rd	High Point	NC	27260	336-883-9111	885-7215
Web: www.presbyterianhomehp.org					

Name / Address	City	State	ZIP	Phone	Fax
Sharon Towers 5100 Sharon Rd *Web:* www.sharontowers.org	Charlotte	NC	28210	704-553-1670	553-1877
Springmoor Life Care Retirement Community 1500 Sawmill Rd *Web:* www.springmoor.com	Raleigh	NC	27615	919-848-7000	848-7392
Breckenridge Village 36855 Ridge Rd	Willoughby	OH	44094	440-942-4342	942-4150
Canton Regency Retirement Center 4515 22nd St NW	Canton	OH	44708	330-477-0456	477-1083
Dorothy Love Retirement Community 3003 W Cisco Rd *Web:* www.dorothylove.com	Sidney	OH	45365	937-498-2391	498-7577
First Community Village 1800 Riverside Dr *TF:* 888-328-9511 ■ *Web:* www.firstcommunityvillage.org	Columbus	OH	43212	614-486-9511	486-5628
Forum at Knightsbridge by Marriott 4590 Knightsbridge Blvd *Web:* www.sunriseseniorliving.com	Columbus	OH	43214	614-451-6793	442-2271
Friendship Village 5800 Forest Hills Blvd *Web:* www.friendshipvillageoh.com	Columbus	OH	43231	614-890-8282	890-2661
Hilltop Village 25900 Euclid Ave *Web:* www.hilltopvillage.com	Euclid	OH	44132	216-261-8383	261-5230
Kendal at Oberlin 600 Kendal Dr *TF Mktg:* 800-548-9469 ■ *Web:* www.kao.kendal.org	Oberlin	OH	44074	440-775-0094	775-9820
Laurel Lake Retirement Community 200 Laurel Lake Dr **Fax Area Code: 330* ■ *TF:* 866-650-0681 ■ *Web:* www.laurellake.com	Hudson	OH	44236	866-650-2100	650-0576*
Llanfair Retirement Community 1701 Llanfair Ave	Cincinnati	OH	45224	513-681-4230	681-0417
Maple Knoll Village 11100 Springfield Pike *TF:* 800-789-6008 ■ *Web:* www.mapleknoll.org	Cincinnati	OH	45246	513-782-2717	782-4324
Marjorie P Lee Retirement Community 3550 Shaw Ave	Cincinnati	OH	45208	513-871-2090	533-5096
Otterbein-Lebanon Retirement Community 585 N SR 741 *Web:* www.otterbein.org	Lebanon	OH	45036	513-932-2020	932-4722
Renaissance The 26376 John Rd	Olmsted Township	OH	44138	440-235-7100	235-7115
Rockynol Retirement Community 1150 W Market St *Web:* www.oprs.org	Akron	OH	44313	330-867-2150	867-1642
Twin Towers 5343 Hamilton Ave	Cincinnati	OH	45224	513-853-2000	853-2703
Wesley Glen Retirement Center 5155 N High St	Columbus	OH	43214	614-888-7492	436-6012
Westlake Village 28550 Westlake Village Dr	Westlake	OH	44145	440-892-4220	892-4756
Westminster-Thurber Community 717 Neil Ave *Web:* www.oprs.org	Columbus	OH	43215	614-228-8888	228-8898
Epworth Villa 14901 N Pennsylvania Ave *TF:* 800-579-8776 ■ *Web:* www.epworthvilla.com	Oklahoma City	OK	73134	405-752-1200	755-4813
Golden Oaks Village 5801 N Oakwood Rd *TF:* 800-259-0914 ■ *Web:* www.goldenoaks.com	Enid	OK	73703	580-234-2817	233-3426
Spanish Cove 11 Palm Ave	Yukon	OK	73099	405-354-1901	354-4429
Capital Manor 1955 Dallas Hwy NW *TF:* 800-637-0327 ■ *Web:* www.capitalmanor.com	Salem	OR	97304	503-362-4101	371-9021
Friendsview Manor 1301 E Fulton St	Newberg	OR	97132	503-538-3144	538-6371
Mennonite Home of Albany 5353 Columbus St SE *Web:* www.mennonitevillage.org	Albany	OR	97322	541-928-7232	917-1399
Rogue Valley Manor 1200 Mira Mar Ave *TF:* 800-848-7868 ■ *Web:* www.retirement.org/rvm	Medford	OR	97504	541-857-7777	857-7590
Terwilliger Plaza 2545 SW Terwilliger Blvd *TF:* 800-875-4211 ■ *Web:* www.terwilligerplaza.com	Portland	OR	97201	503-226-4911	299-4231
Willamette View 12705 SE River Rd *TF:* 800-446-0670 ■ *Web:* www.willametteview.org	Milwaukie	OR	97222	503-654-6581	652-6260
Beaumont at Bryn Mawr 601 N Ithan Ave *Web:* www.beaumontretirement.com	Bryn Mawr	PA	19010	610-526-7000	525-0293
Bethany Village 325 Wesley Dr *Web:* www.bethanyvillage.org	Mechanicsburg	PA	17055	717-766-0279	766-0870
Brethren Home 2990 Carlisle Pike PO Box 128 *Web:* www.brethrenhome.org	New Oxford	PA	17350	717-624-2161	624-5252
Brittany Pointe Estates 1001 Valley Forge Rd *Web:* www.acts-retirement.org	Lansdale	PA	19446	215-855-4109	855-6137
Cathedral Village 600 E Cathedral Rd	Philadelphia	PA	19128	215-487-1300	984-8617
Foulkeways at Gwynedd 1120 Meetinghouse Rd *Web:* www.foulkeways.org	Gwynedd	PA	19436	215-643-2200	646-2917
Foxdale Village 500 E Marylyn Ave *TF:* 800-253-4951	State College	PA	16801	814-238-3322	238-2920
Friendship Village of South Hills 1290 Boyce Rd	Upper Saint Clair	PA	15241	724-941-3100	941-6331
Granite Farms Estates 1343 W Baltimore Pike	Media	PA	19063	610-358-3440	558-9660
Gwynedd Estates 301 Norristown Rd	Ambler	PA	19002	215-628-8840	628-2706
Kendal at Longwood & Crosslands PO Box 100	Kennett Square	PA	19348	610-388-7001	388-5503
LAS Passavant Retirement Community 401 S Main St *Web:* www.lutheranseniorlife.org	Zelienople	PA	16063	724-452-5400	452-5400
Lebanon Valley Brethren Home 1200 Grubb St *Web:* www.lvbh.org	Palmyra	PA	17078	717-838-5406	838-3826
Lima Estates 411 N Middletown Rd	Lima	PA	19037	610-565-7020	565-7425
Logan Square East 2 Franklin Town Blvd *Web:* www.logansquareeast.com	Philadelphia	PA	19103	215-563-1800	563-7976
Lutheran Community at Telford 235 N Washington St *Web:* www.lctelford.org	Telford	PA	18969	215-723-9819	723-8568
Martins Run 11 Martins Run *TF:* 800-327-3875 ■ *Web:* www.martinsrun.com	Media	PA	19063	610-353-7660	353-4928
Meadowood 3205 Skippack Pike PO Box 670 *Web:* www.meadowood.net	Worcester	PA	19490	610-584-1000	584-3645
Menno Village 2075 Scotland Ave *Web:* www.mennohaven.org	Chambersburg	PA	17201	717-263-8545	263-6988
Messiah Village 100 Mt Allen Dr *Web:* www.messiahvillage.com	Mechanicsburg	PA	17055	717-697-4666	790-8200
Moravian Hall Square 175 W North St *Web:* www.moravian.com	Nazareth	PA	18064	610-746-1000	746-1023
Normandy Farms Estates 9000 Twin Silo Dr *Web:* www.acts-retirement.org	Blue Bell	PA	19422	215-699-8721	699-2422
Philadelphia Protestant Home 6500 Tabor Rd	Philadelphia	PA	19111	215-697-8000	697-8137
Pine Run Community 777 Ferry Rd	Doylestown	PA	18901	215-345-9000	340-5128
Quadrangle The 3300 Darby Rd *Web:* www.sunriseseniorliving.com	Haverford	PA	19041	610-642-3000	642-5743
Riddle Village 1048 W Baltimore Pike *Web:* www.riddlevillage.com	Media	PA	19063	610-891-3777	891-3671
Rydal Park 1515 The Fairway *Web:* www.presbyhomes.org/rydal.htm	Rydal	PA	19046	215-885-6800	885-4560
Sherwood Oaks 100 Norman Dr *Web:* www.sherwood-oaks.com	Cranberry Township	PA	16066	724-776-8100	776-8468
Simpson House 2101 Belmont Ave *Web:* www.simpsonhouse.org	Philadelphia	PA	19131	215-878-3600	878-6701
Spring House Estates 728 Norristown Rd	Lower Gwynedd	PA	19002	215-628-8110	628-9701
Waverly Heights 1400 Waverly Rd *Web:* www.waverlyheightsltd.org	Gladwyne	PA	19035	610-645-8600	645-8611
Westminster Village 803 N Wahneta St *Web:* www.wmvallentown.org	Allentown	PA	18109	610-782-8300	782-8398
White Horse Village 535 Gradyville Rd *Web:* www.whitehorsevillage.org	Newtown Square	PA	19073	610-558-5000	558-5001
Willow Valley Lakes Manor 300 Willow Valley Lakes Dr *Web:* www.willowvalleyretirement.com	Willow Street	PA	17584	717-464-0800	464-2560
Bethea Baptist Retirement Community 157 Home Ave	Darlington	SC	29532	843-393-2867	393-2458
Presbyterian Homes of South Carolina Summerville 201 W 9th N St CMR 140	Summerville	SC	29483	843-873-2550	851-2033
Westminster Towers 1330 India Hook Rd	Rock Hill	SC	29732	803-328-5000	328-5140
Alexian Village 100 James Blvd	Signal Mountain	TN	37377	423-886-0101	886-0470
American Retirement Corp 111 Westwood Pl Suite 200 *NYSE: ACR* ■ *TF:* 888-221-7317 ■ *Web:* www.arclp.com	Brentwood	TN	37027	615-221-2250	221-2269
Air Force Village 4917 Ravenswood Dr	San Antonio	TX	78227	210-673-2761	673-1441
Army Residence Community 7400 Crestway Dr *Web:* www.armyresidence.com	San Antonio	TX	78239	210-646-5300	646-5313
Bayou Manor 4141 S Braeswood Blvd	Houston	TX	77025	713-666-2651	660-4800
Capital Senior Living Corp 14160 Dallas Pkwy Suite 300 *NYSE: CSU* ■ *Web:* www.capitalsenior.com	Dallas	TX	75254	972-770-5600	770-5666
Denton Good Samaritan Village 2500 Hinkle Dr	Denton	TX	76201	940-383-2651	382-9306
Forum at Lincoln Heights 311 Nottingham W	San Antonio	TX	78209	210-824-2314	824-6556
Forum at Memorial Woods 777 N Post Oak Rd	Houston	TX	77024	713-956-0870	956-0732
Forum at Park Lane 7831 Park Ln	Dallas	TX	75225	214-369-9902	373-1836
Grace Presbyterian Village 550 E Ann Arbor Ave *Web:* www.gracepresbyterianvillage.org	Dallas	TX	75216	214-376-1701	376-4350
John Knox Village of the Rio Grande Valley 1300 S Border Ave *TF Mktg:* 800-245-6526 ■ *Web:* www.johnknoxvillagergv.com	Weslaco	TX	78596	956-968-4575	968-4570
Manor Park Inc 2208 North Loop 250 W *TF:* 800-523-9898 ■ *Web:* www.manorparkinc.org	Midland	TX	79707	432-689-9898	694-2551
Rolling Meadows 3006 McNiel Ave *Web:* www.rmeadows.com	Wichita Falls	TX	76309	940-691-7511	696-5154
Temple Meridian 4312 S 31st St *Web:* www.meridians.com	Temple	TX	76502	254-771-1226	774-7472
Westminster Manor 4100 Jackson Ave	Austin	TX	78731	512-454-4711	454-1389
Wake Robin 200 Wake Robin Dr *Web:* www.wakerobin.com	Shelburne	VT	05482	802-985-9400	985-8452
Brandermill Woods 14311 Brandermill Woods Trail	Midlothian	VA	23112	804-744-1173	744-4894
Colonnades The 2600 Barracks Rd *Web:* www.sunriseseniorliving.com	Charlottesville	VA	22901	434-971-1892	963-4108
Culpeper Baptist Retirement Community 12425 Village Loop *TF:* 800-894-2411 ■ *Web:* vbh.org/culpeper	Culpeper	VA	22701	540-825-2411	825-5123
Fairfax The 9140 Belvoir Woods Pkwy	Fort Belvoir	VA	22060	703-799-1200	781-2448
Goodwin House 4800 Fillmore Ave *Web:* www.goodwinhouse.org	Alexandria	VA	22311	703-578-1000	824-1379
Goodwin House West 3440 S Jefferson St *Web:* www.goodwinhouse.org	Falls Church	VA	22041	703-820-1488	578-7519
Hermitage The 1600 Westwood Ave *Web:* www.seniorresource.com/hermitag.htm	Richmond	VA	23227	804-355-5721	358-0854
Jefferson The 900 N Taylor St *Web:* www.sunriseseniorliving.com	Arlington	VA	22203	703-516-9455	516-9459
Lakewood Manor 1900 Lauderdale Dr *Web:* vbh.org/lakewood/	Richmond	VA	23238	804-740-2900	740-3774
Shenandoah Valley Westminster-Canterbury 300 Westminster-Canterbury Dr *TF:* 800-492-9463 ■ *Web:* www.svwc.org	Winchester	VA	22603	540-665-5914	665-9781
Virginian The 9229 Arlington Blvd *Web:* www.thevirginian.org	Fairfax	VA	22031	703-385-0555	591-9368
Washington House 5100 Fillmore Ave	Alexandria	VA	22311	703-379-9000	671-0468
Westminster-Canterbury of Lynchburg 501 VES Rd *Web:* www.wclynchburg.org	Lynchburg	VA	24503	434-386-3500	386-3535
Westminster-Canterbury Richmond 1600 Westbrook Ave *TF:* 800-445-9904 ■ *Web:* www.wescanric.org	Richmond	VA	23227	804-264-6000	264-6095
Westminster-Canterbury of Virginia Beach 3100 Shore Dr	Virginia Beach	VA	23451	757-496-1100	496-1122
Williamsburg Landing 5700 Williamsburg Landing Dr	Williamsburg	VA	23185	757-253-0303	565-6537
Bayview Retirement Community 11 W Aloha St	Seattle	WA	98119	206-284-7330	284-9640
Hearthstone The 6720 E Green Lake Way N	Seattle	WA	98103	206-525-9666	522-0190
Horizon House 900 University St *Web:* www.horizonhouse.org	Seattle	WA	98101	206-624-3700	382-3780
Judson Park 23600 Marine View Dr S *TF:* 877-263-8484 ■ *Web:* www.abhow.com/multi/judson_park	Des Moines	WA	98198	206-824-4000	878-6404
Panorama City 1751 Circle Ln SE *Web:* www.panoramacity.org	Lacey	WA	98503	360-456-0111	438-5901
Park Shore 1630 43rd Ave E *Web:* www.parkshore.org	Seattle	WA	98112	206-329-0770	329-0227
Rockwood Retirement Community 2903 E 25th Ave *Web:* www.rockwoodretirement.org	Spokane	WA	99223	509-536-6650	536-6662
Wesley Homes 815 S 216th St *Web:* www.wesleyhomes.org	Des Moines	WA	98198	206-824-5000	870-1209
Cedar Ridge Retirement Campus 113 Cedar Ridge Dr	West Bend	WI	53095	262-334-9487	338-9555
Fairhaven 435 Starin Rd *Web:* www.fairhaven.org	Whitewater	WI	53190	262-473-2140	473-5468
Meriter Retirement Center 110 S Henry St *Web:* www.meriter.com/family/commons/index.htm	Madison	WI	53703	608-283-2000	283-2028
Milwaukee Catholic Home 2462 N Prospect Ave *Web:* www.milwaukeecatholichome.org	Milwaukee	WI	53211	414-224-9700	224-1666
Oakwood Village West 6165 Mineral Point Rd *Web:* www.oakwoodvillage.net	Madison	WI	53705	608-230-4699	230-3286
Saint John's On The Lake 1840 N Prospect Ave *Web:* www.saintjohnsmilw.org	Milwaukee	WI	53202	414-272-2022	291-4979
Village at Manor Park 3023 S 84th St *Web:* www.vmpcares.com	West Allis	WI	53227	414-607-4100	607-4504

676 RETREATS - SPIRITUAL

The facilities listed here offer basic amenities and services such as bed linens, food preparation, maid service, etc. Although physical activity may play a role in the programs offered, the focus is on the spiritual.

Name / Address	City	State	ZIP	Phone	Fax
Ashram The PO Box 8009 *Web:* www.theashram.com	Calabasas	CA	91372	818-222-6900	222-7393
Benedict Inn Retreat & Conference Center 1402 Southern Ave *Web:* www.benedictinn.org	Beech Grove	IN	46107	317-788-7581	782-3142
Bethany Retreat House 2202 Lituanica Ave *Web:* www.bethanyretreathouse.org	East Chicago	IN	46312	219-398-5047	398-9329
Bishop's Ranch 5297 Westside Rd *Web:* www.bishopsranch.org	Healdsburg	CA	95448	707-433-2440	433-3431
Bon Secours Spiritual Center 1525 Marriottsville Rd *Web:* www.bonsecours.org/bssc	Marriottsville	MD	21104	410-442-1320	442-8219
Bridge-Between Retreat Center 4471 Flaherty Ln *Web:* www.bridge-between.org	Denmark	WI	54208	920-864-7230	864-7044
Campion Renewal Center 319 Concord Rd *Web:* www.campioncenter.org	Weston	MA	02493	781-788-6810	894-5864
Cenacle Retreat House & Spirituality Center 29 W 012 Batavia Rd *TF:* 800-240-6702 ■ *Web:* www.cenacle.org	Warrenville	IL	60555	630-393-1231	393-2646
Chopra Center at La Costa Resort & Spa 2013 Costa del Mar Rd *TF:* 888-424-6772 ■ *Web:* www.chopra.com	Carlsbad	CA	92009	760-494-1600	494-1608
Christ the King Retreat Center 621 1st Ave S *Web:* www.kingshouse.com	Buffalo	MN	55313	763-682-1394	682-3453
Conception Abbey PO Box 501 *Web:* www.conceptionabbey.org	Conception	MO	64433	660-944-2821	944-2811

Name / Address	City	State	Zip	Phone	Fax
Coury House Retreat Center 405 N Subiaco Ave	Subiaco	AR	72865	479-934-4411	934-4040
Elat Chayyim 116 Johnson Rd *TF:* 800-398-2630 ■ *Web:* www.elatchayyim.org	Falls Village	CT	06031	860-824-5991	824-7228
Esalen Institute 55000 Hwy 1 *Web:* www.esalen.org	Big Sur	CA	93920	831-667-3000	667-2724
Expanding Light 14618 Tyler Foote Rd *TF:* 800-346-5350 ■ *Web:* www.expandinglight.org	Nevada City	CA	95959	530-478-7518	478-7519
Franciscan Spirituality Center 920 Market St *Web:* www.franciscanspiritualitycenter.org	La Crosse	WI	54601	608-791-5295	
Genesis Spiritual Life Center 53 Mill St *Web:* www.westfield-ma.com/genesis	Westfield	MA	01085	413-562-3627	572-1060
Guelph Centre of Spirituality 5420 Hwy 6 N *Web:* www.loyolahouse.ca	Guelph	ON	N1H6J2	519-824-1250	767-0994
Harbin Hot Springs 18424 Harbin Springs Rd PO Box 782 *Web:* www.harbin.org	Middletown	CA	95461	707-987-2477	987-0616
Hollyhock Box 127 *TF:* 800-933-6339 ■ *Web:* www.hollyhock.bc.ca	Mansons Landing	BC	V0P1K0	250-935-6576	935-6424
Holy Cross Abbey 901 Cool Spring Ln *Web:* www.hcava.org	Berryville	VA	22611	540-955-3124	955-4006
Holy Cross Monastery 1615 Broadway PO Box 99 *Web:* www.holycrossmonastery.com	West Park	NY	12493	845-384-6660	384-6031
Jesuit Center for Spiritual Growth 501 N Church Rd *Web:* www.jesuitspiritualcenter.org/	Wernersville	PA	19565	610-670-3642	670-3650
Jesuit Retreat House 300 Manresa Way *Web:* www.elretiro.org	Los Altos	CA	94022	650-948-4491	948-0640
Kalani Oceanside Retreat RR 2 Box 4500 *TF:* 800-800-6886 ■ *Web:* www.kalani.com	Pahoa	HI	96778	808-965-7828	965-0527
Kirkridge Retreat & Study Center 2495 Fox Gap Rd *Web:* www.kirkridge.org	Bangor	PA	18013	610-588-1793	588-8510
Kordes Retreat Center 841 E 14th St *TF:* 800-880-2777 ■ *Web:* www.thedome.org/kordes	Ferdinand	IN	47532	812-367-2777	367-2313
La Salette Retreat Center 947 Park St *Web:* www.lasalette-shrine.org/centerforchristianliving1.htm	Attleboro	MA	02703	508-222-8530	236-9089
Laity Lodge 719 Earl Garrett St PO Box 290670 *Web:* www.hebuttfoundation.org/LaityLodge	Kerrville	TX	78029	830-792-1230	792-1237
Laurelville Mennonite Church Center 941 Norville Ln *TF:* 800-839-1021 ■ *Web:* www.laurelville.org	Mount Pleasant	PA	15666	724-423-2056	423-2096
Linwood Spiritual Center 50 Linwood Rd *Web:* www.linwoodspiritualctr.org	Rhinebeck	NY	12572	845-876-4178	876-1920
Living Water Worship & Teaching Center 595 N Aspaas St *TF Mktg:* 888-627-5631 ■ *Web:* www.livingwaterretreatcenter.com	Cornville	AZ	86325	928-634-4421	634-0005
Louhelen Baha'i School 3208 S State Rd *TF:* 800-894-9716 ■ *Web:* www.louhelen.org	Davison	MI	48423	810-653-5033	653-7181
Loyola House 5420 Hwy 6 N *Web:* www.loyolahouse.ca	Guelph	ON	N1H6J2	519-824-1250	767-0994
Loyola Retreat House 9270 Loyola Retreat Rd PO Box 9 *Web:* www.loyolaretreat.org	Faulkner	MD	20632	301-870-3515	392-0808
Loyola Retreat House 161 James St *Web:* www.loyola.org	Morristown	NJ	07960	973-539-0740	898-9839
Manna House of Prayer 323 E 5th St *Web:* www.mannahouse.org	Concordia	KS	66901	785-243-4428	243-4321
Marguerite Centre 700 Mackay St *Web:* margueritecentre.com	Pembroke	ON	K8A1G6	613-732-9925	735-2048
Marie Joseph Spiritual Center 10 Evans Rd *Web:* www.presmarymethuen.org/english/mariejo.htm	Biddeford	ME	04005	207-284-5671	286-1371
Marycrest Retreat & Conference Center 2851 W 52nd Ave *Web:* www.marycrest.org/retreat.htm	Denver	CO	80221	303-458-6270	433-5865
Marywood Franciscan Spirituality Center 3560 Hwy 51 N *Web:* www.fspa.org/ministry/marywood.asp	Arbor Vitae	WI	54568	715-385-3750	385-9118
Mercy Center 2300 Adeline Dr *Web:* www.mercy-center.org	Burlingame	CA	94010	650-340-7474	340-1299
Mercy Center for Healing the Whole Person 520 W Buena Ventura *Web:* www.mercycenter.com	Colorado Springs	CO	80907	719-633-2302	633-1031
Mercy Center at Madison 167 Neck Rd PO Box 191 *Web:* www.mercyctrmadison.com	Madison	CT	06443	203-245-0401	245-8718
Milford Spiritual Center 5361 S Milford Rd *Web:* www.milfordspiritualcenter.org	Milford	OH	45150	513-248-3500	248-3503
Monastery of Saint Gertrude 465 Keuterville Rd *Web:* www.rc.net/boise/st_gertrude	Cottonwood	ID	83522	208-962-3224	962-7212
Montserrat Jesuit Retreat House 600 N Shady Shores Dr PO Box 1390 *Web:* www.montserratretreat.org	Lake Dallas	TX	75065	940-321-6020	321-6040
Mount Calvary Retreat House PO Box 1296 *Web:* www.mount-calvary.org	Santa Barbara	CA	93102	805-962-9855	962-4957
Mount Carmel Center 4600 W Davis St *Web:* www.professionalwebs.com/mtcarmel	Dallas	TX	75211	214-331-6224	330-0844
Mount Manresa Jesuit Retreat House 239 Fingerboard Rd *Web:* www.manresasi.org	Staten Island	NY	10305	718-727-3844	727-4881
Mount Saint Alphonsus Retreat Center 1001 Broadway Rt 9W *Web:* www.msaretreathouse.org	Esopus	NY	12429	845-384-8000	384-8088
Omega Institute for Holistic Studies DBA Omega Institute 150 Lake Dr *TF:* 800-944-1001 ■ *Web:* www.eomega.org	Rhinebeck	NY	12572	845-266-4444	266-3769
Omega Retreat and Spirituality Center 216 W Highland *Web:* www.boernebenedictines.com	Boerne	TX	78006	830-816-8471	249-3327
Our Lady of Fatima Retreat House 5353 E 56th St *Web:* www.archindy.org/fatima	Indianapolis	IN	46226	317-545-7681	545-0095
Pecos Benedictine Monastery 143 Cowles Hwy *Web:* www.pecosabbey.org	Pecos	NM	87552	505-757-6415	757-2285
Pendle Hill 338 Plush Mill Rd *TF:* 800-742-3150 ■ *Web:* www.pendlehill.org	Wallingford	PA	19086	610-566-4507	566-3679
Priory Spirituality Center 500 College St NE *Web:* www.stplacid.org	Lacey	WA	98516	360-438-2595	438-9236
Pumpkin Hollow Farm 1184 Rt 11 *TF:* 877-325-3583 ■ *Web:* www.pumpkinhollow.org	Craryville	NY	12521	518-325-3583	325-5633
Quaker Hill Conference Center 10 Quaker Hill Dr *Web:* www.qhcc.org	Richmond	IN	47374	765-962-5741	
Redemptorist Retreat Center 1800 N Timber Trail Ln *Web:* www.redemptoristretreat.org	Oconomowoc	WI	53066	262-567-6900	567-0134
Rowe Camp & Conference Center 22 Kings Hwy Rd Box 273 *Web:* www.rowecenter.org	Rowe	MA	01367	413-339-4954	339-5728
Saint Andrew's Abbey 31001 N Valyermo Rd PO Box 40 *Web:* www.valyermo.com	Valyermo	CA	93563	661-944-2178	944-1076
Saint Anthony Retreat Center 43816 Sierra Dr PO Box 249 *Web:* www.stanthonyretreat.org	Three Rivers	CA	93271	559-561-4595	561-4493
Saint Anthony Retreat Center 300 E 4th St *Web:* www.sarcenter.com	Marathon	WI	54448	715-443-2236	443-2235
Saint Benedict's Retreat & Conference Centre 225 Masters Ave *Web:* www.mts.net/%7Estbens/retreat/index.html	Winnipeg	MB	R4A2A1	204-339-1705	334-8840
Saint Columban Center 6892 Lake Shore Rd PO Box 816 *Web:* www.stcolumbancenter.org	Derby	NY	14047	716-947-4708	947-5759
Saint Edmund's Retreat PO Box 399 *Web:* www.endersisland.com	Mystic	CT	06355	860-536-0565	572-7655
Saint Francis Retreat Center 549 Mission Vineyard Rd *Web:* www.stfrancisretreat.com	San Juan Bautista	CA	95045	831-623-4234	623-9046
Saint Joseph Christian Life Center 18485 Lake Shore Blvd *Web:* www.stjosephchristianlife.org	Cleveland	OH	44119	216-531-7370	531-0629
Saint Meinrad Archabbey 200 Hill Dr *Web:* www.saintmeinrad.edu/monastery_info.aspx	Saint Meinrad	IN	47577	812-357-6585	357-6325
San Damiano Retreat Center 710 Highland Dr PO Box 767 *Web:* www.sandamiano.org	Danville	CA	94526	925-837-9141	837-0522
Satchidananda Ashram Yogaville 180 Yogaville Way Rt 1 Box 1720 **Fax Area Code:* 804 ■ *Web:* www.yogaville.org	Buckingham	VA	23921	434-969-3121	969-1303*
Serra Retreat Center 3401 Serra Rd *Web:* www.serraretreat.com	Malibu	CA	90265	310-456-6631	456-9417
Shalom Prayer Center 840 S Main St *Web:* www.open.org/~shalom	Mount Angel	OR	97362	503-845-6773	845-6585
Shambhala Mountain Center 4921 County Rd 68C *TF:* 888-788-7221 ■ *Web:* www.shambhalamountain.org	Red Feather Lakes	CO	80545	970-881-2184	881-2909
Siena Center 5635 Erie St	Racine	WI	53402	262-639-4100	639-9702
Song of the Morning Yoga Retreat Center 9607 Sturgeon Valley Rd *Web:* www.goldenlotus.org	Vanderbilt	MI	49795	989-983-4107	983-4280
Sophia Spirituality Center 751 S 8th St *Web:* www.mountosb.org/sophia.html	Atchison	KS	66002	913-360-6173	
Spiritual Life Center 7100 E 45th St N *Web:* www.spirituallifecenterwichita.org	Wichita	KS	67226	316-744-0167	744-8072
Spiritual Renewal Center Inc 6400 Coors Rd NW	Albuquerque	NM	87120	505-877-4211	890-4110
Still Life Retreat 394591 Concession 2 RR1 *TF:* 877-584-8880 ■ *Web:* www.spiritual-love-inn.com	Durham	ON	N0G1R0	519-369-3663	369-6676
Tabor Retreat Center 60 Anchor Ave *Web:* www.taborretreatcenter.org	Oceanside	NY	11572	516-536-3004	536-0214
Vivekananda Retreat Ridgely PO Box 321 *Web:* www.ridgely.org	Stone Ridge	NY	12484	845-687-4574	687-4578
Wainwright House 260 Stuyvesant Ave *Web:* www.wainwright.org	Rye	NY	10580	914-967-6080	967-6114
Weber Center 1257 E Siena Heights Dr *Web:* www.adriansisters.org/weber	Adrian	MI	49221	517-266-4000	266-4004
Wisdom House Retreat & Conference Center 229 E Litchfield Rd *Web:* www.wisdomhouse.org	Litchfield	CT	06759	860-567-3163	567-3166
WomanWell 1784 La Crosse Ave *Web:* www.womanwell.org	Saint Paul	MN	55119	651-739-7953	739-7475

677 ROLLING MILL MACHINERY

SEE ALSO Metalworking Machinery p. 1968

Name / Address	City	State	Zip	Phone	Fax
Abbey International Ltd 11140 Avenue Rd *Web:* www.abbeyetna.com	Perrysburg	OH	43551	419-874-4301	874-8200
Ampco-Pittsburgh Corp 600 Grant St Suite 4600 *NYSE:* AP ■ *Web:* www.ampcopittsburgh.com	Pittsburgh	PA	15219	412-456-4400	456-4404
Bonell Mfg Co 13521 S Halsted St *TF:* 800-323-3110	Riverdale	IL	60827	708-849-1770	849-3434
Bradbury Co Inc PO Box 667 *TF:* 800-397-6394 ■ *Web:* www.bradburygroup.net/brad.cfm	Moundridge	KS	67107	620-345-6394	345-6381
Engel Industries Inc 8122 Reilly Ave *TF:* 800-428-6046 ■ *Web:* www.engelind.com	Saint Louis	MO	63111	314-638-0100	638-6514
Fairfield Machine Co Inc 1143 Lower Elkton Rd PO Box 27 *Web:* www.fairfieldmachine.com	Columbiana	OH	44408	330-482-3387	482-5052
Formtek Metal Forming Inc 4899 Commerce Pkwy *TF:* 800-631-0520 ■ *Web:* www.formtekinc.com	Warrensville Heights	OH	44128	216-292-4460	831-7948
Hegenscheidt-MFD Corp 6255 Center Dr *Web:* www.hegenscheidtmfd.com	Sterling Heights	MI	48312	586-274-4900	274-4916
Littell International Inc 145 N Swift Rd *TF:* 800-548-8355 ■ *Web:* www.littell.com	Addison	IL	60101	630-916-6662	916-6663
Morgan Construction Co Rolling Mill Div 15 Belmont St *Web:* www.morganco.com	Worcester	MA	01605	508-755-6111	755-6140
Ruth Corp 3822 Torrey Pines Blvd *Web:* www.ruthcorp.com	Sarasota	FL	34238	941-924-3995	924-5820
Sendzimir T Inc 269 Brookside Rd *Web:* www.sendzimir.com	Waterbury	CT	06708	203-756-4617	756-4610
Stanat Precision Machine Co 9301 W Bernice St	Schiller Park	IL	60176	847-671-6996	671-0537
T Sendzimir Inc 269 Brookside Rd *Web:* www.sendzimir.com	Waterbury	CT	06708	203-756-4617	756-4610
Waterbury Farrel Technologies Inc 200 1st Gulf Blvd *TF:* 800-387-3834 ■ *Web:* www.waterburyfarrel.com	Brampton	ON	L6W4T5	905-455-0402	455-0422
WHEMCO Inc 5 Hot Metal St *TF:* 800-800-7686 ■ *Web:* www.whemco.com	Pittsburgh	PA	15203	412-390-2700	390-2737

678 ROYALTY TRUSTS

Name / Address	City	State	Zip	Phone	Fax
ARC Energy Trust 440 2nd Ave SW Suite 2100 *TSX:* AET.UN ■ *TF:* 888-272-4900 ■ *Web:* www.arcresources.com	Calgary	AB	T2P5E9	403-503-8600	509-6560
Central Coal & Coke Corp 911 Main St Suite 1710	Kansas City	MO	64105	816-842-2430	471-8676
Cross Timbers Royalty Trust 901 Main St Bank of America Plaza 17th Fl *NYSE:* CRT ■ *TF:* 877-228-5084 ■ *Web:* www.crosstimberstrust.com	Dallas	TX	75202	214-209-2400	209-2431
Dominion Resources Black Warrior Trust 901 Main St Bank of America Plaza 17th Fl *NYSE:* DOM ■ *TF:* 800-365-6548	Dallas	TX	75202	214-209-2400	209-2431
Eastern American Natural Gas Trust 700 Lavaca St 2nd Fl *NYSE:* NGT ■ **Fax Area Code:* 312	Austin	TX	78701	512-479-2562	827-8562*
Freehold Royalty Trust 144 4th Ave SW Suite 400 *TF:* 888-257-1873 ■ *Web:* www.freeholdtrust.com	Calgary	AB	T2P3N4	403-221-0800	221-0888
Great Northern Iron Ore Properties 332 Minnesota St Rm W1290 *NYSE:* GNI	Saint Paul	MN	55101	651-224-2385	224-2387
Harvest Energy Trust 330 5th Ave SW Suite 2100 *NYSE:* HTE ■ *TF:* 866-666-1178 ■ *Web:* www.harvestenergy.ca	Calgary	AB	T2P0L4	403-265-1178	266-3490
Hugoton Royalty Trust 901 Main St Bank of America Plaza 17th Fl *NYSE:* HGT ■ *TF:* 877-228-5083 ■ *Web:* www.hugotontrust.com	Dallas	TX	75202	214-209-2400	209-2431
LL & E Royalty Trust 700 Lavaca 2nd Fl *NYSE:* LRT	Austin	TX	78701	512-479-2562	479-2553

	City	State	Zip	Phone	Fax
Marine Petroleum Trust 901 Main St Bank of America Plaza 17th Fl *NASDAQ: MARPS* ■ *TF:* 800-985-0794	Dallas	TX	75202	214-209-2400	
Mesa Royalty Trust 700 Lavaca St 2nd Fl *NYSE: MTR*	Austin	TX	78701	713-216-6369	216-5476
North European Oil Royalty Trust PO Box 456 *NYSE: NRT* ■ *Web:* www.neort.com	Red Bank	NJ	07701	732-741-4008	741-3140
Pengrowth Energy Trust 222 3rd Ave SW Suite 2100 *NYSE: PGH* ■ *TF:* 800-223-4122 ■ *Web:* www.pengrowth.com	Calgary	AB	T2P0B4	403-233-0224	265-6251
Penn West Energy Trust 425 1st St SW Suite 2200 *TF:* 866-693-2707 ■ *Web:* www.pennwest.com	Calgary	AB	T2P3L8	403-777-2500	777-2699
Permian Basin Royalty Trust 901 Main St Suite 1700 Bank of America Plaza *NYSE: PBT* ■ *TF:* 877-228-5085 ■ *Web:* www.pbt-permianbasintrust.com	Dallas	TX	75202	214-209-2400	209-2431
Sabine Royalty Trust 901 Main St 17th Fl Bank of America Plaza *NYSE: SBR* ■ *TF:* 800-365-6541 ■ *Web:* www.sbr-sabineroyalty.com	Dallas	TX	75202	214-209-2400	209-2431
San Juan Basin Royalty Trust 2525 Ridgmar Blvd Suite 100 *NYSE: SJT* ■ **Fax Area Code:* 817 ■ *Web:* www.sjbrt.com	Fort Worth	TX	76116	866-809-4553	735-0936*
Santa Fe Energy Trust 700 Lavaca 2nd Fl *NYSE: SFF*	Austin	TX	78701	512-479-2562	479-2553
TAQA North Ltd 150 6th Ave SW Suite 5100 *TF:* 877-968-7878 ■ *Web:* www.primewestenergy.com/	Calgary	AB	T2P3Y7	403-724-5000	724-5001
TEL Offshore Trust 700 Lavaca 2nd Fl *NASDAQ: TELOZ*	Austin	TX	78701	512-479-2562	479-2553
Texas Pacific Land Trust 1700 Pacific Ave Suite 1670 *NYSE: TPL*	Dallas	TX	75201	214-969-5530	871-7139
Tidelands Royalty Trust PO Box 830650 *TF:* 800-985-0794	Dallas	TX	75202	214-209-2400	209-2431
Torch Energy Royalty Trust 1221 Lamar Suite 1600 *NYSE: TRU* ■ **Fax Area Code:* 713 ■ *Web:* www.torchroyalty.com	Houston	TX	77010	800-536-7453	655-1866*
Williams Coal Seam Gas Royalty Trust 901 Main St Bank of America Plaza 17th Fl *NYSE: WTU* ■ *TF:* 800-365-6544 ■ *Web:* www.wtu-williamscoalseamgastrust.com	Dallas	TX	75202	214-209-2364	209-2431

679 RUBBER GOODS

	City	State	Zip	Phone	Fax
3M Commercial Care Div 3M Center *TF:* 800-847-3021 ■ *Web:* www.3m.com/us/mfg_industrial/commcare	Saint Paul	MN	55144	800-626-8578	
A & A Mfg Co Inc 2300 S Calhoun Rd *Web:* www.gortite.com	New Berlin	WI	53151	262-786-1500	786-3280
Aero Tec Labs Inc 45 Spear Rd Industrial Park *TF:* 800-526-5330 ■ *Web:* www.atlinc.com	Ramsey	NJ	07446	201-825-1400	825-1962
Alliance Rubber Co 210 Carpenter Dam Rd *TF:* 800-626-5940 ■ *Web:* www.rubberband.com	Hot Springs	AR	71901	501-262-2700	262-8192
Apache Mills Inc 18 Passaic Ave Unit 1 *TF:* 800-456-7791	Fairfield	NJ	07004	973-227-9080	808-8330
Barry Controls 82 South St **Fax:* Sales ■ *TF:* 800-227-7962 ■ *Web:* www.barrycontrols.com	Hopkinton	MA	01748	508-417-7000	417-7223*
Biltrite Corp 51 Sawyer Rd *TF:* 800-877-8775 ■ *Web:* www.biltrite.com	Waltham	MA	02454	781-647-1700	647-4205
BRP Mfg Co 637 N Jackson St *TF:* 800-858-0482 ■ *Web:* www.brpmfg.com	Lima	OH	45801	419-228-4441	222-5010
Carlisle Tire & Wheel Mfg 23 Windham Blvd *TF Sales:* 800-827-1001 ■ *Web:* www.carlisletire.com	Aiken	SC	29805	803-643-2900	643-2919
Creative Urethanes Inc 310 N 21st St PO Box 919 *TF Sales:* 800-343-6591 ■ *Web:* www.creativeurethanes.com	Purcellville	VA	20134	540-338-7139	338-5229
Dodge-Regupol Inc 715 Fountain Ave *TF:* 800-322-1923 ■ *Web:* www.regupol.com	Lancaster	PA	17601	717-295-3400	295-3414
Griswold Rubber Co Inc 1 River St PO Box 638 *TF Cust Svc:* 800-472-8788 ■ *Web:* www.griswoldrubber.com	Moosup	CT	06354	860-564-3321	564-5690
HC Lien Rubber Co Inc 1171 E 63rd St *Web:* www.lienrubber.com	Los Angeles	CA	90001	323-846-8880	846-8886
Itran-Tompkins Rubber Corp 375 Metuchen Rd **Fax:* Sales ■ *Web:* www.itran-tompkinsrubber.com	South Plainfield	NJ	07080	908-754-8100	757-1820*
Kent Elastomer Products Inc 1500 St Claire Ave *TF Cust Svc:* 800-331-4762 ■ *Web:* www.kentelastomer.com	Kent	OH	44240	330-673-1011	673-1351
Koneta Inc 1400 Lunar Dr *TF:* 800-331-0775 ■ *Web:* www.konetalrv.com	Wapakoneta	OH	45895	419-739-4200	739-4247
Kraco Enterprises Inc 505 E Euclid Ave *TF:* 800-678-1910 ■ *Web:* www.kraco.com	Compton	CA	90224	310-639-0666	604-9838
Lien HC Rubber Co Inc 1171 E 63rd St *Web:* www.lienrubber.com	Los Angeles	CA	90001	323-846-8880	846-8886
Lot-Ridge Rubber Co 105 Dinsmore St	Botkins	OH	45306	937-693-4611	693-3853
Ludlow Composites Corp 2100 Commerce Dr *TF:* 800-628-5463 ■ *Web:* www.ludlow-comp.com	Fremont	OH	43420	419-332-5531	332-7776
MSM Industries Inc 802 Swan Dr *TF:* 800-648-6648 ■ *Web:* www.msmind.com	Smyrna	TN	37167	615-355-4355	355-6874
Musson RC Rubber Co Inc 1320 E Archwood Ave *TF Cust Svc:* 800-321-2381 ■ *Web:* www.mussonrubber.com	Akron	OH	44306	330-773-7651	773-3254
National Rubber Technologies Corp 35 Cawthra Ave *TF:* 800-387-8501 ■ *Web:* www.nrtna.com	Toronto	ON	M6N5B3	416-657-1111	656-1231
Pawling Corp 157 Charles Colman Blvd *TF:* 800-377-3820 ■ *Web:* www.pawling.com	Pawling	NY	12564	845-855-1000	855-1937
Philpott Rubber Co 1010 Industrial Pkwy *Web:* www.philpottrubber.com	Brunswick	OH	44212	330-225-3344	225-1999
Plasticoid Co 249 W High St *TF:* 800-398-2806 ■ *Web:* www.plasticoid.com	Elkton	MD	21921	410-398-2800	398-2803
R & K Industrial Products Co 1945 N 7th St *TF Cust Svc:* 800-842-7655 ■ *Web:* www.rkwheels.com	Richmond	CA	94801	510-234-7212	234-1923
RC Musson Rubber Co Inc 1320 E Archwood Ave *TF Cust Svc:* 800-321-2381 ■ *Web:* www.mussonrubber.com	Akron	OH	44306	330-773-7651	773-3254
Rex-Hide Inc 705 S Lyons Ave *TF:* 800-527-8403 ■ *Web:* www.rex-hide.com	Tyler	TX	75702	903-593-7387	592-0122
Seismic Energy Products LP 518 Progress Way *TF:* 800-603-8766 ■ *Web:* www.sepbearings.com	Athens	TX	75751	903-675-8571	675-2161
SMR Technologies Inc 93 Nettie Fenwick Rd *TF:* 800-767-6899 ■ *Web:* www.smrtech.com	Fenwick	WV	26202	304-846-2554	846-2024
Star-Glo Industries LLC 2 Carlton Ave *Web:* www.starglo.com	East Rutherford	NJ	07073	201-939-6162	939-4054
Teknor Apex Co 505 Central Ave *TF:* 800-556-3864 ■ *Web:* www.teknorapex.com	Pawtucket	RI	02861	401-725-8000	725-8095
Tennessee Mat Co Inc 1414 4th Ave S *TF:* 800-264-3030 ■ *Web:* www.wearwell.com	Nashville	TN	37210	615-254-8381	255-4428
Vulcan Corp 30 Garfield Pl Suite 1040 *TF Sales:* 800-447-1146 ■ *Web:* www.vulcorp.com	Cincinnati	OH	45202	513-621-2850	241-8199

680 RUBBER GOODS - MECHANICAL

Mechanical rubber goods are rubber components used in machinery, such as o-rings, sprockets, sleeves, roller covers, etc.

	City	State	Zip	Phone	Fax
AGC Inc 106 Evansville Ave *Web:* www.agcincorporated.com	Meriden	CT	06451	203-235-3361	235-6543
AirBoss of America Corp 16441 Yonge St *TSX: BOS* ■ *TF:* 877-395-8071 ■ *Web:* www.airbossofamerica.com	Newmarket	ON	L3X2G8	905-751-1188	751-1101
Alert Mfg & Supply Co 520 S 18th St *TF:* 800-247-4178 ■ *Web:* www.alertmfgsup.com	West Des Moines	IA	50265	515-223-5843	
Allen-Beck Industries Inc 3305 Kellina Ln Hwy 321 N	Granite Falls	NC	28630	828-328-1587	396-5545
Allied-Baltic Rubber Inc 310 Railroad Ave NE	Strasburg	OH	44680	330-878-7800	878-7850
American National Rubber Co Main & High St **Fax:* Sales ■ *TF Cust Svc:* 800-624-3410 ■ *Web:* www.anr-co.com	Ceredo	WV	25507	304-453-1311	453-2347*
American Roller Co 1440 13th Ave *Web:* www.americanroller.com	Union Grove	WI	53182	262-878-2445	878-1932
Ames Rubber Corp 19 Ames Blvd *TF:* 800-697-9101 ■ *Web:* www.amesrubber.com	Hamburg	NJ	07419	973-827-9101	827-8893
Applied Tech Products 565 Swedesford Rd Suite 315 *Web:* www.appliedtechproducts.com	Wayne	PA	19087	610-688-2200	688-1534
Armada Rubber Mfg Co 24586 Armada Ridge Rd PO Box 579 *TF:* 800-842-8311 ■ *Web:* www.armadarubber.com	Armada	MI	48005	586-784-9135	784-5023
Ashtabula Rubber Co 2751 West Ave *Web:* www.ashtabularubber.com	Ashtabula	OH	44004	440-992-2195	992-7829
Atlantic India Rubber Co 1437 Kentucky Rt 1428 *TF:* 800-476-6638 ■ *Web:* www.atlanticindia.com	Hager Hills	KY	41222	606-789-9115	789-9098
Avon Rubber & Plastics Inc 603 W 7th St	Cadillac	MI	49601	231-775-6571	775-8731
Boyd Corp 600 S McClure Rd *TF:* 800-554-0200 ■ *Web:* www.boydcorp.com	Modesto	CA	95357	209-236-1111	236-1154
Buckhorn Rubber Products Inc 5151 Industrial Dr *Web:* www.buckhornrubber.com	Hannibal	MO	63401	573-221-8933	221-7144
Cardinal Rubber Co 939 Wooster Rd N **Fax:* Sales	Barberton	OH	44203	330-745-2191	745-2194*
Chardon Rubber Co 373 Washington St *TF:* 800-322-0193 ■ *Web:* www.chardonrubber.com	Chardon	OH	44024	440-285-2161	286-8422
Chemprene Inc 483 Fishkill Ave *TF:* 800-431-9981 ■ *Web:* www.chemprene.com	Beacon	NY	12508	845-831-2800	831-4639
Chicago Manifold Products Co 171 E Marquardt Dr *TF Sales:* 800-323-7735 ■ *Web:* www.chicagomanifold.com	Wheeling	IL	60090	847-459-6000	459-6277
Colonial Diversified Polymer Products LLC 2055 Forrest St Ext *TF:* 800-303-3606 ■ *Web:* cdpp.colonialdpp.com	Dyersburg	TN	38024	731-287-3636	287-3691
Connor Corp 2701 Dwenger Ave *Web:* www.connorcorp.com	Fort Wayne	IN	46803	260-424-1601	422-7202
Cupples Rubber Industrial Products 903 W 13th St *Web:* www.cupplesrubber.cc	Caruthersville	MO	63830	573-333-1585	333-1585
Custom Fabricated Products LLC 4854 O'Hear Ave	North Charleston	SC	29405	843-744-4200	744-6900
Da/Pro Rubber Inc 601 N Poplar Ave *Web:* www.daprorubber.com	Broken Arrow	OK	74012	918-258-9386	258-3286
Dawson Mfg Co 300 Industrial Park Blvd SE	Dawson	GA	39842	229-995-2191	995-3715
Derby Cellular Products Inc 150 Roosevelt Dr *Web:* www.derbycellularproducts.com	Derby	CT	06418	203-735-4661	735-2984
Fabreeka International Inc 1023 Turnpike St *TF Cust Svc:* 800-322-7352 ■ *Web:* www.fabreeka.com	Stoughton	MA	02072	781-341-3655	341-3983
Finzer Roller Co 129 Rawls Rd *TF:* 888-486-1900 ■ *Web:* www.finzerroller.com	Des Plaines	IL	60018	847-390-6200	390-6201
Flexan Corp 6626 W Dakin St *Web:* www.flexan.com	Chicago	IL	60634	773-685-6446	685-6630
Flexible Products Co 2600 Auburn Ct *Web:* www.flexible-products.com	Auburn Hills	MI	48326	248-852-5500	852-8620
Griffith Rubber Mills 2625 NW Industrial St *TF:* 800-321-9677	Portland	OR	97210	503-226-6971	226-6976
Groendyk Mfg Co Inc 19318 Main St *TF:* 800-879-4395 ■ *Web:* www.groendyk.com	Buchanan	VA	24066	540-254-1010	254-2400
Hiawatha Rubber Co 1700 67th Ave N *TF:* 800-728-3845 ■ *Web:* www.hiawatharubber.com	Minneapolis	MN	55430	763-566-0900	566-9537
Holz Rubber Co Inc 1129 S Sacramento St *TF:* 800-285-1600 ■ *Web:* www.holzrubber.com	Lodi	CA	95240	209-368-7171	368-3246
IER Fujikura 8271 Bavaria Rd *Web:* www.ierfujikura.com	Macedonia	OH	44056	330-425-7121	425-7596
IMCO Inc 1819 W Park Dr PO Box 444 *Web:* www.imcorubber.com	Huntington	IN	46750	260-356-4810	356-7827
Jamak Fabrication Inc 1401 N Bowie Dr *TF:* 800-395-2625 ■ *Web:* www.jamak.com	Weatherford	TX	76086	817-594-8771	594-8324
Jasper Rubber Products Inc 1010 1st Ave W *TF:* 800-457-7457 ■ *Web:* www.jasperrubber.com	Jasper	IN	47546	812-482-3242	481-2702
Johnson Brothers Rubber Inc 42 W Buckeye St	West Salem	OH	44287	419-853-4122	853-4062
Johnson Rubber Co 16025 Johnson St PO Box 67 *TF:* 800-362-1951 ■ *Web:* www.johnsonrubber.com	Middlefield	OH	44062	440-632-1611	
Karman Rubber Co 2331 Copley Rd *Web:* www.karman.com	Akron	OH	44320	330-864-2161	864-2124
Kirkhill Mfg Co 12023 Woodruff Ave *Web:* www.rubbersales.com	Downey	CA	90241	562-803-1117	803-3117
Kirkhill-TA Co 300 E Cypress St *Web:* www.kirkhill-ta.com	Brea	CA	92821	714-529-4901	529-6775
Lauren Mfg 2228 Reiser Ave SE *TF:* 800-683-0676 ■ *Web:* www.lauren.com	New Philadelphia	OH	44663	330-339-3373	339-1515
Lavelle Industries Inc 665 McHenry St *TF:* 800-528-3553 ■ *Web:* www.lavelle.com	Burlington	WI	53105	262-763-2434	763-5607
Linatex Corp of America 1550 Airport Rd *Web:* www.linatex.com	Gallatin	TN	37066	615-230-2100	230-2101
Longwood Elastomers Inc 706 Green Valley Rd Suite 212 *TF:* 800-374-2837 ■ *Web:* www.longwood-elastomers.de	Greensboro	NC	27408	336-272-3710	272-5619
Longwood Industries Inc 325 Columbia Tpke *Web:* www.longwood-industries.de	Florham Park	NJ	07932	973-514-2010	822-3939
Lord Corp 111 Lord Dr *TF:* 800-524-2885 ■ *Web:* www.lord.com	Cary	NC	27511	919-468-5979	
Mantaline Corp 4754 E High St *TF:* 800-321-0948 ■ *Web:* www.mantaline.com	Mantua	OH	44255	330-274-2264	274-8850
Mikron Rubber Products Corp 2600 Homestead Pl *TF:* 800-361-1915 ■ *Web:* www.mikronproducts.com	Rancho Dominguez	CA	90220	310-868-5200	868-5209
Minnesota Rubber 1100 Xenium Ln N **Fax:* Sales ■ *TF:* 800-927-1422 ■ *Web:* www.mnrubber.com/mnrubber	Plymouth	MN	55441	952-927-1400	927-1470*
Minor Rubber Co Inc 49 Ackerman St *TF:* 800-433-6886 ■ *Web:* www.minorrubber.com	Bloomfield	NJ	07003	973-338-6800	893-1399
MOCAP Inc 13100 Manchester Rd *TF:* 800-633-6775 ■ *Web:* www.mocap.com	Saint Louis	MO	63131	314-543-4000	543-4111
Molded Rubber & Plastic Corp 13161 W Glendale Ave *TF:* 888-781-7122 ■ *Web:* www.mrpcorp.com	Butler	WI	53007	262-781-7122	781-5353
Neff-Perkins Co 2950 Industrial Park Dr *Web:* www.neffp.com	Austinburg	OH	44010	440-275-1924	275-3015
Paulstra CRC Corp 460 Fuller Ave NE *Web:* www.paulstracrc.com	Grand Rapids	MI	49503	616-459-4541	459-7053

	City	State	Zip	Phone	Fax
Precision Assoc Inc 740 Washington Ave N *TF Cust Svc:* 800-394-6590 ■ *Web:* www.precisionassoc.com	Minneapolis	MN	55401	612-333-7464	342-2417
Precix Inc 744 Bellville Ave *Web:* www.precixinc.com	New Bedford	MA	02745	508-998-4000	998-4100
Prince Rubber & Plastics Co Inc 137 Arthur St *Web:* www.princerp.com	Buffalo	NY	14207	716-877-7400	877-0743
Quality Synthetic Rubber Inc 1700 Highland Rd *Web:* www.qsr-inc.com	Twinsburg	OH	44087	330-425-8472	425-7976
RotaDyne Corp 8140 Cass Ave *Web:* www.rotadyne.com	Darien	IL	60561	630-769-9700	769-9255
Rubber Engineering 3459 S 700 West PO Box 26188 *TF Cust Svc:* 800-453-6403 ■ *Web:* www.rubeng.com	Salt Lake City	UT	84126	801-530-7887	261-5587
Saint-Gobain Performance Plastics Corp 150 Dey Rd *Web:* www.plastics.saint-gobain.com	Wayne	NJ	07470	973-696-4700	696-4056
SETI Acme Machell Co Inc 2000 Airport Rd	Waukesha	WI	53188	262-521-2870	521-2894
SETI Mold-Ex Co 8052 Armstrong Rd *Web:* www.seti-group.com	Milton	FL	32583	850-626-7211	626-7322
Sperry & Rice Mfg Co LLC 9146 US Hwy 52 *TF:* 800-541-9277 ■ *Web:* www.sperryrubber.com	Brookville	IN	47012	765-647-4141	647-3302
Tepro Inc 590 Baxter Ln	Winchester	TN	37398	931-967-5189	967-3140
Thermodyn Corp 3550 Silica Rd *TF:* 800-654-6518 ■ *Web:* www.thermodyn.com	Sylvania	OH	43560	419-841-7782	841-3139
Triangle Rubber Co Inc 1924 Elkhart Rd *Web:* www.trianglerubberco.com	Goshen	IN	46526	574-533-3118	534-0416
Trostel Ltd 901 Maxwell St *Web:* www.trostel.com	Lake Geneva	WI	53147	262-248-4481	249-8100
Universal Polymer & Rubber Ltd 15730 S Madison Rd *TF:* 800-782-2375 ■ *Web:* www.universalpolymer.com	Middlefield	OH	44062	440-632-1691	632-5761
Vail Rubber Works Inc 521 Langley Ave *Web:* www.vailrubber.com	Saint Joseph	MI	49085	269-983-1595	983-0155
Vernay Laboratories Inc 120 E South College St **Fax:* Sales ■ *TF:* 800-837-6291 ■ *Web:* www.vernay.com	Yellow Springs	OH	45387	937-767-7261	767-7913*
Wabtec Rubber Products 269 Donohue Rd *TF:* 888-867-3539 ■ *Web:* www.wabtec.com/subsidiaries	Greensburg	PA	15601	724-838-1317	832-5630
West American Rubber Co LLC 1413 Braden Ct *Web:* www.westamericanrubber.com	Orange	CA	92868	714-532-3355	532-2238
YUSA Corp 151 Jamison Rd SW *TF:* 800-395-0335	Washington Court House	OH	43160	740-335-0335	335-0330

681 SAFETY EQUIPMENT - MFR

SEE ALSO Medical Supplies - Mfr p. 1955; Personal Protective Equipment & Clothing p. 2105

	City	State	Zip	Phone	Fax
3M Safety Security & Protection Services Div 3M Center *TF:* 800-364-3577 ■ *Web:* www.3m.com	Saint Paul	MN	55144	651-733-1110	
ACR Electronics Inc 5757 Ravenswood Rd *TF:* 800-432-0227 ■ *Web:* www.acrelectronics.com	Fort Lauderdale	FL	33312	954-981-3333	983-5087
Adams Elevator Equipment Co 6310 W Howard St *TF:* 800-323-0796 ■ *Web:* www.adamselevator.com	Niles	IL	60714	847-581-2900	965-9114
Aerial Machine & Tool Corp 4298 Jeb Stuart Hwy *Web:* www.aerialmachineandtool.com	Vesta	VA	24177	276-952-2006	952-2231
Air Cruisers Co PO Box 180 *Web:* www.aircruisers.com	Belmar	NJ	07719	732-681-3527	681-9163
ALP Industries Inc 1229 W Lincoln Hwy *TF:* 800-220-2515 ■ *Web:* www.alpind.com	Coatesville	PA	19320	610-384-1300	384-7300
Amerex Corp 7595 Gadsden Hwy PO Box 81 *Web:* www.amerex-fire.com	Trussville	AL	35173	205-655-3271	655-3279
AmSafe Inc 1043 N 47th Ave *Web:* www.amsafe.com	Phoenix	AZ	85043	602-850-2850	850-2812
Ancra International LLC 4880 W Rosecrans Ave *TF:* 800-973-5091 ■ *Web:* www.ancra-llc.com	Hawthorne	CA	90250	310-973-5000	973-1138
Aristotle Corp 96 Cummings Point Rd *NASDAQ: ARTL* ■ *TF:* 800-558-9595 ■ *Web:* www.aristotlecorp.net	Stamford	CT	06902	203-358-8000	358-0179
Autoliv Inc 3350 Airport Rd *NYSE: ALV* ■ *Web:* www.autoliv.com	Ogden	UT	84405	801-625-9200	625-8236
Badger Fire Protection 4251 Seminole Tr **Fax Area Code:* 800 ■ *TF:* 800-446-3857 ■ *Web:* www.badgerfire.com	Charlottesville	VA	22911	434-973-4361	248-7809*
Bradley Corp W 142 N 9101 Fountain Blvd *TF:* 800-272-3539 ■ *Web:* www.bradleycorp.com	Menomonee Falls	WI	53051	262-251-6000	251-5817
Buckeye Fire Equipment Co 110 Kings Rd *TF:* 800-438-1028 ■ *Web:* www.buckeyef.com	Kings Mountain	NC	28086	704-739-7415	739-7418
Carsonite International Corp 605 Bob Gifford Blvd *TF:* 800-648-7918 ■ *Web:* www.carsonite.com	Early Branch	SC	29916	803-943-9115	943-3375
Central Research Laboratories 3965 Pepin Ave *Web:* www.centres.com	Red Wing	MN	55066	651-388-3565	388-1232
Conax Florida Corp 2801 75th St N *Web:* www.conaxfl.com	Saint Petersburg	FL	33710	727-345-8000	345-4217
DBI/SALA & Protecta 3833 Sala Way *TF:* 800-328-6146 ■ *Web:* www.dbisala.com	Red Wing	MN	55066	651-388-8282	388-5065
Delta Scientific Corp 40355 Delta Ln *Web:* www.deltascientific.com	Palmdale	CA	93551	661-575-1100	575-1109
Encon Safety Products Co 6825 W Sam Houston Pkwy N *TF:* 800-283-6266 ■ *Web:* www.enconsafety.com	Houston	TX	77041	713-466-1449	466-1819
Energy Absorption Systems Inc 35 E Wacker Dr Suite 1100 *Web:* www.energyabsorption.com	Chicago	IL	60601	312-467-6750	467-1356
First Technology Safety Systems 47460 Galleon Dr *Web:* www.ftss.com	Plymouth	MI	48170	734-451-7878	451-9549
Flag Fire Equipment Ltd 1 Stanton St **Fax Area Code:* 800 ■ *Web:* www.flagfire.com	Marinette	WI	54143	715-732-3465	265-0804*
Gemtor Inc 1 Johnson Ave *TF:* 800-405-9048 ■ *Web:* www.gemtor.com	Matawan	NJ	07747	732-583-6200	290-9391
Hawkins Traffic Safety Supply 1255 E Shore Hwy *TF:* 800-772-3995	Berkeley	CA	94710	510-525-4040	525-2861
Herbert S Hiller Corp 401 Commerce Point *TF:* 800-833-5211 ■ *Web:* www.hillercompanies.com/herbert_hiller.html	Harahan	LA	70123	504-736-0008	736-0030
Hiller Herbert S Corp 401 Commerce Point *TF:* 800-833-5211 ■ *Web:* www.hillercompanies.com/herbert_hiller.html	Harahan	LA	70123	504-736-0008	736-0030
Hoover Industries Inc 7260 NW 68th St *Web:* www.hooverindustries.com	Miami	FL	33166	305-888-9791	887-4632
ITW Shippers Products 1203 N Main St *TF:* 800-933-7731 ■ *Web:* www.itwshippers.com	Mount Pleasant	TN	38474	931-379-7731	379-7735
Key Safety Systems Inc 7000 Nineteen Mile Rd *Web:* www.keysafetyinc.com	Sterling Heights	MI	48314	586-726-3800	726-4150
Kidde Fire Fighting 180 Sheree Blvd Suite 390 *Web:* www.kidde-fire.com	Exton	PA	19341	610-363-1400	524-9073
Kidde Safety 1016 Corporate Park Dr *TF:* 800-654-9677 ■ *Web:* www.kiddeus.com	Mebane	NC	27302	919-563-5911	563-3954
Kinedyne Inc 151 Industrial Pkwy *TF:* 800-848-6057 ■ *Web:* www.kinedyne.com	North Branch	NJ	08876	908-231-1800	231-1379
Labock Technologies Inc 1600 N Park Dr *Web:* www.labock.com	Weston	FL	33326	954-335-3535	335-3525
Larsen's Mfg Co 7421 Commerce Ln NE *TF:* 800-527-7367 ■ *Web:* www.larsensmfg.com	Minneapolis	MN	55432	763-571-1181	571-6900
Mercedes Textiles Ltd 5838 Cypihot St *Web:* www.mercedestextiles.com	Ville Saint Laurent	QC	H4S1Y5	514-335-4337	335-9633
Niedner Ltd 675 Merrill St *TF:* 800-567-2703 ■ *Web:* www.wildfire-equipment.com	Coaticook	QC	J1A2S2	819-849-2751	849-7539
North American Fire Hose 910 E Noble Way *Web:* www.northamericanfirehose.com	Santa Maria	CA	93454	805-922-7076	922-0086
Ocenco Inc 10225 82nd Ave *TF:* 800-932-2293 ■ *Web:* www.ocenco.com	Pleasant Prairie	WI	53158	262-947-9000	947-9020
Peck & Hale LLC 180 Division Ave *Web:* www.peckhale.com	West Sayville	NY	11796	631-589-2510	589-2925
Peerless Chain Co 1416 E Sanborn St *TF:* 800-533-8056 ■ *Web:* www.peerlesschain.com	Winona	MN	55987	507-457-9100	457-9252
Plastic Safety Systems Inc 2444 Baldwin Rd *TF:* 800-662-6338 ■ *Web:* www.plasticsafety.com	Cleveland	OH	44104	216-231-8590	231-2702
Potter-Roemer 17451 Hurley St *TF:* 800-366-3473 ■ *Web:* www.potterroemer.com	City of Industry	CA	91744	626-855-4890	937-4777
Quixote Corp 35 E Wacker Dr Suite 1100 *NASDAQ: QUIX* ■ *TF:* 888-323-6374 ■ *Web:* www.quixotecorp.com	Chicago	IL	60601	312-467-6755	467-1356
Reflexite North America 315 South St *TF:* 800-654-7570 ■ *Web:* www.reflexite.com	New Britain	CT	06051	860-223-9297	832-9267
Rite-Hite Corp 8900 N Arbon Dr *TF:* 800-456-0600 ■ *Web:* www.ritehite.com	Milwaukee	WI	53224	414-355-2600	355-9248
Rostra Precision Controls Inc 2519 Dana Dr *TF Cust Svc:* 800-782-3379 ■ *Web:* www.rostra.com	Laurinburg	NC	28352	910-276-4853	276-1354
Safety Components International Inc 41 Stevens St *Web:* www.safetycomponents.com	Greenville	SC	29605	864-240-2600	240-2728
Security Chain Co 16131 SE Harvard St PO Box 949 **Fax Area Code:* 800 ■ *TF:* 800-547-6806 ■ *Web:* www.scc-chain.com	Clackamas	OR	97015	503-656-5400	468-4430*
Simulaids 16 Simulaids Dr *Web:* www.simulaids.com	Saugerties	NY	12477	845-679-2475	679-8996
Survival Systems International Inc 931 Industry Rd PO Box 1567 *Web:* www.survivalsystemsint.net	Kenner	LA	70062	504-469-4545	466-1884
Takata Inc 2500 Takata Dr *Web:* www.takata.com	Auburn Hills	MI	48326	248-373-8040	377-2897
Tread Corp PO Box 13207 *TF:* 800-900-6881 ■ *Web:* www.treadcorp.com	Roanoke	VA	24032	540-982-6881	344-7536

682 SAFETY EQUIPMENT - WHOL

	City	State	Zip	Phone	Fax
Allstar Fire Equipment Inc 12328 Lower Azusa Rd *TF:* 800-425-5787 ■ *Web:* www.allstarfire.com	Arcadia	CA	91006	626-652-0900	652-0920
Alltype Fire Protection Co 9495 Page Ave PO Box 32432 *TF:* 800-369-7101 ■ *Web:* www.alltypefire.com	Saint Louis	MO	63132	314-426-7100	426-7782
American Cleanroom Supply LLC 1042-B El Camino Real Suite 414 **Fax Area Code:* 760 ■ *Web:* www.american-cleanroom.com	Encinitas	CA	92024	888-901-3220	752-3238*
Arbill Glove & Safety Products 10450 Drummond Rd **Fax Area Code:* 800 ■ *TF:* 800-523-5367 ■ *Web:* www.arbill.com	Philadelphia	PA	19154	215-632-2000	426-5808*
Brooks Equipment Co Inc 10926 Davod Tau;pr Dr Siote 3- *TF:* 800-826-3473 ■ *Web:* www.brooksequipment.com	Charlotte	NC	28269	704-596-9438	596-1963
Broward Fire Equipment & Service Inc 101 SW 6th St *TF:* 800-866-3473 ■ *Web:* www.browardfire.com	Fort Lauderdale	FL	33301	954-467-6625	467-6640
Calolympic Glove & Safety Co Inc 1720 Delilah St *TF:* 800-421-6630 ■ *Web:* www.caloly-safety.com	Corona	CA	92879	951-340-2229	340-3337
Choctaw-Kaul Distribution Co 3540 Vinewood Ave *Web:* www.choctawkaul.com	Detroit	MI	48208	313-894-9494	894-7977
Continental Safety Equipment Inc 899 Apollo Rd *TF:* 800-844-7003 ■ *Web:* www.csesafety.com	Eagan	MN	55121	651-454-7233	454-3217
Curtis LN & Sons 1800 Peralta St *TF:* 800-443-3556 ■ *Web:* www.lncurtis.com	Oakland	CA	94607	510-839-5111	839-5325
Dunn Safety Products Inc 37 S Sangamon St *TF:* 800-451-3866	Chicago	IL	60607	312-666-5800	666-5090
Empire Safety & Supply Inc 10624 Industrial Ave **Fax Area Code:* 888 ■ *TF:* 800-376-6337 ■ *Web:* www.empiresafety.com	Roseville	CA	75678	916-781-3003	882-9060*
Fire Equipment Inc 88 Hicks Ave *Web:* www.firefire.com	Medford	MA	02155	781-391-8050	391-8835
Fire Fighters Equipment Co 5638 Commonwealth Ave *TF:* 800-488-8542 ■ *Web:* www.firefightersusa.com	Jacksonville	FL	32232	904-388-8542	384-2610
Fire Protection Service Inc 8050 Harrisburg Blvd	Houston	TX	77012	713-924-9600	923-6272
Industrial Safety & Supply Co Inc 176 Newington Rd *TF:* 800-243-2316 ■ *Web:* www.industrialsafety.com	West Hartford	CT	06110	860-233-9881	236-7603
International Fire Equipment Corp 500 Telser Rd *Web:* www.intlfire.com	Lake Zurich	IL	60047	847-438-2343	438-1869
La Grand Industrial Supply Co PO Box 1959	Portland	OR	97207	503-224-5800	224-0639
Lab Safety Supply Inc PO Box 1368 **Fax Area Code:* 800 ■ *TF:* 800-356-0783 ■ *Web:* www.labsafety.com	Janesville	WI	53547	608-754-2345	543-9910*
LaFrance Equipment Corp 516 Erie St *TF:* 800-873-8808 ■ *Web:* www.lafrance-equipment.com	Elmira	NY	14904	607-733-5511	733-0482
LN Curtis & Sons 1800 Peralta St *TF:* 800-443-3556 ■ *Web:* www.lncurtis.com	Oakland	CA	94607	510-839-5111	839-5325
McLean International Marketing Inc 5300 Elmhurst Rd PO Box 535 *Web:* www.mcleansafety.com	Mequon	WI	53092	262-242-0958	242-6644
Mid-Continent Safety LLC 2909 S Spruce St *TF:* 800-835-7233 ■ *Web:* www.midsafe.com	Wichita	KS	67216	316-522-0900	522-0956
Minnesota Conway 314 W 86th St Suite 101 *TF:* 800-223-2587 ■ *Web:* www.mnconway.com	Bloomington	MN	55420	952-345-3473	345-2499
Nardini Fire Equipment Co Inc 405 County Rd 'E' W *TF:* 888-627-3464 ■ *Web:* www.nardinifire.com	Saint Paul	MN	55126	651-483-6631	483-6945
Orr Safety Corp 11601 Interchange Dr *TF:* 800-726-6789 ■ *Web:* www.orrsafety.com	Louisville	KY	40229	502-774-5791	776-8030
PK Safety Supply 2005 Clement Ave Bldg 9 *TF:* 800-829-9580 ■ *Web:* www.pksafety.com	Alameda	CA	94501	510-337-8880	337-8890
Reliable Fire Equipment Co 12845 S Cicero Ave *Web:* www.reliablefire.com	Alsip	IL	60803	708-597-4600	389-1150
Saf-T-Gard International Inc 205 Huehl Rd *TF:* 800-548-4273 ■ *Web:* www.saftgard.com	Northbrook	IL	60062	847-291-1600	291-1610
Safety Products Inc 3517 Craftsman Blvd **Fax Area Code:* 800 ■ *TF:* 800-248-6860 ■ *Web:* www.spisafety.com	Lakeland	FL	33803	863-665-3601	330-0395*
Safety Solutions Inc 6161 Shamrock Ct PO Box 8100 *TF:* 800-232-7463 ■ *Web:* www.safetysolutions.com	Dublin	OH	43016	614-799-9900	799-9901
Safety Supply South Inc 100 Centrum Dr *TF:* 800-522-8344 ■ *Web:* www.safetysupplysouth.com	Irmo	SC	29063	803-732-1500	732-3696
Safety Today 2425 Speigel Dr Suite A *TF:* 800-837-5900 ■ *Web:* www.safetytoday.com	Groveport	OH	43125	614-409-7200	409-7201
Safeware Inc 3200 Hubbard Rd *TF:* 800-331-6707 ■ *Web:* www.safewareinc.com	Landover	MD	20785	301-683-1234	683-1200
Sanderson Safety Supply Co 1101 SE 3rd Ave *TF:* 800-547-0927 ■ *Web:* www.sandersonsafety.com	Portland	OR	97214	503-238-5700	238-6443

	City	State	Zip	Phone	Fax
Skaggs Cos 3828 S Main St *TF:* 800-879-1787 ■ *Web:* www.skaggscompanies.com	Murray	UT	84115	801-261-4400	261-1580
Stauffer Glove & Safety 361 E 6th St *Web:* www.stauffersafety.com	Red Hill	PA	18076	215-679-4446	679-5053
Sun Devil Fire Equipment Inc 2211 S 3rd Dr. **Fax Area Code:* 602 ■ *TF:* 800-536-3845 ■ *Web:* www.sundevilfire.com	Phoenix	AZ	85003	623-245-0636	495-9291*
United Fire Equipment Co 335 N 4th Ave *TF:* 800-362-0150 ■ *Web:* www.unitedfire.net/uf/	Tucson	AZ	85705	520-622-3639	882-3991
Vallen Corp 521 N Sam Houston Pkwy E Suite 300 *TF:* 800-372-3389 ■ *Web:* www.vallen.com	Houston	TX	77060	281-500-4500	500-4592
Vanguard Distributors Inc 107 NE Lathrop Ave *Web:* www.vanguarddistributors.com	Savannah	GA	31415	912-236-1766	238-3072
Wayest Safety Inc 3750 N I-44 Service Rd *TF:* 800-256-1003 ■ *Web:* www.wayest.com	Oklahoma City	OK	73112	405-942-7101	942-5289
Wenaas AGS Inc 202 E Larkspur St *TF:* 888-576-2668 ■ *Web:* www.wenaasusa.com	Victoria	TX	77904	361-576-2668	576-2674
Wise El Santo Co Inc 11000 Linpage Pl *TF:* 800-727-8541 ■ *Web:* www.wiseelsanto.com	Saint Louis	MO	63132	314-428-3100	428-7017
Zink Safety Equipment 15101 W 110th St *TF:* 800-255-1101 ■ *Web:* www.zinksafety.com	Lenexa	KS	66219	913-492-9444	492-4327

683 SALT

SEE ALSO Food Products - Mfr - Spices, Seasonings, Herbs p. 1657

Companies listed here produce salt that may be used for a variety of purposes, including as a food ingredient or for deicing, water conditioning, or other chemical or industrial applications.

	City	State	Zip	Phone	Fax
Cargill Inc North America 15407 McGinty Rd *TF:* 800-227-4455	Wayzata	MN	55391	952-742-7575	
Cargill Salt Inc 400 S Hwy 169 Suite 600 **Fax:* Sales ■ *TF:* 888-385-7258 ■ *Web:* www.cargillsalt.com	Saint Louis Park	MN	55426	952-984-8280	984-8715*
Compass Minerals International 9900 W 109th St Suite 600 *NYSE: CMP* ■ *TF Cust Svc:* 800-253-7934 ■ *Web:* www.compassminerals.com	Overland Park	KS	66210	913-344-9200	338-7919
Morton Salt Group PO Box 1496 **Fax:* Cust Svc ■ *TF:* 800-551-9086 ■ *Web:* www.mortonsalt.com	New Iberia	LA	70562	337-867-4231	867-4211*
North American Salt Co 8300 College Blvd **Fax:* Mktg ■ *Web:* www.nasalt.com	Overland Park	KS	66210	913-344-9100	345-0309*
United Salt Corp 4800 San Felipe St *TF:* 800-554-8658 ■ *Web:* www.unitedsalt.com	Houston	TX	77056	713-877-2600	877-2604
US Salt Holdings LLC 10955 Lowell Suite 600 *Web:* www.ussaltllc.com	Overland Park	KS	66210	913-253-2200	253-2201

684 SATELLITE COMMUNICATIONS SERVICES

SEE ALSO Cable & Other Pay Television Services p. 1404; Internet Service Providers (ISPs) p. 1872; Telecommunications Services p. 2341

	City	State	Zip	Phone	Fax
ARINC Inc 2551 Riva Rd *TF:* 800-492-2182 ■ *Web:* www.arinc.com	Annapolis	MD	21401	410-266-4000	266-4040
AssureSat Inc 2601 Ocean Pk Blvd Suite 316 *Web:* www.assuresat.com	Santa Monica	CA	90405	310-452-8300	399-7303
Eagle Broadband Inc 101 Courageous Dr. *AMEX: EAG* ■ *TF:* 800-628-3910 ■ *Web:* www.eaglebroadband.com	League City	TX	77573	281-538-6000	334-5302
Ellipso Inc 4410 Massachusetts Ave NW Suite 385 *Web:* www.ellipso.com	Washington	DC	20016	202-466-4488	466-4493
Globalstar LP 461 S Milpitas Blvd Bldg 5 *TF:* 877-245-6225 ■ *Web:* www.globalstar.com	Milpitas	CA	95035	408-933-4000	933-4100
Intelsat Ltd 3400 International Dr NW *Web:* www.intelsat.com	Washington	DC	20008	202-944-6800	944-7898
International Satellite Services Inc 1004 Collier Ctr Way Suite 205 *TF:* 888-511-3403 ■ *Web:* www.issi-us.net	Naples	FL	34110	239-598-2241	598-9343
Iridium Satellite LLC 6701 Democracy Blvd *Web:* www.iridium.com	Bethesda	MD	20817	301-571-6200	571-6250
Level 3 Communications Inc 1 Technology Ctr *TF:* 800-364-0807 ■ *Web:* www.level3.com	Tulsa	OK	74103	918-547-5760	547-1114
Loral Skynet Ltd 500 Hills Dr *Web:* www.loralskynet.com	Bedminster	NJ	07921	908-470-2300	470-2452
Microspace Communications Corp 3100 Highwoods Blvd Suite 120 *Web:* www.microspace.com	Raleigh	NC	27604	919-850-4500	850-4518
Motient Corp 300 Knightsbridge Pkwy **Fax:* Mail Rm ■ *TF:* 800-992-7347 ■ *Web:* www.motient.com	Lincolnshire	IL	60069	847-478-4200	478-4343*
MTN/ATC Teleports 3044 N Commerce Pkwy *TF:* 877-464-4686 ■ *Web:* www.mtnsat.com	Miramar	FL	33025	954-538-4000	431-4077
ORBCOMM LLC 21700 Atlantic Blvd *TF:* 800-672-2666 ■ *Web:* www.orbcomm.com	Dulles	VA	20166	703-433-6300	433-6400
PanAmSat Corp 20 Westport Rd *NYSE: PA* ■ *TF:* 800-726-2672 ■ *Web:* www.panamsat.com	Wilton	CT	06897	203-210-8000	210-8001
SES Americom Inc 4 Research Way **Fax:* Mktg ■ *TF Sales:* 800-273-0329 ■ *Web:* www.ses-americom.com	Princeton	NJ	08540	609-987-4000	987-4312*
SpaceCom Systems Inc 1950 E 71st St **Fax Area Code:* 918 ■ *TF:* 800-950-6690 ■ *Web:* www.spacecom.com	Tulsa	OK	74136	800-950-6690	499-6060*
SpaceNet Inc 1750 Old Meadow Rd *Web:* www.spacenet.com	McLean	VA	22102	703-848-1000	848-1010
StarBand Communciations Inc 1760 Old Meadow Rd *TF Cust Svc:* 800-478-2722 ■ *Web:* www.starband.net	McLean	VA	22102	703-287-3000	287-3010
Stratos Global Corp 6901 Rockledge Dr Suite 900 *TSX: SGB* ■ *Web:* www.stratosglobal.com	Bethesda	MD	20817	301-214-8800	214-8801
Telesat 1601 Telesat Ct *Web:* www.telesat.ca	Gloucester	ON	K1B5P4	613-748-0123	748-8712
ViaSat Inc 6155 El Camino Real *NASDAQ: VSAT* ■ *Web:* www.viasat.com	Carlsbad	CA	92009	760-476-2200	929-3941
XM Satellite Radio Holdings Inc 1500 Eckington Pl NE *NASDAQ: XMSR* ■ *TF:* 877-967-2346 ■ *Web:* www.xmradio.com	Washington	DC	20002	202-380-4000	380-4500

685 SAW BLADES & HANDSAWS

SEE ALSO Tools - Hand & Edge p. 2371

	City	State	Zip	Phone	Fax
Atlanta Sharptech 1594 Evans Dr SW *TF:* 800-241-5296 ■ *Web:* www.sharptech.com	Atlanta	GA	30310	404-752-6000	752-9034
Bairnco Corp 300 Primera Blvd Suite 432 *NYSE: BZ* ■ *Web:* www.bairnco.com	Lake Mary	FL	32746	407-875-2222	875-3398
Blount Outdoor Products Group 4909 SE International Way *TF:* 800-223-5168 ■ *Web:* www.blount.com/Cutsytm.html	Portland	OR	97222	503-653-8881	653-4201
California Saw & Knife Works 721 Brannan St *Web:* www.calsaw.com	San Francisco	CA	94103	415-861-0644	861-0406
Carlton Co 3901 SE Naef Rd	Milwaukie	OR	97267	503-659-8911	659-8616
Contour Saws Inc 1217 Thacker St *TF Sales:* 800-458-9034	Des Plaines	IL	60016	847-824-1146	803-9467
Diamond Saw Works Inc 12290 Olean Rd *TF:* 800-828-1180 ■ *Web:* www.diamondsaw.com	Chaffee	NY	14030	716-496-7417	496-8969
Disston Precision Inc 6795 State Rd *TF Cust Svc:* 800-238-1007 ■ *Web:* www.disstonprecision.com	Philadelphia	PA	19135	215-338-1200	338-7060
Great Neck Saw Mfg Inc 165 E 2nd St *TF Cust Svc:* 800-457-0600 ■ *Web:* www.greatnecksaw.com	Mineola	NY	11501	516-746-5352	746-5358
ICS Blount Inc 4909 SE International Way *TF:* 800-321-1240 ■ *Web:* www.icsbestway.com	Portland	OR	97222	503-653-8881	653-4201
LS Starrett Co 121 Crescent St *NYSE: SCX* ■ *TF:* 888-674-7443 ■ *Web:* www.starrett.com	Athol	MA	01331	978-249-3551	249-8495
Marvel Manufacturing Co Inc 3501 Marvel Dr *TF:* 800-472-9464 ■ *Web:* www.sawing.com	Oshkosh	WI	54902	920-236-7200	236-7209
MK Diamond Products Inc 1315 Storm Pkwy *TF:* 800-421-5830 ■ *Web:* www.mkdiamond.com	Torrance	CA	90501	310-539-5221	539-5158
MK Morse Co 1101 11th St SE *TF:* 800-733-3377 ■ *Web:* www.mkmorse.com	Canton	OH	44707	330-453-8187	453-1111
Simonds International 135 Intervale Rd **Fax Area Code:* 800 ■ *TF:* 800-343-1616 ■ *Web:* www.simonds.cc	Fitchburg	MA	01420	978-343-3731	541-6224*
Vermont American Corp 1961 Bishop Ln *TF:* 800-626-2834 ■ *Web:* www.vermontamerican.com	Louisville	KY	40218	502-625-2000	625-2064

686 SAWMILLS & PLANING MILLS

	City	State	Zip	Phone	Fax
Ainsworth Lumber Co Ltd 1055 Dunsmuir St Suite 3194 *TSX: ANS* ■ *TF:* 877-661-3200 ■ *Web:* www.ainsworth.ca	Vancouver	BC	V7X1L3	604-661-3200	661-3201
Anderson-Tully Co 775 Ridgelake Blvd Suite 1050 *Web:* www.andersontully.com	Memphis	TN	38120	901-576-1400	576-1484
Anthony Forest Products Co 309 N Washington Ave *TF:* 800-221-2326 ■ *Web:* www.anthonyforest.com	El Dorado	AR	71730	870-862-3414	863-4296
Anthony Timberlands Inc 111 S Plum St PO Box 137 *Web:* www.anthonytimberlands.com	Bearden	AR	71720	870-687-3611	687-3712
Armstrong Wood Products Inc 2500 Columbia Ave	Lancaster	PA	17603	717-396-0611	396-6344
Balfour Lumber Co Inc 800 W Clay St PO Box 1337	Thomasville	GA	31799	229-226-0611	226-4297
Beadles Lumber Co Inc 900 6th St NE PO Box 3457 *TF:* 800-763-2400 ■ *Web:* www.beadleslumber.com	Moultrie	GA	31776	229-985-6996	890-6050
Bennett Lumber Products Inc 3759 Hwy 6 PO Box 130 *Web:* www.bennett-lumber.com	Princeton	ID	83857	208-875-1121	875-0191
Bibler Brothers Inc 2401 S Arkansas Ave PO Box 490	Russellville	AR	72811	479-968-4986	968-5281
Bowater Inc 55 E Camper Down Way *NYSE: BOW* ■ **Fax:* Hum Res ■ *TF:* 800-845-6002 ■ *Web:* www.bowater.com	Greenville	SC	29601	864-271-7733	282-9591*
Buse Timber & Sales Inc 3812 28th Pl NE *TF:* 800-305-2577 ■ *Web:* www.busetimber.com	Everett	WA	98205	425-258-2577	259-6956
Buskirk Lumber Co 319 Oak St *TF:* 800-860-9663 ■ *Web:* www.buskirklumber.com	Freeport	MI	49325	616-765-5103	765-3380
California Cedar Products Co 1340 N Washingtron St *Web:* www.calcedar.com	Stockton	CA	95203	209-944-5800	944-9072
Canadian Forest Products Ltd 5162 Northwood Pulp Mill Rd PO Box 6000 *Web:* www.canfor.com	Prince George	BC	V2N2K3	250-962-3500	962-3533
Canfor Corp 1700 W 75th Ave Suite 100 *TSX: CFP* ■ *Web:* www.canfor.com	Vancouver	BC	V6P6G2	604-661-5241	661-5226
Cascade Wood Components Inc 15 Herman Creek Ln PO Box 100	Cascade Locks	OR	97014	509-427-5605	427-5020
Catawissa Lumber & Specialty Co Inc 1 Cemetery St PO Box 176 *Web:* www.catlmbr.com	Catawissa	PA	17820	570-356-2349	356-2485
Cersosimo Lumber Co Inc 1103 Vernon St *TF:* 800-326-5647 ■ *Web:* www.cersosimolumber.com	Brattleboro	VT	05301	802-254-4508	254-5691
Chesterfield Lumber Co 1100 Chesterfield Dr *Web:* www.chesterfieldlumber.com	Darlington	SC	29532	843-393-1211	393-7376
Claude Howard Lumber Co Inc PO Box 1669	Statesboro	GA	30459	912-764-5407	764-6279
Coastal Timbers Inc 1310 Jane St PO Box 10537 *Web:* www.coastaltimbers.com	New Iberia	LA	70562	337-369-3017	365-0003
Coe Mfg Inc 609 Bank St *Web:* www.coemfg.com	Painesville	OH	44077	440-352-9381	352-1487
Collins Cos 1618 SW 1st Ave Suite 500 *TF:* 800-329-1219 ■ *Web:* www.collinswood.com	Portland	OR	97201	503-227-1219	227-5349
Columbia Vista Corp PO Box 489 *Web:* www.columbiavistacorp.com	Vancouver	WA	98666	360-892-0770	944-8229
Cronland Lumber Co 1941 Hwy 73 E *Web:* www.cronlandlumber.com	Iron Station	NC	28080	704-735-6564	736-0284
Cumberland Lumber & Mfg Co 202 Red Rd	McMinnville	TN	37110	931-473-9542	473-6259
David R Webb Co Inc 206 S Holland St PO Box 8 *Web:* www.davidrwebb.com	Edinburgh	IN	46124	812-526-2601	526-5842
Davidson Industries Inc 09766 Hwy 126 PO Box 7	Mapleton	OR	97453	541-268-4422	268-4119
Deltic Timber Corp PO Box 7200 *NYSE: DEL* ■ *Web:* www.deltic.com	El Dorado	AR	71731	870-881-9400	881-6454
Dixon MC Lumber Co Inc 605 W Washington St	Eufaula	AL	36027	334-687-8204	687-8208
Domtar Inc 395 boul de Maisonneuve O *NYSE: DTC* ■ **Fax:* Mktg ■ *TF:* 800-267-2040 ■ *Web:* www.domtar.com	Montreal	QC	H3A1L6	514-848-5400	848-6609*
DR Johnson Lumber Co 1991 Pruner Rd PO Box 66 *Web:* www.drjlumber.com	Riddle	OR	97469	541-874-2231	874-3337
Dwight Lewis Lumber Co Inc Rt 87 PO Box A	Hillsgrove	PA	18619	570-924-3507	924-4233
Feldman Lumber Co Inc 228 Buckeye Rd *TF:* 800-325-0459	Lancaster	KY	40444	859-792-2141	792-2143
Fitzpatrick & Weller Inc 12 Mill St PO Box 490 *Web:* www.fitzweller.com	Ellicottville	NY	14731	716-699-2393	699-2893
Forest Grove Lumber Co 2700 NE Orchard Ave *TF:* 800-647-9663 ■ *Web:* www.fglco.com	McMinnville	OR	97128	503-472-3195	434-5805
Forest Products Mfg Co 51 E 30th St PO Box 606	Jasper	IN	47547	812-482-5625	482-9148
Frank Lumber Co Inc PO Box 79	Mill City	OR	97360	503-897-2371	897-3003
Fulghum Industries Inc 317 S Main St PO Box 909 *TF:* 800-841-5980 ■ *Web:* www.fulghum.com	Wadley	GA	30477	478-252-5223	252-0454
Georgia-Pacific Corp 133 Peachtree St NE *Web:* www.gp.com	Atlanta	GA	30303	404-652-4000	230-5774
Gram Lumber Co 985 NW 2nd St	Kalama	WA	98625	360-673-5231	673-5558
Gray Lumber Co Inc 1350 Gray Hill Rd PO Box 55	Green Pond	AL	35074	205-938-7883	938-2285
Griffin Lumber Co PO Box 237 *Web:* www.griffinlumber.com	Cordele	GA	31010	229-273-3113	273-4909
Gulf Lumber Co Inc 1850 Conception St Rd PO Box 1663 *TF:* 800-496-3307 ■ *Web:* www.gulflumber.com	Mobile	AL	36633	251-457-6872	452-7110
Hampton Affiliates 9600 SW Barnes Rd Sunset Business Park Suite 200 *TF:* 888-310-1464 ■ *Web:* www.hamptonaffiliates.com	Portland	OR	97225	503-297-7691	203-6604

Phone Fax

Hankins Lumber Co Inc 496 Camp McCain Rd PO Box 1397 .... Grenada MS 38902 662-226-2961 226-6404

Hartzell Hardwoods Inc PO Box 919 .... Piqua OH 45356 937-773-7054 773-6160
Web: www.hartzellhardwoods.com

Hassell & Hughes Lumber Co PO Box 68 .... Collinwood TN 38450 931-724-9191 724-4714

Hazlehurst Lumber Co 1077 Lily Rd PO Box 900 .... Hazlehurst MS 39083 601-894-1064 894-1174

Hedstrom Lumber Co Inc 1504 Gunflint Trail .... Grand Marais MN 55604 218-387-2995 387-2204
Web: www.hedstromlumber.com

Hoge Lumber Co 701 S Main St .... New Knoxville OH 45871 419-753-2263 753-2963
Web: www.hoge.com

Hood Distribution McQuesten Group 600 Iron Horse Pk .... North Billerica MA 01862 978-663-3435 667-0934
TF: 800-752-0129 ■ *Web:* www.hoodindustries.com/distribution/mcquesten

Hood Industries Inc 1033 S Reynolds St .... Metcalf GA 31792 229-228-0707 228-0065
Web: www.hoodindustries.com/lumber/

Hunt Forest Products 401 E Reynolds Dr PO Box 1263 .... Ruston LA 71273 318-255-2245 255-4048
TF: 800-390-8589 ■ *Web:* www.huntforpro.com

Idaho Timber Corp 1299 N Orchard St Suite 300 .... Boise ID 83706 208-377-3000 377-1470
Web: www.idahotimber.com

Indian Country Inc 791 Airport Rd .... Deposit NY 13754 607-467-3801 467-4559
TF: 800-414-3801 ■ *Web:* www.indiancountryinc.com

Indiana Hardwoods 7988 Gardner Rd .... Chandler IN 47610 812-925-3343 925-2064
TF: 800-925-3344 ■ *Web:* www.indiana-hardwoods.com

Industrial Timber & Lumber Corp (ITL)
23925 Commerce Park Rd .... Beachwood OH 44122 216-831-3140 831-4734
TF: 800-829-9663 ■ *Web:* www.itlcorp.com

Interfor Pacific 15555 S Hwy 211 .... Molalla OR 97038 503-829-9121 829-5481
Web: www.interfor.com

International Forest Products Ltd (Interfor)
1055 Sunsmuir St Suite 3500 .... Vancouver BC V7X1H7 604-689-6800 688-0313
Web: www.interfor.com

J & J Log & Lumber Corp 528 Old Rt 22 PO Box 1139 .... Dover Plains NY 12522 845-832-6535 832-3757

Jerry G Williams & Sons Inc 524 Brogden Rd PO Box 2430 .... Smithfield NC 27577 919-934-4115 934-4956
Web: www.jerrygwilliamsandsons.com

Johnson DR Lumber Co 1991 Pruner Rd PO Box 66 .... Riddle OR 97469 541-874-2231 874-3337
Web: www.drjlumber.com

Jones JW Lumber Co Inc 1443 Northside Rd .... Elizabeth City NC 27909 252-771-2497 771-8252

Jordan Lumber & Supply Inc 1939 NC Hwy 109 S PO Box 98 .... Mount Gilead NC 27306 910-439-6121 439-6105
Web: www.jordanlumber.com

JW Jones Lumber Co Inc 1443 Northside Rd .... Elizabeth City NC 27909 252-771-2497 771-8252

Keadle Lumber Enterprises Inc 889 Railroad St .... Thomaston GA 30286 706-647-8982 647-1392
Web: www.keadlelumber.com

Keener Lumber Co Inc 1209 W Market St PO Box 2323 .... Smithfield NC 27577 919-934-1087 934-9999

Kitchens Brothers Mfg Co 601 Carpenter St PO Box 217 .... Utica MS 39175 601-885-6001 885-8501

Langdale Forest Products Co 1202 Madison Hwy PO Box 1088 .... Valdosta GA 31603 229-242-7450 333-2533
TF: 800-864-6909 ■ *Web:* www.langdaleforest.com

Lewisohn Sales Co Inc 4001-15 Dell Ave PO Box 192 .... North Bergen NJ 07047 201-864-0300 864-1266
TF Orders: 800-631-3196 ■ *Web:* www.lewisohn.com

Louisiana-Pacific Corp 414 Union St Suite 2000 .... Nashville TN 37219 615-986-5600 986-5666
NYSE: LPX ■ *TF:* 877-744-5600 ■ *Web:* www.lpcorp.com

MacBeath Hardwood Co 2150 Oakdale Ave .... San Francisco CA 94124 415-401-7046 401-8961
TF: 800-233-0782 ■ *Web:* www.macbeath.com

Manke Lumber Co Inc 1717 Marine View Dr .... Tacoma WA 98422 253-572-6252 383-2489
TF: 800-426-8488 ■ *Web:* www.mankelumber.com

Matson Lumber Co Inc 132 Main St .... Brookville PA 15825 814-849-5334 849-3811
Web: www.matsonlumber.com

MC Dixon Lumber Co Inc 605 W Washington St .... Eufaula AL 36027 334-687-8204 687-8208

Merritt Brothers Lumber 5400 E Hwy 54 PO Box 190 .... Athol ID 83801 208-683-3321 683-3328
TF: 800-488-3321 ■ *Web:* www.merrittbros.com

Middleton Building Supply Inc 5 Kings Hwy .... Middleton NH 03887 603-473-2314 473-8531
TF: 800-647-8989 ■ *Web:* www.lavalleys.com

Midwest Hardwood Corp 9540 83rd Ave N .... Maple Grove MN 55369 763-425-8700 391-6740
Web: www.midwesthardwood.com

Miller TR Mill Co Inc 215 Deer St PO Box 708 .... Brewton AL 36427 251-867-4331 867-6882
TF: 800-633-6740 ■ *Web:* www.trmillermill.com

Moose River Lumber Co Inc PO Box 454 .... Jackman ME 04945 207-668-4193 668-5381
Web: www.mooseriverlumber.com

Nagel Lumber Co Inc PO Box 209 .... Land O' Lakes WI 54540 715-547-3361 547-3715
Web: www.nagellumber.com

New South Cos Inc PO Box 9089 .... Myrtle Beach SC 29578 843-236-9399 236-9454
TF: 800-346-8675 ■ *Web:* www.newsouthcompanies.com

Ochoco Lumber Co 200 SE Combs Flat Rd PO Box 668 .... Prineville OR 97754 541-447-6296 447-8992
Web: www.ochocolumber.com

Pacific Lumber Co 125 Main St PO Box 37 .... Scotia CA 95565 707-764-2222 764-4171
Web: www.palco.com

Parton Lumber Co Inc 251 Parton Rd .... Rutherfordton NC 28139 828-287-4257 287-3308
TF: 800-624-1501 ■ *Web:* www.partonlumber.com

Pike Lumber Co Inc PO Box 247 .... Akron IN 46910 574-893-4511 893-7400
TF: 800-356-4554 ■ *Web:* www.pikelumber.com

Plum Creek Timber Co Inc 999 3rd Ave Suite 4300 .... Seattle WA 98104 206-467-3600 467-3795
NYSE: PCL ■ *Web:* www.plumcreek.com

Potlatch Corp 601 W 1st Ave Suite 1600 .... Spokane WA 99201 509-835-1500 835-1555
NYSE: PCH ■ *Web:* www.potlatchcorp.com

Potlatch Corp Wood Products Div 805 Mill Rd PO Box 1388 .... Lewiston ID 83501 208-799-0123 799-1918
Web: www.potlatchcorp.com

Pyramid Mountain Lumber Inc 379 Boy Scout Rd PO Box 549 .... Seeley Lake MT 59868 406-677-2201 677-2509
Web: www.pyramidlumber.com

Rajala Cos PO Box 217 .... Deer River MN 56636 218-246-8277 246-2802
Web: www.rajalacos.com

Reelfoot Lumber Co Inc
205 Henning-Bethlehem Rd PO Box 486 .... Henning TN 38041 731-738-5021 738-5027

Riley Creek Lumber Co 30 Riley Creek Park Dr .... Laclede ID 83841 208-263-7574 265-6530
Web: www.rileycreek.com

Rives & Reynolds Lumber Co 33 Vaughn Dr .... Natchez MS 39120 601-445-8206 442-7301

Robbins Inc 4777 Eastern Ave .... Cincinnati OH 45226 513-871-8988 871-7998
TF: 800-543-1913 ■ *Web:* www.robbinsfloor.com

Robbins Lumber Inc PO Box 9 .... Searsmont ME 04973 207-342-5221 342-5201
TF: 800-287-5067 ■ *Web:* www.rlco.com

Rogers Lumber Co Inc 937 Hwy 7 N .... Camden AR 71701 870-574-0231 574-1206

Rosboro Lumber Co 2509 Main St PO Box 20 .... Springfield OR 97477 541-746-8411 726-8919
Web: www.rosboro.com

Roseburg Forest Products Co PO Box 1088 .... Roseburg OR 97470 541-679-3311
TF: 800-548-5275 ■ *Web:* www.rfpco.com

RSG Forest Products Inc 985 NW 2nd St .... Kalama WA 98625 360-673-2825 673-5558
Web: www.rsgfp.com

Rushmore Forest Products 23848 Hwy 385 PO Box 619 .... Hill City SD 57745 605-574-2512 574-4154
TF: 866-466-5254

Scotch Lumber Co 119 W Main St PO Box 38 .... Fulton AL 36446 334-636-4424 636-7107
TF: 800-936-4424

Scott Industries Inc 1573 Hwy 136 W PO Box 7 .... Henderson KY 42419 270-831-2037 831-2039
TF: 800-951-9276 ■ *Web:* www.scott-mfg.com

Seattle Snohomish Mill Co Inc 9525 Airport Way PO Box 949 .... Snohomish WA 98291 360-568-2171 568-1778
Web: www.sea-sno.com

Sierra Pacific Industries 19794 Riverside Ave .... Anderson CA 96007 530-378-8000 378-8109
Web: www.sierrapacificind.com

Simpson Timber Co 917 E 11th St .... Tacoma WA 98421 253-779-6400 280-9000
Web: www.simpson.com

Smith Flooring Inc 1501 W Hwy 60 PO Box 99 .... Mountain View MO 65548 417-934-2291 934-2295
Web: www.smithflooring.com

South Coast Lumber Co 885 Railroad Ave PO Box 670 .... Brookings OR 97415 541-469-2136 469-9105
Web: www.socomi.com

Southern Forest Products LLC FM 2626 N PO Box 207 .... Bon Wier TX 75928 409-397-4221 397-4880

Stimson Lumber Co 520 SW Yamhill St Suite 700 .... Portland OR 97204 503-222-1676 295-1849
TF: 800-445-9758 ■ *Web:* www.stimsonlumber.com

Swaner Hardwood Co Inc 5 W Magnolia Blvd PO Box 4200 .... Burbank CA 91503 818-953-5350 846-3662
TF: 800-368-1108 ■ *Web:* www.swanerhardwood.com

Taylor-Ramsey Corp PO Box 11888 .... Lynchburg VA 24506 434-929-7443 929-6162
TF: 800-368-3036 ■ *Web:* www.taylorramsey.com

Tembec Inc 800 boul Rene Levesque O Bureau 1050 .... Montreal QC H3B1X1 514-871-0137 397-0896
TSX: TBC ■ *Web:* www.tembec.ca

Tolleson Lumber Co Inc 903 Jernigan St .... Perry GA 31069 478-988-3800 987-0160
TF: 800-768-2105 ■ *Web:* www.tollesonlumber.com

TR Miller Mill Co Inc 215 Deer St PO Box 708 .... Brewton AL 36427 251-867-4331 867-6882
TF: 800-633-6740 ■ *Web:* www.trmillermill.com

Tucker Lumber Cos LLC 601 N Pearl St .... Pageland SC 29728 843-672-6135 672-5393

Universal Forest Products Inc 2801 E Beltline Ave NE .... Grand Rapids MI 49525 616-364-6161 361-7534
NASDAQ: UFPI ■ *TF:* 800-598-9663 ■ *Web:* www.ufpinc.com

Wadena Timberroots 1100 N Jefferson Ave PO Box 109 .... Wadena MN 56482 218-631-2607 631-2513
TF Sales: 800-982-4863

Wagner Woodcraft Inc 10417 S Main St .... Archdale NC 27263 336-431-1197 431-4981

Warm Springs Forest Products Industries
Hwy 26 Bldg 3270 PO Box 810 .... Warm Springs OR 97761 541-553-1131 553-1561
Web: www.wsfpi.com

Webb David R Co Inc 206 S Holland St PO Box 8 .... Edinburgh IN 46124 812-526-2601 526-5842
Web: www.davidrwebb.com

Webster Hardwoods W1038 County Road U .... Bangor WI 54614 608-486-2341 486-2067
TF Sales: 800-284-2173 ■ *Web:* www.websterhardwoods.com

Welco Lumber Co 1218 1st St PO Box 125 .... Marysville WA 98270 360-659-1261 651-1521
TF: 877-261-7239 ■ *Web:* www.skookumcedar.com

Welco Lumber Co Kkookum Div 780 W Hwy 108 .... Shelton WA 98584 360-426-9721 426-1935*
**Fax:* Sales ■ *Web:* www.welcolumberusa.com

West Fraser Timber Co Ltd 858 Beatty St Suite 501 .... Vancouver BC V6B1C1 604-895-2700 681-6061
TSX: WFT ■ *Web:* www.westfraser.com

Western Forest Products Inc 435 Trunk Rd 3rd Fl .... Duncan BC V9L2P9 250-748-3711 748-6630
TSX: WEF ■ *Web:* www.westernforest.com

Westervelt Co 1400 Jack Warner Pkwy NE .... Tuscaloosa AL 35404 205-562-5000 562-5012*
**Fax:* Sales ■ *TF:* 800-633-5983 ■ *Web:* www.westervelt.com

Weyerhaeuser Canada Ltd 925 W Georgia St .... Vancouver BC V6C3L2 604-661-8000

Weyerhaeuser Co 33663 Weyerhaeuser Way S .... Federal Way WA 98003 253-924-2345 924-2685
NYSE: WY ■ *TF:* 800-525-5440 ■ *Web:* www.weyerhaeuser.com

Williams Jerry G & Sons Inc 524 Brogden Rd PO Box 2430 .... Smithfield NC 27577 919-934-4115 934-4956
Web: www.jerrygwilliamsandsons.com

687 SCALES & BALANCES

SEE ALSO Laboratory Apparatus & Furniture p. 1885

Phone Fax

Avery Weigh-Tronix Inc 1000 Armstrong Dr .... Fairmont MN 56031 507-238-4461 238-8258*
**Fax:* Mktg ■ *TF:* 800-533-0456 ■ *Web:* www.wtxweb.com

BRK Brands Inc 3901 Liberty Street Rd .... Aurora IL 60504 630-851-7330 851-9015
TF: 800-323-9005 ■ *Web:* www.firstalert.com

Cardinal Detecto Scale Mfg Co
203 E Dougherty St PO Box 151 .... Webb City MO 64870 417-673-4631 673-5001
TF Cust Svc: 800-641-2008 ■ *Web:* www.cardet.com

Detecto Scale Co 203 E Daugherty St PO Box 151 .... Webb City MO 64870 417-673-4631 673-5001
TF: 800-641-2008 ■ *Web:* www.detectoscale.com

Emery Winslow Scale Co 73 Cogwheel Ln .... Seymour CT 06483 203-881-9333 881-9477
Web: www.emerywinslow.com

Fairbanks Scales Inc 821 Locust St .... Kansas City MO 64106 816-471-0231 471-0241
TF: 800-451-4107 ■ *Web:* www.fairbanks.com

Industrial Data Systems Inc 590 W Freedom Ave .... Orange CA 92865 714-921-9212 998-8656
TF: 800-854-3311 ■ *Web:* www.industrialdata.com

Intercomp Co 3839 CR 116 .... Medina MN 55340 763-476-2531 476-2613
TF: 800-328-3336 ■ *Web:* www.intercompco.com

Johnson Scale Co 235 Fairfield Ave .... West Caldwell NJ 07006 973-226-2100 882-8068
TF: 800-572-2531 ■ *Web:* www.johnsonscale.com

Measurement Specialties Inc 1000 Lucas Way .... Hampton VA 23666 757-766-1500 766-3979
NASDAQ: MEAS ■ *TF:* 800-236-6746 ■ *Web:* www.msiusa.com

Merrick Industries Inc 10 Arthur Dr .... Lynn Haven FL 32444 850-265-3611 265-1707*
**Fax:* Hum Res ■ *TF:* 800-345-8440 ■ *Web:* www.merrick-inc.com

Mettler-Toledo Inc 1900 Polaris Pkwy .... Columbus OH 43240 614-438-4511 438-4518*
NYSE: MTD ■ **Fax:* Sales ■ *TF:* 800-447-9206 ■ *Web:* www.mt.com

Nicol Scales LP 7239 Envoy Ct .... Dallas TX 75247 214-428-8181 428-8127
TF: 800-225-8181 ■ *Web:* www.nicolscales.com

Ohaus Corp 19-A Chapin Rd PO Box 2033 .... Pine Brook NJ 07058 973-377-9000 944-7177
TF: 800-672-7722 ■ *Web:* www.ohaus.com

Pelouze Scale Co 7400 W 100 Pl .... Bridgeview IL 60455 708-598-9100 654-7330*
**Fax Area Code:* 800 ■ *TF:* 800-654-8330 ■ *Web:* www.pelouze.com

Pelstar LLC 7400 W 100th Pl .... Bridgeview IL 60455 708-598-9100 233-5472
TF: 800-638-3722 ■ *Web:* www.pelouze.com

Pennsylvania Scale Co 1042 New Holland Ave .... Lancaster PA 17601 717-295-6935 295-6941
TF: 800-233-0473 ■ *Web:* www.pascale.com

Premier Tech Chronos 1 Premier Ave .... Rivere-du-Loup QC G5R6C1 418-867-8884 862-6642
Web: www.premiertechchronos.com

Rice Lake Weighing Systems 230 W Coleman St .... Rice Lake WI 54868 715-234-9171 234-6967
TF: 800-472-6703 ■ *Web:* www.rlws.com

Scale-Tronix Inc 200 E Post Rd .... White Plains NY 10601 914-948-8117 948-0581
TF: 800-873-2001 ■ *Web:* www.scale-tronix.com

Schenck Trebel Corp 535 Acorn St .... Deer Park NY 11729 631-242-4010 242-5077
TF: 800-873-2357 ■ *Web:* www.schenck-usa.com

Scientech Inc 5649 Arapahoe Ave .... Boulder CO 80303 303-444-1361 444-9229
TF: 800-525-0522 ■ *Web:* www.scientech-inc.com

Setra Systems Inc 159 Swanson Rd .... Boxborough MA 01719 978-263-1400 264-0292
TF: 800-257-3872 ■ *Web:* www.setra.com

SI Technologies Inc 14192 Franklin Ave .... Tustin CA 92780 714-731-1234 731-2019
TF Cust Svc: 800-872-4784 ■ *Web:* www.sitechnologies.com

Sterling Scale Co Inc 20950 Boening Dr .... Southfield MI 48075 248-358-0590 358-2275
TF: 800-331-9931 ■ *Web:* www.sterlingscale.com

Sunbeam Products Inc 2381 Executive Center Dr .... Boca Raton FL 33431 561-912-4100 912-4567
Web: www.sunbeam.com

Tanita Corp of America Inc 2625 S Clearbrook Dr .... Arlington Heights IL 60005 847-640-9241 640-9261
TF: 800-826-4828 ■ *Web:* www.tanita.com

TCI Scales 4208 Russell Rd Unit E .... Mukilteo WA 98275 425-353-4384 347-5845
TF: 800-522-2206 ■ *Web:* www.tciscales.com

Thayer Scale Corp 91 Schoosett St .... Pembroke MA 02359 781-826-8101 826-0072*
**Fax:* Cust Svc ■ *TF:* 800-225-0450 ■ *Web:* www.thayerscale.com

Toroid Corp 225 Wynn Dr NW .... Huntsville AL 35805 256-837-7510 837-7512

				Phone	Fax
Triner Scale & Mfg Co 2842 Sanderwood Dr. *TF:* 800-238-0152 ■ *Web:* www.trinerscale.com	Memphis	TN	38118	901-795-0746	363-3114
Wisconsin Electrical Mfg Co Inc 2501 S Moorland Rd. *Web:* www.yamatocorp.com	New Berlin	WI	53151	262-782-2340	782-2653
Yamato Corp 1775 S Murray Blvd *TF:* 800-538-1762 ■ *Web:* www.yamatocorp.com	Colorado Springs	CO	80916	719-591-1500	591-1045

688 SCHOOL BOARDS (PUBLIC)

				Phone	Fax
Akron Public Schools 70 N Broadway Ave *Web:* www.akronschools.com	Akron	OH	44308	330-761-1661	761-3225
Albuquerque Public Schools 6400 Uptown Blvd NE **Fax:* Hum Res ■ *Web:* ww2.aps.edu	Albuquerque	NM	87110	505-880-3700	889-4883*
Allentown School District 31 S Penn St *Web:* www.allentownsd.org	Allentown	PA	18105	484-765-4000	765-4140
Amarillo Independent School District 7200 I-40 W **Fax:* Hum Res ■ *Web:* www.amaisd.org	Amarillo	TX	79106	806-326-1000	354-4378*
Anchorage School District 5530 E Northern Lights Blvd **Fax:* Hum Res ■ *Web:* www.asdk12.org	Anchorage	AK	99504	907-742-4000	742-4176*
Atlanta Public Schools 130 Trinity Ave SW *Web:* www.atlanta.k12.ga.us	Atlanta	GA	30303	404-802-3500	802-1803
Austin Independent School District 1111 W 6th St *Web:* www.austin.isd.tenet.edu	Austin	TX	78703	512-414-1700	414-1486
Bakersfield City School District 1300 Baker St *Web:* www.bcsd.com	Bakersfield	CA	93305	661-631-4600	326-1485
Baltimore Public Schools 200 E North Ave *Web:* www.baltimorecityschools.org	Baltimore	MD	21202	410-396-8700	545-0897
Birmingham City Schools 2015 Park Pl N *Web:* birmingham.schoolinsites.com/	Birmingham	AL	35203	205-231-4600	231-4761
Boise City Independent School District 8169 W Victory Rd *Web:* www.sd01.k12.id.us	Boise	ID	83709	208-338-3400	338-3487
Boston Public Schools 26 Court St *Web:* www.bostonpublicschools.org	Boston	MA	02108	617-635-9000	635-9059
Broward County Public Schools 600 SE 3rd Ave *Web:* www.browardschools.com	Fort Lauderdale	FL	33301	754-321-0000	321-2701
Brownsville Independent School District 1900 E Price Rd *Web:* www.bisd.us	Brownsville	TX	78521	956-548-8000	548-8010
Buffalo City School District 712 City Hall *Web:* www.buffaloschools.org	Buffalo	NY	14202	716-816-3500	851-3535
Caddo Parish School Board PO Box 32000 **Fax:* Hum Res ■ *Web:* www.caddo.k12.la.us	Shreveport	LA	71130	318-636-0210	603-6559*
Charleston County School District 75 Calhoun St **Fax:* Hum Res ■ *Web:* www.ccsdschools.com	Charleston	SC	29401	843-937-6300	937-6351*
Charlotte-Mecklenburg Schools 701 E 2nd St *Web:* www.cms.k12.nc.us	Charlotte	NC	28202	980-343-3000	343-6270
Chicago Board of Education 125 S Clark St *Web:* www.cps.k12.il.us	Chicago	IL	60603	773-535-8000	553-1045
Cincinnati Public Schools PO Box 5381 *Web:* www.cpsboe.k12.oh.us	Cincinnati	OH	45201	513-363-0123	363-0055
Clark County School District 5100 W Sahara Ave *Web:* www.ccsd.net	Las Vegas	NV	89146	702-799-5311	799-5125
Cleveland Municipal School District 1380 E 6th St **Fax:* Hum Res ■ *Web:* www.cmsdnet.net	Cleveland	OH	44114	216-574-8500	574-8072*
Collier County School Board 5775 Osceola Trail *Web:* www.collier.k12.fl.us	Naples	FL	34109	239-377-0001	377-0336
Colorado Springs School District #11 1115 N El Paso St *Web:* www.cssd11.k12.co.us	Colorado Springs	CO	80903	719-520-2000	577-4546
Columbus Public Schools 270 E State St **Fax:* Hum Res ■ *Web:* www.columbus.k12.oh.us	Columbus	OH	43215	614-365-5000	365-5652*
Corpus Christi Independent School District 801 Leopard St **Fax:* Hum Res ■ *Web:* corpuschristiisd.org	Corpus Christi	TX	78401	361-886-9001	886-9860*
Dallas Independent School District 3700 Ross Ave **Fax:* Hum Res ■ *Web:* www.dallasisd.org	Dallas	TX	75204	972-925-3700	925-4201*
Dayton City Schools 115 S Ludlow St *Web:* www.dps.k12.oh.us	Dayton	OH	45402	937-542-3000	542-3188
Denver Public Schools 900 Grant St *Web:* www.dpsk12.org	Denver	CO	80203	720-423-3200	423-3413
Des Moines Independent School District 1801 16th St **Fax:* Hum Res ■ *Web:* www.dmps.k12.ia.us/	Des Moines	IA	50314	515-242-7911	242-7891*
Detroit Public Schools 3031 W Grand Blvd **Fax:* Hum Res ■ *Web:* www.detroit.k12.mi.us	Detroit	MI	48202	313-873-3111	873-7100*
District of Columbia Public Schools 825 N Capitol St NE 9th Fl *Web:* www.k12.dc.us	Washington	DC	20002	202-442-4289	442-5198
Duval County School System 1701 Prudential Dr *Web:* www.educationcentral.org	Jacksonville	FL	32207	904-390-2000	390-2586
East Baton Rouge Parish School Board 1050 S Foster Dr **Fax:* Hum Res ■ *Web:* www.ebrpss.k12.la.us	Baton Rouge	LA	70806	225-922-5400	922-5688*
El Paso Independent School District 6531 Boeing Dr **Fax:* Hum Res ■ *Web:* www.episd.org	El Paso	TX	79925	915-779-3781	779-4280*
Eugene School District 4J 200 N Monroe St *Web:* www.4j.lane.edu	Eugene	OR	97402	541-687-3123	687-3691
Fayette County Public Schools 701 E Main St **Fax:* Hum Res ■ *Web:* www.fcps.net	Lexington	KY	40502	859-381-4100	381-4271*
Flint Community Schools 923 E Kearsley St *Web:* www.flintschools.org	Flint	MI	48503	810-760-1000	760-6790
Fort Wayne Community Schools 1200 S Clinton St *Web:* www.fwcs.k12.in.us	Fort Wayne	IN	46802	260-467-1000	467-1973
Fort Worth Independent School District 100 N University Dr *Web:* www.fortworthisd.org	Fort Worth	TX	76107	817-871-2389	871-2949
Fresno Unified School District 2309 Tulare St **Fax:* Hum Res ■ *Web:* www.fresno.k12.ca.us	Fresno	CA	93721	559-457-3000	457-3528*
Grand Rapids Public Schools 1331 Franklin St SE *Web:* grps.k12.mi.us	Grand Rapids	MI	49506	616-819-2000	819-3480
Greenville County School District 200 Waddel Rd **Fax:* Hum Res ■ *Web:* www.greenville.k12.sc.us	Taylors	SC	29687	864-241-3100	355-3975*
Guilford County Schools 712 N Eugene St **Fax:* Hum Res ■ *Web:* www.gcsnc.com	Greensboro	NC	27401	336-370-8100	370-8398*
Hamilton County Dept of Education 3074 Hickory Valley Rd **Fax:* Hum Res ■ *Web:* www.hcde.org	Chattanooga	TN	37421	423-209-8400	209-8539*
Hartford Public Schools 960 Main St **Fax:* Hum Res ■ *Web:* www.hartfordschools.org	Hartford	CT	06103	860-695-8000	722-8454*
Hawaii Dept of Education Honolulu District Office 4967 Kilauea Ave *Web:* www.doe.k12.hi.us	Honolulu	HI	96816	808-733-4950	733-4953
Hillsborough County Public Schools 901 E Kennedy Blvd *Web:* www.sdhc.k12.fl.us/	Tampa	FL	33602	813-272-4000	272-4073
Houston Independent School District 4400 W 18th St *Web:* www.houstonisd.org	Houston	TX	77092	713-556-6000	556-6006
Huntsville Board of Education 200 White St *Web:* www.hsv.k12.al.us	Huntsville	AL	35801	256-428-6800	428-6817
Indianapolis Public Schools 120 E Walnut St *Web:* www.headlines.ips.k12.in.us	Indianapolis	IN	46204	317-226-4411	226-4936
Jackson Public School District 662 S President St *Web:* www.jackson.k12.ms.us	Jackson	MS	39201	601-960-8700	960-8713
Jefferson County (KY) Public Schools PO Box 34020 *Web:* www.jefferson.k12.ky.us	Louisville	KY	40232	502-485-3011	485-3991
Kansas City Missouri School District 1211 McGee St *Web:* www.kcmsd.k12.mo.us	Kansas City	MO	64106	816-418-7000	418-7631
Kern County High School District 5801 Sundale Ave *Web:* www.khsd.k12.ca.us	Bakersfield	CA	93309	661-827-3100	827-3300
Knox County Public Schools 912 S Gay St **Fax:* Hum Res ■ *Web:* www.kcs.k12tn.net	Knoxville	TN	37901	865-594-1800	594-3758*
Lafayette Parish School System PO Box 2158 **Fax:* Hum Res ■ *Web:* www.lft.k12.la.us	Lafayette	LA	70502	337-236-6800	236-6963*
Lansing School District 519 W Kalamazoo St **Fax:* Hum Res ■ *Web:* web.lsd.k12.mi.us	Lansing	MI	48933	517-325-6000	325-7345*
Las Cruces Public Schools 505 S Main St Suite 249 **Fax:* Hum Res ■ *Web:* lcps.k12.nm.us	Las Cruces	NM	88001	505-527-5800	527-6658*
Leon County Schools 2757 W Pensacola St **Fax:* Hum Res ■ *Web:* www.leon.k12.fl.us	Tallahassee	FL	32304	850-487-7100	487-7822*
Lincoln Public Schools 5901 'O' St **Fax:* Hum Res ■ *Web:* www.lps.org	Lincoln	NE	68510	402-436-1000	436-1620*
Little Rock School District 810 W Markham St **Fax:* Hum Res ■ *Web:* www.lrsd.org	Little Rock	AR	72201	501-447-1000	447-1162*
Los Angeles Unified School District 333 S Beaudry Ave *Web:* www.lausd.net	Los Angeles	CA	90017	213-241-1000	241-8952
Madison Metropolitan School District 545 W Dayton St **Fax:* Hum Res ■ *Web:* www.madison.k12.wi.us	Madison	WI	53703	608-663-1879	204-0346*
Memphis City Board of Education 2597 Avery Ave *Web:* www.memphis-schools.k12.tn.us	Memphis	TN	38112	901-416-5300	416-5578
Metropolitan Nashville & Davidson County Schools 2601 Bransford Ave *Web:* www.mnps.org	Nashville	TN	37204	615-259-8400	259-8623
Miami-Dade County Public Schools 1450 NE 2nd Ave Rm 912 **Fax:* Hum Res ■ *Web:* www.dadeschools.net	Miami	FL	33132	305-995-1430	995-7401*
Milwaukee Public Schools 5225 W Vliet St **Fax:* Hum Res ■ *Web:* www.milwaukee.k12.wi.us	Milwaukee	WI	53208	414-475-8393	475-8722*
Minneapolis Public Schools 807 NE Broadway **Fax:* Hum Res ■ *Web:* www.mpls.k12.mn.us	Minneapolis	MN	55413	612-668-0000	668-0525*
Mobile County Public Schools PO Box 180069 **Fax:* Hum Res ■ *Web:* www.mcpss.com	Mobile	AL	36618	251-221-4000	221-4545*
Modesto City Schools 426 Locust St **Fax:* Hum Res ■ *Web:* www.monet.k12.ca.us	Modesto	CA	95351	209-576-4011	576-4846*
Montgomery Public Schools 307 S Decatur St *Web:* www.mps.k12.al.us	Montgomery	AL	36104	334-223-6700	269-3076
New Haven Public Schools 54 Meadow St *Web:* www.nhps.net	New Haven	CT	06519	203-946-8811	946-7107
New York City Dept of Education 65 Court St *Web:* schools.nyc.gov	Brooklyn	NY	11201	718-935-2000	
Norfolk Public Schools 800 E City Hall Ave *Web:* www.nps.k12.va.us	Norfolk	VA	23510	757-628-3843	628-3820
Oklahoma City Public Schools 900 N Klein Ave *Web:* www.okcps.org	Oklahoma City	OK	73106	405-587-1000	587-0043
Olympia School District #111 1113 Legion Way SE *Web:* kids.osd.wednet.edu	Olympia	WA	98501	360-596-6117	596-6111
Omaha Public Schools 3215 Cuming St **Fax:* Hum Res ■ *Web:* www.ops.org	Omaha	NE	68131	402-557-2222	557-2319*
Orange County Public Schools 445 W Amelia St **Fax:* Hum Res ■ *Web:* www.ocps.k12.fl.us	Orlando	FL	32801	407-317-3200	317-3392*
Orleans Parish School Board 401 Nashville Ave *Web:* www.nops.k12.la.us	New Orleans	LA	70115	504-304-5680	
Palm Beach County School District 3300 Forest Hill Blvd **Fax:* Hum Res ■ *Web:* www.palmbeach.k12.fl.us	West Palm Beach	FL	33406	561-434-8000	434-8899*
Phoenix Elementary District 1817 N 7th St **Fax:* Hum Res ■ *Web:* www.phxelem.k12.az.us	Phoenix	AZ	85006	602-257-3755	257-6077*
Phoenix Union High School District 4502 N Central Ave **Fax:* Hum Res ■ *Web:* www.phxhs.k12.az.us	Phoenix	AZ	85012	602-271-3100	271-3510*
Pima County School Superintendent 130 W Congress St 4th Fl **Fax:* Hum Res ■ *Web:* www.schools.co.pima.az.us	Tucson	AZ	85701	520-740-8451	623-9308*
Pittsburgh Public Schools 341 S Bellefield Ave **Fax:* Hum Res ■ *Web:* www.pghboe.net	Pittsburgh	PA	15213	412-622-3500	622-7973*
Portland Public Schools 501 N Dixon St *Web:* www.pps.k12.or.us	Portland	OR	97227	503-916-2000	916-3110
Poudre School District 2407 LaPorte Ave *Web:* www.psd.k12.co.us	Fort Collins	CO	80521	970-482-7420	490-3514
Provo School District 280 W 940 North *Web:* www.provo.edu	Provo	UT	84604	801-374-4800	374-4808
Red Clay Consolidated School District 2916 Duncan Rd *Web:* www.redclay.k12.de.us	Wilmington	DE	19808	302-683-6600	636-8775
Richland County School District One 1616 Richland St **Fax:* Hum Res ■ *Web:* www.richlandone.org	Columbia	SC	29201	803-231-7000	231-7417*
Richmond City Public Schools 301 N 9th St *Web:* www.richmond.k12.va.us	Richmond	VA	23219	804-780-7700	780-4122
Richmond County School System 864 Broad St *Web:* www.rcboe.org/home.asp	Augusta	GA	30901	706-826-1000	
Rochester City School District 131 W Broad St *Web:* www.rcsdk12.org	Rochester	NY	14614	585-262-8100	262-5151
Sacramento City Unified School District 5735 47th Ave *Web:* www.scusd.edu	Sacramento	CA	95824	916-643-7400	643-9440
Saint Louis Public Schools 801 N 11th St **Fax:* Hum Res ■ *Web:* www.slps.org/	Saint Louis	MO	63101	314-231-3720	345-2650*
Salem/Keizer School District 2450 Lancaster Dr NE **Fax:* Hum Res ■ *Web:* www.salkeiz.k12.or.us	Salem	OR	97305	503-399-3061	375-7802*
Salt Lake School District 440 E 100 South *Web:* www.slc.k12.ut.us	Salt Lake City	UT	84111	801-578-8599	578-8689
San Antonio Independent School District 141 Lavaca St **Fax:* Hum Res ■ *Web:* www.saisd.net	San Antonio	TX	78210	210-299-5500	299-5600*
San Diego Unified School District 4100 Normal St *Web:* www.sandi.net	San Diego	CA	92103	619-725-8000	725-8001
San Francisco Unified School District 555 Franklin St *Web:* portal.sfusd.edu/template/default.cfm	San Francisco	CA	94102	415-241-6000	241-6429
San Jose Unified School District 855 Lenzen Ave **Fax:* Hum Res ■ *Web:* www.sjusd.k12.ca.us	San Jose	CA	95126	408-535-6000	535-2377*
Savannah-Chatham County Public Schools 208 Bull St **Fax:* Hum Res ■ *Web:* www.savannah.chatham.k12.ga.us	Savannah	GA	31401	912-201-5600	201-7667*
School District of Philadelphia 440 N Broad St *Web:* www.phila.k12.pa.us	Philadelphia	PA	19130	215-400-4000	
Scranton School District 425 N Washington Ave *Web:* www.scrsd.org/ssd/	Scranton	PA	18503	570-348-3402	348-3563
Seattle School District No 1 PO Box 34165 *Web:* www.seattleschools.org	Seattle	WA	98124	206-252-0000	
Sioux Falls School District 201 E 38th St **Fax:* Hum Res ■ *Web:* www.sf.k12.sd.us	Sioux Falls	SD	57105	605-367-7900	367-4637*

				Phone	Fax
Spokane School District #81 200 N Bernard St	Spokane	WA	99201	509-354-7265	354-5963*
*Fax: Hum Res ■ *Web:* www.spokaneschools.org					
Springfield Public School District #186 1900 W Monroe St	Springfield	IL	62704	217-525-3000	525-3005
Web: www.springfield.k12.il.us					
Springfield Public Schools 195 State St	Springfield	MA	01102	413-787-7087	787-7211*
*Fax: Hum Res ■ *Web:* www.sps.springfield.ma.us					
Springfield Public Schools 940 N Jefferson Ave	Springfield	MO	65802	417-523-0000	523-0196*
*Fax: Mail Rm ■ *Web:* sps.k12.mo.us					
Stockton Unified School District 701 N Madison St	Stockton	CA	95202	209-933-7000	933-7071
Web: www.stockton.k12.ca.us					
Syracuse City School District 725 Harrison St	Syracuse	NY	13210	315-435-4499	435-4023*
*Fax: Hum Res ■ *Web:* www.syracusecityschools.com					
Tacoma School District #10 PO Box 1357	Tacoma	WA	98401	253-571-1000	571-1453*
*Fax: Hum Res ■ *Web:* www.tacoma.k12.wa.us					
Toledo Public Schools 420 E Manhattan Blvd	Toledo	OH	43608	419-729-8200	729-8425
Web: www.tps.org					
Topeka School District (USD 501) 624 SW 24th St	Topeka	KS	66611	785-295-3000	575-6162*
*Fax: Hum Res ■ *Web:* www.topeka.k12.ks.us					
Trenton Public School System 108 N Clinton Ave	Trenton	NJ	08609	609-656-4900	989-2682
Web: www.trenton.k12.nj.us					
Tucson Unified School District No 1 1010 E 10th St	Tucson	AZ	85719	520-225-6070	798-8767
Web: www.tusd.k12.az.us					
Tulsa Public Schools 3027 S New Haven Ave	Tulsa	OK	74114	918-746-6800	746-6144*
*Fax: Hum Res ■ *Web:* www.tulsaschools.org					
Wake County Public School System 3600 Wake Forest Rd	Raleigh	NC	27609	919-850-1600	850-1693*
*Fax: Hum Res ■ *Web:* www.wcpss.net					
Washoe County School District PO Box 30425	Reno	NV	89520	775-348-0200	348-0389*
*Fax: Hum Res ■ *Web:* www.washoe.k12.nv.us					
Wichita Unified School District 259 201 N Water St	Wichita	KS	67202	316-973-4553	973-4595
Web: www.usd259.com					
Winston-Salem/Forsyth County Schools 1605 Miller St	Winston-Salem	NC	27103	336-727-2816	727-2008*
*Fax: Hum Res ■ *Web:* wsfcs.k12.nc.us					
Worcester Public Schools 20 Irving St	Worcester	MA	01609	508-799-3115	799-3119
Web: www.wpsweb.com					

689 SCRAP METAL

SEE ALSO Recyclable Materials Recovery p. 2208

				Phone	Fax
A Tenenbaum Co Inc 4500 W Bethany Rd	North Little Rock	AR	72117	501-945-0881	945-3865
Web: www.atenco.net					
Acme Refining 1225 Gifford Rd	Elgin	IL	60120	847-742-9500	742-2375
Adams Steel 3200 E Frontera St	Anaheim	CA	92806	714-630-8901	630-8931
Web: www.adamssteel.com					
Addlestone International Corp PO Drawer 979	Charleston	SC	29402	843-577-9300	577-4141
Allan Industries PO Box 999	Wilkes-Barre	PA	18703	570-826-0123	829-4099
Alma Iron & Metal Co Inc 1431 Williams St	Alma	MI	48801	989-463-2131	463-2135
TF: 800-572-6357					
Alter Trading Corp 689 Craig Rd	Saint Louis	MO	63141	314-872-2400	872-2420
TF: 888-337-2727 ■ *Web:* www.altertrading.com					
Amcep Inc 4484 E Tennessee St	Tucson	AZ	85714	520-748-1900	748-2752
American Iron & Supply Co 2800 Pacific St N	Minneapolis	MN	55411	612-529-9221	529-2548
Web: www.scrappy.com					
AMG Resources Corp 4100 Grand Ave	Pittsburgh	PA	15225	412-331-0770	331-4624*
*Fax: Sales ■ *TF:* 800-633-3606 ■ *Web:* www.amgresources.com					
Auto Shred Recycling LLC PO Box 17188	Pensacola	FL	32522	850-432-0977	433-4814
TF: 800-277-6964					
Azcon Corp 13733 S Ave 'O'	Chicago	IL	60633	773-646-2300	646-4121
Web: www.azcon.net					
Baker Iron & Metal Co Inc 740 Rock Castle Ave	Lexington	KY	40505	859-255-5676	252-3590
TF: 800-398-2537					
Behr Joseph & Sons Inc PO Box 740	Rockford	IL	61105	815-987-2600	987-2606
TF: 800-332-2347 ■ *Web:* www.jbehr.com					
Borg Compressed Steel Corp 1032 N Lewis Ave	Tulsa	OK	74110	918-587-2511	587-2520
Calbag Metals Co PO Box 10067	Portland	OR	97296	503-226-3441	228-0184
TF: 800-398-3441 ■ *Web:* www.calbag.com					
Cohen Brothers Inc PO Box 957	Middletown	OH	45044	513-422-3696	422-9018
TF: 800-878-3697 ■ *Web:* www.cohenbrothersinc.com					
Columbia Iron & Metal Co Inc 6600 Grant Ave	Cleveland	OH	44105	216-883-4972	883-8548
Connell LP 1 International Pl 31st Fl	Boston	MA	02110	617-737-2700	737-1617
TF: 800-276-4746 ■ *Web:* www.connell-lp.com					
CSR Inc PO Box 389	York	PA	17405	717-843-0931	854-4008
TF: 800-839-0931 ■ *Web:* www.consolidatedscrap.com					
Cycle Systems Inc 2580 Broadway SW PO Box 611	Roanoke	VA	24004	540-981-1211	981-0044
TF: 800-542-7000 ■ *Web:* www.cyclesystems.com					
David J Joseph Co 300 Pike St	Cincinnati	OH	45202	513-621-8770	419-6222
Web: www.djj.com					
Davis Industries Inc 9920 Richmond Hwy	Lorton	VA	22079	703-550-7402	550-5576
Duggan Industries Inc 3901 S Lamar St	Dallas	TX	75215	214-428-8336	428-1929
TF: 877-428-8336					
Easton Iron & Metal Co 1100 Bushkill Dr	Easton	PA	18042	610-250-6300	250-6302
Web: www.eastonmetal.com					
ELG Metals Inc 369 River Rd	McKeesport	PA	15132	412-672-9200	672-0824
Web: www.elgmetals.com					
Fairway Salvage Inc 12428 Center St	South Gate	CA	90280	562-630-8766	630-5929
Web: www.fairwaysalvage.com					
Ferrous Processing & Trading Co 9100 John Kronk St	Detroit	MI	48210	313-582-2910	582-1949
FPT Cleveland 3915 E 91st St	Cleveland	OH	44105	216-231-2430	641-9378
FPT Pontiac Div 500 Collier Rd	Pontiac	MI	48340	248-335-8141	335-8714
Franklin Iron & Metal Corp 1939 E 1st St	Dayton	OH	45403	937-253-8184	253-2030
TF: 800-255-8184					
Freedman RK & Son Inc PO Box 1533	Green Island	NY	12183	518-273-1141	273-7735
Web: www.rkfreedman.com					
Gachman Metals & Recycling Co Inc 2600 Shamrock Ave	Fort Worth	TX	76107	817-334-0211	877-1528
TF: 800-749-0423 ■ *Web:* www.gachman.com					
General Iron Industries Inc 1909 N Clifton Ave	Chicago	IL	60614	773-327-9600	327-8732
Gershow Recycling Corp PO Box 526	Medford	NY	11763	631-289-6188	289-6368
Web: www.gershowrecycling.com					
Great Western Recycling Industries Inc 521 Barge Channel Rd	Saint Paul	MN	55107	651-224-4877	224-4870
Grossman Iron & Steel 5 N Market St	Saint Louis	MO	63102	314-231-9423	231-6983
TF: 800-969-9423 ■ *Web:* www.grossmaniron.com					
Hugo Neuschnitzer East 1 Jersey Ave	Jersey City	NJ	07302	201-333-4300	432-5332
Iron & Metals Inc 5555 Franklin St	Denver	CO	80216	303-292-5555	292-0513
TF: 800-776-7910 ■ *Web:* www.ironandmetals.com					
J Solotken & Co Inc PO Box 1645	Indianapolis	IN	46206	317-638-5566	638-5569
Jacobs Iron & Metal Co 3330 Pluto St	Dallas	TX	75212	214-631-6740	631-7224
Joe Krentzman & Son Inc PO Box 508	Lewistown	PA	17044	717-543-5635	543-6299
TF: 800-543-2000					
Joseph Behr & Sons Inc PO Box 740	Rockford	IL	61105	815-987-2600	987-2606
TF: 800-332-2347 ■ *Web:* www.jbehr.com					
Joseph David J Co 300 Pike St	Cincinnati	OH	45202	513-621-8770	419-6222
Web: www.djj.com					
Joseph Simon & Sons Inc 2202 E River St	Tacoma	WA	98421	253-272-9364	838-1998
TF: 800-562-8464 ■ *Web:* www.jsimonandsons.com					
JT Knight & Son Inc PO Box 1259	Columbus	GA	31901	706-322-1685	221-9000
Web: www.jtknight.com					
Kendallville Iron & Metal Inc PO Box 69	Kendallville	IN	46755	260-347-1958	347-1966
TF: 800-530-5564					
Keywell LLC 11900 S Cottage Grove Ave	Chicago	IL	60628	773-660-2060	660-2064
Web: www.keywell.com					
Krentzman Joe & Son Inc PO Box 508	Lewistown	PA	17044	717-543-5635	543-6299
TF: 800-543-2000					
Langley Recycling 503 SE Branner St	Topeka	KS	66607	785-234-2691	354-8019
Web: www.langleyrecycling.com					
Liberty Iron & Metal Co PO Box 1391	Erie	PA	16512	814-453-6758	456-6107
TF: 800-836-0259 ■ *Web:* www.libertyiron.com					
Lipsitz M & Co Inc 100 Elm St	Waco	TX	76704	254-756-6661	754-7954
Web: www.mlipsitzco.com					
Louis Padnos Iron & Metal Co PO Box 1979	Holland	MI	49422	616-396-6521	396-7789
TF: 800-442-3509 ■ *Web:* www.padnos.com					
M Lipsitz & Co Inc 100 Elm St	Waco	TX	76704	254-756-6661	754-7954
Web: www.mlipsitzco.com					
Mayer Pollock Steel Corp PO Box 759	Pottstown	PA	19464	610-323-5500	323-5506
TF: 800-323-5502 ■ *Web:* www.mayerpollock.com					
Mervis Industries Inc 3295 E Main St	Danville	IL	61834	217-442-5300	477-9245
TF: 800-637-3016 ■ *Web:* www.mervis.com					
Metal Exchange Corp 111 West Port Plaza Suite 700	Saint Louis	MO	63146	314-434-3500	434-2196
Web: www.metalexchangecorp.com					
Metal Management 304 W Bankhead St	New Albany	MS	38652	662-538-7104	528-0380
Web: www.mtlm.com					
Metal Management Aerospace Inc 500 Flatbush Ave	Hartford	CT	06106	860-522-3123	951-3367
Metal Management Inc 325 N LaSalle St Suite 550	Chicago	IL	60610	312-645-0700	645-0714
NASDAQ: MTLM ■ *TF:* 888-645-0700 ■ *Web:* www.mtlm.com					
Metal Management NE Inc PO Box 5158	Newark	NJ	07105	973-344-4570	344-8155
Metal Management Pittsburgh Inc 2045 Lincoln Blvd	Elizabeth	PA	15037	412-384-7400	384-7406
Web: www.mtlm.com					
Metalico Annaco Inc PO Box 1148	Akron	OH	44309	330-376-1400	376-9696
TF: 800-394-1300 ■ *Web:* www.annaco.com					
Metalico Inc 186 North Ave E	Cranford	NJ	07016	908-497-9610	497-1097
AMEX: MEA ■ *Web:* www.metalico.com					
Metalsco Inc 11775 Borman Suite 102	Saint Louis	MO	63146	314-997-5200	997-5921
Web: www.metalsco.com					
Mid-City Iron & Metal Corp 2104 E 15th St	Los Angeles	CA	90021	213-747-4281	749-5772
Web: www.adamssteel.com					
Midland Davis Corp 3301 4th Ave	Moline	IL	61265	309-764-6723	764-6729
TF: 800-223-5942					
Miller Compressing Co 1640 W Bruce St	Milwaukee	WI	53204	414-671-5980	671-3658
Web: www.millercompressing.com					
Minkin-Chandler Corp 13501 Sanders Ave	Detroit	MI	48217	313-843-5900	843-6782
Newell Recycling of San Antonio PO Box 830808	San Antonio	TX	78283	210-227-3141	227-8948
OmniSource Corp 7575 W Jefferson Blvd	Fort Wayne	IN	46804	260-422-5541	423-8500
TF: 800-666-4789 ■ *Web:* www.omnisource.com					
Omnisource Corp 2916 Bluff Rd	Indianapolis	IN	46225	317-381-5800	381-5810
Web: www.omnisource.com					
Pacific Coast Recycling Weiner Steel Div 1545 Gage Rd	Montebello	CA	90640	323-723-8327	726-1988
Padnos Louis Iron & Metal Co PO Box 1979	Holland	MI	49422	616-396-6521	396-7789
TF: 800-442-3509 ■ *Web:* www.padnos.com					
Pascap Co Inc 4250 Boston Rd	Bronx	NY	10475	718-325-7200	325-7595
Web: www.pascapco.com					
Progress Rail Services 1600 Progress Dr	Albertville	AL	35950	256-593-1260	593-1249
TF: 800-476-8769 ■ *Web:* www.progressrail.com					
PSC (Philip Services Corp) 51 San Felipe Rd Suite 1600	Houston	TX	77056	713-623-8777	625-7185
TF: 800-726-1300 ■ *Web:* www.contactpsc.com					
PSC Metals Inc 5875 Landerbrook Dr Suite 200	Mayfield Heights	OH	44124	440-753-5400	753-5430
TF: 888-772-6385 ■ *Web:* www.pscmetals.com					
Recycle Metals Corp 407 Allen Wood Rd	Conshohocken	PA	19428	610-828-5553	828-5390
Richman SD Sons Inc 2435 Wheatsheaf Ln	Philadelphia	PA	19137	215-535-5100	288-1043
TF: 800-648-3576 ■ *Web:* www.sdrichmansons.com					
River Metals Recycling PO Box 6521	Louisville	KY	40206	502-585-5331	587-8699
Web: www.rmrecycling.com					
River Recycling Industries Inc 4195 Bradley Rd	Cleveland	OH	44109	216-459-2100	749-8107
Riverside Scrap Iron PO Box 5288	Riverside	CA	92517	951-686-2120	686-8933
TF: 800-399-4766 ■ *Web:* www.riversidemetalrecycling.com					
RK Freedman & Son Inc PO Box 1533	Green Island	NY	12183	518-273-1141	273-7735
Web: www.rkfreedman.com					
Robinson Iron & Metal Co 2735 Brooks St	Houston	TX	77020	713-227-2376	227-2910
Rocky Mountain Recycling 6510 Brighton Blvd	Commerce City	CO	80022	303-288-6867	288-0250
Web: www.mountainrecycling.com					
Rose Metal Processing Inc 2722 Center St	Houston	TX	77007	713-880-7050	880-7011
Sadoff & Rudoy Industries LLP 240 W Arndt St	Fond du Lac	WI	54935	920-921-2070	921-1283
TF: 800-236-5700 ■ *Web:* www.sadoff.com					
Samuels Recycling Co 4400 Sycamore Ave	Madison	WI	53714	608-241-7191	241-2641
Schlafer Iron & Metal Co Inc 1950 Medbury St	Detroit	MI	48211	313-925-8200	925-0133
SD Richman Sons Inc 2435 Wheatsheaf Ln	Philadelphia	PA	19137	215-535-5100	288-1043
TF: 800-648-3576 ■ *Web:* www.sdrichmansons.com					
Segel & Son Inc 107 S South St PO Box 276	Warren	PA	16365	814-723-4900	723-4970
TF: 800-252-1215					
Shredded Products LLC 700 Commerce Rd	Rocky Mount	VA	24151	540-489-7599	489-8431
Simon Joseph & Sons Inc 2202 E River St	Tacoma	WA	98421	253-272-9364	838-1998
TF: 800-562-8464 ■ *Web:* www.jsimonandsons.com					
Simon Resources Inc 2525 Trenton Ave	Williamsport	PA	17701	570-326-9431	326-5028
Sims Bros Inc PO Box 1170	Marion	OH	43301	740-387-9041	387-0083
TF: 800-536-7461 ■ *Web:* www.simsbros.com					
Simsmetal America Inc 600 S 4th St	Richmond	CA	94804	510-412-5300	412-5420
Web: www.sims-group.com					
SLC Recycling Industries Inc 8701 E 8 Mile Rd	Warren	MI	48089	586-759-6600	759-6518
Soave Enterprises LLC 3400 E Lafayette St	Detroit	MI	48207	313-567-7000	567-3331
Web: www.soave.com					
Sol Tick & Co PO Box 1605	Decatur	IL	62525	217-429-4148	429-7565
Solomon Metal Corp 580 Lynnway	Lynn	MA	01905	781-581-7000	599-6130
TF: 800-326-8959					
Solotken J & Co Inc PO Box 1645	Indianapolis	IN	46206	317-638-5566	638-5569
South Bend Scrap & Processing Div Sturgis Iron & Metal Co 1305 Prairie Ave	South Bend	IN	46613	574-287-3311	287-1072
TF: 800-232-2441					
Southern Holdings LLC 109 N Park Dr Suite 320	Covington	LA	70433	985-246-7936	246-7929
TF: 800-467-2727					
Southern Scrap Material Co Inc 6847 Scenic Hwy	Baton Rouge	LA	70807	225-355-4453	355-3167
TF: 800-355-4453					
Sturgis Iron & Metal Co PO Box 579	Sturgis	MI	49091	269-651-7851	651-4189
TF: 800-446-0794					
Sturgis Iron & Metal Co South Bend Scrap & Processing Div 1305 Prairie Ave	South Bend	IN	46613	574-287-3311	287-1072
TF: 800-232-2441					
Sugar Creek Scrap Inc 1201 W National Ave	West Terre Haute	IN	47805	812-533-2147	533-2140
TF: 800-466-7462 ■ *Web:* www.sugarcreekscrap.com					

	City	State	Zip	Phone	Fax
Tenenbaum A Co Inc 4500 W Bethany Rd	North Little Rock	AR	72117	501-945-0881	945-3865
Web: www.atenco.net					
Tennessee Valley Recycling LLC 821 W College St	Pulaski	TN	38478	931-363-3593	363-8065
Thalheimer Brothers Inc 5550 Whitaker Ave	Philadelphia	PA	19124	215-537-5200	533-3993
Web: thalheimerbrothers.com					
Tri-State Iron & Metal Co PO Box 775	Texarkana	AR	75504	870-773-8409	772-3086
TF: 800-773-8409					
Tube City IMS Corp 12 Monongahela Ave	Glassport	PA	15045	412-678-6141	675-8295
TF: 800-225-0478 ■ *Web:* www.tubecity.com					
IMS Division 1155 Business Center Dr	Horsham	PA	19044	215-956-5500	
TF: 800-523-0781 ■ *Web:* www.ims.biz					
Union Processing Inc 3484 S Union St	North Chili	NY	14514	585-594-1600	594-0160
Wabash Alloys LLC PO Box 466	Wabash	IN	46992	260-563-7461	563-5997
TF: 800-348-0571 ■ *Web:* www.wabashalloys.com					
Weiner Steel Div Pacific Coast Recycling 1545 Gage Rd	Montebello	CA	90640	323-723-8327	726-1988
Western Scrap Processing Co 3315 Drennan Industrial Loop S	Colorado Springs	CO	80910	719-390-7986	390-3852
Web: www.westernscrap.com					
Wimco Metals Inc 401 Penn Ave	Pittsburgh	PA	15221	412-243-8000	243-2225
Wise Metals Group 857 Elkridge Landing Rd Suite 600	Linthicum	MD	21090	410-636-6500	636-1564
TF: 800-818-9473 ■ *Web:* www.wisemetals.com					
Yaffe Iron & Metal Co Inc PO Box 916	Muskogee	OK	74402	918-687-7543	687-0053
TF: 800-759-2333 ■ *Web:* www.yaffeco.net					

690 SCREEN PRINTING

	City	State	Zip	Phone	Fax
College House Inc 1400 Chamberlayne Ave	Richmond	VA	23222	804-643-4240	643-4408
TF: 800-888-7606 ■ *Web:* www.thecollegehouse.com					
Designer Decal Inc 1120 E 1st Ave	Spokane	WA	99202	509-535-0267	535-1476
TF: 800-622-6333 ■ *Web:* www.designerdecal.com					
Eagle Eye Screen Printing LLC 8021 S Redwood Rd	West Jordan	UT	84088	801-566-1681	566-7917
Web: www.eagleeyescreenprinting.com					
Empire Screen Printing Inc N5206 Marco Rd PO Box 218	Onalaska	WI	54650	608-783-3301	783-3306
Web: www.empirescreen.com					
Flow-Eze Co 3209 Auburn St	Rockford	IL	61101	815-965-1062	965-1329
TF: 800-435-4873 ■ *Web:* www.flow-eze.com					
Gill Studios Inc 10800 Lackman Rd	Lenexa	KS	66219	913-888-4422	392-4455*
**Fax Area Code:* 800 ■ *TF:* 888-455-4422 ■ *Web:* www.gill-line.com					
Holoubek Inc W 238 N 1800 Rockwood Dr	Waukesha	WI	53188	262-547-0500	547-5847
TF: 800-558-0566 ■ *Web:* www.holoubek.com					
Kay Automotive Graphics 57 Kay Industrial Dr	Lake Orion	MI	48359	248-377-4999	377-2097
TF: 800-443-0190 ■ *Web:* www.kayautomotive.com					
M & M Designs Inc 1981 Quality Blvd	Huntsville	TX	77320	936-295-2682	295-9286
TF: 800-627-0656 ■ *Web:* www.m-mdesigns.com					
Motson Graphics Inc 1717 Bethlehem Pike	Flourtown	PA	19031	215-233-0500	233-5014
TF: 800-972-1986 ■ *Web:* www.motson.com					
Ram Graphics Inc 2408 S Park Ave	Alexandria	IN	46001	800-531-4656	551-6846
Web: www.ramgraphics.com					
Screen Machine Inc 3855 Wabash Ave	San Diego	CA	92104	619-281-3355	281-2033
Serigraph Inc 3801 E Decorah Road	West Bend	WI	53095	262-335-7200	335-7699
TF: 800-279-6060 ■ *Web:* www.serigraph.com					
Stratecom Graphics 235 Conway Dr	Bogart	GA	30622	706-546-8840	354-7815
TF: 800-205-9159					
Technigraph Corp 850 W 3rd St	Winona	MN	55987	507-454-3830	454-6470
Web: www.technigraph.net					
Trau & Loevner Inc 5817 Centre Ave	Pittsburgh	PA	15206	412-361-7700	361-8221
TF: 800-245-6207 ■ *Web:* www.trau-loevner.com					

691 SCREENING - WOVEN WIRE

	City	State	Zip	Phone	Fax
ACS Industries Inc 191 Social St	Woonsocket	RI	02895	401-769-4700	766-2191
TF: 800-237-1939 ■ *Web:* www.acsindustries.com					
Belleville Wire Cloth Inc 18 Rutgers Ave	Cedar Grove	NJ	07009	973-239-0074	239-3985
TF: 800-631-0490 ■ *Web:* www.bwire.com					
Buffalo Wire Works Co 1165 Clinton St	Buffalo	NY	14206	716-826-4666	826-8271
TF: 800-828-7028 ■ *Web:* www.buffalowire.com					
Cleveland Wire Cloth & Mfg Co 3573 E 78th St	Cleveland	OH	44105	216-341-1832	341-1876
TF: 800-321-3234 ■ *Web:* www.wirecloth.com					
Darby Edward J & Son Inc 2200 N 8th St PO Box 50049	Philadelphia	PA	19133	215-236-2203	236-9989
TF: 800-875-6374 ■ *Web:* www.darbywire.com					
Edward J Darby & Son Inc 2200 N 8th St PO Box 50049	Philadelphia	PA	19133	215-236-2203	236-9989
TF: 800-875-6374 ■ *Web:* www.darbywire.com					
Gerard Daniel Worldwide 34 Barnhart Dr	Hanover	PA	17331	717-637-5901	633-7095
TF: 800-233-3017 ■ *Web:* www.gerarddaniel.com					
Halliburton Screen Co 1815 Shearn St	Houston	TX	77007	713-869-5771	869-0728
TF: 800-527-4772 ■ *Web:* www.halliburton.com					
Hanover Wire Cloth 500 E Middle St PO Box 473	Hanover	PA	17331	717-637-3795	637-4766
TF: 800-323-5585 ■ *Web:* www.hanoverwire.com					
Hoyt Wire Cloth Co PO Box 4647	Lancaster	PA	17604	717-394-6871	394-1640
Jelliff Corp 354 Pequot Ave	Southport	CT	06890	203-259-1615	255-7908
TF: 800-364-9502 ■ *Web:* www.jelliff.com					
King Wire Partitions Inc 6044 N Figueroa St	Los Angeles	CA	90042	323-256-4848	256-1950
Web: www.kingwireusa.com					
Metex Corp 970 New Durham Rd	Edison	NJ	08818	732-287-0800	287-8546*
**Fax:* Sales ■ *Web:* www.metexcorp.com					
National-Standard Co 1631 Lake St	Niles	MI	49120	269-683-8100	683-6249
TF: 800-777-1618 ■ *Web:* www.nationalstandard.com					
National Wire Fabric 701 Arkansas St	Star City	AR	71667	870-628-4201	628-3700
TF: 800-643-1558 ■ *Web:* www.nationalwirefabric.com					
New England Fireplace Inc 856 N Main St Ext	Wallingford	CT	06492	203-265-1686	284-8797
TF: 800-448-0409					
New York Wire Co 152 Main St	Mount Wolf	PA	17347	717-266-5626	266-5871
TF: 800-699-4732 ■ *Web:* www.newyorkwire.com					
Newark Wire Cloth Co 160 Verona Ave	Newark	NJ	07013	973-483-7700	483-6315
TF: 800-221-0392 ■ *Web:* www.newarkwire.com					
Phoenix Wire Cloth Inc 585 Stephenson Hwy	Troy	MI	48083	248-585-6350	585-4121
TF: 800-458-3286					
Pittsfield Products Inc PO Box 1027	Ann Arbor	MI	48106	734-665-3771	665-3132
Sherman Wire Co 428 Gibbons Rd	Sherman	TX	75092	903-893-0191	868-9502
TF: 800-527-4637					
Tecknit Inc 129 Dermody St	Cranford	NJ	07016	908-272-5500	272-2741
Web: www.tecknit.com					
TWP Inc 2831 10th St	Berkeley	CA	94710	510-548-4434	548-3073
TF: 800-227-1570 ■ *Web:* www.twpinc.com					
United Capital Corp 9 Park Pl 4th Fl	Great Neck	NY	11021	516-466-6464	829-4301
AMEX: AFP					
Universal Wire Cloth Co 16 N Steel Rd	Morrisville	PA	19067	215-736-8981	736-8994
TF: 800-892-6374 ■ *Web:* www.uwcwirecloth.com					
Wayne Wire Cloth Products Inc 200 E Dresden St	Kalkaska	MI	49646	231-258-9187	258-5504
TF: 800-654-7688					
Western Wire Group 4025 NW Express Ave	Portland	OR	97210	503-222-1644	222-6843
TF: 800-547-9192 ■ *Web:* www.thewesterngroup.com					
Wire Cloth Filter Mfg Co 611 W St Charles Rd	Maywood	IL	60153	708-410-1800	410-1807

692 SEATING - VEHICULAR

	City	State	Zip	Phone	Fax
Advanced Components Technologies Inc 91 S 16th St	Northwood	IA	50459	641-324-2231	324-1231
Web: www.goact.net					
American Metal Fab Inc 55515 Franklin Dr	Three Rivers	MI	49093	269-279-5108	279-5356
Web: www.americanmetalfab.com					
Beloates Aircraft Trim Inc 4408 N Haltom Rd	Haltom City	TX	76117	817-485-5013	485-5014
Bornemann Products Inc 1720 W Dewey St	Bremen	IN	46506	574-546-2881	546-5722
Web: www.bpiseats.com					
Bostrom HO Co Inc 818 Progress Ave	Waukesha	WI	53186	262-542-0222	542-3784
TF: 800-332-5415 ■ *Web:* www.hobostrom.com					
Bostrom Seating Inc 50 Nances Creek Industrial Blvd	Piedmont	AL	36272	256-447-9051	447-2038
TF: 800-459-7328 ■ *Web:* www.bostromseating.com					
Bridgewater Interiors LLC 4617 W Fort St	Detroit	MI	48209	313-842-3300	842-3452
Custom Aircraft Interiors 3701 Industry Ave	Lakewood	CA	90712	562-426-5098	490-0213
Web: www.customaircraftinteriors.com					
Findlay Industries Inc 4000 Fostoria Rd	Findlay	OH	45840	419-422-1302	422-0385
Web: www.findlayindustries.com					
Freedman Seating Co 4545 W Augusta Blvd	Chicago	IL	60651	773-524-2440	252-7450
TF: 800-443-4540 ■ *Web:* www.freedmanseating.com					
HO Bostrom Co Inc 818 Progress Ave	Waukesha	WI	53186	262-542-0222	542-3784
TF: 800-332-5415 ■ *Web:* www.hobostrom.com					
Hoover Industries Inc 7260 NW 68th St	Miami	FL	33166	305-888-9791	887-4632
Web: www.hooverindustries.com					
Johnson Controls Inc Automotive Systems Group 49200 Halyard Dr	Plymouth	MI	48170	734-254-5000	254-5843*
**Fax:* Hum Res ■ *Web:* www.johnsoncontrols.com/asg-intro					
Knoedler Manufacturers Inc 7185 Tower Rd	Battle Creek	MI	49014	269-969-7722	969-7720
Web: www.knoedler.com					
Kustom Fit/Hi-Tech Seating 8990 Atlantic Ave	South Gate	CA	90280	323-564-4481	564-5754
Web: www.kustomfit.com					
Lear Corp 21557 Telegraph Rd	Southfield	MI	48034	248-447-1500	447-1722
NYSE: LEA ■ *Web:* www.lear.com					
Lear Seating Corp 4600 Nancy St	Detroit	MI	48212	313-852-7800	852-7852
Michigan Seat Co 2313 Brooklyn Rd	Jackson	MI	49203	517-787-3650	787-2089
Web: www.mi-seat.com					
Milsco Mfg Co 9009 N 51st St	Brown Deer	WI	53223	414-354-0500	354-0508
TF: 800-645-7261 ■ *Web:* www.milsco.com					
National Seating Co 200 National Dr	Vonore	TN	37885	423-884-6651	884-6166
TF: 800-222-7328 ■ *Web:* www.nationalseating.com					
Precision Pattern Inc 1643 S Maize Rd	Wichita	KS	67209	316-721-3100	721-2053
TF: 800-448-5127 ■ *Web:* www.precision-pattern.com					
Sears Mfg Co 1718 S Concord St PO Box 3667	Davenport	IA	52808	563-383-2800	383-2810
TF Cust Svc: 800-553-3013 ■ *Web:* www.searsseating.com					
Seats Inc 1515 Industrial St PO Box 60	Reedsburg	WI	53959	608-524-4316	524-6004
TF: 800-443-0615 ■ *Web:* www.seatsinc.com					
Sicma Aero Seat Services Inc 22030 20th Ave SE Suite 102	Bothell	WA	98021	425-806-2066	806-2068
Turnbull Enterprises Inc 3100 Viona Ave	Baltimore	MD	21230	410-789-1700	789-1706
Web: www.turnbullenterprises.com					
Villa Furniture Mfg 502 E Julianna St	Anaheim	CA	92801	714-535-7273	535-1271
TF: 888-707-7272 ■ *Web:* www.villainternational.com					
Weber Aircraft LP 2000 Weber Dr	Gainesville	TX	76240	940-668-4100	668-4195
Web: www.weberair.com					
Wise Co Inc 5535 Pleasant View Rd	Memphis	TN	38134	901-388-0155	373-8283
TF: 800-251-2622 ■ *Web:* www.wiseseats.com					

693 SECURITIES BROKERS & DEALERS

SEE ALSO Commodity Contracts Brokers & Dealers p. 1499; Electronic Communications Networks (ECNs) p. 1609; Investment Advice & Management p. 1873; Mutual Funds p. 2010

	City	State	Zip	Phone	Fax
AB Watley Inc 50 Broad St Suite 1728	New York	NY	10004	646-753-9301	202-5204*
**Fax Area Code:* 212 ■ *TF:* 888-229-2853 ■ *Web:* www.abwatley.com					
Accutrade Inc PO Box 2227	Omaha	NE	68103	402-970-4100	243-3768*
**Fax Area Code:* 816 ■ *TF Cust Svc:* 800-228-3011 ■ *Web:* www.accutrade.com					
Adams Harkness Inc 99 High St 12th Fl	Boston	MA	02110	617-371-3900	371-3798
TF: 800-225-6201 ■ *Web:* www.adamsharkness.com					
AG Edwards & Sons Inc 1 N Jefferson Ave	Saint Louis	MO	63103	314-955-3000	955-4536*
**Fax:* Hum Res ■ *Web:* www.agedwards.com					
Allen & Co Inc 711 5th Ave 9th Fl	New York	NY	10022	212-832-8000	832-8023
Ameriprise Brokerage 70400 Ameriprise Financial Center	Minneapolis	MN	55474	612-671-3131	624-2259*
**Fax Area Code:* 800 ■ *TF:* 800-297-7378 ■ *Web:* www.ameriprise.com					
Ameritas Investment Corp PO Box 81889	Lincoln	NE	68501	402-466-4565	467-6945
TF: 800-228-8712 ■ *Web:* www.aicinvest.com					
Aronson + Johnson + Ortiz LP 230 S Broad St 20th Fl	Philadelphia	PA	19102	215-546-7500	546-7506
Web: www.ajopartners.com					
Associated Financial Group Inc 222 N Sepulveda Blvd Suite 1800	El Segundo	CA	90245	310-568-3600	258-6568
Web: www.afgweb.com					
Baird Patrick & Co Inc 305 Plaza 10 Harbor Side Financial Center	Jersey City	NJ	07311	201-680-7300	680-7301
TF: 800-221-7747 ■ *Web:* www.bairdpatrick.com					
Baird Robert W & Co Inc PO Box 672	Milwaukee	WI	53201	414-765-3500	765-3600
TF: 800-792-2473 ■ *Web:* www.rwbaird.com					
Bank of America Securities LLC 600 Montgomery St	San Francisco	CA	94111	415-627-2000	
TF: 800-227-4786 ■ *Web:* www.bofasecurities.com					
Barclays Capital Inc 200 Park Ave	New York	NY	10166	212-412-4000	412-6795*
**Fax:* Hum Res ■ *TF:* 888-227-2275 ■ *Web:* www.barcap.com					
Baum George K & Co 4801 Main St Suite 500 Box 20	Kansas City	MO	64112	816-474-1100	283-5180
TF: 800-821-7195 ■ *Web:* www.gkbaum.com					
BB & T Capital Markets 2 S 9th St	Richmond	VA	23219	804-649-3900	649-3933
TF: 800-476-3819 ■ *Web:* www.bbandt.com					
Beal MR & Co 110 Wall St 6th Fl	New York	NY	10005	212-983-3930	983-4539
Web: www.mrbeal.com					
Bear Stearns & Co Inc 383 Madison Ave	New York	NY	10179	212-272-2000	272-8210*
**Fax:* Hum Res ■ *TF:* 800-999-2000 ■ *Web:* www.bearstearns.com					
Bear Stearns Cos Inc 383 Madison Ave	New York	NY	10179	212-272-2000	272-8210*
NYSE: BSC ■ **Fax:* Hum Res ■ *TF:* 800-999-2000 ■ *Web:* www.bearstearns.com					

Phone | Fax

Bernard L Madoff Investment Securities Co
885 3rd Ave 18th Fl. New York NY 10022 212-230-2424
TF: 800-334-1343 ■ *Web:* www.madoff.com

BISYS Fund Services 3435 Stelzer Rd Suite 1000. Columbus OH 43219 614-470-8000 470-8702
TF: 800-554-3862 ■ *Web:* www.bisys.com/products/fundServices.asp

Blackstone Group 345 Park Ave 31st Fl. New York NY 10154 212-583-5000 583-5712
TF: 800-262-6179 ■ *Web:* www.blackstone.com

Blair William & Co LLC 222 W Adams St. Chicago IL 60606 312-236-1600 236-1875
TF: 800-621-0687 ■ *Web:* www.williamblair.com

Blaylock & Co Inc 780 3rd Ave 44th Fl. New York NY 10017 212-715-6600 715-3300
Web: www.blaylockco.com

BMO Nesbitt Burns Inc 1 First Canadian Pl PO Box 150. Toronto ON M5X1H3 416-359-4000 359-4311
Web: www.bmonesbittburns.com

BNP Paribas 787 7th Ave. New York NY 10019 212-841-3000 841-2146
Web: www.bnpparibas.com

Boston Institutional Services Inc 100 Summer St 16th Fl. Boston MA 02110 617-223-5600 223-5650*
**Fax:* Sales ■ *TF:* 800-325-5323 ■ *Web:* www.bostonis.com

Brean Murray & Co Inc 570 Lexington Ave 11th Fl. New York NY 10022 212-702-6500 702-6649
Web: breanmurray.com

Broadview International 520 Madison Ave. New York NY 10022 212-284-8100 284-8101
TF: 800-346-9616 ■ *Web:* www.broadview.com

Butler Wick & Co Inc 100 Federal Plaza E City Ctr 1. Youngstown OH 44503 330-744-4351 743-7911
TF: 800-229-1643 ■ *Web:* www.butlerwick.com

BUYandHOLD.com Securities Corp PO Box 6498. Edison NJ 08837 800-646-8212 934-3095*
**Fax Area Code:* 732 ■ *Web:* www.buyandhold.com

Cantor Fitzgerald LP 110 E 59th St. New York NY 10022 212-938-5000 829-5280
Web: www.cantor.com

Charles Schwab & Co Inc 211 Main St. San Francisco CA 94105 415-636-7000 636-5970*
**Fax:* PR ■ *TF Cust Svc:* 800-648-5300 ■ *Web:* www.schwab.com

CIBC World Markets 300 Madison Ave. New York NY 10017 212-856-4000
TF: 800-999-6726 ■ *Web:* www.cibcwm.com

Citicorp Venture Capital Ltd 399 Park Ave 14th Fl Zone 4. New York NY 10022 212-559-1127 888-2940
TF: 800-285-3000

CitiStreet PO Box 6723. Summerset NJ 08875 732-514-2000 514-2112*
**Fax:* Hum Res ■ *TF:* 800-537-6517 ■ *Web:* www.citistreetonline.com

City Securities Corp PO Box 44992. Indianapolis IN 46244 317-634-4400 972-7150
TF: 800-800-2489 ■ *Web:* www.citysecurities.com

Comerica Securities 201 W Fort St 3rd Fl. Detroit MI 48226 313-222-5580 222-5098*
**Fax:* Cust Svc ■ *TF:* 800-232-6983 ■ *Web:* www.comerica.com/comerica/default.html

Credit Suisse First Boston Corp 11 Madison Ave. New York NY 10010 212-325-2000
TF: 877-775-2732 ■ *Web:* www.csfb.com

Crowell Weedon & Co
624 S Grand Ave 1 Wilshire Bldg Suite 2600. Los Angeles CA 90017 213-620-1850 622-6525*
**Fax:* Hum Res ■ *TF:* 800-227-0319 ■ *Web:* www.crowellweedon.com

Crown Financial Group Inc 525 Washington Blvd. Jersey City NJ 07303 201-459-9600 332-7495
TF: 800-333-3113

CyberTrader Inc 12401 Research Blvd Bldg 2 Suite 350. Austin TX 78759 888-762-9237 320-1561*
**Fax Area Code:* 512 ■ *TF:* 888-762-9237 ■ *Web:* www.cybertrader.com

DA Davidson & Co Inc 8 3rd St N. Great Falls MT 59401 406-727-4200 791-7380
TF: 800-332-5915 ■ *Web:* www.davidsoncompanies.com/indv

Daiwa Securities America Inc 32 Old Slip Financial Sq. New York NY 10005 212-612-7000 612-7164
Web: www.daiwausa.com

Davenport & Co LLC 901 E Cary St 11th Fl. Richmond VA 23219 804-780-2000 780-2026
TF: 800-846-6666 ■ *Web:* www.davenportllc.com

Davidson DA & Co Inc 8 3rd St N. Great Falls MT 59401 406-727-4200 791-7380
TF: 800-332-5915 ■ *Web:* www.davidsoncompanies.com/indv

Deutsche Bank Securities Inc 60 Wall St. New York NY 10005 800-334-1898

Domestic Securities Inc 160 Summit Ave. Montvale NJ 07645 201-782-0888 782-9090
TF: 877-429-2111 ■ *Web:* www.dom-sec.com

Dougherty & Co LLC 90 S 7th St Suite 4300. Minneapolis MN 55402 612-376-4000 338-7732
TF: 800-328-4085 ■ *Web:* www.doughertymarkets.com

Dresdner Kleinwort Wasserstein 1301 Ave of the Americas. New York NY 10019 212-429-2000 429-2127
TF: 800-457-0245 ■ *Web:* www.drkw.com

Dreyfus Corp 200 Park Ave. New York NY 10166 212-922-6000 922-7533
Web: www.dreyfus.com

Duncan-Williams Inc 6750 Poplar Ave Suite 300. Memphis TN 38138 901-260-6800 260-6994
TF: 800-827-0827 ■ *Web:* www.duncanw.com

E*Trade Financial Corp 4500 Bohannon Dr. Menlo Park CA 94025 650-331-6000 331-6819
NYSE: ET ■ *TF Orders:* 800-786-2575 ■ *Web:* us.etrade.com

Eaton Vance Distributors Inc 255 State St. Boston MA 02109 617-482-8260 482-2396
TF: 800-225-6265 ■ *Web:* www.eatonvance.com

Edward Jones 12555 Manchester Rd. Saint Louis MO 63131 314-515-2000
Web: www.edwardjones.com

Edwards AG & Sons Inc 1 N Jefferson Ave. Saint Louis MO 63103 314-955-3000 955-4536*
**Fax:* Hum Res ■ *Web:* www.agedwards.com

Empire Financial Group Inc 2170 W SR 434 Suite 100. Longwood FL 32779 407-774-1300 834-9995
AMEX: EFH ■ *TF:* 800-569-3337 ■ *Web:* www.empirenow.com

Ferris Baker Watts Inc
1700 Pennsylvania Ave NW Suite 700. Washington DC 20006 202-661-9500 661-9659
TF: 800-227-0308 ■ *Web:* www.fbw.com

Fidelity Brokerage Services Inc 82 Devonshire St. Boston MA 02109 800-343-3548
TF: 800-828-6680 ■ *Web:* www.fidelity.com

Fidelity Personal Investments & Brokerage Group
82 Devonshire St. Boston MA 02109 617-563-7000
TF: 800-828-6680

Fidelity Spartan Brokerage Services Inc 82 Devonshire St. Boston MA 02109 617-563-7000
TF: 800-828-6680

Financial Service Corp 2300 Windy Ridge Pkwy Suite 1100. Atlanta GA 30329 770-916-6500 916-6563*
**Fax:* Mail Rm ■ *TF:* 800-352-4372 ■ *Web:* www.fscorp.com

First Albany Capital Inc 677 Broadway. Albany NY 12207 518-447-8500 447-8115*
**Fax:* Hum Res ■ *TF:* 800-462-6242 ■ *Web:* www.fac.com

First Manhattan Co 437 Madison Ave. New York NY 10022 212-756-3300
Web: www.firstmanhattanco.com

First Southwest Co 325 N Saint Paul St Suite 800. Dallas TX 75201 214-953-4000 953-4065
TF: 800-678-3792 ■ *Web:* www.firstsw.com

Frank Russell Co PO Box 1616. Tacoma WA 98402 253-572-9500 591-3495
TF: 800-426-7969 ■ *Web:* www.russell.com

Franklin Templeton Investments 3344 Quality Dr. Rancho Cordova CA 95670 650-312-2000 463-1125*
**Fax Area Code:* 916 ■ **Fax:* Cust Svc ■ *TF:* 800-632-2350 ■
Web: www.franklintempleton.com

Freedom Investments Inc 375 Raritan Ctr Pkwy. Edison NJ 08837 732-934-3113 934-3095
TF: 800-944-4033 ■ *Web:* www.freedominvestments.com

Friedman Billings Ramsey Group Inc 1001 19th St N 18th Fl. Arlington VA 22209 703-312-9500 312-9501
NYSE: FBR ■ *TF:* 800-846-5050 ■ *Web:* www.fbr.com

Garban Corp 1100 Plaza 5 12th Fl. Jersey City NJ 07311 201-369-5663 369-5678
TF: 800-427-6859 ■ *Web:* www.garban.com

George K Baum & Co 4801 Main St Suite 500 Box 20. Kansas City MO 64112 816-474-1100 283-5180
TF: 800-821-7195 ■ *Web:* www.gkbaum.com

Gilford Securities Inc 777 3rd Ave 17th Fl. New York NY 10017 212-888-6400 826-9738
TF: 800-445-3673 ■ *Web:* www.gilfordsecurities.com

Gleacher & Co LLC 660 Madison Ave 19th Fl. New York NY 10021 212-418-4200 843-3828*
**Fax:* Hum Res ■ *Web:* www.gleacher.com

Glickenhaus & Co 546 5th Ave 7th Fl. New York NY 10036 212-953-7800 983-8436
Web: www.glickenhaus.com

Goldman Sachs & Co 85 Broad St. New York NY 10004 212-902-1000 902-1512*
**Fax:* Mail Rm ■ *TF:* 800-323-5678 ■ *Web:* www.gs.com

Goldman Sachs Group Inc 85 Broad St. New York NY 10004 212-902-1000 902-1513*
NYSE: GS ■ **Fax:* Mail Rm ■ *TF:* 800-323-5678 ■ *Web:* www.gs.com

Greenwich Capital Markets Inc 600 Steamboat Rd. Greenwich CT 06830 203-625-2700
Web: www.gcm.com

Gruss Oscar & Son Inc 74 Broad St 4th Fl. New York NY 10004 212-952-1100 747-0147
Web: www.oscargruss.com

Hambrecht WR & Co 539 Bryant St Suite 100. San Francisco CA 94107 415-551-8600 551-8686
TF Cust Svc: 877-673-6476 ■ *Web:* www.wrhambrecht.com

Hanauer JB & Co 4 Gatehall Dr. Parsippany NJ 07054 973-829-1000 829-0404*
**Fax:* Sales ■ *TF:* 800-631-1094 ■ *Web:* www.jbh.com

HC Wainwright & Co Inc 52 Vanderbilt Ave 12th Fl. New York NY 10017 212-856-5700 856-5753
Web: www.hcwainwright.com

Hilliard JJB WL Lyons Inc 500 W Jefferson St. Louisville KY 40202 502-588-8400 588-4154*
**Fax:* Hum Res ■ *TF:* 800-444-1854 ■ *Web:* www.hilliard.com

Howard Weil 1100 Poydras St Suite 3500. New Orleans LA 70163 504-582-2500 582-2451*
**Fax:* Sales ■ *TF:* 800-322-3005 ■ *Web:* www.howardweil.com

Howe Barnes Investments Inc 222 S Riverside Plaza 7th Fl. Chicago IL 60606 312-655-3000 655-2770*
**Fax:* Cust Svc ■ *TF:* 800-275-4693 ■ *Web:* www.howebarnes.com

Hummer Wayne Investments LLC 300 S Wacker Dr Suite 1500. Chicago IL 60606 312-431-1700 431-0704
TF: 800-621-4477 ■ *Web:* www.whummer.com

ING Altus Group 230 Park Ave 14th Fl. New York NY 10169 212-309-8200 692-9608
TF: 800-621-6626

ING Barings 1325 Ave of the Americas. New York NY 10019 646-424-6000 242-6060
TF: 800-221-5855

Ingalls & Snyder 61 Broadway 31st Fl. New York NY 10006 212-269-7800 269-7893
TF: 800-221-2598 ■ *Web:* www.ingalls.net

Integrated Fund Services Inc 221 E 4th St Suite 300. Cincinnati OH 45202 800-543-8721 362-8086*
**Fax Area Code:* 513 ■ *Web:* www.integratedfundservices.com

Interactive Brokers Group LLC 1 Pickwick Plaza. Greenwich CT 06830 203-618-5700 618-5770
Web: www.interactivebrokers.com

Investec Ernst & Co 1 Battery Park Plaza 2nd Fl. New York NY 10004 212-898-6200 898-6255
Web: www.investecernst.com

Investment Technology Group 380 Madison Ave 4th Fl. New York NY 10017 212-588-4000 444-6292*
NYSE: ITG ■ **Fax:* Hum Res ■ *TF:* 800-215-4484 ■ *Web:* www.itginc.com

Investors Capital Corp 230 Broadway Suite 205. Lynnfield MA 01940 781-593-8565 593-9464
TF: 800-949-1422 ■ *Web:* www.investorscapital.com

Investrade Discount Securities
950 N Milwaukee Ave Suite 102. Glenview IL 60025 847-375-6080 367-8466*
**Fax Area Code:* 877 ■ *TF:* 800-498-7120 ■ *Web:* www.investrade.com

ITG Hoenig 4 International Dr 2nd Fl. Rye Brook NY 10573 914-312-2300 312-2491
TF: 800-999-9558 ■ *Web:* www.itginc.com

ITG Inc 380 Madison Ave 4th Fl. New York NY 10017 212-588-4000 444-6292
TF: 800-215-4484 ■ *Web:* www.itginc.com

Jackson Securities 100 Peachtree St NW Suite 2250. Atlanta GA 30303 404-522-5766 524-1552
TF: 866-888-4574 ■ *Web:* www.jacksonsecurities.com

Janney Montgomery Scott LLC 1801 Market St. Philadelphia PA 19103 215-665-6000 977-8612*
**Fax:* Sales ■ *TF:* 800-526-6397 ■ *Web:* www.janneys.com

JB Hanauer & Co 4 Gatehall Dr. Parsippany NJ 07054 973-829-1000 829-0404*
**Fax:* Sales ■ *TF:* 800-631-1094 ■ *Web:* www.jbh.com

Jefferies & Co Inc 11100 Santa Monica Blvd. Los Angeles CA 90025 310-445-1199 914-1173
TF: 800-421-0160 ■ *Web:* www.jefco.com

Jefferies Group Inc 11100 Santa Monica Blvd. Los Angeles CA 90025 310-445-1199 914-1173
NYSE: JEF ■ *TF:* 800-421-0160 ■ *Web:* www.jefco.com

Jefferson-Pilot Securities Corp PO Box 515. Concord NH 03302 603-226-5000 226-5985
TF: 800-258-3648 ■ *Web:* www.jpsecurities.com

JJB Hilliard WL Lyons Inc 500 W Jefferson St. Louisville KY 40202 502-588-8400 588-4154*
**Fax:* Hum Res ■ *TF:* 800-444-1854 ■ *Web:* www.hilliard.com

Johnston Lemon & Co Inc
1101 Vermont Ave NW Suite 800. Washington DC 20005 202-842-5500 842-7185
TF: 800-424-5158 ■ *Web:* www.johnstonlemon.com

Jones Edward 12555 Manchester Rd. Saint Louis MO 63131 314-515-2000
Web: www.edwardjones.com

Keefe Bruyette & Woods Inc 1 Constitution Plaza 17th Fl. Hartford CT 06103 860-722-5900 722-5919
TF: 800-726-0006 ■ *Web:* www.kbw.com

Kent Financial Services Inc 376 Main St PO Box 74. Bedminster NJ 07921 908-234-0078 234-9355
NASDAQ: KENT ■ *Web:* www.kentfinancialservices.com

Kirkpatrick Pettis Inc 10250 Regency Cir Suite 500. Omaha NE 68114 402-397-5777 392-8335
TF: 800-776-5777 ■ *Web:* www.kirkpatrickpettis.com

Knight Capital Group Inc
525 Washington Blvd Newport Tower 23rd Fl. Jersey City NJ 07310 201-222-9400 557-6853
NASDAQ: NITE ■ *TF:* 800-544-7508 ■ *Web:* www.knight.com

Kohlberg Kravis Roberts & Co 9 W 57th St. New York NY 10019 212-750-8300 750-0003
Web: www.kkr.com

LaBranche & Co Inc 1 Exchange Plaza 25th Fl. New York NY 10006 212-425-1144 344-1469
NYSE: LAB ■ *Web:* www.labranche.com

Ladenburg Thalmann Financial Services Inc
590 Madison Ave. New York NY 10022 212-409-2000 409-2664
AMEX: LTS ■ *TF:* 800-523-8425 ■ *Web:* www.ladenburg.com

Lazard 30 Rockefeller Plaza 59th Fl. New York NY 10020 212-632-6000 632-6051
NYSE: LAZ ■ *Web:* www.lazard.com

Lebenthal & Co Inc 120 Broadway 12th Fl. New York NY 10271 212-425-6116 482-1431
TF: 800-425-6116 ■ *Web:* www.lebenthal.com

Legg Mason Inc 100 Light St. Baltimore MD 21202 410-539-0000 454-3101*
NYSE: LM ■ **Fax:* Hum Res ■ *TF:* 800-368-2558 ■ *Web:* www.leggmason.com

Lehman Brothers Inc 70 Hudson St. Jersey City NJ 07302 201-524-2000
TF: 800-666-2388 ■ *Web:* www.lehman.com

Lepercq de Neuflize & Co 40 W 57th St 19th Fl. New York NY 10019 212-698-0700 262-0144
TF: 800-697-3863 ■ *Web:* www.lepercq.com

Loop Capital Markets LLC 200 W Jackson Blvd 16th Fl. Chicago IL 60606 312-913-4900 913-4928
TF: 888-294-8898 ■ *Web:* www.loopcap.com

LPL Financial Services 1 Beacon St 22nd Fl. Boston MA 02108 617-423-3644
TF: 800-775-4575 ■ *Web:* www.joinlpl.com

Lynch Jones & Ryan Inc 3 Times Sq 8th Fl. New York NY 10036 212-310-9500 223-9082*
**Fax Area Code:* 646 ■ *TF Sales:* 800-992-7526 ■ *Web:* www.ljr.com

Madoff Bernard L Investment Securities 885 3rd Ave 18th Fl. New York NY 10022 212-230-2424
TF: 800-334-1343 ■ *Web:* www.madoff.com

Marshall Miller & Schroeder Inc 150 S 5th St Suite 3000. Minneapolis MN 55402 612-376-1500 376-1548
TF: 800-328-6122 ■ *Web:* www.marshallgroupinc.com

Merrill Lynch & Co Inc
250 Vessey St 4 World Financial Center North Tower. New York NY 10080 212-449-1000 449-8665*
NYSE: MER ■ **Fax:* Mail Rm ■ *TF:* 800-637-7455 ■ *Web:* www.merrilllynch.com

Mesirow Financial Inc 350 N Clark St. Chicago IL 60610 312-595-6000 595-6035*
**Fax:* Hum Res ■ *TF:* 800-453-0600 ■ *Web:* www.mesirowfinancial.com

Miller Johnson Steichen Kinnard Inc
60 S 6th St Suite 3000. Minneapolis MN 55402 612-455-5750 455-5600
TF: 800-444-7884 ■ *Web:* www.mjsk.com

Mizuho Securities USA 111 River St 11th Fl. Hoboken NJ 07030 201-626-1000 626-1577
Web: www.mizuhosecurities.com

Morgan Keegan & Co Inc
50 N Front St Morgan Keegan Tower. Memphis TN 38103 901-524-4100 524-4197
TF: 800-366-7426 ■ *Web:* www.morgankeegan.com

Morgan Stanley 1585 Broadway. New York NY 10036 212-761-4000
NYSE: MWD ■ *TF:* 800-223-2440 ■ *Web:* www.morganstanley.com

Morgan Stanley Investment Management
1221 Ave of the Americas 5th Fl. New York NY 10020 212-762-7400 762-7984
TF: 800-419-2861 ■ *Web:* www.morganstanley.com/im

Company	City	State	ZIP	Phone	Fax
MR Beal & Co 110 Wall St 6th Fl *Web:* www.mrbeal.com	New York	NY	10005	212-983-3930	983-4539
Muriel Siebert & Co Inc 885 3rd Ave Suite 1720 *TF Cust Svc:* 800-872-0444 ■ *Web:* www.siebertnet.com	New York	NY	10022	212-644-2400	486-2784
Natexis Bleichroeder Inc 1345 Ave of the Americas *TF:* 800-435-0336 ■ *Web:* www.asbinc.com	New York	NY	10105	212-698-3000	299-4300
Needham & Co Inc 445 Park Ave 3rd Fl *TF:* 800-903-3268 ■ *Web:* www.needhamco.com	New York	NY	10022	212-371-8300	371-8418
New England Securities Corp 485 E Rt 1 S 4th Fl **Fax Area Code:* 732	Iselin	NJ	08830	800-472-7227	326-4051*
Nikko Securities Co International Inc 7 Times Sq Suite 2502	New York	NY	10036	212-400-4057	400-4058
Nomura Securities International Inc 2 World Financial Ctr Bldg B *Web:* www.nomura.com/usbusiness/	New York	NY	10281	212-667-9300	667-1016
Northern Trust Securities 50 S La Salle St 12th Fl *TF:* 800-621-2253 ■ *Web:* www.northerntrust.com	Chicago	IL	60603	312-557-2000	630-6131
Nuveen Investments Inc 333 W Wacker Dr *NYSE: JNC* ■ *TF:* 800-257-8787 ■ *Web:* www.nuveen.com	Chicago	IL	60606	312-917-7700	
NYLIFE Securities Inc 335 Madison Ave Suite 200 *TF:* 800-695-4785 ■ *Web:* www.nylifesecurities.com	New York	NY	10017	212-351-6000	
Oberweis Securities Inc 3333 Warrenville Rd Suite 500 *TF:* 800-323-6166 ■ *Web:* www.oberweis.net	Lisle	IL	60532	630-577-2300	245-0467
Olympic Cascade Financial Corp DBA National Securities Corp 120 Broadway 27th Fl *Web:* www.nationalsecurities.com	New York	NY	10271	212-417-8000	
Oscar Gruss & Son Inc 74 Broad St 4th Fl *Web:* www.oscargruss.com	New York	NY	10004	212-952-1100	747-0147
Paloma Partners Management Co 2 American Ln	Greenwich	CT	06836	203-862-8000	861-3276
Paulson Capital Corp 811 SW Naito Pkwy Suite 200 *NASDAQ: PLCC* ■ *Web:* www.paulsoninvestment.com	Portland	OR	97204	503-243-6000	243-6018
Paulson Investment Co Inc 811 SW Naito Pkwy Suite 200 *Web:* www.paulsoninvestment.com	Portland	OR	97204	503-243-6000	243-6018
PDI Financial Group 601 N Lynndale Dr *TF:* 800-234-7341 ■ *Web:* www.pdifinancial.com	Appleton	WI	54914	920-739-2303	739-2205
Penson Financial Services Inc 1700 Pacific Ave Suite 1400 *TF:* 800-696-3585 ■ *Web:* www.penson.com	Dallas	TX	75201	214-765-1100	765-1164
People's Securities Inc 1000 Lafayette Blvd **Fax:* Cust Svc ■ *TF:* 800-772-4400	Bridgeport	CT	06601	203-338-0800	338-3218*
Pioneer Investment Management Inc 60 State St 4th Fl **Fax Area Code:* 800 ■ **Fax:* Cust Svc ■ *TF:* 800-225-6292 ■ *Web:* www.pioneerfunds.com	Boston	MA	02109	617-742-7825	225-4240*
Piper Jaffray Cos 800 Nicollet Mall Suite 800 *NYSE: PJC* ■ **Fax:* PR ■ *TF:* 800-333-6000 ■ *Web:* www.piperjaffray.com	Minneapolis	MN	55402	612-303-6000	303-1309*
Ragen Mackenzie Group Inc 999 3rd Ave Suite 4000 **Fax:* Hum Res ■ *TF:* 800-456-4457 ■ *Web:* www.wellsfargo.com/ragen_mackenzie/about	Seattle	WA	98104	206-343-5000	389-8245*
Raymond James Financial Inc 880 Carillon Pkwy *NYSE: RJF* ■ **Fax:* Cust Svc ■ *TF:* 800-248-8863 ■ *Web:* www.rjf.com	Saint Petersburg	FL	33716	727-573-3800	573-8622*
RBC Capital Markets 1 Liberty Plaza **Fax:* Hum Res ■ *TF:* 888-886-8296 ■ *Web:* www.rbccm.com	New York	NY	10006	212-428-6200	428-2329*
RBC Capital Markets 200 Bay St 13th Fl North Tower **Fax:* Hum Res ■ *Web:* www.rbcds.com	Toronto	ON	M5J2J5	416-842-2000	842-8033*
RBC Dain Rauscher Inc 60 S 6th St Dain Rauscher Plaza **Fax:* Hum Res ■ *Web:* www.rbcdain.com	Minneapolis	MN	55402	612-371-2711	371-2777*
Rice Financial Products Co 17 State St 40th Fl *Web:* www.ricefinancialproducts.com	New York	NY	10004	212-908-9200	908-9299
Robeco Investment Management 909 3rd Ave 32nd Fl **Fax:* Hum Res ■ *Web:* www.robeco-usa.com	New York	NY	10022	212-908-9500	908-0109*
Robert W Baird & Co Inc PO Box 672 *TF:* 800-792-2473 ■ *Web:* www.rwbaird.com	Milwaukee	WI	53201	414-765-3500	765-3600
Royal Alliance Assoc Inc One World Financial Center 14th Fl *TF:* 800-821-5100 ■ *Web:* www.royalalliance.com	New York	NY	10281	212-551-5100	551-5671
Ryan Beck & Co 18 Columbia Tpke *TF:* 800-342-2325 ■ *Web:* www.rbeck.com	Florham Park	NJ	07932	973-549-4000	
SBK Brooks Investment Corp 820 Terminal Tower 50 Public Sq *Web:* www.sbkbrooks.com	Cleveland	OH	44113	216-861-6950	861-7619
Schonfeld Securities Inc 1 Jericho Plaza 3rd Fl *Web:* www.schonfeldsecurities.com	Jericho	NY	11753	516-822-0202	822-0590
Schroder Investment Management North America Inc 875 3rd Ave *Web:* www.schroders.com	New York	NY	10022	212-641-3800	641-3979
Schwab Charles & Co Inc 211 Main St **Fax:* PR ■ *TF Cust Svc:* 800-648-5300 ■ *Web:* www.schwab.com	San Francisco	CA	94105	415-636-7000	636-5970*
Scotia Capital Markets 1 Liberty Plaza *TF:* 800-472-6842 ■ *Web:* www.scotiacapital.com	New York	NY	10006	212-225-5000	225-5090
Scott & Stringfellow Inc 909 E Main St *TF:* 800-552-7757 ■ *Web:* www.scottstringfellow.com	Richmond	VA	23219	804-643-1811	649-2916
Seasongood & Mayer LLC 414 Walnut St Suite 300 *TF:* 800-767-7207 ■ *Web:* www.seasongood.com	Cincinnati	OH	45202	513-621-2000	621-5259
Seidler Cos Inc 515 S Figueroa St Suite 1100 **Fax:* Hum Res ■ *TF:* 800-840-1090 ■ *Web:* www.seidlercos.com	Los Angeles	CA	90071	213-683-4500	683-1247*
SG Cowen Securities Corp 1221 Ave of the Americas *TF:* 800-942-7575 ■ *Web:* www.sgcowen.com	New York	NY	10020	212-278-6000	
ShareBuilder Corp 1445 120th Ave NE *TF:* 866-747-2537 ■ *Web:* www.sharebuilder.com	Bellevue	WA	98005	425-451-4440	451-4449
Shelby Cullom Davis & Co 609 5th Ave 11th Fl *TF:* 800-232-0303	New York	NY	10017	212-207-3500	207-3453
Siebert Brandford Shank & Co LLC 100 Wall St Suite 22 *TF:* 800-334-6800 ■ *Web:* www.sbsco.com	New York	NY	10005	646-775-4863	576-9680
Siebert Muriel & Co Inc 885 3rd Ave Suite 1720 *TF Cust Svc:* 800-872-0444 ■ *Web:* www.siebertnet.com	New York	NY	10022	212-644-2400	486-2784
Smith Barney 388 Greenwich St 16th Fl **Fax:* PR ■ *TF:* 800-221-3636 ■ *Web:* www.smithbarney.com	New York	NY	10013	212-816-1641	816-5944*
Standard & Poor's 55 Water St 45th Fl **Fax:* Sales ■ *TF Cust Svc:* 800-344-3014 ■ *Web:* www.standardandpoors.com	New York	NY	10041	212-438-2000	438-3958*
Standard & Poor's Securities Inc 55 Water St **Fax:* Cust Svc	New York	NY	10041	212-438-2000	438-6578*
Stephens Inc 111 Center St **Fax:* Mail Rm ■ *TF:* 800-643-9691 ■ *Web:* www.stephens.com	Little Rock	AR	72201	501-377-2000	377-2666*
Sterne Agee & Leach Inc 800 Shades Creek Pkwy Suite 700 *TF:* 800-240-1438 ■ *Web:* www.sterneagee.com	Birmingham	AL	35209	205-949-3500	949-3607
Stifel Financial Corp 501 N Broadway *NYSE: SF* ■ *TF:* 800-488-0970 ■ *Web:* www.stifel.com	Saint Louis	MO	63102	314-342-2000	342-2051
Stifel Nicolaus & Co Inc 501 N Broadway *TF:* 800-488-0970 ■ *Web:* www.stifel.com	Saint Louis	MO	63102	314-342-2000	342-2051
SunTrust Robinson Humphrey Capital Markets 3333 Peachtree Rd NE Atlanta Financial Ctr *TF:* 877-266-6501 ■ *Web:* www.suntrustrh.com	Atlanta	GA	30326	404-926-5000	
Swiss American Securities Inc 12 E 49th St **Fax:* Hum Res ■ *Web:* www.sasiny.com	New York	NY	10017	212-612-8700	612-8816*
SWS Group Inc 1201 Elm St Suite 3500 *NYSE: SWS* ■ **Fax:* Mail Rm ■ *Web:* www.swst.com	Dallas	TX	75270	214-651-1800	859-6545*
TD Ameritrade Inc 4211 S 102nd St *TF Cust Svc:* 800-237-8692 ■ *Web:* www.ameritrade.com	Omaha	NE	68127	402-331-2744	597-7759
TD Securities (USA) Inc 31 W 52nd St **Fax:* Hum Res ■ *Web:* www.tdsecurities.com	New York	NY	10019	212-827-7000	827-7248*
TradeStation Group Inc 8050 SW 10th St Suite 2000 *NASDAQ: TRAD* ■ *TF:* 800-871-3577 ■ *Web:* www.tradestation.com	Plantation	FL	33324	954-652-7000	652-7899
TradeStation Securities Inc 8050 SW 10th St Suite 2000 *TF:* 800-515-3238 ■ *Web:* www.tradestationsecurities.com	Plantation	FL	33324	954-652-7000	652-7300
Trading Direct 160 Broadway E Bldg 7th Fl *TF:* 800-925-8566 ■ *Web:* www.tradingdirect.com	New York	NY	10038	212-766-0230	766-0914
UBS Capital Markets 111 Pavonia Ave E Newport Financial Ctr *TF:* 800-543-7995 ■ *Web:* www.ubscapitalmarkets.com	Jersey City	NJ	07310	201-963-9100	656-2411
UBS Financial Services Inc 1285 Ave of the Americas *TF:* 800-221-3260 ■ *Web:* financialservicesinc.ubs.com	New York	NY	10019	212-713-2000	
UBS Warburg LLC 677 Washington Blvd *TF:* 800-221-3260 ■ *Web:* www.ubs.com	Stamford	CT	06901	203-719-3000	719-5499
Utendahl Capital Management LP 30 Broad St 21st Fl *TF:* 877-941-4900 ■ *Web:* www.utendahl.com	New York	NY	10004	212-797-2688	425-4199
Vanguard Brokerage Services PO Box 2600 *TF:* 800-992-8327 ■ *Web:* www.vanguard.com	Valley Forge	PA	19482	610-669-1000	669-6366
Veronis Suhler Stevenson 350 Park Ave 7th Fl *Web:* www.vss.com	New York	NY	10022	212-935-4990	381-8168
Wachovia Securities LLC 301 S College St 4th Fl NC 0735 *Web:* www.wachovia.com	Charlotte	NC	28288	704-715-6000	715-6099
Wainwright HC & Co Inc 52 Vanderbilt Ave 12th Fl *Web:* www.hcwainwright.com	New York	NY	10017	212-856-5700	856-5753
Walnut Street Securities Inc 260 Madison Ave 11th Fl *TF:* 800-873-7702	New York	NY	10016	212-354-8800	413-4966
Watley AB Inc 50 Broad St Suite 1728 **Fax Area Code:* 212 ■ *TF:* 888-229-2853 ■ *Web:* www.abwatley.com	New York	NY	10004	646-753-9301	202-5204*
Wayne Hummer Investments LLC 300 S Wacker Dr Suite 1500 *TF:* 800-621-4477 ■ *Web:* www.whummer.com	Chicago	IL	60606	312-431-1700	431-0704
Wedbush Morgan Securities Inc PO Box 30014 **Fax:* Hum Res ■ *Web:* www.wedbush.com	Los Angeles	CA	90030	213-688-8000	688-6652*
Wells Fargo Investments 420 Montgomery St 5th Fl *TF:* 800-621-7609 ■ *Web:* www.wellsfargo.com	San Francisco	CA	94104	415-396-0391	975-7150
William Blair & Co LLC 222 W Adams St *TF:* 800-621-0687 ■ *Web:* www.williamblair.com	Chicago	IL	60606	312-236-1600	236-1875
WM Financial Services Inc 17872 Gillett Ave *Web:* www.wmfinancial.com	Irvine	CA	92614	800-331-3426	
WR Hambrecht & Co 539 Bryant St Suite 100 *TF Cust Svc:* 877-673-6476 ■ *Web:* www.wrhambrecht.com	San Francisco	CA	94107	415-551-8600	551-8686
Ziegler Capital Markets Investment Services 250 E Wisconsin Ave Suite 2000 **Fax Area Code:* 262 ■ **Fax:* Hum Res	Milwaukee	WI	53202	414-978-6400	334-3433*
Ziegler Cos Inc 250 E Wisconsin Ave *Web:* www.ziegler.com	Milwaukee	WI	53202	414-978-6400	978-6401

694 SECURITIES & COMMODITIES EXCHANGES

Company	City	State	ZIP	Phone	Fax
American Stock Exchange (AMEX) 86 Trinity Pl *TF:* 800-843-2639 ■ *Web:* www.amex.com	New York	NY	10006	212-306-1000	
Arbinet-thexchange Inc 120 Albany St Tower II 4th Fl *NASDAQ: ARBX* ■ *TF:* 800-272-4638 ■ *Web:* www.arbinet.com	New Brunswick	NJ	08901	732-509-9100	509-9101
Boston Stock Exchange 100 Franklin St *Web:* www.bostonstock.com	Boston	MA	02110	617-235-2000	235-2200
Bourse de Montreal Inc 800 Victoria Sq PO Box 61 *TF:* 800-361-5353 ■ *Web:* www.m-x.ca	Montreal	QC	H4Z1A9	514-871-2424	871-3514
Chicago Board Options Exchange 400 S La Salle St *TF:* 800-678-4667 ■ *Web:* www.cboe.com	Chicago	IL	60605	312-786-5600	786-7409
Chicago Board of Trade (CBOT) 141 W Jackson Blvd *TF:* 800-572-3276 ■ *Web:* www.cbot.com	Chicago	IL	60604	312-435-3500	341-3150
Chicago Mercantile Exchange (CME) 20 S Wacker Dr *NYSE: CME* ■ *TF:* 800-331-3332 ■ *Web:* www.cme.com	Chicago	IL	60606	312-930-1000	466-4410
Chicago Stock Exchange 440 S LaSalle St *Web:* www.chx.com	Chicago	IL	60605	312-663-2222	663-2058
IntercontinentalExchange Inc 2100 Riverside Pkwy Suite 500 *NYSE: ICE* ■ *Web:* www.theice.com	Atlanta	GA	30328	770-857-4700	951-1307
International Monetary Market 20 S Wacker Dr *TF:* 800-331-3332	Chicago	IL	60606	312-930-3170	
International Securities Exchange (ISE) 60 Broad St *NYSE: ISE* ■ *Web:* www.iseoptions.com	New York	NY	10004	212-943-2400	425-4926
Kansas City Board of Trade 4800 Main St Suite 303 *TF:* 800-821-5228 ■ *Web:* www.kcbt.com	Kansas City	MO	64112	816-753-7500	753-3944
Minneapolis Grain Exchange 400 S 4th St Rm 130 *TF:* 800-827-4746 ■ *Web:* www.mgex.com	Minneapolis	MN	55415	612-321-7101	339-1155
Montreal Exchange 800 Victoria Sq PO Box 61 *TF:* 800-361-5353 ■ *Web:* www.m-x.ca	Montreal	QC	H4Z1A9	514-871-2424	871-3514
Nasdaq Stock Market Inc 165 Broadway 50th Fl *NASDAQ: NDAQ* ■ *Web:* www.nasdaq.com	New York	NY	10006	212-401-8700	
National Stock Exchange (NSX) 440 S LaSalle St Suite 2600 *TF:* 800-843-3924 ■ *Web:* www.nsx.com	Chicago	IL	60605	312-786-8803	939-7239
New York Board of Trade 1 N End Ave 13th Fl *TF:* 800-433-4348 ■ *Web:* www.nybot.com	New York	NY	10282	212-748-4000	742-6981
New York Mercantile Exchange 1 North End Ave *TF:* 800-438-8616 ■ *Web:* www.nymex.com	New York	NY	10282	212-299-2000	301-4570
New York Stock Exchange 11 Wall St *NYSE: NYX* ■ *Web:* www.nyse.com	New York	NY	10005	212-656-3000	656-2126
NSX (National Stock Exchange) 440 S LaSalle St Suite 2600 *TF:* 800-843-3924 ■ *Web:* www.nsx.com	Chicago	IL	60605	312-786-8803	939-7239
NYSE Euronext 11 Wall St *NYSE: NYX* ■ *Web:* www.nyse.com	New York	NY	10005	212-656-3000	656-2126
Pacific Exchange 115 Samsone St 3rd Fl *TF:* 877-729-7291 ■ *Web:* www.pacificex.com	San Francisco	CA	94104	415-393-4000	393-7919
Philadelphia Stock Exchange 1900 Market St *TF:* 800-843-7459 ■ *Web:* www.phlx.com	Philadelphia	PA	19103	215-496-5404	496-5460
Toronto Stock Exchange 130 King St W *TF:* 888-873-8392 ■ *Web:* www.tsx.com	Toronto	ON	M5X1J2	416-947-4700	947-4662

695 SECURITY PRODUCTS & SERVICES

SEE ALSO Audio & Video Equipment p. 1355; Fire Protection Systems p. 1637; Signals & Sirens - Electric p. 2316

Company	City	State	ZIP	Phone	Fax
A4S Security Inc 489 N Denver Ave *NASDAQ: SWAT* ■ **Fax Area Code:* 888 ■ *TF:* 888-825-0247 ■ *Web:* www.shiftwatch.com	Loveland	CO	80537	970-461-0071	837-6765*
ADT Security Systems Inc 14200 E Exposition Ave **Fax:* Hum Res ■ *TF:* 800-662-5378 ■ *Web:* www.adt.com	Aurora	CO	80012	303-338-8200	306-5631*

Phone | Fax

Advantor Systems Corp 1707 Orlando Central Pkwy Suite 350...... Orlando FL 32809 407-859-3350 857-1635*
*Fax: Sales ■ TF Sales: 800-238-2686 ■ Web: www.advantor.com
AFA Protective Systems Inc 519 8th Ave 4th Fl................New York NY 10018 212-279-5000 967-0902
Web: www.afaprotectivesystems.com
Akal Security Inc PO Box 1197............................Santa Cruz NM 87567 505-753-7832 753-8689
TF: 888-325-2527 ■ Web: www.akalsecurity.com
Allied Fire & Security Inc 425 W 2nd Ave.....................Spokane WA 99201 509-624-3152 624-6909
TF: 800-448-8338 ■ Web: www.allied-security.com
AMAG Technology Inc 20701 Manhattan Pl.....................Torrance CA 90501 310-518-2380 834-0685
TF: 800-889-9138 ■ Web: www.amagaccess.com
American Dynamics Corp 6795 Flanders Dr.................. San Diego CA 92121 858-642-2400 642-2440
TF: 800-854-2057 ■ Web: www.americandynamics.net
American Locker Group Inc 608 Allen St...................Jamestown NY 14701 716-664-9600 483-2822
NASDAQ: ALGI ■ TF: 800-828-9118 ■ Web: www.americanlocker.com
American Locker Security Systems Inc 608 Allen St ....Jamestown NY 14701 716-664-9600 664-2949
TF Sales: 800-828-9118 ■ Web: www.americanlocker.com
American Science & Engineering Inc 829 Middlesex Tpke......... Billerica MA 01821 978-262-8700 262-8804
NASDAQ: ASEI ■ TF: 800-225-1608 ■ Web: www.as-e.com
American Security Products Inc 11925 Pacific Ave.............. Fontana CA 92337 951-685-9680 685-9685
TF: 800-421-6142 ■ Web: www.amsecusa.com
APi Systems Group Inc 2609 National Cir........................ Garland TX 75041 214-291-1200 291-1340
TF: 800-223-4922 ■ Web: www.apisystemsgroup.com
Armor Safe Technologies LLC PO Box 560275 ....The Colony TX 75056 972-624-5734 624-5735
TF: 800-487-2766 ■ Web: www.armorsafe.com
Baltimore Alarm & Security Inc 5314 Reistertown Rd .... Baltimore MD 21215 410-358-8600 358-6337
Web: www.baltoalarm.com
BI Inc 6400 Lookout Rd .... Boulder CO 80301 303-218-1000 218-1250
TF: 800-241-2911 ■ Web: www.bi.com
Bosch Security Systems 130 Perinton Pkwy .... Fairport NY 14450 585-223-4060 223-9180
TF: 800-289-0096 ■ Web: www.boschsecurity.us
Brink's Home Security Inc 8880 Esters Blvd .... Irving TX 75063 972-871-3500 871-3317*
*Fax: Hum Res ■ TF: 800-874-1190 ■ Web: www.brinkshomesecurity.com
Brivo Systems LLC 4350 E West Hwy Suite 201 .... Bethesda MD 20814 301-664-5242 664-5264
TF Sales: 866-692-7486 ■ Web: www.brivo.com
Central Signaling Inc 2033 Hamilton Rd ....Columbus GA 31904 706-322-3756 596-8552
TF: 800-554-1104 ■ Web: www.censignal.com
Checkpoint Systems Inc 101 Wolf Dr..........................Thorofare NJ 08086 856-848-1800 848-0937
NYSE: CKP ■ TF: 800-257-5540 ■ Web: www.checkpointsystems.com
Collier Safe Co Inc PO Box 995..............................Odessa FL 33556 813-920-6671 920-5091
Web: www.colliersafe.com
CompuDyne Corp 2530 Riva Rd Suite 201 ....Annapolis MD 21401 410-224-4415
NASDAQ: CDCY ■ Web: www.compudyne.com
Computerized Security Systems Inc 1950 Austin Dr................. Troy MI 48083 248-680-8484 680-8468
TF Sales: 877-272-3565 ■ Web: www.cssmain.com
Corby Industries Inc 1501 E Pennsylvania St................Allentown PA 18109 610-433-1412 435-1963
TF: 800-652-6729 ■ Web: www.corby.com
Detex Corp 302 Detex Dr..............................New Braunfels TX 78130 830-629-2900 620-6711
TF: 800-729-3839 ■ Web: www.detex.com
Diebold Inc 5995 Mayfair Rd ....North Canton OH 44720 330-490-4000
NYSE: DBD ■ TF: 800-999-3600 ■ Web: www.diebold.com
Digital Products of Delaware Inc 625 SW 9th Terr.........Pompano Beach FL 33069 954-941-0903 608-6627*
*Fax Area Code: 888 ■ TF: 800-671-0299 ■ Web: www.digitaltechnologies-2000.com
Digital Security Controls (DSC) 3301 Langstaff Rd ....Concord ON L4K4L2 905-760-3000 760-3004
Web: www.dsc.com
Directed Electronics Inc 1 Viper Way ....Vista CA 92081 760-598-6200 598-6400
NASDAQ: DEIX ■ TF: 800-876-0800 ■ Web: www.directed.com
Doyle Security Systems Inc 792 Calkins Rd...................Rochester NY 14623 585-244-3400 473-4991
TF: 800-836-9538 ■ Web: www.doylesecuritysystems.com
Driven Technologies 2345 S Michigan Ave .... Chicago IL 60616 312-842-1880 842-6225
TF: 877-437-4836 ■ Web: driventechnologiesinc.com
EMERgency 24 Inc 4179 W Irving Park Rd .... Chicago IL 60641 773-777-0707 286-1992
TF: 800-877-3624 ■ Web: www.emergency24.com
Engage Technologies Inc 8419 Sunstate St.......................... Tampa FL 33634 813-885-6615 886-7316
TF: 800-388-2219 ■ Web: www.engagetech.net
Federal APD Inc 42775 Nine-Mile Rd.................................. Novi MI 48375 248-374-9600 374-9610
TF: 800-521-9330 ■ Web: www.federalapd.com
Felts Alarm Co Inc 4000 E Indiana St PO Box 5082 ....Evansville IN 47716 812-473-4008 473-4395
Web: www.feltslock.com/fac_000.html
FireKing Security Group 101 Security Pkwy..................New Albany IN 47150 812-948-8400
TF: 800-457-2424 ■ Web: www.fireking.com
First Action Security Security Team Inc
18702 Crestwood Dr .... Hagerstown MD 21742 301-797-2124 797-2189
TF Cust Svc: 800-342-4243 ■ Web: www.firstactionteam.com
FMJ/Pad.Lock Computer Security Systems Inc
510 W Central Ave Suite D .... Brea CA 92821 310-549-3221 549-2921
TF: 800-322-3365 ■ Web: www.fmjpadlock.com
Force Optical Broadcast Systems 825 Park St .... Christiansburg VA 24073 540-382-0462 381-0392
TF: 800-732-5252 ■ Web: www.forceinc.com
Force Inc 825 Park St...................................... Christiansburg VA 24073 540-382-0462 381-0392
TF: 800-732-5252 ■ Web: www.forceinc.com
Frisco Bay Industries Ltd 160 Graveline St ....Saint-Laurent QC H4T1R7 514-738-7300 735-7039
TF: 800-463-7472 ■ Web: www.friscobay.com
GE Infrastructure 187 Danbury Rd............................... Wilton CT 06897 203-761-1900 761-1924
Web: www.geinfrastructure.com
GE Security 8985 Town Center Pkwy .... Bradenton FL 34202 941-739-4200 302-7557*
*Fax Area Code: 866 ■ TF: 800-655-4497 ■ Web: www.gesecurity.com
Gentex Corp 600 N Centennial St .... Zeeland MI 49464 616-772-1800 772-7348
NASDAQ: GNTX ■ TF: 800-444-4689 ■ Web: www.gentex.com
George Risk Industries Inc 802 S Elm St..........................Kimball NE 69145 308-235-4645 235-2609
TF Sales: 800-523-1227 ■ Web: www.grisk.com
Guardian Alarm Co 20800 Southfield Rd ....Southfield MI 48075 248-423-1000 423-3009
TF: 800-782-9688 ■ Web: www.stayout.com
Henry Brothers Electronics Inc 280 Midland Ave ....Saddle Brook NJ 07663 201-794-6500 794-8341
AMEX: HBE ■ Web: www.hbeonline.net
Honeywell ACS 11 W Spring St .... Freeport IL 61032 815-235-5500
Web: www.honeywell.com/acs
Honeywell Automation & Control Solutions 11 W Spring St .... Freeport IL 61032 815-235-5500
Web: www.honeywell.com/acs
Honeywell Security Inc 165 Eileen Way PO Box 9035............. Syosset NY 11791 516-921-6704 364-5344
TF Cust Svc: 800-573-0154 ■ Web: www.security.honeywell.com
IDenticard Systems Inc 40 Citation Ln........................Lancaster PA 17601 717-569-5797 569-2390
TF: 800-233-0298 ■ Web: www.identicard.com
Integrated Alarm Services Group Inc 99 Pine St 3rd Fl .... Albany NY 12207 518-426-1515 426-0953
NASDAQ: IASG ■ TF: 888-305-4090 ■ Web: www.iasg.us
Intercon Security Ltd 40 Sheppard Ave W Suite 400 .... Toronto ON M2N6K9 416-229-6811 229-1207
Web: www.interconsecurity.com
International Electronics Inc 427 Turnpike St.................... Canton MA 02021 781-821-5566 821-4443
TF: 800-343-9502 ■ Web: www.ieib.com
JAI Pulnix Inc 625 River Oaks Pkwy........................... San Jose CA 95134 408-383-0300 383-0301
TF: 800-445-5444 ■ Web: www.pulnix.com
Johnson Controls Fire & Security Solutions
4100 Gardian St Suite 200...............................Simi Valley CA 93063 805-522-5555 582-7899
TF: 800-229-4076 ■ Web: www.johnsoncontrols.com/security
L-3 Communications Corp Security Systems Div
2005 Gandy Blvd N Suite 600....................... Saint Petersburg FL 33702 727-556-0270 556-0271
Web: www.l-3com.com/secursys
Lane Industries Inc 1200 Shermer Rd ....Northbrook IL 60062 847-498-6789 498-2104

Phone | Fax

Linear LLC 1950 Camino Vida Roble Suite 150 ....Carlsbad CA 92008 760-438-7000 931-1340
TF Cust Svc: 800-421-1587 ■ Web: www.linearcorp.com
LoJack Corp 200 Lowder Brook Dr Suite 1000 .... Westwood MA 02090 781-326-4700 326-7255
NASDAQ: LOJN ■ TF: 800-456-5225 ■ Web: www.lojack.com
Mace Security International Inc 160 Benmont Ave Suite 1 ......Bennington VT 05201 802-447-1503 442-3823
NASDAQ: MACE ■ TF: 800-255-2634 ■ Web: www.mace.com
Matrix Security Systems LLC 109 S Old Dupont Rd .... Wilmington DE 19805 302-683-9101 225-9100
TF: 800-498-5581 ■ Web: www.firstalertsecurity.com/matrix
MAXxess Systems Inc 1515 S Manchester Ave ....Anaheim CA 92802 714-772-1000 780-7999
TF: 800-842-0221 ■ Web: www.maxxesssystems.com
MDI Security Systems Inc 9725 Datapoint Dr Suite 200........San Antonio TX 78229 210-477-5400 477-5401
NASDAQ: MDII ■ TF: 866-435-7634 ■ Web: www.mdisecure.com
MILCOM Systems Corp 532 Viking Dr........................ Virginia Beach VA 23452 757-463-2800 463-3052
TF: 800-967-0966 ■ Web: www.milcomsystems.com
MMF Industries Inc 370 Alice St .... Wheeling IL 60090 847-537-7890 537-1120
TF Cust Svc: 800-445-8293 ■ Web: www.mmfind.com
Monitronics International Inc 2350 Valley View Ln.................Dallas TX 75234 972-243-7443 243-1064*
*Fax: Cust Svc ■ TF Cust Svc: 800-447-9239 ■ Web: www.monitronics.com
MSGI Security Solutions Inc 575 Madison Ave 10th Fl...........New York NY 10022 917-339-7100 339-7111
NASDAQ: MSGI ■ Web: www.msgisecurity.com
NAPCO Security Systems Inc 333 Bayview Ave .... Amityville NY 11701 631-842-9400 842-9137
NASDAQ: NSSC ■ TF: 800-645-9445 ■ Web: www.napcosecurity.com
National Safe Corp 4400 34th St N Unit G.............. Saint Petersburg FL 33714 727-525-7800 528-1209
TF: 800-634-8174 ■ Web: www.nationalsafe.net
National Security Systems Inc 511 Manhasset Woods Rd ....Manhasset NY 11030 516-627-2222
New England Security Inc 10 Industrial Dr PO Box 562 ....Westerly RI 02891 401-596-0660 596-0108
TF: 800-556-7395
Norment Security Group Inc 3224 Mobile Hwy .... Montgomery AL 36108 334-281-8440 288-5485
TF: 800-633-1968 ■ Web: www.normentsecurity.com
Optex America Inc 13661 Benson Ave Bldg C .... Chino CA 91710 909-993-5770 628-5560
TF: 800-966-7839 ■ Web: www.optexamerica.com
OSI Systems Inc 12525 Chadron Ave .... Hawthorne CA 90250 310-978-0516 644-1727
NASDAQ: OSIS ■ Web: www.osi-systems.com
Parking Products Inc 2517 Wyandotte Rd..................Willow Grove PA 19090 215-657-7500 657-4321
Web: www.parkingproducts.com
Per Mar Security 1910 E Kimberly Rd .... Davenport IA 52807 563-326-6291 359-6700
TF: 800-473-7627 ■ Web: www.permarsecurity.com
PerkinElmer Inc 45 William St .... Wellesley MA 02481 781-237-5100 237-9386
NYSE: PKI ■ Web: www.perkinelmer.com
Protection One Inc 1035 N 3rd St Suite 101.................. Lawrence KS 66044 785-856-5500
TF: 800-438-4357 ■ Web: www.protectionone.com
Rapiscan Systems 3232 W El Segundo Blvd .... Hawthorne CA 80250 310-978-1457 349-2491
Web: www.rapiscansystems.com
Schwab Corp PO Box 5088... Lafayette IN 47903 765-447-9470 447-8278
TF: 800-428-7678 ■ Web: www.schwabcorp.com
Seaboard Electronics Co 70 Church St ....New Rochelle NY 10805 914-235-8073 235-8369
Seco-Larm USA Inc 16842 Millikan Ave .... Irvine CA 92606 949-261-2999 261-7326
TF: 800-662-0800 ■ Web: www.seco-larm.com
Securitas Security Services USA Inc 2 Campus Dr............Parsippany NJ 07054 973-267-5300 397-2534
TF: 800-325-6828 ■ Web: www.securitasinc.com
Security Assoc International Inc
2101 S Arlington Heights Rd Suite 150 ....Arlington Heights IL 60005 847-956-8650 956-9360
TF: 800-323-7601 ■ Web: www.sai-inc.com
Security Corp 22325 Roethel Dr... Novi MI 48375 248-374-5700 374-5750
TF: 888-374-5789 ■ Web: www.securitycorp.com
Security Defense Systems Corp 160 Park Ave........................Nutley NJ 07110 973-235-0606 235-0132
TF: 800-325-6339 ■ Web: www.securitydefense.com
Security Services & Technologies
2450 Blvd of the Generals Valley Forge Business Ctr..........Norristown PA 19403 610-630-6790 630-6785
TF: 888-446-7781 ■ Web: www.1sst.com
Security Solutions Inc 5305 Raynor Rd Suite 101............... Garner NC 27529 919-828-1018 560-0458*
*Fax Area Code: 866 ■ TF: 888-531-1018 ■ Web: www.ssisecurity.com
Sensormatic Electronics Corp 6600 Congress Ave .... Boca Raton FL 33487 561-912-6000 912-6097
TF: 800-327-1765 ■ Web: www.sensormatic.com
Sentry Group 900 Linden Ave ....Rochester NY 14625 585-381-4900 381-2940*
*Fax: Cust Svc ■ TF: 800-828-1438 ■ Web: www.sentrysafe.com
Sentry Technology Corp 1881 Lakeland Ave .... Ronkonkoma NY 11779 631-739-2100 739-2124
TF: 800-645-4224 ■ Web: www.sentrytechnology.com
Shiftwatch 489 N Denver Ave............................. Loveland CO 80537 970-461-0071 837-6765*
NASDAQ: SWAT ■ *Fax Area Code: 888 ■ TF: 888-825-0247 ■
Web: www.shiftwatch.com
Siemens Building Technologies Inc 1000 Deerfield Pkwy......Buffalo Grove IL 60089 847-215-1000 215-1093
TF: 800-877-7545 ■ Web: www.us.sbt.siemens.com
SIRCHIE Finger Print Laboratories Inc 100 Hunter Pl .... Youngsville NC 27596 919-554-2244 554-2266
TF: 800-356-7311 ■ Web: www.sirchie.com
Software House 70 Westview St................................Lexington MA 02421 781-466-6660 466-9550
TF: 800-550-6660 ■ Web: www.swhouse.com
Sola Communications Inc 113 N Patch St .... Scott LA 70583 337-235-1515 235-5119
TF: 800-458-8301 ■ Web: www.solacomm.com
Sonitrol Corp 1000 Westlakes Dr Suite 150.........................Berwyn PA 19312 215-238-9090 785-9707*
*Fax Area Code: 610 ■ Web: www.sonitrol.com
Southern Folger Detention Equipment Co 4634 S Presa St .....San Antonio TX 78223 210-533-1231 533-2211
Web: www.southernfolger.com
Synergx Systems Inc 209 Lafayette Dr.......................... Syosset NY 11791 516-433-4700 433-1131
NASDAQ: SYNX ■ Web: www.synergxsystems.com
Techne Electronics Ltd 916 Commercial St..................... Palo Alto CA 94303 650-494-1764 494-0817
Texas Industrial Security 101 Summit Ave Suite 404 ....Fort Worth TX 76102 817-335-3046 335-3048
Web: www.txsecurity.com
Tyco Fire & Security 1 Town Center Rd...................... Boca Raton FL 33486 561-988-7200
Web: www.tycofireandsecurity.com
Unisec Inc 2555 Nicholson St.............................. San Leandro CA 94577 510-352-5610 352-6707
TF: 800-982-4587 ■ Web: www.ultrabarrier.com
Universal Security Instruments Inc 7-A Gwynns Mill Ct .... Owings Mills MD 21117 410-363-3000 363-2218
AMEX: UUU ■ TF: 800-390-4321 ■ Web: www.universalsecurity.com
UTC Fire & Security 9 Farm Springs Rd..........................Farmington CT 06037 860-284-3000 284-3149
Web: www.utcfireandsecurity.com
VASCO Data Security International Inc
1901 S Meyers Rd Suite 210.......................Oakbrook Terrace IL 60181 630-932-8844 932-8852
NASDAQ: VDSI ■ Web: www.vasco.com
Verint Video Solutions 9101 Guilford Rd..................... Columbia MD 21046 301-483-8930 483-9790
TF: 800-638-5969 ■ Web: www.verint.com
William D White Co Inc 3505 Magnolia St...................... Oakland CA 94608 510-658-8167 658-3503
Winner International LLC 32 W State St .... Sharon PA 16146 724-981-1152 981-1034
TF: 800-258-2321 ■ Web: www.winner-intl.com
Xenonics Holdings Inc 2236 Rutherford Rd Suite 123 ....Carlsbad CA 92008 760-438-4004 438-1184
AMEX: XNN ■ Web: www.xenonics.com

696 SECURITY & PROTECTIVE SERVICES

SEE ALSO Investigative Services p. 1873

Phone | Fax

A & R Security Service Inc 2552 W 135th St ....Blue Island IL 60406 708-389-3830 389-3878
Web: www.arsecurity.com

				Phone	Fax
AlliedBarton Security Services 3606 Horizon Dr	King of Prussia	PA	19406	610-239-1100	239-1108
TF: 888-239-1104 ■ *Web:* www.alliedbarton.com					
American Commercial Security Services Inc					
420 Taylor St Suite 200	San Francisco	CA	94102	415-351-4500	351-4593
Brink's Inc 555 Dividend Dr Suite 100	Coppell	TX	75019	469-549-6000	549-6202
Web: www.brinksinc.com					
Command Security Corp PO Box 340	Lagrangeville	NY	12540	845-454-3703	454-0075
Web: www.cscny.com					
Diamond Group 13101 Preston Rd Suite 212	Dallas	TX	75240	972-788-1111	788-0077
Web: www.thediamondgroup.ws					
Diversco Integrated Services Inc 105 Diversco Dr	Spartanburg	SC	29307	864-579-3420	579-9578
TF: 800-277-3420 ■ *Web:* www.diversco.com					
Garda World Security Corp 1390 Barre St	Montreal	QC	H3C1N4	514-281-2811	281-2860
TSX: GW ■ *TF:* 800-334-2732 ■ *Web:* www.garda.ca					
Guard-Systems Inc 12124 Ramona Blvd	El Monte	CA	91732	626-433-4999	433-4988
TF: 800-307-0031 ■ *Web:* www.guardsystemsinc.com					
Guardian Alarm Co 20800 Southfield Rd	Southfield	MI	48075	248-423-1000	423-3009
TF: 800-782-9688 ■ *Web:* www.stayout.com					
Guardsmark Inc 22 S 2nd St	Memphis	TN	38103	901-522-6000	522-6013
TF: 800-238-5878 ■ *Web:* www.guardsmark.com					
Huntleigh USA Corp 10332 Old Olive Street Rd	Saint Louis	MO	63141	314-997-6811	997-0401
Web: www.icts-int.com					
IBI Armored Services Inc 37-06 61st St	Woodside	NY	11377	718-458-4000	458-5371
Web: www.ibiarmored.com					
Initial Security 3355 Cherry Ridge St Suite 200	San Antonio	TX	78230	210-349-6321	344-7770
TF: 800-683-7771 ■ *Web:* www.initialsecurity.com					
Intercon Security Ltd 40 Sheppard Ave W Suite 400	Toronto	ON	M2N6K9	416-229-6811	229-1207
Web: www.interconsecurity.com					
International Claim Specialists 530 W Lockport St	Plainfield	IL	60544	815-254-0600	254-0800
TF: 800-822-8220					
IPC International Corp 2111 Waukegan Rd	Bannockburn	IL	60015	847-444-2000	444-2001
TF: 800-323-1228 ■ *Web:* www.ipcinternational.com					
Levy Security Corp 8750 W Bryn Mawr Ave Suite 1200	Chicago	IL	60631	773-867-9204	714-1318
TF: 800-649-5389 ■ *Web:* www.levysecurity.com					
Loomis Fargo & Co 1655 Vilbig Rd	Dallas	TX	75208	214-742-2554	744-5436
TF: 800-725-7475 ■ *Web:* www.loomisfargo.com					
Maloney Security Inc 1055 Laurel St	San Carlos	CA	94070	650-593-0163	593-1101
Web: www.maloneysecurity.com					
Murray Guard Inc 58 Murray Guard Dr	Jackson	TN	38305	731-668-3400	664-8619
TF: 800-238-3830 ■ *Web:* www.murrayguard.com					
MVM Inc 1593 Spring Hill Rd Suite 700	Vienna	VA	22182	703-790-3138	790-9526
TF: 800-727-1949 ■ *Web:* www.mvminc.com					
Northwest Protective Service Inc 2700 Elliott Ave	Seattle	WA	98121	206-448-4040	448-2461
TF: 888-981-4040 ■ *Web:* www.nwprotective.com					
Pro-Tect Security 3511 S Eastern Ave	Las Vegas	NV	89109	702-735-0110	735-7793
Web: www.pro-tectsecurity.com					
Royce Security Services Inc 3740 Euclid Ave Suite 102	Cleveland	OH	44115	216-426-7752	426-7757
Securitas Security Services USA Inc 2 Campus Dr	Parsippany	NJ	07054	973-267-5300	397-2534
TF: 800-325-6828 ■ *Web:* www.securitasinc.com					
Shield Security 150 W Wardlow Rd	Long Beach	CA	90807	562-283-1100	283-1105
TF: 800-793-3354 ■ *Web:* www.shieldsecurity.com					
Smith Protective Services Inc 8918 John W Carpenter Fwy	Dallas	TX	75247	214-631-4444	631-4241
TF: 800-634-1381 ■ *Web:* www.smithprotective.com					
Trade Show Services DBA Pro-Tect Security					
3511 S Eastern Ave	Las Vegas	NV	89109	702-735-0110	735-7793
Web: www.pro-tectsecurity.com					
Tri-S Security Corp 3700 Mansell Rd Suite 220	Alpharetta	GA	30022	770-625-4945	753-9738
NASDAQ: TRIS					
US Security Assoc Inc 200 Mansell Ct 5th Fl	Roswell	GA	30076	770-625-1400	625-1519
TF: 800-241-0267 ■ *Web:* www.greatguards.com					
UTC Fire & Security 9 Farm Springs Rd	Farmington	CT	06037	860-284-3000	284-3149
Web: www.utcfireandsecurity.com					
Vance 10467 White Granite Dr Suite 210	Oakton	VA	22124	703-592-1400	592-1500
TF: 800-533-6754 ■ *Web:* www.vanceglobal.com					
Wackenhut Airline Services Inc					
4200 Wackenhut Dr Suite 100	Palm Beach Gardens	FL	33410	561-622-5656	691-6795
TF: 800-683-6853 ■ *Web:* www.wackenhut.com					
Wackenhut Corp 4200 Wackenhut Dr Suite 100	Palm Beach Gardens	FL	33410	561-622-5656	691-6591*
**Fax:* Hum Res ■ *TF:* 800-922-6488 ■ *Web:* www.wackenhut.com					
Wackenhut Corp Nuclear Services Div					
4200 Wackenhut Dr Suite 100	Palm Beach Gardens	FL	33410	561-622-5656	691-6795
TF: 800-683-6853 ■ *Web:* www.wackenhut.com					
Wackenhut International Inc					
4200 Wackenhut Dr Suite 100	Palm Beach Gardens	FL	33410	561-622-5656	691-6795
TF: 800-683-6853 ■ *Web:* www.wackenhut.com					
Wackenhut Services Inc					
4200 Wackenhut Dr Suite 100	Palm Beach Gardens	FL	33410	561-622-5656	691-6591*
**Fax:* Hum Res ■ *TF:* 800-922-6488 ■ *Web:* www.wackenhut.com					
Wackenhut Sports Security Inc					
4200 Wackenhut Dr Suite 100	Palm Beach Gardens	FL	33410	561-622-5656	691-6795
TF: 800-683-6853 ■ *Web:* www.wackenhut.com					

697 SEED COMPANIES

SEE ALSO Farm Supplies p. 1634

Seed production and development companies (horticultural and agricultural). or industrial applications.

				Phone	Fax
AgriGold Hybrids RR 1 Box 203	Saint Francisville	IL	62460	618-943-5776	943-7333
TF: 800-262-7333 ■ *Web:* www.agrigold.com					
Albert Lea Seed House 1414 W Main St	Albert Lea	MN	56007	507-373-3161	373-7032
TF: 800-352-5247 ■ *Web:* www.alseed.com					
Ampac Seed Co 32727 Hwy 99 E	Tangent	OR	97389	541-928-1651	928-2430
TF: 800-547-3230 ■ *Web:* www.ampacseed.com					
Applewood Seed Co 5380 Vivian St	Arvada	CO	80002	303-431-7333	467-7886
TF: 888-778-7333 ■ *Web:* www.applewoodseed.com					
Ball Seed Co 622 Town Rd	West Chicago	IL	60185	630-231-3500	231-3605
TF: 800-879-2255 ■ *Web:* www.ballseed.com					
Barenbrug USA Inc 33477 Hwy 99 E	Tangent	OR	97389	541-926-5801	926-9435
TF: 800-547-4101 ■ *Web:* www.barusa.com					
Burpee W Atlee Co 300 Park Ave	Warminster	PA	18974	215-674-4900	674-4170
TF Cust Svc: 800-333-5808 ■ *Web:* www.burpee.com					
Cascade International Seed Co 8483 W Stayton Rd	Aumsville	OR	97325	503-749-1822	749-1824
TF: 800-826-6799					
Circle Grove Seeds Inc 336 Circle Grove Farm Rd PO Box 280	Belhaven	NC	27810	252-943-3141	943-2940
Croplan Genetics PO Box 64281 MS 5850	Saint Paul	MN	55164	651-765-5712	765-5727
TF: 800-328-9680 ■ *Web:* www.croplangenetics.com					
Garst Seed Co 2369 330th St PO Box 500	Slater	IA	50244	515-685-5000	685-5080
TF: 800-831-6630 ■ *Web:* www.garstseed.com					
Gries Seed Farms Inc 2348 N 5th St	Fremont	OH	43420	419-332-5571	332-1817
TF: 800-472-4797 ■ *Web:* www.griesseed.com					
Gurney Seed & Nursery Co Inc 5100 Schenley Pl	Greendale	IN	47025	812-539-2502	354-1484*
**Fax Area Code:* 513 ■ *Web:* www.gurneys.com					
Harris Moran Seed Co 55 Codoni Ave	Modesto	CA	95357	209-579-7333	527-8674
TF: 800-808-7333 ■ *Web:* www.harrismoran.com					
Johnny's Selected Seeds 955 Benton Ave	Winslow	ME	04901	207-861-3900	861-8363
TF: 877-564-6697 ■ *Web:* www.johnnyseeds.com					
Johnston Seed Co 319 W Chestnut St	Enid	OK	73701	580-233-5800	249-5324
TF: 800-375-4613 ■ *Web:* www.johnstonseed.com					
JW Jung Seed Co 335 S High St	Randolph	WI	53956	920-326-3121	692-5864*
**Fax Area Code:* 800 ■ *TF:* 800-297-3123 ■ *Web:* www.jungseed.com					
Latham Seed Co 131 180th St	Alexander	IA	50420	641-692-3258	692-3250
TF: 800-798-3258 ■ *Web:* www.lathamseeds.com					
Lebanon Seaboard Corp 1600 E Cumberland St	Lebanon	PA	17042	717-273-1685	273-9466
TF: 800-233-0628 ■ *Web:* www.lebsea.com					
Loft Seed Inc 9327 US Rt 1 Suite J	Laurel	MD	20723	301-362-5415	362-8548
TF: 800-732-3332					
Monsanto Co 800 N Lindbergh Blvd	Saint Louis	MO	63167	314-694-1000	694-8506
NYSE: MON ■ *Web:* www.monsanto.com					
Mycogen Seeds 9390 Zionsville Rd	Indianapolis	IN	46268	317-337-3000	339-4096
TF: 800-352-6776 ■ *Web:* www.dowagro.com/mycogen/index.htm					
Nunhems USA Inc 1200 Anderson Corner Rd	Parma	ID	83660	208-674-4000	674-4090*
**Fax:* Cust Svc ■ *TF Cust Svc:* 800-733-9505 ■ *Web:* www.nunhemsusa.com					
Olds Seed Solutions 2901 Tackers Ave	Madison	WI	53707	608-249-9291	249-0695
TF: 800-356-7333 ■ *Web:* www.seedsolutions.com					
Park Seed Co 1 Parkton Ave	Greenwood	SC	29647	864-223-8555	941-4502
TF Orders: 800-845-3369 ■ *Web:* www.parkseed.com					
Pennington Seed Inc 1280 AtlantaHwy	Madison	GA	30650	706-342-1234	342-9644
TF: 800-277-1412 ■ *Web:* www.penningtonseed.com					
Red River Commodities Inc 501 42nd St NW	Fargo	ND	58102	701-282-2600	282-5325
TF: 800-437-5539 ■ *Web:* www.redriv.com					
Renee's Garden Seeds Inc 7389 W Zayante Rd	Felton	CA	95018	831-335-7228	335-7227
TF: 888-880-7228 ■ *Web:* www.reneesgarden.com					
Research Seeds Inc DBA Forage Genetics International					
812 1st St S PO Box 339	Nampa	ID	83653	208-466-3568	466-3684
Web: www.foragegenetics.com					
Sakata Seed America Inc 18095 Serene Dr	Morgan Hill	CA	95037	408-778-7758	778-7751
Web: www.sakata.com					
Sand Seed Service Inc 4765 Hwy 143	Marcus	IA	51035	712-376-4135	376-4140
TF: 800-352-2228 ■ *Web:* www.sandsofiowa.com					
Schlessman Seed Co 11513 US Rt 250	Milan	OH	44846	419-499-2572	499-2574
TF: 888-534-7333 ■ *Web:* www.schlessman-seed.com					
Seedway LLC 1734 Railroad Pl	Hall	NY	14463	585-526-6391	526-6832
TF: 800-836-3710 ■ *Web:* www.seedway.com					
Seminis Inc 2700 Camino del Sol	Oxnard	CA	93030	805-647-1572	918-2543*
**Fax:* Cust Svc ■ *TF:* 888-222-1272 ■ *Web:* www.seminis.com					
Sharp Brothers Seed Co 2005 S Sycamore	Healy	KS	67850	620-398-2231	398-2220
TF: 800-462-8483 ■ *Web:* www.sharpseed.com					
Stock Seed Farms 28008 Mill Rd	Murdock	NE	68407	402-867-3771	867-2442
TF: 800-759-1520 ■ *Web:* www.stockseed.com					
Stone Seed Farms Inc 5965 W SR 97	Pleasant Plains	IL	62677	217-546-8006	546-8098
Web: www.stoneseed.com					
Stratton Seed Co 1530 Hwy 79 S PO box 1088	Stuttgart	AR	72160	870-673-4433	672-9837
TF: 800-264-4433 ■ *Web:* www.strattonseed.com					
Syngenta Corp 2200 Concord Pike	Wilmington	DE	19803	302-425-2000	425-2001
TF: 800-759-4500 ■ *Web:* www.syngenta.com					
Syngenta Seeds Inc 7500 Olson Memorial Hwy	Golden Valley	MN	55427	763-593-7333	542-0194
TF: 800-445-0956 ■ *Web:* www.nk-us.com					
Syngenta Seeds Inc Flowers Div 4343 Commerce Ct Suite 500	Lisle	IL	60532	630-969-6300	969-6373
TF: 800-323-7253 ■ *Web:* greendemon.net					
Thorp Seed Co RR 3 Box 257	Clinton	IL	61727	217-935-2171	935-3225
TF: 800-648-2676 ■ *Web:* www.goldenharvestseeds.com					
Triumph Seed Co Hwy 62 Bypass PO Box 1050	Ralls	TX	79357	806-253-2584	253-2820
TF: 800-530-4789 ■ *Web:* www.triumphseed.com					
W Atlee Burpee Co 300 Park Ave	Warminster	PA	18974	215-674-4900	674-4170
TF Cust Svc: 800-333-5808 ■ *Web:* www.burpee.com					
Weeks Seed Co Inc 1050 Moye Blvd	Greenville	NC	27834	252-757-1234	757-0978
TF: 800-322-1234 ■ *Web:* www.weeksseeds.com					
Wetsel Inc 961 Liberty St	Harrisonburg	VA	22802	540-434-6753	434-4894
TF: 800-572-4018 ■ *Web:* www.wetsel.com					

698 SEMICONDUCTOR MANUFACTURING SYSTEMS & EQUIPMENT

				Phone	Fax
Accretech USA Inc 2600 Telegraph Rd Suite 180	Bloomfield Hills	MI	48302	248-332-0100	332-0700
Web: www.accretech.jp/english					
Adcotron EMS Inc 12 Channel St Marine Industrial Pk	Boston	MA	02210	617-598-3000	598-3001
Web: www.adcotron.com					
Advanced Energy Industries Inc 1625 Sharp Pt Dr	Fort Collins	CO	80525	970-221-4670	221-5583
NASDAQ: AEIS ■ *TF:* 800-446-9167 ■ *Web:* www.advanced-energy.com					
Aehr Test Systems 400 Kato Terr	Fremont	CA	94539	510-623-9400	623-9450
NASDAQ: AEHR ■ *TF:* 800-522-7200 ■ *Web:* www.aehr.com					
AIXTRON Inc/Genus 1139 Karlstad Dr	Sunnyvale	CA	94089	408-747-7120	747-7199
TF: 800-366-0989 ■ *Web:* www.genus.com					
Akrion LLC 6330 Hedgewood Dr Suite 150	Allentown	PA	18106	610-391-9200	391-1982*
**Fax:* Sales ■ *Web:* www.akrion.com					
Alphasem Corp 150 E Alamo Dr Suite 7	Chamdler	AZ	85225	480-892-9021	892-9058
Web: www.alphasem.com					
AMI Semiconductor (AMIS) 2300 Buckskin Rd	Pocatello	ID	83201	208-233-4690	234-6796
Web: www.amis.com					
Amistar Corp 237 Via Vera Cruz	San Marcos	CA	92078	760-471-1700	471-9065
Web: www.amistar.com					
Amtech Systems Inc 131 S Clark Dr	Tempe	AZ	85281	480-967-5146	968-3763
NASDAQ: ASYS ■ *Web:* www.amtechsystems.com					
Applied Materials Inc 3050 Bowers Ave	Santa Clara	CA	95054	408-727-5555	748-9943
NASDAQ: AMAT ■ *Web:* www.appliedmaterials.com					
ASM America Inc 3440 E University Dr	Phoenix	AZ	85034	602-470-5700	437-1403
Web: www.asm.com					
ASML 8555 S River Pkwy	Tempe	AZ	85284	480-383-4422	383-3995
NASDAQ: ASML ■ *TF:* 800-227-6462 ■ *Web:* www.asml.com					
Asyst Technologies Inc 46897 Bayside Pkwy	Fremont	CA	94538	510-661-5000	661-5166*
NASDAQ: ASYT ■ **Fax:* Sales ■ *TF:* 800-345-7643 ■ *Web:* www.asyst.com					
ATMI Inc 7 Commerce Dr	Danbury	CT	06810	203-794-1100	792-8040
NASDAQ: ATMI ■ *TF:* 800-766-2681 ■ *Web:* www.atmi.com					
Aviza Technology Inc 440 Kings Valley Rd	Scotts Valley	CA	95066	831-438-2100	439-6223
NASDAQ: AVZA ■ *Web:* www.avizatechnology.com					
Axcelis Technologies Inc 108 Cherry Hill Dr	Beverly	MA	01915	978-787-4000	787-4200
NASDAQ: ACLS ■ *Web:* www.axcelis.com					
BOC Edwards 301 Ballardvale St	Wilmington	MA	01887	978-658-5410	658-7969
TF: 800-848-9800 ■ *Web:* www.bocedwards.com					
Brooks Automation Inc 15 Elizabeth Dr	Chelmsford	MA	01824	978-262-2400	262-2500
NASDAQ: BRKS ■ *Web:* www.brooks.com					

Company / Address	City	State	Zip	Phone	Fax
BTU International Inc 23 Esquire Rd	North Billerica	MA	01862	978-667-4111	667-9068
NASDAQ: BTUI ■ *TF:* 800-998-0666 ■ *Web:* www.btu.com					
Conceptronic Inc 1860 Smithtown Ave	Ronkonkoma	NY	11779	631-981-7081	981-7095
Web: www.conceptronic.com					
Contact Systems Inc 50 Miry Brook Rd	Danbury	CT	06810	203-743-3837	790-6322
Web: www.contactsystems.com					
CVD Equipment Corp 1860 Smithtown Ave	Ronkonkoma	NY	11779	631-981-7081	981-7095
AMEX: CVV ■ *Web:* www.cvdequipment.com					
Cymer Inc 17075 Thornmint Ct	San Diego	CA	92127	858-385-7300	385-7100
NASDAQ: CYMI ■ *Web:* www.cymer.com					
Data I/O Corp 6464 185th Ave NE Suite 101	Redmond	WA	98052	425-881-6444	867-6972
NASDAQ: DAIO ■ *TF:* 800-426-1045 ■ *Web:* www.data-io.com					
DEK USA 8 Bartles Corner Rd	Flemington	NJ	08822	908-782-4140	782-4774
Web: www.dek.com					
Eagle Test Systems Inc 2200 Millbrook Dr	Buffalo Grove	IL	60089	847-367-8282	367-8640
NASDAQ: EGLT ■ *Web:* www.eagletest.com					
Ebara Technologies Inc 51 Main Ave	Sacramento	CA	95838	916-920-5451	925-6654
TF: 800-535-5376 ■ *Web:* www.ebaratech.com					
Electroglas Inc 5729 Fontanoso Way	San Jose	CA	95138	408-528-3000	528-3550
NASDAQ: EGLS ■ *TF:* 800-538-5124 ■ *Web:* www.electroglas.com					
EMCORE Corp 145 Belmont Dr	Somerset	NJ	08873	732-271-9090	271-9686
NASDAQ: EMKR ■ *Web:* www.emcore.com					
Entegris Inc 3500 Lyman Blvd	Chaska	MN	55318	952-556-3131	556-1880
NASDAQ: ENTG ■ *Web:* www.entegris.com					
Entegris, Inc 129 Concord Rd Bldg 2	Billerica	MA	01821	978-436-6500	436-6735
TF: 877-695-7654 ■ *Web:* www.entegris.com					
FormFactor Inc 7005 SouthFront Rd	Livermore	CA	94551	925-290-4000	290-4010
NASDAQ: FORM ■ *Web:* www.formfactor.com					
Fortrend Corp 610 N Mary Ave	Sunnyvale	CA	94089	408-734-9311	734-4299
Web: www.fortrend.com					
FSI International Inc 3455 Lyman Blvd	Chaska	MN	55318	952-448-5440	448-2825
NASDAQ: FSII ■ *TF:* 800-274-5440 ■ *Web:* www.fsi-intl.com					
Goldfinger Technologies LLC 1241 E Dyer Rd Suite 100	Santa Ana	CA	92705	714-445-2000	445-2204
Web: www.akrion.com					
Hittite Microwave Corp 20 Alpha Rd	Chelmsford	MA	01824	978-250-3343	250-3373
NASDAQ: HITT ■ *Web:* www.hittite.com					
Ibis Technology Corp 32 Cherry Hill Dr	Danvers	MA	01923	978-777-4247	777-6570
NASDAQ: IBIS ■ *Web:* www.ibis.com					
Imtec Acculine Inc 1295 Forgewood Ave	Sunnyvale	CA	94089	408-745-7800	734-4883
Web: www.imtecacculine.com					
JMAR Technologies Inc 10905 Technology Pl	San Diego	CA	92127	858-946-6800	946-6899
NASDAQ: JMAR ■ *Web:* www.jmar.com					
Kayex Div SPX Corp 1000 Millstead Way	Rochester	NY	14624	585-235-2524	436-2396
Web: www.kayex.com					
KDF Electronic & Vacuum Services Inc 10 Volvo Dr	Rockleigh	NJ	07647	201-784-5005	784-0202
TF: 877-533-3343 ■ *Web:* www.kdf.com					
KLA-Tencor Corp 160 Rio Robles	San Jose	CA	95134	408-875-3000	875-3030
NASDAQ: KLAC ■ *Web:* www.kla-tencor.com					
Kokusai Semiconductor Equipment Corp					
2450 N 1st St Suite 290	San Jose	CA	95131	408-456-2750	456-2760
TF: 800-800-5321 ■ *Web:* www.ksec.com					
Kulicke & Soffa Industries Inc 100 Virginia Dr	Fort Washington	PA	19034	215-784-6000	784-6001
NASDAQ: KLIC ■ *TF:* 800-445-5671 ■ *Web:* www.kns.com					
Lam Research Corp 4650 Cushing Pkwy	Fremont	CA	94538	510-659-0200	572-1093*
NASDAQ: LRCX ■ **Fax:* Cust Svc ■ *TF:* 800-526-7678 ■ *Web:* www.lamrc.com					
Laurier Inc 10 Tinker Ave	Londonderry	NH	03053	603-626-4700	626-4712
Web: www.besidiehandling.com					
Leadis Technology Inc 800 W California Ave Suite 200	Sunnyvale	CA	94086	408-387-8600	387-8601
NASDAQ: LDIS ■ *Web:* www.leadis.com					
LogicVision Inc 25 Metro Dr 3rd Fl	San Jose	CA	95110	408-453-0146	573-7640
NASDAQ: LGVN ■ *TF:* 888-584-2478 ■ *Web:* www.logicvision.com					
Loranger International Corp 817 4th Ave	Warren	PA	16365	814-723-2250	723-5391
Web: www.loranger.com					
Mattson Technology Inc 47131 Bayside Pkwy	Fremont	CA	94538	510-657-5900	492-5911
NASDAQ: MTSN ■ *TF:* 800-628-8766 ■ *Web:* www.mattson.com					
Micro Component Technology Inc 2340 W County Rd C	Saint Paul	MN	55113	651-697-4000	697-4200
TF: 800-628-1628 ■ *Web:* www.mct.com					
Moore Technologies Inc 1905 N MacArthur Dr	Tracy	CA	95376	209-833-0100	833-0410
Web: www.mooretech.com/moore					
Neutronix-Quintel (NXQ) 685A Jarvis Dr	Morgan Hill	CA	95037	408-776-5190	776-1039
Web: www.neutronixinc.com					
Novellus Systems Inc 4000 N 1st St	San Jose	CA	95134	408-943-9700	943-3422
NASDAQ: NVLS ■ *TF:* 800-800-3079 ■ *Web:* www.novellus.com					
Oerlikon USA Inc 10050 16th St N	Saint Petersburg	FL	33716	727-577-4999	577-7035
Web: www.oerlikon.com					
Rudolph Technologies Inc 550 Clark Dr PO Box 1000	Budd Lake	NJ	07828	973-691-1300	426-1483
NASDAQ: RTEC ■ *TF:* 877-467-8365 ■ *Web:* www.rudolphtech.com					
RVSI Inspection LLC 425 Rabro Dr E	Hauppauge	NY	11788	631-273-9700	273-1167
TF: 800-669-5234 ■ *Web:* www.rvsi.com					
Semitool Inc 655 W Reserve Dr	Kalispell	MT	59901	406-752-2107	752-5522
NASDAQ: SMTL ■ *TF:* 800-548-8495 ■ *Web:* www.semitool.com					
Siemens Dematic Electronics Assembly Systems Inc					
3140 Northwoods Pkwy Suite 300	Norcross	GA	30071	770-797-3000	797-3096
TF: 888-768-4357 ■ *Web:* ea.siemens-dematic.com					
SITE Services Inc 690 Aldo Ave	Santa Clara	CA	95054	408-980-1155	980-1267
Web: www.site.com					
Small Precision Tools Inc 1330 Clegg St	Petaluma	CA	94954	707-765-4545	778-2271
TF: 800-346-4927 ■ *Web:* www.smallprecisiontools.com					
Solid State Equipment Corp 185 Gibraltar Rd	Horsham	PA	19044	215-328-0700	328-9410
Web: www.ssecusa.com					
Solitec Wafer Processing Inc 1777 N Milpitas Blvd Suite 335	Milpitas	CA	95035	408-955-9939	955-0954
TF: 800-648-4040 ■ *Web:* www.solitec-wp.com					
Spire Corp 1 Patriots Pk	Bedford	MA	01730	781-275-6000	275-7470
NASDAQ: SPIR ■ *TF:* 800-510-4815 ■ *Web:* www.spirecorp.com					
SPX Corp Kayex Div 1000 Millstead Way	Rochester	NY	14624	585-235-2524	436-2396
Web: www.kayex.com					
Synetics Solutions Inc 18870 NE Riverside Pkwy	Portland	OR	97230	503-465-6000	465-6393
Web: www.syneticsinc.com					
Tegal Corp 2201 S McDowell Blvd	Petaluma	CA	94954	707-763-5600	765-9311
NASDAQ: TGAL ■ *TF:* 800-828-3425 ■ *Web:* www.tegal.com					
Tek-Vac Industries Inc 176 Express Dr S	Brentwood	NY	11717	631-436-5100	436-5154
Web: www.tekvac.com					
Tokyo Electron America Inc 2400 Grove Blvd	Austin	TX	78741	512-424-1000	424-1001
TF: 800-828-6596 ■ *Web:* www.tel.com/eng/index.html					
Trio-Tech International 14731 Califa St	Van Nuys	CA	91411	818-787-7000	787-9130
AMEX: TRT ■ *Web:* www.triotech.com					
Ultra Clean Technology Systems & Service Inc					
150 Independence Dr	Menlo Park	CA	94025	650-323-4100	326-0929
NASDAQ: UCTT ■ *Web:* www.uct.com					
Ultratech Inc 3050 Zanker Rd	San Jose	CA	95134	408-321-8835	577-3376
NASDAQ: UTEK ■ *TF:* 800-222-1213 ■ *Web:* www.ultratech.com					
Universal Instruments Corp 33 Broome Corporate Park	Conklin	NY	13348	607-779-7522	772-1878
TF: 800-842-9732 ■ *Web:* www.uic.com					
Varian Semiconductor Equipment Assoc Inc 35 Dory Rd	Gloucester	MA	01930	978-282-2000	282-7344
NASDAQ: VSEA ■ *TF:* 800-447-1762 ■ *Web:* www.vsea.com					
Veeco Instruments Inc 1 Terminal Dr	Plainview	NY	11803	516-349-8300	349-8321
NASDAQ: VECO ■ *TF:* 800-645-7566 ■ *Web:* www.veeco.com					

699 SEMICONDUCTORS & RELATED DEVICES

SEE ALSO Electronic Components & Accessories - Mfr p. 1609; Printed Circuit Boards p. 2138

Company / Address	City	State	Zip	Phone	Fax
8x8 Inc 3151 Jay St	Santa Clara	CA	95054	408-727-1885	980-0432
NASDAQ: EGHT ■ *Web:* www.8x8.com					
ABB Semiconductors Inc 575 Epsilon Dr	Pittsburgh	PA	15238	412-967-5858	967-5868
Actel Corp 2061 Stierlin Ct	Mountain View	CA	94043	650-318-4200	318-4600
NASDAQ: ACTL ■ *TF:* 800-262-1060 ■ *Web:* www.actel.com					
Advanced Analogic Technologies Inc DBA AnalogicTech					
830 E Arques Ave	Sunnyvale	CA	94085	408-737-4600	737-4611
NASDAQ: AATI ■ *Web:* www.analogictech.com					
Advanced Micro Devices Inc (AMD) 1 AMD Pl PO Box 3453	Sunnyvale	CA	94088	408-749-4000	749-4291
NYSE: AMD ■ *TF:* 800-538-8450 ■ *Web:* www.amd.com					
Advanced Photonix Inc 1240 Avenida Acaso	Camarillo	CA	93012	805-987-0146	484-9935
AMEX: API ■ *Web:* www.advancedphotonix.com					
Advanced Power Technology Inc 405 SW Columbia St	Bend	OR	97702	541-382-8028	388-0364
NASDAQ: APTI ■ *TF:* 800-522-0809 ■ *Web:* www.advancedpower.com					
Aeroflex Inc 35 S Service Rd	Plainview	NY	11803	516-694-6700	694-6771
NASDAQ: ARXX ■ *TF:* 800-843-1553 ■ *Web:* www.aeroflex.com					
Agere Systems Inc 1110 American Pkwy NE	Allentown	PA	18109	610-712-6011	712-1342
NYSE: AGR ■ *TF:* 800-372-2447 ■ *Web:* www.agere.com					
Agilent Technologies Inc 5301 Stevens Creek Blvd	Santa Clara	CA	95051	877-424-4536	345-8474*
NYSE: A ■ **Fax Area Code:* 408 ■ *TF:* 877-424-4536 ■ *Web:* www.agilent.com					
Allegro Microsystems Inc PO Box 15036	Worcester	MA	01615	508-853-5000	853-8378
Web: www.allegromicro.com					
Alliance Semiconductor Corp 2575 Augustine Dr	Santa Clara	CA	95054	408-855-4900	855-4999
NASDAQ: ALSC ■ *TF:* 888-383-4900 ■ *Web:* www.alsc.com					
Altera Corp 101 Innovation Dr	San Jose	CA	95134	408-544-7000	544-6403*
NASDAQ: ALTR ■ **Fax:* Cust Svc ■ *TF Cust Svc:* 800-767-3753 ■ *Web:* www.altera.com					
AMI Semiconductor Inc 2300 Buckskin Rd	Pocatello	ID	83201	208-233-4690	234-6796
Web: www.amis.com					
Amkor Technology Inc 1900 S Price Rd	Chandler	AZ	85248	480-821-5000	
NASDAQ: AMKR ■ *Web:* www.amkor.com					
ANADIGICS Inc 141 Mt Bethel Rd	Warren	NJ	07059	908-668-5000	668-5068
NASDAQ: ANAD ■ *Web:* www.anadigics.com					
Analog Devices Inc 1 Technology Way PO Box 9106	Norwood	MA	02062	781-329-4700	461-3113
NYSE: ADI ■ *TF:* 800-262-5643 ■ *Web:* www.analog.com					
API Electronics Group Inc 375 Rabro Dr	Hauppauge	NY	11788	631-582-6767	582-6771
Web: www.apielectronics.com					
Apogee Technology Inc 129 Morgan Dr	Norwood	MA	02062	781-551-9450	440-9528
AMEX: ATA ■ *Web:* www.apogeeddx.com					
Applied Micro Circuits Corp 6290 Sequence Dr	San Diego	CA	92121	858-450-9333	450-9885
NASDAQ: AMCC ■ *TF:* 800-935-2622 ■ *Web:* www.amcc.com					
ARM Inc 141 Caspian Ct	Sunnyvale	CA	94089	408-734-5600	734-5050
Web: www.arm.com					
ASAT Inc 490 N McCarthy Blvd Suite 200	Milpitas	CA	95035	408-964-7400	964-5535
NASDAQ: ASTT ■ *Web:* www.asat.com					
Atheros Communications Inc 5480 Great American Pkwy	Santa Clara	CA	95054	408-773-5200	773-9909
NASDAQ: ATHR ■ *Web:* www.atheros.com					
Atmel Corp 2325 Orchard Pkwy	San Jose	CA	95131	408-441-0311	436-4200
NASDAQ: ATML ■ *Web:* www.atmel.com					
AudioCodes Ltd 2099 Gateway Pl Suite 500	San Jose	CA	95110	408-441-1175	451-9520
NASDAQ: AUDC ■ *Web:* www.audiocodes.com					
AuthenTec Inc 709 S Harbor City Blvd Suite 400	Melbourne	FL	32901	321-308-1300	308-1430
Web: www.authentec.com					
Aware Inc 40 Middlesex Tpke	Bedford	MA	01730	781-276-4000	276-4001
NASDAQ: AWRE ■ *Web:* www.aware.com					
AXT Inc 4281 Technology Dr	Fremont	CA	94538	510-683-5900	353-0668
NASDAQ: AXTI ■ *Web:* www.axt.com					
BEI Technologies Inc Duncan Electronics Div 170 Technology Dr	Irvine	CA	92618	949-341-9500	453-2700
Web: www.beiduncan.com					
BI Technologies Corp 4200 Bonita Pl	Fullerton	CA	92835	714-447-2300	447-2745
Web: www.bitechnologies.com					
BP Solar International LLC 630 Solarex Ct	Frederick	MD	21703	301-698-4200	698-4201
Web: www.bpsolar.com					
Broadcom Corp 16215 Alton Pkwy	Irvine	CA	92618	949-450-8700	922-6607
NASDAQ: BRCM ■ *Web:* www.broadcom.com					
California Micro Devices Corp 490 N McCarthy Blvd Suite 100	Milpitas	CA	95035	408-263-3214	263-7846
NASDAQ: CAMD ■ *TF:* 800-325-4966 ■ *Web:* www.calmicro.com					
Catalyst Semiconductor Inc 1250 Borregas Ave	Sunnyvale	CA	94089	408-542-1000	542-1200
NASDAQ: CATS ■ *TF:* 800-258-5991 ■ *Web:* www.catsemi.com					
Celeritek Inc 3236 Scott Blvd	Santa Clara	CA	95054	408-986-5060	986-5095
Web: www.celeritek.com					
Celis Semiconductor Corp					
5475 Mark Dabling Blvd Suite 102	Colorado Springs	CO	80918	719-260-9133	593-8540
Web: www.celis-semi.com					
Centillium Communications Inc 215 Fourier Ave	Fremont	CA	94539	510-771-3700	771-3500
NASDAQ: CTLM ■ *TF:* 877-879-7500 ■ *Web:* www.centillium.com					
Centrovision 2088 Anchor Ct	Newbury Park	CA	91320	805-499-5902	499-7770
TF: 800-700-2088 ■ *Web:* www.centrovision.com					
Chartered Semiconductor Mfg Inc 1450 McCandless Dr	Milpitas	CA	95035	408-941-1100	941-1101
NASDAQ: CHRT ■ *Web:* www.charteredsemi.com					
ChipX 2323 Owen St	Santa Clara	CA	95054	408-988-2445	988-2449
TF: 800-952-4479 ■ *Web:* www.chipx.com					
Cirrus Logic Inc 2901 Via Fortuna	Austin	TX	78746	512-851-4000	851-4977
NASDAQ: CRUS ■ *TF:* 800-888-5016 ■ *Web:* www.cirrus.com					
Clare Inc 78 Cherry Hill Dr	Beverly	MA	01915	978-524-6700	524-4700
Web: www.clare.com					
Conexant Systems Inc 4000 MacArthur Blvd	Newport Beach	CA	92660	949-483-4600	483-4078
NASDAQ: CNXT ■ *TF:* 800-854-8099 ■ *Web:* www.conexant.com					
Cree Inc 4600 Silicon Dr	Durham	NC	27703	919-313-5300	313-5451*
NASDAQ: CREE ■ **Fax:* Sales ■ *TF:* 800-533-2583 ■ *Web:* www.cree.com					
Cypress Semiconductor Corp 3901 N 1st St	San Jose	CA	95134	408-943-2600	943-2741*
NYSE: CY ■ **Fax:* Mktg ■ *TF:* 800-541-4736 ■ *Web:* www.cypress.com					
Dallas Semiconductor Corp 4401 S Beltwood Pkwy	Dallas	TX	75244	972-371-4000	371-4470*
**Fax:* Cust Svc ■ *Web:* www.maxim-ic.com					
DayStar Technologies Inc 13 Corporate Dr	Halfmoon	NY	12065	518-383-4600	383-4900
NASDAQ: DSTI ■ *Web:* www.daystartech.com					
Dialight Corp 1501 Rt 34 S	Farmingdale	NJ	07727	732-919-3119	751-5778
Web: www.dialight.com					
Dialog Semiconductor 7545 Irvine Center Dr Suite 200	Irvine	CA	92618	949-623-8686	623-8305
Web: www.diasemi.com					
Diodes Inc 3050 E Hillcrest Dr Suite 200	Westlake Village	CA	91362	805-446-4800	446-4850
NASDAQ: DIOD ■ *Web:* www.diodes.com					
DPAC Technologies Corp 7321 Lincoln Way	Garden Grove	CA	92841	714-898-0007	897-1772
TF: 800-642-4477 ■ *Web:* www.dpactech.com					
DSP Group Inc 3120 Scott Blvd	Santa Clara	CA	95054	408-986-4300	986-4323
NASDAQ: DSPG ■ *Web:* www.dspg.com					
Duncan Electronics Div BEI Technologies Inc 170 Technology Dr	Irvine	CA	92618	949-341-9500	453-2700
Web: www.beiduncan.com					
EMCORE Corp 145 Belmont Dr	Somerset	NJ	08873	732-271-9090	271-9686
NASDAQ: EMKR ■ *Web:* www.emcore.com					

Phone Fax

Enhanced Memory Systems Inc 1850 Ramtron Dr .... Colorado Springs CO 80921 719-481-7000 481-9170
TF: 800-545-3726 ■ *Web:* www.edram.com

Ensign-Bickford Industries Inc 100 Grist Mill Rd .... Simsbury CT 06070 860-843-2000 843-1510
TF: 800-828-9814 ■ *Web:* www.ensign-bickfordind.com

Epson Electronics America Inc 150 River Oaks Pkwy .... San Jose CA 95134 408-922-0200 922-0238
TF: 800-228-3964 ■ *Web:* www.eea.epson.com

Equator Technologies Inc 520 Pike St Suite 900 .... Seattle WA 98101 206-267-4500 812-1285
Web: www.equator.com

ESS Technology Inc 48401 Fremont Blvd .... Fremont CA 94538 510-492-1088 492-1098
NASDAQ: ESST ■ *Web:* www.esstech.com

Eudyna Devices USA Inc 2355 Zanker Rd .... San Jose CA 95131 408-232-9500 428-9111
Web: www.us.eudyna.com

Evergreen Solar Inc 138 Bartlett St .... Marlborough MA 01752 508-357-2221 229-0747
NASDAQ: ESLR ■ *Web:* www.evergreensolar.com

Exar Corp 48720 Kato Rd .... Fremont CA 94538 510-668-7000 668-7011
NASDAQ: EXAR ■ *Web:* www.exar.com

Fairchild Semiconductor Corp 333 Western Ave .... South Portland ME 04106 207-775-8100 761-6139*
NYSE: FCS ■ **Fax:* Mail Rm ■ *TF:* 800-341-0392 ■ *Web:* www.fairchildsemi.com

Faroudja 180 Baytech Dr Suite 110 .... San Jose CA 95134 408-635-4241 957-0364
Web: www.faroudja.com

FerroTec (USA) Corp 40 Simon St .... Nashua NH 03060 603-883-9800 883-2308
TF: 800-258-1788 ■ *Web:* www.ferrotec.com

Filtronic Compound Semiconductors 10181 Bubb Rd .... Cupertino CA 95014 408-850-5790 850-5725
Web: www.filss.com

Flextronics Semiconductor Inc 2241 Lundy Dr .... San Jose CA 95131 408-576-7429 576-7099
Web: www.flextronicssemi.com

Freescale Semiconductor Inc 6501 William Cannon Dr W .... Austin TX 78735 512-895-2000
NYSE: FSL ■ *TF Tech Supp:* 800-521-6274 ■ *Web:* www.freescale.com

Fujitsu Microelectronics America Inc 1250 E Arques Ave .... Sunnyvale CA 94088 408-737-5600 737-5999
TF: 800-637-0683 ■ *Web:* www.fujitsumicro.com

Genesis Microchip Inc 165 Commerce Valley Dr W .... Thornhill ON L3T7V8 905-889-5400 889-0035
NASDAQ: GNSS ■ *Web:* www.genesis-microchip.com

Gennum Corp 970 Fraser Dr .... Burlington ON L7L5P5 905-632-2996 632-2055
Web: www.gennum.com

GSI Technology Inc 2360 Owen St .... Santa Clara CA 95054 408-980-8388 980-8377
Web: www.gsitechnology.com

HEI Inc 1495 Steiger Lake Ln .... Victoria MN 55386 952-443-2500 443-2668
NASDAQ: HEII ■ *TF:* 866-720-2397 ■ *Web:* www.heii.com

Hifn Inc 750 University Ave .... Los Gatos CA 95032 408-399-3500 399-3501
NASDAQ: HIFN ■ *Web:* www.hifn.com

Hitachi Canada Ltd 2495 Meadowpine Blvd .... Mississauga ON L5N6C3 905-821-4545 821-9435
TF: 800-906-4482 ■ *Web:* www.hitachi.ca

Hitachi High Technologies America Inc
10 N Martingale Rd Suite 500 .... Schaumburg IL 60173 847-273-4141 273-4407
Web: www.hii-hitachi.com

Holt Integrated Circuits Inc 23351 Madero .... Mission Viejo CA 92691 949-859-8800 859-9643
Web: www.holtic.com

Hynix Semiconductor America Inc 3101 N 1st St .... San Jose CA 95134 408-232-8000 232-8115*
**Fax:* Hum Res ■ *Web:* www.us.hynix.com

Ikanos Communications 47669 Fremont Blvd .... Freemont CA 94538 510-979-0400 979-0500
NASDAQ: IKAN ■ *Web:* www.ikanos.com

Infineon Technologies Corp 1730 N 1st St .... San Jose CA 95112 408-501-6000 501-5903*
NYSE: IFX ■ **Fax:* Sales ■ *Web:* www.infineon.com

Innovex Inc 5540 Pioneer Creek Dr .... Maple Plain MN 55359 763-479-5300 479-5395
NASDAQ: INVX ■ *Web:* www.innovexinc.com

Integrated Circuit Systems Inc 2435 Blvd of the Generals .... Norristown PA 19403 610-630-5300 630-5399
NASDAQ: ICST ■ *Web:* www.icst.com

Integrated Device Technology Inc 2975 Stender Way .... Santa Clara CA 95054 408-727-6116 492-8674
NASDAQ: IDTI ■ *TF:* 800-345-7015 ■ *Web:* www.idt.com

Integrated Silicon Solution Inc (ISSI) 2231 Lawson Ln .... Santa Clara CA 95054 408-969-6600 969-7800
NASDAQ: ISSI ■ *TF:* 800-379-4774 ■ *Web:* www.issiusa.com

Intel Corp 2200 Mission College Blvd .... Santa Clara CA 95052 408-765-8080
NASDAQ: INTC ■ *TF Cust Svc:* 800-628-8686 ■ *Web:* www.intel.com

InterDigital Communications Corp 781 3rd Ave .... King of Prussia PA 19406 610-878-7800 992-9432
NASDAQ: IDCC ■ *TF:* 800-669-4737 ■ *Web:* www.interdigital.com

International Rectifier Corp 222 Kansas St .... El Segundo CA 90245 310-322-3331 322-3332
NYSE: IRF ■ *Web:* www.irf.com

Intersil Corp 1001 Murphy Ranch Rd .... Milpitas CA 95035 408-432-8888 434-5351
NASDAQ: ISIL ■ *Web:* www.intersil.com

Intrinsity Inc 11612 Bee Caves Rd Bldg II Suite 200 .... Austin TX 78738 512-421-2100 263-0795
Web: www.intrinsity.com

IQE Inc 119 Technology Dr .... Bethlehem PA 18015 610-861-6930 861-5273
Web: www.iqep.com

Irvine Sensors Corp 3001 Redhill Ave Bldg 3 Suite 108 .... Costa Mesa CA 92626 714-549-8211 557-1260
NASDAQ: IRSN ■ *TF:* 800-468-4612 ■ *Web:* www.irvine-sensors.com

ISSI (Integrated Silicon Solution Inc) 2231 Lawson Ln .... Santa Clara CA 95054 408-969-6600 969-7800
NASDAQ: ISSI ■ *TF:* 800-379-4774 ■ *Web:* www.issiusa.com

IXYS Corp 3540 Bassett St .... Santa Clara CA 95054 408-982-0700 748-9788
NASDAQ: SYXI ■ *Web:* www.ixys.com

Jazz Semiconductor Inc 4321 Jamboree Rd .... Newport Beach CA 92660 949-435-8000 435-8200
Web: www.jazzsemi.com

Judson Technologies LLC 221 Commerce Dr .... Montgomeryville PA 18936 215-368-6900 362-6107
Web: www.judsontechnologies.com

Kopin Corp 200 John Hancock Rd .... Taunton MA 02780 508-824-6696 822-1381
NASDAQ: KOPN ■ *Web:* www.kopin.com

Kulite Semiconductor Products Inc 1 Willow Tree Rd .... Leonia NJ 07605 201-461-0900 461-0990
Web: www.kulite.com

Kyocera America Inc 8611 Balboa Ave .... San Diego CA 92123 858-576-2600 569-9412
Web: americas.kyocera.com/kai/semiparts

Kyocera Solar Inc 7812 E Acoma Dr Suite 2 .... Scottsdale AZ 85260 480-948-8003 483-6431
TF: 800-544-6466 ■ *Web:* www.kyocerasolar.com

Laser Diode Inc 2 Olsen Ave .... Edison NJ 08820 732-549-9001 906-1559
Web: www.laserdiode.com

Lattice Semiconductor Corp 5555 NE Moore Ct .... Hillsboro OR 97124 503-681-0118 268-8347
NASDAQ: LSCC ■ *TF:* 800-327-8636 ■ *Web:* www.latticesemi.com

Legerity Inc 4509 Frederick Ln Suite 200 .... Austin TX 78744 512-228-5400 228-5510
TF: 800-432-4009 ■ *Web:* www.legerity.com

Linear Technology Corp 1630 McCarthy Blvd .... Milpitas CA 95035 408-432-1900 434-0507
NASDAQ: LLTC ■ *Web:* www.linear.com

Logic Devices Inc 395 W Java Dr .... Sunnyvale CA 94089 408-542-5400 542-0080
NASDAQ: LOGC ■ *Web:* www.logicdevices.com

LSI Computer Systems Inc 1235 Walt Whitman Rd .... Melville NY 11747 631-271-0400 271-0405
Web: www.lsicsi.com

LSI Logic Corp 1621 Barber Ln .... Milpitas CA 95035 408-433-8000 433-7715
NYSE: LSI ■ *TF:* 800-433-8778 ■ *Web:* www.lsilogic.com

M Cubed Technologies Inc 921 Main St .... Monroe CT 06468 203-452-2333 452-2335
Web: www.mmmt.com

M/A-COM Inc 1011 Pawtucket Blvd .... Lowell MA 01854 978-442-5000 656-2777
Web: www.macom.com

Macronix America Inc 680 N McCarthy Blvd .... Milpitas CA 95035 408-262-8887 262-8810
Web: www.macronix.com

Marvell Technology Group Ltd 5488 Marvell Ln .... Santa Clara CA 95054 408-222-2500 328-0120
NASDAQ: MRVL ■ *Web:* www.marvell.com

MathStar Inc 5900 Green Oak Dr .... Minnetonka MN 55343 952-746-2200 746-2201
NASDAQ: MATH ■ *Web:* www.mathstar.com

Maxim Integrated Products Inc 120 San Gabriel Dr .... Sunnyvale CA 94086 408-737-7600 737-7194
NASDAQ: MXIM ■ *TF:* 800-659-5909 ■ *Web:* www.maxim-ic.com

Phone Fax

Medtronic Microelectronics Center 2343 W Medtronic Way .... Tempe AZ 85281 480-968-6411 921-6435
TF: 800-633-8766 ■ *Web:* www.medtronic.com/semi

MEMC Electronic Materials Inc 501 Pearl Dr .... Saint Peters MO 63376 636-474-5000 474-5086
NYSE: WFR ■ *Web:* www.memc.com

Micrel Inc 2180 Fortune Dr .... San Jose CA 95131 408-944-0800 474-1000
NASDAQ: MCRL ■ *TF:* 800-800-2045 ■ *Web:* www.micrel.com

Micro Linear Corp 2050 Concourse Dr .... San Jose CA 95131 408-433-5200 432-0363
NASDAQ: MLIN ■ *TF:* 800-998-5200 ■ *Web:* www.microlinear.com

Microchip Technology Inc 2355 W Chandler Blvd .... Chandler AZ 85224 480-792-7200 899-9210
NASDAQ: MCHP ■ *TF:* 800-437-2767 ■ *Web:* www.microchip.com

Microsemi Corp 2381 Morse Ave .... Irvine CA 92614 949-221-7100 756-0308
NASDAQ: MSCC ■ *TF:* 800-713-4113 ■ *Web:* www.microsemi.com

Microtune Inc 2201 10th St .... Plano TX 75074 972-673-1600 673-1602
NASDAQ: TUNE ■ *Web:* www.microtune.com

Mindspeed Technologies Inc 4000 MacArthur Blvd .... Newport Beach CA 92660 949-579-3000 579-3200
NASDAQ: MSPD ■ *Web:* www.mindspeed.com

Mini-Circuits Laboratories Inc PO Box 350166 .... Brooklyn NY 11235 718-934-4500 332-4661
Web: www.minicircuits.com

MIPS Technologies Inc 1225 Charleston Rd .... Mountain View CA 94043 650-567-5000 567-5150
NASDAQ: MIPS ■ *Web:* www.mips.com

Mitsubishi Electric & Electronics USA Inc Semiconductor Div
5201 Great America Pkwy Suite 332 .... Santa Clara CA 95054 408-727-3111 727-2689
Web: www.mitsubishichips.com

Monolithic Power Systems Inc 983 University Ave Bldg A .... Los Gatos CA 95032 408-357-6600 357-6601
NASDAQ: MPWRE ■ *Web:* www.monolithicpower.com

Monolithic System Technology Inc (MoSys)
755 N Matilda Ave Suite 100 .... Sunnyvale CA 94085 408-731-1800 731-1893
NASDAQ: MOSY ■ *Web:* www.mosysinc.com

Mosel Vitelic Inc 3910 N 1st St .... San Jose CA 95134 408-433-6000 433-0952
Web: www.moselvitelic.com

MoSys (Monolithic System Technology Inc)
755 N Matilda Ave Suite 100 .... Sunnyvale CA 94085 408-731-1800 731-1893
NASDAQ: MOSY ■ *Web:* www.mosysinc.com

Motorola Inc 1301 E Algonquin Rd .... Schaumburg IL 60196 847-576-5000 538-3617*
NYSE: MOT ■ **Fax:* Hum Res ■ *TF:* 800-331-6456 ■ *Web:* www.motorola.com

National Semiconductor Corp 2900 Semiconductor Dr .... Santa Clara CA 95051 408-721-5000 732-4880
NYSE: NSM ■ *Web:* www.national.com

NEC Electronics America Inc 2880 Scott Blvd .... Santa Clara CA 95052 408-588-6000 588-6130
TF Tech Supp: 800-366-9782 ■ *Web:* www.am.necel.com

NeoMagic Corp 3250 Jay St .... Santa Clara CA 95054 408-988-7020 988-7036
NASDAQ: NMGC ■ *TF:* 800-838-9924 ■ *Web:* www.neomagic.com

NeoPhotonics Corp 2911 Zanker Rd .... San Jose CA 95134 408-232-9200 456-2971
TF: 800-499-7519 ■ *Web:* www.neophotonics.com

NetLogic Microsystems Inc 1875 Charleston Rd .... Mountain View CA 94043 650-961-6676 961-1092
NASDAQ: NETL ■ *Web:* www.netlogicmicro.com

NetSilicon Inc 411 Waverly Oaks Rd Suite 304 .... Waltham MA 02452 781-647-1234 893-1338
TF: 800-243-2333 ■ *Web:* www.netsilicon.com

Nextest Systems Corp 1901 Monterey Rd .... San Jose CA 95112 408-817-7200 817-7210
NASDAQ: NEXT ■ *Web:* www.nextest.com

Nitto Denko America Inc 48500 Fremont Blvd .... Fremont CA 94538 510-445-5400 445-5480
TF: 800-356-4880 ■ *Web:* www.nittousa.com

O2Micro International Ltd 3118 Patrick Henry Dr .... Santa Clara CA 95054 408-987-5920 987-5929
NASDAQ: OIIM ■ *Web:* www.o2micro.com

Oki Semiconductor 785 N Mary Ave .... Sunnyvale CA 94085 408-720-1900 720-1918
Web: www.okisemi.com

OmniVision Technologies Inc 1341 Orleans Dr .... Sunnyvale CA 94089 408-542-3000 542-3001
NASDAQ: OVTI ■ *Web:* www.ovt.com

Omron Electronics LLC 1 Commerce Dr .... Schaumburg IL 60173 847-843-7900 843-8261
TF: 800-556-6766 ■ *Web:* www.omron247.com

ON Semiconductor Corp 5005 E McDowell Rd .... Phoenix AZ 85008 602-244-6600
NASDAQ: ONNN ■ *TF:* 800-282-9855 ■ *Web:* www.onsemi.com

Optek Technology Inc 1645 Wallace Dr .... Carrollton TX 75006 972-323-2200 323-2396
TF: 800-341-4747 ■ *Web:* www.optekinc.com

OSI Systems Inc 12525 Chadron Ave .... Hawthorne CA 90250 310-978-0516 644-1727
NASDAQ: OSIS ■ *Web:* www.osi-systems.com

Pericom Semiconductor Corp 3545 N 1st St .... San Jose CA 95134 408-435-0800 435-1100
NASDAQ: PSEM ■ *TF:* 800-435-2336 ■ *Web:* www.pericom.com

PerkinElmer Inc 45 William St .... Wellesley MA 02481 781-237-5100 237-9386
NYSE: PKI ■ *Web:* www.perkinelmer.com

PerkinElmer Optoelectronics Inc 44370 Christy St .... Fremont CA 94538 510-979-6500 687-1140
TF: 800-775-6786 ■ *Web:* optoelectronics.perkinelmer.com

Philips Semiconductors 1109 McKay Dr .... San Jose CA 95131 408-434-3000
TF: 800-447-1500 ■ *Web:* www.semiconductors.com

Photronics Inc 15 Secor Rd .... Brookfield CT 06804 203-775-9000 740-5630*
NASDAQ: PLAB ■ **Fax:* Hum Res ■ *Web:* www.photronics.com

Pixelworks Inc 8100 SW Nyberg Rd .... Tualatin OR 97062 503-454-1750 612-0848
NASDAQ: PXLW ■ *Web:* www.pixelworks.com

PLX Technology Inc 870 W Maude Ave .... Sunnyvale CA 94085 408-774-9060 774-2169
NASDAQ: PLXT ■ *TF:* 800-759-3735 ■ *Web:* www.plxtech.com

PMC-Sierra Inc 2700 Production Way Suite 100 .... Burnaby BC V5A4X1 604-415-6000 415-6200
NASDAQ: PMCS ■ *Web:* www.pmc-sierra.com

Power Integrations 5245 Hellyer Ave .... San Jose CA 95138 408-414-9200 414-9201
NASDAQ: POWI ■ *Web:* www.powerint.com

Powerex Inc 173 Pavilion Ln .... Youngwood PA 15697 724-925-7272 925-4393
TF: 800-451-1415 ■ *Web:* www.pwrx.com

Praxair Electronics 542 Rt 303 .... Orangeburg NY 10962 845-359-4200 359-0215
TF: 800-827-4387 ■ *Web:* praxairmrc.com

QLogic Corp 26650 Aliso Viejo Pkwy .... Aliso Viejo CA 92656 949-389-6000 389-6114
NASDAQ: QLGC ■ *TF:* 800-662-4471 ■ *Web:* www.qlogic.com

QuickLogic Corp 1277 Orleans Dr .... Sunnyvale CA 94089 408-990-4000 990-4040
NASDAQ: QUIK ■ *Web:* www.quicklogic.com

Rabbit Semiconductor Inc 2900 Spafford St .... Davis CA 95616 530-757-8400 753-5141*
**Fax:* Mktg ■ *TF:* 888-362-3387 ■ *Web:* www.rabbitsemiconductor.com

Rambus Inc 4440 El Camino Real .... Los Altos CA 94022 650-947-5000 947-5001
NASDAQ: RMBS ■ *TF:* 800-726-2879 ■ *Web:* www.rambus.com

Ramtron International Corp 1850 Ramtron Dr .... Colorado Springs CO 80921 719-481-7000 481-9294
NASDAQ: RMTR ■ *TF:* 800-545-3726 ■ *Web:* www.ramtron.com

Raytek Inc 1201 Shaffer Rd Bldg 2 .... Santa Cruz CA 95060 831-458-1110 458-1239
TF: 800-227-8074 ■ *Web:* www.raytek.com

Raytheon RF Components 350 Lowell St .... Andover MA 01810 978-470-5000 470-9744
Web: www.raytheonrf.com

Renesas Technology Corp 450 Holger Way .... San Jose CA 95134 408-382-7500 382-7501
Web: america.renesas.com

RF Micro Devices Inc 7628 Thorndike Rd .... Greensboro NC 27409 336-664-1233 931-7454
NASDAQ: RFMD ■ *Web:* www.rfmd.com

Samsung Electronics America Inc 105 Challenger Rd .... Ridgefield Park NJ 07660 201-229-4000 229-4029
TF: 800-726-7864 ■ *Web:* www.samsungusa.com

Samsung Semiconductors Inc 3655 N 1st St .... San Jose CA 95134 408-544-4000 544-4980
TF: 800-726-7864 ■ *Web:* www.usa.samsungsemi.com

SANYO Solar USA LLC 970 E 236th St .... Carson CA 90745 310-834-5800 834-0728
Web: www.sanyo.com/aboutsanyo/corp_pro_man_sii.cfm

SatCon Technology Corp 27 Dry Dock Ave .... Boston MA 02210 617-897-2400 897-2401
NASDAQ: SATC ■ *TF:* 888-728-2760 ■ *Web:* www.satcon.com

Seiko Instruments USA Inc 12301 Technology Blvd .... Austin TX 78727 512-349-3800 349-3000
TF: 800-358-0880 ■ *Web:* www.seikoinstruments.com

Phone | Fax

Seiko Instruments USA Inc Electronic Components Div
2990 Lomita Blvd. .... Torrance CA 90505 310-517-7771 517-7709
Web: www.siielectroniccomponents.com

Semtech Corp 200 Flynn Rd .... Camarillo CA 93012 805-498-2111 498-3804
NASDAQ: SMTC ■ *Web:* www.semtech.com

Sharp Microelectronics of the Americas
5700 NW Pacific Rim Blvd. .... Camas WA 98607 360-834-2500 834-8903
Web: www.sharpsma.com

Sheldahl Inc 1150 Sheldahl Rd .... Northfield MN 55057 507-663-8000 663-8545
TF: 800-533-0505 ■ *Web:* www.sheldahl.com

Shell Solar 4650 Adohr Ln .... Camarillo CA 93012 805-482-6800 388-6395
Web: www.shellsolar.com

Showa Denko America Inc 489 5th Ave 18th Fl. .... New York NY 10017 212-370-0033 370-4566
Web: www.sdasf.com

Sigma Designs Inc 1221 California Cir .... Milpitas CA 95035 408-262-9003 957-9740
NASDAQ: SIGM ■ *TF Sales:* 800-845-8086 ■ *Web:* www.sdesigns.com

SigmaTel Inc 1601 S Mo Pac Expy Suite 100 .... Austin TX 78746 512-381-3700 744-1700
NASDAQ: SGTL ■ *Web:* www.sigmatel.com

Silicon Image Inc 1060 E Arques Ave .... Sunnyvale CA 94085 408-616-4000 830-9530
NASDAQ: SIMG ■ *Web:* www.siimage.com

Silicon Laboratories Inc 4635 Boston Ln. .... Austin TX 78735 512-416-8500 416-9669
NASDAQ: SLAB ■ *TF:* 877-444-3032 ■ *Web:* www.silabs.com

Siliconix Inc 2201 Laurelwood Rd .... Santa Clara CA 95056 408-988-8000 567-8950
Web: www.vishay.com

Sipex Corp 233 S Hillview Dr .... Milpitas CA 95035 408-934-7500 935-7600
Web: www.sipex.com

Sirenza Microdevices Inc 303 S Technology Ct. .... Broomfield CO 80021 303-327-3030 410-7088
NASDAQ: SMDI ■ *TF:* 800-764-6642 ■ *Web:* www.sirenza.com

SiRF Technology Holdings Inc 148 E Brokaw Rd. .... San Jose CA 95112 408-467-0410 467-0420
NASDAQ: SIRF ■ *Web:* www.sirf.com

Skyworks Solutions Inc 20 Sylvan Rd .... Woburn MA 01801 781-935-5150 376-3300
NASDAQ: SWKS ■ *Web:* www.skyworksinc.com

Solitron Devices Inc 3301 Electronics Way .... West Palm Beach FL 33407 561-848-4311 863-5946*
**Fax:* Mktg ■ *Web:* www.solitrondevices.com

Sony Semiconductor 3300 Zanker Rd .... San Jose CA 95134 408-432-1600 959-5176
Web: products.sel.sony.com/semi

Southland Micro Systems 9400 Toledo Way .... Irvine CA 92618 949-380-1958 380-0918
TF: 800-255-4200 ■ *Web:* www.southlandmicro.com

Spectrolab Inc 12500 Gladstone Ave .... Sylmar CA 91342 818-365-4611 898-7534
TF: 800-936-4888 ■ *Web:* www.spectrolab.com

SRS Labs Inc 2909 Daimler St .... Santa Ana CA 92705 949-442-1070 852-1099
NASDAQ: SRSL ■ *TF:* 800-243-2737 ■ *Web:* www.srslabs.com

Staktek Holdings Inc 8900 Shoal Creek Blvd Suite 125 .... Austin TX 78757 512-454-9531 454-9409
NASDAQ: STAK ■ *Web:* www.staktek.com

Standard Microsystems Corp 80 Arkay Dr .... Hauppauge NY 11788 631-435-6000 273-5550
NASDAQ: SMSC ■ *TF:* 800-443-7364 ■ *Web:* www.smsc.com

STMicroelectronics Inc 1310 Electronics Dr .... Carrollton TX 75006 972-466-6000 466-7196*
**Fax:* Hum Res ■ *Web:* www.st.com

Summit Microelectronics Inc 1717 Fox Dr .... San Jose CA 95131 408-436-9890 436-9897
Web: www.summitmicro.com

SunPower Corp 430 Indio Way .... Sunnyvale CA 94085 408-991-0900 739-7713
NASDAQ: SPWR ■ *TF:* 877-786-0123 ■ *Web:* www.sunpowercorp.com

Supertex Inc 1235 Bordeaux Dr .... Sunnyvale CA 94089 408-744-0100 222-4800
NASDAQ: SUPX ■ *TF:* 800-487-8737 ■ *Web:* www.supertex.com

Symetrix Corp 5055 Mark Dabling Blvd .... Colorado Springs CO 80918 719-594-6145 598-3437
Web: www.symetrixcorp.com

Taiwan Semiconductor Mfg Co Ltd (TSMC) 2585 Junction Ave .... San Jose CA 95134 408-382-8000 382-8008
NYSE: TSM ■ *Web:* www.tsmc.com

TDK Semiconductor Corp 6440 Oak Canyon. .... Irvine CA 92618 714-508-8800 508-8875
Web: www.tsc.tdk.com

Teccor Electronics Inc 1800 Hurd Dr .... Irving TX 75038 972-580-1515 550-1309*
**Fax:* Sales ■ *Web:* www.teccor.com

Teledyne Electronics & Communications
12964 Panama St. .... Los Angeles CA 90066 310-822-8229 574-2092
Web: www.tet.com

Telephonics Corp 815 Broad Hollow Rd. .... Farmingdale NY 11735 631-755-7000 755-7046
TF: 877-755-7700 ■ *Web:* www.telephonics.com

Tensilica Inc 3255-6 Scott Blvd .... Santa Clara CA 95054 408-986-8000 986-8919
Web: www.tensilica.com

Tessera Technologies Inc 3099 Orchard Dr. .... San Jose CA 95134 408-894-0700 894-0768
NASDAQ: TSRA ■ *Web:* www.tessera.com

Texas Instruments Inc 12500 TI Blvd. .... Dallas TX 75243 972-995-2011 917-7792*
NYSE: TXN ■ **Fax:* Hum Res ■ *TF Cust Svc:* 800-336-5236 ■ *Web:* www.ti.com

Tezzaron Semiconductor Corp 1415 Bond St Suite 111 .... Naperville IL 60563 630-505-0404 505-9292
Web: www.tachyonsemi.com

Toppan Photomasks Inc 131 Old Settlers Blvd .... Round Rock TX 78664 512-310-6500 310-6501
Web: www.photomask.com

Toshiba America Electronic Components Inc
19900 MacArthur Blvd Suite 400. .... Irvine CA 92612 800-879-4963 581-9038*
**Fax Area Code:* 949 ■ **Fax:* Hum Res ■ *TF:* 800-879-4963 ■
Web: www.toshiba.com/taec

Tosoh SMD Inc 3600 Gantz Rd .... Grove City OH 43123 614-875-7912 875-0031
TF: 800-678-8942 ■ *Web:* www.tsmd.com

Transmeta Corp 3990 Freedom Cir .... Santa Clara CA 95054 408-919-3000 919-6540
NASDAQ: TMTA ■ *Web:* www.transmeta.com

TranSwitch Corp 3 Enterprise Dr. .... Shelton CT 06484 203-929-8810 926-9453
NASDAQ: TXCC ■ *Web:* www.transwitch.com

Trident Microsystems Inc 1090 E Arques Ave .... Sunnyvale CA 94085 408-991-8800 733-1087*
NASDAQ: TRID ■ **Fax:* Hum Res ■ *Web:* www.tridentmicro.com

Tripath Technology Inc 2560 Orchard Pkwy .... San Jose CA 95131 408-750-3000 750-3001
TF: 877-874-7284 ■ *Web:* www.tripath.com

TriQuint Semiconductor Inc 2300 NE Brookwood Pkwy .... Hillsboro OR 97124 503-615-9000 615-8904*
NASDAQ: TQNT ■ **Fax:* Hum Res ■ *TF:* 888-258-5873 ■ *Web:* www.tqs.com

Tropian Inc 20813 Stevens Creek Blvd .... Cupertino CA 95014 408-865-1300 865-1385
Web: www.tropian.com

TSMC (Taiwan Semiconductor Mfg Co Ltd) 2585 Junction Ave .... San Jose CA 95134 408-382-8000 382-8008
NYSE: TSM ■ *Web:* www.tsmc.com

Tundra Semiconductor Corp 603 March Rd .... Ottawa ON K2K2M5 613-592-0714 592-1320
TSX: TUN ■ *TF:* 800-267-7231 ■ *Web:* www.tundra.com

Tvia Inc 4001 Burton Dr .... Santa Clara CA 95054 408-982-8588 982-8591
NASDAQ: TVIA ■ *Web:* www.tvia.com

UDT Sensors Inc 12525 Chadron Ave .... Hawthorne CA 90250 310-978-0516 644-1727
Web: www.udt.com

United Microelectronics Corp 488 De Guigne Dr .... Sunnyvale CA 94085 408-523-7800 735-1934
NYSE: UMC ■ *Web:* www.umc.com

Universal Display Corp 375 Phillips Blvd .... Ewing NJ 08618 609-671-0980 671-0995
NASDAQ: PANL ■ *Web:* www.universaldisplay.com

VIA Technologies Inc 940 Mission Ct. .... Fremont CA 94539 510-683-3300 683-3301
Web: www.viatech.com

Virage Logic Corp 47100 Bayside Pkwy .... Fremont CA 94538 510-360-8000 360-8099
NASDAQ: VIRL ■ *TF:* 877-360-6690 ■ *Web:* www.viragelogic.com

Vishay BLH 3 Edgewater Dr. .... Norwood MA 02062 781-298-2200 762-3988
Web: www.blh.com

Vishay Intertechnology Inc 63 Lancaster Ave .... Malvern PA 19355 610-644-1300 296-0657
NYSE: VSH ■ *Web:* www.vishay.com

Vitesse Semiconductor Corp 741 Calle Plano .... Camarillo CA 93012 805-388-3700 987-5896
NASDAQ: VTSS ■ *TF:* 800-848-3773 ■ *Web:* www.vitesse.com

Volterra Semiconductor Corp 3839 Spinnaker Ct .... Fremont CA 94538 510-743-1200 743-1600
NASDAQ: VLTR ■ *Web:* www.volterra.com

Wabash Technologies 1375 Swan St PO Box 829 .... Huntington IN 46750 260-356-8300 355-4265*
**Fax:* Sales ■ *Web:* www.wabashtech.com

Wacker Siltronic Corp 7200 NW Front Ave .... Portland OR 97210 503-243-2020 219-4509*
**Fax:* Sales ■ *TF:* 800-922-5371 ■ *Web:* www.siltronic.com

Wafertech LLC 5509 NW Parker St. .... Camas WA 98607 360-817-3000 817-3590
Web: www.wafertech.com

White Electronic Designs Corp 3601 E University Dr .... Phoenix AZ 85034 602-437-1520 437-9120*
NASDAQ: WEDC ■ **Fax:* Sales ■ *TF:* 800-326-9556 ■ *Web:* www.wedc.com

Winbond Electronics Corp America 2727 N 1st St .... San Jose CA 95134 408-943-6666 474-1600
TF: 800-825-4473 ■ *Web:* www.winbond.com

Xilinx Inc 2100 Logic Dr .... San Jose CA 95124 408-559-7778 559-7114
NASDAQ: XLNX ■ *TF:* 800-494-5469 ■ *Web:* www.xilinx.com

Zarlink Semiconductor Inc 400 March Rd .... Ottawa ON K2K3H4 613-592-0200 592-1010
NYSE: ZL ■ *TF:* 800-325-4927 ■ *Web:* www.zarlink.com

ZiLOG Inc 532 Race St. .... San Jose CA 95126 408-558-8500 558-8300
NASDAQ: ZILG ■ *TF:* 800-662-6211 ■ *Web:* www.zilog.com

Zoran Corp 1390 Kifer Rd .... Sunnyvale CA 94086 408-523-6500 523-6501
NASDAQ: ZRAN ■ *Web:* www.zoran.com

700 SHEET METAL WORK

SEE ALSO Construction - Special Trade Contractors - Plumbing, Heating, Air Conditioning Contractors p. 1544; Construction - Special Trade Contractors - Roofing, Siding, Sheet Metal Contractors p. 1546

Phone | Fax

AB Myr Industries Inc 39635 I-94 S Service Dr. .... Belleville MI 48111 734-941-2200 941-8332
TF: 888-481-0446 ■ *Web:* www.abmyr.com

Abalon Precision Mfg Corp 1040 Home St .... Bronx NY 10459 718-589-5682 589-0300

Abrams Airborne Mfg Inc 3735 N Romero Rd .... Tucson AZ 85705 520-887-1727 293-8807
Web: www.abrams.com

Accurate Metal Fabricators Inc 1011 Seal Beach Blvd .... Seal Beach CA 90740 562-596-4740 596-6799
Web: www.amf1.com

Acme Mfg Co 7601 State Rd. .... Philadelphia PA 19136 215-338-2850 335-1905
TF: 800-899-2850

Aero Trades Mfg Corp 65 Jericho Tpke .... Mineola NY 11501 516-746-3360 746-3417

Air Comfort Corp 2550 Braga Dr. .... Broadview IL 60155 708-345-1900 345-2730
TF: 800-466-3779 ■ *Web:* www.aircomfort.com

Air Conditioning Products Co 30350 Ecorse Rd .... Romulus MI 48174 734-326-0050 326-9632
Web: www.acpshutters.com

Aircom Mfg Inc 6205 E 30th St .... Indianapolis IN 46219 317-545-5383 542-7365
TF: 800-925-2426 ■ *Web:* www.aircommfg.com

Airolite Co 27855 State Route 7 .... Marietta OH 45750 740-373-7676 373-6666
TF: 800-247-6548 ■ *Web:* www.airolite.com

Airtronics Metal Products Inc 1980 Senter Rd .... San Jose CA 95112 408-977-7800 977-7810
Web: www.airtronics.com

Albers Mechanical Contractors Inc 200 W Plato Blvd .... Saint Paul MN 55107 651-224-5428 224-1742
Web: www.albersco.com

Aluminum Line Products Co 24460 Sperry Cir. .... Westlake OH 44145 440-835-8880 835-8879
TF: 800-321-3154 ■ *Web:* www.aluminumline.com

American Warming & Ventilating Inc 7301 International Dr. .... Holland OH 43528 419-865-5000 865-1375
Web: www.american-warming.com

ArcRon Div IEA W 141 N 9501 Fountain Blvd. .... Menomonee Falls WI 53051 262-255-4150 255-7985
TF: 800-886-4151 ■ *Web:* www.arcron.com

Arizona Precision Sheet Metal 2140 W Pinnacle Peak Rd .... Phoenix AZ 85027 623-516-3700 516-3701
TF: 800-443-7039 ■ *Web:* www.apsm-jit.com

Arrow United Industries PO Box 69 .... Wyalusing PA 18853 570-746-1888 746-9286
Web: www.arrowunited.com

ASC Profiles Inc 2110 Enterprise Blvd .... West Sacramento CA 95691 916-372-0933 372-2967
TF Cust Svc: 800-726-2727 ■ *Web:* www.ascprofiles.com

Associated Materials Inc 3773 State Rd .... Cuyahoga Falls OH 44223 330-929-1811 922-2296
TF: 800-257-4335 ■ *Web:* www.associatedmaterials.com

Atlantic Ventilating & Equipment Co 25 Sebethe Dr .... Cromwell CT 06416 860-635-1300 632-7412

Atlas Mfg 2950 Weeks Ave SE .... Minneapolis MN 55414 612-331-2566 331-1295
Web: www.atlasmfg.com

AW Mercer Inc 104 Industrial Dr .... Boyertown PA 19512 610-367-8460 367-7491
Web: www.awmercer.com

Berger Bros Co 805 Pennsylvania Blvd .... Feasterville PA 19053 215-355-1200 355-7738
TF Cust Svc: 800-523-8852 ■ *Web:* www.bergerbros.com

Berger Holdings Ltd 805 Pennsylvania Blvd .... Feasterville PA 19053 215-355-1200 355-7738
TF: 800-523-8852

Bert R Huncilman & Son 115 Security Pkwy .... New Albany IN 47150 812-945-3544 948-2133
Web: www.huncilman.com

BHW Sheet Metal Co 113 Johnson St .... Jonesboro GA 30236 770-471-9303 478-7923

Botner Mfg Inc 10000 Bigge St .... San Leandro CA 94577 510-569-2943 569-2942

Branch Mfg Co 6420 Pine St .... North Branch MN 55056 651-674-4441 674-4442
Web: www.branchmfg.com

Bright Sheet Metal Co Inc 4212 W 71st Suite A .... Indianapolis IN 46268 317-291-7600 291-7604

Cado Fabrications Inc 144 Elm St .... Amesbury MA 01913 978-388-9436 388-6281

Christen Fred & Sons Co 714 George St .... Toledo OH 43608 419-243-4161 243-1292
TF: 800-243-4161

Cinnabar Solution Inc 155 Sunnynoll Ct Suite 300 .... Winston-Salem NC 27106 800-782-2171 722-5198*
**Fax Area Code:* 336 ■ *Web:* www.cinnabarsolutions.com

CL Rieckhoff Co Inc 26265 Northline Rd .... Taylor MI 48180 734-946-8220 946-2004

Clark Specialty Co Inc 8440 Rt 54 .... Hammondsport NY 14840 607-569-2191 569-3694
TF: 888-569-2128 ■ *Web:* www.clarkspecialty.com

Climatemp Inc 315 N May St .... Chicago IL 60607 312-829-3131 829-7510

Cody Co Inc 4200 N I-45 .... Ennis TX 75119 972-875-5884 875-0308
Web: www.codycompany.com

Computer Components Corp 2751 S Hampton Rd .... Philadelphia PA 19154 215-676-7600 464-7876
Web: www.compcomp.com/ccc9

Connell LP 1 International Pl 31st Fl. .... Boston MA 02110 617-737-2700 737-1617
TF: 800-276-4746 ■ *Web:* www.connell-lp.com

Consolidated Systems Inc 650 Rosewood Dr .... Columbia SC 29201 803-771-7920 799-6811
TF: 800-654-1912 ■ *Web:* www.csisteel.com

Contech Construction Products Inc
9025 Centre Pointe Dr Suite 400. .... West Chester OH 45069 513-645-7000 645-7604
TF: 800-338-1122 ■ *Web:* www.contech-cpi.com

Corchran Inc 1340 S State St .... Waseca MN 56093 507-835-3910 835-1382
Web: www.corchran.com

Courtesy Mfg Co 1300 Pratt Blvd .... Elk Grove Village IL 60007 847-437-7500 437-7526
Web: www.cmc-mfg.com

Crown Products Co Inc 6390 Phillips Hwy .... Jacksonville FL 32216 904-665-3609 737-3533
TF: 800-683-7144 ■ *Web:* www.crownproductsco.com

CWR Mfg Corp 7000 Fly Rd .... Syracuse NY 13220 315-437-1032 437-1493
TF Sales: 800-724-0311 ■ *Web:* www.cwronline.com

Dawson Metal Co Inc 825 Allen St. .... Jamestown NY 14701 716-664-3815 664-3485
TF: 877-732-9766 ■ *Web:* www.dawsonmetal.com

Detronic Industries Inc 35800 Beattie Dr. .... Sterling Heights MI 48312 586-977-5660 939-5340
Web: www.detronic.com

Company	City	State	ZIP	Phone	Fax
Du-Mont Co 7800 N Pioneer Ct *Web:* www.du-mont.com	Peoria	IL	61615	309-692-7240	693-2937
Dura-Bilt Products Inc PO Box 188 *TF:* 800-233-4251 ■ *Web:* www.durabilt.com	Wellsburg	NY	14894	570-596-2000	596-3296
Duray/JF Duncan Industries Inc 9301 Stewart & Gray Rd *Web:* www.duraynet.com	Downey	CA	90241	562-862-4269	869-1850
Eagle Cornice Co Inc 89 Pettaconsett Ave *Web:* www.eaglecornice.com	Cranston	RI	02920	401-781-5978	781-6570
Edco & Arrowhead Products Inc 8700 Excelsior Blvd *TF:* 800-333-2580 ■ *Web:* www.edcoproducts.com	Hopkins	MN	55343	952-938-6313	938-4950
Electro-Space Fabricators Inc 300 W High St *Web:* www.esfinc.com	Topton	PA	19562	610-682-7181	682-2133
Elixir Industries Inc 24800 Chrisanta Dr Suite 210 *TF:* 800-421-1942 ■ *Web:* www.elixirind.com	Mission Viejo	CA	92691	949-860-5000	860-5011
Epic Metals Corp 11 Talbot Ave *Web:* www.epicmetals.com	Rankin	PA	15104	412-351-3913	351-2018
Evansville Sheet Metal Works 1901 W Maryland St *Web:* www.esmw.com	Evansville	IN	47712	812-423-7871	423-7353
Experi-Metal Inc 6345 Wall St *Web:* www.experi-metal.com	Sterling Heights	MI	48312	586-977-7800	977-6981
Falstrom Co PO Box 118	Passaic	NJ	07055	973-777-0013	777-6396
Floturn Inc 4236 Thunderbird Ln *Web:* www.floturn.com	Fairfield	OH	45014	513-860-8040	860-8044
Foster LB Co 415 Holiday Dr *NASDAQ: FSTR* ■ **Fax:* Sales ■ *TF:* 800-255-4500 ■ *Web:* www.lbfoster.com	Pittsburgh	PA	15220	412-928-3400	928-3427*
Frank M Booth Inc 222 3rd St *TF:* 800-540-9369 ■ *Web:* www.frankbooth.com	Marysville	CA	95901	530-742-7134	742-8109
Fred Christen & Sons Co 714 George St *TF:* 800-243-4161	Toledo	OH	43608	419-243-4161	243-1292
Gary Metal Mfg LLC 2700 E 5th Ave	Gary	IN	46402	219-885-3232	885-0528
General Sheet Metal Corp 2330 Louisiana Ave N	Minneapolis	MN	55427	763-544-8747	544-6580
Gentek Building Products Inc 3773 State Rd **Fax Area Code:* 330 ■ *Web:* ca.gentekinc.com	Cuyahoga Falls	OH	44223	800-548-4542	922-7688*
Gerome Mfg Co Inc PO Box 1089 *Web:* www.geromemfg.com	Uniontown	PA	15401	724-438-8544	437-5608
Gilbert Mechanical Contractors Inc 4451 W 76th St *TF:* 800-701-0986 ■ *Web:* www.gilbertmech.com	Edina	MN	55435	952-835-3810	835-4765
Global Power Equipment Group Inc 6120 S Yale Ave Suite 1480 *NYSE: GEG* ■ *Web:* www.globalpower.com	Tulsa	OK	74136	918-488-0828	488-8389
Goldberg Brothers Inc PO Box 17048 *Web:* www.goldbergbrothers.bizhosting.com	Denver	CO	80217	303-321-1099	388-0749
Grayd-A Metal Fabricators 13233 E Florence Ave *Web:* www.grayd-a.com	Santa Fe Springs	CA	90670	562-944-8951	944-2326
Greene Metal Products Inc 24500 Capital Blvd	Clinton Township	MI	48036	586-465-6800	465-0136
Greenheck Fan Corp 1100 Industrial Ave PO Box 410 *Web:* www.greenheck.com	Schofield	WI	54476	715-359-6171	355-2399
H & H Industrial Corp 7612 N Rt 130 *TF:* 800-982-0341 ■ *Web:* www.hhindustrial.com	Pennsauken	NJ	08110	856-663-4444	663-4446
Hamilton Form Co Ltd 7009 Midway Rd *Web:* www.hamiltonform.com	Fort Worth	TX	76118	817-590-2111	595-1110
Hi Pro International Inc 5049 S National Dr *TF:* 800-947-0997 ■ *Web:* www.hiprointl.com	Knoxville	TN	37914	865-637-1711	546-9546
HiMEC Inc 1400 7th St NW *TF:* 888-454-4632 ■ *Web:* www.himec.com	Rochester	MN	55901	507-281-4000	281-5206
HM White Inc 12855 Burt Rd *Web:* www.hmwhite.com	Detroit	MI	48223	313-531-8477	531-0522
Huncilman Bert R & Son 115 Security Pkwy *Web:* www.huncilman.com	New Albany	IN	47150	812-945-3544	948-2133
IEA ArcRon Div W 141 N 9501 Fountain Blvd *TF:* 800-886-4151 ■ *Web:* www.arcron.com	Menomonee Falls	WI	53051	262-255-4150	255-7985
IMCO Inc 858 N Lenola Rd	Moorestown	NJ	08057	856-235-7540	727-1637
Industrial Air Inc 428 Edwardia Dr PO Box 8769 *Web:* www.industrialairinc.com	Greensboro	NC	27419	336-292-1030	855-7763
Industrial Louvers Inc 511 7th St S *TF:* 800-328-3421 ■ *Web:* www.industriallouvers.com	Delano	MN	55328	763-972-2981	972-2911
Irving Tool & Mfg Co Inc 2249 Wall St	Garland	TX	75041	972-926-4000	926-4099
Jaquith Industries Inc PO Box 780 *Web:* www.jaquith.com	Syracuse	NY	13205	315-478-5700	478-5707
Jensen Bridge & Supply Co PO Box 151 *Web:* www.jensenbridge.com	Sandusky	MI	48471	810-648-3000	648-3549
John Sykes Co Inc PO Box 5189	Atlantic City	NJ	08404	609-345-1191	344-1952
John W McDougall Co Inc 3731 Amy Lynn Dr *TF:* 800-264-1122 ■ *Web:* www.jwmcd.com	Nashville	TN	37218	615-321-3900	329-9069
Jones Metal Products Inc 3201 3rd Ave *TF:* 800-967-1750 ■ *Web:* www.jonesmetalproducts.com	Mankato	MN	56001	507-625-4436	625-2994
Jor-Mac Co Inc 704 10th Ave *Web:* www.jor-mac.com	Grafton	WI	53024	262-377-5420	377-5606
Juniper Industries Inc 72-15 Metropolitan Ave *TF:* 800-221-4664 ■ *Web:* www.juniperind.com	Middle Village	NY	11379	718-326-2546	326-3786
Kirk Williams Co Inc 2734 Home Rd *Web:* www.kirkwilliamsco.com	Grove City	OH	43123	614-875-9023	875-9214
Klauer Mfg Co PO Box 59 *Web:* www.klauer.com	Dubuque	IA	52004	563-582-7201	582-2022
Knox RF Co Inc PO Box 1337 *TF:* 800-989-7401 ■ *Web:* www.rfknox.com	Smyrna	GA	30081	770-434-7401	433-1783
Krueger Sheet Metal Co 731 N Superior St *TF:* 800-777-9339	Spokane	WA	99202	509-489-0221	489-6539
KSM Industries Inc N 115 W 19025 Edison Dr *Web:* www.ksmindustries.com	Germantown	WI	53022	262-251-9510	251-4865
Kuest Corp PO Box 33007 *Web:* www.kuestcorp.com	San Antonio	TX	78265	210-655-1220	655-8378
LB Foster Co 415 Holiday Dr *NASDAQ: FSTR* ■ **Fax:* Sales ■ *TF:* 800-255-4500 ■ *Web:* www.lbfoster.com	Pittsburgh	PA	15220	412-928-3400	928-3427*
Limco Airepair Inc 5304 S Lawton Ave *Web:* www.limcoairepair.com	Tulsa	OK	74107	918-445-4300	446-8704
Link-Burns Mfg Co Inc 253 American Way	Voorhees	NJ	08043	856-429-6844	429-3734
Livers Bronze Co 4621 E 75th Terr *Web:* www.liversbronze.com	Kansas City	MO	64132	816-300-2828	300-0864
LL Building Products Inc 295 McKoy Rd *Web:* www.llbuildingproducts.com	Burgaw	NC	28425	910-815-2600	259-6383
Maddox Metal Works Inc 4116 Bronze Way *Web:* www.maddoxmetalworks.com	Dallas	TX	75237	214-333-2311	337-8169
Mapes Industries Inc 2929 Cornhusker Hwy *TF:* 800-228-2391 ■ *Web:* www.mapesindustries.com	Lincoln	NE	68504	402-466-1985	466-2790
Mayco Industries LLC 18 W Oxmoor Rd *TF:* 800-749-6061 ■ *Web:* www.maycoindustries.com	Birmingham	AL	35209	205-942-4242	945-8704
Maysteel LLC N89 W14700 Patrita Dr PO Box 1240 *TF:* 800-255-1247 ■ *Web:* www.maysteel.com	Menomonee Falls	WI	53052	262-255-2400	255-2417
McCorvey Sheet Metal Works LP PO Box 405 *TF:* 800-580-7545 ■ *Web:* www.mccorvey.com	Galena Park	TX	77547	713-672-7545	672-0509
McDougall John W Co Inc 3731 Amy Lynn Dr *TF:* 800-264-1122 ■ *Web:* www.jwmcd.com	Nashville	TN	37218	615-321-3900	329-9069
McGill Airflow Corp 1747 E Charter Way *Web:* www.mcgillairflow.com	Stockton	CA	95205	209-466-2351	941-2739
Mech-Tronics Corp 1635 N 25th Ave *Web:* www.mech-tronics.com	Melrose Park	IL	60160	708-344-9823	344-0067
Mechanical Products Mfg Co Inc 8001 S 194th St	Kent	WA	98032	253-395-3000	395-3898
Mercury Aircraft Inc 15-17 Wheeler Ave *Web:* www.mercuryaircraftinc.com	Hammondsport	NY	14840	607-569-4200	569-4634
Metal-Fab Inc 3025 May St *TF:* 800-835-2830 ■ *Web:* www.mtlfab.com	Wichita	KS	67213	316-943-2351	943-2717
Metalcraft of Mayville 1000 Metalcraft Dr	Mayville	WI	53050	920-387-3150	387-0199
Metalcraft Technologies Inc 498 N 2774 West *Web:* www.metalcraft.net	Cedar City	UT	84720	435-586-3871	586-0289
Metaltech Inc 206 Prospect Ave *TF:* 800-325-9986	Kirkwood	MO	63122	314-965-4550	965-4234
Metalworks Inc 902 E 4th St	Ludington	MI	49431	231-845-5136	845-1043
Micro Industries Inc 2990 S Main St *TF:* 800-446-3902 ■ *Web:* www.microindustries.net	Salt Lake City	UT	84115	801-466-2232	466-1441
Mid-Continent Engineering Inc 405 35th Ave NE *Web:* www.mid-continent.com	Minneapolis	MN	55418	612-782-1324	782-1320
Milbank Mfg Co Inc 4801 Deramus Ave *Web:* www.milbankmfg.com	Kansas City	MO	64120	816-483-5314	483-6357
Milcor Inc 484 Thomas Dr *TF:* 800-624-8642 ■ *Web:* www.milcorinc.com	Bensenville	IL	60106	630-595-7320	766-5259
Mitchell Metal Products Inc PO Box 789 *TF:* 800-258-6137	Kosciusko	MS	39090	662-289-7110	289-7112
Modern Tool Inc 1200 Northdale Blvd *Web:* www.moderntoolinc.com	Minneapolis	MN	55448	763-754-7337	754-7557
Morton Metalcraft Co 1021 W Birchwood St *Web:* www.mortongroup.com/metalcraft_index.htm	Morton	IL	61550	309-266-7176	263-1866
Murray Sheet Metal Co Inc 3112 7th St *TF:* 800-464-8801 ■ *Web:* www.murraysheetmetal.com	Parkersburg	WV	26101	304-422-5431	428-4623
Napco Inc 125 McFann Rd *TF:* 800-786-2726 ■ *Web:* www.napcobuildingmaterials.com	Valencia	PA	16059	724-898-1511	898-3357
National Fabtronix Inc 28800 Hesperian Blvd *Web:* www.natfab.com	Hayward	CA	94545	510-785-3135	785-1253
National Metal Fabricators 2395 Greenleaf Ave *TF:* 800-323-8849 ■ *Web:* www.nmfrings.com	Elk Grove Village	IL	60007	847-439-5321	439-4774
New Columbia Joist Co 2093 Old Hwy 15 *TF:* 800-233-3199 ■ *Web:* www.njb-united.com/ncj.htm	New Columbia	PA	17856	570-568-6761	568-1001
New England Sheet Metal Works Inc 2731 S Cherry Ave *Web:* www.nesmw.com	Fresno	CA	93771	559-268-7375	268-5018
Noll Mfg Co 1320 Performance Dr *TF:* 800-235-1014	Stockton	CA	95206	209-234-1600	234-5925
Nu-Way Industries Inc 555 Howard Ave *Web:* www.nu-way.net	Des Plaines	IL	60018	847-298-7710	635-8650
Oakdale Div Tenere Inc 590 Hale Ave N *Web:* www.tenere.com	Oakdale	MN	55128	651-251-4674	251-8594
Owens Corning Fabricating Solutions 426 N Main St *TF:* 877-632-2935	Elkhart	IN	46516	574-522-8473	522-5451
Pemberton Fabricators Inc 30 Indel Ave *TF:* 800-573-6322 ■ *Web:* www.pemfab.com	Rancocas	NJ	08073	609-267-0922	261-2546
Petersen Aluminum Corp 1005 Tonne Rd **Fax Area Code:* 800 ■ *TF:* 800-323-1960 ■ *Web:* www.pac-clad.com	Elk Grove Village	IL	60007	847-228-7150	722-7150*
Platt & Labonia Co 70 Stoddard Ave *TF:* 800-505-9099 ■ *Web:* www.plattlabonia.com	North Haven	CT	06473	203-239-5681	234-7978
Precise Metal Products Co 3839 N 39th Ave	Phoenix	AZ	85019	602-272-2625	233-2123
Quality Metal Products Inc 11500 W 13th Ave *Web:* www.qualitymetalproducts.com	Lakewood	CO	80215	303-232-4242	233-3944
Rangaire Co 501 S Wilhite St	Cleburne	TX	76031	817-556-6500	556-6549
Ready Duct Inc PO Box 101603	Nashville	TN	37224	615-244-2030	259-2936
RF Knox Co Inc PO Box 1337 *TF:* 800-989-7401 ■ *Web:* www.rfknox.com	Smyrna	GA	30081	770-434-7401	433-1783
RG Smith Co PO Box 9067 *Web:* www.rgscontractors.com	Canton	OH	44711	330-456-3415	456-9638
Rieckhoff CL Co Inc 26265 Northline Rd	Taylor	MI	48180	734-946-8220	946-2004
Roll Forming Corp PO Box 369	Shelbyville	KY	40066	502-633-4435	633-5824
Rollex Corp 2001 Lunt Ave *TF Cust Svc:* 800-251-3300 ■ *Web:* www.rollex.com	Elk Grove Village	IL	60007	847-437-3000	437-7561
RTI Tradco 1701 W Main St *Web:* www.fidnet.com/~tradcowa	Washington	MO	63090	636-239-7816	239-3214
RuMar Mfg Corp PO Box 193 *Web:* www.rumar.com	Mayville	WI	53050	920-387-2104	387-2367
Ruskin Mfg Co 3900 Doctor Greaves Rd *Web:* www.ruskin.com	Grandview	MO	64030	816-761-7476	765-8955
S & S Procelain Inc 1410 S 13th St	Louisville	KY	40210	502-635-7421	634-9800
Saint Regis Culvert Inc 202 Morrell St *TF:* 800-527-4604 ■ *Web:* www.stregisculvert.com	Charlotte	MI	48813	517-543-3430	543-2313
Serra Corp 3590 Snell Ave *Web:* www.serracorp.com	San Jose	CA	95136	510-651-7333	657-5860
Service Mfg Group Inc 400 Scajaquada St	Buffalo	NY	14211	716-893-1482	893-1495
Sheet Metal Engineers Inc PO Box 204627	Martinez	GA	30917	706-863-6575	863-8210
Simpson Dura-Vent Inc 877 Cotting Ct *TF:* 800-835-4429 ■ *Web:* www.duravent.com	Vacaville	CA	95688	707-446-1786	446-4740
Smith RG Co PO Box 9067 *Web:* www.rgscontractors.com	Canton	OH	44711	330-456-3415	456-9638
SMT Inc 7300 ACC Blvd *Web:* www.smtcoinc.com	Raleigh	NC	27617	919-782-4804	781-1498
Southbridge Sheet Metal Works Inc 441 Main St	Sturbridge	MA	01566	508-347-7800	347-9118
Southwark Metal Mfg Co Inc 2800 Red Lion Rd *TF:* 800-523-1052 ■ *Web:* www.southwarkmetal.com	Philadelphia	PA	19114	215-735-3401	735-0411
Specialty Engineering Inc 1766 Hwy 36 E *Web:* www.specialtyeng.com	Maplewood	MN	55109	651-777-8311	777-2707
Standex International Corp Air Distribution Products Group 7601 State Rd *TF:* 800-899-2850 ■ *Web:* www.standexadp.com	Philadelphia	PA	19136	215-338-2850	335-1905
Streimer Sheet Metal Works Inc 740 N Knott St *Web:* www.streimer.com	Portland	OR	97227	503-288-9393	288-3327
Structures Unlimited Inc 88 Pine St *TF:* 800-225-3895 ■ *Web:* www.structuresunlimitedinc.com	Manchester	NH	03103	603-645-6539	625-0798
Swift-Cor Precision Inc 344 W 157th St *Web:* www.swiftcor.com	Gardena	CA	90248	310-354-1200	323-2029
Sykes John Co Inc PO Box 5189	Atlantic City	NJ	08404	609-345-1191	344-1952
Tella Tool & Mfg 1015 N Ridge Ave *Web:* www.tellatool.com	Lombard	IL	60148	630-495-0545	495-3056
Tenere Inc Oakdale Div 590 Hale Ave N *Web:* www.tenere.com	Oakdale	MN	55128	651-251-4674	251-8594
Thybar Corp 913 S Kay Ave *TF:* 800-666-2872 ■ *Web:* www.thybar.com	Addison	IL	60101	630-543-5300	543-5309
Trend Technologies LLC 4626 Eucalypus Ave *Web:* www.trendtechnologies.com	Chino	CA	91710	909-597-7861	597-2284
Trinity Industries Inc Highway Safety Products Div 2525 N Stemmons Fwy *TF:* 800-527-6050 ■ *Web:* www.highway-safety.com	Dallas	TX	75207	214-589-8814	589-8423
United McGill Corp 1 Mission Pk *Web:* www.unitedmcgillcorp.com	Groveport	OH	43125	614-836-9981	836-9843
Valley Joist 3019 Gault Ave N *TF:* 800-633-2258 ■ *Web:* www.valleyjoist.com	Fort Payne	AL	35967	256-845-2330	845-2597
Vent-A-Hood Ltd 1000 N Greenville Ave *Web:* www.ventahood.com	Richardson	TX	75081	972-235-5201	231-0663
Vent Products Co Inc 1901 S Kilbourn Ave *TF:* 800-368-8368 ■ *Web:* www.ventprod.com	Chicago	IL	60623	773-521-1900	521-5613
Ventcon Inc 500 Enterprise Dr	Allen Park	MI	48101	313-336-4000	336-5298

Phone Fax

Voisard Mfg Inc 60 Scott St. . . . . Shiloh OH 44878 419-896-3191 896-2127
Web: www.voisard.com
Western Industries Inc Watertown Metal Products Div
1141 S 10th St. . . . . Watertown WI 53094 920-261-0660 261-3832
Web: www.westernind.com
Western Metal Lath & Steel Framing Systems Inc
6510 General Dr. . . . . Riverside CA 92509 951-360-3500 360-3131
TF: 800-365-5284 ■ *Web:* www.wmlinc.com
White HM Inc 12855 Burt Rd . . . . . Detroit MI 48223 313-531-8477 531-0522
Web: www.hmwhite.com
Wisco Products Inc 109 Commercial St. . . . . Dayton OH 45402 937-228-2101 228-2407
TF: 800-367-6570 ■ *Web:* www.wiscoproducts.com
Young & Bertke Air Systems Co 2118 Winchell Ave . . . . . Cincinnati OH 45214 513-241-5566 421-1860
Web: www.youngbertke.com
Young Custom Metal Fabrication 6205 Saint Louis St . . . . . Meridian MS 39307 601-483-6281 693-6529
Web: www.theyounggroup.net

701 SHIP BUILDING & REPAIRING

Phone Fax

Al Larson Boat Shop Inc 1046 S Seaside Ave . . . . . Terminal Island CA 90731 310-514-4100 519-7183
Allied Shipyard Inc PO Box 1240 . . . . . Larose LA 70373 985-693-3323 693-3687
Associated Naval Architects Inc 3400 Shipwright St . . . . . Portsmouth VA 23703 757-484-5320 483-1386
Web: www.anashipyard.com
Atlantic Marine Inc 8500 Heckscher Dr. . . . . Jacksonville FL 32226 904-251-1545 251-3500*
**Fax:* Sales ■ *TF:* 800-395-6446 ■ *Web:* www.atlanticmarine.com
Bath Iron Works Corp 700 Washington St . . . . . Bath ME 04530 207-443-3311 442-1567
Web: www.gdbiw.com
Bay Ship & Yacht Co 310 W Cutting Blvd . . . . . Point Richmond CA 94804 510-237-0140 237-0154
TF: 800-900-6646 ■ *Web:* www.bay-ship.com
Bay Shipbuilding Co 605 N 3rd Ave PO Box 830. . . . . Sturgeon Bay WI 54235 920-743-5524 743-2371
Web: www.manitowocmarine.com
Bender Shipbuilding & Repair 265 S Water St . . . . . Mobile AL 36603 251-431-8000 432-2260
Web: www.bendership.com
Boland Marine & Mfg Co Inc 1000 Tchoupitoulas St . . . . . New Orleans LA 70130 504-581-5800 581-5814
TF: 888-265-2631 ■ *Web:* www.bolandmarine.com
Bollinger Algiers Inc 434 Powder St . . . . . New Orleans LA 70114 504-362-7960 361-1679
Web: www.bollingershipyards.com/BSIAlgiers.htm
Bollinger Gretna 4640 Peters Rd . . . . . Harvey LA 70058 504-367-8080 362-1938
Bollinger Shipyards Inc PO Box 250 . . . . . Lockport LA 70374 985-532-2554 532-7225
Web: www.bollingershipyards.com
Bourg Drydock & Service Co PO Box 1852 . . . . . Houma LA 70361 985-594-5851 594-5992
Braswell Service Group Inc 2007 Cherry Hill Ln . . . . . Charleston SC 29405 843-388-6136
Cascade General Inc 5555 N Channel Ave. . . . . Portland OR 97217 503-285-1111 247-1606*
**Fax:* Hum Res ■ *TF:* 800-505-1930 ■ *Web:* www.casgen.com
Colonna's Shipyard Inc 400 E Indian River Rd . . . . . Norfolk VA 23523 757-545-2414 545-5475
TF: 800-265-6627 ■ *Web:* www.colonnaship.com
Conrad Industries Inc PO Box 790. . . . . Morgan City LA 70381 985-384-3060 385-4090
Web: www.conradindustries.com
Continental Maritime of San Diego Inc 1995 Bay Front St. . . . . San Diego CA 92113 619-234-8851 234-5346
Web: www.continentalmaritime.com
Dakota Creek Industries Inc 820 4th St PO Box 218 . . . . . Anacortes WA 98221 360-293-9575 293-1372
Web: www.dakotacreek.com
Detyens Shipyards Inc
1670 Drydock Ave Bldg 236 Suite 200 . . . . . North Charleston SC 29405 843-308-8000 308-8059
TF: 800-745-2811 ■ *Web:* www.detyens.com
Electric Boat Corp 75 Eastern Pt Rd . . . . . Groton CT 06340 860-433-3000 433-1566*
**Fax:* Hum Res ■ *Web:* www.gdeb.com
Elevating Boats LLC 201 Dean Ct. . . . . Houma LA 70363 985-868-9655 580-7974
Web: www.ebi-inc.com
Elmwood Marine Services 100 James Dr Suite 100 . . . . . Saint Rose LA 70087 504-394-6230 392-8439
Web: www.elmwoodmarine.com
Essex Boat Works Inc Ferry St PO Box 37. . . . . Essex CT 06426 860-767-8276 767-1729
First Wave Marine Inc 2616 South Loop W Suite 665 . . . . . Houston TX 77054 713-847-4600 847-4601
TF: 800-399-9283
Fraser Shipyards Inc 3rd St & Klough Ave PO Box 997 . . . . . Superior WI 54880 715-394-7787 394-2807
Web: www.frasershipyards.com
General Dynamics NASSCO 2798 E Harbor Dr . . . . . San Diego CA 92113 619-544-3400 544-3541
Web: www.nassco.com
Gladding-Hearn Shipbuilding 1 Riverside Ave PO Box 300 . . . . . Somerset MA 02726 508-676-8596 672-1873
Web: www.gladding-hearn.com
Goltens New York Corp 160 Van Brunt St . . . . . Brooklyn NY 11231 718-855-7200 802-1147
TF: 877-204-1088 ■ *Web:* www.goltens.com
Greenbrier Co 1 Centerpointe Dr Suite 200 . . . . . Lake Oswego OR 97035 503-684-7000 684-7553
NYSE: GBX ■ *TF:* 800-343-7188 ■ *Web:* www.gbrx.com
Gulf Craft Inc 3904 Hwy 182 . . . . . Patterson LA 70392 985-395-5254 395-3657
Web: www.gulfcraft.com
Gulf Marine Repair Corp 1200 Sertoma Dr . . . . . Tampa FL 33605 813-247-3153 247-4519
Gunderson Inc 4350 NW Front Ave. . . . . Portland OR 97210 503-972-5700 972-5987
TF: 800-253-4350 ■ *Web:* www.gundersoninc.com
Kvichak Marine Industries 469 NW Bowdoin Pl . . . . . Seattle WA 98107 206-545-8485 545-3504
Web: www.kvichak.com
Lake Union Drydock Co 1515 Fairview Ave E. . . . . Seattle WA 98102 206-323-6400 324-0124
Web: www.ludd.com
Larson Al Boat Shop Inc 1046 S Seaside Ave . . . . . Terminal Island CA 90731 310-514-4100 519-7183
Leevac Shipyards Inc 111 Bunge St. . . . . Jennings LA 70546 337-824-2210 824-2970
MARCO Global 4259 22nd Ave W . . . . . Seattle WA 98199 206-285-3200 282-8520
Web: www.marcoglobal.com
Marine Industries Northwest Inc PO Box 1275. . . . . Tacoma WA 98401 253-627-9136 627-1094
Web: www.mininw.com
Marinette Marine Corp 1600 Ely St . . . . . Marinette WI 54143 715-735-9341 735-3516
Metro Machine Corp 200 Ligon St PO Box 1860. . . . . Norfolk VA 23501 757-543-6801 494-0445*
**Fax:* Hum Res ■ *Web:* www.memach.com
Mitsubishi Heavy Industries America Inc
630 5th Ave Suite 2650. . . . . New York NY 10111 212-969-9000 262-3301
Web: www.mitsubishitoday.com
Newport Shipyard 1 Washington St . . . . . Newport RI 02840 401-846-6000 846-6001
Web: www.newportshipyard.com
Nichols Brothers Boat Builders Inc
5400 S Cameron Rd PO Box 580 . . . . . Freeland WA 98249 360-331-5500 331-7484
Web: www.nicholsboats.com
North Florida Shipyards Inc PO Box 3255. . . . . Jacksonville FL 32206 904-354-3278 353-2665
Northrop Grumman Newport News 4101 Washington Ave. . . . . Newport News VA 23607 757-380-2000 380-3114*
**Fax:* Hum Res ■ *Web:* www.nn.northropgrumman.com/index.asp
Northrop Grumman Ship Systems 1000 Access Rd . . . . . Pascagoula MS 39567 228-935-1122
Web: www.ss.northropgrumman.com
Orange Shipbuilding Co Inc 710 Market St . . . . . Orange TX 77630 409-883-6666 882-0609
Web: www.conradindustries.com
Pacific Fisherman Inc 5351 24th Ave NW. . . . . Seattle WA 98107 206-784-2562 784-1986
Pacific Marine & Navitech Ltd
841 Bishop St Davies Pacific Ctr Suite 1110 . . . . . Honolulu HI 96813 808-531-7001 523-7668

Phone Fax

Pacific Shipyards International LLC
1 Dry Dock Way Pier 41 PO Box 30989 . . . . . Honolulu HI 96820 808-848-6211 848-6279
Web: www.pacificshipyards.com
Pacord Inc 240 W 30th St . . . . . National City CA 91950 619-336-2211 474-3422
Web: www.pacord.com
Robishaw Engineering Inc PO Box 79246 . . . . . Houston TX 77279 713-468-1706 468-5822
Web: www.flexifloat.com
SeaArk Marine Inc PO Box 210 . . . . . Monticello AR 71657 870-367-9755 367-2120
Web: www.seaark.com
Southwest Shipyard 18310 Market Street Rd. . . . . Channelview TX 77530 281-860-3200 860-3215
Swiftships Inc PO Box 2869 . . . . . Morgan City LA 70381 985-384-1700 384-0914
Web: www.swiftships.com
Tecnico Corp 831 Industrial Ave. . . . . Chesapeake VA 23324 757-545-4013 545-4925
TF: 800-786-2207 ■ *Web:* www.tecnicocorp.com
Todd Pacific Shipyards Corp 1801 16th Ave SW. . . . . Seattle WA 98134 206-623-1635 442-8505
Web: www.toddpacific.com
Todd Shipyards Corp 1801 16th Ave SW . . . . . Seattle WA 98134 206-623-1635 442-8506
NYSE: TOD ■ *Web:* www.toddpacific.com
Trinity Industries Inc Inland Barge Group
2525 N Stemmons Fwy . . . . . Dallas TX 75207 214-631-4420 589-8501
Web: www.trinitymarineproducts.com
Trinity Marine Products Inc 2525 N Stemmons Fwy. . . . . Dallas TX 75207 214-631-4420 589-8501
Web: www.trinitymarineproducts.com
VT Halter Marine Inc PO Box 1328 . . . . . Pascagoula MS 39568 228-696-6888 696-6928
Web: www.vthaltermarine.com

702 SHUTTERS - WINDOW (ALL TYPES)

Phone Fax

All Broward Hurricane Panel LLC 450 W McNab Rd. . . . . Fort Lauderdale FL 33309 954-974-3300 973-3928
TF: 800-432-1803 ■ *Web:* www.browardhurricane.com
All Weather Control Inc 4837 Pembroke Rd . . . . . Hollywood FL 33021 954-920-2391 921-1645
Atlantic Shutter Systems 3217 Hwy 301 S . . . . . Latta SC 29565 877-437-0608 752-0111*
**Fax Area Code:* 843 ■ *Web:* www.atlanticshuttersystems.com
Hurst Awning Co Inc 6865 NW 36th Ave . . . . . Miami FL 33147 800-327-0905 634-9078*
**Fax Area Code:* 305 ■ *Web:* www.hurstawning.com
Mastercraft Industries Inc 120 W Allen St . . . . . Rice Lake WI 54868 715-234-8111 234-6370
Web: www.mastercraftindustries.com
Perfect Shutters Inc 12213 Hwy 173. . . . . Hebron IL 60034 815-648-2401 648-4510
TF: 800-548-3336 ■ *Web:* www.shuttersinc.com
Roll-A-Way Inc 10601 Oak St NE . . . . . Saint Petersburg FL 33716 727-576-1143 579-9410
TF: 800-683-9505 ■ *Web:* www.roll-a-way.com
Roll Shutter Systems Inc 21633 N 14th Ave . . . . . Phoenix AZ 85027 623-869-7057 581-3116
TF: 800-551-7655 ■ *Web:* www.rollshuttersystemsusa.com
Rolladen Inc 550 Ansin Blvd. . . . . Hallandale FL 33009 954-921-1522 454-1577
TF: 800-748-8837 ■ *Web:* www.rolladen.com
Rolling Shield Inc 2500 NW 74th Ave . . . . . Miami FL 33122 305-470-9404 470-9405
TF: 800-474-9404 ■ *Web:* www.rollingshield.com
Rolsafe International 5845 Corporation Cir . . . . . Fort Myers FL 33905 239-694-5400 694-8000
TF: 800-833-5486 ■ *Web:* www.rolsafe.com
Shutter Mill Inc 8517 S Perkins Rd . . . . . Stillwater OK 74074 405-377-6455 377-1010
TF: 800-416-6455 ■ *Web:* www.kirtz.com
Storm Safe Shutters 3593 Veronica Shoemaker Blvd. . . . . Fort Myers FL 33916 239-432-9181 337-7315
TF: 800-257-8676 ■ *Web:* www.stormsafeshutters.com
Sunburst Shutters 4094 Ponderosa Way . . . . . Las Vegas NV 89118 702-870-4488 870-6070
Web: www.sunburstshutters.com
Tapco Group 29797 Beck Rd. . . . . Wixom MI 48393 800-521-8486 459-3647*
**Fax Area Code:* 888 ■ *TF:* 800-521-8486 ■ *Web:* www.tapcogroup.com
Vantage Products Corp 960 Almon Rd. . . . . Covington GA 30014 770-788-0136 788-0361
TF: 800-481-3303 ■ *Web:* www.vantageproducts.com

703 SIGNALS & SIRENS - ELECTRIC

Phone Fax

ADDCO Inc 240 Arlington Ave E . . . . . Saint Paul MN 55117 651-488-8600 558-3600
TF: 888-616-4408 ■ *Web:* www.addcoinc.com
ALSTOM Signaling Inc 1025 John St . . . . . West Henrietta NY 14586 585-783-2000 274-8777
TF Cust Svc: 800-717-4477 ■ *Web:* www.alstomsignalingsolutions.com
Cooper Wheelock 273 Branchport Ave. . . . . Long Branch NJ 07740 732-222-6880 222-8707
TF Cust Svc: 800-631-2148 ■ *Web:* www.wheelockinc.com
ECCO 833 W Diamond St. . . . . Boise ID 83705 208-395-8000 688-3226*
**Fax Area Code:* 800 ■ *TF:* 800-635-5900 ■ *Web:* www.eccolink.com
Econolite Control Products Inc 25 Imclone Dr . . . . . Anaheim CA 92806 714-630-3700 630-8576
Web: www.econolite.com
Falcon Safety Products Inc 25 Chubb Way. . . . . Somerville NJ 08876 908-707-4900 707-8855
Web: www.falconsafety.com
Federal Signal Corp Emergency Products Div
2645 Federal Signal Dr. . . . . University Park IL 60466 708-534-3400 534-9050
Web: www.fedsig.com
GE Transportation Rail Global Signaling PO Box 8900. . . . . Melbourne FL 32904 321-435-7000 435-7972*
**Fax:* Cust Svc ■ *TF:* 800-342-5434 ■ *Web:* www.getransportation.com
Harrington Signal Co 2519 4th Ave . . . . . Moline IL 61265 309-762-0731 762-8215
TF: 800-577-5758 ■ *Web:* www.harringtonsignal.com
Jenkins WL Co 1445 Whipple Ave SW . . . . . Canton OH 44710 330-477-3407 477-8404
TF: 800-426-7021 ■ *Web:* www.wljenkinsco.com
Rothenbuhler Engineering 524 Rhodes Rd PO Box 708 . . . . . Sedro Woolley WA 98284 360-856-0836 856-2183
Web: www.rothenbuhlereng.com
Safetran Systems Corp 2400 Nelson Miller Pkwy . . . . . Louisville KY 40223 502-244-7400 244-7444
TF: 800-626-2710 ■ *Web:* www.safetran.com
Safetran Traffic Systems Inc
1485 Garden of the Gods Rd. . . . . Colorado Springs CO 80907 719-599-5600 599-3853
Web: www.safetran-traffic.com
Siemens Intelligent Transportation Systems 8004 Cameron Rd. . . . . Austin TX 78754 512-837-8310 837-0196
TF: 800-388-6882 ■ *Web:* www.itssiemens.com
Traffic Control Corp 780 W Belden Ave Suite D . . . . . Addison IL 60101 630-543-1300 543-5050
TF: 800-996-6511 ■ *Web:* www.trafficcontrolcorp.com
Union Switch & Signal Inc 1000 Technology Dr . . . . . Pittsburgh PA 15219 412-688-2400 688-2399
TF: 800-351-1520 ■ *Web:* www.switch.com
Western Cullen Hayes Inc 2700 W 36th Pl . . . . . Chicago IL 60632 773-254-9600 254-1110
Web: www.wch.com
Whelen Engineering Co Inc Winthrop Rd & Rt 145. . . . . Chester CT 06412 860-526-9504 526-4078
Web: www.whelen.com
WL Jenkins Co 1445 Whipple Ave SW . . . . . Canton OH 44710 330-477-3407 477-8404
TF: 800-426-7021 ■ *Web:* www.wljenkinsco.com

704 SIGNS

SEE ALSO Displays - Exhibit & Trade Show p. 1589; Displays - Point-of-Purchase p. 1589; Signals & Sirens - Electric p. 2316

Company	City	State	Zip	Phone	Fax
ABC Letter Art 1623 S Vermont Ave	Los Angeles	CA	90006	323-733-9141	733-6505
Web: www.abcletterart.com					
Ace Sign Systems Inc 3621 W Royerton Rd	Muncie	IN	47304	765-288-1000	288-1010
TF: 800-607-6010 ■ Web: www.acesign.com					
Advance Corp Braille-Tac Div 8200 97th St S	Cottage Grove	MN	55016	651-771-9297	771-2121
TF: 800-328-9451 ■ Web: www.advancecorp.com					
Allen Industries Inc 6434 Burnt Poplar Rd	Greensboro	NC	27409	336-668-2791	668-7875
TF: 800-967-2553 ■ Web: www.allenindustries.com					
American Porcelain Enamel Co 203 W Church St	Crandall	TX	75114	214-637-4775	631-5424
Web: www.americanporcelain.com					
Artcraft Signs Co 1717 S Acoma St	Denver	CO	80223	303-777-7771	778-7175
TF: 800-278-7771 ■ Web: www.artcraftsign.com					
Atlantic Sign Media Inc 151 McArthur Ln	Burlington	NC	27217	336-584-1375	584-3848
TF: 800-948-3710					
Brady Corp 6555 W Good Hope Rd	Milwaukee	WI	53223	414-358-6600	292-2289*
NYSE: BRC ■ *Fax Area Code: 800 ■ *Fax: Cust Svc ■ TF Cust Svc: 800-537-8791 ■ Web: www.bradycorp.com					
Braille-Tac Div Advance Corp 8200 97th St S	Cottage Grove	MN	55016	651-771-9297	771-2121
TF: 800-328-9451 ■ Web: www.advancecorp.com					
California Neon Products Inc 4530 Mission Gorge Pl	San Diego	CA	92120	619-283-2191	283-9503
TF: 800-822-6366 ■ Web: www.cnpsigns.com					
Century Graphics & Metals Inc 550 S N Lake Blvd Suite 1000	Altamonte Springs	FL	32701	407-262-8290	262-8291
TF: 800-327-5664 ■ Web: www.centurygraphics.com					
Certified Electronic Display Inc 3121 N Adart Rd	Stockton	CA	95215	209-931-7850	931-7856
TF: 800-350-7773 ■ Web: www.certifiedelectronicdisplay.com					
Clearr Corp 6325 Sandburg Rd	Minneapolis	MN	55427	763-398-5400	398-0134
TF: 800-948-3269 ■ Web: www.clearrcorp.com					
CNP Signs & Graphics Inc 4530 Mission Gorge Pl	San Diego	CA	92120	619-283-2191	283-9503
TF: 800-822-6366 ■ Web: www.cnpsigns.com					
Colorado Time Systems 1551 E 11th St	Loveland	CO	80537	970-667-1000	667-5876
TF: 800-279-0111 ■ Web: www.colotime.com					
Couch & Philippi Inc 10680 Fern Ave PO Box A	Stanton	CA	90680	714-527-2261	827-2077
TF Orders: 800-854-3360 ■ Web: www.couchandphilippi.com					
Cummings Signs Inc 4560 Trousdale Dr	Nashville	TN	37204	615-244-5555	782-6699
TF: 800-489-7446 ■ Web: www.cummingssigns.com					
DeeSign Co 7950 Woodley Ave	Van Nuys	CA	91406	800-732-7446	988-4511*
*Fax Area Code: 818 ■ TF: 800-824-2565 ■ Web: www.deesignca.com					
DiAZiT Co Inc 941 US 1 Hwy PO Box 276	Youngsville	NC	27596	919-556-5188	556-3757
TF Cust Svc: 800-334-6641 ■ Web: www.diazit.com					
Douglas Corp 9650 Valley View Rd	Eden Prairie	MN	55344	952-941-2944	942-3124
Web: www.douglascorp.com					
Doyle Signs Inc 232 Interstate Rd	Addison	IL	60101	630-543-9490	543-9493
TF: 800-344-9490 ■ Web: www.doylesigns.com					
Dualite Sales & Service Inc 1 Dualite Ln	Williamsburg	OH	45176	513-724-7100	724-9029
Web: www.dualite.com					
Eastern Metal/USA-SIGN 1430 Sullivan St	Elmira	NY	14901	607-734-2295	734-8783
TF Sales: 800-872-7446 ■ Web: www.usa-sign.com					
Everbrite Inc 4949 S 110th St PO Box 20020	Greenfield	WI	53220	414-529-3500	529-7191
TF: 800-558-3888 ■ Web: www.everbrite.com					
FASTSIGNS International Inc 2542 Highlander Way	Carrollton	TX	75006	972-447-0777	248-8201
TF: 800-827-7446 ■ Web: www.fastsigns.com					
Federal Heath Sign Co 4602 North Ave	Oceanside	CA	92056	760-941-0715	941-0719
Web: www.federalheath.com					
FLOORgraphics Inc 200 American Metro Blvd Suite 120 American Metro Center	Hamilton	NJ	08619	609-528-9200	689-0204
TF: 888-356-6723 ■ Web: www.floorgraphics.com					
GableSigns Inc 7440 Fort Smallwood Rd	Baltimore	MD	21226	410-255-6400	437-5336
TF: 800-854-0568 ■ Web: www.gablesigns.com					
Gemini Inc 103 Mensing Way	Cannon Falls	MN	55009	507-263-3957	263-4887
TF: 800-538-8377 ■ Web: www.signletters.com					
General Sign Co 4857 County Rd 218 PO Box 999	Cape Girardeau	MO	63702	573-334-5041	334-9578
TF Cust Svc: 800-325-0205 ■ Web: www.generalsignco.com					
Globe Transportation Graphics 2097 E Aurora Rd	Twinsburg	OH	44087	330-425-7100	425-9371
TF: 800-321-1496 ■ Web: www.globegrafix.com					
Gopher Sign Co 1310 Randolph Ave	Saint Paul	MN	55105	651-698-5095	699-3727
TF: 800-383-3156 ■ Web: www.gophersign.com					
Gordon Sign 2930 W 9th Ave	Denver	CO	80204	303-629-6121	629-1024
TF: 800-323-6121 ■ Web: www.gordonsign.com					
Grandwell Industries Inc 121 Quantum St	Holly Springs	NC	27540	919-557-1221	552-9830
TF: 800-338-6554 ■ Web: www.grandwell.com					
Graphic Specialties Inc 3110 Washington Ave N	Minneapolis	MN	55411	612-522-5287	287-0952
TF: 800-486-4605 ■ Web: www.signsbygsi.com					
Graphitek Inc 190 North St	Bennington	VT	05201	802-440-8079	442-3184
TF: 800-423-4371 ■ Web: www.graphitek.com					
Hall Signs Inc PO Box 515 Dept 15	Bloomington	IN	47402	812-332-9355	332-9816
TF Cust Svc: 800-284-7446 ■ Web: www.hallsigns.com					
Hawkins Traffic Safety Supply 1255 E Shore Hwy	Berkeley	CA	94710	510-525-4040	525-2861
TF: 800-772-3995					
Hi*Tech Electronic Displays 13900 US Hwy 19N	Clearwater	FL	33764	727-531-4800	524-6655
TF: 800-723-9402 ■ Web: www.hitechled.com					
Hy-Ko Products Co 60 Meadow Ln	Northfield	OH	44067	330-467-7446	467-7442
TF: 800-292-0550 ■ Web: www.hy-ko.com					
Icon Identity Solutions 1418 Elmhurst Rd	Elk Grove Village	IL	60007	847-364-2250	364-1517
TF: 800-633-8181 ■ Web: www.iconid.com					
Image National Inc 16265 Star Rd	Nampa	ID	83687	208-345-4020	336-9886
TF: 800-592-8058 ■ Web: www.imagenational.com					
ImagePoint Inc 445 S Gay St	Knoxville	TN	37902	865-251-1511	
TF: 800-444-7446 ■ Web: www.imagepoint.com					
Insignia Systems Inc 6470 Sycamore Ct N	Maple Grove	MN	55369	763-392-6200	392-6222
NASDAQ: ISIG ■ TF: 800-874-4648 ■ Web: www.insigniasystems.com					
International Display Systems Inc 5008 Veterans Memorial Hwy	Holbrook	NY	11741	631-218-1802	218-1801
TF: 800-542-9779 ■ Web: www.idsmenus.com					
International Patterns Inc 50 Inez Dr	Bay Shore	NY	11706	631-952-2000	952-7602
TF: 800-471-6368 ■ Web: www.internationalpatterns.com					
Interstate Highway Sign Corp 7415 Lindsey Rd	Little Rock	AR	72206	501-490-4242	490-1090
Web: www.interstatesigns.com					
Jarob Inc 2601 Elmridge Dr NW	Grand Rapids	MI	49534	616-453-5419	453-6362
TF: 800-843-2508 ■ Web: www.jarob.com					
JM Stewart Corp 2201 Cantu Ct Suite 217-218	Sarasota	FL	34232	941-378-4242	378-2765
TF: 800-237-3928 ■ Web: www.stewartsigns.com					
Kieffer & Co Inc 3322 Washington Ave	Sheboygan	WI	53081	920-458-4394	451-3360
TF: 800-458-4394 ■ Web: www.kieffersigns.com					
Kux Architectural Products 45065 Michigan Ave	Canton	MI	48188	734-394-0363	394-1846
Web: www.kux.com					
LaFrance Corp 1 LaFrance Way PO Box 5002	Concordville	PA	19331	610-361-4300	361-4301
Web: www.lafrancecorp.com					
Lake Shore Industries Inc 1817 Poplar St PO Box 59	Erie	PA	16512	814-456-4277	453-4293
TF: 800-458-0463 ■ Web: www.lsisigns.com					
Lauretano Sign Group 1 Tremco Dr	Terryville	CT	06786	860-582-0233	583-0949
Web: www.lauretano.com					
Lawrence Sign Inc 945 Pierce Butler Rt	Saint Paul	MN	55104	651-488-6711	488-6715
TF: 800-998-8901 ■ Web: www.lawrencesign.com					
Leotek Electronics USA Corp 1330 Memorex Dr	Santa Clara	CA	95050	408-988-4668	980-0538
TF: 888-806-1188 ■ Web: www.leotek.com					
LSI Industries Inc 10000 Alliance Rd	Cincinnati	OH	45242	513-793-3200	984-1335
NASDAQ: LYTS ■ TF: 800-765-3454 ■ Web: www.lsi-industries.com					
Lyle Signs Inc 6294 Bury Dr	Eden Prairie	MN	55346	952-934-7653	934-0406
TF: 800-367-8560 ■ Web: www.lylesigns.com					
Lynn Sign Co PO Box 1753	Andover	MA	01810	978-470-1194	470-1198
TF: 800-225-5764					
M-R Sign Co Inc 1706 1st Ave N	Fergus Falls	MN	56537	218-736-5681	736-4070
TF: 800-231-5564 ■ Web: www.mrsigncompany.com					
Magnetsigns Advertising Inc 4225 38th St	Camrose	AB	T4V3Z3	780-672-8720	672-8716
TF: 800-219-8977 ■ Web: www.magnetsigns.com					
MCA Industries 6811st St SW	Massillon	OH	44646	330-833-3165	832-9771
Web: www.mcapop.com					
McLoone 75 Sumner St	La Crosse	WI	54603	608-784-1260	782-3711
TF: 800-624-6641 ■ Web: www.mcloone.com					
Mulholland Harper Co Inc 24778 Meeting House Rd PO Box C	Denton	MD	21629	410-479-1300	479-0207
TF: 800-882-3052 ■ Web: www.mulhollandharper.com					
National Print Group Inc 2464 Amnicola Hwy PO Box 5968	Chattanooga	TN	37406	423-622-2254	622-7623
TF: 800-624-0408 ■ Web: www.nationalposters.com					
National Sign Corp 1255 Westlake Ave N	Seattle	WA	98109	206-282-0700	285-3091
Web: www.nationalsigncorp.com					
National Stock Sign Co 1040 El Dorado Ave	Santa Cruz	CA	95062	831-476-2020	476-1734
TF: 800-462-7726					
Nu-Dell Mfg Co Inc 2250 E Devon Ave Suite 349	Des Plaines	IL	60018	847-803-4500	803-4584
Web: www.nudell.com					
Ovation-in-Store 5713 49th Pl	Maspeth	NY	11378	718-628-2600	628-2637
Web: www.ovationadvantage.com					
Pannier Graphics 345 Oak Rd	Gibsonia	PA	15044	724-265-4900	265-4300
TF: 800-544-8428 ■ Web: www.panniergraphics.com					
Pattison Sign Group 555 Ellesmere Rd	Scarborough	ON	M1R4E8	416-759-1111	759-9560
TF: 866-233-2220 ■ Web: www.pattisonsign.com					
Philadelphia Sign Co 707 W Spring Garden St	Palmyra	NJ	08065	856-829-1460	829-8549
TF: 800-355-1460 ■ Web: www.philadelphiasign.com					
Poblocki Sign Co LLC 922 S 70th St	West Allis	WI	53214	414-453-4010	453-3070
TF: 800-776-7064 ■ Web: www.poblocki.com					
Precision Solar Controls Inc 2985 Market St	Garland	TX	75041	972-278-0553	271-9583
TF: 800-686-7414 ■ Web: www.precisionsolarcontrols.com					
Prismaflex Inc 1645 Queens Way E	Mississauga	ON	L4X3A3	905-279-9793	279-1330
TF: 800-526-1488 ■ Web: www.prismaflex.com					
Process Displays Inc 16333 W Rogers Dr	New Berlin	WI	53151	262-782-3600	782-3857
TF: 800-533-1764 ■ Web: www.pdisplays.com					
Protection Services Inc 635 Lucknow Rd	Harrisburg	PA	17110	717-236-9307	236-1281
TF: 866-489-1234 ■ Web: www.protectionservices.com					
Quality Mfg Inc 969 Labore Industrial Ct	Saint Paul	MN	55110	651-483-5473	483-1101
TF: 800-243-5473 ■ Web: www.qualitymanufacturing.com					
Quiel Brothers Sign Co 272 S 'I' St	San Bernardino	CA	92410	909-885-4476	888-2239
Web: www.quielsigns.com					
SA-SO Co 4875 White Bear Pkwy PO Box 64784	Saint Paul	MN	55164	800-527-2450	752-4294
Web: www.sa-so.com					
Safeway Sign Co 9875 Yucca Rd	Adelanto	CA	92301	760-246-7070	246-5512
TF: 800-637-7233 ■ Web: www.safewaysign.com					
Scioto Sign Co Inc 6047 US Rt 68 N	Kenton	OH	43326	419-673-1261	675-3298
TF: 800-572-4686 ■ Web: www.sciotosigns.com					
Scott Sign Systems Inc 7524 Commerce Pl	Sarasota	FL	34243	941-355-5171	351-1787
TF: 800-237-9447 ■ Web: www.scottsigns.com					
Sign-A-Rama 2121 Vista Pkwy	West Palm Beach	FL	33411	561-640-5570	640-5580
TF: 800-776-8105 ■ Web: www.sign-a-rama.com					
Sign Builders Inc 4800 Jefferson Ave PO Box 28380	Birmingham	AL	35221	205-925-9400	923-2124
TF: 800-222-7330 ■ Web: www.signbuilders.com					
Sign Designs Inc 204 Campus Way	Modesto	CA	95350	209-524-4484	521-0272
TF: 800-421-7446 ■ Web: www.signdesigns.com					
Sign Resource Inc 6135 District Blvd	Maywood	CA	90270	323-771-2098	560-7143
TF: 800-423-4283 ■ Web: www.signresource.net					
Signs First PO Box 11569	Memphis	TN	38111	901-682-2264	327-7633
TF: 800-852-2163 ■ Web: www.signsfirst.net					
Signs Now 6976 Professional Pkwy E	Sarasota	FL	34240	941-373-1958	388-9507
TF: 800-356-3373 ■ Web: www.signsnow.com					
Signs by Tomorrow USA Inc 8681 Robert Fulton Dr	Columbia	MD	21046	410-312-3600	312-3520
TF: 800-765-7446 ■ Web: www.signsbytomorrow.com					
Signtex Imaging LP 1225 Alma St Suite C	Tomball	TX	77375	281-351-2776	351-0170
Web: www.signtex.com					
Signtronix 1445 W Sepulveda Blvd	Torrance	CA	90501	800-729-4853	539-3554*
*Fax Area Code: 310 ■ *Fax: Sales ■ TF: 800-729-4853 ■ Web: www.signtronix.com					
Spectrum Corp 10048 Easthaven Blvd	Houston	TX	77075	713-944-6200	944-1290
TF: 800-392-5050 ■ Web: www.specorp.com					
Stout Industries 6425 W Florissant Ave	Saint Louis	MO	63136	314-385-4600	385-9412
TF: 800-325-8530 ■ Web: www.stoutindustries.com					
Total Image 1877 E 17th Ave	Columbus	OH	43219	614-564-1300	564-1399
TF: 800-366-7446 ■ Web: www.totalimagespecialists.com					
Tube Art Displays Inc 1705 4th Ave S	Seattle	WA	98134	206-223-1122	223-1123
TF: 800-562-2854 ■ Web: www.tubeart.com					
Turnroth Sign Co Inc 1207 E Rock Falls Rd	Rock Falls	IL	61071	815-625-1155	625-1158
Visual Graphic Systems Inc 500 10th Ave 7th Fl	New York	NY	10018	212-563-5600	563-9334
TF: 800-203-0301 ■ Web: www.vgs-inc.com					
Vitachrome Graphics Group Inc 11517 Los Nietos Rd	Santa Fe Springs	CA	90670	562-692-9200	692-9055
Web: www.vitachrome.com					
Vomar Products Inc 7800 Deering Ave	Canoga Park	CA	91304	818-610-5115	610-5123
Web: www.vomarproducts.com					
Vomela Specialty Co 380 Saint Peter St Suite 705	Saint Paul	MN	55102	651-228-2200	228-2295
TF: 800-645-1012 ■ Web: www.vomela.com					
Walter Haas & Sons Inc 123 W 23rd St	Hialeah	FL	33010	305-883-2257	883-0598
TF: 800-552-3845 ■ Web: www.haasprint.com					
Wayne Industries 1400 8th St N	Clanton	AL	35045	205-755-5580	755-1516
TF: 800-225-3148 ■ Web: www.wayneindustries.com					
Werner Tool & Mfg Co Inc 12301 E McNichols Rd	Detroit	MI	48205	313-526-6020	526-6070
Web: www.trivision.com					
White Way Sign 451 Kingston Ct	Mount Prospect	IL	60056	847-391-0200	391-0252
TF: 800-621-4122 ■ Web: www.whiteway.com					
Worldwide Sign Systems 446 N Cecil St PO Box 338	Bonduel	WI	54107	715-758-2146	793-4455*
*Fax Area Code: 888 ■ TF: 800-874-3334 ■ Web: www.wwsign.com					
Young Electric Sign Co 2401 Foothill Dr	Salt Lake City	UT	84109	801-464-4600	483-0998
Web: www.yesco.com					
Zumar Industries Inc 9719 Santa Fe Springs Rd PO Box 2883	Santa Fe Springs	CA	90670	562-941-4633	941-4643
TF: 800-654-7446 ■ Web: www.zumar.com					

705 SILVERWARE

SEE ALSO Cutlery p. 1584; Metal Stampings p. 1962

				Phone	Fax
Achievement Products Inc 294 Rt 10 W PO Box 388 Web: www.achievementproducts.com	East Hanover	NJ	07936	973-887-5090	515-0171
Dansk International Designs Ltd 1414 Radcliff St *Fax Area Code: 609 ■ TF Cust Svc: 800-293-2675 ■ Web: www.dansk.com	Bristol PA	NJ	19007	267-525-7800	844-1576*
Empire Silver Co Inc 6520 New Utrecht Ave TF: 800-255-9475 ■ Web: www.empiresilver.com	Brooklyn	NY	11219	718-232-3389	232-0680
Eureka Mfg Co 47 Elm St TF: 800-376-8209 ■ Web: www.woodchest.com	Norton	MA	02766	508-285-9881	285-2205
Great American Products Inc 1661 S Seguin Ave TF: 800-341-4436 ■ Web: www.gap1.com	New Braunfels	TX	78130	830-620-4400	620-8430
Kirk-Stieff Co 100 Lenox Dr	Lawrenceville	NJ	08648	609-896-2800	844-1596
Lenox Inc 100 Lenox Dr TF Cust Svc: 800-635-3669 ■ Web: www.lenox.com	Lawrenceville	NJ	08648	609-896-2800	895-0139
Lunt Silversmiths 298 Federal St TF: 800-242-2774 ■ Web: www.luntsilver.com	Greenfield	MA	01301	413-774-2774	774-4393
Metallics Inc W 7274 County Rd Z PO Box 99 Web: www.metallics.net	Onalaska	WI	54650	608-781-5200	781-2254
Mikasa Inc 100 Plaza Dr TF Cust Svc: 800-833-4681 ■ Web: www.mikasa.com	Secaucus	NJ	07094	201-867-9210	867-0580
Old Newbury Crafters Inc 36 Main St TF: 800-343-1388 ■ Web: www.silvercrafters.com	Amesbury	MA	01913	978-388-0983	388-8430
Olde Country Reproductions Inc 722 W Market St TF Cust Svc: 800-358-3997 ■ Web: www.pewtarex.com	York	PA	17405	717-848-1859	845-7129
Oneida Ltd 163-181 Kenwood Ave TF: 800-877-6667 ■ Web: www.oneida.com	Oneida	NY	13421	315-361-3000	361-3475
Pfaltzgraff Co 140 E Market St *Fax: Cust Svc ■ TF: 800-999-2811 ■ Web: www.pfaltzgraff.com	York	PA	17401	717-848-5500	771-1433*
Reed & Barton Silversmiths Corp 144 W Britannia St TF: 800-822-1824 ■ Web: www.reedbarton.com	Taunton	MA	02780	508-824-6611	822-7269
Rogers Lunt & Bowlen Co DBA Lunt Silversmiths 298 Federal St TF: 800-242-2774 ■ Web: www.luntsilver.com	Greenfield	MA	01301	413-774-2774	774-4393
Salisbury Pewter Co 29085 Airpark Dr TF: 800-824-4708 ■ Web: www.salisburypewter.com	Easton	MD	21601	410-770-4901	770-4904
Towle Silversmiths Mfg Co 175 McClellan Hwy *Fax: Cust Svc ■ Web: www.towlesilver.com	East Boston	MA	02128	617-568-1300	568-9021*
Tropar Mfg Inc 5 Vreeland Rd Web: www.airflyte.com	Florham Park	NJ	07932	973-822-2400	822-2891
Utica Cutlery Co 820 Noyes St TF: 800-888-4223 ■ Web: www.uticastainless.com	Utica	NY	13502	315-733-4663	733-6602
Wallace Silversmiths Inc 175 McClellan Hwy Web: www.wallacesilver.com	East Boston	MA	02128	617-561-2200	569-8484
Woodbury Pewterers Inc 860 Main St S *Fax Area Code: 800 ■ TF: 800-648-2014 ■ Web: www.woodburypewter.com	Woodbury	CT	06798	203-263-2668	819-9492*

706 SIMULATION & TRAINING SYSTEMS

				Phone	Fax
Amherst Systems Inc 1740 Wehrle Dr TF Cust Svc: 800-477-0181	Buffalo	NY	14221	716-631-0610	631-0629
Bemco Inc 2255 Union Pl Web: www.bemcoinc.com	Simi Valley	CA	93065	805-583-4970	583-5033
CACI MTL Systems Inc 3481 Dayton-Xenia Rd Web: www.caci.com/mtl/	Dayton	OH	45432	937-426-3111	426-8301
CAE Inc 8585 Cote de Liesse TSX: CAE ■ TF: 800-760-0667 ■ Web: www.cae.com	Saint Laurent	QC	H4T1G6	514-340-5483	341-7699
Caswell Detroit Armor Corp 720 Industrial Dr Suite 112 Web: www.detroitarmor.com	Cary	IL	60013	847-639-7666	639-7694
Cubic Corp PO Box 85587 AMEX: CUB ■ Web: www.cubic.com	San Diego	CA	92186	858-277-6780	505-1532
Cubic Defense Systems Inc PO Box 85587 Web: www.cubic.com/cda1/	San Diego	CA	92186	858-277-6780	505-1524
Cubic Simulation Systems 2001 W Oakridge Rd TF: 800-327-1020	Orlando	FL	32809	407-859-7410	855-4840
Doron Precision Systems Inc 174 Court St TF: 800-238-6766 ■ Web: www.doronprecision.com	Binghamton	NY	13901	607-772-1610	772-6760
DRS C3 Systems LLC 400 Professional Dr TF: 800-252-4734 ■ Web: www.drs.com	Gaithersburg	MD	20879	301-921-8100	921-8010
DRS Training & Control Systems 645 Anchors St NW *Fax: Hum Res ■ TF: 800-326-6724 ■ Web: www.drs.com	Fort Walton Beach	FL	32548	850-302-3000	302-3371*
Energy Concepts Inc 404 Washington Blvd TF: 800-621-1247 ■ Web: www.energy-concepts-inc.com	Mundelein	IL	60060	847-837-8191	837-8171
Environmental Tectonics Corp 125 James Way AMEX: ETC ■ Web: www.etcusa.com	Southampton	PA	18966	215-355-9100	357-4000
Evans & Sutherland Computer Corp 600 Komas Dr NASDAQ: ESCC ■ *Fax: Hum Res ■ TF Sales: 800-367-7460 ■ Web: www.es.com	Salt Lake City	UT	84108	801-588-1000	588-4517*
Firearms Training Systems Inc 7340 McGinnis Ferry Rd *Fax: Hum Res ■ TF: 800-813-9046 ■ Web: www.fatsinc.com	Suwanee	GA	30024	770-813-0180	622-3505*
FlightSafety International Inc La Guardia Airport Marine Air Terminal TF: 800-877-5343 ■ Web: www.flightsafety.com	Flushing	NY	11371	718-565-4100	565-4134
Frasca International Inc 906 E Airport Rd Web: www.frasca.com	Urbana	IL	61802	217-344-9200	344-9207
IDEAS Simulation Inc 125 Clairemont Ave Suite 570 TF: 800-567-4332 ■ Web: www.ideas-simulation.com	Decatur	GA	30030	404-370-1350	378-3813
Immersion Medical 55 W Watkins Mills Rd TF: 800-929-4709 ■ Web: www.immersion.com	Gaithersburg	MD	20878	301-984-3706	984-2104
Lab-Volt Systems 1710 Hwy 34 PO Box 686 TF: 800-522-9658 ■ Web: www.labvolt.com	Farmingdale	NJ	07727	732-938-2000	774-8573
Malwin Electronics Corp 52 E 22nd St Web: www.malwin.com	Paterson	NJ	07514	973-881-1500	881-1686
Mentor Graphics Corp Mentor Emulation Div 1001 Ridder Park Dr TF: 800-547-3000 ■ Web: www.mentor.com	San Jose	CA	95131	408-436-1500	436-1501
Nida Corp 300 S John Rodes Blvd TF: 800-327-6432 ■ Web: www.nida.com	Melbourne	FL	32904	321-727-2265	727-2655
Sensis Corp 85 Collamer Crossing Web: www.sensis.com	East Syracuse	NY	13057	315-445-0550	445-9401
Ternion Corp 3325 Triana Blvd Web: www.ternion.com	Huntsville	AL	35805	256-881-9933	881-9957
Thales Training & Simulation Inc 5233-A S 122nd East Ave	Tulsa	OK	74146	918-461-1999	461-0064

707 SMART CARDS

				Phone	Fax
ActivCard Inc 6623 Dumbarton Cir NASDAQ: ACTI ■ TF: 800-529-9499 ■ Web: www.activcard.com	Fremont	CA	94555	510-574-0100	574-0101
Alliance Plastics Co 200 W Eight Mile Rd	Ferndale	MI	48220	248-544-6200	544-0973
CardLogix 16 Hughes Suite 100 Web: www.cardlogix.com	Irvine	CA	92618	949-380-1312	380-1428
Clever Devices Ltd 137 Commercial St TF: 800-872-6129 ■ Web: www.cleverdevices.com	Plainview	NY	11803	516-433-6100	433-5088
Credit Card Systems Inc 180 Shepard Ave TF: 800-747-1269 ■ Web: www.ccsplastech.com	Wheeling	IL	60090	847-459-8320	459-1296
DataCard Corp 11111 Bren Rd W TF: 800-328-8623 ■ Web: www.datacard.com	Minnetonka	MN	55343	952-933-1223	933-7971
Gemplus Corp 1350 Old Bayshore Hwy Suite 445 TF: 888-436-7627 ■ Web: www.gemplus.com	Burlingame	CA	94010	650-373-0200	373-0201
Greenwald Industries 212 Middlesex Ave TF: 800-221-0982 ■ Web: www.greenwaldindustries.com	Chester	CT	06412	860-526-0800	526-4205
Indala 6850-B Santa Teresa Blvd TF Sales: 800-779-8663 ■ Web: www.indala.info	San Jose	CA	95119	408-361-4700	361-4701
MDI Security Systems Inc 9725 Datapoint Dr Suite 200 NASDAQ: MDII ■ TF: 866-435-7634 ■ Web: www.mdisecure.com	San Antonio	TX	78229	210-477-5400	477-5401
NexSmart Technologies Inc 188 Technology Dr Suite N *Fax Area Code: 949 ■ Web: www.nexsmart.com	Irvine	CA	92618	626-771-3703	453-8587*
Oberthur Card Systems 3150 E Ana St Web: www.oberthurusa.com	Rancho Dominguez	CA	90221	310-884-7900	884-7904
Perfect Plastic Printing Corp 345 Kautz Rd Web: www.perfectplastic.com	Saint Charles	IL	60174	630-584-1600	584-0648
QualTeq Inc 800 Montros Ave MS CN1037 TF: 800-257-5347 ■ Web: www.qualteq.com	South Plainfield	NJ	07080	908-668-0999	668-7976
Smart Card Integrators Inc 5250 W Century Blvd Suite 442 Web: www.sci-s.com	Los Angeles	CA	90045	310-215-1234	215-1237
SPYRUS Inc 2355 Oakland Rd Suite 1 TF: 800-277-9787 ■ Web: www.spyrus.com	San Jose	CA	95131	408-953-0700	953-9835

708 SNOWMOBILES

SEE ALSO Sporting Goods p. 2323

				Phone	Fax
Arctic Cat Inc 601 Brooks Ave S NASDAQ: ACAT ■ Web: www.arctic-cat.com	Thief River Falls	MN	56701	218-681-8558	681-3162
Bombardier Recreational Products 565 de la Montagne Web: www.brp.com	Valcourt	QC	J0E2L0	450-532-2211	
Polaris Industries Inc 2100 Hwy 55 NYSE: PII ■ Web: www.polarisindustries.com	Medina	MN	55340	763-542-0500	542-0599
Yamaha Motor Corp USA 6555 Katella Ave TF Cust Svc: 800-962-7926 ■ Web: www.yamaha-motor.com	Cypress	CA	90630	714-761-7300	761-7302

SOFTWARE

SEE Computer Software p. 1507

709 SPAS - HEALTH & FITNESS

SEE ALSO Health & Fitness Centers p. 1774; Spas - Hotel & Resort p. 2319; Weight Loss Centers & Services p. 2415

Facilities listed here provide multi-day programs designed to increase health and well-being. Types of programs offered include (but are not limited to) relaxation, smoking cessation, weight loss, and physical fitness.

				Phone	Fax
Agavita Spa at Lajitas - The Ultimate Hideout HC 70 Box 400 Web: www.lajitas.com/Spa.html	Lajitas	TX	79852	432-424-5000	424-5001
AmorePacific Beauty Gallery & Spa 114 Spring St TF: 877-552-6673 ■ Web: us.amorepacific.com	New York	NY	10012	212-966-0400	966-1190
Birdwing Spa 21398 575th Ave Web: www.birdwingspa.com	Litchfield	MN	55355	320-693-6064	693-7026
Black Hills Health & Education Center Box 19 TF: 800-658-5433 ■ Web: www.bhhec.org	Hermosa	SD	57744	605-255-4101	255-4687
Bliss San Francisco 181 3rd St 4th Fl Web: www.blissworld.com/spa	San Francisco	CA	94103	415-281-0990	
Body/Mind Restoration Retreats 56 Lieb Rd Web: www.bodymindretreats.com	Spencer	NY	14883	607-272-0694	277-7801
Breitenbush Hot Springs Retreat & Conference Center 4 Service Rd 46 Mile Post 10 PO Box 578 Web: www.breitenbush.com	Detroit	OR	97342	503-854-3314	854-3319
Cal-a-Vie Spa 29402 Spa Havens Way TF: 866-772-4283 ■ Web: www.cal-a-vie.com	Vista	CA	92084	760-945-2055	630-0074
Calistoga Spa Hot Springs 1006 Washington St TF: 866-822-5772 ■ Web: www.calistogaspa.com	Calistoga	CA	94515	707-942-6269	942-4214
Cooper Wellness Program 12230 Preston Rd TF: 800-444-5192 ■ Web: www.cooperaerobics.com/lif.htm	Dallas	TX	75230	972-386-4777	386-0039
Cornelia Day Resort 663 5th Ave 8th Fl TF: 866-663-1700 ■ Web: www.cornelia.com	New York	NY	10022	212-871-3050	871-1028
Deerfield Spa 650 Resica Falls Rd TF: 800-852-4494 ■ Web: www.deerfieldspa.com	East Stroudsburg	PA	18301	570-223-0160	223-8270
Dr Wilkinson's Hot Springs Resort 1507 Lincoln Ave Web: www.drwilkinson.com	Calistoga	CA	94515	707-942-4102	942-4412
Duke Diet & Fitness Center 804 W Trinity Ave TF: 800-235-3853 ■ Web: www.dukecenter.org/dfc	Durham	NC	27701	919-688-3079	684-6176
El Monte Sagrado Living Resort & Spa 317 Kit Carson Rd TF: 800-828-8267 ■ Web: www.elmontesagrado.com	Taos	NM	87571	505-758-3502	737-2985
French Riviera Health Spa 3908 Veterans Memorial Blvd Web: www.frenchrivieraspa.com	Metairie	LA	70001	504-454-5855	454-7717
Golden Door PO Box 463077 TF: 800-424-0777 ■ Web: www.goldendoor.com	Escondido	CA	92046	760-744-5777	471-2393
Grand Wailea Resort & Spa 3850 Wailea Alanui Dr TF: 800-888-6100 ■ Web: www.grandwailea.com	Wailea	HI	96753	808-875-1234	879-4077

Phone | Fax

Green Mountain at Fox Run PO Box 164 ... Ludlow VT 05149 802-228-8885 228-8887
TF: 800-448-8106 ■ *Web:* www.fitwoman.com
Green Valley Spa 1871 W Canyon View Dr ... Saint George UT 84770 435-628-8060 673-4084
TF: 800-237-1068 ■ *Web:* www.greenvalleyspa.com
Greenhouse Spa The PO Box 1144 ... Arlington TX 76004 817-640-4000 649-0422
Web: www.thegreenhousespa.net
Hawaiian Wellness Holiday PO Box 279 ... Koloa HI 96756 808-332-9244 332-0703
Healing Center of Arizona 25 Wilson Canyon Rd ... Sedona AZ 86336 928-282-7710 282-7710
TF: 877-723-2811 ■ *Web:* www.sedonahealingcenter.com
Heartland Spa 1237 E 1600 North Rd ... Gilman IL 60938 800-545-4853 683-2144*
**Fax Area Code:* 815 ■ *Web:* www.heartlandspa.com
Hills Health Ranch 4871 Caribou Hwy 97 PO Box 26 ... 108 Mile Ranch BC V0K2Z0 250-791-5225 791-6384
TF: 800-668-2233 ■ *Web:* www.spabc.com
Hilton Head Health Institute 14 Valencia Rd ... Hilton Head Island SC 29928 843-785-7292 686-5659
TF: 800-292-2440 ■ *Web:* www.hhhealth.com
Himalayan Institute Center for Health & Healing
952 Bethany Tpke ... Honesdale PA 18431 570-253-5551 253-9078
Web: www.himalayaninstitute.org
Hippocrates Health Institute Life-Change Center
1443 Palmdale Ct ... West Palm Beach FL 33411 561-471-8876 471-9464
TF: 800-842-2125 ■ *Web:* hippocratesinst.org
Kerr House 17777 Beaver St PO Box 363 ... Grand Rapids OH 43522 419-832-1733 832-4303
Web: www.thekerrhouse.com
Kohala Spa 425 Waikoloa Beach Dr ... Waikoloa HI 96738 808-886-2828 886-2953
Web: www.kohalaspa.com
Kripalu Center for Yoga & Health 57 Interlaken Rd ... Stockbridge MA 01262 413-448-3400 448-3384
TF: 800-741-7353 ■ *Web:* www.kripalu.org
La Toscana Resort & Spa 11000 Palm Dr ... Desert Hot Springs CA 92240 760-329-6484 251-8410
TF: 800-635-8660 ■ *Web:* www.latoscanaresorts.com
Lifestyle Center of America Rt 1 Box 4001 ... Sulphur OK 73086 580-993-2327 993-3902
TF: 800-213-8955 ■ *Web:* www.lifestylecenter.org
Lodge & Spa at Cordillera 2205 Cordillera Way ... Edwards CO 81632 970-926-2200 926-2486
TF: 800-877-3529 ■ *Web:* www.cordilleralodge.com
Martyn Tracie Salon 59 5th Ave Suite 1 ... New York NY 10003 212-206-9333 206-8399
Web: www.traciemartyn.com
Miraval Life in Balance 5000 E Via Estancia Miraval ... Catalina AZ 85739 520-825-4000 818-5870
TF: 800-825-4000 ■ *Web:* www.miravalresort.com
Mountain Trek Fitness Retreat & Health Spa Ltd
3800 North St ... Ainsworth Hot Springs BC V0G1A0 250-229-5636 229-5246
TF: 800-661-5161 ■ *Web:* www.hiking.com
New Age Health Spa 7491 SR 55 ... Neversink NY 12765 845-985-7601 985-2467
TF: 800-682-4348 ■ *Web:* www.newagehealthspa.com
New Life Hiking Spa 2617 Killington Rd PO Box 395 ... Killington VT 05751 802-422-4302 422-3690
TF: 800-228-4676 ■ *Web:* www.newlifehikingspa.com
Northern Pines on Crescent Lake Bed & Breakfast Plus
31 Big Pine Rd ... Raymond ME 04071 207-655-7624 935-7574
Web: www.maine.com/norpines
Oaks at Ojai 122 E Ojai Ave ... Ojai CA 93023 805-646-5573 640-1504
TF: 800-753-6257 ■ *Web:* www.oaksspa.com
Ocean Waters Spa 600 N Atlantic Ave ... Daytona Beach FL 32118 386-267-1660 253-9307
TF: 800-767-4471 ■ *Web:* www.oceanwatersspa.com
Ojo Caliente Mineral Springs Resort
50 Los Banos Dr PO Box 68 ... Ojo Caliente NM 87549 505-583-2233 583-2045
TF: 800-222-9162 ■ *Web:* www.ojocalientespa.com
Optimum Health Institute 6970 Central Ave ... Lemon Grove CA 91945 619-464-3346 589-4098
TF: 800-993-4325 ■ *Web:* www.optimumhealth.org
Post Ranch Spa Hwy 1 ... Big Sur CA 93920 831-667-2200 667-2512
Web: www.postranchinn.com/spa.shtml
Pritikin Longevity Center & Spa 19735 Turnberry Way ... Aventura FL 33180 305-935-7131 935-7371*
**Fax:* Resv ■ *TF:* 800-327-4914 ■ *Web:* www.pritikin.com
Raj The 1734 Jasmine Ave ... Fairfield IA 52556 641-472-9580 472-2496
TF: 800-248-9050 ■ *Web:* www.theraj.com
Red Mountain Spa 1275 E Red Mountain Cir ... Ivins UT 84738 435-673-4905 673-1363
TF: 800-407-3002 ■ *Web:* www.redmountainspa.com
Regency House Natural Health Spa 2000 S Ocean Dr ... Hallandale Beach FL 33009 954-454-2220 454-4637
TF: 800-454-0003 ■ *Web:* www.regencyhealthspa.com
Rex Ranch Resort & Spa 131 Alamo Rd ... Amado AZ 85645 520-398-2914 398-8229
TF: 800-547-2696 ■ *Web:* www.rexranch.com
Spa-Atlantis 1350 N Ocean Blvd ... Pompano Beach FL 33062 954-941-6688 590-1001
TF: 800-583-3500 ■ *Web:* www.spaatlantisresort.com
Spa at Coeur d'Alene 115 S 2nd St ... Coeur d'Alene ID 83814 208-765-4000 664-7276
TF: 800-688-5253 ■ *Web:* www.cdaresort.com/spa
Spa Concept Bromont 90 Stanstead St ... Bromont QC J2L1K6 450-534-2717 534-0599
TF: 800-567-7727 ■ *Web:* www.spaconcept.qc.ca/english/entrance.html
Spa at Disney Saratoga Springs Resort
1950-A Broadway ... Lake Buena Vista FL 32830 407-827-4455 827-4585
Web: www.relaxedyet.com
Spa at the Doral Forrestal 100 College Rd E ... Princeton NJ 08540 609-897-7520 897-7237
Web: www.forrestalspa.com
Spa at Grand Lake 1667 Exeter Rd ... Lebanon CT 06249 860-642-4306 642-4799
TF: 800-843-7721 ■ *Web:* www.thespaatgrandlake.com
Spa at Peninsula Beverly Hills 9882 S Santa Monica Blvd ... Beverly Hills CA 90212 310-975-2854 712-5288
Web: beverlyhills.peninsula.com/pbh/fac.html
Spa Radiance 3011 Fillmore St ... San Francisco CA 94123 415-346-6281 346-6170
Web: www.sparadiance.com
Spa at The Setai 2001 Collins Ave ... Miami Beach FL 33139 305-520-6900 520-6600
Web: www.setai.com/spa_philosophy.htm
SpaHalekulani 2199 Kalia Rd ... Honolulu HI 96815 808-923-2311 926-8004
TF: 800-367-2343 ■ *Web:* www.halekulani.com/spa_halekulani/
Sports Core Salon & Day Spa 100 Willow Creek Dr ... Kohler WI 53044 920-457-4746 208-4939
Web: www.destinationkohler.com/location/private/sports_core/sportscore.html
Structure House 3017 Pickett Rd ... Durham NC 27705 919-493-4205 490-0191
TF: 800-553-0052 ■ *Web:* www.structurehouse.com
Tennessee Fitness Spa 299 Natural Bridge Pk Rd ... Waynesboro TN 38485 931-722-5589 722-9113
TF: 800-235-8365 ■ *Web:* www.tfspa.com
Tracie Martyn Salon 59 5th Ave Suite 1 ... New York NY 10003 212-206-9333 206-8399
Web: www.traciemartyn.com
Two Bunch Palms Resort & Spa
67425 Two Bunch Palms Trail ... Desert Hot Springs CA 92240 760-329-8791 329-1874
TF: 800-472-4334 ■ *Web:* www.twobunchpalms.com
Uchee Pines Lifestyle Center 30 Uchee Pines Rd Box 75 ... Seale AL 36875 334-855-4764 855-9014
Web: www.ucheepines.org/lifestylecenter.htm
Vail Cascade Resort & Spa 1300 Westhaven Dr ... Vail CO 81657 970-476-7111 479-7020
TF: 800-420-2424 ■ *Web:* www.vailcascade.com
Vatra Mountain Valley Health Resort Rt 214 Box F ... Hunter NY 12442 518-263-4919 263-4994
TF: 800-232-2772 ■ *Web:* www.vatraspa.com
Westglow Spa 2845 Hwy 221 S ... Blowing Rock NC 28605 828-295-4463 295-5115
TF: 800-562-0807 ■ *Web:* www.westglow.com
White Sulphur Springs Resort & Spa
3100 White Sulphur Springs Rd ... Saint Helena CA 94574 707-963-8588 963-2890
TF: 800-593-8873 ■ *Web:* www.whitesulphursprings.com
Wholistic Life Center 925 Life Ln ... Washburn MO 65772 417-435-2212 435-2211
Web: www.wholisticlifecenter.org
Wiesbaden Hot Springs 625 5th St PO Box 349 ... Ouray CO 81427 970-325-4347 325-4358
Web: www.wiesbadenhotsprings.com

710 SPAS - HOTEL & RESORT

SEE ALSO Spas - Health & Fitness p. 2318

Phone | Fax

100 Fountain Spa at the Pillar & Post Inn
48 John St PO Box 48 ... Niagara-on-the-Lake ON L0S1J0 905-468-0515 468-8646
TF: 888-669-5566 ■ *Web:* www.vintage-hotels.com
Abbey Resort & Fontana Spa 269 Fontana Blvd ... Fontana WI 53125 262-275-6811 275-3264
TF: 800-558-2405 ■ *Web:* www.theabbeyresort.com
Abhasa Waikiki Spa at the Royal Hawaiian Hotel
2259 Kalakaua Ave ... Honolulu HI 96815 808-922-8200 922-3557
Web: www.abhasa.com
Agave the Arizona Spa at the Westin Kierland Resort & Spa
6902 E Greenway Pkwy ... Scottsdale AZ 85254 480-624-1500 624-1130
TF: 888-625-5144 ■ *Web:* www.kierlandresort.com
Allegria Spa at the Park Hyatt Beaver Creek
100 E Thomas Pl ... Beaver Creek CO 81620 970-748-7500 748-7501
TF: 800-233-1234 ■ *Web:* www.allegriaspa.com
Allegria Spa at the Ventana Inn & Spa Hwy 1 ... Big Sur CA 93920 831-667-4222 667-0573
TF: 800-628-6500 ■ *Web:* www.ventanainn.com
Alvadora Spa at the Royal Palms Resort & Spa
5200 E Camelback Rd ... Phoenix AZ 85018 602-977-6400 840-6927
TF: 800-672-6011 ■ *Web:* www.royalpalmshotel.com/spa.htm
Amadeus Spa at the Marriott Napa Valley 3425 Solano Ave ... Napa CA 94558 707-254-3330 254-3333
Web: www.spame.com
Anara Spa at the Hyatt Regency Kauai 1571 Poipu Rd ... Koloa HI 96756 808-240-6440 240-6599
Web: www.anaraspa.com/
Ancient Cedars Spa at the Wickaninnish Inn
Osprey Ln at Chesterman Beach Box 250 ... Tofino BC V0R2Z0 250-725-3113 725-3110
TF: 800-333-4604 ■ *Web:* www.wickinn.com
Aquae Sulis Spa at the JW Marriott Resort Las Vegas
221 N Rampart Blvd ... Las Vegas NV 89145 702-869-7807 869-7772
TF: 877-869-8777 ■ *Web:* www.marriott.com
Aquaterra Spa at the Surf & Sand Resort
1555 S Coast Hwy ... Laguna Beach CA 92651 949-376-2772 376-2773
Web: www.aquaterraspa.com
Aria Spa & Club at the Vail Cascade Resort 1300 Westhaven Dr ... Vail CO 81657 970-479-5942 476-7405
TF: 888-824-5772 ■ *Web:* www.vailcascade.com/spaclub.html
Arizona Biltmore Resort & Spa 2400 E Missouri ... Phoenix AZ 85016 602-955-6600 381-7600
TF: 800-950-0086 ■ *Web:* www.arizonabiltmore.com
Au Naturel Wellness & Medical Spa at the Brookstreet Hotel
525 Legget Dr ... Ottawa ON K2K2W2 613-271-3393 271-3541
TF: 888-826-2220 ■ *Web:* www.brookstreethotel.com
Avanyu Spa at the Equinox Resort
3567 Main St Historic Rt 7-A ... Manchester Village VT 05254 802-362-7881 362-7791
TF: 800-362-4747 ■ *Web:* equinox.rockresorts.com
Avanyu Spa at La Posada de Santa Fe Resort
330 E Palace Ave ... Santa Fe NM 87501 505-954-9630 954-9761
TF: 888-367-7625 ■ *Web:* laposada.rockresorts.com
Avanyu Spa at the Rosario Resort 1400 Rosario Rd ... Eastsound WA 98245 360-376-2222 376-2289
TF: 800-562-8820 ■ *Web:* www.rosarioresort.com
Avanyu Spa at the Snake River Lodge
7710 Granite Loop Rd PO Box 348 ... Teton Village WY 83025 307-732-6070 732-6069
TF: 800-445-4655 ■ *Web:* snakeriverlodge.rockresorts.com
Bathhouse at Calistoga Ranch 580 Lommel Rd ... Calistoga CA 94515 707-254-2820 254-2825
Web: www.calistogaranch.com
Boutique Spa at the Ritz-Carlton Georgetown
3100 South St NW ... Washington DC 20007 202-912-4175 912-4199
TF: 800-241-3333 ■ *Web:* www.ritzcarlton.com
Canyon Ranch SpaClub at the Gaylord Palms Resort
6000 W Osceola Pkwy ... Kissimmee FL 34746 407-586-2051 586-2061
TF: 800-742-9000 ■ *Web:* www.canyonranch.com/spaclubs/gaylord
Canyon Ranch SpaClub at the Venetian
3355 Las Vegas Blvd S Suite 1159 ... Las Vegas NV 89109 702-414-3600 414-3802
TF: 877-220-2688 ■ *Web:* www.canyonranch.com/spaclubs/venetian
Cape Codder Resort & Spa 1225 Iyanough Rd ... Hyannis MA 02601 508-771-3000 790-8145
TF: 888-297-2200 ■ *Web:* www.capecodderresort.com
Centre for Well-Being at the Phoenician
6000 E Camelback Rd ... Scottsdale AZ 85251 480-423-2452 423-2582
TF: 800-843-2392 ■ *Web:* www.centreforwellbeing.com
Century City Fitness Club & Spa 10220 Constellation Blvd ... Century City CA 90067 310-286-2900 286-0208
Web: www.equinoxfitness.com
Chateau Elan Spa at the Chateau Elan Atlanta
Haven Harbour Dr ... Braselton GA 30517 678-425-6064 425-6069
TF: 800-233-9463 ■ *Web:* www.chateauelanatlanta.com
Cheeca Lodge & Spa 81801 Overseas Hwy Mile Marker 82 ... Islamorada FL 33036 305-664-4651 664-2329
TF: 800-327-2888 ■ *Web:* www.cheeca.com
Cliff House Resort & Spa 591 Shore Rd ... Cape Neddick ME 03902 207-361-1000 361-2122
Web: www.cliffhousemaine.com
Cliff Spa at Snowbird Hwy 210 PO Box 929000 ... Snowbird UT 84092 801-933-2225 933-2283
TF: 800-453-3000 ■ *Web:* www.cliffspa.com
Cranwell Resort Spa & Golf Club 55 Lee Rd ... Lenox MA 01240 413-637-1364 637-4364
TF: 800-272-6935 ■ *Web:* www.cranwell.com
Disney's Grand Floridian Spa 4111 N Floridian Way ... Lake Buena Vista FL 32830 407-824-2332 824-2235
Web: www.disneyworld.com
Double Eagle Resort & Spa 5587 Hwy 158 PO Box 736 ... June Lake CA 93529 760-648-7004 648-8225
Web: www.doubleeagleresort.com
Echo Valley Ranch & Spa Clinton PO Box 16 ... Jesmond BC V0K1K0 250-459-2386 459-0086
TF: 800-253-8831 ■ *Web:* www.evranch.com
Elizabeth Arden Red Door Spa at Mystic Marriott Hotel & Spa
625 North Rd ... Groton CT 06340 860-446-2500 446-2696
TF: 866-449-7390 ■ *Web:* www.marriott.com
Elizabeth Arden Red Door Spa at the Seaview Marriott Resort & Spa 400 E Fairway Ln ... Galloway NJ 08205 609-404-4100 404-4110
TF: 800-205-6518 ■ *Web:* www.reddoorspas.com
Emerson Resort & Spa 5368 Rt 28 ... Mount Tremper NY 12457 845-688-7900 688-2789
TF: 877-688-2828 ■ *Web:* www.emersonresortandspa.com
Estancia La Jolla Hotel & Spa 9700 N Torrey Pines Rd ... La Jolla CA 92037 858-550-1000 550-1001
Web: www.estancialajolla.com
Farmhouse Spa at Blackberry Farm 1471 W Millers Cove Rd ... Walland TN 37886 865-379-9819 681-7753
TF: 800-273-6004 ■ *Web:* www.blackberryfarm.com
Felicita Resort 2201 Fishing Creek Valley Rd ... Harrisburg PA 17112 717-599-5301 599-7714
TF: 888-321-3713 ■ *Web:* www.felicitaresort.com
Four Seasons Spa at the Four Seasons Hotel Las Vegas
3960 Las Vegas Blvd S ... Las Vegas NV 89119 702-632-5302 632-5450
TF: 800-332-3442 ■ *Web:* www.fourseasons.com/lasvegas
Four Seasons Spa at the Four Seasons Hotel Los Angeles at Beverly Hills 300 S Doheny Dr ... Los Angeles CA 90048 310-786-2229 860-8966
TF: 800-819-5053 ■ *Web:* www.fourseasons.com/losangeles
Four Seasons Spa at the Four Seasons Resort Aviara
7100 Four Seasons Pt ... Carlsbad CA 92009 760-603-6902 603-3607
TF: 800-819-5053 ■ *Web:* www.fourseasons.com/aviara

	City	State	Zip	Phone	Fax
Four Seasons Spa at the Four Seasons Resort Jackson Hole 7680 Granite Loop Rd PO Box 544	Teton Village	WY	83025	307-732-5120	732-5121
TF: 800-819-5053 ■ *Web:* www.fourseasons.com/jacksonhole					
Four Seasons Spa at the Four Seasons Resort Maui 3900 Wailea Alanui Dr	Wailea	HI	96753	808-874-2925	874-2269
TF: 800-334-6284 ■ *Web:* www.fourseasons.com/maui					
Four Seasons Spa at the Four Seasons Resort Santa Barbara 1260 Channel Dr	Santa Barbara	CA	93108	805-565-8250	565-8451
TF: 800-819-5053 ■ *Web:* www.fourseasons.com/santabarbara					
Four Seasons Spa at the Four Seasons Scottsdale at Troon North 10600 E Crescent Moon Dr	Scottsdale	AZ	85262	480-513-5145	515-5599
TF: 800-819-5053 ■ *Web:* www.fourseasons.com/scottsdale					
Garden Spa at MacArthur Place 29 E MacArthur St	Sonoma	CA	95476	707-933-3193	933-9833
TF: 800-722-1866 ■ *Web:* www.macarthurplace.com					
Glacial Waters Spa at Grand View Lodge 23521 Nokomis Ave	Nisswa	MN	56468	218-963-8700	963-8791
TF: 866-963-8756 ■ *Web:* www.grandviewlodge.com					
Golden Door Spa at the Wyndham Peaks Resort 136 Country Club Dr Box 2702	Telluride	CO	81435	970-728-2590	728-4779
TF: 800-772-5482 ■ *Web:* www.goldendoorspas.com/peaks/					
Green Valley Ranch Resort Casino & Spa 2300 Paseo Verde Pkwy	Henderson	NV	89052	702-617-7777	617-7778
TF: 866-617-0777 ■ *Web:* www.greenvalleyranchresort.com					
Greenbrier The 300 W Main St	White Sulphur Springs	WV	24986	304-536-1110	536-7854
TF: 800-453-4858 ■ *Web:* www.greenbrier.com					
Grove Park Inn Resort & Spa 290 Macon Ave	Asheville	NC	28804	828-252-2711	253-7053
TF: 800-438-5800 ■ *Web:* www.groveparkinn.com					
Health Spa at Meadowood Napa Valley 900 Meadowood Ln	Saint Helena	CA	94574	707-967-1275	967-1270
TF: 800-458-8080 ■ *Web:* www.meadowood.com					
Hibiscus Spa at the Myrtle Beach Marriott Resort at Grande Dunes 8400 Costa Verde Dr	Myrtle Beach	SC	29572	843-692-3730	449-8669
Web: www.csspagroup.com					
Hilton Suites Toronto/Markham Conference Centre & Spa 8500 Warden Ave	Markham	ON	L6G1A5	905-470-8500	415-7633
TF: 800-668-8800 ■ *Web:* www.torontomarkham.hilton.com					
Homestead The 700 N Homestead Dr	Midway	UT	84049	435-654-1102	654-5087
TF: 800-327-7220 ■ *Web:* homesteadresort.com					
Hualalai Sports Club & Spa at the Four Seasons Resort Hualalai 100 Kaupulehu Dr	Kaupulehu-Kona	HI	96740	808-325-8440	325-8451
TF: 800-983-3880 ■ *Web:* www.fourseasons.com/hualalai					
Hyatt Regency Scottsdale Resort at Gainey Ranch 7500 E Doubletree Ranch Rd	Scottsdale	AZ	85258	480-483-5558	483-5544
TF: 800-233-1234 ■ *Web:* scottsdale.hyatt.com					
Indian Springs Resort & Spa 1712 Lincoln Ave	Calistoga	CA	94515	707-942-4913	942-4919
Web: www.indianspringscalistoga.com					
Indies Spa at the Hawks Cay Resort & Marina 61 Hawk's Cay Blvd	Duck Key	FL	33050	305-289-4810	289-4811
TF: 800-432-2232 ■ *Web:* www.hawkscay.com					
Indulgence Spa at Taboo 1209 Muskoka Beach Rd RR 1	Gravenhurst	ON	P1P1R1	705-687-2233	687-7474
TF: 800-461-0236 ■ *Web:* www.tabooresort.com					
Jurlique Spa 4925 N Scottsdale Rd	Scottsdale	AZ	85251	480-424-6072	424-6073
TF: 800-528-7867 ■ *Web:* www.fireskyresort.com/clo-spajurlique/index.html					
Kea Lani Spa at the Fairmont Kea Lani Maui 4100 Wailea Alanui Dr	Maui	HI	96753	808-875-2229	875-1200
TF: 800-659-4100 ■ *Web:* www.fairmont.com					
Kohler Waters Spa 501 Highlands Dr	Kohler	WI	53044	920-457-7777	208-4934
TF: 866-928-3777 ■ *Web:* www.destinationkohler.com/spa/spa_index.html					
La Prairie at the Ritz-Carlton Spa New York (Central Park) 50 Central Pk S 2nd Fl	New York	NY	10019	212-521-6135	521-6124
TF: 800-241-3333 ■ *Web:* www.ritzcarlton.com					
Lafayette Park Hotel 3287 Mt Diablo Blvd	Lafayette	CA	94549	925-283-3700	284-1621
TF: 800-368-2468 ■ *Web:* www.lafayetteparkhotel.com					
Lake Austin Spa Resort 12611 Riverbend Rd	Austin	TX	78732	512-372-7380	372-7382
TF: 800-847-5637 ■ *Web:* www.lakeaustin.com					
Living Spa at El Monte Sagrado 317 Kit Carson Rd	Taos	NM	87571	505-737-9880	737-2990
TF: 800-828-8267 ■ *Web:* www.elmontesagrado.com					
Los Willows Inn & Spa 530 Stewart Canyon Rd	Fallbrook	CA	92028	760-728-8121	728-3622
TF: 888-731-9400 ■ *Web:* www.loswillows.com					
Marriott Starr Pass Resort & Spa 3800 W Starr Pass Blvd	Tucson	AZ	85745	520-792-3500	792-3351
TF: 800-690-8419 ■ *Web:* www.starrpassmarriott.com					
Massage Center at Mohonk Mountain House 1000 Mountain Rest Rd	New Paltz	NY	12561	845-256-2751	256-2737
TF: 800-772-6646 ■ *Web:* www.mohonk.com					
Mauna Lani Spa at Mauna Lani Resort 68-1365 Pauoa Rd	Kohala Coast	HI	96743	808-881-7922	885-4440
TF: 866-877-6982 ■ *Web:* www.maunalani.com					
Mii Amo at Enchantment Resort 525 Boynton Canyon Rd	Sedona	AZ	86336	928-282-2900	282-9249
TF: 888-749-2137 ■ *Web:* www.miiamo.com					
Mirbeau Inn & Spa 851 W Genesee St	Skaneateles	NY	13152	315-685-5006	685-5150
TF: 877-647-2328 ■ *Web:* www.mirbeau.com					
Montage Resort & Spa Laguna Beach 30801 S Coast Hwy	Laguna Beach	CA	92651	949-715-6000	715-6100
Web: www.montagelagunabeach.com					
Moonlight Spa at Moonlight Lodge 1 Mountain Loop Rd	Big Sky	MT	59716	406-995-7700	995-7632
TF: 800-845-4428 ■ *Web:* www.moonlightbasin.com					
Mountain Laurel Spa at Stonewall Resort 940 Resort Dr	Roanoke	WV	26447	304-269-8881	269-4358
TF: 888-278-8150 ■ *Web:* www.stonewallresort.com					
Na Hoola Spa at Hyatt Regency Waikiki Resort 2424 Kalakaua Ave	Honolulu	HI	96815	808-921-6097	237-6339
TF: 800-233-1234 ■ *Web:* www.hyattwaikiki.com					
Nob Hill Spa at the Huntington Hotel 1075 California St	San Francisco	CA	94108	415-345-2888	345-2880
TF: 800-227-4683 ■ *Web:* www.huntingtonhotel.com					
Ojai Valley Inn & Spa 905 Country Club Rd	Ojai	CA	93023	805-646-5511	640-0305
TF: 800-422-6524 ■ *Web:* www.ojairesort.com					
Omni Interlocken Resort 500 Interlocken Blvd	Broomfield	CO	80021	303-438-6600	464-3236
TF: 800-843-6664 ■ *Web:* www.omnihotels.com					
Pala Casino Resort & Spa 11154 Hwy 76 PO Box 40	Pala	CA	92059	760-510-5100	510-5190
TF: 877-946-7252 ■ *Web:* www.palacasino.com					
Peaks Resort & Golden Door Spa 136 Country Club Dr	Telluride	CO	81435	800-789-2220	728-6175*
**Fax Area Code: 970* ■ *TF:* 866-282-4557 ■ *Web:* www.thepeaksresort.com					
Portofino Spa at Portofino Island Resort 10 Portofino Dr	Pensacola	FL	32561	850-916-3455	916-3366
Web: www.portofinoisland.com					
R Spa at the Renaissance ClubSport Walnut Creek Hotel 2805 Jones Rd	Walnut Creek	CA	94597	925-942-6379	942-6348
Web: www.marriott.com					
Radisson Hill Country Resort & Spa 9800 Westover Hills Blvd	San Antonio	TX	78251	210-509-9800	509-9814
TF: 800-333-3333					
Raindance Spa at the Lodge at Sonoma Renaissance Resort 1325 Broadway	Sonoma	CA	95476	707-931-2034	931-2137
TF: 888-710-8008 ■ *Web:* www.thelodgeatsonoma.com					
Red Door Lifestyle Spa 250 Racquet Club Rd	Weston	FL	33326	954-349-5510	349-5667
TF: 800-787-7248 ■ *Web:* www.reddoorlifestylespa.com					
Resort at Squaw Creek 400 Squaw Creek Rd	Olympic Valley	CA	96146	530-583-6300	581-6632
TF: 800-327-3353 ■ *Web:* www.squawcreek.com					
Revive Spa at the JW Marriott Desert Ridge Resort Phoenix 5350 E Marriott Dr	Phoenix	AZ	85054	480-293-3700	293-3725
TF: 866-738-4834 ■ *Web:* www.jwdesertridgeresort.com					
Safety Harbor Resort & Spa 105 N Bayshore Dr	Safety Harbor	FL	34695	727-726-1161	726-4268
TF: 888-237-8772 ■ *Web:* www.safetyharborspa.com					
Scottsdale Resort & Conference Center 7700 E McCormick Pkwy	Scottsdale	AZ	85258	480-991-9000	596-7428
TF: 800-528-0293 ■ *Web:* www.scottsdale-resort.com					
Sea Island Spa at the Cloister 100 Hudson Pl	Sea Island	GA	31561	912-638-5148	638-5894
TF: 800-732-4752 ■ *Web:* www.seaisland.com					
Sea Spa at Loews Coronado Bay Resort 4000 Coronado Bay Rd	Coronado	CA	92118	619-628-8770	628-8775
Web: www.loewshotels.com/hotels/sandiego					
Secret Garden Spa at the Prince of Wales Hotel 6 Picton St PO Box 46	Niagara-on-the-Lake	ON	L0S1J0	905-468-0515	468-9476
TF: 888-669-5566 ■ *Web:* www.vintage-hotels.com					
Senator Inn and Spa of Augusta 284 Western Ave	Augusta	ME	04330	207-622-8800	622-8803
TF: 877-772-2224 ■ *Web:* www.senatorinn.com					
ShaNah Spa at the Bishop's Lodge 1297 Bishop's Lodge Rd	Santa Fe	NM	87501	505-819-4000	983-0832
TF: 800-974-2624 ■ *Web:* www.shanahspa.com					
Shui Spa at Crowne Pointe Historic Inn 82 Bradford St	Provincetown	MA	02657	508-487-6767	487-5554
TF: 877-276-9631 ■ *Web:* www.shuispa.com					
Spa at the Amelia Island Plantation 60 Amelia Village	Amelia Island	FL	32034	904-432-2220	432-2214
TF: 877-843-7722 ■ *Web:* www.spaamelia.com					
Spa at the Arizona Biltmore Resort 2400 E Missouri Ave	Phoenix	AZ	85016	602-955-6600	954-2524
TF: 800-950-0086 ■ *Web:* www.arizonabiltmore.com					
Spa & Athletic Club at the Lodge at Breckinridge 112 Overlook Dr	Breckenridge	CO	80424	970-453-4274	453-0625
TF: 800-736-1607 ■ *Web:* www.thelodgeatbreck.com					
Spa at the Bacara Resort 8301 Hollister Ave	Santa Barbara	CA	93117	805-571-4210	571-3043
Web: www.bacararesort.com					
Spa at the Beau Rivage Resort & Casino 875 Beach Blvd	Biloxi	MS	39530	228-386-7474	386-7918
TF: 888-750-7111 ■ *Web:* www.beaurivage.com					
Spa at Bernardus Lodge 415 W Carmel Valley Rd	Carmel Valley	CA	93924	831-658-3514	659-3529
TF: 888-648-9463 ■ *Web:* www.bernardus.com					
Spa at Big Cedar Lodge 612 Devil's Pool Rd	Ridgedale	MO	65739	417-339-5201	335-2340
Web: www.bigcedar.com					
Spa at the Bodega Bay Lodge 103 Coast Hwy 1	Bodega Bay	CA	94923	707-875-3525	875-2428
TF: 800-368-2468 ■ *Web:* www.bodegabaylodge.com					
Spa at the Breakers 1 S County Rd	Palm Beach	FL	33480	561-653-6656	653-6675
TF: 888-273-2537 ■ *Web:* www.thebreakers.com					
Spa at the Broadmoor 1 Lake Ave	Colorado Springs	CO	80906	719-577-5770	577-5766
TF: 800-634-7711 ■ *Web:* www.broadmoor.com					
Spa at the Buena Vista Palace Resort in the Walt Disney World Resort 1900 Buena Vista Dr PO Box 22206	Lake Buena Vista	FL	32830	407-827-3200	827-3136
Web: www.buenavistapalace.com/resort_activities/spa.cfm					
Spa at the Camelback Inn JW Marriott Resort Golf Club & Spa 5402 E Lincoln Dr	Scottsdale	AZ	85253	480-596-7040	596-7000
TF: 800-922-2635 ■ *Web:* www.camelbackspa.com					
Spa at Carefree Resort & Villas 37220 Mule Train Rd	Carefree	AZ	85377	480-595-3853	595-3857
TF: 888-488-9034 ■ *Web:* www.carefree-resort.com					
Spa at the Carneros Inn 4048 Sonoma Hwy	Napa	CA	94559	707-299-4850	299-4950
Web: www.thecarnerosinn.com					
Spa at the Casa Madrona Hotel 801 Bridgeway	Sausalito	CA	94965	415-354-8308	332-0528
Web: www.casamadrona.com/spa/					
Spa at the Chattanoogan 1201 S Broad St	Chattanooga	TN	37402	423-424-3779	756-3404
TF: 800-619-0018 ■ *Web:* www.chattanooganhotel.com					
Spa at the Chrysalis Inn 804 10th St	Bellingham	WA	98225	360-392-5515	647-0342
TF: 888-808-0005 ■ *Web:* www.thechrysalisinn.com					
Spa Claremont at the Claremont Resort 41 Tunnel Rd	Berkeley	CA	94705	510-549-8566	549-8583
TF: 800-551-7266 ■ *Web:* www.claremontresort.com					
Spa at the CopperWynd Resort & Club 13225 N Eagle Ridge Dr	Fountain Hills	AZ	85268	480-333-1835	333-1901
TF: 877-707-1760 ■ *Web:* www.copperwynd.com					
Spa at Cordillera 2205 Cordillera Way	Edwards	CO	81632	970-926-2200	926-6419
TF: 800-877-3529 ■ *Web:* www.cordilleralodge.com					
Spa at La Costa 2100 Costa del Mar Rd	Carlsbad	CA	92009	760-931-7570	931-7559
TF: 800-729-4772 ■ *Web:* www.lacosta.com					
Spa at the Delta Victoria Ocean Pointe Resort 45 Songhees Rd	Victoria	BC	V9A6T3	250-360-5858	360-5938
TF: 800-575-8882 ■ *Web:* www.deltahotels.com					
Spa at the Diplomat Country Club 501 Diplomat Pkwy	Hallandale	FL	33009	954-883-4905	883-4920
Web: www.diplomatcountryclub.com					
Spa at the Don CeSar Beach Resort 3400 Gulf Blvd	Saint Pete Beach	FL	33706	727-360-1883	360-5036
TF: 866-728-2206 ■ *Web:* www.doncesar.com					
Spa at the Doral Golf Resort 8755 NW 36th St	Doral	FL	33178	305-717-6303	591-6630
TF: 877-773-6725 ■ *Web:* www.marriott.com					
Spa at Eagle Crest Resort 1522 Cline Falls Hwy PO Box 1215	Redmond	OR	97756	541-923-9647	504-1420
TF: 800-682-4786 ■ *Web:* www.eagle-crest.com					
Spa at Eden Roc A Renaissance Resort & Spa 4525 Collins Ave	Miami Beach	FL	33140	305-674-5585	674-5595
TF: 800-327-8337 ■ *Web:* www.marriott.com					
Spa Esmeralda at the Renaissance Esmeralda Resort 44-400 Indian Wells Ln	Indian Wells	CA	92210	760-836-1265	836-1295
TF: 800-214-5524 ■ *Web:* www.renaissanceesmeralda.com					
Spa at the Fairmont Inn Sonoma Mission Inn 100 Boyes Blvd	Sonoma	CA	95476	707-938-9000	938-8012
TF: 877-289-7354 ■ *Web:* www.fairmont.com					
Spa & Fitness Club at the Four Seasons Hotel Washington 2800 Pennsylvania Ave NW	Washington	DC	20007	202-944-2022	944-2072
TF: 800-819-5053 ■ *Web:* www.fourseasons.com/washington					
Spa at Fox Harb'r 1337 Fox Harbour Rd	Wallace	NS	B0K1Y0	902-257-4307	257-1852
TF: 866-257-1801 ■ *Web:* www.foxharbr.com					
Spa Fusion at the Hilton San Francisco 333 O'Farrell St	San Francisco	CA	94102	415-923-5014	202-7776
Web: www.spafusion.com					
Spa Gaucin at the Saint Regis Monarch Beach 1 Monarch Beach Resort	Dana Point	CA	92629	949-234-3367	234-3365
TF: 800-722-1543 ■ *Web:* www.spagaucin.com					
Spa Grande at the Grand Wailea Resort Maui 3850 Wailea Alanui Dr	Wailea	HI	96753	808-875-1234	874-2424
TF: 800-772-1933 ■ *Web:* www.grandwailea.com/spa					
Spa at Gurney's Inn Resort 290 Old Montauk Hwy	Montauk	NY	11954	631-668-1892	668-3689
TF: 800-848-7639 ■ *Web:* www.gurneys-inn.com					
Spa at the Hilton Sedona Resort 10 Ridge View Dr	Sedona	AZ	86351	928-284-6975	284-3825
TF: 877-273-3762 ■ *Web:* www.hiltonsedonaspa.com					
Spa at the Hilton Short Hills Hotel 41 JFK Pkwy	Short Hills	NJ	07078	973-912-7956	379-6870
TF: 800-445-8667 ■ *Web:* www.hiltonshorthills.com					
Spa at the Homestead Rt 220 Main St PO Box 2000	Hot Springs	VA	24445	540-839-7547	839-7668
TF: 800-838-1766 ■ *Web:* www.thehomestead.com					
Spa at the Hotel Hershey 100 Hotel Rd	Hershey	PA	17033	717-520-5888	520-5880
TF: 877-772-9988 ■ *Web:* www.spaathotelhershey.com					
Spa Internazionale at Fisher Island Hotel & Resort 1 Fisher Island Dr	Miami	FL	33109	305-535-6030	535-6032
Web: www.fisherisland.com					
Spa at the JW Marriott Denver at Cherry Creek 2700 E 2nd Ave	Denver	CO	80206	303-320-6012	996-1061
Web: www.marriott.com					
Spa at the JW Marriott Desert Springs Resort Palm Desert 74855 Country Club Dr	Palm Desert	CA	92260	760-341-1856	862-1618
TF: 800-331-3112 ■ *Web:* www.marriott.com					

				Phone	Fax
Spa at the JW Marriott Ihilani Resort 92-1001 Olani St	Kapolei	HI	96707	808-679-3321	679-3871
TF: 800-626-4446 ■ *Web:* www.ihilani.com					
Spa at the Kauai Marriott Resort & Beach Club 3610 Rice St	Lihue	HI	96766	808-246-4918	246-6518
TF: 800-220-2925 ■ *Web:* www.marriott.com					
Spa at Kingsmill Resort 1010 Kingsmill Rd	Williamsburg	VA	23185	757-253-8230	258-1629
TF: 800-965-4772 ■ *Web:* www.kingsmill.com					
Spa at the Laguna Cliffs Marriott Resort 25135 Park Lantern	Dana Point	CA	92629	949-487-7576	661-0874
TF: 866-526-7772 ■ *Web:* lagunacliffspa.com					
Spa at the Lansdowne Resort 44050 Woodridge Pkwy	Leesburg	VA	20176	703-729-4036	729-4096
TF: 877-509-8400 ■ *Web:* www.lansdowneresort.com					
Spa Las Palmas at KSL Rancho Las Palmas 41000 Bob Hope Dr	Rancho Mirage	CA	92270	760-836-3106	837-2341
TF: 800-932-2198 ■ *Web:* www.rancholaspalmas.com/spa/					
Spa Las Palmas at the Marriott Rancho Las Palmas Resort 41000 Bob Hope Dr	Rancho Mirage	CA	92270	760-836-3106	862-4565
TF: 877-843-7720 ■ *Web:* www.spalaspalmas.com					
Spa at the Loews Santa Monica Beach Hotel 1700 Ocean Ave	Santa Monica	CA	90401	310-899-4040	899-4045
Web: www.loewshotels.com/hotels/losangeles					
Spa at the Loews Ventana Canyon Resort 7000 N Resort Dr	Tucson	AZ	85750	520-529-7830	529-7854
Web: www.loewshotels.com/hotels/tucson					
Spa Luana at Turtle Bay Resort 57-091 Kamehameha Hwy	Kahuku	HI	96731	808-293-8811	447-6742
TF: 800-203-3650 ■ *Web:* www.turtlebayresort.com					
Spa at the Mandarin Oriental Miami 500 Brickell Key Dr	Miami	FL	33131	305-913-8332	913-8326
TF: 800-526-6566 ■ *Web:* www.mandarinoriental.com					
Spa at the Marriott Harbor Beach Resort 3030 Holiday Dr	Fort Lauderdale	FL	33316	954-765-3032	766-6101
TF: 866-303-0772 ■ *Web:* www.marriott.com					
Spa at the Marriott Marco Island Resort Golf Club & Spa 400 S Collier Blvd	Marco Island	FL	34145	239-642-2686	389-6938
TF: 800-438-4373 ■ *Web:* marcoislandmarriottspa.com					
Spa at the Marriott Tampa Waterside 700 S Florida Ave	Tampa	FL	33602	813-204-6300	204-6373
TF: 888-268-1616 ■ *Web:* www.marriott.com					
Spa at the Marriott's Grand Hotel & Resort 1 Grand Blvd PO Box 639	Point Clear	AL	36564	251-928-9201	928-1149
TF: 800-544-9933 ■ *Web:* www.marriott.com					
Spa at Le Merigot JW Marriott Beach Hotel Santa Monica 1740 Ocean Ave	Santa Monica	CA	90401	310-395-9700	395-9200
TF: 877-637-4468 ■ *Web:* www.marriott.com					
Spa at Mirror Lake Inn Resort 77 Mirror Lake Dr	Lake Placid	NY	12946	518-523-7834	523-2871
Web: www.mirrorlakeinn.com					
Spa Moana at the Hyatt Regency Maui Resort 200 Nohea Kai Dr	Lahaina	HI	96761	808-667-4725	667-4503
TF: 800-233-1234 ■ *Web:* maui.hyatt.com					
Spa at Montage Resort 30801 S Coast Hwy	Laguna Beach	CA	92651	949-715-6010	715-6014
TF: 866-271-6953 ■ *Web:* www.montagelagunabeach.com					
Spa at Monterey Plaza Hotel 400 Cannery Row	Monterey	CA	93940	831-645-4098	646-0285
TF: 800-334-3999 ■ *Web:* www.woodsidehotels.com					
Spa at the Moody Gardens Hotel 7 Hope Blvd	Galveston	TX	77554	409-683-4440	683-4936
TF: 800-582-4673 ■ *Web:* www.moodygardenshotel.com					
Spa Moulay at Loews Lake Las Vegas Resort 101 Montelago Blvd	Henderson	NV	89011	702-567-6049	567-6067
TF: 800-235-6397 ■ *Web:* www.loewshotels.com					
Spa at Nemacolin Woodlands Resort 1001 Lafayette Dr	Farmington	PA	15437	724-329-6772	329-6922
TF: 800-422-2736 ■ *Web:* www.nwlr.com					
Spa at the Norwich Inn 607 W Thames St	Norwich	CT	06360	860-886-2401	886-9299
TF: 800-275-4772 ■ *Web:* www.thespaatnorwichinn.com					
Spa Olakino at the Waikiki Beach Marriott Resort 2552 Kalakaua Ave	Honolulu	HI	96815	808-924-2121	924-2255
TF: 800-367-5370 ■ *Web:* www.spaolakino.com					
Spa at the Old Edwards Inn 445 Main St	Highlands	NC	28741	828-526-9887	787-2596
Web: www.oldedwardsinn.com					
Spa at the Omni Orlando Resort at Championsgate 1500 Masters Blvd	Champions Gate	FL	33896	407-390-6663	390-6600
TF: 800-843-6664 ■ *Web:* www.omnihotels.com					
Spa at the Omni Tucson National Golf Resort & Spa 2727 W Club Dr	Tucson	AZ	85742	520-877-2367	297-7544
Web: www.tucsonnational.com					
Spa at the Orlando World Center Marriott Resort & Convention Center 8701 World Ctr Dr	Orlando	FL	32821	407-238-8705	238-8777
Web: www.marriott.com					
Spa Pallazo at the Boca Raton Resort & Club 501 E Camino Real	Boca Raton	FL	33432	561-347-4772	447-3183
TF: 877-677-7347 ■ *Web:* www.bocaresort.com					
Spa at Pebble Beach 1518 Cypress Dr	Pebble Beach	CA	93953	831-649-7615	622-6490
TF: 800-654-9300 ■ *Web:* www.pebblebeach.com					
Spa at Pechanga Resort & Casino 45000 Pechanga Pkwy	Temecula	CA	92592	951-719-8501	695-7410
TF: 888-732-4264 ■ *Web:* www.pechanga.com					
Spa at the PGA National Resort 450 Avenue of the Champions	Palm Beach Gardens	FL	33418	561-627-3111	627-6056
TF: 800-633-9150 ■ *Web:* www.pga-resorts.com					
Spa at Pinehurst Resort 180 Barrett Rd E	Pinehurst	NC	28374	910-235-8320	235-8306
TF: 800-487-4653 ■ *Web:* www.pinehurst.com/spa_resort.asp					
Spa at the Ponte Vedra Inn & Club 200 Ponte Vedra Blvd	Ponte Vedra Beach	FL	32082	904-273-7700	273-7706
TF: 800-234-7842 ■ *Web:* www.pvspa.com					
Spa La Quinta at La Quinta Resort 49-499 Eisenhower Dr PO Box 69	La Quinta	CA	92253	760-777-4800	564-5723
TF: 877-527-7721 ■ *Web:* www.laquintaresort.com					
Spa at the Ritz-Carlton Amelia Island 4750 Amelia Island Pkwy	Amelia Island	FL	32034	904-277-1087	277-1071
TF: 800-241-3333 ■ *Web:* www.ritzcarlton.com					
Spa at the Ritz-Carlton Bachelor Gulch 0130 Daybreak Ridge	Avon	CO	81620	970-343-1138	343-1126
TF: 800-241-3333 ■ *Web:* www.ritzcarlton.com					
Spa at the Ritz-Carlton Coconut Grove 3300 SW 27th Ave	Coconut Grove	FL	33133	305-644-4680	644-4681
TF: 800-241-3333 ■ *Web:* www.ritzcarlton.com					
Spa at the Ritz-Carlton Half Moon Bay 1 Miramontes Pt Rd	Half Moon Bay	CA	94019	650-712-7040	712-7070
TF: 800-241-3333 ■ *Web:* www.ritzcarlton.com					
Spa at the Ritz-Carlton Huntington Hotel 1401 S Oak Knoll Ave	Pasadena	CA	91106	626-585-6414	585-6432
TF: 800-241-3333 ■ *Web:* www.ritzcarlton.com					
Spa at the Ritz-Carlton Key Biscayne 455 Grand Bay Dr	Key Biscayne	FL	33149	305-365-4158	365-4515
TF: 800-241-3333 ■ *Web:* ritzcarlton.com					
Spa at the Ritz-Carlton Naples 280 Vanderbilt Beach Rd	Naples	FL	34108	239-514-6100	514-6160
TF: 800-241-3333 ■ *Web:* www.ritzcarlton.com					
Spa at the Ritz-Carlton New Orleans 921 Canal St	New Orleans	LA	70112	504-670-2929	670-2930
TF: 800-241-3333 ■ *Web:* www.ritzcarlton.com					
Spa at the Ritz-Carlton Orlando Grande Lakes 4024 Central Florida Pkwy	Orlando	FL	32837	407-393-4200	393-4022
TF: 800-241-3333 ■ *Web:* www.ritzcarlton.com					
Spa at the Ritz-Carlton Reynolds Plantation 1 Lake Oconee Tr	Greensboro	GA	30642	706-467-7185	467-7188
TF: 800-241-3333 ■ *Web:* www.ritzcarlton.com					
Spa at the Ritz-Carlton Sarasota 1111 Ritz-Carlton Dr	Sarasota	FL	34236	941-309-2000	309-2114
TF: 800-241-3333 ■ *Web:* www.ritzcarlton.com					
Spa at the Ritz-Carlton South Beach 1 Lincoln Rd	Miami Beach	FL	33139	786-276-4090	276-1015
TF: 800-241-3333 ■ *Web:* www.ritzcarlton.com					
Spa at the Ritz-Carlton Tysons Corner 1700 Tysons Blvd	McLean	VA	22102	703-744-3924	744-3990
TF: 800-241-3333 ■ *Web:* www.ritzcarlton.com					
Spa at the Saddlebrook Resort 5700 Saddlebrook Way	Wesley Chapel	FL	33543	813-907-4419	907-4215
TF: 800-729-8383 ■ *Web:* www.saddlebrook.com/spa1.html					
Spa at the Sagamore 110 Sagamore Rd	Bolton Landing	NY	12814	518-743-6081	743-6224
TF: 800-358-3585 ■ *Web:* www.thesagamore.com					
Spa at the Saint Regis Aspen 315 E Dean St	Aspen	CO	81611	970-920-3300	544-7191
TF: 888-625-5144 ■ *Web:* www.stregisaspen.com					
Spa at the Salish Lodge 6501 Railroad Ave PO Box 1109	Snoqualmie	WA	98065	425-831-6535	888-2533
TF: 800-272-5474 ■ *Web:* www.salishlodge.com					
Spa Samadhi at Inn at Sunrise Springs 242 Los Pinos Rd	Santa Fe	NM	87507	505-428-3614	471-7365
TF: 800-955-0028 ■ *Web:* www.sunrisesprings.com					
Spa at the Sanctuary on Camelback Mountain 5700 E McDonald Dr	Paradise Valley	AZ	85253	480-948-2100	607-2335
TF: 800-245-2051 ■ *Web:* www.slh.com/sanctuary					
Spa at the Sanderling Resort 1461 Duck Rd	Duck	NC	27949	252-261-7744	261-1352
TF: 800-701-4111 ■ *Web:* www.thesanderling.com					
Spa at Sanibel Harbour Resort 17260 Harbour Pointe Dr	Fort Myers	FL	33908	239-466-2156	466-2265
Web: www.sanibel-resort.com					
Spa at Saybrook Point Inn 2 Bridge St	Old Saybrook	CT	06475	860-395-3245	388-1504
TF: 800-243-0212 ■ *Web:* www.saybrook.com					
Spa Shiki at the Lodge of Four Seasons Horseshoe Bend Pkwy PO Box 215	Lake Ozark	MO	65049	573-365-8108	365-8101
TF: 800-843-5253 ■ *Web:* www.spashiki.com					
Spa at Silverado 1605 Atlas Peak Rd	Napa	CA	94558	707-257-5555	257-5550
TF: 888-918-4772 ■ *Web:* www.silveradospa.com					
Spa du Soleil at the Auberge du Soleil 180 Rutherford Hill Rd	Rutherford	CA	94573	707-967-3159	967-3171
TF: 800-348-5406 ■ *Web:* www.aubergedusoleil.com/html/spa.shtml					
Spa at the Stoweflake Mountain Resort 1746 Mountain Rd PO Box 369	Stowe	VT	05672	802-760-1083	253-9264
TF: 800-253-2232 ■ *Web:* www.stoweflake.com					
Spa Suites at Kahala Hotel & Resort 5000 Kahala Ave	Honolulu	HI	96816	808-739-8938	739-8939
TF: 800-367-2525 ■ *Web:* www.kahalaresort.com					
Spa Terre at the Hotel Viking 1 Bellevue Ave	Newport	RI	02840	401-848-4848	848-4864
TF: 800-556-7126 ■ *Web:* www.hotelviking.com					
Spa Terre at the Inn & Spa at Loretto 211 Old Santa Fe Trail	Santa Fe	NM	87501	505-984-7997	984-7907
TF: 800-727-5531 ■ *Web:* www.innatloretto.com					
Spa Terre at the Little Palm Island Resort 28500 Overseas Hwy	Little Torch Key	FL	33042	305-515-3028	515-3009
TF: 800-343-8567 ■ *Web:* www.littlepalmisland.com					
Spa Terre at Paradise Point Resort 1404 Vacation Rd	San Diego	CA	92109	858-581-5998	490-6688
TF: 800-344-2626 ■ *Web:* www.paradisepoint.com					
Spa Terre at La Playa Beach Resort & Golf Club 9891 Gulf Shore Dr	Naples	FL	34108	239-598-5117	597-8283
Web: www.laplayaresort.com					
Spa Toccare at Borgata Hotel Casino 1 Borgata Way	Atlantic City	NJ	08401	609-317-7555	317-1039
TF: 866-692-6742 ■ *Web:* www.theborgata.com					
Spa at Topnotch at Stowe Resort 4000 Mountain Rd	Stowe	VT	05672	802-253-6463	253-6415
TF: 800-451-8686 ■ *Web:* www.topnotchresort.com					
Spa Torrey Pines at the Lodge at Torrey Pines 11480 N Torrey Pines Rd	La Jolla	CA	92037	858-777-6690	777-6698
TF: 800-656-0087 ■ *Web:* www.spatorreypines.com					
Spa at the Vail Marriott Mountain Resort 715 W Lionshead Cir	Vail	CO	81657	970-479-5004	477-5671
TF: 800-648-0720 ■ *Web:* www.marriott.com					
Spa at the Vail Mountain Lodge 352 E Meadow Dr	Vail	CO	81657	970-476-7721	477-3225
TF: 866-476-0700 ■ *Web:* www.vailmountainlodge.com					
Spa at the Villagio Inn 6481 Washington St	Yountville	CA	94599	707-948-5050	948-5054
TF: 800-351-1133 ■ *Web:* www.villagio.com					
Spa Vita di Lago at The Ritz Carlton Lake Las Vegas 1610 Lake Las Vegas Pkwy	Henderson	NV	89011	702-567-4600	567-4601
TF: 800-241-3333 ■ *Web:* www.ritzcarlton.com					
Spa at the Watermark Hotel 212 W Crockett St	San Antonio	TX	78205	210-396-5840	396-5880
TF: 866-605-1212 ■ *Web:* www.watermarkhotel.com					
Spa at the Westin Maui Resort 2365 Kaanapali Pkwy	Lahaina	HI	96761	808-661-2588	661-2594
TF: 866-500-8313 ■ *Web:* www.westinmaui.com					
Spa at White Oaks Conference Resort 253 Taylor Rd	Niagara-on-the-Lake	ON	L0S1J0	905-641-2599	641-2623
TF: 800-263-5766 ■ *Web:* www.whiteoaksresort.com					
Spa Without Walls at the Fairmont Orchid Hawaii 1 N Kaniku Dr	Kohala Coast	HI	96743	808-885-2000	887-7317
TF: 800-845-9905 ■ *Web:* www.fairmont.com/orchid					
SpaHalekulani at the Halekulani Hotel 2199 Kalia Rd	Honolulu	HI	96815	808-931-5322	931-5337
TF: 800-367-2343 ■ *Web:* www.halekulani.com					
Stillwater Spa at the Hyatt Regency Coconut Point Resort 5001 Coconut Rd	Bonita Springs	FL	34134	239-390-4360	390-4362
Web: coconutpoint.hyatt.com					
Stillwater Spa at the Hyatt Regency Newport 1 Goat Island	Newport	RI	02840	401-851-3225	851-3299
TF: 800-233-1234 ■ *Web:* www.stillwaterspa.com					
Tamaya Spa at the Hyatt Regency Tamaya Resort 1300 Tuyuna Tr	Santa Ana Pueblo	NM	87004	505-771-6134	771-6232
Web: tamaya.hyatt.com					
Ten Thousand Waves Japanese Health Spa 3451 Hyde Park Rd	Santa Fe	NM	87501	505-992-5025	989-5077
Web: www.tenthousandwaves.com					
The Spa at the Beverly Wilshire 9500 Wilshire Blvd	Beverly Hills	CA	90212	310-385-7023	385-3960
TF: 800-545-4000 ■ *Web:* www.fourseasons.com/beverlywilshire/spa.html					
Turtle Cove Spa at Mountain Harbor Resort 994 Mountain Harbor Rd PO Box 1268	Mount Ida	AR	71957	870-867-1220	867-4678
TF: 800-832-2276 ■ *Web:* www.turtlecovespa.com					
Verandah Club & Spa at the Hilton Anatole 2201 Stemmons Fwy	Dallas	TX	75207	214-761-7878	761-7835
Web: www.verandahclub.com					
Village Bay Spa at Lake Arrowhead Resort 27984 Hwy 189	Lake Arrowhead	CA	92352	909-744-3000	744-3023
TF: 800-800-6792 ■ *Web:* www.laresort.com					
Watermark Hotel & Spa 212 W Crockett St	San Antonio	TX	78205	866-605-1212	226-0389*
**Fax Area Code: 210* ■ *TF:* 866-605-1212 ■ *Web:* www.watermarkhotel.com					
Well Spa at Miramonte Resort 45-000 Indian Wells Ln	Indian Wells	CA	92210	760-837-1652	837-2330
TF: 866-843-9355 ■ *Web:* www.miramonteresort.com					
Westin Kierland Resort & Spa 6902 E Greenway Pkwy	Scottsdale	AZ	85254	480-624-1000	624-1001
TF: 888-625-5144 ■ *Web:* www.kierlandresort.com					
Westin Resort & Spa 4090 Whistler Way	Whistler	BC	V0N1B4	604-905-5000	905-5640
TF: 888-634-5577					
Willow Stream Spa at the Fairmont Banff Springs 405 Spray Ave	Banff	AB	T1L1J4	403-762-1772	762-1766
TF: 800-404-1772 ■ *Web:* www.willowstream.com					
Willow Stream Spa at the Fairmont Empress 633 Humboldt St	Victoria	BC	V8W1A6	250-995-4650	995-4651
TF: 866-854-7444 ■ *Web:* www.fairmont.com					
Willow Stream Spa at Fairmont Scottsdale Princess 7575 E Princess Dr	Scottsdale	AZ	85255	480-585-2732	585-0086
TF: 800-908-9540 ■ *Web:* www.willowstream.com					

	City	State	ZIP	Phone	Fax
Willow Stream Spa at the Turnberry Isle Resort & Club 19999 W Country Club Dr *TF:* 800-327-7028 ■ *Web:* www.fairmont.com	Aventura	FL	33180	305-933-6930	936-2992
Wintergarden Spa & Fitness Center at Wintergreen Resort Rt 664 PO Box 706 *TF:* 800-266-2444 ■ *Web:* www.wintergreenresort.com	Wintergreen	VA	22958	434-325-8185	
ZaSpa at Hotel ZaZa 2332 Leonard St *TF:* 800-597-8399 ■ *Web:* www.hotelzaza.com/	Dallas	TX	75201	214-550-9492	468-8397

711 SPEAKERS BUREAUS

	City	State	ZIP	Phone	Fax
Abacus Speakers Bureau 412 Liberty St PO Box 11669	Knoxville	TN	37939	865-546-0373	673-4680
AEI Speakers Bureau 214 Lincoln St Suite 113 *TF:* 800-447-7325 ■ *Web:* www.aeispeakers.com	Boston	MA	02134	617-782-3111	782-3444
Agricultural Speakers Network 10436 Oak Ridge Dr *TF Sales:* 800-222-1556 ■ *Web:* www.tillergroup.com/_asn	Zionsville	IN	46077	317-873-9797	873-0800
All-Star Agency Speakers Bureau 4829 Powell Rd *TF:* 800-736-0031 ■ *Web:* www.allstaragency.com	Fairfax	VA	22032	703-503-9438	
Ambassador Speakers Bureau 1107 Battlewood St *Web:* www.ambassadoragency.com	Franklin	TN	37069	615-370-4700	661-4344
American Program Bureau Inc 36 Crafts St *TF:* 800-225-4575 ■ *Web:* www.apbspeakers.com	Newton	MA	02458	617-965-6600	965-6610
Atlantic Speakers Bureau 980 Rt 730 *TF:* 866-465-0990 ■ *Web:* www.asb.nb.ca	Scotch Ridge	NB	E3L5L2	506-465-0990	465-0813
Barber & Assoc 412 Liberty St PO Box 11669 *Web:* www.barberusa.com	Knoxville	TN	37939	865-546-0000	673-4680
Barclay Steven Agency 12 Western Ave *TF:* 888-965-7323 ■ *Web:* www.barclayagency.com	Petaluma	CA	94952	707-773-0654	778-1868
Brooks International Speakers Bureau 763 Santa Fe Dr *Web:* www.brooksinternational.com	Denver	CO	80204	303-825-8700	825-8701
Capitol City Speakers Bureau 1620 S 5th St *TF:* 800-397-3183 ■ *Web:* www.capcityspeakers.com	Springfield	IL	62703	217-544-8552	544-1496
Charisma Pros Inc 116 W Osage St *Web:* www.charismapros.com	Greenfield	IN	46140	317-462-4245	
Eagles Talent Connection Inc 57 W South Orange Ave *TF:* 800-345-5607 ■ *Web:* www.eaglestalent.com	South Orange	NJ	07079	973-376-3737	313-0040
Executive Speakers Bureau 8470 Deerfield Ln *TF:* 800-754-9404 ■ *Web:* www.executivespeakers.com	Germantown	TN	38138	901-754-9404	756-4237
Financial Forum 90 N 100 East Suite 4 *TF:* 800-500-5119 ■ *Web:* www.financialspeakers.com	Logan	UT	84321	435-750-0062	750-0064
Five Star Speakers & Trainers LLC 8685 W 96th St *Web:* www.fivestarspeakers.com	Overland Park	KS	66212	913-648-6480	648-6484
Garrett Speakers International Inc PO Box 153448 *TF:* 800-787-2840 ■ *Web:* www.garrettspeakers.com	Irving	TX	75015	972-513-0054	513-0540
Golden Gate International Speakers Bureau Inc 42-335 Washington St Suite 369 *Web:* www.ggisb.com	Palm Desert	CA	92211	760-345-2861	345-9791
Greater Talent Network Inc 437 5th Ave 7th Fl *TF:* 800-326-4211 ■ *Web:* www.greatertalent.com	New York	NY	10016	212-645-4200	627-1471
Harry Walker Agency Inc (HWA) 355 Lexington Ave 21st Fl *Web:* www.harrywalker.com	New York	NY	10017	646-227-4900	227-4901
IMG Speakers 825 7th Ave 8th Fl *Web:* www.imgspeakers.com	New York	NY	10019	212-489-8300	246-1596
International Speakers Bureau Inc 1401 Elm St 41st Fl *TF:* 800-842-4483 ■ *Web:* www.internationalspeakers.com	Dallas	TX	75202	214-744-3885	744-3888
Keppler Assoc Inc 4350 N Fairfax Dr Suite 700 *Web:* www.kepplerspeakers.com	Arlington	VA	22203	703-516-4000	516-4819
Key Speakers Bureau Inc 3500 E Coast Hwy Suite 6 *TF:* 800-675-1175 ■ *Web:* www.keyspeakers.com	Corona del Mar	CA	92625	949-675-7856	675-1478
Leading Authorities Inc 1220 L St NW Suite 850 *TF:* 800-773-2537 ■ *Web:* www.leadingauthorities.com	Washington	DC	20005	202-783-0300	783-0301
National Speakers Bureau 1663 W 7th Ave *TF:* 800-661-4110 ■ *Web:* www.nsb.com	Vancouver	BC	V6J1S4	604-734-3663	734-8906
National Speakers Bureau Inc 14047 W Petronalla Dr Suite 102 *TF:* 800-323-9442 ■ *Web:* www.nationalspeakers.com	Libertyville	IL	60048	847-295-1122	367-5499
Nationwide Speakers Bureau Inc 120 El Camino Dr Suite 104 *Web:* www.nationwidespeakers.com	Beverly Hills	CA	90212	310-273-8807	273-5928
Professional Speakers Bureau PO Box 179 *Web:* www.prospeakers.com	Richmond Hill	ON	L4C4Y2	905-770-1886	
Professional Speakers Network 10436 Oak Ridge Dr *TF:* 800-222-1556 ■ *Web:* tillergroup.com/_psn/	Zionsville	IN	46077	317-873-9797	873-0800
Program Resources PO Box 22307 *Web:* www.programresources.com	Louisville	KY	40252	502-339-1653	339-8085
Santa Barbara Speakers Bureau PO Box 30768 *Web:* www.sbsb.net	Santa Barbara	CA	93130	805-682-7474	563-1028
Speak Inc Speakers Bureau 10680 Treena St Suite 230 *Web:* www.speakinc.com	San Diego	CA	92131	858-228-3771	228-3989
Speakers Guild Inc PO Box 1540 *TF:* 800-343-4530 ■ *Web:* www.speakersguild.com	Sandwich	MA	02563	508-888-6702	888-6771
Speakers Unlimited PO Box 27225 *Web:* www.speakersunlimited.com	Columbus	OH	43227	614-864-3703	864-3876
Speakers.com 130 Lubrano Dr Suite 110 *Web:* www.speakers.com	Annapolis	MD	21401	410-897-1970	897-1971
Steven Barclay Agency 12 Western Ave *TF:* 888-965-7323 ■ *Web:* www.barclayagency.com	Petaluma	CA	94952	707-773-0654	778-1868
Walters International Speakers Bureau PO Box 398 *Web:* www.walters-intl.com	Glendora	CA	91740	626-335-8069	335-6127
Washington Speakers Bureau 1663 Prince St *Web:* www.washspkrs.com	Alexandria	VA	22314	703-684-0555	684-9378
World Class Speakers & Entertainers 5200 Kanan Rd Suite 210 *Web:* www.speak.com	Agoura Hills	CA	91301	818-991-5400	991-2226

712 SPEED CHANGERS, INDUSTRIAL HIGH SPEED DRIVES, GEARS

SEE ALSO Aircraft Parts & Auxiliary Equipment p. 1271; Automotive Parts & Supplies - Mfr p. 1360; Controls & Relays - Electrical p. 1558; Machine Shops p. 1923; Motors (Electric) & Generators p. 1983; Power Transmission Equipment - Mechanical p. 2132

	City	State	ZIP	Phone	Fax
Alten Engineering Div Westerman Cos 245 N Broad St *TF:* 800-338-8265 ■ *Web:* www.westermancompanies.com	Bremen	OH	43107	740-569-4143	569-4111
Altra Industrial Motion Inc 14 Hayward St *NASDAQ: AIMC* ■ *TF Cust Svc:* 888-999-9860 ■ *Web:* www.altramotion.com	Quincy	MA	02171	617-328-3300	479-6238
Altra Holdings Inc DBA Altra Industrial Motion Inc 14 Hayward St *NASDAQ: AIMC* ■ *TF Cust Svc:* 888-999-9860 ■ *Web:* www.altramotion.com	Quincy	MA	02171	617-328-3300	479-6238
Amarillo Gear Co 2401 Sundown Ln *Web:* www.amarillogear.com	Amarillo	TX	79118	806-622-1273	622-3258
Auburn Gear Inc 400 E Auburn Dr *Web:* www.auburngear.com	Auburn	IN	46706	260-925-3200	925-4725
Bison Gear & Engineering Corp 3850 Ohio Ave *TF:* 800-282-4766 ■ *Web:* www.bisongear.com	Saint Charles	IL	60174	630-377-4327	377-6777
Bond Charles Co 11 Green St PO Box 105 *TF Cust Svc:* 800-922-0125	Christiana	PA	17509	610-593-5171	593-5378
Charles Bond Co 11 Green St PO Box 105 *TF Cust Svc:* 800-922-0125	Christiana	PA	17509	610-593-5171	593-5378
Chicago Gear-DO James Corp 2823 W Fulton St	Chicago	IL	60612	773-638-0508	638-7161
Cleveland Gear Co 3249 E 80th St *TF:* 800-423-3169 ■ *Web:* www.clevelandgear.com	Cleveland	OH	44104	216-641-9000	641-2731
Columbia Gear Corp 530 County Rd 50 *TF:* 800-323-9838 ■ *Web:* www.columbiagear.com	Avon	MN	56310	320-356-7301	356-2131
Cone Drive Operations Inc - A Textron Co 240 E 12th St **Fax Area Code:* 888 ■ *TF Sales:* 888-994-2663 ■ *Web:* www.textronpt.com	Traverse City	MI	49685	231-946-8410	907-2663*
Cotta Transmission Co LLC 1301 Prince Hall Dr *Web:* www.cotta.com	Beloit	WI	53511	608-368-5600	368-5605
Dalton Gear Co 212 Colfax Ave N *TF:* 800-328-7485 ■ *Web:* www.daltongear.com	Minneapolis	MN	55405	612-374-2150	374-2467
Danaher Motion 1500 Mittel Blvd *TF:* 866-993-2624 ■ *Web:* www.danahermotion.com	Wood Dale	IL	60191	630-860-7300	694-3305
Designatronics Inc 2101 Jericho Tpke *TF Orders:* 800-345-1144	New Hyde Park	NY	11040	516-328-3300	326-8827
Durst Div Regal-Beloit Corp PO Box 298 *TF:* 800-356-0775 ■ *Web:* www.durstdrives.com	Beloit	WI	53512	608-365-2563	365-2182
Electra-Gear Div Regal-Beloit Corp 1524 15th Ave *TF:* 800-877-4327 ■ *Web:* www.electragear.com	Union Grove	WI	53182	262-878-1221	878-1968
Electro Sales Inc 100 Fellsway W *TF:* 888-789-0500 ■ *Web:* www.electrosales.com	Somerville	MA	02145	617-666-0500	628-2800
Emerson Control Techniques Drives Inc 12005 Technology Dr	Eden Prairie	MN	55344	952-995-8000	
Euclid Universal Corp 30500 Bruce Industrial Pkwy Suite B *TF:* 800-280-2616 ■ *Web:* www.eucliduniversal.com	Solon	OH	44139	440-349-4083	349-4894
Fairchild Industrial Products Co 3920 West Point Blvd **Fax:* Sales ■ *TF:* 800-423-1093 ■ *Web:* www.fairchildproducts.com	Winston-Salem	NC	27103	336-659-3400	659-9323*
Fairfield Mfg Co Inc PO Box 7940 *Web:* www.fairfieldmfg.com	Lafayette	IN	47903	765-772-4000	772-4001
Falk Corp 3001 W Canal St *TF:* 800-852-3255 ■ *Web:* www.falkcorp.com	Milwaukee	WI	53208	414-342-3131	937-4425
Fasco Motors 402 E Haven *Web:* www.fasco.com	Eaton Rapids	MI	48827	517-663-2161	663-1315
Gear Motions Inc 1750 Milton Ave *Web:* www.gearmotions.com	Syracuse	NY	13209	315-488-0100	488-0196
Gear Works The PO Box 80886 *Web:* www.thegearworks.com	Seattle	WA	98108	206-762-3333	762-3704
Geartronics Industries Inc 100 Chelmsford Rd *Web:* www.geartronics.com	North Billerica	MA	01862	978-663-6566	667-3130
Grove Gear Corp 1524 15th Ave *Web:* www.grovegear.com	Union Grove	WI	53182	262-878-1221	878-1730
Hankscraft Inc 300 Wengel Dr *Web:* www.hankscraft-motors.com	Reedsburg	WI	53959	608-524-4341	524-4342
Horsburgh & Scott Co 5114 Hamilton Ave *Web:* www.horsburgh-scott.com	Cleveland	OH	44114	216-431-3900	432-5850
Hub City Inc PO Box 1089 *TF:* 800-482-2489 ■ *Web:* www.hubcityinc.com	Aberdeen	SD	57402	605-225-0360	225-0567
Hurst Mfg 1551 E Broadway **Fax:* Sales ■ *Web:* www.hurstmfg.com	Princeton	IN	47670	812-385-2564	386-7504*
Imperial Electric Co 1503 Exeter Rd *Web:* www.imperialelectric.com	Akron	OH	44306	330-734-3600	734-3601
Industrial Motion Control LLC 1444 S Wolf Rd *Web:* www.camcoindex.com	Wheeling	IL	60090	847-459-5200	459-3064
Kurz Electric Solutions Inc 1325 McMahon Dr *TF:* 800-776-3629 ■ *Web:* www.kurz.com	Neenah	WI	54956	920-886-8200	886-8201
Leedy Mfg Co 210 Hall St SW *Web:* www.leedymfg.com	Grand Rapids	MI	49507	616-245-0517	245-3888
Leeson Electric Corp 2100 Washington St *Web:* www.leeson.com	Grafton	WI	53024	262-377-8810	
Lexel Corp PO Box 508	Franksville	WI	53126	262-886-2002	886-4639
Martin Sprocket & Gear Inc 3100 Sprocket Dr PO Box 91588 *Web:* www.martinsprocket.com	Arlington	TX	76015	817-258-3000	258-3333
Merkle-Korff Industries Inc 1776 Winthrop Dr *Web:* www.merkle-korff.com	Des Plaines	IL	60018	847-296-8800	699-0832
Milwaukee Gear Co 5150 N Port Washington Rd *TF:* 800-959-1142 ■ *Web:* www.milwaukeegear.com	Milwaukee	WI	53217	414-962-3532	962-2774
Molon Motor & Coil Corp 3737 Industrial Ave *TF:* 800-526-6867 ■ *Web:* www.molon.com	Rolling Meadows	IL	60008	847-253-6000	259-5491
Nixon Gear Inc 1750 Milton Ave *Web:* www.gearmotions.com/nixongear.htm	Syracuse	NY	13209	315-488-0100	488-0196
Nuttall Gear LLC 2221 Niagara Falls Blvd *TF:* 800-432-0121 ■ *Web:* www.nuttallgear.com	Niagara Falls	NY	14304	716-298-4100	298-4101
Oliver Gear Inc 1120 Niagara St *Web:* www.gearmotions.com/olivergear.htm	Buffalo	NY	14213	716-885-1080	885-1145
Overton Gear & Tool Corp 530 Westgate Dr *Web:* www.overtongear.com	Addison	IL	60101	630-543-9570	543-7440
Peerless-Winsmith Inc 1401 W Market St *TF:* 800-676-3651 ■ *Web:* www.winsmith.com	Warren	OH	44485	330-399-3651	393-6041
Perfection Gear Inc 9 N Bear Creek Rd *TF:* 800-532-5314	Asheville	NC	28806	828-253-0000	253-2649
Piller Inc 45 Turner Rd *TF:* 800-597-6937 ■ *Web:* www.piller.com	Middletown	NY	10941	845-695-5300	692-0295
Regal-Beloit Corp 200 State St *NYSE: RBC* ■ *Web:* www.regal-beloit.com	Beloit	WI	53511	608-364-8800	364-8818
Regal-Beloit Corp Durst Div PO Box 298 *TF:* 800-356-0775 ■ *Web:* www.durstdrives.com	Beloit	WI	53512	608-365-2563	365-2182
Regal-Beloit Corp Electra-Gear Div 1524 15th Ave *TF:* 800-877-4327 ■ *Web:* www.electragear.com	Union Grove	WI	53182	262-878-1221	878-1968
Rexnord Industries LLC 4701 Greenfield Ave *TF:* 800-852-3255 ■ *Web:* www.rexnord.com	Milwaukee	WI	53214	414-643-3300	643-3078
Richmond Gear PO Box 238 *TF Sales:* 800-476-6446 ■ *Web:* www.richmondgear.com	Liberty	SC	29657	864-843-9231	843-1276
Rush Gears Inc 550 Virginia Dr **Fax Area Code:* 800 ■ *TF:* 800-523-2576 ■ *Web:* www.rushgear.com	Fort Washington	PA	19034	215-542-9000	635-6273*
Schafer Gear Works Inc 4701 Nimtz Pkwy *Web:* www.schafergear.com	South Bend	IN	46628	574-234-4116	234-4115
SEW-Eurodrive Inc 1295 Old Spartanburg Hwy *Web:* www.seweurodrive.com	Lyman	SC	29365	864-439-7537	439-0566
Sewall Gear Mfg Co 705 Raymond Ave *Web:* www.sewallgear.com	Saint Paul	MN	55114	651-645-7721	645-1823
Stature Electric Inc 22543 Fisher Rd PO Box 6660 *Web:* www.statureelectric.com	Watertown	NY	13601	315-782-5910	782-1917
Sterling Electric Inc 7997 Allison Ave *TF Cust Svc:* 800-654-6220 ■ *Web:* www.sterlingelectric.com	Indianapolis	IN	46268	317-872-0471	872-0907

	City	State	Zip	Phone	Fax
Sumitomo Machinery Corp of America 4200 Holland Blvd	Chesapeake	VA	23323	757-485-3355	485-7490
TF: 800-762-9256 ■ *Web:* www.smcyclo.com					
Textron Fluid & Power Inc 40 Westminster St	Providence	RI	02903	401-588-3400	621-5045
Web: www.textron.com					
Toshiba International Corp 13131 W Little York Rd	Houston	TX	77041	713-466-0277	466-8773
TF: 800-231-1412 ■ *Web:* www.tic.toshiba.com					
Westerman Cos Alten Engineering Div 245 N Broad St	Bremen	OH	43107	740-569-4143	569-4111
TF: 800-338-8265 ■ *Web:* www.westermancompanies.com					

713 SPORTING GOODS

SEE ALSO All-Terrain Vehicles p. 1277; Bicycles & Bicycle Parts & Accessories p. 1380; Boats - Recreational p. 1386; Cord & Twine p. 1572; Exercise & Fitness Equipment p. 1628; Firearms & Ammunition (Non-Military) p. 1637; Gym & Playground Equipment p. 1769; Handbags, Totes, Backpacks p. 1769; Motor Vehicles - Commercial & Special Purpose p. 1982; Personal Protective Equipment & Clothing p. 2105; Snowmobiles p. 2318; Swimming Pools p. 2336; Tarps, Tents, Covers p. 2338

	City	State	Zip	Phone	Fax
40-Up Tackle Co 16 Union Ave	Westfield	MA	01085	413-562-3629	562-7328
TF: 800-456-4665 ■ *Web:* www.usline.com					
Abel Automatics Inc 165 Aviador St	Camarillo	CA	93010	805-484-8789	482-0701
TF: 800-848-7335 ■ *Web:* www.abelreels.com					
Acme Tackle Co Inc PO Box 72771	Providence	RI	02907	401-331-6437	272-7821
Web: www.acmetackle.com					
Acushnet Co 333 Bridge St	Fairhaven	MA	02719	508-979-2000	979-3900*
**Fax:* Hum Res ■ *TF:* 800-225-8500 ■ *Web:* www.acushnet.com					
AcuSport Corp 1 Hunter Pl	Bellefontaine	OH	43311	937-593-7010	592-5625*
**Fax:* Sales ■ *TF:* 800-543-3150 ■ *Web:* www.acusport.com					
Adams Golf Inc 300 Delaware Ave Suite 572	Wilmington	DE	19801	302-427-5892	
Web: www.adamsgolf.com					
Adams USA Inc 610 S Jefferson Ave	Cookeville	TN	38501	931-526-2109	526-8357
TF: 800-251-6857 ■ *Web:* www.adamsusa.com					
Air Chair 2175 N Kiowa Blvd Suite 101	Lake Havasu City	AZ	86403	928-505-2226	505-2229
Web: www.airchair.com					
AK Bommer Custom Snowboards PO Box 1444	Valdez	AK	99686	907-835-3846	
Aldila Inc 13450 Stowe Dr	Poway	CA	92064	858-513-1801	513-1870
NASDAQ: ALDA ■ *TF:* 800-854-2786 ■ *Web:* www.aldila.com					
Alpine Archery PO Box 319	Lewiston	ID	83501	208-746-4717	746-1635
Web: www.alpinearchery.com					
American Classic Sales 1142 S 2475 West	Salt Lake City	UT	84104	801-977-3935	977-0529
TF: 888-733-5763 ■ *Web:* www.americanclassic.net					
American Sports 74 Albe Dr Suite 1	Newark	DE	19702	302-369-9480	369-9481
TF: 800-977-6786 ■ *Web:* www.americansports.com					
AMF Bowling Worldwide Inc 8100 AMF Dr	Mechanicsville	VA	23111	804-730-4000	730-0923
TF: 800-342-5263 ■ *Web:* www.amf.com					
Aqua-Cycle International Inc PO Box 2129	Yorba Linda	CA	92885	714-630-1501	630-1503
TF: 800-970-2688 ■ *Web:* www.aqua-cycle.com					
Aqua-Leisure Industries Inc 525 Bodwell St Ext PO Box 239	Avon	MA	02322	508-587-5400	588-4270
TF: 888-807-2998 ■ *Web:* www.aqualeisure.com					
Aqualung America Inc 2340 Cousteau Ct	Vista	CA	92083	760-597-5000	597-4900
TF: 800-635-3483 ■ *Web:* www.aqualung.com					
Arrow Surfboards 1115 Thompson Ave Suite 7	Santa Cruz	CA	95062	831-462-2791	462-5735
Web: www.arrowsurfboards.com					
Atomic USA Inc 9 Columbia Dr	Amherst	NH	03031	603-880-6143	880-6099
TF: 800-258-5020 ■ *Web:* www.atomicski.com					
Austin Surfboards 1244 Jensen Dr Suite 101	Virginia Beach	VA	23451	757-425-6025	
Web: www.austinsurfboards.com					
Bankshot Sports Organization 785 F Rockville Pike Suite 504	Rockville	MD	20852	301-309-0260	309-0263
TF: 800-933-0140 ■ *Web:* www.bankshot.com					
Bare Sportswear Corp 1755 Grant Ave	Blaine	WA	98230	360-332-2700	530-8812*
**Fax Area Code:* 604 ■ *TF:* 800-663-0111 ■ *Web:* www.bare-wetsuits.com					
Bauer Premium Fly Reels PO Box 747	Ashland	OR	97520	541-488-8246	488-8244
TF: 888-484-4165 ■ *Web:* www.bauerflyreel.com					
Bear Creek Canoes Inc 72 Swamp Rd & Rt 107	Sebago	ME	04029	207-647-5850	
TF: 800-241-2268 ■ *Web:* www.bearcreekcanoes.com					
Bell Sports Corp 6225 N State Hwy 161 Suite 300	Irving	TX	75038	469-417-6600	492-1639*
**Fax Area Code:* 214 ■ *TF:* 866-525-2355 ■ *Web:* www.bellsports.com					
Big Rock Sports LLC 173 Hankison Dr	Newport	NC	28570	252-808-3500	726-8352
Web: www.bigrocksports.com					
Biscayne Rod Manufacturing Inc 425 E 9th St	Hialeah	FL	33010	305-884-0808	884-3017
TF: 888-866-7637 ■ *Web:* www.biscaynerod.com					
Bison Inc 603 L St	Lincoln	NE	68508	402-474-3353	638-0698*
**Fax Area Code:* 800 ■ *TF:* 800-247-7668 ■ *Web:* www.bisoninc.com					
Black Knight USA 5355 Sierra Rd	San Jose	CA	95132	408-923-7777	923-7794
TF: 800-535-3300 ■ *Web:* www.bksquash.com					
Bombardier Recreational Products 565 de la Montagne	Valcourt	QC	J0E2L0	450-532-2211	
Web: www.brp.com					
Brass Eagle Inc 1201 SE 30th St	Bentonville	AR	72712	479-464-8700	464-8701
TF: 877-877-4263 ■ *Web:* www.brasseagle.com					
Bravo Sports Corp 12801 Carmenita Rd	Santa Fe Springs	CA	90670	562-484-5100	484-5183
TF Cust Svc: 800-234-9737 ■ *Web:* www.bravosportscorp.com					
Brine Inc 47 Sumner St	Milford	MA	01757	508-478-3250	858-9922*
**Fax Area Code:* 800 ■ *TF:* 800-227-2722 ■ *Web:* www.brine.com					
Brunswick Bowling & Billiards 1 N Field Ct	Lake Forest	IL	60045	847-735-4700	735-4501
Web: www.brunswick.com					
Brunswick Corp 1 N Field Ct	Lake Forest	IL	60045	847-735-4700	735-4765
NYSE: BC ■ *Web:* www.brunswick.com					
Burly Bear Inc DBA ProLine Billiards Etc 700 N Hwy 17-92	Longwood	FL	32750	407-339-8700	339-4326
TF: 800-780-7799 ■ *Web:* www.prolinebilliards.com					
Burton Snowboards Inc 80 Industrial Pkwy	Burlington	VT	05401	802-862-4500	660-3250
TF: 800-881-3138 ■ *Web:* www.burton.com					
Byrne Surfboards 3205 Production Ave Suite J	Oceanside	CA	92054	760-721-6094	721-1098
Web: www.byrnesurf.com					
Callaway Golf Co 2180 Rutherford Rd	Carlsbad	CA	92008	760-931-1771	931-8013
NYSE: ELY ■ *TF:* 800-228-2767 ■ *Web:* www.callawaygolf.com					
Carry-Lite Inc 3601 Jenny Lind Rd	Fort Smith	AR	72901	479-782-8971	783-0234
Web: www.carrylitedecoys.com					
Carstens Industries Inc PO Box 185	Melrose	MN	56352	320-256-3919	256-4052
Web: www.carstensindustries.com					
Cascade Designs Inc 4000 1st Ave S	Seattle	WA	98134	206-624-8573	505-9525
TF Cust Svc: 800-531-9531 ■ *Web:* www.cascadedesigns.com					
Caviness Woodworking Inc 200 N Aycock Ave PO Box 710	Calhoun City	MS	38916	662-628-5195	628-8580
TF: 800-626-5195 ■ *Web:* www.cavinesspaddles.com					
Century Sports Inc 1995 Rutgers University Blvd	Lakewood	NJ	08701	732-905-4422	901-7766
TF Sales: 800-526-7548 ■ *Web:* www.centurysportsinc.com					
Century Tool & Mfg Co Inc 1462 US Rt 20 Bypass PO Box 188	Cherry Valley	IL	61016	815-332-4951	332-2090
TF: 800-435-4525 ■ *Web:* www.centurycamping.com					
Champion Shuffleboard Ltd 7216 Burns St	Richland Hills	TX	76118	817-284-3499	595-1506
TF: 800-826-7856 ■ *Web:* www.championshuffleboard.com					
Channel Islands Surfboards 1160 Mark Ave	Carpinteria	CA	93013	805-963-2678	564-3109
Web: www.cisurfboards.com					
Cleveland Golf Co 5601 Skylab Rd	Huntington Beach	CA	92647	800-999-6263	831-6624
TF Cust Svc: 800-999-6263 ■ *Web:* www.clevelandgolf.com					
Cobra Mfg 7909 E 148th St S PO Box 667	Bixby	OK	74008	918-366-7624	366-3614
TF: 800-352-6272 ■ *Web:* www.cobraarchery.com					
Coleman Co Inc 3600 N Hydraulic	Wichita	KS	67219	316-832-2653	832-3060
TF Cust Svc: 800-835-3278 ■ *Web:* www.coleman.com					
Colorado Classic Co DBA Pappy's Golf Shop 4030 N Sinton Rd	Colorado Springs	CO	80907	719-633-2064	633-2087
Web: www.coloradoclassic.com					
Columbia 300 Inc 5005 West Ave	San Antonio	TX	78213	210-344-9211	349-8672*
**Fax:* Hum Res ■ *TF Cust Svc:* 800-531-5920 ■ *Web:* www.columbia300.com					
Columbia Industries Inc DBA Columbia 300 Inc 5005 West Ave	San Antonio	TX	78213	210-344-9211	349-8672*
**Fax:* Hum Res ■ *TF Cust Svc:* 800-531-5920 ■ *Web:* www.columbia300.com					
Confluence Watersports Co 111 Kayaker Way	Easley	SC	29642	864-859-7518	855-5995
TF: 800-311-7245 ■ *Web:* www.confluencewatersports.com					
Connelly Billiard Mfg 1440 S Euclid Ave	Tucson	AZ	85713	520-624-6000	624-0077
TF: 800-861-8619 ■ *Web:* www.connellybilliards.com					
Connelly Skis Inc 20621 52nd Ave W	Lynnwood	WA	98036	425-775-5416	778-9590
TF: 800-234-7547 ■ *Web:* www.connellyskis.com					
Cortland Line Co Inc 3736 Kellogg Rd	Cortland	NY	13045	607-756-2851	753-8835
TF: 800-847-6787 ■ *Web:* www.cortlandline.com					
Current Designs PO Box 247	Winona	MN	55987	507-454-5430	454-5448
TF: 877-655-1822 ■ *Web:* www.cdkayak.com					
Daisy Outdoor Products 400 W Stribling Dr	Rogers	AR	72756	479-636-1200	636-1601
TF: 800-643-3458 ■ *Web:* www.daisy.com					
Daiwa Corp 12851 Midway Pl	Cerritos	CA	90703	562-802-9589	404-6212
TF: 800-736-4653 ■ *Web:* www.daiwa.com					
DAKINE Hawaii 408 Columbia St Suite 300	Hood River	OR	97031	541-386-3166	386-6199
TF: 800-827-7466 ■ *Web:* www.dakine.com					
DeBeer J & Son Inc 8 Charles Blvd	Guilderland	NY	12084	518-218-7871	218-7993
TF: 800-833-3535 ■ *Web:* www.debeerlacrosse.com					
Diamondback Fly Rods 251 Harrell St	Morrisville	VT	05661	802-888-1854	888-1857
Web: www.diamondbackflyrods.com					
Dolomite USA Corp 5 Commerce Ave	West Lebanon	NH	03784	603-298-5592	298-9872
TF: 800-257-2008 ■ *Web:* www.dolomiteusa.com					
Donek Snowboards Inc 35907 E 88 Ave PO Box 580	Watkins	CO	80137	303-261-0100	261-9988
TF: 877-533-6635 ■ *Web:* www.donek.com					
Douglas Industries Co 3441 S 11th Ave	Eldridge	IA	52748	563-285-4162	285-4163
TF: 800-553-8907 ■ *Web:* www.douglas-sports.com					
Dover Saddlery Inc 525 Great Rd PO Box 1100	Littleton	MA	01460	978-952-8062	952-8063
NASDAQ: DOVR ■ *TF:* 800-406-8204 ■ *Web:* www.doversaddlery.com					
Dynastar/Lange 1441 Ute Blvd Suite 200 PO Box 981060	Park City	UT	84098	435-252-3300	252-3331
TF: 888-243-6722					
E-Force 7920 Arjons Dr Suite A	San Diego	CA	92126	858-547-3720	547-5905
TF: 800-433-6723 ■ *Web:* www.e-force.com					
Eagle Claw Fishing Tackle Co 4245 E 46th Ave	Denver	CO	80216	303-321-1481	321-4750
TF: 800-628-0108 ■ *Web:* www.eagleclaw.com					
Eagle Sports 7223 Wynnwood Ln	Houston	TX	77008	713-861-0427	861-0799
TF: 800-862-4424 ■ *Web:* www.eaglesports.com					
Eastaboga Tackle Mfg Co 261 Mudd St	Eastaboga	AL	36260	256-831-9682	835-2524
Web: www.eastabogatackle.com					
Easton Sports Inc 7855 Haskell Ave Suite 200	Van Nuys	CA	91406	818-782-6445	782-2425
TF: 800-632-7866 ■ *Web:* www.eastonsports.com					
Easton Tru-Flite LLC 2709 S Freeman Rd	Monticello	IN	47960	574-583-5131	583-9271
TF: 800-348-2224					
Easy Rider Canoe & Kayak Co PO Box 88108	Seattle	WA	98138	425-228-3633	277-8778
Web: www.easyriderkayaks.com					
Ebonite International Inc PO Box 746	Hopkinsville	KY	42241	270-881-1200	881-1201
TF: 800-626-8350 ■ *Web:* www.ebonite.com					
EBSCO Industries Inc PRADCO Outdoor Brands Div 3601 Jenny Lind Rd	Fort Smith	AR	72901	479-782-8971	783-0234
TF: 800-531-1201					
Eddyline Kayaks 11977 W Star Ln	Burlington	WA	98233	360-757-2300	757-2302
Web: www.eddyline.com					
Elan USA PO Box 59	Andover	NH	03216	603-735-5650	735-5651
TF: 800-775-8100 ■ *Web:* www.elanskis.com					
Ellett Brothers Inc 267 Columbia Ave	Chapin	SC	29036	803-345-3751	345-1820
TF Sales: 800-845-3711 ■ *Web:* www.ellettbrothers.com					
Eppinger Mfg Co 6340 Schaefer Rd	Dearborn	MI	48126	313-582-3205	582-0110
TF: 888-771-8277 ■ *Web:* www.eppinger.net					
Escalade Inc DBA Escalade Sports PO Box 889	Evansville	IN	47706	812-467-1200	467-1300
NASDAQ: ESCA ■ *TF Cust Svc:* 800-426-1421 ■ *Web:* www.escaladesports.com					
Everlast Worldwide Inc 1350 Broadway Suite 2300	New York	NY	10018	212-239-0990	239-4261
NASDAQ: EVST ■ *Web:* www.everlast.com					
Fly Logic Inc PO Box 270	Melba	ID	83641	208-495-2090	495-2064
TF: 888-359-5644 ■ *Web:* www.flylogic.com					
FMP International 1800 Industrial Pk Dr PO Box 732	Grand Haven	MI	49417	616-847-9121	847-9337
TF: 800-560-7795 ■ *Web:* www.virtualturf.com					
Folbot Inc 4209 Pace St	Charleston	SC	29405	843-744-3483	744-7783
TF: 800-533-5099 ■ *Web:* www.folbot.com					
Forefront Holdings Inc 835 Bill Jones Industrial Dr	Springfield	TN	37172	615-384-1230	384-1290
TF: 800-247-9651 ■ *Web:* www.forefrontgolf.com					
Forten Corp 7815 Silverton Ave Suite 2-A	San Diego	CA	92126	858-693-9888	673-0888
Web: www.forten.com					
Franklin Sports Inc 17 Campanelli Pkwy	Stoughton	MA	02072	781-344-1111	341-3220
TF: 800-225-8647 ■ *Web:* www.franklinsports.com					
G & H Decoys Inc PO Box 1208	Henryetta	OK	74437	918-652-3314	652-3400
TF Orders: 800-443-3269 ■ *Web:* www.ghdecoys.com					
G Loomis Inc 1359 Down River Dr	Woodland	WA	98674	360-225-6516	225-7169
TF: 800-456-6647 ■ *Web:* www.gloomis.com					
G & S Surfboards Inc 7179 Construction Ct Unit A	San Diego	CA	92121	858-695-2690	695-9428
Web: www.gordonandsmith.com					
Game Country Inc 2403 Commerce Ln	Albany	GA	31707	229-883-4703	883-4766
Web: www.gamecountry.biz					
Gamma Sports 200 Waterfront Dr	Pittsburgh	PA	15222	412-323-0335	323-0317
TF: 800-333-0337 ■ *Web:* www.gammasports.com					
Gared Sports Inc 707 N 2nd St Suite 220	Saint Louis	MO	63102	314-421-0044	421-6014
TF: 800-325-2682 ■ *Web:* www.garedsports.com					
Gen-X Sports Inc - A Forzani Co 25 Vanley Crescent	Toronto	ON	M3J2B7	416-636-9993	636-7373
Web: www.genxsportsinc.com					
Gexco 3460 Vine St PO Box 6514	Norco	CA	92860	951-735-4951	479-5154
TF: 800-829-8222					
Gill Athletics Inc 2808 Gemini Ct	Champaign	IL	61822	217-367-8438	367-8440
TF Cust Svc: 800-637-3090 ■ *Web:* www.gillathletics.com					
Goal Oriented Inc 7935 E 14th Ave	Denver	CO	80220	303-393-6040	
TF: 888-393-0888 ■ *Web:* www.soccergoals.com					
Goal Sporting Goods Inc 37 Industrial Pk Rd Box 236	Essex	CT	06426	860-767-9112	767-9121
TF: 800-334-4625 ■ *Web:* www.goalsports.com					
Goals & Poles 7575 Jefferson Hwy	Baton Rouge	LA	70806	225-923-0622	926-0934
TF: 800-275-0317 ■ *Web:* www.goalsandpoles.com					
Goalsetter Systems Inc 1041 Cordova Ave	Lynnville	IA	50153	641-594-4625	594-3343
TF: 800-362-4625 ■ *Web:* www.goalsettersystems.com					

Phone Fax

Golf Galaxy Inc 7275 Flying Cloud Dr … Eden Prairie MN 55344 952-941-8848 941-8846
NASDAQ: GGXY ■ *Web:* www.golfgalaxy.com

Golf Instruments Co 223 Via El Centro … Oceanside CA 92054 760-722-1129
Web: www.golfinstruments.com

GolfCoach Inc 5060 N Royal Atlanta Dr Suite 28 … Tucker GA 30084 770-414-9508 934-6205
TF: 800-772-3813 ■ *Web:* www.golfcoachinc.com

Golfsmith International Inc 11000 N IH-35 … Austin TX 78753 512-837-4810 837-1245
TF Sales: 800-396-0099 ■ *Web:* www.golfsmith.com

GolfWorks The 4820 Jacksontown Rd … Newark OH 43055 740-328-4193 323-0311
TF: 800-848-8358 ■ *Web:* www.golfworks.com

Green Grass Golf Corp 282 Newbridge Rd … Hicksville NY 11801 516-935-6722 935-7064
Web: www.greengrassgolf.com

H O Sports Inc 17622 NE 67th Ct … Redmond WA 98052 425-885-3505 867-5327
TF: 800-938-4646 ■ *Web:* www.hosports.com

Harlick & Co Inc 893 American St … San Carlos CA 94070 650-593-2093 593-9704
Web: www.harlick.com

Harmony Sports 22 Village Dr … Riverside RI 02915 401-490-9334 438-5419
TF: 800-882-3448 ■ *Web:* www.picskate.com

Harrison Hoge Industries 19 N Columbia St … Port Jefferson NY 11777 631-473-7308 473-7398
TF: 800-852-0925 ■ *Web:* www.seaeagle.com

HEAD USA 1 Selleck St … Norwalk CT 06855 203-855-0631 866-9573
TF: 800-874-3235 ■ *Web:* www.head.com

HEAD/Penn Racquet Sports 306 S 45th Ave … Phoenix AZ 85043 602-269-1492 329-7366*
**Fax Area Code:* 888 ■ **Fax:* Cust Svc ■ *TF:* 800-289-7366 ■
Web: www.pennracquet.com

Hillerich & Bradsby Co Inc 800 W Main St … Louisville KY 40202 502-585-5226 585-1179
TF: 800-282-2287 ■ *Web:* www.slugger.com

Hireko Trading Co Inc 16185 Stephens St … City of Industry CA 91745 626-330-0121 367-8912*
**Fax Area Code:* 888 ■ *TF:* 800-367-8912 ■ *Web:* www.hirekogolf.com

Hobie Cat Co 4925 Oceanside Blvd … Oceanside CA 92056 760-758-9100 758-1841
TF: 800-462-4349 ■ *Web:* www.hobiecat.com

Hoops Sporting Equipment Inc 22047 Lutheran Church Rd … Tomball TX 77377 281-351-9822 357-4822
TF: 800-294-4667 ■ *Web:* www.hoopshouston.com

Hoyt USA 543 N Neil Armstrong Rd … Salt Lake City UT 84116 801-363-2990 537-1470
TF: 800-522-4698 ■ *Web:* www.hoytusa.com

Huffy Sports Inc N 53 W 24700 S Corporate Cir … Sussex WI 53089 262-820-3440 500-9756*
**Fax Area Code:* 256 ■ *TF Cust Svc:* 800-558-5234 ■ *Web:* www.huffysports.com

Hunter Co Inc 3300 W 71st Ave … Westminster CO 80030 303-427-4626 428-3980
TF: 800-676-4868 ■ *Web:* www.huntercompany.com

Hyatt Ball Co Ltd PO Box 342 … Fort Edward NY 12828 518-747-0272 747-2619

Innova Recreational Products 11781 A Watertank Rd … Burlington WA 98233 360-707-2855 707-5435
Web: www.innovakayak.com

International Billiards Inc 2311 Washington Ave … Houston TX 77007 713-869-3237 869-8420
Web: www.intlbilliards.com

Intex Recreation Corp
4000 Via Oro Ave Suite 210 PO Box 1440 … Long Beach CA 90801 310-549-5400 513-6905
TF: 800-234-6839 ■ *Web:* www.intexcorp.com

J DeBeer & Son Inc 8 Charles Blvd … Guilderland NY 12084 518-218-7871 218-7993
TF: 800-833-3535 ■ *Web:* www.debeerlacrosse.com

Jayhawk Bowling Supply Inc 355 N Iowa St … Lawrence KS 66044 785-842-3237 842-9667
TF: 800-255-6436 ■ *Web:* www.jayhawkbowling.com

Jerry's Sport Center Inc PO Box 121 … Forest City PA 18421 570-785-9400 388-8452*
**Fax Area Code:* 800 ■ *TF Sales:* 800-234-2612 ■ *Web:* www.jerryssportscenter.com

JKP Sports Inc 19333 SW 18th Ave … Tualatin OR 97062 503-692-1635 691-1100
TF: 800-547-6843 ■ *Web:* www.thejugscompany.com

Johnson Outdoors Inc 555 Main St … Racine WI 53403 262-631-6600 631-6601
NASDAQ: JOUT ■ *TF:* 800-299-2592 ■ *Web:* www.johnsonoutdoors.com

K-2 Sports 4201 6th Ave S … Seattle WA 98108 206-805-4800 972-4066*
**Fax Area Code:* 800 ■ **Fax:* Cust Svc ■ *TF:* 800-972-1617 ■ *Web:* www.k2sports.com

K2 Inc 5818 El Camino Real … Carlsbad CA 92008 760-494-1000 494-1099
NYSE: KTO ■ *TF:* 888-552-7778 ■ *Web:* www.k2inc.net

Kalispel Case Line PO Box 267 … Cusick WA 99119 509-445-1121 445-1082
TF: 800-398-0338 ■ *Web:* www.kalispelcaseline.com

Kangaroo Products Co 111 Kangaroo Dr PO Box 607 … Columbus NC 28722 828-894-8241 894-2718
TF: 800-438-3011 ■ *Web:* www.kangaroogolf.com

Kawasaki Motors Corp USA PO Box 25252 … Santa Ana CA 92799 949-770-0400 460-5600
Web: www.kawasaki.com

Kent Sporting Goods Co Inc 433 Park Ave S … New London OH 44851 419-929-7021 929-1769
TF: 800-537-2970

KL Industries 1790 Sun Dolphin Dr … Muskegon MI 49444 231-733-2725 739-4502
TF: 800-733-2727 ■ *Web:* www.klindustries.com

Klingbeil Shoe Labs Inc 145-01 Jamaica Ave … Jamaica NY 11435 718-297-6864 658-2396
Web: www.klingbeilskatingboots.com

Knight & Hale Game Calls PO Box 1587 … Fort Smith AR 72901 479-782-8971 783-0234
TF: 800-500-9357 ■ *Web:* www.knightandhale.com

Kolpin Outdoors Inc 205 N Depot St … Fox Lake WI 53933 920-928-3118 928-3687
TF: 877-956-5746 ■ *Web:* www.kolpin.com

Kwik Goal Ltd 140 Pacific Dr … Quakertown PA 18951 215-536-2200 536-4309
TF: 800-531-4252 ■ *Web:* www.kwikgoal.com

Kwikee Kwiver Co 6177 Manor St PO Box 130 … Acme MI 49610 231-938-1690 938-2144
TF: 800-346-7001 ■ *Web:* www.kwikeekwiver.com

Lamartek Inc DBA Dive Right 175 NW Washington St … Lake City FL 32055 386-752-1087 755-0613
TF Orders: 800-495-1046 ■ *Web:* www.diverite.com

Lamiglas Inc 1400 Atlantic Ave … Woodland WA 98674 360-225-9436 225-5050
Web: www.lamiglas.com

Laughing Loon 344 Gardiner Rd … Jefferson ME 04348 207-549-3531
Web: www.laughingloon.com

Life-Link International Inc PO Box 2913 … Jackson WY 83001 307-733-2266 733-8469
TF: 800-443-8620 ■ *Web:* www.life-link.com

Lifetime Products Inc PO Box 160010 Freeport Ctr Bldg D-11 … Clearfield UT 84016 801-776-1532 728-1959
TF: 800-242-3865 ■ *Web:* www.lifetime.com

Linden Surfboards 1027 S Cleveland St … Oceanside CA 92054 760-722-8956 722-8972
Web: www.lindensurfboards.com

Lindy Little Joe Inc 1110 Wright St … Brainerd MN 56401 218-829-1714 829-5426
Web: www.lindylittlejoe.com

Lob-Ster Inc 7340 Fulton Ave … North Hollywood CA 91605 818-764-6000 764-6061
Web: www.lobsterinc.com

Local Motion Inc 424 Sumner St … Honolulu HI 96817 808-523-7873 521-6413
TF: 800-841-7613 ■ *Web:* www.localmotioninc.com

Loomis G Inc 1359 Down River Dr … Woodland WA 98674 360-225-6516 225-7169
TF: 800-456-6647 ■ *Web:* www.gloomis.com

Louisville Golf Club Co 2500 Grassland Dr … Louisville KY 40299 502-491-5490 491-6189
TF: 800-456-1631 ■ *Web:* www.louisvillegolf.com

MacGregor Golf Co Inc 1000 Pecan Grove Dr … Albany GA 31701 229-420-7000 420-7064
TF: 800-841-4358 ■ *Web:* www.macgregorgolf.com

MacNeill Engineering Co Inc 289 Elm St … Marlborough MA 01752 508-481-8830 460-9778
TF: 800-652-4267 ■ *Web:* www.champspikes.com

Manns Bait Co 1111 State Docks Rd … Eufaula AL 36027 334-687-5716 687-4352
TF: 800-841-8435 ■ *Web:* www.mannsbait.com

Maravia Corp of Idaho 602 E 45th St … Boise ID 83714 208-322-4949 322-5016
TF: 800-223-7238 ■ *Web:* www.maravia.com

Marble's Cutlery 420 Industrial Park Dr … Gladstone MI 49837 906-428-3710 428-3711
Web: www.marblesoutdoors.com

Marble's Gunsights Inc 420 Industrial Park Dr … Gladstone MI 49837 906-428-3710 428-3711
Web: www.marblearms.com

Mares America Corp 1 Selleck St … Norwalk CT 06855 203-855-0631 866-9573
TF: 800-874-3236 ■ *Web:* www.mares.com

Phone Fax

Martin Archery Inc 3134 W Hwy 12 … Walla Walla WA 99362 509-529-2554 912-2208*
**Fax Area Code:* 800 ■ *TF:* 800-541-8902 ■ *Web:* www.martinarchery.com

Master Industries Inc 14420 Myford Rd … Irvine CA 92606 949-660-0644 660-1678
TF Cust Svc: 800-854-3794 ■ *Web:* www.masterindustries.com

Master Pitching Machine 4200 NE Birmingham Rd … Kansas City MO 64117 816-452-0228 452-7581
TF: 800-878-8228 ■ *Web:* www.masterpitch.com

Masterfit Golf Ltd 140 Phillips Hwy … Jacksonville Beach FL 32256 904-866-4800 886-4805
TF: 866-915-4800 ■ *Web:* www.masterfitgolfltd.com

McHenry Metals Golf Corp 4502 Marquette Ave … Jacksonville FL 32210 866-410-2544 263-1933*
**Fax Area Code:* 410

Michaels of Oregon 1710 Redsoils Ct … Oregon City OR 97045 503-557-0536 655-7546
TF: 800-962-5757 ■ *Web:* www.michaelsoforegon.com

Mister Twister LLC 1401 Commerce St … Minden LA 71055 318-377-8818
TF: 800-344-6331 ■ *Web:* www.mepps.com/mistertwister

Mitsven Surfboards 5151 Sante Fe St Suite F … Pacific Beach CA 92109 858-581-6220 581-6220
Web: www.mitsvensurfboards.com

Mizuno USA 4925 Avalon Ridge Pkwy … Norcross GA 30071 770-441-5553 448-3234
TF: 800-333-7888 ■ *Web:* www.mizunousa.com

Moultrie Feeders 150 Industrial Rd … Alabaster AL 35007 205-664-6700 664-6706
TF: 800-653-3334 ■ *Web:* www.moultriefeeders.com

Murrey International USA 14150 S Figueroa St … Los Angeles CA 90061 310-532-6091 217-0504
TF: 800-421-1022 ■ *Web:* www.murrey.com

Nash Mfg Inc 315 W Ripy St … Fort Worth TX 76110 817-926-5223 924-5111
TF: 800-433-2901 ■ *Web:* www.nashmfg.com

National Billiard Mfg Co 3315 Eugenia Ave … Covington KY 41015 859-431-4129 431-4179
TF: 800-543-0880 ■ *Web:* nationalbilliard.com

Natural Art Inc 2370 S Atlantic Ave … Cocoa Beach FL 32931 321-783-0764 783-3990
Web: www.naturalart.com

Natural Golf Corp 431 Lakeview Ct Suite B … Mount Prospect IL 60056 847-321-4000 795-0101
TF: 888-628-4653 ■ *Web:* www.naturalgolf.com

Nicklaus Golf Equipment Co 7830 Byron Dr … West Palm Beach FL 33404 561-881-7981 881-8214
TF: 800-322-1872 ■ *Web:* www.nicklaus-golf.com

Nike Bauer Hockey Inc 150 Ocean Rd … Greenland NH 03840 603-430-2111 867-4713*
**Fax Area Code:* 800 ■ *TF:* 800-362-3146 ■ *Web:* www.nikebauer.com

Nitro USA 5 Commerce Ave … West Lebanon NH 03784 603-298-9867 298-9872
TF: 877-648-7666 ■ *Web:* www.nitrousa.com

Nocona Athletic Goods Co 901 East Hwy 82 … Nocona TX 76255 940-825-3326 825-4994
TF: 800-433-0957 ■ *Web:* www.nokona.com

North Face Inc 2013 Farallon Dr … San Leandro CA 94577 510-618-3500 618-3571*
**Fax:* Sales ■ *TF:* 800-535-3331 ■ *Web:* www.thenorthface.com

O'Brien International 14615 NE 91st St … Redmond WA 98052 425-202-2100 202-2199
TF: 800-662-7436 ■ *Web:* www.obrien.com

Ocean Kayak 2460 Salashan Loop … Ferndale WA 98248 360-366-4003 366-2628
TF: 800-852-9257 ■ *Web:* www.oceankayak.com

Ocean Management Systems Inc PO Box 146 … Montgomery NY 12549 845-692-3600 692-3623
Web: www.omsdive.com

Oceanic USA 2002 Davis St … San Leandro CA 94577 510-562-0500 569-5404
TF: 800-435-3483 ■ *Web:* www.oceanicworldwide.com

Old Town Canoe Co PO Box 548 … Old Town ME 04468 207-827-5513 827-2779
TF: 800-343-1555 ■ *Web:* www.oldtowncanoe.com

O'Neill Inc 1071 41st Ave PO Box 6300 … Santa Cruz CA 95063 831-475-7500 475-0544
TF: 800-538-0764 ■ *Web:* www.oneill.com

Orlimar G-5140 Flushing Rd … Flushing MI 48433 810-732-0454 732-6662
TF: 888-502-4653 ■ *Web:* www.orlimar.com

Orvis Co Inc 178 Conservation Way … Sunderland VT 05250 802-362-3622 362-3525
TF: 800-541-3541 ■ *Web:* www.orvis.com

Osborne Innovative Products Inc 2221 Garrett St … Enumclaw WA 98022 360-825-4299 825-0163
TF: 800-325-7238 ■ *Web:* www.oipsports.com

Pappy's Golf Shop 4030 N Sinton Rd … Colorado Springs CO 80907 719-633-2064 633-2087
Web: www.coloradoclassic.com

Paragon Aquatics 1351 Rt 55 West Wing … Lagrangeville NY 12540 845-452-5500 452-5426
Web: www.paragonaquatics.com

Penn Fishing Tackle Mfg Co 3028 W Hunting Pk Ave … Philadelphia PA 19132 215-229-9415 223-3017
Web: www.pennreels.com

Perception Inc 111 Kayaker Way … Easley SC 29642 864-859-7518 859-2600
TF: 800-595-2925 ■ *Web:* www.kayaker.com

Ping Inc 2201 W Desert Cove Ave PO Box 82000 … Phoenix AZ 85071 602-870-5000 687-4482*
**Fax:* Cust Svc ■ *TF:* 800-474-6434 ■ *Web:* www.pinggolf.com

Poolmaster Inc 770 W Del Paso Rd … Sacramento CA 95834 916-567-9800 567-9880
TF: 800-854-1776 ■ *Web:* www.poolmaster.net

Porter Athletic Equipment Co 2500 S 25th Ave … Broadview IL 60155 708-338-2000 338-2060
TF: 800-947-6783 ■ *Web:* www.porter-ath.com

Powell Skate One Corp 30 S La Patera Ln … Santa Barbara CA 93117 805-964-1330 964-0511
TF: 800-884-3813 ■ *Web:* www.skateone.com

PRADCO Outdoor Brands Div EBSCO Industries Inc
3601 Jenny Lind Rd … Fort Smith AR 72901 479-782-8971 783-0234
TF: 800-531-1201

Precision Shooting Equipment Inc 2727 N Fairview Ave … Tucson AZ 85705 520-884-9065 884-1479
TF: 800-477-7789 ■ *Web:* www.pse-archery.com

Prince Sports Inc 1 Advantage Ct … Bordentown NJ 08505 609-291-5800 291-5900
TF: 800-283-6647 ■ *Web:* www.princetennis.com

Pure Fishing America 1900 18th St … Spirit Lake IA 51360 712-336-1520 336-5183
TF: 877-777-3850 ■ *Web:* www.purefishing.com

Pure Fishing USA 1900 18th St … Spirit Lake IA 51360 866-447-8736 548-7836*
**Fax Area Code:* 336 ■ *TF:* 800-243-9700 ■ *Web:* www.stren.com

Quiet Flight Inc 109 N Orlando Ave … Cocoa Beach FL 32931 321-783-1530 799-1643

Rapala-Normark Group 10395 Yellow Circle Dr … Minnetonka MN 55343 952-933-7060 933-0046
TF: 800-874-4451 ■ *Web:* www.rapala.com

Rawlings Sporting Goods Co
510 Maryville University Rd Suite 110 … Saint Louis MO 63141 314-819-2800
TF: 800-729-5464 ■ *Web:* www.rawlings.com

Reebok-CCM Hockey Inc 3400 Raymond Lasnir … Montreal QC H4R3L3 514-461-8000 232-9226*
**Fax Area Code:* 800 ■ *Web:* www.thehockeycompany.com

Resilite Sports Products PO Box 764 … Sunbury PA 17801 570-473-3529 473-8988
TF: 800-326-9307 ■ *Web:* www.resilite.com

Riedell Shoes Inc 122 Cannon River Ave … Red Wing MN 55066 651-388-8251 385-5500
TF: 800-698-6893 ■ *Web:* www.riedellskates.com

RIO Products International Inc 5050 S Yellowstone Hwy … Idaho Falls ID 83402 208-524-7760 524-7763
TF: 800-553-0838 ■ *Web:* www.rioproducts.com

RL Winston Rod Co 500 S Main St … Twin Bridges MT 59754 406-684-5674 684-5533
TF: 866-946-7637 ■ *Web:* www.winstonrods.com

Roller Derby Skate Corp 311 W Edwards St … Litchfield IL 62056 217-324-3961 324-2213
Web: www.rollerderby.com

Rollerblade USA Corp 3705 Quakerbridge Rd Suite 207 … Hamilton NJ 08619 609-249-1700 249-1790
TF: 800-232-7655 ■ *Web:* www.rollerblade.com

Rome Specialty Co Inc Rosco Div 501 W Embargo St … Rome NY 13440 315-337-8200 339-2523
TF: 800-794-8357 ■ *Web:* www.roscoinc.com

Ross Reels 1 Ponderosa Ct … Montrose CO 81401 970-249-1212 249-1834
TF: 800-336-1050 ■ *Web:* www.rossreels.com

Rossignol USA 1441 Ute Blvd Suite 200 PO Box 981060 … Park City UT 84098 435-252-3300 252-3331
TF: 888-243-6722 ■ *Web:* www.rossignol.com

Sage Mfg Corp 8500 NE Day Rd … Bainbridge Island WA 98110 206-842-6608 842-6830
TF: 800-533-3004 ■ *Web:* www.sageflyfish.com

Saint Croix of Park Falls Ltd PO Box 279 … Park Falls WI 54552 715-762-3226 762-3293
TF: 800-826-7042 ■ *Web:* www.stcroixrods.com

Sampo Inc 119 Remsen Rd … Barneveld NY 13304 315-896-2606 896-6575
Web: www.sampoinc.com

	City	State	Zip	Phone	Fax
Saunders Archery Co 1874 14th Ave PO Box 1707	Columbus	NE	68601	402-564-7176	564-3260
TF Cust Svc: 800-228-1408 ■ *Web:* www.sausa.com					
Schutt Sports 1200 E Union Ave PO Box 426	Litchfield	IL	62056	217-324-2712	324-2732
TF: 800-637-2047 ■ *Web:* www.schuttsports.com					
Scott Fly Rod Co 2355 Air Park Way	Montrose	CO	81401	970-249-3180	249-4172
TF: 800-728-7208 ■ *Web:* www.scottflyrod.com					
Scott USA Inc PO Box 2030	Sun Valley	ID	83353	208-622-1000	622-1005
TF: 800-292-5874 ■ *Web:* www.scottusa.com					
SCP Pool Corp 109 Northpark Blvd 4th Fl	Covington	LA	70433	985-892-5521	892-1657
NASDAQ: POOL ■ *Web:* www.scppool.com					
Seeker Fishing Rods 1340 W Cowles St	Long Beach	CA	90813	562-491-0076	435-7599
TF: 800-373-3537 ■ *Web:* www.seekerrod.com					
Shakespeare Fishing Tackle Co 3801 Westmore Dr	Columbia	SC	29223	803-754-7000	754-7342
TF Cust Svc: 800-347-3759 ■ *Web:* www.shakespeare-fishing.com					
Sheldons' Inc 626 Center St	Antigo	WI	54409	715-623-2382	623-3001
Web: www.mepps.com					
Shimano American Corp 1 Holland Dr	Irvine	CA	92618	949-951-5003	768-0920
Web: www.shimano.com					
Sierra Designs Inc 2011 Cherry St Suite 202	Louisville	CO	80027	303-262-3050	262-3051
TF: 800-635-0461 ■ *Web:* www.sierradesigns.com					
Simms Fishing Products Corp 101 Evergreen Dr	Bozeman	MT	59715	406-585-3557	585-3562
TF: 866-585-3570 ■ *Web:* www.simmsfishing.com					
Spalding 150 Brookdale Dr	Springfield	MA	01104	413-735-1400	735-1570
TF Cust Svc: 800-772-5346 ■ *Web:* www.spalding.com					
Sport Supply Group Inc 1901 Diplomat Dr	Dallas	TX	75234	972-484-9484	243-0149
TF: 800-527-7510 ■ *Web:* www.sportsupplygroup.com					
SportRack 700 Bernard	Granby	QC	J2G9H7	800-561-0716	
Web: www.sportrack.com					
Standard Golf Co 6620 Nordic Dr	Cedar Falls	IA	50613	319-266-2638	266-9627
TF: 800-553-1707 ■ *Web:* www.standardgolf.com					
Stearns Inc 1100 Stearns Dr	Sauk Rapids	MN	56379	320-252-1642	252-4425
TF: 800-328-3208 ■ *Web:* www.stearnsinc.com					
Stewart Surfboards 2102 S El Camino Real	San Clemente	CA	92673	949-492-1085	492-2344
Web: www.stewartsurfboards.com					
Stockli Ski USA Inc PO Box 370206	Denver	CO	80237	303-220-9737	220-9745
TF: 800-638-6284 ■ *Web:* www.stockli.com					
Stone Legacy Corp S1075 Westland Dr	Spring Valley	WI	54767	715-778-5079	778-7081
TF Sales: 888-858-4826 ■ *Web:* www.stonelegacy.com					
Storm Products Inc 165 S 800 West	Brigham City	UT	84302	435-723-0403	734-0338
TF: 888-450-6920 ■ *Web:* www.stormbowling.com					
Straight Line Sports LLC 17230 NE Sacramento St	Portland	OR	97230	866-426-7673	869-7673
TF: 800-248-5564 ■ *Web:* www.straightlinewatersports.com					
Strikeforce Bowling LLC 1200 S 54th Ave	Cicero	IL	60804	708-863-1200	222-1400
TF: 800-297-8555 ■ *Web:* www.krstrikeforce.com					
StrikeMaster Corp 17217 198 Ave	Big Lake	MN	55309	763-263-8999	263-8986
Web: www.strikemaster.com					
Summit Treestands LLC 715 Summit Dr	Decatur	AL	35601	256-353-0634	353-9818
Web: www.summitstands.com					
Talon 1552 Down River Dr PO Box 907	Woodland	WA	98674	360-225-8247	225-7737
Web: www.talon-graphite.com					
Tampa G Mfg Co 5105 S Lois Ave	Tampa	FL	33611	813-229-1559	902-1558
TF: 800-365-1559 ■ *Web:* www.tampa-g.com					
TaylorMade - adidas Golf 5545 Fermi Ct	Carlsbad	CA	92008	760-918-6000	918-6014
TF Cust Svc: 800-456-8633 ■ *Web:* www.taylormadegolf.com					
Team Cobra Products 1750 Wadsworth Rd Rear Bldg	Akron	OH	44320	800-336-7784	755-0694*
**Fax Area Code:* 866 ■ *TF:* 800-336-7784 ■ *Web:* www.cobraproducts.com					
Tecnica USA 19 Technology Dr	West Lebanon	NH	03784	603-298-8032	298-5790
TF: 800-258-3897 ■ *Web:* www.tecnicausa.com					
Thomas & Thomas Rodmakers Inc 627 Barton Rd	Greenfield	MA	01301	413-774-5436	774-5437
Web: www.thomasandthomas.com					
Tommy Armour Golf Co 225 Byers Rd	Miamisburg	OH	45342	416-630-4996	799-4337*
**Fax Area Code:* 866 ■ *TF Cust Svc:* 800-723-4653 ■ *Web:* www.tommyarmourgolf.com					
Toobs Inc 349 B Quintana Rd	Morro Bay	CA	93442	805-772-5742	772-5781
TF: 800-795-8662 ■ *Web:* www.toobs.com					
Top-Flite Golf Co 425 Meadow St	Chicopee	MA	01021	413-536-1200	322-2673
TF: 866-834-6532 ■ *Web:* www.topflite.com					
True Temper Sports 8275 Tournament Dr Suite 200	Memphis	TN	38125	901-746-2000	746-2160
TF: 800-355-8783 ■ *Web:* www.truetemper.com					
Tuf-Wear USA 1001 Industrial Ave	North Platte	NE	69101	308-532-0187	532-9133
TF: 800-445-5210					
UK International 13400 Danielson St	Poway	CA	92064	858-513-9100	513-9111
TF: 800-852-7483 ■ *Web:* www.uwkinetics.com					
Victoria Skimboards 2955 Laguna Canyon Rd Suite 1	Laguna Beach	CA	92651	949-494-0059	494-5485
Web: www.vicskim.com					
Virtual Turf 1800 Industrial Pk Dr PO Box 732	Grand Haven	MI	49417	616-847-9121	847-9337
TF: 800-560-7795 ■ *Web:* www.virtualturf.com					
Volkl Sport America 19 Technology Dr	West Lebanon	NH	03784	603-298-0314	298-6134
TF: 800-264-4579 ■ *Web:* www.volkl.com					
We-No-Nah Canoe PO Box 247	Winona	MN	55987	507-454-5430	454-5448
Web: www.wenonah.com					
Weed USA Inc 5780 Harrow Glen Ct	Galena	OH	43021	740-548-3881	548-3882
TF: 800-933-3758 ■ *Web:* www.weedusa.com					
Wileys Custom Water Skis 1417 S Trenton	Seattle	WA	98108	206-762-1300	762-7339
TF: 800-962-0785 ■ *Web:* www.wileyski.com					
Wilson Sporting Goods Co 8700 W Bryn Mawr Ave Suite LL	Chicago	IL	60631	773-714-6400	714-4565
Web: www.wilson.com					
Winston Rods 500 S Main St	Twin Bridges	MT	59754	406-684-5674	684-5533
TF: 866-946-7637 ■ *Web:* www.winstonrods.com					
Wittek Golf Supply Co Inc 3865 N Commercial Ave	Northbrook	IL	60052	773-463-2636	463-2150
TF: 800-869-1800 ■ *Web:* www.wittekgolf.com					
Women's Golf Unlimited Inc 18 Gloria Ln	Fairfield	NJ	07004	973-227-7783	227-7018
TF: 800-526-2250 ■ *Web:* www.womensgolfunlimited.com					
Worth Co PO Box 88	Stevens Point	WI	54481	715-344-6081	344-3021
TF: 800-944-1899 ■ *Web:* www.worthco.com					
Worth Sporting Goods 510 Maryville University Dr	Saint Louis	MO	63141	314-819-2800	
TF Cust Svc: 800-282-9637 ■ *Web:* www.worthsports.com					
Wright & McGill Co DBA Eagle Claw Fishing Tackle Co 4245 E 46th Ave	Denver	CO	80216	303-321-1481	321-4750
TF: 800-628-0108 ■ *Web:* www.eagleclaw.com					
Yakima Bait Co Inc PO Box 310	Granger	WA	98932	509-854-1311	854-2263
Web: www.yakimabait.com					
Yamaha Motor Corp USA 6555 Katella Ave	Cypress	CA	90630	714-761-7300	761-7302
TF Cust Svc: 800-962-7926 ■ *Web:* www.yamaha-motor.com					
Yonex Corp 20140 S Western Ave	Torrance	CA	90501	310-793-3800	793-3899
TF: 800-449-6639 ■ *Web:* www.yonex.com					
Zeagle Systems Inc 37150 Chancey Rd	Zephyrhills	FL	33541	813-782-5568	782-5569
Web: www.zeagle.com					
Zebco Corp 6101 E Apache St	Tulsa	OK	74115	918-836-5581	836-0154
TF: 800-588-9030 ■ *Web:* www.zebco.com					

714 SPORTING GOODS STORES

	City	State	Zip	Phone	Fax
2nd Swing Inc 13031 Ridgedale Dr	Minnetonka	MN	55305	952-546-1906	546-1908
Web: www.2ndswing.com					
Academy Sports & Outdoors 1800 N Mason Rd	Katy	TX	77449	281-646-5200	646-5204
TF: 877-999-9856 ■ *Web:* www.academy.com					
Adventure 16 Inc 4620 Alvarado Canyon Rd	San Diego	CA	92120	619-283-2362	283-7956*
**Fax:* Hum Res ■ *TF:* 800-854-2672 ■ *Web:* www.adventure16.com					
Alpina Sports USA 93 Etna Rd	Lebanon	NH	03766	603-448-3101	448-1586
TF: 800-425-7462 ■ *Web:* www.alpinasports.com					
Altrec.com Inc 725 Umatilla Ave	Redmond	OR	97756	541-316-2400	
TF Cust Svc: 800-369-3949 ■ *Web:* www.altrec.com					
Any Mountain Ltd 71 Tamal Vista Blvd	Corte Madera	CA	94925	415-927-2400	927-3388
TF: 800-992-4844 ■ *Web:* www.anymountain.net					
Aspen Sports Ltd 408 E Cooper Ave	Aspen	CO	81611	970-925-6331	925-2755
TF: 800-544-6648 ■ *Web:* www.aspensports.com					
Athletic Supply Co 16101 NE 87th St	Redmond	WA	98052	425-882-1456	497-4713
Web: www.ascosports.com					
Austad's Golf Inc 2801 E 10th St	Sioux Falls	SD	57103	605-332-3373	332-3373
TF: 800-444-1234 ■ *Web:* www.austads.com					
Backwoods Equipment 221 N Main St Suite 221	Wichita	KS	67202	316-267-4297	267-5631
Web: www.backwoods.com					
Baseball Express Inc 1051 E Nakoma St	San Antonio	TX	78216	210-348-7000	525-9339
TF Cust Svc: 800-937-4824 ■ *Web:* www.baseballexp.com					
Bass Pro Shops Outdoor World 1935 S Campbell Ave	Springfield	MO	65807	417-887-7334	885-0072
Web: www.basspro.com					
Big 5 Sporting Goods Corp 2525 E El Segundo Blvd	El Segundo	CA	90245	310-536-0611	297-7580
NASDAQ: BGFV ■ *TF:* 800-367-2445 ■ *Web:* www.big5sportinggoods.com					
Big Bear Sports Centers Inc 2618 King Ave W	Billings	MT	59102	406-652-5777	652-1220
Bike Line Corp 700 Lawrence Dr	West Chester	PA	19380	610-429-4370	429-4295
Web: www.bikeline.com					
Bob Ward & Sons Inc 3015 Paxson St	Missoula	MT	59801	406-728-3220	728-5230
TF: 800-800-5083 ■ *Web:* www.bobwards.com					
Boyne Country Sports 1200 Bay View Rd	Petoskey	MI	49770	231-439-4906	439-4960
TF: 800-462-6963 ■ *Web:* www.boyne.com/skigolf					
Brady's Sportsman's Surplus Inc 2315 Brooks St	Missoula	MT	59801	406-721-5501	728-1112
TF: 800-473-4867 ■ *Web:* www.sportsmanssurplus.com					
Burly Bear Inc DBA ProLine Billiards Etc 700 N Hwy 17-92	Longwood	FL	32750	407-339-8700	339-4326
TF: 800-780-7799 ■ *Web:* www.prolinebilliards.com					
Busy Body Home Fitness 1000 Studebaker Rd Suite 1	Long Beach	CA	90815	562-296-1095	493-3798
TF: 800-466-3348 ■ *Web:* www.busybody.com					
Cabela's Inc 1 Cabela Dr	Sidney	NE	69160	308-254-5505	254-6102*
NYSE: CAB ■ **Fax:* Mktg ■ *TF:* 800-237-8888 ■ *Web:* www.cabelas.com					
Camping World Inc 650 Three Springs Rd	Bowling Green	KY	42104	270-781-2718	781-3968
TF Cust Svc: 800-626-3636 ■ *Web:* www.campingworld.com					
Campmor Inc 28 Parkway	Upper Saddle River	NJ	07458	201-825-8300	236-3601
TF Orders: 800-526-4784 ■ *Web:* www.campmor.com					
Century Martial Art Supply Inc 1000 Century Blvd	Midwest City	OK	73110	405-732-2226	737-8954
TF Sales: 800-626-2787 ■ *Web:* www.centuryma.com					
Champs Sports 311 Manatee Ave W	Bradenton	FL	34205	941-748-0577	741-7582*
**Fax:* Mktg ■ *TF:* 800-991-6813 ■ *Web:* www.champssports.com					
Chick's Sporting Goods Inc 979 Village Oaks Dr	Covina	CA	91724	626-915-1685	339-1713
Web: www.chickssportinggoods.com					
Christy Sports LLC 875 Parfet St	Lakewood	CO	80215	303-237-6321	233-5946
Web: christysports.com					
Crown Enterprises Inc DBA Sportsman & Ski Haus 40 E Idaho St	Kalispell	MT	59901	406-755-6484	758-7425
Web: www.sportsmanskihaus.com					
D & R Sports Center Inc 8178 W Main St	Kalamazoo	MI	49009	269-372-2277	372-9072
TF: 800-992-1520 ■ *Web:* www.dandrsports.com					
Dick's Sporting Goods Inc 300 Industry Dr	Pittsburgh	PA	15275	724-273-3400	695-2574
NYSE: DKS ■ *TF:* 800-690-7655 ■ *Web:* www.dickssportinggoods.com					
Dixie Bocock Sporting Goods DBA Dixie Sporting Goods 501 Deacon Blvd	Winston-Salem	NC	27105	336-724-2421	724-7496
TF: 888-262-6251 ■ *Web:* www.dixiesport.com					
Dixie Gun Works Inc PO Box 130	Union City	TN	38281	731-885-0700	885-0440
TF Orders: 800-238-6785 ■ *Web:* www.dixiegun.com					
Downtown Athletic Store Inc PO Box 6247	Charlottesville	VA	22906	434-975-0750	975-0754
TF: 888-889-6974 ■ *Web:* www.downtownathletic.com					
Dunham's Sports 5000 Dixie Hwy	Waterford	MI	48329	248-674-4991	674-1407
Web: www.dunhamssports.com					
Eastern Mountain Sports Inc 1 Vose Farm Rd	Peterborough	NH	03458	603-924-9571	924-9138
TF: 888-463-6367 ■ *Web:* www.ems.com					
Ed Shirley & Sons Sports Inc 5802 W Dempster St	Morton Grove	IL	60053	847-966-5900	966-9174
Edwin Watts Golf Shops Inc 20 Hill Ave NW	Fort Walton Beach	FL	32548	850-244-2066	244-5217*
**Fax:* Sales ■ *TF:* 800-874-0146 ■ *Web:* www.edwinwatts.com					
Efinger Sporting Goods Co Inc 513 W Union Ave	Bound Brook	NJ	08805	732-356-0604	805-9860
Web: www.efingersportinggoods.com					
Erie Sport Store Inc 701 State St	Erie	PA	16501	814-452-2289	453-5840
TF: 800-333-6812 ■ *Web:* www.eriesportstore.com					
Fanzz 1832 W 2770 South Suite 10	Salt Lake City	UT	84119	801-325-2788	325-2736
TF: 888-326-9946 ■ *Web:* www.fanzz.com					
Fitness Zone 7540 S Memorial Pkwy Suite D	Huntsville	AL	35802	800-875-9145	883-2115*
**Fax Area Code:* 256 ■ *TF Cust Svc:* 800-875-9145 ■ *Web:* www.fitnesszone.com					
Forzani Group Ltd 824 41st Ave NE	Calgary	AB	T2E3R3	403-717-1400	717-1491
Web: www.forzanigroup.com					
Gander Mountain Co 180 E 5th St Suite 1300	Saint Paul	MN	55101	651-325-4300	
NASDAQ: GMTN ■ *TF:* 888-542-6337 ■ *Web:* www.gandermountain.com					
Gerry Cosby & Co Inc 3 Pennsylvania Plaza	New York	NY	10001	212-563-6464	967-0876
TF: 877-563-6464 ■ *Web:* www.cosbysports.com					
GI Joe's Inc 9805 GW Boeckman Rd	Wilsonville	OR	97070	503-682-2242	682-7200
Web: www.joessports.com					
Golf Etc of America Inc 2201 Commercial Ln	Granbury	TX	76048	817-279-7888	579-1793
TF: 800-806-8633 ■ *Web:* www.golfetc.com					
Golf Shack Inc 1631 N Bell School Rd	Rockford	IL	61107	815-397-3709	397-7593
TF: 888-446-5390 ■ *Web:* www.golfshack.com					
Golf USA 3705 W Memorial Rd Suite 801	Oklahoma City	OK	73134	405-751-0015	755-0065
TF: 800-488-1107 ■ *Web:* www.golfusainc.com					
Golfsmith International Inc 11000 N IH-35	Austin	TX	78753	512-837-4810	837-1245
TF Sales: 800-396-0099 ■ *Web:* www.golfsmith.com					
Gregg's Greenlake Cycle 7007 Woodlawn Ave NE	Seattle	WA	98115	206-523-1822	523-5330
Web: www.greggscycles.com					
Gym Source 40 E 52nd St	New York	NY	10022	212-688-4222	750-2886
TF: 800-496-7687 ■ *Web:* www.gymsource.com					
Hibbett Sporting Goods Inc 451 Industrial Ln	Birmingham	AL	35211	205-942-4292	912-7290
NASDAQ: HIBB ■ *Web:* www.hibbett.com					
Hoigaards Inc 5425 Excelsior Blvd	Saint Louis Park	MN	55416	952-929-1351	929-2669
TF: 800-266-8157 ■ *Web:* www.hoigaards.com					
In The Swim Inc 320 Industrial Dr	West Chicago	IL	60185	630-876-1080	766-5329*
**Fax Area Code:* 800 ■ *TF:* 800-288-7946 ■ *Web:* www.intheswim.com					
Island Water Sports Inc 1985 NE 2nd St	Deerfield Beach	FL	33441	954-427-4929	360-7873
TF: 800-873-0375 ■ *Web:* www.islandwatersports.com					
Jan's Mountain Outfitters 1600 Park Ave PO Box 280	Park City	UT	84060	435-649-4949	649-7511
TF: 800-745-1020 ■ *Web:* www.jans.com					

				Phone	Fax
Jay's Sporting Goods Inc 8800 S Clare Ave	Clare	MI	48617	989-386-3475	386-3496
Web: www.jaysoutdoors.com					
Kittery Trading Post 301 US Rt 1	Kittery	ME	03904	207-439-2700	439-8001
TF: 888-587-6246 ■ *Web:* www.kitterytradingpost.com					
Laacke & Joys Co 1433 N Water St	Milwaukee	WI	53202	414-271-7885	271-2330
Web: www.laackeandjoys.com					
Langhorne Ski Shop 543 Lincoln Hwy	Fairless Hills	PA	19030	215-295-4240	295-5341
TF: 800-523-8850					
Leslie's Swimming Pool Supplies					
3925 E Broadway Rd Suite 100	Phoenix	AZ	85040	602-366-3999	366-3944
TF: 800-233-8063 ■ *Web:* www.lesliespool.com					
Lombardi Sports Inc 1600 Jackson St	San Francisco	CA	94109	415-771-0600	771-1891
Web: www.lombardisports.com					
MC Sports 3070 Shaffer Ave SE	Grand Rapids	MI	49512	616-942-2600	942-2786
TF: 800-626-1762 ■ *Web:* www.mcsports.com					
Mel Cotton's Sales & Rentals Inc 1266 W San Carlos St	San Jose	CA	95126	408-287-5994	298-3536
Web: www.melcottons.com					
Modell's Sporting Goods 498 7th Ave 20th Fl	New York	NY	10018	212-822-1000	822-1090
TF: 800-250-7405 ■ *Web:* www.modells.com					
Nill Brothers Sports 2814 S 44th St	Kansas City	KS	66106	913-384-4242	384-0107
Web: www.nillbros.com					
NRC Sports Inc 603 Pleasant St	Paxton	MA	01612	508-852-8206	852-8206
TF: 800-243-5033 ■ *Web:* www.nrcsports.com					
Olympia Sports 5 Bradley Dr	Westbrook	ME	04092	207-854-2794	854-4168
Web: www.olympiasports.net					
OMNI Fitness Equipment Inc 60 Oxford Dr	Moonachie	NJ	07074	201-334-1100	
TF: 877-875-6664 ■ *Web:* www.omnifitness.com					
Paragon Sporting Goods Corp 867 Broadway	New York	NY	10003	212-255-8036	929-1831
Web: www.paragonsports.com					
Pedigree Ski Shop Inc 355 Mamaroneck Ave	White Plains	NY	10605	914-948-2995	948-1599
Web: www.pedigreeskishop.com					
Performance Inc 1 Performance Way	Chapel Hill	NC	27514	919-933-9113	942-5431
TF Cust Svc: 800-727-2433 ■ *Web:* www.performancebike.com					
Peter Glenn Ski & Sports					
2901 W Oakland Pk Blvd Suite B-12	Fort Lauderdale	FL	33311	954-484-7800	739-5724
TF: 800-818-0946 ■ *Web:* www.peterglenn.com					
Pinch A Penny Inc PO Box 6025	Clearwater	FL	33758	727-531-8913	536-8066
TF: 800-509-5571 ■ *Web:* www.pinchapenny.com					
Play It Again Sports 4200 Dahlberg Dr Suite 100	Minneapolis	MN	55422	763-520-8500	520-8470
TF: 800-433-2540 ■ *Web:* www.playitagainsports.com					
Princeton Ski Shop 380 Saw Mill River Rd	Elmsford	NY	10523	914-592-4141	592-6110
TF: 800-255-7547 ■ *Web:* www.princetonski.com					
Pro Golf Inc 37735 Enterprise Ct Suite 600	Farmington Hills	MI	48331	248-994-0553	489-9334
Web: www.progolfamerica.com					
ProLine Billiards Etc 700 N Hwy 17-92	Longwood	FL	32750	407-339-8700	339-4326
TF: 800-780-7799 ■ *Web:* www.prolinebilliards.com					
Ramsey Outdoor Store 240 SR 17 N	Paramus	NJ	07652	201-261-5000	261-2742
TF: 800-699-5874 ■ *Web:* www.ramseyoutdoor.com					
Recreational Equipment Inc (REI) 6750 S 228th St	Kent	WA	98032	253-395-3780	395-4368
TF Orders: 800-426-4840 ■ *Web:* www.rei.com					
Ron Jon Surf Shop 3850 S Banana River Blvd	Cocoa Beach	FL	32931	321-799-8880	799-8882*
*Fax: Mktg ■ *TF:* 888-757-8737 ■ *Web:* www.ronjons.com					
Ski Market 265 Winter St 2nd Fl	Waltham	MA	02451	781-890-1212	890-1811
Web: www.skimarket.com					
Ski Stop 197 S Service Rd	Plainview	NY	11803	516-249-7980	249-5636
Web: www.skistop.com					
Special Tee Golf of Florida 620 E Altamonte Dr	Altamonte Springs	FL	32701	407-834-1900	834-1689
Web: www.specialteegolf.com					
Sport Chalet Inc 1 Sport Chalet Dr	La Canada	CA	91011	818-790-2717	949-5301
NASDAQ: SPCHB ■ *TF:* 888-801-9162 ■ *Web:* www.sportchalet.com					
Sports Authority Inc 1050 W Hampden Ave	Englewood	CO	80110	303-200-5050	832-4738
NYSE: TSA ■ *TF:* 800-666-8143 ■ *Web:* www.thesportsauthority.com					
Sports Endeavors Inc 431 US Hwy 70-A E	Hillsborough	NC	27278	919-644-6800	644-6808
TF: 800-934-3876 ■ *Web:* www.sportsendeavors.com					
Sportsman's Warehouse 7035 S Hightech Dr	Midvale	UT	84047	801-566-6681	304-4301
Web: www.sportsmanswarehouse.com					
Sun & Ski Sports 4001 Greenbriar St Suite 100	Stafford	TX	77477	281-340-5000	340-5020
Web: www.sunandski.com					
Tri-State Distributors 1104 W Pullman Rd	Moscow	ID	83843	208-882-4555	882-8427
TF: 877-878-2835 ■ *Web:* www.t-state.com					
Turner's Outdoorsman 1041 S Mildred Ave	Ontario	CA	91761	909-923-3009	923-3022
Web: www.turners.com					
Val Surf Inc 4810 Whitsett Ave	Valley Village	CA	91607	818-769-6977	769-4318
TF: 888-825-7873 ■ *Web:* www.valsurf.com					
Wheel & Sprocket Inc 5722 S 108th St	Hales Corners	WI	53130	414-529-6600	529-6605
TF: 800-362-4537 ■ *Web:* wheelandsprocket.com					
Winmark Corp 4200 Dahlberg Dr Suite 100	Minneapolis	MN	55422	763-520-8500	520-8410
NASDAQ: WINA ■ *TF:* 800-433-2540 ■ *Web:* www.winmarkcorporation.com					
World of Golf 4500 Tamiami Trail N	Naples	FL	34103	239-263-4999	263-7423
TF: 800-505-9998 ■ *Web:* www.worldofgolf.com					

715 SPORTS COMMISSIONS & REGULATORY AGENCIES - STATE

				Phone	Fax
Arizona Racing Dept 1110 W Washington St Suite 260	Phoenix	AZ	85007	602-364-1700	364-1703
Web: www.azracing.gov					
Arkansas					
Athletic Commission 9110 Lew Dr	Little Rock	AR	72209	501-666-5544	666-5546
Racing Commission 1515 W 7th St Rm 505	Little Rock	AR	72203	501-682-1467	682-5273
Web: www.state.ar.us/dfa/racing					
California					
Athletic Commission 1424 Howe Ave Suite 33	Sacramento	CA	95825	916-263-2195	263-2197
Web: www.dca.ca.gov/csac					
Horse Racing Board 1010 Hurley Way Rm 300	Sacramento	CA	95825	916-263-6000	263-6042
Web: www.chrb.ca.gov					
Delaware					
Harness Racing Commission 2320 S Dupont Hwy	Dover	DE	19901	302-698-4599	697-6287
Web: www.state.de.us/deptagri/harness					
Thoroughbred Racing Commission 2320 S DuPont Hwy	Dover	DE	19901	302-698-4599	463-1376*
*Fax Area Code: 512 ■ *Web:* www.state.de.us/deptagri/thoroughbred					
Florida State Boxing Commission 1940 N Monroe St	Tallahassee	FL	32399	850-488-8500	922-2249
Web: www.state.fl.us/dbpr/sbc					
Idaho Racing Commission PO Box 700	Meridian	ID	83680	208-884-7080	884-7098
Web: www.isp.state.id.us/race					
Illinois Racing Board 100 W Randolph St Suite 11-100	Chicago	IL	60601	312-814-2600	814-5062
Web: www.state.il.us/agency/irb					
Indiana Horse Racing Commission					
150 W Market St Suite 530	Indianapolis	IN	46204	317-233-3119	233-4470
Web: www.in.gov/ihrc					
Kentucky					
Athletic Commission 100 Airport Rd Suite 300	Frankfort	KY	40601	502-564-7760	564-3969
Web: ppr.ky.gov/kac					
Horse Racing Authority 4063 Iron Works Pkwy Bldg B	Lexington	KY	40602	859-246-2040	246-2039
Web: krc.ppr.ky.gov					
Louisiana Racing Commission					
320 N Carrollton Ave Suite 2-B	New Orleans	LA	70119	504-483-4000	483-4898
Web: horseracing.la.gov					
Maryland					
Racing Commission 500 N Calvert St Rm 201	Baltimore	MD	21202	410-230-6330	333-8308
Web: www.dllr.state.md.us/racing					
State Athletic Commission 500 N Calvert St Rm 304	Baltimore	MD	21202	410-230-6223	333-6314
Web: www.dllr.state.md.us/license/occprof/athlet.html					
Massachusetts					
State Boxing Commission 1 Ashburton Pl Rm 1301	Boston	MA	02108	617-727-3200	727-5732
Web: www.mass.gov/mbc					
State Racing Commission 1 Ashurton Pl Rm 1313	Boston	MA	02108	617-727-2581	227-6062
Web: www.state.ma.us/src					
Michigan Racing Commissioners Office					
525 W Allegan St PO Box 30773	Lansing	MI	48909	517-335-1420	241-3018
Web: www.michigan.gov/horseracing/					
Montana Horse Racing Board PO Box 200512	Helena	MT	59620	406-444-4287	444-4305
Web: www.mt.gov/liv/HorseRacing/index.asp					
Nebraska State Racing Commission					
301 Centennial Mall S 6th Fl PO Box 95014	Lincoln	NE	68509	402-471-4155	471-2339
Web: www.horseracing.state.ne.us					
Nevada State Athletic Commission					
555 E Washington Ave Suite 3300	Las Vegas	NV	89101	702-486-2575	486-2577
Web: boxing.nv.gov					
New Jersey					
Racing Commission 140 E Front St	Trenton	NJ	08625	609-292-0613	599-1785
Web: www.njpublicsafety.org/racing					
State Athletic Control Board 140 E Front St	Trenton	NJ	08625	609-292-0317	292-3756
Web: www.state.nj.us/lps/sacb					
New Mexico Racing Commission					
300 San Mateo NE Suite 110	Albuquerque	NM	87108	505-841-6400	841-6413
Web: nmrc.state.nm.us					
New York (State)					
Athletic Commission 123 William St 20th Fl	New York	NY	10038	212-417-5700	417-4987
TF: 866-269-3769 ■ *Web:* www.dos.state.ny.us/athletic					
Racing & Wagering Board 1 Waterliet Ave Ext Suite 2	Albany	NY	12206	518-453-8460	453-8490
Web: www.racing.state.ny.us					
North Dakota Racing Commission 500 N 9th St	Bismarck	ND	58501	701-328-4290	328-4300
Web: www.ndracingcommission.com					
Ohio Racing Commission 77 S High St 18th Fl	Columbus	OH	43215	614-466-2757	466-1900
Web: www.racing.ohio.gov					
Pennsylvania State Athletic Commission 2601 N 3rd St	Harrisburg	PA	17110	717-787-5720	783-0824
Web: www.dos.state.pa.us/sac					
Rhode Island Racing & Athletics Div 233 Richmond St	Providence	RI	02903	401-222-6541	222-6131
Web: www.dbr.state.ri.us/race-athletics.html					
South Dakota Gaming Commission 221 W Capitol Ave Suite 101	Pierre	SD	57501	605-773-6050	773-6053
Web: www.state.sd.us/drr2/reg/gaming					
Tennessee Boxing & Racing Board					
500 James Robertson Pkwy 2nd Fl	Nashville	TN	37243	615-741-2384	741-5995
Texas Racing Commission 8505 Cross Park Dr Suite 110	Austin	TX	78754	512-833-6699	833-6907
Web: www.txrc.state.tx.us					
Utah Sports Commission 201 S Main St Suite 2002	Salt Lake City	UT	84111	801-328-2372	328-2389
Web: www.utahsportscommission.com					
Virginia Racing Commission 3600 W Broad St	Richmond	VA	23230	804-367-8590	367-2474
Web: www.vrc.virginia.gov					
Washington Horse Racing Commission					
6326 Martin Way Suite 209	Olympia	WA	98516	360-459-6462	459-6461
Web: www.whrc.wa.gov					
West Virginia Racing Commission 106 Dee Dr	Charleston	WV	25311	304-558-2150	558-6319
Web: www.wvf.state.wv.us/racing					

SPORTS FACILITIES

SEE Motor Speedways p. 1980; Racing & Racetracks p. 2161; Stadiums & Arenas p. 2329

716 SPORTS TEAMS - BASEBALL

SEE ALSO Associations & Organizations - General - Sports Organizations p. 1314

				Phone	Fax
Major League Baseball (Office of the Commissioner)					
245 Park Ave 31st Fl	New York	NY	10167	212-931-7800	949-5650*
*Fax: PR ■ *TF Cust Svc:* 800-704-2937 ■ *Web:* www.mlb.com					
Arizona Diamondbacks 401 E Jefferson St	Phoenix	AZ	85004	602-462-6500	462-6600
Web: diamondbacks.mlb.com					
Atlanta Braves PO Box 4064	Atlanta	GA	30302	404-522-7630	614-1329
Web: atlanta.braves.mlb.com					
Baltimore Orioles					
Oriole Park at Camden Yards 333 W Camden St	Baltimore	MD	21201	410-685-9800	547-6279*
*Fax: Sales ■ *TF:* 888-848-2473 ■ *Web:* orioles.mlb.com					
Boston Red Sox Fenway Park 4 Yawkey Way	Boston	MA	02215	617-267-9440	236-6797
Web: redsox.mlb.com					
Chicago Cubs Wrigley Field 1060 W Addison St	Chicago	IL	60613	773-404-2827	404-4129*
*Fax: PR ■ *Web:* chicago.cubs.mlb.com					
Chicago White Sox US Cellular Field 333 W 35th St	Chicago	IL	60616	312-674-1000	674-5109
Web: chicago.whitesox.mlb.com					
Cincinnati Reds Great American Ballpark 100 Main St	Cincinnati	OH	45202	513-765-7000	765-7342
Web: reds.mlb.com					
Cleveland Indians Jacobs Field 2401 Ontario St	Cleveland	OH	44115	216-420-4200	420-4799*
*Fax: Cust Svc ■ *Web:* indians.mlb.com					
Colorado Rockies Coors Field 2001 Blake St	Denver	CO	80205	303-292-0200	296-2066*
*Fax: PR ■ *TF:* 800-388-7625 ■ *Web:* colorado.rockies.mlb.com					
Detroit Tigers Comerica Park 2100 Woodward Ave	Detroit	MI	48201	313-962-4000	471-2138*
*Fax: PR ■ *Web:* tigers.mlb.com					
Florida Marlins Dolphins Stadium 2267 Dan Marino Blvd	Miami	FL	33056	305-626-7400	626-7428
TF: 877-627-5467 ■ *Web:* florida.marlins.mlb.com					
Houston Astros Minute Maid Park 501 Crawford St	Houston	TX	77002	713-259-8000	259-8981*
*Fax: PR ■ *Web:* astros.mlb.com					
Kansas City Royals Kauffman Stadium 1 Royal Way	Kansas City	MO	64129	816-921-8000	921-5775
TF Sales: 800-676-9257 ■ *Web:* kansascity.royals.mlb.com					
Los Angeles Angels of Anaheim					
Angel Stadium 2000 Gene Autry Way	Anaheim	CA	92806	714-940-2000	940-2205*
*Fax: PR ■ *Web:* angels.mlb.com					
Los Angeles Dodgers					
Dodger Stadium 1000 Elysian Park Ave	Los Angeles	CA	90012	323-224-1500	224-1269*
*Fax: PR ■ *Web:* losangeles.dodgers.mlb.com					
Milwaukee Brewers Miller Park 1 Brewers Way	Milwaukee	WI	53214	414-902-4400	902-4732
TF: 800-933-7890 ■ *Web:* brewers.mlb.com					

				Phone	Fax
Minnesota Twins					
Hubert H Humphrey Metrodome 34 Kirby Puckett Pl	Minneapolis	MN	55415	612-375-1366	375-7473
TF: 800-338-9467 ■ *Web:* twins.mlb.com					
New York Mets Shea Stadium 123-01 Roosevelt Ave	Flushing	NY	11368	718-507-6387	507-6395
TF: 800-221-1155 ■ *Web:* mets.mlb.com					
New York Yankees Yankee Stadium 161st St & River Ave	Bronx	NY	10451	718-293-4300	293-8431
Web: newyork.yankees.mlb.com					
Oakland Athletics 7000 Coliseum Way McAphee Stadium	Oakland	CA	94621	510-638-4900	568-3770
Web: athletics.mlb.com					
Philadelphia Phillies					
Citizens Bank Park 1 Citizens Bank Park Way	Philadelphia	PA	19148	215-463-6000	389-3050
Web: philadelphia.phillies.mlb.com					
Pittsburgh Pirates PNC Park 115 Federal St	Pittsburgh	PA	15212	412-323-5000	325-4409
TF: 877-893-2827 ■ *Web:* pirates.mlb.com					
Saint Louis Cardinals 420 S 8th St	Saint Louis	MO	63102	314-345-9600	345-9523
Web: stlouis.cardinals.mlb.com					
San Diego Padres Petco Park 100 Park Blvd	San Diego	CA	92101	619-795-5000	795-5035
Web: padres.mlb.com					
San Francisco Giants AT & T Park 24 Willie Mays Plaza	San Francisco	CA	94107	415-972-2000	947-2646
Web: www.sfgiants.com					
Seattle Mariners Safeco Field 1250 1st Ave S	Seattle	WA	98134	206-346-4000	346-4050
Web: seattle.mariners.mlb.com					
Tampa Bay Devil Rays Tropicana Field 1 Tropicana Dr	Saint Petersburg	FL	33705	727-825-3137	825-3111*
**Fax:* PR ■ *TF:* 800-326-7297 ■ *Web:* tampabay.devilrays.mlb.com					
Texas Rangers					
Rangers Ballpark in Arlington 1000 Ballpark Way	Arlington	TX	76011	817-273-5222	273-5285
TF: 888-968-3927 ■ *Web:* texas.rangers.mlb.com					
Toronto Blue Jays 1 Blue Jays Way Suite 3200	Toronto	ON	M5V1J1	416-341-1000	341-1250*
**Fax:* PR ■ *TF:* 888-654-6529 ■ *Web:* toronto.bluejays.mlb.com					
Washington Nationals RFK Stadium 2400 E Capitol St SE	Washington	DC	20003	202-349-0400	547-0025
Web: washington.nationals.mlb.com					

717 SPORTS TEAMS - BASKETBALL

SEE ALSO Associations & Organizations - General - Sports Organizations p. 1314

717-1 National Basketball Association (NBA)

				Phone	Fax
National Basketball Assn (NBA)					
645 5th Ave Olympic Tower 19th Fl	New York	NY	10022	212-407-8000	832-3861
Web: www.nba.com					
Atlanta Hawks Centennial Tower 101 Marietta St NW Suite 1900	Atlanta	GA	30303	404-828-3800	827-3880
Web: www.nba.com/hawks					
Boston Celtics 226 Causeway St 4th Fl	Boston	MA	02114	617-854-8000	367-4286
Web: www.nba.com/celtics					
Charlotte Bobcats 333 E Trade St	Charlotte	NC	28202	704-688-8600	688-8732
Web: www.nba.com/bobcats					
Chicago Bulls United Center 1901 W Madison St	Chicago	IL	60612	312-455-4000	
Web: www.nba.com/bulls					
Cleveland Cavaliers Quicken Loans Arena 1 Center Ct	Cleveland	OH	44115	216-420-2000	420-2298*
**Fax:* PR ■ *TF:* 800-332-2287 ■ *Web:* www.nba.com/cavs					
Dallas Mavericks The Pavillion 2909 Taylor St	Dallas	TX	75226	214-747-6287	658-7121
Web: www.nba.com/mavericks					
Denver Nuggets Pepsi Center 1000 Chopper Cir	Denver	CO	80204	303-405-1100	575-1920
Web: www.nba.com/nuggets					
Detroit Pistons Palace at Auburn Hills 5 Championship Dr	Auburn Hills	MI	48326	248-377-0100	377-4262
Web: www.nba.com/pistons					
Golden State Warriors 1011 Broadway	Oakland	CA	94607	510-986-2200	452-0132
TF: 888-479-4667 ■ *Web:* www.nba.com/warriors					
Houston Rockets Toyota Center 1510 Polk St	Houston	TX	77002	713-758-7200	758-7396*
**Fax:* Hum Res ■ *Web:* www.nba.com/rockets					
Indiana Pacers Conseco Fieldhouse 125 S Pennsylvania St	Indianapolis	IN	46204	317-917-2500	917-2599
Web: www.nba.com/pacers					
Los Angeles Clippers					
Staples Center 1111 S Figueroa St Suite 1100	Los Angeles	CA	90015	213-742-7100	742-7550
Web: www.nba.com/clippers					
Los Angeles Lakers 555 N Nash St	El Segundo	CA	90245	310-426-6000	426-6105
Web: www.nba.com/lakers					
Memphis Grizzlies FedExForum 191 Beale St	Memphis	TN	38103	901-205-1234	205-1235
Web: www.nba.com/grizzlies					
Miami Heat American Airlines Arena 601 Biscayne Blvd	Miami	FL	33132	786-777-1000	777-1609
Web: www.nba.com/heat					
Milwaukee Bucks Bradley Center 1001 N 4th St	Milwaukee	WI	53203	414-227-0500	227-0543
Web: www.nba.com/bucks					
Minnesota Timberwolves Target Center 600 1st Ave N	Minneapolis	MN	55403	612-673-1600	673-1699
Web: www.nba.com/timberwolves					
New Jersey Nets					
Nets Champion Center 390 Murray Hill Pkwy	East Rutherford	NJ	07073	201-935-8888	935-6691*
**Fax:* PR ■ *TF:* 800-765-6387 ■ *Web:* www.nba.com/nets					
New Orleans Hornets 1250 Poydras St Floor 19	New Orleans	LA	70113	504-593-4900	
Web: www.nba.com/hornets					
New York Knicks					
Madison Square Garden 2 Pennsylvania Plaza 14th Fl	New York	NY	10121	212-465-6471	465-6498*
**Fax:* PR ■ *Web:* www.nba.com/knicks					
Orlando Magic 8701 Maitland Summit Blvd	Orlando	FL	32810	407-916-2400	916-2884
Web: www.nba.com/magic					
Philadelphia 76ers Wachovia Center 3601 S Broad St	Philadelphia	PA	19148	215-339-7600	339-7615
Web: www.nba.com/sixers					
Phoenix Suns US Airways Center 201 E Jefferson St	Phoenix	AZ	85004	602-379-7900	379-7990
Web: www.nba.com/suns					
Portland Trail Blazers 1 Center Ct Suite 200	Portland	OR	97227	503-234-9291	736-2187
Web: www.nba.com/blazers					
Sacramento Kings ARCO Arena 1 Sports Pkwy	Sacramento	CA	95834	916-928-0000	928-0727
Web: www.nba.com/kings					
San Antonio Spurs 1 AT & T Center	San Antonio	TX	78219	210-444-5000	444-5003
Web: www.nba.com/spurs					
Seattle SuperSonics 1201 3rd Ave Suite 1000	Seattle	WA	98101	206-281-5800	281-5839
TF: 800-743-7021 ■ *Web:* www.nba.com/sonics					
Toronto Raptors Air Canada Centre 40 Bay St Suite 400	Toronto	ON	M5J2X2	416-366-3865	359-9198
Web: www.nba.com/raptors					
Utah Jazz					
301 W South Temple St Energy Solutions Arena	Salt Lake City	UT	84101	801-325-2500	325-2578*
**Fax:* PR ■ *TF:* 800-358-7328 ■ *Web:* www.nba.com/jazz					
Washington Wizards Verizon Center 601 F St NW	Washington	DC	20004	202-661-5000	
TF: 800-551-7328 ■ *Web:* www.nba.com/wizards					

717-2 Women's National Basketball Association (WNBA)

				Phone	Fax
Women's National Basketball Assn (WNBA) 645 5th Ave	New York	NY	10022	212-688-9622	750-9622
Web: www.wnba.com					
Chicago Sky 20 W Kinzie St Suite 1000	Chicago	IL	60610	312-828-9550	
Web: www.wnba.com/sky					
Connecticut Sun 1 Mohegan Sun Blvd	Uncasville	CT	06382	860-862-4000	862-4010
TF: 877-786-8499 ■ *Web:* www.wnba.com/sun					
Detroit Shock 5 Championship Dr Palace at Auburn Hills	Auburn Hills	MI	48326	248-377-0100	377-3260
Web: www.wnba.com/shock					
Houston Comets 1730 Jefferson St	Houston	TX	77003	713-739-7442	739-7709*
**Fax:* Hum Res ■ *Web:* www.wnba.com/comets					
Indiana Fever Conseco Fieldhouse 125 S Pennsylvania St	Indianapolis	IN	46204	317-917-2500	917-2899
Web: www.wnba.com/fever					
Los Angeles Sparks 888 S Figueroa St Suite 2010	Los Angeles	CA	90017	213-929-1300	929-1325
Web: www.wnba.com/sparks					
Minnesota Lynx 600 1st Ave N Target Center	Minneapolis	MN	55403	612-673-1600	673-8407
Web: www.wnba.com/lynx					
New York Liberty					
Madison Square Garden 2 Pennsylvania Plaza	New York	NY	10121	212-564-9622	465-6250
Web: www.wnba.com/liberty					
Phoenix Mercury US Airways Center 201 E Jefferson St	Phoenix	AZ	85004	602-514-8333	514-8303
Web: www.wnba.com/mercury					
Sacramento Monarchs ARCO Arena 1 Sports Pkwy	Sacramento	CA	95834	916-928-0000	928-8109
Web: www.wnba.com/monarchs					
San Antonio Silver Stars 1 AT & T Center	San Antonio	TX	78219	210-444-5050	444-5003
Web: www.wnba.com/silverstars					
Seattle Storm 351 Elliott Ave W Suite 500	Seattle	WA	98119	206-281-5800	281-5839
TF: 800-743-7021 ■ *Web:* www.wnba.com/storm					
Washington Mystics 627 N Glebe Rd Suite 850	Arlington	VA	22203	202-266-2200	266-2220
Web: www.wnba.com/mystics					

718 SPORTS TEAMS - FOOTBALL

SEE ALSO Associations & Organizations - General - Sports Organizations p. 1314

718-1 Arena Football League (AFL)

				Phone	Fax
Arena Football League (AFL)					
8700 W Bryn Mawr Ave Suite 120-S	Chicago	IL	60631	773-444-1000	444-1010
Web: www.arenafootball.com					
Arizona Rattlers 320 E McDowell Rd Suite 221	Phoenix	AZ	85004	602-379-2320	379-2323
Web: www.azrattlers.com					
Austin Wranglers 2209 W Braker Ln	Austin	TX	78758	512-491-6600	491-6696
Web: www.austinwranglers.com					
Chicago Rush 1011 E Touhy Suite 400	Des Plaines	IL	60018	773-243-3434	243-3435
TF: 877-787-4849 ■ *Web:* www.chicagorush.com					
Colorado Crush 6202 Dahlia St	Commerce City	CO	80022	303-777-7717	287-4278
Web: www.coloradocrush.com					
Columbus Destroyers 200 W Nationwide Blvd	Columbus	OH	43215	614-246-3530	246-3538
Web: www.columbusdestroyers.com					
Dallas Desperados Cowboys Center 1 Cowboys Pkwy	Irving	TX	75063	972-556-9333	556-9910
Web: www.dallasdesperados.com					
Georgia Force 4400 Falcon Pkwy	Flowery Branch	GA	30542	770-965-4344	965-4345
Web: www.georgiaforce.com					
Grand Rapids Rampage 130 Fulton St W	Grand Rapids	MI	49503	616-559-1871	742-5680
TF: 888-595-4878 ■ *Web:* www.rampagefootball.com					
Kansas City Brigade 5366 W 95th St	Prairie Village	KS	66207	913-383-8020	383-8386
Web: www.kcbrigade.com					
Las Vegas Gladiators 4205 W Tompkins Suite 500 East	Las Vegas	NV	89103	702-731-4977	731-2921
Web: www.lvgladiators.com					
Los Angeles Avengers 12100 W Olympic Blvd Suite 400	Los Angeles	CA	90064	310-788-7744	788-7747
TF: 888-283-6437 ■ *Web:* www.laavengers.com					
Nashville Kats 1 Titans Way	Nashville	TN	37213	615-565-4699	565-4252
Web: www.katsonline.com					
New Orleans VooDoo 5800 Airline Dr	Metairie	LA	70003	504-733-0255	729-5598
Web: www.govoodoo.com					
New York Dragons 1535 Old Country Rd	Plainview	NY	11803	516-501-6700	501-6762
TF: 800-882-4753 ■ *Web:* www.newyorkdragons.com					
Orlando Predators 302 S Graham Ave	Orlando	FL	32803	407-447-7337	999-5299
Web: www.orlandopredators.com					
Philadelphia Soul					
7 Penn Center 1635 Market St Suite 1700	Philadelphia	PA	19103	215-636-0421	636-0933
TF: 888-744-5235 ■ *Web:* www.philadelphiasoul.com					
San Jose SaberCats 600 E Brokaw Rd	San Jose	CA	95112	408-573-5577	573-5588
Web: www.sanjosesabercats.com					
Tampa Bay Storm 401 Channelside Dr	Tampa	FL	33602	813-276-7300	276-7301
Web: www.tampabaystorm.com					
Utah Blaze 405 S Main St Suite 1100	Salt Lake City	UT	84111	801-257-3555	257-3497
Web: www.utahblaze.com					

718-2 Canadian Football League (CFL)

				Phone	Fax
Canadian Football League (CFL) 50 Wellington St E 3rd Fl	Toronto	ON	M5E1C8	416-322-9650	322-9651
Web: www.cfl.ca					
British Columbia Lions 10605 135th St	Surrey	BC	V3T4C8	604-930-5466	583-7882
Web: www.bclions.com					
Calgary Stampeders					
1817 Crowchild Trail NW McMahon Stadium	Calgary	AB	T2M4R6	403-289-0205	289-7850
Web: www.stampeders.com					
Edmonton Eskimos 9023 111th Ave	Edmonton	AB	T5B0C3	780-448-1525	429-3452
TF: 800-667-3757 ■ *Web:* www.esks.com					
Hamilton Tiger-Cats 75 Balsam Ave N Ivor Wynne Stadium	Hamilton	ON	L8L8C1	905-547-2418	549-6610
TF: 800-714-7627 ■ *Web:* www.ticats.ca					
Montreal Alouettes 1260 University St Suite 100	Montreal	QC	H3B3B9	514-871-2266	871-2277
Web: www.montrealalouettes.com					
Saskatchewan Roughriders 1910 Piffles Taylor Way Box 1966	Regina	SK	S4P3E1	306-569-2323	566-4280
TF: 888-474-3377 ■ *Web:* www.saskriders.com					
Toronto Argonauts 1 Blue Jays Way Suite 3300	Toronto	ON	M5V1J3	416-341-2700	341-0550
Web: www.argonauts.ca					
Winnipeg Blue Bombers 1465 Maroons Rd	Winnipeg	MB	R3G0L6	204-784-2583	783-5222
Web: www.bluebombers.com					

718-3 National Football League (NFL)

				Phone	Fax
National Football League (NFL) 280 Park Ave	New York	NY	10017	212-450-2000	681-7599
Web: nfl.com					
Arizona Cardinals 8701 S Hardy Dr	Tempe	AZ	85284	602-379-0101	379-1819
TF: 800-999-1402 ■ *Web:* www.azcardinals.com					

	City	State	Zip	Phone	Fax
Atlanta Falcons 4400 Falcon Pkwy *TF:* 800-241-3489 ■ *Web:* www.atlantafalcons.com	Flowery Branch	GA	30542	770-965-3115	965-3185
Baltimore Ravens 1101 Russell St *Web:* www.baltimoreravens.com	Baltimore	MD	21230	410-261-7283	
Buffalo Bills Ralph Wilson Stadium 1 Bills Dr *TF:* 877-228-4257 ■ *Web:* buffalobills.com	Orchard Park	NY	14127	716-648-1800	649-6446
Carolina Panthers Bank of America Stadium 800 S Mint St *Web:* www.panthers.com	Charlotte	NC	28202	704-358-7000	358-7618
Chicago Bears Halas Hall at Conway Park 1000 Football Dr *Web:* www.chicagobears.com	Lake Forest	IL	60045	847-295-6600	295-8986
Cincinnati Bengals 1 Paul Brown Stadium **Fax:* PR ■ *TF:* 866-621-8383 ■ *Web:* www.bengals.com	Cincinnati	OH	45202	513-621-3550	455-8740*
Cleveland Browns 76 Lou Groza Blvd *Web:* www.clevelandbrowns.com	Berea	OH	44017	440-891-5000	891-5009
Dallas Cowboys 1 Cowboys Pkwy *Web:* www.dallascowboys.com	Irving	TX	75063	972-556-9900	556-9304
Denver Broncos 13655 Broncos Pkwy *Web:* www.denverbroncos.com	Englewood	CO	80112	303-649-9000	649-9354
Detroit Lions 222 Republic Dr *TF:* 800-616-7627 ■ *Web:* www.detroitlions.com	Allen Park	MI	48101	313-216-4000	216-4226
Green Bay Packers 1265 Lombardi Ave PO Box 10628 *Web:* www.packers.com	Green Bay	WI	54307	920-569-7500	569-7301
Houston Texans 2 Reliant Park *Web:* www.houstontexans.com	Houston	TX	77054	832-667-2000	667-2100
Indianapolis Colts 7001 W 56th St *TF:* 800-805-2658 ■ *Web:* www.colts.com	Indianapolis	IN	46254	317-297-2658	297-8971
Jacksonville Jaguars 1 Stadium Pl **Fax:* Mktg ■ *TF:* 877-452-4784 ■ *Web:* www.jaguars.com	Jacksonville	FL	32202	904-633-6000	633-6050*
Kansas City Chiefs Arrowhead Stadium 1 Arrowhead Dr *Web:* www.kcchiefs.com	Kansas City	MO	64129	816-920-9300	920-4315
Miami Dolphins 7500 SW 30th St **Fax:* PR ■ *Web:* www.miamidolphins.com	Davie	FL	33314	954-452-7000	452-7055*
Minnesota Vikings 9520 Viking Dr *Web:* www.vikings.com	Eden Prairie	MN	55344	952-828-6500	828-6540
New England Patriots 1 Patriots Pl *Web:* www.patriots.com	Foxboro	MA	02035	508-543-8200	543-0285
New Orleans Saints 5800 Airline Dr *Web:* www.neworleanssaints.com	Metairie	LA	70003	504-733-0255	731-1768
New York Giants 50 State Hwy 120 Giants Stadium *Web:* www.giants.com	East Rutherford	NJ	07073	201-935-8111	939-4134
New York Jets 1000 Fulton Ave *Web:* www.newyorkjets.com	Hempstead	NY	11550	516-560-8100	560-8198
Oakland Raiders 1220 Harbor Bay Pkwy *TF:* 800-724-3377 ■ *Web:* www.raiders.com	Alameda	CA	94502	510-864-5000	864-5134
Philadelphia Eagles NovaCare Complex 1 NovaCare Way *Web:* www.philadelphiaeagles.com	Philadelphia	PA	19145	215-463-2500	339-5464
Pittsburgh Steelers 3400 S Water St *Web:* www.steelers.com	Pittsburgh	PA	15203	412-432-7800	432-7878
Saint Louis Rams 1 Rams Way *TF Cust Svc:* 800-246-7267 ■ *Web:* www.stlouisrams.com	Earth City	MO	63045	314-982-7267	770-9261
San Diego Chargers 4020 Murphy Canyon Rd *TF:* 877-242-7437 ■ *Web:* www.chargers.com	San Diego	CA	92123	858-874-4500	292-2760
San Francisco 49ers 4949 Centennial Blvd *Web:* www.sf49ers.com	Santa Clara	CA	95054	408-562-4949	727-4937
Seattle Seahawks 11220 NE 53rd St *Web:* www.seahawks.com	Kirkland	WA	98033	425-827-9777	827-9008
Tampa Bay Buccaneers 1 Buccaneer Pl *Web:* www.buccaneers.com	Tampa	FL	33607	813-870-2700	878-0813
Tennessee Titans 460 Great Circle Rd *Web:* www.titansonline.com	Nashville	TN	37228	615-565-4000	565-4006
Washington Redskins 21300 Redskin Park Dr *Web:* www.redskins.com	Ashburn	VA	20147	703-726-7000	726-7086

719 SPORTS TEAMS - HOCKEY

SEE ALSO Associations & Organizations - General - Sports Organizations p. 1314

	City	State	Zip	Phone	Fax
National Hockey League (NHL) 1251 Ave of the Americas 47th Fl *Web:* www.nhl.com	New York	NY	10020	212-789-2000	789-2020
National Hockey League (NHL) 50 Bay St 11th Fl **Fax:* PR ■ *Web:* www.nhl.com	Toronto	ON	M5J2X8	416-981-2777	981-2779*
Anaheim Ducks 2695 Katella Ave *TF:* 877-945-3946 ■ *Web:* ducks.nhl.com	Anaheim	CA	92806	714-704-2700	940-2953
Atlanta Thrashers Centennial Tower 101 Marietta St NW Suite 1900 *Web:* www.atlantathrashers.com	Atlanta	GA	30303	404-878-3800	827-5909
Boston Bruins 100 Legends Way *Web:* www.bostonbruins.com	Boston	MA	02114	617-624-1900	523-7184
Buffalo Sabres HSBC Arena 1 Seymour H Knox III Plaza *TF:* 888-467-2273 ■ *Web:* www.sabres.com	Buffalo	NY	14203	716-855-4444	855-4115
Calgary Flames Pengrowth Saddledome 555 Saddledome Rise SE **Fax:* PR ■ *Web:* www.calgaryflames.com	Calgary	AB	T2G2W1	403-777-2177	777-2195*
Carolina Hurricanes RBC Center 1400 Edwards Mill Rd *Web:* hurricanes.nhl.com	Raleigh	NC	27607	919-467-7825	462-7030
Chicago Blackhawks United Center 1901 W Madison St **Fax:* PR ■ *Web:* www.chicagoblackhawks.com	Chicago	IL	60612	312-455-7000	455-7041*
Colorado Avalanche Pepsi Center 1000 Chopper Cir *Web:* www.coloradoavalanche.com	Denver	CO	80204	303-405-1100	575-1928
Columbus Blue Jackets Nationwide Arena 200 W Nationwide Blvd 3rd Fl *TF:* 800-645-2657 ■ *Web:* www.bluejackets.com	Columbus	OH	43215	614-246-4625	246-4007
Dallas Stars 2601 Ave of the Stars *Web:* www.dallasstars.com	Frisco	TX	75034	214-387-5500	387-5599
Detroit Red Wings Joe Louis Arena 600 Civic Center Dr **Fax:* PR ■ *Web:* www.detroitredwings.com	Detroit	MI	48226	313-396-7544	567-0296*
Edmonton Oilers 11230 110th St *Web:* www.edmontonoilers.com	Edmonton	AB	T5G3H7	780-414-4000	409-5890
Florida Panthers BankAtlantic Center 1 Panther Pkwy **Fax:* Sales ■ *Web:* www.floridapanthers.com	Sunrise	FL	33323	954-835-7000	835-7200*
Los Angeles Kings Staples Center 1111 S Figueroa St *TF:* 888-546-4752 ■ *Web:* www.lakings.com	Los Angeles	CA	90015	213-742-7100	742-4500
Minnesota Wild 317 Washington St *Web:* www.wild.com	Saint Paul	MN	55102	651-222-9453	222-1055
Montreal Canadiens Bell Centre 1260 de la Gauchetiere St W **Fax:* PR ■ *Web:* www.canadiens.com/english	Montreal	QC	H3B5E8	514-932-2582	932-9296*
Nashville Predators 501 Broadway Sommet Center *Web:* www.nashvillepredators.com	Nashville	TN	37203	615-770-7825	770-2341
New Jersey Devils Continental Airlines Arena 50 Rt 120N *TF:* 800-653-3845 ■ *Web:* www.newjerseydevils.com	East Rutherford	NJ	07073	201-935-6050	935-1407
New York Islanders 1535 Old Country Rd *TF:* 800-882-4753 ■ *Web:* www.newyorkislanders.com	Plainview	NY	11803	516-501-6700	501-6729
New York Rangers 2 Pennsylvania Plaza *Web:* www.newyorkrangers.com	New York	NY	10121	212-465-6486	465-6494
Ottawa Senators 1000 Palladium Dr Scotia Bank Place *TF:* 800-444-7367 ■ *Web:* www.ottawasenators.com	Kanata	ON	K2V1A5	613-599-0250	599-0358
Philadelphia Flyers Wachovia Center 3601 S Broad St *Web:* www.philadelphiaflyers.com	Philadelphia	PA	19148	215-465-4500	389-9476
Phoenix Coyotes 6751 N Sunset Blvd Suite 200 *Web:* www.phoenixcoyotes.com	Glendale	AZ	85305	623-772-3200	772-3201
Pittsburgh Penguins 1 Chatham Center Suite 400 *TF:* 800-642-7367 ■ *Web:* www.pittsburghpenguins.com	Pittsburgh	PA	15219	412-642-1300	642-1859
Saint Louis Blues Savvis Center 1401 Clark Ave *Web:* www.stlouisblues.com	Saint Louis	MO	63103	314-622-2500	622-2582
San Jose Sharks HP Pavilion at San Jose 525 W Santa Clara St *TF:* 800-755-5050 ■ *Web:* www.sj-sharks.com	San Jose	CA	95113	408-287-7070	999-5797
Tampa Bay Lightning St Pete Times Forum 401 Channelside Dr *Web:* www.tampabaylightning.com	Tampa	FL	33602	813-301-6600	301-1482
Toronto Maple Leafs Air Canada Center 40 Bay St Suite 400 *Web:* www.mapleleafs.com	Toronto	ON	M5J2X2	416-815-5700	
Vancouver Canucks General Motors Pl 800 Griffiths Way *TF:* 888-672-2229 ■ *Web:* www.canucks.com	Vancouver	BC	V6B6G1	604-899-4600	899-7401
Washington Capitals 627 N Glebe Rd Suite 850 *Web:* www.washingtoncaps.com	Arlington	VA	22203	202-266-2200	266-2210

720 SPORTS TEAMS - SOCCER

SEE ALSO Associations & Organizations - General - Sports Organizations p. 1314

	City	State	Zip	Phone	Fax
Major League Soccer (MLS) 420 5th Ave 7th Fl *Web:* www.mlsnet.com	New York	NY	10018	212-450-1200	
Chicago Fire 7000 S Harlem Ave *TF:* 888-657-3473 ■ *Web:* www.chicago-fire.com	Ridgeview	IL	60455	708-594-7200	496-6050
Club Deportivo Chivas USA Home Depot Ctr 18400 Avalon Blvd Suite 500 *TF:* 877-244-8271 ■ *Web:* chivas.usa.mlsnet.com	Carson	CA	90746	310-630-4550	630-4551
Colorado Rapids 600 Victory Way *Web:* www.coloradorapids.com	Commerce City	CO	80027	303-405-1100	727-3536
Columbus Crew Crew Stadium 1 Black & Gold Blvd *TF:* 800-273-9326	Columbus	OH	43211	614-447-2739	447-4109
DC United 2400 E Capitol St SE *Web:* www.dcunited.com	Washington	DC	20003	202-587-5000	587-5400
FC Dallas 9200 World Cup Way Suite 202 *TF:* 888-323-4625 ■ *Web:* fcdallas.mlsnet.com	Frisco	TX	75034	214-705-6700	705-6799
Houston Dynamo 1415 Louisiana St Suite 3400 *Web:* www.houstondynamo.com	Houston	TX	77002	713-276-7500	276-7580
Kansas City Wizards 8900 State Line Rd *Web:* www.kcwizards.com	Leawood	KS	66206	913-387-3400	387-3401
Los Angeles Galaxy Home Depot Center 18400 Avalon Blvd Suite 200 *TF:* 877-342-5299 ■ *Web:* www.lagalaxy.com	Carson	CA	90746	310-630-2200	630-2250
New England Revolution Gillette Stadium 1 Patriot Pl *TF:* 877-438-7387 ■ *Web:* www.revolutionsoccer.net	Foxboro	MA	02035	508-543-5001	384-9128
New York Red Bulls 1 Harmon Plaza 8th Fl *TF:* 877-727-6223 ■ *Web:* www.newyorkredbulls.com	Secaucus	NJ	07094	201-583-7000	583-7055
Real Salt Lake 515 S 700 East #2R *Web:* www.realsaltlake.com	Salt Lake City	UT	84102	801-924-8585	933-4713
Toronto FC BMO Field 170 Princes' Blvd *Web:* toronto.fc.mlsnet.com	Toronto	ON	M6K3C3	416-360-4625	

721 SPRINGS - HEAVY-GAUGE

	City	State	Zip	Phone	Fax
Associated Spring Barnes Group Inc 80 Scott Swamp Rd *Web:* www.asbg.com	Farmington	CT	06032	860-678-0700	409-4611
Automatic Spring Products Corp 803 Taylor Ave *Web:* www.automaticspring.com	Grand Haven	MI	49417	616-842-7800	842-4380
Barnes Group Inc 123 Main St *NYSE:* B ■ *TF:* 800-877-8803 ■ *Web:* www.barnesgroupinc.com	Bristol	CT	06011	860-583-7070	589-3507
Chestnut Group Inc 115 Bloomingdale Ave *Web:* www.chestnutgroup.com	Wayne	PA	19087	610-688-3300	687-2553
Draco Spring Mfg Co PO Box 266086 *Web:* www.dracospring.com	Houston	TX	77207	713-645-4973	645-0480
General Wire Spring Co 1101 Thompson Ave *TF:* 800-245-6200 ■ *Web:* www.generalwirespring.com	McKees Rocks	PA	15136	412-771-6300	771-6317
HS Spring Group 3805 Business Park Dr *Web:* www.hsspring.com	Louisville	KY	40213	502-962-6464	962-6410
Matthew Warren Inc 500 E Ottawa St *Web:* www.mw-ind.com	Logansport	IN	46947	574-722-8200	722-8241
Pa-Ted Spring Co Inc 137 Vincent P Kelly Rd	Bristol	CT	06010	860-582-6368	583-1044
Perfection Spring & Stamping Corp 1449 E Algonquin Rd *Web:* www.pss-corp.com	Mount Prospect	IL	60056	847-437-3900	437-1322
Rockford Spring Co 3801 S Central Ave *Web:* www.rockfordspring.com	Rockford	IL	61102	815-968-3000	968-3100
Rolex Co 385 Hillside Ave	Hillside	NJ	07205	973-926-0900	926-5626
Southern Spring & Stamping Inc 401 Sub Station Rd *TF:* 800-450-5882 ■ *Web:* www.southernspring.com	Venice	FL	34292	941-488-2276	485-9156
Stanley Spring & Stamping Corp 5050 W Foster Ave *Web:* www.stanleyspring.com	Chicago	IL	60630	773-777-2600	777-3894
Union Spring & Mfg Corp 560 Epsilon Dr	Pittsburgh	PA	15238	412-843-5900	963-7706

722 SPRINGS - LIGHT-GAUGE

	City	State	Zip	Phone	Fax
AJ Kay Co 5406 N Elston Ave	Chicago	IL	60630	773-545-5955	545-2587
Alsco Co 1014 Clarkson Parma Town Ln Rd	Hilton	NY	14468	585-392-2585	
American Coil Spring Co Inc 1041 E Keating Ave	Muskegon	MI	49442	231-726-4021	726-2206
Atlantic Spring 137 Hwy 202 S *Web:* www.chestnutgroup.com/pages/as.html	Ringoes	NJ	08551	908-788-5800	788-0511
Atlas Spring Mfg Corp 150 E 157th St *Web:* www.atlasspring.com	Gardena	CA	90248	310-660-0150	660-0172

Phone | Fax

Century Spring Corp PO Box 15287 Los Angeles CA 90015 213-749-1466 749-3802
TF: 800-237-5225 ■ *Web:* www.centuryspring.com
Chestnut Group Inc 115 Bloomingdale Ave Wayne PA 19087 610-688-3300 687-2553
Web: www.chestnutgroup.com
Connecticut Spring & Stamping Corp 48 Spring Ln Farmington CT 06034 860-677-1341 677-7199*
**Fax:* Cust Svc ■ *TF:* 800-255-8590 ■ *Web:* www.ctspringandstamping.com
Dudek & Bock Spring Mfg Co 5100 W Roosevelt Rd Chicago IL 60644 773-379-4100 379-4715
Web: www.dudek-bock.com
Economy Spring & Stamping Co
29 DePaolo Dr PO Box 651 Southington CT 06489 860-621-7358 621-7882
Web: www.economyspring.com
Evans John & Sons Inc 1 Spring Ave PO Box 885 Lansdale PA 19446 215-368-7700 368-9019
Web: www.springcompany.com
Exacto Spring Corp 1201 Hickory St Grafton WI 53024 262-377-3970 377-3854
Web: www.exacto.com
Fairway Spring Co Inc PO Box 69 Horseheads NY 14845 607-739-3541 739-7601
Flex-O-Lators Inc 1460 Jackson Dr Carthage MO 64836 417-358-4095 358-3019
TF: 800-641-4363
General Spring Inc 245 Warehouse Ln Hartsville TN 37074 615-374-9500 374-9540
General Wire Spring Co 1101 Thompson Ave McKees Rocks PA 15136 412-771-6300 771-6317
TF: 800-245-6200 ■ *Web:* www.generalwirespring.com
Hickory Springs Mfg Co 235 2nd Ave NW Hickory NC 28601 828-328-2201 328-5501
TF: 800-438-5341 ■ *Web:* www.hickorysprings.com
John Evans' Sons Inc 1 Spring Ave PO Box 885 Lansdale PA 19446 215-368-7700 368-9019
Web: www.springcompany.com
Kay AJ Co 5406 N Elston Ave Chicago IL 60630 773-545-5955 545-2587
Lee Spring Co Inc 1462 62nd St Brooklyn NY 11219 718-236-2222 236-3919
TF: 800-426-0272 ■ *Web:* www.leespring.com
Leggett & Platt Inc PO Box 757 Carthage MO 64836 417-358-8131 358-5840*
NYSE: LEG ■ **Fax:* Hum Res ■ *TF:* 800-888-4569 ■ *Web:* www.leggett.com
Maryland Precision Spring Co 8900 Kelso Dr Baltimore MD 21221 410-391-7400 687-9223
Web: www.chestnutgroup.com/pages/mps.html
Mastercoil Spring 4010 W Albany St McHenry IL 60050 815-344-0051 344-0071
Web: www.mastercoil.com
Matthew Warren Inc 500 E Ottawa St Logansport IN 46947 574-722-8200 722-8241
Web: www.mw-ind.com
Michigan Spring Div Precision Products Group
2700 Wickham Dr Muskegon MI 49441 231-755-1691 755-3449
Micromatic Spring & Stamping Co Inc 9325 King St Franklin Park IL 60131 847-671-6600 671-3452
Web: www.micromaticspring.com
Mid-West Spring & Stamping Co 1404 Joliet Rd Unit C Romeoville IL 60446 630-739-3800 643-9781*
**Fax Area Code:* 888 ■ *TF:* 800-838-7812 ■ *Web:* www.mwspring.com
Monticello Spring Corp 3137 Freeman Rd PO Box 705 Monticello IN 47960 574-583-8090 583-9299
Web: www.monticellospring.com
Newcomb Spring Corp 235 Spring St Southington CT 06489 860-621-0111 621-7048
Web: www.kando.com
O & G Spring & Wire Forms Specialty Co 4500 W Division St Chicago IL 60651 773-772-9331 772-6578
Web: www.ogspring.com
Pa-Ted Spring Co Inc 137 Vincent P Kelly Rd Bristol CT 06010 860-582-6368 583-1044
Perfection Spring & Stamping Corp
1449 E Algonquin Rd Mount Prospect IL 60056 847-437-3900 437-1322
Web: www.pss-corp.com
Peterson Spring 21200 Telegraph Rd Southfield MI 48034 248-799-5400 357-3176
Web: www.pspring.com
Plymouth Spring Co Inc PO Box 1358 Bristol CT 06011 860-584-0594 584-0943
Web: www.plymouthspring.com
Precision Coil Spring Co Inc 10107 Rose Ave El Monte CA 91731 626-444-0561 444-3712
Web: www.pcspring.com
Precision Products Group Inc 4205 Galleria Dr Rockford IL 61111 815-636-9800 636-8294
Web: www.precprodgroup.com
Precision Products Group Inc Michigan Spring Div
2700 Wickham Dr Muskegon MI 49441 231-755-1691 755-3449
Quality Spring/Togo Inc 355 Jay St Coldwater MI 49036 517-278-2391 279-8142*
**Fax:* Sales ■ *Web:* www.qsti.com
R & L Spring Co 1097 Geneva Pkwy Lake Geneva WI 53147 262-249-7854 249-7866
Web: www.rlspring.com
Rockford Spring Co 3801 S Central Ave Rockford IL 61102 815-968-3000 968-3100
Web: www.rockfordspring.com
Rowley Spring & Stamping Corp 210 Redstone Hill Rd Bristol CT 06010 860-582-8175 589-8718
Web: www.rowleyspring.com
Southern Spring & Stamping Inc 401 Sub Station Rd Venice FL 34292 941-488-2276 485-9156
TF: 800-450-5882 ■ *Web:* www.southernspring.com
Spring Dynamics Inc 7378 Research Dr Almont MI 48003 810-798-2622 798-2902
Web: www.springdynamics.com
Spring Engineers Inc 9740 Tanner Rd Houston TX 77041 713-690-9488 690-1199
TF: 800-899-9488
Stanley Spring & Stamping Corp 5050 W Foster Ave Chicago IL 60630 773-777-2600 777-3894
Web: www.stanleyspring.com
Sterling Spring Corp 5432 W 54th St Chicago IL 60638 773-582-6464 582-0657
TF: 800-969-7884
Twist Inc 47 S Linestone St PO Box 177 Jamestown OH 45335 937-675-9581 675-6781
Web: www.twistinc.com
Union Spring & Mfg Corp 560 Epsilon Dr Pittsburgh PA 15238 412-843-5900 963-7706
Walker Corp 1555 Vintage Ave Ontario CA 91761 909-390-4300 390-4301
Web: www.walkercorp.com
Wesco Spring Co 4501 S Knox Ave Chicago IL 60632 773-838-3350 838-0018
Web: www.wescospring.com
Winamac Coil Spring Inc 512 N Smith St Kewanna IN 46939 574-653-2186 653-2645
Web: www.winamaccoilspring.com
Wire Products Co Inc 14601 Industrial Pkwy Cleveland OH 44135 216-267-0777 267-7972
Web: www.wire-products.com
Yost Superior Co PO Box 1487 Springfield OH 45501 937-323-7591 323-5180
TF: 800-544-4570 ■ *Web:* www.yostsuperior.com

723 STADIUMS & ARENAS

SEE ALSO Convention Centers p. 1559; Performing Arts Facilities p. 2090

Phone | Fax

1st Mariner Arena 201 W Baltimore St Baltimore MD 21201 410-347-2020 347-2042
Web: www.1stmarinerarena.com
Air Canada Centre 40 Bay St Suite 400 Toronto ON M5J2X2 416-815-5500 359-9332
Web: www.theaircanadacentre.com
Alamodome 100 Montana St San Antonio TX 78203 210-207-3663 207-3646
TF: 800-884-3663 ■ *Web:* www.sanantonio.gov/dome
Albert Lea City Arena 701 Lake Chapeau Dr Albert Lea MN 56007 507-377-4374
Web: www.city.albertlea.org/arena.htm
Alerus Center 1200 42nd St S Grand Forks ND 58201 701-792-1200 746-6511
Web: www.aleruscenter.com
Allen County War Memorial Coliseum 4000 Parnell Ave Fort Wayne IN 46805 260-482-9502 484-1637
Web: www.memorialcoliseum.com
Allstate Arena 6920 N Mannheim Rd Rosemont IL 60018 847-635-6601 635-6606
Web: www.allstatearena.com
Alltel Arena 1 ALLTEL Arena Way North Little Rock AR 72114 501-340-5660 340-5668
Web: www.alltelarena.com
Alltel Stadium 1 Stadium Pl Jacksonville FL 32202 904-633-6000 633-6050
TF: 877-452-4784 ■ *Web:* www.jaguars.com
Aloha Stadium 99-500 Salt Lake Blvd Honolulu HI 96818 808-486-9555 486-9520
Web: www.alohastadium.hawaii.gov
American Airlines Arena 601 Biscayne Blvd Miami FL 33132 786-777-1000 777-1230*
**Fax:* Hum Res ■ *Web:* www.aaarena.com
American Airlines Center 2500 Victory Ave Dallas TX 75219 214-222-3687
Web: www.americanairlinescenter.com
Amway Arena 600 W Amelia St Orlando FL 32801 407-849-2000 849-2329
Web: www.orlandovenues.net
Angel Stadium 2000 Gene Autry Way Anaheim CA 92806 714-940-2000 940-2244
Web: www.angels.mlb.com
ARCO Arena 1 Sports Pkwy Sacramento CA 95834 916-928-0000 928-0727
Web: www.arcoarena.com
Arena at Harbor Yard 600 Main St Bridgeport CT 06604 203-345-2300 333-8811
Web: www.arenaatharboryard.com
Arizona Stadium 1 National Championship Dr Tucson AZ 85721 520-621-4622 621-9690
Arrowhead Stadium 1 Arrowhead Dr Kansas City MO 64129 816-920-9300 923-4719*
**Fax:* PR ■ *Web:* www.kcchiefs.com/arrowhead
AT & T Park 24 Willie Mays Plaza San Francisco CA 94107 415-972-2000 947-2646
TF: 877-473-4849 ■ *Web:* www.sfgiants.com
AT&T Center 1 AT&T Pkwy San Antonio TX 78219 210-444-5000 444-5100
Web: www.attcenter.com
Bank of America Stadium 800 S Mint St Charlotte NC 28202 704-358-7000 358-7615
Web: www.panthers.com
BankAtlantic Center 1 Panther Pkwy Sunrise FL 33323 954-835-8000 835-7200
Web: www.bankatlanticcenter.com
Bell Centre 1260 de la Gauchetiere St W Montreal QC H3B5E8 514-989-2800 989-2895
Web: www.centrebell.ca
BI-LO Center 650 N Academy St Greenville SC 29601 864-241-3800 250-4939
Web: www.bilocenter.com
Big Sandy Superstore Arena 1 Civic Ctr Plaza Huntington WV 25701 304-696-5990 696-4463
Web: www.bigsandyarena.com
Blue Cross Arena at the War Memorial 1 War Memorial Sq Rochester NY 14614 585-758-5300 758-5327
Web: www.bluecrossarena.com
Bradley Center 1001 N 4th St Milwaukee WI 53203 414-227-0400 227-0497
Web: www.bradleycenter.com
British Columbia Place Stadium 777 Pacific Blvd Vancouver BC V6B4Y8 604-669-2300 661-3412
Web: www.bcplacestadium.com
Broome County Veterans Memorial Arena 1 Stuart St Binghamton NY 13901 607-778-1527 778-6041
Busch Stadium 700 Clark St Saint Louis MO 63102 314-345-9600 345-9523
Web: www.stlcardinals.com
Canal Park Stadium 300 S Main St Akron OH 44308 330-253-5151 253-3300
TF: 800-972-3767
Charlotte Bobcats Arena 333 E Trade St Charlotte NC 28202 704-424-4120 333-2340
Web: www.charlottebobcatsarena.com
Chase Field 401 E Jefferson St Phoenix AZ 85004 602-462-6500 462-6600
Web: diamondbacks.mlb.com
Cheney Stadium 2502 S Tyler St Tacoma WA 98405 253-752-7707 752-7135
TF: 800-281-3834 ■ *Web:* www.tacomarainiers.com/cheney.htm
Cincinnati Gardens 2250 Seymour Ave Cincinnati OH 45212 513-631-7793 631-2666
Web: www.cincinnatimightyducks.com
Citizens Bank Park 1 Citizens Bank Park Way Philadelphia PA 19148 215-463-6000 389-3050
Web: philadelphia.phillies.mlb.com
Cleveland Browns Stadium 100 Alfred Lerner Way Cleveland OH 44114 440-891-5000 824-3645
TF Sales: 888-891-1999 ■ *Web:* www.clevelandbrowns.com/stadium
Columbus Civic Center 400 4th St Columbus GA 31901 706-653-4482 653-4481
TF: 800-711-3986 ■ *Web:* www.columbuscivicenter.org
Comerica Park 2100 Woodward Ave Detroit MI 48201 313-962-4000 471-2599
Web: www.detroittigers.com
Commonwealth Stadium 11000 Stadium Rd Edmonton AB T5J2R7 780-944-7561 944-7545
Conseco Fieldhouse 125 S Pennsylvania St Indianapolis IN 46204 317-917-2500 917-2599
Web: www.consecofieldhouse.com
Coors Field 2001 Blake St Denver CO 80205 303-762-5437 312-2115
TF: 800-388-7625 ■ *Web:* www.coloradorockies.com
Cotton Bowl 3750 Midway Plaza Dallas TX 75315 214-939-2222 939-2224
Cowtown Coliseum 121 E Exchange Ave Fort Worth TX 76106 817-625-1025 625-1148
TF: 888-269-8696 ■ *Web:* www.cowtowncoliseum.com
Cricket Arena 2700 E Independence Blvd Charlotte NC 28205 704-372-3600 335-3118
Web: www.cricketarenacharlotte.com
David S Palmer Arena 100 W Main St Danville IL 61832 217-431-2424 431-6444
Web: www.palmerarena.com
DCU Center 50 Foster St Worcester MA 01608 508-755-6800 929-0111
Web: www.centrumcentre.com
Delta Center 301 W South Temple Salt Lake City UT 84101 801-325-2000 325-2578*
**Fax:* PR ■ *Web:* www.deltacenter.com
Denver Coliseum 4600 Humboldt St Denver CO 80216 720-865-2474 865-2467
Web: www.denvercoliseum.com
Dodger Stadium 1000 Elysian Park Ave Los Angeles CA 90012 323-224-1500 224-1269
Web: www.dodgers.com
Dolphins Stadium 2269 Dan Marino Blvd Miami Gardens FL 33056 305-623-6100 624-6403
Web: www.dolphinsstadium.com
Dunkin' Donuts Center 1 LaSalle Sq Providence RI 02903 401-331-0700 751-6792
Web: www.dunkindonutscenter.com
Ed Smith Stadium 2700 12th St Sarasota FL 34237 941-954-4101 365-1587
Edward Jones Dome 701 Convention Plaza Saint Louis MO 63101 314-342-5036 342-5040
Web: www.stlouisrams.com
Ewing M Kauffman Stadium 1 Royal Way Kansas City MO 64129 816-921-8000 921-5775
TF: 800-676-9257 ■ *Web:* www.kcroyals.com
Family Arena 2002 Arena Pkwy Saint Charles MO 63303 636-896-4242 896-4205
Web: www.familyarena.com
FARGODOME 1800 N University Dr Fargo ND 58102 701-241-9100 237-0987
Web: www.fargodome.com
FedEx Field 1600 FedEx Way Landover MD 20785 301-276-6000 276-6001
Web: www.redskins.com
FedEx Forum 191 Beale St Memphis TN 38103 901-888-4667 205-1235
Web: www.nba.com/grizzlies
Fenway Park 4 Yawkey Way Boston MA 02215 617-267-9440 236-6797
Web: www.redsox.com
Ford Center 100 W Reno Oklahoma City OK 73102 405-602-8700
Web: www.okfordcenter.com
Ford Field 2000 Brush St Suite 200 Detroit MI 48226 313-262-2000
Web: www.fordfield.com
Frank Erwin Center 1701 Red River Austin TX 78701 512-471-7744 471-9652
Web: www.uterwincenter.com
Freeman Coliseum 3201 E Houston St San Antonio TX 78219 210-226-1177 226-5081
Web: www.freemancoliseum.com
Garrett Coliseum 1555 Federal Dr Montgomery AL 36107 334-242-5597 240-3242
Web: www.garrett.state.al.us/
General Motors Place 800 Griffiths Way Vancouver BC V6B6G1 604-899-7889 899-7401
Web: www.canucks.com/gm
George M Sullivan Sports Arena 1600 Gambell St Anchorage AK 99501 907-279-0618 274-0676
Web: www.sullivanarena.com
Georgia Dome 1 Georgia Dome Dr NW Atlanta GA 30313 404-223-9200 223-8011
Web: www.gadome.com

Name / Address	City	State	Zip	Phone	Fax
Giants Stadium 50 State Hwy 120	East Rutherford	NJ	07073	201-935-8500	935-4262*
*Fax: Hum Res ■ *Web:* www.giants.com					
Gillette Stadium 1 Patriots Pl	Foxboro	MA	02035	508-543-8200	543-0285
Web: www.gillettestadium.com					
Golden Spike Event Center 1000 N 1200 West	Ogden	UT	84404	801-399-8544	392-1995
TF: 800-442-7362 ■ *Web:* www.goldenspikeeventcenter.com					
Great American Ball Park 100 Main St	Cincinnati	OH	45202	513-765-7000	765-7342
Web: www.reds.mlb.com					
Greensboro Coliseum 1921 W Lee St	Greensboro	NC	27403	336-373-7400	373-2170
Web: www.greensborocoliseum.com					
Greensboro Coliseum Complex 1921 W Lee St	Greensboro	NC	27403	336-373-7400	373-2170
Web: www.greensborocoliseum.com					
Hampton Coliseum 1000 Coliseum Dr PO Box 7309	Hampton	VA	23666	757-838-5650	838-2595
Web: www.hamptoncoliseum.org					
Heinz Field 100 Art Rooney Ave	Pittsburgh	PA	15212	412-697-7181	697-7151
Web: www.pittsburghsteelers.com					
Hersheypark Arena & Stadium 950 W Hersheypark Dr	Hershey	PA	17033	717-534-3911	534-8996
Web: www.hersheyparkstadium.com					
Hi Corbett Field 3400 E Camino Campestre	Tucson	AZ	85716	520-327-9467	318-2816
Honda Center 2695 E Katella Ave	Anaheim	CA	92806	714-704-2400	704-2443
TF: 877-945-3946 ■ *Web:* www.hondacenter.com					
HP Pavilion at San Jose 525 W Santa Clara St	San Jose	CA	95113	408-287-7070	999-5797
TF: 800-755-5050 ■ *Web:* www.hppsj.com					
HSBC Arena 1 Seymour Knox III Plaza	Buffalo	NY	14203	716-855-4100	855-4110
TF: 888-467-2273 ■ *Web:* www.hsbcarena.com					
Hubert H Humphrey Metrodome 900 S 5th St	Minneapolis	MN	55415	612-332-0386	332-8334
Web: www.msfc.com					
Husky Stadium 3800 Mont Lake Blvd	Seattle	WA	98105	206-543-2246	
Independence Stadium 3301 Pershing Blvd	Shreveport	LA	71109	318-673-7758	673-7786
INVESCO Field at Mile High 1701 Bryant St	Denver	CO	80204	720-258-3000	258-3050
Web: www.invescofieldatmilehigh.com					
ipayOne Center at the Sports Arena 3500 Sports Arena Blvd	San Diego	CA	92110	619-224-4171	224-3010
Web: www.sandiegoarena.com					
Izod Center 50 State Hwy 120	East Rutherford	NJ	07073	201-935-8500	
Web: www.meadowlands.com					
Jacksonville Veterans Memorial Arena 300 A Philip Randolph Blvd	Jacksonville	FL	32202	904-630-3900	854-0601
Web: www.jaxevents.com/jacksonvillearena/					
Jacobs Field 2401 Ontario St	Cleveland	OH	44115	216-420-4487	420-4799
TF: 800-388-7423 ■ *Web:* www.indians.com					
Jobing.com Arena 9400 W Maryland Ave	Glendale	AZ	85305	623-772-3200	772-3201
Web: jobingarena.com					
Joe Louis Arena 600 Civic Center Dr	Detroit	MI	48226	313-396-7444	396-7994
Web: www.olympiaentertainment.com/JLA/home.asp					
Joel Lawrence Veterans Memorial Coliseum Complex 2825 University Pkwy	Winston-Salem	NC	27105	336-725-5635	727-2922
Web: www.ljvm.com					
Kansas Coliseum 1229 E 85th St N	Valley Center	KS	67147	316-755-1243	755-2869
Web: www.kansascoliseum.com					
Kauffman Ewing M Stadium 1 Royal Way	Kansas City	MO	64129	816-921-8000	921-5775
TF: 800-676-9257 ■ *Web:* www.kcroyals.com					
Kemper Arena 1800 Genessee St	Kansas City	MO	64102	816-513-4000	513-4001
TF: 800-634-3942 ■ *Web:* www.kemperarenakc.com					
Kentucky Fair & Expo Center 937 Phillips Ln	Louisville	KY	40209	502-367-5000	367-5139
Web: www.kyfairexpo.org					
Key Arena 305 Harrison St	Seattle	WA	98109	206-684-7202	684-7343
Web: www.seattlecenter.com					
King Martin Luther Jr Arena 301 W Oglethorpe Ave	Savannah	GA	31401	912-651-6550	651-6552
Web: www.savannahcivic.com					
Ladd-Peebles Stadium 1621 Virginia St	Mobile	AL	36604	251-208-2500	208-2514
Web: www.laddpeeblesstadium.com					
Lambeau Field 1265 Lombardi Ave	Green Bay	WI	54304	920-569-7500	569-7301
Web: www.packers.com					
Landon Arena Kansas Expocentre 1 Expocentre Dr	Topeka	KS	66612	785-235-1986	235-2967
Web: www.ksexpo.com					
Laredo Entertainment Center 6700 Arena Blvd	Laredo	TX	78041	956-791-9192	729-9393
Web: www.laredoarena.com					
Lawrence Joel Veterans Memorial Coliseum 2825 University Pkwy	Winston-Salem	NC	27105	336-725-5635	727-2922
Web: www.ljvm.com					
Lawrence Joel Veterans Memorial Coliseum Complex 2825 University Pkwy	Winston-Salem	NC	27105	336-725-5635	727-2922
Web: www.ljvm.com					
LC Walker Arena & Conference Center 955 4th St	Muskegon	MI	49440	231-726-2939	726-4620
Web: www.lcwalkerarena.com					
Liberty Bowl Memorial Stadium 335 S Hollywood St	Memphis	TN	38104	901-729-4344	276-2756
Lincoln Financial Field 1 Lincoln Financial Field Way	Philadelphia	PA	19148	215-463-2500	570-4040*
*Fax Area Code: 267 ■ *Web:* www.lincolnfinancialfield.com					
Long Beach Arena 300 E Ocean Blvd	Long Beach	CA	90802	562-436-3636	436-9491
Web: www.longbeachcc.com/arena.htm					
Los Angeles Memorial Coliseum 3911 S Figueroa St	Los Angeles	CA	90037	213-748-6136	748-5828
Web: www.lacoliseum.com					
Los Angeles Memorial Coliseum & Sports Arena 3939 S Figueroa St	Los Angeles	CA	90037	213-748-6136	746-9346
Web: www.lacoliseum.com					
Louis J Tullio Arena 809 French St	Erie	PA	16501	814-452-4857	455-9931
Web: www.erieevents.com/tullio.html					
Louis Joe Arena 600 Civic Center Dr	Detroit	MI	48226	313-396-7444	396-7994
Web: www.olympiaentertainment.com/JLA/home.asp					
Louisiana Superdome 1500 Poydras PO Box 52439	New Orleans	LA	70152	504-587-3663	587-3848
TF: 800-756-7074 ■ *Web:* www.superdome.com					
LP Field 1 Titans Way	Nashville	TN	37213	615-565-4300	565-4444
Web: www.titansonline.com					
Lubbock Municipal Auditorium/Coliseum 2720 Drive of Champions	Lubbock	TX	79409	806-775-2243	775-3240
Web: lmcc.ci.lubbock.tx.us					
Macon Centreplex Coliseum 200 Coliseum Dr	Macon	GA	31217	478-751-9152	751-9154
TF: 877-532-6144 ■ *Web:* www.maconcentreplex.com					
Madison Square Garden 2 Pennsylvania Plaza	New York	NY	10121	212-465-6000	465-6092*
*Fax: Sales ■ *Web:* www.thegarden.com					
Mark of the Quad Cities 1201 River Dr	Moline	IL	61265	309-764-2001	764-2192
Web: www.themark.org					
Martin Luther King Jr Arena 301 W Oglethorpe Ave	Savannah	GA	31401	912-651-6550	651-6552
Web: www.savannahcivic.com					
McMahon Stadium 1817 Crowchild Tr NW	Calgary	AB	T2M4R6	403-289-0205	282-2018
Web: www.stampeders.com					
Meadowlands Sports Complex 50 State Hwy 120	East Rutherford	NJ	07073	201-935-8500	935-4262
Web: www.meadowlands.com					
Mellon Arena 66 Mario Lemieux Pl	Pittsburgh	PA	15219	412-642-1800	642-1925
Web: www.mellonarena.com					
Memorial Stadium 200 E Florida Ave	Champaign	IL	61820	217-333-1000	
MetraPark Arena 308 6th Ave N	Billings	MT	59101	406-256-2400	254-7991
TF: 800-366-8538 ■ *Web:* www.metrapark.com					
MetroCentre Arena 300 Elm St	Rockford	IL	61101	815-968-5600	968-5451
Web: www.centreevents.com/MetroCentre/					
Metrodome 900 S 5th St	Minneapolis	MN	55415	612-332-0386	332-8334
Web: www.msfc.com					
MGM Grand Garden Arena 3799 Las Vegas Blvd S	Las Vegas	NV	89109	702-891-1111	891-3036
Web: www.mgmgrand.com					
Michigan Stadium 1201 S Main St University of Michigan	Ann Arbor	MI	48104	734-647-2583	647-1188
TF: 866-296-6849 ■ *Web:* www.mgoblue.com					
Miller Park 1 Brewers Way	Milwaukee	WI	53214	414-902-4400	902-4058
Web: www.milwaukeebrewers.com					
Minute Maid Park 501 Crawford St	Houston	TX	77002	713-259-8000	259-8981
Web: www.astros.com					
Mississippi Veterans Memorial Stadium 2531 N State St	Jackson	MS	39216	601-354-6021	354-6019
Web: www.ms-veteransstadium.com					
Monster Park Jamestown Ave & Harney Way	San Francisco	CA	94124	415-467-1994	467-3049
Web: www.sf49ers.com					
M&T Bank Stadium 1101 Russell St	Baltimore	MD	21230	410-261-7283	
Web: www.baltimoreravens.com					
Mullins Center 200 Commonwealth Ave University of Massachusetts	Amherst	MA	01003	413-545-3001	545-3005
Web: www.mullinscenter.com					
Municipal Auditorium Arena 201 W 13th St	Kansas City	MO	64105	816-513-5000	513-5002
TF: 800-821-7060 ■ *Web:* www.kcconvention.com					
Nassau Veterans Memorial Coliseum 1255 Hempstead Tpke	Uniondale	NY	11553	516-794-9300	794-9389
Web: www.nassaucoliseum.com					
Nationwide Arena 200 W Nationwide Blvd	Columbus	OH	43215	614-246-4625	246-4300
TF: 800-645-2657 ■ *Web:* www.nationwidearena.com					
Neil S Blaisdell Center Arena 777 Ward Ave	Honolulu	HI	96814	808-527-5400	527-5433
Web: www.blaisdellcenter.com					
New Orleans Arena 1501 Girod St	New Orleans	LA	70113	504-587-3663	587-3848
TF: 800-756-7074 ■ *Web:* www.neworleansarena.com					
Norfolk Scope Arena 201 E Brambleton Ave Scope Arena	Norfolk	VA	23510	757-664-6464	664-6990
Web: www.norfolkscope.com					
North Charleston Coliseum & Convention Center 5001 Coliseum Dr	North Charleston	SC	29418	843-529-5050	529-5010
Web: www.coliseumpac.com					
Oakland Arena & McAfee Coliseum 7000 Coliseum Way	Oakland	CA	94621	510-569-2121	569-4246
Web: www.coliseum.com					
Ohio Stadium 411 Woody Hayes Dr	Columbus	OH	43210	614-292-7572	292-0506
Web: www.ohiostatebuckeyes.com					
Olympic Center Arena 2634 Main St	Lake Placid	NY	12946	518-523-1655	523-9275
TF: 800-462-6236 ■ *Web:* www.orda.org					
Olympic Stadium 4549 Pierre-de-Coubertin Ave	Montreal	QC	H1V3N7	514-252-4679	252-9401
TF: 800-463-9767					
Orange Bowl Stadium 1501 NW 3rd St	Miami	FL	33125	305-643-7100	643-7115
Web: www.orangebowlstadium.com					
Oriole Park at Camden Yards 333 W Camden St	Baltimore	MD	21201	410-576-0300	547-9800
TF: 888-848-2473 ■ *Web:* www.orioles.mlb.com					
Palace of Auburn Hills 5 Championship Dr	Auburn Hills	MI	48326	248-377-0100	377-3260*
*Fax: PR ■ *Web:* www.palacenet.com					
Palmer David S Arena 100 W Main St	Danville	IL	61832	217-431-2424	431-6444
Web: www.palmerarena.com					
Paul Brown Stadium 1 Paul Brown Stadium	Cincinnati	OH	45202	513-621-8383	621-3570
Web: www.bengals.com/paulbrownstadium					
Pengrowth Saddledome 555 Saddledome Rise SE	Calgary	AB	T2G2WI	403-777-2177	777-2171*
*Fax: Hum Res					
Peoria Civic Center Arena 201 SW Jefferson St	Peoria	IL	61602	309-673-8900	673-9223
Web: www.peoriaciviccenter.com					
Pepsi Center 1000 Chopper Cir	Denver	CO	80204	303-405-1111	405-1315
Web: www.pepsicenter.com					
Perani Arena & Event Center 3501 Lapeer Rd	Flint	MI	48503	810-744-0580	744-2906
Web: www.peraniarena.com					
Percival Molson Memorial Stadium 475 Pine Ave W	Montreal	QC	H2W1S4	514-871-2266	871-2277
Web: www.montrealalouettes.com					
Petco Park 100 Park Blvd	San Diego	CA	92101	619-795-5000	795-5049
Web: sandiego.padres.mlb.com					
PGE Park 1844 SW Morrison St	Portland	OR	97205	503-553-5400	553-5405
Web: www.pgepark.com					
Philips Arena 1 Philips Dr	Atlanta	GA	30303	404-878-3000	878-3055
Web: www.philipsarena.com					
PNC Park 115 Federal St	Pittsburgh	PA	15212	412-321-2827	325-4404
TF: 800-289-2827 ■ *Web:* pittsburgh.pirates.mlb.com					
Pontiac Silverdome 1200 Featherstone Rd	Pontiac	MI	48342	248-858-7358	456-1691
Web: www.silverdome.com					
Pyramid Arena 1 Auction Ave	Memphis	TN	38105	901-521-9675	528-0153
Web: www.pyramidarena.com					
Qualcomm Stadium 9449 Friars Rd	San Diego	CA	92108	619-641-3100	283-0460
Web: www.sandiego.gov/qualcomm					
Quicken Loans Arena 1 Center Ct	Cleveland	OH	44115	216-420-2000	420-2298
TF: 800-332-2287 ■ *Web:* www.theqarena.com					
Qwest Arena 233 S Capitol Blvd	Boise	ID	83702	208-424-2200	424-2222
Web: www.qwestarenaidaho.com					
Qwest Field 800 Occidental Ave S Suite 200	Seattle	WA	98134	206-381-7555	381-7555
Web: www.seahawks.com/stadium.aspx?SecID=31					
Rabobank Arena Theater & Convention Center 1001 Truxtun Ave	Bakersfield	CA	93301	661-852-7300	861-9904
Web: www.rabobankarena.com					
Ralph Wilson Stadium 1 Bills Dr	Orchard Park	NY	14127	716-648-1800	649-6446
Web: buffalobills.com					
Rangers Ballpark in Arlington 1000 Ballpark Way Suite 400	Arlington	TX	76011	817-273-5222	273-5285
TF: 888-968-3927 ■ *Web:* www.texasrangers.com					
Raymond James Stadium 4201 N Dale Mabry Hwy	Tampa	FL	33607	813-350-6500	673-4308
Web: www.tampasportsauthority.com/rjs					
RBC Center 1400 Edwards Mill Rd	Raleigh	NC	27607	919-467-7825	861-2310
Web: www.rbccenter.com					
RCA Dome 100 S Capitol Ave	Indianapolis	IN	46225	317-262-3410	262-3685
Web: www.iccrd.com					
Reliant Astrodome 1 Reliant Park	Houston	TX	77054	832-667-1400	667-1748
Web: www.reliantpark.com					
Reliant Park 1 Reliant Park	Houston	TX	77054	832-667-1400	
Web: www.reliantpark.com					
Reliant Stadium 2 Reliant Park	Houston	TX	77054	832-667-2000	667-2100
Web: www.reliantpark.com					
Reunion Arena 777 Sports St	Dallas	TX	75207	214-800-3000	800-3040
Web: www.reunionarena.org					
Rexall Place 7300 116th Ave	Edmonton	AB	T5B4X5	780-471-7210	471-8195
Web: www.northlands.com/facilities/rp_main.html					
RFK Stadium 2400 E Capitol St SE	Washington	DC	20003	202-547-9077	547-7460
Web: washington.nationals.mlb.com/NASApp/mlb/index.jsp?c_id=was					
Richmond Coliseum 601 E Leigh St	Richmond	VA	23219	804-780-4970	780-4606
Web: www.richmondcoliseum.net					
Roanoke Civic Center 710 Williamson Rd	Roanoke	VA	24016	540-853-2241	853-2748
Web: www.roanokeciviccenter.com					
Robert F Kennedy Stadium 2400 E Capitol St SE	Washington	DC	20003	202-547-9077	547-7460
Web: washington.nationals.mlb.com/NASApp/mlb/index.jsp?c_id=was					
Roberts Stadium 2600 Division St	Evansville	IN	47711	812-476-1383	476-1881
Web: www.smgevansville.com/roberts.html					
Roger Dean Stadium 4751 Main St	Jupiter	FL	33458	561-775-1818	691-6886
Web: www.rogerdeanstadium.com					
Rogers Centre 1 Blue Jays Way Suite 3000	Toronto	ON	M5V1J3	416-341-3663	341-3101
Web: www.rogerscentre.com					

Phone Fax

Rose Bowl 1001 Rose Bowl Dr .... Pasadena CA 91103 626-577-3100 405-0992
Web: www.rosebowlstadium.com
Rose Garden 1 Center Ct .... Portland OR 97227 503-797-9619 736-2191
TF: 877-789-7673
Rose Quarter Facilities 1 Center Ct Suite 200 .... Portland OR 97227 503-235-8771 736-2187
Web: www.rosequarter.com
Rupp Arena 430 W Vine St .... Lexington KY 40507 859-233-4567 253-2718
Web: www.rupparena.com
Safeco Field 1250 1st Ave S .... Seattle WA 98134 206-346-4000 346-4300
Web: seattle.mariners.mlb.com
San Jose Municipal Stadium 588 E Alma Ave .... San Jose CA 95112 408-297-1435 297-1453
Web: www.sjgiants.com
Savvis Center 1401 Clark Ave .... Saint Louis MO 63103 314-622-5400 622-5410
Web: www.savviscenter.net
Scotiabank Place 1000 Palladium Dr .... Kanata ON K2V1A5 613-599-0100 599-0358
TF: 800-444-7367 ■ Web: www2.scotiabankplace.com
Scottsdale Stadium 7408 E Osborn Rd .... Scottsdale AZ 85251 480-312-2856 312-7729
Web: www.scottsdaleaz.gov/stadium/
Seattle Center 305 Harrison St .... Seattle WA 98109 206-684-7200 684-7342
Web: www.seattlecenter.com
Selland Arena 700 M St .... Fresno CA 93721 559-445-8100 445-8110
Web: www.fresnoconventioncenter.com
Shea Stadium 123-01 Roosevelt Ave .... Flushing NY 11368 718-507-6387 507-6395
Web: www.mets.com
Show Me Center 1333 N Sprigg St .... Cape Girardeau MO 63701 573-651-2297 651-5054
Web: www.showmecenter.biz
Silverdome 1200 Featherstone Rd .... Pontiac MI 48342 248-858-7358 456-1691
Web: www.silverdome.com
Sioux Falls Arena 1201 N West Ave .... Sioux Falls SD 57104 605-367-7288 338-1463
TF: 800-338-3177 ■ Web: www.sfarena.com
Sky Sox Stadium 4385 Tutt Blvd .... Colorado Springs CO 80922 719-597-1449 597-2491
Web: www.skysox.com
Soldier Field 1410 S Museum Campus Dr .... Chicago IL 60605 312-235-7000 235-7030
Web: www.soldierfield.net
Sommet Center 501 Broadway .... Nashville TN 37203 615-770-2000 770-2010
Web: www.sommetcenter.com
Sovereign Bank Arena 81 Hamilton Ave .... Trenton NJ 08611 609-656-3200 656-3201
TF: 888-722-8499 ■ Web: www.sovereignbankarena.com
Spartan Stadium 1257 S 10th St .... San Jose CA 95192 408-924-1850 924-1169
TF: 877-757-8859 ■ Web: www.spartanshops.com/stadium
Spokane Arena 720 W Mallon Ave .... Spokane WA 99201 509-279-7000 279-7050
Web: www.spokanearena.com
St Pete Times Forum 401 Channelside Dr .... Tampa FL 33602 813-301-6600 301-1481
Web: www.sptimesforum.com
Staples Center 1111 S Figueroa St .... Los Angeles CA 90015 213-742-7100 742-7296
Web: www.staplescenter.com
State Fair Arena 333 Gordon Cooper Blvd .... Oklahoma City OK 73107 405-948-6700 948-6828
Sullivan George M Sports Arena 1600 Gambell St .... Anchorage AK 99501 907-279-0618 274-0676
Web: www.sullivanarena.com
Sun Bowl Stadium 2701 Sun Bowl Dr .... El Paso TX 79902 915-747-5265 747-5228
Web: www.sunbowl.org/sbstadium.htm
Sun Devil Stadium 500 E Valley Way Arizona State University .... Tempe AZ 85287 480-965-3482 965-1261
Web: www.asu.edu/tour/main/stad.html
Superdome 1500 Poydras PO Box 52439 .... New Orleans LA 70152 504-587-3663 587-3848
TF: 800-756-7074 ■ Web: www.superdome.com
Taco Bell Arena 1401 Bronco Ln .... Boise ID 83725 208-426-1900 426-1998
Web: www.tacobellarena.com
Tacoma Dome Arena & Exhibition Hall 2727 E 'D' St .... Tacoma WA 98421 253-272-3663 593-7620*
*Fax: Mktg ■ Web: www.tacomadome.org
Target Center Arena 600 1st Ave N .... Minneapolis MN 55403 612-673-1300 673-1370
Web: www.targetcenter.com
TD Banknorth Garden 100 Legends Way .... Boston MA 02114 617-624-1050 624-1818
Web: www.tdbanknorthgarden.com
Texas Stadium 2401 E Airport Fwy .... Irving TX 75062 972-785-4000 785-4709
Web: www.dallascowboys.com/stadium.cfm
Thomas & Mack Center/Sam Boyd Stadium
4505 Maryland Pkwy .... Las Vegas NV 89154 702-895-3761 895-1099
Web: www.thomasandmack.com
Times Union Center 51 S Pearl St .... Albany NY 12207 518-487-2000 487-2020
Web: timesunioncenter-albany.com
Toyota Center 1510 Polk St .... Houston TX 77002 713-758-7200 758-7315
Web: www.houstontoyotacenter.com
Tropicana Field 1 Tropicana Dr .... Saint Petersburg FL 33705 727-825-3120 825-3204
TF: 888-326-7297 ■ Web: tampabay.devilrays.mlb.com
Turner Field 755 Hank Aaron Dr .... Atlanta GA 30315 404-522-7630 614-1329
Web: www.atlantabraves.com
United Center 1901 W Madison St .... Chicago IL 60612 312-455-4500 455-4511
Web: www.unitedcenter.com
University of Phoenix Stadium 1 Cardinals Dr .... Glendale AZ 85305 623-433-7100 433-7199
Web: www.azcardinalsstadium.com
US Airways Center 201 E Jefferson St .... Phoenix AZ 85004 602-379-2000 379-2093
Web: www.usairwayscenter.com
US Cellular Center 370 1st Ave NE .... Cedar Rapids IA 52401 319-398-5211 362-2102
Web: www.uscellularcenter.com
US Cellular Field 333 W 35th St .... Chicago IL 60616 312-674-1000 674-5104*
*Fax: Hum Res ■ Web: www.chisox.com
US Olympic Training Center
1750 E Boulder St 1 Olympic Plaza .... Colorado Springs CO 80909 719-632-5551 866-4677*
*Fax: PR ■ Web: www.usolympicteam.com
US Olympic Training Center 196 Old Military Rd .... Lake Placid NY 12946 518-523-2600 523-1570
Web: www.olympic-usa.org
Van Andel Arena 130 Fulton St W .... Grand Rapids MI 49503 616-742-6600 742-6197
Web: www.vanandelarena.com
Verizon Center 601 F St NW .... Washington DC 20004 202-628-3200 661-5083
Web: www.verizoncenter.com
Verizon Wireless Arena 555 Elm St .... Manchester NH 03101 603-644-5000 644-1575
Web: www.verizonwirelessarena.com
Wachovia Center 3601 S Broad St .... Philadelphia PA 19148 215-336-3600 389-9506
Web: www.comcast-spectacor.com
Wachovia Spectrum 3601 S Broad St .... Philadelphia PA 19148 215-336-3600 389-9506
Web: www.comcast-spectacor.com
War Memorial Stadium 1 Stadium Dr .... Little Rock AR 72205 501-663-6385 663-6387
Web: www.arkansas.gov/wms
Will Rogers Memorial Center 3401 W Lancaster Ave .... Fort Worth TX 76107 817-392-7469 392-8170
Web: www.fortworthgov.org/publicevents/wrmc
Wilson Ralph Stadium 1 Bills Dr .... Orchard Park NY 14127 716-648-1800 649-6446
Web: buffalobills.com
Winnipeg Stadium 1465 Maroons Rd .... Winnipeg MB R3G0L6 204-784-2583 783-5222
Web: www.bluebombers.com
Wrigley Field 1060 W Addison St .... Chicago IL 60613 773-404-2827 404-4129
Web: www.cubs.com
Xcel Energy Center 175 W Kellogg Blvd Suite 501 .... Saint Paul MN 55102 651-265-4800 265-4899
Web: www.xcelenergycenter.com
Yankee Stadium 161st St & River Ave .... Bronx NY 10451 718-293-4300 293-8431
Web: www.yankees.com

724 STAFFING SERVICES

SEE ALSO Employment Offices - Government p. 1617; Employment Services - Online p. 1618; Executive Recruiting Firms p. 1627; Modeling Agencies p. 1975; Professional Employer Organizations (PEOs) p. 2142; Talent Agencies p. 2337

Phone Fax

Ablest Inc 1511 N Westshore Blvd Suite 900 .... Tampa FL 33607 813-830-7700 830-7029
AMEX: AIH ■ Web: www.ablest.com
Accountemps Div Robert Half International Inc
2884 Sand Hill Rd Suite 200 .... Menlo Park CA 94025 650-234-6000 234-6930*
*Fax: Mktg ■ Web: www.accountemps.com
Accounting Principals 1 Independent Dr Suite 215 .... Jacksonville FL 32202 904-360-2400 360-2394
Web: www.accountingprincipals.com
Ace Personnel 7932 Santa Fe .... Overland Park KS 66204 913-901-2410 901-2435
Web: www.acepersonnel.com
Acsys Inc 111 Anza Blvd Suite 400 .... Burlingame CA 94010 650-579-1111 579-1927
Web: www.acsysinc.com
Act-1 Group 1999 W 190th St .... Torrance CA 90504 310-750-3400 750-1100
Web: www.act-1.com
Adecco Inc 175 Broad Hollow Rd .... Melville NY 11747 631-844-7800 844-7022*
NYSE: ADO ■ *Fax: Mktg ■ TF: 877-632-9169 ■ Web: www.adecco.com
Aerotek Inc 7301 Parkway Dr .... Hanover MD 21076 410-540-7000 540-7532
TF: 800-435-2029 ■ Web: www.aerotek.com
All Medical Personnel 4651 Sheridan St .... Hollywood FL 33021 954-922-9696 927-0590
TF: 800-706-2378 ■ Web: www.allmedstaffing.com
Allegis Group Inc 7301 Parkway Dr .... Hanover MD 21076 410-579-3000 540-7709
TF: 800-927-6052 ■ Web: www.allegisgroup.com
Allied Health Group 145 Technology Pkwy NW .... Norcross GA 30092 770-246-9191 246-0882
TF: 800-741-4674 ■ Web: alliedhealth.com
AllStates Technical Services 1900 International Dr .... Birmingham AL 35243 877-972-5401 213-6892*
*Fax Area Code: 888 ■ TF: 800-432-8006 ■ Web: www.allstatestech.com
ALTRES Inc 967 Kapiolani Blvd .... Honolulu HI 96814 808-591-4900 591-4914
TF: 800-373-1955 ■ Web: www.altres.com
American Healthcare Services LLC 1000 John R Suite 250 .... Troy MI 48083 248-588-9700 588-2828
TF: 866-227-9998 ■ Web: www.americanhealthcareservices.net
AMN Healthcare Services Inc 12400 High Bluff Dr Suite 100 .... San Diego CA 92130 858-792-0711 282-1211*
NYSE: AHS ■ *Fax Area Code: 800 ■ TF: 866-510-1904 ■ Web: www.amnhealthcare.com
APEX Systems Inc 4400 Cox Rd .... Richmond VA 23060 804-254-2600 254-7290
TF: 800-452-7391 ■ Web: www.apexsystemsinc.com
AppleOne Employment Services Inc 327 W Broadway .... Glendale CA 91204 818-240-8688 265-5514
TF: 800-872-2677 ■ Web: www.appleone.com
AppleOne Employment Services Inc 50 Paxman Rd Unit 8 .... Etobicoke ON M9C1B7 416-622-0100 622-6327
TF: 800-564-5644 ■ Web: www.appleone.com
Aquent LLC 711 Boylston St .... Boston MA 02116 617-535-6000 535-5004
TF: 800-878-0900 ■ Web: www.aquent.com
ARC Industries Inc 2879 Johnstown Rd .... Columbus OH 43219 614-475-7007 342-5680
TF: 800-734-7007 ■ Web: www.arcind.com
Aspire Group 52 2nd Ave 1st Fl .... Waltham MA 02451 781-522-8390 890-1810
TF: 800-487-2967 ■ Web: www.aspiregroup.net
ATC Healthcare Inc 1983 Marcus Ave Suite E122 .... Lake Success NY 11042 516-750-1655 750-1756
AMEX: AHN ■ Web: www.atchealthcare.com
ATC Travelers 1983 Marcus Ave Suite E122 .... Lake Success NY 11042 866-562-7667 546-5616*
*Fax Area Code: 800 ■ Web: www.atctravelers.com
Atlantic Group 5426 Robin Hood Rd .... Norfolk VA 23513 757-857-6400 233-7441
TF: 800-446-8131 ■ Web: www.atlanticgroup.com
ATS Services Inc 9700 Phillips Hwy Suite 101 .... Jacksonville FL 32256 904-645-9505 645-0390
TF: 800-346-5574 ■ Web: www.ats-services.com
Attorney Resource 750 N Saint Paul St Suite 540 .... Dallas TX 75201 214-922-8050 871-3041
Web: www.attorneyresource.com
Bartech Group 17199 N Laurel Park Dr Suite 224 .... Livonia MI 48152 734-953-5050 953-5075
TF: 800-828-4410 ■ Web: www.thebartechgroup.com
Bartech Technical Services 3980 Chicago Dr .... Grandville MI 49418 616-532-5555 532-6119
TF: 800-968-5776 ■ Web: www.bartechgroup.com
Bay Area Anesthesia Inc 617 S State St PO Box 1547 .... Ukiah CA 95482 707-462-1557 462-5208
TF: 800-327-8427 ■ Web: www.wwmedical.com/bayarea.html
Brown-Eagle Corp 5330 Dijon Dr .... Baton Rouge LA 70808 225-769-1111 769-1175
Butler International Inc 110 Summit Ave .... Montvale NJ 07645 201-573-8000 573-9723
NASDAQ: BUTLE ■ TF: 888-773-4357 ■ Web: www.butlerintl.com
C & A Industries Inc 11825 Q St .... Omaha NE 68137 402-891-0009 891-9161
TF: 800-574-9829 ■ Web: www.ca-industries.com
Calian Technology Ltd 2 Beaverbrook Rd .... Kanata ON K2K1L1 613-599-8600 599-8650
TSX: CTY ■ TF: 877-225-4264 ■ Web: www.calian.com
Career Blazers Inc 590 5th Ave 6th Fl .... New York NY 10036 212-719-3232 221-0452
Web: www.careerblazers.com
CareerBuilder.com 200 N LaSalle St Suite 1100 .... Chicago IL 60601 773-527-3600 349-4467*
*Fax Area Code: 877 ■ TF: 800-638-4212 ■ Web: www.careerbuilder.com
CareerStaff Unlimited Inc 13105 Northwest Fwy .... Houston TX 77063 713-297-9000
TF: 800-443-1221 ■ Web: www.careerstaff.com
CDI Corp 1717 Arch St 35th Fl .... Philadelphia PA 19103 215-569-2200 569-1300
NYSE: CDI ■ Web: www.cdicorp.com
Cejka Search Inc 222 S Central Ave Suite 400 .... Saint Louis MO 63105 314-726-1603 726-0026
TF: 800-678-7858 ■ Web: www.cejkasearch.com
COMFORCE Corp 415 Crossways Park Dr .... Woodbury NY 11797 516-437-3300 437-3392
AMEX: CFS ■ TF: 877-266-3672 ■ Web: www.comforce.com
CompHealth Inc 4021 S 700 East Suite 300 .... Salt Lake City UT 84107 801-264-6400 264-6464
TF: 800-453-3030 ■ Web: www.comphealth.com
Compunnel Software Group Inc 1000 Rt 9 N Suite 102 .... Woodbridge NJ 07095 732-636-1999 636-1747
Web: www.compunnel.com
Computer Consulting Assoc International Inc
200 Pequot Ave .... Southport CT 06480 203-255-8966 255-8501
Web: www.ccaii.com
Compuware Corp Professional Services Div
11095 Viking Dr Suite 430 .... Eden Prairie MN 55344 612-851-2200 851-2300
TF Cust Svc: 800-358-3048 ■ Web: www.compuware.com/services
Comsys IT Partners Inc 4400 Post Oak Pkwy Suite 1800 .... Houston TX 77027 713-386-1400 961-0719
NASDAQ: CITP ■ TF: 877-626-6797 ■ Web: www.comsys.com
Consultis 4401 N Federal Hwy Suite 100 .... Boca Raton FL 33431 561-362-9104 367-9802
TF: 800-275-2667 ■ Web: www.consultis.com
Continuum Legal 1700 Old Meadow Rd Suite 100 .... McLean VA 22102 703-734-7474 734-8839
Web: www.continuumlegal.com
CORESTAFF Services 1775 St James Place Suite 300 .... Houston TX 77056 713-438-1400 438-1763*
*Fax: Mktg ■ Web: www.corestaff.com
CPC Logistics Inc 14528 S Outer 40 Rd Suite 210 .... Chesterfield MO 63017 314-542-2266 542-0666
TF: 800-274-3746 ■ Web: www.callcpc.com
Cross Country Healthcare Inc
6551 Park of Commerce Blvd Suite 200 .... Boca Raton FL 33487 561-998-2232 998-8533
NASDAQ: CCRN ■ TF: 800-347-2264 ■ Web: www.crosscountryhealthcare.com
CyberStaff America Ltd 3-E 28th St 9th Fl .... New York NY 10016 212-244-2300 244-1025
TF: 888-244-2300 ■ Web: cyberstaff.com
Davis Cos 33 Boston Post Rd W .... Marlborough MA 01752 508-481-9500 481-8519
TF: 800-482-9494 ■ Web: www.daviscos.com
Design Group Staffing Services Inc 10012 Jasper Ave .... Edmonton AB T5J1R2 780-428-1505 428-7095
TF: 800-770-1228 ■ Web: www.designgroupstaffing.com

	City	State	ZIP	Phone	Fax
Devon Consulting 950 W Valley Rd Suite 2602 *TF:* 800-229-5709 ■ *Web:* www.devonconsulting.com	Wayne	PA	19087	610-964-2700	964-2708
Diversco Integrated Services Inc 105 Diversco Dr *TF:* 800-277-3420 ■ *Web:* www.diversco.com	Spartanburg	SC	29307	864-579-3420	579-9578
Diversified Corporate Resources Inc 10670 N Central Expy Suite 600 **Fax Area Code:* 866 ■ *Web:* www.dcri.net	Dallas	TX	75231	972-458-8500	280-8908*
Diversified Medical Staffing LLC 3410 Belle Chase Way Suite 600 *TF:* 800-881-3205 ■ *Web:* www.dmshome.com	Lansing	MI	48911	517-702-4030	702-4093
Durham Cos Inc 6300 Transit Rd *TF:* 800-633-7724 ■ *Web:* www.durhamstaffing.com	Depew	NY	14043	716-684-3333	681-7408
Durham Exchange Club Industries Inc 1717 E Lawson St *Web:* www.deci.org	Durham	NC	27703	919-596-1341	596-6380
Eagle Professional Resources Inc 67 Yonge St Suite 200 *TF:* 800-281-2339 ■ *Web:* www.eagleonline.com	Toronto	ON	M5E1J8	416-861-0636	861-8401
EmCare 1717 Main St Suite 5200 *TF:* 800-527-2145 ■ *Web:* www.emcare.com	Dallas	TX	75201	214-712-2000	712-2444
Emergency Consultants Inc 4075 Copper Ridge Dr *TF:* 800-253-1795 ■ *Web:* www.eci-med.cc	Traverse City	MI	49684	231-946-8970	946-1730
EmployBridge LLC 222 W Las Colinas Blvd Suite 1250E *TF:* 800-787-6750 ■ *Web:* www.employbridge.net	Irving	TX	75039	214-296-6700	296-6812
enherent Corp 80 Lamberton Rd 1st Fl *TF:* 877-778-4768 ■ *Web:* www.enherent.com	Windsor	CT	06095	860-687-2200	687-2210
Ensearch Management Consultants 905 E Cotati Ave *TF:* 800-473-6776 ■ *Web:* www.ensearch.com	Cotati	CA	94931	707-795-3800	795-6200
Entech Personnel Services Inc 363 W Big Beaver Rd *TF:* 800-333-6832 ■ *Web:* www.entechpersonnel.com	Troy	MI	48084	248-528-1444	528-6982
EuroSoft Inc 1705 S Capital of Texas Hwy Suite 200 *TF:* 888-329-8100 ■ *Web:* www.eurosoft-inc.com	Austin	TX	78746	512-329-8100	329-6776
Express Personnel Services 8516 NW Expressway *TF:* 800-222-4057 ■ *Web:* www.expresspersonnel.com	Oklahoma City	OK	73162	405-840-5000	717-5665
First Assist Inc 4720 Montgomery Ln Suite 300 *TF:* 800-426-1724 ■ *Web:* www.firstassist.com	Bethesda	MD	20814	301-718-2210	654-9204
G&A Partners 4801 Woodway Dr Suite 210W *TF:* 800-253-8562 ■ *Web:* www.gnapartners.com	Houston	TX	77056	713-784-1181	784-2705
General Employment Enterprises Inc 1 Tower Ln Suite 2200 *AMEX: JOB* ■ *Web:* www.generalemployment.com	Oakbrook Terrace	IL	60181	630-954-0400	954-0447
Gibson Arnold & Assoc 1776 Yorktown St Suite 350 *TF:* 800-879-2007 ■ *Web:* www.gibsonarnold.com	Houston	TX	77056	713-572-3000	572-4664
Gonzer LJ Assoc Inc 1225 Raymond Blvd *TF:* 800-631-4218 ■ *Web:* www.gonzer.com	Newark	NJ	07102	973-624-5600	624-7170
Half Robert International Inc 2884 Sand Hill Rd Suite 200 *NYSE: RHI* ■ *Web:* www.rhii.com	Menlo Park	CA	94025	650-854-9700	234-6930
Headway Corporate Resources Inc 317 Madison Ave 18th Fl *Web:* www.headwaycorp.com	New York	NY	10017	212-672-6600	672-6599
Info Technologies Inc 187 Rt 36 Bldg A Suite 220 *Web:* www.infotechnologiesinc.com	West Long Branch	NJ	07764	732-222-1250	222-4050
InteliStaf Healthcare Inc 18 W 140 Butterfield Rd Suite 600 *Web:* www.intelistaf.com	Oakbrook Terrace	IL	60181	630-916-3950	916-3998
Interim HealthCare Inc 1601 Sawgrass Corporate Pkwy *TF:* 800-338-7786 ■ *Web:* www.interimhealthcare.com	Sunrise	FL	33323	954-858-6000	858-2820
Joule Inc 1235 US Rt 1 S *TF:* 800-906-0906 ■ *Web:* www.jouleinc.com	Edison	NJ	08837	732-548-5444	603-0898
Judge Group Inc 300 Conshohocken State Rd Suite 300 *TF:* 888-228-7162 ■ *Web:* www.judge.com	West Conshohocken	PA	19428	610-667-7700	667-1058
Kelly Law Registry Inc 999 W Big Beaver Rd *Web:* www.thelawregistry.com	Troy	MI	48084	248-362-4444	822-3376
Kelly Services Inc 999 W Big Beaver Rd *NASDAQ: KELYA* ■ **Fax:* Mail Rm ■ *Web:* www.kellyservices.com	Troy	MI	48084	248-362-4444	244-5292*
Kforce Inc 1001 E Palm Ave *NASDAQ: KFRC* ■ *TF:* 888-663-3626 ■ *Web:* www.kforce.com	Tampa	FL	33605	813-552-5000	552-2588
Kimco Staffing Services Inc 17872 Cowan Ave *TF:* 800-649-5627 ■ *Web:* www.kimco.com	Irvine	CA	92614	949-752-6996	752-1126
Labor Finders International Inc 11426 N Jog Rd *Web:* www.laborfinders.com	Palm Beach Gardens	FL	33418	561-627-6507	627-6556
Labor Ready Inc PO Box 2910 *NYSE: LRW* ■ **Fax Area Code:* 800 ■ *TF:* 800-991-4991 ■ *Web:* www.laborready.com	Tacoma	WA	98401	253-383-9101	850-9810*
Lakeshore Staffing Inc 1 N Franklin St Suite 600 *Web:* www.lakeshorestaffing.com	Chicago	IL	60606	312-251-7575	251-7580
LJ Gonzer Assoc Inc 1225 Raymond Blvd *TF:* 800-631-4218 ■ *Web:* www.gonzer.com	Newark	NJ	07102	973-624-5600	624-7170
Lumen Legal 1025 N Campbell Rd *TF:* 877-933-1330 ■ *Web:* www.lumenlegal.com	Royal Oak	MI	48067	248-597-0400	597-0410
Major Legal Services 1111 Chester Ave 510 Park Plaza *TF:* 800-808-3097 ■ *Web:* www.lawplacement.com	Cleveland	OH	44114	216-579-9782	579-1662
Manpower Inc 5301 N Ironwood Rd *NYSE: MAN* ■ *Web:* www.manpower.com	Milwaukee	WI	53217	414-961-1000	906-7945
Med-Emerg International Inc 6711 Mississauga Rd Suite 404 *TF:* 800-265-3429 ■ *Web:* www.med-emerg.com	Mississauga	ON	L5N2W3	905-858-1368	858-1399
Medical Staffing Assoc Inc 6731 Whittier Ave Suite A300 *TF:* 800-235-5105 ■ *Web:* www.medstaffer.com	McLean	VA	22101	703-893-1773	893-7358
Medical Staffing Network Holdings Inc 901 Yamato Rd Suite 110 *NYSE: MRN* ■ *Web:* www.msnhealth.com	Boca Raton	FL	33431	561-322-1300	322-1200
Medstaff National Medical Staffing Inc 170 Southport Dr *TF:* 800-476-3275 ■ *Web:* www.medstafflt.com	Morrisville	NC	27560	919-383-4075	655-1343
Midcom Corp 1056 N Tustin Ave *TF:* 800-737-1632 ■ *Web:* www.midcom.com	Anaheim	CA	92807	714-630-1999	459-7061
Minute Men Staffing Services 3740 Carnegie Ave *Web:* www.minutemeninc.com	Cleveland	OH	44115	216-426-9675	426-2246
MPS Group Inc 1 Independent Dr *NYSE: MPS* ■ *TF:* 800-852-2281 ■ *Web:* www.mpsgroup.com	Jacksonville	FL	32202	904-360-2000	360-2972
National Engineering Service Corp 72 Mirona Rd **Fax Area Code:* 800 ■ *TF:* 800-562-3463 ■ *Web:* www.nesc.com	Portsmouth	NH	03801	603-431-9740	637-2562*
North Star Communications Group Inc 1900 International Park Dr *TF:* 877-862-8682 ■ *Web:* www.northstar.net	Birmingham	AL	35243	205-972-5300	972-6918
Nursefinders Inc 524 E Lamar Blvd Suite 300 *TF:* 800-445-0459 ■ *Web:* www.nursefinders.com	Arlington	TX	76011	817-460-1181	462-9128
OfficeTeam Div Robert Half International Inc 2884 Sand Hill Rd Suite 200 **Fax:* Mktg ■ *Web:* www.officeteam.com	Menlo Park	CA	94025	650-234-6000	234-6930*
On Assignment Inc 26651 W Agoura Rd *NASDAQ: ASGN* ■ *TF:* 800-995-7378 ■ *Web:* www.assignment.net	Calabasas	CA	91302	818-878-7900	878-7930
Orion International Consulting Group Inc 912 Capital of Texas Hwy S Bldg 1 Suite 220 *TF:* 800-336-7466 ■ *Web:* www.orioninternational.com	Austin	TX	78746	512-327-7111	327-4286
Oxford Global Resources Inc 100 Cummings Center Suite 206L *TF:* 800-426-9196 ■ *Web:* www.oxfordcorp.com	Beverly	MA	01915	978-236-1182	236-1077
PDS Technical Services 1925 John Carpenter Fwy Suite 550 *TF:* 800-270-4737 ■ *Web:* www.pdstech.com	Dallas	TX	75063	214-647-9600	647-9636
Peak Technical Services Inc 300 Penn Center Blvd Suite 800 *TF:* 800-825-8088 ■ *Web:* www.peaktechnical.com	Pittsburgh	PA	15235	412-824-2000	829-7941
Personnel Management Inc 1499 Windhorst Way Suite 220 *TF:* 888-967-5764 ■ *Web:* www.workpmi.com	Greenwood	IN	46143	317-888-4400	885-3755
Plus Group Inc 555 E Butterfield Rd Suite 330 *TF:* 800-782-3346 ■ *Web:* www.theplusgroup.com	Lombard	IL	60148	630-515-0500	515-0510
Pomeroy IT Solutions Inc 1020 Petersburg Rd *NASDAQ: PMRY* ■ *TF:* 800-846-8727 ■ *Web:* www.pomeroy.com	Hebron	KY	41048	859-586-1515	586-4414
Principal Technical Services Inc 9960 Research Dr Suite 200 *TF:* 888-787-3711 ■ *Web:* www.ptsstaffing.com	Irvine	CA	92618	949-268-4000	268-4040
Pro Staff Personnel Services 50 S 10th St Suite 500 *TF:* 800-829-5369 ■ *Web:* www.prostaff.com	Minneapolis	MN	55403	612-373-2600	339-2611
Productive Data Systems Inc 6160 S Syracuse Way Suite B-160 *TF:* 800-404-7165 ■ *Web:* www.pdsinc.com	Greenwood Village	CO	80111	303-220-7165	220-7425
Professional Placement Resources 333 1st St N Suite 200 **Fax Area Code:* 888 ■ *TF:* 888-909-5038 ■ *Web:* www.pprjobs.com	Jacksonville Beach	FL	32250	904-241-9231	794-5038*
Professional Staffing Group 89 Devonshire St *Web:* www.psgstaffing.com	Boston	MA	02109	617-250-1000	250-1099
PRWT Services Inc 1835 Market St 8th Fl *Web:* www.prwt.com	Philadelphia	PA	19103	215-569-8810	569-9893
Quantum Resources 300 Arboretum Pl Suite 500 *TF:* 800-446-9852 ■ *Web:* www.quantumresources.net	Richmond	VA	23236	804-320-4800	272-3195
Randstad North America 2015 S Park Rd	Atlanta	GA	30339	770-937-7000	
RCM Technologies Inc 2500 McClellan Ave Suite 350 *NASDAQ: RCMT* ■ *Web:* www.rcmt.com	Pennsauken	NJ	08109	856-486-1777	488-8833
RehabCare Group Inc 7733 Forsyth Blvd Suite 2300 *NYSE: RHB* ■ *TF:* 800-677-1238 ■ *Web:* www.rehabcare.com	Saint Louis	MO	63105	314-863-7422	863-0769
Remedy Temp Inc 101 Enterprise Suite 100 *NASDAQ: REMX* ■ *TF:* 800-828-3726 ■ *Web:* www.remedystaff.com	Aliso Viejo	CA	92656	949-425-7600	425-7980
Research Pharmaceutical Services Inc 610 W Germantown Pike Suite 200 **Fax Area Code:* 866 ■ *TF:* 866-777-1151 ■ *Web:* www.rpsweb.com	Plymouth Meeting	PA	19462	215-540-0700	777-1156*
Resources Global Professionals 695 Town Center Dr Suite 600 *NASDAQ: RECN* ■ *TF:* 800-900-1131 ■ *Web:* www.resourcesglobal.com	Costa Mesa	CA	92626	714-430-6400	428-6090
Right at Home Inc 11949 Q St Suite 100 *TF:* 877-697-7537 ■ *Web:* www.rightathome.net	Omaha	NE	68137	402-697-7537	697-0289
Robert Half International Inc 2884 Sand Hill Rd Suite 200 *NYSE: RHI* ■ *Web:* www.rhii.com	Menlo Park	CA	94025	650-854-9700	234-6930
Robert Half International Inc Accountemps Div 2884 Sand Hill Rd Suite 200 **Fax:* Mktg ■ *Web:* www.accountemps.com	Menlo Park	CA	94025	650-234-6000	234-6930*
Robert Half International Inc Affiliates Div 2884 Sand Hill Rd Suite 200 *Web:* www.roberthalflegal.com	Menlo Park	CA	94025	650-854-9700	234-6930
Robert Half International Inc OfficeTeam Div 2884 Sand Hill Rd Suite 200 **Fax:* Mktg ■ *Web:* www.officeteam.com	Menlo Park	CA	94025	650-234-6000	234-6930*
Roth Staffing Cos LP 333 City Blvd W Suite 100 *TF:* 888-304-4684 ■ *Web:* www.rothstaffing.com	Orange	CA	92868	714-939-8600	939-8688
Salem Group The 2 TransAm Plaza Dr Suite 170 *Web:* www.saleminc.com	Oakbrook Terrace	IL	60181	630-932-7000	932-7010
Sigma Systems Inc 201 Boston Post Rd Suite 201 *TF:* 888-867-4462 ■ *Web:* www.sigmainc.com	Marlborough	MA	01752	508-357-6300	357-6301
Silicon Valley Staffing 2200 Powell St Suite 510 *TF:* 877-660-6000 ■ *Web:* www.siliconvalleystaffing.com	Emeryville	CA	94608	510-923-9898	923-9313
Snelling Personnel Services 12801 N Central Expy Suite 700 **Fax:* Cust Svc ■ *TF:* 800-766-5556 ■ *Web:* www.snelling.com	Dallas	TX	75243	972-239-7575	239-6879*
Softworld Inc 281 Winter St Suite 301 *TF:* 877-899-1166 ■ *Web:* www.softworldinc.com	Waltham	MA	02451	781-466-8882	466-8885
Solomon-Page Group LLC 1140 Ave of the Americas 9th Fl *TF:* 800-296-7646 ■ *Web:* www.spgjobs.com	New York	NY	10036	212-403-6100	764-9260
SOS Staffing Services Inc 2650 S Decker Lake Blvd Suite 500 *TF:* 800-474-1722 ■ *Web:* www.sosstaffing.com	Salt Lake City	UT	84119	801-484-4400	483-4283
Southwest Medical Assoc Inc 1325 Broadway PO Box 2168 *TF:* 800-929-4854 ■ *Web:* www.swmed.com	Rockport	TX	78382	361-729-0646	729-0954
Special Counsel Inc 1 Independent Dr Suite 112 *TF:* 800-737-3436 ■ *Web:* www.specialcounsel.com	Jacksonville	FL	32202	904-737-3436	360-2350
Spherion Corp 2050 Spectrum Blvd *NYSE: SFN* ■ **Fax:* Hum Res ■ *TF:* 866-435-7456 ■ *Web:* www.spherion.com	Fort Lauderdale	FL	33309	954-308-7600	308-7666*
Spherion Corp Technology Group 2050 Spectrum Blvd *Web:* www.spherion.com	Fort Lauderdale	FL	33309	954-938-7600	308-7775
Staffing Now Inc 4600 Westown Pkwy Regency W 6 Suite 113 *Web:* www.staffingnow.com	West Des Moines	IA	50266	515-222-6350	222-6360
Staffmark 111 Center St *Web:* www.staffmark.com	Little Rock	AR	72201	501-235-1100	235-1199
Stivers Staffing Services Inc 200 W Monroe St Suite 1300 *Web:* www.stivers.com	Chicago	IL	60606	312-558-3550	558-1007
Strategic Workforce Solutions Legal Division 500 5th Ave Suite 2520 *Web:* www.strategicworkforce.com	New York	NY	10110	212-944-9112	944-8448
Stratus Services Group Inc 149 Ave at the Common Suite 4 *TF:* 800-777-1557 ■ *Web:* www.stratusservices.com	Shrewsbury	NJ	07702	732-866-0300	653-0292
Stride & Assoc Inc 206 Newbury St 3rd Fl *Web:* www.stridea.com	Boston	MA	02116	617-585-6500	536-9154
Superior Design International Inc 6365 NW 6th Way Suite 360 *TF:* 800-850-4222 ■ *Web:* www.sdintl.com	Fort Lauderdale	FL	33309	954-938-5400	772-5061
Superior Technical Resources Inc 250 International Dr *TF:* 800-568-8310 ■ *Web:* www.superior-sdc.com	Williamsville	NY	14231	716-631-8310	633-2026
Surgical Staff Inc 120 St Matthews Ave PO Box 192 *TF:* 800-339-9599 ■ *Web:* www.surgicalstaff.com	San Mateo	CA	94401	650-558-3999	558-3949
TAC Worldwide Cos 888 Washington St **Fax:* Hum Res ■ *TF:* 800-588-0707 ■ *Web:* www.tacworldwide.com	Dedham	MA	02026	781-251-8000	251-8064*
Talent Tree 9703 Richmond Ave **Fax:* Mktg ■ *TF:* 800-999-1555 ■ *Web:* www.talenttree.com	Houston	TX	77042	713-789-1818	974-0462*
Tandem Staffing Solutions Inc 5901 Broken Sound Pkwy Suite 450 *TF:* 800-275-5000 ■ *Web:* www.tandemstaffingsolutions.com	Boca Raton	FL	33487	561-226-8110	
Team Health Inc 1900 Winston Rd Suite 300 *TF:* 800-342-2898 ■ *Web:* www.teamhealth.com	Knoxville	TN	37919	865-693-1000	539-8030
TeamStaff Inc 300 Atrium Dr *NASDAQ: TSTF* ■ *TF:* 800-374-1001 ■ *Web:* www.teamstaff.com	Somerset	NJ	08873	732-748-1700	748-3253
TeamStaff Rx 18167 US Hwy 19 N Suite 400 **Fax Area Code:* 800 ■ *TF:* 800-345-9642 ■ *Web:* www.teamstaffrx.com	Clearwater	FL	33764	727-329-5555	955-8326*
Technisource Inc 425 W Capitol Ave Suite 3600 *TF:* 877-664-1101 ■ *Web:* www1.technisource.com	Little Rock	AR	72201	501-664-1100	537-4518
Technology & Management Staffing Inc 15245 Shady Grove Rd Suite 350 *Web:* www.t-msi.com	Rockville	MD	20850	301-840-8054	840-0828

Phone Fax

TeleSec CORESTAFF 1775 St James Pl Suite 300 .... Houston TX 77056 713-438-1400 438-1763
Web: www.corestaff.com/telesec.html
Temporary Solutions Inc 10515 Crestwood Dr. .... Manassas VA 20109 703-368-3800 368-3594
TF: 888-874-5627 ■ *Web:* www.tsijobs.com
Thinkpath Inc 201 W Creek Blvd .... Brampton ON L6T5S6 905-460-3040 460-3050
TF: 800-334-3911 ■ *Web:* www.thinkpath.com
Thompson Technologies Inc 114 Townpark Dr Suite 100 .... Kennesaw GA 30144 770-794-8380 794-8381
TF: 888-794-7947 ■ *Web:* www.ttinc.net
Todays Staffing Inc 18111 Preston Rd Suite 700 .... Dallas TX 75252 972-380-9380 713-4195
Web: www.todays.com
TRC Staffing Services Inc 100 Ashford Center N Suite 500 .... Atlanta GA 30338 770-392-1411 393-2742
TF: 800-488-8008 ■ *Web:* www.trcstaff.com
TSR Inc 400 Oser Ave Suite 150 .... Hauppauge NY 11788 631-231-0333 435-1428
NASDAQ: TSRI ■ *Web:* www.tsrconsulting.com
UltraStaff 1818 Memorial Dr .... Houston TX 77007 713-522-7100 522-0744
TF: 800-522-7707 ■ *Web:* www.ultrastaff.com
US Legal Support Inc 363 N Sam Houston Pkwy E Suite 900 .... Houston TX 77060 713-653-7100 653-7171
TF: 800-567-8757 ■ *Web:* www.uslegalsupport.com
Vedior North America 60 Harvard Mill Sq .... Wakefield MA 01880 781-213-1500 213-1520
TF: 800-648-2469 ■ *Web:* www.vediorna.com
VMC Consulting Corp 11611 Willows Rd NE .... Redmond WA 98052 425-558-7700 558-7703
Web: www.vmc-consulting.com
Volt Services Group 477 Madison Ave .... New York NY 10022 212-719-7800 719-7850
TF: 800-367-8658 ■ *Web:* www.volt.com/staffing/profile.cfm
Westaff Inc 298 N Wiget Ln .... Walnut Creek CA 94598 925-930-5300 256-1515
NASDAQ: WSTF ■ *TF:* 800-872-8367 ■ *Web:* www.westaff.com
Winston Resources Inc 122 E 42nd St 3rd Fl .... New York NY 10168 212-557-5000 682-1056
TF: 800-494-6786 ■ *Web:* www.winstonresources.com
Wontawk 25 W 43rd St Suite 812 .... New York NY 10036 212-869-3348 997-1127
Web: www.wontawk.com
Workstream Inc 2600 Lake Lucien Dr Suite 410 .... Maitland FL 32751 407-475-5500
NASDAQ: WSTM ■ *TF:* 866-953-8800 ■ *Web:* www.workstreaminc.com

725 STAGE EQUIPMENT & SERVICES

Phone Fax

Angstrom Lighting 837 N Cahuenga Blvd .... Hollywood CA 90038 323-462-4246 462-8190
TF: 866-275-9211 ■ *Web:* www.angstromlighting.com
Apollo Design Technology Inc 4130 Fourier Dr .... Fort Wayne IN 46818 260-497-9191 497-9192
TF: 800-288-4626 ■ *Web:* www.internetapollo.com
ARTEC Consultants Inc 114 W 26th St 12th Fl .... New York NY 10001 212-242-0120 645-8635
Web: www.artec-usa.com
Audio Visual Services Corp 111 W Ocean Blvd Suite 1110 .... Long Beach CA 90802 562-366-0620 366-0628
Web: www.avservicescorp.com
BlueScreen LLC 137 N Larchmont Blvd Suite 508 .... Los Angeles CA 90004 323-467-7572 220-2195*
**Fax Area Code: 707* ■ *Web:* www.bluescreen.com
Chapman/Leonard Studio Equipment Inc
12950 Raymer St .... North Hollywood CA 91605 818-764-6726 764-6730
TF: 888-883-6559 ■ *Web:* www.chapman-leonard.com
Clair Brothers Audio Systems Inc 1 Ellen Ave .... Lititz PA 17543 717-626-4000 625-4900
Web: www.clair-audio.com
Creative Stage Lighting Co Inc 149 Rt 28 N PO Box 567 .... North Creek NY 12853 518-251-3302 251-2908
Web: www.creativestagelighting.com
Dreamworld Backdrops 6450 Lusk Blvd Suite E-106 .... San Diego CA 92121 858-452-4922 453-2783
TF: 800-737-9869 ■ *Web:* www.dreamworldbackdrops.com
Fisher Dachs Associates 22 W 19th St 6th Fl .... New York NY 10011 212-691-3020 633-1644
Web: www.fda-online.com
Gerriets International 29 Hutchinson Rd .... Allentown NJ 08501 609-758-9121 758-9596
TF: 800-369-3695 ■ *Web:* www.gi-info.com
Grosh Scenic Rentals 4114 Sunset Blvd .... Hollywood CA 90029 323-662-1134 664-7526
TF: 877-363-7998 ■ *Web:* www.grosh.com
High End Systems Inc 2105 Gracy Farms Ln .... Austin TX 78758 512-836-2242 837-5290
TF: 800-890-8989 ■ *Web:* www.highend.com
Hoffend & Sons Inc 66 School St .... Victor NY 14564 585-924-5000 924-0545
Web: www.hoffend.net
Hollywood Rentals Production Services 19731 Nordhoff St .... Northridge CA 91324 818-407-7800 407-7875
TF: 800-233-7830 ■ *Web:* www.hollywoodrentals.com
Holzmueller Productions Corp 1000 25th St .... San Francisco CA 94107 415-826-8383 826-2608
Web: www.holzmueller.com
Janson Industries 1200 Garfield Ave SW .... Canton OH 44706 330-455-7029 455-5919
TF: 800-548-8982 ■ *Web:* www.jansonindustries.com
Lycian Stage Lighting Kings Hwy PO Box D .... Sugar Loaf NY 10981 845-469-2285 469-5355
Web: www.lycian.com
Musson Theatrical Inc 890 Walsh Ave .... Santa Clara CA 95050 408-986-0210 986-9552
TF: 800-843-2837 ■ *Web:* musson.com
Panavision Inc 6219 DeSoto Ave .... Woodland Hills CA 91367 818-316-1000 316-1111
TF: 800-367-7262 ■ *Web:* www.panavision.com
Production Resource Group LLC 539 Temple Hill Rd .... New Windsor NY 12553 845-567-5700 567-5800
Web: www.prg.com
Rosco Laboratories Inc 52 Harbor View Ave .... Stamford CT 06902 203-708-8900 708-8919
TF: 800-767-2669 ■ *Web:* www.rosco.com
Schuler & Shook 750 N Orleans St Suite 400 .... Chicago IL 60610 312-944-8230 944-8297
Web: www.schulershook.com
Screen Works 2201 W Fulton St .... Chicago IL 60612 312-243-8265 243-8290
TF: 800-294-8111 ■ *Web:* www.thescreenworks.com
Secoa Inc 8650 109th Ave N .... Champlin MN 55316 763-506-8800 506-8844
TF: 800-328-5519 ■ *Web:* www.secoa.com
Syracuse Scenery & Stage Lighting Co Inc 101 Monarch Dr .... Liverpool NY 13088 315-453-8096 453-7897
TF: 800-453-7775 ■ *Web:* www.syracusescenery.com
Triangle Scenery Drapery & Lighting Co 1215 Bates Ave .... Los Angeles CA 90029 323-662-8129 662-8120
Web: www.tridrape.com
Vari-Lite 10911 Petal St .... Dallas TX 75238 214-647-7880 647-8030
TF: 800-827-4548 ■ *Web:* www.vari-lite.com

726 STEEL - MFR

Phone Fax

A Finkl & Sons Co 2011 N Southport Ave .... Chicago IL 60614 773-975-2500 348-5347
TF: 800-343-2562 ■ *Web:* www.finkl.com
AK Steel Corp 703 Curtis St .... Middletown OH 45043 513-425-6541
Web: www.aksteel.com
AK Steel Holding Corp 703 Curtis St .... Middletown OH 45043 513-425-5000 425-2115*
NYSE: AKS ■ **Fax: Sales* ■ *TF:* 800-331-5050 ■ *Web:* www.aksteel.com
Aleris International Inc 25825 Science Park Dr Suite 400 .... Beachwood OH 44122 216-910-3400 910-3650
TF: 866-266-2586 ■ *Web:* www.aleris.com
Algoma Steel Inc 105 West St .... Sault Sainte Marie ON P6A7B4 705-945-2351 945-2270*
TSX: AGA ■ **Fax: Hum Res* ■ *TF:* 800-387-9495 ■ *Web:* www.algoma.com
Allegheny Ludlum Corp 1357 E Rodney French Blvd .... New Bedford MA 02744 508-996-5691 984-8900
Web: www.alleghenyrodney.com
Allegheny Ludlum Corp 100 River Rd .... Brackenridge PA 15014 412-394-2800 394-2805
TF Sales: 800-258-3586 ■ *Web:* www.alleghenyludlum.com
Allegheny Technologies Inc 6 PPG Pl Suite 1000 .... Pittsburgh PA 15222 412-394-2800 395-2804*
NYSE: ATI ■ **Fax: Hum Res* ■ *TF Sales:* 800-258-3586 ■
Web: www.alleghenytechnologies.com
ArcelorMittal 3210 Watling St .... East Chicago IN 46312 219-399-1200 399-7164*
**Fax: Cust Svc* ■ *TF:* 800-422-9422 ■ *Web:* www.mittalsteel.com
Baron Drawn Steel Corp 7505 Baron Dr .... Canton MI 48187 734-354-8100 354-8112
TF: 800-537-8850 ■ *Web:* www.baronsteel.com
Bayou Steel Corp PO Box 5000 .... LaPlace LA 70069 985-652-0370 652-8450
TF: 800-535-7692 ■ *Web:* www.bayousteel.com
BCS Cuyahoga LLC 31000 Solon Rd .... Solon OH 44139 440-248-0290 349-4922
TF: 800-362-9132
Border Steel Inc PO Box 12843 .... El Paso TX 79913 915-886-2000 886-2218
Calumet Steel Co 317 E 11th St .... Chicago Heights IL 60411 708-757-7300 757-7901
Carlson GO Inc 350 Marshallton Thorndale Rd .... Downingtown PA 19335 610-384-2800 383-3429
TF: 800-338-5622 ■ *Web:* www.gocarlson.com
Carpenter Specialty Alloys Operations 101 W Bern St .... Reading PA 19601 610-208-2000 208-3716
TF: 800-654-6543 ■ *Web:* www.cartech.com/sao_products
Carpenter Technology Corp 2 Meridian Blvd 3rd Fl .... Wyomissing PA 19610 610-208-2000 208-3882*
NYSE: CRS ■ **Fax: Hum Res* ■ *TF Sales:* 800-654-6543 ■ *Web:* www.cartech.com
Cascade Steel Rolling Mills Inc 3200 N Hwy 99 W .... McMinnville OR 97128 503-472-4181 434-5739
TF: 800-283-2776 ■ *Web:* www.csrm.com
Central Illinois Steel Co 21050 Rt 4 PO Box 78 .... Carlinville IL 62626 217-854-3251 854-4771
Chaparral Steel Co Inc 300 Ward Rd .... Midlothian TX 76065 972-775-8241 775-1930
NASDAQ: CHAP ■ *TF:* 800-527-7979 ■ *Web:* www.chaparralsteel.com
Charleston Steel & Metal Co 107 Brigade St .... Charleston SC 29402 843-722-7278 722-7287
Charter Mfg Co Inc 1212 W Glen Oaks Ln .... Mequon WI 53092 262-243-4700 243-4767
Web: www.chartermfg.com
Chicago Heights Steel Acquisition Corp 211 E Main St .... Chicago Heights IL 60411 708-754-0410 756-5628
TF: 800-424-4487 ■ *Web:* www.chs.com
Commercial Metals Co (CMC) 6565 N MacArthur Blvd Suite 800 .... Irving TX 75039 214-689-4300 689-5886
NYSE: CMC ■ *Web:* www.commercialmetals.com
Corey Steel Co 2800 S 61st Ct .... Cicero IL 60804 708-735-8000 735-8100
TF: 800-323-2750 ■ *Web:* www.coreysteel.com
Crucible Compaction Metals 1001 Robb Hill Rd .... Oakdale PA 15071 412-923-2670 788-4240
TF: 888-923-2670 ■ *Web:* www.cruciblecompaction.com
Crucible Materials Corp 575 State Fair Blvd .... Syracuse NY 13209 315-487-4111 470-9358*
**Fax: Sales* ■ *TF:* 800-365-1180 ■ *Web:* www.crucible.com
Crucible Materials Corp Specialty Metals Div PO Box 977 .... Syracuse NY 13201 315-487-4111 470-9358*
**Fax: Sales* ■ *TF:* 800-365-1180 ■ *Web:* www.crucible.com
D-M-E Co 70 E Hillis St .... Youngwood PA 15697 724-925-7291 925-2424
TF: 800-626-6653
Dofasco Inc 1330 Burlington St E PO Box 2460 .... Hamilton ON L8N3J5 905-544-3761 548-4935*
TSX: DFS ■ **Fax: PR* ■ *TF:* 800-363-2726 ■ *Web:* www.dofasco.ca
Dunkirk Specialty Steel Corp 830 Brigham Rd PO Box 319 .... Dunkirk NY 14048 716-366-1000 366-0478
TF: 800-916-9133 ■ *Web:* www.dunkirkspecialtysteel.com
Electralloy Corp 175 Main St .... Oil City PA 16301 814-678-4100 676-5876
TF: 800-458-7273 ■ *Web:* www.electralloy.com
F & D Head Co 3040 E Peden Rd .... Fort Worth TX 76179 817-236-8773 236-1061
TF: 800-451-2684 ■ *Web:* www.fwfdhead.com
Finkl A & Sons Co 2011 N Southport Ave .... Chicago IL 60614 773-975-2500 348-5347
TF: 800-343-2562 ■ *Web:* www.finkl.com
Geneva Steel Holdings Corp PO Box 2500 .... Provo UT 84603 801-796-0920 227-9090
TF: 800-877-9990 ■ *Web:* www.geneva.com
Georgetown Steel Corp 420 S Hazard St .... Georgetown SC 29440 843-546-2525 527-3134*
**Fax: Sales* ■ *TF Sales:* 800-472-7637
Gerdau AmeriSteel Corp 4221 W Boy Scout Blvd Suite 600 .... Tampa FL 33607 813-286-8383 207-2251
NYSE: GNA ■ *TF Sales:* 800-637-8144 ■ *Web:* www.gerdauameristeel.com
Gibraltar Industries Inc 3556 Lakeshore Rd .... Buffalo NY 14219 716-826-6500 826-1589*
NASDAQ: ROCK ■ **Fax: Sales* ■ *TF:* 800-777-0675 ■ *Web:* www.gibraltar1.com
Gibraltar Metals Corp 1050 Military Rd .... Buffalo NY 14217 716-875-7920 875-7381
TF: 800-873-6322
GO Carlson Inc 350 Marshallton Thorndale Rd .... Downingtown PA 19335 610-384-2800 383-3429
TF: 800-338-5622 ■ *Web:* www.gocarlson.com
Greer Steel Co 624 Boulevard .... Dover OH 44622 330-343-8811 343-1700
TF Sales: 800-388-2868 ■ *Web:* www.greersteel.com
Group Canam Inc 11505 1st Ave Bureau 500 .... Saint-Georges QC G5Y7X3 418-228-8031 228-1750
TSX: CAM ■ *TF:* 877-499-6049 ■ *Web:* www.canammanac.com
Gulf Coast Machine & Supply Co Inc 6817 Industrial Rd .... Beaumont TX 77705 409-842-1311 842-4621
TF: 800-231-3032 ■ *Web:* www.gulfco.com
Heckett Multiserv North America
8050 Rowan Rd Suite 600 .... Cranberry Twp PA 16066 724-741-6600 741-2033
TF: 800-999-7524 ■ *Web:* www.heckettmultiserv.com
Heidtman Steel Products Inc 2401 Front St .... Toledo OH 43605 419-691-4646 698-1150
Web: www.heidtman.com
Huron Valley Steel Corp 41000 E Huron River Dr .... Belleville MI 48111 734-697-3400 697-4445
TF: 800-783-3404
Hutchens Industries Inc Steel Process Div
215 N Patterson Ave .... Springfield MO 65802 417-935-2276 935-2932
TF: 800-654-8824 ■ *Web:* www.hutchensindustries.com
I/N Kote 30755 Edison Rd .... New Carlisle IN 46552 574-654-1000 654-1008
I/N Tek 30755 Edison Rd .... New Carlisle IN 46552 574-654-1000 654-1008
Interstate Steel Co 401 E Touhy Ave .... Des Plaines IL 60017 847-827-3210 827-7216
TF: 800-323-9800 ■ *Web:* www.interstatesteelco.com
IPSCO Inc PO Box 1670 .... Regina SK S4P3C7 306-924-7700 924-7500
NYSE: IPS ■ *TF:* 800-667-1616 ■ *Web:* www.ipsco.com
JFE Steel Corp 350 Park Ave 27th Fl .... New York NY 10022 212-310-9320 308-9292
Web: www.jfe-steel.co.jp
Kentucky Electric Steel LLC PO Box 2119 .... Ashland KY 41105 606-929-1200 929-1219
TF: 800-333-3012 ■ *Web:* www.kentuckyelectricsteel.com
Keystone Steel & Wire Co 7000 SW Adams St .... Peoria IL 61641 309-697-7020 697-7487
Web: www.redbrand.com
Kobe Steel USA Inc 535 Madison Ave 5th Fl .... New York NY 10022 212-751-9400 355-5564
TF: 888-562-3872 ■ *Web:* www.kobelco.co.jp/indexe.htm
LeTourneau Inc PO Box 2307 .... Longview TX 74606 903-237-7000 237-7032
Web: www.letourneau-inc.com
Lone Star Steel Co 15660 N Dallas Pkwy Suite 500 .... Dallas TX 75248 972-386-3981 770-6409
TF: 800-527-4615 ■ *Web:* www.lonestarsteel.com
MACSTEEL 1 Jackson Sq Suite 500 .... Jackson MI 49201 517-782-0415 782-8736*
**Fax: Sales* ■ *TF Sales:* 800-888-7833 ■ *Web:* www.macsteel.com
MAGNATRAX Corp 1220 Old Alpharetta Rd Suite 310 .... Alpharetta GA 30005 678-455-3360 455-3366
Web: www.magnatrax.com
Marion Steel Co 912 Cheney Ave .... Marion OH 43302 740-383-4011 383-6429
TF: 800-333-4011
Metalex Corp 1530 Artaius Pkwy PO Box 399 .... Libertyville IL 60048 847-362-8300 362-7939
TF: 800-323-0792 ■ *Web:* www.metlx.com
Middle Steel USA 4020 Kinross Lakes Pkwy .... Richfield OH 44286 330-659-9100 659-9135
TF: 866-474-8808 ■ *Web:* www.intlsteel.com
Mill Steel Co 5116 36th St SE .... Grand Rapids MI 49512 616-949-6700 977-9300
TF: 800-247-6455 ■ *Web:* www.millsteel.com
Neilsen Mfg Inc 3501 Portland Rd NE .... Salem OR 97303 503-585-0040 362-3814
TF: 800-292-2495 ■ *Web:* www.neilsenmfg.com
New Technology Steel 12301 Hubbell St .... Detroit MI 48227 313-653-4746 653-4916
Web: www.newtechnologysteel.com
Niagara Corp 667 Madison Ave 11th Fl .... New York NY 10021 212-317-1000 317-1001
Web: www.niag.com

				Phone	Fax
Niagara LaSalle Corp 1412 150th St *TF:* 877-289-2277 ■ *Web:* www.niag.com	Hammond	IN	46327	219-853-6000	853-6081
Nisshin USA LLC 1701 Golf Rd Suite 1004 Continental Tower 3 *Web:* www.nisshin-steel.co.jp	Rolling Meadows	IL	60008	847-290-5100	290-0826
NS Group Inc 530 W 9th St *NYSE: NSS* ■ *TF:* 800-348-7751 ■ *Web:* www.nsgrouponline.com	Newport	KY	41071	859-292-6809	292-0593
Nucor Corp 1915 Rexford Rd *NYSE: NUE* ■ *Web:* www.nucor.com	Charlotte	NC	28211	704-366-7000	362-4208
Nucor Corp Cold Finish Div 2800 N Governor Williams Hwy **Fax:* Sales ■ *TF:* 800-333-0590 ■ *Web:* www.nucor.com	Darlington	SC	29540	843-395-8689	395-8759*
Nucor Corp Steel Div 1455 Hagan Ave **Fax:* Sales ■ *TF:* 888-466-8267 ■ *Web:* www.nucorsteel.com	Huger	SC	29450	843-336-6000	336-6150*
Nucor-Yamato Steel Co PO Box 1228 *TF:* 800-289-6977 ■ *Web:* www.nucoryamato.com	Blytheville	AR	72316	870-762-5500	762-1130
Oregon Steel Mills Inc 1000 SW Broadway Suite 2200 *NYSE: OS* ■ *TF:* 800-547-9451 ■ *Web:* www.oregonsteel.com	Portland	OR	97205	503-223-9228	240-5232
Outokumpu Stainless 425 N Martingale Rd Suite 1600 *TF:* 800-833-8703 ■ *Web:* www.outokumpu.com	Schaumburg	IL	60173	847-517-4050	517-2950
Precision Rolled Products Inc 306 Columbia Tpke *TF:* 800-321-0135	Florham Park	NJ	07932	973-822-9100	822-0932
Prudential Steel Ltd 140 4th Ave SW Suite 1800 *TF:* 800-661-1050 ■ *Web:* www.prudentialsteel.com	Calgary	AB	T2P3N3	403-267-0300	265-3426
Quanex Corp 1900 West Loop S Suite 1500 *NYSE: NX* ■ *TF:* 800-231-8176 ■ *Web:* www.quanex.com	Houston	TX	77027	713-961-4600	439-1016
Republic Engineered Products Inc 3770 Embassy Pkwy *TF:* 800-232-7157 ■ *Web:* www.republicengineered.com	Akron	OH	44333	330-670-3000	670-7011
Richfield Iron Works Inc 3313 Richfield Rd	Flint	MI	48506	810-736-2110	736-0300
Roanoke Electric Steel Corp 102 Westside Blvd NW *NASDAQ: RESC* ■ *TF:* 800-765-6567 ■ *Web:* www.roanokesteel.com	Roanoke	VA	24017	540-342-1831	342-9437
Rocky Mountain Steel Mills PO Box 316 **Fax:* Sales ■ *Web:* www.osm.com/RMSM/index.htm	Pueblo	CO	81002	719-561-6000	561-6037*
Rome Strip Steel Co Inc 530 Henry St PO Box 189 *Web:* www.romestripsteel.com	Rome	NY	13442	315-336-5500	336-5510
Samuel Son & Co Ltd 20001 Sherwood St *TF:* 800-521-0870 ■ *Web:* www.samuel.com	Detroit	MI	48234	313-893-5000	893-8422
Sandmeyer Steel Co 1 Sandmeyer Ln *TF:* 800-523-3663 ■ *Web:* www.sandmeyer.com	Philadelphia	PA	19116	215-464-7100	677-1430
Sandvik Materials Technology 982 Griffin Pond Rd *Web:* www.smt.sandvik.com	Clarks Summit	PA	18411	570-585-7500	585-7523
Schnitzer Steel Industries Inc 3200 NW Yeon Ave *NASDAQ: SCHN* ■ *TF:* 800-666-2992 ■ *Web:* www.schnitzersteel.com	Portland	OR	97210	503-224-9900	323-2804
Scion Steel Inc 23800 Blackstone St *TF:* 800-288-2127 ■ *Web:* www.scionsteel.com	Warren	MI	48089	586-755-4000	755-4064
Scot Industries Inc 2277 North St *Web:* www.thomasregister.com/olc/scot	East Troy	WI	53120	262-642-4600	642-4608
Shalmet Corp 116 Pinedale Industrial Rd *TF:* 888-278-1414 ■ *Web:* www.shalmet.com	Orwigsburg	PA	17961	570-366-1414	366-9209
Sheffield Steel Corp 2300 Hwy S 97 *TF:* 800-331-3304 ■ *Web:* www.sheffieldsteel.com	Sand Springs	OK	74063	918-245-1335	241-6931
SMI Steel Alabama 101 S 50th St *TF:* 800-621-0262 ■ *Web:* www.smi-birmingham.com	Birmingham	AL	35212	205-592-8981	591-4554
Standard Steel Div Freedom Forge Corp 500 N Walnut St *Web:* www.standardsteel.com	Burnham	PA	17009	717-248-4911	248-8050
Standard Steel LLC 500 N Walnut St *Web:* www.standardsteel.com	Burnham	PA	17009	717-248-4911	248-8050
Steel Dynamics Inc 6714 Pointe Inverness Way Suite 200 *NASDAQ: STLD* ■ *Web:* www.steeldynamics.com	Fort Wayne	IN	46804	260-459-3553	969-3590
Steel Technologies Inc 15415 Shelbyville Rd *NASDAQ: STTX* ■ *TF:* 800-828-2170 ■ *Web:* www.steeltechnologies.com	Louisville	KY	40245	502-245-2110	244-0182
Steel of West Virginia Inc 17th St & 2nd Ave *TF:* 800-624-3492 ■ *Web:* www.swvainc.com	Huntington	WV	25703	304-696-8200	529-1479
Stelco Inc PO Box 2030 *TSX: STE.a* ■ *TF:* 800-263-9305 ■ *Web:* www.stelco.com	Hamilton	ON	L8N3T1	905-528-2511	308-7011
Tempel Steel Co 5500 N Wolcott Ave **Fax:* Cust Svc ■ *TF:* 800-621-7700 ■ *Web:* www.tempel.com	Chicago	IL	60640	773-250-8000	250-8928*
Texas Industries Inc 1341 W Mockingbird Ln Suite 700W *NYSE: TXI* ■ *Web:* www.txi.com	Dallas	TX	75247	972-647-6700	647-3878
Thomas Steel Strip Corp Delaware Ave NW *TF:* 800-321-7778 ■ *Web:* www.corusspecialstrip.com/tss/	Warren	OH	44485	330-841-6111	841-6187
Thompson Steel Co Inc 120 Royall St *Web:* www.thompsonsteelco.com	Canton	MA	02021	781-828-8800	828-5082
ThyssenKrupp Materials NA Inc 22355 W 11-Mile Rd *Web:* www.tincna.com	Southfield	MI	48034	248-233-5600	233-5699
Timken Co 1835 Dueber Ave SW *NYSE: TKR* ■ *TF:* 800-223-1954 ■ *Web:* www.timken.com	Canton	OH	44706	330-438-3000	471-3810
Timken Latrobe Steel Co 2626 Ligonier St PO Box 31 *TF:* 800-245-7856 ■ *Web:* www.timken.com/products/specialtysteel/	Latrobe	PA	15650	724-537-7711	532-6439
Tube Products Corp 14420 Ewing Ave S	Burnsville	MN	55306	952-894-2817	
TWB Co 1600 Nadeau Rd *Web:* www.twbcompany.com	Monroe	MI	48162	734-289-6400	289-6555
Ulbrich Stainless Steels & Special Metals Inc 57 Dodge Ave **Fax:* Sales ■ *TF:* 800-243-1676 ■ *Web:* www.ulbrich.com	North Haven	CT	06473	203-239-4481	239-7479*
Union Electric Steel Corp 726 Bell Ave *Web:* www.uniones.com	Carnegie	PA	15106	412-429-7655	276-1711
United Foundries Inc 1400 Grace Ave NE *Web:* www.ufirolls.com	Canton	OH	44705	330-456-2761	456-2085
US Steel Corp 600 Grant St *NYSE: X* ■ **Fax:* Hum Res ■ *Web:* www.ussteel.com	Pittsburgh	PA	15219	412-433-1121	433-6779*
USS-POSCO Industries PO Box 471 **Fax:* Sales ■ *TF:* 800-877-7672 ■ *Web:* www.ussposco.com	Pittsburg	CA	94565	925-439-6000	439-6506*
WCI Steel Inc 1040 Pine Ave SE *Web:* www.wcisteel.com	Warren	OH	44483	330-841-8000	841-8322
Wheeling Corrugating Co 1134 Market St **Fax:* Sales ■ *TF Sales:* 800-922-3325 ■ *Web:* www.wheelingcorrugating.com	Wheeling	WV	26003	304-234-2300	234-2330*
Wheeling-Pittsburgh Corp 1134 Market St *NASDAQ: WPSC* ■ *TF:* 800-441-8190	Wheeling	WV	26003	304-234-2400	234-2213
Wheeling-Pittsburgh Steel Corp 1134 Market St **Fax:* Hum Res ■ *Web:* www.wpsc.com	Wheeling	WV	26003	304-234-2400	234-2213*
WHX Corp 444 Theodore Fremd Ave *Web:* www.whxcorp.com	Rye	NY	10580	914-925-4413	925-4498
Worthington Industries Inc 200 Old Wilson Bridge Rd *NYSE: WOR* ■ *TF:* 800-944-2255 ■ *Web:* www.worthingtonindustries.com	Columbus	OH	43085	614-438-3210	438-3256
Worthington Specialty Processing 4905 S Meridian Rd PO Box 1068	Jackson	MI	49204	517-789-0200	789-0209
Worthington Steel Co 1127 Dearborn Dr **Fax:* Sales ■ *TF:* 800-944-3733	Columbus	OH	43085	614-438-3205	438-3283*

727 STONE (CUT) & STONE PRODUCTS

				Phone	Fax
Adam Ross Cut Stone Co 1003 Broadway *Web:* www.adamrosscutstone.com	Albany	NY	12204	518-463-6674	463-0710
Benson Stone Co 1100 11th St *Web:* www.bensonstone.com	Rockford	IL	61104	815-227-2000	227-2001
Biesanz Stone Co Inc 4600 Goodview Rd *TF:* 800-247-8322 ■ *Web:* www.biesanzstone.com	Winona	MN	55987	507-454-4336	454-8140
Briar Hill Stone Co 12470 SR 520 *Web:* www.briarhillstone.com	Glenmont	OH	44628	330-377-5100	377-5110
Bristol Memorial Works Inc 508 Farmington Ave *TF:* 877-225-7626 ■ *Web:* www.rockofages.com	Bristol	CT	06010	860-583-1654	583-1655
Bybee Stone Co Inc 6293 N Matthews Dr *TF:* 800-457-4530 ■ *Web:* www.bybeestone.com	Ellettsville	IN	47429	812-876-2215	876-6329
C & H Stone Co Inc 4000 S Rockport Rd	Bloomington	IN	47403	812-336-2560	331-7292
Cold Spring Granite Inc 202 S 3rd Ave *TF:* 800-328-5040 ■ *Web:* www.coldspringgranite.com	Cold Spring	MN	56320	320-685-3621	685-8490
Columbus Marble Works Corp 2415 Hwy 45 N PO Box 791 *TF:* 800-647-1055	Columbus	MS	39703	662-328-1477	328-5002
Continental Cast Stone Mfg Inc 22001 W 83rd St *TF:* 800-989-7866 ■ *Web:* www.continentalcaststone.com	Shawnee	KS	66227	913-422-7575	422-7272
Dakota Granite Co 14964 484th Ave PO Box 1351 *TF:* 800-843-3333 ■ *Web:* www.dakgran.com	Milbank	SD	57252	605-432-5580	432-6155
Dakota Marble Inc 902 W 19th St *TF:* 800-697-7241 ■ *Web:* www.dakotamarble.com	Yankton	SD	57078	605-665-7241	665-4870
Dally Slate Co 500 Railroad Ave *Web:* www.dallyslate.com	Pen Argyl	PA	18072	610-863-4172	863-8388
Daprato Rigali Inc 6030 N Northwest Hwy *Web:* www.dapratorigali.com	Chicago	IL	60631	773-763-5511	763-5522
Finger Lakes Stone Co 33 Quarry Rd *Web:* www.fingerlakesstone.net	Ithaca	NY	14850	607-273-4646	273-4692
Glenrock International Inc 985 E Linden Ave *TF:* 800-442-6374 ■ *Web:* glenrock.com	Linden	NJ	07036	908-862-3433	862-0430
Harmony Blue Granite Co Inc 583 Harmony Dr PO Box 958 *TF:* 800-241-7000 ■ *Web:* www.harmonybluegranite.com	Elberton	GA	30635	706-283-3111	283-1008
Hilltop Slate Inc PO Box 201 Rt 22 A *Web:* www.hilltopslate.com	Middle Granville	NY	12849	518-642-2270	642-1220
Intercontinental Marble Corp 8228 NW 56th St *Web:* www.intercontinentalmarble.com/	Miami	FL	33166	305-591-2207	477-3237
Kollmann Monumental Works Inc 1915 W Division St *TF:* 800-659-8010 ■ *Web:* www.kollmann.com	Saint Cloud	MN	56301	320-251-8010	251-8019
Kotecki-Rock of Ages Inc 3636 Pearl Rd *TF:* 800-753-2880 ■ *Web:* www.rockofages.com	Cleveland	OH	44109	216-749-2880	749-7221
LeSueur-Richmond Slate Corp PO Box 8 Rt 675 *TF:* 800-235-8921	Arvonia	VA	23004	434-581-3214	581-1130
Little Falls Granite Works 10802 Hwy 10 PO Box 240	Little Falls	MN	56345	320-632-9277	632-3342
Mankato-Kasota Stone Inc 818 N Willow St *TF:* 800-437-7059 ■ *Web:* www.mankato-kasota-stone.com	Mankato	MN	56001	507-625-2746	625-2748
Marshall RJ Co 26776 W 12-Mile Road Suite 201 *TF Cust Svc:* 800-338-7900 ■ *Web:* www.rjmarshallco.com	Southfield	MI	48034	248-353-4100	948-6460
Milwaukee Marble & Granite Co Inc 4535 W Mitchell St *TF:* 877-645-6272 ■ *Web:* www.milwaukeemarble.com	Milwaukee	WI	53214	414-645-0305	645-2620
Monumental Sales Inc 537 22nd Ave N *TF:* 800-442-1660 ■ *Web:* www.sunburstgranites.com	Saint Cloud	MN	56303	320-251-6585	251-6547
Neal WE Slate Co 2840 Hwy 25 *Web:* www.nealslate.com	Watertown	MN	55388	952-955-3340	955-3341
North Carolina Granite Corp 151 Granite Quarry Trail PO Box 151 *TF:* 800-227-6242 ■ *Web:* www.ncgranite.com	Mount Airy	NC	27030	336-786-5141	719-2623
Northwestern Marble & Granite Co 7705 Bush Lake Rd Suite A *Web:* www.northwesternmarble.com	Edina	MN	55439	952-941-8601	941-0994
Owatonna Granite Rock of Ages 1300 Hoffman Dr *TF:* 800-422-2397	Owatonna	MN	55060	507-451-4882	451-3034
RJ Marshall Co 26776 W 12-Mile Road Suite 201 *TF Cust Svc:* 800-338-7900 ■ *Web:* www.rjmarshallco.com	Southfield	MI	48034	248-353-4100	948-6460
Rock of Ages Corp 560 Graniteville Rd *NASDAQ: ROAC* ■ *TF:* 800-421-0166 ■ *Web:* www.rockofages.com	Graniteville	VT	05654	802-476-3115	476-4767
Ross Adam Cut Stone Co 1003 Broadway *Web:* www.adamrosscutstone.com	Albany	NY	12204	518-463-6674	463-0710
Royal Melrose Granite Co 202 S 3rd Ave **Fax Area Code:* 800 ■ *TF:* 800-328-7021	Cold Spring	MN	56320	320-685-5101	473-4881*
Starrett Tru-Stone Technologies Div 1101 Prosper Dr PO Box 430 *TF:* 800-959-0517 ■ *Web:* www.tru-stone.com	Waite Park	MN	56387	320-251-7171	259-5073
Taylor Industries Inc 35 Anderson Rd *Web:* www.tere-stone.com	Parker Ford	PA	19457	610-495-5261	495-5934
Tri-State Cut Stone & Brick Co 10333 Van's Dr *Web:* www.tscutstonebrick.com	Frankfort	IL	60423	815-469-7550	464-5096
Tru-Stone Technologies Div Starrett 1101 Prosper Dr PO Box 430 *TF:* 800-959-0517 ■ *Web:* www.tru-stone.com	Waite Park	MN	56387	320-251-7171	259-5073
Vermont Structural Slate Co Inc 3 Prospect St PO Box 98 *TF:* 800-343-1900 ■ *Web:* www.vermontstructuralslate.com	Fair Haven	VT	05743	802-265-4933	265-3865
Vetter Stone Co 23894 3rd Ave *TF:* 800-878-2850 ■ *Web:* www.vetterstone.com	Mankato	MN	56001	507-345-4568	345-4777
Waller Brothers Stone Co 744 McDermott Rushtown Rd *Web:* www.wallerbrothersstone.com	McDermott	OH	45652	740-259-2356	259-2308
WE Neal Slate Co 2840 Hwy 25 *Web:* www.nealslate.com	Watertown	MN	55388	952-955-3340	955-3341
Winona Monument Co Inc 174 W 3rd St *TF:* 800-657-4411	Winona	MN	55987	507-452-4672	
WS Hampshire Inc 365 Keyes Ave *TF:* 800-541-0251 ■ *Web:* www.wshampshire.com	Hampshire	IL	60140	847-683-4400	683-4407

728 STUDENT ASSISTANCE PROGRAMS

				Phone	Fax
Alabama					
Commission on Higher Education PO Box 302000 *Web:* www.ache.state.al.us/StudentAsst/Programs.htm	Montgomery	AL	36130	334-242-1998	242-0268
Prepaid Affordable College Tuition (PACT) Program 100 N Union St Suite 660 *TF:* 800-252-7228 ■ *Web:* www.treasury.state.al.us	Montgomery	AL	36130	334-242-7514	242-7041
Alaska Student Aid Office PO Box 110505 *TF:* 800-441-2962 ■ *Web:* alaskaadvantage.state.ak.us	Juneau	AK	99811	907-465-2962	465-5316
Arkansas Financial Aid Office 114 E Capitol St *TF:* 800-547-8839 ■ *Web:* www.arkansashighered.com/financial.html	Little Rock	AR	72201	501-371-2013	371-2001
California Student Aid Commission PO Box 419027 *TF:* 888-224-7268 ■ *Web:* www.csac.ca.gov	Rancho Cordova	CA	95741	916-526-8999	526-8002
Coca-Cola Scholars Foundation 1 Coca-Cola Plaza Bldg NAT 7th Fl PO Box 442 *TF:* 800-306-2653 ■ *Web:* www.coca-colascholars.org	Atlanta	GA	30301	404-733-5420	733-5439
College Savings Plans Network 2670 Research Park Dr PO Box 11910 *Web:* www.collegesavings.org	Lexington	KY	40578	859-244-8175	244-8053
Colorado CollegeInvest 1801 Broadway Suite 1300 *TF:* 800-478-5651 ■ *Web:* www.prepaidtuition.org	Denver	CO	80202	303-295-1981	296-4811

Phone Fax

Connecticut Student Financial Aid Office 61 Woodland St .... Hartford CT 06105 860-947-1800 947-1310
Web: www.ctdhe.org/SFA

Council for Opportunity in Education
1025 Vermont Ave NW Suite 900 .... Washington DC 20005 202-347-7430 347-0786
Web: www.trioprograms.org

District of Columbia Tuition Assistance Grant Program
441 4th St NW Rm 350N .... Washington DC 20001 202-727-2824 727-2834
TF: 877-485-6751 ■ *Web:* www.tuitiongrant.dc.gov

Dollars for Scholars Scholarship America 1 Scholarship Way..... Saint Peter MN 56082 507-931-1682 931-9168
TF: 800-248-8080 ■ *Web:* www.scholarshipamerica.org/dfs

eStudentLoan Inc 9477 Waples St Suite 100.................. San Diego CA 92121 858-320-6799
TF Cust Svc: 800-869-1538 ■ *Web:* estudentloan.com

FastWeb Inc 444 N Michigan Ave Suite 3000 .... Chicago IL 60611 312-832-2312 467-0638
TF: 800-327-8932 ■ *Web:* www.fastweb.com

FinAid Page LLC PO Box 2056 Suite 9-134 .... Cranberry Township PA 16066 724-538-4500 538-4502
Web: www.finaid.org

Florida
Prepaid College Board PO Box 6567 .... Tallahassee FL 32314 850-488-8514 309-1766*
**Fax:* Cust Svc ■ *TF:* 800-552-4723 ■ *Web:* www.florida529plans.com
Student Financial Assistance Office
1940 N Monroe St Suite 70.......................... Tallahassee FL 32303 850-410-5200 488-3612
TF: 888-827-2004 ■ *Web:* www.floridastudentfinancialaid.org

Free Application for Federal Student Aid (FAFSA)
US Federal Student Aid Program PO Box 7001........... Mount Vernon IL 62864 319-337-5665
TF: 800-433-3243 ■ *Web:* www.fafsa.ed.gov

Georgia Student Finance Commission
2082 E Exchange Pl Suite 200.................................. Tucker GA 30084 770-724-9000 724-9004
TF: 800-505-4732 ■ *Web:* www.gsfc.org

Harry S Truman Scholarship Foundation
712 Jackson Pl NW .... Washington DC 20006 202-395-4831 395-6995
Web: www.truman.gov

Hawaii Postsecondary Education Commission
2444 Dole St Bachman Hall Rm 209........................... Honolulu HI 96822 808-956-8213 956-5156

Hispanic Scholarship Fund 55 2nd St Suite 1500 .... San Francisco CA 94105 415-808-2300 808-2301
TF: 877-473-4636 ■ *Web:* www.hsf.net

Idaho Scholarship Office PO Box 83720 .... Boise ID 83720 208-334-2270 334-2632
Web: www.idahoboardofed.org/scholarships.asp

Illinois Student Assistance Commission 1755 Lake Cook Rd........ Deerfield IL 60015 847-948-8500 831-8549*
**Fax:* Cust Svc ■ *TF:* 800-899-4722 ■ *Web:* www.collegezone.com

Indiana Students Assistance Commission
150 W Market St Suite 500............................ Indianapolis IN 46204 317-232-2350 232-3260
TF: 888-528-4719 ■ *Web:* www.in.gov/ssaci

Iowa College Student Aid Commission 200 10th St 4th Fl...... Des Moines IA 50309 515-281-3501 725-3401
TF: 800-383-4222 ■ *Web:* www.iowacollegeaid.org

James Madison Memorial Fellowship Foundation
2000 K St NW Suite 303 .... Washington DC 20006 202-653-8700 653-6045
Web: www.jamesmadison.com

Kansas Student Financial Aid Div
1000 SW Jackson St Suite 520................................. Topeka KS 66612 785-296-3518 296-0983
Web: www.kansasregents.org/financial_aid

Kentucky Higher Education Assistance Authority PO Box 798 .... Frankfort KY 40602 502-696-7200 696-7345
TF: 800-928-8926 ■ *Web:* www.kheaa.com

Louisiana Student Financial Assistance Office
PO Box 91202 .... Baton Rouge LA 70821 225-922-1011 922-1089
TF: 800-259-5626 ■ *Web:* www.osfa.state.la.us

Maine (FAME) Finance Authority of Maine PO Box 949........... Augusta ME 04332 207-623-3263 623-0095
TF: 800-228-3734 ■ *Web:* www.famemaine.com

Maryland Student Financial Assistance Office
839 Bestgate Rd Suite 400 .... Annapolis MD 21401 410-260-4565 260-3200
TF: 800-974-0203 ■ *Web:* www.mhec.state.md.us

Massachusetts Educational Financing Authority
125 Summer St Suite 300....................................... Boston MA 02110 617-261-9760 261-9765
TF: 800-449-6332 ■ *Web:* www.mefa.org

Michigan
Education Trust PO Box 30198 .... Lansing MI 48909 517-335-4767 373-6967
TF: 800-638-4543 ■ *Web:* www.michigan.gov/treasury
Student Financial Services Bureau
Austin Bldg 430 West Allegan .... Lansing MI 48922 517-373-4897
TF: 800-642-5626 ■ *Web:* www.michigan.gov/mistudentaid

Minnesota Office of Higher Education
1450 Energy Park Dr Suite 350............................ Saint Paul MN 55108 651-642-0567 642-0675
TF: 800-657-3866 ■ *Web:* www.ohe.state.mn.us

Mississippi
Prepaid Affordable College Tuition Program (MPACT)
501 N West St PO Box 120.................................... Jackson MS 39205 601-359-5255 359-5234
TF: 800-987-4450 ■ *Web:* www.collegesavingsmississippi.com
Student Financial Aid Office 3825 Ridgewood Rd............... Jackson MS 39211 601-432-6997 432-6527
TF: 800-327-2980 ■ *Web:* www.ihl.state.ms.us/financialaid

Missouri Student Assistance Resource Services (MOSTARS)
3515 Amazonas Dr.................................... Jefferson City MO 65109 573-751-2361 751-6635
TF: 800-473-6757 ■ *Web:* www.dhe.mo.gov

Montana Higher Education Board of Regents
46 N Last Change Gulch PO Box 203201 .... Helena MT 59620 406-444-6570 444-1469
Web: www.montana.edu/wwwbor

Morris K Udall Foundation 130 S Scott Ave .... Tucson AZ 85701 520-670-5529 670-5530
Web: www.udall.gov

National Merit Scholarship Corp 1560 Sherman Ave Suite 200 .... Evanston IL 60201 847-866-5100 866-5113
Web: www.nationalmerit.org

Nebraska Coordinating Commission for Postsecondary Education
140 N 8th St Suite 300 PO Box 95005.......................... Lincoln NE 68509 402-471-2847 471-2886
Web: www.ccpe.state.ne.us

New Hampshire Postsecondary Education Commission
3 Barrell Ct Suite 300 .... Concord NH 03301 603-271-2555 271-2696
TF: 800-735-2964 ■ *Web:* www.nh.gov/postsecondary

New Jersey Higher Education Student Assistance Authority
4 Quakerbridge Plaza PO Box 540.............................. Trenton NJ 08625 609-588-7944 588-7389
TF: 800-792-8670 ■ *Web:* www.hesaa.org

New Mexico Financial Aid & Student Services Unit
1068 Cerrillos Rd.. Santa Fe NM 87505 505-476-6500 476-6511
TF: 800-279-9777 ■ *Web:* hed.state.nm.us

New York (State) Higher Education Services Corp
99 Washington Ave .... Albany NY 12255 518-473-1574 473-3749
TF: 888-697-4372 ■ *Web:* www.hesc.com

North Carolina State Education Assistance
Authority PO Box 14103 .... Research Triangle Park NC 27709 919-549-8614 549-8481
TF: 800-700-1775 ■ *Web:* www.ncseaa.edu

North Dakota Student Financial Assistance Program
600 E Boulevard Ave 10th Fl Dept 215 .... Bismarck ND 58505 701-328-2960 328-2961
Web: www.ndus.nodak.edu

Office of Federal Student Aid
Union Center Plaza 830 1st St NE.......................... Washington DC 20202 202-377-3000 275-5000
TF: 800-433-3243 ■ *Web:* www.ed.gov/about/offices/list/fsa
Federal Student Aid Information Center PO Box 84 .... Washington DC 20044 800-433-3243
Web: studentaid.ed.gov

Ohio
State Grants & Scholarships Office
30 E Broad St 36th Fl PO Box 182452 .... Columbus OH 43218 614-466-7420 752-5903
TF: 888-833-1133 ■ *Web:* regents.ohio.gov/sgs
Tuition Trust Authority 580 S High St Suite 208.............. Columbus OH 43215 614-752-9400 466-4486
TF Cust Svc: 800-233-6734 ■ *Web:* www.collegeadvantage.com

Oklahoma State Regents for Higher Education
655 Research Pkwy Suite 200......................... Oklahoma City OK 73104 405-225-9100 225-9235
Web: www.okhighered.org

Oregon Student Assistance Commission
1500 Valley River Dr Suite 100.............................. Eugene OR 97401 541-687-7400 687-7419
TF: 800-452-8807 ■ *Web:* www.osac.state.or.us

Pennsylvania
Higher Education Assistance Agency 1200 N 7th St........... Harrisburg PA 17102 717-720-2860 720-3644
TF: 800-692-7392 ■ *Web:* www.pheaa.org
Tuition Account Plan (TAP 529) PO Box 55463 .... Boston MA 02205 800-440-4000 707-8981*
**Fax Area Code:* 781 ■ *TF:* 800-440-4000 ■ *Web:* tap529.com

Rhode Island Higher Education Assistance Authority
560 Jefferson Blvd.. Warwick RI 02886 401-736-1100 732-3541
TF: 800-922-9855 ■ *Web:* www.riheaa.org

Scholarship America 1 Scholarship Way .... Saint Peter MN 56082 507-931-1682 931-9168
TF: 800-537-4180 ■ *Web:* www.scholarshipamerica.org

Scholarship Resource Network Inc 600 Lexington Ave 3rd Fl...... New York NY 10022 800-926-2619 753-1190*
**Fax Area Code:* 212 ■ *Web:* www.srnexpress.com

South Carolina Higher Education Tuition Grants Commission
101 Business Park Blvd Suite 2100......................... Columbia SC 29203 803-896-1120 896-1126
Web: www.sctuitiongrants.com

SRN Express 600 Lexington Ave 3rd Fl......................... New York NY 10022 800-926-2619 753-1190*
**Fax Area Code:* 212 ■ *Web:* www.srnexpress.com

Tennessee
Baccalaureate Education System Trust (BEST)
PO Box 198786 .... Nashville TN 37219 615-532-8056 734-6467
TF: 888-486-2378 ■ *Web:* www.treasury.state.tn.us/best.htm
Student Assistance Corp
404 James Robertson Pkwy Suite 1510 .... Nashville TN 37243 615-741-1346 741-6101
TF: 800-257-6526 ■ *Web:* state.tn.us/tsac

Texas Higher Education Coordinating Board PO Box 12788.......... Austin TX 78711 512-427-6101 427-6169
Web: www.thecb.state.tx.us

Thurgood Marshall Scholarship Fund
80 Maiden Ln Suite 2204.................................... New York NY 10038 212-573-8888 573-8497
Web: www.thurgoodmarshallfund.org

United Negro College Fund Inc (UNCF)
8260 Willow Oaks Corporate Dr Suite 400 .... Fairfax VA 22031 703-205-3400 205-3507
TF: 800-331-2244 ■ *Web:* www.uncf.org

Utah Higher Education Assistance Authority
60 S 400 West.. Salt Lake City UT 84101 801-321-7294 366-8431
TF: 877-336-7378 ■ *Web:* www.uheaa.org

Vermont Student Assistance Corp PO Box 2000 .... Winooski VT 05404 802-655-9602 654-3765
TF: 800-642-3177 ■ *Web:* www.vsac.org

Virginia
College Savings Plan PO Box 607............................ Richmond VA 23218 804-786-0719 786-2453
TF: 888-567-0540 ■ *Web:* www.virginia529.com
State Council of Higher Education 101 N 14th St 9th Fl........ Richmond VA 23219 804-225-2600 225-2604
Web: www.schev.edu

Washington Higher Education Coordinating Board
917 Lakeridge Way PO Box 43430 .... Olympia WA 98504 360-753-7800 753-7808
Web: www.hecb.wa.gov

West Virginia Higher Education Policy Commission
1018 Kanawha Blvd E Suite 700 .... Charleston WV 25301 304-558-2101 558-5719
TF: 888-825-5707 ■ *Web:* www.hepc.wvnet.edu/students

Wisconsin
Education Investment Program PO Box 7871 .... Madison WI 53707 608-264-7899 266-2647
TF: 888-338-3789 ■ *Web:* www.edvest.com
Higher Educational Aids Board PO Box 7885 .... Madison WI 53707 608-267-2206 267-2808
Web: heab.state.wi.us

Wyoming Community College Commission
2020 Carey Ave 8th Fl .... Cheyenne WY 82002 307-777-7763 777-6567
Web: www.commission.wcc.edu

729 SUBSTANCE ABUSE TREATMENT CENTERS

SEE ALSO Associations & Organizations - General - Self-Help Organizations p. 1314; Hospitals - General Hospitals - Canada p. 1800; Hospitals - General Hospitals - US p. 1802; Hospitals - Psychiatric Hospitals p. 1824

Phone Fax

AdCare Hospital of Worcester 107 Lincoln St................. Worcester MA 01605 508-799-9000 453-3064
TF: 800-345-3552 ■ *Web:* www.adcare.com

Alcohol & Drug Abuse Treatment Center 1003 12th St .... Butner NC 27509 919-575-7928 575-7260

Anchor Hospital 5454 Yorktowne Dr.............................. Atlanta GA 30349 770-991-6044 991-3843
Web: www.anchorhospital.com

Anthony Louis Center 1000 Paul Pkwy............................ Blaine MN 55434 763-757-2906 757-2059
Web: www.anthonylouiscenter.com

Areba Casriel Institute 500 W 57th St....................... New York NY 10019 212-293-3000 293-3020
TF: 800-724-4444 ■ *Web:* www.acirehab.org

Arms Acres 75 Seminary Hill Rd.................................. Carmel NY 10512 845-225-3400 225-7581
TF: 800-989-2676 ■ *Web:* www.armsacres.com

Baltimore Behavioral Health 200 S Arlington Ave............... Baltimore MD 21223 410-962-7180 962-7194

Bethesda Alcohol & Drug Treatment 619 Oak St .... Cincinnati OH 45206 513-569-6116 569-6110

Betty Ford Center 39000 Bob Hope Dr................. Rancho Mirage CA 92270 760-773-4100 773-4126
TF: 800-854-9211 ■ *Web:* www.bettyfordcenter.org

Blue Hills Hospital 500 Vine St .... Hartford CT 06112 860-293-6400 293-6470

Boniface Human Services 5886 W Fort St.......................... Detroit MI 48209 313-842-5741 554-2039
Web: comnet.org/local/orgs/boniface

Bradford Health Services 2101 Magnolia Ave S Suite 518 ...... Birmingham AL 35205 205-251-7753 251-7760
TF: 800-217-2849 ■ *Web:* www.bradfordhealth.com

Brighton Hospital 12851 E Grand River Ave...................... Brighton MI 48116 810-227-1221 227-1869
TF: 800-523-8198 ■ *Web:* www.brightonhospital.org

Central Dupage Hospital's Behavioral Health Services
27 W 350 High Lake Rd .... Winfield IL 60190 630-653-4000 933-1933
Web: www.cdh.org

Central Street Health Center 26 Central St .... Somerville MA 02143 617-591-6033 591-6452

Clear Brook Lodge 890 Bethel Hill Rd .... Shickshinny PA 18655 570-864-3116 864-2812
Web: www.clearbrookinc.com

Clear Brook Manor 1100 E Northampton St.................... Wilkes-Barre PA 18706 570-823-1171 823-1582
TF: 800-582-6241 ■ *Web:* www.clearbrookinc.com

Conifer Park 79 Glenridge Rd.................................. Glenville NY 12302 518-399-6446 952-8228
TF: 800-989-6446 ■ *Web:* www.coniferpark.com

Cornell Interventions 2221 W 64th St .... Woodridge IL 60517 630-968-6477 968-8945
Web: www.cornellcompanies.com

Cornerstone Medical Arts Center Hospital 57 W 57th St......... New York NY 10019 212-755-0200 755-0915
TF: 800-233-9999 ■ *Web:* www.cornerstoneny.com

Cove Forge Behavioral Health Rt 1 .... Williamsburg PA 16693 814-832-2131 832-2133
TF: 800-873-2131

	City	State	ZIP	Phone	Fax
Eagleville Hospital 100 Eagleville Rd TF: 800-255-2019 ■ Web: www.eaglevillehospital.com	Eagleville	PA	19408	610-539-6000	539-6249
Fairbanks Hospital 8102 Clearvista Pkwy TF: 800-225-4673 ■ Web: www.fairbankscd.org	Indianapolis	IN	46256	317-849-8222	849-1455
Family Recovery Inc 555 SW 148th Ave TF: 800-417-6237 ■ Web: www.thefamilyrecovery.com	Sunrise	FL	33325	954-370-0200	915-0812
Fellowship Hall Inc 5140 Dunstan Rd TF: 800-659-3381 ■ Web: www.fellowshiphall.com	Greensboro	NC	27405	336-621-3381	621-7513
Florida Center for Addictions & Dual Disorders 100 W College Dr Web: www.tchsonline.com	Avon Park	FL	33825	863-452-3858	452-3863
Focus Healthcare at High Point 5960 SW 106th Ave TF: 800-523-7773 ■ Web: www.focushealthcare.com/Highpoint.html	Cooper City	FL	33328	954-680-2700	680-9941
Friary of Lakeview Center 4400 Hickory Shores Blvd TF: 800-332-2271 ■ Web: www.thefriary.org	Gulf Breeze	FL	32563	850-932-9375	934-1281
Gateway Foundation Inc 55 E Jackson St Suite 1500 Web: www.gatewayfoundation.org	Chicago	IL	60604	312-663-1130	663-0504
Gaudenzia Inc Common Ground 2835 N Front St TF: 888-237-8984	Harrisburg	PA	17110	717-238-5553	232-7362
Glenbeigh Health Source 2863 SR 45 TF: 800-234-1001 ■ Web: www.glenbeigh.com	Rock Creek	OH	44084	440-563-3400	563-9619
Greenleaf Center 2209 Pineview Dr	Valdosta	GA	31602	229-247-4357	244-6194
Griffin Memorial Hospital PO Box 151 TF: 877-580-5044	Norman	OK	73070	405-321-4880	573-6652
Hanley Center 5200 East Ave TF: 800-444-7008 ■ Web: www.hanleycenter.org	West Palm Beach	FL	33407	561-841-1000	841-1100
Hazelden Center for Youth & Families 11505 36th Ave N TF: 800-257-7800 ■ Web: www.hazelden.org	Plymouth	MN	55441	763-509-3800	559-0149
Hazelden Chicago 867 N Dearborn St TF: 800-257-7810 ■ Web: www.hazelden.org	Chicago	IL	60610	312-943-3534	943-3530
Hazelden Foundation 15245 Pleasant Valley Rd TF: 800-257-7810 ■ Web: www.hazelden.org	Center City	MN	55012	651-213-4200	213-4411
Hazelden New York 322 8th Ave 12th Fl TF: 800-257-7800 ■ Web: www.hazelden.org	New York	NY	10001	212-420-9520	420-9664
Hazelden Springbrook 1901 Esther St TF Admissions: 800-257-7800 ■ Web: www.hazelden.org	Newberg	OR	97132	503-537-7000	537-7007
HealthSource Saginaw 3340 Hospital Rd TF: 800-662-6848	Saginaw	MI	48603	989-790-7700	790-9297
Highland Ridge Hospital 7309 S 180 W Web: www.highlandridgehospital.com	Midvale	UT	84047	801-569-2153	567-9006
Impact Drug & Alcohol Treatment Center 1680 N Fair Oaks Ave TF: 888-400-4222 ■ Web: www.impacthouse.com	Pasadena	CA	91103	626-798-0884	798-6970
Jefferson Alcohol & Drug Abuse Center 600 S Preston St	Louisville	KY	40202	502-583-3951	581-9234
Julian F Keith Alcohol & Drug Abuse Treatment Center 201 Tabernacle Rd Web: www.jfkadatc.net	Black Mountain	NC	28711	828-669-3400	669-3451
Kent Community Hospital 750 Fuller Ave NE	Grand Rapids	MI	49503	616-486-3000	486-2419
Keystone Center 2001 Providence Ave TF: 800-558-9600 ■ Web: www.keystonecenter.net	Chester	PA	19013	610-876-9000	876-5441
La Hacienda Treatment Center 145 La Hacienda Way PO Box 1 TF: 800-749-6160 ■ Web: www.lahacienda.com	Hunt	TX	78024	830-238-4222	238-3120
Livengrin Foundation 4833 Hulmeville Rd TF: 800-245-4746 ■ Web: www.livengrin.org	Bensalem	PA	19020	215-638-5200	638-2603
Malvern Institute 940 King Rd TF: 888-643-3869 ■ Web: www.malverninstitute.com	Malvern	PA	19355	610-647-0330	647-2572
Mental Health Institute Iowa Residential Treatment Center 1200 E Washington St	Mount Pleasant	IA	52641	319-385-7231	
Mount Regis Center 405 Kimball Ave TF: 800-477-3447 ■ Web: www.mtregis.com	Salem	VA	24153	540-389-4761	389-6539
Mountain Manor Treatment Center 9701 Keysville Rd PO Box 136 TF: 800-537-3422	Emmitsburg	MD	21727	301-447-2361	447-6504
New Directions Inc 30800 Chagrin Blvd TF: 800-750-6709 ■ Web: www.newdirect.org	Cleveland	OH	44124	216-591-0324	591-1243
Phoenix House Foundation Inc 164 W 74th St TF: 800-262-2463 ■ Web: www.phoenixhouse.org	New York	NY	10023	212-595-5810	496-6035
Providence Behavioral Health Hospital 1233 Main St TF: 800-274-7724 ■ Web: mercycares.com/pages.asp?id=514	Holyoke	MA	01040	413-536-5111	539-2992
Redgate Memorial Recovery Center 1775 Chestnut Ave	Long Beach	CA	90813	562-599-8444	591-6134
Rimrock Foundation 1231 N 29th St TF: 800-227-3953 ■ Web: www.rimrock.org	Billings	MT	59101	406-248-3175	248-3821
Riverside General Hospital Houston Recovery Center 4514 Lyons Ave Web: riversidehospital.fifthwardhouston.org	Houston	TX	77020	713-331-2500	526-2441
Rivervalley Behavioral Health Hospital 1000 Industrial Dr TF: 800-755-8477 ■ Web: www.rvbh.com/rvvip.htm	Owensboro	KY	42301	270-689-6800	689-6799
Rubicon Inc 1300 MacTavish Ave Web: www.rubiconrehab.com	Richmond	VA	23230	804-359-3255	359-5137
Saint Josephs Villa of Rochester 3300 Dewey Ave Web: www.stjosephsvilla.com	Rochester	NY	14616	585-865-1550	865-5219
Samaritan Village 138-02 Queens Blvd Web: samvill.org	Briarwood	NY	11435	718-206-2000	206-2399
Schick Shadel Hospital 12101 Ambaum Blvd SW TF: 800-272-8464 ■ Web: www.schick-shadel.com	Seattle	WA	98146	206-244-8100	431-9142
Self Help Addiction Rehabilitation Corp 1852 W Grand Blvd	Detroit	MI	48208	313-894-8444	894-2712
Serenity Lane 616 E 16th Ave TF: 800-543-9905 ■ Web: www.serenitylane.org	Eugene	OR	97401	541-687-1110	687-9041
Sierra Tucson Inc 39580 S Lago Del Oro Pkwy TF: 800-842-4487 ■ Web: www.sierratucson.com	Tucson	AZ	85739	520-624-4000	818-5888
Spectrum Programs Inc 11031 NE 6th Ave Web: www.spectrumprograms.com	Miami	FL	33161	305-757-0602	757-2387
Spencer Recovery Centers Inc 1316 S Coast Hwy TF: 800-334-0394 ■ Web: www.spencerrecovery.com	Laguna Beach	CA	92651	949-376-3705	376-6862
Starlite Recovery Center 230 Mesa Verde Dr PO Box 317 TF: 800-292-0148 ■ Web: www.starliterecovery.com	Center Point	TX	78010	830-634-2212	634-2532
Substance Abuse Foundation 3125 E 7th St TF: 888-476-2743 ■ Web: www.safinc.org	Long Beach	CA	90804	562-439-7755	438-6891
Talbott Recovery Campus 5448 Yorktowne Dr TF: 800-445-4232 ■ Web: www.talbottcampus.com	Atlanta	GA	30349	770-994-0185	994-2024
Turning Point Hospital 3015 Veterans Pkwy TF: 800-342-1075 ■ Web: www.turningpointcare.com	Moultrie	GA	31788	229-985-4815	890-1614
Turning Point of Tampa 6227 Sheldon Rd TF: 800-397-3006 ■ Web: www.tptampa.com	Tampa	FL	33615	813-882-3003	885-6974
Twin Town Treatment Center 1706 University Ave	Saint Paul	MN	55104	651-645-3661	645-0959
Valley Forge Medical Center & Hospital 1033 W Germantown Pike TF: 888-539-8500	Norristown	PA	19403	610-539-8500	539-0910
Village South Inc 3180 Biscayne Blvd TF: 800-443-3784 ■ Web: www.villagesouth.com	Miami	FL	33137	305-573-3784	576-1348
Wabash Valley Hospital 2900 N River Rd Web: www.wvhmhc.org	West Lafayette	IN	47906	765-463-2555	497-3960
Wake County Alcoholism Treatment Center 3000 Falstaff Rd	Raleigh	NC	27610	919-250-1500	250-1597
Walter B Jones Alcohol & Drug Abuse Treatment Center 2577 W 5th St	Greenville	NC	27834	252-830-3426	830-8585
Warwick Manor Behavioral Health 3680 Warwick Rd TF: 800-344-6423	East New Market	MD	21631	410-943-8108	943-3976
Willingway Hospital 311 Jones Mill Rd TF: 800-242-9455 ■ Web: www.willingway.com	Statesboro	GA	30458	912-764-6236	764-7063
Wilmington Treatment Center 2520 Troy Dr TF: 800-992-3671 ■ Web: www.wilmtreatment.com	Wilmington	NC	28401	910-762-2727	762-7923

730 SURVEYING, MAPPING, RELATED SERVICES

SEE ALSO Engineering & Design p. 1619

	City	State	ZIP	Phone	Fax
Abrams Aerial Survey Corp 9659 W Grand Ledge Hwy Suite 1 TF: 800-826-7518 ■ Web: www.abramsaerial.com	Sunfield	MI	48890	517-372-8100	372-8112
Analytical Surveys Inc (ASI) 9725 Datapoint Dr Suite 300-B NASDAQ: ANLT ■ Web: www.anlt.com	San Antonio	TX	78229	210-657-1500	599-3162
ASI (Analytical Surveys Inc) 9725 Datapoint Dr Suite 300-B NASDAQ: ANLT ■ Web: www.anlt.com	San Antonio	TX	78229	210-657-1500	599-3162
Bowman Consulting Group 3863 Centerview Dr Suite 300 Web: www.bowmanconsulting.com	Chantilly	VA	20151	703-464-1000	481-8410
C-MAP USA Inc 133 Falmouth Rd TF: 800-424-2627 ■ Web: www.c-map.com	Mashpee	MA	02649	508-477-8010	539-4381
Day & Zimmermann Group Inc 1818 Market St TF: 800-523-0786 ■ Web: www.dayzim.com	Philadelphia	PA	19103	215-299-8000	299-8030
Fugro Chance Inc 6100 Hillcroft St Suite 300 Web: www.fugrochance.com	Houston	TX	77081	713-346-3700	346-3671
Fugro Pelagos Inc 3738 Ruffin Rd Web: www.fugro-pelagos.com	San Diego	CA	92123	858-292-8922	292-5308
Greenhorne & O'Mara Inc 6110 Frost Pl TF: 866-322-8905 ■ Web: www.g-and-o.com	Laurel	MD	20707	301-982-2800	220-2483
Huitt-Zollars Inc 3131 McKinney Ave Suite 600 Web: www.huitt-zollars.com	Dallas	TX	75204	214-871-3311	871-0757
KCI Technologies Inc 10 N Park Dr TF: 800-572-7496 ■ Web: www.kci.com/tech	Hunt Valley	MD	21030	410-316-7800	316-7817
Kimball L Robert & Assoc Inc 615 W Highland Ave Web: www.lrkimball.com	Ebensburg	PA	15931	814-472-7700	472-7712
L Robert Kimball & Assoc Inc 615 W Highland Ave Web: www.lrkimball.com	Ebensburg	PA	15931	814-472-7700	472-7712
Landiscor Inc 1710 E Indian School Rd Suite 201 Web: www.landiscor.com	Phoenix	AZ	85016	602-248-8989	266-8116
MacDonald Dettwiler & Assoc Ltd 13800 Commerce Pkwy TSX: MDA ■ Web: www.mda.ca	Richmond	BC	V6V2J3	604-278-3411	278-2117
Markhurd Corp 13400 68th Ave N TF: 800-627-4873 ■ Web: www.markhurd.com	Maple Grove	MN	55311	763-420-9606	420-9584
Schoor DePalma Inc PO Box 900 Web: www.schoordepalma.com	Manalapan	NJ	07726	732-577-9000	577-9888
Sidwell Co Inc 675 Sidwell Ct Web: www.sidwellco.com	Saint Charles	IL	60174	630-549-1000	549-1111
Space Imaging Inc 12076 Grant St *Fax: Mktg ■ TF: 800-697-4454 ■ Web: www.spaceimaging.com	Thornton	CO	80241	303-254-2000	254-2215*
Spot Image Corp 14595 Avion Pkwy Suite 500 TF: 800-275-7768 ■ Web: www.spot.com	Chantilly	VA	20151	703-715-3100	715-3120
Wade-Trim Group Inc 25251 Northline Rd TF: 800-482-2864 ■ Web: www.wadetrim.com	Taylor	MI	48180	734-947-9700	947-9726

731 SWIMMING POOLS

	City	State	ZIP	Phone	Fax
Anthony & Sylvan Pools Corp PO Box 1449 TF: 800-366-7958 ■ Web: www.anthony-sylvan.com	Doylestown	PA	18901	215-489-5600	489-5610
Aquasports LLC 999 Jersey Ave	New Brunswick	NJ	08901	732-247-6298	828-0609
Delair Group LLC 8600 River Rd TF: 800-235-0185 ■ Web: www.delairgroup.com	Delair	NJ	08110	856-663-2900	663-1297
Fox Pool Corp 3490 Board Rd TF: 800-723-1011 ■ Web: www.foxpool.com	York	PA	17402	717-764-8581	764-4293
Gary Pools Inc 438 Sandau Rd TF: 800-966-9605 ■ Web: www.garypools.com	San Antonio	TX	78216	210-341-5153	341-5154
Hoffinger Industries Inc 6914 Autumn Oaks Dr Suite B Web: www.hoffinger.com	Olive Branch	MS	38654	662-890-7930	890-7930
Imperial Pools Inc 33 Wade Rd TF: 800-444-9977 ■ Web: www.imperialpools.com	Latham	NY	12110	518-786-1200	786-0954
Morgan Building Systems Inc 2800 McCree Rd TF: 800-935-0321 ■ Web: www.morganusa.com	Garland	TX	75041	972-864-7300	864-7307
Paddock Pools 6525 E Thomas Rd *Fax: Hum Res ■ Web: www.paddockpoolsandspas.com	Scottsdale	AZ	85251	480-947-7261	970-7432*
Radiant Pools Div Trojan Leisure Products LLC 440 N Pearl St TF: 866-697-5870 ■ Web: www.radiantpools.com/	Albany	NY	12207	518-434-4161	432-6554
Vogue Pool Products 7050 Saint-Patrick St TF: 800-363-3232 ■ Web: www.voguepools.com	LaSalle	QC	H8N1V2	514-363-3232	363-1772
Wagner Pool Co Inc 750 Wordin Ave Web: www.wagnerswimmingpools.com	Bridgeport	CT	06605	203-335-3960	331-9430

732 SWITCHGEAR & SWITCHBOARD APPARATUS

SEE ALSO Transformers - Power, Distribution, Specialty p. 2377; Wiring Devices - Current-Carrying p. 2416

	City	State	ZIP	Phone	Fax
American Solenoid Co Inc 760 New Brunswick Rd TF: 800-526-3966	Somerset	NJ	08873	732-560-1240	560-8823
Atkinson Industries Inc 1801 E 27th St Terr Web: www.atkinsonindustries.com	Pittsburg	KS	66762	620-231-6900	231-7154
Automatic Switch Co 50-60 Hanover Rd TF: 800-524-1023 ■ Web: www.asco.com	Florham Park	NJ	07932	973-966-2000	966-2628
AZZ Inc 1300 S University Dr Suite 200 NYSE: AZZ ■ Web: www.azz.com	Fort Worth	TX	76107	817-810-0095	336-5354
Bel Fuse Inc 206 Van Vorst St NASDAQ: BELFA ■ TF: 800-235-3873 ■ Web: www.belfuse.com	Jersey City	NJ	07302	201-432-0463	432-9542
Cole Instrument Corp 2650 S Croddy Way *Fax: Sales ■ Web: www.cole-switches.com	Santa Ana	CA	92704	714-556-3100	241-9061*
Components Corp of America 717 N Harwood St Suite 2660 Web: www.components-corp-amer.com	Dallas	TX	75201	214-969-0166	969-5905
CW Industries 130 James Way Web: www.cwind.com	Southampton	PA	18966	215-355-7080	355-1088

Phone Fax

Eaton Cutler-Hammer Inc 1 Tuscarawas Rd ..... Beaver PA 15009 724-775-2000 773-1593
TF: 800-354-2070 ■ *Web:* www.cutler-hammer.com
Electroswitch Corp 180 King Ave ..... Weymouth MA 02188 781-335-5200 335-4253
Web: www.electroswitch.com
Ferraz Shawmut Inc 374 Merrimac St ..... Newburyport MA 01950 978-462-6662 462-7934
Web: www.ferrazshawmut.com
Grayhill Inc 561 Hillgrove Ave ..... La Grange IL 60525 708-354-1040 354-2820
TF: 800-244-0559 ■ *Web:* www.grayhill.com
Guardian Electric Mfg Co Inc 1425 Lake Ave ..... Woodstock IL 60098 815-337-0050 337-0377
TF: 800-762-0369 ■ *Web:* www.guardian-electric.com
Indak Mfg Corp 1915 Techny Rd ..... Northbrook IL 60062 847-272-0343 272-0697
Web: www.indak.com
InPlay Technologies Inc 234 S Extension Rd Suite 103 ..... Mesa AZ 85210 480-586-3300 844-9625
NASDAQ: NPLA ■ *TF:* 800-729-3132 ■ *Web:* www.inplaytechnologies.com
Instruments Inc 7263 Engineer Rd Suite G ..... San Diego CA 92111 858-571-1111 571-0188
Web: www.instrumentsinc.com
ITW Switches 2550 Mill Brook Dr ..... Buffalo Grove IL 60089 847-876-9400 876-9440
TF: 800-544-3354 ■ *Web:* www.itwswitches.com
K-R Automation Corp 2000 Centerwood Dr ..... Warren MI 48091 586-756-3131 756-4333
Web: www.krauto.com
Korry Electronics Co 901 Dexter Ave N ..... Seattle WA 98109 206-281-1300 281-1365
TF: 800-257-8921 ■ *Web:* www.korry.com
Littelfuse Inc 800 E Northwest Hwy ..... Des Plaines IL 60016 847-824-1188 824-3024*
NASDAQ: LFUS ■ **Fax:* Sales ■ *Web:* www.littelfuse.com
Mac Products Inc 60 Pennsylvania Ave PO Box 469 ..... Kearny NJ 07032 973-344-0700 344-5368
Web: www.macproducts.net
Meter Devices Co Inc
3359 Bruening Ave SW PO Box 6382 Stn B ..... Canton OH 44706 330-455-0301 455-1461
TF: 888-367-6383 ■ *Web:* www.meter-devices.com
Otto Engineering Inc 2 E Main St ..... Carpentersville IL 60110 847-428-7171 428-4160
Web: www.ottoeng.com
Pacs Industries Inc 61 Steamboat Rd ..... Great Neck NY 11024 516-829-9060 829-9557
Web: www.pacsind.com
Powell Industries Inc 8550 Mosely Dr ..... Houston TX 77075 713-944-6900 947-4453
NASDAQ: POWL ■ *Web:* www.powellind.com
Russelectric Inc 99 Industrial Park Rd ..... Hingham MA 02043 781-749-6000 749-8077
TF: 800-225-5250 ■ *Web:* www.russelectric.com
Satin American Corp 40 Oliver Terr ..... Shelton CT 06484 203-929-6363 929-9684
TF: 800-272-7711 ■ *Web:* www.satinamerican.com
Siemens Energy & Automation Inc 3333 Old Milton Pkwy ..... Alpharetta GA 30005 770-751-2000 740-2534
TF: 800-964-4114 ■ *Web:* automation.usa.siemens.com
Siemens Power Transmission & Distribution Inc
7000 Siemens Rd ..... Wendell NC 27591 919-365-2200 365-2201
TF: 800-347-6659 ■ *Web:* www.ptd.siemens.com
SPD Technologies 13500 Roosevelt Blvd ..... Philadelphia PA 19116 215-677-4900 677-1504
Web: www.spdtech.com
Square D Schneider Electric 1415 S Roselle Rd ..... Palatine IL 60067 847-397-2600 925-7500
TF: 888-778-2733 ■ *Web:* www.squared.com
Tapeswitch Corp 100 Schmitt Blvd ..... Farmingdale NY 11735 631-630-0442 630-0454
TF: 800-234-8273 ■ *Web:* www.tapeswitch.com
Texas Instruments Inc Sensors & Controls Group
529 Pleasant St PO Box 2964 ..... Attleboro MA 02703 508-236-3800
Web: www.ti.com/snc
TopWorx Inc 3300 Fern Valley Rd ..... Louisville KY 40213 502-969-8000 969-5911
TF: 800-969-9020 ■ *Web:* www.topworx.com
USCO Power Equipment Corp 8100 Churchill Ave ..... Leeds AL 35094 205-699-0840 699-0858*
**Fax:* Sales ■ *Web:* www.uscopower.com

733 TABLE & KITCHEN SUPPLIES - CHINA & EARTHENWARE

Phone Fax

Buffalo China Inc 500 Bailey Ave ..... Buffalo NY 14210 716-824-8515 824-1378
TF Cust Svc: 800-828-7033
Dansk International Designs Ltd 1414 Radcliff St ..... Bristol PA NJ 19007 267-525-7800 844-1576*
**Fax Area Code:* 609 ■ *TF Cust Svc:* 800-293-2675 ■ *Web:* www.dansk.com
Fitz & Floyd Corp Inc 501 Corporate Dr ..... Lewisville TX 75057 972-874-3480 353-7718
TF: 800-243-2058 ■ *Web:* www.fitzandfloyd.com
Frankoma Pottery 9549 Frankoma Rd ..... Sapulpa OK 74066 918-224-5511 227-3117
TF: 800-331-3650 ■ *Web:* www.frankoma.com
Hall China Co 1 Anna St PO Box 989 ..... East Liverpool OH 43920 330-385-2900 837-4950*
**Fax Area Code:* 800 ■ *TF Cust Svc:* 800-445-4255 ■ *Web:* www.hallchina.com
Hartstone Pottery Inc 1719 Dearborn St PO Box 2310 ..... Zanesville OH 43701 740-452-9000 452-5369
TF: 800-339-4278 ■ *Web:* www.hartstonepottery.com
Heartland China Inc PO Box 8156 ..... Topeka KS 66608 785-354-8080 242-8090
TF: 888-383-3163 ■ *Web:* www.heartlandchina.com
Hollohaza USA 920 E Colorado Blvd Suite 542 ..... Pasadena CA 91106 626-666-1431 568-3275
Web: www.hollohaza.com
Homer Laughlin China Co 672 Fiesta Dr ..... Newell WV 26050 304-387-1300 387-4265
TF: 800-452-4462 ■ *Web:* www.hlchina.com
Laughlin Homer China Co 672 Fiesta Dr ..... Newell WV 26050 304-387-1300 387-4265
TF: 800-452-4462 ■ *Web:* www.hlchina.com
Lenox Inc 100 Lenox Dr ..... Lawrenceville NJ 08648 609-896-2800 895-0139
TF Cust Svc: 800-635-3669 ■ *Web:* www.lenox.com
Lipper International Inc 235 Washington St ..... Wallingford CT 06492 203-269-8588 284-8637
TF: 800-243-3129 ■ *Web:* www.lipperinternational.com
Luna Garcia 201 San Juan Ave ..... Venice CA 90291 310-396-8026
TF: 800-905-9975 ■ *Web:* www.lunagarcia.com
Martin's Herend Imports Inc 21440 Pacific Blvd ..... Sterling VA 20167 703-450-1601 450-1605
TF: 800-643-7363 ■ *Web:* www.herendusa.com
Mikasa Inc 100 Plaza Dr ..... Secaucus NJ 07094 201-867-9210 867-0580
TF Cust Svc: 800-833-4681 ■ *Web:* www.mikasa.com
Noritake Co Inc 15-22 Fair Lawn Ave ..... Fair Lawn NJ 07410 201-475-5200 796-2269
TF: 888-296-3423 ■ *Web:* www.noritake.com
Oneida Ltd 163-181 Kenwood Ave ..... Oneida NY 13421 315-361-3000 361-3475
TF: 800-877-6667 ■ *Web:* www.oneida.com
Pfaltzgraff Co 140 E Market St ..... York PA 17401 717-848-5500 771-1433*
**Fax:* Cust Svc ■ *TF:* 800-999-2811 ■ *Web:* www.pfaltzgraff.com
Royal China & Porcelain Cos Inc 1265 Glen Ave ..... Moorestown NJ 08057 856-866-2900 866-2499
TF Orders: 800-631-7120
Royal Doulton USA Inc 200 Cottontail Ln ..... Somerset NJ 08873 732-356-7880 764-4974
TF: 800-682-4462 ■ *Web:* www.royaldoulton.com
Syracuse China Co 2801 Court St ..... Syracuse NY 13208 315-455-5671 455-4532
TF: 800-448-5711 ■ *Web:* www.libbey.com
True West 8549 PR 2414 PO Box 441 ..... Royse City TX 75189 972-636-7922 635-2059
Web: www.truewesthome.com
Waterford Wedgwood USA Inc 1330 Campus Pkwy ..... Wall NJ 07719 732-938-5800 938-6915
Web: www.wwusa.com
World Kitchen Inc 11911 Freedom Dr Suite 600 ..... Reston VA 20190 703-456-4700 456-2020
TF Cust Svc: 800-999-3436 ■ *Web:* www.worldkitchen.com

734 TALENT AGENCIES

SEE ALSO Literary Agents p. 1916; Modeling Agencies p. 1975

Phone Fax

3 Arts Entertainment 9460 Wilshire Blvd Suite 415 ..... Beverly Hills CA 90212 310-888-3200 888-3210
Agency for the Performing Arts 405 S Beverly Dr ..... Beverly Hills CA 90212 310-888-4200 888-4242
Web: www.apa-agency.com
Artists Group 3345 Wilshire Blvd Suite 915 ..... Los Angeles CA 90010 310-552-1100 531-0006*
**Fax Area Code:* 213
Artists Group 1650 Broadway Suite 610 ..... New York NY 10019 212-586-1452 586-0037
Bauman Redanty & Shaul 5757 Wilshire Blvd Suite 473 ..... Los Angeles CA 90036 323-857-6666 857-0368
Blitz Models & Talents 487 Adelaide St W Suite 305 ..... Toronto ON M5V1T4 416-703-5799 703-6232
Brillstein Grey Entertainment 9150 Wilshire Blvd Suite 350 ..... Beverly Hills CA 90212 310-275-6135 275-6180
Brookside Artist Management 250 W 57th St Suite 2303 ..... New York NY 10107 212-489-4929 489-9056
Buddy Lee Attractions Inc 38 Music Sq East Suite 300 ..... Nashville TN 37203 615-244-4336 726-0429
Web: www.buddyleeattractions.com
CAA (Creative Artists Agency Inc) 2000 Ave of the Stars ..... Los Angeles CA 90067 424-288-2000 288-2900
Web: www.caa.com
CAA LLC 3310 West End Ave 5th Fl ..... Nashville TN 37203 615-383-8787 383-4937
Web: www.caa.com
CAA Sports 801 W 47th St Suite 219 ..... Kansas City MO 64112 816-531-5777 753-2332
Web: www.caa.com
Capital Sports & Entertainment 98 San Jacinto Blvd Suite 430 ..... Austin TX 78701 512-370-1919 470-1920
Web: www.planetcse.com
CESD Talent Agency Inc
10635 Santa Monica Blvd Suites 130/135 ..... Los Angeles CA 90025 310-475-2111 475-1929
Web: www.cedtalent.com
CESD Voices 10635 Santa Monica Blvd Suites 130/135 ..... Los Angeles CA 90025 310-475-2111 475-1929
Web: www.cedvoices.com
CKX Inc 650 Madison Ave ..... New York NY 10022 212-838-3100 872-1473
NASDAQ: CKXE ■ *Web:* ir.ckx.com
CM Artists New York 127 W 96th St Suite 13 B ..... New York NY 10025 212-864-1005 864-1066
Web: www.cmartists.com
Columbia Artists Management LLC 1790 Broadway ..... New York NY 10019 212-841-9500 841-9744
Web: www.cami.com
Creative Artists Agency Inc (CAA) 2000 Ave of the Stars ..... Los Angeles CA 90067 424-288-2000 288-2900
Web: www.caa.com
Don Buchwald & Assoc 6500 Wilshire Blvd Suite 2200 ..... Los Angeles CA 90048 323-655-7400 655-7470
Web: www.buchwald.com
Endeavor Agency 9601 Wilshire Blvd 3rd Fl ..... Beverly Hills CA 90210 310-248-2000 248-2020
Endeavor Agency 152 W 57th St 25th Fl ..... New York NY 10019 212-625-2500 625-2552
Finkel Shelly Management 60 E 42nd St Suite 464 ..... New York NY 10165 212-682-9400 983-9028
Web: www.shellyfinkel.com
Firm The 9465 Wilshire Blvd Suite 600 ..... Beverly Hills CA 90212 310-860-8000 860-8100
Gaylord Sports Management
13845 N Northsight Blvd Suite 200 ..... Scottsdale AZ 85260 480-483-9500 483-9598
Web: www.gaylordsports.com
Gersh Agency 232 N Canon Dr ..... Beverly Hills CA 90210 310-274-6611 274-3923
Web: www.gershcomedy.com
Gersh Agency 41 Madison Ave 33rd Fl ..... New York NY 10010 212-997-1818 997-1978
Web: www.gershcomedy.com
Gorfaine/Schwartz Agency 4111 W Alameda Ave Suite 509 ..... Burbank CA 91505 818-260-8500 260-8522
Web: www.gsamusic.com
Great North Artists Management 350 Dupont St ..... Toronto ON M5R1V9 416-925-2051 925-3904
Hartig Hilepo Agency Ltd 54 W 21st St Suite 610 ..... New York NY 10010 212-929-1772 929-1266
HS International 9871 Irvine Center Dr ..... Irvine CA 92618 949-753-9153 753-9253
Web: www.hsi.net
IFA Talent Agency 8730 Sunset Blvd Suite 490 ..... Los Angeles CA 90069 310-659-5522 659-3344
IMG Artists Carnegie Hall Tower 152 W 57th St 5th Fl ..... New York NY 10019 212-994-3500 994-3550
Web: www.imgartists.com
IMG Inc 1360 E 9th St IMG Center Suite 100 ..... Cleveland OH 44114 216-522-1200 522-1145
Web: www.imgworld.com
IMG Tennis IMG Center 1360 E 9th St Suite 100 ..... Cleveland OH 44114 216-522-1200 522-1145
Web: www.imgworld.com
Immortal Entertainment
10585 Santa Monica Blvd Suite 120 ..... Los Angeles CA 90025 310-481-1800 474-5872
Innovative Artists 1505 10th St ..... Santa Monica CA 90401 310-656-0400 656-0456
International Creative Management Inc (ICM)
10250 Constellation Blvd ..... Century City CA 90067 310-550-4000 550-4100
Web: www.icmtalent.com
International Creative Management Inc (ICM)
825 8th Ave 26th Fl ..... New York NY 10019 212-556-5600 556-5665
Web: www.icmtalent.com
Iris Burton Agency 8916 Ashcroft Ave ..... Los Angeles CA 90048 310-288-0121
John Crosby Management 1310 N Spaulding Ave ..... Los Angeles CA 90046 323-874-2400 874-2500
Kraft-Engel Management 15233 Ventura Blvd Suite 200 ..... Sherman Oaks CA 91403 818-380-1918 380-2609
Legacy Sports Group 500 Newport Ctr Dr Suite 800 ..... Newport Beach CA 92660 949-721-6200 720-1331
Management 360 9111 Wilshire Blvd ..... Beverly Hills CA 90210 310-272-7000 272-0084
Media Talent Group 9200 Sunset Blvd Suite 550 ..... West Hollywood CA 90069 310-275-7900 275-7910
Metropolitan Talent Agency 4500 Wilshire Blvd ..... Los Angeles CA 90010 323-857-4500 857-4599
Web: www.mta.com
Monterey International 200 W Superior St Suite 202 ..... Chicago IL 60610 312-640-7500 640-7515
Web: www.montereyinternational.net
Monterey Peninsula Artists/Paradigm 509 Hartnell St ..... Monterey CA 93940 831-375-4889 375-2623
Web: www.montereypeninsulaartists.com
Monterey Peninsula Artists/Paradigm
124 12th Ave S Suite 410 ..... Nashville TN 37203 615-251-4400 251-4401
Web: www.montereypeninsulaartists.com
Nettwerk 1650 W 2nd Ave ..... Vancouver BC V6J4R3 604-654-2929 654-1993
Web: www.nettwerk.com
Nettwerk 1545 Wilcox Ave Suite 200 ..... Hollywood CA 90028 323-301-4200 301-4199
Web: www.nettwerk.com
Nettwerk 345 7th Ave 24th Fl ..... New York NY 10001 212-760-1540 760-9719
Web: www.nettwerk.com
Octagon 1751 Pinnacle Dr Suite 1500 ..... McLean VA 22102 703-905-3300 905-4495
Web: www.octagon.com
One Entertainment 12 W 57th St PH ..... New York NY 10019 212-974-3900
Original Artists 826 Broadway 4th Fl ..... New York NY 10003 212-254-1234 254-3121
Panacea Entertainment 13587 Andalusia Dr ..... Camarillo CA 93012 805-491-9400 491-0406
Paradigm Talent & Literary Agency
360 N Crescent Dr North Bldg ..... Beverly Hills CA 90210 310-288-8000 288-2000
Parseghian/Planco Management 23 E 22nd St 3rd Fl ..... New York NY 10010 212-777-7786 777-8642
Peter Strain & Assoc 5455 Wilshire Blvd Suite 1812 ..... Los Angeles CA 90036 323-525-3391 525-0881
Peter Strain & Assoc 321 W 44th St Suite 805 ..... New York NY 10036 212-391-0380 391-1405
PMK/HBH 700 San Vicente Blvd Suite G910 ..... West Hollywood CA 90069 310-289-6200 289-6677
Prince Marketing Group 454 Prospect Ave Suite 74 ..... West Orange NJ 07052 973-325-0800 243-0037
TF: 800-987-7462 ■ *Web:* www.princemarketinggroup.com
Progressive Artists Agency 400 S Beverly Dr Suite 216 ..... Beverly Hills CA 90212 310-553-8561 553-4726
Rigberg Entertainment Group 1180 S Beverly Dr Suite 601 ..... Los Angeles CA 90035 310-712-0712 712-0717
Rogers & Cowan PR
Pacific Design Center 8687 Melrose Ave 7th Fl ..... Los Angeles CA 90069 310-854-8100 854-8101
Web: www.rogersandcowan.com
Rosebud Agency PO Box 170429 ..... San Francisco CA 94117 415-386-3456 386-0599
Web: www.rosebudus.com

Company / Address	City	State	ZIP	Phone	Fax
SFX Sports Group 5335 Wisconsin Ave NW Suite 850	Washington	DC	20015	202-686-2000	686-5050
TF: 800-776-7378 ■ *Web:* sfxsports.com					
Shapiro/West & Assoc 141 El Camino Dr Suite 205	Beverly Hills	CA	90212	310-278-8896	278-7238
Shelly Finkel Management 60 E 42nd St Suite 464	New York	NY	10165	212-682-9400	983-9028
Web: www.shellyfinkel.com					
Smith Susan Co 1344 N Wetherly Dr	Los Angeles	CA	90069	310-276-4224	276-4343
SMS Talent Agency 8730 Sunset Blvd Suite 440	Los Angeles	CA	90069	310-289-0909	289-0990
Special Artists Agency 9465 Wilshire Blvd Suite 890	Beverly Hills	CA	90212	310-859-9688	859-1842
Stone Manners Agency 6500 Wilshire Blvd Suite 550	Los Angeles	CA	90048	323-655-1313	655-7676
Susan Smith Co 1344 N Wetherly Dr	Los Angeles	CA	90069	310-276-4224	276-4343
TalentWorks 3500 W Olive Ave Suite 1400	Burbank	CA	91505	818-972-4300	955-6411
United Talent Agency Inc 9560 Wilshire Blvd Suite 500	Beverly Hills	CA	90212	310-273-6700	247-1111
Web: www.unitedtalent.com					
William Morris Agency 1 William Morris Pl	Beverly Hills	CA	90212	310-859-4000	859-4462
Web: www.wma.com					
William Morris Agency 119 Washington Ave Suite 400	Miami Beach	FL	33139	305-938-2000	938-2002
Web: www.wma.com					
William Morris Agency 1325 Ave of the Americas	New York	NY	10019	212-586-5100	246-3583
Web: www.wma.com					
William Morris Agency 1600 Division St Suite 300	Nashville	TN	37203	615-963-3000	963-3090
Web: www.wma.com					

TAPE - ADHESIVE

SEE Medical Supplies - Mfr p. 1955

735 TAPE - CELLOPHANE, GUMMED, MASKING, PRESSURE SENSITIVE

SEE ALSO Medical Supplies - Mfr p. 1955

Company / Address	City	State	ZIP	Phone	Fax
3M Adhesives & Tapes Div 3M Ctr Bldg 21-1W-01	Saint Paul	MN	55144	800-362-3550	778-4244*
**Fax Area Code:* 651 ■ **Fax:* Cust Svc					
3M Automotive Aftermarket Div 3M Center Bldg 223-6N-01	Saint Paul	MN	55144	651-737-6515	699-7840*
**Fax Area Code:* 800 ■ *TF:* 800-364-3577 ■ *Web:* www.3m.com/us/auto_marine_aero/aad					
3M Canada Co PO Box 5757	London	ON	N6A4T1	519-451-2500	452-4714*
**Fax:* Library ■ *TF:* 800-265-1840 ■ *Web:* www.3m.com/ca/					
3M Consumer & Office Div 3M Ctr	Saint Paul	MN	55144	651-733-1110	736-2133
TF: 800-364-3577					
3M Display & Graphics Div 3M Ctr	Saint Paul	MN	55144	651-733-1110	733-9973
TF: 800-364-3577					
3M Personal Care Div 3M Center Bldg 220-3W-10	Saint Paul	MN	55144	866-212-5083	736-9780*
**Fax Area Code:* 651 ■ *Web:* www.3m.com/us/healthcare/personal_care					
Adchem Corp 1852 Old Country Rd	Riverhead	NY	11901	631-727-6000	727-6010
Web: www.adchem.com					
American Biltrite Inc 57 River St	Wellesley Hills	MA	02481	781-237-6655	237-6880
AMEX: ABL ■ *Web:* ambilt.com					
American Biltrite Inc Tape Products Div 105 Whittendale Dr	Moorestown	NJ	08057	856-778-0700	778-7485
Web: www.abitape.com					
Argent Automotive Systems 41016 Concept Dr	Plymouth	MI	48170	734-582-9800	582-9999
TF: 800-223-9890 ■ *Web:* www.argent-automotive.com					
Avery Dennison Corp 150 N Orange Grove Blvd	Pasadena	CA	91103	626-304-2000	304-2192
NYSE: AVY ■ *TF Cust Svc:* 800-252-8379 ■ *Web:* www.averydennison.com					
Avery Dennison Specialty Tapes Div 205 Chester St Bldg 5	Painesville	OH	44077	440-358-6000	358-3295
Web: www.averydennison.com					
Beiersdorf North America 187 Danbury Rd	Wilton	CT	06897	203-563-5800	854-8112*
**Fax:* Hum Res ■ *TF:* 800-233-2340 ■ *Web:* www.beiersdorf.com					
Bemis Co Inc 1 Neenah Center 4th Fl PO Box 669	Neenah	WI	54957	920-727-4100	
NYSE: BMS ■ *Web:* www.bemis.com					
Brady Coated Products 6555 W Good Hope Rd	Milwaukee	WI	53223	414-358-6600	292-2289*
**Fax Area Code:* 800 ■ *TF:* 800-635-7557 ■ *Web:* www.coatedproducts.com					
Brite-Line Technologies Inc 104 Revere St	Canton	MA	02021	781-828-0220	828-6041
TF: 800-458-0336 ■ *Web:* www.brite-line.com					
Canada Vibac Tape Corp 12250 Industrial Blvd	Montreal	QC	H1B5M5	514-640-1599	640-1630
TF: 800-557-0192 ■ *Web:* www.vibacgroup.com					
Cantec Industries Inc 455 Cote Vertu Rd	Montreal	QC	H4N1E8	514-334-1510	745-0764
TF Orders: 800-334-1567 ■ *Web:* www.cttgroup.com					
Compac Corp 103 Bilby Rd	Hackettstown	NJ	07840	908-498-0660	850-0272
TF: 800-631-9350 ■ *Web:* www.compaccorp.com					
Covalence Adhesives 25 Forge Pkwy	Franklin	MA	02038	508-918-1600	328-4822*
**Fax Area Code:* 800 ■ *TF:* 800-248-7659 ■ *Web:* covalenceadhesives.com					
Crowell Corp 1 Coral Rd PO Box 3227	Newport	DE	19804	302-998-0557	998-0626
TF: 800-441-7525 ■ *Web:* www.crowellcorp.com					
Custom Tapes Inc 7125 W Gunnison St	Harwood Heights	IL	60706	708-867-6060	867-0522
TF: 800-621-7994					
Decker Tape Products Inc 6 Stewart Pl	Fairfield	NJ	07004	973-227-5350	808-9418
TF: 800-227-5252 ■ *Web:* www.deckertape.com					
DeWAL Industries Inc 15 Ray Trainor Dr	Narragansett	RI	02882	401-789-9736	783-6780
TF: 800-366-8356 ■ *Web:* www.dewal.com					
Dielectric Polymers Inc 218 Race St	Holyoke	MA	01040	413-532-3288	533-9316
TF: 800-628-9007 ■ *Web:* www.dipoly.com					
Eternabond 75 E Division St	Mundelein	IL	60060	847-837-9400	837-9449
TF: 888-336-2663 ■ *Web:* www.eternabond.com					
FiberMark Inc 161 Wellington Rd	Brattleboro	VT	05301	802-257-0365	257-5907*
**Fax:* Sales ■ *Web:* www.fibermark.com					
Forbo Adhesives LLC 523 Davis Dr Suite 400	Durham	NC	27713	919-433-1300	433-1301
TF: 800-213-4805 ■ *Web:* www.forbo.com					
Gaska-Tape Inc 1810 W Lusher Ave	Elkhart	IN	46517	574-294-5431	293-4504
TF: 800-423-1571 ■ *Web:* www.gaska.com					
Harris Industries Inc 5181 Argosy Ave	Huntington Beach	CA	92649	714-898-8048	898-7108
TF: 800-222-6866 ■ *Web:* www.harrisind.com					
Hawkeye International Ltd PO Box 451485	Los Angeles	CA	90045	310-324-4047	324-6461
Web: www.hawkeyeintl.com					
Henkel Corp 32150 Just Imagine Dr	Avon	OH	44011	440-937-7000	937-7077
TF: 800-321-1733 ■ *Web:* www.henkelca.com					
Holland Mfg Co Inc 15 Main St PO Box 404	Succasunna	NJ	07876	973-584-8141	584-6845
TF: 800-345-0492 ■ *Web:* www.hollandmfg.com					
Intertape Polymer Group Inc 3647 Cortez Rd W Suite 102	Bradenton	FL	34210	941-727-5788	727-1568
NYSE: ITP ■ *TF:* 800-474-8273 ■ *Web:* www.intertapepolymer.com					
JHL Industries 10012 Nevada Ave	Chatsworth	CA	91311	818-882-2233	882-4350
TF: 800-255-6636 ■ *Web:* www.jhlindustries.com					
Kruse Adhesive Tape Inc 16582 Burke Ln	Huntington Beach	CA	92647	714-596-0707	596-4887
TF: 800-992-7702 ■ *Web:* www.krusetape.com					
M & C Specialties Co 90 James Way	Southampton	PA	18966	215-322-1600	322-1620
TF Cust Svc: 800-441-6996 ■ *Web:* www.mcspecialties.com					
MACtac 4560 Darrow Rd	Stow	OH	44224	330-688-1111	688-2540
TF: 800-762-2822 ■ *Web:* www.mactac.com					
Morgan Adhesives Co DBA MACtac 4560 Darrow Rd	Stow	OH	44224	330-688-1111	688-2540
TF: 800-762-2822 ■ *Web:* www.mactac.com					
Neptco Inc 30 Hamlet St	Pawtucket	RI	02861	401-722-5500	722-6378
TF: 800-354-5445 ■ *Web:* www.neptco.com					
Permacel Box 671	New Brunswick	NJ	08903	732-418-2400	418-2474
TF: 800-755-8273 ■ *Web:* www.permacel.com					
Plymouth Bishop Div Plymouth Rubber Co Inc 104 Revere St	Canton	MA	02021	781-828-0220	828-6041
TF: 800-458-0336 ■ *Web:* www.plymouthrubber.com					
Plymouth Rubber Co Inc 104 Revere St	Canton	MA	02021	781-828-0220	828-6041
TF: 800-458-0336 ■ *Web:* www.plymouthrubber.com					
Plymouth Rubber Co Inc Plymouth Bishop Div 104 Revere St	Canton	MA	02021	781-828-0220	828-6041
TF: 800-458-0336 ■ *Web:* www.plymouthrubber.com					
PolyMask Corp 500 Thornburg Dr	Conover	NC	28613	828-465-3053	465-2404
TF: 800-624-4772 ■ *Web:* www.polymask.com					
Presto Tape Inc 1626 Bridgewater Rd	Bensalem	PA	19020	215-245-8555	245-8554
TF: 800-331-1373 ■ *Web:* www.prestotape.com					
Pro Tapes & Specialties 100 Northfield Ave	Edison	NJ	08837	732-346-0900	346-0777
TF: 800-345-0234 ■ *Web:* www.protapes.com					
Quik-Tape Inc 6558 Holiday Rd	Buford	GA	30518	770-804-1244	698-0717
TF: 800-462-8273 ■ *Web:* www.quik-tape.com					
Scapa Tapes North America 746 Gotham Pkwy	Carlstadt	NJ	07072	201-939-0565	939-0437
TF: 800-801-0323 ■ *Web:* www.scapana.com					
Shurtape Technologies Inc 1506 Highland Ave NE	Hickory	NC	28601	828-322-2700	322-4419
TF: 800-438-5779 ■ *Web:* www.shurtape.com					
STA Overlaminations DBA SEKISUI TA Industries 100 S Puente St	Brea	CA	92821	714-255-7888	990-6851
Web: www.sta-overlamination.com					
Stik-II Products Inc 41 O'Neill St	Easthampton	MA	01027	413-527-7120	527-7249
TF: 800-356-3572 ■ *Web:* www.stik-2.com					
TapeSouth Inc 10302 Deerwood Pk Suite 125	Jacksonville	FL	32256	904-642-1800	642-7006
Web: www.tapesouth.com					
Tesa Tape Inc 5825 Carnegie Blvd	Charlotte	NC	28209	704-554-0707	852-8831*
**Fax Area Code:* 800 ■ **Fax:* Cust Svc ■ *TF:* 800-873-8825 ■ *Web:* www.tesatape.com					
Thomas Tape Co PO Box 207	Springfield	OH	45501	937-325-6414	325-2850
Web: www.thomastape.com					
Tommy Tape Mfg Inc 135 Redstone St	Southington	CT	06489	860-378-0111	378-0113
Web: www.tommytape.com					
Venture Tape Corp 30 Commerce Rd	Rockland	MA	02370	781-331-5900	871-0065
TF: 800-343-1076 ■ *Web:* www.venturetape.com					
WTP Inc 100 Klitchman Dr PO Box 938	Coloma	MI	49038	269-468-3399	468-3391
TF: 800-521-0731 ■ *Web:* www.wtp-inc.com					
Zepak Corp 26755 SW 95th Ave PO Box 789	Wilsonville	OR	97070	503-682-1248	682-3599
TF: 800-248-7732 ■ *Web:* www.zepak.com					

736 TARPS, TENTS, COVERS

SEE ALSO Bags - Textile p. 1367; Sporting Goods p. 2323

Company / Address	City	State	ZIP	Phone	Fax
Aero Industries Inc 4243 W Bradbury Ave	Indianapolis	IN	46241	317-244-2433	244-1311
TF Sales: 800-535-9545 ■ *Web:* www.aeroindustries.com					
American Pavilion Co 1706 Warrington Ave	Danville	IL	61832	217-443-0800	443-9619
Web: www.americanpavilion.com					
American Recreation Products Inc 1224 Fern Ridge Pkwy	Saint Louis	MO	63141	314-576-8000	576-8072
TF: 800-325-4121					
Anchor Industries Inc 1100 Burch Dr	Evansville	IN	47725	812-867-2421	867-1429
TF: 800-544-4445 ■ *Web:* www.anchorinc.com					
Bailey & Staub Inc 1 Bailey Cir	New London	CT	06320	860-442-5621	444-6622
Canvas Products Co 2340 Lafayette Blvd W	Detroit	MI	48216	313-496-1000	496-1001
TF Cust Svc: 800-624-6671 ■ *Web:* www.canvaspc.com					
Canvas Specialty 7344 E Bandini Blvd	Los Angeles	CA	90040	323-722-1156	724-3848
Web: www.can-spec.com					
Carefree of Colorado 2145 W 6th Ave	Broomfield	CO	80020	303-469-3324	731-8600*
**Fax Area Code:* 800 ■ *TF:* 800-621-2617 ■ *Web:* www.carefreeofcolorado.com					
Clamshell Structures Inc DBA Clamshell Buildings 1990 Knoll Dr	Ventura	CA	93003	805-650-1700	650-1733
TF: 800-360-8853 ■ *Web:* www.clamshell.com					
Commonwealth Canvas Corp 411 Electronics Ave	Danvers	MA	01923	978-646-9400	646-9260
TF: 877-922-6827 ■ *Web:* www.commonwealthcanvas.com					
CR Daniels Inc 3451 Ellicott Ctr Dr	Ellicott City	MD	21043	410-461-2100	461-2987
TF: 800-933-2638 ■ *Web:* www.crdaniels.com					
DC Humphrys Inc 5744 Woodland Ave	Philadelphia	PA	19143	215-724-8181	724-8706
TF Sales: 800-523-4503					
Detroit Cover Co 274 Waterman St	Detroit	MI	48209	313-898-9202	496-0252
Diamond Brand Canvas Products 145 Cane Creek Industrial Pk Rd Suite 1	Fletcher	NC	28732	828-684-9848	687-0965
TF Sales: 800-258-9811 ■ *Web:* www.diamondbrand.com					
Eide Industries Inc 16215 Piuma Ave	Cerritos	CA	90703	562-402-8335	924-2233
TF: 800-422-6827 ■ *Web:* www.eideindustries.com					
Estex Mfg Co Inc 402 E Broad St PO Box 368	Fairburn	GA	30213	770-964-3322	964-7534
TF: 800-749-1224 ■ *Web:* www.estexmfg.com					
Fisher Canvas Products Inc 415 Saint Mary St	Burlington	NJ	08016	609-239-2733	239-2728
TF: 800-892-6688 ■ *Web:* www.fishercanvas.com					
Harry Miller Co Inc 850 Albany St	Boston	MA	02119	617-427-2300	442-1152
TF: 800-225-5598 ■ *Web:* www.harrymiller.com					
John Johnson Co 274 Waterman St	Detroit	MI	48209	313-496-0600	496-0252
TF: 800-991-1394 ■ *Web:* www.jjcompany.com					
Johnson Outdoors Inc 555 Main St	Racine	WI	53403	262-631-6600	631-6601
NASDAQ: JOUT ■ *TF:* 800-299-2592 ■ *Web:* www.johnsonoutdoors.com					
Loop-Loc Ltd 390 Motor Pkwy	Hauppauge	NY	11788	631-582-2626	582-2636
TF: 800-562-5667 ■ *Web:* www.looploc.com					
M Putterman & Co Inc 4834 S Oakley St	Chicago	IL	60609	773-927-4120	650-6028
TF: 800-621-0146 ■ *Web:* www.mputterman.com					
Mauritzon Inc 3939 W Belden Ave	Chicago	IL	60647	773-235-6000	235-1479
TF: 800-621-4352 ■ *Web:* www.mauritzononline.com					
Midwest Canvas Corp 4635 W Lake St	Chicago	IL	60644	773-287-4400	854-2017
TF: 800-433-4701 ■ *Web:* www.midwestcanvas.com					
Miller Harry Canvas Co Inc 850 Albany St	Boston	MA	02119	617-427-2300	442-1152
TF: 800-225-5598 ■ *Web:* www.harrymiller.com					
North Sails Group LLC 125 Old Gate Ln	Milford	CT	06460	203-877-7621	874-6059
Web: www.northsails.com					
Outdoor Venture Corp Hwy 1651 PO Box 337	Stearns	KY	42647	606-376-5021	376-3341
Rainier Industries Ltd 18435 Olympic Ave S	Tukwila	WA	98188	425-251-1800	251-5065
TF: 800-869-7162 ■ *Web:* www.rainierindustries.com					
Robertson Mfg Inc 112 Woodland Ave	West Grove	PA	19390	610-869-9600	869-6365
TF: 800-260-5423					
Shur-Co Inc 2309 Shur-Lok St PO Box 713	Yankton	SD	57078	605-665-6000	665-0501
TF: 800-437-4172 ■ *Web:* www.shurco.com					
Steele Canvas Basket Corp 201 William St PO Box 6267 IMCN	Chelsea	MA	02150	617-889-0202	889-0524
TF: 800-541-8929 ■ *Web:* www.steele-canvas.com					
Sullivan & Brampton Inc 1688 Abram Ct	San Leandro	CA	94577	510-483-7771	483-7723
TF: 800-257-5900 ■ *Web:* www.sullivanandbrampton.com					
Trimaco LLC 2800 Meridian Pkwy Suite 185	Durham	NC	27713	919-433-4010	433-4011
TF: 866-874-6226 ■ *Web:* www.trimaco.com					

Phone Fax

Troy Sunshade Co 607 Riffle Ave .... Greenville OH 45331 937-548-2466 548-6102
TF: 800-833-8769 ■ *Web:* www.troysunshade.com
Universal Fabric Structures Inc 2200 Kumry Rd .... Quakertown PA 18951 215-529-9921 529-9936
TF: 800-634-8368 ■ *Web:* www.ufsinc.com
Webb Mfg Co 1241 Carpenter St .... Philadelphia PA 19147 215-336-5570 336-4422
TF: 800-932-2634 ■ *Web:* www.webbmfg.com

737 TAX PREPARATION SERVICES

Phone Fax

DuCharme McMillen & Assoc Inc 6610 Mutual Dr .... Fort Wayne IN 46825 260-484-8631 482-8152
Web: www.dmainc.com
EconoTax Inc 5946 Ridgewood Rd Suite B-101 .... Jackson MS 39211 601-956-0500 956-0583
TF: 800-748-9106 ■ *Web:* www.taxproinc.net
Express Tax Franchise Corp 3030 Hartley Rd Suite 320 .... Jacksonville FL 32257 904-262-0031 262-2864
TF: 888-417-4461 ■ *Web:* www.expresstaxservice.com
Fiducial 1370 Ave of the Americas 31st Fl .... New York NY 10019 212-207-4700 308-2613
TF: 866-343-8242 ■ *Web:* www.fiducial.com
Fiducial Columbia Turel 13909 SE Stark St .... Portland OR 97233 503-252-1415 252-4257
Fiducial Franchising 10480 Little Patuxent Pkwy 3rd Fl .... Columbia MD 21044 410-910-5885 910-5903
TF: 800-323-9000 ■ *Web:* www.fiducial.com/franchise
H & R Block Tax Services Inc 4400 Main St .... Kansas City MO 64111 816-753-6900 753-5346
TF: 800-869-9220 ■ *Web:* www.hrblock.com
Jackson Hewitt Inc 7 Sylvan Way .... Parsippany NJ 07054 973-496-1040 229-8935*
NYSE: JTX ■ **Fax Area Code:* 605 ■ *TF:* 800-234-1040 ■ *Web:* www.jacksonhewitt.com
Liberty Tax Service Inc 1716 Corporate Landing Pkwy .... Virginia Beach VA 23454 757-493-8855 493-0169
TF: 800-790-3863 ■ *Web:* www.libertytax.com
RSM McGladrey Inc 1185 Ave of the Americas .... New York NY 10036 212-372-1000 372-1001
TaxPro Inc DBA EconoTax Inc
5946 Ridgewood Rd Suite B-101 .... Jackson MS 39211 601-956-0500 956-0583
TF: 800-748-9106 ■ *Web:* www.taxproinc.net

738 TELECOMMUNICATIONS EQUIPMENT & SYSTEMS

SEE ALSO Computer Equipment - Modems p. 1502; Radio & Television Broadcasting & Communications Equipment p. 2194

Phone Fax

Able Communications Ltd 2931 W Central Ave Suite F .... Santa Ana CA 92704 714-979-7893 979-6117
Web: www.able.com
ACE*COMM Corp 704 Quince Orchard Rd Suite 100 .... Gaithersburg MD 20878 301-721-3000 721-3001
NASDAQ: ACEC ■ *TF:* 800-989-5566 ■ *Web:* www.acecomm.com
ADC Telecommunications Inc 13625 Technology Dr .... Eden Prairie MN 55344 952-938-8080 917-1717
NASDAQ: ADCT ■ *TF:* 800-366-3891 ■ *Web:* www.adc.com
ADTRAN Inc 901 Explorer Blvd .... Huntsville AL 35806 256-963-8000 963-8004
NASDAQ: ADTN ■ *TF:* 800-923-8726 ■ *Web:* www.adtran.com
AirNet Communications Corp 3950 Dow Rd .... Melbourne FL 32934 321-984-1990 676-6734
NASDAQ: ANCC ■ *TF:* 800-984-1990 ■ *Web:* www.aircom.com
Airspan Networks Inc 777 Yamato Rd Suite 105 .... Boca Raton FL 33431 561-893-8670 893-8671
NASDAQ: AIRN ■ *Web:* www.airspan.com
Alcatel Canada Inc 600 March Rd .... Ottawa ON K2K2E6 613-591-3600 591-3680
TF: 888-662-3425 ■ *Web:* www.alcatel.ca
Alcatel USA Inc 3400 W Plano Pkwy .... Plano TX 75075 972-519-3000
TF: 800-252-2835 ■ *Web:* www.usa.alcatel.com
AltiGen Communications Inc 4555 Cushing Pkwy .... Fremont CA 94538 510-252-9712 252-9738
NASDAQ: ATGN ■ *TF:* 888-258-4436 ■ *Web:* www.altigen.com
Alvarion Inc 2495 Leghorn St .... Mountain View CA 94043 650-314-2500 967-3966
NASDAQ: ALVR ■ *Web:* www.alvarion.com
AML Communications Inc 1000 Avenida Acaso .... Camarillo CA 93012 805-388-1345 484-2191
Web: www.amlj.com
Amtelco 4800 Curtin Dr .... McFarland WI 53558 608-838-4194 838-8367
TF: 800-356-9148 ■ *Web:* www.amtelco.com
APA Enterprises Inc 2950 NE 84th Ln .... Blaine MN 55449 763-784-4995 784-2038
NASDAQ: APAT ■ *Web:* www.apaenterprises.com
Applied Innovation Inc 5800 Innovation Dr .... Dublin OH 43016 614-798-2000 798-1770
NASDAQ: AINN ■ *TF:* 800-247-9482 ■ *Web:* www.aiinet.com
Argon ST Inc 12701 Fair Lakes Cir Suite 800 .... Fairfax VA 22033 703-322-0881 322-0885
NASDAQ: STST ■ *Web:* www.argonst.com
Aspect Software Inc 1310 Ridder Park Dr .... San Jose CA 95131 408-325-2200 325-2260
TF: 800-391-2341 ■ *Web:* www.aspect.com
Astrocom Corp 2950 Xenium Ln N Suite 140 .... Plymouth MN 55441 763-694-9949 551-0664
TF: 800-669-6242 ■ *Web:* www.astrocorp.com
AT & T Inc 175 E Houston St .... San Antonio TX 78205 210-821-4105 351-2274*
NYSE: T ■ **Fax:* Hum Res ■ *TF:* 888-875-6388 ■ *Web:* www.att.com
Audiovox Corp 150 Marcus Blvd .... Hauppauge NY 11788 631-231-7750 434-3995
NASDAQ: VOXX ■ *TF:* 800-645-4994 ■ *Web:* www.audiovox.com
Axesstel Inc 6815 Flanders Dr Suite 210 .... San Diego CA 92121 858-625-2100 625-2110
AMEX: AFT ■ *Web:* www.axesstel.com
Bo-Sherrel Co Inc 3340 Tree Swallow Pl .... Fremont CA 94555 510-792-0354 797-2038
Broadwing Corp 1122 Capital of Texas Hwy S .... Austin TX 78746 512-742-3700
NASDAQ: BWNG ■ *TF:* 800-847-5705 ■ *Web:* www.broadwing.com
Carrier Access Corp 5395 Pearl Pkwy .... Boulder CO 80301 303-442-5455 443-5908
NASDAQ: CACS ■ *Web:* www.carrieraccess.com
Casabyte Inc 222 Williams Ave S .... Renton WA 98055 425-254-9925 254-9926
TF Cust Svc: 888-352-9527 ■ *Web:* www.casabyte.com
Casio Inc 570 Mt Pleasant Ave .... Dover NJ 07801 973-361-5400 537-8910*
**Fax:* Hum Res ■ *TF Cust Svc:* 800-634-1895 ■ *Web:* www.casio.com
Catapult Communications Corp 160 S Whisman Rd .... Mountain View CA 94041 650-960-1025 960-1029
NASDAQ: CATT ■ *Web:* www.catapult.com
Ceragon Networks Inc 10 Forest Ave .... Paramus NJ 07652 201-845-6955 845-5665
NASDAQ: CRNT ■ *TF Tech Supp:* 877-342-3247 ■ *Web:* www.ceragon.com
Charles Industries Ltd 5600 Apollo Dr .... Rolling Meadows IL 60008 847-806-6300 806-6231
TF: 800-458-4747 ■ *Web:* www.charlesindustries.com
CiDRA Corp 50 Barnes Park N .... Wallingford CT 06492 203-265-0035 294-4211
TF: 877-243-7277 ■ *Web:* www.cidra.com
CIENA Corp 1201 Winterson Rd .... Linthicum MD 21090 410-694-5700 694-5750
NASDAQ: CIEN ■ *TF:* 800-921-1144 ■ *Web:* www.ciena.com
ClearOne Communications Inc 5225 Wiley Post Way .... Salt Lake City UT 84116 801-975-7200 977-0087
TF: 800-945-7730 ■ *Web:* www.clearone.com
CMG Wireless Data Solutions 10375 Richman Ave Suite 1000 .... Houston TX 77042 713-954-7000 785-4918
Web: www.logicacmg.com
COM DEV International Ltd 155 Sheldon Dr .... Cambridge ON N1R7H6 519-622-2300 622-1691
TSX: CDV ■ *Web:* www.comdev.ca
Comarco Inc 25541 Commerce Center Dr .... Lake Forest CA 92630 949-599-7400 599-1415
NASDAQ: CMRO ■ *Web:* www.comarco.com
Comarco Wireless Technologies Inc
25541 Commerce Center Dr .... Lake Forest CA 92630 949-599-7400 599-1415
TF Cust Svc: 800-697-1500 ■ *Web:* www.comarco.com

Phone Fax

Command Communications Inc 7025 S Fulton St Suite 120 .... Centennial CO 80112 303-792-0890 792-0855
TF: 800-288-3491 ■ *Web:* www.command-comm.com
Communication Technologies Inc DBA COMTek
14151 Newbrook Dr Suite 400 .... Chantilly VA 20151 703-961-9080 961-1330
TF: 888-266-8358 ■ *Web:* www.comtechnologies.com
Communications Systems Inc 213 S Main St .... Hector MN 55342 320-848-6231 848-2702
AMEX: JCS ■ *Web:* www.commsystems.com
Communications Test Design Inc 1373 Enterprise Dr .... West Chester PA 19380 610-436-5203 436-6890
TF: 800-223-3910 ■ *Web:* www.ctdi.com
Compunetix Inc 2420 Mosside Blvd .... Monroeville PA 15146 412-373-8110 373-2720
TF: 800-879-4266 ■ *Web:* www.compunetix.com
COMTek 14151 Newbrook Dr Suite 400 .... Chantilly VA 20151 703-961-9080 961-1330
TF: 888-266-8358 ■ *Web:* www.comtechnologies.com
Comverse Network Systems Inc 100 Quannapowitt Pkwy .... Wakefield MA 01880 781-246-9000 224-8135
Web: www.comverse.com
Comverse Technology Inc 100 Quannapowitt Pkwy .... Wakefield MA 01880 781-246-9000 224-8135
NASDAQ: CMVT ■ *Web:* www.cmvt.com
Concerto Software 6 Technology Pk Dr .... Westford MA 01886 978-952-0200 952-0201
TF: 800-999-4458 ■ *Web:* www.concerto.com
Conklin Corp 199 West Rd .... Pleasant Valley NY 12569 845-635-2136 635-2510
TF: 800-266-5546 ■ *Web:* www.conklincorp.com
Convergent Networks Inc 9 Executive Park Dr .... North Billerica MA 01862 978-323-3300 323-3500
Web: www.convergentnet.com
CopperCom Inc 3600 FAU Blvd .... Boca Raton FL 33431 561-322-4000 322-4050
TF: 866-267-7371 ■ *Web:* www.coppercom.com
CopyTele Inc 900 Walt Whitman Rd .... Melville NY 11747 631-549-5900 549-5974
Web: www.copytele.com
Cyber Digital Inc 400 Oser Ave Suite 1650 .... Hauppauge NY 11788 631-231-1200 231-1446
Web: www.cyberdigitalinc.com
Digital Lightwave Inc 5575 Rio Vista Dr .... Clearwater FL 33760 727-442-6677 442-5660
TF: 800-548-9283 ■ *Web:* www.lightwave.com
Digital Voice Corp 1201 S Beltline Rd .... Coppell TX 75019 469-635-6500 635-6580
TF Cust Svc: 800-777-8329 ■ *Web:* www.digitalvoicecorp.com
Ditech Communications Corp 825 E Middlefield Rd .... Mountain View CA 94043 650-623-1300 564-9599
NASDAQ: DITC ■ *TF:* 800-234-0884 ■ *Web:* www.ditechcom.com
DynaMetric Inc 717 S Myrtle Ave .... Monrovia CA 91016 626-358-2559 359-5701
TF: 800-525-6925 ■ *Web:* www.dynametric.com
Dynamic Concepts Inc 1730 17th St NE .... Washington DC 20002 202-944-8787 526-7233
Web: www.dcihq.com
Eagle Telephonics Inc 3880 Veterans Memorial Hwy Suite 203 .... Bohemia NY 11716 631-471-3600 471-6595
Web: www.eagletelephonics.com
ECI Telecom Ltd 1201 W Cypress Creek Rd .... Fort Lauderdale FL 33309 954-772-3070 351-4404
NASDAQ: ECIL ■ *Web:* www.ecitele.com
Electronic Tele-Communications Inc 1915 MacArthur Rd .... Waukesha WI 53188 262-542-5600 542-1524
TF: 888-746-4382 ■ *Web:* www.etcia.com
Emblaze VCON Americas 2 University Plaza Suite 201 .... Hackensack NJ 07601 201-883-1220 883-1229
Web: www.emblazevcon.com
EMS Technologies Inc
660 Engineering Dr Technology Park Atlanta .... Norcross GA 30092 770-263-9200 263-9207
NASDAQ: ELMG ■ *Web:* www.elmg.com
Endwave Corp 130 Baytech Dr .... San Jose CA 95112 408-522-3100 522-3102
NASDAQ: ENWV ■ *Web:* www.endwave.com
eOn Communications Corp 4105 Royal Dr Suite 100 .... Kennesaw GA 30144 770-423-2200 423-2228
NASDAQ: EONC ■ *TF:* 800-955-5321 ■ *Web:* www.eoncc.com
Ericsson Inc 6300 Legacy Dr .... Plano TX 75024 972-583-0000
TF: 800-234-0730 ■ *Web:* www.ericsson.com/US
FiberNet Telecom Group Inc 570 Lexington Ave 3rd Fl .... New York NY 10022 212-405-6200 421-8860
NASDAQ: FTGX ■ *TF:* 800-342-3768 ■ *Web:* www.ftgx.com
Franklin Wireless Corp 9853 Pacific Heights Blvd Suite N .... San Diego CA 92121 858-623-0000 623-0050
Web: www.fklt.com
Fujitsu America Inc 1250 E Arques Ave .... Sunnyvale CA 95085 408-746-6200 746-6260
TF: 800-538-8460 ■ *Web:* www.fujitsu.com
GAI-Tronics Corp PO Box 1060 .... Reading PA 19607 610-777-1374 775-6540
TF: 800-492-1212 ■ *Web:* www.gai-tronics.com
General DataComm Inc 6 Rubber Ave .... Naugatuck CT 06770 203-729-0271 729-2883
Web: www.gdc.com
Genesys Telecommunications Laboratories Inc
2001 Junipero Serra Blvd .... Daly City CA 94014 650-466-1100 466-1260
TF: 888-436-3797 ■ *Web:* www.genesyslab.com
Glenayre Electronics Inc 11360 Lakefield Dr .... Duluth GA 30097 770-283-1000 497-3982
TF Tech Supp: 800-866-4002 ■ *Web:* www.glenayre.com
Glenayre Technologies Inc 11360 Lakefield Dr .... Duluth GA 30097 770-283-1000 497-3982
NASDAQ: GEMS ■ *TF:* 800-866-4002 ■ *Web:* www.glenayre.com
GN US Inc 77 Northeastern Blvd .... Nashua NH 03062 603-598-1100 598-1122
TF: 800-327-2230 ■ *Web:* www.jabra.com
Harmonic Inc 549 Baltic Way .... Sunnyvale CA 94089 408-542-2500 542-2511
NASDAQ: HLIT ■ *TF:* 800-788-1330 ■ *Web:* www.harmonicinc.com
Harris Corp 1025 W NASA Blvd .... Melbourne FL 32919 321-727-9100
NYSE: HRS ■ *TF:* 800-442-7747 ■ *Web:* www.harris.com
Harris Stratex Networks Inc
Research Triangle Park 637 Davis Dr .... Morrisville NC 27560 919-767-3250 767-3231
NASDAQ: HSTX ■ *Web:* www.harrisstratex.com
Hitachi Telecom USA Inc 3617 Parkway Ln .... Norcross GA 30092 770-446-8821 242-1418
Web: www.hitel.com
Hughes Network Systems LLC 11717 Exploration Ln .... Germantown MD 20876 301-428-5500 428-1868
Web: www.hns.com
iDEN Group Motorola Inc 8000 W Sunrise Blvd .... Plantation FL 33322 954-723-5000
Web: idenphones.motorola.com
iDirect Technologies Inc 13865 Sunrise Valley Dr Suite 100 .... Herndon VA 20171 703-648-8080 648-8014
TF: 888-362-5475 ■ *Web:* www.idirect.net
ILEX Systems 246 Industrial Way W .... Eatontown NJ 07724 732-380-9400 380-9401
Web: www.ilex.com
InnoMedia Inc 128 Baytech Dr .... San Jose CA 95134 408-432-5400 432-5404
TF: 888-251-6250 ■ *Web:* www.innomedia.com
Inter-Tel Inc 1615 S 52nd St .... Tempe AZ 85281 480-449-8900 449-8919
NASDAQ: INTL ■ *TF:* 800-669-5858 ■ *Web:* www.inter-tel.com
Intervoice Inc 17811 Waterview Pkwy .... Dallas TX 75252 972-454-8000 454-8707
NASDAQ: INTV ■ *TF:* 800-955-3675 ■ *Web:* www.intervoice.com
InterWorks Systems Inc 70 Corbin St Suite M .... Bayshore NY 11706 631-424-9757 424-9774
TF: 800-814-9757 ■ *Web:* www.interworks.com
ISCO International Inc 1001 Cambridge Dr .... Elk Grove Village IL 60007 847-391-9400 299-9609
AMEX: ISO ■ *TF:* 888-472-3458 ■ *Web:* www.iscointl.com
Iwatsu America Inc 8001 Jetstar Dr Suite 100 .... Irving TX 75063 972-929-0242 929-8919
Web: www.iwatsu.com
Jabra North America 700 E Butterfield Rd Suite 150 .... Lombard IL 60148 630-442-6900 371-2628
Web: www.jabra.com
JDS Uniphase Corp DBA JDSU 430 N McCarthy Blvd .... Milpitas CA 95035 408-546-5000 546-4300
NASDAQ: JDSU ■ *TF:* 800-543-1550 ■ *Web:* www.jdsu.com
JDSU 430 N McCarthy Blvd .... Milpitas CA 95035 408-546-5000 546-4300
NASDAQ: JDSU ■ *TF:* 800-543-1550 ■ *Web:* www.jdsu.com
JTech Communications Inc 6413 Congress Ave Suite 150 .... Boca Raton FL 33487 561-997-0772 997-0773
TF: 800-321-6221 ■ *Web:* www.jtech.com
Kyocera Wireless Corp 10300 Campus Point Dr .... San Diego CA 92121 858-882-2000 882-2010
Web: www.kyocera-wireless.com
L-3 Communications Corp 600 3rd Ave 34-35 Fl .... New York NY 10016 212-697-1111 867-5249
NYSE: LLL ■ *TF:* 866-463-6555 ■ *Web:* www.l-3com.com

Company	City	State	ZIP	Phone	Fax
L-3 Communications ILEX Systems 246 Industrial Way W	Eatontown	NJ	07724	732-380-9400	380-9401
Web: www.ilex.com					
Lantronix Corp 15353 Barranca Pkwy	Irvine	CA	92618	949-453-3990	453-3995
NASDAQ: LTRX ■ *TF Orders:* 800-422-7055 ■ *Web:* www.lantronix.com					
LCC International Inc 7925 Jones Branch Dr	McLean	VA	22102	703-873-2000	873-2100
NASDAQ: LCCI ■ *Web:* www.lcc.com					
Lucent Technologies Inc 600 Mountain Ave	Murray Hill	NJ	07974	908-582-8500	508-2576
NYSE: LU ■ *Web:* www.lucent.com					
Luminent Inc 20550 Nordhoff St	Chatsworth	CA	91311	818-773-9044	576-9486
Web: www.luminentoic.com					
Magnasync Corp 1135 N Mansfield Ave	Hollywood	CA	90038	323-962-0382	962-8601
TF: 800-366-3564 ■ *Web:* www.magnasync.com					
Matsushita Communication Industrial Corp of USA					
776 Hwy 74 S	Peachtree City	GA	30269	770-487-3356	487-3357
Web: www.panasonic.com					
Metro-Tel Corp 11640 Arbor St Suite 100	Omaha	NE	68144	402-498-2964	493-5100
TF: 888-998-8300 ■ *Web:* www.metrotelcorp.com					
Microlog Corp 20270 Goldenrod Ln	Germantown	MD	20876	301-540-5500	540-5557
Web: www.mlog.com					
Micronetics Inc 26 Hampshire Dr	Hudson	NH	03051	603-883-2900	882-8987
NASDAQ: NOIZ ■ *Web:* www.micronetics.com					
Microphase Corp 587 Connecticut Ave	Norwalk	CT	06854	203-866-8000	866-6727
Web: www.microphase.com					
Midcom Inc 121 Airport Dr	Watertown	SD	57201	605-886-4385	886-4486
TF: 800-643-2661 ■ *Web:* www.midcom-inc.com					
MILCOM Systems Corp 532 Viking Dr	Virginia Beach	VA	23452	757-463-2800	463-3052
TF: 800-967-0966 ■ *Web:* www.milcomsystems.com					
Mitel Networks Corp 350 Legget Dr	Kanata	ON	K2K2W7	613-592-2122	592-4784
TF: 800-267-6244 ■ *Web:* www.mitel.com					
Mobile Telesystems Inc 205 Perry Pkwy Suite 14	Gaithersburg	MD	20877	301-963-5970	963-4140
Web: www.mti-usa.com					
Molex Premise Networks 2222 Wellington Ct	Lisle	IL	60532	630-969-4550	969-1352
TF: 800-866-3827 ■ *Web:* www.molexpn.com					
Moseley Assoc Inc 111 Castilian Dr	Santa Barbara	CA	93117	805-968-9621	685-9638
Web: www.moseleysb.com					
Motorola Canada Ltd 8133 Warden Ave	Markham	ON	L6G1B3	905-948-5200	948-5250
TF: 800-268-3395 ■ *Web:* www.motorola.ca/					
Motorola Inc 1301 E Algonquin Rd	Schaumburg	IL	60196	847-576-5000	538-3617*
NYSE: MOT ■ **Fax:* Hum Res ■ *TF:* 800-331-6456 ■ *Web:* www.motorola.com					
Motorola Inc Cellular Subscriber Sector 600 N US Hwy 45	Libertyville	IL	60048	847-523-5000	525-4348
TF: 800-331-6456					
Motorola Inc iDEN Group 8000 W Sunrise Blvd	Plantation	FL	33322	954-723-5000	
Web: idenphones.motorola.com					
Motorola Inc Land Mobile Products Sector					
1301 E Algonquin Rd	Schaumburg	IL	60196	847-576-5000	538-3617
TF: 800-247-2346					
NDS Americas 3500 Highland Ave	Costa Mesa	CA	92626	714-434-2100	434-2105
NASDAQ: NNDS ■ *TF:* 866-398-8749 ■ *Web:* www.nds.com					
NEC America Inc 6555 N State Hwy 161	Irving	TX	75039	214-262-2000	262-2114
TF Cust Svc: 800-338-9549 ■ *Web:* www.necus.com/necam					
NEC USA Inc 101 E 52nd St	New York	NY	10022	212-326-2400	326-2419
TF Hum Res: 800-338-9549 ■ *Web:* www.necus.com					
Network Equipment Technologies Inc 6900 Paseo Padre Pkwy	Fremont	CA	94555	510-713-7300	574-4000
NYSE: NWK ■ *TF:* 888-828-8080 ■ *Web:* www.net.com					
NICE Systems Inc 301 Rt 17 N 10th Fl	Rutherford	NJ	07070	201-964-2600	964-2610
TF: 888-577-6423 ■ *Web:* www.nice.com					
NightHawk Systems Inc 8200 E Pacific Pl Suite 204	Denver	CO	80231	303-337-4811	337-3084
TF Sales: 800-735-7650 ■ *Web:* www.nighthawksystems.com					
NMS Communications 100 Crossing Blvd	Framingham	MA	01702	508-271-1000	271-1300
NASDAQ: NMSS ■ *TF Sales:* 800-533-6120 ■ *Web:* www.nmscommunications.com					
Nokia Inc 6000 Connection Dr	Irving	TX	75039	972-894-5000	894-5050
NYSE: NOK ■ *TF:* 800-547-9810 ■ *Web:* www.nokia.com					
Norsat International Inc 110-4020 Viking Way	Richmond	BC	V6V2N2	604-821-2800	821-2801
TF: 888-830-4223 ■ *Web:* www.norsat.com					
Nortel Networks Corp 8200 Dixie Rd Suite 100	Brampton	ON	L6T5P6	905-863-7000	863-9166
NYSE: NT ■ *TF Cust Svc:* 800-466-7835 ■ *Web:* www.nortel.com					
Nortel Networks Corp 2221 Lakeside Blvd	Richardson	TX	75082	972-684-1000	684-3801
Web: www.nortelnetworks.com					
Notify Technology Corp 1054 S De Anza Blvd Suite 105	San Jose	CA	95129	408-777-7920	996-7405
Web: www.notifycorp.com					
NSGDatacom Inc 3863 Centerview Dr	Chantilly	VA	20151	703-793-2000	793-2001
Web: www.nsgdata.com					
Numerex Corp 1600 Parkwood Cir Suite 500	Atlanta	GA	30339	770-693-5950	693-5951
NASDAQ: NMRX ■ *TF:* 800-665-5686 ■ *Web:* www.nmrx.com					
Occam Networks Inc 77 Robin Hill Rd	Santa Barbara	CA	93117	805-692-2900	692-2999
Web: www.occamnetworks.com					
Oki America Inc 785 N Mary Ave	Sunnyvale	CA	94085	408-720-1900	720-1918
TF: 800-654-3282 ■ *Web:* www.oki.com					
Oki Network Technologies 785 N Mary Ave	Sunnyvale	CA	94085	408-737-6477	737-6441
TF: 800-641-8909 ■ *Web:* www.okint.com					
Oplink Communications Inc 46335 Landing Pkwy	Fremont	CA	94538	408-433-0606	433-0608
NASDAQ: OPLK ■ *Web:* www.oplink.com					
Optelecom Inc 12920 Cloverleaf Ctr Dr	Germantown	MD	20874	301-444-2200	444-2299
NASDAQ: OPTC ■ *TF:* 800-293-4237 ■ *Web:* www.optelecom.com					
Optical Communication Products Inc 6101 Variel Ave	Woodland Hills	CA	91367	818-251-7100	251-7111
NASDAQ: OCPI ■ *Web:* www.ocp-inc.com					
Orion Systems Inc 602 Masons Mill Business Park	Huntingdon Valley	PA	19006	215-659-1207	659-4234
Web: www.orionsystemsinc.net					
OSRAM Sylvania Inc 100 Endicott St	Danvers	MA	01923	978-777-1900	750-2152
Web: www.sylvania.com					
Panasonic Communications & Systems Co 1 Panasonic Way	Secaucus	NJ	07094	201-348-7000	392-6007*
**Fax:* Hum Res ■ *TF Cust Svc:* 800-211-7262 ■ *Web:* www.panasonic.com					
Panasonic Consumer Electronics Co 1 Panasonic Way	Secaucus	NJ	07094	201-348-7000	392-6168
TF: 888-275-2595 ■ *Web:* www.panasonic.com/consumer_electronics/home					
Philips Electronics North America Corp					
1251 Ave of the Americas 20th Fl	New York	NY	10020	212-536-0500	536-0559*
**Fax:* Hum Res ■ *TF:* 800-223-1828 ■ *Web:* www.philips.com					
Plantronics Inc PO Box 635	Santa Cruz	CA	95061	831-426-5858	426-6098
NYSE: PLT ■ *TF:* 800-544-4660 ■ *Web:* www.plantronics.com					
Polycom Inc 4750 Willow Rd	Pleasanton	CA	94588	925-924-6000	924-6101*
NASDAQ: PLCM ■ **Fax:* Hum Res ■ *TF:* 866-476-5926 ■ *Web:* www.polycom.com					
Porta Systems Corp 6851 Jericho Tpke Suite 170	Syosset	NY	11791	516-364-9300	682-4655
TF: 800-937-6782 ■ *Web:* www.portasystems.com					
Protel Inc 4150 Kidron Rd	Lakeland	FL	33811	863-644-5558	646-5855
TF: 800-925-8882 ■ *Web:* www.protelinc.com					
Proxim Wireless Corp 2115 O'Nel Dr	San Jose	CA	95131	408-731-2700	731-3670
TF: 800-229-1630 ■ *Web:* www.proxim.com					
Pulse Communications Inc 2900 Towerview Rd	Herndon	VA	20171	703-471-2900	471-2951*
**Fax:* Cust Svc ■ *TF Cust Svc:* 800-381-1997 ■ *Web:* www.pulse.com					
Qualcomm Inc 5775 Morehouse Dr	San Diego	CA	92121	858-587-1121	658-2100
NASDAQ: QCOM ■ *Web:* www.qualcomm.com					
Quintron Systems Inc 2105 S Blosser Rd	Santa Maria	CA	93458	805-928-4343	928-5775
Web: www.quintron.com					
QuorTech Solutions Ltd 7777 10th St NE Suite 110	Calgary	AB	T2E8X2	403-516-2600	516-2666
Web: www.quortech.com					
RAD Data Communications Ltd 900 Corporate Dr	Mahwah	NJ	07430	201-529-1100	529-1157
TF: 800-444-7234 ■ *Web:* www.rad.com					
Radian Communications Services Corp					
461 Cornwall Rd PO Box 880	Oakville	ON	L6J5C5	905-844-1242	844-8837
TF: 866-472-3126 ■ *Web:* www.radiancorp.com					
Redback Networks Inc 300 Holger Way	San Jose	CA	95134	408-750-5000	750-5599
NASDAQ: RBAK ■ *TF:* 866-727-5400 ■ *Web:* www.redback.com					
Redback Networks Systems Canada Inc					
4190 Still Creek Dr Suite 200	Burnaby	BC	V5C6C6	604-629-7000	294-8830
TF: 877-922-2847 ■ *Web:* www.redback.com					
Redcom Laboratories Inc 1 Redcom Ctr	Victor	NY	14564	585-924-7550	924-6572
Web: www.redcom.com					
RFL Electronics Inc 353 Powerville Rd	Boonton	NJ	07005	973-334-3100	334-3863
Web: www.rflelect.com					
Riverstone Networks Inc 5200 Great America Pkwy	Santa Clara	CA	95054	408-878-6500	878-6501
TF: 888-924-6797 ■ *Web:* www.riverstonenet.com					
Rochelle Communications Inc 8906 Wall St Suite 205	Austin	TX	78754	512-339-8188	339-1299
Web: www.rochelle.com					
SAJE Technology LLC 765 Dixon Ct	Hoffman Estates	IL	60195	847-756-7603	496-4515
Web: www.saje-tech.com					
Samsung Electronics America Inc 105 Challenger Rd	Ridgefield Park	NJ	07660	201-229-4000	229-4029
TF: 800-726-7864 ■ *Web:* www.samsungusa.com					
Samsung Telecommunications America LLP					
1301 E Lookout Dr	Richardson	TX	75082	972-761-7000	761-7001
TF: 800-726-7864 ■ *Web:* www.samsung.com					
Sanyo Fisher Co 21605 Plummer St	Chatsworth	CA	91311	818-998-7322	701-4194
Web: us.sanyo.com					
Shared Technologies Inc 1405 S Beltline Rd	Coppell	TX	75019	972-462-5800	462-5808
TF: 888-835-4444 ■ *Web:* www.stfi.com					
Siemens Canada Ltd 2185 Derry Rd W	Mississauga	ON	L5N7A6	905-819-8000	819-5777
Web: www.siemens.ca					
Siemens Communications Inc 900 Broken Sound Pkwy	Boca Raton	FL	33487	561-923-5000	
Web: www.icn.siemens.com					
SmarTrunk Systems Inc 401 W 35th St Bldg B	National City	CA	91950	619-426-6440	426-3788
TF: 866-870-9052 ■ *Web:* www.smartrunk.com					
Sola Communications Inc 113 N Patch St	Scott	LA	70583	337-235-1515	235-5119
TF: 800-458-8301 ■ *Web:* www.solacomm.com					
Solunet Inc 7703 Technology Dr Suite 100	West Melbourne	FL	32904	321-676-7947	676-0809
TF: 888-765-8638 ■ *Web:* www.solunet.com					
Sonetronics Inc PO Box L	West Belmar	NJ	07719	732-681-5016	681-5216
Web: www.sonetronics.com					
Sonus Networks Inc 7 Technology Dr	Westford	MA	01886	978-614-8100	614-8101
NASDAQ: SONS ■ *Web:* www.sonusnet.com					
SpectraLink Corp 5755 Central Ave	Boulder	CO	80301	303-440-5330	440-5331
NASDAQ: SLNK ■ *TF:* 800-676-5465 ■ *Web:* www.spectralink.com					
SPL Integrated Solutions 9180 Rumsey Rd Suite D-4	Columbia	MD	21045	410-992-0998	992-0758
TF: 800-292-4125 ■ *Web:* www.splis.com					
SR Telecom Inc 8150 Trans-Canada Hwy	Saint-Laurent	QC	H4S1M5	514-335-1210	334-7783
TSX: SRX ■ *Web:* www.srtelecom.com					
Star Dynamics Corp 100 Outwater Ln	Garfield	NJ	07026	973-340-3883	340-1530
Web: www.stardynamic.com					
Startel Corp 17661 Cowan Ave	Irvine	CA	92614	949-863-8700	863-9650
TF: 800-782-7835 ■ *Web:* www.startelcorp.com					
STEP Communications Inc 1066 Saratoga Ave Suite 220	San Jose	CA	95129	408-261-8818	261-0880
Web: www.sybersay.com					
STM Wireless Inc 2 Faraday	Irvine	CA	92618	949-753-7864	753-1122
Web: www.stmi.com					
Sunrise Telecom Inc 302 Enzo Dr	San Jose	CA	95138	408-363-8000	363-8313
NASDAQ: SRTI ■ *Web:* www.sunrisetelecom.com					
Superior Essex Communications LLC 150 Interstate North Pkwy	Atlanta	GA	30339	770-657-6000	303-8807
TF: 800-685-4887 ■ *Web:* www.superioressex.com					
Suttle PO Box 548	Hector	MN	55342	320-848-6711	848-6218
TF: 800-852-8662 ■ *Web:* www.suttleonline.com					
Symetrics Industries Inc 1615 W NASA Blvd	Melbourne	FL	32901	321-254-1500	259-4122
Web: www.symetrics.com					
Symmetricom Inc 2300 Orchard Pkwy	San Jose	CA	95131	408-433-0910	428-7998
NASDAQ: SYMM ■ *TF:* 888-367-7966 ■ *Web:* www.symmetricom.com					
Syntellect Inc 16610 N Black Canyon Hwy Suite 100	Phoenix	AZ	85053	602-789-2800	789-2899
TF: 800-788-9733 ■ *Web:* www.syntellect.com					
T-Systems Inc 701 Warrenville Rd	Lisle	IL	60532	630-493-6100	493-6111
Web: www.t-systems.com					
TAG Solutions 12 Elmwood Rd	Albany	NY	12204	518-292-6500	292-6510
Web: www.tagsolutions.com					
Technical Communications Corp 100 Domino Dr	Concord	MA	01742	978-287-5100	371-1280
Web: www.tccsecure.com					
Tekelec 5200 Paramount Pkwy	Morrisville	NC	27560	919-460-5500	460-0877
NASDAQ: TKLC ■ *TF:* 800-835-3532 ■ *Web:* www.tekelec.com					
Tel Electronics Inc 705 E Main St	American Fork	UT	84003	801-756-9606	756-9135
TF: 800-564-9424 ■ *Web:* www.tel-electronics.com					
Telco Systems Inc 2 Hampshire St Suite 3A	Foxboro	MA	02038	781-255-2120	255-2122
TF: 800-227-0937 ■ *Web:* www.telco.com					
Telecommunications Analysis Group Inc 12 Elmwood Rd	Albany	NY	12204	518-292-6500	292-6510
Web: www.tagsolutions.com					
Telect Inc 1730 N Madson St	Liberty Lake	WA	99019	509-926-6000	926-1553
TF: 800-551-4567 ■ *Web:* www.telect.com					
Telegenix Inc 1930 Olney Ave Bldg 32	Cherry Hill	NJ	08034	856-424-5220	424-0889
TF: 800-424-5220 ■ *Web:* www.telegenix.com					
Telekenex Inc 3221 20th St	San Francisco	CA	94110	415-869-9000	726-1739*
**Fax Area Code:* 866 ■ *TF:* 888-469-5100 ■ *Web:* www.telekenex.com					
Telephonics Corp 815 Broad Hollow Rd	Farmingdale	NY	11735	631-755-7000	755-7046
TF: 877-755-7700 ■ *Web:* www.telephonics.com					
Tellabs Inc 1415 W Diehl Rd	Naperville	IL	60563	630-798-8800	798-2000
NASDAQ: TLAB ■ *TF:* 888-290-8377 ■ *Web:* www.tellabs.com					
Telrad Connegy Inc 400 Crossways Park Dr	Woodbury	NY	11797	516-730-3310	
TF Cust Svc: 800-628-3038 ■ *Web:* www.telradusa.com					
Teltone Corp PO Box 945	Bothell	WA	98041	425-487-1515	487-2288
TF: 800-426-3926 ■ *Web:* www.teltone.com					
Teltronics Inc 2150 Whitfield Industrial Way	Sarasota	FL	34243	941-753-5000	751-7724
TF: 800-486-7685 ■ *Web:* www.teltronics.com					
Telular Corp 311 W Wacker Dr Suite 4300	Chicago	IL	60606	847-247-9400	247-0021
NASDAQ: WRLS ■ *Web:* www.telular.com					
Terabeam Inc 2115 O'Nel Dr	San Jose	CA	95131	408-731-2700	731-3675
NASDAQ: TRBM ■ *TF:* 800-229-1630 ■ *Web:* www.terabeam.com					
Texcom Inc 600 Washington St	Portsmouth	VA	23704	757-397-0035	397-2813
Web: www.texcominc.com					
Thales Antennas PO Box 540	Totowa	NJ	07511	973-812-9000	812-9050
ThinkEngine Networks Inc 100 Nickerson Rd	Marlborough	MA	01752	508-624-7600	624-0289
AMEX: THN ■ *TF:* 888-228-5061 ■ *Web:* www.thinkengine.com					
Tollgrade Communications Inc 493 Nixon Rd	Cheswick	PA	15024	412-820-1400	820-1530
NASDAQ: TLGD ■ *TF Cust Svc:* 800-878-3399 ■ *Web:* www.tollgrade.com					
Tone Commander Systems Inc 11609 49th Pl W	Mukilteo	WA	98275	425-349-1000	349-1010
TF: 800-524-0024 ■ *Web:* www.tonecommander.com					
Toshiba America Inc 1251 Ave of the Americas Suite 4100	New York	NY	10020	212-596-0600	593-3875
TF: 800-457-7777 ■ *Web:* www.toshiba.com					
Toshiba America Information Systems Inc 9740 Irvine Blvd	Irvine	CA	92618	949-583-3000	
TF Cust Svc: 800-457-7777 ■ *Web:* www.tais.com					
Tut Systems Inc 6000 SW Meadows Rd Suite 200	Lake Oswego	OR	97035	971-217-0400	217-0495
NASDAQ: TUTS ■ *TF:* 877-225-7255 ■ *Web:* www.tutsys.com					

				Phone	Fax
Tyco Telecommunications 60 Columbia Rd	Morristown	NJ	07960	973-656-8000	656-8990
Web: www.tycotelecom.com					
Uniden America Corp 4700 Amon Carter Blvd	Fort Worth	TX	76155	817-858-3300	858-3605*
**Fax:* Hum Res ■ *TF Cust Svc:* 800-297-1023 ■ *Web:* www.uniden.com					
UTStarcom Inc 1275 Harbor Bay Pkwy	Alameda	CA	94502	510-864-8800	864-8802
NASDAQ: UTSI ■ *Web:* www.utstar.com					
Vanco USA - Chicago 200 S Wacker Dr Suite 1600	Chicago	IL	60606	312-660-5000	660-5050
TF: 888-482-4669 ■ *Web:* www.vanco-usa.com					
Vela Research LP 5540 Rio Vista Dr	Clearwater	FL	33760	727-507-5300	507-5311
Web: www.vela.com					
Veramark Technologies Inc 3750 Monroe Ave	Pittsford	NY	14534	585-381-6000	383-6800
Web: www.veramark.com					
Verint Systems Inc 330 S Service Rd	Melville	NY	11747	631-962-9600	962-9300
NASDAQ: VRNT ■ *TF:* 800-967-1028 ■ *Web:* www.verintsystems.com					
Viseon Inc 17103 Preston Rd Suite 150-N	Dallas	TX	75248	972-220-1500	
Web: www.viseonvideo.com					
Vodavi Technology Inc 4717 E Hilton Ave Suite 400	Phoenix	AZ	85034	480-443-6000	443-6150
NASDAQ: VTEK ■ *TF:* 800-843-4863 ■ *Web:* www.vodavi.com					
VTech Innovations LP 9590 SW Gemini Dr Suite 120	Beaverton	OR	97008	503-596-1200	644-9887
TF: 800-835-8023 ■ *Web:* www.vtechphones.com					
Vyyo Inc 6625 The Corners Pkwy Suite 100	Norcorss	GA	30092	678-282-8000	447-2405*
NASDAQ: VYYO ■ **Fax Area Code:* 770 ■ *Web:* www.vyyo.com					
Westell Technologies Inc 750 N Commons Dr	Aurora	IL	60504	630-898-2500	375-4931*
NASDAQ: WSTL ■ **Fax:* Sales ■ *TF:* 800-323-6883 ■ *Web:* www.westell.com					
Wireless Telecom Group Inc 25 Eastmans Rd	Parsippany	NJ	07054	973-386-9696	386-9191
AMEX: WTT ■ *Web:* www.noisecom.com					
XETA Technologies Inc 1814 W Tacoma St	Broken Arrow	OK	74012	918-664-8200	664-6876
NASDAQ: XETA ■ *TF Cust Svc:* 800-845-9145 ■ *Web:* www.xeta.com					
Zhone Technologies Inc 7001 Oakport St	Oakland	CA	94621	510-777-7000	777-7001
NASDAQ: ZHNE ■ *TF:* 877-946-6320 ■ *Web:* www.zhone.com					

739 TELECOMMUNICATIONS SERVICES

				Phone	Fax
AboveNet Inc 360 Hamilton Ave 7th Fl	White Plains	NY	10601	914-421-6700	421-6777
TF: 866-859-6971 ■ *Web:* www.above.net					
Acceris Communications Inc 9530 Padgett St Suite 101	San Diego	CA	92126	858-547-5700	547-5621*
**Fax Area Code:* 877 ■ *Web:* www.acceris.com					
Access America 673 Emery Valley Rd	Oak Ridge	TN	37830	865-482-2140	482-2306
TF: 800-860-2140 ■ *Web:* www.accessam.com					
Access Integrated Technologies Inc DBA AccessIT					
55 Madison Ave Suite 300	Morristown	NJ	07960	973-290-0080	290-0081
AMEX: AIX ■ *Web:* www.accessitx.com					
AccessIT 55 Madison Ave Suite 300	Morristown	NJ	07960	973-290-0080	290-0081
AMEX: AIX ■ *Web:* www.accessitx.com					
ACT Teleconferencing Inc 1526 Cole Blvd Bldg 3 Suite 300	Golden	CO	80401	303-235-9000	238-0096
TF: 800-228-2554 ■ *Web:* www.acttel.com					
Alaska Communications Systems Group Inc					
600 Telephone Ave	Anchorage	AK	99503	907-297-3000	297-3100
NASDAQ: ALSK ■ *TF:* 800-478-7121 ■ *Web:* www.acsalaska.com					
Allstream Corp 200 Wellington St W	Toronto	ON	M5V3G2	416-345-2000	345-2840
TF: 877-288-2345 ■ *Web:* www.allstream.com					
Alltel Corp 1 Allied Dr	Little Rock	AR	72202	501-905-8000	905-8487
NYSE: AT ■ *TF:* 800-255-8351 ■ *Web:* www.alltel.com					
Amanda Co 4079 Govenor Dr Suite 320	San Diego	CA	92122	800-410-2745	396-7218
Web: www.taa.com					
AmeriCom Inc 870 E 9400 S	Sandy	UT	84094	801-571-2446	257-6643*
**Fax Area Code:* 775 ■ *TF:* 800-820-6296 ■ *Web:* www.americom.com					
AT & T Inc 175 E Houston St	San Antonio	TX	78205	210-821-4105	351-2274*
NYSE: T ■ **Fax:* Hum Res ■ *TF:* 888-875-6388 ■ *Web:* www.att.com					
ATI 30575 Trabuco Canyon Rd Suite 200	Trabuco Canyon	CA	92679	949-265-2000	265-2001
TF: 877-757-0000 ■ *Web:* www.ati1.com					
ATSI Communications Inc 3201 Cherry Ridge	San Antonio	TX	78230	210-614-7240	614-7264
Web: www.atsi.net					
ATX Communications Inc 2100 Renaissance Blvd	King of Prussia	PA	19406	610-755-4000	755-3290
TF: 800-220-2891 ■ *Web:* www.atx.com					
ATX Group Inc 8550 Freeport Pkwy	Irving	TX	75063	972-753-6200	753-6300
Web: www.atxg.com					
Bell Aliant Regional Communications					
6 S Maritime Centre 1505 Barrington St	Halifax	NS	B3J2W3	902-487-4609	425-0708
TSX: BA.UN ■ *Web:* bell.aliant.ca					
Bell Canada 1000 rue de la Gauchetiere O Bureau 3700	Montreal	QC	H3B4Y7	514-870-8777	786-3962
TF: 888-932-6666 ■ *Web:* www.bell.ca					
BellSouth Corp 1155 Peachtree St NE	Atlanta	GA	30309	404-249-2000	
NYSE: BLS ■ *Web:* bellsouthcorp.com					
BellSouth Long Distance Inc					
400 Perimeter Center Terr Suite 400	Atlanta	GA	30346	770-352-3000	352-3200*
**Fax:* Hum Res ■ *TF:* 877-271-7795 ■ *Web:* www.bellsouth.com					
BestNet Communications Corp					
5075 Cascade Rd SE Suite A	Grand Rapids	MI	49546	616-977-9933	977-9955
Web: www.bestnetcom.com					
Birch Telecom Inc 2300 Main St Suite 2300	Kansas City	MO	64108	816-300-3000	300-3291
TF: 888-422-4724 ■ *Web:* www.birch.com					
Bluegrass Cellular Inc 2902 Ring Rd	Elizabethtown	KY	42701	270-769-0339	766-1161
TF: 800-928-2355 ■ *Web:* www.bluecell.com					
Boston Communications Group Inc 55 Middlesex Tpke	Bedford	MA	01730	781-904-5000	904-5601
NASDAQ: BCGI ■ *Web:* www.bcgi.net					
Broadcast International Inc 7050 Union Pk Ctr Suite 650	Midvale	UT	84047	801-562-2252	562-1773
TF: 800-722-0400 ■ *Web:* www.brin.com					
Broadview Networks Holdings Inc					
800 Westchester Ave Suite N-501	Rye Brook	NY	10573	914-922-7000	922-7001
TF: 800-260-8766 ■ *Web:* www.broadviewnet.com					
BT Americas Inc 350 Madison Ave	New York	NY	10017	646-487-7400	487-3370
Web: www.btglobalservices.com					
CallWave Inc 136 W Canon Perdido St Suite A	Santa Barbara	CA	93101	805-690-4000	690-4200
NASDAQ: CALL ■ *Web:* www.callwave.com					
Cavalier Telephone LLC 2134 W Laburnum Ave	Richmond	VA	23227	804-422-4100	422-4392
TF: 800-683-3944 ■ *Web:* www.cavtel.com					
Cbeyond Communications LLC					
320 Interstate North Pkwy SE Suite 300	Atlanta	GA	30339	678-424-2400	424-2500
NASDAQ: CBEY ■ *TF:* 866-424-2600 ■ *Web:* www.cbeyond.net					
Cellular One Group (Licensing Management Office)					
3650 131St Ave SE Suite 600	Bellevue	WA	98006	425-586-8700	586-8666
TF: 800-545-5982 ■ *Web:* www.cellularone.com					
Centennial Communications Corp 3349 Rt 138 Building A	Wall	NJ	07719	732-556-2200	556-2243
NASDAQ: CYCL ■ *Web:* www.centennialcom.com					
Century Interactive LLC 7502 Greenville Ave Suite 300	Dallas	TX	75231	214-360-6280	360-6283
TF: 800-256-3159 ■ *Web:* www.centuryinteractive.com					
Cincinnati Bell Inc 221 E 4th St	Cincinnati	OH	45202	513-397-9900	241-1264
NYSE: CBB ■ *TF:* 800-422-1199 ■ *Web:* www.cincinnatibell.com					
Cincinnati Bell Telephone Co 201 E 4th St	Cincinnati	OH	45202	513-397-9900	241-9360
Web: www.cincinnatibell.com					
Citizens Communications Co 3 High Ridge Pk	Stamford	CT	06905	203-614-5600	614-4602
NYSE: CZN ■ *TF:* 800-877-4390 ■ *Web:* www.czn.net					
ClearTel Communications Inc 2855 S Congress Ave	Delray Beach	FL	33455	561-454-5000	
TF Cust Svc: 888-389-1400 ■ *Web:* www.cleartel.com					
Coastal Communications 100 Ryon Ave	Hinesville	GA	31313	912-369-9000	368-0625
TF: 877-702-3030 ■ *Web:* www.coastalnow.com					
Comcast Business Communications Inc 650 Centerton Rd	Moorestown	NJ	08057	856-638-4000	638-4051
TF: 888-262-7300 ■ *Web:* www.comcast-ccs.com					
Commonwealth Telephone Co 100 CTE Dr	Dallas	PA	18612	570-675-1121	675-4205
TF: 800-544-1530 ■ *Web:* www.ct-enterprises.com/ct.html					
Commonwealth Telephone Enterprises Inc 100 CTE Dr	Dallas	PA	18612	570-631-2700	631-8005
NASDAQ: CTCO ■ *Web:* www.ct-enterprises.com					
Comporium Communications 332 E Main St	Rock Hill	SC	29730	803-324-9011	326-5708
TF: 866-922-5922 ■ *Web:* www.comporium.com					
Consolidated Communications Inc 121 S 17th St	Mattoon	IL	61938	217-235-3311	234-9600
TF: 800-553-9981 ■ *Web:* www.consolidated.com					
Convergent Media Systems Corp					
190 Bluegrass Valley Pkwy 1 Convergent Ctr	Alpharetta	GA	30005	770-369-9000	369-9100
TF: 800-254-7463 ■ *Web:* www.convergent.com					
Cooperative Communications Inc 412-420 Washington Ave	Belleville	NJ	07109	973-759-8100	531-0150*
**Fax Area Code:* 201 ■ *TF:* 800-833-2700 ■ *Web:* www.cooperativenet.com					
Corporate Telephone 56 Roland St	Boston	MA	02129	617-625-1200	625-1201
TF: 800-274-1211 ■ *Web:* www.corporatetelephone.com					
Covista Communications Inc 4803 Hwy 58 N	Chattanooga	TN	37416	423-648-9700	648-9705
TF: 800-805-1000 ■ *Web:* www.covista.com					
CT Communications Inc 1000 Progress Pl	Concord	NC	28025	704-722-2500	722-2558
NASDAQ: CTCI ■ *TF Cust Svc:* 800-617-8595 ■ *Web:* www.ctc.net					
Cypress Communications Inc 4 Piedmont Ctr Suite 600	Atlanta	GA	30305	404-869-2500	869-2525
TF: 888-205-6912 ■ *Web:* www.cypresscom.net					
D & E Communications Inc 124 E Main St	Ephrata	PA	17522	717-733-4101	721-9865
NASDAQ: DECC ■ *TF Cust Svc:* 800-321-6112 ■ *Web:* www.decommunications.com					
Dakota Central Telecommunications Co-op 630 5th St N	Carrington	ND	58421	701-652-3184	674-8121
TF: 800-771-0974 ■ *Web:* www.daktel.com					
DataWave Systems Inc 13575 Commerce Pkwy Suite 110	Richmond	BC	V6V2L1	604-295-1800	295-1801
Web: www.datawave.ca					
Davel Communications Inc 200 Public Sq Suite 700	Cleveland	OH	44114	216-241-2555	241-2574
TF: 800-333-9920 ■ *Web:* www.davelgroup.com					
Deltacom Inc 7037 Old Madison Pike	Huntsville	AL	35806	256-382-5900	
Web: www.deltacom.com					
deltathree Inc 75 Broad St 31st Fl	New York	NY	10004	212-500-4850	500-4888
NASDAQ: DDDC ■ *TF:* 888-335-8230 ■ *Web:* corp.deltathree.com					
Deutsche Telekom Inc 600 Lexington Ave 17th Fl	New York	NY	10022	212-424-2900	424-2989
NYSE: DT ■ *TF:* 888-382-4872 ■ *Web:* www.telekom.de/english					
Dobson Communications Corp 14201 Wireless Way	Oklahoma City	OK	73134	405-529-8500	529-8515
NASDAQ: DCEL ■ *TF Cust Svc:* 800-522-9404 ■ *Web:* www.dobson.net					
Dynegy Global Communications 1000 Louisiana St Suite 5800	Houston	TX	77002	713-507-6400	767-0872
TF: 800-922-2104 ■ *Web:* www.dynegy.com					
Eagle Broadband Inc 101 Courageous Dr	League City	TX	77573	281-538-6000	334-5302
AMEX: EAG ■ *TF:* 800-628-3910 ■ *Web:* www.eaglebroadband.com					
EATELCORP Inc 913 S Burnside Ave	Gonzales	LA	70737	225-621-4300	621-4352
TF: 800-621-4211 ■ *Web:* www.eatel.com					
eircom (US) Ltd 1 Landmark Sq Suite 1105	Stamford	CT	06901	203-363-7171	363-7176
TF: 888-387-6731 ■ *Web:* www.eircomus.com					
Elantic Networks Inc 2134 W Laburnum Ave	Richmond	VA	23227	804-422-4100	422-4392
TF: 888-854-2138 ■ *Web:* www.elantictelecom.com					
Enventis Telecom Inc 21 W Superior St Suite 200	Duluth	MN	55802	218-740-6111	720-2765
TF: 888-436-8683 ■ *Web:* www.enventistelecom.com					
Eschelon Telecom Inc 730 2nd Ave S Suite 900	Minneapolis	MN	55402	612-376-4400	376-4411
NASDAQ: ESCH ■ *Web:* www.eschelon.com					
Excel Telecommunications 433 Las Colinas Blvd Suite 1300	Irving	TX	75039	972-910-1900	853-8832*
**Fax Area Code:* 800 ■ *TF Tech Supp:* 800-589-5884 ■ *Web:* www.excel.com					
Excell Services 5302 Ave Q	Lubbock	TX	79412	806-747-2474	747-5047
TF: 800-658-6041 ■ *Web:* www.excellsvcs.com					
FairPoint Communications Inc 521 E Morehead St Suite 250	Charlotte	NC	28202	704-344-8150	344-8121
NYSE: FRP ■ *Web:* www.fairpoint.com					
Farmers Telephone Co-op Inc 1101 E Main St	Kingstree	SC	29556	843-382-2333	382-3909
TF: 888-218-5050 ■ *Web:* www.ftc-i.net					
Faxaway 417 2nd Ave W	Seattle	WA	98119	206-301-7000	301-7500
TF: 800-906-4329 ■ *Web:* www.faxaway.com					
FaxBack Inc 7409 SW Tech Ctr Dr Suite 100	Tigard	OR	97223	503-645-1114	597-5399
TF: 800-329-2225 ■ *Web:* www.faxback.com					
FDN Communications 2301 Lucien Way Suite 200	Maitland	FL	32751	407-835-0300	835-1437
TF: 877-433-6435 ■ *Web:* www.fdn.com					
FiberTower Corp 185 Berry St Suite 4800	San Francisco	CA	94107	415-659-3500	659-0007
NASDAQ: FTWR ■ *Web:* www.fibertower.com					
France Telecom North America LLC					
1270 Ave of the Americas Suite 2800	New York	NY	10020	212-332-2100	245-8605
Frontier Corp 180 S Clinton Ave	Rochester	NY	14646	585-777-1000	
TF: 800-836-0342 ■ *Web:* www.frontieronline.com					
Fusion Telecommunications International Inc					
420 Lexington Ave Suite 518	New York	NY	10170	212-201-2400	972-7884
AMEX: FSN ■ *Web:* www.fusiontel.com					
General Communication Inc 2550 Denali St Suite 1000	Anchorage	AK	99503	907-265-5600	868-5676
NASDAQ: GNCMA ■ *TF:* 800-770-7886 ■ *Web:* www.gci.com					
Genesys Conferencing Inc 9139 S Ridgeline Blvd	Highlands Ranch	CO	80129	303-267-1272	267-1287
TF: 800-685-1995 ■ *Web:* www.genesys.com					
Global Crossing Conferencing 1499 W 121 Ave	Westminster	CO	80234	303-633-3000	633-3001
TF: 800-525-8244 ■ *Web:* net.globalcrossing.com/conferencing					
GlobeTel Communications Corp					
9050 Pines Blvd Suite 255	Pembroke Pines	FL	33024	954-241-0590	272-0380
AMEX: GTE ■ *Web:* www.globetel.net					
Golden State Cellular 17400 High School Rd	Jamestown	CA	95327	209-533-8844	533-8400
TF: 800-453-8255 ■ *Web:* www.goldenstatecellular.com					
Golden West Telecommunications Co-op Inc					
415 Crown St PO Box 411	Wall	SD	57790	605-279-2161	279-2727
TF: 866-279-2161 ■ *Web:* www.goldenwest.com					
Graphnet Inc 40 Fultron St 28th Fl	New York	NY	10038	212-994-1100	994-1150
TF: 800-327-1800 ■ *Web:* www.graphnet.com					
Guadalupe Valley Telephone Co-op 36101 FM 3159	New Braunfels	TX	78132	830-885-4411	885-2400
TF: 800-367-4882 ■ *Web:* www.gvtc.com					
Hargray Communications PO Box 5986	Hilton Head Island	SC	29938	843-686-5000	686-1152
TF: 800-726-1266 ■ *Web:* www.hargray.com					
Harrisonville Telephone Co 213 S Main St PO Box 149	Waterloo	IL	62298	618-939-6112	939-4826
TF: 888-482-8353 ■ *Web:* portal.htc.net					
Horry Telephone Co-op Inc 3480 Hwy 701 N	Conway	SC	29526	843-365-2151	365-1999
TF: 800-824-6779 ■ *Web:* www.htcinc.net					
Hungarian Telephone & Cable Corp 1201 3rd Ave Suite 3400	Seattle	WA	98101	206-654-0204	652-2911
AMEX: HTC ■ *Web:* www.htcc.hu					
iBasis Inc 20 2nd Ave	Burlington	MA	01803	781-505-7500	505-7300
Web: www.ibasis.net					
IDT Corp 520 Broad St	Newark	NJ	07102	973-438-1000	438-1453
NYSE: IDT ■ *TF:* 800-225-5438 ■ *Web:* www.idt.net					
ILD Telecommunications Inc 16200 Addison Rd Suite 180	Addison	TX	75001	972-267-0100	267-0105
TF: 800-749-1229 ■ *Web:* www.ildtelecommunications.com					
InfoHighway Communications 39 Broadway 19th Fl	New York	NY	10006	212-566-2100	404-5199
TF: 877-375-4636 ■ *Web:* www.infohighway.com					
Integra Telecom Inc 1201 NE Lloyd Blvd Suite 500	Portland	OR	97232	503-453-8000	453-8221
TF: 800-727-8484 ■ *Web:* www.integratelecom.com					

				Phone	Fax
Intercall Inc 8420 W Bryn Mawr Suite 400 *Web:* www.intercall.com	Chicago	IL	60631	773-399-1600	399-1588
Intrado Inc 1601 Dry Creek Dr *NASDAQ: TRDO* ■ *Web:* www.intrado.com	Longmont	CO	80503	720-494-5800	494-6600
Iowa Telecommunications Services Inc 115 S 2nd Ave W *NYSE: IWA* ■ *TF:* 877-901-4692 ■ *Web:* www.iowatelecom.com	Newton	IA	50208	641-787-2000	787-2001
Iridium Satellite LLC 6701 Democracy Blvd *Web:* www.iridium.com	Bethesda	MD	20817	301-571-6200	571-6250
IVCi LLC 180 Adams Ave *TF:* 800-224-7083 ■ *Web:* www.ivci.com	Hauppauge	NY	11788	631-273-5800	273-7277
j2 Global Communications Inc 6922 Hollywood Blvd 8th Fl *NASDAQ: JCOM* ■ *TF Sales:* 888-718-2000 ■ *Web:* www.j2global.com	Hollywood	CA	90028	323-860-9200	
Japan Telecom America Inc 100 Wall St Suite 1803 *Web:* www.jt-america.com	New York	NY	10020	212-422-4650	422-4653
KDDI America Inc 825 3rd Ave 3rd Fl *Web:* www.kddia.com/eng	New York	NY	10022	212-295-1200	295-1080
Knology Inc 1241 OG Skinner Dr *NASDAQ: KNOL* ■ *Web:* www.knology.com	West Point	GA	31833	706-645-8553	645-1446
LCC International Inc 7925 Jones Branch Dr *NASDAQ: LCCI* ■ *Web:* www.lcc.com	McLean	VA	22102	703-873-2000	873-2100
Leap Wireless International Inc 10307 Pacific Center Ct *NASDAQ: LEAP* ■ *TF:* 877-977-5327 ■ *Web:* www.leapwireless.com	San Diego	CA	92121	858-882-6000	882-6010
Lexcom Inc DBA Lexcom Communications PO Box 808 *TF:* 888-234-1663 ■ *Web:* www.lexcominc.net	Lexington	NC	27293	336-249-9901	243-3026
Lexent Inc 90 White St *Web:* www.lexent.net	New York	NY	10013	212-981-0700	334-0847
Liberty Global Inc 12300 Liberty Blvd *NASDAQ: LBTYA* ■ *Web:* www.lgi.com	Englewood	CO	80112	303-220-6600	220-6601
Lightpath 1111 Stewart Ave *Web:* www.optimumlightpath.com	Bethpage	NY	11714	516-803-2300	
Locus Telecommunications Inc 111 Sylvan Ave *TF:* 888-823-7587 ■ *Web:* www.locus.net	Englewood Cliffs	NJ	07632	201-585-3600	947-6108
Lynch Interactive Corp 401 Theodore Fremd Ave *Web:* www.lynchinteractivecorp.com	Rye	NY	10580	914-921-8821	921-6410
Madison River Communications Corp 103 S 5th St *Web:* www.madisonriver.net	Mebane	NC	27302	919-563-1500	563-4993
Manitoba Telecom Services Inc 333 Main St *TSX: MBT* ■ *TF:* 800-565-1936	Winnipeg	MB	R3C3V6	204-941-8244	772-6391
Matanuska Telephone Assn Inc 1740 S Chugach St *Web:* www.mta-telco.com	Palmer	AK	99645	907-745-3211	761-2481
McLeodUSA Inc 6400 C St SW *TF:* 800-790-7767 ■ *Web:* www.mcleodusa.com	Cedar Rapids	IA	52406	319-364-0000	790-7767
MediaRing.com Inc 262 Santa Ana Ct *Web:* www.mediaring.com	Sunnyvale	CA	94085	408-962-1251	962-1252
MetroPCS Communications Inc 8144 Walnut Hill Ln Suite 800 *TF Cust Svc:* 888-863-8768 ■ *Web:* www.metropcs.com	Dallas	TX	75231	214-265-2550	265-2570
Midcontinent Communications 5111 S Louise Ave **Fax:* Cust Svc ■ *TF:* 800-888-1300 ■ *Web:* www.midcocomm.com	Sioux Falls	SD	57106	605-229-1775	330-4089*
Millington Telephone Co Inc 4880 Navy Rd *Web:* www.millingtononline.com	Millington	TN	38053	901-872-3311	873-0022
Multi-Link Communications Inc 2460 W 26th Ave Suite 380-C *TF:* 888-968-5465 ■ *Web:* www.multilinkcom.com	Denver	CO	80211	303-831-1977	831-1988
Multiband Corp 9449 Science Ctr Dr *NASDAQ: MBND* ■ *TF:* 866-577-6263 ■ *Web:* www.multibandusa.com	New Hope	MN	55428	763-504-3000	504-3060
Net2Phone Inc 520 Broad St *NASDAQ: NTOP* ■ *TF:* 800-225-5438 ■ *Web:* www.net2phone.com	Newark	NJ	07102	973-438-3111	438-1829
NetLojix Communications Inc 81 David Love Pl *Web:* www.netlojix.com	Goleta	CA	93117	805-884-6300	884-6311
Network Communications International Corp 606 E Magrill St *TF:* 888-686-3699 ■ *Web:* www.ncic.com	Longview	TX	75601	903-757-4455	757-4899
Network Services LLC 525 S Douglas St Suite 250 **Fax Area Code:* 800 ■ *TF:* 800-536-0700 ■ *Web:* www.networkservices.net	El Segundo	CA	90245	310-615-6500	536-0900*
Nextel Partners Inc 4500 Carillon Point Rd *NASDAQ: NXTP* ■ *TF:* 888-566-6111 ■ *Web:* www.nextelpartners.com	Kirkland	WA	98033	425-576-3600	576-3650
NII Holdings Inc 10700 Parkridge Blvd Suite 600 *NASDAQ: NIHD* ■ *Web:* www.nii.com	Reston	VA	20191	703-390-5100	390-5149
North State Communications 111 N Main St *Web:* www.northstate.net	High Point	NC	27260	336-886-3600	887-7418
NSTAR Communications Inc 800 Boylston St *TF:* 800-592-2000	Boston	MA	02199	617-424-2000	
NTELOS Holdings Corp 401 Spring Ln Suite 300 PO Box 1990 *NASDAQ: NTLS* ■ *TF:* 877-468-3567 ■ *Web:* www.ntelos.com	Waynesboro	VA	22980	540-946-3500	946-3595
NTT America Inc 101 Park Ave 41st Fl *Web:* www.nttamerica.com	New York	NY	10178	212-661-0810	661-1078
NTT DoCoMo USA Inc 461 5th Ave 24th Fl *NYSE: DCM* ■ *Web:* www.docomo-usa.com	New York	NY	10017	212-994-7222	994-7219
NuVox Communications Inc 16090 Swingley Ridge Rd Suite 500 **Fax:* Sales ■ *TF:* 800-800-9681 ■ *Web:* www.nuvox.com	Chesterfield	MO	63017	636-537-5700	331-7102*
One Communications Corp 100 Chestnut St *Web:* www.onecommunications.com	Rochester	NY	14604	585-246-4231	
Otelco Inc 505 3rd Ave E *AMEX: OTT* ■ *TF:* 800-286-4600 ■ *Web:* www3.otelco.net	Oneonta	AL	35121	205-625-3591	625-3523
Pac-West Telecomm Inc 4210 Coronado Ave *NASDAQ: PACW* ■ **Fax Area Code:* 877 ■ *TF:* 800-399-3389 ■ *Web:* www.pacwest.com	Stockton	CA	95204	209-926-3300	926-4820*
PaeTec Communications Inc 1 PaeTec Plaza 600 Willowbrook Office Pk *TF:* 877-472-3832 ■ *Web:* www.paetec.com	Fairport	NY	14450	585-340-2500	340-2801
Panhandle Telecommunication Systems Inc 2224 NW Hwy 64 *TF:* 800-327-7525 ■ *Web:* www.ptsi.net	Guymon	OK	73942	580-338-7525	338-4200
Pioneer Telephone Co-op 1304 Main St PO Box 631 *TF:* 888-929-1014 ■ *Web:* www.pioneertelephonecoop.com	Philomath	OR	97370	541-929-3135	929-1221
Pioneer Telephone Co-op Inc 108 E Roberts Ave PO Box 539 **Fax:* Mktg ■ *Web:* www.ptci.com	Kingfisher	OK	73750	405-375-4111	699-3053*
Powercom Corp 1807 N Center St *TF Cust Svc:* 800-444-4014 ■ *Web:* www.powercom.net	Beaver Dam	WI	53916	920-887-3148	885-2879
Premiere Global Services Inc 3399 Peachtree Rd NE Suite 700 *NYSE: PGI* ■ *Web:* www.premiereglobal.com	Atlanta	GA	30326	404-262-8400	
Primus Telecommunications 7901 Jones Ranch Dr Suite 900 *NASDAQ: PRTL* ■ *TF:* 800-226-4884 ■ *Web:* www.primustel.com	McLean	VA	22102	703-902-2800	902-2814
Proximity Inc 1526 Cole Blvd Suite 300 *TF:* 800-433-2900 ■ *Web:* www.proximity.com	Golden	CO	80401	303-235-3500	
Puerto Rico Telephone Co PO Box 360998 *Web:* www.telefonicapr.com	San Juan	PR	00936	787-782-8282	792-8877
PVT Networks Inc 4011 Main St *TF:* 866-746-9844 ■ *Web:* www.pvt.com	Artesia	NM	88210	505-746-9844	746-9747
Q Comm International Inc 510 E Technology Ave Bldg C *AMEX: QMM* ■ *TF:* 800-626-9941 ■ *Web:* www.qcomm.com	Orem	UT	84097	801-226-4222	222-9555
Questar InfoComm Inc 180 E 100 South PO Box 45433 *TF:* 800-729-6790 ■ *Web:* www.questarinfo.com	Salt Lake City	UT	84145	801-324-5856	324-5510
Qwest Communications International Inc 1801 California St *NYSE: Q* ■ *TF:* 800-899-7780 ■ *Web:* www.qwest.com	Denver	CO	80202	303-992-1400	992-1724
Rapid Link Inc 17383 Sunset Blvd Suite 350 *TF:* 800-378-9045 ■ *Web:* www.dialthru.com	Pacific Palisades	CA	90272	310-566-1700	573-9435
RCN Corp 196 Van Buren St Suite 300 *NASDAQ: RCNI* ■ *TF Cust Svc:* 800-746-4726 ■ *Web:* www.rcn.com	Herndon	VA	20170	703-434-8200	434-8462
Rogers Communications Inc 333 Bloor St E 10th Fl *NYSE: RCI* ■ *TF:* 888-620-7777 ■ *Web:* www.rogers.com	Toronto	ON	M4W1G9	416-935-7777	935-3599
Rogers Wireless Communications Inc 1 Mount Pleasant Rd *TF:* 800-268-7347 ■ *Web:* www.rogers.com	Toronto	ON	M4Y2Y5	416-935-1100	935-3339
Rural Cellular Corp 3905 Dakota St SW PO Box 2000 *NASDAQ: RCCC* ■ *Web:* www.ruralcellular.com	Alexandria	MN	56308	320-762-2000	808-2102
Satellink Communications Inc PO Box 2099 **Fax Area Code:* 757 ■ *TF:* 800-426-2283 ■ *Web:* www.satellink.net	Grafton	VA	23692	800-426-2283	890-2691*
Securus Technologies Inc 14651 Dallas Pkwy Suite 600 *TF:* 800-559-1539 ■ *Web:* www.securustech.net	Dallas	TX	75254	972-277-0300	277-0301
Shenandoah Telecommunications Co PO Box 459 *NASDAQ: SHEN* ■ *TF:* 800-743-6835 ■ *Web:* www.shentel.com	Edinburg	VA	22824	540-984-4141	984-4816
SkyTel Corp PO Box 2469 **Fax:* Hum Res ■ *TF Cust Svc:* 800-759-8737 ■ *Web:* www.skytel.com	Jackson	MS	39225	601-944-1300	460-8736*
Smart City Networks 3720 Howard Hughes Pkwy Suite 190 *TF:* 888-446-6911 ■ *Web:* www.smartcitynetworks.com	Las Vegas	NV	89109	702-943-6000	943-6001
Solarus 440 E Grand Ave *TF:* 800-421-9282 ■ *Web:* portal.wctc.net	Wisconsin Rapids	WI	54494	715-421-8111	
Southern Communications Services Inc DBA Southern LINC 5555 Glenridge Connector Suite 500 *TF:* 800-406-0151 ■ *Web:* www.southernlinc.com	Atlanta	GA	30342	678-443-1500	443-1596
Southern LINC 5555 Glenridge Connector Suite 500 *TF:* 800-406-0151 ■ *Web:* www.southernlinc.com	Atlanta	GA	30342	678-443-1500	443-1596
Sprint PCS Group 6391 Sprint Pkwy *Web:* www.sprintpcs.com	Overland Park	KS	66251	800-829-0965	
SunCom Wireless Holdings Inc 1100 Cassatt Rd *NYSE: TPC* ■ *TF Cust Svc:* 800-786-7378 ■ *Web:* www.suncom.com	Berwyn	PA	19312	610-651-5900	993-2687
SureWest Communications 211 Lincoln St *NASDAQ: SURW* ■ *TF:* 866-787-3937 ■ *Web:* www.surewest.com	Roseville	CA	95678	916-786-6141	786-7170
T-Mobile USA Inc 12920 SE 38th St *TF:* 800-318-9270 ■ *Web:* www.t-mobile.com	Bellevue	WA	98006	425-383-4000	378-4040
T-Systems Inc 701 Warrenville Rd *Web:* www.t-systems.com	Lisle	IL	60532	630-493-6100	493-6111
TDS Telecommunications Corp 525 Junction Rd *TF:* 800-358-3648 ■ *Web:* www.tdstelecom.com	Madison	WI	53717	608-664-4000	664-4809
Telefonica Data USA 1111 Brickell Ave Suite 1000 *NYSE: TEF* ■ **Fax Area Code:* 786 ■ *Web:* www.us.telefonica.com	Miami	FL	33131	305-925-5473	425-1764*
Teletouch Communications Inc 5718 Airport Freeway *AMEX: TLL* ■ *Web:* www.teletouch.com	Fort Worth	TX	76117	817-654-6225	
Teligent Inc PO Box 105451 *TF:* 888-411-1175 ■ *Web:* www.teligent.com	Atlanta	GA	30348	888-411-1175	841-1957
TELUS Corp 3777 Kingsway Ave *NYSE: TU* ■ **Fax:* Hum Res ■ *TF:* 888-811-2323 ■ *Web:* www.telus.com	Burnaby	BC	V5H3Z7	604-432-2151	436-1352*
Time Warner Telecom Inc 10475 Park Meadow Dr *NASDAQ: TWTC* ■ *TF:* 800-565-8982 ■ *Web:* www.twtelecom.com	Littleton	CO	80124	303-566-1000	516-1011
TippingPoint Technologies Inc 7501-B N Capital of Texas Hwy *TF:* 888-648-9663 ■ *Web:* www.tippingpoint.com	Austin	TX	78731	512-681-8000	681-8099
TNS Inc DBA Transaction Network Services 1939 Roland Clarke Pl *NYSE: TNS* ■ *TF:* 800-240-2824 ■ *Web:* www.tnsi.com	Reston	VA	20191	703-453-8300	453-8599
Trans National Communications International Inc 2 Charlesgate W Suite 500 *TF:* 800-900-5210 ■ *Web:* www.tncii.com	Boston	MA	02215	617-369-1000	369-1111
Transaction Network Services 1939 Roland Clarke Pl *NYSE: TNS* ■ *TF:* 800-240-2824 ■ *Web:* www.tnsi.com	Reston	VA	20191	703-453-8300	453-8599
Trinsic Inc 601 S Harbour Island Blvd Suite 220 *TF:* 800-511-4572 ■ *Web:* www.trinsic.com	Tampa	FL	33602	813-273-6261	273-6861
Twin Lakes Telephone Co-op 201 W Gore Ave *TF Cust Svc:* 800-644-8582 ■ *Web:* www.twlakes.net	Gainesboro	TN	38562	931-268-2151	268-2734
UbiquiTel Inc 1 W Elm St Suite 400 *NASDAQ: UPCS* ■ *Web:* www.ubiquitelpcs.com	Conshohocken	PA	19428	610-832-3300	832-3400
United Systems Access Inc 5 Bragdon Ln Suite 200 *TF:* 877-872-2800 ■ *Web:* www.savewithusa.com	Kennebunk	ME	04043	207-467-8000	467-8008
Universal Service Administrative Co 2000 L St NW Suite 200 *TF:* 888-641-8722 ■ *Web:* www.universalservice.org	Washington	DC	20036	202-776-0200	776-0080
Universal Service Administrative Co Rural Health Care Div 100 S Jefferson Rd *TF:* 800-229-5476 ■ *Web:* www.rhc.universalservice.org	Whippany	NJ	07981	973-581-5010	599-6514
Universal Service Administrative Co Schools & Libraries Div 2000 L St NW Suite 200 **Fax Area Code:* 703 ■ *Web:* www.sl.universalservice.org	Washington	DC	20036	888-203-8100	653-7419*
uReach Technologies Inc 2137 Hwy 35 N *TF:* 888-506-7790 ■ *Web:* www.ureach.com	Holmdel	NJ	07733	732-335-5400	335-8129
US Cellular Corp (USCC) 8410 W Bryn Mawr Ave Suite 700 *AMEX: USM* ■ *Web:* www.uscc.com	Chicago	IL	60631	773-399-8900	399-8936
US LEC Corp 6801 Morrison Blvd 3 Morrocroft Ctr *NASDAQ: CLEC* ■ *TF:* 800-588-7380 ■ *Web:* www.uslec.com	Charlotte	NC	28211	704-319-1000	319-1040
USA Mobility Inc 6677 Richmond Hwy *NASDAQ: USMO* ■ *Web:* www.usamobility.com	Alexandria	VA	22306	703-660-6677	660-6994
USCC (US Cellular Corp) 8410 W Bryn Mawr Ave Suite 700 *AMEX: USM* ■ *Web:* www.uscc.com	Chicago	IL	60631	773-399-8900	399-8936
VarTec Telecom Inc 433 Las Colinas Blvd E Suite 1300 **Fax Area Code:* 214 ■ *TF:* 800-583-8832 ■ *Web:* www.vartec.com	Irving	TX	75039	800-779-2239	424-1144*
VeriSign Inc 487 E Middlefield Rd *NASDAQ: VRSN* ■ *TF Sales:* 866-893-6565 ■ *Web:* www.verisign.com	Mountain View	CA	94043	650-961-7500	961-7300
Verizon Airfone 2809 Butterfield Rd *TF Cust Svc:* 800-247-3663 ■ *Web:* www22.verizon.com/airfone	Oak Brook	IL	60522	630-572-1800	573-9456
Verizon Business 1 Verizon Way *TF Cust Svc:* 866-232-4282 ■ *Web:* www.verizonbusiness.com	Basking Ridge	NJ	07920	800-339-9911	
Verizon Communications Inc 140 West St *NYSE: VZ* ■ *Web:* www.verizon.com	New York	NY	10036	212-395-2121	869-3265
Verizon Network Services Group 140 West St	New York	NY	10007	212-395-2121	
Verizon Wireless 180 Washington Valley Rd **Fax:* Hum Res ■ *TF:* 800-922-0204 ■ *Web:* www.verizonwireless.com	Bedminster	NJ	07921	908-306-7000	306-6839*
Voice Power Telecommunications Inc PO Box 187 *TF:* 800-613-6470 ■ *Web:* www.vptnet.com	Austin	TX	78767	512-419-4600	419-4601
Voicecom 5900 Windward Pkwy Suite 500 **Fax Area Code:* 877 ■ *TF:* 800-384-4357 ■ *Web:* www.voicecom.com	Alpharetta	GA	30005	800-384-4357	761-1173*
Vonage Holdings Corp 23 Main St *NYSE: VG* ■ *Web:* www.vonage.com	Holmdel	NJ	07733	732-528-2600	834-0189
Vycera Communications Inc 12750 High Bluff Dr Suite 200 *TF Cust Svc:* 800-705-3500 ■ *Web:* www.vycera.com	San Diego	CA	92130	858-792-2400	794-0050
Warwick Valley Telephone Co DBA WVT Communications 47 Main St PO Bo 592 *NASDAQ: WWVY* ■ *TF Cust Svc:* 800-952-7642 ■ *Web:* www.wvtc.com	Warwick	NY	10990	845-986-8080	986-3299
Windstream Corp 4001 Rodney Parham Rd *NYSE: WIN* ■ *Web:* www.windstream.com	Little Rock	AR	72212	501-748-7000	
Working Assets Long Distance Service 101 Market St Suite 700 *TF Cust Svc:* 800-788-0898 ■ *Web:* www.workingforchange.com	San Francisco	CA	94105	415-369-2000	371-1048
WQN Inc 14911 Quorum Dr Suite 140 *NASDAQ: WQNI* ■ *TF:* 866-661-6176 ■ *Web:* www.wqn.com	Dallas	TX	75254	972-361-1980	980-8996
WVT Communications 47 Main St PO Bo 592 *NASDAQ: WWVY* ■ *TF Cust Svc:* 800-952-7642 ■ *Web:* www.wvtc.com	Warwick	NY	10990	845-986-8080	986-3299

Phone Fax

XO Communications Inc 11111 Sunset Hills Rd ... Reston VA 20190 703-547-2000 547-2881
TF: 800-900-6398 ■ Web: www.xo.com

Yak Communications Inc 300 Consillium Pl Suite 500 ... Scarborough ON M1H3G2 647-722-2752 722-2763
NASDAQ: YAKC ■ TF: 877-878-1100 ■ Web: www.yak.ca

740 TELEMARKETING & OTHER TELE-SERVICES

Both inbound and outbound telephone marketing as well as other tele-services are included here.

Phone Fax

Access Worldwide Communications Inc
1820 N Fort Myer Dr Suite 400 ... Arlington VA 22209 703-292-5210 465-8642
Web: www.accessww.com

Accretive Commerce 13801 Reese Blvd W ... Huntersville NC 28078 704-370-5000 370-5050
TF: 800-713-5519 ■ Web: www.accretivecommerce.com

Aegis Communications Group Inc 8001 Bent Branch Dr ... Irving TX 75063 972-830-1800 830-1851
TF: 800-830-1800 ■ Web: www.aegiscomgroup.com

AFFINA 2001 Ruppman Plaza ... Peoria IL 61614 309-685-5901 679-4431*
*Fax: Hum Res ■ TF: 800-787-7626 ■ Web: www.affina.com

Alta Resources 120 N Commercial St ... Neenah WI 54958 920-727-9925 727-9954
TF: 877-464-2582 ■ Web: www.altaresources.com

AmeriCall Group Inc 550 E Diehl Rd ... Naperville IL 60563 630-955-9100 955-9955
TF: 800-688-0078 ■ Web: www.americallgroup.com

American Home Base 428 Childers St ... Pensacola FL 32534 850-857-0860 484-8661
TF: 800-422-4663 ■ Web: www.amhomebase.com

AnswerNet Network 345 Witherspoon St ... Princeton NJ 08542 609-921-7450 921-7632
TF: 800-411-5777 ■ Web: www.answernet.com

APAC Customer Services Inc 6 Parkway N ... Deerfield IL 60015 847-374-4980 374-4991
NASDAQ: APAC ■ TF: 800-776-2722 ■ Web: www.apaccustomerservices.com

Calling Solutions By Phone Power Inc
2200 McCullough Ave ... San Antonio TX 78212 210-822-7400 581-6541
TF: 800-321-8582 ■ Web: www.callingsolutions.com

Carlson Marketing Group 1405 Xenium Ln ... Plymouth MN 55441 763-212-4000 212-1896
TF: 888-521-2200 ■ Web: www.carlsonmarketing.com

Connection The 11351 Rupp Dr ... Burnsville MN 55337 952-948-5488 948-5498
TF Sales: 800-883-5777 ■ Web: www.the-connection.com

Consolidated Market Response
700 W Lincoln Ave Suite 200 ... Charleston IL 61920 217-348-7050 348-7060
TF: 800-500-6006 ■ Web: www.cmresponse.com

Convergys Corp 201 E 4th St ... Cincinnati OH 45202 513-723-7000
NYSE: CVG ■ TF: 888-284-9900 ■ Web: www.convergys.com

Data Services Direct LLC 959 US 46 Suite 302 ... Parsippany NJ 07054 973-331-8101 331-8108
Web: www.dataservicesdirect.com

DialAmerica Marketing Inc 960 MacArthur Blvd ... Mahwah NJ 07495 201-327-0200 818-6242
TF Cust Svc: 800-526-4679 ■ Web: www.dialamerica.com

EBSCO TeleServices 4150 Belden Village Ave NW Suite 401 ... Canton OH 44718 330-492-5105 492-5205
TF: 800-456-5105 ■ Web: www.call-ets.com

Faneuil Group 363 Broadway Suite 906 ... Winnipeg MB R3C3N9 204-934-1900
TF: 866-326-3845 ■ Web: www.faneuil.com

Gage 10000 Hwy 55 ... Minneapolis MN 55441 763-595-3800 595-3871
Web: www.gage.com

Global Response Corp 777 S SR-7 ... Margate FL 33068 954-973-7300 969-2407
TF: 800-537-8000 ■ Web: www.globalresponse.com

Greene Henry M & Assoc Inc
300 Tri State International Suite 272 ... Lincolnshire IL 60045 847-948-7400 948-0400
TF: 800-356-1300 ■ Web: www.greeneassoc.com

Harte-Hanks Direct Marketing 55 5th Ave 14th Fl ... New York NY 10003 212-889-5000 696-9151
TF: 800-543-2212 ■ Web: www.harte-hanks.com

Harte-Hanks Response Management 2800 Wells Branch Pkwy ... Austin TX 78728 512-434-1100 244-9222
TF: 800-333-3383 ■ Web: www.harte-hanks.com

Henry M Greene & Assoc Inc
300 Tri State International Suite 272 ... Lincolnshire IL 60045 847-948-7400 948-0400
TF: 800-356-1300 ■ Web: www.greeneassoc.com

Holden MSS 5000 Lima St ... Denver CO 80239 720-374-3700 374-3720
TF: 888-714-3700 ■ Web: www.holdenmss.com

ICT Group Inc 100 Brandywine Blvd ... Newtown PA 18940 215-757-0200 685-5718*
NASDAQ: ICTG ■ *Fax Area Code: 267 ■ TF: 800-799-6880 ■ Web: www.ictgroup.com

InfoCision Management Corp 325 Springside Dr ... Akron OH 44333 330-668-1400 668-1401
TF: 800-210-6269 ■ Web: www.infocision.com

Integretel Inc 5883 Rue Ferrari ... San Jose CA 95138 408-362-4000 362-2795
TF: 888-302-2750 ■ Web: www.integretel.com

InterMedi@ Marketing Solutions 204 Carter Dr ... West Chester PA 19382 610-696-4646 429-5137
TF: 800-835-3466 ■ Web: www.intermediamarketing.com

iSky Inc 6100 Frost Pl ... Laurel MD 20707 240-456-4300 456-4335
TF: 800-351-5055 ■ Web: www.isky.com

King TeleServices 140 58th St Suite 6-I ... Brooklyn NY 11220 718-361-4100 439-4265

Lester Inc 19 Business Park Dr ... Branford CT 06405 203-488-5265 483-0408
TF: 800-999-5265 ■ Web: www.lesterusa.com

Lexicon Marketing Corp 640 S San Vicente Blvd ... Los Angeles CA 90048 323-782-7400 782-7410
TF: 800-722-8888 ■ Web: www.lexiconmarketing.com

LiveBridge Inc 7303 SE Lake Rd ... Portland OR 97267 503-652-6000 653-3994
TF: 800-783-6000 ■ Web: www.livebridge.com

Meyer Assoc Inc DBA Meyer Teleservices 14 7th Ave N ... Saint Cloud MN 56303 320-259-4000 259-4044
TF: 800-676-9233 ■ Web: www.callmeyer.com

Midco Call Center Services 4901 E 26th St ... Sioux Falls SD 57110 605-330-4125 910-5655*
*Fax Area Code: 800 ■ TF: 800-843-8800 ■ Web: www.midcocall.com

Millennium Teleservices LLC 425 Raritan Center Pkwy ... Edison NJ 08837 877-877-7698 417-4435*
*Fax Area Code: 888 ■ Web: www.mmtel.com

NOVO 1 Inc 4301 Cambridge Rd ... Fort Worth TX 76155 817-355-8200 355-8505
TF: 800-325-2580 ■ Web: www.novo1.com

OKS-Ameridial Inc 4535 Strausser St NW ... North Canton OH 44720 330-497-4888 497-5500
TF: 800-445-7128 ■ Web: www.oksameridial.com

One Call Systems Inc 115 Evergreen Heights Dr ... Pittsburgh PA 15229 412-415-5000 415-5023
Web: www.1-call.com

Philadelphia Direct 2577A Interplex Dr ... Trevose PA 19053 215-244-8835 244-9447
TF: 800-222-2765

PRC LLC 8151 Peters Rd Suite 3000 ... Plantation FL 33324 954-693-3700 693-3767
TF: 800-866-4443 ■ Web: www.prcnet.com

ProCom Inc 28838 US Hwy 69 PO Box 27 ... Lamoni IA 50140 641-784-8841 784-4100
TF: 800-433-9893 ■ Web: www.procom-inc.com

Prosodie Interactive 855 SW 78th Ave Suite 100 ... Plantation FL 33324 954-343-5588 776-7634*
*Fax Area Code: 866 ■ TF: 877-453-5700 ■ Web: www.prosodieinteractive.com

Protocol Marketing Group 600 W Chicago Ave Suite 600 ... Chicago IL 60610 312-245-3140 245-3141
Web: www.protocolusa.com

Reese Teleservices Inc 925 Penn Ave ... Pittsburgh PA 15222 412-355-0800 765-0356
TF: 800-365-3500 ■ Web: www.reeseteleservices.com

Results Telemarketing Inc 499 Sheridan St 4th Fl ... Dania Beach FL 33004 954-921-2400 923-8070
TF: 800-284-5318 ■ Web: www.resultstel.com

SITEL Corp 7277 World Communication Dr ... Omaha NE 68122 402-963-6810 963-3097
NYSE: SWW ■ TF: 800-445-6600 ■ Web: www.sitel.com

TCIM Services Inc 1013 Centre Rd Suite 400 ... Wilmington DE 19805 302-633-3000 633-3039
TF: 800-333-2255 ■ Web: www.tcim.com

Tele Business USA 1945 Techny Rd Suite 3 ... Northbrook IL 60062 847-480-1560 509-8459
TF: 800-228-8353 ■ Web: www.tbiz.com

Tele-Serve 409 Main St ... Eau Claire WI 54701 715-834-3442 834-5991
TF Cust Svc: 800-428-8159 ■ Web: www.tele-serve.net

Telemarketing Co DBA TTC Marketing Solutions
3945 N Neenah Ave ... Chicago IL 60634 773-545-0407 545-4034
TF: 800-777-6340 ■ Web: www.thetelemktgco.com

TeleNational Marketing 2918 N 72nd St ... Omaha NE 68134 402-548-1100 391-2044
TF Cust Svc: 800-333-6106 ■ Web: www.telenational.com

Teleperformance USA 1991 S 4650 West ... Salt Lake City UT 84104 801-257-5800 257-6246
Web: www.teleperformance.com/USA

Telerx 723 Dresher Rd ... Horsham PA 19044 215-347-5700 347-5800
TF: 800-283-5379 ■ Web: valueofx.telerx.com

TeleServices Direct 5305 Lakeview Pkwy S Dr ... Indianapolis IN 46268 317-216-2240 216-2248
TF: 888-646-6626 ■ Web: www.teleservicesdirect.com

TeleSystems Marketing Inc 3600 S Gessner St Suite 250 ... Houston TX 77063 713-784-3439 780-5931
TF: 800-622-0190 ■ Web: www.telesystemsmarketing.com

TeleTech Holdings Inc 9197 S Peoria St ... Englewood CO 80112 303-397-8100 397-8695
NASDAQ: TTEC ■ TF: 800-835-3832 ■ Web: www.teletech.com

TRG Customer Solutions 1700 Pennsylvania Ave NW ... Washington DC 20006 202-289-9898
TF: 888-767-1051 ■ Web: www.trgcustomersolutions.com

USA 800 Inc 9808 E 66th Terr PO Box 16795 ... Raytown MO 64133 816-358-1303 358-8845
TF: 800-821-7539 ■ Web: www.usa-800.com

West Corp 9910 Maple St ... Omaha NE 68134 402-571-7700 573-1030*
NASDAQ: WSTC ■ *Fax: Hum Res ■ TF: 800-542-1000 ■ Web: www.west.com

Working Solutions 1820 Preston Park Blvd Suite 2000 ... Plano TX 75093 972-964-4800 964-4802
Web: www.workingsol.com

Young America Corp 717 Faxon Rd ... Young America MN 55397 952-467-3366 294-8496
TF: 800-533-4529 ■ Web: www.young-america.com

TELEVISION - CABLE

SEE Cable & Other Pay Television Services p. 1404; Television Networks - Cable p. 2344

741 TELEVISION COMPANIES

Phone Fax

Acme Communications Inc 2101 E 4th St Suite 202 ... Santa Ana CA 92705 714-245-9499 245-9494
NASDAQ: ACME ■ Web: www.acmecommunications.com

Allbritton Communications Co 1000 Wilson Blvd Suite 2700 ... Arlington VA 22209 703-647-8700 647-8707

Barrington Broadcasting 2500 W Higgins Rd Suite 155 ... Hoffman Estates IL 60169 847-884-1178 755-3045
Web: www.barringtontv.com

Bell Globemedia Inc 9 Channel Nine Ct ... Toronto ON M1S4B5 416-332-5700 291-5537
Web: www.bellglobemedia.ca

Belo Corp Television Group 400 S Record St ... Dallas TX 75202 214-977-6606 977-6603
TF: 800-431-0010 ■ Web: www.belo.com/companies/tvgroup.x2

BlueStone Television 8415 E 21st St N Suite 120 ... Wichita KS 67206 316-315-0076 315-0345
Web: www.bluestonetv.com

Caballero Television 3310 Keller Springs Rd Suite 105 ... Carrollton TX 75006 972-788-0533 980-4842
TF: 888-299-9910

California Oregon Broadcasting Inc 125 S Fir St ... Medford OR 97501 541-779-5555 779-1151

CanWest Global Communications Corp
201 Portage Ave 31st Fl CanWest Global Pl ... Winnipeg MB R3B3L7 204-956-2025 947-9841
NYSE: CWG ■ Web: www.canwestglobal.com

Capitol Broadcasting Co Inc 2619 Western Blvd ... Raleigh NC 27606 919-890-6000 890-6095
Web: www.cbc-raleigh.com

Chambers Communications Corp 2975 Chad Dr ... Eugene OR 97408 541-485-5611 342-1568
Web: www.cmc.net/~chambers

Charleston Television Inc 210 W Coleman Blvd ... Mount Pleasant SC 29464 843-884-4141 881-3410

Christian Television Network Inc 6922 142nd Ave N ... Largo FL 33771 727-535-5622 531-2497
Web: www.ctnonline.com

Cisneros Group of Cos 36 E 61st St ... New York NY 10065 212-355-0620 838-1836
Web: www.cisneros.com

Citadel Communications Co 44 Pondfield Rd Suite 12 ... Bronxville NY 10708 914-793-3400 793-3693

Clear Channel Television 200 E Basse Rd ... San Antonio TX 78209 210-822-2828 822-2299
TF: 888-937-6131 ■ Web: www.clearchannel.com/television

Communications Corp of America
700 Saint John St Suite 300 ... Lafayette LA 70501 337-237-1142 237-1373
TF: 800-237-1142

Community Communications Inc 11510 E Colonial Dr ... Orlando FL 32817 407-273-2300 273-3613

Community Educational Television 10902 Wilcrest Dr ... Houston TX 77099 281-561-5828 561-9793
Web: www.communityedtv.org

Cox Broadcasting Inc Cox Television Div
6205 Peachtree Dunwoody Rd ... Atlanta GA 30328 404-843-5000 847-6469
Web: www.coxenterprises.com

CTV Globe Media 1331 Yonge St ... Toronto ON M4T1Y1 416-925-6666 926-4026
Web: www.chumlimited.com

CTV Television Inc 9 Channel Nine Ct ... Toronto ON M1S4B5 416-332-5000 291-5337
Web: www.ctv.ca

Diversified Business Communications 121 Free St ... Portland ME 04101 207-842-5400 842-5505
TF: 800-842-5404 ■ Web: www.divbusiness.com

Drewry Communications PO Box 708 ... Lawton OK 73502 580-355-7000 357-3811

Duhamel Broadcasting Enterprises Inc 518 St Joseph St ... Rapid City SD 57701 605-342-2000 342-7305

Eagle Communications Inc 340 W Main St ... Missoula MT 59802 406-721-2063 721-2083
Web: www.nbcmontana.com

Education Broadcasting 450 W 33rd St ... New York NY 10001 212-560-1313 560-1314

Emmis Communications Corp
40 Monument Cir 1 Emmis Plaza Suite 700 ... Indianapolis IN 46204 317-266-0100 631-3750
NASDAQ: EMMS ■ Web: www.emmis.com

Entravision Communications Corp
2425 Olympic Blvd Suite 6000 W ... Santa Monica CA 90404 310-447-3870 447-3899
NYSE: EVC ■ Web: www.entravision.com

Equity Broadcasting Corp 1 Shackleford Dr Suite 400 ... Little Rock AR 72211 501-219-2400 228-8000
Web: www.ebcorp.net

Evening Post Publishing Co 134 Columbus St ... Charleston SC 29403 843-577-7111 937-5579

EW Scripps Co 312 Walnut St Suite 2800 ... Cincinnati OH 45202 513-977-3000 977-3720*
NYSE: SSP ■ *Fax: Hum Res ■ TF: 800-888-3000 ■ Web: www.scripps.com

Fisher Communications Inc 100 4th Ave N Suite 510 ... Seattle WA 98109 206-404-7000 404-6037
NASDAQ: FSCI ■ TF: 800-443-0073 ■ Web: www.fsci.com

Flinn Broadcasting 6080 Mt Moriah Rd Ext ... Memphis TN 38115 901-375-9324 795-4454
Web: www.flinn.com

Forum Communications Co 101 5th St N ... Fargo ND 58102 701-235-7311 241-5406
TF: 800-747-7311 ■ Web: www.forumcomm.com

Fox Television Stations Inc 1999 S Bundy Dr ... Los Angeles CA 90025 310-584-2000 584-2024
Web: www.myfoxla.com

Freedom Communications Inc 17666 Fitch ... Irvine CA 92614 949-553-9292 474-7675
Web: www.freedom.com

Gannett Broadcasting Co 7950 Jones Branch Dr ... McLean VA 22107 703-854-6000
Web: www.gannett.com

Phone Fax

Gannett Co Inc 7950 Jones Branch Dr McLean VA 22107 703-854-6000
NYSE: GCI ■ *Web:* www.gannett.com
Granite Broadcasting Corp 767 3rd Ave 34th Fl New York NY 10017 212-826-2530 826-2858
Web: www.granitetv.com
Grant Communications Inc
915 Middle River Dr Suite 409 Fort Lauderdale FL 33304 954-568-2000 568-2015
Gray Television Inc 4370 Peachtree Rd NE Atlanta GA 30319 404-504-9828 261-9607
NYSE: GTN ■ *Web:* www.graycommunications.com
Griffin Television Inc 7401 N Kelley Ave Oklahoma City OK 73111 405-843-6641 841-9989*
**Fax:* News Rm
Groupe TVA Inc 1600 de Maisonneuve Blvd E Montreal QC H2L4P2 514-526-9251 598-6085
Web: tva.canoe.com
Hearst-Argyle Television Inc 300 W 57th St 39th Fl New York NY 10019 212-887-6800 887-6835
NYSE: HTV ■ *Web:* www.hearstargyle.com
Hearst Corp 1345 6th Ave New York NY 10105 212-649-2000 280-1045*
**Fax Area Code:* 646 ■ **Fax:* Hum Res ■ *Web:* www.hearstcorp.com
Hoak Media Corp 500 Crescent Ct Suite 220 Dallas TX 75201 972-960-4848 960-4899
Web: www.hoak.net
Hubbard Broadcasting Inc 3415 University Ave Saint Paul MN 55114 651-646-5555 642-4314*
**Fax:* Hum Res
ION Media Networks Inc 601 Clearwater Park Rd West Palm Beach FL 33401 561-659-4122 659-4252
AMEX: ION ■ *TF:* 800-646-7296 ■ *Web:* www.ionmedia.tv
Jim Pattison Media Group 1067 W Cordova St Suite 1800 Vancouver BC V6C1C7 604-688-6764 694-6900
Web: www.jimpattison.com/medi/me__index.htm
Journal Broadcast Group Inc 720 E Capitol Dr Milwaukee WI 53212 414-332-9611 967-5400
Web: www.journalbroadcastgroup.com
LeSea Broadcasting 61300 S Ironwood Rd South Bend IN 46614 574-291-8200 291-9043
TF: 800-365-3732 ■ *Web:* www.lesea.com
Liberty Corp 135 Main St PO Box 502 Greenville SC 29602 864-241-5400 241-5401*
**Fax:* Hum Res ■ *Web:* www.libertycorp.com
LIN TV Corp 1 Richmond Sq Suite 230-E Providence RI 02906 401-454-2880 454-0089
NYSE: TVL ■ *TF:* 800-772-4546 ■ *Web:* www.lintv.com
Lincoln Financial Media 100 N Greene St PO Box 21008 Greensboro NC 27420 336-691-3000 691-3938*
**Fax Area Code:* 704 ■ *Web:* www.lincolnfinancialmedia.com
Max Media LLC 2200 Stephens Ave Missoula MT 59801 406-542-8900 728-4800
TF: 800-926-9952 ■ *Web:* www.maxmontana.com
McGraw-Hill Cos Inc Broadcasting Group 4600 Air Way San Diego CA 92102 619-237-6211 262-2275
Web: www.mcgraw-hill.com
McKinnon Broadcasting Co PO Box 719051 San Diego CA 92171 858-571-5151 571-4852
Media General Broadcast Group 111 N 4th St Richmond VA 23219 804-649-6000 775-4601
Web: www.mgbg.com
Meredith Corp 1716 Locust St Des Moines IA 50309 515-284-3000 284-3806
NYSE: MDP ■ *Web:* www.meredith.com
Mission Broadcasting Inc 62 S Franklin St Wilkes-Barre PA 18701 570-961-2222 823-4523
Morgan Murphy Broadcasting Group 7025 Raymond Rd Madison WI 53719 608-271-4321 271-6111
Morris Multimedia Inc 27 Abercorn St Savannah GA 31401 912-233-1281 232-4639
Web: www.morrismultimedia.com
New York Times Co Broadcast Group 803 Channel Three Dr Memphis TN 38103 901-543-2333 543-2198
Web: www.nytco.com/company.html
Newfoundland Broadcasting Co Ltd 446 Logy Bay Rd Saint Johns NL A1C5S2 709-722-5015 726-5107
Web: www.ntv.ca
News Corp Ltd 1211 Ave of the Americas 7th Fl New York NY 10036 212-852-7000 852-7145*
NYSE: NWS ■ **Fax:* Investor Rel ■ *Web:* www.newscorp.com
Nexstar Broadcasting Group Inc 509 S Neil St Champaign IL 61824 217-356-8333 373-3608
NASDAQ: NXST ■ *Web:* www.nexstar.tv
Northwest Television Inc PO Box 1313 Eugene OR 97440 541-342-4965 342-5436
Pappas Telecasting Cos 500 S Chinowth Rd Visalia CA 93277 559-733-7800 733-7878
Web: www.pappastv.com
Pegasus Communications Corp 225 E City Line Ave Bala Cynwyd PA 19004 610-934-7000 934-7121
TF: 888-438-7488 ■ *Web:* www.pgtv.com
Piedmont Television 7621 Little Ave Suite 506 Charlotte NC 28226 704-341-0944 341-0945
Web: www.piedmonttv.com
Post-Newsweek Stations Inc 550 W Lafayette Blvd Detroit MI 48226 313-223-2260 223-2263
Web: www.washpostco.com/bcast.htm
Prime Time Christian Broadcasting Inc PO Box 61000 Midland TX 79711 432-563-0420 563-1736
TF: 800-707-0420 ■ *Web:* www.godslearningchannel.com
Quincy Newspapers Inc 130 S 5th St Quincy IL 62301 217-223-5100 223-9757
TF: 800-373-9444 ■ *Web:* www.whig.com
Ramar Communications Inc 9800 University Ave Lubbock TX 79423 806-745-3434 748-1949
Raycom Media Inc 201 Monroe St RSA Tower 20th Fl Montgomery AL 36104 334-206-1400 206-1555
Web: www.raycommedia.com
Red River Broadcasting Corp PO Box 9115 Fargo ND 58106 701-277-1515 277-1830
Reiten Television Inc 3425 S Broadway Minot ND 58702 701-852-2104 838-1050
Roberts Broadcasting Co
1408 N Kingshighway Blvd Suite 300 Saint Louis MO 63113 314-367-4600 367-0174
Web: www.robertstower.com
Rockfleet Broadcasting Inc 7669 S 45 Rd Cadillac MI 49601 231-775-9813 775-1898
Saga Communications Inc 73 Kercheval Ave Grosse Pointe Farms MI 48236 313-886-7070 886-7150
NYSE: SGA ■ *TF:* 888-886-7070 ■ *Web:* www.sagacommunications.com
Sarkes Tarzian Inc PO Box 62 Bloomington IN 47402 812-332-7251 331-4575
Schurz Communications Inc 225 W Colfax Ave South Bend IN 46626 574-287-1001 287-2257
Web: www.schurz.com
Sinclair Broadcast Group Inc 10706 Beaver Dam Rd Hunt Valley MD 21030 410-568-1500 568-1533
NASDAQ: SBGI ■ *Web:* www.sbgi.net
Smith Broadcasting Group Inc 2315 Red Rose Way Santa Barbara CA 93109 805-965-0400
Web: www.smithtelevision.com
Sunbeam Television Corp 1401 79th Street Cswy Miami FL 33141 305-751-6692 795-2746
TF: 800-845-7777
Sunbelt Broadcasting Co 1500 Foremaster Ln Las Vegas NV 89101 702-642-3333 657-3423
Tampa Television Inc 200 S Parker St Tampa FL 33606 813-228-8888 221-5794
TBN (Trinity Broadcasting Network) PO Box A Santa Ana CA 92711 714-832-2950 665-2156
TF: 888-731-1000 ■ *Web:* www.tbn.org
TCT Ministries Inc 111 Airway Dr PO Box 1010 Marion IL 62959 618-997-9333 997-1859
Web: www.tct.tv
Telemundo Communications Group Inc 2290 W 8th Ave Hialeah FL 33010 305-884-8200
TF: 800-688-8851 ■ *Web:* www.telemundo.com
Tribune Broadcasting Co 435 N Michigan Ave Suite 1800 Chicago IL 60611 312-222-9100 329-0611
Web: www.tribune.com
Tribune Co 435 N Michigan Ave Chicago IL 60611 312-222-9100 329-0611
NYSE: TRB ■ *Web:* www.tribune.com
Trinity Broadcasting Network (TBN) PO Box A Santa Ana CA 92711 714-832-2950 665-2156
TF: 888-731-1000 ■ *Web:* www.tbn.org
Univision Television Group Inc 5999 Center Dr Los Angeles CA 90045 310-216-3434 348-5674
Web: www.univision.com
Viacom Television Stations Group 4200 Bradford Ave Studio City CA 91604 818-655-2000 655-2221
Web: www.viacom.com
Weigel Broadcasting 26 N Halstead St Chicago IL 60661 312-705-2600 705-2656
White Knight Broadcasting Inc 700 Saint John St Suite 301 Lafayette LA 70501 337-237-9965 235-5872
Wicks Group of Cos LLC 405 Park Ave Suite 702 New York NY 10022 212-838-2100 223-2109
Web: www.wicksgroup.com
Withers Broadcasting Co PO Box 1508 Mount Vernon IL 62864 618-242-3500 242-2490
TF: 800-333-1577
WYOMedia Inc 1856 Skyview Dr Casper WY 82601 307-577-5923 577-5928
Young Broadcasting Inc 599 Lexington Ave 47th Fl New York NY 10022 212-688-5100 758-1229
NASDAQ: YBTVA ■ *Web:* www.youngbroadcasting.com
ZGS Communications 2000 N 14th St Suite 400 Arlington VA 22201 703-528-5656 526-0879
Web: www.zgsgroup.com

742 TELEVISION NETWORKS - BROADCAST

Phone Fax

ABC Inc 77 W 66th St New York NY 10023 212-456-7777 456-2795
Web: abc.go.com
CBS Broadcasting Inc 51 W 52nd St New York NY 10019 212-975-4321 975-7934*
**Fax:* Mktg ■ *Web:* www.cbs.com
CBS Corp 51 W 52nd St New York NY 10019 212-975-4321 975-4516
NYSE: CBS ■ *Web:* www.cbscorporation.com
CSTV Networks Inc 2035 Corte Del Nogal Suite 250 Carlsbad CA 92011 760-431-8221 431-8108
Web: www.cstv.com
Fox Broadcasting Co 10201 W Pico Blvd Los Angeles CA 90035 310-369-1000
Web: www.fox.com
NBC Television Network 30 Rockefeller Plaza New York NY 10112 212-664-4444 664-4085
Web: www.nbc.com
Public Broadcasting Service (PBS) 2100 Crystal Dr Arlington VA 22202 703-739-5000 739-0775
Web: www.pbs.org
Telemundo Communications Group Inc 2290 W 8th Ave Hialeah FL 33010 305-884-8200
TF: 800-688-8851 ■ *Web:* www.telemundo.com
United Paramount Network (UPN) 11800 Wilshire Blvd Los Angeles CA 90025 310-575-7000 575-7280*
**Fax:* PR ■ *Web:* www.upn.com
Univision Communications Inc
1999 Ave of the Stars Suite 3050 Los Angeles CA 90067 310-556-7600 556-7615
NYSE: UVN ■ *Web:* www.univision.com
WB Television Network 4000 Warner Blvd Bldg 34-R Burbank CA 91522 818-977-5000 977-2282*
**Fax:* PR ■ *Web:* thewb.warnerbros.com

743 TELEVISION NETWORKS - CABLE

Phone Fax

@MAX 1100 Ave of the Americas New York NY 10036 212-512-1000
Web: www.cinemax.com
5StarMAX 1100 Ave of the Americas New York NY 10036 212-512-1000
Web: www.cinemax.com
A & E Television Networks 235 E 45th St New York NY 10017 212-210-1400 210-9755
Web: www.aetv.com
ABC Family Channel 500 S Buena Vista St Burbank CA 91521 818-560-1000
Web: abcfamily.go.com
ABS-CBN Global Ltd DBA Filipino Channel
150 Shoreline Dr Redwood City CA 94065 650-508-6000 508-6003
TF: 800-345-2465 ■ *Web:* www.abs-cbn.com/international
Accent Health 5440 Beaumont Ctr Blvd Suite 400 Tampa FL 33634 813-349-7100 349-7200
TF: 800-791-8756 ■ *Web:* www.accenthealth.com
ACCESS - The Education Station 10212 Jaspaer Ave Edmonton AB T5J5A3 780-440-7777 440-8899
Web: www.accesstv.ca
Access Media Group 10212 Jasper Ave Edmonton AB T5J5A3 780-440-7777 440-8899
Web: www.accesslearning.com
ActionMAX 1100 Ave of the Americas New York NY 10036 212-512-1000 512-5570
Web: www.cinemax.com
American Movie Classics (AMC) 200 Jericho Quadrangle Jericho NY 11753 516-803-4300
Web: www.amctv.com
AmericanLife TV Network 650 Massachusetts Ave NW Washington DC 20001 202-289-6633 289-6632
TF: 800-446-6388 ■ *Web:* www.americanlifetv.com
Animal Planet 8516 Georgia Ave Silver Spring MD 20910 240-662-2000
Web: animal.discovery.com
Animal Planet Canada 9 Channel Nine Ct Scarborough ON M1S4B5 416-332-5000 332-4275
Web: animalplanet.ca
Arts & Entertainment Network (A & E) 235 E 45th St 9th Fl New York NY 10017 212-210-1400 210-9755
Web: www.aetv.com
Artv 1400 Rene-Levesque Blvd E Bureau A-53-1 Montreal QC H2L2M2 514-597-3788 597-3633
Web: www.artv.ca
Asian Television Network 130 Pony Dr Newmarket ON L3Y7B6 905-836-6460 853-5212
Web: www.asiantelevision.com
Astral Television Networks 181 Bay St Suite 100 Toronto ON M5J2T3 416-956-2010 956-2018
Web: www.astralmedia.com
Auto Channel 332 W Broadway Suite 1604 Louisville KY 40202 502-992-0200 992-0201
Web: www.theautochannel.com
AZN Television 4100 E Dry Creek Rd Suite A300 Littleton CO 80122 303-712-5400 712-5401
Web: azntv.com
BBC America 747 3rd Ave 6th Fl New York NY 10017 212-705-9300 888-0576
Web: www.bbcamerica.com
BBC Canada 121 Bloor St E Suite 200 Toronto ON M4W3M5416-967-0022 967-0044
Web: www.bbccanada.com
BET Inc 1235 W Pl NE Washington DC 20018 202-608-2000 608-2599
TF: 800-626-9911 ■ *Web:* www.bet.com
Biography Channel 235 E 45th St 11th Fl New York NY 10017 212-210-1400 210-9755
Web: www.biography.com
Black Entertainment Television Networks 1235 W Pl NE Washington DC 20018 202-608-2000 608-2599
TF: 800-626-9911 ■ *Web:* www.bet.com
Black Family Channel 800 Forrest St NW Atlanta GA 30318 404-350-2509 350-0356
Web: www.blackfamilychannel.com
Black Starz! 8900 Liberty Cir Englewood CO 80112 720-852-7700 852-7710
Web: www.starz.com
Bloomberg Television 1731 Lexington Ave New York NY 10022 212-318-2000 617-5999
TF: 800-955-4003 ■ *Web:* www.bloomberg.com/tv
Boating Channel PO Box 1148 Sag Harbor NY 11963 631-725-4440
Web: www.boatingchannel.com
Book Television 10212 Jasper Ave Edmonton AB T5J5A3 780-440-7777 440-8899
Web: www.booktelevision.com
Bpm:tv 115 Gordon Baker Rd 8th Fl Toronto ON M2H3R6 416-756-2404 756-5526
Web: www.bpmtv.com
Bravo 30 Rockefeller Plaza 14th Fl New York NY 10112 212-664-4444
Web: www.bravotv.com
Bravo! Canada 299 Queen St W Toronto ON M5V2Z5 416-591-5757 591-6619
Web: www.bravo.ca
C-SPAN3 400 N Capitol St NW Suite 650 Washington DC 20001 202-737-3220 737-6626
Web: www.c-span.org
C-SPAN (Cable Satellite Public Affairs Network)
400 N Capitol St NW Suite 650 Washington DC 20001 202-737-3220 737-3323
Web: www.c-span.org
C-SPAN Extra 400 N Capitol St NW Suite 650 Washington DC 20001 202-737-3220 737-3323
Web: www.c-span.org
Cable News Network (CNN) 1 CNN Center Atlanta GA 30303 404-827-1500 827-1784
Web: www.cnn.com
Cable Public Affairs Channel (CPAC) 45 O'Connor St Suite 1750 Ottawa ON K1P1A4 613-567-2722 567-2741
TF: 877-287-2722 ■ *Web:* www.cpac.ca
Cable Radio Networks Inc (CRN) 10487 Sunland Blvd Sunland CA 91040 818-352-7152 352-3229
TF: 800-336-2225 ■ *Web:* www.crni.net
Cable Satellite Public Affairs Network (C-SPAN)
400 N Capitol St NW Suite 650 Washington DC 20001 202-737-3220 737-3323
Web: www.c-span.org

	City	State	ZIP	Phone	Fax
Canadian Learning Television (CLT) 10212 Jasper Ave *Web:* www.clt.ca	Edmonton	AB	T5J5A3	780-440-7777	440-8899
Canadian Learning Television (CLT) 299 Queen St W *Web:* www.clt.ca	Toronto	ON	M5V2Z5	780-440-7777	440-8899
Canal D 2100 Rue Sainte-Catherine O Bureau 700 *TF:* 800-361-5194 ■ *Web:* www.canald.com	Montreal	QC	H3H2T3	514-939-3150	939-3151
Canal Indigo 2100 Rue Sainte-Catherine O Bureau 1000 *Web:* www.canalindigo.com	Montreal	QC	H3H2T3	514-939-5090	939-5098
Canal Savoir 4750 Ave Henri Julien Bureau 100 *TF:* 888-640-2626 ■ *Web:* www.canal.qc.ca	Montreal	QC	H2T3E4	514-841-2626	841-0822
Canal Vie 2100 Rue Sainte-Catherine O Bureau 700 *TF:* 800-361-5194 ■ *Web:* www.canalvie.com	Montreal	QC	H3H2T3	514-939-3150	939-3151
Cartoon Network 1050 Techwood Dr *Web:* www.cartoonnetwork.com	Atlanta	GA	30318	404-885-2263	
Christian Broadcasting Network (CBN) 977 Centerville Tpke CBN Ctr. *TF:* 800-759-0700 ■ *Web:* www.cbn.com	Virginia Beach	VA	23463	757-226-7000	226-2017
Christian Television Network Inc 6922 142nd Ave N *Web:* www.ctnonline.com	Largo	FL	33771	727-535-5622	531-2497
Cinemax 1100 Ave of the Americas *Web:* www.cinemax.com	New York	NY	10036	212-512-1000	
Classic Arts Showcase PO Box 828 *Web:* www.classicartsshowcase.org	Burbank	CA	91503	323-878-0283	878-0329
CLT (Canadian Learning Television) 10212 Jasper Ave *Web:* www.clt.ca	Edmonton	AB	T5J5A3	780-440-7777	440-8899
CLT (Canadian Learning Television) 299 Queen St W *Web:* www.clt.ca	Toronto	ON	M5V2Z5	780-440-7777	440-8899
CMT (Country Music Television) 330 Commerce St *Web:* www.cmt.com	Nashville	TN	37201	615-335-8400	335-8628
CNBC Inc 900 Sylvan Ave *TF:* 800-788-2622 ■ *Web:* www.cnbc.com	Englewood Cliffs	NJ	07632	201-735-2622	
CNBC World 900 Sylvan Ave	Englewood Cliffs	NJ	07632	201-735-2622	346-6527
CNN Headline News 1 CNN Center *Web:* www.cnn.com/HLN	Atlanta	GA	30303	404-827-1500	878-0891
CNN International 1 CNN Center *Web:* www.cnn.com/CNNI	Atlanta	GA	30303	404-827-1500	
College Sports Television 85 10th Ave 3rd Fl *Web:* www.cstv.com	New York	NY	10011	212-342-8700	342-8899
Comedy Central 1775 Broadway 10th Fl. **Fax:* PR ■ *Web:* www.comedycentral.com	New York	NY	10019	212-767-8600	767-8592*
Comedy Network PO Box 9 Stn O *Web:* www.thecomedynetwork.ca	Toronto	ON	M4A2M9	416-332-5300	332-5301
Cool TV 1 Lombard Pl Suite 2100 *Web:* www.canada.com	Winnipeg	MB	R3B8Y1	204-926-4800	926-4853
Corus Entertainment Inc 181 Bay St Suite 1630 *NYSE: CJR* ■ *TF:* 877-772-3770 ■ *Web:* www.corusent.com	Toronto	ON	M5J2T3	416-642-3770	642-3779
Country Music Television (CMT) 330 Commerce St *Web:* www.cmt.com	Nashville	TN	37201	615-335-8400	335-8628
Country Music Television Canada 64 Jefferson Ave Unit 18 *Web:* www.cmtcanada.com	Toronto	ON	M6K3H4	416-534-1191	
Court TV Canada 10212 Jasper Ave *Web:* www.courttvcanada.ca	Edmonton	AB	T5J5A3	780-440-7777	440-8899
CPAC (Cable Public Affairs Channel) 45 O'Connor St Suite 1750 *TF:* 877-287-2722 ■ *Web:* www.cpac.ca	Ottawa	ON	K1P1A4	613-567-2722	567-2741
CRN (Cable Radio Networks Inc) 10487 Sunland Blvd. *TF:* 800-336-2225 ■ *Web:* www.crni.net	Sunland	CA	91040	818-352-7152	352-3229
Cross TV 370 W Camino Gardens Blvd 3rd Fl *Web:* www.crosstv.com	Boca Raton	FL	33432	561-367-7454	750-7959
Crown Media Holdings Inc 6430 S Fiddlers Green Cir Suite 225 *NASDAQ: CRWN* ■ *TF:* 800-820-7990 ■ *Web:* www.hallmarkchannel.com	Greenwood Village	CO	80111	303-220-7990	220-7660
CTV Television Inc 9 Channel Nine Ct *Web:* www.ctv.ca	Toronto	ON	M1S4B5	416-332-5000	291-5337
CTV Travel 9 Channel Nine Ct *Web:* www.ctvtravel.ca	Toronto	ON	M1S4B5	416-332-5000	332-4571
Daystar Television Network PO Box 612066 *TF:* 800-329-0029 ■ *Web:* www.daystar.com	Dallas	TX	75261	817-571-1229	571-7458
Deep Dish TV 339 Lafayette St 3rd Fl *Web:* www.deepdishtv.org	New York	NY	10012	212-473-8933	420-8332
DejaView 1 Lombard Pl Suite 2100 *Web:* www.canada.com	Winnipeg	MB	R3B8Y1	204-926-4800	926-4853
Discovery Channel 8516 Georgia Ave *Web:* dsc.discovery.com	Silver Spring	MD	20910	240-662-2000	
Discovery Channel Canada 9 Channel Nine Ct *Web:* discoverychannel.ca	Scarborough	ON	M1S4B5	416-332-5000	332-4230
Discovery Civilization Canada 9 Channel Nine Ct *Web:* discoverycivilization.ca	Scarborough	ON	M1S4B5	416-332-5000	
Discovery Communications Inc 1 Discovery Pl **Fax Area Code:* 301 ■ *TF:* 800-762-2189 ■ *Web:* www.discovery.com	Silver Spring	MD	20910	859-342-8439	986-4826*
Discovery Health Canada 121 Bloor St E Suite 200 *Web:* www.discoveryhealth.ca	Toronto	ON	M4W3M5	416-967-0022	967-0044
Discovery Health Channel 8516 Georgia Ave *Web:* health.discovery.com	Silver Spring	MD	20910	240-662-2000	
Discovery Home Channel 8516 Georgia Ave. *Web:* home.discovery.com	Silver Spring	MD	20910	240-662-2000	
Discovery Kids Channel 8516 Georgia Ave. *Web:* kids.discovery.com	Silver Spring	MD	20910	240-662-2000	
Discovery Latin America 6505 Blue Lagoon Dr Suite 300	Miami	FL	33126	786-273-4700	
Discovery Times Channel 1 Discovery Pl *Web:* times.discovery.com	Silver Spring	MD	20910	240-662-2000	
Discovery Wings Channel 8516 Georgia Ave *Web:* www.disneychannel.com	Silver Spring	MD	20910	240-662-2000	
Disney Channel 3800 W Alameda Ave *Web:* www.disneychannel.com	Burbank	CA	91505	818-569-7500	569-3193
Do-It-Yourself Network 9721 Sherrill Blvd *Web:* www.diynet.com	Knoxville	TN	37932	865-694-2700	531-8933
Documentary Channel 64 Jefferson Ave Unit 18 *Web:* www.documentarychannel.com	Toronto	ON	M6K3H4	416-534-1191	
Drive-In Classics 299 Queen St W *Web:* www.driveinclassics.ca	Toronto	ON	M5V2Z5	416-591-5757	591-6619
E! Entertainment Television 5750 Wilshire Blvd *Web:* www.eonline.com	Los Angeles	CA	90036	323-954-2400	954-2660
Employment & Career Channel 253 W 51st St 3rd Fl *Web:* www.employ.com	New York	NY	10019	212-445-0754	445-0760
Encore 8900 Liberty Cir. *Web:* www.encoretv.com	Englewood	CO	80112	720-852-7700	852-7710
ESPN 545 Middle St *Web:* espn.go.com	Bristol	CT	06010	860-585-2000	766-2213
ESPN Classic Canada 9 Channel Nine Ct *Web:* www.tsn.ca	Scarborough	ON	M1S4B5	416-332-5000	
ESPN Classic Sports 545 Middle St *Web:* espn.go.com/classic	Bristol	CT	06010	860-585-2000	766-7273
ESPN Deportes 77 W 66th St **Fax Area Code:* 212 ■ *TF:* 800-337-6783 ■ *Web:* espndeportes.espn.go.com	New York	NY	10023	800-337-6783	456-0236*
ESPNEWS 545 Middle St **Fax:* Hum Res ■ *Web:* sports.espn.go.com/espn/espnews	Bristol	CT	06010	860-585-2000	585-2425*
Eternal Word Television Network (EWTN) 5817 Old Leeds Rd *Web:* www.ewtn.com	Irondale	AL	35210	205-271-2900	271-2939
Family Channel 181 Bay St Suite 100 PO Box 787 *Web:* www.familychannel.ca	Toronto	ON	M5J2T3	416-956-2030	956-2035
FamilyNet 6350 West Fwy *TF:* 800-292-2287 ■ *Web:* www.familynet.com	Fort Worth	TX	76116	817-737-4011	737-8209
Fashion Television Channel 299 Queen St W *Web:* www.ftchannel.com	Toronto	ON	M5V2Z5	416-591-5757	
Fine Living Network 9721 Sherrill Blvd **Fax Area Code:* 310 ■ *Web:* www.fineliving.com	Knoxville	TN	37932	865-694-2700	931-0708*
FitTV 1 Discovery Pl *Web:* fittv.discovery.com	Silver Spring	MD	20910	240-662-2000	662-1845
Food Network 75 9th Ave *Web:* www.foodnetwork.com	New York	NY	10011	212-398-8836	736-7716
Food Network Canada 121 Bloor St E Suite 200 *Web:* www.foodtv.ca	Toronto	ON	M4W3M5	416-967-0022	967-0022
Fox Movie Channel PO Box 900 *Web:* www.thefoxmoviechannel.com	Beverly Hills	CA	90213	310-369-1000	369-0468
FOX News Channel 1211 Ave of the Americas **Fax:* News Rm ■ *Web:* www.foxnews.com	New York	NY	10036	212-301-3000	301-8274*
Fox Sports en Espanol PO Box 900 *Web:* espanol.sports.yahoo.com	Beverly Hills	CA	90213	310-369-1000	
FOX Sports Net 10201 W Pico Blvd *Web:* msn.foxsports.com	Los Angeles	CA	90035	310-369-1000	
Fox Sports World Canada 1 Lombard Pl Suite 2100 *Web:* www.canada.com	Winnipeg	MB	R3B8Y1	204-926-4800	926-4853
Free Speech TV PO Box 6060 *Web:* www.freespeech.org	Boulder	CO	80306	303-442-8445	442-6472
FreMantle Media Ltd 4000 W Alameda Ave 3rd Fl *Web:* www.fremantlemedia.com	Burbank	CA	91505	818-748-1110	563-6410
Fuel TV Inc 1440 Sepulveda Blvd Suite 1900 *Web:* www.fuel.tv	Los Angeles	CA	90025	310-369-1000	444-8559
Fuse 11 Penn Plaza 17th Fl *Web:* www.fuse.tv	New York	NY	10001	212-324-3400	324-3445
FX Networks LLC 10201 W Pico Blvd Bldg 103 Rm 4144 *Web:* www.fxnetworks.com	Los Angeles	CA	90035	310-369-1000	969-4688
G4 Media Inc 12100 W Olympic Blvd Suite 200 *Web:* www.g4tv.com	West Los Angeles	CA	90064	310-979-5000	979-5100
Galavision 605 3rd Ave 12th Fl *TF:* 877-412-8852 ■ *Web:* www.univision.net	New York	NY	10158	212-455-5200	867-6710
Gemstar-TV Guide International Inc 6922 Hollywood Blvd *NASDAQ: GMST* ■ *Web:* www.gemstartvguide.com	Hollywood	CA	90028	323-817-4600	817-4629
Global Television Network 81 Barber Greene Rd *TF:* 800-387-8001	Toronto	ON	M3C2A2	416-446-5311	446-5449
Golf Channel 7580 Commerce Center Dr *Web:* www.thegolfchannel.com	Orlando	FL	32819	407-363-4653	363-7976
GolTV Inc 1666 JFK Cswy Suite 402 *Web:* www.goltv.tv	North Bay Village	FL	33141	305-864-9799	864-7299
Great American Country 49 Music Sq W Suite 301 **Fax Area Code:* 615 ■ *TF:* 800-727-5663 ■ *Web:* www.gactv.com	Nashville	TN	37203	865-694-2700	329-8770*
GSN 2150 Colorado Ave Suite 100 *Web:* www.gsn.com	Santa Monica	CA	90404	310-255-6800	255-6810
Hallmark Channel 12700 Ventura Blvd Suite 200 *TF:* 888-390-7474 ■ *Web:* www.hallmarkchannel.com	Studio City	CA	91604	818-755-2400	755-2564
HBO (Home Box Office Inc) 1100 Ave of the Americas *Web:* www.hbo.com	New York	NY	10036	212-512-1000	
HBO Comedy 1100 Ave of the Americas *Web:* www.hbo.com/comedyplex	New York	NY	10036	212-512-1000	512-5570
HBO Family 1100 Ave of the Americas *Web:* www.hbofamily.com	New York	NY	10036	212-512-1000	
HBO Latino 1100 Ave of the Americas *Web:* www.hbolatino.com	New York	NY	10036	212-512-1000	512-5570
HGTV (Home & Garden Television) 9721 Sherrill Blvd *Web:* www.hgtv.com	Knoxville	TN	37932	865-694-2700	531-8933
Hispanic Information & Telecommunications Network Inc 63 Flushing Ave Unit 281 *Web:* www.hitn.org	Brooklyn	NY	11205	212-966-5660	966-5725
Historia 2100 Rue Sainte-Catherine O Bureau 700 *TF:* 800-361-5194 ■ *Web:* www.historiatv.com	Montreal	QC	H3H2T3	514-939-3150	939-3151
History Channel 235 E 45th St 8th Fl **Fax:* PR ■ *Web:* www.historychannel.com	New York	NY	10017	212-210-1400	210-9755*
History International 235 E 45th St 12th Fl *Web:* www.historyinternational.com	New York	NY	10017	212-210-1400	907-9476
History Television 121 Bloor St E Suite 1500 *Web:* www.historytelevision.ca	Toronto	ON	M4W3M5	416-967-1174	960-0971
Home Box Office Inc (HBO) 1100 Ave of the Americas *Web:* www.hbo.com	New York	NY	10036	212-512-1000	
Home & Garden Television (HGTV) 9721 Sherrill Blvd *Web:* www.hgtv.com	Knoxville	TN	37932	865-694-2700	531-8933
Home & Garden Television Canada 121 Bloor St E Suite 200 *Web:* www.hgtv.ca	Toronto	ON	M4W3M5	416-967-0022	967-0044
HSN LP 1 HSN Dr. **Fax:* Cust Svc ■ *TF:* 800-284-3900 ■ *Web:* www.hsn.com	Saint Petersburg	FL	33729	727-872-1000	872-4133*
i Channel 115 Gordon Baker Rd 8th Fl *Web:* www.ichannel.ca	Toronto	ON	M2H3R6	416-756-2404	756-5526
i network 601 Clearwater Park Rd **Fax:* PR ■ *TF:* 800-646-7296 ■ *Web:* www.ionline.tv	West Palm Beach	FL	33401	561-659-4122	655-7343*
Idea Channel 2002 Filmore Ave Suite 1 *TF:* 800-388-0662 ■ *Web:* www.ideachannel.com	Erie	PA	16506	814-833-7107	833-7415
ImaginAsian TV 19 W 44th St 9th Fl *Web:* www.iatv.tv	New York	NY	10036	212-869-4288	869-4285
iN DEMAND 345 Hudson St 17th Fl *Web:* www.indemand.com	New York	NY	10014	646-638-8200	486-0855
Independent Film Channel 200 Jericho Quadrangle *Web:* www.ifctv.com	Jericho	NY	11753	516-803-3000	803-4506
Independent Film Channel Canada 1649 Brunswick St Suite 103 *Web:* www.ifctv.ca	Halifax	NS	B3J2G3	902-423-2662	423-7862
Inspirational Network The (INSP) 7910 Crescent Executive Dr Suite 500 *TF:* 800-725-4677 ■ *Web:* www.insp.com	Charlotte	NC	28217	704-525-9800	561-7971
Le Canal Nouvelles TVA 1600 de Maisonneuve E *Web:* www.lcn.canoe.com	Montreal	QC	H2L4P2	514-598-2869	598-6073
Learning Channel The (TLC) 8516 Georgia Ave *TF:* 888-404-5969 ■ *Web:* tlc.discovery.com	Silver Spring	MD	20910	240-662-2000	
Les Chaines Tele Astral 2100 Rue Sainte-Catherine O Bureau 700 *Web:* www.astralmedia.com	Montreal	QC	H3H2T3	514-939-3150	939-3151
Liberty Channel PO Box 10352 *Web:* www.libertychannel.com	Lynchburg	VA	24506	434-582-2742	582-2741
Life Network 121 Bloor St E Suite 1500 *Web:* www.lifenetwork.ca	Toronto	ON	M4W3M5	416-967-1174	960-0971
Lifetime Entertainment Services 309 W 49th St *Web:* www.lifetimetv.com	New York	NY	10019	212-424-7000	957-4110
Lifetime Real Women 309 W 49th St *Web:* www.lifetimetv.com/lrw	New York	NY	10019	212-424-7000	957-4110
Lonestar 1 Lombard Pl Suite 2100 *Web:* www.canada.com/globaltv	Winnipeg	MB	R3B8Y1	204-926-4800	926-4853
Lottery Channel Inc 600 Vine St Suite 400 *Web:* www.gamesinc.net	Cincinnati	OH	45202	513-381-0777	721-6035

Name / Address	City	State	Zip	Phone	Fax
Mentv 1 Lombard Pl Suite 2100	Winnipeg	MB	R3B8Y1	204-926-4800	926-4853
Web: www.canada.com					
Mescape 181 Bay St Suite 100	Toronto	ON	M5J2T3	416-956-2010	956-5415
MeteoMedia 1755 Boul Rene-Levesque E Bureau 251	Montreal	QC	H2K4P6	514-597-1700	597-2981
TF: 800-461-8368 ■ *Web:* www.meteomedia.com					
MExcess 181 Bay St Suite 100	Toronto	ON	M5J2T3	416-956-2010	956-5415
Web: www.themovienetwork.ca/MExcess					
MFest 181 Bay St Suite 100	Toronto	ON	M5J2T3	416-956-2010	956-5415
Web: www.themovienetwork.ca/MFest					
MFun! 181 Bay St Suite 100	Toronto	ON	M5J2T3	416-956-2010	956-5415
Web: www.themovienetwork.ca/MFun					
MMore 181 Bay St Suite 100	Toronto	ON	M5J2T3	416-956-2010	956-5415
Web: www.themovienetwork.ca/MMore					
MoreMAX 1100 Ave of the Americas	New York	NY	10036	212-512-1000	512-5570
Web: www.cinemax.com					
Movie Central 42 Pardee Ave	Toronto	ON	M6K3H5	416-534-1191	437-3188*
**Fax Area Code:* 780 ■ *Web:* www.moviecentral.ca					
Movie Network 181 Bay St Suite 100	Toronto	ON	M5J2T3	416-956-2010	956-5415
Web: www.themovienetwork.ca					
MOVIEplex 8900 Liberty Cir	Englewood	CO	80112	720-852-7700	852-7710
Web: www.starz.com					
Mpix 181 Bay St Suite 100	Toronto	ON	M5J2T3	416-956-2010	956-5415
Web: mpix.ca					
MSG Network 4 Penn Plaza	New York	NY	10001	212-465-6000	465-6024
Web: www.msgnetwork.com					
MSNBC 1 MSNBC Plaza	Secaucus	NJ	07094	201-583-5000	583-5590
TF: 800-813-8255 ■ *Web:* www.msnbc.msn.com					
MTV (MTV Networks) 1515 Broadway	New York	NY	10036	212-258-8000	258-8100
Web: www.mtv.com					
MTV Networks (MTV) 1515 Broadway	New York	NY	10036	212-258-8000	258-8100
Web: www.mtv.com					
MTV Networks On Campus Inc (mtvU) 1633 Broadway 31st Fl	New York	NY	10019	212-654-3600	
Web: www.mtvu.com					
MTV Networks Latin America 1111 Lincoln Rd 6th Fl	Miami Beach	FL	33139	305-535-3700	672-5204
Web: www.mtvla.com					
MTV2 1515 Broadway 10th Fl	New York	NY	10036	212-258-8000	
Web: www.mtv2.com					
MuchLoud 299 Queen St W	Toronto	ON	M5V2Z5	416-591-5757	591-6824
Web: www.muchloud.com					
MuchMoreMusic 299 Queen St W	Toronto	ON	M5V2Z5	416-591-5757	
Web: www.muchmoremusic.com					
MuchMoreRetro 299 Queen St W	Toronto	ON	M5V2Z5	416-591-5757	
Web: www.muchmoreretro.com					
MuchMusic 299 Queen St W	Toronto	ON	M5V2Z5	416-591-5757	
Web: www.muchmusic.com					
MuchVibe 299 Queen St W	Toronto	ON	M5V2Z5	416-591-5757	
Web: www.muchvibe.ca					
Mun2 TV 2470 W 8th Ave	Hialeah	FL	33010	305-882-8700	889-7205
Web: www.mun2tv.com					
Musimax 355 Rue Sainte-Catherine O	Montreal	QC	H3B1A5	514-284-7587	284-1889
Web: www.musimax.com					
Musiqueplus 355 Rue Sainte-Catherine O	Montreal	QC	H3B1A5	514-284-7587	284-1889
Web: www.musiqueplus.com					
Mystery 1 Lombard Pl Suite 2100	Winnipeg	MB	R3B8Y1	204-926-4800	926-4853
Web: www.canada.com					
NASA TV NASA Headquarters 300 'E' St SW	Washington	DC	20546	202-358-0001	358-3469
Web: www.nasa.gov/ntv					
National Geographic Channel 1145 17th St NW	Washington	DC	20036	202-912-6500	912-6603
Web: www.nationalgeographic.com/channel					
National Geographic Channel Canada 121 Bloor St E Suite 1500	Toronto	ON	M4W3M5	416-967-1174	960-0971
Web: www.nationalgeographic.ca					
New England Cable News (NECN) 160 Wells Ave	Newton	MA	02459	617-630-5000	630-5055
Web: www.boston.com/news/necn/					
New England Sports Network 480 Arsenal St	Watertown	MA	02472	617-536-9233	536-7814
Web: www.boston.com/sports/nesn					
News Central 10706 Beaver Dam Rd	Hunt Valley	MD	21030	410-568-1500	568-2121
Web: www.newscentral.tv					
NFL Network 280 Park Ave	New York	NY	10017	212-450-2000	681-7599
Web: www.nfl.com/nflnetwork					
NHL Network 9 Channel Nine Ct	Scarborough	ON	M1S4B5	416-332-5000	
Web: www.tsn.ca/nhl_network					
Nick at Nite 1515 Broadway 42nd Fl	New York	NY	10036	212-258-8000	258-7676
Web: www.tvland.com/nickatnite					
Nickelodeon 1515 Broadway 38th Fl	New York	NY	10036	212-258-8000	258-7705
Web: www.nick.com					
Noggin LLC 1633 Broadway 7th Fl	New York	NY	10019	212-654-7707	654-4879
Web: www.noggin.com					
Oasis TV Inc 1875 Century Pk E Suite 600	Los Angeles	CA	90067	310-553-4300	553-1159
Web: www.oasistv.com					
One: The Body, Mind & Spirit Channel 171 Liberty St Suite 230	Toronto	ON	M6K3P6	416-368-3194	368-9774
Web: www.onebodymindspirit.com					
Outdoor Channel 43445 Business Park Dr Suite 103	Temecula	CA	92590	951-699-6991	699-6313
NASDAQ: OUTD ■ *TF:* 800-770-5750 ■ *Web:* www.outdoorchannel.com					
Outdoor Life Network Canada 9 Channel Nine Ct	Scarborough	ON	M1S4B5	416-332-5000	
Web: www.tsn.ca/oln					
OuterMAX 1100 Ave of the Americas	New York	NY	10036	212-512-1000	
Web: www.cinemax.com					
Ovation The Arts Network 2850 Ocean Park Blvd	Santa Monica	CA	90405	800-682-8466	813-6336*
**Fax Area Code:* 703 ■ *TF:* 800-682-8466 ■ *Web:* www.ovationtv.com					
Oxygen Media Inc 75 9th Ave 7th Fl	New York	NY	10011	212-651-2000	651-2099
Web: www.oxygen.com					
Pet Network 115 Gordon Baker Rd 8th Fl	Toronto	ON	M2H3R6	416-756-2404	756-5526
Web: www.mypetnetwork.tv					
Playboy Entertainment 2706 Media Center Dr	Los Angeles	CA	90065	323-276-4000	276-4500
Prime Time Christian Broadcasting Inc PO Box 61000	Midland	TX	79711	432-563-0420	563-1736
TF: 800-707-0420 ■ *Web:* www.godslearningchannel.com					
PRIME TV 1 Lombard Pl Suite 2100	Winnipeg	MB	R3B8Y1	204-926-4800	926-4853
Web: www.canada.com					
Product Information Network 2600 Michelson Dr Suite 1650	Irvine	CA	92612	949-263-9900	757-1526
Web: www.pinnet.com					
QVC Inc 1200 Wilson Dr	West Chester	PA	19380	484-701-1000	701-1138*
**Fax:* Cust Svc ■ *TF:* 800-367-9444 ■ *Web:* www.qvc.com					
Rainbow Media Holdings Inc 200 Jericho Quadrangle	Jericho	NY	11753	516-803-3000	803-3003
Web: www.rainbow-media.com					
RDS (Reseau des Sports) 1755 Boul Rene-Levesque E Bureau 300	Montreal	QC	H2K4P6	514-599-2244	599-2299
Web: www.rds.ca					
Report on Business Television 720 King St W 10th Fl	Toronto	ON	M5V2T3	416-957-8100	957-8180
TF: 877-284-7878 ■ *Web:* www.robtv.com					
Reseau des Sports (RDS) 1755 Boul Rene-Levesque E Bureau 300	Montreal	QC	H2K4P6	514-599-2244	599-2299
Web: www.rds.ca					
Resort Sports Network PO Box 7528	Portland	ME	04112	207-772-5000	775-3658
TF: 800-653-0697 ■ *Web:* www.rsn.com					
Rogers Sportsnet Inc DBA Sportsnet 9 Channel Nine Ct	Scarborough	ON	M1S4B5	416-332-5600	332-5767
Web: www.sportsnet.ca					
Sci-Fi Channel 30 Rockefeller Plaza 21st Fl	New York	NY	10112	212-664-4444	
Web: www.scifi.com					
Science Channel 8516 Georgia Ave	Silver Spring	MD	20910	240-662-2000	
Web: science.discovery.com					
SCOLA 21557 270th St	McClelland	IA	51548	712-566-2202	566-2502
Web: www.scola.org					
Score The 370 King St W Suite 304	Toronto	ON	M5V1J9	416-977-6787	977-0238
Web: www.thescore.ca					
Scream 64 Jefferson Ave Unit 18	Toronto	ON	M6K3H4	416-534-1191	
Web: www.screamtelevision.ca					
Series+ 2100 Rue Sainte-Catherine O Bureau 700	Montreal	QC	H3H2T3	514-939-3150	939-3151
TF: 800-361-5194 ■ *Web:* www.seriesplus.com					
Shop at Home LLC 5388 Hickory Hollow Pkwy	Antioch	TN	37013	615-263-8000	263-8905
TF: 800-224-9739 ■ *Web:* www.shopathometv.com					
ShopNBC 6740 Shady Oak Rd	Eden Prairie	MN	55344	952-943-6000	943-6711*
**Fax:* Hum Res ■ *TF:* 800-676-5523 ■ *Web:* www.shopnbc.com					
Shopping Channel 59 Ambassador Dr	Mississauga	ON	L5T2P9	905-362-2020	362-7702
Web: www.theshoppingchannel.com					
Showcase 121 Bloor St E Suite 1500	Toronto	ON	M4W3M5	416-967-1174	960-0971
Web: www.showcase.ca					
Showcase Action 121 Bloor St E Suite 1500	Toronto	ON	M4W3M5	416-967-1174	960-0971
Web: www.showcase.ca/action					
Showcase Diva 121 Bloor St E Suite B-1	Toronto	ON	M4W3M5	416-967-0022	967-0044
Web: www.showcase.ca/diva					
Showtime Networks Inc 1633 Broadway 15th Fl	New York	NY	10019	212-708-1600	708-1530
Web: www.sho.com					
Si TV 3030 Andrita St	Los Angeles	CA	90065	323-256-8900	256-9888
Web: www.sitv.com					
SoapNet LLC 3800 W Alameda Ave	Burbank	CA	91505	818-560-1000	
Web: soapnet.go.com					
Space: The Imagination Station 299 Queen St W	Toronto	ON	M5V2Z5	416-591-5757	591-6619
Web: www.spacecast.com					
Speed Channel Inc 9711 Southern Pine Blvd	Charlotte	NC	28273	704-731-2222	731-2222
Web: www.speedtv.com					
Spike TV 1775 Broadway 9th Fl	New York	NY	10019	212-767-4001	
Web: www.spiketv.com					
Sports Network Canada 9 Channel Nine Ct	Toronto	ON	M4A2M9	416-332-5000	
Web: www.tsn.ca					
Star! The Entertainment Information Station 299 Queen St W	Toronto	ON	M5V2Z5	416-591-5757	
Web: www.star-tv.com					
Starz Encore Group LLC 8900 Liberty Cir	Englewood	CO	80112	720-852-7700	852-7710
Web: www.starz.com					
Starz! 8900 Liberty Cir	Englewood	CO	80112	720-852-7700	852-7710
Web: www.starz.com					
Starz! Family 8900 Liberty Cir	Englewood	CO	80112	720-852-7700	852-7710
Web: www.starz.com					
Style 121 W Lexington Dr Suite 300	Glendale	CA	91203	818-480-3170	480-3180
Web: www.eonline.com/Style					
Sun Sports 1000 Legion Pl Suite 1600	Orlando	FL	32801	407-648-1150	245-2571
Web: www.sunsportstv.com					
Sundance Channel 1633 Broadway 8th Fl	New York	NY	10019	212-708-1500	654-4724
Web: www.sundancechannel.com					
Super Ecran 2100 Rue Sainte-Catherine O Bureau 1000	Montreal	QC	H3H2T3	514-939-5090	939-5098
Web: www.superecran.com					
Superstation WGN 220 E 42nd St Suite 400	New York	NY	10017	212-210-5900	210-5905
Web: wgnsuperstation.trb.com					
Talktv 9 Channel Nine Ct	Toronto	ON	M4A2M9	416-332-5000	
Web: www.talktv.ca					
TBN (Trinity Broadcasting Network) PO Box A	Santa Ana	CA	92711	714-832-2950	665-2156
TF: 888-731-1000 ■ *Web:* www.tbn.org					
TBS (Turner Broadcasting System Inc) 1 CNN Center	Atlanta	GA	30303	404-827-1700	885-4326
Web: www.turner.com					
TBS Superstation 1050 Techwood Dr NW	Atlanta	GA	30318	404-827-1717	
Web: www.superstation.com					
TCT Ministries Inc 111 Airway Dr PO Box 1010	Marion	IL	62959	618-997-9333	997-1859
Web: www.tct.tv					
Telelatino Network Inc (TLN) 5125 Steeles Ave W	Toronto	ON	M9L1R5	416-744-8200	744-0966
TF: 800-551-8401 ■ *Web:* www.tlntv.com					
TELETOON Canada Inc 181 Bay St Suite 100 PO Box 787	Toronto	ON	M5J2T3	416-956-2060	956-2070
Web: www.teletoon.com					
Tennis Channel 2850 Ocean Park Blvd Suite 150	Santa Monica	CA	90405	310-314-9400	314-9433
Web: www.thetennischannel.com					
ThrillerMAX 1100 Ave of the Americas	New York	NY	10036	212-512-1000	512-5570
Web: www.cinemax.com					
TLN (Telelatino Network Inc) 5125 Steeles Ave W	Toronto	ON	M9L1R5	416-744-8200	744-0966
TF: 800-551-8401 ■ *Web:* www.tlntv.com					
Toon Disney 3800 W Alameda Ave	Burbank	CA	91505	818-569-7500	567-4375
Web: www.toondisney.com					
Total Living Network 2880 Vision Ct	Aurora	IL	60506	630-801-3838	801-3839
Web: www.tln.com					
Travel Channel 8516 Georgia Ave	Silver Spring	MD	20910	240-662-2000	
TF: 888-404-5969 ■ *Web:* travel.discovery.com					
Treehouse TV Inc 64 Jefferson Ave Unit 18	Toronto	ON	M6K3H4	416-534-1191	
Web: www.treehousetv.com					
Trinity Broadcasting Network (TBN) PO Box A	Santa Ana	CA	92711	714-832-2950	665-2156
TF: 888-731-1000 ■ *Web:* www.tbn.org					
truTV 600 3rd Ave 2nd Fl	New York	NY	10016	212-973-2800	973-3355*
**Fax:* News Rm ■ *Web:* www.courttv.com					
Turner Broadcasting System Inc (TBS) 1 CNN Center	Atlanta	GA	30303	404-827-1700	885-4326
Web: www.turner.com					
Turner Classic Movies 1050 Techwood Dr NW	Atlanta	GA	30318	404-827-1717	
Web: www.tcm.turner.com					
Turner Network Television (TNT) 1050 Techwood Dr NW	Atlanta	GA	30318	404-827-1717	
Web: www.tnt.tv					
TV Asahi America Inc 875 3rd Ave 3rd Fl	New York	NY	10022	212-644-6300	644-0003
TF: 800-272-4467 ■ *Web:* www.tv-asahi.net/html/english.html					
TV Guide Channel 7140 S Lewis Ave	Tulsa	OK	74136	918-488-4000	488-4594
TF: 800-447-7388 ■ *Web:* www.tvguide.com					
TV Guide Inc 6922 Hollywood Blvd	Hollywood	CA	90028	323-817-4600	817-4629
NASDAQ: GMST ■ *Web:* www.gemstartvguide.com					
TV Land 1515 Broadway 48th Fl	New York	NY	10036	212-846-2550	
Web: www.tvland.com					
TV One 1010 Wayne Ave 10th Fl	Silver Spring	MD	20910	301-755-0400	755-2833
Web: www.tv-one.tv					
USA Network 30 Rockefeller Plaza	New York	NY	10112	212-664-4444	413-6509
Web: www.usanetwork.com					
ValueVision Media Inc 6740 Shady Oak Rd	Eden Prairie	MN	55344	952-943-6000	943-6711
NASDAQ: VVTV ■ *Web:* www.shopnbc.com					
VERSUS 281 Tresser Blvd 2 Stamford Plaza 9th Fl	Stamford	CT	06901	203-406-2500	406-2530
Web: www.versus.com					
VH1 Classic 1633 Broadway 9th Fl	New York	NY	10019	212-654-8900	654-4743
Web: www.vh1.com					
Video Hits One (VH1) 1515 Broadway 20th Fl	New York	NY	10036	212-258-8000	846-1753*
**Fax:* Hum Res ■ *Web:* www.vh1.com					

Phone Fax

VideoSeat Pay-Per-View 546 E Main St — Lexington KY 40508 859-226-4678 226-4391
Web: www.hostcommunications.com
Viewers Choice Pay Per View 181 Bay St Suite 100 — Toronto ON M2J2T3 416-956-2010 956-5415
Web: www.viewerschoice.ca
VisionTV 171 E Liberty St Suite 230 — Toronto ON M6K3P6 416-368-3194 368-9774
Web: www.visiontv.ca
Voy Network 330 Madison Ave 6th Fl — New York NY 10017 212-204-8331 202-5240
Web: www.voy.tv
VRAK-TV 2100 Rue Sainte-Catherine O Bureau 700 — Montreal QC H3H2T3 514-939-3150 939-3151
TF: 800-361-5194 ■ *Web:* www.vrak.tv
W Network 64 Jefferson Ave Unit 18 — Toronto ON M6K3H4 416-534-1191
Web: www.wnetwork.com
WAM! America's Kidz Network 8900 Liberty Cir — Englewood CO 80112 720-852-7700 852-7710
Web: www.starz.com
Weather Channel 300 Interstate N Pkwy — Atlanta GA 30339 770-226-0000 226-2702
Web: www.weather.com
Weather Network 2655 Bristol Cir — Oakville ON L6H7W1 905-829-1159 829-5800
Web: www.theweathernetwork.com
WMAX 1100 Ave of the Americas — New York NY 10036 212-512-1000
Web: www.cinemax.com
Women's Entertainment LLC 200 Jericho Quadrangle — Jericho NY 11753 516-803-2300 803-4113*
**Fax:* Mktg ■ *Web:* we.tv
Worship Network PO Box 428 — Safety Harbor FL 34695 727-536-0036 479-1427
TF: 877-296-7744 ■ *Web:* www.worship.net
Xtreme Sports 1 Lombard Pl Suite 2100 — Winnipeg MB R3B8Y1 204-926-4800 926-4853
Web: www.canada.com
YTV Canada Inc 64 Jefferson Ave Unit 18 — Toronto ON M6K3H4 416-534-1191
Web: www.ytv.com
Z 2100 Rue Sainte-Catherine O Bureau 700 — Montreal QC H3H2T3 514-939-3150 939-3151
TF: 800-361-5194 ■ *Web:* www.ztele.com

744 TELEVISION STATIONS

SEE ALSO Internet Broadcasting p. 1870

ABC	American Broadcasting Co	**PBS**	Public Broadcasting Service
CBC	Canadian Broadcasting Corp	**QS**	Television Quatre Saisons
CBS	Columbia Broadcasting System	**SRC**	Societe Radio-Canada
CTV	Canadian Television Network	**TBN**	Trinity Broadcasting Network
Fox	Fox Broadcasting Co	**Tele**	Telemundo Communications Group
GTN	Global Television Network	**TVA**	Groupe TVA
Ind	Independent	**Uni**	Univision Television Network
NBC	National Broadcasting Co	**UPN**	United Paramount Network
PAX	Paxson Communications Corp	**WB**	Warner Bros Television

744-1 Abilene, TX

Phone Fax

KIDZ-TV Ch 42 (MNT) 500 Chestnut St Suite 804 — Abilene TX 79602 325-672-5606 676-2437
Web: www.kidzabilene.com
KRBC-TV Ch 9 (NBC) 4510 S 14th St — Abilene TX 79605 325-692-4242 692-8265
Web: www.krbctv.com
KTAB-TV Ch 32 (CBS) 4510 S 14th St — Abilene TX 79605 325-695-2777 695-9922
Web: www.ktabtv.com
KTXS-TV Ch 12 (ABC) 4420 N Clack St — Abilene TX 79601 325-677-2281 672-5307*
**Fax:* News Rm ■ *TF:* 800-588-5897 ■ *Web:* www.ktxs.com
KXVA-TV Ch 15 (Fox) 500 Chestnut St Suite 804 — Abilene TX 79602 325-672-5606 673-8437

744-2 Albany, NY

Phone Fax

WCWN-TV Ch 45 (CW) 14 Corporate Woods Blvd Suite 201 — Albany NY 12211 518-431-3150 431-3155
Web: capitalregionscw.trb.com
WMHT-TV Ch 17 (PBS) 4 Global View — Troy NY 12180 518-880-3400 880-3409
TF: 800-477-9648 ■ *Web:* www.wmht.org
WNYT-TV Ch 13 (NBC) 15 N Pearl St — Albany NY 12204 518-436-4791 434-0659
TF: 800-999-9698 ■ *Web:* www.wnyt.com
WRGB-TV Ch 6 (CBS) 1400 Balltown Rd — Schenectady NY 12309 518-346-6666 346-6249
Web: www.wrgb.com
WTEN-TV Ch 10 (ABC) 341 Northern Blvd — Albany NY 12204 518-436-4822 426-4792*
**Fax:* News Rm ■ *Web:* www.wten.com
WXXA-TV Ch 23 (Fox) 28 Corporate Cir — Albany NY 12203 518-862-2323 862-0930*
**Fax:* News Rm ■ *TF:* 800-999-2882 ■ *Web:* www.fox23tv.com
WYPX-TV Ch 55 (I) 1 Charles Blvd — Guilderland NY 12084 518-464-9842 464-0633

744-3 Albuquerque/Santa Fe, NM

Phone Fax

KASA-TV Ch 2 (Fox) 1377 University Blvd NE — Albuquerque NM 87102 505-246-2222 764-2456
Web: www.kasa.com
KASY-TV Ch 50 (MNT) 8341 Washington St NE — Albuquerque NM 87113 505-797-1919 344-1145
Web: www.upn50tv.com
KCHF-TV Ch 11 (Ind) 27556 I-25 E Frontage Rd — Santa Fe NM 87508 505-473-1111 474-4998
TF: 800-831-9673 ■ *Web:* www.kchf.com
KLUZ-TV Ch 41 (Uni) 2725 F Broadbent Pkwy NE — Albuquerque NM 87107 505-344-5589 344-0891
KNAT-TV Ch 23 (TBN) 1510 Coors Blvd NW — Albuquerque NM 87121 505-836-6585 831-8725
Web: www.tbn.org
KNME-TV Ch 5 (PBS)
1130 University Blvd NE University of New Mexico — Albuquerque NM 87131 505-277-2121 277-2191
TF: 800-328-5663 ■ *Web:* www.knmetv.org
KOAT-TV Ch 7 (ABC) 3801 Carlisle Blvd NE — Albuquerque NM 87107 505-884-7777 884-6354
TF: 800-421-6159 ■ *Web:* www.koat.com
KOB-TV Ch 4 (NBC) 4 Broadcast Plaza SW — Albuquerque NM 87104 505-243-4411 764-2522
Web: www.kobtv.com
KRQE-TV Ch 13 (CBS) 13 Broadcast Plaza SW — Albuquerque NM 87104 505-243-2285 842-8483
TF: 800-283-4227 ■ *Web:* www.krqe.com
KTFQ-TV Ch 14 (Uni) 2725 F Broadbent Pkwy NE — Albuquerque NM 87107 505-344-5589 344-0891
KWBQ-TV Ch 19 (CW) 8341 Washington St NE — Albuquerque NM 87113 505-797-1919 344-1145
Web: www.wb19tv.com

744-4 Amarillo, TX

Phone Fax

KACV-TV Ch 2 (PBS) PO Box 447 — Amarillo TX 79178 806-371-5222 371-5258
TF: 800-999-9243 ■ *Web:* www.kacvtv.org
KAMR-TV Ch 4 (NBC) 1015 S Fillmore St — Amarillo TX 79101 806-383-3321 381-2943
Web: www.kamr.com
KCIT-TV Ch 14 (Fox) 1015 S Fillmore St — Amarillo TX 79101 806-374-1414 381-0912
Web: www.fox14.tv
KCPN-TV Ch 31 (Ind) 1015 S Fillmore St — Amarillo TX 79101 806-374-1414 371-0408
Web: www.fox14.tv
KFDA-TV Ch 10 (CBS) 7900 Broadway — Amarillo TX 79105 806-383-1010 381-9859
Web: www.newschannel10.com
KVII-TV Ch 7 (ABC) 1 Broadcast Center — Amarillo TX 79101 806-373-1787 371-7329
TF: 800-777-5844 ■ *Web:* www.kvii.com

744-5 Anchorage, AK

Phone Fax

KAKM-TV Ch 7 (PBS) 3877 University Dr — Anchorage AK 99508 907-563-7070 273-9192
Web: www.publicbroadcasting.net/apti/news.newsmain
KIMO-TV Ch 13 (ABC) 2700 E Tudor Rd — Anchorage AK 99507 907-561-1313 561-8934
TF: 877-304-1313 ■ *Web:* www.aksuperstation.com
KTBY-TV Ch 4 (Fox) 440 E Benson Blvd Suite 1 — Anchorage AK 99503 907-274-0404 264-5180
Web: www.fox4ktby.com
KTUU-TV Ch 2 (NBC) 701 E Tudor Rd Suite 220 — Anchorage AK 99503 907-762-9202 563-3318
Web: www.ktuu.com
KTVA-TV Ch 11 (CBS) 1007 W 32nd Ave — Anchorage AK 99503 907-562-3456 273-3189
Web: www.ktva.com
KYES-TV Ch 5 (MNT) 3700 Woodland Dr Suite 800 — Anchorage AK 99517 907-248-5937 339-3889
Web: www.kyes.com

744-6 Asheville, NC/Greenville, SC/Spartanburg, SC

Phone Fax

WGGS-TV Ch 16 (Ind) 3409 Rutherford Rd Ext — Taylors SC 29687 864-244-1616 292-8481
TF: 800-849-3683 ■ *Web:* www.wggs16.com
WHNS-TV Ch 21 (Fox) 21 Interstate Ct — Greenville SC 29615 864-288-2100 297-0728
Web: www.whns.com
WLOS-TV Ch 13 (ABC) 110 Technology Dr — Asheville NC 28803 828-684-1340 651-4618
TF: 800-288-8813 ■ *Web:* www.wlos.com
WMYA-TV Ch 40 (MNT) 110 Technology Dr — Asheville NC 28803 828-684-1340 297-8085*
**Fax Area Code:* 864 ■ *TF:* 800-288-8813 ■ *Web:* www.my40.tv
WNEG-TV Ch 32 (CBS) 100 North Blvd — Toccoa GA 30577 706-886-0032 886-7033
Web: www.wneg32.com
WRET-TV Ch 49 (PBS) PO Box 4069 — Spartanburg SC 29305 864-503-9371 503-3615
WSPA-TV Ch 7 (CBS) PO Box 1717 — Spartanburg SC 29304 864-576-7777 587-5430
TF: 800-207-6397 ■ *Web:* www.wspa.com
WYCW-TV Ch 62 (CW) PO Box 1717 — Spartanburg SC 29304 864-576-7777 587-5430
Web: www.wasv.com
WYFF-TV Ch 4 (NBC) 505 Rutherford St — Greenville SC 29609 864-242-4404 240-5305
Web: www.thecarolinachannel.com

744-7 Atlanta, GA

Phone Fax

WAGA-TV Ch 5 (Fox) 1551 Briarcliff Rd NE — Atlanta GA 30306 404-875-5555 898-0169*
**Fax:* News Rm ■ *Web:* www.fox5atlanta.com
WATL-TV Ch 36 (MNT) 1 Monroe Pl NE — Atlanta GA 30324 404-881-3600 881-3635
Web: wb36.trb.com
WDCO-TV Ch 29 (PBS) 260 14th St NW — Atlanta GA 30318 404-685-2400 685-2417
TF: 800-222-6006 ■ *Web:* www.gpb.org/gptv
WGCL-TV Ch 46 (CBS) 425 14th St NW — Atlanta GA 30318 404-325-4646 327-3003
Web: www.wgcltv.com
WGTV-TV Ch 8 (PBS) 260 14th St NW — Atlanta GA 30318 404-685-2400 685-2417
TF: 800-222-6006 ■ *Web:* www.gpb.org/gptv
WJSP-TV Ch 28 (PBS) 260 14th St NW — Atlanta GA 30318 404-685-2400 685-2591
TF: 800-222-4788 ■ *Web:* www.gpb.org/gptv
WPBA-TV Ch 30 (PBS) 740 Bismark Rd NE — Atlanta GA 30324 678-686-0321 686-0356
Web: www.wpba.org
WPXA-TV Ch 14 (I) 200 N Cobb Pkwy Suite 114 — Marietta GA 30062 770-919-0575 919-9621
WSB-TV Ch 2 (ABC) 1601 W Peachtree St NE — Atlanta GA 30309 404-897-7000 897-7370
Web: www.wsbtv.com
WTBS-TV Ch 17 (Ind) 1050 Techwood Dr NW — Atlanta GA 30318 404-827-1717 827-1947
Web: tbssuperstation.com/tbs17
WUPA-TV Ch 69 (CW) 2700 Northeast Expy Bldg A — Atlanta GA 30345 404-325-6929 633-4567
Web: cwatlantatv.com
WVAN-TV Ch 9 (PBS) 260 14th St NW — Atlanta GA 30318 404-685-2400 685-2431
TF: 800-222-6006 ■ *Web:* www.gpb.org/gptv
WXIA-TV Ch 11 (NBC) 1611 W Peachtree St NE — Atlanta GA 30309 404-892-1611 881-0675*
**Fax:* News Rm ■ *Web:* www.11alive.com

744-8 Augusta, GA

Phone Fax

WAGT-TV Ch 26 (NBC) PO Box 1526 — Augusta GA 30903 706-826-0026 724-4028
TF: 800-924-8639 ■ *Web:* www.nbc26news.com
WCES-TV Ch 20 (PBS) 260 14th St NW — Atlanta GA 30318 404-685-2400 685-2684
Web: www.gpb.org/gptv
WFXG-TV Ch 54 (Fox) 3933 Washington Rd — Augusta GA 30907 706-650-5400 650-8411
Web: www.wfxg.com
WJBF-TV Ch 6 (ABC) 1001 Reynolds St — Augusta GA 30901 706-722-6664 722-0022
Web: www.wjbf.com
WRDW-TV Ch 12 (CBS) PO Box 1212 — Augusta GA 30903 803-278-1212 279-8316
Web: www.wrdw.com

744-9 Austin, TX

Phone Fax

KEYE-TV Ch 42 (CBS) 10700 Metric Blvd — Austin TX 78758 512-835-0042 837-6753
TF: 800-563-9742 ■ *Web:* www.keyetv.com
KLRU-TV Ch 18 (PBS) 2504-B Whitis Ave — Austin TX 78712 512-471-4811 475-9090
Web: www.klru.org
KNVA-TV Ch 54 (CW) 908 W ML King Jr Blvd — Austin TX 78701 512-478-5400 476-1520
Web: www.knva.com
KTBC-TV Ch 7 (Fox) 119 E 10th St — Austin TX 78701 512-476-7777 495-7060
Web: www.fox7.com
KVUE-TV Ch 24 (ABC) 3201 Steck Ave — Austin TX 78757 512-459-6521 533-2233*
**Fax:* News Rm ■ *Web:* www.kvue.com
KXAN-TV Ch 36 (NBC) 908 W ML King Jr Blvd — Austin TX 78701 512-476-3636 469-0630
Web: www.kxan.com

744-10 Bakersfield, CA

Station	City	State	ZIP	Phone	Fax
KABE-TV Ch 31 (Uni) 5801 Truxtun Ave	Bakersfield	CA	93309	661-324-0031	334-2693
Web: www.univision.com					
KBAK-TV Ch 29 (CBS) 1901 Westwind Dr	Bakersfield	CA	93301	661-327-7955	327-5603
TF: 800-229-6397 ■ *Web:* www.eyeoutforyou.com					
KERO-TV Ch 23 (ABC) 321 21st St	Bakersfield	CA	93301	661-637-2323	323-5538*
**Fax:* News Rm ■ *Web:* www.turnto23.com					
KGET-TV Ch 17 (NBC) 2120 L St	Bakersfield	CA	93301	661-283-1700	283-1855
Web: www.kget.com					
KUVI-TV Ch 45 (MNT) 5801 Truxtun Ave	Bakersfield	CA	93309	661-324-0045	334-2693
Web: www.kuvi45.com					

744-11 Baltimore, MD

Station	City	State	ZIP	Phone	Fax
WBAL-TV Ch 11 (NBC) 3800 Hooper Ave	Baltimore	MD	21211	410-467-3000	338-6460
TF: 800-677-9225 ■ *Web:* www.thewbalchannel.com					
WBFF-TV Ch 45 (Fox) 2000 W 41st St	Baltimore	MD	21211	410-467-4545	467-5090
Web: www.foxbaltimore.com					
WBOC-TV Ch 16 (CBS) 1729 N Salisbury Blvd	Salisbury	MD	21801	410-749-1111	742-5190
Web: www.wboc.com					
WCPB-TV CH 28 (PBS) 11767 Owings Mills Blvd	Owings Mills	MD	21117	410-581-4097	581-4338
Web: www.mpt.org					
WJZ-TV Ch 13 (CBS) 3725 Malden Ave	Baltimore	MD	21211	410-466-0013	578-7502
Web: www.wjz.com					
WMAR-TV Ch 2 (ABC) 6400 York Rd	Baltimore	MD	21212	410-377-2222	377-0493
Web: www.insidebaltimore.com/wmar					
WMDT-TV Ch 47 (ABC) 202 Downtown Plaza	Salisbury	MD	21801	410-742-4747	742-5767
Web: www.wmdt.com					
WMPT-TV Ch 22 (PBS) 11767 Owings Mills Blvd	Owings Mills	MD	21117	410-356-5600	581-4338
TF: 800-223-3678 ■ *Web:* www.mpt.org					
WMPT-TV Ch 67 (PBS) 11767 Owings Mills Blvd	Owings Mills	MD	21117	410-356-5600	
TF: 800-223-3678 ■ *Web:* www.mpt.org					
WNUV-TV Ch 54 (CW) 2000 W 41st St	Baltimore	MD	21211	410-467-4545	467-5090
Web: www.wbbaltimore.com					
WUTB-TV Ch 24 (MNT) 4820 Seton Dr	Baltimore	MD	21215	410-358-2400	764-7232
Web: www.upn24.com					

744-12 Bangor, ME

Station	City	State	ZIP	Phone	Fax
WABI-TV Ch 5 (CBS) 35 Hildreth St	Bangor	ME	04401	207-947-8321	941-9378
Web: www.wabi.tv					
WLBZ-TV Ch 2 (NBC) 329 Mt Hope Ave	Bangor	ME	04401	207-942-4821	942-2109
TF: 800-244-6306 ■ *Web:* www.wlbz.com					
WMEB-TV Ch 12 (PBS) 65 Texas Ave	Bangor	ME	04401	207-941-1010	942-2857
Web: www.mainepbs.org					
WVII-TV Ch 7 (ABC) 371 Target Industrial Cir	Bangor	ME	04401	207-945-6457	945-6864
TF: 800-499-9844 ■ *Web:* www.localmaine.com					

744-13 Baton Rouge, LA

Station	City	State	ZIP	Phone	Fax
KLPB-TV Ch 24 (PBS) 7733 Perkins Rd	Baton Rouge	LA	70810	225-767-5660	767-4421
TF: 800-272-8161 ■ *Web:* www.lpb.org					
KLTS-TV Ch 24 (PBS) 7733 Perkins Rd	Baton Rouge	LA	70810	225-767-5660	767-4299
Web: www.lpb.org					
KZUP-TV 19 (Ind) 10000 Perkins Rd	Baton Rouge	LA	70810	225-766-3233	768-9293
WAFB-TV Ch 9 (CBS) 844 Government St	Baton Rouge	LA	70802	225-383-9999	379-7980*
**Fax:* News Rm ■ *TF:* 800-223-9232 ■ *Web:* www.wafb.com					
WBRL-TV Ch 21 (CW) 10000 Perkins Rd	Baton Rouge	LA	70810	225-769-0044	923-2822
WBRZ-TV Ch 2 (ABC) 1650 Highland Rd	Baton Rouge	LA	70802	225-387-2222	336-2347*
**Fax:* News Rm ■ *Web:* www.2theadvocate.com					
WGMB-TV Ch 44 (Fox) 10000 Perkins Rd	Baton Rouge	LA	70810	225-769-0044	768-9293
Web: www.fox44.com					
WLPB-TV Ch 27 (PBS) 7733 Perkins Rd	Baton Rouge	LA	70810	225-767-5660	767-4421*
**Fax:* News Rm ■ *TF:* 800-272-8161 ■ *Web:* www.lpb.org					
WVLA-TV Ch 33 (NBC) 10000 Perkins Rd	Baton Rouge	LA	70810	225-766-3233	768-9191
Web: www.nbc33tv.com					

744-14 Billings, MT

Station	City	State	ZIP	Phone	Fax
KHMT-TV Ch 4 (Fox) 445 S 24th St W	Billings	MT	59102	406-652-7366	652-6963
Web: www.khmt.com					
KSVI-TV Ch 6 (ABC) 445 S 24th St W	Billings	MT	59102	406-652-4743	652-6963
Web: www.ksvi.com					
KTVQ-TV Ch 2 (CBS) 3203 3rd Ave N	Billings	MT	59101	406-252-5611	252-9938
Web: www.ktvq.com					
KULR-TV Ch 8 (NBC) 2045 Overland Ave	Billings	MT	59102	406-656-8000	652-8207
Web: www.kulr8.com					

744-15 Birmingham, AL

Station	City	State	ZIP	Phone	Fax
WABM-TV Ch 68 (MNT) 651 Beacon Pkwy W Suite 105	Birmingham	AL	35209	205-943-2168	290-2114
Web: www.wabm68.com					
WBIQ-TV Ch 10 (PBS) 2112 11th Ave S Suite 400	Birmingham	AL	35205	205-328-8756	251-2192
TF: 800-239-5233 ■ *Web:* www.aptv.org					
WBRC-TV Ch 6 (Fox) PO Box 6	Birmingham	AL	35201	205-322-6666	583-4356
Web: www.wbrc.com					
WCFT-TV Ch 33 (ABC) 800 Concourse Pkwy Suite 200	Birmingham	AL	35244	205-403-3340	982-3942*
**Fax:* News Rm ■ *Web:* www.abc3340.com					
WEIQ-TV Ch 42 (PBS) 2112 11th Ave S Suite 400	Birmingham	AL	35205	205-328-8756	251-2192
TF: 800-239-5233 ■ *Web:* www.aptv.org					
WHIQ-TV Ch 25 (PBS) 2112 11th Ave S Suite 400	Birmingham	AL	35205	205-328-8756	251-2192
TF: 800-239-5233 ■ *Web:* www.aptv.org					
WIAT-TV Ch 42 (CBS) PO Box 59496	Birmingham	AL	35259	205-322-4200	320-2713
Web: www.wiat.com					
WPXH-TV Ch 44 (I) 2085 Golden Crust Dr	Birmingham	AL	35209	205-870-4404	870-0744
WTJP-TV Ch 60 (TBN) 313 Rosedale Ave	Gadsden	AL	35901	256-546-8860	543-8623
Web: www.tbn.org					
WTTO-TV Ch 21 (CW) 651 Beacon Pkwy W Suite 105	Birmingham	AL	35209	205-943-2168	290-2114
Web: www.wtto21.com/birmingham_al/					
WVTM-TV Ch 13 (NBC) 1732 Valley View Dr	Birmingham	AL	35209	205-933-1313	323-3314
Web: www.nbc13.com					

744-16 Bismarck, ND

Station	City	State	ZIP	Phone	Fax
KBMY-TV Ch 17 (ABC) 3128 E Broadway Ave	Bismarck	ND	58501	701-223-1700	250-7244
TF: 877-563-9369 ■ *Web:* www.abc17.tv					
KFYR-TV Ch 5 (NBC) 200 N 4th St	Bismarck	ND	58501	701-255-5757	255-8220
Web: www.kfyrtv.com					
KNDX-TV Ch 26 (Fox) 3130 E Broadway Ave	Bismarck	ND	58501	701-355-0026	250-7244
TF: 877-563-9369 ■ *Web:* www.westdakotafox.com					
KXMB-TV Ch 12 (CBS) 1811 N 15th St	Bismarck	ND	58501	701-223-9197	223-3320
TF: 800-223-9197 ■ *Web:* www.kxmb.com					

744-17 Boise, ID

Station	City	State	ZIP	Phone	Fax
KAID-TV Ch 4 (PBS) 1455 N Orchard St	Boise	ID	83706	208-373-7220	373-7245
TF: 800-543-6868 ■ *Web:* www.idahoptv.org					
KBCI-TV Ch 2 (CBS) 140 N 16th St	Boise	ID	83702	208-336-5222	472-2212
Web: www2.kbcitv.com					
KIVI-TV Ch 6 (ABC) 1866 E Chisholm Dr	Nampa	ID	83687	208-336-0500	381-6682
Web: www.6onyourside.com					
KNIN-TV Ch 9 (MNT) 816 W Bannock St Suite 402	Boise	ID	83702	208-331-0909	344-0119
Web: www.knin.com					
KTRV-TV Ch 12 (Fox) 1 6th St N	Nampa	ID	83687	208-466-1200	467-6958
Web: www.fox12news.com					
KTVB-TV Ch 7 (NBC) PO Box 7	Boise	ID	83707	208-375-7277	378-1762
TF: 800-559-7277 ■ *Web:* www.ktvb.com					

744-18 Boston, MA

Station	City	State	ZIP	Phone	Fax
WBPX-TV Ch 68 (I) 1120 Soldiers Field Rd	Boston	MA	02134	617-787-6868	787-4114
Web: www.ionline.tv					
WBZ-TV Ch 4 (CBS) 1170 Soldiers Field Rd	Boston	MA	02134	617-787-7000	254-6383
Web: www.wbz4.com					
WCVB-TV Ch 5 (ABC) 5 TV Pl	Needham	MA	02494	781-449-0400	449-6681
Web: www.thebostonchannel.com					
WENH-TV Ch 11 (PBS) 268 Mast Rd	Durham	NH	03824	603-868-1100	868-7552
Web: www.nhptv.org					
WFXT-TV Ch 25 (Fox) 25 Fox Dr	Dedham	MA	02026	781-467-2525	467-7213
Web: www.fox25.com					
WGBH-TV Ch 2 (PBS) 125 Western Ave	Boston	MA	02134	617-300-2000	300-1026
TF: 800-300-2000 ■ *Web:* www.wgbh.org					
WHDH-TV Ch 7 (NBC) 7 Bulfinch Pl	Boston	MA	02114	617-725-0777	723-6117
Web: www2.whdh.com					
WLVI-TV Ch 56 (CW) 75 Morrissey Blvd	Boston	MA	02125	617-265-5656	287-2872*
**Fax:* News Rm ■ *Web:* bostonscw.trb.com					
WMUR-TV Ch 9 (ABC) 100 S Commercial St	Manchester	NH	03101	603-669-9999	641-9005
Web: www.thewmurchannel.com					
WSBK-TV Ch 38 (Ind) 1170 Soldiers Field Rd	Allston	MA	02134	617-787-7000	254-6383
Web: www.upn38.com					
WUNI-TV Ch 27 (Uni) 33 4th Ave	Needham	MA	02494	781-433-2727	433-2750
Web: www.wunitv.com					
WZMY-TV Ch 50 (Ind) 11 A St	Derry	NH	03038	603-434-8850	434-8627
Web: www.mytvstation.tv					

744-19 Brownsville, TX

Station	City	State	ZIP	Phone	Fax
KGBT-TV Ch 4 (CBS) 9201 W Expy 83	Harlingen	TX	78552	956-421-4444	366-4494
Web: www.team4news.com					
KLUJ-TV Ch 44 (TBN) 1920 Al Conway Dr Suite 117	Brownsville	TX	78550	956-425-4225	412-1740
KMBH-TV Ch 60 (PBS) 1701 Tennessee St	Harlingen	TX	78550	956-421-4111	421-4150
Web: www.kmbh.org					
KNVO-TV Ch 48 (Uni) 801 N Jackson Rd	McAllen	TX	78501	956-687-4848	687-7784
KRGV-TV Ch 5 (ABC) PO Box 5	Weslaco	TX	78599	956-968-5555	973-5016
Web: www.newschannel5.tv					
KTLM-TV Ch 40 (Tele) 3900 N 10th St 7th Fl	McAllen	TX	78501	956-686-0040	686-0770
KVEO-TV Ch 23 (NBC) 394 North Expy	Brownsville	TX	78521	956-544-2323	544-4636
Web: www.kveo.com					

744-20 Buffalo, NY

Station	City	State	ZIP	Phone	Fax
WGRZ-TV Ch 2 (NBC) 259 Delaware Ave	Buffalo	NY	14202	716-849-2200	849-7602
TF: 877-849-2200 ■ *Web:* www.wgrz.com					
WIVB-TV Ch 4 (CBS) 2077 Elmwood Ave	Buffalo	NY	14207	716-874-4410	874-8173*
**Fax:* News Rm ■ *Web:* www.wivb.com					
WKBW-TV Ch 7 (ABC) 7 Broadcast Plaza	Buffalo	NY	14202	716-845-6100	856-8784*
**Fax:* News Rm ■ *TF:* 800-234-9529 ■ *Web:* www.wkbw.com					
WNED-TV Ch 17 (PBS) 140 Lower Terr Horizons Plaza	Buffalo	NY	14202	716-845-7000	845-7036
Web: www.wned.org					
WNGS-TV Ch 67 (Ind) 9279 Dutch Hill Rd	West Valley	NY	14171	716-942-3000	942-3010
Web: www.wngstv.com					
WNYO-TV Ch 49 (MNT) 699 Hertel Ave Suite 100	Buffalo	NY	14207	716-875-4949	875-4919
Web: www.wb49.net/					
WUTV-TV Ch 29 (Fox) 951 Whitehaven Rd	Grand Island	NY	14072	716-773-7531	773-5753
Web: www.wutv.com					

744-21 Calgary, AB

Station	City	State	ZIP	Phone	Fax
CBRT-TV Ch 9 (CBC) PO Box 2640	Calgary	AB	T2P2M7	403-521-6000	521-6079
Web: www.cbc.ca					
CFCN-TV Ch 4 (CTV) 80 Patina Rise SW	Calgary	AB	T3H2W4	403-240-5600	240-5689
Web: www.cfcn.ca					
CICT-TV Ch 7 (GTN) 222 23rd St NE	Calgary	AB	T2E7N2	403-235-7709	248-3842*
**Fax:* News Rm ■ *Web:* www.canada.com/globaltv/calgary/					
CKAL-TV Ch 5 (Ind) 535 7th Ave SW	Calgary	AB	T2P0Y4	403-508-2222	508-2224
Web: www.a-channel.com					

744-22 Casper, WY

Station	City	State	ZIP	Phone	Fax
KCWC-TV Ch 4 (PBS) 2660 Peck Ave	Riverton	WY	82501	307-856-6944	856-3893
Web: www.wyoptv.org					
KCWY-TV Ch 13 (NBC) 141 Progress Cir	Mills	WY	82644	307-577-0013	577-5251
Web: www.nbcforwyoming.com					

	City	State	Zip	Phone	Fax
KFNB-TV Ch 20 (Fox) 1856 Skyview Dr.	Casper	WY	82601	307-577-5923	577-5928
KGWC-TV Ch 14 (CBS) 1856 Skyview Dr.	Casper	WY	82601	307-234-1111	234-4005
KLWY-TV Ch 27 (Fox) 1856 Skyview Dr	Casper	WY	82601	307-577-5923	577-5928
KTWO-TV Ch 2 (ABC) 1896 Skyview Dr.	Casper	WY	82609	307-237-3711	234-9866
Web: www.k2tv.com					

744-23 Cedar Rapids, IA

	City	State	Zip	Phone	Fax
KCRG-TV Ch 9 (ABC) 501 2nd Ave SE	Cedar Rapids	IA	52401	319-398-8422	398-8378
TF: 800-332-5443 ■ *Web:* www.kcrg.com					
KFXA-TV Ch 28 (Fox) 600 Old Marion Rd NE	Cedar Rapids	IA	52402	319-393-2800	395-7028
TF: 800-642-6140 ■ *Web:* www.fox2840.com					
KGAN-TV Ch 2 (CBS) 600 Old Marion Rd NE	Cedar Rapids	IA	52402	319-395-9060	395-0987
TF: 800-642-6140 ■ *Web:* www.kgan.com					
KPXR-TV Ch 48 (I) 1957 Blairs Ferry Rd NE	Cedar Rapids	IA	52402	319-378-1260	378-0076
KWKB-TV Ch 20 (CW) 1547 Baker Ave	West Branch	IA	52358	319-643-5952	643-3124
Web: www.kwkb.com					
KWWL-TV Ch 7 (NBC) 500 E 4th St.	Waterloo	IA	50703	319-291-1200	291-1255
Web: www.kwwl.com					

744-24 Charleston, SC

	City	State	Zip	Phone	Fax
WCBD-TV Ch 2 (NBC) 210 W Coleman Blvd	Mount Pleasant	SC	29464	843-884-2222	881-3410
Web: www.wcbd.com					
WCIV-TV Ch 4 (ABC) PO Box 22165	Charleston	SC	29413	843-881-4444	849-2519*
**Fax:* News Rm ■ *Web:* www.abcnews4.com					
WCSC-TV Ch 5 (CBS) 2126 Charlie Hall Blvd.	Charleston	SC	29414	843-577-6397	402-5744
Web: www.wcsc.com					
WITV-TV Ch 7 (PBS) 1101 Geroge Rogers Blvd	Columbia	SC	29201	803-737-3200	737-3476
Web: www.scetv.org					
WJWJ-TV Ch 16 (PBS) PO Box 1165	Beaufort	SC	29901	843-524-0808	524-1016
Web: www.wjwj.org					
WMMP-TV Ch 36 (MNT) 4301 Arco Ln	North Charleston	SC	29418	843-744-2424	554-9649
Web: www.wmmp36.com					
WTAT-TV Ch 24 (Fox) 4301 Arco Ln	North Charleston	SC	29418	843-744-2424	554-9649
Web: www.wtat24.com					

744-25 Charleston, WV

	City	State	Zip	Phone	Fax
WCHS-TV Ch 8 (ABC) 1301 Piedmont Rd	Charleston	WV	25301	304-346-5358	346-4765
TF: 888-696-9247 ■ *Web:* www.wchstv.com					
WLPX-TV Ch 29 (I) 600-C Prestige Park Dr Suite C	Hurricane	WV	25526	304-760-1029	760-1036
WOWK-TV Ch 13 (CBS) 555 5th Ave	Huntington	WV	25701	304-525-1313	523-0545
TF: 800-234-9695 ■ *Web:* www.wowktv.com					
WPBY-TV Ch 33 (PBS) 600 Capitol St.	Charleston	WV	25301	304-696-6630	556-4980
Web: www.wvpubcast.org					
WQCW-TV Ch 30 (CW) 800 Gallia St Suite 430	Portsmouth	OH	45662	740-353-3391	353-3372
Web: www.whcp-tv.com					
WSAZ-TV Ch 3 (NBC) PO Box 2115	Huntington	WV	25721	304-697-4780	690-3066
TF: 800-834-8515 ■ *Web:* www.wsaz.com					
WVAH-TV Ch 11 (Fox) 11 Broadcast Plaza	Hurricane	WV	25526	304-757-0011	757-7533
Web: www.wvah.com					

744-26 Charlotte, NC

	City	State	Zip	Phone	Fax
WAXN-TV Ch 64 (ABC) 1901 N Tryon St.	Charlotte	NC	28206	704-338-9999	335-4736*
**Fax:* News Rm ■ *TF:* 800-367-9762 ■ *Web:* www.wsoctv.com/action64					
WBTV-TV Ch 3 (CBS) 1 Julian Price Pl	Charlotte	NC	28208	704-374-3500	374-3671
Web: www.wbtv.com					
WCCB-TV Ch 18 (Fox) 1 Television Pl	Charlotte	NC	28205	704-372-1800	358-4841
Web: www.foxcharlotte.tv					
WCNC-TV Ch 6 (NBC) 1001 Wood Ridge Center Dr	Charlotte	NC	28217	704-329-3636	357-4975
Web: www.nbc6.com					
WHKY-TV Ch 14 (Ind) PO Box 1059	Hickory	NC	28603	828-322-5115	322-8256
Web: www.whky.com					
WJZY-TV Ch 46 (CW) 3501 Performance Rd.	Charlotte	NC	28214	704-398-0046	393-8407
Web: www.upn46.com					
WMYT-TV Ch 12 (MNT) 3501 Performance Rd	Charlotte	NC	28214	704-398-0046	393-8407
Web: www.wb55.com					
WSOC-TV Ch 9 (ABC) 1901 N Tryon St.	Charlotte	NC	28206	704-338-9999	335-4736
TF: 800-367-9762 ■ *Web:* www.wsoctv.com					
WTVI-TV Ch 42 (PBS) 3242 Commonwealth Ave	Charlotte	NC	28205	704-372-2442	335-1358
Web: www.wtvi.org					

744-27 Chattanooga, TN

	City	State	Zip	Phone	Fax
WDEF-TV Ch 12 (CBS) 3300 Broad St	Chattanooga	TN	37408	423-785-1200	785-1271
Web: www.wdef.com					
WDSI-TV Ch 61 (Fox) 1101 E Main St.	Chattanooga	TN	37408	423-265-0061	265-3636
Web: www.fox61tv.com					
WELF-TV Ch 23 (TBN) 384 S Campus Rd	Lookout Mountain	GA	30750	706-820-1663	820-1735
Web: www.tbn.org					
WFLI-TV Ch 53 (CW) 6024 Shallowford Rd Suite 100	Chattanooga	TN	37421	423-893-9553	893-9853
Web: www.thecwchattanooga.com					
WRCB-TV Ch 3 (NBC) 900 Whitehall Rd	Chattanooga	TN	37405	423-267-5412	756-3148*
**Fax:* News Rm ■ *Web:* www.wrcbtv.com					
WTCI-TV Ch 45 (PBS) 7540 Bonnie Shire Dr.	Chattanooga	TN	37416	423-629-0045	698-8557
Web: www.wtci-tv45.com					
WTVC-TV Ch 9 (ABC) PO Box 60028	Chattanooga	TN	37406	423-757-7320	757-7401
Web: www.newschannel9.com					

744-28 Cheyenne, WY

	City	State	Zip	Phone	Fax
KCWY-TV Ch 13 (NBC) 141 Progress Cir.	Mills	WY	82644	307-577-0013	577-5251
Web: www.nbcforwyoming.com					
KGWN-TV Ch 5 (CBS) 2923 E Lincolnway	Cheyenne	WY	82001	307-634-7755	638-0182
TF: 877-672-8019 ■ *Web:* www.kgwn.tv					
KKTU-TV Ch 33 (ABC) 4200 E 2nd St	Casper	WY	82609	307-638-8738	237-3713
Web: www.k2tv.com					

744-29 Chicago, IL

	City	State	Zip	Phone	Fax
WBBM-TV Ch 2 (CBS) 630 N McClurg Ct	Chicago	IL	60611	312-202-2222	202-3878
Web: cbs2chicago.com					
WCIU-TV Ch 26 (Ind) 26 N Halsted St.	Chicago	IL	60661	312-705-2600	660-8323
Web: www.wciu.com					
WCPX-TV Ch 38 (I) NBC Tower 454 N Columbus Dr	Chicago	IL	60611	312-836-5669	595-9813
Web: www.ionline.tv					
WFLD-TV Ch 32 (Fox) 205 N Michigan Ave.	Chicago	IL	60601	312-565-5532	819-1332
Web: www.foxchicago.com					
WGBO-TV Ch 66 (Uni) 541 N Fairbanks Ct 11th Fl	Chicago	IL	60611	312-670-1000	494-6492
WGN-TV Ch 9 (CW) 2501 W Bradley Pl.	Chicago	IL	60618	773-528-2311	528-6050
Web: wgntv.trb.com					
WJYS-TV Ch 62 (Ind) 18600 S Oak Park Ave	Tinley Park	IL	60477	708-633-0001	633-0040
Web: www.wjystv62.com					
WLS-TV Ch 7 (ABC) 190 N State St.	Chicago	IL	60601	312-750-7777	899-8019
Web: abclocal.go.com/wls					
WMAQ-TV Ch 5 (NBC) 454 N Columbus Dr NBC Tower	Chicago	IL	60611	312-836-5555	527-5925
Web: www.nbc5.com					
WPWR-TV Ch 50 (Fox) 205 N Michigan Ave.	Chicago	IL	60601	312-565-5532	819-1332
WSNS-TV Ch 44 (Tele) 454 N Columbus Dr	Chicago	IL	60611	312-836-3000	836-3232
WTTW-TV Ch 11 (PBS) 5400 N St Louis Ave	Chicago	IL	60625	773-583-5000	583-3046
Web: www.wttw.com					
WYCC-TV Ch 20 (PBS) 7500 S Pulaski Rd	Chicago	IL	60652	773-838-7878	581-2071
Web: www.wycc.org					

744-30 Cincinnati, OH

	City	State	Zip	Phone	Fax
WCET-TV Ch 48 (PBS) 1223 Central Pkwy	Cincinnati	OH	45214	513-381-4033	381-7520
Web: www.wcet.org					
WCPO-TV Ch 9 (ABC) 1720 Gilbert Ave.	Cincinnati	OH	45202	513-721-9900	721-7717
Web: www.wcpo.com					
WKRC-TV Ch 12 (CBS) 1906 Highland Ave	Cincinnati	OH	45219	513-763-5500	421-3820
Web: www.wkrc.com					
WLWT-TV Ch 5 (NBC) 1700 Young St.	Cincinnati	OH	45202	513-412-5000	412-6121
Web: www.channelcincinnati.com					
WSTR-TV Ch 64 (MNT) 5177 Fishwick Dr	Cincinnati	OH	45216	513-641-4400	242-2633
Web: www.wb64.net					
WXIX-TV Ch 19 (Fox) 635 W 7th St 19 Broadcast Plaza	Cincinnati	OH	45203	513-421-1919	421-3022
Web: www.wxix.com					

744-31 Cleveland/Akron, OH

	City	State	Zip	Phone	Fax
WBNX-TV Ch 55 (CW) 2690 State Rd	Cuyahoga Falls	OH	44223	330-922-5500	929-2410
TF: 800-367-8855 ■ *Web:* www.wbnx.com					
WDLI-TV Ch 17 (TBN) 1764 Wadsworth Rd.	Akron	OH	44320	330-753-5542	753-4563
Web: www.tbn.org					
WEAO-TV Ch 49 (PBS) 1750 Campus Center Dr	Kent	OH	44240	330-677-4549	678-0688
TF: 800-544-4549 ■ *Web:* www.pbs4549.org					
WEWS-TV Ch 5 (ABC) 3001 Euclid Ave	Cleveland	OH	44115	216-431-5555	431-3666
Web: www.newsnet5.com					
WJW-TV Ch 8 (Fox) 5800 S Marginal Rd	Cleveland	OH	44103	216-431-8888	391-9559
Web: www.fox8cleveland.com					
WKYC-TV Ch 3 (NBC) 1333 Lakeside Ave E	Cleveland	OH	44114	216-344-3333	344-3326
Web: www.wkyc.com					
WNEO-TV Ch 45 (PBS) 1750 Campus Center Dr	Kent	OH	44240	330-677-4549	678-0688
TF: 800-554-4549 ■ *Web:* www.pbs4549.org					
WOIO-TV Ch 19 (CBS) 1717 E 12th St.	Cleveland	OH	44114	216-771-1943	436-5460
TF: 877-929-1943 ■ *Web:* www.woio.com					
WQHS-TV Ch 61 (Uni) 2861 W Ridgewood Dr.	Cleveland	OH	44134	440-888-0061	888-7023
WUAB-TV Ch 43 (MNT) 1717 E 12th St.	Cleveland	OH	44114	216-771-1943	515-7152
TF: 800-929-0132 ■ *Web:* www.wuab.com					
WVIZ-TV Ch 25 (PBS) 1375 Euclid Ave	Cleveland	OH	44115	216-916-6100	916-6090
Web: www.wviz.org					

744-32 Colorado Springs, CO

	City	State	Zip	Phone	Fax
KKTV-TV Ch 11 (CBS) 3100 N Nevada Ave	Colorado Springs	CO	80907	719-634-2844	634-3741
Web: www.kktv.com					
KOAA-TV Ch 5/30 (NBC) 2200 7th Ave	Pueblo	CO	81003	719-544-5781	295-6655
Web: www.koaa.com					
KRDO-TV Ch 13 (ABC) 399 S 8th St	Colorado Springs	CO	80905	719-632-1515	475-0815
Web: www.krdotv.com					
KTSC-TV Ch 8 (PBS) 2200 Bonforte Blvd	Pueblo	CO	81001	719-543-8800	549-2208
Web: www.ktsc.org					
KXRM-TV Ch 21 (Fox) 560 Wooten Rd	Colorado Springs	CO	80915	719-596-2100	591-4180
Web: www.kxrm.com					

744-33 Columbia, SC

	City	State	Zip	Phone	Fax
WACH-TV Ch 57 (Fox) 1400 Pickens St Suite 6	Columbia	SC	29201	803-252-5757	212-7270
Web: www.wach.com					
WHMC-TV Ch 23 (PBS) 1101 George Rogers Blvd	Columbia	SC	29201	803-737-3200	737-3417
Web: www.scetv.org					
WIS-TV Ch 10 (NBC) 1111 Bull St.	Columbia	SC	29201	803-758-1218	758-1155
Web: www.wistv.com					
WKTC-TV Ch 63 (MNT) 120-A Pontiac Business Center Dr.	Elgin	SC	29045	803-419-6363	419-6399
Web: www.wktctv.com/					
WLTX-TV Ch 19 (CBS) 6027 Garner's Ferry Rd	Columbia	SC	29209	803-776-3600	695-3714
Web: www.wltx.com					
WOLO-TV Ch 25 (ABC) 5807 Shakespeare Rd	Columbia	SC	29223	803-754-7525	754-6147
Web: www.wolo.com					
WRLK-TV Ch 35 (PBS) 1101 George Rogers Blvd.	Columbia	SC	29201	803-737-3200	737-3526
TF: 800-922-5437 ■ *Web:* www.scetv.org					

744-34 Columbus, GA

	City	State	Zip	Phone	Fax
WLGA-TV Ch 66 (CW) 1800 Pepperell Pkwy	Opelika	AL	36801	334-749-5766	749-5768
Web: www.wlgatv.com					
WLTZ-TV Ch 38 (NBC) 6140 Buena Vista Rd	Columbus	GA	31907	706-561-3838	563-8467
Web: www.wltz.com					
WRBL-TV Ch 3 (CBS) 1350 13th Ave.	Columbus	GA	31901	706-323-3333	323-0841
Web: www.wrbl.com					

Columbus, GA (Cont'd)

Station	City	State	ZIP	Phone	Fax
WTVM-TV Ch 9 (ABC) 1909 Wynnton Rd *Web:* www.wtvm.com	Columbus	GA	31906	706-324-6471	322-7527
WXTX-TV Ch 54 (Fox) 6524 Buena Vista Rd *Web:* www.wtvm.com	Columbus	GA	31907	706-568-2900	561-5965

744-35 Columbus, OH

Station	City	State	ZIP	Phone	Fax
WBNS-TV Ch 10 (CBS) 770 Twin Rivers Dr **Fax:* News Rm ■ *Web:* www.wbns10tv.com	Columbus	OH	43215	614-460-3700	460-2891*
WCMH-TV Ch 4 (NBC) 3165 Olentangy River Rd *Web:* www.nbc4i.com	Columbus	OH	43202	614-263-4444	263-0166
WOSU-TV Ch 34 (PBS) 2400 Olentangy River Rd *Web:* www.wosu.org/tv	Columbus	OH	43210	614-292-9678	292-7625
WOUC-TV Ch 44 (PBS) Ohio University Telecommunications Center 9 S College St *Web:* www.woub.org	Athens	OH	45701	740-593-1771	593-0240
WSFJ-TV Ch 51 (I) 3948 Townsfair Way Suite 220 *TF:* 800-517-5151 ■ *Web:* www.pax51.com	Columbus	OH	43219	614-416-6080	416-6345
WSYX-TV Ch 6 (ABC) 1261 Dublin Rd **Fax:* News Rm ■ *Web:* www.wsyx6.com	Columbus	OH	43215	614-481-6666	481-6624*
WTTE-TV Ch 28 (Fox) 1261 Dublin Rd *Web:* www.wtte28.com	Columbus	OH	43215	614-481-6666	481-6624
WWHO-TV Ch 53 (CW) 1160 Dublin Rd Suite 500 *Web:* www.wwhotv.com	Columbus	OH	43215	614-485-5300	485-5339

744-36 Corpus Christi, TX

Station	City	State	ZIP	Phone	Fax
KAJA-TV Ch 68 (Tele) 409 S Staples St *Web:* www.kristv.com	Corpus Christi	TX	78401	361-886-6101	886-6116
KDF-TV Ch 47 (Fox) 409 S Staples St *Web:* www.kristv.com	Corpus Christi	TX	78401	361-886-6100	886-6116
KEDT-TV Ch 16 (PBS) 4455 S Padre Island Dr Suite 38 *TF:* 800-307-5338 ■ *Web:* www.kedt.org	Corpus Christi	TX	78411	361-855-2213	855-3877
KIII-TV Ch 3 (ABC) 5002 S Padre Island Dr *TF:* 800-874-5705 ■ *Web:* www.kiiitv.com	Corpus Christi	TX	78411	361-986-8300	986-8311
KORO-TV Ch 28 (Uni) 102 N Mesquite St	Corpus Christi	TX	78401	361-883-2823	883-2931
KRIS-TV Ch 6 (NBC) 409 S Staples St *Web:* www.kristv.com	Corpus Christi	TX	78401	361-886-6100	886-6175
KZTV-TV Ch 10 (CBS) 301 Artesian St *Web:* www.cbs10kztv.com	Corpus Christi	TX	78401	361-883-7070	882-8553

744-37 Dallas/Fort Worth, TX

Station	City	State	ZIP	Phone	Fax
KDAF-TV Ch 33 (CW) 8001 John Carpenter Fwy *TF:* 877-252-8233 ■ *Web:* wb33.trb.com	Dallas	TX	75247	214-252-9233	252-3379
KDFI-TV Ch 27 (Fox) 400 N Griffin St *Web:* www.kdfi27.com	Dallas	TX	75202	214-637-2727	720-3355
KDFW-TV Ch 4 (Fox) 400 N Griffin St *Web:* www.kdfwfox4.com	Dallas	TX	75202	214-720-4444	720-3263
KDTX-TV Ch 58 (TBN) 2823 W Irving Blvd *Web:* www.tbn.org	Irving	TX	75062	972-313-1333	790-5853
KERA-TV Ch 13 (PBS) 3000 Harry Hines Blvd *Web:* www.kera.org/tv	Dallas	TX	75201	214-871-1390	754-6035
KFWD-TV Ch 52 (Ind) 606 Young St *Web:* www.kfwd.tv	Dallas	TX	75202	214-977-6780	977-6544
KPXD-TV Ch 68 (I) 3900 Barnett St *Web:* www.ionline.tv	Fort Worth	TX	76103	817-654-6467	
KSTR-TV Ch 49 (Uni) 2323 Bryan St Suite 1900 **Fax Area Code:* 214	Dallas	TX	75201	972-579-4900	954-4920*
KTVT-TV Ch 11 (CBS) 5233 Bridge St *Web:* www.cbs11tv.com	Fort Worth	TX	76103	817-451-1111	496-7739
KTXA-TV Ch 21 (Ind) 1011 N Central Expy *Web:* www.upn21.com	Dallas	TX	75231	214-743-2100	743-2150
KUVN-TV Ch 23 (Uni) 2323 Bryan St Suite 1900	Dallas	TX	75201	214-758-2300	758-2324
KXAS-TV Ch 5 (NBC) 3900 Barnett St *TF:* 800-232-5927 ■ *Web:* www.nbc5i.com	Fort Worth	TX	76103	817-429-5555	654-6325
KXTX-TV Ch 39 (Tele) 3100 McKinnon St Suite 800 *Web:* www.telemundodallas.com	Dallas	TX	75021	214-521-3900	523-5946
WFAA-TV Ch 8 (ABC) 606 Young St Communications Center *Web:* www.wfaa.com	Dallas	TX	75202	214-748-9631	977-6585

744-38 Dayton, OH

Station	City	State	ZIP	Phone	Fax
WBDT-TV Ch 26 (CW) 2589 Corporate Pl *Web:* www.daytonswb.com	Miamisburg	OH	45342	937-384-9226	384-7392
WDTN-TV Ch 2 (NBC) 4595 S Dixie Ave *Web:* www.wdtn.com	Dayton	OH	45439	937-293-2101	296-7147
WHIO-TV Ch 7 (CBS) 1414 Wilmington Ave *Web:* www.whiotv.com	Dayton	OH	45420	937-259-2111	259-2005
WKEF-TV Ch 22 (ABC) 1731 Soldiers Home Rd *Web:* www.wkef22.com	Dayton	OH	45418	937-263-2662	263-9537
WPTD-TV Ch 16 (PBS) 110 S Jefferson St *TF:* 800-247-1614 ■ *Web:* www.thinktv.org	Dayton	OH	45402	937-220-1600	220-1642
WRGT-TV Ch 45 (Fox) 45 Broadcast Plaza *Web:* www.wkef22.com/dayton_oh/	Dayton	OH	45408	937-263-4500	268-5265

744-39 Denver, CO

Station	City	State	ZIP	Phone	Fax
KBDI-TV Ch 12 (PBS) 2900 Welton St 1st Fl *TF:* 800-727-8812 ■ *Web:* www.kbdi.org	Denver	CO	80205	303-296-1212	296-6650
KCEC-TV Ch 50 (Uni) 777 Grant St Suite 500	Denver	CO	80203	303-832-0050	832-3410
KCNC-TV Ch 4 (CBS) 1044 Lincoln St *Web:* www.cbs4denver.com	Denver	CO	80203	303-861-4444	830-6380
KDVR-TV Ch 31 (Fox) 100 E Speer Blvd *TF:* 888-369-4762 ■ *Web:* www.fox31news.com	Denver	CO	80203	303-595-3131	566-2931
KMGH-TV Ch 7 (ABC) 123 Speer Blvd *Web:* www.thedenverchannel.com	Denver	CO	80203	303-832-7777	832-0119
KPXC-TV Ch 59 (I) 3001 S Jamaica Ct Suite 200 *Web:* www.ionline.tv	Aurora	CO	80014	303-751-5959	751-5993
KRMA-TV Ch 6 (PBS) 1089 Bannock St *TF:* 800-274-6666 ■ *Web:* www.krma.org	Denver	CO	80204	303-892-6666	620-5600
KUSA-TV Ch 9 (NBC) 500 Speer Blvd *Web:* www.kusa.com	Denver	CO	80203	303-871-9999	698-4700
KWGN-TV Ch 2 (CW) 6160 S Wabash Way *Web:* cw2.trb.com	Greenwood Village	CO	80111	303-740-2222	740-2847
KWHD-TV Ch 53 (Ind) 12999 E Adams Aircraft Cir *TF:* 866-576-5353 ■ *Web:* www.kwhdtv53.com	Englewood	CO	80112	303-799-8853	792-5303

744-40 Des Moines, IA

Station	City	State	ZIP	Phone	Fax
KCCI-TV Ch 8 (CBS) 888 9th St *Web:* www.kcci.com	Des Moines	IA	50309	515-247-8888	244-0202
KDIN-TV Ch 11 (PBS) 6450 Corporate Dr *TF:* 800-532-1290 ■ *Web:* www.iptv.org	Johnston	IA	50131	515-242-3100	242-5830
KDSM-TV Ch 17 (Fox) 4023 Fleur Dr *Web:* www.kdsm.com	Des Moines	IA	50321	515-287-1717	287-0064
KFPX-TV Ch 39 (I) 4570 114th St *Web:* www.ionmedia.tv	Urbandale	IA	50322	515-331-3939	331-1312
KIIN-TV Ch 12 (PBS) 6450 Corporate Dr *TF:* 800-532-1290 ■ *Web:* www.iptv.org	Johnston	IA	50131	515-242-3100	242-4113
WHO-TV Ch 13 (NBC) 1801 Grand Ave **Fax:* News Rm ■ *TF:* 800-835-1313 ■ *Web:* www.whotv.com	Des Moines	IA	50309	515-242-3500	242-3796*
WOI-TV Ch 5 (ABC) 3903 Westown Pkwy **Fax:* Sales ■ *Web:* www.woi-tv.com	West Des Moines	IA	50266	515-457-9645	457-1034*

744-41 Detroit, MI

Station	City	State	ZIP	Phone	Fax
CBET-TV Ch 9 (CBC) 825 Riverside Dr W *Web:* www.cbc.ca/windsor	Windsor	ON	N9A5K9	519-255-3411	255-3412
WADL-TV Ch 38 (Fox) 22590 15-Mile Rd *Web:* www.wadldetroit.com	Clinton Township	MI	48035	586-790-3838	790-3841
WDIV-TV Ch 4 (NBC) 550 W Lafayette Blvd *TF:* 800-654-8221 ■ *Web:* www.clickondetroit.com	Detroit	MI	48226	313-222-0500	222-0592
WJBK-TV Ch 2 (Fox) PO Box 2000 *Web:* www.wjbk.com	Southfield	MI	48037	248-557-2000	557-1199
WKBD-TV Ch 50 (CW) 26905 W 11-Mile Rd *Web:* cw50detroit.com	Southfield	MI	48034	248-355-7000	355-7000
WMYD-TV Ch 20 (MNT) 27777 Franklin Rd Suite 1220 *Web:* www.tv20detroit.com	Southfield	MI	48034	248-355-2020	355-0368
WPXD-TV Ch 31 (I) 3975 Varsity Dr *Web:* www.ionline.tv	Ann Arbor	MI	48108	734-973-7900	973-7906
WTVS-TV Ch 56 (PBS) 7441 2nd Ave *Web:* www.wtvs.org	Detroit	MI	48202	313-873-7200	876-8118
WWJ-TV Ch 62 (CBS) 26905 W 11-Mile Rd *Web:* www.wwjtv.com	Southfield	MI	48034	248-355-7000	355-6292
WXYZ-TV Ch 7 (ABC) 20777 W Ten-Mile Rd *Web:* www.detnow.com	Southfield	MI	48037	248-827-7777	827-4454

744-42 Duluth, MN

Station	City	State	ZIP	Phone	Fax
KBJR-TV Ch 6 (NBC) 246 S Lake Ave *Web:* www.kbjr.com	Duluth	MN	55802	218-727-8484	720-9699
KDLH-TV Ch 3 (CBS) 246 S Lake Ave *Web:* www.kdlh.com	Duluth	MN	55802	218-720-9600	720-9660
KQDS-TV Ch 21 (Fox) 2001 London Rd	Duluth	MN	55812	218-728-1622	728-1557
WDIO-TV Ch 10 (ABC) 10 Observation Rd *TF:* 800-477-1013 ■ *Web:* www.wdio.com	Duluth	MN	55811	218-727-6864	727-4415
WDSE-TV Ch 8 (PBS) 632 Niagara Ct *TF:* 888-563-9373 ■ *Web:* www.wdse.org	Duluth	MN	55811	218-724-8568	724-4269

744-43 Edmonton, AB

Station	City	State	ZIP	Phone	Fax
CBXFT-TV Ch 11 (SRC) PO Box 555 *Web:* www.radio-canada.ca/television	Edmonton	AB	T5J2P4	780-468-7500	468-7779
CBXT-TV Ch 5 (CBC) 123 Edmonton City Center *Web:* www.cbc.ca/edmonton	Edmonton	AB	T5J2Y8	780-468-7555	468-7510
CFRN-TV Ch 3 (CTV) 18520 Stony Plain Rd *Web:* www.cfrntv.ca	Edmonton	AB	T5S1A8	780-483-3311	489-5883
CITV-TV Ch 13 (GTN) 5325 Allard Way	Edmonton	AB	T6H5B8	780-436-1250	438-8438
CKEM-TV Ch 51 (Ind) 10212 Jasper Ave **Fax:* News Rm	Edmonton	AB	T5J5A3	780-412-2783	412-2799*

744-44 El Paso, TX

Station	City	State	ZIP	Phone	Fax
KCOS-TV Ch 13 (PBS) 9050 Viscount Blvd Suite A-440 *Web:* www.kcostv.org	El Paso	TX	79925	915-590-1313	594-5394
KDBC-TV Ch 4 (CBS) 2201 Wyoming Ave *Web:* www.kdbc.com	El Paso	TX	79903	915-496-4444	496-4593
KFOX-TV Ch 14 (Fox) 6004 N Mesa St *Web:* www.kfoxtv.com	El Paso	TX	79912	915-833-8585	833-8717
KINT-TV Ch 26 (Uni) 5426 N Mesa St *Web:* www.univision26.com	El Paso	TX	79912	915-581-1126	585-4642
KRWG-TV Ch 22 (PBS) Jordan St PO Box 30001 MSC TV 22 *TF:* 866-457-9488 ■ *Web:* www.krwg-tv.org	Las Cruces	NM	88003	505-646-2222	646-1924
KTFN-TV Ch 65 (Uni) 5426 N Mesa St *Web:* www.univision.com	El Paso	TX	79912	915-581-1126	585-4642
KTSM-TV Ch 9 (NBC) 801 N Oregon St *Web:* www.ktsm.com	El Paso	TX	79902	915-532-5421	544-0536
KTYO-TV Ch 48 (Tele) 10033 Carnegie Ave	El Paso	TX	79925	915-591-9595	591-9896
KVIA-TV Ch 7 (ABC) 4140 Rio Bravo St **Fax:* News Rm ■ *TF:* 800-580-5842 ■ *Web:* www.kvia.com	El Paso	TX	79902	915-496-7777	532-0505*

744-45 Erie, PA

Station	City	State	ZIP	Phone	Fax
WFXP-TV Ch 66 (Fox) 8455 Peach St *TF:* 888-989-9538 ■ *Web:* www.fox66.tv	Erie	PA	16509	814-864-2400	864-5393
WICU-TV Ch 12 (NBC) 3514 State St *Web:* www.wicu12.com	Erie	PA	16508	814-454-5201	454-3753
WJET-TV Ch 24 (ABC) 8455 Peach St *Web:* www.wjettv.com	Erie	PA	16509	814-864-2400	868-3041
WQLN-TV Ch 54 (PBS) 8425 Peach St *TF:* 800-727-8854 ■ *Web:* www.wqln.org	Erie	PA	16509	814-864-3001	864-4077

Station	City	State	Zip	Phone	Fax
WSEE-TV Ch 35 (CBS) 1220 Peach St	Erie	PA	16501	814-455-7575	454-5541
Web: www.35wsee.com					

744-46 Eugene, OR

Station	City	State	Zip	Phone	Fax
KEZI-TV Ch 9 (ABC) PO Box 7009	Eugene	OR	97401	541-485-5611	343-9664
Web: www.kezi.com					
KLSR-TV Ch 34 (Fox) 2940 Chad Dr	Eugene	OR	97408	541-683-2525	683-8016
Web: www.klsrtvfox.com					
KMTR-TV Ch 16 (NBC) 3825 International Ct	Springfield	OR	97477	541-746-1600	747-0866
Web: www.kmtr.com					
KVAL-TV Ch 13 (CBS) PO Box 1313	Eugene	OR	97440	541-342-4961	342-2635
Web: www.kval.com					

744-47 Evansville, IN

Station	City	State	Zip	Phone	Fax
WAZE-TV Ch 19 (CW) 1277 N St Joseph Ave	Evansville	IN	47720	812-425-1900	423-3405
TF: 888-488-1900 ■ *Web:* www.wazetv.com					
WEHT-TV Ch 25 (ABC) 800 Marywood Dr	Henderson	KY	42420	270-826-9566	827-0561
TF: 800-879-8549 ■ *Web:* www.abc25.com					
WEVV-TV Ch 44 (CBS) 44 Main St	Evansville	IN	47708	812-464-4444	465-9450
Web: www.wevv.com					
WFIE-TV Ch 14 (NBC) 1115 Mt Auburn Rd	Evansville	IN	47720	812-426-1414	426-1945
TF: 800-832-0014 ■ *Web:* www.14wfie.com					
WNIN-TV Ch 9 (PBS) 405 Carpenter St	Evansville	IN	47708	812-423-2973	428-7548
Web: www.wnin.org					
WTSN-TV Ch 63 (MNT) 44 Main St	Evansville	IN	47708	812-464-4463	465-4559
WTVW-TV Ch 7 (Fox) 477 Carpenter St	Evansville	IN	47708	812-424-7777	421-4040
TF: 800-511-6009 ■ *Web:* www.wtvw.com					

744-48 Fairbanks, AK

Station	City	State	Zip	Phone	Fax
KATN-TV Ch 2 (ABC) 516 2nd Ave Suite 400	Fairbanks	AK	99701	907-452-2125	456-8225
Web: www.aksuperstation.com					
KFXF-TV Ch 7 (Fox) 3650 Bradock St Suite 2	Fairbanks	AK	99701	907-452-3697	456-3428
Web: www.tvtv.com					
KTVF-TV Ch 11 (NBC) 3528 International Way	Fairbanks	AK	99701	907-452-5121	458-1820
KUAC-TV Ch 9 (PBS) PO Box 755620 University of Alaska	Fairbanks	AK	99775	907-474-7491	474-5064
Web: www.alaskaone.org					
KXD-TV Ch 13 (CBS) 3650 Bradock St Suite 2	Fairbanks	AK	99701	907-452-3697	456-3428

744-49 Fargo/Grand Forks, ND

Station	City	State	Zip	Phone	Fax
KBME-TV Ch 3 (PBS) 207 N 5th St	Fargo	ND	58102	701-241-6900	239-7650
TF: 800-359-6900 ■ *Web:* www.prairiepublic.org					
KFME-TV Ch 13 (PBS) 207 N 5th St	Fargo	ND	58102	701-241-6900	239-7650
TF: 800-359-6900 ■ *Web:* www.prairiepublic.org					
KGFE-TV Ch 2 (PBS) 207 N 5th St	Fargo	ND	58102	701-241-6900	239-7650
TF: 800-359-6900 ■ *Web:* www.prairiepublic.org					
KVLY-TV Ch 11 (NBC) 1350 21st Ave S	Fargo	ND	58103	701-237-5211	232-0493
TF: 800-450-5844 ■ *Web:* www.kvlytv11.com					
KVRR-TV Ch 15 (Fox) PO Box 9115	Fargo	ND	58106	701-277-1515	277-1830
KXJB-TV Ch 4 (CBS) 1350 21st Ave S	Fargo	ND	58103	701-237-5211	237-5396
Web: www.kx4.com					
WDAY-TV Ch 6 (ABC) 301 S 8th St	Fargo	ND	58103	701-237-6500	241-5358
Web: www.in-forum.com/wday					
WDAZ-TV Ch 8 (ABC) 2220 S Washington St	Grand Forks	ND	58201	701-775-2511	746-4507
TF: 800-732-4361 ■ *Web:* www.wdaz.com					

744-50 Flint, MI

Station	City	State	Zip	Phone	Fax
WAQP-TV Ch 49 (Ind) 2865 Trautner Dr	Saginaw	MI	48604	989-249-5969	249-1220
WEYI-TV Ch 25 (NBC) 2225 W Willard Rd	Clio	MI	48420	810-687-1000	687-4925
Web: www.nbc25.net					
WFUM-TV Ch 28 (PBS) 303 E Kearsley St University of Michigan	Flint	MI	48502	810-762-3028	233-6017
TF: 800-728-9386 ■ *Web:* www.wfum.org					
WJRT-TV Ch 12 (ABC) 2302 Lapeer Rd	Flint	MI	48503	810-233-3130	257-2812*
**Fax:* News Rm ■ *Web:* abclocal.go.com/wjrt					
WNEM-TV Ch 5 (CBS) 107 N Franklin St	Saginaw	MI	48607	989-755-8191	758-2110
TF: 800-522-9636 ■ *Web:* www.wnem.com					
WSMH-TV Ch 66 (Fox) 3463 W Pierson Rd	Flint	MI	48504	810-785-8866	785-8963
TF: 800-244-4664 ■ *Web:* www.wsmh66.com					

744-51 Fort Smith, AR

Station	City	State	Zip	Phone	Fax
KAFT-TV Ch 13 (PBS) 350 S Donaghey Ave	Conway	AR	72034	501-682-2386	682-4122
TF: 800-662-2386 ■ *Web:* www.aetn.org					
KFSM-TV Ch 5 (CBS) 318 N 13th St	Fort Smith	AR	72902	479-783-3131	783-3295
Web: www.kfsm.com					
KHBS-TV Ch 40 (ABC) 2415 N Albert Pike	Fort Smith	AR	72904	479-783-4040	785-5375
TF: 800-821-9170 ■ *Web:* www.thehometownchannel.com					
KNWA-TV Ch 24 (NBC) 15 S Block St Suite 101	Fayetteville	AR	72701	479-571-5100	571-8914
Web: www.knwa.com					
KPBI-TV Ch 46 (Fox) 523 N Greenwood Ave	Fort Smith	AR	72901	479-785-4600	785-4844

744-52 Fort Wayne, IN

Station	City	State	Zip	Phone	Fax
WANE-TV Ch 15 (CBS) 2915 W State Blvd	Fort Wayne	IN	46808	260-424-1515	424-6054
Web: www.wane.com					
WFFT-TV Ch 55 (Fox) 3707 Hillegas Rd	Fort Wayne	IN	46808	260-471-5555	484-4331
Web: www.wfft.com					
WFWA-TV Ch 39 (PBS) 2501 E Coliseum Blvd	Fort Wayne	IN	46805	260-484-8839	482-3632
TF: 888-484-8839 ■ *Web:* www.wfwa.org					
WISE-TV Ch 33 (NBC) 2633 W State Blvd	Fort Wayne	IN	46808	260-422-7474	422-7702
Web: www.wise33.com					
WPTA-TV Ch 21 (ABC) 3401 Butler Rd	Fort Wayne	IN	46808	260-483-0584	483-2568
Web: www.wpta.com					

744-53 Fresno, CA

Station	City	State	Zip	Phone	Fax
KAIL-TV Ch 53 (MNT) 1590 Alluvial Ave	Clovis	CA	93611	559-299-9753	299-1523
Web: www.kail.tv					
KFSN-TV Ch 30 (ABC) 1777 G St	Fresno	CA	93706	559-442-1170	266-5024
Web: abclocal.go.com/kfsn					
KFTV-TV Ch 21 (Uni) 3239 W Ashlan Ave	Fresno	CA	93722	559-222-2121	222-2890
TF: 800-733-5388					
KGPE-TV Ch 47 (CBS) 4880 N 1st St	Fresno	CA	93726	559-222-2411	225-5305*
**Fax:* News Rm ■ *Web:* www.47cbs.com					
KMPH-TV Ch 26 (Fox) 5111 E McKinley Ave	Fresno	CA	93727	559-453-8850	255-9626
Web: www.kmph.com					
KNXT-TV Ch 49 (Ind) 1550 N Fresno St	Fresno	CA	93703	559-488-7440	488-7444
Web: www.knxt.tv					
KSEE-TV Ch 24 (NBC) 5035 E McKinley Ave	Fresno	CA	93727	559-454-2424	454-2485
TF: 800-234-5733 ■ *Web:* www.ksee24.com					
KVPT-TV Ch 18 (PBS) 1544 Van Ness Ave	Fresno	CA	93721	559-266-1800	650-1880
Web: www.kvpt.org					

744-54 Grand Rapids, MI

Station	City	State	Zip	Phone	Fax
WGVU-TV Ch 35 (PBS) 301 W Fulton St	Grand Rapids	MI	49504	616-331-6666	331-6625
TF: 800-442-2771 ■ *Web:* www.wgvu.org					
WLLA-TV Ch 64 (Ind) PO Box 3157	Kalamazoo	MI	49003	269-345-6421	345-5665
Web: www.wlla.com					
WOOD-TV Ch 8 (NBC) 120 College Ave SE	Grand Rapids	MI	49503	616-456-8888	456-5755
Web: www.woodtv.com					
WOTV-TV Ch 41 (ABC) 120 College Ave	Grand Rapids	MI	49503	616-456-8880	235-4323
Web: www.wotv.com					
WTLJ-TV Ch 54 (Ind) 10290 48th Ave	Allendale	MI	49401	616-895-4154	892-4401
Web: www.tct-net.org					
WWMT-TV Ch 3 (CBS) 590 W Maple St	Kalamazoo	MI	49008	269-388-3333	388-8322
TF: 800-875-3333 ■ *Web:* www.wwmt.com					
WXMI-TV Ch 17 (Fox) 3117 Plaza Dr NE	Grand Rapids	MI	49525	616-364-8722	364-8506
Web: fox17.trb.com					
WZPX-TV Ch 43 (I) 2610 Horizon Dr SE Suite E	Grand Rapids	MI	49546	616-222-4343	493-2677
TF: 877-729-8843 ■ *Web:* www.wzpxtv.com					
WZZM-TV Ch 13 (ABC) 645 Three-Mile Rd NW	Grand Rapids	MI	49544	616-785-1313	784-8367
Web: www.wzzm13.com					

744-55 Great Falls, MT

Station	City	State	Zip	Phone	Fax
KFBB-TV Ch 5 (ABC) PO Box 1139	Great Falls	MT	59403	406-453-4377	727-9703
TF: 800-854-7720 ■ *Web:* www.kfbb.com					
KRTV-TV Ch 3 (CBS) PO Box 2989	Great Falls	MT	59403	406-453-2433	791-5479
Web: www.krtv.com					
KTGF-TV Ch 16 (NBC) 118 6th St S	Great Falls	MT	59405	406-761-8816	454-3484
TF: 800-926-5401 ■ *Web:* www.ktgf.com					

744-56 Green Bay, WI

Station	City	State	Zip	Phone	Fax
WACY-TV Ch 32 (MNT) 1391 North Rd	Green Bay	WI	54313	920-490-0320	494-7071
TF: 800-800-6619 ■ *Web:* www.mynew32.com					
WBAY-TV Ch 2 (ABC) 115 S Jefferson St	Green Bay	WI	54301	920-432-3331	432-1190
TF: 800-261-9229 ■ *Web:* www.wbay.com					
WFRV-TV Ch 5 (CBS) 1181 E Mason St	Green Bay	WI	54301	920-437-5411	437-4576
Web: www.wfrv.com					
WGBA-TV Ch 26 (NBC) 1391 North Rd	Green Bay	WI	54313	920-494-2626	490-2500
Web: www.wgba.com					
WIWB-TV Ch 14 (CW) 975 Parkview Rd Suite 4	Green Bay	WI	54304	920-983-9014	983-9424
TF: 877-352-1000 ■ *Web:* www.wb14tv.com					
WLUK-TV Ch 11 (Fox) 787 Lombardi Ave	Green Bay	WI	54304	920-494-8711	494-8782
TF: 800-242-8067 ■ *Web:* www.wluk.com					
WPNE-TV Ch 38 (PBS) 821 University Ave	Madison	WI	53706	608-263-2121	263-1952
Web: www.wpt.org					

744-57 Halifax, NS

Station	City	State	Zip	Phone	Fax
CBHT-TV Ch 3 (CBC) 1840 Bell Rd PO Box 3000	Halifax	NS	B3J3E9	902-420-4100	420-4137
Web: www.cbc.ca					
CIHF-TV Ch 8 (GTN) PO Box 1643 CRO	Halifax	NS	B3J2Z1	902-481-7400	481-7427
CJCH-TV Ch 5 (Ind) 2885 Robie St	Halifax	NS	B3J2Z4	902-454-3200	454-3280

744-58 Harrisburg, PA

Station	City	State	Zip	Phone	Fax
WGAL-TV Ch 8 (NBC) 1300 Columbia Ave	Lancaster	PA	17604	717-393-5851	393-9484
Web: www.thewgalchannel.com					
WGCB-TV Ch 49 (Ind) PO Box 88	Red Lion	PA	17356	717-246-1681	244-9316
Web: www.wgcbtv.com					
WHP-TV Ch 21 (CBS) 3300 N 6th St	Harrisburg	PA	17110	717-238-2100	238-4903
Web: www.whptv.com					
WHTM-TV Ch 27 (ABC) 3235 Hoffman St PO Box 5860	Harrisburg	PA	17110	717-236-2727	236-1263
Web: www.whtm.com					
WITF-TV Ch 33 (PBS) 1982 Locust Ln	Harrisburg	PA	17109	717-236-6000	236-4628
TF: 800-366-9483 ■ *Web:* www.witf.org					
WLYH-TV Ch 15 (CW) 3300 N 6th St	Harrisburg	PA	17110	717-238-2100	238-4903
Web: www.cw15.com					
WPMT-TV Ch 43 (Fox) 2005 S Queen St	York	PA	17403	717-843-0043	843-9741
Web: fox43.trb.com					

744-59 Hartford, CT

Station	City	State	Zip	Phone	Fax
WCTX-TV Ch 59 (MNT) 8 Elm St	New Haven	CT	06510	203-782-5900	782-5995
Web: ww2.myupn9.com					
WEDH-TV Ch 24 (PBS) 1049 Asylum Ave	Hartford	CT	06105	860-278-5310	275-7406
Web: www.cptv.org					
WFSB-TV Ch 3 (CBS) 333 Capital Blvd	Rocky Hill	CT	06062	860-244-1740	728-0263
Web: www.wfsb.com					
WHPX-TV Ch 26 (I) Shaws Cove 3 Suite 226	New London	CT	06320	860-444-2626	440-2601
Web: www.paxhartford.tv					

Hartford, CT (Cont'd)

Station / Address	City	State	Zip	Phone	Fax
WTIC-TV Ch 61 (Fox) 1 Corporate Center	Hartford	CT	06103	860-527-6161	293-0178*
**Fax:* News Rm ■ *Web:* fox61.trb.com					
WTNH-TV Ch 8 (ABC) 8 Elm St	New Haven	CT	06510	203-784-8888	789-2010*
**Fax:* Mktg ■ *Web:* www.wtnh.com					
WTXX-TV Ch 20 (CW) 1 Corporate Center	Hartford	CT	06103	860-527-6161	293-0178
Web: cw20.trb.com					
WUVN-TV Ch 18 (Uni) 1 Constitution Plaza 7th Fl	Hartford	CT	06103	860-278-1818	278-1811
Web: www.wuvntv.com					
WVIT-TV Ch 30 (NBC) 1422 New Britain Ave	West Hartford	CT	06110	860-521-3030	521-3110
TF: 800-523-9848 ■ *Web:* www.nbc30.com					

744-60 Helena, MT

Station / Address	City	State	Zip	Phone	Fax
KMTF-TV Ch 10 (CW) 100 W Lyndale Ave Suite B	Helena	MT	59601	406-457-1010	442-5106
KTVH-TV Ch 12 (NBC) 100 W Lyndale Ave	Helena	MT	59601	406-457-1212	442-5106
Web: www.ktvh.com					
KUSM-TV Ch 9 (PBS) Visual Communications Bldg Rm 183	Bozeman	MT	59717	406-994-3437	994-6545
TF: 800-426-8243 ■ *Web:* montanapbs.org					
KWYB-TV Ch 18 (ABC) 505 W Park St	Butte	MT	59701	406-782-7185	723-9269
Web: www.kwyb.com					
KXLF-TV Ch 4 (CBS) 1003 S Montana St	Butte	MT	59701	406-782-0444	782-8906
Web: www.montanasnewsstation.com					

744-61 Honolulu, HI

Station / Address	City	State	Zip	Phone	Fax
KBFD-TV Ch 32 (Ind) 1188 Bishop St Suite PH 1	Honolulu	HI	96813	808-521-8066	521-5233
Web: www.kbfd.com					
KFVE-TV Ch 8 (NBC) 150-B Puuhale Rd	Honolulu	HI	96819	808-847-3246	845-3616
KGMB-TV Ch 9 (CBS) 1534 Kapiolani Blvd	Honolulu	HI	96814	808-973-5462	944-5252
Web: www.kgmb.com/kgmb					
KHET-TV Ch 11 (PBS) 2350 Dole St	Honolulu	HI	96822	808-973-1000	973-1090
Web: www.pbshawaii.org					
KHNL-TV Ch 13 (NBC) 150-B Puuhale Rd	Honolulu	HI	96819	808-847-3246	845-3616
Web: www.khnl.com					
KHON-TV Ch 2 (Fox) 88 Piikoi St	Honolulu	HI	96814	808-591-4278	593-2418
Web: www.khon2.com					
KIKU-TV Ch 20 (Ind) 737 Bishop St Mauka Tower Suite 1430	Honolulu	HI	96813	808-847-2021	841-3326
Web: www.kikutv.com					
KITV-TV Ch 4 (ABC) 801 S King St	Honolulu	HI	96813	808-535-0400	536-8993
Web: www.thehawaiichannel.com					
KPXO-TV Ch 66 (I) 875 Waimanu St Suite 630	Honolulu	HI	96813	808-591-1275	591-1409
KWHE-TV Ch 14 (Ind) 1188 Bishop St Suite 502	Honolulu	HI	96813	808-538-1414	526-0326
TF: 800-218-1414 ■ *Web:* www.kwhe.com					

744-62 Houston, TX

Station / Address	City	State	Zip	Phone	Fax
KETH-TV Ch 14 (TBN) 10902 S Wilcrest Dr	Houston	TX	77009	281-561-5828	561-9793
Web: www.communityedtv.org					
KHOU-TV Ch 11 (CBS) 1945 Allen Pkwy	Houston	TX	77019	713-526-1111	520-7763
Web: www.khou.com					
KHWB-TV Ch 39 (CW) 7700 Westpark Dr	Houston	TX	77063	713-781-3939	787-0528
Web: khwbtv.trb.com					
KNWS-TV Ch 51 (Ind) 8440 Westpark Dr	Houston	TX	77063	713-974-5151	974-5188
Web: knws51.com					
KPRC-TV Ch 2 (NBC) PO Box 2222	Houston	TX	77252	713-222-2222	771-4930
Web: www.click2houston.com					
KPXB-TV Ch 49 (I) 256 N Sam Houston Pkwy E Suite 49	Houston	TX	77060	281-820-4900	820-3016
Web: www.ionline.tv					
KRIV-TV Ch 26 (Fox) 4261 Southwest Fwy	Houston	TX	77027	713-479-2600	479-2859*
**Fax:* News Rm ■ *Web:* www.fox26.com					
KTBU-TV Ch 55 (Ind) 7026 Old Katy Rd Suite 201	Houston	TX	77024	713-864-0455	864-1993
Web: www.thetube.net					
KTMD-TV Ch 47 (Tele) 1235 North Loop W Suite 125	Houston	TX	77008	713-974-4848	266-6397
Web: www.ktmd.com					
KTRK-TV Ch 13 (ABC) 3310 Bissonnet St	Houston	TX	77005	713-666-0713	664-0013
Web: abclocal.go.com/ktrk					
KTXH-TV Ch 20 (MNT) 4261 Southwest Fwy	Houston	TX	77027	713-661-2020	479-2859
Web: www.ktxh.com					
KUHT-TV Ch 8 (PBS) 4343 Elgin St	Houston	TX	77204	713-748-8888	743-8867
TF: 800-364-5848 ■ *Web:* www.houstonpbs.org					
KXLN-TV Ch 45 (Uni) 5100 SW Freeway	Houston	TX	77056	713-965-2600	965-2701

744-63 Huntsville, AL

Station / Address	City	State	Zip	Phone	Fax
WAAY-TV Ch 31 (ABC) 1000 Monte Sano Blvd SE	Huntsville	AL	35801	256-533-3131	533-5191*
**Fax:* News Rm ■ *TF:* 877-799-9229 ■ *Web:* www.waaytv.com					
WAFF-TV Ch 48 (NBC) 1414 Memorial Pkwy N	Huntsville	AL	35801	256-533-4848	534-4101
Web: www.waff.com					
WHDF-TV Ch 15 (CW) 200 Andrew Jackson Way	Huntsville	AL	35801	256-536-1550	536-8286
Web: www.thevalleyscw.tv					
WHNT-TV Ch 19 (CBS) PO Box 19	Huntsville	AL	35804	256-533-1919	536-9468
TF: 800-533-8819 ■ *Web:* www.whnt.com					
WZDX-TV Ch 54 (Fox) 1309 N Memorial Pkwy	Huntsville	AL	35801	256-533-5454	533-5315
Web: www.fox54.com					

744-64 Indianapolis, IN

Station / Address	City	State	Zip	Phone	Fax
WFYI-TV Ch 20 (PBS) 1401 N Meridian St	Indianapolis	IN	46202	317-636-2020	633-7418
Web: www.wfyi.org					
WHMB-TV Ch 40 (Ind) 10511 Greenfield Ave	Noblesville	IN	46060	317-773-5050	776-4051
Web: www.whmbtv.com					
WIPX-TV Ch 63 (I) 1000 N Merdian St	Indianapolis	IN	46204	317-655-5840	655-5848
WISH-TV Ch 8 (CBS) 1950 N Meridian St	Indianapolis	IN	46202	317-923-8888	931-2242
Web: www.wishtv.com					
WNDY-TV Ch 23 (MNT) 1950 N Meridian	Indianapolis	IN	46202	317-956-8888	931-2242
Web: www.wndy.com					
WRTV-TV Ch 6 (ABC) 1330 N Meridian St	Indianapolis	IN	46202	317-635-9788	269-1445*
**Fax:* News Rm ■ *Web:* www.theindychannel.com					
WTHR-TV Ch 13 (NBC) 1000 N Meridian St	Indianapolis	IN	46204	317-636-1313	636-3717
Web: www.wthr.com					
WTIU-TV Ch 30 (PBS) 1229 E 7th St	Bloomington	IN	47405	812-855-5900	855-0729
TF: 800-662-3311 ■ *Web:* www.wtiu.indiana.edu					
WTTV-TV Ch 4 (CW) 6910 Network Pl	Indianapolis	IN	46278	317-632-5900	715-6251*
**Fax:* Hum Res ■ *Web:* thecw4.trb.com					
WXIN-TV Ch 59 (Fox) 6910 Network Pl	Indianapolis	IN	46278	317-632-5900	715-6251
Web: fox59.trb.com					

744-65 Jackson, MS

Station / Address	City	State	Zip	Phone	Fax
WAPT-TV Ch 16 (ABC) 7616 Channel 16 Way	Jackson	MS	39209	601-922-1607	922-1663
Web: www.wapt.com					
WCBI-TV Ch 4 (CBS) 201 5th St S	Columbus	MS	39701	662-327-4444	329-1004
Web: wcbi.com					
WDAM-TV Ch 7 (NBC) PO Box 16269	Hattiesburg	MS	39404	601-544-4730	584-9302
TF: 800-844-9326 ■ *Web:* www.wdam.com					
WHLT-TV Ch 22 (CBS) 5912 Hwy 49 Cloverleaf Mall Suite A	Hattiesburg	MS	39401	601-545-2077	545-3589
Web: www.cbs22thehub.com					
WJTV-TV Ch 12 (CBS) 1820 TV Rd	Jackson	MS	39204	601-372-6311	372-8798
Web: www.wjtv.com					
WLBT-TV Ch 3 (NBC) 715 S Jefferson St	Jackson	MS	39201	601-948-3333	355-7830
Web: www.wlbt.com					
WLOV-TV Ch 27 (Fox) PO Box 350	Tupelo	MS	38802	662-842-7620	844-7061
Web: www.wlov.com					
WMAE-TV Ch 12 (PBS) 3825 Ridgewood Rd	Jackson	MS	39211	601-432-6565	432-6746
TF: 800-922-9698 ■ *Web:* www.mpbonline.org					
WMAH-TV Ch 19 (PBS) 3825 Ridgewood Rd	Jackson	MS	39211	601-432-6565	432-6135
TF: 800-922-9698 ■ *Web:* www.mpbonline.org					
WMPN-TV Ch 29 (PBS) 3825 Ridgewood Rd	Jackson	MS	39211	601-432-6565	432-6135
TF: 866-262-9643 ■ *Web:* www.mpbonline.org					
WRBJ-TV Ch 34 (CW) PO Box 6905	Jackson	MS	39282	601-922-1234	922-0268
WTVA-TV Ch 9 (NBC) PO Box 350	Tupelo	MS	38802	662-842-7620	844-7061
Web: www.wtva.com					
WUFX-TV Ch 35 (Fox) 1 Great Pl	Jackson	MS	39209	601-922-1234	922-0268
Web: www.gomiss.com					

744-66 Jacksonville, FL

Station / Address	City	State	Zip	Phone	Fax
WAWS-TV Ch 30 (Fox) 11700 Central Pkwy	Jacksonville	FL	32224	904-642-3030	642-5665
Web: www.fox30online.com					
WCWJ-TV Ch 17 (CW) 9117 Hogan Rd	Jacksonville	FL	32216	904-641-1700	641-0306
Web: www.wjwb.com					
WJCT-TV Ch 7 (PBS) 100 Festival Park Ave	Jacksonville	FL	32202	904-353-7770	354-6846
Web: www.wjct.org					
WJXT-TV Ch 4 (Ind) 4 Broadcast Pl	Jacksonville	FL	32207	904-399-4000	393-9822*
**Fax:* News Rm ■ *Web:* www.news4jax.com					
WJXX-TV Ch 25 (ABC) 1070 E Adams St	Jacksonville	FL	32202	904-354-1212	633-8899*
**Fax:* News Rm ■ *TF:* 800-352-8812 ■ *Web:* www.firstcoastnews.com					
WPXC-TV Ch 21 (I) 7434 Blythe Island Hwy	Brunswick	GA	31523	912-262-6397	261-9582
Web: www.paxjacksonville.tv					
WTEV-TV Ch 47 (CBS) 11700 Central Pkwy	Jacksonville	FL	32224	904-642-3030	642-5665
Web: www.wtev.com					
WTLV-TV Ch 12 (NBC) 1070 E Adams St	Jacksonville	FL	32202	904-354-1212	633-8899*
**Fax:* News Rm ■ *TF:* 800-352-8812 ■ *Web:* www.firstcoastnews.com					

744-67 Jefferson City, MO

Station / Address	City	State	Zip	Phone	Fax
KMIZ-TV Ch 17 (ABC) 501 Business Loop 70 E	Columbia	MO	65201	573-449-0917	875-7078
TF: 800-441-4485 ■ *Web:* www.kmiz.com					
KMOS-TV Ch 6 (PBS) Central Missouri State University	Warrensburg	MO	64093	660-543-4134	543-8863
TF: 800-753-3436 ■ *Web:* www.kmos.org					
KNLJ-TV Ch 25 (Ind) 9810 SR-AE	New Bloomfield	MO	65063	573-896-5105	896-4376
TF: 800-228-5284 ■ *Web:* www.hereshelpnet.org					
KOMU-TV Ch 8 (NBC) 5550 Hwy 63 S	Columbia	MO	65201	573-884-6397	884-5353
TF: 800-409-0292 ■ *Web:* www.komu.com					
KRCG-TV Ch 13 (CBS) PO Box 659	Jefferson City	MO	65102	573-896-5144	896-5193
Web: www.krcg.com					

744-68 Johnson City, TN

Station / Address	City	State	Zip	Phone	Fax
WAPK-TV Ch 36 (MNT) 222 Commerce St	Kingsport	TN	37660	423-246-9578	246-1863
Web: www.wapktv.com/					
WCYB-TV Ch 5 (NBC) 101 Lee St	Bristol	VA	24201	276-645-1555	645-1554
Web: www.wcyb.tv					
WEMT-TV Ch 39 (Fox) 101 Lee St	Bristol	VA	24201	276-821-9296	645-1510
TF: 800-376-3939 ■ *Web:* www.wemt39.com					
WJHL-TV Ch 11 (CBS) 338 E Main St	Johnson City	TN	37601	423-926-2151	434-4537
TF: 800-606-9545 ■ *Web:* www.wjhl.com					
WKPT-TV Ch 19 (ABC) 222 Commerce St	Kingsport	TN	37660	423-246-9578	246-1863
Web: www.wkpttv.com					

744-69 Juneau, AK

Station / Address	City	State	Zip	Phone	Fax
KATH-TV Ch 5 (NBC) 1107 W 8th St	Juneau	AK	99801	907-586-8384	586-8394
KJUD-TV Ch 8 (ABC) 175 S Franklin St Suite 320	Juneau	AK	99801	907-586-3145	463-3041
Web: www.aksuperstation.com					
KTNL-TV Ch 13 (CBS/I) 520 Lake St	Sitka	AK	99835	907-747-5749	747-8440
Web: www.ktnl.tv					
KTOO-TV Ch 3 (PBS) 360 Egan Dr	Juneau	AK	99801	907-586-1670	586-3612
TF: 800-870-5866 ■ *Web:* www.ktoo.org					

744-70 Kansas City, KS & MO

Station / Address	City	State	Zip	Phone	Fax
KCPT-TV Ch 19 (PBS) 125 E 31st St	Kansas City	MO	64108	816-756-3580	931-2500
Web: www.kcpt.org					
KCTV-TV Ch 5 (CBS) 4500 Shawnee Mission Pkwy	Fairway	KS	66205	913-677-5555	677-7243
Web: www.kctv.com					
KCWE-TV Ch 29 (CW) 1049 Central St	Kansas City	MO	64105	816-221-2900	760-9149*
**Fax:* Sales ■ *Web:* www.thekansascitychannel.com					
KMBC-TV Ch 9 (ABC) 655 Winchester Ave	Kansas City	MO	64133	816-221-9999	421-4163
Web: www.thekansascitychannel.com					
KMCI-TV Ch 38 (Ind) 4720 Oak St	Kansas City	MO	64112	816-753-4141	932-4145
Web: www.kmci.com					

Station	City	State	ZIP	Phone	Fax
KPXE-TV Ch 50 (I) 4720 Oak St	Kansas City	MO	64112	816-924-5050	
TF: 800-646-7296					
KSHB-TV Ch 41 (NBC) 4720 Oak St.	Kansas City	MO	64112	816-753-4141	932-4145
Web: www.kshb.com					
KSMO-TV Ch 62 (MNT) 4500 Shawnee Mission Pkwy	Fairway	KS	66205	913-677-5555	621-4703
Web: www.myksmotv.com/					
WDAF-TV Ch 4 (Fox) 3030 Summit St.	Kansas City	MO	64108	816-753-4567	561-4181
Web: www.wdaftv4.com					

744-71 Knoxville, TN

Station	City	State	ZIP	Phone	Fax
WATE-TV Ch 6 (ABC) 1306 N Broadway NE	Knoxville	TN	37917	865-637-6666	525-4091
Web: www.wate.com					
WBIR-TV Ch 10 (NBC) 1513 Hutchinson Ave.	Knoxville	TN	37917	865-637-1010	637-6380
Web: www.wbir.com					
WBXX-TV Ch 20 (CW) 10427 Cogdill Rd Suite 100	Knoxville	TN	37932	865-777-9220	777-9221
Web: www.wb20tv.com					
WETP-TV Ch 2 (PBS) 1611 E Magnolia Ave	Knoxville	TN	37917	865-595-0220	595-0220
TF: 800-595-0220					
WKOP-TV Ch 15 (PBS) 1611 E Magnolia Ave	Knoxville	TN	37917	865-595-0220	595-0300
TF: 800-595-0220 ■ *Web:* www.etptv.org					
WTNZ-TV Ch 43 (Fox) 9000 Executive Park Dr Bldg D Suite 300	Knoxville	TN	37923	865-693-4343	691-6904
Web: www.wtnzfox43.com					
WVLT-TV Ch 8 (CBS) 6450 Papermill Dr	Knoxville	TN	37919	865-450-8888	450-8869
Web: www.volunteertv.com					

744-72 Lafayette, LA

Station	City	State	ZIP	Phone	Fax
KADN-TV Ch 15 (Fox) 1500 Eraste Landry Rd.	Lafayette	LA	70506	337-237-1500	237-2237
TF: 800-738-6736					
KATC-TV Ch 3 (ABC) 1103 Eraste Landry Rd	Lafayette	LA	70506	337-235-3333	235-9363
Web: www.katc.com					
KLFY-TV Ch 10 (CBS) 1808 Eraste Landry Rd.	Lafayette	LA	70506	337-981-4823	984-8323*
**Fax:* Sales ■ *Web:* www.klfy.com					
KPLC-TV Ch 7 (NBC) PO Box 1490	Lake Charles	LA	70602	337-439-9071	437-7600
Web: www.kplctv.com					

744-73 Lansing, MI

Station	City	State	ZIP	Phone	Fax
WILX-TV Ch 10 (NBC) 500 American Rd	Lansing	MI	48911	517-393-0110	393-8555
TF: 800-968-9180 ■ *Web:* www.wilx.com					
WKAR-TV Ch 23 (PBS) MSU 283 Communications Arts Bldg	East Lansing	MI	48824	517-432-9527	353-7124
Web: wkar.org/tv					
WLAJ-TV Ch 53 (ABC) 5815 S Pennsylvania Ave	Lansing	MI	48911	517-394-5300	887-0077
Web: www.wlaj.com					
WLNS-TV Ch 6 (CBS) 2820 E Saginaw St	Lansing	MI	48912	517-372-8282	374-7610
Web: www.wlns.com					
WSYM-TV Ch 47 (Fox) 600 W Saint Joseph St Suite 47	Lansing	MI	48933	517-484-7747	484-3144
Web: www.fox47news.com					

744-74 Las Vegas, NV

Station	City	State	ZIP	Phone	Fax
KBLR-TV Ch 39 (Tele) 73 Spectrum Blvd	Las Vegas	NV	89101	702-258-0039	259-0580
Web: www.kblr39.com					
KFBT-TV Ch 33 (Ind) 3830 S Jones Blvd	Las Vegas	NV	89103	702-873-0033	382-1351
Web: www.kfbt33.com					
KINC-TV Ch 15 (Uni) 500 Pilot Rd Suite D	Las Vegas	NV	89119	702-434-0015	434-0527
Web: www.entravision.com					
KLAS-TV Ch 8 (CBS) 3228 Channel 8 Dr	Las Vegas	NV	89109	702-792-8888	792-2977*
**Fax:* News Rm ■ *Web:* www.klas-tv.com					
KLVX-TV Ch 10 (PBS) 4210 Channel 10 Dr.	Las Vegas	NV	89119	702-799-1010	799-5586
Web: www.klvx.org					
KTNV-TV Ch 13 (ABC) 3355 S Valley View Blvd	Las Vegas	NV	89102	702-876-1313	876-2237
TF: 800-463-9713 ■ *Web:* www.ktnv.com					
KVBC-TV Ch 3 (NBC) PO Box 44169	Las Vegas	NV	89116	702-642-3333	657-3152
Web: www.kvbc.com					
KVCW-TV Ch 21 (CW) 3830 S Jones Blvd.	Las Vegas	NV	89103	702-382-2121	382-1351
Web: www.wblasvegas.com					
KVVU-TV Ch 5 (Fox) 25 TV 5 Dr	Henderson	NV	89014	702-435-5555	436-2507
Web: www.kvvu.com					

744-75 Lexington, KY

Station	City	State	ZIP	Phone	Fax
WDKY-TV Ch 56 (Fox) 836 Euclid Ave Suite 201	Lexington	KY	40502	859-269-5656	269-3774
Web: www.wdky56.com					
WKLE-TV Ch 46 (PBS) 600 Cooper Dr.	Lexington	KY	40502	859-258-7000	258-7399
TF: 800-432-0951					
WKYT-TV Ch 27 (CBS) 2851 Winchester Rd	Lexington	KY	40509	859-299-0411	293-1578*
**Fax:* News Rm ■ *Web:* www.wkyt.com					
WLEX-TV Ch 18 (NBC) PO Box 1457	Lexington	KY	40588	859-259-1818	254-2217*
**Fax:* News Rm ■ *TF:* 800-255-4566 ■ *Web:* www.wlextv.com					
WTVQ-TV Ch 36 (ABC) 6940 Man O War Blvd	Lexington	KY	40509	859-294-3636	293-5002
Web: www.wtvq.com					

744-76 Lincoln, NE

Station	City	State	ZIP	Phone	Fax
KLKN-TV Ch 8 (ABC) 3240 S 10th St	Lincoln	NE	68502	402-434-8000	436-2236
Web: www.klkntv.com					
KOLN-TV Ch 10 (CBS) PO Box 30350	Lincoln	NE	68503	402-467-4321	467-9210
TF: 800-475-1011 ■ *Web:* www.kolnkgin.com					
KUON-TV Ch 12 (PBS) 1800 N 33rd St	Lincoln	NE	68583	402-472-3611	472-1785
TF: 800-698-3426 ■ *Web:* mynptv.org/nptv					

744-77 Little Rock, AR

Station	City	State	ZIP	Phone	Fax
KARK-TV Ch 4 (NBC) 1401 W Capitol Ave Suite 104	Little Rock	AR	72201	501-340-4444	376-2957
Web: www.kark.com					
KATV-TV Ch 7 (ABC) 401 S Main St	Little Rock	AR	72201	501-372-7777	324-7852
Web: www.katv.com					
KETG-TV Ch 9 (PBS) 350 S Donaghey Ave	Conway	AR	72034	501-682-2386	682-4122
TF: 800-662-2386 ■ *Web:* www.aetn.org					
KETS-TV Ch 2 (PBS) 350 S Donaghey Ave	Conway	AR	72032	501-682-2386	682-4122
TF: 800-662-2386 ■ *Web:* www.aetn.org					
KLRT-TV Ch 16 (Fox) 10800 Colonel Glenn Rd	Little Rock	AR	72204	501-225-0016	225-0428
Web: www.klrt.com					
KTHV-TV Ch 11 (CBS) PO Box 269	Little Rock	AR	72203	501-376-1111	376-1645
Web: www.todaysthv.com					
KWBF-TV Ch 42 (MNT) 1 Shackleford Dr Suite 400	Little Rock	AR	72211	501-219-2400	604-8000
Web: www.wb42.com					

744-78 Los Angeles, CA

Station	City	State	ZIP	Phone	Fax
KABC-TV Ch 7 (ABC) 500 Circle Seven Dr.	Glendale	CA	91201	818-863-7777	863-7080
Web: abclocal.go.com/kabc					
KBEH-TV Ch 63 (Ind) 950 Flynn Rd	Camarillo	CA	93012	805-388-0081	383-1063
Web: www.canal63.com					
KCAL-TV Ch 9 (Ind) 6121 Sunset Blvd	Los Angeles	CA	90028	323-460-3000	460-3767
Web: www.kcal9.com					
KCBS-TV Ch 2 (CBS) 6121 Sunset Blvd.	Los Angeles	CA	90028	323-460-3000	460-3733
Web: www.cbs2.com					
KCET-TV Ch 28 (PBS) 4401 Sunset Blvd	Los Angeles	CA	90027	323-666-6500	953-5523
Web: www.kcet.org					
KCOP-TV Ch 13 (MNT) 1999 S Bundy Dr	Los Angeles	CA	90025	310-584-2000	584-2024
Web: www.upn13.com					
KDOC-TV Ch 56 (Ind) 18021 Cowan	Irvine	CA	92614	949-442-9800	261-5956
Web: www.kdoctv.net					
KESQ-TV Ch 3 (ABC) 42650 Melanie Pl	Palm Desert	CA	92211	760-568-6830	773-5107
TF: 877-564-9729 ■ *Web:* www.kesq.com					
KHIZ-TV Ch 64 (Ind) 15605 Village Dr	Victorville	CA	92394	760-241-6464	241-0056
Web: www.khiztv.com					
KJLA-TV Ch 57 (Ind) 2323 Corinth Ave	Los Angeles	CA	90064	310-943-5288	943-5299
TF: 800-588-5788 ■ *Web:* www.kjla.com					
KLCS-TV Ch 58 (PBS) 1061 W Temple St	Los Angeles	CA	90012	213-241-4000	481-1019
Web: www.klcs.org					
KMEX-TV Ch 34 (Uni) 5999 Center Dr.	Los Angeles	CA	90045	310-216-3434	348-3493*
**Fax:* News Rm ■ *Web:* www.kmex.com					
KMIR-TV Ch 6 (NBC) 72920 Parkview Dr	Palm Desert	CA	92260	760-568-3636	568-1176
Web: www.kmir6.com					
KNBC-TV Ch 4 (NBC) 3000 W Alameda Ave	Burbank	CA	91523	818-840-4444	840-3535
Web: www.nbc4.tv					
KPXN-TV Ch 30 (I) 10880 Wilshire Blvd Suite 1200	Los Angeles	CA	90024	310-234-2215	474-7095
KRCA-TV Ch 62 (Ind) 1845 Empire Ave.	Burbank	CA	91504	818-563-5722	972-2694
Web: www.krca62.tv					
KSCI-TV Ch 18 (Ind) 1990 S Bundy Dr Suite 850	Los Angeles	CA	90025	310-478-1818	442-2388
TF: 800-841-1818 ■ *Web:* www.kscitv.com					
KTBN-TV Ch 40 (TBN) 2442 Michelle Dr	Tustin	CA	92780	714-832-2950	665-2191
TF: 888-731-1000 ■ *Web:* www.tbn.org					
KTLA-TV Ch 5 (CW) 5800 Sunset Blvd	Los Angeles	CA	90028	323-460-5500	460-5333
Web: ktla.trb.com					
KTTV-TV Ch 11 (Fox) 1999 S Bundy Dr	Los Angeles	CA	90025	310-584-2000	584-2024
Web: www.fox11la.com					
KVEA-TV Ch 52 (Tele) 3000 W Alameda Ave	Burbank	CA	91523	818-260-5700	260-5730
Web: www.telemundola.com					

744-79 Louisville, KY

Station	City	State	ZIP	Phone	Fax
WAVE-TV Ch 3 (NBC) 725 S Floyd St	Louisville	KY	40203	502-585-2201	561-4105
Web: www.wave3.com					
WBKI-TV Ch 34 (CW) 1601 Alliant Ave	Louisville	KY	40299	502-809-3400	266-6262
TF: 877-541-3434 ■ *Web:* www.wbki.tv					
WBNA-TV Ch 21 (I) 3701 Fern Valley Rd.	Louisville	KY	40219	502-964-2121	966-9692
Web: www.wbna-21.com					
WDRB-TV Ch 41 (Fox) 624 W Muhammad Ali Blvd	Louisville	KY	40203	502-584-6441	589-5559
Web: www.fox41.com					
WHAS-TV Ch 11 (ABC) PO Box 1100.	Louisville	KY	40201	502-582-7840	582-7279
Web: www.whas11.com					
WKMJ-TV Ch 68 (PBS) 600 Cooper Dr	Lexington	KY	40502	859-258-7000	258-7399
TF: 800-432-0951 ■ *Web:* www.ket.org					
WKPC-TV Ch 15 (PBS) 600 Cooper Dr	Lexington	KY	40502	859-258-7000	258-7399
TF: 800-432-0951 ■ *Web:* www.ket.org					
WLKY-TV Ch 32 (CBS) 1918 Mellwood Ave.	Louisville	KY	40206	502-893-3671	896-0725
Web: www.thelouisvillechannel.com					

744-80 Lubbock, TX

Station	City	State	ZIP	Phone	Fax
KAMC-TV Ch 28 (ABC) 7403 S University Ave	Lubbock	TX	79423	806-745-2828	748-2212
Web: www.kamc28.tv					
KCBD-TV Ch 11 (NBC) 5600 Ave A	Lubbock	TX	79404	806-744-1414	749-1111
Web: www.kcbd.com					
KJTV-TV Ch 34 (Fox) 9800 University Ave	Lubbock	TX	79423	806-745-3434	748-1949
Web: www.foxkjtv34.com					
KLBK-TV Ch 13 (CBS) 7403 S University Ave	Lubbock	TX	79423	806-745-2345	748-2250
Web: www.klbk.com					
KTXT-TV Ch 5 (PBS) Texas Tech Univ Box 42161	Lubbock	TX	79409	806-742-2209	742-1274
Web: www.ktxt.org					
KUPT-TV Ch 22 (CW) 9800 University Ave	Lubbock	TX	79423	806-745-3434	748-1949

744-81 Macon, GA

Station	City	State	ZIP	Phone	Fax
WGNM-TV Ch 64 (Ind) 178 Steven Dr	Macon	GA	31210	478-474-8400	474-4777
Web: www.wgnm.com					
WGXA-TV Ch 24 (Fox) 599 ML King Jr Blvd	Macon	GA	31201	478-745-2424	750-4347
TF: 800-592-4240 ■ *Web:* www.fox24.com					
WMAZ-TV Ch 13 (CBS) 1314 Gray Hwy.	Macon	GA	31211	478-752-1313	752-1331
Web: www.13wmaz.com					
WMGT-TV Ch 41 (NBC) 301 Poplar St.	Macon	GA	31201	478-745-4141	742-2626
TF: 866-901-6397 ■ *Web:* www.wmgt.com					
WPGA-TV Ch 58 (ABC) 1691 Forsyth St	Macon	GA	31201	478-745-5858	745-5800
TF: 800-225-5222 ■ *Web:* www.58abc.com					

744-82 Madison, WI

Station	City	State	ZIP	Phone	Fax
WBUW-TV Ch 57 (CW) 2814 Syene Rd	Madison	WI	53713	608-270-5700	270-5717
Web: www.wb57.com					

Madison, WI (Cont'd)

Station	City	State	ZIP	Phone	Fax
WHA-TV Ch 21 (PBS) 821 University Ave	Madison	WI	53706	608-263-2121	263-1952
Web: www.wpt.org					
WISC-TV Ch 3 (CBS) PO Box 44965	Madison	WI	53744	608-271-4321	271-0800
Web: www.channel3000.com					
WKOW-TV Ch 27 (ABC) 5727 Tokay Blvd	Madison	WI	53719	608-274-1234	274-9514
Web: www.wkowtv.com					
WMSN-TV Ch 47 (Fox) 7847 Big Sky Dr	Madison	WI	53719	608-833-0047	274-9569
Web: www.fox47.com					
WMTV-Ch 15 (NBC) 615 Forward Dr	Madison	WI	53711	608-274-1515	271-5194
TF: 800-894-4222 ■ *Web:* nbc15.madison.com					

744-83 Memphis, TN

Station	City	State	ZIP	Phone	Fax
WBUY-TV Ch 40 (TBN) 3447 Cazassa St	Memphis	TN	38116	901-396-9541	396-9585
WHBQ-TV Ch 13 (Fox) 485 S Highland St	Memphis	TN	38111	901-320-1313	320-1366
Web: www.foxmemphis.com					
WKNO-TV Ch 10 (PBS) 900 Getwell Rd	Memphis	TN	38111	901-458-2521	325-6505
Web: www.wkno.org					
WLMT-TV Ch 30 (CW) 2701 Union Ave Ext	Memphis	TN	38112	901-323-2430	452-1820
Web: www.upn30memphis.com					
WMC-TV Ch 5 (NBC) 1960 Union Ave	Memphis	TN	38104	901-726-0555	278-7633
Web: www.wmctv.com					
WPTY-TV Ch 24 (ABC) 2701 Union Ave Ext	Memphis	TN	38112	901-323-2430	452-1820
Web: www.abc24.com					
WREG-TV Ch 3 (CBS) 803 Channel Three Dr	Memphis	TN	38103	901-543-2333	543-2167
Web: www.wreg.com					

744-84 Miami/Fort Lauderdale, FL

Station	City	State	ZIP	Phone	Fax
WBFS-TV Ch 33 (MNT) 8900 NW 18th Terr	Miami	FL	33172	305-621-3333	628-3448
Web: upn33.com					
WBZL-TV Ch 39 (CW) 2055 Lee St	Hollywood	FL	33020	954-925-3939	922-3965
Web: cwsfl.trb.com					
WEYS-TV Ch 22 (CBS) 525 Southard St	Key West	FL	33040	305-296-4969	296-1669
WFOR-TV Ch 4 (CBS) 8900 NW 18th Terr	Miami	FL	33172	305-591-4444	477-3040
Web: www.wfor.com					
WHFT-TV Ch 45 (TBN) 3324 Pembroke Rd	Pembroke Park	FL	33021	954-962-1700	962-2817
TF: 888-731-1000					
WLRN-TV Ch 17 (PBS) 172 NE 15th St	Miami	FL	33132	305-995-1717	995-2299
Web: www.wlrn.org					
WLTV-TV Ch 23 (Uni) 9405 NW 41st St	Miami	FL	33178	305-470-2323	471-4236
WPBT-TV Ch 2 (PBS) 14901 NE 20th Ave	Miami	FL	33181	305-949-8321	949-9772*
**Fax:* News Rm ■ *TF:* 800-222-9728 ■ *Web:* www.channel2.org					
WPLG-TV Ch 10 (ABC) 3900 Biscayne Blvd	Miami	FL	33137	305-576-1010	325-2480*
**Fax:* News Rm ■ *Web:* www.local10.com					
WPXM-TV Ch 35 (I) 15000 SW 27th St	Miramar	FL	33027	954-622-6835	622-6843
WSCV-TV Ch 51 (NBC) 15000 SW 27th St	Miramar	FL	33027	954-622-6000	622-7700
Web: www.telemundo51.com					
WSVN-TV Ch 7 (Fox) 1401 79th St Cswy	Miami	FL	33141	305-751-6692	757-2266
Web: www.wsvn.com					
WTVJ-TV Ch 6 (NBC) 15000 SW 27th St	Miramar	FL	33027	954-622-6000	622-6107
Web: www.nbc6.net					

744-85 Milwaukee, WI

Station	City	State	ZIP	Phone	Fax
WCGV-TV Ch 24 (MNT) 4041 N 35th St	Milwaukee	WI	53216	414-874-1824	874-1899
Web: www.upn24.net					
WDJT-TV Ch 58 (CBS) 809 S 60th St	Milwaukee	WI	53214	414-777-5800	777-5802
Web: www.cbs58.com					
WISN-TV Ch 12 (ABC) PO Box 402	Milwaukee	WI	53201	414-342-8812	342-7505
Web: www.themilwaukeechannel.com					
WITI-TV Ch 6 (Fox) 9001 N Green Bay Rd	Milwaukee	WI	53209	414-355-6666	586-2141*
**Fax:* News Rm ■ *Web:* www.fox6milwaukee.com					
WJJA-TV Ch 49 (Ind) 4311 E Oakwood Rd	Oak Creek	WI	53154	414-764-4953	764-5190
WMVS-TV Ch 10 (PBS) 1036 N 8th St	Milwaukee	WI	53233	414-271-1036	297-7536
Web: www.mptv.org					
WMVT-TV Ch 36 (PBS) 1036 N 8th St	Milwaukee	WI	53233	414-271-1036	297-7536
Web: www.mptv.org					
WPXE-TV Ch 55 (I) 6161 N Flint Rd Suite F	Milwaukee	WI	53209	414-247-0117	247-1302
Web: www.ionmedia.tv					
WTMJ-TV Ch 4 (NBC) 720 E Capitol Dr	Milwaukee	WI	53212	414-332-9611	967-5378
Web: www.touchtmj4.com					
WVCY-TV Ch 30 (Ind) 3434 W Kilbourn Ave	Milwaukee	WI	53208	414-935-3000	935-3015
TF: 800-729-9829 ■ *Web:* www.vcyamerica.org					
WVTV-TV Ch 18 (CW) 4041 N 35th St	Milwaukee	WI	53216	414-874-1824	874-1899
Web: www.wvtv18.com/milwaukee_wi/					

744-86 Minneapolis/Saint Paul, MN

Station	City	State	ZIP	Phone	Fax
KARE-TV Ch 11 (NBC) 8811 Olson Memorial Hwy	Golden Valley	MN	55427	763-546-1111	546-8606
Web: www.kare11.com					
KMSP-TV Ch 9 (Fox) 11358 Viking Dr	Eden Prairie	MN	55344	952-944-9999	942-0455
Web: www.kmsp.com					
KPXM-TV Ch 41 (I) 22601 176th St	Big Lake	MN	55309	763-263-8666	
TF: 800-646-7246 ■ *Web:* www.ionline.tv					
KSTP-TV Ch 5 (ABC) 3415 University Ave W	Saint Paul	MN	55114	651-646-5555	642-4409
Web: www.kstp.com					
KTCA-TV Ch 2 (PBS) 172 E 4th St	Saint Paul	MN	55101	651-222-1717	229-1282
Web: www.ktca.org					
KTCI-TV Ch 17 (PBS) 172 E 4th St	Saint Paul	MN	55101	651-222-1717	229-1282
Web: www.tpt.org					
WCCO-TV Ch 4 (CBS) 90 S 11th St	Minneapolis	MN	55403	612-339-4444	330-2767
TF: 800-444-9226 ■ *Web:* www.wcco.com					
WFTC-TV Ch 29 (MNT) 11358 Viking Dr	Eden Prairie	MN	55344	952-944-9999	942-0455
Web: www.upn29.com					
WUCW-TV Ch 23 (CW) 1640 Como Ave	Saint Paul	MN	55108	651-646-2300	646-1220
Web: www.kmwb23.com					

744-87 Mobile, AL

Station	City	State	ZIP	Phone	Fax
WALA-TV Ch 10 (Fox) 1501 Satchel Paige Dr	Mobile	AL	36606	251-434-1010	434-1073
Web: www.fox10tv.com					
WBPG-TV Ch 55 (CW) 1501 Satchel Paige Dr	Mobile	AL	36606	251-434-1010	434-1073
WEAR-TV Ch 3 (ABC) 4990 Mobile Hwy	Pensacola	FL	32506	850-456-3333	455-8972
TF: 866-856-9327 ■ *Web:* www.weartv.com					
WJTC-TV Ch 44 (Ind) 661 Azalea Rd	Mobile	AL	36609	251-602-1544	602-1547
Web: www.wjtc.com					
WKRG-TV Ch 5 (CBS) 555 Broadcast Dr	Mobile	AL	36606	251-479-5555	473-8130
Web: www.wkrg.com					
WLOX-TV Ch 13 (ABC) 208 Debuys Rd	Biloxi	MS	39531	228-896-1313	896-2596*
**Fax:* News Rm ■ *Web:* www.wlox.com					
WMPV-TV Ch 21 (TBN) 1668 W I-65 Service Rd S	Mobile	AL	33693	251-661-2101	661-7121
Web: www.tbn.org					
WPMI-TV Ch 15 (NBC) 661 Azalea Rd	Mobile	AL	36609	251-602-1500	602-1550
Web: www.wpmi.com					
WSRE-TV Ch 23 (PBS) 1000 College Blvd	Pensacola	FL	32504	850-484-1200	484-1255
Web: www.wsre.org					
WXXV-TV Ch 25 (Fox) 14351 Hwy 49 N	Gulfport	MS	39503	228-832-2525	832-4442
Web: www.wxxv25.com					

744-88 Monterey, CA

Station	City	State	ZIP	Phone	Fax
KCAH-TV Ch 25 (PBS) 1585 Schallenberger Rd	San Jose	CA	95131	408-795-5400	995-5446
Web: www.kteh.org					
KCBA-TV Ch 35 (Fox) 1550 Moffett St	Salinas	CA	93905	831-422-3500	422-9365
TF: 800-321-5222 ■ *Web:* www.kcba.com					
KION-TV Ch 46 (CBS) 1550 Moffett St	Salinas	CA	93905	831-422-3500	422-9365
TF: 800-321-5222 ■ *Web:* www.kion46.com					
KSBW-TV Ch 8 (NBC) 238 John St	Salinas	CA	93901	831-758-8888	424-3750
Web: www.theksbwchannel.com					
KSMS-TV Ch 67 (Uni) 67 Garden Ct	Monterey	CA	93940	831-373-6767	373-6700

744-89 Montgomery, AL

Station	City	State	ZIP	Phone	Fax
WAIQ-TV Ch 26 (PBS) 1255 Madison Ave	Montgomery	AL	36107	334-264-9900	264-7045
TF: 800-239-5239 ■ *Web:* www.aptv.org					
WAKA-TV Ch 8 (CBS) 3020 Eastern Blvd	Montgomery	AL	36116	334-271-8888	244-7859
TF: 800-467-0401 ■ *Web:* www.waka.com					
WCOV-TV Ch 20 (Fox) PO Box 250045	Montgomery	AL	36111	334-288-7020	288-5414
Web: www.wcov.com					
WNCF-TV Ch 32 (ABC) 3251 Harrison Rd	Montgomery	AL	36109	334-270-3200	271-2972
Web: www.abc32.com					
WSFA-TV Ch 12 (NBC) 12 E Delano Ave	Montgomery	AL	36105	334-288-1212	613-8303*
**Fax:* News Rm ■ *Web:* www.wsfa.com					

744-90 Montpelier/Burlington, VT

Station	City	State	ZIP	Phone	Fax
WCAX-TV Ch 3 (CBS) 30 Joy Dr	South Burlington	VT	05403	802-658-6300	652-6399
Web: www.wcax.com					
WETK-TV Ch 33 (PBS) 204 Ethan Allen Ave	Colchester	VT	05446	802-655-4800	655-6593
TF: 800-639-7811 ■ *Web:* www.vpt.org					
WFFF-TV Ch 44 (Fox) 298 Mountain View Dr	Colchester	VT	05446	802-660-9333	660-8673
TF: 888-400-4855 ■ *Web:* www.fox44.net					
WNNE-TV Ch 31 (NBC) PO Box 1310	White River Junction	VT	05001	802-295-3100	295-9056*
**Fax:* News Rm ■ *Web:* www.thechamplainchannel.com/wnne					
WPTZ-TV Ch 5 (NBC) 5 Television Dr	Plattsburgh	NY	12901	518-561-5555	561-5940
Web: www.thechamplainchannel.com					
WVNY-TV Ch 22 (ABC) 298 Mountain View Dr	Colchester	VT	05446	802-658-8022	863-2422
Web: www.abc22.com					

744-91 Montreal, QC

Station	City	State	ZIP	Phone	Fax
CBFT-TV Ch 2 (SRC) 1400 Rene-Levesque Blvd E	Montreal	QC	H2L2M2	514-597-6000	597-5404
CBMT-TV Ch 6 (CBC) 1400 Rene-Levesque Blvd E	Montreal	QC	H2L2M2	514-597-6000	597-6354
Web: www.cbc.ca/montreal					
CBVE-TV Ch 5 (CBC) 1400 Rene-Levesque Blvd E	Montreal	QC	H2L2M2	514-597-6000	597-6354
CFCF-TV Ch 12 (CTV) 1205 Papineau Ave	Montreal	QC	H2K4R2	514-273-6311	276-9399
Web: www.cfcf12.ca					
CFJP-TV Ch 35 (QS) 612 Saint Jacques St Suite 100	Montreal	QC	H3C5R1	514-390-6035	390-0773
CFTM-TV Ch 10 (TVA) 1600 de Maisonneuve Blvd E	Montreal	QC	H2L4P2	514-526-9251	598-6073
CFTU-TV Ch 29 (Ind) 4750 Henri-Julien Ave Bureau 100	Montreal	QC	H2T3E4	514-841-2626	284-9363
Web: www.canal.qc.ca					
CIVM-TV Ch 17 (Ind) 1000 Fullum St	Montreal	QC	H2K3L7	514-521-2424	873-7464
Web: www.telequebec.qc.ca					

744-92 Myrtle Beach, SC

Station	City	State	ZIP	Phone	Fax
WBTW-TV Ch 13 (CBS) 101 McDonald Ct	Myrtle Beach	SC	29588	843-293-1301	293-7701
Web: www.wbtw.com					
WECT-TV Ch 6 (NBC) 322 Shipyard Blvd	Wilmington	NC	28412	910-791-8070	791-9535
Web: www.wect.com					
WFXB-TV Ch 43 (Fox) 3364 Huger St	Myrtle Beach	SC	29577	843-828-4300	828-4343
Web: www.wfxb.com					
WPDE-TV Ch 15 (ABC) 1194 Atlantic Ave	Conway	SC	29526	843-234-9733	234-9739
TF: 800-698-9733 ■ *Web:* www.wpdetv15.com					
WWMB-TV Ch 21 (CW) 1194 Atlantic Ave	Conway	SC	29526	843-234-9733	234-9739
TF: 800-698-9733					

744-93 Naples/Fort Myers, FL

Station	City	State	ZIP	Phone	Fax
WBBH-TV Ch 20 (NBC) 3719 Central Ave PO Box 7578	Fort Myers	FL	33901	239-939-2020	936-7771
Web: www.nbc-2.com					
WFTX-TV Ch 36 (Fox) 621 SW Pine Island Rd	Cape Coral	FL	33991	239-574-3636	574-2025
Web: www.fox4florida.com					
WGCU-TV Ch 30 (PBS) 10501 FGCU Blvd	Fort Myers	FL	33965	239-590-2300	590-2310
TF: 888-824-0030 ■ *Web:* www.wgcu.org					
WINK-TV Ch 11 (CBS) 2824 Palm Beach Blvd	Fort Myers	FL	33916	239-334-1111	332-0767
Web: www.winktv.com					
WTVK-TV Ch 46 (CW) 2824 Palm Beach Blvd	Fort Myers	FL	33916	239-334-1111	498-0146
WZVN-TV Ch 26 (ABC) 3719 Central Ave PO Box 7578	Fort Myers	FL	33901	239-939-2020	936-7771
TF: 800-741-8820 ■ *Web:* www.wzvn.com					

744-94 Nashville, TN

Station	City	State	ZIP	Phone	Fax
WKRN-TV Ch 2 (ABC) 441 Murfreesboro Rd *TF:* 800-242-9576 ■ *Web:* www.wkrn.com	Nashville	TN	37210	615-369-7222	369-7329
WNAB-TV Ch 58 (CW) 631 Mainstream Dr PO Box 17 *Web:* www.cw58.tv	Nashville	TN	37228	615-259-5617	259-3962
WNPT-TV Ch 8 (PBS) 161 Rains Ave *Web:* www.wnpt.net	Nashville	TN	37203	615-259-9325	248-6120
WNPX-TV Ch 28 (I) 1281 N Mt Juliet Rd Suite L	Mount Juliet	TN	37122	615-773-6100	758-4105
WSMV-TV Ch 4 (NBC) 5700 Knob Rd *Web:* www.wsmv.com	Nashville	TN	37209	615-353-4444	353-2343
WTVF-TV Ch 5 (CBS) 474 James Robertson Pkwy **Fax:* News Rm ■ *Web:* www.newschannel5.com	Nashville	TN	37219	615-244-5000	244-9883*
WUXP-TV Ch 30 (MNT) 631 Mainstream Dr PO Box 17 *Web:* www.wuxp.com	Nashville	TN	37228	615-259-5630	259-3962
WZTV-TV Ch 17 (Fox) 631 Mainstream Dr PO Box 17 *Web:* www.fox17.com	Nashville	TN	37228	615-244-1717	259-3962

744-95 New Orleans, LA

Station	City	State	ZIP	Phone	Fax
WDSU-TV Ch 6 (NBC) 846 Howard Ave *Web:* www.wdsu.com	New Orleans	LA	70113	504-679-0600	679-0733
WGNO-TV Ch 26 (ABC) 365 Canal St Suite B-100 *Web:* abc26.trb.com	New Orleans	LA	70130	504-525-3838	619-6332
WHNO-TV Ch 20 (Ind) 839 St Charles Ave *Web:* www.whno.com	New Orleans	LA	70130	504-681-0120	681-0180
WLAE-TV Ch 32 (PBS) 3330 N Causeway Blvd *Web:* www.pbs.org/wlae	Metairie	LA	70002	504-866-7411	840-9838
WNOL-TV Ch 38 (CW) 365 Canal St *Web:* neworleanscw38.trb.com	Covington	LA	70433	504-525-3838	569-0908
WPXL-TV Ch 49 (I) 3900 Veterans Blvd Suite 202	Metairie	LA	70002	504-887-9795	887-1518
WUPL-TV Ch 54 (MNT) 1024 N Rampart St *Web:* wupltv.com	New Orleans	LA	70116	504-529-4444	529-6472
WVUE-TV Ch 8 (Fox) 1025 S Jefferson Davis Pkwy *Web:* www.fox8live.com	New Orleans	LA	70125	504-486-6161	483-1543
WWL-TV Ch 4 (CBS) 1024 N Rampart St *Web:* www.wwltv.com	New Orleans	LA	70116	504-529-4444	529-6472
WYES-TV Ch 12 (PBS) 708-B Phosphor Ave *Web:* www.wyes.org	Metairie	LA	70005	504-486-5511	483-8408

744-96 New York, NY

Station	City	State	ZIP	Phone	Fax
WABC-TV Ch 7 (ABC) 7 Lincoln Sq **Fax:* News Rm ■ *Web:* abclocal.go.com/wabc	New York	NY	10023	212-456-1000	456-2381*
WCBS-TV Ch 2 (CBS) 524 W 57th St *Web:* www.cbs2ny.com	New York	NY	10019	212-975-4321	975-9387
WLIW-TV Ch 21 (PBS) 1 Channel 21 Dr PO Box 21 *Web:* www.wliw.org	Plainview	NY	11803	516-367-2100	349-0760
WLNY-TV Ch 55 (Ind) 270 S Service Rd Suite 55 *Web:* www.wlnytv.com	Melville	NY	11747	631-777-8855	420-4822
WNBC-TV Ch 4 (NBC) 30 Rockefeller Plaza *Web:* www.wnbc.com	New York	NY	10112	212-664-4444	664-2994
WNET-TV Ch 13 (PBS) 450 W 33rd St *Web:* www.thirteen.org	New York	NY	10001	212-560-1313	560-1314
WNJU-TV Ch 47 (Tele) 2200 Fletcher Ave 6th Fl *Web:* www.telemundo47.com	Fort Lee	NJ	07024	201-969-4247	969-4111
WNYE-TV Ch 25 (PBS) 112 Tillary St *Web:* www.wnye.org	Brooklyn	NY	11201	718-250-5800	
WNYW-TV Ch 5 (Fox) 205 E 67th St *Web:* www.myfoxny.com	New York	NY	10065	212-452-5555	249-1182
WPIX-TV Ch 11 (CW) 220 E 42nd St **Fax:* News Rm ■ *Web:* cw11.trb.com	New York	NY	10017	212-949-1100	210-2591*
WPXN-TV Ch 31 (I) 1330 Ave of the Americas 32nd Fl *TF:* 800-646-7296	New York	NY	10019	212-757-3100	956-0920
WRNN-TV Ch 62 (Ind) 437 5th Ave 11th Fl *TF:* 800-824-3302 ■ *Web:* www.rnntv.com	New York	NY	10016	212-725-2666	481-2802
WTBY-TV Ch 54 (TBN) 11 Merritt Blvd *Web:* www.tbn.org	Fishkill	NY	12524	845-896-4610	896-4614
WWOR-TV Ch 9 (MNT) 9 Broadcast Plaza *Web:* www.upn9.com	Secaucus	NJ	07096	201-348-0009	330-3777
WXTV-TV Ch 41 (Uni) 500 Frank W Burr Blvd 6th Fl	Teaneck	NJ	07666	201-287-4141	287-9427

744-97 Norfolk/Virginia Beach, VA

Station	City	State	ZIP	Phone	Fax
WAVY-TV Ch 10 (NBC) 300 Wavy St *Web:* www.wavy.com	Portsmouth	VA	23704	757-393-1010	397-8279
WGNT-TV Ch 27 (CW) 1318 Spratley St *Web:* cw27.com	Portsmouth	VA	23704	757-393-2501	399-3303
WHRO-TV Ch 15 (PBS) 5200 Hampton Blvd *Web:* www.whro.org	Norfolk	VA	23508	757-889-9400	489-0007
WPXV-TV Ch 49 (I) 230 Clearfield Ave Suite 104	Virginia Beach	VA	23462	757-499-1261	499-1679
WSKY-TV Ch 4 (Ind) 1417 N Battlefield Blvd Suite 160 *TF:* 800-414-0911 ■ *Web:* www.wsky4.com	Chesapeake	VA	23320	757-382-0004	382-0365
WTKR-TV Ch 3 (CBS) 720 Boush St *TF:* 800-375-0901 ■ *Web:* www.wtkr.com	Norfolk	VA	23510	757-446-1000	446-1376
WTVZ-TV Ch 33 (MNT) 900 Granby St *Web:* www.wtvz33.com	Norfolk	VA	23510	757-622-3333	623-1541
WVBT-TV Ch 43 (Fox) 243 Wythe St *Web:* www.wvbt.com	Portsmouth	VA	23704	757-393-4343	397-8279
WVEC-TV Ch 13 (ABC) 613 Woodis Ave *Web:* www.wvec.com	Norfolk	VA	23510	757-625-1313	628-5855

744-98 Oklahoma City, OK

Station	City	State	ZIP	Phone	Fax
KAUT-TV Ch 43 (MNT) 11901 N Eastern Ave *Web:* www.ok43.com	Oklahoma City	OK	73131	405-478-4300	516-4343
KETA-TV Ch 13 (PBS) PO Box 14190 *Web:* www.oeta.onenet.net	Oklahoma City	OK	73113	405-848-8501	841-9216
KFOR-TV Ch 4 (NBC) 444 E Britton Rd *Web:* www.kfor.com	Oklahoma City	OK	73114	405-478-1212	478-6337
KOCB-TV Ch 34 (CW) 1228 E Wilshire Blvd *Web:* www.kocb.com	Oklahoma City	OK	73111	405-843-2525	475-9120
KOCO-TV Ch 5 (ABC) 1300 E Britton Rd *Web:* www.channeloklahoma.com	Oklahoma City	OK	73131	405-478-3000	478-6675
KOKH-TV Ch 25 (Fox) 1228 E Wilshire Blvd *Web:* www.kokh25.com/oklahoma_ok/	Oklahoma City	OK	73111	405-843-2525	478-4343
KOPX-TV Ch 62 (I) 13424 Railway Dr *Web:* www.ionline.tv	Oklahoma City	OK	73114	405-478-9562	751-6867
KSBI-TV Ch 52 (Ind) 1350 SE 82nd St *Web:* www.ksbitv.com	Oklahoma City	OK	73149	405-631-7335	631-7367
KWTV-TV Ch 9 (CBS) 7401 N Kelley Ave **Fax:* News Rm ■ *Web:* www.newsok.com	Oklahoma City	OK	73111	405-843-6641	841-9989*

744-99 Omaha, NE

Station	City	State	ZIP	Phone	Fax
KETV-TV Ch 7 (ABC) 2665 Douglas St *TF:* 800-279-5388 ■ *Web:* www.ketv.com	Omaha	NE	68131	402-345-7777	522-7740
KMTV-TV Ch 3 (CBS) 10714 Mockingbird Dr *Web:* www.km3news.com	Omaha	NE	68127	402-592-3333	592-4714
KPTM-TV Ch 42 (Fox) 4625 Farnam St *Web:* www.kptm.com	Omaha	NE	68132	402-558-4200	554-4290
KXVO-TV Ch 15 (CW) 4625 Farnam St *Web:* www.kxvo.com	Omaha	NE	68132	402-554-1500	554-4290
KYNE-TV Ch 26 (PBS) 6001 Dodge St	Omaha	NE	68182	402-472-3611	554-2440
WOWT-TV Ch 6 (NBC) 3501 Farnam St *TF:* 800-688-2431 ■ *Web:* www.wowt.com	Omaha	NE	68131	402-346-6666	233-7880

744-100 Orlando, FL

Station	City	State	ZIP	Phone	Fax
WCEU-TV Ch 15 (PBS) 1200 W International Speedway Blvd Bldg 400 *TF:* 800-638-9238 ■ *Web:* www.wceu.org	Daytona Beach	FL	32114	386-506-4415	506-4427
WESH-TV Ch 2 (NBC) 1021 N Wymore Rd *Web:* www.wesh.com/	Winter Park	FL	32789	407-645-2222	539-7948
WFTV-TV Ch 9 (ABC) 490 E South St *Web:* www.wftv.com	Orlando	FL	32801	407-841-9000	481-2891
WKCF-TV Ch 18 (CW) 31 Skyline Dr *TF:* 877-411-2899 ■ *Web:* www.wb18.com	Lake Mary	FL	32746	407-670-3018	647-4163
WKMG-TV Ch 6 (CBS) 4466 N John Young Pkwy *TF:* 888-853-6060 ■ *Web:* www.local6.com	Orlando	FL	32804	407-291-6000	298-2122
WMFE-TV Ch 24 (PBS) 11510 E Colonial Dr *Web:* www.wmfe.org	Orlando	FL	32817	407-273-2300	273-3613
WOFL-TV Ch 35 (Fox) 35 Skyline Dr *Web:* www.wofl.com	Lake Mary	FL	32746	407-644-3535	741-5189
WOPX-TV Ch 56 (I) 7091 Grand National Dr Suite 100 *Web:* www.ionmedia.tv	Orlando	FL	32819	407-370-5600	363-1759
WOTF-TV Ch 43 (Uni) 739 North Dr Suite C *Web:* www.univision.com	Melbourne	FL	32934	321-254-4343	254-9343
WRBW-TV Ch 65 (MNT) 35 Skyline Dr *Web:* www.wrbw.com	Lake Mary	FL	32746	407-248-6500	741-5189
WTGL-TV Ch 52 (Ind) 653 W Michigan St *Web:* tv52.org	Orlando	FL	32805	407-423-5200	422-0120

744-101 Ottawa, ON

Station	City	Prov	Postal Code	Phone	Fax
CBOFT-TV Ch 9 (SRC) 250 Lanark Ave CP 3220 Succ C **Fax:* News Rm	Ottawa	ON	K1Y1E4	613-724-5550	724-5074*
CBOT-TV Ch 4 (CBC) PO Box 3220 Stn C *Web:* www.cbc.ca/ottawa	Ottawa	ON	K1Y1E4	613-288-6000	288-6423
CFGS-TV Ch 34 (QS) 171 Jean Proulx St	Gatimeau	QC	J8Z1W5	819-770-1040	770-1490
CHOT-TV Ch 40 (TVA) 171 Jean Proulx St	Gatimeau	QC	J8Z1W5	819-770-1040	770-1490
CHRO-TV Ch 5 (Ind) 87 George St *TF:* 800-461-2476	Ottawa	ON	K1N9H7	613-789-0606	789-6590
CJOH-TV Ch 13 (CTV) 1500 Merivale Rd PO Box 5813 *Web:* www.cjoh.com	Ottawa	ON	K2C3G6	613-224-1313	274-4215

744-102 Peoria, IL

Station	City	State	ZIP	Phone	Fax
WAOE-TV Ch 59 (MNT) 2907 Springfield Rd *Web:* www.upn59tv.com	East Peoria	IL	61602	309-698-2525	674-5959
WEEK-TV Ch 25 (NBC) 2907 Springfield Rd *Web:* www.week.com	East Peoria	IL	61611	309-698-2525	698-9335
WHOI-TV Ch 19 (ABC) 500 N Stewart St *Web:* www.hoinews.com	Creve Coeur	IL	61610	309-698-1919	698-4817
WMBD-TV Ch 31 (CBS) 3131 N University St *Web:* www.wmbd.com	Peoria	IL	61604	309-688-3131	686-8650
WTVP-TV Ch 47 (PBS) PO Box 1347 *TF:* 800-837-4747 ■ *Web:* www.wtvp.org	Peoria	IL	61654	309-677-4747	677-4730
WYZZ-TV Ch 43 (Fox) 2714 E Lincoln St *Web:* www.wyzz43.com	Bloomington	IL	61704	309-662-4373	663-6943

744-103 Philadelphia, PA

Station	City	State	ZIP	Phone	Fax
KYW-TV Ch 3 (CBS) 1555 Hamilton St *Web:* www.kyw.com	Philadelphia	PA	19130	215-238-4700	238-4783
WCAU-TV Ch 10 (NBC) 10 Monument Rd *Web:* www.nbc10.com	Bala Cynwyd	PA	19004	610-668-5510	668-3700
WFMZ-TV Ch 69 (Ind) 300 E Rock Rd *Web:* www.wfmz.com	Allentown	PA	18103	610-797-4530	791-2288
WGTW-TV Ch 48 (Ind) 960 Ashland Ave	Folcroft	PA	19032	610-583-1370	
WHYY-TV Ch 12 (PBS) 150 N 6th St *Web:* whyy.org	Philadelphia	PA	19106	215-351-1200	351-3352
WMGM-TV Ch 40 (NBC) 1601 New Rd *Web:* www.wmgmtv.com	Linwood	NJ	08221	609-927-4440	927-7014
WNJT-TV Ch 52 (PBS) PO Box 777 *Web:* www.njn.net/television	Trenton	NJ	08625	609-777-5000	633-2927
WPHL-TV Ch 17 (MNT) 5001 Wynnefield Ave **Fax:* News Rm ■ *Web:* myphl17.trb.com/	Philadelphia	PA	19131	215-878-1700	879-7682*
WPPX-TV Ch 61 (I) 3901 B Main St Suite 301 *Web:* www.ionmedia.tv	Philadelphia	PA	19127	215-482-4770	482-4777
WPSG-TV Ch 57 (CW) 1555 Hamilton St *Web:* cwphilly.com	Philadelphia	PA	19130	215-977-5700	977-5300
WPVI-TV Ch 6 (ABC) 4100 City Line Ave *Web:* abclocal.go.com/wpvi	Philadelphia	PA	19131	215-878-9700	581-4530
WTXF-TV Ch 29 (Fox) 330 Market St *Web:* www.foxphiladelphia.com	Philadelphia	PA	19106	215-925-2929	925-2420
WYBE-TV Ch 35 (Ind) 8200 Ridge Ave *Web:* www.wybe.org	Philadelphia	PA	19128	215-483-3900	483-6908

744-104 Phoenix, AZ

Station	City	State	ZIP	Phone	Fax
KAET-TV Ch 8 (PBS) PO Box 871405 *Web:* www.kaet.asu.edu	Tempe	AZ	85287	480-965-3506	965-1000
KASW-TV Ch 61 (CW) 5555 N 7th Ave	Phoenix	AZ	85013	480-661-6161	207-3277
KAZT-TV Ch 27 (Ind) 3211 Tower Rd *Web:* www.kaz.tv	Prescott	AZ	86305	928-778-6770	445-5210
KFPH-TV Ch 13 (Uni) 2158 N 4th St	Flagstaff	AZ	86004	928-527-1300	527-1394
KNAZ-TV Ch 2 (NBC) 2201 N Vicky St	Flagstaff	AZ	86004	928-526-2232	526-8110
KNXV-TV Ch 15 (ABC) 515 N 44th St *TF:* 800-803-3277 ■ *Web:* www.knxv.com	Phoenix	AZ	85008	602-273-1500	685-3000
KPAZ-TV Ch 21 (TBN) 3551 E McDowell Rd *Web:* www.tbn.org	Phoenix	AZ	85008	602-273-1477	267-9427
KPHO-TV Ch 5 (CBS) 4016 N Black Canyon Hwy *Web:* www.kpho.com	Phoenix	AZ	85017	602-264-1000	650-0761
KPNX-TV Ch 12 (NBC) 1101 N Central Ave *Web:* www.azcentral.com/12news/	Phoenix	AZ	85004	602-257-1212	257-6619
KPPX-TV Ch 51 (I) 2777 E Camelback Rd Suite 220 *TF:* 888-467-2988	Phoenix	AZ	85016	602-340-1466	808-8864
KSAZ-TV Ch 10 (Fox) 511 W Adams St *TF:* 888-369-4762 ■ *Web:* www.fox10.com	Phoenix	AZ	85003	602-257-1234	262-0177
KTVK-TV Ch 3 (Ind) 5555 N 7th Ave *Web:* www.azfamily.com	Phoenix	AZ	85013	602-207-3333	207-3477
KTVW-TV Ch 33 (Uni) 6006 S 30th St	Phoenix	AZ	85042	602-243-3333	276-8658
KUTP-TV Ch 45 (MNT) 511 W Adams *Web:* www.kutp.com	Phoenix	AZ	85003	602-257-1234	626-0181

744-105 Pittsburgh, PA

Station	City	State	ZIP	Phone	Fax
KDKA-TV Ch 2 (CBS) 1 Gateway Center *Web:* www.kdka.com	Pittsburgh	PA	15222	412-575-2200	575-2871
WPGH-TV Ch 53 (Fox) 750 Ivory Ave **Fax:* News Rm ■ *Web:* www.wpgh53.com/pittsburgh_pa	Pittsburgh	PA	15214	412-931-5300	931-4284*
WPMY-TV Ch 22 (MNT) 750 Ivory Ave *Web:* www.wcwb22.com	Pittsburgh	PA	15214	412-931-5300	931-4284
WPXI-TV Ch 11 (NBC) 4145 Evergreen Rd *TF:* 800-237-9794 ■ *Web:* www.wpxi.com	Pittsburgh	PA	15214	412-237-1100	237-4900
WQED-TV Ch 13 (PBS) 4802 5th Ave *TF:* 800-876-1316 ■ *Web:* www.wqed.org	Pittsburgh	PA	15213	412-622-1300	622-6413
WTAE-TV Ch 4 (ABC) 400 Ardmore Blvd **Fax:* News Rm ■ *Web:* www.thepittsburghchannel.com	Pittsburgh	PA	15221	412-242-4300	244-4628*

744-106 Pocatello, ID

Station	City	State	ZIP	Phone	Fax
KFXP-TV Ch 31 (Fox) 902 E Sherman St *Web:* www.kfxp.com	Pocatello	ID	83201	208-232-3141	232-8032
KIDK-TV Ch 3 (CBS) 1255 E 17th St *Web:* www.kidktv.com	Idaho Falls	ID	83403	208-522-5100	535-0946
KIFI-TV Ch 8 (ABC) 150 S Main St Suite C PO Box 1001 *Web:* www.localnews8.com	Pocatello	ID	83204	208-233-8888	233-8932
KISU-TV Ch 10 (PBS) Idaho State University CB 8111 921 S 8th Ave *TF:* 800-543-6868 ■ *Web:* www.idahoptv.org	Pocatello	ID	83209	208-282-2857	282-2848
KPVI-TV Ch 6 (NBC) 902 E Sherman St *TF:* 800-366-5784 ■ *Web:* www.kpvi.com	Pocatello	ID	83201	208-232-6666	233-6678

744-107 Portland, ME

Station	City	State	ZIP	Phone	Fax
WCBB-TV Ch 10 (PBS) 1450 Lisbon St *TF:* 800-884-1717 ■ *Web:* www.mpbc.org	Lewiston	ME	04240	207-783-9101	783-5193
WCSH-TV Ch 6 (NBC) 1 Congress Sq *TF:* 800-464-1213 ■ *Web:* www.wcsh6.com	Portland	ME	04101	207-828-6666	828-6620
WGME-TV Ch 13 (CBS) 1335 Washington Ave *TF:* 800-766-9330 ■ *Web:* www.wgme.com	Portland	ME	04103	207-797-1313	878-3505
WMTW-TV Ch 8 (ABC) PO Box 8 *TF:* 800-248-6397 ■ *Web:* www.wmtw.com	Auburn	ME	04211	207-782-1800	783-7371
WPME-TV Ch 35 (MNT) 4 Ledgeview Dr *Web:* www.mainesupn.com	Westbrook	ME	04092	207-774-0051	774-6849
WPXT-TV Ch 12 (CW) 4 Ledgeview Dr *Web:* www.maineswb.com	Westbrook	ME	04092	207-774-0051	774-6849

744-108 Portland, OR

Station	City	State	ZIP	Phone	Fax
KATU-TV Ch 2 (ABC) 2153 NE Sandy Blvd *TF:* 800-447-6397 ■ *Web:* www.katu.com	Portland	OR	97232	503-231-4222	231-4263
KEPB-TV Ch 28 (PBS) 7140 SW Macadam Ave *Web:* www.opb.org	Portland	OR	97219	503-244-9900	293-1919
KGW-TV Ch 8 (NBC) 1501 SW Jefferson St *TF:* 800-288-5498 ■ *Web:* www.kgw.com	Portland	OR	97201	503-226-5000	226-5059
KOIN-TV Ch 6 (CBS) 222 SW Columbia St *Web:* www.koin.com	Portland	OR	97201	503-464-0600	464-0717
KOPB-TV Ch 10 (PBS) 7140 SW Macadam Ave *Web:* www.opb.org	Portland	OR	97219	503-244-9900	293-1919
KPDX-TV Ch 49 (MNT) 14975 NW Greenbrier Pkwy *TF:* 866-906-1249 ■ *Web:* www.kpdx.com	Beaverton	OR	97006	503-906-1249	548-6920
KPTV-TV Ch 12 (Fox) 14975 NW Greenbrier Pkwy *TF:* 866-906-1249 ■ *Web:* www.kptv.com	Beaverton	OR	97006	503-906-1249	548-6920
KPXG-TV Ch 22 (I) 811 SW Naito Pkwy **Fax:* Sales ■ *Web:* www.ionmedia.tv	Portland	OR	97204	503-222-2221	222-3732*
KWBP-TV Ch 32 (CW) 10255 SW Arctic Dr *Web:* portlandscw.trb.com	Beaverton	OR	97005	503-644-3232	626-3576

744-109 Providence, RI

Station	City	State	ZIP	Phone	Fax
WJAR-TV Ch 10 (NBC) 23 Kenney Dr *Web:* www.turnto10.com	Cranston	RI	02920	401-455-9100	455-9140
WLNE-TV Ch 6 (ABC) 10 Orms St *Web:* www.abc6.com	Providence	RI	02904	401-453-8000	331-4431
WLWC-TV Ch 28 (CW) 1 State St Suite 100 *Web:* cw28tv.com	Providence	RI	02908	401-351-8828	351-0222
WNAC-TV Ch 64 (Fox) 25 Catamore Blvd	East Providence	RI	02914	401-438-7200	431-1012
WPRI-TV Ch 12 (CBS) 25 Catamore Blvd *Web:* www.wpri.com	East Providence	RI	02914	401-438-7200	431-1012
WPXQ-TV Ch 69 (I) 3 Shaws Cove	New London	CT	06320	860-444-2626	440-2601
WSBE-TV Ch 36 (PBS) 50 Park Ln *Web:* www.wsbe.org	Providence	RI	02907	401-222-3636	222-3407

744-110 Quebec City, QC

Station	City	State	ZIP	Phone	Fax
CBVT-TV Ch 11 (CBC) PO Box 18800	Quebec	QC	G1K9L4	418-654-1341	656-8567
CFAP-TV Ch 2 (QS) 330 Saint Vallier St E Office 025	Quebec	QC	G1K9C5	418-624-2222	624-0162
CFCM-TV Ch 4 (TVA) 1000 Myrand Ave	Sainte-Foy	QC	G1V2W3	418-688-9330	681-1252
CKMI-TV Ch 20 (GTN) 1000 Myrand Ave *TF:* 800-521-4323	Sainte-Foy	QC	G1V2W3	418-682-2020	682-2620

744-111 Raleigh/Durham, NC

Station	City	State	ZIP	Phone	Fax
WFPX-TV Ch 62 (I) Drawer 62	Lumber Bridge	NC	28357	910-843-3884	843-2873
WLFL-TV Ch 22 (CW) 3012 Highwoods Blvd Suite 101 *Web:* www.wb22tv.com	Raleigh	NC	27604	919-872-9535	878-3877
WNCN-TV Ch 17 (NBC) 1205 Front St *Web:* www.nbc17.com	Raleigh	NC	27609	919-836-1717	836-1747
WRAL-TV Ch 5 (CBS) 2619 Western Blvd *TF:* 800-245-9725 ■ *Web:* www.wral.com	Raleigh	NC	27606	919-821-8555	821-8541
WRAZ-TV Ch 50 (Fox) 512 S Mangum St *TF:* 877-369-5050 ■ *Web:* www.fox50.com	Durham	NC	27701	919-595-5050	595-5028
WRDC-TV Ch 28 (MNT) 3012 Highwoods Blvd Suite 101 *Web:* www.wrdc28.com	Raleigh	NC	27604	919-872-2854	878-3697
WRPX-TV Ch 47 (I) 3209 Gresham Lake Rd Suite 151	Raleigh	NC	27615	919-876-1642	876-1415
WTVD-TV Ch 11 (ABC) 411 Liberty St *TF:* 800-467-4440 ■ *Web:* abclocal.go.com/wtvd	Durham	NC	27701	919-683-1111	687-4373
WUNC-TV Ch 4 (PBS) PO Box 14900 **Fax:* News Rm ■ *TF:* 800-906-5050 ■ *Web:* www.unctv.org	Research Triangle Park	NC	27709	919-549-7000	549-7043*
WUNL-TV Ch 26 (PBS) PO Box 14900 *Web:* www.unctv.org	Research Triangle Park	NC	27709	919-549-7000	549-7043
WUVC-TV Ch 40 (Uni) 230 Donaldson St	Fayetteville	NC	28301	910-323-4040	323-3924

744-112 Rapid City, SD

Station	City	State	ZIP	Phone	Fax
KBHE-TV Ch 9 (PBS) PO Box 5000 *TF:* 800-456-0766 ■ *Web:* www.sdpb.org	Vermillion	SD	57069	605-677-5861	677-5010
KCLO-TV Ch 15 (CBS) 1719 W Main St *Web:* www.keloland.com	Rapid City	SD	57702	605-341-1500	348-5518
KEVN-TV Ch 7 (Fox) 2000 Skyline Dr PO Box 677 *Web:* www.kevn.com	Rapid City	SD	57709	605-394-7777	348-9128
KNBN-TV Ch 27 (NBC) 2424 S Plaza Dr *Web:* www.newscenter1.com	Rapid City	SD	57702	605-355-0024	355-9274
KOTA-TV Ch 3 (ABC) 518 Saint Joseph St *Web:* www.kotatv.com	Rapid City	SD	57701	605-342-2000	342-7305
KPLO-TV Ch 6 (CBS) 501 S Phillips Ave *TF:* 800-888-5356	Sioux Falls	SD	57104	605-336-1100	336-0202
KTSD-TV Ch 10 (PBS) PO Box 5000 *TF:* 800-456-0766 ■ *Web:* www.sdpb.org	Vermillion	SD	57069	605-677-5861	677-5010

744-113 Reno/Carson City, NV

Station	City	State	ZIP	Phone	Fax
KAME-TV Ch 21 (MNT) 4920 Brookside Ct *Web:* www.foxreno.com	Reno	NV	89502	775-856-2121	856-2116
KNPB-TV Ch 5 (PBS) 1670 N Virginia St *Web:* www.knpb.org	Reno	NV	89503	775-784-4555	784-1438
KOLO-TV Ch 8 (ABC) PO Box 10000 **Fax:* News Rm ■ *Web:* www.kolotv.com	Reno	NV	89510	775-858-8888	858-8855*
KREN-TV Ch 27 (CW) 5166 Meadow Wood Mall Cir *Web:* www.kren.com	Reno	NV	89502	775-333-2727	327-6827
KRNV-TV Ch 4 (NBC) 1790 Vassar St *TF:* 877-377-0122 ■ *Web:* www.krnv.com	Reno	NV	89502	775-322-4444	785-1250
KRXI-TV Ch 11 (Fox) 4920 Brookside Ct *Web:* www.foxreno.com	Reno	NV	89502	775-856-1100	
KTVN-TV Ch 2 (CBS) 4925 Energy Way *Web:* www.ktvn.com	Reno	NV	89502	775-858-2222	861-4298

744-114 Richmond, VA

Station	City	State	ZIP	Phone	Fax
WCVE-TV Ch 23 (PBS) 23 Sesame St *TF:* 800-476-8440 ■ *Web:* www.wcve.org	Richmond	VA	23235	804-320-1301	320-8729
WRIC-TV Ch 8 (ABC) 301 Arboretum Pl *Web:* www.wric.com	Richmond	VA	23236	804-330-8888	330-8883
WRLH-TV Ch 35 (Fox) 1925 Westmoreland St *Web:* www.fox35.com	Richmond	VA	23230	804-358-3535	358-1495
WTVR-TV Ch 6 (CBS) 3301 W Broad St *Web:* www.wtvr.com	Richmond	VA	23230	804-254-3600	254-3697
WUPV-TV Ch 65 (CW) 3301 W Broad St *Web:* www.cwrichmond.tv	Richmond	VA	23230	804-254-3600	342-5746
WWBT-TV Ch 12 (NBC) 5710 Midlothian Tpke *Web:* www.nbc12.com	Richmond	VA	23225	804-230-1212	230-2793

744-115 Roanoke, VA

Station	City	State	ZIP	Phone	Fax
WBRA-TV Ch 15 (PBS) 1215 McNeil Dr *TF:* 800-221-0991 ■ *Web:* www.wbra.org	Roanoke	VA	24015	540-344-0991	344-2148
WDBJ-TV Ch 7 (CBS) 2807 Hershberger Rd NW *TF:* 800-777-9325 ■ *Web:* www.wdbj7.com	Roanoke	VA	24017	540-344-7000	344-5097
WDRL-TV Ch 24 (Ind) 5002 Airport Rd NW *Web:* www.wdrl-tv.com	Roanoke	VA	24012	540-366-1825	366-7530
WFXR-TV Ch 27 (Fox) 2618 Colonial Ave SW *Web:* www.fox2127.com	Roanoke	VA	24015	540-344-2127	345-1912
WPXR-TV Ch 38 (I) 401 3rd St SW	Roanoke	VA	24011	540-857-0038	345-8568
WSET-TV Ch 13 (ABC) 2320 Langhorne Rd *Web:* www.wset.com	Lynchburg	VA	24501	434-528-1313	847-0448
WSLS-TV Ch 10 (NBC) PO Box 10 *TF:* 800-800-9757 ■ *Web:* www.wsls.com	Roanoke	VA	24022	540-981-9110	343-2059

744-116 Rochester, MN

Station	City	State	ZIP	Phone	Fax
KAAL-TV Ch 6 (ABC) 1701 10th Pl NE *TF:* 800-234-0776 ■ *Web:* www.kaaltv.com	Austin	MN	55912	507-437-6666	433-9560
KIMT-TV Ch 3 (CBS) 112 N Pennsylvania Ave. *TF:* 800-323-4883 ■ *Web:* www.kimt.com	Mason City	IA	50401	641-423-2540	423-9309
KSMQ-TV Ch 15 (PBS) 2000 8th Ave NW *Web:* www.ksmq.org	Austin	MN	55912	507-433-0678	433-0670
KTTC-TV Ch 10 (NBC) 6301 Bandel Rd NW *TF:* 800-288-1656 ■ *Web:* www.kttc.com	Rochester	MN	55901	507-288-4444	288-6324
KXLT-TV Ch 47 (Fox) 6301 Bandel Rd NW *TF:* 877-369-4788 ■ *Web:* www.fox47kxlt.com	Rochester	MN	55901	507-252-4747	252-5050

744-117 Rochester, NY

Station	City	State	ZIP	Phone	Fax
WHAM-TV Ch 13 (ABC) PO Box 20555 *Web:* www.13wham.com	Rochester	NY	14602	585-334-8700	334-8719
WHEC-TV Ch 10 (NBC) 191 East Ave. *TF:* 800-284-9432 ■ *Web:* www.whec.com	Rochester	NY	14604	585-546-5670	546-5688
WROC-TV Ch 8 (CBS) 201 Humboldt St. **Fax:* News Rm ■ *Web:* www.wroctv.com	Rochester	NY	14610	585-288-8400	288-1505*
WUHF-TV Ch 31 (Fox) 201 Humbolt St. **Fax:* News Rm ■ *Web:* www.foxrochester.com	Rochester	NY	14610	585-232-3700	288-1505*
WXXI-TV Ch 21 (PBS) PO Box 30021 *Web:* www.wxxi.org	Rochester	NY	14603	585-325-7500	258-0335

744-118 Rockford, IL

Station	City	State	ZIP	Phone	Fax
WIFR-TV Ch 23 (CBS) 2523 N Meridian Rd. *Web:* www.wifr.com	Rockford	IL	61101	815-987-5300	965-0981
WQRF-TV Ch 39 (Fox) 1917 N Meridian Rd *Web:* www.fox39.com	Rockford	IL	61101	815-963-5413	963-6113
WREX-TV Ch 13 (NBC) 10322 Auburn Rd. **Fax:* News Rm ■ *Web:* www.wrex.com	Rockford	IL	61103	815-335-2213	335-2297*
WTVO-TV Ch 17 (ABC) 1917 N Meridian Rd *Web:* www.wtvo.com	Rockford	IL	61101	815-963-5413	963-6113

744-119 Sacramento, CA

Station	City	State	ZIP	Phone	Fax
KCRA-TV Ch 3 (NBC) 3 Television Cir *Web:* www.kcra.com	Sacramento	CA	95814	916-446-3333	446-3333
KMAX-TV Ch 31 (CBS) 2713 KOVR Dr	West Sacramento	CA	95605	916-925-3100	374-1304
KOVR-TV Ch 13 (CBS) 2713 KOVR Dr. *Web:* www.kovr13.com	West Sacramento	CA	95605	916-374-1313	374-1304
KQCA-TV Ch 58 (MNT) 58 Television Cir. *Web:* www.my58.com/	Sacramento	CA	95814	916-447-5858	554-4658
KSPX-TV Ch 29 (I) 3352 Mather Field Rd *TF:* 888-467-2988	Rancho Cordova	CA	95670	916-368-2929	368-0225
KTXL-TV Ch 40 (Fox) 4655 Fruitridge Rd *Web:* fox40.trb.com	Sacramento	CA	95820	916-454-4422	739-0559
KUVS-TV Ch 19 (Uni) 1710 Arden Way	Sacramento	CA	95815	916-927-1900	614-1906
KVIE-TV Ch 6 (PBS) 2595 Capitol Oaks Dr *TF:* 800-347-5843 ■ *Web:* www.kvie.org	Sacramento	CA	95833	916-929-5843	929-7215
KXTV-TV Ch 10 (ABC) 400 Broadway *Web:* www.news10.net	Sacramento	CA	95818	916-441-2345	447-6107

744-120 Saint Louis, MO

Station	City	State	ZIP	Phone	Fax
KDNL-TV Ch 30 (ABC) 1215 Cole St *Web:* www.abcstlouis.com	Saint Louis	MO	63106	314-436-3030	
KETC-TV Ch 9 (PBS) 3655 Olive St *Web:* www.ketc.org	Saint Louis	MO	63108	314-512-9000	512-9005
KMOV-TV Ch 4 (CBS) 1 Memorial Dr. *TF:* 800-477-5668 ■ *Web:* www.kmov.com	Saint Louis	MO	63102	314-621-4444	621-4775
KNLC-TV Ch 24 (Ind) 1411 Locust St *Web:* www.knlc.tv	Saint Louis	MO	63103	314-436-2424	436-2434
KPLR-TV Ch 11 (CW) 2250 Ball Dr *Web:* wb11tv.trb.com/	Saint Louis	MO	63146	314-447-1111	447-6480
KSDK-TV Ch 5 (NBC) 1000 Market St **Fax:* News Rm ■ *Web:* www.ksdk.com	Saint Louis	MO	63101	314-421-5055	444-5164*
KTVI-TV Ch 2 (Fox) 5915 Berthold Ave. **Fax:* News Rm ■ *TF:* 800-920-0222 ■ *Web:* www.fox2ktvi.com	Saint Louis	MO	63110	314-647-2222	644-7419*

744-121 Salt Lake City, UT

Station	City	State	ZIP	Phone	Fax
KBYU-TV Ch 11 (PBS) 2000 Ironton Blvd Brigham Young University *TF:* 800-298-5298 ■ *Web:* www.kbyutv.org	Provo	UT	84606	801-422-8450	422-8478
KJZZ-TV Ch 14 (Ind) 5181 Amelia Earhart Dr **Fax:* Sales ■ *Web:* www.kjzz.com	Salt Lake City	UT	84116	801-537-1414	238-6415*
KPNZ-TV Ch 24 (Ind) 150 N Wright Bros Dr Suite 520 *Web:* www.z24tv.com	Salt Lake City	UT	84116	801-519-2424	359-1272
KSL-TV Ch 5 (NBC) PO Box 1160 *Web:* www.ksl.com	Salt Lake City	UT	84110	801-575-5555	575-5560
KSTU-TV Ch 13 (Fox) 5020 W Amelia Earhart Dr *Web:* www.fox13.com	Salt Lake City	UT	84116	801-532-1300	537-5335
KTVX-TV Ch 4 (ABC) 2175 W 1700 South *Web:* www.abc4.tv	Salt Lake City	UT	84104	801-975-4444	973-4176
KUED-TV Ch 7 (PBS) 101 Wasatch Dr Rm 215 *TF:* 800-477-5833 ■ *Web:* www.kued.org	Salt Lake City	UT	84112	801-581-7777	585-5096
KUPX-TV Ch 16 (I) 466C Lawndale Dr. *TF:* 888-467-2988	Salt Lake City	UT	84115	801-474-0016	463-9667
KUTV-TV Ch 2 (CBS) 299 S Main St Suite 150 **Fax:* News Rm ■ *Web:* www.kutv.com	Salt Lake City	UT	84111	801-973-3000	973-3349*
KUWB-TV Ch 30 (CW) 2175 W 1700 South *Web:* www.cw30.com	Murray	UT	84104	801-975-4444	975-4442

744-122 San Antonio, TX

Station	City	State	ZIP	Phone	Fax
KABB-TV Ch 29 (Fox) 4335 NW Loop 410 *Web:* www.kabb.com	San Antonio	TX	78229	210-366-1129	442-6333
KENS-TV Ch 5 (CBS) 5400 Fredericksburg Rd *Web:* www.mysanantonio.com	San Antonio	TX	78229	210-366-5000	377-0740
KLRN-TV Ch 9 (PBS) 501 Broadway St *TF:* 800-627-8193 ■ *Web:* www.klrn.org	San Antonio	TX	78215	210-270-9000	270-9078
KMYS-TV Ch 35 (MNT) 4335 NW Loop 410 **Fax:* News Rm ■ *Web:* www.krrt.com	San Antonio	TX	78229	210-366-1129	442-6333*
KSAT-TV Ch 12 (ABC) 1408 N Saint Mary's St **Fax:* News Rm ■ *Web:* www.ksat.com	San Antonio	TX	78215	210-351-1200	351-1310*
KVDA-TV Ch 60 (Tele) 6234 San Pedro Ave **Fax:* News Rm	San Antonio	TX	78216	210-340-8860	341-2051*
KWEX-TV Ch 41 (Uni) 411 E Durango Blvd **Fax:* News Rm	San Antonio	TX	78204	210-227-4141	226-0131*
WOAI-TV Ch 4 (NBC) 1031 Navarro St. *Web:* www.woai.com	San Antonio	TX	78205	210-226-4444	224-9898

744-123 San Diego, CA

Station	City	State	ZIP	Phone	Fax
KFMB-TV Ch 8 (CBS) 7677 Engineer Rd *Web:* www.kfmb.com	San Diego	CA	92111	858-571-8888	560-0627
KGTV-TV Ch 10 (ABC) PO Box 85347 *Web:* www.10news.com	San Diego	CA	92186	619-237-1010	262-1302
KNSD-TV Ch 39 (NBC) 225 Broadway *Web:* www.nbcsandiego.com	San Diego	CA	92101	619-231-3939	578-0202
KPBS-TV Ch 15 (PBS) 5200 Campanile Dr *TF:* 888-399-5727 ■ *Web:* www.kpbs.org	San Diego	CA	92182	619-594-1515	594-3812
KSWB-TV Ch 69 (CW) 7191 Engineer Rd. **Fax:* News Rm ■ *Web:* kswbtv.trb.com	San Diego	CA	92111	858-492-9269	573-6600*
KUSI-TV Ch 51 (Ind) 4575 Viewridge Ave *Web:* www.kusi.com	San Diego	CA	92123	858-571-5151	576-9317
XETV-TV Ch 6 (Fox) 8253 Ronson Rd *Web:* www.fox6.com	San Diego	CA	92111	858-279-6666	268-9388

744-124 San Francisco, CA

Station	City	State	ZIP	Phone	Fax
KBHK-TV Ch 44 (CW) 855 Battery St 4th Fl. **Fax:* PR ■ *Web:* kbcwtv.com	San Francisco	CA	94111	415-765-8144	397-2841*
KBWB-TV Ch 20 (Ind) 2500 Marin St *Web:* www.yourtv20.com	San Francisco	CA	94124	415-821-2020	821-9158
KDTV-TV Ch 14 (Uni) 50 Fremont St 41st Fl. *Web:* www.univision.com	San Francisco	CA	94105	415-538-8000	538-8053
KGO-TV Ch 7 (ABC) 900 Front St. *Web:* abclocal.go.com/kgo	San Francisco	CA	94111	415-954-7777	956-6402
KICU-TV Ch 36 (Ind) 2102 Commerce Dr *TF:* 800-464-5428 ■ *Web:* www.ktvu.com/kicu	San Jose	CA	95131	408-953-3636	953-3610
KNTV-TV Ch 11 (NBC) 2450 N 1st St *Web:* www.nbc11.com	San Jose	CA	95131	408-432-6221	
KPIX-TV Ch 5 (CBS) 855 Battery St. *Web:* www.cbs5.com	San Francisco	CA	94111	415-765-4444	765-8916
KQED-TV Ch 9 (PBS) 2601 Mariposa St. *Web:* www.kqed.org	San Francisco	CA	94110	415-864-2000	553-2241
KRON-TV Ch 4 (Ind) 1001 Van Ness Ave. *Web:* www.kron4.com	San Francisco	CA	94109	415-441-4444	561-8136
KSTS-TV Ch 48 (Tele) 2349 Bering Dr *Web:* www.ksts.com	San Jose	CA	95131	408-944-4848	433-5921
KTEH-TV Ch 54 (PBS) 1585 Schallenberger Rd. *Web:* www.kteh.org	San Jose	CA	95131	408-795-5400	995-5446
KTNC-TV Ch 42 (Ind) 1700 Montgomery St Suite 400 *Web:* www.ktnc.com	San Francisco	CA	94111	415-398-4242	352-1800
KTSF-TV Ch 26 (Ind) 100 Valley Dr. *TF:* 800-488-6226 ■ *Web:* www.ktsf.com	Brisbane	CA	94005	415-468-2626	467-7559
KTVU-TV Ch 2 (Fox) 2 Jack London Sq. *Web:* www.ktvu.com	Oakland	CA	94607	510-834-1212	272-9957

744-125 San Juan, PR

Station	City	State	ZIP	Phone	Fax
WKAQ-TV Ch 2 (Tele) PO Box 009366222 **Fax:* News Rm	San Juan	PR	00936	787-758-2222	641-2179*

744-126 Savannah, GA

Station	City	State	ZIP	Phone	Fax
WGSA-TV Ch 34 (CW) 401 Mall Blvd Suite 201-B	Savannah	GA	31406	912-692-8000	692-0400
WJCL-TV Ch 22 (ABC) 10001 Abercorn St *Web:* www.abc22tv.com	Savannah	GA	31406	912-925-0022	921-2235
WSAV-TV Ch 3 (NBC) 1430 E Victory Dr *Web:* www.wsav.com	Savannah	GA	31404	912-651-0300	651-0304
WTGS-TV Ch 28 (Fox) 10001 Abercorn St. *Web:* www.wtgs.com	Savannah	GA	31406	912-925-2287	925-7026
WTOC-TV Ch 11 (CBS) PO Box 8086 **Fax:* News Rm ■ *Web:* www.wtoctv.com	Savannah	GA	31412	912-234-1111	232-4945*

744-127 Scranton, PA

Station	City	State	ZIP	Phone	Fax
WBRE-TV Ch 28 (NBC) 62 S Franklin St *TF:* 800-294-7261 ■ *Web:* www.wbre.com	Wilkes-Barre	PA	18701	570-823-2828	829-0440
WNEP-TV Ch 16 (ABC) 16 Montage Mountain Rd. **Fax:* News Rm ■ *TF:* 800-982-4374 ■ *Web:* www.wnep.com	Moosic	PA	18507	570-346-7474	341-1344*
WOLF-TV Ch 56 (Fox) 1181 Hwy 315	Plains	PA	18702	570-970-5600	970-5601
WQPX-TV Ch 64 (I) 409 Lackawanna Ave Suite 700	Scranton	PA	18503	570-344-6400	344-3303
WSWB-TV Ch 38 (CW) 1181 Hwy 315	Plains	PA	18702	570-970-5600	970-5601
WVIA-TV Ch 44 (PBS) 100 WVIA Way *Web:* www.wvia.org/tv	Pittston	PA	18640	570-344-1244	655-1180
WYOU-TV Ch 22 (CBS) 62 S Franklin St *TF:* 800-422-9968 ■ *Web:* www.wyou.com	Wilkes-Barre	PA	18701	570-961-2222	829-0440

744-128 Seattle/Tacoma, WA

Station	City	State	ZIP	Phone	Fax
KBTC-TV Ch 28 (PBS) 2320 S 19th St *TF:* 888-596-5282 ■ *Web:* www.kbtc.org	Tacoma	WA	98405	253-680-7700	680-7725
KCPQ-TV Ch 13 (Fox) 1813 Westlake Ave N *Web:* q13.trb.com	Seattle	WA	98109	206-674-1313	674-1713
KCTS-TV Ch 9 (PBS) 401 Mercer St *TF:* 800-443-9991 ■ *Web:* www.kcts.org	Seattle	WA	98109	206-728-6463	443-6691

Seattle/Tacoma, WA (Cont'd)

Station	City	State	ZIP	Phone	Fax
KING-TV Ch 5 (NBC) 333 Dexter Ave N *Web:* www.king5.com	Seattle	WA	98109	206-448-5555	448-4525
KIRO-TV Ch 7 (CBS) 2807 3rd Ave *Web:* www.kirotv.com	Seattle	WA	98121	206-728-7777	441-4840
KMYQ-TV Ch 22 (MNT) 1813 Westlake Ave N *Web:* myq2.trb.com/	Seattle	WA	98109	206-674-1313	674-1713
KOMO-TV Ch 4 (ABC) 140 4th Ave N *Web:* www.komotv.com	Seattle	WA	98109	206-404-4000	404-4422
KONG-TV Ch 16 (Ind) 333 Dexter Ave N *Web:* www.kongtv.com	Seattle	WA	98109	206-448-3166	448-4525
KSTW-TV Ch 11 (CW) 602 Oakesdale Ave SW *TF:* 866-313-5789 ■ *Web:* www.kstw.com	Renton	WA	98055	206-441-1111	441-1116
KVOS-TV Ch 12 (Ind) 1151 Ellis St *TF:* 800-488-5867 ■ *Web:* www.kvos.com	Bellingham	WA	98225	360-671-1212	647-0824
KWPX-TV Ch 33 (I) 8112 304th Ave SW PO Box 426 *TF:* 888-467-2988	Preston	WA	98050	425-222-6010	222-6032

744-129 Shreveport, LA

Station	City	State	ZIP	Phone	Fax
KMSS-TV Ch 33 (Fox) 3519 Jewella Ave *TF:* 800-631-5677 ■ *Web:* www.kmsstv.com	Shreveport	LA	71109	318-631-5677	631-4195
KSHV-TV Ch 45 (MNT) 3519 Jewella Ave *Web:* www.kshv.com	Shreveport	LA	71109	318-631-4545	631-4195
KSLA-TV Ch 12 (CBS) 1812 Fairfield Ave *Web:* www.ksla.com	Shreveport	LA	71101	318-222-1212	677-6705
KTAL-TV Ch 6 (NBC) 3150 N Market St *TF:* 866-665-6000 ■ *Web:* www.newschannel6.tv	Shreveport	LA	71107	318-629-6000	629-7171
KTBS-TV Ch 3 (ABC) 312 E Kings Hwy *Web:* www.ktbs.com	Shreveport	LA	71104	318-861-5800	219-4601

744-130 Sioux Falls, SD

Station	City	State	ZIP	Phone	Fax
KDLT-TV Ch 46 (NBC) 3600 S Westport Ave *TF:* 800-727-5358 ■ *Web:* www.kdlt.com	Sioux Falls	SD	57106	605-361-5555	361-3982
KELO-TV Ch 11 (CBS) 501 S Phillips Ave **Fax:* News Rm ■ *TF:* 800-888-5356 ■ *Web:* www.keloland.com	Sioux Falls	SD	57104	605-336-1100	336-0202*
KSFY-TV Ch 13 (ABC) 300 N Dakota Ave Suite 100 *Web:* www.ksfy.com	Sioux Falls	SD	57104	605-336-1300	336-7936
KTTW-TV Ch 17 (Fox) 2817 W 11th St *TF:* 800-759-8352 ■ *Web:* www.kttw.com	Sioux Falls	SD	57104	605-338-0017	338-7173
KUSD-TV Ch 2 (PBS) PO Box 5000 *TF:* 800-456-0766 ■ *Web:* www.sdpb.org	Vermillion	SD	57069	605-677-5861	677-5010

744-131 South Bend, IN

Station	City	State	ZIP	Phone	Fax
WBND-TV Ch 57 (Ind) 3665 Park Pl W Suite 200 *Web:* www.abc57.com	Mishawaka	IN	46545	574-243-4316	243-4326
WNDU-TV Ch 16 (NBC) 54516 933 N *TF:* 800-631-6397 ■ *Web:* www.wndu.com	South Bend	IN	46637	574-631-1616	631-1639
WNIT-TV Ch 34 (PBS) 2300 Charger Blvd *Web:* www.wnit.org	Elkhart	IN	46514	574-674-5961	262-8497
WSBT-TV Ch 22 (CBS) 300 W Jefferson Blvd *TF:* 800-872-3141 ■ *Web:* www.wsbt.com	South Bend	IN	46601	574-233-3141	288-6630
WSJV-TV Ch 28 (Fox) PO Box 28 *TF:* 800-975-8881 ■ *Web:* www.fox28.com	South Bend	IN	46624	574-679-9758	294-1267

744-132 Spokane, WA

Station	City	State	ZIP	Phone	Fax
KAYU-TV Ch 28 (Fox) 4600 S Regal St *Web:* www.kayutv.com	Spokane	WA	99223	509-448-2828	448-0926
KHQ-TV Ch 6 (NBC) 1201 W Sprague Ave *Web:* www.khq.com	Spokane	WA	99201	509-448-6000	448-4644
KREM-TV Ch 2 (CBS) 4103 S Regal St *TF:* 800-753-2220 ■ *Web:* www.krem.com	Spokane	WA	99223	509-448-2000	448-6397
KSKN-TV Ch 22 (CW) 4103 S Regal St *Web:* www.krem.com/wb22	Spokane	WA	99223	509-448-2000	448-6397
KSPS-TV Ch 7 (PBS) 3911 S Regal St *TF:* 800-735-2377 ■ *Web:* www.ksps.org	Spokane	WA	99223	509-354-7800	354-7757
KXLY-TV Ch 4 (ABC) 500 W Boone Ave *Web:* www.kxly.com	Spokane	WA	99201	509-324-4000	327-3932

744-133 Springfield, IL

Station	City	State	ZIP	Phone	Fax
WAND-TV Ch 17 (ABC) 904 South Side Dr *Web:* www.wandtv.com	Decatur	IL	62521	217-424-2500	424-2583
WBUI-TV Ch 23 (CW) 2510 Parkway Ct *TF:* 888-440-9223 ■ *Web:* www.wb23tv.com	Decatur	IL	62526	217-428-2323	428-6455
WCIA-TV Ch 3 (CBS) PO Box 20 *TF:* 800-929-3559 ■ *Web:* www.wcia.com	Champaign	IL	61824	217-356-8333	373-3663
WICD-TV Ch 15 (NBC) 250 S Country Fair Dr *Web:* www.wicd15.com	Champaign	IL	61821	217-351-8500	351-6056
WICS-TV Ch 20 (NBC) 2680 E Cook St **Fax:* News Rm ■ *TF:* 800-263-9720 ■ *Web:* www.wics.com	Springfield	IL	62703	217-753-5620	753-5681*
WILL-TV Ch 12 (PBS) 300 N Goodwin Ave *TF:* 800-528-7980 ■ *Web:* www.will.uiuc.edu	Urbana	IL	61801	217-333-1070	244-6386
WRSP-TV Ch 55 (Fox) 3003 Old Rochester Rd *Web:* www.wrsptv.com	Springfield	IL	62703	217-523-8855	523-4410
WSEC-TV Ch 14 (PBS) PO Box 6248 *TF:* 800-232-3605 ■ *Web:* www.tkn.tv	Springfield	IL	62708	217-483-7887	483-1112

744-134 Springfield, MA

Station	City	State	ZIP	Phone	Fax
WGBY-TV Ch 57 (PBS) 44 Hampden St *Web:* www.wgby.org	Springfield	MA	01103	413-781-2801	731-5093
WGGB-TV Ch 40 (ABC) 1300 Liberty St *Web:* www.wggb.com	Springfield	MA	01104	413-733-4040	788-7640
WWLP-TV Ch 22 (NBC) PO Box 2210 *Web:* www.wwlp.com	Springfield	MA	01102	413-786-2200	377-2261

744-135 Springfield, MO

Station	City	State	ZIP	Phone	Fax
KDEB-TV Ch 27 (Fox) 2650 E Division St *Web:* www.fox27.com	Springfield	MO	65803	417-862-2727	862-6439
KOLR-TV Ch 10 (CBS) 2650 E Division St *Web:* www.kolr10.com	Springfield	MO	65803	417-862-1010	862-6439
KOZK-TV Ch 21 (PBS) 901 S National Ave *TF:* 866-684-5695 ■ *Web:* www.optv.org	Springfield	MO	65804	417-836-3500	836-3569
KSPR-TV Ch 33 (ABC) 1359 Saint Louis St *TF:* 800-220-8222 ■ *Web:* www.springfield33.com	Springfield	MO	65802	417-831-1333	831-4125
KWBM-TV Ch 31 (MNT) 1736 E Sunshine Suite 815	Springfield	MO	65804	417-336-0031	336-3199
KYTV-TV Ch 3 (NBC) PO Box 3500 *TF:* 800-492-4335 ■ *Web:* www.ky3.com	Springfield	MO	65808	417-268-3000	268-3364

744-136 Syracuse, NY

Station	City	State	ZIP	Phone	Fax
WCNY-TV Ch 24 (PBS) PO Box 2400 *TF:* 800-451-9269 ■ *Web:* www.wcny.org	Syracuse	NY	13220	315-453-2424	451-8824
WNYS-TV Ch 43 (MNT) 1000 James St *Web:* www.wnys43.com	Syracuse	NY	13203	315-472-6800	471-8889
WSPX-TV Ch 56 (I) 6508-B Basile Rowe	East Syracuse	NY	13057	315-414-0178	414-0482
WSTM-TV Ch 3 (NBC) 1030 James St *Web:* www.wstm.com	Syracuse	NY	13203	315-474-5000	474-5122
WSYR-TV Ch 9 (ABC) 5904 Bridge St *Web:* www.wsyr.com	East Syracuse	NY	13057	315-446-9999	446-9283
WSYT-TV Ch 68 (Fox) 1000 James St *Web:* www.wsyt68.com	Syracuse	NY	13203	315-472-6800	471-8889
WTVH-TV Ch 5 (CBS) 980 James St *Web:* www.wtvh.com	Syracuse	NY	13203	315-425-5555	425-0129

744-137 Tallahassee, FL

Station	City	State	ZIP	Phone	Fax
WCTV-TV Ch 6 (CBS) 4000 County Rd 12 *TF:* 800-375-4204 ■ *Web:* www.wctv6.com	Tallahassee	FL	32312	850-893-6666	668-3851
WFSU-TV Ch 11 (PBS) 1600 Red Barber Plaza *TF:* 800-322-9378 ■ *Web:* www.wfsu.org	Tallahassee	FL	32310	850-487-3170	487-3093
WFXU-TV Ch 57 (CW) 950 Commerce Blvd	Midway	FL	32343	850-576-4990	576-0200
WTLH-TV Ch 49 (Fox) 950 Commerce Blvd *Web:* www.fox49.com	Midway	FL	32343	850-576-4990	576-0200
WTWC-TV Ch 40 (NBC) 8440 Deerlake Rd S *Web:* www.wtwc40.com	Tallahassee	FL	32312	850-893-4140	893-6974
WTXL-TV Ch 27 (ABC) 1620 Commerce Pkwy *Web:* www.wtxl.com	Midway	FL	32343	850-893-3127	668-0423

744-138 Tampa/Saint Petersburg, FL

Station	City	State	ZIP	Phone	Fax
WCLF-TV Ch 22 (Ind) PO Box 6922 *Web:* www.ctnonline.com	Clearwater	FL	33758	727-535-5622	531-2497
WEDU-TV Ch 3 (PBS) 1300 North Blvd *Web:* www.wedu.org	Tampa	FL	33607	813-254-9338	253-0826
WFLA-TV Ch 8 (NBC) 200 S Parker St *TF:* 800-348-9352 ■ *Web:* www.wfla.com	Tampa	FL	33606	813-228-8888	225-2770
WFTS-TV Ch 28 (ABC) 4045 N Himes Ave *TF:* 800-234-9387 ■ *Web:* www.wfts.com	Tampa	FL	33607	813-354-2800	870-2828
WMOR-TV Ch 32 (Ind) 7201 E Hillsborough Ave *Web:* www.moretv32.com	Tampa	FL	33610	813-626-3232	626-1961
WTOG-TV Ch 44 (CW) 365 105th Terr NE *Web:* cw44.com	Saint Petersburg	FL	33716	727-576-4444	576-6155
WTSP-TV Ch 10 (CBS) 11450 Gandy Blvd N *TF:* 800-393-6610 ■ *Web:* www.wtsp.com	Saint Petersburg	FL	33702	727-577-1010	576-6924
WTTA-TV Ch 38 (MNT) 7622 Bald Cypress Pl *Web:* www.wtta38.com	Tampa	FL	33614	813-886-9882	880-8100
WTVT-TV Ch 13 (Fox) 3213 W Kennedy Blvd *Web:* www.wtvt.com	Tampa	FL	33609	813-876-1313	871-3135
WUSF-TV Ch 16 (PBS) 4202 E Fowler Ave *TF:* 800-654-3703 ■ *Web:* www.wusftv.usf.edu	Tampa	FL	33620	813-974-4000	974-4806
WXPX-TV Ch 66 (I) 14444 66th St N *Web:* www.ionmedia.tv	Clearwater	FL	33764	727-479-1053	479-1055

744-139 Toledo, OH

Station	City	State	ZIP	Phone	Fax
WGTE-TV Ch 30 (PBS) PO Box 30 *TF:* 800-243-9483 ■ *Web:* www.wgte.org	Toledo	OH	43614	419-380-4600	380-4710
WLMB-TV Ch 40 (Ind) 26693 Eckel Rd PO Box 908 *Web:* www.wlmb.org	Perrysburg	OH	43552	419-874-8862	874-8867
WNWO-TV Ch 24 (NBC) 300 S Byrne Rd *Web:* www.wnwo.com	Toledo	OH	43615	419-535-0024	535-0202
WTOL-TV Ch 11 (CBS) 730 N Summit St *Web:* www.wtol.com	Toledo	OH	43604	419-248-1111	244-7104
WTVG-TV Ch 13 (ABC) 4247 Dorr St *Web:* abclocal.go.com/wtvg	Toledo	OH	43607	419-531-1313	534-3898
WUPW-TV Ch 36 (Fox) 4 Seagate *TF:* 866-369-6397 ■ *Web:* www.foxtoledo.com	Toledo	OH	43604	419-244-3600	725-1636

744-140 Topeka, KS

Station	City	State	ZIP	Phone	Fax
KSNT-TV Ch 27 (NBC) 6835 NW Hwy 24 *Web:* www.ksnt.com	Topeka	KS	66618	785-582-4000	582-5283
KTKA-TV Ch 49 (ABC) 2121 SW Chelsea Dr *TF:* 800-279-3128 ■ *Web:* www.ktka.tv	Topeka	KS	66614	785-273-4949	273-7811
KTMJ-TV Ch 43 (Fox) 4100 SW Southgate Dr *TF:* 866-954-7100 ■ *Web:* www.fox43topeka.com	Topeka	KS	66609	785-272-4350	272-0422
KTWU-TV Ch 11 (PBS) 1700 SW College Ave *TF:* 800-866-5898 ■ *Web:* ktwu.wuacc.edu	Topeka	KS	66621	785-231-1111	231-1112
WIBW-TV Ch 13 (CBS) 631 SW Commerce Pl *Web:* www.wibw.com	Topeka	KS	66615	785-272-6397	272-1363

744-141 Toronto, ON

Station	City	State	ZIP	Phone	Fax
CBLT-TV Ch 5 (CBC) 250 Front St W *TF:* 866-306-4636 ■ *Web:* www.cbc.ca/toronto	Toronto	ON	M5W1E6	416-205-3311	205-7166

				Phone	Fax
CFMT-TV Ch 47 (Ind) 545 Lake Shore Blvd W	Toronto	ON	M5V1A3	416-260-0047	260-3621
Web: www.omni1.ca					
CFTO-TV Ch 9 (CTV) 9 Channel 9 Ct	Toronto	ON	M4A2M9	416-332-5000	299-2273
TF: 800-668-0060 ■ *Web:* www.cftonews.com					
CICA-TV Ch 19 (Ind) 2180 Yonge St Box 200 Stn Q	Toronto	ON	M4T2T1	416-484-2600	484-4234
TF: 800-613-0513 ■ *Web:* www.tvo.org					
CITY-TV Ch 57 (Ind) 299 Queen St W	Toronto	ON	M5V2Z5	416-591-7400	593-6391
Web: www.citytv.com/toronto					
CKVR-TV Ch 3 (Ind) 33 Beacon Rd PO Box 519	Barrie	ON	L4M4T9	705-734-3300	733-0302
Web: www.thenewvr.com					

744-142 Tucson, AZ

				Phone	Fax
KGUN-TV Ch 9 (ABC) 7280 E Rosewood St	Tucson	AZ	85710	520-722-5486	733-7050
Web: www.kgun9.com					
KHRR-TV Ch 40 (Tele) 5151 E Broadway Blvd Suite 600	Tucson	AZ	85711	520-396-2600	396-2640
KMSB-TV Ch 11 (Fox) 1855 N 6th Ave	Tucson	AZ	85705	520-770-1123	629-7185
Web: www.fox11az.com/news					
KOLD-TV Ch 13 (CBS) 7831 N Business Park Dr	Tucson	AZ	85743	520-744-1313	744-5235
Web: www.kold.com					
KTTU-TV Ch 18 (MNT) 1855 N 6th Ave	Tucson	AZ	85705	520-624-0180	629-7185
Web: www.kttu.com					
KUAT-TV Ch 6 (PBS) University of Arizona PO Box 210067	Tucson	AZ	85721	520-621-5828	621-4122*
**Fax:* News Rm ■ *Web:* kuat.org					
KVOA-TV Ch 4 (NBC) 209 W Elm PO Box 5188	Tucson	AZ	85703	520-792-2270	620-1309
Web: www.kvoa.com					
KWBA-TV Ch 58 (CW) 3481 E Michigan St	Tucson	AZ	85714	520-889-5800	889-5855
Web: www.kwba.com					

744-143 Tulsa, OK

				Phone	Fax
KJRH-TV Ch 2 (NBC) 3701 S Peoria Ave	Tulsa	OK	74105	918-743-2222	748-1436
Web: www.kjrh.com					
KOKI-TV Ch 23 (Fox) 2625 S Memorial Dr	Tulsa	OK	74129	918-491-0023	491-6650
Web: www.fox23.com					
KOTV-TV Ch 6 (CBS) PO Box 6	Tulsa	OK	74101	918-732-6000	732-6016
Web: www.kotv.com					
KQCW-TV Ch 12 (CW) 233 S Detroit Ave Suite 100	Tulsa	OK	74120	918-280-7400	280-0019
Web: www.wb19.com					
KTFO-TV Ch 41 (MNT) 2625 S Memorial Dr	Tulsa	OK	74129	918-491-0023	388-0516
Web: www.upn41.com					
KTUL-TV Ch 8 (ABC) PO Box 8	Tulsa	OK	74101	918-445-8888	445-9316
Web: www.ktul.com					
KWHB-TV Ch 47 (Ind) 8835 S Memorial Dr	Tulsa	OK	74133	918-254-4701	254-5614
Web: www.kwhb.com					

744-144 Vancouver, BC

				Phone	Fax
CBUFT-TV Ch 26 (SRC) 700 Hamilton St	Vancouver	BC	V6B4A2	604-662-6212	662-6229
CBUT-TV Ch 2 (CBC) 700 Hamilton St PO Box 4600	Vancouver	BC	V6B4A2	604-662-6000	662-6878
Web: www.cbc.ca/bc					
CHAN-TV Ch 8 (GTN) 7850 Enterprise St	Vancouver	BC	V5A1V7	604-420-2288	421-9427
Web: www.canada.com/vancouver					
CIVI-TV Ch 12 (Ind) 1420 Broad St	Victoria	BC	V8W2B1	250-381-2484	381-2485
TF: 866-242-2484 ■ *Web:* www.achannel.ca/victoria					
CIVT-TV Ch 9 (CTV) 750 Burrard St Suite 300	Vancouver	BC	V6Z1X5	604-608-2868	608-2698
Web: www.bcctv.ca					
CKVU-TV Ch 10 (Ind) 180 W 2nd Ave	Vancouver	BC	V5Y3T9	604-876-1344	876-2476
TF: 888-336-9978 ■ *Web:* www.citytv.com/vancouver					

744-145 Washington, DC

				Phone	Fax
WDCA-TV Ch 20 (MNT) 5151 Wisconsin Ave NW	Washington	DC	20016	202-895-3050	895-3340
Web: www.upn20wdca.com					
WDCW-TV Ch 50 (CW) 2121 Wisconsin Ave NW Suite 350	Washington	DC	20007	202-965-5050	965-0050
Web: thecwdc.trb.com					
WETA-TV Ch 26 (PBS) 2775 S Quincy St	Arlington	VA	22206	703-998-1801	998-3401
Web: www.weta.org					
WHUT-TV Ch 32 (PBS) 2222 4th St NW	Washington	DC	20059	202-806-3200	806-3300
Web: www.howard.edu/tv/					
WJLA-TV Ch 7 (ABC) 1100 Wilson Blvd	Arlington	VA	22209	703-236-9552	236-2331
Web: www.wjla.com					
WPXW-TV Ch 66 (I) 6199 Old Arrington Ln	Fairfax Station	VA	22039	703-503-7966	503-1225
WRC-TV Ch 4 (NBC) 4001 Nebraska Ave NW	Washington	DC	20016	202-885-4000	885-4104
Web: www.nbc4.com					
WTTG-TV Ch 5 (Fox) 5151 Wisconsin Ave NW	Washington	DC	20016	202-244-5151	895-3132*
**Fax:* News Rm ■ *TF:* 800-988-4885 ■ *Web:* www.fox5dc.com					
WUSA-TV Ch 9 (CBS) 4100 Wisconsin Ave NW	Washington	DC	20016	202-895-5999	364-6163
Web: www.wusatv9.com					

744-146 West Palm Beach, FL

				Phone	Fax
WFGC-TV Ch 61 (Ind) 1900 S Congress Ave Suite A	West Palm Beach	FL	33406	561-642-3361	967-5961
Web: www.wfgc.com					
WFLX-TV Ch 29 (Fox) 4119 W Blue Heron Blvd	West Palm Beach	FL	33404	561-845-2929	863-1238
Web: www.wflxfox29.com					
WPBF-TV Ch 25 (ABC) 3970 RCA Blvd Suite 7007	Palm Beach Gardens	FL	33410	561-694-2525	624-1089
Web: www.wpbfnews.com					
WPEC-TV Ch 12 (CBS) 1100 Fairfield Dr	West Palm Beach	FL	33407	561-844-1212	842-1212
Web: www.wpecnews12.com					
WPTV-TV Ch 5 (NBC) 1100 Banyan Blvd	West Palm Beach	FL	33401	561-655-5455	653-5719*
**Fax:* News Rm ■ *Web:* www.wptv.com					
WPXP-TV Ch 67 (I) 601 Clearwater Park Rd	West Palm Beach	FL	33401	561-659-4122	659-4252
TF: 800-646-7296 ■ *Web:* www.ionline.tv					
WTVX-TV Ch 34 (CW) 1700 Palm Beach Lakes Blvd	West Palm Beach	FL	33401	561-681-3434	684-9193
Web: www.upn34.com					
WXEL-TV Ch 42 (PBS) PO Box 6607	West Palm Beach	FL	33405	561-737-8000	369-3067
TF: 800-915-9935 ■ *Web:* www.wxel.org					

744-147 Wheeling, WV

				Phone	Fax
WNPB-TV Ch 24 (PBS) 191 Scott Ave	Morgantown	WV	26508	304-284-1440	284-1454
TF: 888-596-9729					
WTOV-TV Ch 9 (NBC) 9 Red Donley Plaza	Mingo Junction	OH	43938	740-282-0911	282-0439
TF: 800-288-0799 ■ *Web:* www.wtov9.com					
WTRF-TV Ch 7 (CBS) 96 16th St	Wheeling	WV	26003	304-232-7777	233-5822*
**Fax:* News Rm ■ *TF:* 800-777-9873 ■ *Web:* www.wtrf.com					

744-148 Wichita, KS

				Phone	Fax
KAKE-TV Ch 10 (ABC) 1500 N West St	Wichita	KS	67203	316-943-4221	943-5374
Web: www.kake.com					
KPTS-TV Ch 8 (PBS) 320 W 21 St	Wichita	KS	67203	316-838-3090	838-8586
TF: 800-794-8498 ■ *Web:* www.kpts.org					
KSAS-TV Ch 24 (Fox) 316 N West St	Wichita	KS	67203	316-942-2424	942-8927
Web: www.foxkansas.com					
KSCC-TV Ch 36 (MNT) 316 N West St	Wichita	KS	67203	316-941-1036	942-8927
Web: www.mytvwichita.com					
KSCW-TV Ch 33 (CW) 200 W Douglas Ave 7th Fl	Wichita	KS	67202	316-303-0700	303-0160
Web: www.kansascw.com					
KSNW-TV Ch 3 (NBC) 833 N Main St	Wichita	KS	67203	316-265-3333	292-1195
TF: 800-949-5769 ■ *Web:* www.ksn.com					
KWCH-TV Ch 12 (CBS) 2815 E 37th St North	Wichita	KS	67219	316-838-1212	831-6193
TF: 888-512-6397 ■ *Web:* www.kwch.com					

744-149 Winnipeg, MB

				Phone	Fax
CBWF-TV Ch 3 (SRC) 541 Portage Ave	Winnipeg	MB	R3C2H1	204-788-3222	788-3255
TF: 866-306-4636					
CBWT-TV Ch 6 (CBC) 541 Portage Ave	Winnipeg	MB	R3C2H1	204-788-3222	788-3643
TF: 866-306-4636 ■ *Web:* www.cbc.ca/manitoba					
CHMI-TV Ch 13 (Ind) 8 Forks Market Rd	Winnipeg	MB	R3C4Y3	204-947-9613	956-0811
Web: www.achannel.com					
CKND-TV Ch 9 (GTN) 603 St Mary's Rd	Winnipeg	MB	R2M3L8	204-233-3304	233-5615
Web: www.canada.com/winnipeg					
CKY-TV Ch 5 (CTV) Polo Park	Winnipeg	MB	R3G0L7	204-788-3300	780-3297*
**Fax:* News Rm ■ *Web:* www.cky.com					

744-150 Winston-Salem, NC

				Phone	Fax
WCWG-TV Ch 20 (CW) 622G Guilford College Rd	Greensboro	NC	27409	336-547-0020	547-8144
Web: www.wtwb.com					
WFMY-TV Ch 2 (CBS) 1615 Phillips Ave	Greensboro	NC	27405	336-379-9369	273-9433
Web: www.wfmy.com					
WGHP-TV Ch 8 (Fox) HP-8	High Point	NC	27261	336-841-8888	841-5169
Web: www.fox8wghp.com					
WGPX-TV Ch 16 (I) 1114 N O' Henry Blvd	Greensboro	NC	27405	336-272-9227	703-6138
WMYV-TV Ch 48 (MNT) 3500 Myer Lee Dr	Winston-Salem	NC	27101	336-274-4848	723-8217
Web: www.upn48.com					
WXII-TV Ch 12 (NBC) 700 Coliseum Dr	Winston-Salem	NC	27106	336-721-9944	721-0856
Web: www.wxii12.com					
WXLV-TV Ch 45 (ABC) 3500 Myer Lee Dr	Winston-Salem	NC	27101	336-722-4545	723-8217
Web: www.abc45.com					

744-151 Youngstown, OH

				Phone	Fax
WFMJ-TV Ch 21 (NBC) 101 W Boardman St	Youngstown	OH	44503	330-744-8611	742-2472
TF: 800-488-9365 ■ *Web:* www.wfmj.com					
WKBN-TV Ch 27 (CBS) 3930 Sunset Blvd	Youngstown	OH	44512	330-782-1144	782-3504
Web: www.wkbn.com					
WYFX-TV Ch 62 (Fox) 3930 Sunset Blvd	Youngstown	OH	44512	330-782-1114	782-3504
WYTV-TV Ch 33 (ABC) 3800 Shady Run Rd	Youngstown	OH	44502	330-783-2930	782-8154
TF: 800-686-2930 ■ *Web:* www.wytv.com					

745 TELEVISION SYNDICATORS

Television syndicators are companies that produce programming in-house and market and distribute the programs to networks on a national or regional basis.

				Phone	Fax
A Taste of New York Inc 10 Roberta Ln	Syosset	NY	11791	516-677-0239	677-9278
Web: www.tasteofny.com					
ABC NewsOne 47 W 66th St 2nd Fl	New York	NY	10023	212-456-4110	456-2771
Access Television Network Inc 2600 Michelson Dr Suite 1650	Irvine	CA	92612	949-263-9900	757-1526
Web: www.accesstv.com					
American Public Television (APT) 55 Summer St 4th Fl	Boston	MA	02110	617-338-4455	338-5369
Web: www.aptvs.org					
AP Broadcast Services 1825 K St NW Suite 800	Washington	DC	20006	202-736-1100	736-1199
TF: 800-821-4747 ■ *Web:* apbroadcast.com					
Babe Winkelman Productions PO Box 407	Brainerd	MN	56401	218-822-4424	822-7436
TF: 800-333-0471 ■ *Web:* www.winkelman.com					
Buena Vista Television 500 S Buena Vista St	Burbank	CA	91521	818-460-6552	563-2178
CBS Newspath 524 W 57th St	New York	NY	10019	212-975-2881	541-8630
Web: www.newspath.cbs.com					
CF Entertainment Inc 9903 Santa Monica Blvd Suite 418	Beverly Hills	CA	90212	310-277-3500	277-3511
Web: www.entertainmentstudios.com					
Dick Clark Productions Inc 9200 Sunset Blvd 10th Fl	Los Angeles	CA	90069	310-786-8900	777-2187
Web: www.dickclarkproductions.com					
Five Star Productions 430 S Congress Ave	Delray Beach	FL	33445	561-279-7827	279-4808
Web: www.fivestarproductions.com					
Georgia Public Broadcasting (GPB) 260 14th St NW	Atlanta	GA	30318	404-685-4788	685-2431
TF: 800-222-6006 ■ *Web:* www.gpb.org					
GRTV (Guthy-Renker Television Network)					
3340 Ocean Pk Suite 3055	Santa Monica	CA	90405	310-581-6250	581-3232
Web: www.guthy-renker.com					
Guthy-Renker Television Network (GRTV)					
3340 Ocean Pk Suite 3055	Santa Monica	CA	90405	310-581-6250	581-3232
Web: www.guthy-renker.com					
Harpo Productions Inc 110 N Carpenter	Chicago	IL	60607	312-633-1000	633-1976
Web: www.oprah.com					
Hearst Entertainment & Syndication Group 300 W 57th St	New York	NY	10019	212-649-2500	245-2306
Web: www.hearstcorp.com/entertainment					
Independent Television Service (ITVS)					
651 Brannan St Suite 410	San Francisco	CA	94107	415-356-8383	356-8391
Web: www.itvs.org					

Phone Fax

Information Television Network 621 NW 53rd St Suite 350 Boca Raton FL 33487 561-997-5433 997-5208
TF: 800-463-6488 ■ *Web:* www.itvisus.com
Initiative Corp 5700 Wilshire Blvd Suite 400 Los Angeles CA 90036 323-370-8000 370-8965
Web: www.im-na.com
Inside Albany Productions Inc Capitol Stn PO Box 7328 Albany NY 12224 518-426-3771 426-5396
Web: www.insidealbany.com
Ivanhoe Broadcast News 2745 W Fairbanks Ave Winter Park FL 32789 407-740-0789 740-5320
Web: www.ivanhoe.com
Jameson Broadcast Inc 1644 Hawthorne St Sarasota FL 34239 941-906-8800 906-8801
Web: www.jamesonbroadcast.com
King World Productions Inc 2401 Colorado Ave Suite 110 Santa Monica CA 90404 310-264-3300 264-3301
Web: www.kingworld.com
KJD Teleproductions 30 Whyte Dr Voorhees NJ 08043 856-751-3500 751-7729
Litton Entertainment 790 Johnnie Dodds Blvd Suite 201 Mount Pleasant SC 29464 843-883-5060 883-9957
Web: www.litton.tv
Medstar Television Inc 5920 Hamilton Blvd Allentown PA 18106 610-395-1300 391-1556
Web: www.medstar.com
National Educational Telecommunications Assn (NETA)
PO Box 50008 Columbia SC 29250 803-799-5517 771-4831
Web: www.netaonline.org
NBC Enterprises 3000 W Alameda Ave Burbank CA 91523 818-526-6900 526-6922
Web: www.nbcenterprises.com
Oliver Productions Inc
1717 Rhode Island Ave NW Suite 640 Washington DC 20036 202-457-0870 296-2285
Web: www.mclaughlin.com
Program Resources Group (PRG) 450 W 33rd St 7th Fl New York NY 10001 212-974-2121 560-4921
Web: www.programresourcesgroup.com
RCTV International 4380 NW 128th St Miami FL 33054 305-688-7475 685-5697
Web: www.rctvintl.com
Reuters Television International Ltd
3 Times Sq Reuters Bldg 4th Fl New York NY 10036 646-223-4000
Web: www.reuters.com
Telepictures Productions 3500 W Olive Ave Suite 1000 Burbank CA 91505 818-972-0777 972-0864
Web: www.telepicturestv.com
Tribune Entertainment Co 5800 Sunset Blvd Los Angeles CA 90028 323-460-5800 460-5892
Web: www.tribtv.com
TV Japan 100 Broadway 15th Fl New York NY 10005 212-262-3377 262-5577
TF Cust Svc: 877-885-2726 ■ *Web:* www.tvjapan.net
TVA Productions 3950 Vantage Ave Studio City CA 91604 818-505-8300 505-8370
Web: www.tvaproductions.com
UniWorld Entertainment 100 Ave of the Americas 16th Fl New York NY 10013 212-219-1600 274-8565
Web: www.uniworldgroup.com
Warner Bros Domestic Television Distribution
4000 Warner Blvd Burbank CA 91522 818-954-6000
WPT Enterprises Inc 5700 Wilshire Blvd Suite 350 Los Angeles CA 90036 323-330-9900 850-2870
NASDAQ: WPTE ■ *Web:* www.worldpokertour.com

746 TESTING FACILITIES

Phone Fax

ABC Research Corp 3437 SW 24th Ave Gainesville FL 32607 352-372-0436 378-6483
Web: www.abcr.com
Accutest Laboratories 2235 Rt 130 Bldg B Dayton NJ 08810 732-329-0200 329-3499
TF: 800-329-0204 ■ *Web:* www.accutest.com
Acuren Inspection Inc 101 Old Underwood Rd Bldg J La Porte TX 77571 281-842-3350 842-3370
TF: 800-853-4417 ■ *Web:* www.acuren.com
Adamson Analytical Laboratories Inc 2200 Crouse Dr Corona CA 92879 951-549-9657 549-9659
Web: www.adamsonlab.com
Aguirre Engineering LLC 13276 E Fremont Pl Centennial CO 80112 303-799-8378 799-8392
TF: 800-403-7066
Air Force Flight Test Center
AFFTC/PA 1 S Rosamond Blvd Edwards AFB CA 93524 661-277-3510 277-2732
Web: www.edwards.af.mil
Aircraft X-Ray Labs Inc 5216 Pacific Blvd Huntington Park CA 90255 323-587-4141 588-6410
Web: www.aircraftxray.com
All Metals Processing of Orange County Inc
8401 Standustrial St Stanton CA 90680 714-828-8238 828-4552
TF: 800-894-4489 ■ *Web:* www.allmetalsprocessing.com
Altran Corp 451 D St Boston MA 02210 617-204-1000 204-1010
TF: 800-281-2506 ■ *Web:* www.altran.com
Alucid Solutions Inc 5887 Glenridge Dr Suite 350 Atlanta GA 30328 678-904-9490 904-9490
Web: www.usabilitysystems.com
American Standards Testing Bureau Inc PO Box 583 New York NY 10274 212-943-3160 825-2250
TF: 800-221-5170
Analysts Inc 2441 W 205 St Suite C-100 Torrance CA 90501 310-320-0070 320-0970
TF: 800-336-3637 ■ *Web:* www.analystsinc.com
Animal & Plant Health Inspection Service (APHIS) National Veterinary Services Laboratories 1800 Dayton Ave PO Box 844 Ames IA 50010 515-663-7200 663-7402
Web: www.aphis.usda.gov/vs/nvsl
AppLabs Inc 387 S 520 W Suite 100 Lindon UT 84042 801-852-9500 852-9501
Web: www.applabs.com
Arnold Engineering Development Center (AEDC)
AEDC Public Affairs 100 Kindell Dr Suite B-213 Arnold AFB TN 37389 931-454-4204 454-6086*
**Fax: Hum Res* ■ *Web:* www.arnold.af.mil
Astro Pak Corp 270 E Baker St Suite 100 Costa Mesa CA 92626 949-270-0400 540-0627*
**Fax Area Code: 714* ■ *TF:* 800-743-5444 ■ *Web:* www.astropakcorp.com
Atlas Testing Labs Inc 6929 E Slauson Ave Commerce CA 90040 323-722-8810 888-1493
Ballantine Laboratories Inc 9 Saddle Rd Cedar Knolls NJ 07927 973-984-1900 984-1479
Web: www.ballantinelabs.com
Bioanalytical Systems Inc Clinical Research Unit
302 W Fayette St Baltimore MD 21201 410-385-4500 385-1957
TF: 800-787-7800 ■ *Web:* www.pharmakinetics.com
Bosch Automotive Proving Grounds 32104 State Rd 2 New Carlisle IN 46552 574-654-4000 654-8755
Web: www.bosch.us
Brook Environmental & Engineering Corp
11419 Cronridge Dr Suite 10 Owings Mills MD 21117 410-356-4875 356-5073
TF: 800-381-4434 ■ *Web:* www.brookeng.com
Brown Dayton T Inc 1175 Church St Bohemia NY 11716 631-589-6300 589-4046
TF: 800-232-6300 ■ *Web:* www.daytontbrown.com
Camin Cargo Control Inc 230 Marion Ave Linden NJ 07036 908-862-1899 523-0616*
**Fax: Hum Res* ■ *TF:* 800-756-8798 ■ *Web:* www.camincargo.com
Cedtech Testing Labs 10708 S Garfield Ave South Gate CA 90280 323-773-7835 773-4362
Celsis International 6200 S Lindbergh Blvd Saint Louis MO 63123 314-487-6776 487-8991
Web: www.celsis.com
Center for Devices & Radiological Health
9200 Corporate Blvd Suite 100G Rockville MD 20850 800-638-2041 443-8818*
**Fax Area Code: 301* ■ *Web:* www.fda.gov/cdrh
Construction Technology Laboratories Inc 5400 Old Orchard Rd Skokie IL 60077 847-965-7500 965-6541
TF: 800-522-2285 ■ *Web:* www.ctlgroup.com
Construction Testing & Engineering Inc 242 W Larch Rd Suite F Tracy CA 95304 209-839-2890 839-2895
TF: 800-576-2271 ■ *Web:* www.cte-inc.net
Dayton T Brown Inc 1175 Church St Bohemia NY 11716 631-589-6300 589-4046
TF: 800-232-6300 ■ *Web:* www.daytontbrown.com

Phone Fax

Defiance Testing & Engineering Services Inc 1628 Northwood St Troy MI 48084 248-458-5900 458-5901
Web: www.defiancetest.com
Detroit Testing Lab Inc 27485 George Merrelli Dr Warren MI 48092 586-754-9000 754-9045
TF: 800-820-7009 ■ *Web:* www.dtl-inc.com
Dryden Flight Research Center PO Box 273 Edwards CA 93523 661-276-3311 276-3566
Web: www.dfrc.nasa.gov
EDO Technical Services Operations 254 E Ave K-4 Lancaster CA 93535 661-723-7368 948-7003
Web: www.edotso.com
Engineering Dynamics Inc 3925 S Kalamath St Englewood CO 80110 303-761-4367 761-4379
Web: www.engdynamics.com
Environmental Enterprises Inc 10163 Cincinnati Dayton Rd Cincinnati OH 45241 513-772-2818 782-8950
TF: 800-722-2818 ■ *Web:* www.eeienv.com
Evans Analytical Group 810 Kifer Rd Sunnyvale CA 94086 408-530-3500 530-3501
Web: www.eaglabs.com
FDA (Food & Drug Administration) Center for Devices & Radiological Health 9200 Corporate Blvd Suite 100G Rockville MD 20850 800-638-2041 443-8818*
**Fax Area Code: 301* ■ *Web:* www.fda.gov/cdrh
Food & Drug Administration (FDA) Center for Devices & Radiological Health 9200 Corporate Blvd Suite 100G Rockville MD 20850 800-638-2041 443-8818*
**Fax Area Code: 301* ■ *Web:* www.fda.gov/cdrh
Froehling & Robertson Inc 3015 Dumbarton Rd Richmond VA 23228 804-264-2701 264-1202
Web: www.fandr.com
GZA GeoEnvironmental Inc 1 Edgewater Dr Norwood MA 02062 781-278-3700 278-5701
Web: www.gza.com
Hunt Robert W Co Inc
580 Waters Edge Oak Creek Ctr Suite 210 Lombard IL 60148 630-691-4333 691-1688
Web: www.rwhunt.com
Idaho National Laboratory (INL) PO Box 1625 Idaho Falls ID 83415 866-495-7440 526-5408*
**Fax Area Code: 208* ■ *TF:* 800-708-2680 ■ *Web:* www.inl.gov
InformationWEEK Labs 600 Community Dr Manhasset NY 11030 516-562-5000 562-5036
Web: www.informationweek.com
Infoworld Test Center 501 2nd St Suite 120 San Francisco CA 94107 415-243-4344 543-2200
Web: www.infoworld.com/testcenter
Institute For Clean And Secure Energy
University of Utah 155 S 1452 E Rm 380 Salt Lake City UT 84112 801-585-1233 585-1456
Web: www.ices.utah.edu
Intertek Automotive Research 5404 Bandera Rd San Antonio TX 78238 210-684-2310 684-6074
Web: www.intertek-cb.com/newsitetest/services/ARL/index.shtml
Intertek Testing Services North America Inc 3933 US Rt 11 Cortland NY 13045 607-753-6711 756-9891
TF: 800-345-3851 ■ *Web:* www.intertek-etlsemko.com
Keweenaw Research Center
Michigan Technological University 1400 Townsend Dr Houghton MI 49931 906-487-2750 487-2202
Web: www.mtukrc.org
Lancaster Laboratories Inc
2425 New Holland Pike PO Box 12425 Lancaster PA 17605 717-656-2301 656-2681
Web: www.lancasterlabs.com
Laucks Testing Laboratories Inc 940 S Harney St Seattle WA 98108 206-767-5060 767-5063
Web: www.laucksslabs.com
Ledoux & Co Inc 359 Alfred Ave Teaneck NJ 07666 201-837-7160 837-1235
Web: www.ledoux.com
LFR Inc 194 Forbes Rd Suite 100 Braintree MA 02184 781-356-7300 356-2211
Web: www.lfr.com
Magna Chek Inc 32701 Edward Ave Madison Heights MI 48071 248-597-0089 597-0440
TF: 800-582-8947 ■ *Web:* www.magnachek.com
Magnetic Inspection Laboratory Inc
1401 Greenleaf Ave Elk Grove Village IL 60007 847-437-4488 437-4538
Web: www.milinc.com
Metcut Research Inc 3980 Rosslyn Dr Cincinnati OH 45209 513-271-5100 271-9511
TF: 800-966-2888 ■ *Web:* www.metcut.com
Modern Industries Inc 613 W 11th St Erie PA 16501 814-455-8061 453-4382
Web: www.mi-erie.com
MSE Technology Applications Inc PO Box 4078 Butte MT 59702 406-494-7100 494-7230
Web: www.mse-ta.com
Nanomaterials & Nanomanufacturing Research Center
University of South Florida Dept of Engineering 4202 E Fowler Ave ENB 118 Tampa FL 33620 813-974-2096 974-3610
Web: nnrc.eng.usf.edu
National Air & Radiation Environmental Laboratory (NAREL)
US Environmental Protection Agency 540 S Morris Ave Montgomery AL 36115 334-270-3400 270-3454
Web: www.epa.gov/narel
National Highway Traffic Safety Administration (NHTSA) Vehicle Research & Test Center 10820 SR 347 PO Box B37 East Liberty OH 43319 937-666-4511 666-3590
TF: 800-262-8309 ■ *Web:* www.nhtsa.gov
National Technical Systems Inc
24007 Ventura Blvd Suite 200 Calabasas CA 91302 818-591-0776 591-0899
NASDAQ: NTSC ■ *TF:* 800-759-2687 ■ *Web:* www.ntscorp.com
Naval Air Warfare Center Weapons Div 575 I Ave Suite 1 Point Mugu CA 93042 805-989-7113 989-8829
Web: www.nawcwpns.navy.mil
New Mexico State University Physical Science Laboratory
Stewart & Espina Sts Las Cruces NM 88003 505-646-9100 646-9434
Northwest Labs of Seattle 241 S Holden St Seattle WA 98108 206-763-6252 763-3949
Web: www.nwlabs1896.com
NU Laboratories Inc 312 Old Allerton Rd Annandale NJ 08801 908-713-9300 713-9001
Web: www.nulabs.com
Owensby & Kritikos Inc 671 Whitney Ave Bldg B Gretna LA 70056 504-368-3122 362-4546
TF: 800-749-3122 ■ *Web:* www.ok-insp.com
Penniman & Browne Inc PO Box 65309 Baltimore MD 21209 410-825-4131 321-7384
Web: www.pandbinc.com
Performance Validation LLC
2601 Fortune Cir Suite 200-C 1 Park Fletcher Indianapolis IN 46241 317-248-8848 248-0464
TF: 800-875-8897 ■ *Web:* www.perfval.com
Perry Technologies 100 East 17th St Riviera Beach FL 33404 561-842-5261 842-5303
Web: www.perrytech.com
Pittsburgh Testing Lab Div Professional Service Industries Inc
850 Poplar St Pittsburgh PA 15220 412-922-4000 922-4014
Web: www.psiusa.com
PPD Development Inc 929 N Front St Wilmington NC 28401 910-251-0081 762-5820
Web: www.ppdi.com
Professional Service Industries Inc Pittsburgh Testing Lab Div
850 Poplar St Pittsburgh PA 15220 412-922-4000 922-4014
Web: www.psiusa.com
Qore Property Science 11420 Johns Creek Pkwy Duluth GA 30097 770-476-3555 476-0213
TF: 877-767-3462 ■ *Web:* www.qore.net
Radiometrics Midwest Corp 12 E Devonwood Ave Romeoville IL 60446 815-293-0772 293-0820
Web: www.radiomet.com
Retlif Inc Testing Laboratories 795 Marconi Ave Ronkonkoma NY 11779 631-737-1500 737-1497
Web: www.retlif.com
Robert W Hunt Co Inc
580 Waters Edge Oak Creek Ctr Suite 210 Lombard IL 60148 630-691-4333 691-1688
Web: www.rwhunt.com
Rothe Development Inc 4614 Sinclair Rd San Antonio TX 78222 210-648-3131 648-4091
TF: 800-229-5209 ■ *Web:* www.rothe.com
SGS Canada Inc 6275 Northam Dr Unit 2 Mississauga ON L4V1Y8 905-676-9595 676-9362
TF: 800-636-0847 ■ *Web:* www.ca.sgs.com
SGS Life Science Services 310 Brunel Rd Mississauga ON L4Z2C2 905-890-4880 890-4890
Web: www.sgs.com/life_sciences

				Phone	Fax
SGS US Testing Co Inc 291 Fairfield Ave	Fairfield	NJ	07004	973-575-5252	575-7175
TF Cust Svc: 800-777-8378 ■ *Web:* www.us.sgs.com					
Sigma Test Labs 1480 W 178th St	Gardena	CA	90248	310-324-9465	532-6216
Web: www.sigmatestlabs.com					
Smith-Emery Co 781 E Washington Blvd	Los Angeles	CA	90021	213-749-3411	741-8620
TF: 800-734-9747 ■ *Web:* www.smithemery.com					
Southern Petroleum Lab Inc 8880 Interchange Dr	Houston	TX	77054	713-660-0901	660-8975
TF: 800-969-6775 ■ *Web:* www.spl-inc.com					
Specialized Technology Resources Inc 10 Water St	Enfield	CT	06082	860-749-8371	749-7533
TF: 800-729-8371 ■ *Web:* www.strlab.com					
Stennis Space Center Blach Blvd Bldg 1100	Stennis Space Center	MS	39529	228-688-2211	688-1094*
**Fax:* PR ■ *Web:* www.nasa.gov/centers/stennis					
STERIS-Isomedix Services Inc 2500 Commerce Dr	Libertyville	IL	60048	847-247-0970	247-0882
Web: www.steris.com/isomedix/isomedix.cfm					
Stork Herron Testing Laboratories Inc 5405 E Schaaf Rd	Cleveland	OH	44131	216-524-1450	524-1459
Web: www.stork-herron.com					
Sypris Test & Measurement 6120 Hanging Moss Rd	Orlando	FL	32807	407-678-6900	671-0664
TF: 800-775-2550 ■ *Web:* www.sypris.com/stm					
Teledyne Brown Engineering Environmental Services					
PO Box 070007	Huntsville	AL	35807	256-726-1000	726-1010*
**Fax:* Hum Res ■ *TF:* 800-933-2091 ■ *Web:* www.tbe.com/businessUnits/environmental					
Terra Tek Inc 1935 S Fremont Dr	Salt Lake City	UT	84104	801-584-2400	584-2406
TF: 800-372-2522 ■ *Web:* www.terratek.com					
TestAmerica Laboratories Inc 122 Lyman St	Asheville	NC	28801	828-258-3746	258-1292*
**Fax:* Sales ■ *TF:* 800-344-5759 ■ *Web:* www.testamericainc.com					
Tolly Group 3701 Sau Blvd Suite 100	Boca Raton	FL	33431	561-391-5610	391-5810
Web: www.tolly.com					
Transportation Research Center Inc (TRC Inc)					
10820 Rt 347 PO Box B-67	East Liberty	OH	43319	937-666-2011	666-5066
TF: 800-837-7872 ■ *Web:* www.trcpg.com					
Transportation Technology Center Inc					
55500 DOT Rd PO Box 11130	Pueblo	CO	81001	719-584-0750	584-0711
Web: www.aar.com					
Truesdail Laboratories Inc 14201 Franklin Ave	Tustin	CA	92780	714-730-6239	730-6462
Web: www.truesdail.com					
Turner-Fairbank Highway Research Center					
6300 Georgetown Pike	McLean	VA	22101	202-493-3165	493-3170
Web: www.tfhrc.gov					
Twin City Testing 662 Cromwell Ave	Saint Paul	MN	55114	651-645-3601	659-7348
TF: 888-645-8378 ■ *Web:* www.twincitytesting.com					
Twining Laboratories of Southern California Inc					
3310 Airport Way	Long Beach	CA	90806	562-426-3355	426-6424
Web: www.twininglabs.com					
Underwriters Laboratories Inc 333 Pfingsten Rd	Northbrook	IL	60062	847-272-8800	272-8129
Web: www.ul.com					
US Army Aviation Technical Test Center					
Cairns Army Air Field Bldg 30601	Fort Rucker	AL	36362	334-255-8000	255-8005
TF: 888-838-1306 ■ *Web:* www.attc.army.mil					
US Army Dugway Proving Ground	Dugway	UT	84022	435-831-2151	831-2420
US Army Electronic Proving Ground CSTE-DTC-EP-CO	Fort Huachuca	AZ	85613	520-533-8267	538-6361
Web: www.epg.army.mil					
US Army Space & Missile Defense Command HELFSTF Directorate SMDC-AC-H US Hwy					
70 MM 186	White Sands Missile Range	NM	88002	505-679-5041	679-5068
US Army White Sands Missile Range	White Sands	NM	88002	505-678-2121	
Web: www.wsmr.army.mil					
US Army Yuma Proving Ground 301 C St	Yuma	AZ	85365	928-328-2163	328-6249
Web: www.yuma.army.mil					
US Biosystems Inc 3231 NW 7th Ave	Boca Raton	FL	33431	561-447-7373	447-6136
TF: 888-862-5227 ■ *Web:* www.usbiosystems.com					
Valley Lea Laboratories 4609 Grape Rd Suite D-4	Mishawaka	IN	46545	574-272-8484	272-8485
TF: 800-822-1283					
Vehicle Research & Test Center					
10820 SR 347 PO Box B37	East Liberty	OH	43319	937-666-4511	666-3590
TF: 800-262-8309 ■ *Web:* www.nhtsa.gov					
VeriTest 1050 Winter St Suite 2300	Waltham	MA	02451	781-434-6000	434-6064
TF: 877-342-5334 ■ *Web:* www.veritest.com					
Wadsworth Center					
Biggs Laboratory New York Department of Health Empire State Plaza PO Box 509	Albany	NY	12201	518-474-2160	
Web: www.wadsworth.org					
Wallops Flight Facility Office of Public Affairs	Wallops Island	VA	23337	757-824-1579	824-1971
Web: www.wff.nasa.gov/					
WIL Research Laboratories Inc 1407 George Rd	Ashland	OH	44805	419-289-8700	289-3650
TF Cust Svc: 800-221-9610 ■ *Web:* www.wilresearch.com					
Wyle Laboratories 128 Maryland St	El Segundo	CA	90245	310-322-1763	322-3603
Web: www.wylelabs.com					

747 TEXTILE MACHINERY

				Phone	Fax
AB Carter Inc 4801 York Hwy PO Box 518	Gastonia	NC	28053	704-865-1201	864-8870
Web: www.abcarter.com					
Advanced Innovative Technologies LLC 530 Wilbanks Dr	Ball Ground	GA	30107	770-479-1900	479-4179
Web: www.aitequipment.com					
Barudan America Inc 29500 Fountain Pkwy	Solon	OH	44139	440-248-8770	248-8856
TF: 800-627-4776 ■ *Web:* www.barudan.com					
Baxter Corp 211 N Poston St PO Box 1766	Shelby	NC	28150	704-482-2476	487-1216
Belmont Textile Machinery Co					
1212 W Catawba St PO Box 568	Mount Holly	NC	28120	704-827-5836	827-8551
Web: www.btmc.com					
Bowman Hollis Mfg Inc 2925 Old Steele Creek Rd	Charlotte	NC	28208	704-374-1500	333-5520
TF: 888-269-2358 ■ *Web:* www.bowmanhollis.com					
Carter AB Inc 4801 York Hwy PO Box 518	Gastonia	NC	28053	704-865-1201	864-8870
Web: www.abcarter.com					
Cobble/Tufting Machine Co Inc 1731 Kimberly Park Dr	Dalton	GA	30720	706-278-1857	226-8223
Web: www.cobbleusa.com					
Custom Industries Inc 6106 W Market St	Greensboro	NC	27409	336-299-2885	294-2472
Web: www.customindustries.com					
Day International Inc 130 W 2nd St Suite 1700	Dayton	OH	45401	937-224-4000	226-1466
Web: www.dayintl.com					
DR Kenyon & Son Inc PO Box 6200	Bridgewater	NJ	08807	908-722-0001	722-0002
Eastman Machine Co 779 Washington St	Buffalo	NY	14203	716-856-2200	856-1140
TF: 800-872-5571 ■ *Web:* www.eastmancuts.com					
Elliott Metal Works Inc 210 Old Piedmont Hwy PO Box 8675	Greenville	SC	29604	864-269-8930	269-8932
TF: 800-726-1542 ■ *Web:* www.elliottmetalworks.com					
Embroidery Store 2035 Soapstone Mountain Rd	Staley	NC	27355	336-622-1688	622-0854
TF Cust Svc: 800-727-4244 ■ *Web:* www.embstore.com					
Entec Composite Machines Inc 300 W 2975 South	Salt Lake City	UT	84115	801-486-8107	484-4363
Web: www.entec.com					
Fenner Dunlop Americas 21 Laredo Dr	Scottdale	GA	30079	404-297-3170	296-5165*
**Fax:* Sales ■ *Web:* www.gaduck.com					
Gaston County Dyeing Machine Co PO Box 308	Stanley	NC	28164	704-822-5000	827-0476
Web: www.gaston-county.com					
Gerber Technology Inc 24 Industrial Park Rd W	Tolland	CT	06084	860-871-8082	871-3779*
**Fax:* Mktg ■ *TF:* 800-826-3243 ■ *Web:* www.gerbertechnology.com					
Gribetz International Inc 13800 NW 4th St	Sunrise	FL	33325	954-846-0300	846-0381
TF: 800-326-4742 ■ *Web:* gsgcompanies.com/gribetz.htm					
GTP Inc 1801 Rutherford Rd	Greenville	SC	29609	864-288-5475	297-5081
Web: www.globaltextilepartner.com					
Handy/Kenlin Group 1750 N 25th Ave	Melrose Park	IL	60160	708-450-9000	450-9047
Web: www.handykenlin.com					
HH Arnold Co Inc 529 Liberty St	Rockland	MA	02370	781-878-0346	878-7944
Web: www.hharnold.com					
Hirsch International Corp 50 Engineers Rd	Hauppauge	NY	11738	631-436-7100	772-1788*
NASDAQ: HRSH ■ **Fax Area Code:* 800 ■ *TF:* 800-394-4426 ■ *Web:* www.hirschintl.com					
Hix Corp 1201 E 27th Terr	Pittsburg	KS	66762	620-231-8568	231-1598
TF: 800-835-0606 ■ *Web:* www.hixcorp.com					
Ioline Corp 14140 NE 200th St	Woodinville	WA	98072	425-398-8282	398-8383
TF: 800-598-0029 ■ *Web:* www.ioline.com					
KMSCO Inc 1257 Westfield Ave	Clark	NJ	07066	732-382-9898	382-9479
TF: 877-898-2900 ■ *Web:* www.logoknits.com					
Kuesters Corp 101 Zima Park Dr	Spartanburg	SC	29301	864-576-0660	587-5761
Web: www.kuesters.com					
Lawson-Hemphill Inc 1658 G A R Hwy	Swansea	MA	02777	508-679-5364	679-5396
Web: www.lawsonhemphill.com					
LHP Corp 487 Leard St PO Box 448	Hartwell	GA	30643	706-376-8028	376-6844
Lummus Corp 1 Lummus Dr PO Box 4259	Savannah	GA	31407	912-447-9000	447-9250
TF: 800-458-6687 ■ *Web:* www.lummus.com					
Mayer Industries Inc 3777 Industrial Blvd	Orangeburg	SC	29118	803-536-3500	536-2545
Mayer Textile Machine Corp Inc 310 Brighton Rd PO Box 1240	Clifton	NJ	07012	973-773-3350	473-3463
MB Industries Inc Hwy 64 W PO Box 1118	Rosman	NC	28772	828-862-4201	862-4297
McCoy-Ellison Inc 1101 Curtis St PO Box 967	Monroe	NC	28111	704-289-5413	283-0480
TF: 800-811-5348 ■ *Web:* www.mccoy-ellison.com					
Morrison Berkshire Inc 865 S Church St	North Adams	MA	01247	413-663-6501	664-8738
Web: www.morrisonberkshire.com					
Mullen Testers Div Standex International Corp					
939 Chicopee St	Chicopee	MA	01013	413-536-1311	536-1367
Web: www.mullenbursttesters.com					
Petty Machine Co Inc 2403 Forbes Rd	Gastonia	NC	28056	704-864-3254	861-1937
TF: 800-343-0960					
Pneumafil Corp Textile Systems Div					
440-A Chesapeake Dr PO Box 16348	Charlotte	NC	28297	704-399-7441	398-7516
TF: 800-525-1560 ■ *Web:* www.pneumafil.com/td					
Rando Machine Corp 1071 Rt 31 PO Box 614	Macedon	NY	14502	315-986-2761	986-7943
Web: www.randomachine.com					
Saco Lowell Parts LLC 115 Saco Lowell Rd PO Box 307	Easley	SC	29641	864-850-4400	859-2908
TF: 800-845-0103 ■ *Web:* www.sacolowell.com					
Saurer Inc 8801 South blvd	Charlotte	NC	28273	704-588-0072	554-7350
Web: saurerinclive.oca.ch/					
Standex International Corp Mullen Testers Div					
939 Chicopee St	Chicopee	MA	01013	413-536-1311	536-1367
Web: www.mullenbursttesters.com					
Stork Prints America Inc 3201 Rotary Dr	Charlotte	NC	28269	704-598-7171	569-0858
Web: www.storktextile.com					
Thermopatch Corp 2204 Erie Blvd E	Syracuse	NY	13224	315-446-8110	445-8046
TF Cust Svc: 800-252-6555 ■ *Web:* www.thermopatch.com					
Tidland Corp 2305 SE 8th Ave	Camas	WA	98607	360-834-2345	834-5865
TF: 800-426-1000 ■ *Web:* www.tidland.com					
Tompkins Brothers Co Inc 623 Oneida St	Syracuse	NY	13202	315-475-9925	475-5733
Web: www.tompkinsbros.com					
TrimMaster 4860 N 5th St Hwy	Temple	PA	19560	610-921-0203	929-8833
TF: 800-356-4237 ■ *Web:* www.trimmaster.com					
Tubular Textile Machinery 113 Woodside Dr PO Box 2097	Lexington	NC	27293	336-956-6444	956-1795
TF: 800-531-3715 ■ *Web:* www.tubetex.com					
Tuftco Corp 2318 S Holtzclaw Ave	Chattanooga	TN	37408	423-698-8601	698-0842
TF: 800-288-3826 ■ *Web:* www.tuftco.com					
Tuftco Finishing Systems 100 W Industrial Blvd	Dalton	GA	30720	706-277-1110	277-4334
Vanguard Supreme 601 MacArthur Cir	Monroe	NC	28110	704-283-8171	283-9257
TF: 800-222-1971 ■ *Web:* www.vanguardsupreme.com					
VITA Link Machine Group DBA Embroidery Store					
2035 Soapstone Mountain Rd	Staley	NC	27355	336-622-1688	622-0854
TF Cust Svc: 800-727-4244 ■ *Web:* www.embstore.com					
Wardwell Braiding Machine Co 1211 High St	Central Falls	RI	02863	401-724-8800	723-2690
Web: www.wardwell.com					
West Point Foundry & Machine Co					
2021 Stateline Rd PO Box 589	West Point	GA	31833	706-643-2127	643-2100
Web: www.westpoint.com					
Whirlaway Corp 720 Shiloh Ave	Wellington	OH	44090	440-647-4711	647-3962
Web: www.whirlawaycorporation.com					

748 TEXTILE MILLS

748-1 Broadwoven Fabric Mills

				Phone	Fax
Alice Mfg Co Inc 208 E 1st Ave	Easley	SC	29640	864-859-6323	859-6328
TF: 800-695-2542 ■ *Web:* www.alicemfgco.com					
American Cotton Growers Textile Div 1926 FM 54	Littlefield	TX	79339	806-385-6401	385-5155
TF: 800-333-8011 ■ *Web:* www.pcca.com/Divisions/Textile					
American Silk Mills Corp 75 Stark St	Plains	PA	18705	570-822-7147	829-7044
Web: www.americansilk.com					
American Velvet Co 22 Bayview Ave	Stonington	CT	06378	860-535-1050	535-4398
Belding Hausman Inc 2130 E Main St	Lincolnton	NC	28092	704-735-2581	748-9863
TF: 800-350-2353 ■ *Web:* www.beldinghausman.com					
Bloomsburg Mills Inc 111 W 40th St 10th Fl	New York	NY	10018	212-221-6114	354-9375
Web: www.bloomsburgmills.net					
Burlington WorldWide Apparel Fabrics Group					
804 Green Valley Rd Suite 300	Greensboro	NC	27408	336-379-2000	379-6470
TF: 800-763-0123					
Carolina Mills Inc 618 Carolina Ave	Maiden	NC	28650	828-428-9911	428-2335
Web: www.carolinamills.com					
Carpostan Industries Inc 205 W 12th Ave	Lake View	SC	29563	843-759-2105	759-2594
Carthage Fabrics Corp 261 Niagara-Carthage Rd PO Box 398	Carthage	NC	28327	910-947-2211	947-5352
TF: 800-541-4877					
Central Textiles Inc 237 Mill Ave	Central	SC	29630	864-639-2491	639-4513
Circa 1801 1 Jacquard Dr	Connelly Springs	NC	28612	828-397-7003	397-1867
TF Cust Svc: 800-462-9295					
Cone Denim LLC 804 Green Valley Rd Suite 300	Greensboro	NC	27408	336-379-6220	379-6043
TF: 800-763-0123					
Cone Jacquards 3400 Hwy 221 A	Cliffside	NC	28024	828-657-9662	657-4941
Copland Fabrics Inc PO Box 1208	Burlington	NC	27216	336-226-0272	229-9551
Web: www.coplandfabrics.com					
Covington Industries Inc 386 Park Ave S 18th Fl	New York	NY	10016	212-689-2200	576-1167
Web: www.covington-industries.com					

Broadwoven Fabric Mills (Cont'd)

Company	City	State	ZIP	Phone	Fax
Covington Upholstery Fabrics Inc 317 W High St 7th Fl.	High Point	NC	27260	336-883-4141	889-6387
Web: www.covington-industries.com					
Craftex Mills Inc 450 Sentry Pkwy E	Blue Bell	PA	19422	610-941-1212	941-7171
TF: 866-992-5684 ■ Web: www.craftex.com					
Culp Inc 1823 E Chester Dr.	High Point	NC	27265	336-889-5161	881-8615
NYSE: CFI ■ Web: www.culpinc.com					
Culp Woven Velvets Inc 414 W Hampton St	Anderson	SC	29624	864-226-2857	225-9006
Dan River Inc 700 Lanier Ave	Danville	VA	24541	434-799-7000	799-2984
TF: 800-645-0880 ■ Web: www.danriver.com					
Delta Woodside Industries Inc 700 N Woods Dr.	Fountain Inn	SC	29644	864-255-4100	255-4165
Web: www.deltawoodside.com					
DeRoyal Textiles Inc 125 E York St	Camden	SC	29020	803-432-2403	425-4566
TF Sales: 800-845-1062 ■ Web: www.deroyal.com/OEM/textiles/					
Dicey Mills Inc 430 Neisler St	Shelby	NC	28151	704-487-6324	482-1972
Faribault Mills 1500 NW 2nd Ave PO Box 369	Faribault	MN	55021	507-334-6444	332-2936
TF: 800-533-0444 ■ Web: www.faribaultmills.com					
Fortune Fabrics Inc 315 Simpson St	Swoyersville	PA	18704	570-288-3666	283-2124
Web: www.fortunefabrics.net					
Galey & Lord Inc 7736 McCloud Rd Suite 300	Greensboro	NC	27409	336-665-3000	665-3106
TF Cust Svc: 800-527-9548					
Glass Henry & Co 49 W 37th St 14th Fl.	New York	NY	10018	212-213-8500	213-0076
TF: 800-845-5933 ■ Web: www.henryglassfabrics.com					
Glen Raven Inc 1831 N Park Ave	Glen Raven	NC	27217	336-227-6211	226-8133
TF: 800-788-4413 ■ Web: www.glenraven.com					
Greenwood Mills Inc 300 Morgan Ave	Greenwood	SC	29646	864-229-2571	229-1111
TF: 800-847-5929					
Hamrick Mills Inc 515 W Buford St PO Box 48	Gaffney	SC	29342	864-489-4731	487-9946
TF: 800-297-6306 ■ Web: www.mvmills.com					
Henry Glass & Co 49 W 37th St 14th Fl.	New York	NY	10018	212-213-8500	213-0076
TF: 800-845-5933 ■ Web: www.henryglassfabrics.com					
Hoffman Mills Inc 470 Park Ave S 7th Fl	New York	NY	10016	212-684-3700	779-1299
Inman Mills 300 Park Rd PO Box 207	Inman	SC	29349	864-472-2121	472-0261
Web: inmanmills.com					
Interface Fabric Inc 9 Oak St	Guilford	ME	04443	207-876-3331	876-4352
TF: 800-762-3331 ■ Web: www.interfacefabrics.com					
JB Martin Co 10 E 53rd St	New York	NY	10022	212-421-2020	421-1460
TF: 800-223-0525 ■ Web: www.jbmartin.com					
Johnston Textiles Inc 3101 23rd Dr.	Valley	AL	36854	334-768-1000	768-1047
TF: 800-227-0192 ■ Web: www.johnstontextiles.com					
Juniata Fabrics Inc PO Box 1806	Altoona	PA	16603	814-944-9381	944-1938
TF: 800-654-2666 ■ Web: www.juniatafabrics.com					
Keystone Weaving Mills Inc 1349 W Cumberland St	Lebanon	PA	17042	717-272-4665	272-4840
KM Fabrics Inc 2 Waco St	Greenville	SC	29611	864-295-2550	295-3356
Kuraray America Inc 101 E 52nd St 26th Fl.	New York	NY	10022	212-986-2230	867-3543
TF: 800-879-1676 ■ Web: www.kurarayamerica.com					
La France Industries Div Mount Vernon Mills Inc					
290 Old Anderson Rd	La France	SC	29656	864-646-3213	646-4235*
*Fax: Hum Res ■ TF: 800-845-9728					
Lantal Textiles Inc 1300 Langenthal Dr PO Box 965	Rural Hall	NC	27045	336-969-9551	969-3810*
*Fax: Hum Res ■ TF: 800-334-3309 ■ Web: www.lantal.com					
Leggett & Platt Inc Textile & Fiber Products Group					
1410 Donelson Pike	Nashville	TN	37217	615-367-8900	360-8451
TF: 800-888-4136 ■ Web: www.lpfiber.com					
LW Packard & Co Inc 6 Mill St	Ashland	NH	03217	603-968-3351	968-7649
Web: www.lwpackard.com					
Martin JB Co 10 E 53rd St	New York	NY	10022	212-421-2020	421-1460
TF: 800-223-0525 ■ Web: www.jbmartin.com					
Milliken & Co 920 Milliken Rd	Spartanburg	SC	29303	864-503-2020	503-2100*
*Fax: Hum Res ■ Web: www.milliken.com					
Mount Vernon Mills Inc 503 S Main St PO Box 100	Mauldin	SC	29662	864-688-7100	688-7215
TF: 800-845-8857 ■ Web: www.mvmills.com					
Mount Vernon Mills Inc La France Industries Div					
290 Old Anderson Rd	La France	SC	29656	864-646-3213	646-4235*
*Fax: Hum Res ■ TF: 800-845-9728					
Packard LW & Co Inc 6 Mill St.	Ashland	NH	03217	603-968-3351	968-7649
Web: www.lwpackard.com					
Polartec LLC 46 Stafford St	Lawrence	MA	01841	978-685-6341	975-2595
TF: 800-252-6688 ■ Web: www.polartec.com					
Polymer Group Inc 9335 Harris Corners Pkwy	Charlotte	NC	28269	704-697-5100	697-5116
Web: www.polymergroupinc.com					
Precision Fabrics Group Inc 301 N Elm St Suite 600	Greensboro	NC	27401	336-510-8000	510-8004
TF: 800-284-8001 ■ Web: www.precisionfabrics.com					
Pure Silk Fabrics 700 Hwy W 46	Clifton	NJ	07013	973-546-7888	546-8813
Quaker Fabric Corp 941 Grinnell St	Fall River	MA	02721	508-678-1951	679-2580
NASDAQ: QFAB ■ Web: www.quakerfabric.com					
Ramtex Inc 1259 Foushee Rd	Ramseur	NC	27316	336-824-5600	824-5689
Web: www.ramtex.com					
Raxon Fabrics Corp 261 5th Ave Suite 501	New York	NY	10016	212-532-6816	481-9361
Reeves Brothers Inc 790 Reeves St	Spartanburg	SC	29301	864-576-1210	595-2270
Web: www.reevesbrothers.com					
Scalamandre Silks Inc 300 Trade Zone Dr.	Ronkonkoma	NY	11779	631-467-8800	467-9448
TF: 800-932-4361 ■ Web: www.scalamandre.com/contents.htm					
Schneider Mills Inc 1430 Broadway 7th Fl.	New York	NY	10018	212-768-7500	768-0909
Somerset Industries Inc 68 Harrison St	Gloversville	NY	12078	518-773-7383	773-8978
TF: 800-262-0606					
Springs Global US Inc 205 N White St	Fort Mill	SC	29715	803-547-1500	547-1579*
*Fax: Mktg ■ TF: 888-926-7888 ■ Web: www.springs.com					
Stanwood Mills Inc 570 7th Ave.	New York	NY	10018	212-944-4826	944-6485
Stonecutter Mills Corp 400 Spindale St	Spindale	NC	28160	828-286-2341	287-7280
Web: www.stonecuttermills.com					
Sunbury Textile Mills Inc 1200 Miller St PO Box 768	Sunbury	PA	17801	570-286-3800	286-8530
Tweave Inc 138 Barrows St	Norton	MA	02766	508-285-6701	285-2904
Web: www.tweave.com					
Unifi Inc 7201 W Friendly Ave	Greensboro	NC	27410	336-294-4410	316-5422
NYSE: UFI ■ Web: www.unifi-inc.com					
Valdese Weavers LLC 1000 Perkins Rd SE	Valdese	NC	28690	828-874-2181	874-3920
Web: www.valdeseweavers.com					
Warm Co 5529 186th Pl SW	Lynnwood	WA	98037	425-248-2424	248-2422
TF: 800-234-9276 ■ Web: www.warmcompany.com					
Weave Corp 433 Hackensack Ave	Hackensack	NJ	07601	201-646-1500	343-6297
Web: www.weavecorp.com					
WestPoint Home Inc 28 E 28th St 8th Fl	New York	NY	10016	212-930-2000	
TF: 800-533-8229 ■ Web: www.martex.com					

748-2 Coated Fabric

Company	City	State	ZIP	Phone	Fax
Alpha Assoc Inc 2 Amboy Ave	Woodbridge	NJ	07095	732-634-5700	634-1430
TF: 800-563-3136 ■ Web: www.alphainc.com					
Archer Rubber Co 213 Central St	Milford	MA	01757	508-473-1870	478-7078
Web: www.archerrubber.com					
Beckmann Converting Inc 14 Park Dr PO Box 390	Amsterdam	NY	12010	518-842-0073	842-0282
Web: www.beckmannconverting.com					
Bradford Industries Inc 1857 Middlesex St	Lowell	MA	01851	978-459-4100	459-8725
Web: www.bradfordind.com					
Brookwood Laminating Inc 1425 Kingstown Rd	Peace Dale	RI	02883	401-789-5862	789-1450
Web: www.brookwoodcos.com					
Bryant Industries Corp 276 5th Ave	New York	NY	10001	212-689-6655	689-6348
Cellusuede Products Inc 500 N Madison St	Rockford	IL	61107	815-964-8619	964-7949
Web: www.cellusuede.com					
Coaters Inc 305 Nash Rd	New Bedford	MA	02746	508-996-6787	997-0959
Cooley Group 50 Esten Ave	Pawtucket	RI	02860	401-724-9000	726-8620
TF Cust Svc: 800-333-3048 ■ Web: www.cooleygroup.com					
Dazian Inc 124 Enterprise Ave S	Secaucus	NJ	07094	201-549-1000	549-1055
Web: www.dazian.com					
Deccofelt Corp 555 S Vermont Ave	Glendora	CA	91740	626-963-8511	963-4981
TF Cust Svc: 800-543-3226 ■ Web: www.deccofelt.com					
Der-Tex Corp 1 Lehner Rd	Saco	ME	04072	207-284-5931	669-9026
TF: 800-669-0364 ■ Web: www.dertexcorp.com					
Duracote Corp 350 N Diamond St	Ravenna	OH	44266	330-296-9600	296-5102
TF: 800-321-2252 ■ Web: www.duracote.com					
Emtex Inc 42B Cherry Hill Dr	Danvers	MA	01923	978-907-4500	907-4555
Web: www.emtexinc.com					
Engineered Fabrics Corp 669 Goodyear St	Rockmart	GA	30153	770-684-7855	684-7438
Web: www.engfabrics.com					
Fabrite Laminating Corp 70 Passaic St	Wood Ridge	NJ	07075	973-777-1406	777-6707
Web: www.fabrite.com					
Flexfirm Products Inc 2300 N Chico Ave	South El Monte	CA	91733	626-448-7627	579-5116
Web: www.flexfirmproducts.com					
Gore WL & Assoc Inc 551 Papermill Rd	Newark	DE	19711	302-738-4880	738-7710
Web: www.gore.com					
Haartz Corp 87 Hayward Rd	Acton	MA	01720	978-264-2600	264-2601
Web: www.haartz.com					
Herculite Products Inc 105 E Sinking Springs Ln	Emigsville	PA	17318	717-764-1192	764-5211
TF: 800-772-0036					
ICG/Holliston 905 Holliston Mills Rd PO Box 478	Kingsport	TN	37662	423-357-6141	325-0351*
*Fax Area Code: 800 ■ TF: 800-251-0251 ■ Web: www.icgholliston.com					
John Boyle & Co Inc 1803 Salisbury Rd	Statesville	NC	28677	704-872-8151	878-0572
TF Cust Svc: 800-438-1061 ■ Web: www.johnboyle.com					
Middlesex Research Mfg Co Inc 27 Apsley St.	Hudson	MA	01749	978-562-3697	562-7446
TF: 800-424-5188 ■ Web: www.middlesexresearch.com					
OMNOVA Solutions Inc 175 Ghent Rd	Fairlawn	OH	44333	330-869-4200	869-4288
NYSE: OMN ■ Web: www.omnova.com					
OMNOVA Solutions Inc Decorative & Building Products Div					
175 Ghent Rd	Fairlawn	OH	44333	330-869-4200	869-4288
Web: www.omnova.com					
Reflexite Corp 120 Darling Dr.	Avon	CT	06001	860-676-7100	676-7199
TF: 800-654-7570 ■ Web: www.reflexite.com					
SanduskyAthol International 100 22nd St PO Box 105	Butner	NC	27509	919-575-6523	575-9344
TF: 800-282-6523 ■ Web: www.sanduskyathol.com					
Sauquoit Industries LLC 300 Palm St	Scranton	PA	18505	570-348-2751	348-0920
TF: 800-858-5552 ■ Web: www.sauquoit.com					
Seaman Corp 1000 Venture Blvd	Wooster	OH	44691	330-262-1111	263-6950
TF: 800-927-8578 ■ Web: www.seamancorp.com					
Swift Textile Metalizing LLC 23 Britton Dr PO Box 66	Bloomfield	CT	06002	860-243-1122	243-0848
Web: www.swift-textile.com					
Taconic 136 Coonbrook Rd PO Box 69	Petersburgh	NY	12138	518-658-3202	658-3204
TF: 800-833-1805 ■ Web: www.4taconic.com					
Twitchell Corp 4031 Ross Clark Cir NW	Dothan	AL	36304	334-792-0002	673-4120
TF: 800-633-7550 ■ Web: www.twitchellcorp.com					
Uniroyal Engineered Products LLC 501 S Water St	Stoughton	WI	53589	608-873-6631	873-3355
TF: 800-873-8800 ■ Web: www.naugahyde.com					
Vintex Inc 1 Mount Forest Dr	Mount Forest	ON	N0G2L2	519-323-0100	323-0333*
*Fax: Sales ■ TF Sales: 800-846-8399 ■ Web: www.vintex.com					
Vulplex Inc DBA Coaters Inc 305 Nash Rd	New Bedford	MA	02746	508-996-6787	997-0959
WL Gore & Assoc Inc 551 Papermill Rd	Newark	DE	19711	302-738-4880	738-7710
Web: www.gore.com					

748-3 Industrial Fabrics

Company	City	State	ZIP	Phone	Fax
Acme Group 1750 Telegraph Rd	Bloomfield Hills	MI	48302	248-203-2000	454-9658
TF: 800-521-8565 ■ Web: www.acmemills.com					
Albany International Corp 1373 Broadway PO Box 1907	Albany	NY	12201	518-445-2200	445-6292
NYSE: AIN ■ TF: 800-833-3836 ■ Web: www.albint.com					
Albany International Corp Appleton Wire Div 435 6th St	Menasha	WI	54952	920-725-2600	729-7357
TF: 800-558-3526 ■ Web: www.albint.com					
Albany International Corp Engineered Fabrics Div					
214 Kirby Dr	Portland	TN	37148	615-325-6767	325-1082
TF: 800-833-3836 ■ Web: www.albint.com					
Amatex Corp 1032 Stambridge St	Norristown	PA	19404	610-277-6100	277-6106
TF: 800-441-9680 ■ Web: www.amatex.com					
AMETEK Inc Chemical Products Div 455 Corporate Blvd	Newark	DE	19702	302-456-4400	456-4444
TF Orders: 800-441-7777 ■ Web: www.ametekhaveg.com					
AstenJohnson 4399 Corporate Rd	Charleston	SC	29405	843-747-7800	202-6278
Web: www.astenjohnson.com					
Belton Industries Inc 1205 Hanby Rd PO Box 127	Belton	SC	29627	864-338-5711	338-5594
TF: 800-845-8753 ■ Web: www.beltonindustries.com					
BGF Industries Inc 3802 Robert Porcher Way	Greensboro	NC	27410	336-545-0011	545-0233
TF: 800-476-4845 ■ Web: www.bgf.com					
Bonn FH Co 4300 Gateway Blvd	Springfield	OH	45502	937-323-7024	323-0388
TF: 800-323-0143 ■ Web: www.fhbonn.com					
Carthage Mills 4243 Hunt Rd	Cincinnati	OH	45242	513-794-1600	794-3434
TF Sales: 800-543-4430 ■ Web: www.carthagemills.com					
Elk Technolgies Inc 14911 Quorom Dr Suite 600	Dallas	TX	75254	972-851-0500	851-0550
Web: technologies.elkcorp.com					
Fablok Mills Inc 140 Spring St	Murray Hill	NJ	07974	908-464-1950	464-6520
Web: www.fablokmills.com					
FH Bonn Co 4300 Gateway Blvd	Springfield	OH	45502	937-323-7024	323-0388
TF: 800-323-0143 ■ Web: www.fhbonn.com					
Firestone Fibers & Textiles Co 100 Firestone Ln	Kings Mountain	NC	28086	704-734-2100	734-2196
TF: 800-441-1336 ■ Web: www.firestonefibers.com					
HFI Corp 2421 McGaw Rd	Columbus	OH	43207	614-491-0700	491-1899
Web: www.ait-hfi.com					
Highland Industries Inc 650 Chesterfield Rd	Cheraw	SC	29520	843-537-2121	537-8274
Web: www.takata.com					
Industrial Fabrics Corp 7160 Northland Cir N	Minneapolis	MN	55428	763-535-3220	535-6040
TF: 800-328-3036 ■ Web: www.ifcfabrics.com					
Kordsa USA 17780 Armstrong Rd	Laurel Hill	NC	28351	910-462-2051	462-5040
Web: www.kordsa.us					
LINQ Industrial Fabrics Inc 2550 W 5th North St	Summerville	SC	29483	843-873-5800	875-8237
TF Cust Svc: 888-705-8424 ■ Web: www.linqind.com					
Mutual Industries Inc 707 W Grange St	Philadelphia	PA	19120	215-927-6000	927-3388
TF: 800-523-0888 ■ Web: www.mutualindustries.com					
Newtex Industries Inc 8050 Victor Mendon Rd	Victor	NY	14564	585-924-9135	924-4645
TF: 800-836-1001 ■ Web: www.newtex.com					
Sefar Printing Solutions Inc 120 Mt Holly Bypass	Lumberton	NJ	08048	609-613-5000	267-1750
TF: 800-289-8385 ■ Web: www.sefar.com					
Sherman Textile Co Inc 800 E Main St PO Box 596	Dallas	NC	28034	704-922-5254	922-5411

Company	City	State	Zip	Phone	Fax
Stern & Stern Industries Inc 708 3rd Ave 30th Fl *Web:* www.sternandstern.com	New York	NY	10017	212-972-4040	818-9230
TenCate Industrial Fabrics North America 365 S Holland Dr *TF:* 888-795-0808 ■ *Web:* www.tencate.com	Pendergrass	GA	30567	706-693-2226	693-4400
TenCate Geosynthetics North America 365 S Holland Dr *TF:* 888-795-0808 ■ *Web:* www.tencate.com	Pendergrass	GA	30567	706-693-2226	693-4400
TenCate Protective Fabrics USA 6501 Mall Blvd *TF:* 800-241-8630 ■ *Web:* www.tencate.com	Union City	GA	30291	770-969-1000	969-6846
Tex-Tech Industries Inc 105 N Main St PO Box 8 *TF:* 800-441-7089 ■ *Web:* www.textechindustries.com	North Monmouth	ME	04265	207-933-4404	933-9266
Ultrafabrics LLC 400 Executive Blvd *TF:* 888-361-9216 ■ *Web:* www.ultrafabricsllc.com	Elmsford	NY	10523	914-460-1730	347-1591
Weavexx Corp 14101 Capital Blvd *TF:* 800-932-8399 ■ *Web:* www.weavexx.com	Youngsville	NC	27596	919-556-7235	556-1063
Wellstone Mills 856 S Pleasantburg Dr *TF:* 877-867-6455 ■ *Web:* www.wellstonemills.com	Greenville	SC	29607	864-242-1293	242-1927
Wendell Fabrics Corp 108 E Church St *Web:* www.wendellfabrics.com	Blacksburg	SC	29702	864-839-6341	839-2911

748-4 Knitting Mills

Company	City	State	Zip	Phone	Fax
Alamac American Knits LLC 1885 Alamac Rd PO Box 1347 *Web:* www.alamacusa.com	Lumberton	NC	28359	910-618-2200	618-2292
Ames Textile Corp 710 Chelmsford St *Web:* www.amestextile.com	Lowell	MA	01851	978-458-3321	454-9149
Apex Mills Corp 168 Doughty Blvd *TF:* 800-989-2739 ■ *Web:* www.apexmills.com	Inwood	NY	11096	516-239-4400	239-4951
Asheboro Elastics Corp 150 N Park St *Web:* www.asheboroelastics.com	Asheboro	NC	27203	336-629-2626	629-3782
Bloomsburg Mills Inc 1 W 40th St 10th Fl *Web:* www.bloomsburgmills.net	New York	NY	10018	212-221-6114	354-9375
Cellunet Mfg Co 1002 Jacksonville Rd	Burlington	NJ	08016	609-386-1147	386-8978
Charbert Inc 299 Church St *TF:* 800-570-2184 ■ *Web:* www.charbert.com	Alton	RI	02894	401-364-7751	364-3390
Clover Knits Inc 1075 Jackson Heights	Clover	SC	29710	803-222-3021	222-4105
Contempora Fabrics Inc 351 Contempora Dr *TF:* 800-346-3650 ■ *Web:* www.contemporafabrics.com	Lumberton	NC	28358	910-738-7131	738-9575
Darlington Fabrics Corp 1407 Broadway Suite 1220 *TF:* 800-556-7152 ■ *Web:* www.darlingtonfabrics.com	New York	NY	10018	212-938-1054	938-1025
Draper Knitting Co 28 Draper Ln *Web:* www.draperknitting.com	Canton	MA	02021	781-828-0029	828-3034
Elastic Fabrics of America 3112 Pleasant Garden Rd *Web:* www.elasticfabrics.com	Greensboro	NC	27406	336-275-9401	378-2631
Fab Industries Corp 98 Cutter Mill Rd Suite 412-N *Web:* www.fab-industries.com	Great Neck	NY	11021	516-498-3200	829-0783
Fairystone Fabrics LLC 2247 N Park Ave	Burlington	NC	27217	336-228-1771	228-8042
Flexlon Fabrics Inc 174 Trollingwood Rd	Haw River	NC	27258	336-578-0111	578-8247
Gehring Textiles Inc 1225 Franklin Ave Suite 300 *Web:* www.gehringtextiles.com	Garden City	NY	11530	516-747-4555	747-8885
Glenoit LLC 1 Linde Dr *TF:* 800-223-1999	Goldsboro	NC	27530	919-735-7111	713-7209
Guilford Mills Inc 6001 W Market St *TF Cust Svc:* 800-277-0987 ■ *Web:* www.guilfordproducts.com	Greensboro	NC	27409	336-316-4000	316-4059
Guilford Mills Inc Automotive Div 1754 NC State Hwy 903 **Fax:* Sales ■ *Web:* www.guilfordproducts.com	Kenansville	NC	28349	910-296-5200	296-6338*
H Warshow & Sons Inc 1375 Broadway 26th Fl	New York	NY	10018	212-921-9200	944-5704
Hornwood Inc 766 Hailey's Ferry Rd *Web:* www.hornwoodinc.com	Lilesville	NC	28091	704-848-4121	848-4555
Klauber Brothers Inc 980 Ave of the Americas 2nd Fl	New York	NY	10018	212-686-2531	481-7194
Lebcor International Inc 110 W 40th St Suite 803	New York	NY	10018	212-354-8500	354-4938
McMurray Fabrics Inc 152 Madison Ave 15th Fl	New York	NY	10016	212-684-3100	683-8093
Minnesota Knitting Mills 1450 Mendota Heights Rd *Web:* www.mnknit.com	Saint Paul	MN	55120	651-452-2240	452-8915
MoCaro Industries Inc 2201 Mocaro Dr *Web:* www.mocaro.com	Statesville	NC	28677	704-878-6645	873-6139
Monterey Mills Inc 1725 E Delavan Dr *TF:* 800-255-9665 ■ *Web:* www.montereymills.com	Janesville	WI	53546	608-754-2866	754-3750
Paris Lace Inc 1500 Main Ave *TF:* 800-533-5223	Clifton	NJ	07011	973-478-9035	478-9186
Roman Knit Inc 957 N Main St **Fax:* Sales	Norwood	NC	28128	704-474-4123	474-4127*
Russ-Knits Inc Hwy 211 E	Candor	NC	27229	910-974-4114	974-4023
Titone Joseph & Sons Inc 1002 Jacksonville Rd	Burlington	NJ	08016	609-386-1147	386-8978
Warshow H & Sons Inc 1375 Broadway 26th Fl	New York	NY	10018	212-921-9200	944-5704
Westchester Lace Inc 3901 Liberty Ave *TF:* 800-699-5223 ■ *Web:* www.westchesterlace.com	North Bergen	NJ	07047	201-864-2150	864-2116

748-5 Narrow Fabric Mills

Company	City	State	Zip	Phone	Fax
Advance Fiber Technologies Corp 344 Lodi St *TF:* 800-631-1930	Hackensack	NJ	07601	201-488-2700	489-5656
American Cord & Webbing Co 88 Century Dr *Web:* www.acw1.com	Woonsocket	RI	02895	401-762-5500	762-5514
Avery Dennison 950 German St PO Box 735 *TF:* 800-528-9591 ■ *Web:* www.paxar.com	Lenoir	NC	28645	828-758-2338	758-2038
Bally Ribbon Mills 23 N 7th St *Web:* www.ballyribbon.com	Bally	PA	19503	610-845-2211	845-8013
Bo-Buck Mills Inc 921 East Blvd *TF:* 800-690-7474 ■ *Web:* www.bobuckmills.com	Chesterfield	SC	29709	843-623-2158	623-6849
Carolina Narrow Fabric Co 1100 Patterson Ave *Web:* www.carolinanarrowfabric.com	Winston-Salem	NC	27101	336-631-3000	631-3060
Carson & Gebel Ribbon Co 17 Green Pond Rd *TF:* 800-223-8283 ■ *Web:* www.cgribbon.com	Rockaway	NJ	07866	973-627-4200	627-1175
Conrad-Jarvis Corp 217 Conant St **Fax:* Orders	Pawtucket	RI	02860	401-722-8700	726-8860*
CT-Nassau Corp 4101 S NC 62	Alamance	NC	27201	336-570-0091	570-1519
ELC Industries 1439 Dave Lyle Blvd Suite 16-C *TF Sales:* 800-765-7423 ■ *Web:* www.ahrice.com	Rock Hill	SC	29730	803-980-7600	980-7676
Fulflex Inc 701 E Church St *TF:* 800-283-2500 ■ *Web:* www.fulflex.com	Greenville	TN	37745	423-638-5722	638-1298
Georgia Narrow Fabrics LLC 2050 Sunset Blvd *TF:* 800-245-5350	Jesup	GA	31545	912-427-6961	427-3396
Glencairn Mfg Co 5 Saunders St	Pawtucket	RI	02860	401-723-9871	724-5340
Gudebrod Inc 274 Shoemaker Rd *TF:* 877-249-2211 ■ *Web:* www.gudebrod.com	Pottstown	PA	19464	610-327-4050	327-4588
Hickory Brands Inc 429 27th St NW *TF:* 800-438-5777 ■ *Web:* www.griffinshine.com	Hickory	NC	28601	828-322-2600	328-1700
Hope Global Engineered Textile Solutions 50 Martin St *TF:* 800-634-1335 ■ *Web:* www.hopeglobal.com	Cumberland	RI	02864	401-333-8990	334-6442
Ideal Bias Binding Corp 372 Kilburn St *TF:* 800-532-6600	Fall River	MA	02724	508-673-3212	677-2626
JRM Industries Inc 1 Mattimore St *TF:* 800-533-2697 ■ *Web:* www.jrm.com	Passaic	NJ	07055	973-779-9340	779-8017
Julius Koch USA Inc 387 Church St *TF Sales:* 800-522-3652 ■ *Web:* www.jkusa.com	New Bedford	MA	02745	508-995-9565	995-8434
Koch Julius USA Inc 387 Church St *TF Sales:* 800-522-3652 ■ *Web:* www.jkusa.com	New Bedford	MA	02745	508-995-9565	995-8434
Mitchellace Inc 830 Murray St *TF:* 800-848-8696 ■ *Web:* www.mitchellace.com	Portsmouth	OH	45662	740-354-2813	353-4669
Moore Co 36 Beach St *Web:* www.darlingtonfabrics.com	Westerly	RI	02891	401-596-2816	596-6801
Murdock Webbing Co 27 Foundry St *TF:* 800-375-2052 ■ *Web:* www.murdockwebbing.com	Central Falls	RI	02863	401-724-3000	722-9730
Name Maker Inc 4450 Commerce Cir PO Box 43821 **Fax Area Code:* 404 ■ **Fax:* Orders ■ *TF:* 800-241-2890 ■ *Web:* www.namemaker.com	Atlanta	GA	30336	800-241-2890	691-7711*
Narricot Industries LP 928 Jaymore Rd Suite C150 *Web:* www.narricot.com	Southampton	PA	18966	215-322-3900	322-3905
Narrow Fabric Industries Inc 701 Reading Ave *TF:* 800-523-8118 ■ *Web:* www.narrowfabric.com	West Reading	PA	19611	610-376-2891	376-2869
NFA Corp 850 Boylston St Suite 428	Chestnut Hill	MA	02467	617-232-6060	
Paxar Corp Woven Labels Group 1600 Pollitt Dr	Fair Lawn	NJ	07410	201-956-6100	956-6020
Pittsfield Weaving Co Inc 55 Barnstead Rd *Web:* www.pwcolabel.com	Pittsfield	NH	03263	603-435-8301	435-6753
Premier Narrow Fabrics 455 Hwy 70 W *TF:* 800-633-4538 ■ *Web:* www.premiernf.com	Columbiana	AL	35051	205-669-3101	669-8672
Rhode Island Textile Co 211 Columbus Ave *TF:* 800-556-6488 ■ *Web:* www.ritextile.com	Pawtucket	RI	02861	401-722-3700	726-2840
Ross Matthews Mills Inc 657 Quarry St *TF:* 800-753-7677	Fall River	MA	02723	508-677-0601	676-9663
Sequins International Inc 60-01 31st Ave *Web:* www.sequins.com	Woodside	NY	11377	718-204-0002	204-0999
Shelby Elastics Inc 639 N Post Rd *TF:* 800-562-4507 ■ *Web:* www.shelbyelastics.com	Shelby	NC	28150	704-487-4301	481-9348
South Carolina Elastic Co 201 South Carolina Elastic Rd *TF:* 800-845-6700 ■ *Web:* www.scelastic.com	Landrum	SC	29356	864-457-3388	457-3579
Southern Weaving Co 1005 W Bramlett Rd *TF:* 800-849-8962 ■ *Web:* www.southernweaving.com	Greenville	SC	29611	864-233-1635	240-9302
Star Binding & Trimming Corp 1109 Grand Ave *TF:* 800-782-7150 ■ *Web:* www.starnj.com	North Bergen	NJ	07047	201-864-2220	864-1051
State Narrow Fabrics Inc 2902 Borden Ave *TF:* 800-221-7288 ■ *Web:* www.statenarrow.com	Long Island City	NY	11101	718-392-8787	392-9421
Sturges Mfg Co Inc 2030 Sunset Ave *Web:* www.sturgesmfg.com	Utica	NY	13502	315-732-6159	732-2314
Sullivan-Carson Inc 1018 Laurel Oak Rd Suite 12	Voorhees	NJ	08043	856-784-4222	784-1151
Tape Craft Corp 200 Tape Craft Dr *TF Cust Svc:* 800-521-1783 ■ *Web:* www.tapecraft.com	Oxford	AL	36203	256-236-2535	236-6718
Trimtex Co Inc 400 Park Ave *TF:* 800-326-9135 ■ *Web:* www.trimtex.com	Williamsport	PA	17701	570-326-9135	326-4250
Wayne Mills Co Inc 130 W Berkley St *TF:* 800-220-8053 ■ *Web:* www.waynemills.com	Philadelphia	PA	19144	215-842-2134	438-8599
Wiener Laces Inc 98 Cutter Mill Rd Suite 412-N	New York	NY	10021	516-498-3200	829-0783
William Wright Co 85 South St *TF:* 800-545-5740 ■ *Web:* www.wrights.com	West Warren	MA	01092	413-436-7732	436-9785
Worldtex Inc PO Box 2187	Hickory	NC	28603	828-322-2242	327-6417
Wright William E Ltd 85 South St *TF:* 800-545-5740 ■ *Web:* www.wrights.com	West Warren	MA	01092	413-436-7732	436-9785

748-6 Nonwoven Fabrics

Company	City	State	Zip	Phone	Fax
Acme Felt Works Co 6500 Stanford Ave	Los Angeles	CA	90001	323-752-3778	752-7164
Aetna Felt Corp 2401 W Emaus Ave *TF:* 800-526-4451 ■ *Web:* www.aetnafelt.com	Allentown	PA	18103	610-791-0900	791-5791
Airtex Consumer Products a Division of Federal Foam Technologies 150 Industrial Park Blvd *TF:* 800-851-8887 ■ *Web:* www.airtex.com	Cokato	MN	55321	320-286-2696	286-2428
American Felt & Filter Co DBA AFFCO 361 Walsh Ave *Web:* www.affco.com	New Windsor	NY	12553	845-561-3560	563-4422
American Nonwovens Corp 221 Fabritek Dr *TF:* 800-628-7961 ■ *Web:* www.amerinon.com	Columbus	MS	39702	662-327-0745	327-8317
Bacon Felt Co Inc 395 W Water St *Web:* www.baconfelt.com	Taunton	MA	02780	508-823-0791	823-2855
BBA Fiberweb 70 Old Hickory Blvd *TF:* 800-847-7000 ■ *Web:* www.bbafiberweb.com	Old Hickory	TN	37138	615-847-7000	847-7068
BBA Nonwovens 70 Old Hickory Blvd *TF:* 800-847-7000 ■ *Web:* www.bbanonwovens.com	Old Hickory	TN	37138	615-847-7000	847-7068
Berwick Offray LLC 2015 W Front St *TF:* 800-327-0350 ■ *Web:* www.berwickindustries.com	Berwick	PA	18603	570-752-5934	759-0889
Boston Felt Co Inc 31 Front St PO Box 6258 *Web:* www.bostonfelt.com	East Rochester	NH	03868	603-332-7000	332-6049
Buffalo Batt & Felt 3307 Walden Ave *Web:* www.buffalobatt.com	Depew	NY	14043	716-683-4100	683-8928
Clark-Cutler-McDermott Co 5 Fisher St PO Box 269 *TF:* 800-922-3019 ■ *Web:* www.ccmcd.com	Franklin	MA	02038	508-528-1200	528-1406
Cumulus Fibres Inc 1101 Tarhill Rd *TF:* 800-888-4569	Charlotte	NC	28208	704-394-2229	394-2650
Elk Performance Nonwoven Fabrics 14911 Quorom Dr Suite 600 *Web:* nonwovens.elkcorp.com	Dallas	TX	75254	972-851-0500	851-0550
Elk Premium Building Products Inc 14911 Quorum Dr Suite 600 *Web:* www.elkcorp.com	Dallas	TX	75254	972-851-0500	851-0550
Felters Group Inc 41 Peachview Blvd	Gaffney	SC	29341	864-488-0701	488-3008
Fiberbond Corp 110 Menke Rd *Web:* www.fiberbond.net	Michigan City	IN	46360	219-879-4541	874-7502
Fisher Textiles Inc 139 Business Park Dr *TF:* 800-554-8886 ■ *Web:* www.fishertextiles.com	Indian Trail	NC	28079	704-821-8870	821-8880
Foss Mfg Co LLC 11 Merrill Industrial Dr PO Box 5000 *TF:* 800-343-3277 ■ *Web:* www.fossmfg.com	Hampton	NH	03843	603-929-6000	929-6010
Freudenberg Nonwovens Ltd 2975 Pembroke Rd *TF:* 800-542-2804 ■ *Web:* www.nonwovens-group.com	Hopkinsville	KY	42240	270-886-0204	890-0743
Hobbs Bonded Fibers Inc 200 S Commerce St *TF:* 800-433-3357 ■ *Web:* www.hobbsbondedfibers.com	Waco	TX	76710	254-741-0040	772-7238
Leggett & Platt Inc Textile & Fiber Products Group 1410 Donelson Pike *TF:* 800-888-4136 ■ *Web:* www.lpfiber.com	Nashville	TN	37217	615-367-8900	360-8451
Lydall Inc Thermal Acoustical Group 1241 Buck Shoals Rd *TF:* 800-353-2996	Hamptonville	NC	27020	336-468-8522	468-8555
National Nonwovens 180 Pleasant St *TF:* 800-333-3469 ■ *Web:* www.nationalnonwovens.com	Easthampton	MA	01027	413-527-3445	527-0456
Orr Felt Co 750 S Main St *Web:* www.orrfelt.com	Piqua	OH	45356	937-773-0551	778-9670
PGI Nonwovens/Chicopee Inc 1203 S Chicopee Rd *TF:* 800-631-5594 ■ *Web:* www.chixtowels.com	Benson	NC	27504	919-894-4111	207-3140
Sellars Nonwovens 808 Valley Ave *Web:* www.sellarsnonwovens.com	Atglen	PA	19310	610-593-5145	593-7000
Tietex International 3010 N Blackstock Rd *TF:* 800-843-8390 ■ *Web:* www.tietex.com	Spartanburg	SC	29301	864-574-0500	574-9440

Nonwoven Fabrics (Cont'd)

	City	State	Zip	Phone	Fax
Trenton Mills LLC 400 Factory St PO Box 107 *Web:* www.trentonmills.com	Trenton	TN	38382	731-855-1323	855-9000

748-7 Textile Dyeing & Finishing

	City	State	Zip	Phone	Fax
Advanced Textile Composites 700 E Parker St *Web:* www.advtextile.com	Scranton	PA	18509	570-207-7000	207-7070
Albert Screen Print Inc 3704 Summit Rd *TF:* 800-759-2774 ■ *Web:* www.albertinc.com	Norton	OH	44203	330-753-1252	753-1612
Amerbelle Textiles LLC 104 E Main St PO Box 30 *Web:* www.amerbelle.com	Vernon	CT	06066	860-979-0070	797-0072
Aurora Textile Finishing Co 911 N Lake St PO Box 70 *TF:* 800-864-0303 ■ *Web:* www.auroratextile.com/	Aurora	IL	60507	630-892-7651	892-3215
Bettilee Industries Inc 615 N Elm St	Dalton	GA	30721	706-278-5455	278-2120
Blumenthal Print Works Inc 905 S Broad St *TF:* 800-535-8590 ■ *Web:* www.blumenthalprintworks.com	New Orleans	LA	70125	504-822-4620	822-2147
Bradford Dyeing Assoc Inc 460 Bradford Rd *Web:* www.bdadye.com	Bradford	RI	02808	401-377-2231	377-2234
Brittany Dyeing & Printing Corp 1357 E Rodney French Blvd *Web:* www.brittanyusa.com	New Bedford	MA	02744	508-999-3281	996-6623
Buckeye Fabric Finishing Co 1260 E Main St PO Box 216 *Web:* www.buckeyefabric.com	Coshocton	OH	43812	740-622-3251	622-9317
Carlisle Finishing 3863 Carlisle Chester Hwy *Web:* www.itg-global.com/companies/carlisle_finishing.html	Carlisle	SC	29031	864-427-6221	429-0330
Como Textile Prints Inc 191-195 E Railway Ave	Paterson	NJ	07503	973-279-2950	881-8450
Coral Dyeing & Finishing Corp 555 E 31st St	Paterson	NJ	07513	973-278-0272	278-9490
Cranston Print Works Co 1381 Cranston St *TF:* 800-876-2756 ■ *Web:* www.cranstonvillage.com	Cranston	RI	02920	401-943-4800	943-3971
Crystal Springs Print Works Inc 100 Longstreet Ave PO Box 750 *Web:* www.cspwi.com	Chickamauga	GA	30707	706-375-2121	375-5585
Deep River Dyeing & Finishing Co Inc 225 Poplar St PO Box 217	Randleman	NC	27317	336-498-4181	498-7252
DFP Acquisition LLC 1150 Center St *TF:* 800-735-6257 ■ *Web:* www.diversifiedflock.com	Easton	PA	18042	610-252-6181	559-9152
Dixon William J Co Inc 756 Springdale Dr *Web:* www.wjdixon.com	Exton	PA	19341	610-524-1131	524-7964
Duro Textiles LLC 110 Chace St *Web:* www.duroindustries.com	Fall River	MA	02724	508-675-0101	677-6791
GJ Littlewood & Son Inc 4045 Main St *Web:* www.littlewooddyers.com	Philadelphia	PA	19127	215-483-3970	483-6129
Globe Dye Works Co 4500 Worth St	Philadelphia	PA	19124	215-535-3301	831-8223
Graphic Prints Inc 16540 S Main St	Gardena	CA	90248	310-768-0474	515-1164
Hanes Cos Inc 600 Northwest Blvd *Web:* www.hanesfinishing.com	Winston-Salem	NC	27101	336-725-1391	777-3375
Hanes Dye & Finish Inc 600 Northwest Blvd *Web:* www.hanesfinishing.com	Winston-Salem	NC	27101	336-725-1391	777-3375
Harodite Industries Inc 66 South St *TF:* 800-328-5656 ■ *Web:* www.harodite.com	Taunton	MA	02780	508-824-6961	880-0696
Holt Sublimation Printing & Products 2208 Air Park Dr *TF:* 800-544-4658 ■ *Web:* www.holtsublimation.com	Burlington	NC	27215	336-222-3600	229-7580
Huffman Finishing Co 4919 Hickory Blvd PO Box 170	Granite Falls	NC	28630	828-396-1741	396-4235
International Veiling Corp 244 Hazel St	Clifton	NJ	07011	973-772-3100	772-3863
Kenyon Industries Inc 36 Sherman Ave *Web:* www.kenyonindustries.net	Shannock	RI	02875	401-364-7761	364-6130
Mastex Industries Inc 2-3 Bigelow St PO Box 1160	Holyoke	MA	01040	413-536-3614	532-6639
Meridian Dyed Yarn Group 312 Colombo St *Web:* www.meridiandyedyarn.com	Valdese	NC	28690	828-874-2151	874-2189
Microfibres Inc 1 Moshassuck St *Web:* www.microfibres.com	Pawtucket	RI	02860	401-725-4883	722-8520
Parthenon Prints Inc 909 W 39th St *Web:* www.parthenonprints.com	Panama City	FL	32405	850-769-8321	769-5374
Rockland Industries Inc 1601 Edison Hwy *TF Cust Svc:* 800-876-2566 ■ *Web:* www.roc-lon.com	Baltimore	MD	21213	410-522-2505	522-2545
Royal Carolina Corp 7305 Old Friendly Rd *Web:* www.royalcarolina.com	Greensboro	NC	27410	336-292-8845	294-2396
Russell Corp Fabrics Div 755 Lee St *Web:* www.russellcorp.com	Alexander City	AL	35010	256-500-4000	500-4474
Santee Print Works 19 Progress St	Sumter	SC	29153	803-773-1461	773-0227
Southampton Textile Co 520 Reese St	Emporia	VA	23847	434-634-2159	634-0056
Starensier Inc 10 Mulliken Way *Web:* www.starensier.com	Newburyport	MA	01950	978-462-7311	465-6223
Synthetics Finishing Co 515 23rd St SW *Web:* www.tsgfinishing.com	Hickory	NC	28602	828-328-5522	328-2179
TSG Inc 1400 Welsh Rd PO Box 1400	North Wales	PA	19454	215-628-2000	641-1325
Wade Mfg Co Hwy 74 E	Wadesboro	NC	28170	704-694-2131	694-6621
Western Piece Dyers & Finishers Inc 2845 W 48th Pl *TF:* 866-493-7839 ■ *Web:* www.westexinc.com	Chicago	IL	60632	773-523-7000	523-0965
William J Dixon Co Inc 756 Springdale Dr *Web:* www.wjdixon.com	Exton	PA	19341	610-524-1131	524-7964
Wolfe Dye & Bleach Works Inc 25 Ridge Rd	Shoemakersville	PA	19555	610-562-7639	562-4462
Yates Bleachery Co 503 Flintstone Rd *Web:* www.yatesbleachery.com	Flintstone	GA	30725	706-820-1531	820-9459

748-8 Textile Fiber Processing Mills

	City	State	Zip	Phone	Fax
A Sheftel & Sons Inc 2121 31st St SW *TF Cust Svc:* 800-542-2426	Allentown	PA	18103	610-797-9420	797-7272
Acordis Celluosic Fibers Ltd US Hwy 43 N PO Box 171 *TF:* 800-633-6720 ■ *Web:* www.acordis.com	Axis	AL	36505	251-679-2200	679-2229
Buffalo Industries Inc 99 S Spokane St *Web:* www.buffaloind.com	Seattle	WA	98134	206-682-9900	682-9907
Charles House & Sons Inc 235 Singleton St *TF:* 800-243-7063	Woonsocket	RI	02895	401-769-0189	769-0192
Claremont Flock Corp 107 Scott Dr *Web:* www.claremontflock.com	Leominster	MA	01453	978-534-6191	534-8924
Fabri-Tech Inc 8236 N 600 W *TF Cust Svc:* 800-332-4797	McCordsville	IN	46055	317-335-9412	335-9413
Fiber Conversion Inc 15 E Elm St	Broadalbin	NY	12025	518-883-3431	883-8748
Herndon JE Co Inc 1020 J E Herndon Access Rd *TF:* 800-277-0500	Kings Mountain	NC	28086	704-739-4711	734-0621
House Charles & Sons Inc 235 Singleton St *TF:* 800-243-7063	Woonsocket	RI	02895	401-769-0189	769-0192
International Cellulose Inc 3110 W 28th St	Chicago	IL	60623	773-847-8000	847-0436
JE Herndon Co Inc 1020 J E Herndon Access Rd *TF:* 800-277-0500	Kings Mountain	NC	28086	704-739-4711	734-0621
Leggett & Platt Inc Textile & Fiber Products Group 1410 Donelson Pike *TF:* 800-888-4136 ■ *Web:* www.lpfiber.com	Nashville	TN	37217	615-367-8900	360-8451
Leigh Fibers Inc 1101 Syphrit Rd *TF:* 800-274-7707 ■ *Web:* www.leighfibers.com	Wellford	SC	29385	864-439-4111	439-4116
Lewis Industrial Supply Co 3307 N 6th St *TF:* 800-929-2400 ■ *Web:* www.lewisindustrialsupply.com	Harrisburg	PA	17110	717-234-2409	233-4380
Newco Fibre Co Inc 430 E 36th St *Web:* www.newcofibre.com	Charlotte	NC	28205	704-333-0751	332-2425
Norman W Paschall Co Inc 1 Paschall Rd *TF:* 800-849-1820 ■ *Web:* www.paschall.com	Peachtree City	GA	30269	770-487-7945	487-0840
Oklahoma Waste & Wiping Rag Co Inc 2013 SE 18th St *TF Cust Svc:* 800-232-4433	Oklahoma City	OK	73129	405-670-3100	670-3993
Roddie Wool Scouring Co Inc 201 A L Reed St PO Box 30	Brady	TX	76825	325-597-2138	597-2797
Royal Processing Co 5710 Old Concord Rd	Charlotte	NC	28213	704-599-2804	599-2805
RSM Co 811 Pressley Rd *Web:* www.rsmcompany.com	Charlotte	NC	28217	704-525-6851	525-8368
Sheftel A & Sons Inc 2121 31st St SW *TF Cust Svc:* 800-542-2426	Allentown	PA	18103	610-797-9420	797-7272
Slosman Corp 100 Fairview Rd *TF:* 800-544-9387 ■ *Web:* www.slosman.com	Asheville	NC	28803	828-274-2100	274-0000
Triangle Textiles Ltd 1320 E Division St *TF:* 800-622-8299 ■ *Web:* www.triangletextiles.com	Slaton	TX	79364	806-828-6573	828-5198

748-9 Yarn & Thread Mills

	City	State	Zip	Phone	Fax
American & Efird Inc 22 American St PO Box 507 **Fax Area Code:* 800 ■ *TF:* 800-438-6781 ■ *Web:* www.amefird.com	Mount Holly	NC	28120	704-827-4311	453-9060*
Amital Spinning Corp 197 Bosch Blvd *TF:* 800-548-1922	New Bern	NC	28562	252-636-3435	637-8043
Artee-Wrap Spun 105 Metrolina Dr	Shelby	NC	28150	704-482-3826	482-0735
Brodnax Mills 2 Kerr Dr PO Box A *Web:* www.brodnaxmills.com	Brodnax	VA	23920	434-729-2325	729-9581
Burke Mills Inc 191 Sterling St NW *Web:* www.burkemills.com	Valdese	NC	28690	828-874-6341	879-7188
Carolina Mills Inc 618 Carolina Ave *Web:* www.carolinamills.com	Maiden	NC	28650	828-428-9911	428-2335
Chargeurs Wool USA 178 Wool Rd	Jamestown	SC	29453	843-257-2212	257-4579
Charles Craft Inc 21381 Charles Craft Ln PO Box 1049 *TF:* 800-277-1009 ■ *Web:* www.charlescraft.com	Laurinburg	NC	28352	910-844-3521	844-9846
Cheraw Yarn Mills Inc PO Box 807 *Web:* www.cym.com	Cheraw	SC	29520	843-537-7846	537-7665
Chesterfield Yarn Mills Inc 201 N Maple St *Web:* www.chesterfieldwraps.com	Pageland	SC	29728	843-672-7211	672-7210
Clasgens J & H Co Inc 2383 SR-132	New Richmond	OH	45157	513-553-4177	
Clover Yarns Inc 1030 Tanyard Branch Trail	Clover	VA	24534	434-454-7151	454-6725
Coats & Clark Inc 3430 Toringdon Way Suite 301	Charlotte	NC	28227	704-329-5800	329-5025
Coats North America 3430 Toringdon Way Suite 301 *TF:* 800-631-0965 ■ *Web:* www.coats.com	Charlotte	NC	28277	704-329-5800	329-5899
Crescent Spinning Co 100 Main St *Web:* www.pharryarns.com	McAdenville	NC	28101	704-824-3551	825-7302
Crescent Woolen Mills Co 1016 School St	Two Rivers	WI	54241	920-793-3331	793-3818
Dillon Yarn Inc 1019 Titan Rd	Dillon	SC	29536	843-774-7353	774-0338
DMC Corp Port Kearny Bldg 10F *Web:* www.dmc-usa.com	South Kearny	NJ	07032	973-589-0606	589-8931
EAM Inc 398 W Memorial Dr	Dallas	GA	30132	770-445-2776	445-2777
Eddington Thread Mfg Co 3222 Knights Rd *TF:* 800-220-8901 ■ *Web:* www.edthread.com	Bensalem	PA	19020	215-639-8900	639-1420
Elmore-Pisgah Inc 204 Oak St *TF:* 800-633-7829 ■ *Web:* www.elmore-pisgah.com	Spindale	NC	28160	828-286-3665	287-0655
Fred Whitaker Co 941 Industry Ave SE *TF:* 800-336-5717	Roanoke	VA	24013	540-427-4343	427-3052
Glen Raven Inc 1831 N Park Ave *TF:* 800-788-4413 ■ *Web:* www.glenraven.com	Glen Raven	NC	27217	336-227-6211	226-8133
Grover Industries Inc 219 Laurel Ave *Web:* www.groverindustries.com	Grover	NC	28073	704-937-7434	937-7507
Guilford Mills Inc Fibers Div 200 Dickens Rd	Fuquay-Varina	NC	27526	919-552-5667	552-6094
Hickory Yarns Inc 1025 10th St NE *Web:* www.hickoryyarns.com	Hickory	NC	28601	828-322-1550	322-1627
Interstock Premium Cabinets LLC 915 Pennsylvania Blvd *Web:* www.interstockcabinets.com	Feasterville	PA	19053	267-288-1200	288-1206
J & H Clasgens Co Inc 2383 SR-132	New Richmond	OH	45157	513-553-4177	
Jagger Brothers Inc 5 Water St PO Box 188 *Web:* www.jaggeryarn.com	Springvale	ME	04083	207-324-5622	490-2661
Jefferson Mills Inc 27 Valley St *TF Sales:* 800-574-0069 ■ *Web:* www.jeffersonmills.com	Pulaski	VA	24301	540-980-1530	980-6388
Jones Cos Ltd 312 S 14th St *Web:* www.jonesyarn.com	Humboldt	TN	38343	731-784-2832	784-7131
Kent Mfg Co 671 Runnymede Rd	Pickens	SC	29671	864-878-6367	878-2723
Liberty Throwing Co Inc 214 Pringle St PO Box 1387 *Web:* www.libertythrowing.com	Kingston	PA	18704	570-287-1114	283-3531
Lion Brand Yarn Co 34 W 15th St *TF:* 800-795-5466 ■ *Web:* www.lionbrand.com	New York	NY	10011	212-243-8995	627-8154
Lorenzo Textile Mills Inc 417 Fillmore St	Lorenzo	TX	79343	806-634-5506	634-5775
Ludlow Textiles Co Inc 50 State St PO Box 559 *TF:* 800-628-9048 ■ *Web:* www.ludlowtextiles.com	Ludlow	MA	01056	413-583-5051	589-1415
Meridian Dyed Yarn Group 312 Colombo St *Web:* www.meridiandyedyarn.com	Valdese	NC	28690	828-874-2151	874-2189
Meridian Specialty Yarns 40 Rex Ave *Web:* www.meridiandyedyarn.com	Gastonia	NC	28054	704-824-7880	824-7870
Middleburg Yarn Processing Co 909 N Orange St *TF:* 800-728-9376	Selinsgrove	PA	17870	570-374-1284	374-1283
National Spinning Co Inc 111 W 40th St 28th Fl *TF:* 800-868-7764 ■ *Web:* www.natspin.com	New York	NY	10018	212-382-6400	382-6450
Oakdale Cotton Mills 710 Oakdale Rd *Web:* www.oakdalecotton.com	Jamestown	NC	27282	336-454-1144	454-4935
Parkdale Mills Inc 531 Cotton Blossom Cir *TF:* 800-331-1843 ■ *Web:* www.parkdalemills.com	Gastonia	NC	28054	704-864-8761	874-5170
Perfect Thread Co Inc 10 E Merrick Rd *TF:* 800-645-3500	Valley Stream	NY	11580	516-825-6565	825-6568
Pharr Yarns Inc 100 Main St *Web:* www.pharryarns.com	McAdenville	NC	28101	704-824-3551	824-0072
Pisgah Yarn & Dyeing Co Inc 550 Orchard St	Old Fort	NC	28762	828-668-7667	668-4960
Regal Mfg Co Inc 990 3rd Ave SE PO Box 2363 *Web:* www.regalmfgcoinc.com	Hickory	NC	28603	828-328-5381	328-4936
Richmond Yarns Inc 1748 Hwy 220	Ellerby	NC	28338	910-652-5554	652-2203
RL Stowe Mills Inc 100 N Main St *TF:* 800-880-5314 ■ *Web:* www.rlstowe.com	Belmont	NC	28012	704-825-5314	825-7414
Robison-Anton Textile Co 175 Bergen Blvd *TF:* 800-932-0250 ■ *Web:* www.robison-anton.com	Fairview	NJ	07022	201-941-0500	941-8994
Roselon Industries Inc 18 S 5th St	Quakertown	PA	18951	215-536-3275	536-7284
Sapona Mfg Co Inc 2478 Cedar Falls Rd *Web:* www.saponamfg.com	Cedar Falls	NC	27230	336-625-2727	626-0876
Shuford Mills Inc 1985 Tate Blvd SE **Fax:* Cust Svc ■ *TF:* 800-633-7649 ■ *Web:* www.shufordmills.com	Hickory	NC	28601	828-328-2131	328-5792*

Company	City	State	Zip	Phone	Fax
Spectrum Dyed Yarns Inc 136 Patterson Rd *TF:* 800-221-9456 ■ *Web:* www.sdy.com	Kings Mountain	NC	28086	704-739-7401	739-4754
Stowe RL Mills Inc 100 N Main St *TF:* 800-880-5314 ■ *Web:* www.rlstowe.com	Belmont	NC	28012	704-825-5314	825-7414
Supreme Corp 325 Spence Rd *TF:* 888-604-6975 ■ *Web:* www.ukisupreme.com	Conover	NC	28613	828-322-6975	322-7881
Tuscarora Yarns Inc 8760 E Franklin St *TF:* 800-849-6527 ■ *Web:* www.tuscarorayarns.com	Mount Pleasant	NC	28124	704-436-6527	436-9461
Unifi Inc 7201 W Friendly Ave *NYSE: UFI* ■ *Web:* www.unifi-inc.com	Greensboro	NC	27410	336-294-4410	316-5422
Universal Fibers Inc PO Box 8930 *TF Cust Svc:* 800-457-4759 ■ *Web:* www.universalfibers.com	Bristol	VA	24203	276-669-1161	669-3304
Waverly Mills Inc 23 3rd St *TF Cust Svc:* 800-496-9276 ■ *Web:* www.waverlymills.com	Laurinburg	NC	28352	910-276-1441	276-5826
Wehadkee Yarn Mills Inc 802 3rd Ave *TF:* 800-996-9276 ■ *Web:* www.wehadkee.com	West Point	GA	31833	706-645-1331	645-1373
Whitaker Fred Co 941 Industry Ave SE *TF:* 800-336-5717	Roanoke	VA	24013	540-427-4343	427-3052
Wyndmoor Industries Inc 104 Industrial Park Rd	Lincolnton	NC	28093	704-732-1171	732-4831

749 TEXTILE PRODUCTS - HOUSEHOLD

Company	City	State	Zip	Phone	Fax
1888 Mills 1581 Southern Dr PO Box 797	Griffin	GA	30224	770-229-2361	228-4732
Ado Corp 851 Simuel Rd *TF Cust Svc:* 800-845-0918 ■ *Web:* www.ado-usa.com	Spartanburg	SC	29301	864-574-2731	574-5835
Amana Woolen Mill 800 48th Ave *TF:* 800-222-6430 ■ *Web:* www.amanawoolenmill.com	Amana	IA	52203	319-622-3432	622-6018
American Textile Co 10 N Linden St *TF Cust Svc:* 800-289-2826 ■ *Web:* www.americantextile.com	Duquesne	PA	15110	412-948-1020	948-1002
American Woolen Co 4000 NW 30th Ave	Miami	FL	33142	305-635-4000	633-4997
Arden Cos 18000 W Nine-Mile Rd Suite 700 *Web:* www.ardencompanies.com	Southfield	MI	48075	248-355-1101	355-1230
Arlee Home Fashions Inc 261 5th Ave 6th Fl	New York	NY	10016	212-689-0020	532-6428
Arley Corp 1115 W Chestnut St *TF Cust Svc:* 800-628-7872 ■ *Web:* www.arley.com	Brockton	MA	02301	508-580-4245	580-1264
Ascot Enterprises Inc 503 S Main St *Web:* www.ascotent.com	Nappanee	IN	46550	574-773-7751	773-2894
Avante Bedspreads Co 900 Conroy Pl	Easton	PA	18040	610-438-2418	258-2791
Bardwil Industries Inc 1071 Ave of the Americas 4th Fl *Web:* www.bardwilhome.com	New York	NY	10018	212-944-1870	869-3599
Beacon Looms Inc 411 Alfred Ave *Web:* www.beaconlooms.com	Teaneck	NJ	07666	201-833-1600	833-4053
Biddeford Blankets 300 Terrace Dr *TF:* 800-789-6441 ■ *Web:* biddefordblankets.com	Mundelein	IL	60060	847-566-7442	566-6431
Biederlack of America 11501 Bedford Rd NE *Web:* www.biederlack.com	Cumberland	MD	21502	301-759-3633	759-3837
Blair Mills LP 115 Little St *TF Cust Svc:* 800-458-8038	Belton	SC	29627	864-338-6611	338-4238
Brentwood Originals Inc 20639 S Fordyce Ave *Web:* www.brentwoodoriginals.com	Long Beach	CA	90810	310-637-6804	639-9710
Cadillac Curtain Corp 230 5th Ave Suite 707	New York	NY	10001	212-684-0410	213-9821
Carole Fabrics Inc 633 NW Frontage Rd *TF:* 800-241-0920 ■ *Web:* www.carolefabrics.com	Augusta	GA	30907	706-863-4742	863-8186
Carpenter Co Morning Glory Div 302 Highland Dr **Fax Area Code: 512* ■ *Web:* www.carpenter.com	Taylor	TX	76574	800-234-9105	352-6025*
Charles Craft Inc 21381 Charles Craft Ln PO Box 1049 *TF:* 800-277-1009 ■ *Web:* www.charlescraft.com	Laurinburg	NC	28352	910-844-3521	844-9846
CHF Industries Inc 1 Park Ave 9th Fl *TF:* 800-243-7090 ■ *Web:* www.chfindustries.com	New York	NY	10016	212-951-7800	951-8001
Corona Curtain Mfg Co Inc 401 Neponset St	Canton	MA	02021	617-350-6970	439-4393
Cotton Goods Mfg Co 259 N California Ave *Web:* www.cottongoodsmfg.com	Chicago	IL	60612	773-265-0088	265-0096
Creative Bath Products 250 Creative Dr *Web:* www.creativebath.com	Central Islip	NY	11722	631-582-8000	582-2020
Creative Home Furnishings Inc 530 Park Ln **Fax: Sales* ■ *TF Cust Svc:* 800-261-1315 ■ *Web:* www.dakotah.com	Webster	SD	57274	605-345-4646	345-2399*
Croscill Home Inc 261 5th Ave 25th Fl *Web:* www.croscill.com	New York	NY	10016	212-689-7222	481-8656
Crown Crafts Inc 916 S Burnside *TF:* 800-433-9560 ■ *Web:* www.crowncrafts.com	Gonzales	LA	70737	225-647-9100	647-8331
CS Brooks Inc 9 Benedict Pl *Web:* www.csbrooks.com	Greenwich	CT	06830	203-622-4171	622-4172
Curtain & Drapery Fashions Inc 100 Curtain Way *Web:* www.curtainanddraperyfashions.com	Lowell	NC	28098	704-823-1266	823-1270
Custom Drapery Blinds & Shutters 3900 Polk St *TF:* 800-929-9211 ■ *Web:* www.cdbas.com	Houston	TX	77023	713-225-9211	227-0808
Dan River Inc 700 Lanier Ave *TF:* 800-645-0880 ■ *Web:* www.danriver.com	Danville	VA	24541	434-799-7000	799-2984
Decorator Industries Inc 10011 Pines Blvd Suite 201 *AMEX: DII* ■ *Web:* www.decoratorindustries.com	Pembroke Pines	FL	33024	954-436-8909	436-1778
Dorothy's Ruffled Originals Inc 6721 Market St **Fax Area Code: 877* ■ *TF:* 800-367-6849 ■ *Web:* www.dorothysoriginals.com	Wilmington	NC	28405	910-791-1298	569-9024*
Earle Industries Inc 17539 Hwy 64 PO Box 28 *TF:* 888-944-8667	Earle	AR	72331	870-792-8694	792-7100
Echota Fabrics Inc 1394 US 41 N *Web:* www.echotafabrics.com	Calhoun	GA	30701	706-629-9750	629-5229
Elrene Home Fashions Inc 261 5th Ave 10th Fl	New York	NY	10016	212-889-6376	481-1738
Ex-Cell Home Fashion Inc 295 5th Ave Rm 612 *TF:* 800-223-1999	New York	NY	10016	212-213-8000	213-5591
F Schumacher & Co 79 Madison Ave *TF:* 800-523-1200 ■ *Web:* www.fschumacher.com	New York	NY	10016	212-213-7900	213-7848
Fashion Industries Inc 1120 Everee Inn Rd	Griffin	GA	30224	770-228-3010	412-1124
Franco Mfg Co Inc 555 Prospect St *TF:* 800-631-4663 ■ *Web:* www.francomfg.com	Metuchen	NJ	08840	732-494-0500	494-8270
Haleyville Drapery PO Box 695	Haleyville	AL	35565	205-486-9257	486-4788
Hedaya Home Fashions Inc 1111 Jefferson Ave	Elizabeth	NJ	07201	908-352-0808	352-4060
Hollander Home Fashions Corp 6560 W Rogers Cir Suite 19 *TF:* 800-233-7666 ■ *Web:* www.hollander.com	Boca Raton	FL	33487	561-997-6900	997-8738
Hornick Louis & Co Inc 261 5th Ave *Web:* www.louishornick.com	New York	NY	10016	212-679-2448	779-7098
Kaslen Textiles 5899 Downey Rd *TF:* 800-423-4448 ■ *Web:* www.kaslentextiles.com	Vernon	CA	90058	323-589-5337	588-7799
Kay Dee Designs Inc 177 Skunk Hill Rd **Fax Area Code: 800* ■ *TF:* 800-537-3433 ■ *Web:* www.kaydeedesigns.com	Hope Valley	RI	02832	401-539-2405	272-0724*
Kellwood Co 600 Kellwood Pkwy *NYSE: KWD* ■ *Web:* www.kellwood.com	Chesterfield	MO	63017	314-576-3100	576-3462
Kennebunk Home Inc 25 Canal St *TF:* 800-242-1537 ■ *Web:* www.kennebunkhome.com	Suncook	NH	03275	603-485-7511	485-2054
Klear-Vu Corp 135 Alden St *TF:* 800-732-8723 ■ *Web:* www.klearvu.com	Fall River	MA	02723	508-674-5723	672-2027
Lafayette Venetian Blind Inc 3000 Klondike Rd *TF:* 800-342-5523 ■ *Web:* www.lafvb.com	West Lafayette	IN	47906	765-464-2500	464-2680
Leggett & Platt Inc Vantage Div 5070 Phillip Lee Dr PO Box 43944	Atlanta	GA	30336	404-691-9500	691-9149
Lichtenberg S & Co Inc 295 5th Ave Rm 918 *TF Cust Svc:* 800-682-1959 ■ *Web:* www.lichtenberg.com	New York	NY	10016	212-689-4510	689-4517
Lincoln Textile Products Co Inc 900 Conroy Pl	Easton	PA	18040	610-438-2418	258-2791
Louis Hornick & Co Inc 261 5th Ave *Web:* www.louishornick.com	New York	NY	10016	212-679-2448	779-7098
Louisville Bedding Co 10400 Bunsen Way *TF:* 800-626-2594 ■ *Web:* www.loubed.com	Louisville	KY	40299	502-491-3370	495-5346
Manual Woodworkers & Weavers Inc 3737 Howard Gap Rd *TF:* 800-542-3139 ■ *Web:* www.manualww.com	Hendersonville	NC	28792	828-692-7333	696-2961
Marietta Drapery & Window Coverings Co 22 Trammel St *TF:* 800-241-7974 ■ *Web:* www.mariettadrapery.com	Marietta	GA	30064	770-428-3335	425-8129
Miller Curtain Co Inc 1734 Centennial St PO Box 240790 *TF:* 800-741-9020 ■ *Web:* www.millercurtain.com	San Antonio	TX	78224	210-483-1000	483-1509
Miller Industries Inc PO Box 97 *Web:* www.mjblankets.com	Lisbon Falls	ME	04252	207-353-4371	353-5900
Newport Layton Home Fashions Inc 14546 N Lombard St *TF:* 800-752-2225	Portland	OR	97203	503-283-4864	283-4895
Oxford Drapery Inc 230 5th Ave Suite 707	New York	NY	10001	212-684-0410	213-9821
Pacific Coast Feather Co 1964 4th Ave S *Web:* www.pacificcoast.com	Seattle	WA	98134	206-624-1057	625-9783
Paramount Industrial Cos Inc 1112 Kingwood Ave *TF:* 800-777-5337	Norfolk	VA	23502	757-855-3321	855-2029
Pendleton Woolen Mills Inc 220 NW Broadway *TF:* 800-760-4844 ■ *Web:* www.pendleton-usa.com	Portland	OR	97209	503-226-4801	535-5502
Perfect Fit Industries Inc 261 5th Ave Suite 1901 *TF Cust Svc:* 800-438-1516 ■ *Web:* www.perfectfitindustries.com	New York	NY	10016	212-679-6656	545-7241
Phoenix Down Corp 85 Rt 46 W *TF:* 800-255-3696 ■ *Web:* www.phoenixdown.com	Totowa	NJ	07512	973-812-8100	812-9077
Quip Industries Inc 191 Methodist St *TF:* 800-851-4013 ■ *Web:* www.quipindustries.com	Carlyle	IL	62231	618-594-2437	594-4707
Riegel Consumer Products 51 Riegel Rd PO Box E *TF:* 800-845-3251 ■ *Web:* www.riegellinen.com	Johnston	SC	29832	803-275-2541	275-2219
Riverdale Decorative Products 18 Beaver St	Newark	NJ	07102	973-286-1800	286-1801
Royal Home Fashions Inc Fay & Eastview Sts	Durham	NC	27704	919-683-8011	688-8268
S Lichtenberg & Co Inc 295 5th Ave Rm 918 *TF Cust Svc:* 800-682-1959 ■ *Web:* www.lichtenberg.com	New York	NY	10016	212-689-4510	689-4517
Samson Mfg Co 231 E 13th St PO Box 807 *TF:* 800-682-1959	Waynesboro	GA	30830	706-554-2129	554-6857
Saturday Knight Ltd 2100 Section Rd	Cincinnati	OH	45237	513-641-1400	242-2805
Springs Global US Inc 205 N White St **Fax: Mktg* ■ *TF:* 888-926-7888 ■ *Web:* www.springs.com	Fort Mill	SC	29715	803-547-1500	547-1579*
Standard Textile Co Inc Decorative Products One Knollcrest Dr *TF:* 800-888-5000 ■ *Web:* www.standardtextile.com	Cincinnati	OH	45237	513-761-9255	761-0467
Surefit Inc 6575 Snowdrift Rd Suite 101 *TF:* 800-305-5856 ■ *Web:* www.surefit.net	Allentown	PA	18106	610-264-7300	266-2690
TexStyle Inc 5555 Murray Ave Suite A *TF:* 800-875-8001	Cincinnati	OH	45227	513-272-1800	272-1817
Town & Country Linen Corp 475 Oberlin Ave S *TF:* 800-285-1950	Lakewood	NJ	08701	732-364-2000	364-8492
Tweel Home Furnishings Inc 18 Beaver St *Web:* www.tweelhome.com	Newark	NJ	07102	973-286-1800	286-1801
United Feather & Down Inc 414 E Golf Rd *TF:* 800-932-3696 ■ *Web:* www.ufandd.com	Des Plaines	IL	60016	847-296-6500	296-6616
Vantage Div Leggett & Platt Inc 5070 Phillip Lee Dr PO Box 43944	Atlanta	GA	30336	404-691-9500	691-9149
Wesco Fabrics Inc 4001 Forest St *TF:* 800-950-9372 ■ *Web:* www.wescofabrics.com	Denver	CO	80216	303-388-4101	388-3908
WestPoint Home Inc 28 E 28th St 8th Fl *TF:* 800-533-8229 ■ *Web:* www.martex.com	New York	NY	10016	212-930-2000	
Whisper Soft Mills Inc 127 Rockfish Plaza PO Box 997	Wallace	NC	28466	910-285-8200	285-4374

750 THEATERS - BROADWAY

SEE ALSO Performing Arts Facilities p. 2090; Performing Arts Organizations - Theater Companies p. 2103; Theaters - Resident p. 2366

Company	City	State	Zip	Phone	Fax
Al Hirschfeld Theatre 302 W 45th St *TF:* 800-432-7250 ■ *Web:* www.telecharge.com	New York	NY	10036	212-239-6200	239-5801
Ambassador Theatre 215 W 49th St *TF:* 800-432-7250 ■ *Web:* www.telecharge.com	New York	NY	10019	212-239-6200	239-5801
American Airlines Theatre 227 W 42nd St *Web:* www.roundabouttheatre.org	New York	NY	10036	212-719-1300	869-8817
Barrymore Theatre 243 W 47th St *TF:* 800-432-7250	New York	NY	10036	212-239-6200	239-5801
Belasco Theatre 111 W 44th St *TF:* 800-432-7250	New York	NY	10036	212-239-6200	
Biltmore Theatre 261 W 47th St *Web:* www.manhattantheatreclub.com	New York	NY	10036	212-399-3000	399-4329
Booth Theatre 222 W 45th St *TF:* 800-432-7250 ■ *Web:* www.telecharge.com	New York	NY	10036	212-239-6200	239-5801
Broadhurst Theatre 235 W 44th St *TF:* 800-432-7250 ■ *Web:* www.telecharge.com	New York	NY	10036	212-239-6200	239-5801
Broadway Theatre 1681 Broadway *TF:* 800-432-7250	New York	NY	10019	212-239-6200	239-5801
Brooks Atkinson Theatre 256 W 47th St *TF:* 800-755-4000	New York	NY	10036	212-307-4100	
Cadillac Winter Garden Theatre 1634 Broadway *TF:* 800-432-7250	New York	NY	10019	212-239-6200	239-5801
Circle in the Square Theatre 1633 Broadway *TF:* 800-432-7250 ■ *Web:* www.telecharge.com	New York	NY	10019	212-239-6200	239-5801
Cort Theatre 138 W 48th St *TF:* 800-432-7250	New York	NY	10036	212-239-6200	239-5801
Eugene O'Neill Theatre 230 W 49th St *TF:* 800-432-7250	New York	NY	10019	212-239-6200	239-5801
Ford Center for the Performing Arts 213 W 42nd St *TF:* 800-755-4000	New York	NY	10036	212-307-4100	
Gershwin Theatre 222 W 51st St *TF:* 800-755-4000	New York	NY	10019	212-307-4100	
Golden Theatre 252 W 45th St *TF:* 800-432-7250 ■ *Web:* www.telecharge.com	New York	NY	10036	212-239-6200	239-5801
Helen Hayes Theatre 240 W 44th St *TF:* 800-432-7250 ■ *Web:* www.telecharge.com	New York	NY	10036	212-239-6200	239-5801
Imperial Theatre 249 W 45th St *TF:* 800-432-7250 ■ *Web:* www.telecharge.com	New York	NY	10036	212-239-6200	239-5801
Jacob Theatre 242 W 45th St *TF:* 800-432-7250 ■ *Web:* www.telecharge.com	New York	NY	10036	212-239-6200	239-5801
Longacre Theatre 220 W 48th St *TF:* 800-432-7250 ■ *Web:* www.telecharge.com	New York	NY	10036	212-239-6200	239-5801

	City	State	Zip	Phone	Fax
Lunt-Fontanne Theatre 205 W 46th St *TF:* 800-755-4000	New York	NY	10036	212-307-4100	
Lyceum Theatre 149 W 45th St *TF:* 800-432-7250 ■ *Web:* www.telecharge.com	New York	NY	10036	212-239-6200	239-5801
Majestic Theatre 245 W 44th St *TF:* 800-432-7250 ■ *Web:* www.telecharge.com	New York	NY	10036	212-239-6200	239-5801
Marquis Theatre 211 W 45th St *TF:* 800-755-4000	New York	NY	10036	212-307-4100	
Minskoff Theatre 200 W 45th St *TF:* 800-755-4000	New York	NY	10036	212-307-4100	
Music Box Theatre 239 W 45th St *TF:* 800-432-7250 ■ *Web:* www.telecharge.com	New York	NY	10036	212-239-6200	239-5801
Nederlander Theatre 208 W 41st St *TF:* 800-755-4000	New York	NY	10036	212-307-4100	
Neil Simon Theatre 250 W 52nd St *TF:* 800-755-4000	New York	NY	10019	212-307-4100	
New Amsterdam Theatre 214 W 42nd St *TF:* 800-755-4000	New York	NY	10036	212-307-4100	
Palace Theatre 1564 Broadway *TF:* 800-755-4000	New York	NY	10036	212-307-4100	
Richard Rodgers Theatre 226 W 46th St *TF:* 800-755-4000	New York	NY	10036	212-307-4100	
Roundabout Theatre Co 231 W 39th St Suite 1200 *Web:* www.roundabouttheatre.org	New York	NY	10018	212-719-9393	869-8817
Saint James Theatre 246 W 44th St *TF:* 800-432-7250 ■ *Web:* www.telecharge.com	New York	NY	10036	212-239-6200	239-5801
Schoenfeld Theatre 236 W 45th St *TF:* 800-432-7250	New York	NY	10036	212-239-6200	239-5801
Shubert Theatre 225 W 44th St *TF:* 800-432-7250 ■ *Web:* www.telecharge.com	New York	NY	10036	212-239-6200	239-5801
Snapple Theater Center 1627 Broadway	New York	NY	10039	212-695-3401	921-7928
Studio 54 Theatre 254 W 54th St *Web:* www.roundabouttheatre.org	New York	NY	10019	212-719-1300	956-9254
Virginia Theatre 245 W 52nd St *TF:* 800-432-7250	New York	NY	10019	212-239-6200	239-5801
Vivian Beaumont Theatre 150 W 65th St *TF:* 800-432-7250	New York	NY	10023	212-239-6200	239-5801
Walter Kerr Theatre 219 W 48th St *TF:* 800-432-7250 ■ *Web:* www.telecharge.com	New York	NY	10036	212-239-6200	239-5801

751 THEATERS - MOTION PICTURE

	City	State	Zip	Phone	Fax
Allen Theaters 133 Wyatt Dr Suite 3 *Web:* www.allentheaters.com	Las Cruces	NM	88001	505-524-7933	527-0068
AMC Entertainment Inc 920 Main St *TF:* 800-326-2432 ■ *Web:* www.amctheatres.com	Kansas City	MO	64105	816-221-4000	480-4617
American Multi-Cinema Inc 920 Main St *TF:* 800-326-2432 ■ *Web:* www.amctheatres.com	Kansas City	MO	64105	816-221-4000	480-4617
BlueGrass Theatres Inc 3304 Gondola Ct	Lexington	KY	40513	859-296-5998	296-4817
Carmike Cinemas Inc 1301 1st Ave *NASDAQ: CKEC* ■ *TF:* 800-241-0431 ■ *Web:* www.carmike.com	Columbus	GA	31901	706-576-3400	576-3880
Celebration! Cinema 2121 Celebration Ave *Web:* www.celebrationcinema.com	Grand Rapids	MI	49525	616-447-4200	447-4201
Century Theatres LP 150 Pelican Way *Web:* www.centurytheatres.com	San Rafael	CA	94901	415-448-8400	448-8358
Chakeres Theatres Inc 222 N Murray St *Web:* www.chakerestheatres.com	Springfield	OH	45503	937-323-6447	325-1100
Cinemark USA Inc 3900 Dallas Pkwy Suite 500 *TF:* 800-950-2872 ■ *Web:* www.cinemark.com	Plano	TX	75093	972-665-1000	665-1004
CinemaStar Luxury Theaters Inc 1949 Avenida del Oro Suite 100 *Web:* www.cinemastar.com	Oceanside	CA	92056	760-945-2500	945-2510
Cineplex Entertainment LP 1303 Yonge St *TSX: CGX.un* ■ *TF:* 800-333-4461 ■ *Web:* www.cineplex.com	Toronto	ON	M4T2Y9	416-323-6600	323-7228
Classic Cinemas 603 Rogers St *Web:* www.classiccinemas.com	Downers Grove	IL	60515	630-968-1600	968-1626
Clearview Cinema Group Inc 97 Main St *Web:* www.clearviewcinemas.com	Chatham	NJ	07928	908-918-2000	273-7157
Colorado Cinema Holdings 6696 S Parker Rd *Web:* www.coloradocinemas.net	Aurora	CO	80016	303-766-7900	766-9865
Consolidated Theatres Inc 5970 Fairview Rd Suite 600 *Web:* www.consolidatedmovies.com	Charlotte	NC	28210	704-554-1695	554-1696
De Anza Land & Leisure Corp 1615 Cordova St	Los Angeles	CA	90007	323-734-9951	734-2531
Dickinson Theatres Inc 6801 W 107th St *Web:* www.dtmovies.com	Overland Park	KS	66212	913-432-2334	432-9507
Eastern Federal Corp 901 East Blvd **Fax:* Mktg ■ *TF:* 800-394-7368 ■ *Web:* www.easternfederal.com	Charlotte	NC	28203	704-377-3495	358-8427*
Empire Theatres Ltd 610 E River Rd Suite 205 *Web:* www.empiretheatres.com	New Glasgow	NS	B2H3S2	902-755-7620	755-7640
Goodrich Quality Theaters Inc 4417 Broadmoor Ave SE *TF:* 800-473-3523 ■ *Web:* www.gqti.com	Kentwood	MI	49512	616-698-7733	698-7220
Harkins Amusement Enterprises Inc 7511 E McDonald Dr *Web:* www.harkinstheatres.com	Scottsdale	AZ	85250	480-627-7777	443-0950
Hollywood Theater Holdings Inc 919 SW Taylor St Suite 800 *Web:* www.wallacetheaters.com	Portland	OR	97205	503-221-7090	796-0229
IMAX Corp 2525 Speakman Dr Sheridan Science & Technology Pk *NASDAQ: IMAX* ■ *Web:* www.imax.com	Mississauga	ON	L5K1B1	905-403-6500	403-6450
Iwerks Entertainment Inc 4520 W Valerio St *TF:* 800-388-8628 ■ *Web:* www.iwerks.com	Burbank	CA	91505	818-841-7766	840-6104
Kerasotes ShowPlace Theatres LLC 224 N Des Plaines Ave Suite 200 *TF:* 877-293-2000 ■ *Web:* www.kerasotes.com	Chicago	IL	60661	312-775-3160	777-0480
Landmark Theaters 2222 S Barrington Ave *Web:* www.landmarktheatres.com	Los Angeles	CA	90064	310-473-6701	312-2364
Larry H Miller MEGAPLEX Theatres 9273 S State St *Web:* www.megaplextheatres.com	Sandy	UT	84070	801-304-4577	
Loews Cineplex Entertainment Corp 711 5th Ave 12th Fl *Web:* www.enjoytheshow.com	New York	NY	10022	646-521-6000	521-6277
Malco Theatres Inc 5851 Ridgeway Center Pkwy *Web:* www.malco.com	Memphis	TN	38120	901-761-3480	681-2044
Mann Theatres Corp of California 16530 Ventura Blvd Suite 500 *Web:* www.manntheatres.com	Encino	CA	91436	818-784-6266	784-8717
Mann Theatres Inc 711 Hennepin Ave *Web:* www.manntheatresmn.com	Minneapolis	MN	55403	612-332-3303	332-3305
Marcus Corp 100 E Wisconsin Ave *NYSE: MCS* ■ *TF:* 800-274-0099 ■ *Web:* www.marcuscorp.com	Milwaukee	WI	53202	414-905-1000	905-2129
Marcus Theatres Corp 100 E Wisconsin Ave Suite 19 *TF Cust Svc:* 800-274-0099 ■ *Web:* www.marcustheaters.com	Milwaukee	WI	53202	414-905-1000	905-2189
Metropolitan Theaters Corp 8727 W 3rd St *Web:* www.metrotheatres.com	Los Angeles	CA	90048	310-858-2800	858-2860
Muvico Theaters 3101 N Federal Hwy 6th Fl *TF:* 800-294-6585 ■ *Web:* www.muvico.com	Fort Lauderdale	FL	33306	954-564-6550	564-6553
National Amusements Inc 200 Elm St **Fax:* Mktg ■ *Web:* www.national-amusements.com	Dedham	MA	02026	781-461-1600	329-4670*
Northeast Cinemas LLC 500 Franklin Village Dr Suite 204 **Fax Area Code: 508*	Franklin	MA	02038	774-235-2300	520-3196*
Pacific Theatres Corp 120 N Robertson Blvd *Web:* www.pacifictheatres.com	Los Angeles	CA	90048	310-657-8420	855-9837
Rave Motion Pictures 3333 Welborn St Suite 100 *Web:* www.ravemotionpictures.com	Dallas	TX	75219	972-692-1700	692-1708
Reading International Inc 500 Citadel Dr Suite 300 *AMEX: RDI* ■ *Web:* www.readingrdi.com	Commerce	CA	90040	213-235-2240	235-2229
Regal Entertainment Group 7132 Regal Ln *NYSE: RGC* ■ *TF:* 877-835-5734 ■ *Web:* www.regalcinemas.com	Knoxville	TN	37918	865-922-1123	922-3188
Star Theatres 25333 W 12-Mile Rd *Web:* www.startheatres.com	Southfield	MI	48034	248-357-1140	357-1151
WF Cinema Holdings LP DBA Mann Theatres Corp of California 16530 Ventura Blvd Suite 500 *Web:* www.manntheatres.com	Encino	CA	91436	818-784-6266	784-8717
Wometco Enterprises Inc 3195 Ponce De Leon Blvd	Coral Gables	FL	33134	305-529-1400	529-1499

752 THEATERS - RESIDENT

SEE ALSO Performing Arts Facilities p. 2090; Performing Arts Organizations - Theater Companies p. 2103; Theaters - Broadway p. 2365

All of the theaters listed here are members of the League of Resident Theatres (LORT). In order to become a member of LORT, each theater must be incorporated as a non-profit, IRS-approved organization; must rehearse each self-produced production for a minimum of three weeks; must have a playing season of 12 weeks or more; and must operate under a LORT-Equity contract.

	City	State	Zip	Phone	Fax
ACT Theatre 700 Union St Kreielsheimer Pl *Web:* www.acttheatre.org	Seattle	WA	98101	206-292-7660	292-7670
Actors Theatre of Louisville 316 W Main St *TF:* 800-428-5849 ■ *Web:* www.actorstheatre.org	Louisville	KY	40202	502-584-1265	561-3300
Alabama Shakespeare Festival 1 Festival Dr *TF:* 800-841-4273 ■ *Web:* www.asf.net	Montgomery	AL	36117	334-271-5300	271-5348
Alley Theatre 615 Texas Ave *Web:* www.alleytheatre.org	Houston	TX	77002	713-228-9341	222-6542
Alliance Theatre Co 1280 Peachtree St NE Woodruff Arts Center *Web:* www.alliancetheatre.org	Atlanta	GA	30309	404-733-4650	733-4625
American Conservatory Theater 30 Grant Ave 6th Fl *Web:* www.act-sfbay.org	San Francisco	CA	94108	415-834-3200	834-3360
American Repertory Theatre 64 Brattle St *Web:* www.amrep.org	Cambridge	MA	02138	617-495-2668	495-1705
Arden Theatre Co 40 N 2nd St *Web:* www.ardentheatre.org	Philadelphia	PA	19106	215-922-8900	922-7011
Arena Stage 1101 6th St SW *Web:* www.arenastage.org	Washington	DC	20024	202-554-9066	488-4056
Arizona Theatre Co 343 S Scott Ave *TF:* 888-772-9449 ■ *Web:* www.aztheatreco.org	Tucson	AZ	85701	520-884-8210	628-9129
Arkansas Repertory Theatre 601 Main St *TF:* 866-684-3737 ■ *Web:* www.therep.org	Little Rock	AR	72201	501-378-0445	378-0012
Asolo Theatre Co 5555 N Tamiami Tr *TF:* 800-361-8388 ■ *Web:* www.asolo.org	Sarasota	FL	34243	941-351-9010	351-5796
Barter Theatre 133 W Main St *Web:* www.bartertheatre.com	Abingdon	VA	24210	276-628-2281	619-3335
Berkeley Repertory Theatre 2025 Addison St *TF:* 888-427-8849 ■ *Web:* www.berkeleyrep.org	Berkeley	CA	94704	510-647-2900	647-2976
Berkshire Theatre Festival PO Box 797 *TF:* 866-811-4111 ■ *Web:* www.berkshiretheatre.org	Stockbridge	MA	01262	413-298-5536	298-3368
Brown Clarence Theatre 206 McClung Tower *Web:* www.clarencebrowntheatre.com	Knoxville	TN	37996	865-974-6011	974-4867
Capital Repertory Theatre 111 N Pearl St Market Street Theater *Web:* www.capitalrep.org	Albany	NY	12207	518-462-4531	465-0213
Center Stage 700 N Calvert St *Web:* www.centerstage.org	Baltimore	MD	21202	410-986-4000	539-3912
Center Theatre Group 601 W Temple St *Web:* www.taperahmanson.com	Los Angeles	CA	90012	213-628-2772	972-7402
Cincinnati Playhouse in the Park 962 Mt Adams Cir *TF:* 800-582-3208 ■ *Web:* www.cincyplay.com	Cincinnati	OH	45202	513-345-2242	345-2250
City Theatre Co 1300 Bingham St *Web:* www.citytheatrecompany.org	Pittsburgh	PA	15203	412-431-4400	431-5535
Clarence Brown Theatre 206 McClung Tower *Web:* www.clarencebrowntheatre.com	Knoxville	TN	37996	865-974-6011	974-4867
Cleveland Play House 8500 Euclid Ave *Web:* www.clevelandplayhouse.com	Cleveland	OH	44106	216-795-7010	795-7005
Court Theatre 5535 S Ellis Ave *Web:* www.courttheatre.org	Chicago	IL	60637	773-702-7005	834-1897
Dallas Theater Center 3636 Turtle Creek Blvd *Web:* www.dallastheatercenter.org	Dallas	TX	75219	214-526-8210	521-7666
Delaware Theatre Co 200 Water St *Web:* www.delawaretheatre.com	Wilmington	DE	19801	302-594-1104	594-1107
Denver Center Theatre Co 1101 13th St *TF:* 800-641-1222 ■ *Web:* www.denvercenter.org	Denver	CO	80204	303-893-4000	595-9634
Florida Stage 262 S Ocean Blvd *TF:* 800-514-3837 ■ *Web:* www.floridastage.org	Manalapan	FL	33462	561-585-3404	588-4708
Ford's Theatre 511 10th St NW *TF:* 800-899-2367 ■ *Web:* www.fordstheatre.org	Washington	DC	20004	202-638-2941	347-6269
Geffen Playhouse 10886 Le Conte Ave *Web:* www.geffenplayhouse.com	Los Angeles	CA	90024	310-208-6500	208-0341
George Street Playhouse 9 Livingston Ave *Web:* www.georgestplayhouse.org	New Brunswick	NJ	08901	732-246-7717	247-9151
Georgia Shakespeare 4484 Peachtree Rd NE *Web:* www.gashakespeare.org	Atlanta	GA	30319	404-504-3400	504-3414
Geva Theatre Center 75 Woodbury Blvd *Web:* www.gevatheatre.org	Rochester	NY	14607	585-232-1366	232-4031
Goodman Theatre 170 N Dearborn St *Web:* www.goodman-theatre.org	Chicago	IL	60601	312-443-3811	443-3821
Goodspeed Musicals PO Box A *Web:* www.goodspeed.org	East Haddam	CT	06423	860-873-8664	873-2329
Great Lakes Theater Festival 1501 Euclid Ave Suite 300 *TF:* 800-766-6048 ■ *Web:* www.greatlakestheater.org	Cleveland	OH	44115	216-241-5490	241-6315
Guthrie Theater 818 S 2nd St *TF:* 877-447-8243 ■ *Web:* www.guthrietheater.org	Minneapolis	MN	55415	612-225-6000	225-6004
Hartford Stage Co 50 Church St *Web:* www.hartfordstage.org	Hartford	CT	06103	860-525-5601	525-4420
Huntington Theatre Co 264 Huntington Ave Boston University Theatre *Web:* www.huntingtontheatre.org	Boston	MA	02115	617-266-7900	353-8300
Indiana Repertory Theatre 140 W Washington St *Web:* www.indianarep.com	Indianapolis	IN	46204	317-635-5277	236-0767

Name / Address	City	State	Zip	Phone	Fax
Intiman Theatre 201 Mercer St Seattle Ctr	Seattle	WA	98109	206-269-1901	269-1928
Web: www.intiman.org					
Kansas City Repertory Theatre 4949 Cherry St	Kansas City	MO	64110	816-235-2727	235-2704
TF: 888-502-2700 ■ *Web:* www.kcrep.org					
La Jolla Playhouse PO Box 12039	La Jolla	CA	92039	858-550-1070	550-1075
Web: www.lajollaplayhouse.com					
Laguna Playhouse 606 Laguna Canyon Rd	Laguna Beach	CA	92651	949-497-2787	497-6948
Web: www.lagunaplayhouse.com					
Lincoln Center Theater 150 W 65th St	New York	NY	10023	212-362-7600	873-0761
Web: www.lct.org					
Long Wharf Theatre 222 Sargent Dr	New Haven	CT	06511	203-787-4284	776-2287
TF: 800-782-8497 ■ *Web:* www.longwharf.org					
Maltz Jupiter Theatre 1001 E Indiantown Rd	Jupiter	FL	33477	561-743-2666	743-0107
TF: 800-445-1666 ■ *Web:* www.jupitertheatre.org					
Manhattan Theatre Club Inc 311 W 43rd St 8th Fl	New York	NY	10036	212-399-3000	399-4329
Web: www.manhattantheatreclub.com					
McCarter Theatre 91 University Pl	Princeton	NJ	08540	609-258-6500	497-0369
Web: www.mccarter.org					
Merrimack Repertory Theatre 50 E Merrimack St	Lowell	MA	01852	978-454-6324	
Web: www.merrimackrep.org					
Milwaukee Repertory Theater 108 E Wells St	Milwaukee	WI	53202	414-224-1761	224-9097
Web: www.milwaukeerep.com					
Northlight Theatre 9501 Skokie Blvd	Skokie	IL	60077	847-679-9501	679-1879
Web: www.northlight.org					
Old Globe Theatre 1363 Old Globe Way	San Diego	CA	92101	619-231-1941	231-5879
Web: www.oldglobe.org					
Pasadena Playhouse 39 S El Molino Ave	Pasadena	CA	91101	626-792-8672	792-6142
Web: www.pasadenaplayhouse.org					
People's Light & Theatre Co 39 Conestoga Rd	Malvern	PA	19355	610-647-1900	640-9521
Web: www.peopleslight.org					
Philadelphia Theatre Co 230 S 15th St 4th Fl	Philadelphia	PA	19102	215-985-1400	985-5800
Web: www.phillytheatreco.com					
Pittsburgh Public Theater 621 Penn Ave	Pittsburgh	PA	15222	412-316-8200	316-8219
Web: www.ppt.org					
PlayMakers Repertory Co					
University of North Carolina Center for Dramatic Art CB #3235	Chapel Hill	NC	27599	919-962-7529	904-8396*
**Fax Area Code:* 866 ■ *Web:* www.playmakersrep.org					
Portland Center Stage 1111 SW Broadway Ave	Portland	OR	97205	503-248-6309	228-7058
Web: www.pcs.org					
Portland Stage Co PO Box 1458	Portland	ME	04104	207-774-1043	774-0576
Web: www.portlandstage.com					
Prince Music Theater 1412 Chestnut St	Philadelphia	PA	19102	215-972-1000	972-1020
Web: www.princemusictheater.org					
Repertory Theatre of Saint Louis 130 Edgar Rd PO Box 191730	Saint Louis	MO	63119	314-968-7340	968-9638
Web: www.repstl.org					
Roundabout Theatre Co 231 W 39th St Suite 1200	New York	NY	10018	212-719-9393	869-8817
Web: www.roundabouttheatre.org					
San Jose Repertory Theatre 101 Paseo de San Antonio	San Jose	CA	95113	408-367-7266	367-7237
Web: www.sjrep.com					
Seattle Repertory Theatre 155 Mercer St PO Box 900923	Seattle	WA	98109	206-443-2210	443-2379
TF: 877-900-9285 ■ *Web:* www.seattlerep.org					
Shakespeare Theatre 516 8th St SE	Washington	DC	20003	202-547-3230	547-0226
TF: 877-487-8849 ■ *Web:* www.shakespearetheatre.org					
South Coast Repertory 655 Town Ctr Dr	Costa Mesa	CA	92626	714-708-5500	708-5576
Web: www.scr.org					
Studio Arena Theatre 710 Main St	Buffalo	NY	14202	716-856-8025	856-3415
TF: 800-777-8243 ■ *Web:* www.studioarena.org					
Syracuse Stage 820 E Genesee St	Syracuse	NY	13210	315-443-4008	443-9846
Web: www.syracusestage.org					
Theatre For A New Audience 154 Christopher St #3D	New York	NY	10014	212-229-2819	229-2911
Web: www.tfana.org					
TheatreWorks PO Box 50458	Palo Alto	CA	94303	650-463-1950	463-1963
Web: theatreworks.org					
Trinity Repertory Co 201 Washington St	Providence	RI	02903	401-521-1100	751-5577
Web: www.trinityrep.com					
Virginia Stage Co Monticello & Tazewell Sts	Norfolk	VA	23514	757-627-6988	628-5958
Web: www.vastage.com					
Wilma Theater 265 S Broad St	Philadelphia	PA	19107	215-893-9456	893-0895
Web: www.wilmatheater.org					
Yale Repertory Theatre 1120 Chapel St PO Box 1257	New Haven	CT	06505	203-432-1234	432-6423
Web: www.yale.edu/yalerep					

753 TICKET BROKERS

Name / Address	City	State	Zip	Phone	Fax
Acteva.com 1 Bush St 15th Fl	San Francisco	CA	94104	415-374-8222	374-8233
TF Cust Svc: 877-855-8646 ■ *Web:* www.acteva.com					
All American Ticket Service 2616 Philadelphia Pike Suite E	Claymont	DE	19703	302-798-8556	798-6552
TF: 800-669-0571 ■ *Web:* www.alltickets.com					
Americana Tickets NY 115 W 45th St 8th Fl	New York	NY	10036	212-581-6660	262-9627
TF: 800-833-3121 ■ *Web:* www.americanatickets.com					
Broadway.com 727 7th Ave 6th Fl	New York	NY	10019	212-541-8457	541-4892
TF: 800-276-2392 ■ *Web:* www.broadway.com					
Front Row USA Entertainment Inc					
18170 W Dixie Hwy 2nd Fl	North Miami Beach	FL	33160	305-940-8499	936-2438
TF: 800-446-8499 ■ *Web:* www.frontrowusa.com					
GetTix.net 4909 E McDowell Rd Suite 104	Phoenix	AZ	85008	480-994-0772	994-0759
Web: www.gettix.net					
Global Entertainment Ticketing 4909 E McDowell Rd Suite 104	Phoenix	AZ	85008	480-994-0772	994-0759
Web: www.gettix.net					
Good Time Tickets Inc 38 Hadden Field Rd	Palmyra	NJ	08065	856-829-3900	829-2797
TF: 800-774-8499 ■ *Web:* www.goodtimetickets.com					
GoTickets.com 201 Shannon Oaks Cir	Cary	NC	27512	919-481-4868	481-9101
TF: 800-775-1617 ■ *Web:* www.gotickets.com					
Great Seats Inc 7338 Baltimore Ave Suite 108A	College Park	MD	20740	301-985-6250	985-6254
TF: 800-664-5056 ■ *Web:* www.greatseats.com					
HMR Enterprises Inc DBA VIP Tickets					
14515 Ventura Blvd Suite 210	Sherman Oaks	CA	91403	818-907-1548	784-2359
TF: 800-328-4253 ■ *Web:* www.viptickets.com					
Moviefone Inc 333 Westchester Ave 2nd Fl	White Plains	NY	10604	914-872-0333	872-0066
TF Cust Svc: 800-745-0009 ■ *Web:* www.moviefone.com					
Pacific Northwest Ticket Service 2864 77th Ave SE	Mercer Island	WA	98040	206-232-0150	232-0159
TF: 800-281-0753 ■ *Web:* www.nwtickets.com					
Premiere Tickets & Tours Inc 201 Shannon Oaks Cir	Cary	NC	27512	919-481-4868	481-9101
TF: 800-775-1617 ■ *Web:* www.gotickets.com					
Select-A-Ticket Inc 25 Rt 23 S	Riverdale	NJ	07457	973-839-6100	839-0870
TF: 800-735-3288 ■ *Web:* www.selectaticket.com					
Shubert Ticketing Services 234 W 44th St	New York	NY	10036	212-944-3700	944-4170
TF: 800-545-2559 ■ *Web:* www.telecharge.com					
Theatre Development Fund 1501 Broadway 21st Fl	New York	NY	10036	212-221-0885	768-1563
Web: www.tdf.org					
Ticket Box 2125 Center Ave Suite 509	Fort Lee	NJ	07024	201-461-8771	461-4606
TF: 800-842-5440 ■ *Web:* www.theticketbox.com					
Ticket Heaven 600 S County Farm Rd Suite 144	Wheaton	IL	60187	630-260-0626	260-4831
TF: 800-260-6616 ■ *Web:* www.ticketheaven.com					
Ticket Pros USA 245 Peachtree Ctr Ave Suite M-39	Atlanta	GA	30303	404-524-8491	614-0420
TF: 800-962-2985 ■ *Web:* www.ticketmall.com					
Ticket Source Inc 5516 E Mockingbird Ln Suite 100	Dallas	TX	75206	214-821-9011	821-9060
TF: 800-557-6872 ■ *Web:* www.ticketsource.com					
Ticketfinder.com 236 W Portal Ave Suite 360	San Francisco	CA	94127	650-757-3514	
TF: 800-523-1515 ■ *Web:* www.ticketfinder.com					
Ticketmall.com 245 Peachtree Ctr Ave Suite M-39	Atlanta	GA	30303	404-524-8491	614-0420
TF: 800-962-2985 ■ *Web:* www.ticketmall.com					
Ticketmaster 3701 Wilshire Blvd 7th Fl	Los Angeles	CA	90010	213-381-2000	386-1244
TF: 800-366-8652 ■ *Web:* www.ticketmaster.com					
Ticketmonster Inc 303 Frederick Rd	Catonsville	MD	21228	410-719-0030	719-0082*
**Fax:* Sales ■ *TF:* 800-637-3719 ■ *Web:* www.ticketmonster.com					
Tickets Galore Inc 33 Haddon Ave	Westmont	NJ	08108	856-869-8499	869-2258
TF: 888-849-9663 ■ *Web:* www.ticketsgalore.com					
Tickets.com Inc 555 Anton Blvd 11th Fl	Costa Mesa	CA	92626	714-327-5400	327-5410
TF: 800-352-0212 ■ *Web:* www.tickets.com					
TicketWeb Inc PO Box 77250	San Francisco	CA	94103	800-965-4827	649-9218*
**Fax Area Code:* 510 ■ *TF Cust Svc:* 866-468-7630 ■ *Web:* www.ticketweb.com					
TNT Tickets Inc 23881 Via Fabricante Suite 505	Mission Viejo	CA	92691	949-458-5744	830-4504
TF: 800-425-5849 ■ *Web:* www.tnttickets.com					
Total Travel & Tickets Inc 6250 N Andrews Ave Suite 205	Fort Lauderdale	FL	33309	954-493-9151	493-8195
TF: 800-493-8499 ■ *Web:* www.total-tickets.com					
Up Front Tickets 915 Druid Hill Ave	Pasadena	MD	21122	410-384-9104	384-9106
Web: www.upfronttickets.com					
VIP Tickets 14515 Ventura Blvd Suite 210	Sherman Oaks	CA	91403	818-907-1548	784-2359
TF: 800-328-4253 ■ *Web:* www.viptickets.com					
Western States Ticket Service 143 W McDowell Rd	Phoenix	AZ	85003	602-254-3300	254-3387
TF: 800-326-0331 ■ *Web:* www.wstickets.com					
Who Needs Two? 707 Lake Cook Rd Suite 115	Deerfield	IL	60015	847-564-8499	564-8855
TF: 888-246-8499					

754 TILE - CERAMIC (WALL & FLOOR)

Name / Address	City	State	Zip	Phone	Fax
American Marazzi Tile 359 Clay Rd	Sunnyvale	TX	75182	972-226-0110	226-2263
TF: 888-420-8453 ■ *Web:* www.marazzitile.com					
Ann Sacks Tile & Stone Inc 8120 NE 33rd Dr	Portland	OR	97211	503-281-7751	287-8807
TF: 800-278-8453 ■ *Web:* www.annsackstile.com					
Architectural Shapes & Colors Custom Tile 1201 Millerton St SE	Canton	OH	44707	330-484-0429	484-0480
TF: 877-497-4273					
Armstrong World Industries Inc 2500 Columbia Ave	Lancaster	PA	17603	717-397-0611	396-6133*
**Fax:* Hum Res ■ *TF Cust Svc:* 800-233-3823 ■					
Web: www.armstrong.com/armstrong_home.jsp					
B & W Tile Mfg Co Inc 14600 S Western Ave	Gardena	CA	90249	310-538-9579	538-2190
Web: www.bwtile.com					
BolArt Custom Tile 6 Terrace St	Alfred	NY	14802	607-587-9771	587-9110
Web: www.bolarttile.com					
Crossville Porcelain Stone/USA 346 Sweeney Dr	Crossville	TN	38555	931-484-2110	456-3993
Web: www.crossville-ceramics.com					
Curran Group Inc 7502 S Main St	Crystal Lake	IL	60014	815-455-5100	455-7894
Web: www.currangroup.com					
Dal-Tile International Inc 7834 Hawn Fwy	Dallas	TX	75217	214-398-1411	309-4553
TF: 800-933-8453 ■ *Web:* www.daltile.com					
Deutsche Steinzeug America Inc (DSA) 367 Curie Dr	Alpharetta	GA	30005	770-442-5500	442-5502
Web: www.dsa-ceramics.com					
Ege Seramik America Inc 5600 Oakbrook Pkwy Suite 280	Norcross	GA	30093	678-291-0888	291-0832
Web: www.egeseramik-usa.com					
Endicott Clay Products Co 57120 707 Rd	Endicott	NE	68350	402-729-3315	729-5804
TF: 800-927-9179 ■ *Web:* www.endicott.com					
Endicott Tile LLC 57120 707 Rd	Endicott	NE	68350	402-729-3315	729-5804
TF: 800-927-9179 ■ *Web:* www.endicott.com					
Epro Inc 10890 E CR 6	Bloomville	OH	44818	419-426-3561	343-8453*
**Fax Area Code:* 866 ■ *TF:* 866-818-3776 ■ *Web:* www.eprotile.com					
Florida Tile Industries Inc 1 Sikes Blvd	Lakeland	FL	33815	863-687-7171	683-8936
TF: 800-352-8453 ■ *Web:* www.floridatile.com					
Interceramic USA 2333 S Jupiter Rd	Garland	TX	75041	214-503-5500	503-4890
Web: www.interceramicusa.com					
Interstyle Ceramics & Glass Ltd 3625 Brighton Ave	Burnaby	BC	V5A3H5	604-421-7229	421-7544
TF: 800-667-1566 ■ *Web:* www.interstyle.bc.ca					
Ironrock Capital Inc 1201 Millerton St SE	Canton	OH	44707	330-484-4887	484-4880
TF: 800-325-3945 ■ *Web:* www.ironrockcapital.com					
Jefferson Ceramic Tile Co Inc 405 S Main St	Jefferson	WI	53549	920-674-5725	674-3677
Web: www2.jctc.com					
Laufen USA 4244 Mt Pleasant St NW Suite 100	North Canton	OH	44720	330-649-5000	649-5055
TF: 800-321-0684 ■ *Web:* www.laufenusa.com					
ME Tile Co Inc 6463 Waveland Ave	Hammond	IN	46320	219-554-1877	554-1880
Web: www.metile.com					
Meredith Collection 1201 Millerton St SE	Canton	OH	44707	330-484-1656	484-9380
TF: 800-325-3945 ■ *Web:* www.meredithtile.com					
Metropolitan Ceramics 1201 Millerton St SE	Canton	OH	44707	330-484-4887	484-4880
TF: 800-325-3945 ■ *Web:* www.metroceramics.com					
Monarch Ceramic Tile 834 Richwood Ave	Florence	AL	35630	256-764-6181	718-4148
TF Cust Svc: 800-289-8453 ■ *Web:* www.monarchceramictile.com					
Sacks Ann Tile & Stone Inc 8120 NE 33rd Dr	Portland	OR	97211	503-281-7751	287-8807
TF: 800-278-8453 ■ *Web:* www.annsackstile.com					
Summitville Tiles Inc SR-644	Summitville	OH	43962	330-223-1511	223-1414
Web: www.summitville.com					
Talisman Handmade Tiles 4401 N Ravenswood Ave	Chicago	IL	60640	773-784-2628	784-2656
Web: members.aol.com/talismant/index.htm					
US Ceramic Tile Co 4244 Mt Pleasant St NW Suite 100	North Canton	OH	44720	330-649-5000	649-5055
TF: 800-321-0684 ■ *Web:* www.usctco.com					

755 TIMBER TRACTS

Name / Address	City	State	Zip	Phone	Fax
American Wilderness Resources 350 Flat Rock Rd	Lake George	NY	12845	518-668-4600	668-4929
Web: www.american-wilderness.com					
Boething Treeland Farms Inc 23475 Long Valley Rd	Woodland Hills	CA	91367	818-883-1222	592-4955
Boise Cascade LLC 1111 W Jefferson St	Boise	ID	83702	208-384-6161	384-7189
Web: www.bc.com					
Bowater Inc 55 E Camper Down Way	Greenville	SC	29601	864-271-7733	282-9591*
NYSE: BOW ■ **Fax:* Hum Res ■ *TF:* 800-845-6002 ■ *Web:* www.bowater.com					
Crescent Resources Inc 400 S Tryon St Suite 1300	Charlotte	NC	28202	980-321-6000	
Web: www.crescent-resources.com					
Deltic Timber Corp PO Box 7200	El Dorado	AR	71731	870-881-9400	881-6454
NYSE: DEL ■ *Web:* www.deltic.com					
Haida Corp PO Box 89	Hydaburg	AK	99922	907-285-3721	285-3944
TF: 800-478-3721 ■ *Web:* www.haidacorp.com					

	City	State	Zip	Phone	Fax
Holiday Tree Farms Inc 800 NW Cornell Ave *TF:* 800-289-3684 ■ *Web:* www.holidaytreefarm.com	Corvallis	OR	97330	541-753-3236	757-8028
Huber JM Corp 333 Thornall St *Fax: Hum Res ■ *Web:* www.huber.com	Edison	NJ	08837	732-549-8600	549-2239*
Industrial Timber & Lumber Corp (ITL) 23925 Commerce Park Rd *TF:* 800-829-9663 ■ *Web:* www.itlcorp.com	Beachwood	OH	44122	216-831-3140	831-4734
JM Huber Corp 333 Thornall St *Fax: Hum Res ■ *Web:* www.huber.com	Edison	NJ	08837	732-549-8600	549-2239*
Lester Group Inc 101 E Commerce Pkwy *Web:* www.lestergroup.com	Barnesville	VA	24102	276-632-2195	632-2117
Martin Roy O Lumber Co Inc 2189 Memorial Dr *Web:* www.martco.com	Alexandria	LA	71301	318-448-0405	443-0159
MAXXAM Group Inc 5847 San Felipe St Suite 2600	Houston	TX	77057	713-975-7600	267-3703
McShan Lumber Co Inc PO Box 27 *TF:* 800-882-3712 ■ *Web:* www.mcshanlumber.com	McShan	AL	35471	205-375-6277	375-2773
MeadWestvaco Forest Resources 180 W Westvaco Rd	Summerville	SC	29483	843-871-5000	873-2654
Murray Pacific Corp 1201 Pacific Ave Suite 1750	Tacoma	WA	98402	253-383-4911	383-3261
Musser Forests Inc 1800 119 Hwy N *Web:* www.musserforests.com	Indiana	PA	15701	724-465-5685	465-9893
Olympic Resource Management 19245 10th Ave NE *Web:* www.orminc.com	Poulsbo	WA	98370	360-697-6626	697-1156
Pike Lumber Co Inc PO Box 247 *TF:* 800-356-4554 ■ *Web:* www.pikelumber.com	Akron	IN	46910	574-893-4511	893-7400
Plum Creek Timber Co Inc 999 3rd Ave Suite 4300 *NYSE: PCL* ■ *Web:* www.plumcreek.com	Seattle	WA	98104	206-467-3600	467-3795
Roy O Martin Lumber Co Inc 2189 Memorial Dr *Web:* www.martco.com	Alexandria	LA	71301	318-448-0405	443-0159
Sierra Pacific Industries 19794 Riverside Ave *Web:* www.sierrapacificind.com	Anderson	CA	96007	530-378-8000	378-8109
Starker Forests Inc 7240 SW Philomath Blvd *Web:* www.starkerforests.com	Corvallis	OR	97333	541-929-2477	929-2178
Timber Resource Services 6400 Hwy 66	Klamath Falls	OR	97601	541-884-2240	880-5472
Westervelt Co 1400 Jack Warner Pkwy NE *Fax: Sales ■ *TF:* 800-633-5983 ■ *Web:* www.westervelt.com	Tuscaloosa	AL	35404	205-562-5000	562-5012*
Weyerhaeuser Co 33663 Weyerhaeuser Way S *NYSE: WY* ■ *TF:* 800-525-5440 ■ *Web:* www.weyerhaeuser.com	Federal Way	WA	98003	253-924-2345	924-2685
Yule Tree Farms PO Box 429 *Web:* www.yuletreefarm.com	Aurora	OR	97002	503-678-2101	651-2663

756 TIMESHARE COMPANIES

SEE ALSO Hotels & Hotel Companies p. 1832

	City	State	Zip	Phone	Fax
Bluegreen Corp 4960 Conference Way N Suite 100 *NYSE: BXG* ■ *TF:* 800-456-2582 ■ *Web:* www.bluegreenonline.com	Boca Raton	FL	33431	561-912-8000	912-8100
Celebrity Resorts 2800 N Poinciana Blvd *TF:* 800-423-8604 ■ *Web:* www.celebrityresorts.com	Kissimmee	FL	34746	407-997-5000	997-5225
Central Florida Investments Inc 5601 Windhover Dr *TF:* 800-925-9999 ■ *Web:* www.westgateresorts.com	Orlando	FL	32819	407-351-3383	352-8935
Club Intrawest 375 Water St Suite 326 *TF:* 800-767-2166 ■ *Web:* www.clubintrawest.com	Vancouver	BC	V6B5C6	604-689-8816	682-7842
Diamond Resorts International 3745 Las Vegas Blvd S *TF:* 866-309-7318 ■ *Web:* www.diamondresorts.com	Las Vegas	NV	89109	702-261-1000	
Disney Vacation Club 200 Celebration Pl *TF:* 800-500-3990 ■ *Web:* dvc.disney.go.com/dvc/index	Celebration	FL	34747	407-566-3100	566-3393
Fairfield Resorts Inc 8427 S Park Cir *TF Cust Svc:* 800-251-8736 ■ *Web:* www.efairfield.com	Orlando	FL	32819	407-370-5200	370-5258
Fairmont Vacation Villas PO Box 127 *TF Resv:* 800-663-6333 ■ *Web:* www.fairmontvillas.com	Fairmont Hot Springs	BC	V0B1L0	250-345-6321	345-6446
Festiva Resorts 1 Vance Gap Rd *TF Resv:* 877-933-7848 ■ *Web:* www.festivaresorts.com	Asheville	NC	28805	828-254-3378	254-2285
Four Seasons Vacation Ownership 1165 Leslie St *TF:* 800-332-3442 ■ *Web:* www.fourseasons.com/residence_clubs	Toronto	ON	M3C2K8	416-449-1750	441-4374
Grand Pacific Resorts 5900 Pasteur Ct Suite 200 *TF:* 800-444-3515 ■ *Web:* www.grandpacificresorts.com	Carlsbad	CA	92008	760-431-8500	431-4580
Hilton Grand Vacations Co LLC 6355 Metro West Blvd Suite 180 *TF:* 800-521-3144 ■ *Web:* www.hgvc.com	Orlando	FL	32835	407-521-3100	521-3112
Hyatt Vacation Ownership Inc 450 Carillon Pkwy Suite 210 *TF Resv:* 800-926-4447 ■ *Web:* www.hyatt.com/hvc	Saint Petersburg	FL	33716	727-803-9400	803-9401
ILX Resorts Inc 2111 E Highland Ave Suite 210 *AMEX: ILX* ■ *TF:* 800-822-2589 ■ *Web:* www.ilxinc.com	Phoenix	AZ	85016	602-957-2777	957-2780
Interval International Inc 6262 Sunset Dr PH 1 *TF:* 800-828-8200 ■ *Web:* www.intervalworld.com	Miami	FL	33143	305-666-1861	667-5321
Island One Resorts 2345 Sand Lake Rd Suite 100 *TF:* 800-892-7523 ■ *Web:* www.islandone.com	Orlando	FL	32809	407-859-8900	240-9506
Marriott Vacation Club International 10400 Fernwood Rd *Fax: Mail Rm ■ *TF:* 800-845-5279 ■ *Web:* www.vacationclub.com	Bethesda	MD	20817	301-380-3000	380-7752*
Monarch Grand Vacations 23091 Mill Creek Dr *TF:* 800-828-4200 ■ *Web:* www.monarchgrandvacations.com	Laguna Hills	CA	92653	949-609-2400	587-2499
One Napili Way 5355 Lower Honoapiilani Hwy *TF:* 800-841-6284 ■ *Web:* www.onenapiliway.com	Lahaina	HI	96761	808-669-2007	669-5103
Resort Condominiums International (RCI) 9998 N Michigan Rd *Fax: Cust Svc ■ *TF:* 800-481-5738 ■ *Web:* www.rci.com	Carmel	IN	46032	317-805-9000	805-9677*
Royal Aloha Vacation Club 1505 Dillingham Blvd Suite 212 *TF:* 800-367-5212 ■ *Web:* www.ravc.com	Honolulu	HI	96817	808-847-8050	841-5467
Shell Vacations Club 40 Skokie Blvd Suite 350 *Web:* www.shellvacationsclub.com	Northbrook	IL	60062	847-564-4600	564-0703
Silverleaf Resorts Inc 1221 Riverbend Dr *AMEX: SVL* ■ *TF:* 800-613-0310 ■ *Web:* www.silverleafresorts.com	Dallas	TX	75247	214-631-1166	630-5715
Starwood Vacation Ownership Inc 8800 Vistana Center Dr *TF:* 800-847-8262 ■ *Web:* www.starwoodvo.com	Orlando	FL	32821	407-239-3000	239-3111
Sunterra Corp 3865 W Cheyenne Ave *NASDAQ: SNRR* ■ *TF:* 800-411-9922 ■ *Web:* www.sunterra.com	North Las Vegas	NV	89032	702-804-8600	543-4772
Tempus Resorts International 7380 Sand Lake Rd Suite 600 *TF:* 800-463-7256 ■ *Web:* www.tempusresorts.com	Orlando	FL	32819	407-226-1000	
Trendwest Resorts Inc 9805 Willows Rd NE *TF:* 800-722-3487 ■ *Web:* www.trendwestresorts.com	Redmond	WA	98052	425-498-2500	498-3051
Vacation Internationale 1417 116th Ave NE *TF:* 800-444-6633 ■ *Web:* www.vacationinternationale.com	Bellevue	WA	98004	425-454-3065	454-4339
Westgate Resorts 5601 Windhover Dr *TF:* 800-925-9999 ■ *Web:* www.westgateresorts.com	Orlando	FL	32819	407-351-3383	352-8935
WorldMark The Club 9805 Willows Rd NE *TF:* 800-722-3487 ■ *Web:* www.worldmarktheclub.com	Redmond	WA	98052	425-498-1950	498-1968

757 TIRES - MFR

	City	State	Zip	Phone	Fax
AirBoss of America Corp 16441 Yonge St *TSX: BOS* ■ *TF:* 877-395-8071 ■ *Web:* www.airbossofamerica.com	Newmarket	ON	L3X2G8	905-751-1188	751-1101
Bandag Inc 2905 N Hwy 61 *NYSE: BDG* ■ *TF:* 800-233-2205 ■ *Web:* www.bandag.com	Muscatine	IA	52761	563-262-1400	262-1069
Bridgestone Americas Holding Inc 535 Marriott Dr *TF Cust Svc:* 800-543-7522 ■ *Web:* www.bridgestone-firestone.com	Nashville	TN	37214	615-937-5000	937-3621
Carlisle Tire & Wheel Mfg 23 Windham Blvd *TF Sales:* 800-827-1001 ■ *Web:* www.carlisletire.com	Aiken	SC	29805	803-643-2900	643-2919
Continental Tire North America Inc 1800 Continental Blvd *Fax: Hum Res ■ *TF:* 800-478-1254 ■ *Web:* www.conti-online.com	Charlotte	NC	28273	704-583-3900	583-8540*
Cooper Tire & Rubber Co 701 Lima Ave *NYSE: CTB* ■ *TF Cust Svc:* 800-854-6288 ■ *Web:* www.coopertires.com	Findlay	OH	45840	419-423-1321	424-4108
Dayton Tire Co PO Box 24011 *Fax: Hum Res	Oklahoma City	OK	73124	405-280-3000	280-3309*
Denman Tire Corp 400 Diehl South Rd *TF Cust Svc:* 800-334-5543 ■ *Web:* www.denmantire.com	Leavittsburg	OH	44430	330-675-4242	675-4232
Dunlop Tire Corp PO Box 1109 *Fax: Hum Res ■ *TF:* 800-828-7428 ■ *Web:* www.dunloptire.com	Buffalo	NY	14240	716-639-5200	639-5017*
Falcon Wheel Tri-State Rubber 974 N 6th St	Steubenville	OH	43952	740-283-2255	283-4422
Galaxy Tire & Wheel Inc 730 Eastern Ave *TF Sales:* 800-343-3276 ■ *Web:* www.galaxytire.com	Malden	MA	02148	781-321-3910	322-2147
Goodyear Tire & Rubber Co 1144 E Market St *NYSE: GT* ■ *Fax: Cust Svc ■ *TF Cust Svc:* 800-321-2136 ■ *Web:* www.goodyear.com	Akron	OH	44316	330-796-2121	796-3753*
Hankook Tire America Corp 1450 Valley Rd *TF:* 800-426-5665 ■ *Web:* www.hankooktireusa.com	Wayne	NJ	07470	973-633-9000	633-0028
Hercules Tire & Rubber Co 16380 US 224 E Suite 200 *TF:* 800-677-9535 ■ *Web:* www.herculestire.com	Findlay	OH	45840	419-425-6400	425-6403
Kelly-Springfield Tire Co 12501 Willow Brook Rd SE *Web:* www.kelly-springfield.com	Cumberland	MD	21502	301-777-6000	777-6008
Maine Industrial Tires Ltd 9 Laurence Rd *TF Sales:* 800-782-2371 ■ *Web:* www.industrialtires.com	Gorham	ME	04038	207-856-6381	854-1029
Martin Wheel Co Inc 342 West Ave *TF:* 800-462-7846	Tallmadge	OH	44278	330-633-3278	633-3303
McCarthy Tire Co Inc 1004 Stony Battery Rd *Web:* www.mccarthytire.com	Lancaster	PA	17601	717-898-0947	898-0949
Michelin North America Inc 1 Parkway S PO Box 19001 *Fax Area Code: 800 ■ *Fax: Cust Svc ■ *TF Cust Svc:* 800-847-3435 ■ *Web:* www.michelin.com	Greenville	SC	29602	864-458-5000	423-2987*
Mickey Thompson Tires 4600 Prosper Dr *TF:* 800-222-9092 ■ *Web:* www.mickeythompsontires.com	Stow	OH	44224	330-928-9092	928-0503
Mitchell Industrial Tire Co 2915 8th Ave PO Box 71839 *Fax: Sales ■ *TF:* 800-251-7226 ■ *Web:* www.mitco.com	Chattanooga	TN	37407	423-698-4442	697-7143*
Pirelli Tire North America 100 Pirelli Dr PO Box 700 *TF:* 800-747-3554 ■ *Web:* www.us.pirelli.com	Rome	GA	30161	706-368-5800	368-5832
Purcell Tire & Rubber Co 301 N Hall St *Fax: Hum Res ■ *TF:* 800-326-8410 ■ *Web:* www.purcelltire.com	Potosi	MO	63664	573-438-2133	438-2151*
Robbins LLC PO Box 60 *Fax: Acctg ■ *TF:* 800-633-3312 ■ *Web:* www.robbinsllc.com	Tuscumbia	AL	35674	256-383-5441	383-9424*
SolidBoss Worldwide Inc 200 Veterans Blvd *TF:* 888-258-7252 ■ *Web:* www.airbosspolymer.com	South Haven	MI	49090	269-637-2181	637-8955
Specialty Tires of America Inc 1600 Washington St *TF:* 800-622-7327	Indiana	PA	15701	724-349-9010	349-8192
Stratham Tire Inc 355 Rt 125 *TF:* 800-427-7217 ■ *Web:* www.strathamtire.com	Brentwood	NH	03833	603-679-5840	679-9875
Superior Tire & Rubber Corp 1818 Pennsylvania Ave W PO Box 308 *TF Cust Svc:* 800-289-1456 ■ *Web:* www.superiortire.com	Warren	PA	16365	814-723-2370	723-5123
Tech International 200 E Coshocton St *TF:* 800-336-8324 ■ *Web:* www.techtirerepairs.com	Johnstown	OH	43031	740-967-9015	967-1039
Tech Supply 28300 Industrial Blvd Suite D PO Box 56747 *TF:* 800-245-8324 ■ *Web:* www.gotechsupply.com	Hayward	CA	94545	510-783-7085	783-8741
Titan Tire Co 2345 E Market St *TF:* 800-872-2327 ■ *Web:* www.titan-intl.com	Des Moines	IA	50317	515-265-9200	265-9301
Toyo Tire USA Corp 6261 Katella Ave Suite 2B *Fax: Mktg ■ *TF:* 800-678-3250 ■ *Web:* www.toyo.com	Cypress	CA	90630	714-236-2080	229-6184*
Trelleborg Wheel Systems America Inc 61 State Rt 43 N *TF:* 800-666-8473 ■ *Web:* tws.trelleborg.com	Hartville	OH	44632	330-877-1211	877-1831
Trintex Corp PO Box 309 *Web:* www.trintex.com	Bowdon	GA	30108	770-258-5551	258-3901
Vogue Tire & Rubber Co Inc 1101 Feehanville Dr *TF:* 800-323-1466 ■ *Web:* www.vogue-tyre.com	Mount Prospect	IL	60056	847-297-1900	375-9367
Yokohama Tire Corp 601 S Acacia Ave *TF:* 800-423-4544 ■ *Web:* www.yokohamatire.com	Fullerton	CA	92831	714-870-3800	870-3853

758 TIRES & TUBES - WHOL

	City	State	Zip	Phone	Fax
Allied Oil & Supply Inc 2209 S 24th St *TF:* 800-333-3717 ■ *Web:* www.allied-oil.com	Omaha	NE	68103	402-344-4343	344-4360
Am-Pack Tasco Distributing Ltd PO Box 20305 *TF:* 800-548-1075	Waco	TX	76702	254-772-9144	751-7764
American Tire Distributors Inc 12200 Herbert Wayne Ct Suite 150 *Fax: Cust Svc ■ *TF:* 800-277-8473 ■ *Web:* www.americantiredistributors.com	Huntersville	NC	28078	704-992-2000	992-1382*
Ampac Tire North Inc 29987 Ahern Ave *Web:* www.tirepros.com	Union City	CA	94587	510-441-0322	441-0351
Ball Tire & Gas Inc 620 S Ripley Blvd *TF:* 800-322-3016 ■ *Web:* www.balltire.com	Alpena	MI	49707	989-354-4186	356-2080
Barron's Wholesale Tire Inc 1302 Eastport Rd *TF:* 800-245-1899 ■ *Web:* www.barrontire.com	Jacksonville	FL	32218	904-751-2449	751-2506
Bauer Built Inc PO Box 248 *TF:* 800-999-0123 ■ *Web:* www.bauerbuilt.com	Durand	WI	54736	715-672-4295	672-8452
Ben Tire Distributors Ltd 203 E Madison St PO Box 158 *TF:* 800-252-8961 ■ *Web:* www.bentire.com	Toledo	IL	62468	217-849-3519	849-3019
Bob Sumerel Tires & Service Inc 3646 E Broad St *TF:* 800-858-0421 ■ *Web:* www.bobsumereltire.com	Columbus	OH	43213	614-237-6325	237-6328
Burggraf Corp 322 Main St *TF:* 800-331-2617 ■ *Web:* www.burggraftire.com	Quapaw	OK	74363	918-674-2281	674-2283
Capital Tire Inc 1001-17 Cherry St *TF:* 800-537-0190	Toledo	OH	43608	419-241-5111	241-7902
Clark Tire & Auto Supply Co Inc 220 S Center St *TF:* 800-968-3092 ■ *Web:* www.clarktire.com	Hickory	NC	28602	828-322-2303	327-2783
Cross-Midwest Tire Inc 3570 Gardener Ave *Web:* www.crossmidwest.com	Kansas City	MO	64120	816-231-6511	231-6393
Dapper Tire Co Inc 4025 Lockridge St *TF:* 800-266-7172 ■ *Web:* www.dappertire.com	San Diego	CA	92102	619-266-1397	266-2384
Dunlap & Kyle Co Inc PO Box 720 *TF:* 800-647-6133 ■ *Web:* www.dktire.com	Batesville	MS	38606	662-563-7601	563-0019
East Bay Tire Co 2200 Huntington Dr Unit C *TF:* 800-831-8473 ■ *Web:* www.eastbaytire.com	Fairfield	CA	94533	707-437-4700	437-4800
Eddie's Tire Service Inc 3077 Valley Rd	Berkeley Springs	WV	25411	304-258-1368	258-1777
Falken Tire Corp 10404 6th St *TF:* 800-723-2553 ■ *Web:* www.falkentire.com	Rancho Cucamonga	CA	91730	909-466-1116	466-1169
Free Service Tire Co Inc 126 Buffalo St *Web:* www.freeservicetire.com	Johnson City	TN	37604	423-979-2250	979-2263

				Phone	Fax
Friend Tire Co 11 N Industrial Dr	Monett	MO	65708	417-235-7836	235-3062
TF: 800-950-8473 ■ *Web:* www.friendtire.com					
Gateway Tire Co Inc 4 W Crescentville Rd	Cincinnati	OH	45246	513-874-2500	874-7412
TF: 800-837-1405					
Haas TO Tire Co Inc 2400 'O' St PO Box 81067	Lincoln	NE	68501	402-323-4220	474-0336
Web: www.tohaastire.com					
Hanco Corp 3650 Dodd Rd	Eagan	MN	55123	651-456-5600	456-9709
TF Cust Svc: 800-328-7400 ■ *Web:* www.hancomn.com					
Harris Tire Co PO Drawer 888	Troy	AL	36081	334-566-2691	566-9511
Web: www.harristire.com					
Hesselbein Tire Co Inc 4299 Industrial Dr	Jackson	MS	39209	601-974-5959	974-5977
TF: 800-685-6462					
Intercity Tire Export Corp 5975 NW 82nd Ave	Miami	FL	33166	305-592-9211	477-1757
Jones Ken Tire Inc PO Box 782	Worcester	MA	01613	508-755-5255	755-4397
TF: 800-225-9513 ■ *Web:* www.kenjones.com					
Ken Jones Tire Inc PO Box 782	Worcester	MA	01613	508-755-5255	755-4397
TF: 800-225-9513 ■ *Web:* www.kenjones.com					
Kenda USA 7095 Americana Pkwy	Reynoldsburg	OH	43068	614-866-9803	866-9805
TF: 866-536-3287 ■ *Web:* www.kendausa.com					
Kost Tire Distributors Inc 335 Court St	Binghamton	NY	13904	607-723-1230	771-8443
TF: 800-622-6672 ■ *Web:* www.kosttire.com					
Kramer Tire Co Inc 1369 Azalea Garden Rd	Norfolk	VA	23502	757-857-1234	857-7339
Web: www.kramertire.com					
Kumho Tire USA Inc 14605 Miller Ave	Fontana	CA	92336	909-428-3999	428-3988
TF: 800-445-8646 ■ *Web:* www.kumhotireusa.com					
Lakin Tire West Inc 15305 Spring Ave	Santa Fe Springs	CA	90670	562-802-2752	802-7584
TF: 800-488-2752 ■ *Web:* www.lakintire.com					
Laramie Tire Distributors Inc 2000 Campus Ln	East Norristown	PA	19403	610-615-8000	615-8001
TF: 800-523-0430					
Michelin North America Inc 1 Parkway S PO Box 19001	Greenville	SC	29602	864-458-5000	423-2987*
**Fax Area Code:* 800 ■ **Fax:* Cust Svc ■ *TF Cust Svc:* 800-847-3435 ■ *Web:* www.michelin.com					
Parrish Tire Co Inc 5130 Indiana Ave	Winston-Salem	NC	27106	336-767-0202	744-2716
TF: 800-849-8473 ■ *Web:* www.parrishtire.com					
Phillips Tire Co Inc 1123 W Commonwealth Ave	Fullerton	CA	92833	714-525-2306	525-1297
Web: www.phillipstire.com					
Pomps Tire Service Inc 1123 Cedar St	Green Bay	WI	54302	920-435-8301	431-7614
TF: 800-236-8911 ■ *Web:* www.pompstire.com					
Pueblo Super Tire Co 74 Fabrication Dr	Pueblo West	CO	81007	719-543-1609	
Raben Tire Co Inc 400 NW 4th St	Evansville	IN	47708	812-465-5566	465-5554
TF: 800-322-6247 ■ *Web:* www.rabentire.com					
Radial Tire Wholesale Corp PO Box 204	West Sacramento	CA	95691	916-371-5190	371-0614
Reliable Tire Co 805 N Blackhorse Pike PO Box 39	Blackwood	NJ	08012	856-232-0700	232-6583
TF: 800-342-3426 ■ *Web:* www.reliabletire.com					
Rott-Keller Supply Co Inc 6520 8th St PO Box 390	Fargo	ND	58107	701-235-0563	232-7900
TF: 800-342-4709 ■ *Web:* www.rottkeller.com					
Sehman Tire Service Inc 814 Atlantic Ave PO Box 889	Franklin	PA	16323	814-437-7878	432-7578
TF: 800-895-8663 ■ *Web:* www.sehmantire.com					
Service Tire Co 2737 W Vernor Hwy	Detroit	MI	48216	313-237-0050	237-0075
Snyder Wholesale Tire Co 401 Cadiz Rd	Wintersville	OH	43953	740-264-5543	264-1489
TF: 800-967-8473					
Southeastern Wholesale Tire Co 4721 Trademark Dr	Raleigh	NC	27610	919-832-3900	861-4357
TF: 800-849-9215					
Steepleton Tire Co 777 S Lauderdale St	Memphis	TN	38126	901-774-6440	774-6445
Sumerel Bob Tires & Service Inc 3646 E Broad St	Columbus	OH	43213	614-237-6325	237-6328
TF: 800-858-0421 ■ *Web:* www.bobsumereltire.com					
TBC Corp 4770 Hickory Hill Rd	Memphis	TN	38141	901-363-8030	541-3625
TF: 800-238-6469 ■ *Web:* www.tbccorp.com					
Terry's Tire Town Inc 2360 W Main St	Alliance	OH	44601	330-821-5022	829-1913
TF: 800-235-2921					
Tire Centers LLC 310 Inglesby Pkwy	Duncan	SC	29334	864-329-2700	329-2900
TF: 800-603-2430 ■ *Web:* www.tirecenters.com					
Tire Group International Inc 6695 NW 36th Ave	Miami	FL	33147	305-696-0096	696-5926
Web: www.tiregroup.com					
Tire Rack 7101 Vorden Pkwy	South Bend	IN	46628	574-287-2345	236-7707
TF: 800-428-8359 ■ *Web:* www.tirerack.com					
Tire-Rama Inc 1401 Industrial Ave PO Box 23509	Billings	MT	59104	406-245-4006	245-0257
TF: 800-828-1642 ■ *Web:* www.tirerama.com					
Tire Warehouse Inc 7300 NW 41st St	Miami	FL	33166	305-592-9280	592-9280
Web: www.tirewarehouse.com					
Tire Wholesalers Co Inc 1783 E 14-Mile Rd	Troy	MI	48083	248-589-9910	589-9919
Tire's Warehouse Inc 240 Teller St	Corona	CA	92879	951-808-0111	808-9062
TO Haas Tire Co Inc 2400 'O' St PO Box 81067	Lincoln	NE	68501	402-323-4220	474-0336
Web: www.tohaastire.com					
Traction Wholesale Center Inc 1515 Parkway Ave	Trenton	NJ	08628	609-771-9383	771-4311
TF: 800-846-8847					
Tyres International Inc 619 E Tallmadge Ave	Akron	OH	44310	330-374-1000	374-0038
TF: 800-321-0941					
University Wholesalers Inc 1945 Main St	Colchester	VT	05446	802-655-8030	655-8036
TF: 800-852-5222					
Valley Tire & Auto Parts Inc 500 New Babcock St	Buffalo	NY	14206	716-856-7055	
WD Tire Warehouse Inc 3805 E Livingston Ave	Columbus	OH	43227	614-461-8944	461-0136
TF: 800-634-7883					
Wheels Etc 15186 Foothill Blvd	Fontana	CA	92335	909-350-8200	350-4630
TF: 800-758-4737 ■ *Web:* www.wheels-etc.com					
White Tire Distributors Inc 1513 Seibel Dr NE	Roanoke	VA	24012	540-342-3183	342-2341
TF: 800-476-9448 ■ *Web:* www.whitetire.com					
Wholesale Tire Co PO Box 1637	Victoria	TX	77902	361-578-2945	578-2967
TF: 800-950-8119					
Wholesale Tire Inc PO Box 1660	Clarksburg	WV	26302	304-624-8465	624-8468*
**Fax:* Sales ■ *TF:* 800-772-5752					
Woody Tire Co Inc 1606 50th St	Lubbock	TX	79412	806-747-4556	747-7507
TF: 800-530-4818 ■ *Web:* www.woodytire.com					

759 TOBACCO & TOBACCO PRODUCTS

				Phone	Fax
800-JR Cigar Inc 301 Rt 10 E	Whippany	NJ	07981	973-884-9555	457-3299*
**Fax Area Code:* 800 ■ **Fax:* Orders ■ *TF:* 800-572-4427 ■ *Web:* www.jrcigars.com					
Abel Cigar Co 165 Aviador St	Camarillo	CA	93010	805-484-8789	482-0701
TF: 800-848-7335 ■ *Web:* www.cigarrolling.com					
Albert H Notini & Sons Inc 225 Aiken St	Lowell	MA	01854	978-459-7151	458-7692
TF: 800-366-8464 ■ *Web:* www.ahnotini.com					
Alliance One International Inc 512 Bridge St PO Box 681	Danville	VA	24541	434-792-7511	791-6769
NYSE: AOI ■ *Web:* www.aointl.com					
Altadis USA 5900 N Andrews Ave Suite 1100	Fort Lauderdale	FL	33309	954-772-9000	938-7811
TF Orders: 800-446-5797 ■ *Web:* www.altadisusa.com					
AMCON Distributing Co 7405 Irvington Rd	Omaha	NE	68122	402-331-3727	331-4834
AMEX: DIT ■ *TF:* 800-369-6200 ■ *Web:* www.amcon.com					
AW Marshall Co PO Box 16127	Salt Lake City	UT	84116	801-328-4713	328-9600
TF: 800-273-4713					
Burklund Distributors Inc 2500 N Main St Suite 3	East Peoria	IL	61611	309-694-1900	694-6788
TF: 800-322-2876 ■ *Web:* www.burklund.com					
Carolina Group 714 Green Valley Rd	Greensboro	NC	27408	336-335-7000	335-7414
NYSE: CG ■ *TF:* 888-278-1133					
Cigar.com Inc 6771 Chrisphalt Dr	Bath	PA	18014	800-357-9800	281-1025*
**Fax Area Code:* 484 ■ *TF:* 800-357-9800 ■ *Web:* www.cigar.com					
Conwood Co 813 Ridge Lake Blvd	Memphis	TN	38101	901-685-7267	727-0949*
**Fax Area Code:* 800 ■ *TF:* 800-238-2409 ■ *Web:* www.conwoodco.com					
Conwood Co LP 46 Keel Ave PO Box 217	Memphis	TN	38101	901-248-1700	526-3527
TF: 800-238-2409 ■ *Web:* www.cwdlp.com					
Core-Mark International Inc 395 Oyster Point Blvd Suite 415	South San Francisco	CA	94080	650-589-9445	952-4284
TF: 800-622-1713 ■ *Web:* www.coremark.com					
Domestic Tobacco Co 830 N Prince St	Lancaster	PA	17603	717-393-0613	397-2381
Web: www.amishcigar.com					
Eby-Brown Co 280 W Shuman Blvd Suite 280	Naperville	IL	60563	630-778-2800	778-2831
TF: 800-553-8249 ■ *Web:* www.eby-brown.com					
Finck Cigar Co 414 Vera Cruz St	San Antonio	TX	78207	210-226-4191	226-2825
TF Orders: 800-221-0638 ■ *Web:* www.finckcigarcompany.com					
Flue-Cured Tobacco Cooperative 1304 Annapolis Dr	Raleigh	NC	27608	919-821-4560	821-4564
Web: www.ustobaccofarmer.com					
General Cigar Co Inc 387 Park Ave S	New York	NY	10016	212-448-3800	679-1450
TF: 800-273-8044 ■ *Web:* www.cigarworld.com					
George Melhado & Co 10 Merchant St	Sharon	MA	02067	781-784-5550	784-8870
TF: 800-635-4236					
Holts Cigar Co 1522 Walnut St	Philadelphia	PA	19102	215-732-8500	732-4988
TF: 800-523-1641 ■ *Web:* www.holts.com					
House of Windsor Inc Orchard St PO Box 68	Dallastown	PA	17313	717-244-4501	244-0305
TF Cust Svc: 800-237-4715 ■ *Web:* www.houseofwindsortobacco.com					
J Polep Distribution Services Inc 705 Meadow St	Chicopee	MA	01013	413-592-4141	592-5870
TF: 800-447-6537 ■ *Web:* www.jpolep.com					
JC Newman Cigar Co 2701 16th St	Tampa	FL	33605	813-248-2124	247-2135
TF Orders: 800-477-1884 ■ *Web:* www.cigarfamily.com					
John Middleton Inc 418 W Church Rd	King of Prussia	PA	19406	610-265-1400	337-7546
TF: 800-523-1126					
Keilson-Dayton Co 107 Commerce Park Dr	Dayton	OH	45404	937-236-1070	236-2124
TF: 800-759-3174					
Liggett Group Inc 100 Maple Ln	Mebane	NC	27302	919-304-7700	304-7797
TF: 800-334-1686 ■ *Web:* www.liggettgroup.com					
Lorillard Tobacco Co 714 Green Valley Rd	Greensboro	NC	27408	336-335-7000	335-7550
TF: 877-703-0386 ■ *Web:* www.lorillard.net					
Macon Cigar & Tobacco Co Inc DBA MCT Wholesale 575 12th St	Macon	GA	31201	478-743-2236	744-0903
TF: 800-637-0190 ■ *Web:* www.mctweb.com					
Mafco Worldwide Corp 3rd St & Jefferson Ave	Camden	NJ	08104	856-964-8840	964-6029
Marshall AW Co PO Box 16127	Salt Lake City	UT	84116	801-328-4713	328-9600
TF: 800-273-4713					
MCT Wholesale 575 12th St	Macon	GA	31201	478-743-2236	744-0903
TF: 800-637-0190 ■ *Web:* www.mctweb.com					
Middleton John Inc 418 W Church Rd	King of Prussia	PA	19406	610-265-1400	337-7546
TF: 800-523-1126					
National Cigar Corp 407 N main St PO Box 97	Frankfort	IN	46041	765-659-3326	654-6932
TF: 800-321-0247 ■ *Web:* www.broadleafcigars.com					
National Tobacco Co LP 3029 W Muhammad Ali Blvd	Louisville	KY	40212	502-778-4421	774-9235
TF Cust Svc: 800-331-5964					
Newman JC Cigar Co 2701 16th St	Tampa	FL	33605	813-248-2124	247-2135
TF Orders: 800-477-1884 ■ *Web:* www.cigarfamily.com					
Notini Albert H & Sons Inc 225 Aiken St	Lowell	MA	01854	978-459-7151	458-7692
TF: 800-366-8464 ■ *Web:* www.ahnotini.com					
Owens RC Co 310 N Blythe St	Gallatin	TN	37066	615-452-5658	452-0107
TF: 800-821-2933					
Philip Morris USA 615 Maury St	Richmond	VA	23224	804-274-2000	
TF Cust Svc: 800-343-0975 ■ *Web:* www.philipmorrisusa.com					
Polep J Distribution Services Inc 705 Meadow St	Chicopee	MA	01013	413-592-4141	592-5870
TF: 800-447-6537 ■ *Web:* www.jpolep.com					
RC Owens Co 310 N Blythe St	Gallatin	TN	37066	615-452-5658	452-0107
TF: 800-821-2933					
Reynolds American Inc 401 N Main St PO Box 2959	Winston-Salem	NC	27102	336-741-5000	741-4238
NYSE: RAI ■ *Web:* www.reynoldsamerican.com					
RJ Reynolds Tobacco Co 401 N Main St	Winston-Salem	NC	27102	336-741-5000	741-4238
Web: www.rjrt.com					
Rothmans Inc 1500 Don Mills Rd	Toronto	ON	M3B3L1	416-449-5525	449-4486
TSX: ROC ■ *Web:* www.rothmansinc.ca					
Saint Joe Distributing 5808 Corporate Dr	Saint Joseph	MO	64507	816-233-8213	233-5525
TF: 800-892-9072					
Saint Joseph Tobacco Co Inc DBA Saint Joe Distributing 5808 Corporate Dr	Saint Joseph	MO	64507	816-233-8213	233-5525
TF: 800-892-9072					
Sledd Co 100 E Cove Ext	Wheeling	WV	26003	304-243-1820	243-1209
TF: 800-333-0374 ■ *Web:* www.sleddco.com					
Stanlou Tobacco Inc 86 Alexander St	Yonkers	NY	10701	914-969-0378	969-0612
Star Scientific Inc 801 Liberty Way	Chester	VA	23836	804-530-0535	530-8474
NASDAQ: STSI ■ *TF:* 800-867-6653 ■ *Web:* www.starscientific.com					
Swedish Match Inc 7300 Beaufont Springs Dr Suite 400	Richmond	VA	23225	804-302-1700	302-1760
Web: www.swedishmatch.com					
Swisher International Group Inc 459 E 16th St PO box 2230	Jacksonville	FL	32203	904-353-4311	353-9175
TF: 800-843-3731 ■ *Web:* www.swisher.com					
Taylor Brothers Div Conwood Co LP 2415 Stratford Rd SW	Winston-Salem	NC	27103	336-768-4630	768-4677
Tobacco Exporters International USA Ltd 2280 Mountain Industrial Blvd	Tucker	GA	30084	770-934-8540	938-9473
TF: 800-221-4134					
Tobacco Superstores Inc PO Box 1219	Forrest City	AR	72336	870-633-0099	633-8279
Web: www.tobaccosuper.com					
Universal Leaf Tobacco Co Inc 1501 N Hamilton St	Richmond	VA	23230	804-359-9311	254-3560*
**Fax:* Hum Res ■ *Web:* www.universalcorp.com					
US Smokeless Tobacco Co 100 W Putnam Ave	Greenwich	CT	06830	203-661-1100	863-7226
Web: www.ussmokelesstobacco.com					

760 TOOL & DIE SHOPS

				Phone	Fax
A Finkl & Sons Co 2011 N Southport Ave	Chicago	IL	60614	773-975-2500	348-5347
TF: 800-343-2562 ■ *Web:* www.finkl.com					
A & M Tool & Die Co Inc 64 Mill St	Southbridge	MA	01550	508-764-3241	765-1377
TF: 800-848-4628 ■ *Web:* www.am-tool.com					
ABA-PGT Inc 10 Gear Dr	Manchester	CT	06040	860-649-4591	643-7619
Web: www.abapgt.com					
Abrasive-Form Inc 454 Scott Dr	Bloomingdale	IL	60108	630-893-7800	893-6313
Web: www.abrasive-form.com					
Ahaus Tool & Engineering Inc PO Box 280	Richmond	IN	47375	765-962-3571	962-3426
TF: 800-962-3571 ■ *Web:* www.ahaus.com					
AIP Inc 1290 Maplelawn St	Troy	MI	48084	248-649-7300	649-8079
TF: 800-247-5551 ■ *Web:* www.aippunch.com					

	City	State	ZIP	Phone	Fax
Alco Industries Inc 820 Adams Ave Suite 130	Norristown	PA	19403	610-666-0930	666-0752
Web: www.alcoind.com					
Alcona Tool & Machine Inc PO Box 340	Lincoln	MI	48742	989-736-8151	736-6717
Web: www.alconatool.com					
Alden Tool Co Inc 199 New Park Dr	Berlin	CT	06037	860-828-3556	828-8872
Web: www.aldentool.com					
Alliance Carolina Tool & Mold Corp 125 Glenn Bridge Rd	Arden	NC	28704	828-684-7831	687-0808
TF: 800-684-7831 ■ *Web:* www.alliance-carolina.com					
Alliance Precision Plastics Corp 595 Trabold Rd	Rochester	NY	14624	585-426-2630	247-2954
Web: www.allianceppc.com					
Anchor Lamina Inc 311 Pinebush Rd	Cambridge	ON	H1T1B2	519-740-6623	740-8213
Web: www.anchorlamina.com					
Anchor Tool & Die Co 11830 Brookpark Rd	Cleveland	OH	44130	216-362-1850	265-7833
Web: www.anchor-mfg.com					
Apex Tool Works Inc 3200 Tollview Dr	Rolling Meadows	IL	60008	847-394-5810	394-2739
Web: www.apextool.com					
Armin Industries 1500 N La Fox St	South Elgin	IL	60177	847-742-1864	742-0253
TF: 800-427-3607 ■ *Web:* www.armin-ind.com					
Armstrong Mold Corp 6910 Manlius Ctr Rd	East Syracuse	NY	13057	315-437-1517	437-9198
Web: www.armstrongmold.com					
Astro Tool & Machine Co Inc 810 Martin St	Rahway	NJ	07065	732-382-2454	382-6394
Web: www.astrotoolco.com					
Atlas Tool Inc 29880 Groesbeck Hwy	Roseville	MI	48066	586-778-3570	778-3931
Web: www.atlastool.com					
Austro Mold Inc 3 Rutter St	Rochester	NY	14606	585-458-1410	458-0963
Web: www.austromold.com/austromold					
Bermer Precision Products 94 Ashland Ave	Southbridge	MA	01550	508-764-2521	765-1173
Bilco Tool Corp 30076 Dequindre Rd	Warren	MI	48092	586-574-9300	574-9340
Web: www.bilcotool.com					
Birdsall Tool & Gage Co 24735 Crestview Ct	Farmington Hills	MI	48335	248-474-5150	474-5600
Web: www.birdsalltool.com					
Brinkman Tool & Die Inc 325 Kiser St	Dayton	OH	45404	937-222-1161	222-2079
Web: www.brinkmantool.com					
Burr Oak Tool & Gauge Co Inc PO Box 338	Sturgis	MI	49091	269-651-9393	651-4324
Web: www.burroak.com					
CA Spalding Co 1011 Cedar Ave	Croydon	PA	19021	267-550-9000	550-9008
Web: www.caspalding.com					
Caco-Pacific Corp 813 N Cummings Rd	Covina	CA	91724	626-331-3361	966-4219
Web: www.cacopacific.com					
Capitol Technologies Inc 3615 W Voorde Dr	South Bend	IN	46628	574-232-3311	233-7082
TF: 800-270-5222 ■ *Web:* www.capitoltech.com					
Carlson Tool & Mfg Corp W 57 N 14386 Doerr PO Box 85	Cedarburg	WI	53012	262-377-2020	377-1751
TF: 800-532-2252 ■ *Web:* www.carlsontool.com					
Carr Lane Mfg 4200 Carr Lane Ct	Saint Louis	MO	63119	314-647-6200	647-5736
Web: www.carrlane.com					
Chicago Cutting Die Co 3555 Woodhead Dr	Northbrook	IL	60062	847-509-5800	509-0355
TF: 800-747-3437 ■ *Web:* www.chicagocuttingdie.com					
Chicago Mold Engineering Co 615 Stetson Ave	Saint Charles	IL	60174	630-584-1311	584-8695
Web: www.chicagomold.com					
Cleveland Punch & Die Co 666 Pratt St PO Box 769	Ravenna	OH	44266	330-296-4342	451-6877*
**Fax Area Code:* 888 ■ *TF:* 888-451-4342 ■ *Web:* www.clevelandpunch.com					
Clifty Engineering & Tool Co Inc 2949 Clifty Dr	Madison	IN	47250	812-273-3272	273-4841
Web: www.cliftyengineering.com					
Cole Tool & Die Co PO Box 187	Mansfield	OH	44901	419-522-1272	522-5506
Web: www.coletool.com					
Colonial Machine Co PO Box 650	Kent	OH	44240	330-673-5859	673-6687
Web: www.colonial-machine.com					
Comet Die & Engraving Co 909 N Larch Ave	Elmhurst	IL	60126	630-833-5600	833-2644
Web: www.cometdie.com					
Cook Technologies Inc N 2nd St	Green Lane	PA	18054	215-234-4535	234-5015
TF: 800-755-2856 ■ *Web:* www.cooktechnologies.com					
Crown Mold & Machine Inc 16959 Munn Rd	Chagrin Falls	OH	44023	440-543-5090	543-4582
Web: www.crownmold.net					
Custom Mold Engineering Inc 9780 S Franklin Dr	Franklin	WI	53132	800-448-2005	421-2430*
**Fax Area Code:* 414 ■ *Web:* www.custommold.com					
D & D Mfg Inc 500 Territorial Dr	Bolingbrook	IL	60440	630-759-0015	759-0043
Web: www.ddmfg.com					
D-M-E Co 29111 Stephenson Hwy	Madison Heights	MI	48071	248-398-6000	544-5705
TF: 800-626-6653 ■ *Web:* www.dme.net					
Danly IEM 6779 Engle Rd Suite F	Middleburg Heights	OH	44130	440-239-7600	833-2659*
**Fax Area Code:* 800 ■ *TF:* 800-243-2659 ■ *Web:* www.danly.com					
Danly IEM Punchrite Div 16065 Industrial Ln SW	Cleveland	OH	44135	216-267-1444	267-1470
TF: 800-232-2659 ■ *Web:* www.danly.com					
Dayton Progress Corp 500 Progress Rd	Dayton	OH	45449	937-859-5111	859-5353
Web: www.daytonprogress.com					
Decatur Mold Tool & Engineering Inc 3330 N State Rd 7	North Vernon	IN	47265	812-346-5188	346-7357
Web: www.decaturmold.com					
Delaware Machinery & Tool PO Box 2665	Muncie	IN	47307	765-284-3335	289-7185
Web: www.delawaremachinery.com					
Delva Tool & Machine Corp PO Box 2249	Cinnaminson	NJ	08077	856-786-8700	786-8708
Web: www.delvatool.com					
Demmer Corp 3525 Capital City Blvd	Lansing	MI	48906	517-321-3600	321-7449
Web: www.demmercorp.com					
Detroit Tool & Engineering Co 441 W Elm St	Lebanon	MO	65536	417-532-2141	532-8367
Web: www.detroittool.com					
Diamond Die & Mold Co 35401 Groesbeck Hwy	Clinton Township	MI	48035	586-791-0700	791-5419
Web: www.diamond-die.com					
Diamond Tool & Die Inc 508 29th Ave	Oakland	CA	94601	510-534-7050	534-0454
TF: 800-227-1084 ■ *Web:* www.dtdjobshop.com					
Die-Namic Inc 12700 Delta Dr	Taylor	MI	48180	734-946-6150	946-8787
TF: 800-817-1270 ■ *Web:* www.die-namic.com					
Diemasters Mfg Inc 2100 Touhy Ave	Elk Grove Village	IL	60007	847-640-9900	640-6292
Web: www.diemasters.net					
Dixie Tool & Die Co Inc PO Box 327	Gadsden	AL	35902	256-442-3220	442-3927
Web: www.dtdal.com					
Dominion Technologies Inc 15736 Sturgeon St	Roseville	MI	48066	586-773-3303	773-2730
Web: www.dominiontec.com					
Ehrhardt Tool & Machine Co 25 Central Industrial Dr	Granite City	IL	62040	618-452-5749	436-6905*
**Fax Area Code:* 314 ■ *Web:* www.ehrhardttool.com					
Electro-Magnetic Products Inc 355 Crider Ave	Moorestown	NJ	08057	856-235-3011	722-0566
TF: 800-234-0071 ■ *Web:* www.empmags.com/					
Elizabeth Carbide Die Co Inc PO Box 95	McKeesport	PA	15135	412-751-3000	754-0755
Web: www.eliz.com/Locations/ecarbide.php					
Estee Mold & Die Inc 1467 Stanley Ave	Dayton	OH	45404	937-224-7853	228-0257
Web: www.esteemold.com					
Excel Tool Inc 2020 1st Ave	Seymour	IN	47274	812-522-6880	522-6524
Web: www.exceleti.com					
F & G Tool & Die Co 3024 Dryden Rd	Dayton	OH	45439	937-294-1405	294-3862
Web: www.fgtool.com					
Ferriot Inc 1000 Arlington Cir	Akron	OH	44306	330-786-3000	786-3001
Web: www.ferriot.com					
Finkl A & Sons Co 2011 N Southport Ave	Chicago	IL	60614	773-975-2500	348-5347
TF: 800-343-2562 ■ *Web:* www.finkl.com					
First Tool Corp 612 Linden Ave	Dayton	OH	45403	937-254-6197	254-0625
Web: www.firsttoolcorp.com					
Fort Wayne Wire Die Inc 2424 American Way	Fort Wayne	IN	46809	260-747-1681	747-4269
Web: www.fwwd.com					
Frizzelle & Parsons Die Sinking Co 6602 John Deere Rd	Moline	IL	61265	309-796-1030	796-2935
Web: www.frizzelle-parsons.com					
Futuramic Tool & Engineering Co 24680 Gibson Dr	Warren	MI	48089	586-758-2200	758-0641
Web: www.futuramic.com					
Future Products Tool Corp 885 N Rochester Rd	Clawson	MI	48017	248-588-1060	588-7303
TF: 800-237-5754 ■ *Web:* www.future-products.com					
Genca 9600 18th St N	Saint Petersburg	FL	33716	727-524-3622	531-5700
TF: 800-237-5448 ■ *Web:* www.genca.com					
General Carbide Corp PO Box C	Greensburg	PA	15601	724-836-3000	547-2659*
**Fax Area Code:* 800 ■ *TF:* 800-245-2465 ■ *Web:* www.generalcarbide.com					
General Tool Co 101 Landy Ln	Cincinnati	OH	45215	513-733-5500	733-5604
TF: 800-472-4406 ■ *Web:* www.gentool.com					
Gillette Machine & Tool Co 955 Millstead Way	Rochester	NY	14624	585-436-0058	235-0016
Web: www.gillettemachine.com					
GlobalDie 1130 Minot Ave PO Box 1120	Auburn	ME	04211	800-910-3747	910-9187
Web: www.globaldie.com					
Goodrich Corp Sterling Die Div 5565 Venture Dr Suite D	Parma	OH	44130	216-267-1300	267-3356
TF: 800-533-1300					
Greenville Tool & Die Co PO Box 310	Greenville	MI	48838	616-754-5693	754-5500
Web: www.gtd.com					
Guill Tool & Engineering Co Inc 10 Pike St	West Warwick	RI	02893	401-828-7600	823-5310
Web: www.guilltool.com					
H & J Tool & Die Co Inc 1565 Ocean Ave	Bohemia	NY	11716	631-589-7500	589-2951
Web: www.h-j.com					
Hammill Mfg Co Inc PO Box 6680	Toledo	OH	43612	419-476-0789	476-8653
Web: www.hammillmfg.com					
Harig Mfg Corp 5757 W Howard St	Niles	IL	60714	847-647-9500	647-8351
Web: www.harigmfg.com					
Hercules Machine Tool & Die Co 13920 E Ten-Mile Rd	Warren	MI	48089	586-778-4120	778-0070
Web: www.hmtd.com					
Hill Engineering Inc 930 N Villa Ave	Villa Park	IL	60181	630-834-4430	834-4755
Web: www.hillengr.com					
Hoppe Tool Inc 107 1st Ave	Chicopee	MA	01020	413-592-9213	592-4688
TF Sales: 800-742-6571 ■ *Web:* www.hoppetool.com					
Howmet TMP Corp 3960 S Marginal Rd	Cleveland	OH	44114	216-391-3885	391-4842
Web: www.alcoa.com/howmet					
HPM Div Taylor's Industrial Services LLC 820 Marion Rd	Mount Gilead	OH	43338	419-946-0222	946-2473
Web: www.taylorsind.com/2003/hpm/index.php					
Hudson Tool & Die Co 1327 N US 1	Ormond Beach	FL	32174	386-672-2000	676-6212*
**Fax:* Sales ■ *Web:* www.hudsontool.com					
Hudson Tool & Die Co 3845 Carnation St	Franklin Park	IL	60131	847-678-8710	678-0526
Hydro Carbide PO Box 363	Latrobe	PA	15650	724-539-9701	539-8140
TF: 800-245-2476 ■ *Web:* www.hydrocarbide.com					
Hygrade Precision Technologies Inc 329 Cooke St	Plainville	CT	06062	860-747-5773	747-3179
TF: 800-457-1666 ■ *Web:* www.hygrade.com					
Incoe Corp 1740 E Maple Rd	Troy	MI	48083	248-616-0220	616-0225
Web: www.incoe.com					
Independent Dies Div Western Supply 2930 Cass Ave	Saint Louis	MO	63106	314-531-4300	531-4401
Web: www.wsids.com					
Ivanhoe Tool & Die Co Inc PO Box 218	Thompson	CT	06277	860-923-9541	923-2497
Web: www.ivanhoetool.com					
Jade Corp 3063 Philmont Ave	Huntingdon Valley	PA	19006	215-947-3333	947-6838
TF: 800-628-4370 ■ *Web:* www.jadecorp.com					
Jasco Tools Inc 1390 Mt Read Blvd PO Box 60497	Rochester	NY	14606	585-254-7000	254-2655
TF: 800-724-5497 ■ *Web:* www.jascotools.com					
Jennings International Corp 3 Blue Heron Dr	Collegeville	PA	19426	610-272-1600	272-1737
Web: www.jenningsinternational.com					
Jo-Ad Industries Inc 31465 Stephenson Hwy	Madison Heights	MI	48071	248-588-4810	588-3448
Web: www.jo-ad.com					
Jones Metal Products Co 200 N Center St	West Lafayette	OH	43845	740-545-6381	545-9690
TF: 800-552-3468					
Kell-Strom Tool Co Inc 214 Church St	Wethersfield	CT	06109	860-529-6851	257-9694
TF: 800-851-6851 ■ *Web:* www.kell-strom.com					
Keller O Tool Engineering Co 12701 Inkster Rd	Livonia	MI	48150	734-425-4500	
Kenmode Tool & Engineering Co 820 W Algonquin Rd	Algonquin	IL	60102	847-658-5041	658-9150
Kennedy Tool & Die Inc 325 W Main St	Birdsboro	PA	19508	610-582-8735	582-3150
Web: www.ktdmold.com					
Kirby Machine Co 1709 E Cherry St PO Box 1776	Noblesville	IN	46061	317-773-6700	773-8031
Web: www.wckirby.com					
L & F Industries Corp Div of Erie Press Systems					
1253 W 12th St PO Box 4061	Erie	PA	16512	814-455-3941	456-4819
TF: 800-222-3608 ■ *Web:* www.lfindustries.com					
Lane Punch Corp 281 Lane Pkwy	Salisbury	NC	28146	704-633-3900	227-6725*
**Fax Area Code:* 800 ■ *Web:* www.lanepunch.com					
Lansing Tool & Engineering Inc 1313 S Waverly Rd	Lansing	MI	48917	517-372-2550	372-1703
Web: www.lansingtool.com					
Leech Tool & Die Works Inc 13144 Dickson Rd	Meadville	PA	16335	814-336-2141	337-0354
Web: www.leechind.com					
Leicester Die & Tool Inc PO Box 156	Leicester	MA	01524	508-892-3893	892-3015
Lenhardt Tool & Die Co PO Box 279	Alton	IL	62002	618-462-1075	462-6306
Web: www.lenhardttool.com					
Lou-Rich Machine Tool Inc 505 W Front St	Albert Lea	MN	56007	507-377-8910	373-7110
Web: www.lou-rich.com					
LTC Inc 330 N 7th Ave	Lebanon	PA	17046	717-273-3711	273-4310
Luick Quality Gage & Tool 4401 S Delaware Dr	Muncie	IN	47302	765-288-1818	288-2346
Web: www.luick.com					
Mate Precision Tooling Inc 1295 Lund Blvd	Anoka	MN	55303	763-421-0230	421-0285
TF: 800-328-4492 ■ *Web:* www.matept.com					
MBtech Autodie LLC 44 Coldbrook St NW	Grand Rapids	MI	49503	616-454-9361	356-1410*
**Fax:* Acctg					
McAfee Tool & Die Inc 1717 Boettler Rd	Uniontown	OH	44685	330-896-9555	896-9549
Web: www.mcafeetool.com					
Metco Mfg Co Inc 1993 County Line Rd	Warrington	PA	18976	215-343-1993	343-7703
TF: 888-343-1993 ■ *Web:* www.metcomfg.com					
Mid-State Machine Products Inc 83 Verti Dr	Winslow	ME	04901	207-873-6136	872-2017
TF: 800-341-4672 ■ *Web:* www.mid-statemachine.com					
Midwest Tool & Engineering Co 112 Webster St	Dayton	OH	45402	937-224-0756	224-0757
Web: www.themidwesttool.com					
Millcraft SMS Services LLC PO Box 1107	Oil City	PA	16301	814-677-9400	677-9431
TF: 800-394-4862					
Moeller Mfg Co Inc Punch & Die Div					
43938 Plymouth Oaks Blvd	Plymouth	MI	48170	734-416-0000	416-2200
TF: 800-521-7613 ■ *Web:* moeller.com					
Mold-A-Matic Corp DBA MAMCO 147 River St	Oneonta	NY	13820	607-433-2121	432-7861
TF: 800-486-8611 ■ *Web:* www.mamcomolding.com					
Mold Base Industries Inc 7501 Derry St	Harrisburg	PA	17111	717-564-7960	564-2250
TF: 800-241-6656 ■ *Web:* www.moldbase.com					
MS Willett Inc PO Box 266	Cockeysville	MD	21030	410-771-0460	771-6972
Web: www.mswillett.com					
MTD Technologies Inc 5201 102nd Ave N	Pinellas Park	FL	33782	727-546-2446	541-3684
Web: www.mtd-tech.com					
Mutual Tool & Die Inc 725 Lilac Ave	Dayton	OH	45427	937-268-6713	268-4688
Web: www.mutualtool.com					
National Tool & Mfg Co Inc 100-124 N 12th St	Kenilworth	NJ	07033	908-276-1600	276-8616
TF: 800-223-0926 ■ *Web:* www.ntm.com					
Northwestern Tools Inc 3130 Valleywood Dr	Dayton	OH	45429	937-298-9994	298-3715
Web: www.northwesterntools.com					

Phone Fax

O Keller Tool Engineering Co 12701 Inkster Rd .... Livonia MI 48150 734-425-4500
Oberg Industries Inc 2301 Silverville Rd .... Freeport PA 16229 724-295-2121 295-2588
TF: 800-286-1275 ■ *Web:* www.oberg.com
OMCO Mould Inc 1 Omco Sq .... Winchester IN 47394 765-584-4000 584-4982
Ontario Die Co of America 2735 20th St .... Port Huron MI 48060 810-987-5060 987-3688
Web: www.ontariodie.com
Ort Tool & Die Corp 6555 S Dixie Hwy .... Erie MI 48133 734-848-6845 848-4308
Web: www.orttool.com
OTC Div SPX Corp 655 Eisenhower Dr .... Owatonna MN 55060 507-455-7000 455-7300*
**Fax:* Hum Res ■ *TF:* 800-533-6127 ■ *Web:* www.otctools.com
Outokumpu Livernois Engineering Co 25315 Kean St .... Dearborn MI 48124 313-278-0200 278-5992
TF: 800-900-0200
Paragon Die & Engineering Co 5225 33rd St SE .... Grand Rapids MI 49512 616-949-2220 949-2536
Web: www.paragondie.com
Paslin Co 25411 Ryan Rd .... Warren MI 48091 586-758-0200 758-3322
TF: 877-972-7546 ■ *Web:* www.paslin.com
PCS Co 34488 Doreka Dr .... Fraser MI 48026 586-294-7780 294-7799
TF: 800-521-0546 ■ *Web:* www.pcs-company.com
Peddinghaus Corp 300 N Washington Ave .... Bradley IL 60915 815-937-3800 937-4003
TF: 800-786-2448 ■ *Web:* www.peddinghaus.com
Penn State Tool & Die Corp 7590 Rt 30 .... North Huntingdon PA 15642 724-864-2626 864-5300
Web: www.pennstatetool.com
Penn United Technology Inc 799 N Pike Rd .... Cabot PA 16023 724-352-1507 352-4970
Web: www.pennunited.com
Pennsylvania Tool & Gages Inc PO Box 534 .... Meadville PA 16335 814-336-3136 333-9131
TF: 877-827-8285 ■ *Web:* www.patool.com
PHB Inc 7900 W Ridge Rd .... Fairview PA 16415 814-474-5511 474-2063
Web: www.phbcorp.com
Phinney Tool & Die Co PO Box 270 .... Medina NY 14103 585-798-3000 798-5612
Web: www.phinneytool.com
Plasidyne Engineering & Mfg Inc 3230 E 59th St .... Long Beach CA 90805 562-531-0510 531-1377
Web: www.plasidyne.com
Porter Precision Products Inc 2734 Banning Rd .... Cincinnati OH 45239 513-923-3777 923-1111
TF: 800-543-7041 ■ *Web:* www.porterpunch.com
Power Brake Dies Inc 263 W 154th St .... South Holland IL 60473 708-339-5951 339-7737
Web: www.powerbrakedies.com
Precision Component Industries 5325 Southway St SW .... Canton OH 44706 330-477-6287 477-1052
Web: www.precision-component.com
Precision Fasteners Tooling Inc 11530 Western Ave .... Stanton CA 90680 714-898-8558 891-4988
Precision Tool Die & Machine Co Inc 6901 Preston Hwy .... Louisville KY 40219 502-479-0800 635-2636
Prikos & Becker Tool Co 8109 N Lawndale Ave .... Skokie IL 60076 847-675-3910 675-3913
Product Engineering Co 1480 14th St .... Columbus IN 47201 812-372-4421 372-2837
Producto Machine Co 800 Union Ave .... Bridgeport CT 06607 203-367-8675 368-2597
TF Cust Svc: 800-243-9898
Prospect Mold Inc 1100 Main St .... Cuyahoga Falls OH 44221 330-929-3311 920-1338
TF: 800-683-3312 ■ *Web:* www.prospect-akromold.com
Quality Metalcraft Inc 33355 Glendale St .... Livonia MI 48150 734-261-6700 261-5180
Web: www.qualitymetalcraft.com
Rapid Die & Engineering Inc 2031 Calvin Ave SE .... Grand Rapids MI 49507 616-241-5406 241-4002
Web: www.rapiddie.biz
Ready Machine Tool & Die Corp PO Box 285 .... Connersville IN 47331 765-825-3108 825-1176
Web: www.readymachine.com
Reddog Industries Inc 2012 E 33rd St .... Erie PA 16510 814-898-4321 899-5671
Web: www.reddog-erie.com
Reed City Tool & Die Inc 603 E Church St .... Reed City MI 49677 231-832-5504 832-5270
Web: www.reedcitytool.com
Reliance Tool & Mfg Co 617 N State St .... Elgin IL 60123 847-695-1234 695-0931
Web: www.reliancetool.com
Remmele Engineering Inc 10 Old Hwy 8 SW .... New Brighton MN 55112 651-635-4100 635-4168
TF: 800-222-7737 ■ *Web:* www.remmele.com
Republic Die & Tool Co 45000 Van Born Rd PO Box 339 .... Belleville MI 48112 734-699-3400 699-4081
Reuther Mold & Mfg Co 1225 Munroe Falls Ave .... Cuyahoga Falls OH 44221 330-923-5266 923-9930
Web: www.reuthermold.com
Reynolds Mfg Co 501 38th St .... Rock Island IL 61201 309-788-7443 788-7715
Web: www.reynoldsmfg.com
Richardson Mfg Co 2209 Old Jacksonville Rd .... Springfield IL 62704 217-546-2249 546-9433
Web: www.rmc-bigcnc.com
Rocheleau Tool & Die Co Inc 117 Industrial Rd .... Fitchburg MA 01420 978-345-1723 345-5972
Web: www.rocheleautool.com
Rocon Mfg Corp 606 Hague St .... Rochester NY 14606 585-436-8189 436-2188
Web: www.roconmfg.com
Rome Tool & Die Co Inc 113 Hemlock St .... Rome GA 30161 706-234-6743 234-1242
TF: 800-241-3369 ■ *Web:* www.rometool.com
Ronart Industries Inc 19365 Sherwood St .... Detroit MI 48234 313-893-4800 893-1440
Web: www.ronart.com
RotoMetrics Group 800 Howerton Ln .... Eureka MO 63025 636-587-3600 587-3701
TF: 800-325-3851 ■ *Web:* www.rotometrics.com
Sarcol Inc 3050 W Taylor St .... Chicago IL 60612 773-533-3000 533-3004
Web: www.sarcolinc.com
SB Whistler & Sons Inc PO Box 207 .... Akron NY 14001 716-542-4141 542-4226
TF: 800-828-1010 ■ *Web:* www.sbwhistler.com
Schoitz Engineering Inc PO Box 546 .... Waterloo IA 50704 319-234-6615 234-0368
Web: www.schoitz.com
Schroeder & Bogardus Die Co Inc 1130 Red Gum St .... Anaheim CA 92806 714-630-2270 630-1739
Web: www.schroederinc.com
Select Tool & Die Corp 60 Heid Ave .... Dayton OH 45404 937-233-9191 233-7640
TF: 800-797-4150 ■ *Web:* www.selecttoolcorp.com
Sidney Tool & Die Inc PO Box 849 .... Sidney OH 45365 937-492-6121 498-9601
Skill Tool & Die Corp 16151 Puritas Ave .... Cleveland OH 44135 216-267-8866 267-3858
Smith Tom Industries 500 Smith Dr .... Clayton OH 45315 937-832-1555 832-1577
Web: www.tomsmithindustries.com
Spalding CA Co 1011 Cedar Ave .... Croydon PA 19021 267-550-9000 550-9008
Web: www.caspalding.com
Specialty Design & Mfg Co PO Box 4039 .... Reading PA 19606 610-779-1357 370-0269
Web: www.specialtydesign.com
SPX Corp OTC Div 655 Eisenhower Dr .... Owatonna MN 55060 507-455-7000 455-7300*
**Fax:* Hum Res ■ *TF:* 800-533-6127 ■ *Web:* www.otctools.com
Sterling Die Div Goodrich Corp 5565 Venture Dr Suite D .... Parma OH 44130 216-267-1300 267-3356
TF: 800-533-1300
Superior Die Set Corp 900 W Drexel Ave .... Oak Creek WI 53154 414-764-4900 657-0855*
**Fax Area Code:* 800 ■ *TF:* 800-558-6040 ■ *Web:* www.supdie.com
Superior Die Tool & Machine Co 2301 Fairwood Ave .... Columbus OH 43207 614-444-2181 444-8712
TF: 800-292-2181 ■ *Web:* www.superior-dietool.com
Superior Jig Inc 1540 N Orangethorpe Way .... Anaheim CA 92801 714-525-4777 525-8798
Web: www.sji.net
Swan Engineering & Machine Co 2611 State St .... Bettendorf IA 52722 563-355-2671 355-5380
Synergis Technologies Corp 3755 36th St SE .... Grand Rapids MI 49512 616-245-4400 475-3204
Web: www.synergis.us
Taylor's Industrial Services LLC HPM Div 820 Marion Rd ..... Mount Gilead OH 43338 419-946-0222 946-2473
Web: www.taylorsind.com/2003/hpm/index.php
Tipp Machine & Tool Inc PO Box 280 .... Tipp City OH 45371 937-667-8481 667-2818
Web: www.tippmachine.com
Tom Smith Industries 500 Smith Dr .... Clayton OH 45315 937-832-1555 832-1577
Web: www.tomsmithindustries.com
Toolcraft Products Inc PO Box 482 .... Dayton OH 45404 937-223-8271 223-1408
Web: www.toolcraftproducts.com

Phone Fax

Tools & Production Co 4924 N Encinita Ave .... Temple City CA 91780 626-286-0213 286-3398
Web: www.toolsandproduction.com
Triangle Tool Corp 8609 W Port Ave .... Milwaukee WI 53224 414-357-7117 357-7610
Tru-Cut Inc 1145 Allied Dr .... Sebring OH 44672 330-938-9806 938-9342
Web: www.trucut.com
Uniloy Milacron Inc 5550 Occidental Hwy Suite B .... Tecumseh MI 49286 517-424-8900 424-8992
TF: 800-419-7771 ■ *Web:* www.uniloymilacron.com
Unipunch Products Inc 370 Babcock St .... Buffalo NY 14206 716-825-7960 825-0581
TF Sales: 800-828-7061 ■ *Web:* www.unipunch.com
United Tool & Engineering Co 4095 Prairie Hill Rd .... South Beloit IL 61080 815-389-3021 389-1968
Walker Tool & Die Inc 2411 Walker Ave NW .... Grand Rapids MI 49544 616-453-5471 453-3765
TF: 888-925-5377 ■ *Web:* www.walkertool.com
Wand Tool Co Inc 852 Seton Ct .... Wheeling IL 60090 847-459-2400 459-2421
Web: www.wandtool.com
Western Supply Independent Dies Div 2930 Cass Ave .... Saint Louis MO 63106 314-531-4300 531-4401
Web: www.wsids.com
Westland Corp 1735 S Maize Rd .... Wichita KS 67209 316-721-1144 721-1495
TF: 800-247-1144 ■ *Web:* www.westlandusa.com
Whistler SB & Sons Inc PO Box 207 .... Akron NY 14001 716-542-4141 542-4226
TF: 800-828-1010 ■ *Web:* www.sbwhistler.com
Willett MS Inc PO Box 266 .... Cockeysville MD 21030 410-771-0460 771-6972
Web: www.mswillett.com
Wirtz Mfg Co Inc 1105 24th St .... Port Huron MI 48061 810-987-4700 987-8135
Web: www.wirtzusa.com
Wright Industries 1520 Elm Hill Pike .... Nashville TN 37210 615-361-6600 366-5978
Web: www.wrightind.com
Yarema Die & Engineering Co Inc 300 Minnesota Rd .... Troy MI 48083 248-585-2830 616-1422
TF: 800-989-2830 ■ *Web:* www.yarema.com

761 TOOLS - HAND & EDGE

SEE ALSO Lawn & Garden Equipment p. 1888; Metalworking Devices & Accessories p. 1967; Saw Blades & Handsaws p. 2303

Phone Fax

Acorn Products Inc 390 W Nationwide Blvd .... Columbus OH 43215 614-222-4400 221-8397
TF: 800-888-4196
Adjustable Clamp Co 404 N Armour St .... Chicago IL 60622 312-666-0640 666-2723
Web: www.adjustableclamp.com
Allway Tools Inc 1255 Seabury Ave .... Bronx NY 10462 718-792-3636 823-9640
TF: 800-422-5592 ■ *Web:* www.allwaytools.com
Ames Taping Tools Inc 3305 Breckenridge Blvd Suite 122 .... Duluth GA 30096 770-243-2637 243-2658
TF Cust Svc: 800-408-2801 ■ *Web:* www.amestools.com
Ames True Temper Inc 465 Railroad Ave .... Camp Hill PA 17011 717-737-1500 730-2550
TF: 800-393-1846 ■ *Web:* www.ames.com
Apex Div Cooper Tools Inc 762 W Stewart St .... Dayton OH 45408 937-222-7871 228-0422
Web: www.coopertools.com/brands/apex
Applied Concepts Inc 4607 Forge Rd .... Colorado Springs CO 80907 719-598-5070 265-2521
TF: 800-466-5028 ■ *Web:* www.robogrip.com
Arrow Fastener Co Inc 271 Mayhill St .... Saddle Brook NJ 07663 201-843-6900 843-3911
Web: www.arrowfastener.com
ATI Tools Div Snap-on Inc 2425 W Vineyard Ave .... Escondido CA 92029 760-746-8301 746-4295
TF: 800-284-4460 ■ *Web:* www.atitools.com
Baltimore Tool Works PO Box 27149 .... Baltimore MD 21230 410-752-5297 752-0528
TF: 800-752-5533 ■ *Web:* www.baltimoretool.com
BARCO Industries Inc 1020 MacArthur Rd .... Reading PA 19605 610-374-3117 374-6320
TF Cust Svc: 800-234-8665 ■ *Web:* www.barcotools.com
Bondhus Corp 1400 E Broadway St .... Monticello MN 55362 763-295-2162 295-4440
TF Cust Svc: 800-328-8310 ■ *Web:* www.bondhus.com
Brunner & Lay Inc 9300 King Ave .... Franklin Park IL 60131 847-678-3232 678-0642
TF: 800-872-6899 ■ *Web:* www.brunnerlay.com
Cal-Van Tools 4300 Waterleaf Ct .... Greensboro NC 27410 336-294-3259 299-4003
TF: 800-537-1077 ■ *Web:* www.calvantools.com
Channellock Inc 1306 S Main St .... Meadville PA 16335 814-724-8700 337-3616
TF Cust Svc: 800-724-3018 ■ *Web:* www.channellock.com
Charles GG Schmidt & Co Inc 301 W Grand Ave .... Montvale NJ 07645 201-391-5300 391-3565
TF: 800-724-6438 ■ *Web:* www.cggschmidt.com
Consolidated Devices Inc 19220 San Jose Ave .... City of Industry CA 91748 626-965-0668 810-2759
TF: 800-525-6319 ■ *Web:* www.cditorque.com
Cooper Industries 600 Travis St Suite 5800 .... Houston TX 77002 713-209-8400 209-8995
NYSE: CBE ■ *Web:* www.cooperindustries.com
Cooper Tools Inc 3535 Glenwood Ave .... Raleigh NC 27612 919-781-7200 783-2007
Web: www.coopertools.com
Cooper Tools Inc Apex Div 762 W Stewart St .... Dayton OH 45408 937-222-7871 228-0422
Web: www.coopertools.com/brands/apex
Cooper Tools Inc Hand Tools Div 1000 Lufkin Rd .... Apex NC 27539 919-362-1670 387-0415*
**Fax Area Code:* 800 ■ *Web:* www.cooperhandtools.com
Cornwell Quality Tools Co 667 Seville Rd .... Wadsworth OH 44281 330-336-3506 336-3337
TF Cust Svc: 800-321-8356 ■ *Web:* www.cornwelltools.com
CS Osborne & Co Inc 125 Jersey St .... Harrison NJ 07029 973-483-3232 484-3621
Web: www.csosborne.com
CTA Mfg Corp 263 Veterans Blvd .... Carlstadt NJ 07072 201-896-1000 896-0529
Web: www.ctatools.com
Danaher Corp 2099 Pennsylvania Ave NW 12th Fl .... Washington DC 20006 202-828-0850 828-0860
NYSE: DHR ■ *Web:* www.danaher.com
Danaher Tool Group 14600 York Rd Suite A .... Sparks MD 21152 410-773-7800 234-0472*
**Fax Area Code:* 800 ■ *TF:* 800-688-8949
Dasco Pro Inc 340 Blackhawk Park Ave .... Rockford IL 61104 815-962-3727
TF: 800-327-2690
Duo-Fast Corp 2400 Galvin Dr .... Elgin IL 60123 847-783-5500 783-5501
TF Cust Svc: 888-386-3278 ■ *Web:* www.duo-fast.com
Empire Level Mfg Corp 929 Empire Dr .... Mukwonago WI 53149 262-368-2000 368-2127
TF: 800-558-0722 ■ *Web:* www.empirelevel.com
Emporium Specialties Co Inc 94 Foster St PO Box 65 .... Austin PA 16720 814-647-8661 647-5536
Web: www.empspec.com
Enderes Tool Co Inc 14925 Energy Way .... Apple Valley MN 55124 952-891-1200 891-1202
TF: 800-874-7776 ■ *Web:* www.enderes.com
Estwing Mfg Co 2647 8th St .... Rockford IL 61109 815-397-9521 397-8665
Web: www.estwing.com
Everhard Products Inc 1016 9th St SW .... Canton OH 44707 330-453-7786
Web: www.everhard.com
Fiskars Brands Inc 2537 Daniels St .... Madison WI 53718 608-259-1649 294-4790
TF: 800-500-4849 ■ *Web:* www.fiskars.com
Fletcher-Terry Co Inc 65 Spring Ln .... Farmington CT 06032 860-677-7331 676-8858
TF Cust Svc: 800-843-3826 ■ *Web:* www.fletcher-terry.com
General Machine Products Co Inc 3111 Old Lincoln Hwy .... Trevose PA 19053 215-357-5500 357-6216
TF Tech Supp: 800-345-6009 ■ *Web:* www.gmptools.com
General Tools Mfg Co LLC 80 White St .... New York NY 10013 212-431-6100 431-6499
TF: 800-697-8665 ■ *Web:* www.generaltools.com
Greenfield Disston Co 7345-G W Friendly Ave .... Greensboro NC 27410 336-852-9220 299-0616
Grobet File Co of America Inc 750 Washington Ave .... Carlstadt NJ 07072 201-939-6700 939-5067
TF: 800-847-4188 ■ *Web:* www.grobetusa.com

Phone | Fax

Harrington Tools Inc
5440 San Fernando Rd W PO Box 39879 Los Angeles CA 90039 323-245-2142 500-8378*
*Fax Area Code: 818 ■ TF: 800-331-6291 ■ Web: www.harringtontools.com

Hastings Fiber Glass Products Inc 770 Cook Rd PO Box 218 Hastings MI 49058 269-945-9541 945-4623
Web: www.hfgp.com

Hexacon Electric Co 161 W Clay Ave Roselle Park NJ 07204 908-245-6200 245-6176
TF: 888-439-2266 ■ Web: www.hexaconelectric.com

Huther Brothers Inc 1290 University Ave Rochester NY 14607 585-473-9462 473-9476
TF: 888-448-8437 ■ Web: www.hutherbros.com

Hyde Mfg Co 54 Eastford Rd Southbridge MA 01550 508-764-4344 765-5250
TF: 800-872-4933 ■ Web: www.hydetools.com

Irwin Tools Div Newell Rubbermaid Inc
8935 Northpointe Executive Dr Huntersville NC 28078 704-987-4555 987-4506
TF: 800-866-5740 ■ Web: www.irwin.com

Johnson Level & Tool Mfg Co Inc 6333 W Donges Bay Rd Mequon WI 53092 262-242-1161 242-0189
Web: www.johnsonlevel.com

Jonard Industries Corp 134 Marbledale Rd Tuckahoe NY 10707 914-793-0700 793-4527
Web: www.jonard.com

Jore Corp 45000 Hwy 93 Ronan MT 59864 406-528-4350 676-4901
TF: 888-809-5673 ■ Web: www.jorecorporation.com

Kastar Inc 5501 21st St PO 1616 Racine WI 53401 262-554-2300 554-7503
TF Cust Svc: 800-645-1142 ■ Web: www.kastar.com

Ken-Tool Co 768 E North St Akron OH 44305 330-535-7177 872-4929*
*Fax Area Code: 800 ■ Web: www.kentool.com

Klein Tools Inc 7200 N McCormick Blvd PO Box 599033 Skokie IL 60659 847-677-9500 677-4476
TF Cust Svc: 800-553-4676 ■ Web: www.kleintools.com

Leatherman Tool Group Inc 12106 NE Ainsworth Cir Portland OR 97220 503-253-7826 253-7830
TF: 800-847-8665 ■ Web: www.leatherman.com

Lisle Corp 807 E Main St Clarinda IA 51632 712-542-5101 542-6591
Web: www.lislecorp.com

LS Starrett Co 121 Crescent St Athol MA 01331 978-249-3551 249-8495
NYSE: SCX ■ TF: 888-674-7443 ■ Web: www.starrett.com

Mac Tools Inc 505 N Cleveland Ave Westerville OH 43082 614-755-7000 622-3295
TF: 800-622-8665 ■ Web: www.mactools.com

Malco Products Inc 14080 State Hwy 55 NW Annandale MN 55302 320-274-8246 274-2269
TF: 800-328-3530 ■ Web: www.malcotools.com

Mann Edge Tool Co PO Box 351 Lewistown PA 17044 717-248-9628 248-4846
TF Sales: 800-248-8303 ■ Web: www.mannedge.com

Marshalltown Co 104 S 8th Ave Marshalltown IA 50158 641-753-5999 753-6341
TF: 800-888-0127 ■ Web: www.marshalltown.com

Matco Tools 4403 Allen Rd Stow OH 44224 330-929-4949 926-5320
TF: 800-368-6651 ■ Web: www.matcotools.com

Mayhew Steel Products Inc 199 Industrial Blvd Turners Falls MA 01376 413-863-4860 863-8464
TF: 800-872-0037 ■ Web: www.mayhew.com

MIBRO Group 111 Sinnott Rd Toronto ON M1L4S6 416-285-9000 285-9500
Web: www.mibro.com

Newell Rubbermaid Inc Irwin Tools Div
8935 Northpointe Executive Dr Huntersville NC 28078 704-987-4555 987-4506
TF: 800-866-5740 ■ Web: www.irwin.com

Newell Rubbermaid Inc Tools & Hardware Group
10B Glenlake Pkwy Suite 600 Atlanta GA 30328 770-407-3800 407-3970
Web: www.newellrubbermaid.com

Olympia Group Inc 505 S 7th Ave City of Industry CA 91746 626-336-4999 336-4899
TF: 800-888-8782 ■ Web: www.olympiaweb.com

QEP Co Inc 1001 Broken Sound Pkwy NW Suite A Boca Raton FL 33487 561-994-5550 241-2830
NASDAQ: QEPC ■ TF: 800-777-8665 ■ Web: www.qep.com

Red Devil Inc 1437 S Boulder Suite 750 Boulder Towers Tulsa OK 74361 918-585-8111 585-8120
TF: 800-423-3845 ■ Web: www.reddevil.com

Reed Mfg Co 1425 W 8th St Erie PA 16502 814-452-3691 455-1697
TF: 800-456-1697 ■ Web: www.reedmfgco.com

Relton Corp 317 Rolyn Dr PO Box 60019 Arcadia CA 91066 626-446-8201 446-9671
TF Cust Svc: 800-423-1505 ■ Web: www.relton.com

Ridge Tool Co 400 Clark St Elyria OH 44035 440-323-5581 329-4853
Web: www.ridgid.com

Ripley Co 46 Nooks Hill Rd Cromwell CT 06416 860-635-2200 635-3631
TF: 800-528-8665 ■ Web: www.ripley-tools.com

Schmidt Charles GG & Co Inc 301 W Grand Ave Montvale NJ 07645 201-391-5300 391-3565
TF: 800-724-6438 ■ Web: www.cggschmidt.com

Seymour Mfg Co Inc 500 N Broadway St Seymour IN 47274 812-522-2900 522-6109
TF: 800-457-1909 ■ Web: www.seymourmfg.com

SK Hand Tool Corp 3535 W 47th St Chicago IL 60632 773-523-1300 523-2103
TF: 800-822-5575 ■ Web: www.skhandtool.com

Skyo Industries Inc 171 Brook Ave Deer Park NY 11729 631-586-4702 586-4126
TF: 800-645-5535

Snap-on Inc 2801 80th St Kenosha WI 53143 262-656-5200 656-5577
NYSE: SNA ■ Web: www.snapon.com

Snap-on Inc ATI Tools Div 2425 W Vineyard Ave Escondido CA 92029 760-746-8301 746-4295
TF: 800-284-4460 ■ Web: www.atitools.com

Snow & Nealley Co PO Box 876 Bangor ME 04402 207-947-6642 941-0857
TF: 800-933-6642 ■ Web: www.snowandnealley.com

Stabila Inc 332 Industrial Dr South Elgin IL 60177 847-488-0050 488-0051
TF: 800-869-7460 ■ Web: www.stabila.com

Stanley Fastening Systems LP Rt 2 East Greenwich RI 02818 401-884-2500 884-3122
Web: www.stanleybostitch.com

Stanley Mechanics Tools 12827 Valley Branch Ln Dallas TX 75234 972-247-1367 919-7436
TF Orders: 877-435-7337

Stanley Supply & Services Inc 335 Willow St North Andover MA 01845 978-682-2000 743-8141*
*Fax Area Code: 800 ■ TF Cust Svc: 888-887-9473 ■
Web: www.stanleysupplyservices.com

Stanley Tools Inc 480 Myrtle St New Britain CT 06053 860-225-5111 643-3756*
*Fax Area Code: 800 ■ TF Cust Svc: 800-262-2161 ■ Web: www.stanleytools.com

Stanley Tools Worldwide 480 Myrtle St New Britain CT 06053 860-225-5111 643-3756*
*Fax Area Code: 800 ■ TF Cust Svc: 800-262-2161 ■ Web: www.stanleytools.com

Stanley Works 1000 Stanley Dr New Britain CT 06053 860-225-5111 827-3895
NYSE: SWK ■ TF Cust Svc: 800-262-2161 ■ Web: www.stanleyworks.com

Stride Tool Inc 46 E Washington St Ellicottville NY 14731 716-945-4991 699-2490
TF: 888-467-8665 ■ Web: www.stridetool.com

Stride Tool Inc Imperial Div 6300 W Howard St Niles IL 60714 847-581-3300 581-3380
TF: 888-467-8665 ■ Web: stridetool.com/imperial

Stride Tool Inc Milbar Div 530 E Washington St Chagrin Falls OH 44022 440-247-4600 247-3998
TF: 877-225-8858 ■ Web: www.milbar.com

Superior Tool Co 100 Hayes Dr Unit C Brooklyn Heights OH 44131 216-398-8600 398-8691
TF: 800-533-3244 ■ Web: www.superiortool.com

Tamco Inc PO Box 371 Monongahela PA 15063 724-258-6622 258-6692
TF: 800-826-2672 ■ Web: www.tamcotools.com

Ullman Devices Corp 664 Danbury Rd Ridgefield CT 06877 203-438-6577 431-9064
Web: users.ntplx.net/~ullman

UnionTools Inc 390 W Nationwide Blvd Columbus OH 43215 614-222-4400 221-8397
TF: 800-848-6657 ■ Web: www.uniontools.com

Vaughan & Bushnell Mfg Co 11414 Maple Ave Hebron IL 60034 815-648-2446 648-4300
TF: 800-435-6000 ■ Web: www.vaughanmfg.com

Vermont American Corp 1961 Bishop Ln Louisville KY 40218 502-625-2000 625-2064
TF: 800-626-2834 ■ Web: www.vermontamerican.com

Wall Lenk Corp PO Box 3049 Kinston NC 28502 252-527-4186 527-4189
TF: 888-527-4186 ■ Web: www.wlenk.com

Warner Mfg Co 13435 Industrial Park Blvd Minneapolis MN 55441 763-559-4740 559-1364
TF: 800-234-7708 ■ Web: www.warnertool.com

Western Forge Corp 4607 Forge Rd Colorado Springs CO 80907 719-598-5070 260-3500

Wheeler-Rex 3744 Jefferson Rd PO Box 688 Ashtabula OH 44005 440-998-2788 992-2925
TF: 800-321-7950 ■ Web: www.wheelerrex.com

Wilton Tool Group 2420 Vantage Dr Elgin IL 60123 847-851-1000 934-6730
TF: 800-519-7381 ■ Web: www.wiltontool.com

WMH Tool Group Inc 2420 Vantage Dr Elgin IL 60123 847-649-3010 851-1045
TF: 800-274-6848 ■ Web: www.wmhtoolgroup.com

Wolfcraft Inc 333 Swift Rd Addison IL 60101 630-773-4777 268-9476
Web: www.wolfcraft.com

Wright Tool Co 1 Wright Dr Barberton OH 44203 330-848-3702 848-0619
TF: 800-321-2902 ■ Web: www.wrighttool.com

Zephyr Mfg Co PO Box 759 Inglewood CA 90307 310-410-4907 410-2913
TF: 800-624-3944 ■ Web: www.zephyrtool.com

TOOLS - MACHINE

SEE Machine Tools - Metal Cutting Types p. 1924; Machine Tools - Metal Forming Types p. 1925

762 TOOLS - POWER

SEE ALSO Lawn & Garden Equipment p. 1888; Metalworking Devices & Accessories p. 1967

Phone | Fax

Actuant Corp 6100 N Baker Rd Milwaukee WI 53209 414-352-4160 247-5550
NYSE: ATU ■ TF: 800-624-5242 ■ Web: www.actuant.com

Air Tool Service Co (ATSCO) 7722 Metric Dr Mentor OH 44060 440-942-4475 942-6387
TF: 800-321-3554 ■ Web: www.atsco.com

American Pneumatic Tool Inc 14710 S Maple Ave Gardena CA 90248 310-538-2600 323-6656
TF: 800-532-7402 ■ Web: www.apt-tools.com

Atlas Copco Tools & Assembly Systems 2998 Dutton Rd Auburn Hills MI 48326 248-373-3000 373-3001
TF: 800-859-3746 ■ Web: www.atlascopco.com/tools/us

Biesemeyer Mfg Corp 216 S Alma School Rd Suite 1 Mesa AZ 85210 480-835-9300 834-8515
TF: 800-782-1831 ■ Web: www.biesemeyer.com

Black & Decker Corp 701 E Joppa Rd Towson MD 21286 410-716-3900 716-2996*
NYSE: BDK ■ *Fax: Mktg ■ Web: www.bdk.com

Blackstone Industries Inc 16 Stoney Hill Rd Bethel CT 06801 203-792-8622 796-7861
TF: 800-441-0625 ■ Web: www.blackstoneind.com

Blount Inc Oregon Cutting Systems Div
4909 SE International Way Portland OR 97222 503-653-8881 653-4201
TF: 800-223-5168 ■ Web: www.oregonchain.com

Chicago Pneumatic Tool Co 1800 Overview Dr Rock Hill SC 29730 803-817-7000 817-7036*
*Fax: Hum Res ■ TF: 800-367-2442 ■ Web: www.chicagopneumatic.com

Cooper Industries 600 Travis St Suite 5800 Houston TX 77002 713-209-8400 209-8995
NYSE: CBE ■ Web: www.cooperindustries.com

Cooper Tools Inc 3535 Glenwood Ave Raleigh NC 27612 919-781-7200 783-2007
Web: www.coopertools.com

DESA International 2701 Industrial Dr Bowling Green KY 42101 270-781-9600 745-7800
TF Cust Svc: 800-432-5212 ■ Web: www.desaint.com

Dremel Inc 4915 21st St Racine WI 53406 262-554-1390 554-7654
TF: 800-437-3635 ■ Web: www.dremel.com

Dynabrade Inc 8989 Sheridan Dr Clarence NY 14031 716-631-0100 631-2073
TF Cust Svc: 800-828-7333 ■ Web: www.dynabrade.com

Enerpac 6101 N Baker Rd Milwaukee WI 53209 262-781-6600 781-1049*
*Fax: Cust Svc ■ TF Cust Svc: 800-433-2766 ■ Web: www.enerpac.com

Florida Pneumatic Mfg Corp 851 Jupiter Park Ln Jupiter FL 33458 561-744-9500 575-9134
TF: 800-327-9403 ■ Web: www.florida-pneumatic.com

Greenlee Textron Inc 4455 Boeing Dr Rockford IL 61109 815-397-7070 397-8289
TF: 800-435-0786 ■ Web: www.greenlee.textron.com

Hilti Inc 5400 S 122nd East Ave Tulsa OK 74146 918-252-6000 252-0522
TF Cust Svc: 800-879-8000 ■ Web: www.us.hilti.com

Hougen Mfg Inc 3001 Hougen Dr Swartz Creek MI 48473 810-635-7111 635-8277
TF Orders: 800-462-7818 ■ Web: www.hougen.com

Hydratight Sweeney Products Inc
12508 E Briarwood Ave Unit 1-A Englewood CO 80112 303-749-6000 749-6001
TF Cust Svc: 800-448-2524 ■ Web: www.hydratightsweeney.com

International Staple & Machine Co 629 E Butler Rd Butler PA 16002 724-287-7711 287-2811
TF: 800-378-3430 ■ Web: www.ismsys.com

Makita USA Inc 14930 Northam St Suite C La Mirada CA 90638 714-522-8088 522-8133
TF: 800-462-5482 ■ Web: www.makitausa.com

Master Appliance Corp 2420 18th St Racine WI 53403 262-633-7791 633-9745
TF: 800-558-9413 ■ Web: www.masterappliance.com

Milwaukee Electric Tool Corp 13135 W Lisbon Rd Brookfield WI 53005 262-781-3600 638-9582*
*Fax Area Code: 800 ■ *Fax: Orders ■ TF: 800-729-3878 ■
Web: www.milwaukeetool.com

Newell Rubbermaid Inc Tools & Hardware Group
10B Glenlake Pkwy Suite 600 Atlanta GA 30328 770-407-3800 407-3970
Web: www.newellrubbermaid.com

Oregon Cutting Systems Div Blount Inc
4909 SE International Way Portland OR 97222 503-653-8881 653-4201
TF: 800-223-5168 ■ Web: www.oregonchain.com

P & F Industries Inc 300 Smith St Farmingdale NY 11735 631-694-1800 694-1836
NASDAQ: PFIN ■ Web: www.pfina.com

Paslode 888 Forest Edge Dr Vernon Hills IL 60061 847-634-1900 634-6602
TF: 800-682-3428 ■ Web: www.paslode.com

Pioneer Tool & Forge Inc 101 6th St New Kensington PA 15068 724-337-4700 337-4707
TF: 800-359-6408 ■ Web: www.breakersteel.com

Pneutek Inc 17 Friars Dr Hudson NH 03051 603-883-1660 882-9165
TF: 800-431-8665 ■ Web: www.pneutek.com

Porter-Cable Corp 4825 Hwy 45 N Jackson TN 38305 731-668-8600 664-0525
TF: 800-321-9443 ■ Web: www.porter-cable.com

Powernail Co 1300 Rose Rd Lake Zurich IL 60047 847-634-3000 634-4943
TF: 800-323-1653 ■ Web: www.powernail.com

Precision Twist Drill Co 301 Industrial Ave Crystal Lake IL 60012 815-459-2040 459-2804
TF: 800-877-3745 ■ Web: www.precisiontwistdrill.com

Ridge Tool Co 400 Clark St Elyria OH 44035 440-323-5581 329-4853
Web: www.ridgid.com

Robert Bosch LLC 2800 S 25th Ave Broadview IL 60155 708-865-5200 865-6430
Web: www.boschusa.com

Robert Bosch Tool Corp 1800 W Central Rd Mount Prospect IL 60056 224-223-2000 232-2368
TF: 800-301-8255 ■ Web: www.boschtools.com

Ryobi Technologies Inc 1428 Pearman Dairy Rd Anderson SC 29625 864-226-6511 261-9435
TF: 800-525-2579 ■ Web: www.ryobitools.com

SENCO Products Inc 8485 Broadwell Rd Cincinnati OH 45244 513-388-2000 388-2026
TF Tech Supp: 800-543-4596 ■ Web: www.senco.com

Shopsmith Inc 6530 Poe Ave Dayton OH 45414 937-898-6070 722-3965*
*Fax Area Code: 800 ■ TF Cust Svc: 800-543-7586 ■ Web: www.shopsmith.com

				Phone	Fax
Sioux Tools Inc 250 Snap-on Dr. *TF Orders:* 800-722-7290 ■ *Web:* www.siouxtools.com	Murphy	NC	28906	828-835-9765	835-9685
Speedgrip Chuck Inc 2000 E Industrial Pkwy. *Web:* www.speedgrip.com	Elkhart	IN	46516	574-294-1506	294-2465
Stanley Assembly Technologies Div 5335 Avion Park Dr *Web:* www.stanleyworks.com/bu_airtools.asp	Highland Heights	OH	44143	440-461-5500	461-2710
Stanley Fastening Systems LP Rt 2 *Web:* www.stanleybostitch.com	East Greenwich	RI	02818	401-884-2500	884-3122
Stanley Hydraulic Tools Div 3810 SE Naef Rd. *Web:* www.stanleyworks.com/bu_hydraulic.asp	Milwaukie	OR	97267	503-659-5660	652-1780
Stihl Inc 536 Viking Dr **Fax Area Code:* 888 ■ *TF Cust Svc:* 888-784-8575 ■ *Web:* www.stihlusa.com	Virginia Beach	VA	23452	757-486-9100	784-8576*
Suhner Mfg Inc PO Box 1234 *TF:* 800-323-6886 ■ *Web:* www.suhnerusa.com	Rome	GA	30162	706-235-8047	235-8045
Thomas C Wilson Inc 21-11 44th Ave *TF:* 800-230-2636 ■ *Web:* www.tcwilson.com	Long Island City	NY	11101	718-729-3360	361-2872
WMH Tool Group Inc 2420 Vantage Dr. *TF:* 800-274-6848 ■ *Web:* www.wmhtoolgroup.com	Elgin	IL	60123	847-649-3010	851-1045

763 TOUR OPERATORS

SEE ALSO Bus Services - Charter p. 1399; Travel Agencies p. 2380

				Phone	Fax
Abercrombie & Kent International Inc 1520 Kensington Rd Suite 212 *TF:* 800-323-7308 ■ *Web:* www.abercrombiekent.com	Oak Brook	IL	60523	630-954-2944	954-3324
Academy Bus Tours Inc 111 Paterson Ave. *TF:* 800-442-7272 ■ *Web:* www.academybus.com	Hoboken	NJ	07030	201-339-6000	420-8087
ACIS Educational Tours 343 Congress St Suite 3100 *TF:* 800-888-2247 ■ *Web:* www.acis.com	Boston	MA	02210	617-236-2051	450-5601
Adventure Alaska Tours Inc PO Box 64 *TF:* 800-365-7057 ■ *Web:* www.adventurealaskatours.com	Hope	AK	99605	907-782-3730	782-3725
Adventure Center 40 N Main St *TF:* 800-444-2819 ■ *Web:* www.raftingtours.com	Ashland	OR	97520	541-488-2819	482-5139
Adventure Center Inc 1311 63rd St Suite 200. *TF:* 800-227-8747 ■ *Web:* www.adventurecenter.com	Emeryville	CA	94608	510-654-1879	654-4200
Adventure Challenge 8225 Oxer Rd *Web:* adventurechallenge.com	Richmond	VA	23235	804-276-7600	222-1709
Adventure Connection PO Box 475 *TF:* 800-556-6060 ■ *Web:* www.raftcalifornia.com	Coloma	CA	95613	530-626-7385	626-9268
Adventure Discovery Tours Inc 3602 El Paso Dr. *Web:* www.rivertrips.net	Cottonwood	AZ	86326	928-634-5363	
Adventure Life South America 1655 S 3rd St W Suite 1 *TF:* 800-344-6118 ■ *Web:* www.adventure-life.com	Missoula	MT	59801	406-541-2677	541-2676
Adventures Out West 15001 N 74th St. **Fax Area Code:* 602 ■ *TF:* 800-755-0935 ■ *Web:* www.advoutwest.com	Scottsdale	AZ	85260	800-755-0935	996-4890*
Africa Adventure Co 5353 N Federal Hwy Suite 300 *TF:* 800-882-9453 ■ *Web:* www.africa-adventure.com	Fort Lauderdale	FL	33308	954-491-8877	491-9060
African Travel Inc 1100 E Broadway 2nd Fl. *TF:* 800-421-8907 ■ *Web:* www.africantravelinc.com	Glendale	CA	91205	818-507-7893	507-5802
Agape Tours Inc 1210 US Hwy 281 **Fax:* Sales ■ *TF:* 800-460-2641 ■ *Web:* www.agapetoursinc.com	Wichita Falls	TX	76310	940-767-4935	692-8477*
AHI International Corp 6400 Shafer Ct. *TF:* 800-323-7373 ■ *Web:* www.ahitravel.com	Rosemont	IL	60018	847-384-4500	318-5000
Alaska! Bus Charters & Tours Inc PO Box 190735 *Web:* www.alaskabus.com	Anchorage	AK	99519	706-743-5509	743-5929
Alpha Omega Tours & Charters 419 N Jefferson St PO Box 97 *TF:* 800-351-1060 ■ *Web:* www.alphaomegatoursandcharters.com	Medical Lake	WA	99022	509-299-5595	299-5545
Alpine Adventure Trails Tours Inc 7495 Lower Thomaston Rd. *TF:* 888-478-4004 ■ *Web:* www.swisshiking.com	Macon	GA	31220	478-477-4004	477-4117
Alyson Adventures Inc 923 White St *TF:* 800-825-9766 ■ *Web:* www.alysonadventures.com	Key West	FL	33040	305-296-9935	292-9665
Ambassadors Group Inc DBA People to People Ambassador Programs Inc 110 S Ferrall St. *NASDAQ: EPAX* ■ *TF:* 800-669-7882 ■ *Web:* www.ambassadorsgroup.com	Spokane	WA	99202	509-534-6200	534-5245
American Coach Lines Inc 2328 10th Ave N Suite 501 *Web:* www.americancoachlines.com	Lake Worth	FL	33460	561-721-1170	721-2390
American Trails West 92 Middle Neck Rd *TF:* 800-645-6260 ■ *Web:* www.americantrailswest.com	Great Neck	NY	11021	516-487-2800	487-2855
AmericanTours International Inc (ATI) 6053 W Century Blvd. *TF:* 800-800-8942 ■ *Web:* www.americantours.com	Los Angeles	CA	90045	310-641-9953	216-5807
Ameritours 5018 William Flynn Hwy *TF:* 800-466-3868 ■ *Web:* www.ameritours.com	Gibsonia	PA	15044	724-443-5600	443-7447
Anderson Coach & Travel 1 Anderson Plaza *TF:* 800-345-3435 ■ *Web:* www.goanderson.com	Greenville	PA	16125	724-588-8310	588-0257
Atlantis Adventures 210 W 6th Ave Suite 200 *Web:* www.atlantisadventures.com	Vancouver	BC	V5Y1K8	604-875-1367	875-0833
Atlantis Submarines International Inc DBA Atlantis Adventures 210 W 6th Ave Suite 200 *Web:* www.atlantisadventures.com	Vancouver	BC	V5Y1K8	604-875-1367	875-0833
ATS Tours 300 Continental Blvd Suite 350 *TF:* 800-423-2880 ■ *Web:* www.atstours.com	El Segundo	CA	90245	310-643-0044	643-0032
Australian Pacific Touring (USA) Ltd 4605 Lankershim Blvd Suite 712 *TF:* 888-299-1428 ■ *Web:* www.aptouring.com	North Hollywood	CA	91602	818-755-6392	755-6396
Backroads 801 Cedar St *TF:* 800-462-2848 ■ *Web:* www.backroads.com	Berkeley	CA	94710	510-527-1555	527-1444
Badger Coaches Inc 5501 Femrite Dr. *TF:* 800-442-8259 ■ *Web:* www.badgerbus.com	Madison	WI	53718	608-255-1511	258-3484
Banff Adventures Unlimited 211 Bear St *TF:* 800-644-8888 ■ *Web:* www.banffadventures.com	Banff	AB	T1L1A8	403-762-4554	760-3196
Bestway Tours & Safaris 8678 Greenall Ave Suite 206 *TF:* 800-663-0844 ■ *Web:* www.bestway.com	Burnaby	BC	V5J3M6	604-264-7378	264-7774
Big Five Tours & Expeditions 1551 SE Palm Ct *TF:* 800-244-3483 ■ *Web:* www.bigfive.com	Stuart	FL	34994	772-287-7995	287-5990
Big Red Balloon Sightseeing Adventures 8710 W Hillsborough Ave Suite 189 *Web:* www.bigredballoon.com	Tampa	FL	33615	813-969-1518	886-5538
Bigfoot Adventure Tours Inc 360 Edworthy Way Suite 104 *TF:* 888-244-6673 ■ *Web:* www.bigfoottours.com	New Westminster	BC	V3L5T8	604-777-9905	777-9906
Blue Grass Tours Inc 817 Enterprise Dr. *TF:* 800-755-6956 ■ *Web:* www.bluegrasstours.com	Lexington	KY	40510	859-233-2152	255-4748
Bombard Society Inc 333 Pershing Way *TF:* 800-862-8537 ■ *Web:* www.buddybombard.com	West Palm Beach	FL	33401	561-837-6610	837-6623
Bonaventure Tours 8 Boudreau Ln *TF:* 800-561-1213 ■ *Web:* www.aboutbonaventuretours.com	Haute-Aboujagane	NB	E4P5N1	506-532-3674	532-6487
Borderland Tours 2550 W Calle Padilla. *TF:* 800-525-7753 ■ *Web:* www.borderland-tours.com	Tucson	AZ	85745	520-882-7650	792-9205
Branson Vacation Tours 1972 SR 165 Suite J. *Web:* www.bvtamerica.com	Branson	MO	65616	417-336-6122	336-6126
Breakaway Tours 10 Kingsbridge Garden Cir Suite 400 *TF:* 800-465-4257 ■ *Web:* www.breakawaytours.com	Mississauga	ON	L5R3K6	905-501-9774	501-9979
Brendan Worldwide Vacations 21625 Prairie St *TF:* 800-421-8446 ■ *Web:* www.brendanvacations.com	Chatsworth	CA	91311	818-428-6000	772-6492
Brennan Vacations 5301 S Federal Cir. *TF:* 800-237-7249 ■ *Web:* www.brennanvacations.com	Littleton	CO	80123	303-703-7549	703-7601
Brewster Rocky Mountain Adventures 208 Caribou St *TF:* 800-691-5085 ■ *Web:* www.brewsteradventures.com	Banff	AB	T1L1A9	403-762-5454	762-2970
Brewster Transport Co Ltd 100 Gopher St PO Box 1140 *TF:* 800-661-1152 ■ *Web:* www.brewster.ca	Banff	AB	T1L1J3	403-762-6700	762-6750
Brown Tours 50 Venner Rd *TF:* 800-424-4700 ■ *Web:* www.browntours.com	Amsterdam	NY	12010	518-843-4700	843-3600
Burke International Tours Inc DBA Christian Tours Inc PO Box 890 *TF:* 800-476-3900 ■ *Web:* www.burkechristiantours.com	Newton	NC	28658	828-465-3900	465-3912
Butterfield & Robinson 70 Bond St Suite 300 *TF:* 800-678-1147 ■ *Web:* www.butterfield.com	Toronto	ON	M5B1X3	416-864-1354	864-0541
California Parlor Car Tours 1255 Post St Suite 1011 *TF:* 800-227-4250 ■ *Web:* www.calpartours.com	San Francisco	CA	94109	415-474-7500	673-1539
CampAlaska Tours PO Box 872247 *TF:* 800-376-9438 ■ *Web:* www.campalaska.com	Wasilla	AK	99687	907-376-9438	376-2353
CEA (Cultural Experiences Abroad Inc) 1400 E Southern Ave Suite B-108 *TF:* 800-266-4441 ■ *Web:* www.gowithcea.com	Tempe	AZ	85282	480-557-7900	557-7926
Centennial Travelers 1532 E Mulberry St Suite G *TF:* 800-223-0675 ■ *Web:* www.centennialtravel.com	Fort Collins	CO	80524	970-484-4988	484-0022
Chicago Supernatural Tours PO Box 557544 *Web:* www.ghosttours.com	Chicago	IL	60655	708-499-0300	
Christian Tours Inc PO Box 890 *TF:* 800-476-3900 ■ *Web:* www.burkechristiantours.com	Newton	NC	28658	828-465-3900	465-3912
Churchill Nature Tours PO Box 429 *Web:* www.churchillnaturetours.com	Erickson	MB	R0J0P0	204-636-2968	636-2557
Classic Student Tours 7026 Corporate Way Suite 116 *TF:* 800-860-0246	Dayton	OH	45459	937-439-0032	439-0041
Club Europa 802 W Oregon St *TF:* 800-331-1882 ■ *Web:* clubeuropatravel.com	Urbana	IL	61801	217-344-5863	344-4072
Coach Tours Ltd 475 Federal Rd. *TF:* 800-822-6224 ■ *Web:* www.coachtour.com	Brookfield	CT	06804	203-740-1118	775-6851
Coach USA Inc 160 S Rt 17 N **Fax:* Sales ■ *TF:* 800-877-1888 ■ *Web:* www.coachusa.com	Paramus	NJ	07652	201-225-7500	225-7502*
Collette Travel Service Inc 162 Middle St. *TF:* 800-832-4656 ■ *Web:* www.collettevacations.com	Pawtucket	RI	02860	401-728-3805	728-1380
Columbia Rafting Adventures Ltd 4985 Hot Springs Rd Unit 2 *TF:* 877-706-7238 ■ *Web:* www.columbiarafting.com	Fairmont Hot Springs	BC	V0B1L2	250-345-4550	345-6155
Columbia River Safaris PO Box 2292 *TF:* 866-344-4931 ■ *Web:* www.columbiariversafaris.ca	Golden	BC	V0A1H0	250-344-4931	344-6140
Contemporary Tours 1400 Old Country Rd Suite 100 *TF:* 800-627-8873 ■ *Web:* www.contemporarytours.com	Westbury	NY	11590	516-484-5032	
Contiki Holidays 801 E Katella Ave 3rd Fl *TF:* 888-266-8454 ■ *Web:* www.contiki.com	Anaheim	CA	92805	714-935-0808	935-2579
Cox & Kings 25 Davis Blvd *TF:* 800-999-1758 ■ *Web:* www.coxandkingsusa.com	Tampa	FL	33606	813-258-3323	258-3852
Cultural Experiences Abroad Inc (CEA) 1400 E Southern Ave Suite B-108 *TF:* 800-266-4441 ■ *Web:* www.gowithcea.com	Tempe	AZ	85282	480-557-7900	557-7926
Cyr Bus Tours 153 Gilman Falls Ave *TF:* 800-244-2335 ■ *Web:* www.cyrbustours.com/#tours	Old Town	ME	04468	207-827-2335	827-6763
Dash Tours 1024 Winnipeg St. *TF:* 800-265-0000 ■ *Web:* www.dashtours.com	Regina	SK	S4R8P8	306-352-2222	757-4126
Dipert Travel & Transportation Ltd PO Box 580 *TF:* 800-433-5335 ■ *Web:* www.dandipert.com	Arlington	TX	76004	817-543-3710	543-3728
Discovery Charter & Tours 1558 Broughton Blvd *TF:* 888-468-6877 ■ *Web:* www.discoverycharters.bc.ca	Port McNeil	BC	V0N2R0	250-956-3167	956-4285
Earthwatch Institute 3 Clock Tower Pl Suite 100 PO Box 75 *TF:* 800-776-0188 ■ *Web:* www.earthwatch.org	Maynard	MA	01754	978-461-0081	461-2332
Educational Tours 1123 Sterling Rd. *TF:* 800-343-9003 ■ *Web:* www.edtours-us.com	Inverness	FL	34450	352-344-3589	344-0067
Educational Tours Inc PO Box 828. *TF:* 800-962-0060 ■ *Web:* www.et-educationaltours.com	Northbrook	IL	60065	847-509-0088	509-0011
Educational Travel Consultants PO Box 1580 *TF:* 800-247-7969 ■ *Web:* www.educationaltravelconsultants.com	Hendersonville	NC	28793	828-693-0412	692-1591
Educational Travel Tours Inc PO Box 9028 *TF:* 800-959-9833 ■ *Web:* www.educationaltraveltours.com	Trenton	NJ	08650	609-587-1550	587-1550
EF Tours 1 Education St *TF:* 800-872-8439 ■ *Web:* www.eftours.com	Cambridge	MA	02141	617-619-1000	619-1901
Especially 4-U Tours & Travel 7165 E University Dr Suite 15 Sun Valley Office Park *TF:* 800-331-4968 ■ *Web:* www.especially4utours.com	Mesa	AZ	85207	480-985-4200	355-4128
Esplanade Tours 160 Commonwealth Ave Suite L3 *TF:* 800-426-5492 ■ *Web:* www.esplanadetours.com	Boston	MA	02116	617-266-7465	262-9829
Explorica Inc 145 Tremont St. *Web:* www.explorica.com	Boston	MA	02111	888-310-7120	310-7088
Fantastic Tours & Travel 6143 Jericho Tpke *TF:* 800-552-6262 ■ *Web:* www.fantastictours.com	Commack	NY	11725	631-462-6262	462-2311
Flack Tours PO Box 725 *TF:* 800-842-9747	Waddington	NY	13694	315-393-7160	388-4207
Friendly Excursions Inc PO Box 69	Sunland	CA	91041	818-353-7726	353-3903
Frontier Tours Inc 1923 N Carson St Suite 105 *TF:* 800-648-0912 ■ *Web:* www.frontiertours.com	Carson City	NV	89701	775-882-2100	882-0208
Frontiers International Travel PO Box 959 *TF:* 800-245-1950 ■ *Web:* www.frontierstravel.com	Wexford	PA	15090	724-935-1577	935-5388
Gadabout Tours Inc 700 E Tahquitz Canyon Way *TF:* 800-952-5068 ■ *Web:* www.gadabouttours.com	Palm Springs	CA	92262	760-325-5556	325-5127
GAP Adventures 19 Charlotte St *TF:* 800-465-5600 ■ *Web:* www.gapadventures.com	Toronto	ON	M5V2H5	416-260-0999	260-1888
General Tours 53 Summer St *TF:* 800-221-2216 ■ *Web:* www.generaltours.com	Keene	NH	03431	603-357-5033	357-4548
Geographic Expeditions 1008 Gen Kennedy Ave PO Box 29902 *TF:* 800-777-8183 ■ *Web:* www.geoex.com	San Francisco	CA	94129	415-922-0448	346-5535
Gerber Tours Inc 1400 Old Country Rd Suite 100 *TF:* 800-645-9145 ■ *Web:* www.gerbertours.com	Westbury	NY	11590	516-826-5000	826-5044
Global Educational Tours 3510 S Keystone Ave Suite B *TF:* 888-508-6877 ■ *Web:* www.globaledtours.com	Indianapolis	IN	46227	317-787-2787	787-2765
GlobalQuest Journeys Ltd 185 Willis Ave 2nd Fl *TF:* 800-221-3254 ■ *Web:* www.globalquesttravel.com	Mineola	NY	11501	516-739-3690	739-8022
Globus Cosmos & Monograms 5301 S Federal Cir. *TF:* 800-221-0090 ■ *Web:* www.globusjourneys.com	Littleton	CO	80123	303-797-2800	798-5441
Globus DBA Globus Cosmos & Monograms 5301 S Federal Cir. *TF:* 800-221-0090 ■ *Web:* www.globusjourneys.com	Littleton	CO	80123	303-797-2800	798-5441
Go Ahead Tours 1 Education St *TF:* 800-242-4686 ■ *Web:* www.goaheadtours.com	Cambridge	MA	02141	617-619-1000	619-1901

				Phone	Fax
Go Next 8000 W 78th St Suite 345	Minneapolis	MN	55439	952-918-8950	918-8975
TF: 800-842-9023 ■ *Web:* www.gonext.com					
Go West Adventures Inc PO Box 882319	Los Angeles	CA	90009	310-216-2522	216-2638
Web: www.gowestadventures.com					
Go Wild Tours	Ainsworth Hot Springs	BC	V0G1A0	250-229-5374	
Web: www.gowildtours.com					
Go...With Jo! Tours & Travel Inc 910 Dixieland Rd	Harlingen	TX	78552	956-423-1446	421-5787
TF: 800-999-1446 ■ *Web:* www.gowithjo.com					
Golden Age Festival Travel 5501 New Jersey Ave	Wildwood Crest	NJ	08260	609-522-6316	729-8606
TF: 800-257-8920 ■ *Web:* www.festiveholidays.com					
Good Time Tours 455 Corday St	Pensacola	FL	32503	850-476-0046	476-7637
TF: 800-446-0886 ■ *Web:* www.goodtimetours.com					
Good Times Travel Inc 17132 Magnolia St	Fountain Valley	CA	92708	714-848-1255	848-2855
TF: 888-488-2287 ■ *Web:* www.goodtimestravel.com					
Grand European Tours 6000 Meadows Rd Suite 520	Lake Oswego	OR	97035	503-718-2262	718-5198
TF: 800-552-5545 ■ *Web:* www.getours.com					
Grand Expeditions 4800 N Federal Hwy Suite 307-D	Boca Raton	FL	33431	561-347-7654	
Web: www.grandex.com					
Gray Line Worldwide 1835 Gaylord St	Denver	CO	80206	303-394-6920	394-6950
Web: www.grayline.com					
Green Tortoise Adventure Travel 494 Broadway	San Francisco	CA	94133	415-956-7500	956-4900
TF: 800-867-8647 ■ *Web:* www.greentortoise.com					
Greene Coach Charters & Tours Inc 126 Bohannon Ave	Greeneville	TN	37745	423-638-8271	638-5541
TF: 800-338-5469 ■ *Web:* www.greenecoach.com					
Group Leaders of America Inc 420 E State St PO Box 129	Salem	OH	44460	330-337-1027	337-1118
TF: 800-628-0993 ■ *Web:* www.glamer.com					
Gutsy Women Travel 101 Limekiln Pike	Glenside	PA	19038	215-572-7676	886-2228
TF Resv: 866-464-8879 ■ *Web:* www.gutsywomentravel.com					
Hesselgrave International PO Box 30768	Bellingham	WA	98228	360-734-3570	734-3588
TF: 800-457-5522 ■ *Web:* www.hesselgrave.com					
Historic Tours of America Inc 201 Front St Suite 224	Key West	FL	33040	305-296-3609	292-8902
TF: 800-868-7482 ■ *Web:* www.historictours.com					
Holiday Expeditions 544 East 3900 South	Salt Lake City	UT	84107	801-266-2087	266-1448
TF: 800-624-6323 ■ *Web:* www.holidayexpeditions.com					
Holiday Tours Inc 10367 Randleman Rd	Randleman	NC	27317	336-498-9000	498-2204
TF: 800-733-9011 ■ *Web:* www.holidaytoursinc.com					
Holiday Travel Inc DBA Holiday Vacations 2727 Henry Ave	Eau Claire	WI	54701	715-834-5555	834-8554
TF: 800-826-2266 ■ *Web:* www.holidayvacation.com					
Holiday Vacations 2727 Henry Ave	Eau Claire	WI	54701	715-834-5555	834-8554
TF: 800-826-2266 ■ *Web:* www.holidayvacation.com					
Insight Vacations Inc 801 Katella Ave	Anaheim	CA	92805	800-582-8380	937-4910*
*Fax Area Code: 714 ■ *Web:* www.insightvacations.com/us					
International Expeditions Inc 1 Environs Pk	Helena	AL	35080	205-428-1700	428-1714
TF: 800-633-4734 ■ *Web:* www.internationalexpeditions.com					
International Student Tours 999 W Broadway Ave Suite 720	Vancouver	BC	V5Z1K5	604-714-1244	738-4080
TF: 888-472-3933 ■ *Web:* www.istours.com					
Intrav Inc 11969 Westline Industrial Dr	Saint Louis	MO	63146	314-655-6700	655-6670
TF: 800-825-2900 ■ *Web:* www.intrav.com					
Isram World of Travel 233 Park Ave S 10th Fl	New York	NY	10003	212-661-1193	370-1477
TF: 800-223-7460 ■ *Web:* www.isram.com					
ISTours 999 W Broadway Ave Suite 720	Vancouver	BC	V5Z1K5	604-714-1244	738-4080
TF: 888-472-3933 ■ *Web:* www.istours.com					
JALPAK International Hawaii Inc					
2270 Kalakaua Ave Suite 1600	Honolulu	HI	96815	808-926-4500	924-6797
Janssen's Charters & Tours 1623 Woods Rd E	Port Orchard	WA	98366	360-871-2446	871-0245
TF: 800-922-5044					
Jasmine's China Adventure Tours 6044 Laguna Villa Way	Elk Grove	CA	95758	916-683-1790	683-1790
Web: www.jasminechina.com					
Julian Tours 1500 N Beauregard St Suite 110	Alexandria	VA	22311	703-379-2300	379-5030
TF: 800-541-7936 ■ *Web:* www.juliantours.com					
Katmai Coastal Bear Tours PO Box 1503	Homer	AK	99603	907-235-8337	
TF: 800-532-8338 ■ *Web:* www.katmaibears.com					
KE Adventure Travel PO Box 8910	Avon	CO	81620	970-949-0606	547-3768*
*Fax Area Code: 303 ■ *TF:* 800-497-9675 ■ *Web:* www.keadventure.com					
Ker & Downey Inc 6703 Highway Blvd	Katy	TX	77494	281-371-2500	371-2514
TF: 800-423-4236 ■ *Web:* www.kerdowney.com					
Kincaid Coach Lines Inc 9207 Woodend Rd	Edwardsville	KS	66111	913-441-6200	441-0068
TF: 800-998-1901 ■ *Web:* www.kincaidcoach.com					
Knight Inlet Grizzly Bear Adventure Tours					
8841 Driftwood Rd	Black Creek	BC	V9J1A8	250-337-1953	337-1914
Web: www.grizzlytours.com					
Kootenay River Runners PO Box 81	Edgewater	BC	V0A1E0	250-347-9210	347-6595
TF: 800-599-4399 ■ *Web:* www.raftingtherockies.com					
Lamers Tour & Travel 1126 W Boden Ct	Milwaukee	WI	53221	414-281-2002	281-9826
TF: 800-236-8687 ■ *Web:* www.lamerstour.com					
Landmark Tours Inc 164 Demar Ave	Saint Paul	MN	55126	651-490-5408	490-1454
Lindblad Expeditions 96 Morton St 9th Fl	New York	NY	10014	212-765-7740	265-3770
TF: 800-397-3348 ■ *Web:* www.expeditions.com					
M & M Tours Inc 17 Spaulding Ln	Saugerties	NY	12477	845-246-3196	246-4450
Macy's Travel 700 Nicollet Mall	Minneapolis	MN	55402	612-375-2884	375-3830
TF: 800-316-6166 ■ *Web:* www.macystravel.com					
Magic Bus Co 520 Lakeshore Blvd E	Toronto	ON	M5A1C3	416-516-7433	516-6774
TF: 877-371-8747 ■ *Web:* www.magicbuscompany.com					
Martz Group 239 Old River Rd	Wilkes-Barre	PA	18702	570-821-3838	821-3835
TF: 800-334-9608 ■ *Web:* www.martzgroup.com					
Martz Tours 239 Old River Rd	Wilkes-Barre	PA	18702	570-821-3849	821-3811
TF: 800-432-8069 ■ *Web:* www.martztours.com					
Maupintour Inc 2688 S Rainbow Suite D	Las Vegas	NV	89146	702-260-3600	
TF: 800-255-4266 ■ *Web:* www.maupintour.com					
Mayflower Tours Inc 1225 Warren Ave PO Box 490	Downers Grove	IL	60515	630-435-8500	960-3575
TF: 800-323-7604 ■ *Web:* www.mayflowertours.com					
McKinzie Tours Inc 7835 W 151st St PO Box 23559	Overland Park	KS	66283	913-681-2202	681-2685
Web: www.mckinzietours.com					
Meline's Lodge and Guide Service PO Box 82	Nestor Falls	ON	P0X1K0	807-484-2483	
TF: 800-561-3166 ■ *Web:* www.canadafishingtrips.com					
Micato Safaris 15 W 26th St 11th Fl	New York	NY	10010	212-545-7111	545-8297
TF: 800-642-2861 ■ *Web:* www.micato.com					
Mid-American Coaches Inc PO Box 1609	Washington	MO	63090	636-239-4700	239-9542
TF: 866-316-9508 ■ *Web:* www.mid-americancoaches.com					
Midnight Sun Adventure Travel 1845-B Fort St	Victoria	BC	V8R1J6	250-480-9409	483-7422
TF: 800-255-5057 ■ *Web:* www.midnightsuntravel.com					
Monograms 5301 S Federal Cir	Littleton	CO	80123	303-797-2800	798-5441
TF: 866-270-9841 ■ *Web:* www.monogramstravel.com					
Montana River Outfitters 923 10th Ave N	Great Falls	MT	59401	406-761-1677	452-3833
TF: 800-800-8218 ■ *Web:* www.montanariveroutfitters.com					
Mount Saint Helens Tours Inc PO Box 350	Toutle	WA	98649	360-274-7007	
Web: www.ecoparkresort.com/tours.htm					
Mountain Travel Sobek 1266 66th St Suite 4	Emeryville	CA	94608	510-594-6000	594-6001
TF: 888-687-6235 ■ *Web:* www.mtsobek.com					
Musiker Discovery Programs Inc 1326 Old Northern Blvd	Roslyn	NY	11576	516-621-3939	625-3438
TF: 888-878-6637 ■ *Web:* www.summerfun.com					
Natural Habitat Adventures 2945 Center Green Ct	Boulder	CO	80301	303-449-3711	449-3712
TF: 800-543-8917 ■ *Web:* www.nathab.com					
New Horizons Tour & Travel Inc 2727 Spring Arbor Rd	Jackson	MI	49203	517-788-6822	788-6847
TF: 800-327-4695 ■ *Web:* www.nhtt.com					
New York Tours 1414 Grand St	Hoboken	NJ	07030	800-735-8530	653-5498*
*Fax Area Code: 201 ■ *Web:* www.newyorktoursnyc.com					

				Phone	Fax
Nichols Five Star Charters & Tours PO Box 709	Fond du Lac	WI	54936	920-929-8030	929-8039
Northern Light Balloon Expeditions PO Box 1695	Sedona	AZ	86339	928-282-2274	282-6173
TF: 800-230-6222					
Northern Tours 2740 Bauer St	Eau Claire	WI	54701	715-834-1463	834-8222
TF: 800-735-8687 ■ *Web:* www.gonortherntours.com					
Off the Beaten Path 7 E Beall St	Bozeman	MT	59715	406-586-1311	587-4147
TF: 800-445-2995 ■ *Web:* www.offthebeatenpath.com					
Old West Tours 3432 Limestone Dr	Rosamond	CA	93560	661-256-4091	256-6512
TF: 800-868-7777					
Olivia Cruises & Resorts 434 Brannan St	San Francisco	CA	94107	415-962-5700	962-5710
TF: 800-631-6277 ■ *Web:* www.olivia.com					
On Tour 201 Cortsen Rd	Pleasant Hill	CA	94523	925-930-9135	945-8931
Web: www.ontourca.com					
Onondaga Coach Corp PO Box 277	Auburn	NY	13021	315-255-2216	255-0925
TF: 800-451-1570 ■ *Web:* www.onondagacoach.com					
Orange Belt Stages 2134 E Mineral King Ave	Visalia	CA	93292	559-733-4408	733-0538
TF: 800-266-7433 ■ *Web:* www.orangebelt.com					
Overseas Adventure Travel 347 Congress St	Boston	MA	02210	800-221-0814	346-6700*
*Fax Area Code: 617 ■ *Web:* www.oattravel.com					
Pacific Delight Tours Inc 3 Park Ave 38th Fl	New York	NY	10016	212-818-1781	818-1743
TF: 800-221-7179 ■ *Web:* www.pacificdelighttours.com					
Panorama Balloon Tours	Del Mar	CA	92014	760-271-3467	
TF: 800-455-3592 ■ *Web:* www.gohotair.com					
Paragon Tours 21 Father DeValles Blvd Suite 204	Fall River	MA	02723	508-379-1976	379-1979
TF: 800-999-5050 ■ *Web:* www.paragontours.com					
ParkEast Tours 1 Environs Park	Helena	AL	35080	205-428-1700	428-1714
TF: 800-223-6078 ■ *Web:* www.parkeast.com					
People to People Ambassador Programs Inc 110 S Ferrall St	Spokane	WA	99202	509-534-6200	534-5245
NASDAQ: EPAX ■ *TF:* 800-669-7882 ■ *Web:* www.ambassadorsgroup.com					
Perillo Tours 577 Chestnut Ridge Rd	Woodcliff Lake	NJ	07677	201-307-1234	307-1808
TF: 800-431-1515 ■ *Web:* www.perillotours.com					
Pilgrim Tours & Travel Inc 3821 Main St PO Box 268	Morgantown	PA	19543	610-286-0788	286-6262
TF: 800-322-0788 ■ *Web:* www.pilgrimtours.com					
Pitmar Tours 7549 140th St Suite 9	Surrey	BC	V3W5J9	604-531-3442	596-3444
Web: www.pitmartours.com					
PML Travel & Tours 750 Rt 73 S Suite 204	Marlton	NJ	08053	856-983-1866	983-8434
TF: 800-872-4868 ■ *Web:* www.pmltours.com					
Polynesian Adventure Tours Inc 1049 Kikowaena Pl	Honolulu	HI	96819	808-833-3000	836-0692
TF: 800-622-3011 ■ *Web:* www.polyad.com					
Premier Tours 1430 Walnut St 2nd Fl	Philadelphia	PA	19102	215-893-9966	893-0357
TF: 800-545-1910 ■ *Web:* www.premiertours.com					
Presley Tours Inc 16 Presley Park Dr PO Box 58	Makanda	IL	62958	618-549-0704	549-0404
TF: 800-621-6100 ■ *Web:* www.presleytours.com					
Princess Tours 2815 2nd Ave Suite 400	Seattle	WA	98121	206-336-6000	336-6100
TF: 800-426-0442 ■ *Web:* www.princess.com					
Rail Europe Group 44 S Broadway 11th Fl	White Plains	NY	10601	914-682-2999	681-3287*
*Fax: Sales ■ *TF:* 800-848-7245 ■ *Web:* www.raileurope.com					
Raz Transportation 11655 SW Pacific Hwy	Portland	OR	97223	503-684-3322	968-3223
TF: 888-684-3322 ■ *Web:* www.raztrans.com					
Red Sail Sports Inc 1 Ferry Bldg Suite 255	San Francisco	CA	94111	415-981-4411	981-6203
TF: 877-733-7245 ■ *Web:* www.redsail.com					
REI Adventures PO Box 1938	Sumner	WA	98390	253-437-1100	395-8160
TF: 800-622-2236 ■ *Web:* www.rei.com/adventures					
Richmond Tours 1828 Hylan Blvd	Staten Island	NY	10305	718-979-3111	979-7143
TF: 800-766-3868 ■ *Web:* www.richmond-tours.com					
Rivers Oceans & Mountains Adventures Inc (ROAM)					
7025 Beggs Rd	Nelson	BC	V1L5P6	250-229-2115	229-2119
TF: 877-271-7626 ■ *Web:* www.iroamtheworld.com					
Roberts Hawaii Inc 680 Iwilei Rd Dole Office Bldg Suite 700	Honolulu	HI	96817	808-523-7750	522-7872
TF: 800-831-5541 ■ *Web:* www.robertshawaii.com					
Royal Coach Tours 630 Stockton Ave	San Jose	CA	95126	408-279-4801	286-1410
TF: 800-927-6925 ■ *Web:* www.royal-coach.com					
Royal Tours Inc PO Box 998	Randleman	NC	27317	336-629-9080	629-9011
TF: 800-997-6925 ■ *Web:* www.royaltours.org					
RSVP Vacations 2535 25th Ave S	Minneapolis	MN	55406	612-729-1113	729-2809
TF: 800-328-7787 ■ *Web:* www.rsvpvacations.com					
Sanborn Tours Inc 2015 S 10th St	McAllen	TX	78503	956-682-9872	682-0016
TF: 800-395-8482 ■ *Web:* www.sanborns.com					
Scenic Airlines Inc 2705 Airport Dr	North Las Vegas	NV	89032	702-638-3300	638-3275
TF: 800-634-6801 ■ *Web:* www.scenicairlines.com					
Scholastic Tours Inc 3841 Nostrand Ave	Brooklyn	NY	11235	718-934-9400	891-8681
TF: 800-221-6209					
Senior Tours Canada Inc 225 Eglinton Ave W	Toronto	ON	M4R1A9	416-322-1529	322-1166
TF: 800-268-3492 ■ *Web:* www.seniortours.ca					
Seniority Adventures PO Box 709	Sugar Land	TX	77487	281-313-6565	277-6565
Seniors Unlimited LLC 53 W Huron St	Pontiac	MI	48342	248-338-1333	338-2637
TF: 800-837-1333					
Shoreline Tours & Travel 1 Main St W Unit 8	Kingsville	ON	N9Y1H2	519-733-6583	733-8052
TF: 800-265-0818 ■ *Web:* www.shorelinetours.com					
Short Hills Tours PO Box 310	Short Hills	NJ	07078	973-467-2113	467-3353
TF: 800-348-6871 ■ *Web:* www.shorthillstours.com					
Silver Fox Tours & Motorcoaches 3 Silver Fox Dr	Millbury	MA	01527	508-865-6000	865-4660
TF: 800-342-5998 ■ *Web:* www.silverfoxcoach.com					
Silverado Stages Inc 241 Prado Rd	San Luis Obispo	CA	93401	805-544-7658	544-7675
TF: 800-781-4699 ■ *Web:* www.silveradotours.com					
Sky High Red Rock Balloon Adventures 105 Canyon Diablo	Sedona	AZ	86351	928-284-0040	284-1760
TF: 800-258-3754 ■ *Web:* www.redrockballoons.com					
Smithsonian Journeys PO Box 23182	Washington	DC	20026	202-357-4700	633-6099
TF: 877-338-8687 ■ *Web:* www.smithsonianjourneys.org					
South of the Border Tours 7937 E Coronado Rd	Tucson	AZ	85750	520-760-4000	760-3999
Web: www.azcoachtours.com					
Southern Coach Co 1300 E Pettigrew St	Durham	NC	27701	919-688-1230	688-5305
TF: 800-222-4793 ■ *Web:* www.southerncoach.com					
Specialty Tours Inc 3095 S Parker Rd Suite 150	Aurora	CO	80014	303-337-7488	337-9257
TF: 800-342-4299 ■ *Web:* www.specialtytours.com					
Sports Leisure Vacations 9521-H Folsom Blvd	Sacramento	CA	95827	916-361-2051	361-7995
TF: 800-951-5556 ■ *Web:* www.sportsleisure.com					
Sports Travel Inc 60 Main St PO Box 50	Hatfield	MA	01038	413-247-7678	247-5700
TF: 800-662-4424 ■ *Web:* www.sportstravelandtours.com					
Storm Chasing Adventure Tours 4775 Deer Cr	Island Park	ID	83429	303-888-8629	
Web: www.stormchasing.com					
Straight A Tours & Travel 6881 Kingspointe Pkwy Suite 18	Orlando	FL	32819	407-896-1242	896-1151
TF: 800-237-5440 ■ *Web:* straightatours.com					
Student Tours Inc 60 West Ave	Vineyard Haven	MA	02568	508-693-5078	693-8627
TF: 800-331-7093 ■ *Web:* www.studenttoursinc.com					
Student Travel Services Inc 1413 Madison Pk Dr	Glen Burnie	MD	21061	410-859-4200	787-9580
TF: 800-648-4849 ■ *Web:* www.ststravel.com					
Sundial Special Vacations Inc 2609 Hwy 101 N Suite 103	Seaside	OR	97138	503-738-3324	738-3369
TF: 800-547-9198 ■ *Web:* www.sundialtour.com					
Sunny Land Tours Inc 166 Main St1 Corporate Dr Suite 1-F	Palm Coast	FL	32127	386-449-0059	449-0060
TF: 800-783-7839 ■ *Web:* www.sunnylandtours.com					
Sunrise Fantasy Flights Inc DBA Big Red Balloon Sightseeing					
Adventures 8710 W Hillsborough Ave Suite 189	Tampa	FL	33615	813-969-1518	886-5538
Web: www.bigredballoon.com					
Suntrek Tours Inc 77 W 3rd St	Santa Rosa	CA	95401	707-523-1800	523-1911
TF: 800-786-8735 ■ *Web:* www.suntrek.com					

Phone Fax

Super Holiday Tours 116 Gatlin Ave .... Orlando FL 32806 407-851-0060 851-0071
TF: 800-327-2116 ■ Web: www.superholiday.com

Tag-A-Long Expeditions 452 N Main St .... Moab UT 84532 435-259-8946 259-8990
TF: 800-453-3292 ■ Web: tagalong.com

Talbot Tours Inc 1952 Camden Ave .... San Jose CA 95124 408-879-0101 879-0183
TF: 800-662-9933 ■ Web: www.talbottours.com

Tauck World Discovery 10 Norden Pl .... Norwalk CT 06855 203-899-6500 899-6612*
*Fax: Hum Res ■ TF: 800-468-2825 ■ Web: www.tauck.com

TCS Expeditions 710 2nd Ave Suite 840 .... Seattle WA 98104 206-727-7300 727-7309
TF: 800-727-7477 ■ Web: www.tcs-expeditions.com

Timberwolf Tours Ltd 51404 RR 264 Suite 34 .... Spruce Grove AB T7Y1E4 780-470-4966 339-3960*
*Fax Area Code: 866 ■ TF: 888-467-9697 ■ Web: www.timberwolftours.com

Toto Tours Ltd 1326 W Albion Ave .... Chicago IL 60626 773-274-8686 274-8695
TF: 800-565-1241 ■ Web: www.tototours.com

Tourco Inc 16 E Pond Rd .... Nobleboro ME 04555 207-563-2288 563-3335
TF: 800-537-5378 ■ Web: www.tourco.com

Trafalgar Tours 801 E Katella Ave .... Anaheim CA 92805 714-937-4900 935-2579
TF: 866-544-4434 ■ Web: www.trafalgartours.com

Trans-Bridge Tours 1155 MacArthur Rd .... Whitehall PA 18052 610-776-8687
TF: 800-962-9135 ■ Web: www.transbridgebus.com/transb.htm

Transat AT Inc 5959 Cote Vertu .... Montreal QC H4S2E6 514-906-0330 906-5131
TSX: TRZ ■ TF: 877-470-1011 ■ Web: www.transat.com

Travcoa 4340 Von Karman Ave Suite 400 .... Newport Beach CA 92660 949-476-2800 476-2538
TF: 800-992-2003 ■ Web: www.travcoa.com

Travel Adventures Inc 1175 S Lapeer Rd .... Lapeer MI 48446 810-664-1777 664-1913
TF: 800-356-2737 ■ Web: www.traveladventures.com

Travel Mates of Virginia Inc PO Box 2 .... Harrisonburg VA 22803 540-434-4155 434-8724
TF: 888-262-4863 ■ Web: www.tmates.com

Travel Tours Inc 2111 W Hwy 51 PO Box 40 .... Wagoner OK 74477 918-485-4595 485-8216
TF: 800-331-3192 ■ Web: www.traveltoursinc.com

TravelQuest International 305 Double D Dr .... Prescott AZ 86303 928-445-7754
TF: 800-830-1998 ■ Web: www.tq-international.com

TrekAmerica PO Box 189 .... Rockaway NJ 07866 973-983-1144 983-8551
TF: 800-221-0596 ■ Web: www.trekamerica.com

Tri-State Travel Inc PO Box 307 .... Galena IL 61036 815-777-0820 777-8128
TF: 800-779-4869 ■ Web: www.tristatetravel.com

Tumlare Corp 2128 Bellmore Ave .... Bellmore NY 11710 516-781-0322 781-0896
TF: 800-223-4664 ■ Web: www.tumlare.com

Upstate Tours & Travel 207 Geyser Rd .... Saratoga Springs NY 12866 518-584-5252 584-1092
TF: 800-237-5252 ■ Web: www.upstatetours.com

USA Student Travel 5080 Robert J Mathews Pkwy .... El Dorado Hills CA 95762 916-939-6805 939-6806
TF: 800-448-4444 ■ Web: www.usastudenttravel.com

VBT Bicycle Vacations 614 Monkton Rd .... Bristol VT 05443 802-453-4811 453-4806
TF: 800-245-3868 ■ Web: www.vbt.com

VentureOut 575 Pierce St Suite 604 .... San Francisco CA 94117 415-626-5678 626-5679
TF: 888-431-6789 ■ Web: www.venture-out.com

VIP Tour & Charter Bus Co 129-137 Fox St .... Portland ME 04101 207-772-4457 772-7020
TF: 800-337-4457 ■ Web: www.vipchartercoaches.com

Visit America Inc 330 7th Ave 20th Fl .... New York NY 10001 212-683-8082 683-8501
Web: www.visitamerica.com

Wade Tours Inc 797 Burdeck St .... Schenectady NY 12306 518-355-4500 355-4942
TF: 800-955-9233 ■ Web: www.wadetours.com

Walking Adventures International PO Box 871000 .... Vancouver WA 98687 360-260-9393 260-1131
TF: 800-779-0353 ■ Web: www.walkingadventures.com

West Coast Connection 318 Indian Trace Suite 336 .... Weston FL 33326 954-888-9780 888-9781
TF: 800-767-0227 ■ Web: www.westcoastconnection.com

Western Discovery International 507 Casazza Dr Suite C .... Reno NV 89502 775-329-9933 329-1045
TF: 800-843-5061 ■ Web: www.westerndiscovery.com

Westwego Swamp Adventures 501 Laroussini St .... Westwego LA 70094 504-581-4501 581-1957
TF: 800-633-0503 ■ Web: www.westwegoswampadventures.com

White Mountain Adventures 122 A Eagle Crescent PO Box 4259 .... Banff AB T1L1E6 403-760-4403 760-4409
TF: 800-408-0005 ■ Web: www.whitemountainadventures.com

White Star Tours 26 E Lancaster Ave .... Reading PA 19607 610-775-5000 775-7155
TF: 800-437-2323 ■ Web: www.whitestartours.com

Wilderness Travel 1102 9th St .... Berkeley CA 94710 510-558-2488 558-2489
TF: 800-368-2794 ■ Web: www.wildernesstravel.com

Wings Tours Inc 11350 McCormick Rd Suite 703 .... Hunt Valley MD 21031 410-771-0925 771-0928
TF: 800-869-4647 ■ Web: www.wingsegypt.com

Wisconsin Coach Lines Inc 1520 Arcadian Ave .... Waukesha WI 53186 262-542-8861 542-2036
TF: 877-324-7767 ■ Web: www.wisconsincoach.com

WorldPass Travel Group LLC
5080 Robert J Matthews Pkwy .... El Dorado Hills CA 95838 916-939-6805 939-6806
TF: 888-877-4445 ■ Web: www.goworldpass.com

WorldStrides 590 Peter Jefferson Pkwy Suite 300 .... Charlottesville VA 22911 434-982-8600 982-8748
TF: 800-468-5899 ■ Web: www.worldstrides.com

764 TOY STORES

Phone Fax

A2Z Science & Nature Store 57 King St .... Northampton MA 01060 413-586-1611 584-7253
TF: 877-261-6171 ■ Web: www.a-two-z.com

Build-A-Bear Workshop Inc
1954 Innerbelt Business Center Dr .... Saint Louis MO 63114 314-423-8000 423-8188
NYSE: BBW ■ TF: 888-560-2327 ■ Web: www.buildabear.com

Creative Kid Stuff 4313 Upton Ave S .... Minneapolis MN 55410 612-929-2431 929-6770
TF Orders: 800-353-0710 ■ Web: www.creativekidstuff.com

Discount School Supplies 2 Lower Ragsdale Rd Suite 200 .... Monterey CA 93940 831-333-2000 333-3610
TF: 800-293-9314 ■ Web: www.smarterkids.com

Electronics Boutique Holdings Corp 931 S Matlack St .... West Chester PA 19382 610-430-8100 430-6574
Web: www.ebworld.com

FAO Schwarz 875 Avenue of the Americas 20th Fl .... New York NY 10001 800-426-8697 276-0170
Web: www.fao.com

Galt Toys 900 N Michigan Ave .... Chicago IL 60611 312-440-9550 440-9258
Web: galttoysgaltbaby.com

Hobbytown USA 6301 S 58th St .... Lincoln NE 68516 402-434-5385
TF: 800-869-0424 ■ Web: www.hobbytown.com

HobbyTron.com 1053 S 1675 W .... Orem UT 84058 801-434-7664 437-1714
TF: 800-494-1778 ■ Web: www.hobbytron.com

KB Toys 100 West St .... Pittsfield MA 01201 413-496-3000 496-3630*
*Fax: Cust Svc ■ Web: www.kbtoys.com

Learning Express Inc 29 Buena Vista St .... Devens MA 01434 978-889-1000 889-1010
TF: 800-924-2296 ■ Web: www.learningexpress.com

Pun's Toy Shop 839 1/2 Lancaster Ave .... Bryn Mawr PA 19010 610-525-9789 527-5514

Right Start Inc 23622 Calabasas Rd Suite 339 .... Calabasas CA 91302 818-707-7100
Web: www.rightstart.com

Toys 'R' Us Inc 1 Geoffrey Way .... Wayne NJ 07470 973-617-3500 617-4006
TF: 800-869-7787 ■ Web: www.toysrus.com

765 TOYS, GAMES, HOBBIES

SEE ALSO Baby Products p. 1366; Bicycles & Bicycle Parts & Accessories p. 1380; Computer Software - Games & Entertainment Software p. 1512

Phone Fax

Action Products International Inc 1101 N Keller Rd Suite E .... Orlando FL 32810 407-481-8007 481-2781
NASDAQ: APII ■ TF: 800-772-2846 ■ Web: www.apii.com

Airmate Co Inc 16280 County Rd D .... Bryan OH 43506 419-636-3184 636-4210
TF: 800-544-3614 ■ Web: www.airmatecompany.com

Alexander Doll Co Inc DBA Madame Alexander
615 W 131st St .... New York NY 10027 212-283-5900 283-4263
TF: 800-229-5192 ■ Web: www.madamealexander.com

American Girl Inc 8400 Fairway Pl .... Middleton WI 53562 608-836-4848 836-0761
TF Orders: 800-845-0005 ■ Web: www.americangirl.com

American Plastic Toys Inc 799 Ladd Rd .... Walled Lake MI 48390 248-624-4881 624-4918
TF: 800-521-7080 ■ Web: www.americanplastictoys.com

Annalee Mobilitee Dolls Inc 50 Reservoir Rd .... Meredith NH 03253 603-279-6544 279-6659
TF Cust Svc: 800-433-6557 ■ Web: www.annalee.com

Atari Inc 417 5th Ave 8th Fl .... New York NY 10016 212-726-6500 252-8603
NASDAQ: ATAR ■ TF: 800-898-1438 ■ Web: www.atari.com

Atlas Model Railroad Co Inc 378 Florence Ave .... Hillside NJ 07205 908-687-0880 687-8857
TF Orders: 800-872-2521 ■ Web: www.atlasrr.com

Baby Einstein Co LLC 500 S Buena Vista St .... Burbank CA 91521 800-793-1454 549-2060*
*Fax Area Code: 818 ■ Web: www.babyeinstein.com

Bachmann Industries Inc 1400 E Erie Ave .... Philadelphia PA 19124 215-533-1600 744-4699
TF Cust Svc: 800-356-3910 ■ Web: www.bachmanntrains.com

Ball Bounce and Sport Inc/Hedstrom Plastics
1401 Jacobson Ave .... Ashland OH 44805 419-289-9310 281-3371*
*Fax: Sales ■ TF: 800-765-9665 ■ Web: www.hedstrom.com

Binney & Smith Inc 1100 Church Ln .... Easton PA 18044 610-253-6271 250-5768
TF: 800-272-9652 ■ Web: www.binney-smith.com

Bravo Sports Corp 12801 Carmenita Rd .... Santa Fe Springs CA 90670 562-484-5100 484-5183
TF Cust Svc: 800-234-9737 ■ Web: www.bravosportscorp.com

Cardinal Industries Inc 21-01 51st Ave .... Long Island City NY 11101 718-784-3000 482-7877
Web: www.cardinalgames.com

Charles Craft Inc 21381 Charles Craft Ln PO Box 1049 .... Laurinburg NC 28352 910-844-3521 844-9846
TF: 800-277-1009 ■ Web: www.charlescraft.com

Commonwealth Toy & Novelty Co 45 W 25th St 5th Fl .... New York NY 10010 212-242-4070 645-4279

Community Products LLC DBA Community Playthings
359 Gibson Hill Rd .... Chester NY 10918 845-572-3410 336-5948*
*Fax Area Code: 800 ■ *Fax: Cust Svc ■ TF: 800-777-4244 ■
Web: www.communityplaythings.com

Creativity for Kids 9450 Allen Dr .... Cleveland OH 44125 216-643-4660 643-4663
TF: 800-311-8684 ■ Web: www.creativityforkids.com

Crisloid Inc 55 Porter St .... Providence RI 02905 401-461-7200 785-3750

Daisy Outdoor Products 400 W Stribling Dr .... Rogers AR 72756 479-636-1200 636-1601
TF: 800-643-3458 ■ Web: www.daisy.com

Dimensions Inc 1801 N 12th St .... Reading PA 19604 610-939-9900 939-9666
TF: 800-523-8452 ■ Web: www.dimensions-crafts.com

Douglas Cuddle Toys Co Inc 69 Krif Rd PO Box D .... Keene NH 03431 603-352-3414 352-1248
TF: 800-992-9002 ■ Web: www.douglascuddletoy.com

Effanbee Doll Co 459 Hurley Ave .... Hurley NY 12443 845-339-8246 339-8326
TF: 888-362-3655 ■ Web: www.effanbeedoll.com

Electronic Arts Inc (EA) 209 Redwood Shores Pkwy .... Redwood City CA 94065 650-628-1500 628-1414
NASDAQ: ERTS ■ TF Sales: 877-324-2637 ■ Web: www.ea.com

Erapro/Paris Co Inc 2500 Guenette St .... Saint Laurent QC H4R2H2 514-335-0550 335-0571
TF: 877-372-9273 ■ Web: eragroup.ca

Estes-Cox Corp 1295 H St .... Penrose CO 81240 719-372-6565 372-3419
TF: 800-525-7561 ■ Web: www.estesrockets.com

Fisher-Price Inc 636 Girard Ave .... East Aurora NY 14052 716-687-3000 687-3476
TF: 800-432-5437 ■ Web: www.fisher-price.com

Gayla Industries Inc 6401 Antoine Dr .... Houston TX 77091 713-681-2411 682-1357
TF: 800-231-7508 ■ Web: www.gaylainc.com

Goffa International Corp 930 Flushing Ave .... Brooklyn NY 11206 718-361-8883 361-0506
TF: 800-969-7864 ■ Web: www.goffausa.com

Goldberger Doll Mfg Co Inc 538 Johnson Ave .... Brooklyn NY 11237 718-366-5800 417-5587
TF: 800-452-3655 ■ Web: www.goldbergerdoll.com

Great Planes Model Distributors Co 1608 Interstate Dr .... Champaign IL 61826 217-398-6300 398-1104
TF: 800-637-7660 ■ Web: www.greatplanes.com

Guidecraft USA 66 Grand Ave Suite 207 .... Englewood NJ 07631 201-894-5401 894-5405
TF: 800-544-6526 ■ Web: www.guidecraft.com

Guillow Paul K Inc 40 New Salem St .... Wakefield MA 01880 781-245-5255 245-4738
Web: www.guillow.com

Gund Inc 1 Runyons Ln .... Edison NJ 08817 732-248-1500 248-1968
TF Cust Svc: 800-448-4863 ■ Web: www.gund.com

Hanover Accessories Inc 3500 Holly Ln N Suite 10 .... Plymouth MN 55447 763-509-6100 551-9992
TF: 888-509-6100 ■ Web: www.hanoveraccessories.com

Hasbro Inc 1027 Newport Ave .... Pawtucket RI 02861 401-431-8697 431-8082*
NYSE: HAS ■ *Fax: Cust Svc ■ TF: 800-242-7276 ■ Web: www.hasbro.com

Hasbro Inc Parker Brothers Div 200 Narragansett Park Dr .... Pawtucket RI 02862 888-836-7025 431-8082*
*Fax Area Code: 401 ■ Web: www.hasbro.com/games

Hasbro Inc Playskool Div 1027 Newport Ave .... Pawtucket RI 02861 401-431-8697 431-8082
TF: 800-242-7276 ■ Web: www.playskool.com

Hasbro Inc Tiger Electronics Div 1027 Newport Ave .... Pawtucket RI 02861 401-431-8697 431-8082
TF: 800-844-3733 ■ Web: www.hasbro.com/tigertoys

Imperial Toy Corp 2060 E 7th St .... Los Angeles CA 90021 213-489-2100 489-4467
Web: www.imperialtoy.com

International Playthings Inc 75D Lackawanna Ave .... Parsippany NJ 07054 973-316-2500 316-5883
TF: 800-631-1272 ■ Web: www.intplay.com

JAKKS Pacific Inc 22619 Pacific Coast Hwy Suite 250 .... Malibu CA 90265 310-456-7799 317-8527
NASDAQ: JAKK ■ TF: 877-875-2557 ■ Web: www.jakkspacific.com

Klutz 450 Lambert Ave .... Palo Alto CA 94306 650-857-0888 857-9110
TF: 800-737-4123 ■ Web: klutz.com

K'NEX Industries Inc 2990 Bergey Rd .... Hatfield PA 19440 215-997-7722 996-4225
TF: 800-543-5639 ■ Web: www.brio.net

LeapFrog Enterprises Inc 6401 Hollis St Suite 150 .... Emeryville CA 94608 510-420-5000 420-5001
NYSE: LF ■ TF: 800-701-5327 ■ Web: www.leapfrog.com

Learning Curve International Inc 1111 W 22nd St Suite 320 .... Oak Brook IL 60523 630-573-7200 573-7575
TF: 800-704-8697 ■ Web: www.learningcurve.com

Learning Resources 380 N Fairway Dr .... Vernon Hills IL 60061 847-573-8400 573-8425
TF: 800-222-3909 ■ Web: www.learningresources.com

Lee Middleton Original Dolls Inc
480 Olde Worthington Rd Suite 110 .... Westerville OH 43082 614-901-0604 901-0517
TF: 800-242-3285 ■ Web: www.leemiddleton.com

LEGO Systems Inc 555 Taylor Rd .... Enfield CT 06082 860-749-2291 763-6800
TF: 800-243-4870 ■ Web: www.lego.com

Lionel LLC 26750 23 Mile Rd .... Chesterfield MI 48051 586-949-4100 949-6757*
*Fax: Hum Res ■ TF: 800-454-6635 ■ Web: www.lionel.com

Little Tikes Co 2180 Barlow Rd .... Hudson OH 44236 330-650-3000 650-3877
TF Cust Svc: 800-321-0183 ■ Web: www.littletikes.com

Lovee Doll & Toy Co Inc 200 5th Ave Suite 1210 .... New York NY 10010 212-242-1545 242-4596

Mag-Nif Inc 8820 East Ave .... Mentor OH 44060 440-946-4308 974-0449
TF: 800-869-5463 ■ Web: www.magnif.com

				Phone	Fax
Maple City Rubber Co 55 Newton St TF: 800-841-9434 ■ Web: www.maplecityrubber.com	Norwalk	OH	44857	419-668-8261	668-1275
Marvel Enterprises Inc 417 5th Ave NYSE: MVL ■ TF: 800-217-9158 ■ Web: www.marvel.com	New York	NY	10016	212-576-4000	
Mattel Inc 333 Continental Blvd NYSE: MAT ■ TF Cust Svc: 800-524-8697 ■ Web: www.mattel.com	El Segundo	CA	90245	310-252-2000	252-2180
Mega Brands America Inc 6 Regent St TF: 800-272-9667 ■ Web: www.megabloks.com	Livingston	NJ	07039	973-535-1313	533-9447
Mega Brands Inc 4505 Hickmore TF Cust Svc: 800-465-6342 ■ Web: www.megabloks.com	Montreal	QC	H4T1K4	514-333-5555	333-4470
Midwest Products Co Inc 400 S Indiana St *Fax: Sales ■ TF Orders: 800-348-3497 ■ Web: www.midwestproducts.com	Hobart	IN	46342	219-942-1134	947-2347*
Model Rectifier Corp 80 Newfield Ave Web: www.modelrec.com	Edison	NJ	08837	732-225-2100	225-0091
Newell Rubbermaid Inc Home & Family Group 10B Glenlake Pkwy Suite 300 TF: 800-434-4314 ■ Web: www.newellrubbermaid.com	Atlanta	GA	30328	770-407-3800	407-3970
Nintendo of America Inc 4820 150th Ave NE TF Cust Svc: 800-255-3700 ■ Web: www.nintendo.com	Redmond	WA	98052	425-882-2040	882-3585
Ohio Art Co 1 Toy St TF: 800-641-6226 ■ Web: www.world-of-toys.com	Bryan	OH	43506	419-636-3141	636-7614
Original Appalachian Artworks Inc 1721 Hwy 75 S Web: www.cabbagepatchkids.com	Cleveland	GA	30528	706-865-2171	865-5862
Overbreak LLC 9420 Chivers Ave TF: 888-537-6520 ■ Web: www.overbreak.com	Sun Valley	CA	91352	818-252-3425	252-3892
Parker Brothers Div Hasbro Inc 200 Narragansett Park Dr *Fax Area Code: 401 ■ Web: www.hasbro.com/games	Pawtucket	RI	02862	888-836-7025	431-8082*
Patch Products Inc 1400 E Inman Pkwy TF: 800-524-4263 ■ Web: www.patchproducts.com	Beloit	WI	53511	608-362-6896	362-8178
Paul K Guillow Inc 40 New Salem St Web: www.guillow.com	Wakefield	MA	01880	781-245-5255	245-4738
PDP (Performance Designed Products) 1840 E 27th St TF: 800-331-3844 ■ Web: www.pdp-usa.com	Vernon	CA	90058	323-234-9911	234-9922
Performance Designed Products (PDP) 1840 E 27th St TF: 800-331-3844 ■ Web: www.pdp-usa.com	Vernon	CA	90058	323-234-9911	234-9922
Pioneer National Latex Co 246 E 4th St TF: 800-537-6723 ■ Web: www.pioneernational.com	Ashland	OH	44805	419-289-3300	289-7118
Plaid Enterprises Inc 3225 Westech Dr TF: 800-842-4197 ■ Web: www.plaidonline.com	Norcross	GA	30092	678-291-8100	291-8383
Playmates Toys Inc 611 Anton Blvd Suite 600 Web: www.playmatestoys.com	Costa Mesa	CA	92626	714-428-2000	428-2200
Playmobil USA Inc 26 Commerce Dr TF: 800-752-9662 ■ Web: www.playmobil.com	Cranbury	NJ	08512	609-395-5566	409-1288
Playskool Div Hasbro Inc 1027 Newport Ave TF: 800-242-7276 ■ Web: www.playskool.com	Pawtucket	RI	02861	401-431-8697	431-8082
Poof-Slinky Inc 45400 Helm St PO Box 701394 TF: 800-829-9502 ■ Web: www.poof-slinky.com	Plymouth	MI	48170	734-454-9552	454-9540
Pop Rocket Inc 6330 San Vicente Blvd TF: 800-238-0798 ■ Web: www.poprocket.com	Los Angeles	CA	90048	323-932-4300	932-4400
Pressman Toy Corp 121 New England Ave TF Cust Svc: 800-800-0298 ■ Web: www.pressmantoy.com	Piscataway	NJ	08854	732-562-1590	562-8407
Princess Soft Toys 7664 W 78th St TF: 800-252-7638 ■ Web: www.princesstoys.com	Minneapolis	MN	55439	952-829-5772	829-5596
Radica USA Ltd 13628-A Beta Rd NASDAQ: RADA ■ TF Cust Svc: 800-803-9611 ■ Web: www.radicagames.com	Dallas	TX	75244	972-490-4247	490-0765
Radio Flyer Inc 6515 W Grand Ave TF: 800-621-7613 ■ Web: www.radioflyer.com	Chicago	IL	60707	773-637-7100	637-8874
RC2 Corp 1111 W 22nd St Suite 320 NASDAQ: RCRC ■ TF: 800-704-8697 ■ Web: www.rc2corp.com	Oak Brook	IL	60523	630-573-7200	573-7575
Revell-Monogram LLC 725 Landwehr Rd TF: 800-833-3570 ■ Web: www.revell-monogram.com	Northbrook	IL	60062	847-770-6100	770-6101
Russ Berrie US Gift Inc 111 Bauer Dr NYSE: RUS ■ TF Cust Svc: 800-272-7877 ■ Web: www.russberrie.com	Oakland	NJ	07436	201-337-9000	405-7355
Scholastic Corp 557 Broadway NASDAQ: SCHL ■ TF Cust Svc: 800-724-6527 ■ Web: www.scholastic.com	New York	NY	10012	212-343-6100	
SEGA of America Inc 650 Townsend St Suite 650 Web: www.sega.com	San Francisco	CA	94103	415-701-6000	701-6018
SIG Mfg Co Inc 401 S Front St TF Sales: 800-247-5008 ■ Web: www.sigmfg.com	Montezuma	IA	50171	641-623-5154	623-3922
Sony Computer Entertainment America Inc 919 E Hillsdale Blvd 2nd Fl Web: www.playstation.com	Foster City	CA	94404	650-655-8000	655-8001
Spin Master Ltd 450 Front St W TF: 800-622-8339 ■ Web: www.spinmaster.com	Toronto	ON	M5V1B6	416-364-6002	364-8005
Steiff North America 425 Paramont Dr TF: 800-830-0429 ■ Web: www.steiffusa.com	Raynham	MA	02767	508-828-2377	821-4477
Swibco Inc 4810 Venture Rd *Fax Area Code: 800 ■ TF: 877-794-2261 ■ Web: www.swibco.com	Lisle	IL	60532	630-968-8900	367-7943*
Tara Toy Corp 40 Adams Ave TF: 800-899-8272 ■ Web: www.taratoy.com	Hauppauge	NY	11788	631-273-8697	273-8583
Team Losi Inc 4710 E Guasti Rd TF: 800-338-4639 ■ Web: www.teamlosi.com	Ontario	CA	91761	909-390-9595	390-5356
Testor Corp 440 Blackhawk Park Ave TF: 800-962-3741 ■ Web: www.testors.com	Rockford	IL	61104	815-962-6654	962-7401
Tiger Electronics Div Hasbro Inc 1027 Newport Ave TF: 800-844-3733 ■ Web: www.hasbro.com/tigertoys	Pawtucket	RI	02861	401-431-8697	431-8082
Tonner Doll Co 459 Hurley Ave TF: 888-362-3655 ■ Web: www.tonnerdoll.com	Hurley	NY	12443	845-339-9537	339-1259
Trinity Products Inc 36 Meridian Rd Web: www.teamtrinity.com	Edison	NJ	08820	732-635-1600	635-1640
Troxel Co 11495 Hwy 57 Web: www.troxel.com	Moscow	TN	38057	901-877-6875	877-3439
Twin Hills Inc 70 Hickory Rd TF: 800-210-8230 ■ Web: www.twinhills.com	Hickory	KY	42051	270-856-2277	856-2249
Ty Inc 280 Chestnut Ave *Fax: Cust Svc ■ TF Cust Svc: 800-876-8000 ■ Web: www.ty.com	Westmont	IL	60559	630-920-1515	920-1980*
Uncle Milton Industries Inc 5717 Corsa Ave TF: 800-869-7555 ■ Web: www.unclemilton.com	Westlake Village	CA	91362	818-707-0800	707-0878
Universal Mfg Co Inc 5450 Deramus Ave TF: 800-821-2724	Kansas City	MO	64120	816-231-2771	483-6842
University Games Corp 2030 Harrison St TF: 800-347-4818 ■ Web: www.ugames.com	San Francisco	CA	94110	415-503-1600	503-0085
Upper Deck Co LLC 5909 Sea Otter Pl TF Cust Svc: 800-873-7332 ■ Web: www.upperdeck.com	Carlsbad	CA	92008	760-929-6500	929-6548
US Playing Card Co 4590 Beech St *Fax: Mktg ■ TF: 800-832-0523 ■ Web: www.usplayingcard.com	Cincinnati	OH	45212	513-396-5700	396-5878*
Vermont Teddy Bear Co Inc 6655 Shelburne Rd TF: 800-988-8277 ■ Web: www.vermontteddybear.com	Shelburne	VT	05482	802-985-3001	985-1304
VTech Electronics North America LLC 1155 W Dundee St Suite 130 TF: 800-521-2010 ■ Web: www.vtechkids.com	Arlington Heights	IL	60004	847-400-3600	400-3601
Walthers William K Inc 5601 W Florist Ave TF: 800-877-7171 ■ Web: www.walthers.com	Milwaukee	WI	53218	414-527-0770	527-4423
Wham-O Inc 5903 Christie Ave TF: 888-942-6650 ■ Web: www.wham-o.com	Emeryville	CA	94608	510-596-4202	596-4292
Wiffle Ball Inc 275 Bridgeport Ave Web: www.wiffle.com	Shelton	CT	06484	203-924-4643	924-9433
William K Walthers Inc 5601 W Florist Ave TF: 800-877-7171 ■ Web: www.walthers.com	Milwaukee	WI	53218	414-527-0770	527-4423
Wizards of the Coast Inc 1801 Land Ave SW *Fax: Cust Svc ■ TF Cust Svc: 800-324-6496 ■ Web: www.wizards.com	Renton	WA	98055	425-226-6500	204-5818*
World Wide Press Inc 801 River Dr S TF: 800-548-9888	Great Falls	MT	59405	406-727-7812	453-3711

TRAILERS - TRUCK

SEE Truck Trailers p. 2386

766 TRAILERS (TOWING) & TRAILER HITCHES

				Phone	Fax
Big-Tex Trailers 12400 W I-20 E Web: www.bigtextrailers.com	Midland	TX	79711	432-563-0300	563-0310
Bright Coop Inc 803 W Seale St TF: 800-562-0730 ■ Web: www.brightcoop.com	Nacogdoches	TX	75964	936-564-8378	564-3281
Cequent Towing Products 47774 Anchor Ct W TF: 800-521-0510 ■ Web: www.draw-tite.com	Plymouth	MI	48170	734-656-3000	656-3009
Cequent Trailer Products 1050 Indianhead Dr TF: 800-604-9466 ■ Web: www.fultonperformance.com	Mosinee	WI	54455	715-693-1700	693-1799
CM Trailers Inc 200 County Rd PO Box 680 TF: 888-268-7577 ■ Web: www.cmtrailers.com	Madill	OK	73446	580-795-5536	795-7263
Com-Fab Inc 4657 Price Hilliards Rd Web: www.comfab-inc.com	Plain City	OH	43064	740-857-1107	857-1757
Creek Hill Welding 50 Mill St TF: 866-593-8188 ■ Web: www.creekhillwelding.com	Christiana	PA	17509	610-593-8188	593-5321
Dethmers Mfg Co Inc 4010 320th St TF: 800-543-3626 ■ Web: www.demco-products.com/index.html	Boyden	IA	51234	712-725-2302	725-2380
Eagle Trailers Inc 300 S Elm St Web: www.eagletrailer.com	Homer	MI	49245	517-568-5372	568-5399
Exiss Aluminum Trailers Inc 900 Exiss Blvd Box D TF: 877-993-9477 ■ Web: www.exiss.com	El Reno	OK	73036	405-262-6471	262-9277
EZ Loader Boat Trailers Inc 717 N Hamilton St TF: 800-398-5623 ■ Web: www.ezloader.com/default.asp	Spokane	WA	99202	509-489-0181	489-5729
Featherlite Inc PO Box 320 NASDAQ: FTHR ■ TF: 800-800-1230 ■ Web: www.fthr.com	Cresco	IA	52136	563-547-6000	547-6100
Gooseneck Trailer Mfg Co 4400 E Hwy 21 TF: 800-688-5490 ■ Web: www.gooseneck.net	Bryan	TX	77808	979-778-0034	778-0615
H & H Trailer Co 222 N 1st St Web: www.hhtrailer.com	Clarinda	IA	51632	712-542-2618	542-2707
Hawkeye Leisure Trailers Ltd 1419 11th St N TF: 888-874-9943 ■ Web: www.yachtclubtrailers.com	Humboldt	IA	50548	515-332-1802	332-1833
Karavan Trailers Inc 100 Karavan Dr Web: www.karavantrailer.com	Fox Lake	WI	53933	920-928-6200	928-6201
Load Rite Trailers Inc 265 Lincoln Hwy TF: 800-562-3783 ■ Web: www.loadrite.com	Fairless Hills	PA	19030	215-949-0500	949-1385
Mac-Lander Inc 925 Furnas Dr Web: www.mac-lander.com	Osceola	IA	50213	641-342-6036	342-3508
Midwest Industries Inc PO Box 235 TF: 800-859-3028 ■ Web: www.shorelandr.com	Ida Grove	IA	51445	712-364-3365	364-3361
Performance Trailers Inc 6430 47th St N Web: www.performancetrailers.com	Pinellas Park	FL	33781	727-527-8829	521-3701
Quality S Mfg Inc 3801 N 43rd Ave TF: 800-521-8181 ■ Web: www.quality-s.com	Phoenix	AZ	85019	602-233-3499	233-9110
Reese Products Inc 2602 College Ave TF: 800-326-1090 ■ Web: www.reeseprod.com	Goshen	IN	46528	574-537-6800	537-6986
Rigid Hitch Inc 3301 W Burnsville Pkwy TF Cust Svc: 800-624-7630 ■ Web: www.rigidhitch.com	Burnsville	MN	55337	952-895-5001	895-9150
Sooner Trailer Mfg Co 1515 McCurdy Rd Web: www.soonertrailers.com	Duncan	OK	73533	580-255-6979	255-9783
Sundowner Trailers Inc 9805 S State Hwy 48 TF: 800-654-3879 ■ Web: www.sundownertrailer.com	Coleman	OK	73432	580-937-4255	937-4440
Take 3 Trailers Inc 2007 Longwood Dr TF: 866-428-2533 ■ Web: www.take3trailers.com	Brenham	TX	77833	979-337-9568	337-9122
TriMas Corp 39400 Woodward Ave Suite 130 Web: www.trimascorp.com	Bloomfield Hills	MI	48304	248-631-5450	631-5455
Unique Functional Products Corp 135 Sunshine Ln TF: 800-854-1905 ■ Web: www.ufpnet.com	San Marcos	CA	92069	760-744-1610	744-4709
Valley Automotive Inc 32501 Dequindre Rd TF Cust Svc: 800-344-3112 ■ Web: www.valleyoem.com	Madison Heights	MI	48071	248-588-6900	588-0027

767 TRAINING & CERTIFICATION PROGRAMS - COMPUTER & INTERNET

				Phone	Fax
Canterbury Consulting Group Inc 352 Stokes Rd Suite 200 TF: 800-873-2040 ■ Web: www.canterburyconsultinggroup.com	Medford	NJ	08055	609-953-0044	953-0062
DSI Inc PO Box 162652 Web: www.dsiinc.com	Austin	TX	78716	512-327-6800	327-6838
Element K LLC 500 Canal View Blvd TF: 800-434-3466 ■ Web: www.elementk.com	Rochester	NY	14623	585-240-7500	240-7760
Global Knowledge Network Corp 9000 Regency Pkwy Suite 500 TF: 800-268-7737 ■ Web: www.globalknowledge.com	Cary	NC	27512	919-461-8600	461-8646
Intellinex LLC 925 Euclid Ave Suite 1800 TF: 866-835-3276 ■ Web: www.intellinex.com	Cleveland	OH	44115	216-685-6000	685-6116
Learning Tree International Inc 400 N Continental Blvd Suite 200 NASDAQ: LTRE ■ TF Cust Svc: 800-843-8733 ■ Web: www.learningtree.com	El Segundo	CA	90245	310-417-9700	414-9344
MeasureUp Inc 2325 Lakeview Pkwy Suite 175 *Fax Area Code: 770 ■ TF: 800-649-1687 ■ Web: www.measureup.com	Alpharetta	GA	30004	678-356-5000	777-0732*
MindLeaders.com Inc 5500 Glendon Ct Suite 200 TF: 800-223-3732 ■ Web: www.mindleaders.com	Dublin	OH	43016	614-781-7300	781-6510
MSI/Canterbury Inc 200 Lanidex Plaza *Fax Area Code: 973 ■ Web: www.msicanterbury.com	Parsippany	NJ	07054	800-638-2252	781-0939*
NETg Inc 14624 Scottsdale Rd TF Cust Svc: 800-265-1900 ■ Web: www.netg.com	Scottsdale	AZ	85254	480-315-4000	315-4003
New Horizons Computer Learning Centers Inc 1900 S State College Blvd Suite 100 *Fax: Sales ■ TF: 888-222-3380 ■ Web: www.newhorizons.com	Anaheim	CA	92806	714-712-1000	938-6002*
New Horizons Worldwide Inc 1900 S State College Blvd Suite 200 TF: 800-725-3276 ■ Web: www.newhorizons.com	Anaheim	CA	92806	714-940-8000	938-6002
Productivity Point International Inc 2950 Gateway Center Blvd *Fax Area Code: 919 ■ Web: www.propoint.com	Morrisville	NC	27560	800-774-2727	379-5602*

Phone | Fax

ProsoftTraining 410 N 44th St Suite 600 .... Phoenix AZ 85008 602-794-4199 794-4198
TF: 888-776-7638 ■ *Web:* www.prosofttraining.com
Sento Corp 420 E South Temple .... Salt Lake City UT 84111 801-431-9200 532-2173
NASDAQ: SNTO ■ *TF:* 800-868-8448 ■ *Web:* www.sento.com
SkillSoft PLC 107 Northeastern Blvd .... Nashua NH 03062 603-324-3000 821-5151
NASDAQ: SKIL ■ *TF:* 877-545-5763 ■ *Web:* www.skillsoft.com

768 TRAINING PROGRAMS - CORPORATE

Phone | Fax

AchieveGlobal Inc 8875 Hidden River Pkwy Suite 400 .... Tampa FL 33637 813-631-5500 631-5796
TF: 800-659-6090 ■ *Web:* www.achieveglobal.com
ActionCOACH 5670 Wynn Rd Suite C .... Las Vegas NV 89118 702-795-3188 795-3183
TF: 888-483-2828 ■ *Web:* www.actioncoach.com
Alternative Board 1640 Grant St Suite 200 .... Denver CO 80203 303-839-1200 839-0012
TF: 800-727-0126 ■ *Web:* www.tabboards.com
American Management Assn (AMA) 1601 Broadway .... New York NY 10019 212-586-8100 903-8168
TF: 800-262-9699 ■ *Web:* www.amanet.org
American Management Assn International Keye Productivity Center Div 600 AMA Way .... Saranac Lake NY 12983 518-891-1500 891-0368
TF Cust Svc: 800-262-9699 ■ *Web:* www.amanet.org
Avalar Network Inc PO Box 82010 .... Las Vegas NV 89180 702-895-8988 895-8998
TF: 877-895-8988 ■ *Web:* www.avalar.biz
Baker Communications Inc 2400 Augusta Dr Suite 369 .... Houston TX 77057 713-627-7700 587-2051
Web: www.bakercommunications.com
Bankers Training & Certification Center
12250 Weber Hill Rd Suite 200 .... Saint Louis MO 63127 314-843-5656 843-0166
TF: 800-264-7600 ■ *Web:* www.bankerstraining.com
Bob Pike Group 7620 W 78th St .... Edina MN 55439 952-829-1954 829-0260
TF: 800-383-9210 ■ *Web:* www.bobpikegroup.com
Breakthrough Learning Inc 17800 Woodland Ave .... Morgan Hill CA 95037 408-779-0701 779-5158
TF: 800-221-3637 ■ *Web:* www.blearning.com
Canterbury Consulting Group Inc 352 Stokes Rd Suite 200 .... Medford NJ 08055 609-953-0044 953-0062
TF: 800-873-2040 ■ *Web:* www.canterburyconsultinggroup.com
Carlson Marketing Group 1405 Xenium Ln .... Plymouth MN 55441 763-212-4000 212-1896
TF: 888-521-2200 ■ *Web:* www.carlsonmarketing.com
Center for Creative Leadership
1 Leadership Pl PO Box 26300 .... Greensboro NC 27438 336-545-2810 282-3284
Web: www.ccl.org
Center for Professional Advancement
44 W Ferris St Box 7077 .... East Brunswick NJ 08816 732-238-1600 238-9113
Web: www.cfpa.com
Corpedia Corp DBA Corpedia Education
2020 N Central Ave Suite 1050 .... Phoenix AZ 85004 602-712-9919 712-0019
TF: 877-629-8724 ■ *Web:* www.corpedia.com
Creative Training Techniques International Inc 7620 W 78th St .... Edina MN 55439 952-829-1954 829-0260
TF: 800-383-9210 ■ *Web:* www.bobpikegroup.com
Crestcom International Ltd
6900 E Belleview Ave Suite 300 .... Greenwood Village CO 80111 303-267-8200 267-8207
TF: 888-273-7826 ■ *Web:* www.crestcom.com
Dale Carnegie Training & Assoc Inc 290 Motor Pkwy .... Hauppauge NY 11788 631-415-9300 415-9390
Web: www.dale-carnegie.com
Don Hutson Organization 516 Tennessee St Suite 219 .... Memphis TN 38103 901-767-0000 767-5959
TF: 800-647-9166 ■ *Web:* www.donhutson.com
Elite Business Services PO Box 9630 .... Rancho Santa Fe CA 92067 800-204-3548 756-4781*
**Fax Area Code:* 858 ■ *TF:* 800-204-3548 ■ *Web:* www.elitebusinessservices.com
Executive Enterprises Institute 2 Shaw's Cove Suite 205 .... New London CT 06320 860-701-5900 250-3861*
**Fax Area Code:* 800 ■ *TF:* 800-831-8333 ■ *Web:* www.eeiconferences.com
Forum Corp 265 Franklin St 4th Fl .... Boston MA 02110 617-523-7300 371-3300
TF: 800-367-8611 ■ *Web:* www.forum.com
Franklin Covey Co 2200 W Parkway Blvd .... Salt Lake City UT 84119 801-975-1776 817-8411*
NYSE: FC ■ **Fax:* Cust Svc ■ *TF:* 800-827-1776 ■ *Web:* www.franklincovey.com
Fred Pryor Seminars 9757 Metcalf Ave .... Overland Park KS 66212 800-780-8476 967-8842*
**Fax Area Code:* 913 ■ *TF:* 800-780-8476 ■ *Web:* www.pryor.com
Frontline Group of Texas LLC
14550 Torrey Chase Blvd Suite 330 .... Houston TX 77014 281-453-6000 453-8000
TF: 800-285-5512 ■ *Web:* www.frontline-group.com
General Physics Corp 6095 Marshalee Dr Suite 300 .... Elkridge MD 21075 410-379-3600 540-5302
TF: 800-727-6677 ■ *Web:* www.gpworldwide.com
Growth Coach 10700 Montgomery Rd Suite 300 .... Cincinnati OH 45242 513-563-8339 563-2691
TF: 888-292-7992 ■ *Web:* www.thegrowthcoach.com
HealthStream Inc 209 10th Ave S Suite 450 .... Nashville TN 37203 615-301-3100 301-3200
NASDAQ: HSTM ■ *TF:* 800-933-9293 ■ *Web:* www.healthstream.com
Hinda Incentives Inc 2440 W 34th St .... Chicago IL 60608 773-890-5900 890-4606
TF: 800-621-4412 ■ *Web:* www.hinda.com
Insight Information 214 King St W Suite 300 .... Toronto ON M5H3S6 416-777-2020 777-1292*
**Fax Area Code:* 866 ■ *TF:* 888-777-1707 ■ *Web:* www.insightinfo.com
ITC Learning Corp 1616 Anderson Rd Suite 109 .... McLean VA 22102 703-286-0756 852-7174
TF: 800-638-3757 ■ *Web:* www.itclearning.com
Jones Knowledge Inc 9697 E Mineral Ave .... Centennial CO 80112 303-792-3111 799-0966
TF: 800-453-5663 ■ *Web:* www.jonesknowledge.com
Keye Productivity Center Div American Management Assn International 600 AMA Way .... Saranac Lake NY 12983 518-891-1500 891-0368
TF Cust Svc: 800-262-9699 ■ *Web:* www.amanet.org
Leadership Management Inc 4567 Lake Shore Dr .... Waco TX 76710 254-776-2060 772-9588
TF: 800-568-1241 ■ *Web:* www.lmi-bus.com
Learning Communications LLC 38 Discovery Suite 250 .... Irvine CA 92618 949-788-9209 727-4323
TF: 800-622-3610 ■ *Web:* www.learncom.com
Levinson Institute Inc 28 Main St Suite 100 .... Jaffrey NH 03452 603-532-4700 532-4750
TF: 800-290-5735 ■ *Web:* www.levinsoninst.com
Linkage Inc 16 New England Executive Pk Suite 205 .... Burlington MA 01803 781-402-5400 402-5556
Web: www.linkageinc.com
MSI/Canterbury Inc 200 Lanidex Plaza .... Parsippany NJ 07054 800-638-2252 781-0939*
**Fax Area Code:* 973 ■ *Web:* www.msicanterbury.com
National Businesswomen's Leadership Assn
PO Box 419107 .... Kansas City MO 64141 913-432-7755 432-0824
TF: 800-258-7246 ■ *Web:* www.nationalseminarstraining.com
National Seminars Group 6901 W 63rd St .... Shawnee Mission KS 66202 913-432-7755 432-0824
TF: 800-258-7246 ■ *Web:* www.nationalseminarstraining.com
Nelson Motivation Inc 12245 World Trade Dr Suite C .... San Diego CA 92128 858-487-1046 487-0259
TF: 800-575-5521 ■ *Web:* www.nelson-motivation.com
Novations Group Inc 10 Guest St Suite 300 .... Boston MA 02135 617-254-7600 254-7117
TF: 888-652-9975 ■ *Web:* www.novations.com
NTL Institute for Applied Behavioral Science
300 N Lee St Suite 300 .... Alexandria VA 22314 703-548-8840 684-1256
TF: 800-777-5227 ■ *Web:* www.ntl.org
Pacific Institute 1709 Harbor Ave SW .... Seattle WA 98126 206-628-4800 587-6007
TF: 800-426-3660 ■ *Web:* www.thepacificinstitute.com
Priority Management Systems Inc 13251 Delf Pl Suite 420 .... Richmond BC V6V2A2 604-214-7772 214-7773
TF: 800-665-5448 ■ *Web:* www.prioritymanagement.com
Productivity Inc 4 Armstrong Rd 3rd Fl .... Shelton CT 06484 203-225-0451 225-0771
TF: 800-966-5423 ■ *Web:* www.productivityinc.com

Phone | Fax

Productivity Point International Inc
2950 Gateway Center Blvd .... Morrisville NC 27560 800-774-2727 379-5602*
**Fax Area Code:* 919 ■ *Web:* www.propoint.com
Rockhurst University Continuing Education Center Inc
PO Box 419107 .... Kansas City MO 64141 913-432-7755 432-0824
TF: 800-258-7246
Sandler Sales Institute 10411 Stevenson Rd .... Stevenson MD 21153 410-653-1993 358-7858
TF: 800-638-5686 ■ *Web:* www.sandler.com
Schiller Center 801 Duke St .... Alexandria VA 22314 703-684-4735 684-4738
Web: www.schiller.org
Six Sigma Academy 15210 N Scottsdale Rd Suite 250 .... Scottsdale AZ 85254 480-515-9501 515-9507
Web: www.6-sigma.com
SkillPath Seminars 6900 Squibb Rd .... Shawnee Mission KS 66202 913-362-3900 362-4241
TF: 800-873-7545 ■ *Web:* www.skillpath.com
SkillSoft PLC 107 Northeastern Blvd .... Nashua NH 03062 603-324-3000 821-5151
NASDAQ: SKIL ■ *TF:* 877-545-5763 ■ *Web:* www.skillsoft.com
SmartPros Ltd 12 Skyline Dr .... Hawthorne NY 10532 914-345-2620 345-2603
AMEX: PED ■ *TF:* 800-621-0043 ■ *Web:* www.smartpros.com
Speakeasy Inc 1180 W Peachtree St Suite 600 .... Atlanta GA 30309 404-541-4800 541-4848
Web: www.speakeasyinc.com
TAB Boards International Inc 1640 Grant St Suite 200 .... Denver CO 80203 303-839-1200 839-0012
TF: 800-727-0126 ■ *Web:* www.tabboards.com
TeamSource Technical Services
1930 S Austin Ave Suite 101 .... Georgetown TX 78626 512-931-2787 931-2650
TF: 800-489-0585 ■ *Web:* www.teamsource.com
Toastmasters International 23182 Arroyo Vista .... Rancho Santa Margarita CA 92688 949-858-8255 858-1207
Web: www.toastmasters.org
TWL Knowledge Group Inc 4101 International Pkwy .... Carrollton TX 75007 972-309-4000 309-4706*
**Fax:* Cust Svc ■ *TF:* 800-624-2272 ■ *Web:* www.twlk.com
US Learning Inc 516 Tennessee St Suite 219 .... Memphis TN 38103 901-767-5700 767-5959
TF: 800-647-9166 ■ *Web:* www.uslearning.com
Wilson Learning Corp 8000 W 78th St Suite 200 .... Edina MN 55439 952-944-2880 828-8835
TF: 800-328-7937 ■ *Web:* www.wilsonlearning.com

769 TRAINING PROGRAMS (MISC)

SEE ALSO Children's Learning Centers p. 1445; Training & Certification Programs - Computer & Internet p. 2376; Training Programs - Corporate p. 2377

Phone | Fax

Academy for Guided Imagery Inc
30765 Pacific Coast Hwy Suite 369 .... Malibu CA 90265 800-726-2070 727-2070
Web: www.academyforguidedimagery.com
American College of Orgonomy 4419 Rt 27 PO Box 490 .... Princeton NJ 08542 732-821-1144 821-0174
Web: www.orgonomy.org
Audio-Digest Foundation DBA Cme Unlimited; Infomedix
1577 E Chevy Chase Dr .... Glendale CA 91206 818-240-7500 845-4375*
**Fax Area Code:* 800 ■ *TF:* 800-423-2308 ■ *Web:* www.audio-digest.org
Canter & Assoc Inc 12975 Coral Tree Pl .... Los Angeles CA 90066 310-578-4700 578-4710
TF Cust Svc: 800-733-1711 ■ *Web:* www.canter.net
Ed Necco & Assoc 307 County Rd 120 S .... South Point OH 45680 740-894-7180 894-1132
TF: 877-506-3226 ■ *Web:* www.necco.org
Executive Protection Institute
276 Journey's End Way PO Box 802 .... Berryville VA 22611 540-554-2540 554-2558
Web: www.personalprotection.com
Feng Shui Institute of America LLC 7547 Bruns Ct .... Canal Winchester OH 43110 614-837-8370 834-9760
Web: www.windwater.com
FlightSafety International Inc
La Guardia Airport Marine Air Terminal .... Flushing NY 11371 718-565-4100 565-4134
TF: 800-877-5343 ■ *Web:* www.flightsafety.com
Francis J Curry National Tuberculosis Center
3180 18th St Suite 102 .... San Francisco CA 94110 415-502-4600 502-4620
TF: 877-390-6682 ■ *Web:* www.nationaltbcenter.edu
Global University 1211 S Glenstone Ave .... Springfield MO 65804 417-862-9533 865-7167
TF: 800-443-1083 ■ *Web:* www.globaluniversity.edu
Institute for Integral Development PO Box 2172 .... Colorado Springs CO 80901 719-634-7943 630-7025
TF: 800-544-9562 ■ *Web:* www.institutefortraining.com
Learn.com Inc 14000 NW 4th St .... Sunrise FL 33325 954-233-4000 233-4001
TF: 800-544-1023 ■ *Web:* www.learn.com
Megatech Corp 555 Woburn St .... Tewksbury MA 01876 978-937-9600 453-9936
TF: 800-767-6342 ■ *Web:* www.megatechcorp.com
National Tuberculosis Center 3180 18th St Suite 102 .... San Francisco CA 94110 415-502-4600 502-4620
TF: 877-390-6682 ■ *Web:* www.nationaltbcenter.edu
Natural Golf Corp 431 Lakeview Ct Suite B .... Mount Prospect IL 60056 847-321-4000 795-0101
TF: 888-628-4653 ■ *Web:* www.naturalgolf.com
Outward Bound USA 100 Mystery Point Rd .... Garrison NY 10524 845-424-4000 424-4121
TF: 800-243-8520 ■ *Web:* www.outwardbound.org
Penland School of Crafts 67 Dora's Trail PO Box 37 .... Penland NC 28765 828-765-2359 765-7389
Web: www.penland.org
Res-Care Inc 10140 Linn Station Rd .... Louisville KY 40223 502-394-2100 394-2408
NASDAQ: RSCR ■ *TF:* 800-866-0860 ■ *Web:* www.rescare.com
Smith & Wesson Academy 299 Page Blvd .... Springfield MA 01104 413-846-6461 736-0776
Web: academy.smith-wesson.com
Yamaha Music Education System 6600 Orangethorpe Ave .... Buena Park CA 90620 858-621-2222
Web: www.yamaha.com/musiced/newmusiced/main.html

770 TRANSFORMERS - POWER, DISTRIBUTION, SPECIALTY

Phone | Fax

Active Power Inc 2128 W Breaker Ln .... Austin TX 78758 512-836-6464 836-4511
NASDAQ: ACPW ■ *Web:* www.activepower.com
Advance Transformer Co 10275 W Higgins Rd .... Rosemont IL 60018 847-390-5000 423-1882*
**Fax Area Code:* 888 ■ *TF:* 800-322-2086 ■ *Web:* www.advancetransformer.com
AFP Transformers Inc 206 Talmadge Rd .... Edison NJ 08817 732-248-0305 248-0542
TF: 800-843-1215 ■ *Web:* www.afp-transformers.com
Bodine Co 236 S Mount Pleasant Rd .... Collierville TN 38027 901-853-7211 853-5009
TF: 800-223-5778 ■ *Web:* www.bodine.com
Central Moloney Inc PO Box 6608 .... Pine Bluff AR 71611 870-534-5332 536-4002
Web: www.centralmoloneyinc.com
Cherokee International Corp 2841 Dow Ave .... Tustin CA 92780 714-544-6665 838-4742
NASDAQ: CHRK ■ *Web:* www.cherokeellc.com
Cooper Power Systems Inc 2300 Badger Dr .... Waukesha WI 53187 262-896-2400 896-2313
Web: www.cooperpower.com
Daykin Electric Corp 34425 Schoolcraft Rd .... Livonia MI 48150 734-261-3310 261-3352
Web: www.daykin.com
Delta Star Inc 270 Industrial Rd .... San Carlos CA 94070 650-508-2850 593-0658
TF: 800-892-8673 ■ *Web:* www.deltastar.com

Phone Fax

Ensign Corp 201 Ensign Rd .... Bellevue IA 52031 563-872-3900 872-4575
Web: www.ensigncorp.com
Federal Pacific Transformer Co PO Box 8200 .... Bristol VA 24203 276-669-4084 669-1869
Web: www.electro-mechanical.com/trans.html
Howard Industries Inc PO Box 1588 .... Laurel MS 39441 601-425-3151 649-8090*
**Fax:* Mktg ■ *Web:* www.howard-ind.com
Hunterdon Transformer Co 75 Industrial Dr .... Alpha NJ 08865 908-454-2400 454-6266
Web: www.hunterdontransformer.com
Johnson Electric Coil Co 821 Watson St .... Antigo WI 54409 715-627-4367 623-2812
TF: 800-826-9741 ■ *Web:* www.johnsoncoil.com
Lamination Specialties Corp 235 N Artesian Ave .... Chicago IL 60612 312-243-2181 243-2873
Web: www.laminationspecialties.com
MGM Transformer Co 5701 Smithway St .... Commerce CA 90040 323-726-0888 726-8224
TF: 800-423-4366 ■ *Web:* www.mgm-transformer.com
MTE Corp PO Box 9013 .... Menomonee Falls WI 53051 262-253-8200 253-8222
TF: 800-253-8210 ■ *Web:* www.mtecorp.com
Niagara Transformer Corp 1747 Dale Rd .... Buffalo NY 14225 716-896-6500 896-8871
TF: 800-817-5652 ■ *Web:* www.niagaratransformer.com
Norlake Mfg Co PO Box 215 .... Elyria OH 44036 440-353-3200 353-3232
Web: www.norlakemfg.com
Olsun Electrics Corp 10901 Commercial St .... Richmond IL 60071 815-678-2421 678-4909
TF: 800-336-5786 ■ *Web:* www.olsun.com
Pauwels Transformers 1 Pauwels Dr .... Washington MO 63090 636-239-6783 239-1926
TF: 800-833-6582 ■ *Web:* www.pauwels.com
RE Uptegraff Mfg Co PO Box 182 .... Scottdale PA 15683 724-887-7700 887-4748
Web: www.uptegraff.com
Shape LLC 2105 Corporate Dr .... Addison IL 60101 630-620-8394 620-0784
TF: 800-367-5811 ■ *Web:* www.shapellc.com/
Siemens Power Transmission & Distribution Inc
7000 Siemens Rd .... Wendell NC 27591 919-365-2200 365-2201
TF: 800-347-6659 ■ *Web:* www.ptd.siemens.com
SMC Electrical Products Inc 6072 Ohio River Rd .... Huntington WV 25702 304-736-8933 736-4541
Web: www.smcelectrical.com
Square D Schneider Electric 1415 S Roselle Rd .... Palatine IL 60067 847-397-2600 925-7500
TF: 888-778-2733 ■ *Web:* www.squared.com
T & R Electric Supply Co Inc PO Box 180 .... Colman SD 57017 605-534-3555 534-3861
TF: 800-843-7994 ■ *Web:* www.t-r.com
Tech-Tran Corp 50 Indel Ave PO Box 232 .... Rancocas NJ 08073 609-267-6750 267-6751
TF: 800-257-9420 ■ *Web:* www.tech-tran.com
Uptegraff RE Mfg Co PO Box 182 .... Scottdale PA 15683 724-887-7700 887-4748
Web: www.uptegraff.com
VanTran Industries Inc PO Box 20128 .... Waco TX 76702 254-772-9740 772-0016
TF Sales: 800-433-3346 ■ *Web:* www.vantran.com
Victor Products USA PO Box 1980 .... Cranberry Township PA 16066 724-776-4900 776-3855
Web: www.victorproductsusa.com
Virginia Transformer Corp 220 Glade View Dr .... Roanoke VA 24012 540-345-9892 342-7694
TF: 800-882-3944 ■ *Web:* www.vatransformer.com
Ward Transformer Sales & Service Inc PO Box 90609 .... Raleigh NC 27675 919-787-3553 787-1683
TF: 800-334-9600 ■ *Web:* www.wardtransformer.com
Warner Power LLC 40 Depot St .... Warner NH 03278 603-456-3111 456-3754
Web: www.warnerpower.com
Waukesha Electric Systems Inc 400 S Prairie Ave .... Waukesha WI 53186 262-547-0121 521-0198
TF: 800-835-2732 ■ *Web:* www.waukeshaelectric.com

771 TRANSLATION SERVICES

SEE ALSO Language Schools p. 1885

Phone Fax

AltaVista Translation 701 1st Ave .... Sunnyvale CA 94089 408-349-3300 349-3301
Web: babelfish.altavista.com
Berlitz International Inc 400 Alexander Pk .... Princeton NJ 08540 609-514-9650 514-9648
TF: 800-257-9449 ■ *Web:* www.berlitz.com
Boston Language Institute Inc 648 Beacon St 3rd Fl .... Boston MA 02215 617-262-3500 262-3595
Web: www.boslang.com
Cosmopolitan Translation Bureau Inc
53 W Jackson Blvd Suite 1260 .... Chicago IL 60604 312-726-2610 427-8591
Language Line Services 1 Lower Ragsdale Dr Bldg 2 .... Monterey CA 93940 831-648-7541
TF: 877-886-3885 ■ *Web:* www.languageline.com
Linguistics Systems Inc 201 Broadway .... Cambridge MA 02139 617-864-3900 864-5186
TF: 800-654-5006 ■ *Web:* www.linguist.com
Lionbridge Technologies Inc 1050 Winter St Suite 2300 .... Waltham MA 02451 781-434-6000 434-6034
NASDAQ: LIOX ■ *Web:* www.lionbridge.com
OmniTranslations 41-29 41st St Suite 6A .... Sunnyside NY 11104 718-729-6115
Web: www.omnitr.com
Professional Translating Services Inc
44 W Flagler St Suite 1800 .... Miami FL 33130 305-371-7887 381-9824
Web: www.protranslating.com
SDL International 5700 Granite Pkwy Suite 560 .... Plano TX 75024 214-387-8500 387-9120
Web: www.sdl.com
SimulTrans LLC 1804 N Shoreline Blvd .... Mountain View CA 94043 650-605-1300 605-1301
Web: www.simultrans.com
Spanish-American Translating 330 Eagle Ave .... West Hempstead NY 11552 516-481-3339 481-7905
Translation Group LTD 30 Washington Ave .... Haddonfield NJ 08033 856-354-4755 354-1856
TransPerfect Translations Inc 3 Park Ave 39th Fl .... New York NY 10016 212-689-5555 689-1059
Web: www.transperfect.com
TripleInk 60 S 6th St Suite 2600 .... Minneapolis MN 55402 612-342-9800 342-9745
TF: 800-632-1388 ■ *Web:* www.tripleink.com

772 TRANSPLANT CENTERS - BLOOD STEM CELL

Phone Fax

Alfred I duPont Hospital for Children Blood & Bone Marrow Transplantation Div 1600 Rockland Rd .... Wilmington DE 19803 302-651-5572 651-5575
All Children's Hospital Bone Marrow Transplant Program
801 6th St S Dept 6630 .... Saint Petersburg FL 33701 727-767-6856 767-4803
Web: www.allkids.org
Arthur G James Cancer Hospital & Richard J Solove Research Institute Bone Marrow Transplant Program 300 W 10th Ave Rm 326 .... Columbus OH 43210 614-293-3153 293-6868
Web: www.jamesline.com
Barbara Ann Karmanos Cancer Institute Bone Marrow/Stem Cell Transplant Program 4100 John R Rm 1308-A .... Detroit MI 48201 313-576-9096 576-8422
TF: 800-527-6266 ■ *Web:* www.karmanos.org
Barnes-Jewish Hospital Bone Marrow & Stem Cell Transplant Program 660 E Euclid Ave CB 8007 .... Saint Louis MO 63110 314-454-8304 454-5656
TF: 800-635-2371 ■ *Web:* www.barnesjewish.org

Phone Fax

Baylor University Medical Center at Dallas Blood & Marrow Transplant Services 3409 Worth St Suite 600 .... Dallas TX 75246 214-820-8764 820-7346
Web: www.baylorhealth.com/Locations/Hospitals/BUMC
Beth Israel Deaconess Medical Center Bone Marrow Transplantation Program 330 Brookline Ave .... Boston MA 02215 617-667-9920 667-9922
Web: www.bidmc.harvard.edu
Blood & Marrow Transplant Group of Georgia
5670 Peachtree Dunwoody Rd Suite 1000 .... Atlanta GA 30342 404-255-1930 255-1939
Web: www.bmtga.com
Brown Cancer Center Blood & Marrow Transplant Program
529 S Jackson St .... Louisville KY 40202 502-562-4363 562-4374
Web: browncancercenter.org
Cedars-Sinai Medical Center Blood & Marrow Transplant Program 8635 W 3rd St Suite 590W .... Los Angeles CA 90048 310-423-5351
TF: 800-233-2771 ■ *Web:* www.cedars-sinai.edu/bloodmarrow
Children's Healthcare of Atlanta at Egleston AFLAC Cancer Center & Blood Disorders Service 1405 Clifton Rd NE .... Atlanta GA 30322 404-785-1200 785-6288
Web: www.choa.org/OurServices/Transplant/BMT
Children's Hospital Bone Marrow Transplant Program
1056 E 19th Ave Rm B-115 .... Denver CO 80218 303-861-6892 837-2831
Web: www.thechildrenshospital.org
Children's Hospital Bone Marrow Transplant Program
LSU Health Science Ctr 200 Henry Clay Ave .... New Orleans LA 70118 504-896-9740 896-9758
Web: www.chnola.org
Children's Hospital of Los Angeles Research Immunology/Bone Marrow Transplant Div 4650 Sunset Blvd MS 62 .... Los Angeles CA 90027 323-669-2546 906-8185
Web: chla.usc.edu
Children's Hospital of New York-Presbyterian Pediatric Blood & Marrow Transplantation Program 3959 Broadway 11 Central .... New York NY 10032 212-305-5593 305-8428
Web: www.childrensnyp.org
Children's Hospital of Orange County Blood & Donor Services
505 S Main St .... Orange CA 92868 714-532-8339 532-8830
Web: www.choc.org
Children's Hospital of Philadelphia Stem Cell Transplant Program 3405 Civic Ctr Blvd Wood Bldg Rm 4324 .... Philadelphia PA 19104 215-590-2141 590-4744
Web: www.chop.edu
Children's Hospital & Research Center at Oakland Blood & Marrow Transplantation Program 747 52nd St .... Oakland CA 94609 510-428-3000 601-3916
Web: www.childrenshospitaloakland.org/t_healthcare.cfm?id=253
Children's Hospital of Wisconsin Bone Marrow Transplant Clinic 9000 W Wisconsin Ave PO Box 1997 .... Milwaukee WI 53201 414-266-2420 266-2426
Web: www.chw.org
Children's Medical Center of Dallas Center for Cancer & Blood Disorders 1935 Motor St .... Dallas TX 75235 214-456-2382 456-6133
Web: www.childrens.com
Children's Memorial Hospital Stem Cell Transplant Program
2300 Children's Plaza Box 30 .... Chicago IL 60614 773-880-4562 880-3053
Web: www.childrensmemorial.org
Children's National Medical Center Hematology/Oncology Dept 111 Michigan Ave NW .... Washington DC 20010 202-884-2800
Web: www.dcchildrens.com
Christiana Hospital Bone Marrow Transplant Unit
4755 Ogletown-Stanton Rd Rm 6126 .... Newark DE 19713 302-733-6156 733-6159
Web: www.christianacare.org
Cincinnati Children's Hospital Medical Center Blood & Marrow Transplantation Program 3333 Burnet Ave .... Cincinnati OH 45229 513-636-7609
Web: www.cincinnatichildrens.org
City of Hope at Banner Good Samaritan Bone Marrow Transplantation 1111 E McDowell Rd Suite 12B .... Phoenix AZ 85006 602-239-4526 747-9739
City of Hope National Medical Center Hematology & Hematopoietic Cell Transplantation Div 1500 E Duarte Rd .... Duarte CA 91010 626-256-4673 301-8888
TF: 800-535-7119 ■ *Web:* www.cityofhope.org/HCT
Cleveland Clinic Bone Marrow Transplantation Program
9500 Euclid Ave Rm R32 .... Cleveland OH 44195 216-445-4941 445-7444
TF: 800-223-2273 ■ *Web:* www.clevelandclinic.org/cancer
Cook Children's Medical Center Bone Marrow Transplant Unit
801 7th Ave .... Fort Worth TX 76104 682-885-1405 885-7190
Web: www.cookchildrens.org
Dana-Farber Cancer Institute Stem Cell/Bone Marrow Transplant Program 44 Binney St Dana Bldg 1B Rm 30 .... Boston MA 02115 617-632-2434 632-4139
Web: www.dana-farber.org
DeVos Children's Hospital Pediatric Hematology/Oncology Program 100 Michigan St NE MC 85 .... Grand Rapids MI 49503 616-391-9127 391-9430
Web: www.devoschildrens.org
Duke University Medical Center Bone Marrow & Stem Cell Transplant Program 2400 Pratt St Suite 9100 Box 3961 .... Durham NC 27710 919-668-1002 668-1091
Web: bmt.mc.duke.edu
Fairview University Medical Center Blood & Marrow Transplant Clinic 420 Delaware St SE MMC 803 .... Minneapolis MN 55455 612-273-2800 626-2664
Web: www.fairviewbmt.org
Fox Chase Cancer Center Bone Marrow Transplant Program
7604 Central Ave Friends Hall Physicians Bldg .... Philadelphia PA 19111 215-214-3122 214-3131
Web: www.fccc.edu/clinical/bonemarrow
Froedtert Hospital Bone Marrow Transplant Program
9200 W Wisconsin Ave .... Milwaukee WI 53226 414-805-3666
TF: 800-272-3666 ■ *Web:* www.froedtert.com
H Lee Moffitt Cancer Center & Research Institute Blood & Marrow Transplantation Program 12902 Magnolia Dr .... Tampa FL 33612 813-979-7202
Web: www.moffitt.usf.edu
Hackensack University Medical Center Bone Marrow Transplantation Div 30 Prospect Ave .... Hackensack NJ 07601 201-996-5600
Web: www.humed.com/cancercenter/trans.shtml
Hahnemann University Hospital Bone Marrow Transplant Program 230 N Broad St .... Philadelphia PA 19102 215-762-7510 762-4406
Web: www.hahnemannhospital.com
Henry Ford Hospital Bone Marrow Transplant Program
2799 W Grand Blvd .... Detroit MI 48202 313-916-2767
Web: www.henryfordhealth.org
Hospital for Sick Children Blood & Marrow Transplant Program
555 University Ave Rm 3677 .... Toronto ON M5G1X8 416-813-6800
Web: www.sickkids.ca/bonemarrowtransplant
Hospital of the University of Pennsylvania Bone Marrow & Stem Cell Transplant Program 3400 Spruce St Rhoads Pavillion 7th Fl .... Philadelphia PA 19104 215-662-3800 662-4064
Web: www.penncancer.com
Indiana Blood & Marrow Transplantation
Saint Francis Hospital 1600 Albany St 6th Tower .... Beech Grove IN 46107 317-782-7355 782-6316
TF: 800-361-0016 ■ *Web:* www.ibmtindy.com
Indiana University Cancer Center Bone Marrow & Stem Cell Transplant Team 550 N University Blvd Suite 5630 .... Indianapolis IN 46202 317-274-1114 274-4342
TF: 877-814-7594 ■ *Web:* cancer.iu.edu/programs/bmt
INOVA Fairfax Hospital Transplant Center
8503 Arlington Blvd Suite 200 .... Fairfax VA 22031 703-970-3178 970-3179
TF: 800-358-8831 ■ *Web:* www.inova.org

				Phone	Fax
Jewish Hospital Blood & Marrow Transplant Program 4777 E Galbraith Rd 5th Fl	Cincinnati	OH	45236	513-686-5482	686-5483
Web: www.health-alliance.com/jewish					
Kansas City Blood & Marrow Transplant Program 4320 Wornall Rd Suite 220	Kansas City	MO	64111	816-531-1417	932-8247
Karmanos Cancer Institute Bone Marrow/Stem Cell Transplant Program 4100 John R Rm 1308-A	Detroit	MI	48201	313-576-9096	576-8422
TF: 800-527-6266 ■ *Web:* www.karmanos.org					
Lombardi Comprehensive Cancer Center at Georgetown University Bone Marrow Transplantation Program 3800 Reservoir Rd NW	Washington	DC	20057	202-444-7253	
Web: lombardi.georgetown.edu/clinicalcare					
Loyola University Medical Center Bone Marrow Transplant Unit 2160 S 1st Ave Bldg 112 Rm D29	Maywood	IL	60153	708-327-3216	327-3075
Web: www.lumc.edu/svcline/cancer					
Mayo Clinic Bone Marrow Transplant Program 200 1st St SW	Rochester	MN	55905	507-284-4100	266-2855
Web: www.mayoclinic.org/bonemarrowtransplant					
MCV Hospital Bone Marrow Transplant Program 1300 E Marshall St 10th Fl PO Box 980157	Richmond	VA	23298	804-828-9000	828-7825
Web: www.vcuhealth.org/programs.asp					
MD Anderson Cancer Center Blood & Marrow Transplantation Program 1515 Holcombe Blvd	Houston	TX	77030	713-792-2687	
Web: www.mdanderson.org					
Medical City Hospital Transplant Center 7777 Forest Ln Bldg A 12 S	Dallas	TX	75230	972-566-6547	566-3897
TF: 800-348-4318 ■ *Web:* www.medicalcityhospital.com					
Medical University of South Carolina Blood & Marrow Transplant Program 86 Jonathan Lucas St 3rd Fl Hollings Cancer Center	Charleston	SC	29425	843-792-9300	792-1407
Web: hcc.musc.edu/patient/multidisciplinary					
Memorial Sloan-Kettering Cancer Center Bone Marrow Transplant Service 1275 York Ave	New York	NY	10021	212-639-7432	744-2245
Web: www.mskcc.org					
Miami Children's Hospital Bone Marrow Transplant Program 3100 SW 62nd Ave	Miami	FL	33155	305-669-6466	663-8511
Web: www.mch.com					
Mount Sinai Hospital Bone Marrow Transplant Program 19 E 98th St Suite 3-D	New York	NY	10029	212-241-6021	410-0978
Web: www.mountsinai.org					
New York Presbyterian Hospital Stem Cell Transplantation Program 525 E 68th St Payson Rm 3	New York	NY	10021	212-746-2119	746-9853
Web: www.cornellphysicians.com/StemCells					
North Shore-Long Island Jewish Health System Bone Marrow & Blood Cell Transplant Program 300 Community Dr	Manhasset	NY	11030	516-562-8973	562-8924
Web: www.northshorelij.com					
Northwestern Memorial Hospital Stem Cell Transplant Program 222 E Superior Rm 600	Chicago	IL	60611	312-926-5400	
Web: www.nmh.org					
Oregon Health & Science University Bone Marrow Transplant Program 3181 SW Sam Jackson Park Rd	Portland	OR	97239	503-494-1617	494-7086
Web: www.ohsucancer.com					
OU Medical Center Bone Marrow Transplant Program 920 SL Young Blvd WP-2040	Oklahoma City	OK	73104	405-271-6369	271-4221
Web: www.oumedcenter.com					
Penn State Milton S Hershey Medical Center Bone Marrow Transplantation Program 500 University Dr	Hershey	PA	17033	717-531-1657	531-1656
Web: www.hmc.psu.edu					
Presbyterian-Saint Luke's Medical Center Blood & Marrow Transplant Program 1719 E 19th Ave	Denver	CO	80218	303-839-6953	
TF: 877-268-9300 ■ *Web:* www.pslmc.com					
Roper Cancer Center Bone Marrow Transplant Program 316 Calhoun St	Charleston	SC	29401	843-724-2296	724-1977
Web: www.ropersaintfrancis.com/cancer					
Roswell Park Cancer Institute Blood & Marrow Transplantation Program Elm & Carlton Sts	Buffalo	NY	14263	716-845-3516	845-8564
TF: 800-685-6825 ■ *Web:* www.roswellpark.org					
Rush Cancer Institute Bone Marrow Transplant Center Rush University Medical Ctr 1725 W Harrison St Suite 864	Chicago	IL	60612	312-942-3049	942-6863
Web: www.bone-marrow-transplant.org					
Saint Francis Medical Center Bone Marrow Transplant Program 2228 Liliha St Suite 102-B	Honolulu	HI	96820	808-547-6154	547-6979
Web: www.stfrancishawaii.org					
Saint Joseph's Regional Medical Center Marrow & Stem Cell Transplant Center 703 Main St	Paterson	NJ	07503	973-754-4360	
Web: www.stjosephshealth.org					
Saint Jude Children's Research Hospital Stem Cell Transplantation Div 332 N Lauderdale St	Memphis	TN	38105	901-495-2721	
Web: www.stjude.org					
Saint Louis University Cancer Center Hematology & Oncology Div 3655 Vista Ave 3rd Fl	Saint Louis	MO	63110	314-577-8689	773-1167
Web: cancercenter.slu.edu					
Schneider Children's Hospital Bone Marrow Transplant Program 269-01 76th Ave	New Hyde Park	NY	11040	718-470-3470	343-4642
Web: www.schneiderchildrenshospital.org					
Scripps Green Hospital Blood & Marrow Transplant Center 10666 N Torrey Pines Rd	La Jolla	CA	92037	858-554-2814	
Web: www.scripps.org/41_613.asp					
Seattle Cancer Care Alliance 825 Eastlake Ave E PO Box 19023	Seattle	WA	98109	206-288-1024	288-1025
TF: 800-804-8824 ■ *Web:* www.seattlecca.org					
Shands Hospital at the University of Florida Blood & Bone Marrow Transplant Program 1600 SW Archer Rd Box 100403	Gainesville	FL	32610	352-265-0062	265-0525
TF: 800-749-7424 ■ *Web:* www.shands.org					
Sidney Kimmel Comprehensive Cancer Center at Johns Hopkins Bone Marrow Transplant Program 401 N Broadway Suite 1100	Baltimore	MD	21231	410-955-0432	502-1153
Web: www.hopkinskimmelcancercenter.org					
SSM Cardinal Glennon Children's Hospital Stem Cell Transplant Unit 1465 S Grand Blvd	Saint Louis	MO	63104	314-577-5638	
Web: www.cardinalglennon.com					
Stanford University School of Medicine Blood & Marrow Transplant Program 300 Pasteur Dr Room H-3249 MC 5623	Stanford	CA	94305	650-723-0822	725-8950
Web: bmt.stanford.edu					
Strong Memorial Hospital Stem Cell Transplantation Center 601 Elmwood Ave Box 610	Rochester	NY	14642	585-275-1941	275-5590
Web: www.stronghealth.com					
Texas Children's Hospital Stem Cell & Bone Marrow Transplant Program 6621 Fannin St MC3-3320	Houston	TX	77030	832-826-5059	
Web: www.texaschildrenshospital.org/carecenters					
Texas Transplant Institute 7700 Floyd Curl Dr	San Antonio	TX	78229	210-575-3817	575-4113
TF: 800-298-7824 ■ *Web:* www.texastransplant.org					
Thomas Jefferson University Hospital Blood & Marrow Transplant Unit 125 S 9th St Suite 801	Philadelphia	PA	19107	215-955-6612	935-9791
Web: www.jefferson.edu					
Tufts-New England Medical Center Bone Marrow Transplant Program 750 Washington St Box 542	Boston	MA	02111	617-636-0154	636-2520
TF: 866-636-5001 ■ *Web:* www.nemc.org/home					
Tulane University Hospital & Clinic Bone Marrow Transplant Program 1415 Tulane Ave HC-62	New Orleans	LA	70112	504-988-6326	988-8860
Web: www2.tulane.edu/hsc/tuhc.cfm					
UCLA Bone Marrow Transplantation Program Jonsson Comprehensive Cancer Ctr 10833 LeConte Ave Suite 42121CHS	Los Angeles	CA	90095	310-206-5755	206-5511
Web: www.healthcare.ucla.edu/institution/groups-detail?group_id=13252					
UCSF Medical Center Bone Marrow Transplant Program 400 Parnassus Ave 5th Fl Box 0324	San Francisco	CA	94143	415-353-2220	353-2545
Web: www.ucsfhealth.org					
UMass Memorial Medical Center Bone Marrow Transplant Program 55 Lake Ave N	Worcester	MA	01655	508-856-6255	334-7983
Web: www.umassmemorial.org					
UNC Lineberger Comprehensive Cancer Center Bone Marrow Transplant Program 3009 Old Clinic Bldg CB 7305	Chapel Hill	NC	27599	919-966-0931	
Web: cancer.med.unc.edu					
University of Alabama at Birmingham Bone Marrow Transplant Program 619 S 19th St P302 West Pavilion	Birmingham	AL	35249	205-934-1911	975-2670
TF: 800-822-6478 ■ *Web:* www.bonemarrow.uab.edu					
University of Arkansas for Medical Sciences Bone Marrow Transplantation Center 4301 W Markham Ave Slot 816	Little Rock	AR	72205	501-686-8250	526-2273
Web: www.uams.edu/medcenter/special/BoneMar.asp					
University of California Davis Cancer Center Blood Marrow Transplant Program 4501 X Street Suite 3016	Sacramento	CA	95817	916-734-3771	734-7946
Web: www.ucdmc.ucdavis.edu/cancer					
University of California San Diego Medical Center Blood & Marrow Transplantation Program 3855 Health Sciences Dr Suite 0960 Moores UCSD Cancer Ctr	La Jolla	CA	92093	858-822-6842	822-6844
Web: health.ucsd.edu/transplant/bmt					
University of Chicago Hospitals Stem Cell Transplant Program 5841 S Maryland Ave MC2115 Rm E212F	Chicago	IL	60637	773-834-5358	
Web: www.uchospitals.edu					
University Hospitals of Cleveland Blood & Marrow Transplant Program 11100 Euclid Ave	Cleveland	OH	44106	216-844-7859	
Web: www.irelandcancercenter.org					
University of Illinois Medical Center Stem Cell Transplant Unit 1740 W Taylor St 8th Fl	Chicago	IL	60612	312-355-1102	
Web: uillinoismedcenter.org					
University of Iowa Hospitals & Clinics Blood & Marrow Transplantation Program 200 Hawkins Dr C332 General Hospital	Iowa City	IA	52242	319-356-3337	353-6585
TF: 800-944-8220 ■ *Web:* www.int-med.uiowa.edu/clinical/BoneMarrow					
University of Kansas Medical Center Bone Marrow/Hematopoietic Stem Cell Transplant Program 3901 Rainbow Blvd Rm 1417	Kansas City	KS	66160	913-588-6077	588-3996
Web: www.marrow.org/cgi-bin/NETWORK/tc_idx.pl?ctr_id=593&p_src=state					
University of Kentucky Chandler Medical Center Blood & Marrow Transplant Program 800 Rose St Rm CC 301	Lexington	KY	40536	859-323-5768	323-8990
University of Maryland Greenebaum Cancer Center Blood & Marrow Transplant Program Univ of Maryland 22 S Greene St Gudelsky Bldg Rm N9E11	Baltimore	MD	21201	410-328-1299	328-1971
TF: 800-888-8823 ■ *Web:* www.umm.edu/cancer/canc_stem.html					
University Medical Center					
Blood & Marrow Transplantation Program 1501 N Campbell Ave PO Box 245176	Tucson	AZ	85724	520-694-9043	694-0230
TF: 800-831-9205 ■ *Web:* www.azumc.com					
Bone Marrow & Blood Stem Cell Transplant Program 602 Indiana Ave	Lubbock	TX	79415	806-743-3178	775-9981
Web: www.teamumc.org					
University of Miami Sylvester Comprehensive Cancer Center Blood & Marrow Transplant Program 1475 NW 12th Ave	Miami	FL	33136	305-243-1000	243-1129
TF: 800-545-2292 ■ *Web:* www.sylvester.org					
University of Michigan Cancer Center Blood & Marrow Transplantation Program 1500 E Medical Center Dr B2-352 CCGC	Ann Arbor	MI	48109	734-936-8785	
Web: www.cancer.med.umich.edu					
University of Mississippi Medical Center Bone Marrow Transplant Program 2500 N State St	Jackson	MS	39216	601-984-5617	984-5621
University of Nebraska Medical Center					
Bone Marrow Transplantation Program (Adults) 985164 Nebraska Medical Center	Omaha	NE	68198	402-559-6406	559-6888
Web: www.nebraskamed.com/cancer/stemcell.cfm					
Bone Marrow Transplantation Program (Pediatrics) 985164 Nebraska Medical Center	Omaha	NE	68198	402-559-8229	559-6888
Web: www.nebraskamed.com					
University of Pittsburgh Medical Center Stem Cell Transplantation Program 515 Centre Ave	Pittsburgh	PA	15232	412-648-6430	
Web: www.upmccancercenters.com/stemcell					
University of Texas Southwestern Medical Center Dallas Hematopoietic Cell Transplant Program 2201 Inwood Rd 2nd Fl	Dallas	TX	75390	214-645-4673	645-2661*
**Fax:* Hum Res ■ *Web:* www.utsouthwestern.edu					
University of Utah Hospital & Clinics Blood & Marrow Transplant Program 50 N Medical Dr	Salt Lake City	UT	84132	801-585-2044	585-5825
TF: 800-664-8268 ■ *Web:* uuhsc.utah.edu/bmt					
University of Wisconsin Hospital & Clinics Hematology & Bone Marrow Transplant Clinic 600 Highland Ave	Madison	WI	53792	608-263-1836	262-1982
Web: www.uwhealth.org					
Vanderbilt University Medical Center Stem Cell Transplant Program 1301 22nd Ave S 2665 TVC	Nashville	TN	37232	615-936-1803	936-1812
Web: www.mc.vanderbilt.edu/transplant					
Veterans Affairs Puget Sound Medical Center Marrow Transplant Unit 1660 S Columbian Way	Seattle	WA	98108	206-762-1010	
TF: 800-329-8387 ■ *Web:* www1.va.gov/psmtu					
Wake Forest University Baptist Medical Center Comprehensive Cancer Center Medical Center Blvd	Winston-Salem	NC	27157	336-713-5433	716-5687
Web: www1.wfubmc.edu					
West Virginia University Hospitals Blood & Marrow Transplant Program 1 Medical Center Dr PO Box 9162	Morgantown	WV	26506	304-293-6859	293-2134
Web: www.hsc.wvu.edu/mbrcc/bmt					
Westchester Medical Center Bone Marrow/Stem Cell Program 19 Bradhurst Ave Suite 2100	Hawthorne	NY	10532	914-493-1448	493-2428
Web: www.wcmc.com					
Western Pennsylvania Hospital Hematology/Oncology Patient Care Unit 4800 Friendship Ave Suite 2303 NT	Pittsburgh	PA	15224	412-578-4707	578-4391
TF: 866-680-0004 ■ *Web:* www.wpahs.org/wph					
Winship Cancer Institute Bone Marrow Transplant/Hematology/Leukemia Clinic Emory Univ School of Medicine 1365 Clifton Rd NE Plaza Level Winship	Atlanta	GA	30322	404-778-4342	778-1930
TF: 888-946-7447 ■ *Web:* www.winshipcancerinstitute.org					
Yale-New Haven Hospital Blood Stem Cell Transplant Unit 20 York St 8 W Pavilion	New Haven	CT	06510	203-688-7557	
Web: www.ynhh.org					

773 TRANSPORTATION EQUIPMENT & SUPPLIES - WHOL

Phone Fax

A & K Railroad Materials Inc PO Box 30076 Salt Lake City UT 84130 801-974-5484 972-2041*
*Fax: Sales ■ TF: 800-453-8812 ■ Web: www.akrailroad.com

AAR Aircraft Turbine Center
1100 N Wood Dale Rd 1 AAR Pl Wood Dale IL 60191 630-227-2000
TF: 800-422-2213

AAR Corp 1100 N Wood Dale Rd 1 AAR Pl Wood Dale IL 60191 630-227-2000 227-2019
NYSE: AIR ■ TF: 800-422-2213 ■ Web: www.aarcorp.com

AAR Defense Systems 1100 N Wood Dale Rd 1 AAR Pl Wood Dale IL 60191 630-227-2000
Web: www.aarcorp.com/airframe/defense.html

AAR Distribution 1100 N Wood Dale Rd 1 AAR Pl Wood Dale IL 60191 630-227-2000
TF: 800-422-2213

Aero Hardware & Parts Co Inc 130 Business Park Dr Armonk NY 10504 914-273-8550 273-8612
Web: www.aerohardwareparts.com

Aerotech World Trade Corp 11 New King St White Plains NY 10604 914-681-3000 428-3621
TF: 800-499-2982 ■ Web: www.aerotechworld.com

Africair Inc 13691 SW 145th Ct Miami FL 33186 305-255-6973 255-4064
Web: www.africair.com

AIRCO Group 1853 S Eisenhower Ct Wichita KS 67209 316-945-0445 945-8014
TF: 800-835-2243 ■ Web: www.airco-ict.com

Aircraft Trading Center Inc 17885 SE Federal Hwy Tequesta FL 33469 561-747-3500 744-6000
Web: www.atcjets.com

AirLiance Materials LLC 450 Medinah Rd Roselle IL 60172 847-233-5800 233-5900
TF: 877-233-5800 ■ Web: www.airliance.com

Airline Spares America Inc 1022 E Newport Ctr Dr Deerfield Beach FL 33442 954-429-8600 429-8388
Web: www.asaspares.com

Airparts Co Inc 2310 NW 55th Ct Fort Lauderdale FL 33309 954-739-3575 739-9514
TF: 800-392-4999 ■ Web: www.airpartsco.com

Alamo Aircraft Ltd 2538 SW 36th St PO Box 37343 San Antonio TX 78237 210-434-5577 434-1030
Web: www.alamoaircraft.com

Alexander/Ryan Marine & Safety Co of Louisiana
120 Pintail St Saint Rose LA 70087 504-496-0151 496-0160
TF: 800-496-0151 ■ Web: www.armsnola.com

Allied International Corp 7 Hill St Bedford Hills NY 10507 914-241-6900 241-6985
Web: www.alliedinter.com

American Equipment Co 621 NW 53rd St Suite 360 Boca Raton FL 33487 561-997-2080 997-2110
Web: www.ameco.net

American General Supplies Inc 7840 Airpark Rd Gaithersburg MD 20879 301-590-9200 590-3069
Web: www.agsusa.com

Argo International Corp 140 Franklin St New York NY 10013 212-431-1700 226-9072
TF: 877-274-6468 ■ Web: www.argointl.com

Arrow Trading Inc 5290 NW 20th Terr Hangar 57-101 Fort Lauderdale FL 33309 954-771-9366 771-8966
Web: www.arrowtrading.com

ASC Industries Inc 1227 Corporate Dr W Arlington TX 76006 817-640-1300 649-2685
TF: 800-733-1580 ■ Web: www.ascintl.com

Atlantic Track & Turnout Co 270 Broad St PO Box 1589 Bloomfield NJ 07003 973-748-5885 748-4520
TF Cust Svc: 800-631-1274 ■ Web: www.atlantictrack.com

Aviall Inc 2750 Regent Blvd DFW Airport TX 75261 972-586-1000 586-1361
NYSE: AVL ■ TF: 800-284-2551 ■ Web: www.aviall.com

Aviation Power & Marine 3030 SW 13th Pl Boynton Beach FL 33426 561-732-6000 732-6562

Aviojet Corp 76 Brookside Dr Upper Saddle River NJ 07458 201-825-3111 825-6950
Web: www.aviojet.com

Banner Aerospace Inc 1750 Tysons Blvd Suite 1400 McLean VA 22102 703-478-5800 478-5767
Web: www.banner.com

Birmingham Rail & Locomotive Co Inc PO Box 530157 Birmingham AL 35253 205-424-7245 424-7436
TF: 800-241-2260 ■ Web: www.bhamrail.com

Boat Owners Warehouse 311 SW 24th St Fort Lauderdale FL 33315 954-522-7998 463-3199
TF: 888-262-8799 ■ Web: www.boatownerswarehouse.com

C Melchers & Co America Inc 222 Juana Ave San Leandro CA 94577 510-618-1600 618-1605
Web: www.melchers.com

Chand LLC 157 Hwy 654 Mathews LA 70375 985-532-2512 532-2571
Web: www.chand.com

Core Inc 6590 W Rogers Cir Suites 1 & 2 Boca Raton FL 33487 561-241-4580 241-4582
Web: www.core-aerospace.com

DAC International Inc 6702 McNeil Dr Austin TX 78729 512-331-5323 331-4516
TF: 800-527-2531 ■ Web: www.dacint.com

Defender Industries Inc 42 Great Neck Rd Waterford CT 06385 860-701-3400 701-3424
TF: 800-628-8225 ■ Web: www.defender.com

Dodson Aviation Inc 2110 Montana Rd Ottawa KS 66067 785-242-4000 242-9227
TF: 800-255-0034 ■ Web: www.dodson.com

Donovan Marine Inc 6316 Humphreys St Harahan LA 70123 504-488-5731 486-3258
TF: 800-347-4464

Dreyfus-Cortney & Lowery Brothers Rigging
4400 N Galvez St New Orleans LA 70117 504-944-3366 947-8557
TF: 800-228-7660 ■ Web: www.dcl-usa.com

Dunlop Aerospace Braking Systems
5673 Old Dixie Hwy Suite 120 Forest Park GA 30297 404-362-9900 362-9911
Web: www.dunlop-aerospace.com

Dutch Valley Supply Co Inc (DVS)
970 Progress Center Ave Lawrenceville GA 30043 770-513-0612 513-0716
Web: www.dutchvalley.com

East Air Corp 337 2nd St Hackensack NJ 07601 201-487-6060 487-5938
Web: www.eastaircorp.com

Edmo Distributors Inc 12830 E Mirabeau Pkwy Spokane WA 99216 509-535-8280 828-0623*
*Fax Area Code: 800 ■ TF: 800-235-3300 ■ Web: www.edmo.com

ERS Industries Inc 1005 Indian Church Rd West Seneca NY 14224 716-675-2040 675-0300
TF: 800-993-6446 ■ Web: www.ersindustries.com

Fairchild Corp 1750 Tysons Blvd Suite 1400 McLean VA 22102 703-478-5800 478-5767
NYSE: FA ■ Web: www.fairchild.com

Fatair Inc 17033 Evergreen Pl City of Industry CA 91745 626-839-7513 839-7523

First Aviation Services Inc 15 Riverside Ave Westport CT 06880 203-291-3300 291-3330
NASDAQ: FAVS ■ Web: www.firstaviation.com

Fisheries Supply Co 1900 N Northlake Way Seattle WA 98103 206-632-4462 634-4600
TF: 800-426-6930 ■ Web: www.fisheriessupply.com

Freundlich Supply Co Inc 2200 Arthur Kill Rd Staten Island NY 10309 718-356-1500 356-3661
TF: 800-221-0260 ■ Web: www.fresupco.com

GC Supply Inc 3587 Clover Ln New Castle PA 16105 724-658-1741 658-2940
TF: 800-248-4653 ■ Web: www.golfcarsupply.com

General Aviation Services Inc 430 Telser Rd Lake Zurich IL 60047 847-726-5000 726-7668
TF: 800-382-3658 ■ Web: www.genav.com

Gulf Marine & Industrial Supplies Inc
401 Saint Joseph St New Orleans LA 70130 504-525-6252 525-4761
Web: www.gulfmarine.net

Hawker Pacific Aerospace 11240 Sherman Way Sun Valley CA 91352 818-765-6201 765-8073
Web: www.hawker.com

Heli-Mart Inc 3184 Airway Ave Suite E Costa Mesa CA 92626 714-755-2999 755-2995
TF: 800-826-6899 ■ Web: www.helimart.com

Helicopter Support Inc (HSI) 124 Quarry Rd PO Box 111068 Trumbull CT 06611 203-416-4000 416-4291
TF: 800-795-6051 ■ Web: www.hsius.com

HSI (Helicopter Support Inc) 124 Quarry Rd PO Box 111068 Trumbull CT 06611 203-416-4000 416-4291
TF: 800-795-6051 ■ Web: www.hsius.com

IHI Inc 280 Park Ave West Bldg 30th Fl New York NY 10017 212-599-8100 599-8111

Industry-Railway Suppliers Inc 811 Golf Ln Bensenville IL 60106 630-766-5708 766-0017
TF: 800-728-0029 ■ Web: www.industryrailway.com

Phone Fax

J-H Supply Co Inc 2132 Osuna Rd NE Suite A Albuquerque NM 87113 505-344-6006 345-2116

Jerry's Marine Service 100 SW 16th St Fort Lauderdale FL 33315 954-525-0311 525-0361*
*Fax: Sales ■ TF: 800-432-2231 ■ Web: www.jerrysmarine.com

Jet Turbine Service Inc 620 NW 35th St Boca Raton FL 33431 561-417-4537 417-0772
Web: www.jetturbine.com

JMA Railroad Supply Co 381 S Main Pl Carol Stream IL 60188 630-653-9224 653-9040
TF: 800-874-0643 ■ Web: www.jmarail.com

Kampi Components Co Inc 88 Canal Rd Fairless Hills PA 19030 215-736-2000 736-9000
Web: www.kampi.com

KAPCO/VALTEC 3120 E Enterprise St Brea CA 92821 714-223-5400 996-3490
TF: 800-825-8321 ■ Web: www.kapcousa.com

Kellogg Marine Supply Inc 5 Enterprise Dr Old Lyme CT 06371 860-434-6002 628-1304*
*Fax Area Code: 800 ■ TF: 800-243-9303 ■ Web: www.kelloggmarine.com

Kellstrom Industries 3701 Flamingo Rd Miramar FL 33027 954-538-2000 538-6626
Web: www.kellstrom.com

Land 'N' Sea Distributing Inc 3131 N Andrews Ave Ext Pompano Beach FL 33064 954-792-5436 792-9971
TF: 800-432-7652 ■ Web: www.landnsea.net

Lewis Marine Supply Co Inc 220 SW 32nd St Fort Lauderdale FL 33315 954-523-4371 463-7715*
*Fax: Sales ■ TF Sales: 800-327-3792 ■ Web: www.lewismarine.com

M & M Aerospace Hardware Inc 10000 NW 15th Terr Miami FL 33172 305-592-5155 507-7191
TF: 800-533-5155 ■ Web: www.mmaero.com

Memphis Group Inc 3900 Willow Lake Blvd Memphis TN 38118 901-362-8600 365-1482
Web: www.memphisgrp.com

Meridian Aerospace Group Ltd 3796 Vest Mill Rd Winston-Salem NC 27103 336-765-5454 765-5577
TF: 800-538-7767 ■ Web: www.meridianaerospacegroup.com

National Salvage & Service Corp 6755 Old SR 37 S Bloomington IN 47401 812-339-9000 331-8235
TF: 800-769-8437

Octagon Aerospace Inc 511 5th St Unit A San Fernando CA 91340 818-898-2200 898-2221
Web: www.octagonaero.com

Omni Jet Trading Center 9415 Jet Ln Hangar 3 Easton MD 21601 410-820-7300 820-5082
Web: www.omnijet.com

Ottosen Propeller & Accessories Inc 105 S 28th St Phoenix AZ 85034 602-275-8514 275-8594
TF: 800-528-7551

Pacific Meridian Group 222 Juana Ave San Leandro CA 94577 510-618-1600 618-1605
Web: www.melchers.com

Parker Hannifin Corp Aircraft Wheel & Brake Div 1160 Center Rd Avon OH 44011 440-937-6211 937-5409
TF: 800-272-5464

PartsBase Inc 905 Clint Moore Rd Boca Raton FL 33487 561-953-0700 953-0795
TF: 888-322-6896 ■ Web: www.partsbase.com

Paxton Co 1111 Ingleside Rd Norfolk VA 23502 757-853-6781 853-7709
TF: 800-234-7290 ■ Web: www.paxtonco.com

Rails Co 101 Newark Way Maplewood NJ 07040 973-763-4320 763-2585
TF: 800-217-2457 ■ Web: www.railsco.com

Relli Technology Inc 1200 S Rogers Circle Boca Raton FL 33487 561-886-0200 886-0201
Web: www.relli.com

RS Aviation Inc 7901 W 25th Ct Hialeah FL 33016 305-825-4667 362-7584

Sabine Universal Products Inc PO Box 295 Port Arthur TX 77641 409-982-9446 982-0420
TF: 800-482-9446

Satair USA Inc 3993 Trade Port Blvd Suite 100 Atlanta GA 30354 404-675-6333 675-6311
Web: www.satair.com

Shorty's Truck & Railroad Car Parts Inc
7744 Alabama Hwy 144 PO Box 270 Alexandria AL 36250 256-892-3131 892-3190
TF: 800-227-7995

SkyTech Inc
Martin State Airport 701 Wilson Point Rd Hanger 3 Baltimore MD 21220 410-574-4144 687-2927
TF: 888-386-3596 ■ Web: www.skytechinc.com

Spencer Industries Inc 19308 68th Ave S Kent WA 98032 253-796-1100 796-1101*
*Fax: Sales ■ TF: 800-367-5646 ■ Web: www.spencer-ind.com

Steiner Shipyard Inc PO Box 742 Bayou La Batre AL 36509 251-824-7488 824-4178
Web: www.steinershipyard.com

Summit Aviation Supply 1008 Teaneck Rd Teaneck NJ 07666 201-837-3644 837-9464
Web: www.summitradio.com

Sun Aviation Inc 10010 E 87th St Kansas City MO 64138 816-358-4925 737-0658
Web: www.sunav.com

Taos Industries Inc 480 Production Ave Madison AL 35758 256-772-7743 772-7789
Web: www.taos-inc.com

TPS Aviation Inc 1515 Crocker Ave Hayward CA 94544 510-475-1010 475-8817

Transaero Inc 80 Crossways Park Dr Woodbury NY 11797 516-921-7400 921-7407
Web: www.transaeroinc.com

Turbo Resources International Inc 5780 W Oakland St Chandler AZ 85226 480-961-3600 961-1775
Web: www.turboresources.com

Unical Aviation Inc 4775 Irwindale Ave Irwindale CA 91706 626-813-1901 813-1908
TF: 800-813-1901 ■ Web: www.unical.com

Unirex Inc 9310 E 37th St N Wichita KS 67226 316-636-1228 636-5482
TF: 800-397-1257 ■ Web: www.unirexinc.com

United Aerospace Corp 9800 Premier Pkwy Miramar FL 33025 954-364-0085 364-0089

United Marine Inc 490 NW South River Dr Miami FL 33128 305-545-8445 325-1241
TF: 800-432-8575 ■ Web: www.unitedmarinewholesale.com

US Airways Leasing & Sales Inc 2345 Crystal Dr Arlington VA 22227 703-872-7500 872-7515

Valley Power Systems Inc 425 S Hacienda Blvd City of Industry CA 91745 626-333-1243 369-7096
TF: 800-924-4265 ■ Web: www.valleypowersystems.com

Van Bortel Aircraft Inc 4900 S Collins St Arlington TX 76018 817-468-7788 468-7886
TF: 800-759-4295 ■ Web: www.vanbortel.com

Volvo Aero Services 645 Park of Commerce Way Boca Raton FL 33487 561-998-9330 998-9719
Web: www.volvo.com/volvoaero/global/en-gb/

Washington Chain & Supply Inc 2901 Utah Ave S PO Box 3645 Seattle WA 98124 206-623-8500 621-9834
TF: 800-851-3429 ■ Web: www.wachain.com

West Marine Inc 500 Westridge Dr Watsonville CA 95076 831-728-2700 728-4360
NASDAQ: WMAR ■ TF: 800-538-0775 ■ Web: www.westmarine.com

Western Branch Diesel Inc 3504 Shipwright St Portsmouth VA 23703 757-673-7000 673-7190
Web: www.wbdiesel.com

Yingling Aircraft Inc 2010 Airport Rd Wichita KS 67209 316-943-3246 943-2484
TF: 800-835-0083 ■ Web: www.yinglingaircraft.com

ZAP 501 4th St Santa Rosa CA 95401 707-525-8658 525-8692
TF Orders: 800-251-4555 ■ Web: www.zapworld.com

774 TRAVEL AGENCIES

SEE ALSO Tour Operators p. 2373; Travel Agency Networks p. 2383

Phone Fax

A1SuperCruises.com 3380 Fairline Farms Rd Suite 7 West Palm Beach FL 33414 561-204-2669 753-3141
TF: 866-878-8785 ■ Web: www.a1supercruises.com

AAA (American Automobile Assn) 1000 AAA Dr Heathrow FL 32746 407-444-4240 444-4247
Web: www.aaa.com

AAA (American Automobile Assn) 1000 AAA Dr Heathrow FL 32746 407-444-4240 444-4247
Web: www.aaa.com

ABC Corporate Services 6400 Shafer Ct Suite 310 Rosemont IL 60018 847-384-6868 318-1448
TF: 800-722-5179 ■ Web: www.abccst.com

Abracadabra! Cruises 1735 Roswell Rd Suite 100 Marietta GA 30062 770-509-8080 509-7229
TF: 800-474-5678 ■ Web: www.cruisemagic.com

Adelman Travel Group 6980 N Port Washington Rd Milwaukee WI 53217 414-352-7600 352-3900
TF: 800-231-3999 ■ Web: www.adelmantravel.com

				Phone	Fax
ADTRAV Travel Management 4555 S Lake Pkwy	Birmingham	AL	35244	205-444-4800	444-4808
TF: 800-476-2952 ■ *Web:* www.adtrav.com					
AESU Travel Inc 3922 Hickory Ave	Baltimore	MD	21211	410-366-5494	366-6999
TF: 800-638-7640 ■ *Web:* www.aesu.com					
Alamo Travel Group Inc 9000 Wurzbach Rd	San Antonio	TX	78240	210-593-0084	614-2448
TF: 800-692-5266 ■ *Web:* www.alamotravel.com					
Alaska Tour & Travel 9170 Jewel Lake Rd Suite 202	Anchorage	AK	99502	907-245-0200	245-0400
TF: 800-208-0200 ■ *Web:* www.alaskatravel.com					
Alaska Travel Adventures Inc 18384 Redmond Way	Redmond	WA	98052	425-497-1212	882-2479
TF: 800-323-5757 ■ *Web:* www.alaskarv.com					
Alaska Vacation Packages PO Box 622	Palmer	AK	99645	907-745-8872	745-8873
TF: 888-745-8872 ■ *Web:* www.alaskavacationpackages.com					
All Aboard Cruise Center PO Box 540685	Grand Prairie	TX	75054	972-262-4638	
TF: 800-567-5379 ■ *Web:* www.cruisingfun.com					
All Aboard Cruises Inc 11114 SW 127th Ct	Miami	FL	33186	305-385-8657	419-4873*
**Fax Area Code:* 786 ■ *TF:* 800-883-8657 ■ *Web:* www.allaboardcruises.com					
All About Honeymoons 7887 E Belleview	Englewood	CO	80110	720-259-4546	753-1796*
**Fax Area Code:* 303 ■ *TF:* 888-845-4488 ■ *Web:* www.aahfranchise.com					
All Cruise Travel 1213 Lincoln Ave Suite 205	San Jose	CA	95125	408-295-1200	295-2254
TF: 800-227-8473 ■ *Web:* www.allcruise.com					
All-Inclusive Vacations Inc 1595 Iris St	Lakewood	CO	80215	303-980-6483	233-1597
TF: 866-980-6483 ■ *Web:* www.all-inclusivevacations.com					
All-Waves Cruise & Travel 20381 Lake Forest Dr Suite B-3	Lake Forest	CA	92630	949-829-8031	829-8394
TF: 800-449-0767 ■ *Web:* www.allwaves.com					
Altour-Classic Cruise & Travel 19720 Ventura Blvd Suite A	Woodland Hills	CA	91364	818-346-8747	346-1492
TF: 800-688-8500 ■ *Web:* www.classic-cruise.com					
American Automobile Assn (AAA) 1000 AAA Dr	Heathrow	FL	32746	407-444-4240	444-4247
Web: www.aaa.com					
American Automobile Assn (AAA) 1000 AAA Dr	Heathrow	FL	32746	407-444-4240	444-4247
Web: www.aaa.com					
American Express Business Travel 5000 Atrium Way	Mount Laurel	NJ	08054	856-222-3900	222-3939
American Express Travel Service Co 200 Vesey St American Express Tower C 3 World Financial Ctr	New York	NY	10285	212-640-2000	640-9365
Web: www134.americanexpress.com/travel/					
Anchors Away Cruise Center 3702 Independence Pl	Rocklin	CA	95677	916-625-0722	625-0724
TF: 888-516-6306 ■ *Web:* www.mustcruise.com					
Anchors Away Cruise Outlet 3750 Caribou St PO Box 871723	Wasilla	AK	99687	907-373-3494	373-3498
TF: 800-580-3494 ■ *Web:* www.1anchorsaway.com					
Andavo Travel Inc 5325 S Valentia Way	Greenwood Village	CO	80111	303-694-3322	741-6329
TF: 800-685-0038 ■ *Web:* www.andavotravel.com					
Apple Vacations Inc 101 NW Point Blvd	Elk Grove Village	IL	60007	847-640-1150	640-1950
TF: 800-365-2775 ■ *Web:* www.applevacations.com					
Austin Travel 265 Spagnoli Rd	Melville	NY	11747	516-465-1000	390-6940
TF: 800-645-7466 ■ *Web:* www.austintravel.com					
Avanti Destinations Inc 851 SW 6th St	Portland	OR	97204	503-295-1100	422-9505*
**Fax Area Code:* 800 ■ *TF:* 800-422-5053 ■ *Web:* www.avantidestinations.com					
Azumano Travel Service Inc 400 SW 4th Ave	Portland	OR	97204	503-294-2000	221-6349
TF: 800-777-2018 ■ *Web:* www.azumano.com					
Balboa Travel Management Inc 5414 Oberlin Dr Suite 300	San Diego	CA	92121	858-678-3700	678-3399
TF: 800-359-8773 ■ *Web:* www.balboa.com					
Best Price Cruises 8930 S Federal Hwy	Port Saint Lucie	FL	34952	772-344-3330	398-1505
TF: 800-672-7485 ■ *Web:* www.bestpricecruises.com					
Best Travel Inc 8600 W Bryn Mawr Ave	Chicago	IL	60631	773-380-0150	693-1689
TF: 800-323-3015 ■ *Web:* www.besttravel.com					
Bob's Cruises 635 Fourth Line	Oakville	ON	L6L5W4	905-338-2077	842-8081
TF: 800-361-6688 ■ *Web:* www.bobscruises.com					
Boeing Travel Management Co 325 JS McDonnell Blvd Bldg 303 M-S3069236	Hazelwood	MO	63042	314-551-4025	551-4098
TF: 800-243-8292 ■ *Web:* www.boeingtravel.com					
Bon Voyage Travel 1640 E River Rd Suite 115	Tucson	AZ	85718	520-797-1110	797-2408
TF: 800-439-7963 ■ *Web:* www.bvtravel.com					
Branson Deals 152 Christie Ln	Walnut Shade	MO	65771	800-221-5692	
Web: bdr-llc.com/bransondeals					
Brennco Travel Services Inc 6600 College Blvd Suite 130	Overland Park	KS	66211	913-660-0121	660-0160
TF: 800-955-1909 ■ *Web:* www.brennco.com					
Bridge Travel Alliance 2200 Powell St Suite 130	Emeryville	CA	94608	510-496-8266	652-8572
TF: 800-762-5885 ■ *Web:* www.bridgetravelalliance.com					
Brownell World Travel 813 Shades Creek Pkwy Suite 100	Birmingham	AL	35209	205-802-6222	414-7167
TF: 800-999-3960 ■ *Web:* www.brownelltravel.com					
BTS Travel & Tours 323 Silvergrove Dr NW	Calgary	AB	T3B4M4	403-286-1205	247-6722
TF: 877-929-9019 ■ *Web:* www.btstravel.com					
Campbell Travel 14800 Landmark Blvd Suite 155	Dallas	TX	75254	972-716-2500	392-9256
TF: 800-357-7972 ■ *Web:* www.campbelltravel.com					
Caravelle Travel Management Inc 1900 E Golf Rd Suite 1100	Schaumburg	IL	60173	847-619-8300	619-8375
TF: 800-323-0902 ■ *Web:* www.caravelle-travel.com					
Carefree Vacations Inc 9710 Scranton Rd Suite 300	San Diego	CA	92121	858-450-4060	450-0628
TF: 800-800-8505 ■ *Web:* www.carefreevacations.com					
Cass Tours 109 N Maple St Suite B	Corona	CA	92880	951-371-3511	371-3530
TF: 800-593-6510 ■ *Web:* www.casstours.com					
Casto Travel Inc 900 Lafayette St Suite 105	Santa Clara	CA	95050	408-984-7000	984-7007
TF: 800-832-3445 ■ *Web:* www.casto.com					
Certified Vacations Group Inc 110 E Broward Blvd	Fort Lauderdale	FL	33301	954-522-1440	357-4604
TF: 800-233-7260					
CI Travel 101 W Main St Suite 800	Norfolk	VA	23510	757-627-8000	626-0536
TF: 800-222-3577 ■ *Web:* www.citravel.com					
City Escape Holidays 13470 Washington Blvd Suite 101	Marina del Rey	CA	90292	310-827-5031	827-5575
TF: 800-222-0022 ■ *Web:* www.cityescapeholidays.com					
Classic Custom Vacations 5893 Rue Ferrari	San Jose	CA	95138	408-287-4550	287-9272
TF: 800-221-3949 ■ *Web:* www.classiccustomvacations.com					
Club Med Inc 75 Valencia Ave	Coral Gables	FL	33134	305-925-9000	443-0562*
**Fax:* Mail Rm ■ *TF:* 800-258-2633 ■ *Web:* www.clubmed.com					
Collette Vacations 162 Middle St	Pawtucket	RI	02860	401-727-9000	728-1380
TF: 800-340-5158 ■ *Web:* www.collettevacations.com					
Conlin Travel Inc 3270 Washtenaw Ave	Ann Arbor	MI	48104	734-677-0900	677-0901
TF: 800-426-6546 ■ *Web:* www.conlintravel.com					
Consolidated Cruises 300 Market St	Kingston	PA	18704	570-283-8480	288-3699
TF: 800-732-2628 ■ *Web:* www.consolidatedcruises.com					
Coral Beach Travel & Tours Inc 9600 W Sample Rd Suite 402	Coral Springs	FL	33065	954-345-7504	
Web: www.coralbeachtravel.com					
Corporate Travel Management Group 450 E 22nd St Suite 100	Lombard	IL	60148	630-691-9100	691-8136*
**Fax:* Mktg ■ *TF:* 800-323-3800 ■ *Web:* www.corptrav.com					
Cosmos 5301 S Federal Cir	Littleton	CO	80123	303-797-2800	798-5441
TF: 800-276-1241 ■ *Web:* www.cosmos.com					
Costamar Travel Inc 1421 E Oakland Park Blvd	Fort Lauderdale	FL	33334	954-630-0060	630-0703
TF: 800-444-7171 ■ *Web:* www.costamar.com					
Covington International Travel 4401 Dominion Blvd	Glen Allen	VA	23060	804-747-7077	273-0009
TF: 800-922-9238 ■ *Web:* www.covingtontravel.com					
Creative Leisure International 951 Transport Way	Petaluma	CA	94954	707-778-1800	778-1223
TF: 800-426-6367 ■ *Web:* www.creativeleisure.com					
Crown Travel & Cruises 240 Newton Rd Suite 106	Raleigh	NC	27615	919-870-1986	870-1666
TF: 800-869-7447 ■ *Web:* www.crowncruise.com					
Cruise Brokers 4802 Gunn Hwy Suite 141	Tampa	FL	33624	813-288-9597	264-5736
TF: 800-409-1919 ■ *Web:* www.cruisebrokers.com					
Cruise Center The 11713 101st Ave E	Puyallup	WA	98373	253-845-5330	845-5338
TF: 800-454-7174 ■ *Web:* www.thecruisecenter.com					
Cruise Concepts 34034 US Hwy 19 N	Palm Harbor	FL	34684	727-784-7245	789-5398
TF: 800-752-7963 ■ *Web:* www.cruiseconcepts.com					
Cruise Connection LLC 7932 N Oak Suite 210	Kansas City	MO	64118	816-420-8688	420-8667
TF: 800-572-0004 ■ *Web:* www.cruiseconnectionllc.com					
Cruise Connections Inc 1422 S Stratford Rd	Winston-Salem	NC	27103	336-659-9772	701-1156*
**Fax Area Code:* 215 ■ *TF:* 800-248-7447 ■ *Web:* www.cruiseconnections.com					
Cruise Holidays International Inc 701 Carlson Pkwy	Minnetonka	MN	55305	800-866-7245	212-5266*
**Fax Area Code:* 763 ■ *Web:* www.cruiseholidays.com					
Cruise Marketing International 3401 Investment Blvd Suite 3	Hayward	CA	94545	510-784-8500	784-8989
TF: 800-578-7742 ■ *Web:* www.cruiserussia.com					
Cruise People Inc 10191 W Sample Rd Suite 215	Coral Springs	FL	33065	954-753-0069	340-1968
TF: 800-642-2469 ■ *Web:* www.cruisepeople.com					
Cruise People Ltd 1252 Lawrence Ave E Suite 210	Don Mills	ON	M3A1C3	416-444-2410	447-2628
TF: 800-268-6523 ■ *Web:* www.thecruisepeople.ca					
Cruise Shop The 700 Pasquinelli Dr Suite C	Westmont	IL	60559	630-325-7447	321-1669
TF: 800-622-6456 ■ *Web:* www.cruise-shop.com					
Cruise & Travel Inc 26212 Carmel St	Laguna Hills	CA	92656	949-360-8081	305-1774
TF: 888-484-3732 ■ *Web:* www.cruiseandtravel.com					
Cruise & Travel Shoppe 5809 NW 48th Ave	Coconut Creek	FL	33073	954-427-3216	
TF: 800-957-4477 ■ *Web:* www.cruiseandtravelshoppe.com					
Cruise Vacation Center PO Box 12304	Huntsville	AL	35815	256-880-6700	880-6785
TF: 800-239-9997 ■ *Web:* www.cruisevacationinc.com					
Cruise Vacation Center 2042 Central Pk Ave	Yonkers	NY	10710	914-337-8500	337-8672
TF: 800-803-7245 ■ *Web:* www.cruisevacationcenter.com					
Cruise Value Center 6 Edgeboro Rd	East Brunswick	NJ	08816	732-257-4545	257-4599
TF: 800-231-7447 ■ *Web:* www.cruisevalue.com					
Cruise Ventures DBA CI Travel 101 W Main St Suite 800	Norfolk	VA	23510	757-627-8000	626-0536
TF: 800-222-3577 ■ *Web:* www.citravel.com					
Cruise Web Inc 8100 Corporate Dr Suite 300	Landover	MA	20785	240-487-0155	487-0154
TF: 800-377-9383 ■ *Web:* www.cruiseweb.com					
CruiseOne Inc 1415 NW 62nd St Suite 205	Fort Lauderdale	FL	33309	954-958-3700	958-3703
TF: 800-832-3592 ■ *Web:* www.cruiseone.com					
Cruises Cruises 6604 Antoine Dr	Houston	TX	77091	713-681-9866	957-2076
TF: 800-245-9806 ■ *Web:* www.cruisescruises.net					
Cruises Inc 1415 SW 62nd St	Fort Lauderdale	FL	33309	954-958-3700	958-3703
TF Cust Svc: 800-854-0500 ■ *Web:* www.cruisesinc.com					
Cruises by Kay 306 Shore Dr	Bremerton	WA	98310	360-782-9600	479-3025
TF: 800-938-2602 ■ *Web:* www.cruisesbykay.com					
CruisesOnly 100 Sylvan Rd Suite 600	Woburn	MA	01801	617-424-7990	424-1943
TF: 800-278-4737 ■ *Web:* www.cruisesonly.com					
CTS Corporate Travel Solutions 340 Cedar St Suite 1200	Saint Paul	MN	55101	651-287-4900	287-1312
TF: 800-635-5488 ■ *Web:* www.ctsinc.com					
Cutting Edge Cruises & Tours 32 Toms Way	Lagrangeville	NY	12540	845-227-2660	689-3311
TF: 888-345-6100 ■ *Web:* www.thecuttingedgecruises.com					
Delta Vacations 110 E Broward Blvd	Fort Lauderdale	FL	33301	954-522-1440	468-4775
TF: 800-654-6559 ■ *Web:* www.deltavacations.com					
Direct Travel 860 Wyckoff Ave	Mahwah	NJ	07430	201-847-9000	847-2102
Web: www.vtstraveldirect.com					
E Tour & Travel 3626 Quadrangle Blvd Suite 400	Orlando	FL	32817	407-658-8285	658-1768
TF: 800-339-5120 ■ *Web:* www.etourandtravel.com					
Elegant Voyages 6348 Skywalker Dr	San Jose	CA	95135	408-239-0300	239-0304
TF: 800-555-3534 ■ *Web:* www.elegantvoyages.com					
Euro Lloyd Travel Inc 1640 Hempstead Tpke	East Meadow	NY	11554	516-228-4970	228-8258
TF: 800-334-2724 ■ *Web:* www.eurolloyd.com					
European Travel Inc 301 Howard St 4th Fl	San Francisco	CA	94105	415-981-5518	986-5166
TF: 800-635-6463					
Fantasy Holidays 400 Jericho Tpke Suite 301	Jericho	NY	11753	516-935-8500	932-4622
TF: 800-645-2555 ■ *Web:* www.fantasyholidays.com					
First Class International 27156 Burbank	Foothill Ranch	CA	92610	949-829-5300	829-5333
TF: 800-222-9968					
Fox World Travel Inc 7936 Sheridan Rd	Kenosha	WI	53143	262-654-9116	654-0220
TF Resv: 800-236-8475 ■ *Web:* www.gofox.com					
Freighter World Cruises Inc 180 South Lake Ave Suite 335	Pasadena	CA	91101	626-449-3106	449-9573
TF: 800-531-7774 ■ *Web:* www.freighterworld.com					
Friendly Cruises Inc 3081 S Sycamore Village Dr	Superstition Mountain	AZ	85218	888-842-1786	358-1498*
**Fax Area Code:* 480 ■ *TF:* 800-842-1786 ■ *Web:* www.friendlycruises.com					
Fugazy International Travel 6006 SW 18th St Suite B3	Boca Raton	FL	33433	954-481-2888	
TF: 800-852-7613 ■ *Web:* www.fugazytravel.com					
Funjet Vacations 8907 N Port Washington Rd	Milwaukee	WI	53217	414-351-3553	351-1453
TF: 800-558-6654 ■ *Web:* www.funjet.com					
Future Vacations Inc 110 E Broward Blvd 11th Fl	Fort Lauderdale	FL	33301	954-522-1440	357-4672
TF: 800-456-2323 ■ *Web:* www.futurevacations.com					
Gant Travel Management 304 W Kirkwood Ave Suite 1	Bloomington	IN	47404	800-742-4198	332-6263*
**Fax Area Code:* 812 ■ *TF:* 800-742-4198 ■ *Web:* www.ganttravel.com					
Garber Travel Service Inc 27 Boylston St	Chestnut Hill	MA	02467	617-739-2200	965-8937
TF: 800-359-4272 ■ *Web:* www.garber.com					
Gateway Travel Management 1501 Ardmore Blvd Suite 400	Pittsburgh	PA	15221	412-244-3740	731-1580
TF: 800-553-0093 ■ *Web:* www.gtmtravel.com					
GE Perfect Getaways PO Box 5007	Carol Stream	IL	60197	800-452-7118	328-5333*
**Fax Area Code:* 727 ■ **Fax:* Cust Svc ■ *TF:* 800-621-5505 ■ *Web:* www.geperfectgetaways.com					
Giselle's Travel Inc 1300 Ethan Way Suite 100	Sacramento	CA	95825	916-922-5500	679-3090
TF: 800-782-5545 ■ *Web:* www.globaltrav.com					
Global Experts in Travel 1441 E Maple St	Troy	MI	48083	248-528-8000	528-3774
Web: www.globalconnected.net/english/index2.asp					
Global Travel 900 W Jefferson St	Boise	ID	83702	208-387-1000	338-6042
TF: 800-584-8888 ■ *Web:* www.globaltrav.com					
GOGO WorldWide Vacations 69 Spring St	Ramsey	NJ	07446	201-934-3500	934-3764
TF: 800-899-9800 ■ *Web:* www.gogowwv.com					
Golden Bear Travel Inc 16 Digital Dr	Novato	CA	94949	415-382-8900	382-9086
TF: 800-551-1000 ■ *Web:* www.goldenbeartravel.com					
Golden Sports Tours 301 W Parker Rd Suite 206	Plano	TX	75023	972-578-1166	578-0786
TF: 800-966-8258 ■ *Web:* www.goldensports.com					
Golf Packages of the Carolinas 218 Main St	North Myrtle Beach	SC	29582	877-732-6999	
TF: 877-833-2255 ■ *Web:* www.golfvacationpackages.com					
Gwin's Travel Planners Inc 212 N Kirkwood Rd	Kirkwood	MO	63122	314-822-1957	835-1107
TF: 800-325-1904 ■ *Web:* www.gwins.com					
GWV International 300 1st Ave	Needham	MA	02494	781-449-6500	449-7582
TF: 800-225-5498 ■ *Web:* www.gwvtravel.com					
Hanin Travel 3345 Wilshire Blvd Suite 510	Los Angeles	CA	90012	213-388-4949	388-4946
TF: 800-839-5929					
HRG 16 E 34th St 3rd Fl	New York	NY	10016	212-689-9525	481-2933
TF: 800-622-6622 ■ *Web:* www.hrgworldwide.com					
ICE Gallery 10030 N 25th Ave	Phoenix	AZ	85021	602-395-1995	395-0030
TF: 888-320-4234 ■ *Web:* www.icegallery.com					
InnovAsian Travel Inc 10 North Ln	Armonk	NY	10504	914-273-6716	273-6719
TF: 800-553-4665 ■ *Web:* www.innovasian.com					
International Cruise & Excursion Gallery DBA ICE Gallery 10030 N 25th Ave	Phoenix	AZ	85021	602-395-1995	395-0030
TF: 888-320-4234 ■ *Web:* www.icegallery.com					
Islands in the Sun Cruises & Tours 348 Thompson Creek Mall Suite 107	Stevensville	MD	21666	301-251-4457	315-6027
TF: 800-278-7786 ■ *Web:* www.crus-sun.com					

				Phone	Fax
Japan Travel Bureau USA Inc 156 W 56th St 3rd Fl	New York	NY	10019	212-698-4900	586-9686
TF: 800-235-3523 ■ *Web:* www.jtbusa.com					
JourneyCorp 350 Madison Ave 15th Fl	New York	NY	10016	212-753-5511	644-8171
TF: 800-305-4911 ■ *Web:* www.journeycorp.com					
Kintetsu International 1325 Ave of the Americas Suite 2001	New York	NY	10019	212-259-9585	259-9545
Web: www.kintetsu.com					
Lawyers' Travel Service 71 5th Ave 10th Fl	New York	NY	10003	212-679-1166	679-4629
TF: 800-431-1112 ■ *Web:* www.wtsg.com/LawyersTravel.htm					
Liberty Travel Inc 69 Spring St	Ramsey	NJ	07446	201-934-3500	934-3651
TF: 800-899-9800 ■ *Web:* www.libertytravel.com					
Link to Travel PO Box 30907	Great Falls	VA	22066	703-757-4088	
Web: www.mindspring.com/~link.to.travel					
Lorraine Travel 377 Alhambra Cir	Coral Gables	FL	33134	305-446-4433	441-9444*
**Fax:* Sales ■ *TF:* 800-666-8911 ■ *Web:* www.lorrainetravel.com					
Maine Windjammer Assn 251 Jefferson St MS-06	Waldoboro	ME	04572	800-807-9463	
Web: www.sailmainecoast.com					
Mark Travel Corp 8907 N Port Washington Rd	Milwaukee	WI	53217	414-228-7472	351-5256
TF: 800-558-3060 ■ *Web:* www.marktravel.com					
Marshall Field's Travel Service 700 Nicollet Mall	Minneapolis	MN	55402	612-375-2884	375-3830
TF: 800-316-6166 ■ *Web:* www.travel.fields.com					
Martz Travel 239 Old River Rd	Wilkes-Barre	PA	18702	570-821-3860	
TF: 800-822-1727 ■ *Web:* www.martztravel.com					
MC & A Inc 615 Piikoi St Suite 1000	Honolulu	HI	96814	808-589-5500	589-5500
TF: 877-589-5501					
Menno Travel Service Inc DBA MTS Travel Inc					
124 E Main St 4th Fl	Ephrata	PA	17522	717-733-4131	733-1909
TF: 800-642-8315 ■ *Web:* www.mtstravel.com					
Merit Travel Group Inc 145 King St W Suite 2020	Toronto	ON	M5H1J8	416-364-3775	364-5117
TF: 800-268-5940 ■ *Web:* www.merit.ca					
MLT Vacations 4660 W 77th St	Edina	MN	55435	952-474-2540	367-8420*
**Fax Area Code:* 651 ■ *TF:* 800-362-3520 ■ *Web:* www.worryfreevacations.com					
Montrose Travel 2355 Honolulu Ave	Montrose	CA	91020	818-553-3210	248-7364
TF: 800-766-4687 ■ *Web:* www.montrosetravel.com					
More Hawaii for Less Inc 1200 Quail St Suite 290	Newport Beach	CA	92660	949-724-5050	724-5046
TF: 800-967-6687 ■ *Web:* www.hawaii4less.com					
Morris Murdock Travel 240 E Morris Ave Suite 400	Salt Lake City	UT	84115	801-487-9731	483-6677
TF: 800-888-6699 ■ *Web:* www.morrismurdock.com					
MTS Travel Inc 124 E Main St 4th Fl	Ephrata	PA	17522	717-733-4131	733-1909
TF: 800-642-8315 ■ *Web:* www.mtstravel.com					
National Discount Cruise Co					
1401 N Cedar Crest Blvd Suite 56	Allentown	PA	18104	610-439-4883	439-8086
TF: 800-788-8108 ■ *Web:* www.nationaldiscountcruise.com					
National Leisure Group (NLG) 100 Sylvan Rd Suite 600	Woburn	MA	01801	617-424-7990	424-1943
Web: www.nlg.com					
Navigant International Canada					
2810 Matheson Blvd E 3rd FL	Mississauga	ON	L4W4X7	905-629-9975	629-0361
TF: 800-668-1116 ■ *Web:* www.navigant.ca					
Navigant Luxury Vacations					
2810 Matheson Blvd E Suite 101	Mississauga	ON	L4W4X7	905-206-8244	206-8286
Web: www.navigantvacations.ca					
Nippon Express Travel USA 22 Center Point Dr Suite 110	La Palma	CA	90623	714-521-2050	521-0155
TF: 800-654-8228 ■ *Web:* www.nipponexpresstravel.us					
Nippon Travel Agency America Inc DBA NTA America					
1025 W 190th St Suite 300	Gardena	CA	90248	310-768-3119	323-6235
Web: www.ntaamerica.com					
NLG (National Leisure Group) 100 Sylvan Rd Suite 600	Woburn	MA	01801	617-424-7990	424-1943
Web: www.nlg.com					
Northstar Cruises 80 Bloomfield Ave Suite 102	Caldwell	NJ	07006	973-228-5005	228-5014
TF: 800-249-9360 ■ *Web:* www.northstarcruises.com					
NTA America 1025 W 190th St Suite 300	Gardena	CA	90248	310-768-3119	323-6235
Web: www.ntaamerica.com					
NWA WorldVacations 2915 N Broadway	Minot	ND	58703	701-839-5555	420-6287
TF: 800-727-1111 ■ *Web:* www.nwaworldvacations.com					
Ocean One Cruise Outlet 3264 Marilynn St	Lancaster	CA	93536	661-949-2873	949-3311
TF: 877-362-7770 ■ *Web:* www.oceanone.com					
Omega World Travel Inc 3102 Omega Office Pk Dr Suite 100	Fairfax	VA	22031	703-359-8888	359-8887
TF: 800-756-6342 ■ *Web:* www.owt.net					
Outdoor Connection Inc 424 Neosho	Burlington	KS	66839	620-364-5500	364-5563
Web: www.outdoor-connection.com					
Ovation Travel Group 71 5th Ave 11th Fl	New York	NY	10003	212-679-1600	679-4629
TF: 800-431-1112 ■ *Web:* www.ovationtravel.com					
Paradise Island Vacations 2000 S Pine Island Rd Suite 800	Plantation	FL	33324	954-809-2000	713-2098*
**Fax:* Cust Svc ■ *TF:* 800-722-7466 ■ *Web:* www.atlantis.com					
Patterson TravelStore 855 Howe Ave Suite 5	Sacramento	CA	95825	916-929-5555	649-3633
TF: 800-283-2772 ■ *Web:* www.pattravel.com					
Pleasant Holidays LLC 2404 Townsgate Rd	Westlake Village	CA	91361	818-991-3390	495-4972*
**Fax Area Code:* 805 ■ *TF:* 800-242-9244 ■ *Web:* www.pleasantholidays.com					
Premier Golf 4355 River Green Pkwy	Duluth	GA	30096	770-291-4100	291-5157
TF: 800-283-4653 ■ *Web:* www.premiergolf.com					
Prestige Travel & Cruises Inc 6175 Spring Mountain Rd	Las Vegas	NV	89146	702-251-5552	253-6316
TF: 800-553-0204 ■ *Web:* www.prestigecruises.com					
Pro Golf Travel 515 Madison Ave 10th Fl	New York	NY	10022	212-775-4550	593-4907
TF: 888-227-1059 ■ *Web:* www.protravelinc.com					
Professional Travel Inc					
25000 Country Club Blvd Suite 170	North Olmsted	OH	44070	440-734-8800	734-4528
TF: 800-247-0060 ■ *Web:* www.protrav.com					
Protravel International Inc 515 Madison Ave 10th Fl	New York	NY	10022	212-755-4550	593-4907
TF: 800-227-1059 ■ *Web:* www.protravelinc.com					
Provident Travel Corp 11309 Montgomery Rd	Cincinnati	OH	45249	513-247-1100	247-1121
TF: 800-543-2120 ■ *Web:* www.providenttravel.com					
Qantas Vacations 300 Continental Blvd Suite 350	El Segundo	CA	90245	310-322-6359	535-1057
TF: 800-348-8145 ■ *Web:* www.qantasvacations.com					
Regal Travel 720 Iwilei Rd Suite 101	Honolulu	HI	96817	808-566-7000	566-7498
TF: 800-817-9920 ■ *Web:* www.regaltravel.com					
Rich Worldwide Travel Inc 500 Mamaroneck Ave	Harrison	NY	10528	914-835-7600	835-1666
TF: 800-431-1130 ■ *Web:* www.richtravel.com					
Rocky Mountain Escape PO Box 5029	Hinton	AB	T7V1X3	780-865-0124	865-5029
Web: www.ecolodge.com					
SatoTravel 511 Shaw Rd	Sterling	VA	20166	703-708-9400	
TF: 800-776-7286 ■ *Web:* www.satotravel.com					
Scheduled Airlines Traffic Offices Inc DBA SatoTravel					
511 Shaw Rd	Sterling	VA	20166	703-708-9400	
TF: 800-776-7286 ■ *Web:* www.satotravel.com					
SeaEurope Holidays Inc 6801 Lake Worth Rd Suite 107	Lake Worth	FL	33467	561-432-4100	432-2550
TF: 800-533-3755 ■ *Web:* www.seaeurope.com					
SGH Golf Inc 9403 Kenwood Rd Suite C110	Cincinnati	OH	45242	513-984-0414	984-9648
TF: 800-284-8884 ■ *Web:* www.sghgolf.com					
Ship N Shore 100 Sylvan Rd Suite 600	Woburn	MA	01801	800-892-5537	
TF Cust Svc: 866-711-7447 ■ *Web:* www.cruisesonly.com/p/co/sns					
Simply Cruises Inc 3814 Hampton Ave	Saint Louis	MO	63109	314-832-8880	832-8182
TF: 888-367-9398 ■ *Web:* www.simplycruises.com					
Ski-Pak Inc 110Roessler Rd	Pittsburgh	PA	15220	800-446-4688	729-8201*
**Fax Area Code:* 206 ■ *TF:* 800-446-4688 ■ *Web:* www.ski-pak.com					
Spectacular Sport Specials Inc 5813 Citrus Blvd	New Orleans	LA	70123	504-734-9511	734-7075
TF: 800-451-5772 ■ *Web:* www.spectacularsport.com					
Sports Empire PO Box 6169	Lakewood	CA	90714	562-920-2350	920-1828
TF: 800-255-5258 ■ *Web:* www.sports-empire.com					
Star Travel Services Inc 301 N Morton St	Bloomington	IN	47404	812-336-6811	331-6670
Sterling Cruises & Travel 8700 W Flagler St Suite 105	Miami	FL	33174	305-592-2522	592-7442
TF: 800-435-7967 ■ *Web:* www.cruisewin.com					
Stevens Travel Management Inc 119 W 40th St 14th Fl	New York	NY	10018	212-696-4300	679-5072
TF: 800-275-7400 ■ *Web:* www.stevenstravel.com					
Stratton Travel Management 860 Wyckoff Ave	Mahwah	NJ	07430	201-405-1999	405-1199
TF: 800-223-0599 ■ *Web:* www.strattontravel.com					
Sun Holidays Inc 7208 Sand Lake Rd Suite 207	Orlando	FL	32819	800-422-8000	
Web: www.sunholidaytours.com					
Sun Islands Hawaii Inc 2299 Kuhio Ave 1st Fl	Honolulu	HI	96815	808-926-3888	922-6951
TF: 800-560-3338 ■ *Web:* www.sunislandshawaii.com					
Sunburst Vacations 310 1st Ave	Needham Heights	MA	02494	781-707-2668	707-5899
TF: 800-786-2877 ■ *Web:* www.sunburstvacations.com					
SunQuest Vacations 77-6435 Kuakini Hwy	Kailua-Kona	HI	96740	808-329-6438	329-5480
TF: 800-367-5168 ■ *Web:* www.sunquest-hawaii.com					
Sunsational Cruises 710 W Elliot Rd	Tempe	AZ	85284	480-491-6248	491-6251
TF: 800-239-6252 ■ *Web:* www.sunsationalcruises.com					
SunSpots International 1918 NE 181st Ave	Portland	OR	97230	503-666-3893	661-7771
TF: 800-334-5623 ■ *Web:* www.sunspotsintl.com					
SunTrips Inc 2350 Paragon Dr	San Jose	CA	95131	408-432-1101	436-7902*
**Fax:* Hum Res ■ *TF Resv:* 800-786-8747 ■ *Web:* www.suntrips.com					
Tenenbaum's Vacation Stores Inc 300 Market St	Kingston	PA	18704	570-288-8747	283-0918
TF: 800-545-7099 ■ *Web:* www.tenenbaums.com					
Thomas Cook Canada 130 Merton St	Toronto	ON	M4S1A4	416-485-1700	485-1700
TF: 800-387-8438 ■ *Web:* www.thomascook.com					
TNT Vacations 2 Charlesgate W	Boston	MA	02215	617-262-9200	
Web: www.tntvacations.com					
Tower Travel Management 1 Tower Ln Suite 2520	Oakbrook Terrace	IL	60181	630-954-3000	954-3040
TF: 800-542-9700 ■ *Web:* www.towertravel.com					
TQ3Navigant 84 Inverness Cir E	Englewood	CO	80112	303-706-0800	706-0770
TF: 877-628-4426 ■ *Web:* www.tq3navigant.com					
TQ3NavigantVacations.com 84 Inverness Cir E	Englewood	CO	80112	303-706-0800	706-0881
TF: 800-783-9200 ■ *Web:* www.tq3navigantvacations.com					
Transat Holidays USA Inc 140 S Federal Hwy	Dania	FL	33004	954-920-0090	920-0190
TF: 866-828-4872 ■ *Web:* athusa.com					
Transat AT Inc 5959 Cote Vertu	Montreal	QC	H4S2E6	514-906-0330	906-5131
TSX: TRZ ■ *TF:* 877-470-1011 ■ *Web:* www.transat.com					
TransGlobal Vacations 8907 N Port Washington Rd	Milwaukee	WI	53217	414-228-7472	351-5256
TF: 800-699-2080 ■ *Web:* www.tgvacations.com					
Travel Advisors 7930 Lee Blvd	Leawood	KS	66206	913-649-6266	649-0179
TF: 800-745-6260 ■ *Web:* www.traveladvisors.org					
Travel Authority Inc 702 N Shore Dr Suite 300	Jeffersonville	IN	47130	812-206-5100	206-5400
TF: 800-626-2717 ■ *Web:* www.thetravelauthority.com					
Travel Destinations Management Group Inc					
110 Painters Mill Rd Suite 36	Owings Mills	MD	21117	410-363-3111	363-1816
TF: 800-635-7307 ■ *Web:* www.traveldest.com					
Travel Impressions Ltd 465 Smith St	Farmingdale	NY	11735	631-845-8000	845-8095
TF: 800-284-0044 ■ *Web:* www.travelimpressions.com					
Travel Inc 4355 River Green Pkwy	Duluth	GA	30096	770-291-4100	291-5232*
**Fax:* Hum Res ■ *TF:* 800-452-6575 ■ *Web:* www.travelinc.com					
Travel-Rite International 3000 Dundee Rd Suite 309	North Brooke	IL	60062	847-412-1420	412-0438
TF: 877-880-3033					
Travel Team Inc 2495 Main St	Buffalo	NY	14214	716-862-7600	862-7650
TF: 800-633-6782 ■ *Web:* www.thetravelteam.com					
Travel & Transport Inc 2120 S 72nd St	Omaha	NE	68124	402-399-4500	398-9950*
**Fax:* Hum Res ■ *TF:* 800-228-2545 ■ *Web:* www.tandt.com					
TraveLeaders Group Inc 1701 Ponce de Leon Blvd	Coral Gables	FL	33134	305-445-2999	448-8290
TF: 800-327-0180 ■ *Web:* www.traveleaders.com					
Travelennium Inc 5050 Poplar Ave Suite 115	Memphis	TN	38157	901-767-0761	766-0126
TF: 800-844-4924 ■ *Web:* www.travelennium.com					
Traveline Travel Agencies Inc 4074 Erie St	Willoughby	OH	44094	440-946-4040	946-3613
TF: 888-700-8747 ■ *Web:* www.travelinetravel.com					
Travelmore/Carlson-Wagonlit Travel 212 W Colfax Ave	South Bend	IN	46601	574-232-3061	251-3027
TF: 877-543-5752 ■ *Web:* www.travelmore.com					
Travelong Inc 225 W 35th St Suite 1501	New York	NY	10001	212-736-2166	736-6161
TF: 800-537-6043 ■ *Web:* www.travelong.com					
TravelStore Inc 11601 Wilshire Blvd	Los Angeles	CA	90025	310-575-5540	575-5541
TF: 800-343-9779 ■ *Web:* www.travelstoreusa.com					
TravelVisions 1000 Heritage Ctr Cir	Round Rock	TX	78664	512-238-3166	238-3001
TF: 800-452-2256 ■ *Web:* www.travelvisions.com					
Travizon Inc 10 State St 2nd Fl	Woburn	MA	01801	781-994-1200	343-6128
TF: 888-781-5200 ■ *Web:* www.travizon.com					
TripQuest Inc 786 N Beal Pkwy Suite 7A	Fort Walton Beach	FL	32548	850-862-8999	862-7021
TF: 888-459-8747 ■ *Web:* www.trip-quest.com					
Tzell Travel Group 119 W 40th St 14th Fl	New York	NY	10018	212-944-2121	944-7100
Web: www.tzell.com					
Ultramar Travel Management International					
14 E 47th St 5th Fl	New York	NY	10017	212-856-5600	856-0129
TF: 888-856-2929 ■ *Web:* www.ultramartravel.com					
United Vacations 8907 N Port Washington Rd	Milwaukee	WI	53217	414-351-8470	351-2831*
**Fax:* Cust Svc ■ *TF:* 800-377-1816 ■ *Web:* www.unitedvacations.com					
User-Friendly Group Inc DBA Friendly Cruises Inc					
3081 S Sycamore Village Dr	Superstition Mountain	AZ	85218	888-842-1786	358-1498*
**Fax Area Code:* 480 ■ *TF:* 800-842-1786 ■ *Web:* www.friendlycruises.com					
Vacation Express Inc 301 Perimeter Center N NE Suite 500	Atlanta	GA	30346	404-315-4848	248-1237
TF: 800-309-4717 ■ *Web:* www.vacationexpress.com					
Valerie Wilson Travel Inc 475 Park Ave S	New York	NY	10016	212-532-3400	779-7073
TF: 800-776-1116 ■ *Web:* www.vwti.com					
VE Holdings Inc DBA Vacation Express Inc					
301 Perimeter Center N NE Suite 500	Atlanta	GA	30346	404-315-4848	248-1237
TF: 800-309-4717 ■ *Web:* www.vacationexpress.com					
Virtuoso 505 Main St Suite 5	Fort Worth	TX	76102	817-870-0300	870-1050
TF: 800-401-4274 ■ *Web:* www.virtuoso.com					
Wilson Valerie Travel Inc 475 Park Ave S	New York	NY	10016	212-532-3400	779-7073
TF: 800-776-1116 ■ *Web:* www.vwti.com					
World Travel Bureau Inc 620 N Main St	Santa Ana	CA	92701	714-835-8111	835-8124
TF: 800-899-3370 ■ *Web:* www.wtbtvl.com					
World Travel Inc 1724 W Schuylkill Rd	Douglassville	PA	19518	610-327-9000	327-8222
TF: 800-341-2014 ■ *Web:* www.worldtravelinc.com					
WorldTravel BTI 1055 Lenox Park Blvd Suite 420	Atlanta	GA	30319	404-841-6600	814-2983
TF: 800-342-3234 ■ *Web:* www.worldtravel.com					
Worldwide Holidays Inc 7800 Red Rd Suite 112	South Miami	FL	33143	305-665-0841	661-1457
TF: 800-327-9854 ■ *Web:* www.galapagoscruises.net					
Worldwide Travel & Cruise Assoc Inc					
150 S University Dr Suite E	Plantation	FL	33324	954-452-8800	474-7629
TF: 800-881-8484 ■ *Web:* www.cruiseco.com					
Wright Travel Inc 2505 21st Ave S Suite 500	Nashville	TN	37212	615-783-1111	783-1100
TF: 800-643-5992 ■ *Web:* www.wrighttravel.net					
YMT Vacations 8831 Aviation Blvd	Inglewood	CA	90301	310-649-3820	649-2118
TF: 800-922-9000 ■ *Web:* www.ymtvacations.com					

775 TRAVEL AGENCY NETWORKS

SEE ALSO Travel Agencies p. 2380

A travel agency network is a consortium of travel agencies in which a host agency provides technology, marketing, distribution, customer support, and other services to the network member agencies in exchange for a percentage of the member agencies' profits.

				Phone	Fax
Algonquin Travel Corp 130 Merton St *TF Cust Svc:* 888-599-0789 ■ *Web:* www.algonquintravel.com	Toronto	ON	M4S1A4	416-485-1700	482-5901
American Express Co Inc World Financial Center 200 Vesey St *NYSE: AXP* ■ *TF:* 800-666-1775 ■ *Web:* home.americanexpress.com	New York	NY	10285	212-640-2000	640-0128
BTI Canada 370 King St W Suite 700 *TF:* 800-668-6623 ■ *Web:* www.rider.ca	Toronto	ON	M5V1J9	416-593-8866	593-7158
Carlson Leisure Group 12755 State Hwy 55 *TF:* 800-335-8747 ■ *Web:* www.carlsontravel.com	Plymouth	MN	55441	763-212-5000	212-5458
Carlson Wagonlit Travel Inc 701 Carlson Pkwy *TF:* 800-335-8747 ■ *Web:* www.carlsonwagonlit.com	Minnetonka	MN	55305	763-212-5000	212-5458
CP Franchising LLC DBA Cruise Planners 3300 University Dr Suite 602 *TF:* 800-683-0206 ■ *Web:* www.cruiseplanners.com	Coral Springs	FL	33065	954-344-8060	344-4479
Cruise Planners 3300 University Dr Suite 602 *TF:* 800-683-0206 ■ *Web:* www.cruiseplanners.com	Coral Springs	FL	33065	954-344-8060	344-4479
CruiseOne Inc 1415 NW 62nd St Suite 205 *TF:* 800-832-3592 ■ *Web:* www.cruiseone.com	Fort Lauderdale	FL	33309	954-958-3700	958-3703
CTS Cruise & Travel 5435 Scotts Valley Dr *TF:* 800-287-0684 ■ *Web:* www.e-travco.com	Scotts Valley	CA	95066	831-438-8844	438-8855
Design Travel Management Group Inc 2168 Lake Shore Cir *TF:* 800-773-7930 ■ *Web:* www.dtmgi.com	Arlington Heights	IL	60004	847-577-7930	577-7917
Ensemble Travel 29 W 36th St 8th Fl *TF:* 800-442-6871 ■ *Web:* www.ensembletravel.com	New York	NY	10018	212-545-7460	545-7428
eTravCo Inc 100 Oakwood Ave Suite 100 *Web:* www.e-travco.com	State College	PA	16803	814-238-2860	231-0709
Global Travel International 2600 Lake Lucien Dr Suite 201 *TF:* 800-715-4440 ■ *Web:* www.globaltravel.com	Maitland	FL	32751	407-660-7800	875-0711
GTM Travel Group 100 Executive Way Suite 202 *Web:* www.gtmtravelgroup.com	Ponte Vedra	FL	32082	904-285-4600	285-4620
Hickory Travel Systems Inc Park 80 Plaza East *TF:* 800-448-0350 ■ *Web:* www.hickorytravelsystems.com	Saddle Brook	NJ	07663	201-221-4463	843-4764
IT Group Inc 100 Executive Way Suite 202 *TF:* 888-482-4636 ■ *Web:* www.itgroupnetwork.com	Ponte Vedra Beach	FL	32082	904-285-9796	285-9794
MAST Vacation Partners Inc (MAST) 17 W 635 Butterfield Rd Suite 150 *Web:* www.mvptravel.com	Oakbrook Terrace	IL	60181	630-889-9817	889-9832
Navigant International Inc 84 Inverness Cir E *NASDAQ: FLYR* ■ *TF:* 877-628-4426 ■ *Web:* www.navigant.com	Englewood	CO	80112	303-706-0800	706-0770
Nexion 1 E Kirkwood Blvd Suite E *TF:* 800-747-6813 ■ *Web:* www.nexionnet.com	Southlake	TX	76092	408-280-6410	271-2039
RADIUS® 4330 East-West Hwy Suite 1100 *TF:* 800-989-3059 ■ *Web:* www.radiustravel.com	Bethesda	MD	20814	301-718-9500	718-4290
Results Travel 701 Carlson Pkwy *TF:* 800-523-2200 ■ *Web:* www.resultstravel.com	Minnetonka	MN	55305	763-212-5000	212-2302
REZconnect Technologies Inc 560 Sylvan Ave *TF:* 800-669-9000	Englewood Cliffs	NJ	07632	201-567-8500	567-4405
Riverside Travel Group Inc 13343 SE Stark St Suite 200 *TF:* 800-772-2228 ■ *Web:* www.riversidetravel.com	Portland	OR	97233	503-255-2950	255-7268
Sabre Travel Network 3150 Sabre Dr *Web:* www.sabretravelnetwork.com	Southlake	TX	76092	682-605-1000	
SYNERGI Global Travel Management 140 Broadway 46th Fl *TF:* 800-622-6622 ■ *Web:* www.synergitravel.com	New York	NY	10005	212-208-1422	208-1447
Thor Inc 382 S Arthur Ave *TF:* 800-862-2111 ■ *Web:* www.thor24.com	Louisville	CO	80027	303-876-4100	876-4101
Tix Travel & Ticket Agency Inc 201 Main St **Fax Area Code:* 845 ■ *Web:* www.tixtravel.com	Nyack	NY	10960	800-269-6849	358-1266*
TQ3 Travel Solutions 84 Inverness Cir E *TF:* 877-628-4426 ■ *Web:* www.tq3.com	Englewood	CO	80112	303-706-0800	706-0770
Travel Society Inc 600 S Cherry St Suite 100 *Web:* www.travelsociety.com	Denver	CO	80246	303-321-0900	321-0025
Travelex International Inc 2500 W Higgins Rd Suite 1065 *TF:* 800-882-0499 ■ *Web:* www.excapes.com	Hoffman Estates	IL	60169	847-882-0400	882-1212
Travelsavers Inc 71 Audrey Ave *Web:* www.travelsavers.com	Oyster Bay	NY	11771	516-624-0500	624-0308
UNIGLOBE Travel USA LLC 18662 MacArthur Blvd Suite 100 *TF:* 800-863-1606 ■ *Web:* www.uniglobetravelusa.com	Irvine	CA	92612	949-623-9000	623-9008
Vacation.com Inc 1650 King St Suite 450 *TF:* 800-843-0733 ■ *Web:* www.vacation.com	Alexandria	VA	22314	703-535-5505	548-6815
Virtuoso 505 Main St Suite 5 *TF:* 800-401-4274 ■ *Web:* www.virtuoso.com	Fort Worth	TX	76102	817-870-0300	870-1050
Western Assn of Travel Agencies (WESTA) 5933 NE Win Sivers Dr Suite 202 *TF:* 800-288-8191 ■ *Web:* www.westa1.org	Portland	OR	97220	503-251-8170	251-8174
WorldClass Travel Network 4300 Marke Pointe Dr Suite 240 *TF:* 800-234-3576 ■ *Web:* www.worldclassnetwork.net	Bloomington	MN	55435	952-835-8636	835-2340
Worldtek Travel Inc 111 Water St *TF:* 800-243-1723 ■ *Web:* www.worldtek.com	New Haven	CT	06511	203-772-0470	865-2034
WorldTravel BTI 1055 Lenox Park Blvd Suite 420 *TF:* 800-342-3234 ■ *Web:* www.worldtravel.com	Atlanta	GA	30319	404-841-6600	814-2983

TRAVEL INFORMATION - CITY

SEE Convention & Visitors Bureaus p. 1563

776 TRAVEL SERVICES - ONLINE

SEE ALSO Hotel Reservations Services p. 1829

				Phone	Fax
4Deals.com 3102 Omega Office Park *Web:* www.4deals.com	Fairfax	VA	22031	703-359-0200	359-8880
11th Hour.com 1200 Lake Hearn Dr Suite 300 *TF:* 888-740-1998 ■ *Web:* www.11thhourvacations.com	Atlanta	GA	30319	404-256-6620	256-6679
AirGorilla LLC 579 Orange Ave *Web:* www.airgorilla.com	Coronado	CA	92118	619-435-2147	
Away.com Inc 702 H St NW Suite 200 *Web:* away.com	Washington	DC	20001	202-654-8000	654-8081
BedandBreakfast.com 700 Brazos St Suite B-700 *TF Sales:* 800-462-2632 ■ *Web:* www.bedandbreakfast.com	Austin	TX	78701	512-322-2700	320-0883
Best Fares USA Inc 1301 S Bowen Rd Suite 400 *TF:* 800-880-1234 ■ *Web:* www.bestfares.com	Arlington	TX	76013	817-860-5573	795-2901
BigEasy.com 610 S Peter St **Fax:* Hum Res ■ *TF:* 800-543-6332 ■ *Web:* www.bigeasy.com	New Orleans	LA	70130	504-587-1600	587-1617*
Bombardier Skyjet 3040 Williams Dr Suite 404 *TF Cust Svc:* 888-275-9538 ■ *Web:* www.skyjet.com	Fairfax	VA	22031	703-584-3330	584-3361
Car Rental Express 2817 138th St *TF:* 888-557-8188 ■ *Web:* www.carrentalexpress.com	Surrey	BC	V4P1T6	604-714-5911	731-5772
Cheap Tickets Inc 7 Sylvan Way *Web:* www.cheaptickets.com	Parsippany	NJ	07054	888-922-8849	
Cheapseats.com 11145 Tampa Ave Suite 17-B *Web:* www.cheapseats.com	Northridge	CA	91326	800-243-2773	
Cheaptickets.com 7 Sylvan Way *Web:* www.cheaptickets.com	Parsippany	NJ	07054	888-922-8849	
Cruise.com 1701 Eller Dr *TF:* 888-333-3116 ■ *Web:* www.cruise.com	Fort Lauderdale	FL	33316	954-763-6828	
Cruises.com 100 Sylvan Rd Suite 600 *TF:* 800-288-6006 ■ *Web:* www.cruises.com	Woburn	MA	01801	617-424-7990	424-1943
DiscountHotels.com 1200 Lake Hearn Dr Suite 300 *TF Cust Svc:* 800-291-9960 ■ *Web:* www.discounthotels.com	Atlanta	GA	30319	404-256-6620	
Elegant Small Hotels Lanier Publishing International 514 Petaluma Blvd S *Web:* www.elegantsmallhotel.com	Petaluma	CA	94953	707-763-0271	763-5762
Excursia.com PO Box 936 **Fax Area Code:* 706 ■ *Web:* excursia.com	Augusta	GA	30903	800-622-6358	828-4304*
Expedia Inc 3150 139th Ave SE *NASDAQ: EXPE* ■ *TF:* 800-397-3342 ■ *Web:* www.expedia.com	Bellevue	WA	98005	425-679-7200	679-7240
FamilyTravelGuides.com Lanier Publishing International 514 Petaluma Blvd S *Web:* www.familytravelguides.com	Petaluma	CA	94953	707-763-0271	763-5762
Flights.com 96 Engle St *Web:* www.flights.com	Englewood	NJ	07631	516-228-4972	228-8258
Fodors.com 1745 Broadway *TF:* 888-264-1745 ■ *Web:* www.fodors.com	New York	NY	10019	212-782-9000	940-7352
Frommer's.com 111 River St 5th Fl *Web:* www.frommers.com	Hoboken	NJ	07030	201-748-6000	748-5612
GetThere LP 3150 Sabre Dr *TF:* 800-850-3906 ■ *Web:* www.getthere.com	Southlake	TX	76092	682-605-1000	
Hidden America PO Box 4262 *Web:* hiddenamerica.com	River Edge	NJ	07661	201-967-7853	986-1373
History Travel 3307 Northland Dr Suite 220 *TF:* 877-238-6877 ■ *Web:* www.historytravel.com	Austin	TX	78731	512-244-9883	857-0077
Hotwire.com 333 Market St Suite 100 *TF:* 877-468-9473 ■ *Web:* www.hotwire.com	San Francisco	CA	94105	415-343-8400	343-8401
iExplore Inc 954 W Washington Blvd Suite 3E *TF:* 800-439-7567 ■ *Web:* www.iexplore.com	Chicago	IL	60607	312-492-9443	
IgoUgo Inc 530 Broadway 11th Fl *Web:* www.igougo.com	New York	NY	10012	917-237-0223	237-0185
Kayak.com 27 Ann St Suite 300 *Web:* www.kayak.com	Norwalk	CT	06854	203-899-3120	899-3125
Lanier TravelGuides Network Lanier Publishing International 514 Petaluma Blvd S *Web:* www.travelguides.com	Petaluma	CA	94953	707-763-0271	763-5762
LastMinuteTravel.com Inc 220 E Central Pkwy Suite 4010 *TF:* 800-442-0568 ■ *Web:* www.lastminutetravel.com	Altamonte Springs	FL	32701	407-667-8700	667-8850
Lonely Planet Online 150 Linden St *TF:* 800-275-8555 ■ *Web:* www.lonelyplanet.com	Oakland	CA	94607	510-893-8555	893-8563
MapQuest Inc 3710 Hempland Rd PO Box 601 *Web:* www.mapquest.com	Mountville	PA	17554	717-285-8500	285-8411
Mobissimo 984 Folsom St *Web:* www.mobissimo.com	San Francisco	CA	94109	415-344-0838	348-1496
National Park Service Reservation Center 12501 Willowbrook Rd **Fax Area Code:* 301 ■ *Web:* www.recreation.gov	Cumberland	MD	21502	800-365-2267	784-9079*
National Recreation Reservation Service PO Box 140 *TF:* 877-444-6777 ■ *Web:* www.recreation.gov	Ballston Spa	NY	12020	518-885-3639	
New Orleans Hospitality Enterprises Inc DBA BigEasy.com 610 S Peter St **Fax:* Hum Res ■ *TF:* 800-543-6332 ■ *Web:* www.bigeasy.com	New Orleans	LA	70130	504-587-1600	587-1617*
OneTravel.com 258 Main St 3rd Fl *TF:* 800-929-2523 ■ *Web:* www.onetravel.com	East Greenville	PA	18041	215-541-1030	541-1060
OnlineCityGuide.com LLC 1940 Elm Hill Pike *TF:* 800-467-1218 ■ *Web:* www.onlinecityguide.com	Nashville	TN	37210	615-259-4500	777-5500
Orbitz LLC 200 S Wacker Dr Suite 1900 *TF:* 888-656-4546 ■ *Web:* www.orbitz.com	Chicago	IL	60606	312-894-5000	894-5001
Pamela Lanier's Bed & Breakfast Guide Lanier Publishing International 514 Petaluma Blvd S *Web:* www.lanierbb.com	Petaluma	CA	94953	707-763-0271	763-5762
Pamela Lanier's Family Travel Guides Lanier Publishing International 514 Petaluma Blvd S *Web:* www.familytravelguides.com	Petaluma	CA	94953	707-763-0271	763-5762
Priceline.com Inc 800 Connecticut Ave *NASDAQ: PCLN* ■ **Fax:* Mktg ■ *TF:* 800-774-2354 ■ *Web:* www.priceline.com	Norwalk	CT	06854	203-299-8000	299-8955*
ReserveAmerica 2480 Meadowvale Blvd Suite 120 *TF:* 800-695-4636 ■ *Web:* www.reserveamerica.com	Mississauga	ON	L5N8M6	905-286-6600	286-0371
Resorts OnLine 400 E 59th St Suite 12B *Web:* www.resortsonline.com	New York	NY	10022	212-744-6586	744-6823
Roadside America PO Box 429 *Web:* www.roadsideamerica.com	Middletown	NJ	07748	732-957-0080	957-0514
SideStep Inc 3131 Jay St Suite 210 *Web:* www.sidestep.com	Santa Clara	CA	95054	408-235-1700	235-1717
Spa Finder Inc 257 Park Ave S 10th Fl *TF:* 800-255-7727 ■ *Web:* www.spafinder.com	New York	NY	10010	212-924-6800	924-7240
TravelNow.com Inc 4124 S McCann Ct *TF:* 800-568-1972 ■ *Web:* www.travelnow.com	Springfield	MO	65804	417-864-3600	864-8811
Travelocity.com LP 11603 Crosswinds way Suite 125 *TF:* 888-709-5983 ■ *Web:* www.travelocity.com	San Antonio	TX	78233	682-605-3000	
Travelzoo Inc 590 Madison Ave 21st Fl *NASDAQ: TZOO* ■ *Web:* www.travelzoo.com	New York	NY	10022	212-521-4200	521-4230
TripAdvisor LLC 464 Hillside Ave Suite 304 *Web:* www.tripadvisor.com	Needham	MA	02494	781-444-1113	444-1146
Vacation.com Inc 1650 King St Suite 450 *TF:* 800-843-0733 ■ *Web:* www.vacation.com	Alexandria	VA	22314	703-535-5505	548-6815
Yahoo! Maps 701 1st Ave *Web:* maps.yahoo.com	Sunnyvale	CA	94089	408-349-3300	349-3301
Yahoo! Travel 701 1st Ave *Web:* travel.yahoo.com	Sunnyvale	CA	94089	408-349-3300	349-3301

777 TRAVEL & TOURISM INFORMATION - CANADIAN

Phone Fax

Canadian Tourism Commission
1055 Dunsmuir St Suite 1400 4 Bentall Center Box 49220 ..... Vancouver BC V7X1L2 604-638-8300
Web: www.canadatourisme.com

Newfoundland & Labrador Tourism PO Box 8730 .... Saint John's NL A1B4K2 709-729-2830 729-0057
TF: 800-563-6353 ■ *Web:* www.newfoundlandandlabradortourism.com

Nova Scotia Dept of Tourism & Culture 1800 Argyle St .... Halifax NS B3J3N8 902-424-5000 424-2668
TF: 800-565-0000 ■ *Web:* www.NovaScotia.com

Nunavut Tourism PO Box 1450 .... Iqaluit NU X0A0H0 867-979-6551 979-1261
TF: 800-491-7910 ■ *Web:* www.nunavuttourism.com

NWT Tourism Box 610 .... Yellowknife NT X1A2N5 867-873-7200 873-4059
TF: 800-661-0788 ■ *Web:* www.explorenwt.com

Ontario Tourism Marketing Partnership Corp
900 Bay St Hearst Block 10th Fl .... Toronto ON M7A2E1 905-282-1721 282-7433
TF: 800-668-2746 ■ *Web:* www.ontariotravel.net

Prince Edward Island Tourism PO Box 2000 .... Charlottetown PE C1A7N8 902-368-4441 368-4438
TF: 888-734-7529 ■ *Web:* www.gov.pe.ca

Tourism New Brunswick 19 Aberdeen St PO Box 12345 .... Campbellton NB E3N2J6 506-789-4982 789-2044
TF: 800-561-0123 ■ *Web:* www.tourismnewbrunswick.ca

Tourism Saskatchewan 1922 Park St .... Regina SK S4N7M4 306-787-9600 787-0715
TF: 877-237-2273 ■ *Web:* www.sasktourism.com

Tourism Yukon PO Box 2703 .... Whitehorse YT Y1A2C6 867-667-5036 393-7005
TF: 800-661-0494 ■ *Web:* www.touryukon.com

Tourisme Quebec 1255 Peel St Office 100 .... Montreal QC H3B4V4 514-873-2015 864-3838
Web: www.tourisme.gouv.qc.ca/anglais/index.html

Travel Alberta 999 8th St SW Suite 500 .... Calgary AB T2R1J5 403-297-2700 297-5068
TF: 800-252-3782 ■ *Web:* www.travelalberta.com

Travel Manitoba 155 Carlton St 7th Fl .... Winnipeg MB R3C3H8 204-927-7800 927-7828
TF: 800-665-0040 ■ *Web:* www.travelmanitoba.com

travel.bc.ca 3697 Quadra St .... Victoria BC V8X1H5 866-810-6645 768-1899
Web: travel.bc.ca

York Region Tourism 17250 Young St Box 147 4th Fl .... Newmarket ON L3Y6Z1 905-883-3442 895-3482
TF: 888-448-0000 ■ *Web:* www.yorktourism.com

778 TRAVEL & TOURISM INFORMATION - FOREIGN TRAVEL

SEE ALSO Embassies & Consulates - Foreign, in the US p. 1612

Phone Fax

Anguilla Tourist Marketing Office 246 Central Ave .... White Plains NY 10606 914-287-2400 287-2404
TF: 877-426-4845 ■ *Web:* www.anguilla-vacation.com

Antigua & Barbuda Dept of Tourism & Trade 25 SE 2nd Ave Suite 300 ... Miami FL 33131 305-381-6762 381-7908
TF: 888-268-4227 ■ *Web:* www.antigua-barbuda.org

Antigua & Barbuda Dept of Tourism & Trade 305 E 47th St 6th Fl .... New York NY 10007 212-541-4117 541-4789
TF: 888-268-4227 ■ *Web:* www.antigua-barbuda.org

Argentina National Tourist Office
1101 Brickell Ave Suite 901 South Tower .... Miami FL 33131 305-442-1366 441-7029
Web: www.sectur.gov.ar

Argentina National Tourist Office 12 W 56th St .... New York NY 10019 212-603-0443 586-1786
Web: www.sectur.gov.ar

Aruba Tourism Authority 1 Financial Plaza Suite 2508 .... Fort Lauderdale FL 33394 954-767-6477 767-0432
TF: 800-862-7822 ■ *Web:* www.aruba.com

Aruba Tourism Authority 1750 Powder Springs Rd Suite 190 .... Marietta GA 30064 404-892-7822 873-2193
Web: www.aruba.com

Aruba Tourism Authority 1144 E State St Suite A-300 .... Geneva IL 60134 630-262-5580 262-5581
TF: 800-862-7822 ■ *Web:* www.aruba.com

Aruba Tourism Authority 1200 Harbor Blvd .... Weehawken NJ 07086 201-330-0800 330-8757
TF: 800-862-7822 ■ *Web:* www.aruba.com

Aruba Tourism Authority 10655 Six Pines Dr Suite 145 ..... The Woodlands TX 77380 281-362-1616 362-1644
TF: 800-862-7822 ■ *Web:* www.aruba.com

Austrian Tourist Office PO Box 1142 .... New York NY 10108 212-944-6880 730-4568
Web: www.austria.info/us

Bahamas Tourism Office 11400 W Olympic Blvd Suite 204 ..... Los Angeles CA 90064 310-312-9544 445-8800
TF: 800-439-6993 ■ *Web:* www.bahamas.com

Bahamas Tourism Office 1200 S Pine Island Rd Suite 750 .... Plantation FL 33324 954-236-9292 236-9282
TF: 800-224-3681 ■ *Web:* www.bahamas.com

Bahamas Tourism Office 8600 W Bryn Mawr Ave Suite 580 N ...... Chicago IL 60631 773-693-1500 693-1114
Web: www.bahamas.com

Bahamas Tourism Office 60 E 42nd St Suite 1850 .... New York NY 10165 212-758-2777 753-6531
TF: 800-823-3136 ■ *Web:* www.bahamas.com

Barbados Tourism Authority 3440 Wilshire Blvd Suite 1207 ..... Los Angeles CA 90010 213-380-2198 384-2763
Web: barbados.org/barbados2

Barbados Tourism Authority 150 Alhambra Cir Suite 1000 ..... Coral Gables FL 33134 305-442-7471 774-9497
TF: 800-221-9831 ■ *Web:* barbados.org/barbados2

Barbados Tourism Authority 800 2nd Ave 2nd Fl .... New York NY 10017 212-986-6516 573-9850
TF: 800-221-9831 ■ *Web:* barbados.org/barbados2

Belgian Tourist Office 220 E 42nd St Suite 3402 .... New York NY 10017 212-758-8130 355-7675
Web: www.visitbelgium.com

Bermuda Dept of Tourism 675 3rd Ave 20th Fl .... New York NY 10017 212-818-9800 983-5289
TF: 800-223-6106 ■ *Web:* www.bermudatourism.com

Bonaire Government Tourist Office 10 Rockefeller Plaza Suite 900 ... New York NY 10020 212-956-5911 956-5913
TF: 800-266-2473 ■ *Web:* www.infobonaire.com

British Virgin Islands Tourist Board
3450 Wilshire Blvd Suite 1202 .... Los Angeles CA 90010 213-736-8931 736-8935
TF: 800-835-8530 ■ *Web:* www.bvitourism.com

British Virgin Islands Tourist Board
1270 Broadway Suite 705 .... New York NY 10001 212-696-0400 563-2263
TF: 800-835-8530 ■ *Web:* www.bvitourism.com

Canadian Tourism Commission
1055 Dunsmuir St Suite 1400 4 Bentall Center Box 49220 ..... Vancouver BC V7X1L2 604-638-8300
Web: www.canadatourisme.com

Caribbean Tourism Organization 80 Broad St 32nd Fl .... New York NY 10004 212-635-9530 635-9511
Web: www.doitcaribbean.com

Cayman Islands Dept of Tourism 8300 NW 53rd St Suite 103 .... Miami FL 33166 305-599-9033 599-3766
Web: www.caymanislands.ky

Cayman Islands Dept of Tourism
18 W 140 Butterfield Rd Suite 920 .... Oakbrook Terrace IL 60181 630-705-0650 705-1383
Web: www.caymanislands.ky

Cayman Islands Dept of Tourism 3 Park Ave 39th Fl .... New York NY 10016 212-889-9009 889-9125
TF: 877-422-9626 ■ *Web:* www.caymanislands.ky

Cayman Islands Dept of Tourism 820 Gessner Rd Suite 1335 ...... Houston TX 77024 713-461-1317 461-7409
Web: www.caymanislands.ky

China National Tourist Office 550 N Brand Blvd Suite 910 .... Glendale CA 91203 818-545-7507 545-7506
TF: 800-670-2228 ■ *Web:* www.cnto.org

China National Tourist Office 350 5th Ave Suite 6413 .... New York NY 10118 212-760-8218
Web: www.cnto.org

Corporation Tourisme et Congres de Trois-Rivieres
1457 rue Notre Dame .... Trois-Rivieres QC G9A4X4 819-375-1122 375-0022
TF: 800-313-1123 ■ *Web:* www.tourismetroisrivieres.com

Phone Fax

Croatian National Tourist Office 350 5th Ave Suite 4003 .... New York NY 10118 212-279-8672 279-8683
TF: 800-829-4416 ■ *Web:* www.croatia.hr

Curacao Tourist Board 3361 SW 3rd Ave Suite 102 .... Miami FL 33145 305-285-0511 285-0535
TF: 800-328-7222 ■ *Web:* www.curacao-tourism.com

Cyprus Tourism Organization 13 E 40th St .... New York NY 10016 212-683-5280 683-5282
Web: www.cyprustourism.org

Czech Center New York 1109 Madison Ave .... New York NY 10028 212-288-0830 288-0971
Web: www.czechcenter.com

Czech Center & Tourist Authority 1109 Madison Ave .... New York NY 10028 212-288-0830 288-0971
Web: www.czechcenter.com

Danish Tourist Board 655 3rd Ave 18th Fl .... New York NY 10017 212-885-9700 885-9710
Web: www.visitdenmark.com

Dominican Republic Tourist Board 848 Brickell Ave Suite 405 .... Miami FL 33131 305-358-2899 358-4185
Web: www.dominicanrepublic.com

Dominican Republic Tourist Board 136 E 57th St Suite 803 .... New York NY 10022 212-588-1012 588-1015
TF: 888-374-6361 ■ *Web:* www.dominicanrepublic.com

Egyptian Tourist Authority 630 5th Ave Suite 2305 .... New York NY 10111 212-332-2570 956-6439
TF: 877-773-4978 ■ *Web:* www.egypttourism.org

Fiji Visitors Bureau 5777 W Century Blvd Suite 220 .... Los Angeles CA 90045 310-568-1616 670-2318
TF: 800-932-3454 ■ *Web:* www.bulafiji.com

Finnish Tourist Board 655 3rd Ave 18th Fl .... New York NY 10017 212-885-9700 885-9710
Web: www.gofinland.org

French Government Tourist Office
9454 Wilshire Blvd Suite 210 .... Beverly Hills CA 90212 310-271-6665 276-2835
Web: www.franceguide.com

French Government Tourist Office
205 N Michigan Ave Suite 3770 .... Chicago IL 60601 312-327-0290
Web: www.franceguide.com

French Government Tourist Office 444 Madison Ave 16th Fl ...... New York NY 10022 212-838-7800 838-7855
Web: us.franceguide.com

French West Indies Tourist Board 444 Madison Ave 16th Fl ...... New York NY 10022 212-838-7800 838-7855

Gabon Tourist Information Office 347 5th Ave Suite 805 .... New York NY 10016 212-447-6700 447-1532

German National Tourist Office 122 E 42nd St 20th Fl .... New York NY 10168 212-661-7200 661-7174
Web: www.visits-to-germany.com

Greek National Tourist Organization 645 5th Ave Suite 903 .... New York NY 10022 212-421-5777 826-6940
Web: www.gnto.gr

Grenada Board of Tourism PO Box 1668 .... Lake Worth FL 33460 561-588-8176 588-7267
TF: 800-927-9554 ■ *Web:* www.grenadagrenadines.com

Grenada Board of Tourism 305 Madison Ave Suite 2145 .... New York NY 10165 212-687-9554 682-4748
Web: www.grenadagrenadines.com

Honduras Tourism Institute 299 Alhambra Cir Suite 226 .... Coral Gables FL 33134 305-461-0601 461-0602
TF: 800-410-9608 ■ *Web:* www.letsgohonduras.com

Hong Kong Tourism Board 10940 Wilshire Blvd Suite 2050 ..... Los Angeles CA 90024 310-208-4582 208-1869
TF: 800-282-4582 ■ *Web:* www.discoverhongkong.com

Hong Kong Tourism Board 115 E 54th St 2nd Fl .... New York NY 10022 212-421-3382 421-8428
Web: www.discoverhongkong.com

Hungarian National Tourist Office 350 5th Ave Suite 7107 .... New York NY 10118 212-695-1221 695-0809
Web: www.gotohungary.com

Icelandic Tourist Board PO Box 4649 .... Grand Central Station NY 10163 212-885-9700 885-9710
Web: www.icelandtouristboard.com

India Tourist Office 3550 Wilshire Blvd Suite 204 .... Los Angeles CA 90010 213-380-8855 380-6111
TF: 800-422-4634 ■ *Web:* www.tourismofindia.com

India Tourist Office 1270 Ave of the Americas Suite 1808 .... New York NY 10020 212-586-4901 582-3274
TF: 800-953-9399 ■ *Web:* www.tourismofindia.com

Irish Tourist Board 345 Park Ave 17th Fl .... New York NY 10154 212-418-0800 371-9052
TF: 800-669-9967 ■ *Web:* www.tourismireland.com

Israel Government Tourist Office
6380 Wilshire Blvd Suite 1700 .... Los Angeles CA 90048 323-658-7463 658-6543
Web: www.goisrael.com

Israel Government Tourist Office 800 2nd Ave 16th Fl .... New York NY 10017 212-499-5660 499-5645
TF: 888-774-7723 ■ *Web:* www.goisrael.com

Italian Government Tourist Board
12400 Wilshire Blvd Suite 550 .... Los Angeles CA 90025 310-820-1898 820-6357
Web: www.italiantourism.com

Italian Government Tourist Board
500 N Michigan Ave Suite 2240 .... Chicago IL 60611 312-644-0996 644-3019
Web: www.italiantourism.com

Italian Government Tourist Board 630 5th Ave Suite 1565 .... New York NY 10111 212-245-5618 586-9249
Web: www.italiantourism.com

Jamaica Tourist Board 5201 Blue Lagoon Dr Suite 1101 .... Miami FL 33126 305-665-0557 666-7239
TF: 800-233-4582 ■ *Web:* www.visitjamaica.com

Japan National Tourist Organization
515 S Figueroa St Suite 1470 .... Los Angeles CA 90071 213-623-1952 623-6301
Web: www.japantravelinfo.com

Japan National Tourist Organization
1 Rockefeller Plaza Suite 1250 .... New York NY 10020 212-757-5640 307-6754
Web: www.japantravelinfo.com

Jordan Tourism Board 6867 Elm St Suite 102 .... McLean VA 22101 703-243-7404 243-7406
TF: 877-733-5673 ■ *Web:* www.seejordan.org

Kenya Tourism Board
c/o Carlson Destinationa Marketing Services PO
Box 59159 .... Minneapolis MN 55459 866-445-3692 212-2533*
**Fax Area Code: 763 ■ *TF:* 866-445-3692 ■ *Web:* www.magicalkenya.com

Korea National Tourism Organization
5509 Wilshire Blvd Wilshire Blvd Suite 103 .... Los Angeles CA 90036 323-634-0280 634-0281
TF: 800-868-7567 ■ *Web:* english.tour2korea.com

Korea National Tourism Organization
737 N Michigan Ave Suite 910 .... Chicago IL 60611 312-981-1717 981-1721
TF: 800-868-7567 ■ *Web:* english.tour2korea.com

Korea National Tourism Organization 2 Executive Dr Suite 750 ..... Fort Lee NJ 07024 201-585-0909 585-9041
TF: 800-868-7567 ■ *Web:* english.tour2korea.com

Luxembourg National Tourist Office 17 Beekman Pl .... New York NY 10022 212-935-8888 935-5896
Web: www.ont.lu

Macau Government Tourist Office
1334 Parkview Ave Suite 300 .... Manhattan Beach CA 90266 310-545-3430 545-4221
TF: 866-656-2228 ■ *Web:* www.macautourism.gov.mo

Martinique Promotion Bureau 444 Madison Ave 16th Fl .... New York NY 10022 800-391-4909
Web: www.martinique.org

Mexico Tourism Board 5975 Sunset Dr Suite 305 .... Miami FL 33143 786-621-2909 621-2907
TF: 800-446-3942 ■ *Web:* www.visitmexico.com

Mexico Tourism Board 225 N Michigan Ave Suite 1850 .... Chicago IL 60601 312-228-0517 228-0515
TF: 800-446-3942 ■ *Web:* www.visitmexico.com

Mexico Tourism Board 400 Madison Ave Suite 11-C .... New York NY 10017 212-308-2110 308-9060
TF: 800-446-3942 ■ *Web:* www.visitmexico.com

Mexico Tourism Board 4507 San Jacinto Suite 308 .... Houston TX 77004 713-772-2581 772-6058
TF: 800-446-3942 ■ *Web:* www.visitmexico.com

Monaco Government Tourist Office 565 5th Ave 23rd Fl .... New York NY 10017 212-286-3330 286-9890
TF: 800-753-9696 ■ *Web:* www.visitmonaco.com

Moroccan National Tourist Office
7208 Sand Lake Rd Suite 204 .... Orlando FL 32819 407-264-0133 264-0134
Web: www.tourism-in-morocco.com

Moroccan National Tourist Office 20 E 46th St Suite 1201 .... New York NY 10017 212-557-2520 949-8148
Web: www.tourism-in-morocco.com

Netherlands Board of Tourism & Conventions
355 Lexington Ave 19th Fl .... New York NY 10017 212-370-7360 370-9507
TF: 888-464-6552 ■ *Web:* www.holland.com

	City	State	ZIP	Phone	Fax
New Zealand Tourism Board					
501 Santa Monica Blvd Suite 300	Santa Monica	CA	90401	310-395-7480	395-5453
TF: 866-639-9325 ■ *Web:* www.newzealand.com/travel					
Norwegian Tourist Board 655 3rd Ave 18th Ave	New York	NY	10017	212-885-9700	885-9710
Web: www.visitnorway.com					
Peru Tourist Office 495 Biltmore Way Suite 404	Coral Gables	FL	33134	305-476-1220	
TF: 866-661-7378 ■ *Web:* www.peru.info/perueng.asp					
Philippine Dept of Tourism 556 5th Ave 1st Fl Mezzanine	New York	NY	10036	212-575-7915	302-6759
Web: www.tourism.gov.ph					
Polish National Tourist Office 5 Marine View Plaza Suite 208	Hoboken	NJ	07030	201-420-9910	584-9153
Web: www.polandtour.org					
Portuguese Trade & Tourism Office 590 5th Ave 4th Fl	New York	NY	10036	646-723-0200	575-4737*
**Fax Area Code:* 212 ■ *TF:* 800-767-8842 ■ *Web:* www.visitportugal.com					
Portuguese Trade & Tourist Office					
88 Kearny St Suite 1770	San Francisco	CA	94108	415-391-7080	391-7147
Web: www.visitportugal.com					
Puerto Rico Tourism Co 3575 W Cahuenga Blvd Suite 620	Los Angeles	CA	90068	323-874-5991	874-7257
TF: 800-874-1230 ■ *Web:* www.gotopuertorico.com					
Puerto Rico Tourism Co					
901 Ponce de Leon Blvd Suite 101	Coral Gables	FL	33134	305-445-9112	445-9450
TF: 800-866-7827 ■ *Web:* www.gotopuertorico.com					
Puerto Rico Tourism Co 666 5th Ave 15th Fl	New York	NY	10103	212-586-6262	586-1212
TF: 800-223-6530 ■ *Web:* www.gotopuertorico.com					
Puerto Rico Tourism Co					
Paseo La Princesa PO Box 902-3960	Old San Juan	PR	00902	787-721-2400	722-6238
Web: www.gotopuertorico.com					
Romanian National Tourist Office 355 Lexington Ave 19th Fl	New York	NY	10017	212-545-8484	
Web: www.romaniatourism.com					
Russian National Group 224 W 30th St Suite 701	New York	NY	10001	646-473-2233	473-2205
TF: 877-221-7120 ■ *Web:* www.russia-travel.com					
Russian National Tourist Office 224 W 30th St Suite 701	New York	NY	10001	646-473-2233	473-2205
TF: 877-221-7120 ■ *Web:* www.russia-travel.com					
Saint Barthelemy Tourist Office 444 Madison Ave 16th Fl	New York	NY	10022	212-838-7800	838-7855
Web: us.franceguide.com					
Saint Kitts Tourism Authority 414 E 75th St Suite 5	New York	NY	10021	212-535-1234	734-6511
TF: 800-582-6208 ■ *Web:* www.stkitts-tourism.com					
Saint Lucia Tourist Board 800 2nd Ave 9th Fl	New York	NY	10017	212-867-2950	867-2795
TF: 800-456-3984 ■ *Web:* www.stlucia.org					
Saint Maarten Tourist Office 675 3rd Ave Suite 1807	New York	NY	10017	212-953-2084	953-2145
TF: 800-786-2278 ■ *Web:* www.st-maarten.com					
Saint Martin Tourist Office 675 3rd Ave Suite 1807	New York	NY	10017	212-475-8970	260-8481
TF: 877-956-1234 ■ *Web:* www.st-martin.org					
Saint Vincent & the Grenadines Tourist Information Office					
801 2nd Ave 21st Fl	New York	NY	10017	212-687-4981	949-5946
TF: 800-729-1726 ■ *Web:* www.svgtourism.com					
Scandinavian Tourism Inc 655 3rd Ave 18th Fl	New York	NY	10017	212-885-9700	885-9764
Web: www.visitsweden.com					
Scandinavian Tourist Boards 655 3rd Ave	New York	NY	10017	212-885-9700	885-9710
Web: www.goscandinavia.com					
Senegal Tourist Office 350 5th Ave Suite 3118	New York	NY	10118	212-279-1953	279-1958
Web: www.senegal-tourism.com					
Singapore Tourism Board 5670 Wilshire Blvd Suite 1550	Los Angeles	CA	90036	323-677-0808	677-0801
TF: 800-283-9595 ■ *Web:* www.visitsingapore.com					
Singapore Tourism Board 1156 Ave of Americas Suite 702	New York	NY	10036	212-302-4861	302-4801
Web: www.visitsingapore.com					
South African Tourism Board					
500 5th Ave 20th Fl Suite 2040	New York	NY	10110	212-730-2929	764-1980
TF: 800-593-1318 ■ *Web:* www.southafrica.net/index.cfm					
Swedish Travel & Tourism Council 655 3rd Ave 18th Fl	New York	NY	10017	212-885-9700	885-9764
Web: www.visitsweden.com					
Switzerland Tourism 608 5th Ave Suite 202	New York	NY	10020	212-757-5944	262-6116
TF: 800-794-7795 ■ *Web:* www.myswitzerland.com					
Tahiti Tourism 300 Continental Blvd Suite 160	El Segundo	CA	90245	310-414-8484	414-8490
Web: www.tahiti-tourisme.com					
Taiwan Visitors Assn 3731 Wilshire Blvd Suite 780	Los Angeles	CA	90010	213-389-1158	389-1094
Web: www.taiwan.net.tw					
Taiwan Visitors Assn 555 Montgomery St Suite 505	San Francisco	CA	94111	415-989-8677	989-7242
Web: www.taiwan.net.tw					
Taiwan Visitors Assn 405 Lexington Ave 37th Fl	New York	NY	10174	212-867-1632	867-1635
Web: www.taiwan.net.tw					
Tourism Australia 6100 Center Dr Suite 1150	Los Angeles	CA	90045	310-695-3200	695-3201
TF: 800-369-6863 ■ *Web:* www.australia.com					
Tourism Authority of Thailand					
611 N Larchmont Blvd 1st Fl	Los Angeles	CA	90004	323-461-9814	461-9834
TF: 800-842-4526 ■ *Web:* www.tourismthailand.org					
Tourism Authority of Thailand 61 Broadway Suite 2810	New York	NY	10006	212-432-0433	269-2588
TF: 800-842-4526 ■ *Web:* www.tourismthailand.org					
Tourism Malaysia 818 W 7th St Suite 970	Los Angeles	CA	90017	213-689-9702	689-1530
TF: 800-336-6842 ■ *Web:* www.tourism.gov.my					
Tourism Malaysia 120 E 56th St Suite 810	New York	NY	10022	212-754-1113	754-1116
TF: 800-558-6787 ■ *Web:* www.tourism.gov.my					
Tourism New Zealand 501 Santa Monica Blvd Suite 300	Santa Monica	CA	90401	310-395-7480	395-5453
TF: 866-639-9325 ■ *Web:* www.newzealand.com/travel					
Tourist Office of Spain 8383 Wilshire Blvd Suite 960	Beverly Hills	CA	90211	323-658-7188	658-1061
Web: www.okspain.org					
Tourist Office of Spain 1395 Brickell Ave Suite 1130	Miami	FL	33131	305-358-1992	358-8223
Web: www.okspain.org					
Tourist Office of Spain 845 N Michigan Ave Suite 915-E	Chicago	IL	60611	312-642-1992	642-9817
Web: www.okspain.org					
Tourist Office of Spain 666 5th Ave 35th Fl	New York	NY	10103	212-265-8822	265-8864
Web: www.okspain.org					
Turkish Tourist Office 5055 Wilshire Blvd Suite 850	Los Angeles	CA	90036	323-937-8066	937-1271
Web: www.tourismturkey.org					
Turkish Tourist Office 821 UN Plaza 1st Fl	New York	NY	10017	212-687-2194	599-7568
TF: 877-367-8875 ■ *Web:* www.tourismturkey.org					
Turks & Caicos Islands Tourism Office					
60 E 42nd St Suite 2817	New York	NY	10165	646-375-8830	375-8835
TF: 800-241-0824 ■ *Web:* www.turksandcaicostourism.com					
Turks & Caicos Islands Tourism Office					
60 E 42nd St Suite 2817	New York	NY	10165	646-375-8830	375-8835
TF: 800-241-0824 ■ *Web:* www.turksandcaicostourism.com					
US Virgin Islands Dept of Tourism					
3460 Wilshire Blvd Suite 412	Los Angeles	CA	90010	213-739-0138	739-2005
Web: www.usvitourism.vi					
US Virgin Islands Dept of Tourism					
444 N Capitol St NW Suite 305	Washington	DC	20001	202-624-3590	624-3594
TF: 800-372-8784 ■ *Web:* www.usvitourism.vi					
US Virgin Islands Dept of Tourism					
2655 S LeJeune Rd Suite 907	Coral Gables	FL	33134	305-442-7200	445-9044
TF: 800-372-8784 ■ *Web:* www.usvitourism.vi					
US Virgin Islands Dept of Tourism					
245 Peachtree Center Ave Suite MB-05	Atlanta	GA	30303	404-688-0906	525-1102
Web: www.usvitourism.vi					
US Virgin Islands Dept of Tourism					
500 N Michigan Ave Suite 2030	Chicago	IL	60611	888-656-8784	670-8788*
**Fax Area Code:* 312 ■ *Web:* www.usvitourism.vi					
US Virgin Islands Dept of Tourism					
1270 Ave of the Americas Suite 2108	New York	NY	10020	212-332-2222	332-2223
Web: www.usvitourism.vi					
US Virgin Islands Dept of Tourism PO Box 6400	Saint Thomas	VI	00804	340-774-8784	774-4390
TF: 800-372-8784 ■ *Web:* www.usvitourism.vi					
VisitBritain 551 5th Ave Suite 701	New York	NY	10176	212-986-2266	986-1188
TF: 800-462-2748 ■ *Web:* www.visitbritain.com					
VisitDenmark 655 3rd Ave 18th Fl	New York	NY	10017	212-885-9700	885-9710
Web: www.visitdenmark.com					

779 TREE SERVICES

SEE ALSO Landscape Design & Related Services p. 1885

	City	State	ZIP	Phone	Fax
Asplundh Tree Expert Co 708 Blair Mill Rd	Willow Grove	PA	19090	215-784-4200	784-4405
TF: 800-248-8733 ■ *Web:* www.asplundh.com					
Asplundh Tree Services 708 Blair Mill Rd	Willow Grove	PA	19090	215-784-4200	784-4493
TF: 800-248-8733					
Bartlett FA Tree Expert Co 1290 E Main St	Stamford	CT	06902	203-323-1131	323-1129
TF: 877-227-8538 ■ *Web:* www.bartlett.com					
Care of Trees Inc 2371 Foster Ave	Wheeling	IL	60090	847-394-4220	394-3376
Web: www.thecareoftrees.com					
Davey Tree Expert Co 1500 N Mantua St	Kent	OH	44240	330-673-9511	673-1037*
**Fax:* Hum Res ■ *TF:* 800-445-8733 ■ *Web:* www.davey.com					
FA Bartlett Tree Expert Co 1290 E Main St	Stamford	CT	06902	203-323-1131	323-1129
TF: 877-227-8538 ■ *Web:* www.bartlett.com					
Lewis Tree Service Inc 300 Lucius Gordon Dr	West Henrietta	NY	14586	585-436-3208	235-5864
TF: 800-333-1593 ■ *Web:* www.lewistree.com					
Nelson Tree Service Inc 3300 Office Park Dr Suite 205	Dayton	OH	45439	937-294-1313	294-8673
TF: 800-522-4311 ■ *Web:* www.nelsontree.com					
Shade Tree Service Co Inc 520 S Highway Dr	Fenton	MO	63026	636-343-1212	343-5660
Web: www.stsco.net					
Townsend Tree PO Box 128	Parker City	IN	47368	765-468-3007	468-3131
TF: 800-428-8128 ■ *Web:* www.townsendtree.com					
Trees Inc 650 N Sam Houston Pkwy E Suite 209	Houston	TX	77060	281-447-1327	447-5045
TF: 800-260-0728 ■ *Web:* www.treesinc.com					
West Tree Service Inc 6300 Forbing Rd	Little Rock	AR	72209	501-568-5111	562-9378
TF: 800-779-2967 ■ *Web:* www.westtree.com					
Wright Tree Service Inc PO Box 1718	Des Moines	IA	50306	515-277-6291	
TF: 800-882-1216 ■ *Web:* www.wrighttree.com					

780 TROPHIES, PLAQUES, AWARDS

	City	State	ZIP	Phone	Fax
Architectural Bronze Aluminum Corp					
655 Deerfield Rd Suite 100	Deerfield	IL	60015	847-266-7300	266-7301
TF: 800-339-6581 ■ *Web:* www.architecturalbronze.com					
Au Sable Woodworking Co PO Box 108	Frederic	MI	49733	989-348-7086	348-5246
TF: 800-248-9261					
Award Products Inc 4830 N Front St	Philadelphia	PA	19120	215-324-0414	324-0417
Web: www.amprostrophy.com					
Bruce Fox Inc 1909 McDonald Ln	New Albany	IN	47150	812-945-3511	945-0275
TF: 800-289-3699 ■ *Web:* www.brucefox.com					
Champion Awards Inc 3649 Winplace Rd	Memphis	TN	38118	901-365-4830	365-2796
TF: 800-242-6781 ■ *Web:* www.champion-awards.com					
Classic Medallics Inc 2-15 Borden Ave	Long Island City	NY	11101	718-392-5410	784-1757
Web: www.classic-medallics.com					
Crown Trophy 9 Skyline Dr	Hawthorne	NY	10532	800-583-8228	347-0211*
**Fax Area Code:* 914 ■ *Web:* www.crowntrophy.com					
F & H Ribbon Co Inc PO Box 1338	Hurst	TX	76053	817-283-5891	344-3010*
**Fax Area Code:* 800 ■ *TF:* 800-877-5775 ■ *Web:* www.fhribbon.com					
Fox Bruce Inc 1909 McDonald Ln	New Albany	IN	47150	812-945-3511	945-0275
TF: 800-289-3699 ■ *Web:* www.brucefox.com					
Hand Industries/Dirilyte Line 315 S Hand Ave	Warsaw	IN	46580	574-267-3525	267-7349
Web: www.dirilyte.com					
Jostens Inc 3601 Minnesota Ave Suite 400	Minneapolis	MN	55435	952-830-3300	830-3309*
**Fax:* Hum Res ■ *TF:* 800-235-4774 ■ *Web:* www.jostens.com					
Metallic Arts Inc 914 N Lake Rd	Spokane	WA	99212	509-489-7173	483-1759
TF: 800-541-3200 ■ *Web:* www.metallicarts.com					
Neff Athletic Lettering Co 645 Pine St PO Box 218	Greenville	OH	45331	937-548-3194	544-9030*
**Fax Area Code:* 800 ■ *TF Cust Svc:* 800-232-6333 ■ *Web:* www.neffco.com					
Owens RS & Co 5535 N Lynch Ave	Chicago	IL	60630	773-282-6000	545-4501
TF: 800-282-6200 ■ *Web:* www.rsowens.com					
Perma Plaque Corp 29 W Easy St	Simi Valley	CA	93065	805-520-8600	520-8618
Plastic Dress-Up Co 11077 E Rush St	South El Monte	CA	91733	626-442-7711	442-1814
TF: 800-800-7711 ■ *Web:* www.pdu.com					
Regalia Mfg Co PO Box 4448	Rock Island	IL	61204	309-788-7471	788-0788
TF: 800-798-7471					
RS Owens & Co 5535 N Lynch Ave	Chicago	IL	60630	773-282-6000	545-4501
TF: 800-282-6200 ■ *Web:* www.rsowens.com					
Tropar Mfg Inc 5 Vreeland Rd	Florham Park	NJ	07932	973-822-2400	822-2891
Web: www.airflyte.com					
Trophyland USA Inc 7001 W 20th Ave	Hialeah	FL	33014	800-327-5820	823-4836*
**Fax Area Code:* 305 ■ *TF:* 800-327-5820 ■ *Web:* www.trophyland.com/					
Tuff-Weld Wood Specialties 7569 Woodman Pl	Van Nuys	CA	91405	818-988-0991	782-6697
TF Cust Svc: 800-223-2955 ■ *Web:* www.tuffweld.com					
US Bronze Sign Co 811 2nd Ave	New Hyde Park	NY	11040	516-352-5155	352-1761
TF: 800-872-5155 ■ *Web:* www.usbronze.com					
Western Badge & Trophy Co 1716 W Washington Blvd	Los Angeles	CA	90007	323-735-1201	735-8571
TF: 800-367-4332 ■ *Web:* www.westernbadge.com					
Wilson Trophy Co 1724 Frienza Ave	Sacramento	CA	95815	916-927-9733	927-9955
TF: 800-325-4911 ■ *Web:* www.wilsontrophy.com					

TRUCK BODIES

SEE Motor Vehicles - Commercial & Special Purpose p. 1982

781 TRUCK RENTAL & LEASING

	City	State	ZIP	Phone	Fax
Brody Transportation Co Inc 621 S Bentalou St	Baltimore	MD	21223	410-947-5800	947-5858

Company	City	State	Zip	Phone	Fax
Carco National Lease Inc 2905 N 32nd St. *TF:* 800-643-2596	Fort Smith	AR	72904	479-441-3200	441-3212
DeCarolis Truck Rental Inc 333 Colfax St *TF:* 800-666-1169 ■ *Web:* www.decarolis.com	Rochester	NY	14606	585-254-1169	458-4072
GE Trailer Fleet Services 530 E Swedesford Rd *TF Cust Svc:* 800-333-2030 ■ *Web:* www.trailerservices.com	Wayne	PA	19087	484-254-0100	
Hale Trailer Brake & Wheel Service Inc 5361 Oakview Dr. *TF:* 800-383-8894 ■ *Web:* www.haletrailer.com	Allentown	PA	18104	610-395-0371	395-7868
Idealease Inc 430 N Rand Rd. *Web:* www.idealease.com	North Barrington	IL	60010	847-304-6000	304-0076
Interstate NationaLease 2700 Palmyra Rd.	Albany	GA	31702	229-883-7250	888-9251
Lily Transportation Corp 145 Rosemary St *Web:* www.lily.com	Needham	MA	02494	781-449-8811	449-7128
Mendon Leasing Corp 362 Kingsland Ave *Web:* www.mendonleasing.com	Brooklyn	NY	11222	718-391-5300	349-2514
National Truck Leasing System DBA NationaLease 1 S 450 Summit Ave Suite 300 *TF:* 800-729-6857 ■ *Web:* www.ntls.com	Oakbrook Terrace	IL	60181	630-953-8878	953-0040
NationaLease 1 S 450 Summit Ave Suite 300 *TF:* 800-729-6857 ■ *Web:* www.ntls.com	Oakbrook Terrace	IL	60181	630-953-8878	953-0040
PACCAR Leasing Corp 777 106th Ave NE PO Box 1518 *TF:* 800-426-1420 ■ *Web:* www.paclease.com	Bellevue	WA	98009	425-468-7400	468-8211
Penske Corp Rt 10 Green Hills PO Box 563 **Fax:* Acctg ■ *TF:* 800-222-0277 ■ *Web:* www.penske.com	Reading	PA	19603	610-775-6000	775-5064*
Penske Truck Leasing Co LP Rt 10 Green Hills PO Box 563 **Fax:* Acctg ■ *TF:* 800-222-0277 ■ *Web:* www.pensketruckleasing.com	Reading	PA	19603	610-775-6000	775-5064*
Rapid Ways Truck Leasing Inc 3900 Great Midwest Dr. *TF:* 800-962-7322 ■ *Web:* www.rapidwaysleasing.com	Kansas City	MO	64161	816-455-7262	459-3221
Rush Enterprises Inc 555 IH 35 S Suite 500 *NASDAQ: RUSHA* ■ *TF:* 800-973-7874 ■ *Web:* www.rushenterprises.com	New Braunfels	TX	78130	830-626-5200	626-5310
Ryder System Inc 11690 NW 105th St *NYSE: R* ■ *TF:* 800-327-3399 ■ *Web:* www.ryder.com	Miami	FL	33178	305-500-3726	500-4599
Salem Leasing Corp PO Box 24788 *TF:* 800-877-2536 ■ *Web:* www.salemleasing.com	Winston-Salem	NC	27114	336-768-6800	760-9644
Star Truck Rentals Inc 3940 Eastern Ave SE *TF:* 800-748-0468 ■ *Web:* www.starlease.com	Grand Rapids	MI	49508	616-243-7033	243-7498
U-Haul International Inc PO Box 21502 *TF:* 800-468-4285 ■ *Web:* www.uhaul.com	Phoenix	AZ	85036	602-263-6011	
XTRA Intermodal 100 Tower Dr *TF:* 800-344-9872 ■ *Web:* www.xtraintermodal.com	Burr Ridge	IL	60527	630-789-3200	789-8826

782 TRUCK TRAILERS

SEE ALSO Motor Vehicles - Commercial & Special Purpose p. 1982

Company	City	State	Zip	Phone	Fax
4-Star Trailers Inc 10000 NW 10th St *TF:* 800-848-3095 ■ *Web:* www.4startrailers.com	Oklahoma City	OK	73127	405-324-7827	324-8423
American Carrier Equipment Corp 2285 E Date Ave *TF:* 800-344-2174 ■ *Web:* www.trailer1.com	Fresno	CA	93706	559-442-1500	442-3618
Arkansas Trailer Mfg Co 3200 S Elm St *TF:* 800-666-5417	Little Rock	AR	72204	501-666-5417	666-1787
Barrett Trailers Inc 1831 Hardcastle Blvd *TF:* 888-405-4050 ■ *Web:* www.barrett-trailers.com	Purcell	OK	73080	405-527-5050	527-3206
Beall Corp 8801 N Vancouver Ave *Web:* www.beallcorp.com	Portland	OR	97217	503-735-2110	735-2601
Boydstun Metal Works Inc 9002 N Sever Ct *Web:* www.boydstun.com	Portland	OR	97203	503-285-3515	285-9082
Brenner Tank LLC 450 Arlington Ave *TF:* 800-558-9750 ■ *Web:* www.brennertank.com	Fond du Lac	WI	54935	920-922-5020	922-3303
Bri-Mar Mfg LLC 1080 S Main St *TF:* 800-732-5845 ■ *Web:* www.bri-mar.com	Chambersburg	PA	17201	717-263-6116	263-6479
Clement Industries Inc PO Box 914 *TF Cust Svc:* 800-562-5948 ■ *Web:* www.clementind.com	Minden	LA	71058	318-377-2776	371-4370
CM Trailers Inc 200 County Rd PO Box 680 *TF:* 888-268-7577 ■ *Web:* www.cmtrailers.com	Madill	OK	73446	580-795-5536	795-7263
Cottrell Inc 2125 Candler Rd *TF Sales:* 800-827-0132 ■ *Web:* www.cottrelltrailers.com	Gainesville	GA	30507	770-532-7251	535-2831
Dakota Mfg Co Inc 1909 S Rowley St *TF:* 800-232-5682	Mitchell	SD	57301	605-996-5571	996-5572
Dan Hill & Assoc Inc DBA Flow Boy Mfg PO Box 720660 *TF:* 800-580-3260 ■ *Web:* www.flowboy.com	Norman	OK	73070	405-329-3765	329-8588
Delavan Industries 199 Lein Rd *TF:* 888-508-0700 ■ *Web:* www.delavan.net	West Seneca	NY	14224	716-677-4080	677-4085
Dexter Chassis Group 501 S Miller Dr *TF:* 800-669-7681 ■ *Web:* www.dexterchassisgroup.com	White Pigeon	MI	49099	269-483-7681	483-9089
Doonan Trailer Corp PO Box 1466 *Web:* www.doonan.com	Great Bend	KS	67530	620-792-6222	792-3308
Eager Beaver 14893 Hwy 27 *TF:* 800-257-8163 ■ *Web:* www.eagerbeavertrailers.com	Lake Wales	FL	33853	863-638-1421	638-3705
East Mfg Corp 1871 State Rt 44 PO Box 277 *TF:* 888-405-3278 ■ *Web:* www.eastmfg.com	Randolph	OH	44265	330-325-9921	325-7851
Everlite Inc 607 Fisher Rd **Fax:* Sales ■ *TF:* 800-600-3867 ■ *Web:* www.everlite.net	Longview	TX	75604	903-297-3444	295-1474*
Featherlite Inc PO Box 320 *NASDAQ: FTHR* ■ *TF:* 800-800-1230 ■ *Web:* www.fthr.com	Cresco	IA	52136	563-547-6000	547-6100
Florig Equipment Inc 906 W Ridge Pike *Web:* www.florig.com	Conshohocken	PA	19428	610-825-0900	825-0909
Flow Boy Mfg PO Box 720660 *TF:* 800-580-3260 ■ *Web:* www.flowboy.com	Norman	OK	73070	405-329-3765	329-8588
Fontaine Trailer Co 430 Letson Rd PO Box 619 *TF:* 800-821-6535 ■ *Web:* fontainetrailer.com	Haleyville	AL	35565	205-486-5251	486-7291
General Trailer Parts LLC 1420 S B St *TF:* 800-452-9532 ■ *Web:* www.generaltrailerparts.com	Springfield	OR	97477	541-746-8218	726-4707
Great Dane Trailers Inc 602 E Lathrop Ave *Web:* www.greatdanetrailers.com	Savannah	GA	31415	912-644-2100	644-2166
Heil Trailer International 5741 Cornelison Rd Bldg A **Fax:* Sales ■ *TF:* 800-400-6913 ■ *Web:* www.heiltrailer.com	Chattanooga	TN	37411	423-499-1300	855-6389*
Hesse Inc 6700 St John Ave *TF:* 800-821-5562 ■ *Web:* www.grouphesse.com	Kansas City	MO	64123	816-483-7808	241-9010
Hill Dan & Assoc Inc DBA Flow Boy Mfg PO Box 720660 *TF:* 800-580-3260 ■ *Web:* www.flowboy.com	Norman	OK	73070	405-329-3765	329-8588
Hudson Brothers Trailer Mfg inc 1508 Hwy 218 W *Web:* www.hudsontrailers.com	Indian Trail	NC	28079	704-753-4393	753-2011
J & L's Cargo Express Inc 405 Kesco Dr *Web:* www.cargoexpress.com	Bristol	IN	46507	574-848-7441	848-1407
K-Dee Supply Inc 621 E Lake St *TF:* 800-221-6417	Lake Mills	WI	53551	920-648-8202	648-8138
Kalyn/Siebert LP 1505 W Main St *TF:* 800-525-9689 ■ *Web:* www.kalynsiebert.com	Gatesville	TX	76528	254-865-7235	865-7234
Kentucky Trailer 2601 S 3rd St *TF:* 888-598-7245 ■ *Web:* www.kytrailer.com	Louisville	KY	40208	502-637-2551	636-3675
Kentucky Trailer Technologies 1240 Pontiac Trail *TF:* 800-521-9700 ■ *Web:* www.kytrailers.com	Walled Lake	MI	48390	248-960-9700	960-7775
Kiefer Built Inc 305 E 1st St *TF:* 888-254-3337 ■ *Web:* www.kieferbuiltinc.com	Kanawha	IA	50447	641-762-3201	762-3425
LBT Inc 11502 'I' St.	Omaha	NE	68137	402-333-4900	333-0685
LBT Stainless Inc 1799 Ram Bay Rd	Manning	SC	29102	803-473-5283	473-5284
Ledwell & Son Enterprises 3300 Waco St **Fax:* Sales ■ *Web:* www.ledwell.com	Texarkana	TX	75501	903-838-6531	831-2719*
Liddell Trailers 100 Industrial Dr *TF:* 800-662-9216 ■ *Web:* www.liddelltrailers.com	Springville	AL	35146	205-467-3990	467-3937
Load King Div Terex Corp 701 E Rose St PO Box 427 *TF:* 800-264-5522 ■ *Web:* www.loadkingtrailers.com	Elk Point	SD	57025	605-356-3301	356-3268
Loadcraft Industries Inc 3811 N Bridge St PO Box 1429 *Web:* www.hri-rig.com	Brady	TX	76825	325-597-2911	597-0781
Lufkin Industries Inc 601 S Raguet St *NASDAQ: LUFK* ■ *Web:* www.lufkin.com	Lufkin	TX	75902	936-634-2211	637-5474
Mac Trailer Mfg Inc 14599 Commerce St NE *TF:* 800-795-8454 ■ *Web:* www.mactrailer.com	Alliance	OH	44601	330-823-9900	823-0232
MCT Industries Inc 7451 Pan American Fwy NE *Web:* www.mct-ind.com	Albuquerque	NM	87109	505-345-8651	345-8659
Merritt Equipment Co 9339 Hwy 85 *TF:* 800-634-3036 ■ *Web:* www.merritt-equip.com	Henderson	CO	80640	303-289-2286	227-1083
Mickey Truck Bodies Inc 1305 Trinity Ave PO Box 2044 *TF:* 800-334-9061 ■ *Web:* www.mickeybody.com	High Point	NC	27261	336-882-6806	882-6856
Mobilized Systems Inc 1032 Seabrook Way *Web:* www.gomsi.com	Cincinnati	OH	45245	513-943-1111	943-1113
Nu Van Technology Inc 2155 Hwy 1187 PO Box 759 **Fax:* Orders ■ *TF:* 800-487-1734 ■ *Web:* www.nuvan.com	Mansfield	TX	76063	817-477-1734	473-3942*
Pace American Inc 11550 Harter Dr *TF:* 800-247-5767 ■ *Web:* www.paceamerican.com	Middlebury	IN	46540	574-825-7223	825-7393
Parco-Hesse Corp 1060 Andre-Line Rd *TF:* 800-363-5975 ■ *Web:* www.grouphesse.com	Granby	QC	J2J1J9	450-378-4696	378-3614
Pines Trailer Corp 2555 S Blue Island Ave	Chicago	IL	60608	773-254-5533	254-7610
Polar Service Centers 7600 E Sam Houston Pkwy N *TF:* 800-955-8558 ■ *Web:* www.polartank.com	Houston	TX	77049	281-459-6400	459-5382
Polar Tank Trailer Inc 12810 CR 17 *TF:* 800-826-6589 ■ *Web:* www.polartank.com	Holdingford	MN	56340	320-746-2255	746-2937
Red River Mfg Inc 202 8th St W *TF:* 800-762-5557 ■ *Web:* www.redrivermfg.com	West Fargo	ND	58078	701-282-3013	282-3039
Reliance Trailer Mfg Co 7911 Redwood Dr *TF:* 800-339-7911 ■ *Web:* www.reliancetrailer.com	Cotati	CA	94931	707-795-0081	795-9305
Road Systems Inc 2001 S Benton St *Web:* www.cnf.com/road_systems.asp	Searcy	AR	72143	501-279-0991	279-2644
Rogers Brothers Corp 100 Orchard St *TF:* 800-441-9880 ■ *Web:* www.rogerstrailers.com	Albion	PA	16401	814-756-4121	756-4830
Steco Mfg 2215 S Van Buren St *TF:* 800-627-8326 ■ *Web:* www.stecoinc.com	Enid	OK	73703	580-237-7433	242-1635
Stoughton Trailers LLC 416 S Academy St *Web:* www.stoughton-trailers.com	Stoughton	WI	53589	608-873-2500	873-2575
Strick Corp 225 Lincoln Hwy	Fairless Hills	PA	19030	215-949-3600	949-4779
Summit Trailer Sales Inc 1 Summit Plaza *TF:* 800-437-3729 ■ *Web:* www.summittrailer.com	Summit Station	PA	17979	570-754-3511	754-7025
Talbert Mfg Inc 1628 W SR-114 *TF Cust Svc:* 800-348-5232 ■ *Web:* www.talbertmfg.com	Rensselaer	IN	47978	219-866-7141	866-5437
Terex Corp Load King Div 701 E Rose St PO Box 427 *TF:* 800-264-5522 ■ *Web:* www.loadkingtrailers.com	Elk Point	SD	57025	605-356-3301	356-3268
Thiele Manufacturing LLC 309 Spruce St *Web:* www.thielebody.com	Windber	PA	15963	814-467-4504	467-4172
Timpte Inc 1827 Industrial Dr *TF:* 888-256-4884 ■ *Web:* www.timpte.com	David City	NE	68632	402-367-3056	367-4340
Towmaster Inc 61381 US Hwy 12 *TF:* 800-462-4517 ■ *Web:* www.towmastertrailers.com	Litchfield	MN	55355	320-693-7900	693-7921
Trail King Industries Inc 147 Industrial Pk Rd *TF:* 800-545-1549 ■ *Web:* www.trailking.com	Brookville	PA	15825	814-849-2342	849-5063
Trailmobile Corp 1101 Skokie Blvd Suite 350 *TF:* 800-877-4990 ■ *Web:* www.trailmobile.com	Northbrook	IL	60062	847-504-2000	480-9262
Trailmobile Trailer LLC 1101 Skokie Blvd Suite 350 *TF:* 800-877-4990 ■ *Web:* www.trailmobile.com	Northbrook	IL	60062	847-504-2000	480-9262
Trailstar Mfg Corp 20700 Harrisburg-Westville Rd *TF:* 800-235-5635 ■ *Web:* www.trailstar-trailers.com	Alliance	OH	44601	330-821-9900	821-6941
Transcraft Corp 110 Florsheim Dr *TF:* 800-950-2995 ■ *Web:* www.transcraft.com	Anna	IL	62906	618-833-5151	833-3885
Travis Body & Trailer Inc 13955 Furman Rd FM 529 *TF:* 800-535-4372 ■ *Web:* www.travistrailers.com	Houston	TX	77041	713-466-5888	466-3238
Truck Equipment Service Co 800 Oak St *TF:* 800-869-0363 ■ *Web:* www.cornhusker800.com	Lincoln	NE	68521	402-476-3225	476-3726
Utility Tool & Body Co 151 E 16th St *Web:* www.utilitytoolandbody.com	Clintonville	WI	54929	715-823-3167	823-5274
Utility Trailer Mfg Co 17295 E Railroad St *Web:* www.utilitytrailer.com	City of Industry	CA	91748	626-965-1541	965-2790
Vanco USA Trailer Mfg 1170 Florence Rd PO Box 430 *Web:* www.vancotrailers.com	Columbus	NJ	08022	609-499-4141	499-8865
Vantage Trailers Inc 29335 Hwy 90 *TF:* 800-826-8245 ■ *Web:* www.vantagetrailer.com	Katy	TX	77494	281-391-2664	391-2668
VE Enterprises Inc PO Box 369 *Web:* www.veenterprises.com	Springer	OK	73458	580-653-2171	653-2773
Wabash National Corp PO Box 6129 *NYSE: WNC* ■ *TF Sales:* 800-937-4784 ■ *Web:* www.wabashnational.com	Lafayette	IN	47903	765-771-5300	771-5474
Wells Cargo Inc 1503 W McNaughton St *TF:* 800-348-7553 ■ *Web:* www.wellscargo.com	Elkhart	IN	46514	574-264-9661	264-5938
Western Trailer Co 6700 Business Way *TF:* 888-344-2539 ■ *Web:* www.westerntrailer.com	Boise	ID	83716	208-344-2539	344-1521
Western World Inc 312 Simplot Blvd W *TF:* 800-247-2535 ■ *Web:* www.circlejtrailers.com	Caldwell	ID	83605	208-459-0842	459-0106
Wilson Trailer Co 4400 S Lewis Blvd *TF:* 800-798-2002 ■ *Web:* www.wilsontrailer.com	Sioux City	IA	51106	712-252-6500	252-6510
Witzco Trailers Inc 6101 McIntosh Rd *TF:* 888-922-9900 ■ *Web:* www.witzco.com	Sarasota	FL	34238	941-922-5301	924-2402
WW Trailer Mfg Inc PO Box 807	Madill	OK	73446	580-795-5571	
X-L Specialized Trailers Inc 201 4th St SW *Web:* www.xlspecializedtrailer.com	Oelwein	IA	50662	319-283-4852	283-5312

783 TRUCKING COMPANIES

SEE ALSO Logistics Services (Transportation & Warehousing) p. 1918; Moving Companies p. 1984

Company	City	State	Zip	Phone	Fax
A-1 Fargo International 7700 SW 100th St *Web:* www.a1fargo.com	Miami	FL	33156	305-670-9501	670-1208
A-P-A Transport Corp 2100 85th St	North Bergen	NJ	07047	201-869-6600	869-5472
AAA Cooper Transportation 1751 Kinsey Rd *TF:* 800-633-7571 ■ *Web:* www.aaacooper.com	Dothan	AL	36303	334-793-2284	793-1063

Company	City	State	Zip	Phone	Fax
ABF Freight Systems Inc 3801 Old Greenwood Rd *Fax: Cust Svc ■ *Web:* www.abfs.com	Fort Smith	AR	72903	479-785-8700	785-8800*
Ace Doran Hauling & Rigging Co Inc 1601 Blue Rock St *TF:* 800-829-0929 ■ *Web:* www.acedoran.com	Cincinnati	OH	45223	513-681-7900	853-3188
Ace Transportation Inc PO Box 91714	Lafayette	LA	70509	337-837-4567	837-1423
Acme Truck Line Inc 121 Pailet Dr *TF:* 800-825-6246 ■ *Web:* www.acmetruck.com	Harvey	LA	70058	504-368-2510	368-2510
Admiral-Merchants Motor Freight Inc 215 S 11th St *TF:* 800-972-8864 ■ *Web:* www.ammf.com	Minneapolis	MN	55403	612-332-4819	332-4765
Aetna Freight Lines Inc PO Box 350 *TF:* 800-837-4995	Warren	OH	44482	330-369-5201	369-5204
Alan Ritchey Inc 740 S I-35 E Frontage Rd *TF:* 800-877-0273 ■ *Web:* www.alanritchey.com	Valley View	TX	76272	940-726-3276	726-5335
Allied Automotive Group 160 Clairemont Ave *Web:* www.aag1.com	Decatur	GA	30030	404-371-0379	370-4216
Alvan Motor Freight Inc 3600 Alvan Rd *TF:* 800-632-4172 ■ *Web:* www.alvanmotor.com	Kalamazoo	MI	49001	269-382-1500	345-3888
American Transfer & Storage Co 1735 W Crosby Rd Suite 100A *Web:* www.americantransfer.com	Carrollton	TX	75006	972-466-1111	242-0440
Anderson Trucking Service Inc 755 Opportunity St PO Box 1377 *TF:* 800-328-2307 ■ *Web:* www.ats-inc.com	Saint Cloud	MN	56302	320-255-7400	255-7412
Apgar Bros Inc PO Box 631	Bound Brook	NJ	08805	732-356-3900	356-2557
ARG Trucking Corp 369 Bostwick Rd *Fax: Sales ■ *TF:* 800-334-1314	Phelps	NY	14532	315-789-8871	789-8879*
Arkansas Best Corp PO Box 10048 *NASDAQ: ABFS* ■ *Fax: Sales ■ *Web:* www.arkbest.com	Fort Smith	AR	72917	479-785-6000	785-8927*
Armellini Express Lines Inc 3446 SW Armellini Ave *Fax: Cust Svc ■ *TF:* 800-626-1815 ■ *Web:* www.armellini.com	Palm City	FL	34990	772-287-0575	221-3284*
Arnold Transportation Services Inc 9523 Florida Mining Blvd *TF:* 800-388-8320 ■ *Web:* www.arnoldtrans.com	Jacksonville	FL	32257	904-262-4285	260-0628
Art Pape Transfer Inc 1080 E 12th St	Dubuque	IA	52001	563-588-1435	588-1527
Associated Petroleum Carriers Inc PO Box 2808 *TF:* 800-573-9301	Spartanburg	SC	29304	864-573-9301	573-9305
Atkinson Freight Lines Co 2950 State Rd PO Box 984 *TF:* 800-345-8052 ■ *Web:* www.atkinsonfreight.com	Bensalem	PA	19020	215-638-1130	638-9375
Autolog Corp 1701 E Linden Ave *TF:* 800-526-6078 ■ *Web:* www.autolog.net	Linden	NJ	07036	908-587-9400	587-9685
Automotive Carrier Services Co LLC 402 S Main St 7th Fl *TF:* 800-685-7904 ■ *Web:* www.acstransport.com	Joplin	MO	64801	417-206-5900	206-5997
Autumn Industries Inc 518 Perkins-Jones Rd *TF:* 800-447-2116 ■ *Web:* www.autumnindustries.com	Warren	OH	44483	330-372-5002	372-3699
Averitt Express Inc PO Box 3166 *Fax: Mail Rm ■ *TF:* 800-283-7488 ■ *Web:* www.averittexpress.com	Cookeville	TN	38502	931-526-3306	528-7804*
Baer Howard F Inc 1301 Foster Ave *TF:* 800-447-7430	Nashville	TN	37210	615-255-7351	726-1529
Baggett Transportation Co 2 S 32nd St *TF:* 800-633-8982 ■ *Web:* www.baggetttransport.com	Birmingham	AL	35233	205-322-6501	320-2329
Barry Trucking Inc 3073 S Chase Ave Suite 100 *TF:* 800-279-8395	Milwaukee	WI	53207	414-274-6150	274-6140
Beaver Express Service LLC PO Box 1147 *TF:* 800-593-2328 ■ *Web:* www.beaverexpress.com	Woodward	OK	73802	580-256-6460	256-6239
Beelman Truck Co 1 Racehorse Dr *TF Sales:* 800-541-5918	East Saint Louis	IL	62205	618-646-5300	646-5400
Benton Express Inc PO Box 16709 *TF:* 888-423-6866 ■ *Web:* www.benton-express.com	Atlanta	GA	30321	404-267-2200	267-2201
Besl Transfer Co 5700 Este Ave *TF:* 800-456-2375 ■ *Web:* www.besl.com	Cincinnati	OH	45232	513-242-3456	242-4013
Bilkays Express Co 400 S 2nd St *TF:* 800-526-4006 ■ *Web:* www.bilkays.com	Elizabeth	NJ	07206	908-289-2400	289-6364
BJJ Co Inc PO Box 30010 *TF:* 800-776-2551	Stockton	CA	95213	209-941-8361	941-0476
Black Hills Trucking Inc PO Drawer 2360 *TF:* 800-253-8080	Casper	WY	82602	307-237-9301	266-0252
Blue & Gray Transportation Co Inc 1111 Commerce Rd *TF:* 800-368-2583	Richmond	VA	23234	804-232-2324	233-7383
Boyd Bros Transportation Inc 3275 Hwy 30 *TF:* 800-338-2693 ■ *Web:* www.boydbros.com	Clayton	AL	36016	334-775-1400	775-9310
Britt Trucking Co Inc PO Drawer 707 *TF:* 800-448-9098	Lamesa	TX	79331	806-872-3353	872-2673
Bulkmatic Transport Co 2001 N Cline Ave *TF:* 800-535-8505 ■ *Web:* www.bulkmatic.com	Griffith	IN	46319	219-972-7630	972-7655
Bunning John Transfer Co Inc PO Box 128 *TF:* 800-443-2753	Rock Springs	WY	82902	307-362-3791	362-9040
Burns Motor Freight Inc PO Box 149 *TF:* 800-598-5674 ■ *Web:* www.burns-motor-freight.com	Marlinton	WV	24954	304-799-6106	799-4257
Butler & Co Inc PO Box 570 *TF:* 800-633-8988	Vernon	AL	35592	205-695-7132	695-9500
Butler Trucking Co PO Box 88 *TF:* 800-458-3777	Woodland	PA	16881	814-857-7644	857-5186
Caldwell Freight Lines Inc PO Box 1950 *TF:* 800-438-8244 ■ *Web:* www.caldwellfreight.com	Lenoir	NC	28645	828-728-9231	728-7072
California Cartage Co Inc 3545 Long Beach Blvd 5th Fl *TF:* 888-537-1432 ■ *Web:* www.calcartage.com	Long Beach	CA	90807	562-427-1143	427-6855
CAR Transportation Brokerage Co PO Box 712 *TF:* 800-648-6588	Springdale	AR	72765	479-751-8747	751-6921
Carlile Transportation Services Inc 1800 E 1st Ave *TF:* 800-478-1853 ■ *Web:* www.carlilekw.com	Anchorage	AK	99501	907-276-7797	278-7301
Carroll Fulmer Logistics Corp 8340 American Way *Fax: Mktg ■ *TF:* 800-468-9400	Groveland	FL	34736	352-429-5000	429-0350*
Cassens Transport Co 145 N Kansas St *Web:* www.cassens.com/transport	Edwardsville	IL	62025	618-656-3006	692-7316
Celadon Trucking Services Inc 9503 E 33rd St *TF:* 800-235-2366 ■ *Web:* www.celadontrucking.com	Indianapolis	IN	46235	317-972-7000	890-1922
CenTra 12225 Stephens Rd *TF:* 800-334-4883 ■ *Web:* www.centraltransportint.com	Warren	MI	48089	586-939-7000	759-3631
Central Freight Lines Inc PO Box 2638 *NASDAQ: CENF* ■ *TF:* 800-233-9226 ■ *Web:* www.centralfreight.com	Waco	TX	76702	254-772-2120	741-5370
Central Petroleum Transport Inc 4036 Southgate Dr *TF Sales:* 800-798-6357 ■ *Web:* www.cptrans.com	Sioux City	IA	51111	712-258-6357	258-8592
Central Transport International Inc 12225 Stephens Rd *TF:* 800-334-4883 ■ *Web:* www.centraltransportint.com	Warren	MI	48089	586-939-7000	759-3631
Chadderton Trucking Inc PO Box 687 *TF:* 800-942-8074 ■ *Web:* www.chaddertontrucking.com	Sharon	PA	16146	724-981-5050	981-1615
Cimarron Express Inc 21611 SR-51 PO Box 185 *TF:* 800-759-8979 ■ *Web:* www.cimarronexpress.com	Genoa	OH	43430	419-855-7713	855-7510
Clipper Americas Inc 2500 City West Blvd Suite 500 *Web:* www.clipper-group.com	Houston	TX	77042	713-953-2200	953-2201
Clipper Exxpress Inc 9014 Heritage Pkwy Suite 300 *TF:* 800-678-2547 ■ *Web:* www.clippergroup.com	Woodridge	IL	60517	630-739-0700	739-1817
Coastal Transport Co Inc 5714 Star Ln *TF:* 800-256-8897 ■ *Web:* www.coastaltransport.net	Houston	TX	77057	713-784-1010	784-1302
Colonial Freight Systems Inc 10924 McBride Ln *TF:* 800-826-1402 ■ *Web:* www.cfsi.com	Knoxville	TN	37932	865-966-9711	966-3649
Colorado-Denver Delivery Inc 7170 Dahlia St *TF:* 800-488-3077 ■ *Web:* www.codi.com	Commerce City	CO	80022	303-289-5577	289-1261
Combined Transport Inc 5656 Crater Lake Ave *TF:* 800-547-2870 ■ *Web:* www.combinedtransport.com	Central Point	OR	97502	541-734-7418	826-2001
Comcar Industries Inc 502 E Bridgers Ave *TF Cust Svc:* 800-524-1101 ■ *Web:* www.comcar.com	Auburndale	FL	33823	863-967-1101	965-1023
Commercial Storage & Distribution Co 432 Richmond Rd	Texarkana	TX	75503	903-794-2202	793-4295
Con-Way Central Express Inc 4880 Venture Dr *TF:* 800-421-4007 ■ *Web:* www.con-way.com/aboutcts/ccx.html	Ann Arbor	MI	48108	734-994-6600	663-2966
Con-way Inc 2855 Campus Dr Suite 300 *NYSE: CNW* ■ *Web:* www.con-way.com	San Mateo	CA	94403	650-378-5200	357-9160
Con-Way Southern Express 14500 Trinity Blvd Suite 118 *TF:* 800-525-3117 ■ *Web:* www.con-way.com/aboutcts/cse.html	Fort Worth	TX	76155	817-358-3600	358-3715
Con-Way Transportation Services Inc 110 Parkland Plaza *Web:* www.con-way.com	Ann Arbor	MI	48103	734-769-0203	214-5650
Con-Way Western Express 6301 Beach Blvd Suite 300 *TF:* 800-545-9683 ■ *Web:* www.con-way.com/aboutcts/cwx.html	Buena Park	CA	90621	714-562-0110	562-0761
Container Freight Corp 6150 Paramount Blvd *TF:* 800-252-7208	Long Beach	CA	90805	562-220-2433	220-2522
Contract Freighters Inc PO Box 2547 *Fax: Mktg ■ *TF:* 800-641-4747 ■ *Web:* www.cfi-us.com	Joplin	MO	64803	417-623-5229	623-0532*
Cooper Jack Transport Co Inc 2345 Grand Blvd Suite 400 *TF:* 866-449-6301 ■ *Web:* www.jackcooper.com	Kansas City	MO	64108	816-983-4000	983-5000
Covenant Transport Inc 400 Birmingham Hwy *NASDAQ: CVTI* ■ *TF:* 800-334-9686 ■ *Web:* www.covenanttransport.com	Chattanooga	TN	37419	423-821-1212	821-5442
CR England & Sons Inc 4701 W 2100 South *TF:* 800-453-8826 ■ *Web:* www.crengland.com	Salt Lake City	UT	84120	801-972-2712	
Crescent Truck Lines 2480 Whipple Rd *TF:* 800-722-3171 ■ *Web:* www.crnt.com	Hayward	CA	94544	510-471-8900	471-8990
Cresco Lines Inc 15220 S Halsted St *TF:* 800-323-4476 ■ *Web:* www.crescolines.com	Harvey	IL	60426	708-596-8310	596-9759
Crete Carrier Corp 400 NW 56th St *Fax: Mktg ■ *TF:* 800-998-4095 ■ *Web:* www.cretecarrier.com	Lincoln	NE	68528	402-475-9521	479-2073*
CRST International Inc 3930 16th Ave SW PO Box 68 *Fax: Sales ■ *TF:* 800-366-8460 ■ *Web:* www.crst.com	Cedar Rapids	IA	52406	319-396-4400	390-2649*
CS Henry Transfer Inc PO Box 2306 *TF:* 800-849-6400 ■ *Web:* www.cshenry.com/transfer_index.html	Rocky Mount	NC	27802	252-446-5116	446-3468
CTI PO Box 397 *TF:* 800-362-4952 ■ *Web:* www.cti-az.com	Rillito	AZ	85654	520-624-2348	682-3509
CTL Distribution Inc PO Drawer 437 *TF:* 800-237-9088 ■ *Web:* www.drivectl.com	Mulberry	FL	33860	863-428-2373	428-1731
Curtiss Arlin Trucking Inc PO Box 26 *TF:* 800-328-8940	Montevideo	MN	56265	320-269-5581	269-9417
Daggett Truck Line Inc PO Box 158 *TF:* 800-262-9393	Frazee	MN	56544	218-334-3711	334-2566
Dahlsten Truck Line Inc 101 W Edgar PO Box 95 *TF:* 800-228-4313 ■ *Web:* www.dahlsten.com	Clay Center	NE	68933	402-762-3511	762-3592
Daily Express Inc 1072 Harrisburg Pike *TF:* 800-735-3136 ■ *Web:* www.dailyexp.com	Carlisle	PA	17013	717-243-5757	240-2103
Dallas & Mavis Specialized Carrier Co 625 55th St *Web:* www.dallas-mavis.com	Kenosha	WI	53140	888-878-2504	
Dana Transport Inc 210 Essex Ave E *TF:* 800-733-3262 ■ *Web:* www.danacompanies.com	Avenel	NJ	07001	732-750-9100	
Dart Transit Co Inc PO Box 64110 *TF:* 800-366-9000 ■ *Web:* www.dartadvantage.com	Saint Paul	MN	55164	651-688-2000	683-1600
Daylight Transport 1501 Hughes Way *TF:* 800-468-9999 ■ *Web:* www.dylt.com	Long Beach	CA	90810	310-507-8200	507-8310
Decker Truck Line 3584 5th Ave S *Web:* www.deckercompanies.com/decker.htm	Fort Dodge	IA	50501	515-576-4141	576-4158
Del Monte Trucking Operations 2 Nestle Way *TF:* 800-634-6300	Lathrop	CA	95330	209-547-7275	547-7247
Dennis Trucking Co Inc 630 Parkway Run *Fax Area Code: 215 ■ *TF:* 800-333-4961	Brook	PA	19008	800-333-4961	492-9148*
Devine Intermodal 3870 Channel Dr *TF:* 800-371-4430 ■ *Web:* www.devineintermodal.com	West Sacramento	CA	95691	916-371-4430	371-0355
Diamond Transportation System Inc 5021 21st St *TF:* 800-927-5702 ■ *Web:* www.diamondtrans.net	Racine	WI	53406	262-554-5400	554-5412
Distribution Technologies Inc DBA DistTech 14841 Sperry Rd *TF:* 800-321-3143 ■ *Web:* www.disttech.com	Newbury	OH	44065	440-338-1010	338-1256
DistTech 14841 Sperry Rd *TF:* 800-321-3143 ■ *Web:* www.disttech.com	Newbury	OH	44065	440-338-1010	338-1256
Doudell Trucking Co 555 E Capitol Ave	Milpitas	CA	95035	408-263-7300	263-2266
Duffy Brothers Inc PO Box 250 *TF:* 800-242-1887	Columbus	WI	53925	920-623-4160	623-4199
Dun Transportation & Stringing Inc 304 Reynolds Ln *Web:* www.duntrans.com	Sherman	TX	75092	903-891-9660	891-9665
Duncan Machinery Movers Inc 2004 Duncan Machinery Dr *TF:* 800-331-0116 ■ *Web:* www.dmmlex.com	Lexington	KY	40504	859-233-7333	233-7365
E & L Transport Co LLC 35005 W Michigan Ave *Fax: Hum Res ■ *TF:* 800-833-8322 ■ *Web:* www.eltrans.com	Wayne	MI	48184	734-729-9500	729-9780*
ECL Group of Cos Ltd 7100 44th St SE *Web:* www.eclgroup.com	Calgary	AB	T2C2V7	403-720-5000	720-5060
EL Farmer & Co PO Box 3512 *TF:* 800-592-4753	Odessa	TX	79760	432-332-1496	334-6057
Ennis Transportation Co Inc PO Drawer 715 *TF:* 800-527-6772	Ennis	TX	75120	972-878-5801	878-4560
Enterprise Truck Line Inc 336 W US Hwy 30 Suite 201	Valparaiso	IN	46385	219-476-1300	476-1385
Epes Carriers Inc 3400 Edgefield Ct *TF:* 800-869-3737 ■ *Web:* www.epestransport.com	Greensboro	NC	27409	336-668-3358	668-7005
Erickson Transport Corp PO Box 10068 *TF:* 800-641-4595	Springfield	MO	65808	417-862-6741	862-4992
Esparza Enterprises Inc 7201 Schirra Ct Suite A	Bakersfield	CA	93313	661-323-3772	831-0040
Estes Express Lines Inc 3901 W Broad St *Fax: Sales ■ *TF:* 800-569-0920 ■ *Web:* www.estes-express.com	Richmond	VA	23230	804-353-1900	353-8001*
EW Wylie Corp 222 40th St SW *TF Cust Svc:* 800-437-4132 ■ *Web:* www.wylietrucking.com	Fargo	ND	58103	701-282-5550	281-0415
Ewell HR Inc 4635 Division Hwy *TF:* 800-233-0161 ■ *Web:* www.hrewell.com	East Earl	PA	17519	717-354-4556	355-9184
Farmer EL & Co PO Box 3512 *TF:* 800-592-4753	Odessa	TX	79760	432-332-1496	334-6057
FedEx Freight East PO Box 840 *TF:* 800-874-4723 ■ *Web:* www.fedexfreight.fedex.com	Harrison	AR	72602	870-741-9000	741-3002
FedEx Freight West 6411 Guadalupe Mines Rd *Fax: Cust Svc ■ *TF:* 800-845-4647 ■ *Web:* www.fedexfreight.fedex.com	San Jose	CA	95120	408-268-9600	748-0701*
FFE Transportation Services Inc 1145 Empire Central Pl *Fax: Sales ■ *TF:* 800-569-9200 ■ *Web:* www.ffeinc.com	Dallas	TX	75247	214-630-8090	819-5625*
Finch NE Co 1925 S Darst St	Peoria	IL	61607	309-671-1433	671-1474
Five Star Trucking Inc 4380 Glenbrook Rd *TF:* 800-321-3658 ■ *Web:* www.fivestartrucking.com	Willoughby	OH	44094	440-953-9300	953-1863
Floyd & Beasley Transfer Co Inc PO Box 8 *TF:* 800-952-7599 ■ *Web:* www.fbtcinc.com	Sycamore	AL	35149	256-245-4385	249-3002
Fort Edward Express Co Inc PO Box 394 *TF:* 800-342-1233	Fort Edward	NY	12828	518-792-6571	792-6985
Forward Air Corp 420 Airport Rd PO Box 1058 *NASDAQ: FWRD* ■ *TF:* 800-726-6654 ■ *Web:* www.forwardair.com	Greeneville	TN	37744	423-636-7100	497-4625
Fredericksen Tank Lines Inc PO Box 235 *TF:* 800-441-2109	West Sacramento	CA	95691	916-371-4655	371-7983

Phone Fax

Fulmer Carroll Logistics Corp 8340 American Way ... Groveland FL 34736 352-429-5000 429-0350*
*Fax: Mktg ■ TF: 800-468-9400
Gabler Trucking Inc 1580 Gabler Rd PO Box 220 ... Chambersburg PA 17201 717-261-1492 264-8967
Web: www.hcgabler.com
Gainey Transportation Services Inc 6000 Clay Ave SW ... Grand Rapids MI 49548 616-530-8551 530-6064
TF: 800-859-4072 ■ Web: www.gaineycorp.com
GI Trucking Co 14727 Alondra Blvd ... La Mirada CA 90638 714-523-1122 523-2575
TF: 800-541-1670 ■ Web: www.gi-trucking.com
Gibco Motor Express Inc PO Box 18 ... Elberfeld IN 47613 812-867-0069 867-4962
TF: 800-333-4285
Gordon Trucking Inc 151 Stewart Rd SW ... Pacific WA 98047 253-863-7777 863-8497
TF: 800-426-8486 ■ Web: www.gordontrucking.com
Gra-Bell Truck Line Inc PO Box 1019 ... Holland MI 49422 616-396-1453 396-3882
TF: 800-632-5300 ■ Web: www.gra-bell.com
Gray Jack Transport Inc 4600 E 15th Ave ... Gary IN 46403 219-938-7020 938-6866
Gray Truck Line Co PO Box 1406 ... Lake Alfred FL 33850 863-956-3431 956-5226
TF: 800-282-6884
Great Lakes Cartage Co PO Box 4704 ... Youngstown OH 44515 330-793-9331 793-6505
TF Cust Svc: 800-228-4274
Green Transfer & Storage Co 10099 N North Portland Rd ... Portland OR 97203 503-286-0673 286-0676
Groendyke Transport Inc 2510 Rock Island Blvd ... Enid OK 73701 580-234-4663 234-1216
TF: 800-843-2103 ■ Web: www.groendyke.com
Gully Transportation Inc 3820 Wismann Ln ... Quincy IL 62305 217-224-0770 224-9885
Web: www.gullyicx.com
H & W Trucking Co Inc 1772 N Andy Griffith Pkwy PO Box 1545 ... Mount Airy NC 27030 336-789-2188 789-7973
TF: 800-334-9181 ■ Web: www.hwtrucking.com
Hallamore Motor Transportation Inc 795 Plymouth St ... Holbrook MA 02343 781-767-2000 767-0845
TF: 800-242-1300 ■ Web: www.hallamore.com
Heartland Express Inc 2777 Heartland Dr ... Coralville IA 52241 319-545-2728 545-1349
NASDAQ: HTLD ■ TF: 800-553-1201 ■ Web: www.heartlandexpress.com
Heartland Express Inc 1515 Wherebottom Springs Rd ... Chester VA 23836 804-768-0016 768-4686
TF: 800-444-4929 ■ Web: www.heartlandexpress.com
Henry CS Transfer Inc PO Box 2306 ... Rocky Mount NC 27802 252-446-5116 446-3468
TF: 800-849-6400 ■ Web: www.cshenry.com/transfer_index.html
Higgins Erectors & Haulers Inc 7715 Lockport Rd ... Niagara Falls NY 14304 716-297-2600 205-0159
Highway Transport Inc PO Box 50068 ... Knoxville TN 37950 865-584-8631 584-2851
Web: www.hytt.com
Hirschbach Motor Lines Inc 920 W 21st St PO Box 9 ... South Sioux City NE 68776 402-494-5000 772-2500*
*Fax Area Code: 800 ■ TF: 800-554-2969 ■ Web: www.hirschbach.com
Hodges Trucking Co Inc 4050 W I-40 ... Oklahoma City OK 73108 405-947-7764 942-5636
TF: 800-733-7765 ■ Web: www.hodgestruckandcrane.com
Houff Transfer Inc PO Box 220 ... Weyers Cave VA 24486 540-234-9233 234-9011
TF: 800-476-4683 ■ Web: www.houff.com
Howard F Baer Inc 1301 Foster Ave ... Nashville TN 37210 615-255-7351 726-1529
TF: 800-447-7430
Howard Sheppard Inc PO Box 797 ... Sandersville GA 31082 478-552-5127 552-6973
Web: www.howardsheppard.com
Howard's Express Inc 369 Bostwick Rd ... Phelps NY 14532 315-789-8871 789-0279
TF: 800-274-1100
HR Ewell Inc 4635 Division Hwy ... East Earl PA 17519 717-354-4556 355-9184
TF: 800-233-0161 ■ Web: www.hrewell.com
Hribar Trucking Inc 1521 Waukesha Rd ... Caledonia WI 53108 262-835-4401 835-4043
Web: www.hribarcompanies.com
HTL Inc PO Box 988DTS ... Omaha NE 68101 712-328-2393 322-8667
TF: 800-877-4136
Interstate Distributor Co 11707 21st Ave S ... Tacoma WA 98444 253-537-9455 795-1050*
*Fax Area Code: 800 ■ TF: 800-426-8560 ■ Web: www.intd.com
Irvin Dick Inc 475 Wilson Ave ... Shelby MT 59474 406-434-5583 434-5505
TF: 800-332-5131
J & J Motor Service Inc 2338 S Indiana Ave ... Chicago IL 60616 312-225-3323 225-9873
Jack B Kelley Inc 8101 W 34th Ave ... Amarillo TX 79121 806-353-3553 353-9611
TF: 800-225-5525 ■ Web: www.jackbkelley.com
Jack Cooper Transport Co Inc 2345 Grand Blvd Suite 400 ... Kansas City MO 64108 816-983-4000 983-5000
TF: 866-449-6301 ■ Web: www.jackcooper.com
Jack Gray Transport Inc 4600 E 15th Ave ... Gary IN 46403 219-938-7020 938-6866
Jerry Lipps Trucking Inc 3888 Nash Rd PO Drawer F ... Cape Girardeau MO 63702 573-335-8204 335-4483
TF Cust Svc: 800-325-3331 ■ Web: www.jerrylippsinc.com
Jevic Transportation Inc 700 Creek Rd ... Delanco NJ 08075 856-461-7111 764-6734*
*Fax: Hum Res ■ TF: 800-257-0427 ■ Web: www.jevic.com
JH Walker Trucking Co Inc 152 N Hollywood Rd ... Houma LA 70364 985-868-8330 873-5210
TF: 800-535-5992 ■ Web: www.jhwalkertrucking.com
Jones Motor Co Inc 900 W Bridge St PO Box 137 ... Spring City PA 19475 610-948-7900 948-5660
TF: 800-825-6637 ■ Web: www.jonesmotor.com
KAG West 4076 Seaport Blvd ... West Sacramento CA 95691 916-371-8241 677-0810
Web: www.kagwest.com
Kahului Trucking & Storage Inc 140 Hobron Ave ... Kahului HI 96732 808-877-5001 877-0572
Kaplan Trucking Co 6600 Bessemer Ave ... Cleveland OH 44127 216-341-3322 341-3348
Web: www.kaplantrucking.com
Kauai Commercial Co Inc 1811 Leleiona St ... Lihue HI 96766 808-245-1985 245-2079
Keller Transfer Line Inc 5635 Clay Ave SW ... Grand Rapids MI 49548 616-531-1850 531-0810
TF: 800-666-0701
Kelley Jack B Inc 8101 W 34th Ave ... Amarillo TX 79121 806-353-3553 353-9611
TF: 800-225-5525 ■ Web: www.jackbkelley.com
Kenan Advantage Group Inc 4895 Dressler Rd NW ... Canton OH 44718 330-491-0474 491-1471
TF: 800-969-5149 ■ Web: www.kenanadvantagegroup.com
Kenan Transport Co 100 Europa Ctr Suite 320 ... Chapel Hill NC 27517 919-967-8221 929-5295
TF: 800-768-8765
Key Energy 2210 W Broadway ... Sweetwater TX 79556 325-236-6611 236-6106
TF: 800-749-6613 ■ Web: www.keyenergy.com
Kings County Truck Lines 754 S Blackstone ... Tulare CA 93275 559-686-2857 685-4649
TF: 800-842-5285
Kinnie Annex Cartage Co 32097 Hollingsworth Ave ... Warren MI 48092 586-939-2880 939-3705
TF: 888-546-6432
KLLM Transport Services Inc 135 Riverview Dr ... Richland MS 39218 601-939-2545 936-5496*
*Fax: Mktg ■ TF: 800-925-1000 ■ Web: www.kllm.com
Knight Transportation Inc 5601 W Buckeye Rd ... Phoenix AZ 85043 602-269-2000 269-8409
NYSE: KNX ■ TF: 800-489-2000 ■ Web: www.knighttransportation.com
Kruepke Trucking Inc 2881 Hwy P ... Jackson WI 53037 262-677-3155 677-3206
TF: 800-798-5000
La Rosa Del Monte Express Inc 1133-35 Tiffany St ... Bronx NY 10459 718-991-3300 893-1948
TF: 800-452-7672 ■ Web: www.larosadelmonte.com
Land Span Inc 1120 W Griffin Rd ... Lakeland FL 33805 863-688-1102 683-2190
TF: 800-248-4847 ■ Web: www.landspan.com
Land Transportation 1901 Phoenix Blvd Suite 210 ... Atlanta GA 30349 678-251-2500 251-2534
TF: 888-831-4448 ■ Web: www.landtrans.net
Landair Corp 1110 Myers St ... Greeneville TN 37743 423-783-1300 783-1354*
*Fax: Cust Svc ■ TF: 888-526-3247 ■ Web: www.landair.com
Landstar Express America Inc 13410 Sutton Park Dr S ... Jacksonville FL 32224 800-872-3278 390-1216*
*Fax Area Code: 904 ■ *Fax: Hum Res
Landstar Gemini Inc 13410 Sutton Park Dr S ... Jacksonville FL 32224 800-862-9232
Landstar Inway Inc 1000 Simpson Rd ... Rockford IL 61102 815-972-5000 972-5270*
*Fax: Hum Res ■ TF: 800-435-4373
Landstar Ligon Inc 13410 Sutton Park Dr S ... Jacksonville FL 32224 904-306-2440 235-1991*
*Fax Area Code: 800 ■ TF: 800-235-4466
Landstar Ranger Inc 13410 Sutton Pk Dr S ... Jacksonville FL 32224 904-398-9400 872-1216*
*Fax Area Code: 800 ■ *Fax: Hum Res ■ TF: 800-872-9400

Landstar System Inc 13410 Sutton Park Dr S ... Jacksonville FL 32224 904-398-9400 390-1437
NASDAQ: LSTR ■ TF: 800-872-9400 ■ Web: www.landstar.com
Langer Transport Corp 420 Rt 440 N ... Jersey City NJ 07305 201-434-1600 434-1120
Lanter Co PO Box 68 ... Madison IL 62060 618-452-9500 452-9510
TF: 800-966-6137 ■ Web: www.lanter.com
Lawrence Transportation Systems PO Box 7667 ... Roanoke VA 24019 540-966-4000 966-4555
TF: 800-336-9626 ■ Web: www.lawrencetransportation.com
LCT Transportation Services 26444 County Rd 33 ... Okahumpka FL 34762 352-326-8900 365-1181
TF: 800-874-3344
Lee & Eastes Tank Lines Inc 2418 Airport Way S ... Seattle WA 98134 206-623-5403 623-3611
TF: 800-552-7496
Linden Bulk Transportation Co Inc 4200 Tremley Point Rd ... Linden NJ 07036 908-862-3883 986-5090*
*Fax: Sales ■ TF: 800-333-2855 ■ Web: www.lindenbulk.com
Linden Motor Freight Co Inc 1300 Lower Rd ... Linden NJ 07036 908-862-1400 862-1526
Web: www.lindenmotorfreight.com
Linden Warehouse & Distribution Co Inc 1300 Lower Rd ... Linden NJ 07036 908-862-1400 862-1526
Web: www.lindenwarehouse.com
Lipps Jerry Trucking Inc 3888 Nash Rd PO Drawer F ... Cape Girardeau MO 63702 573-335-8204 335-4483
TF Cust Svc: 800-325-3331 ■ Web: www.jerrylippsinc.com
Liquid Transport Corp 8470 Allison Pointe Blvd Suite 400 ... Indianapolis IN 46250 317-841-4200 841-8259
TF: 800-942-3175 ■ Web: www.liquidtransport.com
Lisa Motor Lines Inc PO Box 4529 ... Fort Worth TX 76164 817-336-2900 336-2816
TF: 800-569-9234 ■ Web: www.lisamtc.com
LL Smith Trucking Inc PO Box 987 ... Riverton WY 82501 307-856-2491 856-7432
LoBiondo Brothers Motor Express Inc PO Box 550 ... Rosenhayn NJ 08352 856-451-2410 451-6923
Lockwood Bros Inc 220 Salters Creek Rd ... Hampton VA 23661 757-722-1946 722-3699
TF: 800-367-5295 ■ Web: www.lockwoodbros.com
Lodi Truck Service Inc PO Box 1120 ... Lodi CA 95241 209-334-4100 333-0609
Lynden Transport Inc 3027 Rampart Dr ... Anchorage AK 99501 907-276-4800 257-5160
TF: 800-327-9390 ■ Web: www.ltia.lynden.com
Mail Contractors of America
3800 N Rodney Parham Rd Suite 331 ... Little Rock AR 72212 501-280-0500 280-0111
TF: 800-294-7743 ■ Web: www.mcalogistics.com
Mainliner Motor Express Inc PO Box 7439 ... Omaha NE 68107 402-734-3500 733-7813
TF: 800-228-9887
Malone Freight Lines 1901 Floyd Bradford Rd ... Trussville AL 35173 205-951-1900 951-5957
TF: 800-366-6350 ■ Web: www.malonefreightlines.com
Market Transport Ltd 110 N Marine Dr ... Portland OR 97217 503-283-2405 289-8453
TF: 800-547-0781 ■ Web: www.markettransport.com
Marten Transport Ltd 129 Marten St ... Mondovi WI 54755 715-926-4216 926-5609
NASDAQ: MRTN ■ TF: 800-395-3000 ■ Web: www.marten.com
Martin Howard Inc 4315 Meyer Rd ... Fort Wayne IN 46806 260-447-5591 447-4026
TF: 800-348-4759
Martin Trucking Inc PO Box M ... Hugoton KS 67951 620-544-4920 544-4990
TF: 800-737-0047
Matheson Trucking Inc 10519 E Stockton Blvd Suite 125 ... Elk Grove CA 95624 916-685-2330 685-8875
TF: 800-455-7678 ■ Web: www.mathesoninc.com
Maust Transportation 21848 76th Ave S ... Kent WA 98032 253-479-0261 479-0399
TF: 800-446-2878 ■ Web: www.maustcorp.com
Maverick Transportation Inc PO Box 15428 ... Little Rock AR 72231 501-945-6130 955-1500*
*Fax: Sales ■ TF: 800-289-6600 ■ Web: www.maverickusa.com
May Trucking Co 4185 Brooklake Rd PO Box 9039 ... Salem OR 97305 503-393-7030 642-0105*
*Fax Area Code: 208 ■ TF: 800-547-9169 ■ Web: www.maytrucking.com
Mayfield Transfer Co Inc 3200 W Lake St ... Melrose Park IL 60160 708-681-4440 681-4483
TF: 800-222-2959 ■ Web: www.mfld.net
McClendon Transportation Group PO Box 641 ... Lafayette AL 36862 334-864-9311 864-0028
TF: 800-633-7710 ■ Web: www.mccl.com
McDermott Inc PO Box 544 ... Enosburg Falls VT 05450 802-933-2144 933-2867
McKenzie Tank Lines Inc PO Box 1200 ... Tallahassee FL 32302 850-576-1221 574-2351
Web: www.mckenzietank.com
McLeod Trucking & Rigging PO Box 790376 ... Charlotte NC 28206 704-372-3611 372-3611
TF: 800-438-0330
McQuaide WC Inc 153 Macridge Ave ... Johnstown PA 15904 814-269-6000 269-6092
TF: 800-456-0292 ■ Web: www.mcquaide.com
Melton Truck Lines Inc 808 N 161 East Ave ... Tulsa OK 74116 918-234-8000 234-1004
TF: 800-545-6651 ■ Web: www.meltontruck.com
Mercer Transportation Co PO Box 35610 ... Louisville KY 40232 502-584-2301 648-2859*
*Fax Area Code: 800 ■ TF: 800-626-5375 ■ Web: www.mercer-trans.com
MGM Transport Corp 1 Railroad Ave ... Ridgefield NJ 07657 201-840-1340 840-9985
TF: 800-646-8726
Midwest Coast Transport 1600 E Benson Rd ... Sioux Falls SD 57104 605-339-8400 339-8407
TF Cust Svc: 800-843-6699 ■ Web: www.midwest-coast.com
Midwest Motor Express Inc 5015 E Main Ave ... Bismarck ND 58502 701-223-1880 224-1405
TF: 800-741-4097 ■ Web: www.mmeinc.com
Milan Express Co Inc 1091 Kefauver Dr PO Box 699 ... Milan TN 38358 731-686-7428 686-8829
TF: 800-231-7303 ■ Web: www.milanexpress.com
Miller Transporters Inc 5500 Hwy 80 W ... Jackson MS 39209 601-922-8331 923-2535
TF Cust Svc: 800-645-5378 ■ Web: www.millert.com
Motor Cargo Industries Inc 845 W Center St ... North Salt Lake UT 84054 801-936-1111 299-5225
TF: 800-922-4099 ■ Web: www.motorcargo.com
Murrows Transfer Inc PO Box 4095 ... High Point NC 27263 336-475-6101 475-1240
TF Cust Svc: 800-669-2928 ■ Web: www.murrows.com
National Carriers Inc PO Box 1358 ... Liberal KS 67905 620-624-1621 626-0627
TF: 800-835-9180 ■ Web: www.nationalcarriers.com
Navajo Express Inc PO Box 17880 ... Denver CO 80217 303-287-3800 286-9661*
*Fax: Sales ■ TF: 800-525-1969 ■ Web: www.navajo.com
NE Finch Co 1925 S Darst St ... Peoria IL 61607 309-671-1433 671-1474
Neely Ross Systems Inc 1500 2nd St ... Birmingham AL 35214 205-798-1137 798-0751
Web: www.rossneely.com
New England Motor Freight Inc 1-71 North Ave East ... Elizabeth NJ 07201 908-965-0100 965-1881
Web: www.nemf.com
New Penn Motor Express Inc 625 S 5th Ave ... Lebanon PA 17042 717-274-2521 274-5593
TF Cust Svc: 800-285-5000 ■ Web: www.newpenn.com
Nick Strimbu Inc 3500 Parkway Rd ... Brookfield OH 44403 330-448-4071 448-1672
TF: 800-446-8785 ■ Web: www.nickstrimbu.com
North Shore Central Illinois Freight Co 5101 S Lawndale Ave ... Summit IL 60501 708-496-8222 496-8449
Web: www.northshorelogistics.net
Nussbaum Trucking Inc 2200 N Main St ... Normal IL 61761 309-452-4426 452-4431
TF: 800-322-7305 ■ Web: www.nussbaum.com
Old Dominion Freight Line Inc 500 Old Dominion Way ... Thomasville NC 27360 336-889-5000 802-5229
NASDAQ: ODFL ■ TF: 800-432-6335 ■ Web: www.odfl.com
Oliver Trucking Co Inc PO Box 53 ... Winchester KY 40392 859-744-6373 744-6016
TF: 800-354-7421
Osborn Transportation Inc PO Box 1830 ... Gadsden AL 35902 256-442-2514 413-0002
Web: www.osborntransportation.com
Ozark Motor Lines Inc 3934 Homewood Rd ... Memphis TN 38118 901-251-9711 251-0222
TF: 800-264-4100 ■ Web: www.ozark.com
PAM Transportation Services Inc PO Box 188 ... Tontitown AR 72770 479-361-9111 361-5335
NASDAQ: PTSI ■ TF: 800-879-7261 ■ Web: www.pamt.com
Pape Art Transfer Inc 1080 E 12th St ... Dubuque IA 52001 563-588-1435 588-1527
Patriot Transportation Holding Inc 1801 Art Museum Dr 3rd Fl ... Jacksonville FL 32207 904-396-5733 396-0258
NASDAQ: PATR ■ TF: 877-704-1776 ■ Web: www.patriottrans.com
Peet Frate Line Inc 650 S Eastwood Dr PO Box 1129 ... Woodstock IL 60098 815-338-5500 338-1052
TF: 800-435-6909 ■ Web: www.peetfrateline.com
Perkins Specialized Transportation Inc 5502 W 73rd St ... Indianapolis IN 46268 317-297-3550 298-2071
TF: 800-428-3762 ■ Web: www.perkinsspecialized.com
Peters Truck Lines PO Box 218 ... Yreka CA 96097 530-842-4134 842-4765

Phone Fax

Petron Inc PO Box 8718 Alexandria LA 71306 318-445-5685 448-1727
TF: 800-551-6678
Pitt Ohio Express 15 27th St Pittsburgh PA 15222 412-281-9883 232-3392
TF Cust Svc: 800-366-7488 ■ Web: www.pittohio.com
Powers Transportation Systems Inc PO Box 103 Savannah GA 31402 912-966-2198 966-2791
TF: 888-673-1287 ■ Web: www.ptran.com
Pozas Brothers Trucking Co Inc 8130 Enterprise Dr Newark CA 94560 510-742-9939 742-9979
TF: 800-874-8383
Prestera Trucking PO Box 399 South Point OH 45680 740-894-4770 894-5051
TF: 800-759-9555
Prime Inc PO Box 4208 Springfield MO 65808 417-866-0001 521-6850*
*Fax: Sales ■ TF Cust Svc: 800-848-4560 ■ Web: www.primeinc.com
Puget Sound Truck Lines Inc 3720 Airport Way S Seattle WA 98134 206-623-1600 621-7793
TF: 800-638-2254 ■ Web: www.psfl.com
Quality Carriers Inc PO Box 580129 Pleasant Prairie WI 53158 262-857-2341 857-7497
Quality Distribution Inc 3802 Corporex Pk Dr Suite 200 Tampa FL 33619 813-630-5826 630-9637
NASDAQ: QLTY ■ TF: 800-282-2031 ■ Web: www.qualitydistribution.com
Raven Transport Co Inc 6800 Broadway Ave Jacksonville FL 32254 904-880-1515 880-1913
Web: www.raventrans.com
Redwood Coast Trucking 2210 Peninsula Dr Arcata CA 95521 707-443-0857 443-1247
Refrigerated Food Express Inc PO Box 347 Avon MA 02322 508-587-4600 588-9655
TF: 800-225-2350 ■ Web: www.refrigeratedfood.com
Reliable Trucking Inc 5141 Commercial Cir Concord CA 94520 925-681-6500 449-6234
TF: 800-952-3344
RFK Transportation 5650 6th St SW Cedar Rapids IA 52404 319-364-8102 364-8339
TF: 800-322-8412 ■ Web: www.rfktrans.com
Ritchey Alan Inc 740 S I-35 E Frontage Rd Valley View TX 76272 940-726-3276 726-5335
TF: 800-877-0273 ■ Web: www.alanritchey.com
Roadway Express Inc 1077 Gorge Blvd Akron OH 44310 330-384-1717 258-6068
TF: 800-762-3929 ■ Web: www.roadway.com
Roehl Transport Inc 1916 E 29th St PO Box 750 Marshfield WI 54449 715-591-3795 387-1942
TF: 800-826-8367 ■ Web: www.roehl.net
Ross Neely Systems Inc 1500 2nd St Birmingham AL 35214 205-798-1137 798-0751
Web: www.rossneely.com
Rountree Transport & Rigging Inc 2640 N Lane Ave Jacksonville FL 32254 904-781-1033 786-6229
TF: 800-342-5036 ■ Web: www.rountreetransport.com
Roy Bros Inc 764 Boston Rd Billerica MA 01821 978-667-1921 667-5091
TF Cust Svc: 800-225-0830
RTI Transport Inc 5635 Clay Ave SW Grand Rapids MI 49548 616-531-1467 531-0810
TF: 800-666-0701
Sagara Trucking Inc PO Box 1345 Woodland CA 95776 530-662-9611 662-5863
Saia Motor Freight Line Inc 11456 Johns Creek Pkwy Suite 400 Duluth GA 30097 770-232-4050 232-4055*
*Fax: Cust Svc ■ TF: 800-950-7242 ■ Web: www.saia.com
Sammons Trucking 3665 W Broadway Missoula MT 59808 406-728-2600 549-4989
TF: 800-548-9276 ■ Web: www.sammonstrucking.com
Schilli Transportation Services Inc 6358 W US 24 Remington IN 47977 219-261-2101 261-2879
TF: 800-759-2101 ■ Web: www.schilli.com
Schneider National Inc 3101 S Packerland Dr PO Box 2545 Green Bay WI 54306 920-592-2000 592-3565*
*Fax: Mktg ■ TF Cust Svc: 800-558-6767 ■ Web: www.schneider.com
SCS Transportation Inc 4435 Main St Suite 930 Kansas City MO 64111 816-960-3664 714-5920
NASDAQ: SCST ■ TF: 800-533-9643 ■ Web: www.scstransportation.com
Seaboard Tank Lines Inc 124 Monahan Ave Dunmore PA 18512 570-343-2491 963-7625
TF: 800-338-4221
Shaffer Trucking Inc 49 E Main St PO Box 418 New Kingstown PA 17072 717-766-4708 795-5550
TF Cust Svc: 800-742-3337 ■ Web: www.shaffertrucking.com
Shaw Trucking Inc 7804 Belvedere Rd West Palm Beach FL 33411 800-930-7263 731-7627*
*Fax Area Code: 954 ■ Web: www.shawtrucking.com
Shaw Willis Express Inc 201 N Elm St Elm Springs AR 72728 479-248-7261 248-1967
TF: 800-643-3540 ■ Web: www.willisshaw.com
Sheedy Drayage Co Inc 1215 Michigan St San Francisco CA 94107 415-648-7171 648-1535
TF: 800-792-2984 ■ Web: www.sheedycrane.com
Shippers Express Co 1651 Kerr Dr Jackson MS 39204 601-948-4251 948-5232
TF: 800-647-2480
Short Freight Lines Inc 459 S River Rd Bay City MI 48708 989-893-3505 893-3151
TF: 800-248-0625
Shuster's Transportation Inc 750 E Valley St Willits CA 95490 707-459-4131 459-1855
Smithway Motor Xpress Inc 2031 Quail Ave Fort Dodge IA 50501 515-576-7418 576-6106
NASDAQ: SMXC ■ TF: 800-247-4972 ■ Web: www.smxc.com
South Shore Transportation Inc 4010 Columbus Ave Sandusky OH 44870 419-626-6267 626-9640
TF: 800-418-9726 ■ Web: www.sshoretrans.com
Southeastern Freight Lines Inc 420 Davega Rd Lexington SC 29073 803-794-7300 939-3462*
*Fax: Cust Svc ■ TF: 800-637-7335 ■ Web: www.sefl.com
Southwestern Motor Transport Inc 4600 Goldfield San Antonio TX 78218 210-661-6791 662-3295
TF: 800-531-1071 ■ Web: www.smtlines.com
Spectraserv Inc 75 Jacobus Ave South Kearny NJ 07032 973-589-0277 589-0415
TF: 800-445-4436 ■ Web: www.spectraserv.com
Stahly Cartage Co 119 S Main St Edwardsville IL 62025 618-656-5070 656-0293
TF: 800-851-5553
Star Transportation Inc 1116 Polk Ave Nashville TN 37210 615-256-4336 256-2330
TF: 800-333-3060 ■ Web: www.startransportation.com
Stevens Transport PO Box 279010 Dallas TX 75227 972-216-9000 289-7002
TF: 800-233-9369 ■ Web: www.stevenstransport.com
Strimbu Nick Inc 3500 Parkway Rd Brookfield OH 44403 330-448-4071 448-1672
TF: 800-446-8785 ■ Web: www.nickstrimbu.com
Sullivan RM Transportation 649 Cottage St Springfield MA 01104 413-739-2558 739-1955
TF: 800-628-1064
Sunbelt Furniture Express Inc PO Box 487 Hickory NC 28603 828-464-7240 465-3560
TF: 800-766-1117
Sunco Carriers Inc 1025 N Chestnut Rd Lakeland FL 33805 863-688-1948 680-1759
TF: 800-237-8288 ■ Web: www.suncocarriers.com
Sunflower Carriers Inc PO Box 9 York NE 68467 402-362-7491 362-9495
TF Cust Svc: 800-775-5000
Superior Carriers Inc 711 Jory Blvd Suite 101-N Oak Brook IL 60523 630-573-2555 573-2570
TF: 800-654-7707 ■ Web: www.superior-carriers.com
Swift Transportation Co Inc 2200 S 75th Ave Phoenix AZ 85043 602-269-9700 907-7380*
NASDAQ: SWFT ■ *Fax Area Code: 623 ■ TF: 800-800-2200 ■ Web: www.swifttrans.com
T & T Trucking Inc 11396 N Hwy 99 Lodi CA 95240 209-368-3629 931-6156
TF: 800-692-3457 ■ Web: www.tttrucking.com
Tank Lines Inc 1357 Diamond Springs Rd Virginia Beach VA 23455 757-464-9349 464-0685
TF: 800-969-1357
Tankstar USA Inc PO Box 736 Milwaukee WI 53201 414-671-1600 647-7947
TF: 800-338-5699 ■ Web: www.tankstar.com
Tauro Brothers Trucking Co 1775 N State St Girard OH 44420 330-545-9763 545-2276
TF: 800-860-9763
Telfer Oil Co 211 Foster St Martinez CA 94553 925-228-1515 229-3955
TF: 800-624-9917 ■ Web: www.telferoil.com
Teresi Trucking Inc PO Box 1270 Lodi CA 95241 209-368-2472 369-2830
TF: 800-692-3431 ■ Web: www.teresitrucking.com
Thomas WS Transfer Inc 1854 Morgantown Ave Fairmont WV 26554 304-363-8050 363-8052
TF: 800-624-8062
Tiona Truck Line Inc PO Box 90 Butler MO 64730 660-679-4197 679-3616
TF: 800-821-3046 ■ Web: www.trucktiona.com
Tower Central Inc PO Box 6010 Wheeling WV 26003 304-277-1000 277-1572
Trailer Bridge Inc 10405 New Berlin Rd E Jacksonville FL 32226 904-751-7100 751-7444
NASDAQ: TRBR ■ TF: 800-554-1589 ■ Web: www.trailerbridge.com
TransAm Trucking Inc 15910 S 169th Hwy Olathe KS 66051 913-782-5300 324-7194
TF: 800-573-0588 ■ Web: www.transamtruck.com

Phone Fax

Transport Corp of America Inc 1715 Yankee Doodle Rd Eagan MN 55121 651-686-2500 686-2566
TF: 800-328-3927 ■ Web: www.transportamerica.com
Transport Inc PO Box 400 Moorhead MN 56561 218-236-6300 236-0352
TF: 800-598-7267 ■ Web: www.transport-inc.com
Transport Service Co 908 N Elm St Suite 101 Hinsdale IL 60521 630-920-5800 920-6806
TF Sales: 800-323-5561 ■ Web: www.transportserviceco.com
TransWood Inc 2565 St Marys Ave Omaha NE 68105 402-346-8092 341-2112
Web: www.transwood.com
Trimac Transportation System PO Box 3000 Rapid City SD 57709 605-348-1063 341-0649
TF: 800-843-4012 ■ Web: www.trimac.com
Trinity Industries Transportation Inc 2525 N Stemmons Fwy Dallas TX 75207 214-631-4420 589-8501
Web: www.trinitytrucking.com
Triple Crown Services 2720 Dupont Commerce Ct Suite 200 Fort Wayne IN 46825 260-416-3600 416-3771
TF: 800-325-6510 ■ Web: www.triplecrownsvc.com
Truck Transport Inc 2280 Cassens Dr Fenton MO 63026 636-343-1877 343-3042
TF: 800-274-5995
Truckers Express 3501 W Broadway Missoula MT 59808 406-721-6002 721-9380
Web: www.truckersexpress.com
Turner Brothers Trucking Co Inc PO Box 83017 Oklahoma City OK 73148 405-680-5100 681-6968
Underwood Machinery Transport Inc 940 W Troy Ave Indianapolis IN 46225 317-783-9235 782-2769
TF: 800-428-2372 ■ Web: www.underwoodcompanies.com
United Road Services Inc 10701 Middlebelt Rd Romulus MI 48174 734-947-7900
TF: 888-730-7797 ■ Web: www.unitedroad.com
Universal Truckload Services Inc 12755 E Nine Mile Rd Warren MI 48089 586-920-0100 920-0258
NASDAQ: UACL ■ TF: 800-233-9445 ■ Web: www.uacl.com
US Cargo & Courier Service 900 Williams Ave Columbus OH 43212 614-552-2746 358-1368
TF: 800-234-8608 ■ Web: www.us-cargo.com
US Xpress Enterprises Inc 4080 Jenkins Rd Chattanooga TN 37421 423-510-3000 510-4006
NASDAQ: XPRSA ■ TF: 800-251-6291 ■ Web: www.usxpress.com
USA Truck Inc 3200 Industrial Pk Rd Van Buren AR 72956 479-471-2500 471-2577
NASDAQ: USAK ■ TF: 800-872-8782 ■ Web: www.usa-truck.com
USF Bestway Inc 17200 N Perimeter Dr Scottsdale AZ 85255 480-760-1675 760-3005
TF: 800-274-1250 ■ Web: www.usfc.com/ltl/home/bestway.jsp
USF Glen Moore Inc 1711 Shearer Dr Carlisle PA 17013 717-245-0788 245-9848*
*Fax: Cust Svc ■ Web: www.usfc.com/truckload/home
USF Holland Inc 750 E 40th St Holland MI 49423 616-395-5000 392-3104
TF: 800-456-6322 ■ Web: www.usfc.com/ltl/home/holland.jsp
USF Reddaway Inc PO Box 1035 Clackamas OR 97015 503-650-1286 722-3673
TF: 800-395-1360 ■ Web: www.usfc.com/ltl/home/reddaway.jsp
Vitran Corp Inc 185 The West Mall Suite 701 Toronto ON M9C5L5 416-596-7664 596-8039
NASDAQ: VTNC ■ Web: www.vitran.com
Vitran Express Inc 6500 E 30th St Indianapolis IN 46219 317-803-6400 543-1228
TF: 800-366-0150 ■ Web: www.vitranexpress.com
Waggoners Trucking PO Box 31357 Billings MT 59107 406-248-1919 248-7557
TF: 800-999-9097 ■ Web: www.waggonerstrucking.com
Ward Trucking Corp PO Box 1553 Altoona PA 16603 814-944-0803 944-5470
TF: 800-458-3625 ■ Web: www.wardtrucking.com
Warren Transport Inc PO Box 420 Waterloo IA 50704 319-233-6113 233-7459
TF: 800-553-2792 ■ Web: www.warrentransport.com
WC McQuaide Inc 153 Macridge Ave Johnstown PA 15904 814-269-6000 269-6092
TF: 800-456-0292 ■ Web: www.mcquaide.com
Weaver Brothers Inc 2230 Spar Ave Anchorage AK 99501 907-278-4526 276-4316
TF: 800-478-4600 ■ Web: www.wbialaska.com
Werner Enterprises Inc PO Box 45308 Omaha NE 68145 402-895-6640 894-3927*
NASDAQ: WERN ■ *Fax: Hum Res ■ TF: 800-228-2240 ■ Web: www.werner.com
Western Co-op Transport Assn PO Box 327 Montevideo MN 56265 320-269-5531 269-5532
TF: 800-992-8817 ■ Web: www.westernco-op.com
White Brothers Trucking Co PO Box 82 Wasco IL 60183 630-584-3810 584-3816
TF: 800-323-4762
Wildwood Express Trucking 12416 E Swanson Ave Kingsburg CA 93631 559-897-1035 897-1038
TF: 800-627-3115
Wilhelm Trucking Co PO Box 10363 Portland OR 97296 503-227-0561 241-4913
TF Cust Svc: 800-275-3974 ■ Web: www.wilhelmtruck.com
Willis Shaw Express Inc 201 N Elm St Elm Springs AR 72728 479-248-7261 248-1967
TF: 800-643-3540 ■ Web: www.willisshaw.com
Wilson Trucking Corp PO Box 200 Fishersville VA 22939 540-949-3200 949-3205
TF: 800-494-5766 ■ Web: www.wilsontrucking.com
Wispak Transport Inc 11225 W County Line Rd Milwaukee WI 53224 414-410-8282 357-6234
TF: 800-558-0560
Womeldorf Inc PO Box 829 Du Bois PA 15801 814-849-8347 849-8340
TF: 800-245-6339
Wynne Transport Service Inc 2222 N 11th St Omaha NE 68108 402-342-4001 342-4608
TF: 800-383-9330 ■ Web: www.wynnetr.com
Yanke Group of Cos 2815 Lorne Ave Saskatoon SK S7J0S5 306-955-4221 955-5663
TF: 800-667-7988 ■ Web: www.yanke.ca
Yeatts Transfer Co PO Box 687 Altavista VA 24517 434-369-5695 369-5705
TF: 800-446-0939
Yellow Freight System Inc 10990 Roe Ave Overland Park KS 66211 913-344-3000 344-4909*
*Fax: Sales ■ TF: 800-458-3323
Young's Commercial Transfer 44 S Lotas St Porterville CA 93257 559-784-6651 784-5280
TF: 800-289-1639
Yourga Trucking Inc 154 JH Yourga Pl Wheatland PA 16161 724-981-3600 981-3603
TF: 800-245-1722 ■ Web: www.yourga.com

784 TYPESETTING & RELATED SERVICES

SEE ALSO Graphic Design p. 1767; Printing Companies - Commercial Printers p. 1503

Phone Fax

A-1 Composition Co 208 S Jefferson St Chicago IL 60661 312-236-8733 373-6399
Acitronics 746 E Main St Branford CT 06405 203-481-0308 481-5901
Ano-Coil Corp 60 E Main St Rockville CT 06066 860-871-1200 872-0534
TF: 800-492-7286 ■ Web: www.anocoil.com
Aptara Inc 3110 Fairview Park Dr Falls Church VA 22042 703-352-0001 352-8862
Web: www.aptaracorp.com
Artisan Press 726 Jefferson Ave Ashland OR 97520 541-482-3373 482-3379
TF: 800-424-9364 ■ Web: www.artisanpress.net
Auto-Graphics Inc 3201 Temple Ave Pomona CA 91768 909-595-7204 595-3506
TF: 800-776-6939 ■ Web: www4.auto-graphics.com
Banta Premedia Services 18790 W 78th St Chanhassen MN 55317 952-937-5005 937-5034
Web: www.bantadigital.com
BeaconPMG 1797 Seddon Ct Ashland OH 44805 419-289-0558 289-8923
Web: www.beacon.com
Black Dot Group 6115 Official Rd Crystal Lake IL 60014 815-459-8520 459-7259
Web: www.blackdot.com
Blanks Color Imaging 2343 N Beckley Ave Dallas TX 75208 214-741-3905 741-6105
TF: 800-325-7651 ■ Web: www.blanks.com
Carey Digital 1718 Central Pkwy Cincinnati OH 45214 513-241-5210 241-2205
TF: 800-767-6071 ■ Web: www.careydigital.com
Casablanca Printing Inc 2716 S Grand Ave Santa Ana CA 92705 714-662-2250 662-2825
Web: www.casablancaprinting.com

Company / Address	City	State	ZIP	Phone	Fax
Cenveo Colorhouse 13010 County Rd 6 *TF:* 800-328-8046 ■ *Web:* www.cenveocolorhouse.com	Plymouth	MN	55441	763-553-0100	550-3600
Chakra Communications 644 Ellicott St *Web:* www.chakracentral.com	Buffalo	NY	14203	716-505-7300	505-7301
Citiplate Inc 1600 Stewart Ave Suite 201 **Fax:* Orders ■ *TF:* 800-280-9778 ■ *Web:* www.citiplate.com	Westbury	NY	11590	516-484-2000	484-9778*
Cohber Press PO Box 93100 *TF:* 800-724-3032 ■ *Web:* www.cohber.com	Rochester	NY	14692	585-475-9100	475-9406
Color Communication Inc 4000 W Fillmore St *TF:* 800-458-5743 ■ *Web:* www.ccicolor.com	Chicago	IL	60624	773-638-1400	638-0887
Composing Room of Michigan Inc 678 Front Ave NW Suite 135 *Web:* www.comproom.com	Grand Rapids	MI	49504	616-776-7940	776-7944
Computer Composition Corp 1401 W Girard Ave *Web:* www.computercomposition.com	Madison Heights	MI	48071	248-545-4330	544-1611
Container Graphics Corp 113 Edinburgh Dr S Suite 110 *Web:* www.containergraphics.com	Cary	NC	27511	919-481-4200	469-4897
Continental Colorcraft 1166 W Garvey Ave *Web:* www.continentalcolorcraft.com	Monterey Park	CA	91754	323-283-3000	283-3206
CSW Inc 1723 Canton Ave *TF:* 800-837-4221	Toledo	OH	43604	419-243-4221	243-7509
Dix Type Inc 200-B Gateway Park Dr *Web:* www.dixtype.com	North Syracuse	NY	13212	315-478-4700	478-4946
Dixie Graphics Co 636 Grassmere Park *Web:* www.dixiegraphics.com	Nashville	TN	37211	615-832-7000	832-7621
Donnelley Financial 201 S College St Suite 2250 **Fax:* Sales ■ *Web:* www.rrdonnelley.com/wwwrrd/Markets/Financial/Financial.asp	Charlotte	NC	28244	704-335-6600	344-9694*
ET Lowe Publishing Co 2920 Sidco Dr *Web:* www.etlowe.com	Nashville	TN	37204	615-254-8866	254-8867
Fine Arts Engraving Co 109 Shore Dr *Web:* www.faec.com	Burr Ridge	IL	60527	630-920-9300	920-1524
G & S Typesetters Inc 410 Baylor St *Web:* www.gstype.com	Austin	TX	78703	512-478-5341	476-4756
GGS Information Services Inc 3265 Farmtrail Rd *TF:* 800-927-4474 ■ *Web:* www.ggsinc.com	York	PA	17409	717-764-2222	767-1132
Graphics Group 2800 Taylor St *Web:* www.graphicsgroup.com	Dallas	TX	75226	214-749-2222	749-2252
Imaging Technologies Services Inc 655 Lambert Dr NE *Web:* www.itrepro.com	Atlanta	GA	30324	404-874-8400	872-1215
In Sync Media 550 N Oak St *Web:* www.insyncmedia.com	Inglewood	CA	90302	310-680-2200	680-2595
IPC Communications Services 501 Colonial Dr *TF:* 888-563-3220 ■ *Web:* www.ipc-world.com	Saint Joseph	MI	49085	269-983-7105	983-5736
IPP Lithoplate Corp 1313 W Randolph St 2nd Fl *Web:* www.ipplitho.com	Chicago	IL	60607	312-243-0465	243-6318
Jackson Typesetting Co Inc 1820 W Ganson St	Jackson	MI	49202	517-784-0576	784-1200
KC Photo Engraving Co 2666 E Nina St *TF:* 800-660-4127	Pasadena	CA	91107	323-681-0203	681-6506
Kreber Graphics Inc 2580 Westbelt Dr *TF:* 800-777-3501 ■ *Web:* www.kreber.com	Columbus	OH	43228	614-529-5701	777-4890
Lake Shore Imaging Inc 815 25th Ave	Bellwood	IL	60104	312-427-8216	427-4949
Lasergraphics Inc 4 Squire Rd *Web:* www.laserg.com	Revere	MA	02151	781-289-2022	289-2027
Ligature 4909 Alcoa Ave *TF:* 800-944-5440 ■ *Web:* www.theligature.com	Los Angeles	CA	90058	323-585-6000	585-1737
Lowe ET Publishing Co 2920 Sidco Dr *Web:* www.etlowe.com	Nashville	TN	37204	615-254-8866	254-8867
Mark Trece Inc 112 Connolly Rd *TF:* 800-638-1464 ■ *Web:* www.marktrece.com	Fallston	MD	21047	410-893-3903	893-3906
Maryland Composition Co 14880 Sweitzer Rd *Web:* www.marylandcomp.com	Laurel	MD	20707	410-760-7900	760-5295
MATRIX Publishing Co 1920 Bank Ln *Web:* www.matrixpublishing.com	York	PA	17404	717-764-9673	764-9672
Matthews Packing Graphics 1851 Harbor Bay Pkwy Suite 1000 *Web:* www.matthewsgsd.com	Alameda	CA	94502	510-263-1840	337-0177
Memphis Engraving Co 5120 Elmore Rd *TF:* 800-426-6803 ■ *Web:* www.goimec.com	Memphis	TN	38134	901-388-8200	377-2739
National Engraving Co 248 Oxmoor Ct *TF:* 800-633-8613	Birmingham	AL	35209	205-942-2809	942-2363
New England Typographic Service Inc 206 W Newberry Rd *Web:* www.netype.com	Bloomfield	CT	06002	860-242-2251	242-9350
Newtype Inc 447 Rt 10E Suite 14 *Web:* www.newtypeinc.com	Randolph	NJ	07869	973-361-6000	361-6005
Pal Graphics Inc 2525 Braga Dr *Web:* www.palgraphics.com	Broadview	IL	60155	708-344-8500	344-8503
Para Plate & Plastics Inc 15910 Shoemaker Ave *TF:* 800-788-1556	Cerritos	CA	90701	562-404-3434	404-2496
Pine Tree Composition Inc 26 Forrestal St *Web:* www.pinetreecomposition.com	Lewiston	ME	04240	207-786-2113	786-3509
Presstek Inc 55 Executive Dr *NASDAQ: PRST* ■ *TF:* 877-862-2227 ■ *Web:* www.presstek.com	Hudson	NH	03051	603-595-7000	594-8575
Printing Prep Inc 12 E Tupper St *TF:* 877-878-7114 ■ *Web:* www.printleader.us	Buffalo	NY	14203	716-852-5011	852-3150
Pro Image Corp 517 Carlisle Ave *TF:* 800-245-7259 ■ *Web:* www.proimagecorp.com	York	PA	17404	717-845-5300	845-5301
Progressive Information Technologies 315 Busser Rd *TF:* 800-673-2500 ■ *Web:* www.pit-magnus.com	Emigsville	PA	17318	717-764-5908	767-4092
Regency Infographics Inc 2867 E Allegheny Ave	Philadelphia	PA	19134	215-425-8810	634-0780
Richards Graphic Communications Inc 2700 Van Buren St *Web:* www.rgcnet.com	Bellwood	IL	60104	708-547-6000	547-6044
Ridgways Inc 6300 Gulfton St *Web:* www.ridgways.com	Houston	TX	77081	713-782-8580	782-2862
Riverpoint Media Group 150 Eva St *Web:* www.riverpointmedia.com	Saint Paul	MN	55107	651-227-4037	227-7368
Schawk Inc 1600 E Sherwin Ave *TF:* 800-621-1909 ■ *Web:* www.schawk.com	Des Plaines	IL	60018	847-296-6000	296-9466
Schawk Inc 2626 2nd St NE *Web:* www.schawk.com	Minneapolis	MN	55418	612-789-8514	789-5424
Southern Colortype Co Inc 2927 Sidco Dr	Nashville	TN	37204	615-256-1631	726-2320
Southern Graphic Systems Inc 2823 S Floyd St *TF:* 800-228-3720	Louisville	KY	40209	502-637-5443	624-5299
Southern Graphics Systems 7435 Empire Dr	Florence	KY	41042	859-525-1190	647-8205
Spectragraphic Inc 4 Brayton Ct *Web:* www.spectragraphic.com	Commack	NY	11725	631-499-3100	499-5255
ST Assoc Inc One Teal Rd *Web:* www.stassoc.com	Wakefield	MA	01880	781-246-4700	246-4218
Stevenson The Color Co Inc 535 Wilmer Ave *Web:* www.stevensoncolor.com	Cincinnati	OH	45226	513-321-7500	321-7502
Stratford Textech 70 Landmark Hill Dr *TF:* 800-451-4328 ■ *Web:* www.stratfordpublishing.com	Brattleboro	VT	05301	802-254-6073	254-5240
Studio Image Inc 3110 N Clybourn Ave	Burbank	CA	91505	818-848-1300	848-0974
T & R Graphic Imaging Inc 2535 17th St *TF:* 800-525-2497 ■ *Web:* www.tandrinc.com	Denver	CO	80211	303-458-0626	455-8905
Texas Graphics Resource 1601 Prudential Dr	Dallas	TX	75235	214-630-2800	630-0713
Thomas Technology Solutions Inc 1 Progress Dr *TF:* 800-872-2828 ■ *Web:* www.thomastechsolutions.com	Horsham	PA	19044	215-682-5000	682-5200
Total Works Inc 2222 N Elston Ave *TF:* 866-489-4313 ■ *Web:* www.totalworks.net	Chicago	IL	60614	773-489-4313	489-0482
Trece Mark Inc 112 Connolly Rd *TF:* 800-638-1464 ■ *Web:* www.marktrece.com	Fallston	MD	21047	410-893-3903	893-3906
TSI Graphics Inc 520 Spirit of St Louis Blvd *Web:* www.tsigraphics.com	Chesterfield	MO	63005	636-532-1393	532-7301
Typesetting Inc 1144 S Robertson Blvd *TF:* 800-794-8973	Los Angeles	CA	90035	310-273-3330	273-0733
Unity Engraving Co Inc 210 S Van Brunt Ave	Englewood	NJ	07631	201-569-6400	569-2956
VT Graphics Inc 465 Penn St PO Box 5334 *Web:* www.vtgraph.com	Yeadon	PA	19050	610-259-4090	259-7235
West Essex Graphics Inc 305 Fairfield Ave *TF:* 800-221-5859 ■ *Web:* www.westessexgraphics.com	Fairfield	NJ	07004	973-227-2400	227-2906
Yaeger Graphics Inc 935 W 3rd Ave	Columbus	OH	43212	614-294-6326	294-7363
Zenith Engraving Co 731 Wilson St PO Box 870 *TF:* 800-551-7535 ■ *Web:* www.zenithengraving.com	Chester	SC	29706	803-377-1911	581-1998

785 ULTRASONIC CLEANING EQUIPMENT

SEE ALSO Dental Equipment & Supplies - Mfr p. 1586

Company / Address	City	State	ZIP	Phone	Fax
Branson Ultrasonics Corp 41 Eagle Rd *Web:* www.branson-plasticsjoin.com	Danbury	CT	06813	203-796-0400	796-9838
Crest Ultrasonics Corp PO Box 7266 *TF:* 800-992-7378 ■ *Web:* www.crest-ultrasonics.com	Trenton	NJ	08628	609-883-4000	883-6452
L & R Mfg Co 577 Elm St *Web:* www.lrultrasonics.com/	Kearny	NJ	07032	201-991-5330	991-5870
Sonicor Instrument Corp 14 Connor Ln *TF:* 800-864-5022 ■ *Web:* www.sonicor.com	Deer Park	NY	11729	631-842-3344	842-3389
Sonics & Materials Inc 53 Church Hill Rd *TF:* 800-745-1105 ■ *Web:* www.sonicsandmaterials.com	Newtown	CT	06470	203-270-4600	270-4610
Sterigenics 2015 Spring Rd Suite 650 *TF:* 800-472-4508 ■ *Web:* www.sterigenics.com	Oak Brook	IL	60523	630-928-1700	928-1701

786 UNITED NATIONS AGENCIES, ORGANIZATIONS, PROGRAMS

Organization / Address	City	State	ZIP	Phone	Fax
United Nations UN Plaza **Fax:* PR ■ *Web:* www.un.org	New York	NY	10017	212-963-1234	963-0071*
Food & Agriculture Organization of the UN (FAO) 1 UN Plaza Suite DC1-1125 *Web:* www.fao.org	New York	NY	10017	212-963-6036	963-5425
Inter-American Development Bank 1300 New York Ave NW *Web:* www.iadb.org	Washington	DC	20577	202-623-1000	623-3096
International Atomic Energy Agency (IAEA) 1 UN Plaza Suite DC1-1155 **Fax Area Code:* 917 ■ *Web:* www.iaea.org	New York	NY	10017	212-963-6010	367-4046*
International Fund for Agricultural Development (IFAD) 1775 K St NW Suite 410 *Web:* www.ifad.org	Washington	DC	20006	202-331-9099	331-9366
International Labour Organization (ILO) 220 E 42nd St Suite 3101 *Web:* www.ilo.org	New York	NY	10017	212-697-0150	697-5218
International Monetary Fund 700 19th St NW *Web:* www.imf.org	Washington	DC	20431	202-623-7000	623-4661
International Tsunami Information Center 737 Bishop St Suite 2200 *Web:* www.tsunamiwave.info	Honolulu	HI	96813	808-532-6422	532-5569
United Nations Children's Fund (UNICEF) 3 UN Plaza *TF Orders:* 800-553-1200 ■ *Web:* www.unicef.org	New York	NY	10017	212-326-7000	888-7465
United Nations Development Programme 1 UN Plaza *Web:* www.undp.org	New York	NY	10017	212-906-5000	906-5364
United Nations Educational Scientific & Cultural Organization (UNESCO) 2 UN Plaza Suite 900 *Web:* www.unesco.org	New York	NY	10017	212-963-5995	963-8014
United Nations Environment Programme 2 UN Plaza Suite DC2-803 *Web:* www.unep.org	New York	NY	10017	212-963-8210	963-7341
United Nations Industrial Development Organization (UNIDO) 1 UN Plaza Suite DC1-1110 *Web:* www.unido.org	New York	NY	10017	212-963-6890	963-7904
World Bank Group 1818 H St NW *Web:* www.worldbank.org	Washington	DC	20433	202-473-1000	477-6391
World Food Programme North America 2 UN Plaza DC-2 Rm 2500 *Web:* www.wfp.org	New York	NY	10017	212-963-8364	963-8019
World Health Organization (WHO) 2 UN Plaza Suite DC2-0970 *Web:* www.who.int	New York	NY	10017	212-963-4388	963-8565
World Intellectual Property Organization (WIPO) 2 UN Plaza Room 2525 *Web:* www.wipo.int	New York	NY	10017	212-963-6813	963-4801

787 UNITED NATIONS MISSIONS

SEE ALSO Embassies & Consulates - Foreign, in the US p. 1612

All of the missions listed here are permanent missions except the Holy See, which has the status of Permanent Observer Mission to the UN. Two member states, Kiribati and Palau, are not listed because they do not maintain offices in New York. Another member state, Guinea Bissau, has a New York office but is excluded from this list because no telephone number was available for it.

Mission / Address	City	State	ZIP	Phone	Fax
Afghanistan 360 Lexington Ave 11th Fl	New York	NY	10017	212-972-1212	972-1216
Albania 320 E 79th St	New York	NY	10021	212-249-2059	535-2917
Algeria 326 E 48th St *Web:* www.algeria-un.org	New York	NY	10017	212-750-1960	759-9538
Andorra 2 UN Plaza 27th Fl	New York	NY	10017	212-750-8064	750-6630
Angola 125 E 73rd St	New York	NY	10021	212-861-5656	861-9295
Antigua & Barbuda 305 E 47th St 6th Fl *Web:* www.un.int/antigua	New York	NY	10017	212-541-4117	757-1607
Argentina 1 UN Plaza 25th Fl *Web:* www.un.int/argentina	New York	NY	10017	212-688-6300	980-8395
Armenia 119 E 36th St *Web:* www.un.int/armenia	New York	NY	10016	212-686-9079	686-3934

				Phone	Fax
Australia 150 E 42nd St 33rd Fl	New York	NY	10017	212-351-6600	351-6610
Web: www.australianyc.org					
Austria 600 3rd Ave 31st Fl	New York	NY	10016	917-542-8400	949-1840*
**Fax Area Code:* 212 ■ *Web:* www.un.int/austria					
Azerbaijan 866 UN Plaza Suite 560	New York	NY	10017	212-371-2559	371-2784
Bahamas 231 E 46th St	New York	NY	10017	212-421-6925	759-2135
Bahrain 866 2nd Ave 14th Fl	New York	NY	10017	212-223-6200	319-0687
Web: www.un.int/bahrain					
Bangladesh 227 E 45th St	New York	NY	10017	212-867-3434	972-4038
Web: www.un.int/bangladesh					
Barbados 800 2nd Ave 2nd Fl	New York	NY	10017	212-867-8431	986-1030
TF: 800-221-9831					
Belarus 136 E 67th St 4th Fl	New York	NY	10021	212-535-3420	734-4810
Web: www.un.int/belarus					
Belgium 823 UN Plaza 4th Fl	New York	NY	10017	212-378-6300	681-7618
Web: www.un.int/belgium					
Belize 675 3rd Ave Suite 1911	New York	NY	10017	212-593-0999	593-0932
Web: www.belizemission.com					
Benin 125 E 38th St	New York	NY	10016	212-684-1339	684-2058
Web: www.un.int/benin					
Bhutan 763 UN Plaza	New York	NY	10017	212-682-2268	661-0551
Bolivia 211 E 43rd St Rm 802	New York	NY	10017	212-682-8132	687-4642
Bosnia & Herzegovina 866 UN Plaza Suite 585	New York	NY	10017	212-751-9015	751-9019
Botswana 154 E 46th St	New York	NY	10017	212-889-2277	725-5061
Brazil 747 3rd Ave 9th Fl	New York	NY	10017	212-372-2600	371-5716
Web: www.un.int/brazil					
Brunei Darussalam 771 1st Ave	New York	NY	10017	212-697-3465	697-9889
Bulgaria 11 E 84th St	New York	NY	10028	212-737-4790	472-9865
Web: www.un.int/bulgaria					
Burkina Faso 866 UN Plaza Suite 326	New York	NY	10017	212-308-4720	308-4690
Burundi 336 E 45th St 12th Fl	New York	NY	10017	212-499-0001	499-0006
Cambodia 866 UN Plaza Suite 420	New York	NY	10017	212-223-0676	223-0425
Web: www.un.int/cambodia					
Cameroon 22 E 73rd St	New York	NY	10021	212-794-2296	249-0533
Canada 885 2nd Ave 14th Fl	New York	NY	10017	212-848-1100	848-1195
Web: www.un.int/canada					
Cape Verde 27 E 69th St	New York	NY	10021	212-472-0333	794-1398
Central African Republic 51 Clifton Ave Suite 2008	Newark	NJ	07104	973-482-9161	350-1174
Chad 211 E 43rd St Suite 1703	New York	NY	10017	212-986-0980	986-0152
Chile 855 2nd Ave Suite 44	New York	NY	10017	212-832-3323	832-0236
Web: www.un.int/chile					
China People's Republic of 350 E 35th St	New York	NY	10016	212-655-6100	634-7626
Web: www.china-un.org					
Colombia 140 E 57th St 5th Fl	New York	NY	10022	212-355-7776	371-2813
Web: www.colombiaun.org					
Comoros 866 UN Plaza Suite 418	New York	NY	10017	212-750-1637	750-1657
Web: www.un.int/comoros					
Congo Democratic Republic of the 866 UN Plaza Suite 511	New York	NY	10017	212-319-8061	319-8232
Web: www.un.int/drcongo					
Congo Republic of the 866 2nd Ave 2nd Fl	New York	NY	10017	212-832-6553	832-6558
Web: www.un.int/congo					
Costa Rica 211 E 43rd St Rm 903	New York	NY	10017	212-986-6373	986-6842
Web: un.cti.depaul.edu/cgi-bin/spider.py					
Cote D'Ivoire 46 E 74th St	New York	NY	10021	212-717-5555	717-4492
Web: www.un.int/cotedivoire					
Croatia 820 2nd Ave 19th Fl	New York	NY	10017	212-986-1585	986-2011
Web: www.un.int/croatia					
Cuba 315 Lexington Ave	New York	NY	10016	212-689-7215	689-9073
Web: www.un.int/cuba					
Cyprus 13 E 40th St	New York	NY	10016	212-481-6023	685-7316
Web: www.un.int/cyprus					
Czech Republic 1109 Madison Ave	New York	NY	10028	646-981-4000	981-4099
Web: www.czechembassy.org					
Denmark 885 2nd Ave 18th Fl	New York	NY	10017	212-308-7009	308-3384
Web: www.un.int/denmark					
Djibouti 866 UN Plaza Suite 4011	New York	NY	10017	212-753-3163	223-1276
Dominica 800 2nd Ave Suite 400H	New York	NY	10017	212-949-0853	808-4975
Dominican Republic 144 E 44th St 4th Fl	New York	NY	10017	212-867-0833	986-4694
Web: www.un.int/dr					
East Timor 866 UN Plaza Suite 1201	New York	NY	10017	212-759-3675	759-4196
Web: www.un.int/timor-leste					
Ecuador 866 UN Plaza Suite 516	New York	NY	10017	212-935-1680	935-1835
Egypt 304 E 44th St	New York	NY	10017	212-503-0300	949-5999
El Salvador 46 Park Ave 3rd Fl	New York	NY	10016	212-679-1616	725-3467
Equatorial Guinea 242 E 51st St	New York	NY	10022	212-223-2324	223-2366
Eritrea 800 2nd Ave 18th Fl	New York	NY	10017	212-687-3390	687-3138
Web: www.un.int/eritrea					
Estonia 600 3rd Ave 26th Fl	New York	NY	10016	212-883-0640	883-0648
Ethiopia 866 2nd Ave 3rd Fl	New York	NY	10017	212-421-1830	754-0360
Web: www.un.int/ethiopia					
Fiji 630 3rd Ave 7th Fl	New York	NY	10017	212-687-4130	687-3963
Finland 866 UN Plaza Suite 222	New York	NY	10017	212-355-2100	759-6156
Web: www.un.int/finland					
France 245 E 47th St 44th Fl	New York	NY	10017	212-308-5700	421-6889
Web: www.un.int/france					
Gabon 18 E 41st St 9th Fl	New York	NY	10017	212-686-9720	689-5769
Web: www.un.int/gabon					
Gambia 800 2nd Ave Rm 400F	New York	NY	10017	212-949-6640	856-9820
Georgia 1 UN Plaza 26th Fl	New York	NY	10017	212-759-1949	759-1823
Web: www.un.int/georgia					
Germany 871 UN Plaza	New York	NY	10017	212-940-0400	940-0402
Web: www.germany-info.org/UN					
Ghana 19 E 47th St	New York	NY	10017	212-832-1300	751-6743
Web: www.un.int/ghana					
Greece 866 2nd Ave 13th Fl	New York	NY	10017	212-888-6900	888-4440
Web: www.greeceun.org					
Grenada 800 2nd Ave Suite 400-K	New York	NY	10017	212-599-0301	599-1540
Guatemala 57 Park Ave	New York	NY	10016	212-679-4760	685-8741
Web: www.un.int/guatemala					
Guinea 140 E 39th St	New York	NY	10016	212-687-8115	687-8248
Web: www.un.int/guinea					
Guyana 801 2nd Ave 5th Fl	New York	NY	10017	212-573-5828	573-6225
Haiti 801 2nd Ave Rm 600	New York	NY	10017	212-370-4840	661-8698
Holy See 25 E 39th St	New York	NY	10016	212-370-7885	370-9622
Web: www.holyseemission.org					
Honduras 866 UN Plaza Suite 417	New York	NY	10017	212-752-3370	223-0498
Web: www.un.int/honduras					
Hungary 227 E 52nd St	New York	NY	10022	212-752-0209	755-5395
Web: www.un.int/hungary					
Iceland 800 3rd Ave 36th Fl	New York	NY	10022	212-593-2700	593-6269
Web: www.iceland.org/un/nyc					
India 235 E 43rd St	New York	NY	10017	212-490-9660	490-9656
Web: www.un.int/india					
Indonesia 325 E 38th St	New York	NY	10016	212-972-8333	972-9780
Web: www.indonesiamission-ny.org					
Iran Islamic Republic of 622 3rd Ave 34th Fl	New York	NY	10017	212-687-2020	867-7086
Web: www.un.int/iran					
Iraq 14 E 79th St	New York	NY	10021	212-737-4433	772-1794
Ireland 885 2nd Ave 19th Fl	New York	NY	10017	212-421-6934	752-4726
Web: www.un.int/ireland					
Israel 800 2nd Ave	New York	NY	10017	212-499-5510	499-5515
Web: www.israel-un.org/					
Italy 2 UN Plaza 24th Fl	New York	NY	10017	212-486-9191	486-1036
Web: www.italyun.org					
Jamaica 767 3rd Ave 9th Fl	New York	NY	10017	212-935-7509	935-7607
Web: www.un.int/jamaica					
Japan 866 UN Plaza 2nd Fl	New York	NY	10017	212-223-4300	751-1966
Web: www.un.int/japan					
Kazakhstan 866 UN Plaza Suite 586	New York	NY	10017	212-230-1900	230-1172
Web: www.un.int/kazakhstan					
Kenya 866 UN Plaza Rm 486	New York	NY	10017	212-421-4740	486-1985
Web: www.un.int/kenya					
Korea Democratic People's Republic of 820 2nd Ave 13th Fl	New York	NY	10017	212-972-3105	972-3154
Korea Republic of 335 E 45th St	New York	NY	10017	212-439-4000	986-1083
Web: www.un.int/korea					
Kuwait 321 E 44th St	New York	NY	10017	212-973-4300	370-1733
Web: www.kuwaitmission.com					
Kyrgyzstan 866 UN Plaza Suite 477	New York	NY	10017	212-486-4214	486-5259
Lao People's Democratic Republic 317 E 51st St	New York	NY	10022	212-832-2734	750-0039
Web: www.un.int/lao					
Latvia 333 E 50th St	New York	NY	10022	212-838-8877	838-8920
Lebanon 866 UN Plaza Rm 531-533	New York	NY	10017	212-355-5460	838-2819
Lesotho 204 E 39th St	New York	NY	10016	212-661-1690	682-4388
Web: www.un.int/lesotho					
Liberia 820 2nd Ave Suite 1300	New York	NY	10017	212-687-1033	687-1035
Libyan Arab Jamahiriya 309-315 E 48th St	New York	NY	10017	212-752-5775	593-4787
Web: www.libya-un.org					
Liechtenstein 633 3rd Ave 27th Fl	New York	NY	10017	212-599-0220	599-0064
Lithuania 420 5th Ave 3rd Fl	New York	NY	10018	212-354-7820	354-7833
Web: www.un.int/lithuania/lithuania.html					
Luxembourg 17 Beekman Pl	New York	NY	10022	212-935-3589	935-5896
Web: www.un.int/luxembourg					
Macedonia Republic of 866 UN Plaza Suite 517	New York	NY	10017	212-308-8504	308-8724
Web: www.un.int/macedonia					
Madagascar 820 2nd Ave Suite 800	New York	NY	10017	212-986-9491	986-6271
Malawi 600 3rd Ave 21st Fl	New York	NY	10016	212-317-8738	317-8729
Malaysia 313 E 43rd St	New York	NY	10017	212-986-6310	490-8576
Web: www.un.int/malaysia					
Maldives 800 2nd Ave Suite 400-E	New York	NY	10017	212-599-6194	661-6405
Web: www.un.int/maldives					
Mali 111 E 69th St	New York	NY	10021	212-737-4150	472-3778
Web: www.un.int/mali					
Malta 249 E 35th St	New York	NY	10016	212-725-2345	779-7097
Marshall Islands 800 2nd Ave 18th Fl	New York	NY	10017	212-983-3040	983-3202
Mauritania 116 E 38th St	New York	NY	10016	212-252-0113	252-0175
Mauritius 211 E 43rd St 15th Fl	New York	NY	10017	212-949-0190	697-3829
Mexico 2 UN Plaza 28th Fl	New York	NY	10017	212-752-0220	688-8862
Web: www.un.int/mexico					
Micronesia Federated States of 820 2nd Ave Suite 17A	New York	NY	10017	212-697-8370	697-8295
Web: www.fsmgov.org/fsmun					
Moldova 35 E 29th St	New York	NY	10016	212-447-1867	447-4067
Web: www.un.int/moldova					
Monaco 866 UN Plaza Suite 520	New York	NY	10017	212-832-0721	832-5358
Web: www.un.int/monaco					
Mongolia 6 E 77th St	New York	NY	10021	212-861-9460	861-9464
Web: www.un.int/mongolia					
Morocco 866 2nd Ave 6th & 7th Fl	New York	NY	10017	212-421-1580	980-1512
Web: www.un.int/morocco					
Mozambique 420 E 50th St	New York	NY	10022	212-644-6800	644-5972
Web: www.un.int/mozambique					
Myanmar 10 E 77th St	New York	NY	10021	212-744-1271	744-1290
Namibia 360 Lexington Ave Suite 1502	New York	NY	10017	212-685-2003	685-1561
Web: www.un.int/namibia					
Nauru 800 2nd Ave Suite 400-A	New York	NY	10017	212-937-0074	937-0079
Nepal 820 2nd Ave Suite 17B	New York	NY	10017	212-370-3988	953-2038
Web: www.un.int/nepal					
Netherlands 235 E 45th St 16th Fl	New York	NY	10017	212-697-5547	370-1954
Web: www.pvnewyork.org					
New Zealand 1 UN Plaza 25th Fl	New York	NY	10017	212-826-1960	758-0827
Web: nzmissionny.org					
Nicaragua 820 2nd Ave Suite 801	New York	NY	10017	212-490-7997	286-0815
Web: www.un.int/nicaragua					
Niger 417 E 50th St	New York	NY	10022	212-421-3260	753-6931
Web: www.un.int/niger					
Nigeria 828 2nd Ave	New York	NY	10017	212-953-9130	697-1970
Norway 825 3rd Ave 39th Fl	New York	NY	10022	212-421-0280	688-0554
Web: www.norway-un.org					
Oman 866 UN Plaza Suite 540	New York	NY	10017	212-355-3505	644-0070
Pakistan 8 E 65th St	New York	NY	10021	212-879-8600	744-7348
Web: www.un.int/pakistan					
Panama 866 UN Plaza Suite 4030	New York	NY	10017	212-421-5420	421-2694
Papua New Guinea 201 E 42nd St Suite 405	New York	NY	10017	212-557-5001	557-5009
Paraguay 211 E 43rd St Suite 400	New York	NY	10017	212-687-3490	818-1282
Web: www.un.int/paraguay					
Peru 820 2nd Ave Suite 1600	New York	NY	10017	212-687-3336	972-6975
Philippines 556 5th Ave 5th Fl	New York	NY	10036	212-764-1300	840-8602
Web: www.un.int/philippines					
Poland 9 E 66th St	New York	NY	10021	212-744-2506	517-6771
Web: www.polandun.org					
Portugal 866 2nd Ave 9th Fl	New York	NY	10017	212-759-9444	355-1124
Web: www.un.int/portugal					
Qatar 809 UN Plaza 4th Fl	New York	NY	10017	212-486-9335	758-4952
Romania 573-577 3rd Ave	New York	NY	10016	212-682-3274	682-9746
Web: www.un.int/romania					
Russian Federation 136 E 67th St	New York	NY	10021	212-861-4900	628-0252
Web: www.un.int/russia					
Rwanda 124 E 39th St	New York	NY	10016	212-679-9010	679-9133
Saint Kitts & Nevis 414 E 75th St Suite 5	New York	NY	10021	212-535-1234	535-6854
Web: www.stkittsnevis.org/unmission.html					
Saint Lucia 800 2nd Ave 9th Fl	New York	NY	10017	212-697-9360	697-4993
Web: www.un.int/stlucia					
Saint Vincent & the Grenadines 800 2nd Ave 4th Fl	New York	NY	10017	212-599-0950	599-1020
Samoa 800 2nd Ave Suite 400J	New York	NY	10017	212-599-6196	599-0797
San Marino 327 E 50th St	New York	NY	10022	212-751-1234	751-1436
Sao Tome & Principe 400 Park Ave 7th Fl	New York	NY	10022	212-317-0533	317-0580
Senegal 238 E 68th St	New York	NY	10021	212-517-9030	517-3032
Web: www.un.int/senegal					
Serbia & Montenegro 854 5th Ave	New York	NY	10021	212-879-8700	879-8705
Web: www.un.int/serbia-montenegro					
Seychelles 800 2nd Ave Suite 400C	New York	NY	10017	212-972-1785	972-1786
Sierra Leone 245 E 49th St	New York	NY	10017	212-688-1656	688-4924
Singapore 231 E 51st St	New York	NY	10022	212-826-0840	826-2964
Web: www.mfa.gov.sg/newyork					

	City	State	Zip	Phone	Fax
Slovakia 801 2nd Ave 12th Fl *Web:* www.un.int/slovakia	New York	NY	10017	212-286-8418	286-8419
Slovenia 600 3rd Ave 24th Fl *Web:* www.un.int/slovenia	New York	NY	10016	212-370-3007	370-1824
Solomon Islands 800 2nd Ave Suite 400L	New York	NY	10017	212-599-6192	661-8925
Somalia 425 E 61nd St Suite 702	New York	NY	10021	212-688-9410	759-0651
South Africa 333 E 38th St 9th Fl *Web:* www.southafrica-newyork.net	New York	NY	10016	212-213-5583	692-2498
Spain 245 E 47th St 36th Fl *Web:* www.spainun.org	New York	NY	10017	212-661-1050	949-7247
Sri Lanka 630 3rd Ave 20th Fl	New York	NY	10017	212-986-7040	986-1838
Sudan 305 E 47th St 4th Fl	New York	NY	10017	212-573-6033	573-6160
Suriname 866 UN Plaza Suite 320 *Web:* www.un.int/suriname	New York	NY	10017	212-826-0660	980-7029
Swaziland 408 E 50th St	New York	NY	10022	212-371-8910	754-2755
Sweden 885 2nd Ave 46th Fl *Web:* www.un.int/sweden	New York	NY	10017	212-583-2500	832-0389
Switzerland 633 3rd Ave 29th Fl *Web:* www.eda.admin.ch/newyork_miss/e	New York	NY	10011	212-286-1540	286-1555
Syrian Arab Republic 820 2nd Ave 15th Fl	New York	NY	10017	212-661-1313	983-4439
Tajikistan Republic of 136 E 67th St	New York	NY	10021	212-744-2196	472-7645
Tanzania United Republic of 201 E 42nd St Suite 1700	New York	NY	10017	212-972-9160	682-5232
Thailand 351 E 52nd St	New York	NY	10022	212-754-2230	688-3029
Timor-Leste 866 UN Plaza Suite 1201 *Web:* www.un.int/timor-leste	New York	NY	10017	212-759-3675	759-4196
Togo 112 E 40th St	New York	NY	10016	212-490-3455	983-6684
Tonga 250 E 51st St	New York	NY	10022	917-369-1025	369-1024
Trinidad & Tobago 820 2nd Ave 5th Fl	New York	NY	10017	212-697-7620	682-3580
Tunisia 31 Beekman Pl	New York	NY	10022	212-751-7503	751-0569
Turkey 821 UN Plaza 10th Fl *Web:* www.un.int/turkey	New York	NY	10017	212-949-0150	949-0086
Turkmenistan 866 UN Plaza Suite 424	New York	NY	10017	212-486-8908	486-2521
Tuvalu 800 2nd Ave Suite 400-D	New York	NY	10017	212-490-0534	808-4975
Uganda 336 E 45th St	New York	NY	10017	212-949-0110	687-4517
Ukraine 220 E 51st St *Web:* www.un.int/ukraine	New York	NY	10022	212-759-7003	355-9455
United Arab Emirates 305 E 47th St 7th Fl	New York	NY	10017	212-371-0480	371-4923
United Kingdom of Great Britain & Northern Ireland 885 2nd Ave 28th Fl *Web:* www.ukun.org	New York	NY	10017	212-745-9200	745-9316
United States of America 799 UN Plaza *Web:* www.un.int/usa	New York	NY	10017	212-415-4000	415-4443
Uruguay 866 UN Plaza Suite 322 *Web:* www.un.int/uruguay	New York	NY	10017	212-752-8240	593-0935
Uzbekistan 801 2nd Ave 20th Fl	New York	NY	10017	212-486-4242	486-7998
Vanuatu 800 E 2nd Ave	New York	NY	10004	212-920-5700	
Vatican City 25 E 39th St *Web:* www.holyseemission.org	New York	NY	10016	212-370-7885	370-9622
Venezuela 335 E 46th St *Web:* www.un.int/venezuela	New York	NY	10017	212-557-2055	557-3528
Vietnam 866 UN Plaza Suite 435 *Web:* www.un.int/vietnam	New York	NY	10017	212-644-0594	644-5732
Yemen 413 E 51st St	New York	NY	10022	212-355-1730	750-9613
Zambia 237 E 52nd St *Web:* www.un.int/zambia	New York	NY	10022	212-888-5770	888-5213
Zimbabwe 128 E 56th St	New York	NY	10022	212-980-9511	308-6705

788 UNIVERSITIES - CANADIAN

	City	Prov	Postal Code	Phone	Fax
Acadia University 15 University Ave *Web:* www.acadiau.ca	Wolfville	NS	B4P2R6	902-542-2201	585-1081
Alberta College of Art & Design 1407 14th Ave NW *TF:* 800-251-8290 ■ *Web:* www.acad.ab.ca	Calgary	AB	T2N4R3	403-284-7600	289-6682
Athabasca University 1 University Dr *TF:* 800-788-9041 ■ *Web:* www.athabascau.ca	Athabasca	AB	T9S3A3	780-675-6111	675-6174
Atlantic Baptist University 333 Gorge Rd *TF:* 888-968-6228 ■ *Web:* www.abu.nb.ca	Moncton	NB	E1G3H9	506-858-8970	858-9694
Bethany Bible College 26 Western St *TF:* 888-432-4444 ■ *Web:* www.bbc.ca	Sussex	NB	E4E1E6	506-432-4400	432-4425
Bishop's University 2600 College St *TF:* 800-567-2792 ■ *Web:* www.ubishops.ca	Sherbrooke	QC	J1M0C8	819-822-9600	822-9661
Brandon University 270 18th St *Web:* www.brandonu.ca	Brandon	MB	R7A6A9	204-728-9520	726-4573
Brescia University College 1285 Western Rd *Web:* www.brescia.uwo.ca	London	ON	N6G1H2	519-432-8353	858-5137
Brock University 500 Glenridge Ave *Web:* www.brocku.ca	Saint Catharines	ON	L2S3A1	905-688-5550	988-5488
Campion College at the University of Regina 3737 Wascana Pkwy *TF:* 800-667-7282 ■ *Web:* www.campioncollege.sk.ca	Regina	SK	S4S0A2	306-586-4242	359-1200
Canadian College of Naturopathic Medicine 1255 Sheppard Ave E *TF:* 866-241-2266 ■ *Web:* www.ccnm.edu	Toronto	ON	M2K1E2	416-498-1255	498-1576
Canadian Memorial Chiropractic College 6100 Leslie St *Web:* www.cmcc.ca	Toronto	ON	M2H3J1	416-482-2340	482-9745
Cape Breton University 1250 Grand Lake Rd *TF:* 888-959-9995 ■ *Web:* www.cbu.ca	Sydney	NS	B1P6L2	902-539-5300	562-0119
Carleton University 1125 Colonel By Dr *Web:* www.carleton.ca	Ottawa	ON	K1S5B6	613-520-7400	520-3847
Columbia Bible College 2940 Clearbrook Rd *Web:* www.columbiabc.edu	Abbotsford	BC	V2T2Z8	604-853-3358	853-3063
Concordia University 1455 de Maisonneuve Blvd W *Web:* www.concordia.ca	Montreal	QC	H3G1M8	514-848-2424	848-2621
Concordia University College of Alberta 7128 Ada Blvd NW *TF:* 866-479-5200 ■ *Web:* www.concordia.ab.ca	Edmonton	AB	T5B4E4	780-479-8481	378-8460
Dalhousie University 6299 South St C-300 Henry Hix Academic *Web:* www.dal.ca	Halifax	NS	B3H4H6	902-494-2211	494-1630
Dominican University College 96 Empress Ave *Web:* www.collegedominicain.ca	Ottawa	ON	K1R7G3	613-233-5696	233-6064
Emmanuel Bible College 100 Fergus Ave *Web:* www.ebcollege.on.ca	Kitchener	ON	N2A2H2	519-894-8900	894-5331
First Nations University of Canada					
Northern 1301 Central Ave *Web:* www.firstnationsuniversity.ca	Prince Albert	SK	S6V4W1	306-763-0066	764-3511
Regina 1 First Nations Way *Web:* www.firstnationsuniversity.ca	Regina	SK	S4S7K2	306-790-5950	790-5999
Saskatoon 710 Duke St *TF:* 800-267-6303 ■ *Web:* www.firstnationsuniversity.ca	Saskatoon	SK	S7K0P8	306-931-1800	665-0175
Heritage College & Seminary 175 Holiday Inn Dr *TF:* 800-465-1961 ■ *Web:* www.heritage-theo.edu	Cambridge	ON	N3C3T2	519-651-2869	651-2870
Huntington University 935 Ramsey Lake Rd *TF:* 800-461-6366 ■ *Web:* www.huntington.laurentian.ca	Sudbury	ON	P3E2C6	705-673-4126	673-6917
Huron University College 1349 Western Rd *Web:* www.huronuc.on.ca	London	ON	N6G1H3	519-438-7224	438-3938
International Academy of Design & Technology Toronto 39 John St **Fax:* Admissions ■ *TF:* 800-361-6664 ■ *Web:* www.iadt.ca	Toronto	ON	M5V3G6	416-922-3666	922-7835*
King's University College 9125 50th St *TF:* 800-661-8582 ■ *Web:* www.kingsu.ab.ca	Edmonton	AB	T6B2H3	780-465-3500	465-3534
King's University College 266 Epworth Ave *TF:* 800-265-4406 ■ *Web:* www.uwo.ca/kings	London	ON	N6A2M3	519-433-3491	433-2227
Kwantlen University College 12666 72nd Ave *Web:* www.kwantlen.ca	Surrey	BC	V3W2M8	604-599-2100	599-2068
Lakehead University 955 Oliver Rd *Web:* www.lakeheadu.ca	Thunder Bay	ON	P7B5E1	807-343-8110	343-8023
Laurentian University 935 Ramsey Lake Rd *Web:* www.laurentian.ca	Sudbury	ON	P3E2C6	705-675-4843	675-4891
McGill University 845 Sherbrooke St W **Fax:* Admissions ■ *Web:* www.mcgill.ca	Montreal	QC	H3A2T5	514-398-4455	398-8939*
McMaster University 1280 Main St W *Web:* www.mcmaster.ca	Hamilton	ON	L8S4L8	905-525-9140	527-1105
Memorial University of Newfoundland PO Box 4200 *Web:* www.mun.ca	Saint John's	NL	A1C5S7	709-737-8000	737-4569
Mount Allison University 65 York St *Web:* www.mta.ca	Sackville	NB	E4L1E4	506-364-2300	364-2299
Mount Royal College 4825 Mount Royal Gate SW *TF:* 877-440-5001 ■ *Web:* www.mtroyal.ab.ca	Calgary	AB	T3E6K6	403-440-6111	440-6339
Mount Saint Vincent University 166 Bedford Hwy *Web:* www.msvu.ca	Halifax	NS	B3M2J6	902-457-6117	457-6600
Nipissing University 100 College Dr Box 5002 *Web:* www.nipissingu.ca	North Bay	ON	P1B8L7	705-474-3450	495-4421
Brantford 67 Darling St *Web:* www.nipissingu.ca/brantford	Brantford	ON	N3T2K6	519-756-8228	720-9996
Muskoka 440 Ecclestone Dr *Web:* www.nipissingu.ca/muskoka	Bracebridge	ON	P1L1Z6	705-645-2921	645-2922
NSCAD University 5163 Duke St *TF:* 888-444-5989 ■ *Web:* www.nscad.ns.ca	Halifax	NS	B3J3J6	902-444-9600	425-2420
Ontario College of Art & Design 100 McCaul St *Web:* www.ocad.on.ca	Toronto	ON	M5T1W1	416-977-6000	977-6006
Prairie Bible Institute Box 4000 330 6th Ave N *TF:* 800-661-2425 ■ *Web:* www.prairie.edu	Three Hills	AB	T0M2N0	403-443-5511	443-5540
Queen's University 74 Union St Gordon Hall *Web:* www.queensu.ca	Kingston	ON	K7L3N6	613-533-2000	533-2068
Redeemer University College 777 Garner Rd E *TF:* 877-779-0913 ■ *Web:* www.redeemer.on.ca	Ancaster	ON	L9K1J4	905-648-2131	648-2134
Royal Military College of Canada PO Box 17000 Stn Forces *Web:* www.rmc.ca	Kingston	ON	K7K7B4	613-541-6000	541-6599
Royal Roads University 2005 Sooke Rd *TF:* 800-788-8028 ■ *Web:* www.royalroads.ca	Victoria	BC	V9B5Y2	250-391-2550	391-2500
Ryerson University 350 Victoria St *Web:* www.ryerson.ca	Toronto	ON	M5B2K3	416-979-5027	979-5221
Saint Frances Xavier University PO Box 5000 **Fax:* Admissions ■ *TF Admissions:* 877-867-7839 ■ *Web:* www.stfx.ca	Antigonish	NS	B2G2W5	902-863-3300	867-2329*
Saint Jerome's University 290 Westmount Rd N *Web:* www.sju.ca	Waterloo	ON	N2L3G3	519-884-8110	884-5759
Saint Mary's University 923 Robie St *Web:* www.stmarys.ca	Halifax	NS	B3H3C3	902-420-5400	496-8100
Saint Paul University 223 Main St *TF:* 800-637-6859 ■ *Web:* www.ustpaul.ca	Ottawa	ON	K1S1C4	613-236-1393	782-3014
Saint Thomas More College 1437 College Dr *TF:* 800-667-2019 ■ *Web:* www.stmcollege.ca	Saskatoon	SK	S7N0W6	306-966-8900	966-8904
Saint Thomas University 51 Dineen Dr *Web:* w3.stu.ca	Fredericton	NB	E3B5G3	506-452-0640	452-0617
Simon Fraser University					
Burnaby 8888 University Dr *Web:* www.sfu.ca	Burnaby	BC	V5A1S6	778-782-3111	
Harbour Centre 515 W Hastings St *Web:* www.harbour.sfu.ca	Vancouver	BC	V6B5K3	778-782-6930	782-5219
Surrey 2400 Central City 10153 King George Hwy *Web:* www.surrey.sfu.ca	Surrey	BC	V3T2W1	604-268-7500	
Taylor University College & Seminary 11525 23rd Ave *TF:* 800-567-4988 ■ *Web:* www.taylor-edu.ca	Edmonton	AB	T6J4T3	780-431-5200	436-9416
Thompson Rivers University Box 3010 900 McGill Rd **Fax:* Admissions ■ *TF:* 800-663-1663 ■ *Web:* www.tru.ca	Kamloops	BC	V2C5N3	250-828-5000	371-5960*
Thorneloe University 935 Ramsey Lake Rd *TF:* 866-846-7635 ■ *Web:* www.thorneloe.laurentian.ca	Sudbury	ON	P3E2C6	705-673-1730	673-4979
Toronto Baptist Seminary & Bible College 130 Gerrard St E *Web:* www.tbs.edu	Toronto	ON	M5A3T4	416-925-3263	925-8305
Toronto School of Theology 47 Queen's Park Crescent E *Web:* www.tst.edu	Toronto	ON	M5S2C3	416-978-4039	978-7821
Trent University 1600 W Bank Dr *TF:* 888-739-8885 ■ *Web:* www.trentu.ca	Peterborough	ON	K9J7B8	705-748-1011	748-1629
Trinity Western University 7600 Glover Rd **Fax:* Admissions ■ *TF:* 888-468-6898 ■ *Web:* www.twu.ca	Langley	BC	V2Y1Y1	604-888-7511	513-2064*
Universite Laval Pavillion Bonensant *TF:* 877-785-2825 ■ *Web:* www.ulaval.ca	Quebec	QC	G1K7P4	418-656-2131	656-5216
Universite de Moncton Campus de Moncton *TF:* 800-363-8336 ■ *Web:* www.umoncton.ca	Moncton	NB	E1A3E9	506-858-4000	858-4544
Edmundston 165 boulevard Hebert *TF:* 888-736-8623 ■ *Web:* www.umce.ca	Edmundston	NB	E3V2S8	506-737-5051	737-5373
Shippagan 218 boulevard JD Gauthier *TF:* 800-363-8336 ■ *Web:* www.umcs.ca	Shippagan	NB	E8S1P6	506-336-3400	336-3604
Universite de Montreal CP 6128 Succursale Centre Ville **Fax:* Admissions ■ *Web:* www.umontreal.ca	Montreal	QC	H3C3J7	514-343-6111	343-5788*
Universite du Quebec 475 rue du Parvis *Web:* www.uquebec.ca	Quebec	QC	G1K9H7	418-657-3551	657-2132
Ecole de Technologie Superieure 1100 Notre-Dame St W *Web:* www.etsmtl.ca	Montreal	QC	H3C1K3	514-396-8800	396-8950
Universite du Quebec a Montreal CP 8888 Succursale Centre-Ville *Web:* www.uqam.ca	Montreal	QC	H3C3P8	514-987-3000	987-8932
Universite du Quebec a Trois-Rivieres 3351 Boul des Forges CP 500 *Web:* www.uqtr.ca	Trois-Rivieres	QC	G9A5H7	819-376-5011	376-5210
Universite Sainte Anne 1695 Rt 1 *Web:* www.usainteanne.ca	Pointe-de-l'Eglise	NS	B0W1M0	902-769-2114	769-2930
Universite de Sherbrooke 2500 boul de l'Universite *Web:* www.usherbrooke.ca	Sherbrooke	QC	J1K2R1	819-821-8000	821-7966
Longueil 1111 rue Saint Charles O Tour O 5 étage bureau 500 *Web:* www.usherbrooke.ca/longueuil	Longueil	QC	J4K5G4	450-463-1835	670-3689
University of Alberta 89th Ave & 114th St 201 Administration Bldg. *TF:* 800-852-8434 ■ *Web:* www.ualberta.ca	Edmonton	AB	T6G2M7	780-492-3111	492-7172
Augustana 4901 46th Ave *TF:* 800-661-8714 ■ *Web:* www.augustana.ab.ca	Camrose	AB	T4V2R3	780-679-1100	679-1129
University of British Columbia 2016-1874 East Mall *TF:* 877-272-1422 ■ *Web:* www.ubc.ca	Vancouver	BC	V6T1Z1	604-822-9836	822-3599
Okanagan 3333 University Way *Web:* web.ubc.ca/okanagan	Kelowna	BC	V1V1V7	250-491-6500	
University of Calgary 2500 University Dr NW *Web:* www.ucalgary.ca	Calgary	AB	T2N1N4	403-220-5110	282-7298

Phone Fax

University of Guelph 50 Stone Rd E ... Guelph ON N1G2W1 519-824-4120 766-9481
Web: www.uoguelph.ca
University of Lethbridge 4401 University Dr ... Lethbridge AB T1K3M4 403-320-5700 329-5159*
**Fax:* Admissions ■ *Web:* www.uleth.ca
University of Manitoba 65 Chancellors Cir 424 University Center ... Winnipeg MB R3T2N2 204-474-8880 474-7554
TF Admissions: 800-224-7713 ■ *Web:* www.umanitoba.ca
University of New Brunswick PO Box 4400 ... Fredericton NB E3B5A3 506-453-4666 453-5016
Web: www.unb.ca
Saint John 100 Tucker Park Rd PO Box 5050 ... Saint John NB E2L4L5 506-648-5500 648-5528
Web: www.unbsj.ca
University of Northern British Columbia 3333 University Way ... Prince George BC V2N4Z9 250-960-5555 960-6330
Web: www.unbc.ca
University of Ottawa 550 Cumberland St ... Ottawa ON K1N6N5 613-562-5800 562-5323
TF: 877-868-8292 ■ *Web:* www.uottawa.ca
University of Prince Edward Island 550 University Ave ... Charlottetown PE C1A4P3 902-566-0400 628-4311
TF: 800-606-8734 ■ *Web:* www.upei.ca
University of Regina 3737 Wascana Pkwy ... Regina SK S4S0A2 306-585-4111 585-4591
Web: www.uregina.ca
Luther College 3737 Wascana Pkwy ... Regina SK S4S0A2 306-585-5333 585-5267
Web: www.luthercollege.edu
University of Saskatchewan 105 Administration Pl ... Saskatoon SK S7N5A2 306-966-4343 966-6730
Web: www.usask.ca
Saint Thomas More College 1437 College Dr ... Saskatoon SK S7N0W6 306-966-8900 966-8904
TF: 800-667-2019 ■ *Web:* www.stmcollege.ca
University of Sudbury 935 Ramsey Lake Rd ... Sudbury ON P3E2C6 705-673-5661 673-4912
Web: www.usudbury.com
University of Toronto 315 Bloor St W ... Toronto ON M5S1A3 416-978-2011 978-7022*
**Fax:* Admissions ■ *Web:* www.utoronto.ca
Mississauga 3359 Mississauga Rd N ... Mississauga ON L5L1C6 905-828-5399 569-4301
Web: www.utm.utoronto.ca
Scarborough 1265 Military Trail ... Toronto ON M1C1A4 416-287-8872 978-7022
Web: www.utsc.utoronto.ca
University of Trinity College 6 Hoskin Ave ... Toronto ON M5S1H8 416-978-2522 978-2797
Web: www.trinity.utoronto.ca
Victoria University 140 Charles St ... Toronto ON M5S1K9 416-585-4524 585-4524
Web: www.vicu.utoronto.ca
University of Victoria PO Box 1700 Stn CSC ... Victoria BC V8W2Y2 250-721-7211 721-6225*
**Fax:* Admissions ■ *Web:* www.uvic.ca
University of Waterloo 200 University Ave W ... Waterloo ON N2L3G1 519-885-1211 746-3242
Web: www.uwaterloo.ca
University of Western Ontario 1151 Richmond St ... London ON N6A5B8 519-661-2111 850-2394
Web: www.uwo.ca
King's University College 266 Epworth Ave ... London ON N6A2M3 519-433-3491 433-2227
TF: 800-265-4406 ■ *Web:* www.uwo.ca/kings
University of Windsor 401 Sunset Ave ... Windsor ON N9B3P4 519-253-3000 973-7070
Web: athena.uwindsor.ca
University of Winnipeg 515 Portage Ave ... Winnipeg MB R3B2E9 204-786-7811 786-8656
Web: www.uwinnipeg.ca
Vancouver Film School 198 W Hastings St 2nd Fl ... Vancouver BC V6B1H2 604-685-5808 685-5830
TF: 800-661-4101 ■ *Web:* www.vfs.com
Victoria Motion Picture School Ltd 775 Topaz Ave Suite 101 ... Victoria BC V8T4Z7 250-381-3032
TF: 888-522-3456 ■ *Web:* www.vicfilm.com
Victoria University 140 Charles St ... Toronto ON M5S1K9 416-585-4524 585-4524
Web: www.vicu.utoronto.ca
Wilfrid Laurier University 75 University Ave W ... Waterloo ON N2L3C5 519-884-1970 884-8826
Web: www.wlu.ca
York University 4700 Keele St ... Toronto ON M3J1P3 416-736-2100 736-5741
Web: www.yorku.ca

789 UNIVERSITY SYSTEMS

Listings are organized by state names.

Phone Fax

Alabama Higher Education Commission
100 N Union St PO Box 302000 ... Montgomery AL 36130 334-242-1998 242-0268
Web: www.ache.state.al.us
University of Alabama System 401 Queen City Ave ... Tuscaloosa AL 35401 205-348-5861 348-9788
Web: www.uasystem.ua.edu
University of Alaska System 910 Yukon Dr PO Box 775000 ... Fairbanks AK 99775 907-450-8000 450-8012
Web: www.alaska.edu
Arkansas Higher Education Dept 114 E Capitol Ave ... Little Rock AR 72201 501-371-2000 371-2001
Web: www.arkansashighered.com
University of Arkansas System 2404 N University Ave ... Little Rock AR 72207 501-686-2500 686-2507
Web: www.uasys.edu
California State University System 401 Golden Shore ... Long Beach CA 90802 562-951-4000 951-4899
Web: www.calstate.edu
University of California System 1111 Franklin St 12th Fl ... Oakland CA 94607 510-987-9074 987-9086
Web: www.ucop.edu
Colorado State University System 410 17th St Suite 2440 ... Denver CO 80202 303-534-6290 534-6298
Web: www.csusystem.edu
University of Colorado System 1800 Grant St Suite 800 ... Denver CO 80203 303-860-5600 860-5610
Web: www.cusys.edu
Connecticut State University System 39 Woodland St ... Hartford CT 06105 860-493-0000 493-0085
Web: w3.sysoff.ctstateu.edu
Delaware Higher Education Commission 820 N French St 5th Fl ... Wilmington DE 19801 302-577-3240 577-6765
TF: 800-292-7935 ■ *Web:* www.doe.state.de.us/high-ed
State University System of Florida
325 W Gaines St Suite 1614 ... Tallahassee FL 32399 850-245-0466 245-9685
Web: www.fldcu.org
University System of Georgia 270 Washington St SW ... Atlanta GA 30334 404-656-2250 657-6979
Web: www.usg.edu
University of Hawaii System 2444 Dole St ... Honolulu HI 96822 808-956-8111 956-3952
Web: www.hawaii.edu
Illinois Higher Education Board 431 E Adams St 2nd Fl ... Springfield IL 62701 217-782-2551 782-8548
Web: www.ibhe.org
University of Illinois System 506 S Wright St Suite 352 ... Urbana IL 61801 217-333-1920 244-2282
Web: www.uillinois.edu
Indiana Higher Education Commission 101 W Ohio St Suite 550 ... Indianapolis IN 46204 317-464-4400 464-4410
Web: www.che.state.in.us
Louisiana State University System 3810 W Lakeshore Dr ... Baton Rouge LA 70808 225-578-2111 578-5524
Web: www.lsusystem.lsu.edu
Southern University System JS Clark Administrative Bldg 4th Fl ... Baton Rouge LA 70813 225-771-4500 771-5522
Web: www.sus.edu
University of Louisiana System 1201 N 3rd St Suite 7-300 ... Baton Rouge LA 70802 225-342-6950 342-6473
Web: www.uls.state.la.us
University of Maine System 16 Central St ... Bangor ME 04401 207-973-3200 973-3296
Web: www.maine.edu
University System of Maryland 3300 Metzerott Rd ... Adelphi MD 20783 301-445-2740 445-1931
TF: 800-477-8437 ■ *Web:* www.ums.edu
Massachusetts Higher Education Board 1 Ashburton Pl Rm 1401 ... Boston MA 02108 617-994-6950 727-6397
Web: www.mass.edu
University of Massachusetts System 225 Franklin St ... Boston MA 02110 617-287-7000 287-7044
Web: www.massachusetts.edu
Minnesota State Colleges & Universities
Wells Fargo Pl 30 7th St E Suite 350 ... Saint Paul MN 55101 651-296-8012 297-5550
TF: 888-667-2848 ■ *Web:* www.mnscu.edu
University of Missouri System 321 University Hall ... Columbia MO 65211 573-882-2011 882-2721
TF: 800-225-6075 ■ *Web:* www.umsystem.edu
Montana University System
46 N Last Chance Gulch PO Box 203201 ... Helena MT 59620 406-444-6570 444-1469
Web: www.montana.edu/mus
Nebraska State College System 1445 K St PO Box 94605 ... Lincoln NE 68509 402-471-2505 471-2669
Web: www.nscs.edu
University of Nebraska System 3835 Holdrege St Varner Hall ... Lincoln NE 68583 402-472-2111 472-1237
TF: 800-542-1602 ■ *Web:* www.nebraska.edu
Nevada System of Higher Education 2601 Enterprise Rd ... Reno NV 89512 775-784-4905 784-1127
Web: system.nevada.edu
University System of New Hampshire 25 Concord Rd Dunlap Center ... Durham NH 03824 603-862-1800 862-0946
Web: www.usnh.unh.edu
New Jersey Higher Education Commission
20 W State St PO Box 542 ... Trenton NJ 08625 609-292-4310 292-7225
Web: www.state.nj.us/highereducation
New Mexico Higher Education Department 1068 Cerrillos Rd ... Santa Fe NM 87505 505-476-1100 476-6511
TF: 800-279-9777 ■ *Web:* hed.state.nm.us
City University of New York (CUNY) 535 E 80th St ... New York NY 10075 212-794-5555 794-5397
TF: 800-286-9937 ■ *Web:* www.cuny.edu
New York (State) Higher Education Office
State Education Bldg 2nd Fl West Mezzanine ... Albany NY 12234 518-474-3862 486-2175
Web: www.highered.nysed.gov
State University of New York (SUNY) State University Plaza ... Albany NY 12246 518-443-5555 443-5322
Web: www.suny.edu
North Carolina Community College System 200 W Jones St ... Raleigh NC 27603 919-807-7100 807-7164
Web: www.ncccs.cc.nc.us
University of North Carolina 910 Raleigh Rd PO Box 2688 ... Chapel Hill NC 27515 919-962-1000 962-6725
Web: www.northcarolina.edu
North Dakota University System
600 E Boulevard Ave Dept 215 10th Fl ... Bismarck ND 58505 701-328-2960 328-2961
Web: www.ndus.edu
Ohio State University System
190 N Oval Mall 205 Bricker Hall ... Columbus OH 43210 614-292-2424 292-1231
Web: www.osu.edu
Oklahoma State System of Higher Education
655 Research Pkwy Suite 200 ... Oklahoma City OK 73104 405-225-9120 225-9235
Web: www.okhighered.org
Oregon University System
506 SW Mill St Suite 530 PO Box 751 ... Portland OR 97207 503-725-5700 725-5709
Web: www.ous.edu
Pennsylvania State System of Higher Education
2986 N 2nd St ... Harrisburg PA 17110 717-720-4000 720-4011
TF: 800-457-7743 ■ *Web:* www.passhe.edu
Pennsylvania State University Commonwealth College System 111 Old Main ... University Park PA 16802 814-863-0327 865-3692
Web: campuses.psu.edu/uc.htm
Rhode Island Higher Education Office 301 Promenade St ... Providence RI 02908 401-455-9300 455-9314
Web: www.ribghe.org
South Carolina Commission on Higher Education
1333 Main St Suite 200 ... Columbia SC 29201 803-737-2260 737-2297
Web: www.che400.state.sc.us
Tennessee Higher Education Commission
404 James Robertson Pkwy Suite 1900 ... Nashville TN 37243 615-741-3605 741-6230
Web: state.tn.us/thec
University of Tennessee System 800 Andy Holt Tower 8th Fl ... Knoxville TN 37996 865-974-2241 974-3753
Web: www.utk.edu/system
Texas A & M University System
200 Technology Way Suite 2043 ... College Station TX 77845 979-458-6000 458-6044
Web: www.tamus.edu
Texas State University System 200 E 10th St Suite 600 ... Austin TX 78701 512-463-1808 463-1816
Web: www.tsus.edu
Texas Tech University System
Texas Tech University Administration Bldg Suite 124 ... Lubbock TX 79409 806-742-0012 742-8050
Web: www.texastech.edu
University of Texas System 601 Colorado St ... Austin TX 78701 512-499-4200 499-4215
Web: www.utsystem.edu
Utah System of Higher Education 60 S 400 West ... Salt Lake City UT 84101 801-321-7101 366-8405
Web: www.utahsbr.edu
Vermont State Colleges
1 Park St Stanley Hall 3rd Fl PO Box 359 ... Waterbury VT 05676 802-241-2520 241-3369
Web: web.vsc.edu
Virginia Community College System 101 N 14th St 15th Fl ... Richmond VA 23219 804-819-4901 819-4766
Web: www.vccs.edu
Washington Higher Education Coordinating Board
917 Lakeridge Way PO Box 43430 ... Olympia WA 98504 360-753-7800 753-7808
Web: www.hecb.wa.gov
West Virginia Higher Education Policy Commission
1018 Kanawha Blvd E Suite 700 ... Charleston WV 25301 304-558-2101 558-5719
TF: 888-825-5707 ■ *Web:* www.hepc.wvnet.edu/students
University of Wisconsin System
1220 Linden Dr 1720 Van Hise Hall ... Madison WI 53706 608-262-2321 262-3985
Web: www.uwsa.edu
Wyoming Community College Commission
2020 Carey Ave 8th Fl ... Cheyenne WY 82002 307-777-7763 777-6567
Web: www.commission.wcc.edu

790 UTILITY COMPANIES

SEE ALSO Electric Companies - Cooperatives (Rural) p. 1595; Gas Transmission - Natural Gas p. 1688

Types of utilities included here are electric companies, water supply companies, and natural gas companies.

Phone Fax

AEP Public Service Co of Oklahoma PO Box 24404 ... Canton OH 44701 888-216-3523
Web: www.aepcustomer.com
AEP Texas North Co 1 Riverside Plaza ... Columbus OH 43215 614-716-1000 716-1823
TF: 866-322-5563 ■ *Web:* www.aeptexas.com
AES Corp 4300 Wilson Blvd 11th Fl ... Arlington VA 22203 703-522-1315 528-4510
NYSE: AES ■ *Web:* www.aes.com
AGL Resources Inc 10 Peachtree Pl ... Atlanta GA 30309 404-584-4000 584-4210*
NYSE: ATG ■ **Fax:* Hum Res ■ *TF Cust Svc:* 800-427-5463 ■ *Web:* www.aglc.com
Alabama Gas Corp (Alagasco)
605 Richard Arrington Jr Blvd N ... Birmingham AL 35203 205-326-8100 326-2617
TF: 800-292-4005 ■ *Web:* www.alagasco.com

Company	City	State	Zip	Phone	Fax
Alabama Power Co PO Box 2641 *Fax: Cust Svc ■ TF: 800-245-2244 ■ Web: www.southernco.com/site/alapower	Birmingham	AL	35291	205-257-1000	226-1988*
Alaska Power & Telephone Co 193 Otto St PO Box 3222 TF Cust Svc: 800-982-0136 ■ Web: www.aptalaska.com	Port Townsend	WA	98368	360-385-1733	385-5177
Allegheny Power 800 Cabin Hill Dr TF Cust Svc: 800-255-3443 ■ Web: www.alleghenypower.com	Greensburg	PA	15601	724-837-3000	
Alliant Energy Corp 4902 N Biltmore Ln PO Box 77007 NYSE: LNT ■ TF Cust Svc: 800-255-4268 ■ Web: www.alliantenergy.com	Madison	WI	53707	608-458-3311	458-0100
AmerenUE PO Box 66149 *Fax: Hum Res ■ TF: 800-552-7583 ■ Web: www.ameren.com	Saint Louis	MO	63166	314-621-3222	554-4535*
American Electric Power 1 Riverside Plaza Web: www.aep.com	Columbus	OH	43215	614-716-1000	716-1823
American National Power Inc 62 Forest St Suite 102	Marlborough	MA	01752	508-382-9300	382-9400
APS (Arizona Public Service Co) 400 N 5th St *Fax: Cust Svc ■ TF Cust Svc: 800-253-9405 ■ Web: www.aps.com	Phoenix	AZ	85024	602-250-1000	944-8208*
Aqua America Inc 762 W Lancaster Ave NYSE: WTR ■ *Fax: Hum Res ■ TF: 877-987-2782 ■ Web: www.aquaamerica.com	Bryn Mawr	PA	19010	610-525-1400	525-7658*
Aquarion Co 835 Main St TF: 800-732-9678 ■ Web: www.aquarion.com	Bridgeport	CT	06604	203-336-7624	336-7775
Aquila Inc 20 W 9th St NYSE: ILA ■ TF: 800-303-0752 ■ Web: www.aquila.com	Kansas City	MO	64105	816-421-6600	467-3591
AREVA Inc 4800 Hampden Ln Suite 1100 Web: www.areva.com	Bethesda	MD	20814	301-652-9197	652-5691
Arizona Public Service Co (APS) 400 N 5th St *Fax: Cust Svc ■ TF Cust Svc: 800-253-9405 ■ Web: www.aps.com	Phoenix	AZ	85024	602-250-1000	944-8208*
Arkansas Western Gas Co 1001 Sain St TF: 800-773-2113 ■ Web: www.awgonline.com	Fayetteville	AR	72703	479-521-5400	582-4747
ATCO Ltd 909 11th Ave SW Suite 1400 TSX: ACO.X ■ Web: www.atco.ca	Calgary	AB	T2R1N6	403-292-7550	292-7532
Atlantic City Electric 800 King St Web: www.atlanticcityelectric.com	Wilmington	DE	19899	302-429-3011	429-3018
Atmos Energy 5430 LBJ Fwy Suite 1800 TF: 888-363-7427 ■ Web: www.atmosenergy.com	Dallas	TX	75240	972-934-9227	855-3040
Avista Corp 1411 E Mission St NYSE: AVA ■ TF: 800-727-9170 ■ Web: www.avistacorp.com	Spokane	WA	99202	509-495-4817	495-8725
Avista Utilities 1411 E Mission St *Fax: Cust Svc ■ TF: 800-227-9187 ■ Web: www.avistautilities.com	Spokane	WA	99252	509-495-4817	495-4184*
Baltimore Gas & Electric Co 39 W Lexington St *Fax: Cust Svc ■ TF: 800-685-0123 ■ Web: www.bge.com	Baltimore	MD	21201	410-234-5000	234-7406*
Bangor Hydro Electric Co 21 Telcom Dr TF: 800-499-6600 ■ Web: www.bhe.com	Bangor	ME	04402	207-945-5621	990-6954
Bay State Gas Co 300 Friberg Pkwy TF: 800-882-5454 ■ Web: www.baystategas.com	Westborough	MA	01581	508-836-7000	836-7070
Berkshire Gas Co Inc 115 Cheshire Rd TF: 800-292-5012 ■ Web: www.berkshiregas.com	Pittsfield	MA	01201	413-442-1511	443-0546
BIW Ltd 230 Beaver St AMEX: BIW ■ TF: 800-481-0141	Ansonia	CT	06401	203-735-1888	732-2616
Bonneville Power Administration 905 NE 11th Ave Web: www.bpa.gov	Portland	OR	97232	503-230-3000	
Cabot Oil & Gas Corp 1200 Enclave Pkwy NYSE: COG ■ *Fax: Hum Res ■ TF: 800-434-3985 ■ Web: www.cabotog.com	Houston	TX	77077	281-589-4600	589-4910*
Cadiz Inc 777 S Figueroa St Suite 4250 NASDAQ: CDZI ■ Web: www.cadizinc.com	Los Angeles	CA	90017	213-271-1600	271-1614
CalEnergy a MidAmerican Energy Holdings Co 302 S 36th St Suite 400 Web: www.calenergy.com	Omaha	NE	68131	402-341-4500	231-1558
California Water Service Group 1720 N 1st St NYSE: CWT ■ TF: 800-750-8200 ■ Web: www.calwater.com	San Jose	CA	95112	408-367-8200	367-8430
Calpine Corp 50 W San Fernando St 5th Fl TF: 800-359-5115 ■ Web: www.calpine.com	San Jose	CA	95113	408-995-5115	995-0505
Canadian Utilities Ltd 909 11th Ave SW Suite 1400 TSX: CU ■ Web: www.canadian-utilities.com	Calgary	AB	T2R1N6	403-292-7500	292-7532
Cap Rock Energy Corp 500 W Wall St Suite 400 AMEX: RKE ■ *Fax: Cust Svc ■ TF: 800-442-8688 ■ Web: www.caprockenergy.com	Midland	TX	79701	432-683-5422	756-2866*
Cascade Natural Gas Corp 222 Fairview Ave N NYSE: CGC ■ Web: www.cngc.com	Seattle	WA	98109	206-624-3900	624-7215
CenterPoint Energy Arkla PO Box 751 TF: 800-992-7552 ■ Web: arkla.centerpointenergy.com	Little Rock	AR	72203	501-377-4556	377-4590
Central Hudson Gas & Electric Corp 284 South Ave *Fax: Hum Res ■ TF: 800-527-2714 ■ Web: www.centralhudson.com	Poughkeepsie	NY	12601	845-452-2000	486-5415*
Central Maine Power Co 83 Edison Dr TF: 800-565-0121 ■ Web: www.cmpco.com	Augusta	ME	04336	207-623-3521	623-5908
Central Vermont Public Service Corp 77 Grove St NYSE: CV ■ *Fax Area Code: 802 ■ TF: 800-649-2877 ■ Web: www.cvps.com	Rutland	VT	05701	800-649-2877	747-2199*
Chesapeake Utilities Corp 909 Silver Lake Blvd NYSE: CPK ■ Web: www.chpk.com	Dover	DE	19904	302-734-6799	734-6750
Cheyenne Light Fuel & Power Co 108 W 18th St Web: www.cheyennelight.com	Cheyenne	WY	82001	307-638-3361	778-2106
Chubu Electric Power Co Inc 900 17th St NW Suite 1220 Web: www.chuden.co.jp/english/index.html	Washington	DC	20006	202-775-1960	331-9256
Cinergy/PSI 139 E 4th St *Fax Area Code: 317 ■ TF Cust Svc: 800-544-6900 ■ Web: www.cinergypsi.com	Cincinnati	OH	45202	513-421-9500	838-2292*
Citizens Gas & Coke Utility 2020 N Meridian St TF: 800-427-4217 ■ Web: www.citizensgas.com	Indianapolis	IN	46202	317-924-3341	927-4395
City Public Service Board 145 Navarro St TF: 800-773-3077 ■ Web: www.citypublicservice.com	San Antonio	TX	78296	210-353-2222	353-4633
Cleco Power LLC 2030 Donahue Ferry Rd *Fax: Hum Res ■ TF Cust Svc: 800-622-6537 ■ Web: www.cleco.com	Pineville	LA	71361	318-484-7400	484-7488*
CMS Electric & Gas Co 1 Energy Plaza TF: 888-477-5050 ■ Web: www.cmsenergy.com	Jackson	MI	49201	517-788-0550	
Colorado Springs Utilities 111 S Cascade Ave TF: 800-238-5434 ■ Web: www.csu.org	Colorado Springs	CO	80903	719-448-4800	668-3400
Columbia Gas of Kentucky Inc 2001 Mercer Rd TF: 800-432-9345 ■ Web: www.columbiagasky.com	Lexington	KY	40511	859-288-0210	288-6349
Columbia Gas of Maryland Inc 501 Technology Dr *Fax: Mktg ■ TF Cust Svc: 888-460-4332 ■ Web: www.columbiagaspamd.com	Canonsburg	PA	15317	724-416-6300	416-6383*
Columbia Gas of Ohio Inc 200 Civic Center Dr TF: 800-282-3044 ■ Web: www.columbiagasohio.com	Columbus	OH	43215	614-460-6000	460-4947
Columbia Gas of Pennsylvania Inc 501 Technology Dr *Fax: Mktg ■ TF Cust Svc: 888-460-4332 ■ Web: www.columbiagaspamd.com	Canonsburg	PA	15317	724-416-6300	416-6383*
Columbia Gas of Virginia Inc 1809 Coyote Dr TF Cust Svc: 800-543-8911 ■ Web: www.columbiagasva.com	Chester	VA	23836	804-323-5300	323-5338
ComEd An Exelon Co PO Box 87522 TF: 800-334-7661 ■ Web: www.ceco.com	Chicago	IL	60680	312-394-4321	394-3110
Commerce Energy Group Inc 600 Anton Blvd Suite 2000 AMEX: EGR ■ Web: www.commerceenergy.com	Costa Mesa	CA	92626	714-259-2500	259-2559
Connecticut Light & Power Co 107 Selden St *Fax: PR ■ TF Cust Svc: 800-286-2000 ■ Web: www.cl-p.com	Berlin	CT	06037	860-665-5000	665-2032*
Connecticut Natural Gas Corp PO Box 1500 *Fax: Mktg ■ Web: www.cngcorp.com	Hartford	CT	06144	860-727-3000	727-3326*
Consolidated Edison Co of New York 4 Irving Pl *Fax: Hum Res ■ TF: 800-752-6633 ■ Web: www.coned.com	New York	NY	10003	212-460-4600	260-8647*
Consumers Energy Co 1 Energy Plaza *Fax: Hum Res ■ TF Cust Svc: 800-477-5050 ■ Web: www.consumersenergy.com	Jackson	MI	49201	517-788-0550	788-2451*
Covanta Energy Corp 40 Lane Rd TF: 866-268-2682 ■ Web: www.covantaenergy.com	Fairfield	NJ	07004	973-882-9000	882-7234
CrossCountry Energy LLC 5444 Westheimer Rd Web: www.crosscountryenergy.com	Houston	TX	77056	713-989-7000	
Dakota Gasification Co 420 County Rd 26 Web: www.dakotagas.com	Beulah	ND	58523	701-873-2100	873-6404
Dayton Power & Light Co PO Box 1247 TF: 800-433-8500 ■ Web: www.waytogo.com	Dayton	OH	45401	937-331-3900	259-7385
Delmarva Power 800 King St TF Cust Svc: 800-375-7117 ■ Web: www.delmarva.com	Wilmington	DE	19899	302-434-0300	
Delta Natural Gas Co Inc 3617 Lexington Rd NASDAQ: DGAS ■ TF: 800-262-2012 ■ Web: www.deltagas.com	Winchester	KY	40391	859-744-6171	744-3623
Detroit Edison Co 2000 2nd Ave TF Cust Svc: 800-477-4747 ■ Web: utilities.dteenergy.com	Detroit	MI	48226	313-235-8000	235-8828
Direct Energy LP 2225 Sheppard Ave E 4th Fl *Fax Area Code: 800 ■ Web: www.directenergy.com	Toronto	ON	M2J5C2	888-305-3828	346-2233*
Dominion East Ohio PO Box 26785 TF Cust Svc: 800-573-1153 ■ Web: www.dom.com/about/companies/eohio/index.jsp	Richmond	VA	23261	800-362-7557	
Dominion Hope PO Box 26783 *Fax: Cust Svc ■ TF: 888-667-3000 ■ Web: www.dom.com/about/companies/hope	Richmond	VA	23261	304-623-8600	623-8603*
Dominion North Carolina Power 701 E Cary St TF: 888-667-3000 ■ Web: www.dom.com	Richmond	VA	23219	804-771-3000	
Dominion Peoples 625 Liberty Ave TF: 800-764-0111 ■ Web: www.dom.com/about/companies/peoples	Pittsburgh	PA	15222	412-244-2626	
Dominion Virginia Power 701 E Cary St TF: 888-667-3000 ■ Web: www.dom.com	Richmond	VA	23219	804-771-3000	
Duke Energy Kentucky Inc 139 E 4th St *Fax: Cust Svc ■ TF Cust Svc: 800-544-6900 ■ Web: www.duke-energy.com	Cincinnati	OH	45202	513-421-9500	287-2376*
Duke Energy North America 5400 Westheimer Ct TF: 800-873-3853 ■ Web: www.dena.duke-energy.com	Houston	TX	77056	713-627-5400	627-6577
Duke Energy Services Group 5400 Westheimer Ct TF: 800-873-3853 ■ Web: www.duke-energy.com	Houston	TX	77056	713-627-5400	627-4145
Duke Energy Trading & Marketing 5400 Westheimer Ct TF: 800-873-3853 ■ Web: www.duke-energy.com	Houston	TX	77056	713-260-1800	627-4145
Duke Power Co 526 S Church St TF: 800-777-9898 ■ Web: www.dukepower.com	Charlotte	NC	28202	800-777-9896	
Duke Power Co Nantahala Power & Light Div 301 NP & L Loop Web: www.nantahalapower.com	Franklin	NC	28734	828-524-2121	369-4608
Duquesne Light Co 411 7th Ave TF Cust Svc: 888-393-7100 ■ Web: www.dqe.com	Pittsburgh	PA	15219	412-393-6000	393-6448
Eastern Shore Natural Gas Co 417 Bank Ln	Dover	DE	19904	302-734-6720	
Edison Sault Electric Co 725 E Portage Ave TF: 800-562-4960 ■ Web: www.edisonsault.com	Sault Sainte Marie	MI	49783	906-632-2221	632-8444
El Paso Electric Co 123 W Mills St NYSE: EE ■ TF: 800-351-1621 ■ Web: www.epelectric.com	El Paso	TX	79901	915-543-5711	543-2299
Elizabethtown Gas Co 1 Elizabethtown Plaza TF: 800-242-5830 ■ Web: www.elizabethtowngas.com	Union	NJ	07083	908-289-5000	289-0301
Empire District Electric Co 602 Joplin St NYSE: EDE ■ *Fax: Hum Res ■ TF: 800-639-0077 ■ Web: www.empiredistrict.com	Joplin	MO	64801	417-625-5100	625-5146*
Enbridge Inc 425 1st St SW Suite 3000 NYSE: ENB ■ Web: www.enbridge.com	Calgary	AB	T2P3L8	403-231-3900	231-3920
Endesa SA 410 Park Ave 4th Fl Suite 410 NYSE: ELE ■ Web: www.endesa.es	New York	NY	10022	212-750-7200	750-7433
Energy West Inc 1 First Ave S NASDAQ: EWST ■ TF: 800-570-5688 ■ Web: www.energywest.com	Great Falls	MT	59401	406-791-7500	791-7560
EnergyUSA-TPC Corp 1500 165th St TF: 800-531-1193 ■ Web: www.energyusa-tpc.com	Hammond	IN	46324	219-853-5929	853-5951
EnergyWorks North America LLC 124 Riverbreeze Pl Web: www.energyworks.com	Arnold	MD	21012	410-647-0479	647-0588
Enron Corp 1221 Lamar St TF: 800-973-6766 ■ Web: www.enron.com	Houston	TX	77010	713-853-6161	853-3129
ENSTAR Natural Gas Co PO Box 196289 Web: www.enstargas.com	Anchorage	AK	99519	907-277-5551	276-6696
Entergy Arkansas Inc 425 W Capitol Ave TF: 800-368-3749 ■ Web: www.entergy-arkansas.com	Little Rock	AR	72201	501-377-4000	
Entergy Louisiana Inc 639 Loyola Ave *Fax: Cust Svc ■ TF Cust Svc: 800-368-3749 ■ Web: www.entergy-louisiana.com	New Orleans	LA	70113	504-529-5262	576-2509*
Entergy Mississippi Inc PO Box 1640 *Fax: Hum Res ■ Web: www.entergy-mississippi.com	Jackson	MS	39215	601-368-5000	351-4464*
Entergy New Orleans Inc 639 Loyola Ave *Fax: Cust Svc ■ TF Cust Svc: 800-368-3749 ■ Web: www.entergy-neworleans.com	New Orleans	LA	70113	504-529-5262	576-2509*
Entergy Texas Inc 350 Pine St TF: 800-368-3749 ■ Web: www.entergy-texas.com	Beaumont	TX	77701	409-838-6631	
Environmental Power Corp 1 Cate St 4th Fl AMEX: EPG ■ TF: 888-430-3082 ■ Web: www.environmentalpower.com	Portsmouth	NH	03801	603-431-1780	431-2650
Equitable Gas Co 225 N Shore Dr TF: 800-654-6335 ■ Web: www.eqt.com	Pittsburgh	PA	15212	412-395-3000	395-3290
Equitable Resources Inc 225 N Shore Dr NYSE: EQT ■ Web: www.eqt.com	Pittsburgh	PA	15212	412-395-3200	553-5757
Equitable Utilities 225 N Shore Dr TF: 800-654-6335 ■ Web: www.eqt.com	Pittsburgh	PA	15212	412-395-3000	395-3155
Florida City Gas 955 E 25th St TF: 800-993-7546 ■ Web: www.floridacitygas.com	Hialeah	FL	33013	305-691-8710	694-9337
Florida Power & Light Co 700 Universe Blvd Web: www.fpl.com	Juno Beach	FL	33408	561-691-7171	691-7177
Florida Public Utilities Co 401 S Dixie Hwy AMEX: FPU ■ TF: 800-427-7712 ■ Web: www.fpuc.com	West Palm Beach	FL	33401	561-832-0872	833-0151
FPL Energy Inc 700 Universe Blvd TF: 888-867-3050 ■ Web: www.fplenergy.com	Juno Beach	FL	33408	561-691-7171	691-7177
Gas Co The 515 Kamakee St Web: www.hawaiigas.com	Honolulu	HI	96814	808-535-5933	535-5932
Gaz Metro LP 1717 rue du Havre TSX: GZM.un ■ TF: 800-567-1313 ■ Web: www.gazmetro.com	Montreal	QC	H2K2X3	514-598-3444	598-3144
Georgia Power Co 241 Ralph McGill Blvd NE TF Cust Svc: 888-660-5890 ■ Web: www.southernco.com/gapower/	Atlanta	GA	30308	404-506-6526	506-3771
Green Mountain Energy Co 3815 Capital of Texas Hwy S Suite 100 TF Cust Svc: 800-286-5856 ■ Web: www.greenmountain.com	Austin	TX	78704	512-691-6100	691-6151
Green Mountain Power Corp 163 Acorn Ln NYSE: GMP ■ TF: 888-835-4672 ■ Web: www.gmpvt.com	Colchester	VT	05446	802-864-5731	655-8419
Gulf Power Co 1 Energy Pl *Fax: Hum Res ■ TF: 800-487-6937 ■ Web: www.southernco.com/gulfpower/	Pensacola	FL	32520	850-444-6111	444-6238*
Hawaiian Electric Co Inc PO Box 3978 Web: www.heco.com	Honolulu	HI	96812	808-548-7311	543-4680
Hydro One Inc 483 Bay St TF: 888-664-9376 ■ Web: www.hydroone.com	Toronto	ON	M5G2P5	416-345-5000	345-6060
Idaho Power Co 1221 W Idaho St *Fax: Hum Res ■ TF: 800-488-6151 ■ Web: www.idahopower.com	Boise	ID	83702	208-388-2200	388-6695*
Illuminating Co 76 S Main St *Fax Area Code: 877 ■ *Fax: Cust Svc ■ TF: 800-646-0400 ■ Web: www.firstenergycorp.com	Akron	OH	44308	216-622-9800	289-3674*
Indianapolis Power & Light Co PO Box 1595 TF Cust Svc: 888-261-8222 ■ Web: www.iplpower.com	Indianapolis	IN	46206	317-261-8261	
Intermountain Gas Co Inc 555 S Cole Rd TF Cust Svc: 800-548-3679 ■ Web: www.intgas.com	Boise	ID	83709	208-377-6000	377-6097
Kansas City Power & Light Co 1201 Walnut St *Fax: Cust Svc ■ Web: www.kcpl.com/home.htm	Kansas City	MO	64106	816-556-2200	654-1125*

Phone | Fax

Kansas Gas Service 7421 W 129th St ... Overland Park KS 66213 913-319-8600 319-8668*
*Fax: Hum Res ■ TF: 800-794-4780 ■ Web: www.kansasgasservice.com

Kentucky Utilities Co 1 Quality St ... Lexington KY 40507 859-255-2100
TF: 800-981-0600 ■ Web: www.eon-us.com/ku/

KeySpan Energy Delivery 1 Metrotech Ctr ... Brooklyn NY 11201 718-403-2000 488-1762*
*Fax: Hum Res ■ Web: delivery.keyspanenergy.com

Kinder Morgan Inc 500 Dallas St Suite 1000 ... Houston TX 77002 713-369-9000 369-9100
NYSE: KMI ■ TF: 800-525-3752 ■ Web: www.kne.com

Kinder Morgan Inc KN Energy Retail Div 370 Van Gordon St ... Lakewood CO 80228 303-989-1740
TF: 800-232-1627 ■ Web: www.kindermorgan.com

KN Energy Retail Div Kinder Morgan Inc 370 Van Gordon St ... Lakewood CO 80228 303-989-1740
TF: 800-232-1627 ■ Web: www.kindermorgan.com

Kokomo Gas & Fuel Co Inc 900 East Blvd ... Kokomo IN 46904 765-459-4101 459-0526
Web: www.kokomogas.com

Laclede Gas Co 720 Olive St ... Saint Louis MO 63101 314-342-0500 588-0615*
*Fax: Hum Res ■ TF: 800-887-4173 ■ Web: www.lacledegas.com

Lampton-Love Inc 2829 Lakeland Dr Suite 1505 ... Jackson MS 39232 601-933-3400 933-3420
Web: www.lamptonlove.com

Long Island Power Authority
333 Earle Ovington Blvd Suite 403 ... Uniondale NY 11553 516-222-7700 222-9137
TF Cust Svc: 877-275-5472 ■ Web: www.lipower.org

Louisville Gas & Electric Co 220 W Main St ... Louisville KY 40202 502-627-2000 627-2690*
*Fax: Cust Svc ■ TF: 800-331-7370 ■ Web: www.lgeenergy.com

Madison Gas & Electric Co 133 S Blair St ... Madison WI 53703 608-252-7000 252-7098
TF: 800-245-1125 ■ Web: www.mge.com

Maine & Maritimes Corp 209 State St PO Box 789 ... Presque Isle ME 04769 207-760-2499
AMEX: MAM ■ TF: 877-272-1523 ■ Web: www.maineandmaritimes.com

Memphis Light Gas & Water PO Box 430 ... Memphis TN 38101 901-528-4011 528-4758
Web: www.mlgw.com

Merrill Lynch Commodities 20 E Greenway Plaza Suite 700 ... Houston TX 77046 713-544-6222 544-4121
TF: 866-820-6000 ■ Web: www.entergykoch.com

Metretek Technologies Inc 303 E 17th Ave Suite 660 ... Denver CO 80203 303-785-8080 785-8085
AMEX: MEK ■ TF: 800-394-8169 ■ Web: www.metretek.com

Metromedia Energy Inc 6 Industrial Way W Suite F ... Eatontown NJ 07724 732-542-7575 542-8655
TF: 800-828-9427 ■ Web: www.metromediaenergy.com

Metropolitan Utilities District 1723 Harney St ... Omaha NE 68102 402-449-8155 449-8166
TF: 800-732-5864 ■ Web: www.mudomaha.com

Michigan Consolidated Gas Co 2000 2nd Ave ... Detroit MI 48226 313-235-4000 256-5825
TF Cust Svc: 800-477-4747 ■ Web: utilities.dteenergy.com

MidAmerican Energy Co 666 Grand Ave ... Des Moines IA 50309 515-242-4300 281-2981
TF: 800-338-8007 ■ Web: www.midamericanenergy.com

Middle Tennessee Natural Gas Utility District
1036 W Broad St ... Smithville TN 37166 615-597-4300 597-4260
TF: 800-880-6373 ■ Web: www.mtng.com

Middlesex Water Co 1500 Ronson Rd ... Iselin NJ 08830 732-634-1500 750-5981
NASDAQ: MSEX ■ TF: 800-729-4030 ■ Web: www.middlesexwater.com

Minnesota Power Inc 30 W Superior St ... Duluth MN 55802 218-722-2641 723-3944
TF: 800-228-4966 ■ Web: www.mnpower.com

Mirant Corp 1155 Perimeter Ctr W ... Atlanta GA 30338 678-579-5000 579-5001
NYSE: MIR ■ TF: 800-334-2726 ■ Web: www.mirant.com

Mississippi Power Co Inc 2992 W Beach Blvd ... Gulfport MS 39501 228-864-1211 865-5606
TF: 800-353-9777 ■ Web: www.southernco.com/mspower

Missouri Gas Energy 3420 Broadway ... Kansas City MO 64111 816-360-5500 360-5630
TF: 800-582-1234 ■ Web: www.missourigasenergy.com

Mobile Gas Service Corp 2828 Dauphin St ... Mobile AL 36606 251-476-2720 471-2588*
*Fax: Mktg ■ Web: www.mobile-gas.com

Montana-Dakota Utilities Co 122 E Broadway ... Bismarck ND 58502 701-222-7900 222-4329
TF: 800-638-3278 ■ Web: www.mdu.com

Mount Carmel Public Utility Co 316 Market St ... Mount Carmel IL 62863 618-262-5151
Web: www.mtcpu.com

Nashville Gas Co Div Piedmont Natural Gas Co
665 Mainstream Dr ... Nashville TN 37228 615-734-0734 734-1753*
*Fax: Mktg ■ TF: 800-752-7504 ■ Web: www.nashvillegas.com

National Fuel Gas Distribution Corp 6363 Main St ... Williamsville NY 14221 716-857-7000 857-7310
TF: 800-365-3234 ■ Web: www.natfuel.com

National Fuel Gas Supply Corp 6363 Main St ... Williamsville NY 14226 716-857-7000 857-7206
TF Cust Svc: 800-365-3234 ■ Web: nfg.natfuel.com/gsweb1

National Fuel Resources Inc
165 Lawrence Bell Dr Suite 120 ... Williamsville NY 14221 716-630-6786 630-6798
TF: 800-839-9993 ■ Web: www.nfrinc.com

National Grid 25 Research Dr ... Westborough MA 01582 508-389-2000 389-2028*
*Fax: Hum Res ■ TF: 888-424-2113 ■ Web: www.nationalgridus.com

Nevada Power Co 6226 W Sahara Ave ... Las Vegas NV 89146 702-367-5000 367-5535
TF Cust Svc: 800-331-3103 ■ Web: www.nevadapower.com

New England Gas Co 100 Weybosset St ... Providence RI 02903 401-272-5040 421-6760
TF: 800-227-8000 ■ Web: www.negasco.com

New Jersey Natural Gas Co 1415 Wyckoff Rd ... Wall NJ 07719 732-938-1000 938-7350*
*Fax: Cust Svc ■ Web: www2.njng.com

New York Power Authority 123 Main St ... White Plains NY 10601 914-681-6200 681-6515
Web: www.nypa.gov

New York State Electric & Gas Corp
Corporate Dr PO Box 5240 ... Binghamton NY 13902 800-572-1111
Web: www.nyseg.com

Nicor Gas 1844 Ferry Rd ... Naperville IL 60563 630-983-8888 983-4229
TF: 888-642-6748 ■ Web: www.nicor.com

NIPSCO (Northern Indiana Public Service Co)
801 E 86th Ave ... Merrillville IN 46410 219-853-5200 647-5589*
*Fax: Hum Res ■ TF Cust Svc: 800-464-7726 ■ Web: www.nipsco.nisource.com

North Shore Gas Co 3001 Grand Ave ... Waukegan IL 60085 866-556-6004 336-8815*
*Fax Area Code: 847 ■ *Fax: Mktg

Northern Indiana Fuel & Light Co Inc 220 E 7th St ... Auburn IN 46706 260-925-2700 925-5255
Web: www.nifl co.com

Northern Indiana Public Service Co (NIPSCO)
801 E 86th Ave ... Merrillville IN 46410 219-853-5200 647-5589*
*Fax: Hum Res ■ TF Cust Svc: 800-464-7726 ■ Web: www.nipsco.nisource.com

Northern Utilities Inc 300 Friberg Pkwy ... Westborough MA 01581 508-836-7000 836-7070
TF: 800-882-5454 ■ Web: www.northernutilities.com

Northwest Natural Gas Co DBA NW Natural 220 NW 2nd Ave ... Portland OR 97209 503-226-4211 220-2584
NYSE: NWN ■ TF: 800-422-4012 ■ Web: www.nwnatural.com

NorthWestern Energy 600 Market St W ... Huron SD 57350 605-352-8411 353-8361
TF: 800-245-6977 ■ Web: www.northwesternonline.com

Nova Scotia Power Inc PO Box 910 ... Halifax NS B3J2W5 902-428-6230 428-6108
TF: 800-428-6230 ■ Web: www.nspower.ca

NRG Energy Inc 211 Carnegie Ctr ... Princeton NJ 08540 609-524-4500 524-4501
NYSE: NRG ■ TF: 800-241-4674 ■ Web: www.nrgenergy.com

NRG Texas LLC PO Box 4710 ... Houston TX 77210 713-795-6000 795-7431
Web: www.txgenco.com

NSTAR Electric 1 Nstar Way ... Westwood MA 02090 781-441-8000 441-8025
TF Cust Svc: 800-592-2000 ■ Web: www.nstaronline.com

NSTAR Gas 1 NSTAR Way ... Westwood MA 02090 800-592-2000
Web: www.nstaronline.com

NW Natural 220 NW 2nd Ave ... Portland OR 97209 503-226-4211 220-2584
NYSE: NWN ■ TF: 800-422-4012 ■ Web: www.nwnatural.com

OG & E Electric Services 3220 S High ... Oklahoma City OK 73124 405-553-3000 553-3165
TF: 800-272-9741 ■ Web: www.oge.com

Ohio Edison Co 76 S Main St PO Box 3637 ... Akron OH 44309 800-646-0400 384-4796*
*Fax Area Code: 330 ■ *Fax: Cust Svc ■ TF Cust Svc: 800-633-4766

Oklahoma Natural Gas Co 401 N Harvey ... Oklahoma City OK 73101 405-551-6500 551-6610
TF: 800-664-5463 ■ Web: www.ong.com

ONEOK Inc 100 W 5th St ... Tulsa OK 74103 918-588-7000 588-7145
NYSE: OKE ■ Web: www.oneok.com

Orange & Rockland Utilities Inc 1 Blue Hill Plaza ... Pearl River NY 10965 845-352-6000 577-2958
TF Cust Svc: 877-434-4100 ■ Web: www.oru.com

Osaka Gas Co Ltd 375 Park Ave Suite 2109 ... New York NY 10152 212-980-1666 832-0946
Web: www.osakagas.co.jp/indexe.htm

Otter Tail Power Co 215 S Cascade St ... Fergus Falls MN 56537 218-739-8200 739-8218
TF: 800-551-3593 ■ Web: www.otpco.com

Oxbow Power Corp 1601 Forum Pl Suite 1400 ... West Palm Beach FL 33401 561-697-4300 640-8847
Web: www.oxbow.com

Pacific Gas & Electric Co 77 Beale St ... San Francisco CA 94105 415-973-7000 543-0841*
*Fax: Hum Res ■ TF Cust Svc: 800-743-5000 ■ Web: www.pge.com

Pacific Power & Light 825 NE Multnomah St ... Portland OR 97232 503-813-5000 800-2851*
*Fax Area Code: 888 ■ *Fax: Cust Svc ■ TF Cust Svc: 888-221-7070 ■
Web: www.pacificpower.net

PacifiCorp 825 NE Multnomah St ... Portland OR 97232 503-813-5000 813-5023*
*Fax: Hum Res ■ TF: 877-722-5001 ■ Web: www.pacificorp.com

Park Water Co 9750 Washburn Rd ... Downey CA 90241 562-923-0711 861-5902
TF: 800-727-5987 ■ Web: www.parkwater.com

Pennichuck Corp 25 Manchester St ... Merrimack NH 03054 603-882-5191 913-2362
NASDAQ: PNNW ■ TF: 800-553-5191 ■ Web: www.pennichuck.com

Pennsylvania Power Co 76 S Main St ... Akron OH 44308 800-646-0400 384-3866*
*Fax Area Code: 330 ■ TF Cust Svc: 800-720-3600

Peoples Gas Light & Coke Co 130 E Randolph Dr ... Chicago IL 60601 312-240-4000 240-4120
TF: 866-556-6001

Pepco Energy Services Inc 1300 N 17th St Suite 1600 ... Arlington VA 22209 703-253-1800 253-1698
TF: 800-363-7499 ■ Web: www.pepco.com

Pepco Holdings Inc 701 9th St NW ... Washington DC 20068 202-872-2000 833-7610
NYSE: POM ■ Web: www.pepco.com

Philadelphia Gas Works 800 W Montgomery Ave ... Philadelphia PA 19122 215-236-0500 684-6500*
*Fax: Hum Res ■ Web: www.pgworks.com

Piedmont Natural Gas 1915 Rexford Rd ... Charlotte NC 28211 704-364-3120 365-3849
NYSE: PNY ■ TF: 800-752-7504 ■ Web: www.piedmontng.com

Piedmont Natural Gas Co Nashville Gas Co Div
665 Mainstream Dr ... Nashville TN 37228 615-734-0734 734-1753*
*Fax: Mktg ■ TF: 800-752-7504 ■ Web: www.nashvillegas.com

Pike Natural Gas Co 144 Bowers Ave PO Box 249 ... Hillsboro OH 45133 937-393-1901 393-1075

Pinnacle West Energy Corp 400 N 5th St Suite 800 ... Phoenix AZ 85004 602-379-2500 250-3007

Portland General Electric 121 SW Salmon St ... Portland OR 97204 503-464-8000 464-2676*
*Fax: Hum Res ■ TF: 800-542-8818 ■ Web: www.portlandgeneral.com

PPL Electric Utilities Corp 2 N 9th St ... Allentown PA 18101 610-774-5151 774-5408*
*Fax: Cust Svc ■ TF Cust Svc: 800-342-5775 ■ Web: www.pplweb.com

PPL EnergyPlus LLC 2 N 9th St ... Allentown PA 18101 610-774-5151 774-3484
TF Cust Svc: 800-342-5775 ■ Web: www.pplenergyplus.com

PPL Gas Utilities Corp PO Box 508 ... Lock Haven PA 17745 800-652-0550
TF: 800-959-7366 ■ Web: www.pplgas.com

PPL Generation LLC 2 N 9th St ... Allentown PA 18101 610-774-5151 774-3484
TF Cust Svc: 800-342-5775

PPL Global LLC 2 N 9th St ... Allentown PA 18101 610-774-5151 774-6043
Web: www.pplweb.com/pplglobal/index.htm

ProGas Ltd 240 4th Ave SW 11th Fl ... Calgary AB T2P4H4 403-233-1301 233-5655
Web: www.progas.com

Progress Energy Florida Inc 100 Central Ave ... Saint Petersburg FL 33701 727-820-5151
TF Cust Svc: 800-700-8744 ■ Web: www.progress-energy.com

ProLiance Energy LLC 111 Monument Circle Suite 2200 ... Indianapolis IN 46204 317-231-6800 231-6900
Web: www.proliance.com

PS Energy Group Inc 2987 Clairmont Rd Suite 450 ... Atlanta GA 30329 404-321-5711 321-3938
TF: 800-334-7548 ■ Web: www.psenergy.com

PSEG Power LLC 80 Park Plaza ... Newark NJ 07101 973-430-7000 824-5382
TF: 800-436-7734 ■ Web: www.pseg.com

PSNC Energy 800 Gaston Rd ... Gastonia NC 28056 704-864-6731 834-6547*
*Fax: Hum Res ■ TF: 800-222-1034 ■ Web: www.scana.com

Public Service Electric & Gas Co 80 Park Plaza ... Newark NJ 07102 973-430-7000 824-5382*
*Fax: Hum Res ■ TF Cust Svc: 800-436-7734 ■ Web: www.pseg.com/companies/pseandg

Public Service of New Hampshire 780 N Commercial St ... Manchester NH 03105 603-669-4000
TF: 800-662-7764 ■ Web: www.psnh.com

Puget Sound Energy Inc 10885 NE 4th St ... Bellevue WA 98009 425-454-6363 424-6537
TF: 888-225-5773 ■ Web: www.pse.com

Questar Gas Co PO Box 45841 ... Salt Lake City UT 84139 801-324-5111 324-5483
TF: 800-323-5517 ■ Web: www.questargas.com

Reliant Energy Inc 1000 Main St ... Houston TX 77002 713-497-3000 488-5925
NYSE: RRI ■ TF: 866-872-6646 ■ Web: www.reliant.com

Richardson Sid Carbon & Energy Cos 201 Main St ... Fort Worth TX 76102 817-390-8600
Web: www.sidrich.com

Roanoke Gas Co 519 Kimball Rd ... Roanoke VA 24030 540-777-3800 777-3957
TF: 800-552-6514 ■ Web: www.roanokegas.com

Rochester Gas & Electric Corp 89 East Ave ... Rochester NY 14649 800-743-2110 771-2895*
*Fax Area Code: 585 ■ TF: 888-253-8888 ■ Web: www.rge.com

Rockland Electric Co 1 Blue Hill Plaza ... Pearl River NY 10965 845-352-6000 577-2958
TF: 877-434-4100

Salt River Project (SRP) 1521 N Project Dr ... Tempe AZ 85281 602-236-5900 236-2442
TF: 800-258-4777 ■ Web: www.srpnet.com

San Diego Gas & Electric Co 101 Ash St ... San Diego CA 92101 619-696-2000 654-1755*
*Fax Area Code: 858 ■ *Fax: Cust Svc ■ TF: 800-411-7343 ■ Web: www.sdge.com

Savannah Electric & Power Co 600 E Bay St ... Savannah GA 31401 800-437-3890
Web: www.savannahelectric.com

SCANA Energy Marketing Inc 1426 Main St MC 092 ... Columbia SC 29201 803-217-1300 217-1329
TF: 800-472-1051 ■ Web: www.scana.com

SemCanada Energy Co 530 8th Ave SW Suite 1000 ... Calgary AB T2P3S8 403-213-6000 213-6224
Web: www.semcanadaenergy.com

SEMCO Energy Gas Co 1411 3rd St Suite A ... Port Huron MI 48060 810-987-2200 987-7286
TF: 800-624-2019 ■ Web: www.semcoenergy.com

Shell Trading DBA Coral Energy LP
909 Fannin St Plaza Level 1 ... Houston TX 77010 713-767-5400
Web: www.coral-energy.com

Sid Richardson Carbon & Energy Cos 201 Main St ... Fort Worth TX 76102 817-390-8600
Web: www.sidrich.com

Sierra Pacific Power Co 6100 Neil Rd ... Reno NV 89511 775-834-4011 834-4202*
*Fax: Cust Svc ■ TF: 800-962-0399 ■ Web: www.sierrapacific.com

South Carolina Electric & Gas Co 1426 Main St ... Columbia SC 29218 803-748-3000
Web: www.scana.com/sceg

South Florida Natural Gas 4090 S Ridgewood Ave ... Port Orange FL 32121 386-428-5721 427-6663
Web: www.fpuc.com

South Jersey Gas Co 1 S Jersey Plaza Rt 54 ... Folsom NJ 08037 609-561-9000 561-8225
TF: 888-766-9900 ■ Web: www.sjindustries.com/sjg.htm

Southern California Edison Co 2244 Walnut Grove Ave ... Rosemead CA 91770 626-302-1212 302-8984
TF: 800-655-4555 ■ Web: www.sce.com

Southern California Gas Co 555 W 5th St ... Los Angeles CA 90013 213-244-1200 244-8293
TF: 800-427-2200 ■ Web: www.socalgas.com

Southern California Water Co 630 E Foothill Blvd ... San Dimas CA 91773 909-394-3600 394-1382
Web: www.aswater.com

Southern Connecticut Gas Co 855 Main St ... Bridgeport CT 06604 203-382-8111 382-8120
Web: www.soconngas.com

Southern Union Co 417 Lackawanna Ave ... Scranton PA 18503 570-614-5000 820-2401
NYSE: SUG ■ Web: www.southernunionco.com

Company	City	State	Zip	Phone	Fax
SouthStar Energy Services LLC 817 W Peachtree St NW Suite 1000 *TF:* 888-442-7288 ■ *Web:* www.southstarenergy.com	Atlanta	GA	30308	404-685-4000	685-4030
Southwest Gas Corp 4300 W Tropicana Ave *NYSE: SWX* ■ *TF:* 800-748-5539 ■ *Web:* www.swgas.com	Las Vegas	NV	89103	702-365-1555	365-2368
Southwest Gas Corp Central Arizona Div 10851 N Black Canyon Hwy *TF Cust Svc:* 800-873-2440 ■ *Web:* www.swgas.com	Phoenix	AZ	85029	602-395-4080	861-3361
Southwest Gas Corp Northern Nevada Div 400 Eagle Station Ln *TF:* 800-832-2555 ■ *Web:* www.swgas.com	Carson City	NV	89701	775-887-2706	884-3027
Southwest Gas Corp Southern Arizona Div 3401 E Gas Rd *TF:* 800-428-7324 ■ *Web:* www.swgas.com	Tucson	AZ	85714	520-794-6596	295-1991
Southwest Gas Corp Southern California Div 13471 Mariposa Rd *TF:* 800-443-8093 ■ *Web:* www.swgas.com	Victorville	CA	92395	760-951-4021	951-4081
Southwest Gas Corp Southern Nevada Div 4300 W Tropicana Ave *Web:* www.swgas.com	Las Vegas	NV	89103	702-365-2185	365-2368
Southwest Water Co 624 S Grand Ave Suite 2900 *NASDAQ: SWWC* ■ *Web:* www.southwestwater.com	Los Angeles	CA	90017	213-929-1800	929-1888
Southwestern Energy Co 2350 N Sam Houston Pkwy E Suite 300 *NYSE: SWN* ■ *Web:* www.swn.com	Houston	TX	77032	281-618-4700	618-4757
Split Rock Energy LLC 301 4th Ave S Suite 860N *Web:* www.splitrockenergy.com	Minneapolis	MN	55415	612-851-1300	851-2000
SUEZ Energy North America Inc 1990 Post Oak Blvd Suite 1900 *Web:* www.suezenergyna.com	Houston	TX	77056	713-636-0000	636-1364
Superior Water Light & Power 2915 Hill Ave *TF:* 800-227-7957 ■ *Web:* www.mnpower.com/about_mp/swlp/	Superior	WI	54880	715-394-2200	395-6300
SWEPCo 1 Riverside Plaza *Web:* www.swepco.com	Columbus	OH	43215	888-216-3523	
TECO Energy Inc Tampa Electric Co Div PO Box 111 *Web:* www.tampaelectric.com	Tampa	FL	33601	813-228-1111	
Tenaska Inc 1044 N 115th St Suite 400 *Web:* www.tenaska.com	Omaha	NE	68154	402-691-9500	691-9526
Terasen Inc 16705 Fraser Hwy *TSX: TER* ■ *TF:* 800-224-9376 ■ *Web:* www.terasen.com	Surrey	BC	V4N0E8	604-576-7000	592-7677
Texas Gas Service Co 1301 South MoPac Expwy Suite 400 *TF:* 800-700-2443 ■ *Web:* www.texasgasservice.com	Austin	TX	78746	512-477-5852	465-1124
Texas-New Mexico Power Co 4100 International Plaza Tower 2 9th Fl *TF:* 800-435-2822 ■ *Web:* www.tnpe.com/aboutcorpprofile2.asp	Fort Worth	TX	76109	817-731-0099	737-1392
Tokyo Electric Power Co Inc 1901 L St NW Suite 720 *Web:* www.tepco.co.jp/en/index-e.html	Washington	DC	20036	202-457-0790	457-0810
Toledo Edison Co 76 S Main St **Fax Area Code:* 419 ■ *TF:* 800-447-3333	Akron	OH	44308	800-447-3333	249-5345*
TransAlta Corp 110 12th Ave SW *NYSE: TAC* ■ *Web:* www.transalta.com	Calgary	AB	T2P2M1	403-267-7110	
Tucson Electric Power Co PO Box 711 **Fax:* Cust Svc ■ *TF Cust Svc:* 800-328-8853 ■ *Web:* www.tucsonelectric.com	Tucson	AZ	85702	520-571-4000	770-2004*
Tuscarora Gas Pipeline Co 1140 Financial Blvd Suite 900	Reno	NV	89502	775-834-4011	834-3886
TXU Electric 1601 Bryan St *TF:* 800-242-9113 ■ *Web:* www.txu.com/us/ourbus/elecgas	Dallas	TX	75201	214-812-4600	812-5453
UGI Utilities Inc 225 Morgantown Rd PO Box 13009 *TF:* 800-276-2722 ■ *Web:* www.ugi.com	Reading	PA	19612	610-796-3400	736-5803
United Illuminating Co 157 Church St **Fax:* Hum Res ■ *TF Cust Svc:* 800-722-5584 ■ *Web:* www.uinet.com	New Haven	CT	06510	203-499-2000	499-5906*
Upper Peninsula Power Co 18494 Canal Rd **Fax Area Code:* 906 ■ *Web:* www.uppco.wpsr.com	Houghton	MI	49931	800-562-7680	483-4544*
Utah Power & Light 825 NE Multnomah St **Fax Area Code:* 888 ■ *TF Cust Svc:* 888-221-7070 ■ *Web:* www.utahpower.net	Portland	OR	97232	503-813-5000	800-2851*
Vectren Corp 411 NW Riverside Dr *NYSE: VVC* ■ *TF:* 800-227-1376 ■ *Web:* www.vectren.com	Evansville	IN	47708	812-491-4000	
Virginia American Water Co 2223 Duke St *Web:* www.vawc.com	Alexandria	VA	22314	703-549-7080	836-6652
Virginia Natural Gas Inc 5100 E Virginia Beach Blvd *TF Cust Svc:* 866-229-3578 ■ *Web:* vng.aglr.com	Norfolk	VA	23502	757-466-5400	466-5437
Washington Gas & Light Co 6801 Industrial Road **Fax Area Code:* 202 ■ *TF:* 800-752-7520 ■ *Web:* www.washgas.com	Springfield	VA	22151	703-750-4440	624-6010*
We Energies PO Box 2046 **Fax:* Mktg ■ *TF:* 800-242-9437 ■ *Web:* www.we-energies.com	Milwaukee	WI	53201	414-221-2345	221-3853*
Westar Energy 818 S Kansas Ave *TF:* 800-794-4780 ■ *Web:* www.wr.com	Topeka	KS	66612	785-575-6300	575-1796
Western Kentucky Gas Co Inc PO Box 650205 *TF:* 888-954-4321	Dallas	TX	75265	972-934-9227	855-4039
Western Massachusetts Electric Co 1 Federal St Bldg 111-4 *TF:* 800-286-2000 ■ *Web:* www.wmeco.com	Springfield	MA	01105	413-785-5871	787-9352
Western Water Co 705 Mission Ave *TF:* 877-928-9282 ■ *Web:* www.wwtr.com	San Rafael	CA	94901	415-256-8800	256-8803
Wisconsin Power & Light Co 4902 N Biltmore Ln PO Box 77007 **Fax Area Code:* 608	Madison	WI	53718	800-255-4268	758-1466*
Wisconsin Public Service Corp PO Box 19001 **Fax Area Code:* 920 ■ **Fax:* Mktg ■ *Web:* www.wisconsinpublicservice.com	Green Bay	WI	54307	800-450-7260	433-1527*
Xcel Energy Inc PO Box 840 *TF:* 800-772-7858 ■ *Web:* www.xcelenergy.com	Denver	CO	80201	303-571-7511	294-8533
Xcel Energy Inc 414 Nicollet Mall *NYSE: XEL* ■ *TF:* 800-328-8226 ■ *Web:* www.xcelenergy.com	Minneapolis	MN	55401	612-330-5500	330-2900
Yankee Energy System Inc 107 Selden St *TF:* 800-286-5000 ■ *Web:* www.yankeeenergy.com	Berlin	CT	06037	203-639-4000	
York Water Co 130 E Market St PO Box 15089 *NASDAQ: YORW* ■ *TF:* 800-750-5561 ■ *Web:* www.yorkwater.com	York	PA	17405	717-845-3601	852-0058

791 VACUUM CLEANERS - HOUSEHOLD

SEE ALSO Appliances - Small - Mfr p. 1280

Company	City	State	Zip	Phone	Fax
Beam Industries 1700 W 2nd St *TF:* 800-369-2326 ■ *Web:* www.beamvac.com	Webster City	IA	50595	515-832-4620	832-6659
Bissell Inc 2345 Walker NW **Fax:* Hum Res ■ *Web:* www.bissell.com	Grand Rapids	MI	49544	616-453-4451	453-3485*
Black & Decker Corp 701 E Joppa Rd *NYSE: BDK* ■ **Fax:* Mktg ■ *Web:* www.bdk.com	Towson	MD	21286	410-716-3900	716-2996*
CentralVac International Inc 1525 E 5th St *TF:* 800-666-3133 ■ *Web:* www.centralvac.com	Kimball	NE	69145	308-235-4139	235-4687
Electrolux LLC 5420 LBJ Fwy Suite 800 *TF Cust Svc:* 800-243-9078 ■ *Web:* www.electroluxusa.com	Dallas	TX	75240	214-361-4300	378-7561
Eureka Co 807 N Main St *TF Cust Svc:* 800-843-4324 ■ *Web:* www.eureka.com	Bloomington	IL	61701	309-828-2367	823-5203
HMI Industries Inc 13325 Darice Pkwy Unit A *TF Cust Svc:* 800-344-1840 ■ *Web:* www.filterqueen.com	Strongsville	OH	44149	440-846-7800	
Hoover Co 7005 Cochran Rd **Fax:* Mail Rm ■ *TF:* 888-321-1134 ■ *Web:* www.hoovercompany.com	Glenwillow	OH	44139	330-499-9200	497-5845*
Kirby Co 1920 W 114th St *TF:* 800-437-7170 ■ *Web:* www.kirby.com	Cleveland	OH	44102	216-228-2400	221-3162
Lindsay Mfg Inc PO Box 1708 *TF:* 800-546-3729 ■ *Web:* www.lindsaymfg.com	Ponca City	OK	74602	580-762-2457	762-9547
Metropolitan Vacuum Cleaner Co Inc 1 Ramapo Ave PO Box 149 *TF:* 800-822-1602 ■ *Web:* www.metrovacworld.com	Suffern	NY	10901	845-357-1600	357-1640
Oreck Corp 100 Plantation Rd *TF Orders:* 800-535-8810 ■ *Web:* www.oreck.com	New Orleans	LA	70123	504-733-8761	733-6709
Panasonic Consumer Electronics Co 1 Panasonic Way *TF:* 888-275-2595 ■ *Web:* www.panasonic.com/consumer_electronics/home	Secaucus	NJ	07094	201-348-7000	392-6168
Rexair Inc 50 W Big Beaver Rd Suite 350 *Web:* www.rainbowsystem.com	Troy	MI	48084	248-643-7222	643-7676
Royal Appliance Mfg Co 7005 Cochran Rd *TF:* 888-321-1134 ■ *Web:* www.royalappliance.com	Glenwillow	OH	44139	440-996-2000	996-2025
Sanyo Fisher Co 21605 Plummer St *Web:* us.sanyo.com	Chatsworth	CA	91311	818-998-7322	701-4194
Sequoia Vacuum Systems Inc 164 Jefferson Dr *TF:* 800-994-0494 ■ *Web:* www.sequoiavacuum.com	Menlo Park	CA	94025	650-322-7281	322-8745

792 VALVES - INDUSTRIAL

Company	City	State	Zip	Phone	Fax
American Cast Iron Pipe Co (ACIPCO) 2916 16th St N *TF:* 800-442-2347 ■ *Web:* www.acipco.com	Birmingham	AL	35207	205-325-7701	307-2747
Anderson Brass Co 1629 W Bobo Newsome Hwy *TF:* 800-476-9876 ■ *Web:* www.andersonbrass.com	Hartsville	SC	29550	843-332-4111	332-3752
Anderson Greenwood/Crosby Inc 43 Kendrick St *Web:* www.andersongreenwood.com/SrvProd.asp	Wrentham	MA	02093	508-384-3121	384-3152
Armstrong International Inc 2081 SE Ocean Blvd 4th Fl *Web:* www.armintl.com	Stuart	FL	34996	772-286-7175	286-1001
Automatic Machine Products Co 17 Wall St *Web:* www.ampcomp.com	Attleboro	MA	02703	508-222-2300	222-2307
Automatic Switch Co 50-60 Hanover Rd *TF:* 800-524-1023 ■ *Web:* www.asco.com	Florham Park	NJ	07932	973-966-2000	966-2628
Automatic Valve Corp 41144 Vincenti Ct *Web:* www.automaticvalve.com	Novi	MI	48375	248-474-6700	474-6732
AY McDonald Mfg Co 4800 Chavenelle Rd *TF Cust Svc:* 800-292-2737 ■ *Web:* www.aymcdonald.com	Dubuque	IA	52002	563-583-7311	588-0720
Balon Corp 3245 S Hattie Ave *Web:* www.balon.com	Oklahoma City	OK	73129	405-677-3321	
Barksdale Inc 3211 Fruitland Ave *TF:* 800-835-1060 ■ *Web:* www.barksdale.com	Los Angeles	CA	90058	323-589-6181	589-3463
Bonney Forge Corp US Rt 522 S *TF Cust Svc:* 800-345-7546 ■ *Web:* www.bonneyforge.com	Mount Union	PA	17066	814-542-2545	542-9977
Circle Seal Controls Inc 2301 Wardlow Cir *Web:* www.circle-seal.com	Corona	CA	92880	951-270-6200	270-6201
Clow Valve Co 902 S 2nd St *TF:* 800-829-2569 ■ *Web:* www.clowvalve.com	Oskaloosa	IA	52577	641-673-8611	673-8269
Conbraco Industries Inc 701 Matthews-Mint Hill Rd *Web:* www.conbraco.com	Matthews	NC	28105	704-847-9191	841-6021
Continental Disc Corp 3160 W Heartland Dr *Web:* www.contdisc.com	Liberty	MO	64068	816-792-1500	792-2277
Control Components Inc 22591 Avenida Empresa *TF:* 800-788-8762 ■ *Web:* www.ccivalve.com	Rancho Santa Margarita	CA	92688	949-858-1877	858-1878
Conval Inc 265 Field Rd *Web:* www.conval.com	Somers	CT	06071	860-749-0761	763-3557
Cook Manley 12950 Royal Dr *Web:* www.cookmanley.com	Stafford	TX	77477	281-261-5700	403-1027
Crane Co 100 1st Stamford Pl 4th Fl *NYSE: CR* ■ *Web:* www.craneco.com	Stamford	CT	06902	203-363-7300	363-7295
Crane Co Stockham Div 2129 3rd Ave SE *TF:* 800-786-2542 ■ *Web:* www.stockham.com	Cullman	AL	35055	256-775-3800	775-3860
Crane Valve Group North America 9200 New Trails Dr Suite 200 *Web:* www.cranevalve.com	The Woodlands	TX	77381	281-298-5463	298-1920
Cross Mfg Inc 11011 King St Suite 210 *TF:* 800-542-7677 ■ *Web:* www.crossmfg.com	Overland Park	KS	66210	913-451-1233	451-1235
Curtiss-Wright Flow Control Target Rock Div 1966 Broadhollow Rd *Web:* www.curtisswright.com	Farmingdale	NY	11735	631-293-3800	293-6144
DeZurik Water Controls 250 Riverside Ave N *TF:* 800-788-0288 ■ *Web:* www.dezurik.com	Sartell	MN	56377	320-259-2000	259-2227
Dresser Flow Solutions 16240 Port St NW *TF:* 800-847-1099 ■ *Web:* www.dresser.com	Houston	TX	77041	832-590-2300	590-2331
Dynex Rivett Inc 770 Capitol Dr *Web:* www.dynexhydraulics.com	Pewaukee	WI	53072	262-691-0300	691-0312
Engineered Controls International Inc 100 Rego Dr *Web:* www.regoproducts.com	Elon	NC	27244	336-449-7707	449-6594
Engineered Valves Div ITT Industries Inc 33 Centerville Rd *TF:* 800-366-1111 ■ *Web:* www.engvalves.com	Lancaster	PA	17603	717-291-1901	509-2336
Fike Corp 704 SW 10th St *TF:* 877-342-3453 ■ *Web:* www.fike.com	Blue Springs	MO	64015	816-229-3405	228-9277
Fisher Controls International Inc 205 S Center St PO Box 190 *Web:* www.emersonprocess.com/fisher	Marshalltown	IA	50158	641-754-3011	754-2830
Fleck Controls Inc 20580 Enterprise Ave *TF Cust Svc:* 888-784-9065 ■ *Web:* www.fleckcontrols.com	Brookfield	WI	53045	262-784-4490	784-7794
Flowserve Corp 5215 N O'Connor Blvd Suite 2300 *NYSE: FLS* ■ *Web:* www.flowserve.com	Irving	TX	75039	972-443-6500	443-6800
FMC Technologies Inc 1803 Gears Rd *NYSE: FTI* ■ *TF:* 800-869-6999 ■ *Web:* www.fmctechnologies.com	Houston	TX	77067	281-591-4000	591-4102
GA Industries Inc 9025 Marshall Rd *Web:* www.gaindustries.com	Cranberry Township	PA	16066	724-776-1020	776-1254
Gemini Valve Inc 2 Otter Ct *TF:* 800-370-0936 ■ *Web:* www.geminivalve.com	Raymond	NH	03077	603-895-4761	895-6785
Goulds Pumps Inc Goulds Water Technologies Group 2881 E Bayard St Ext *TF:* 800-327-7700	Seneca Falls	NY	13148	315-568-2811	568-7973
Groth Corp 13650 N Promenade Blvd *TF:* 800-531-3140 ■ *Web:* www.grothcorp.com	Stafford	TX	77477	281-295-6800	295-6999
Halkey-Roberts Corp 2700 Halkey-Roberts Pl N *TF Sales:* 800-303-4384 ■ *Web:* www.halkey-roberts.com	Saint Petersburg	FL	33716	727-577-1300	563-0275
High Vacuum Apparatus LLC 12880 Moya Blvd *TF:* 800-551-4422 ■ *Web:* www.highvac.com	Reno	NV	89506	775-359-4442	359-1369
Hilton Valve Inc 14520 NE 91st Ct *Web:* www.hiltonvalve.com	Redmond	WA	98052	425-883-7000	883-8080
Hoerbiger Corp of America Inc 3350 Gateway Dr *TF:* 800-327-8961 ■ *Web:* www.hoerbigercorp.com	Pompano Beach	FL	33069	954-974-5700	974-0964

Company	City	State	ZIP	Phone	Fax
Hudson Valve Co Inc 5301 Office Park Dr Suite 330 *Fax Area Code: 800 ■ *TF:* 800-748-6218 ■ *Web:* www.hudsonvalve.com	Bakersfield	CA	93309	661-869-1126	607-8731*
Humphrey Products Co 5070 East N Ave *TF:* 800-477-8707 ■ *Web:* www.humphrey-products.com	Kalamazoo	MI	49048	269-381-5500	381-4113
Hunt Valve Co Inc DBA Hunt Engineering 1913 E State St *TF:* 800-321-2757 ■ *Web:* www.huntvalve.com	Salem	OH	44460	330-337-9535	337-3754
Hydroseal Valve Co Inc 1500 SE 89th St *TF:* 800-654-4842 ■ *Web:* www.hydroseal.com	Oklahoma City	OK	73149	405-631-1533	644-2575
Hyson Products 10367 Brecksville Rd *TF:* 800-876-4976 ■ *Web:* www.asbg.com/default_hyson.html	Brecksville	OH	44141	440-526-5900	838-7684
ITT Fluid Technology Corp 10 Mountainview Rd 3rd Fl *Web:* www.ittfluidtechnology.com/home.html	Upper Saddle River	NJ	07458	201-760-9800	760-9692
ITT Goulds Pumps Industries/Goulds Industrial Pumps Group 240 Fall St *TF:* 800-327-7700 ■ *Web:* www.gouldspumps.com	Seneca Falls	NY	13148	315-568-2811	568-2418
ITT Industries Inc Engineered Valves Div 33 Centerville Rd *TF:* 800-366-1111 ■ *Web:* www.engvalves.com	Lancaster	PA	17603	717-291-1901	509-2336
Jarecki Valves 6910 W Ridge Rd	Fairview	PA	16415	814-474-2666	474-3645
Jerguson Gage & Valve Co 16633 Foltz Industrial Pkwy *Web:* www.clark-reliance.com	Strongsville	OH	44149	440-572-7400	238-8828
Kennedy Valve 1021 E Water St *TF:* 800-782-5831 ■ *Web:* www.kennedyvalve.com	Elmira	NY	14902	607-734-2211	734-3288
Kerotest Mfg Corp 5500 2nd Ave *TF:* 800-825-8371 ■ *Web:* www.kerotest.com	Pittsburgh	PA	15207	412-521-4200	521-5990
KF Industries Inc 1500 SE 89th St *TF:* 800-654-4842 ■ *Web:* www.kfvalves.com	Oklahoma City	OK	73149	405-631-1533	631-5034
Lee Co 2 Pellitaug Rd PO Box 424 *Fax: Sales ■ *TF:* 800-533-7584 ■ *Web:* www.theleeco.com	Westbrook	CT	06498	860-399-6281	399-7058*
Leonard Valve Co 1360 Elmwood Ave *TF:* 888-797-4456 ■ *Web:* www.leonardvalve.com	Cranston	RI	02910	401-461-1200	941-5310
Leslie Controls Inc 12501 Telecom Dr *TF:* 800-253-7543 ■ *Web:* www.lesliecontrols.com	Tampa	FL	33637	813-978-1000	978-0984
Mac Valves Inc 30569 Beck Rd *TF:* 800-622-8587 ■ *Web:* www.macvalves.com	Wixom	MI	48393	248-624-7700	624-0549
Marotta Controls Inc 78 Boonton Ave PO Box 427 *TF:* 888-627-6882 ■ *Web:* www.marotta.com	Montville	NJ	07045	973-334-7800	334-1219
Marshall Gas Controls Inc 1000 Civic Center Loop *TF:* 800-447-9513 ■ *Web:* www.mgc-mbc.com	San Marcos	TX	78666	512-396-2257	396-2217
Maxon Corp 201 E 18th St *Web:* www.maxoncorp.com	Muncie	IN	47302	765-284-3304	286-8394
McDonald AY Mfg Co 4800 Chavenelle Rd *TF Cust Svc:* 800-292-2737 ■ *Web:* www.aymcdonald.com	Dubuque	IA	52002	563-583-7311	588-0720
McKenzie Valve & Machining Co 145 Airport Rd *Web:* www.mckenzievalve.com	McKenzie	TN	38201	731-352-5027	352-3029
McWane Inc 2900 Hwy 280 Suite 300 *Web:* www.mcwane.com	Birmingham	AL	35223	205-414-3100	414-3170
Metso Automation 44 Bowditch Dr Box 8044 *Web:* www.metsoautomation.com	Shrewsbury	MA	01545	508-852-0200	852-8172
Milwaukee Valve Co Inc 16550 W Stratton Dr *TF:* 800-348-6544 ■ *Web:* www.milwaukeevalve.com	New Berlin	WI	53151	262-432-2800	432-2801
Mueller Co 500 W Eldorado St *Fax: Cust Svc ■ *Web:* www.muellerflo.com	Decatur	IL	62522	217-423-4471	425-7537*
Mueller Refrigeration Co Inc 121 Rogers St PO Box 239 *TF Cust Svc:* 800-251-8983 ■ *Web:* www.muellerindustries.com	Hartsville	TN	37074	615-374-2124	374-2080
Newport News Industrial Corp 182 Enterprise Dr *TF:* 800-627-0353	Newport News	VA	23603	757-380-7053	688-3841
NIBCO Inc 1516 Middlebury St *TF:* 800-234-0227 ■ *Web:* www.nibco.com	Elkhart	IN	46515	574-295-3000	295-3307
Ogontz Corp 2835 Terwood Rd *TF:* 800-523-2478 ■ *Web:* www.ogontz.com	Willow Grove	PA	19090	215-657-4770	657-0460
OPW Fueling Components PO Box 405003 *TF:* 800-422-2525 ■ *Web:* www.opw-fc.com	Cincinnati	OH	45240	513-870-3100	874-1231
Pacific Valves 3201 Walnut Ave *Web:* www.cranevalve.com	Signal Hill	CA	90755	562-426-2531	595-9717
Parker Hannifin Corp Hydraulic Valve Div 520 Ternes Ave *Fax: Sales ■ *TF:* 800-272-7537 ■ *Web:* www.parker.com/hydraulicvalve	Elyria	OH	44035	440-366-5200	366-5253*
Parker Hannifin Corp Sporlan Div 711 Industrial Ave	Washington	MO	63090	636-239-6524	239-5042
Parker Hannifin Fluid Control Div 95 Edgewood Ave *TF:* 800-825-8305 ■ *Web:* www.parker.com/sc	New Britain	CT	06051	860-827-2300	827-2384
Parker Instrumentation Group 6035 Parkland Blvd *TF:* 800-272-7537 ■ *Web:* www.parker.com/instrumentation	Cleveland	OH	44124	216-896-3000	896-4022
Peter Paul Electronics Co Inc 480 John Downey Dr *Web:* www.peterpaul.com	New Britain	CT	06051	860-229-4884	223-1734
PGI International 16101 Vallen Dr *TF:* 800-231-0233 ■ *Web:* www.pgiint.com	Houston	TX	77041	713-466-0056	744-9892
Plast-O-Matic Valves Inc 1384 Pompton Ave *Web:* www.plastomatic.com	Cedar Grove	NJ	07009	973-256-3000	256-4745
Plattco Corp 7 White St *TF:* 800-352-1731 ■ *Web:* www.plattco.com	Plattsburgh	NY	12901	518-563-4640	563-4892
Powell William Co 2503 Spring Grove Ave *TF:* 800-888-2583 ■ *Web:* www.powellvalves.com	Cincinnati	OH	45214	513-852-2000	852-2997
Primore Inc 2304 W Beecher Rd *Web:* www.primore.com	Adrian	MI	49221	517-265-6168	265-6160
Richards Industries Inc 3170 Wasson Rd *Fax: Sales ■ *TF Cust Svc:* 800-543-7311 ■ *Web:* www.richardsind.com	Cincinnati	OH	45209	513-533-5600	871-0105*
Robert H Wager Co 570 Montroyal Rd *TF:* 800-562-7024 ■ *Web:* www.wagerusa.com	Rural Hall	NC	27045	336-969-6909	969-6375
Sedco 2304 W Beecher Rd PO Box 624 *Web:* www.sedco-prv.com	Adrian	MI	49221	517-263-2220	263-2546
Servotronics Inc 1110 Maple St PO Box 300 *AMEX: SVT* ■ *Web:* www.servotronics.com	Elma	NY	14059	716-655-5990	655-6012
Shan-Rod Inc 7308 Driver Rd PO Box 380 *Web:* www.shanrod.com	Berlin Heights	OH	44814	419-588-2066	588-3310
Sherwood 2111 Liberty Dr *Web:* www.sherwoodvalve.com	Niagara Falls	NY	14304	800-438-2916	
Snap-Tite Inc 8325 Hessinger Dr *Web:* www.snap-tite.com	Erie	PA	16509	814-838-5700	833-0145
Spence Engineering Co Inc 150 Coldenham Rd *Web:* www.spenceengineering.com	Walden	NY	12586	845-778-5566	778-1072
Sporlan Valve Co Inc 206 Lange Dr	Washington	MO	63090	636-239-1111	239-9130
Standard Machine & Mfg Co Inc 10014 Big Bend Blvd	Saint Louis	MO	63122	314-966-4500	966-2532
Starflo Corp 940 Crosscreek Rd SE *TF:* 800-888-2583	Orangeburg	SC	29115	803-536-9660	534-8813
Stockham Div Crane Co 2129 3rd Ave SE *TF:* 800-786-2542 ■ *Web:* www.stockham.com	Cullman	AL	35055	256-775-3800	775-3860
Storm Mfg Group Inc 23201 Normandie Ave *TF:* 800-210-2525 ■ *Web:* www.storm-manufacturing.com	Torrance	CA	90501	310-326-8287	326-8310
Swagelok Co 29500 Solon Rd *Web:* www.swagelok.com	Solon	OH	44139	440-248-4600	519-1089
T-3 Energy Services Inc 7135 Ardmore St *NASDAQ: TTES* ■ *Web:* www.t3energyservices.com	Houston	TX	77054	713-996-4110	996-4123
Tapco International 11307 W Little York Rd *TF:* 866-827-2660 ■ *Web:* www.tapcointernational.com	Houston	TX	77041	713-466-0300	466-8425
Target Rock Div Curtiss-Wright Flow Control 1966 Broadhollow Rd *Web:* www.curtisswright.com	Farmingdale	NY	11735	631-293-3800	293-6144
Transtech Industries Inc 200 Centennial Ave Suite 202 *Web:* hometown.aol.com/arttrti/index.html	Piscataway	NJ	08854	732-564-3122	981-1856
Tri-Clover Inc 9560 58th Pl Suite 300	Kenosha	WI	53144	262-605-2600	605-2664
United Brass Works Inc 714 S Main St *TF:* 800-334-3035 ■ *Web:* www.ubw.com	Randleman	NC	27317	336-498-2661	498-4267
Valcor Engineering Corp 2 Lawrence Rd *Web:* www.valcor.com	Springfield	NJ	07081	973-467-8400	467-8382
Velan Valve Corp 94 Ave C Griswold Industrial Park *Web:* www.velan.com	Williston	VT	05495	802-863-2562	862-4014
Wager Robert H Co 570 Montroyal Rd *TF:* 800-562-7024 ■ *Web:* www.wagerusa.com	Rural Hall	NC	27045	336-969-6909	969-6375
Watson McDaniel Co 428 Jones Blvd *Web:* www.watsonmcdaniel.com	Pottstown	PA	19464	610-495-5131	495-5134
Watts Regulator Co 815 Chestnut St *Fax: Cust Svc ■ *Web:* www.wattsreg.com	North Andover	MA	01845	978-688-1811	689-2457*
Watts Water Technologies Inc 815 Chestnut St *NYSE: WTS* ■ *Fax: Cust Svc ■ *Web:* www.wattsind.com	North Andover	MA	01845	978-688-1811	689-2457*
Weir Slurry North America 2701 S Stoughton Rd *Web:* www.weirslurry.com	Madison	WI	53716	608-221-2261	221-5807
William Powell Co 2503 Spring Grove Ave *TF:* 800-888-2583 ■ *Web:* www.powellvalves.com	Cincinnati	OH	45214	513-852-2000	852-2997
Xomox Corp 4444 Cooper Rd *Fax: Hum Res ■ *Web:* www.xomox.com	Cincinnati	OH	45242	513-745-6000	745-6044*
Zimmermann & Jansen Inc 620 N Houston Ave *Web:* www.zjinc.com	Humble	TX	77338	281-446-8000	446-8126

793 VALVES & HOSE FITTINGS - FLUID POWER

SEE ALSO Carburetors, Pistons, Piston Rings, Valves p. 1407

Company	City	State	ZIP	Phone	Fax
A-1 Components Corp 625 W 18th St *Fax Area Code: 800 ■ *TF:* 800-759-2872 ■ *Web:* www.a-1components.com	Hialeah	FL	33010	305-885-1911	759-9299*
Air-Way Mfg Co 586 N Main St *TF Cust Svc:* 800-253-1036 ■ *Web:* www.air-way.com	Olivet	MI	49076	269-749-2161	749-3161
Arkwin Industries Inc 686 Main St *Web:* www.arkwin.com	Westbury	NY	11590	516-333-2640	997-4053
Bettis Actuators & Controls 18703 GH Cir PO Box 508 *Web:* www.emersonprocess.com/valveautomation/bettis	Waller	TX	77484	281-727-5300	727-5353
Bosch Rexroth Corp 5150 Prairie Stone Pkwy *TF:* 800-860-1055 ■ *Web:* www.boschrexroth-us.com	Hoffman Estates	IL	60192	847-645-3600	645-6201
Bosch Rexroth Corp Mobile Hydraulics Div PO Box 394 *TF:* 866-230-2790 ■ *Web:* www.boschrexroth-us.com	Wooster	OH	44691	330-263-3300	263-3333
Cameron Valves & Measurement 3250 Briarpark Dr Suite 300 *Web:* www.c-a-m.com	Houston	TX	77042	281-499-8511	261-3588
Cashco Inc PO Box 6 *Web:* www.cashco.com	Ellsworth	KS	67439	785-472-4461	472-3539
Civacon 4304 N Mattox Rd *TF Sales:* 888-526-5657 ■ *Web:* www.civacon.com	Riverside	MO	64150	816-741-6600	741-1061
Clippard Instrument Lab 7390 Colerain Ave *TF:* 877-245-6247 ■ *Web:* www.clippard.com	Cincinnati	OH	45239	513-521-4261	521-4464
Continental Hydraulics Div Continental Machines Inc 5502 W 123rd St *Web:* www.continentalhydraulics.com	Savage	MN	55378	952-894-8900	895-6444
Continental Machines Inc Continental Hydraulics Div 5502 W 123rd St *Web:* www.continentalhydraulics.com	Savage	MN	55378	952-894-8900	895-6444
Crissair Inc PO Box 4000 *Web:* www.crissair.com	Palmdale	CA	93550	661-273-5411	273-1280
Delta Power Co 4484 Boeing Dr *Web:* www.delta-power.com	Rockford	IL	61109	815-397-6628	397-2526
Deltrol Fluid Products 3001 Grant Ave *Fax: Sales ■ *Web:* www.deltrolfluid.com	Bellwood	IL	60104	708-547-0500	547-6881*
Dixon Valve & Coupling Co 800 High St *TF:* 800-876-3822	Chestertown	MD	21620	410-778-2000	778-4702
Dynaquip Controls 10 Harris Industrial Pk *TF:* 800-545-3636 ■ *Web:* www.dynaquip.com	Saint Clair	MO	63077	636-629-3700	629-5528
EA Patten Co 303 Wetherell St	Manchester	CT	06040	860-649-2851	649-6230
EKK Eagle America 33 Plan Way Bldg 5 *TF:* 800-314-9246 ■ *Web:* www.eagle-america.net	Warwick	RI	02886	401-732-0333	732-2201
Essex Mfg Inc 6 Sunnen Dr *Web:* www.essexind.com/manufac_frame.htm	Saint Louis	MO	63143	314-644-3000	644-3857
Faber Enterprises Inc 6606 Variel Ave *Web:* www.faberent.com	Canoga Park	CA	91303	818-999-1300	712-0512
Gar-KenyonTechnologies 238 Water St PO Box 559 *Web:* www.garkenyon.com	Naugatuck	CT	06770	203-729-4900	729-4950
Gould JD Co Inc 4707 Massachusetts Ave *TF:* 800-634-6853 ■ *Web:* www.gouldvalve.com	Indianapolis	IN	46218	317-547-5289	547-5234
Hays Fluid Controls PO Box 580 *TF:* 800-354-4297 ■ *Web:* www.haysfluidcontrols.com	Dallas	NC	28034	704-922-9565	922-9595
Henry Pratt Co 401 S Highland Ave *TF:* 877-436-7728 ■ *Web:* www.henrypratt.com	Aurora	IL	60506	630-844-4000	844-4124
Hoke Inc 405 Centura Ct *Web:* www.hoke.com	Spartanburg	SC	29305	864-574-7966	574-0998
Hunt Valve Co Inc DBA Hunt Engineering 1913 E State St *TF:* 800-321-2757 ■ *Web:* www.huntvalve.com	Salem	OH	44460	330-337-9535	337-3754
HUSCO International Inc PO Box 257 *Web:* www.huscointl.com	Waukesha	WI	53187	262-513-4200	513-4514
Hyson Products 10367 Brecksville Rd *TF:* 800-876-4976 ■ *Web:* www.asbg.com/default_hyson.html	Brecksville	OH	44141	440-526-5900	838-7684
ITT Aerospace Controls 28150 Industry Dr *Web:* www.ittaerospace.com	Valencia	CA	91355	661-295-4000	295-4155
ITT Fluid Technology Corp 10 Mountainview Rd 3rd Fl *Web:* www.ittfluidtechnology.com/home.html	Upper Saddle River	NJ	07458	201-760-9800	760-9692
ITT Industries Inc 4 W Red Oak Ln *NYSE: ITT* ■ *Web:* www.itt.com	White Plains	NY	10604	914-641-2000	696-2950
JD Gould Co Inc 4707 Massachusetts Ave *TF:* 800-634-6853 ■ *Web:* www.gouldvalve.com	Indianapolis	IN	46218	317-547-5289	547-5234
Jetstream of Houston LLP 4930 Cranswick *TF:* 800-231-8192 ■ *Web:* www.waterblast.com	Houston	TX	77041	713-462-7000	462-5387
Kepner Products Co 995 N Ellsworth Ave *Web:* www.kepner.com	Villa Park	IL	60181	630-279-1550	279-9669
Kimray Inc 52 NW 42nd St *Web:* www.kimray.com	Oklahoma City	OK	73118	405-525-6601	525-7520
Leggitt SH Co 1000 Civic Center Loop *TF:* 800-877-2495 ■ *Web:* www.marshallgas.com	San Marcos	TX	78666	512-396-0707	396-2619
Mead Fluid Dynamics Inc 4114 N Knox Ave *Web:* www.meadfluiddynamics.com	Chicago	IL	60641	773-685-6800	685-7002
Midland Mfg Corp 7733 Gross Point Rd *Web:* www.midlandmfg.net	Skokie	IL	60077	847-677-0333	677-0138
Morrison Brothers Co PO Box 238 *TF Cust Svc:* 800-553-4840 ■ *Web:* www.morbros.com	Dubuque	IA	52004	563-583-5701	583-5028

Company	City	State	Zip	Phone	Fax
Norgren 5400 S Delaware St *Fax: Mktg ■ Web: www.norgren.com/usa	Littleton	CO	80120	303-794-5000	795-9487*
Oilgear Co PO Box 343924 NASDAQ: OLGR ■ TF Sales: 800-276-5356 ■ Web: www.oilgear.com	Milwaukee	WI	53234	414-327-1700	327-0532
Parker Climate & Industrial Controls Group 6035 Parkland Blvd Web: www.parker.com/cig	Cleveland	OH	44124	216-896-3000	896-4007
Parker Fluid Connectors Group 6035 Parkland Blvd TF: 800-272-7537 ■ Web: www.parker.com/fcg	Cleveland	OH	44124	216-896-3000	896-4000
Parker Hannifin Corp Brass Products Div 300 Parker Dr TF: 800-272-7537 ■ Web: www.parker.com/brassprod	Otsego	MI	49078	269-694-9411	694-4614
Parker Hannifin Corp Fluid Power Systems Div 595 Shelter Rd TF: 800-401-5015 ■ Web: www.parker.com	Lincolnshire	IL	60069	847-821-9478	383-8900
Parker Hannifin Corp General Valve Div 26 Clinton Dr Unit 103 TF: 800-482-8258 ■ Web: www.parker.com	Hollis	NH	03049	603-545-1500	585-8080
Parker Hannifin Corp Hydraulics Valve Div 520 Ternes Ave	Elyria	OH	44035	440-366-5100	366-5253
Parker Hannifin Corp Instrumentation Pneutronics Div 26 Clinton Dr Suite 103 Web: www.pneutronics.com	Hollis	NH	03049	603-595-1500	595-8080
Parker Hannifin Corp Pneumatic Div 8676 East M 89	Richland	MI	49083	269-629-5000	629-5385
Parker Hannifin Corp Skinner Valve Div 95 Edgewood Ave TF: 800-825-8305 ■ Web: www.parker.com/skinner	New Britain	CT	06051	860-827-2300	827-2384
Patten EA Co 303 Wetherell St	Manchester	CT	06040	860-649-2851	649-6230
PBM Inc 1070 Sandy Hill Rd TF: 800-967-4726 ■ Web: www.pbmvalve.com	Irwin	PA	15642	724-863-0550	864-9255
PerkinElmer Inc 45 William St NYSE: PKI ■ Web: www.perkinelmer.com	Wellesley	MA	02481	781-237-5100	237-9386
Pima Valve Inc 6525 W Allison Rd Web: www.pimavalve.com	Chandler	AZ	85226	520-796-1095	796-4012
Plattco Corp 7 White St TF: 800-352-1731 ■ Web: www.plattco.com	Plattsburgh	NY	12901	518-563-4640	563-4892
Pratt Henry Co 401 S Highland Ave TF: 877-436-7728 ■ Web: www.henrypratt.com	Aurora	IL	60506	630-844-4000	844-4124
Precision Dynamics Inc 60 Production Ct TF: 888-840-1230 ■ Web: www.predyne.com	New Britain	CT	06051	860-229-3753	827-0223
Rexarc Inc PO Box 7 Web: www.rexarc.com	West Alexandria	OH	45381	937-839-4604	839-5897
Richards Industries Inc 3170 Wasson Rd *Fax: Sales ■ TF Cust Svc: 800-543-7311 ■ Web: www.richardsind.com	Cincinnati	OH	45209	513-533-5600	871-0105*
Ritter Technology LLC 100 Williams Dr TF: 800-374-8837 ■ Web: www.ritter1.com	Zelienople	PA	16063	724-452-6000	452-0766
Rocker Industries 1500 W 240th St	Harbor City	CA	90710	310-534-5660	534-4285
Ross Controls PO Box 7015 Web: www.rosscontrols.com	Troy	MI	48007	248-764-1800	764-1850
SafeWay Hydraulics Inc 4040 Norex Dr TF Cust Svc: 800-222-1169 ■ Web: www.safewayhyd.com	Chaska	MN	55318	952-448-2600	448-3466
Sargent Controls & Aerospace 5675 W Burlingame Rd TF: 800-932-5273 ■ Web: www.sargentcontrols.com	Tucson	AZ	85743	520-744-1000	744-9290
Sedco 2304 W Beecher Rd PO Box 624 Web: www.sedco-prv.com	Adrian	MI	49221	517-263-2220	263-2546
SH Leggitt Co 1000 Civic Center Loop TF: 800-877-2495 ■ Web: www.marshallgas.com	San Marcos	TX	78666	512-396-0707	396-2619
Skinner Valve Div Parker Hannifin Corp 95 Edgewood Ave TF: 800-825-8305 ■ Web: www.parker.com/skinner	New Britain	CT	06051	860-827-2300	827-2384
SMC Pneumatics Inc 3011 N Franklin Rd PO Box 26646 TF: 800-762-7621 ■ Web: www.smcusa.com	Indianapolis	IN	46226	317-899-4440	899-3102
Specialty Mfg Co 5858 Centerville Rd Web: www.specialtymfg.com	Saint Paul	MN	55127	651-653-0599	653-0989
Sterling Hydraulics Inc 850 Arthur Ave Web: www.sterling-hyd.com	Elk Grove Village	IL	60007	847-690-1333	690-1335
Sun Hydraulics Corp 1500 W University Pkwy NASDAQ: SNHY ■ Web: www.sunhydraulics.com	Sarasota	FL	34243	941-355-2983	355-4497
Teleflex Fluid Systems Inc One Firestone Dr TF: 800-225-9077 ■ Web: www.teleflexhose.com	Suffield	CT	06078	860-668-1285	668-2353
Versa Products Co Inc 22 Spring Valley Rd Web: www.versavalves.com	Paramus	NJ	07652	201-843-2400	843-2931
Watts Fluidair Inc 9 Cutts Rd *Fax: Cust Svc ■ TF: 877-467-4323 ■ Web: www.wattsfluidair.com	Kittery	ME	03904	207-439-9511	475-4010*
Watts Regulator Co 815 Chestnut St *Fax: Cust Svc ■ Web: www.wattsreg.com	North Andover	MA	01845	978-688-1811	689-2457*
Watts Water Technologies Inc 815 Chestnut St NYSE: WTS ■ *Fax: Cust Svc ■ Web: www.wattsind.com	North Andover	MA	01845	978-688-1811	689-2457*
Weir Valves & Controls USA 285 Canal St Web: www.weirvalves.com	Salem	MA	01970	978-744-5690	740-9668
Young & Franklin Inc 942 Old Liverpool Rd Web: www.yf.com	Liverpool	NY	13088	315-457-3110	457-9204

794 VARIETY STORES

Company	City	State	Zip	Phone	Fax
99 Cents Only Stores 4000 Union Pacific Ave NYSE: NDN ■ Web: www.99only.com	Commerce	CA	90023	323-980-8145	980-8160
Alaska Commercial Co 550 W 64th Ave Suite 200 TF: 800-478-4484 ■ Web: www.alaskacommercial.com	Anchorage	AK	99518	907-273-4600	273-4800
Andersons Inc Retail Group 480 W Dussel Dr TF: 800-537-3370 ■ Web: www.andersonsstore.com	Maumee	OH	43537	419-893-5050	891-6452
Army & Air Force Exchange Service (AAFES) 3911 S Walton Walker Blvd TF: 800-527-6790 ■ Web: www.aafes.com	Dallas	TX	75236	214-312-2011	
B & B Sales Inc 712 S Broadway Web: www.bbdsales.com	Oklahoma City	OK	73109	405-232-3578	232-2848
Ben Franklin Stores Promotions Unlimited Corp 087601 Web: www.benfranklinstores.com	Racine	WI	53408	262-681-7000	
Big Lots Inc 300 Phillipi Rd NYSE: BLI ■ TF: 800-877-1253 ■ Web: www.biglots.com	Columbus	OH	43228	614-278-6800	278-6739
Bomgaars 323 Water St Web: www.bomgaars.com	Sioux City	IA	51103	712-277-2000	277-1247
Building No 19 Inc 319 Lincoln St TF: 800-225-5061 ■ Web: www.building19.com	Hingham	MA	02043	781-749-6900	749-3691
Buy.com Inc 85 Enterprise St TF: 877-880-1030 ■ Web: www.buy.com	Aliso Viejo	CA	92656	949-389-2000	389-2800
Dollar Discount Stores of America Inc 1362 Naamans Creek Rd TF: 800-227-5314 ■ Web: www.dollardiscount.com	Boothwyn	PA	19061	610-497-1991	485-6439
Dollar General Corp 100 Mission Ridge NYSE: DG ■ Web: www.dollargeneral.com	Goodlettsville	TN	37072	615-855-4000	855-4139
Dollar Tree Stores Inc 500 Volvo Pkwy NASDAQ: DLTR ■ Web: www.dollartree.com	Chesapeake	VA	23320	757-321-5000	321-5292
Duckwall-ALCO Stores Inc 401 Cottage Ave NASDAQ: DUCK ■ TF: 800-334-2526 ■ Web: www.duckwall.com	Abilene	KS	67410	785-263-3350	263-7531
Dueber's Inc 300 Industrial Blvd	Norwood Young America	MN	55397	952-467-3085	467-3001
Family Dollar Stores Inc 10401 Monroe Rd NYSE: FDO ■ Web: www.familydollar.com	Matthews	NC	28105	704-847-6961	847-0189
Fred Meyer Inc PO Box 42121 *Fax: Cust Svc ■ TF: 800-858-9202 ■ Web: www.fredmeyer.com	Portland	OR	97242	503-232-8844	797-5395*
Glassman Marc Inc 5841 W 130th St Web: www.marcs.com	Parma	OH	44130	216-265-7700	267-0088
Hand Stores 1310 Long Beach Blvd Web: www.handstores.com	Beach Haven	NJ	08008	609-207-1755	
Internet Shopping Outlet Inc 55 John St 11th Fl TF: 800-757-3015 ■ Web: www.shoplet.com	New York	NY	10038	212-619-3353	619-3389
JWT Stores Inc DBA Hand Stores 1310 Long Beach Blvd Web: www.handstores.com	Beach Haven	NJ	08008	609-207-1755	
Marc Glassman Inc 5841 W 130th St Web: www.marcs.com	Parma	OH	44130	216-265-7700	267-0088
Marden's Inc 184 College Ave TF: 800-564-3337 ■ Web: www.mardenssurplus.com	Waterville	ME	04901	207-873-6112	873-6680
Meyer Fred Inc PO Box 42121 *Fax: Cust Svc ■ TF: 800-858-9202 ■ Web: www.fredmeyer.com	Portland	OR	97242	503-232-8844	797-5395*
Navy Exchange Service Command (NEXCOM) 3280 Virginia Beach Blvd TF: 800-628-3924 ■ Web: www.navy-nex.com	Virginia Beach	VA	23452	757-463-6200	
Orvis Co Inc 178 Conservation Way TF: 800-541-3541 ■ Web: www.orvis.com	Sunderland	VT	05250	802-362-3622	362-3525
Overstock.com Inc 6322 S 3000 East Suite 100 NASDAQ: OSTK ■ TF Cust Svc: 800-843-2446 ■ Web: www.overstock.com	Salt Lake City	UT	84121	801-947-3100	944-4629
Super Dollar Stores 3401 Gresham Lake Rd TF: 800-366-9144	Raleigh	NC	27615	919-876-6000	790-9572
Swain's General Store Inc 602 E 1st St Web: www.swainsinc.com	Port Angeles	WA	98362	360-452-2357	452-7561
Unclaimed Baggage Center 509 W Willow St Web: www.unclaimedbaggage.com	Scottsboro	AL	35768	256-259-1525	259-0818
Variety Wholesalers Inc 3401 Gresham Lake Rd TF: 800-366-9144 ■ Web: www.vwstores.com	Raleigh	NC	27615	919-876-6000	790-9570

795 VENTURE CAPITAL FIRMS

Companies listed here are investors, not lenders.

Company	City	State	Zip	Phone	Fax
@Ventures 187 Ballardvale St Suite A-260 Web: www.ventures.com	Wilmington	MA	01887	978-658-8980	658-8981
3i North America 275 Middlefield Rd Suite 200 Web: www.3ius.com	Menlo Park	CA	94025	650-470-3200	470-3201
4C Ventures 21 E 94th St 3rd Fl Web: www.4cventures.com	New York	NY	10028	212-996-3133	996-4644
AAVIN Equity Partners LP 118 3rd Ave SE Suite 630 Web: www.aavin.com	Cedar Rapids	IA	52401	319-247-1072	363-9519
Abbott Capital Management LLC 1211 Ave of the Americas Suite 4300 Web: www.abbottcapital.com	New York	NY	10036	212-757-2700	757-0835
Aberdare Ventures One Embarcadero Center Suite 4000 Web: www.aberdare.com	San Francisco	CA	94111	415-392-7442	392-4264
ABS Capital Partners 400 E Pratt St Suite 910 Web: www.abscapital.com	Baltimore	MD	21202	410-246-5600	246-5606
ABS Ventures 890 Winter St Suite 225 Web: www.absventures.com	Waltham	MA	02451	781-250-0400	250-0345
Acacia Venture Partners 101 California St Suite 3160 Web: www.acaciavp.com	San Francisco	CA	94111	415-433-4200	433-4250
Accel Partners 428 University Ave Web: www.accel.com	Palo Alto	CA	94301	650-614-4800	614-4880
Accuitive Medical Ventures LLC 2750 Premiere Pkwy Suite 200 TF: 888-935-4411 ■ Web: www.amvpartners.com	Duluth	GA	30097	678-812-1101	417-7325
Adams Capital Management Inc 500 Blackburn Ave Web: www.acm.com	Sewickley	PA	15143	412-749-9454	749-9459
Adams Harkness Techventures 99 High St Web: www.ahventures.com	Boston	MA	02110	617-788-1670	788-1663
Adams Street Partners LLC 1 N Wacker Dr Suite 2200 Web: www.adamsstreetpartners.com	Chicago	IL	60606	312-553-7890	553-7891
Adena Ventures 20 E Circle Dr Web: www.adenaventures.com	Athens	OH	45701	740-597-1470	597-1399
Adobe Ventures LP 345 Park Ave Web: www.adobe.com	San Jose	CA	95110	408-536-6000	537-6000
Advanced Technology Ventures 485 Ramona St Web: www.atvcapital.com	Palo Alto	CA	94301	650-321-8601	321-0934
Advanced Technology Ventures 1000 Winter St Suite 3700 Web: www.atvcapital.com	Waltham	MA	02451	781-290-0707	684-0045
Advantage Capital Partners 16750 Gulf Blvd Web: www.advantagecap.com	North Redington Beach	FL	33708	813-261-5040	282-3381
Advent International Corp 75 State St 29th Fl Web: www.adventinternational.com	Boston	MA	02109	617-951-9400	951-0566
Agilent Technologies Inc 5301 Stevens Creek Blvd NYSE: A ■ *Fax Area Code: 408 ■ TF: 877-424-4536 ■ Web: www.agilent.com	Santa Clara	CA	95051	877-424-4536	345-8474*
Alerion Partners 105 Rowayton Ave Web: www.alerionpartners.com	Rowayton	CT	06853	203-838-6700	838-6712
Alexander Hutton Venture Partners 999 3rd Ave Suite 3700 Web: www.ahvp.com	Seattle	WA	98104	206-341-9800	341-9810
Allegis Capital 130 Lytton Ave Suite 210 Web: www.allegiscapital.com	Palo Alto	CA	94301	650-687-0500	687-0234
Allegra Partners 320 Park Ave 18th Fl Web: www.allegrapartners.com	New York	NY	10022	212-277-1526	277-1533
Allied Capital Corp 1919 Pennsylvania Ave NW 3rd Fl NYSE: ALD ■ TF: 888-818-5298 ■ Web: www.alliedcapital.com	Washington	DC	20006	202-721-6100	659-2053
Alloy Ventures 400 Hamilton Ave 4th floor Web: www.alloyventures.com	Palo Alto	CA	94301	650-687-5000	687-5010
Allstate Insurance Co Private Equity Div 3075 Sanders Rd Suite Q5D	Northbrook	IL	60062	847-402-6029	402-4726
Alpha Capital Partners Ltd 122 S Michigan Ave Suite 1700 Web: www.alphacapital.com	Chicago	IL	60603	312-322-9800	322-9808
Alta Communications Inc 200 Clarendon St 51st Fl Web: www.altacomm.com	Boston	MA	02116	617-262-7770	262-9779
Alta Partners 1 Embarcadero Ctr 37th Fl Web: www.altapartners.com	San Francisco	CA	94111	415-362-4022	362-6178
Altira Group LLC 1625 Broadway Suite 2450 Web: www.altiragroup.com	Denver	CO	80202	303-592-5500	592-5519
Altos Ventures 2882 Sand Hill Rd Suite 100 Web: www.altosvc.com	Menlo Park	CA	94025	650-234-9771	233-9821
Altotech Ventures LLC 205 De Anza Blvd Suite 14 Web: www.altotechventures.com	San Mateo	CA	94402	650-574-1870	
AM Pappas & Assoc 2520 Meridian Pkwy Web: www.ampappas.com	Durham	NC	27713	919-998-3300	998-3301
American Capital Group Inc 175 Technology Dr Suite 100 TF: 800-305-0224 ■ Web: www.americancapitalgroup.com	Irvine	CA	92618	949-271-5800	271-5850
American River Ventures 2270 Douglas Blvd Suite 212 Web: www.arventures.com	Roseville	CA	95661	916-780-2828	780-5443

Firm / Address	City	State	Zip	Phone	Fax
Ampersand Venture Management Corp					
55 William St Suite 240	Wellesley	MA	02481	781-239-0700	239-0824
Web: www.ampersandventures.com					
Antares Capital Corp 9999 NE 2nd Ave Suite 306	Miami Shores	FL	33138	305-894-2888	894-3227
Web: www.antarescapital.com					
Apax Partners Inc 153 E 53rd St 53rd Fl	New York	NY	10022	212-753-6300	319-6155
TF: 800-220-2526 ■ *Web:* www.apax.com					
Aperture Venture Partners 645 Madison Ave 20th Fl	New York	NY	10022	212-758-7325	319-8779
Web: www.aperturevp.com					
Apex Investment Partners 225 W Washington St Suite 1500	Chicago	IL	60606	312-857-2800	857-1800
Web: www.apexvc.com					
Appian Ventures 1512 Larimer St Suite 200-A	Denver	CO	80202	303-830-2450	830-2449
Web: www.appianvc.com					
Arbor Partners LLC 130 S 1st St	Ann Arbor	MI	48104	734-668-9000	669-4195
Web: www.arborpartners.com					
Arboretum Ventures 334 E Washington St	Ann Arbor	MI	48104	734-998-3688	998-3689
Web: www.arboretumvc.com					
ARCH Development Partners LLC 20 N Wacker Dr Suite 2000	Chicago	IL	60606	312-442-4400	263-0724
Web: www.archdevelopmentpartners.com					
ARCH Venture Partners 8725 W Higgins Rd Suite 290	Chicago	IL	60631	773-380-6600	380-6606
Web: www.archventure.com					
Arete Corp PO Box 1299	Center Harbor	NH	03226	603-253-9797	253-9799
Web: www.arete-microgen.com					
Ascension Health Ventures LLC					
11775 Borman Dr Suite 310	Saint Louis	MO	63146	314-733-8113	733-8678
Web: www.ascensionhealthventures.org					
Ascent Venture Partners 255 State St 5th Fl	Boston	MA	02109	617-720-9400	720-9401
Web: www.ascentvp.com					
Asset Management Co 2100 Geng Rd Suite 200	Palo Alto	CA	94303	650-494-7400	856-1826
Web: www.assetman.com					
Associated Venture Investors Management					
130 Lytton Ave Suite 210	Palo Alto	CA	94301	650-687-0235	687-0234
Web: www.avicapital.com					
ATA Ventures 203 Redwood Shores Pkwy Suite 550	Redwood City	CA	94065	650-594-0189	594-0257
Web: www.ataventures.com					
Atlas Venture 890 Winter St Suite 320	Waltham	MA	02451	781-622-1700	622-1701
Web: www.atlasventure.com					
August Capital 2480 Sand Hill Rd Suite 101	Menlo Park	CA	94025	650-234-9900	234-9910
Web: www.augustcap.com					
Aurora Funds 2525 Meridian Pkwy Suite 220	Durham	NC	27713	919-484-0400	484-0444
Web: www.aurorafunds.com					
Austin Ventures 300 W 6th St Suite 2300	Austin	TX	78701	512-485-1900	476-3952
Web: www.austinventures.com					
Avansis Ventures LLC 12010 Sunset Hills Rd Suite 830	Reston	VA	20190	703-796-0222	935-0574
Web: www.avansis.com					
AVI Management 130 Lytton Ave Suite 210	Palo Alto	CA	94301	650-687-0235	687-0234
Web: www.avicapital.com					
Axiom Venture Partners LP CityPlace II 17th Fl 185 Asylum St	Hartford	CT	06103	860-548-7799	548-7797
Web: www.axiomventures.com					
Bachow & Assoc Inc 3 Bala Plaza E 5th Fl	Bala Cynwyd	PA	19004	610-660-4900	660-4930
Web: www.bachow.com					
Bain Capital Inc 111 Huntington Ave	Boston	MA	02199	617-516-2000	516-2010
Web: www.baincap.com					
Battelle Ventures 103 Carnegie Center Suite 100	Princeton	NJ	08540	609-921-1456	921-8703
Web: www.battelleventures.com					
Battery Ventures 20 William St Suite 200	Wellesley	MA	02481	781-577-1000	577-1001
Web: www.battery.com					
Bay Partners 10600 N De Anza Blvd Suite 100	Cupertino	CA	95014	408-725-2444	446-4502
Web: www.baypartners.com					
BCM Technologies 11 Greenway Plaza Suite 2900	Houston	TX	77046	713-795-0105	795-4602
Web: www.bcmtechnologies.com					
Beecken Petty O'Keefe & Co 131 S Dearborn St Suite 2800	Chicago	IL	60603	312-435-0300	435-0371
Web: www.beeckenpetty.com					
Benchmark Capital 2480 Sand Hill Rd Suite 200	Menlo Park	CA	94025	650-854-8180	854-8183
Web: www.benchmark.com					
Beringea LLC 32330 W 12 Mile Rd	Farmington Hills	MI	48334	248-489-9000	489-8819
Web: www.beringea.com					
Berkeley International Capital Corp					
650 California St 26th Fl	San Francisco	CA	94108	415-249-0450	249-0553
Web: www.berkeleyvc.com					
Bessemer Venture Partners 83 Walnut St	Wellesley Hills	MA	02481	781-237-6050	235-7576
Web: www.bessemervp.com					
BioAdvance 3701 Market St	Philadelphia	PA	19104	215-966-6214	966-6215
Web: www.bioadvance.com					
Bioventures Investors 101 Main St Suite 1750	Cambridge	MA	02142	617-252-3443	621-7993
Web: www.bioventuresinvestors.com					
Blue Chip Venture Co 250 E 5th St 1100 Chiquita Ctr	Cincinnati	OH	45202	513-723-2300	723-2306
TF: 800-775-1812 ■ *Web:* www.bcvc.com					
Blue Point Capital Partners 127 Public Sq Suite 5100	Cleveland	OH	44114	216-535-4700	535-4701
TF: 866-837-2048 ■ *Web:* www.bluepointcapital.com					
Blueprint Ventures 601 Gateway Blvd Suite 1140	South San Francisco	CA	94080	415-901-4000	901-4035
Web: www.blueprintventures.com					
BlueRun Ventures 545 Middlefield Rd Suite 210	Menlo Park	CA	94025	650-462-7250	462-7252
Web: www.bluerunventures.com					
BNP Paribas Capital Funding LLC 787 7th Ave 33rd Fl	New York	NY	10019	212-841-2000	841-2146
Web: www.bnpparibas.com/en/home					
Boldcap Ventures LLC 969 3rd Ave Suite 4-C	New York	NY	10022	212-730-5498	591-0880*
**Fax Area Code:* 917 ■ *Web:* www.boldcap.com					
Borealis Ventures 10 Allen St	Hanover	NH	03755	603-643-1500	643-7600
Web: www.borealisventures.com					
Boston Capital Ventures 114 State St 6th Fl	Boston	MA	02109	617-227-6550	227-3847
Web: www.bcv.com					
Boston Millennia Partners 30 Rowes Wharf Suite 500	Boston	MA	02110	617-428-5150	428-5160
Web: www.millenniapartners.com					
Boston Ventures Management Inc 125 High St 17 Fl	Boston	MA	02110	617-350-1500	350-1509
Web: www.bostonventures.com					
Braemar Energy Ventures 340 Madison Ave 18th Fl	New York	NY	10017	212-697-0900	682-9439
Web: www.braemarenergy.com					
Brantley Partners 3201 Enterprise Pkwy Suite 350	Beachwood	OH	44122	216-464-8400	464-8405
Web: www.brantleypartners.com					
Brentwood Venture Capital					
11150 Santa Monica Blvd Suite 1200	Los Angeles	CA	90025	310-477-7678	312-1868
Web: www.brentwoodvc.com					
BTG International Inc 300 Barr Harbor Dr 7th Fl	West Conshohocken	PA	19428	610-278-1660	278-1605
Web: www.btgplc.com					
Buerk Dale Victor LLC 1200 5th Ave Suite 1800	Seattle	WA	98101	206-956-0898	956-0863
Web: www.bdvllc.com					
Burrill & Co 1 Embarcadero Ctr Suite 2700	San Francisco	CA	94111	415-591-5400	591-5401
Web: www.burrillandco.com					
BV Cornerstone Ventures LP 11001 W 120th Ave Suite 310	Broomfield	CO	80021	303-410-2500	466-9316
Web: www.bvcv.com					
Cambridge Innovations Inc 1 Broadway 14th Fl	Cambridge	MA	02142	617-758-4200	758-4101
Web: www.cambridgeincubator.com					
Cambridge Light Partners 955 Massachusetts Ave Suite 304	Cambridge	MA	02139	617-497-6310	
Web: www.cambridgelight.com					
Camp Ventures LLC 309 1st St Suite 1	Los Altos	CA	94022	650-949-0841	618-1719
Web: www.campventures.com					
Canaan Partners 285 Riverside Ave Suite 250	Westport	CT	06880	203-855-0400	854-9117
Web: www.canaan.com					
Capital Network Inc (TCN) PO Box 39	Groton	MA	01450	978-846-3972	
Web: www.thecapitalnetwork.org					
Capital Resource Partners 200 State St 13th Fl	Boston	MA	02109	617-478-9600	478-9605
Web: www.crp.com					
Capital Southwest Corp 12900 Preston Rd Suite 700	Dallas	TX	75230	972-233-8242	233-7362
NASDAQ: CSWC ■ *Web:* www.capitalsouthwest.com					
Cardinal Partners 600 Alexander Park Suite 204	Princeton	NJ	08540	609-924-6452	683-0174
Web: www.cardinalpartners.com					
Cardinal Venture Capital 1010 El Camino Real Suite 250	Menlo Park	CA	94025	650-289-4700	614-4865
Web: www.cardinalvc.com					
Cargill Ventures 1200 Park Pl Suite 300	San Mateo	CA	94403	650-356-7060	356-7077
Web: www.cargillventures.com					
Castile Ventures 930 Winter St Suite 500	Waltham	MA	02451	781-890-0060	890-0065
Web: www.castileventures.com					
Catamount Ventures 400 Pacific Ave 3rd Floor	San Francisco	CA	94133	415-277-0300	277-0301
Web: www.catamountventures.com					
Catterton Partners 599 W Putnam Ave Suite 200	Greenwich	CT	06830	203-629-4901	629-4903
Web: www.cpequity.com					
CB Health Ventures 360 Madison Ave 5th Fl	New York	NY	10017	212-869-5600	869-6418
Web: www.health-ventures.com					
CCG Venture Partners LLC 14405 Brown Rd	Tomball	TX	77375	281-290-8331	290-8332
Web: www.ccgvp.com					
CEI Ventures Inc 2 Portland Fish Pier Suite 206	Portland	ME	04101	207-772-5356	772-5503
Web: www.ceiventures.com					
CenterPoint Ventures 6300 Bridge Pt Pkwy Bldg 1 Suite 500	Austin	TX	78730	512-795-5800	795-5849
Web: www.cpventures.com					
Chaney R & Co Inc 6363 Woodway Dr Suite 960	Houston	TX	77057	713-356-7555	750-0021
Web: www.rchaney.com					
Charles River Ventures					
1000 Winter St Bay Colony Corporate Ctr Suite 3300	Waltham	MA	02451	781-768-6000	768-6100
TF: 866-278-3278 ■ *Web:* www.crv.com					
Charter Venture Capital 525 University Ave Suite 1400	Palo Alto	CA	94301	650-325-6953	325-4762
Web: www.charterventures.com					
Cherry Tree Investment Co 301 Carlson Pkwy Suite 103	Minnetonka	MN	55305	952-893-9012	893-9036
Web: www.cherrytree.com					
Chevron Texaco Technology Venture Investments LLC					
3901 Briar Park Rd	Houston	TX	77042	713-954-6974	954-6388
Web: www.chevron.com/technologyventures					
Chisholm Private Capital Partners					
800 Research Pkwy Suite 385	Oklahoma City	OK	73104	405-605-1111	605-1115
Web: www.chisholmvc.com					
CHL Medical Partners 1055 Washington Blvd 6th Fl	Stamford	CT	06901	203-324-7700	324-3636
Web: www.chlmedical.com					
Chrysalis Ventures 101 S 5th St 1650 National City Tower	Louisville	KY	40202	502-583-7644	583-7648
Web: www.chrysalisventures.com					
Churchill Capital Inc 333 S 7th St Suite 2400	Minneapolis	MN	55402	612-673-6633	673-6630
TF: 888-782-3328 ■ *Web:* www.churchillnet.com					
CIBC Wood Gundy Capital 425 Lexington Ave	New York	NY	10017	212-856-6500	
TF: 800-999-6726 ■ *Web:* www.cibcwm.com					
CID Capital Inc 1 American Sq Suite 2850	Indianapolis	IN	46282	317-269-2350	269-2355
Web: www.cidequity.com					
CIVC Partners 191 N Wacker Dr Suite 1100	Chicago	IL	60606	312-873-7300	873-7301
Web: www.civc.com					
Clarion Capital Corp 3690 Orange Place Suite 400	Beachwood	OH	44122	216-896-1260	896-1261
Clearstone Venture Partners 1351 4th St 4th Fl	Santa Monica	CA	90401	310-460-7900	460-7901
Web: www.clearstone.com					
CMEA Ventures 1 Embarcadero Center Suite 3250	San Francisco	CA	94111	415-352-1520	352-1524
Web: www.cmeaventures.com					
Code Hennessy & Simmons Inc 10 S Wacker Dr Suite 3175	Chicago	IL	60606	312-876-1840	876-3854
Web: www.chsonline.com					
Columbia Capital 201 N Union St Suite 300	Alexandria	VA	22314	703-519-2000	519-5870
TF: 800-247-7727 ■ *Web:* www.colcap.com					
Comcast Interactive Capital 1500 Market St	Philadelphia	PA	19102	215-981-8450	981-8429
Web: www.civentures.com					
Comdisco Ventures Group 5600 N River Rd Suite 800	Rosemont	IL	60018	847-698-3000	518-5440
TF: 800-321-1111 ■ *Web:* www.comdisco.com/ventures.asp					
Commons Capital LP 320 Washington St 4th Fl	Brookline	MA	02445	617-739-3500	
Web: www.commonscapital.com					
Commonwealth Capital Ventures 950 Winter St Suite 4100	Waltham	MA	02451	781-890-5554	890-3414
Web: www.commonwealthvc.com					
Compass Technology Partners LP					
261 Hamilton Ave Suite 200	Palo Alto	CA	94301	650-322-7595	322-0588
Web: www.compasstechpartners.com					
ComVentures 305 Lytton Ave	Palo Alto	CA	94301	650-325-9600	325-9608
Web: www.comventures.com					
Connecticut Innovations Inc 200 Corporate Pl 3rd Fl	Rocky Hill	CT	06067	860-563-5851	563-4877
TF: 888-337-5454 ■ *Web:* www.ctinnovations.com					
Conning Capital Partners (CCP) 100 Pearl St 17th Fl	Hartford	CT	06103	860-761-8200	761-8299
Web: www.conningcapital.com					
Consolidated Mercantile Inc 106 Avenue Rd	Toronto	ON	M5R2H3	416-920-0500	920-7851
NASDAQ: CSLMF ■ *Web:* www.consolidatedmercantile.com					
Cordova Ventures 2500 Northwinds Pkwy Suite 475	Alpharetta	GA	30004	678-942-0300	942-0301
Web: www.cordovaventures.com					
Core Capital Partners 901 15th St NW Suite 950	Washington	DC	20005	202-589-0090	589-0091
Web: www.core-capital.com					
Cornerstone Equity Investors LLC					
355 Lexington Ave Suite 1400	New York	NY	10017	212-753-0901	826-6798
Web: www.cornerstone-equity.com					
Court Square Ventures 0 Court Sq	Charlottesville	VA	22902	434-817-3300	817-3299
Web: www.courtsquareventures.com					
Cravey Green & Wahlen Inc 12 Piedmont Ctr Suite 210	Atlanta	GA	30305	404-816-3255	816-3258
TF: 800-249-6669 ■ *Web:* www.cgwlp.com					
Crescendo Ventures 480 Cowper St Suite 300	Palo Alto	CA	94301	650-470-1200	470-1201
Web: www.crescendoventures.com					
Cross Atlantic Capital Partners					
5 Radnor Corporate Ctr Suite 555 100 Matsonford Rd	Radnor	PA	19087	610-995-2650	971-2062
Web: www.xacp.com					
Cross Atlantic Partners Inc 551 Madison Ave 7th Fl	New York	NY	10022	646-521-7500	497-0061
Web: www.crossatlanticpartners.com					
Crossbow Ventures 1 N Clematis St Suite 510	West Palm Beach	FL	33401	561-838-9005	838-4105
TF: 866-831-3454 ■ *Web:* www.crossbowventures.com					
Crosslink Capital 2 Embarcadero Ctr Suite 2200	San Francisco	CA	94111	415-617-1800	
Web: www.crosslinkcapital.com					
Crosspoint Venture Partners 2925 Woodside Rd	Woodside	CA	94062	650-851-7600	851-7661
Web: www.crosspointvc.com					
Crown Advisors International Ltd					
60 E 42nd St Lincoln Bldg Suite 1835	New York	NY	10165	212-808-5278	351-8556*
**Fax Area Code:* 646 ■ *Web:* www.crownadvisors.com					
Cutlass Capital 84 State St Suite 1040	Boston	MA	02109	617-624-0363	624-9669
Web: www.cutlasscapital.com					
CW Group 1041 3rd Ave 2nd Fl	New York	NY	10021	212-308-5266	644-0354
Web: www.cwventures.com					
Cypress Ventures 535 Middlefield Rd Suite 100	Menlo Park	CA	94025	650-325-6699	325-7799
Web: www.cypressventures.com					

Firm / Address	City	State	Zip	Phone	Fax
Davis, Tuttle Venture Partners LP 110 W 7th St Suite 1000 *Web:* www.davistuttle.com	Tulsa	OK	74119	918-584-7272	582-3403
Defta Partners 111 Pine St Suite 1410 *Web:* www.deftapartners.com	San Francisco	CA	94111	415-433-2262	433-2264
Delphi Ventures 3000 Sand Hill Rd Bldg 1 Suite 135 *Web:* www.delphiventures.com	Menlo Park	CA	94025	650-854-9650	854-2961
DeMuth Folger & Wetherill 300 Frank W Burr Blvd 5th Fl Glenpointe Ctr E *Web:* www.dfwcapital.com	Teaneck	NJ	07666	201-836-6000	836-5666
Desai Capital Management Inc 410 Park Ave *TF:* 800-337-2484 ■ *Web:* www.desaicapital.com	New York	NY	10022	212-838-9191	838-9807
Digital Power Capital LLC 411 W Putnam Ave Suite 125 *Web:* www.digitalpower.com	Greenwich	CT	06830	203-862-7045	862-7345
DoCoMo Capital 3240 Hillview Ave *Web:* www.docomo-capital.com	Palo Alto	CA	94304	650-493-9600	493-9664
Doll Capital Management 2420 Sand Hill Rd Suite 200 *Web:* www.dcm.com	Menlo Park	CA	94025	650-233-1400	854-9159
Dolphin Equity Partners 750 Lexington Ave 16th Floor *TF:* 800-838-1207 ■ *Web:* www.dolphinequity.com	New York	NY	10022	212-446-1600	446-1638
Domain Assoc 1 Palmer Sq Suite 515 *TF:* 800-241-1901 ■ *Web:* www.domainvc.com	Princeton	NJ	08542	609-683-5656	683-9789
Dominion Ventures Inc 1656 N California Blvd Suite 300 *TF:* 800-875-4890 ■ *Web:* www.dominion.com	Walnut Creek	CA	94596	925-280-6300	280-6338
Draper Fisher Jurvetson 2882 Sand Hill Rd *Web:* www.dfj.com	Menlo Park	CA	94025	650-233-9000	233-9233
Duchossois Technology Partners 845 Larch Ave *Web:* www.duchtec.com	Elmhurst	IL	60126	630-530-6105	993-8644
Earlybird Venture Capital 2061 Avy Ave Suite 201 *Web:* www.earlybird.com	Menlo Park	CA	94025	650-461-8050	461-8051
East Gate Capital Management 514 High St Suite 5 *Web:* www.eg-group.com	Palo Alto	CA	94301	650-325-5077	325-5072
Edelson Technology Partners 300 Tice Blvd *Web:* www.edelsontech.com	Woodcliff Lake	NJ	07677	201-930-9898	930-8899
EDF Ventures 425 N Main St *Web:* www.edfvc.com	Ann Arbor	MI	48104	734-663-3213	663-7358
Edison Venture Fund 1009 Lenox Dr Bldg 4 *Web:* www.edisonventure.com	Lawrenceville	NJ	08648	609-896-1900	896-0066
EGL Holdings 3495 Piedmont Rd 11 Piedmont Center Suite 412 *Web:* www.eglholdings.com	Atlanta	GA	30305	404-949-8300	949-8311
El Dorado Ventures 2440 Sand Hill Rd Suite 200 *Web:* www.eldorado.com	Menlo Park	CA	94025	650-854-1200	854-1202
Electra Partners Inc 708 3rd Ave 21st Fl	New York	NY	10017	212-818-0421	818-0010
Empire Ventures 1020 SW Taylor St Suite 415 *Web:* www.empireventures.com	Portland	OR	97205	503-222-1556	222-1607
Endeavor Capital Management 49 Richmondville Ave Suite 215 *Web:* www.endeavorcap.com	Westport	CT	06880	203-341-7788	341-7799
EnerTech Capital Partners 435 Devon Park Dr Bldg 700 *Web:* www.enertechcapital.com	Wayne	PA	19087	610-254-4141	254-4188
Enterprise Partners 2223 Avenida de la Playa Suite 300 *Web:* www.epvc.com	La Jolla	CA	92037	858-454-8833	454-9069
Entrepia Ventures Inc 5201 Great American Pkwy Suite 456 *Web:* www.entrepia.com	Santa Clara	CA	95054	408-492-9040	492-9540
Envest Ventures 2101 Parks Ave Suite 401 *Web:* www.envestventures.com	Virginia Beach	VA	23451	757-437-3000	437-3884
Equus Capital Corp 2727 Allen Pkwy 13th Fl *TF:* 800-856-0901 ■ *Web:* www.equuscap.com	Houston	TX	77019	713-529-0900	529-9545
Essex Woodlands Health Ventures 21 Waterway Ave Suite 225 *Web:* www.essexwoodlands.com	The Woodlands	TX	77380	281-364-1555	364-9755
Euclid SR Partners 45 Rockefeller Plaza Suite 3240 *Web:* www.euclidsr.com	New York	NY	10111	212-218-6880	218-6877
Ferrer Freeman & Co LLC 10 Glenville St The Mill *Web:* www.ffandco.com	Greenwich	CT	06831	203-532-8011	532-8016
Fidelity Ventures 82 Devonshire St Suite E27A *Web:* www.fidelityventures.com	Boston	MA	02109	617-392-2448	476-9023
Financial Technology Ventures 555 California St Suite 2900 *Web:* www.ftventures.com	San Francisco	CA	94108	415-229-3000	229-3005
Finaventures 3000 Ocean Park Blvd Suite 1022 *Web:* www.finaventures.com	Santa Monica	CA	90405	310-399-5011	452-5492
First Analysis Corp 1 S Wacker Dr Suite 3900 *Web:* www.facvc.com	Chicago	IL	60606	312-258-1400	258-0334
Fisher Lynch Capital 2929 Campus Dr Suite 410 **Fax Area Code:* 810 ■ *Web:* www.fisherlynch.com	San Mateo	CA	94403	650-233-8015	222-6386*
FLAG Capital Management LLC 1 Beacon St 23rd Fl *Web:* www.flagcapital.com	Boston	MA	02108	617-557-0028	557-0029
Flagship Ventures 1 Memorial Dr 7th Fl *Web:* www.flagshipventures.com	Cambridge	MA	02142	617-868-1888	868-1115
Fletcher Spaght Inc 222 Berkeley St 20th Fl *Web:* www.fletcherspaght.com	Boston	MA	02116	617-247-6700	247-7757
Flywheel Ventures 400 Montgomery St Suite 1040 **Fax Area Code:* 877 ■ *Web:* www.flywheelventures.com	San Francisco	CA	94104	800-750-7870	866-4107*
Focus Ventures 525 University Ave Suite 1400 *Web:* www.focusventures.com	Palo Alto	CA	94301	650-325-7400	325-8400
Formative Ventures 2061 Avy Ave *Web:* www.formativeventures.com	Menlo Park	CA	94025	650-461-8000	461-8010
Forward Ventures 9393 Towne Centre Dr Suite 200 *Web:* www.forwardventures.com	San Diego	CA	92121	858-677-6077	452-8799
Foundation Capital 70 Willow Rd Suite 200 *Web:* www.foundationcapital.com	Menlo Park	CA	94025	650-614-0500	614-0505
Foundation Medical Partners 105 Rowayton Ave *Web:* www.foundmed.com	Rowayton	CT	06853	203-851-3900	831-8289
Frazier & Co 601 Union St Suite 3200 *TF:* 800-411-4499 ■ *Web:* www.frazierco.com	Seattle	WA	98101	206-621-7200	621-1848
Frontenac Co 135 S La Salle St Suite 3800 *TF:* 800-368-3681 ■ *Web:* www.frontenac.com	Chicago	IL	60603	312-368-0044	368-9520
G-51 Capital Management 901 S Mo Pac Expy Bldg 3 Suite 410 *Web:* www.g51.com	Austin	TX	78746	512-929-5151	732-0886
Gabriel Venture Partners 350 Marine Pkwy Suite 200 *Web:* www.gabrielvp.com	Redwood Shores	CA	94065	650-551-5000	551-5001
Garage Technology Ventures 3300 Hillview Ave Suite 150 *Web:* www.garage.com	Palo Alto	CA	94304	650-354-1800	354-1801
Gazelle Techventures 11611 N. Meridian St Suite 310 *Web:* www.gazellevc.com	Carmel	IN	46032	317-275-6800	275-1100
Gefinor Ventures Management Inc 375 Park Ave Suite 2401 *Web:* www.gefinorventures.com	New York	NY	10152	212-308-1111	308-1182
General Atlantic LLC 3 Pickwick Plaza Suite 200 *Web:* www.generalatlantic.com	Greenwich	CT	06830	203-629-8600	622-8818
Geocapital Partners 1 Executive Dr Suite 160 *Web:* www.geocapital.com	Fort Lee	NJ	07024	201-461-9292	461-7793
GIV Venture Partners 1 Delaware Technology Park Suite 400 Rm 428 *Web:* www.givventurepartners.com	Newark	DE	19711	703-442-3300	442-3388
GKM Ventures 11150 Santa Monica Blvd Suite 825 *Web:* www.gkmventures.com	Los Angeles	CA	90025	310-268-2610	268-0870
Globespan Capital Partners 1 Boston Pl Suite 2810 *Web:* www.globespancapital.com	Boston	MA	02108	617-305-2300	305-2301
GrandBanks Capital 10 Langley Rd Suite 403 *Web:* www.grandbankscapital.com	Newton Center	MA	02459	617-928-9314	928-9305
Granite Global Ventures 2494 Sand Hill Rd Suite 100 *Web:* www.ggvc.com	Menlo Park	CA	94025	650-475-2150	475-2151
Granite Ventures LLC 1 Bush St Suite 1350 *Web:* www.granitevc.com	San Francisco	CA	94104	415-591-7700	591-7720
Great Hill Partners LLC 1 Liberty Sq *Web:* www.greathillpartners.com	Boston	MA	02109	617-790-9400	790-9401
Greer Capital Advisors LLC 2200 Woodcrest Pl Suite 309 *Web:* www.greercap.com	Birmingham	AL	35209	205-445-0800	445-1013
Greylock 880 Winter St Suite 300 *TF:* 800-289-5525 ■ *Web:* www.greylock.com	Waltham	MA	02451	781-622-2200	622-2300
Grosvenor Funds 57 Old Post Rd #2 2nd Floor *Web:* www.grosvenorfund.com	Greenwich	CT	06830	203-629-8337	629-8506
Grotech Capital Group 9690 Deereco Rd Suite 800 *Web:* www.grotech.com	Timonium	MD	21093	410-560-2000	560-1910
Grove Street Advisors 20 William St Suite 230 *Web:* www.grovestreetadvisors.com	Wellesley	MA	02481	781-263-6100	263-6101
GRP Partners 2121 Ave of the Stars Suite 1630 *Web:* www.grpvc.com	Los Angeles	CA	90067	310-785-5100	785-5111
GTCR Golder Rauner LLC 6100 Sears Tower *Web:* www.gtcr.com	Chicago	IL	60606	312-382-2200	382-2201
Guide Ventures 12509 Bel-Red Rd Suite 201-B *Web:* www.guideventures.com	Bellevue	WA	98005	425-450-0062	
Hamilton BioVentures 12555 High Bluff Dr Suite 310 *Web:* www.hamiltonbioventures.com	San Diego	CA	92130	858-314-2350	314-2355
HarbourVest Partners LLC 1 Financial Ctr 44th Fl *Web:* www.harbourvest.com	Boston	MA	02111	617-348-3707	350-0305
Harvard Management Co Inc 600 Atlantic Ave 16th Fl **Fax:* Hum Res ■ *TF:* 800-723-0044	Boston	MA	02210	617-523-4400	367-1361*
Harvest Partners 280 Park Ave 33rd Fl *TF:* 866-427-8727 ■ *Web:* www.harvpart.com	New York	NY	10017	212-599-6300	812-0100
HC Wainwright & Co Inc 52 Vanderbilt Ave 12th Fl *Web:* www.hcwainwright.com	New York	NY	10017	212-856-5700	856-5753
HealthCare Ventures LLC 44 Nassau St *Web:* www.hcven.com	Princeton	NJ	08542	609-430-3900	430-9525
Hercules Technology Growth Capital Inc 400 Hamilton Ave Suite 310 *NASDAQ: HTGC* ■ *Web:* www.herculestech.com	Palo Alto	CA	94301	650-289-3060	473-9194
Hickory Venture Group 301 Washington St NW Suite 301 *Web:* www.hvcc.com	Huntsville	AL	35801	256-539-1931	539-5130
Highland Capital Partners 92 Hayden Ave *Web:* www.hcp.com	Lexington	MA	02421	781-861-5500	861-5499
HLM Venture Partners 222 Berkeley St 21st Fl *Web:* www.hlmvp.com	Boston	MA	02116	617-266-0030	266-3619
HMS Hawaii 841 Bishop St Suite 860 *Web:* www.hmshawaii.com	Honolulu	HI	96813	808-545-3755	531-2611
HO2 Partners 2 Galleria Tower Suite 1670 *Web:* www.ho2.com	Dallas	TX	75240	972-702-1144	702-8234
Housatonic Partners 111 Huntington Ave Suite 2850 *Web:* www.housatonicpartners.com	Boston	MA	02199	617-399-9200	267-5565
Hummer Winblad Venture Partners 2 S Park 2nd Fl *Web:* www.humwin.com	San Francisco	CA	94107	415-979-9600	979-9601
Hunt Ventures LP 1445 Ross at Field Suite 1400 *Web:* www.huntventures.com	Dallas	TX	75202	214-978-8200	
Idanta Partners Ltd 12526 High Bluff Dr Suite 160 *Web:* www.idanta.com	San Diego	CA	92130	858-356-0150	356-0152
Idealab 130 W Union St *TF:* 888-433-3522 ■ *Web:* www.idealab.com	Pasadena	CA	91103	626-585-6900	535-2701
IDG Ventures Pacific 650 California St 24th Floor *Web:* www.idgvusa.com	San Francisco	CA	94108	415-439-4420	439-4428
IGNITE Group 255 Shoreline Dr Suite 510 *Web:* www.ignitegroup.com	Redwood City	CA	94065	650-622-2000	622-2015
In-Q-Tel Inc PO Box 12407 *Web:* www.in-q-tel.org	Arlington	VA	22219	703-248-3000	248-3001
Inflection Point Ventures 1 Innovation Way Suite 500 *Web:* www.inflectpoint.com	Newark	DE	19711	302-452-1120	452-1122
Information Technology Ventures (ITV) 480 Cowper St Suite 200 *Web:* www.itventures.com	Palo Alto	CA	94301	650-462-8400	462-8415
InnoCal LP 600 Anton Blvd Suite 1270 *Web:* www.innocal.com	Costa Mesa	CA	92626	714-850-6784	850-6798
Innovation Works Inc 2000 Technology Dr Suite 250 *Web:* www.innovationworks.org	Pittsburgh	PA	15219	412-681-1520	681-2625
Institutional Venture Partners 3000 Sand Hill Rd Bldg 2 Suite 250 *Web:* www.ivp.com	Menlo Park	CA	94025	650-854-0132	854-2009
Intelligent Systems Corp 4355 Shackleford Rd *AMEX: INS* ■ *Web:* www.intelsys.com	Norcross	GA	30093	770-381-2900	381-2808
Internet Capital Group Inc 690 Lee Rd Suite 310 *NASDAQ: ICGE* ■ *Web:* www.internetcapital.com	Wayne	PA	19087	610-989-0111	727-6901
Intersouth Partners 406 Blackwell St Suite 200 *Web:* www.intersouth.com	Durham	NC	27701	919-493-6640	493-6649
InterWest Partners 2710 Sand Hill Rd 2nd Fl *Web:* www.interwest.com	Menlo Park	CA	94025	650-854-8585	854-4706
INVESCO Private Capital Inc 1166 Ave of the Americas 26th Fl *Web:* www.invesco.com	New York	NY	10036	212-278-9000	278-9822
Ironside Ventures 161 Worcester Rd Suite 602 *Web:* www.ironsideventures.com	Framingham	MA	01701	781-622-5800	622-5801
iSherpa Capital LLC 6400 S Fidler's Green Circle Suite 650 *Web:* www.isherpa.com	Greenwood Village	CO	80111	303-645-0500	645-0501
Jafco Ventures Inc 505 Hamilton Ave Suite 310 *Web:* www.jafco.com	Palo Alto	CA	94301	650-463-8800	463-8801
JatoTech Ventures 6300 Bridgepoint Pkwy Bldg 1 Suite 500 *Web:* www.jatotech.com	Austin	TX	78730	512-795-5860	692-2868
JEGI Capital LLC 150 E 52nd St 18th Fl *Web:* www.jegi.com	New York	NY	10022	212-754-0710	754-0337
JH Whitney & Co LLC 130 Main St *TF:* 800-881-6085 ■ *Web:* www.jhwhitney.com	New Canaan	CT	06840	203-716-6100	716-6122
JK&B Capital 180 N Stetson Ave Suite 4500 *Web:* www.jkbcapital.com	Chicago	IL	60601	312-946-1200	946-1103
Johnson & Johnson Development Corp 1 Johnson & Johnson Plaza *Web:* www.jnj.com	New Brunswick	NJ	08933	732-524-3218	247-5309
Johnston Assoc Inc 48 Elm Ridge Rd *Web:* www.jaivc.com	Pennington	NJ	08534	609-737-0314	737-2935
KB Partners LLC 1101 Skokie Blvd Suite 260 *Web:* www.kbpartners.com	Northbrook	IL	60062	847-714-0444	714-0445
KBL Healthcare Ventures 757 3rd Ave 12th Fl *Web:* www.kblvc.com	New York	NY	10017	212-319-5555	319-5591
Key Principal Partners 50 California St Suite 2424 *Web:* www.key.com/keyprincipalpartners	San Francisco	CA	94111	415-692-4660	402-0472

Firm	City	State	ZIP	Phone	Fax
Kinetic Ventures 2 Wisconsin Cir Suite 620	Chevy Chase	MD	20815	301-652-8066	652-8310
Web: www.kineticventures.com					
Kitty Hawk Capital 2901 Coltsgate Rd Suite 100	Charlotte	NC	28211	704-362-3909	362-2774
Kleiner Perkins Caufield & Byers 2750 Sand Hill Rd	Menlo Park	CA	94025	650-233-2750	233-0300
Web: www.kpcb.com					
Kodiak Venture Partners 1000 Winter St Suite 3800	Waltham	MA	02451	781-672-2500	672-2501
Web: www.kodiakvp.com					
L Capital Partners SBIC LP 10 E 53rd St 37th Fl	New York	NY	10022	212-675-7755	206-9156
Web: www.lcapital.us					
Labrador Ventures 101 University Ave 4th Floor	Palo Alto	CA	94301	650-366-6000	366-6430
Web: www.labrador.com					
Lancet Capital 100 Technology Dr Suite 200	Pittsburgh	PA	15219	412-471-7107	
Web: www.lancetcapital.com					
Latterell Venture Partners					
1 Embarcadero Center Suite 4050	San Francisco	CA	94111	415-399-9880	399-9879
Web: www.lvpcapital.com					
Lecensohn Venture Partners 260 Townsend St Suite 600	San Francisco	CA	94107	415-217-4710	217-4727
Web: www.levp.com					
Lee Munder Venture Partners LLC 200 Clarendon St 28th Fl	Boston	MA	02116	617-380-5600	380-5601
Web: www.leemunder.com					
Legacy Venture 550 Lytton Ave 2nd Fl	Palo Alto	CA	94301	650-324-5980	324-5982
Web: www.legacyventure.com					
Life Sciences Greenhouse 225 Market St 5th Fl	Harrisburgh	PA	17101	717-635-2100	635-2010
Web: www.lsgpa.com					
Lighthouse Capital Partners 500 Drake's Landing Rd	Greenbrae	CA	94904	415-464-5900	925-3387
Web: www.lcpartners.com					
Lightspeed Venture Partners 2200 Sand Hill Rd Suite 100	Menlo Park	CA	94025	650-234-8300	234-8333
Web: www.lightspeedvp.com					
Lilly BioVentures DC 1089 Lilly Corporate Ctr	Indianapolis	IN	46285	317-651-3050	651-3051
Web: www.lillyventures.com					
Lubar & Co 700 N Water St Suite 1200	Milwaukee	WI	53202	414-291-9000	291-9061
Web: www.lubar.com					
Madison Dearborn Partners 3 1st National Plaza Suite 3800	Chicago	IL	60602	312-895-1000	895-1001
Web: www.mdcp.com					
Markpoint Venture Partners 15770 Dallas Pkwy Suite 800	Dallas	TX	75248	972-490-1976	490-1980
Web: www.markpt.com					
Mason Wells Biomedical Fund					
411 E Wisconsin Ave Suite 1280	Milwaukee	WI	53202	414-727-6400	727-6410
Web: www.masonwells.com					
Massachusetts Capital Resource Co 420 Boylston St 5th Fl	Boston	MA	02116	617-536-3900	536-7930
Web: www.masscapital.com					
Massachusetts Technology Development Corp (MTDC)					
40 Broad St	Boston	MA	02109	617-723-4920	723-5983
Web: www.mtdc.com					
Matrix Partners					
1000 Winter St Bay Colony Corporate Ctr Suite 4500	Waltham	MA	02451	781-890-2244	890-2288
Web: www.matrixpartners.com					
Maveron LLC 505 5th Ave S Suite 600	Seattle	WA	98104	206-288-1700	288-1777
Web: www.maveron.com					
Mayfield Fund 2800 Sand Hill Rd Suite 250	Menlo Park	CA	94025	650-854-5560	854-5712
Web: www.mayfield.com					
Mayflower Group 558 Clapboardtree St	Westwood	MA	02090	617-267-9000	266-6666
MCG Capital Corp 1100 Wilson Blvd Suite 3000	Arlington	VA	22209	703-247-7500	247-7505
NASDAQ: MCGC ■ *TF:* 877-624-2733 ■ *Web:* www.mcgcapital.com					
McKellar & Co 311 E Rose Ln	Phoenix	AZ	85012	602-277-1800	217-1512*
**Fax Area Code:* 503					
MDT Advisors Inc 125 Cambridgepark Dr	Cambridge	MA	02140	617-234-2200	234-2210
Web: www.mdtai.com					
Mediphase Venture Partners					
3 Newton Executive Park Suite 104	Newton	MA	02462	617-332-3408	332-8463
Web: www.mediphaseventure.com					
Menlo Ventures 3000 Sand Hill Rd Bldg 4 Suite 100	Menlo Park	CA	94025	650-854-8540	854-7059
Web: www.menloventures.com					
Mesirow Financial Private Equity 350 N Clark St	Chicago	IL	60610	312-595-6000	595-4246
TF: 800-453-0600 ■ *Web:* www.mesirowfinancial.com					
Mid-Atlantic Venture Funds 125 Goodman Dr	Bethlehem	PA	18015	610-865-6550	865-6427
Web: www.mavf.com					
MidCoast Capital 259 N Radnor-Chester Rd Suite 210	Radnor	PA	19087	610-687-8580	971-2154
Web: www.midcoastcapital.com					
Milestone Venture Partners 551 Madison Ave 7th Fl	New York	NY	10022	212-223-7400	223-0315
Web: www.milestonevp.com					
Mission Ventures 11455 El Camino Real Suite 450	San Diego	CA	92130	858-350-2100	350-2101
Web: www.missionventures.com					
Mitsui & Co Venture Partners 2180 Sand Hill Rd Suite 345	Menlo Park	CA	94025	650-234-5000	233-9205
Web: www.mitsuivp.com					
Mohr Davidow Ventures					
3000 Sand Hill Rd Bldg 3 Suite 290	Menlo Park	CA	94025	650-854-7236	854-7365
Web: www.mdv.com					
Montagu Newhall Associates Inc					
100 Painters Mill Rd Suite 700	Owings Mills	MD	21117	410-363-2725	356-9937
Web: www.montagunewhall.com					
Montreux Equity Partners					
3000 Sand Hill Rd Bldg 1 Suite 260	Menlo Park	CA	94025	650-234-1200	234-1250
Web: www.montreuxequity.com					
Monumental Venture Partners LLC					
8201 Greensboro Dr Suite 216	McLean	VA	22102	703-821-0400	821-0281
Web: www.mvpfunds.com					
Morgan Stanley Venture Partners 1585 Broadway 38th Fl	New York	NY	10036	212-761-6003	761-9580
TF: 800-419-2861 ■ *Web:* www.morganstanley.com/institutional/venturepar					
Morgenthaler 2710 Sand Hill Rd Suite 100	Menlo Park	CA	94025	650-388-7600	388-7601
Web: www.morgenthaler.com					
Morgenthaler Ventures 50 Public Sq Suite 2700	Cleveland	OH	44113	216-416-7500	416-7501
Web: www.morgenthaler.com					
Mountaineer Capital LP 107 Capital St Suite 300	Charleston	WV	25301	304-347-7525	347-0072
Web: www.mtncap.com					
MPM Capital Offices 200 Clarendon St 54th Fl	Boston	MA	02116	617-425-9200	425-9201
TF: 888-799-6245 ■ *Web:* www.mpmcapital.com					
MRV Communications Inc 20415 Nordhoff St	Chatsworth	CA	91311	818-773-0900	773-0906
NASDAQ: MRVC ■ *TF Sales:* 800-858-7815 ■ *Web:* www.mrv.com					
MTDC (Massachusetts Technology Development Corp)					
40 Broad St	Boston	MA	02109	617-723-4920	723-5983
Web: www.mtdc.com					
MVC Capital Inc 287 Bowman Ave 2nd Fl	Purchase	NY	10577	914-701-0310	701-0315
NYSE: MVC ■ *Web:* www.mvccapital.com					
National Healthcare Services					
120 Golden Shore Ave Suite 320	Long Beach	CA	90802	562-432-0047	432-0091
Web: www.nationalhealthcareservices.com					
Nautic Partners LLC 50 Kennedy Plaza 12th Fl	Providence	RI	02903	401-278-6770	278-6387
Web: www.nauticpartners.com					
Nazem & Co 220 W 42nd St 23rd Fl	New York	NY	10036	212-371-7900	371-2150
Web: www.nazem.com					
NCIC Capital Fund 900 Kettering Tower	Dayton	OH	45423	937-222-4422	222-1323
Web: www.ncicfund.com					
NCT Ventures PO Box 2790	Westerville	OH	43086	614-794-2732	794-2738
Web: www.nctventures.com					
Needham & Co 445 Park Ave	New York	NY	10022	212-705-0385	371-2311
TF: 866-691-8263 ■ *Web:* www.needhamcapital.com					
Neocarta Ventures Inc 45 Fairfield St 4th Fl	Boston	MA	02116	617-239-9000	266-4107
Web: www.neocarta.com					
NeuroVentures Capital LLC 0 Court Sq	Charlottesville	VA	22902	434-297-1000	297-1001
Web: www.neuroventures.com					
New Capital Partners 312 23rd St N	Birmingham	AL	35203	205-939-8400	939-8402
Web: www.newcapitalpartners.com					
New Enterprise Assoc 2490 Sand Hill Rd	Menlo Park	CA	94025	650-854-9499	854-9397
Web: www.nea.com					
New Venture Partners LLC 98 Floral Ave	Murray Hill	NJ	07974	908-464-0900	464-8131
Web: www.newventurepartners.com					
New York Life Venture Capital 51 Madison Ave	New York	NY	10010	212-576-7000	
Newbury Ventures 4 Orinda Way Suite 200 Bldg B	Orinda	CA	94563	925-258-1400	258-1404
Web: www.newburyven.com					
NewSpring Capital 555 E Lancaster Ave Suite 520	Radnor	PA	19087	610-567-2380	567-2388
Web: www.newspringcapital.com					
Newtek Business Services Inc 1440 Broadway 17th Fl	New York	NY	10018	212-356-9500	643-1006
NASDAQ: NKBS ■ *TF:* 866-639-1835 ■ *Web:* www.newtekbusinessservices.com					
Newton Technology Partners 555 Bryant St Suite 584	Palo Alto	CA	94301	650-331-3990	745-1222
Web: www.newtontp.com					
NGEN Partners LLC 1114 State St Suite 247	Santa Barbara	CA	93101	805-564-3156	564-1669
Web: www.ngenpartners.com					
NIF Ventures USA Inc 2300 Geng Rd Suite 220	Palo Alto	CA	94303	650-461-5000	858-0892
Web: www.nifusa.com					
NJTC Venture Fund 1001 Briggs Rd Suite 280	Mount Laurel	NJ	08054	856-273-6800	273-0990
Web: www.njtcvc.com					
Noro-Moseley Partners 4200 Northside Pkwy NW Bldg 9	Atlanta	GA	30327	404-233-1966	239-9280
TF: 800-648-0520 ■ *Web:* www.noro-moseley.com					
North American Business Development Co Ltd					
135 S La Salle St Suite 4000	Chicago	IL	60603	312-332-4950	332-1540
Web: www.northamericanfund.com					
North Atlantic Capital 2 City Ctr 5th Fl	Portland	ME	04101	207-772-4470	772-3257
Web: www.northatlanticcapital.com					
North Bridge Venture Partners 950 Winter St Suite 4600	Waltham	MA	02451	781-290-0004	290-0999
Web: www.nbvp.com					
North Coast Technology Investors LP					
206 S 5th Ave Suite 550	Ann Arbor	MI	48104	734-662-7667	662-6261
Web: www.northcoastvc.com					
North Hill Ventures 10 Post Office Sq 11th Fl	Boston	MA	02109	617-788-2150	788-2152
Web: www.northhillventures.com					
Northwood Ventures 485 Underhill Blvd Suite 205	Syosset	NY	11791	516-364-5544	364-0879
Web: www.northwoodventures.com					
Norwest Equity Partners 80 S 8th St Suite 3600	Minneapolis	MN	55402	612-215-1600	215-1601
Web: www.nep.com					
Norwest Venture Partners 525 University Ave Suite 800	Palo Alto	CA	94301	650-321-8000	321-8010
Web: www.norwestvc.com					
Novak Biddle Venture Partners					
7501 Wisconsin Ave East Tower Suite 1380	Bethesda	MD	20814	240-497-1910	223-0255
Web: www.novakbiddle.com					
NTH Power Technologies Inc 50 California St Suite 840	San Francisco	CA	94111	415-983-9983	983-9984
Web: www.nthpower.com					
Oak Investment Partners 1 Gorham Island 1st Fl	Westport	CT	06880	203-226-8346	227-0372
Web: www.oakinv.com					
OAS (Omron Advanced Systems Inc)					
3945 Freedom Cir Suite 1070	Santa Clara	CA	95054	408-970-1150	727-5540
Web: www.oas.net					
OCA Ventures LLC 141 W Jackson Blvd 39th Fl	Chicago	IL	60604	312-542-8954	542-8952
Web: www.ocaventures.com					
Olympic Venture Partners 1010 Market St	Kirkland	WA	98033	425-889-9192	889-0152
Web: www.ovp.com					
Olympus Partners 1 Station Pl Metro Ctr 4th Fl N	Stamford	CT	06902	203-353-5900	353-5910
Web: www.olympuspartners.com					
Omron Advanced Systems Inc (OAS)					
3945 Freedom Cir Suite 1070	Santa Clara	CA	95054	408-970-1150	727-5540
Web: www.oas.net					
ONCAP 161 Bay St Suite 4800	Toronto	ON	M5J2S1	416-214-4300	214-6160
Web: www.oncap.com					
One Equity Partners 320 Park Ave 18th Fl	New York	NY	10022	212-277-1500	277-1533
Web: www.oneequity.com					
Onset Ventures 2400 Sand Hill Rd Suite 150	Menlo Park	CA	94025	650-529-0700	529-0777
Web: www.onset.com					
Oxford Bioscience Partners 650 Town Center Dr Suite 880	Costa Mesa	CA	92626	714-754-5719	754-6802
Web: www.oxbio.com					
Oxford Bioscience Partners 315 Post Rd W	Westport	CT	06880	203-341-3300	341-3309
Web: www.oxbio.com					
Pacific Horizon Ventures 701 5th Ave Suite 4970	Seattle	WA	98104	206-682-1181	682-8077
Web: www.pacifichorizon.com					
Palo Alto Venture Partners 151 Lytton Ave	Palo Alto	CA	94301	650-462-1221	462-1227
Web: www.pavp.com					
Palomar Ventures 100 Wilshire Blvd Suite 1700	Santa Monica	CA	90401	310-260-6050	656-4150
Web: www.palomarventures.com					
Pappajohn Capital Resources 2116 Financial Ctr	Des Moines	IA	50309	515-244-5746	244-2346
Web: www.pappajohn.com					
Partech International 50 California St Suite 3200	San Francisco	CA	94111	415-788-2929	788-6763
Web: www.partechintl.com					
Path4 Ventures 4030 W Braker Ln Suite 360	Austin	TX	78759	512-344-3300	344-3350
Web: www.path4ventures.com					
Paul Capital Partners 50 California St Suite 3000	San Francisco	CA	94111	415-283-4300	283-4301
Web: www.paulcapital.com					
Peck's Management Partners Ltd					
1 Rockefeller Plaza Suite 1730	New York	NY	10020	212-332-1333	332-1334
Web: www.pecks.com					
Peninsula Equity Partners					
3000 Sand Hill Rd Bldg 2 Suite 100	Menlo Park	CA	94025	650-854-0314	854-0670
Web: www.peninsulaequity.com					
Pennell Venture Partners LLC 332 Bleecker St Suite K-67	New York	NY	10014	917-345-4134	365-3195*
**Fax Area Code:* 646 ■ *Web:* www.pennell.com					
Pfingsten Partners LLC					
520 Lake Cook Rd Corporate 500 Ctr Suite 375	Deerfield	IL	60015	847-374-9140	374-9150
Web: www.pfingstenpartners.com					
Phoenix Partners 1000 2nd Ave Suite 3950	Seattle	WA	98104	206-624-8968	624-1907
Web: www.phoenixvc.com					
Pitango Venture Capital 2929 Campus Dr Suite 410	San Mateo	CA	94403	650-357-9088	357-9088
Web: www.pitango.com					
PNC Equity Management Group					
249 5th Ave 1 PNC Plaza 8th Fl	Pittsburgh	PA	15222	412-768-8661	762-6233
Web: www.pncequity.com					
Polaris Venture Partners 1000 Winter St Suite 3355	Waltham	MA	02451	781-290-0770	290-0880
Web: www.polarisventures.com					
Pomona Capital 780 3rd Ave 44th Fl	New York	NY	10017	212-593-3639	593-3987
Web: www.pomonacapital.com					
Posco BioVentures 2710 Loker Ave W Suite 360	Carlsbad	CA	92010	760-448-2848	448-2840
Web: www.poscobioventures.com					
Primus Venture Partners 5900 Landerbrook Dr Suite 200	Cleveland	OH	44124	440-684-7300	684-7342
Web: www.primusventure.com					
Prince Ventures 6475 Bold Venture Tr	Tallahassee	FL	32309	850-321-3353	668-7223
Web: www.princeventures.com					

Firm	City	State	ZIP	Phone	Fax
Prism Venture Partners 100 Lowder Brook Dr Suite 2500 *Web:* www.prismventure.com	Westwood	MA	02098	781-302-4000	302-4040
Prolog Ventures LLC 7733 Forsyth Blvd Suite 1440 *Web:* www.prologventures.com	Saint Louis	MO	63105	314-743-2400	743-2403
Prospect Venture Partners 435 Tasso St Suite 200 *Web:* www.prospectventures.com	Palo Alto	CA	94301	650-327-8800	324-8838
Provco Group 795 E Lancaster Ave Suite 200 *Web:* www.provcogroup.com	Villanova	PA	19085	610-520-2010	520-1905
Providence Equity Partners Inc 50 Kennedy Plaza 18th Fl *Web:* www.provequity.com	Providence	RI	02903	401-751-1700	751-1790
Psilos Group Managers LLC 625 Ave of the Americas 4th Fl *Web:* www.psilos.com	New York	NY	10011	212-242-8844	242-8855
PureTech Ventures 222 Berkeley St Suite 1040 *Web:* www.puretechventures.com	Boston	MA	02116	617-482-2333	482-3337
Quaker BioVentures 2929 Arch St Cira Centre *Web:* www.quakerbio.com	Philadelphia	PA	19104	215-988-6800	988-6801
Quellos 601 Union St 56th Fl *Web:* www.quellos.com	Seattle	WA	98101	206-613-6700	613-6710
R Chaney & Co Inc 6363 Woodway Dr Suite 960 *Web:* www.rchaney.com	Houston	TX	77057	713-356-7555	750-0021
Radius Ventures LLC 400 Madison Ave 8th Fl *Web:* www.radiusventures.com	New York	NY	10017	212-897-7778	397-2656
Redhills Ventures 2620 Regatta Dr Suite 208 *Web:* www.redhillsventures.com	Las Vegas	NV	89128	702-233-2160	233-2167
RedShift Ventures 11911 Freedom Dr 1 Fountain Sq Suite 500 *Web:* www.redshiftventures.com	Reston	VA	20190	703-904-9800	904-0571
Rembrandt Venture Partners 2200 Sand Hill Rd Suite 160 *Web:* www.rembrandtvc.com	Menlo Park	CA	94025	650-326-7070	326-3780
Research Corp Technologies 101 N Wilmot Rd Suite 600 *Web:* www.rctech.com	Tucson	AZ	85711	520-748-4400	748-0025
Reynolds Dewitt & Co 300 Main St *TF:* 800-877-3344	Cincinnati	OH	45202	513-241-8716	421-3602
Rho Capital Partners Inc 152 W 57th St 23rd Fl *Web:* www.rho.com	New York	NY	10019	212-751-6677	751-3613
Rice Sangalis Toole & Wilson 5847 San Felipe Rd Suite 2929	Houston	TX	77057	713-783-7770	783-9750
Richland Ventures 1201 16th Ave S *Web:* www.richlandventures.com	Nashville	TN	37212	615-383-8030	269-0463
Ridgewood Capital 947 Linwood Ave *TF:* 800-942-5550 ■ *Web:* ridgewoodcapital.com	Ridgewood	NJ	07450	201-447-9000	447-0474
Riordan Lewis & Haden 10900 Wilshire Blvd Suite 850 *Web:* www.rlhinvestors.com	Los Angeles	CA	90024	310-405-7200	405-7222
RiverVest Venture Partners 7733 Forsyth Blvd Suite 1650 *Web:* www.rivervest.com	Saint Louis	MO	63105	314-726-6700	726-6715
RockMapleVentures 40 Williams St Suite G-20 *Web:* www.rockmapleventures.com	Wellesley	MA	02481	617-262-8501	687-0050
Rockport Capital Partners 160 Federal St 18th Fl *Web:* www.rockportcap.com	Boston	MA	02110	617-912-1420	912-1449
Rocky Mountain Capital Partners LLP 7887 E Belleville Ave Suite 1100 *Web:* www.rockycapital.com	Englewood	CO	80111	303-297-1701	557-0677
Rosewood Capital 1 Maritime Plaza Suite 1401 *Web:* www.rosewoodcap.com	San Francisco	CA	94111	415-362-5526	362-1192
RRE Ventures 126 E 56th St *Web:* www.rre.com	New York	NY	10022	212-418-5100	
Rustic Canyon Partners 2425 Olympic Blvd Suite 6050 W *Web:* www.rusticcanyon.com	Santa Monica	CA	90404	310-998-8000	998-8001
Safeguard Scientifics Inc 435 Devon Park Dr Suite 800 *NYSE: SFE* ■ *TF:* 877-506-7371 ■ *Web:* www.safeguard.com	Wayne	PA	19087	610-293-0600	293-0601
Sail Venture Partners LP 600 Anton Blvd Suite 1750 **Fax Area Code: 815* ■ *Web:* www.sailvc.com	Costa Mesa	CA	92626	714-241-7500	642-0271*
Saints Ventures LLC 475 Sansome St Suite 1850 *Web:* www.saintsvc.com	San Francisco	CA	94111	415-773-2080	835-5970
Sanderling 400 S El Camino Real Suite 1200 *Web:* www.sanderling.com	San Mateo	CA	94402	650-401-2000	375-7077
SAP Ventures 3410 Hillview Ave *Web:* www.sapventures.com	Palo Alto	CA	94304	650-849-4000	849-4240
Sapient Capital Management LLC PO Box 1590 *Web:* www.sapientcapital.com	Wilson	WY	83014	307-733-3806	733-4630
Saugatuck Capital Co 1 Canterbury Green *Web:* www.saugatuckcapital.com	Stamford	CT	06901	203-348-6669	324-6995
Scale Venture Partners 950 Tower Ln Suite 700 *Web:* www.scalevp.com	Foster City	CA	94404	650-378-6000	378-6040
Seaflower Ventures 1000 Winter St Suite 1000 *Web:* www.seaflower.com	Waltham	MA	02451	781-466-9552	466-9553
SeaPoint Ventures 719 2nd Ave Suite 1405 *Web:* www.seapointventures.com	Seattle	WA	98104	206-438-1880	438-1886
Selby Venture Partners 3500 Alameda de las Pulgas Suite 200 *Web:* www.selbyventures.com	Menlo Park	CA	94025	650-854-7399	854-7039
Select Capital Ventures 4718 Old Gettysburg Rd Suite 405 *Web:* www.selectcapitalventures.com	Mechanicsburg	PA	17055	717-972-1316	
Sequel Venture Partners 4430 Arapahoe Ave Suite 220 *Web:* www.sequelvc.com	Boulder	CO	80303	303-546-0400	546-9728
Sequoia Capital 3000 Sand Hill Rd Bldg 4 Suite 180 *Web:* www.sequoiacap.com	Menlo Park	CA	94025	650-854-3927	854-2957
Sevin Rosen Funds 13455 Noel Rd Suite 1670 *Web:* www.srfunds.com	Dallas	TX	75240	972-702-1100	702-1103
Shasta Ventures 2440 Sand Hill Rd Suite 300 *Web:* www.shastaventures.com	Menlo Park	CA	94025	650-543-1700	543-1799
Shaw Venture Partners 400 SW 6th Ave Suite 1100	Portland	OR	97204	503-228-4884	227-2471
Shelton Cos 5955 Carnegie Blvd Suite 225	Charlotte	NC	28209	704-557-2200	557-2260
Shepherd Ventures 12250 El Camino Real Suite 116 *Web:* www.shepherdventures.com	San Diego	CA	92130	858-509-4744	509-3662
SI Ventures 12600 Gateway Blvd *Web:* www.siventures.com	Fort Meyers	FL	33913	239-561-4760	561-4916
Sienna Ventures 2330 Marinship Way Suite 130 *Web:* www.siennaventures.com	Sausalito	CA	94965	415-339-2800	339-2808
Sierra Ventures 2884 Sand Hill Rd Suite 100 *TF:* 800-819-9665 ■ *Web:* www.sierraven.com	Menlo Park	CA	94025	650-854-1000	854-5593
Sigma Partners 1600 El Camino Real Suite 280 *Web:* www.sigmapartners.com	Menlo Park	CA	94025	650-853-1700	853-1717
Signature Capital LLC 100 Commercial St Suite 410 *Web:* www.signaturecapital.com	Portland	ME	04101	207-773-8123	773-8128
Siguler Guff & Co LLC 825 3rd Ave 10th Fl *Web:* www.sigulerguff.com	New York	NY	10022	212-332-5100	332-5130
Sloan Ventures LLC 430 N Old Woodward Ave *Web:* www.sloanventures.com	Birmingham	MI	48009	248-540-9660	540-5461
SmartForest Ventures 319 SW Washington St Suite 720 *Web:* www.smartforest.com	Portland	OR	97204	503-222-2552	222-2834
Sofinnova Ventures 140 Geary St 10th Fl *Web:* www.sofinnova.com	San Francisco	CA	94108	415-228-3380	228-3390
SOFTBANK Inc 1188 Centre St *Web:* www.softbank.com	Newton Center	MA	02459	617-928-9300	928-9304
Solstice Capital 6245 E Broadway Blvd Suite 620 *Web:* www.solcap.com	Tucson	AZ	85711	520-514-8000	
South Atlantic Capital Inc 614 W Bay St *Web:* www.southatlantic.com	Tampa	FL	33606	813-253-2500	253-2360
Southeast Interactive Technology Funds 630 Davis Dr Suite 220 *Web:* www.seinteractive.com	Morrisville	NC	27560	919-558-8324	558-2025
Space Center Ventures Inc 2501 Rosegate *Web:* www.scvinc.com	Roseville	MN	55113	651-604-4201	
Spectrum Equity Investors LP 1 International Pl 29th Fl *Web:* www.spectrumequity.com	Boston	MA	02110	617-464-4600	464-4601
Split Rock Partners 1600 El Camino Real Suite 290 *Web:* www.splitrock.com	Menlo Park	CA	94025	650-617-1500	617-1510
Sprout Group 11 Madison Ave 13th Fl *Web:* www.sproutgroup.com	New York	NY	10010	212-538-3600	538-8245
SR One Ltd 200 Barr Harbor Dr 4 Tower Bridge Suite 250	West Conshohocken	PA	19428	610-567-1000	567-1039
Steamboat Ventures 3601 W Olive Ave Suite 650 *Web:* steamboatvc.disney.go.com	Burbank	CA	91505	818-566-7400	566-7490
Sterling Venture Partners 6225 Smith Ave Suite 210 *Web:* www.sterlingpartners.us	Baltimore	MD	21209	443-703-1700	703-1750
Storm Ventures 2440 Sand Hill Rd Suite 301 *Web:* www.stormventures.com	Menlo Park	CA	94025	650-926-8800	926-8888
Strategic Investments & Holdings Inc 369 Franklin St Cyclorama Bldg *Web:* www.sihi.net	Buffalo	NY	14202	716-857-6000	857-6490
Summit Partners 222 Berkeley St 18th Fl *Web:* www.summitpartners.com	Boston	MA	02116	617-824-1000	824-1100
Sutter Hill Ventures 755 Page Mill Rd Suite A-200 *Web:* www.shv.com	Palo Alto	CA	94304	650-493-5600	858-1854
SV Life Sciences 60 State St Suite 3650 *Web:* www.svlsa.com	Boston	MA	02109	617-367-8100	367-1590
T Rowe Price Threshold Partnerships 100 E Pratt St 10th Fl *TF:* 877-804-2315 ■ *Web:* www.troweprice.com	Baltimore	MD	21202	410-345-2000	345-3618
TA Assoc Inc 200 Clarendon St 56th Fl *TF:* 800-836-8873 ■ *Web:* www.ta.com	Boston	MA	02116	617-574-6700	574-6728
TAT Capital Partners Ltd PO Box 23326 *Web:* www.tatcapital.com	San Jose	CA	95153	408-270-9200	270-4140
TD Capital 79 Wellington St W 6th Fl TD Waterhouse *Web:* www.tdcapital.com	Toronto	ON	M5K1A2	416-307-8470	982-5045
Techfarm 2275 E Bayshore Rd Suite 150 *Web:* www.techfarm.com	Palo Alto	CA	94303	650-934-0900	934-0910
Technology Crossover Ventures 528 Ramona St *Web:* www.tcv.com	Palo Alto	CA	94301	650-614-8200	614-8222
Technology Funding Inc 460 St Michael's Dr Suite 1000 *TF:* 800-821-5323 ■ *Web:* www.techfunding.com	Santa Fe	NM	87505	505-982-2200	820-6900
Technology Partners 550 University Ave *Web:* www.technologypartners.com	Palo Alto	CA	94301	650-289-9000	289-9001
Techxas Ventures 4401 Westgate Blvd Suite 300-W *Web:* www.techxas.com	Austin	TX	78745	512-334-3140	334-3121
Telecommunications Development Fund 1850 K St NW Suite 1075 *Web:* www.tdfund.com	Washington	DC	20006	202-293-8840	293-8850
TeleSoft Partners 950 Tower Ln Suite 1600 *Web:* www.telesoftvc.com	Foster	CA	94404	650-358-2500	358-2501
TEOCO Corp 12150 Monument Dr Suite 400 *TF:* 888-868-3626 ■ *Web:* www.teoco.com	Fairfax	VA	22033	703-322-9200	259-2131
Texas Growth Fund 111 Congress Ave Suite 2900 *Web:* www.tgfmanagement.com	Austin	TX	78701	512-322-3100	322-3101
TGap Ventures 259 E Michigan Ave Suite 208 *Web:* www.tgapventures.com	Kalamazoo	MI	49007	269-217-1999	381-5453
Thoma Cressey Bravo Inc 600 Montgomery St 32nd Fl *Web:* www.tcb.com	San Francisco	CA	94111	415-263-3660	392-6480
Thomas Weisel Partners Group LLC 1 Montgomery St *NASDAQ: TWPG* ■ *TF:* 800-933-3445 ■ *Web:* www.tweisel.com	San Francisco	CA	94104	415-364-2500	364-2695
Thomas, McNerney & Partners 263 Tresser Blvd 16th Fl *Web:* www.tm-partners.com	Stamford	CT	06901	203-978-2000	978-2005
TL Ventures 435 Devon Pk Dr 700 Bldg *Web:* www.tlventures.com	Wayne	PA	19087	610-971-1515	975-9330
TMVP (Triathlon Medical Ventures) 250 E 5th St 1100 Chiquita Ctr *Web:* www.tmvp.com	Cincinnati	OH	45202	513-723-2600	723-2615
Topspin Partners LP 3 Expy Plaza *Web:* www.topspinpartners.com	Roslyn Heights	NY	11577	516-625-9400	625-9499
Tortoise Energy Capital Corp 10801 Mastin Blvd Suite 222 *NYSE: TYY* ■ *Web:* www.tortoiseadvisors.com	Overland Park	KS	66210	913-981-1020	981-1021
Trellis Partners 2600 Via Fortuna Suite 150 *Web:* www.trellis.com	Austin	TX	78746	512-330-9200	330-9400
Trelys Funds LP PO Box 545 *Web:* www.trelys.com	Columbia	SC	29202	919-484-0400	484-0444
Triathlon Medical Ventures (TMVP) 250 E 5th St 1100 Chiquita Ctr *Web:* www.tmvp.com	Cincinnati	OH	45202	513-723-2600	723-2615
Trident Capital 505 Hamilton Ave Suite 200 *Web:* www.tridentcap.com	Palo Alto	CA	94301	650-289-4400	289-4444
Trillium Group LLC 1221 Pittsford Victor Rd *Web:* www.trillium-group.com	Pittsford	NY	14534	585-383-5680	383-0042
Trinity Ventures 3000 Sand Hill Rd Bldg 4 Suite 160 *Web:* www.trinityventures.com	Menlo Park	CA	94025	650-854-9500	854-9501
Triton Ventures 6300 Bridge Point Pkwy Bldg 1 Suite 500 *Web:* www.tritonventures.com	Austin	TX	78730	512-795-5820	795-5828
Tullis Dickerson & Co Inc 2 Greenwich Plaza 4th Fl *Web:* www.tullisdickerson.com	Greenwich	CT	06830	203-629-8700	629-9293
TVM Techno Venture Management LP 101 Arch St Suite 1950 *Web:* www.tvmvc.com	Boston	MA	02110	617-345-9320	345-9377
Union Square Ventures 915 Broadway Suite 1408 *Web:* www.unionsquareventures.com	New York	NY	10010	212-994-7880	994-7399
UPS Strategic Enterprise Fund 55 Glenlake Pkwy NE Bldg 1 4th Fl *Web:* www.ups.com/sef	Atlanta	GA	30328	404-828-8814	828-8088
US Venture Partners 2735 Sand Hill Rd Suite 300 *TF:* 877-773-8787 ■ *Web:* www.usvp.com	Menlo Park	CA	94025	650-854-9080	854-3018
UV Partners 2755 E Cottonwood Pkwy Suite 520 *Web:* www.utahventures.com	Salt Lake City	UT	84121	801-365-0262	365-0233
Valhalla Partners 8000 Towers Crescent Dr Suite 1050 *Web:* www.valhallapartners.com	Vienna	VA	22182	703-448-1400	448-1441
Vanguard Venture Partners 505 Hamilton Ave Suite 300 *Web:* www.vanguardventures.com	Palo Alto	CA	94301	650-321-2900	321-2902
VantagePoint Venture Partners 1001 Bayhill Dr Suite 300 *Web:* www.vpvp.com	San Bruno	CA	94066	650-866-3100	869-6078
Vector Capital 456 Montgomery St 19th Fl *Web:* www.vectorcapital.com	San Francisco	CA	94104	415-293-5000	293-5100
Venrock Assoc 30 Rockefeller Plaza Suite 5508 *Web:* www.venrock.com	New York	NY	10112	212-649-5600	649-5788
Ventana Growth Fund 18881 Von Karman Ave Tower 17 Suite 330 *Web:* www.ventanaglobal.com	Irvine	CA	92612	949-476-2204	752-0223

Name / Address	City	State	Zip	Phone	Fax
Venture Capital Fund of America 509 Madison Ave Suite 1400	New York	NY	10022	212-838-5577	838-7614
Web: www.vcfa.com					
Venture Investors LLC 505 S Rosa Rd Suite 201	Madison	WI	53719	608-441-2700	441-2727
Web: www.ventureinvestors.com					
VentureVest Capital Corp 2530 W Long Cir	Littleton	CO	80120	303-730-7939	730-7947
Web: www.venturevest.com					
Vertical Group 25 DeForest Ave	Summit	NJ	07901	908-277-3737	273-9434
Web: www.vertical-group.com					
Vesbridge Partners LLC 1700 W Park Dr	Westboro	MA	01581	508-475-2300	475-2399
Web: www.vesbridge.com					
Village Ventures Inc 430 Main St Suite 1	Williamstown	MA	01267	413-458-1100	458-0338
Web: www.villageventures.com					
Vimac Ventures 177 Milk St	Boston	MA	02109	617-350-9800	350-9899
Web: www.vimac.com					
Vision Capital 1350 Old Bayshore Hwy Suite 360	Burlingame	CA	94010	650-373-2720	373-2727
Web: www.visioncap.com					
Vista Ventures 1011 Walnut St 4th Fl	Boulder	CO	80302	303-543-5716	543-5717
Web: www.vistavc.com					
VS & A Communications Partners 350 Park Ave 7th Fl	New York	NY	10022	212-935-4990	381-8168
TF: 800-935-4990 ■ *Web:* www.vss.com					
VSP (VSP Capital) 201 Post St Suite 1100	San Francisco	CA	94118	415-558-8600	558-8686
Web: www.vspcapital.com					
VSP Capital (VSP) 201 Post St Suite 1100	San Francisco	CA	94118	415-558-8600	558-8686
Web: www.vspcapital.com					
vSpring Capital 2795 E Cottonwood Pkwy Suite 360	Salt Lake City	UT	84121	801-942-8999	942-1636
Web: www.vspring.com					
Wainwright HC & Co Inc 52 Vanderbilt Ave 12th Fl	New York	NY	10017	212-856-5700	856-5753
Web: www.hcwainwright.com					
Walden Group of Venture Capital 750 Battery St Suite 700	San Francisco	CA	94111	415-391-7225	391-7262
Web: www.waldenvc.com					
Walden International 1 California St Suite 2800	San Francisco	CA	94111	415-765-7100	765-7200
Web: www.waldenintl.com					
Warburg Pincus Ventures Co Inc 466 Lexington Ave 10th Fl	New York	NY	10017	212-878-0600	878-9351
Web: www.warburgpincus.com					
Washington Research Foundation 2815 Eastlake Ave E Suite 300	Seattle	WA	98102	206-336-5600	336-5615
Web: www.wrfcapital.com					
WayPoint Ventures 320 N Main St Suite 400	Ann Arbor	MI	48104	734-332-1700	332-1900
Web: www.wpvc.com					
Weisel Thomas Partners Group LLC 1 Montgomery St	San Francisco	CA	94104	415-364-2500	364-2695
NASDAQ: TWPG ■ *TF:* 800-933-3445 ■ *Web:* www.tweisel.com					
WestBridge Capital Partners 950 Tower Ln Suite 1020	Foster City	CA	94404	650-854-3927	357-7075
Web: www.wbcp.com					
Western Technology Investment (WTI) 2010 North 1st St Suite 310	San Jose	CA	95131	408-436-8577	436-8625
Web: www.westerntech.com					
Weston Presidio Capital 200 Clarendon St 50th Fl	Boston	MA	02116	617-988-2500	988-2515
Web: www.westonpresidio.com					
Wicks Group of Cos LLC 405 Park Ave Suite 702	New York	NY	10022	212-838-2100	223-2109
Web: www.wicksgroup.com					
Willowridge Inc 25 E 86th St	New York	NY	10028	212-369-4700	369-5661
Web: www.willowridgeinc.com					
Wind Point Partners 676 N Michigan Ave Suite 3700	Chicago	IL	60611	312-255-4800	255-4820
Web: www.wppartners.com					
Windjammer Capital Investors 610 Newport Ctr Dr Suite 1100	Newport Beach	CA	92660	949-721-9944	720-4222
TF: 800-314-2644 ■ *Web:* www.windjammercapital.com					
Windspeed Ventures 52 Waltham St	Lexington	MA	02421	781-860-8888	863-1874
Web: www.windspeed.com					
Woodside Fund 350 Marine Pkwy Suite 300	Redwood Shores	CA	94065	650-610-8050	610-8051
TF: 888-368-5545 ■ *Web:* www.woodsidefund.com					
Worldview Technology Partners 435 Tasso St Suite 120	Palo Alto	CA	94301	650-322-3800	322-3880
Web: www.worldview.com					
WTI (Western Technology Investment) 2010 North 1st St Suite 310	San Jose	CA	95131	408-436-8577	436-8625
Web: www.westerntech.com					
Zanett Inc 635 Madison Ave 15th Fl	New York	NY	10022	212-583-0300	
NASDAQ: ZANE ■ *Web:* www.zanettinc.com					
Zon Capital Partners 5 Vaughn Dr Suite 302	Princeton	NJ	08540	609-452-1653	452-1693
Web: www.zoncapital.com					
Zone Venture Capital 241 S Figueroa St Suite 340	Los Angeles	CA	90012	213-628-2400	628-2433
Web: www.zonevc.com					
ZS Fund LP 1133 Ave of the Americas	New York	NY	10036	212-398-6200	398-1808
TF: 888-386-3573 ■ *Web:* www.zsfundlp.com					

796 VETERANS NURSING HOMES - STATE

SEE ALSO Hospitals - Veterans Hospitals p. 1828

Name / Address	City	State	Zip	Phone	Fax
Arizona State Veterans Home 4141 N 3rd St	Phoenix	AZ	85012	602-248-1550	222-6687
Arkansas State Veterans Home 4701 W 20th St	Little Rock	AR	72204	501-296-1885	296-1888
Baldomero Lopez State Veterans' Nursing Home 6919 Parkway Blvd	Land O'Lakes	FL	34639	813-558-5000	558-5021
Barboursville Veterans Home 512 Water St	Barboursville	WV	25504	304-736-1027	736-1093
Bill Nichols State Veterans Home 1784 Elkahatchee Rd	Alexander City	AL	35010	256-329-3311	329-1101
Charlotte Hall Veterans Home 29449 Charlotte Hall Rd	Charlotte Hall	MD	20622	301-884-8171	884-4964
Chelsea Soldiers Home 91 Crest Ave	Chelsea	MA	02150	617-884-5660	884-1162
Colorado State Veterans Nursing Home-Florence 903 Moore Dr	Florence	CO	81226	719-784-6331	784-5335
Colorado State Veterans Nursing Home-Homelake 3749 Sherman Ave	Monte Vista	CO	81144	719-852-5118	852-3881
TF: 888-838-2687					
Colorado State Veterans Nursing Home-Rifle 851 E 5th St	Rifle	CO	81650	970-625-0842	625-3706
Colorado State Veterans Nursing Home-Walsenburg 23500 US Hwy 160	Walsenburg	CO	81089	719-738-5133	738-5138
TF: 800-645-8387					
DJ Jacobetti Home for Veterans 425 Fisher St	Marquette	MI	49855	906-226-3576	226-2380
Eastern Montana Veterans Home 2000 Montana Ave	Glendive	MT	59330	406-345-8855	345-8121
Emory L Bennett Memorial Veterans' Nursing Home 1920 Mason Ave	Daytona Beach	FL	32117	386-274-3460	274-3487
Floyd E "Tut" Fann State Veterans Home 2701 Meridian St	Huntsville	AL	35811	256-851-2807	859-4115
Georgia War Veterans Home 2249 Vinson Hwy	Milledgeville	GA	31061	478-445-5582	445-1701
Georgia War Veterans Nursing Home 1101 15th St	Augusta	GA	30901	706-721-2824	721-3892
Grand Island Veterans' Home 2300 W Capital Ave	Grand Island	NE	68803	308-385-6252	385-6257*
**Fax: Acctg*					
Grand Rapids Home for Veterans 3000 Monroe Ave NW	Grand Rapids	MI	49505	616-364-5300	364-5397*
**Fax: Hum Res*					
Hastings Veterans Home 1200 E 18th St	Hastings	MN	55033	651-438-8504	437-2012
TF: 877-838-3803 ■ *Web:* www.mvh.state.mn.us/hastings.html					
Hollidaysburg Veterans Home PO Box 319	Hollidaysburg	PA	16648	814-696-5201	696-5260
Holyoke Soldiers Home 110 Cherry St	Holyoke	MA	01040	413-532-9475	538-7968
Idaho State Veterans Home-Boise 320 Collins Rd	Boise	ID	83702	208-334-5000	334-4753
Idaho State Veterans Home-Lewiston 821 21st Ave	Lewiston	ID	83501	208-799-3422	799-3414
Idaho State Veterans Home-Pocatello 1957 Alvin Ricken Dr	Pocatello	ID	83201	208-236-6340	236-6343
Illinois Veterans Home-Anna 792 N Main St	Anna	IL	62906	618-833-6302	833-3603
Illinois Veterans Home-Manteno 1 Veterans Dr	Manteno	IL	60950	815-468-6581	468-7001
Illinois Veterans Home-Quincy 1707 N 12th St	Quincy	IL	62301	217-222-8641	222-9621
Illinois Veterans Home-La Salle 1015 O'Connor Ave	La Salle	IL	61301	815-223-0303	223-5815
Indiana Veterans Home 3851 N River Rd	West Lafayette	IN	47906	765-463-1502	497-8568
Iowa Veterans Home 1301 Summit St	Marshalltown	IA	50158	641-752-1501	753-4278
Kansas Soldiers' Home 201 Custer St	Fort Dodge	KS	67843	620-227-2121	225-6331
Kansas Veterans' Home 1220 World War II Memorial Dr	Winfield	KS	67156	620-221-9479	221-9053
Long Island State Veterans Home 100 Patriots Rd	Stony Brook	NY	11790	631-444-8500	444-8575
Louisiana War Veterans' Home 4739 Hwy 10	Jackson	LA	70748	225-634-5265	634-4057
Luverne Veterans Home 1300 N Kniss Ave	Luverne	MN	56156	507-283-1100	283-1127
Web: www.mvh.state.mn.us/luverne.html					
Maine Veterans Home-Augusta 310 Cony Rd	Augusta	ME	04330	207-622-2454	626-2957
Web: www.maineveteranshomes.org					
Maine Veterans Home-Bangor 44 Hogan Rd	Bangor	ME	04401	207-942-2333	942-4810
TF: 888-684-4665 ■ *Web:* www.maineveteranshomes.org					
Maine Veterans Home-Caribou 163 Van Buren Rd Suite 2	Caribou	ME	04736	207-498-6074	498-3037
TF: 888-684-4667 ■ *Web:* www.maineveteranshomes.org					
Maine Veterans Home-Scarborough 290 US Rt 1	Scarborough	ME	04074	207-883-7184	883-7852
TF: 888-684-4666 ■ *Web:* www.maineveteranshomes.org					
Maine Veterans Home-South Paris 477 High St	South Paris	ME	04281	207-743-6300	743-7595
TF: 888-684-4668 ■ *Web:* www.maineveteranshomes.org					
Menlo Park Veterans Memorial Home 132 Evergreen Rd PO Box 3013	Edison	NJ	08818	732-452-4100	603-3192
Michael J Fitzmaurice Veterans Home 2500 Minnekahta Ave	Hot Springs	SD	57747	605-745-5127	745-5547
Minnesota Veterans Home-Fergus Falls 1821 N Park St	Fergus Falls	MN	56537	218-736-0400	739-7686
Web: www.mvh.state.mn.us/ff.html					
Minnesota Veterans Home-Minneapolis 5101 Minnehaha Ave S	Minneapolis	MN	55407	612-721-0600	721-0604
TF: 877-838-6757 ■ *Web:* www.mvh.state.mn.us/mpls.html					
Minnesota Veterans Home-Silver Bay 45 Banks Blvd	Silver Bay	MN	55614	218-226-6300	226-6336
TF: 877-729-8387 ■ *Web:* www.mvh.state.mn.us/sbay.html					
Mississippi State Veterans' Home Collins 3261 Hwy 49 S	Collins	MS	39428	601-765-0403	765-0336
Mississippi State Veterans' Home Jackson 4607 Lindbergh Dr	Jackson	MS	39209	601-353-6142	969-1386
Mississippi State Veterans' Home Kosciusko 310 Autumn Ridge Dr	Kosciusko	MS	39090	662-289-7769	289-7803
Mississippi State Veterans' Home Oxford 120 Veterans Dr	Oxford	MS	38655	662-236-7641	236-2129
Missouri Veterans Home-Cape Girardeau 2400 Veterans Memorial Dr	Cape Girardeau	MO	63701	573-290-5870	290-5909
Missouri Veterans Home-Mexico 1 Veterans Dr	Mexico	MO	65265	573-581-1088	581-5356
Missouri Veterans Home-Mount Vernon 600 N Main St	Mount Vernon	MO	65712	417-466-7103	466-4040
Web: www.sofnet.com/~movet					
Missouri Veterans Home-Saint James 620 N Jefferson St	Saint James	MO	65559	573-265-3271	265-5771
Missouri Veterans Home-Saint Louis 10600 Lewis & Clark Blvd	Saint Louis	MO	63136	314-340-6389	340-6379
Montana Veterans Home PO Box 250	Columbia Falls	MT	59912	406-892-3256	892-0256
New Hampshire Veterans Home 139 Winter St	Tilton	NH	03276	603-527-4400	527-4402
Web: www.nh.gov/veterans					
New Jersey Veterans Memorial Home 524 N West Blvd	Vineland	NJ	08360	856-696-6400	696-6885
New Jersey Veterans Paramus Home 1 Veterans Dr	Paramus	NJ	07652	201-634-8200	
New Mexico State Veterans Center 992 S Broadway St	Truth or Consequences	NM	87901	505-894-9081	894-4229
TF: 800-964-3976					
New York State Veterans Home at Batavia 220 Richmond Ave	Batavia	NY	14020	585-345-2000	345-9030
New York State Veterans Home at Oxford 4211 State Hwy 220	Oxford	NY	13830	607-843-3100	843-3194
New York State Veterans Home at Saint Albans 178-50 Linden Blvd	Jamaica	NY	11434	718-481-6268	481-6860
Norfolk Veterans Home 600 E Benjamin Ave	Norfolk	NE	68701	402-370-3330	370-3190
North Carolina Veterans Nursing Home 214 Cochran Ave	Fayetteville	NC	28301	910-630-4257	630-0868
North Dakota State Veterans Home 1400 Rose St	Lisbon	ND	58054	701-683-6500	683-6550
Northeast Louisiana War Veterans' Home 6700 Hwy 165 N	Monroe	LA	71203	318-362-4206	362-4241
Ohio Veterans Home 3416 Columbus Ave	Sandusky	OH	44870	419-625-2454	609-2544*
**Fax: Admitting* ■ *TF Admissions:* 800-572-7934					
Oklahoma Veterans Center Ardmore 1015 S Commerce	Ardmore	OK	73401	580-223-2266	221-5606
Web: www.odva.state.ok.us					
Oklahoma Veterans Center Claremore PO Box 988	Claremore	OK	74018	918-342-5432	342-0835
Web: www.odva.state.ok.us					
Oklahoma Veterans Center Clinton PO Box 1209	Clinton	OK	73601	580-331-2200	323-4834
Web: www.odva.state.ok.us					
Oklahoma Veterans Center Norman PO Box 1668	Norman	OK	73070	405-360-5600	364-8432
Web: www.odva.state.ok.us					
Oklahoma Veterans Center Sulphur 200 E Fairlane	Sulphur	OK	73086	580-622-2144	622-5881
Web: www.odva.state.ok.us					
Oklahoma Veterans Center Talihina Hwy 63 A PO Box 1168	Talihina	OK	74571	918-567-2251	567-2950
Oregon Veterans' Home 700 Veterans Dr	The Dalles	OR	97058	541-296-7190	296-7862
TF: 800-846-8460 ■ *Web:* www.oregonveteranshome.com					
Rhode Island Veterans' Home 480 Metacom Ave	Bristol	RI	02809	401-253-8000	254-1340
Richard M Campbell State Nursing Home 4605 Belton Hwy	Anderson	SC	29621	864-261-6734	261-0453
Rocky Hill Veterans Home & Healthcare Center 287 West St	Rocky Hill	CT	06067	860-721-5891	721-5904
Tennessee State Veterans Home-Humboldt 2865 Main St	Humboldt	TN	38343	731-784-8405	784-2448
Tennessee State Veterans Home-Murfreesboro 345 Compton Rd	Murfreesboro	TN	37130	615-895-8850	895-5091
Thomas Fitzgerald Veterans' Home 15345 W Maple Rd	Omaha	NE	68116	402-595-2180	595-2234
Thomson-Hood Veterans Center 100 Veterans Dr	Wilmore	KY	40390	859-858-2814	858-4039
TF: 800-928-4838 ■ *Web:* www.kdva.net/					
Utah Veterans Nursing Home 700 S Foothill Blvd	Salt Lake City	UT	84113	801-584-1900	584-1960
Vermont Veterans Home 325 North St	Bennington	VT	05201	802-442-6353	447-2757
Veterans Care Center 4550 Shenandoah Ave	Roanoke	VA	24017	540-982-2860	982-8667
Web: www.vdva.vipnet.org/carecenter_main.htm					
Veterans Home of California-Barstow 100 E Veterans Pkwy	Barstow	CA	92311	760-252-6200	252-6333
TF: 800-746-0606 ■ *Web:* www.cdva.ca.gov/homes/barstow.asp					
Veterans Home of California-Chula Vista 700 E Naples Ct	Chula Vista	CA	91911	619-482-6010	205-1903
TF: 888-857-2146					
Veterans Home of California-Yountville PO Box 1200	Yountville	CA	94599	707-944-4541	944-4542
TF: 800-404-8387 ■ *Web:* www.co.san-joaquin.ca.us/veterans/yount.htm					
Veterans' Home of Wyoming 700 Veterans Ln	Buffalo	WY	82834	307-684-5511	684-7636
Washington Veterans Home PO Box 698	Retsil	WA	98378	360-895-4700	895-4719
William F Green State Veterans Home 300 Faulkner Dr	Bay Minette	AL	36507	251-937-8049	937-2472
Wisconsin Veterans Home N2665 County Rd QQ	King	WI	54946	715-258-5586	258-5736

797 VETERINARY HOSPITALS

Name / Address	City	State	Zip	Phone	Fax
Animal Hospital Inc 5001 N 12th Ave	Pensacola	FL	32504	850-479-2900	479-3322
Web: www.petcarehospital.com					
Banfield The Pet Hospital 11815 NE Glenn Widing Dr	Portland	OR	97220	503-256-7299	256-7636
TF: 800-838-6738 ■ *Web:* www.banfield.net					
National PetCare Centers (NPC) 3540 JFK Pkwy	Fort Collins	CO	80525	970-226-6632	239-0201
TF: 877-738-4677 ■ *Web:* www.nationalpet.com					

	City	State	Zip	Phone	Fax
Noah's Animal Hospitals 5510 Millersville Rd *Web:* www.noahshospitals.com	Indianapolis	IN	46226	317-253-1327	726-2404
Pet Vet Animal Hospitals 4543 Post Oak Pl Suite 110 *Web:* www.petvethospitals.com	Houston	TX	77027	713-629-7521	629-7737
Radiocat 32-A Mellor Ave *TF:* 800-323-9729 ■ *Web:* www.radiocat.com	Baltimore	MD	21228	410-788-5200	788-5201
VCA Antech Inc 12401 W Olympic Blvd *NASDAQ: WOOF* ■ *TF:* 800-966-1822 ■ *Web:* www.vcaantech.com	Los Angeles	CA	90064	310-571-6500	571-6700
Veterinary Specialists of the Southeast 3169 W Montague Ave. *Web:* www.vss.org	North Charleston	SC	29418	843-566-0023	
VetSelect Animal Hospital 2150 Old Novi Rd *Web:* www.vetselect.com	Novi	MI	48377	248-624-1100	624-6542

798 VETERINARY MEDICAL ASSOCIATIONS - STATE

	City	State	Zip	Phone	Fax
Alabama PO Box 3514 *Web:* www.alvma.com	Montgomery	AL	36109	334-395-0086	270-3399
Alaska 12641 Alpine Dr. *Web:* www.akvma.org	Anchorage	AK	99516	907-563-3701	
Arizona 100 W Coolidge St *Web:* www.azvma.org	Phoenix	AZ	85013	602-242-7936	249-3828
Arkansas PO Box 17687 *Web:* www.arkvetmed.org	Little Rock	AR	72222	501-868-3036	868-3034
California 1400 River Park Dr Suite 100 *TF:* 800-655-2862 ■ *Web:* www.cvma.net	Sacramento	CA	95815	916-649-0599	646-9156
Colorado 191 Yuma St *TF:* 800-228-5429 ■ *Web:* www.colovma.com	Denver	CO	80223	303-318-0447	318-0450
Connecticut 100 Roscommon Dr Suite 320 *Web:* www.ctvet.org	Middletown	CT	06457	860-635-7770	635-6400
Delaware 937 Monroe Terr *Web:* www.devma.org	Dover	DE	19904	302-674-8581	674-8581
District of Columbia PO Box 710477 *Web:* www.dcavm.org	Herndon	VA	20171	703-733-0556	742-8745
Florida 7131 Lake Ellenor Dr. *TF:* 800-992-3862 ■ *Web:* www.fvma.com	Orlando	FL	32809	407-851-3862	240-3710
Georgia 2814 Spring Rd Suite 217 *TF:* 800-853-1625 ■ *Web:* www.gvma.net	Atlanta	GA	30339	678-309-9800	309-3361
Hawaii PO Box 61309	Honolulu	HI	96839	808-733-8828	733-8829
Idaho 1841 W Secluded Ct *Web:* www.ivma.org	Kuna	ID	83634	208-922-9431	922-9435
Illinois 133 S 4th St Suite 202 *Web:* www.isvma.org	Springfield	IL	62701	217-523-8387	523-7981
Indiana 201 S Capitol Ave Suite 405 *Web:* www.invma.org	Indianapolis	IN	46225	317-974-0888	974-0985
Iowa 1605 N Ankeny Blvd Suite 110 *Web:* www.iowavma.org	Ankeny	IA	50023	515-965-9237	965-9239
Kansas 816 SW Tyler St Suite 200 *Web:* www.ksvma.org	Topeka	KS	66612	785-233-4141	233-2534
Kentucky 108 Consumer Ln *Web:* www.kvma.org	Frankfort	KY	40601	502-226-5862	226-6177
Louisiana 8550 United Plaza Blvd Suite 1001 *TF:* 800-524-2996 ■ *Web:* www.lvma.org	Baton Rouge	LA	70809	225-928-5862	408-4422
Maine 97-A Exchange St Suite 305 **Fax Area Code:* 888 ■ *Web:* mainevma.org	Portland	ME	04101	207-752-1392	612-0941*
Maryland 8015 Corporate Dr Suite A *TF:* 888-884-6862 ■ *Web:* www.mdvma.org	Baltimore	MD	21236	410-931-3332	931-2060
Massachusetts 163Lakeside Ave. *Web:* www.massvet.org	Marlborough	MA	01752	508-460-9333	460-9969
Michigan (MVMA) 2144 Commons Pkwy *Web:* www.michvma.org	Okemos	MI	48864	517-347-4710	347-4666
Minnesota 101 Bridgepoint Way Suite 100 *Web:* www.mvma.org	South Saint Paul	MN	55075	651-645-7533	645-7539
Mississippi 209 S Lafayette St *Web:* www.msvet.org	Starkville	MS	39759	662-324-9380	324-9380
Missouri 2500 Country Club Dr. *Web:* www.mvma.us	Jefferson City	MO	65109	573-636-8612	659-7175
Montana PO Box 6322 *Web:* www.mtvma.org	Helena	MT	59604	406-447-4259	442-8018
Nebraska 2727 W 2nd St Suite 227 *Web:* www.nvma.org	Hastings	NE	68901	402-463-4704	463-4705
Nevada PO Box 34420 *Web:* www.nevadavma.org	Reno	NV	89533	775-324-5344	747-9170
New Hampshire PO Box 616	Concord	NH	03302	603-224-2432	228-7048
New Jersey 203 Towne Centre Dr *Web:* www.njvma.org	Hillsborough	NJ	08844	908-359-1184	359-7619
New Mexico 60 Placitas Trails Rd. *Web:* www.nmvma.org	Placitas	NM	87043	505-867-6373	771-8963
New York 9 Highland Ave *TF:* 800-876-9867 ■ *Web:* www.nysvms.org	Albany	NY	12205	518-437-0787	437-0957
North Carolina 1611 Jones Franklin Rd Suite 108 *TF:* 800-446-2862 ■ *Web:* www.ncvma.org	Raleigh	NC	27606	919-851-5850	851-5859
North Dakota 921 S 9th St Suite 120 *TF:* 877-637-6386 ■ *Web:* www.ndvma.com	Bismarck	ND	58504	701-221-7740	258-9005
Ohio (OVMA) 3168 Riverside Dr *TF:* 800-662-6862 ■ *Web:* www.ohiovma.org	Columbus	OH	43221	614-486-7253	486-1325
Oklahoma PO Box 14521 *Web:* www.okvma.org	Oklahoma City	OK	73113	405-478-1002	478-7193
Oregon 1880 Lancaster Dr NE Suite 118 *TF:* 800-235-3502 ■ *Web:* www.oregonvma.org	Salem	OR	97305	503-399-0311	363-4218
Pennsylvania 12 Briarcrest Sq *TF:* 888-550-7862 ■ *Web:* www.pavma.org	Hershey	PA	17033	717-533-7934	533-4761
Puerto Rico 352 San Claudio Ave Suite 248 *Web:* www.cmvpr.org	San Juan	PR	00926	787-283-2840	761-3440
Rhode Island 302 Pearl St Suite 108 *Web:* www.rivma.org	Providence	RI	02907	401-751-0944	780-0940
South Carolina PO Box 11766 *TF:* 800-441-7228 ■ *Web:* www.scav.org	Columbia	SC	29211	803-254-1027	254-3773
South Dakota South Dakota State University Box 2175	Brookings	SD	57007	605-688-6649	688-6003
Tennessee PO Box 803 *TF:* 800-697-3587 ■ *Web:* www.tvmanet.org	Fayetteville	TN	37334	931-438-0070	433-6289
Texas 8104 Exchange Dr *Web:* www.tvma.org	Austin	TX	78754	512-452-4224	452-6633
Vermont 88 Beech St. *Web:* www.vtvets.org	Essex Junction	VT	05452	802-878-6888	878-2871
Virginia 2314-C Commerce Ctr Dr *TF:* 800-937-8862 ■ *Web:* www.vvma.org	Rockville	VA	23146	804-749-8058	749-8003
Washington PO Box 962 *TF:* 800-399-7862 ■ *Web:* www.wsvma.org	Bellevue	WA	98009	425-454-8381	454-8382
West Virginia 201 Virginia St W *Web:* www.wvvma.org	Charleston	WV	25302	304-437-0497	346-0589
Wisconsin 301 N Broom St. *TF:* 888-254-5202 ■ *Web:* www.wvma.org	Madison	WI	53703	608-257-3665	257-8989
Wyoming 1841 W Secluded Ct *TF:* 800-272-1813 ■ *Web:* www.wyvma.org	Kuna	ID	83634	208-922-9431	922-9435

799 VIATICAL SETTLEMENT COMPANIES

A viatical settlement is the sale of an existing life insurance policy by a terminally ill person to a third party in return for a percentage of the face value of the policy paid immediately.

	City	State	Zip	Phone	Fax
AmeriFirst Funding Group Inc 2015-A Osborne Rd *Web:* www.amerifirstinc.com	Saint Marys	GA	31558	912-882-8851	882-9461
AMG/Neuma Inc 7366 N Lincoln Ave Suite 202 *TF:* 800-457-7828	Lincolnwood	IL	60712	847-674-1150	674-1165
Ardan Group Ltd 111 St Joseph's Terr *TF:* 800-699-3522 ■ *Web:* www.ardangroup.com	Woodbridge	NJ	07095	732-855-0670	855-0659
CMG Surety LLC 1016 Collier Ctr Way Suite 100 *Web:* www.cmgsurety.com	Naples	FL	34110	239-597-0128	597-1977
Coventry First LLC 7111 Valley Green Rd. *TF:* 877-836-8300 ■ *Web:* www.coventry.com	Fort Washington	PA	19034	215-233-5100	233-3201
Habersham Funding LLC 415 E Paces Ferry Rd NE Terrace Level *TF:* 888-874-2402 ■ *Web:* www.habershamfunding.com	Atlanta	GA	30305	404-233-8275	233-9394
Independent Funding LLC 997 Old Eagle School Rd Suite 201	Wayne	PA	19087	610-647-1229	
Legacy Benefits Corp 350 5th Ave Suite 4320 *TF:* 800-875-1000 ■ *Web:* www.legacybenefits.com	New York	NY	10118	212-643-1190	643-1180
Life Equity LLC 85 Executive Pkwy Suite 100 *Web:* www.lifeequity.net	Hudson	OH	44236	330-342-7772	342-7782
Life Partners Holdings Inc 204 Woodhew Dr. *NASDAQ: LPHI* ■ *TF:* 800-368-5569 ■ *Web:* www.lifepartnersinc.com	Waco	TX	76712	254-751-7797	751-1025
Life Settlement Providers LLC 6302A North Point Rd *Web:* www.lifesettlementproviders.com	Baltimore	MD	21210	410-477-1976	477-1978
Life Settlement Solutions Inc 9201 Spectrum Center Blvd Suite 105 *Web:* www.lss-corp.com	San Diego	CA	92123	858-576-8067	576-9329
Life Trust LLC 330 Madison Ave 6th Fl. *Web:* www.life-trust.net	New York	NY	10017	212-653-0840	653-0844
Lifeline Program 1979 Lakeside Pkwy Suite 925 **Fax Area Code:* 954 ■ *TF:* 800-572-4346 ■ *Web:* www.thelifeline.com	Tucker	GA	30084	800-252-5282	568-5970*
Magna Administrative Services Inc Life Settlement Div 1320 S Dixie Hwy *Web:* www.viamagna.com	Coral Gables	FL	33146	305-443-2898	668-1880
Milestone Providers LLC 600-G Eden Rd Suite A *TF:* 888-877-5686 ■ *Web:* www.milestonesettlements.com	Lancaster	PA	17601	717-560-6383	560-3970
Page & Assoc Inc DBA Lifeline Program 1979 Lakeside Pkwy Suite 925 **Fax Area Code:* 954 ■ *TF:* 800-572-4346 ■ *Web:* www.thelifeline.com	Tucker	GA	30084	800-252-5282	568-5970*
Peachtree Life Settlements 6501 Park of Commerce Blvd Suite 140-B *TF:* 866-730-4411 ■ *Web:* www.peachtreelifesettlements.com	Boca Raton	FL	33487	561-962-3900	962-7205
Phoenix Rising Enterprises LLC 304 E 2nd Ave Suite A *Web:* www.phoenixfirerise.com	Rome	GA	30161	706-235-8530	235-9353
Portsmouth Settlement Co Inc 1724 Phoenix Pkwy	Atlanta	GA	30349	770-997-1733	997-4588
Secondary Life Capital LLC 1010 Wisconsin Ave Suite 620 **Fax Area Code:* 202 ■ *Web:* www.secondarylifecapital.com	Washington	DC	20007	888-600-5433	464-1068*
Senior Settlements LLC 303 Harper Dr. *Web:* www.seniorsettlementsllc.com	Moorestown	NJ	08057	856-235-2133	235-1294
Vespers Financial Group 3210 Grace St Suite 1150 *TF:* 888-777-5432 ■ *Web:* vespersfinancialgroup.com	Washington	DC	20007	202-333-4100	333-4662

800 VIDEO STORES

SEE ALSO Book, Music, Video Clubs p. 1388

	City	State	Zip	Phone	Fax
Amazon.com Inc 1200 12th Ave S Suite 1200 *NASDAQ: AMZN* ■ **Fax:* Hum Res ■ *TF Cust Svc:* 800-201-7575 ■ *Web:* www.amazon.com	Seattle	WA	98144	206-266-1000	266-7601*
Archambault Group Inc 500 rue Sainte-Catherine E *TF:* 877-849-8589 ■ *Web:* www.archambault.ca	Montreal	QC	H2L2C6	514-849-6206	849-0764
Best Buy Co Inc 7601 Penn Ave S *NYSE: BBY* ■ **Fax Area Code:* 952 ■ **Fax:* Cust Svc ■ *TF:* 800-369-5050 ■ *Web:* www.bestbuy.com	Richfield	MN	55423	612-291-1000	238-3160*
Blockbuster Inc 1201 Elm St Suite 2100 *NYSE: BBI* ■ **Fax Area Code:* 972 ■ *Web:* www.blockbuster.com	Dallas	TX	75270	214-854-3000	683-8165*
Border Entertainment LLC 206 E Northern Lights Blvd	Anchorage	AK	99503	907-277-8525	277-8532
CD Universe 101 N Plains Industrial Rd *TF:* 800-231-7937 ■ *Web:* www.cduniverse.com	Wallingford	CT	06492	203-294-1648	294-0391
CinemaNow 4553 Glencoe Ave Suite 200 *TF:* 800-432-5216 ■ *Web:* www.cinemanow.com	Marina del Rey	CA	90292	310-314-3015	314-3050
Circuit City Group 9950 Mayland Dr. **Fax:* Acctg ■ *TF:* 800-251-2665 ■ *Web:* www.circuitcity.com	Richmond	VA	23233	804-527-4000	527-4171*
Coconuts Music & Movies 38 Corporate Cir *TF:* 800-540-1242 ■ *Web:* www.coconuts.com	Albany	NY	12203	518-452-1242	869-4819
DVD Avenue PO Box 820 *TF:* 800-990-4159 ■ *Web:* www.dvdavenue.com	Clinton	MD	20735	301-856-4159	856-4153
DVD Empire 2140 Woodland Rd *TF:* 888-383-1880 ■ *Web:* www.dvdempire.com	Warrendale	PA	15086	724-776-9090	625-6623
Endless Video 300 Oak St Suite 750	Pembroke	MA	02359	781-826-1200	826-1561
Facets Multimedia Inc 1517 W Fullerton Ave *TF:* 800-331-6197 ■ *Web:* www.facets.org	Chicago	IL	60614	773-281-9075	929-5437
Gameznflix Inc 1535 Blackjack Rd **Fax Area Code:* 270 ■ *Web:* www.gameznflix.com	Franklin	KY	42134	888-542-6817	778-0025*
Half.com Inc PO Box 1469 **Fax Area Code:* 877 ■ *TF:* 800-545-9857 ■ *Web:* www.half.ebay.com	Draper	UT	84020	800-545-9857	349-5782*
Hollywood Entertainment Corp DBA Hollywood Video 9275 SW Peyton Ln. *TF:* 877-325-8687 ■ *Web:* www.hollywoodvideo.com	Wilsonville	OR	97070	503-570-1600	570-1680
Hollywood Video 9275 SW Peyton Ln *TF:* 877-325-8687 ■ *Web:* www.hollywoodvideo.com	Wilsonville	OR	97070	503-570-1600	570-1680
Intelliflix Inc 1401 Forum Way Suite 503 *Web:* www.intelliflix.com	West Palm Beach	FL	33401	561-697-8325	697-8320
Movie Exchange Inc PO Box 394 *Web:* www.movieexchange.com	Oaks	PA	19456	610-631-9180	631-9359
Movie Gallery Inc 900 W Main St *NASDAQ: MOVI* ■ *TF Cust Svc:* 866-209-5533 ■ *Web:* www.moviegallery.com	Dothan	AL	36301	334-677-2108	677-1169
Musicland Group Inc 10400 Yellow Circle Dr. *TF Cust Svc:* 800-538-3465 ■ *Web:* www.musicland.com	Minnetonka	MN	55343	952-931-8000	931-8300

				Phone	Fax
NetFlix Inc 100 Winchester Cir *NASDAQ: NFLX* ■ **Fax Area Code:* 408 ■ *TF:* 888-638-3549 ■ *Web:* www.netflix.com	Los Gatos	CA	95032	888-638-3549	317-3737*
SightSound Technologies Inc 311 S Craig St Suite 205 *Web:* www.sightsound.com	Pittsburgh	PA	15213	412-621-6100	341-2442
Strawberries Music & Video 38 Corporate Cir *TF:* 800-540-1242 ■ *Web:* www.twec.com/corpsite/stores	Albany	NY	12203	518-452-1242	869-4819
Suncoast Motion Picture Co 10400 Yellow Circle Dr *TF:* 800-538-3465 ■ *Web:* www.suncoast.com	Minnetonka	MN	55343	952-931-8000	931-8300
Tower Records 2500 Del Monte St Bldg C *TF:* 800-225-0880 ■ *Web:* www.towerrecords.com	West Sacramento	CA	95691	916-373-2500	373-3012
Videoflicks Canada 1701 Avenue Rd *Web:* www.myvideoflicks.ca	Toronto	ON	M5M3Y3	416-782-1883	782-1265
Wherehouse Music 2330 Carson St **Fax Area Code:* 310 ■ *Web:* www.wherehouse.com	Carson	CA	90810	518-452-1242	516-9057*

801 VISION CORRECTION CENTERS

				Phone	Fax
Arrowsmith Eye Institute 210 25th Ave N Suite 900 *TF:* 800-844-2019 ■ *Web:* www.arrowsmith-eye.com	Nashville	TN	37203	615-327-2020	321-3175
Barnet-Dulaney Eye Center 4800 N 22nd St *TF:* 800-966-7000 ■ *Web:* www.goodeyes.com	Phoenix	AZ	85016	602-955-1000	508-4700
Carolina Eye Assoc PA 2170 Midland Rd *Web:* www.carolinaeye.com	Southern Pines	NC	28387	910-295-2100	295-5339
Chicago Cornea Consultants Ltd 806 S Central Ave Suite 300 *Web:* www.chicagocornea.com	Highland Park	IL	60035	847-882-5900	882-6028
Eye Centers of Florida 4101 Evans Ave *TF:* 800-226-3377 ■ *Web:* www.see-your-best.com	Fort Myers	FL	33901	239-939-3456	936-8776
Gordon Binder Vision Institute 8910 University Ctr Ln Suite 800 *Web:* www.gbvision.com	San Diego	CA	92122	858-455-6800	455-0244
Hunkeler Eye Institute 4321 Washington St Suite 6000 *Web:* www.hunkeler.com	Kansas City	MO	64111	816-931-4733	931-9498
John-Kenyon Eye Center 1305 Wall St Suite 200 *TF:* 800-342-5393 ■ *Web:* www.johnkenyon.com	Jeffersonville	IN	47130	812-288-9011	288-7479
Jones Eye Clinic 4405 Hamilton Blvd PO Box 3246 *TF:* 800-334-2015	Sioux City	IA	51104	712-239-3937	239-1305
Laser Vision Centers Inc 540 Maryville Centre Dr Suite 200 *TF:* 800-852-1033 ■ *Web:* www.laservision.com	Saint Louis	MO	63141	314-434-6900	434-2424
LaserSight of Wisconsin 240 1st St *TF:* 888-774-3937 ■ *Web:* www.lasersightwi.com	Neenah	WI	54956	920-729-6600	729-6603
LaserVue Eye Center 3540 Mendocino Ave Suite 200 *TF:* 888-527-3745 ■ *Web:* www.laservue.com	Santa Rosa	CA	95403	707-522-6200	522-6213
LCA-Vision Inc 7840 Montgomery Rd *NASDAQ: LCAV* ■ *TF:* 888-529-2020	Cincinnati	OH	45236	513-792-9292	792-5620
Maryland Regional Eye Assoc 800 Prince Frederick Blvd *Web:* www.marylandcataracts.com	Prince Frederick	MD	20678	410-535-2270	535-9549
Millennium Laser Eye Centers 1750 Tysons Blvd Suite 120 *TF:* 888-565-2737 ■ *Web:* www.millenniumlaser.com	McLean	VA	22102	703-761-4999	761-4960
Minnesota Eye Consultants PA 710 E 24th St Suite 106 *TF:* 800-526-7632 ■ *Web:* www.mn-eye.com	Minneapolis	MN	55404	612-813-3600	813-3601
NovaMed Inc 980 N Michigan Ave Suite 1620 *NASDAQ: NOVA* ■ *TF:* 800-388-4133 ■ *Web:* www.novamed.com	Chicago	IL	60611	312-664-4100	664-4250
Ophthalmology Consultants The Center for LASIK 5800 Colonial Dr Suite 100 *TF:* 800-448-8770 ■ *Web:* www.bestvision.com	Margate	FL	33063	954-977-8770	977-8774
Pacific Cataract & Laser Institute 2517 NE Kresky Ave *TF:* 800-224-7254 ■ *Web:* www.pcli.com	Chehalis	WA	98532	360-748-8632	748-3869
Prado Vision Center 7522 N Himes Ave *TF:* 877-455-2745 ■ *Web:* www.pradovision.com	Tampa	FL	33614	813-931-0500	935-4055
South Penn Eye Care Surgeons (SPECS) 250 E Walnut St	Hanover	PA	17331	717-632-6063	632-8337
Southwestern Eye Center 2610 E University Dr *TF:* 800-425-8404 ■ *Web:* uw-prod-01.sweye.com	Mesa	AZ	85213	480-892-8400	892-9533
SPECS (South Penn Eye Care Surgeons) 250 E Walnut St	Hanover	PA	17331	717-632-6063	632-8337
Swinger Vision Center 205 W End Ave Suite 10R *Web:* www.swingervision.com	New York	NY	10021	212-579-5500	787-7867
TLC Vision Corp 5280 Solar Dr Suite 300 *NASDAQ: TLCV* ■ *TF:* 888-225-5852 ■ *Web:* www.lzr.com	Mississauga	ON	L4W5M8	905-602-2020	602-2025
Vista Alliance Eye Care Assoc 160 E 56th St 9th Fl *TF:* 888-695-2745 ■ *Web:* www.nylasik.com	New York	NY	10022	212-758-3838	758-4175
Will Vision & Laser Centers 8100 NE Pkwy Dr Suite 125 *TF:* 877-542-3937 ■ *Web:* www.willvision.com	Vancouver	WA	98662	360-885-1327	885-1333

802 VITAMINS & NUTRITIONAL SUPPLEMENTS

SEE ALSO Food Products - Mfr - Diet & Health Foods p. 1646; Medicinal Chemicals & Botanical Products p. 1957; Pharmaceutical Companies p. 2109; Pharmaceutical Companies - Generic Drugs p. 2111

				Phone	Fax
Access Business Group 7575 Fulton St E *TF Cust Svc:* 800-253-6500 ■ *Web:* www.accessbusinessgroup.com	Ada	MI	49355	616-787-5358	
ADM Natural Health & Nutrition 4666 E Faries Pkwy **Fax:* PR ■ *TF:* 800-510-2178 ■ *Web:* www.admworld.com	Decatur	IL	62526	217-451-4450	451-4510*
Amazon Herb Co 1002 Jupiter Park Ln Suite 1 *TF:* 800-835-0850 ■ *Web:* www.amazonherb.net/Corporate	Jupiter	FL	33458	561-575-7663	575-7935
American Biologics 1180 Walnut Ave *TF:* 800-227-4473 ■ *Web:* americanbiologics.com	Chula Vista	CA	91911	619-429-8200	429-8004
American Sports Nutrition Inc 1800 Silas Deane Hwy Unit 224 *TF:* 888-462-5671 ■ *Web:* www.americanwhey.com	Rocky Hill	CT	06067	860-563-0300	563-0301
Aspen Group Inc 10325 N Rt 47 *TF:* 888-227-7361 ■ *Web:* www.aspennutrients.com	Hebron	IL	60034	815-648-2001	648-2095
AST Sports Science Inc 120 Capitol Dr *TF:* 800-627-2788 ■ *Web:* www.ast-ss.com	Golden	CO	80401	303-278-1420	278-1417
Bactolac Pharmaceutical Inc 7 Oser Ave *Web:* www.bactolac.com	Hauppage	NY	11788	631-951-4908	951-4749
Beehive Botanicals Inc 16297 W Nursery Rd *TF:* 800-233-4483 ■ *Web:* www.beehive-botanicals.com	Hayward	WI	54843	715-634-4274	634-3523
Celex Laboratories Inc 115-21600 Westminster Hwy *Web:* www.celexlaboratories.com	Richmond	BC	V6V0A2	604-231-6077	231-6078
Champion Nutrition 1301 Sawgrass Corp Pkwy *TF:* 800-752-7873 ■ *Web:* www.champion-nutrition.com	Sunrise	FL	33323	954-233-3300	
Chattem Inc 1715 W 38th St *NASDAQ: CHTT* ■ *TF:* 800-366-6077 ■ *Web:* www.chattem.com	Chattanooga	TN	37409	423-821-4571	821-0395
CV Technologies Inc 9604 20th Ave *TF:* 888-843-7239 ■ *Web:* www.herbtech.com	Edmonton	AB	T6N1G1	780-432-0022	432-7772
CytoSport Inc 4795 Industrial Way **Fax Area Code:* 707 ■ *TF:* 888-298-6629 ■ *Web:* www.cytosport.com	Benicia	CA	94510	925-685-6600	748-5732*
Douglas Laboratories Inc 600 Boyce Rd *TF:* 800-245-4440 ■ *Web:* www.douglaslabs.com	Pittsburgh	PA	15205	412-494-0122	494-0155
DuPont Agriculture & Nutrition 1007 Market St DuPont Bldg *TF:* 800-441-7515	Wilmington	DE	19898	302-774-1000	999-4399
EAS Inc 625 Cleveland Ave **Fax Area Code:* 303 ■ *TF:* 800-297-9776 ■ *Web:* www.eas.com	Columbus	OH	43215	614-624-7677	279-7358*
Edom Laboratories Inc 100-M E Jeffryn Blvd *Web:* www.edomlaboratories.com	Deer Park	NY	11729	631-586-2266	
Enzymatic Therapy 825 Challenger Dr *TF:* 800-783-2286 ■ *Web:* www.enzy.com	Green Bay	WI	54311	920-469-1313	469-4400
Foodscience Corp 20 New England Dr Suite 1000 *TF:* 800-451-5190 ■ *Web:* www.foodsciencecorp.com	Essex Junction	VT	05452	802-878-5508	878-0549
Futurebiotics LLC 70 Commerce Dr *TF:* 800-367-5433 ■ *Web:* www.futurebiotics.com	Hauppauge	NY	11788	631-273-6300	273-1165
Garden of Life Inc 5500 Zillage Blvd Suite 202 *TF Orders:* 888-622-8986 ■ *Web:* www.gardenoflifeusa.com	West Palm Beach	FL	33407	561-748-2477	472-9298
Garden State Nutritionals 8 Henderson Dr *TF:* 800-526-9095 ■ *Web:* www.gardenstatenutritionals.com	West Caldwell	NJ	07006	973-575-9200	575-6782
GeoPharma Inc 6950 Bryan Dairy Rd *NASDAQ: GORX* ■ *TF:* 800-654-2347	Largo	FL	33777	727-544-8866	544-4386
Ginco International 725 E Cochran St Unit C *TF:* 800-284-2598 ■ *Web:* www.ginsengcompany.com	Simi Valley	CA	93065	805-520-2592	520-7509
GNC Corp 300 6th Ave **Fax:* Cust Svc ■ *TF Cust Svc:* 888-462-2548 ■ *Web:* www.gnc.com	Pittsburgh	PA	15222	412-288-4600	338-8905*
Great Earth Companies 200 Adams Blvd *Web:* www.greatearth.com	Farmingdale	NY	11735	800-284-8243	
Hammer Nutrition Ltd 4952 Whitefish Stage Rd *TF Cust Svc:* 800-336-1977 ■ *Web:* www.e-caps.com	Whitefish	MT	59937	406-862-1877	862-4543
Health Products Corp 1060 Nepperhan Ave *Web:* www.hpc7.com	Yonkers	NY	10703	914-423-2900	963-6001
Herbalist The 2106 NE 65th St *TF:* 800-694-3727 ■ *Web:* www.theherbalist.com	Seattle	WA	98115	206-523-2600	522-3253
Idea Sphere Inc 600 E Quality Dr *TF:* 800-645-5626 ■ *Web:* www.twinlab.com	American Fork	UT	74003	801-763-0700	763-0789
Integrated BioPharma Inc 225 Long Ave *AMEX: INB* ■ *TF:* 888-319-6962 ■ *Web:* www.ibiopharma.com	Hillside	NJ	07205	973-926-0816	926-1735
Irwin Naturals 5310 Beethoven St *TF:* 800-841-8448 ■ *Web:* www.omninutra.com	Los Angeles	CA	90066	310-306-3636	301-1546
Jamieson Laboratories Ltd 2 St Clair Ave W Suite 1600 *TF:* 800-265-5053 ■ *Web:* www.jamiesonvitamins.com	Toronto	ON	M4V1L5	416-960-0052	960-4803
Jo Mar Laboratories 583-B Division St *TF:* 800-538-4545 ■ *Web:* www.jomarlabs.com	Campbell	CA	95008	408-374-5920	374-5922
Labrada Nutrition 403 Century Plaza Dr Suite 440 *TF:* 800-832-9948 ■ *Web:* www.labrada.com	Houston	TX	77073	281-209-2137	209-2135
Mannatech Inc 600 S Royal Ln Suite 200 *NASDAQ: MTEX* ■ *TF:* 800-281-4469 ■ *Web:* www.mannatech-inc.com	Coppell	TX	75019	972-471-7400	471-8135
Matol Botanical International Ltd 290 La Brosse Ave *TF:* 800-363-1890 ■ *Web:* www.matol.com	Pointe-Claire	QC	H9R6R6	514-426-2865	693-3405
Maxam Nutraceutics 1020 Wasco St Suite D *TF:* 800-800-9119 ■ *Web:* www.maxamlabs.com	Hood River	OR	97031	541-387-4500	387-4503
Maximum Human Performance Inc (MHP Inc) 21 Dwight Pl *TF:* 888-783-8844 ■ *Web:* www.maxperformance.com	Fairfield	NJ	07004	973-785-9055	785-9159
McNeil Nutritionals 601 Office Center Dr	Fort Washington	PA	19034	215-273-7000	273-4074
Mega-Pro International Inc 251 W Hilton Dr *TF:* 800-541-9469 ■ *Web:* www.mega-pro.com	Saint George	UT	84770	435-673-1001	673-1007
MET-Rx Nutrition Inc 2100 Smithtown Ave *TF:* 800-926-3879 ■ *Web:* www.met-rx.com	Ronkonkoma	NY	11779	800-556-3879	303-6457
MHP Inc (Maximum Human Performance Inc) 21 Dwight Pl *TF:* 888-783-8844 ■ *Web:* www.maxperformance.com	Fairfield	NJ	07004	973-785-9055	785-9159
National Vitamin Co 1145 W Gila Bend Hwy *TF:* 800-538-5828 ■ *Web:* www.nationalvitamin.com	Casa Grande	CA	85222	520-426-3100	426-3005
Natrol Inc 21411 Prairie St *NASDAQ: NTOL* ■ *TF:* 800-326-1520 ■ *Web:* www.natrol.com	Chatsworth	CA	91311	818-739-6000	739-6001
Naturade Products Inc 2099 S State College Blvd Suite 210 *TF:* 800-367-2880 ■ *Web:* www.naturade.com	Anaheim	CA	92806	714-860-7600	935-9837
Natural Alternatives International Inc 1185 Linda Vista Dr *NASDAQ: NAII* ■ *TF:* 800-848-2646 ■ *Web:* www.nai-online.com	San Marcos	CA	92078	760-744-7340	744-9589
Natural Factors Nutritional Products Inc 1111 80th St SW Suite 100 *TF:* 800-322-8704 ■ *Web:* www.naturalfactors.com	Everett	WA	98203	425-513-8800	348-9050
Natural Factors Nutritional Products Ltd 1550 United Blvd **Fax Area Code:* 800 ■ *TF:* 800-663-8900 ■ *Web:* www.naturalfactors.com	Coquitlam	BC	V3K6Y7	604-420-4229	663-2115*
Natural Organics Inc 548 Broadhollow Rd *TF:* 800-645-9500 ■ *Web:* www.natplus.com	Melville	NY	11747	631-293-0030	293-0349
Naturally Vitamins 4404 E Elwood St *TF:* 888-766-4406 ■ *Web:* www.naturallyvitamins.com	Phoenix	AZ	85040	480-991-0200	991-0551
Nature's Life 900 Larkspur Landing Cir Suite 105 **Fax Area Code:* 800 ■ *TF:* 800-247-6997 ■ *Web:* www.natlife.com	Larkspur	CA	94939	435-655-6790	643-7195*
Nature's Sunshine Products Inc 75 E 1700 South *NASDAQ: NATRE* ■ **Fax:* Mail Rm ■ *TF Cust Svc:* 800-223-8225 ■ *Web:* www.naturessunshine.com	Provo	UT	84606	801-342-4300	342-4305*
Nature's Way 1375 Mountain Springs Pkwy *TF:* 800-962-8873 ■ *Web:* www.naturesway.com	Springville	UT	84663	801-489-1500	489-1700
NBTY Inc 90 Orville Dr *NYSE: NTY* ■ **Fax:* Cust Svc ■ *TF:* 800-348-0090 ■ *Web:* www.nbty.com	Bohemia	NY	11716	631-567-9500	244-1709*
Next Proteins International 2283 Cosmos Ct *TF:* 800-468-6398 ■ *Web:* www.designerprotein.com	Carlsbad	CA	92009	760-431-8152	431-0323
Nickers International Ltd PO Box 50066 *TF:* 800-642-5377 ■ *Web:* www.nickint.com	Staten Island	NY	10305	718-448-6283	448-6298
Nutraceutical International Corp 1400 Kearns Blvd 2nd Fl *NASDAQ: NUTR* ■ **Fax Area Code:* 800 ■ *TF:* 800-669-8877 ■ *Web:* www.nutraceutical.com	Park City	UT	84060	435-655-6000	767-8541*
Nutrilite Products Inc 5600 Beach Blvd PO Box 5940 *Web:* www.nutrilite.com	Buena Park	CA	90621	714-562-6200	736-7610
Pacific Health Laboratories Inc 100 Matawan Rd Suite 420 *TF:* 800-397-7683 ■ *Web:* www.pacifichealthlabs.com	Matawan	NJ	07747	732-739-2900	739-4360
Paragon Laboratories 20433 Earl St *TF:* 800-231-3670 ■ *Web:* www.paralabs.com	Torrance	CA	90503	310-370-1563	370-7354
Peak Nutrition 1097 11th St *TF:* 800-600-2069 ■ *Web:* www.peaknutrition.com	Syracuse	NE	68446	402-269-2825	269-2649
Peak Nutrition DBA Peak Nutrition 1097 11th St *TF:* 800-600-2069 ■ *Web:* www.peaknutrition.com	Syracuse	NE	68446	402-269-2825	269-2649
Perrigo Co 515 Eastern Ave *NASDAQ: PRGO* ■ *TF:* 800-253-3606 ■ *Web:* www.perrigo.com	Allegan	MI	49010	269-673-8451	673-9128
Pharmanex Inc 75 W Center St *TF:* 888-742-7626 ■ *Web:* www.pharmanex.com	Provo	UT	84601	801-345-9800	345-2850
Pharmavite LLC 8510 Balboa Blvd Suite 300 *TF:* 800-423-2405 ■ *Web:* www.vitamin.com	Northridge	CA	91325	818-221-6200	
Phibro Animal Health Corp 65 Challenger Rd 3rd Fl *TF:* 800-223-0434 ■ *Web:* www.phibrochem.com	Ridgefield Park	NJ	07660	201-329-7300	329-7399
Power Organics 301 S Old Stage Rd *TF:* 800-327-1956 ■ *Web:* www.klamathbluegreen.com	Mount Shasta	CA	96067	530-926-6684	926-6685

	City	State	Zip	Phone	Fax
Prolab Nutrition 21411 Prairie St	Chatsworth	CA	91311	818-739-6000	739-6001
TF: 800-776-5221 ■ *Web:* www.prolab.com					
Randal Nutritional Products Inc					
1595 Hampston Way PO Box 7328	Santa Rosa	CA	95407	707-528-1800	528-0924
TF: 800-221-1697 ■ *Web:* www.randalnutritional.com					
Rexall Sundown Inc 851 Broken Sound Pkwy NW	Boca Raton	FL	33487	561-241-9400	
TF: 800-327-0908 ■ *Web:* www.rexallsundown.com					
Santa Cruz Nutritionals 2200 Delaware Ave	Santa Cruz	CA	95060	831-457-3200	460-0610*
**Fax:* Sales ■ *Web:* www.scnutr.com					
Schiff Nutrition International Inc 2002 S 5070 West	Salt Lake City	UT	84104	801-975-5000	436-3444
NYSE: WNI ■ *TF:* 800-453-9542 ■ *Web:* www.weider.com					
Solae Co 4300 Dunkin Ave	Saint Louis	MO	63110	314-659-3000	659-5730*
**Fax:* Cust Svc ■ *TF:* 800-325-7108 ■ *Web:* www.protein.com					
SportPharma Inc 2 Terminal Rd	New Brunswick	NJ	08901	732-545-3130	214-1210
Web: www.sportpharma.com					
Tahitian Noni International 333 W Riverpark Dr	Provo	UT	84604	801-431-6000	234-1007
TF: 800-445-2969 ■ *Web:* www.tahitiannoni.com					
Thayers Natural Pharmaceuticals Inc 20 Catbrier Rd	Westport	CT	06883	203-226-0940	227-8183
TF: 888-842-9371 ■ *Web:* www.thayers.com					
Tishcon Corp 30 New York Ave	Westbury	NY	11590	516-333-3050	997-3660
TF: 800-848-8442 ■ *Web:* www.tishcon.com					
TSN Labs Inc PO Box 38	Midvale	UT	84047	801-261-2252	261-4774
TF: 800-769-7290 ■ *Web:* www.tsn2000.com					
Ultra-Lab Nutrition Inc 7491 N Federal Hwy Suite C5-148	Boca Raton	FL	33487	561-367-1474	367-1707
TF: 800-800-0267 ■ *Web:* www.ultra-lab.com					
USANA Health Sciences Inc 3838 W Parkway Blvd	Salt Lake City	UT	84120	801-954-7100	954-7300
NASDAQ: USNA ■ *TF:* 888-950-9595 ■ *Web:* www.usanahealthsciences.com					
Vitamins Inc 200 E Randolph Dr Suite 5130	Chicago	IL	60601	312-861-0700	861-0708
Web: www.vitamins-inc.com					
Wachters' Organic Sea Products Corp 550 Sylvan St	Daly City	CA	94014	650-757-9851	757-9858
TF: 800-682-7100 ■ *Web:* www.wachters.com					
Wakunaga of America Co Ltd 23501 Madero	Mission Viejo	CA	92691	949-855-2776	458-2764
TF: 800-421-2998 ■ *Web:* www.kyolic.com					
Windmill Health Products 100 Lehigh Dr	Fairfield	NJ	07004	973-575-6591	882-3256
TF: 800-822-4320 ■ *Web:* www.windmillvitamins.com					
XELR8 Holdings Inc 480 S Holly St	Denver	CO	80246	303-316-8577	316-8078
AMEX: PRH ■ *TF:* 888-935-7808 ■ *Web:* www.xelr8.com					
XELR8 Inc DBA XELR8 Holdings Inc 480 S Holly St	Denver	CO	80246	303-316-8577	316-8078
AMEX: PRH ■ *TF:* 888-935-7808 ■ *Web:* www.xelr8.com					

803 VOCATIONAL & TECHNICAL SCHOOLS

SEE ALSO Children's Learning Centers p. 1445; Colleges & Universities - Four-Year p. 1475; Colleges - Community & Junior p. 1459; Colleges - Culinary Arts p. 1471; Colleges - Fine Arts p. 1472; Language Schools p. 1885; Military Service Academies p. 1970; Universities - Canadian p. 2392

Listings in this category are organized alphabetically by states.

	City	State	Zip	Phone	Fax
Enterprise-Ozark Community College 1975 Ave C	Mobile	AL	36615	251-438-2816	438-2836
Web: www.eocc.edu/mobile/index.htm					
Ozark Aviation 3405 S US Hwy 231	Ozark	AL	36360	334-774-5113	774-6399
Web: www.eocc.edu/ozark/index.htm					
H Councill Trenholm State Technical College					
1225 Air Base Blvd	Montgomery	AL	36108	334-832-9000	420-4206
Web: www.trenholmtech.cc.al.us					
Patterson 3920 Troy Hwy	Montgomery	AL	36116	334-288-1080	420-4201
Web: www.trenholmtech.cc.al.us					
Herzing College Birmingham 280 W Valley Ave	Birmingham	AL	35209	205-916-2800	916-2807*
**Fax:* Admissions ■ *TF:* 800-425-9432 ■ *Web:* www.herzing.edu/birmingham					
ITT Technical Institute Birmingham 6270 Park South Dr	Bessemer	AL	35022	205-497-5700	497-5799
TF: 800-488-7033 ■ *Web:* www.itt-tech.edu					
JF Drake State Technical College 3421 Meridian St N	Huntsville	AL	35811	256-539-8161	539-6439
TF: 888-413-7253 ■ *Web:* www.drakestate.edu					
Lawson State Community College 3060 Wilson Rd SW	Birmingham	AL	35221	205-925-2515	923-7106*
**Fax:* Admissions ■ *Web:* www.ls.cc.al.us					
Bessemer 1100 9th Ave SW	Bessemer	AL	35022	205-428-6391	929-3605*
**Fax:* Admissions ■ *Web:* www.lawsonstate.edu					
Lurleen B Wallace Community College MacAurthur					
1708 N Main St PO Drawer 910	Opp	AL	36467	334-493-3573	493-7003
Web: www.lbwcc.edu					
Reid State Technical College I-65 & Hwy 83 PO Box 588	Evergreen	AL	36401	251-578-1313	578-5355
TF: 866-578-1313 ■ *Web:* www.rstc.cc.al.us					
Trenholm State Technical College 1225 Air Base Blvd	Montgomery	AL	36108	334-832-9000	420-4206
Web: www.trenholmtech.cc.al.us					
Virginia College					
Birmingham 65 Bagby Dr Suite 100	Birmingham	AL	35209	205-802-1200	943-3940
TF: 877-812-8428 ■ *Web:* www.vc.edu					
Huntsville 2800-A Bob Wallace Ave	Huntsville	AL	35805	256-533-7387	533-7785
TF: 866-314-5635 ■ *Web:* www.vc.edu/huntsville					
Wallace Community College Selma 3000 Earl Goodwin Pkwy	Selma	AL	36703	334-876-9227	876-9250
Web: wccs.edu					
DeVry University Calgary 2700 3rd Ave SE	Calgary	AB	T2A7W4	403-235-3450	207-6225
TF: 800-363-5558 ■ *Web:* www.devry.edu/calgary					
Brown Mackie College 4585 E Speedway Blvd Suite 204	Tucson	AZ	85712	520-327-6866	325-0108
Web: www.edmc.edu					
DeVry University Phoenix 2149 W Dunlap Ave	Phoenix	AZ	85021	602-870-9222	331-1494
TF Cust Svc: 800-528-0250 ■ *Web:* www.phx.devry.edu					
ITT Technical Institute					
Tempe 5005 S Wendler Dr	Tempe	AZ	85282	602-437-7500	437-7505
TF: 800-879-4881 ■ *Web:* www.itt-tech.edu					
Tucson 1455 W River Rd	Tucson	AZ	85704	520-408-7488	292-9899
TF: 800-870-9730 ■ *Web:* www.itt-tech.edu					
Lamson College 1126 N Scottsdale Rd Suite 17	Tempe	AZ	85281	480-898-7000	967-6645
TF: 800-898-7017 ■ *Web:* www.lamsoncollege.com					
RainStar University 8370 E Via De Ventura St Bldg K-100	Scottsdale	AZ	85258	480-423-0375	990-8854
Web: www.rainstaruniversity.com					
Southwest Institute of Healing Arts 1100 E Apache Blvd	Tempe	AZ	85281	480-994-9244	994-3228
TF: 888-504-9106 ■ *Web:* www.swiha.org					
Universal Technical Institute Inc 10695 W Pierce St	Avondale	AZ	85323	623-245-4600	245-4601
NYSE: UTI ■ *TF:* 800-859-1202 ■ *Web:* www.uticorp.com					
Remington College 19 Remington Rd	Little Rock	AR	72204	501-312-0007	225-3819
Web: www.remingtoncollege.edu					
Argosy University Santa Monica 3910 31st St	Santa Monica	CA	90405	310-866-4000	452-2950
TF: 866-505-0332 ■ *Web:* www.argosyu.edu					
Bryan College of Court Reporting					
3580 Wilshire Blvd Suite 4000	Los Angeles	CA	90010	213-484-8850	483-3936
TF: 877-484-8850 ■ *Web:* www.bryancollege.edu					
Concorde Career Colleges					
Garden Grove 12951 Euclid St Suite 101	Garden Grove	CA	92840	714-703-1900	530-4737
Web: www.concordecareercolleges.com/garden					
North Hollywood 12412 Victory Blvd	North Hollywood	CA	91606	818-766-8151	766-1587
TF: 800-852-8434 ■ *Web:* www.concordecareercolleges.com/hollywood					
San Bernardino 201 E Airport Dr Suite A	San Bernardino	CA	92408	909-884-8891	384-1768
TF: 800-852-8434 ■ *Web:* www.concordecareercolleges.com/sanbern					
San Diego 4393 Imperial Ave Suite 100	San Diego	CA	92113	619-688-0800	220-4177
Web: www.concordecareercolleges.com/sandiego					
DeVry University					
Fremont 6600 Dumbarton Cir	Fremont	CA	94555	510-574-1200	742-0866*
**Fax:* Admissions ■ *TF:* 888-201-9941 ■ *Web:* www.fre.devry.edu					
Long Beach 3880 Kilroy Airport Way	Long Beach	CA	90806	562-997-5422	997-5371*
**Fax:* Admissions ■ *TF:* 800-597-1333 ■ *Web:* www.lb.devry.edu					
Pomona 901 Corporate Center Dr University Center	Pomona	CA	91768	909-622-9800	868-4165
TF: 800-243-3660 ■ *Web:* www.pom.devry.edu					
West Hills 22801 Roscoe Blvd	West Hills	CA	91304	818-713-8111	713-8118
Web: www.devry.edu					
Everest College					
Alhambra 2215 W Mission Rd	Alhambra	CA	91803	626-979-4940	979-4960
TF: 800-722-7337 ■ *Web:* www.everest.edu					
Anaheim 511 N Brookhurst Suite 300	Anaheim	CA	92801	714-953-6500	953-4163
Web: www.everest.edu					
City of Industry 12801 Crossroads Parkway S	City of Industry	CA	91746	562-908-2500	908-7656
TF: 866-463-4997 ■ *Web:* www.everest.edu					
Los Angeles 3000 S Robertson Blvd Suite 300	Los Angeles	CA	90034	310-840-5777	287-2344
Web: www.everest.edu					
San Bernardino 217 Club Center Dr Suite A	San Bernardino	CA	92408	909-777-3300	777-3313
Web: www.everest.edu					
San Jose 1245 S Winchester Blvd Suite 102	San Jose	CA	95128	408-246-4171	557-9874
TF: 877-246-4124 ■ *Web:* www.everest.edu					
Golden Gate University					
Monterey Bay 500 8th St	Marina	CA	93933	831-884-0900	884-0913
Web: www.ggu.edu					
Roseville 7 Sierra Gate Plaza Suite 101	Roseville	CA	95678	916-648-1446	780-2797
Web: www.ggu.edu					
San Francisco 536 Mission St	San Francisco	CA	94105	415-442-7000	442-7807*
**Fax:* Admissions ■ *TF:* 800-448-4968 ■ *Web:* www.ggu.edu					
San Jose 50 Airport Pkwy Suite 150	San Jose	CA	95110	408-573-7300	573-0890
Web: www.ggu.edu					
Heald College					
Concord 5130 Commercial Cir	Concord	CA	94520	925-288-5800	288-5896
TF: 800-755-3550 ■ *Web:* www.heald.edu					
Fresno 255 W Bullard Ave	Fresno	CA	93704	559-438-4222	438-0948*
**Fax:* Admissions ■ *TF:* 800-284-0844 ■ *Web:* www.heald.edu					
Hayward 25500 Industrial Blvd	Hayward	CA	94545	510-783-2100	783-3287
TF: 800-884-3253 ■ *Web:* www.heald.edu					
Rancho Cordova 2910 Prospect Park Dr	Rancho Cordova	CA	95670	916-638-1616	853-8282
Web: www.heald.edu					
Roseville 7 Sierra Gate Plaza	Roseville	CA	95678	916-789-8600	789-8616
TF: 800-884-3253 ■ *Web:* www.heald.edu					
Salinas 1450 N Main St	Salinas	CA	93906	831-443-1700	443-1050
TF: 800-755-3550 ■ *Web:* www.heald.edu					
San Francisco 350 Mission St	San Francisco	CA	94102	415-808-3000	808-3005*
**Fax:* Admissions ■ *Web:* www.heald.edu					
San Jose 341 Great Mall Pkwy	Milpitas	CA	95035	408-934-4900	934-7777
TF: 800-884-3253 ■ *Web:* www.heald.edu					
Stockton 1605 E March Ln	Stockton	CA	95210	209-473-5200	477-2739
TF: 800-884-3253 ■ *Web:* www.heald.edu					
ITT Technical Institute					
Anaheim 525 N Muller Ave	Anaheim	CA	92801	714-535-3700	535-1802
Web: www.itt-tech.edu					
Lathrop 16916 S Harlan Rd	Lathrop	CA	95330	209-858-0077	858-0277*
**Fax:* Admissions ■ *TF:* 800-346-1786 ■ *Web:* www.itt-tech.edu					
Oxnard 2051 Solar Dr Suite 150	Oxnard	CA	93036	805-988-0143	988-1813
TF: 800-530-1582 ■ *Web:* www.itt-tech.edu					
Rancho Cordova 10863 Gold Center Dr	Rancho Cordova	CA	95670	916-851-3900	851-9225
TF: 800-488-8466 ■ *Web:* www.itt-tech.edu					
San Bernardino 670 E Carnegie Dr	San Bernardino	CA	92408	909-806-4600	806-4699
TF: 800-888-3801 ■ *Web:* www.itt-tech.edu					
San Diego 9680 Granite Ridge Dr	San Diego	CA	92123	858-571-8500	571-1277
TF: 800-883-0380 ■ *Web:* www.itt-tech.edu					
San Dimas 650 W Cienega Ave	San Dimas	CA	91773	909-971-2300	971-2350
TF: 800-414-6522 ■ *Web:* www.itt-tech.edu					
Sylmar 12669 Encinitas Ave	Sylmar	CA	91342	818-364-5151	364-5150
TF: 800-363-2086 ■ *Web:* www.itt-tech.edu					
Torrance 20050 S Vermont Ave	Torrance	CA	90502	310-380-1555	380-1557
Web: www.itt-tech.edu					
National Institute of Technology Long Beach					
2161 Technology Pl	Long Beach	CA	90810	562-624-9530	432-3721
Web: www.nitschools.com					
National Polytechnic College of Engineering & Oceaneering					
272 S Fries Ave	Wilmington	CA	90744	310-834-2501	834-7132*
**Fax:* Admissions ■ *TF:* 800-432-3483 ■ *Web:* www.natpoly.edu					
Shasta College 11555 Old Oregon Trail	Redding	CA	96049	530-225-4600	225-4995
Web: www.shastacollege.edu					
West Orange College 12541 Brookhurst St Suite 104	Garden Grove	CA	92840	714-530-5000	530-5003*
**Fax:* Admissions ■ *Web:* www.westorangecollege.com					
Westwood College					
Inland Empire 20 W 7th St	Upland	CA	81786	909-931-7550	931-9195
Web: www.westwood.edu					
Los Angeles 3250 Wilshire Blvd Suite 400	Los Angeles	CA	90010	213-739-9999	382-2468*
**Fax:* Admissions ■ *TF:* 877-377-4600 ■ *Web:* www.westwood.edu					
Wyotech					
Fremont 200 Whitney Pl	Fremont	CA	94539	510-490-6900	490-8599
Web: www.wyotech.com					
Oakland 9636 Earhart Rd	Oakland	CA	94621	510-569-8436	635-3936
Web: www.wyotech.com					
Sacramento 980 Riverside Pkwy	West Sacramento	CA	95605	916-376-8888	239-0060*
**Fax Area Code:* 877 ■ *TF:* 877-433-8800 ■ *Web:* www.wyotech.com					
Bel-Rea Institute of Animal Technology 1681 S Dayton St	Denver	CO	80247	303-751-8700	751-9969
TF: 800-950-8001 ■ *Web:* www.bel-rea.com					
Colorado Technical University Denver					
5775 Denver Tech Center Blvd Suite 100	Greenwood Village	CO	80111	303-694-6600	694-6673
TF: 866-888-5616 ■ *Web:* www.ctudenver.com					
Concorde Career Colleges Denver 111 N Havana St	Aurora	CO	80010	303-861-1151	839-5478
Web: www.concordecareercolleges.com/denver					
Denver Academy of Court Reporting					
9051 Harlan St Suite 20	Westminster	CO	80031	303-427-5292	427-5383
Web: www.dacr.org					
DeVry University					
Colorado Springs 1175 Kelly Johnson Blvd	Colorado Springs	CO	80920	719-632-3000	866-6770
TF: 877-691-3002 ■ *Web:* www.devry.edu					
Denver 6312 S Fiddlers Green Circle Suite 150	Englewood	CO	80111	303-329-3000	329-4486
TF: 877-773-3879 ■ *Web:* www.devry.edu					
Everest College 1815 Jet Wing Dr	Colorado Springs	CO	80916	719-638-6580	638-6818
Web: everest-college.com					

	City	State	Zip	Phone	Fax
Aurora 14280 E Jewell Ave Suite 100 Web: www.everest.edu	Aurora	CO	80012	303-745-6244	745-6245
Thornton 9065 Grant St TF: 800-611-2101 ■ Web: www.everest.edu	Thornton	CO	80229	303-457-2757	457-4030
ITT Technical Institute Thornton 500 E 84th Ave TF: 800-395-4488 ■ Web: www.itt-tech.edu	Thornton	CO	80229	303-288-4488	288-8166
Jones International University Ltd 9697 E Mineral Ave *Fax: Admissions ■ TF: 800-811-5663 ■ Web: www.jonesinternational.edu	Centennial	CO	80112	303-784-8200	799-0966*
Lincoln College of Technology 460 S Lipan St TF: 800-347-3232 ■ Web: www.lincolnedu.com/campus/denver-co	Denver	CO	80223	303-722-5724	778-8264
Westwood College					
Aviation Technology - Denver 10851 W 120th Ave TF: 888-889-3505 ■ Web: www.westwood.edu	Broomfield	CO	80021	303-466-1714	469-3797
Denver 7350 N Broadway TF: 800-992-5050 ■ Web: www.westwood.edu	Denver	CO	80221	303-650-5050	426-1832
North Denver 7350 N Broadway TF: 800-992-5050 ■ Web: www.westwood.edu	Denver	CO	80221	303-426-7000	426-1832
Gibbs College Norwalk 10 Norden Pl TF: 800-845-5333 ■ Web: www.gibbsnorwalk.edu	Norwalk	CT	06855	203-838-4173	899-0788
International College of Hospitality Management 1760 Mapleton Ave TF: 800-955-0809 ■ Web: www.ichm.edu	Suffield	CT	06078	860-668-3515	668-7369
Delaware Technical & Community College					
Owens PO Box 610 Web: www.dtcc.edu/owens	Georgetown	DE	19947	302-856-5400	855-5961
Stanton 400 Stanton-Christiana Rd *Fax: Admissions ■ Web: www.dtcc.edu/stanton-wilmington	Newark	DE	19713	302-454-3900	453-3084*
Terry 100 Campus Dr Web: www.dtcc.edu/terry	Dover	DE	19904	302-857-1000	857-1094
Acupuncture & Massage College 10506 N Kendall Dr *Fax: Admissions ■ Web: www.amcollege.edu	Miami	FL	33176	305-595-9500	595-2622*
Argosy University Tampa 4401 W Himes Ave Suite 150 TF: 800-850-6488 ■ Web: www.argosyu.edu	Tampa	FL	33614	813-393-5290	874-1989
ATI Health Education Center 1395 NW 167th St Suite 200 TF: 800-275-2725	Miami	FL	33169	305-628-1000	628-1461
Brown Mackie College Miami 1501 Biscayne Blvd *Fax: Admissions ■ TF: 866-505-0335 ■ Web: www.brownmackie.edu	Miami	FL	33132	305-341-6600	428-5836*
Concorde Career Colleges Jacksonville 7960 Arlington Expy Web: www.concordecareercolleges.com/jacksonville	Jacksonville	FL	32211	904-725-0525	721-9944
Concorde Career Institute					
Lauderdale Lakes 4000 N SR-7 Web: www.concordecareercolleges.com/lauderdale	Lauderdale Lakes	FL	33319	954-731-8880	485-2961
Tampa 4202 W Spruce St Web: www.concordecareercolleges.com/tampa	Tampa	FL	33607	813-874-0094	872-6884
Crane Institute of America Inc 3880 St Johns Pkwy TF: 800-832-2726 ■ Web: www.craneinstitute.com	Sanford	FL	32771	407-322-6800	330-0660
DeVry University					
Miramar 2300 SW 145th Ave Web: www.devry.edu	Miramar	FL	33027	954-499-9800	499-9730
Orlando 4000 Millenia Blvd *Fax: Admissions ■ TF: 888-857-5757 ■ Web: www.devry.edu	Orlando	FL	32839	407-370-3131	370-3198*
First Coast Technical Institute 2980 Collins Ave TF: 866-462-3284 ■ Web: www.fcti.org	Saint Augustine	FL	32084	904-824-4401	824-6750
Florida Metropolitan University					
Brandon 3924 Coconut Palm Dr *Fax: Admissions ■ TF: 877-338-0068 ■ Web: www.fmu.edu	Tampa	FL	33619	813-621-0041	628-0919*
Jacksonville 8226 Phillips Hwy TF: 800-611-2101 ■ Web: www.fmu.edu	Jacksonville	FL	32256	904-731-4949	731-0599
Lakeland 995 E Memorial Blvd Suite 110 Web: www.fmu.edu	Lakeland	FL	32256	863-686-1444	688-9881
Melbourne 2401 N Harbor City Blvd Web: www.fmu.edu	Melbourne	FL	32935	321-253-2929	255-2017
North Orlando 5421 Diplomat Cir *Fax: Admissions ■ TF: 800-628-5870 ■ Web: www.fmu.edu	Orlando	FL	32810	407-628-5870	628-1344*
Orange Park 805 Wells Rd Web: www.fmu.edu	Orange Park	FL	32073	904-264-9122	264-9952
Pinellas 2471 McMullen Booth Rd Suite 200 TF: 800-353-3687 ■ Web: www.fmu.edu	Clearwater	FL	33759	727-725-2688	725-3827
Pompano Beach 225 N Federal Hwy TF: 800-468-0168 ■ Web: www.fmu.edu	Pompano Beach	FL	33062	954-783-7339	783-7964
South Orlando 9200 Southpark Center Loop TF: 800-611-2101 ■ Web: www.fmu.edu	Orlando	FL	32819	407-851-2525	851-1477
Tampa 3319 W Hillsborough Ave TF: 877-225-0009 ■ Web: www.fmu.edu	Tampa	FL	33614	813-879-6000	871-2483
Florida Technical College 12689 Challenger Pkwy Suite 130 TF: 888-678-2929 ■ Web: www.flatech.edu	Orlando	FL	32826	407-447-7300	447-7301
Full Sail Real World Education 3300 University Blvd Suite 160 TF: 800-226-7625 ■ Web: www.fullsail.com	Winter Park	FL	32792	407-679-6333	678-0070
Herzing College Winter Park 1595 S Semoran Blvd Suite 1501 TF: 800-492-1664 ■ Web: www.herzing.edu	Winter Park	FL	32792	407-478-0500	478-0501
ITT Technical Institute					
Fort Lauderdale 3401 S University Dr TF: 800-488-7797 ■ Web: www.itt-tech.edu	Fort Lauderdale	FL	33328	954-476-9300	476-6889
Jacksonville 6600 Youngerman Cir Suite 10 TF: 800-318-1264 ■ Web: www.itt-tech.edu	Jacksonville	FL	32244	904-573-9100	573-0512
Miami 7955 NW 12th St Suite 119 *Fax: Admissions ■ Web: www.itt-tech.edu	Miami	FL	33126	305-477-3080	477-7561*
Tampa 4809 Memorial Hwy TF: 800-825-2831 ■ Web: www.itt-tech.edu	Tampa	FL	33634	813-885-2244	888-8451
Kaplan University 6301 Kaplan University Ave *Fax Area Code: 888 ■ TF: 866-527-5268 ■ Web: www.kaplan.edu/ku	Fort Lauderdale	FL	33309	954-515-3000	243-9880*
Keiser College Melbourne 900 S Babcock St Web: www.keisercollege.edu	Melbourne	FL	32901	321-409-4800	725-3766
Keiser University					
Daytona Beach 1800 Business Park Blvd Web: www.keiseruniversity.edu	Daytona Beach	FL	32114	386-274-5060	274-2725
Fort Lauderdale 1500 NW 49th St *Fax: Admissions ■ TF: 800-749-4456 ■ Web: www.keisercollege.edu	Fort Lauderdale	FL	33309	954-776-4456	351-4043*
Sarasota 6151 Lake Osprey Dr TF: 866-534-7372 ■ Web: www.keisercollege.edu	Sarasota	FL	34240	941-907-3900	907-2016
Lincoln College of Technology 2410 Metro Centre Blvd TF: 800-826-9986 ■ Web: www.lincolncollegeoftechnology.com	West Palm Beach	FL	33407	561-842-8324	842-9503
Remington College					
Jacksonville 7011 AC Skinner Pkwy Suite 140 Web: www.remingtoncollege.edu	Jacksonville	FL	32256	904-296-3435	296-9097
Largo 8550 Ulmerton Rd Suite 100 TF: 888-900-2343 ■ Web: www.remingtoncollege.edu	Largo	FL	33771	727-532-1999	530-7710
Tampa 2410 E Busch Blvd TF: 800-992-4850 ■ Web: www.remingtoncollege.edu	Tampa	FL	33612	813-935-5700	935-7415
Stenotype Institute of Jacksonville 3986 Boulevard Center Dr Bldg 1200 Suite 200 TF: 800-273-5090 ■ Web: www.stenotypeinstitute.net	Jacksonville	FL	32207	904-398-4141	398-7878
Wackenhut Training Institute 4200 Wackenhut Dr Suite 100 TF: 800-506-6265	Palm Beach Gardens	FL	33410	561-622-5656	691-6700
Athens Technical College 800 US Hwy 29 N Web: www.athenstech.edu	Athens	GA	30601	706-355-5000	369-5756
Augusta Technical College 3200 Augusta Tech Dr *Fax: Admissions ■ Web: www.augustatech.edu	Augusta	GA	30906	706-771-4000	771-4034*
Bauder College 384 N Yards Blvd NW Suite 190 *Fax: Admissions ■ TF: 800-241-3797 ■ Web: www.bauder.edu	Atlanta	GA	30313	404-237-7573	237-1619*
Brown College of Court Reporting & Medical Transcription 1740 Peachtree St NW TF: 800-849-0703 ■ Web: www.browncollege.com	Atlanta	GA	30309	404-876-1227	876-4415
Brown Mackie College Atlanta 6600 Peachtree Dunwoody NE 600 Embassy Row Suite 130 Web: www.brownmackie.edu	Atlanta	GA	30328	770-510-2310	
Central Georgia Technical College 3300 Macon Tech Dr TF: 866-430-0135 ■ Web: www.centralgatech.edu	Macon	GA	31206	478-757-3400	757-3454
Columbus Technical College 928 Manchester Expy Web: www.columbustech.org	Columbus	GA	31904	706-649-1800	649-1804
DeVry University Georgia 250 N Arcadia Ave *Fax: Admissions ■ TF: 800-221-4771 ■ Web: www.atl.devry.edu	Decatur	GA	30030	404-292-7900	292-7011*
Gupton-Jones College of Funeral Service 5141 Snapfinger Woods Dr TF: 800-848-5352 ■ Web: www.gupton-jones.edu	Decatur	GA	30035	770-593-2257	593-1891
Herzing College Atlanta 3393 Peachtree Rd Suite 1003 TF: 800-573-4533 ■ Web: www.herzing.edu/atlanta	Atlanta	GA	30326	404-816-4533	816-5576
ITT Technical Institute Kennesaw 1000 Cobb Place Blvd NW Web: www.itt-tech.edu	Kennesaw	GA	30144	770-426-2300	426-2350
Savannah Technical College 5717 White Bluff Rd TF: 800-769-6362 ■ Web: www.savannahtech.edu	Savannah	GA	31405	912-443-5700	443-5705
Westwood College Atlanta Northlake 2309 Parklake Dr NE *Fax Area Code: 770 ■ Web: www.westwood.edu	Atlanta	GA	30345	404-962-2999	934-9539*
Argosy University Miami 1001 Bishop St 400 ASB Tower TF: 888-323-2777 ■ Web: www.argosy.edu/	Honolulu	HI	96813	808-536-5555	536-5505
Heald College Honolulu 1500 Kapiolani Blvd *Fax: Admissions ■ TF: 800-940-0530 ■ Web: www.heald.edu	Honolulu	HI	96814	808-955-1500	955-6964*
Remington College Honolulu 1111 Bishop St Suite 400 Web: www.remingtoncollege.edu	Honolulu	HI	96813	808-942-1000	533-3064
Eastern Idaho Technical College 1600 S 25th E TF: 800-662-0261 ■ Web: www.eitc.edu	Idaho Falls	ID	83404	208-524-3000	525-7026
ITT Technical Institute Boise 12302 W Explorer Dr TF: 800-666-4888 ■ Web: www.itt-tech.edu	Boise	ID	83713	208-322-8844	322-0173
Brown Mackie College Moline 1527 47th Ave Web: www.brownmackie.edu	Moline	IL	61265	309-762-2100	762-2374
DeVry University					
Addison 1221 N Swift Rd TF: 800-346-5420 ■ Web: www.devry.edu/addison	Addison	IL	60101	630-953-1300	543-2196
Chicago 3300 N Campbell Ave *Fax: Admissions ■ Web: www.chi.devry.edu	Chicago	IL	60618	773-929-8500	697-2710*
Tinley Park 18624 W Creek Dr Web: www.devry.edu	Tinley Park	IL	60477	708-342-3300	
Gem City College 700 State St Web: www.gemcitycollege.com	Quincy	IL	62301	217-222-0391	222-1557
ITT Technical Institute					
Burr Ridge 7040 High Grove Blvd TF: 877-488-0001 ■ Web: www.itt-tech.edu	Burr Ridge	IL	60527	630-455-6470	455-6476
Matteson 600 Holiday Plaza Dr Web: www.itt-tech.edu	Matteson	IL	70443	708-747-2571	747-0023
Mount Prospect 1401 Feehanville Dr Web: www.itt-tech.edu	Mount Prospect	IL	60056	847-375-8800	375-9022
Lexington College 310 S Peoria St Suite 512 *Fax: Admissions ■ Web: www.lexingtoncollege.edu	Chicago	IL	60607	312-226-6294	226-6405*
MacCormac College 29 E Madison Ave Web: www.maccormac.edu	Chicago	IL	60602	312-922-1884	922-4286
Midstate College 411 W Northmoor Rd TF: 800-251-4299 ■ Web: www.midstate.edu	Peoria	IL	61614	309-692-4092	692-3893
Morrison Institute of Technology 701 Portland Ave Web: www.morrison.tec.il.us	Morrison	IL	61270	815-772-7218	772-7584
Northwestern Business College 4829 N Lipps Ave TF: 888-205-2283 ■ Web: www.northwesternbc.edu	Chicago	IL	60630	773-777-4220	777-2861
Westwood College					
O'Hare Airport 8501 W Higgins Rd Suite 100 TF: 877-877-8857 ■ Web: www.westwood.edu	Chicago	IL	60631	773-380-6800	714-0828
River Oaks 80 River Oaks Center Suite 111 Web: www.westwood.edu	Calumet City	IL	60409	708-832-1988	832-9623
Worsham College of Mortuary Science 495 Northgate Pkwy Web: www.worshamcollege.com	Wheeling	IL	60090	847-808-8444	808-8493
Brown Mackie College					
Fort Wayne 3000 E Coliseum Blvd TF: 866-433-2289 ■ Web: www.brownmackie.edu	Fort Wayne	IN	46805	260-484-4400	484-2678
Merrillville 1000 E 80th Pl Suite 101N TF: 800-258-3321 ■ Web: www.brownmackie.edu	Merrillville	IN	46410	219-769-3321	738-1076
Michigan City 325 E US Hwy 20 TF: 800-519-2416 ■ Web: www.brownmackie.edu	Michigan City	IN	46360	219-877-3100	877-3110
South Bend 1030 E Jefferson Blvd TF: 800-743-2447 ■ Web: www.brownmackie.edu	South Bend	IN	46617	574-237-0774	237-3585
College of Court Reporting Inc 111 W 10th St Suite 111 TF: 866-294-3974 ■ Web: www.ccr.edu	Hobart	IN	46342	219-942-1459	942-1631
Indiana Business College 550 E Washington St TF: 800-999-9229 ■ Web: www.ibcschools.edu	Indianapolis	IN	46204	317-264-5656	264-5650
International Business College 5699 Coventry Ln TF: 800-589-6363 ■ Web: www.ibcfortwayne.edu	Fort Wayne	IN	46804	260-459-4500	436-1896
ITT Technical Institute					
Fort Wayne 2810 Dupont Commerce Ct TF: 800-866-4488 ■ Web: www.itt-tech.edu	Fort Wayne	IN	46825	260-497-6200	497-6299
Indianapolis 9511 Angola Ct TF: 800-937-4488 ■ Web: www.itt-tech.edu	Indianapolis	IN	46268	317-875-8640	875-8641
Newburgh 10999 Stahl Rd TF: 800-832-4488 ■ Web: www.itt-tech.edu	Newburgh	IN	47630	812-858-1600	858-0646
Ivy Tech Columbus College Columbus 4475 Central Ave TF: 800-922-4838 ■ Web: www.ivytech.edu/columbus	Columbus	IN	47203	812-372-9925	372-0311
Ivy Tech Community College					
Bloomington 200 Daniels Way TF: 866-447-0700 ■ Web: www.bloomington.ivytech.edu	Bloomington	IN	47404	812-332-1559	330-6106
Central Indiana 50 W Fall Creek Pkwy North Dr TF: 800-732-1470 ■ Web: www.ivytech.edu/Indianapolis	Indianapolis	IN	46208	317-921-4882	921-4753
East Central 4301 S Cowan Rd TF: 800-589-8324 ■ Web: www.ivytech.edu/eastcentral	Muncie	IN	47302	765-289-2291	289-2292
Kokomo 1815 E Morgan St TF: 800-459-0561 ■ Web: www.ivytech.edu/kokomo	Kokomo	IN	46901	765-459-0561	454-5111
Lafayette PO Box 6299 Web: www.laf.ivytech.edu	Lafayette	IN	47903	765-772-9100	772-9214
North Central 220 Dean Johnson Blvd TF: 888-489-3478 ■ Web: www.ivytech.edu/southbend	South Bend	IN	46601	574-289-7001	236-7177
Northeast 3800 N Anthony Blvd TF: 800-859-4882 ■ Web: www.ivytech.edu/fortwayne	Fort Wayne	IN	46805	260-482-9171	480-2053

	City	State	Zip	Phone	Fax
Northwest 1440 E 35th Ave	Gary	IN	46409	219-981-1111	981-4415
TF: 800-843-4882 ■ Web: www.gary.ivytech.edu					
Richmond 2359 Chester Blvd	Richmond	IN	47374	765-966-2656	962-8741
TF: 800-659-4562 ■ Web: www.ivytech.edu/richmond					
Southeast 590 Ivy Tech Dr	Madison	IN	47250	812-265-2579	265-4028
Web: www.ivytech.edu/southeast					
Southern Indiana 8204 Hwy 311	Sellersburg	IN	47172	812-246-3301	246-9905
TF: 800-321-9021 ■ Web: www.ivytech.edu/sellersburg					
Southwest Indiana 3501 N 1st Ave	Evansville	IN	47710	812-426-2865	429-9878
Web: www.ivytech.edu/evansville					
Wabash Valley 7999 S US 41 S	Terre Haute	IN	47802	812-299-1121	299-5723
TF: 800-377-4882 ■ Web: ivytech7.cc.in.us					
Lincoln College of Technology 7225 Winton Dr Bldg 128	Indianapolis	IN	46268	317-632-5553	687-0475
TF: 800-554-4465 ■ Web: www.lincolnedu.com/campus/indianapolis-in					
Mid-America College of Funeral Science					
3111 Hamburg Pike	Jeffersonville	IN	47130	812-288-8878	288-5942
TF: 800-221-6158 ■ Web: www.mid-america.edu					
AIB College of Business 2500 Fleur Dr	Des Moines	IA	50321	515-244-4221	244-6773
TF: 800-444-1921 ■ Web: www.aib.edu					
Western Iowa Tech Community College 4647 Stone Ave	Sioux City	IA	51106	712-274-6400	274-6412
TF: 800-352-4649 ■ Web: www.witcc.com					
Brown Mackie College					
Lenexa 9705 Lenexa Dr	Lenexa	KS	66215	913-768-1900	495-9555
TF: 800-635-9101 ■ Web: www.brownmackie.edu					
Salina 2106 S 9th St	Salina	KS	67401	785-825-5422	827-7623
TF: 800-365-0433 ■ Web: www.brownmackie.com					
Concorde Career Colleges 5800 Foxridge Dr Suite 500	Mission	KS	66202	913-831-9977	831-6556
NASDAQ: CCDC ■ TF: 800-515-1007 ■ Web: www.concorde.edu					
Wichita Area Technical College 301 S Grove St Bldg A	Wichita	KS	67211	316-677-9400	677-9555
TF: 866-296-4031 ■ Web: www.watc.edu					
Bowling Green Technical College 1845 Loop Dr	Bowling Green	KY	42101	270-901-1000	901-1144
Web: www.bowlinggreen.kctcs.edu					
Brown Mackie College					
Hopkinsville 4001 Ft Campbell Blvd	Hopkinsville	KY	42240	270-886-1302	886-3544
TF: 800-359-4753 ■ Web: www.brownmackie.edu					
Louisville 3605 Fern Valley Rd	Louisville	KY	40219	502-968-7191	357-9956
TF: 800-999-7387 ■ Web: www.bmcaec.com					
Northern Kentucky 309 Buttermilk Pike	Fort Mitchell	KY	41017	859-341-5627	341-6483
Web: www.brownmackie.edu					
Daymar College 3361 Buckland Sq	Owensboro	KY	42301	270-926-4040	685-4090
TF: 800-960-4090 ■ Web: www.daymarcollege.edu					
Gateway Community & Technical College					
300 Buttermilk Pike	Fort Mitchell	KY	41017	859-441-4500	426-3385
Web: www.gateway.kctcs.edu					
ITT Technical Institute Louisville 10509 Timberwood Cir	Louisville	KY	40223	502-327-7424	327-7624
TF: 888-790-7427 ■ Web: www.itt-tech.edu					
Louisville Technical Institute 3901 Atkinson Square Dr	Louisville	KY	40218	502-456-6509	456-2341
TF: 800-844-6528 ■ Web: www.louisvilletech.com					
National College Lexington 2376 Sir Barton Way	Lexington	KY	40509	859-253-0621	254-7664
Web: www.ncbt.edu					
National College of Business & Technology					
Danville 115 E Lexington Ave	Danville	KY	40422	859-236-6991	236-1063
Web: www.ncbt.edu					
Florence 7627 Ewing Blvd	Florence	KY	41042	859-525-6510	525-8961
Web: www.ncbt.edu					
Louisville 4205 Dixie Hwy	Louisville	KY	40216	502-447-7634	447-2442
Web: www.ncbt.edu					
Pikeville 50 National College Blvd	Pikeville	KY	41501	606-478-7200	478-7209
TF: 800-664-1886 ■ Web: www.ncbt.edu					
Richmond 125 S Killarney Ln	Richmond	KY	40475	859-623-8956	624-5544
Web: www.ncbt.edu					
Owensboro Community & Technical College					
4800 New Hartford Rd	Owensboro	KY	42303	270-686-4400	686-4496
TF: 866-755-6282 ■ Web: www.octc.kctcs.edu					
Southwestern College Florence 8095 Connector Dr	Florence	KY	41042	859-282-9999	282-7940
Web: www.swcollege.net					
Remington College Lafayette 303 Rue Louis XIV	Lafayette	LA	70508	337-981-4010	983-7130
TF: 800-736-2687 ■ Web: www.remingtoncollege.edu					
Andover College 901 Washington Ave	Portland	ME	04103	207-774-6126	774-1715
TF: 800-639-3110 ■ Web: www.andovercollege.com					
Beal College 99 Farm Rd	Bangor	ME	04401	207-947-4591	947-0208
TF: 800-660-7351 ■ Web: www.bealcollege.edu					
Central Maine Community College 1250 Turner St	Auburn	ME	04210	207-755-5100	755-5493
TF Admissions: 800-891-2002 ■ Web: www.cmcc.edu					
Central Maine Medical Center School of Nursing					
29 Lowell St	Lewiston	ME	04240	207-795-2720	795-2849
Web: www.cmmcson.org					
Eastern Maine Community College 354 Hogan Rd	Bangor	ME	04401	207-974-4600	974-4608
Web: www.emcc.edu					
Northern Maine Community College 33 Edgemont Dr	Presque Isle	ME	04769	207-768-2700	768-2831
Web: www.nmcc.edu					
Southern Maine Community College 2 Fort Rd	South Portland	ME	04106	207-741-5500	741-5760
TF: 877-282-2182 ■ Web: www.smccme.edu					
Broadcasting Institute of Maryland 7200 Harford Rd	Baltimore	MD	21234	410-254-2770	254-5357
TF: 800-942-9246 ■ Web: www.bim.org					
Hagerstown Business College 18618 Crestwood Dr	Hagerstown	MD	21742	301-739-2670	791-7661
TF: 800-422-2670 ■ Web: www.hagerstownbusinesscol.org					
ITT Technical Institute Owings Mills 11301 Red Run Blvd	Owings Mills	MD	21117	443-394-7115	394-7715
TF: 877-411-6782 ■ Web: www.itt-tech.edu					
Maryland Bartending Academy 209 New Jersey Ave NE	Glen Burnie	MD	21060	410-787-0020	787-0402
Web: www.marylandbartending.com					
National Labor College 10000 New Hampshire Ave	Silver Spring	MD	20903	301-431-6400	431-5411
TF: 866-863-7293 ■ Web: www.nlc.edu					
Bay State College 122 Commonwealth Ave	Boston	MA	02116	617-236-8000	536-1735
TF: 800-815-3276 ■ Web: www.baystate.edu					
Benjamin Franklin Institute of Technology 41 Berkeley St	Boston	MA	02116	617-423-4630	482-3706
Web: www.bfit.edu					
Boston Architectural Center 320 Newbury St	Boston	MA	02115	617-262-5000	585-0121*
*Fax: Admissions ■ TF: 877-585-0100 ■ Web: www.the-bac.edu					
FINE Mortuary College LLC 150 Kerry Pl	Norwood	MA	02062	781-762-1211	762-7177
Web: www.fine-ne.com					
Franklin Institute of Technology 41 Berkeley St	Boston	MA	02116	617-423-4630	482-3706
Web: www.bfit.edu					
Gibbs College Boston 126 Newbury St	Boston	MA	02116	617-578-7100	578-7163
TF: 888-309-0444 ■ Web: www.gibbsboston.edu					
ITT Technical Institute Woburn 10 Forbes Rd	Woburn	MA	01801	781-937-8324	937-3402
TF: 800-430-5097 ■ Web: www.itt-tech.edu					
Laboure College 2120 Dorchester Ave	Boston	MA	02124	617-296-8300	296-7947
Web: www.laboure.edu					
New England College of Finance 10 High St Suite 204	Boston	MA	02110	617-951-2350	951-2533
TF: 888-696-6323 ■ Web: www.finance.edu					
Wyotech Bedford 150 Hanscom Dr	Bedford	MA	01730	781-274-8448	274-8490
Web: www.wyotech.com					
Academy of Court Reporting Clawson 1330 W 14-Mile Rd	Clawson	MI	48017	248-435-9030	
Web: www.acr.edu					
Cleary University 3601 Plymouth Rd	Ann Arbor	MI	48105	734-332-4477	332-4646
TF: 800-589-1979 ■ Web: www.cleary.edu					
Livingston 3750 Cleary Dr	Howell	MI	48843	800-686-1883	548-2170*
*Fax Area Code: 517 ■ Web: www.cleary.edu					
Everest Institute 26111 Evergreen Rd Suite 201	Southfield	MI	48076	248-799-9933	799-2912*
*Fax: Admissions ■ TF: 800-611-2101 ■ Web: www.everest-institute.com					
ITT Technical Institute					
Canton 1905 S Haggerty Rd	Canton	MI	48188	734-397-7800	397-1945
TF: 800-247-4477 ■ Web: www.itt-tech.edu					
Grand Rapids 4020 Sparks Dr SE	Grand Rapids	MI	49546	616-956-1060	956-5606
TF: 800-632-4676 ■ Web: www.itt-tech.edu					
Troy 1522 E Big Beaver Rd	Troy	MI	48083	248-524-1800	524-1965
TF: 800-832-6817 ■ Web: www.itt-tech.edu					
Lewis College of Business 17370 Meyers Rd	Detroit	MI	48235	313-862-6300	862-1027*
*Fax: Admissions ■ Web: www.lewiscollege.edu					
Anoka Technical College 1355 W Hwy 10	Anoka	MN	55303	763-576-4700	576-4756*
*Fax: Admissions ■ TF: 800-247-5588 ■ Web: www.ank.tec.mn.us					
Brown College 1440 Northland Dr	Mendota Heights	MN	55120	651-905-3400	905-3540
TF: 800-574-3777 ■ Web: www.browncollege.edu					
Dakota County Technical College 1300 E 145th St	Rosemount	MN	55068	651-423-8000	423-8775
TF: 877-937-3282 ■ Web: www.dctc.edu					
Duluth Business University 4724 Mike Colalilo Dr	Duluth	MN	55807	218-722-4000	628-2127
TF: 800-777-8406 ■ Web: www.dbumn.edu					
Dunwoody College of Technology 818 Dunwoody Blvd	Minneapolis	MN	55403	612-374-5800	374-4128
TF: 800-292-4625 ■ Web: www.dunwoody.edu					
Hennepin Technical College 9000 Brooklyn Blvd	Brooklyn Park	MN	55445	952-995-1300	488-2944*
*Fax Area Code: 763 ■ *Fax: Admissions ■ TF: 800-345-4655 ■ Web: www.hennepintech.edu					
Northwest Technical Institute 950 Blue Gentian Rd Suite 500	Eagan	MN	55121	952-944-0080	944-9274
TF: 800-443-4223 ■ Web: www.nti.edu					
Ridgewater College					
Hutchinson 2 Century Ave SE	Hutchinson	MN	55350	320-587-3636	587-9019*
*Fax: Admissions ■ TF: 800-222-4424 ■ Web: www.ridgewater.edu					
Willmar 2101 15th Ave NW PO Box 1097	Willmar	MN	56201	320-231-5114	231-7677*
*Fax: Admissions ■ TF: 800-722-1151 ■ Web: www.ridgewater.edu					
Saint Cloud Technical College 1540 Northway Dr	Saint Cloud	MN	56303	320-308-5089	308-5981
TF: 800-222-1009 ■ Web: www.sctc.edu					
Saint Paul College 235 Marshall Ave	Saint Paul	MN	55102	651-846-1666	846-1703
TF: 800-227-6029 ■ Web: www.saintpaul.edu					
Virginia College					
Gulf Coast 920 Cedar Lake Rd	Biloxi	MS	39532	228-392-2994	392-2039
TF: 888-208-6932 ■ Web: www.vc.edu/gulfcoast					
Jackson 5360 I-55 N	Jackson	MS	39211	601-977-0960	956-4325
Web: www.vc.edu/jackson					
Concorde Career Colleges Kansas City 3239 Broadway	Kansas City	MO	64111	816-531-5223	756-3231
Web: www.concordecareercolleges.com/kansas					
DeVry University Kansas City 11224 Holmes Rd	Kansas City	MO	64131	816-941-0430	942-8169
TF: 800-821-3766 ■ Web: www.kc.devry.edu					
Everest College 1010 W Sunshine St	Springfield	MO	65807	417-864-7220	864-5697
TF: 800-475-2669 ■ Web: www.everest-college.com					
ITT Technical Institute					
Arnold 1930 Meyer Drury Dr	Arnold	MO	63010	636-464-6600	464-6611
TF: 888-488-1082 ■ Web: www.itt-tech.edu					
Earth City 3640 Corporate Trail Dr	Earth City	MO	63045	314-298-7800	513-5750
TF: 800-235-5488 ■ Web: www.itt-tech.edu					
Kansas City 9150 E 41st Terr	Kansas City	MO	64133	816-276-1400	276-1410
TF: 877-488-1442 ■ Web: www.itt-tech.edu					
Vatterott College 8580 Evans Ave	Berkley	MO	63134	314-264-1500	
Web: www.vatterott-college.com					
Joplin 5898 N Main	Joplin	MO	64801	417-781-5633	781-6437
Web: www.vatterott-college.edu					
Kansas City 8955 E 38th Terr	Kansas City	MO	64129	816-861-1000	861-1400*
*Fax: Admissions ■ TF: 800-466-3997 ■ Web: www.vatterott-college.edu					
Saint Ann 3925 Industrial Dr	Saint Ann	MO	63074	314-428-5900	428-5956
TF: 888-370-7955 ■ Web: www.vatterott-college.edu					
Saint Joseph 3131 Frederick Ave	Saint Joseph	MO	64506	816-364-5399	364-1593
TF: 800-282-5327 ■ Web: www.vatterott-college.edu					
South County 12970 Maurer Industrial Dr	Sunset Hills	MO	63127	314-843-4200	843-1709
TF: 888-828-8376 ■ Web: www.vatterott-college.edu					
Springfield 3850 S Campbell	Springfield	MO	65807	417-831-8116	831-5099*
*Fax: Admissions ■ TF: 866-314-6454 ■ Web: www.vatterott-college.edu					
University of Montana					
College of Technology 909 South Ave W	Missoula	MT	59801	406-243-7811	243-7899
Web: www.cte.umt.edu					
Helena College of Technology 1115 N Roberts St	Helena	MT	59601	406-444-6800	444-6892
TF: 800-241-4882 ■ Web: www.umhelena.edu					
Hamilton College					
Lincoln 1821 K St	Lincoln	NE	68508	402-474-5315	474-0896
TF: 800-742-7738 ■ Web: www.hamiltonlincoln.com					
Omaha 3350 N 90th St	Omaha	NE	68134	402-572-8500	573-1341
TF: 800-642-1456 ■ Web: www.hamiltonomaha.com					
ITT Technical Institute Omaha 9814 M St	Omaha	NE	68127	402-331-2900	452-3512
TF: 800-677-9260 ■ Web: www.itt-tech.edu					
Nebraska College of Technical Agriculture RR 3 Box 23A	Curtis	NE	69025	308-367-4124	367-5203
TF: 800-328-7847 ■ Web: ncta.unl.edu					
Southeast Community College Milford 600 State St	Milford	NE	68405	402-761-2131	761-2324
TF: 800-933-7223 ■ Web: www.southeast.edu					
Vatterott College Omaha 11818 I St	Omaha	NE	68137	402-392-1300	891-9413
TF: 888-886-3856 ■ Web: www.vatterott-college.edu					
ITT Technical Institute Henderson 168 N Gibson Rd	Henderson	NV	89014	702-558-5404	558-5412
TF: 800-488-8459 ■ Web: www.itt-tech.edu					
McIntosh College 23 Cataract Ave	Dover	NH	03820	603-742-1234	743-0060
TF: 800-624-6867 ■ Web: www.mcintoshcollege.edu					
Berkeley College					
Garrett Mountain 44 Rifle Camp Rd	West Paterson	NJ	07424	973-278-5400	278-9141
TF: 800-446-5400 ■ Web: www.berkeleycollege.edu					
Paramus 64 E Midland Ave	Paramus	NJ	07652	201-967-9667	265-6446
TF: 800-446-5400 ■ Web: www.berkeleycollege.edu					
Woodbridge 430 Rahway Ave	Woodbridge	NJ	10601	732-750-1800	750-0652
TF: 800-446-5400 ■ Web: www.berkeleycollege.edu					
DeVry University North Brunswick 630 US Hwy 1	North Brunswick	NJ	08902	732-435-4880	435-4851
TF: 800-333-3879 ■ Web: www.nj.devry.edu					
Divers Academy International 1500 Liberty Pl	Erial	NJ	08081	856-404-6100	404-6104
Web: www.diversacademy.com					
Gibbs College Livingston 630 W Mt Pleasant Ave	Livingston	NJ	07039	973-369-1360	369-1416
TF: 877-442-2765 ■ Web: www.gibbsnj.edu					
Central New Mexico Community College					
525 Buena Vista Dr SE	Albuquerque	NM	87106	505-224-3000	224-3237
Web: www.cnm.edu					
Crownpoint Institute of Technology PO Box 849	Crownpoint	NM	87313	505-786-4100	786-5644
Web: www.cit.cc.nm.us					
ITT Technical Institute Albuquerque 5100 Masthead St NE	Albuquerque	NM	87109	505-828-1114	828-1849
TF: 800-636-1114 ■ Web: www.itt-tech.edu					
Southwestern Indian Polytechnic Institute					
9169 Coors Rd NW PO Box 10146	Albuquerque	NM	87184	505-346-2346	346-2373
TF: 800-586-7474 ■ Web: www.sipi.bia.edu					
American Academy McAllister Institute of Funeral Service					
619 W 54th St 6th Fl	New York	NY	10019	212-757-1190	765-5923
Web: www.funeraleducation.org					

	City	State	Zip	Phone	Fax
Berkeley College					
New York City 3 E 43rd St	New York	NY	10017	212-986-4343	818-1079
TF: 800-446-5400 ■ Web: www.berkeleycollege.edu					
White Plains 99 Church St	White Plains	NY	10601	914-694-1122	328-9469
TF: 800-446-5400 ■ Web: www.berkeleycollege.edu					
Bramson ORT College 69-30 Austin St	Forest Hills	NY	11375	718-261-5800	575-5119
Web: www.bramsonort.org					
Bryant & Stratton College					
Albany 1259 Central Ave	Albany	NY	12205	518-437-1802	437-1048
Web: www.bryantstratton.edu					
Amherst 40 Hazelwood Dr	Amherst	NY	14228	716-691-0012	691-6716*
*Fax: Admissions ■ Web: www.bryantstratton.edu					
Buffalo 465 Main St	Buffalo	NY	14203	716-884-9120	884-0091
Web: www.bryantstratton.edu					
Greece 150 Bellwood Dr	Rochester	NY	14606	585-720-0660	720-9226
Web: www.bryantstratton.edu					
Henrietta 1225 Jefferson Rd	Rochester	NY	14623	585-292-5627	292-6015
Web: www.bryantstratton.edu					
Southtowns 200 Red Tail Dr	Orchard Park	NY	14127	716-677-9500	677-9599
Web: www.bryantstratton.edu					
Syracuse 953 James St	Syracuse	NY	13203	315-472-6603	474-4383
Web: www.bryantstratton.edu					
Syracuse North 8687 Carling Rd	Liverpool	NY	13090	315-652-6500	652-5500
Web: www.bryantstratton.edu					
Cochran School of Nursing 967 N Broadway	Yonkers	NY	10701	914-964-4283	964-4796
Web: www.riversidehealth.org					
College of Westchester 325 Central Ave	White Plains	NY	10606	914-948-4442	948-8015*
*Fax: Admissions ■ TF: 800-333-4924 ■ Web: www.cw.edu					
Commercial Driver Training 600 Patton Ave	West Babylon	NY	11704	631-249-1330	249-0428
Web: www.cdtschool.com					
DeVry University Long Island City 3020 Thomson Ave	Long Island City	NY	11101	718-472-2728	269-4432*
*Fax: Admissions ■ TF: 888-713-3879 ■ Web: www.devry.edu					
Helene Fuld College of Nursing 24 E 120th St	New York	NY	10035	212-616-7200	616-7299
Web: www.helenefuld.edu					
Institute of Design & Construction 141 Willoughby St	Brooklyn	NY	11201	718-855-3661	852-5889
Web: www.idc.edu					
Interboro Institute 450 W 56th St	New York	NY	10019	212-399-0091	246-9614*
*Fax: Admissions ■ Web: www.interboro.com					
ITT Technical Institute					
Albany 13 Airline Dr	Albany	NY	12205	518-452-9300	452-9393
TF: 800-489-1191 ■ Web: www.itt-tech.edu					
Getzville 2295 Millersport Hwy	Getzville	NY	14068	716-689-2200	689-2828
TF: 800-469-7593 ■ Web: www.itt-tech.edu					
Liverpool 235 Greenfield Pkwy	Liverpool	NY	13088	315-461-8000	461-8008
Web: www.itt-tech.edu					
Jamestown Business College 7 Fairmount Ave	Jamestown	NY	14701	716-664-5100	664-3144
Web: www.jbcny.org					
Katharine Gibbs School					
Melville 320 S Service Rd	Melville	NY	11747	631-370-3300	293-1763*
*Fax Area Code: 516 ■ Web: www.gibbsmelville.edu					
New York 50 W 40th St	New York	NY	10018	212-867-9300	973-8379*
*Fax: Admissions ■ TF: 800-843-0738 ■ Web: www.gibbsmelville.edu					
Long Island College Hospital School of Nursing 340 Court St	Brooklyn	NY	11231	718-780-1071	780-1936
Web: www.futurenurselich.org					
Monroe College 2501 Jerome Ave	Bronx	NY	10468	718-933-6700	364-3552*
*Fax: Admissions ■ TF: 800-556-6676 ■ Web: www.monroecollege.edu					
New York Career Institute 11 Park Pl 4th Fl	New York	NY	10007	212-962-0002	385-7574
Web: www.nyci.com					
Olean Business Institute 301 N Union St	Olean	NY	14760	716-372-7978	372-2120
Web: www.obi.edu					
Phillips Beth Israel School of Nursing					
776 Ave of the Americas 4th Fl	New York	NY	10001	212-614-6110	614-6109
Web: www.futurenursebi.org					
Plaza College 74-09 37th Ave	Jackson Heights	NY	11372	718-779-1430	779-7423
Web: www.plazacollege.edu					
Simmons Institute of Funeral Service 1828 South Ave	Syracuse	NY	13207	315-475-5142	475-3817
TF: 800-727-3536 ■ Web: www.simmonsinstitute.com					
TCI College of Technology 320 W 31st St	New York	NY	10001	212-594-4000	330-0891*
*Fax: Admissions ■ TF: 800-878-8246 ■ Web: www.tcicollege.edu					
Technical Career Institute 320 W 31st St	New York	NY	10001	212-594-4000	330-0891*
*Fax: Admissions ■ TF: 800-878-8246 ■ Web: www.tcicollege.edu					
Utica School of Commerce 201 Bleecker St	Utica	NY	13501	315-733-2307	733-9281
TF: 800-321-4872 ■ Web: www.uscny.edu					
Wood Tobe-Coburn School 8 E 40th St	New York	NY	10016	212-686-9040	686-9171
TF: 800-394-9663 ■ Web: www.woodtobecoburn.edu					
Forsyth Technical Community College					
2100 Silas Creek Pkwy	Winston-Salem	NC	27103	336-723-0371	761-2399
Web: www.forsythtech.edu					
South College - Asheville 29 Turtle Creek Dr	Asheville	NC	28803	828-277-5521	277-6151
Web: www.southcollegenc.com					
Stanly Community College 141 College Dr	Albemarle	NC	28001	704-982-0121	982-0819
Web: www.stanly.edu					
United Tribes Technical College 3315 University Dr	Bismarck	ND	58504	701-255-3285	530-0640
Web: www.uttc.edu					
Academy of Court Reporting					
Akron 2930 W Market St	Akron	OH	44333	330-867-4030	867-3432
Web: www.acr.edu					
Cleveland 2044 Euclid Ave	Cleveland	OH	44115	216-861-3222	861-4517
TF: 888-203-7265 ■ Web: www.acr.edu					
Columbus 150 E Gay St	Columbus	OH	43215	614-221-7770	221-8429
Web: www.acr.edu					
Antonelli College 124 E 7th St	Cincinnati	OH	45202	513-241-4338	241-9396
TF: 800-505-4338 ■ Web: www.antonellic.com					
Belmont Technical College 120 Fox Shannon Pl	Saint Clairsville	OH	43950	740-695-9500	695-2247
Web: www.btc.edu					
Bradford School 2469 Stelzer Rd	Columbus	OH	43219	614-416-6200	416-6210*
*Fax: Admissions ■ TF: 800-678-7981 ■ Web: www.bradfordschoolcolumbus.edu					
Brown Mackie College					
Akron 755 White Pond Dr	Akron	OH	44320	330-733-8766	869-3650
Web: www.brownmackie.edu					
Canton 4300 Munson Ave NW	North Canton	OH	44718	330-494-1214	494-8112
Web: www.brownmackie.edu					
Cincinnati 1011 Glendale-Milford Rd	Cincinnati	OH	45215	513-771-2424	771-3413
TF: 800-888-1455 ■ Web: www.brownmackie.edu					
Findlay 1700 Fostoria Ave Suite 100	Findlay	OH	45840	419-423-2211	423-0725
TF: 800-842-3687 ■ Web: www.brownmackie.edu					
Bryant & Stratton College					
Cleveland 1700 E 13th St	Cleveland	OH	44114	216-771-1700	771-7787
Web: www.bryantstratton.edu					
Parma 12955 Snow Rd	Parma	OH	44130	216-265-3151	265-0325
Web: www.bryantstratton.edu					
Willoughby Hills 27557 Chardon Rd	Willoughby Hills	OH	44092	440-944-6800	944-9260
Web: www.bryantstratton.edu					
Central Ohio Technical College 1179 University Dr	Newark	OH	43055	740-366-1351	364-9531
Web: www.cotc.edu					

	City	State	Zip	Phone	Fax
Cincinnati College of Mortuary Science					
645 W North Bend Rd	Cincinnati	OH	45224	513-761-2020	761-3333
TF: 888-377-8433 ■ Web: www.ccms.edu					
Cleveland Institute of Electronics 1776 E 17th St	Cleveland	OH	44114	216-781-9400	781-0331
TF: 800-243-6446 ■ Web: www.cie-wc.edu					
Davis College 4747 Monroe St	Toledo	OH	43623	419-473-2700	473-2472
TF: 800-477-7021 ■ Web: www.daviscollege.edu					
DeVry University Columbus 1350 Alum Creek Dr	Columbus	OH	43209	614-253-7291	253-0843*
*Fax: Admissions ■ TF: 800-426-2206 ■ Web: www.devrycols.edu					
ETI Technical College of Niles 2076 Youngstown-Warren Rd	Niles	OH	44446	330-652-9919	652-4399
Web: eticollege.edu					
Hocking College 3301 Hocking Pkwy	Nelsonville	OH	45764	740-753-3591	753-7065
TF: 877-462-5464 ■ Web: www.hocking.edu					
ITT Technical Institute					
Dayton 3325 Stop Eight Rd	Dayton	OH	45414	937-454-2267	264-7799
TF: 800-568-3241 ■ Web: www.itt-tech.edu					
Norwood 4750 Wesley Ave	Norwood	OH	45212	513-531-8300	531-8368
TF: 800-314-8324 ■ Web: www.itt-tech.edu					
Strongsville 14955 Sprague Rd	Strongsville	OH	44136	440-234-9091	234-7694
TF: 800-331-1488 ■ Web: www.itt-tech.edu					
Warrensville Heights 4700 Richmond Rd	Warrensville Heights	OH	44128	216-896-6500	896-6599
TF: 800-741-3494 ■ Web: www.itt-tech.edu					
Youngstown 1030 N Meridian Rd	Youngstown	OH	44509	330-270-1600	270-8333
TF: 800-832-5001 ■ Web: www.itt-tech.edu					
James A Rhodes State College 4240 Campus Dr	Lima	OH	45804	419-221-1112	221-0450
Web: www.rhodesstate.edu					
Jefferson Community College 4000 Sunset Blvd	Steubenville	OH	43952	740-264-5591	264-1338
TF: 800-682-6553 ■ Web: www.jcc.edu					
Marion Technical College 1467 Mt Vernon Ave	Marion	OH	43302	740-389-4636	389-6136
Web: www.mtc.edu					
Miami-Jacobs Career College 110 N Patterson Blvd	Dayton	OH	45402	937-222-7337	461-3384
TF: 888-461-3384 ■ Web: www.miamijacobs.edu					
North Central State College 2441 Kenwood Circle	Mansfield	OH	44906	419-755-4800	755-4750
TF: 888-755-4899 ■ Web: www.ncstatecollege.edu					
Northwest State Community College 22600 SR-34	Archbold	OH	43502	419-267-5511	267-3688
Web: www.northweststate.edu					
Ohio Institute of Photography & Technology 2029 Edgefield Rd	Dayton	OH	45439	937-294-6155	294-2259
TF: 800-932-9698 ■ Web: www.oipt.com					
Remington College Cleveland 14445 Broadway Ave	Cleveland	OH	44125	216-475-7520	475-6055
Web: www.remingtoncollege.edu					
RETS Tech Center 555 E Alex Bell Rd	Centerville	OH	45459	937-433-3410	435-6516
TF: 800-837-7387 ■ Web: www.retstechcenter.com					
Southwestern College					
Dayton 111 W 1st St	Dayton	OH	45402	937-224-0061	224-0065
Web: www.swcollege.net					
Franklin 201 E 2nd St	Franklin	OH	45005	937-746-6633	746-6754
Web: www.swcollege.net					
Tri-county 149 Northland Blvd	Cincinnati	OH	45246	513-874-0432	874-1330
Web: www.swcollege.net					
Stark State College of Technology 6200 Frank Ave NW	North Canton	OH	44720	330-494-6170	497-6313
TF: 800-797-8275 ■ Web: www.starkstate.edu					
University of Northwestern Ohio 1441 N Cable Rd	Lima	OH	45805	419-227-3141	229-6926
Web: www.unoh.edu					
Zane State College 1555 Newark Rd	Zanesville	OH	43701	740-454-2501	454-0035
TF: 800-686-8324 ■ Web: www.zanestate.edu					
Oklahoma State University Okmulgee 1801 E 4th St	Okmulgee	OK	74447	918-293-4678	293-4650
TF: 800-722-4471 ■ Web: www.osu-okmulgee.edu					
Spartan College of Aeronautics & Technology 8820 E Pine St	Tulsa	OK	74115	918-836-6886	831-5287
TF Admissions: 800-331-1204 ■ Web: www.spartan.edu					
Heald College Portland 625 SW Broadway 2nd Fl	Portland	OR	97205	503-229-0492	229-0498
TF: 800-432-5344 ■ Web: www.heald.edu					
ITT Technical Institute Portland 6035 NE 78th Ct	Portland	OR	97218	503-255-6500	255-8381
TF: 800-234-5488 ■ Web: www.itt-tech.edu					
American College 270 S Bryn Mawr Ave	Bryn Mawr	PA	19010	610-526-1000	526-1300*
*Fax: Admissions ■ TF: 888-263-7265 ■ Web: www.theamericancollege.edu					
Aviation Institute of Maintenance 3001 Grant Ave	Philadelphia	PA	19114	215-676-7700	671-0566
Web: www.aviationmaintenance.edu					
Berean Institute 1901 W Girard Ave	Philadelphia	PA	19130	215-763-4833	236-6011
Web: www.bereaninstitute.edu					
Cambria-Rowe Business College 221 Central Ave	Johnstown	PA	15902	814-536-5168	536-5160
Web: www.crbc.net					
Central Pennsylvania College College Hill Rd	Summerdale	PA	17093	717-732-0702	732-5254
TF: 800-759-2727 ■ Web: www.centralpenn.edu					
CHI Institute					
Broomall 1991 Sproul Rd Suite 42	Broomall	PA	19008	610-353-7630	359-1370
Web: www.chitraining.com					
Southampton 520 Street Rd	Southampton	PA	18966	215-357-5100	357-4212
TF: 866-357-5100 ■ Web: www.chitraining.com					
Dean Institute of Technology 1501 W Liberty Ave	Pittsburgh	PA	15226	412-531-4433	531-4435
Web: www.deantech.edu					
DeVry University Fort Washington 1140 Virginia Dr	Fort Washington	PA	19034	215-591-5700	591-5745
Web: www.devry.edu					
DuBois Business College 1 Beaver Dr	Du Bois	PA	15801	814-371-6920	371-3974
TF: 800-692-6213 ■ Web: www.dbcollege.com					
Education Direct 925 Oak St	Scranton	PA	18515	570-961-4033	343-8462
Web: www.educationdirect.com					
Erie Business Center					
Erie 246 W 9th St	Erie	PA	16501	814-456-7504	456-4882
TF: 800-352-3743 ■ Web: www.eriebc.com					
New Castle 170 Cascade Galleria	New Castle	PA	16101	724-658-9066	658-3083
TF: 800-722-6227 ■ Web: www.eriebc.com					
Everest Institute 100 Forbes Ave Suite 1200	Pittsburgh	PA	15222	412-261-4520	261-4546
TF: 888-279-3314 ■ Web: www.everest-institute.com/					
ITT Technical Institute					
Bensalem 3330 Tillman Dr	Bensalem	PA	19020	215-244-8871	244-8872
TF: 866-488-8324 ■ Web: www.itt-tech.edu					
King of Prussia 760 Moore Rd	King of Prussia	PA	19406	610-491-8004	491-9047
TF: 866-902-8324 ■ Web: www.itt-tech.edu					
Mechanicsburg 5020 Louise Dr	Mechanicsburg	PA	17055	717-691-9263	691-9273
TF: 800-847-4756 ■ Web: www.itt-tech.edu					
Pittsburgh 10 Parkway Center	Pittsburgh	PA	15220	412-937-9150	937-9425
TF: 800-353-8324 ■ Web: www.itt-tech.edu					
Johnson College 3427 N Main Ave	Scranton	PA	18508	570-342-6404	348-2181*
*Fax: Admissions ■ TF: 800-293-9675 ■ Web: www.johnson.edu					
Kaplan Career Institute 5650 Derry St	Harrisburg	PA	17111	717-558-1300	
TF: 800-272-4632					
ICM Campus 10 Wood St	Pittsburgh	PA	15222	412-261-2647	261-0998
TF: 800-441-5222					
Lansdale School of Business 201 Church Rd	North Wales	PA	19454	215-699-5700	699-8770
Web: www.lsbonline.com					
Lehigh Valley College 2809 E Saucon Valley Rd	Center Valley	PA	18034	610-791-5100	791-7810
TF: 888-330-6999 ■ Web: www.lehighvalley.edu					
Lincoln Technical Institute 5151 Tilghman St	Allentown	PA	18104	610-398-5301	395-2706
TF: 877-533-2592 ■ Web: www.lincolntech.com/c_allentown_pa.php					
Lincoln Technical Institute 9191 Torresdale Ave	Philadelphia	PA	19136	215-335-0800	335-1443
TF: 877-606-6581 ■ Web: www.lincolntech.com/c_philadelphia_pa.php					

Phone *Fax*

McCann School of Business & Technology 47 S Main St ..... Mahanoy City PA 17948 570-773-1820 773-0483
Web: www.mccannschool.com
Mixology Wine Institute 77 W Broad St. ..... Bethlehem PA 18018 610-814-2900
Web: www.mixologywine.com
Newport Business Institute
Lower Burrell 945 Greensburg Rd ..... Lower Burrell PA 15068 724-339-7542 339-2950
TF: 800-752-7695 ■ Web: www.nbi.edu
Williamsport 941 W 3rd St ..... Williamsport PA 17701 570-326-2869 326-2136
TF: 800-962-6971 ■ Web: www.newportbusiness.com
Penn Commercial Inc 242 Oak Spring Rd ..... Washington PA 15301 724-222-5330 222-4722
TF: 888-309-7484 ■ Web: www.penncommercial.edu
Pennco Tech 3815 Otter St ..... Bristol PA 19007 215-824-3200 785-1945
TF: 800-575-9399 ■ Web: www.penncotech.com
Pennsylvania College of Technology 1 College Ave ..... Williamsport PA 17701 570-326-3761 321-5551
TF Admissions: 800-367-9222 ■ Web: www.pct.edu
Pennsylvania Institute of Technology 800 Manchester Ave ..... Media PA 19063 610-892-1500 892-1533*
*Fax: Admissions ■ TF: 800-422-0025 ■ Web: www.pit.edu
Pittsburgh Institute of Aeronautics PO Box 10897 ..... Pittsburgh PA 15236 412-346-2100 466-0513
TF: 800-444-1440 ■ Web: www.pia.edu/aviation/
Pittsburgh Institute of Mortuary Science Inc
5808 Baum Blvd ..... Pittsburgh PA 15206 412-362-8500 362-1684
TF: 800-933-5808 ■ Web: www.pims.edu
Pittsburgh Technical Institute 1111 McKee Rd ..... Oakdale PA 15071 412-809-5100 809-5121*
*Fax: Admissions ■ TF: 800-905-9985 ■ Web: www.pti.edu
Thaddeus Stevens College of Technology 750 E King St ..... Lancaster PA 17602 717-299-7701 391-6929
TF: 800-842-3832 ■ Web: www.stevenstech.org
Triangle Tech Inc 1940 Perrysville Ave ..... Pittsburgh PA 15214 412-359-1000 359-1012
TF: 800-874-8324 ■ Web: www.triangle-tech.edu
Du Bois PO Box 551 ..... Du Bois PA 15801 814-371-2090 371-9227
TF: 800-874-8324 ■ Web: www.triangle-tech.com
Erie 2000 Liberty St ..... Erie PA 16502 814-453-6016 454-2818
TF: 800-874-8324 ■ Web: www.triangle-tech.com
Greensburg 222 E Pittsburgh St ..... Greensburg PA 15601 724-832-1050 834-0325
TF: 800-533-4224 ■ Web: www.triangle-tech.com
Welder Training & Testing Institute 1144 N Graham St ..... Allentown PA 18109 610-820-9551 820-0271
TF: 800-223-9884 ■ Web: www.welderinstitute.com
Williamson Free School of Mechanical Trades
106 S New Middletown Rd ..... Media PA 19063 610-566-1776 566-6502
Web: www.williamson.edu
Wyotech Blairsville 500 Innovation Dr ..... Blairsville PA 15717 724-459-9500 459-6499
Web: www.wyotech.com
New England Institute of Technology 2500 Post Rd ..... Warwick RI 02886 401-467-7744 738-5122
TF: 800-736-7744 ■ Web: www.neit.edu
Central Carolina Technical College 506 N Guignard Dr ..... Sumter SC 29150 803-778-1961 778-6696
Web: www.sum.tec.sc.us
Denmark Technical College 500 Solomon Blatt Blvd ..... Denmark SC 29042 803-793-5175 793-5942*
*Fax: Admissions ■ Web: www.denmarktech.edu
Florence-Darlington Technical College 2715 W Lucas St ..... Florence SC 29501 843-661-8324 661-8041
TF: 800-228-5745 ■ Web: www.fdtc.edu
Horry-Georgetown Technical College 2050 Hwy 501 E ..... Conway SC 29526 843-347-3186 347-4207
Web: www.hgtc.edu
Myrtle Beach 743 Hemlock Ave ..... Myrtle Beach SC 29577 843-477-0808 477-0775
Web: www.hgtc.edu/campusesnmb.htm
ITT Technical Institute Greenville
6 Independence Pointe Independence Corporate Park ..... Greenville SC 29615 864-288-0777 297-0930
TF: 800-932-4488 ■ Web: www.itt-tech.edu
Piedmont Technical College 620 N Emerald Rd ..... Greenwood SC 29646 864-941-8324 941-8555
TF: 800-868-5528 ■ Web: www.ptc.edu
Spartanburg Technical College PO Box 4386 ..... Spartanburg SC 29305 864-592-4800 592-4564
TF: 866-591-3700 ■ Web: www.stcsc.edu
Technical College of the Lowcountry 921 Ribaut Rd ..... Beaufort SC 29901 843-525-8324 525-8285
TF: 800-768-8252 ■ Web: www.tclonline.org
Tri-County Technical College PO Box 587 ..... Pendleton SC 29670 864-646-8361 646-1890*
*Fax: Admissions ■ Web: www.tctc.edu
Trident Technical College 7000 Rivers Ave PO Box 118067 ..... Charleston SC 29423 843-574-6111 574-6483*
*Fax: Admissions ■ TF: 877-349-7184 ■ Web: www.tridenttech.edu
Southeast Technical Institute 2320 N Career Ave ..... Sioux Falls SD 57107 605-367-8355 367-4372*
*Fax: Admissions ■ TF: 800-247-0789 ■ Web: www.southeasttech.com
Concorde Career Colleges Memphis
5100 Poplar Ave Suite 132 ..... Memphis TN 38137 901-761-9494 761-3293
TF: 800-464-1212 ■ Web: www.concordecareercolleges.com/memphis
Draughons Junior College 340 Plus Park Blvd ..... Nashville TN 37217 615-361-7555 367-2736
TF: 866-888-9070 ■ Web: www.draughons.edu
Fountainhead College of Technology 3203 Tazewell Pike ..... Knoxville TN 37918 865-688-9422 688-2419
TF: 888-218-7335 ■ Web: www.fountainheadcollege.edu
Gupton John A College 1616 Church St ..... Nashville TN 37203 615-327-3927 321-4518
Web: www.guptoncollege.com
ITT Technical Institute
Cordova 7260 Goodlett Farms Pkwy ..... Cordova TN 38016 901-381-0200 381-0299
TF: 866-444-5141 ■ Web: www.itt-tech.edu
Knoxville 10208 Technology Dr ..... Knoxville TN 37932 865-671-2800 671-2811
TF: 800-671-2801 ■ Web: www.itt-tech.edu
Nashville 2845 Elm Hill Pike ..... Nashville TN 37214 615-889-8700 872-7209
TF: 800-331-8386 ■ Web: www.itt-tech.edu
John A Gupton College 1616 Church St ..... Nashville TN 37203 615-327-3927 321-4518
Web: www.guptoncollege.com
Nashville State Community College 120 White Bridge Rd ..... Nashville TN 37209 615-353-3333 353-3243*
*Fax: Admissions ■ TF: 800-272-7363 ■ Web: www.nscc.edu
National College of Business & Technology
Bristol 1328 Hwy 11 W ..... Bristol TN 37620 423-878-4440 793-1060
Web: www.ncbt.edu
Nashville 3748 Nolensville Rd ..... Nashville TN 37211 615-333-3344 333-3429
TF: 800-986-1800 ■ Web: www.ncbt.edu
Northeast State Technical Community College
2425 Hwy 75 PO Box 246 ..... Blountville TN 37617 423-323-3191 279-7636
TF: 800-836-7822 ■ Web: www.nstcc.cc.tn.us
Remington College Memphis 2710 Nonconnah Blvd ..... Memphis TN 38132 901-345-1000 396-8310
Web: www.remingtoncollege.edu
South College 3904 Lonas Dr ..... Knoxville TN 37909 865-251-1800 584-7339
Web: www.southcollegetn.edu
Aviation Institute of Maintenance Houston
8880 Telephone Rd ..... Houston TX 77061 713-645-4444 644-0902
TF: 888-349-5387 ■ Web: www.aviationmaintenance.edu
Concorde Career Colleges Arlington
601 Ryan Plaza Dr Suite 200 ..... Arlington TX 76011 817-261-1594 461-3443
Web: www.concordecareercolleges.com/arlington
Court Reporting Institute of Dallas
1341 W Mockingbird Ln Suite 200-E ..... Dallas TX 75247 214-350-9722 631-0143
TF: 866-382-1284 ■ Web: www.crid.com
Court Reporting Institute of Houston
13101 Northwest Fwy Suite 100 ..... Houston TX 77040 713-996-8300 996-8360
TF: 866-996-8300 ■ Web: www.crid.com/html/houston/houstoncampus.html
Dallas Institute of Funeral Service 3909 S Buckner Blvd ..... Dallas TX 75227 214-388-5466 388-0316
TF: 800-235-5444 ■ Web: www.dallasinstitute.edu

Phone *Fax*

DeVry University
Houston 11125 Equity Dr ..... Houston TX 77041 713-973-3000 896-7650*
*Fax: Admissions ■ TF: 866-703-3879 ■ Web: www.devry.edu
Irving 4800 Regent Blvd ..... Irving TX 75063 972-929-6777 929-6778
TF: 800-633-3879 ■ Web: www.dal.devry.edu
Everest Institute San Antonio 6550 First Park Ten Blvd ..... San Antonio TX 78213 210-732-7800 731-9313*
*Fax: Admissions ■ TF: 800-327-8765 ■ Web: www.everest-institute.com
ITT Technical Institute
Arlington 551 Ryan Plaza Dr ..... Arlington TX 76011 817-794-5100 275-8446*
*Fax: Admissions ■ TF: 888-288-4950 ■ Web: www.itt-tech.edu
Austin 6330 Hwy 290 E Suite 150 ..... Austin TX 78723 512-467-6800 467-6677
TF: 800-431-0677 ■ Web: www.itt-tech.edu
Houston 15651 North Fwy ..... Houston TX 77090 281-873-0512 873-0518*
*Fax: Admissions ■ TF: 800-879-6486 ■ Web: www.itt-tech.edu
Richardson 2101 Waterview Pkwy ..... Richardson TX 75080 972-690-9100 690-0853
TF: 888-488-5761 ■ Web: www.itt-tech.edu
San Antonio 5700 Northwest Pkwy ..... San Antonio TX 78249 210-694-4612 694-4651*
*Fax: Admissions ■ TF: 800-880-0570 ■ Web: www.itt-tech.edu
Iverson Business School & Court Reporting
1600 E Pioneer Pkwy Suite 200 ..... Arlington TX 76010 817-274-6465 548-7607
Web: www.iversonschool.edu
Remington College
Dallas 1800 Eastgate Dr ..... Garland TX 75041 972-686-7878 686-5116
Web: www.remingtoncollege.edu
Fort Worth 300 E Loop 820 ..... Fort Worth TX 76112 817-451-0017 496-1257
TF: 800-336-6668 ■ Web: www.remingtoncollege.edu
South Texas Vocational Technical Institute
2419 E Haggar Ave ..... Weslaco TX 78596 956-969-1564 969-1887
TF: 888-279-3556 ■ Web: www.stvt.edu
Virginia College Austin 6301 E Hwy 290 ..... Austin TX 78723 512-371-3500 371-3502
TF: 888-420-2048 ■ Web: www.vc.edu/austin
Wade College 1950 Stemmons Fwy Suite 2026 ..... Dallas TX 75207 214-637-3530 637-0827
TF: 800-624-4850 ■ Web: www.wadecollege.edu
Westwood College
Dallas 8390 LBJ Fwy ..... Dallas TX 75243 214-570-0100 570-2229*
*Fax: Admissions ■ TF: 800-803-3140 ■ Web: www.westwood.edu
Fort Worth 4232 North Fwy ..... Fort Worth TX 76137 817-547-9600 547-9602*
*Fax: Admissions ■ TF: 866-553-9998 ■ Web: www.westwood.edu
ITT Technical Institute Murray 920 W Levoy Dr ..... Murray UT 84123 801-263-3313 263-3497
TF: 800-365-2136 ■ Web: www.itt-tech.edu
Latter Day Saints Business College 95 N 300 West ..... Salt Lake City UT 84101 801-524-8100 524-1900
TF: 800-999-5767 ■ Web: www.ldsbc.edu
Sterling College PO Box 72 ..... Craftsbury Common VT 05827 802-586-7711 586-2596
TF: 800-648-3591 ■ Web: www.sterlingcollege.edu
Vermont Technical College PO Box 500 ..... Randolph Center VT 05061 802-728-1445 728-1321
TF: 800-442-8821 ■ Web: www.vtc.vsc.edu
AKS Massage School 462 Herndon Pkwy Suite 208 ..... Herndon VA 20170 703-464-0333
TF: 877-306-3422 ■ Web: www.aksmassageschool.com
Bryant & Stratton College
Richmond 8141 Hull St Rd ..... Richmond VA 23235 804-745-2444 745-6884
TF: 800-735-2420 ■ Web: www.bryantstratton.edu
Virginia Beach 301 Center Point Dr ..... Virginia Beach VA 23462 757-499-7900 499-9977
Web: www.bryantstratton.edu
DeVry University Crystal City 2450 Crystal Dr ..... Arlington VA 22202 703-414-4000 414-4040
Web: www.devry.edu
Everest College 1430 Spring Hill Rd Suite 200 ..... McLean VA 22102 703-288-3131 288-3757
Web: www.everest.edu
ITT Technical Institute
Norfolk 863 Glenrock Rd Suite 100 ..... Norfolk VA 23502 757-466-1260 466-7630
TF: 888-253-8324 ■ Web: www.itt-tech.edu
Richmond 300 Gateway Centre Pkwy ..... Richmond VA 23235 804-330-4992 330-4993
TF: 888-330-4888 ■ Web: www.itt-tech.edu
Springfield 7300 Boston Blvd ..... Springfield VA 22153 703-440-9535 440-9561
TF: 866-817-8324 ■ Web: www.itt-tech.edu
Jefferson College of Health Sciences
920 S Jefferson St PO Box 13186 ..... Roanoke VA 24031 540-985-8483 224-6703
TF: 888-985-8483 ■ Web: www.jchs.edu
National College of Business & Technology
Bluefield 100 Logan St ..... Bluefield VA 24605 276-326-3621 322-5731
Web: www.ncbt.edu
Charlottesville 1819 Emmet St ..... Charlottesville VA 22901 434-295-0136 979-8061
Web: www.ncbt.edu
Danville 336 Old Riverside Dr ..... Danville VA 24540 434-793-6822 793-3634
Web: www.ncbt.edu
Harrisonburg 51 B Burgess Rd ..... Harrisonburg VA 22801 540-432-0943 432-1133
Web: www.ncbt.edu
Lynchburg 104 Candlewood Court ..... Lynchburg VA 24502 434-239-3500 239-3948
Web: www.ncbt.edu
Martinsville 10 Church St ..... Martinsville VA 24114 276-632-5621 632-7915
Web: www.ncbt.edu
Roanoke Valley 1813 E Main St ..... Salem VA 24153 540-986-1800 444-4198
TF: 800-664-1886 ■ Web: www.ncbt.edu
Westwood College Arlington Ballston 1901 N Fort Myer Dr ..... Arlington VA 22209 703-243-3900 243-1644
Web: www.westwood.edu
DeVry University Federal Way 3600 S 344th Way ..... Federal Way WA 98001 253-943-2800 943-3291*
*Fax: Admissions ■ TF: 877-923-3879 ■ Web: www.devry.edu
Highline Community College 2400 S 240th St ..... Des Moines WA 98198 206-878-3710
Web: www.highline.edu
ITT Technical Institute
Seattle 12720 Gateway Dr Suite 100 ..... Seattle WA 98168 206-244-3300 246-7635
TF: 800-422-2029 ■ Web: www.itt-tech.edu
Spokane 13518 E Indiana Ave ..... Spokane WA 99216 509-926-2900 926-2908
TF: 800-777-8324 ■ Web: www.itt-tech.edu
Everest Institute 5514 Big Tyler Rd ..... Cross Lanes WV 25313 304-776-6290 776-6262
Web: www.everest.edu
Huntington Junior College 900 5th Ave ..... Huntington WV 25701 304-697-7550 697-7554
TF: 800-344-4522 ■ Web: www.huntingtonjuniorcollege.com
West Virginia Junior College 176 Thompson Dr ..... Bridgeport WV 26330 304-842-4007 842-8191
Web: www.wvjc.com
Charleston 1000 Virginia St E ..... Charleston WV 25301 304-345-2820 345-1425
TF: 800-924-5208 ■ Web: www.wvjc.com
Morgantown 148 Willey St ..... Morgantown WV 26505 304-296-8282 581-6990
Web: www.wvjc.com
Blackhawk Technical College 6004 Prairie Rd ..... Janesville WI 53547 608-756-4121 743-4407
Web: www.blackhawk.edu
Bryant & Stratton College Milwaukee
310 W Wisconsin Ave Suite 500-E ..... Milwaukee WI 53203 414-276-5200 276-3930
Web: www.bryantstratton.edu
Chippewa Valley Technical College 620 W Clairemont Ave ..... Eau Claire WI 54701 715-833-6200 833-6470
TF: 800-547-2882 ■ Web: www.cvtc.edu
Fox Valley Technical College
1825 N Bluemound Dr PO Box 2277 ..... Appleton WI 54912 920-735-5600 735-2484
TF: 800-735-3882 ■ Web: www.fvtc.edu
Gateway Technical College 3520 30th Ave ..... Kenosha WI 53144 262-564-2200 564-2201
TF: 800-247-7122 ■ Web: www.gtc.edu

	City	State	Zip	Phone	Fax
Herzing College Madison 5218 E Terrace Dr	Madison	WI	53718	608-249-6611	249-8593*
**Fax:* Admissions ■ *TF:* 800-582-1227 ■ *Web:* www.herzing.edu/madison					
ITT Technical Institute Greenfield 6300 W Layton Ave	Greenfield	WI	53220	414-282-9494	282-9698
Web: www.itt-tech.edu					
Lakeshore Technical College 1290 North Ave	Cleveland	WI	53015	920-693-1000	693-3561
TF: 800-443-2129 ■ *Web:* www.gotoltc.com					
Madison Area Technical College 3550 Anderson St	Madison	WI	53704	608-246-6100	246-6880
TF: 800-322-6282 ■ *Web:* matcmadison.edu/matc					
Mid-State Technical College 500 32nd St N	Wisconsin Rapids	WI	54494	715-422-5444	422-5440
TF: 888-575-6782 ■ *Web:* www.mstc.edu					
Milwaukee Area Technical College 700 W State St	Milwaukee	WI	53233	414-297-6600	297-7990
TF: 800-720-6282 ■ *Web:* www.matc.edu					
Moraine Park Technical College 235 N National Ave	Fond du Lac	WI	54935	920-922-8611	924-3421
TF: 800-472-4554 ■ *Web:* www.morainepark.edu					
Northcentral Technical College 1000 W Campus Dr	Wausau	WI	54401	715-675-3331	675-9776
TF: 888-682-7144 ■ *Web:* www.ntc.edu					
Northeast Wisconsin Technical College 2740 W Mason St	Green Bay	WI	54307	920-498-5400	498-6882
TF: 800-422-6982 ■ *Web:* www.nwtc.edu					
Southwest Wisconsin Technical College 1800 Bronson Blvd	Fennimore	WI	53809	608-822-3262	822-6019
TF: 800-362-3322 ■ *Web:* www.swtc.edu					
Waukesha County Technical College 800 Main St	Pewaukee	WI	53072	262-691-5275	695-3460
Web: www.wctc.edu					
Western Wisconsin Technical College 304 6th St N	La Crosse	WI	54602	608-785-9200	
TF: 800-322-9982 ■ *Web:* www.wwtc.edu					
Wisconsin Indianhead Technical College					
Ashland Campus 2100 Beaser Ave	Ashland	WI	54806	715-682-4591	682-8040
TF: 800-243-9482 ■ *Web:* www.witc.edu/ash					
New Richmond Campus 1019 S Knowles Ave	New Richmond	WI	54017	715-246-6561	246-2777
TF: 800-243-9482 ■ *Web:* www.witc.edu/nrich					
Rice Lake Campus 1900 College Dr	Rice Lake	WI	54868	715-234-7082	234-5172
TF: 800-243-9482 ■ *Web:* www.witc.edu/rlake					
Superior Campus 600 N 21 St	Superior	WI	54880	715-394-6677	394-3771
TF: 800-243-9482 ■ *Web:* www.witc.edu/sup					
WyoTech 4373 N 3rd St	Laramie	WY	82072	307-742-3776	742-4354
TF: 800-521-7158 ■ *Web:* www.wyotech.com					

804 VOTING SYSTEMS & SOFTWARE

	City	State	Zip	Phone	Fax
Avante International Technology Inc					
70 Washington Rd	Princeton Junction	NJ	08550	609-799-8896	799-9308
Web: www.aitechnology.com					
Diebold Inc 5995 Mayfair Rd	North Canton	OH	44720	330-490-4000	
NYSE: DBD ■ *TF:* 800-999-3600 ■ *Web:* www.diebold.com					
Election Data Corp 29751 Valley Center Rd	Valley Center	CA	92082	760-751-1131	751-1141
Web: www.inkavote.com					
Election Data Direct Inc PO Box 302021	Escondido	CA	92030	760-751-9900	751-9901
TF: 800-233-9953 ■ *Web:* www.eddvote.com					
Election Services Corp 70 Trade Zone Ct	Ronkonkoma	NY	11779	516-248-4200	248-4770
Election Systems & Software Inc 11208 John Galt Blvd	Omaha	NE	68137	402-593-0101	593-8107
TF: 800-247-8683 ■ *Web:* www.essvote.com					
Election Works Inc 3N840 Trotter Ln	Saint Charles	IL	60175	630-377-1973	377-9268
TF: 888-619-0500 ■ *Web:* www.electionworks.com					
Elections USA Inc 1927 E Saw Mill Rd	Quakertown	PA	18951	215-538-0779	538-3283
TF: 800-789-8683 ■ *Web:* www.electionsusainc.com					
Fidlar Technologies 4450 48th Ave Ct	Rock Island	IL	61201	309-794-3200	794-3201
TF: 800-747-4600 ■ *Web:* www.fidlar.com					
Guardian Voting Systems 1675 Delany Rd	Gurnee	IL	60031	800-888-9527	662-6633*
**Fax Area Code:* 847 ■ *TF:* 800-888-9527 ■ *Web:* www.controls-online.com/gvs					
Hart InterCivic 15500 Wells Port Dr PO Box 80649	Austin	TX	78708	512-252-6400	831-1485*
**Fax Area Code:* 800 ■ *TF:* 800-223-4278 ■ *Web:* www.hartintercivic.com					
MicroVote General Corp 6366 Guilford Ave	Indianapolis	IN	46220	317-257-4900	254-3269
TF: 800-257-4901 ■ *Web:* www.microvote.com					
Sequoia Voting Systems 7677 Oak Port St Suite 800	Oakland	CA	94621	510-875-1200	875-1226
Web: www.sequoiavote.com					
UniLect Corp PO Box 3026	Danville	CA	94526	925-833-8660	833-8874
Web: www.unilect.com					

805 WALLCOVERINGS

	City	State	Zip	Phone	Fax
Blue Mountain Wallcoverings Inc 15 Akron Rd	Toronto	ON	M8W1T3	416-251-1678	251-8968
TF: 800-219-2424 ■ *Web:* www.ihdg.com					
Butler Printing & Laminating Inc					
250 Hamburg Tpke PO Box 836	Butler	NJ	07405	973-838-8550	838-1767
TF: 800-524-0786 ■ *Web:* www.butlerprinting.com					
F Schumacher & Co 79 Madison Ave	New York	NY	10016	212-213-7900	213-7848
TF: 800-523-1200 ■ *Web:* www.fschumacher.com					
Fashion Wallcoverings 4005 Carnegie Ave	Cleveland	OH	44103	216-432-1600	432-0800
TF Orders: 800-362-9930 ■ *Web:* www.fashionwallcoverings.com					
Goldcrest Wallcoverings 1526 New Scotland Rd	Slingerlands	NY	12159	518-478-7214	478-7216
TF: 800-535-9513 ■ *Web:* www.wallcovering.com					
Hunter & Co of North Carolina Inc 1945 W Green Dr	High Point	NC	27261	336-883-4161	889-3270
TF: 800-523-8387 ■ *Web:* www.hunterwallpaper.com					
J Josephson Inc 35 Horizon Blvd	South Hackensack	NJ	07606	201-440-7000	440-7109*
**Fax:* Cust Svc ■ *Web:* www.jjosephson.com					
Seabrook Wallcoverings Inc 1325 Farmville Rd	Memphis	TN	38122	901-320-3500	320-3673*
**Fax:* Cust Svc ■ *TF:* 800-238-9152 ■ *Web:* www.seabrookwallcoverings.com					
Sellers & Josephson Inc 111 Commerce Rd	Carlstadt	NJ	07072	201-567-1353	567-8179
TF: 800-274-3385					
Thibaut Inc 480 Frelinghuysen Ave	Newark	NJ	07114	973-643-1118	643-3050
TF: 800-223-0704 ■ *Web:* www.thibautdesign.com					
Warner Wallcoverings 9201 W Belmont Ave	Franklin Park	IL	60131	847-737-8000	737-0089
TF: 800-621-1143 ■ *Web:* www.thewarnerco.com					
York Wallcoverings Inc 750 Linden Ave PO Box 5166	York	PA	17405	717-846-4456	843-5624
TF: 800-453-9281 ■ *Web:* www.yorkwall.com					

806 WAREHOUSING & STORAGE

SEE ALSO Logistics Services (Transportation & Warehousing) p. 1918

806-1 Commercial Warehousing

	City	State	Zip	Phone	Fax
Acme Distribution Centers Inc 18101 E Colfax Ave	Aurora	CO	80011	303-340-2100	340-2424
TF: 800-444-3614 ■ *Web:* www.acmedistribution.com					
American Warehouses Inc 1918 Collingsworth St	Houston	TX	77009	713-228-6381	228-5913
Web: www.americanwarehouses.com					
ArchivesOne 1625 Straits Tpke Suite 211	Middleburg	CT	06762	203-757-7654	757-7894
Web: www.archivesone.com					
Columbian Distribution Services Inc 900 Hall St SW	Grand Rapids	MI	49503	616-514-6000	514-5990
TF: 888-609-8542 ■ *Web:* www.columbian.us					
D & D Distribution Services Inc 789 Kings Mill Rd	York	PA	17403	717-845-1646	846-0414
Web: www.dd-dist.com					
Dart Warehouse Corp 1430 S Eastman Ave	Los Angeles	CA	90023	323-264-1011	
TF: 800-963-3278 ■ *Web:* www.dartentities.com					
Day Willis Storage Co 4100 Bennett Rd PO Box 676	Toledo	OH	43697	419-476-8000	476-1087
DD Jones Transfer & Warehouse Co Inc 2115 Portlock Rd	Chesapeake	VA	23324	757-494-0200	494-0204
TF: 800-335-4787 ■ *Web:* www.ddjones.com					
Dependable Distribution Services Inc 1301 Union Ave	Pennsauken	NJ	08110	856-665-1700	488-6332
Distribution Technology Inc 1701 Continental Blvd	Charlotte	NC	28273	704-588-2867	588-6831
Web: www.distributiontechnology.com					
Dixie Warehouse Services 6001 National Tpke PO Box 36158	Louisville	KY	40233	502-368-6564	366-6133
Web: www.dixiewarehouse.com					
Edler & Co Inc 3500 Oakton St	Skokie	IL	60076	847-675-1900	675-2042
Elston-Richards Inc 3701 Patterson Ave SE	Grand Rapids	MI	49512	616-698-2698	698-8090
Web: www.elstonrichards.com					
Evans Distribution Systems 18765 Seaway Dr	Melvindale	MI	48122	313-388-3200	388-0136
TF: 888-361-9850 ■ *Web:* www.evansdist.com					
Federal Warehouse Co 101 National Rd	East Peoria	IL	61611	309-694-4500	282-0442
TF: 800-747-4100					
File Keepers LLC 6277 E Slauson Ave	Los Angeles	CA	90040	323-728-3151	728-1349
TF: 800-332-3453 ■ *Web:* www.filekeepers.com					
Gulf Compress 201 N 19th St	Corpus Christi	TX	78408	361-882-5489	882-8081
Web: www.gulfcompress.com					
Hansen Storage Co 2880 N 112th St	Milwaukee	WI	53222	414-476-9221	476-0646
Web: www.hansenstorage.com					
Hartford Despatch Moving & Storage Inc 225 Prospect St	East Hartford	CT	06108	860-528-9551	282-1224
TF: 800-678-9000 ■ *Web:* www.hartforddespatch.com					
Hollister Moving & Storage PO Box 1987	Hollister	CA	95024	831-637-6250	636-5029
TF: 800-696-6250					
Holman Distribution Center of Oregon Inc 2300 SE Beta St	Milwaukie	OR	97222	503-652-1912	652-1970
Web: www.holmandc.com					
Iron Mountain 745 Atlantic Ave	Boston	MA	02111	800-935-6966	350-7881*
NYSE: IRM ■ **Fax Area Code:* 617 ■ *TF:* 800-899-4766 ■ *Web:* www.ironmountain.com					
Jones DD Transfer & Warehouse Co Inc 2115 Portlock Rd	Chesapeake	VA	23324	757-494-0200	494-0204
TF: 800-335-4787 ■ *Web:* www.ddjones.com					
Keller Transfer/Commerce Distribution Center					
31750 Enterprise Dr	Livonia	MI	48151	734-458-5116	458-9103
TF: 800-933-0950 ■ *Web:* www.krclogistics.com					
Kenco Group Inc 2001 Riverside Dr	Chattanooga	TN	37406	423-756-5552	756-1529
TF: 800-365-7189 ■ *Web:* www.kencogroup.com					
Linden Warehouse & Distribution Co Inc 1300 Lower Rd	Linden	NJ	07036	908-862-1400	862-1526
Web: www.lindenwarehouse.com					
Mid-West Terminal Warehouse Co Inc					
1700 N Universal Ave	Kansas City	MO	64120	816-231-8811	231-0020
Web: www.mwtco.com					
Murphy Warehouse Co 701 24th Ave SE	Minneapolis	MN	55414	612-623-1200	623-9108
Web: www.murphywarehouse.com					
National Terminals Corp 250 S Northwest Hwy Suite 300	Park Ridge	IL	60668	847-655-7700	655-7701
Pacific Coast Warehouse Service Inc 5125 Schaefer Ave	Chino	CA	91710	909-590-1743	
Web: www.pcwc.com					
Recall Corp 1 Recall Center 180 Technology Pkwy	Norcross	GA	30092	770-776-1200	
TF: 888-732-2556 ■ *Web:* www.recall.com					
Robinson Terminal Warehouse Corp 2 Duke St	Alexandria	VA	22314	703-836-8300	836-8307
TF: 800-331-6593 ■ *Web:* www.robinsonterminal.com					
Security Storage Co 1701 Florida Ave NW	Washington	DC	20009	202-234-5600	234-3513
TF: 800-736-6825 ■ *Web:* www.sscw.com					
SOPAKCO Inc 102 Coile St	Greeneville	TN	37745	423-639-1163	639-7270
Web: www.sopakco.com					
Southern Warehousing & Distribution LP					
3232 N Pan Am Expy	San Antonio	TX	78219	210-224-7771	226-9485
Web: www.southernwd.com					
Southern Warehousing & Distribution Ltd					
102 W Pineloch Ave Suite 10	Orlando	FL	32806	407-859-3550	859-4307
Web: www.southernwarehouse.com					
Tejas Logistics System 324 Pleasant St	Waco	TX	76704	254-752-9241	752-8950
TF: 800-535-9786 ■ *Web:* www.tejaswarehouse.com					
Willis Day Storage Co 4100 Bennett Rd PO Box 676	Toledo	OH	43697	419-476-8000	476-1087

806-2 Refrigerated Storage

	City	State	Zip	Phone	Fax
American Growers Cooling Co 1569 Abbott St PO Box 10100	Salinas	CA	93912	831-753-6555	757-3233
Atlas Cold Storage 1731 Morrow St PO Box 220	Green Bay	WI	54305	920-468-8311	468-0210
Web: www.atlascold.com/					
Berkshire Refrigerated Warehousing 4550 S Packers Ave	Chicago	IL	60609	773-254-2424	254-5141
Burris Logistics 501 SE 5th St	Milford	DE	19963	302-839-4531	839-5175
TF: 800-805-8135 ■ *Web:* www.burrislogistics.com					
Genesee Valley Cold Storage Co					
40 Lackawanna Ave PO Box 250	Mount Morris	NY	14510	585-658-3322	658-3427
Merchants Terminal Corp 501 N Kresson St	Baltimore	MD	21224	410-342-9300	522-1163
Web: www.merchantsterminal.com					
Mid-Florida Freezer Warehouses Ltd					
9025 N Atlantic Ave	Port Canaveral	FL	32920	321-783-9623	783-5513
Web: www.mffreezer.com					
New Orleans Cold Storage & Warehouse Co Inc					
3411 Jourdan Rd	New Orleans	LA	70126	504-944-4400	944-8539
TF: 800-782-2653 ■ *Web:* www.nocs.com					
Perley-Halladay Assoc Inc 1442 Phoenixville Pike	West Chester	PA	19380	610-296-5800	647-1711
TF: 800-248-5800 ■ *Web:* www.perleyhalladay.com					
Reddy Ice & Cassco Refrigerated Services					
610 Pleasant Valley Rd PO Box 548	Harrisonburg	VA	22801	540-433-2751	433-7870
TF: 800-999-4231 ■ *Web:* www.reddyice.com					
Total Logistic Control 8300 Logistic Dr	Zeeland	MI	49464	616-772-9009	772-1407*
**Fax:* Sales ■ *TF:* 800-333-5599 ■ *Web:* www.totallogistic.com					
United Freezer & Storage Co 650 N Meridian Rd	Youngstown	OH	44509	330-792-1739	792-2299
Web: www.unitedfreezer.com					

Refrigerated Storage (Cont'd)

Phone Fax

US Cold Storage Inc 100 Dobbs Ln Suite 102 .... Cherry Hill NJ 08034 856-354-8181 354-8199
Web: www.uscoldstorage.com

806-3 Self-Storage Facilities

Phone Fax

A-American Self Storage Management Co Inc
11560 Tennessee Ave .... Los Angeles CA 90064 310-914-4022 914-4042
TF: 800-499-3524 ■ *Web:* www.aamericanselfstorage.com
American Storage 945 E Main St .... Spartanburg SC 29302 864-585-6178 591-2299
Web: www.americanstoragerentalspaces.com/
Derrel's Mini Storage 3265 W Ashlan Ave .... Fresno CA 93722 559-224-9900 224-1884
Web: www.derrels.com
Devon Self Storage Holdings LLC 2000 Powell St Suite 1240 ..... Emeryville CA 94068 510-450-1300 450-1325
TF: 800-995-4480 ■ *Web:* www.devonselfstorage.com
Executive Self Storage Assoc Inc
5353 W Dartmouth Ave Suite 401 .... Denver CO 80227 303-703-1290 703-1289
Web: www.executiveselfstorage.com
Extra Space Storage Inc
2795 E Cottonwood Pkwy Suite 400 .... Salt Lake City UT 84121 801-562-5556 562-5579
NYSE: EXR ■ *Web:* www.extraspace.com
Hendry Investments DBA Lock-N-Key Mini-Storage
402 E Ramsey Rd .... San Antonio TX 78216 210-341-2227 341-2369
Web: www.lock-n-key.com
Lock-N-Key Mini-Storage 402 E Ramsey Rd .... San Antonio TX 78216 210-341-2227 341-2369
Web: www.lock-n-key.com
Lock Up Storage Centers 800 Frontage Rd .... Northfield IL 60093 847-441-7760 441-7732
Web: www.thelockup.com
Lock Up Development Corp DBA Lock Up Storage Centers
800 Frontage Rd .... Northfield IL 60093 847-441-7760 441-7732
Web: www.thelockup.com
Metro Storage LLC 13528 Boulton Blvd .... Lake Forest IL 60045 847-235-8900 235-8901
TF Cust Svc: 888-498-1660 ■ *Web:* www.metrostorage.com
National Self Storage Management Inc
1610 E River Rd Suite 117 .... Tucson AZ 85718 520-577-9777 577-0824
TF: 877-648-9512 ■ *Web:* www.nationalselfstorage.com
Private Mini Storage 10575 Westoffice Dr .... Houston TX 77042 713-464-6944 464-6313*
**Fax:* Cust Svc ■ *Web:* www.private-mini.com
Public Storage Inc 701 Western Ave .... Glendale CA 91201 818-244-8080 291-1015*
NYSE: PSA ■ **Fax:* Mail Rm ■ *TF Cust Svc:* 800-567-0759 ■
Web: www.publicstorage.com
Sentry Storage 12233 Folsom Blvd .... Rancho Cordova CA 95742 916-351-0110 351-1803
Web: www.sentrystorage.com
Sentry-Tech Enterprises DBA Sentry Storage
12233 Folsom Blvd .... Rancho Cordova CA 95742 916-351-0110 351-1803
Web: www.sentrystorage.com
Shader Brothers Corp DBA Personal Mini Storage Management Co 6327 Edgewater Dr .... Orlando FL 32810 407-297-3683 578-0400
Web: www.personalministorage.com/
Sovran Self Storage Inc DBA Uncle Bob's Self Storage
6467 Main St .... Buffalo NY 14221 716-633-1850 633-3397
NYSE: SSS ■ *Web:* www.sovranss.com
Stor-All Systems Inc 1375 W Hillsboro Blvd .... Deerfield Beach FL 33442 954-421-7888 426-1108
TF: 800-937-8673 ■ *Web:* www.stor-all.com
Storage Inns Inc 9909 Clayton Rd Suite 205 .... Saint Louis MO 63124 314-997-6603 997-0376
Storage Solutions 65 S Sycamore St Suite 2 .... Mesa AZ 85202 480-844-3900 844-3939
Web: www.storage-solutions.org
U-Haul International Inc PO Box 21502 .... Phoenix AZ 85036 602-263-6011
TF: 800-468-4285 ■ *Web:* www.uhaul.com
U-Store-It Trust 50 Public Sq Suite 2800 .... Cleveland OH 44113 216-274-1340 274-1360
NYSE: YSI ■ *TF:* 800-234-4494 ■ *Web:* www.u-store-it.com
Uncle Bob's Self Storage 6467 Main St .... Buffalo NY 14221 716-633-1850 633-3397
NYSE: SSS ■ *Web:* www.sovranss.com

807 WASTE MANAGEMENT

SEE ALSO Recyclable Materials Recovery p. 2208; Remediation Services p. 2210

Phone Fax

Allied Waste Industries Inc
15880 N Greenway Hayden Loop Suite 100 .... Scottsdale AZ 85260 480-627-2700 627-2701
NYSE: AW ■ *Web:* www.alliedwaste.com
Allied Waste Service Inc 6449 Valley Dr .... Bettendorf IA 52722 563-332-0050 332-4464
TF: 800-233-9634 ■ *Web:* investor.alliedwaste.com
ARC Disposal & Recycling Co 2101 S Busse Rd .... Mount Prospect IL 60056 847-981-0091 981-9180
Web: www.arcdisposal.com
Arlington Disposal Co 1212 Harrison Ave .... Arlington TX 76011 817-317-2000 860-0330
Web: www.duncandisposal.com
Athens Disposal Co Inc 14048 Valley Blvd .... City of Industry CA 91746 626-336-3636 330-4686
TF Cust Svc: 888-336-6100 ■ *Web:* www.athensservices.com
Automated Waste Disposal Inc 307 White St .... Danbury CT 06810 203-743-0405 794-1631
Web: www.automatedwaste.com
Avalon Holdings Corp 1 American Way .... Warren OH 44484 330-856-8800 856-8480
AMEX: AWX ■ *Web:* avalonholdings.com
Bend Garbage & Recycling Inc
20835 NE Montana St PO Box 504 .... Bend OR 97709 541-382-2263 383-3640
Bluebonnet Waste Control PO Box 223845 .... Dallas TX 75222 214-748-5221 748-6886
Web: www.bluebonnetwaste.com
Burrtec Waste Industries Inc 9890 Cherry Ave .... Fontana CA 92335 909-429-4200 429-4291
Web: www.burrtec.com
CalMet Services Inc 9821 Downey Norwalk Rd .... Downey CA 90241 562-869-0901 529-7688
Web: www.calmetservices.com
CalMet Services Inc 7202 Peterson Ln .... Paramount CA 90723 323-721-8120 529-7688*
**Fax Area Code:* 562 ■ *TF:* 800-990-6387 ■ *Web:* www.calmetservices.com
Canadian Waste Services Inc 5045 S Service Rd Suite 300 .... Burlington ON L7L5Y7 905-633-3999 633-3970
Web: www.wm.com/canada
Casella Waste Systems Inc 25 Greens Hill Ln PO Box 866 .... Rutland VT 05702 802-775-0325 775-3290
NASDAQ: CWST ■ *TF:* 800-227-3552 ■ *Web:* www.casella.com
Community Waste Disposal Inc 2010 California Crossing .... Dallas TX 75220 972-392-9300 392-9301
Web: www.communitywastedisposal.com
Consolidated Disposal Services Inc
12949 Telegraph Rd .... Santa Fe Springs CA 90670 800-299-4898 906-0251*
**Fax Area Code:* 562 ■ *TF:* 800-299-4898
Coulter Cos Inc DBA Peoria Disposal Co PO Box 9071 .... Peoria IL 61612 309-688-0760 688-0881
TF: 888-988-0760
Crown Disposal Inc 9189 De Garmo Ave .... Sun Valley CA 91352 818-767-0675 768-3930
Web: www.crowndisposal.com

Phone Fax

Curtis Bay Energy 3200 Hawkins Point Rd .... Baltimore MD 21226 410-354-3228 354-3591
Web: www.curtisbayenergy.com
Deffenbaugh Industries Inc 18181 W 53rd St PO Box 3220 .... Shawnee KS 66203 913-631-3300 248-0267
TF: 800-631-3301 ■ *Web:* www.deffenbaughindustries.com
Edco Disposal Corp 6670 Federal Blvd .... Lemon Grove CA 91945 619-287-7555 287-4073
Web: www.edco-corp.com
EL Harvey & Sons Inc 68 Hopkinton Rd .... Westborough MA 01581 508-836-3000 836-3040
TF: 800-321-3002 ■ *Web:* www.elharvey.com
EnergySolutions LLC 423 W 300 South Suite 200 .... Salt Lake City UT 84116 801-649-2000 321-0453
Web: www.energysolutions.com
EnerTech Environmental Inc 675 Seminole Ave Suite 207 .... Atlanta GA 30307 404-355-3390 355-3292
Web: www.enertech.com
EQ-The Environmental Quality Co 36255 Michigan Ave .... Wayne MI 48184 734-329-8000 329-8140
TF: 800-592-5489 ■ *Web:* www.eqonline.com
Gilton Solid Waste Management 1722 Mono Dr .... Modesto CA 95354 209-527-3781 527-0422
TF: 800-894-8980 ■ *Web:* www.gilton.com
Green Valley Disposal 644 N Santa Cruz Ave Unit 4 .... Los Gatos CA 95032 408-354-2100 354-2101
Harold LeMay Enterprises Inc 13502 Pacific Ave .... Tacoma WA 98444 253-537-8687 537-8689
TF: 800-345-3629 ■ *Web:* www.lemayinc.com
Harris Waste Management Group Inc
200 Clover Reach Dr .... Peachtree City GA 30269 770-631-7290 631-7299
TF: 800-468-5657 ■ *Web:* www.harriswaste.com
Harrison Industries Inc 5275 Colt St PO Box 4009 .... Ventura CA 93007 805-647-1414 644-7751
TF: 800-418-7274 ■ *Web:* www.ejharrison.com
Headwaters Inc 10653 Riverfront Pkwy Suite 300 .... South Jordan UT 84095 801-984-9400 984-9407
NYSE: HW ■ *Web:* www.hdwtrs.com
Heritage Environmental Services Inc 7901 W Morris St .... Indianapolis IN 46231 317-243-0811 486-5085
TF: 877-436-8778 ■ *Web:* www.heritage-enviro.com
Homewood Disposal Service Inc 1501 W 175th St .... Homewood IL 60430 708-798-1004 798-7193
Web: www.homewooddisposal.com
Industrial Services of America Inc 7100 Grade Ln .... Louisville KY 40213 502-368-1661 368-1440
NASDAQ: IDSA ■ *TF:* 800-824-2144 ■ *Web:* www.isa-inc.com
Instate Waste Services 375 Rt 1 & 9 S .... Jersey City NJ 07306 201-547-4100 451-1144
TF: 800-386-7783
JC Duncan Co Inc DBA Arlington Disposal Co
1212 Harrison Ave .... Arlington TX 76011 817-317-2000 860-0330
Web: www.duncandisposal.com
Jet-A-Way 47 Kemble St .... Roxbury MA 02119 617-541-4000 541-4015
Web: www.jet-a-way.com
JP Mascaro Inc 600 W Neversink Rd .... Reading PA 19606 610-779-8807 779-8919
TF: 800-334-3403
Kaiser Ventures LLC 3633 E Inland Empire Blvd Suite 480 .... Ontario CA 91764 909-483-8500 944-6605
TF: 800-889-3652 ■ *Web:* www.kaiserventures.com
Kimmins Corp 1501 2nd Ave E .... Tampa FL 33605 813-248-3878 247-0183
Web: www.kimmins.com
LeMay Harold Enterprises Inc 13502 Pacific Ave .... Tacoma WA 98444 253-537-8687 537-8689
TF: 800-345-3629 ■ *Web:* www.lemayinc.com
Modern Corp 4746 Model City Rd .... Model City NY 14107 716-754-8226 754-8964
TF: 800-662-0012 ■ *Web:* www.moderncorporation.com
N-Viro International Corp 3450 W Central Ave Suite 328 .... Toledo OH 43606 419-535-6374 535-7008
TF: 800-666-8476 ■ *Web:* www.nviro.com
Napa Recycling & Waste Services 820 Levitin Way PO Box 239 .... Napa CA 94559 707-256-3500 256-3565
Web: www.naparecycling.com
National Serv-All Inc 6231 McBeth Rd .... Fort Wayne IN 46809 260-747-4117 478-4903
TF: 800-876-9001
Norcal Waste Systems Inc 160 Pacific Ave Suite 200 .... San Francisco CA 94111 415-875-1000 875-1124
TF: 800-652-1275 ■ *Web:* www.norcalwaste.com
Oakleaf Waste Management LLC
800 Connecticut Blvd 1 Oakleaf Center .... East Hartford CT 06108 860-290-1250 290-1251
TF: 888-625-5323 ■ *Web:* www.oakleafwastemgmt.com
Palm Springs Disposal Co 4690 E Mesquite Ave .... Palm Springs CA 92264 760-327-1351 323-5132
TF: 800-973-3873 ■ *Web:* www.palmspringsdisposal.com
Peoria Disposal Co PO Box 9071 .... Peoria IL 61612 309-688-0760 688-0881
TF: 888-988-0760
Rabanco Ltd 54 S Dawson St .... Seattle WA 98134 206-332-7700 332-7627
Web: www.rabanco.com
Republic Services Inc 110 SE 6th St Suite 2800 .... Fort Lauderdale FL 33301 954-769-2400 769-2647*
NYSE: RSG ■ **Fax:* Hum Res ■ *TF:* 877-241-8396 ■ *Web:* www.republicservices.com
Richmond Sanitary Group 3260 Blume Dr .... Richmond CA 94806 510-262-1610 222-1032*
**Fax:* Cust Svc
Rubatino Refuse Removal Inc 2812 Hoyt Ave .... Everett WA 98201 425-259-0044 339-4196
Web: www.rubatino.com
Rumpke Consolidated Cos Inc 10795 Hughes Rd .... Cincinnati OH 45251 513-851-0122 385-9634
TF: 800-582-3107 ■ *Web:* www.rumpke.com
San Luis Garbage Co 2925 McMillan St Suite 202 .... San Luis Obispo CA 93401 805-543-0875 543-0620
Sanitary Services Co Inc 1001 Roeder Ave .... Bellingham WA 98227 360-734-3490 671-0239
Web: www.ssc-inc.com
Shaw Environmental & Infrastructure Inc 4171 Essen Ln .... Baton Rouge LA 70809 225-932-2500 932-2618
TF: 800-747-3322 ■ *Web:* www.shawgrp.com/ShawEandI/
Silver State Disposal Inc 770 E Sahara Ave .... Las Vegas NV 89193 702-735-5151 599-5586
Web: www.republicservices.com
Solid Waste Services Inc DBA JP Mascaro Inc
600 W Neversink Rd .... Reading PA 19606 610-779-8807 779-8919
TF: 800-334-3403
South Tahoe Refuse Co 2140 Ruth Ave .... South Lake Tahoe CA 96150 530-541-5105 544-2608
Web: www.southtahoerefuse.com
Stericycle Inc 28161 N Keith Dr .... Lake Forest IL 60045 847-367-5910 367-9493
NASDAQ: SRCL ■ *TF:* 800-355-8773 ■ *Web:* www.stericycle.com
Sunset Scavenger Co 250 Executive Park Suite 2100 .... San Francisco CA 94134 415-330-1300 330-1338
Web: www.sunsetscavenger.com
Synagro Technologies Inc 1800 Bering Dr Suite 1000 .... Houston TX 77057 713-369-1700 369-1750
NASDAQ: SYGR ■ *TF:* 800-370-0035 ■ *Web:* www.synagro.com
Tahoe Truckee Disposal Co PO Box 6479 .... Tahoe City CA 96145 530-583-0148 583-0804
Taormina Industries Inc 1131 N Blue Gum St .... Anaheim CA 92806 714-238-3300 238-3307*
**Fax:* Hum Res ■ *Web:* www.taormina.com
Texas Disposal Systems Inc 12200 Carl Rd .... Creedmoor TX 78610 512-392-1515 243-4123
TF: 800-375-8375 ■ *Web:* www.texasdisposal.com
Urban Services Systems Corp
2041 ML King Ave SE Suite 236 .... Washington DC 20012 202-678-7393 678-7397
TF: 800-766-0635 ■ *Web:* www.urbanssc.com
Veolia Environmental Services 1525 Kautz Rd Suite 1000 .... West Chicago IL 60185 630-762-7721 587-1144
Web: veoliaes.com
Veolia Industrial Services 1980 N Hwy 146 .... La Porte TX 77571 713-307-2100 307-7600
TF: 877-719-5086 ■ *Web:* veoliaes-is.com
VFL Technology Corp 16 Hagerty Blvd .... West Chester PA 19382 610-918-1100 918-7222
TF: 800-882-8358 ■ *Web:* www.vfltech.com
Waste Connections Inc 35 Iron Pt Cir Suite 200 .... Folsom CA 95630 916-608-8200 608-8290
NYSE: WCN ■ *TF:* 877-288-8200 ■ *Web:* www.wcnx.org
Waste Industries Inc 3301 Benson Dr Suite 601 .... Raleigh NC 27609 919-325-3000 325-3013*
**Fax:* Mktg ■ *TF:* 800-647-9946 ■ *Web:* www.waste-ind.com
Waste Management Inc 1001 Fannin St Suite 4000 .... Houston TX 77002 713-512-6200 512-6299
NYSE: WMI ■ *TF:* 800-633-7871 ■ *Web:* www.wastemanagement.com
Waste Services Inc 1122 International Blvd Suite 601 .... Burlington ON L7L6Z8 905-319-1237 319-9050
NASDAQ: WSII ■ *Web:* www.wasteservicesinc.com
Waste Stream Environmental Inc 9289 Bonta Bridge Rd .... Jordan NY 13080 315-689-1380 689-1359
WCA Waste Corp 1 Riverway Suite 1400 .... Houston TX 77056 713-292-2400 292-2455
NASDAQ: WCAA ■ *Web:* www.wcamerica.com

	City	State	ZIP	Phone	Fax
Wheelabrator Technologies Inc 4 Liberty Ln W *TF:* 800-682-0026 ■ *Web:* www.wheelabrator.com	Hampton	NH	03842	603-929-3000	929-3139
York Disposal Inc PO Box 1401	York	PA	17405	717-845-1557	764-1944

808 WATER - BOTTLED

	City	State	ZIP	Phone	Fax
Abita Springs Water Co 101 Airline Dr *Web:* www.abitasprings.com	Metairie	LA	70001	504-828-2222	828-2520
Absopure Water Co 8835 General Dr **Fax:* Cust Svc ■ *TF:* 800-422-7678 ■ *Web:* www.absopure.com	Plymouth	MI	48170	734-459-8000	451-0055*
Beverage Corp International 3505 NW 107th St *TF:* 800-226-5061 ■ *Web:* www.bcibeverages.com	Miami	FL	33167	305-714-7000	
Calistoga Mineral Water Co 777 W Putnam Ave *Web:* www.calistogawater.com	Greenwich	CT	06830	203-531-4100	863-0298
Canadian Springs Ltd 1200 Britannia Rd E *Web:* www.sparklingsprings.com	Mississauga	ON	L4W4T5	905-795-6500	670-3628
Carolina Mountain Water Co 150 Central Ave *TF:* 800-643-1501 ■ *Web:* www.mountainvalleyspring.com	Hot Springs	AR	71901	501-623-6671	623-5135
Clearly Canadian Beverage Corp 2267 10th Ave W *TF:* 800-735-7180 ■ *Web:* www.clearly.ca	Vancouver	BC	V6K2J1	604-742-5300	922-8195
Coca-Cola Enterprises Inc 2500 Windy Ridge Pkwy *NYSE: CCE* ■ *Web:* www.cokecce.com	Atlanta	GA	30339	770-989-3000	989-3597
Crystal Geyser Water Co 501 Washington St *TF Cust Svc:* 800-443-9737 ■ *Web:* www.crystalgeyser.com	Calistoga	CA	94515	707-942-0500	942-0647
Culligan International Co 1 Culligan Pkwy *TF:* 800-285-5442 ■ *Web:* www.culligan.com	Northbrook	IL	60062	847-205-6000	205-6030
Deep Rock Water Co 2640 California St *TF:* 800-695-2020 ■ *Web:* www.deeprockwater.com	Denver	CO	80205	303-292-2020	296-8812
Deer Park Spring Water 777 W Putnam Ave *Web:* www.deerparkwater.com	Greenwich	CT	06830	203-531-4100	863-0298
Distillata Co 1608 E 24th St *TF Cust Svc:* 800-999-2906 ■ *Web:* www.distillata.com	Cleveland	OH	44114	216-771-2900	771-1672
DS Waters of America Inc 5660 New Northside Dr Suite 500 **Fax Area Code:* 770 ■ *Web:* www.water.com	Atlanta	GA	30328	800-444-7873	965-5011*
Fountainhead Water Co 3280 Green Point Pkwy *TF:* 800-874-8595 ■ *Web:* www.fountainheadwater.com	Norcross	GA	30040	678-820-6016	805-5562
Glacier Clear Enterprises Inc 3291 Thomas St *TF Cust Svc:* 800-668-5118 ■ *Web:* www.glacierclear.com	Innisfil	ON	L9S3W3	705-436-6363	436-4949
Great Spring Waters of America Inc 777 W Putnam Ave *Web:* www.nestle-watersna.com	Greenwich	CT	06836	203-531-4100	863-0298
Klarbrunn Inc 860 West St *TF:* 800-910-2837 ■ *Web:* www.klarbrunn.com	Watertown	WI	53094	920-262-6300	262-9273
Miscoe Springs Inc 89 Northbridge Rd	Mendon	MA	01756	508-473-0550	473-3971
Mountain Valley Spring Co 150 Central Ave *TF:* 800-643-1501 ■ *Web:* www.mountainvalleyspring.com	Hot Springs	AR	71901	501-623-6671	623-5135
Natural Springs Water Group LLC 128 LP Auer Rd *Web:* www.naturalspringsllc.com	Johnson City	TN	37604	423-926-7905	926-8210
Nestle Waters North America Inc 2767 E Imperial Hwy *TF:* 800-950-9393 ■ *Web:* www.nestle-watersna.com	Brea	CA	92821	714-792-2100	792-2600
Nicolet Forest Bottling Co Inc 561 Plate Dr Suite 1 *TF:* 888-928-3756 ■ *Web:* www.nicoletwater.com	East Dundee	IL	60118	847-382-2950	382-2959
PepsiCo Beverages North America 700 Anderson Hill Rd *Web:* www.pepsi.com	Purchase	NY	10577	914-253-2000	253-2070
Perrier Group of North America 777 W Putnam Ave *Web:* www.nestle-watersna.com	Greenwich	CT	06836	203-531-4100	863-0298
Poland Spring Water 777 W Putnam Ave *Web:* www.polandspring.com	Greenwich	CT	06830	203-531-4100	863-0298
Polar Beverages Inc 1001 Southbridge St *TF Cust Svc:* 800-225-7410 ■ *Web:* www.polarbev.com	Worcester	MA	01610	508-753-4300	793-0813
Pure-Flo Water Co 7737 Mission Gorge Rd *TF Cust Svc:* 800-787-3356 ■ *Web:* www.pureflo.com	Santee	CA	92071	619-448-5120	596-4154
Talking Rain Beverage Co 30520 SE 84th St *TF Cust Svc:* 800-734-0748 ■ *Web:* www.talkingrain.com	Preston	WA	98050	425-222-4900	222-4901
Universal Beverages PO Box 448 *TF:* 888-426-7936	Ponte Vedra Beach	FL	32004	904-280-7795	280-7794
Vermont Pure Holdings Ltd 1050 Buckingham St *AMEX: VPS* ■ **Fax Area Code:* 860 ■ *TF Cust Svc:* 800-939-9119 ■ *Web:* www.vermontpure.com	Watertown	CT	06795	800-525-0070	274-0397*
Zephyrhills Natural Spring Water 777 W Putnam Ave *TF:* 800-950-9398 ■ *Web:* www.zephyrhillswater.com	Greenwich	CT	06830	203-531-4100	863-0298

809 WATER TREATMENT & FILTRATION PRODUCTS & EQUIPMENT

	City	State	ZIP	Phone	Fax
Aqua-Aerobic Systems Inc 6306 N Alpine Rd *TF:* 800-940-5008 ■ *Web:* www.aqua-aerobic.com	Rockford	IL	61111	815-654-2501	654-2508
AquaCell Technologies Inc 10410 Trademark St *AMEX: AQA* ■ *TF:* 800-326-5222 ■ *Web:* www.aquacell.com	Rancho Cucamonga	CA	91730	909-987-0456	987-6306
Aquion Water Treatment Products LLC 2080 E Lunt Ave *Web:* www.aquionwater.com	Elk Grove Village	IL	60007	847-437-9400	437-1594
Aquion Water Treatment Products LLC ClearWater Tech Div PO Box 15330 *TF:* 800-262-0203 ■ *Web:* www.cwtozone.com	San Luis Obispo	CA	93406	805-549-9724	
Aquion Water Treatment Products LLC Rainsoft Div 2080 E Lunt Ave *TF:* 800-860-7638 ■ *Web:* www.rainsoft.com	Elk Grove Village	IL	60007	847-437-9400	437-1594
Brentwood Industries Inc Polychem Systems Div 651 Brentwood Dr *Web:* www.polychemsys.com	Reading	PA	19611	484-651-1300	651-1499
Brita Products Co PO Box 24305 *TF:* 800-242-7482 ■ *Web:* www.brita.com	Oakland	CA	94623	510-271-7000	832-1463
Clack Corp 4462 Duraform Ln *Web:* www.clackcorp.com/	Windsor	WI	53598	608-846-3010	846-2586
ClearWater Tech Div Aquion Water Treatment Products LLC PO Box 15330 *TF:* 800-262-0203 ■ *Web:* www.cwtozone.com	San Luis Obispo	CA	93406	805-549-9724	
Court Thomas Wingert 11800 Monarch St *Web:* www.jlwingert.com	Garden Grove	CA	92841	714-379-5519	379-5549
Crane Environmental 2600 Eisenhower Ave Bldg 100A *TF:* 800-633-7435 ■ *Web:* www.cranenv.com	Trooper	PA	19403	610-631-7700	631-6800
Culligan International Co 1 Culligan Pkwy *TF:* 800-285-5442 ■ *Web:* www.culligan.com	Northbrook	IL	60062	847-205-6000	205-6030
Dow Liquid Separations PO Box 1206 *TF:* 800-447-4369 ■ *Web:* www.dow.com/liquidseps	Midland	MI	48642	989-832-1311	832-1465
EcoWater Systems LLC PO Box 64420 *TF Cust Svc:* 800-942-5415 ■ *Web:* www.ecowater.com	Saint Paul	MN	55164	651-739-5330	739-4547
Everpure Inc 1040 Muirfield Dr *TF:* 800-323-7873 ■ *Web:* www.everpure.com	Hanover Park	IL	60133	630-307-3000	307-3030
FB Leopold Co Inc ITT Advanced Water Treatment 227 S Division St *Web:* www.fbleopold.com	Zelienople	PA	16063	724-452-6300	452-1377
Filterspun 624 N Fairfield St *TF:* 800-432-0108 ■ *Web:* www.filterspun.com	Amarillo	TX	79107	806-383-3840	383-3842
GE Water & Process Technologies 4636 Somerton Rd *Web:* www.gewater.com	Trevose	PA	19053	215-355-3300	
Glacier Clear Enterprises Inc 3291 Thomas St *TF Cust Svc:* 800-668-5118 ■ *Web:* www.glacierclear.com	Innisfil	ON	L9S3W3	705-436-6363	436-4949
Graver Technologies Inc 200 Lake Dr *TF:* 800-249-1990 ■ *Web:* www.gravertech.com	Glasgow	DE	19702	302-731-1700	731-1707
Graver Water Systems Inc 750 Walnut Ave *TF:* 877-472-8379 ■ *Web:* www.graver.com	Cranford	NJ	07016	908-653-4200	653-4300
Hungerford & Terry Inc 226 Atlantic Ave *Web:* www.hungerfordterry.com	Clayton	NJ	08312	856-881-3200	881-6859
Industrial Filter & Pump Mfg Co 5900 W Ogden Ave *Web:* www.industrialfilter.com	Cicero	IL	60804	708-656-7800	656-7806
Infilco Degremont Inc PO Box 71390 8007 Discovery Dr *TF:* 800-446-1150 ■ *Web:* www.infilcodegremont.com	23229	VA	23294	804-756-7600	756-7643
Integrated Separation Solutions Inc (ISS) 6333 Odana Rd *Web:* www.isepsol.com	Madison	WI	53719	608-276-6850	276-6856
ITT Advanced Water Treatment 14125 S Bridge Cir *Web:* www.ittadvancedwatertreatment.com	Charlotte	NC	28273	704-716-7600	716-7610
ITT Advanced Water Treatment FB Leopold Co Inc 227 S Division St *Web:* www.fbleopold.com	Zelienople	PA	16063	724-452-6300	452-1377
Keystone Filter Div Met-Pro Corp 2385 N Penn Rd *TF:* 800-811-4424 ■ *Web:* www.keystone-filter.com	Hatfield	PA	19440	215-723-9300	997-1839
KX Industries 269 S Lambert Rd *TF:* 800-462-8745 ■ *Web:* www.kxindustries.com	Orange	CT	06477	203-799-9000	799-7000
Lancaster Pump Co 1340 Manheim Pike *Web:* www.lancasterpump.com	Lancaster	PA	17601	717-397-3521	392-0266
McNish Corp 840 N Russell Ave *TF:* 800-992-5537	Aurora	IL	60506	630-892-7921	892-7951
Met-Pro Corp Keystone Filter Div 2385 N Penn Rd *TF:* 800-811-4424 ■ *Web:* www.keystone-filter.com	Hatfield	PA	19440	215-723-9300	997-1839
Met-Pro Corp Systems Div 1555 Bustard Rd Box 325 *Web:* www.met-prosystems.com	Kulpsville	PA	19443	215-631-9500	631-1801
MSC Liquid Filtration Corp 198 Freshwater Blvd *TF Cust Svc:* 800-237-7359 ■ *Web:* www.mscliquidfiltration.com	Enfield	CT	06082	860-745-7475	745-7477
National Filter Media Corp 691 N 400 West *TF:* 800-777-4248 ■ *Web:* www.nfm-filter.com	Salt Lake City	UT	84103	801-363-6736	531-1293
National Water Purifiers Corp 1065 E 14th St	Hialeah	FL	33010	305-887-7065	887-6209
Pall Corp 2200 Northern Blvd *NYSE: PLL* ■ *TF:* 800-645-6532 ■ *Web:* www.pall.com	East Hills	NY	11548	516-484-5400	484-5228
Pentair Inc 5500 Wayzata Blvd Suite 800 *NYSE: PNR* ■ *TF:* 800-328-9626 ■ *Web:* www.pentair.com	Golden Valley	MN	55416	763-545-1730	656-5400
Pentair Water Pool & Spa 1620 Hawkins Ave *TF:* 800-831-7133 ■ *Web:* www.pentairpool.com	Sanford	NC	27330	919-566-8000	566-8910
PEP Filters Inc 322 Rolling Hills Rd *TF:* 800-243-4586 ■ *Web:* www.pepfilters.com	Mooresville	NC	28117	704-662-3133	662-3155
Polaris Pool Systems Inc 2620 Commerce Way *TF Cust Svc:* 800-822-7933 ■ *Web:* www.polarispoolsystems.com	Vista	CA	92081	760-599-9600	597-1235
Polychem Systems Div Brentwood Industries Inc 651 Brentwood Dr *Web:* www.polychemsys.com	Reading	PA	19611	484-651-1300	651-1499
Pristine Water Solutions Inc 1570 S Lakeside Dr *TF:* 800-562-1537 ■ *Web:* www.pristinewatersolutions.com	Waukegan	IL	60085	847-689-1100	689-9289
Pure & Secure LLC 4120 NW 44th St *TF Cust Svc:* 800-875-5915 ■ *Web:* www.mypurewater.com	Lincoln	NE	68524	402-467-9300	467-9393
Schreiber LLC 100 Schreiber Dr *Web:* www.schreiberwater.com	Trussville	AL	35173	205-655-7466	655-7669
Severn Trent Services Inc 580 Virginia Dr Suite 300 **Fax:* Mktg ■ *TF:* 866-646-9201 ■ *Web:* www.severntrentservices.com	Fort Washington	PA	19034	215-646-9201	283-3487*
Siemens Water Technologies 181 Thorn Hill Rd *TF:* 800-525-0658 ■ *Web:* www.industry.siemens.com/Water/en	Warrendale	PA	15086	724-772-0044	
Slickbar Products Corp 18 Beach St *TF:* 800-322-2666 ■ *Web:* www.slickbar.com	Seymour	CT	06483	203-888-7700	888-7720
Taylor Technologies Inc 31 Loveton Cir *TF Cust Svc:* 800-837-8548 ■ *Web:* www.taylortechnologies.com	Sparks	MD	21152	410-472-4340	771-4291
Walker Process Equipment 840 N Russell Ave *TF:* 800-992-5537 ■ *Web:* www.walker-process.com	Aurora	IL	60506	630-892-7921	892-7951
Waterco USA Inc 21420 N 15th Ln *TF:* 800-884-0048 ■ *Web:* www.waterco.com	Phoenix	AZ	85027	623-434-4703	434-4704
Waterco USA Inc 1864 Tobacco Rd *TF:* 800-247-7291 ■ *Web:* www.waterco.com	Augusta	GA	30906	706-793-7291	790-5688
Watts Water Technologies Inc 815 Chestnut St *NYSE: WTS* ■ **Fax:* Cust Svc ■ *Web:* www.wattsind.com	North Andover	MA	01845	978-688-1811	689-2457*
Westech Engineering Inc 3625 S West Temple *Web:* www.westech-inc.com	Salt Lake City	UT	84115	801-265-1000	265-1080
Zodiac Pool Care Inc 2620 Commerce Way **Fax Area Code:* 877 ■ *TF:* 800-822-7933 ■ *Web:* www.zodiacpoolcare.com	Vista	CA	92081	760-599-9600	327-1403*

810 WEAPONS & ORDNANCE (MILITARY)

SEE ALSO Firearms & Ammunition (Non-Military) p. 1637; Missiles, Space Vehicles, Parts p. 1974; Simulation & Training Systems p. 2318

	City	State	ZIP	Phone	Fax
Aerojet Hwy 50 Aerojet Rd *Web:* www.aerojet.com	Rancho Cordova	CA	95742	916-355-1000	351-8667
Allied Defense Group Inc 8000 Towers Crescent Dr Suite 260 *AMEX: ADG* ■ *TF:* 800-847-5322 ■ *Web:* www.alliedefensegroup.com	Vienna	VA	22182	703-847-5268	847-5334
Amron LLC 920 Amron Ave	Antigo	WI	54409	715-623-4176	623-5231
Armtec Defense Products Co 85-901 Ave 53 *Web:* www.armtecdefense.com	Coachella	CA	92236	760-398-0143	398-4609
CIC International Ltd 5 Marine View Plaza *Web:* www.cic-international.com	Hoboken	NJ	07030	201-792-1800	792-5755
Ensign-Bickford Industries Inc 100 Grist Mill Rd *TF:* 800-828-9814 ■ *Web:* www.ensign-bickfordind.com	Simsbury	CT	06070	860-843-2000	843-1510
Essex Industries Inc 7700 Gravois Ave *Web:* www.essexind.com	Saint Louis	MO	63123	314-832-4500	832-1633
General Dynamics Armament & Technical Products 128 Lakeside Ave *Web:* www.gdatp.com	Burlington	VT	05401	802-657-6346	657-6633
General Dynamics Corp 2941 Fairview Park Dr Suite 100 *NYSE: GD* ■ *Web:* www.gendyn.com	Falls Church	VA	22042	703-876-3000	876-3125
General Dynamics Land Systems 38500 Mound Rd *Web:* www.gdls.com	Sterling Heights	MI	48310	586-825-4000	825-4013
General Dynamics Ordnance & Tactical Systems 1010 Dr ML King Jr Blvd N *Web:* www.gd-ots.com	Saint Petersburg	FL	33716	727-578-8100	578-8119

	City	State	Zip	Phone	Fax
Kaman Aerospace Corp Old Windsor Rd PO Box 2 *Web:* www.kamanaero.com	Bloomfield	CT	06002	860-242-4461	243-7514
Marvin Engineering Co 260 W Beach Ave **Fax Area Code:* 310 ■ *Web:* www.marvineng.com	Inglewood	CA	90302	323-678-1281	673-9472*
NAPCO International Inc 11055 Excelsior Blvd *Web:* www.napcointl.com	Hopkins	MN	55343	952-931-2400	931-2402
Textron Marine & Land Systems 19401 Chef Menteur Hwy *Web:* www.systems.textron.com	New Orleans	LA	70129	504-245-6600	254-8000
Textron Systems Corp 201 Lowell St *Web:* www.systems.textron.com	Wilmington	MA	01887	978-657-5111	657-1843

811 WEB HOSTING SERVICES

SEE ALSO Internet Service Providers (ISPs) p. 1872

Companies listed here are engaged primarily in hosting web sites for companies and individuals. Although many Internet Service Providers (ISPs) also provide web hosting services, they are not included among these listings.

	City	State	Zip	Phone	Fax
@INR.net 379 Amherst St Suite 218 *TF:* 877-880-8120 ■ *Web:* www.inr.net	Nashua	NH	03063	603-880-8120	880-8783
1 2 3 HostMe! 3864 Courtney St Suite 130 *TF:* 888-321-3278 ■ *Web:* www.fast.net	Bethlehem	PA	18017	610-266-6700	266-8653
50megs.com 1253 N Research Way Suite Q-2500 *Web:* www.50megs.com	Orem	UT	84097	801-437-6000	
About Web Services 1253 N Research Way Suite Q-2500 *TF:* 800-396-1999	Orem	UT	84097	801-437-6000	
Affinity Internet Inc 3250 Commercial Blvd Suite 200 *Web:* www.affinity.net	Fort Lauderdale	FL	33309	954-334-8000	334-8001
Altura International 1 Lower Ragsdale Dr Bldg 1 Suite 210 *Web:* www.altura.com	Monterey	CA	93940	831-649-2489	644-9280
Angelfire 100 5th Ave *Web:* angelfire.lycos.com	Waltham	MA	02451	781-370-2700	370-2600
BCE Emergis Inc 1000 rue de Serigny Bureau 600 *TSX: IFM* ■ *TF:* 866-363-7447 ■ *Web:* www.emergis.com	Longueuil	QC	J4K5B1	450-928-6000	928-6344
Broadspire Services 1200 W 7th St Suite 340 *Web:* www.broadspire.com	Los Angeles	CA	90017	213-986-1050	688-7791
Catalog.com Inc 6404 International Pkwy Suite 2200 *TF:* 888-932-4376 ■ *Web:* www.catalog.com	Plano	TX	75093	972-380-2202	380-0911
Chapel Services Inc 1212 W Main St *TF:* 888-747-4949 ■ *Web:* www.chpl.net	Richmond	KY	40475	859-623-1500	624-3019
CI Host 1901 Central Dr Suite 750 **Fax Area Code:* 888 ■ *TF Tech Supp:* 888-820-0688 ■ *Web:* www.cihost.com	Bedford	TX	76021	817-868-6999	242-7557*
Classified Ventures LLC 175 W Jackson Blvd Suite 800 *Web:* www.classifiedventures.com	Chicago	IL	60604	312-575-2700	645-0201
CommuniTech.Net Inc 303 Peachtree Ctr Ave Suite 500 *TF:* 877-467-8464 ■ *Web:* www.communitech.net	Atlanta	GA	30303	404-260-2477	260-2712
DataPipe 80 River St *TF:* 877-773-3306 ■ *Web:* www.datapipe.com	Hoboken	NJ	07030	201-792-4847	792-3090
DataRealm Internet Services LLC PO Box 1616 *TF:* 877-227-3783 ■ *Web:* www.serve.com	Hudson	WI	54016	602-850-4044	850-3660
E-Access Inc 840 6th Ave *Web:* www.e-access.net	Huntington	WV	25701	304-697-0437	
EarthLink Inc 1375 Peachtree St NE *NASDAQ: ELNK* ■ **Fax:* Sales ■ *TF:* 800-332-4892 ■ *Web:* www.earthlink.net	Atlanta	GA	30309	404-815-0770	888-9210*
eStoreManager.com c/o American Digital Network Inc 9725 Scranton Rd *TF:* 877-928-9376 ■ *Web:* www.estoremanager.com	San Diego	CA	92121	858-427-2400	576-0148
Express Technologies Inc DBA Hosting.com PO Box 22789 *TF:* 800-284-9391 ■ *Web:* www.expresstech.net	Louisville	KY	40252	502-214-4100	214-4141
FortuneCity Inc 322 8th Ave 11th Fl *TF:* 866-638-2489 ■ *Web:* www.fortunecity.com	New York	NY	10001	212-981-8600	981-8125
Freeservers.com 1253 N Research Way Suite Q-2500 *TF:* 800-396-1999 ■ *Web:* www.freeservers.com	Orem	UT	84097	801-437-6000	437-6020
FreeYellow.com 70 Blanchard Rd 3rd Fl **Fax Area Code:* 425 ■ *Web:* www.freeyellow.com	Burlington	MA	01803	866-434-5563	201-6163*
FullWeb Inc 201 Robert S Kerr Ave Suite 210 *TF:* 888-826-4687 ■ *Web:* www.fullweb.com	Oklahoma City	OK	73102	405-236-8200	236-8201
Global Knowledge Group Inc (GKG) 2700 Earl Rudder Fwy S Suite 1300 *TF:* 800-617-0412 ■ *Web:* www.gkg.net	College Station	TX	77845	979-693-5447	694-7060
Homestead Technologies Inc 3375 Edison Way *TF:* 800-797-2958 ■ *Web:* www.homestead.com	Menlo Park	CA	94025	650-549-3100	364-7329
HomeStore Inc 30700 Russell Ranch Rd *NASDAQ: HOMS* ■ *TF Cust Svc:* 800-878-4166 ■ *Web:* www.homestore.com	Westlake Village	CA	91362	805-557-2300	557-2680
Host Depot Inc 12524 W Atlantic Blvd *TF:* 888-340-3527 ■ *Web:* www.hostdepot.com	Coral Springs	FL	33071	954-340-3527	340-3539
Hostcentric Inc 70 Blanchard Rd 3rd Fl **Fax Area Code:* 781 ■ *TF:* 800-467-8669 ■ *Web:* www.hostcentric.com	Burlington	MA	01803	800-467-8669	998-8340*
Hostedware Corp 16 Technology Dr Suite 116 *TF:* 800-211-6967 ■ *Web:* www.hostedware.com	Irvine	CA	92618	949-585-1500	585-0050
Hosting.com PO Box 22789 *TF:* 800-284-9391 ■ *Web:* www.expresstech.net	Louisville	KY	40252	502-214-4100	214-4141
Hostway Corp 1 N State St 12th Fl *TF:* 866-467-8929 ■ *Web:* www.hostway.com	Chicago	IL	60602	312-236-2132	236-1958
Hurricane Electric Internet Services 760 Mission Ct *Web:* www.he.com	Fremont	CA	94539	510-580-4100	580-4151
Hypermart 730 Blanchard Rd **Fax Area Code:* 781 ■ *Web:* www.hypermart.net	Burlington	MA	01803	877-287-5929	998-8586*
INetU Inc 744 Roble Rd Suite 70 *TF:* 888-664-6388 ■ *Web:* www.inetu.net	Allentown	PA	18109	610-266-7441	266-7434
Interland Inc 303 Peachtree Ctr Ave Suite 500 *NASDAQ: INLD* ■ *TF:* 800-214-1460 ■ *Web:* www.interland.net	Atlanta	GA	30303	404-260-2477	720-3707
Knight Ridder Digital 35 S Market St *TF:* 877-732-5248 ■ *Web:* www.knightridderdigital.com	San Jose	CA	95113	408-938-6000	938-6098
Media3 Technologies LLC 33 Riverside Dr N River Commerce Pk *TF:* 800-903-9327 ■ *Web:* www.media3.net	Pembroke	MA	02359	781-826-1213	826-1513
Microserve Inc 276 5th Ave Suite 1011 *Web:* www.mserve.com	New York	NY	10001	212-683-2811	696-0123
NetNation Communications Inc 550 Burrard St Suite 200 *TF:* 888-277-0000 ■ *Web:* www.netnation.com	Vancouver	BC	V6C2B5	604-688-8946	688-8934
New York Times Digital 500 7th Ave *Web:* www.nytco.com/company.html	New York	NY	10018	646-698-8000	698-8344
OLM LLC 4 Trefoil Dr **Fax Area Code:* 800 ■ *TF:* 877-265-6638 ■ *Web:* www.olm.net	Trumbull	CT	06611	203-445-7700	570-7696*
Pacific Internet 105 W Clay St *NASDAQ: PCNTF* ■ *TF:* 888-722-8638 ■ *Web:* www.pacific.net	Ukiah	CA	95482	707-468-1005	468-5822
Pegasus Web Technologies Inc PO Box 939 *TF:* 888-734-9320 ■ *Web:* www.pwebtech.com	Clifton	NJ	07014	973-572-1070	267-9450
Power Surge Technologies Inc 220 W Ridgeway Ave Suite 105 *TF:* 800-867-5055 ■ *Web:* www.powersurge.net	Waterloo	IA	50701	319-233-1412	233-1569
Quik Internet 3151 Airway Ave Suite M-3 *Web:* www.quik.com	Costa Mesa	CA	92626	714-429-1040	429-1038
Rackspace Ltd 9725 Datapoint Dr Suite 100 *TF:* 800-961-2888 ■ *Web:* www.rackspace.com	San Antonio	TX	78229	210-447-4000	447-4100
Radiant Communications Corp 1050 W Pender St Suite 1600 *TF:* 888-219-2111 ■ *Web:* www.radiant.net	Vancouver	BC	V6E4T3	604-257-0500	608-0999
Real Cities Network 35 S Market St *TF:* 877-732-5248 ■ *Web:* www.realcities.com	San Jose	CA	95113	408-938-6000	938-6048
Salon Media Group Inc 101 Spear St Suite 203 *Web:* www.salon.com	San Francisco	CA	94105	415-645-9200	645-9204
ServInt Internet Services 6861 Elm St Suite 4E *TF:* 800-573-7846 ■ *Web:* www.servint.net	McLean	VA	22101	703-847-1381	847-1383
Solo Web Hosting 10350 Barnes Canyon Rd *TF:* 877-275-8763 ■ *Web:* www.websolo.com	San Diego	CA	92121	858-410-6929	410-6928
Stargate Holdings Corp 2805 Butterfield Rd Suite 100 *TF:* 800-282-6541 ■ *Web:* www.stargateinc.com	Oak Brook	IL	60523	630-572-2242	
Superb Internet Corp 700 W Pender St Suite 1400 *TF:* 888-354-6128 ■ *Web:* www.superb.net	Vancouver	BC	V6C1G8	604-638-2525	638-2953
TierraNet Inc 9573 Chesapeake Dr 1st Fl *TF:* 877-843-7721 ■ *Web:* www.tierranet.com	San Diego	CA	92123	858-560-9416	560-9417
Tripod 100 5th Ave *Web:* www.tripod.lycos.com	Waltham	MA	02451	781-370-2700	370-2600
ValueWeb 3250 W Commercial Blvd Suite 200 *TF:* 800-934-6788 ■ *Web:* www.valueweb.net	Fort Lauderdale	FL	33309	954-429-3449	334-8001
Verio Inc 8005 S Chester St Suite 200 *Web:* home.verio.com	Centennial	CO	80112	303-645-1900	792-3869
Virtual Web Servers Inc 122 W Bay St **VPOP Technologies Inc**	Savannah	GA	31401	912-525-2500	525-2502
365 E Avenida de los Arboles PMB 374 **Fax Area Code:* 213 ■ *TF Sales:* 888-811-8767 ■ *Web:* www.vpop.net	Thousand Oaks	CA	91360	805-529-9374	477-2113*
Vstore.com c/o Vcommerce Corp 10001 N 92nd St Suite 120 *TF:* 800-821-6034 ■ *Web:* www.vstore.com	Scottsdale	AZ	85258	480-922-9922	922-9921
Walt Disney Internet Group 5161 Lankershim Blvd *Web:* corporate.disney.go.com/wdig	North Hollywood	CA	91601	818-623-3200	623-3577
Web Communications LLC 8005 S Chester St Suite 200 **Fax Area Code:* 801 ■ *TF:* 888-893-2266 ■ *Web:* www.webcom.com	Englewood	CO	80112	888-893-2266	437-0202*
WorldPort Communications Inc 2626 Warrenville Rd Suite 400 **Fax Area Code:* 847 ■ *Web:* www.wrdp.com	Downers Grove	IL	60515	312-456-2536	537-3797*
WorldPost Technologies Inc 603 Navarro St Suite 605 *Web:* www.worldpost.com	San Antonio	TX	78205	210-212-5600	212-5800
Yahoo! Small Business 701 1st Ave *Web:* smallbusiness.yahoo.com	Sunnyvale	CA	94089	408-349-3300	349-3301
Yahoo! Website Services 701 1st Ave *Web:* website.yahoo.com	Sunnyvale	CA	94089	408-349-3300	349-3301
ZDNet Inc 235 2nd St *Web:* www.zdnet.com	San Francisco	CA	94105	415-344-2000	

812 WEB SITE DESIGN SERVICES

SEE ALSO Advertising Agencies p. 1257; Advertising Services - Online p. 1260; Computer Systems Design Services p. 1520

	City	State	Zip	Phone	Fax
415 Productions Inc 2507 Bryant St *Web:* www.415.com	San Francisco	CA	94110	415-642-4200	642-4210
Acro Media Inc 103-2303 Leckie Rd *Web:* www.acromediainc.com	Kelowna	BC	V1X6Y5	250-763-8884	763-6936
Active Web Corp 512 Woolrich St *TF:* 866-837-2711 ■ *Web:* www.activeweb.net	Guelph	ON	N1H3X7	519-837-2711	837-3408
AKQA Inc 1055 Thomas Jefferson St NW Suite 680 *Web:* www.akqa.com	Washington	DC	20007	202-551-9900	551-9930
Aptinet Inc 130 W 42nd St 20th Fl *Web:* www.aptinet.com	New York	NY	10035	212-725-7255	730-2980
Ariesnet Inc 15950 N Dallas Pkwy Suite 400 *TF:* 888-932-3375 ■ *Web:* www.ariesnet.com	Dallas	TX	75248	214-932-3900	932-1222
Bigstep 101 Continental Blvd 3rd Fl **Fax Area Code:* 310 ■ *Web:* go.bigstep.com	El Segundo	CA	90245	866-499-2799	388-1335*
Bixler Inc 2000 N 14th St Suite 600 *Web:* www.bixler.com	Arlington	VA	22201	703-894-3000	894-3001
Blue Dingo Digital 520 Broadway 4th Fl *Web:* www.bluedingo.com	New York	NY	10012	212-358-8200	358-8210
bx.com Inc 3 Davol Sq *TF:* 800-344-8487 ■ *Web:* bx.com	Providence	RI	02903	401-274-8991	274-8949
Digital West Media Inc PO Box 270219 *Web:* www.dwmi.com	San Diego	CA	92198	760-740-1787	737-9874
Duffy & Partners 50 S 6th St Suite 2800 *Web:* www.duffy.com	Minneapolis	MN	55402	612-321-2333	321-2334
Forum One Communications Corp 2200 Mt Vernon Ave *Web:* www.forumone.com	Alexandria	VA	22301	703-548-1855	995-4937
Fry Inc 650 Avis Dr *TF:* 800-379-6858 ■ *Web:* www.frymulti.com	Ann Arbor	MI	48108	734-741-0640	769-9918
Fusebox Inc 36 W 20th St PH *Web:* www.fusebox.com	New York	NY	10011	212-929-7644	929-7947
G2 Interactive 101 E County Line Rd Suite 200 *Web:* www.g2.com/interactive	Hatboro	PA	19040	267-615-5200	615-5201
Genex Interactive 10003 Washington Blvd *Web:* www.genex.com	Los Angeles	CA	90232	310-736-2000	736-2001
GotData.com Inc 26895 Aliso Creek Rd Suite B606 *Web:* www.gotdata.com	Aliso Viejo	CA	92656	949-458-8602	716-7500
Grizzly Web Designers 154 Marina Bay Ct *Web:* www.grizzly-internet.com	Sylvan Lake	AB	T4S1E9	866-493-8326	
Headquarters.Com Inc 625 Walnut Ridge Dr Suite 108 *TF:* 800-788-1298 ■ *Web:* www.headquarters.com	Hartland	WI	53029	262-369-0600	369-0800
Idea Integration Corp 1 Independent Dr 2nd Fl *TF:* 800-433-2206 ■ *Web:* www.idea.com	Jacksonville	FL	32202	904-360-2700	360-2509
IMC2 12404 Park Central Suite 400 *Web:* www.imc2.com	Dallas	TX	75251	214-224-1000	224-1100
Intercosmos Media Group Inc 650 Poydras St Suite 1150 *Web:* www.intercosmos.com	New Orleans	LA	70130	504-679-5170	
ISITE Design Inc 615 SW Broadway Suite 200 *TF:* 888-269-9103 ■ *Web:* www.isitedesign.com	Portland	OR	97205	503-221-9860	212-0239
Logical Design Solutions Inc 131 Madison Ave *TF:* 800-275-5374 ■ *Web:* www.lds.com	Morristown	NJ	07960	973-971-0100	971-0103
Paloma Systems Inc 11250 Waples Mill Rd *Web:* www.palomasys.com	Fairfax	VA	22030	703-563-2060	591-0985
Sapient Corp 25 1st St 4th Fl *NASDAQ: SAPE* ■ *Web:* www.sapient.com	Cambridge	MA	02141	617-621-0200	621-1300
uSight 727 N 1550 E *TF:* 800-544-9459 ■ *Web:* www.usight.com	Orem	UT	84097	801-356-3131	356-3003

Phone Fax

Website Pros Inc 12735 Grand Bay Pkwy W Bldg 200 .... Jacksonville FL 32258 904-680-6600 880-0350
NASDAQ: WSPI ■ *TF:* 800-438-7483 ■ *Web:* www.websitepros.com

813 WEIGHT LOSS CENTERS & SERVICES

SEE ALSO Health & Fitness Centers p. 1774; Spas - Health & Fitness p. 2318

Phone Fax

Barix Clinics 135 S Prospect St .... Ypsilanti MI 48198 734-547-4700 547-1281
TF: 800-282-0066 ■ *Web:* www.barixinfo.com
Fit America MD 2201 Stirling Rd .... Fort Lauderdale FL 33312 800-221-1186 570-8608*
**Fax Area Code: 954* ■ *TF:* 800-940-7546 ■ *Web:* www.fitamericamd.com
Forest Health Services LLC 135 S Prospect St .... Ypsilanti MI 48198 800-282-0066 547-1281*
**Fax Area Code: 734* ■ *TF:* 800-282-0066 ■ *Web:* www.foresthealth.com
Inches-A-Weigh North America Inc 4320 Alpine Ct.............. Rockford IL 61107 815-227-4623
TF: 800-241-8663 ■ *Web:* www.inchesaweigh.com
Jazzercise Inc 2460 Impala Dr .... Carlsbad CA 92010 760-476-1750 602-7180
TF Cust Svc: 800-348-4748 ■ *Web:* www.jazzercise.com
Jenny Craig International Inc 5770 Fleet St .... Carlsbad CA 92008 760-696-4000 696-4506
TF: 800-443-2331 ■ *Web:* www.jennycraig.com
LA Weight Loss Centers 747 Dresher Rd Suite 100............ Horsham PA 19044 215-346-4400
TF: 877-524-3571 ■ *Web:* www.laweightloss.com
NutriSystem Inc 300 Welsh Rd Bldg 1 .... Horsham PA 19044 215-706-5300 706-5388
NASDAQ: NTRI ■ *TF:* 800-585-5483 ■ *Web:* www.nutrisystem.com
Physicians Weight Loss Centers of America Inc
395 Springside Dr .... Akron OH 44333 330-666-7952 666-2197
TF: 800-205-7887 ■ *Web:* www.pwlc.com
Weight Management Centers 2605 W Swann Ave Suite 600 .... Tampa FL 33609 813-876-7073 877-1277
Web: www.weightmanagement.com
Weight Watchers International Inc 175 Crossways Pk W........ Woodbury NY 11797 516-390-1400 390-1334
NYSE: WTW ■ *TF:* 800-651-6000 ■ *Web:* www.weightwatchers.com

814 WELDING & SOLDERING EQUIPMENT

Phone Fax

Acro Automation Systems Inc 2900 W Green Tree Rd .... Milwaukee WI 53209 414-352-4540 352-1609
Web: www.acro.com
AGM Industries Inc 16 Jonathan Dr .... Brockton MA 02301 508-587-3900 587-3283
TF: 800-225-9990 ■ *Web:* www.agmind.com
Alliance Winding Equipment Inc 3939 Vanguard Dr .... Fort Wayne IN 46809 260-478-2200
Web: www.alliance-winding.com
American Ultraviolet Co 40 Morristown Rd Suite 2-B......... Bernardsville NJ 07924 908-696-1130 696-1131
Web: www.americanultraviolet.com
Applied Fusion Inc 1915 Republic Ave.................... San Leandro CA 94577 510-351-4511 351-0692
Web: www.appliedfusioninc.com
Arc Machines Inc 10500 Orbital Way........................ Pacoima CA 91331 818-896-9556 890-3724
Web: www.arcmachines.com
Arcos Industries 1 Arcos Dr .... Mount Carmel PA 17851 570-339-5200 339-5206
TF: 800-233-8460 ■ *Web:* www.arcos.us
Argus International Ltd
108 Whispering Pines Dr Suite 110 .... Scotts Valley CA 95066 831-461-4700 461-4701
TF: 800-862-7487 ■ *Web:* www.argusinternational.com
Automation International Inc 1020 Bahls St .... Danville IL 61832 217-446-9500 446-6855
Web: www.automation-intl.com
Banner Welder Inc N 117 W 18200 Fulton Dr .... Germantown WI 53022 262-253-2900 253-2919
Web: www.bannerweld.com
CK Worldwide Inc 3501 C St NE PO Box 1638 .... Auburn WA 98071 253-854-5820 939-1746
TF: 800-426-0877 ■ *Web:* www.ckworldwide.com
Esab Welding & Cutting Products Inc
411 S Ebenezer Rd PO Box 100545 .... Florence SC 29501 843-669-4411 664-4258*
**Fax: Hum Res* ■ *TF:* 800-372-2123 ■ *Web:* www.esabna.com
Eureka Welding Alloys Inc 2000 E Avis Dr .... Madison Heights MI 48071 248-588-0001 585-7711
TF: 800-962-8560 ■ *Web:* www.eurekaweldingalloys.com
Eutectic Corp N 94 W 14355 Garwin Mace Dr........... Menomonee Falls WI 53051 262-255-5520 255-5542
TF: 800-558-8524
Forney Industries Inc 1830 LaPorte Ave PO Box 563 .... Fort Collins CO 80522 970-482-7271 498-9505
TF: 800-521-6038 ■ *Web:* www.forneyind.com
Goss Inc 1511 Rt 8 .... Glenshaw PA 15116 412-486-6100 486-6844
TF: 800-367-4677 ■ *Web:* www.gossonline.com
Harris Products Group 4501 Quality Pl.......................... Mason OH 45040 513-754-2000 754-8778*
**Fax: Sales* ■ *TF:* 800-733-4043 ■ *Web:* www.harrisproductsgroup.com
Hobart Brothers Co 400 Trade Sq E.............................. Troy OH 45373 937-332-4000 332-5178*
**Fax: Hum Res* ■ *Web:* www.hobartbrothers.com
Industrial Welders & Machinists Inc PO Box 16720.............. Duluth MN 55806 218-628-1011 624-3319
TF: 800-689-9520
Jetline Engineering 15 Goodyear St .... Irvine CA 92618 949-951-1515 951-9237
TF: 800-499-4471 ■ *Web:* www.jetline.com
Kuka Flexible Production Systems Corp
6600 Center Dr.. Sterling Heights MI 48312 586-795-2000 978-0429
Web: www.kukausa.com
Lincoln Electric Co 22801 St Clair Ave .... Cleveland OH 44117 216-481-8100 486-1751
Web: www.lincolnelectric.com
Manufacturing Technology Inc 1702 W Washington St .... South Bend IN 46628 574-233-9490 233-9489
Web: www.mtiwelding.com
Merrill Mfg Corp 236 Genesee St PO Box 566.................... Merrill WI 54452 715-536-5533 536-5590
TF: 800-826-5300 ■ *Web:* www.merrill-mfg.com
Milco Mfg Co 2147 E 10-Mile Rd.............................. Warren MI 48091 586-755-7320 755-7442
TF: 800-697-6452 ■ *Web:* www.milcomfg.com
Miller Electric Mfg Co 1635 W Spencer St...................... Appleton WI 54914 920-734-9821 735-4134*
**Fax: Sales* ■ *Web:* www.millerwelds.com
Newcor Inc 4850 Coolidge Hwy Suite 100 .... Royal Oak MI 48073 248-435-4269 435-5385
Web: www.newcor.com
NLC Inc 100 Block S Oklahoma St PO Box 348 .... Jackson MO 63755 573-243-3141 243-7122
TF: 800-747-4743
Northern Stamping Corp 6600 Chapek Pkwy .... Cuyahoga Heights OH 44125 216-883-8888 883-8237
Ogden Welding Systems Inc 372 Division St................. Schererville IN 46375 219-322-5252 865-1825
Web: www.ogdenwelding.com
Palomar Technologies 2728 Loker Ave W........................ Carlsbad CA 92010 760-931-3600 931-5191
TF: 800-854-3467 ■ *Web:* www.palomartechnologies.com
Pandjiris Inc 5151 Northrup Ave.............................. Saint Louis MO 63110 314-776-6893 776-8763
TF: 800-237-2006 ■ *Web:* www.pandjiris.com
Research Inc 7128 Shady Oak Rd .... Eden Prairie MN 55344 952-941-3300 941-3628
Web: www.researchinc.com
RoMan Mfg Inc 861 47th St SW.......................... Grand Rapids MI 49509 616-530-8641 530-8953
Web: www.romanmfg.com
RWC Inc 2105 S Euclid Ave.. Bay City MI 48706 989-684-4030 684-3960
Web: www.rwcinc.com
Savair Inc 48500 Structural Dr .... Chesterfield Township MI 48051 586-949-9353 949-4493

Phone Fax

Sciaky Inc 4915 W 67th St.. Chicago IL 60638 708-594-3800 594-9213
Web: www.sciaky.com
Smith Equipment Mfg Co 2601 Lockheed Ave .... Watertown SD 57201 605-882-3200 685-3370*
**Fax Area Code: 800* ■ *TF Cust Svc:* 800-328-3363 ■ *Web:* www.smithequipment.com
Sonobond Ultrasonics Inc 1191 McDermott Dr .... West Chester PA 19380 610-696-4710 692-0674
TF: 800-323-1269 ■ *Web:* www.sonobondultrasonic.com
Stulz-Sickles Steel Co 929 Julia St PO Box 273 .... Elizabeth NJ 07207 908-351-1776 351-8231
TF: 800-351-1776 ■ *Web:* www.stulzsicklessteel.com
Systematics Inc 1025 Saunders Ln PO Box 2429 .... West Chester PA 19380 610-696-9040 430-8714
TF: 800-222-9353
Taylor-Winfield Corp PO Box 500.............................. Brookfield OH 44403 330-448-4464 448-3538
Web: www.taylor-winfield.com
Thermadyne Holdings Corp
16052 Swingley Ridge Rd Suite 300...................... Saint Louis MO 63017 636-728-3000
Web: www.thermadyne.com
Thermatool Corp 31 Commerce St PO Box 120769............ East Haven CT 06512 203-468-4100 468-4284*
**Fax:* Cust Svc ■ *Web:* www.thermatool.com
Tuffaloy Products Inc 1400 S Batesville Rd...................... Greer SC 29650 864-879-0763 877-2212
TF: 800-521-3722 ■ *Web:* www.tuffaloy.com
Unitek Miyachi Corp 1820 S Myrtle Ave .... Monrovia CA 91017 626-303-5676 358-8048
Web: www.unitekmiyachi.com
Uniweld Products Inc 2850 Ravenswood Rd .... Fort Lauderdale FL 33312 954-584-2000 587-0109
TF: 800-323-2111 ■ *Web:* www.uniweld.com
Vitronics Soltec Inc 2 Marin Way............................ Stratham NH 03885 603-772-7778 772-7776
Web: www.vitronics-soltec.com
Weld Mold Co 750 Rickett Rd.................................... Brighton MI 48116 810-229-9521 229-9580
TF: 800-521-9755 ■ *Web:* www.weldmold.com
Weld Tooling Corp 3001 W Carson St .... Pittsburgh PA 15204 412-331-1776 331-0383
TF: 800-245-3186 ■ *Web:* www.bugo.com
Weldmation Inc 31720 Stephenson Hwy .... Madison Heights MI 48071 248-585-0010 585-0016
Web: www.weldmation.com/corp
Weltronic 24775 Crestview Ct.......................... Farmington Hills MI 48335 248-987-1218 987-1226
Western Enterprises Inc 875 Bassett Rd .... Westlake OH 44145 800-783-7890 835-8283*
**Fax Area Code: 440* ■ *TF:* 800-783-7890 ■ *Web:* www.westernenterprises.com

815 WHOLESALE CLUBS

Phone Fax

BJ's Wholesale Club 1 Mercer Rd .... Natick MA 01760 508-651-7400 651-6251
NYSE: BJ ■ *TF:* 800-257-2582 ■ *Web:* www.bjs.com
Cost-U-Less Inc 3633 136th Pl SE Suite 110................... Bellevue WA 98006 425-945-0213 945-0214
NASDAQ: CULS ■ *Web:* www.costuless.com
Costco Wholesale Corp 999 Lake Dr .... Issaquah WA 98027 425-313-8100 313-8103
NASDAQ: COST ■ *TF Cust Svc:* 800-774-2678 ■ *Web:* www.costco.com
Costco Wholesale Corp International Div 999 Lake Dr........... Issaquah WA 98027 425-313-8100 313-8103
Web: www.costco.com
Marukai Wholesale Mart 2310 Kamehameha Hwy.............. Honolulu HI 96819 808-845-5051 841-2379
PriceSmart Inc 9740 Scranton Rd .... San Diego CA 92121 858-404-8800
NASDAQ: PSMT ■ *Web:* www.pricesmart.com
Sam's Club Div Wal-Mart Stores Inc 608 SW 8th St........... Bentonville AR 72712 479-277-7000
TF: 888-746-7726 ■ *Web:* www.samsclub.com
Wal-Mart Stores Inc Sam's Club Div 608 SW 8th St........... Bentonville AR 72712 479-277-7000
TF: 888-746-7726 ■ *Web:* www.samsclub.com

816 WIRE & CABLE

Phone Fax

AFC Cable Systems Inc 272 Duchaine Blvd .... New Bedford MA 02745 508-998-1131 998-1447
TF: 800-757-6996 ■ *Web:* www.afcweb.com
Alcan Cable 3 Ravinia Dr Suite 1600 .... Atlanta GA 30346 770-394-9886 395-9053
Web: www.cable.alcan.com
Allwire Inc 16395 Ave 24 1/2 PO Box 1000.................. Chowchilla CA 93610 559-665-4893 665-7389
TF: 800-255-3828 ■ *Web:* www.allwire.com
AmerCable Inc 350 Bailey Rd .... El Dorado AR 71730 870-862-4919 862-9613
TF: 800-643-1516 ■ *Web:* www.amercable.com
APA Enterprises Inc 2950 NE 84th Ln .... Blaine MN 55449 763-784-4995 784-2038
NASDAQ: APAT ■ *Web:* www.apaenterprises.com
Astro Industries Inc 4403 Dayton-Xenia Rd...................... Dayton OH 45432 937-429-5900 429-4054*
**Fax: Sales* ■ *TF:* 800-543-5810 ■ *Web:* www.astro-ind.com
Bekaert Corp 3200 W Market St Suite 303 .... Akron OH 44333 330-867-3325 873-3424
Web: www.bekaert.com
BIW Connector Systems LLC 500 Tesconi Cir .... Santa Rosa CA 95401 707-523-2300 523-3567
Web: www.biwconsys.com
Capro Inc 300 S Cochran St PO Box 588................................ Willis TX 77378 936-856-2971 856-4328
Web: www.capro.com
Cargill Ferrous International 12700 Whitewater Rd 4th Fl ...... Minnetonka MN 55343 952-984-3377 984-3326
Web: www.cargillsteel.com
Cerro Wire & Cable Co Inc 1099 Thompson Rd SE .... Hartselle AL 35640 256-773-2522
TF: 800-523-3869 ■ *Web:* www.cerrowire.com
Charter Wire 114 N Jackson St .... Milwaukee WI 53202 414-390-3000 390-3031
TF: 800-436-9074 ■ *Web:* www.charterwire.com
Coleman Cable Systems Inc 1530 Shields Dr .... Waukegan IL 60085 847-672-2300 689-1192
TF: 800-323-9355 ■ *Web:* www.colemancable.com
Cooner Wire Co 9265 Owensmouth Ave......................... Chatsworth CA 91311 818-882-8311 709-8281
Web: www.coonerwire.com
Cove Four-Slide & Stamping Corp 195 E Merrick Rd .... Freeport NY 11520 516-379-4232 379-4563
Web: www.covefour.com
Dekko Technologies LLC
8645 E Backwater Rd PO Box 337 .... North Webster IN 46555 574-834-2818 834-2794
Web: www.dekkotech.com
Draka Cableteq USA 22 Joseph E Warner Blvd .... North Dighton MA 02764 508-822-5444 822-1944
TF: 800-333-4248 ■ *Web:* www.drakacabletequsa.com
Elektrisola Inc 126 High St...................................... Boscawen NH 03303 603-796-2114 796-2111
TF: 800-325-2022 ■ *Web:* www.elektrisola.com
Encore Wire Corp 1410 Millwood Rd PO Box 1149.............. McKinney TX 75069 972-562-9473 562-3644
NASDAQ: WIRE ■ *TF:* 800-962-9473 ■ *Web:* www.encorewire.com
Eubanks Engineering Co 3022 Inland Empire Blvd .... Ontario CA 91764 909-483-2456 483-2498
Web: www.eubanks.com
Gehr Industries 7400 E Slauson Ave.......................... Los Angeles CA 90040 323-728-5558 725-0864
TF: 800-688-6606 ■ *Web:* www.gehr.com/gehr/
Hendrix Wire & Cable Inc 53 Old Wilton Rd .... Milford NH 03055 603-673-2040 673-0449
Web: www.hendrix-wc.com
Insteel Industries Inc 1373 Boggs Dr .... Mount Airy NC 27030 336-786-2141 786-2144
NASDAQ: IIIN ■ *TF:* 800-334-9504 ■ *Web:* www.insteel.com
International Wire Group Inc 12 Masonic Ave...................... Camden NY 13316 315-245-2000 245-1916
Web: www.mills-partners.com/operating/wire.htm
International Wire Group Omega Wire Div PO Box 131 .... Camden NY 13316 315-964-2217 245-0737
Ivy Steel & Wire Co 6933 Clinton Dr .... Houston TX 77020 713-674-8431 674-5931
Web: www.ivysteel.com

Phone Fax

Kalas Mfg Inc 25 Main St PO Box 328 Denver PA 17517 717-336-5575 336-4248
Web: www.kalaswire.com
Kerite Co 49 Day St. Seymour CT 06483 203-888-2591 888-1987
TF: 800-777-7483 ■ *Web:* www.kerite.com
Keystone Consolidated Industries Inc 7000 SW Adams St. Peoria IL 61641 309-697-7020 697-7120
TF Sales: 800-447-6444 ■ *Web:* www.redbrand.com
Leggett Wire Co 1 Leggett Rd Carthage MO 64836 417-358-8131 358-6904
TF: 800-888-4569 ■ *Web:* www.leggett.com
Marine Industrial Cable Corp PO Box 29207 New Orleans LA 70189 504-254-0754 254-3930
TF: 800-831-7534
Mercury Wire Products Inc 1 Mercury Dr Spencer MA 01562 508-885-6363 885-3316
Web: www.mercurywire.com
Mid-South Wire Co Inc 1070 Visco Dr Nashville TN 37210 615-244-5258 256-5836
TF: 800-714-7800 ■ *Web:* www.midsouthwire.com
Nichols Wire 1547 Helton Dr Florence AL 35630 256-764-4271 767-5152
TF: 800-633-3156 ■ *Web:* www.nicholswire.com
Okonite Co 102 Hilltop Rd. Ramsey NJ 07446 201-825-0300 825-3524
Web: www.okonite.com
Owl Wire & Cable Inc 3127 Seneca Turnpike Canastota NY 13032 315-697-2011 697-2123
TF: 800-765-9473 ■ *Web:* www.owlwire.com
Rea Magnet Wire Co Inc 3600 E Pontiac St Fort Wayne IN 46803 260-421-7321 422-4246
TF: 800-732-9473 ■ *Web:* www.reawire.com
Ribbon Technology Corp 825 Taylor Station Rd PO Box 30758 Gahanna OH 43230 614-864-5444 864-5305
TF: 800-848-0477 ■ *Web:* www.ribtec.com
Rochester Corp 751 Old Brandy Rd Culpeper VA 22701 540-825-2111 825-2238
Web: www.rochestercables.com
S & S Industries Inc 32-00 Skillman Ave Long Island City NY 11101 718-585-1333 292-2132
Santa Fe Textiles Inc 17370 Mt Herrmann St Fountain Valley CA 92708 949-251-1960 863-9788
Web: www.barcel.com/link5.htm
Seneca Wire & Mfg Co 319 S Vine St Fostoria OH 44830 419-435-9261 435-9265
TF Sales: 800-537-9537 ■ *Web:* www.senecawire.com
Shaped Wire Inc 30000 Solon Rd. Solon OH 44139 440-248-7600 248-5491
Web: www.shapedwire.com
Sivaco Wire Group 800 rue Ouellette Marieville QC J3M1P5 450-658-8741 460-0310
TF: 800-876-9473 ■ *Web:* www.sivaco.com
Southwire Co 1 Southwire Dr Carrollton GA 30119 770-832-4242 838-6462
TF: 800-444-1700 ■ *Web:* www.southwire.com
Sumitomo Electric USA Inc 21221 S Western Ave Suite 200 Torrance CA 90501 310-782-0227 782-0211
Web: www.sumitomo.com
Superior Essex Inc Magnet Wire/Winding Wire Div
1601 Wall St PO Box 1601 Fort Wayne IN 46802 260-461-4633 461-4690
TF Cust Svc: 800-551-8948 ■ *Web:* www.superioressex.com
Techalloy Co Inc 370 Franklin Tpke Mahwah NJ 07430 201-529-0900 529-1074
TF: 800-882-1006 ■ *Web:* www.techalloy.com
Techalloy Co Inc Baltimore Wire Div 2310 Chesapeake Ave. Baltimore MD 21222 410-633-9300 633-2033
TF: 800-638-1458 ■ *Web:* www.techalloy.com
TI Wire 12459 Arrow Rt PO Box 4464 Rancho Cucamonga CA 91729 909-899-1673 899-4533
TF: 800-843-9561 ■ *Web:* www.tiwireusa.com
Times Fiber Communications Inc 358 Hall Ave. Wallingford CT 06492 203-265-8500 265-8628
TF: 800-677-2288 ■ *Web:* www.timesfiber.com
Tuthill Corp 8500 S Madison St Burr Ridge IL 60527 630-382-4900 382-4999
TF: 800-888-4455 ■ *Web:* www.tuthill.com
Wire Rope Corp of America Inc
609 N 2nd St PO Box 288 Saint Joseph MO 64502 816-233-0287 236-5000
TF: 800-343-2808 ■ *Web:* www.wrca.com
Wirerope Works Inc 100 Maynard St Williamsport PA 17701 570-326-5146 327-4274
TF Cust Svc: 800-541-7673 ■ *Web:* www.wwwrope.com
Wrap-On Co Inc 5550 W 70th Pl. Bedford Park IL 60638 708-496-2150 496-2154
TF: 800-621-6947 ■ *Web:* www.wrapon.com

817 WIRE & CABLE - ELECTRONIC

Phone Fax

Alpha Wire Co 711 Lidgerwood Ave Elizabeth NJ 07207 908-925-8000 541-4402*
**Fax Area Code:* 800 ■ **Fax:* Sales ■ *TF:* 800-522-5742 ■ *Web:* www.alphawire.com
American Insulated Wire Corp 260 Forbes Blvd Mansfield MA 02048 508-964-1200 964-1192
TF: 800-366-2492 ■ *Web:* www.aiwc.com
Belden Inc 7701 Forsyth Blvd Suite 800. Saint Louis MO 63105 314-854-8000 854-8001
NYSE: BDC ■ *Web:* www.belden.com
Belden Inc Americas Div 2200 US Hwy 27 S PO Box 1980 Richmond IN 47375 765-983-5200 983-5294
TF: 800-235-3362 ■ *Web:* www.belden.com
C & M Corp 51 S Walnut St PO Box 348 Wauregan CT 06387 860-774-4812 774-7330
Web: www.cm-corp.com
Cable USA Inc 2584 S Horseshoe Dr Naples FL 34104 239-643-6400 643-4230
Web: www.cableusainc.com
Cables to Go Inc 1501 Webster St Dayton OH 45404 937-224-8646 496-2666
TF: 800-826-7904 ■ *Web:* www.cablestogo.com
Champlain Cable Corp 175 Hercules Dr Colchester VT 05446 802-654-4200 654-4224*
**Fax:* Sales ■ *TF:* 800-451-5162 ■ *Web:* www.champcable.com
Cicoil Corp 24960 Ave Tibbitts Valencia CA 91355 661-295-1295 295-0813
Web: www.cicoil.com
CommScope Inc 1100 Commscope Pl SE PO Box 1729 Hickory NC 28603 828-324-2200 328-3400*
NYSE: CTV ■ **Fax:* Cust Svc ■ *TF:* 800-982-1708 ■ *Web:* www.commscope.com
Comprehensive Video Group 55 Ruta Ct South Hackensack NJ 07606 201-229-4270 814-0510
TF: 800-526-0242 ■ *Web:* www.compvideo.com
Comtran Corp 1 Main St Whitinsville MA 01588 508-234-6256 234-7132
TF: 800-842-7809 ■ *Web:* www.comtrancorp.com
Consolidated Electronic Wire & Cable Co 11044 King St. Franklin Park IL 60131 847-455-8830 455-8837
TF: 800-621-4278 ■ *Web:* www.conwire.com
Corning Cable Systems 800 17th St NW PO Box 489 Hickory NC 28603 828-901-5000 325-5060
TF: 800-743-2671 ■ *Web:* www.siecor.com
CXtec 5404 S Bay Rd PO Box 4799 Syracuse NY 13212 315-476-3000 455-1800
TF Orders: 800-767-3282 ■ *Web:* www.cxtec.com
Dekoron Wire & Cable 1300 Industrial Blvd. Mount Pleasant TX 75455 903-572-3475 572-1331
Web: www.dekoroncable.com
Draka Cableteq USA 22 Joseph E Warner Blvd North Dighton MA 02764 508-822-5444 822-1944
TF: 800-333-4248 ■ *Web:* www.drakacabletequsa.com
Draka Comteq Americas 2512 Penny Rd PO Box 39. Claremont NC 28610 828-459-9821 459-8444
TF: 800-879-9862 ■ *Web:* www.drakacomteq.us
Electro Products Inc 26601 79th Ave S Kent WA 98032 253-859-0575 859-9101
TF: 800-423-0646 ■ *Web:* www.electro-products.com
Fujikura America Inc 280 Interstate North Cir SE Suite 530 Atlanta GA 30339 770-956-7200 956-9854
TF: 888-385-4587 ■ *Web:* www.fujikura.com
Furukawa America Inc 200 Westpark Dr Suite 190 Peachtree City GA 30269 770-487-1234 487-9910
Web: www.furukawaamerica.com
General Cable Corp 4 Tesseneer Dr Highland Heights KY 41076 859-572-8000 572-8458
NYSE: BGC ■ *TF:* 800-572-8000 ■ *Web:* www.biccgeneral.com
Harbour Industries Inc 4744 Shelburne Rd PO Box 188 Shelburne VT 05482 802-985-3311 985-9534
Web: www.harbourind.com
Judd Wire Inc 124 Turnpike Rd Turners Falls MA 01376 413-863-4357 863-4362
TF Cust Svc: 800-545-5833 ■ *Web:* www.juddwire.com
Madison Cable Corp 125 Goddard Memorial Dr. Worcester MA 01603 508-752-2884 752-4230
TF: 877-623-4766 ■ *Web:* www.madisoncable.com

Phone Fax

MNM Group Inc 3235 Sunset Ln. Hatboro PA 19040 215-672-9600 674-5380
TF: 800-645-3477 ■ *Web:* www.themnmgroup.com
Mohawk Div of Belden Inc 9 Mohawk Dr. Leominster MA 01453 978-537-9961 537-4358
TF: 800-422-9961 ■ *Web:* www.mohawk-cable.com
National Wire & Cable Corp 136 San Fernando Rd Los Angeles CA 90031 323-225-5611 225-4630
Web: www.nationalwire.com
Nehring Electric Works Inc 813 E Locust St DeKalb IL 60115 815-756-2741 756-7048
TF: 800-435-4481 ■ *Web:* www.nehringwire.com
Oleco Inc 18683 Trimble Ct PO Box 463 Spring Lake MI 49456 616-842-6790 842-5886
Web: www.olecoinc.com
Optical Cable Corp 5290 Concourse Dr Roanoke VA 24019 540-265-0690 265-0724
NASDAQ: OCCF ■ *TF:* 800-622-7711 ■ *Web:* www.occfiber.com
Paige Electric Corp 1160 Springfield Rd Union NJ 07083 908-687-7810 687-2722
TF: 800-327-2443 ■ *Web:* www.paigeelectric.com
Parlex Corp 1 Parlex Place Methuen MA 01844 978-685-4341 685-8809
Web: www.parlex.com
Phelps Dodge Industries 1 N Central Ave. Phoenix AZ 85004 602-366-8100 366-7300
Web: www.phelpsdodge.com
Pirelli Cables & Systems 700 Industrial Dr Lexington SC 29072 803-951-4800 951-4022*
**Fax:* Mktg ■ *TF Cust Svc:* 800-845-8507 ■ *Web:* www.pirelli.com/cables
Prestolite Wire Corp 200 Galleria Officentre Suite 212 Southfield MI 48034 248-355-4422 386-4462
TF: 800-498-3132 ■ *Web:* www.prestolitewire.com
Rockbestos-Surprenant Cable Corp 20 Bradley Park Rd East Granby CT 06026 860-653-8300 653-8410
Web: www.r-scc.com
Siemon Co 101 Siemon Co Dr. Watertown CT 06795 860-945-4200 945-4225
TF: 866-548-5814 ■ *Web:* www.siemon.com
Superior Essex Inc 150 Interstate North Pkwy Atlanta GA 30339 770-657-6000 303-8883
NASDAQ: SPSX ■ *TF:* 800-551-8948 ■ *Web:* www.superioressex.com
Tensolite Co 100 Tensolite Dr. Saint Augustine FL 32092 904-829-5600 829-3447
TF: 800-458-9960 ■ *Web:* www.tensolite.com
Trilogy Communications Inc 2910 Hwy 80 E Pearl MS 39208 601-932-4461 939-6637
TF: 800-874-5649 ■ *Web:* www.trilogycoax.com
Tyco Telecommunications 60 Columbia Rd Morristown NJ 07960 973-656-8000 656-8990
Web: www.tycotelecom.com

818 WIRING DEVICES - CURRENT-CARRYING

Phone Fax

Aerospace Optics Inc 3201 Sandy Ln Fort Worth TX 76112 817-451-1141 654-3405
TF: 888-848-4786 ■ *Web:* www.vivisun.com
ALP Lighting Components Inc 6333 Gross Point Rd Niles IL 60714 773-774-9550 594-3874
TF: 877-257-5841 ■ *Web:* www.alp-ltg.com
AMI DODUCO Inc 1003 Corporate Ln. Export PA 15632 724-733-8332 733-2880
Web: www.amidoduco.com
Amphenol Corp 358 Hall Ave. Wallingford CT 06492 203-265-8900 265-8628
NYSE: APH ■ *TF:* 877-267-4366 ■ *Web:* www.amphenol.com
Ark-Les Corp 95 Mill St. Stoughton MA 02072 781-297-6000 297-6160
TF: 800-342-6472 ■ *Web:* www.ark-les.com
Arlington Industries Inc 1 Stauffer Industrial Park. Scranton PA 18517 570-562-0270 562-0646
TF: 800-233-4717 ■ *Web:* www.aifittings.com
AVA Electronics Corp 4000 Bridge St. Drexel Hill PA 19026 610-284-2500 259-8379
TF Sales: 800-331-8838
AVCON Corp 4640 Ironwood Dr. Franklin WI 53132 414-817-6160 817-6161
TF: 800-433-7642 ■ *Web:* www.avconev.com
Brainin Advance Industries Inc 48 Frank Mossberg Dr. Attleboro MA 02703 508-222-3151 226-8703
Web: www.brainin.com
Carling Technologies Inc 60 Johnson Ave. Plainville CT 06062 860-793-9281 793-9231
TF: 800-243-8556 ■ *Web:* www.carlingtech.com
Charles E Gillman Co 907 E Frontage Rd Rio Rico AZ 85648 520-281-1141 281-1372
Web: www.gillman.com
Checon Corp 30 Larsen Way. North Attleboro MA 02763 508-809-5100 809-5163
Web: www.checon.com
Cherry Corp 11200 88th Ave Pleasant Prairie WI 53158 262-942-6500 942-6577
TF: 800-898-3966 ■ *Web:* www.cherrycorp.com
Cinch Connectors Inc 1700 Findley Rd Lombard IL 60148 630-705-6000 705-6060
TF: 800-323-9612 ■ *Web:* www.cinch.com
Cole Hersee Co 20 Old Colony Ave. Boston MA 02127 617-268-2100 268-9490
TF: 800-365-2653 ■ *Web:* www.colehersee.com
Component Enterprises Co 235-275 E Penn St Norristown PA 19401 610-272-7900 272-7040
Connector Mfg Co 3501 Symmes Rd Hamilton OH 45015 513-860-4455 860-6114
Web: www.cmclugs.com
Control Concepts Corp 328 Water St Binghamton NY 13901 607-724-2484 722-8713
TF: 800-288-6169 ■ *Web:* www.control-concepts.com
Cooper Bussmann Inc 114 Old State Rd. Ellisville MO 63021 636-394-2877 544-2570*
**Fax Area Code:* 800 ■ *Web:* www.bussmann.com
Cooper Crouse-Hinds Wolf & 7th North St PO Box 4999 Syracuse NY 13221 315-477-5531 477-5179
TF: 866-764-5454 ■ *Web:* www.crouse-hinds.com
Cooper Industries 600 Travis St Suite 5800. Houston TX 77002 713-209-8400 209-8995
NYSE: CBE ■ *Web:* www.cooperindustries.com
Cooper Wiring Devices Inc 203 Cooper Cir Peachtree City GA 30269 770-631-2100 329-3055*
**Fax Area Code:* 800 ■ *TF Cust Svc:* 800-441-3177 ■ *Web:* www.cooperwiringdevices.com
Cord Sets Inc 1015 5th St N. Minneapolis MN 55411 612-337-9700 337-0800
TF: 800-752-0580 ■ *Web:* www.cordsetsinc.com
Cord Specialties Co 10632 W Grand Ave. Franklin Park IL 60131 847-455-3503 455-0916
Web: www.cordspecialties.com
Crouse-Hinds Div Cooper Industries Ltd
Wolf & 7th North St PO Box 4999 Syracuse NY 13221 315-477-5531 477-5179
TF: 866-764-5454 ■ *Web:* www.crouse-hinds.com
Curtis Industries Inc 2400 S 43rd St Milwaukee WI 53219 414-649-4200 649-4279
TF: 800-657-0853 ■ *Web:* www.curtisind.com
Delta-Unibus Corp 515 N Railroad Ave. North Lake IL 60164 708-409-1200 409-1211
Web: www.deltaunibus.com
Deutsch Engineered Connecting Devices 5733 W Whittier Ave Hemet CA 92545 951-765-2200 922-1544
Web: www.deutschecd.com
Dossert Corp 500 Captain Neville Dr. Waterbury CT 06705 203-573-1616 753-0178
TF: 800-890-8878 ■ *Web:* www.dossert.com
Duraline Div JB Nottingham & Co Inc 75 Hoffman Ln Islandia NY 11749 631-234-2002 234-2360
Web: www.jbn-duraline.com
Edwin Gaynor Corp 200 Charles St. Stratford CT 06615 203-378-5545 381-9019
TF: 800-342-9667 ■ *Web:* www.egaynor.com
EECO Switch 880 Columbia St Brea CA 92821 714-835-6000 482-9429
TF: 800-854-3808 ■ *Web:* www.eecoswitch.com
EFI Electronics Corp 1751 S 4800 West Salt Lake City UT 84104 801-977-9009 977-0200
TF: 800-877-1174 ■ *Web:* www.efinet.com
Electri-Cord Mfg Co Inc 312 E Main St Westfield PA 16950 814-367-2265 367-2314
Web: www.electri-cord.com
Electronic Systems Packaging LLC
1175 W Victoria St. Rancho Dominguez CA 90220 310-639-2535 632-6666
Web: www.espbus.com
Electroswitch Electronic Products 2010 Yonkers Rd Raleigh NC 27604 919-833-0707 833-8016
TF: 888-768-2797 ■ *Web:* www.electro-nc.com
ERICO International Corp 30575 Bainbridge Rd Suite 300. Solon OH 44139 440-349-2630 349-2996
TF: 800-800-9301 ■ *Web:* www.erico.com

Company	City	State	Zip	Phone	Fax
ERICO Products Inc 34600 Solon Rd *TF:* 800-813-3378 ■ *Web:* www.erico.com	Solon	OH	44139	440-248-0100	248-0723
ETCO Inc 25 Bellows St *Web:* www.etco.com	Warwick	RI	02888	401-467-2400	467-9230
Eureka Electrical Products Inc 79 Clay St	North East	PA	16428	814-725-9638	725-3670
FTZ Industries Inc 515 Palmetto Dr *TF:* 800-336-8989 ■ *Web:* www.ftzind.com	Simpsonville	SC	29681	864-963-5000	963-5352
G & W Electric Co 3500 W 127th St *Web:* www.gwelec.com	Blue Island	IL	60406	708-388-5010	388-0755
Gaynor Edwin Corp 200 Charles St *TF:* 800-342-9667 ■ *Web:* www.egaynor.com	Stratford	CT	06615	203-378-5545	381-9019
Glenair Inc 1211 Air Way *Web:* www.glenair.com	Glendale	CA	91201	818-247-6000	500-9912
Group Dekko Services LLC 6928 N 400 E *TF:* 800-829-0700 ■ *Web:* www.dekko.com	Kendallville	IN	46755	260-347-0700	347-2028
Hi-Stat Mfg Co Inc 345 S Mill St *Web:* www.histat.com	Lexington	OH	44904	419-884-1219	884-4196
Hoffman Products 20700 Hubbell Ave **Fax Area Code:* 800 ■ *TF:* 800-645-2014 ■ *Web:* www.hoffmanproducts.com	Oak Park	MI	48237	248-395-8462	908-1295*
Hoyt Corp 520 S Dean St *TF:* 800-255-4698 ■ *Web:* www.hoyt-corp.com	Englewood	NJ	07631	201-894-0707	894-0916
Hubbell Inc 584 Derby-Milford Rd *NYSE:* HUBB ■ *Web:* www.hubbell.com	Orange	CT	06477	203-799-4100	799-4205
Hubbell Premise Wiring Inc 14 Lord's Hill Rd **Fax Area Code:* 860 ■ *Web:* www.hubbell-premise.com	Stonington	CT	06378	800-626-0005	535-8328*
Hubbell Wiring Device-Kellems 185 Plains Rd **Fax Area Code:* 800 ■ **Fax:* Cust Svc ■ *Web:* www.hubbell-wiring.com	Milford	CT	06460	203-882-4800	255-1031*
ILSCO 4730 Madison Rd *TF Sales:* 800-776-9775 ■ *Web:* www.ilsco.com	Cincinnati	OH	45227	513-533-6200	533-6226
Independent Protection Co Inc 1607 S Main St *TF:* 800-860-8388 ■ *Web:* www.ipclp.com	Goshen	IN	46526	574-533-4116	534-3719
ITT Neo-Dyn Industrial Switch 28150 Industry Dr **Fax:* Mktg ■ *Web:* www.neodyn.com	Valencia	CA	91355	661-295-4000	294-1750*
JB Nottingham & Co Inc Duraline Div 75 Hoffman Ln *Web:* www.jbn-duraline.com	Islandia	NY	11749	631-234-2002	234-2360
Joslyn Electronics 5900 Eastport Blvd *TF:* 800-238-5000 ■ *Web:* www.joslynsurge.com	Richmond	VA	23231	804-236-3300	236-4040
Joslyn High Voltage Corp 4000 E 116th St *TF:* 800-621-5875 ■ *Web:* www.joslynhivoltage.com	Cleveland	OH	44105	216-271-6600	341-3615
KDI Precision Products Inc 3975 McMann Rd *TF:* 800-377-3334 ■ *Web:* www.kdi-ppi.com	Cincinnati	OH	45245	513-943-2000	943-2321
Kemlon Products & Development Co 1424 N Main St *Web:* www.kemlon.com	Pearland	TX	77581	281-997-3300	997-1300
Keystone Cable Corp 8200 Lynch Rd *TF:* 800-223-2996 ■ *Web:* www.keystonecable.net	Detroit	MI	48234	313-924-9720	924-0050
Lamcor Inc 2025 E Orangewood Ave *Web:* www.lamcorinc.com	Anaheim	CA	92806	714-634-2950	634-4713
Leviton Mfg Co Inc 59-25 Little Neck Pkwy *TF Tech Supp:* 800-824-3005 ■ *Web:* www.leviton.com	Little Neck	NY	11362	718-229-4040	281-6102
Liebert Corp 1050 Dearborn Dr *TF Tech Supp:* 800-543-2778 ■ *Web:* www.liebert.com	Columbus	OH	43085	614-888-0246	841-6022
Lighting Components & Design Inc 692 S Military Tr *Web:* www.lightingcomponents.com	Deerfield Beach	FL	33442	954-425-0123	425-0110
LL Rowe Co 66 Holton St *Web:* www.llrowe.com	Woburn	MA	01801	781-729-7860	721-7264
McGill Electrical Product Group 9377 W Higgins Rd **Fax Area Code:* 800 ■ *TF:* 888-832-0660 ■ *Web:* www.mcgillelectrical.com	Rosemont	IL	60018	847-268-6000	356-4714*
Mill-Max Mfg Corp 190 Pine Hollow Rd *TF:* 800-294-8027 ■ *Web:* www.mill-max.com	Oyster Bay	NY	11771	516-922-6000	922-9253
Nexus Inc 50 Sunnyside Ave *Web:* www.nexus.com	Stamford	CT	06904	203-327-7300	324-7623
Ohio Associated Enterprises LLC 1382 W Jackson St *TF:* 800-863-9014	Painesville	OH	44077	440-354-3148	354-0687
Omnetics Connector Corp 7260 Commerce Cir E *TF Cust Svc:* 800-343-0025 ■ *Web:* www.omnetics.com	Minneapolis	MN	55432	763-572-0656	572-3925
Panduit Corp 17301 S Ridgeland Ave *TF:* 888-506-5400 ■ *Web:* www.panduit.com	Tinley Park	IL	60477	708-532-1800	532-1811
Pass & Seymour/Legrand 50 Boyd Ave PO Box 4822 *TF:* 800-223-4185 ■ *Web:* www.passandseymour.com	Syracuse	NY	13221	315-468-6211	468-6296
Penn-Union Corp 229 Waterford St *Web:* www.penn-union.com	Edinboro	PA	16412	814-734-1631	734-4946
Philips Accessories 13895 Industrial Park Blvd Suite 110 *TF:* 800-639-7646	Plymouth	MN	55441	763-559-0841	557-0884
Philips Accessories Power Sentry Div 13895 Industrial Park Blvd Suite 110 *TF:* 800-852-4312 ■ *Web:* www.powersentry.com	Plymouth	MN	55441	763-559-0841	557-0884
Phoenix Co of Chicago Inc 555 Pond Dr *Web:* www.phoenixofchicago.com	Wood Dale	IL	60191	630-595-2300	595-6579
PolyPhaser Corp 2225 Park Pl *TF Cust Svc:* 800-325-7170 ■ *Web:* www.polyphaser.com	Minden	NV	89423	775-782-2511	782-4476
Power Connect Devices Inc 7232 Aviation Blvd Suite 202	Redondo Beach	CA	90278	310-322-6580	322-8130
Preformed Line Products 660 Beta Dr *NASDAQ:* PLPC ■ *TF:* 888-773-3676 ■ *Web:* www.preformed.com	Mayfield Village	OH	44143	440-461-5200	442-8816
Rowe LL Co 66 Holton St *Web:* www.llrowe.com	Woburn	MA	01801	781-729-7860	721-7264
Shape LLC 2105 Corporate Dr *TF:* 800-367-5811 ■ *Web:* www.shapellc.com/	Addison	IL	60101	630-620-8394	620-0784
SL Industries Inc 520 Fellowship Rd Suite A114 *AMEX:* SLI ■ *Web:* slindustries.com	Mount Laurel	NJ	08054	856-727-1500	727-1683
Springfield Wire Inc 243 Cottage St *Web:* www.springfield-wire.com	Springfield	MA	01104	413-781-6950	739-3809
Storm Products Co 501 Santa Monica Blvd Suite 703 *Web:* www.stormproducts.com	Santa Monica	CA	90401	310-319-5388	319-5394
Technitrol Inc 1210 Northbrook Dr Suite 470 *NYSE:* TNL ■ *Web:* www.technitrol.com	Trevose	PA	19053	215-355-2900	355-7397
Technology Research Corp 5250 140th Ave N *NASDAQ:* TRCI ■ *TF Mktg:* 800-483-2000 ■ *Web:* www.trci.net	Clearwater	FL	33760	727-535-0572	535-4828
Tower Mfg Corp 25 Reservoir Ave *Web:* www.towermfg.com	Providence	RI	02907	401-467-7550	461-2710
Transtector Systems Inc 10701 Airport Dr **Fax:* Sales ■ *TF:* 800-882-9110 ■ *Web:* www.transtector.com	Hayden Lake	ID	83835	208-772-8515	762-6117*
Tripp Lite Inc 1111 W 35th St *Web:* www.tripplite.com	Chicago	IL	60609	773-869-1111	869-1329
Veetronix Inc 1311 W Pacific Ave *TF:* 800-445-0007 ■ *Web:* www.veetronix.com	Lexington	NE	68850	308-324-6661	324-4985
Vitrus Inc 881 Main St *Web:* www.vitrus.com	Pawtucket	RI	02860	401-724-9350	728-4620
Volex Inc 915 Tate Blvd SE Suite 130 *Web:* www.volex.com	Hickory	NC	28602	828-485-4500	485-4501
Weidmuller Inc 821 Southlake Blvd *TF Cust Svc:* 800-849-9343 ■ *Web:* www.weidmuller.com	Richmond	VA	23236	804-794-2877	379-2593
Wells-CTI Inc 2102 W Quail Ave Suite 2 *TF:* 800-348-2505 ■ *Web:* www.wellscti.com	Phoenix	AZ	85027	623-581-5330	780-3987
Wiremold Co 60 Woodlawn St *TF Sales:* 800-621-0049 ■ *Web:* www.wiremold.com	West Hartford	CT	06110	860-233-6251	232-2062
Wiremold Co Brooks Electronics Div 13200 Townsend Rd *TF:* 800-523-0130	Philadelphia	PA	19154	215-969-3803	969-3858
Woodhead Industries Inc 333 Knightsbridge Pkwy Suite 200 *NASDAQ:* WDHD ■ *Web:* www.woodhead.com	Lincolnshire	IL	60069	847-353-2500	883-8732
Woodhead LP 3411 Woodhead Dr *TF Mktg:* 800-225-7724 ■ *Web:* www.danielwoodhead.com	Northbrook	IL	60062	847-272-7990	272-8133
Woods Industries Canada Inc 375 Kennedy Rd *TF:* 800-561-4321	Toronto	ON	M1K2A3	416-267-4610	267-5211
Woods Industries Inc 5541 W 74th St *TF:* 800-428-6168 ■ *Web:* www.woodsltd.com	Indianapolis	IN	46268	317-844-7261	843-1675
WPI Inc 90 W Broadway *Web:* www.wpi-interconnect.com	Salem	NJ	08079	856-935-7370	935-3093

819 WIRING DEVICES - NONCURRENT-CARRYING

Company	City	State	Zip	Phone	Fax
Active Industries Inc 20 Solar Dr *TF:* 800-403-2284 ■ *Web:* www.activeind.com	Clifton Park	NY	12065	518-371-2020	371-0434
Adalet 4801 W 150th St **Fax:* Sales ■ *Web:* www.adalet.com	Cleveland	OH	44135	216-267-9000	267-1681*
Allied Moulded Products Inc 222 N Union St *Web:* www.alliedmoulded.com	Bryan	OH	43506	419-636-4217	636-2450
Aluma-Form Inc 3625 Old Getwell Rd *Web:* www.alumaform.com	Memphis	TN	38118	901-362-0100	794-9515
Bedford Materials Co Inc 7676 Allegheny Rd *TF:* 800-773-4276 ■ *Web:* www.bedfordmaterials.com	Manns Choice	PA	15550	814-623-9014	623-9199
Bridgeport Fittings Inc 705 Lordship Blvd *Web:* www.bptfittings.com	Stratford	CT	06615	203-377-5944	381-3488
Chalfant Mfg Co 11525 Madison Ave *Web:* www.chalfantcabletray.com	Cleveland	OH	44102	216-521-7922	521-6854
Chase & Sons Inc 19 Highland Ave *TF:* 800-323-4182 ■ *Web:* www.chasecorp.com/chasesons.html	Randolph	MA	02368	781-963-2600	986-1445
Conduit Pipe Products Co 1501 W Main St *TF:* 800-848-6125 ■ *Web:* www.conduitpipe.com	West Jefferson	OH	43162	614-879-9114	879-5185
Cooper B-Line Inc 509 W Monroe St **Fax Area Code:* 800 ■ *TF:* 800-851-7415 ■ *Web:* www.b-line.com	Highland	IL	62249	618-654-2184	356-1438*
Cope TJ Inc 11500 Norcom Rd *TF:* 800-426-4293 ■ *Web:* www.tjcope.com	Philadelphia	PA	19154	215-961-2570	961-2580
Cottrell Paper Co Inc 1135 Rock City Rd PO Box 35 *TF:* 800-948-3559 ■ *Web:* www.cottrellpaper.com	Rock City Falls	NY	12863	518-885-1702	885-0741
Curlee Mfg Co 13639 Aldine Westfield Rd *TF:* 800-631-6815 ■ *Web:* www.egs-curlee.com	Houston	TX	77039	281-774-3700	774-3761
EGS Electrical Group LLC 9377 W Higgins Rd *TF:* 800-621-1506 ■ *Web:* www.egseg.com	Rosemont	IL	60018	847-268-6000	268-6060
Electri-Flex Co 222 W Central Ave *TF Cust Svc:* 800-323-6174 ■ *Web:* www.electriflex.com	Roselle	IL	60172	630-529-2920	529-0482
Electric & Gas Technology Inc 3233 W Kingsley Rd **Fax:* Acctg ■ *Web:* www.elgt.com	Garland	TX	75041	972-840-3223	271-8925*
Electro-Term/Hollingsworth 90 Memorial Dr *TF:* 800-638-8376 ■ *Web:* www.hollingsworth.com	Springfield	MA	01104	413-734-6469	733-0827
Flex-Cable 20 W Huron St *TF:* 800-245-3539 ■ *Web:* www.flexcable.com	Pontiac	MI	48342	248-332-6900	332-4828
Gaylord Mfg Co 1730 E Whitmore Ave PO Box 547 *TF:* 800-375-0091 ■ *Web:* www.gaylordmfg.com	Ceres	CA	95307	209-538-3313	
Gund Co 2121 Walton Rd *Web:* www.thegundcompany.com	Saint Louis	MO	63114	314-423-5200	423-9009
Hoffman Enclosures Inc 2100 Hoffman Way *Web:* www.hoffmanonline.com	Anoka	MN	55303	763-421-2240	422-2600
Homaco Inc 125 Eugene O'Neil Ct *TF:* 800-934-5432 ■ *Web:* www.homaco.com	New London	CT	06320	860-445-3800	405-2992
Hubbell Killark 3940 ML King Dr *TF:* 800-545-5275 ■ *Web:* www.hubbell-killark.com	Saint Louis	MO	63113	314-531-0460	531-7164
Hubbell Premise Wiring Inc 14 Lord's Hill Rd **Fax Area Code:* 860 ■ *Web:* www.hubbell-premise.com	Stonington	CT	06378	800-626-0005	535-8328*
Hubbell RACO 3902 W Sample St *TF:* 800-722-6437 ■ *Web:* www.hubbell-raco.com	South Bend	IN	46619	574-234-7151	283-4244
Hubbell Wiegmann 501 W Apple St *Web:* www.hubbell-wiegmann.com	Freeburg	IL	62243	618-539-3193	539-5794
Hughes Brothers Inc 210 N 13th St PO Box 159 *Web:* www.hughesbros.com	Seward	NE	68434	402-643-2991	643-2149
ICO-RALLY Corp 2575 E Bayshore Rd **Fax Area Code:* 800 ■ *Web:* www.icorally.com	Palo Alto	CA	94303	650-856-9900	856-2006*
Icore International Inc 3780 Flightline Dr *Web:* www.icoregroup.com	Santa Rosa	CA	95403	707-535-2700	521-2524
Ideal Industries Inc 1 Becker Pl **Fax:* Mktg ■ *TF Cust Svc:* 800-435-0705 ■ *Web:* www.idealindustries.com	Sycamore	IL	60178	815-895-5181	899-7712*
Joslyn Sunbank Co LLC 1740 Commerce Way **Fax:* Cust Svc ■ *TF:* 800-275-8777 ■ *Web:* www.sunbankcorp.com	Paso Robles	CA	93446	805-238-2840	238-0241*
Kortick Mfg Co 2230 Davis Ct *Web:* www.kortick.com	Hayward	CA	94545	510-856-3600	856-3606
Lamson & Sessions Co 25701 Science Park Dr *NYSE:* LMS ■ *TF:* 800-321-1970 ■ *Web:* www.lamson-sessions.com	Cleveland	OH	44122	216-464-3400	464-1455
LoDan Electronics Inc 3311 N Kennicott Ave *TF:* 800-401-4995 ■ *Web:* www.lodan.com	Arlington Heights	IL	60004	847-398-5311	398-5340
MacLean Power Systems 11411 Addison St **Fax:* Sales ■ *Web:* www.macleanpower.com	Franklin Park	IL	60131	847-455-0014	455-0029*
Monti Inc 333 W Seymour Ave *Web:* www.monti-inc.com	Cincinnati	OH	45216	513-761-7775	948-6858
MP Husky Corp 204 Old Piedmont Hwy PO Box 16749 *TF:* 800-277-4810 ■ *Web:* www.mphusky.com	Greenville	SC	29606	864-234-4800	234-4822
Mulberry Metal Products Inc 2199 Stanley Terr *Web:* www.mulberrymetal.com	Union	NJ	07083	908-688-8850	688-7294
O-Z/Gedney 9377 W Higgins Rd **Fax Area Code:* 800 ■ *TF:* 800-621-1506 ■ *Web:* www.o-zgedney.com	Rosemont	IL	60018	847-268-6000	356-4714*
Ohio Brass Co 1850 Richland Ave E *Web:* www.hubbellpowersystems.com	Aiken	SC	29801	803-648-8386	642-2959
Opti-Com Mfg Network Co Inc 259 Plauche St *TF:* 800-345-8774 ■ *Web:* www.omni-opti.com	Harahan	LA	70123	504-736-0331	733-9046
P-W Industries Inc 9415 Kruse Rd *TF:* 800-452-3023 ■ *Web:* www.pwcabletray.com	Pico Rivera	CA	90660	562-463-9055	463-9062
Rittal Corp 1 Rittal Pl *TF:* 800-477-4000 ■ *Web:* www.rittal-corp.com	Springfield	OH	45504	937-399-0500	390-5599
Robroy Industries Inc 10 River Rd *Web:* www.robroy.com	Verona	PA	15147	412-828-2100	828-8934
Saginaw Control & Engineering Inc 95 Midland Rd *TF:* 800-234-6871 ■ *Web:* www.saginawcontrol.com	Saginaw	MI	48638	989-799-6871	799-4524
Southwire Co 2630 El Presidio St **Fax:* Sales ■ *TF:* 800-444-1700 ■ *Web:* www.southwire.com	Long Beach	CA	90810	310-886-8300	631-3602*
Thomas & Betts Corp 8155 T & B Blvd *NYSE:* TNB ■ *TF:* 800-858-6022 ■ *Web:* www.tnb.com	Memphis	TN	38125	901-252-8000	252-1306
TJ Cope Inc 11500 Norcom Rd *TF:* 800-426-4293 ■ *Web:* www.tjcope.com	Philadelphia	PA	19154	215-961-2570	961-2580

Company	City	State	Zip	Phone	Fax
US Samica Inc 477 Windcrest Rd PO Box 848 *TF:* 800-248-5528 ■ *Web:* www.ussamica.com	Rutland	VT	05702	802-775-5528	775-5935
Varflex Corp 512 W Court St PO Box 551 *TF:* 800-648-4014 ■ *Web:* www.varflex.com	Rome	NY	13442	315-336-4400	336-0005
Virginia Plastics Co Inc 3453 Aerial Way Dr *TF:* 888-905-2225 ■ *Web:* www.vaplastics.com	Roanoke	VA	24018	540-981-9700	981-2022
Weidmann Electrical Technology 1 Gordon Mills Way PO Box 903 *TF:* 800-242-6748 ■ *Web:* www.weidmann-electrical.com	Saint Johnsbury	VT	05819	802-748-8106	748-8029

820 WOOD MEMBERS - STRUCTURAL

Company	City	State	Zip	Phone	Fax
AC Houston Lumber Co 2912 E La Madre Way *Web:* www.achoustonlumber.com	North Las Vegas	NV	89081	702-633-5100	633-5111
Alpine Engineered Products Inc 1200 Park Central Blvd S PO Box 2225 *TF:* 800-735-8055 ■ *Web:* www.alpeng.com	Pompano Beach	FL	33061	954-781-3333	977-3149
American Laminators 600 Applegate St PO Box 297 *Web:* www.americanlaminators.com	Drain	OR	97435	541-836-2000	836-7144
Armstrong Lumber Co Inc 2709 Auburn Way N *TF:* 800-868-9066 ■ *Web:* www.armstrong-homes.com	Auburn	WA	98002	253-833-6666	833-5878
Automated Building Components Inc 2359 Grant Rd *Web:* www.abctruss.com	North Baltimore	OH	45872	419-257-2152	257-2779
Automated Products Inc 1812 Karau Dr	Marshfield	WI	54449	715-387-3426	387-6588
Best Homes Inc 1230 W 171st St	Hazel Crest	IL	60429	708-335-2000	335-4891
Bradco Supply Corp 13 Production Way *TF:* 877-427-2320 ■ *Web:* www.bradcosupply.com	Avenel	NJ	07001	732-382-3400	382-6577
Buettner Brothers Lumber Co 700 7th Ave SW *TF:* 800-500-0669	Cullman	AL	35055	256-734-4221	737-8102
Burns Construction Inc 6676 S Old US Hwy 31 *TF:* 800-552-3309	Macy	IN	46951	574-382-2315	382-2522
Citation Homes Inc 1100 Lake St *TF:* 800-831-5090 ■ *Web:* www.citationhomes.com	Spirit Lake	IA	51360	712-336-2156	336-4779
Columbia Forest Products Inc 222 SW Columbia St Suite 1575 *TF:* 800-547-4261 ■ *Web:* www.columbiaforestproducts.com	Portland	OR	97201	503-224-5300	224-5294
Columbus Roof Trusses Inc 2525 Fisher Rd	Columbus	OH	43204	614-272-6464	272-6469
Cox Lumber Co 3300 Fairfield Ave S *Web:* www.coxlumber.com	Saint Petersburg	FL	33712	727-327-4503	327-5393
Dura-Bilt Truss Co 3312 Patterson Rd PO Box 796	Riverbank	CA	95367	209-869-4545	869-3886
East Coast Lumber & Supply Co 308 Ave A *Web:* www.eastcoastlumber.com	Fort Pierce	FL	34950	772-466-1700	465-8678
Engineered Building Component Co 146 Washington Ave S *Web:* www.ebcotruss.com	Hopkins	MN	55343	952-935-4902	935-4901
Enwood Structures Inc 5724 McCrimmon Pkwy *TF:* 800-777-8648 ■ *Web:* www.enwood.com	Morrisville	NC	27560	919-467-6155	469-2536
Evergreen Truss Co Inc 6302 NE 127th Ave	Vancouver	WA	98682	360-256-2300	892-0017
Fabricated Wood Products Inc 6150 W Frontage Rd	Medford	MN	55049	507-451-1019	451-5103
Fagen's Building Centers Inc 2515 Pebble Ave *Web:* www.fagens.com	Pittsburgh	PA	15233	412-323-2100	323-9509
Frank Calandra Co Inc 134 Pfeister Ave	Cresson	PA	16630	814-886-4121	886-8143
Fullerton Building Systems Inc 34620 250th St *TF:* 800-450-9782 ■ *Web:* www.fullertonbldg.com	Worthington	MN	56187	507-376-3128	376-9530
Gang Nail Truss Co of Visalia 1440 N Shirk Rd *Web:* www.gangnailtruss.com	Visalia	CA	93291	559-651-2121	651-1832
HM Stauffer & Sons Inc 33 Glenola Dr	Leola	PA	17540	717-656-2811	656-4392
Houston AC Lumber Co 2912 E La Madre Way *Web:* www.achoustonlumber.com	North Las Vegas	NV	89081	702-633-5100	633-5111
iLevel by Weyerhaeuser 200 E Mallard Dr *TF Cust Svc:* 800-338-0515 ■ *Web:* www.ilevel.com	Boise	ID	83706	208-364-1200	364-1300
Laminators Inc 3255 Souderton Pike *TF:* 800-523-2347 ■ *Web:* www.signboards.com	Hatfield	PA	19440	215-723-8107	721-4669
Molpus Co 502 Valley View Dr *Web:* www.molpus.com	Philadelphia	MS	39350	601-656-3373	656-4947
Montgomery Truss & Panel Inc 803 W Main St *TF:* 800-245-0334	Grove City	PA	16127	724-458-7500	458-0765
Olympic Structures Inc 1850 93rd Ave SW *TF:* 800-562-6066	Olympia	WA	98512	360-943-5433	352-1529
Oso Lumber & Hardware Inc 21015 State Rd 9 NE *Web:* www.osolumber.com	Arlington	WA	98223	360-435-8397	435-6035
Perfection Truss Inc 5305 Williams St	Albuquerque	NM	87105	505-877-0770	873-2438
Powell Structural Systems Inc 130 Johnson Dr *TF:* 800-351-7176 ■ *Web:* www.powelltruss.com	Delaware	OH	43015	740-549-0465	549-0474
Ram Building Components Co 9500 Henry Ct *TF:* 800-827-5434	Zeeland	MI	49464	616-875-8157	875-8229
Robbins Mfg Co 13001 N Nebraska Ave PO Box 17939 *TF:* 800-282-9336	Tampa	FL	33682	813-971-3030	972-3980
Roof Structures Inc 3333 Yale Way *Web:* www.roofstructures.com	Fremont	CA	94538	510-226-7171	226-8989
Sentinel Structures Inc 477 S Peck Ave *Web:* www.sentinelstructures.com	Peshtigo	WI	54157	715-582-4544	582-4932
Shelter Systems Ltd 1025 Meadow Branch Rd *Web:* www.sheltersystems.com	Westminster	MD	21158	410-876-3900	857-5754
Shook Builder Supply Co 1400 16th St NE *TF:* 800-968-0758	Hickory	NC	28601	828-328-2051	328-2425
Southern Components Inc 7360 Julie Frances Rd *TF:* 800-256-2144 ■ *Web:* www.southerncomponents.com	Shreveport	LA	71129	318-687-3330	686-5159
Standard Structures Inc 5900 Pruitt Ave *TF:* 800-862-4936 ■ *Web:* www.standardstructures.com	Windsor	CA	95492	707-836-8100	836-8109
Stark Truss Co Inc 109 Miles Ave SW *TF:* 800-933-2258 ■ *Web:* www.starktruss.com	Canton	OH	44710	330-478-2100	478-9413
Stauffer HM & Sons Inc 33 Glenola Dr	Leola	PA	17540	717-656-2811	656-4392
Structural Wood Corp 4000 Labore Rd *TF:* 800-652-9058 ■ *Web:* www.structural-wood.com	Saint Paul	MN	55110	651-426-8111	426-6859
Structural Wood Systems 321 Dohrimier St *Web:* www.structuralwood.com	Greenville	AL	36037	334-382-6534	382-4260
Tacoma Truss Systems Inc 20617 Mountain Hwy E *Web:* www.tacomatruss.com	Spanaway	WA	98387	253-847-2204	847-2207
Timber Truss Housing Systems Inc 525 McClelland St PO Box 996 *TF:* 800-766-9072 ■ *Web:* www.timbertruss.com	Salem	VA	24153	540-387-0273	389-0849
Trusco Inc 12527 Porr Rd *TF:* 800-847-5841 ■ *Web:* www.truscoinc.com	Doylestown	OH	44230	330-658-2027	658-4979
Truss Mfg Co Inc 17317 Westfield Park Rd *TF:* 800-467-4525	Westfield	IN	46074	317-896-2571	896-3776
Truss-Span Corp 3136 B St NW *TF:* 800-842-8256	Auburn	WA	98001	253-833-1050	735-1126
Trussway Ltd 9411 Alcorn Rd *Web:* www.trussway.com	Houston	TX	77093	713-691-6900	691-2064
Unadilla Silo Co Inc 18 Clifton St PO Box K	Unadilla	NY	13849	607-369-9341	369-3608
Universal Forest Products Inc 2801 E Beltline Ave NE *NASDAQ: UFPI* ■ *TF:* 800-598-9663 ■ *Web:* www.ufpinc.com	Grand Rapids	MI	49525	616-364-6161	361-7534

Company	City	State	Zip	Phone	Fax
Valley Best-Way Building Supply 118 S Union Rd *TF:* 800-722-4491 ■ *Web:* www.valleybest-way.com	Spokane	WA	99206	509-924-1250	922-5420
Villaume Industries Inc 2926 Lone Oak Cir *TF Cust Svc:* 800-488-3610 ■ *Web:* www.villaume.com	Saint Paul	MN	55121	651-454-3610	454-8556
Windquest Co Inc 3311 Windquest Dr *TF:* 800-562-4257 ■ *Web:* www.windquestco.com	Holland	MI	49424	616-399-3311	399-8784
Wood Structures Inc 20 Pomerleau St *TF:* 800-341-9612 ■ *Web:* www.wsitruss.com	Biddeford	ME	04005	207-282-7556	282-2423

821 WOOD PRESERVING

Company	City	State	Zip	Phone	Fax
Appalachian Timber Services Inc 393 Edgar Given Pkwy *Web:* www.atstimber.com	Sutton	WV	26601	304-765-7393	765-3788
Atlantic Wood Industries Inc PO Box 1608 *Web:* www.atlanticwood.com	Savannah	GA	31402	912-964-1234	964-1331
Bell Lumber & Pole Co 778 1st St NW PO Box 120786 *TF:* 877-633-4334 ■ *Web:* www.bellpole.com	New Brighton	MN	55112	651-633-4334	633-8852
Brooks Mfg Co 2120 Pacific St PO Box 7 *Web:* www.brooksmfg.com	Bellingham	WA	98227	360-733-1700	734-6668
Brown Wood Preserving Co Inc 6201 Camp Ground Rd *TF:* 800-537-1765	Louisville	KY	40216	502-448-2337	448-9944
Building Products Plus 12317 Almeda Rd *TF:* 800-460-8627 ■ *Web:* www.buildingproductsplus.com	Houston	TX	77045	713-434-8008	433-7068
Burke-Parsons-Bowlby Corp Rt 21 S *TF:* 800-745-7095 ■ *Web:* www.bpbcorp.com	Ripley	WV	25271	304-372-2211	372-1211
Colfax Creosoting Co PO Box 1110	Alexandria	LA	71309	318-442-2467	445-9144
Cox Industries Inc 860 Cannon Bridge Rd PO Box 1124 *TF:* 800-476-4401 ■ *Web:* www.coxwood.com	Orangeburg	SC	29116	803-534-7467	534-1410
Ellijay Lumber & Wood Preserving Co 143 S Oldy Hwy 5 PO Box 526	Ellijay	GA	30540	706-889-8010	635-4753
Great Southern Wood Preserving Inc 1100 Hwy 431 N PO Box 610 *TF:* 800-633-7539 ■ *Web:* www.greatsouthernwood.com	Abbeville	AL	36310	334-585-2291	585-4353
Hoover Treated Wood Products Inc 154 Wire Rd *Web:* www.frtw.com	Thomson	GA	30824	706-595-5058	595-8462
Idaho Cedar Sales Inc 221 N Main St PO Box 399	Troy	ID	83871	208-835-2161	835-2772
JH Baxter & Co 1700 El Camino Real Suite 407 PO Box 5902 *TF:* 800-780-7073 ■ *Web:* www.jhbaxter.com	San Mateo	CA	94402	650-349-0201	570-6878
Koppers Inc 436 7th Ave *NYSE: KOP* ■ *TF:* 800-321-9876 ■ *Web:* www.koppers.com	Pittsburgh	PA	15219	412-227-2001	227-2333
Land O'Lakes Wood Preserving Co 171 3rd Ave N PO Box 87	Tenstrike	MN	56683	218-586-2203	586-2005
McFarland Cascade 1640 E Marc St *TF Cust Svc:* 800-426-8430 ■ *Web:* www.ldm.com	Tacoma	WA	98421	253-572-3033	627-0764
Osmose Inc 980 Ellicott St *TF:* 800-877-7653 ■ *Web:* www.osmose.com	Buffalo	NY	14209	716-882-5905	882-5139
Pearson Lumber Co 1511 Hargrove Rd PO Box 1548	Tuscaloosa	AL	35403	205-345-5516	345-5518
Perma Treat Corp 74 Airline Dr	Durham	CT	06422	860-349-1133	349-1365
Professional Coaters Inc 2148 Port of Tacoma Rd	Tacoma	WA	98421	253-627-1141	627-1150
Robbins Mfg Co 13001 N Nebraska Ave PO Box 17939 *TF:* 800-282-9336	Tampa	FL	33682	813-971-3030	972-3980
Seaman Timber Co Inc PO Box 372 1051 Hwy 25 S *TF:* 800-782-8155 ■ *Web:* www.seamantimber.com	South Montevallo	AL	35115	205-665-2536	665-2545
Shenandoah Wood Preserving Co PO Box 310	Scotland Neck	NC	27874	252-826-4151	826-3369
Sumter Wood Preserving Co Inc Hwy 378 & 76 By-pass PO Box 637	Sumter	SC	29151	803-775-5301	773-1522
Tolleson Lumber Co Inc 903 Jernigan St *TF:* 800-768-2105 ■ *Web:* www.tollesonlumber.com	Perry	GA	31069	478-988-3800	987-0160
Western Wood Preserving Co 1310 Zehnder St PO Box 1250 *TF:* 800-472-7714 ■ *Web:* www.westernwoodpreserving.com	Sumner	WA	98390	253-863-8191	863-9129
Wood Preservers Inc 15939 Historyland Hwy PO Box 158 *TF:* 800-368-2536 ■ *Web:* www.woodpreservers.com	Warsaw	VA	22572	804-333-4022	333-9269

822 WOOD PRODUCTS - RECONSTITUTED

Company	City	State	Zip	Phone	Fax
Collins Cos 1618 SW 1st Ave Suite 500 *TF:* 800-329-1219 ■ *Web:* www.collinswood.com	Portland	OR	97201	503-227-1219	227-5349
Component Concepts Inc 200 Mason Way *Web:* www.componentconceptsnc.com	Thomasville	NC	27360	336-475-1331	475-3551
Duraflame Inc 2894 Mt Diablo Ave PO Box 1230 *Web:* www.duraflame.com	Stockton	CA	95201	209-461-6600	462-9412
Homasote Co 932 Lower Ferry Rd PO Box 7240 *TF:* 800-257-9491 ■ *Web:* www.homasote.com	West Trenton	NJ	08628	609-883-3300	883-3497
Panel Processing Inc 120 N Industrial Hwy *TF:* 800-433-7142 ■ *Web:* www.panel.com	Alpena	MI	49707	989-356-9007	356-9000
Panolam Industries International Inc 20 Progress Dr *TF:* 800-672-6652 ■ *Web:* www.panolam.com	Shelton	CT	06484	203-925-1556	225-0051
Pasquier Panel Products Inc 1510 Puyallup St PO Box 1170 *Web:* www.pasquierpanel.com	Sumner	WA	98390	253-863-6323	891-7993
Potlatch Corp 601 W 1st Ave Suite 1600 *NYSE: PCH* ■ *Web:* www.potlatchcorp.com	Spokane	WA	99201	509-835-1500	835-1555
Potlatch Corp Wood Products Div 805 Mill Rd PO Box 1388 *Web:* www.potlatchcorp.com	Lewiston	ID	83501	208-799-0123	799-1918
Tectum Inc 105 S 6th St *TF:* 888-977-9691 ■ *Web:* www.tectum.com	Newark	OH	43055	740-345-9691	349-9305
Temple-Inland Inc 1300 S Mopac Expy *NYSE: TIN* ■ *TF:* 800-826-8807 ■ *Web:* www.temple-inland.com	Austin	TX	78746	512-434-5800	434-8723
West Fraser Timber Co Ltd 858 Beatty St Suite 501 *TSX: WFT* ■ *Web:* www.westfraser.com	Vancouver	BC	V6B1C1	604-895-2700	681-6061

823 WOOD PRODUCTS - SHAPED & TURNED

Company	City	State	Zip	Phone	Fax
Brown Wood Products Co 7040 N Lawndale Ave **Fax Area Code:* 800 ■ *TF:* 800-328-5858 ■ *Web:* www.brownwoodprod.com	Lincolnwood	IL	60712	847-673-4780	884-0423*
Burroughs-Ross-Colville Co 301 Depot St *Web:* www.brclumber.com	McMinnville	TN	37110	931-473-2111	473-5350
Chicago Dowel Co Inc 4700 W Grand Ave *TF:* 800-333-6935 ■ *Web:* www.chicagodowel.com	Chicago	IL	60639	773-622-2000	622-2047
Cowee WJ LLC 28 Taylor Ave *TF:* 800-862-6933 ■ *Web:* www.cowee.com	Berlin	NY	12022	518-658-9000	658-2244
Davidson Plyforms Inc 5505 33rd St SE *Web:* www.plyforms.com	Grand Rapids	MI	49512	616-956-0033	956-0041

				Phone	Fax
Dellen Wood Products Inc 3014 N Flora Rd	Spokane	WA	99216	509-928-1397	926-4261
Frank A Edmunds & Co 6111 S Sayre Ave	Chicago	IL	60638	773-586-2772	586-2783
TF: 800-447-3516					
Gateway Corp 100 E 5th St	Corinth	MS	38834	662-286-3351	286-3353
Web: www.gatewayhandles.com					
Hudson River Inlay 34 State Street	Ossining	NY	10562	914-762-1134	762-9508
TF: 800-745-0744 ■ *Web:* www.hudsonriverinlay.com					
Jarden Home Brands 345 South High St Suite 201	Mincie	IN	47305	765-281-5000	281-5450
TF Cust Svc: 800-428-8150 ■ *Web:* www.jardenhomebrands.com					
Michigan Maple Block Co 1420 Standish Ave	Petoskey	MI	49770	231-347-4170	347-7975
Web: www.mapleblock.com					
Moldwood Products Co 104 Mallard Dr	York	AL	36925	205-392-5256	392-5914
Web: www.moldwood.com					
Owens Handle Co Inc 4200 N Frazier St	Conroe	TX	77303	936-856-2981	856-2260
Saunders Brothers Inc 170 Forest St	Westbrook	ME	04092	207-854-2551	854-1243
TF: 800-343-0675 ■ *Web:* www.saundersbros.com					
Seymour Mfg Co 219 Handle St	Sequatchie	TN	37374	423-942-5901	942-6806
TF: 800-221-3419					
WJ Cowee LLC 28 Taylor Ave	Berlin	NY	12022	518-658-9000	658-2244
TF: 800-862-6933 ■ *Web:* www.cowee.com					

824 WOODWORKING MACHINERY

				Phone	Fax
Acrowood Corp 4425 S 3rd Ave PO Box 1028	Everett	WA	98203	425-258-3555	252-7622
Web: www.acrowood.com					
Baker Products Hwy 21 N PO Box 128	Ellington	MO	63638	573-663-7711	663-2787
TF: 800-548-6914 ■ *Web:* www.baker-online.com					
Capital Machine Co Inc 2801 Roosevelt Ave	Indianapolis	IN	46218	317-638-6661	636-5122
Web: www.capitalmachineco.com					
Coe Mfg Inc 609 Bank St	Painesville	OH	44077	440-352-9381	352-1487
Web: www.coemfg.com					
Corley Mfg Co 2900 Crescent Cir PO Box 471	Chattanooga	TN	37401	423-698-0284	622-3258
Web: www.corleymfg.com					
Diehl Machines 981 S Wabash St	Wabash	IN	46992	260-563-2102	563-0206
Web: www.diehlmachines.com					
HMC Corp 284 Maple St	Contoocook	NH	03229	603-746-4691	746-4819
Web: www.hmccorp.com					
ITW Amp 100 Fairway Dr Suite 114	Vernon Hills	IL	60061	847-918-1970	426-7019*
**Fax Area Code:* 800 ■ *TF:* 800-322-4204 ■ *Web:* www.itwamp.com					
James L Taylor Mfg Co 108 Parker Ave	Poughkeepsie	NY	12601	845-452-3780	452-0764
TF: 800-952-1321 ■ *Web:* www.jamesltaylor.com					
Jenkins Systems LLC 2803 S Taylor Dr	Sheboygan	WI	53081	920-452-2110	452-2338
Web: www.jenkins-systems.com					
Kimwood Corp 77684 Hwy 99 S PO Box 97	Cottage Grove	OR	97424	541-942-4401	942-0719
TF: 800-942-4401 ■ *Web:* www.kimwood.com					
KVAL Inc 825 Petaluma Blvd S	Petaluma	CA	94952	707-762-7367	762-0621
TF: 800-553-5825 ■ *Web:* www.kvalinc.com					
McDonough Mfg Co 2320 Melby St PO Box 510	Eau Claire	WI	54702	715-834-7755	834-3968
Web: mcdonough-mfg.com					
Memphis Machinery & Supply Co Inc 2881 Directors Cove	Memphis	TN	38131	901-527-4443	529-9663
TF: 800-388-4485 ■ *Web:* www.memphismachinery.com					
Mereen-Johnson Machine Co 4401 Lyndale Ave N	Minneapolis	MN	55412	612-529-7791	529-0120
TF: 888-465-7297 ■ *Web:* www.mereen-johnson.com					
Newman Whitney 507 Jackson St	Greensboro	NC	27403	336-273-8261	273-6939
Web: www.newmanwhitney.com					
Newman Machine Co Inc 507 Jackson St	Greensboro	NC	27403	336-273-8261	273-6939
Web: www.newmanwhitney.com					
Oliver Machinery Co 1210 Andover Park E	Tukwila	WA	98188	206-575-2722	575-2723
TF: 800-559-5065 ■ *Web:* www.olivermachinery.net					
Pacific Hoe Co 2700 SE Tacoma St PO Box 82155	Portland	OR	97202	503-234-9501	234-3506
TF: 800-547-5537 ■ *Web:* www.pacific-hoe.com					
Pendu Mfg Inc 718 N Shirk Rd	New Holland	PA	17557	717-354-4348	355-2148
TF: 800-233-0471 ■ *Web:* www.pendu.com					
Premier Gear & Machine Works Inc 1700 NW Thurman St	Portland	OR	97209	503-227-3514	227-1611
Web: www.premier-gear.com					
Safety Speed Cut Mfg Co Inc 13943 Lincoln St NE	Ham Lake	MN	55304	763-755-1600	755-6080
TF: 800-772-2327 ■ *Web:* www.panelsaw.com					
Thermwood Corp 904 Buffaloville Rd	Dale	IN	47523	812-937-4476	937-2956
TF Mktg: 800-533-6901 ■ *Web:* www.thermwood.com					
USNR Inc 558 Robinson Rd PO Box 310	Woodland	WA	98674	360-225-8267	225-8017
TF: 800-289-8767 ■ *Web:* www.usnr.com					
Viking Engineering & Development Inc 5750 Main St NE	Fridley	MN	55432	763-571-2400	586-1319
TF Sales: 800-328-2403 ■ *Web:* www.vikingeng.com					
Voorwood Co 2350 Barney St	Anderson	CA	96007	530-365-3311	365-3315
TF: 800-826-0089 ■ *Web:* www.voorwood.com					
Yates-American Machine Co Inc 2880 Kennedy Dr	Beloit	WI	53511	608-364-0333	364-0481
TF: 800-752-6377 ■ *Web:* www.yatesamerican.com					

825 WORLD TRADE CENTERS

				Phone	Fax
Atlantic Canada World Trade Centre 1800 Argyle St Suite 4126	Halifax	NS	B3J2V9	902-428-7233	420-8308
Web: www.acwtc.com					
Bay Area World Trade Center 544 Water St	Oakland	CA	94607	510-251-5900	251-5902
Web: www.bawtc.com					
Dallas World Trade Center 2100 N Stemmons Fwy	Dallas	TX	75207	214-655-6100	637-6833*
**Fax Area Code:* 800 ■ *TF:* 800-325-6587					
Greater Kansas City World Trade Center					
911 Main St Suite 2600	Kansas City	MO	64105	816-374-5483	274-6483
Web: www.kctrade.com					
Greater Philadelphia World Trade Center					
900 3rd Ave 33rd Fl	New York	NY	10022	212-909-8400	980-2631
Greenville-Spartanburg World Trade Center					
315 Old Boiling Springs Rd	Greer	SC	29650	864-297-8600	
Houston World Trade Assn					
Greater Houston Partnership 1200 Smith St Suite 700	Houston	TX	77002	713-844-3639	844-0635
Hudson Valley World Trade Center					
33 Airport Center Dr Suite 105	New Windsor	NY	12553	845-567-3670	567-3671
Jacksonville World Trade Center 3 Independent Dr	Jacksonville	FL	32202	904-366-6658	353-6343
Kansas World Trade Center 111 S Market St	Wichita	KS	67202	316-264-5982	264-5983
Web: www.kansaswtc.org					
Kentucky World Trade Center 333 W Vine St Suite 1600	Lexington	KY	40507	859-258-3139	233-0658
Web: www.kwtc.org					
Minnesota World Trade Center 30 E 7th St Suite 110	Saint Paul	MN	55101	651-296-2383	
Montana World Trade Center					
Gallagher Business Bldg University of Montana Suite 257	Missoula	MT	59812	406-243-6982	243-5259
TF: 888-773-2703 ■ *Web:* www.mwtc.org					
Northern California World Trade Center 917 7th St	Sacramento	CA	95814	916-319-4277	443-2672
Web: www.norcalwtc.org					
Ronald Reagan Building & International Trade Center					
1300 Pennsylvania Ave NW	Washington	DC	20004	202-312-1300	312-1310
TF: 888-393-3306 ■ *Web:* www.itcdc.com					
San Diego World Trade Center 1250 6th Ave Suite 100	San Diego	CA	92101	619-615-0868	615-0876
Web: www.wtcsd.org					
South Carolina World Trade Center 1 Poston Rd Suite 103	Charleston	SC	29407	843-852-9880	852-9890
Web: www.scwtc.org					
State of Hawaii World Trade Center					
Business Development & Marketing Div 250 S Hotel St 5th Fl	Honolulu	HI	96813	808-587-2750	586-2589
Wisconsin World Trade Center 750 N Memorial Lincoln Dr	Milwaukee	WI	53202	414-274-3840	274-3846
Web: www.wistrade.org					
World Trade Center Alaska 431 W 7th Ave Suite 108	Anchorage	AK	99501	907-278-7233	278-2982
Web: www.wtcak.org					
World Trade Center Assn Los Angeles-Long Beach					
350 S Figueroa St Suite 172	Los Angeles	CA	90071	213-680-1888	680-1878
Web: www.wtcanet.org/					
World Trade Center Atlanta					
303 Peachtree St NE Lower Lobby 100	Atlanta	GA	30308	404-880-9595	880-1564
Web: www.wtcatlanta.com					
World Trade Center Baltimore 401 E Pratt St Suite 232	Baltimore	MD	21202	410-576-0022	576-0751
Web: www.wtci.org					
World Trade Center Boston 200 Seaport Blvd Suite 50	Boston	MA	02210	617-385-5000	385-5090
TF: 800-367-9822 ■ *Web:* www.seaportboston.com					
World Trade Center Cleveland 1768 E 25th St	Cleveland	OH	44114	216-391-7002	391-7004
TF: 888-304-4769 ■ *Web:* www.wtccleveland.org					
World Trade Center Delaware 702 West St	Wilmington	DE	19801	302-656-7905	656-7956
Web: www.wtcde.com					
World Trade Center Denver 1625 Broadway Suite 680	Denver	CO	80202	303-592-5760	592-5228
Web: www.wtcdn.com					
World Trade Center Detroit/Windsor					
16630 Southfield Rd PO Box 637	Allen Park	MI	48101	313-388-2345	388-9945
Web: www.wtcdw.com					
World Trade Center Edmonton 9990 Jasper Ave Suite 600	Edmonton	AB	T5J1P7	780-426-4620	424-7946
World Trade Center El Paso/Juarez					
123 Mills St Centre Bldg Suite 200	El Paso	TX	79901	915-544-0022	544-0030
Web: www.wtcinternational.org					
World Trade Center Illinois 200 E Randolph St Suite 2200	Chicago	IL	60601	312-467-0550	467-0615
Web: www.wtcc.org					
World Trade Center Miami 1007 N America Way Suite 500	Miami	FL	33132	305-871-7910	871-7904
Web: www.worldtrade.org					
World Trade Center Montreal					
380 Saint-Antoine St W Suite 6000	Montreal	QC	H2Y3X7	514-871-4002	871-1255
Web: www.wtcmontreal.com					
World Trade Center of New Orleans 2 Canal St Suite 2900	New Orleans	LA	70130	504-529-1601	529-1691
Web: www.wtc-no.org					
World Trade Center Norfolk 101 W Main St	Norfolk	VA	23510	757-627-9440	627-1548
World Trade Center North Carolina					
10900 World Trade Blvd Suite 112	Raleigh	NC	27617	919-281-2740	281-2741
Web: www.wtcnc.org/					
World Trade Center Orlando 736-A N Magnolia Ave 2nd Fl	Orlando	FL	32803	407-649-1899	649-1486
Web: www.worldtradecenterorlando.org					
World Trade Center Ottawa 130 Slater St Suite 750	Ottawa	ON	K1P6E2	613-598-4666	594-8705
World Trade Center Palm Beach					
777 S Flagler Dr Suite 800	West Palm Beach	FL	33401	561-712-1443	712-1445
Web: www.wtcpalmbeach.com					
World Trade Center Pittsburgh 425 6th Ave Suite 1100	Pittsburgh	PA	15219	412-392-1000	642-2217
TF: 877-392-1300					
World Trade Center Portland 121 SW Salmon St Suite 250	Portland	OR	97204	503-464-8888	464-8880
Web: www.wtcpd.com					
World Trade Center Rhode Island					
Chaffee Center for International Business 1150 Douglas Pike	Smithfield	RI	02917	401-232-6407	232-6416
World Trade Center Rio Grande Valley at McAllen					
1901 S Taylor Rd	McAllen	TX	78503	956-686-1982	631-2971
World Trade Center Saint Louis					
121 S Meramec Ave Suite 1111	Saint Louis	MO	63105	314-615-8141	862-0102
Web: www.worldtradecenter-stl.com					
World Trade Center San Antonio 118 Broadway Suite 324	San Antonio	TX	78205	210-978-7600	978-7610
Web: www.newpro.net/wtcsa					
World Trade Center Seattle 2200 Alaskan Way Suite 410	Seattle	WA	98121	206-441-5144	770-7923
Web: www.wtcseattle.com					
World Trade Center Tacoma 950 Pacific Ave Suite 310	Tacoma	WA	98402	253-396-1022	396-1033
Web: www.wtcta.org					
World Trade Center Tampa Bay 1101 Channel Side Dr	Tampa	FL	33602	813-864-3000	864-3100
Web: www.wtctampa.com					
World Trade Center Toronto 1 First Canadian Pl PO Box 60	Toronto	ON	M5X1C1	416-366-6811	366-2483
Web: www.bot.com					
World Trade Center Vancouver 999 Canada Pl Suite 515	Vancouver	BC	V6C3E1	604-683-7959	682-5359

826 ZOOS & WILDLIFE PARKS

SEE ALSO Aquariums - Public p. 1282; Botanical Gardens & Arboreta p. 1391

				Phone	Fax
Abilene Zoological Gardens 2070 Zoo Ln Nelson Park	Abilene	TX	79602	325-676-6085	676-6084
Web: www.abilenetx.com/zoo/zoo.htm					
Acadia Zoo Park 446 Bar Harbor Rd	Trenton	ME	04605	207-667-3244	
Web: www.acadiazoo.org					
Admiralty Island & Pack Creek Bear Preserve					
USDA Forest Service 709 W 9th St	Juneau	AK	99801	907-586-8806	586-7892
African Lion Safari & Game Farm RR 1	Cambridge	ON	N1R5S2	519-623-2620	623-9542
TF: 800-461-9453 ■ *Web:* www.lionsafari.com					
African Safari Wildlife Park 267 Lightner Rd	Port Clinton	OH	43452	419-732-3606	734-1919
TF: 800-521-2660 ■ *Web:* www.africansafariwildlifepark.com					
Akron Zoological Park 500 Edgewood Ave	Akron	OH	44307	330-375-2550	375-2575
Web: www.akronzoo.org					
Alameda Park Zoo 1021 N White Sands Blvd	Alamogordo	NM	88310	505-439-4290	439-4103
Web: ci.alamogordo.nm.us/coa/coaALAMEDAPARKZOO.html					
Alaska Wildlife Conservation Center					
Milepost 79 Seward Hwy	Portage Glacier	AK	99587	907-783-2025	783-2370
TF: 866-773-2025 ■ *Web:* www.alaskawildlife.org					
Alaska Zoo 4731 O'Malley Rd	Anchorage	AK	99507	907-346-3242	346-2673
Web: www.alaskazoo.org					
Alexandria Zoological Park 3016 Masonic Dr	Alexandria	LA	71301	318-473-1143	473-1149
Web: www.thealexandriazoo.com					

	City	State	Zip	Phone	Fax
Alligator Adventure					
4604 Hwy 17 S Barefoot Landing	North Myrtle Beach	SC	29598	843-361-0789	361-0742
Web: www.alligatoradventure.com					
Amarillo Zoo Hwy 287 N Thompson Park	Amarillo	TX	79105	806-381-7911	381-7901
Animal Ark Wildlife Sanctuary & Nature Center					
1265 Deerlodge Rd	Reno	NV	89506	775-970-3111	
Web: www.animalark.org					
Arizona-Sonora Desert Museum 2021 N Kinney Rd	Tucson	AZ	85743	520-883-1380	883-2500
Web: www.desertmuseum.org					
Arkansas Alligator Farm & Petting Zoo					
847 Whittington Ave	Hot Springs	AR	71901	501-623-6172	
TF: 800-750-7891 ■ *Web:* www.hotspringsusa.com/gatorfarm					
Assiniboine Park Zoo 460 Assiniboine Park Dr	Winnipeg	MB	R3P2N7	204-986-2327	832-5420
Web: www.zoosociety.com					
Audubon Zoo 6500 Magazine St	New Orleans	LA	70118	504-581-4629	861-2486
TF: 800-774-7394 ■ *Web:* www.auduboninstitute.org/zoo					
Austin Zoo 10807 Rawhide Trail	Austin	TX	78736	512-288-1490	
TF: 800-291-1490 ■ *Web:* www.austinzoo.org					
Aviary & Zoo of Naples 9824 Immokalee Rd	Naples	FL	34120	239-353-2215	353-1188
Web: www.aviaryofnaples.com					
Ball John Zoological Garden 1300 W Fulton	Grand Rapids	MI	49504	616-336-4301	336-3907
Beardsley Zoo 1875 Noble Ave	Bridgeport	CT	06610	203-394-6565	394-6566
Web: www.beardsleyzoo.org					
Bergen County Zoological Park 216 Forest Ave	Paramus	NJ	07652	201-262-3771	986-1788
Bever Park Zoo 2700 Bever Ave SE	Cedar Rapids	IA	52403	319-286-5761	286-5758
Binder Park Zoo 7400 Division Dr	Battle Creek	MI	49014	269-979-1351	979-8834
Web: www.binderparkzoo.org					
Binghampton Zoo at Ross Park 60 Morgan Rd	Binghamton	NY	13903	607-724-5461	724-5454
Web: www.rossparkzoo.com					
Birmingham Zoo 2630 Cahaba Rd	Birmingham	AL	35223	205-879-0409	879-9426
TF: 888-966-2426 ■ *Web:* www.birminghamzoo.com					
Blank Park Zoo 7401 SW 9th St	Des Moines	IA	50315	515-285-4722	285-1487
Web: www.blankparkzoo.com					
Bolsa Chica Ecological Reserve 3842 Warner Ave	Huntington Beach	CA	92649	714-846-1114	846-4065
Web: www.bolsachica.org					
Bowmanville Zoological Park Ltd 340 King St E	Bowmanville	ON	L1C3K5	905-623-5655	623-0957
Web: www.bowmanvillezoo.com					
Bramble Park Zoo 800 10th St NW PO Box 910	Watertown	SD	57201	605-882-6269	882-5232
Web: www.brambleparkzoo.com					
Brandywine Zoo 1001 North Park Dr	Wilmington	DE	19802	302-571-7747	571-7787
Web: www.brandywinezoo.org					
BREC's Baton Rouge Zoo 3601 Thomas Rd	Baton Rouge	LA	70807	225-775-3877	775-3931
Web: www.brzoo.org					
Brevard Zoo 8225 N Wickham Rd	Melbourne	FL	32940	321-254-9453	259-5966
Web: www.brevardzoo.org					
British Columbia Wildlife Park 9077 Dallas Dr	Kamloops	BC	V2C6V1	250-573-3242	573-2406
Web: www.bczoo.org					
Bronx Zoo 2300 Southern Blvd	Bronx	NY	10460	718-220-5100	220-2685
TF: 800-234-5128 ■ *Web:* www.bronxzoo.com					
Brookfield Zoo 3300 Golf Rd	Brookfield	IL	60513	708-485-2200	485-3532
Web: www.brookfieldzoo.org					
Buffalo Zoological Gardens 300 Parkside Ave	Buffalo	NY	14214	716-837-3900	837-0738
Web: www.buffalozoo.org					
Busch Gardens Tampa Bay 3605 Bougainvillea Ave	Tampa	FL	33612	813-987-5082	987-5111
TF: 888-800-5447 ■ *Web:* www.buschgardens.com					
Busch Gardens Williamsburg 1 Busch Gardens Blvd	Williamsburg	VA	23187	800-343-7946	253-3399*
*Fax Area Code: 757 ■ *Fax: Mktg ■ *TF:* 800-343-7946 ■ *Web:* www.buschgardens.com					
Butterfly Pavilion & Insect Center 6252 W 104th Ave	Westminster	CO	80020	303-469-5441	657-5944
Web: www.butterflies.org					
Buttonwood Park Zoo 425 Hawthorn St	New Bedford	MA	02740	508-991-6178	979-1731
Web: www.bpzoo.org					
Caldwell Zoo 2203 ML King Blvd PO Box 4785	Tyler	TX	75712	903-593-0121	595-5083
Web: www.caldwellzoo.org					
Calgary Zoo Botanical Garden & Prehistoric Park					
1300 Zoo Rd NE	Calgary	AB	T2E7V6	403-232-9300	237-7582
TF: 800-661-1678 ■ *Web:* www.calgaryzoo.ab.ca					
Cameron Park Zoo 1701 N 4th St	Waco	TX	76707	254-750-8400	750-8430
Web: www.cameronparkzoo.com					
Cape May County Park & Zoo 4 Moore Rd	Cape May Court House	NJ	08210	609-465-5271	465-5421
Capron Park Zoo 201 County St	Attleboro	MA	02703	508-222-3047	223-2208
Web: www.capronparkzoo.com					
Caribbean Gardens 1590 Goodlette-Frank Rd	Naples	FL	34102	239-262-5409	262-6866
TF: 888-520-3756 ■ *Web:* www.caribbeangardens.com					
Cat Tales Zoological Park N 17020 Newport Hwy	Mead	WA	99021	509-238-4126	238-4126
Web: www.cattales.org					
Central Florida Zoological Park					
3755 NW Hwy 17-92 & I-4 PO Box 470309	Lake Monroe	FL	32747	407-323-4450	321-0900
Web: www.centralfloridazoo.org					
Central Park Zoo 5th Ave & 64th St	New York	NY	10021	212-439-6500	
Web: www.centralparkzoo.com					
Chahinkapa Zoo & Prairie Rose Carousel					
1004 RJ Hughes Dr	Wahpeton	ND	58075	701-642-8709	642-9285
Web: www.chahinkapazoo.com					
Charles Paddock Zoo 9305 Pismo Ave	Atascadero	CA	93422	805-461-5080	461-7625
Web: www.charlespaddockzoo.org					
Chattanooga Zoo 1101 McCallie Ave	Chattanooga	TN	37404	423-697-1322	697-1329
Web: zoo.chattanooga.org					
Cherry Brook Zoo 901 Foster Thurston Dr	Saint John	NB	E2K5H9	506-634-1440	634-0717
Web: www.cherrybrookzoo.com					
Cheyenne Mountain Zoological Park					
4250 Cheyenne Mountain Zoo Rd	Colorado Springs	CO	80906	719-633-9925	633-2254
Web: www.cmzoo.org					
Cincinnati Zoo & Botanical Garden 3400 Vine St	Cincinnati	OH	45220	513-281-4701	559-7790
TF: 800-944-4776 ■ *Web:* www.cincyzoo.org					
Claws 'n' Paws Wild Animal Park Rt 590	Lake Ariel	PA	18436	570-698-6154	698-2957
Web: www.clawsnpaws.com					
Cleveland Metroparks Zoo 3900 Wildlife Way	Cleveland	OH	44109	216-661-6500	661-3312
Web: www.clemetzoo.com					
Clyde Peeling's Reptiland 18628 US Rt 15	Allenwood	PA	17810	570-538-1869	538-1714
TF: 800-737-8452 ■ *Web:* www.reptiland.com					
Columbian Park Zoo 1915 Scott St	Lafayette	IN	47904	765-771-2231	807-1547
Web: www.city.lafayette.in.us/park/Zoo.htm					
Columbus Zoo & Aquarium 9990 Riverside Dr PO Box 400	Powell	OH	43065	614-645-3400	645-3465
TF: 800-666-5397 ■ *Web:* www.colszoo.org					
Como Zoo & Conservatory 1225 Estabrook Dr	Saint Paul	MN	55103	651-487-8200	487-8254
Web: www.ci.stpaul.mn.us/depts/parks/comopark/					
Cosley Zoo 1356 N Gary Ave	Wheaton	IL	60187	630-665-5534	260-6408
Web: www.cosleyzoo.org					
Cougar Mountain Zoo 19525 SE 54th	Issaquah	WA	98027	425-392-6278	392-1076
Web: www.cougarmountainzoo.org					
Dakota Zoo Sertoma Park Riverside Park Rd PO Box 711	Bismarck	ND	58502	701-223-7543	258-8350
Web: www.dakotazoo.org					
Dallas Zoo 650 S RL Thornton Fwy	Dallas	TX	75203	214-670-6826	670-7450
Web: www.dallas-zoo.org					
David Traylor Zoo of Emporia 75 Soden Rd	Emporia	KS	66801	620-342-6558	342-8820
Web: www.emporiazoo.org					
Denver Zoo 2300 Steele St	Denver	CO	80205	303-376-4800	376-4801
Web: www.denverzoo.org					
Detroit Zoological Institute 8450 W Ten-Mile Rd	Royal Oak	MI	48067	248-398-0903	541-0344
Web: www.detroitzoo.org					
Dickerson Park Zoo 3043 N Fort	Springfield	MO	65803	417-833-1570	833-4459
Web: www.dickersonparkzoo.org					
Discovery Cove 6000 Discovery Cove Way Suite B	Orlando	FL	32821	407-370-1280	586-8046
TF: 877-434-7268 ■ *Web:* www.discoverycove.com					
Disney's Animal Kingdom 2901 Osceola Pkwy	Lake Buena Vista	FL	32830	407-938-3000	938-4799
Web: disneyworld.disney.go.com					
Dreher Park Zoo 1301 Summit Blvd	West Palm Beach	FL	33405	561-533-0887	585-6085
Web: www.palmbeachzoo.org					
Ecomuseum 21125 ch Sainte-Marie	Sainte-Anne-de-Bellevue	QC	H9X3Y7	514-457-9449	457-0769
Web: www.ecomuseum.ca					
El Paso Zoo 4001 E Paisano St	El Paso	TX	79905	915-521-1850	
Web: www.elpasozoo.org					
Ellen Trout Zoo 402 Zoo Circle	Lufkin	TX	75904	936-633-0399	633-0311
Web: www.ellentroutzoo.com					
Elmwood Park Zoo 1661 Harding Blvd	Norristown	PA	19401	610-277-3825	292-0332
Web: www.elmwoodparkzoo.org/					
Erie Zoo 423 W 38th St	Erie	PA	16508	814-864-4091	864-1140
Web: www.eriezoo.org					
Everglades Alligator Farm 40351 SW 192nd Ave	Homestead	FL	33034	305-247-2628	248-9711
Web: www.everglades.com					
Everglades Safari Park 26700 Tamiami Trail	Miami	FL	33144	305-226-6923	554-5666
Web: www.evsafaripark.com					
Felix Neck Wildlife Sanctuary 100 Felix Neck Dr	Edgartown	MA	02539	508-627-4850	627-6052
For-Mar Nature Preserve & Arboretum 2142 N Genesee Rd	Burton	MI	48509	810-789-8567	743-0541
Web: www.geneseecountyparks.org/formar.htm					
Fort Wayne Children's Zoo 3411 Sherman Blvd	Fort Wayne	IN	46808	260-427-6800	427-6820
Web: www.kidszoo.com					
Fort Worth Zoological Park 1989 Colonial Pkwy	Fort Worth	TX	76110	817-871-7000	759-7501
Web: www.fortworthzoo.com					
Fossil Rim Wildlife Center 2155 CR 2008	Glen Rose	TX	76043	254-897-2960	897-3785
Web: www.fossilrim.com					
Franklin Park Zoo 1 Franklin Park Rd	Boston	MA	02121	617-541-5466	989-2025
Web: www.zoonewengland.com					
Fresno Chaffee Zoo 894 W Belmont Ave	Fresno	CA	93728	559-498-2671	264-9226
Web: www.fresnochaffeezoo.com					
Gator Park 24050 SW 8th St	Miami	FL	33184	305-559-2255	559-2844
TF: 800-559-2205 ■ *Web:* www.gatorpark.com					
Gatorland 14501 S Orange Blossom Trail	Orlando	FL	32837	407-855-5496	240-9389
TF: 800-393-5297 ■ *Web:* www.gatorland.com					
Gibbon Conservation Center PO Box 800249	Santa Clarita	CA	91380	661-296-2737	296-1237
Web: www.gibboncenter.org					
Gifford Rosamond Zoo at Burnet Park 1 Conservation Pl	Syracuse	NY	13204	315-435-8511	435-8517
Web: rosamondgiffordzoo.com					
Gladys Porter Zoo 500 Ringgold St	Brownsville	TX	78520	956-546-7187	541-4940
Web: www.gpz.org					
Glen Oak Zoo 2218 N Prospect Rd	Peoria	IL	61603	309-686-3365	685-6240
Web: www.glenoakzoo.org					
Global Wildlife Center 26389 Hwy 40	Folsom	LA	70437	985-796-3585	796-9487
Web: www.globalwildlife.com					
Good Zoo & Benedum Planetarium Rt 88 N Oglebay Park	Wheeling	WV	26003	304-243-4030	243-4110
TF: 800-624-6988 ■ *Web:* www.oglebay-resort.com/goodzoo					
Granby Zoo & Amazoo Water Park 525 Saint-Hubert St	Granby	QC	J2G5P3	450-372-9113	372-5531
TF: 877-472-6299 ■ *Web:* www.zoogranby.ca					
Great Plains Zoo 805 S Kiwanis Ave	Sioux Falls	SD	57104	605-367-7059	367-8340
Web: www.gpzoo.org					
Greenville Zoo 150 Cleveland Park Dr	Greenville	SC	29601	864-467-4300	467-4314
Web: www.greenvillezoo.com					
Grizzly & Wolf Discovery Center 201 S Canyon	West Yellowstone	MT	59758	406-646-7001	646-7004
TF: 800-257-2570 ■ *Web:* www.grizzlydiscoveryctr.com					
Happy Hollow Park & Zoo 1300 Senter Rd Kelley Park	San Jose	CA	95112	408-277-3000	277-4470
Web: www.happyhollowparkandzoo.org					
Harmony Park Safari 431 Clouds Cove Rd	Huntsville	AL	35803	877-726-4625	
Hattiesburg Zoo 107 S 17th Ave Kamper Park	Hattiesburg	MS	39401	601-545-4576	545-4653
Web: www.hattiesburgms.com/przoo.html					
Have Trunk Will Travel 27575 Hwy 74	Perris	CA	92570	951-943-9227	943-9563
Web: www.havetrunkwilltravel.com					
Hazel & Bill Rutherford Wildlife Prairie State Park					
3826 N Taylor Rd	Hanna City	IL	61536	309-676-0998	676-7783
Web: www.wildlifeprairiestatepark.org					
Henry Doorly Zoo 3701 S 10th St	Omaha	NE	68107	402-733-8401	733-7868
Web: www.omahazoo.com					
Henry Vilas Park Zoo 702 S Randall Ave	Madison	WI	53715	608-266-4733	266-5923
Web: www.vilaszoo.org					
Henson Robinson Zoo 1100 E Lake Dr	Springfield	IL	62712	217-753-6217	529-8748
Web: www.hensonrobinsonzoo.org					
Hogle Zoological Gardens 2600 E Sunnyside Ave	Salt Lake City	UT	84108	801-582-1631	584-1770
Web: www.hoglezoo.org					
Honolulu Zoo 151 Kapahulu Ave	Honolulu	HI	96815	808-971-7171	971-7173
Web: www.honoluluzoo.org					
Houston Zoological Gardens 1513 N MacGregor Dr	Houston	TX	77030	713-533-6500	533-6755
Web: www.houstonzoo.org					
Hutchinson Zoo 6 Emerson Loop E Carey Park	Hutchinson	KS	67501	620-694-2693	
Indianapolis Zoo 1200 W Washington St	Indianapolis	IN	46222	317-630-2001	630-5153
Web: www.indianapoliszoo.com					
International Exotic Feline Sanctuary PO Box 637	Boyd	TX	76023	940-433-5091	433-5092
Web: www.bigcat.org					
Jackson Zoological Park 2918 W Capitol St	Jackson	MS	39209	601-352-2580	352-2594
Web: jacksonzoo.org					
Jacksonville Zoological Gardens 370 Zoo Pkwy	Jacksonville	FL	32218	904-757-4463	757-4315
Web: www.jaxzoo.org					
John Ball Zoological Garden 1300 W Fulton	Grand Rapids	MI	49504	616-336-4301	336-3907
Jungle Adventures 26205 E Hwy 50	Christmas	FL	32709	407-568-1354	568-0038
TF: 877-424-2867 ■ *Web:* www.jungleadventures.com					
Jungle Cat World Inc 3667 Concession 6	Orono	ON	L0B1M0	905-983-5016	983-9858
Web: www.junglecatworld.com					
Jungle Island 1111 Parrot Jungle Trail	Miami	FL	33132	305-400-7000	400-7290
Web: www.jungleisland.com					
Kangaroo Conservation Center 222 Bailey-Waters Rd	Dawsonville	GA	30534	706-265-6100	265-6261
Web: www.kangaroocenter.com					
Kansas City Zoo 6800 Zoo Dr	Kansas City	MO	64132	816-513-5700	784-3909
Web: www.kansascityzoo.org					
Kansas Wildlife Exhibit 700 N Nims St Central Riverside Park	Wichita	KS	67203	316-337-9211	
Web: www.gpnc.org/kansas.htm					
Kentucky Horse Park 4089 Iron Works Pkwy	Lexington	KY	40511	859-233-4303	254-0253
TF: 800-678-8813 ■ *Web:* www.imh.org/khp/hp1.html					
Knoxville Zoological Gardens Inc 3500 Knoxville Zoo Dr	Knoxville	TN	37914	865-637-5331	637-1943
Web: www.knoxville-zoo.org					
Lake Superior Zoological Gardens 7210 Fremont St	Duluth	MN	55807	218-723-3748	723-3750
Web: www.lszoo.org					
Lee Richardson Zoo 312 E Finnup Dr	Garden City	KS	67846	620-276-1250	276-1259
Web: www.garden-city.org/zoo					
Lincoln Children's Zoo 1222 S 27th St	Lincoln	NE	68502	402-475-6741	475-6742
Web: www.lincolnzoo.org					

				Phone	Fax
Lincoln Park Zoo 2001 N Clark St	Chicago	IL	60614	312-742-2000	742-2317
Web: www.lpzoo.com					
Lion Country Safari 2003 Lion Country Safari Rd	Loxahatchee	FL	33470	561-793-1084	793-9603
Web: www.lioncountrysafari.com					
Little Rock Zoo 1 Jonesboro Dr	Little Rock	AR	72205	501-666-2406	666-7040
Web: www.littlerockzoo.com					
Living Desert Zoo & Gardens 47900 Portola Ave	Palm Desert	CA	92260	760-346-5694	568-9685
Web: www.livingdesert.org					
Living Desert Zoo & Gardens 1504 Miehls Dr	Carlsbad	NM	88220	505-887-5516	885-4478
Los Angeles Zoo & Botanical Gardens 5333 Zoo Dr	Los Angeles	CA	90027	323-644-4200	662-9786
Web: www.lazoo.org					
Louisville Zoo 1100 Trevilian Way	Louisville	KY	40213	502-459-2181	459-2196
Web: www.louisvillezoo.org					
Lowry Park Zoo 7530 North Blvd	Tampa	FL	33604	813-935-8552	935-9486
Web: www.lowryparkzoo.com					
Magnetic Hill Zoo 100 Worthington Ave	Moncton	NB	E1C9Z3	506-384-0303	853-3569
Maryland Zoo in Baltimore Druid Hill Park	Baltimore	MD	21217	410-396-7102	396-6464
Web: www.marylandzoo.org					
Maymont 1700 Hampton St	Richmond	VA	23220	804-358-7166	358-9994
Web: www.maymont.org					
Memphis Zoo 2000 Galloway Ave	Memphis	TN	38104	901-333-6500	333-6501
Web: www.memphiszoo.org					
Mesker Park Zoo 2421 Bement Ave	Evansville	IN	47720	812-435-6143	435-6140
Web: www.meskerparkzoo.com					
Miami Metrozoo 12400 SW 152nd St	Miami	FL	33177	305-251-0400	378-6381
Web: www.miamimetrozoo.com					
Micke Grove Zoo 11793 N Micke Grove Rd	Lodi	CA	95240	209-953-8840	331-7271
Web: www.co.san-joaquin.ca.us/mgzoo					
Mill Mountain Zoo 2404 Prospect Rd Mill Mountain Park	Roanoke	VA	24014	540-343-3241	343-8111
Web: www.mmzoo.org					
Miller Park Zoo 1020 S Morris Ave	Bloomington	IL	61701	309-434-2250	434-2823
Web: www.millerparkzoo.org					
Milwaukee County Zoo 10001 W Blue Mound Rd	Milwaukee	WI	53226	414-771-3040	256-5410
Web: www.milwaukeezoo.org					
Minnesota Zoo 13000 Zoo Blvd	Apple Valley	MN	55124	952-431-9200	431-9300
TF: 800-366-7811 ■ *Web:* www.mnzoo.com					
Mobile Zoo 15161 Ward Rd W	Wilmer	AL	36587	251-649-1845	649-0434
Web: www.mobilezoo.cc					
Monkey Jungle 14805 SW 216th St	Miami	FL	33170	305-235-1611	235-4253
Web: www.monkeyjungle.com					
Montgomery Zoo 2301 Coliseum Pkwy	Montgomery	AL	36110	334-240-4900	240-4916
Web: www.montgomeryzoo.com					
Nashville Zoo 3777 Nolensville Rd	Nashville	TN	37211	615-833-1534	333-0728
Web: www.nashvillezoo.org					
National Zoological Park (Smithsonian Institution)					
3001 Connecticut Ave NW	Washington	DC	20008	202-633-4800	673-4836
Web: nationalzoo.si.edu					
Natural Bridge Wildlife Ranch					
26515 Natural Bridge Caverns Rd	San Antonio	TX	78266	830-438-7400	438-3494
Web: wildliferanchtexas.com					
New York State Zoo 1 Thompson Park	Watertown	NY	13601	315-782-6180	782-6192
Web: www.nyslivingmuseum.org					
North Carolina Zoological Park 4401 Zoo Pkwy	Asheboro	NC	27205	336-879-7000	879-2891
TF: 800-488-0444 ■ *Web:* www.nczoo.org					
Northeastern Wisconsin Zoo 4418 Reforestation Rd	Green Bay	WI	54313	920-448-4466	434-4162
Web: www.co.brown.wi.us/parks/newzoo					
Northwest Trek Wildlife Park 11610 Trek Dr E	Eatonville	WA	98328	360-832-6117	832-6118
Web: www.nwtrek.org					
Oakland Zoo 9777 Golf Links Rd	Oakland	CA	94605	510-632-9525	635-5719
Web: www.oaklandzoo.org					
Oklahoma City Zoological Park & Botanical Gardens					
2101 NE 50th St	Oklahoma City	OK	73111	405-424-3344	425-0207
Web: www.okczoo.com					
Omaha's Henry Doorly Zoo 3701 S 10th St	Omaha	NE	68107	402-733-8401	733-7868
Web: www.omahazoo.com					
Orange County Zoo 1 Irvine Park Rd	Orange	CA	92862	714-973-6847	
Web: www.ocparks.com/oczoo					
Oregon Zoo 4001 SW Canyon Rd	Portland	OR	97221	503-226-1561	226-6836
Web: www.oregonzoo.org					
Out of Africa Wildlife Park 4020 N Cherry Rd	Camp Verde	AZ	86322	928-567-2840	567-2839
Web: www.outofafricapark.com					
Palm Beach Zoo at Dreher Park 1301 Summit Blvd	West Palm Beach	FL	33405	561-533-0887	585-6085
Web: www.palmbeachzoo.org					
Parc Safari 850 Rt 202	Hemmingford	QC	J0L1H0	450-247-2727	247-3563
Web: www.parcsafari.com					
Parks at Chehaw 105 Chehaw Park Rd	Albany	GA	31701	229-430-5275	430-3035
Web: www.parksatchehaw.org					
Paul E Zollman Zoo 5731 County Rd 105 NW	Byron	MN	55920	507-775-2451	775-2544
Philadelphia Zoo 3400 W Girard Ave	Philadelphia	PA	19104	215-243-1100	243-5385
Web: www.phillyzoo.org					
Phoenix Zoo 455 N Galvin Pkwy	Phoenix	AZ	85008	602-273-1341	273-7078
Web: www.phoenixzoo.org					
Pittsburgh Zoo & PPG Aquarium 1 Wild Pl	Pittsburgh	PA	15206	412-665-3639	665-3661
TF: 800-474-4966 ■ *Web:* www.pittsburghzoo.com					
Pocatello Zoo 3101 Ave of the Chiefs	Pocatello	ID	83204	208-234-6264	234-6265
Web: www.pocatellozoo.org					
Point Defiance Zoo & Aquarium 5400 N Pearl St	Tacoma	WA	98407	253-591-5337	591-5448
Web: www.pdza.org					
Porter Gladys Zoo 500 Ringgold St	Brownsville	TX	78520	956-546-7187	541-4940
Web: www.gpz.org					
Potter Park Zoo 1301 S Pennsylvania Ave	Lansing	MI	48912	517-483-4221	483-6065
Web: www.potterparkzoo.org					
Prospect Park Zoo 450 Flatbush Ave	Brooklyn	NY	11225	718-399-7339	399-7337
Web: wcs.org/home/zoos/prospectpark					
Provincial Wildlife Park 149 Creighton Rd	Shubenacadie	NS	B0N2H0	902-758-2040	758-7011
Web: wildlifepark.gov.ns.ca					
Pueblo Zoo 3455 Nuckolls Ave	Pueblo	CO	81005	719-561-1452	561-8686
Web: www.pueblozoo.org					
Queens Zoo 53-51 111th St	Flushing	NY	11368	718-271-1500	
Web: wcs.org/home/zoos/queenswildlifecenter					
Racine Zoo 2131 N Main St	Racine	WI	53402	262-636-9189	636-9307
Web: www.racinezoo.org					
Red River Zoo 4220 21st Ave S	Fargo	ND	58104	701-277-9240	277-9238
Web: www.redriverzoo.org					
Reid Park Zoo 1100 S Randolph Way	Tucson	AZ	85716	520-791-3204	791-5378
Web: www.tucsonzoo.org					
Richardson Lee Zoo 312 E Finnup Dr	Garden City	KS	67846	620-276-1250	276-1259
Web: www.garden-city.org/zoo					
Rio Grande Zoo					
Albuquerque Biological Park 903 10th St SW	Albuquerque	NM	87102	505-764-6200	764-6281
Web: www.cabq.gov/biopark/zoo					
Riverbanks Zoo & Botanical Garden 500 Wildlife Pkwy	Columbia	SC	29210	803-779-8717	253-6381
Web: www.riverbanks.org					
Riverside Zoo 1600 S Beltline Hwy W	Scottsbluff	NE	69361	308-630-6236	632-2953
Web: www.riversidezoo.org					
Riverview Park & Zoo 1230 Water St N	Peterborough	ON	K9H7G4	705-748-9301	745-6866
Web: www.puc.org/files/zoo/zoo.html					
Robinson Henson Zoo 1100 E Lake Dr	Springfield	IL	62712	217-753-6217	529-8748
Web: www.hensonrobinsonzoo.org					
Roger Williams Park Zoo 1000 Elmwood Ave	Providence	RI	02907	401-785-3510	941-3988
Web: www.rogerwilliamsparkzoo.org					
Rolling Hills Wildlife Adventure 625 N Hedville Rd	Salina	KS	67401	785-827-9488	827-3738
Web: www.rhrwildlife.com					
Roosevelt Park Zoo 1219 Burdick Expy E	Minot	ND	58701	701-857-4166	857-4169
Web: www.rpzoo.com					
Rosamond Gifford Zoo at Burnet Park 1 Conservation Pl	Syracuse	NY	13204	315-435-8511	435-8517
Web: rosamondgiffordzoo.com					
Sacramento Zoo 3930 W Land Park Dr	Sacramento	CA	95822	916-808-5888	264-5887
Web: www.saczoo.com					
Safari West Wildlife Preserve & Tent Camp					
3115 Porter Creek Rd	Santa Rosa	CA	95404	707-579-2551	579-8777
TF: 800-616-2695 ■ *Web:* www.safariwest.com					
Saint Augustine Alligator Farm 999 Anastasia Blvd	Saint Augustine	FL	32084	904-824-3337	829-6677
Web: www.alligatorfarm.com					
Saint Louis Zoological Park 1 Government Dr	Saint Louis	MO	63110	314-781-0900	647-7969
Web: www.stlzoo.org					
Salisbury Zoological Park 755 S Park Dr	Salisbury	MD	21804	410-548-3188	860-0919
Web: www.salisburyzoo.org					
Salmonier Nature Park PO Box 190	Holyrood	NL	A0A2R0	709-729-6974	229-7078
Web: www.gov.nf.ca/snp					
San Antonio Zoological Gardens & Aquarium					
3903 N Saint Mary's St	San Antonio	TX	78212	210-734-7184	734-7291
Web: www.sazoo-aq.org					
San Diego Wild Animal Park 15500 San Pasqual Valley Rd	Escondido	CA	92027	760-747-8702	746-7081
Web: www.wildanimalpark.org					
San Diego Zoo 2920 Zoo Dr	San Diego	CA	92101	619-231-1515	231-0249
Web: www.sandiegozoo.org					
San Francisco Zoo 1 Zoo Rd	San Francisco	CA	94132	415-753-7080	681-2039
Web: www.sfzoo.org					
Santa Ana Zoo 1801 E Chestnut Ave	Santa Ana	CA	92701	714-835-7484	
Web: www.santaanazoo.org					
Santa Barbara Zoological Gardens 500 Ninos Dr	Santa Barbara	CA	93103	805-962-5339	962-1673
Web: www.santabarbarazoo.org					
Santa Fe Community College Teaching Zoo					
3000 NW 83rd St	Gainesville	FL	32606	352-395-5604	395-7365
Web: inst.sfcc.edu/~zoo/					
Sarasota Jungle Gardens 3701 Bay Shore Rd	Sarasota	FL	34234	941-355-5305	355-1222
TF: 877-861-6547 ■ *Web:* www.sarasotajunglegardens.com					
Scovill Zoo 71 S Country Club Rd	Decatur	IL	62521	217-421-7435	422-7330
Web: www.decatur-parks.org					
Sedgwick County Zoo 5555 Zoo Blvd	Wichita	KS	67212	316-660-9453	942-3781
Web: www.scz.org					
Seneca Park Zoo 2222 Saint Paul St	Rochester	NY	14621	585-266-6846	342-1477
Web: senecaparkzoo.org					
Sequoia Park Zoo 3414 W St	Eureka	CA	95503	707-442-6552	441-4237
Web: www.eurekawebs.com/zoo/					
Sierra Safari Zoo 10200 N Virginia St	Reno	NV	89506	775-677-1101	677-7874
Web: www.sierrasafarizoo.com					
Silver Springs 5656 E Silver Springs Blvd	Silver Springs	FL	34488	352-236-2121	236-2860
Web: www.silversprings.com					
Southern Nevada Zoological-Botanical Park					
1775 N Rancho Dr	Las Vegas	NV	89106	702-648-5955	648-5955
Web: www.lasvegaszoo.org/					
Spring River Park & Zoo 1306 E College Blvd	Roswell	NM	88201	505-624-6760	624-6941*
**Fax:* Parks Dept ■ *Web:* www.roswellcvb.com/zoo.htm					
Staten Island Zoo 614 Broadway	Staten Island	NY	10310	718-442-3101	981-8711
Web: www.statenislandzoo.org					
Sunset Zoo 2333 Oak St	Manhattan	KS	66502	785-587-2737	587-2730
Web: www.ci.manhattan.ks.us/sunsetzoo					
Tautphaus Park Zoo 2725 Carnival Way	Idaho Falls	ID	83402	208-612-8552	528-6256
Web: www.idahofallszoo.org					
Texas Zoo 110 Memorial Dr	Victoria	TX	77901	361-573-7681	576-1094
Web: www.texaszoo.org					
Toledo Zoo 2700 Broadway	Toledo	OH	43609	419-385-5721	389-8670
Web: www.toledozoo.org					
Topeka Zoological Park 635 SW Gage Blvd	Topeka	KS	66606	785-368-9180	368-9152
Web: www.topeka.org/zoo					
Toronto Zoo 361-A Old Finch Ave	Scarborough	ON	M1B5K7	416-392-5900	392-5934
Web: www.torontozoo.com					
Tracy Aviary 600 E 900 South	Salt Lake City	UT	84105	801-596-8500	596-7325
Web: www.tracyaviary.org					
Trevor Zoo 131 Millbrook School Rd	Millbrook	NY	12545	845-677-3704	677-3774
Trout Ellen Zoo 402 Zoo Circle	Lufkin	TX	75904	936-633-0399	633-0311
Web: www.ellentroutzoo.com					
Tulsa Zoo 6421 E 36th St North	Tulsa	OK	74115	918-669-6600	669-6610
Web: www.tulsazoo.com					
Tupelo Buffalo Park & Zoo 2272 N Coley Rd	Tupelo	MS	38803	662-844-8709	844-8850
TF: 866-272-4766 ■ *Web:* www.tupelobuffalopark.com					
Utica Zoo 99 Steele Hill Rd	Utica	NY	13501	315-738-0472	738-0475
Web: www.uticazoo.org					
Valley Zoo 13315 Buena Vista Rd	Edmonton	AB	T5R5R1	780-496-6912	944-7529
Vilas Henry Park Zoo 702 S Randall Ave	Madison	WI	53715	608-266-4733	266-5923
Web: www.vilaszoo.org					
Virginia Zoological Park 3500 Granby St	Norfolk	VA	23504	757-441-2706	441-5408
Web: www.virginiazoo.org					
Waccatee Zoological Farm 8500 Enterprise Rd	Myrtle Beach	SC	29575	843-650-8500	
Web: www.waccateezoo.com					
Washington Park Zoological Gardens 115 Lakeshore Dr	Michigan City	IN	46360	219-873-1510	873-1539
Web: www.washingtonparkzoo.com					
West Virginia State Wildlife Center Rt 20 S	French Creek	WV	26218	304-924-6211	924-6781
Wild Animal Safari 1300 Oak Grove Rd	Pine Mountain	GA	31822	706-663-8744	663-8880
TF: 800-367-2751 ■ *Web:* www.animalsafari.com					
Wildlife Safari 16406 N 292nd St	Ashland	NE	68003	402-944-9453	
Web: www.omahazoo.com					
Wildlife Safari 1790 Safari Rd	Winston	OR	97496	541-679-6761	679-9210
Web: www.wildlifesafari.org					
Wildlife Sanctuary of Northwest Florida 105 N 'S' St	Pensacola	FL	32505	850-433-9453	438-6168
Web: members.aol.com/wildlifenwfl/					
Wildlife West Nature Park 87 N Frontage Rd	Edgewood	NM	87015	505-281-7655	281-7170
Web: www.wildlifewest.org					
Wildlife World Zoo 16501 W Northern Ave	Litchfield Park	AZ	85340	623-935-9453	935-7499
Web: www.wildlifeworld.com					
Wilds The 14000 International Rd	Cumberland	OH	43732	740-638-5030	638-2287
Web: www.thewilds.org					
Wonders of Wildlife 500 W Sunshine St	Springfield	MO	65807	417-890-9453	890-9278
Web: www.wondersofwildlife.org					
Woodland Park Zoo 601 N 59th St	Seattle	WA	98103	206-684-4800	615-0290
Web: www.zoo.org					
World of Reptiles & Birds Park					
Edgartown-Vineyard Haven Rd	Edgartown	MA	02539	508-627-5634	
Web: www.reptilesandbirds.com					
Zollman Paul E Zoo 5731 County Rd 105 NW	Byron	MN	55920	507-775-2451	775-2544
Zoo The 5701 Gulf Breeze Pkwy	Gulf Breeze	FL	32563	850-932-2229	932-3278
Web: www.the-zoo.com					

	City	State	Zip	Phone	Fax
Zoo of Acadiana Rue Zoo St Hwy 90 E *Web:* www.zooofacadiana.org	Broussard	LA	70518	337-837-4325	837-4253
Zoo Atlanta 800 Cherokee Ave *Web:* www.zooatlanta.org	Atlanta	GA	30315	404-624-5600	627-7514
Zoo Boise 355 N Julia Davis Dr *Web:* www.cityofboise.org/parks/zoo	Boise	ID	83702	208-384-4260	384-4194
Zoo in Forest Park Sumner Ave *Web:* www.forestparkzoo.org	Springfield	MA	01138	413-733-2251	733-2330
Zoo Sauvage de Saint-Felicien 2230 boul du Jardin *TF:* 800-667-5687 ■ *Web:* www.zoosauvage.qc.ca	Saint-Felicien	QC	G8K2P8	418-679-0543	679-3647
ZooAmerica North American Wildlife Park 100 W Hersheypark Dr. *TF:* 800-437-7439 ■ *Web:* www.hersheypa.com/attractions/zooAmerica	Hershey	PA	17033	717-534-3860	534-3151
ZooMontana & Botanical Gardens 2100 S Shiloh Rd *Web:* www.zoomontana.org	Billings	MT	59106	406-652-8100	652-9281
ZooQuarium 674 Rte 28 *Web:* www.zooquariumcapecod.net	West Yarmouth	MA	02673	508-775-8883	

Area Code and Zip Code Guide

The information provided in this Guide is organized **alphabetically by city name**, with area code(s) and zip code(s) shown to the right of the city name.

A

City	Area Code(s)	Zip Code(s)
Abbeville, AL	334	36310
Abbeville, GA	229	31001
Abbeville, LA	337	70510–70511
Abbeville, SC	864	29620
Abbotsford, WI	715	54405
Abbott Park, IL	224, 847	60064
Aberdeen, ID	208	83210
Aberdeen, MD	410	21001
Aberdeen, MS	662	39730
Aberdeen, NC	910	28315
Aberdeen, SD	605	57401–57402
Aberdeen, WA	360	98520
Aberdeen Proving Ground, MD	410	21005, 21010
Abernathy, TX	806	79311
Abilene, KS	785	67410
Abilene, TX	915	79601–79608, 79697–79699
Abingdon, VA	276	24210–24212
Abington, MA	339, 781	02351
Abington, PA	215, 267	19001
Accident, MD	301	21520
Accokeek, MD	301	20607
Accomac, VA	757	23301
Accord, NY	845	12404
Ackerman, MS	662	39735
Acme, MI	231	49610
Acton, MA	351, 978	01718–01720
Acworth, GA	470, 770	30101–30102
Ada, MI	616	49301, 49355–49357
Ada, MN	218	56510
Ada, OH	419, 567	45810
Ada, OK	580	74820–74821
Adairsville, GA	470, 770	30103
Adams, MA	413	01220
Adams, OR	541	97810
Adamstown, MD	301	21710
Adamstown, PA	717	19501
Adamsville, TN	731	38310
Addison, AL	256	35540
Addison, IL	331, 630	60101
Addison, TX	469, 972	75001
Addison, VT	802	05491
Adel, GA	229	31620
Adel, IA	515	50003
Adelanto, CA	760	92301
Adelphi, MD	301	20783, 20787
Adrian, GA	478	31002
Adrian, MI	517	49221
Advance, NC	336	27006
Affton, MO	314	63123
Afton, OK	918	74331
Afton, WY	307	83110
Agawam, MA	413	01001
Agoura Hills, CA	818	91301, 91376–91377
Aguadilla, PR	787, 939	00603–00605
Ahoskie, NC	252	27910
Aiea, HI	808	96701
Aiken, SC	803	29801–29808
Ainsworth, NE	402	69210
Airway Heights, WA	509	99001
Aitkin, MN	218	56431
Ajo, AZ	520	85321
Akron, CO	970	80720
Akron, IN	574	46910
Akron, NY	585	14001
Akron, OH	234, 330	44301–44328, 44333–44334*
Akron, PA	717	17501
Alabaster, AL	205	35007, 35144
Alachua, FL	386	32615–32616
Alamance, NC	336	27201
Alameda, CA	510	94501–94502
Alamo, CA	925	94507
Alamo, GA	912	30411
Alamo, TN	731	38001
Alamo, TX	956	78516
Alamogordo, NM	505	88310–88311
Alamosa, CO	719	81101–81102
Albany, CA	510	94706, 94710
Albany, GA	229	31701–31708
Albany, KY	606	42602
Albany, MN	320	56307
Albany, MO	660	64402
Albany, NY	518	12201–12214, 12220–12262*
Albany, OR	541	97321
Albany, TX	915	76430
Albemarle, NC	704, 980	28001–28002
Albert Lea, MN	507	56007
Alberta, VA	434	23821
Albertson, NY	516	11507
Albertville, AL	256	35950–35951
Albia, IA	641	52531
Albion, IL	618	62806
Albion, IN	260	46701
Albion, MI	517	49224
Albion, NE	402	68620
Albion, NY	585	14411
Albion, PA	814	16401, 16475
Albuquerque, NM	505	87101–87125, 87131, 87153*
Alcoa, TN	865	37701
Alcorn State, MS	601, 769	39096
Alden, NY	585	14004
Alderson, WV	304	24910
Aledo, IL	309	61231
Alexander, AR	501	72002
Alexander, IA	641	50420
Alexander, NY	585	14005
Alexander City, AL	256	35010–35011
Alexandria, AL	256	36250
Alexandria, IN	765	46001
Alexandria, LA	318	71301–71309, 71315
Alexandria, MN	320	56308
Alexandria, SD	605	57311
Alexandria, TN	615	37012
Alexandria, VA	571, 703	22301–22315, 22320–22321*
Alexandria Bay, NY	315	13607
Alfred, ME	207	04002
Alfred, NY	607	14802
Algoma, WI	920	54201
Algona, IA	515	50511
Algona, WA	253	98001
Algonquin, IL	224, 847	60102, 60156
Alhambra, CA	626	91801–91804, 91841, 91896*
Alice, TX	361	78332–78333, 78342
Aliceville, AL	205	35442
Aliquippa, PA	724, 878	15001
Aliso Viejo, CA	949	92653–92656, 92698
Alledonia, OH	740	43902
Allegan, MI	616	49010
Allen, TX	469, 972	75002, 75013
Allen Park, MI	313	48101
Allendale, MI	616	49401
Allendale, NJ	201, 551	07401
Allendale, SC	803	29810
Allenhurst, NJ	732, 848	07709–07711
Allenstown, NH	603	03275
Allentown, NJ	609	08501
Allentown, PA	484, 610	18101–18109, 18175, 18195
Allenwood, NJ	732, 848	08720
Allenwood, PA	570	17810
Allgood, AL	205	35013
Alliance, NE	308	69301
Alliance, OH	234, 330	44601
Allison, IA	319	50602
Allison Park, PA	412, 878	15101
Allston, MA	617, 857	02134
Alma, GA	912	31510
Alma, KS	785	66401, 66501
Alma, MI	989	48801–48802
Alma, NE	308	68920
Alma, WI	608	54610
Almena, WI	715	54805
Almo, ID	208	83312
Almont, MI	810	48003
Alpena, MI	989	49707
Alpha, NJ	908	08865
Alpharetta, GA	470, 678, 770	30004–30005, 30009, 30022*
Alpine, CA	619	91901–91903
Alpine, TX	915	79830–79832
Alpine, UT	801	84004
Alsip, IL	708	60803
Alta, UT	801	84092
Altadena, CA	626	91001–91003
Altamahaw, NC	336	27202
Altamont, KS	620	67330
Altamont, TN	931	37301
Altamonte Springs, FL	321, 407	32701, 32714–32716
Altavista, VA	434	24517
Alto, GA	706, 762	30510, 30596
Alton, IL	618	62002
Alton, MO	417	65606
Altona, NY	518	12910
Altoona, IA	515	50009
Altoona, PA	814	16601–16603
Alturas, CA	530	96101
Altus, OK	580	73521–73523
Altus AFB, OK	580	73523
Alva, OK	580	73717
Alvarado, TX	682, 817	76009
Alvin, TX	281, 832	77511–77512
Alviso, CA	408	95002
Amado, AZ	520	85640, 85645
Amana, IA	319	52203–52204
Amarillo, TX	806	79101–79124, 79159, 79163*
Ambler, PA	215, 267	19002
Amboy, IL	815	61310
Amboy, WA	360	98601
Ambridge, PA	724, 878	15003
Amelia Court House, VA	804	23002
Amelia Island, FL	904	32034
American Falls, ID	208	83211
American Fork, UT	801	84003
Americus, GA	229	31709–31710
Ames, IA	515	50010–50014
Amesbury, MA	351, 978	01913
Amherst, MA	413	01002–01004, 01059
Amherst, NH	603	03031
Amherst, NY	716	14051, 14068, 14221, 14226*
Amherst, TX	806	79312
Amherst, VA	434	24521
Amidon, ND	701	58620
Amite, LA	985	70422
Amityville, NY	631	11701, 11708
Amlin, OH	614	43002
Amory, MS	662	38821
Amsterdam, NY	518	12010
Anaconda, MT	406	59711
Anacortes, WA	360	98221–98222
Anadarko, OK	405	73005
Anaheim, CA	714	92801–92817, 92825, 92850*
Anaheim Hills, CA	714	92807–92809, 92817
Anahuac, TX	409	77514
Analomink, PA	570	18320
Anamosa, IA	319	52205
Anchorage, AK	907	99501–99524, 99540, 99599*
Ancora, NJ	609	08037
Andalusia, AL	334	36420
Anderson, CA	530	96007
Anderson, IN	765	46011–46018

*Partial list of zip codes, including main range

City	Area Code(s)	Zip Code(s)
Anderson, MO	417	64831
Anderson, SC	864	29621–29626
Anderson, TX	936	77830, 77875
Andersonville, GA	229	31711
Andover, KS	316	67002
Andover, ME	207	04216
Andover, MA	351, 978	01810–01812, 01899, 05501*
Andover, NJ	862, 973	07821
Andover, OH	440	44003
Andrews, TX	915	79714
Andrews AFB, MD	240, 301	20762
Angel Fire, NM	505	87710
Angels Camp, CA	209	95221–95222
Angie, LA	985	70426, 70467
Angleton, TX	979	77515–77516
Angola, IN	260	46703
Angola, LA	225	70712
Angoon, AK	907	99820
Angwin, CA	707	94508, 94576
Ankeny, IA	515	50015, 50021
Ann Arbor, MI	734	48103–48109, 48113
Anna, IL	618	62906
Annandale, MN	320	55302
Annandale, NJ	908	08801
Annandale, VA	571, 703	22003
Annapolis, MD	410, 443	21401–21405, 21411–21412
Annapolis Junction, MD	301	20701
Anniston, AL	256	36201–36207
Annona, TX	903	75550
Annville, PA	717	17003
Anoka, MN	763	55303–55304
Anson, TX	915	79501
Ansonia, CT	203	06401
Ansonia, OH	937	45303
Ansted, WV	304	25812
Anthony, KS	620	67003
Anthony, TX	915	79821
Antigo, WI	715	54409
Antioch, CA	925	94509, 94531
Antioch, IL	224, 847	60002
Antioch, TN	615	37011–37013
Antlers, OK	580	74523
Antonito, CO	719	81120
Antrim, NH	603	03440
Anza, CA	951	92539
Apache, OK	580	73006
Apache Junction, AZ	480	85217–85220, 85278, 85290
Apalachicola, FL	850	32320, 32329
Apex, NC	919	27502
Apopka, FL	321, 407	32703–32704, 32712
Apple Valley, CA	760	92307–92308
Apple Valley, MN	952	55124
Appleton, WI	920	54911–54915, 54919
Appomattox, VA	434	24522
Aptos, CA	831	95001–95003
Aquebogue, NY	631	11931
Arab, AL	256	35016
Arapaho, OK	580	73620
Arbor Vitae, WI	715	54568
Arbuckle, CA	530	95912
Arcade, NY	585	14009
Arcadia, CA	626	91006–91007, 91066, 91077
Arcadia, FL	863	34265–34269
Arcadia, LA	318	71001
Arcadia, SC	864	29320
Arcadia, WI	608	54612
Arcata, CA	707	95518–95521
Archbold, OH	419, 567	43502
Archdale, NC	336	27263
Archer, FL	352	32618
Archer City, TX	940	76351
Arco, ID	208	83213
Arcola, IL	217	61910
Arcola, TX	281, 832	77583
Arden, NC	828	28704
Arden Hills, MN	651	55112
Ardmore, OK	580	73401–73403
Ardmore, PA	484, 610	19003
Ardsley, NY	914	10502
Arecibo, PR	787, 939	00612–00614
Argonne, IL	331, 630	60439
Argyle, MN	218	56713
Arkadelphia, AR	870	71923, 71998–71999
Arkansas City, AR	870	71630
Arkansas City, KS	620	67005
Arlington, MA	339, 781	02474–02476
Arlington, MN	507	55307
Arlington, TN	901	38002
Arlington, TX	682, 817	76001–76019, 76094–76096
Arlington, VT	802	05250
Arlington, VA	571, 703	22201–22230, 22234, 22240*
Arlington, WA	360	98223
Arlington Heights, IL	224, 847	60004–60006
Armada, MI	586	48005
Armonk, NY	914	10504
Armour, SD	605	57313
Armstrong, IA	712	50514
Arnett, OK	580	73832
Arnold, MD	410	21012
Arnold, MO	636	63010
Arnold, PA	724, 878	15068
Arnold AFB, TN	931	37389
Aromas, CA	831	95004
Arroyo Grande, CA	805	93420–93421
Artesia, CA	562	90701–90703
Artesia, NM	505	88210–88211
Artesian, SD	605	57314
Arthur, IL	217	61911
Arthur, NE	308	69121
Arthurdale, WV	304	26520
Arvada, CO	303, 720	80001–80007, 80021, 80403
Arvilla, ND	701	58214
Arvin, CA	661	93203
Arvonia, VA	434	23004
Asbury, NJ	908	08802
Asbury Park, NJ	732, 848	07712
Ash Flat, AR	870	72513
Ashaway, RI	401	02804
Ashburn, GA	229	31714
Ashburn, VA	571, 703	20146–20149, 22093
Ashdown, AR	870	71822
Asheboro, NC	336	27203–27205
Asheville, NC	828	28801–28806, 28810–28816
Ashford, AL	334	36312
Ashford, WA	360	98304
Ashippun, WI	920	53003
Ashland, AL	256	36251
Ashland, KS	620	67831
Ashland, KY	606	41101–41105, 41114
Ashland, ME	207	04732, 04737, 04759
Ashland, MA	508, 774	01721
Ashland, MS	662	38603
Ashland, MT	406	59003–59004
Ashland, NE	402	68003
Ashland, NH	603	03217
Ashland, OH	419, 567	44805
Ashland, OR	541	97520
Ashland, PA	570	17921
Ashland, VA	804	23005
Ashland, WI	715	54806
Ashland City, TN	615	37015
Ashley, ND	701	58413
Ashtabula, OH	440	44004–44005
Ashton, ID	208	83420, 83447
Ashton, IL	815	61006
Ashville, AL	205	35953
Ashville, NY	716	14710
Ashville, OH	740	43103
Asotin, WA	509	99402
Aspen, CO	970	81611–81612
Aspermont, TX	940	79502
Assumption, IL	217	62510
Aston, PA	484, 610	19014
Astoria, NY	347, 718	11101–11106
Astoria, OR	503	97103
Atascadero, CA	805	93422–93423
Atchison, KS	913	66002
Atco, NJ	856	08004
Atglen, PA	484, 610	19310
Athens, AL	256	35611–35614
Athens, GA	706, 762	30601–30612
Athens, OH	740	45701
Athens, TN	423	37303, 37371
Athens, TX	903	75751–75752
Athens, WV	304	24712
Atherton, CA	650	94027
Athol, ID	208	83801
Athol, MA	351, 978	01331, 01368
Atkinson, NH	603	03811
Atlanta, GA	404, 470, 678	30301–30380, 30384–30399*
Atlanta, MI	989	49709
Atlanta, TX	903	75551
Atlantic, IA	712	50022
Atlantic, NC	252	28511
Atlantic Beach, FL	904	32224, 32233
Atlantic Beach, NC	252	28512
Atlantic City, NJ	609	08400–08406
Atmore, AL	251	36502–36504
Atoka, OK	580	74525, 74542
Attalla, AL	256	35954
Attica, IN	765	47918
Attica, NY	585	14011
Attica, OH	419, 567	44807
Attleboro, MA	508, 774	02703
Attleboro Falls, MA	508, 774	02763
Atwater, CA	209	95301, 95342
Atwood, KS	785	67730
Au Gres, MI	989	48703
Auburn, AL	334	36830–36832
Auburn, CA	530	95602–95604
Auburn, IL	217	62615
Auburn, IN	219	46706
Auburn, KY	270	42206
Auburn, ME	207	04210–04212
Auburn, MA	508, 774	01501
Auburn, NE	402	68305
Auburn, NY	315	13021–13024
Auburn, WA	253	98001–98003, 98023, 98047*
Auburn University, AL	334	36849
Auburndale, FL	863	33823
Auburndale, MA	617, 857	02466
Audubon, IA	712	50025
Audubon, PA	484, 610	19403, 19407
Augusta, AR	870	72006
Augusta, GA	706, 762	30901–30919, 30999
Augusta, KS	316	67010
Augusta, ME	207	04330–04338
Augusta, MI	616	49012
Augusta, MT	406	59410
Auke Bay, AK	907	99821
Aumsville, OR	503, 971	97325
Aurora, CO	303, 720	80002, 80010–80019*
Aurora, IL	331, 630	60504–60507, 60568, 60572*
Aurora, IN	812	47001
Aurora, MN	218	55705
Aurora, MO	417	65605
Aurora, NE	402	68818
Aurora, NY	315	13026
Aurora, OH	234, 330	44202
Aurora, OR	503, 971	97002
Austell, GA	470, 770	30106, 30168
Austin, IN	812	47102
Austin, MN	507	55912
Austin, PA	814	16720
Austin, TX	512	73301, 73344, 78701, 78774*
Austinburg, OH	440	44010
Autaugaville, AL	334	36003
Ava, MO	417	65608
Avalon, CA	310, 424	90704
Avenal, CA	559	93204
Avenel, NJ	732, 848	07001
Aventura, FL	305, 786	33160, 33180, 33280
Avery Island, LA	337	70513
Avoca, PA	570	18641
Avon, CO	970	81620
Avon, CT	860	06001
Avon, MA	508, 774	02322
Avon, MN	320	56310
Avon, OH	440	44011
Avon Lake, OH	440	44012
Avon Park, FL	863	33825–33826
Avondale, AZ	623	85323
Avondale, PA	484, 610	19311

Partial list of zip codes, including main range

City	Area Code(s)	Zip Code(s)
Axis, AL	251	36505
Axtell, KS	785	66403
Axtell, NE	308	68924
Ayer, MA	351, 978	01432
Azle, TX	682, 817	76020, 76098
Aztec, NM	505	87410
Azusa, CA	626	91702

B

City	Area Code(s)	Zip Code(s)
Babson Park, FL	863	33827
Babson Park, MA	339, 781	02457
Babylon, NY	631	11702–11707
Bad Axe, MI	989	48413
Bagdad, KY	502	40003
Bagley, MN	218	56621
Baileys Harbor, WI	920	54202
Bainbridge, GA	229	31717–31718
Bainbridge Island, WA	206	98110
Baird, TX	915	79504
Baker, LA	225	70704, 70714
Baker, MT	406	59313, 59354
Baker, NV	775	89311
Baker City, OR	541	97814
Bakersfield, CA	661	93301–93313, 93380–93390
Bakerstown, PA	724, 878	15007
Bakersville, NC	828	28705
Bal Harbour, FL	305, 786	33154
Bala Cynwyd, PA	484, 610	19004
Baldwin, GA	706, 762	30511
Baldwin, LA	337	70514
Baldwin, MI	231	49304
Baldwin, NY	516	11510
Baldwin, WI	715	54002
Baldwin City, KS	785	66006
Baldwin Park, CA	626	91706
Baldwinsville, NY	315	13027
Ball Ground, GA	470, 770	30107
Ballinger, TX	915	76821
Ballston Spa, NY	518	12020
Ballwin, MO	636	63011, 63021–63024
Bally, PA	484, 610	19503
Balsam Lake, WI	715	54810
Baltimore, MD	410, 443	21075, 21201–21244*
Bamberg, SC	803	29003
Bandera, TX	830	78003
Bangor, ME	207	04401–04402
Bangor, PA	484, 610	18010–18013, 18050
Bangor, WI	608	54614
Banner Elk, NC	828	28604, 28691
Banning, CA	951	92220
Bannock, OH	740	43972
Bannockburn, IL	224, 847	60015
Bar Harbor, ME	207	04609
Baraboo, WI	608	53913
Baraga, MI	906	49908
Barberton, OH	234, 330	44203
Barboursville, WV	304	25504
Barbourville, KY	606	40906
Bardstown, KY	502	40004
Bardwell, KY	270	42023
Barker, NY	716	14012
Barksdale AFB, LA	318	71110
Barnard, VT	802	05031
Barnardsville, NC	828	28709
Barnesville, GA	470, 770	30204
Barneveld, NY	315	13304
Barnstable, MA	508, 774	02630, 02634
Barnwell, SC	803	29812–29813
Barre, MA	351, 978	01005
Barre, VT	802	05641
Barrington, IL	224, 847	60010–60011
Barrington, NH	603	03825
Barrington, NJ	856	08007
Barron, WI	715	54812
Barrow, AK	907	99723, 99734, 99759, 99789*
Barstow, CA	760	92310–92312
Bartlesville, OK	918	74003–74006
Bartlett, IL	331, 630	60103, 60108, 60133
Bartlett, NE	308	68622
Bartlett, TN	901	38133–38135, 38184
Bartlett, TX	254	76511
Bartow, FL	863	33830–33831
Basalt, CO	970	81621
Basin, WY	307	82410
Basking Ridge, NJ	908	07920, 07939
Bassett, NE	402	68714
Bassett, VA	276	24055
Bastrop, LA	318	71220–71221
Bastrop, TX	512	78602
Batavia, IL	331, 630	60510, 60539
Batavia, NY	585	14020–14021
Batavia, OH	513	45103
Batesburg, SC	803	29006
Batesville, AR	870	72501–72503
Batesville, IN	812	47006
Batesville, MS	662	38606
Bath, ME	207	04530
Bath, NY	607	14810
Bath, OH	234, 330	44210
Bath, PA	484, 610	18014
Bath, SD	605	57427
Baton Rouge, LA	225	70801–70827, 70831–70837*
Battle Creek, MI	616	49014–49018
Battle Creek, NE	402	68715
Battle Ground, WA	360	98604
Battle Mountain, NV	775	89820
Baudette, MN	218	56623
Baxley, GA	912	31513–31515
Bay City, MI	989	48706–48708
Bay City, TX	979	77404, 77414
Bay Harbor, MI	231	49770
Bay Harbor Islands, FL	305, 786	33154
Bay Minette, AL	251	36507
Bay Pines, FL	727	33744
Bay Saint Louis, MS	228	39520–39521, 39525
Bay Shore, NY	631	11706
Bay Springs, MS	601, 769	39422
Bay Village, OH	440	44140
Bayamon, PR	787, 939	00956–00961
Bayard, NE	308	69334
Bayboro, NC	252	28515
Bayfield, WI	715	54814
Bayonne, NJ	201, 551	07002
Bayou La Batre, AL	251	36509
Bayport, MN	651	55003
Bayport, NY	631	11705
Bayside, NY	347, 718	11359–11361
Baytown, TX	281, 832	77520–77522
Bayville, NJ	732, 848	08721
Beach, ND	701	58621
Beach Lake, PA	570	18405
Beachwood, OH	216	44122
Beacon, NY	845	12508
Beale AFB, CA	530	95903
Bean Station, TN	865	37708
Bear Creek, WI	715	54922
Bear Mountain, NY	845	10911
Bearden, AR	870	71720
Beatrice, NE	402	68310
Beattyville, KY	606	41311
Beaufort, NC	252	28516
Beaufort, SC	843	29901–29906
Beaumont, CA	951	92223
Beaumont, TX	409	77657, 77701–77713*
Beaumont, VA	804	23014
Beaver, OK	580	73932
Beaver, PA	724, 878	15009
Beaver, UT	435	84713
Beaver, WV	304	25813
Beaver City, NE	308	68926
Beaver Creek, CO	970	81620
Beaver Dam, KY	270	42320
Beaver Dam, WI	920	53916–53917
Beaver Dams, NY	607	14812
Beaver Falls, NY	315	13305
Beaver Falls, PA	724, 878	15010
Beavercreek, OH	937	45410, 45430–45434
Beaverton, OR	503, 971	97005–97008, 97075–97078
Bechtelsville, PA	484, 610	19505
Beckley, WV	304	25801–25802, 25926
Bedford, IN	812	47421
Bedford, IA	712	50833
Bedford, KY	502	40006
Bedford, MA	339, 781	01730–01731
Bedford, NH	603	03110
Bedford, OH	440	44146
Bedford, PA	814	15522
Bedford, TX	682, 817	76021–76022, 76095
Bedford, VA	540	24523
Bedford Heights, OH	216	44128, 44146
Bedford Hills, NY	914	10507
Bedford Park, IL	708	60455–60459, 60499–60501*
Bedminster, NJ	908	07921
Beebe, AR	501	72012
Beech Creek, PA	570	16822
Beech Grove, IN	317	46107
Beeville, TX	361	78102–78104
Bel Air, MD	410	21014–21015
Belcamp, MD	410	21017
Belcourt, ND	701	58316
Belding, MI	616	48809, 48887
Belfast, ME	207	04915
Belgrade, MT	406	59714
Belhaven, NC	252	27810
Bell, CA	323	90201–90202, 90270
Bell Gardens, CA	562	90201–90202
Bella Vista, AR	479	72714–72715
Bellaire, MI	231	49615
Bellaire, TX	713, 832	77401–77402
Belle Chasse, LA	504	70037
Belle Fourche, SD	605	57717
Belle Glade, FL	561	33430
Belle Mead, NJ	908	08502
Belle Plaine, MN	952	56011
Belle Vernon, PA	724, 878	15012
Bellefontaine, OH	937	43311
Bellefonte, PA	814	16823
Bellerose, NY	347, 718	11426
Belleview, FL	352	34420–34421
Belleville, IL	618	62220–62226
Belleville, KS	785	66935
Belleville, MI	734	48111–48112
Belleville, NJ	862, 973	07109
Belleville, PA	717	17004
Belleville, WI	608	53508
Bellevue, IA	563	52031
Bellevue, NE	402	68005, 68123, 68147, 68157
Bellevue, OH	419, 567	44811
Bellevue, WA	425	98004–98009, 98015
Bellflower, CA	562	90706–90707
Bellingham, MA	508, 774	02019
Bellingham, WA	360	98225–98228
Bellmawr, NJ	856	08031, 08099
Bellmore, NY	516	11710
Bellows Falls, VT	802	05101
Bellport, NY	631	11713
Bells, TN	731	38006
Bellville, OH	419, 567	44813
Bellville, TX	979	77418
Bellvue, CO	970	80512
Bellwood, IL	708	60104
Bellwood, PA	814	16617
Belmont, CA	650	94002–94003
Belmont, MA	617, 857	02478–02479
Belmont, MS	662	38827
Belmont, NH	603	03220
Belmont, NY	585	14813
Belmont, NC	704, 980	28012
Beloit, KS	785	67420
Beloit, WI	608	53511–53512
Belpre, OH	740	45714
Belton, SC	864	29627
Belton, TX	254	76513
Beltsville, MD	301	20704–20705
Belvidere, IL	815	61008
Belvidere, NJ	908	07823
Belzoni, MS	662	39038
Bemidji, MN	218	56601, 56619
Bend, OR	541	97701–97702, 97707–97709
Benicia, CA	707	94510
Benjamin, TX	940	79505
Benkelman, NE	308	69021

*Partial list of zip codes, including main range

City	Area Code(s)	Zip Code(s)
Bennettsville, SC	843	29512
Bennington, NH	603	03442
Bennington, VT	802	05201
Bensalem, PA	215, 267	19020–19021
Bensenville, IL	331, 630	60105–60106, 60399
Benson, AZ	520	85602
Benson, MN	320	56215
Benson, NC	919	27504
Benton, AR	501	72015–72018, 72022, 72158
Benton, IL	618	62812
Benton, KY	270	42025
Benton, LA	318	71006
Benton, MO	573	63736
Benton, PA	570	17814
Benton, TN	423	37307
Benton Harbor, MI	616	49022–49023
Bentonville, AR	479	72712, 72716
Berea, KY	859	40403–40404
Berea, OH	440	44017
Bergenfield, NJ	201, 551	07621
Berkeley, CA	510	94701–94712, 94720
Berkeley, IL	708	60163
Berkeley, MO	314	63134, 63140
Berkeley Heights, NJ	908	07922
Berkeley Springs, WV	304	25411
Berlin, CT	860	06037
Berlin, MD	410	21811
Berlin, NH	603	03570
Berlin, NJ	856	08009
Berlin, NY	518	12022
Berlin, OH	234, 330	44610
Berlin, PA	814	15530
Berlin, WI	920	54923
Berlin Heights, OH	419, 567	44814
Bernalillo, NM	505	87004
Bernardsville, NJ	908	07924
Berne, IN	260	46711, 46769
Berrien Springs, MI	616	49103–49104
Berryville, AR	870	72616
Berryville, VA	540	22611
Berwick, PA	570	18603
Berwyn, IL	708	60402
Berwyn, PA	484, 610	19312
Beryl, UT	435	84714
Bessemer, AL	205	35020–35023
Bessemer, MI	906	49911
Bessemer City, NC	704, 980	28016
Bethany, CT	203	06524
Bethany, MO	660	64424
Bethany, OK	405	73008
Bethany, WV	304	26032
Bethany Beach, DE	302	19930
Bethel, AK	907	99559, 99637, 99679, 99680*
Bethel, CT	203	06801
Bethel, ME	207	04217, 04286
Bethel, MN	763	55005
Bethel, VT	802	05032
Bethel Park, PA	412, 878	15102
Bethesda, MD	240, 301	20810–20817, 20824–20827*
Bethlehem, GA	470, 770	30620
Bethlehem, PA	484, 610	18015–18020, 18025
Bethpage, NY	516	11714
Bettendorf, IA	563	52722
Beulah, MI	231	49617
Beulah, ND	701	58523
Beverly, MA	351, 978	01915
Beverly, NJ	609	08010
Beverly, OH	740	45715, 45721
Beverly Hills, CA	310, 323, 424	90209–90213
Bexley, OH	614	43209
Biddeford, ME	207	04005–04007
Big Bear Lake, CA	909	92315
Big Bend National Park, TX	915	79834
Big Cabin, OK	918	74332
Big Island, VA	434	24526
Big Lake, AK	907	99652
Big Lake, MN	763	55309
Big Lake, TX	915	76932
Big Pine Key, FL	305, 786	33043
Big Rapids, MI	231	49307
Big Rock, IL	331, 630	60511
Big Sky, MT	406	59716
Big Spring, TX	915	79720–79721
Big Stone Gap, VA	276	24219
Big Sur, CA	831	93920
Big Timber, MT	406	59011
Bigfork, MN	218	56628, 56639
Bigfork, MT	406	59911
Biglerville, PA	717	17307
Billerica, MA	351, 978	01821–01822, 01862
Billings, MT	406	59101–59117
Billings, OK	580	74630
Biloxi, MS	228	39530–39535, 39540
Bingen, WA	509	98605
Binger, OK	405	73009
Bingham Farms, MI	248, 947	48025
Binghamton, NY	607	13901–13905
Bird-in-Hand, PA	717	17505
Birdsboro, PA	484, 610	19508
Birmingham, AL	205	35201–35249, 35253–35255*
Birmingham, MI	248, 947	48009–48012
Birmingham, NJ	609	08011
Bisbee, AZ	520	85603
Biscoe, NC	910	27209
Bishop, CA	760	93512–93515
Bishopville, SC	803	29010
Bismarck, ND	701	58501–58507
Bison, SD	605	57620
Bixby, OK	918	74008
Black Butte Ranch, OR	541	97759
Black Creek, NC	252	27813
Black Earth, WI	608	53515
Black Hawk, CO	303, 720	80403, 80422
Black Mountain, NC	828	28711
Black River Falls, WI	715	54615
Blackfoot, ID	208	83221
Blacksburg, SC	864	29702
Blacksburg, VA	540	24060–24063
Blackshear, GA	912	31516
Blackwell, OK	580	74631
Blackwood, NJ	856	08012
Bladensburg, MD	301	20710
Blaine, MN	763	55014, 55434, 55449
Blaine, WA	360	98230–98231
Blair, NE	402	68008–68009
Blairsville, GA	706, 762	30512–30514
Blairsville, PA	724, 878	15717
Blakely, GA	229	31723
Blakeslee, PA	570	18610
Blanchester, OH	937	45107
Bland, VA	276	24315
Blanding, UT	435	84511
Blandon, PA	484, 610	19510
Blasdell, NY	716	14219
Blauvelt, NY	845	10913
Blissfield, MI	517	49228
Blomkest, MN	320	56216
Bloomfield, CT	860	06002
Bloomfield, IN	812	47424
Bloomfield, IA	641	52537–52538
Bloomfield, MO	573	63825
Bloomfield, NJ	862, 973	07003
Bloomfield Hills, MI	248, 947	48301–48304
Bloomingdale, IL	331, 630	60108, 60117
Bloomingdale, IN	765	47832
Bloomington, CA	909	92316
Bloomington, IL	309	61701–61704, 61709–61710*
Bloomington, IN	812	47401–47408, 47490
Bloomington, MN	952	55420, 55425, 55431, 55435*
Bloomsburg, PA	570	17815, 17839
Bloomsbury, NJ	908	08804
Blountstown, FL	850	32424
Blountville, TN	423	37617
Blowing Rock, NC	828	28605
Blue Anchor, NJ	609	08037
Blue Ash, OH	513	45242
Blue Ball, PA	717	17506
Blue Bell, PA	215	19422–19424
Blue Earth, MN	507	56013
Blue Hill, ME	207	04614
Blue Island, IL	708	60406, 60827
Blue Mounds, WI	608	53517
Blue Mountain, MS	662	38610
Blue Ridge, GA	706, 762	30513
Blue Springs, MO	816	64013–64015
Bluefield, VA	276	24605
Bluefield, WV	304	24701
Bluegrove, TX	940	76352
Bluffton, IN	260	46714
Bluffton, OH	419, 567	45817
Bluffton, SC	843	29910
Blunt, SD	605	57522
Blythe, CA	760	92225–92226, 92280
Blytheville, AR	870	72315–72319
Blythewood, SC	803	29016
Boardman, OH	234, 330	44512–44513
Boardman, OR	541	97818
Boaz, AL	256	35956–35957
Boca Raton, FL	561	33427–33434, 33464, 33481*
Bodega Bay, CA	707	94923
Boerne, TX	830	78006, 78015
Bogalusa, LA	985	70427–70429
Bogart, GA	706, 762	30622
Bogota, NJ	201, 551	07603
Bohemia, NY	631	11716
Boiling Springs, NC	704, 980	28017
Boise, ID	208	83701–83735, 83744, 83756*
Boise City, OK	580	73933
Boley, OK	918	74829
Bolingbrook, IL	331, 630	60439–60440, 60490
Bolivar, MO	417	65613, 65727
Bolivar, TN	731	38008, 38074
Bolivia, NC	910	28422
Bolton, CT	860	06043
Bolton, MA	351, 978	01740
Bolton Landing, NY	518	12814
Bon Air, VA	804	23235
Bon Secour, AL	251	36511
Bon Wier, TX	409	75928
Bonham, TX	903	75418
Bonifay, FL	850	32425
Bonita, CA	619	91902, 91908
Bonita Springs, FL	239	34133–34136
Bonner Springs, KS	913	66012
Bonners Ferry, ID	208	83805
Bono, AR	870	72416
Boone, IA	515	50036–50037
Boone, NC	828	28607–28608
Booneville, AR	479	72927
Booneville, KY	606	41314
Booneville, MS	662	38829
Boonton, NJ	862, 973	07005
Boonville, IN	812	47601
Boonville, MO	660	65233
Boothbay Harbor, ME	207	04536–04538, 04570
Boothwyn, PA	484, 610	19061
Borden, IN	812	47106
Bordentown, NJ	609	08505
Borger, TX	806	79007–79008
Boring, OR	503, 971	97009
Borrego Springs, CA	760	92004
Boscawen, NH	603	03303
Boscobel, WI	608	53805
Bossier City, LA	318	71111–71113, 71171–71172
Boston, MA	617, 857	02101–02137, 02163, 02196*
Bothell, WA	425	98011–98012, 98021, 98028*
Botkins, OH	937	45306
Bottineau, ND	701	58318
Bouckville, NY	315	13310
Boulder, CO	303, 720	80301–80310, 80314, 80321*
Boulder, MT	406	59632
Boulder City, NV	702	89005–89006
Bound Brook, NJ	732, 848	08805
Bountiful, UT	801	84010–84011
Bourbon, MO	573	65441
Bourbonnais, IL	815	60914
Bovey, MN	218	55709
Bow, NH	603	03304
Bow, WA	360	98232
Bowbells, ND	701	58721
Bowdon, GA	470, 770	30108
Bowerston, OH	740	44695
Bowie, AZ	520	85605

Partial list of zip codes, including main range

City	Area Code(s)	Zip Code(s)
Bowie, MD	301	20715–20721
Bowie, TX	940	76230
Bowling Green, FL	863	33834
Bowling Green, KY	270	42101–42104
Bowling Green, MO	573	63334
Bowling Green, OH	419, 567	43402–43403
Bowling Green, VA	804	22427–22428
Bowman, ND	701	58623
Bowmansville, NY	716	14026
Box Elder, MT	406	59521
Boxborough, MA	351, 978	01719
Boyden, IA	712	51234
Boydton, VA	434	23917
Boyertown, PA	484, 610	19512
Boylston, MA	508, 774	01505
Boyne Falls, MI	231	49713
Boynton Beach, FL	561	33424–33426, 33435–33437*
Boys Town, NE	402	68010
Bozeman, MT	406	59715–59719, 59771–59773
Bozrah, CT	860	06334
Brackenridge, PA	724, 878	15014
Brackettville, TX	830	78832
Bradbury, CA	626	91010
Braddock, PA	412, 878	15104
Bradenton, FL	941	34201–34212, 34280–34282
Bradford, PA	814	16701
Bradford, VT	802	05033
Bradley, IL	815	60915
Bradley, ME	207	04411
Bradley, WV	304	25818
Brady, TX	915	76825
Braham, MN	320	55006
Braidwood, IL	815	60408
Brainard, NE	402	68626
Brainerd, MN	218	56401, 56425
Braintree, MA	339, 781	02184–02185
Braithwaite, LA	504	70040, 70046
Branchburg, NJ	908	08876
Branchville, NJ	862, 973	07826–07827, 07890
Brandenburg, KY	270	40108
Brandon, FL	813	33508–33511
Brandon, MS	601, 769	39042–39043, 39047, 39232
Brandon, VT	802	05733
Branford, CT	203	06405
Branson, MO	417	65615–65616
Braselton, GA	470, 678, 770	30517
Brattleboro, VT	802	05301–05304
Brawley, CA	760	92227
Braymer, MO	660	64624
Brazil, IN	812	47834
Brea, CA	714	92821–92823
Breckenridge, CO	970	80424
Breckenridge, MN	218	56520
Breckenridge, TX	254	76424
Brecksville, OH	440	44141
Breese, IL	618	62230
Breezy Point, MN	218	56472
Bremen, GA	470, 770	30110
Bremen, IN	574	46506
Bremen, OH	740	43107
Bremerton, WA	360	98310–98314, 98337
Brenham, TX	979	77833–77834
Brent, AL	205	35034
Brentwood, NH	603	03833
Brentwood, NY	631	11717
Brentwood, TN	615	37024–37027
Bretton Woods, NH	603	03575
Brevard, NC	828	28712
Brewer, ME	207	04412
Brewerton, NY	315	13029
Brewster, MA	508, 774	02631
Brewster, NE	308	68821
Brewster, NY	845	10509
Brewster, OH	234, 330	44613
Brewster, WA	509	98812
Brewton, AL	251	36426–36427
Briarcliff Manor, NY	914	10510
Briarwood, NY	347, 718	11435
Brick, NJ	732, 848	08723–08724
Brickeys, AR	870	72320
Bridgeport, AL	256	35740

City	Area Code(s)	Zip Code(s)
Bridgeport, CA	760	93517
Bridgeport, CT	203	06601–06615, 06650, 06673*
Bridgeport, NE	308	69336
Bridgeport, NJ	856	08014
Bridgeport, PA	484, 610	19405
Bridgeport, WV	304	26330
Bridgeton, MO	314	63044–63045
Bridgeton, NJ	856	08302
Bridgeview, IL	708	60455
Bridgeville, PA	412, 878	15017
Bridgewater, MA	508, 774	02324–02325
Bridgewater, NJ	908	08807
Bridgewater, VA	540	22812
Bridgewater Corners, VT	802	05035
Bridgman, MI	616	49106
Bridgton, ME	207	04009
Brigantine, NJ	609	08203
Brigham City, UT	435	84302
Brighton, CO	303, 720	80601–80603
Brighton, MA	617, 857	02135
Brighton, MI	810	48114–48116
Brighton, UT	801	84121
Brillion, WI	920	54110
Brimfield, IL	309	61517
Brinkley, AR	870	72021
Brinson, GA	229	31725
Brisbane, CA	415, 650	94005
Bristol, CT	860	06010–06011
Bristol, FL	850	32321
Bristol, IN	574	46507
Bristol, PA	215, 267	19007
Bristol, RI	401	02809
Bristol, TN	423	37620–37621, 37625
Bristol, VT	802	05443
Bristol, VA	276	24201–24203, 24209
Bristol, WI	262	53104
Britton, SD	605	57430
Broadalbin, NY	518	12025
Broadus, MT	406	59317
Broadview, IL	708	60153–60155
Broadview Heights, OH	440	44147
Broadway, VA	540	22815
Brockport, NY	585	14420
Brockton, MA	508, 774	02301–02305
Brockway, PA	814	15824
Brocton, NY	716	14716
Brodhead, WI	608	53520
Brodnax, VA	434	23920
Broken Arrow, OK	918	74011–74014
Broken Bow, NE	308	68822
Broken Bow, OK	580	74728
Bronson, FL	352	32621
Bronwood, GA	229	31726
Bronx, NY	347, 718	10451–10475, 10499
Bronxville, NY	914	10708
Brook Park, OH	216	44142
Brookfield, CT	203	06804
Brookfield, IL	708	60513
Brookfield, MO	660	64628
Brookfield, OH	234, 330	44403
Brookfield, WI	262	53005–53008, 53045
Brookhaven, MS	601, 769	39601–39603
Brookhaven, PA	484, 610	19015
Brookings, OR	541	97415
Brookings, SD	605	57006–57007
Brookline, MA	617, 857	02445–02447
Brooklyn, CT	860	06234
Brooklyn, IA	641	52211
Brooklyn, MI	517	49230
Brooklyn, NY	347, 718	11201–11256
Brooklyn Center, MN	763	55428–55430, 55443–55444
Brooklyn Heights, OH	216	44109, 44131
Brooklyn Park, MN	763	55428–55429, 55443–55445
Brooks AFB, TX	210	78235
Brookshire, TX	281, 832	77423
Brooksville, FL	352	34601–34614
Brooksville, KY	606	41004
Brookville, IN	765	47012
Brookville, OH	937	45309
Brookville, PA	814	15825
Brookwood, AL	205	35444

City	Area Code(s)	Zip Code(s)
Broomall, PA	484, 610	19008
Broomfield, CO	303, 720	80020–80021, 80038, 80234
Broussard, LA	337	70518
Brown Deer, WI	414	53209, 53223
Brownfield, TX	806	79316, 79376
Browning, MT	406	59417
Browns Mills, NJ	609	08015
Brownsboro, AL	256	35741
Brownsburg, IN	317	46112
Brownstown, IN	812	47220
Brownsville, KY	270	42210
Brownsville, PA	724, 878	15417
Brownsville, TN	731	38012
Brownsville, TX	956	78520–78526
Brownsville, VT	802	05037
Brownsville, WI	920	53006
Brownville, NY	315	13615
Brownwood, TX	915	76801–76804
Bruce, SD	605	57220
Bruceton Mills, WV	304	26525
Brunswick, GA	912	31520–31527, 31561
Brunswick, ME	207	04011, 04053
Brunswick, NC	910	28424
Brunswick, OH	234, 330	44212
Brush, CO	970	80723
Brusly, LA	225	70719
Bryan, OH	419, 567	43506
Bryan, TX	979	77801–77808
Bryantown, MD	301	20617
Bryce Canyon, UT	435	84717
Bryn Athyn, PA	215, 267	19009
Bryn Mawr, PA	484, 610	19010
Bryson City, NC	828	28713
Buchanan, GA	470, 770	30113
Buchanan, MI	616	49107
Buchanan, VA	540	24066
Buckeye, AZ	623	85326
Buckhannon, WV	304	26201
Buckingham, VA	434	23921
Bucyrus, OH	419, 567	44820
Buda, TX	512	78610
Budd Lake, NJ	862, 973	07828
Buellton, CA	805	93427
Buena, NJ	856	08310
Buena Park, CA	714	90620–90624
Buena Vista, CO	719	81211
Buena Vista, GA	229	31803
Buena Vista, VA	540	24416
Buffalo, MN	763	55313
Buffalo, MO	417	65622
Buffalo, NY	716	14201–14233, 14240–14241*
Buffalo, OK	580	73834
Buffalo, SD	605	57720
Buffalo, WY	307	82834, 82840
Buffalo Gap, TX	915	79508
Buffalo Grove, IL	224, 847	60089
Buford, GA	470, 678, 770	30515–30519
Buhl, ID	208	83316
Buies Creek, NC	910	27506
Bullhead City, AZ	928	86426–86430, 86439–86442*
Bunker Hill, IN	765	46914
Bunker Hill, KS	785	67626
Bunn, NC	919	27508
Bunnell, FL	386	32110
Buras, LA	504	70041
Burbank, CA	818	91501–91510, 91521–91526
Burbank, IL	708	60459
Burgaw, NC	910	28425
Burgettstown, PA	724, 878	15021
Burien, WA	206	98146–98148, 98166–98168
Burke, SD	605	57523
Burke, VA	571, 703	22009, 22015
Burkesville, KY	270	42717
Burkeville, VA	434	23922
Burleigh, NJ	609	08210
Burleson, TX	682, 817	76028, 76097
Burley, ID	208	83318
Burlingame, CA	650	94010–94012
Burlington, CO	719	80807
Burlington, IL	224, 847	60109
Burlington, IA	319	52601

Partial list of zip codes, including main range

City	Area Code(s)	Zip Code(s)
Burlington, KS	620	66839
Burlington, KY	859	41005
Burlington, MA	339, 781	01803–01805
Burlington, NJ	609	08016
Burlington, NC	336	27215–27220
Burlington, VT	802	05401–05407
Burlington, WA	360	98233
Burlington, WI	262	53105
Burnet, TX	512	78611
Burnham, PA	717	17009
Burns, OR	541	97710, 97720
Burnsville, MN	952	55306, 55337
Burnsville, NC	828	28714
Burr Ridge, IL	331, 630	60525–60527
Burton, MI	810	48509, 48519, 48529
Burton, OH	440	44021
Burtonsville, MD	301	20866
Burwell, NE	308	68823
Bushkill, PA	570	18324, 18371–18373
Bushnell, FL	352	33513
Bushnell, IL	309	61422
Butler, AL	205	36904
Butler, GA	478	31006
Butler, IN	260	46721
Butler, MD	410	21023
Butler, MO	660	64730
Butler, NJ	862, 973	07405
Butler, PA	724, 878	16001–16003
Butler, WI	262	53007
Butner, NC	919	27509
Butte, MT	406	59701–59703, 59707, 59750
Butte, NE	402	68722
Butterfield, MN	507	56120
Buxton, NC	252	27920
Buzzards Bay, MA	508, 774	02532, 02542
Byfield, MA	351, 978	01922
Byhalia, MS	662	38611
Byrdstown, TN	931	38549
Byron, IL	815	61010
Byron, MN	507	55920
Byron Center, MI	616	49315

C

City	Area Code(s)	Zip Code(s)
Cabazon, CA	951	92230, 92282
Cabot, AR	501	72023
Cabot, PA	724, 878	16023
Cadillac, MI	231	49601
Cadiz, KY	270	42211
Cadiz, OH	740	43907
Cahokia, IL	618	62206
Cairo, GA	229	31728
Cairo, IL	618	62914
Calabasas, CA	818	91301–91302, 91372
Calabasas Hills, CA	818	91301
Calais, ME	207	04619
Caldwell, ID	208	83605–83607
Caldwell, NJ	862, 973	07006–07007
Caldwell, OH	740	43724
Caldwell, TX	979	77836
Caledonia, MN	507	55921
Caledonia, NY	585	14423
Caledonia, WI	262	53108
Calexico, CA	760	92231–92232
Calhoun, GA	706, 762	30701–30703
Calhoun, KY	270	42327
Calhoun, TN	423	37309
Calhoun City, MS	662	38916, 38955
Calico Rock, AR	870	72519
California, MD	301	20619
California, MO	573	65018, 65042
California, PA	724, 878	15419
Calipatria, CA	760	92233
Calistoga, CA	707	94515
Callery, PA	724, 878	16024
Callicoon, NY	845	12723
Calmar, IA	563	52132
Calumet, MI	906	49913, 49918, 49942
Calumet City, IL	708	60409
Calumet Park, IL	708	60643, 60827
Camarillo, CA	805	93010–93012

City	Area Code(s)	Zip Code(s)
Camas, WA	360	98607
Cambria, CA	805	93428
Cambridge, IL	309	61238
Cambridge, MD	410	21613
Cambridge, MA	617, 857	02138–02142, 02163, 02238*
Cambridge, MN	763	55008
Cambridge, NE	308	69022
Cambridge, OH	740	43725, 43750
Cambridge, WI	608	53523
Cambridge City, IN	765	47327
Cambridge Springs, PA	814	16403
Camden, AL	334	36726
Camden, AR	870	71701, 71711
Camden, DE	302	19934
Camden, IN	574	46917
Camden, ME	207	04843, 04847
Camden, MI	517	49232
Camden, NJ	856	08100–08110
Camden, NY	315	13316
Camden, NC	252	27921
Camden, SC	803	29020
Camden, TN	731	38320
Camdenton, MO	573	65020
Cameron, LA	337	70631
Cameron, MO	816	64429
Cameron, MT	760	59720
Cameron, TX	254	76520
Cameron Park, CA	530	95682
Camilla, GA	229	31730
Camillus, NY	315	13031
Camp Douglas, WI	608	54618, 54637
Camp Hill, PA	717	17001, 17011–17012*
Camp Lejeune, NC	910	28542, 28547
Camp Pendleton, CA	760	92054–92055
Camp Point, IL	217	62320
Camp Shelby, MS	601, 769	39401, 39407
Camp Springs, MD	301	20746–20748
Camp Verde, AZ	928	86322
Campbell, CA	408	95008–95011
Campbell Hall, NY	845	10916
Campbellsville, KY	270	42718–42719
Campton, KY	606	41301, 41342
Canadian, TX	806	79014
Canal Winchester, OH	614	43110
Canandaigua, NY	585	14424–14425
Canastota, NY	315	13032
Candler, NC	828	28715
Cando, ND	701	58324
Candor, NC	910	27229
Canfield, OH	234, 330	44406
Cannon AFB, NM	505	88101–88103
Cannon Beach, OR	503	97110
Cannon Falls, MN	507	55009
Canoga Park, CA	818	91303–91309, 91396
Canon City, CO	719	81212–81215, 81246
Canonsburg, PA	724, 878	15317
Canterbury, NH	603	03224
Canton, GA	470, 770	30114–30115
Canton, IL	309	61520
Canton, MA	339, 781	02021
Canton, MI	734	48187–48188
Canton, MS	601, 769	39046
Canton, MO	573	63435
Canton, NY	315	13617
Canton, OH	234, 330	44701–44714, 44718–44721*
Canton, PA	570	17724, 17743
Canton, SD	605	57013
Canton, TX	903	75103
Canyon, TX	806	79015–79016
Canyon City, OR	541	97820
Canyonville, OR	541	97417
Cape Canaveral, FL	321	32920
Cape Charles, VA	757	23310
Cape Coral, FL	239	33904, 33909–33910*
Cape Elizabeth, ME	207	04107
Cape Girardeau, MO	573	63701–63705
Cape May, NJ	609	08204
Cape May Court House, NJ	609	08210
Cape Vincent, NY	315	13618
Capitol Heights, MD	301	20731, 20743, 20753, 20790*
Capitola, CA	831	95010, 95062

City	Area Code(s)	Zip Code(s)
Capron, VA	434	23829
Captain Cook, HI	808	96704
Captiva, FL	239	33924
Capulin, NM	505	88414
Carbondale, IL	618	62901–62903
Carbondale, PA	570	18407
Carefree, AZ	480	85377
Carey, OH	419, 567	43316
Caribou, ME	207	04736
Carle Place, NY	516	11514
Carlinville, IL	217	62626
Carlisle, IN	812	47838
Carlisle, KY	859	40311, 40350
Carlisle, PA	717	17013
Carlisle, SC	864	29031
Carlsbad, CA	760	92008–92009, 92013, 92018
Carlsbad, NM	505	88220–88221
Carlstadt, NJ	201, 551	07072
Carlton, MN	218	55718
Carlyle, IL	618	62231
Carmel, CA	831	93921–93923
Carmel, IN	317	46032–46033, 46082
Carmel, NY	845	10512
Carmel Valley, CA	831	93924
Carmi, IL	618	62821
Carmichael, CA	916	95608–95609
Carnegie, PA	412, 878	15106
Carnesville, GA	706, 762	30521
Carneys Point, NJ	856	08069
Caro, MI	989	48723
Carol Stream, IL	331, 630	60116, 60125–60128*
Carolina, PR	787, 939	00979–00988
Carpentersville, IL	224, 847	60110
Carpinteria, CA	805	93013–93014
Carrabassett Valley, ME	207	04947
Carrington, ND	701	58421
Carrizo Springs, TX	830	78834
Carrizozo, NM	505	88301
Carroll, IA	712	51401
Carroll Valley, PA	717	17320
Carrollton, AL	205	35447
Carrollton, GA	470, 770	30112, 30116–30119
Carrollton, IL	217	62016
Carrollton, KY	502	41008, 41045
Carrollton, MS	662	38917
Carrollton, MO	660	64633
Carrollton, OH	234, 330	44615
Carrollton, TX	469, 972	75006–75011
Carson, CA	310, 424	90745–90749, 90810
Carson, ND	701	58529
Carson City, MI	989	48811
Carson City, NV	775	89701–89706, 89711–89714*
Carter Lake, IA	712	51510
Carteret, NJ	732, 848	07008
Cartersville, GA	470, 770	30120–30121
Carterville, IL	618	62918
Carthage, IL	217	62321
Carthage, MS	601, 769	39051
Carthage, MO	417	64836
Carthage, NC	910	28327
Carthage, TN	615	37030
Carthage, TX	903	75633
Caruthersville, MO	573	63830
Carver, MA	508, 774	02330, 02355, 02366
Cary, IL	224, 847	60013
Cary, NC	919	27511–27513, 27518–27519
Casa Grande, AZ	520	85222, 85230
Cascade, ID	208	83611
Cascade Locks, OR	509	97014
Casey, IL	217	62420
Cashiers, NC	828	28717
Cashmere, WA	509	98815
Casper, WY	307	82601–82605, 82609, 82615*
Casselberry, FL	321, 407	32707–32708, 32718–32719*
Cassopolis, MI	616	49031
Cassville, MO	417	65623–65625
Castaic, CA	661	91310, 91384
Castine, ME	207	04420–04421
Castle Dale, UT	435	84513
Castle Point, NY	845	12511
Castle Rock, CO	303, 720	80104

*Partial list of zip codes, including main range

City	Area Code(s)	Zip Code(s)
Castleton, VT	802	05735
Castro Valley, CA	510	94546, 94552
Castroville, CA	831	95012
Catalina, AZ	520	85738–85739
Catasauqua, PA	484, 610	18032
Catawba, VA	540	24070
Catawissa, PA	570	17820
Cathedral City, CA	760	92234–92235
Cathlamet, WA	360	98612
Catlettsburg, KY	606	41129
Catonsville, MD	410	21228
Catoosa, OK	918	74015
Catskill, NY	518	12414
Cavalier, ND	701	58220
Cave Junction, OR	541	97523, 97531
Cayce, SC	803	29033
Cazenovia, NY	315	13035
Cedar City, UT	435	84720–84721
Cedar Crest, NM	505	87008
Cedar Falls, IA	319	50613–50614
Cedar Falls, NC	336	27230
Cedar Grove, NJ	862, 973	07009
Cedar Grove, WI	920	53013
Cedar Hill, TX	469, 972	75104–75106
Cedar Knolls, NJ	862, 973	07927
Cedar Park, TX	512	78613, 78630
Cedar Rapids, IA	319	52401–52411, 52497–52499
Cedar Springs, GA	229	31732
Cedar Springs, MI	616	49319
Cedar Vale, KS	620	67024
Cedarburg, WI	262	53012
Cedartown, GA	470, 770	30125
Cedarville, OH	937	45314
Celebration, FL	321, 407	34747
Celina, OH	419, 567	45822, 45826
Celina, TN	931	38551
Centennial, CO	303, 720	80015–80016, 80111–80112*
Center, NE	402	68724
Center, ND	701	58530
Center, TX	936	75935
Center City, MN	651	55002, 55012
Center Hill, FL	352	33514
Center Line, MI	586	48015
Center Moriches, NY	631	11934
Center Point, TX	830	78010
Center Valley, PA	484, 610	18034
Centerburg, OH	740	43011
Centerport, NY	631	11721
Centerville, IA	641	52544
Centerville, MA	508, 774	02632–02636
Centerville, MO	573	63633
Centerville, OH	937	45458–45459
Centerville, TN	931	37033
Centerville, TX	903	75833
Centerville, UT	801	84014
Central, SC	864	29630
Central City, CO	303, 720	80427
Central City, KY	270	42330
Central City, NE	308	68826
Central Falls, RI	401	02863
Central Islip, NY	631	11722, 11749, 11760
Central Point, OR	541	97502
Centralia, IL	618	62801
Centralia, MO	573	65240
Centralia, WA	360	98531
Centre, AL	256	35960
Centre Hall, PA	814	16828
Centreville, AL	205	35042
Centreville, IL	618	62207
Centreville, MD	410	21617
Centreville, MI	616	49032
Centreville, MS	601, 769	39631
Centreville, VA	571, 703	20120–20122
Centuria, WI	715	54824
Century, FL	850	32535
Ceres, CA	209	95307
Cerritos, CA	562	90701–90703
Chadds Ford, PA	484, 610	19317
Chadron, NE	308	69337
Chaffee, NY	585	14030
Chagrin Falls, OH	440	44022–44023
Chalfont, PA	215, 267	18914
Challis, ID	208	83226–83229
Chalmette, LA	504	70043–70044
Chama, NM	505	87520
Chamberlain, SD	605	57325–57326
Chambersburg, PA	717	17201
Chamblee, GA	470, 770	30341, 30366
Champaign, IL	217	61820–61826
Champion, PA	814	15622
Chandler, AZ	480	85224–85226, 85244–85249
Chandler, IN	812	47610
Chandler, OK	405	74834
Chandlerville, IL	217	62627
Chanhassen, MN	952	55317
Channahon, IL	815	60410
Channelview, TX	281, 832	77530
Channing, TX	806	79018, 79058
Chantilly, VA	571, 703	20151–20153
Chanute, KS	620	66720
Chapel Hill, NC	919	27514–27517, 27599
Chapin, SC	803	29036
Chapmanville, WV	304	25508
Chappell, NE	308	69129
Chardon, OH	440	44024
Chariton, IA	641	50049
Charleroi, PA	724, 878	15022
Charles City, IA	641	50616, 50620
Charles City, VA	804	23030
Charles Town, WV	304	25414
Charleston, IL	217	61920
Charleston, ME	207	04422
Charleston, MS	662	38921, 38958
Charleston, MO	573	63834
Charleston, SC	843	29401–29425, 29492
Charleston, WV	304	25301–25339, 25350, 25356*
Charleston AFB, SC	843	29404
Charlestown, IN	812	47111
Charlestown, MA	617, 857	02129
Charlestown, NH	603	03603
Charlevoix, MI	231	49711, 49720
Charlotte, MI	517	48813
Charlotte, NC	704, 980	28201–28290, 28296–28299
Charlotte, TN	615	37036
Charlotte, VT	802	05445
Charlotte Court House, VA	434	23923
Charlotte Hall, MD	301	20622
Charlottesville, VA	434	22901–22911
Charlton City, MA	508, 774	01508
Chase City, VA	434	23924
Chaska, MN	952	55318
Chateaugay, NY	518	12920
Chatfield, MN	507	55923
Chatham, IL	217	62629
Chatham, MA	508, 774	02633
Chatham, NJ	862, 973	07928
Chatham, NY	518	12037
Chatham, VA	434	24531
Chatom, AL	251	36518
Chatsworth, CA	818	91311–91313
Chatsworth, GA	706, 762	30705
Chatsworth, IL	815	60921
Chattahoochee, FL	850	32324
Chattanooga, TN	423	37343, 37401–37424
Chautauqua, NY	716	14722
Chauvin, LA	985	70344
Cheboygan, MI	231	49721
Checotah, OK	918	74426
Cheektowaga, NY	716	14043, 14206, 14211, 14215*
Chehalis, WA	360	98532
Chelan, WA	509	98816
Chelmsford, MA	351, 978	01824
Chelsea, MA	617, 857	02150
Chelsea, MI	734	48118
Chelsea, VT	802	05038
Cheltenham, PA	215, 267	19012
Cheney, KS	316	67025
Cheney, WA	509	99004
Cheraw, SC	843	29520
Cherokee, IA	712	51012
Cherokee, NC	828	28719
Cherokee, OK	580	73728
Cherry Hill, NJ	856	08002–08003, 08034
Cherry Point, NC	252	28533
Cherry Valley, IL	815	61016
Cherry Valley, MA	508, 774	01611
Cherryfield, ME	207	04622
Cherryville, NC	704, 980	28021
Chesapeake, VA	757	23320–23328
Chesapeake City, MD	410	21915
Cheshire, CT	203	06408–06411
Chester, CT	860	06412
Chester, GA	478	31012
Chester, IL	618	62233
Chester, MD	410	21619
Chester, MT	406	59522
Chester, NH	603	03036
Chester, NJ	908	07930
Chester, NY	845	10918
Chester, PA	484, 610	19013–19016, 19022
Chester, SC	803	29706
Chester, VA	804	23831, 23836
Chester, WV	304	26034
Chester Springs, PA	484, 610	19425
Chesterbrook, PA	484, 610	19087
Chesterfield, MI	586	48047, 48051
Chesterfield, MO	314, 636	63005–63006, 63017
Chesterfield, SC	843	29709
Chesterfield, VA	804	23832, 23838
Chesterfield Township, MI	586	48047, 48051
Chesterland, OH	440	44026
Chesterton, IN	219	46304
Chestertown, MD	410	21620, 21690
Chestertown, NY	518	12817
Chestnut Hill, MA	617, 857	02467
Chestnut Ridge, NY	845	10952, 10965, 10977
Cheswick, PA	724, 878	15024
Cheverly, MD	301	20781–20785
Chevy Chase, MD	301	20813–20815, 20825
Cheyenne, OK	580	73628
Cheyenne, WY	307	82001–82010
Cheyenne Wells, CO	719	80810
Cheyney, PA	484, 610	19319
Chicago, IL	312, 773	60601–60701, 60706–60707*
Chicago Heights, IL	708	60411–60412
Chickamauga, GA	706, 762	30707
Chickasaw, AL	251	36611
Chickasha, OK	405	73018, 73023
Chico, CA	530	95926–95929, 95973–95976
Chicopee, MA	413	01013–01014, 01020–01022
Chiefland, FL	352	32626, 32644
Childersburg, AL	256	35044
Childress, TX	940	79201
Chillicothe, IL	309	61523
Chillicothe, MO	660	64601
Chillicothe, OH	740	45601
Chilton, WI	920	53014
Chincoteague Island, VA	757	23336–23337
Chinle, AZ	928	86503, 86507, 86538, 86545*
Chino, CA	909	91708–91710
Chinook, MT	406	59523, 59535
Chipley, FL	850	32428
Chippewa Falls, WI	715	54729, 54774
Chisholm, MN	218	55719
Chocorua, NH	603	03817
Choteau, MT	406	59422
Chowchilla, CA	559	93610
Christiana, PA	484, 610	17509
Christiansburg, VA	540	24068, 24073
Christmas, FL	321, 407	32709
Chuckey, TN	423	37641
Chula Vista, CA	619	91909–91915, 91921
Cicero, IL	708	60804
Cimarron, KS	620	67835
Cincinnati, OH	513	45201–45258, 45262–45280*
Cinnaminson, NJ	856	08077
Circle, MT	406	59215
Circle Pines, MN	763	55014
Circleville, OH	740	43113
Cisco, TX	254	76437
Citrus Heights, CA	916	95610–95611, 95621, 95662
City of Commerce, CA	323	90040, 90091
City of Industry, CA	626	90601, 91714–91716*

*Partial list of zip codes, including main range

City	Area Code(s)	Zip Code(s)
Clackamas, OR	503, 971	97015
Clairton, PA	412, 878	15025
Clallam Bay, WA	360	98326
Clanton, AL	205	35045–35046
Clare, MI	989	48617
Claremont, CA	909	91711
Claremont, NH	603	03743
Claremont, NC	828	28610
Claremore, OK	918	74017–74018
Clarence, NY	716	14031, 14221
Clarendon, AR	870	72029
Clarendon, TX	806	79226
Clarendon Hills, IL	331, 630	60514, 60527
Clarinda, IA	712	51632
Clarion, IA	515	50525–50526
Clarion, PA	814	16214
Clarissa, MN	218	56440
Clark, CO	970	80428
Clark, NJ	732, 848	07066
Clark, SD	605	57225
Clarkdale, AZ	928	86324
Clarkesville, GA	706, 762	30523
Clarks Summit, PA	570	18411
Clarksburg, MD	240, 301	20871
Clarksburg, WV	304	26301–26302, 26306, 26461
Clarksdale, MS	662	38614, 38669
Clarkston, MI	248, 947	48346–48348
Clarksville, AR	479	72830
Clarksville, IN	812	47129–47131
Clarksville, TN	931	37040–37044
Clarksville, TX	903	75426
Claude, TX	806	79019
Clawson, MI	248, 947	48017, 48398
Claxton, GA	912	30414–30417, 30438
Clay, WV	304	25043
Clay Center, KS	785	67432
Clay Center, NE	402	68933
Claymont, DE	302	19703
Clayton, AL	334	36016
Clayton, CA	925	94517
Clayton, DE	302	19938
Clayton, GA	706, 762	30525
Clayton, MO	314	63105, 63124
Clayton, NJ	856	08312
Clayton, NM	505	88415
Clayton, NC	919	27520
Clear Brook, VA	540	22624
Clear Creek, IN	812	47426
Clear Lake, IA	641	50428
Clear Lake, SD	605	57226
Clearfield, PA	814	16830
Clearfield, UT	801	84015–84016, 84089
Clearwater, FL	727	33755–33769
Clearwater Beach, FL	727	33767
Cleburne, TX	682, 817	76031–76033
Cleghorn, IA	712	51014
Clementon, NJ	856	08021
Clements, CA	209	95227
Clements, MN	507	56224
Clemson, SC	864	29631–29634
Clermont, FL	352	34711–34713
Cleveland, GA	706, 762	30528
Cleveland, MS	662	38732–38733
Cleveland, OH	216, 440	44101–44149, 44177–44199
Cleveland, OK	918	74020
Cleveland, TN	423	37311–37312, 37320–37323*
Cleveland, TX	281, 832	77327–77328
Cleveland, WI	920	53015
Cleveland Heights, OH	216	44106, 44112, 44118, 44121
Clewiston, FL	863	33440
Clifford, PA	570	18413
Cliffside, NC	828	28024
Cliffside Park, NJ	201, 551	07010
Cliffwood Beach, NJ	732, 848	07735
Clifton, AZ	928	85533
Clifton, KS	785	66937
Clifton, NJ	862, 973	07011–07015
Clifton, TN	931	38425
Clifton, TX	254	76634, 76644
Clifton Forge, VA	540	24422
Clifton Heights, PA	484, 610	19018
Clifton Park, NY	518	12065
Clifton Springs, NY	315	14432
Clines Corners, NM	505	87070
Clinton, AR	501	72031
Clinton, CT	860	06413
Clinton, IL	217	61727
Clinton, IN	765	47842
Clinton, IA	563	52732–52736, 52771
Clinton, KY	270	42031
Clinton, LA	225	70722
Clinton, ME	207	04927
Clinton, MD	301	20735
Clinton, MA	351, 978	01510
Clinton, MI	517	49236
Clinton, MN	320	56225
Clinton, MS	601, 769	39056–39060
Clinton, MO	660	64735
Clinton, NJ	908	08809
Clinton, NY	315	13323
Clinton, NC	910	28328–28329
Clinton, OK	580	73601
Clinton, SC	864	29325
Clinton, TN	865	37716–37717
Clinton Township, MI	586	48035–48038
Clintonville, WI	715	54929
Clintwood, VA	276	24228
Clio, MI	810	48420
Clive, IA	515	50325
Cloquet, MN	218	55720
Closter, NJ	201, 551	07624
Cloudcroft, NM	505	88317, 88350
Clover, SC	803	29710
Clover, VA	434	24534
Cloverdale, VA	540	24077
Clovis, CA	559	93611–93613
Clovis, NM	505	88101–88103
Clute, TX	979	77531
Clyde, NY	315	14433
Clyde, NC	828	28721
Clyde Park, MT	406	59018
Coachella, CA	760	92236
Coal Township, PA	570	17866
Coalgate, OK	580	74538
Coalinga, CA	559	93210
Coalmont, TN	931	37313
Coalville, UT	435	84017
Coatesville, PA	484, 610	19320
Cobleskill, NY	518	12043
Coburg, OR	541	97408
Cochran, GA	478	31014
Cochranton, PA	814	16314
Cockeysville, MD	410	21030–21031
Cocoa, FL	321	32922–32927
Cocoa Beach, FL	321	32931–32932
Coconut Creek, FL	754, 954	33063–33066, 33073, 33097
Coconut Grove, FL	305, 786	33133–33134, 33146
Cody, WY	307	82414
Coeburn, VA	276	24230
Coeur d'Alene, ID	208	83814–83816
Coffeyville, KS	620	67337
Cogan Station, PA	570	17728
Cohasset, MA	339, 781	02025
Cohoes, NY	518	12047
Cokato, MN	320	55321
Coker, AL	205	35452
Colby, KS	785	67701
Colchester, CT	860	06415, 06420
Colchester, IL	309	62326
Colchester, VT	802	05439, 05446–05449
Cold Spring, KY	859	41076
Cold Spring, MN	320	56320
Cold Spring, NY	845	10516
Cold Spring Harbor, NY	516	11724
Cold Springs, NV	775	89506
Coldspring, TX	936	77331
Coldwater, KS	620	67029
Coldwater, MI	517	49036
Coldwater, OH	419, 567	45828
Coleman, FL	352	33521
Coleman, MI	989	48618
Coleman, OK	580	73432
Coleman, TX	915	76834
Colfax, IA	515	50054
Colfax, LA	318	71417
Colfax, WA	509	99111
College Corner, OH	513	45003
College Park, GA	404, 470	30337
College Park, MD	301	20740–20742
College Place, WA	509	99324
College Point, NY	347, 718	11356
College Station, TX	979	77840–77845
Collegedale, TN	423	37315
Collegeville, MN	320	56321
Collegeville, PA	484, 610	19426, 19473
Colleyville, TX	682, 817	76034
Collierville, TN	901	38017, 38027
Collingswood, NJ	856	08108
Collins, MS	601, 769	39428
Collins, NY	716	14034
Collinsville, IL	618	62234
Collinsville, OK	918	74021
Collinsville, VA	276	24078
Collinwood, TN	931	38450
Colman, SD	605	57017
Colmar, PA	215, 267	18915
Coloma, CA	530	95613
Coloma, MI	616	49038–49039
Colon, MI	616	49040
Colonial Heights, VA	804	23834
Colorado City, AZ	928	86021
Colorado City, TX	915	79512
Colorado Springs, CO	719	80901–80950, 80960–80962*
Colquitt, GA	229	31737
Colstrip, MT	406	59323
Colt, AR	870	72326
Colton, CA	909	92313, 92324
Columbia, IL	618	62236
Columbia, KY	270	42728, 42735
Columbia, LA	318	71418
Columbia, MD	410, 443	21044–21046
Columbia, MS	601, 769	39429
Columbia, MO	573	65201–65205, 65211–65218*
Columbia, NC	252	27925
Columbia, PA	717	17512
Columbia, SC	803	29201–29230, 29240, 29250*
Columbia, TN	931	38401–38402
Columbia City, IN	260	46725
Columbia Falls, MT	406	59912
Columbia Heights, MN	763	55421
Columbia Station, OH	440	44028
Columbiana, AL	205	35051
Columbiana, OH	234, 330	44408
Columbus, GA	706, 762	31829, 31901–31909*
Columbus, IN	812	47201–47203
Columbus, KS	620	66725
Columbus, MS	662	39701–39705, 39710
Columbus, MT	406	59019
Columbus, NE	402	68601–68602
Columbus, NC	828	28722
Columbus, ND	701	58727
Columbus, OH	614	43085, 43201–43236*
Columbus, TX	979	78934
Columbus, WI	920	53925
Columbus AFB, MS	662	39701
Columbus Grove, OH	419, 567	45830
Colusa, CA	530	95932
Colville, WA	509	99114
Comanche, TX	915	76442
Combined Locks, WI	920	54113
Commack, NY	631	11725
Commerce, CA	323	90040, 90091
Commerce, GA	706, 762	30529–30530, 30599
Commerce, TX	903	75428–75429
Commerce City, CO	303, 720	80022, 80037
Commerce Township, MI	248, 947	48382, 48390
Compton, CA	310, 424	90220–90224
Comstock, NY	518	12821
Comstock Park, MI	616	49321
Conception, MO	660	64433
Concord, CA	925	94518–94529
Concord, MA	351, 978	01742
Concord, NH	603	03301–03305

*Partial list of zip codes, including main range

City	Area Code(s)	Zip Code(s)
Concord, NC	704, 980	28025–28027
Concord, OH	440	44060, 44077
Concordia, KS	785	66901
Concordville, PA	484, 610	19331, 19339–19340
Condon, OR	541	97823
Conejos, CO	719	81129
Conestoga, PA	717	17516
Congers, NY	845	10920
Conklin, NY	607	13748
Conneaut, OH	440	44030
Connell, WA	509	99326
Connellsville, PA	724, 878	15425
Connersville, IN	765	47331
Conover, NC	828	28613
Conrad, IA	641	50621
Conrad, MT	406	59425
Conroe, TX	936	77301–77306, 77384–77385
Conshohocken, PA	484, 610	19428–19429
Contoocook, NH	603	03229
Convent, LA	225	70723
Conway, AR	501	72032–72035
Conway, NH	603	03818
Conway, SC	843	29526–29528
Conyers, GA	470, 770	30012–30013, 30094
Cook, MN	218	55723
Cookeville, TN	931	38501–38506
Coolidge, AZ	520	85228
Coolidge, GA	229	31738
Coolidge, TX	254	76635
Coon Rapids, MN	763	55433, 55448
Cooper, TX	903	75432
Cooper City, FL	754, 954	33024–33026, 33328–33330
Coopersburg, PA	484, 610	18036
Cooperstown, NY	607	13326
Cooperstown, ND	701	58425
Coopersville, MI	616	49404
Coos Bay, OR	541	97420
Copiague, NY	631	11726
Copley, OH	234, 330	44321
Coppell, TX	469, 972	75019, 75099
Copper Center, AK	907	99573
Copper Mountain, CO	970	80443
Copperas Cove, TX	254	76522
Coquille, OR	541	97423
Cora, WY	307	82925
Coral Gables, FL	305, 786	33114, 33124, 33133, 33134*
Coral Springs, FL	754, 954	33065–33067, 33071, 33075*
Coralville, IA	319	52241
Coraopolis, PA	412, 878	15108
Corbett, OR	503, 971	97019
Corbin, KY	606	40701–40702
Corcoran, CA	559	93212, 93282
Cordele, GA	229	31010, 31015
Cordell, OK	580	73632
Cordova, AK	907	99574, 99677
Cordova, TN	901	38016–38018, 38088
Core, WV	304	26529
Corinne, UT	435	84307
Corinth, MS	662	38834–38835
Corinth, TX	940	76208–76210
Cornelia, GA	706, 762	30531
Cornelius, NC	704, 980	28031
Cornelius, OR	503, 971	97113
Cornell, WI	715	54732
Corning, AR	870	72422
Corning, CA	530	96021, 96029
Corning, IA	712	50841
Corning, NY	607	14830–14831
Cornish, NH	603	03745
Cornville, AZ	928	86325
Cornwall, NY	845	12518
Cornwall Bridge, CT	860	06754
Corona, CA	951	92877–92883
Corona, NY	347, 718	11368
Corona del Mar, CA	949	92625
Coronado, CA	619	92118, 92178
Corpus Christi, TX	361	78350, 78401–78419*
Corry, PA	814	16407
Corsicana, TX	903	75109–75110, 75151
Corte Madera, CA	415	94925, 94976
Cortez, CO	970	81321
Cortland, NY	607	13045
Cortlandt Manor, NY	845	10567
Corunna, MI	989	48817
Corvallis, MT	406	59828
Corvallis, OR	541	97330–97333, 97339
Corydon, IN	812	47112
Corydon, IA	641	50060
Cos Cob, CT	203	06807
Coshocton, OH	740	43812
Costa Mesa, CA	714, 949	92626–92628
Cotati, CA	707	94926–94931
Cottage Grove, OR	541	97424, 97472
Cottonport, LA	318	71327
Cottonwood, AZ	928	86326
Cottonwood, CA	530	96022
Cottonwood, ID	208	83522, 83533
Cottonwood, MN	507	56229
Cottonwood Falls, KS	620	66845
Cotuit, MA	508, 774	02635
Cotulla, TX	830	78001, 78014
Coudersport, PA	814	16915
Coulee City, WA	509	99115
Coulee Dam, WA	509	99116
Council, ID	208	83612
Council Bluffs, IA	712	51501–51503
Council Grove, KS	620	66846, 66873
Countryside, IL	708	60525
Coupeville, WA	360	98239
Courtland, VA	757	23837
Coushatta, LA	318	71019
Coventry, RI	401	02816
Covina, CA	626	91722–91724
Covington, GA	470, 770	30014–30016
Covington, IN	765	47932
Covington, KY	859	41011–41019
Covington, LA	985	70433–70435
Covington, TN	901	38019
Covington, VA	540	24426
Cowiche, WA	509	98923
Coxsackie, NY	518	12051, 12192
Cozad, NE	308	69130
Craftsbury Common, VT	802	05827
Craig, CO	970	81625–81626
Craigsville, VA	540	24430
Cranberry Township, PA	724, 878	16066
Cranbury, NJ	609	08512, 08570
Crandall, TX	469, 972	75114
Crandon, WI	715	54520
Crane, TX	915	79731
Cranford, NJ	908	07016
Cranston, RI	401	02823, 02905–02910*
Craryville, NY	518	12521
Crater Lake, OR	541	97604
Crawfordsville, IN	765	47933–47939
Crawfordville, FL	850	32326–32327
Crawfordville, GA	706, 762	30631
Crazy Horse, SD	605	57730
Creede, CO	719	81130
Creedmoor, NC	919	27522, 27564
Creighton, NE	402	68729
Crescent City, CA	707	95531–95532, 95538
Crescent Springs, KY	859	41017
Cresco, IA	563	52136
Cresco, PA	570	18326
Cresskill, NJ	201, 551	07626
Cresson, PA	814	16630, 16699
Cresson, TX	682, 817	76035
Cressona, PA	570	17929
Creston, IA	641	50801
Crestview, FL	850	32536–32539
Crestview Hills, KY	859	41017
Creswell, OR	541	97426
Crete, IL	708	60417
Crete, NE	402	68333
Creve Coeur, IL	309	61610
Creve Coeur, MO	314	63141
Crewe, VA	434	23930
Cripple Creek, CO	719	80813
Crisfield, MD	410	21817
Crockett, CA	510	94525
Crockett, TX	936	75835
Crofton, MD	410	21114
Cromwell, CT	860	06416
Crookston, MN	218	56716
Crosby, ND	701	58730
Crosbyton, TX	806	79322
Cross City, FL	352	32628
Cross Lanes, WV	304	25313, 25356
Cross Plains, WI	608	53528
Crossett, AR	870	71635
Crossville, TN	931	38555–38558, 38571–38572
Croswell, MI	810	48422
Crow Agency, MT	406	59022
Crowell, TX	940	79227
Crowley, CO	719	81033–81034
Crowley, LA	337	70526–70527
Crown Point, IN	219	46307–46308
Crownsville, MD	410	21032
Croydon, PA	215, 267	19021
Crum Lynne, PA	484, 610	19022
Crystal, MN	763	55422, 55427–55429
Crystal Bay, NV	775	89402
Crystal City, MO	636	63019
Crystal City, TX	830	78839
Crystal Falls, MI	906	49920
Crystal Lake, IL	815	60012–60014, 60039
Crystal River, FL	352	34423, 34428–34429
Crystal Springs, MS	601, 769	39059
Cuba, NY	585	14727
Cudahy, CA	323	90201
Cudahy, WI	414	53110
Cuddy, PA	412, 878	15031
Cuero, TX	361	77954
Cullman, AL	256	35055–35058
Cullowhee, NC	828	28723
Culpeper, VA	540	22701
Culver, OR	541	97734
Culver City, CA	310, 424	90230–90233
Cumberland, KY	606	40823
Cumberland, MD	301	21501–21505
Cumberland, OH	740	43732
Cumberland, RI	401	02864
Cumberland, VA	804	23040
Cumberland Gap, TN	423	37724, 37752
Cumming, GA	470, 770	30028, 30040–30041
Cupertino, CA	408	95014–95015
Currie, NC	910	28435
Currituck, NC	252	27929
Curtis, NE	308	69025
Cushing, OK	918	74023
Cusick, WA	509	99119
Cusseta, GA	706, 762	31805
Custer, SD	605	57730
Cut Bank, MT	406	59427
Cuthbert, GA	229	31740
Cuyahoga Falls, OH	234, 330	44221–44224
Cuyahoga Heights, OH	216	44105, 44125–44127
Cynthiana, KY	859	41031
Cypress, CA	714	90630
Cypress, TX	281, 832	77410, 77429, 77433

D

City	Area Code(s)	Zip Code(s)
Dade City, FL	352	33523–33526
Dadeville, AL	256	36853
Dafter, MI	906	49724
Dahlgren, VA	540	22448
Dahlonega, GA	706, 762	30533, 30597
Daingerfield, TX	903	75638
Dakota, IL	815	61018
Dakota City, IA	515	50529
Dakota City, NE	402	68731
Dakota Dunes, SD	605	57049
Dale, IN	812	47523
Dalhart, TX	806	79022
Dallas, GA	470, 770	30132, 30157
Dallas, NC	704, 980	28034
Dallas, OR	503, 971	97338
Dallas, PA	570	18612, 18690
Dallas, TX	214, 469, 972	75201–75254, 75258–75270*
Dallastown, PA	717	17313
Dalton, GA	706, 762	30719–30722

*Partial list of zip codes, including main range

City	Area Code(s)	Zip Code(s)
Dalton, MA	413	01226–01227
Dalton, OH	234, 330	44618
Daly City, CA	650	94013–94017
Damariscotta, ME	207	04543
Dammeron Valley, UT	435	84783
Dana Point, CA	949	92624, 92629
Danboro, PA	215, 267	18916
Danbury, CT	203	06810–06817
Danbury, NC	336	27016
Dandridge, TN	865	37725
Dania Beach, FL	754, 954	33004, 33312
Daniel, WY	307	83115
Danielson, CT	860	06239
Danielsville, GA	706, 762	30633
Dannemora, NY	518	12929
Danube, MN	320	56230
Danvers, MA	351, 978	01923
Danville, AR	479	72833
Danville, CA	925	94506, 94526
Danville, IL	217	61832–61834
Danville, IN	317	46122
Danville, IA	319	52623
Danville, KY	859	40422–40423
Danville, PA	570	17821–17822
Danville, VA	434	24540–24544
Daphne, AL	251	36526
Darby, MT	406	59829
Dardanelle, AR	479	72834
Darien, CT	203	06820
Darien, GA	912	31305
Darien, IL	331, 630	60561
Darien Center, NY	585	14040
Darlington, SC	843	29532, 29540
Darlington, WI	608	53530
Darrow, LA	225	70725
Dartmouth, MA	508, 774	02714, 02747–02748
Dassel, MN	320	55325
Dauphin Island, AL	251	36528
Davenport, FL	863	33836–33837, 33896–33897
Davenport, IA	563	52801–52809
Davenport, WA	509	99122
David City, NE	402	68632
Davidson, NC	704, 980	28035–28036
Davie, FL	754, 954	33024, 33312–33317*
Davis, CA	530	95616–95618
Davis, WV	304	26260
Davison, MI	810	48423
Daviston, AL	256	36256
Davisville, WV	304	26142
Dawson, GA	229	31742
Dawsonville, GA	706, 762	30534
Dayton, IA	515	50530
Dayton, NV	775	89403
Dayton, NJ	732, 848	08810
Dayton, OH	937	45390, 45401–45441*
Dayton, TN	423	37321
Dayton, TX	936	77535
Dayton, WA	509	99328
Daytona Beach, FL	386	32114–32129, 32198
Daytona Beach Shores, FL	386	32116
Dayville, CT	860	06241
De Funiak Springs, FL	850	32433–32435
De Kalb, MS	601, 769	39328
De Pere, WI	920	54115
De Queen, AR	870	71832
De Smet, SD	605	57231
De Witt, AR	870	72042
De Witt, IA	563	52742
Deadwood, SD	605	57732
Dearborn, MI	313	48120–48128
Dearborn Heights, MI	313	48125–48127
Death Valley, CA	760	92328
Decatur, AL	256	35601–35603, 35609, 35699
Decatur, AR	479	72722
Decatur, GA	404, 470	30030–30037
Decatur, IL	217	62521–62527
Decatur, IN	260	46733
Decatur, MS	601, 769	39327
Decatur, TN	423	37322
Decatur, TX	940	76234
Decaturville, TN	731	38329
Deckerville, MI	810	48427
Declo, ID	208	83323
Decorah, IA	563	52101
Dedham, MA	339, 781	02026–02027
Deer Harbor, WA	360	98243
Deer Lodge, MT	406	59722
Deer Park, CA	707	94576
Deer Park, NY	631	11729
Deer Park, TX	281, 832	77536
Deer River, MN	218	56636
Deerfield, IL	224, 847	60015
Deerfield, MA	413	01342
Deerfield, WI	608	53531
Deerfield Beach, FL	754, 954	33064, 33441–33443
Deerwood, MN	218	56444
Defiance, OH	419, 567	43512
DeForest, WI	608	53532
DeGraff, OH	937	43318
DeKalb, IL	815	60115
Del City, OK	405	73115, 73135, 73165
Del Mar, CA	858	92014
Del Norte, CO	719	81132
Del Rey, CA	559	93616
Del Rio, TX	830	78840–78843, 78847
Delair, NJ	856	08110
Delanco, NJ	856	08075
DeLand, FL	386	32720–32724
Delano, CA	661	93215–93216
Delano, MN	763	55328
Delavan, MN	507	56023
Delavan, WI	262	53115
Delaware, OH	740	43015
Delaware City, DE	302	19706
Delaware Water Gap, PA	570	18327
Delbarton, WV	304	25670
DeLeon Springs, FL	386	32130
Delhi, NY	607	13753
Dellroy, OH	234, 330	44620
Delmar, MD	410	21875
Delmar, NY	518	12054
Delmont, NJ	856	08314
Delmont, PA	724, 878	15626
Delphi, IN	765	46923
Delphos, OH	419, 567	45833
Delray Beach, FL	561	33444–33448, 33482–33484
Delta, CO	970	81416
Delta, UT	435	84624
Deming, NM	505	88030–88031
Demopolis, AL	334	36732
Demorest, GA	706, 762	30535, 30544
Demotte, IN	219	46310
Denham Springs, LA	225	70706, 70726–70727
Denison, IA	712	51442
Denison, TX	903	75020–75021
Denmark, SC	803	29042
Denmark, WI	920	54208
Denton, MD	410	21629
Denton, NC	336	27239
Denton, TX	940	76201–76210
Denver, CO	303, 720	80002, 80010–80014*
Denver, IA	319	50622
Denver, NC	704, 980	28037
Denver, PA	717	17517
Denville, NJ	862, 973	07834
Depew, NY	716	14043
Depoe Bay, OR	541	97341
Deposit, NY	607	13754
Dequincy, LA	337	70633
Derby, CT	203	06418
Derby, KS	316	67037
Derby, NY	716	14047
DeRidder, LA	337	70634
Dermott, AR	870	71638
Derry, NH	603	03038
Derwent, OH	740	43733
Des Allemands, LA	504	70030
Des Arc, AR	870	72040
Des Moines, IA	515	50301–50340, 50347–50350*
Des Moines, WA	206	98148, 98198
Des Plaines, IL	224, 847	60016–60019
Descanso, CA	760	91916
Desert Hot Springs, CA	760	92240–92241
Deshler, NE	402	68340
DeSoto, KS	913	66018
DeSoto, TX	469, 972	75115, 75123
Destin, FL	850	32540–32541, 32550
Destrehan, LA	985	70047
Detroit, MI	313, 734	48201–48244, 48255, 48260*
Detroit, OR	503, 971	97342
Detroit Lakes, MN	218	56501–56502
Devault, PA	484, 610	19432
Devens, MA	351, 978	01432
Devils Lake, ND	701	58301
Devils Tower, WY	307	82714
Devon, PA	484, 610	19333
Dewey, OK	918	74029
Dewey Beach, DE	302	19971
DeWitt, NY	315	13214
Dexter, MI	734	48130
Dexter, MO	573	63841
Diamond, MO	417	64840
Diamond Bar, CA	909	91765
Diamond Point, NY	518	12824
Diboll, TX	936	75941
Dickens, TX	806	79229
Dickinson, ND	701	58601–58602
Dickinson, TX	281, 832	77539
Dickson, TN	615	37055–37056
Dighton, KS	620	67839
Dighton, MA	508, 774	02715
Dillingham, AK	907	99576
Dillon, MT	406	59725
Dillon, SC	843	29536
Dillwyn, VA	434	23936
Dimmitt, TX	806	79027
Dinosaur, CO	970	81610, 81633
Dinuba, CA	559	93618
Dinwiddie, VA	804	23841
Dix Hills, NY	631	11746
Dixie, GA	229	31629
Dixmoor, IL	708	60406, 60426
Dixon, CA	707	95620
Dixon, IL	815	61021
Dixon, KY	270	42409
Dixon, MO	573	65459
Dobbs Ferry, NY	914	10522
Dobson, NC	336	27017
Dodge Center, MN	507	55927
Dodge City, KS	620	67801
Dodgeville, WI	608	53533, 53595
Dolgeville, NY	315	13329
Dolton, IL	708	60419
Donaldson, IN	574	46513
Donaldsonville, LA	225	70346
Donalsonville, GA	229	31745
Dongola, IL	618	62926
Doniphan, MO	573	63935
Dorado, PR	787, 939	00646
Doraville, GA	470, 770	30340, 30360–30362
Dorchester, MA	617, 857	02121–02125
Dorchester, NE	402	68343
Doswell, VA	804	23047
Dothan, AL	334	36301–36305
Double Springs, AL	205	35553
Douglas, AK	907	99824
Douglas, AZ	520	85607–85608, 85655
Douglas, GA	912	31533–31535
Douglas, MI	616	49406
Douglas, WY	307	82633
Douglassville, PA	484, 610	19518
Douglassville, TX	903	75560
Douglaston, NY	347, 718	11362–11363
Douglasville, GA	470, 770	30133–30135, 30154
Dove Creek, CO	970	81324
Dover, DE	302	19901–19906
Dover, FL	813	33527
Dover, NH	603	03820–03822
Dover, NJ	862, 973	07801–07806, 07869
Dover, OH	234, 330	44622
Dover, TN	931	37058
Dover AFB, DE	302	19902
Dover Plains, NY	845	12522

*Partial list of zip codes, including main range

City	Area Code(s)	Zip Code(s)
Dowagiac, MI	616	49047
Downers Grove, IL	331, 630	60515–60517
Downey, CA	562	90239–90242
Downieville, CA	530	95936
Downingtown, PA	484, 610	19335, 19372
Doylestown, OH	234, 330	44230
Doylestown, PA	215, 267	18901, 18933
Doyline, LA	318	71023
Dracut, MA	351, 978	01826
Dragoon, AZ	520	85609
Drain, OR	541	97435
Draper, UT	801	84020
Dravosburg, PA	412, 878	15034
Dresden, TN	731	38225
Dresher, PA	215, 267	19025
Dresser, WI	715	54009
Drexel Hill, PA	484, 610	19026
Driggs, ID	208	83422
Drummond Island, MI	906	49726
Dry Ridge, KY	859	41035
Dryden, NY	607	13053
Du Bois, PA	814	15801
Duarte, CA	626	91009–91010
Dublin, CA	925	94568
Dublin, GA	478	31021, 31027, 31040
Dublin, NH	603	03444
Dublin, NC	910	28332
Dublin, OH	614	43016–43017
Dublin, VA	540	24084
Dubois, ID	208	83423, 83446
Dubois, WY	307	82513
Dubuque, IA	563	52001–52004, 52099
Duchesne, UT	435	84021
Duck, NC	252	27949
Duck Hill, MS	662	38925
Duck Key, FL	305, 786	33050
Dudley, GA	478	31022
Dudley, MA	508, 774	01571
Dudley, MO	573	63936
Dudley, NC	919	28333
Due West, SC	864	29639
Dugway, UT	435	84022
Dulles, VA	571, 703	20101–20104, 20163–20166*
Duluth, GA	470, 678, 770	30026–30029, 30095–30099
Duluth, MN	218	55701, 55801–55816
Dumas, TX	806	79029
Dunbar, PA	724, 878	15431
Dunbar, WV	304	25064
Dunbar, WI	715	54119
Dunbridge, OH	419, 567	43414
Duncan, AZ	928	85534
Duncan, OK	580	73533–73536, 73575
Duncan, SC	864	29334, 29390–29391
Duncannon, PA	717	17020
Duncansville, PA	814	16635
Duncanville, TX	469, 972	75116, 75137–75138
Dundalk, MD	410	21222
Dundee, FL	863	33838
Dundee, IL	224, 847	60118
Dundee, NY	607	14837
Dundee, OR	503, 971	97115
Dunedin, FL	727	34697–34698
Dunkirk, IN	765	47336
Dunkirk, MD	301	20754
Dunkirk, NY	716	14048, 14166
Dunlap, IL	309	61525
Dunlap, TN	423	37327
Dunmore, PA	570	18509–18512
Dunn, NC	910	28334–28335
Dunnell, MN	507	56127
Dunnellon, FL	352	34430–34434
Dunning, NE	308	68833
Dunseith, ND	701	58329
Dupont, WA	253	98327
Dupree, SD	605	57623
DuQuoin, IL	618	62832
Durand, MI	989	48429
Durand, WI	715	54736
Durango, CO	970	81301–81303
Durant, OK	580	74701–74702
Durham, CT	860	06422
Durham, NH	603	03824
Durham, NC	919	27701–27717, 27722
Duryea, PA	570	18642
Dushore, PA	570	18614
Duxbury, MA	339, 781	02331–02332
Dwight, IL	815	60420
Dyer, NV	760	89010
Dyersburg, TN	731	38024–38025
Dyersville, IA	563	52040
Dyess AFB, TX	915	79607

E

City	Area Code(s)	Zip Code(s)
Eads, CO	719	81036
Eagan, MN	651	55120–55123
Eagle, CO	970	81631
Eagle, WI	262	53119
Eagle Creek, OR	503, 971	97022
Eagle Grove, IA	515	50533
Eagle Nest, NM	505	87710, 87718
Eagle Pass, TX	830	78852–78853
Eagle River, AK	907	99577
Eagle River, MI	906	49950
Eagle River, WI	715	54521
Eagle Rock, CA	323	90041
Eagleville, PA	484, 610	19403, 19408, 19415
Earle, AR	870	72331
Earlville, IL	815	60518
Early Branch, SC	803	29916
Earth City, MO	314	63045
Easley, SC	864	29640–29642
East Alton, IL	618	62024
East Amherst, NY	716	14051
East Aurora, NY	585	14052
East Bend, NC	336	27018
East Berlin, CT	860	06023
East Bernstadt, KY	606	40729
East Bloomfield, NY	585	14443, 14469
East Boston, MA	617, 857	02128, 02228
East Brunswick, NJ	732, 848	08816
East Canton, OH	234, 330	44730
East Chicago, IN	219	46312
East Cleveland, OH	216	44110–44112, 44118
East Derry, NH	603	03041
East Dubuque, IL	815	61025
East Dundee, IL	224, 847	60118
East Durham, NY	518	12423
East Earl, PA	717	17519
East Elmhurst, NY	347, 718	11369–11371
East Falmouth, MA	508, 774	02536
East Farmingdale, NY	631	11735
East Granby, CT	860	06026
East Grand Forks, MN	218	56721
East Grand Rapids, MI	616	49506, 49546
East Greenville, PA	215, 267	18041
East Greenwich, RI	401	02818
East Haddam, CT	860	06423
East Hampstead, NH	603	03826
East Hampton, CT	860	06424, 06447
East Hampton, NY	631	11937
East Hanover, NJ	862, 973	07936
East Hartford, CT	860	06108, 06118, 06128, 06138
East Haven, CT	203	06512–06513
East Hazel Crest, IL	708	60429
East Hills, NY	516	11548, 11576–11577
East Jordan, MI	231	49727
East Lansing, MI	517	48823–48826
East Liberty, OH	937	43074, 43319
East Liverpool, OH	234, 330	43920
East Longmeadow, MA	413	01028, 01116
East Meadow, NY	516	11554
East Millstone, NJ	732, 848	08873–08875
East Moline, IL	309	61244
East Montpelier, VT	802	05651
East New Market, MD	410	21631
East Northport, NY	631	11731
East Norwalk, CT	203	06855
East Orange, NJ	862, 973	07017–07019
East Palatka, FL	386	32131
East Palestine, OH	234, 330	44413
East Palo Alto, CA	650	94303
East Pembroke, NY	585	14056
East Peoria, IL	309	61611
East Petersburg, PA	717	17520
East Point, GA	404, 470	30344, 30364
East Providence, RI	401	02914–02916
East Rochester, NH	603	03868
East Rutherford, NJ	201, 551	07073
East Saint Louis, IL	618	62201–62208
East Stroudsburg, PA	570	18301
East Syracuse, NY	315	13057
East Taunton, MA	508, 774	02718
East Tawas, MI	989	48730
East Templeton, MA	351, 978	01438
East Texas, PA	484, 610	18046
East Troy, WI	262	53120
East Walpole, MA	508, 774	02032
East Weymouth, MA	339, 781	02189
East Windsor, CT	860	06016, 06088
East Windsor, NJ	609	08512, 08520
Eastaboga, AL	256	36260
Easthampton, MA	413	01027
Eastlake, MI	231	49626
Eastlake, OH	440	44095–44097
Eastland, TX	254	76448
Eastman, GA	478	31023
Easton, MD	410	21601, 21606
Easton, PA	484, 610	18040–18045
Eastpointe, MI	586	48021
Eastport, ME	207	04631
Eastsound, WA	360	98245
Eastville, VA	757	23347
Eaton, CO	970	80615
Eaton, IN	765	47338
Eaton, OH	937	45320
Eaton Rapids, MI	517	48827
Eatonton, GA	706, 762	31024
Eatontown, NJ	732, 848	07724, 07799
Eatonville, WA	360	98328
Eau Claire, WI	715	54701–54703
Ebensburg, PA	814	15931
Edcouch, TX	956	78538
Eddyville, KY	270	42038
Eden, NC	336	27288–27289
Eden Prairie, MN	952	55343–55347
Edenton, NC	252	27932
Edgartown, MA	508, 774	02539
Edgefield, SC	803	29824
Edgeley, ND	701	58433
Edgerton, MN	507	56128
Edgerton, OH	419, 567	43517
Edgerton, WI	608	53534
Edgewater, FL	386	32132, 32141
Edgewater, MD	410, 443	21037
Edgewater, NJ	201, 551	07020
Edgewood, IA	563	52042–52044
Edgewood, MD	410	21040
Edgewood, NY	631	11717
Edgewood, WA	253	98371–98372, 98390
Edina, MN	952	55343, 55410, 55416, 55424*
Edina, MO	660	63537
Edinboro, PA	814	16412, 16444
Edinburg, TX	956	78539–78540
Edinburg, VA	540	22824
Edinburgh, IN	812	46124
Edison, CA	661	93220
Edison, NJ	732, 848	08817–08820, 08837, 08899
Edisto Beach, SC	843	29438
Edmeston, NY	607	13335
Edmond, OK	405	73003, 73013, 73034, 73083
Edmonds, WA	425	98020, 98026
Edmonton, KY	270	42129
Edmore, MI	989	48829
Edna, TX	361	77957
Edon, OH	419, 567	43518
Edwards, CA	661	93523–93524
Edwards, CO	970	81632
Edwardsburg, MI	616	49112, 49130
Edwardsville, IL	618	62025–62026
Edwardsville, KS	913	66111–66113
Edwardsville, PA	570	18704
Effingham, IL	217	62401

*Partial list of zip codes, including main range

City	Area Code(s)	Zip Code(s)
Egg Harbor, WI	920	54209
Egg Harbor City, NJ	609	08215
Egg Harbor Township, NJ	609	08234
Eglin AFB, FL	850	32542
Eielson AFB, AK	907	99702
Eighty Four, PA	724, 878	15330
Ekalaka, MT	406	59324
El Cajon, CA	619	92019–92022, 92090
El Campo, TX	979	77437
El Centro, CA	760	92243–92244
El Cerrito, CA	510	94530
El Dorado, AR	870	71730–71731, 71768
El Dorado, KS	316	67042
El Dorado Hills, CA	916	95762
El Dorado Springs, MO	417	64744
El Monte, CA	626	91731–91735
El Paso, IL	309	61738
El Paso, TX	915	79821, 79901–79961*
El Reno, OK	405	73036
El Segundo, CA	310, 424	90245
El Sobrante, CA	510	94803, 94820
Elba, AL	334	36323
Elba, NY	585	14058
Elberfeld, IN	812	47613
Elberton, GA	706, 762	30635
Elbow Lake, MN	218	56531
Eldora, IA	641	50627
Eldorado, IL	618	62930
Eldorado, TX	915	76936
Eldorado Springs, CO	303, 720	80025
Eldridge, CA	707	95431
Eldridge, IA	563	52748
Eleele, HI	808	96705
Elephant Butte, NM	505	87935
Elgin, IL	224, 847	60120–60123
Elgin, SC	803	29045
Elizabeth, IL	815	61028
Elizabeth, IN	812	47117
Elizabeth, NJ	908	07201–07202, 07206–07208
Elizabeth, PA	412, 878	15037
Elizabeth, WV	304	26143
Elizabeth City, NC	252	27906–27909
Elizabethton, TN	423	37643–37644
Elizabethtown, IL	618	62931
Elizabethtown, KY	270	42701–42702
Elizabethtown, NY	518	12932
Elizabethtown, NC	910	28337
Elizabethtown, PA	717	17022
Elizabethville, PA	717	17023
Elk City, OK	580	73644, 73648
Elk Grove, CA	916	95624, 95758–95759
Elk Grove Village, IL	224, 847	60007–60009
Elk Point, SD	605	57025
Elk Rapids, MI	231	49629
Elk River, MN	763	55330
Elkader, IA	563	52043
Elkhart, IN	574	46514–46517
Elkhart, KS	620	67950
Elkhart Lake, WI	920	53020
Elkhorn, NE	402	68022
Elkhorn, WI	262	53121
Elkin, NC	336	28621
Elkins, WV	304	26241
Elkins Park, PA	215, 267	19027
Elkland, PA	814	16920
Elko, MN	952	55020
Elko, NV	775	89801–89803, 89815
Elkridge, MD	410	21075
Elkton, KY	270	42220
Elkton, MD	410	21921–21922
Elkton, OH	234, 330	44415
Ellaville, GA	229	31806
Ellendale, ND	701	58436
Ellensburg, WA	509	98926, 98950
Ellenville, NY	845	12428
Ellenwood, GA	404, 470	30294
Ellettsville, IN	812	47429
Ellicott City, MD	410	21041–21043
Ellicottville, NY	716	14731
Ellijay, GA	706, 762	30540
Ellington, CT	860	06029

City	Area Code(s)	Zip Code(s)
Ellinwood, KS	620	67526
Ellis, KS	785	67637
Ellisville, MS	601, 769	39437
Ellisville, MO	636	63011, 63021, 63038
Ellsworth, KS	785	67439
Ellsworth, ME	207	04605
Ellsworth, WI	715	54003, 54010–54011
Ellsworth AFB, SD	605	57706
Ellwood City, PA	724, 878	16117
Elm Grove, WI	262	53122
Elm Springs, AR	479	72728
Elma, NY	585	14059
Elma, WA	360	98541
Elmendorf AFB, AK	907	99505–99506
Elmer, NJ	856	08318
Elmhurst, IL	331, 630	60126
Elmhurst, NY	347, 718	11373, 11380
Elmira, NY	607	14901–14905, 14925
Elmira, OR	541	97437
Elmira Heights, NY	607	14903
Elmont, NY	516	11003
Elmore, AL	334	36025
Elmore, OH	419, 567	43416
Elmsford, NY	914	10523
Elmwood, CT	860	06110, 06133
Elmwood Park, IL	708	60707
Elmwood Park, NJ	201, 551	07407
Elon, NC	336	27244
Elsah, IL	618	62028
Elsmere, KY	859	41018
Elverson, PA	484, 610	19520
Elwood, IN	765	46036
Elwood, NE	308	68937
Ely, MN	218	55731
Ely, NV	775	89301, 89315
Elyria, OH	440	44035–44039
Elysburg, PA	570	17824
Emerado, ND	701	58228
Emeryville, CA	510	94608, 94662
Emigrant, MT	406	59027
Emigsville, PA	717	17318
Eminence, KY	502	40019
Eminence, MO	573	65466
Emlenton, PA	724, 878	16373
Emmaus, PA	484, 610	18049, 18098–18099
Emmetsburg, IA	712	50536
Emmett, ID	208	83617
Emmitsburg, MD	301	21727
Emory, TX	903	75440
Emory, VA	276	24327
Empire, MI	231	49630
Emporia, KS	620	66801
Emporia, VA	434	23847
Emporium, PA	814	15834
Encinitas, CA	760	92023–92024
Encino, CA	818	91316, 91335, 91416, 91426*
Endicott, NY	607	13760–13763
Enfield, CT	860	06082–06083
Enfield, NH	603	03748
Enfield, NC	252	27823
Engelhard, NC	252	27824
England, AR	501	72046
Englewood, CO	303, 720	80110–80112, 80150–80155*
Englewood, FL	941	34223–34224, 34295
Englewood, NJ	201, 551	07631–07632
Englewood, OH	937	45315, 45322
Englewood Cliffs, NJ	201, 551	07632
English, IN	812	47118
Englishtown, NJ	732, 848	07726
Enid, OK	580	73701–73706
Ennis, MT	406	59729
Ennis, TX	469, 972	75119–75120
Enola, PA	717	17025
Enon, OH	937	45323
Enoree, SC	864	29335
Enosburg Falls, VT	802	05450
Enterprise, AL	334	36330–36331
Enterprise, OR	541	97828
Enumclaw, WA	360	98022
Ephraim, UT	435	84627
Ephrata, PA	717	17522

City	Area Code(s)	Zip Code(s)
Ephrata, WA	509	98823
Epping, NH	603	03042
Epps, LA	318	71237
Epworth, IA	563	52045
Erdenheim, PA	215, 267	19038
Erie, CO	303, 720	80516
Erie, IL	309	61250
Erie, KS	620	66733
Erie, MI	734	48133
Erie, PA	814	16501–16515, 16522, 16530*
Erin, TN	931	37061
Erlanger, KY	859	41017–41018
Erving, MA	351, 978	01344
Erwin, TN	423	37650
Escalon, CA	209	95320
Escanaba, MI	906	49829
Escondido, CA	760	92025–92033, 92046
Esopus, NY	845	12429
Espanola, NM	505	87532–87533
Essex, CT	860	06426
Essex, MD	410	21221
Essex Junction, VT	802	05451–05453
Essexville, MI	989	48732
Essington, PA	484, 610	19029
Estancia, NM	505	87009, 87016
Estero, FL	239	33928
Estes Park, CO	970	80511, 80517
Estherville, IA	712	51334
Estill, SC	803	29918, 29939
Euclid, OH	216	44117–44119, 44123, 44132*
Eudora, AR	870	71640
Eufaula, AL	334	36027, 36072
Eufaula, OK	918	74432, 74461
Eugene, OR	541	97401–97408, 97412, 97440*
Euless, TX	682, 817	76039–76040
Eunice, LA	337	70535
Eureka, CA	707	95501–95503, 95534
Eureka, IL	309	61530
Eureka, KS	620	67045
Eureka, MO	636	63025
Eureka, MT	406	59917
Eureka, NV	775	89316
Eureka Springs, AR	479	72631–72632
Eustis, FL	352	32726–32727, 32736
Eutaw, AL	205	35462
Evans, GA	706, 762	30809
Evans City, PA	724, 878	16033
Evanston, IL	224, 847	60201–60204, 60208–60209
Evanston, WY	307	82930–82931
Evansville, IN	812	47701–47750
Evansville, WI	608	53536
Evansville, WY	307	82636
Eveleth, MN	218	55734
Everett, MA	617, 857	02149
Everett, PA	814	15537
Everett, WA	425	98201–98208
Evergreen, AL	251	36401
Evergreen, CO	303, 720	80437–80439
Evergreen Park, IL	708	60805
Ewa Beach, HI	808	96706
Ewing, NJ	609	08618, 08628, 08638
Excelsior, MN	952	55331
Excelsior Springs, MO	816	64024
Exeter, CA	559	93221
Exeter, NH	603	03833
Exeter, PA	570	18643
Exeter, RI	401	02822
Export, PA	724, 878	15632
Exton, PA	484, 610	19341, 19353
Eynon, PA	570	18403

F

City	Area Code(s)	Zip Code(s)
Fabens, TX	915	79838
Fair Haven, VT	802	05731, 05743
Fair Lawn, NJ	201, 551	07410
Fair Oaks, CA	916	95628
Fairbanks, AK	907	99701–99716, 99767, 99775*
Fairborn, OH	937	45324, 45431
Fairburn, GA	470, 770	30213
Fairbury, NE	402	68352

*Partial list of zip codes, including main range

City	Area Code(s)	Zip Code(s)
Fairchild AFB, WA	509	99011
Fairfax, SC	803	29827
Fairfax, VA	571, 703	20151–20153, 22030–22039
Fairfax Station, VA	571, 703	22039
Fairfield, AL	205	35064
Fairfield, CA	707	94533–94535, 94585
Fairfield, CT	203	06430–06432
Fairfield, ID	208	83322, 83327
Fairfield, IL	618	62837
Fairfield, IA	641	52556–52557
Fairfield, ME	207	04937
Fairfield, MT	406	59436
Fairfield, NJ	862, 973	07004
Fairfield, OH	513	45011–45014, 45018
Fairfield, PA	717	17320
Fairfield, TX	903	75840
Fairfield, VT	802	05455
Fairfield Glade, TN	931	38555–38558
Fairgrove, MI	989	48733
Fairhaven, MA	508, 774	02719
Fairhope, AL	251	36532–36533
Fairlawn, OH	234, 330	44313, 44333–44334
Fairlee, VT	802	05045
Fairless Hills, PA	215, 267	19030
Fairmont, MN	507	56031, 56075
Fairmont, MT	406	59711
Fairmont, WV	304	26554–26555
Fairplay, CO	719	80432, 80440, 80456
Fairport, NY	585	14450
Fairport Harbor, OH	440	44077
Fairton, NJ	856	08320
Fairview, NJ	201, 551	07022
Fairview, OK	580	73737
Fairview, OR	503, 971	97024
Fairview, PA	814	16415
Fairview Heights, IL	618	62208, 62232
Fairview Park, OH	440	44126
Fairview Village, PA	484, 610	19409
Fajardo, PR	787, 939	00738
Falconer, NY	716	14733
Falfurrias, TX	361	78355
Fall Creek, WI	715	54742
Fall River, MA	508, 774	02720–02726
Fall River, WI	920	53932
Fallbrook, CA	760	92028, 92088
Fallon, NV	775	89406–89407, 89496
Falls Church, VA	571, 703	22040–22047
Falls City, NE	402	68355
Fallsburg, NY	845	12733
Fallston, MD	410	21047
Falmouth, KY	859	41040
Falmouth, ME	207	04105
Falmouth, MA	508, 774	02540–02543
Fanwood, NJ	908	07023
Far Hills, NJ	908	07931
Far Rockaway, NY	347, 718	11096, 11690–11697
Fargo, ND	701	58102–58109, 58121–58126
Faribault, MN	507	55021
Farina, IL	618	62838
Farmers Branch, TX	469, 972	75234, 75244
Farmerville, LA	318	71241
Farmingdale, NJ	732, 848	07727
Farmingdale, NY	631	11735–11737, 11774
Farmington, CT	860	06030–06034, 06085
Farmington, ME	207	04911, 04938
Farmington, MI	248, 947	48331–48336
Farmington, MN	651	55024
Farmington, MO	573	63640
Farmington, NH	603	03835
Farmington, NM	505	87401–87402, 87499
Farmington, NY	585	14425
Farmington, PA	724, 878	15437
Farmington, UT	801	84025
Farmington Hills, MI	248, 947	48331–48336
Farmingville, NY	631	11738
Farmville, NC	252	27828
Farmville, VA	434	23901, 23909, 23943
Farnhamville, IA	515	50538
Farragut, TN	865	37922
Farwell, TX	806	79325
Faulkner, MD	301	20632
Faulkton, SD	605	57438
Fayette, AL	205	35555
Fayette, IA	563	52142
Fayette, MS	601, 769	39069, 39081
Fayette, MO	660	65248
Fayetteville, AR	479	72701–72704
Fayetteville, GA	470, 770	30214–30215, 30232
Fayetteville, NY	315	13066
Fayetteville, NC	910	28301–28314
Fayetteville, PA	717	17222
Fayetteville, TN	931	37334
Fayetteville, WV	304	25840
Feasterville, PA	215, 267	19053
Federal Way, WA	253	98001–98003, 98023, 98063*
Federalsburg, MD	410	21632
Feeding Hills, MA	413	01030
Felton, DE	302	19943
Fennimore, WI	608	53809
Fenton, MI	810	48430
Fenton, MO	636	63026, 63099
Fenwick, WV	304	26202
Ferdinand, IN	812	47532
Fergus Falls, MN	218	56537–56538
Ferguson, MO	314	63135–63136, 63145
Fernandina Beach, FL	904	32034–32035
Ferndale, CA	707	95536
Ferndale, MI	248, 947	48220
Ferndale, WA	360	98248
Ferriday, LA	318	71334
Ferrisburg, VT	802	05456
Ferrum, VA	540	24088
Ferrysburg, MI	616	49409
Fessenden, ND	701	58438
Festus, MO	636	63028
Fillmore, UT	435	84631
Fincastle, VA	540	24090
Findlay, OH	419, 567	45839–45840
Finksburg, MD	410	21048
Finley, ND	701	58230
Finleyville, PA	724, 878	15332
Firebaugh, CA	559	93622
Firth, ID	208	83236
Fisher Island, FL	305, 786	33109, 33139
Fishers, IN	317	46038
Fishersville, VA	540	22939
Fishkill, NY	845	12524
Fiskeville, RI	401	02823
Fitchburg, MA	351, 978	01420
Fitzgerald, GA	229	31750
Flagler Beach, FL	386	32136, 32151
Flagstaff, AZ	928	86001–86004, 86011, 86015*
Flanders, NJ	862, 973	07836
Flandreau, SD	605	57028
Flasher, ND	701	58535
Flat Rock, NC	828	28731
Flatonia, TX	361	78941
Fleetwood, PA	484, 610	19522
Flemingsburg, KY	606	41041
Flemington, NJ	908	08822
Fletcher, NC	828	28732
Fletcher, OH	937	45326
Flint, MI	810	48501–48509, 48519, 48529*
Flintstone, GA	706, 762	30725
Flippin, AR	870	72634
Flora, IL	618	62839
Flora, MS	601, 769	39071
Floral Park, NY	516	11001–11005
Florence, AL	256	35630–35634
Florence, AZ	520	85232, 85279
Florence, CO	719	81226, 81290
Florence, KY	859	41022, 41042
Florence, MA	413	01062
Florence, MS	601, 769	39073
Florence, NJ	609	08518
Florence, OR	541	97439
Florence, SC	843	29501–29506
Florence, WI	715	54121
Floresville, TX	830	78114
Florham Park, NJ	862, 973	07932
Florida, NY	845	10921
Florida City, FL	305, 786	33034
Florien, LA	318	71429
Florissant, CO	719	80816
Florissant, MO	314	63031–63034
Flourtown, PA	215, 267	19031
Flower Mound, TX	469, 972	75022, 75027–75028
Flowery Branch, GA	470, 770	30542
Flowood, MS	601, 769	39208, 39232
Floyd, VA	540	24091
Floydada, TX	806	79235
Flushing, MI	810	48433
Flushing, NY	347, 718	11351–11381, 11385–11386*
Fogelsville, PA	484, 610	18051
Folcroft, PA	484, 610	19032
Foley, AL	251	36535–36536
Foley, MN	320	56329, 56357
Folkston, GA	912	31537
Folsom, CA	916	95630, 95762–95763
Folsom, LA	985	70437
Folsom, NJ	609	08037
Fond du Lac, WI	920	54935–54937
Fonda, NY	518	12068
Fontana, CA	951	92334–92337
Fontana, WI	262	53125
Fontana Dam, NC	828	28733
Foothill Ranch, CA	949	92610
Ford, KS	620	67842
Fordland, MO	417	65652
Fords, NJ	732, 848	08863
Fordyce, AR	870	71742
Forest, MS	601, 769	39074
Forest, OH	419, 567	45843
Forest, VA	434	24551
Forest City, IA	641	50436
Forest City, NC	828	28043
Forest City, PA	570	18421
Forest Grove, OR	503, 971	97116
Forest Hill, MD	410	21050
Forest Hills, NY	347, 718	11375
Forest Lake, MN	651	55025
Forest Park, GA	404, 470	30297–30298
Forest Park, IL	708	60130
Forestville, CA	707	95436
Forestville, CT	860	06010
Forked River, NJ	609	08731
Forks, WA	360	98331
Forksville, PA	570	18616
Forman, ND	701	58032
Forrest City, AR	870	72335–72336
Forsyth, GA	478	31029
Forsyth, MO	417	65653
Forsyth, MT	406	59327
Fort Atkinson, WI	920	53538
Fort Belvoir, VA	571, 703	22060
Fort Benning, GA	706, 762	31905, 31995
Fort Benton, MT	406	59442
Fort Bliss, TX	915	79906–79908, 79916–79918
Fort Bragg, CA	707	95437, 95488
Fort Bragg, NC	910	28307–28310
Fort Buchanan, PR	787, 939	00920–00922, 00934–00936
Fort Calhoun, NE	402	68023
Fort Campbell, KY	270	42223
Fort Carson, CO	719	80913
Fort Collins, CO	970	80521–80528, 80553
Fort Davis, TX	915	79734
Fort Defiance, AZ	928	86504, 86549
Fort Deposit, AL	334	36032
Fort Dix, NJ	609	08640
Fort Dodge, IA	515	50501
Fort Dodge, KS	620	67801
Fort Drum, NY	315	13602–13603
Fort Edward, NY	518	12828
Fort Eustis, VA	757	23604
Fort Gaines, GA	229	31751
Fort Gibson, OK	918	74434
Fort Gordon, GA	706, 762	30905
Fort Harrison, MT	406	59636
Fort Hood, TX	254	76544
Fort Huachuca, AZ	520	85613, 85670
Fort Irwin, CA	760	92310
Fort Jackson, SC	803	29207
Fort Jones, CA	530	96032

*Partial list of zip codes, including main range

City	Area Code(s)	Zip Code(s)
Fort Kent, ME	207	04741–04743
Fort Knox, KY	502	40121
Fort Laramie, WY	307	82212
Fort Lauderdale, FL	754, 954	33301–33340, 33345–33351*
Fort Leavenworth, KS	913	66027
Fort Lee, NJ	201, 551	07024
Fort Lee, VA	804	23801
Fort Leonard Wood, MO	573	65473
Fort Lewis, WA	253	98433
Fort Loramie, OH	937	45845
Fort Madison, IA	319	52627
Fort McPherson, GA	404, 470	30310, 30330
Fort Meade, MD	301	20755
Fort Meade, SD	605	57741
Fort Mill, SC	803	29708, 29715–29716
Fort Mitchell, KY	859	41017
Fort Monmouth, NJ	732, 848	07703
Fort Monroe, VA	757	23651
Fort Morgan, CO	970	80701, 80705, 80742
Fort Myer, VA	571, 703	22211
Fort Myers, FL	239	33901–33919, 33965, 33994
Fort Myers Beach, FL	239	33931–33932
Fort Oglethorpe, GA	706, 762	30742
Fort Payne, AL	256	35967–35968
Fort Pierce, FL	772	34945–34954, 34979–34988
Fort Pierre, SD	605	57532
Fort Polk, LA	337	71459
Fort Recovery, OH	419, 567	45846
Fort Richardson, AK	907	99504–99505
Fort Riley, KS	785	66442
Fort Rucker, AL	334	36362
Fort Sam Houston, TX	210	78234
Fort Scott, KS	620	66701
Fort Shafter, HI	808	96858
Fort Sill, OK	580	73503
Fort Smith, AR	479	72901–72908, 72913–72919
Fort Smith, MT	406	59035
Fort Snelling, MN	612	55111
Fort Stewart, GA	912	31313–31315
Fort Stockton, TX	915	79735
Fort Story, VA	757	23459
Fort Sumner, NM	505	88119
Fort Supply, OK	580	73841
Fort Thomas, KY	859	41075
Fort Totten, ND	701	58335
Fort Valley, GA	478	31030
Fort Wainwright, AK	907	99703
Fort Walton Beach, FL	850	32547–32549
Fort Washington, MD	301	20744, 20749–20750
Fort Washington, PA	215, 267	19034, 19048–19049
Fort Wayne, IN	260	46801–46809, 46814–46819*
Fort Worth, TX	682, 817	76101–76140, 76147–76150*
Fort Yates, ND	701	58538
Fortine, MT	406	59918
Fortuna, CA	707	95540
Forty Fort, PA	570	18704
Fossil, OR	541	97830
Foster City, CA	650	94404
Fostoria, OH	419, 567	44830
Fountain Hills, AZ	480	85268–85269
Fountain Inn, SC	864	29644
Fountain Valley, CA	714	92708, 92728
Four Oaks, NC	919	27524
Fowler, CA	559	93625
Fowler, IN	765	47944, 47984–47986
Fowlerville, MI	517	48836
Fox Lake, WI	920	53933
Foxboro, MA	508, 774	02035
Foxborough, MA	508, 774	02035
Frackville, PA	570	17931–17932
Framingham, MA	508, 774	01701–01705
Francesville, IN	219	47946
Frankenmuth, MI	989	48734, 48787
Frankfort, IL	815	60423
Frankfort, IN	765	46041
Frankfort, KY	502	40601–40604, 40618–40622
Frankfort, MI	231	49635
Frankfort, NY	315	13340
Franklin, GA	706, 762	30217
Franklin, ID	208	83237
Franklin, IN	317	46131
Franklin, KY	270	42134–42135
Franklin, LA	337	70538
Franklin, MA	508, 774	02038
Franklin, NE	308	68939
Franklin, NH	603	03235
Franklin, NJ	862, 973	07416
Franklin, NC	828	28734, 28744
Franklin, OH	513	45005, 45342
Franklin, PA	814	16323
Franklin, TN	615	37064–37069
Franklin, TX	979	77856
Franklin, VA	757	23851
Franklin, WV	304	26807
Franklin, WI	414	53132
Franklin Furnace, OH	740	45629
Franklin Lakes, NJ	201, 551	07417
Franklin Park, IL	224, 847	60131, 60398
Franklin Springs, GA	706, 762	30639
Franklin Square, NY	516	11010
Franklinton, LA	985	70438
Franklinton, NC	919	27525
Franklinville, NY	585	14737
Franksville, WI	262	53126
Frankton, IN	765	46044
Franktown, CO	303, 720	80116
Fraser, MI	586	48026
Frazee, MN	218	56544
Frazer, PA	484, 610	19355
Frazeysburg, OH	740	43822
Frederic, MI	989	49733
Frederica, DE	302	19946
Frederick, CO	303, 720	80504, 80516, 80530
Frederick, MD	301	21701–21705, 21709
Frederick, OK	580	73542
Fredericksburg, PA	717	17026
Fredericksburg, TX	830	78624
Fredericksburg, VA	540	22401–22408, 22412
Fredericktown, MO	573	63645
Fredericktown, OH	740	43019
Fredonia, AZ	928	86022, 86052
Fredonia, KS	620	66736
Fredonia, NY	716	14063
Fredonia, WI	262	53021
Freeburg, IL	618	62243
Freeburg, MO	573	65035
Freedom, WY	307	83120
Freehold, NJ	732, 848	07728
Freeland, MI	989	48623
Freeland, PA	570	18224
Freeland, WA	360	98249
Freeport, IL	815	61032
Freeport, ME	207	04032–04034
Freeport, MI	616	49325
Freeport, NY	516	11520
Freeport, PA	724, 878	16229
Freeport, TX	979	77541–77542
Fremont, CA	510	94536–94539, 94555
Fremont, IN	260	46737
Fremont, MI	231	49412–49413
Fremont, NE	402	68025–68026
Fremont, OH	419, 567	43420
French Camp, CA	209	95231
French Creek, WV	304	26218–26219
French Lick, IN	812	47432
Frenchburg, KY	606	40322
Frenchtown, NJ	908	08825
Fresh Meadows, NY	347, 718	11365–11366
Fresno, CA	559	93650, 93701–93729*
Friday Harbor, WA	360	98250
Fridley, MN	763	55421, 55432
Friendship, WI	608	53927, 53934
Friendswood, TX	281, 832	77546–77549
Friona, TX	806	79035
Frisco, CO	970	80443
Frisco, TX	469, 972	75034–75035
Fritch, TX	806	79036
Front Royal, VA	540	22630
Frostburg, MD	301	21532
Frostproof, FL	863	33843
Fruita, CO	970	81521
Fruitland, ID	208	83619
Fruitport, MI	231	49415
Fullerton, CA	714	92831–92838
Fullerton, NE	308	68638
Fulton, AL	334	36446
Fulton, IL	815	61252
Fulton, MS	662	38843
Fulton, MO	573	65251
Fulton, NY	315	13069
Fultonville, NY	518	12016, 12072
Fuquay-Varina, NC	919	27526

G

City	Area Code(s)	Zip Code(s)
Gabriels, NY	518	12939
Gadsden, AL	256	35901–35907
Gaffney, SC	864	29340–29342
Gahanna, OH	614	43230
Gail, TX	806	79738
Gainesboro, TN	931	38562
Gainesville, FL	352	32601–32614, 32627, 32635*
Gainesville, GA	470, 678, 770	30501–30507
Gainesville, MO	417	65655
Gainesville, TX	940	76240–76241
Gaithersburg, MD	240, 301	20877–20886, 20898–20899
Galax, VA	276	24333
Galena, IL	815	61036
Galena, KS	620	66739
Galena, MD	410	21635
Galena, MO	417	65624, 65656
Galena Park, TX	713, 832	77547
Galesburg, IL	309	61401–61402
Galesburg, KS	620	66740
Galion, OH	419, 567	44833
Gallatin, MO	660	64640
Gallatin, TN	615	37066
Gallatin Gateway, MT	406	59730
Gallaway, TN	901	38036
Galliano, LA	985	70354
Gallipolis, OH	740	45631
Gallitzin, PA	814	16641
Galloway, NJ	609	08201, 08205
Gallup, NM	505	87301–87305, 87310, 87317*
Galt, CA	209	95632
Galveston, TX	409	77550–77555
Gambier, OH	740	43022
Ganado, AZ	928	86505, 86540
Gann Valley, SD	605	57341
Gap, PA	717	17527
Garden City, GA	912	31405–31408, 31415–31418
Garden City, KS	620	67846, 67868
Garden City, MI	734	48135–48136
Garden City, NY	516	11530–11531, 11535–11536*
Garden City, TX	915	79739
Garden City Park, NY	516	11040
Garden Grove, CA	714	92840–92846
Gardena, CA	310, 323, 424	90247–90249
Gardiner, ME	207	04345
Gardner, IL	815	60424
Gardner, KS	913	66030–66031
Gardner, MA	351, 978	01440
Gardners, PA	717	17324
Gardnerville, NV	775	89410
Garfield, NJ	862, 973	07026
Garfield Heights, OH	216	44105, 44125–44128
Garland, NC	910	28441
Garland, TX	469, 972	75040–75049
Garner, IA	641	50438
Garner, NC	919	27529
Garnett, KS	785	66032
Garretson, SD	605	57030
Garrett, IN	260	46738
Garrettsville, OH	234, 330	44231
Garrison, NY	845	10524
Garrison, ND	701	58540
Garwood, NJ	908	07027
Gary, IN	219	46401–46411
Garyville, LA	985	70051, 70076
Gaston, OR	503, 971	97119
Gastonia, NC	704, 980	28052–28056
Gate City, VA	276	24251
Gatesville, NC	252	27938

**Partial list of zip codes, including main range*

City	Area Code(s)	Zip Code(s)
Gatesville, TX	254	76528, 76596–76599
Gatlinburg, TN	865	37738
Gautier, MS	228	39553
Gaylord, MI	989	49734–49735
Gaylord, MN	507	55334
Gearhart, OR	503, 971	97138
Geismar, LA	225	70734
Geneseo, IL	309	61254
Geneseo, NY	585	14454
Geneva, AL	334	36340
Geneva, IL	331, 630	60134
Geneva, NE	402	68361
Geneva, NY	315	14456
Geneva, OH	440	44041
Genoa, OH	419, 567	43430
Genoa City, WI	262	53128
Gentry, AR	479	72734
George, IA	712	51237
George West, TX	361	78022
Georgetown, CO	303, 720	80444
Georgetown, DE	302	19947
Georgetown, GA	229	31754
Georgetown, KY	502	40324
Georgetown, MA	351, 978	01833
Georgetown, NY	315	13072, 13129
Georgetown, OH	937	45121
Georgetown, SC	843	29440–29442
Georgetown, TX	512	78626–78628
Gering, NE	308	69341
Germantown, MD	301	20874–20876
Germantown, OH	937	45325–45327
Germantown, TN	901	38138–38139, 38183
Germantown, WI	262	53022
Gervais, OR	503, 971	97026
Gettysburg, PA	717	17325–17326
Gettysburg, SD	605	57442
Getzville, NY	716	14068
Geyserville, CA	707	95441
Gibbon, MN	507	55335
Gibbon, NE	308	68840
Gibbsboro, NJ	856	08026
Gibbstown, NJ	856	08027
Gibson, GA	706, 762	30810
Gibson City, IL	217	60936
Gibsonia, PA	724, 878	15044
Gibsonville, NC	336	27249
Giddings, TX	979	78942
Gig Harbor, WA	253	98329–98335
Gilbert, AZ	480	85233–85234, 85296–85299
Gilbertsville, KY	270	42044
Gilford, NH	603	03247–03249
Gillett, AR	870	72055
Gillette, WY	307	82716–82718, 82731–82732
Gilman, CT	860	06336
Gilmer, TX	903	75644–75645
Gilmore City, IA	515	50541
Gilroy, CA	408	95020–95021
Girard, KS	620	66743
Girard, OH	234, 330	44420
Girard, PA	814	16417
Girdwood, AK	907	99587, 99693
Gladstone, MI	906	49837
Gladstone, MO	816	64116–64119, 64155–64156*
Gladstone, NJ	908	07934
Gladwin, MI	989	48624
Gladwyne, PA	484, 610	19035
Glasgow, KY	270	42141–42142, 42156
Glasgow, MT	406	59230–59231
Glassboro, NJ	856	08028
Glassport, PA	412, 878	15045
Glastonbury, CT	860	06033
Glen Allen, VA	804	23058–23060
Glen Arbor, MI	231	49636
Glen Arm, MD	410	21057
Glen Burnie, MD	410	21060–21062
Glen Cove, NY	516	11542
Glen Dale, WV	304	26038
Glen Echo, MD	301	20812
Glen Ellen, CA	707	95442
Glen Ellyn, IL	331, 630	60137–60138
Glen Gardner, NJ	908	08826
Glen Head, NY	516	11545
Glen Jean, WV	304	25846
Glen Lyn, VA	540	24093
Glen Raven, NC	336	27215
Glen Riddle, PA	484, 610	19037, 19063
Glen Ridge, NJ	862, 973	07028
Glen Rock, NJ	201, 551	07452
Glen Rock, PA	717	17327
Glen Rose, TX	254	76043
Glencoe, IL	224, 847	60022
Glencoe, MN	320	55336
Glendale, AZ	623	85301–85313, 85318
Glendale, CA	818	91201–91210, 91214, 91221*
Glendale, CO	303, 720	80246
Glendale, NY	347, 718	11385
Glendale, WI	414	53209–53212, 53217
Glendale Heights, IL	331, 630	60139
Glendive, MT	406	59330
Glendora, CA	626	91740–91741
Glendora, NJ	856	08029
Gleneden Beach, OR	541	97388
Glenelg, MD	410	21737
Glenmont, OH	234, 330	44628
Glenmoore, PA	484, 610	19343
Glennallen, AK	907	99588
Glennville, GA	912	30427
Glens Falls, NY	518	12801–12804
Glenshaw, PA	412, 878	15116
Glenside, PA	215, 267	19038
Glenview, IL	224, 847	60025–60026
Glenville, NY	518	12302, 12325
Glenville, WV	304	26351
Glenwillow, OH	440	44139
Glenwood, IL	708	60425
Glenwood, IA	712	51534
Glenwood, MN	320	56334
Glenwood Springs, CO	970	81601–81602
Glidden, IA	712	51443
Glide, OR	541	97443
Globe, AZ	928	85501–85502
Glorieta, NM	505	87535
Gloucester, MA	351, 978	01930–01931
Gloucester, NJ	856	08030–08031
Gloucester, VA	804	23061
Gloucester Point, VA	804	23062
Gloversville, NY	518	12078
Gnadenhutten, OH	740	44629
Godfrey, IL	618	62035
Godwin, NC	910	28344
Goffstown, NH	603	03045–03046
Golconda, IL	618	62938
Golconda, NV	480	89414
Gold Beach, OR	541	97444
Gold Canyon, AZ	480	85218–85219
Gold Hill, NV	775	89440
Gold Hill, OR	541	97525
Gold River, CA	916	95670
Golden, CO	303, 720	80401–80403, 80419
Golden, MS	662	38847
Golden Valley, MN	763	55416, 55422, 55426, 55427
Goldendale, WA	509	98620
Goldfield, NV	775	89013
Goldsboro, NC	919	27530–27534
Goldthwaite, TX	915	76844
Goleta, CA	805	93110–93111, 93116–93118*
Golf, IL	224, 847	60029
Goliad, TX	361	77963
Gonzales, CA	831	93926
Gonzales, LA	225	70707, 70737
Gonzales, TX	830	78629
Goochland, VA	804	23063
Goodfellow AFB, TX	915	76908
Goodfield, IL	309	61742
Gooding, ID	208	83330
Goodland, KS	785	67735
Goodlettsville, TN	615	37070–37072
Goodman, MS	662	39079
Goodrich, MI	810	48438
Goodwell, OK	580	73939
Goodyear, AZ	623	85338
Gordo, AL	205	35466
Gordon, NE	308	69343
Gordonsville, VA	540	22942
Gordonville, TX	903	76245
Gore, OK	918	74435
Gorham, ME	207	04038
Gorham, NH	603	03581
Goshen, IN	574	46526–46528
Goshen, NY	845	10924
Goulds, FL	305, 786	33170
Gouverneur, NY	315	13642
Gove, KS	785	67736
Gowanda, NY	716	14070
Grabill, IN	260	46741
Graceville, FL	850	32440
Gracewood, GA	706, 762	30812
Grady, AR	870	71644
Grafton, IL	618	62037
Grafton, MA	508, 774	01519
Grafton, ND	701	58237
Grafton, OH	440	44044
Grafton, WV	304	26354
Grafton, WI	262	53024
Graham, NC	336	27253
Graham, TX	940	76450
Grain Valley, MO	816	64029
Grambling, LA	318	71245
Gramercy, LA	225	70052
Gramling, SC	864	29348
Grampian, PA	814	16838
Granada Hills, CA	818	91344, 91394
Granbury, TX	682, 817	76048–76049
Granby, CO	970	80446
Granby, CT	860	06035, 06090
Grand Blanc, MI	810	48439
Grand Canyon, AZ	928	86023
Grand Chenier, LA	337	70643
Grand Forks, ND	701	58201–58208
Grand Forks AFB, ND	701	58204–58205
Grand Haven, MI	616	49417
Grand Island, NE	308	68801–68803
Grand Island, NY	716	14072
Grand Junction, CO	970	81501–81506
Grand Junction, MI	616	49056
Grand Ledge, MI	517	48837
Grand Marais, MN	218	55604
Grand Marsh, WI	608	53936
Grand Portage, MN	218	55605
Grand Prairie, TX	469, 972	75050–75054
Grand Rapids, MI	616	49501–49518, 49523–49525*
Grand Rapids, MN	218	55730, 55744–55745
Grand Rapids, OH	419, 567	43522
Grand Terrace, CA	909	92313, 92324
Grandview, MO	816	64030
Grandview, WA	509	98930
Grandville, MI	616	49418, 49468
Granger, IN	574	46530
Granger, WA	509	98932
Grangeville, ID	208	83530–83531
Granite, OK	580	73547
Granite City, IL	618	62040
Granite Falls, MN	320	56241
Granite Falls, NC	828	28630
Granite Quarry, NC	704, 980	28072
Graniteville, SC	803	29829
Graniteville, VT	802	05654
Grant, CO	303, 720	80448
Grant, MI	231	49327
Grant, NE	308	69140
Grant City, MO	660	64456
Grantham, PA	717	17027
Grants, NM	505	87020
Grants Pass, OR	541	97526–97528, 97543
Grantsboro, NC	252	28529
Grantsburg, WI	715	54840
Grantsville, MD	301	21536
Grantsville, WV	304	26147
Grantville, PA	717	17028
Granville, IL	815	61326
Granville, MA	413	01034
Granville, NY	518	12832
Granville, OH	740	43023

*Partial list of zip codes, including main range

City	Area Code(s)	Zip Code(s)
Grapevine, TX	682, 817	76051, 76092, 76099
Grass Valley, CA	530	95945, 95949
Graterford, PA	484, 610	19426
Gratz, PA	717	17030
Grawn, MI	231	49637
Gray, GA	478	31032
Gray, KY	606	40734
Gray, LA	985	70359
Grayling, MI	989	49738–49739
Grayslake, IL	224, 847	60030
Grayson, KY	606	41143
Grayville, IL	618	62844
Great Barrington, MA	413	01230
Great Bend, KS	620	67530
Great Falls, MT	406	59401–59406
Great Falls, VA	571, 703	22066
Great Lakes, IL	224, 847	60088
Great Neck, NY	516	11020–11027
Greeley, CO	970	80631–80634, 80638–80639
Greeley, NE	308	68842
Green Bay, WI	920	54301–54313, 54324, 54344
Green Brook, NJ	732, 848	08812
Green Cove Springs, FL	904	32043
Green Forest, AR	870	72638
Green Island, NY	518	12183
Green Lake, WI	920	54941
Green Lane, PA	215, 267	18054
Green Pond, AL	205	35074
Green River, UT	435	84515, 84525, 84540
Green River, WY	307	82935–82938
Green Springs, OH	419, 567	44836
Green Valley, AZ	520	85614, 85622
Greenbelt, MD	301	20768–20771
Greenbrae, CA	415	94904, 94914
Greencastle, IN	765	46135
Greencastle, PA	717	17225
Greendale, WI	414	53129
Greene, NY	607	13778
Greeneville, TN	423	37743–37745
Greenfield, IN	317	46140
Greenfield, IA	641	50849
Greenfield, MA	413	01301–01302
Greenfield, MO	417	65661
Greenfield, NH	603	03047
Greenfield, OH	937	45123, 45165
Greenfield, WI	414	53219–53221, 53227–53228
Greenland, NH	603	03840
Greenlawn, NY	631	11740
Greenport, NY	631	11944
Greens Farms, CT	203	06436
Greensboro, AL	334	36744
Greensboro, GA	706, 762	30642
Greensboro, NC	336	27401–27420, 27425–27429*
Greensburg, IN	812	47240
Greensburg, KS	620	67054
Greensburg, KY	270	42743
Greensburg, LA	225	70441
Greensburg, PA	724, 878	15601, 15605–15606
Greenup, KY	606	41144
Greenvale, NY	516	11548
Greenville, AL	334	36037
Greenville, DE	302	19807
Greenville, GA	706, 762	30222
Greenville, IL	618	62246
Greenville, KY	270	42345
Greenville, MI	616	48838
Greenville, MS	662	38701–38704, 38731
Greenville, MO	573	63944
Greenville, NC	252	27833–27836, 27858
Greenville, OH	937	45331
Greenville, PA	724, 878	16125
Greenville, RI	401	02828
Greenville, SC	864	29601–29617, 29698
Greenville, TX	903	75401–75404
Greenwell Springs, LA	225	70739
Greenwich, CT	203	06830–06832, 06836
Greenwood, AR	479	72936
Greenwood, DE	302	19950
Greenwood, IN	317	46142–46143
Greenwood, MS	662	38930, 38935
Greenwood, SC	864	29646–29649

City	Area Code(s)	Zip Code(s)
Greenwood, WI	715	54437
Greenwood Village, CO	303, 720	80110–80112, 80121, 80150*
Greer, SC	864	29650–29652
Gregory, SD	605	57533
Grenada, MS	662	38901–38902
Grenloch, NJ	856	08032
Gresham, OR	503, 971	97030, 97080
Gretna, LA	504	70053–70056
Gretna, NE	402	68028
Gretna, VA	434	24557
Greybull, WY	307	82426
Greystone Park, NJ	862, 973	07950
Griffin, GA	470, 770	30223–30224
Griffith, IN	219	46319
Griggsville, IL	217	62340
Grinnell, IA	641	50112, 50177
Groesbeck, TX	254	76642
Grosse Pointe, MI	313	48224, 48230, 48236
Grosse Pointe Farms, MI	313	48230, 48236
Grosse Pointe Park, MI	313	48215, 48224, 48230, 48236
Grosse Pointe Shores, MI	313	48230, 48236
Groton, CT	860	06340, 06349
Groton, MA	351, 978	01450, 01470–01471
Groton, VT	802	05046
Grove, OK	918	74344–74345
Grove City, OH	614	43123
Grove City, PA	724, 878	16127
Grove Hill, AL	251	36451
Groveland, FL	352	34736
Groveport, OH	614	43125, 43195–43199
Grover, NC	704, 980	28073
Grover Beach, CA	805	93433, 93483
Groves, TX	409	77619
Groveton, TX	936	75845
Grovetown, GA	706, 762	30813
Grundy, VA	276	24614
Grundy Center, IA	319	50638
Gruver, TX	806	79040
Guayama, PR	787, 939	00784–00785
Guerneville, CA	707	95446
Guilderland, NY	518	12084
Guildhall, VT	802	05905
Guilford, CT	203	06437
Guilford, ME	207	04443
Guin, AL	205	35563
Gulf Breeze, FL	850	32561–32566
Gulf Shores, AL	251	36542, 36547
Gulfport, FL	727	33707, 33711, 33737
Gulfport, MS	228	39501–39507
Gun Barrel City, TX	903	75147
Gunnison, CO	970	81230–81231, 81247
Gunnison, UT	435	84634
Guntersville, AL	256	35976
Guntown, MS	662	38849
Gurdon, AR	870	71743
Gurnee, IL	224, 847	60031
Gustavus, AK	907	99826
Guthrie, OK	405	73044
Guthrie, TX	806	79236
Guthrie Center, IA	641	50115
Guymon, OK	580	73942
Gwynedd, PA	215, 267	19436
Gwynedd Valley, PA	215, 267	19437

H

City	Area Code(s)	Zip Code(s)
Hackensack, NJ	201, 551	07601–07602
Hackettstown, NJ	908	07840
Haddam, CT	860	06438
Haddonfield, NJ	856	08033
Hadley, MA	413	01035
Hagerman, ID	208	83332
Hagerman, NM	505	88232
Hagerstown, MD	240, 301	21740–21742, 21746–21749
Hahnville, LA	985	70057
Hailey, ID	208	83333
Haines, AK	907	99827
Haines City, FL	863	33844–33845
Hainesport, NJ	609	08036
Haledon, NJ	862, 973	07508, 07538
Hales Corners, WI	414	53130–53132

City	Area Code(s)	Zip Code(s)
Haleyville, AL	205	35565
Half Moon Bay, CA	650	94019
Halifax, MA	339, 781	02338
Halifax, NC	252	27839
Halifax, PA	717	17032
Halifax, VA	434	24558
Hall, NY	585	14463
Hallandale, FL	754, 954	33008–33009
Hallettsville, TX	361	77964
Hallock, MN	218	56728, 56740, 56755
Hallowell, ME	207	04347
Halls, TN	731	38040
Halstad, MN	218	56548
Halstead, KS	316	67056
Haltom City, TX	682, 817	76111, 76117, 76137, 76148*
Ham Lake, MN	763	55304
Hamburg, AR	870	71646
Hamburg, NJ	862, 973	07419
Hamburg, NY	716	14075, 14219
Hamburg, PA	484, 610	19526
Hamden, CT	203	06514–06518
Hamel, MN	763	55340
Hamer, ID	208	83425
Hamilton, AL	205	35570
Hamilton, GA	706, 762	31811
Hamilton, IL	217	62341
Hamilton, MT	406	59840
Hamilton, NJ	609	08609–08611, 08619–08620*
Hamilton, NY	315	13346
Hamilton, OH	513	45011–45026
Hamilton, TX	254	76531
Hamilton Square, NJ	609	08690
Hamlet, NC	910	28345
Hamlin, NY	585	14464
Hamlin, TX	915	79520
Hamlin, WV	304	25523
Hammond, IN	219	46320–46327
Hammond, LA	985	70401–70404
Hammond, WI	715	54002, 54015
Hammondsport, NY	607	14840
Hammonton, NJ	609	08037
Hampden-Sydney, VA	434	23943
Hampshire, IL	224, 847	60140
Hampstead, MD	410	21074
Hampstead, NH	603	03841
Hampton, AR	870	71744
Hampton, GA	470, 770	30228
Hampton, IA	641	50441
Hampton, NH	603	03842–03843
Hampton, SC	803	29913, 29924
Hampton, VA	757	23605, 23630–23631*
Hampton Falls, NH	603	03844
Hamptonville, NC	336	27020
Hamtramck, MI	313	48211–48212
Hana, HI	808	96713
Hanahan, SC	843	29406, 29410
Hanceville, AL	256	35077
Hancock, MI	906	49930
Hancock, MN	320	56244
Hancock, WI	715	54943
Hanford, CA	559	93230–93232
Hannibal, MO	573	63401
Hannibal, OH	740	43931
Hanover, IN	812	47243
Hanover, MD	410	21075–21076, 21098
Hanover, NH	603	03755
Hanover, PA	717	17331–17334
Hanover, VA	804	23069
Hanover Park, IL	331, 630	60108, 60133
Hanscom AFB, MA	339, 781	01731
Hanson, MA	339, 781	02341, 02350
Harahan, LA	504	70123
Harbor Beach, MI	989	48441
Harbor City, CA	310, 424	90710
Harbor Springs, MI	231	49737–49740
Harborcreek, PA	814	16421
Harcourt, IA	515	50544
Hardin, IL	618	62047
Hardin, MT	406	59034
Hardinsburg, KY	270	40143
Hardwick, GA	478	31034

*Partial list of zip codes, including main range

City	Area Code(s)	Zip Code(s)
Hardwick, VT	802	05843
Hardy, VA	540	24101
Harkers Island, NC	252	28531
Harlan, IA	712	51537, 51593
Harlan, KY	606	40831, 40840
Harlem, GA	706, 762	30814
Harlem, MT	406	59526
Harleysville, PA	215, 267	19438–19441
Harlingen, TX	956	78550–78553
Harlowton, MT	406	59036
Harpers Ferry, IA	563	52146
Harpers Ferry, WV	304	25425
Harrells, NC	910	28444
Harriman, NY	845	10926
Harriman, TN	865	37748
Harrington, DE	302	19952
Harrington Park, NJ	201, 551	07640
Harris, MN	651	55032
Harris, NY	845	12742
Harrisburg, AR	870	72432
Harrisburg, IL	618	62946
Harrisburg, NE	308	69345
Harrisburg, NC	704, 980	28075
Harrisburg, PA	717	17101–17113, 17120–17130*
Harrison, AR	870	72601–72602
Harrison, ID	208	83833, 83842
Harrison, MI	989	48625
Harrison, NE	308	69346
Harrison, NJ	862, 973	07029
Harrison, NY	914	10528
Harrison, OH	513	45030
Harrison Township, MI	586	48045
Harrisonburg, LA	318	71340
Harrisonburg, VA	540	22801–22803, 22807
Harrisonville, MO	816	64701
Harrisville, MI	989	48740
Harrisville, WV	304	26362
Harrodsburg, KY	859	40330
Harrogate, TN	423	37707, 37752
Hart, MI	231	49420
Hartford, AL	334	36344
Hartford, CT	860	06101–06156, 06160–06161*
Hartford, KY	270	42347
Hartford, WI	262	53027
Hartford City, IN	765	47348
Hartington, NE	402	68739
Hartland, ME	207	04943
Hartland, WI	262	53029
Hartsdale, NY	914	10530
Hartselle, AL	256	35640
Hartsville, SC	843	29550–29551
Hartsville, TN	615	37074
Hartville, MO	417	65667
Hartville, OH	234, 330	44632
Hartwell, GA	706, 762	30643
Hartwick, NY	607	13348
Harvard, IL	815	60033
Harvey, IL	708	60426
Harvey, LA	504	70058–70059
Harwich, MA	508, 774	02645
Harwood Heights, IL	708	60656, 60706
Hasbrouck Heights, NJ	201, 551	07604
Haskell, NJ	862, 973	07420
Haskell, TX	940	79521
Hastings, MI	616	49058
Hastings, MN	651	55033
Hastings, NE	402	68901–68902
Hastings-on-Hudson, NY	914	10706
Hatboro, PA	215, 267	19040
Hatfield, MA	413	01038
Hatfield, PA	215, 267	19440
Hato Rey, PR	787, 939	00917–00919
Hattiesburg, MS	601, 769	39401–39407
Haughton, LA	318	71037
Hauppauge, NY	631	11749, 11760, 11788
Havana, IL	309	62644
Haverford, PA	484, 610	19041
Haverhill, MA	351, 978	01830–01835
Haverstraw, NY	845	10927
Havertown, PA	484, 610	19083
Haviland, KS	620	67059
Havre, MT	406	59501
Havre de Grace, MD	410	21078
Haw River, NC	336	27258
Hawaii National Park, HI	808	96718
Hawaiian Gardens, CA	562	90716
Hawesville, KY	270	42348
Hawkins, TX	903	75765
Hawkins, WI	715	54530
Hawkinsville, GA	478	31036
Hawthorn Woods, IL	224, 847	60047
Hawthorne, CA	310, 424	90250–90251
Hawthorne, NV	775	89415
Hawthorne, NJ	862, 973	07506–07507
Hawthorne, NY	914	10532
Hay Springs, NE	308	69347, 69367
Hayden, AZ	520	85235
Hayden, ID	208	83835
Hayden Lake, ID	208	83835
Hayes Center, NE	308	69032
Hayesville, NC	828	28904
Hayesville, OH	419, 567	44838
Haynesville, VA	804	22472
Hayneville, AL	334	36040
Hays, KS	785	67601, 67667
Haysville, KS	316	67060
Hayti, MO	573	63851
Hayti, SD	605	57241
Hayward, CA	510	94540–94546, 94552, 94557
Hayward, WI	715	54843
Hazard, KY	606	41701–41702
Hazel Crest, IL	708	60429
Hazel Park, MI	248, 947	48030
Hazelwood, MO	314	63042–63045, 63135
Hazen, ND	701	58545
Hazlehurst, GA	912	31539
Hazlehurst, MS	601, 769	39083
Hazlet, NJ	732, 848	07730
Hazleton, PA	570	18201–18202
Healdsburg, CA	707	95448
Healy, AK	907	99743, 99755
Healy, KS	620	67850
Heartwell, NE	308	68945
Heath, OH	740	43056
Heathrow, FL	321, 407	32746
Heathsville, VA	804	22473
Hebbronville, TX	361	78361
Heber, CA	760	92249
Heber City, UT	435	84032
Heber Springs, AR	501	72543–72545
Hebron, IL	815	60034
Hebron, KY	859	41048
Hebron, NE	402	68370
Hebron, OH	740	43025, 43098
Hector, MN	320	55342
Hedgesville, WV	304	25427
Heflin, AL	256	36264
Helen, GA	706, 762	30545
Helena, AL	205	35080
Helena, AR	870	72342
Helena, GA	229	31037
Helena, MT	406	59601–59604, 59620–59626
Helena, OK	580	73741
Helenwood, TN	423	37755
Hellertown, PA	484, 610	18055
Hemet, CA	951	92543–92546
Hemphill, TX	409	75948
Hempstead, NY	516	11549–11551
Hempstead, TX	979	77445
Henderson, CO	303, 720	80640
Henderson, KY	270	42419–42420
Henderson, NE	402	68371
Henderson, NV	702	89009–89016, 89052–89053*
Henderson, NC	252	27536–27537
Henderson, TN	731	38340
Henderson, TX	903	75652–75654, 75680
Hendersonville, NC	828	28739, 28791–28793
Hendersonville, TN	615	37075–37077
Hennepin, IL	815	61327
Henniker, NH	603	03242
Henning, TN	731	38041
Henrietta, NY	585	14467
Henrietta, TX	940	76365
Henry, TN	731	38231
Henryetta, OK	918	74437
Henryville, IN	812	47126
Heppner, OR	541	97836
Hercules, CA	510	94547
Hereford, AZ	520	85615
Hereford, TX	806	79045
Herkimer, NY	315	13350
Hermann, MO	573	65041
Hermiston, OR	541	97838
Hermitage, MO	417	65668
Hermitage, PA	724, 878	16148
Hermitage, TN	615	37076
Hermleigh, TX	915	79526
Hermon, ME	207	04401
Hermosa, SD	605	57744
Hernando, FL	352	34442
Hernando, MS	662	38632
Herndon, PA	570	17830
Herndon, VA	571, 703	20170–20172, 20190–20195*
Herrin, IL	618	62948
Hershey, PA	717	17033
Hertford, NC	252	27930, 27944
Hesperia, CA	760	92340, 92345
Hesston, KS	620	67062
Hettinger, ND	701	58639
Heuvelton, NY	315	13654
Hewitt, NJ	862, 973	07421
Hewitt, TX	254	76643
Heyburn, ID	208	83336
Hialeah, FL	305, 786	33002, 33010–33018
Hialeah Gardens, FL	305, 786	33010, 33016–33018
Hiawassee, GA	706, 762	30546
Hiawatha, IA	319	52233
Hiawatha, KS	785	66434
Hibbing, MN	218	55746–55747
Hickam AFB, HI	808	96853
Hickman, KY	270	42050
Hickory, KY	270	42051
Hickory, NC	828	28601–28603
Hicksville, NY	516	11801–11804, 11815, 11819*
Hidden Valley, PA	814	15502
Higginsville, MO	660	64037
High Point, NC	336	27260–27265
High Ridge, MO	636	63049
High Shoals, GA	706, 762	30645
Highgate Springs, VT	802	05460
Highland, CA	909	92346
Highland, IL	618	62249
Highland, IN	219	46322, 47854
Highland, KS	785	66035
Highland, NY	845	12528
Highland Heights, KY	859	41076
Highland Heights, OH	440	44143
Highland Hills, OH	216	44122, 44128
Highland Park, IL	224, 847	60035–60037
Highland Park, MI	313	48203
Highland Springs, VA	804	23075
Highlands, NJ	732, 848	07732
Highlands Ranch, CO	303, 720	80124–80130, 80163
Highmore, SD	605	57345
Hightstown, NJ	609	08520
Hildebran, NC	828	28637
Hill AFB, UT	801	84056
Hill City, KS	785	67642
Hill City, SD	605	57745
Hilliard, OH	614	43026
Hillsboro, IL	217	62049
Hillsboro, KS	620	67063
Hillsboro, MO	636	63050
Hillsboro, NH	603	03244
Hillsboro, ND	701	58045
Hillsboro, OH	937	45133
Hillsboro, OR	503, 971	97123–97124
Hillsboro, TX	254	76645
Hillsboro, WV	304	24946
Hillsboro, WI	608	54634
Hillsboro Beach, FL	754, 954	33062
Hillsborough, NJ	908	08844
Hillsborough, NC	919	27278

*Partial list of zip codes, including main range

City	Area Code(s)	Zip Code(s)
Hillsdale, MI	517	49242
Hillsdale, NJ	201, 551	07642, 07676
Hillsgrove, PA	570	18619
Hillside, IL	708	60162–60163
Hillside, NJ	973	07205
Hillsville, VA	276	24343
Hilmar, CA	209	95324
Hilo, HI	808	96720–96721
Hilton, NY	585	14468
Hilton Head Island, SC	843	29915, 29925–29928
Hinckley, MN	320	55037
Hinckley, OH	234, 330	44233
Hindman, KY	606	41822
Hines, IL	708	60141
Hinesville, GA	912	31310–31315
Hingham, MA	339, 781	02018, 02043–02044
Hinsdale, IL	331, 630	60521–60523, 60570
Hinsdale, NH	603	03451
Hinton, OK	405	73047
Hinton, WV	304	25951
Hiram, OH	234, 330	44234
Hixson, TN	423	37343
Hobart, IN	219	46342
Hobart, OK	580	73651
Hobbs, IN	765	46047
Hobbs, NM	505	88240–88244
Hobe Sound, FL	772	33455, 33475
Hoboken, NJ	201, 551	07030
Hockessin, DE	302	19707
Hodgenville, KY	270	42748
Hodgkins, IL	708	60525
Hoffman, NC	910	28347
Hoffman Estates, IL	224, 847	60173, 60179, 60192, 60195
Hohenwald, TN	931	38462
Hoisington, KS	620	67544
Holbrook, AZ	928	86025–86031
Holbrook, MA	339, 781	02343
Holbrook, NY	631	11741
Holden, MA	508, 774	01520
Holdenville, OK	405	74848
Holdingford, MN	320	56340
Holdrege, NE	308	68949, 68969
Holland, IN	812	47541
Holland, MI	616	49422–49424
Holland, NY	716	14080
Holland, OH	419, 567	43528
Hollandale, MS	662	38748
Hollidaysburg, PA	814	16648
Hollis, NH	603	03049
Hollis, OK	580	73550
Hollister, CA	831	95023–95024
Hollister, MO	417	65672–65673
Holliston, MA	508, 774	01746
Holloman AFB, NM	505	88330
Hollsopple, PA	814	15935
Holly, MI	248, 947	48442
Holly Hill, FL	386	32117
Holly Springs, MS	662	38634–38635, 38649
Hollywood, CA	323	90027–90028, 90038, 90068*
Hollywood, FL	754, 954	33019–33029, 33081–33084*
Holmdel, NJ	732, 848	07733, 07777
Holmen, WI	608	54636
Holstein, IA	712	51025
Holt, MI	517	48842
Holton, KS	785	66436
Holtsville, NY	631	00501, 00544, 11742
Holyoke, CO	970	80734
Holyoke, MA	413	01040–01041
Homer, AK	907	99603
Homer, GA	706, 762	30547
Homer, LA	318	71040
Homerville, GA	912	31634
Homestead, FL	305, 786	33030–33035, 33039, 33090*
Homestead, PA	412, 878	15120
Homewood, AL	205	35209, 35219, 35259
Homewood, IL	708	60430
Hominy, OK	918	74035
Homosassa Springs, FL	352	34447
Honaunau, HI	808	96726
Hondo, TX	830	78861
Honea Path, SC	864	29654
Honeoye, NY	585	14471
Honesdale, PA	570	18431
Honolulu, HI	808	96801–96830, 96835–96850
Hood River, OR	541	97031
Hooker, OK	580	73945
Hooper, NE	402	68031
Hoosick Falls, NY	518	12090
Hoover, AL	205	35216, 35226, 35236, 35244
Hopatcong, NJ	862, 973	07843
Hope, AK	907	99605
Hope, AR	870	71801–71802
Hope Hull, AL	334	36043
Hope Valley, RI	401	02832
Hopedale, MA	508, 774	01747
Hopewell, VA	804	23860
Hopewell Junction, NY	845	12533
Hopkins, MI	616	49328
Hopkins, MN	952	55305, 55343–55345
Hopkins, SC	803	29061
Hopkinsville, KY	270	42240–42241
Hopkinton, MA	508, 774	01748
Hopkinton, NH	603	03229
Hopland, CA	707	95449
Hoquiam, WA	360	98550
Horn Lake, MS	662	38637
Hornell, NY	607	14843
Hornick, IA	712	51026
Horse Cave, KY	270	42749
Horseheads, NY	607	14844–14845
Horseshoe Bay, TX	830	78654–78657
Horsham, PA	215, 267	19044
Horton, KS	785	66439
Hot Springs, AR	501	71901–71903, 71909–71914
Hot Springs, SD	605	57747
Hot Springs, VA	540	24445
Hot Springs National Park, AR	501	71901–71903, 71909–71914*
Hot Sulphur Springs, CO	970	80451
Houghton, IA	319	52631
Houghton, MI	906	49921, 49931
Houghton, NY	585	14744
Houghton Lake, MI	989	48629
Houlka, MS	662	38850
Houlton, ME	207	04730, 04761
Houma, LA	985	70360–70364
Houston, MS	662	38851
Houston, MO	417	65483
Houston, TX	281, 713, 832	77001–77099, 77201–77293*
Houtzdale, PA	814	16651, 16698
Howard, KS	620	67349
Howard, SD	605	57349
Howard Lake, MN	320	55349, 55575
Howell, MI	517	48843–48844, 48863
Howell, NJ	732, 848	07731
Howes Cave, NY	518	12092
Howey in the Hills, FL	352	34737
Hoxie, KS	785	67740
Hubbard, OR	503, 971	97032
Huber Heights, OH	937	45424
Hudson, FL	727	34667–34669, 34674
Hudson, KS	620	67545
Hudson, MA	351, 978	01749
Hudson, MI	517	49247
Hudson, NH	603	03051
Hudson, NY	518	12534
Hudson, NC	828	28638
Hudson, OH	234, 330	44236–44238
Hudson, WI	715	54016, 54082
Hudson Falls, NY	518	12839
Hueytown, AL	205	35022–35023
Hughesville, MD	301	20637
Hughson, CA	209	95326
Hugo, CO	719	80821
Hugo, MN	651	55038
Hugo, OK	580	74743
Hugoton, KS	620	67951
Hulbert, OK	918	74441
Hull, IA	712	51239
Hull, MA	339, 781	02045
Humacao, PR	787, 939	00791–00792
Humble, TX	281, 832	77325, 77338–77339*
Humboldt, IA	515	50548
Humboldt, KS	620	66748
Humboldt, TN	731	38343
Hummelstown, PA	717	17036
Hunlock Creek, PA	570	18621
Hunt, TX	830	78024
Hunt Valley, MD	410	21030–21031, 21065
Hunter, NY	518	12442
Huntersville, NC	704, 980	28070, 28078
Huntertown, IN	260	46748
Huntingburg, IN	812	47542
Huntingdon, PA	814	16652–16654
Huntingdon, TN	731	38344
Huntingdon Valley, PA	215, 267	19006
Huntington, IN	260	46750
Huntington, NY	631	11743
Huntington, UT	435	84528
Huntington, VT	802	05462
Huntington, WV	304	25701–25729, 25755, 25770*
Huntington Beach, CA	714	92605, 92615, 92646, 92649
Huntington Park, CA	323	90255
Huntington Station, NY	631	11746–11750
Huntley, IL	224, 847	60142
Huntley, MT	406	59037
Huntsville, AL	256	35801–35816, 35824, 35893*
Huntsville, AR	479	72740
Huntsville, MO	660	65259
Huntsville, TN	423	37756
Huntsville, TX	936	77320, 77340–77344*
Hurley, WI	715	54534, 54565
Huron, CA	559	93234
Huron, OH	419, 567	44839
Huron, SD	605	57350, 57399
Hurricane, WV	304	25526
Hurst, TX	682, 817	76053–76054
Hutchins, TX	469, 972	75141
Hutchinson, KS	620	67501–67505
Hutchinson, MN	320	55350
Huttonsville, WV	304	26273
Hyannis, MA	508, 774	02601
Hyannis, NE	308	69350
Hyattsville, MD	301	20781–20788
Hydaburg, AK	907	99922
Hyde Park, MA	617, 857	02136–02137
Hyde Park, NY	845	12538
Hyde Park, VT	802	05655
Hyden, KY	606	41749, 41762
Hyrum, UT	435	84319
Hysham, MT	406	59038, 59076

I

City	Area Code(s)	Zip Code(s)
Ida Grove, IA	712	51445
Idabel, OK	580	74745
Idaho City, ID	208	83631
Idaho Falls, ID	208	83401–83406, 83415
Idaho Springs, CO	303, 720	80452
Idyllwild, CA	951	92549
Imlay City, MI	810	48444
Immaculata, PA	484, 610	19345
Immokalee, FL	239	34142–34143
Imperial, CA	760	92251
Imperial, MO	636	63052–63053
Imperial, NE	308	69033
Imperial Beach, CA	619	91932–91933
Ina, IL	618	62846
Incline Village, NV	775	89450–89452
Independence, CA	760	93526
Independence, IA	319	50644
Independence, KS	620	67301
Independence, KY	859	41051
Independence, MO	816	64050–64058
Independence, OH	216	44131
Independence, OR	503, 971	97351
Independence, VA	276	24348
Indian, AK	907	99540
Indian Orchard, MA	413	01151
Indian Springs, NV	702	89018, 89070
Indian Trail, NC	704, 980	28079
Indian Wells, CA	760	92210
Indiana, PA	724, 878	15701, 15705

*Partial list of zip codes, including main range

City	Area Code(s)	Zip Code(s)
Indianapolis, IN	317	46201–46260, 46266–46268*
Indianola, IA	515	50125
Indianola, MS	662	38749–38751
Indianola, PA	412, 878	15051
Indiantown, FL	772	34956
Indio, CA	760	92201–92203
Inez, KY	606	41224
Ingalls, KS	620	67853
Inglewood, CA	310, 424	90301–90313, 90397–90398
Ingomar, PA	412, 878	15127
Inkster, MI	313	48141
Inman, SC	864	29349
Institute, WV	304	25112
Intercourse, PA	717	17534
Interior, SD	605	57750
Interlochen, MI	231	49643
International Falls, MN	218	56649
Inver Grove Heights, MN	651	55076–55077
Inverness, FL	352	34450–34453
Inwood, NY	516	11096
Iola, KS	620	66749
Iola, WI	715	54945, 54990
Ione, CA	209	95640
Ionia, MI	616	48846
Iowa City, IA	319	52240–52246
Iowa Falls, IA	641	50126
Ipswich, MA	351, 978	01938
Ipswich, SD	605	57451
Irma, WI	715	54442
Irmo, SC	803	29063
Iron Mountain, MI	906	49801–49802, 49831
Iron River, WI	715	54847
Irondale, AL	205	35210
Ironton, MO	573	63650
Ironton, OH	740	45638
Ironwood, MI	906	49938
Irvine, CA	949	92602–92606, 92612–92623*
Irvine, KY	606	40336, 40472
Irvine, PA	814	16329
Irving, TX	214, 469, 972	75014–75017, 75037–75039*
Irvington, NJ	862, 973	07111
Irvington, NY	914	10533
Irvington, VA	804	22480
Irwin, PA	724, 878	15642
Irwindale, CA	626	91706
Irwinton, GA	478	31042
Iselin, NJ	732, 848	08830
Ishpeming, MI	906	49849, 49865
Islamorada, FL	305, 786	33036, 33070
Islandia, NY	631	11749, 11760
Isle of Palms, SC	843	29451
Isle of Wight, VA	757	23397
Islip, NY	631	11751
Isola, MS	662	38754
Issaquah, WA	425	98027–98029, 98075
Itasca, IL	331, 630	60143
Itasca, TX	254	76055
Ithaca, MI	989	48847
Ithaca, NY	607	14850–14853, 14882
Itta Bena, MS	662	38941
Iuka, MS	662	38852
Ivanhoe, CA	559	93235
Ivanhoe, MN	507	56142
Ivel, KY	606	41642
Ivins, UT	435	84738
Ivoryton, CT	860	06442
Ivyland, PA	215, 267	18974
Ixonia, WI	920	53036

J

City	Area Code(s)	Zip Code(s)
Jackman, ME	207	04945
Jackpot, NV	775	89825
Jacksboro, TN	423	37757
Jacksboro, TX	940	76458
Jackson, AL	251	36501, 36515, 36545
Jackson, CA	209	95642, 95654
Jackson, GA	470, 770	30233
Jackson, KY	606	41307, 41339
Jackson, LA	225	70748
Jackson, MI	517	49201–49204
Jackson, MN	507	56143
Jackson, MS	601, 769	39201–39218, 39225, 39232*
Jackson, MO	573	63755
Jackson, NH	603	03846
Jackson, NJ	732, 848	08527
Jackson, NC	252	27845
Jackson, OH	740	45640
Jackson, SC	803	29831
Jackson, TN	731	38301–38308, 38314
Jackson, WI	262	53037
Jackson, WY	307	83001–83002, 83025
Jackson Center, OH	937	45334
Jackson Heights, NY	347, 718	11372
Jackson Hole, WY	307	83001–83002
Jacksonville, AL	256	36265
Jacksonville, AR	501	72076–72078
Jacksonville, FL	904	32099, 32201–32250*
Jacksonville, IL	217	62650–62651
Jacksonville, NC	910	28540–28546
Jacksonville, TX	903	75766
Jacksonville Beach, FL	904	32227, 32240, 32250
Jaffrey, NH	603	03452
Jamaica, NY	347, 718	11405, 11411–11439*
Jamaica Plain, MA	617, 857	02130
Jamesburg, NJ	732, 848	08831
Jamestown, CA	209	95327
Jamestown, KY	270	42629
Jamestown, NY	716	14701–14704
Jamestown, NC	336	27282
Jamestown, ND	701	58401–58405
Jamestown, OH	937	45335
Jamestown, RI	401	02835
Jamestown, SC	843	29453
Jamestown, TN	931	38556
Janesville, IA	319	50647
Janesville, WI	608	53545–53547
Jarratt, VA	434	23867–23870
Jasper, AL	205	35501–35504
Jasper, AR	870	72641
Jasper, FL	386	32052
Jasper, GA	706, 762	30143
Jasper, IN	812	47546–47549
Jasper, MN	507	56144
Jasper, TN	423	37347
Jasper, TX	409	75951
Jay, FL	850	32565
Jay, ME	207	04239, 04262
Jay, OK	918	74346
Jay, VT	802	05859
Jayton, TX	806	79528
Jean, NV	702	89019, 89026
Jeanerette, LA	337	70544
Jeannette, PA	724, 878	15644
Jefferson, AR	870	72079
Jefferson, GA	706, 762	30549
Jefferson, IA	515	50129
Jefferson, LA	504	70121
Jefferson, NC	336	28640
Jefferson, OH	440	44047
Jefferson, OR	541	97352
Jefferson, SD	605	57038
Jefferson, TX	903	75657
Jefferson, WI	920	53549
Jefferson City, MO	573	65101–65111
Jefferson City, TN	865	37760
Jefferson Valley, NY	914	10535
Jeffersontown, KY	502	40269, 40299
Jeffersonville, GA	478	31044
Jeffersonville, IN	812	47129–47134, 47144, 47199
Jeffersonville, NY	845	12748
Jeffersonville, OH	740	43128
Jekyll Island, GA	912	31527
Jelm, WY	970	82063, 82070–82072
Jena, LA	318	71342
Jenison, MI	616	49428–49429
Jenkintown, PA	215, 267	19046
Jenks, OK	918	74037
Jennerstown, PA	814	15547
Jennings, LA	337	70546
Jericho, NY	516	11753, 11853
Jermyn, PA	570	18433
Jerome, ID	208	83338
Jersey City, NJ	201, 551	07097, 07302–07311
Jerseyville, IL	618	62052
Jessup, MD	410, 443	20794
Jesup, GA	912	31545–31546, 31598–31599
Jetersville, VA	804	23083
Jetmore, KS	620	67854
Jewell, IA	515	50130
Jewett, TX	903	75846
Jim Thorpe, PA	570	18229
Johnson, KS	620	67855
Johnson, VT	802	05656
Johnson City, NY	607	13790
Johnson City, TN	423	37601–37605, 37614–37615
Johnson City, TX	830	78636
Johnston, IA	515	50131
Johnston, RI	401	02919
Johnston, SC	803	29832
Johnston City, IL	618	62951
Johnstown, NY	518	12095
Johnstown, OH	740	43031
Johnstown, PA	814	15901–15909, 15915, 15945
Joliet, IL	815	60431–60436
Jonesboro, AR	870	72401–72404
Jonesboro, GA	470, 770	30236–30238
Jonesboro, IL	618	62952
Jonesboro, LA	318	71251
Jonesborough, TN	423	37659
Jonesburg, MO	636	63351
Jonestown, MS	662	38639
Jonesville, LA	318	71343, 71377
Jonesville, VA	276	24263
Joplin, MO	417	64801–64804
Joppa, MD	410	21085
Jordan, MN	952	55352, 56071
Jordan, MT	406	59337
Jordan, NY	315	13080
Joshua Tree, CA	760	92252
Jourdanton, TX	830	78026
Julesburg, CO	970	80737
Junction, TX	915	76849
Junction, UT	435	84740
Junction City, KS	785	66441–66442
Junction City, OR	541	97448
Juneau, AK	907	99801–99803, 99811, 99821*
Juneau, WI	920	53039
Juno Beach, FL	561	33408
Jupiter, FL	561	33458, 33468–33469*

K

City	Area Code(s)	Zip Code(s)
Kadoka, SD	605	57543
Kahoka, MO	660	63445
Kahuku, HI	808	96731
Kahului, HI	808	96732–96733
Kailua, HI	808	96734
Kailua-Kona, HI	808	96739–96740, 96745
Kaiser, MO	573	65047
Kalaheo, HI	808	96741
Kalama, WA	360	98625
Kalamazoo, MI	616	49001–49009, 49019, 49024*
Kalaupapa, HI	808	96742
Kalida, OH	419, 567	45853
Kalispell, MT	406	59901–59904
Kalkaska, MI	231	49646
Kalona, IA	319	52247
Kamuela, HI	808	96743
Kanab, UT	435	84741
Kanawha, IA	641	50447
Kane, PA	814	16735
Kaneohe, HI	808	96744
Kankakee, IL	815	60901–60902
Kannapolis, NC	704, 980	28081–28083
Kansas City, KS	913	66101–66119, 66160
Kansas City, MO	816	64101–64173, 64179–64199*
Kapaa, HI	808	96746
Kapolei, HI	808	96707–96709
Karnes City, TX	830	78118
Karthaus, PA	814	16845
Kasson, MN	507	55944
Katonah, NY	914	10536

*Partial list of zip codes, including main range

City	Area Code(s)	Zip Code(s)
Katy, TX	281, 832	77449–77450, 77491–77494
Kaufman, TX	469, 972	75142
Kaukauna, WI	920	54130–54131
Kaumakani, HI	808	96747
Keaau, HI	808	96749
Kealakekua, HI	808	96750
Kearney, MO	816	64060
Kearney, NE	308	68845–68849
Kearneysville, WV	304	25429–25430
Kearny, NJ	201, 551	07032, 07099
Keene, CA	661	93531
Keene, NH	603	03431, 03435
Keene, TX	682, 817	76059
Keesler AFB, MS	228	39534
Keizer, OR	503, 971	97303, 97307
Keller, TX	682, 817	76244, 76248
Kellogg, ID	208	83837
Kelly, WY	307	83011
Kelseyville, CA	707	95451
Kelso, WA	360	98626
Kemmerer, WY	307	83101
Kenai, AK	907	99611, 99635
Kenansville, NC	910	28349
Kendall, FL	305, 786	33156–33158, 33173–33176*
Kendallville, IN	260	46720, 46755
Kenedy, TX	830	78119, 78125
Kenilworth, NJ	908	07033
Kenmare, ND	701	58746
Kenmore, NY	716	14217, 14223
Kenmore, WA	425	98028
Kennebec, SD	605	57544
Kennebunk, ME	207	04043
Kennebunkport, ME	207	04046
Kennedy Space Center, FL	321	32815
Kenner, LA	504	70062–70065
Kennesaw, GA	470, 770	30144, 30152, 30156, 30160
Kennett, MO	573	63857
Kennett Square, PA	484, 610	19348
Kennewick, WA	509	99336–99338
Kenosha, WI	262	53140–53144, 53158
Kenova, WV	304	25530
Kensington, CT	860	06037
Kensington, MD	301	20891, 20895
Kent, CT	860	06757
Kent, OH	234, 330	44240–44243
Kent, WA	253	98031–98035, 98042, 98064
Kentfield, CA	415	94904, 94914
Kentland, IN	219	47951
Kenton, OH	419, 567	43326
Kentwood, MI	616	49506–49508, 49512, 49518*
Kenwood, CA	707	95452
Kenyon, MN	507	55946
Keokuk, IA	319	52632
Keosauqua, IA	319	52565
Kermit, TX	915	79745
Kernersville, NC	336	27284–27285
Kernville, CA	760	93238
Kerrville, TX	830	78028–78029
Kershaw, SC	803	29067
Keshena, WI	715	54135
Keswick, VA	434	22947
Ketchikan, AK	907	99901–99903, 99918–99919*
Ketchum, ID	208	83340
Kettering, OH	937	45409, 45419–45420*
Keuka Park, NY	315	14478
Kew Gardens, NY	347, 718	11415–11418
Kewanee, IL	309	61443
Kewanna, IN	574	46935, 46939
Kewaskum, WI	262	53040
Kewaunee, WI	920	54216
Key Biscayne, FL	305, 786	33149
Key Largo, FL	305, 786	33037
Key West, FL	305, 786	33040–33041, 33045
Keyser, WV	304	26726
Keystone, CO	970	80435
Keystone, SD	605	57751
Keystone Heights, FL	352	32656
Keytesville, MO	660	65261
Kiamesha Lake, NY	845	12751
Kiawah Island, SC	843	29455
Kidron, OH	234, 330	44636

City	Area Code(s)	Zip Code(s)
Kiel, WI	920	53042
Kihei, HI	808	96753
Kilgore, TX	903	75662–75663
Kill Devil Hills, NC	252	27948
Killbuck, OH	234, 330	44637
Killeen, TX	254	76540–76549
Killington, VT	802	05751
Kimball, NE	308	69145
Kimberly, OR	541	97848
Kimberly, WI	920	54136
Kincheloe, MI	906	49784–49788
Kinder, LA	337	70648
Kinderhook, NY	518	12106
Kindred, ND	701	58051
King, NC	336	27021
King, WI	715	54946
King City, CA	831	93930
King Ferry, NY	315	13081
King George, VA	540	22485
King of Prussia, PA	484, 610	19406, 19487
King Salmon, AK	907	99549, 99613
King William, VA	804	23086
Kingfisher, OK	405	73750
Kingman, AZ	928	86401–86402, 86411–86413*
Kingman, KS	620	67068
Kings Bay, GA	912	31547
Kings Mountain, NC	704, 980	28086
Kings Point, NY	516	11024
Kingsburg, CA	559	93631
Kingsford, MI	906	49801–49802
Kingsport, TN	423	37660–37665, 37669
Kingston, MA	339, 781	02364
Kingston, MO	816	64650
Kingston, NJ	609	08528
Kingston, NY	845	12401–12402
Kingston, OK	580	73439
Kingston, PA	570	18704
Kingston, RI	401	02881
Kingston, TN	865	37763
Kingston, WA	360	98346
Kingstree, SC	843	29556
Kingsville, MD	410	21087
Kingsville, MO	816	64061
Kingsville, TX	361	78363–78364
Kingwood, TX	281, 832	77325, 77339, 77345, 77346
Kingwood, WV	304	26519, 26537
Kinnelon, NJ	862, 973	07405
Kinsale, VA	804	22488
Kinsley, KS	620	67547
Kinsman, OH	234, 330	44428
Kinston, NC	252	28501–28504
Kiowa, CO	303, 720	80117
Kirbyville, TX	409	75956
Kirkland, WA	425	98033–98034, 98083
Kirksville, MO	660	63501
Kirkville, NY	315	13082
Kirkwood, MO	314	63122
Kirtland, OH	440	44094
Kirtland AFB, NM	505	87116–87118
Kissimmee, FL	321, 407	34741–34747, 34758–34759
Kittanning, PA	724, 878	16201, 16215
Kittery, ME	207	03904
Klamath Falls, OR	541	97601–97603, 97625
Knights Landing, CA	530	95645
Knightstown, IN	765	46148
Knox, IN	574	46534
Knoxville, IA	641	50138, 50197–50198
Knoxville, TN	865	37901–37902, 37909–37933*
Kodiak, AK	907	99615, 99619, 99697
Kohler, WI	920	53044
Kokomo, IN	765	46901–46904
Koloa, HI	808	96756
Kosciusko, MS	662	39090
Koshkonong, MO	417	65692
Kotzebue, AK	907	99752
Kountze, TX	409	77625
Kreamer, PA	570	17833
Kula, HI	808	96790
Kulpsville, PA	215, 267	19443
Kuna, ID	208	83634
Kurten, TX	979	77862

City	Area Code(s)	Zip Code(s)
Kutztown, PA	484, 610	19530

L

City	Area Code(s)	Zip Code(s)
L'Anse, MI	906	49946
La Belle, FL	863	33935
La Canada, CA	818	91011–91012
La Conner, WA	360	98257
La Crescenta, CA	818	91214, 91224
La Crosse, KS	785	67548, 67553
La Crosse, WI	608	54601–54603
La Fayette, GA	706, 762	30728
La Follette, TN	423	37729, 37766
La France, SC	864	29656
La Grande, OR	541	97850
La Grange, IL	708	60525
La Grange, TX	979	78945
La Grange Park, IL	708	60526
La Habra, CA	562	90631–90633
La Jolla, CA	858	92037–92039, 92092–92093
La Junta, CO	719	81050
La Mesa, CA	619	91941–91944
La Mesa, NM	505	88044
La Mirada, CA	562, 714	90637–90639
La Moure, ND	701	58458
La Palma, CA	714	90623
La Pine, OR	541	97739
La Plata, MD	301	20646
La Plume, PA	570	18440
La Porte, IN	574	46350–46352
La Porte, TX	281, 832	77571–77572
La Puente, CA	626	91744–91749
La Quinta, CA	760	92253
La Rue, OH	740	43332
La Salle, IL	815	61301
La Union, NM	505	88021
La Vergne, TN	615	37086–37089
La Verne, CA	909	91750
La Veta, CO	719	81055
Lac du Flambeau, WI	715	54538
Lacey, WA	360	98503–98509, 98513–98516
Lackawanna, NY	716	14218
Lackland AFB, TX	210	78236
Laclede, ID	208	83841
Lacon, IL	309	61540
Laconia, NH	603	03246–03249
Ladd, IL	815	61329
Ladysmith, WI	715	54848
Lafayette, AL	334	36862
Lafayette, CA	925	94549, 94596
Lafayette, CO	303, 720	80026
Lafayette, IN	765	47901–47909, 47996
Lafayette, LA	337	70501–70509, 70593–70598
Lafayette, NJ	862, 973	07848
Lafayette, TN	615	37083
LaFox, IL	331, 630	60147
Lago Vista, TX	512	78645
LaGrange, GA	706, 762	30240–30241, 30261
LaGrange, IN	260	46761
LaGrange, KY	502	40031
Lagrangeville, NY	845	12540
Laguna Beach, CA	949	92607, 92637, 92651, 92656*
Laguna Hills, CA	949	92637, 92653–92656
Laguna Niguel, CA	949	92607, 92677
Lahaina, HI	808	96761, 96767
Laie, HI	808	96762
Lake Alfred, FL	863	33850
Lake Andes, SD	605	57356
Lake Ariel, PA	570	18436
Lake Bluff, IL	224, 847	60044
Lake Buena Vista, FL	321, 407	32830
Lake Butler, FL	386	32054
Lake Charles, LA	337	70601–70616, 70629
Lake City, CO	970	81235
Lake City, FL	386	32024–32025, 32055–32056
Lake City, IA	712	51449
Lake City, MI	231	49651
Lake City, MN	651	55041
Lake City, PA	814	16423
Lake City, SC	843	29560
Lake Crystal, MN	507	56055

*Partial list of zip codes, including main range

City	Area Code(s)	Zip Code(s)
Lake Dallas, TX	940	75065
Lake Delton, WI	608	53940
Lake Elsinore, CA	951	92530–92532
Lake Forest, CA	949	92609, 92630
Lake Forest, IL	224, 847	60045
Lake Geneva, WI	262	53147
Lake George, CO	719	80827
Lake George, NY	518	12845
Lake Grove, NY	631	11755
Lake Harmony, PA	570	18624
Lake Havasu City, AZ	928	86403–86406
Lake Helen, FL	386	32744
Lake Hiawatha, NJ	862, 973	07034
Lake Isabella, CA	760	93240
Lake Jackson, TX	979	77566
Lake Junaluska, NC	828	28745
Lake Lillian, MN	320	56253
Lake Lure, NC	828	28746
Lake Mary, FL	321, 407	32746, 32795
Lake Mills, WI	920	53551
Lake Monroe, FL	321, 407	32747
Lake Odessa, MI	616	48849
Lake Orion, MI	248, 947	48359–48362
Lake Oswego, OR	503, 971	97034–97035
Lake Ozark, MO	573	65049
Lake Park, GA	229	31636
Lake Placid, FL	863	33852, 33862
Lake Placid, NY	518	12946
Lake Pleasant, NY	518	12108
Lake Powell, UT	435	84533
Lake Providence, LA	318	71254
Lake Saint Louis, MO	636	63367
Lake Stevens, WA	425	98258
Lake Success, NY	516	11020, 11042
Lake Toxaway, NC	828	28747
Lake View, SC	843	29563
Lake Village, AR	870	71653
Lake Wales, FL	863	33853–33859, 33867, 33898
Lake Worth, FL	561	33454, 33460–33467
Lake Zurich, IL	224, 847	60047
Lakehurst, NJ	732, 848	08733, 08755, 08759
Lakeland, FL	863	33801–33815
Lakeland, GA	229	31635
Lakeland, LA	225	70752
Lakeport, CA	707	95453
Lakeside, AZ	928	85929
Lakeside, CA	619	92040
Laketon, IN	260	46943
Lakeview, AR	870	72642
Lakeview, CA	909	92567
Lakeview, OR	541	97630
Lakeville, CT	860	06039
Lakeville, MN	952	55044
Lakeville, PA	570	18438
Lakeway, TX	512	78734, 78738
Lakewood, CA	562	90711–90716, 90805
Lakewood, CO	303, 720	80033, 80123, 80214, 80215*
Lakewood, NJ	732, 848	08701
Lakewood, NY	716	14750
Lakewood, OH	216	44107
Lakewood, WA	253	98439, 98492, 98497, 98499
Lakin, KS	620	67860
Lakota, ND	701	58344
Lamar, CO	719	81052
Lamar, MO	417	64759
Lamberton, MN	507	56152
Lambertville, NJ	609	08530
Lame Deer, MT	406	59043
Lamesa, TX	806	79331
Lamoni, IA	641	50140
Lamont, CA	661	93241
Lampasas, TX	512	76550
Lanai City, HI	808	96763
Lanark, IL	815	61046
Lancaster, CA	661	93534–93539, 93584–93586
Lancaster, KY	859	40444–40446
Lancaster, MO	660	63548
Lancaster, NH	603	03584
Lancaster, NY	716	14043, 14086
Lancaster, OH	740	43130
Lancaster, PA	717	17601–17608, 17699
Lancaster, SC	803	29720–29722
Lancaster, TX	469, 972	75134, 75146
Lancaster, VA	804	22503
Lancaster, WI	608	53813
Lander, WY	307	82520
Landisburg, PA	717	17040
Landisville, PA	717	17538
Landover, MD	301	20785
Landrum, SC	864	29356
Lanett, AL	334	36863
Langdon, ND	701	58249
Langhorne, PA	215, 267	19047, 19053
Langley, WA	360	98260
Langley AFB, VA	757	23665
Langston, OK	405	73050
Lanham, MD	301	20703–20706, 20784
Lanham Seabrook, MD	301	20703–20706
Lansdale, PA	215, 267	19446
Lansdowne, PA	484, 610	19050
Lansford, PA	570	18232
Lansing, IL	708	60438
Lansing, KS	913	66043
Lansing, MI	517	48901, 48906–48924*
Lantana, FL	561	33460–33465
Lapeer, MI	810	48446
LaPlace, LA	985	70068–70069
Laporte, PA	570	18626
Laramie, WY	307	82051, 82063, 82070, 82073
Larchmont, NY	914	10538
Laredo, TX	956	78040–78049
Largo, FL	727	33770–33779
Largo, MD	301	20774
Larkspur, CA	415	94939, 94977
Larned, KS	620	67550
Larose, LA	985	70373–70374
Las Animas, CO	719	81054
Las Cruces, NM	505	88001–88006, 88011–88012
Las Vegas, NV	702	89101–89164, 89170–89173*
Las Vegas, NM	505	87701, 87745
Latham, NY	518	12110–12111, 12128
Lathrop, CA	209	95330
Latrobe, PA	724, 878	15650
Latta, SC	843	29565
Latty, OH	419, 567	45855
Lauderdale-by-the-Sea, FL	754, 954	33062, 33308
Lauderhill, FL	754, 954	33311–33313, 33319–33321*
Laughlin, NV	702	89028–89029
Laughlin AFB, TX	830	78840–78843
Laurel, MD	240, 301	20707–20709, 20723–20726
Laurel, MS	601, 769	39440–39443
Laurel Hill, NC	910	28351
Laurelton, NY	347, 718	11413
Laurens, IA	712	50554
Laurens, SC	864	29360
Laurinburg, NC	910	28352–28353
Lava Hot Springs, ID	208	83246
LaVale, MD	301	21502–21504
Lawndale, CA	310, 424	90260–90261
Lawrence, KS	785	66044–66049
Lawrence, MA	351, 978	01840–01843
Lawrence, MI	616	49064
Lawrence, NY	516	11559
Lawrence, PA	724, 878	15055
Lawrenceburg, IN	812	47025
Lawrenceburg, KY	502	40342
Lawrenceburg, TN	931	38464
Lawrenceville, GA	470, 678, 770	30042–30049
Lawrenceville, IL	618	62439
Lawrenceville, NJ	609	08648
Lawrenceville, VA	434	23868
Lawton, MI	616	49065
Lawton, OK	580	73501–73507, 73558
Layton, NJ	862, 973	07851
Layton, UT	801	84040–84041
Le Center, MN	507	56057
Le Grand, IA	641	50142
Le Mars, IA	712	51017, 51031
Le Roy, NY	585	14482
Le Sueur, MN	507	56058
Lead, SD	605	57754
Leadville, CO	719	80429, 80461
League City, TX	281, 832	77573–77574
Leakesville, MS	601, 769	39451
Leakey, TX	830	78873
Leander, TX	512	78641, 78645–78646
Leavenworth, KS	913	66043, 66048
Leavittsburg, OH	234, 330	44430
Leawood, KS	913	66206–66211, 66224
Lebanon, CT	860	06249
Lebanon, IL	618	62254
Lebanon, IN	765	46052
Lebanon, KY	270	40033
Lebanon, MO	417	65536
Lebanon, NH	603	03756, 03766
Lebanon, NJ	908	08833
Lebanon, OH	513	45036
Lebanon, OR	541	97355
Lebanon, PA	717	17042, 17046
Lebanon, TN	615	37087–37090
Lebanon, VA	276	24266
Lebec, CA	661	93243
Lecanto, FL	352	34460–34461
Lee, MA	413	01238, 01264
Lee's Summit, MO	816	64063–64065, 64081–64082*
Leechburg, PA	724, 878	15656
Leeds, AL	205	35094
Leeds, MA	413	01053
Leesburg, FL	352	34748–34749, 34788–34789
Leesburg, GA	229	31763
Leesburg, NJ	856	08327
Leesburg, VA	571, 703	20175–20178
Leesville, LA	337	71446, 71459, 71496
Leesville, SC	803	29070
Lehi, UT	801	84043
Lehigh Acres, FL	239	33936, 33970–33972
Lehigh Valley, PA	484, 610	18001–18003
Lehighton, PA	484, 610	18235
Lehman, PA	570	18627
Leicester, MA	508, 774	01524
Leicester, NY	585	14481
Leitchfield, KY	270	42754–42755
Leland, MI	231	49654
Leland, NC	910	28451
Lemmon, SD	605	57638
Lemon Grove, CA	619	91945–91946
Lemont, IL	331, 630	60439–60440, 60490
Lemoore, CA	559	93245–93246
Lemoyne, PA	717	17043
Lena, IL	815	61048
Lenexa, KS	913	66210–66220, 66227, 66285*
Lenni, PA	484, 610	19052
Lenoir, NC	828	28633, 28645
Lenoir City, TN	865	37771–37772
Lenox, MA	413	01240
Leola, PA	717	17540
Leola, SD	605	57456
Leominster, MA	351, 978	01453
Leon, IA	641	50144
Leonardtown, MD	301	20650
Leonia, NJ	201, 551	07605
Leoti, KS	620	67861
Lester, PA	484, 610	19029, 19113
Lester Prairie, MN	320	55354
Levelland, TX	806	79336–79338
Leverett, MA	413	01054
Levittown, NY	516	11756
Levittown, PA	215, 267	19054–19059
Lewes, DE	302	19958
Lewis Center, OH	740	43035
Lewis Run, PA	814	16738
Lewisberry, PA	717	17339
Lewisburg, PA	570	17837
Lewisburg, TN	931	37091
Lewisburg, WV	304	24901
Lewiston, ID	208	83501
Lewiston, ME	207	04240–04243
Lewiston, MI	989	49756
Lewiston, MN	507	55952
Lewiston, NY	716	14092
Lewiston, NC	252	27849
Lewistown, IL	309	61542
Lewistown, MO	573	63452

*Partial list of zip codes, including main range

City	Area Code(s)	Zip Code(s)
Lewistown, MT	406	59457
Lewistown, PA	717	17044
Lewisville, AR	870	71845
Lewisville, ID	208	83431
Lewisville, NC	336	27023
Lewisville, TX	469, 972	75022, 75027–75029*
Lexington, GA	706, 762	30648
Lexington, KY	859	40502–40517, 40522–40526*
Lexington, MA	339, 781	02420–02421
Lexington, MI	810	48450
Lexington, MS	662	39095
Lexington, MO	660	64067
Lexington, NE	308	68850
Lexington, NC	336	27292–27295
Lexington, OH	419, 567	44904
Lexington, OK	405	73051
Lexington, SC	803	29071–29073
Lexington, TN	731	38351
Lexington, VA	540	24450
Lexington Park, MD	301	20653
Libby, MT	406	59923
Liberal, KS	620	67901, 67905
Liberty, IN	765	47353
Liberty, KY	606	42539
Liberty, MS	601, 769	39645
Liberty, MO	816	64068–64069, 64087
Liberty, NC	336	27298
Liberty, SC	864	29657
Liberty, TX	936	77575
Liberty Corner, NJ	908	07938
Liberty Lake, WA	509	99019
Libertyville, IL	224, 847	60048, 60092
Licking, MO	573	65542
Lightfoot, VA	757	23090
Lighthouse Point, FL	754, 954	33064, 33074
Ligonier, PA	724, 878	15658
Lihue, HI	808	96766
Lilburn, GA	470, 770	30047–30048
Lillington, NC	910	27546
Lima, NY	585	14485
Lima, OH	419, 567	45801–45809, 45819, 45854
Lima, PA	484, 610	19037
Limerick, PA	484, 610	19468
Limon, CO	719	80826–80828
Lincoln, CA	916	95648
Lincoln, IL	217	62656
Lincoln, KS	785	67455
Lincoln, ME	207	04457
Lincoln, MA	339, 781	01773
Lincoln, MI	989	48742
Lincoln, NE	402	68501–68532, 68542, 68583*
Lincoln, RI	401	02802, 02865
Lincoln City, IN	812	47552
Lincoln City, OR	541	97367
Lincoln Park, MI	313	48146
Lincoln Park, NJ	862, 973	07035
Lincoln University, PA	484, 610	19352
Lincolnshire, IL	224, 847	60069
Lincolnton, GA	706, 762	30817
Lincolnton, NC	704, 980	28092–28093
Lincolnwood, IL	224, 847	60645–60646, 60659, 60712
Lincroft, NJ	732, 848	07738
Linden, AL	334	36748
Linden, IN	765	47955
Linden, NJ	908	07036
Linden, TN	931	37096
Linden, TX	903	75563
Lindenhurst, NY	631	11757
Lindenwood, IL	815	61049
Lindon, UT	801	84042
Lindsay, CA	559	93247
Lindsay, NE	402	68644
Lindsay, OK	405	73052
Lindsborg, KS	785	67456
Lindstrom, MN	651	55045
Linesville, PA	814	16424
Lingle, WY	307	82223
Linn, MO	573	65051
Linneus, MO	660	64653
Lino Lakes, MN	651	55014, 55038, 55110, 55126
Linthicum, MD	410	21090
Linthicum Heights, MD	410	21090
Linton, IN	812	47441
Linton, ND	701	58552
Linville, NC	828	28646
Linwood, KS	913	66052
Linwood, NJ	609	08221
Linwood, PA	484, 610	19061
Lionville, PA	484, 610	19353
Lipscomb, TX	806	79056
Lisbon, NH	603	03585
Lisbon, ND	701	58054
Lisbon, OH	234, 330	44432
Lisbon Falls, ME	207	04252
Lisle, IL	331, 630	60532
Litchfield, CT	860	06750, 06759
Litchfield, IL	217	62056
Litchfield, MI	517	49252
Litchfield, MN	320	55355
Litchfield Park, AZ	623	85340
Lithia, FL	813	33547
Lithia Springs, GA	470, 770	30122
Lithonia, GA	470, 770	30038–30039, 30058
Lititz, PA	717	17543
Little Chute, WI	920	54140
Little Compton, RI	401	02801, 02837
Little Elm, TX	469, 972	75068
Little Falls, MN	320	56345
Little Falls, NJ	862, 973	07424
Little Falls, NY	315	13365
Little Ferry, NJ	201, 551	07643
Little Neck, NY	347, 718	11362–11363
Little River, SC	843	29566
Little Rock, AR	501	72201–72227, 72231, 72260*
Little Rock AFB, AR	501	72076
Little Silver, NJ	732, 848	07739
Little Torch Key, FL	305, 786	33042
Little Valley, NY	716	14755
Littlefield, TX	806	79339
Littlerock, WA	360	98556
Littlestown, PA	717	17340
Littleton, CO	303, 720	80120–80130, 80160–80166
Littleton, MA	351, 978	01460
Live Oak, CA	530	95953
Live Oak, FL	386	32060, 32064
Livermore, CA	925	94550–94551
Livermore, CO	970	80536
Liverpool, NY	315	13088–13090
Livingston, AL	205	35470
Livingston, CA	209	95334
Livingston, LA	225	70754
Livingston, MT	406	59047
Livingston, NJ	862, 973	07039
Livingston, TN	931	38570
Livingston, TX	936	77351, 77399
Livingston Manor, NY	845	12758
Livonia, MI	734	48150–48154
Llano, TX	915	78643
Loa, UT	435	84747
Loch Sheldrake, NY	845	12759
Lock Haven, PA	570	17745
Lockhart, TX	512	78644
Lockport, IL	815	60441, 60446
Lockport, LA	985	70374
Lockport, NY	716	14094–14095
Locust Grove, VA	540	22508
Lodi, CA	209	95240–95242
Lodi, NJ	862, 973	07644
Logan, IA	712	51546, 51550
Logan, OH	740	43138
Logan, UT	435	84321–84323, 84341
Logan, WV	304	25601
Logansport, IN	574	46947
Loganville, GA	470, 770	30052
Loma Linda, CA	909	92350, 92354–92357
Lombard, IL	331, 630	60148
Lompoc, CA	805	93436–93438
London, KY	606	40741–40745
London, OH	740	43140
Londonderry, NH	603	03053
Lone Tree, CO	303, 720	80112, 80124
Lone Tree, IA	319	52755
Lone Wolf, OK	580	73655
Long Beach, CA	562	90745–90749, 90801–90815*
Long Beach, MS	228	39560
Long Beach, NY	516	11561
Long Beach, WA	360	98631
Long Branch, NJ	732, 848	07740
Long Grove, IL	224, 847	60047–60049
Long Island City, NY	347, 718	11101–11109, 11120
Long Pond, PA	570	18334
Long Prairie, MN	320	56347
Long Valley, NJ	908	07853
Longboat Key, FL	941	34228
Longmeadow, MA	413	01106, 01116
Longmont, CO	303, 720	80501–80504
Longview, TX	903	75601–75608, 75615
Longview, WA	360	98632
Longwood, FL	321, 407	32750–32752, 32779, 32791
Lonoke, AR	501	72086
Lookout Mountain, GA	706, 762	30750
Lookout Mountain, TN	423	37350
Loomis, CA	916	95650
Lorain, OH	440	44052–44055
Lordsburg, NM	505	88009, 88045, 88055
Lorenzo, TX	806	79343
Loretto, KY	270	40037
Loretto, PA	814	15940
Loretto, TN	931	38469
Loris, SC	843	29569
Lorman, MS	601, 769	39096
Lorton, VA	571, 703	22079, 22199
Los Alamitos, CA	562, 714	90720–90721
Los Alamos, NM	505	87544–87545
Los Altos, CA	650	94022–94024
Los Altos Hills, CA	650	94022–94024
Los Angeles, CA	213, 310, 323, 424	90001–90103, 90174, 90185*
Los Angeles AFB, CA	310, 424	90009
Los Banos, CA	209	93635
Los Gatos, CA	408	95030–95033
Los Lunas, NM	505	87031
Lostine, OR	541	97857
Lotus, CA	530	95651
Loudon, NH	603	03307
Loudon, TN	865	37774
Loudonville, NY	518	12211
Loudonville, OH	419, 567	44842
Louisa, KY	606	41201, 41230
Louisa, VA	540	23093
Louisburg, NC	919	27549
Louisville, CO	303, 720	80027–80028
Louisville, GA	478	30434
Louisville, IL	618	62858
Louisville, KY	502	40201–40233, 40241–40245*
Louisville, MS	662	39339
Louisville, OH	234, 330	44641
Louisville, TN	865	37777
Loup City, NE	308	68853
Loveland, CO	970	80537–80539
Loveland, OH	513	45111, 45140
Lovell, WY	307	82431
Lovelock, NV	775	89419
Loves Park, IL	815	61111, 61130–61132
Lovingston, VA	434	22949
Lovington, NM	505	88260
Low Moor, VA	540	24457
Lowell, AR	479	72745
Lowell, FL	352	32663
Lowell, IN	219	46356
Lowell, MA	351, 978	01850–01854
Lowell, MI	616	49331
Lowellville, OH	234, 330	44436
Lower Burrell, PA	724, 878	15068
Lower Gwynedd, PA	215, 267	19002
Lower Waterford, VT	802	05848
Lowville, NY	315	13367
Loxahatchee, FL	561	33470
Loysville, PA	717	17047
Lubbock, TX	806	79401–79416, 79423–79424*
Lubec, ME	207	04652
Lucas, KY	270	42156
Lucasville, OH	740	45648, 45699
Lucedale, MS	601, 769	39452

**Partial list of zip codes, including main range*

City	Area Code(s)	Zip Code(s)
Ludington, MI	231	49431
Ludlow, MA	413	01056
Ludlow, VT	802	05149
Ludowici, GA	912	31316
Lufkin, TX	936	75901–75904, 75915
Lugoff, SC	803	29078
Luke AFB, AZ	623	85307–85309
Lula, MS	662	38644
Luling, LA	985	70070
Lumber Bridge, NC	910	28357
Lumberton, NJ	856	08048
Lumberton, NC	910	28358–28360
Lumberton, TX	409	77657
Lumpkin, GA	229	31815
Lunenburg, MA	351, 978	01462
Lunenburg, VT	802	05906
Lunenburg, VA	434	23952
Luray, VA	540	22835
Lusk, WY	307	82225
Lutherville, MD	410	21093–21094
Lutsen, MN	218	55612
Luttrell, TN	865	37779
Luverne, AL	334	36049
Luverne, MN	507	56156
Luxemburg, WI	920	54217
Lykens, PA	717	17048
Lyman, SC	864	29365
Lyme, NH	603	03768
Lynbrook, NY	516	11563–11564
Lynchburg, TN	931	37352
Lynchburg, VA	434	24501–24506, 24512–24515
Lyndhurst, NJ	201, 551	07071
Lyndon, KS	785	66451
Lyndonville, NY	585	14098
Lyndonville, VT	802	05851
Lynn, IN	765	47355
Lynn, MA	339, 781	01901–01905, 01910
Lynn Haven, FL	850	32444
Lynnfield, MA	339, 781	01940
Lynnwood, WA	425	98036–98037, 98046
Lynwood, CA	310, 424	90262
Lyon, MS	662	38645
Lyon Mountain, NY	518	12952–12955
Lyon Station, PA	484, 610	19536
Lyons, CO	303, 720	80540
Lyons, GA	912	30436
Lyons, KS	620	67554
Lyons, NJ	908	07939
Lyons, NY	315	14489
Lyons, OR	503, 971	97358

M

City	Area Code(s)	Zip Code(s)
Mableton, GA	404, 470	30126
Macclenny, FL	386	32063
MacDill AFB, FL	813	33608
Macedon, NY	315	14502
Macedonia, OH	234, 330	44056
Machesney Park, IL	815	61115
Machias, ME	207	04654, 04686
Machiasport, ME	207	04655
Mackay, ID	208	83251
Mackinac Island, MI	906	49757
Mackinaw City, MI	231	49701
Macomb, IL	309	61455
Macomb, MI	586	48042–48044
Macomb Township, MI	586	48042–48044
Macon, GA	478	31201–31221, 31294–31299
Macon, MS	662	39341
Macon, MO	660	63552
Macungie, PA	484, 610	18062
Macy, IN	574	46951
Macy, NE	402	68039
Maddock, ND	701	58348
Madeira Beach, FL	727	33708, 33738
Madelia, MN	507	56062
Madera, CA	559	93637–93639
Madill, OK	580	73446
Madison, AL	256	35756–35758
Madison, CT	203	06443
Madison, FL	850	32340–32341
Madison, GA	706, 762	30650
Madison, IL	618	62060
Madison, IN	812	47250
Madison, ME	207	04950
Madison, MN	320	56256
Madison, MS	601, 769	39110, 39130
Madison, NE	402	68748
Madison, NJ	862, 973	07940
Madison, NC	336	27025
Madison, OH	440	44057
Madison, SD	605	57042
Madison, TN	615	37115–37116
Madison, VA	540	22719, 22727
Madison, WV	304	25130
Madison, WI	608	53562, 53593, 53701, 53719*
Madison Heights, MI	248, 947	48071
Madisonville, KY	270	42431
Madisonville, LA	985	70447
Madisonville, TN	423	37354
Madisonville, TX	936	77864
Madras, OR	541	97741
Maggie Valley, NC	828	28751
Magna, UT	801	84044
Magnolia, AR	870	71753–71754
Magnolia, MS	601, 769	39652
Mahanoy City, PA	570	17948
Mahnomen, MN	218	56557
Mahomet, IL	217	61853
Mahopac, NY	845	10541
Mahwah, NJ	201, 551	07430, 07495–07498
Maiden, NC	828	28650
Maiden Rock, WI	715	54750
Maitland, FL	321, 407	32751, 32794
Makanda, IL	618	62958
Makawao, HI	808	96768
Malad City, ID	208	83252
Malden, MA	339, 781	02148
Malden, MO	573	63863
Malibu, CA	310, 424	90263–90265
Malinta, OH	419, 567	43535
Malone, FL	850	32445
Malone, NY	518	12953
Malta, ID	208	83342
Malta, IL	815	60150
Malta, MT	406	59538
Malta, NY	518	12020
Malvern, AR	501	72104–72105
Malvern, OH	234, 330	44644
Malvern, PA	484, 610	19355
Malverne, NY	516	11565
Mamaroneck, NY	914	10543
Mammoth Cave, KY	270	42259
Mammoth Lakes, CA	760	93546
Mamou, LA	337	70554
Manahawkin, NJ	609	08050
Manalapan, FL	561	33462
Manalapan, NJ	732, 848	07726
Manasquan, NJ	732, 848	08736
Manassas, VA	571, 703	20108–20113
Manassas Park, VA	571, 703	20111
Manawa, WI	920	54949
Manchester, CT	860	06040–06045
Manchester, IA	563	52057
Manchester, KY	606	40962
Manchester, ME	207	04351
Manchester, MI	734	48158
Manchester, NH	603	03101–03111
Manchester, TN	931	37349, 37355
Manchester, VT	802	05254
Manchester Center, VT	802	05255
Manchester Village, VT	802	05254
Mancos, CO	970	81328
Mandan, ND	701	58554
Mandeville, LA	985	70448, 70470–70471
Mangum, OK	580	73554
Manhasset, NY	516	11030
Manhattan, KS	785	66502–66506
Manhattan Beach, CA	310, 424	90266–90267
Manheim, PA	717	17545
Manila, UT	435	84046
Manistee, MI	231	49660
Manistique, MI	906	49854
Manitou, OK	580	73555
Manitou Springs, CO	719	80829
Manitowoc, WI	920	54220–54221
Mankato, KS	785	66956
Mankato, MN	507	56001–56006
Manlius, NY	315	13104
Manning, IA	712	51455
Manning, ND	701	58642
Manning, SC	803	29102
Manor, TX	512	78653
Mansfield, AR	479	72944
Mansfield, CT	860	06250, 06268
Mansfield, LA	318	71052
Mansfield, MA	508, 774	02031, 02048
Mansfield, MO	417	65704
Mansfield, OH	419, 567	44901–44907, 44999
Mansfield, PA	570	16933
Mansfield, TX	682, 817	76063
Manson, NC	252	27553
Manteca, CA	209	95336–95337
Manteno, IL	815	60950
Manteo, NC	252	27954
Manti, UT	435	84642
Mantorville, MN	507	55955
Mantua, NJ	856	08051
Mantua, OH	234, 330	44255
Many, LA	318	71449
Maple Glen, PA	215, 267	19002
Maple Grove, MN	763	55311, 55369, 55569
Maple Heights, OH	216	44137
Maple Park, IL	331, 630	60151
Maple Plain, MN	763	55348, 55359, 55393, 55570*
Maple Shade, NJ	856	08052
Maple Valley, WA	425	98038
Mapleton, OR	541	97453
Mapleville, RI	401	02839
Maplewood, MN	651	55109, 55117–55119
Maplewood, NJ	862, 973	07040
Maplewood, NY	518	12189
Mappsville, VA	757	23407
Maquoketa, IA	563	52060
Marana, AZ	520	85653
Marathon, FL	305, 786	33050–33052
Marathon, WI	715	54448
Marble City, OK	918	74945
Marble Falls, TX	830	78654–78657
Marblehead, MA	339, 781	01945
Marblehead, OH	419, 567	43440
Marceline, MO	660	64658
Marcellus, NY	315	13108
Marco Island, FL	239	34145–34146
Marcus, IA	712	51035
Marcy, NY	315	13403
Marengo, IL	815	60152
Marengo, IA	319	52301
Marfa, TX	915	79843
Margate, FL	754, 954	33063–33068, 33073, 33093
Marianna, AR	870	72360
Marianna, FL	850	32446–32448
Maricopa, AZ	520	85239
Marietta, GA	470, 678, 770	30006–30008, 30060–30069*
Marietta, OH	740	45750
Marietta, OK	580	73448
Marietta, PA	717	17547
Marina, CA	831	93933
Marina del Rey, CA	310, 424	90291–90295
Marine City, MI	810	48039
Marinette, WI	715	54143
Marion, AL	334	36756
Marion, AR	870	72364
Marion, IL	618	62959
Marion, IN	765	46952–46953
Marion, IA	319	52302
Marion, KS	620	66861
Marion, KY	270	42064
Marion, MA	508, 774	02738
Marion, NY	315	14505
Marion, NC	828	28737, 28752
Marion, OH	740	43301–43302, 43306–43307
Marion, SC	843	29571

*Partial list of zip codes, including main range

City	Area Code(s)	Zip Code(s)
Marion, SD	605	57043
Marion, VA	276	24354
Marion, WI	715	54950
Mariposa, CA	209	95338
Marissa, IL	618	62257
Marked Tree, AR	870	72365
Markham, IL	708	60426
Markle, IN	260	46770
Markleeville, CA	530	96120
Marks, MS	662	38646
Marksville, LA	318	71351
Marlboro, NJ	732, 848	07746
Marlboro, VT	802	05344
Marlborough, MA	508, 774	01752
Marlin, TX	254	76661
Marlinton, WV	304	24954
Marlow Heights, MD	301	20746–20748
Marlton, NJ	856	08053
Marquette, MI	906	49855
Marrero, LA	504	70072–70073
Marriottsville, MD	410	21104
Mars, PA	724, 878	16046
Mars Hill, NC	828	28754
Marshall, AR	870	72650
Marshall, IL	217	62441
Marshall, MI	616	49068–49069
Marshall, MN	507	56258
Marshall, MO	660	65340
Marshall, NC	828	28753
Marshall, TX	903	75670–75672
Marshall, WI	608	53559
Marshalls Creek, PA	570	18335
Marshalltown, IA	641	50158
Marshfield, MA	339, 781	02020, 02041, 02047, 02051*
Marshfield, MO	417	65706
Marshfield, WI	715	54404, 54441, 54449, 54472
Marshville, NC	704, 980	28103
Marstons Mills, MA	508, 774	02648
Martin, SD	605	57551
Martin, TN	731	38237–38238
Martinez, CA	925	94553
Martinez, GA	706, 762	30907
Martins Ferry, OH	740	43935
Martinsburg, WV	304	25401–25402
Martinsdale, MT	406	59053
Martinsville, IN	765	46151
Martinsville, VA	276	24112–24115
Maryland Heights, MO	314	63043
Marylhurst, OR	503, 971	97036
Marysville, CA	530	95901–95903
Marysville, KS	785	66508, 66555
Marysville, MI	810	48040
Marysville, OH	937	43040–43041
Marysville, PA	717	17053
Marysville, WA	360	98270–98271
Maryville, IL	618	62062
Maryville, MO	660	64468
Maryville, TN	865	37801–37804
Mascot, TN	865	37806
Mashantucket, CT	860	06339
Mashpee, MA	508, 774	02649
Mason, MI	517	48854
Mason, OH	513	45040
Mason, TX	915	76856
Mason City, IA	641	50401–50402, 50467
Maspeth, NY	347, 718	11378
Massapequa, NY	516	11758
Massena, IA	712	50853
Massena, NY	315	13662
Massillon, OH	234, 330	44646–44648
Matador, TX	806	79244
Matawan, NJ	732, 848	07747
Mather, CA	916	95655
Mathews, LA	985	70375
Mathews, VA	804	23109
Matteson, IL	708	60443
Matthews, NC	704, 980	28104–28106
Mattoon, IL	217	61938
Mattoon, WI	715	54450
Mauldin, SC	864	29662
Maumee, OH	419, 567	43537
Maumelle, AR	501	72113, 72118
Maunaloa, HI	808	96770
Maury, NC	252	28554
Mauston, WI	608	53948
Maxton, NC	910	28364
Maxwell AFB, AL	334	36112–36113
Mayaguez, PR	787, 939	00680–00682
Maybrook, NY	845	12543
Mayersville, MS	662	39113
Mayetta, KS	785	66509
Mayfield, KY	270	42066
Mayfield, PA	570	18433
Mayfield Heights, OH	440	44124
Mayfield Village, OH	440	44143
Mayhill, NM	505	88339
Maynard, IA	563	50655
Maynard, MA	351, 978	01754
Maynardville, TN	865	37807
Mayo, FL	386	32066
Mayport, FL	904	32227–32228
Mays Landing, NJ	609	08330
Maysville, KY	606	41056
Maysville, MO	816	64469
Mayville, NY	716	14757
Mayville, ND	701	58257
Mayville, WI	920	53050
Maywood, CA	323	90270
Maywood, IL	708	60153–60155
Maywood, NE	308	69038
Maywood, NJ	201, 551	07607
Mazama, WA	509	98833
Mazomanie, WI	608	53560
McAdenville, NC	704, 980	28101
McAfee, NJ	862, 973	07428
McAlester, OK	918	74501–74502
McAllen, TX	956	78501–78505
McArthur, OH	740	45651
McBee, SC	843	29101
McCall, ID	208	83635–83638
McCalla, AL	205	35111
McCaysville, GA	706, 762	30555
McChord AFB, WA	253	98438–98439, 98499
McClelland, IA	712	51548
McCloud, CA	530	96057
McClusky, ND	701	58463
McComb, MS	601, 769	39648–39649
McComb, OH	419, 567	45858
McConnell AFB, KS	316	67221
McConnellsburg, PA	717	17233
McConnellsville, NY	315	13401
McConnelsville, OH	740	43756
McCook, IL	708	60525
McCook, NE	308	69001
McCordsville, IN	317	46055
McCormick, SC	864	29835
McDermott, OH	740	45652
McDonough, GA	470, 770	30252–30253
McEwen, TN	931	37101
McFarland, WI	608	53558
McGraw, NY	607	13101
McGregor, IA	563	52157
McGregor, MN	218	55760
McGregor, TX	254	76657
McGuire AFB, NJ	609	08641
McHenry, IL	815	60050–60051
McHenry, MD	301	21541
McIntosh, SD	605	57641
McKee, KY	606	40447
McKees Rocks, PA	412, 878	15136
McKeesport, PA	412, 878	15130
McKenzie, TN	731	38201
McKinleyville, CA	707	95519–95521
McKinney, TX	469, 972	75069–75071
McLean, TX	806	79057
McLean, VA	571, 703	22101–22106
McLeansboro, IL	618	62859
McLeansville, NC	336	27301
McLeod, MT	406	59052
McLoud, OK	405	74851
McLouth, KS	913	66054
McMinnville, OR	503, 971	97128
McMinnville, TN	931	37110–37111
McMurray, PA	724, 878	15317
McPherson, KS	620	67460
McRae, GA	229	31055
McShan, AL	205	35471
McSherrystown, PA	717	17344
Mead, WA	509	99021
Meade, KS	620	67864
Meadow Lands, PA	724, 878	15347
Meadowbrook, PA	215, 267	19046
Meadville, MS	601, 769	39653
Meadville, PA	814	16335, 16388
Mebane, NC	919	27302
Mechanicsburg, IL	217	62545
Mechanicsburg, PA	717	17050, 17055
Mechanicsville, VA	804	23111, 23116
Mechanicville, NY	518	12118
Medaryville, IN	219	47957
Medfield, MA	508, 774	02052
Medford, MA	339, 781	02153–02156
Medford, NJ	609	08055
Medford, NY	631	11763
Medford, OK	580	73759
Medford, OR	541	97501–97504
Medford, WI	715	54451
Media, PA	484, 610	19037, 19063–19065*
Medical Lake, WA	509	99022
Medicine Lake, MT	406	59247
Medicine Lodge, KS	620	67104
Medina, MN	763	55340, 55357–55359
Medina, NY	585	14103
Medina, OH	234, 330	44215, 44256–44258
Medley, FL	305, 786	33166, 33178
Medora, ND	701	58645
Medway, MA	508, 774	02053
Meeker, CO	970	81641
Mehoopany, PA	570	18629
Melba, ID	208	83641
Melbourne, AR	870	72556
Melbourne, FL	321	32901–32912, 32919, 32934*
Melbourne Beach, FL	321	32951
Melfa, VA	757	23410
Melrose, MA	339, 781	02176–02177
Melrose, MN	320	56352
Melrose Park, IL	708	60160–60165
Melrose Park, PA	215, 267	19027
Melville, NY	516, 631	11747, 11775
Melvin, IL	217	60952
Melvindale, MI	313	48122
Memphis, MO	660	63555
Memphis, TN	901	37501, 38101–38152*
Memphis, TX	806	79245
Mena, AR	479	71953
Menahga, MN	218	56464
Menan, ID	208	83434
Menard, IL	618	62259
Menard, TX	915	76859
Menasha, WI	920	54952
Mendenhall, MS	601, 769	39114
Mendham, NJ	862, 973	07945
Mendocino, CA	707	95460
Mendon, IL	217	62351
Mendon, MA	508, 774	01756
Mendota, CA	559	93640
Mendota, IL	815	61342
Mendota Heights, MN	651	55118–55120
Menlo, GA	706, 762	30731
Menlo Park, CA	650	94025–94029
Menominee, MI	906	49858
Menomonee Falls, WI	262	53051–53052
Menomonie, WI	715	54751
Mentone, CA	909	92359
Mentone, IN	574	46539
Mentone, TX	915	79754
Mentor, OH	440	44060–44061
Mequon, WI	262	53092, 53097
Merced, CA	209	95340–95344, 95348
Mercedes, TX	956	78570
Mercer, PA	724, 878	16137
Mercer Island, WA	206	98040
Mercersburg, PA	717	17236

*Partial list of zip codes, including main range

City	Area Code(s)	Zip Code(s)
Mercerville, NJ	609	08619
Meredith, NH	603	03253
Meriden, CT	203	06450–06454
Meridian, GA	912	31319
Meridian, ID	208	83642, 83680
Meridian, MS	601, 769	39301–39309
Meridian, TX	254	76665
Merion, PA	484, 610	19066
Merkel, TX	915	79536
Merriam, KS	913	66202–66204
Merrick, NY	516	11566
Merrifield, VA	571, 703	22081–22082, 22116–22120
Merrill, MI	989	48637
Merrill, WI	715	54452
Merrillville, IN	219	46410–46411
Merrimac, MA	351, 978	01860
Merrimac, WI	608	53561
Merrimack, NH	603	03054
Merritt Island, FL	321	32952–32954
Mertzon, TX	915	76941
Mertztown, PA	484, 610	19539
Mesa, AZ	480	85201–85216, 85274–85277
Mesa Verde National Park, CO	970	81330
Mesilla Park, NM	505	88047
Mesquite, NV	702	89024–89027
Mesquite, TX	469, 972	75149–75150, 75180–75187
Metairie, LA	504	70001–70011, 70033, 70055*
Metamora, IL	309	61548
Metcalf, GA	229	31792
Methuen, MA	351, 978	01844
Metlakatla, AK	907	99926
Metropolis, IL	618	62960
Metter, GA	912	30439
Metuchen, NJ	732, 848	08840
Mexia, TX	254	76667
Mexico, MO	573	65265
Mexico, NY	315	13114
Meyersdale, PA	814	15552
Miami, FL	305, 786	33010–33018, 33054–33056*
Miami, OK	918	74354–74355
Miami, TX	806	79059
Miami Beach, FL	305, 786	33109, 33119, 33139, 33141*
Miami Lakes, FL	305, 786	33014–33018
Miami Shores, FL	305, 786	33138, 33150–33153*
Miami Springs, FL	305, 786	33166, 33266
Miamisburg, OH	937	45342–45343
Micanopy, FL	352	32667
Micaville, NC	828	28755
Michigan City, IN	219	46360–46361
Middle Granville, NY	518	12849
Middle Island, NY	631	11953
Middle River, MD	410	21220
Middle Village, NY	347, 718	11379
Middleboro, MA	508, 774	02344–02349
Middlebourne, WV	304	26149
Middleburg, PA	570	17842
Middleburg, VA	540	20117–20118
Middleburg Heights, OH	440	44130
Middlebury, CT	203	06762
Middlebury, IN	574	46540
Middlebury, VT	802	05753
Middlefield, CT	860	06455
Middlefield, OH	440	44062
Middleport, NY	585	14105
Middlesboro, KY	606	40965
Middlesex, NJ	732, 848	08846
Middleton, MA	351, 978	01949
Middleton, NH	603	03887
Middleton, WI	608	53562
Middletown, CA	707	95461
Middletown, CT	860	06457–06459
Middletown, DE	302	19709
Middletown, NJ	732, 848	07748
Middletown, NY	845	10940–10943
Middletown, OH	513	45042–45044
Middletown, PA	717	17057
Middletown, RI	401	02840–02842
Middletown, VA	540	22645, 22649
Midland, GA	706, 762	31820
Midland, MI	989	48640–48642, 48667–48670*
Midland, NC	704, 980	28107
Midland, TX	915	79701–79712
Midland, VA	540	22728
Midland Park, NJ	201, 551	07432
Midlothian, IL	708	60445
Midlothian, TX	469, 972	76065
Midlothian, VA	804	23112–23114
Midvale, UT	801	84047
Midway, FL	850	32343
Midway, GA	912	31320
Midway, KY	859	40347
Midway, UT	435	84049
Midwest City, OK	405	73110, 73130, 73140, 73145
Mifflinburg, PA	570	17844
Mifflintown, PA	717	17059
Milaca, MN	320	56353
Milan, GA	229	31060
Milan, IL	309	61264
Milan, MI	734	48160
Milan, MO	660	63556
Milan, OH	419, 567	44846
Milan, TN	731	38358
Milbank, SD	605	57252–57253
Milbridge, ME	207	04658
Miles City, MT	406	59301
Milford, CT	203	06460
Milford, DE	302	19963
Milford, IN	574	46542
Milford, IA	712	51351
Milford, MA	508, 774	01757
Milford, MI	248, 947	48380–48381
Milford, NE	402	68405
Milford, NH	603	03055
Milford, OH	513	45150
Milford, PA	570	18337
Mililani, HI	808	96789
Mill City, OR	503, 971	97360
Mill Run, PA	724, 878	15464
Mill Valley, CA	415	94941–94942
Millboro, VA	540	24460
Millbrae, CA	650	94030–94031
Millbrook, NY	845	12545
Millburn, NJ	862, 973	07041
Millbury, MA	508, 774	01527, 01586
Millbury, OH	419, 567	43447
Milldale, CT	860	06467
Milledgeville, GA	478	31059–31062
Millen, GA	478	30442
Miller, SD	605	57362
Millersburg, OH	234, 330	44654
Millersburg, PA	717	17061
Millersville, MD	410	21108
Millersville, PA	717	17551
Millersville, TN	615	37072
Millerton, NY	518	12546
Milligan College, TN	423	37682
Millington, TN	901	38053–38055, 38083
Millinocket, ME	207	04462
Millis, MA	508, 774	02054
Mills, WY	307	82604, 82644
Millville, NJ	856	08332
Millwood, VA	540	22646
Milpitas, CA	408	95035–95036
Milroy, IN	765	46156
Milton, FL	850	32570–32572, 32583
Milton, MA	617, 857	02186
Milton, NY	845	12547
Milton, PA	570	17847
Milton, WV	304	25541
Milton, WI	608	53563
Milton-Freewater, OR	541	97862
Milwaukee, WI	414	53201–53228, 53233–53237*
Milwaukie, OR	503, 971	97222, 97267–97269
Minden, LA	318	71055–71058
Minden, NE	308	68959
Minden, NV	775	89423
Mineola, NY	516	11501
Mineral, CA	530	96061–96063
Mineral Point, MO	573	63660
Mineral Wells, TX	940	76067–76068
Mineral Wells, WV	304	26120–26121, 26150
Minersville, PA	570	17954
Minerva, OH	234, 330	44657
Mineville, NY	518	12956
Mingo Junction, OH	740	43938
Minneapolis, KS	785	67467
Minneapolis, MN	612, 763, 952	55401–55450, 55454–55460*
Minnesota Lake, MN	507	56068
Minnetonka, MN	763, 952	55305, 55343–55345
Minnewaukan, ND	701	58351
Minonk, IL	309	61760
Minooka, IL	815	60447
Minot, ND	701	58701–58707, 58768
Minot AFB, ND	701	58704–58705
Minster, OH	419, 567	45865
Mio, MI	989	48647
Mira Loma, CA	951	91752
Miramar, FL	754, 954	33023–33029, 33083
Misenheimer, NC	704, 980	28109
Mishawaka, IN	574	46544–46546
Mishicot, WI	920	54228
Mission, KS	913	66201–66205, 66222
Mission, SD	605	57555
Mission, TX	956	78572–78573
Mission Hills, CA	818	91345–91346, 91395
Mission Viejo, CA	949	92675, 92690–92694
Mission Woods, KS	913	66205
Mississippi State, MS	662	39762
Missoula, MT	406	59801–59808, 59812
Missouri City, TX	281, 832	77459, 77489
Mitchell, IN	812	47446
Mitchell, NE	308	69357
Mitchell, SD	605	57301
Mitchells, VA	540	22729
Mitchellville, IA	515	50169
Mitchellville, MD	301	20716–20717, 20721
Moab, UT	435	84532
Moberly, MO	660	65270
Mobile, AL	251	36601–36633, 36640–36644*
Mocksville, NC	336	27028
Model City, NY	716	14107
Modesto, CA	209	95350–95358, 95397
Moffett Field, CA	650	94035
Mogadore, OH	234, 330	44260
Mohall, ND	701	58761
Mohawk, NY	315	13407
Mohnton, PA	484, 610	19540
Mojave, CA	661	93501–93502, 93519
Mokena, IL	708	60448
Molalla, OR	503, 971	97038
Moline, IL	309	61265–61266
Monaca, PA	724, 878	15061
Monahans, TX	915	79756
Monarch, CO	719	81227
Moncks Corner, SC	843	29430, 29461
Mondovi, WI	715	54755, 54764
Monee, IL	708	60449
Monessen, PA	724, 878	15062
Monett, MO	417	65708
Monitor, WA	509	98836
Monmouth, IL	309	61462
Monmouth, OR	503, 971	97361
Monmouth Junction, NJ	732, 848	08852
Monona, IA	563	52159
Monongahela, PA	724, 878	15063
Monroe, CT	203	06468
Monroe, GA	470, 770	30655–30656
Monroe, IA	641	50170
Monroe, LA	318	71201–71203, 71207–71213
Monroe, MI	734	48161–48162
Monroe, NC	704, 980	28110–28112
Monroe, OH	513	45050, 45073, 45099
Monroe, WA	360	98272
Monroe, WI	608	53566
Monroe Township, NJ	609	08831
Monroeville, AL	251	36460–36462
Monroeville, PA	412, 878	15140, 15146
Monrovia, CA	626	91016–91017
Monsey, NY	845	10952
Mont Alto, PA	717	17237
Montague, MI	231	49437
Montague, TX	940	76251
Montauk, NY	631	11954

Partial list of zip codes, including main range

City	Area Code(s)	Zip Code(s)
Montclair, CA	909	91763
Montclair, NJ	862, 973	07042–07043
Monte Vista, CO	719	81135, 81144
Montebello, CA	323	90640
Montebello, NY	845	10901
Montecito, CA	805	93108, 93150
Montello, WI	608	53949
Monterey, CA	831	93940–93944
Monterey, VA	540	24465
Monterey Park, CA	323, 626	91754–91756
Montesano, WA	360	98563
Montevallo, AL	205	35115
Montevideo, MN	320	56265
Montezuma, IA	641	50171
Montezuma, KS	620	67867
Montgomery, AL	334	36101–36125, 36130–36135*
Montgomery, IL	331, 630	60538
Montgomery, NY	845	12549
Montgomery, PA	570	17752
Montgomery, TX	936	77316, 77356
Montgomery, WV	304	25136
Montgomery City, MO	573	63361
Montgomery Village, MD	301	20877–20879, 20886
Montgomeryville, PA	215, 267	18936
Monticello, AR	870	71655–71657
Monticello, FL	850	32344–32345
Monticello, GA	706, 762	31064
Monticello, IL	217	61856
Monticello, IN	574	47960
Monticello, IA	319	52310
Monticello, KY	606	42633
Monticello, MN	763	55362–55365, 55561–55565*
Monticello, MS	601, 769	39654
Monticello, MO	573	63457
Monticello, NY	845	12701, 12777
Monticello, UT	435	84535
Montour Falls, NY	607	14865
Montoursville, PA	570	17754
Montpelier, IN	765	47359
Montpelier, OH	419, 567	43543
Montpelier, VT	802	05601–05604, 05609, 05620*
Montreat, NC	828	28757
Montrose, CA	818	91020–91021
Montrose, CO	970	81401–81402
Montrose, MI	810	48457
Montrose, NY	845	10548
Montrose, PA	570	18801
Montross, VA	804	22520
Montvale, NJ	201, 551	07645
Montville, NJ	862, 973	07045
Monument, OR	541	97864
Moodus, CT	860	06469
Moody, AL	205	35004
Moon Township, PA	412, 878	15108
Moonachie, NJ	201, 551	07074
Moore, OK	405	73153, 73160, 73170
Moore Haven, FL	863	33471
Moorefield, WV	304	26836
Moorestown, NJ	856	08057
Mooresville, IN	317	46158
Mooresville, NC	704, 980	28115–28117
Moorhead, MN	218	56560–56563
Moorhead, MS	662	38761
Moorpark, CA	805	93020–93021
Moose, WY	307	83012
Moose Lake, MN	218	55767
Mooseheart, IL	331, 630	60539
Moosic, PA	570	18507
Moosup, CT	860	06354
Mora, MN	320	55051
Mora, NM	505	87732
Moraga, CA	925	94556, 94570, 94575
Moran, WY	307	83013
Moravia, NY	315	13118
Morehead, KY	606	40351
Morehead City, NC	252	28557
Morenci, AZ	928	85540
Morenci, MI	517	49256
Moreno Valley, CA	951	92551–92557
Morgan, GA	229	31766
Morgan, MN	507	56266
Morgan, UT	801	84050
Morgan City, LA	985	70380–70381
Morgan Hill, CA	408	95037–95038
Morganfield, KY	270	42437
Morganton, NC	828	28655, 28680
Morgantown, KY	270	42261
Morgantown, PA	484, 610	19543
Morgantown, WV	304	26501–26508
Moro, OR	541	97039
Moroni, UT	435	84646
Morrilton, AR	501	72110
Morris, AL	205	35116
Morris, IL	815	60450
Morris, MN	320	56267
Morris Plains, NJ	862, 973	07950
Morrison, CO	303, 720	80465
Morrison, IL	815	61270
Morristown, IN	765	46161
Morristown, NJ	862, 973	07960–07963
Morristown, OH	740	43759
Morristown, TN	423	37813–37816
Morrisville, NY	315	13408
Morrisville, NC	919	27560
Morrisville, PA	215, 267	19067
Morrisville, VT	802	05657, 05661
Morro Bay, CA	805	93442–93443
Morrow, GA	470, 770	30260, 30287
Morton, IL	309	61550
Morton, MN	507	56270
Morton, MS	601, 769	39117
Morton, TX	806	79346
Morton Grove, IL	224, 847	60053
Mosca, CO	719	81146
Moscow, ID	208	83843–83844
Moscow, TN	901	38057
Moselle, MS	601, 769	39459
Moses Lake, WA	509	98837
Mosinee, WI	715	54455
Mosquero, NM	505	87733
Moss Beach, CA	650	94038
Moss Landing, CA	831	95039
Moss Point, MS	228	39562–39563, 39581
Motley, MN	218	56466
Mott, ND	701	58646
Moulton, AL	256	35650
Moultrie, GA	229	31768, 31776
Mound City, IL	618	62963
Mound City, KS	913	66056
Mound City, SD	605	57646
Moundridge, KS	620	67107
Mounds View, MN	763	55112
Moundsville, WV	304	26041
Mount Airy, NC	336	27030–27031
Mount Angel, OR	503, 971	97362
Mount Arlington, NJ	862, 973	07856
Mount Ayr, IA	641	50854
Mount Berry, GA	706, 762	30149
Mount Carmel, IL	618	62863
Mount Carmel, PA	570	17851
Mount Carroll, IL	815	61053
Mount Clemens, MI	586	48043–48046
Mount Crawford, VA	540	22841
Mount Crested Butte, CO	970	81225
Mount Dora, FL	352	32756–32757
Mount Freedom, NJ	862, 973	07970
Mount Gay, WV	304	25637
Mount Gilead, NC	910	27306
Mount Gilead, OH	419, 567	43338
Mount Holly, NJ	609	08060
Mount Holly, NC	704, 980	28120
Mount Hope, OH	234, 330	44660
Mount Ida, AR	870	71957
Mount Jackson, VA	540	22842
Mount Joy, PA	717	17552
Mount Juliet, TN	615	37121–37122
Mount Kisco, NY	914	10549
Mount Laurel, NJ	856	08054
Mount Lebanon, PA	412, 878	15228
Mount Marion, NY	845	12456
Mount Meigs, AL	334	36057
Mount Morris, IL	815	61054
Mount Morris, NY	585	14510
Mount Olive, MS	601, 769	39119
Mount Olive, NJ	862, 973	07828
Mount Olive, NC	919	28365
Mount Olive, WV	304	25185
Mount Olivet, KY	606	41064
Mount Pleasant, IA	319	52641
Mount Pleasant, MI	989	48804, 48858–48859
Mount Pleasant, NC	704, 980	28124
Mount Pleasant, PA	724, 878	15666
Mount Pleasant, SC	843	29464–29466
Mount Pleasant, TN	931	38474
Mount Pleasant, TX	903	75455–75456
Mount Pocono, PA	570	18344
Mount Prospect, IL	224, 847	60056
Mount Pulaski, IL	217	62548
Mount Royal, NJ	856	08061
Mount Shasta, CA	530	96067
Mount Solon, VA	540	22843
Mount Sterling, IL	217	62353
Mount Sterling, KY	859	40353
Mount Sterling, OH	740	43143
Mount Vernon, AL	251	36560
Mount Vernon, GA	912	30445
Mount Vernon, IL	618	62864
Mount Vernon, IN	812	47620
Mount Vernon, IA	319	52314
Mount Vernon, KY	606	40456
Mount Vernon, MO	417	65712
Mount Vernon, NY	914	10550–10553, 10557–10558
Mount Vernon, OH	740	43050
Mount Vernon, TX	903	75457
Mount Vernon, VA	571, 703	22121
Mount Vernon, WA	360	98273–98274
Mount Washington, KY	502	40047
Mount Wolf, PA	717	17347
Mountain City, TN	423	37683
Mountain Grove, MO	417	65711
Mountain Home, AR	870	72653–72654
Mountain Home, ID	208	83647
Mountain Home, TN	423	37684
Mountain Home AFB, ID	208	83648
Mountain Lakes, NJ	862, 973	07046
Mountain Pass, CA	760	92366
Mountain Pine, AR	501	71956
Mountain Top, PA	570	18707
Mountain View, AR	870	72533, 72560
Mountain View, CA	650	94035, 94039–94043
Mountain View, MO	417	65548
Mountain View, WY	307	82939
Mountainair, NM	505	87036
Mountainside, NJ	908	07092
Mountlake Terrace, WA	425	98043
Moville, IA	712	51039
Moxee, WA	509	98936
Muenster, TX	940	76252
Mukilteo, WA	425	98275
Mukwonago, WI	262	53149
Mulberry, FL	863	33860
Muleshoe, TX	806	79347
Mullen, NE	308	69152
Mullica Hill, NJ	856	08062
Muncie, IN	765	47302–47308
Muncy, PA	570	17756
Mundelein, IL	224, 847	60060
Munfordville, KY	270	42765
Munhall, PA	412, 878	15120
Munising, MI	906	49862
Munroe Falls, OH	234, 330	44262
Munster, IN	219	46321
Murdo, SD	605	57559
Murdock, NE	402	68407
Murfreesboro, AR	870	71958
Murfreesboro, NC	252	27855
Murfreesboro, TN	615	37127–37133
Murphy, ID	208	83650
Murphy, NC	828	28906
Murphysboro, IL	618	62966
Murray, KY	270	42071
Murray, UT	801	84107, 84117, 84121, 84123*
Murray Hill, NJ	908	07974

Partial list of zip codes, including main range

City	Area Code(s)	Zip Code(s)
Murrells Inlet, SC	843	29576
Murrieta, CA	951	92562–92564
Murrysville, PA	724, 878	15668
Muscatine, IA	563	52761
Muscle Shoals, AL	256	35661–35662
Muskego, WI	262	53150
Muskegon, MI	231	49440–49445
Muskegon Heights, MI	231	49444
Muskogee, OK	918	74401–74403
Mustang, OK	405	73064
Myerstown, PA	717	17067
Myrtle Beach, SC	843	29572–29579, 29587–29588
Mystic, CT	860	06355, 06388

N

City	Area Code(s)	Zip Code(s)
Nacogdoches, TX	936	75961–75965
Nageezi, NM	505	87037
Nags Head, NC	252	27959
Nahunta, GA	912	31553
Naknek, AK	907	99633
Nampa, ID	208	83651–83653, 83686–83687
Nanticoke, MD	410	21840
Nanticoke, PA	570	18634
Nantucket, MA	508, 774	02554, 02564, 02584
Nanuet, NY	845	10954
Napa, CA	707	94558–94559, 94581
Napanoch, NY	845	12458
Naperville, IL	331, 630	60540, 60563–60567
Naples, FL	239	34101–34120
Naples, NY	585	14512
Napoleon, ND	701	58561
Napoleon, OH	419, 567	43545
Napoleonville, LA	985	70390
Nappanee, IN	574	46550
Narberth, PA	484, 610	19072
Narragansett, RI	401	02874, 02879–02882
Naselle, WA	360	98638
Nashotah, WI	262	53058
Nashua, NH	603	03060–03064
Nashville, AR	870	71852
Nashville, GA	229	31639
Nashville, IL	618	62263
Nashville, IN	812	47448
Nashville, NC	252	27856
Nashville, TN	615	37201–37250
Nassau, NY	518	12123
Nassau Bay, TX	281, 832	77058, 77258
Nassawadox, VA	757	23413
Natchez, MS	601, 769	39120–39122
Natchitoches, LA	318	71457–71458, 71497
Nathrop, CO	719	81236
Natick, MA	508, 774	01760
National City, CA	619	91950–91951
Natrona Heights, PA	724, 878	15065
Natural Bridge Station, VA	540	24579
Naugatuck, CT	203	06770
Navarre, MN	952	55392
Navarre, OH	234, 330	44662
Navasota, TX	936	77868–77869
Navesink, NJ	732, 848	07752
Nazareth, PA	484, 610	18064
Nebo, NC	828	28761
Nebraska City, NE	402	68410
Nederland, TX	409	77627
Nedrow, NY	315	13120
Needham, MA	339, 781	02492–02494
Needham Heights, MA	339, 781	02494
Neenah, WI	920	54956–54957
Neillsville, WI	715	54456
Neligh, NE	402	68756
Nellis AFB, NV	702	89191
Nelson, NE	402	68961
Nelsonville, OH	740	45764
Neodesha, KS	620	66757
Neosho, MO	417	64850–64853
Nephi, UT	435	84648
Neponset, IL	309	61345
Neptune, NJ	732, 848	07753–07754
Neptune Beach, FL	904	32266
Nespelem, WA	509	99155
Nesquehoning, PA	570	18240
Ness City, KS	785	67560
Netcong, NJ	862, 973	07857
Nettleton, MS	662	38858
Nevada, IA	515	50201
Nevada, MO	417	64772
Nevada City, CA	530	95959
Neversink, NY	845	12765
New Albany, IN	812	47150–47151
New Albany, MS	662	38652
New Albany, OH	614	43054
New Augusta, MS	601, 769	39462
New Baltimore, MI	586	48047, 48051
New Bedford, MA	508, 774	02740–02746
New Berlin, NY	607	13411
New Berlin, WI	262	53146, 53151
New Bern, NC	252	28560–28564
New Bethlehem, PA	814	16242
New Bloomfield, PA	717	17068
New Boston, TX	903	75570
New Braunfels, TX	830	78130–78135
New Bremen, OH	419, 567	45869
New Brighton, MN	651	55112
New Brighton, PA	724, 878	15066
New Britain, CT	860	06050–06053
New Brunswick, NJ	732, 848	08901–08906, 08922, 08933*
New Canaan, CT	203	06840–06842
New Carlisle, IN	574	46552
New Carlisle, OH	937	45344
New Castle, CO	970	81647
New Castle, DE	302	19720–19721
New Castle, IN	765	47362
New Castle, KY	502	40050
New Castle, PA	724, 878	16101–16108
New Castle, VA	540	24127
New Century, KS	913	66031
New City, NY	845	10956
New Columbia, PA	570	17856
New Concord, OH	740	43762
New Cumberland, PA	717	17070
New Cumberland, WV	304	26047
New England, ND	701	58647
New Enterprise, PA	814	16664
New Era, MI	231	49446
New Fairfield, CT	203	06812
New Freedom, PA	717	17349
New Glarus, WI	608	53574
New Gretna, NJ	609	08224
New Hampton, IA	641	50659–50661
New Hampton, NY	845	10958
New Harbor, ME	207	04554, 04558
New Hartford, CT	860	06057
New Hartford, NY	315	13413
New Haven, CT	203	06501–06525, 06530–06540
New Haven, IN	260	46774
New Haven, MI	586	48048–48050
New Hill, NC	919	27562
New Holland, PA	717	17557
New Hope, MN	763	55427–55428
New Hope, PA	215, 267	18938
New Hyde Park, NY	516	11040–11044, 11099
New Iberia, LA	337	70560–70563
New Kensington, PA	724, 878	15068–15069
New Kent, VA	804	23124
New Kingstown, PA	717	17072
New Knoxville, OH	419, 567	45871
New Lebanon, NY	518	12125
New Lenox, IL	815	60451
New Lexington, OH	740	43764
New Lisbon, NJ	609	08064
New Lisbon, WI	608	53950
New London, CT	860	06320
New London, IA	319	52645
New London, MO	573	63459
New London, NH	603	03257
New London, OH	419, 567	44851
New London, WI	920	54961
New Madrid, MO	573	63869
New Market, VA	540	22844
New Martinsville, WV	304	26155
New Milford, CT	860	06776
New Milford, NJ	201, 551	07646
New Orleans, LA	504	70112–70131, 70139–70190*
New Oxford, PA	717	17350
New Paltz, NY	845	12561
New Paris, IN	574	46553
New Philadelphia, OH	234, 330	44663
New Port Richey, FL	727	34652–34656
New Providence, NJ	908	07974
New Richmond, OH	513	45157
New Richmond, WI	715	54017
New Roads, LA	225	70760
New Rochelle, NY	914	10801–10805
New Rockford, ND	701	58356
New Sharon, IA	641	50207
New Smyrna Beach, FL	386	32168–32170
New Springfield, OH	234, 330	44443
New Tazewell, TN	423	37824–37825
New Town, ND	701	58763
New Ulm, MN	507	56073
New Wilmington, PA	724, 878	16142, 16172
New Windsor, MD	410	21776
New Windsor, NY	845	12553
New York, NY	212, 646, 917	10001–10048, 10055, 10060*
New York Mills, MN	218	56567
New York Mills, NY	315	13417
Newark, CA	510	94560
Newark, DE	302	19702, 19711–19718*
Newark, NJ	862, 973	07101–07108, 07112–07114*
Newark, NY	315	14513
Newark, OH	740	43055–43058, 43093
Newaygo, MI	231	49337
Newberg, OR	503, 971	97132
Newberry, MI	906	49868
Newberry, SC	803	29108
Newburg, WI	262	53060
Newburgh, IN	812	47629–47630
Newburgh, NY	845	12550–12555
Newbury, OH	440	44065
Newbury Park, CA	805	91319–91320
Newburyport, MA	351, 978	01950–01951
Newcastle, WY	307	82701, 82715
Newcomerstown, OH	740	43832
Newell, SD	605	57760
Newell, WV	304	26050
Newfane, VT	802	05345
Newhall, CA	661	91321–91322, 91381–91382
Newington, CT	860	06111, 06131
Newington, NH	603	03801
Newington, VA	571, 703	22122
Newkirk, OK	580	74647
Newland, NC	828	28657
Newman Grove, NE	402	68758
Newnan, GA	470, 678, 770	30263–30265, 30271
Newport, AR	870	72112
Newport, DE	302	19804
Newport, IN	765	47966
Newport, KY	859	41071–41076, 41099
Newport, MN	651	55055
Newport, NH	603	03773
Newport, NC	252	28570
Newport, OR	541	97365–97366
Newport, RI	401	02840–02841
Newport, TN	423	37821–37822
Newport, VT	802	05855
Newport, WA	509	99156
Newport Beach, CA	949	92657–92663
Newport News, VA	757	23600–23612, 23628
Newton, GA	229	31770
Newton, IL	618	62448
Newton, IA	641	50208
Newton, KS	316	67114–67117
Newton, MA	617, 857	02456–02468, 02495
Newton, NJ	862, 973	07860
Newton, NC	828	28658
Newton, TX	409	75966
Newton Center, MA	617, 857	02459
Newton Falls, OH	234, 330	44444
Newton Grove, NC	910	28366
Newton Upper Falls, MA	617, 857	02464
Newtonville, NY	518	12110, 12128
Newtown, CT	203	06470

Partial list of zip codes, including main range

City	Area Code(s)	Zip Code(s)
Newtown, PA	215, 267	18940
Newtown Square, PA	484, 610	19073
Nezperce, ID	208	83543
Niagara Falls, NY	716	14301–14305
Niagara University, NY	716	14109
Niantic, CT	860	06357
Niceville, FL	850	32578, 32588
Nicholasville, KY	859	40340, 40356
Niles, IL	224, 847	60714
Niles, MI	616	49120–49121
Niles, OH	234, 330	44446
Ninety Six, SC	864	29666
Niota, TN	423	37826
Nipomo, CA	805	93444
Niskayuna, NY	518	12309
Nisswa, MN	218	56468
Nixon, TX	830	78140
Noble, OK	405	73068
Noblesville, IN	317	46060–46061
Nocona, TX	940	76255
Nogales, AZ	520	85621, 85628, 85648, 85662
Nokomis, FL	941	34274–34275
Nome, AK	907	99762
Norco, CA	951	92860
Norcross, GA	470, 678, 770	30003, 30010, 30071, 30091*
Norfolk, CT	860	06058
Norfolk, MA	508, 774	02056
Norfolk, NE	402	68701–68702
Norfolk, VA	757	23500–23523, 23529–23530*
Normal, AL	256	35762
Normal, IL	309	61761, 61790
Norman, OK	405	73019, 73026, 73069, 73072
Norridge, IL	708	60634, 60656, 60706
Norristown, PA	484, 610	19401–19409, 19488–19489
North Adams, MA	413	01247
North Amityville, NY	631	11701
North Andover, MA	351, 978	01845
North Anson, ME	207	04958
North Attleboro, MA	508, 774	02760–02763
North Augusta, SC	803	29841–29842, 29860–29861
North Aurora, IL	331, 630	60542
North Babylon, NY	631	11703
North Baltimore, OH	419, 567	45872
North Barrington, IL	224, 847	60010
North Bay Village, FL	305, 786	33141
North Bend, OR	541	97459
North Bend, WA	425	98045
North Bergen, NJ	201, 551	07047
North Berwick, ME	207	03906
North Billerica, MA	351, 978	01862
North Branch, MN	651	55056
North Branch, NJ	908	08876
North Branford, CT	203	06471
North Brookfield, MA	508, 774	01535
North Brunswick, NJ	732, 848	08902
North Canton, OH	234, 330	44709, 44720
North Charleston, SC	843	29405–29406, 29410, 29415*
North Chelmsford, MA	351, 978	01863
North Chicago, IL	224, 847	60064, 60086–60088
North Chili, NY	585	14514
North Clarendon, VT	802	05759
North Conway, NH	603	03860
North Dartmouth, MA	508, 774	02747
North Dighton, MA	508, 774	02764
North East, MD	410	21901
North East, PA	814	16428
North Easton, MA	508, 774	02356–02357
North Falmouth, MA	508, 774	02556, 02565
North Fort Myers, FL	239	33903, 33917–33918
North Grafton, MA	508, 774	01536
North Grosvenordale, CT	860	06255
North Haledon, NJ	862, 973	07508, 07538
North Haven, CT	203	06473
North Haverhill, NH	603	03774
North Hero, VT	802	05474
North Highlands, CA	916	95660
North Hills, CA	818	91343, 91393
North Hollywood, CA	818	91601–91618
North Huntingdon, PA	724, 878	15642
North Judson, IN	574	46366
North Kansas City, MO	816	64116

City	Area Code(s)	Zip Code(s)
North Kingstown, RI	401	02852–02854, 02874
North Kingsville, OH	440	44068
North Lake, WI	262	53064
North Las Vegas, NV	702	89030–89036, 89084–89086
North Liberty, IA	319	52317
North Lima, OH	234, 330	44452
North Little Rock, AR	501	72113–72120, 72124, 72190*
North Logan, UT	435	84341
North Manchester, IN	260	46962
North Mankato, MN	507	56002–56003
North Miami, FL	305, 786	33161–33162, 33167–33169*
North Miami Beach, FL	305, 786	33160–33162, 33169, 33179*
North Monmouth, ME	207	04265
North Myrtle Beach, SC	843	29582, 29597–29598
North Newton, KS	316	67117
North Olmsted, OH	440	44070
North Palm Beach, FL	561	33403, 33408–33410
North Pekin, IL	309	61554
North Plains, OR	503, 971	97133
North Platte, NE	308	69101–69103
North Providence, RI	401	02904, 02908–02911
North Quincy, MA	617, 857	02171
North Redington Beach, FL	727	33708
North Richland Hills, TX	682, 817	76118, 76180–76182
North Ridgeville, OH	440	44035, 44039
North Riverside, IL	708	60546
North Royalton, OH	440	44133
North Saint Paul, MN	651	55109
North Salt Lake, UT	801	84054
North Scituate, RI	401	02857
North Sioux City, SD	605	57049
North Smithfield, RI	401	02824, 02896
North Springfield, VT	802	05150
North Stonington, CT	860	06359
North Syracuse, NY	315	13212
North Tonawanda, NY	716	14120
North Vernon, IN	812	47265
North Versailles, PA	412, 878	15137
North Wales, PA	215, 267	19436, 19454–19455
North Warren, PA	814	16365
North Webster, IN	574	46555
North White Plains, NY	914	10603
North Wilkesboro, NC	336	28656–28659, 28674
Northampton, MA	413	01060–01063
Northampton, PA	484, 610	18067
Northborough, MA	508, 774	01532
Northbrook, IL	224, 847	60062–60065
Northeast Harbor, ME	207	04662
Northfield, IL	224, 847	60093
Northfield, MN	507	55057
Northfield, NJ	609	08225
Northfield, OH	234, 330	44056, 44067
Northfield, VT	802	05663
Northford, CT	203	06472
Northlake, IL	708	60164
Northport, AL	205	35473–35476
Northport, NY	631	11768
Northridge, CA	818	91324–91330, 91343
Northumberland, PA	570	17857
Northvale, NJ	201, 551	07647
Northville, MI	248	48167
Northwood, IA	641	50459
Northwood, OH	419, 567	43605, 43619
Norton, KS	785	67654
Norton, MA	508, 774	02766
Norton, OH	234, 330	44203
Norton, VA	276	24273
Norton Shores, MI	231	49441
Norwalk, CA	562	90650–90652, 90659
Norwalk, CT	203	06850–06860
Norwalk, OH	419, 567	44857
Norway, IA	319	52318
Norwell, MA	339, 781	02018, 02061
Norwich, CT	860	06351, 06360, 06365
Norwich, KS	620	67118
Norwich, NY	607	13815
Norwich, OH	740	43767
Norwood, MA	339, 781	02062
Norwood, MN	952	55368, 55383, 55554, 55583
Norwood, NJ	201, 551	07648
Norwood, NC	704, 980	28128

City	Area Code(s)	Zip Code(s)
Norwood, OH	513	45207, 45212
Notre Dame, IN	574	46556
Nottingham, PA	484, 610	19362
Nottoway, VA	434	23955
Novato, CA	415	94945–94949, 94998
Novi, MI	248, 947	48374–48377
Nowata, OK	918	74048
Nucla, CO	970	81424
Nuevo, CA	951	92567
Nutley, NJ	862, 973	07110
Nyack, NY	845	10960
Nyssa, OR	541	97913

O

City	Area Code(s)	Zip Code(s)
O'Fallon, MO	636	63366–63367
O'Neill, NE	402	68763
Oak Brook, IL	331, 630	60521–60523, 60527, 60561
Oak Creek, WI	414	53154
Oak Forest, IL	708	60452
Oak Grove, LA	318	71263
Oak Grove, OR	503, 971	97222, 97267–97268
Oak Grove, VA	804	22443
Oak Harbor, WA	360	98277–98278
Oak Hill, WV	304	25901
Oak Lawn, IL	708	60453–60459
Oak Park, IL	708	60301–60304
Oak Park, MI	248, 947	48237
Oak Ridge, NJ	862, 973	07438
Oak Ridge, TN	865	37830–37831
Oakbrook Terrace, IL	331, 630	60181
Oakdale, CA	209	95361
Oakdale, LA	318	71463
Oakdale, MN	651	55042, 55128
Oakdale, NY	631	11769
Oakdale, PA	412, 878	15071
Oakdale, WI	608	54649
Oakham, MA	508, 774	01068
Oakhurst, CA	559	93644
Oakhurst, NJ	732, 848	07755
Oakland, CA	510	94601–94627, 94643, 94649*
Oakland, MD	301	21550
Oakland, NJ	201, 551	07436
Oakland, TN	901	38060
Oakland City, IN	812	47660
Oakland Park, FL	754, 954	33304–33311, 33334
Oakley, CA	925	94513, 94561
Oakley, KS	785	67748
Oakmont, PA	412, 878	15139
Oaks, PA	484, 610	19456
Oakton, VA	571, 703	22124
Oakville, CA	707	94562
Oakville, IA	319	52646
Oakwood, GA	470, 770	30502, 30566
Oakwood, OH	419, 567	45409, 45419, 45873
Oakwood, VA	276	24631
Oakwood Village, OH	440	44146
Oberlin, KS	785	67749
Oberlin, LA	337	70655
Oberlin, OH	440	44074
Oblong, IL	618	62449
Ocala, FL	352	34470–34483
Ocean, NJ	732, 848	07712
Ocean City, MD	410	21842–21843
Ocean City, NJ	609	08226
Ocean Shores, WA	360	98569
Ocean Springs, MS	228	39564–39566
Oceano, CA	805	93445
Oceanport, NJ	732, 848	07757
Oceanside, CA	760	92049–92058
Oceanside, NY	516	11572
Oceanville, NJ	609	08231
Ochopee, FL	239	34141
Ocilla, GA	229	31774
Ocoee, FL	321, 407	34761
Oconomowoc, WI	262	53066
Oconto, WI	920	54153
Oconto Falls, WI	920	54154
Odenton, MD	410	21113
Odessa, FL	813	33556
Odessa, MO	816	64076

*Partial list of zip codes, including main range

City	Area Code(s)	Zip Code(s)
Odessa, TX	915	79760–79769
Odessa, WA	509	99144, 99159
Odon, IN	812	47562
Odum, GA	912	31555
Oelwein, IA	319	50662
Offutt AFB, NE	402	68113
Ogallala, NE	308	69153
Ogden, UT	801	84201, 84244, 84401, 84415
Ogdensburg, NY	315	13669
Oglesby, IL	815	61348
Oglethorpe, GA	478	31068
Ogunquit, ME	207	03907
Oil City, PA	814	16301
Ojai, CA	805	93023–93024
Ojo Caliente, NM	505	87549
Ojus, FL	305, 786	33163, 33180
Okahumpka, FL	352	34762
Okanogan, WA	509	98840
Okarche, OK	405	73762
Okeechobee, FL	863	34972–34974
Okemah, OK	918	74859
Okemos, MI	517	48805, 48864
Oklahoma City, OK	405	73101–73173, 73177–73180*
Okmulgee, OK	918	74447
Olathe, KS	913	66051, 66061–66063
Old Bethpage, NY	631	11804
Old Bridge, NJ	732, 848	08857
Old Brookville, NY	516	11545–11548
Old Chatham, NY	518	12136
Old Forge, PA	570	18518
Old Fort, NC	828	28762
Old Greenwich, CT	203	06870
Old Hickory, TN	615	37138
Old Lyme, CT	860	06371
Old Orchard Beach, ME	207	04064
Old Saybrook, CT	860	06475
Old Town, ME	207	04468
Old Westbury, NY	516	11568
Oldwick, NJ	908	08858
Olean, NY	585	14760
Olive Branch, MS	662	38654
Olive Hill, KY	606	41164
Olivet, MI	616	49076
Olivet, SD	605	57052
Olivia, MN	320	56277
Olney, IL	618	62450
Olney, MD	301	20830–20832
Olney, TX	940	76374
Olustee, FL	386	32072
Olympia, WA	360	98501–98516, 98599
Olympia Fields, IL	708	60461
Olympic Valley, CA	530	96146
Olyphant, PA	570	18447–18448
Omaha, NE	402	68046, 68101–68147*
Omak, WA	509	98841
Onalaska, WI	608	54650
Onamia, MN	320	56359
Onawa, IA	712	51040
Onaway, MI	989	49765
Oneida, NY	315	13421
Oneida, TN	423	37841
Oneida, WI	920	54155
Oneonta, AL	205	35121
Oneonta, NY	607	13820
Onida, SD	605	57564
Onley, VA	757	23418
Only, TN	931	37140
Onsted, MI	517	49265
Ontario, CA	909	91758–91764, 91798
Ontario, NY	585	14519
Ontario, OR	541	97914
Ontonagon, MI	906	49953
Ooltewah, TN	423	37363
Opa Locka, FL	305, 786	33014, 33054–33056
Opelika, AL	334	36801–36804
Opelousas, LA	337	70570–70571
Opheim, MT	406	59250
Opp, AL	334	36467
Oquawka, IL	309	61469
Oracle, AZ	520	85623
Oradell, NJ	201, 551	07649
Orange, CA	714	92856–92869
Orange, CT	203	06477
Orange, MA	351, 978	01355, 01364, 01378
Orange, NJ	862, 973	07050–07051
Orange, TX	409	77630–77632
Orange, VA	540	22960
Orange Beach, AL	251	36561
Orange City, IA	712	51041
Orange Cove, CA	559	93646, 93675
Orange Park, FL	904	32003–32006, 32065–32067*
Orange Village, OH	216	44022, 44122, 44128, 44146
Orangeburg, NY	845	10962
Orangeburg, SC	803	29115–29118
Orangevale, CA	916	95662
Orchard Lake, MI	248, 947	48323–48324
Orchard Park, NY	716	14127
Ord, NE	308	68862
Ordway, CO	719	81063
Orefield, PA	484, 610	18069
Oregon, IL	815	61061
Oregon, MO	660	64473
Oregon, OH	419, 567	43605, 43616–43618
Oregon, WI	608	53575
Oregon City, OR	503, 971	97045
Orem, UT	801	84057–84059, 84097
Orestes, IN	765	46063
Orient, OH	614	43146
Oriental, NC	252	28571
Orinda, CA	925	94563
Orion, MI	248, 947	48359–48362
Oriskany, NY	315	13424
Orland, CA	530	95963
Orland Park, IL	708	60462, 60467
Orlando, FL	321, 407	32801–32839, 32853–32862*
Orleans, IN	812	47452
Orleans, MA	508, 774	02653
Ormond Beach, FL	386	32173–32176
Orofino, ID	208	83544
Orondo, WA	509	98843
Orono, ME	207	04469, 04473
Orosi, CA	559	93647
Oroville, CA	530	95915, 95940, 95965, 95966*
Orrtanna, PA	717	17353
Orrville, OH	234, 330	44667
Ortonville, MI	248, 947	48462
Ortonville, MN	320	56278
Orwigsburg, PA	570	17961
Osage, IA	641	50454, 50461
Osage Beach, MO	573	65065
Osage City, KS	785	66523
Osawatomie, KS	913	66064
Osborne, KS	785	67473
Osceola, AR	870	72370
Osceola, IA	641	50213
Osceola, MO	417	64776
Osceola, NE	402	68651
Osceola, WI	715	54020
Osceola Mills, PA	814	16666
Oscoda, MI	989	48750
Osgood, IN	812	47037
Osgood, OH	419, 567	45351
Oshkosh, NE	308	69154, 69190
Oshkosh, WI	920	54901–54906
Oskaloosa, IA	641	52577
Oskaloosa, KS	785	66066
Osseo, MN	763	55311, 55369, 55569
Ossining, NY	914	10562
Ossipee, NH	603	03864
Osterville, MA	508, 774	02655
Oswego, IL	331, 630	60543
Oswego, KS	620	67356
Oswego, NY	315	13126
Otisville, NY	845	10963
Otsego, MI	616	49078
Ottawa, IL	815	61350
Ottawa, KS	785	66067
Ottawa, OH	419, 567	45875
Ottawa Lake, MI	734	49267
Otter River, MA	351, 978	01436
Otter Rock, OR	541	97369
Ottsville, PA	484, 610	18942
Ottumwa, IA	641	52501
Ouray, CO	970	81427
Overland Park, KS	913	66202–66215, 66221–66225*
Overton, NV	702	89040
Oviedo, FL	321, 407	32762–32766
Owasso, OK	918	74055, 74073
Owatonna, MN	507	55060
Owego, NY	607	13827
Owen, WI	715	54460
Owensboro, KY	270	42301–42304
Owensville, MO	573	65066
Owenton, KY	502	40359
Owings Mills, MD	410	21117
Owingsville, KY	606	40360
Owosso, MI	989	48841, 48867
Oxford, AL	256	36203
Oxford, CT	203	06478
Oxford, GA	470, 770	30054
Oxford, ME	207	04270
Oxford, MI	248, 947	48370–48371
Oxford, MS	662	38655
Oxford, NY	607	13830
Oxford, NC	919	27565
Oxford, OH	513	45056
Oxford, PA	484, 610	19363
Oxford, WI	608	53952
Oxnard, CA	805	93030–93035
Oyster Bay, NY	516	11771
Ozark, AL	334	36360–36361
Ozark, AR	479	72949
Ozark, MO	417	65721
Ozawkie, KS	785	66070
Ozona, TX	915	76943
Ozone Park, NY	347, 718	11416–11417

P

City	Area Code(s)	Zip Code(s)
Pablo, MT	406	59855
Pace, FL	850	32571
Pacheco, CA	925	94553
Pacific, MO	636	63069
Pacific, WA	253	98047
Pacific Beach, CA	858	92109
Pacific Grove, CA	831	93950
Pacific Palisades, CA	310, 424	90272
Pacifica, CA	650	94044–94045
Packwood, IA	319	52580
Pacoima, CA	818	91331–91334
Paden City, WV	304	26159
Paducah, KY	270	42001–42003
Paducah, TX	806	79248
Page, AZ	928	86036, 86040
Pageland, SC	843	29728
Pagosa Springs, CO	970	81147, 81157
Pahoa, HI	808	96778
Pahokee, FL	561	33476
Pahrump, NV	775	89041, 89048, 89060, 89061
Paicines, CA	831	95043
Paincourtville, LA	985	70391
Painesville, OH	440	44077
Paint Rock, TX	915	76866
Painted Post, NY	607	14870
Paintsville, KY	606	41240
Palatine, IL	224, 847	60038, 60055, 60067, 60074*
Palatine Bridge, NY	518	13428
Palatka, FL	386	32177–32178
Palestine, TX	903	75801–75803, 75882
Palisade, NE	308	69040
Palisades, NY	845	10964
Palisades Park, NJ	201, 551	07650
Palm Bay, FL	321	32905–32911
Palm Beach, FL	561	33480
Palm Beach Gardens, FL	561	33403, 33408–33412*
Palm Beach Shores, FL	561	33404
Palm City, FL	772	34990–34991
Palm Coast, FL	386	32135–32137, 32142, 32164
Palm Desert, CA	760	92210–92211, 92255, 92260*
Palm Harbor, FL	727	34682–34685
Palm Springs, CA	760	92262–92264, 92292
Palmdale, CA	661	93550–93552, 93590–93591*
Palmer, AK	907	99645

*Partial list of zip codes, including main range

City	Area Code(s)	Zip Code(s)
Palmer, MA	413	01069
Palmerton, PA	484, 610	18071
Palmetto, FL	941	34220–34221
Palmetto, GA	470, 770	30268
Palmyra, IN	812	47164
Palmyra, MO	573	63461
Palmyra, NJ	856	08065
Palmyra, NY	315	14522
Palmyra, PA	717	17078
Palmyra, VA	434	22963
Palmyra, WI	262	53156
Palo Alto, CA	650	94301–94310
Palo Pinto, TX	940	76484
Palos Heights, IL	708	60463
Palos Hills, IL	708	60465
Palos Verdes Peninsula, CA	310, 424	90274–90275
Pampa, TX	806	79065–79066
Pana, IL	217	62557
Panama City, FL	850	32401–32413, 32417, 32461
Panama City Beach, FL	850	32401, 32407–32408*
Panguitch, UT	435	84759
Panhandle, TX	806	79068
Panorama City, CA	818	91402, 91412
Pantego, NC	252	27860
Paola, KS	913	66071
Paoli, IN	812	47454
Paoli, PA	484, 610	19301
Paonia, CO	970	81428
Papaikou, HI	808	96781
Papillion, NE	402	68046, 68133, 68157
Paradise, CA	530	95967–95969
Paradise, PA	717	17562
Paragould, AR	870	72450–72451
Paramount, CA	562	90723
Paramus, NJ	201, 551	07652–07653
Parchman, MS	662	38738
Paris, ID	208	83261, 83287
Paris, IL	217	61944
Paris, KY	859	40361–40362
Paris, MO	660	65275
Paris, TN	731	38242
Paris, TX	903	75460–75462
Park City, KY	270	42160
Park City, UT	435	84060, 84068, 84098
Park Falls, WI	715	54552
Park Forest, IL	708	60466
Park Hill, OK	918	74451
Park Hills, MO	573	63601, 63653
Park Rapids, MN	218	56470
Park Ridge, IL	224, 847	60068
Park Ridge, NJ	201, 551	07656
Parker, AZ	928	85344
Parker, CO	303, 720	80134, 80138
Parker, SD	605	57053
Parker, WA	509	98939
Parker City, IN	765	47368
Parker Ford, PA	484, 610	19457
Parkersburg, WV	304	26101–26106
Parksley, VA	757	23421
Parkville, MO	816	64151–64152
Parlier, CA	559	93648
Parlin, NJ	732, 848	08859
Parma, ID	208	83660
Parma, OH	216, 440	44129–44134
Parowan, UT	435	84761
Parshall, CO	970	80468
Parsippany, NJ	862, 973	07054
Parsons, KS	620	67357
Parsons, TN	731	38363
Parsons, WV	304	26287
Pasadena, CA	626	91050–91051, 91101–91110*
Pasadena, MD	410	21122–21123
Pasadena, TX	281, 713, 832	77501–77508
Pascagoula, MS	228	39562–39563, 39567–39569*
Pasco, WA	509	99301–99302
Pascoag, RI	401	02859
Paso Robles, CA	805	93446–93447
Passaic, NJ	862, 973	07055
Patagonia, AZ	520	85624
Patchogue, NY	631	11772
Paterson, NJ	862, 973	07501–07514, 07522–07524*
Paterson, WA	509	99345
Patrick AFB, FL	321	32925
Patterson, CA	209	95363
Patterson, GA	912	31557
Patterson, LA	985	70392
Patterson, NY	845	12563
Patton, CA	909	92369
Patuxent River, MD	301	20670
Paul, ID	208	83347
Paulding, OH	419, 567	45879
Pauls Valley, OK	405	73075
Paw Paw, MI	616	49079
Pawcatuck, CT	860	06379
Pawhuska, OK	918	74009, 74056
Pawleys Island, SC	843	29585
Pawling, NY	845	12564
Pawnee, OK	918	74058
Pawnee City, NE	402	68420
Pawtucket, RI	401	02860–02862
Paxton, IL	217	60957
Paxton, MA	508, 774	01612
Payette, ID	208	83661
Paynesville, MN	320	56362
Payson, AZ	928	85541, 85547
Payson, UT	801	84651
Peabody, MA	351, 978	01960–01961
Peace Dale, RI	401	02879, 02883
Peach Glen, PA	717	17375
Peachtree City, GA	470, 770	30269
Peapack, NJ	908	07977
Pearce, AZ	520	85625
Pearisburg, VA	540	24134
Pearl, MS	601, 769	39208, 39218, 39232, 39288
Pearl City, HI	808	96782
Pearl Harbor, HI	808	96860
Pearl River, NY	845	10965
Pearland, TX	281, 832	77581–77584, 77588
Pearsall, TX	830	78061
Pearson, GA	912	31642
Pebble Beach, CA	831	93953
Pecos, NM	505	87552
Pecos, TX	915	79772
Peculiar, MO	816	64078
Peekskill, NY	845	10566
Pekin, IL	309	61554–61558
Pekin, IN	812	47165
Pelham, AL	205	35124
Pelham, GA	229	31779
Pelham, NH	603	03076
Pelham, NY	845	10803
Pelham Manor, NY	845	10803
Pelican Rapids, MN	218	56572
Pell City, AL	205	35125–35128
Pella, IA	641	50219
Pelzer, SC	864	29669
Pemberton, NJ	609	08068
Pembroke, GA	912	31321
Pembroke, MA	339, 781	02327, 02358–02359
Pembroke, NH	603	03275
Pembroke, NC	910	28372
Pembroke, VA	540	24136
Pembroke Park, FL	754, 954	33009, 33021–33023
Pembroke Pines, FL	754, 954	33019–33029, 33081–33084*
Pen Argyl, PA	484, 610	18072
Penacook, NH	603	03303
Penasco, NM	505	87553
Pender, NE	402	68047
Pendergrass, GA	706, 762	30567
Pendleton, IN	765	46064
Pendleton, OR	541	97801
Pendleton, SC	864	29670
Penfield, NY	585	14526
Penfield, PA	814	15849
Peninsula, OH	234, 330	44264
Penland, NC	828	28765
Penn Yan, NY	315	14527
Penndel, PA	215, 267	19047
Pennington, NJ	609	08534
Pennsauken, NJ	856	08109–08110
Pennsburg, PA	215, 267	18073
Pennsville, NJ	856	08070
Penrose, CO	719	81240
Pensacola, FL	850	32501–32516, 32520–32526*
Pensacola Beach, FL	850	32561
Pentwater, MI	231	49449
Peoria, AZ	623	85345, 85380–85385
Peoria, IL	309	61601–61616, 61625–61644*
Peoria Heights, IL	309	61614–61616
Peosta, IA	563	52068
Peotone, IL	708	60468
Pepper Pike, OH	216	44122–44124
Pequannock, NJ	862, 973	07440
Perdue Hill, AL	251	36470
Perham, MN	218	56573
Perkasie, PA	215, 267	18944
Perkinston, MS	601, 769	39573
Perris, CA	951	92570–92572, 92599
Perry, FL	850	32347–32348
Perry, GA	478	31069
Perry, IA	515	50220
Perry, KS	785	66073
Perry, OH	440	44081
Perry, OK	580	73077
Perrysburg, OH	419, 567	43551–43552
Perrysville, OH	419, 567	44864
Perryton, TX	806	79070
Perryville, AR	501	72126
Perryville, MO	573	63747, 63775–63776
Perth Amboy, NJ	732, 848	08861–08863
Peru, IL	815	61354
Peru, IN	765	46970–46971
Peru, NE	402	68421
Pescadero, CA	650	94060
Peshastin, WA	509	98847
Peshtigo, WI	715	54157
Petal, MS	601, 769	39465
Petaluma, CA	707	94952–94955, 94975, 94999
Peterborough, NH	603	03458
Petersburg, AK	907	99833
Petersburg, IL	217	62659, 62675
Petersburg, IN	812	47567
Petersburg, TX	806	79250
Petersburg, VA	804	23801–23806
Petersburg, WV	304	26847
Petersburgh, NY	518	12138
Peterson AFB, CO	719	80914
Petoskey, MI	231	49770
Pewaukee, WI	262	53072
Pewee Valley, KY	502	40056
Pflugerville, TX	512	78660, 78691
Pharr, TX	956	78577
Phelps, NY	315	14532
Phenix City, AL	334	36867–36870
Phil Campbell, AL	256	35581
Philadelphia, MS	601, 769	39350
Philadelphia, PA	215, 267	19019, 19092–19093*
Philip, SD	605	57567
Philippi, WV	304	26416
Philipsburg, MT	406	59858
Philipsburg, PA	814	16866
Phillips, WI	715	54555
Phillipsburg, KS	785	67661
Phillipsburg, NJ	908	08865
Philmont, NY	518	12565
Philomath, OR	541	97370
Philpot, KY	270	42366
Phoenix, AZ	480, 602	85001–85055, 85060–85087*
Phoenix, OR	541	97535
Phoenixville, PA	484, 610	19453, 19460
Picayune, MS	601, 769	39466
Pickens, SC	864	29671
Pickerington, OH	614	43147
Pico Rivera, CA	562	90660–90665
Piedmont, AL	256	36272
Pierce, NE	402	68767
Pierre, SD	605	57501
Pierz, MN	320	56364
Piffard, NY	585	14533
Pigeon, MI	989	48755
Pigeon Forge, TN	865	37862–37864, 37868, 37876
Piggott, AR	870	72454
Pikesville, MD	410	21208, 21282

*Partial list of zip codes, including main range

City	Area Code(s)	Zip Code(s)
Pikeville, KY	606	41501–41502
Pikeville, TN	423	37367
Pilot Grove, IA	319	52648
Pima, AZ	928	85535, 85543
Pinckneyville, IL	618	62274
Pinconning, MI	989	48650
Pine Bluff, AR	870	71601–71603, 71611–71613
Pine Bluffs, WY	307	82082
Pine Brook, NJ	862, 973	07058
Pine City, MN	320	55063
Pine City, NY	607	14871
Pine Island, MN	507	55963
Pine Mountain, GA	706, 762	31822
Pine Plains, NY	518	12567
Pine River, MN	218	56456, 56474
Pinedale, WY	307	82941
Pinehurst, NC	910	28370, 28374
Pinellas Park, FL	727	33780–33782
Pinetops, NC	252	27864
Pineville, KY	606	40977
Pineville, LA	318	71359–71361
Pineville, MO	417	64856
Pineville, NC	704, 980	28134
Pineville, WV	304	24859, 24874
Piney Flats, TN	423	37686, 37699
Pinole, CA	510	94564
Pioche, NV	775	89043
Pioneer, OH	419, 567	43554
Pipersville, PA	215, 267	18947
Pipestem, WV	304	25979
Pipestone, MN	507	56164
Pippa Passes, KY	606	41844
Piqua, OH	937	45356
Piru, CA	805	93040
Piscataway, NJ	732, 848	08854–08855
Pismo Beach, CA	805	93420, 93433, 93448, 93449
Pitman, NJ	856	08071
Pittsboro, MS	662	38951
Pittsboro, NC	919	27228, 27312
Pittsburg, CA	925	94565
Pittsburg, KS	620	66762–66763
Pittsburg, TX	903	75686
Pittsburgh, PA	412, 878	15122–15123, 15201–15244*
Pittsfield, IL	217	62363
Pittsfield, ME	207	04967
Pittsfield, MA	413	01201–01203
Pittsfield, NH	603	03263
Pittsford, NY	585	14534
Pittston, PA	570	18640–18644
Pittstown, NJ	908	08867
Pittsville, WI	715	54466
Placentia, CA	714	92870–92871
Placerville, CA	530	95667
Plain, WI	608	53577
Plain City, OH	614	43064
Plainfield, IL	815	60544
Plainfield, IN	317	46168
Plainfield, NJ	908	07060–07063, 07069
Plainfield, VT	802	05667
Plainfield, WI	715	54966
Plains, GA	229	31780
Plains, PA	570	18702–18705
Plains, TX	806	79355
Plainsboro, NJ	609	08536
Plainview, MN	507	55964
Plainview, NY	516	11803
Plainview, TX	806	79072–79073
Plainville, CT	860	06062
Plainville, KS	785	67663
Plainville, MA	508, 774	02762
Plainville, NY	315	13137
Plainwell, MI	616	49080
Plankinton, SD	605	57368
Plano, IL	331, 630	60545
Plano, TX	469, 972	75023–75026, 75074–75075*
Plant City, FL	813	33564–33567
Plantation, FL	754, 954	33311–33313, 33317–33318*
Plantsville, CT	860	06479
Plaquemine, LA	225	70764–70765
Plato, MN	320	55370
Platte City, MO	816	64079
Platteville, WI	608	53818
Plattsburg, MO	816	64477
Plattsburgh, NY	518	12901–12903
Plattsmouth, NE	402	68048
Pleasant Gap, PA	814	16823
Pleasant Grove, UT	801	84062
Pleasant Hill, CA	925	94523
Pleasant Plains, IL	217	62677
Pleasant Prairie, WI	262	53142–53143, 53158
Pleasant Valley, NY	845	12569
Pleasanton, CA	925	94566–94568, 94588
Pleasanton, TX	830	78064
Pleasantville, NJ	609	08232–08234
Pleasantville, NY	914	10570–10572
Plentywood, MT	406	59254
Plover, WI	715	54467
Plymouth, IN	574	46563
Plymouth, MA	508, 774	02345, 02360–02362
Plymouth, MI	734	48170
Plymouth, MN	763	55441–55442, 55447
Plymouth, NH	603	03264
Plymouth, NC	252	27962
Plymouth, VT	802	05056
Plymouth, WI	920	53073
Plymouth Meeting, PA	484, 610	19462
Pocahontas, AR	870	72455
Pocahontas, IA	712	50574
Pocatello, ID	208	83201–83209
Pocomoke City, MD	410	21851
Pocono Manor, PA	570	18349
Point Clear, AL	334	36564
Point Comfort, TX	361	77978
Point Lookout, MO	417	65726
Point Lookout, NY	516	11569
Point Marion, PA	724, 878	15474
Point of Rocks, MD	301	21777
Point Pleasant, WV	304	25550
Point Pleasant Beach, NJ	732, 848	08742
Point Richmond, CA	510	94801
Poland, OH	234, 330	44514
Polk City, FL	863	33868
Polk City, IA	515	50226
Polkton, NC	704, 980	28135
Pollocksville, NC	252	28573
Polson, MT	406	59860
Pomeroy, OH	740	45769
Pomeroy, WA	509	99347
Pomfret, CT	860	06258
Pomfret Center, CT	860	06259
Pomona, CA	909	91765–91769, 91797–91799
Pomona, NJ	609	08240
Pomona, NY	845	10970
Pompano Beach, FL	754, 954	33060–33077, 33093, 33097
Pompton Lakes, NJ	862, 973	07442
Pompton Plains, NJ	862, 973	07444
Ponca, NE	402	68770
Ponca City, OK	580	74601–74604
Ponce Inlet, FL	386	32127
Ponchatoula, LA	985	70454
Ponte Vedra Beach, FL	904	32004, 32082
Pontiac, IL	815	61764
Pontiac, MI	248, 947	48340–48343
Pontotoc, MS	662	38863
Pooler, GA	912	31322
Pope AFB, NC	910	28308
Poplar, MT	406	59255
Poplar Bluff, MO	573	63901–63902
Poplarville, MS	601, 769	39470
Poquoson, VA	757	23662
Port Allen, LA	225	70767
Port Angeles, WA	360	98362–98363
Port Aransas, TX	361	78373
Port Arthur, TX	409	77640–77643
Port Charlotte, FL	941	33948–33954, 33980–33983
Port Chester, NY	914	10573
Port Clinton, OH	419, 567	43452
Port Ewen, NY	845	12466
Port Gibson, MS	601, 769	39150
Port Hueneme, CA	805	93041–93044
Port Huron, MI	810	48060–48061
Port Isabel, TX	956	78578, 78597
Port Jefferson, NY	631	11777
Port Jefferson Station, NY	631	11776–11777
Port Jervis, NY	845	12771, 12785
Port Lavaca, TX	361	77972, 77979
Port Ludlow, WA	360	98365
Port Neches, TX	409	77651
Port Orange, FL	386	32118–32119, 32124–32129
Port Orchard, WA	360	98366–98367
Port Orford, OR	541	97465
Port Saint Joe, FL	850	32410, 32456–32457
Port Saint Lucie, FL	772	34952–34953, 34983–34988
Port Sulphur, LA	504	70083
Port Tobacco, MD	301	20677
Port Townsend, WA	360	98368
Port Washington, NY	516	11050–11055
Port Washington, WI	262	53074
Portage, IN	219	46368
Portage, MI	616	49002, 49024, 49081
Portage, WI	608	53901
Portageville, MO	573	63873
Portales, NM	505	88123, 88130
Porter, IN	219	46304
Porterville, CA	559	93257–93258
Portland, AR	870	71663
Portland, CT	860	06480
Portland, IN	260	47371
Portland, ME	207	04101–04112, 04116, 04122*
Portland, MI	517	48875
Portland, OR	503, 971	97201–97242, 97251–97259*
Portland, TN	615	37148
Portola, CA	530	96122, 96129
Portola Valley, CA	650	94028
Portsmouth, NH	603	03801–03804
Portsmouth, OH	740	45662–45663
Portsmouth, RI	401	02871–02872
Portsmouth, VA	757	23701–23709
Portville, NY	585	14770
Post, TX	806	79356
Post Falls, ID	208	83854, 83877
Post Mills, VT	802	05058
Postville, IA	563	52162
Poteau, OK	918	74953
Potomac, MD	301	20854, 20859
Potosi, MO	573	63664
Potsdam, NY	315	13676, 13699
Pottsboro, TX	903	75076
Pottstown, PA	484, 610	19464–19465
Pottsville, PA	570	17901
Poughkeepsie, NY	845	12601–12604
Poughquag, NY	845	12570
Poulsbo, WA	360	98370
Poultney, VT	802	05741, 05764
Pound, VA	276	24279
Poway, CA	858	92064, 92074
Powderhorn, CO	970	81243
Powell, OH	614	43065
Powell, TN	865	37849
Powell, WY	307	82435
Powhatan, VA	804	23139
Prairie City, IL	309	61470
Prairie du Chien, WI	608	53821
Prairie du Sac, WI	608	53578
Prairie Grove, IL	815	60012, 60050
Prairie View, TX	936	77446
Prairie Village, KS	913	66202–66208
Prairieville, LA	225	70769
Pratt, KS	620	67124
Prattville, AL	334	36066–36068
Preble, IN	260	46782
Prentiss, MS	601, 769	39474
Prescott, AZ	928	86301–86305, 86313, 86330
Prescott, AR	870	71857
Prescott, WA	509	99348
Prescott, WI	715	54021
Prescott Valley, AZ	928	86312–86314
Presidio of San Francisco, CA	415	94129
Presque Isle, ME	207	04769
Preston, GA	229	31824
Preston, ID	208	83263
Preston, MN	507	55965
Preston, WA	425	98050

*Partial list of zip codes, including main range

City	Area Code(s)	Zip Code(s)
Prestonsburg, KY	606	41653
Price, UT	435	84501
Prichard, AL	251	36610, 36617
Prides Crossing, MA	617, 857	01965
Primghar, IA	712	51245
Primm, NV	702	89019
Primos, PA	484, 610	19018
Prince Frederick, MD	410	20678
Prince George, VA	804	23875
Prince William, VA	571, 703	22193
Princess Anne, MD	410	21853
Princeton, ID	208	83857
Princeton, IL	815	61356
Princeton, IN	812	47670
Princeton, KY	270	42445
Princeton, MN	763	55371
Princeton, MO	660	64673
Princeton, NJ	609	08540–08544
Princeton, WV	304	24740
Princeton Junction, NJ	609	08550
Princeville, HI	808	96714, 96722
Princeville, IL	309	61559
Prineville, OR	541	97754
Prinsburg, MN	320	56281
Prior Lake, MN	952	55372
Proctor, MN	218	55810
Proctor, VT	802	05765
Prophetstown, IL	815	61277
Prospect, CT	203	06712
Prospect, ME	207	04981
Prospect Harbor, ME	207	04669
Prospect Heights, IL	224, 847	60070
Prospect Hill, NC	336	27314
Prosperity, SC	803	29127
Prosser, WA	509	99350
Providence, RI	401	02901–02912, 02918, 02940
Provincetown, MA	508, 774	02657
Provo, UT	801	84601–84606
Pryor, OK	918	74361–74362
Pueblo, CO	719	81001–81015
Pueblo West, CO	719	81007
Puerto Nuevo, PR	787, 939	00920–00921
Pulaski, NY	315	13142
Pulaski, TN	931	38478
Pulaski, VA	540	24301
Pulaski, WI	920	54162
Pullman, WA	509	99163–99165
Punta Gorda, FL	941	33950–33951, 33955, 33980*
Punxsutawney, PA	814	15767
Purcell, OK	405	73080
Purcellville, VA	540	20132–20134, 20160
Purchase, NY	914	10577
Purvis, MS	601, 769	39475
Put-in-Bay, OH	419, 567	43456
Putnam, CT	860	06260
Putney, VT	802	05346
Puunene, HI	808	96784
Puyallup, WA	253	98371–98375
Pyote, TX	915	79777

Q

City	Area Code(s)	Zip Code(s)
Quakertown, PA	215, 267	18951
Quanah, TX	940	79252
Quantico, VA	571, 703	22134–22135
Quapaw, OK	918	74363
Quarryville, PA	717	17566
Queens Village, NY	347, 718	11427–11429
Queensbury, NY	518	12801–12804
Queenstown, MD	410	21658
Quimby, IA	712	51049
Quinault, WA	360	98575
Quincy, CA	530	95971
Quincy, FL	850	32351–32353
Quincy, IL	217	62301, 62305–62306
Quincy, MA	617, 857	02169–02171, 02269
Quincy, PA	717	17247
Quincy, WA	509	98848
Quinlan, TX	903	75474
Quinter, KS	785	67752
Quitman, GA	229	31643
Quitman, MS	601, 769	39355
Quitman, TX	903	75783

R

City	Area Code(s)	Zip Code(s)
Racine, WI	262	53401–53408, 53490
Radcliff, KY	270	40159–40160
Radcliffe, IA	515	50230
Radford, VA	540	24141–24143
Radisson, WI	715	54867
Radnor, PA	484, 610	19087
Raeford, NC	910	28361, 28376
Rahway, NJ	732, 848	07065
Raiford, FL	386, 904	32026, 32083
Rainsville, AL	256	35986
Raleigh, MS	601, 769	39153
Raleigh, NC	919	27601–27629, 27634–27636*
Ralls, TX	806	79357
Ralston, IA	712	51459
Ralston, NE	402	68127
Ramah, NM	505	87321, 87357
Ramona, CA	760	92065
Ramona, OK	918	74061
Ramseur, NC	336	27316
Ramsey, MN	763	55303
Ramsey, NJ	201, 551	07446
Rancho Cordova, CA	916	95670, 95741–95743
Rancho Cucamonga, CA	909	91701, 91729–91730*
Rancho Dominguez, CA	310, 424	90220, 90224
Rancho Mirage, CA	760	92270
Rancho Palos Verdes, CA	310, 424	90275
Rancho Santa Fe, CA	858	92067, 92091
Rancho Santa Margarita, CA	949	92688
Rancho Viejo, TX	956	78575
Rancocas, NJ	609	08073
Randallstown, MD	410	21133
Randleman, NC	336	27317
Randolph, MA	339, 781	02368
Randolph, NJ	862, 973	07869
Randolph, UT	435	84064
Randolph, VT	802	05060
Randolph, WI	920	53956–53957
Randolph AFB, TX	210	78148–78150
Randolph Center, VT	802	05061
Random Lake, WI	920	53075
Rangely, CO	970	81648
Ranger, TX	254	76470
Rankin, PA	412, 878	15104
Rankin, TX	915	79778
Rantoul, IL	217	61866
Rapid City, SD	605	57701–57703, 57709
Rapidan, VA	540	22733
Raritan, NJ	908	08869, 08896
Raton, NM	505	87740
Ravenna, MI	231	49451
Ravenna, OH	234, 330	44266
Ravenswood, WV	304	26164
Rawlins, WY	307	82301, 82310
Ray Brook, NY	518	12977
Raymond, ME	207	04071
Raymond, MS	601, 769	39154
Raymond, NH	603	03077
Raymond, WA	360	98577
Raymondville, TX	956	78580, 78598
Raymore, MO	816	64083
Rayne, LA	337	70578
Raynham, MA	508, 774	02767
Raytown, MO	816	64129, 64133, 64138
Rayville, LA	318	71269
Readfield, ME	207	04355
Reading, MA	339, 781	01867
Reading, PA	484, 610	19601–19612, 19640
Readville, MA	617, 857	02136–02137
Reamstown, PA	717	17567
Red Bank, NJ	732, 848	07701–07704
Red Bay, AL	256	35582
Red Bluff, CA	530	96080
Red Bud, IL	618	62278
Red Cloud, NE	402	68970
Red Feather Lakes, CO	970	80536, 80545
Red Hill, PA	215, 267	18073–18076
Red Lake Falls, MN	218	56750
Red Lion, PA	717	17356
Red Lodge, MT	406	59068
Red Oak, IA	712	51566, 51591
Red River, NM	505	87558
Red Rock, AZ	520	85245
Red Springs, NC	910	28377
Red Wing, MN	651	55066
Redding, CA	530	96001–96003, 96049, 96099
Redding, CT	203	06896
Redfield, SD	605	57469
Redford, MI	313	48239–48240
Redlands, CA	909	92373–92375
Redmond, OR	541	97756
Redmond, WA	425	98052–98053, 98073–98074
Redondo Beach, CA	310, 424	90277–90278
Redstone, CO	970	81623
Redstone Arsenal, AL	256	35808–35809
Redwood, NY	315	13679
Redwood City, CA	650	94059–94065
Redwood Falls, MN	507	56283
Reed City, MI	231	49677
Reedley, CA	559	93654
Reedsburg, WI	608	53958–53959
Refugio, TX	361	78377
Rego Park, NY	347, 718	11374
Rehoboth Beach, DE	302	19971
Reidsville, GA	912	30453, 30499
Reidsville, NC	336	27320–27323
Reinbeck, IA	319	50669
Reisterstown, MD	410	21071, 21136
Rembert, SC	803	29128
Remington, IN	219	47977
Remus, MI	989	49340
Renick, WV	304	24966
Reno, NV	775	89501–89515, 89520–89523*
Rensselaer, IN	219	47978
Rensselaer, NY	518	12144
Renton, WA	425	98055–98059
Renville, MN	320	56284
Represa, CA	916	95671
Republic, MO	417	65738
Republic, WA	509	99166
Research Triangle Park, NC	919	27709
Reseda, CA	818	91335–91337
Reserve, NM	505	87830
Reston, VA	571, 703	20190–20196, 22096
Retsil, WA	360	98378
Revere, MA	339, 781	02151
Rexburg, ID	208	83440–83441, 83460
Reynolds, GA	478	31076
Reynoldsburg, OH	614	43068
Rhinebeck, NY	845	12572
Rhinelander, WI	715	54501
Rhodes, MI	989	48652
Rialto, CA	909	92376–92377
Rice Lake, WI	715	54868
Riceboro, GA	912	31323
Rich Square, NC	252	27869
Richardson, TX	214, 469, 972	75080–75085
Richfield, MN	612	55423
Richfield, OH	234, 330	44286
Richfield, UT	435	84701
Richfield, WI	414	53076
Richland, MI	616	49083
Richland, MS	601, 769	39208, 39218, 39232
Richland, PA	717	17087
Richland, WA	509	99352–99353
Richland Center, WI	608	53581
Richland Hills, TX	682, 817	76118, 76180
Richlands, VA	276	24641
Richmond, CA	510	94801–94808, 94820, 94850
Richmond, IL	815	60071
Richmond, IN	765	47374–47375
Richmond, KY	859	40475–40476
Richmond, MO	816	64085
Richmond, TX	281, 832	77406, 77469
Richmond, VA	804	23173, 23218–23242*
Richmond Heights, MO	314	63117
Richmond Heights, OH	216	44143
Richmond Hill, NY	347, 718	11418

*Partial list of zip codes, including main range

City	Area Code(s)	Zip Code(s)
Richvale, CA	530	95974
Rickreall, OR	503, 971	97371
Riddle, OR	541	97469
Riderwood, MD	410	21139
Ridge, NY	631	11961
Ridge Spring, SC	803	29129
Ridgecrest, CA	760	93555–93556
Ridgedale, MO	417	65739
Ridgefield, CT	203	06877–06879
Ridgefield, NJ	201, 551	07657
Ridgefield Park, NJ	201, 551	07660
Ridgeland, MS	601, 769	39157–39158
Ridgeland, SC	843	29912, 29936
Ridgeville, SC	843	29472
Ridgeway, SC	803	29130
Ridgeway, VA	276	24148
Ridgewood, NJ	201, 551	07450–07452
Ridgewood, NY	347, 718	11385–11386
Ridgway, CO	970	81432
Ridgway, PA	814	15853
Ridley Park, PA	484, 610	19078
Rifle, CO	970	81650
Rigby, ID	208	83442
Rillito, AZ	520	85654
Rindge, NH	603	03461
Ringgold, GA	706, 762	30736
Ringoes, NJ	908	08551
Ringwood, NJ	862, 973	07456
Rio, WI	920	53960
Rio Grande, NJ	609	08242
Rio Grande, OH	740	45674
Rio Grande City, TX	956	78582
Rio Rancho, NM	505	87124, 87174
Rio Rico, AZ	520	85648
Rio Verde, AZ	480	85263
Rio Vista, CA	707	94571
Ripley, MS	662	38663
Ripley, TN	731	38063
Ripley, WV	304	25271
Ripon, CA	209	95366
Ripon, WI	920	54971
Ririe, ID	208	83443
Rising Sun, IN	812	47040
Rising Sun, MD	410	21911
Rison, AR	870	71665
Ritzville, WA	509	99169
River Edge, NJ	201, 551	07661
River Falls, WI	715	54022
River Forest, IL	708	60305
River Grove, IL	708	60171
River Rouge, MI	313	48218
Riverbank, CA	209	95367, 95390
Riverdale, GA	470, 770	30274, 30296
Riverdale, IL	708	60827
Riverdale, MD	301	20737–20738
Riverdale, NJ	862, 973	07457
Riverdale, NY	347, 718	10463, 10471
Riverdale, UT	801	84405
Riverhead, NY	631	11901
Riverside, CA	951	92501–92509, 92513–92522
Riverside, MI	616	49084
Riverside, MO	816	64150–64151, 64168
Riverside, NJ	856	08075
Riverton, NJ	856	08076–08077
Riverton, UT	801	84065, 84095
Riverton, WY	307	82501
Riverview, FL	813	33568–33569
Riverwoods, IL	224, 847	60015
Riviera Beach, FL	561	33403–33407, 33418–33419
Roanoke, IN	260	46783
Roanoke, VA	540	24001–24050
Roanoke Rapids, NC	252	27870
Roaring Spring, PA	814	16673
Robbins, NC	910	27325
Robbinsdale, MN	763	55422
Robbinsville, NJ	609	08691
Robbinsville, NC	828	28771
Robert Lee, TX	915	76945
Roberta, GA	478	31078
Roberts, IL	217	60962
Robertsdale, AL	251	36567, 36574
Robesonia, PA	484, 610	19551
Robins AFB, GA	478	31098
Robinson, IL	618	62454
Robinsonville, MS	662	38664
Robstown, TX	361	78380
Roby, TX	915	79543
Rochdale, MA	508, 774	01542
Rochelle, IL	815	61068
Rochelle Park, NJ	201, 551	07662
Rochester, IN	574	46975
Rochester, MI	248, 947	48306–48309
Rochester, MN	507	55901–55906
Rochester, NH	603	03839, 03866–03868
Rochester, NY	585	14601–14627, 14638–14653*
Rochester, PA	724, 878	15074
Rochester, VT	802	05767
Rochester, WA	360	98579
Rochester, WI	262	53167
Rochester Hills, MI	248, 947	48306–48309
Rock City Falls, NY	518	12863
Rock Creek, OH	440	44084
Rock Falls, IL	815	61071
Rock Hill, NY	845	12775
Rock Hill, SC	803	29730–29734
Rock Island, IL	309	61201–61204, 61299
Rock Port, MO	660	64482
Rock Rapids, IA	712	51246
Rock Spring, GA	706, 762	30739
Rock Springs, WY	307	82901–82902, 82942
Rockaway, NJ	862, 973	07866
Rockaway Beach, NY	347, 718	11693
Rockaway Park, NY	347, 718	11694
Rockford, AL	256	35136
Rockford, IL	815	61101–61114, 61125–61126
Rockford, MI	616	49341, 49351
Rockford, MN	763	55373
Rockford, TN	865	37853
Rockingham, NC	910	28379–28380
Rockland, ME	207	04841
Rockland, MA	339, 781	02370
Rockledge, FL	321	32955–32956
Rockleigh, NJ	201, 551	07647
Rocklin, CA	916	95677, 95765
Rockmart, GA	470, 770	30153
Rockport, IN	812	47635
Rockport, ME	207	04856
Rockport, MA	351, 978	01966
Rockport, TX	361	78381–78382
Rocksprings, TX	830	78880
Rockton, IL	815	61072
Rockville, CT	860	06066
Rockville, IN	765	47872
Rockville, MD	240, 301	20847–20859
Rockville Centre, NY	516	11570–11572, 11592
Rockwall, TX	469, 972	75032, 75087
Rockwell, NC	704, 980	28138
Rockwell City, IA	712	50579
Rockwood, MI	734	48173
Rocky Ford, CO	719	81067
Rocky Hill, CT	860	06067
Rocky Mount, NC	252	27801–27804
Rocky Mount, VA	540	24151
Roebuck, SC	864	29376
Rogers, AR	479	72756–72758
Rogers, CT	860	06263
Rogers City, MI	989	49779
Rogersville, AL	256	35652
Rogersville, TN	423	37857
Rogue River, OR	541	97537
Rohnert Park, CA	707	94927–94928
Roland, AR	501	72135
Roland, IA	515	50236
Rolla, MO	573	65401–65402, 65409
Rolla, ND	701	58367
Rolling Fork, MS	662	39159
Rolling Hills Estates, CA	310, 424	90274–90275
Rolling Meadows, IL	224, 847	60008
Rome, GA	706, 762	30149, 30161–30165
Rome, NY	315	13440–13442, 13449
Romeo, MI	586	48065
Romeoville, IL	815	60441, 60446
Romney, WV	304	26757
Romulus, MI	734	48174
Romulus, NY	315	14541
Ronceverte, WV	304	24970
Ronkonkoma, NY	631	11749, 11779
Roodhouse, IL	217	62082
Roosevelt, AZ	928	85545
Roosevelt, UT	435	84066
Rootstown, OH	234, 330	44272
Rosamond, CA	661	93560
Roscoe, IL	815	61073
Roscoe, PA	412, 878	15477
Roscommon, MI	989	48653
Rose Hill, NC	910	28458
Roseau, MN	218	56751
Rosebud, TX	254	76570
Roseburg, OR	541	97470
Rosedale, MS	662	38769
Roseland, NJ	862, 973	07068
Roselle, IL	331, 630	60172
Roselle, NJ	908	07203
Roselle Park, NJ	908	07204
Rosemead, CA	626	91770–91772
Rosemont, IL	224, 847	60018
Rosemont, PA	484, 610	19010
Rosemount, MN	651	55068
Rosenberg, TX	281, 832	77471
Rosendale, WI	920	54974
Rosenhayn, NJ	856	08352
Roseville, CA	916	95661, 95678, 95746, 95747
Roseville, MI	586	48066
Roseville, MN	651	55112–55113, 55126
Roseville, OH	740	43777
Rosiclare, IL	618	62982
Roslindale, MA	617, 857	02131
Roslyn, NY	516	11576
Roslyn Heights, NY	516	11577
Rosman, NC	828	28772
Rosslyn, VA	571, 703	22209
Rossville, GA	706, 762	30741–30742
Roswell, GA	470, 678, 770	30075–30077
Roswell, NM	505	88201–88203
Rothschild, WI	715	54474
Round Lake, IL	224, 847	60073
Round Rock, TX	512	78664, 78680–78683
Roundup, MT	406	59072–59073
Rouses Point, NY	518	12979
Rowayton, CT	203	06853
Rowe, MA	413	01367
Rowlett, TX	469, 972	75030, 75088–75089
Rowley, MA	351, 978	01969
Roxboro, NC	336	27573
Roxbury, MA	617, 857	02118–02120
Roxbury Crossing, MA	617, 857	02120
Roy, NM	505	87743
Roy, UT	801	84067
Roy, WA	360	98580
Royal Oak, MI	248, 947	48067–48068, 48073
Royal Palm Beach, FL	561	33411–33412, 33421
Royersford, PA	484, 610	19468
Rugby, ND	701	58368
Ruidoso Downs, NM	505	88346
Rumford, RI	401	02916
Running Springs, CA	909	92382
Rupert, ID	208	83343, 83350
Rural Hall, NC	336	27045, 27094, 27098, 27099
Rush, NY	585	14543
Rush City, MN	320	55067–55069
Rushford, MN	507	55971
Rushville, IL	217	62681
Rushville, IN	765	46173
Rushville, NE	308	69360
Rusk, TX	903	75785
Ruskin, FL	813	33570–33573
Russell, KS	785	67665
Russellville, AL	256	35653–35654
Russellville, AR	479	72801–72802, 72811–72812
Russellville, KY	270	42276
Russia, OH	937	45363
Rustburg, VA	434	24588
Ruston, LA	318	71270–71273

*Partial list of zip codes, including main range

City	Area Code(s)	Zip Code(s)
Rutherford, CA	707	94573
Rutherford, NJ	201, 551	07070
Rutherfordton, NC	828	28139
Rutland, MA	508, 774	01543
Rutland, VT	802	05701–05702
Rutledge, TN	865	37861
Rydal, PA	215, 267	19046
Rye, NY	914	10580
Rye Brook, NY	914	10573
Ryegate, MT	406	59074

S

City	Area Code(s)	Zip Code(s)
Sabetha, KS	785	66534
Sac City, IA	712	50583
Saco, ME	207	04072
Sacramento, CA	916	94203–94211, 94229–94263*
Saddle Brook, NJ	201, 551	07663
Saegertown, PA	814	16433
Safety Harbor, FL	727	34695
Safford, AZ	928	85546–85548
Sag Harbor, NY	631	11963
Saginaw, MI	989	48601–48609, 48663
Sagle, ID	208	83809, 83860
Saguache, CO	719	81149
Sahuarita, AZ	520	85629
Saint Albans, VT	802	05478–05479
Saint Albans, WV	304	25177
Saint Ann, MO	314	63074
Saint Ansgar, IA	641	50472, 50481
Saint Anthony, ID	208	83445
Saint Anthony, MN	612	55418–55421
Saint Augustine, FL	904	32080, 32084–32086*
Saint Bonaventure, NY	585	14778
Saint Bonifacius, MN	952	55375
Saint Catharine, KY	859	40061
Saint Charles, IL	331, 630	60174–60175
Saint Charles, MI	989	48655
Saint Charles, MO	636	63301–63304
Saint Clair, MI	810	48079
Saint Clair, MN	507	56080
Saint Clair, MO	636	63077
Saint Clair, PA	570	17970
Saint Clair Shores, MI	586	48080–48082
Saint Clairsville, OH	740	43950
Saint Cloud, FL	321, 407	34769–34773
Saint Cloud, MN	320	56301–56304, 56372, 56387*
Saint Croix Falls, WI	715	54024
Saint Davids, PA	484, 610	19087
Saint Francis, KS	785	67756
Saint Francis, WI	414	53207, 53235
Saint Francisville, IL	618	62460
Saint Francisville, LA	225	70775
Saint Gabriel, LA	225	70776
Saint George, SC	843	29477
Saint George, UT	435	84770–84771, 84782–84783*
Saint Helena, CA	707	94574
Saint Helena Island, SC	843	29920
Saint Helens, OR	503, 971	97051
Saint Henry, OH	419, 567	45883
Saint Hilaire, MN	218	56754
Saint Ignace, MI	906	49781
Saint James, LA	225	70086
Saint James, MN	507	56081
Saint James, MO	573	65559
Saint James, NY	631	11780
Saint Joe, IN	260	46785
Saint John, KS	620	67576
Saint Johns, AZ	928	85936
Saint Johns, MI	989	48879
Saint Johnsbury, VT	802	05819
Saint Joseph, LA	318	71366
Saint Joseph, MI	616	49085
Saint Joseph, MN	320	56374–56375
Saint Joseph, MO	816	64501–64508
Saint Leo, FL	352	33574
Saint Louis, MI	989	48880
Saint Louis, MO	314	63101–63151, 63155–63171*
Saint Louis Park, MN	952	55416, 55424–55426
Saint Maries, ID	208	83861
Saint Martin, OH	513	45118
Saint Martinville, LA	337	70582
Saint Marys, GA	912	31558
Saint Marys, OH	419, 567	45885
Saint Marys, PA	814	15857
Saint Marys, WV	304	26170
Saint Matthews, SC	803	29135
Saint Meinrad, IN	812	47577
Saint Michael, MN	763	55376
Saint Michaels, MD	410	21624, 21647, 21663
Saint Nazianz, WI	920	54232
Saint Paul, MN	651	55101–55129, 55133, 55144*
Saint Paul, NE	308	68873
Saint Pauls, NC	910	28384
Saint Pete Beach, FL	727	33706, 33736
Saint Peter, MN	507	56082
Saint Peters, MO	636	63303–63304, 63376
Saint Petersburg, FL	727	33701–33716, 33728–33743*
Saint Rose, LA	504	70087
Saint Simons Island, GA	912	31522
Sainte Genevieve, MO	573	63670
Salamanca, NY	716	14779
Salem, AR	870	72576
Salem, IL	618	62881
Salem, IN	812	47167
Salem, MA	351, 978	01970–01971
Salem, MO	573	65560
Salem, NH	603	03079
Salem, NJ	856	08079
Salem, OH	234, 330	44460
Salem, OR	503, 971	97301–97314
Salem, SC	864	29676
Salem, SD	605	57058
Salem, VA	540	24153–24157
Salem, WV	304	26426
Salida, CA	209	95368
Salida, CO	719	81201, 81227–81228*
Salina, KS	785	67401–67402
Salinas, CA	831	93901–93908, 93912–93915*
Saline, MI	734	48176
Salineville, OH	234, 330	43945
Salisbury, CT	860	06068, 06079
Salisbury, MD	410	21801–21804
Salisbury, MA	351, 978	01952
Salisbury, NC	704, 980	28144–28147
Sallisaw, OK	918	74955
Salmon, ID	208	83467
Salt Flat, TX	915	79847
Salt Lake City, UT	801	84101–84153, 84157–84158*
Saltillo, MS	662	38866
Saltsburg, PA	724, 878	15681
Saluda, SC	864	29138
Saluda, VA	804	23149
Salyersville, KY	606	41465
San Andreas, CA	209	95249–95250
San Angelo, TX	915	76901–76909
San Anselmo, CA	415	94960, 94979
San Antonio, FL	352	33576
San Antonio, TX	210	78201–78270, 78275–78299
San Augustine, TX	936	75972
San Benito, TX	956	78586
San Bernardino, CA	909	92401–92427
San Bruno, CA	650	94066–94067, 94096–94098
San Carlos, CA	650	94070–94071
San Clemente, CA	949	92672–92674
San Diego, CA	619, 858	92101–92199
San Dimas, CA	909	91773
San Fernando, CA	818	91340–91346
San Francisco, CA	415	94101–94177, 94188
San Gabriel, CA	626	91775–91778
San Gregorio, CA	650	94074
San Jacinto, CA	951	92581–92583
San Joaquin, CA	559	93660
San Jose, CA	408	95101–95142, 95148–95164*
San Juan, PR	787, 939	00901–00902, 00906–00940*
San Juan Bautista, CA	831	95045
San Juan Capistrano, CA	949	92675, 92690–92694
San Leandro, CA	510	94577–94579
San Lorenzo, CA	510	94580
San Luis, CO	719	81134, 81152
San Luis Obispo, CA	805	93401–93412
San Marcos, CA	760	92069, 92078–92079
San Marcos, TX	512	78666–78667
San Marino, CA	626	91108, 91118
San Mateo, CA	650	94401–94409, 94497
San Pablo, CA	510	94806
San Pedro, CA	310, 424	90731–90734
San Quentin, CA	415	94964, 94974
San Rafael, CA	415	94901–94904, 94912–94915
San Ramon, CA	925	94583
San Saba, TX	915	76877
San Ysidro, CA	619	92143, 92173
Sanborn, NY	716	14132
Sand Point, AK	907	99661
Sand Springs, OK	918	74063
Sanderson, FL	386	32087
Sanderson, TX	915	79848
Sandersville, GA	478	31082
Sandia Park, NM	505	87047
Sandpoint, ID	208	83862–83864, 83888
Sandston, VA	804	23150
Sandstone, MN	320	55072
Sandusky, MI	810	48471
Sandusky, OH	419, 567	44870–44871
Sandwich, MA	508, 774	02563, 02644
Sandy, UT	801	84070, 84090–84094
Sandy Hook, CT	203	06482
Sandy Hook, KY	606	41171
Sandy Lake, PA	724, 878	16145
Sandy Spring, MD	301	20860
Sanford, FL	321, 407	32771–32773
Sanford, ME	207	04073
Sanford, NC	919	27237, 27330–27332
Sanger, CA	559	93657
Sangerfield, NY	315	13455
Sanibel, FL	239	33957
Santa Ana, CA	714, 949	92701–92712, 92725–92728*
Santa Ana Pueblo, NM	505	87004
Santa Barbara, CA	805	93101–93111, 93116–93121*
Santa Clara, CA	408	95050–95056
Santa Clarita, CA	661	91310, 91321–91322*
Santa Claus, IN	812	47579
Santa Cruz, CA	831	95060–95067
Santa Cruz, NM	505	87567
Santa Fe, NM	505	87500–87509, 87592–87594
Santa Fe Springs, CA	562	90605, 90670–90671
Santa Maria, CA	805	93454–93458
Santa Monica, CA	310, 424	90401–90411
Santa Paula, CA	805	93060–93061
Santa Rosa, CA	707	95401–95409
Santa Rosa, NM	505	88435
Santa Rosa, TX	956	78593
Santa Rosa Beach, FL	850	32459
Santa Teresa, NM	505	88008, 88063
Santa Ynez, CA	805	93460
Santee, CA	619	92071–92072
Santurce, PR	787, 939	00907–00916, 00936, 00940
Sapulpa, OK	918	74066–74067
Saraland, AL	251	36571
Saranac Lake, NY	518	12983
Sarasota, FL	941	34230–34243, 34260, 34276*
Saratoga, CA	408	95070–95071
Saratoga, WY	307	82331
Saratoga Springs, NY	518	12866
Sardinia, OH	937	45171
Sardis, MS	662	38666
Sarita, TX	361	78385
Sartell, MN	320	56377
Sasabe, AZ	520	85633
Satanta, KS	620	67870
Satsuma, AL	251	36572
Saugerties, NY	845	12477
Sauget, IL	618	62201
Saugus, CA	661	91350, 91390
Saugus, MA	339, 781	01906
Sauk Centre, MN	320	56378, 56389
Sauk City, WI	608	53583
Sauk Rapids, MN	320	56379
Saukville, WI	262	53080
Sault Sainte Marie, MI	906	49783, 49788
Sausalito, CA	415	94965–94966
Savage, MD	410, 443	20763
Savage, MN	952	55378

**Partial list of zip codes, including main range*

City	Area Code(s)	Zip Code(s)
Savanna, IL	815	61074
Savannah, GA	912	31401–31422, 31498–31499
Savannah, MO	816	64485
Savannah, TN	731	38372
Savoy, IL	217	61874
Saxonburg, PA	724, 878	16056
Sayre, OK	580	73662
Sayre, PA	570	18840
Sayreville, NJ	732, 848	08871–08872
Scandia, KS	785	66966
Scandinavia, WI	715	54977
Scappoose, OR	503, 971	97056
Scarborough, ME	207	04070, 04074
Scarsdale, NY	914	10583
Schaefferstown, PA	717	17088
Schaumburg, IL	224, 847	60159, 60168, 60173, 60192*
Schenectady, NY	518	12008, 12301–12309*
Schererville, IN	219	46375
Schertz, TX	210	78154
Schiller Park, IL	224, 847	60176
Schnecksville, PA	484, 610	18078
Schofield, WI	715	54476
Schoharie, NY	518	12157
Schoolcraft, MI	616	49087
Schuyler, NE	402	68661
Schuylkill Haven, PA	570	17972
Schwertner, TX	254	76573
Scituate, MA	339, 781	02040, 02055, 02060, 02066
Scobey, MT	406	59263
Scooba, MS	662	39358
Scotch Plains, NJ	908	07076
Scotia, CA	707	95565
Scotia, NY	518	12302
Scotland Neck, NC	252	27874
Scotrun, PA	570	18355
Scott, AR	501	72142
Scott, LA	337	70583
Scott, MS	662	38772
Scott AFB, IL	618	62225
Scott City, KS	620	67871
Scott City, MO	573	63780
Scott Depot, WV	304	25560
Scottdale, GA	404, 470	30079
Scottdale, PA	724, 878	15683
Scotts Valley, CA	831	95060, 95066–95067
Scottsbluff, NE	308	69361–69363
Scottsboro, AL	256	35768–35769
Scottsburg, IN	812	47170
Scottsdale, AZ	480	85250–85271
Scottsville, KY	270	42164
Scottsville, NY	585	14546
Scottsville, TX	903	75688
Scottville, MI	231	49454
Scranton, PA	570	18501–18522, 18540, 18577
Sea Island, GA	912	31561
Seabrook, NH	603	03874
Seabrook, NJ	856	08302
Seabrook, TX	281, 832	77586
Seabrook Island, SC	843	29455
Seaford, DE	302	19973
Seagoville, TX	469, 972	75159
Seal Beach, CA	562	90740
Seale, AL	334	36875
Searcy, AR	501	72143–72145, 72149
Searsmont, ME	207	04973
Searsport, ME	207	04974
Seaside, CA	831	93955
Seaside, OR	503	97138
Seaside Heights, NJ	732, 848	08751
Seattle, WA	206	98101–98138, 98144–98191*
Sebastian, FL	772	32958, 32976–32978
Sebastopol, CA	707	95472–95473
Sebastopol, MS	601, 769	39359
Sebring, FL	863	33870–33876
Sebring, OH	234, 330	44672
Secaucus, NJ	201, 551	07094–07096
Sedalia, CO	303, 720	80135
Sedalia, MO	660	65301–65302
Sedalia, NC	336	27342
Sedan, KS	620	67361
Sedona, AZ	928	86336–86341, 86351
Sedro Woolley, WA	360	98284
Seeley Lake, MT	406	59868
Seffner, FL	813	33583–33584
Seguin, TX	830	78155–78156
Selah, WA	509	98942
Selby, SD	605	57472
Selden, NY	631	11784
Selinsgrove, PA	570	17870
Selkirk, NY	518	12158
Sellersburg, IN	812	47172
Sellersville, PA	215, 267	18960
Sells, AZ	520	85634
Selma, AL	334	36701–36703
Selma, CA	559	93662
Selma, TX	210	78154
Selmer, TN	731	38375
Seminole, FL	727	33772–33778
Seminole, OK	405	74818, 74868
Seminole, TX	915	79360
Semmes, AL	251	36575
Senatobia, MS	662	38665–38668
Seneca, KS	785	66538
Seneca, SC	864	29672, 29678–29679
Seneca Falls, NY	315	13148
Sequatchie, TN	423	37374
Seven Hills, OH	216	44131
Severn, MD	410	21144
Severn, NC	252	27877
Severna Park, MD	410	21146
Sevierville, TN	865	37862–37864, 37868, 37876
Seville, OH	234, 330	44273
Sewanee, TN	931	37375, 37383
Seward, AK	907	99664
Seward, NE	402	68434
Sewell, NJ	856	08080
Sewickley, PA	412, 878	15143, 15189
Seymour, CT	203	06478, 06483
Seymour, IN	812	47274
Seymour, TX	940	76380
Seymour Johnson AFB, NC	919	27531
Shady Grove, PA	717	17256
Shadyside, OH	740	43947
Shafter, CA	661	93263
Shaftsbury, VT	802	05262
Shaker Heights, OH	216	44118–44122
Shakopee, MN	952	55379
Shallotte, NC	910	28459, 28467–28470
Shamokin, PA	570	17872
Shamokin Dam, PA	570	17876
Shannock, RI	401	02875
Sharon, CT	860	06069
Sharon, MA	339, 781	02067
Sharon, PA	724, 878	16146–16148
Sharon, WI	262	53585
Sharon Center, OH	234, 330	44274
Sharon Springs, KS	785	67758
Sharonville, OH	513	45241
Sharpsburg, MD	301	21782
Sharpsville, PA	724, 878	16150
Sharptown, MD	410	21861
Shavertown, PA	570	18708
Shaw AFB, SC	803	29152
Shawano, WI	715	54166
Shawnee, CO	303, 720	80448, 80475
Shawnee, KS	913	66203, 66214–66220*
Shawnee, OK	405	74801–74804
Shawnee Mission, KS	913	66201–66227, 66250, 66276*
Shawnee on Delaware, PA	570	18356
Shawneetown, IL	618	62984
Sheboygan, WI	920	53081–53083
Sheboygan Falls, WI	920	53085
Sheffield, AL	256	35660
Sheffield, IA	641	50475
Sheffield, MA	413	01257
Sheffield, PA	814	16347
Sheffield, TX	915	79781
Shelbina, MO	573	63468
Shelburne, VT	802	05482
Shelburne Falls, MA	413	01370
Shelby, MI	231	49455
Shelby, MT	406	59474
Shelby, NE	402	68662
Shelby, NC	704, 980	28150–28152
Shelby, OH	419, 567	44875
Shelby Township, MI	586	48315–48318
Shelbyville, IL	217	62565
Shelbyville, IN	317	46176
Shelbyville, KY	502	40065–40066
Shelbyville, MO	573	63469
Shelbyville, TN	931	37160–37162
Sheldon, IA	712	51201
Shell, WY	307	82441
Shell Lake, WI	715	54871
Shelley, ID	208	83274
Shellman, GA	229	31786
Shelocta, PA	724, 878	15774
Shelton, CT	203	06484
Shelton, NE	308	68876
Shelton, WA	360	98584
Shenandoah, IA	712	51601–51603
Shenandoah, PA	570	17976
Shepherdstown, WV	304	25443
Shepherdsville, KY	502	40165
Sheppard AFB, TX	940	76311
Sherburne, NY	607	13460
Sheridan, AR	870	72150
Sheridan, IN	317	46069
Sheridan, MI	989	48884
Sheridan, OR	503, 971	97378
Sheridan, WY	307	82801
Sherman, MS	662	38869
Sherman, TX	903	75090–75092
Sherman Oaks, CA	818	91401–91403, 91411–91413*
Sherwood, AR	501	72116–72120, 72124
Sherwood, OR	503, 971	97140
Shickshinny, PA	570	18655
Shillington, PA	484, 610	19607
Shiloh, OH	419, 567	44878
Shiloh, TN	731	38376
Shiner, TX	361	77984
Ship Bottom, NJ	609	08008
Shippensburg, PA	717	17257
Shippenville, PA	814	16254
Shiprock, NM	505	87420, 87461
Shipshewana, IN	260	46565
Shirley, MA	351, 978	01464
Shirley, NY	631	11967
Shoals, IN	812	47581
Shoemakersville, PA	484, 610	19555
Shoreline, WA	206	98133, 98155, 98177
Shoreview, MN	651	55126
Shorewood, IL	815	60431, 60435–60436
Short Hills, NJ	862, 973	07078
Shoshone, ID	208	83324, 83352
Show Low, AZ	928	85901–85902, 85911
Shreveport, LA	318	71101–71110, 71115–71120*
Shrewsbury, MA	508, 774	01545–01546
Shrewsbury, NJ	732, 848	07702
Shrub Oak, NY	914	10588
Sibley, IA	712	51249
Sibley, MO	816	64088
Sidney, IA	712	51652
Sidney, MI	989	48885
Sidney, MT	406	59270
Sidney, NE	308	69160–69162
Sidney, NY	607	13838
Sidney, OH	937	45365–45367
Sierra Blanca, TX	915	79851
Sierra Madre, CA	626	91024–91025
Sierra Vista, AZ	520	85613, 85635–85636*
Signal Hill, CA	562	90804–90807
Signal Mountain, TN	423	37377
Sigourney, IA	641	52591
Sikeston, MO	573	63801
Siler City, NC	919	27344
Siloam Springs, AR	479	72761
Silsbee, TX	409	77656
Silver Bay, MN	218	55614
Silver City, NM	505	88022, 88036, 88053, 88061*
Silver Creek, NE	308	68663
Silver Creek, NY	716	14136
Silver Lake, IN	260	46982

Partial list of zip codes, including main range

City	Area Code(s)	Zip Code(s)
Silver Lake, NH	603	03875
Silver Spring, MD	301	20901–20918, 20997
Silver Spring, PA	717	17575
Silver Springs, FL	352	34488–34489
Silverdale, WA	360	98315, 98383
Silverton, CO	970	81433
Silverton, OH	513	45236
Silverton, OR	503, 971	97381
Silverton, TX	806	79257
Silvis, IL	309	61282
Simi Valley, CA	805	93062–93065, 93093–93094*
Simpson, PA	570	18407
Simpsonville, KY	502	40067
Simpsonville, SC	864	29680–29681
Simsbury, CT	860	06070, 06081, 06089, 06092
Singer Island, FL	561	33404
Sinking Spring, PA	484, 610	19608
Sinton, TX	361	78387
Sioux Center, IA	712	51250
Sioux City, IA	712	51101–51111
Sioux Falls, SD	605	57101–57110, 57117–57118*
Siren, WI	715	54872
Sisseton, SD	605	57262
Sisters, OR	541	97759
Sitka, AK	907	99835–99836
Skagway, AK	907	99840
Skaneateles Falls, NY	315	13119, 13153
Skillman, NJ	908	08558
Skokie, IL	224, 847	60076–60077
Skowhegan, ME	207	04976
Sky Valley, GA	706, 762	30537
Skytop, PA	570	18357
Slater, CO	970	81653
Slater, IA	515	50244
Slatersville, RI	401	02876
Slaton, TX	806	79364
Slayton, MN	507	56172
Sleepy Eye, MN	507	56085
Slidell, LA	985	70458–70461, 70469
Slippery Rock, PA	724, 878	16057
Smackover, AR	870	71762
Smethport, PA	814	16749
Smith Center, KS	785	66967
Smithfield, NC	919	27577
Smithfield, RI	401	02828, 02917
Smithfield, VA	757	23430–23431
Smithland, KY	270	42081
Smithton, PA	724, 878	15479
Smithtown, NY	631	11745, 11787–11788
Smithville, MO	816	64089
Smithville, OH	234, 330	44677
Smithville, TN	615	37166
Smithville, TX	512	78957
Smyrna, DE	302	19977
Smyrna, GA	404, 770	30080–30082, 30339
Smyrna, TN	615	37167
Sneads, FL	850	32460
Sneedville, TN	423	37869
Snellville, GA	770	30039, 30078
Snohomish, WA	360	98290–98291, 98296
Snoqualmie, WA	425	98065–98068
Snow Hill, MD	410	21863
Snow Hill, NC	252	28580
Snowbird, UT	801	84092
Snowflake, AZ	928	85937, 85942
Snowmass Village, CO	970	81615
Snowshoe, WV	304	26209
Snyder, NE	402	68664
Snyder, TX	915	79549–79550
Social Circle, GA	470, 770	30025
Socorro, NM	505	87801
Soda Springs, ID	208	83230, 83276, 83285
Sodus, NY	315	14551
Solana Beach, CA	858	92075
Soldotna, AK	907	99669
Soledad, CA	831	93960
Solitude, UT	801	84121
Solomon, KS	785	67480
Solomons, MD	410	20688
Solon, OH	440	44139
Solvang, CA	805	93463–93464
Somers, CT	860	06071
Somers, NY	914	10589
Somers Point, NJ	609	08244
Somerset, KY	606	42501–42503, 42564
Somerset, MA	508, 774	02725–02726
Somerset, NJ	732, 848	08873–08875
Somerset, PA	814	15501, 15510
Somerton, AZ	928	85350
Somerville, MA	617, 857	02143–02145
Somerville, NJ	908	08876
Somerville, TN	901	38060, 38068
Sonoita, AZ	520	85637
Sonoma, CA	707	95476
Sonora, CA	209	95370–95373
Sonora, TX	915	76950
Sonyea, NY	585	14556
Soperton, GA	912	30457
Sorrento, LA	225	70778
Souderton, PA	215, 267	18964
South Attleboro, MA	508, 774	02703
South Barre, VT	802	05670
South Barrington, IL	224, 847	60010
South Bay, FL	561	33493
South Beloit, IL	815	61080
South Bend, IN	574	46601–46604, 46612–46620*
South Bend, WA	360	98586
South Boston, VA	434	24592
South Brunswick, NJ	732, 848	08810
South Burlington, VT	802	05401–05407
South Canaan, PA	570	18459
South Carver, MA	508, 774	02366
South Casco, ME	207	04077
South Charleston, WV	304	25303, 25309
South Chicago Heights, IL	708	60411
South Deerfield, MA	413	01373
South Easton, MA	508, 774	02375
South El Monte, CA	626	91733
South Elgin, IL	224, 847	60177
South Euclid, OH	216	44118–44121
South Fallsburg, NY	845	12779
South Fork, PA	814	15956
South Fulton, TN	731	38257
South Gate, CA	323, 562	90280
South Hackensack, NJ	201, 551	07606
South Hadley, MA	413	01075
South Haven, MI	616	49090
South Hill, VA	434	23970
South Holland, IL	708	60473
South Houston, TX	713, 832	77587
South Jordan, UT	801	84065, 84095
South Kearny, NJ	862, 973	07032
South Laguna, CA	949	92651
South Lake Tahoe, CA	530	96150–96158
South Lancaster, MA	351, 978	01561
South Lee, MA	413	01260
South Lyon, MI	248, 947	48178
South Miami, FL	305, 786	33143–33146, 33155–33156*
South Milwaukee, WI	414	53172
South Mountain, PA	717	17261
South Natick, MA	508, 774	01760
South Norwalk, CT	203	06854
South Orange, NJ	862, 973	07079
South Otselic, NY	315	13155
South Padre Island, TX	956	78597
South Paris, ME	207	04281
South Pasadena, CA	626	91030–91031
South Pittsburg, TN	423	37380
South Plainfield, NJ	908	07080
South Plymouth, NY	607	13844
South Point, OH	740	45680
South Portland, ME	207	04106, 04116
South River, NJ	732, 848	08877, 08882
South Saint Paul, MN	651	55075–55077
South Salt Lake, UT	801	84107, 84115, 84119, 84123*
South San Francisco, CA	650	94080–94083, 94099
South Sioux City, NE	402	68776
South Weymouth, MA	339, 781	02190
South Whitley, IN	260	46787
South Williamson, KY	606	41503
South Williamsport, PA	570	17702
South Windham, CT	860	06266
South Windham, ME	207	04082
South Windsor, CT	860	06074
South Yarmouth, MA	508, 774	02664, 02673
Southampton, NY	631	11968–11969
Southampton, PA	215, 267	18954, 18966
Southaven, MS	662	38671–38672
Southborough, MA	508, 774	01745, 01772
Southbridge, MA	508, 774	01550
Southbury, CT	203	06488
Southern Pines, NC	910	28387–28388
Southfield, MI	248, 947	48034–48037, 48075–48076*
Southgate, MI	734	48195
Southington, CT	860	06489
Southlake, TX	682, 817	76092
Southold, NY	631	11971
Southport, CT	203	06490
Southport, NC	910	28461, 28465
Southwest Harbor, ME	207	04656, 04679
Southwick, MA	413	01077
Spalding, ID	208	83540, 83551
Spanaway, WA	253	98387
Spanish Fort, AL	251	36527, 36577
Sparkill, NY	845	10976
Sparks, MD	410	21152
Sparks, NV	775	89431–89436
Sparta, GA	706, 762	31087
Sparta, MI	616	49345
Sparta, NJ	862, 973	07871
Sparta, NC	336	28675
Sparta, TN	931	38583
Sparta, WI	608	54656
Spartanburg, SC	864	29301–29307, 29316–29319
Spearfish, SD	605	57783, 57799
Spearman, TX	806	79081
Spearville, KS	620	67876
Speedway, IN	317	46224
Spencer, IN	812	47460
Spencer, IA	712	51301, 51343
Spencer, MA	508, 774	01562
Spencer, NY	607	14883
Spencer, NC	704, 980	28159
Spencer, TN	931	38585
Spencer, WV	304	25276
Spencerport, NY	585	14559
Spencerville, OH	419, 567	45887
Spiceland, IN	765	47385
Spindale, NC	828	28160
Spirit Lake, IA	712	51360
Spokane, WA	509	99201–99224, 99228, 99251*
Spotsylvania, VA	540	22553
Spring, TX	281, 832	77373, 77379–77393
Spring Arbor, MI	517	49283
Spring City, PA	484, 610	19475
Spring City, UT	435	84662
Spring Green, WI	608	53588
Spring Grove, IL	815	60081
Spring Hill, FL	352	34604–34611
Spring Hill, TN	931	37174
Spring Hope, NC	252	27882
Spring House, PA	215, 267	19477
Spring Lake, MI	231, 616	49456
Spring Lake, NJ	732, 848	07762
Spring Lake Park, MN	612, 763	55432
Spring Mills, PA	814	16875
Spring Valley, CA	619	91976–91979
Spring Valley, IL	815	61362
Spring Valley, MN	507	55975
Spring Valley, NY	845	10977
Spring Valley, WI	715	54767
Springboro, OH	513	45066
Springdale, AR	479	72762–72766
Springdale, OH	513	45246
Springdale, PA	724, 878	15144
Springdale, UT	435	84767, 84779
Springer, NM	505	87729, 87747
Springer, OK	580	73458
Springfield, CO	719	81073
Springfield, GA	912	31329
Springfield, IL	217	62701–62709, 62713–62726*
Springfield, KY	859	40069
Springfield, MA	413	01101–01119, 01128–01129*

Partial list of zip codes, including main range

City	Area Code(s)	Zip Code(s)
Springfield, MN	507	56087
Springfield, MO	417	65721, 65742, 65801, 65810*
Springfield, NJ	862, 973	07081
Springfield, OH	937	45501–45506
Springfield, OR	541	97477–97478, 97482
Springfield, PA	484, 610	19064, 19118
Springfield, SD	605	57062
Springfield, TN	615	37172
Springfield, VT	802	05156
Springfield, VA	571, 703	22009, 22015, 22150, 22161
Springfield Gardens, NY	347, 718	11413
Springs, PA	814	15562
Springtown, TX	682, 817	76082
Springvale, ME	207	04083
Springview, NE	402	68778
Springville, AL	205	35146
Springville, UT	801	84663
Spruce Pine, NC	828	28777
Stafford, TX	281, 832	77477, 77497
Stafford, VA	540	22554–22555
Stafford Springs, CT	860	06076
Stamford, CT	203	06901–06914, 06920–06928
Stamford, NY	607	12167
Stamps, AR	870	71860
Stanardsville, VA	434	22973
Stanberry, MO	660	64489
Standish, ME	207	04084
Standish, MI	989	48658
Stanfield, AZ	520	85272
Stanford, CA	650	94305, 94309
Stanford, KY	606	40484
Stanford, MT	406	59479
Stanhope, NJ	862, 973	07874
Stanley, NC	704, 980	28164
Stanley, ND	701	58784
Stanleytown, VA	276	24168
Stanton, CA	714	90680
Stanton, KY	606	40380
Stanton, MI	989	48888
Stanton, NE	402	68779
Stanton, ND	701	58571
Stanton, TX	915	79782
Stanwood, WA	360	98282, 98292
Staples, MN	218	56479
Stapleton, NE	308	69163
Star, NC	910	27356
Star City, AR	870	71667
Starbuck, MN	320	56381
Starke, FL	904	32091
Starkville, MS	662	39759–39760
State Center, IA	641	50247
State College, PA	814	16801–16805
State Farm, VA	804	23160
State University, AR	870	72467
Stateline, NV	775	89449
Staten Island, NY	347, 718	10301–10314
Statenville, GA	229	31648
Statesboro, GA	912	30458–30461
Statesville, NC	704, 980	28625, 28677, 28687
Staunton, VA	540	24401–24402, 24407
Stayton, OR	503, 971	97383
Steamboat Springs, CO	970	80477, 80487–80488
Stearns, KY	606	42647
Steele, ND	701	58482
Steeleville, IL	618	62288
Steelville, MO	573	65565–65566
Steilacoom, WA	253	98388
Stennis Space Center, MS	228	39522, 39529
Stephenville, TX	254	76401–76402
Sterling, CO	970	80751
Sterling, IL	815	61081
Sterling, KS	620	67579
Sterling, VA	571, 703	20163–20167
Sterling City, TX	915	76951
Sterling Heights, MI	586	48310–48314
Steubenville, OH	740	43952–43953
Stevens Point, WI	715	54481, 54492
Stevensburg, VA	540	22741
Stevenson, AL	256	35772
Stevenson, CT	203	06491
Stevenson, MD	410	21153

City	Area Code(s)	Zip Code(s)
Stevenson, WA	509	98648
Stevensville, MD	410	21666
Stevensville, MI	616	49127
Stewart, MN	320	55385
Stewartville, MN	507	55976
Stigler, OK	918	74462
Stillwater, ME	207	04489
Stillwater, MN	651	55082–55083
Stillwater, NY	518	12170
Stillwater, OK	405	74074–74078
Stilwell, OK	918	74960
Stinnett, TX	806	79083
Stirling, NJ	908	07980
Stockbridge, GA	470, 770	30281
Stockbridge, MA	413	01262–01263
Stockton, CA	209	95201–95215, 95219, 95267*
Stockton, KS	785	67669
Stockton, MO	417	65785
Stockville, NE	308	69042
Stone Creek, OH	234, 330	43840
Stone Mountain, GA	470, 770	30083–30088
Stone Ridge, NY	845	12484
Stoneham, MA	339, 781	02180
Stoneville, MS	662	38776
Stonington, CT	860	06378
Stony Brook, NY	631	11790, 11794
Stony Creek, VA	434	23882
Stony Point, NY	845	10980
Storm Lake, IA	712	50588
Stormville, NY	845	12582
Storrs, CT	860	06268
Stoughton, MA	339, 781	02072
Stoughton, WI	608	53589
Stow, OH	234, 330	44224
Stowe, PA	484, 610	19464
Stowe, VT	802	05672
Stoystown, PA	814	15563
Strafford, MO	417	65757
Strasburg, CO	303, 720	80136
Strasburg, OH	234, 330	44680
Strasburg, VA	540	22641, 22657
Stratford, CA	559	93266
Stratford, CT	203	06497, 06614–06615
Stratford, NJ	856	08084
Stratford, TX	806	79084
Stratford, WI	715	54484
Stratham, NH	603	03885
Stratton, CO	719	80836
Stratton Mountain, VT	802	05155
Strausstown, PA	484, 610	19559
Strawberry Point, IA	563	52076
Streamwood, IL	331, 630	60107
Streator, IL	815	61364
Streetsboro, OH	234, 330	44241
Stringtown, OK	580	74569
Stromsburg, NE	402	68666
Strongsville, OH	440	44136, 44149
Stroudsburg, PA	570	18360
Stryker, OH	419, 567	43557
Stuart, FL	772	34994–34997
Stuart, VA	276	24171
Stuarts Draft, VA	540	24477
Studio City, CA	818	91602–91607, 91614
Sturbridge, MA	508, 774	01518, 01566
Sturgeon Bay, WI	920	54235
Sturgis, MI	616	49091
Sturgis, SD	605	57785
Sturtevant, WI	262	53177
Stuttgart, AR	870	72160
Subiaco, AR	479	72865
Sublette, KS	620	67877
Sublimity, OR	503, 971	97385
Succasunna, NJ	862, 973	07876
Sudbury, MA	351, 978	01776
Suffern, NY	845	10901
Suffield, CT	860	06078–06080, 06093
Suffolk, VA	757	23432–23439
Sugar Grove, IL	331, 630	60554
Sugar Land, TX	281, 832	77478–77479, 77487, 77496
Sugar Valley, GA	706, 762	30746
Sugarcreek, OH	234, 330	44681

City	Area Code(s)	Zip Code(s)
Suitland, MD	301	20746, 20752
Sullivan, IL	217	61951
Sullivan, IN	812	47864, 47882
Sullivan, MO	573	63080
Sullivans Island, SC	843	29482
Sulphur, LA	337	70663–70665
Sulphur, OK	580	73086
Sulphur Springs, TX	903	75482–75483
Sultan, WA	360	98294
Summerdale, AL	251	36580
Summerdale, PA	717	17093
Summersville, WV	304	26651
Summerville, GA	706, 762	30747
Summerville, SC	843	29483–29485
Summit, IL	708	60501
Summit, MS	601, 769	39666
Summit, NJ	908	07901–07902
Summit, NY	518	12175
Summit Station, PA	570	17979
Summitville, OH	234, 330	43962
Sumner, WA	253	98352, 98390
Sumter, SC	803	29150–29154
Sumterville, FL	352	33585
Sun City, AZ	623	85351, 85372–85379
Sun City, CA	951	92584–92587
Sun City, FL	813	33586
Sun City Center, FL	813	33570–33573
Sun City West, AZ	623	85374–85379, 85387
Sun Lakes, AZ	480	85248
Sun Prairie, WI	608	53590–53591, 53596
Sun Valley, CA	818	91352–91353
Sun Valley, ID	208	83353–83354
Sunbury, OH	740	43074
Sunbury, PA	570	17801, 17877
Suncook, NH	603	03275
Sundance, WY	307	82729
Sunland, CA	818	91040–91041
Sunland Park, NM	505	88008, 88063
Sunman, IN	812	47041
Sunny Isles Beach, FL	305, 786	33160
Sunnyside, NY	347, 718	11104
Sunnyside, WA	509	98944
Sunnyvale, CA	408	94085–94090
Sunnyvale, TX	469, 972	75182
Sunrise, FL	754, 954	33304, 33313, 33319, 33326*
Sunriver, OR	541	97707
Superior, AZ	520	85273
Superior, MT	406	59872
Superior, WI	715	54880
Supply, NC	910	28462
Surfside, FL	305, 786	33154
Surfside Beach, SC	843	29575, 29587
Surgoinsville, TN	423	37873
Surry, VA	757	23883
Susanville, CA	530	96127–96130
Sussex, NJ	862, 973	07461
Sussex, VA	434	23884
Sussex, WI	262	53089
Sutherlin, OR	541	97479
Sutter, CA	530	95982
Sutton, MA	508, 774	01590
Sutton, WV	304	26601
Suttons Bay, MI	231	49682
Suwanee, GA	470, 678, 770	30024
Swainsboro, GA	478	30401
Swampscott, MA	339, 781	01907
Swannanoa, NC	828	28778
Swanquarter, NC	252	27885
Swansea, IL	618	62220–62226
Swansea, MA	508, 774	02777
Swanton, OH	419, 567	43558
Swanton, VT	802	05488
Swarthmore, PA	484, 610	19081
Swartz Creek, MI	810	48473
Swea City, IA	515	50590
Swedesboro, NJ	856	08085
Sweet Briar, VA	434	24595
Sweet Home, OR	541	97386
Sweetwater, TN	423	37874
Sweetwater, TX	915	79556
Swepsonville, NC	336	27359

Partial list of zip codes, including main range

City	Area Code(s)	Zip Code(s)
Swiftwater, PA	570	18370
Swissvale, PA	412, 878	15218
Swords Creek, VA	276	24649
Swoyersville, PA	570	18704
Sycamore, AL	256	35149
Sycamore, IL	815	60178
Sykesville, MD	410	21784
Sylacauga, AL	256	35150–35151
Sylmar, CA	818	91342, 91392
Sylva, NC	828	28779
Sylvania, GA	912	30467
Sylvania, OH	419, 567	43560
Sylvester, GA	229	31791
Syosset, NY	516	11773, 11791
Syracuse, IN	574	46567
Syracuse, KS	620	67878
Syracuse, NE	402	68446
Syracuse, NY	315	13201–13225, 13235, 13244*

T

City	Area Code(s)	Zip Code(s)
Tabor, SD	605	57063
Tabor City, NC	910	28463
Tacoma, WA	253	98401–98424, 98431–98433*
Taft, CA	661	93268
Taft, OK	918	74463
Taftville, CT	860	06380
Tahlequah, OK	918	74464–74465
Tahoe City, CA	530	96145–96146
Tahoka, TX	806	79373
Takoma Park, MD	301	20903, 20912–20913
Talbotton, GA	706, 762	31827
Talihina, OK	918	74571
Talladega, AL	256	35160–35161
Tallahassee, FL	850	32301–32318, 32395, 32399
Tallapoosa, GA	470, 770	30176
Tallassee, AL	334	36023, 36045, 36078
Tallevast, FL	941	34270
Tallmadge, OH	234, 330	44278
Tallulah, LA	318	71282–71284
Talmage, PA	717	17580
Taloga, OK	580	73667
Tama, IA	641	52339
Tamaqua, PA	570	18252
Tamarac, FL	754, 954	33309, 33319–33323*
Tamiment, PA	570	18371
Tamms, IL	618	62988, 62993
Tampa, FL	813	33601–33637, 33647–33651*
Taneytown, MD	410	21787
Tangent, OR	541	97389
Tannersville, PA	570	18372
Taos, NM	505	87571
Tappahannock, VA	804	22560
Tarboro, NC	252	27886
Tarentum, PA	724, 878	15084
Tarpon Springs, FL	727	34688–34691
Tarrytown, NY	914	10591
Tarzana, CA	818	91335, 91356–91357
Taunton, MA	508, 774	02718, 02780–02783
Tavares, FL	352	32778
Tavernier, FL	305, 786	33070
Tawas City, MI	989	48763–48764
Taylor, MI	313, 734	48180
Taylor, NE	308	68879
Taylor, PA	570	18517
Taylor, TX	512	76574
Taylors, SC	864	29687
Taylorsville, KY	502	40071
Taylorsville, MS	601, 769	39168
Taylorsville, NC	828	28681
Taylorville, IL	217	62568
Tazewell, TN	423	37879
Tazewell, VA	276	24608, 24651
Teaneck, NJ	201, 551	07666
Teays, WV	304	25569
Tecumseh, MI	517	49286
Tecumseh, NE	402	68450
Tecumseh, OK	405	74873
Tehachapi, CA	661	93561, 93581
Tekamah, NE	402	68061
Telford, PA	215, 267	18969
Tell City, IN	812	47586
Telluride, CO	970	81435
Temecula, CA	951	92589–92593
Tempe, AZ	480, 602	85280–85289
Temperance, MI	734	48182
Temple, PA	484, 610	19560
Temple, TX	254	76501–76508
Temple City, CA	626	91780
Temple Hills, MD	301	20748, 20752, 20757, 20762
Temple Terrace, FL	813	33617, 33637, 33687
Templeton, CA	805	93465
Tenafly, NJ	201, 551	07670
Tenino, WA	360	98589
Tenstrike, MN	218	56683
Tequesta, FL	561	33469
Terminal Island, CA	310, 424	90731
Terra Bella, CA	559	93270
Terre Haute, IN	812	47801–47814
Terrell, TX	469, 972	75160–75161
Terry, MT	406	59349
Terryville, CT	860	06786
Teterboro, NJ	201, 551	07608
Teton Village, WY	307	83025
Teutopolis, IL	217	62467
Tewksbury, MA	351, 978	01876
Texarkana, AR	870	71854
Texarkana, TX	903	75501–75507, 75599
Texas City, TX	409	77590–77592
Thatcher, AZ	928	85552
The Colony, TX	469, 972	75034, 75056
The Dalles, OR	541	97058
The Sea Ranch, CA	707	95445, 95497
The Villages, FL	352	32159–32162
The Woodlands, TX	281, 832	77380–77387, 77393
Thedford, NE	308	69166
Theodore, AL	251	36582, 36590, 36619
Thermopolis, WY	307	82443
Thibodaux, LA	985	70301–70302, 70310
Thief River Falls, MN	218	56701
Thiensville, WI	262	53092, 53097
Thomaston, CT	860	06778, 06787
Thomaston, GA	706, 762	30286
Thomaston, ME	207	04861
Thomasville, AL	334	36762, 36784
Thomasville, GA	229	31757–31758, 31792, 31799
Thomasville, NC	336	27360–27361
Thomasville, PA	717	17364
Thompson, CT	860	06277
Thompson, IA	641	50478
Thompson Falls, MT	406	59873
Thompsons Station, TN	615	37179
Thompsonville, MI	231	49683
Thomson, GA	706, 762	30824
Thorndale, PA	484, 610	19372
Thornton, CO	303, 720	80020, 80221, 80229, 80233*
Thornton, IL	708	60476
Thornville, OH	740	43076
Thornwood, NY	914	10594
Thorofare, NJ	856	08086
Thousand Oaks, CA	805	91319–91320, 91358–91362
Three Lakes, WI	715	54562
Three Rivers, CA	559	93271
Three Rivers, MI	616	49093
Three Rivers, TX	361	78060, 78071
Throckmorton, TX	940	76483
Thurmont, MD	301	21788
Tiburon, CA	415	94920
Tie Siding, WY	307	82084
Tierra Amarilla, NM	505	87575
Tierra Verde, FL	727	33715
Tiffin, OH	419, 567	44883
Tifton, GA	229	31793–31794
Tigard, OR	503, 971	97223–97224, 97281
Tigerville, SC	864	29688
Tilden, TX	361	78072
Tillamook, OR	503	97141
Tillery, NC	252	27887
Tilton, NH	603	03276, 03298–03299
Timber Lake, SD	605	57656
Timberline Lodge, OR	503, 971	97028
Timmonsville, SC	843	29161
Timonium, MD	410	21093–21094
Tinker AFB, OK	405	73145
Tinley Park, IL	708	60477
Tinton Falls, NJ	732, 848	07724
Tionesta, PA	814	16353
Tipp City, OH	937	45371
Tipton, IN	765	46072
Tipton, IA	563	52772
Tipton, MO	660	65081
Tipton, OK	580	73570
Tipton, PA	814	16684
Tiptonville, TN	731	38079
Tishomingo, OK	580	73460
Titusville, FL	321	32780–32783, 32796
Titusville, NJ	609	08560
Titusville, PA	814	16354
Toa Baja, PR	787, 939	00949–00951
Toccoa, GA	706, 762	30577
Toccoa Falls, GA	706, 762	30598
Togo, MN	218	55723
Tok, AK	907	99776–99780
Tokeland, WA	360	98590
Toledo, IL	217	62468
Toledo, IA	641	52342
Toledo, OH	419, 567	43601–43624, 43635, 43652*
Tolland, CT	860	06084
Tolleson, AZ	623	85353
Tollhouse, CA	559	93667
Tolono, IL	217	61880
Toluca, IL	815	61369
Tomah, WI	608	54660
Tomball, TX	281, 832	77337, 77375–77377
Tombstone, AZ	520	85638
Tompkinsville, KY	270	42167
Toms River, NJ	732, 848	08753–08757
Tonalea, AZ	928	86044, 86053–86054
Tonawanda, NY	716	14150–14151, 14217, 14223
Tonkawa, OK	580	74653
Tonopah, NV	775	89049
Tontitown, AR	479	72770
Tooele, UT	435	84074
Topeka, IN	260	46571
Topeka, KS	785	66601–66629, 66634–66638*
Toppenish, WA	509	98948
Topsfield, MA	351, 978	01983
Topsham, ME	207	04086
Topton, PA	484, 610	19562
Torrance, CA	310, 424	90501–90510
Torrance, PA	724, 878	15779
Torrey, UT	435	84775
Torrington, CT	860	06790–06791
Torrington, WY	307	82240
Totowa, NJ	862, 973	07511–07512
Tougaloo, MS	601, 769	39174
Toulon, IL	309	61483
Toutle, WA	360	98645, 98649
Towaco, NJ	862, 973	07082
Towanda, PA	570	18848
Towner, ND	701	58788
Townsend, MA	351, 978	01469, 01474
Townsend, MT	406	59644
Townsend, TN	865	37882
Towson, MD	410	21204, 21284–21286
Tracy, CA	209	95304, 95376–95378*
Travelers Rest, SC	864	29690
Traverse City, MI	231	49684–49686, 49696
Travis AFB, CA	707	94535
Tremonton, UT	435	84337
Trenton, FL	352	32693
Trenton, GA	706, 762	30752
Trenton, ME	207	04605
Trenton, MI	734	48183
Trenton, MO	660	64683
Trenton, NE	308	69044
Trenton, NJ	609	08601–08611, 08618–08620*
Trenton, NC	252	28585
Trenton, OH	513	45067
Trenton, SC	803	29847
Trenton, TN	731	38382
Trevor, WI	262	53102, 53179
Trevose, PA	215, 267	19053

*Partial list of zip codes, including main range

City	Area Code(s)	Zip Code(s)
Triangle, VA	571, 703	22172
Tribune, KS	620	67879
Trinidad, CO	719	81074, 81082
Trinity, AL	256	35673
Trinity, NC	336	27370
Trinity Center, CA	530	96091
Trion, GA	706, 762	30753
Trotwood, OH	937	45406, 45415–45418*
Troutdale, OR	503, 971	97060
Troy, AL	334	36079–36082
Troy, ID	208	83871
Troy, IL	618	62294
Troy, KS	785	66087
Troy, MI	248, 947	48007, 48083–48085*
Troy, MO	636	63379
Troy, NY	518	12179–12183
Troy, NC	910	27371
Troy, OH	937	45373–45374
Troy, VA	434	22974
Truckee, CA	530	96160–96162
Truman, MN	507	56088
Trumann, AR	870	72472
Trumbauersville, PA	215, 267	18970
Trumbull, CT	203	06611
Trussville, AL	205	35173
Truth or Consequences, NM	505	87901
Tryon, NE	308	69167
Tryon, NC	828	28782
Tsaile, AZ	928	86556
Tualatin, OR	503, 971	97062
Tuba City, AZ	928	86045
Tuckahoe, NY	914	10707
Tucker, AR	501	72168
Tucker, GA	470, 678, 770	30084–30085
Tucson, AZ	520	85701–85754, 85775–85777
Tucumcari, NM	505	88401, 88416
Tukwila, WA	206, 425	98108, 98138, 98168, 98178*
Tulare, CA	559	93274–93275
Tulelake, CA	530	96134
Tulia, TX	806	79088
Tullahoma, TN	931	37388–37389
Tullytown, PA	215, 267	19007
Tulsa, OK	918	74101–74121, 74126–74137*
Tumacacori, AZ	520	85640, 85645–85646
Tumwater, WA	360	98501, 98511–98512
Tunica, MS	662	38676
Tunkhannock, PA	570	18657
Tupelo, MS	662	38801–38804
Turbeville, SC	843	29162
Turlock, CA	209	95380–95382
Turner, OR	503, 971	97359, 97392
Turners Falls, MA	413	01349, 01376
Turnersville, NJ	856	08012
Turpin, OK	580	73950
Turtle Creek, PA	412, 878	15145
Turtle Lake, WI	715	54004, 54889
Tuscaloosa, AL	205	35401–35407, 35485–35487
Tuscola, IL	217	61953
Tuscola, TX	915	79562
Tuscumbia, AL	256	35674
Tuscumbia, MO	573	65082
Tuskegee, AL	334	36083
Tuskegee Institute, AL	334	36083, 36087–36088
Tustin, CA	714	92780–92782
Twentynine Palms, CA	760	92277–92278
Twin Bridges, MT	406	59754
Twin Falls, ID	208	83301–83303
Twinsburg, OH	234, 330	44087
Two Harbors, MN	218	55616
Two Rivers, WI	920	54241
Tybee Island, GA	912	31328
Tyler, MN	507	56178
Tyler, TX	903	75701–75713, 75798–75799
Tylertown, MS	601, 769	39667
Tyndall, SD	605	57066
Tyndall AFB, FL	850	32403
Tyngsboro, MA	351, 978	01879
Tyrone, GA	470, 770	30290
Tyrone, PA	814	16686

U

City	Area Code(s)	Zip Code(s)
Ubly, MI	989	48475
Uhrichsville, OH	740	44683
Ukiah, CA	707	95418, 95482
Ullin, IL	618	62992
Ulm, MT	406	59485
Ulysses, KS	620	67880
Umatilla, OR	541	97882
Una, SC	864	29378
Unadilla, GA	478	31091
Unadilla, NY	607	13849
Unalakleet, AK	907	99684
Unalaska, AK	907	99547, 99685, 99692
Uncasville, CT	860	06382
Union, IL	815	60180
Union, MO	636	63084
Union, NJ	908	07083
Union, SC	864	29379
Union, WA	360	98592
Union, WV	304	24983
Union City, CA	510	94587
Union City, GA	470, 770	30291
Union City, IN	765	47390
Union City, NJ	201, 551	07086–07087
Union City, PA	814	16438
Union City, TN	731	38261, 38281
Union Gap, WA	509	98901–98903
Union Grove, WI	262	53182
Union Lake, MI	248, 947	48387
Union Springs, AL	334	36089
Uniondale, NY	516	11553–11556, 11588
Uniontown, AL	334	36786
Uniontown, OH	234, 330	44685
Uniontown, PA	724, 878	15401
Unionville, MO	660	63565
Unity, ME	207	04988
Universal City, CA	818	91608, 91618
Universal City, TX	210	78148–78150
University, MS	662	38677
University Center, MI	989	48710
University City, MO	314	63124, 63130
University Heights, OH	216	44118, 44122
University of Richmond, VA	804	23173
University Park, IL	708	60466
University Park, IA	641	52595
University Park, PA	814	16802
Upland, CA	909	91784–91786
Upland, IN	765	46989
Upland, PA	484, 610	19013–19015
Upper Arlington, OH	614	43220–43221
Upper Black Eddy, PA	484, 610	18972
Upper Marlboro, MD	301	20772–20775, 20792
Upper Montclair, NJ	862, 973	07043
Upper Saddle River, NJ	201, 551	07458
Upper Saint Clair, PA	724, 878	15241
Upper Sandusky, OH	419, 567	43351
Upperville, VA	540	20184–20185
Upton, MA	508, 774	01568
Upton, NY	631	11973
Urbana, IL	217	61801–61803
Urbana, IN	260	46990
Urbana, IA	319	52345
Urbana, OH	937	43078
Urbandale, IA	515	50322–50323
Ursa, IL	217	62376
USAF Academy, CO	719	80841
Utica, MI	586	48315–48318
Utica, MS	601, 769	39175
Utica, NY	315	13501–13505, 13599
Uvalde, TX	830	78801–78802

V

City	Area Code(s)	Zip Code(s)
Vacaville, CA	707	95687–95688, 95696
Vail, CO	970	81657–81658
Valdese, NC	828	28690
Valdez, AK	907	99686
Valdosta, GA	229	31601–31606, 31698–31699
Vale, OR	541	97918
Valencia, CA	661	91354–91355, 91380, 91385
Valencia, PA	724, 878	16059
Valentine, NE	402	69201
Valhalla, NY	914	10595
Vallejo, CA	707	94503, 94589–94592
Valley, AL	334	36854, 36872
Valley Center, CA	760	92082
Valley Center, KS	316	67147
Valley City, ND	701	58072
Valley City, OH	234, 330	44280
Valley Cottage, NY	845	10989
Valley Falls, NY	518	12185
Valley Forge, PA	484, 610	19481–19485, 19493–19496
Valley Park, MO	636	63088
Valley Stream, NY	516	11580–11583
Valley View, OH	216	44125, 44131
Valley View, TX	940	76272
Valley Village, CA	818	91607, 91617
Valparaiso, IN	219	46383–46385
Valyermo, CA	661	93563
Van Alstyne, TX	903	75495
Van Buren, AR	479	72956–72957
Van Buren, MO	573	63965
Van Horn, TX	915	79855
Van Nuys, CA	818	91316, 91388, 91401, 91416*
Van Wert, OH	419, 567	45891
Vanceburg, KY	606	41179
Vancouver, WA	360	98660–98668, 98682–98687
Vandalia, IL	618	62471
Vandalia, OH	937	45377
Vandenberg AFB, CA	805	93437
Vanderbilt, MI	989	49795
Vandergrift, PA	724, 878	15690
Vansant, VA	276	24656
Vashon, WA	206	98013, 98070
Vassar, MI	989	48768–48769
Vega, TX	806	79092
Vega Alta, PR	787, 939	00692
Velva, ND	701	58790
Venice, CA	310, 424	90291–90296
Venice, FL	941	34284–34293
Ventura, CA	805	93001–93009
Verdi, NV	775	89439
Vergennes, VT	802	05491
Vermillion, SD	605	57069
Vernal, UT	435	84078–84079
Vernon, AL	205	35592
Vernon, CA	323	90058
Vernon, CT	860	06066
Vernon, IN	812	47282
Vernon, NJ	862, 973	07462
Vernon, NY	315	13476
Vernon, TX	940	76384–76385
Vernon Hills, IL	224, 847	60061
Vernonia, OR	503, 971	97064
Vero Beach, FL	772	32960–32969
Verona, MS	662	38879
Verona, NY	315	13478
Verona, PA	412, 878	15147
Verona, VA	540	24482
Verona, WI	608	53593
Versailles, IN	812	47042
Versailles, KY	859	40383–40386
Versailles, MO	573	65084
Vesta, VA	276	24177
Vestal, NY	607	13850–13851
Vevay, IN	812	47043
Vicksburg, MI	616	49097
Vicksburg, MS	601, 769	39180–39183
Victor, ID	208	83455
Victor, NY	585	14564
Victoria, MN	952	55386
Victoria, TX	361	77901–77905
Victoria, VA	434	23974
Vidalia, GA	912	30474–30475
Vidalia, LA	318	71373
Vienna, GA	229	31092
Vienna, IL	618	62995
Vienna, MO	573	65582
Vienna, OH	234, 330	44473
Vienna, VA	571, 703	22027, 22124, 22180, 22185
Vienna, WV	304	26101, 26105
Viera, FL	321	32940, 32955
Villa Park, IL	331, 630	60181
Villanova, PA	484, 610	19085

*Partial list of zip codes, including main range

City	Area Code(s)	Zip Code(s)
Ville Platte, LA	337	70586
Vinalhaven, ME	207	04863
Vincennes, IN	812	47591
Vincent, AL	205	35178
Vineland, NJ	856	08360–08362
Vineyard Haven, MA	508, 774	02568, 02573
Vinita, OK	918	74301
Vinton, IA	319	52349
Vinton, LA	337	70668
Vinton, VA	540	24179
Virginia, IL	217	62691
Virginia, MN	218	55777, 55792
Virginia Beach, VA	757	23450–23471, 23479
Virginia City, MT	406	59755
Virginia City, NV	775	89440
Viroqua, WI	608	54665
Visalia, CA	559	93277–93279, 93290–93292
Vista, CA	760	92083–92085
Vivian, LA	318	71082
Vonore, TN	423	37885
Voorhees, NJ	856	08043
Voorheesville, NY	518	12186

W

City	Area Code(s)	Zip Code(s)
Wabash, IN	260	46992
Wabasha, MN	651	55981
Wabasso, FL	772	32970
Waco, TX	254	76701–76716, 76795–76799
Waconia, MN	952	55375, 55387
Waddington, NY	315	13694
Wadena, MN	218	56482
Wadesboro, NC	704, 980	28170
Wadley, AL	256	36276
Wadley, GA	478	30477
Wadsworth, OH	234, 330	44281–44282
Wagoner, OK	918	74467, 74477
Wahoo, NE	402	68066
Wahpeton, ND	701	58074–58076
Waianae, HI	808	96792
Waikoloa, HI	808	96738
Wailea, HI	808	96753
Wailuku, HI	808	96793
Waimanalo, HI	808	96795
Waipahu, HI	808	96797
Waite Park, MN	320	56387–56388
Wakarusa, IN	574	46573
Wake Forest, NC	919	27587–27588
WaKeeney, KS	785	67672
Wakefield, MA	339, 781	01880
Wakefield, MI	906	49968
Wakefield, RI	401	02879–02883
Wakulla Springs, FL	850	32327
Walbridge, OH	419, 567	43465
Walcott, IA	563	52773
Walden, CO	970	80430, 80480
Walden, NY	845	12586
Waldorf, MD	301	20601–20604
Waldron, AR	479	72924, 72958
Wales, WI	262	53183
Waleska, GA	470, 770	30183
Walhalla, SC	864	29691
Walker, MI	616	49544
Walker, MN	218	56484
Walkerton, IN	574	46574
Wall, NJ	732, 848	07719
Wall, SD	605	57790
Walla Walla, WA	509	99362
Wallace, ID	208	83873–83874
Wallace, NC	910	28466
Wallace, SC	843	29596
Walland, TN	865	37886
Walled Lake, MI	248, 947	48390–48391
Waller, TX	281, 832	77484
Wallingford, CT	203	06492–06495
Wallingford, PA	484, 610	19086
Wallington, NJ	862, 973	07057
Wallkill, NY	845	12589
Walls, MS	662	38680, 38686
Walnut, CA	909	91788–91789, 91795
Walnut, IL	815	61376
Walnut Creek, CA	925	94595–94598
Walnut Creek, OH	234, 330	44687
Walnut Ridge, AR	870	72476
Walpole, MA	508, 774	02032, 02071, 02081
Walpole, NH	603	03608
Walsenburg, CO	719	81089
Walstonburg, NC	252	27888
Walterboro, SC	843	29488
Walters, OK	580	73572
Walthall, MS	662	39771
Waltham, MA	339, 781	02451–02455
Walthourville, GA	912	31333
Walton, IN	574	46994
Walton Hills, OH	440	44146
Walworth, WI	262	53184
Wamego, KS	785	66547
Wampsville, NY	315	13163
Wanamingo, MN	507	55983
Wanatah, IN	219	46390
Wantagh, NY	516	11793
Wapakoneta, OH	419, 567	45819, 45895
Wapato, WA	509	98951
Wapello, IA	319	52653
Wapiti, WY	307	82450
Wappingers Falls, NY	845	12590
Ward, CO	303, 720	80481
Ward Hill, MA	351, 978	01835
Warden, WA	509	98857
Ware, MA	413	01082
Wareham, MA	508, 774	02571
Warfordsburg, PA	301	17267
Warm Springs, GA	706, 762	31830
Warm Springs, MT	406	59756
Warm Springs, OR	541	97761
Warm Springs, VA	540	24484
Warminster, PA	215, 267	18974, 18991
Warner, NH	603	03278
Warner, OK	918	74469
Warner Robins, GA	478	31088, 31093–31099
Warren, AR	870	71671
Warren, MI	586	48088–48093, 48397
Warren, MN	218	56762
Warren, NJ	908	07059
Warren, OH	234, 330	44481–44488
Warren, PA	814	16365–16369
Warren, RI	401	02885
Warren, VT	802	05674
Warrendale, PA	724, 878	15086, 15095–15096
Warrensburg, MO	660	64093
Warrensville Heights, OH	216	44122, 44128
Warrenton, GA	706, 762	30828
Warrenton, MO	636	63383
Warrenton, NC	252	27589
Warrenton, OR	503	97146
Warrenton, VA	540	20186–20188
Warrenville, IL	331, 630	60555
Warrington, PA	215, 267	18976
Warrior, AL	205	35180
Warroad, MN	218	56741, 56763
Warsaw, IN	574	46580–46582
Warsaw, KY	859	41095
Warsaw, MO	660	65355
Warsaw, NY	585	14569
Warsaw, NC	910	28398
Warsaw, VA	804	22572
Wartburg, TN	423	37887
Warwick, NY	845	10990
Warwick, RI	401	02818, 02886–02889
Wasco, IL	331, 630	60183
Waseca, MN	507	56093
Washburn, MO	417	65772
Washburn, ND	701	58577
Washburn, WI	715	54891
Washington, CT	860	06777, 06793–06794
Washington, DC	202	20001–20020, 20024–20082*
Washington, GA	706, 762	30673
Washington, IL	309	61571
Washington, IN	812	47501
Washington, IA	319	52353
Washington, KS	785	66968
Washington, MO	636	63090
Washington, NJ	908	07882
Washington, NC	252	27889
Washington, PA	724, 878	15301
Washington, VA	540	22747
Washington, WV	304	26181
Washington Court House, OH	740	43160
Washington Green, CT	860	06793
Washington Island, WI	920	54246
Washington Navy Yard, DC	202	20374–20376, 20388–20391*
Washingtonville, NY	845	10992
Washougal, WA	360	98671
Wasilla, AK	907	99652–99654, 99687, 99694
Wassaic, NY	845	12592
Watauga, TX	682, 817	76148
Water Valley, MS	662	38965
Waterbury, CT	203	06701–06712, 06716, 06720*
Waterbury, VT	802	05671, 05676
Waterbury Center, VT	802	05677
Waterford, CT	860	06385–06386
Waterford, MI	248, 947	48327–48330
Waterford, NY	518	12188
Waterford, PA	814	16441
Waterford, WI	262	53185
Waterloo, IL	618	62298
Waterloo, IN	260	46793
Waterloo, IA	319	50701–50707, 50799
Waterloo, NY	315	13165
Waterloo, WI	920	53594
Watertown, CT	860	06779, 06795
Watertown, MA	617, 857	02471–02472, 02477
Watertown, MN	952	55388
Watertown, NY	315	13601–13603
Watertown, SD	605	57201
Watertown, WI	920	53094, 53098
Waterville, ME	207	04901–04903
Waterville, OH	419, 567	43566
Waterville, WA	509	98858
Waterville Valley, NH	603	03215
Watervliet, NY	518	12189
Watford City, ND	701	58854
Watkins Glen, NY	607	14891
Watkinsville, GA	706, 762	30677
Watonga, OK	580	73772
Watrous, NM	505	87750–87753
Watseka, IL	815	60970
Watsonville, CA	831	95076–95077
Wauchula, FL	863	33873
Waucoma, IA	563	52171
Wauconda, IL	224, 847	60084
Waukegan, IL	224, 847	60079, 60085–60087
Waukesha, WI	262	53146, 53151, 53186, 53189
Waukon, IA	563	52172
Waunakee, WI	608	53597
Waupaca, WI	715	54981
Waupun, WI	920	53963
Wauregan, CT	860	06387
Waurika, OK	580	73573
Wausau, WI	715	54401–54403
Wauseon, OH	419, 567	43567
Wautoma, WI	920	54982
Wauwatosa, WI	414	53210–53213, 53222, 53226
Waverly, FL	863	33877
Waverly, IA	319	50677
Waverly, OH	740	45690
Waverly, TN	931	37185
Waverly, VA	804	23890–23891
Wawaka, IN	260	46794
Waxahachie, TX	469, 972	75165–75168
Waycross, GA	912	31501–31503
Wayland, MA	508, 774	01778
Wayland, MI	616	49348
Wayland, NY	585	14572
Waymart, PA	570	18472
Wayne, MI	734	48184
Wayne, NE	402	68787
Wayne, NJ	862, 973	07470, 07474–07477
Wayne, PA	484, 610	19080, 19087–19089
Wayne, WV	304	25570
Waynesboro, GA	706, 762	30830
Waynesboro, MS	601, 769	39367
Waynesboro, PA	717	17268

*Partial list of zip codes, including main range

City	Area Code(s)	Zip Code(s)
Waynesboro, TN	931	38485
Waynesboro, VA	540	22980
Waynesburg, PA	724, 878	15370
Waynesville, MO	573	65583
Waynesville, NC	828	28738, 28785–28786
Wayzata, MN	763, 952	55391
Weatherford, OK	580	73096
Weatherford, TX	682, 817	76085–76088
Weaverville, CA	530	96093
Weaverville, NC	828	28787
Webb City, MO	417	64870
Webberville, MI	517	48892
Webster, MA	508, 774	01570
Webster, NY	585	14580
Webster, SD	605	57274
Webster, TX	281, 832	77598
Webster City, IA	515	50595
Webster Groves, MO	314	63119
Webster Springs, WV	304	26288
Wedowee, AL	256	36278
Weed, CA	530	96094
Weehawken, NJ	201, 551	07086–07087
Weidman, MI	989	48893
Weimar, CA	530	95736
Weirsdale, FL	352	32195
Weirton, WV	304	26062
Weiser, ID	208	83672
Welch, WV	304	24801
Welches, OR	503, 971	97067
Weldon, NC	252	27890
Wellesley, MA	339, 781	02457, 02481–02482
Wellesley Hills, MA	339, 781	02481
Wellesley Island, NY	315	13640
Wellfleet, MA	508, 774	02667
Wellington, CO	970	80549
Wellington, FL	561	33414, 33421, 33467
Wellington, KS	620	67152
Wellington, OH	440	44090
Wellington, TX	806	79095
Wells, ME	207	04090
Wells, MN	507	56097
Wells, NV	775	89835
Wellsboro, PA	570	16901
Wellsburg, NY	570	14894
Wellsburg, WV	304	26070
Wellsville, NY	585	14895
Wellsville, OH	234, 330	43968
Wellton, AZ	928	85356
Wenatchee, WA	509	98801–98802, 98807
Wendell, NC	919	27591
Wenham, MA	351, 978	01984
Wentworth, NC	336	27375
Wernersville, PA	484, 610	19565
Weslaco, TX	956	78596–78599
Wesley Chapel, FL	813	33543–33544
Wessington Springs, SD	605	57382
Wesson, MS	601, 769	39191
West Alexandria, OH	937	45381
West Allis, WI	414	53214, 53219, 53227
West Atlantic City, NJ	609	08232
West Babylon, NY	631	11704–11707
West Barnstable, MA	508, 774	02668
West Bath, ME	207	04530
West Belmar, NJ	732, 848	07719
West Bend, IA	515	50597
West Bend, WI	262	53090, 53095
West Bethesda, MD	301	20817, 20827
West Bloomfield, MI	248, 947	48322–48325
West Boylston, MA	508, 774	01583
West Branch, IA	319	52358
West Branch, MI	989	48661
West Brentwood, NY	631	11717
West Bridgewater, MA	508, 774	02379
West Burlington, IA	319	52655
West Caldwell, NJ	862, 973	07006–07007
West Carrollton, OH	937	45439, 45449
West Chester, OH	513	45069–45071
West Chester, PA	484, 610	19380–19383
West Chicago, IL	331, 630	60185–60186
West Columbia, SC	803	29033, 29169–29172
West Columbia, TX	979	77486
West Conshohocken, PA	484, 610	19428
West Covina, CA	626	91790–91793
West Deptford, NJ	856	08066
West Des Moines, IA	515	50265–50266, 50398
West Dover, VT	802	05351, 05356
West Dundee, IL	224, 847	60118
West Falmouth, MA	508, 774	02574
West Fargo, ND	701	58078
West Frankfort, IL	618	62896
West Franklin, NH	603	03235
West Glacier, MT	406	59921, 59936
West Greenwich, RI	401	02817
West Grove, PA	484, 610	19390
West Hartford, CT	860	06107–06110, 06117–06119*
West Haven, CT	203	06516
West Haverstraw, NY	845	10993
West Hazleton, PA	570	18202
West Helena, AR	870	72390
West Hempstead, NY	516	11552
West Henrietta, NY	585	14586
West Hills, CA	818	91304–91308
West Hollywood, CA	310, 323, 424	90038, 90046–90048
West Homestead, PA	412, 878	15120
West Hurley, NY	845	12491
West Islip, NY	631	11795
West Jefferson, OH	614	43162
West Jordan, UT	801	84084, 84088
West Kennebunk, ME	207	04094
West Kingston, RI	401	02892
West Lafayette, IN	765	47906–47907, 47996
West Lafayette, OH	740	43845
West Lebanon, IN	765	47991
West Lebanon, NH	603	03784
West Liberty, IA	319	52776
West Liberty, KY	606	41472
West Liberty, WV	304	26074
West Long Branch, NJ	732, 848	07764
West Los Angeles, CA	310, 424	90025
West Mansfield, OH	937	43358
West Melbourne, FL	321	32904, 32912
West Memphis, AR	870	72301–72303
West Middlesex, PA	724, 878	16159
West Mifflin, PA	412, 878	15122–15123, 15236
West Milford, NJ	862, 973	07480
West Monroe, LA	318	71291–71294
West New York, NJ	201, 551	07093
West Nyack, NY	845	10994
West Olive, MI	616	49460
West Orange, NJ	862, 973	07052
West Palm Beach, FL	561	33401–33422
West Park, NY	845	12493
West Paterson, NJ	862, 973	07424
West Pittsburg, PA	724, 878	16160
West Plains, MO	417	65775–65776
West Point, GA	706, 762	31833
West Point, MS	662	39773
West Point, NE	402	68788
West Point, NY	845	10996–10997
West Point, PA	215, 267	19486
West Point, VA	804	23181
West Redding, CT	203	06896
West Roxbury, MA	617, 857	02132
West Sacramento, CA	916	95605, 95691, 95798, 95799
West Saint Paul, MN	651	55107, 55118
West Salem, OH	419, 567	44287
West Salem, WI	608	54669
West Sayville, NY	631	11796
West Seneca, NY	716	14206, 14210, 14218, 14220*
West Springfield, MA	413	01089–01090
West Tawakoni, TX	903	75474
West Terre Haute, IN	812	47885
West Trenton, NJ	609	08628
West Union, IA	563	52175
West Union, OH	937	45693
West Union, WV	304	26456
West Valley, NY	716	14171
West Valley City, UT	801	84118–84120, 84128
West Warren, MA	413	01092
West Warwick, RI	401	02893
West Yellowstone, MT	406	59758
Westampton, NJ	609	08060
Westborough, MA	508, 774	01580–01582
Westbrook, CT	860	06498
Westbrook, ME	207	04092, 04098
Westbury, NY	516	11568, 11590–11597
Westby, WI	608	54667
Westchester, IL	708	60154
Westcliffe, CO	719	81252
Westerlo, NY	518	12055, 12193
Westerly, RI	401	02808, 02891
Westerville, OH	614	43081–43082, 43086
Westfield, IN	317	46074
Westfield, MA	413	01085–01086
Westfield, NJ	908	07090–07091
Westfield, NY	716	14787
Westfield, PA	814	16927, 16950
Westfield, VT	802	05874
Westfield Center, OH	234, 330	44251
Westford, MA	351, 978	01886
Westhampton Beach, NY	631	11978
Westlake, LA	337	70669
Westlake, OH	440	44145
Westlake, TX	682, 817	76262
Westlake Village, CA	805, 818	91359–91363
Westland, MI	734	48185–48186
Westminster, CA	714	92683–92685
Westminster, CO	303, 720	80003–80005, 80020–80021*
Westminster, MD	410	21157–21158
Westminster, MA	351, 978	01441, 01473
Westminster Station, VT	802	05159
Westmont, IL	331, 630	60559–60561
Westmont, NJ	856	08108
Westmoreland, KS	785	66426, 66549
Weston, CT	203	06883
Weston, FL	754, 954	33326–33327, 33331–33332
Weston, MA	339, 781	02493
Weston, MO	816	64098
Weston, WV	304	26452
Westover, MD	410	21871, 21890
Westport, CT	203	06880–06881, 06888–06889
Westport, MA	508, 774	02790
Westport, WA	360	98595
Westville, IN	574	46391
Westwego, LA	504	70094–70096
Westwood, KS	913	66205
Westwood, MA	339, 781	02090
Westwood, NJ	201, 551	07675–07677
Wethersfield, CT	860	06109, 06129
Wetumpka, AL	334	36092–36093
Wewahitchka, FL	850	32465
Wewoka, OK	405	74884
Wexford, PA	724, 878	15090
Weyers Cave, VA	540	24486
Weymouth, MA	339, 781	02188–02191
Wharton, TX	979	77488
Whately, MA	413	01093, 01373
Wheat Ridge, CO	303, 720	80002, 80033–80034*
Wheatland, IA	563	52777
Wheatland, PA	724, 878	16161
Wheatland, WY	307	82201
Wheaton, IL	331, 630	60187–60189
Wheaton, MD	301	20902, 20906, 20915
Wheaton, MN	320	56296
Wheeler, TX	806	79096
Wheeling, IL	224, 847	60090
Wheeling, WV	304	26003
Whippany, NJ	862, 973	07981–07983, 07999
Whiskeytown, CA	530	96095
White Bear Lake, MN	651	55110, 55115
White Castle, LA	225	70788
White City, OR	541	97503
White Cloud, MI	231	49349
White Deer, PA	570	17887
White Haven, PA	570	18661
White Lake, MI	248, 947	48383–48386
White Oak, PA	412, 878	15131
White Oak, TX	903	75693
White Pigeon, MI	616	49099
White Plains, NY	914	10601–10610, 10650
White River, SD	605	57579
White River Junction, VT	802	05001, 05009
White Sands, NM	505	88002

Partial list of zip codes, including main range

City	Area Code(s)	Zip Code(s)
White Sands Missile Range, NM	505	88002
White Stone, VA	804	22578
White Sulphur Springs, MT	406	59645
White Sulphur Springs, WV	304	24986
Whitefish, MT	406	59937
Whitehall, MI	231	49461–49463
Whitehall, PA	484, 610	18052
Whitehall, WI	715	54773
Whitehouse, NJ	908	08888
Whitehouse, OH	419, 567	43571
Whitehouse Station, NJ	908	08889
Whitesburg, KY	606	41858
Whitestone, NY	347, 718	11357
Whiteville, NC	910	28472
Whiteville, TN	901	38075
Whitewater, WI	262	53190
Whitfield, MS	601, 769	39193
Whiting, IN	219	46394
Whiting, NJ	732, 848	08759
Whitinsville, MA	508, 774	01588
Whitley City, KY	606	42653
Whitsett, NC	336	27377
Whittier, AK	907	99693
Whittier, CA	562	90601–90612
Wibaux, MT	406	59353
Wichita, KS	316	67201–67236, 67251, 67256*
Wichita Falls, TX	940	76301–76311
Wickenburg, AZ	928	85358, 85390
Wickliffe, KY	270	42087
Wickliffe, OH	440	44092
Wiggins, MS	601, 769	39577
Wilber, NE	402	68465
Wilberforce, OH	937	45384
Wilbraham, MA	413	01095
Wilburton, OK	918	74578
Wilder, KY	859	41071, 41076
Wilder, VT	802	05088
Wildomar, CA	951	92595
Wildorado, TX	806	79098
Wildwood, FL	352	34785
Wildwood, NJ	609	08260
Wildwood Crest, NJ	609	08260
Wilkes-Barre, PA	570	18701–18711, 18761–18769*
Wilkesboro, NC	336	28697
Willard, OH	419, 567	44888–44890
Willard, UT	435	84340
Willcox, AZ	520	85643–85644
Williams Bay, WI	262	53191
Williamsburg, IA	319	52361
Williamsburg, KY	606	40769
Williamsburg, OH	513	45176
Williamsburg, PA	814	16693
Williamsburg, VA	757	23081, 23185–23188
Williamson, WV	304	25661
Williamsport, IN	765	47993
Williamsport, MD	301	21795
Williamsport, PA	570	17701–17705
Williamston, MI	517	48895
Williamston, NC	252	27892
Williamstown, KY	859	41097
Williamstown, MA	413	01267
Williamstown, NJ	856	08094
Williamstown, WV	304	26187
Williamsville, NY	716	14221, 14231
Willimantic, CT	860	06226
Willingboro, NJ	609	08046
Willis, TX	936	77318, 77378
Williston, FL	352	32696
Williston, ND	701	58801–58802
Williston, SC	803	29853
Williston, VT	802	05495
Willits, CA	707	95429, 95490
Willmar, MN	320	56201
Willoughby, OH	440	44094–44097
Willow Grove, PA	215, 267	19090
Willow Springs, MO	417	65793
Willow Street, PA	717	17584
Willowbrook, IL	331, 630	60527
Willows, CA	530	95988
Willsboro, NY	518	12996
Wilmerding, PA	412, 878	15148
Wilmette, IL	224, 847	60091
Wilmington, CA	310, 424	90744, 90748
Wilmington, DE	302	19801–19810, 19850, 19880*
Wilmington, MA	978	01887
Wilmington, NC	910	28401–28412
Wilmington, OH	937	45177
Wilmore, KY	859	40390
Wilson, NY	716	14172
Wilson, NC	252	27893–27896
Wilson, WY	307	83014
Wilsonville, OR	503, 971	97070
Wilton, CT	203	06897
Wilton, IA	563	52778
Wilton, ME	207	04294
Wilton, NH	603	03086
Wilton, NY	518	12831
Wimberley, TX	512	78676
Winamac, IN	574	46996
Winchester, IL	217	62694
Winchester, IN	765	47394
Winchester, KY	859	40391–40392
Winchester, MA	339, 781	01890
Winchester, NH	603	03470
Winchester, TN	931	37398
Winchester, VA	540	22601–22604, 22638
Wind Gap, PA	484, 610	18091
Windber, PA	814	15963
Winder, GA	470, 770	30680
Windermere, FL	321, 407	34786
Windham, NH	603	03087
Windom, MN	507	56101, 56118
Window Rock, AZ	928	86515
Windsor, CA	707	95492
Windsor, CT	860	06006, 06095
Windsor, NC	252	27983
Windsor, VT	802	05089
Windsor, VA	757	23487
Windsor, WI	608	53598
Windsor Locks, CT	860	06096
Winfield, AL	205	35594
Winfield, IL	331, 630	60190
Winfield, KS	620	67156
Winfield, WV	304	25213
Wingate, NC	704, 980	28174
Winlock, WA	360	98596
Winn, ME	207	04495
Winnebago, WI	920	54985
Winneconne, WI	920	54986
Winnemucca, NV	775	89445–89446
Winner, SD	605	57580
Winnetka, CA	818	91306, 91396
Winnett, MT	406	59084–59087
Winnfield, LA	318	71483
Winnsboro, LA	318	71295
Winnsboro, SC	803	29180
Winona, MN	507	55987–55988
Winona, MS	662	38967
Winona, MO	573	65588
Winona Lake, IN	219	46590
Winooski, VT	802	05404
Winslow, AZ	928	86047
Winslow, ME	207	04901
Winslow, NJ	609	08095
Winsted, CT	860	06063, 06094, 06098
Winston, OR	541	97496
Winston-Salem, NC	336	27101–27109, 27113–27117*
Winter Garden, FL	321, 407	34777–34778, 34787
Winter Haven, FL	863	33880–33888
Winter Park, CO	970	80482
Winter Park, FL	321, 407	32789–32793
Winters, CA	530	95694
Winters, TX	915	79567
Winterset, IA	515	50273
Wintersville, OH	740	43952–43953
Winterthur, DE	302	19735
Winthrop, ME	207	04364
Winthrop, WA	509	98862
Winton, NC	252	27986
Wiscasset, ME	207	04578
Wisconsin Dells, WI	608	53965
Wisconsin Rapids, WI	715	54494–54495
Wisdom, MT	406	59761
Wise, VA	276	24293
Wixom, MI	248, 947	48393
Woburn, MA	781	01801, 01806–01808*
Wolcott, CT	203	06716
Wolcott, IN	219	47995
Wolcott, NY	315	14590
Wolf, WY	307	82844
Wolf Point, MT	406	59201
Wolfe City, TX	903	75496
Wolfeboro, NH	603	03894
Womelsdorf, PA	484, 610	19567
Wood Dale, IL	331, 630	60191
Wood River, IL	618	62095
Woodbine, GA	912	31569
Woodbine, IA	712	51579
Woodbine, MD	301	21797
Woodbourne, NY	845	12788
Woodbridge, CT	203	06525
Woodbridge, NJ	732, 848	07095
Woodbridge, VA	571, 703	22191–22195
Woodburn, IN	260	46797
Woodburn, OR	503, 971	97071
Woodbury, CT	203	06798
Woodbury, MN	651	55125, 55129
Woodbury, NJ	856	08096–08097
Woodbury, NY	516	11797
Woodbury, TN	615	37190
Woodcliff Lake, NJ	201, 551	07677
Woodhaven, MI	734	48183
Woodhaven, NY	347, 718	11421
Woodinville, WA	425	98072
Woodland, CA	530	95695, 95776
Woodland, PA	814	16881
Woodland, WA	360	98674
Woodland Hills, CA	818	91302–91303, 91364–91367*
Woodridge, IL	331, 630	60517, 60540
Woodruff, SC	864	29388
Woodruff, WI	715	54568
Woods Cross, UT	801	84010, 84087
Woods Hole, MA	508, 774	02543
Woodsfield, OH	740	43793
Woodside, CA	650	94062
Woodside, NY	347, 718	11377
Woodstock, CT	860	06281
Woodstock, GA	470, 770	30188–30189
Woodstock, IL	815	60098
Woodstock, NY	845	12498
Woodstock, VT	802	05091
Woodstock, VA	540	22664
Woodstown, NJ	856	08098
Woodville, MS	601, 769	39669
Woodville, OH	419, 567	43469
Woodville, TX	409	75979, 75990
Woodville, WI	715	54028
Woodward, IA	515	50276
Woodward, OK	580	73801–73802
Woolrich, PA	570	17779
Woonsocket, RI	401	02895
Woonsocket, SD	605	57385
Wooster, OH	234, 330	44691
Worcester, MA	508, 774	01601–01615, 01653–01655
Worcester, PA	484, 610	19490
Worland, WY	307	82401, 82430
Wormleysburg, PA	717	17043
Worth, IL	708	60482
Worthington, MN	507	56187
Worthington, OH	614	43085
Wrangell, AK	907	99929
Wray, CO	970	80758
Wrens, GA	706, 762	30818, 30833
Wrentham, MA	508, 774	02070, 02093
Wright, WY	307	82732
Wright City, MO	636	63390
Wright-Patterson AFB, OH	937	45433
Wrightstown, NJ	609	08562
Wrightsville, AR	501	72183
Wrightsville, GA	478	31096
Wrightsville, PA	717	17368
Wrightsville Beach, NC	910	28480
Wyalusing, PA	570	18853

Partial list of zip codes, including main range

City	Area Code(s)	Zip Code(s)
Wyandanch, NY	631	11798
Wyandotte, MI	734	48192
Wyckoff, NJ	201, 551	07481
Wye Mills, MD	410	21679
Wylliesburg, VA	434	23976
Wyncote, PA	215, 267	19095
Wyndmoor, PA	215, 267	19038
Wynne, AR	870	72396
Wynnewood, PA	484, 610	19096
Wyoming, MI	616	49418, 49508–49509
Wyoming, MN	651	55092
Wyoming, PA	570	18644
Wyomissing, PA	484, 610	19610
Wysox, PA	570	18854
Wytheville, VA	276	24382

X

City	Area Code(s)	Zip Code(s)
Xenia, OH	937	45385

Y

City	Area Code(s)	Zip Code(s)
Yabucoa, PR	787, 939	00767
Yacolt, WA	360	98675
Yadkinville, NC	336	27055
Yakima, WA	509	98901–98909
Yakutat, AK	907	99689
Yale, IA	641	50277
Yanceyville, NC	336	27379
Yankton, SD	605	57078–57079
Yardley, PA	215, 267	19067
Yardville, NJ	609	08620
Yarmouth, ME	207	04096
Yates Center, KS	620	66783
Yazoo City, MS	662	39194
Yeadon, PA	484, 610	19050
Yellow Springs, OH	937	45387
Yellowstone National Park, WY	307	82190
Yellville, AR	870	72687
Yelm, WA	360	98597
Yerington, NV	775	89447
Yoakum, TX	361	77995
Yonkers, NY	914	10701–10710
Yorba Linda, CA	714	92885–92887
York, AL	205	36925
York, NE	402	68467
York, PA	717	17315, 17401–17407
York, SC	803	29745
York Harbor, ME	207	03910–03911
York Haven, PA	717	17370
York Springs, PA	717	17372
Yorktown, VA	757	23690–23693
Yorktown Heights, NY	914	10598
Yorkville, IL	331, 630	60560
Yorkville, NY	315	13495
Young America, MN	952	55394–55399, 55473, 55550*
Young Harris, GA	706, 762	30582
Youngstown, OH	234, 330	44501–44515, 44555, 44598*
Youngsville, LA	337	70592
Youngsville, NC	919	27596
Youngsville, PA	814	16371
Youngwood, PA	724, 878	15697
Yountville, CA	707	94599
Ypsilanti, MI	734	48197–48198
Yreka, CA	530	96097
Yuba City, CA	530	95991–95993
Yucaipa, CA	909	92399
Yucca Valley, CA	760	92284–92286
Yukon, OK	405	73085, 73099
Yuma, AZ	928	85364–85369
Yuma, CO	970	80759

Z

City	Area Code(s)	Zip Code(s)
Zachary, LA	225	70791
Zachow, WI	715	54182
Zanesville, OH	740	43701–43702
Zapata, TX	956	78076
Zebulon, GA	470, 770	30295
Zebulon, NC	919	27597
Zeeland, MI	616	49464
Zelienople, PA	724, 878	16063
Zellwood, FL	321, 407	32798
Zenda, WI	262	53195
Zephyrhills, FL	813	33539–33544
Zillah, WA	509	98953
Zion, IL	224, 847	60099
Zionsville, IN	317	46077
Zionsville, PA	484, 610	18092
Zolfo Springs, FL	863	33890
Zumbrota, MN	507	55992

Partial list of zip codes, including main range

Index to Classified Headings

Citations given in this index refer to the subject headings under which listings are organized in the Classified Section. The page numbers given for each citation refer to the page on which a particular subject category begins rather than to a specific company or organization name. "See" and "See also" references are included to help in the identification of appropriate subject categories.

A

B

D

E

F

G

I

J

M

N

O

S

T

U

V

X

Y

Z